DIRECTORY OF
LIBRARY &
INFORMATION
PROFESSIONALS™

published in collaboration with

AMERICAN LIBRARY ASSOCIATION

Special participating organizations
American Society for Information Science
Canadian Library Association
Information Industry Association
Medical Library Association
Special Libraries Association

Volume 2
Indexes

rp®

research publications
Woodbridge, Connecticut

The Library of Congress has cataloged this serial publication as follows:
ISSN 0894-7031
ISBN 0-89235-125-X

Computerized Laser Page Imaging by May & Speh
Manufactured in the United States of America

Table of Contents

VOLUME 1 — LISTINGS

Foreword iv

Introduction v

Advisory and Editorial Committees vii

User's Guide viii
    Key to Biographical Listing xi
    Key to Specialty Index xii
    Key to Employer Index xiii
    Key to Consulting/Freelance Index xiv
    Key to Geographical Index xv

Table of Abbreviations and Acronyms xvi

Biographical Listings . . . . 1 - 1392

VOLUME 2 — INDEXES

Foreword xxii

Introduction xxiii

Advisory and Editorial Committees xxv

User's Guide xxvi
    Key to Biographical Listing xxix
    Key to Specialty Index xxx
    Key to Employer Index xxxi
    Key to Consulting/Freelance Index xxxii
    Key to Geographical Index xxxiii

Table of Abbreviations and Acronyms xxxiv

Specialty Index . . . . 1393 - 2004
    Professionals are indexed under alphabetically-sorted keywords with their self-defined professional expertise or subject specialty and further sorted by state (Canadian province or country).

Employer Index . . . . 2005 - 2240
    Professionals, with their current positions, are indexed by employers. Employers are listed alphabetically and further sorted by state (Canadian province or country).

Consulting/Freelance Index . . . . 2241 - 2562
    Professionals, with their phone numbers, are indexed by their consulting/freelance availability, arranged by state (Canadian province or country) and city.

Geographical Index . . . . 2563 - 2735
    Professionals are indexed by state (Canadian province or country) and city, grouped by employers' names.

Foreword

The need for current biographical information on members of the library and information professions has for many years been a concern of the American Library Association (ALA), but is a need which has not always been easy to meet. ALA's past efforts have included the publications of *A Biographical Directory of Librarians in the United States and Canada* (1970) and *Who's Who in Library and Information Services* (1982), as well as annual publication of its membership directory. However, the dynamic nature of the field and the more rapid rate at which it has grown and changed have created new challenges in developing new biographical tools.

ALA has been fortunate to work with Research Publications, Inc., through its Directory and Database Division, to create a new information resource that would respond effectively to the demand for biographical information about our expanding and diverse profession. Our objective has been to develop a powerful research tool that will meet a variety of information needs of publishers, associations, librarians, and many others who seek information about their peers. We wished to use this project as an opportunity to define and characterize more broadly the profession as it has changed since earlier works were published. We have sought to make the best possible use of current information technologies to produce not only the print version of the *Directory,* but also a CD-ROM version. We envision the *Directory* as an ongoing program, with future editions continuing to expand and improve.

Critical to the success of the project has been the co-sponsorship of several key associations in the library profession and information industry, along with more than twenty additional organizations whose membership lists formed the basis of our canvass of the profession. This has truly been a collaborative effort, one which has resulted, we believe, in the most comprehensive compilation of biographical data ever achieved in this field, a rich source of data supporting a wide range of practical and research needs for demographic, market, geographic, and many other kinds of analysis of the information professions.

We appreciate the field's positive response to this project, and are confident that the *Directory of Library & Information Professionals*™ will respond effectively to many information needs.

Thomas J. Galvin, Ph.D.
Executive Director
American Library Association

Introduction

The decision to publish the **Directory of Library & Information Professionals**™ *(DLIP)* was made in response to the need expressed by information professionals for a tool to facilitate communication and exchange of information within the information profession. *DLIP* in both CD-ROM and print form provides such a tool. Prior to *DLIP* the most current information available on people in the information field was *Who's Who in Library and Information Services* published by the American Library Association in 1982. The need for an expanded and up-to-date version was evident. Not only had the biographical data changed but the field had changed dramatically as well — new technologies, new theories and new markets had expanded the focus and growth of the information services field.

With the enthusiastic collaboration of the American Library Association and special participation of other leading information professional organizations, editorial work on the *Directory* began in earnest September 1986. An Advisory Committee was formed made up of the executive directors of the American Library Association, American Society for Information Science, Canadian Library Association, Information Industry Association, Medical Library Association and Special Libraries Association. In addition, five individuals, selected to represent a cross-section of knowledge and experience in the information field, agreed to serve on the Editorial Committee. Both committees were intricately involved in the formulation of editorial policies and the compilative process of the *Directory*. Together, they formulated the purpose of the *DLIP* project — to compile an authoritative and comprehensive biographical resource of current reference value. To that end, directory development proceeded to:

- secure data on as many professionals as possible;
- include more than an individual's career and education facts by gathering data such as areas of product, subject and consulting expertise;
- provide multiple indexes to enable users to locate individuals by various types of expertise, geographical area and employer without knowing a specific name;
- publish in both CD-ROM and print format.

Scope and Coverage:

The *Directory of Library & Information Professionals*™ presents biographical data on nearly 43,000 individuals. These listings reflect diverse educational backgrounds, career paths, professional activities, job titles and work environments. However, to warrant inclusion in *DLIP,* an individual had to meet one or more of the following four critera:

1. work and/or participate in the information field at a *professional level;*
2. work with information systems which capture, store and retrieve information of relevance to a variety of users;
3. work in education or training, non-library information services or library work fields;
4. ally themselves personally and participate in the information field through membership in national professional associations and societies.

Compilation:

A master mailing list was compiled by merging membership lists of twenty North American library and information-related associations and societies. A questionnaire, cover letter and brochure were sent to approximately 80,000 professionals in February 1987. In addition, announcements of the project were made in the library press and many individuals who did not receive a questionnaire in the mail requested copies by phone. Questionnaires were also distributed at professional trade shows. Incoming questionnaires were checked against the mailing list and eight weeks after the initial mailing a "final call" mailing was sent to all those who had not yet responded.

To further the objective of providing a directory of current reference value, the Editorial and Advisory Committees identified categories of information professionals who merited inclusion in the work (whether or not they responded to a mailing) because of significant employment position, significant association office, records of achievements, or major contributions to the field. Names and addresses of these essential individuals were secured and two more mailings were made. Finally, for those who still did not respond, telephone calls and data garnered from publicly available printed materials resulted in staff-compiled entries for these individuals, noted by asterisks at the ends of these sketches in Volume 1.

In addition, to assure breadth of coverage, the ALA agreed to supply current name, employer and address data for selected categories of their members who did not respond to the data request form or individuals who became members after the mailings (approximately 20,000 names). These "referral entries" appear exactly as they reside in the ALA membership file and are noted by a dagger in Volume 1.

Our data editors prepared a full biographical profile for each respondent according to "house" standards of style and list of abbreviations. Individuals were given an option to receive a proof of their entry to check for accuracy and completeness. Approximately 80% of respondents requested a proof. Compilation of the *Directory* was scheduled to permit as much up-to-date information as possible.

To ensure accuracy and thoroughness, our editorial plan called for data obtained directly from the individual biographees. Thus, we were unable to include individuals who, though active in the information field, did not respond to our data request, did not receive one of our mailings, was not chosen as an essential reference name by our Advisory & Editorial Committees, or requested not to be listed in the *Directory*. Any assistance users can provide in identifying candidates for the next edition or general comments and suggestions about the *Directory* are invited. Such information will assist our editors to assure future depth and breadth of coverage to provide a simple and practical way to find information professionals.

Related Products:

To provide greater access to the data collected for the *Directory of Library & Information Professionals*™, a CD-ROM version of the *Directory* is also available. For more information about the CD-ROM version contact:

> Joel M. Lee, Senior Manager, ALA Information Technology Publishing, 50 East Huron Street, Chicago, Illinois 60611. (312) 944-6780.
> Toll-free: in the US: 1-800-545-2433; in Illinois: 1-800-545-2444; in Canada: 1-800-545-2455. Operator on duty 8:15 AM to 4:45 PM CST.

In addition, twin directories, *CD-ROM Current Users* and *CD-ROM Potential Users* are available. These directories were compiled using information provided by the professionals listed in *DLIP*. For more information about these directories contact:

> John H. Dick, Research Publications, 900 Armour Drive, Lake Bluff, Illinois 60044. (312) 234-1220.

Acknowledgements:

The *Directory of Library & Information Professionals*™ is compiled, edited and printed by the Directory and Database Division of Research Publications, 900 Armour Drive, Lake Bluff, Illinois 60044. John H. Dick is the Publisher and the Editorial Manager is Ann J. Shenassa. Editorial assistance was provided by:

Sue Aker	Janet McClain
James Elrod	Maura Harrigan
Mark Hawkins	Divina Rouse
Kathryn Wacker	Shana Wingard

Brenda Barrera and Joe Dickman provided editorial research. Mary Jane Anderson reviewed and cross-referenced the computer-generated specialty index.

The following individuals are due special thanks for their contributions to the *Directory:* Judy Freeman, Jean Hsieh, Gene Kent, Joe Manusos, Kathy Milewski and Claire Rendall.

The idea to publish an updated biographical directory of information professionals was first generated by Robert F. Asleson. Gary Facente, John H. Dick and Joel M. Lee initiated the collaboration between the ALA and Research Publications and laid out the basic project plan. Joel Lee has been our primary liaison with the ALA and we are grateful for his assistance.

Research Publications also wishes to express thanks to a number of ALA staff members who contributed to the development of the project and whose assistance at various stages made this *Directory* possible: Dr. Thomas J. Galvin, Edgar S. McLarin, Patricia Scarry, Richard Roman, Rob Carlson, Mary Mills, and Paul A. Kobasa.

The Editors

Advisory and Editorial Committees

Advisory Committee

Research Publications gratefully acknowledges the following individuals for their cooperation in securing mailing lists and making themselves available for review, evaluation and general comment on the *Directory of Library & Information Professionals*™.

Thomas J. Galvin
Executive Director
American Library Association

Jane Cooney
Executive Director
Canadian Library Association

David R. Bender
Executive Director
Special Libraries Association

Raymond A. Palmer
Executive Director
Medical Library Association

Linda Resnik
Executive Director
American Society for Information Science

Paul G. Zurkowski
President
Information Industry Association

Editorial Committee

The following individuals assisted in the development of the data collection form, substance and format of the indexes, and the content and format of the biographical listings. They further made themselves available throughout the production process, sharing their expertise and network of knowledgeable colleagues.

Joel M. Lee
Senior Manager
Information Technology Publishing
American Library Association

Mary Jo Lynch
Director
Office for Research
American Library Association

T. Brian Nielsen
Head of Reference Department,
Coordinator of Research
Northwestern University

Sandy Whiteley
Editor
Reference Books Bulletin
American Library Association

Melissa B. Mickey
Database Specialist
Schiff, Hardin & Waite

User's Guide

The *Directory of Library & Information Professionals*™ profiles information specialists in the private sector, government, academia and other institutions. Biographies submitted biographical data to us by completing a data request form. The form was designed to elicit accurate responses that would highlight an individual's professional life. If particular categories were inappropriate to an individual, those sectors were left blank. Biographical listings in alphabetical order are provided in Volume 1.

Each individual who responded to our questionnaire and provided the relevant information is indexed four ways in Volume 2: by professional expertise or subject specialty; employer; consulting/freelance availability; and geographic location. A full description of the indexes is included in this user's guide.

Editorial Practices:

Alphabetizing is in accordance with the following rules:

All names, keywords and phrases are alphabetized letter for letter up to a space and thereafter letter by letter for the next group of characters until another space is reached, and so on. The only exception is that a space within a surname is ignored.

Hyphens, apostrophes and other punctuation are ignored.

Abbreviations and acronyms are alphabetized as the full words they represent. They are explained in the Table of Abbreviations.

Numerals sort according to the spelling of the words they represent.

Words with multiple spellings (e.g., catalog, catalogue) are alphabetized under the common American spelling.

Data sorted geographically is presented alphabetically in the following sequence:

1. US states and territories
2. Canadian provinces
3. Countries other than Canada and the United States

Information provided by a biographee in a non-English language was anglicized as much as possible except in titles of publications or other areas where it would be inappropriate or confusing to do so.

An asterisk at the end of a biographical listing denotes data prepared by our editors based on information obtained directly by telephone or through publicly available sources. These listings are indexed in Volume 2.

A dagger symbol at the end of a biographical listing denotes data provided by the American Library Association. These listings (approximately 20,000 names) appear exactly as they reside in the ALA membership file. They are not indexed in Volume 2.

Biographical listings were prepared using "house" standards of style and abbreviation. To assure accurate content and preference of the respondent, data provided directly by the biographee underwent minor if any, editing.

Data Request Form:

There are three elements of information which were included on the data request form but which are not printed in this directory. This information is provided, when submitted by the biographee, on the CD-ROM version only.

1. Sex

2. Date and Place of Birth

3. Employer Type: Respondents could identify one category from the following list that best describes their employing organization.

Employer Type Categories

INDEPENDENT INFORMATION SERVICES

Consulting Firm
Information Broker/Supplier

CORPORATE

Abstracting/Indexing Service
Bookseller
Corporate Archives/Records Center
Corporate Information Center
Database Producer
Database Vendor
Independent Research Firm, For Profit
Independent Research Firm, Nonprofit
Information Services Vendor
Library Services Vendor
Library Supplies/Equipment Vendor
Publisher
Special Library, For Profit
Special Library, Nonprofit
Technical/Research Information Center

LAW

Law Firm
Law School/Department

MEDICAL

Hospital/Clinic
Medical School/Department
Dental School/Department

EDUCATION

School of Library/Information Science
University
College
Community/Junior College
Research Center/Laboratory
School Library/Media Center

PUBLIC AND GOVERNMENT LIBRARIES AND/OR AGENCIES

Armed Forces
Federal
State/Provincial
Municipal/County/Regional

OTHER ORGANIZATIONS

Archives
Association/Society/Club
Church
Foundation
International
Museum
Network/Consortium/Utility

UNAFFILIATED

Retired
Self-employed

Biographee's Name: The style of name indicated or preferred by the biographee is the form presented.

Current Position: Respondents were asked to provide their current job title and the year they started in that position. For those individuals with more than one current position, their additional employment is included in the Previous Positions section and can be identified by an open date.

Employer and Address: Respondents were asked to list their employer and delineate as appropriate the Organization, Company or University name; the Division, Department, Unit or Branch name; and the Library Name. The Organization or Library name is the data that is listed in the Employer and Geographical Indexes.

Although we specifically requested the employer's address, some respondents preferred to use a different mailing address and we honored those requests.

Previous Positions: Respondents were asked to summarize employment history including position, organization and years of employment.

Education: Respondents could list up to three post-secondary degrees including earned degree and major field, institution and year awarded. Information related to advanced or continuing education that did not culminate in a degree can be found in the Achievements section. The name of the institution reflects the name supplied by the biographee; this may be the name of a college or school within a university, or a school having multiple locations where the biographee has not identified a specific location.

Publications: Respondents were asked to provide information on books, journal articles, monographs or special papers. The title, publisher, and year of publication are provided. Respondent's role is assumed as author unless specified otherwise (i.e., editor, co-editor). We asked respondents to submit a maximum of three of their most important publications, but as data field space permitted, we included as many as provided.

Achievements: Respondents were asked to provide information on three of the most important achievements of their professional career. We included as much information as space permitted.

Honors: Respondents were asked to provide information on three of the most significant honors in their professional career. This information includes prizes, awards, fellowships, and grants, as well as offices and board or honorary society memberships. We included as much information as space permitted and made no editorial judgments regarding data being best suited to this section or the previous section, Achievements.

Memberships: Respondents were asked to provide the names of professional organizations of which they are a member. Originally this section was limited to only national memberships but was revised to include regional and local organizations and division membership within a larger organization. Offices or committee memberships are included in the previous section, Honors.

Professional Expertise/Subject Specialty: Respondents could list up to three phrases that best describe the specific areas in which they are most active. Professionals are indexed by these phrases in the Specialty Index.

Languages: Respondents were asked to list a maximum of four non-English languages and their relevant proficiency in each (i.e., read, write, speak and/or translate).

Consulting/Freelance Availability: Respondents could choose up to six areas from the following list in which they are available to do consulting or freelance work. The Consulting/Freelance Index is organized by these areas.

Abstracter	Proofreader
Academic Library Consultant	Public Library Consultant
Archivist	Public Relations Consultant
Bibliographer	Records Management Consultant
Cataloger	Researcher
Collection Development/	Reviewer
Evaluation Consultant	Speaker (free)
Database/Systems Consultant	Speaker (honorarium)
General Library/Information Consultant	Special Library Consultant
Indexer	Staff Development Consultant
Library Automation Consultant	Trainer
Library Building Consultant	Translator (by language)
Online Searcher	Writer/Editor

In addition, respondents were asked to provide the address and phone number where they should be contacted for consulting/freelance work (if different from the employer address and phone). This information is included in the Consulting/Freelance Index.

Key to Biographical Listing

① **WOOD, ELIZABETH FOY**
② Mgr Info Srvs, ③ Computer Testing Inc, Commercial Lib Srvs, McGovern Lib, ④ 1985—, ⑤ PO Box 62 Ashe Turnpike, Brunson SC 29911 (803)572-1182 ⑥ **Career:** Syst Design & Implementation, BLSI Inc, 1980-85; Operations Mgr, Roosevelt Research Ctr, 1972-80; Info Spclst, Modern Info Systems, 1968-72 ⑦ **Education:** MLS Info Retrieval, Syracuse Univ, 1978; BA Communications, Univ of SC, 1968 ⑧ **Publications:** "The Added Value of Information Analysis Centers," Syracuse Lib Qtly, 1983 ⑨ **Achievements:** Designed and implemented labor statistics bibliographic information system ⑩ **Honors:** Distinguished Service Award, ASIS SC Chpt; Pres, SC Socty of Info Mgrs ⑪ **Memberships:** ASIS; SLA ⑫ **Specialties:** Information processing; Information retrieval; Statistical databases ⑬ **Languages:** German: read ⑭ **Available As:** Database/systems consult; ⑮ 119 Lakeview Terr, Lake Vernon SC 29912 (803)457-1923

- ① Name
- ② Current business position
- ③ Current business affiliation name/department/library
- ④ Years in current position
- ⑤ Business affiliation address and phone
- ⑥ Previous positions: position, employer, years (beginning with most recent)
- ⑦ Post-secondary education: degree and major field, institution, degree year (beginning with most recent)
- ⑧ Most important publications
- ⑨ Major professional achievements
- ⑩ Most significant prizes, awards, fellowships, grants or offices
- ⑪ Professional memberships
- ⑫ Professional expertise and/or subject specialties
- ⑬ Non-English language proficiency
- ⑭ Consulting/freelance availability
- ⑮ Consulting/freelance address and phone number (only if different from business address and phone)

* staff-compiled entry

† referral entry from ALA membership file

Names are arranged alphabetically without regard to punctuation and/or spaces within surnames or given names. The only exception is that surnames beginning with "Saint" or "St." are interfiled and then alphabetized by the remaining portion of the surname. Each biographical listing is presented in a uniform order as shown in the foregoing fictional listing. Abbreviations are explained in the Table of Abbreviations.

Key to Specialty Index

Most full biographical listings include a field of information labeled **Specialties.** In this field information professionals list, in their own terminology, their areas of professional expertise and/or subject specialization. By computer, these specialty phrases were analyzed word by word resulting in over 3500 unique keywords. These keywords were edited for meaningful content and reclassified with their phrases into 1657 keyword index headings which are cross-referenced in the Specialty Index. When several professionals have used the same phraseology to describe their expertise, a stacked citation format further sorted by state (Canadian province or country) is used. The Specialty Index contains over 85,700 listings.

Example:

Under the keyword heading CATALOGING, are the names of professionals who specialize in various aspects of cataloging. Within the same phrase, they are sorted by US state (Canadian province or country).

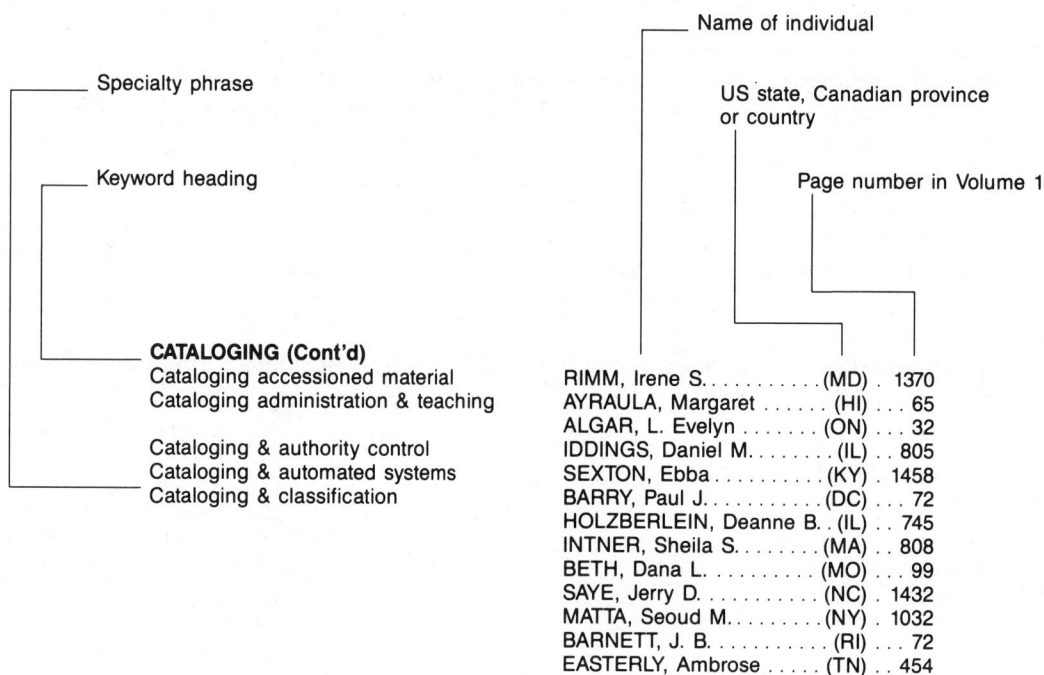

Name of individual

Specialty phrase

US state, Canadian province
or country

Keyword heading

Page number in Volume 1

CATALOGING (Cont'd)
Cataloging accessioned material
Cataloging administration & teaching

Cataloging & authority control
Cataloging & automated systems
Cataloging & classification

RIMM, Irene S. . . . . (MD) . 1370
AYRAULA, Margaret . . . . . . (HI) . . . 65
ALGAR, L. Evelyn . . . . (ON) . . . 32
IDDINGS, Daniel M. . . . . (IL) . . 805
SEXTON, Ebba . . . . (KY) . 1458
BARRY, Paul J. . . . . (DC) . . . 72
HOLZBERLEIN, Deanne B. . (IL) . . 745
INTNER, Sheila S. . . . . (MA) . . 808
BETH, Dana L. . . . . (MO) . . . 99
SAYE, Jerry D. . . . . (NC) . 1432
MATTA, Seoud M. . . . . (NY) . 1032
BARNETT, J. B. . . . . (RI) . . . 72
EASTERLY, Ambrose . . . . . (TN) . . 454

States, provinces and countries are alphabetically sorted by their abbreviations.

Key to Employer Index

Professionals who provided an employer name are listed with their current position and Volume 1 page location. A stacked citation format is used for multiple professionals working for one employer. Employers are listed alphabetically and further sorted by state.

Name of individual

Current position

Employer name

Employer state (province, country)

Page number in Volume 1

Downers Grove Pub Lib (IL)   BALCOM, Kathleen M. (Lib Dir) 70
NEAL, Karen Fencl (Ref Libn) 1195
SCHULTZ, Lois B. (Chlds Libn) 1444

Downington Area Sch District (PA)
AMICONE, Janice L. (Libn) 33
GREBEY Betty H. (Libn) 635
JAFFE, Lawrence L. (Lib Dept Head) 812

Downs Rachlin & Martin (VT)
BROWNE, Wynne W. (Libn) 188
Drake Univ (IA)   EDWARDS, John D. (Law Lib Dir & Assoc Prof) 458
SKEERS, Timothy M. (Serials Libn) 1500
STOPPLE, Ellen K. (Assoc Law Libn & Prof) 1563

Draughons Junior Coll (TN)   TURNER, Deborah M. (Libn) 1648
Dresser Industries Inc (NJ)   GIBSON, Timothy T. (Sr Tax Libn) 602
Dresser Industries Inc (TX)   SZE, Melanie C. (Info Spclst) 1605
Dres Univ (NJ)   DOPELAND, Alice T. (Catlgng Dept Head) . . . 314
COUGHLIN, Caroline M. (Lib Dir) 316
FERRIBY, Peter G. (Catlgr) 507
FRIEDMAN, Ruth (Ref Libn) 545
JONES, Arthur E. (Dir Emeritus/Spcl Cols Libn) 83

States, provinces and countries are alphabetically sorted by their abbreviations. "The" is ignored as the first word in the alphabetical sorting of employer names.

Key to Consulting/Freelance Index

Professionals are indexed by consulting/freelance availability. They are grouped by state (Canadian province or country) and city with telephone number and Volume 1 page location following their name. The state, city and phone listed in this index is the one provided by the professional to be used for consulting/freelance purposes.

Consulting/freelance availability areas appearing in this index are:

Abstracter
Academic Library Consultant
Archivist
Bibliographer
Cataloger
Collection Development/
    Evaluation Consultant
Database/Systems Consultant
General Library/Information
Consultant
Indexer
Library Building Consultant
Library Automation Consultant
Online Searcher

Proofreader
Public Library Consultant
Public Relations Consultant
Records Management Consultant
Researcher
Reviewer
Speaker (free)
Speaker (honorarium)
Special Library Consultant
Staff Development Consultant
Trainer
Translator (by language)
Writer/Editor

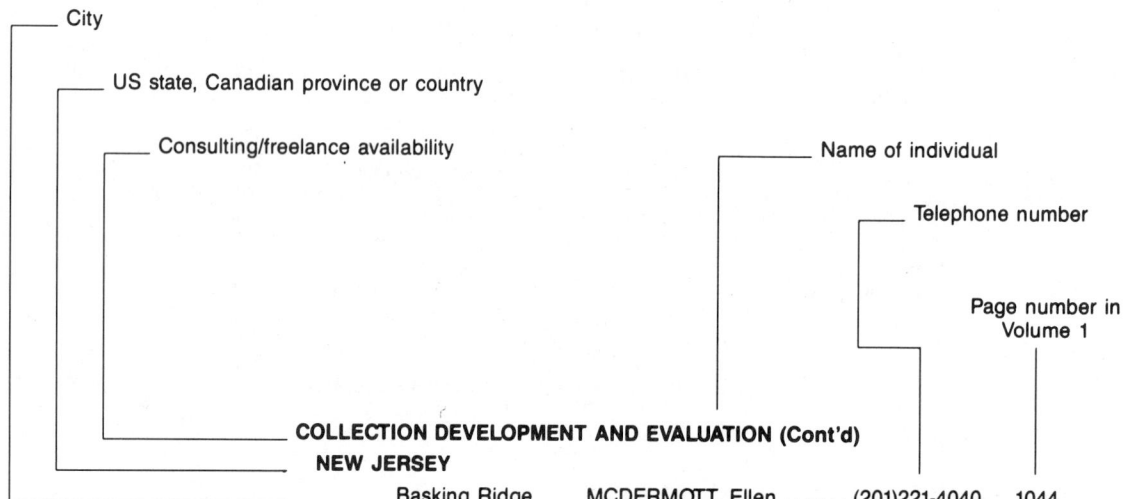

City

US state, Canadian province or country

Consulting/freelance availability

Name of individual

Telephone number

Page number in
Volume 1

COLLECTION DEVELOPMENT AND EVALUATION (Cont'd)
NEW JERSEY

City	Name	Phone	Page
Basking Ridge	MCDERMOTT, Ellen	(201)221-4040	1044
	THOMPSON, Melia M.	(201)953-3326	1621
Belleville	BRYANT, David S.	(201)450-3434	186
	COHEN, Adrea G.	(201)450-3434	314
Bridgewater	ROMANASKY, Maria C.	(201)218-0400	1386
	STEVENS, Sharon G.	(201)218-3819	1564
Caldwell	HODGE, Patricia A.	(201)288-4424	741
Dover	RYAN, Mary E.	(201)989-3079	1419
Fairfield	GUIDA, Pat	(201)227-7418	645
Fort Monmouth	MICHAL, Judith A.	(201)532-3172	1083

States, provinces and countries are alphabetically sorted by their abbreviations.

Key to Geographical Index

Professionals are indexed by the US state (Canadian province or country) and city of their employer. They are listed by alphabetically-sorted employers names with a Volume 1 page location following their name.

Employer name

City

US state, Canadian province or country

Name of individual

Page number in Volume 1

CALIFORNIA (Cont'd)

SAN FRANCISCO (Cont'd

Arthur Anderson & Co	FOX, Marylou P.	536
Bank of America	POLLACH, Karen F.	1298
Bay Area Air Quality Management District	LENSCHAU, Jane A.	1621
Bay Area Reference Center	SHOUSE, Richard	1458
Bechtel Power Corp	MAH, Jeffery	1030
Chevron Corp	BROWN, Barbara L.	186
	WOO, Winnie H.	1743
City & County of San Francisco Libs	GUARINO, John P.	646
	SCHMIDT, Robert R.	1444
City Coll of San Francisco	FEW, JOHN E.	507

"The" is ignored as the first word in the alpahbetical sorting of employer names.

Table of Abbreviations

The following abbreviations are frequently found in this directory.

* staff-compiled entry

† referral entry from ALA membership file

AAAI American Association for Artificial Intelligence
AAAS American Association for the Advancement of Science
AALL American Association of Law Libraries
AALS Association of American Library Schools
AAMSI American Association for Medical Systems and Informatics
AAP Association of American Publishers
AASL American Association of School Librarians
AAUP American Association of University Professors
AAUW American Association of University Women
AB Alberta
ABA American Bar Association
Abstctng Abstracting
Abstctr Abstracter
Abstrc(s) Abstract(s)
Acad Academy, Academic
Acq(s) Acquisition(s)
ACRL Association of College and Research Libraries
Actg Acting
Admin Administration
Adminstr(s) Administrator(s)
Adminstrv Administrative
ACT Australian Capital Territory
Adv Adviser
Advsy Advisory
AECT Association for Educational Communication
AFB Air Force Base
Agy Agency
AIC American Institute of Conservation
AIM Association of Information Managers
AJL Association of Jewish Libraries
AK Alaska
AL Alabama
ALA American Library Association
ALG Algeria
ALISE Association for Library and Information Science Education
ALSC Association for Library Service to Children
ALTA American Library Trustee Association
Am American
Amer America
Appl(s) Application(s)
Apr April
Apt Apartment
AR Arkansas
Arch(s) Archive(s)
Archvl Archival
Archvst(s) Archivist(s)
ARG Argentina
ARL Association of Research Libraries
ARLIS/NA Art Libraries Society/North America
ARMA Association of Records Managers and Administrators
ARSC Association for Recorded Sound Collections
AS American Samoa
ASCLA Association of Specialized and Cooperative Library Agencies
ASI American Society of Indexers
ASIDIC Association of Information and Dissemination Centers
ASIS American Society for Information Science
Assn Association
Assoc(s) Associate(s)
Assocd Associated
Asst(s) Assistant(s)
AST Austria
ASTED Association pour l'Advancement des Science et des Techniques de la Documentation

ATLA American Theological Library Association
Aug August
AUS Australia
Aut Autumn
Auth Author
AV Audiovisual
Ave Avenue
AZ Arizona
BAH Bahamas
BC British Columbia
Bd Board
BEL Belgium
BER Bermuda
Bibl Bibliography
Biblgph Bibliographical
Biblgphr Bibliographer
Bio Biology
Biog Biography
Biogph Biographical
Bk(s) Book(s)
Bldg Building
Bltn Bulletin
Blvd Boulevard
BOT Botswana
BRA Brazil
BRN Bahrain
Bro Brother
BSA Bibliographical Society of America
Bus Business
CA California
CAIS/ASCI Canadian Association for Information Science
CALS Canadian Association of Library Schools
CAML Canadian Association of Music Libraries
CAN Canada
CAN ALL Canadian Association of Law Libraries
Canadn Canadian
CARL Canadian Association of Research Libraries
Cath Catholic
Catlg(s) Catalog(s)
Catlgng Cataloging
Catlgr Cataloger
CEGEP College d'Enseignement General et Professional
Centl Central
Cert Certified
Certft Certificate
Certftn Certification
CHE Chile
Chem Chemistry
CHI People's Republic of China
ChLA Children's Literature Association
CHLA Canadian Health Libraries Association
Chld(s) Children(s)
CHNAMLA Chinese-American Library Association
Chpt Chapter
Cir Circle
Circ Circulation
CISTI Canadian Institute for Science and Technology
CLA Canadian Library Association
Classftn Classification
CLENE Continuing Library Education Network and Exchange
CM Northern Mariannas Islands
CMO Camaroon
Cmplr Compiler
CNLIA Council of National Library and Information Associations
Cnsrvtry Conservatory
Cnstrm Consortium
Cnty County
Co(s) Company(ies)
CO Colorado
COL Columbia
Col(s) Collection(s)
Coll(s) College(s)
Com(s) Committee(s)
Comm(s) Communications(s)
Comp Computer

Comptng Computing
Comunty Community
Conf Conference
Consltn Consultation
Consltng Consulting
Consult Consultant
Contng Continuing
Contrib Contribute
Contribr Contributor
Contribtn Contribution
Contribtng Contributing
Coop Cooperative
Cooprtn Cooperation
Coord Coordinate
Coordntn Coordination
Coordntr Coordinator
Corp Corporation
Corprt Corporate
COSLA Chief Officers of State Library Agencies
CSLA Church and Synagogue Library Association
CSR Costa Rica
CT Connecticut
Ctl Control
Ctr(s) Center(s)
CUB Cuba
CUNY City University of New York
Cur Curator
Curr Curriculum
CZ Canal Zone
CZC Czechoslovakia
DC District of Columbia
DE Delaware
Dec December
DEN Denmark
Dept Department
Dev Develop
Devlpd Developed
Devlpmnt Development
Devlpmntl Developmental
Devlpng Developing
Devlpr Developer
Dir(s) Director(s)
Dirctry Directory
Dist District
Div Division
Divsnl Divisional
Docum(s) Document(s)
Documtn Documentation
DOE Department of Energy
Dr Doctor, Drive
E East
Econ Economics
Ed Edition
Edit Editor
Editd Edited
Editrl Editorial
Educ Education
Eductnl Educational
Eductr(s) Educator(s)
EFLA Educational Film Library Association (now American Film and Video Association)
EGY Egypt
Elem Elementary
ELS El Salvador
ENG England
Engl English
Engrng Engineering
Environ Environmental
ERT Exhibits Round Table
Exec Executive
Feb February
Fed Federal
FIJ Fiji
FL Florida
FLC Federal Library Committee
FLRT Federal Librarians Round Table
Flwship Fellowship
Fndtn Foundation

Fr Father
FRN France
Ft Fort
GA Georgia
Gen General
Geol Geology
GODORT Government Documents Round Table
Govt(s) Government(s)
Govtl Governmental
GRE Greece
Grad Graduate
GU Guam
GUA Guatamala
HEA Higher Education Act
HI Hawaii
Hist History
Histl Historical
Histn Historian
Histns Historians
Histrc Historic
HKG Hong Kong
Hlth Health
HSLN Health Science Library Network
Hts Heights
Hum Humanities
HUN Hungary
IA Iowa
IBM International Business Machines
ID Idaho
IDN Indonesia
IFLA International Federation of Library Associations and Institutions
IFRT Intellectual Freedom Round Table
IIA Information Industry Association
IL Illinois
IN Indiana
Inc Incorporated
IND India
Indxr(s) Indexer(s)
Info Information
Inst(s) Institute(s)
Instn(s) Institution(s)
Instnl Institutional
Instr(s) Instructor(s)
Instrc Instruction
Instrcl Instructional
Interlib Interlibrary
Intgrtd Integrated
Intl International
IRE Ireland
IRN Iran
IRRT International Relations Round Table
ISR Israel
ITL Italy
ITT International Telephone and Telegraph
JAM Jamaica
Jan January
JAP Japan
JMRT Junior Members Round Table
Jnl(s) Jnl(s)
Jnlsm Journalism
Jr Junior
Jul July
Jun June
KEN Kenya
KS Kansas
KWT Kuwait
KY Kentucky
L(s) Library(ies)
LA Louisiana
Lab(s) Laboratory(ies)
LAMA Library Administration and Management Association
Lang Language
LEB Lebanon
Lect Lecture
Lectr Lecturer
LES Lesotho
LHRT Library History Round Table
Lib(s) Library(ies)
Libn(s) Librarian(s)
Libnshp Librarianship
LIRT Library Instruction Round Table
Lit Literature

LITA Library and Information Technology Association
Litcy Literacy
LJ Library Journal
Ln Lane
Ln(s) Librarian(s)
Lnship Librarianship
Lrng Learning
LRRT Library Research Round Table
LUX Luxembourg
MA Massachusetts
Mag Magazine
MAGERT Map and Geography Round Table
MAL Malawi
Mar March
MARBI Machine-Readable Form of Bibliographic Information
Math Mathematics
MB Manitoba
MD Maryland
ME Maine
Med Medical
Medcn Medicine
Mem Member
Memrl Memorial
Memshp Membership
MEX Mexico
MFLA Midwest Federation of Library Associations
Mgmt Management
Mgr(s) Manager(s)
MI Michigan
MIT Massachusetts Institute of Technology
Mktg Marketing
MLA Medical Library Association
MLY Malaysia
MN Minnesota
Mncpl Municipal
MO Missouri
Ms(s) Manuscript(s)
MS Mississippi
Mt Mount
MT Montana
Mtg Meeting
Mtrls Materials
Musm Museum
N North
NAACP National Association for the Advancement of Colored People
NAGARA National Association of Government Archives and Record Administrators
NAS National Academy of Sciences
NASA National Aeronautics and Space Administration
Natl National
NB New Brunswick
NC North Carolina
NCLIS National Commission on Libraries and Information Science
ND North Dakota
NDEA National Defense Education Act
NE Nebraska
NEA National Education Association
NET Netherlands
Netwk(s) Network(s)
NF Newfoundland
NFAIS National Federation of Abstracting and Indexing Services
NGR Nigeria
NGU New Guinea
NH New Hampshire
NIR Northern Ireland
NJ New Jersey
NKO North Korea
NLA National Librarians Association
NM New Mexico
NO New Orleans
NOAA National Oceanic and Atmospheric Administration
NOR Norway
Nov November
NS Nova Scotia
NSW New South Wales
NT Northwest Territories

NV Nevada
NW Northwest
Nwsltr Newsletter
NY New York
NZD New Zealand
Oct October
Ofc Office
Ofcr(s) Officer(s)
OH Ohio
OHA Oral History Association
OK Oklahoma
OLUG Online Users Group
OMA Oman
ON Ontario
OR Oregon
Organz Organization
Orgnznl Organizational
PA Pennsylvania
PAK Pakistan
PAN Panama
PE Prince Edward Island
Perdcl(s) Periodical(s)
Persnl Personnel
Pgmr Programmer
Phila Philadelphia
Philos Philosophy
PHP Phillipines
Pk Park
Pkwy Parkway
Pl Place
PLA Public Library Association
Plng Planning
Pol Political
POL Poland
PQ Quebec
PR Puerto Rico
Prcdngs Proceedings
Prcsng Processing
Pres President
Prodctn Production
Prof(s) Professor(s)
Profsnl(s) Professional(s)
Prog(s) Program(s)
Proj(s) Project(s)
Psy Psychology
PTG Portugal
Pub Public
Publshg Publishing
Publshr(s) Publisher(s)
Pubn(s) Publication(s)
QLD Queensland
Qtly Quarterly
RASD Reference and Adult Services Division
Rd Road
Ref Reference
REFORMA National Association for Library Service to the Spanish Speaking
Regnl Regional
Rep Representative
Resrc(s) Resource(s)
Resrch Research
Resrchng Researching
Resrchr Researcher
Retrvl Retrieval
RI Rhode Island
RR Rural route
RSTD Resources and Technical Services Division
Rsv(s) Reserves
Rvw(s) Review(s)
S South
SAA Society of American Archivists
SAF South Africa
SBPR Sociedad de Bibliotecarios de Puerto Rico
SC South Carolina
Sch(s) School(s)
Schlrshp Scholarship
Sci(s) Science(s)
Scintfc Scientific
Scitst Scientist
SCT Scotland
SD South Dakota
SDA Saudi Arabia

Sec Secondary
SEC Security and Exchange Commission
Sect Section
Secy Secretary
SELA Southeastern Library Association
Sem Seminary
Sep September
SIN Singapore
SK Saskatchewan
SKO South Korea
SLA Special Libraries Association
Soc Social
Soclgy Sociology
Socty Society
SOLINET Southeastern Library Network
SORT Staff Organizations Round Table
Spcl Special
Spclst Specialist
SPN Spain
Spr Spring
Sq Square
Sr Senior, sister
Srch Search
Srchng Searching
Srchr Searcher
SRRT Social Responsibilities Round Table
Srv(s) Service(s)
SSP Society for Scholarly Publications
St Saint, Street
Stan(s) Standard(s)
Statscl Statistical
Std Studies
Ste Suite
Sum Summer

SUNY State University of New York
Supvsng Supervising
Supvsr Supervisor
SW Southwest
SWE Sweden
SWLA Southwest Library Association
SWZ Switzerland
Syst(s) System(s)
TAI Federal Republic of China (Taiwan)
TAN Tanzania
Tchg Teaching
Tchr Teacher
Tech Technology
Techgst Technologist
Technl Technical
Terr Terrace
TESLA Technical Standards for Library Automation
THA Thailand
Theol Theology
TKY Turkey
TLA Theatre Library Association
TN Tennessee
Treas Treasurer
TRN Trinidad
Trng Training
TT Trust Territories
TUA Tunisia
TWA Trans World Airlines
TX Texas
UAE United Arab Emirates
UCLA University of California at Los Angeles
UGN Uganda

ULC Urban Libraries Council
UMI University Microfilms International
UN United Nations
UNESCO United Nations Educational, Scientific and Cultural Organization
UNICEF United Nations Childrens Fund
Univ(s) University(ies)
US United States
USA Unites States
USC University of Southern California
USOE US Office of Education
UT Utah
VA Virginia
VEN Venezuela
VI Virgin Islands
Vol Volume
VT Vermont
W West
WA Washington
WAL Wales
WGR Federal Republic of Germany
WI Wisconsin
Wint Winter
WLB Wilson Library Bulletin
WV West Virginia
WY Wyoming
YASD Young Adult Services Division
YMCA Young Mens Christian Association
Yng young
YT Yukon Territory
YWCA Young Womens Christian Association
ZAI Zaire
ZAM Zambia
ZIM Zimbabwe

Specialty Index

Professionals are listed under alphabetically-sorted keywords with their self-defined professional expertise or subject specialty and further sorted by state (Canadian province or country).

ABSTRACTING

Abstract & indexing services
Abstracting

WERLING, Anita L.	. . . .	(MI)	1324
HUNG, Joanne Y.	. . . . . .	(CA)	574
KLEIMAN, Helen M.	. . . .	(DC)	659
FEINBERG, Hilda W.	. . . .	(GA)	368
ZIMMERMAN, Brenda M.	(IN)	1388
DAVIS, Margo	. . . .	(LA)	280
ANDREWS, Peter J.	. . . . .	(MA)	27
LUKOS, Geraldine F.	. . .	(MA)	748
NATOLI, Dorothy L.	. . . .	(MA)	889
TIBBO, Helen R.	. . . . . .	(MD)	1244
WORDEN, Diane D.	. . . .	(MI)	1369
CUMMINGS, Charles F.	. .	(NJ)	264
KUSHINKA, Kerry L.	. . .	(NJ)	685
GUILER, Paula J.	. . . . . .	(NY)	476
PRESCHEL, Barbara M.	. .	(NY)	991
SULOUFF, Patricia T.	. . .	(NY)	1208
RYERSON, George D.	. . .	(OH)	1071
LINDBERG, Richard L.	. .	(PA)	728
WEBER, A C.	. . . .	(PA)	1313
FRANKUM, Katherine H.	.	(TX)	398
CRAVEN, Timothy C.	. . .	(ON)	256

Abstracting & abstract editing
Abstracting & indexing

HOFFMAN, Allen	. . . . . .	(NY)	547
GATLING, James L.	. . . .	(AL)	422
SPIGAI, Fran	. . . .	(CA)	1174
ALSOP, Robyn J.	. . . . . .	(CO)	18
LUEVANE, Marsha A.	. . .	(CO)	747
KASCUS, Marie A.	. . . . .	(CT)	628
FRAULINO, Philip S.	. . .	(DC)	399
THURONYI, Geza T.	. . .	(DC)	1243
HALASZ, Marilynn J.	. . .	(IL)	484
VALAUSKAS, Edward J.	.	(IL)	1271
HENSON, Jane E.	. . . . .	(IN)	529
JAMES, Bonnie B.	. . . . .	(KY)	592
BOYCE, Bert R.	. . . .	(LA)	122
TETTEH, Joseph A.	. . . .	(LA)	1233
BATES, Ruthann I.	. . . . .	(MD)	64
GENUARDI, Michael T.	. .	(MD)	427
WALL, Eugene	. . . .	(MD)	1297
MAXWELL, Bonnie J.	. . .	(MI)	788
SMITH, Catherine A.	. . .	(MI)	1153
AMIRZAFARI, Jamileh A.	.	(NJ)	20
HOGAN, Thomas H.	. . .	(NJ)	549
MANY, Florence L.	. . . . .	(NJ)	767
OLSON, Lucie M.	. . . . . .	(NJ)	923
HLAVA, Marjorie M.	. . . .	(NM)	544
BIDDEN, Julia E.	. . . . . .	(NY)	94
BRISFJORD, Inez S.	. . .	(NY)	136
COCHRANE, Pauline A.	. .	(NY)	226
GOODSELL, Joan W.	. . . .	(NY)	450
MINOR, Barbara B.	. . . .	(NY)	846
MUTTER, Letitia N.	. . . .	(NY)	883
PISTILLI, Susan A.	. . . . .	(NY)	976
SPERR BRISFJORD, Inez L.	. . . .	(NY)	1173
WINDSOR, Donald A.	. .	(NY)	1354
WOODS, Lawrence J.	. .	(NY)	1367
COPENHAVER, Ida L.	. .	(OH)	244
SHELLENBERGER, Dawn M.	. . . .	(PA)	1126
CHOI, Jin M.	. . . .	(SC)	210
BURT, Eugene C.	. . . . . .	(TX)	164
BRZUSTOWICZ, Richard J.	. . . .	(WA)	152

ABSTRACTING (Cont'd)

Abstracting & indexing

BERTRAND-GASTALDY, Suzanne	. . . .	(PQ)	91
GAULIN, S D.	. . . .	(PQ)	422
LUSSIER, Richard	. . . . .	(PQ)	749
PELLETIER, Rosaire	. . . .	(PQ)	955
SATYANARAYANA, Vadhri V.	. . . .	(IND)	1084
AFOLAYAN, Matthew A.	.	(NGR)	7

Abstracting & indexing databases
Abstracting & indexing service
Abstracting & indexing services

GOLDENBERG, Joan M.	.	(VA)	445
LAWRENCE, Philip D.	. .	(VA)	704
MARCACCIO, Kathleen Y.	(MI)	768
DENIGER, Constant	. . . .	(PQ)	292

Abstracting & indexing technical data
Abstracting & research
Abstracting & technical writing
Abstracting & translating
Abstracting current-medical literature
Abstracting, editing, translation
Abstracting, indexing
Abstracting, indexing & cataloging
Abstracting, indexing, bibliography
Abstracting, indexing, editing
Abstracting newsletter publications
Abstracts
Abstracts & information services admin

AGRAWAL, Surendra P.	.	(IND)	7
HOWARD, Susanna J.	. .	(NC)	564
HADDERMAN, Margaret .	(OR)	482
FISHER, Daphne V.	. . . .	(PA)	380
SPRY, Patricia	. . . .	(ON)	1176
SHIPLEY, Ruth M.	. . . . .	(MO)	1131
REITH, Louis J.	. . . .	(DC)	1022
HALPERN, Marilyn	. . . . .	(NJ)	489
HART, Patricia H.	. . . . . .	(MI)	507
OREJANA, Rebecca D.	. .	(PHP)	925
HYSLOP, Marjorie R.	. . .	(OH)	580
KOVITZ, Nancy R.	. . . . . .	(IL)	674
SILVA, Mary E.	. . . .	(WA)	1138
PLATAU, Gerard O.	. . . .	(OH)	977

Agricultural information abstracting
Bibliography, abstracting, indexing
Biomedical indexing & abstracting
Brief bank indexing & abstracting
Cataloging, abstracting & indexing
Chemical abstracts searching
Daily news abstracting
Editing & abstracting
Index & abstract technical reports
Indexing, abstracting & editing
Indexing, abstracting & retrieval
Indexing, abstracting & thesaurus bldg
Indexing & abstracting

ASIS, Moises	. . . .	(CUB)	36
FALK, Joyce D.	. . . .	(CA)	362
JOHNSON, Hilary C.	. . .	(DE)	605
FRANKS, Janice	. . . . . .	(AL)	398
CAN, Hung V.	. . . .	(PQ)	177
BOLEK, Ann D.	. . . .	(OH)	112
LEVINTON, Juliette	. . . .	(NY)	721
TAKACS, Sharon N.	. . . .	(IL)	1220
CIBULSKIS, Elizabeth R.	.	(IL)	214
DOUVILLE, Judith A.	. . .	(CT)	314
JOHNSON, David K.	. . . .	(NJ)	603
SUIDAN, Randa H.	. . . .	(IL)	1207
KACZOROWSKI, Monice M.	. . . .	(CA)	621
WHITBY, Thomas J.	. . . .	(CO)	1330
JOY, Patricia L.	. . . .	(CT)	618
SENKUS, Linda J.	. . . . .	(CT)	1115
DEARNBARGER, Dennis	. .	(DC)	284
PICCIANO, Laura	. . . . . .	(DC)	970
MISRA, Jayasri T.	. . . . .	(GA)	847
BEATTY, William K.	. . . .	(IL)	70
DAVIS, Richard A.	. . . . .	(IL)	280
HURD, Albert E.	. . . .	(IL)	577
KIENE, Andrea L.	. . . . . .	(IL)	647
KOWITZ, Aletha A.	. . . .	(IL)	674
PERTELL, Grace M.	. . . .	(IL)	961
STEVENSON, Katherine .	(IL)	1191
EISENMANN, Laura M.	.	(MA)	341
GIBSON, Sarah S.	. . . . .	(MA)	432
KING, Laurie L.	. . . .	(MA)	651
SCHWARTZ, Candy S.	. .	(MA)	1104
KNICKERBOCKER, Wendy	. . . .	(MD)	664
SAGAR, Mary B.	. . . . . .	(MI)	1074
VAN ALLEN, Neil K.	. . . .	(MI)	1271

ABSTRACTING (Cont'd)

Indexing & abstracting

JOB, Rose A.	(MO)	601
FERRIGNO, Helen F.	(NH)	373
AMRON, Irving	(NJ)	20
CONLEY, Gail D.	(NJ)	236
ESKA, Dorothy I.	(NJ)	354
GLADSTONE, Mark A.	(NJ)	439
THIRD, Bettie J.	(NJ)	1235
ASTIFIDIS, Maria	(NY)	37
BELLI, Frank G.	(NY)	78
BRENNER, Everett H.	(NY)	133
FRIED, Suzanne C.	(NY)	403
GAMAL, Sandra H.	(NY)	416
GREENGRASS, Alan R.	(NY)	464
HOLMES, Harvey L.	(NY)	553
ISGANITIS, Jamie C.	(NY)	585
LEWICKY, George I.	(NY)	722
LIPETZ, Ben A.	(NY)	732
MATTA, Seoud M.	(NY)	785
MEAGHER, Anne E.	(NY)	819
POLAND, Jean A.	(OK)	980
LARSON, Signe E.	(OR)	700
CUTRONA, Cheryl	(PA)	268
PILKINGTON, James P.	(TN)	973
BAGHAL-KAR, Vali E.	(TX)	45
GRACY, David B.	(TX)	455
JACKSON, Eugene B.	(TX)	587
JACKSON, Ruth L.	(TX)	588
SCHLESSINGER, Bernard S.	(TX)	1094
SELWYN, Laurie	(TX)	1114
WILLIAMS, Suzi	(TX)	1346
RODRIGUEZ, Robert D.	(VA)	1048
DYKSTRA, Mary E.	(NS)	331
BOJIN, Minda A.	(ON)	111
SCHABAS, Ann H.	(ON)	1088
DUMONT, Monique	(PQ)	325
GOODELL, Paulette M.	(AUS)	448
HUEMER, Christina G.	(ITL)	570

Indexing & abstracting analysis	TAN, Elizabeth L.	(IL)	1222
Japanese technl literature abstracting	FOWELLS, Fumi T.	(MI)	393
Journal abstracting	PANGALLO, Karen L.	(MA)	938
Legislative abstracting	OVERTON, Kathryn R.	(DC)	931
Medical abstracting & indexing	CARVER, Mary	(NY)	191
Monthly abstracting services	RUBINSTEIN, Ed	(NY)	1065
Music literature abstracting	HOLMES, John H.	(PA)	553
Online abstracting	HORNE, Ernest L.	(MI)	560
Online database searching & abstracting	HOYT, Henry M.	(NY)	566
Patent abstracting	CIERZNIEWSKI, Robert J.	(MI)	214
Periodicals, abstracting & indexing	RICHARD, Marie F.	(PQ)	1028
Reviews & abstracts articles	GABBIANELLI, Patrice A.	(NJ)	411
Selecting & abstracting articles	HASSAN, Abe H.	(CA)	511
Technical indexing & abstracting	WILLS, Luella G.	(VA)	1349
Training, abstracting & indexing	AUSTON, Ione	(VA)	40
Video cataloging, indexing & abstracting	LOFTHOUSE, Patricia A.	(IL)	737

ACADEMIC (See also Campus, College, University)

Academic administration	KLATT, Melvin J.	(IL)	658
	ORAM, Robert W.	(TX)	925
Academic & research libraries	DAIN, Phyllis	(NJ)	270
Academic & research libraries book sales	SCHRIFT, Leonard B.	(NY)	1100
Academic & special lib administration	BOWDEN, Philip L.	(IL)	120
Academic & special library management	PHINNEY, Hartley K.	(CO)	969
Academic archives	SWEENEY, Shelley T.	(SK)	1215
Academic bibliographic instruction	ENGLE, Michael O.	(OR)	349
Academic branch libraries	SEAL, Robert A.	(TX)	1109
Academic competition	CORNWELL, Linda L.	(IN)	247
Academic computing	CLINE, Nancy M.	(PA)	222
Academic databases	KAHN, Martin F.	(NY)	622
Academic departmental libraries	DARLING, John B.	(NC)	275
Academic information systems	JENKIN, Michael A.	(FL)	596
	WILSON, Marjorie P.	(MD)	1352
Academic, junior & senior highs	COLLINS, Judith A.	(CA)	232

ACADEMIC (Cont'd)

Academic librarian status	KELLOGG, Rebecca B.	(AZ)	637
	HOSEL, Harold V.	(CA)	561
Academic librarianship	KELLOGG, Rebecca B.	(AZ)	637
	WEISS, William B.	(CA)	1320
	UYEHARA, Harry Y.	(GU)	1270
	WHITELEY, Sandra M.	(IL)	1333
	CLARK, Georgia A.	(MI)	217
	REELING, Patricia G.	(NJ)	1016
	VASSALLO, Paul	(NM)	1279
	HELLING, James T.	(OH)	524
	BELL, Carole R.	(RI)	76
	VOCINO, Michael C.	(RI)	1286
	WILKINSON, Eoin H.	(AUS)	1340
Academic librarianship, administration	POLLARD, Frances M.	(IL)	981
Academic librarianship & administration	DE PEW, John N.	(FL)	293
Academic librarianship & reference	SINGH, Swarn L.	(KS)	1143
Academic libraries	HERON, David W.	(CA)	532
	STEVENS, Frank A.	(DC)	1190
	BRYNTESON, Susan	(DE)	152
	ALLISON, Anne M.	(FL)	17
	DALLMAN, Glenn R.	(FL)	270
	GOGGIN, Margaret K.	(FL)	444
	DAVIS, Maryellen K.	(IL)	280
	FORREST, Charles G.	(IL)	390
	SINEATH, Timothy W.	(KY)	1143
	PATTERSON, Charles D.	(LA)	948
	BENENFELD, Alan R.	(MA)	80
	MONSMA, Marvin E.	(MI)	855
	CARROLL, C E.	(MO)	187
	PATRICK, Ruth J.	(MT)	947
	HOLLEY, Edward G.	(NC)	551
	MORAN, Barbara B.	(NC)	862
	FREAUF, Louis E.	(NE)	399
	DAVIS, Hiram L.	(NM)	279
	CURLEY, Elmer F.	(NV)	265
	BOBINSKI, George S.	(NY)	108
	LANG, Jovian P.	(NY)	695
	BUTTLAR, Lois J.	(OH)	167
	LEE, Sul H.	(OK)	711
	CROWE, Virginia M.	(PA)	261
	TOWNLEY, Charles T.	(PA)	1253
	MUNOZ-SOLA, Haydee	(PR)	879
	THOMPSON, Annie F.	(PR)	1239
	PEMBERTON, J M.	(TN)	956
	MARCHANT, Maurice P.	(UT)	768
	DENDY, Adele S.	(VA)	291
	KELLY, Ardie L.	(VA)	637
	ROTHSTEIN, Samuel	(BC)	1060
	MCCALLUM, David L.	(ON)	793
Academic libraries administration	KATZ, Ruth M.	(NC)	630
Academic libraries consulting	MCDONOUGH, Kathleen C.	(NH)	803
Academic libraries planning	QUERY, Lance D.	(IL)	999
Academic library	WALTER, Maria	(NY)	1300
	PIERCE, Miriam D.	(PA)	971
Academic library administration	GIBBS, Robert C.	(AL)	431
	BRIL, Patricia L.	(CA)	136
	GALLOWAY, R D.	(CA)	415
	MIRSKY, Phyllis S.	(CA)	847
	SESSIONS, Judith A.	(CA)	1117
	TRUJILLO, Roberto G.	(CA)	1259
	BREIVIK, Patricia S.	(CO)	132
	LANDRUM, Margaret C.	(CO)	693
	GUNN, Thomas H.	(FL)	477
	MCNEAL, Archie L.	(FL)	816
	RODGERS, Frank	(FL)	1047
	BEARD, Charles E.	(GA)	69
	GRISHAM, Frank P.	(GA)	471
	HUNTER, Julie V.	(GA)	576
	PETERSON, Fred M.	(IL)	963
	WELCH, Theodore F.	(IL)	1321
	MOBLEY, Emily R.	(IN)	851
	KIRK, Thomas G.	(KY)	654
	WILSON, William G.	(MD)	1353
	GOLUB, Andrew J.	(ME)	447
	PARKS, George R.	(ME)	943
	CHURCHWELL, Charles	(MI)	213
	CORY, Kenneth A.	(MI)	248

ACADEMIC (Cont'd)

Academic library administration
	FRANKIE, Suzanne O.	(MI)	397
	MONSMA, Marvin E.	(MI)	855
	WIEMERS, Eugene L.	(MI)	1336
	DELZELL, Robert F.	(MO)	290
	GOVAN, James F.	(NC)	454
	HEWITT, Joe A.	(NC)	535
	PARK, Leland M.	(NC)	941
	RODNEY, Mae L.	(NC)	1048
	DU BOIS, Paul Z.	(NJ)	322
	HODGE, Patricia A.	(NJ)	546
	YUEH, Norma N.	(NJ)	1384
	CLUNE, John R.	(NY)	223
	MOORE, Jane R.	(NY)	859
	ESHELMAN, William R.	(OH)	354
	MADAUS, J R.	(OK)	758
	JOSEY, E J.	(PA)	618
	MUNDAY, Robert S.	(PA)	878
	WALSH, Carolyn C.	(PA)	1299
	HUNT, Donald R.	(TN)	575
	STOWERS, Joel A.	(TN)	1199
	CARGILL, Jennifer S.	(TX)	181
	DAHLSTROM, Joe F.	(TX)	269
	SPEARS, Norman L.	(TX)	1172
	HASKELL, John D.	(VA)	510
	THOMAS, Lawrence E.	(WA)	1237
	AMAN, Mohammed M.	(WI)	19
	BRUNDIN, Robert E.	(AB)	150
	BULAONG, Grace F.	(ON)	156
	HOFFMANN, Ellen J.	(ON)	548
	KATZ, Bernard M.	(ON)	630
	HAMMERLY, Hernan D.	(ARG)	493
	SIBAI, Mohamed M.	(SDA)	1134

Academic library admin & management
| VEANER, Allen B. | (ON) | 1280 |

Academic library & media administration
| PARKS, Gary D. | (MO) | 943 |

Academic library book jobber
| NAGEL, Lawrence D. | (CA) | 886 |

Academic library budgeting & planning
| SMITH, Gordon W. | (CA) | 1155 |

Academic library building planning
ELLSWORTH, Ralph E.	(CO)	345
MCDONALD, John P.	(CT)	802
GALVIN, Hoyt R.	(NC)	415
PARK, Leland M.	(NC)	941
ROUSE, Roscoe	(OK)	1061
SIEGMANN, Starla C.	(WI)	1136

Academic library buildings
MIRSKY, Phyllis S.	(CA)	847
KASER, David	(IN)	628
PARKS, George R.	(ME)	943
ENGELKE, Hans	(MI)	349
CLEMMER, Joel G.	(MN)	221
ESHELMAN, William R.	(OH)	354

Academic library collection development
| MURRAY, Lucia M. | (OR) | 882 |

Academic library construction
| RICHARDS, James H. | (NM) | 1028 |

Academic library cooperation
| LEMKE, Darrell H. | (DC) | 715 |

Academic library evaluation
| NEUHOFE, M D. | (FL) | 897 |
| WILLIAMS-JENKINS, Barbara J. | (SC) | 1347 |

Academic library experience
| CALHOUN, Margie B. | (AL) | 172 |

Academic library jobbers & acquisitions
| BERKNER, Dimity S. | (NY) | 87 |

Academic library management
RENEKER, Maxine H.	(AZ)	1023
HOSEL, Harold V.	(CA)	561
KOYAMA, Janice T.	(CA)	674
WEBER, David C.	(CA)	1314
MCDONALD, John P.	(CT)	802
LEE, Hwa W.	(OH)	710
WATSON, Tom G.	(TN)	1310
JENNERICH, Elaine Z.	(VA)	598
SWEETLAND, James H.	(WI)	1215
FRANCIS, Derek R.	(BC)	396
BONNELLY, Claude	(PQ)	114

Academic library organization
| RICHARDS, James H. | (NM) | 1028 |

Academic library public services
HOSEL, Harold V.	(CA)	561
DAVID, Indra M.	(MI)	276
CRANE, John G.	(NH)	255

Academic library reference
| NELSON, Michael L. | (WY) | 894 |

Academic library reference service
| WEIMER, Sally W. | (CA) | 1317 |

ACADEMIC (Cont'd)

Academic library reference services	GREENE, Cathy C.	(MA)	463
Academic library relations	KOYAMA, Janice T.	(CA)	674
Academic library reorganization	SZILASSY, Sandor	(NJ)	1218
Academic library standards	KANIA, Antoinette M.	(NY)	625
	BORCHUCK, Fred P.	(TN)	116
Academic library system	MOSBORG, Stella F.	(IL)	870
Academic library system administration	SMITH, Gordon W.	(CA)	1155
Academic periodical department	KEIST, Sandra H.	(NM)	635
Academic public service	ADELMAN, Jean S.	(PA)	6
Academic reference	ROBAR, Terri J.	(FL)	1038
	LAUDERDALE, Diane S.	(IL)	702
	VOGEL, Jane G.	(NC)	1286
	BUDGE, William D.	(NY)	155
	EISENBERG, Phyllis B.	(VA)	340
	OLIVETTI, L J.	(VA)	921
Academic reference services	LEHMAN, Douglas K.	(FL)	712
Academic reference work	BOPP, Richard E.	(IL)	116
Academic, research, & special libraries	YASSA, Lucie M.	(CA)	1378
Academic research libraries	STEINKE, Cynthia A.	(MN)	1186
Academic science & technology reference	COHEN, Jackson B.	(NY)	228
Academic science librarianship	WANAT, Camille A.	(CA)	1302
Academic science libraries	YOCUM, Patricia B.	(MI)	1380
Academic science library design	STANKUS, Tony	(MA)	1180
Academic staff professional development	WHEELER, Helen R.	(CA)	1329
Academic status	HOBBINS, Alan J.	(PQ)	545
Administration, academic libraries	BRENNAN, Terrence F.	(NE)	133
Administration of small academic libs	LANCASTER, Edith E.	(ID)	691
Administrative academic libraries	STEPHENS, Jerry W.	(AL)	1188
Building planning, academic libraries	DORR, Ralze W.	(KY)	313
Formula funding of academic libraries	SMITH, Gordon W.	(CA)	1155
Friends of academic libraries	ORAM, Robert W.	(TX)	925
General academic reference	OPPENHEIM, Michael R.	(CA)	925
International profsnl & academic publshg	SMITH, Richard A.	(CA)	1159
Library administration, academic library	QUICK, Richard C.	(NY)	999
Management in academic libraries	LEONHARDT, Thomas W.	(CA)	717
Medical & academic collection devlpmnt	INGRAHAM-SWETS, Leonoor	(OR)	582
Professional conditions of academic libs	VINE, Rita F.	(AB)	1285
Public & private academic libraries	EASTERLY, Ambrose	(TN)	333
Records management in academia	SCHULTZ, Charles R.	(TX)	1101
Reference & instruction academic support	VERNON, Christie D.	(VA)	1283
Role of academic librarians	EKLAND, Patricia A.	(BC)	341
School & academic administration	SPENCER, Albert F.	(GA)	1173
Small academic building design	LUCAS, Linda L.	(CA)	746
Small academic library management	DALY, Simeon	(IN)	271
Steady-state academic libraries	SAVAGE, Daniel A.	(ON)	1085
Teaching academic library services	TRYON, Jonathan S.	(RI)	1259
Upgrading foreign academic libraries	SIEMENS, Bessie M.	(MEX)	1136
West European academic monographs	JAGER, Conradus	(MA)	591

ACADEMY

| Academy Awards research | STOCKSTILL, Patrick E. | (CA) | 1195 |

ACADIAN

| Bibliographies of Acadian works | POTVIN, Claude | (NB) | 987 |

ACCESS (See also Barriers, OPAC, PAC)

Access	PICCIANO, Jacqueline L.	(NY)	970
Access policies	POSTAR, Adeen J.	(DC)	986
Access review & coordination	GRAF, Thomas H.	(DC)	456
Access review databases	GRAF, Thomas H.	(DC)	456
Access services	LEVIN, Marc A.	(CA)	720
	WILSON, Karen A.	(CA)	1351
	MOODY, Marilyn K.	(IA)	857
	HICKLING, Jeanne	(IN)	536
	REIMER, Sylvia D.	(KS)	1021

ACCESS (Cont'd)
Access services

	MORNER, Claudia J. . . .	(MA)	865
	PALO, Eric E.	(NC)	937
	METZ, Ray E.	(NY)	828
	TOYAMA, Ryoko	(NY)	1253
	RADER, Joe C.	(TN)	1002
	BRADT, Elizabeth J.	(WA)	126
Access to information	WEBRECK, Susan J. . . .	(PA)	1314
Bibliographic & information access	DEL CERVO, Diane M. . .	(CT)	289
Bibliographic searching & access	MARTIN, Noelene P. . . .	(PA)	777
Cable television public access	PEARSON, Roger L. . . .	(IL)	953
Circulation, access services	EDWARDS, Dana S. . . .	(IL)	337
Collection access & networks	JOHNSON, Carolynn K. .	(WA)	603
Computers & public access	HERMAN, Felicia G.	(CT)	531
End-user access	LEVY, Louise R.	(NJ)	721
Government information access	JOHNSON, Veronica A. .	(MI)	609
Government publications, access to info	WHITAKER, Constance C.	(OH)	1329
Handicapped access to libraries	SMITH, Ann M.	(MA)	1152
Health sciences literature access	FLEMMING, Tom	(ON)	384
Information access	RUBY, Carmela M.	(CA)	1065
Information access & reference	LARY, Marilyn S.	(GA)	700
Information access instruction	GROVER, Iva S.	(WA)	474
Job access for handicapped	SOMERS, Betty J.	(NY)	1166
Legal access litigation	WELCH, Steven J.	(IL)	1321
Management of access services	DEVLIN, Margaret K. . . .	(PA)	297
Microcomputer public access centers	LARSON, Teresa B.	(IA)	700
Microcomputers & public access	RAPPAPORT, Susan E. . .	(NY)	1008
Non-print acquisition & access	KRANZ, Ralph	(UT)	676
Online database access	LOGAN, Elisabeth L.	(FL)	737
Online public access catalogs	BISOM, Diane B.	(CA)	99
	DRIVER, Linda A.	(CA)	320
	GLASSMAN, Penny L. . .	(MA)	440
	STERLING, Judith K. . . .	(MD)	1189
	FABIAN, William M.	(MO)	360
	HOWE, Ernest A.	(AB)	565
Online subject access interfaces	BATES, Marcia J.	(CA)	64
Prisoner's access law	WARNER, Marnie M. . . .	(MA)	1305
Privacy & access policies	NASH, Cherie A.	(UT)	888
Public access & local cable	BARNETT, Donald E. . . .	(OR)	57
Public access catalogs	SHAPTON, Gregory B. . .	(CA)	1122
Public access computers	MCCOY, Judy I.	(TX)	799
	BLUME, Scott	(WA)	107
Public access law	WARNER, Marnie M. . . .	(MA)	1305
Public access microcomputer services	BROWN, Janis F.	(CA)	144
Public access microcomputers	MUDD, Isabelle G.	(AK)	875
	LEWIS, Jean R.	(AZ)	723
	HARRIS, Roger L.	(CA)	506
	FORREST, Charles G. . .	(IL)	390
	MILLS, Elaine L.	(KS)	844
	UPPGARD, Jeannine . . .	(MA)	1269
	MCCANN, Susan F.	(NH)	794
	POLLY, Jean A.	(NY)	981
	RIVERA, Gregorio	(NY)	1037
	HOFFACKER, Antoinette C.	(PA)	547
	PIELE, Linda J.	(WI)	971
Public access online catalogs	PHENIX, Katharine J. . . .	(LA)	967
Public access to information	HALLINAN, Patricia R. . .	(NY)	489
Public access to law	DUNN, Mary B.	(NY)	327
Public circulation & access services	DREW, Wilfred E.	(NY)	319
Public microcomputer access	SMITH, Valerie M.	(OH)	1161
Public services & access	STROUP, Elizabeth F. . .	(DC)	1203
Reference & access	PROSSER, Judy A.	(CO)	995
	JACOBS, Richard A. . . .	(DC)	590
	RUSH, James S.	(DC)	1068
	WALLER, M C.	(KY)	1298
	CREW, Roger T.	(VA)	258
Regulatory information access	MCRAE, Alexander D. . .	(MD)	818
Remote access online catalogs	KALIN, Sarah G.	(PA)	623
Subject access	COLLANTES, Lourdes Y.	(NY)	232
	MANDEL, Carol A.	(NY)	764
	WALKER, M G.	(NY)	1296
	LYTLE, Richard H.	(PA)	753
	MICCO, Helen M.	(PA)	831
Subject access to ethnomusicology	SCHUURSMA, Ann B. . .	(NET)	1103
Subject access to information	COLLINS, William P. . . .	(ISR)	233
Telecommunications access	WRIGHT, Bernell	(NY)	1370
Videotaping for public access	ASHFORD, Richard K. . .	(MD)	36

ACCESSIONS

Accessions	ZEAGER, Lloyd	(PA)	1387
	TISSING, Robert W.	(TX)	1247
Appraisal & accessioning	WALLER, M C.	(KY)	1298
Cataloging accessioned material	RHEAUME, Irene M. . . .	(MD)	1025
Cataloging & accessions	WEISS, Susan	(FL)	1320
Processing accessioned material	RHEAUME, Irene M. . . .	(MD)	1025
Records accessioning & processing	SCOTT, Paul R.	(TX)	1108

ACCIDENTS (See also Safety)

Accident prevention research	BISSON, Jacques	(PQ)	100
Transportation accidents	BARTH, Nancy L.	(CA)	61

ACCOUNTING (See also Allocations, Auditing, Budget, Cost, Expenditure, Fund, Invoice, Payable)

Account management	BROWN, Sandra S.	(IN)	147
Account support	FOUSER, Jane G.	(IL)	393
Accounting	HEIDKA, Patricia L.	(IL)	521
	LEE, Lynda M.	(LA)	710
	FISHER, Jean K.	(MA)	381
	HATFIELD, Philip A.	(MA)	511
	SCANLAN, Jean M.	(MA)	1087
	KILBERG, Jacqueline L. .	(NY)	648
	MCMURRAY, Sallylou . .	(OH)	815
	CARTELLI, Alessandra J.	(PA)	188
	PLEFKA, Cathleen S. . .	(PA)	978
	PENDRAK, Eileen	(TX)	956
Accounting & audit reference	MCDEVITT-PARKS, Kathryn B.	(CA)	802
Accounting & auditing	SHEERAN, Carole A. . . .	(DC)	1125
Accounting & auditing literature	DOSER, Virginia A.	(CA)	313
Accounting & auditing research	VEASLEY, Mignon M. . . .	(CA)	1280
	EMERSON, Beth A.	(TX)	347
Accounting & business	BEHAR, Evelyn W.	(NY)	74
Accounting & business bibliography	NELOMS, Karen H.	(NY)	893
Accounting & management consulting	WONG, Mabel K.	(IL)	1363
Accounting & statistics	RZECZKOWSKI, Eugene M.	(DC)	1072
Accounting & tax	BLAIR, William W.	(PA)	103
Accounting & tax research	KLOPPER, Susan M. . . .	(GA)	662
	HAYWARD, Sheila S. . . .	(MA)	517
	SNAY, Sylvia A.	(MI)	1162
Accounting & taxation	TICE, Kathleen A.	(CA)	1244
Accounting & taxation research	FROST, Roxanna	(WA)	406
Accounting, auditing & taxation ref	HETZLER, Jill K.	(WA)	534
Accounting auditing reference	SWANTEK, Kathleen M. .	(IL)	1214
Accounting, budgeting	LLOYD, H R.	(PA)	735
Accounting databases	ROSENFELD, Lillian E. . .	(NY)	1056
Accounting firm libraries	MURRAY, Marilyn R. . . .	(IL)	882
Accounting libraries	KOENDERINCK, Myrla J.	(AB)	668
Accounting reference	HENEKS, Julia A.	(DC)	528
	FLEISHMAN, Lauren Z. .	(NY)	384
	DUPUIS, Marcel	(PQ)	327
Accounting research	GROFT, Mary L.	(IL)	471
	DINGLEY, Doris A.	(MN)	305
	ROSENBERGER, Constance G.	(PA)	1056
	HOPKINS, Terry F.	(TX)	558
	SMITH, Kraleen S.	(TX)	1156
Accounting, tax research	STEPHENS, Stefanie N. .	(AZ)	1188
Accounts	TRIMINGHAM, Robert . .	(CA)	1256
Auditing, accounting	MCCALLUM, Anita J. . . .	(ON)	793
Budget & accounts payable	VOIT, Irene E.	(NV)	1287
Business, finance & accounting databases	KILBERG, Jacqueline L. .	(NY)	648
Business, industry, accounting info	WELLS, Nancy E.	(ON)	1322
Chartered accounting	PORTER, David E.	(ON)	984
Cost accounting	REDRICK, Miriam J.	(NJ)	1014
Develop & design accounting systems	CHRISTIANSON, Ellory J.	(MN)	212
Fund accounting systems	FRIEDMAN, Barbara S. .	(NY)	403
Grant accounting systems	FRIEDMAN, Barbara S. .	(NY)	403
Legal & accounting library services	SMOTHERS, Alyce A. . .	(LA)	1162
Legal & accounting reference	ROESCH, Gay E.	(CO)	1049
Library accounting	ANDERSON, Karen T. . .	(IL)	23
Management accounting	REDRICK, Miriam J.	(NJ)	1014
Management & cost accounting	FRANKLIN, Brinley R. . . .	(DC)	397
Professional reference accounting pubns	HALPIN, Gerard B.	(ON)	490

ACCOUNTING (Cont'd)
Receivable & payable accounts	CHAPP, Debra R.	(IL)	202
Tax & accounting reference	BLUM, Linda C.	(CA)	107
Tax & accounting research	WHITTLESEY, Jane M. . .	(TX)	1334
Trademarks, banking, accounting services	FLEMING, Jack C.	(ON)	384

ACCREDITATION
Accreditation	ELINOR, Yungmeyer . . .	(IL)	342
	FORTIER, Jan M.	(MA)	391
	JARAMILLO, Juana S. . .	(PR)	594
	DOVE, Herbert P.	(SC)	314
Accreditation & program evaluation	MITCHELL, Joan M.	(PA)	849
College & school accreditation	FITZPATRICK, Kelly . . .	(MD)	383
Evaluation & accreditation	GORCHELS, Clarence C.	(OR)	451
Library accreditation	WROTENBERY, Carl R. .	(TX)	1373
Library accreditation committees	JOHNSON, Jean L.	(MA)	606
Library school accreditation	FRANKIE, Suzanne O. . .	(MI)	397
	GREENE, Richard L.	(PQ)	464

ACID
Acid rain	STOSS, Frederick W. . . .	(NY)	1198

ACQUISITIONS (See also Approval, Buying, Continuations, Exchange, Gifts, Orders, Procurement, Purchasing)
Academic library jobbers & acquisitions	BERKNER, Dimity S. . . .	(NY)	87
Acquisition	ATKINSON, Calberta O. .	(AL)	38
	RAFAEL, Ruth K.	(CA)	1003
	CARROON, Robert G. . .	(CT)	187
	CLARY, Ann R.	(DC)	219
	TRIPP-MELBY, Pamela .	(DC)	1257
	SHAW, Craig S.	(IA)	1123
	TIMMER, Julia B.	(IN)	1246
	ADAMS, Deborah L.	(MI)	4
	SOPER, Marley H.	(MI)	1168
	TUCKWOOD, Jo A.	(MO)	1262
	RUCKMAN, Stanley N. . .	(NM)	1065
	DOBRZYNSKI, Terenita .	(NY)	307
	KOUO, Lily W.	(NY)	673
	GLAUS, Roberta I.	(TN)	440
	HARRISON, Karen M. . .	(TX)	507
	NOLAN, Edward W.	(WA)	907
Acquisition & cataloging serials	CHANG, Min M.	(CA)	200
Acquisition & evaluation of rare records	WAXMAN, Jack	(FL)	1311
Acquisition & maintenance	DATUS, Marie B.	(NE)	275
Acquisition & organization	FILIATRAULT, Andre Y. .	(PQ)	376
Acquisition, cataloging of record col	MECHTENBERG, Paul . .	(IL)	820
Acquisition development	CHANIN, Leah F.	(GA)	201
Acquisition non-print media	SPEIRS, Gilmary	(PA)	1172
Acquisition of Americana	MCCORISON, Marcus A.	(MA)	798
Acquisition of eductnl motion pictures	CHAVES, Francisco M. . .	(FL)	204
Acquisition of library materials	BRADFORD, Daniel	(DC)	125
Acquisition of manuscripts	HODSON, Sara S.	(CA)	546
	GORDON, Robert S.	(ON)	451
Acquisition of materials on Japan	MAKINO, Yasuko	(IL)	762
Acquisition of motion pictures & videos	TALIT, Lynn	(CT)	1221
Acquisition of rare books	BUFF, Iva M.	(NY)	155
Acquisition reference technical service	WIENER, Sylvia B.	(NY)	1336
Acquisition services	MURDEN, Steven H. . . .	(VA)	879
Acquisition systems	FAUST, Mary H.	(IN)	366
Acquisitions	NICOLSON, Mary C. . . .	(AK)	903
	STEPHENS, Dennis J. . .	(AK)	1187
	BATTISTELLA, Maureen S.	(AL)	65
	DUNMIRE, Raymond V. .	(AL)	326
	NELSON, Barbara K. . . .	(AL)	893
	O'NEAL, Kenneth W. . . .	(AL)	924
	PRUITT, Paul M.	(AL)	996
	SMITH, Julia L.	(AL)	1156
	ALSMEYER, Henry L. . . .	(AR)	18
	BLAND, Janet A.	(AR)	103
	DUDEK, Robert J.	(AR)	323
	HAMBY, Tracy A.	(AR)	491

ACQUISITIONS (Cont'd)
Acquisitions			
	PIERSON, Betty	(AR)	972
	PITTS, Cynthia F.	(AR)	976
	FAHY, Terry W.	(AZ)	361
	WOLFSON, Catherine L.	(AZ)	1361
	ALIPRAND, Joan M. . . .	(CA)	13
	ALLABACK, Patricia G. .	(CA)	13
	ALLISON, Terry L.	(CA)	17
	ANDERSON, David C. . .	(CA)	22
	ASAWA, Edward E.	(CA)	35
	ASHLEY, Elizabeth	(CA)	36
	BRISCOE, Georgia K. . . .	(CA)	136
	CATER, Judy J.	(CA)	194
	CELLE, Deborah A.	(CA)	196
	CLINE, Cheryl L.	(CA)	222
	CRANFORD, Theodore N.	(CA)	255
	DAVIS, Charles E.	(CA)	278
	DUNKEL, Lisa M.	(CA)	326
	EARHART, Marilyn N. . .	(CA)	332
	ELDREDGE, Mary	(CA)	342
	FRANCISCO, Marylynn .	(CA)	396
	FREUDENBERGER, Elsie L.	(CA)	402
	GATES, Jane P.	(CA)	421
	GIBSON, Harold R.	(CA)	432
	HALBROOK, Anne M. . .	(CA)	485
	HARDIN, Betty N.	(CA)	500
	HEATHER, Joleen	(CA)	519
	HELFER, Doris S.	(CA)	523
	HERDMAN, Elena	(CA)	530
	HUFF-DUFF, Barbara . . .	(CA)	570
	KRAMER, Helen A.	(CA)	675
	KRIKORIAN, Rosanne . .	(CA)	678
	LEONHARDT, Thomas W.	(CA)	717
	LUKE, Keye L.	(CA)	747
	MANKE, Merrill E.	(CA)	765
	MARCUS, Sharon F. . . .	(CA)	769
	MILLS, Denise Y.	(CA)	844
	MOKRZYCKI, Karen M. .	(CA)	852
	MOORE, Evia B.	(CA)	859
	MORRIS, George H.	(CA)	866
	MULE, Gabriel	(CA)	876
	OKA, Susan Y.	(CA)	919
	REILLY, James H.	(CA)	1020
	SONIN, Hille	(CA)	1167
	VRATNY-WATTS, Janet M.	(CA)	1289
	WHITE, Kathleen M.	(CA)	1331
	WICKEY, Marjorie J. . . .	(CA)	1335
	WILSON, Marilyn J.	(CA)	1352
	CHERVENAK, Joseph F.	(CO)	206
	HOFFMAN, Ann M.	(CO)	547
	CARNEGLIA, Anna L. . .	(CT)	183
	ICHINOSE, Mitsuko	(CT)	581
	LAWRENCE, Carol A. . .	(CT)	704
	LYNCH, M W.	(CT)	751
	ROSS, Carole L.	(CT)	1058
	SHORE, Julia M.	(CT)	1132
	STUEHRENBERG, Paul F.	(CT)	1205
	WARZALA, Martin L. . . .	(CT)	1307
	ALBIN, Michael W.	(DC)	10
	BAILEY, Marian C.	(DC)	46
	BAUMGARDNER, Sandra A.	(DC)	66
	BRIDGE, Peter H.	(DC)	135
	CHAPMAN, Susan E. . . .	(DC)	202
	CUMMING, Leighton H. .	(DC)	264
	ERICSON, Richard J. . . .	(DC)	353
	FALK, Diane M.	(DC)	362
	FILSTRUP, E C.	(DC)	377
	HANFORD, Sally	(DC)	495
	HOLLYFIELD, Diane S. .	(DC)	552
	KAHLER, Mary E.	(DC)	622
	LEWIS, Robert J.	(DC)	724
	MARSHALL, David L. . . .	(DC)	774
	MAYHEW, Eileen G.	(DC)	790
	MORRIS, Timothy J.	(DC)	867
	NEFF, William B.	(DC)	892
	PLETZKE, Linda	(DC)	978

ACQUISITIONS (Cont'd)
Acquisitions

ACQUISITIONS (Cont'd)
Acquisitions

PUGH, Thurman A.	(DC)	997
RAFFERTY, Eve	(DC)	1003
RANDOLPH, Susan E.	(DC)	1007
RILEY, Eileen V.	(DC)	1034
RUSHING, Naomi J.	(DC)	1068
SMITH, Mary P.	(DC)	1158
STACEY, Kathleen M.	(DC)	1177
SULLIVAN, Robert C.	(DC)	1208
UNVER, Amira V.	(DC)	1269
WITHERELL, Julian W.	(DC)	1358
ARMSTRONG, Ruth C.	(FL)	32
BOGGUS, Tamara K.	(FL)	110
COHN, William L.	(FL)	229
CUBBERLEY, Carol W.	(FL)	263
FAIRBANKS, Deborah M.	(FL)	361
FELTZ, Carol	(FL)	370
FROSCHER, Jean L.	(FL)	406
HOMEYARD, Marjorie A.	(FL)	555
JOHNSON, Betty D.	(FL)	602
MALANCHUK, Iona R.	(FL)	762
MIRANDA, Salvador	(FL)	847
ORSER, Frank W.	(FL)	927
PRATT, Darnell D.	(FL)	990
SNYDER, Jean	(FL)	1165
STEINBERG, Celia L.	(FL)	1185
WILLETT, Charles	(FL)	1341
BAKER, Barry B.	(GA)	47
HOWARD, Rachel L.	(GA)	564
JOBSON, Betty S.	(GA)	601
JOHNSON, Jane G.	(GA)	605
OVERBECK, James A.	(GA)	931
PAULK, Betty D.	(GA)	950
SOMERS, Sally W.	(GA)	1167
SWANSON, Joe	(GA)	1213
HASSLER, William B.	(HI)	511
HERRICK, Kenneth R.	(HI)	532
POLANSKY, Patricia A.	(HI)	980
ERTL, Mary R.	(IA)	353
MARSHALL, Jessica A.	(IA)	774
SNIDER, Jacqueline I.	(IA)	1163
SORENSON, Debra J.	(IA)	1168
THEOBALD, Joanice	(IA)	1234
WIESE, Glenda C.	(IA)	1337
FORD, Karin E.	(ID)	389
OSTRANDER, Gloria J.	(ID)	929
TATE, Karen E.	(ID)	1225
WILLIAMS, Brenda M.	(ID)	1342
BRADY, Mary M.	(IL)	127
CARPENTER, Kathryn H.	(IL)	185
COOPER, Susan C.	(IL)	243
HANKES, Janice R.	(IL)	496
HASSERT, Rita M.	(IL)	511
HITCHCOCK, Gail A.	(IL)	544
HOLLI, Melvin G.	(IL)	552
HOPKINS, Jane L.	(IL)	558
JOHNSON, Judith M.	(IL)	606
KARSTEN, Eileen S.	(IL)	628
KLEIN, Richard S.	(IL)	659
LIBBEY, Maurice C.	(IL)	725
LIMAYE, Asha A.	(IL)	727
LINDGREN, Beverly P.	(IL)	729
MADAY, Geraldine	(IL)	758
MANSFIELD, Fred	(IL)	767
MOUW, James R.	(IL)	874
MULLER, Karen	(IL)	877
MURRAY, Theresa A.	(IL)	882
PORCELLA, Brewster	(IL)	984
ROBERTSON, S D.	(IL)	1042
SACHS, Iris P.	(IL)	1073
SCHMIDT, Karen A.	(IL)	1095
BALDWIN, James A.	(IN)	51
CORYA, William L.	(IN)	248
FAUST, Mary H.	(IN)	366
FRANCQ, Carole	(IN)	396
GALE, Sarah E.	(IN)	413
HUFFORD, Gordon L.	(IN)	571
KUDRYK, Oleg	(IN)	682
MAXWELL, Jan C.	(IN)	788
MCGINNIS, Mildred M.	(IN)	806
MILLS, Richard E.	(IN)	844
READ, Glenn F.	(IN)	1012
SANDSTROM, Pamela E.	(IN)	1081
SCHOCH, Marjorie R.	(IN)	1098
ZEUGNER, Lorenzo A.	(IN)	1387
COOKE, Bette L.	(KS)	241
HANNE, Anna R.	(KS)	497
HATCHER, Marihelen	(KS)	511
MADSEN, Debora L.	(KS)	759
SNYDER, Fritz	(KS)	1164
TANNER, Jane E.	(KS)	1223
BARKSDALE, Milton K.	(KY)	57
CULPEPPER, Jetta C.	(KY)	264
HAWLEY, Mary B.	(KY)	514
MAZUK, Melody	(KY)	791
NILES, Judith F.	(KY)	904
PRITCHARD, Elsie T.	(KY)	994
SELMER, Sylvia A.	(KY)	1114
SEXTON, Ebba J.	(KY)	1118
WOOD, Linda H.	(KY)	1364
CUMLET, Harolyn S.	(LA)	264
GERICKE, Paul W.	(LA)	428
KERN, Elizabeth	(LA)	643
PATTERSON, Trudy J.	(LA)	948
REID, Marion T.	(LA)	1019
STANDEFER, Steven R.	(LA)	1179
ALCORN, Cynthia W.	(MA)	11
BARNHART, Arlene C.	(MA)	58
BELANGER, Janet B.	(MA)	75
BELLO, Susan E.	(MA)	78
BROW, Ellen H.	(MA)	141
CIANFARINI, Margaret	(MA)	214
DI BONA, Leslie F.	(MA)	299
DUFFEK, Elizabeth A.	(MA)	323
GAUDET, Dodie E.	(MA)	422
HALE, Janice L.	(MA)	485
HARDY, Eileen D.	(MA)	500
HILL, Barbara M.	(MA)	539
JUDD, Eleanor M.	(MA)	618
KIRK, Darcy	(MA)	654
KRIER, Mary M.	(MA)	678
MCLAUGHLIN, Lee R.	(MA)	813
MOREN, Harold M.	(MA)	863
NORMAN-CAMP, Melody	(MA)	909
PROUTY, Sharman E.	(MA)	996
RESSMEYER, Ellen H.	(MA)	1024
ROTMAN, Laurie D.	(MA)	1060
SAUER, David A.	(MA)	1084
VAN BEEK, Susan	(MA)	1272
VIDMANIS, Visvaldis E.	(MA)	1283
WALKER, Mary M.	(MA)	1296
WALSH, James E.	(MA)	1299
WELLS, Susan C.	(MA)	1323
BINAU, Myra I.	(MD)	97
BRADLEY, Wanda L.	(MD)	126
COLE, Anna B.	(MD)	230
DENNEY, Christine A.	(MD)	292
DOWD, Frank B.	(MD)	315
EUSTACE, Susan J.	(MD)	356
KINZER, Kathryn	(MD)	653
KUNZ, Margarett N.	(MD)	684
LAFFREY, Laurel W.	(MD)	687
MASON, Pamela R.	(MD)	781
MEYER, William P.	(MD)	830
PETTERSON, Marjorie M.	(MD)	965
PHILLIPS, Lena M.	(MD)	968
POTTER, Andrea K.	(MD)	987
PRATT, Laura C.	(MD)	990
RICE, Rosamond H.	(MD)	1027
STEINHOFF, Cynthia K.	(MD)	1186
THOMAS, Sarah E.	(MD)	1238
CASSERLY, Mary F.	(ME)	193
STANTON, Linda J.	(ME)	1181
APPS, Michelle L.	(MI)	30
CAMMENGA, Cheryl G.	(MI)	175
CARLSON, Susan L.	(MI)	182
CARSON, Claudia A.	(MI)	188

ACQUISITIONS (Cont'd)
Acquisitions

CRAWFORD, Geraldine H. (MI) 256
DOMBROWSKI, Mark A. (MI) 310
FORD, Stephen W. (MI) 390
KNOCH, Daniel L. (MI) 665
MARTIN, Rose M. (MI) 778
PONOMARENKO, Ella (MI) 982
RACZ, Twyla M. (MI) 1001
SANFORD, John D. (MI) 1081
SATTERTHWAITE, Diane A. (MI) 1084
THOMAS, David H. (MI) 1236
VOELZ, Laura D. (MI) 1286
WHEATON, Julie A. (MI) 1328
ANGUS, Jacqueline A. (MN) 28
GALLIGAN, Sara A. (MN) 414
NILES, Ann A. (MN) 904
OLSON, Carol A. (MN) 922
OSTAZEWSKI, Theodore (MN) 928
VAN HORN, Virginia A. (MN) 1275
WENTE, Norman G. (MN) 1324
AYLWARD, Judith A. (MO) 43
BOETTCHER, Joel W. (MO) 110
NODLER, Charles E. (MO) 906
NORTH, Daniel L. (MO) 909
VERBECK, Alison F. (MO) 1282
WINJUM, Roberta J. (MO) 1355
JOHNSON, Max C. (MS) 607
MCMILLAN, Carnette R. (MS) 815
PAYNE, David L. (MS) 951
ROGERS, Margaret N. (MS) 1049
WILLIS, Jan L. (MS) 1348
BEKKEN, Helen L. (MT) 75
GRASMICK, Brenda (MT) 458
ABBOTT, Dorothy D. (NC) 1
CHENG, Chao S. (NC) 206
FARKAS, Doina C. (NC) 364
HOLMES, Elizabeth A. (NC) 553
HUNT, Margaret R. (NC) 575
KAN, Irene E. (NC) 624
MCCONNELL, Judith J. (NC) 797
MEEHAN-BLACK, Elizabeth C. (NC) 821
PARKER, Lanny C. (NC) 942
POWELL, Lucy A. (NC) 988
RICHMOND, Alice S. (NC) 1030
TOMLINSON, Charles E. (NC) 1250
BOONE, Jon A. (ND) 115
VYZRALEK, Dolores E. (ND) 1290
FAWCETT, Georgene E. (NE) 367
HENDRICKSON, Kent H. (NE) 527
JOHNSON, Judy L. (NE) 606
REIDELBACH, John H. (NE) 1019
VAN BAUCOM, Charles (NE) 1272
DUCHIN, Douglas (NH) 322
GEISEL, Ann M. (NH) 425
JACKSON, Patience K. (NH) 588
LANDAU, Cynthia R. (NH) 692
STEARNS, Melissa M. (NH) 1183
TATE, Joanne D. (NH) 1225
ASSENHEIMER, Judy (NJ) 37
AXEL-LUTE, Paul (NJ) 42
BENTON, Mary A. (NJ) 84
BLACK, William R. (NJ) 102
CHAO, Gloria F. (NJ) 201
CHEN, Chiou S. (NJ) 205
CIMBALA, Diane J. (NJ) 214
CONNORS, Linda E. (NJ) 238
DYKEMAN, Amy (NJ) 331
EDWARDS, Susan M. (NJ) 338
KRUSE, Theodore H. (NJ) 681
MALAKOFF, Diane L. (NJ) 762
REISLER, Reina (NJ) 1021
ROUSEK, Marie B. (NJ) 1061
STOCK, Norman (NJ) 1195
TUTTLE, Helen W. (NJ) 1265
ATKINS, Gene D. (NM) 37
KLOPFER, Jerome J. (NM) 662
LEON, Louise B. (NM) 716

SAUNDERS, Laurel B. (NM) 1084
SOHN, Jeanne G. (NM) 1165
DION, Kathleen L. (NV) 305
ABLOVE, Gayle J. (NY) 2
AXTMANN, Margaret M. (NY) 42
BEHRMANN, Christine A. (NY) 75
BOREK, Mary A. (NY) 116
BRESLIN, Ellen R. (NY) 133
BROWN, June E. (NY) 145
BUFF, Iva M. (NY) 155
BURKE, Joseph A. (NY) 160
CHICARELLA, Joseph T. (NY) 207
CHURCH, Virginia K. (NY) 213
CINQUE, Deborah G. (NY) 214
CIOPPA, Lawrence (NY) 214
COLLANTES, Lourdes Y. (NY) 232
DANSKER, Shirley E. (NY) 274
DAVIS, Deborah G. (NY) 278
DAVIS, Susan A. (NY) 281
DOWNING, Elaine L. (NY) 316
DUTIKOW, Irene V. (NY) 329
EARLY, Caroline L. (NY) 332
FEIGER, Cherie S. (NY) 368
FIEGAS, Barbara E. (NY) 375
FOSTER, Selma V. (NY) 392
FRIEDMAN, Judy B. (NY) 404
GALASSO, Nancy (NY) 412
GITNER, Fred J. (NY) 439
GORMAN, Mary B. (NY) 452
GUZMAN, Diane J. (NY) 479
HAYNES, Patricia (NY) 516
HITT, Gail D. (NY) 544
IRONS, Florence E. (NY) 584
JAY, Donald F. (NY) 595
JOHNSON, James G. (NY) 605
JUCHIMEK, Dianne M. (NY) 618
KAHN, Laura (NY) 622
KELLOGG, Marya S. (NY) 637
KELLY, Donald V. (NY) 637
KLINGLE, Philip A. (NY) 662
LEWIS, Gillian H. (NY) 723
LIDSKY, Ella (NY) 725
LOMEN, Nancy L. (NY) 738
LUBETSKI, Edith E. (NY) 745
MACK, Theodore D. (NY) 756
MARGALITH, Helen M. (NY) 770
MARKOWITZ, Lois (NY) 771
MASTRANGELO, Paul J. (NY) 783
MAYER, Mary C. (NY) 789
MILLER, Heather S. (NY) 838
MILLER, Mary F. (NY) 840
NESTA, Frederick N. (NY) 896
NICOL, Margaret W. (NY) 903
NOGA, Susan D. (NY) 907
NUZZO, David J. (NY) 912
O'HALLORAN, James V. (NY) 918
PIDGEON, Alice C. (NY) 971
PLATT, Mary L. (NY) 977
RAJEC, Elizabeth M. (NY) 1004
RAUCH, Theodore G. (NY) 1010
RESCIGNO, Dolores S. (NY) 1024
RITTER, Sally K. (NY) 1037
ROSE, Pamela M. (NY) 1055
SCHNEIDER, Helen S. (NY) 1097
SOKOLOWSKI, Denise G. (NY) 1166
TURIEL, David (NY) 1263
UCHTORFF, Barbara J. (NY) 1267
VAN RIPER, Joy C. (NY) 1277
WEINSTEIN, Ellen B. (NY) 1318
WOOTEN, Jean A. (NY) 1368
ARTZ, Theodora S. (OH) 35
CARPENTER, Eric J. (OH) 184
ESBIN, Martha P. (OH) 354
FRENCH, Thomas R. (OH) 402
FROMMEYER, L R. (OH) 405
JACOBSON, Susan D. (OH) 590
JUNEJA, Derry C. (OH) 620
KOVACIC, Mark E. (OH) 673

ACQUISITIONS (Cont'd)
Acquisitions

ACQUISITIONS (Cont'd)
Acquisitions

KRITZER, Hyman W. . . . (OH) 679
MALUCHNIK, Kathryn K. (OH) 764
MCCOY, Betty J. . . . . . . (OH) 799
MCCROSKY, Janet E. . . (OH) 800
MOORE, Maxwell J. . . . . (OH) 860
SEDLCOK, Barbara J. . . (OH) 1111
SWINEHART, Katharine J. (OH) 1216
TRAMDACK, Philip J. . . . (OH) 1254
COULTER, Cynthia M. . . (OK) 251
DOBBERTEEN, Sara J. . (OK) 307
PARHAM, Kay B. . . . . . . (OK) 940
ROYSTER, Peggy K. . . . (OK) 1063
BENSON, Mary M. . . . . . (OR) 83
BROWN, Patricia L. . . . . (OR) 146
BURNS, Carol J. . . . . . . (OR) 162
DUNN, Carolyn A. . . . . . (OR) 326
PETERSON, Karen L. . . . (OR) 964
SCHENCK, William Z. . . (OR) 1091
SHAW, Elizabeth L. . . . . (OR) 1123
SOOHOO, Terry A. . . . . (OR) 1167
AL SADAT, Amira A. . . . (PA) 17
ARMISTEAD, Henry T. . . (PA) 32
BENYO, John C. . . . . . . (PA) 84
BRADLEY, James S. . . . (PA) 126
BRAUTIGAM, David K. . . (PA) 130
CARINO, Leopoldo C. . . (PA) 181
CHAMBERLAIN, Carol E. (PA) 197
DRAGOTTA, Linda L. . . . (PA) 318
FISHER, Kim N. . . . . . . (PA) 381
GRIFFITHS, June B. . . . . (PA) 469
HARRISON, Susan B. . . (PA) 507
HODGE, Margaret T. . . . (PA) 546
JARVIS, William E. . . . . (PA) 595
JENKS, George M. . . . . (PA) 597
KEISER, Barbara J. . . . . (PA) 635
KOKOLUS, Cait C. . . . . . (PA) 669
KREDEL, Stephen F. . . . (PA) 677
LINKE, Erika C. . . . . . . (PA) 731
MADER, Marion C. . . . . (PA) 759
OGBURN, Joyce L. . . . . (PA) 918
PHALAN, Mary A. . . . . . (PA) 967
RATHBONE, Marjorie A. . (PA) 1009
RICE, Patricia O. . . . . . . (PA) 1027
RICHARDS, Barbara G. . (PA) 1028
RITTER, Ralph E. . . . . . . (PA) 1037
ROBINSON, Agnes F. . . (PA) 1043
SHAPERA, Gladys S. . . . (PA) 1121
SNELGROVE, Pamela S. (PA) 1163
TUCKER, Cornelia A. . . . (PA) 1261
AYALA-ORTIZ, Orietta . . (PR) 42
TORRES-TAPI, Manual A. (PR) 1251
DESMARAIS, Norman P. (RI) 295
DEVIN, Robin B. . . . . . . (RI) 297
LISTOVITCH, Denise A. . (RI) 733
MARSH, Corrie V. . . . . . (RI) 773
DENNIS, Everett J. . . . . . (SC) 292
ELLIS, Janet L. . . . . (SC) 344
JOHNSON, Steven D. . . (SC) 609
PUKL, Joseph M. . . . . . . (SC) 997
STRAUCH, Katina P. . . . (SC) 1200
WASHINGTON, Nancy H. (SC) 1307
MYERS, Nancy L. . . . . . (SD) 884
ABOUSHAMA, Mary F. . (TN) 2
BASKETT, D A. . . . . (TN) 63
BEHRENS, Elizabeth A. . (TN) 75
BULL, Margaret J. . . . . . (TN) 156
DENTON, Ann L. . . . . . . (TN) 293
HUDSON, Earline H. . . . . (TN) 569
HUGGINS, Annelle R. . . . (TN) 571
LEISERSON, Annabelle . (TN) 714
MABBOTT, Deborah D. . (TN) 753
NICOL, Jessie T. . . . . . . (TN) 902
PERRY, Glenda L. . . . . . (TN) 960
SCOTT, Margaret W. . . . (TN) 1107
ALESSI, Dana L. . . . . . . (TX) 11
BAKER, Linda L. . . . . . . (TX) 49
BLAYLOCK, James C. . . (TX) 105
BREWSTER, Olive N. . . . (TX) 134

ACQUISITIONS (Cont'd)
Acquisitions

BROOKS, Ruth H. . . . . . (TX) 140
CARGILL, Jennifer S. . . . (TX) 181
CLEMENTS, Cynthia L. . (TX) 221
COPELAND, David R. . . (TX) 244
CRENSHAW, Jan C. . . . (TX) 258
CRINION, Jacquelyn A. . (TX) 259
DEWBERRY, Betty B. . . (TX) 298
DUNCAN, Lucy E. . . . . . (TX) 325
FACKLER, Naomi P. . . . (TX) 360
HARLOW, Sally S. . . . . . (TX) 502
HILLMAN, Kathy R. . . . . (TX) 541
JACKSON, Marian D. . . . (TX) 588
JOITY, Donna M. . . . . . . (TX) 610
KELLEY, Carol M. . . . . . (TX) 636
KERLEY, Izoro D. . . . . . . (TX) 643
KHADER, Majed J. . . . . (TX) 645
KIM, David U. . . . . (TX) 648
LANGA, Patricia A. . . . . (TX) 695
LUECKENHOFF, Anne F. (TX) 747
LUTZ, Linda A. . . . . (TX) 750
MAGRILL, Rose M. . . . . (TX) 760
MASON, Timothy D. . . . . (TX) 781
MILLER, Rea R. . . . . (TX) 841
MURPHY, Kristine L. . . . (TX) 881
MURPHY, Pency G. . . . . (TX) 881
MURRAY, Kathleen R. . . (TX) 882
MURRAY, Margaret A. . . (TX) 882
NISONGER, Thomas E. . (TX) 905
PARKER, David F. . . . . . (TX) 941
PARTON, William A. . . . (TX) 945
RAMSEY, Donna E. . . . . (TX) 1005
SAULSBURY, Margie M. (TX) 1084
SEAMAN, Helen D. . . . . (TX) 1109
STRICKLAND, Jimmy R. (TX) 1202
WILSON, Craig A. . . . . . (TX) 1350
WORLEY, Larry J. . . . . . (TX) 1369
GELDMACHER, Bonnie R. (UT) 425
HAGGERTY, Maxine R. . (UT) 483
NELSON, Veneese C. . . (UT) 895
BURGESS, Edwin B. . . . (VA) 159
COMPARIN, Ida . . . . (VA) 235
COOK, Charlaine C. . . . . (VA) 239
COSGROVE-DAVIES, Lisa
A. . . . . (VA) 248
EGERTSON, Yvonne L. . (VA) 339
FINCH, Mildred E. . . . . . (VA) 377
FOX, Barbara S. . . . . . . (VA) 394
GRANT, Juanita G. . . . . (VA) 458
HASKELL, Mary B. . . . . . (VA) 510
KAWAGUCHI, Miyako . . (VA) 632
LAINE, Rebecca R. . . . . (VA) 688
LINN, Cynthia S. . . . . . . (VA) 731
MCCLAIN, Deborah C. . . (VA) 795
MCLAUGHLIN, Elaine C. (VA) 813
MILLER, Nancy M. . . . . . (VA) 841
MONK, Joanne . . . . (VA) 855
TATUM, George M. . . . . (VA) 1225
TEAL, Erika U. . . . . (VA) 1229
ULBRICH, David E. . . . . (VA) 1268
WEEKS, Linda F. . . . . . . (VA) 1315
WHITE, Ardeen L. . . . . . (VA) 1330
THOMPSON, Judith H. . . (VT) 1240
BEN-SIMON, Julie E. . . . (WA) 83
FEATHERS, John E. . . . . (WA) 367
MCBRIDE, Anne . . . . . . (WA) 792
MURRAY, James M. . . . (WA) 882
PACKER, Donna E. . . . . (WA) 933
STEVENS, Peter H. . . . . (WA) 1190
STRONG, Sunny A. . . . . (WA) 1203
CRAWFORD, Josephine . (WI) 256
DELAUCHE, Jean E. . . . (WI) 289
DEWEY, Gene L. . . . . . . (WI) 298
HOUKOM, Susan L. . . . . (WI) 563
JONES, Richard E. . . . . . (WI) 614
MEERDINK, Richard E. . (WI) 821
MILLER, Julia E. . . . . . . (WI) 839
POPESCU, Constantin C. (WI) 983
SCOFIELD, Constance V. (WI) 1106

ACQUISITIONS (Cont'd)

Acquisitions

	LANGER, Frank A.	(WV)	695
	LYLE, Heather A.	(WV)	751
	POWELL, Ruth A.	(WV)	988
	SCOTT, John E.	(WV)	1107
	THACKER, Timothy M.	(WV)	1233
	STEWART, William L.	(WY)	1193
	ALLISON, Scott	(AB)	17
	FELL, Anthony M.	(AB)	370
	HOBBS, Brian	(AB)	545
	ROONEY, Sieglinde E.	(AB)	1053
	STARR, Jane E.	(AB)	1182
	ZIEGLER, Fred	(AB)	1388
	BENSON, Theodore L.	(MB)	83
	BLANCHARD, Jim	(MB)	103
	LINCOLN, Robert S.	(MB)	728
	REID, Marion I.	(MB)	1019
	LEBLANC, Amedee	(NB)	708
	TIFFANY, William C.	(NF)	1244
	ALBURGER, Thomas P.	(ON)	11
	GARLOCK, Gayle N.	(ON)	419
	JARVIS, A W.	(ON)	595
	KAVANAGH, Susan E.	(ON)	631
	LAWLESS, Ruthmary G.	(ON)	704
	LUTZ, Linda J.	(ON)	750
	MCCUBBIN, George M.	(ON)	800
	PORTEUS, Andrew C.	(ON)	985
	RAY, Cathy J.	(ON)	1011
	SEBANC, Mark F.	(ON)	1110
	URQUHART, Dawn M.	(ON)	1270
	WILSON, Valerie E.	(ON)	1353
	AUGER, Claudette	(PQ)	39
	BERARDINUCCI, Heather R.	(PQ)	84
	BOUDREAU, Gerald E.	(PQ)	118
	DAUNAIS, Marie J.	(PQ)	275
	HOBBINS, Alan J.	(PQ)	545
	LESSARD, Josee	(PQ)	718
	FU, Ting W.	(HKG)	407
	ALI, Farooq M.	(SDA)	13
Acquisitions & bibliographic control	LINDGREN, Arla M.	(NY)	729
Acquisitions & budget	JARABEK, Leona T.	(OH)	594
Acquisitions & budgeting	CHANG, Min M.	(CA)	200
	PARISI, Judith A.	(CT)	940
Acquisitions & cataloging	LAPOLT, Margaret B.	(CT)	697
	LOOMIS, Barbara	(IL)	740
	SADLER, Shirley L.	(IL)	1073
	BROWN, Sandra S.	(IN)	147
	LUNG, Chan S.	(NY)	748
	TASNADI, Deborah L.	(WI)	1224
Acquisitions & collection development	POTTER, William G.	(AZ)	987
	WINTER, Eugenia B.	(CA)	1356
	KASCUS, Marie A.	(CT)	628
	WOLFE, Susan J.	(DC)	1361
	DANNECKER, Joyce H.	(FL)	274
	LOCKE, John W.	(IL)	736
	SOTO, Donna G.	(LA)	1169
	TATELMAN, Susan D.	(MA)	1225
	BEARSS, Daniel H.	(MD)	69
	TURKOS, Joseph A.	(MD)	1263
	ARNDT, Arleen	(MI)	33
	IRVING, Ophelia M.	(NC)	584
	JARRELL, James R.	(NC)	594
	GRABE, Lauralee F.	(NE)	455
	MCADOO, Jannifer C.	(NJ)	792
	THORSON, Connie C.	(NM)	1242
	BIDDEN, Julia E.	(NY)	94
	DESSER, Darrilyn	(NY)	296
	DEUTSCH, Karen A.	(NY)	296
	O'BRIEN, Elmer J.	(OH)	914
	GRILIKHES, Sandra B.	(PA)	470
	RIEKE, Judith L.	(TN)	1033
	CARROLL, Dewey E.	(TX)	187
	HOLLOWAY, Geraldine B.	(TX)	552
	DIERCKS, Thelma C.	(VA)	302
	KALABUS, Robert L.	(WY)	622
	ENGLESAKIS, Marina F.	(AB)	350
	SNYDER, Lisa A.	(MAL)	1165
Acquisitions & collection management	KNAUFF, Elisabeth S.	(DC)	663

ACQUISITIONS (Cont'd)

Acquisitions & editing	BATES, Barbara S.	(PA)	63
Acquisitions & information retrieval	MOORE, Virginia B.	(DC)	861
Acquisitions & interlibrary loan	TERRY, Susan N.	(DC)	1232
	RUST, Roxy J.	(SC)	1070
Acquisitions & lesson plans	JORDAN, Sharon L.	(WA)	617
Acquisitions & materials processing	LESNIK, Pauline	(NY)	718
Acquisitions & product development	YANNOTTA, Peter J.	(NJ)	1377
Acquisitions & serials	TAYLOR, Patricia A.	(AZ)	1228
	PETRY, Robyn E.	(IL)	965
Acquisitions & serials automation	MCCALLISTER, Myrna J.	(ME)	793
Acquisitions & serials technical srvs	KARASICK, Alice W.	(CA)	627
Acquisitions, archival & law field	SHEPARD, E L.	(VA)	1126
Acquisitions automation	LOWELL, Gerald R.	(CT)	744
	PRESLEY, Roger L.	(GA)	991
	CHAMBERLAIN, Carol E.	(PA)	197
Acquisitions bibliography	PINES, Doralynn	(NY)	974
Acquisitions, books & serials	MIRANDA, Cecilia	(TX)	847
Acquisitions, bks, records, music scores	SILVER, Martin A.	(CA)	1138
Acquisitions cataloging	OLMSTEAD, Nancy L.	(CA)	921
	MIRANDA, Esmeralda C.	(MN)	847
	SULLIVAN, Stephen W.	(NY)	1208
Acquisitions, cataloging, circulation	TODD, Hal W.	(FL)	1248
Acquisitions, children's materials	CORLEE, Lisa	(OK)	246
Acquisitions, circulation, print media	GOODWYN, Betty R.	(AL)	450
Acquisitions, collection building	CADLE, Dean	(NC)	170
Acquisitions, collection development	WALSH, Lynn R.	(FL)	1299
	CHANG, Robert H.	(TX)	201
	UMBERGER, Sheila S.	(VA)	1268
Acquisitions department management	LEBEL, Clement	(PQ)	707
Acquisitions, gifts & exchanges	EASTERLY, Ambrose	(TN)	333
Acquisitions, including Third World	HENN, Barbara J.	(IN)	528
Acquisitions, interlibrary loan	NEILL, Sharon E.	(ON)	892
Acquisitions management	GREGORY, Joan A.	(AZ)	466
Acquisitions, monographic & audiovisual	WILLIAMS, Charles M.	(IL)	1342
Acquisitions, monographic & serials	BENNETT, Lee L.	(IL)	82
Acquisitions, monographs & serials	WACHEL, Kathleen B.	(IA)	1290
Acquisitions, monographs, serials	BARKER, Joseph W.	(CA)	56
Acquisitions of books & serials	WARD, Dorothy S.	(AL)	1303
Acquisitions of information companies	KEON, Edward F.	(NJ)	643
Acquisitions of legal materials	STOPPEL, Ellen K.	(IA)	1198
Acquisitions of materials	ZULA, Floyd M.	(LA)	1391
Acquisitions of monographic notes	MAGLADRY, George C.	(CA)	759
Acquisitions on microcomputer	MILLS, Elaine L.	(KS)	844
Acquisitions, physical sciences	MERRYMAN, Margaret M.	(VA)	827
Acqs, processing print, non-print	FRENCH, Janet D.	(PA)	402
Acquisitions, serials	TAYLOR, Trish A.	(AZ)	1229
	MERRITT, Betty A.	(CA)	827
Acquisitions, serials & proceedings	LEFEBVRE, Veronica A.	(MD)	712
Acquisitions, serials maintenance	PICQUET, D C.	(TN)	971
Acquisitions software development	LAREW, Christian K.	(NJ)	697
Acquisitions specialization	MACDONALD, Wayne D.	(MA)	754
Acquisitions systems	SALGAT, Anne M.	(PA)	1076
Acquisitions, technical services	BATTAGLIA, Bonnie J.	(CA)	64
	MORGAN, Linda M.	(CA)	864
	COFFEY, James R.	(NJ)	227
Acquisitions work	CAHALANE, Edmond P.	(DC)	171
Acquisitions, young adult materials	CORLEE, Lisa	(OK)	246
Administration & acquisitions	KAPNICK, Laura B.	(NY)	626
	FU, Paul S.	(OH)	407
	RAVE, David A.	(SD)	1010
Archival acquisition projects	MORRISSEY, Charles T.	(VT)	869
Archives acquisition	SUMNERS, Bill F.	(TN)	1209
Art books acquisitions	RICE, Ralph A.	(TX)	1027
Art history acquisition	CICCONE, Amy N.	(VA)	214
Asian materials acquisition	CHAN, Moses C.	(NC)	199
Audiovisual acquisition	WILCOX, Carolyn G.	(CT)	1338
Audiovisual cataloging & acquisitions	SPIEGELMAN, Barbara M.	(PA)	1174
Audiovisual librarianship & acquisitions	EARL, Susan R.	(NC)	332
Automated acquisitions	FRYMIRE, Jane K.	(MN)	407
Automated acquisitions control	DE LUISE, Alexandra	(PQ)	290
Automated acquisitions systems	BARKER, Joseph W.	(CA)	56
	TRIMINGHAM, Robert	(CA)	1256
	KAPOOR, Jagdish C.	(NH)	626
	HUDSON, Gary A.	(SD)	569
Automated serials & acquisitions	ROYLE, Maryanne	(IL)	1063
Automation of serials & acquisitions	WAN, William W.	(TX)	1302

ACQUISITIONS (Cont'd)

Biomedical data acquisitions	PEETERS, Marc D.	(BEL)	954
Book acquisition	KRAMER, William J.	(DC)	675
	PATTERSON, Anne S.	(MD)	948
Book acquisitions	FARKAS, Charles R.	(NY)	364
	JOHNSON, Joan E.	(PA)	606
	LASATER, Mary C.	(TN)	700
Book & journal acquisitions	GREGORY, Melissa R.	(IL)	466
Book selection & acquisition	LANGEVIN, Ann T.	(NV)	695
	GRAY, Patricia B.	(VA)	460
	MEHRAD, Jafar	(IRN)	821
Book selection & acquisitions	HARRINGTON, Charles W.	(LA)	504
Books & serials acquisitions	OSIER, Donald V.	(SDA)	928
Business resrch, acquisitions, & instrc	CAMERON, Constance B.	(RI)	174
Cataloging & acquisition	PHILLIPS, Patricia A.	(TN)	968
	FUN, Winnie W.	(VA)	409
Cataloging & acquisitions	HAYES, Linda J.	(CA)	516
	CHAPMAN, Elwynda K.	(DC)	202
	ELDER, Richard H.	(MD)	342
	LIU, David T.	(TX)	734
	RIEPMA, Helen J.	(TX)	1033
	PARKER, Charles G.	(PQ)	941
Children's srvs, teaching, acquisitions	BACHAND, Alice J.	(KS)	43
Circulation & acquisitions	ROSS, Theodosia B.	(GA)	1059
Collection development, acquisitions	LEICH, Harold M.	(DC)	713
Collection development & acquisition	DILUCIA, Samuel J.	(HI)	303
Collection development & acquisitioning	HAYES, Bonaventure F.	(NY)	515
Collection development & acquisitions	WILSON, Jacqueline B.	(CA)	1351
	MEIKAMP, Kathie D.	(DC)	822
	NICHTER, Alan	(FL)	902
	TERNAK, Armand T.	(FL)	1232
	COVER, Teresa A.	(MN)	252
	MASON, Michael L.	(NJ)	781
	GILLESPIE, Gerald V.	(NY)	435
	KASPAR, Eileen	(NY)	629
	BLOMQUIST, Laura G.	(OH)	106
	HOLLOWAY, Johnna H.	(VA)	552
	KRAEHE, Mary A.	(VA)	674
Complete book acquisition service	ABRAMOFF, Lawrence J.	(MA)	3
Computer applications to acquisitions	DELONG, Douglas A.	(IL)	290
Computerized acquisitions	BOYCE, Harold W.	(IN)	122
Corporate acquisitions	HYLAND, Barbara	(ON)	580
Current book acquisitions	DE LUISE, Alexandra	(PQ)	290
Database searching & acquisitions	HERMAN, Marsha	(NY)	531
Document acquisitions	STEVENS, Marjorie	(MI)	1190
Documentation acquisition	ARROWOOD, Nina R.	(NJ)	35
Economics & finance acquisitions	MAYNARD, Elizabeth	(OH)	790
Economics & psychological acquisitions	RICHARDSON, Linda B.	(VA)	1029
Federal acquisition regulations	SMITH, David A.	(VA)	1153
Film & video acquisition	HUGHES, Rolanda L.	(IN)	572
	HAYNES, Jean	(NY)	516
Foreign language acquisitions	MCELWAIN, William	(IL)	804
Foreign law book acquisition	KREH, Fritz	(WGR)	677
Foreign title acquisitions	SIEVERS, Arlene M.	(IN)	1136
Foreign-language acquisitions	BELL, Irena L.	(ON)	77
Gift acquisitions	COOMBS, Elisabeth G.	(CT)	241
Gift & exchange acquisitions	DECKER, Leola M.	(MD)	286
Government documents acquisitions	MARSHALL, Marion B.	(DC)	774
Government library material acquisitions	BLACKBURN, Clayton E.	(NY)	102
Health sciences acquisitions	GRIMES, Maxyne M.	(FL)	470
Humanities acquisition	HOWARD-HILL, Trevor	(SC)	564
Information acquisition & analysis	CARSON, Bonnie L.	(MO)	188
Information & material acquisitions	CARPENTER, Dale	(NY)	184
Info services, acq diversification	REEDY, Martha J.	(MA)	1015
Journal acquisitions	PRITCHARD, Robert W.	(MA)	994
Knowledge acquisition for expert systems	MUSEN, Mark A.	(CA)	883
Latin American acquisitions	MAKUCH, Andrew L.	(AZ)	762
Latin American materials acquisitions	BALLANTYNE, Lygia M.	(FL)	53
Law acquisitions	GARCIA, Mary E.	(CA)	417
Law book acquisitions	WALSH, Sharon T.	(PA)	1300
Law firm acquisitions	SNYDER, Elizabeth A.	(ENG)	1164
Law library acquisitions	EICHER, Thomas E.	(IA)	339

ACQUISITIONS (Cont'd)

Library acquisitions	MONTGOMERY, John W.	(CA)	856
	SORGENFREI, Robert K.	(CA)	1168
	FLYNN, Kathleen M.	(MA)	386
	EAGLEN, Audrey B.	(OH)	331
Library acquisitions & development	JONSON, Laurence F.	(IA)	616
Library acquisitions & library budgeting	KELLY, Glen J.	(ON)	637
Lib material, acquisition, preservation	KALRA, Bhupinder S.	(IL)	623
Library materials acquisition	SHABOWICH, Stanley A.	(TX)	1118
Library systems & acquisitions	BREWER, Joseph	(NY)	134
Manufacturing technology acquisition	STEVENS, Michael	(IL)	1190
Manuscript acquisitions	MCCULLOH, Judith M.	(IL)	801
Manuscripts & publications acquisitions	VIOL, Robert W.	(OH)	1285
Map acquisitions	GALNEDER, Mary H.	(WI)	415
Materials acquisition	FELDER, Jimmie R.	(AL)	369
	KAUFENBERG, Jane M.	(MN)	630
	RUSSELL, Sharon A.	(NB)	1069
Media acquisitions	SCHREFFLER, Lynne W.	(PA)	1099
Medical acquisitions	WAKEFORD, Paul J.	(CA)	1293
	RENNIE, Margaret C.	(LA)	1023
Medical collection acquisitions	PHILLIPS, Donna M.	(IA)	968
Medical serials acquisitions & control	WOODBURN, Judy I.	(NC)	1366
Merger & acquisition reference	ANTONETZ, Dolores	(NY)	29
Merger & acquisition reporting	GREEN, Randall N.	(DC)	462
Mergers & acquisitions	GOLDSTEIN, Bernard	(NJ)	446
	SLUSSER, W P.	(NY)	1150
Mergers & acquisitions in publishing	BODDORF, James E.	(NY)	109
	DRONZEK, Ronald	(NY)	320
	HADLEY, J M.	(NY)	482
	HALE, Paul E.	(NY)	485
	HUNNEWELL, Walter	(NY)	574
	LAMB, David C.	(NY)	689
	SCHULTE, Anthony M.	(NY)	1101
	SHAPIRO, Marvin L.	(NY)	1121
	STEVENSON, Jeffery T.	(NY)	1191
	SUHLER, John S.	(NY)	1207
	VERONIS, John J.	(NY)	1283
Microforms acquisition & cataloging	HUGHES, Frances M.	(CT)	571
Middle grade fiction & nonfiction acqs	BUCKLEY, Virginia L.	(NY)	154
Monograph acquisitions	BILYEU, David D.	(CA)	97
	SCHUSTER, Bonnie H.	(MT)	1103
	HAMILTON, Marsha J.	(OH)	492
Monographic acquisition	ERICKSON, Lynda L.	(VA)	352
Monographic acquisitions	ORR, Margaret H.	(IA)	926
	DELONG, Douglas A.	(IL)	290
	STIFFLEAR, Allan J.	(MA)	1194
	COOK, Kay A.	(MI)	240
	JASPER, Richard P.	(MI)	595
	FLOWERS, Janet L.	(NC)	386
	STETSON, Keith R.	(NC)	1190
	RITCHIE, David G.	(NY)	1036
	D'ANDRAIA, Dana D.	(OR)	272
	HUDSON, Gary A.	(SD)	569
Monographic & serials acquisitions	PERRYMAN, Wayne R.	(TX)	961
	WAN, William W.	(TX)	1302
Monographs acquisition	MARCINKO, Dorothy K.	(AL)	769
	GEMPELER, Constance M.	(AZ)	426
Music acquisitions for college libraries	SMILEY, Marilynn J.	(NY)	1151
Music materials acquisitions	FALCONER, Joan O.	(IA)	362
Newspaper acquisition & cataloging	DANKY, James P.	(WI)	274
Non-print acquisition & access	KRANZ, Ralph	(UT)	676
NOTIS acquisitions system	GALE, Sarah E.	(IN)	413
Online acquisitions	GIBBS, Nancy J.	(AL)	431
Periodicals acquisition	RINE, Joseph L.	(MN)	1035
Periodicals acquisition & check-in	KESSINGER, Pamela C.	(IL)	644
Periodicals, acquisitions	ROBICHAUD, Marcel J.	(NY)	1042
Procurement & acquisitions	ROY, Alice R.	(VA)	1063
Product, publication acquisition	QUINLIN, Margaret M.	(MD)	1000
Purchase & acquisition	COMRAS, Rema	(FL)	235
Purchasing & acquisitions	RICHARD, Marie F.	(PQ)	1028
Rare book acquisition & cataloging	COX, Shelley M.	(IL)	253
Record acquisition & cataloging	BARGAR, Arthur W.	(CT)	56
Reference, acquisitions librarianship	ENGLAND, Ellen M.	(VA)	349
Reference & acquisitions	FENLON, Mary P.	(KS)	371
Reference, cataloging & acquisitions	KOPAN, Ellen K.	(CA)	671
Religious acquisitions	REYNOLDS, Dorsey	(PA)	1025
Science acquisitions	FLICK, Frances J.	(IA)	385

ACQUISITIONS (Cont'd)

Selection & acquisition	MISENHEIMER, Paula S.	(AR)	847
	MASTERS, Robin J.	(CA)	782
	NICHOLS, Dolores D.	(TN)	901
Selection & acquisition of library mtrls	SMITH, Cynthia A.	(OH)	1153
Selection & acquisitions	STAYNER, Delsie A.	(CA)	1183
	WILSON, Memory A.	(OH)	1352
	GILMORE, Carolyn	(PQ)	437
Selection & acquisitions of materials	MORRIS, Trisha A.	(OH)	867
Selection of acquisition materials	BIANCHI, Karen F.	(WA)	93
Serial acquisitions	WILLMERING, William J.	(MD)	1348
	SCHUSTER, Bonnie H.	(MT)	1103
Serial & monograph acquisitions	WETZBARGER, Cecilia G.	(MD)	1328
Serials acquisition	GASKINS, Betty	(KY)	421
	GELENTER, Winifred H.	(MD)	426
	LEWIS, Diane M.	(VA)	723
	DOI, Makiko	(WA)	309
Serials acquisition & cataloging	GRIFFITH, Joan C.	(NH)	469
Serials acquisition & control	KHOURY, Nancy L.	(LA)	646
Serials acquisitions	PALM, Miriam W.	(CA)	935
	LONBERGER, Jana L.	(GA)	738
	ERTL, Mary R.	(IA)	353
	BAIRD, Lynn N.	(ID)	47
	DELONG, Douglas A.	(IL)	290
	SIEVERS, Arlene M.	(IN)	1136
	WINJUM, Roberta J.	(MO)	1355
	TAYLOR, David C.	(NC)	1226
	TUTTLE, Marcia L.	(NC)	1266
	SHROUT, Sally J.	(OK)	1133
	D'ANDRAIA, Dana D.	(OR)	272
	SWEARINGEN, Wilba S.	(TX)	1214
Serials acquisitions & control	SCHWARTZ, Marla J.	(VA)	1105
Serials acquisitions & preservation	IRVIN, Judy C.	(LA)	584
Serials & acquisitions	LI, Dorothy W.	(IL)	724
Serials binding & acquisitions	GOLIAN, Linda M.	(FL)	447
Spanish language acquisitions	PETERSON, Anita R.	(CA)	962
Technical information acquisition	RICE, Gerald W.	(NH)	1027
Technical information acquisitions	MONTGOMERY, Suzanne L.	(VA)	856
Technical processing & acquisitions	BOGGESS, John J.	(MD)	110
Technical services, acquisitions	SMITH, Kathleen S.	(DC)	1156
	DOLAN, Robert T.	(IN)	309
	SANTIAGO, Maria	(PR)	1082
Technical services, acqs & cataloging	MAZZEI, Peter J.	(NJ)	791
Visual & sound material acquisition	DRIESSEN, Karen C.	(MT)	320
Worldwide scientific acquisitions	SNIDER, Elizabeth M.	(OH)	1163
Young adult books, acquisition & editing	JACKSON, Nancy D.	(NY)	588
Young adult fiction & nonfiction acqs	BUCKLEY, Virginia L.	(NY)	154

ACTING (See also Theater)

American actors & actresses	ARCHER, Stephen M.	(MO)	31
Director & actor	NIEHAUS, Barbara J.	(IL)	903
Professional acting	MYERS, Maria P.	(NY)	884

ACTUARIAL

Actuarial science research	CHAPA, Joan I.	(IL)	201

ACUPUNCTURE

Acupuncture	DIAL, Zona P.	(AZ)	299

ADLER

Adlerian psychology references	KAHN, Paul J.	(CA)	622
Complete collections of Adlerian jnls	KAHN, Paul J.	(CA)	622

ADMINISTRATION (See also Directing, Executive, Head, Leadership, Management, Organization, Supervision)

Abstracts & information services admin	PLATAU, Gerard O.	(OH)	977
Academic administration	KLATT, Melvin J.	(IL)	658
	ORAM, Robert W.	(TX)	925
Academic & special lib administration	BOWDEN, Philip L.	(IL)	120
Academic librarianship, administration	POLLARD, Frances M.	(IL)	981
Academic librarianship & administration	DE PEW, John N.	(FL)	293

ADMINISTRATION (Cont'd)

Academic libraries administration	KATZ, Ruth M.	(NC)	630
Academic library administration	GIBBS, Robert C.	(AL)	431
	BRIL, Patricia L.	(CA)	136
	GALLOWAY, R D.	(CA)	415
	MIRSKY, Phyllis S.	(CA)	847
	SESSIONS, Judith A.	(CA)	1117
	TRUJILLO, Roberto G.	(CA)	1259
	BREIVIK, Patricia S.	(CO)	132
	LANDRUM, Margaret C.	(CO)	693
	GUNN, Thomas H.	(FL)	477
	MCNEAL, Archie L.	(FL)	816
	RODGERS, Frank	(FL)	1047
	BEARD, Charles E.	(GA)	69
	GRISHAM, Frank P.	(GA)	471
	HUNTER, Julie V.	(GA)	576
	PETERSON, Fred M.	(IL)	963
	WELCH, Theodore F.	(IL)	1321
	MOBLEY, Emily R.	(IN)	851
	KIRK, Thomas G.	(KY)	654
	WILSON, William G.	(MD)	1353
	GOLUB, Andrew J.	(ME)	447
	PARKS, George R.	(ME)	943
	CHURCHWELL, Charles	(MI)	213
	CORY, Kenneth A.	(MI)	248
	FRANKIE, Suzanne O.	(MI)	397
	MONSMA, Marvin E.	(MI)	855
	WIEMERS, Eugene L.	(MI)	1336
	DELZELL, Robert F.	(MO)	290
	GOVAN, James F.	(NC)	454
	HEWITT, Joe A.	(NC)	535
	PARK, Leland M.	(NC)	941
	RODNEY, Mae L.	(NC)	1048
	DU BOIS, Paul Z.	(NJ)	322
	HODGE, Patricia A.	(NJ)	546
	YUEH, Norma N.	(NJ)	1384
	CLUNE, John R.	(NY)	223
	MOORE, Jane R.	(NY)	859
	ESHELMAN, William R.	(OH)	354
	MADAUS, J R.	(OK)	758
	JOSEY, E J.	(PA)	618
	MUNDAY, Robert S.	(PA)	878
	WALSH, Carolyn C.	(PA)	1299
	HUNT, Donald R.	(TN)	575
	STOWERS, Joel A.	(TN)	1199
	CARGILL, Jennifer S.	(TX)	181
	DAHLSTROM, Joe F.	(TX)	269
	SPEARS, Norman L.	(TX)	1172
	HASKELL, John D.	(VA)	510
	THOMAS, Lawrence E.	(WA)	1237
	AMAN, Mohammed M.	(WI)	19
	BRUNDIN, Robert E.	(AB)	150
	BULAONG, Grace F.	(ON)	156
	HOFFMANN, Ellen J.	(ON)	548
	KATZ, Bernard M.	(ON)	630
	HAMMERLY, Hernan D.	(ARG)	493
	SIBAI, Mohamed M.	(SDA)	1134
Academic library admin & management	VEANER, Allen B.	(ON)	1280
Academic library & media administration	PARKS, Gary D.	(MO)	943
Academic library system administration	SMITH, Gordon W.	(CA)	1155
Administer circulation, processing	STAINBROOK, Lynn M.	(WI)	1178
Administer law library	CONNORS, Jean M.	(OR)	238
Administering budget	ROGERS, William F.	(OH)	1050
Administering library services	BROWN, Atlanta T.	(DE)	142
Administering local history collection	CARTER, Susan M.	(IN)	190
Administering nursing book collection	DAUGHERTY, Carolyn M.	(MD)	275
Administering school library programs	JACKSON, Gloria D.	(CA)	587
Administering university archives	MATTHEW, Jeannette M.	(IN)	785
Administration	COLSON, Marcia B.	(AK)	234
	CRANE, Karen R.	(AK)	255
	JENKINS, Joyce K.	(AK)	597
	KINNEY, John M.	(AK)	653
	LESH, Nancy L.	(AK)	718
	BENHAM, Frances	(AL)	80
	CANTRELL, Clyde H.	(AL)	179
	CARTER, Selina J.	(AL)	190
	DANCE, Betty A.	(AL)	272

ADMINISTRATION (Cont'd)
Administration

HAND, Linda M.	(AL)	494
LEWIS, Timothy A.	(AL)	724
OSBURN, Charles B.	(AL)	927
RUSSELL, Lisa R.	(AL)	1069
SELLEN, Mary K.	(AL)	1114
SOUTER, Thomas A.	(AL)	1169
SPENCE, Paul H.	(AL)	1173
STEPHENS, Alice G.	(AL)	1187
ALSMEYER, Henry L.	(AR)	18
CLEVENGER, Judy B.	(AR)	221
HOUGHTON, Sally L.	(AR)	563
MILLS, Peggy	(AR)	844
VAN ARSDALE, Dennis G.	(AR)	1272
ZUMWALT, George M.	(AR)	1391
CULL, Roberta	(AZ)	263
DANIELS, Delores E.	(AZ)	273
DOHERTY, Walter E.	(AZ)	309
FRIEDMAN, Zena K.	(AZ)	404
GILSON, Myral A.	(AZ)	437
GROSSNICKLE, Jane L.	(AZ)	473
HAZLETT, Florence E.	(AZ)	517
LAIRD, W D.	(AZ)	688
REICHEL, Mary	(AZ)	1018
SCHNEIDER, Elizabeth K.	(AZ)	1097
SHACKELFORD, Eileen R.	(AZ)	1118
ANDRUS, Eloise A.	(CA)	27
BARKEY, Patrick T.	(CA)	56
BENNETT, Carson W.	(CA)	81
BERGSING, Patricia M.	(CA)	87
BIEK, David E.	(CA)	95
BOORKMAN, Jo A.	(CA)	115
BRANDT, Steven R.	(CA)	128
BRUDVIG, Glenn L.	(CA)	149
CARPIO, Virginia A.	(CA)	185
CHAN, Carl C.	(CA)	199
CLINTWORTH, William A.	(CA)	222
CONMY, Peter T.	(CA)	236
CONNOLLY, Betty F.	(CA)	237
COOPER, Richard S.	(CA)	243
DEGOOD, S K.	(CA)	288
DIENER, Margaret M.	(CA)	302
DONALDSON, Maryanne T.	(CA)	311
FRY, Stephen M.	(CA)	407
FRY, Thomas K.	(CA)	407
GATES, Jane P.	(CA)	421
GIBSON, Harold R.	(CA)	432
GILMAN, Nelson J.	(CA)	436
GOODRICH, Jeanne D.	(CA)	449
GRANGER, Dorothy J.	(CA)	457
GRIEDER, Elmer M.	(CA)	467
GUIDINGER, Delmar J.	(CA)	476
HESSEL, William H.	(CA)	534
HOUSEL, Mary B.	(CA)	563
HUCKINS, Barbara W.	(CA)	569
KELSH, Virginia J.	(CA)	639
LACHENDRO, Leonard L.	(CA)	686
LEFF, Barbara Y.	(CA)	712
LEO, Karen A.	(CA)	716
MACLEOD, June F.	(CA)	757
MARCUS, Sharon F.	(CA)	769
MAWDSLEY, Katherine F.	(CA)	787
MCQUOWN, Eloise	(CA)	817
MOKRZYCKI, Karen M.	(CA)	852
MOORE, Everett L.	(CA)	859
MORGAN, Linda M.	(CA)	864
O'BRIEN, Philip M.	(CA)	915
PAGE, Kathryn	(CA)	934
PANDOLFO, Steven P.	(CA)	937
PELLE, Catherine A.	(CA)	955
POOLE, Jay M.	(CA)	983
REVEAL, Arlene H.	(CA)	1024
SAWYER, Anne R.	(CA)	1086
SHAFFER, Dallas Y.	(CA)	1119
SHARROW, Marilyn J.	(CA)	1122
SIMON, Vaughn L.	(CA)	1141
SPINKS, Paul	(CA)	1175
TANIS, Norman E.	(CA)	1222

ADMINISTRATION (Cont'd)
Administration

THOMPSON, Don K.	(CA)	1239
THORNE, Marco G.	(CA)	1242
TROTTA, Victoria K.	(CA)	1258
VANVUREN, Darcy D.	(CA)	1277
WIGLEY, Marylou	(CA)	1337
WILLIAMS, Leonette M.	(CA)	1344
WILSON, Linda L.	(CA)	1351
WINTER, Eugenia B.	(CA)	1356
BOTHMER, A J.	(CO)	118
BRAGDON, Lynn	(CO)	127
CAMPBELL, Frances D.	(CO)	176
CONNOR, Evelyn	(CO)	238
GEHRES, Eleanor M.	(CO)	425
GOODYEAR, Mary L.	(CO)	450
JOHNSON, K S.	(CO)	606
LAZARUS, Josephine G.	(CO)	706
LEITNER, Lavonne	(CO)	714
MYERS, Sara J.	(CO)	885
NICKEL, Robbie L.	(CO)	902
ARCARI, Ralph D.	(CT)	30
BALMER, Mary	(CT)	53
BIRCH, Grace M.	(CT)	97
COHEN, Morris L.	(CT)	228
CUSTER, Deborah P.	(CT)	267
FARADAY, Joanna	(CT)	363
JACOB, William	(CT)	589
KIJANKA, Dorothy M.	(CT)	647
LAMB, Gertrude	(CT)	690
ORLOSKE, Margaret Q.	(CT)	926
PIERCE, Anne L.	(CT)	971
PORTER, Stuart T.	(CT)	985
ROGERS, Brian D.	(CT)	1049
SCHIMMEL, Louise S.	(CT)	1093
SHOLTZ, Katherine J.	(CT)	1132
STEVENS, Norman D.	(CT)	1190
WALSH, Kathryn A.	(CT)	1299
WALTER, Kenneth G.	(CT)	1300
WREGE, Ann S.	(CT)	1370
ALBIN, Michael W.	(DC)	10
BARDE, Karla I.	(DC)	56
BURNS, Dean A.	(DC)	162
BYERS, Laura T.	(DC)	168
CHILD, Margaret S.	(DC)	208
CHIN, Cecilia H.	(DC)	208
CLARY, Ann R.	(DC)	219
COCKE, Lucy S.	(DC)	226
COLETTI, Jeannette D.	(DC)	231
COOK, Marilyn M.	(DC)	240
CROSS, Dorothy A.	(DC)	260
CYLKE, Frank K.	(DC)	268
DELANCEY, James F.	(DC)	288
FIFER-CANBY, Susan M.	(DC)	376
FLYNN, Richard M.	(DC)	387
HAITH, Dorothy M.	(DC)	484
JACKSON, Elisabeth S.	(DC)	587
KALKUS, Stanley	(DC)	623
KEHOE, Patrick E.	(DC)	634
MARTIN, Kathleen S.	(DC)	777
MCDERMOTT, Patricia M.	(DC)	802
MCLEMORE, Roberta T.	(DC)	814
MUSSEHL, Allan A.	(DC)	883
OSTROVE, Geraldine E.	(DC)	929
PANZERA, Donald P.	(DC)	938
PATEL, Patricia C.	(DC)	947
RATHER, Lucia J.	(DC)	1009
ROGERS, Sharon J.	(DC)	1050
ROSENBERG, Jane A.	(DC)	1056
SCULLY, Mark F.	(DC)	1109
STANHOPE, Charles V.	(DC)	1180
STOCKTON, Sue T.	(DC)	1196
STONE, Elizabeth W.	(DC)	1197
STUBBS, Linda T.	(DC)	1204
SWEETLAND, Loraine F.	(DC)	1215
TOWELL, Jane M.	(DC)	1252
WALLACE, Michael T.	(DC)	1298
BEACH, Rose M.	(DE)	68
DANIEL, Alfred I.	(DE)	272
JAMISON, Susan C.	(DE)	593

ADMINISTRATION (Cont'd)
Administration

PUFFER, Yvonne L. . . . . (DE) 997
BURDICK, Lois B. . . . . . (FL) 158
BURROWS, Suzetta C. . (FL) 163
BUSTETTER, Stanley R. (FL) 166
COHN, William L. . . . . . . (FL) 229
COMRAS, Rema . . . . . . (FL) 235
DOWNS, Antonie B. . . . . (FL) 317
DRAKE, Grady . . . . (FL) 318
EZQUERRA, Isabel . . . . (FL) 360
FARKAS, Andrew . . . . . . (FL) 364
GLASS, Nellie L. . . . . . . (FL) 440
GRANT, George C. . . . . (FL) 458
HARKNESS, Mary L. . . . (FL) 501
HARRIS, Frank D. . . . . . (FL) 504
HENSON, Llewellyn L. . . (FL) 529
HOUCK, Catherine M. . . (FL) 562
JONES, Linda L. . . . . . . (FL) 613
LABRAKE, Orlyn B. . . . . (FL) 686
MORSE, Pat B. . . . . (FL) 869
ROSEN, Bettylou . . . . . . (FL) 1055
SCHROEDER, Edwin M. . (FL) 1100
STABLER, William H. . . . (FL) 1177
TAYLOR, Betty W. . . . . . (FL) 1226
TREYZ, Joseph H. . . . . . (FL) 1256
WILLIAMS, Thomas L. . . (FL) 1347
ALLEN, William R. . . . . . (GA) 16
BAIN, Michael L. . . . . . . (GA) 47
BAKER, Barry B. . . . . . . (GA) 47
BASLER, Thomas G. . . . (GA) 63
BROCKMEIER, Kristina C. (GA) 138
CHAMBERS, Shirley M. . (GA) 198
CLARK, Tommy A. . . . . . (GA) 218
DEES, Anthony R. . . . . . (GA) 287
FENNELL, Janice C. . . . . (GA) 371
HENDERSON, Mary E. . . (GA) 526
JOHNSON, Nancy P. . . . (GA) 608
LANDRAM, Christina L. . (GA) 693
LAWSON, A V. . . . . (GA) 705
LAZENBY, Gail R. . . . . . (GA) 706
LINKER, Rita S. . . . . (GA) 731
LUCHSINGER, Arlene E. (GA) 746
MANCINI, Donna D. . . . . (GA) 764
MC LAIN, Swan M. . . . . (GA) 813
MILLS, Robin K. . . . . (GA) 844
MORTON, Ann W. . . . . . (GA) 870
MOSLEY, Mary M. . . . . . (GA) 871
WILSON, David C. . . . . . (GA) 1350
AKAO, Pamela S. . . . . . . (HI) 9
HAAK, John R. . . . . (HI) 480
MITCHELL, Jeanette E. . (HI) 848
PLADERA, Lucretia . . . . (HI) 977
TANAKA, Momoe . . . . . . (HI) 1222
BENTZ, Dale M. . . . . (IA) 84
BLACK, William K. . . . . . (IA) 102
BROWN, Jeanine B. . . . . (IA) 144
JOHNSON, Anne C. . . . . (IA) 602
MARQUARDT, Larry D. . (IA) 772
SEGER, Robert M. . . . . . (IA) 1112
SIEBERSMA, Lois R. . . . (IA) 1135
STOPPEL, William A. . . . (IA) 1198
BOLLES, Charles A. . . . . (ID) 112
HANSEN, Ralph W. . . . . (ID) 498
AUFDENKAMP, Joann . . (IL) 39
BEAN, Janet R. . . . . (IL) 69
BOAST, Carol . . . . (IL) 108
BOWEN, Christopher F. . (IL) 120
CARY, Jan E. . . . . (IL) 191
CICHON, Marilyn T. . . . . (IL) 214
COLLINS, Janet . . . . (IL) 232
CRISPEN, Joanne . . . . . (IL) 259
CULBERTSON, Lillian D. (IL) 263
DAWOOD, Rosemary . . . (IL) 282
DELANA, Genevieve A. . (IL) 288
DEUEL, Marlene R. . . . . (IL) 296
DOYLE, Francis R. . . . . . (IL) 317
DUFF, John B. . . . . (IL) 323
FAUST, Julia B. . . . . (IL) 366
FEATHER, Pamela P. . . . (IL) 367

ADMINISTRATION (Cont'd)
Administration

FORD, Jennifer D. . . . . . (IL) 389
FOSTER, Eloise C. . . . . . (IL) 392
FRANKLIN, Annette E. . . (IL) 397
FREDERICKSEN, Grant A. (IL) 400
GASKELL, Judith A. . . . . (IL) 421
GERDES, Neil W. . . . . . . (IL) 428
GILLFILLAN, Nancy M. . (IL) 435
GRAY, Karen S. . . . . (IL) 460
GRIFFIN, Thelma J. . . . . (IL) 469
GRUMBLING, Dennis K. . (IL) 474
HALE, Charles E. . . . . . . (IL) 485
HAMILTON, Beth A. . . . . (IL) 491
HANNON, Bobbie A. . . . (IL) 497
HENRY, Nancy J. . . . . . . (IL) 529
HESSLER, Nancy R. . . . (IL) 534
HINTZ, Jeanne E. . . . . . . (IL) 543
HOPKINS, Jane L. . . . . . (IL) 558
HURD, Albert E. . . . . (IL) 577
JANSSON, John F. . . . . (IL) 594
KINGERY, Victor P. . . . . (IL) 652
KLEIN, Richard S. . . . . . (IL) 659
KNUDTSON, Gail L. . . . . (IL) 666
KUBIAK, Matthew C. . . . (IL) 682
LAMB, Sara G. . . . . (IL) 690
LAMONT, Bridget L. . . . . (IL) 691
LARSON, Carol . . . . (IL) 699
LINDGREN, William D. . . (IL) 729
LINDVALL, Robert J. . . . (IL) 730
LYNCH, Beverly P. . . . . . (IL) 751
MCGOWAN, John P. . . . (IL) 807
MOORMAN, John A. . . . (IL) 862
MORRISON, Samuel F. . (IL) 868
NAPSHA, Cheryl A. . . . . (IL) 887
NOURIE, Alan R. . . . . . . (IL) 910
NOVELLI, Jean L. . . . . . (IL) 911
OCHSNER, Renata E. . . (IL) 915
PERTELL, Grace M. . . . . (IL) 961
PETERSON, Kenneth G. . (IL) 964
PORCELLA, Brewster . . . (IL) 984
PRIOR, Janice L. . . . . . . (IL) 993
RABAI, Terezia . . . . (IL) 1001
RAYMAN, Ronald A. . . . (IL) 1011
RECKS, Dorcas E. . . . . . (IL) 1013
REID, Margaret L. . . . . . (IL) 1019
RETTIG, James R. . . . . . (IL) 1024
ROZANSKI, Barbara . . . (IL) 1064
SCOTT, Alice H. . . . . (IL) 1106
SHERMAN, Janice E. . . (IL) 1128
SHOTWELL, Richard T. . (IL) 1133
STEVENSON, Katherine . (IL) 1191
STRYCK, B C. . . . . (IL) 1203
SUGDEN, Barbara L. . . . (IL) 1206
SVENSSON, C G. . . . . . (IL) 1212
THOMPSON, Richard E. . (IL) 1241
TZE-CHUNG, Li . . . . (IL) 1267
WATSON, Robert E. . . . (IL) 1310
WICKS, Jerry R. . . . . (IL) 1335
WOZNY, Jay . . . . (IL) 1370
WRIGHT, Donald E. . . . . (IL) 1371
BAKER, Donald E. . . . . . (IN) 48
BRADLEY, Johanna . . . . (IN) 126
DAGNESE, Joseph M. . . (IN) 269
ELLIOTT, Barbara J. . . . . (IN) 343
EWICK, Charles R. . . . . (IN) 359
FISCHLER, Barbara B. . . (IN) 380
GILL, John H. . . . . (IN) 435
GNAT, Jean M. . . . . (IN) 442
HOVISH, Joseph J. . . . . (IN) 563
JOHNSON, Marjorie J. . . (IN) 607
KRULL, Jeffrey R. . . . . . (IN) 680
MCCARTNEY, Shirley R. (IN) 795
MULLINS, James L. . . . . (IN) 878
PERRY, Margaret . . . . . . (IN) 960
SANER, Eileen K. . . . . . (IN) 1081
SCHOCH, Marjorie R. . . (IN) 1098
SEDLACK, Ellen M. . . . . (IN) 1111
SHEETS, Michael T. . . . . (IN) 1125
STUSSY, Susan A. . . . . . (IN) 1205

ADMINISTRATION (Cont'd)
Administration

THOMPSON, Susan J. . . .	(IN)	1241
WOOD, Michael B.	(IN)	1364
BENNETT, Samuel J. . . .	(KS)	82
BINGHAM, James L. . . .	(KS)	97
BRADEN, Jan	(KS)	125
DOMBOURIAN MOORE, Ann	(KS)	310
EICHELBERGER, Marianne	(KS)	339
HALE, Martha L.	(KS)	485
HANNE, Anna R.	(KS)	497
MCIRVIN, Jane P.	(KS)	809
RADEMACHER, Richard J.	(KS)	1002
SCHRAG, Dale R.	(KS)	1099
WHITE, George R.	(KS)	1331
WIEBE, Margaret A.	(KS)	1336
ANDERSON, Patricia E. .	(KY)	25
BENNETT, Donna S. . . .	(KY)	81
BRINKMAN, Carol S. . . .	(KY)	136
DARE, Philip N.	(KY)	274
WILLIAMS, Danby O. . . .	(KY)	1342
WOOD, Linda H.	(KY)	1364
CURTIS, Robert L.	(LA)	267
DOMBOURIAN, Sona J. .	(LA)	310
GERICKE, Paul W.	(LA)	428
HAGEDORN, Dorothy L. .	(LA)	482
JARRED, Ada D.	(LA)	594
JONES, Stephanie R. . . .	(LA)	615
KHOURY, Nancy L.	(LA)	646
LEINBACH, Philip E.	(LA)	714
PATTERSON, Trudy J. . . .	(LA)	948
PHILLIPS, Faye	(LA)	968
PICKETT, Joanne H. . . .	(LA)	970
REEDY, Ruth C.	(LA)	1015
SALTER, Jeffrey L.	(LA)	1077
SMITH, Richard J.	(LA)	1160
STANDEFER, Steven R. .	(LA)	1179
SWEAT, Mary L.	(LA)	1214
WILSON, C D.	(LA)	1350
ANDERSON, Cheryl M. .	(MA)	22
BENENFELD, Alan R. . . .	(MA)	80
BERNIER, Esta S.	(MA)	89
BOZONE, Billie R.	(MA)	124
BRIDEGAM, Willis E. . . .	(MA)	135
BURKETT, Nancy H. . . .	(MA)	161
CHANNING, Rhoda K. . .	(MA)	201
CHEVES, Vera L.	(MA)	207
CODAIR, Frederick R. . .	(MA)	226
CORNELL, Barbara M. . .	(MA)	246
CORNWALL, Scot J. . . .	(MA)	247
CRAIG, James L.	(MA)	254
CURLEY, Arthur	(MA)	265
DYER, Victor E.	(MA)	330
EDMONDS, Anne C. . . .	(MA)	336
ERICKSON, Alan E.	(MA)	352
FOSTER, Joan	(MA)	392
FREEHLING, Dan J.	(MA)	400
FREITAG, Wolfgang M. .	(MA)	401
FRIEDMAN, Fred T.	(MA)	403
GILLIES, Irene B.	(MA)	436
GUSTAFSON, Eleanor A.	(MA)	478
HAMANN, Edmund G. . .	(MA)	490
HELO, Martin	(MA)	525
HILL, Barbara M.	(MA)	539
HOLMBERG, Olga S. . . .	(MA)	553
HUGGINS, Dean A.	(MA)	571
KANE, Lois B.	(MA)	625
KING, Patricia M.	(MA)	652
LADD, Dorothy P.	(MA)	687
LEE, Marilyn M.	(MA)	710
LEWIS, David D.	(MA)	722
MONTANA, Edward J. . .	(MA)	855
MOORACHIAN, Rose . . .	(MA)	858
MOULTON, Catherine A.	(MA)	873
NORTON, Linda N.	(MA)	910
NOYES, Suzanne N. . . .	(MA)	911
O'NEAL, Ellis E.	(MA)	923

ADMINISTRATION (Cont'd)
Administration

PAPADEMETRIOU, George C.	(MA)	938
PILLSBURY, Mary J. . . .	(MA)	973
REEVE, Russell J.	(MA)	1016
SAKEY, Joseph G.	(MA)	1076
STANTON, Martha	(MA)	1181
STITT, Walter B.	(MA)	1195
TUCHMAN, Maurice S. .	(MA)	1261
WARNER, Marnie M. . . .	(MA)	1305
WILLIAMS, Carole C. . . .	(MA)	1342
WILLS, Lynda J.	(MA)	1349
BLEGEN, John C.	(MD)	105
BROWN, Florence S. . . .	(MD)	144
CHU, Ellen M.	(MD)	212
COLAIANNI, Lois A. . . .	(MD)	229
COLBORN, Robert J. . . .	(MD)	230
COLE, Anna B.	(MD)	230
CUMMINGS, John P. . . .	(MD)	264
GALLAGHER, Charles F.	(MD)	413
GLOCK, Martha H.	(MD)	441
HALL, Mary A.	(MD)	488
HARRAR, H J.	(MD)	503
HOWARD, Joseph H. . . .	(MD)	564
LARSEN, Lida L.	(MD)	698
MCKAY, Eleanor	(MD)	809
MCKEAN, Joan M.	(MD)	810
NEAL, Robert L.	(MD)	890
NEKRITZ, Leah K.	(MD)	893
PINDER, Jo A.	(MD)	974
RAY, John G.	(MD)	1011
RUSSELL, Keith W. . . .	(MD)	1069
SLATER, Susan B.	(MD)	1148
SUTTON, Sharan D. . . .	(MD)	1212
SZCZCPANIAK, Adam S.	(MD)	1218
TARAN, Nadia P.	(MD)	1223
THOMAS, Sarah E.	(MD)	1238
YUILLE, Willie K.	(MD)	1384
ALBRIGHT, Elaine M. . . .	(ME)	10
BILODEAU, Judith M. . . .	(ME)	97
CROSBY, Barbara A. . . .	(ME)	260
HOLMES, Richard C. . . .	(ME)	553
NICHOLS, J G.	(ME)	901
BEDUNAH, Virginia M. . .	(MI)	74
BEST, Donald A.	(MI)	92
CHAPIN, Richard E.	(MI)	201
DOERR, Jane P.	(MI)	308
DOMBROWSKI, Mark A.	(MI)	310
DOUBLESTEIN, Judith A.	(MI)	313
DRABENSTOTT, Jon D. .	(MI)	317
DYKI, Judy	(MI)	331
FLAHERTY, Kevin C. . . .	(MI)	383
GALIK, Barbara A.	(MI)	413
GAMBLE, Marian L. . . .	(MI)	416
GOSLING, William A. . . .	(MI)	453
HAKA, Clifford H.	(MI)	484
HARPER, Nancy L.	(MI)	503
HOUGH, Carolyn A.	(MI)	562
JENSEN, David P.	(MI)	598
JONES, Clifton H.	(MI)	612
KIRBY, Frederick J. . . .	(MI)	654
KLEIN, Michele S.	(MI)	659
KRUUT, Evald	(MI)	681
KULBERG, Gretchen S. .	(MI)	683
LEARY, Margaret R. . . .	(MI)	707
MARTIN, Rose M.	(MI)	778
MIKA, Joseph J.	(MI)	834
NIETHAMMER, Leslee . .	(MI)	904
OLDENBURG, Joseph F.	(MI)	920
PARK, Janice R.	(MI)	941
PINKHAM, Eleanor H. . .	(MI)	974
PRETZER, Dale H.	(MI)	992
SMITH, Paul M.	(MI)	1159
SMITH, William K.	(MI)	1161
SPYERS-DURAN, Peter .	(MI)	1177
VAN TOLL, Faith	(MI)	1277
WERLING, Anita L.	(MI)	1324
ANDERSON, Margaret J.	(MN)	24
EBRO, Diane C.	(MN)	334

ADMINISTRATION (Cont'd)
Administration

FOSTER, Veo G. . . . . . . (MN) 393
GALT, Francis E. . . . . . . (MN) 415
HAEUSER, Michael J. . . (MN) 482
HAYS, Robert M. . . . . . . (MN) 517
HOLT, Constance W. . . . (MN) 554
JANZEN, Deborah K. . . . (MN) 594
KIMBROUGH, Joseph . . (MN) 649
KISHEL, Deane A. . . . . . (MN) 656
MCDIARMID, Errett W. . . (MN) 802
WENTE, Norman G. . . . . (MN) 1324
WOLF, Joy G. . . . . (MN) 1360
ALLEN, Ronald . . . . (MO) 16
ATHY, Doris J. . . . . (MO) 37
ELLIOTT, Dorothy G. . . . (MO) 344
GIBSON, Patricia A. . . . . (MO) 432
GUENTHER, Charles J. . (MO) 475
HESS, Stanley W. . . . . . (MO) 534
KNORR, Martin R. . . . . . (MO) 665
PAGE, Jacqueline M. . . . (MO) 934
SCHELL, Rosalie F. . . . . (MO) 1091
SMITH, Nancy M. . . . . . . (MO) 1159
SPALDING, Helen H. . . . (MO) 1171
SULLIVAN, Marilyn G. . . (MO) 1208
TIPSWORD, Thomas N. . . (MO) 1246
VAN BLAIR, Betty A. . . . (MO) 1272
WOLF, Constance P. . . . (MO) 1360
BURKS, Alvin L. . . . . (MS) 161
MACON, Myra . . . . (MS) 758
MITCHELL, Deborah S. . . (MS) 848
MOMAN, Orthella P. . . . . (MS) 854
REID, Thomas G. . . . . . . (MS) 1019
WOODBURN, David M. . . (MS) 1366
CHANDLER, Devon . . . . (MT) 199
CLARK, Robert M. . . . . . (MT) 218
MEADOWS, Judith A. . . (MT) 819
NERODA, Edward W. . . . (MT) 895
ARMITAGE, Katherine Y. (NC) 32
BUTSON, Linda C. . . . . . (NC) 167
DRUESEDOW, John E. . (NC) 320
ESTES, Elizabeth W. . . . (NC) 355
GERMAIN, Claire M. . . . (NC) 429
HADDEN, Linda W. . . . . (NC) 481
HOLMES, Elizabeth A. . . (NC) 553
LEE, Charles D. . . . . (NC) 709
MASSEY, Nancy O. . . . . (NC) 782
MATOCHIK, Michael J. . (NC) 784
MCLEOD, Herbert E. . . . (NC) 814
METZGER, Eva C. . . . . . (NC) 829
OLENDER, Karen L. . . . . (NC) 920
OPLINGER, Mary P. . . . . (NC) 925
PERRY, Douglas F. . . . . (NC) 960
ROBERTSON, W D. . . . . (NC) 1042
SLOCUM, Charlotte A. . . (NC) 1150
SMITH, Merrill F. . . . . . . (NC) 1158
SOUTHERLAND, Carol A. (NC) 1169
THIBODEAU, Patricia L. . (NC) 1235
THOMAS, John B. . . . . . (NC) 1237
VAN HOVEN, William D. (NC) 1276
WRIGHT, Barbara A. . . . (NC) 1370
BIRDSALL, Douglas G. . . (ND) 98
GILL, Bernard I. . . . . (ND) 435
PEDERSEN, Lila . . . . . . (ND) 954
GARDNER, Charles A. . . (NE) 417
JACKA, David C. . . . . . . (NE) 586
MAYESKI, John K. . . . . . (NE) 790
NEWCOMER, Audrey P. (NE) 898
SCHULZ, Stanley D. . . . (NE) 1102
VAN BAUCOM, Charles . (NE) 1272
WISE, Sally H. . . . . (NE) 1357
GEISEL, Ann M. . . . . (NH) 425
HARDSOG, Ellen L. . . . . (NH) 500
HARE, William J. . . . . . . (NH) 501
HIGGINS, Matthew J. . . . (NH) 538
MARSHALL, Margaret E. . (NH) 774
PRIDHAM, Sherman C. . . (NH) 993
SHERWOOD, Janet R. . . (NH) 1129
ANDERMAN, Lynea . . . . (NJ) 21
BRANAN, Julia D. . . . . . (NJ) 127

ADMINISTRATION (Cont'd)
Administration

BRODMAN, Estelle . . . . . (NJ) 139
BURDEN, Geraldine R. . . (NJ) 158
BURNS, John A. . . . . . . (NJ) 162
CHELARIU, Ana R. . . . . (NJ) 204
COUGHLIN, Caroline M. . (NJ) 250
CROCKER, Jane L. . . . . (NJ) 259
DONOHUE, Nancy W. . . (NJ) 312
EBELING, Elinor H. . . . . (NJ) 334
EDWARDS, Susan M. . . (NJ) 338
GILHEANY, Rosary S. . . (NJ) 434
GRANT, George E. . . . . (NJ) 458
GREENBERG, Evelyn . . . (NJ) 463
GREENBERG, Ruth S. . . (NJ) 463
HIGGINS, Flora T. . . . . . (NJ) 537
HURLEY, John . . . . (NJ) 577
JIULIANO, Margaret C. . . (NJ) 600
KARETZKY, Stephen . . . (NJ) 627
KLATH, Nancy S. . . . . . . (NJ) 657
LADOF, Nina S. . . . . (NJ) 687
LUXNER, Ann F. . . . . . . (NJ) 750
MCADOO, Jannifer C. . . (NJ) 792
MEYER, Mary L. . . . . . . (NJ) 830
MULLINS, Lynn S. . . . . . (NJ) 878
NELSON, Louise H. . . . . (NJ) 894
OGONEK, Donna L. . . . . (NJ) 918
PAULLIN, William D. . . . (NJ) 950
ROSS, Robert D. . . . . . . (NJ) 1058
SCHUBACK COHN, Judith (NJ) 1101
SCHUT, Grace W. . . . . . (NJ) 1103
SCHWARTZ, Lawrence C. (NJ) 1104
SEARLE, Jo A. . . . . (NJ) 1110
SMITH, Reginald W. . . . . (NJ) 1159
ZULEWSKI, Gerald J. . . . (NJ) 1391
DOWLIN, C E. . . . . (NM) 316
GODFREY, Lois E. . . . . . (NM) 442
HUMPHREY, Thomas W. (NM) 573
LANCASTER, Kevin M. . (NM) 692
NEWTON, Barbara I. . . . (NM) 900
SABATINI, Joseph D. . . . (NM) 1072
SAUNDERS, Laurel B. . . (NM) 1084
SEISER, Virginia . . . . . . (NM) 1113
SOHN, Jeanne G. . . . . . (NM) 1165
DONOVAN, Ruth H. . . . . (NV) 312
GRAY, Robert G. . . . . . . (NV) 460
MANLEY, Charles W. . . . (NV) 765
ZENAN, Joan S. . . . . . . (NV) 1387
ANDREWS, Charles R. . . (NY) 26
BAILIE, Donna L. . . . . . . (NY) 47
BALDWIN, Geraldine S. . (NY) 51
BALKEMA, John B. . . . . (NY) 52
BARTLE, Matthew W. . . . (NY) 61
BECKER, Jeanne . . . . . . (NY) 72
BENNIN, Cheryl S. . . . . . (NY) 82
BIRNBAUM, Henry . . . . . (NY) 98
BONK, Sharon C. . . . . . . (NY) 114
BRANDEAU, John H. . . . (NY) 128
BRIGHAM, Jeffrey L. . . . (NY) 136
CABEEN, Samuel K. . . . (NY) 170
CALVANO, Margaret . . . (NY) 174
CHICCO, Giuliano . . . . . (NY) 208
CHICKERING, F W. . . . . (NY) 208
CLOUDSLEY, Donald H. . (NY) 223
CONRAD, Frances M. . . (NY) 238
COPLEN, Ron . . . . (NY) 244
COTY, Patricia A. . . . . . . (NY) 250
CROWLEY, John V. . . . . (NY) 261
CUMMINS, A B. . . . . (NY) 264
DAVIS, Deborah G. . . . . (NY) 278
DAVIS, Mary B. . . . . (NY) 280
DECANDIDO, Graceanne
A. . . . . (NY) 285
DEUTSCH, Karen A. . . . (NY) 296
DORN, Robert J. . . . . . . (NY) 313
EDSALL, Shirley A. . . . . (NY) 336
EDWARDS, Harriet M. . . (NY) 337
EISENBERG, Debra . . . . (NY) 340
ELLENBERGER, Jack S. (NY) 343
FORCE, Stephen . . . . . . (NY) 389

ADMINISTRATION (Cont'd)
Administration

FOWLER, Carole F. . . . . (NY) 393
FRANCK, Jane P. . . . . . (NY) 396
FRASENE, Joanne R. . . . (NY) 399
FRIEDLAND, Rhoda W. . (NY) 403
GARVEY, Jeffrey M. . . . . (NY) 421
GATNER, Elliott S. . . . . . (NY) 422
GILLESPIE, John T. . . . . (NY) 435
GILLIGAN, Mary A. . . . . (NY) 436
GLASER, June E. . . . . . . (NY) 439
GOODMAN, Rhonna A. . . (NY) 449
GRUNDT, Leonard . . . . . (NY) 475
HENDERSON, Janice E. . (NY) 526
HERNANDEZ, Tamsen M. (NY) 532
HEWITT, Vivian D. . . . . . (NY) 535
HIGGINBOTHAM, Barbra
    B. . . . . (NY) 537
HOOVER, James L. . . . . (NY) 557
HORNICK-LOCKARD,
    Barbara A. . . . . (NY) 560
HUMPHRY, John A. . . . . (NY) 574
HUTCHINSON, Ann P. . . (NY) 579
JANIAK, Jane M. . . . . . . (NY) 593
JAY, Donald F. . . . . (NY) 595
KENDRICK, Curtis L. . . . (NY) 640
KENSELAAR, Robert . . . (NY) 642
KING, Charles L. . . . . . . (NY) 650
KINYATTI, Njoki W. . . . . (NY) 653
KLEIN, Stephen C. . . . . . (NY) 659
KLINGLE, Philip A. . . . . . (NY) 662
KRANICH, Nancy C. . . . (NY) 676
KRIEGER, Tillie . . . . (NY) 678
KUCSMA, Susan P. . . . . (NY) 682
LACKS, Bernice K. . . . . . (NY) 686
LANE, Elizabeth J. . . . . . (NY) 694
LEWIS, David W. . . . . . . (NY) 723
LEWIS, Margaret S. . . . . (NY) 723
LINDNER, Charlotte K. . . (NY) 729
LOCHER, Cornelia E. . . . (NY) 736
LUBETSKI, Edith E. . . . . (NY) 745
MATZEK, Richard A. . . . (NY) 786
MAUTINO, Patricia H. . . . (NY) 787
MILNES, Patricia C. . . . . (NY) 845
MORAN, Sylvia J. . . . . . (NY) 862
MORRISON, J M. . . . . . (NY) 868
MURDOCK, William J. . . (NY) 880
NAYLOR, Richard J. . . . (NY) 890
NEESE, Janet A. . . . . . . (NY) 892
NYREN, Dorothy E. . . . . (NY) 913
OPATOW, Dave . . . . (NY) 924
OVERGAARD, Lynn H. . (NY) 931
PALMER, Paul R. . . . . . . (NY) 936
PANELLA, Deborah S. . . (NY) 938
PARKE, Kathryn E. . . . . . (NY) 941
PARR, Mary Y. . . . . (NY) 944
PATTISON, Frederick W. (NY) 948
PERKUS, Paul C. . . . . . . (NY) 959
PICCIANO, Jacqueline L. (NY) 970
PILLAI, Karlye A. . . . . . . (NY) 973
PRESCHEL, Barbara M. . (NY) 991
RICHTER, Kathleen A. . . (NY) 1031
RISH, Jennifer G. . . . . . . (NY) 1035
ROBBINS, Diane D. . . . . (NY) 1038
ROTH, Claire J. . . . . (NY) 1059
ROWELL, Margaret K. . . (NY) 1062
ROWLAND, Eileen . . . . . (NY) 1062
SAHLEM, James R. . . . . (NY) 1075
SANDERS, Robin S. . . . (NY) 1080
SCIOLINO, Elaine T. . . . (NY) 1106
SEER, Gitelle . . . . (NY) 1111
SELVAR, Jane C. . . . . . . (NY) 1114
SHANNON, Michael O. . (NY) 1120
SHAPIRO, June R. . . . . . (NY) 1121
SHELANDER, Frances R. (NY) 1125
SIMONIS, James J. . . . . (NY) 1141
SIMPSON, Charles W. . . (NY) 1141
SMITH, Frederick E. . . . . (NY) 1155
SPAIN, Frances L. . . . . . (NY) 1170
SPORE, Stuart . . . . (NY) 1175

ADMINISTRATION (Cont'd)
Administration

STAHL, J N. . . . . (NY) 1178
STANTON, Lee W. . . . . (NY) 1181
STEFANI, Carolyn R. . . . (NY) 1185
STEIN, Arlene B. . . . . . . (NY) 1185
STEIN, Marsha . . . . (NY) 1185
SUMMERS, Ruth O. . . . . (NY) 1209
SWERDLOVE, Dorothy L. (NY) 1215
TANZER, Barbara . . . . . (NY) 1223
TELATNIK, George M. . . (NY) 1230
TOMLIN, Anne C. . . . . . (NY) 1250
VAJDA, Elizabeth A. . . . (NY) 1271
VANNORTWICK, Barbara
    L. . . . . (NY) 1276
VAN ZANTEN, Frank V. . (NY) 1278
WISHART, H L. . . . . (NY) 1357
WOOD, Thor E. . . . . (NY) 1365
WYDEN, Elaine S. . . . . . (NY) 1374
ANDERSON, Carl A. . . . (OH) 21
BELVIN, Robert J. . . . . . (OH) 78
BRITTON, Constance J. . (OH) 137
BUCK, Jeremy R. . . . . . . (OH) 153
BURKE, Ambrose L. . . . . (OH) 160
BURLINGAME, Dwight F. (OH) 161
CAIN, Linda B. . . . . (OH) 171
CONNERS, Margaret S. . (OH) 237
CROWE, William J. . . . . (OH) 261
DRAPP, Laureen . . . . . . (OH) 318
DUFFETT, Gorman L. . . . (OH) 323
ELWELL, Pamela M. . . . (OH) 347
EMRICK, Nancy J. . . . . . (OH) 348
ESBIN, Martha P. . . . . . . (OH) 354
FELLOWS, Barbara G. . . (OH) 370
FINET, Scott . . . . (OH) 378
GARTEN, Edward D. . . . (OH) 420
GILROY, Dorothy A. . . . . (OH) 437
HUNT, James R. . . . . . . (OH) 575
JONES, Robert M. . . . . . (OH) 614
KIRBAWY, Barbara L. . . (OH) 653
KRITZER, Hyman W. . . . (OH) 679
LESLIE, Camille J. . . . . . (OH) 718
LOWELL, Virginia L. . . . (OH) 744
MACKENZIE, Alberta E. . (OH) 756
MAURER, Charles B. . . . (OH) 787
MCCAULEY, Hannah V. . (OH) 795
MCCONNELL, Pamela J. (OH) 798
MCNEER, Elizabeth J. . . (OH) 816
MEAD, Catherine S. . . . (OH) 819
MILLER, Ruth G. . . . . . . (OH) 842
MOFFETT, William A. . . . (OH) 852
MULHERN, Raymond A. . (OH) 876
PETTY, Sue W. . . . . (OH) 965
PIETY, John S. . . . . (OH) 972
RADER, Hannelore B. . . (OH) 1002
SCHAEFGEN, Susan M. . (OH) 1089
SMITH, Robert S. . . . . . . (OH) 1160
STORCK, John N. . . . . . (OH) 1198
VALENTE, Elda C. . . . . . (OH) 1271
VARGA, Carol C. . . . . . . (OH) 1278
ZAPOROZHETZ, Laurene
    E. . . . . (OH) 1386
BUTHOD, J C. . . . . (OK) 166
CALLARD, Joanne C. . . (OK) 173
CURTIS, Ronald A. . . . . (OK) 267
DICKSON, Theresa J. . . (OK) 301
JUDKINS, Timothy C. . . . (OK) 619
KEENE, Janis C. . . . . . . (OK) 634
KIMBLE, Valerie F. . . . . (OK) 649
KIRKBRIDE, Rebecca M. (OK) 654
SARK, Sue . . . . (OK) 1083
STEWART, Vicki . . . . . . (OK) 1193
WALLEN, Joyce M. . . . . (OK) 1298
BROWNE, Joseph P. . . . (OR) 148
JURKINS, Jacquelyn J. . (OR) 620
KNUDSON, June . . . . . . (OR) 666
SUGGS, Wayne L. . . . . . (OR) 1206
BANDEMER, June E. . . . (PA) 54
BARD, Nelson P. . . . . . . (PA) 56
BARRY, James W. . . . . . (PA) 60

ADMINISTRATION (Cont'd)
Administration

ADMINISTRATION (Cont'd)
Administration

BERK, Jack M.	(PA)	87
BLACK, Dorothy M.	(PA)	101
BRYANT, Lillian D.	(PA)	152
CAMPBELL, Susan M.	(PA)	177
CARLSON, Rena M.	(PA)	182
CORRIGAN, John T.	(PA)	247
DOLE, Wanda V.	(PA)	309
DUCK, Patricia M.	(PA)	322
GODDARD, Burton L.	(PA)	442
HABER, Walter H.	(PA)	481
HANSON, Eugene R.	(PA)	498
HOFFMAN, Elizabeth P.	(PA)	547
JACOBS, Mark D.	(PA)	589
KAGER, Jeffrey F.	(PA)	621
KEANE, John J.	(PA)	633
KNAPP, Mabel J.	(PA)	663
KRIVDA, Marita J.	(PA)	679
LAZARUS, Karin	(PA)	706
LYNESS, Ann L.	(PA)	752
MAYOVER, Steven J.	(PA)	791
MCKOWN, Cornelius J.	(PA)	812
MECH, Terrence F.	(PA)	820
MINES, Denise C.	(PA)	846
MYERS, James N.	(PA)	884
NEWPORT, Dorothea D.	(PA)	900
NISTA, Ann S.	(PA)	905
PAUL, Suzanne	(PA)	949
POWERS, Beverly A.	(PA)	989
REED, Gertrude	(PA)	1015
ROBBINS, Stephen L.	(PA)	1039
ROBINSON, Agnes F.	(PA)	1043
ROSENSTEEL, J R.	(PA)	1057
RYAN, Patricia M.	(PA)	1071
SAFFORD, Herbert D.	(PA)	1074
SALVAYON, Connie	(PA)	1078
SAUNDERS, William B.	(PA)	1085
SMALL, Sally S.	(PA)	1151
SNELGROVE, Pamela S.	(PA)	1163
STEWART, Barbara R.	(PA)	1192
STILLMAN, Mary E.	(PA)	1194
STRAUSS, Richard F.	(PA)	1201
SULLIVAN, Jennifer B.	(PA)	1207
TABORSKY, Theresa	(PA)	1219
TRIPP, Audrey J.	(PA)	1257
WHITTAKER, Edward L.	(PA)	1334
WILSON, Martin P.	(PA)	1352
WOLFE, Gary D.	(PA)	1360
WOODSWORTH, Anne	(PA)	1367
MOMBILLE, Pedro	(PR)	854
MUNOZ-SOLA, Haydee	(PR)	879
PEREZ, Sarai	(PR)	958
AYLWARD, James F.	(RI)	42
HULL, Catherine C.	(RI)	572
LLOYD, Lynn A.	(RI)	735
LOXLEY, Donna J.	(RI)	745
PERRY, Beth I.	(RI)	960
SHERIDAN, Jean	(RI)	1127
BAND, Richard A.	(SC)	53
BOONE, Shirley W.	(SC)	115
CUBBEDGE, Frankie H.	(SC)	262
EISENSTADT, Rosa M.	(SC)	341
GILBERT, Sybil M.	(SC)	434
GORDON, Clara B.	(SC)	451
HIPPS, Gary M.	(SC)	543
LANGSTON, William E.	(SC)	696
MCAULAY, Louise S.	(SC)	792
MCMASTER, Sarah D.	(SC)	815
MEYER, Richard W.	(SC)	830
OLINGER, Elizabeth B.	(SC)	920
SLIFE, Joye D.	(SC)	1149
TARLTON, Shirley M.	(SC)	1224
WASHINGTON, Nancy H.	(SC)	1307
WILLIAMS-JENKINS, Barbara J.	(SC)	1347
DERTIEN, James L.	(SD)	294
HULKONEN, David A.	(SD)	572
LANG, Elizabeth A.	(SD)	695
ADAMS, Paul R.	(TN)	5
AUD, Thomas L.	(TN)	39
BERWIND, Anne M.	(TN)	91
BLAIR, Lynne M.	(TN)	102
DENTON, A W.	(TN)	293
DRESCHER, Judith A.	(TN)	319
FANCHER, Evelyn P.	(TN)	363
FULTON, Dixie W.	(TN)	409
HELGUERA, Byrd S.	(TN)	524
HODGES, Terence M.	(TN)	546
JETT, Don W.	(TN)	600
KARL, Roger M.	(TN)	627
MCFARLAND, Jane E.	(TN)	805
MCHOLLIN, Mattie L.	(TN)	809
MEREDITH, Don L.	(TN)	825
PARKS, Dorothy R.	(TN)	943
WALDEN, Winston A.	(TN)	1294
WALKER, Mary E.	(TN)	1296
WELLS, Paul F.	(TN)	1323
WILSON, Florence J.	(TN)	1351
WORLEY, Joan H.	(TN)	1369
WRIGHT, David A.	(TN)	1371
ALFORD, Mary A.	(TX)	13
BIGLEY, John E.	(TX)	96
BLAYLOCK, James C.	(TX)	105
BUCKNALL, Carolyn F.	(TX)	154
CANALES, Herbert G.	(TX)	178
CARRINGTON, Samuel M.	(TX)	186
CHAPMAN, Katherine	(TX)	202
CLUFF, E D.	(TX)	223
COCHRAN, Carolyn	(TX)	225
COOK, C C.	(TX)	239
CRENSHAW, Jan C.	(TX)	258
CRISSINGER, John D.	(TX)	259
ELAM, Craig S.	(TX)	341
FARMER, David	(TX)	364
FERRIER, Douglas M.	(TX)	373
FORD, Barbara J.	(TX)	389
GARAZA, Noemi	(TX)	417
GRAY, Wayne D.	(TX)	460
HAMBLETON, James E.	(TX)	490
HARVILL, Melba S.	(TX)	509
HENINGTON, David M.	(TX)	528
HUGHES, Sue M.	(TX)	572
KIM, David U.	(TX)	648
MCCORD, Stanley J.	(TX)	798
MCCURDY, Sandra A.	(TX)	801
MCKAY, Mary F.	(TX)	810
MEARS, William F.	(TX)	820
MERSKY, Roy M.	(TX)	827
MILLS, Helen L.	(TX)	844
MOLTZAN, Janet R.	(TX)	854
MONCLA, Carolyn S.	(TX)	854
MULLER, Mary M.	(TX)	877
ORR, Joella A.	(TX)	926
PARTON, William A.	(TX)	945
PROGAR, Dorothy R.	(TX)	995
RAMSEY, Donna E.	(TX)	1005
RICKLEFS, Dale L.	(TX)	1032
ROBERSON, Janis L.	(TX)	1039
SARGENT, Charles W.	(TX)	1082
SCHUMANN, Iris T.	(TX)	1103
SHIPMAN, Natalie W.	(TX)	1131
SIMS, Phillip W.	(TX)	1142
SNELL, Marykay H.	(TX)	1163
THOMAS, Greg	(TX)	1236
VELA-CREIXELL, Mary I.	(TX)	1281
WERKING, Richard H.	(TX)	1324
WILBUR, Sharon F.	(TX)	1338
WYGANT, Larry J.	(TX)	1375
YAPLE, Marilyn V.	(TX)	1378
MARCHANT, Maurice P.	(UT)	768
MAYFIELD, David M.	(UT)	790
THOMSON, Ralph D.	(UT)	1242
TOMLIN, Celia K.	(UT)	1250
ZEIDNER, Christine M.	(UT)	1387
CHAMBERLAIN, William R.	(VA)	197
DARDEN, Sue E.	(VA)	274

ADMINISTRATION (Cont'd)
Administration

FRANTZ, Ray W. . . . . . . (VA) 398
GRANT, Juanita G. . . . . (VA) 458
HANNA, Jill C. . . . . . (VA) 496
HOLLOWAY, Johnna H. . . (VA) 552
HUETER, Eike . . . . (VA) 570
KIEWITT, Eva L. . . . . . (VA) 647
LUH, Lydia Y. . . . . (VA) 747
MACLEOD, James M. . . (VA) 757
MCKELVEY, Mary J. . . . (VA) 810
MILLER, Richard A. . . . (VA) 841
OGDEN, Howard A. . . . (VA) 918
ROBISON, Dennis E. . . . (VA) 1045
SCHNEIDER, Holle E. . . . (VA) 1097
TAI, Elizabeth L. . . . . . (VA) 1220
TERWILLIGER, Gloria P. . (VA) 1232
VAZQUEZ, Martha W. . . (VA) 1280
WAGENKNECHT, Robert
    E. . . . . (VA) 1291
WIANT, Sarah K. . . . . . (VA) 1335
SOUFFRONT, Blanche L. . (VI) 1169
BATTEY, Jean D. . . . . . (VT) 64
KNEELAND, Marjorie H. . (VT) 664
REED, Sally G. . . . . . . (VT) 1015
REIT, Janet W. . . . . . . (VT) 1022
RUCKER, Ronald E. . . . (VT) 1065
SHERMAN, Jacob R. . . . (VT) 1128
BAUMANN, Charles H. . . (WA) 66
BODKIN, Sharon C. . . . (WA) 109
CHRISTIANSEN, Claire B. (WA) 211
FOLEY, Katherine E. . . . (WA) 387
HAZELTON, Penelope A. (WA) 517
HENINGER, Irene C. . . . (WA) 528
KREIMEYER, Vicki R. . . . (WA) 677
LIPTON, Laura E. . . . . . (WA) 732
MCBRIDE, Anne . . . . . (WA) 792
MCCOOL, Donna L. . . . (WA) 798
MURRAY, James M. . . . (WA) 882
MUTSCHLER, Herbert F. (WA) 883
ROBERTS, Elizabeth P. . (WA) 1039
SLIVKA, Enid M. . . . . . (WA) 1149
STEWART, Jane . . . . . (WA) 1192
BLACKWELDER, Mary B. (WI) 102
BRENNEN, Patrick W. . . (WI) 133
CARMACK, Bob . . . . . (WI) 183
CARR, Jo A. . . . . (WI) 185
EGGUM, Janet M. . . . . (WI) 339
FENNESSEY, Mary D. . . (WI) 371
FLYNN, Kathryn J. . . . . (WI) 386
GILLETTE, Meredith . . . (WI) 435
HAWLEY, Joann C. . . . (WI) 514
HEITKEMPER, Elsie M. . (WI) 523
JENSEN, Hans W. . . . . (WI) 598
KOSLOV, Marcia J. . . . (WI) 672
MEERDINK, Richard E. . . (WI) 821
MULLER, H N. . . . . . . (WI) 877
NAESETH, Gerhard B. . . (WI) 886
PATANE, John R. . . . . (WI) 946
PROCES, Stephen L. . . . (WI) 994
SHARMA, Ravindra N. . . (WI) 1122
TURNER, Judith C. . . . (WI) 1264
ANTIGO, Dolores A. . . . (WV) 29
DANNUNZIO, Rebecca T. (WV) 274
GAUMOND, George R. . . (WV) 423
GRAHAM, Robert J. . . . (WV) 456
RULE, Judy K. . . . . . . (WV) 1067
SCOTT, John E. . . . . . (WV) 1107
SHILL, Harold B. . . . . . (WV) 1130
SIZEMORE, William C. . . (WV) 1145
COTTAM, Keith M. . . . . (WY) 250
HEUER, William J. . . . . (WY) 535
HIGBY, Helen E. . . . . . (WY) 537
HOFF, Vickie J. . . . . . . (WY) 547
IVERSON, Deborah P. . . (WY) 585
SIMPSON, Susan M. . . . (WY) 1142
BAYRAK, Bettie . . . . . . (AB) 68
INGIBERGSSON, Asgeir (AB) 582
JORDAHL, Ronald I. . . . (AB) 616
KISSAU, Arlene M. . . . . (AB) 656

ADMINISTRATION (Cont'd)
Administration

MOFFAT, N L. . . . . (AB) 852
RAND, Duncan D. . . . . (AB) 1006
SEYEDMAHMOUD, Donna
    A. . . . . (AB) 1118
BARTON, Joan A. . . . . (BC) 62
CAPES, Judy L. . . . . . (BC) 179
HARRIS, Winifred E. . . . (BC) 506
INSELBERG, Diana E. . . (BC) 583
LEVESQUE, Nancy B. . . (BC) 719
MANSBRIDGE, John . . . (BC) 767
MOONEY, Shirley E. . . . (BC) 858
PLETT, Katherine . . . . . (BC) 978
WIEBE, Frieda . . . . . . (BC) 1336
EAGLETON, Kathleen M. (MB) 331
REID, Marion I. . . . . . . (MB) 1019
CHIASSON, Gilles . . . . (NB) 207
EADIE, Tom . . . . (NB) 331
GAUTHIER, Rose M. . . . (NB) 423
ELLIS, Richard H. . . . . . (NF) 345
PENNEY, Pearce J. . . . (NF) 957
BIRDSALL, William F. . . (NS) 98
HUANG, Paul T. . . . . . (NS) 568
LEWIS, Aileen M. . . . . (NS) 722
LYNCH, Darrell B. . . . . (NS) 751
BALL, John L. . . . . (ON) 52
BRIGGS, Geoffrey H. . . (ON) 135
BROOKING, Ruth P. . . . (ON) 140
CADA, Elizabeth J. . . . . (ON) 170
DARBY, Janet M. . . . . . (ON) 274
GIBSON, Mary B. . . . . . (ON) 432
GILLHAM, Virginia A. . . (ON) 436
HAUCK, Danuta . . . . . (ON) 512
HEARDER-MOAN, Wendy
    P. . . . . (ON) 518
ISRAEL, Fred C. . . . . . (ON) 585
LORENTOWICZ, Genia . (ON) 741
MEHTA, Subbash C. . . . (ON) 821
MOORE, Heather J. . . . (ON) 859
MORRIS, Sandra M. . . . (ON) 867
PULLEYBLANK, Mildred
    C. . . . . (ON) 997
RIPLEY, Victoria E. . . . . (ON) 1035
RYAN, Noel . . . . (ON) 1071
SCHWENGER, Frances S. (ON) 1105
SKEITH, Mary E. . . . . . (ON) 1145
WYMAN, Kathleen M. . . (ON) 1375
ALLARD, Serge . . . . . . (PQ) 14
BOULET, Paul E. . . . . . (PQ) 119
CHEVRIER, Francine . . . (PQ) 207
CLEMENT, Clarie . . . . . (PQ) 221
COTE, Claire . . . . (PQ) 249
DARBON, Ginette . . . . . (PQ) 274
DEMERS, Madeleine M. . (PQ) 291
DENOMMEE, Celine . . . (PQ) 293
EVANS, Calvin D. . . . . (PQ) 356
GELINAS, Michel R. . . . (PQ) 426
LAMBERT, Yvan . . . . . (PQ) 690
LAMONTAGNE,
    Jacqueline . . . . (PQ) 691
LAMOUREUX, Michele . . (PQ) 691
LEBEL, Anne . . . . (PQ) 707
LONDON, Eleanor . . . . (PQ) 738
LYDON, Rosemary E. . . . (PQ) 751
MACKEY, Laurette . . . . (PQ) 756
MATE, Albert V. . . . . . (PQ) 783
MCKENZIE, Donald R. . . (PQ) 811
NAGY, Cecile . . . . (PQ) 886
RIOPEL, Jean M. . . . . . (PQ) 1035
ROY, Christine . . . . . . (PQ) 1063
SIMON, Marie L. . . . . . (PQ) 1140
SOKOV, Asta M. . . . . . (PQ) 1166
CALEF, Daniel C. . . . . . (SK) 172
INGLES, Ernie B. . . . . . (SK) 582
KEASCHUK, Michael J. . (SK) 633
TURNBULL, Keith . . . . . (SK) 1264
SMITH, Lindsay L. . . . . (AUS) 1157
SMITH, Margit J. . . . . . (ENG) 1157
DEROODE, Clifford H. . . (FRN) 294

ADMINISTRATION (Cont'd)

Administration

	WACHTER, Margery C.	(FRN)	1290
	JOLING, Carole G.	(ITL)	610
	RODRIGUEZ, Serafin L.	(MEX)	1048
	MARTIN, Nannette	(SDA)	777
	TAMEEM, Jamal A.	(SDA)	1221
Administration, academic libraries	BRENNAN, Terrence F.	(NE)	133
Administration & acquisitions	KAPNICK, Laura B.	(NY)	626
	FU, Paul S.	(OH)	407
	RAVE, David A.	(SD)	1010
Administration & book selection	SNYDER, Esther M.	(ISR)	1164
Administration & building consulting	KUHN, Warren B.	(IA)	682
Admin & collection development	LEISTER, Jack	(CA)	714
	NAIRN, Charles E.	(MI)	886
	PICQUET, D C.	(TN)	971
Administration & consulting	KASPER, Barbara	(CT)	629
Administration & finance	BRYAN, Arthur L.	(NH)	151
Administration & fundraising	HEINZ, Catharine F.	(DC)	522
Administration & library design	LISZEWSKI, Edward H.	(VA)	733
Administration & management	FRANK, Donald G.	(AZ)	396
	HIEB, Louis A.	(AZ)	537
	APPEL, Anne M.	(CA)	29
	ELLSWORTH, Dianne J.	(CA)	345
	KIRBY, Barbara L.	(CA)	653
	MONROE, Shula H.	(CA)	855
	NICKERSON, Susan L.	(CA)	902
	OLMSTEAD, Nancy L.	(CA)	921
	ROSE, Melissa M.	(CA)	1055
	SCHWARZMANN, Diane D.	(CA)	1105
	SMITH, Elizabeth M.	(CA)	1154
	WOOD, Linda M.	(CA)	1364
	MOBLEY, Arthur B.	(DC)	851
	WEIHER, Claudine J.	(DC)	1316
	BOWER, Beverly L.	(FL)	120
	BRANDON, Alfred N.	(FL)	128
	MILLER, Charles E.	(FL)	836
	LARY, Marilyn S.	(GA)	700
	TYLER, Audrey Q.	(GA)	1266
	WOODLEE, Rick G.	(GA)	1366
	DUJSIK, Gerald	(IL)	324
	HORST, Stanley E.	(IL)	561
	KLINGBERG, Susan	(IL)	661
	MACKAMAN, Frank H.	(IL)	756
	PARENT, Roger H.	(IL)	940
	SHAW, Joyce M.	(IL)	1123
	SIMON, Ralph C.	(IN)	1141
	MOORE, Grace E.	(LA)	859
	MUSSER, Egbert G.	(MA)	883
	POLLARD, Russell O.	(MA)	981
	FLOWER, Kenneth E.	(MD)	386
	HUMPHREYS, Betsy L.	(MD)	573
	JOHNSON, Emily P.	(MD)	604
	SANDS, George A.	(MD)	1081
	CLARK, Georgia A.	(MI)	217
	HERNANDEZ, Ramon R.	(MI)	532
	LEE, Lucy W.	(MI)	710
	PORTER, Jean F.	(MI)	984
	SMITH, Nancy J.	(MI)	1158
	ZARYCZNY, Wlodzimierz A.	(MI)	1386
	BROGAN, Martha L.	(MN)	139
	ROHLF, Robert H.	(MN)	1050
	CAMPBELL, Jerry D.	(NC)	176
	HANSEL, Patsy J.	(NC)	497
	ISACCO, Jeanne M.	(NC)	584
	WAGNER, Rod G.	(NE)	1292
	PERLUNGHER, Jane R.	(NH)	959
	HESS, Jayne L.	(NJ)	534
	KELSEY, Ann L.	(NJ)	639
	LYNN-NELSON, Gayle	(NJ)	752
	STRONG, Moira O.	(NJ)	1203
	KRAEMER, Mary P.	(NM)	674
	BATES, Ellen	(NY)	63
	CADE, Roberta G.	(NY)	170
	KASPAR, Eileen	(NY)	629
	NEWMAN, Jerald C.	(NY)	899
	REID, Carolyn A.	(NY)	1018
	ALBRECHT, Cheryl C.	(OH)	10

ADMINISTRATION (Cont'd)

Administration & management

	BLACK, Larry D.	(OH)	101
	BREWER, Karen L.	(OH)	134
	DUANE, Carol A.	(OH)	321
	DU MONT, Rosemary R.	(OH)	325
	GARDNER, John R.	(OH)	418
	NEWCOMBE, Jack A.	(PA)	898
	POSES, June A.	(PA)	985
	VANN, John D.	(PA)	1276
	TOWELL, Fay J.	(SC)	1252
	HEYMAN, Berna L.	(VA)	536
	SCHEITLE, Janet M.	(VA)	1091
	KEMP, Barbara E.	(WA)	639
	BANNEN, Carol A.	(WI)	54
	BEHR, Alice S.	(WV)	75
	OSBORN, Lucie P.	(WY)	927
	WURBS, Sue A.	(WY)	1374
	VAN REENEN, Johannes A.	(BC)	1277
	BASSNETT, Peter J.	(ON)	63
	KENDALL, Sandra A.	(ON)	640
	BARLOW, Elizabeth A.	(SK)	57
Administration & organization	WOODBURY, Marda	(CA)	1366
	MEDEIROS, Joseph	(NY)	820
	FEDRICK, Mary A.	(PA)	368
	BOYLAN, Merle N.	(WA)	123
	CAMERON, Bruce	(SK)	174
Administration & personal manuscript col	CUMMINGS, Hilary A.	(OR)	264
Administration & personnel	FORTIER, Jan M.	(MA)	391
	ROCK, Sue W.	(NJ)	1046
Administration & personnel management	HAGLE, Claudette S.	(TX)	483
Administration & planning	WATSON, Ellen I.	(AR)	1309
	DUNKLY, James W.	(MA)	326
	TRICARICO, Mary A.	(MA)	1256
	GUY, Wendell A.	(NY)	479
	NICHOLS, James T.	(OH)	901
	SEKERAK, Robert J.	(VT)	1113
	DAHLGREN, Anders C.	(WI)	269
Administration & policy development	DILUCIA, Samuel J.	(HI)	303
Administration & public library	BROWN, Lucinda A.	(KY)	145
Administration & public relations	GARDINER, Judith R.	(NJ)	417
Administration & public services	HORRELL, Jeffrey L.	(NY)	560
Administration & reference	PENNER, Elaine C.	(TX)	957
	GLENN, Lucy D.	(VA)	441
Administration & research	CARROLL, Dewey E.	(TX)	187
Administration & staff development	HOGAN, Patricia M.	(IL)	549
	ALLDREDGE, Noreen S.	(MT)	14
	LIN, John T.	(VA)	727
Administration & staff supervision	IRONS, Carol A.	(IL)	584
Administration & supervision	MILLER, Suzanne M.	(CA)	842
	MOORE, Phyllis C.	(CA)	861
	LOSEY, Doris C.	(FL)	742
	BOLEF, Doris	(IL)	112
	BRAZILE, Orella R.	(LA)	130
	BROOKS, Jerrold L.	(NC)	140
	JACKSON, Nancy G.	(VA)	588
	JORDAN, Ervin L.	(VA)	616
Admin, bibliographic instruction	COSTELLO, Janice M.	(WI)	249
Administration board relationships	MEADOWS, Donald F.	(BC)	819
Administration, branch library	BRACKNEY, Kathryn S.	(GA)	125
Administration, budgeting	MEYERS, Duane H.	(OK)	830
Administration, collection & development	RAFAEL, Ruth K.	(CA)	1003
Administration, collection development	BAREFOOT, Gary F.	(NC)	56
Administration, community college libs	HELLER, Nancy M.	(NY)	524
Administration community library service	WECHTLER, Stephen R.	(NJ)	1315
Administration, especially labor unions	LANDRY, Mary E.	(MD)	693
Administration in archives	WINN, Carolyn P.	(MA)	1355
Administration in hospital libraries	MALMGREN, Terri L.	(CA)	763
Administration in libraries	CHRISTOPHER, Irene	(MA)	212
Administration including grant writing	LYNCH, Mary D.	(PA)	752
Administration, law library	GIANNATTASI, Gerard E.	(NY)	430
Administration, libraries	VINT, Patricia A.	(MI)	1285

ADMINISTRATION (Cont'd)

Administration, management	SULLIVAN, Suzanne E. . .	(CA)	1208
	CHATFIELD, Michele R. . .	(DC)	203
	LOVE, Erika	(NM)	743
	KROAH, Larry A.	(PA)	679
	CURRAN, William M. . . .	(PQ)	266
Administration, management & instruction	QUIRING, Virginia M. . . .	(KS)	1000
Administration management techniques	BENOIT, Anthony H.	(LA)	82
Administration, medical education	KERR, Audrey M.	(MB)	644
Administration, middle management	TONGATE, John T.	(TX)	1250
Administration, middle school library	GERLACH, Gretchen J. . .	(IL)	429
Administration of a new library	DERMODY, Rita R.	(TX)	294
Administration of central & main branch	APPELBAUM, Sara B. . .	(FL)	29
Administration of children's department	GREENFIELD, Judith C. . .	(NY)	464
Administration of college libraries	MCKEE, Christopher	(IA)	810
Administration of college library	MCVEY, Susan C.	(OK)	818
Administration of departmental library	SHANKLAND, Anne H. . .	(ME)	1120
Administration of government records	WALCH, Victoria I.	(VA)	1293
Administration of information agencies	SHANK, Russell	(CA)	1120
Administration of information services	RUTHERFORD, Virginia L.	(GA)	1070
Administration of law firm library	D'AMORE, Denice M. . . .	(OH)	272
Administration of learning resource ctr	BOOK, Imogene I.	(SC)	115
Administration of library & info srvs	RODAWALT, Valarie J. . .	(TX)	1046
Administration of library service	LYDERS, Josette A.	(TX)	750
Administration of library services	NEWTON, Stephanne K. .	(DC)	900
	JOHNSON, Stephen C. . .	(OH)	609
Administration of non-profit corporation	TREBBY, Janis G.	(WI)	1255
Administration of periodicals collection	SMITH, Cynthia A.	(OH)	1153
Administration of public services	ROBINSON, Margaret G. .	(CA)	1044
Administration of research libraries	FORTH, Stuart	(PA)	391
Administration of school libraries	LENOX, Mary F.	(MO)	715
	EGAN, Mary J.	(NY)	338
	SHAPIRO, Lillian L.	(NY)	1121
	ADRIAN, Donna J.	(PQ)	7
Administration of school lib media progs	KLASING, Jane P.	(FL)	657
Administration of small academic libs	LANCASTER, Edith E. . .	(ID)	691
Administration of small libraries	VIGEANT, Robert J.	(IN)	1284
	HAY, Linda A.	(VT)	515
Administration of subscriptions	SMITH, Cynthia A.	(OH)	1153
Administration of system	HERSTAND, Joellen	(OK)	533
Administration of technical services	ANDERSON, David C. . .	(CA)	22
	GLEIM, David E.	(NC)	441
	LANGE, Elizabeth A. . . .	(SC)	695
Administration of university libraries	JENNERICH, Edward J. .	(WA)	598
Administration of user services	WILSON, Lizabeth A. . . .	(IL)	1351
Administration of visual collections	SHAW, Renata V.	(DC)	1123
Administration on regional level	PURCELL, Marcia L. . . .	(NY)	998
Administration organization, personnel	HEISE, George F.	(NJ)	522
Administration, personnel, budget	DAVID, Indra M.	(MI)	276
Administration, personnel, budget, space	ROSENFELD, Mary A. . .	(DC)	1056
Administration, personnel management	MCCARTHY, Germaine A.	(MA)	794
Administration planning & development	ZIPKOWITZ, Fay	(RI)	1389
Administration plus unions	DONAHUGH, Robert H. .	(OH)	310
Administration, public services	MORAN, William S.	(NH)	862
	UVA, Peter A.	(NY)	1270
Administration, purchasing, cataloging	HEDGES, Bonnie L.	(VA)	520
Administration reference	O'CONNELL, Susan	(NY)	915
Administration, reference, research	KNIGHT, Shirley D.	(NJ)	664
Administration, reference services	BURGESS, Rita N.	(PA)	159
Administration systems analysis	CHRISTNER, Deborah S.	(CA)	212
Administration, systems, planning	LARKIN, Patrick J.	(NY)	698
Administration, training & development	BOAZ, Martha T.	(CA)	108
Administration training & staff mgmt	NANTON-COMISSIONG, Barbara L.	(TRN)	887
Administrative	VOSS, Ruth A.	(AR)	1289
	DYER, Charles R.	(CA)	330
	BERARD, Sue A.	(KS)	84
	GROSSHANS, Maxine Z.	(MD)	473
	CAMMENGA, Cheryl G. .	(MI)	175
	GOLDSTEIN, Doris R. . .	(MI)	446

ADMINISTRATION (Cont'd)

Administrative	HEMPHILL, Frank A. . . .	(MI)	525
	CARRINGTON, Ruth . . .	(NY)	186
	HARKINS, Anna W.	(PA)	501
	GARDNER, Linda	(TX)	418
	GLAZER, Frederic J. . . .	(WV)	440
Administrative academic libraries	STEPHENS, Jerry W. . . .	(AL)	1188
Administrative & communications systems	MEADOWS, Donald F. . .	(BC)	819
Administrative & technical systems	KNIGHTLY, John J.	(TN)	664
Administrative assistance	RZECZKOWSKI, Eugene M.	(DC)	1072
Administrative leadership	GOULD, Douglas A.	(UT)	454
Administrative library work	SOBKOWIAK, Emily J. . .	(IL)	1165
Administrative management	FREEDMAN, Jack A. . . .	(MS)	400
Administrative networking	PELLEY, Shirley N.	(OK)	955
Administrative operations	BRANN, Andrew R.	(OH)	128
Administrative planning & evaluation	TERNAK, Armand T. . . .	(FL)	1232
Administrative planning & organization	SIMON, Bradley A.	(OK)	1140
Administrative policy for command	ROY, Alice R.	(VA)	1063
Administrative reference	PADUA, Flores N.	(PR)	934
Administrative responsibilities	SCHUERMANN, Lois J. .	(DC)	1101
Administrative services	NELSON, William N.	(AL)	895
	LA FOGG, Mary C.	(CT)	688
	NELSON, Norman L. . . .	(OK)	895
	MYERS, Marcia J.	(TN)	884
	HAYWARD, Edith C. . . .	(AB)	517
Administrative services & library mgmt	LEVIN, Marc A.	(CA)	720
Administrative special programs	FELLA, Sarah C.	(OR)	370
Administrative, supervising	MARK, Ronnie J.	(NY)	770
Administrative supervision	BUTTERWORTH, Donald Q.	(KY)	167
	HIRSCH, Dorothy K.	(MD)	543
Administrative support	CASSEDY, Barbara S. . .	(DC)	193
	SKLODOSKI, Terrance E.	(KY)	1147
	OKUDA, Sachiko E.	(ON)	920
Administrative system design	CLARKE, Elba C.	(GA)	218
Administrator	LAWSON, Venable A. . .	(GA)	705
	EVERINGHAM, Joyce D.	(NY)	358
	SVENNINGSEN, Karen L.	(NY)	1212
	WOODRUFF, Brenda B. .	(OH)	1366
	JONES, Faye E.	(WA)	613
Administrator, film & video library	MORRISON, George J. .	(NY)	868
Administrator, school library system	MORRISON, George J. .	(NY)	868
Advocacy of archival administration	SANTORO, Corrado A. .	(MB)	1082
Americana collection administration	JACKSON, Richard H. . .	(NY)	588
Archival administration	BRIDGES, Edwin C.	(AL)	135
	OETTING, Edward C. . . .	(AZ)	917
	BONFIELD, Lynn A.	(CA)	114
	NEWHALL, Ann C.	(CT)	898
	BURKE, Frank G.	(DC)	160
	JACOBS, Richard A. . . .	(DC)	590
	PINKETT, Harold T.	(DC)	974
	MAYER, Dale C.	(IA)	789
	STEWART, Virginia R. . .	(IL)	1193
	REDMON, Sherrill	(KY)	1014
	PAPENFUSE, Edward C.	(MD)	939
	DUVAL, Marjorie A.	(ME)	329
	COIR, Mark A.	(MI)	229
	HONHART, Frederick L. .	(MI)	556
	JONES, Clifton H.	(MI)	612
	SHAFER, Steven I.	(MI)	1119
	DANIELS, Paul A.	(MN)	273
	YOUNG, Julia M.	(MS)	1382
	MEVERS, Frank C.	(NH)	829
	DENSMORE, Christopher	(NY)	293
	LACHATANERE, Diana .	(NY)	686
	BAUMANN, Roland M. . .	(OH)	66
	CORNELL, Alice M.	(OH)	246
	GOERLER, Raimund E. .	(OH)	443
	HILAND, Gerard P.	(OH)	538
	REILLY, Sara L.	(PA)	1020
	SUMNERS, Bill F.	(TN)	1209
	HOWINGTON, Tad C. . .	(TX)	566
	KENAMORE, Jane A. . . .	(TX)	640
	SCHULTZ, Charles R. . .	(TX)	1101
	WILSON, Michael E.	(TX)	1352
	MANARIN, Louis H.	(VA)	764

ADMINISTRATION (Cont'd)

Archival administration

CLINE, Robert S.	(WA)	222
EASTWOOD, Terence M.	(BC)	333
WALSH, G M.	(ON)	1299
WOLVSKY, Haya S.	(ISR)	1362

Archival & photographic administration — DENSKY, Lois R. (NJ) 293

Archive, museum, & library admin — WRIGHT, John C. (HI) 1371

Archives administration

DABRISHUS, Michael J.	(AR)	269
BUTLER, Randall R.	(CA)	167
OKEEFE, Julia C.	(CA)	919
BRADSHER, James G.	(DC)	126
CRAWFORD, Elva B.	(DC)	256
HEISS, Harry G.	(DC)	523
SAHLI, Nancy A.	(DC)	1075
ELZY, Martin I.	(GA)	347
SCHEWE, Donald B.	(GA)	1092
GAYNON, David B.	(IL)	424
CONNELLY, James T.	(IN)	237
HARING, Jacqueline K.	(MA)	501
HOLDEN, Harley P.	(MA)	550
HORN, David E.	(MA)	559
MCLAIN, Guy A.	(MA)	813
O'TOOLE, James M.	(MA)	930
BOEDER, Thelma B.	(MN)	109
JESSEE, W S.	(MN)	600
SHOPTAUGH, Terry L.	(MN)	1132
WURL, Joel F.	(MN)	1374
HAVENER, Ralph S.	(MO)	513
JONES, Martin J.	(NY)	614
SERBACKI, Mary	(NY)	1116
SVIBRUCK, Jonathan	(NY)	1212
WHEELER, Elaine	(NY)	1328
FLAHIVE, Mary E.	(OH)	383
STOLT, Wilbur A.	(OK)	1196
THELEN, Richard L.	(OR)	1234
TURNBAUGH, Roy C.	(OR)	1264
ANDERSON, R J.	(PA)	25
LYTLE, Richard H.	(PA)	753
SPENCER, Catherine K.	(TX)	1173
WACHTER-NELSON, Ruth M.	(TX)	1290
EDWARDS, Steven M.	(WA)	338
RHOADS, James B.	(WA)	1026
BEYEA, Marion L.	(NB)	93
TAYLOR, Hugh A.	(NS)	1227
CAYA, Marcel	(PQ)	195
ORTIZ MONASTERIO, Leonor	(MEX)	927

Archives administration & operations — ROTHMAN, John (NY) 1060

Archives administration, land records — TEMPLE, Wayne C. (IL) 1230

Archives & manuscripts administration

PARHAM, Robert B.	(AK)	940
LATOUR, Terry S.	(MS)	701
KOVAN, Allan S.	(WI)	673

Archives management & administration — DUNN, Lucia S. (IL) 327

Art collections & museum administration — SOMMER, Ursula M. (NJ) 1167

Art library administration — SCHMIDT, Mary M. (NJ) 1095

Arts administration

MYERS, Maria P.	(NY)	884
HECK, Thomas F.	(OH)	519
LEWIS, Marjorie B.	(PA)	724

Assisting administrative duties — CHAPP, Debra R. (IL) 202

Assisting in library administration — KIBREAH, Golam (IN) 646

Audiovisual administration — CONOVER, Kathryn H. (FL) 238

Audiovisual equipment administration — WALTERS, Corky (WY) 1301

Audiovisual services administration — LATZEE, Henry R. (IL) 702

Automated administrative systems — ARROWOOD, Donna J. (CA) 34

Automation administration

RAWLEY, Wayne	(IA)	1010
BULAONG, Grace F.	(ON)	156

Bibliographic instruction, admin — BAUNER, Ruth E. (IL) 67

Branch administration

BROCKMAN, B D.	(GA)	138
RODERICK, Mary P.	(TX)	1047
VIIERANS, Mary P.	(BC)	1284

Branch adminstrv & supervisory skills — SMITH-EPPS, E P. (GA) 1161

Branch libraries administration — RAWLES-HEISER, Carolyn (IN) 1010

ADMINISTRATION (Cont'd)

Branch library administration

CRAIG, Susan V.	(KS)	254
SEABORN, Frances L.	(PA)	1109
GOLDBERG, Rhoda L.	(TX)	444
GREEN, Carol C.	(WA)	461

Budget administration

PANZERA, Donald P.	(DC)	938
KAUFFMAN, Betty G.	(NJ)	631
BONAMICI, Andrew R.	(OR)	113
ROY, Helene	(PQ)	1063

Budget & administration — FRALEY, Ruth A. (NY) 395

Budget & personnel administration — HEMPHILL, Jean F. (CO) 525

Budget, personnel actions administration — CURTIS, George H. (MO) 267

Budgeting & administration — MACFARLANE, Judy A. (PQ) 755

Budgeting & fiscal administration — ALMONY, Robert A. (MO) 17

Building & staff administration — BALCOM, William T. (IL) 51

Business administration

HICKS, Mary F.	(CA)	537
TEMPLETON, Mary E.	(GA)	1231
RUSIEWSKI, Charles B.	(IL)	1068
FERRERE, Cathy M.	(NY)	373
SIMONIS, James J.	(NY)	1141

Business archives administration — KING, Eleanor M. (PA) 650

Business development, mgmt & admin — PATRICIU, Florin S. (MD) 947

Catalog administration — MONTEE, Monty L. (CT) 856

Cataloging administration & teaching — AYRAULT, Margaret W. (HI) 43

Cataloging administrative records — WHEELER, Elaine (NY) 1328

Children's services administration

GUTHRIE, Chab C.	(OH)	479
FASICK, Adele M.	(ON)	366

Collection development, administration — ANTHONY, Paul L. (IL) 29

College & library administration — VEIT, Fritz (IL) 1281

College & school library administration — BROWN, Thomas M. (WV) 148

College & university library admin

GITLER, Robert L.	(CA)	438
KONDELIK, John P.	(IN)	670
YOUNG, Tommie M.	(NC)	1383
ALEXANDER, Shirley B.	(TX)	12

College library administration

ROSS, Rosemary E.	(AK)	1058
BOUSFIELD, Humphrey G.	(FL)	119
HARDESTY, Larry L.	(FL)	499
SIMMONS, Randall C.	(ID)	1140
FARBER, Evan I.	(IN)	363
MORRILL, Walter D.	(IN)	866
DAVIS, Mavis W.	(MD)	280
PARKS, James F.	(MS)	943
JONES, Plummer A.	(NC)	614
KROBER, Alfred C.	(NY)	679
MCGOWAN, Sarah M.	(WI)	807

Community college administration — MCCRACKEN, Barbara L. (TX) 799

Computer system administration — PETERSON, Barbara E. (PA) 962

Computers for administrative purposes — FOLEY, Mary D. (KY) 387

Conservation administration

BAKER, John P.	(NY)	48
HOGAN, Kristine K.	(NY)	549

Construction project administration — WALTERS, Daniel L. (WA) 1301

Consulting on administrative issues — RICH, Marcia A. (MA) 1027

Consulting on archival administration — BEHRND-KLODT, Menzi L. (WI) 75

Contract administration

SLOCA, Sue E.	(DC)	1150
BOGGESS, John J.	(MD)	110

Coordinating & administrating branches — ALGAZE, Selma B. (FL) 13

Corporate administration support — HOOTKIN, Neil M. (WI) 557

Cost analysis, library administration — ANDERSON, Sherry (NC) 25

County library administration

TRAVER, Dorothy A.	(CA)	1254
HALL, Edward B.	(MD)	487

County records administration & archives — WEAVER, Clifton W. (AL) 1312

Data administration

DENNISON, Lynn C.	(CA)	292
REED, Patricia A.	(DC)	1015
BREWER, Christina A.	(MD)	134
MCDONALD, David R.	(MI)	802

Database administration

TRIMBLE, Kathy W.	(CA)	1256
CURRAN, George L.	(NY)	266
MCCLURE, Margaret R.	(TX)	797
MOONEY, Shirley E.	(BC)	858
LEWIS, Leslie	(ON)	723

Database & systems administration — KINLEY, Jo H. (DC) 652

Database design & administration — JONES, Anne (NY) 611

Database management & administration — SLEETER, Ellen L. (CA) 1148

Departmental administration — BENDER, Cynthia F. (MD) 79

ADMINISTRATION (Cont'd)

Departmental management & administration	BOELKE, Joanne H.	(IL)	110
District school library administration	CURRIE, Bertha B.	(NS)	266
Divisional administration	TAGGART, William R.	(BC)	1220
Docket, conflict administration	KERN, Sharon P.	(IA)	643
East Asian library administration	KANEKO, Hideo	(CT)	625
Educational administration	BOISSE, Joseph A.	(CA)	111
	BRAUDE, Robert M.	(NY)	129
	SCHERDIN, Mary J.	(WI)	1092
Electronic mail administration	BEDARD, Bernard J.	(PQ)	73
Elementary school libraries admin	ZUCKER, Blanche M.	(NV)	1391
Federal program administration	CROCKETT, Martha L.	(DC)	259
Film & video library administration	THOMAS, Fred	(MD)	1236
Finance & administration	WASCHLER, Merl E.	(AZ)	1307
	COTE, Susan J.	(OH)	249
Financial administration	EIDSON, Alreeta	(CO)	340
	THOMPSON, Mary A.	(DC)	1240
	GALLOWAY, Margaret E.	(TX)	415
	SKELTON, W M.	(ON)	1146
Foundation administration	THOMPSON, Mary A.	(DC)	1240
General administration	DAY, Janeth N.	(AL)	282
	LIEBERMAN, Lucille N.	(CT)	726
	THOMPSON, Bert A.	(IL)	1239
	CAROLLO, Michael T.	(NV)	184
	SUHRE, Carol A.	(OH)	1207
	DEDAS, Madelyn W.	(WA)	286
General administration & management	EASTMAN, Ann H.	(VA)	333
General administration, public libraries	KRALISZ, Victor F.	(TX)	675
General administration, univ libraries	DORR, Ralze W.	(KY)	313
General administrative responsibilities	STARK, Li S.	(NY)	1181
General library administration	SKOGLUND, Susan E.	(MI)	1147
General library management, admin	DOLAN, Mary M.	(MN)	309
General management & administration	FREEDMAN, Bernadette	(PA)	400
Geoscience collections & administration	WICK, Constance S.	(MA)	1335
Government records administration	OLSON, David J.	(NC)	922
Grant administration	THOMPSON, Mary A.	(DC)	1240
	DAHLEN, Roger W.	(MD)	269
Grant program administration	LEWIS, Alan D.	(MN)	722
Grant proposals & administration	CABEZAS, Sue A.	(MA)	170
Grant writing, administration	SARLES, Christie V.	(NH)	1083
Grants administration	SMITH, George V.	(AK)	1155
	LINSLEY, Priscilla M.	(CO)	731
	JACOBS, Richard A.	(DC)	590
	SAHLI, Nancy A.	(DC)	1075
	MOUNCE, Marvin W.	(FL)	873
	BRONSON, Diane A.	(GA)	140
Grants administration & program devlpmnt	WRIGHT, Paul L.	(KY)	1372
Health administration	PINKOWSKI, Patricia E.	(IL)	975
	SAHYOUN, Naim K.	(MI)	1075
Health administration databases	RICHARDSON, Alice W.	(PA)	1029
Health administration literature	POOLE, Connie	(IL)	983
	SCHWARTZ, Dorothy D.	(NY)	1104
Health care administration & management	PATTERSON, Jennifer J.	(TN)	948
Health care administration reference srv	HAMILTON, Elizabeth J.	(VA)	492
Health science library administration	FULLER, Sherrilynne S.	(MN)	409
Health sciences library administration	EATON, Elizabeth K.	(MA)	333
	ANDERSON, Rachael K.	(NY)	25
	RICHARDS, Daniel T.	(NY)	1028
Health services administration	ACKERMAN, F C.	(DC)	3
Health services administration research	PLOTSKY, Andrea G.	(CA)	978
High school administration	BOULA, Lillian Y.	(FL)	119
High school library administration	GOZEMBA, Frances E.	(MA)	455
Higher education administration	FUSTUKJIAN, Samuel Y.	(FL)	410
	KATZ, Ruth M.	(NC)	630
	PERSON, Ruth J.	(PA)	961
Historical society, library admin	MILLER, Irene K.	(CT)	838
Hospital administration	TOVREA, Roxanna L.	(IA)	1252
	LARKIN, Virgil C.	(NY)	698
	CREELAN, Marilee M.	(OH)	257
	PIPER, Paula	(PA)	975
	KAKOSCHKE, Mona S.	(ON)	622
Hospital administration databases	MAHOVLIC, Leanne M.	(OH)	761
Hospital administration reference	SCHULTZ, Therese A.	(IL)	1102
Hospital administration resources	BRETSCHER, Susan M.	(NY)	134

ADMINISTRATION (Cont'd)

Hospital libraries administration	O'CONNOR, Elizabeth W.	(NJ)	916
Hospital library administration	STRUB, Jeane E.	(NM)	1203
	WALLER, Carolyn A.	(RI)	1298
	TAYLOR, Margaret P.	(ON)	1227
Hospital library administration & mgmt	WALES, Patricia L.	(CT)	1294
Information center administration	BONACORDA, James J.	(NY)	113
	BROOME, Diana M.	(BC)	141
	BELLEFONTAINE, Gillian	(ON)	78
Information policy administration	DE TONNANCOUR, P R.	(TX)	296
Installation & administration	REILLY, Dayle A.	(MA)	1020
Internal database administration	LUNAS, Leslie K.	(NJ)	748
K-12 school administration	REMKIEWICZ, Frank L.	(CA)	1022
Large high school library administration	SPICER, Orlin C.	(MO)	1174
Law administration	MAZZA, Joanne C.	(CA)	791
Law firm library administration	YALLER, Loretta O.	(DE)	1376
	VARGAS, Gwen S.	(PA)	1278
Law libraries administration	MARKE, Julius J.	(NY)	771
Law library administration	CLAPP, Laurel R.	(AL)	216
	ADAN, Adrienne	(CA)	6
	CASTETTER, Karla M.	(CA)	194
	HAYTHORN, Joseph D.	(CA)	517
	NEMCHEK, Lee R.	(CA)	895
	MCGUIRL, Marlene C.	(DC)	808
	PREBLE, Leverett L.	(DC)	990
	DANIELS, Westwell R.	(FL)	273
	EFRON, Muriel C.	(FL)	338
	WOODARD, Joseph L.	(FL)	1365
	JACOBS, Roger F.	(IN)	590
	FISHER, Collette J.	(LA)	380
	DUNN, Donald J.	(MA)	326
	MATZ, Ruth G.	(MA)	786
	MURRAY, Lynn T.	(MA)	882
	TRUBEY, Cornelia	(MA)	1258
	POOLEY, Beverly J.	(MI)	983
	SEARLS, Eileen H.	(MO)	1110
	GASAWAY, Laura N.	(NC)	421
	WILLIAMS, Lisa W.	(NC)	1344
	GIANNATTASI, Gerard E.	(NY)	430
	HAMMOND, Jane L.	(NY)	493
	PAGEL, Scott B.	(NY)	934
	NISSENBAUM, Robert J.	(OH)	905
	FLYNN, Lauri R.	(OR)	387
	BEYER, Robyn L.	(PA)	93
	SMITH, Linda D.	(PA)	1157
	CHAMPION, Walter T.	(TX)	198
	EDMONDS, Edmund P.	(VA)	336
	RAE, E A.	(ON)	1002
Law library administration for courts	WELKER, Kathy J.	(OH)	1321
Law library management administration	HERNANDEZ, Marilyn J.	(MB)	531
Learning resource center administration	BOROWSKI, Joseph F.	(IL)	117
Learning resources administration	BOONE, Morell D.	(MI)	115
	JASSAL, Raghbir S.	(NM)	595
Legal administrative support systems	CROCKETT, Denise J.	(NY)	259
Legal library management administration	HERNANDEZ, Marilyn J.	(MB)	531
Librarianship, administration	PETERSON, Randall T.	(IL)	964
Library activities administration	COLEMAN, L Z.	(AL)	231
Library administration	SCHORR, Alan E.	(AK)	1099
	SMITH, George V.	(AK)	1155
	WEILAND, Karen B.	(AK)	1317
	BIVINS, Hulen E.	(AL)	100
	DAMICO, James A.	(AL)	271
	HAMILTON, Ann H.	(AL)	491
	LASETER, Ernest P.	(AL)	700
	PARSLEY, Brantley H.	(AL)	944
	PENNINGTON, Walter W.	(AL)	957
	RAGSDALE, Kate W.	(AL)	1003
	LARSON, Larry	(AR)	699
	MCCOY, Evelyn G.	(AR)	799
	ROYAL, Selvin W.	(AR)	1063
	SANDERS, Kathryn A.	(AR)	1080
	WOODS, L B.	(AR)	1367
	YOUNG, Juana R.	(AR)	1382
	BOROVANSKY, Vladimir T.	(AZ)	117
	BUXTON, David T.	(AZ)	168

ADMINISTRATION (Cont'd)
Library administration

EDWARDS, Ralph M.	(AZ)	337
POWELL, Lawrence C.	(AZ)	988
TEVIS, Raymond H.	(AZ)	1233
ADENIRAN, Dixie D.	(CA)	6
ALFORD, Thomas E.	(CA)	13
AMRHEIN, John K.	(CA)	20
BIRCH, Tobeylynn	(CA)	98
BIRKEL, Paul E.	(CA)	98
BIRNIE, Elizabeth B.	(CA)	98
BLANK, Karen L.	(CA)	104
BOISSE, Joseph A.	(CA)	111
BONNET, Janice M.	(CA)	114
BOOKHEIM, Louis W.	(CA)	115
BOONE, Mary L.	(CA)	115
BRITTON, Helen H.	(CA)	137
CONDON, Erika M.	(CA)	236
CRAMPON, Jean E.	(CA)	255
CREAGHE, Norma S.	(CA)	257
DAILEY, Kazuko M.	(CA)	270
DOLVEN, Mary	(CA)	310
DUNKEL, Lisa M.	(CA)	326
FERGUSON, Chris D.	(CA)	372
GALLEGO, Bert H.	(CA)	414
GAY, Elizabeth K.	(CA)	423
GINSBURG, Helen W.	(CA)	438
GOLD, Anne M.	(CA)	444
HAIKALIS, Peter D.	(CA)	484
HAMMER, Sharon A.	(CA)	493
HEARTH, Fred E.	(CA)	519
HELLUM-BERMAN, Bertha D.	(CA)	524
HINCKLEY, Ann T.	(CA)	542
HOWATT, Helen C.	(CA)	565
IAMELE, Richard T.	(CA)	581
KLECKER, Anita N.	(CA)	658
KUCZMA, Michelle	(CA)	682
LAICH, Katherine	(CA)	688
LEE, Lydia H.	(CA)	710
LEVY, Mary J.	(CA)	722
MARTIN, Rebecca R.	(CA)	778
MELTZER, Ellen J.	(CA)	823
MEYER, Cynthia K.	(CA)	830
MORRIS, Jacquelyn M.	(CA)	866
MULE, Gabriel	(CA)	876
MULLER, Malinda S.	(CA)	877
PABST, Kahleen T.	(CA)	933
PALMER, Catherine C.	(CA)	936
PANTAGES, Sandra K.	(CA)	938
PARSONS, Jerry L.	(CA)	945
PETTAS, William A.	(CA)	965
RAMIREZ, William L.	(CA)	1005
RICHARDS, Marcia M.	(CA)	1028
ROSASCHI, Jim P.	(CA)	1054
RUHL, Taylor D.	(CA)	1066
SALZER, Elizabeth M.	(CA)	1078
SCHLOSSER, Anne G.	(CA)	1094
SIEGEL, Ernest	(CA)	1136
SMITH, Marvin E.	(CA)	1158
STEINMANN, Lois S.	(CA)	1186
STEUBEN, Raymond L.	(CA)	1190
SVIHRA, S J.	(CA)	1212
TANNO, John W.	(CA)	1223
TESTA, Elizabeth M.	(CA)	1233
THOMPSON, James C.	(CA)	1240
VEGA, Carolyn L.	(CA)	1281
VOIGT, Melvin J.	(CA)	1287
WALTERS, Mary D.	(CA)	1301
WAY, Kathy A.	(CA)	1311
WERNER, Gloria	(CA)	1324
WERNER, O J.	(CA)	1325
WIERZBA, Heidemarie B.	(CA)	1337
WILSON, Barbara A.	(CA)	1350
WILSON, Wayne V.	(CA)	1353
WONG, Clark C.	(CA)	1362
WOODWARD, Daniel	(CA)	1368
BOWERS, Sandra L.	(CO)	121
CHAMBERS, Joan L.	(CO)	198
CUMMING, Linda L.	(CO)	264

ADMINISTRATION (Cont'd)
Library administration

FIELD, Oliver T.	(CO)	375
GARYPIE, Renwick	(CO)	421
GREEN, Nancy W.	(CO)	462
HANSON, Elana L.	(CO)	498
HENDRICKSON, Charles R.	(CO)	527
MITCHELL, Marilyn J.	(CO)	849
MOFFEIT, Tony A.	(CO)	852
ROBERTS, Francis X.	(CO)	1040
BERBERICH, Patricia L.	(CT)	84
BERRY, Louise P.	(CT)	90
BERSON, Bella Z.	(CT)	90
BRADBERRY, Richard P.	(CT)	125
BRYAN, Barbara D.	(CT)	151
BURGAN, John S.	(CT)	159
LAWRENCE, Scott W.	(CT)	705
LEVINE, Marion H.	(CT)	720
SCHERER, Leslie C.	(CT)	1092
SELVERSTONE, Harriet S.	(CT)	1114
SIGGINS, Jack A.	(CT)	1137
SIMON, William H.	(CT)	1141
TRAINER, Karin A.	(CT)	1253
CAREY, Marsha C.	(DC)	181
FORK, Donald J.	(DC)	390
GEHRINGER, Michael E.	(DC)	425
JONES, Catherine A.	(DC)	611
LOMAX, Denise W.	(DC)	738
OAKLEY, Robert L.	(DC)	913
PAGE, John S.	(DC)	934
PILGRIM, Auriel J.	(DC)	973
QUINN, Susan	(DC)	1000
SHEELER, Harva L.	(DC)	1125
SHELAR, James W.	(DC)	1125
STACKPOLE, Laurie E.	(DC)	1178
STEWART, Ruth A.	(DC)	1193
TABB, Winston	(DC)	1219
TARR, Susan M.	(DC)	1224
TRIPP-MELBY, Pamela	(DC)	1257
TURTELL, Neal T.	(DC)	1265
WALKER, Heather C.	(DC)	1295
WANG, Chi	(DC)	1302
WELSH, William J.	(DC)	1323
WOLTER, John A.	(DC)	1362
COONS, Daniel E.	(DE)	242
TITUS, H M.	(DE)	1247
ULRICH, Sue	(DE)	1268
ALLEN, Francis P.	(FL)	15
ALLISON, Anne M.	(FL)	17
BARTHE, Margaret R.	(FL)	61
BROWN, Lyn S.	(FL)	145
CANELAS, Dale B.	(FL)	178
CORNELL, Sylvia C.	(FL)	247
DALLMAN, Glenn R.	(FL)	270
DEWAR, Jo E.	(FL)	298
EVANS, Josephine K.	(FL)	357
MAPP, Erwin E.	(FL)	768
METCALF, Davinci C.	(FL)	828
MILLIKEN, Ruth L.	(FL)	843
NEUHOFE, M D.	(FL)	897
SEBRIGHT, Terence F.	(FL)	1110
SESSA, Frank B.	(FL)	1116
SHINN, Sydniciel	(FL)	1131
SKALLERUP, Harry R.	(FL)	1145
SUMMERS, Lorraine S.	(FL)	1209
TEW, Robin L.	(FL)	1233
WALTON, Terence M.	(FL)	1302
BAUSCH, Donna K.	(GA)	67
BECHAM, Gerald C.	(GA)	71
BISSO, Arthur J.	(GA)	100
BRONSON, Diane A.	(GA)	140
BROWN, Edna E.	(GA)	143
BUDLONG, Thomas F.	(GA)	155
CALHOUN, Wanda J.	(GA)	172
FISTE, David A.	(GA)	382
HAMMOND, Elizabeth D.	(GA)	493
HEFFINGTON, Carl O.	(GA)	520
HEID, Gregory G.	(GA)	521
LISI, Susan C.	(GA)	732

ADMINISTRATION (Cont'd)
Library administration

MCIVER, Stephanie P. . .	(GA)	809
WILTSE, Helen C.	(GA)	1353
WEINGARTH, Darlene . .	(GU)	1318
ASHFORD, Marguerite K.	(HI)	36
HOEFLER, Barbara B. . .	(HI)	547
WILSON, Deetta C.	(HI)	1350
BERNING, Robert W. . . .	(IA)	89
DUNLAP, Leslie W.	(IA)	326
EDWARDS, John D.	(IA)	337
JENSEN, Janet L.	(IA)	598
POTTER, Corinne J.	(IA)	987
SCHEETZ, George H. . . .	(IA)	1090
ABRAHAM, Terry	(ID)	3
BECK, Richard J.	(ID)	71
COVINGTON, Eddis E. . .	(ID)	252
DOWNEY, Howard R. . . .	(ID)	316
ALLEY, Brian	(IL)	16
ANDERSON, Karen T. . .	(IL)	23
ANES, Joy R.	(IL)	27
BLOOM, Stephen C.	(IL)	106
BROWN, Doris R.	(IL)	143
CHESLEY, Thea B.	(IL)	207
CLARK, Barton M.	(IL)	216
COX, James C.	(IL)	253
DAVIS, Richard A.	(IL)	280
DOWNS, Robert B.	(IL)	317
ELDER, Nancy J.	(IL)	342
FUNK, Carla J.	(IL)	409
GARDNER, Trudy A.	(IL)	418
GIBBS, Margareth	(IL)	431
GOEHNER, Donna M. . .	(IL)	443
GROSS, Dorothy E.	(IL)	472
GUINEE, Andrea M.	(IL)	476
HORNY, Karen L.	(IL)	560
HOUDEK, Frank G.	(IL)	562
JENKINS, Darrell L.	(IL)	597
JOHNSTON, James R. . .	(IL)	610
KAGANN, Laurie K.	(IL)	621
KOWITZ, Aletha A.	(IL)	674
LI, Richard T.	(IL)	725
MADDEN, Michael J. . . .	(IL)	758
MCCOY, Ralph E.	(IL)	799
MEACHEN, Edward W. .	(IL)	819
MICHAELSON, Robert C.	(IL)	832
MONTANELLI, Dale S. . .	(IL)	855
O'BRIEN, Nancy P.	(IL)	915
OPEM, John D.	(IL)	925
O'SHEA, Cornelius M. . .	(IL)	928
PALMER, Raymond A. . .	(IL)	936
PHILLIPS, Dorothy E. . . .	(IL)	968
PIRON, Alice M.	(IL)	975
PIZER, Irwin H.	(IL)	977
ROBERTSON, S D.	(IL)	1042
RUBIN, Richard E.	(IL)	1065
SANDERS, Charlene R. .	(IL)	1079
SCHWERIN, Kurt	(IL)	1106
SIMPSON, Donald B. . . .	(IL)	1141
STARRATT, Joseph A. . .	(IL)	1182
TITUS, Elizabeth M.	(IL)	1247
TODD, Alexander W. . . .	(IL)	1248
VLCEK, Randall	(IL)	1286
VOLKMANN, Carl W. . . .	(IL)	1287
WAGNER, Ralph D.	(IL)	1292
WAITE, Ellen J.	(IL)	1293
WEECH, Terry L.	(IL)	1315
WHIPPLE, Caroline B. . .	(IL)	1329
WICKREMERATNE, Swarna	(IL)	1335
WILLSON, Richard E. . . .	(IL)	1349
BABBITT, Dennis L.	(IN)	43
COOPER, David L.	(IN)	242
EISEN, David J.	(IN)	340
FARRELL, David	(IN)	365
GALBRAITH, Leslie R. . .	(IN)	413
HAVLIK, Robert J.	(IN)	513
HOLICKY, Bernard H. . . .	(IN)	550
HOOK-SHELTON, Sara A.	(IN)	556
LOGSDON, Robert L. . . .	(IN)	737

ADMINISTRATION (Cont'd)
Library administration

MILLER, Robert C.	(IN)	841
SLOAN, Elaine F.	(IN)	1149
TUCKER, Dennis C.	(IN)	1261
WHITE, Herbert S.	(IN)	1331
BRAND, Alice A.	(KS)	127
BROWN, Mary A.	(KS)	146
BURICH, Nancy J.	(KS)	160
JOHNSON, Duane F. . . .	(KS)	603
RIDDLE, Raymond E. . . .	(KS)	1032
SCHANCK, Peter C. . . .	(KS)	1090
SNOKE, Elizabeth R. . . .	(KS)	1163
BESANT, Larry X.	(KY)	91
BIRCHFIELD, Martha J. .	(KY)	98
DEERING, Ronald F. . . .	(KY)	287
EDDY, Leonard M.	(KY)	335
FAUPEL, David W.	(KY)	366
GILMER, Wesley	(KY)	437
HELLARD, Ellen G.	(KY)	524
SUTHERLAND, Thomas A.	(KY)	1211
YOUNG, Sandra C.	(KY)	1383
BUCHANAN, William C. .	(LA)	153
LOUBIERE, Sue	(LA)	742
POSTELL, William D. . . .	(LA)	986
RAMBO, Gloria P.	(LA)	1005
REID, Marion T.	(LA)	1019
SKINNER, Robert E.	(LA)	1146
TAYLOR, Rebecca A. . . .	(LA)	1228
WICKER, W W.	(LA)	1335
BANDER, Edward J.	(MA)	54
CORCORAN, Dennis R. .	(MA)	245
DACHS, Jerald K.	(MA)	269
DAVY, Edgar W.	(MA)	281
DVORAK, Robert	(MA)	330
GROSE, B D.	(MA)	472
HOPKINS, Benjamin	(MA)	557
KEENAN, Elizabeth L. . . .	(MA)	634
KISSNER, Arthur J.	(MA)	656
LEAHY, Lynda C.	(MA)	706
LEEDS, Pauline R.	(MA)	711
MARTIN, Murray S.	(MA)	777
MCDONALD, Stanley M.	(MA)	803
MCDOWELL, Sylvia A. . .	(MA)	804
MCLELLAN, Mary T. . . .	(MA)	814
MICHAUD, Charles A. . .	(MA)	832
MOLTZ, Sandra S.	(MA)	854
MOSS, Karen M.	(MA)	872
PERCY, Theresa R.	(MA)	958
ROSE, Christine P.	(MA)	1054
SCHATZ, Natalie M.	(MA)	1090
TASHJIAN, Virginia A. . .	(MA)	1224
WINN, Carolyn P.	(MA)	1355
ZIMPFER, William E. . . .	(MA)	1389
BOGGESS, John J.	(MD)	110
BROWN, Carolyn P.	(MD)	142
GILLESPIE, David M. . . .	(MD)	435
GOETZ, Arthur H.	(MD)	443
GOLDSTEIN, Helene B. .	(MD)	446
HERIN, Nancy J.	(MD)	531
LACROIX, Eve M.	(MD)	686
MARTIN, Susan K.	(MD)	778
PISA, Maria G.	(MD)	975
SMITH, Jessie C.	(MD)	1156
WATERS, Samuel T. . . .	(MD)	1309
WILKINSON, Billy R. . . .	(MD)	1340
ALEXANDER, William D.	(ME)	12
FRIDLEY, Russell W. . . .	(ME)	403
PHIPPS, Bert L.	(ME)	969
VIGLE, John B.	(ME)	1284
ADAMS, Deborah L.	(MI)	4
ALLEN, Nancy H.	(MI)	15
AMES, Kay L.	(MI)	20
AMES, Mark J.	(MI)	20
BOONE, Morell D.	(MI)	115
ESTRY, Donna S.	(MI)	355
FRY, James W.	(MI)	406
GREEN, Katherine A. . . .	(MI)	462
GRIMM, Ann C.	(MI)	470
HANSON, Charles D. . . .	(MI)	498

ADMINISTRATION (Cont'd)
Library administration

KOLLMORGEN, Rose M.	(MI)	669
MARQUIS, Rollin P.	(MI)	773
MLODZIANOWSKI, Mary L.	(MI)	850
MONSMA, Marvin E.	(MI)	855
NDENGA, Viola W.	(MI)	890
OBERG, Larry R.	(MI)	914
RAZ, Robert E.	(MI)	1012
RIZZO, John R.	(MI)	1037
SHAPIRO, Beth J.	(MI)	1121
STOFFLE, Carla J.	(MI)	1196
TUCKER, Florence R.	(MI)	1261
WAGMAN, Frederick H.	(MI)	1291
WARNER, Robert M.	(MI)	1305
WILLIAMS, James F.	(MI)	1343
ANDERSON, Anita M.	(MN)	21
CARRISON, Dale K.	(MN)	187
COLLINS, Mary F.	(MN)	233
DUNN, Jamie N.	(MN)	326
HAASE, Gretchen E.	(MN)	480
HOPP, Ralph H.	(MN)	558
METZ, T J.	(MN)	828
OZOLINS, Karl L.	(MN)	933
SCHULZETENBERG, Anthony C.	(MN)	1102
BURCKEL, Nicholas C.	(MO)	158
CANN, Cheryle J.	(MO)	178
CRAWFORD, Susan Y.	(MO)	257
HALBROOK, Barbara	(MO)	485
HANKS, Nancy C.	(MO)	496
HOWERTON, Betty J.	(MO)	565
KAISER, Patricia L.	(MO)	622
KEMP, Charles H.	(MO)	639
MARTIN, Louis E.	(MO)	777
MARTIN, Mason G.	(MO)	777
MEADOR, John M.	(MO)	819
MILLER, William C.	(MO)	843
MULTER, Ell P.	(MO)	878
RACINE, John D.	(MO)	1001
REAMS, Bernard D.	(MO)	1013
STRAUSE, Robert C.	(MO)	1200
ANDERSON, James F.	(MS)	23
BLACKLEDGE, Theresa P.	(MS)	102
PAYNE, David L.	(MS)	951
SELTZER, Ada M.	(MS)	1114
WEST, Carol C.	(MS)	1326
WILLIAMSON, Phyllis B.	(MT)	1348
AHLERS, Glen P.	(NC)	8
BARKER, Richard T.	(NC)	56
BARTON, Phillip K.	(NC)	62
BERTHRONG, Merrill G.	(NC)	91
BIRD, Warren P.	(NC)	98
BOYCE, Emily S.	(NC)	122
BYRD, Gary D.	(NC)	168
CANNON, Robert E.	(NC)	179
FRANKLE, Raymond A.	(NC)	397
GAUGHAN, Thomas M.	(NC)	422
GRENDLER, Marcella	(NC)	467
HALL, Frances H.	(NC)	487
LACROIX, Michael J.	(NC)	686
LITTLETON, Isaac T.	(NC)	734
NUTTER, Susan K.	(NC)	912
SEIBERT, Karen S.	(NC)	1112
SHEARY, Edward J.	(NC)	1124
SPEER, Susan C.	(NC)	1172
TAYLOR, Raymond M.	(NC)	1228
WILKINS, Alice L.	(NC)	1340
KARAIM, Betty J.	(ND)	627
KAUP, Jermain A.	(ND)	631
ZINK, Esther L.	(ND)	1389
BOYER, Janice S.	(NE)	123
FORSMAN, Avis B.	(NE)	391
HANWAY, Wayne E.	(NE)	499
PETERSON, Vivian A.	(NE)	964
PHIPPS, Michael C.	(NE)	969
THOMAS, Jacquelyn H.	(NH)	1236
ANDERSON, Janelle E.	(NJ)	23
BULMAN, Learned T.	(NJ)	156

ADMINISTRATION (Cont'd)
Library administration

COHN, John M.	(NJ)	229
FIELD, Jack	(NJ)	375
GARVEY, Nancy G.	(NJ)	421
KOEPP, Donald W.	(NJ)	668
MALLALIEU, Robert K.	(NJ)	763
MONTAVON, Victoria A.	(NJ)	855
ODELL, Glendon T.	(NJ)	916
POLACH, Frank	(NJ)	980
SCHNEIDER, Lynette C.	(NJ)	1097
STEPHEN, Ross G.	(NJ)	1187
VARIEUR, Normand L.	(NJ)	1278
WHITING, Elaine M.	(NJ)	1333
DAVIS, Hiram L.	(NM)	279
GIBSON, Julie A.	(NM)	432
JASSAL, Raghbir S.	(NM)	595
TUBESING, Richard L.	(NM)	1261
JONYNAS, Aldona I.	(NV)	616
MCNEAL, Betty	(NV)	816
SOUTHWICK, Susan A.	(NV)	1170
ATKIN, Shifra	(NY)	37
BARRIE, John L.	(NY)	59
BERNTSEN, Robert M.	(NY)	90
BIDDLE, Stanton F.	(NY)	94
BOBINSKI, Mary F.	(NY)	108
BRAUDE, Robert M.	(NY)	129
BREEN, M F.	(NY)	131
BROWN, June E.	(NY)	145
BURSTEIN, Rose A.	(NY)	164
CASTRO, Julio E.	(NY)	194
CAVINESS, Ann N.	(NY)	195
CIPOLLA, Wilma R.	(NY)	215
COOVER, James B.	(NY)	244
DANSKER, Shirley E.	(NY)	274
DESCIORA, Susan O.	(NY)	294
DUCHAC, Kenneth F.	(NY)	322
EVANS, Robert W.	(NY)	358
EYMAN, David H.	(NY)	359
FINCH, C H.	(NY)	377
GAFFNEY, Ellen E.	(NY)	412
GLOECKNER, Donna S.	(NY)	441
GRECO, Gloria T.	(NY)	461
HARVEY, John F.	(NY)	509
HAYWARD, Diane J.	(NY)	517
HOROWITZ, Cyma M.	(NY)	560
JAFFE, Steven	(NY)	591
JAHR, Joanne B.	(NY)	591
JOHNSON, Richard D.	(NY)	608
JUNG, Norman O.	(NY)	620
KANSFIELD, Norman J.	(NY)	625
KING, Dennis W.	(NY)	650
KRATZ, Charles E.	(NY)	676
LASH, David B.	(NY)	700
LAUBACHER, Marilyn R.	(NY)	702
LAUER, Jonathan D.	(NY)	702
LAURENCE, Katherine S.	(NY)	703
LUNG, Chan S.	(NY)	748
MARKOWITZ, Lois	(NY)	771
MICHAEL, Douglas O.	(NY)	831
MOLHOLT, Pat	(NY)	852
MOLZ, Redmond K.	(NY)	854
MOORE, Ann L.	(NY)	858
MORGAN, Lynn K.	(NY)	864
MULLER, Claudya B.	(NY)	877
MURPHY, Anne M.	(NY)	880
MURRAY, Suzanne H.	(NY)	882
PALMIERI, Lucien E.	(NY)	937
PANELLA, Nancy M.	(NY)	938
RANDALL, Lawrence E.	(NY)	1006
RANKIN, Carol A.	(NY)	1007
RIGNEY, Janet M.	(NY)	1034
ROECKEL, Alan G.	(NY)	1048
ROWELL, Gordon A.	(NY)	1062
RYAN, Donald L.	(NY)	1070
SHUBERT, Joseph F.	(NY)	1133
SMITHEE, Jeannette P.	(NY)	1161
SORGEN, Herbert J.	(NY)	1168
STEWART, Betty F.	(NY)	1192
SWEENEY, Richard T.	(NY)	1215

ADMINISTRATION (Cont'd)
Library administration

TAYLOR, Patricia A.	(NY)	1228
VON WAHLDE, Barbara .	(NY)	1288
WATERS, Betsy M.	(NY)	1308
WENDT, Mary E.	(NY)	1324
WYATT, James F.	(NY)	1374
BETCHER, William M. . .	(OH)	92
BLOMQUIST, Laura G. . .	(OH)	106
DZIEDZINA, Christine A.	(OH)	331
GARDNER, Frank D. . . .	(OH)	417
GENAWAY, David C. . . .	(OH)	426
HAYNES, Kathleen J. . . .	(OH)	516
HELLING, James T.	(OH)	524
HUBER, Donald L.	(OH)	569
HUNE, Mary G.	(OH)	574
KOBULNICKY, Michael .	(OH)	666
MCPEAK, James J.	(OH)	817
O'BRIEN, Elmer J.	(OH)	914
PARCH, Grace D.	(OH)	939
PASQUAL, Patricia E. . .	(OH)	946
PATIENCE, Alice	(OH)	947
PINKNEY, Helen L.	(OH)	975
REESE, Gregory L.	(OH)	1016
SAWYERS, Elizabeth J. .	(OH)	1086
SCHIRMER, Robert W. . .	(OH)	1093
SCOLES, Clyde S.	(OH)	1106
TERHUNE, R S.	(OH)	1231
WALLACH, John S.	(OH)	1298
WEIDA, William A.	(OH)	1316
WILSON, Lucy	(OH)	1351
COCHENOUR, John J. . .	(OK)	225
HARRINGTON, Sue A. . .	(OK)	504
KENNEDY, James W. . . .	(OK)	641
LAU, Ray D.	(OK)	702
LEE, Sul H.	(OK)	711
MCQUITTY, Jeanette N. .	(OK)	817
ROBIN, Annabeth	(OK)	1043
ROBINSON, Joel M.	(OK)	1044
SAYRE, John L.	(OK)	1087
STOLT, Wilbur A.	(OK)	1196
BURKHOLDER, Sue A. . .	(OR)	161
CHMELIR, Lynn K.	(OR)	209
DUNN, Carolyn A.	(OR)	326
FORCIER, Peggy C.	(OR)	389
GEORGE, Melvin R.	(OR)	427
HILDEBRAND, Carol I. . .	(OR)	538
INGRAHAM-SWETS, Leonoor	(OR)	582
JOHNSON, Millard F. . . .	(OR)	607
KRUPP, Robert A.	(OR)	681
METZENBACHER, Gary W.	(OR)	828
MORGAN, James E. . . .	(OR)	864
MUNGER, Freda R.	(OR)	879
PIPER, Larry W.	(OR)	975
SALMON, Kay H.	(OR)	1077
SHIPMAN, George W. . .	(OR)	1131
WAND, Patricia A.	(OR)	1302
AMICONE, Janice L. . . .	(PA)	20
BOYLAN, Lorena A.	(PA)	123
BRAVARD, Robert S. . . .	(PA)	130
BURNS, Richard K.	(PA)	162
CLEVELAND, Susan E. . .	(PA)	221
COOPER, Joanne S. . . .	(PA)	243
CORRINGAN, John T. . .	(PA)	247
FALGIONE, Joseph F. . .	(PA)	362
FARNY, Diane M.	(PA)	365
FENICHEL, Carol H. . . .	(PA)	371
FORD, Sylverna V.	(PA)	390
FREEMAN, Michael S. . .	(PA)	401
GILBERT, Nancy L.	(PA)	434
GLOVER, Peggy D.	(PA)	442
HERRON, Nancy L.	(PA)	533
HILL, Judith L.	(PA)	540
HOFFMAN, David R. . . .	(PA)	547
HORVATH, Patricia M. . .	(PA)	561
MCCABE, Gerard B. . . .	(PA)	792
MCCABE, James P.	(PA)	793
MILLER, Mary C.	(PA)	840

ADMINISTRATION (Cont'd)
Library administration

NANSTIEL, Barbara L. . . .	(PA)	887
NEMEYER, Carol A.	(PA)	895
NIPPERT, Carolyn C. . . .	(PA)	904
PAGELL, Ruth A.	(PA)	934
PENROSE, Anna M.	(PA)	957
SMITH, Barbara J.	(PA)	1153
STICHA, Denise S.	(PA)	1193
SUMMERS, George V. . .	(PA)	1209
TAMKEVICZ, Julia H. . . .	(PA)	1221
TYCE, Richard	(PA)	1266
WALL, H D.	(PA)	1297
WHITEHURST, Dori A. . .	(PA)	1333
WYATT, Patricia A.	(PA)	1374
SABATER-SOLA, Rigel .	(PR)	1072
CAIRNS, Roberta A.	(RI)	171
LEVESQUE, Janet A. . . .	(RI)	719
TAYLOR, Merrily E.	(RI)	1227
BOWLES, David M.	(SC)	121
CALLAHAM, Betty E. . . .	(SC)	173
CHANDLER, Dorothy S. .	(SC)	199
DOVE, Herbert P.	(SC)	314
DRYDEN, Donald W. . . .	(SC)	321
MITLIN, Laurance R. . . .	(SC)	850
RIDGE, Davy J.	(SC)	1032
SAWYER, Warren A. . . .	(SC)	1086
SEAMAN, Sheila L.	(SC)	1109
TOOMBS, Kenneth E. . . .	(SC)	1251
HILMOE, Deann D.	(SD)	541
THOMPSON, Ronelle K. .	(SD)	1241
BENNETT, Peg E.	(TN)	82
BORCHUCK, Fred P. . . .	(TN)	116
EDWARDS, Rela G.	(TN)	337
GLEAVES, Edwin S.	(TN)	441
GOODALE, Adebonojo L.	(TN)	448
JACKSON, Joseph A. . . .	(TN)	587
JOYCE, Donald F.	(TN)	618
LEWIS, Rosalyn	(TN)	724
MARTIN, Jess A.	(TN)	776
MYERS, Marcia J.	(TN)	884
RICHARDS, Timothy F. . .	(TN)	1028
ROBERTSON, Billy O. . .	(TN)	1041
SMITH, Robert F.	(TN)	1160
VEACH, Lynn H.	(TN)	1280
WARD, James E.	(TN)	1304
ALBERTSON, Christopher A.	(TX)	10
BALDWIN, Joe M.	(TX)	51
BARKAN, Steven M. . . .	(TX)	56
BIGGERSTAFF, Judi L. .	(TX)	95
BILLINGS, Harold W. . . .	(TX)	96
BLACK, Elizabeth A. . . .	(TX)	101
BRESIE, Mayellen	(TX)	133
BREWER, Stanley E. . . .	(TX)	134
BROWN, Steven L.	(TX)	147
BULL, Margarita A.	(TX)	156
CASE, Bonnie N.	(TX)	191
CATES, Susan W.	(TX)	195
CHUANG, Felicia S.	(TX)	213
COTE, Carolee T.	(TX)	249
DEWBERRY, Betty B. . .	(TX)	298
DIXON, Catherine A. . . .	(TX)	306
DOYLE, Patricia L.	(TX)	317
GRAY, Paul W.	(TX)	460
HANES, Fred W.	(TX)	495
HOLIBAUGH, Ralph W. .	(TX)	550
HOWARD, Elizabeth A. . .	(TX)	564
HSU, Patrick K.	(TX)	567
IBACH, Robert D.	(TX)	581
KINGSBERY, Evelyn B. .	(TX)	652
KLAPPERSACK, Dennis .	(TX)	657
KLEIN, Mindy F.	(TX)	659
MOUNCE, Clara B.	(TX)	873
OGDEN, Suzanne M. . . .	(TX)	918
OLM, Jane G.	(TX)	921
SENG, Mary A.	(TX)	1115
SKINNER, Vicki F.	(TX)	1146
SNAPP, Elizabeth M. . . .	(TX)	1162
SOUTHARD, Ruth K. . . .	(TX)	1169

ADMINISTRATION (Cont'd)
Library administration

SVEINSSON, Joan L. . . .	(TX)	1212
TRAFFORD, Susan M. . .	(TX)	1253
WALKER, Constance M. .	(TX)	1295
WIKOFF, Ruth S.	(TX)	1338
WORLEY, Merry P.	(TX)	1369
YANCY, Susan M.	(TX)	1377
HANSON, Roger K.	(UT)	498
SHIRTS, Russell B.	(UT)	1131
ALTHEN, Elsa E.	(VA)	18
BERKELEY, Edmund . . .	(VA)	87
BROWN, Charles M. . . .	(VA)	142
BROWN, William A.	(VA)	148
CALLAHAN, John J. . . .	(VA)	173
DIERCKS, Thelma C. . . .	(VA)	302
FRANKLIN, Robert D. . . .	(VA)	398
GROVE, Pearce S.	(VA)	473
HUBBARD, William J. . .	(VA)	568
HURT, Charlene S.	(VA)	577
LEHMAN, Lois J.	(VA)	713
MARSHALL, Nancy H. . .	(VA)	775
NORDEN, David J.	(VA)	908
SADLER, Graham H. . . .	(VA)	1073
THORKILDSON, Terry A.	(VA)	1242
WARREN, Gail	(VA)	1306
BRONSTEIN, Dorothy J. .	(VI)	140
CHANG, Henry C.	(VI)	200
EATON, Nancy L.	(VT)	334
MOORE, Russell S.	(VT)	861
BAKER, Robert K.	(WA)	49
BLACKABY, Sandra L. . .	(WA)	102
HARBOLD, Mary J.	(WA)	499
HUTTON, Emily A.	(WA)	579
MCCAIN, Claudia J.	(WA)	793
PASTINE, Maureen D. . .	(WA)	946
STEVENS, Peter H.	(WA)	1190
TAYLOR, James B.	(WA)	1227
WEAVER, Carolyn G. . . .	(WA)	1312
YAPLE, Henry M.	(WA)	1377
DANIELS, Jerome P. . . .	(WI)	273
FU, Tina C.	(WI)	407
GOSZ, Kathleen M.	(WI)	453
MARQUARDT, Steve R. .	(WI)	772
PARSONS, Patricia S. . .	(WI)	945
RAAB, Kathleen M.	(WI)	1001
SCHMIDT, Mary A.	(WI)	1095
TASNADI, Deborah L. . .	(WI)	1224
TIETZ, Kathleen E.	(WI)	1244
FAULKNER, Ronnie W. . .	(WV)	366
JULIAN, Charles A.	(WV)	619
JOHNSON, Wayne H. . .	(WY)	609
BATEMAN, Robert A. . . .	(AB)	63
BUSCH, B J.	(AB)	165
HU, Shih S.	(AB)	568
JARVIS, Marylea	(AB)	595
LAVKULICH, Joanne . . .	(AB)	704
MACGOWN, Madge C. .	(AB)	755
MCDOUGALL, Donald B.	(AB)	803
RICHARDS, Vincent P. . .	(AB)	1029
BRIDGES, Douglas W. . .	(BC)	135
HALLIWELL, Dean W. . .	(BC)	489
MCINNES, Douglas N. . .	(BC)	809
RAY, Gordon L.	(BC)	1011
SCOTT, Priscilla R.	(BC)	1108
CONVERSE, Wm R. . . .	(MB)	239
PORTER, Patricia K. . . .	(MB)	985
BAZILLION, Richard J. . .	(ON)	68
BLACK, John B.	(ON)	101
BLACK, Sandra M.	(ON)	101
FOWLIE, Les	(ON)	394
FRAPPIER, Gilles	(ON)	399
GENOE, Murray W.	(ON)	427
GIBSON, Elizabeth A. . .	(ON)	432
JOHNSON, James R. . . .	(ON)	605
KING, Olive E.	(ON)	652
LAND, Reginald B.	(ON)	692
LEBLANC, Jean J.	(ON)	708
MARSHALL, Alexandra P.	(ON)	773
MOORE, Carole I.	(ON)	858

ADMINISTRATION (Cont'd)
Library administration

MURRAY-LACHAPELLE, Rosemary F.	(ON)	882
NICHOLSON, Jill A.	(ON)	902
PAVLIN, Stefanie A.	(ON)	951
RICHER, Yvon	(ON)	1030
SPICER, Erik J.	(ON)	1174
VANDERELST, Wil	(ON)	1274
WALSH, Sandra A.	(ON)	1300
WILKINSON, John P. . . .	(ON)	1340
WONG, Anita	(ON)	1362
AUMONT, Gerard	(PQ)	40
CHASSE, Jules	(PQ)	203
CHENIER, Andre	(PQ)	206
CRAWFORD, David S. . .	(PQ)	256
GARNETT, Joyce C. . . .	(PQ)	419
GREENE, Richard L. . . .	(PQ)	464
ORMSBY, Eric	(PQ)	926
RIDLER, Elizabeth A. . . .	(SK)	1032
VOHRA, Pran	(SK)	1287
RADFORD, Neil	(AUS)	1002
LINE, Maurice B.	(ENG)	730
BALDWIN, Robert D. . . .	(JAM)	52
ERDEL, Timothy P.	(JAM)	352
TOGUCHI, Eiko	(JAP)	1248
BOWEN, Dorothy N.	(KEN)	120
HANHAN, Leila M.	(LEB)	495
OROZCO-TENORIO, Jose M.	(MEX)	926
DE CASTRO, Elinore H. . .	(PHP)	285
MORAN, Teresita C.	(PHP)	862
RUNGSANG, Rebecca J.	(THA)	1067

Library administration, academic library

QUICK, Richard C.	(NY)	999

Library administration & automation

FUNG, Margaret C.	(MA)	409

Library administration & finance

HOWINGTON, Lee R. . .	(GA)	566

Library administration & management

ANDERSON, Herschel V.	(AZ)	23
BENGSTON, Carl E. . . .	(CA)	80
BOSSEAU, Don L.	(CA)	177
MINUDRI, Regina U. . . .	(CA)	847
WALCH, David B.	(CA)	1293
STEERE, Paul J.	(DC)	1184
SIROIS, Julie J.	(HI)	1144
BERRY, John W.	(IL)	90
SPARKS, Marie C.	(IN)	1171
REDDY, Sigrid R.	(MA)	1014
KOSMIN, Linda J.	(MD)	672
NEWMAN, Wilda B.	(MD)	900
DIDIER, Elaine K.	(MI)	301
ENGELKE, Hans	(MI)	349
COGSWELL, James A. . .	(MN)	227
ALBRITTON, Rosie L. . .	(MO)	10
RICKERSON, George T. .	(MO)	1031
HUTCHINSON, Barbara J.	(NJ)	579
CHANG, Daphne Y.	(NY)	200
BURRIER, Donald H. . . .	(OH)	163
MASON, Marilyn G.	(OH)	781
WOOD, Richard J.	(SC)	1365
LOWRY, Charles B.	(TX)	745

Library administration & personnel

ALITO, Martha A.	(DC)	13
SNYDER, Carolyn A. . . .	(IN)	1164

Library administration & planning

AKEROYD, Richard G. . .	(CT)	9
BONE, Larry E.	(NY)	113
CLARK, Robert L.	(OK)	218
BAKER, Douglas	(WI)	48

Library administration & policy

BILLY, George J.	(NY)	97

Library administration & staff

FOWLER, Margaret A. . .	(MB)	394

Library administration & supervision

GUYDON, Janet H.	(IN)	479

Library administration, col development

BROWN, Biraj L.	(SDA)	142

Library administration, online searching

SIARNY, William D.	(IL)	1134

Library administration, public services

HAWKINS, Mary J.	(KS)	514

Library administration, reader services

STWODAH, M I.	(VA)	1206

Library administrative

SKIDMORE, Stephen C. .	(OK)	1146

Library, administrative services

BYNON, George E.	(OR)	168

Library administrator

RITCHESON, Charles R.	(CA)	1036

Library & administrative documents

MEUNIER, Pierre	(PQ)	829

Library & archive administration

DOAK, Wesley A.	(OR)	306

ADMINISTRATION (Cont'd)

Library & data records administration	HURT, Nancy S.	(TX)	578
Library & info center administration	CROSS, Jennie B.	(MI)	260
Library & media administration	RONEY, Raymond G. . . .	(CA)	1053
	BLESH, Tamara E.	(NH)	105
Library & public administration	KERSCHNER, Joan G. . .	(NV)	644
Library automation administration	BRUNELL, David H.	(CO)	150
Library branch administration	FELTON, Barbara M. . . .	(IN)	370
Library budget administration	MURPHY, Joyce	(BC)	880
Library education & administration	BOMAR, Cora P.	(NC)	113
Lib education teaching & administration	SULLIVAN, Peggy A. . . .	(IL)	1208
Library finance & administration	EVERINGHAM, Neil G. . .	(VA)	358
Library management & administration	LEUNG, Shirley W.	(CA)	719
	LOOMIS, Barbara L.	(CA)	740
	STRONG, Gary E.	(CA)	1203
	SITTER, Clara M.	(CO)	1144
	SUNG, Carolyn H.	(DC)	1210
	DEYOUNG, Charles D. . .	(IN)	298
	FLAHERTY, Barbara A. . .	(MA)	383
	KERSHNER, Stephen A. .	(MI)	644
	WILSON, Patricia L.	(MI)	1352
	BRANIN, Joseph J.	(MN)	128
	EUSTER, Joanne R.	(NJ)	356
	SHELSTAD, Kirsten R. . .	(NM)	1126
	GREEN, Judith G.	(NY)	462
	KARRE, David J.	(OH)	628
	CLINE, Nancy M.	(PA)	222
	HELMS, Frank Q.	(PA)	525
	TODD, Fred W.	(TX)	1248
	DUNCAN, Cynthia B. . . .	(VA)	325
	RODGER, Jane	(ON)	1047
Library media administration	WONG, Clark C.	(CA)	1362
	ANDERSON, Della L. . . .	(MD)	22
Library media center administration	BUCKINGHAM, Betty J. . .	(IA)	154
Library, museum & archives admin	HYATT, John D.	(TX)	580
Library network administration	BYRN, James H.	(VA)	169
Library operation & administration	EGAN, Terence W.	(AZ)	338
Library organization & administration	JONES, William G.	(IL)	615
	COLLINS, Evron S.	(OH)	232
	ROUSE, Charlie L.	(OK)	1061
Library personnel administration	NICHOLS, Elizabeth D. . .	(CA)	901
	BOWDEN, Philip L.	(IL)	120
Library planning & administration	STUDER, William J.	(OH)	1204
	KACENA, Carolyn	(TX)	621
Library preservation administration	JONES, Maralyn	(CA)	614
Library project administration	MCCAUGHTRY, Dorothy H.	(CT)	795
Library school administration	LOWE, Mildred	(NY)	744
	WHALEN, Lucille	(NY)	1328
Library science education administration	FOOS, Donald D.	(FL)	388
Library system administration	SWAN, James A.	(KS)	1213
	WU, Harry P.	(MI)	1373
	NETTLES, Jess	(MS)	896
	LANGER, Frank A.	(WV)	695
Library systems administration	WILLIAMS, Susan S. . . .	(MI)	1346
	LIN, Susan T.	(NY)	728
	MILLS, Fiolina B.	(VI)	844
Library technical services admin	NICHOLS, Elizabeth D. . .	(CA)	901
Management administration	EATON, Elizabeth K. . . .	(MA)	333
	SHAUGHNESSY, Thomas W.	(MO)	1123
	CAMPBELL, Joylene E. .	(SK)	177
Management, administration, programs	LEHMAN, Tom	(MN)	713
Management, administration, supervisory	MARSHALL, Kathryn E. .	(IL)	774
Management & administration	HARDIN, Willie	(AR)	500
	FELDMAN, Irwin	(CA)	369
	LUSHINGTON, Nolan . . .	(CT)	749
	WILLSON, Katherine H. . .	(CT)	1349
	DICKSON, Constance P. .	(DC)	301
	FEINBERG, Beryl L.	(DC)	368
	HEAD, Anita K.	(DC)	518
	HOWARD, Mary R.	(GA)	564
	HUNTER, Julie V.	(GA)	576
	TRAINOR, Donna J.	(GA)	1253
	COATSWORTH, Patricia A.	(IL)	224

ADMINISTRATION (Cont'd)

Management & administration

	HANKES, Janice R.	(IL)	496
	FARLEY, Janice S.	(IN)	364
	SCHAD, Jasper G.	(KS)	1088
	BROGDON, Jennie L. . . .	(MD)	139
	HOMAN, J M.	(MI)	555
	SCHROEDER, Janet K. . .	(MN)	1100
	CRAIG, Marian D.	(MO)	254
	SUTTON, Judith K.	(NC)	1211
	STEPHENS, Ann E.	(NE)	1187
	ANSELMO, Edith H.	(NJ)	28
	STEEN, Carol N.	(NJ)	1184
	THRESHER, Jacquelyn E.	(NJ)	1243
	FRIEDMAN, Judy B.	(NY)	404
	NEWMAN, George C. . .	(NY)	899
	PRONIN, Monica	(NY)	995
	SEARS, Carlton A.	(NY)	1110
	BLACK, Frances P.	(OH)	101
	COPENHAVER, Ida L. . .	(OH)	244
	AXAM, John A.	(PA)	42
	DILLEN, Judith A.	(PA)	303
	GUTHRIE, Melinda L. . . .	(TX)	479
	HOADLEY, Irene B.	(TX)	545
	DRESANG, Eliza T.	(WI)	319
	NECHKA, Ada M.	(AB)	891
	PREMONT, Jacques	(PQ)	990
	ROY, Lucille Y.	(PQ)	1063
Management & administrative activities	LAWRENCE, Thomas A.	(NY)	705
Management & personnel administration	JONES, Anne	(NY)	611
Management records administration	AUSTIN, Ralph A.	(NY)	40
Manager & administrator of library	BERGEN, Dessa C.	(NY)	85
Managing, administration	MCCALLUM, Anita J. . . .	(ON)	793
Managing & administering personnel	ROUDEBUSH, Lawanda C.	(IA)	1061
Manuscript administration	LENNON, Donald R.	(NC)	715
Manuscripts & archives administration	HARDWICK, Bonnie S. . .	(CA)	500
Map library administration	COOMBS, James A.	(MO)	241
Media administration	MATHAI, Aleyamma	(NJ)	783
	MICHAEL, Douglas O. . .	(NY)	831
Media & library administration	NEILL, Laquita B.	(MS)	892
Media center administration	CLAVER, M P.	(AL)	219
	KOEPP, Sara H.	(IA)	668
	HELLER, Dawn H.	(IL)	524
	CLEAVER, Betty P.	(OH)	220
Media center operation & administration	EGAN, Terence W.	(AZ)	338
Media, library administration	STRANGE, Elizabeth B. .	(DE)	1200
Medical library administration	WALTERS, Gwen E. . . .	(FL)	1301
	DALRYMPLE, Prudence W.	(IL)	271
	GOLUB, Andrew J.	(ME)	447
	ROSENSTEIN, Philip . . .	(NJ)	1057
	ZUCKER, Blanche M. . . .	(NV)	1391
	ANDERSON, Rachael K.	(NY)	25
	KIRSCH, Anne S.	(NY)	655
	TANNER, Ellen B.	(NY)	1222
	GALLANT, Jennifer J. . . .	(OH)	414
	HALLERBERG, Gretchen A.	(OH)	489
	BOWLBY, Raynna M. . . .	(RI)	121
	FISHER, Janet S.	(TN)	381
	KNOTT, Teresa L.	(TX)	665
	MILLER, Jean K.	(TX)	838
	ROBERTSON, Ann	(WA)	1041
	KIRKWOOD, Brenda S. .	(SDA)	655
Medical reference administration	HEIDENREICH, Fred L. . .	(AZ)	521
Medical school administration	WILSON, Marjorie P. . . .	(MD)	1352
Medium-sized library administration	NEEDHAM, George M. . .	(OH)	891
	HALEY, Anne E.	(WA)	486
Microcomputers & library administration	RAPPAPORT, Susan E. .	(NY)	1008
Microcomputers in library administration	HOFFACKER, Antoinette C.	(PA)	547
Middle school library media center admin	GOZEMBA, Frances E. . .	(MA)	455
Municipal library administration	PERRY, Edward C.	(CA)	960

ADMINISTRATION (Cont'd)

Museum administration	SCHEWE, Donald B. . . .	(GA)	1092
	STEWART, Virginia R. . .	(IL)	1193
	KENAMORE, Jane A. . . .	(TX)	640
	JOHNSON, Kenneth P. . .	(VA)	606
Music administration & reference	HALL, Bonlyn G.	(VA)	487
Music library administration	FISKEN, Patricia B. . . .	(NH)	382
	VELLUCCI, Sherry L. . . .	(NJ)	1282
Music library administration & mgmt	BOGNAR, Dorothy M. . .	(CT)	111
Network administration	MEDINA, Sue O.	(AL)	820
	GRISHAM, Frank P.	(GA)	471
	BANFIELD, Eilzabeth S. .	(NS)	54
Network & consortium administration	NEUFELD, Judith B. . . .	(NY)	897
Non-profit administration	BALL, Alice D.	(DC)	52
Nuclear regulations & quality admin	KING, Betty J.	(WA)	650
Office administration	BOSTON, Mary T.	(CO)	118
One-person library administration	ALFONSI-GIN, Mary A. . .	(IL)	13
Organization & administration	TEANEY, Carol R.	(MO)	1229
	COAN, Mary L.	(NY)	224
	FOLCARELLI, Ralph J. . .	(NY)	387
Organization, planning & administration	HOELLE, Dolores M. . . .	(NJ)	547
Outreach administration	KLAUBER, Julie B.	(NY)	658
Overall administration & management	SHAW, Elizabeth L.	(OR)	1123
Pay & benefit administration	LEBRUN, Marlene M. . . .	(MD)	708
Performing arts administration	BUCK, Richard M.	(NY)	154
Personal computers for library admin	CALHOUN, Ellen	(NJ)	172
Personnel administration	COOLMAN, Jacqueline . .	(CA)	241
	TERRY, Josephine R. . . .	(CA)	1232
	YEH, Irene K.	(CA)	1379
	DIMATTIA, Ernest A. . . .	(CT)	304
	SHOLTZ, Katherine J. . .	(CT)	1132
	PANZERA, Donald P. . . .	(DC)	938
	CANELAS, Dale B.	(FL)	178
	EHRHORN, Jean H.	(HI)	339
	CRETH, Sheila D.	(IA)	258
	JENKINS, Darrell L.	(IL)	597
	LI, Dorothy W.	(IL)	724
	MCCABE, Ronald B. . . .	(IL)	793
	PETERSON, Fred M. . . .	(IL)	963
	VOLKMANN, Carl W. . . .	(IL)	1287
	RAWLES-HEISER, Carolyn	(IN)	1010
	CLOHERTY, Lauretta M.	(MA)	223
	KEOUGH, Francis P. . . .	(MA)	643
	LEBRETON, Jonathan A.	(MD)	708
	WILKINSON, Billy R. . . .	(MD)	1340
	SCHWARTZ, Diane G. . .	(MI)	1104
	SCHRAMM, Betty V. . . .	(MO)	1099
	COGGINS, Timothy L. . .	(NC)	227
	LANEY, Elizabeth J.	(NC)	695
	RODNEY, Mae L.	(NC)	1048
	KARMAZIN, Sharon M. .	(NJ)	627
	KUUSKMAE, Mati	(NY)	685
	ROGERS, Irene	(NY)	1049
	ROSSOFF, Judith H. . . .	(NY)	1059
	WENDT, Mary E.	(NY)	1324
	CUPP, Christian M.	(OH)	265
	GARTEN, Edward D. . . .	(OH)	420
	HELSER, Fred L.	(OH)	525
	BONAMICI, Andrew R. . .	(OR)	113
	HELICHER, Karl W.	(PA)	524
	NEAL, James G.	(PA)	890
	GALLOWAY, Margaret E.	(TX)	415
	GOLDBERG, Rhoda L. . .	(TX)	444
	TODD, Fred W.	(TX)	1248
	OLSEN, Randy J.	(UT)	921
	GHERMAN, Paul M.	(VA)	430
	HASKELL, John D.	(VA)	510
	WEAVER, Carolyn G. . . .	(WA)	1312
	ROOS, Tedine J.	(WY)	1053
	KHOUZAM, Monique . . .	(PQ)	646
Personnel administration & development	SHELDON, L S.	(CO)	1126
Personnel admin, performance appraisal	VEANER, Allen B.	(ON)	1280
Personnel & administration	MILLER, Marcia M.	(IN)	840
Personnel & budgeting administrative	LETTIERI, Robin M.	(NY)	719
Personnel management & administration	SCOTT, Thomas L.	(MN)	1108
	GIORDANO, Frederick S.	(NY)	438

ADMINISTRATION (Cont'd)

Personnel policies & administration	RITTER, Philip W.	(NC)	1036
Photograph collection administration	OKEEFE, Julia C.	(CA)	919
Planning & administration	JANES, Nina	(CO)	593
	PETERSON, Stephen L. .	(CT)	964
Planning & development, administration	WALSH, Lynn R.	(FL)	1299
Planning & personnel administration	PHILLIPS, Carol B.	(TX)	967
Preservation administration	FORTSON, Judith	(CA)	392
	OGDEN, Barclay W. . . .	(CA)	918
	MOON, Myra J.	(CO)	857
	BENNETT, Scott B.	(IL)	82
	BAKER, John P.	(NY)	48
	DARLING, Pamela W. . .	(NY)	275
	ROZENE, Janette B. . . .	(NY)	1064
	SWARTZELL, Ann G. . .	(NY)	1214
	BOOMGAARDEN, Wesley L. .	(OH)	115
	HEIDTMANN, Toby	(OH)	521
	PATTERSON, Robert H. .	(OK)	948
Private law firm administration	SCHIPPER, Joan A.	(CA)	1093
	KLEBBA, Lisa A.	(MO)	658
Program administration	GRAY, Dorothy L.	(DC)	459
Project administration	HORACEK, Paula B. . . .	(CA)	558
Project management & administration	MANBECK, Virginia B. . .	(NY)	764
Public administration	COLSON, Harold G.	(AL)	234
	GOODYEAR, Mary L. . . .	(CO)	450
	BLALOCK, Louise	(CT)	103
	ACKERMAN, F C.	(DC)	3
	JAQUES, Thomas F. . . .	(LA)	594
	GARDNER, Jack I.	(NV)	418
	SHIROMA, Susan G. . . .	(NY)	1131
	SILVER, Linda R.	(OH)	1138
	FOREHAND, Margaret P. .	(VA)	390
	ADAMS, Karen G.	(SK)	5
Public administration & policy	LEISTER, Jack	(CA)	714
Public administration research	ETTER, Constance L. . . .	(IL)	355
Public affairs & administration	FU, Tina C.	(WI)	407
Public affairs & public administration	FERRALL, J E.	(AZ)	373
Public health administration	HORAK, Ellen B.	(CT)	558
Public history administration	PRICE, William S.	(NC)	993
Public libraries administration	OAKS, Claire	(IL)	913
	VOJTECH, Kathryn	(IL)	1287
	CRABB, Elizabeth A. . . .	(TX)	254
	GOLDEN, Helene	(PQ)	445
Public library administration	KELLEY, Sally J.	(AR)	637
	PACK, Nancy C.	(AR)	933
	TROMATER, Raymond B.	(AR)	1257
	BROWN, Donna M.	(CA)	143
	BUCKLEY, James W. . . .	(CA)	154
	CONOVER, Robert W. . .	(CA)	238
	FARRIER, George F. . . .	(CA)	365
	KELLUM-ROSE, Nancy P.	(CA)	637
	KLINE, Victoria E.	(CA)	661
	LANGE, Clifford E.	(CA)	695
	NELSON, Helen M.	(CA)	893
	SHAPTON, Gregory B. . .	(CA)	1122
	STORSTEEN, Linda L. . .	(CA)	1198
	TEMA, William J.	(CA)	1230
	BETTENCOURT, Nancy J.	(CO)	92
	MAGRATH, Lynn L.	(CO)	760
	HOLLOWAY, Patricia W. .	(CT)	552
	JOHMANN, Nancy	(CT)	601
	FRANKLIN, Hardy R. . . .	(DC)	397
	RAPHAEL, Mary E.	(DC)	1008
	BREEDEN, Wendy R. . . .	(FL)	131
	MOUNCE, Marvin W. . . .	(FL)	873
	HUNTER, Julie V.	(GA)	576
	JAMES, Stephen E.	(GA)	592
	STEWART, Carol J.	(GA)	1192
	TOPE, Diana R.	(GA)	1251
	HORNE, Norman P.	(HI)	560
	GEIB, Jerry H.	(IA)	425
	LIND, Beverly F.	(IA)	728
	MINTER, Elizabeth D. . . .	(IA)	846
	BROWN, Diana M.	(IL)	143
	DEMPSEY, Frank J.	(IL)	291
	GOLDHOR, Herbert	(IL)	445
	HARRIS, Robert A.	(IL)	506
	HOFFMANN, Maurine L. .	(IL)	548

ADMINISTRATION (Cont'd)
Public library administration

LARSON, Carol . . . . (IL) 699
LOCASCIO, John F. . . . . (IL) 735
MCCULLY, William C. . . (IL) 801
MECHTENBERG, Paul . . (IL) 820
MEISELS, Henry R. . . . . (IL) 822
NOVAK, Lorrine M. . . . . (IL) 911
OLDERR, Steven . . . . . . (IL) 920
OSERMAN, Stuart . . . . . (IL) 928
PODESCHI, Gwen . . . . . (IL) 979
ROSENFELD, Joel C. . . . (IL) 1056
SCHLIPF, Frederick A. . . (IL) 1094
SHAVIT, David . . . . (IL) 1123
WEST, Barbara G. . . . . . (IL) 1326
ZENKE, Mary H. . . . . . . (IL) 1387
BOLTE, William F. . . . . . (IN) 113
GNAT, Raymond E. . . . . (IN) 442
HOLMAN, Mary J. . . . . . (IN) 553
LAUBE, Lois R. . . . . . . (IN) 702
OZINGA, Connie J. . . . . (IN) 933
ROBLEE, Martha A. . . . . (IN) 1045
BEATTIE, Brian . . . . (KS) 70
MUTH, Thomas J. . . . . . (KS) 883
BAKER, Janet R. . . . . . . (MA) 48
BUSH, Margaret A. . . . . . (MA) 165
DYGERT, Michael H. . . . (MA) 331
HILTON, Robert C. . . . . . (MA) 541
JAMES, Flaherty C. . . . . (MA) 592
LATHAM, Ronald B. . . . . (MA) 701
RAMSAY, John E. . . . . . (MA) 1005
COLLINS, Elizabeth H. . . (MD) 232
CURRY, Anna A. . . . . . . (MD) 266
GALE, Roswita W. . . . . . (MD) 413
GRIFFEN, Agnes M. . . . . (MD) 468
ROBINSON, Charles W. . (MD) 1043
WOODWARD, Robert C. (ME) 1368
HORN, Anna E. . . . . (MI) 559
O'CONNELL, Catherine A. (MI) 915
SHERIDAN, Clare A. . . . (MI) 1127
TATE, David L. . . . . (MI) 1225
WOODFORD, Arthur M. . (MI) 1366
FUGAZZI, Elizabeth B. . . (MN) 408
HOSLETT, Andrea E. . . . (MN) 561
YOUNG, Jerry F. . . . . . . (MN) 1382
ALEXANDER, Susanna . (MO) 12
FRANKLIN, Jill S. . . . . . . (MO) 397
GAERTNER, Donell J. . . (MO) 411
GRAVES, Sid F. . . . . (MS) 459
MACNEILL, Daniel S. . . . (MS) 758
SCHALAU, Robert D. . . . (MS) 1089
SCHLESINGER, Deborah
    L. . . . . (MT) 1094
GADDIS, Dale W. . . . . . . (NC) 411
RITTER, Philip W. . . . . . (NC) 1036
STEPHENS, Doris G. . . . (NC) 1188
TAYLOR, Michael Y. . . . (NC) 1228
WELCH, John T. . . . . . . (NC) 1321
HARRIS, Patricia L. . . . . (ND) 505
REA, Linda M. . . . . (NE) 1012
BECKERMAN, Edwin P. . (NJ) 72
BENNETT, Rowland F. . . (NJ) 82
BOGIS, Nana E. . . . . (NJ) 110
FADLALLA, Gerald J. . . . (NJ) 361
HECHT, James M. . . . . . (NJ) 519
MCCOY, W K. . . . . (NJ) 799
SUDALL, Arthur D. . . . . . (NJ) 1206
HUNSBERGER, Charles
    W. . . . . (NV) 574
CUMMINS, A B. . . . . (NY) 264
EISNER, Joseph . . . . (NY) 341
FLUCKIGER, Adrienne N. (NY) 386
GOLDEN, Fay A. . . . . . . (NY) 445
MITTELGLUCK, Eugene L. (NY) 850
O'CONNOR, William J. . . (NY) 916
ROUNDS, Joseph B. . . . (NY) 1061
STREIT, Ann M. . . . . (NY) 1202
TRUDELL, Robert J. . . . . (NY) 1259
VERBESEY, J R. . . . . . . (NY) 1282
COOK, Charles T. . . . . . (OH) 239

ADMINISTRATION (Cont'd)
Public library administration

                                                    CROMER, Kenneth L. . . . (OH) 260
                                                    FURL, Michael . . . . (OH) 410
                                                    O'CONNOR, Deborah F. . (OH) 916
                                                    REBENACK, John H. . . . (OH) 1013
                                                    BRAWNER, Lee B. . . . . (OK) 130
                                                    MEEKS, James D. . . . . . (OR) 821
                                                    CRONEBERGER, Robert
                                                        B. . . . . (PA) 260
                                                    HORVATH, Robert T. . . . (PA) 561
                                                    KAMPER, Albert F. . . . . . (PA) 624
                                                    KEISER, Barbara J. . . . . (PA) 635
                                                    MULLEN, Francis X. . . . . (PA) 877
                                                    THOMAS, Scott E. . . . . . (PA) 1238
                                                    TYNAN, Laurie F. . . . . . . (PA) 1267
                                                    BUNDY, Annalee M. . . . . (RI) 157
                                                    COOPER, William C. . . . (SC) 244
                                                    HEIMBURGER, Bruce R. . (SC) 521
                                                    LINE, Faith A. . . . . (SC) 730
                                                    NORTON, Tedgina . . . . . (TN) 910
                                                    DOUGLAS, Virginia G. . . (TX) 314
                                                    RASKA, Ginny . . . . (TX) 1009
                                                    GIACOMA, Pete J. . . . . . (UT) 430
                                                    HENDERSON, Harriet . . . (VA) 526
                                                    JOHNSON, Kenneth P. . . (VA) 606
                                                    BRENNAN, Cindy L. . . . . (WA) 132
                                                    WIRT, Michael J. . . . . . . (WA) 1356
                                                    DAWSON, Terry P. . . . . (WI) 282
                                                    LAMB, Donald K. . . . . . . (WI) 689
                                                    PENNINGTON, Jerome G. (WI) 957
                                                    SAGER, Donald J. . . . . . (WI) 1074
                                                    BEWLEY, Lois M. . . . . . . (BC) 93
                                                    FREVE, Reay H. . . . . (NS) 402
                                                    SKRZESZEWSKI, Stan E. (ON) 1147
                                                    BOYER, Denis P. . . . . . . (PQ) 123
                                                    MATTE, Pierre V. . . . . . . (PQ) 785
                                                    SHAW, Shiow J. . . . . . . (TAI) 1124

Public library administration &
    planning

Public library administration, budget

Public library administrative activities

Public library branch administration

Public library development & admin

Public library system administration

Public regional library administration

Public school library administration

Public service administration

Public services administration

STEINFELD, Michael . . . (MA) 1186
NIEMI, Peter G. . . . . (WI) 903
WALSH, Florence C. . . . (NJ) 1299
MOLZ, Jean B. . . . . (MD) 854
PITTMAN, Dorothy E. . . . (MD) 976
POSEL, Nancy R. . . . . . . (PA) 985
JONES, Wyman . . . . (CA) 615
KENT, Charles D. . . . . . (ON) 642
PORMEN, Paul E. . . . . . (OH) 984
JOHNSTON, Judy F. . . . (FL) 610
BALACHANDRAN,
    Sarojini . . . . (MO) 50
OELZ, Erling R. . . . . (MT) 917
SHELTON, Kathryn H. . . (AK) 1126
ADAMS, Judith A. . . . . . (AL) 5
CLARK, Alice S. . . . . (CA) 216
LEWIS, Alfred J. . . . . (CA) 722
MCELROY, Neil J. . . . . . (CA) 804
CLEMENS, Bonnie J. . . . (GA) 220
BINGHAM, Karen H. . . . (IL) 97
VANCIL, David E. . . . . . . (IN) 1273
LIPPINCOTT, Joan K. . . (NY) 732
THOMAS, Deborah A. . . (PA) 1236
JOSEPH, Margaret A. . . . (TX) 617

Publishing administration

Rare book library administration

Rare books administration

Records administration

Reference administration

WEIDA, William A. . . . . . (OH) 1316
KNACHEL, Philip A. . . . . (DC) 663
KENAMORE, Jane A. . . . (TX) 640
ROSS, Rodney A. . . . . . (DC) 1058
KASALKO, Sally G. . . . . (AR) 628
CAIN, Anne H. . . . . (CA) 171
HAHN, Ellen . . . . (DC) 483
WILER, Linda L. . . . . (FL) 1339
BRAUCH, Patricia O. . . . (NY) 129
PHILLIPS, Linda L. . . . . . (TN) 968
DUPUIS, Marcel . . . . (PQ) 327

Reference & library administration

Reference service administration

Reference services administration

Reference unit administration

Reference work, administration

Regional system administration

AYALA, John L. . . . . (CA) 42
TROMBLEY, Patricia A. . (TX) 1258
VIOLETTE, Judith L. . . . . (IN) 1285
APPLEBY, Judith A. . . . . (PQ) 30
HERBST, Linda R. . . . . . (MI) 530
LE BUTT, Katherine L. . . (NB) 708

ADMINISTRATION (Cont'd)

Religious archives administration	JOHNSON, Timothy J.	(IL)	609
Research administration	RIKLI, Arthur E.	(MO)	1034
	POTEAT, James B.	(NY)	986
Research library administration	GRAZIANO, Eugene	(CA)	460
	SCHMIDT, C J.	(CA)	1095
	ROGERS, Rutherford D.	(CT)	1050
	PETERSON, Paul A.	(MO)	964
	NITECKI, Joseph Z.	(NY)	905
Resource person to lib administration	WATSON, Joyce N.	(ON)	1309
Rural library administration	BURNETT, James H.	(CO)	161
School administration	GEIB, Jerry H.	(IA)	425
School & academic administration	SPENCER, Albert F.	(GA)	1173
School & public library administration	VEITCH, Carol J.	(NC)	1281
School district library administration	APPEL MOSESOF, Rhoda S.	(NJ)	29
School library administration	HAWKINS, Nina L.	(CA)	514
	MILLER, Margaret S.	(CA)	840
	HUGHES, Sondra K.	(CO)	572
	DAYTON, Diane	(GA)	283
	WHITE, Carol A.	(GA)	1330
	TRUETT, Carol A.	(HI)	1259
	DONHAM, Jean O.	(IA)	311
	HILAND, Leah F.	(IA)	538
	ADCOCK, Donald C.	(IL)	6
	FISHER, Lois F.	(IL)	381
	KARON, Joyce E.	(IL)	627
	KRAMER, Pamela K.	(IL)	675
	SHAFER, Anne E.	(IL)	1119
	BIANCHINO, Cecelia	(IN)	94
	LITTLE, Robert D.	(IN)	733
	MOSLEY, Mattie J.	(LA)	871
	BARTH, Edward W.	(MD)	61
	DEAN, Frances C.	(MD)	283
	MOLLENKOPF, Carolyn M.	(MO)	853
	RANDAZZO, Corinne O.	(MS)	1006
	SUMRALL, Ada M.	(MS)	1210
	HATHAWAY, Milton G.	(NC)	512
	GREENSPAN, Vivi S.	(NJ)	465
	FREEMAN, Patricia E.	(NM)	401
	CORRY, Emmett	(NY)	247
	ELLIS, Kathleen V.	(NY)	344
	JAFFE, Lawrence J.	(PA)	591
	MIZIK, Judy G.	(PA)	850
	WALKER, Sue A.	(PA)	1296
	FERNANDEZ, Josefina L.	(PR)	373
	MCANALLY, Charlotte L.	(TN)	792
	SCOTT, Willodene A.	(TN)	1108
	BURT, Lesta N.	(TX)	164
	CARDENAS, Martha L.	(TX)	180
	NISBY, Dora R.	(TX)	904
	PARIS, Janelle A.	(TX)	940
	WOLL, Christina B.	(TX)	1361
	KARPISEK, Marian E.	(UT)	628
	YOUNGER, Melinda M.	(VA)	1383
	BUELER, Roy D.	(WA)	155
	CZARNEZKI, Mary E.	(WI)	268
School library & media administration	JOSEPH, Elizabeth T.	(PA)	617
	SKELLEY, Cornelia A.	(WA)	1145
School library media administration	CARTER, Yvonne B.	(DC)	190
	YOUNG, Christina C.	(DC)	1381
	NOONAN, Eileen F.	(IL)	908
	MEANS, E P.	(KS)	820
	KULLESEID, Eleanor R.	(NY)	683
	CHISHOLM, Margaret	(WA)	209
School media administration	BURKE, Grace W.	(GA)	160
	WILSON, Mary S.	(MS)	1352
School media center administration	ROTH, Alvin R.	(MN)	1059
	JOYCE, Robert A.	(NC)	618
	LATROBE, Kathy H.	(OK)	701
	LAUGHLIN, Mildred A.	(OK)	703
Science administration & buildings	SOMERVILLE, Arleen N.	(NY)	1167
Science library administration	HALE, Kay K.	(FL)	485
Scientific library administration	BARKER, Victoria S.	(CO)	56
Selection, admin, reference, cataloging	MALTBY, Florence H.	(MO)	764
Serials administration	KASCUS, Marie A.	(CT)	628
	STOPPEL, Ellen K.	(IA)	1198
	HEPFER, Cynthia K.	(NY)	530
	HEPFER, William E.	(NY)	530

ADMINISTRATION (Cont'd)

Small college library administration	OLSEN, Rowena J.	(KS)	921
	SPICER, Orlin C.	(MO)	1174
	GARRETSON, Henry C.	(NY)	420
Small library administration	LEIDER, Karen S.	(DC)	713
	MORGAN, Sally W.	(HI)	864
	MCCLAREY, Catherine A.	(IL)	796
	PROCTOR, Judy C.	(IN)	995
	JOB, Rose A.	(MO)	601
	BALOG, Rita J.	(OH)	53
	PAKALA, James C.	(PA)	935
	MERCHANT, Thomas L.	(WI)	825
Small library administration & organz	REINGOLD, Judith S.	(NH)	1021
Small lib development & administration	HILL, Susan E.	(TX)	540
Small public library administration	MUDD, Isabelle G.	(AK)	875
	OVERSTREET, Allen J.	(FL)	931
	LINTNER, Barbara J.	(IL)	731
	MOTT, Schuyler L.	(ME)	872
	YOUNG, Lynne M.	(MN)	1382
	WAGGONER, Susan M.	(PA)	1291
	KNODLE, Shirley M.	(WI)	665
	EVANS, Patricia D.	(AB)	357
	KIRKPATRICK, Jane E.	(ON)	655
Small special library administration	CLARK, Jane F.	(GA)	217
Special collection administration	LEACH, Sally S.	(TX)	706
Special collections administration	MULLANE, William H.	(AZ)	877
	ZEIDBERG, David S.	(CA)	1387
	GORDON, Vesta L.	(VA)	452
	KIMBALL, Gregg D.	(VA)	649
	CUTHBERT, John A.	(WV)	267
Special libraries administration	FIRTH, Margaret A.	(MA)	379
	LEONARD, Ruth S.	(MA)	717
	COSKEY, Rosemary B.	(MD)	248
	SIGALA, Stephanie C.	(MO)	1137
	NORTON, Nancy P.	(TN)	910
Special library administration	MINTON, James O.	(AZ)	846
	ELMAN, Stanley A.	(CA)	345
	GOLDMAN, Nancy L.	(CA)	445
	SELZER, Nancy S.	(DE)	1114
	CULBERTSON, Diana L.	(IL)	263
	DAVIS, Elisabeth B.	(IL)	278
	KAYAIAN, Mary S.	(IL)	632
	MCNEILL, Janice M.	(IL)	816
	MOBLEY, Emily R.	(IN)	851
	TUTTLE, Walter A.	(NC)	1266
	VIXIE, Anne C.	(OR)	1286
	BOWLBY, Raynna M.	(RI)	121
	DUMAINE, Paul R.	(RI)	325
	BARLOGA, Carolyn J.	(WI)	57
	SUNDER-RAJ, P E.	(ON)	1210
Special library general administration	AHRENSFELD, Jan	(IL)	8
Special small library administration	BODNAR, Marta	(ON)	109
Specialized database administration	BILES, Mark J.	(NJ)	96
Staff & services administration	ESPER, Elizabeth	(FL)	354
State library administration	TOPE, Diana R.	(GA)	1251
	ROBERTSON, Linda L.	(IA)	1042
	NIX, Larry T.	(WI)	905
State library agency administration	WILKINS, Barratt	(FL)	1340
Supervision & administration	THOMAS, Lucille C.	(NY)	1237
Supervisory administration	HARVEY, Carl G.	(AB)	509
Teacher & administrator	COLYER, Judith A.	(MI)	234
Teaching administration, special libs	HUMPHRY, James	(NY)	574
Teaching & lecturing library admin	GRIFFEN, Agnes M	(MD)	468
Teaching library administration	MCNEAL, Archie L.	(FL)	816
Technical processing center admin	ENGELBERT, Alan M.	(WI)	348
Technical service administration	PERCELLI, Irene M.	(NY)	958
Technical services administration	BIERMAN, Kenneth J.	(AZ)	95
	HENSLEY, Charlotta C.	(CO)	529
	MANNING, Leslie A.	(CO)	766
	DAVIS, Betty B.	(IN)	277
	MUELLER, Jeanne G.	(IN)	875
	WAGAR, Joanna M.	(MI)	1291
	MARION, Phyllis C.	(MN)	770
	RACINE, John D.	(MO)	1001
	BREEDLOVE, Elizabeth A.	(NJ)	131
	HARRINGTON, Sue A.	(OK)	504
	BOYLAN, Lorena A.	(PA)	123
	RICHARDS, Barbara G.	(PA)	1028
	ROHDY, Margaret A.	(PA)	1050

ADMINISTRATION (Cont'd)

Technical services administration

BENGTSON, Betty G. ..	(TN)	80
LYNCH, Frances H.	(TN)	751
BATEMAN, Robert A.	(AB)	63

Technical services organization & admin

JOB, Rose A.	(MO)	601

Technological university library admin	SNYDER, Richard L.	(PA)	1165
Theological library administration	ALDRICH, Willie L.	(NC)	11
Toxicology archive administration	YOUNG, Carolyn K.	(KS)	1381
Trainer, administration	MORRIS, Effie L.	(CA)	866
Training development & administration	WALTERS, Carol G.	(NC)	1301
University administration	TIRRO, Frank P.	(CT)	1247
	SWARTZ, Jon D.	(TX)	1214
University library administration	BLANCHARD, J R.	(CA)	103
	HOLLAND, Harold E.	(CA)	550
	VOSPER, Robert	(CA)	1289
	FUSTUKJIAN, Samuel Y.	(FL)	410
	BISHOP, David F.	(GA)	99
	SMITH, Eldred R.	(MN)	1154
	ORNE, Jerrold	(NC)	926
	DALTON, Jack	(NY)	271
	SMITH, John B.	(NY)	1156
	BOBICK, James E.	(OH)	108
	BRANSCOMB, Lewis C. .	(OH)	129
	PATTERSON, Robert H. ..	(OK)	948
	ROUSE, Roscoe	(OK)	1061
	LYNDEN, Frederick C. ..	(RI)	752
	RANEY, Leon	(SD)	1007
	JAX, John J.	(WI)	595
University research lib administration	RUNKLE, Martin D.	(IL)	1067
UNIX systems administration	SULLIVAN, Edward A. ..	(CA)	1207

ADMIRALTY (See also Maritime)

Admiralty & maritime law	COMBE, David A.	(LA)	234
Admiralty law	RABER, Steven	(NY)	1001

ADMISSIONS

Admissions	NYHAN, Constance W. .	(CA)	912
Admissions & recruiting	ARNOLD, Barbara J. ...	(WI)	33

ADOLESCENT (See also Teenagers, Young, Young Adult, Youth)

Adolescent fiction	SHANNON, Jerry B.	(TX)	1120
Adolescent literature	KIRK, Mary L.	(IA)	654
	LANGHORNE, Mary J. ..	(IA)	696
	GROSE, Rosemary F. ...	(MA)	472
	GIBSON, Robert S.	(VA)	432
	JONES, Sally L.	(WA)	615
Adolescent materials	MCDONALD, Frances B. .	(MN)	802
Literature for adolescents	SADLER, Philip A.	(MO)	1073
Teaching children & adolescent lit	SANDERS, John B.	(MO)	1080
Working with children & adolescents	POLOMSKI, Linda	(CT)	982

ADULTS (See also Aging, Elderly, Older, Senior)

Adult & children literacy	LENGES, Magdelene ...	(IN)	715
Adult & children reference	POTTER, Robert E.	(FL)	987
Adult & children's book selection	GENCO, Barbara A.	(NY)	426
Adult & children's programming	CHRISTNER, Terry A. ...	(KS)	212
	HILDEBRANT, Darrel D. .	(ND)	539
Adult & children's reference service	KAPUR, Geraldine P.	(MI)	626
Adult & children's services	ELGIN, Susan R.	(CA)	342
Adult & juvenile storytelling	MACFARLANE, Francis X.	(TX)	755
Adult & reference specialist	MACK, Phyllis G.	(NY)	756
Adult & young adult collection devlpmnt	STEVENSON, Sheila M. .	(IL)	1191
Adult & young adult readers advisory	TREMBLAY, Carolyn B. .	(NH)	1255
Adult & young adult services	CHALLENER, Marcee M. .	(FL)	197
	SADLER, Shirley L.	(IL)	1073
	STEVENSON, Sheila M. .	(IL)	1191
	REILLY, Deborah D.	(MD)	1020
Adult basic & continuing education	WASSERMAN, Ricki F. .	(NY)	1308
Adult basic education	MARTIN, Brian G.	(NY)	775
Adult book selection	COFFEY, Dorothy A.	(MI)	227
Adult collection development	AMESTOY, Helen M. ...	(CA)	20
	BJORKLUND, Katharine B.	(NM)	100

ADULTS (Cont'd)

Adult education	GUARINO, John P.	(CA)	475
	STEVENSON, Grace T. .	(CA)	1191
	CANAVAN, Roberta N. ..	(NJ)	178
	PULLER, Maryam W.	(PA)	997
	WEBER ROOCHVARG, Lynn E.	(PA)	1314
Adult education, lifelong learning	GANN, Daniel H.	(IN)	416
Adult fiction	ALLENBACH, Norma A. .	(NY)	16
	LEGO, Jane B.	(VA)	712
Adult genre fiction	PENN, Lea M.	(NC)	957
Adult independent learners	MCGRIFF, Mary E.	(NC)	808
Adult librarianship	TSAI, Fu M.	(MI)	1260
	SMITH, Judy S.	(MS)	1156
Adult library programming	KUSZMAUL, Marcia J. ...	(IL)	685
	BURKE, Lauri K.	(RI)	160
Adult library programs	SARLES, Christie V.	(NH)	1083
Adult literacy	THOMAS, Vivian	(CA)	1238
	MCCAFFERY, Laurabelle	(IN)	793
	ARMITAGE, Katherine Y.	(NC)	32
	ROMISHER, Sivya S.	(NJ)	1053
	LYMAN, Helen H.	(NY)	751
	BERLIN, Susan T.	(OH)	87
	GREESON, Judy G.	(TN)	465
	STRAWDER, Maxine S. .	(TN)	1201
Adult literacy materials	GOLDBERG, Rhoda L. ...	(TX)	444
Adult literacy tutor trainer	KORNITSKY, Judith M. ..	(FL)	672
Adult materials selection	NICHTER, Alan	(FL)	902
Adult new reader materials	MCGRIFF, Mary E.	(NC)	808
Adult new readers publishing	RYAN, Jenny L.	(NY)	1071
Adult programming	POIRIER, Maria K.	(CT)	980
	ROEHLING, Steven R. ...	(GA)	1048
	WEISS, Cynthia A.	(IA)	1320
	JACOB, Merle L.	(IL)	589
	ROBY, B D.	(KY)	1045
	MCCORMICK, Emily S. .	(NC)	798
	BRODERICK, Therese L.	(NY)	139
	GILLESPIE, Gerald V.	(NY)	435
	SPYROS, Marsha L.	(NY)	1177
	YEE, J E.	(WA)	1379
Adult programming & instruction	UTSUNOMIYA, Leslie D.	(BC)	1270
Adult programming & services	DEMETRAKAKES, Jennifer B.	(IL)	291
Adult programs	BALCOM, William T.	(IL)	51
	O'BRYANT, Alice A.	(MT)	915
	NYERGES, Michael S. ..	(NY)	912
Adult public services	GREEN, Vera A.	(PA)	462
Adult reading interests & materials	FERSTL, Kenneth L.	(TX)	374
Adult reading services	MULAWKA, Chet	(CT)	876
Adult reference	MURPHY, Patricia A.	(CA)	881
	SIMAS, Therese C.	(CA)	1139
	SMITH, Heather	(CA)	1155
	WALSH, Donamarie F. ..	(CA)	1299
	INGERSOLL, Lyn L.	(DC)	582
	BRYAN, Michael G.	(FL)	151
	AUSTIN, Sandra G.	(IL)	40
	MILLER, Glenda G.	(IL)	838
	NOTOWITZ, Joshua D. ..	(MD)	910
	YERMAN, Roslyn F.	(MI)	1380
	ZARYCZNY, Wlodzimierz A.	(MI)	1386
	FARIAS, Elizabeth H. ...	(NC)	363
	WHITE, Sherry J.	(NC)	1332
	THONER, Jane T.	(NJ)	1242
	ENG, Mamie	(NY)	348
	KRAMPITZ, Barbara E. .	(NY)	676
	KRISTIAN, Alice	(NY)	679
	GRANTS, Yvette M.	(OH)	458
	BRADY, Josiah B.	(TN)	126
	EDWARDS, Susan E. ...	(WA)	338
	WAGNER, Sabina H. ...	(WA)	1292
	WASICK, Mary A.	(WI)	1308
	BROSSEAU, Lise	(PQ)	141
Adult reference & services	LOCKETT, Sandra B. ...	(WI)	736
Adult reference, reader's advisory	GELINAS, Jeanne L.	(MN)	426
Adult reference, reader's services	PORTER, Eva L.	(NJ)	984
Adult reference service	HICKS, Cynthia S.	(CA)	536
	MALLER, Mark P.	(IL)	763

ADULTS (Cont'd)

Adult reference services	GROOMS, Richard O.	(AL)	472
	FARNHAM, Shera M.	(AZ)	365
	HERSH, Daniel	(CA)	533
	ROBINSON, Lois C.	(FL)	1044
	MEYER, Barbara G.	(IL)	829
	MAY, Cecilia J.	(KS)	788
	KUBICK, Dan P.	(NE)	682
	BJORKLUND, Katharine B.	(NM)	100
	MULLEN, Francis X.	(PA)	877
Adult service	SHUEY, Andrea L.	(TX)	1133
Adult services	STEPHENS, Annabel K.	(AL)	1187
	POSSNER, Roger D.	(AZ)	986
	WATT, Mary J.	(AZ)	1310
	ANDERSEN, Leslie N.	(CA)	21
	GOLDMACHER, Sheila L.	(CA)	445
	HARRIS, Roger L.	(CA)	506
	MILO, Albert J.	(CA)	845
	TORKELSON, Jon A.	(CA)	1251
	BROOMALL, Susan G.	(FL)	141
	GREEN, Madonna	(FL)	462
	MITTLEMAN, Marilyn	(FL)	850
	STAMPFL, Barbara A.	(FL)	1179
	TAYLOR, Rose M.	(FL)	1228
	BROCKMAN, B D.	(GA)	138
	CHAUDOIN, Sheila M.	(IA)	204
	COCHRAN, William M.	(IA)	225
	KENAGY, Charles R.	(IA)	640
	NELSON, Mary L.	(IA)	894
	CHENOWETH, Rose M.	(IL)	206
	GREENFIELD, Jane W.	(IL)	464
	GUSS, Emily R.	(IL)	478
	HANKES, Janice R.	(IL)	496
	HINTZ, Jeanne E.	(IL)	543
	LAMB, Sara G.	(IL)	690
	NORWOOD, Pamela Z.	(IL)	910
	PIRES, Priscilla J.	(IL)	975
	PRESSING, Kirk L.	(IL)	991
	REILLY, Jane A.	(IL)	1020
	ROSE, Marta A.	(IL)	1055
	ROZANSKI, Barbara	(IL)	1064
	STROUSE, Roger L.	(IL)	1203
	SUNDELL, Elizabeth B.	(IL)	1210
	THOMAS, Marcia L.	(IL)	1237
	WALKER, Laura L.	(IL)	1295
	DUNCAN, Maureen E.	(IN)	325
	HELLARD, Ellen G.	(KY)	524
	KONTROVITZ, Eileen R.	(LA)	671
	SKIPTON, Iris E.	(MA)	1146
	BENSON, Carol T.	(MI)	83
	HORN, Anna E.	(MI)	559
	WASSERMAN, Sherry T.	(MI)	1308
	BYRNE, Roseanne	(MN)	169
	CLARKE, Charlotte C.	(MN)	218
	HAYS, Robert M.	(MN)	517
	WEIKUM, James M.	(MN)	1317
	HULL, Laurence O.	(NC)	572
	VAN HOY, Catherine S.	(NC)	1276
	WASILICK, Michael J.	(NC)	1308
	SHERWOOD, Janet R.	(NH)	1129
	DENNIS, Deborah E.	(NJ)	292
	HURLEY, John	(NJ)	577
	PARR, Louise M.	(NJ)	943
	PISKORIK, Elizabeth	(NJ)	976
	SCHMITT, Judy	(NJ)	1096
	EDWARDS, Guy P.	(NY)	337
	FRIEDMAN, Estelle Y.	(NY)	403
	HEINEMAN, Stephanie R.	(NY)	522
	MCCLURE, Jean M.	(NY)	797
	MOUSTAFA, Theresa A.	(NY)	874
	O'NEIL, Margaret M.	(NY)	924
	ROSSWURM, K M.	(NY)	1059
	SACCO, Gail A.	(NY)	1073
	SIMON, Patricia B.	(NY)	1140
	WENDOLSKI, Alice D.	(NY)	1323
	DOMBEY, Kathryn W.	(OH)	310
	KUCINSKI, B J.	(OH)	682
	RHODES, Glenda T.	(OH)	1026
	GORDON, Patricia H.	(OR)	451
	GIBLIN, Carol C.	(PA)	431

ADULTS (Cont'd)

Adult services	GLOVER, Peggy D.	(PA)	442
	HARKINS, Anna W.	(PA)	501
	HOFFACKER, Antoinette C.	(PA)	547
	LEE, Janis M.	(PA)	710
	SHEA, Margaret	(RI)	1124
	CHANDLER, Dorothy S.	(SC)	199
	MURDOCK, Everlyne K.	(SC)	879
	SINDEL, Amy C.	(SC)	1143
	MARCHANT, Cathy	(UT)	768
	LEGO, Jane B.	(VA)	712
	PARKER, John A.	(VA)	942
	HIATT, Peter	(WA)	536
	TRUHLER, Judith A.	(WA)	1259
	MONROE, Margaret E.	(WI)	855
	SINGH, Rosemary A.	(WI)	1143
	LAITMAN, Sheila	(ON)	688
Adult services & collection development	TYNES, Jacqueline K.	(NY)	1267
Adult services & programming	BINGHAM, Elizabeth E.	(LA)	97
Adult services & reference	DENNIE, David L.	(DC)	292
	HENSON, Ruby P.	(MI)	530
	GILLESPIE, Gerald V.	(NY)	435
Adult services & resources	LYMAN, Helen H.	(NY)	751
Adult services in public libraries	HAHN, Maureen	(PA)	484
Adult services management	BRYAN, Mila	(IL)	152
Adult services, programming	OLSON, Joann M.	(SC)	922
Adult special services	KRAMPITZ, Barbara E.	(NY)	676
Adult storytelling	VOSS, Joyce M.	(IL)	1289
Adult students	NOLAND, Jon	(CA)	908
Adult trade nonfiction selection	WISOTZKI, Lila B.	(MD)	1358
Adult-level storytelling	POMERANTZ, Bruce F.	(OH)	982
Adults	SALLSTROM, Marilee A.	(CA)	1077
Arts & humanities adult programming	SMOTHERS, Joyce W.	(NJ)	1162
Branch adult book selection	RODGER, Elizabeth A.	(ON)	1047
Children & adult reference & referral	DAYO, Ayo	(TX)	283
Developing programs for adults	FISCHER, Anna M.	(PA)	379
Disabled, older adults	DUPERREAULT, Marilyn J.	(SK)	327
Dyslexic adult students	THOMPSON, Jane K.	(VT)	1240
Film programming for adults	JEFFERY, Phyllis D.	(AL)	596
General adult reference	AMESTOY, Helen M.	(CA)	20
General reference & adult services	FOSTER, Joan	(MA)	392
Guidance for adult learners	O'HARA, Frederic J.	(NY)	919
Impaired older adult services	LEONARD, Gloria J.	(WA)	716
Library adult education programs	REILLY, Jane A.	(IL)	1020
Library services to adults	HANSEN, Andrew M.	(IL)	497
Management & adult public services	SZETO, Dorcas C.	(CA)	1218
Older adult services	KANNER, Elliott E.	(IL)	625
	MILLER, Junelle	(IN)	839
	BOLIN, Nancy C.	(MD)	112
Public libraries, adult programs	WRIGHT, Kathryn D.	(AL)	1372
Public libraries & adult services	FARACE, Virginia K.	(FL)	363
Public library, adult education	BROWN, Freddiemae E.	(TX)	144
Public library adult programming	MEYERS, Arthur S.	(IN)	830
Public library adult reference	DAVIS, Joy V.	(GA)	279
Public library adult services	ROLSTAD, Gary O.	(IL)	1052
Public programming for adults	MACKNIGHT, Judith M.	(NY)	757
Reference & adult materials	FELTON, Barbara M.	(IN)	370
Reference & adult services	BEEBE, Richard J.	(CA)	74
	VANDERLYKE, Barbara A.	(CT)	1274
	WAGNER, George L.	(CT)	1291
	ATWOOD, Virginia W.	(ID)	38
	KALRA, Bhupinder S.	(IL)	623
	WILSEY, Charlotte A.	(MD)	1349
	DESIREY, Janice M.	(MN)	295
	AULD, Hampton M.	(NC)	39
	TAYLOR, Anne C.	(NJ)	1226
	BARRETT, John C.	(NY)	59
	DESCH, Carol A.	(NY)	294
	LA SORTE, Antonia J.	(NY)	700
	ROECKEL, Alan G.	(NY)	1048
	SELVAR, Jane C.	(NY)	1114
	VELA-CREIXELL, Mary I.	(TX)	1281
	WEBER, Joan L.	(WA)	1314
	TALIS, Ross M.	(WI)	1221
Select weed central adult circulation	DOYLE, Patricia A.	(TX)	317
Training for adult services	SPYROS, Marsha L.	(NY)	1177

ADVERTISING (See also Marketing, Public Relations, Publicity)

Advertising	CAROTHERS, Diane F. .	(IL)	184
	LEVINSON, Gail	(MA)	721
	ROSE, Sharon G.	(MI)	1055
	BURKE, J L.	(NY)	160
	FEUERSTEIN, Robin ...	(NY)	374
	NASON, Stanley J.	(NY)	888
	OLEARY, Martha H.	(NY)	920
	PETRUGA, Patricia L.	(ON)	965
Advertising & business information	MASTROIANNI, Richard L.	(MD)	783
Advertising & marketing	DELANEY, Jerry	(IL)	289
	GATES, Carol M.	(IL)	421
	ROSENBERG, Barbra E.	(MA)	1055
	PERECMAN, Carol J.	(MI)	958
	HARNDEN, Donna J. ...	(MN)	502
	COHEN, Marsha C.	(NY)	228
	FENTON, Joan T.	(NY)	371
	MORRIS, Margaret J. ...	(NY)	867
	SANTORO, Tesse F. ...	(NY)	1082
	SCHACHTER, Bert	(NY)	1088
	SWANSON, Mary A. ...	(NY)	1213
	POWERS, Sally J.	(TX)	989
Advertising & marketing databases	ZILAVY, Julie A.	(NY)	1388
Advertising & marketing research	STEINMANN, Lois S. ...	(CA)	1186
	MACIVER, Linda B.	(MA)	756
	ROCHLEN, Rita E.	(MI)	1046
	GESKE, Aina S.	(NY)	430
Advertising & marketing services	BROMLEY, Alice V.	(NY)	140
Advertising & promotional literature	LONGO, Margaret K. ...	(CA)	740
Advertising & public relations	PEARSON, Jo A.	(IA)	952
Advertising copywriter	MITZIGA, Walter J.	(IL)	850
Advertising database	KELLEY, Dennis L.	(NY)	636
Advertising databases	GOODSELL, Joan W. ...	(NY)	450
Advertising databases & publishing	LITTLE, Dean K.	(OH)	733
Advertising information	HUBBARD, Susan E. ...	(NY)	568
Advertising marketing reference service	OWENS, Tina M.	(IL)	932
Advertising, newsletter production	WASERSTEIN, Gina S. .	(PA)	1307
Advertising, public relations consulting	FRISBIE, Richard	(IL)	405
Advertising research	PETRUGA, Patricia L. ...	(ON)	965
Advertising sales management	KOBASA, Paul A.	(IL)	666
Business, advertising & legal research	FISHER, Daphne V.	(PA)	380
Business & advertising reference	BUSSEY, Holly J.	(NY)	165
Business, marketing & advertising resrch	PIDALA, Veronica C. ...	(NY)	971
Electronic advertising	PODWOL, Sharon L. ...	(NY)	979
Industrial advertising	WISE, Eileen M.	(ON)	1356
Marketing, advertising & sales	CORNICK, Ron	(IL)	247
Marketing, advertising, public relations	BETTENCOURT, Nancy J.	(CO)	92
Marketing & advertising	SHIRASAWA, Sharon V.	(CA)	1131
Marketing & advertising databases	BUSSEY, Holly J.	(NY)	165
Public relations & advertising	GAMBRELL, Drucilla S. .	(AL)	416

ADVISING (See also Advisory, Consulting, Guidance)

Advising a student publication	MASON, John A.	(IL)	781
Advising, federal & state government	CASEY, Daniel W.	(DC)	192
Advising readers	EISENSTADT, Rosa M. .	(SC)	341
Career education information advising	LYONS, A J.	(MO)	753
College library advisement	MCCULLOUGH, Jack W.	(NJ)	801
Curriculum advising	DOUGLASS, Charlene K.	(GA)	314
Investment advice	NOBLE, James K.	(NY)	906
Programming & reader advisor	MARCKS, Carol J.	(LA)	769
Publishing advice	ROBLING, John S.	(MI)	1045
Reader advising	CLEMINSHAW, Barbara B.	(NY)	221
	WIRICK, Terry L.	(PA)	1356
Reader advisor	COLEMAN, James M. ...	(AL)	231
Reader's adviser's services	SHEEHAN, Robert C. ..	(NY)	1125
Reference & reader adviser service	ROUSE, Charlie L.	(OK)	1061
Reference, reader advising	ASLESEN, Rosalie V. ...	(SD)	36
Training & advising	BREWER, Helen L.	(VA)	134

ADVISORY (See also Advising, Consulting, Guidance)

Adult & young adult readers advisory	TREMBLAY, Carolyn B. .	(NH)	1255
Adult reference, reader's advisory	GELINAS, Jeanne L. ...	(MN)	426
Audiovisual selection & advisory	ORMOND, Sarah C.	(MI)	926
General reader's advisory work	BURKE, Lauri K.	(RI)	160
Library advisory	SELLERS, Wayne C.	(TX)	1114
Library instruction & reader's advisory	LINDGREN, Beverly P. ..	(IL)	729

ADVISORY (Cont'd)

LSCA advisory board	STEVENSON, Marilyn E. .	(CA)	1191
National advisory bodies	STEELE, Colin R.	(AUS)	1184
OCPL advisory	HAAS, William E.	(NY)	480
Reader advisories	JONES, Mary L.	(IL)	614
Reader advisory	CHAMBERS, Donald A. .	(HI)	198
	GILBERT, Donna J.	(OH)	433
Reader's advisories	KELLOGG, Joanne T. ...	(ME)	637
Reader's advisory	GALLAHAR, Christine M.	(FL)	414
	COLLINS, Eugenia A. ...	(GA)	232
	BROWN, Nancy E.	(IL)	146
	CALTVEDT, Sarah C. ...	(IL)	174
	JACOB, Merle L.	(IL)	589
	GILLIES, Irene B.	(MA)	436
	MCCORMICK, Sheila P. .	(MA)	799
	HIRSCH, Dorothy K.	(MD)	543
	HERTZ, Sylvia	(MI)	533
	ORMOND, Sarah C.	(MI)	926
	YOUNG, Lynne M.	(MN)	1382
	AYLWARD, Judith A.	(MO)	43
	MASSEY, Nancy O.	(NC)	782
	GREENBERG, Ruth S. ...	(NJ)	463
	VAN WIEMOKLY, Jane G.	(NJ)	1277
	ALVAREZ, Ronald	(NY)	19
	DEMARCO, Elizabeth A. .	(NY)	291
	KUCINSKI, B J.	(OH)	682
	JORDAN, Linda K.	(OK)	616
	KITE, Yvonne D.	(UT)	657
	RODGER, Elizabeth A. ..	(ON)	1047
Readers advisory book information	IRGON, Deborah A.	(NJ)	583
Reader's advisory, reference work	CORDUKES, Laura L. ...	(ON)	246
Readers' advisory service	NITZBERG, Dale B.	(MD)	905
Reader's advisory service & reference	HUNTER, Julie A.	(NC)	576
Readers advisory services	LAWRENCE, Scott W. ...	(CT)	705
Reading promotion, advisory	SHANNON, Kathleen L. .	(IL)	1120
Reference & reader advisory	LIGGAN, Mary K.	(VA)	726
Reference & reader's advisory	HOLMES, Nancy M.	(GA)	553
	KELLSTEDT, Jenny	(MA)	637
	BAILEY, Carol A.	(MD)	46
	O'NEIL, Margaret M.	(NY)	924
Reference & readers advisory services	OLENDER, Karen L.	(NC)	920
Young adult readers advisory	BENOIT, Ursula L.	(ON)	83

ADVOCACY (See also Lobbying)

Advocacy	HAGEMEYER, Alice L. ..	(DC)	483
Advocacy & lobbying	FADDEN, Donald M.	(PA)	360
Advocacy of archival administration	SANTORO, Corrado A. ..	(MB)	1082
Advocate library legislation	BEARD, Charles E.	(GA)	69
Arts advocacy	STRAWDER, Maxine S. ..	(TN)	1201
Child advocate, public relations	BANTA, Gratia J.	(OH)	55
Library advocacy	REEVES, Joan R.	(RI)	1016
Library legislation & advocacy	LARSON, Phyllis S.	(PA)	699
Mental health advocacy	COOPER, Joanne S. ...	(PA)	243
Public library advocacy	POSEL, Nancy R.	(PA)	985

AERIAL

| Aerial photography | STARK, Peter L. ...... | (OR) | 1181 |
| Maps, aerial photos, atlases | EASTON, William W. .... | (IL) | 333 |

AERONAUTICS (See also Aviation)

Aeronautical engineering information	AUSTIN, Rhea C.	(MD)	40
Aeronautical history	FOX, Howard A.	(WA)	394
Aeronautical history rare books	BARRETT, Donald J. ...	(CO)	59
Aeronautical indexing	LEVIN, Amy E.	(DC)	720
Aeronautics & aerospace reference	LEONARDO, Joan M. ...	(ON)	717
Military & aeronautics reference	KYSELY, Elizabeth C. ...	(CO)	685

AEROSPACE (See also Space)

Aeronautics & aerospace reference	LEONARDO, Joan M. ...	(ON)	717
Aerospace	MIRONENKO, Rimma ...	(CA)	847
	ZEBROWSKI, Cheryl K. .	(CA)	1387
	MILLIGAN, Steven M. ...	(CO)	843
	BOYLE, Lawrence C. ...	(IL)	124
	LAWRENCE, Barbara ...	(NY)	704

AEROSPACE (Cont'd)

Aerospace

	DOWDELL, Marlene S. . . .	(OH)	315
Aerospace & defense	DEWBERRY, Claire D. . . .	(GA)	298
Aerospace & engineering databases	ANTHONY, Paul L.	(IL)	29
Aerospace, automotive, engineering	YOUNGEN, Gregory K. .	(IN)	1383
Aerospace defense	DELTANO, Pauline T. . . .	(MA)	290
Aerospace industry research	BELL, Karen L.	(GA)	77
Aerospace information	KENNY-SLOAN, Linda . .	(CA)	642
	HALL, Robert G.	(MA)	488
Aerospace information & databases	SMALLWOOD, James R.	(CT)	1151
Aerospace information resources	KITCHENS, Philips H. . . .	(AL)	657
Aerospace intelligence	MAUTER, George A. . . .	(NY)	787
Aerospace library management	PAUL, Donald C.	(CA)	949
Aerospace literature	SCOTT, Catherine D. . .	(DC)	1107
Aerospace related research	JOHNSON, Marlys J. . . .	(MN)	607
Aerospace technical literature	BOYD, Effie W.	(TN)	122
Aviation & aerospace medicine	ROGERS, Ruth T.	(FL)	1050
Defense & aerospace info resources	BARTL, Richard P.	(NY)	61
Online aerospace & defense searching	RICH, Denise A.	(PA)	1027

AFFIRMATIVE

Affirmative action	YEH, Irene K.	(CA)	1379

AFRICA

Africa & Middle East cataloging	LEONARD, Louise F. . . .	(FL)	716
African & Afro-American studies	RHODES, Deborah L. . . .	(NY)	1026
African & Caribbean music	RICHARDSON, Deborra A.	(DC)	1029
African & Middle Eastern research	WITHERELL, Julian W. .	(DC)	1358
African bibliography	KRAEHE, Mary A.	(VA)	674
African libraries	JORDAN, Robert T.	(DC)	617
African library development assistance	PASQUARIELLA, Susan K.	(NY)	946
African literature history & arts	HUTSON, Jean B.	(NY)	579
African studies	MCCLEAN, Vernon E. . .	(NJ)	796
African studies bibliography	KAGAN, Alfred	(CT)	621
	HOWELL, John B.	(IA)	565
Africana	EASTERBROOK, David L.	(IL)	333
	PANOFSKY, Hans E. . .	(IL)	938
	MULLIGAN, William H. . .	(MI)	877
Africana bibliography	FINNEGAN, Gregory A. .	(NH)	378
Africana cataloging	STAMM, Andrea L.	(IL)	1179
Africana libraries	HUTSON, Jean B.	(NY)	579
	BOWEN, Dorothy N. . . .	(KEN)	120
Afro-American & African studies	BATTLE, Thomas C. . . .	(DC)	65
	HALL, Jo A.	(MI)	488
Area studies, African studies	ELSASSER, Katharine K.	(DC)	346
Cataloging Africana materials	NIEKAMP, Dorothy R. . .	(IN)	903
Development issues, African affairs	KOSTINKO, Gail A.	(DC)	673
Education & Africa	WISE, Kenda C.	(AL)	1357
Francophonic African bibliography	SHAYNE, Mette H.	(IL)	1124
Latin America & Africa	WARPHEA, Rita C.	(VA)	1306
Libraries in Sierra Leone West Africa	WATERS, Bill F.	(MO)	1308
South Africa	CASON, Maidel K.	(DE)	193
West African soils & water resources	CANDELMO, Emily	(NY)	178
Women in Africa	CASON, Maidel K.	(DE)	193

AFRO-AMERICAN (See also Black)

African & Afro-American studies	RHODES, Deborah L. . . .	(NY)	1026
African-American studies	MCCLEAN, Vernon E. . .	(NJ)	796
Afro-American, American lit resrch	BAKISH, David J.	(NY)	50
Afro-American & African studies	BATTLE, Thomas C. . . .	(DC)	65
	HALL, Jo A.	(MI)	488
Afro-American bibliography	BULLOCK, Penelope L. .	(GA)	156
	SCOTT, Sharon E.	(IL)	1108
	GUNN, Arthur C.	(MI)	477
	WRAY, Wendell L.	(PA)	1370
Afro-American children's literature	ELAM, Barbara C.	(MA)	341
Afro-American collection development	MARSHALL, Albert P. . .	(MI)	773
	WRIGHT, Catherine A. . .	(OR)	1370
Afro-American collections	HAZEL, Debora E.	(NC)	517
	SHOCKLEY, Ann A. . . .	(TN)	1132
Afro-American history	KNOX, Jo E.	(MD)	666
	MACK, Phyllis G.	(NY)	756
	LOTZ, Rainer E.	(WGR)	742

AFRO-AMERICAN (Cont'd)

Afro-American literature & art	HUTSON, Jean B.	(NY)	579
Afro-American music	RICHARDSON, Deborra A.	(DC)	1029
Afro-American studies	BALDWIN, Claudia A. . .	(CA)	51
	BULLOCK, Penelope L. .	(GA)	156
	SEARCY, David L.	(GA)	1109
Afro-Americana	JORDAN, Casper L. . . .	(GA)	616
Collection development, Afro-American	BELCHER, Emily M. . . .	(NJ)	76
Reserve & Afro-American librarianship	GENTRY, Etherlene H. . .	(MS)	427
Southwest Afro-American	STEPHENS, Alonzo T. . .	(TN)	1187
Teaching Afro-American literature	PERRY, Margaret	(IN)	960
Tennessee Afro-American	STEPHENS, Alonzo T. . .	(TN)	1187
Writing about Afro-American literature	PERRY, Margaret	(IN)	960

AGING (See also Elderly, Geriatrics, Gerontology, Older, Senior)

Aging & libraries	BEDIENT, Douglas	(IL)	73
Educational films on aging	YAHNKE, Robert E.	(MN)	1376
Library programs for aging	KRAMER, Mollie W.	(NY)	675
Library service to aging	PETERSON, Vivian A. . .	(NE)	964
	MONROE, Margaret E. . .	(WI)	855
Library services to the aging	FERSTL, Kenneth L.	(TX)	374
Reference & aging issues	TABER, Sally A.	(DC)	1219
Service to the aging	CASEY, Genevieve M. . .	(MI)	192
	KLEIMAN, Allan M.	(NY)	658
Services for the aged	SHEPHERD, Antoinette . .	(TX)	1127
Services for the aging	FOOS, Donald D.	(FL)	388
Services to aging, elderly	NEALE, Marilee	(TX)	891
Services to an aging population	MOORE, Bessie B.	(DC)	858

AGREEMENTS

Cooperative library agreements	MARTIN, Robert A.	(FL)	778
Cooperative serials agreements	ROBERTS, Elizabeth P. .	(WA)	1039
Worldwide exchange agreements	SNIDER, Elizabeth M. . . .	(OH)	1163

AGRIBUSINESS

Agribusiness research	BLUMENFELD, Judith K.	(MN)	107

AGRICULTURAL (See also Agribusiness, Crops, Farm)

Agricultural & scientific databases	PORTA, Maria A.	(IL)	984
Agricultural bibliography	STUBBAN, Vanessa L. . .	(KS)	1204
Agricultural biotechnology	LARSON, Jean A.	(MD)	699
Agricultural database	SPARKS, Richard M. . . .	(DC)	1171
Agricultural database searching	BARBER, Helen M.	(NM)	55
Agricultural databases	RUSS, Pamela K.	(FL)	1068
	CRAWFORD, Sherrida J.	(GA)	257
	LEDFORD, Carole L. . . .	(GA)	708
	MATHEWS, Eleanor R. . .	(IA)	784
	THOMPSON, Michael E. .	(MD)	1240
	BLUMENFELD, Judith K.	(MN)	107
	PETERSON, Julia C. . . .	(MN)	963
	GIBSON, Marianne	(MO)	432
	LAVOY, Constance J. . . .	(NC)	704
	BRITTON, Constance J. .	(OH)	137
	NOGA, Dolores A.	(AB)	907
	COOK, Elaine	(ENG)	239
	JOLING, Carole G.	(ITL)	610
Agricultural economics	CASEMENT, Susan D. . .	(CA)	192
	SCHULTZ, Susan	(IL)	1102
	LETNES, Louise M.	(MN)	718
Agricultural economics reference	PERMAN, Karen A.	(IL)	959
	REEDMAN, M R.	(MB)	1015
Agricultural engineering databases	MCNAUGHT, Hugh W. . .	(ON)	816
Agricultural information	HARRIS, Susan C.	(CA)	506
	KENNEDY, Amy J.	(MA)	640
	IRURIA, Daniel M.	(KEN)	584
Agricultural information abstracting	ASIS, Moises	(CUB)	36
Agricultural information dissemination	SINHA, Pramod K.	(IND)	1143
Agricultural information services	MLYNAR, Mary	(OH)	850
	WOODWARD, Anthony M.	(ENG)	1367
Agricultural information systems	BURTON, Hilary D.	(CA)	164
	OLSEN, Wallace C.	(NY)	922
	LUMANDE, Edward	(ZAM)	748
Agricultural libraries	LEDFORD, Carole L. . . .	(GA)	708
Agricultural, plant science information	MITCHELL, Steve	(CA)	849

AGRICULTURAL (Cont'd)

Agricultural reference	MATHEWS, Eleanor R. . .	(IA)	784
	DECKER, Leola M.	(MD)	286
	KINCH, Michael P.	(OR)	649
Agricultural research	NOGA, Dolores A.	(AB)	907
Agricultural resources	PEARSON, Jo A.	(IA)	952
Agricultural science reference	GAGE, Marilyn K.	(OK)	412
Agricultural sciences	SIBIA, Tejinder S.	(CA)	1134
Agricultural sciences reference & bibl	MANNARINO, Elizabeth R.	(OR)	766
Agricultural veterinary databases	NEELEY, Dana M.	(TX)	891
Agriculture	DEW, Stephen H.	(AR)	297
	JONES, Douglas E.	(AZ)	612
	SCHINDLER, Jo A.	(HI)	1093
	HUDSON, Rosetta A.	(MO)	570
	MOUREY, Deborah A. . .	(NY)	874
	KOSTER, Lieuwien M. . .	(NET)	673
Agriculture & biology online searching	GRAINGER, Bruce	(PQ)	457
Agriculture & food	BATEMAN, Robert A. . . .	(AB)	63
Agriculture & medicine online searching	STUBBAN, Vanessa L. . .	(KS)	1204
Agriculture collection development	MILLER, Susan E.	(LA)	842
	HARPER, Judy A.	(MB)	503
Agriculture databases	CURTIS, Susan C.	(GA)	267
	ADAM, Anthony J.	(WI)	4
Agriculture reference	HARPER, Judy A.	(MB)	503
	SIMUNDSSON, Elva D. . .	(MB)	1142
Banking & agriculture reference	PHILLIPS, Lena M.	(MD)	968
Biological & agricultural databases	CACCESE, Vincent	(CA)	170
	JOHNSON, Deanna L. . . .	(CA)	603
	SHAH, Syed M.	(NY)	1119
Biological & agricultural journals	SHAH, Syed M.	(NY)	1119
Biology, agriculture & environment	LANE, David M.	(NH)	694
Biology & agriculture bibliography	BLANCHARD, J R.	(CA)	103
Chemical & agriculture databases	CLARK, Wendolyn H. . . .	(AL)	218
Collection development, agriculture	NIPP, Deanna	(NJ)	904
Controlled environment agriculture	LAKE, Mary S.	(AZ)	689
Food, agriculture, nutrition information	JOHNSON, Sheila A. . . .	(NY)	609

AGRONOMY

Chemical & agronomy research	GAMBRELL, Drucilla S. .	(AL)	416

AI (See also Artificial, CAI, Expert, Intelligence)

AI expert systems	SIEGEL, Elliot R.	(MD)	1136
CAD/CAM & AI research	POLK, Diana B.	(IL)	981
Expert systems & AI	PITT, William B.	(MD)	976

AIR

Air & space law	FOX, James R.	(PA)	394
Air pollution	SMITH, Shirley M.	(NV)	1161
Map & air photo collections	SUTHERLAND, Johnnie D.	(GA)	1211
Water & air analysis	LEE, Diana W.	(AB)	709

AIR FORCE (See also Armed Forces)

Air Force libraries	NELSON, Marie L.	(CO)	894

ALASKA

Alaska & arctic information reference	SOKOLOV, Barbara J. . .	(AK)	1165
Alaska & polar regions reference service	LAKE, Gretchen L.	(AK)	688
Alaska collection development project	INNES-TAYLOR, Catherine E.	(AK)	583
Alaska environmental databases	SOKOLOV, Barbara J. . .	(AK)	1165

ALCOHOL (See also Substances)

Alcohol & drug abuse	KING, Karen P.	(SK)	651
Alcohol & drug use & abuse	MITCHELL, Andrea L. . .	(CA)	848
Alcohol & drugs	REIMER, Bette J.	(AB)	1020
Alcohol information online	MITCHELL, Andrea L. . .	(CA)	848
Alcohol studies	PAGE, Penny B.	(NJ)	934
Alcohol studies indexing	WEGLARZ, Catherine R.	(NJ)	1316
Alcoholism & substance abuse reference	WEINBERG, Gail B. . . .	(MN)	1317
Alcoholism, Mental hygiene	GILSON, Robert	(NY)	437
Substance & alcohol abuse	ROLETT, Virginia V.	(NH)	1051

ALLOCATIONS (See also Accounting)

Allocations	MONGAN, Janet	(OH)	854
Building planning & space allocation	RAWLEY, Wayne	(IA)	1010
Library indirect cost allocations	FRANKLIN, Brinley R. . .	(DC)	397
Resource allocation	LITTLE, Paul L.	(OK)	733
Resource allocations	MILLER, Richard T.	(MO)	841

ALTERNATIVE

Alternate forms of energy	JESKE, Margo	(ON)	600
Alternative careers	SIMONE-HOHE, M J. . . .	(PA)	1141
Alternative library, special collection	ANDREWS, Margaret . . .	(MA)	27
Alternative press	TSANG, Daniel C.	(CA)	1260
	EMBARDO, Ellen E.	(CT)	347
Alternative press publication	FROST, Michelle	(CA)	406
Alternatives to test animals	THURSTON, Ethel H. . . .	(NY)	1243
Health sciences including alternative	WOODBURY, Marda . . .	(CA)	1366
Science fiction alternative histories	COLLINS, William J.	(CA)	233

AMC (See also Cataloging)

AMC & MARC format manuscripts	ROBINSON, Christie M. .	(KY)	1043
AMC format	CLOUD, Patricia D.	(IL)	223
Cataloging manuscripts, using AMC format	CARTLEDGE, Connie L. .	(DC)	190
Cataloging with MARC AMC	BOYD, Sandra E.	(MS)	123

AMERICAN (See also Canada, Central (America), Latin America, South (America), United States, Western)

Acquisition of Americana	MCCORISON, Marcus A.	(MA)	798
Afro-American, American lit resrch	BAKISH, David J.	(NY)	50
American actors & actresses	ARCHER, Stephen M. . .	(MO)	31
American & English literature	ELDREDGE, Mary	(CA)	342
	DAVIS, Sandra B.	(IL)	281
American & English lit bibliography	BAKY, John S.	(PA)	50
American & European history	GRIPPO, Christopher F. .	(WA)	471
American & foreign language literature	SHIRES, Nancy P.	(NC)	1131
American & local history	LEERHOFF, Ruth E.	(CA)	712
American architecture slides	ROMEO, Sheryl R.	(DC)	1052
American art	WEIDMAN, Jeffrey	(OH)	1316
	BUSHNELL, Marietta P. .	(PA)	165
American art bibliography	WALKER, William B. . . .	(NY)	1296
American art history	BRUNK, Thomas W.	(MI)	150
American art reference	FALK, Peter H.	(CT)	362
	LYNAGH, Patricia M. . . .	(DC)	751
American art song	SHERIDAN, Margaret G.	(PA)	1127
American Black Catholic history	HOGAN, Peter E.	(MD)	549
American cultural history	MOSS, Roger W.	(PA)	872
American culture	WILLIAMS, Martin T. . . .	(DC)	1345
American decorative arts	LANTZ, Louise K.	(MD)	697
American diplomatic history	MCDONALD, Ellen J. . . .	(MA)	802
American ethnic collections	SUTTON, David H.	(PA)	1211
American figurative sculpture	SALMON, Robin R.	(SC)	1077
American folk arts	LIND, Judith Y.	(NJ)	728
American folklife indexing	OLSON, Eric J.	(NC)	922
American government	CHANCE, Truett L.	(TX)	199
American history	ALLAN, Nancy P.	(IL)	14
	BRIGGS, Martha T.	(IL)	135
	O'TOOLE, James M. . . .	(MA)	930
	PETTIT, Marilyn H.	(NY)	965
	VAN HORNE, John C. . .	(PA)	1275
	BLACK, J A.	(TX)	101
American history & biography	HANKAMER, Roberta A.	(MA)	496
American history bibliography	GETCHELL, Charles M. .	(NC)	430
American history collection development	VYHNANEK, Louis	(WA)	1290
American history consulting	SCHEIPS, Paul J.	(MD)	1091
American Indian archives	SPOTTED EAGLE, Joy .	(MT)	1175
	THIEL, Mark G.	(WI)	1235
American Indian bibliography	WEEKS, John M.	(MN)	1315
American Indian special collections	THIEL, Mark G.	(WI)	1235
American Indians	DAVIS, Mary B.	(NY)	280
American Jewish history	CLINE, Robert S.	(WA)	222
American law	RIEMANN, Frederick A. .	(TX)	1033
American Library Association chapters	GESSNER, Marianne . . .	(MI)	430
American library history	HOLLEY, Edward G.	(NC)	551
American literacy history	ABBOTT, Craig S.	(IL)	1

AMERICAN (Cont'd)

American literature — DOSER, Virginia A. . . . . . (CA) 313
FLYNN, Richard M. . . . . (DC) 387
MORTON, Bruce . . . . . . (MT) 870
WHITTINGTON, Erma P. (NC) 1334
BROWAR, Lisa M. . . . . . (NY) 141
DAVIS, Inez W. . . . . (TN) 279
American literature, romanticism — FISHER, Benjamin F. . . . (MS) 380
American music — ANDERSON, Gillian B. . . (DC) 23
BARNHILL, Georgia B. . . (MA) 58
COOLIDGE, Arlan R. . . . (RI) 241
American music bibliography — CARNOVALE, A N. . . . . (MS) 184
American music development — JERDE, Curtis D. . . . . . (LA) 599
American music reference — JACKSON, Richard H. . . (NY) 588
American musical theatre archives — ROSENBURG, Betsy R. . . (CT) 1056
American popular entertainments — LOMONACO, Martha S. . (NY) 738
American popular music — WELLS, Paul F. . . . . . . (TN) 1323
American presidency history — ELZY, Martin I. . . . . . . (GA) 347
American religion — SHUSTER, Robert D. . . . (IL) 1134
American science — ELLIOTT, Clark A. . . . . (MA) 343
American social history — ANDERSON, R J. . . . . . (PA) 25
American Southwest — KLIMIADES, Mario N. . . (AZ) 661
American studies — CHOJNACKA, Jadwiga . (POL) 210
American theatre history — ARCHER, Stephen M. . . (MO) 31
American 20th century records — ASHKENAS, Bruce F. . . (VA) 36
American women's studies — DICKSON, Katherine M. . (MD) 301
Americana — LABUDDE, Kenneth J. . . (MO) 686
FLAKE, Chad J. . . . . . . (UT) 383
PLITT, Jeanne G. . . . . . (VA) 978
PRESGRAVES, Jim . . . . (VA) 991
Americana collection administration — JACKSON, Richard H. . . (NY) 588
Americana, famous American autographs — STRINGFELLOW, William T. . . . . (NY) 1202
Americana, Old Northwest Territory — MULLIGAN, William H. . . (MI) 877
Anglo-American literature — WIENER, Paul B. . . . . . (NY) 1336
Bibliography of American art — SMITH, Raymond W. . . . (CT) 1159
Black American culture — SCOTT, Lydia E. . . . . . (PA) 1107
Black American history manuscripts — WEST, Donald . . . . (MI) 1326
Buying & selling of American literature — MARTIN, John W. . . . . (IL) 776
Catholic Americana — AMES, Charlotte A. . . . (IN) 19
Collection devlpmnt, Western Americana — CLARK, Robert M. . . . . (MT) 218
Consultation on American Catholic hist — THOMAS, Evangeline M. (KS) 1236
Contemporary American crafts — POLSTER, Joanne . . . . (NY) 982
Contemporary American drama — DACE, Tish . . . . (MA) 269
Contemporary American Jewish issues — HOROWITZ, Cyma M. . . (NY) 560
Contemporary American music — BOZIWICK, George E. . . (NY) 124
Contemporary American music bibliography — HARTSOCK, Ralph M. . . (PA) 508
Early American history & culture — MONTGOMERY, Michael S. . . . . (NJ) 856
Early American history 1492-1800 — ADAMS, Thomas R. . . . (RI) 6
18th century American history — GROVE, Pearce S. . . . . (VA) 473
English & American literature — MCPHERON, William . . . (CA) 817
KING, Judith D. . . . . . (CT) 651
STEBELMAN, Scott D. . . (DC) 1183
ELLIS, Marie C. . . . . . . (GA) 345
NAIMAN, Sandra M. . . . (IL) 886
BRACKEN, James K. . . . (IN) 124
IMMLER, Frank . . . . . . (MN) 582
BROCKMAN, William S. . (NJ) 138
JONES, Arthur E. . . . . . (NJ) 611
FRALEY, David B. . . . . (WA) 395
European & American history — THOMPSON, Janet A. . . (NM) 1240
History, American West — EMERSON, Tamsen L. . . (WY) 347
History of American libraries — MCMULLEN, Charles H. . (VA) 815
History of American printing — MCCORISON, Marcus A. (MA) 798
Libraries & American society — VANCE, Kenneth E. . . . (MI) 1273
Literature of American Southwest — BROGDEN, Stephen R. . (IA) 139
Native American — BLACK, Lea J. . . . . . . (ND) 101
SUMNER, Delores T. . . . (OK) 1209
Native American collection — CULL, Roberta . . . . . . (AZ) 263
Native American genealogy — AUTRY, Brick . . . . (TX) 41
Native American libraries — MCCRACKEN, John R. . (CA) 799
Native American music — ROBERTS, Donald L. . . (IL) 1039
Native Americans collections — MITTEN, Lisa A. . . . . . (PA) 850

AMERICAN (Cont'd)

Native Americans research — YOUNKIN, C G. . . . . . . (TX) 1383
New American religions — SMITH, Robert E. . . . . (IN) 1160
19th century American religious music — CHRISTENSON, Donald E. (OH) 211
19th century British & American lit — COLEY, Betty A. . . . . . (TX) 231
North American geology — WEST, Barbara F. . . . . (TX) 1326
North American periodicals — NOBLE, Jean E. . . . . . (CA) 906
Pacific Northwest Americana — REESE, Gary F. . . . . . (WA) 1016
Promoting regional American history — REINSTEIN, Julia B. . . . (NY) 1021
Rare books, Americana — REESE, William S. . . . (CT) 1016
Rare books, West Americana — DOBBERTEEN, Sara J. . (OK) 307
Recent American history — ELZY, Martin I. . . . . . . (GA) 347
Reference, American ethnic studies — RENKIEWICZ, Frank A. . (MI) 1023
Research, American Indian studies — BLUMER, Thomas J. . . . (DC) 107
Research & writing American history — SCHEIPS, Paul J. . . . . (MD) 1091
Research in American literature — BRODERICK, John C. . . (DC) 138
Services to Mexican Americans — NEALE, Marilee . . . . . (TX) 891
South American literature — WELCH, Thomas L. . . . . (DC) 1321
20th century American history — BARTHELL, Daniel W. . . (DC) 61
20th century American popular music — SPECHT, Joe W. . . . . . (TX) 1172
20th century American theater — LOMONACO, Martha S. . (NY) 738
USSR, Asia, South American, Europe art — BLAIR, Madeline S. . . . (DC) 102
Western American Jewish history — ARONER, Miriam D. . . . (CA) 34

ANABAPTIST

Anabaptist history — MARNET, Carole M. . . . (PA) 772

ANALOGUE (See also Recordings)

Analogue disc preservation — WAYLAND, Terry T. . . . (TX) 1311

ANALYSIS

Administration systems analysis — CHRISTNER, Deborah S. (CA) 212
Analyses of book industry — APPELBAUM, Judith P. . (PA) 29
Analysis design information systems — DEBONS, Anthony . . . . (PA) 285
Analysis of information needs — HOSONO, Kimio . . . . . (JAP) 562
Analysis of library systems — GOODFELLOW, Marjorie E. . . . . (PQ) 448
Analysis of medical information — LAMPORT, Bernard . . . (NY) 691
Analysis of science library functions — ALEXANDER, Carol G. . (VA) 12
Analyst — ELWELL, Christopher S. . (CT) 347
Analytic catalog — HOFFMAN, Herbert H. . (CA) 548
Analytical bibliography of music — BOORMAN, Stanley H. . (NY) 115
Analytical software — ZURBRIGG, Lyn E. . . . (ON) 1391
Analyze business opportunities — KIESER, Scott P. . . . . (NY) 647
Analyzing finances & budgeting — BENDER, Betty W. . . . (WA) 79
Automated text analyses — VON KEITZ, Wolfgang . . (WGR) 288
Automation & work analysis — WEAVER-MEYERS, Pat L. (OK) 1313
Automation, systems analysis — STAMBOULIEH, Nora . (PQ) 1179
Benefits analysis & evaluation — DUFORE, Thomas H. . . (AZ) 324
Bibliographic product analysis — FARINA, Robert A. . . . (DC) 363
Bibliometric analyses — FETTERMAN, Nelma I. . . (AB) 374
Biotechnology search analyst — FRANZELLO, Joseph J. . (TX) 398
Broker analysis research — HEFFRON, Betsy A. . . . (NY) 520
Business analysis & forecasting — BRINNER, Roger E. . . . (MA) 136
Business information analysis — MILLS, Catherine H. . . . (RI) 843
Business research analysis — JACKSON, Craig A. . . . (ON) 587
Cataloging & subject analysis — TAYLOR, Arlene G. . . . (NY) 1226
Cataloging, subject analysis — SOPER, Mary E. . . . . (WA) 1168
Classification & subject analysis — DYKSTRA, Mary E. . . . (NS) 331
Collection analysis — KRABBE, Natalie . . . . . (OR) 674
ROUSSEAU, Denis . . . (PQ) 1061
Collection analysis & development — RINGER, Sarah A. . . . . (AR) 1035
MACNEILL, Daniel S. . . (MS) 758
Community analysis — MILLER, Edward P. . . . (AZ) 837
STINES, Joe R. . . . . . (FL) 1194
LUEDER, Dianne B. . . . (IL) 747
HALE, Martha L. . . . . . (KS) 485
SUMLER, Claudia B. . . (MD) 1209
SMITHEE, Jeannette P. . (NY) 1161
VERBESEY, J R. . . . . . (NY) 1282
SAULMON, Sharon A. . . (OK) 1084
Company/industry competitive analysis — WARNER, Claudette S. . (IL) 1305

ANALYSIS (Cont'd)

Competitive analysis	MILLER, Ralph D.	(CA)	841
	CARR, Sallyann	(DC)	186
	MCDANIEL, Sara H.	(GA)	801
	BRAIMON, Margie S.	(NJ)	127
	MOUREY, Deborah A.	(NY)	874
	BORUCKI, Jennifer A.	(OH)	117
Competitive research, analyses	SOUDER, Edith I.	(PA)	1169
Competitor analysis & evaluation	PICKETT, Doyle C.	(NJ)	970
Computer systems analysis	CHRISTY, Ann K.	(DC)	212
Conducting & analyzing surveys	CANTWELL, Mickey A.	(NY)	179
Cost analysis, library administration	ANDERSON, Sherry	(NC)	25
Cost-benefit analysis	GOODFELLOW, Marjorie E.	(PQ)	448
Data analysis & retrieval	YACOUBY, Ray S.	(MA)	1376
Database analysis	DE ARMAN, Charles L.	(DC)	284
	WHITMAN, Jean A.	(MD)	1333
	GARCIA, Joseph E.	(MI)	417
	HARDIN, Nancy E.	(TN)	500
Database analysis & design	TAYLOR, Alice J.	(CA)	1226
Database & systems analysis	ROCHELEAU, Kathleen D.	(MA)	1046
Database systems design & analysis	KAVANAGH, Janette R.	(CO)	631
Document analysis	THACH, Phat V.	(PQ)	1233
Document analysis & generic coding	KNOERDEL, Joan E.	(MD)	665
Documentation analysis & coordination	HACKMAN, Larry J.	(NY)	481
Economic & industry analysis	FELDMAN, Stanley J.	(MA)	369
Economic research & analysis	COOPER, J P.	(MA)	243
End-user needs analysis	SHELBURNE, Elizabeth C.	(DC)	1125
Financial analysis	JONES, Jennifer R.	(NY)	613
Financial analysis research	HEFFRON, Betsy A.	(NY)	520
Financial market analysis	PHILLIPS, Steven G.	(MA)	969
Flexable packaging information analysis	MILLS, Catherine H.	(RI)	843
Grants analysis	HEDLIN, Ethel W.	(DC)	520
Graphic information analysis	PECK, Brian T.	(FL)	953
Health risk analysis research	MUNRO, Nancy B.	(TN)	879
Indexing & abstracting analysis	TAN, Elizabeth L.	(IL)	1222
Indexing, database analysis	MOOMEY, Margaret M.	(CO)	857
Industry analysis	BAKST, Shelley D.	(MA)	50
	HUSSEY, Laurie L.	(MA)	578
Information acquisition & analysis	CARSON, Bonnie L.	(MO)	188
Information analysis	PAUSLEY, Barbara H.	(OH)	950
Information delivery systems & analysis	GRIMES, A R.	(DC)	470
Information management analysis	BUSSEY, Holly J.	(NY)	165
Information needs evaluations & analysis	HOLDEN, Douglas H.	(ND)	550
Information retrieval & analysis	OWEN, Beth C.	(MA)	931
Information systems analysis & design	BORKO, Harold	(CA)	116
	WILLIAMS, James G.	(PA)	1344
Information systems design, analysis	SYPERT, Clyde F.	(CA)	1217
Job analysis & evaluation	DUFORE, Thomas H.	(AZ)	324
Legislative analysis	COAKLEY, Dorothy J.	(CA)	224
Library automation & systems analysis	MAURA-SARDO, Mariano A.	(PR)	787
Library cost analysis	SAYRE, Edward C.	(NM)	1087
Library cost analysis studies	FRANKLIN, Brinley R.	(DC)	397
Library policy analysis	DOWDING, Martin R.	(ON)	315
Library system analysis	ROHLF, Robert H.	(MN)	1050
Library system analysis & design	MORGAN, Ferrell	(CA)	864
Library systems analysis	HEINRITZ, Fred J.	(CT)	522
	PARKS, Amy N.	(CT)	943
	SILVESTER, June P.	(MD)	1139
	MULLINER, Kent	(OH)	878
	LEUNG, Frank F.	(ON)	719
Library systems analysis & automation	ALBERTUS, Donna M.	(NY)	10
Library systems & analysis	ANDERSON, Thomas G.	(GA)	25
	TODD, Fred W.	(TX)	1248
Library usage analysis	HUESTIS, Jeffrey C.	(MO)	570
Management analysis	ORTIZ, Diane	(NV)	927
Market analysis business reports	KASE-MCLAREN, Karen A.	(NY)	628
Market research & analysis	ROE, Georgeanne T.	(MA)	1048
Marketing research & analysis	EVANS, Shirley A.	(OH)	358
Mathematical analysis	ROBB, Thomas W.	(DC)	1038
Medical info system analysis & design	HENDRICKSON, Maria F.	(NY)	527
New media market analysis	KLOPFENSTEIN, Bruce C.	(OH)	662

ANALYSIS (Cont'd)

Online analysis	MATTOX, Rosemary S.	(KS)	786
Online analysis of labor	ANDERSEN, H F.	(MI)	21
Online database search analyst	JOHNSON, Stephen C.	(OH)	609
Online search analysis	WILLIAMS, Elizabeth L.	(TN)	1343
Policy analysis	PEYTON, David	(DC)	966
	SLATER, Susan B.	(MD)	1148
	WILLETT, Holly G.	(WI)	1341
Procedural systems analysis	NYBERG, Lelia J.	(CA)	912
Public library systems analysis	SHELTON, John L.	(GA)	1126
Quantitative analysis	FRETWELL, Gordon E.	(MA)	402
Real estate analysis	LEVINE, Linda A.	(NY)	720
Records management systems analysis	BALON, Brett J.	(SK)	53
Research & analytical report writing	MEYER, Andrea P.	(CO)	829
Research design & analysis	CHOBOT, Mary C.	(VA)	210
	LUECHT, Richard M.	(WI)	747
Research methods & cost analysis	WEBRECK, Susan J.	(PA)	1314
Research methods & systems analysis	FENSKE, Ruth E.	(IL)	371
Researcher, consultant, & analyst	KNIGHTLY, John J.	(TN)	664
Salary & compensation analysis	FRETWELL, Gordon E.	(MA)	402
Statistical analysis	COMPTON, Joan C.	(CA)	235
	RINGWALT, Arthur	(CA)	1035
	PIGGFORD, Roland	(MA)	972
	BUNCE, Catherine J.	(ON)	157
Strategic corporate information analysis	BEICHMAN, John C.	(MI)	75
Subject analysis	MICHEL, Dee A.	(CA)	832
	WEINTRAUB, D K.	(CA)	1318
	HARGRAVE, Charles W.	(DC)	501
	CLACK, Doris H.	(FL)	215
	WILSON, Betty R.	(IL)	1350
	LEWICKY, George I.	(NY)	722
	VIZINE-GOETZ, Diane	(OH)	1286
	DAILY, Jay E.	(PA)	270
	FUJIMOTO, Jan D.	(UT)	408
	PORTEUS, Andrew C.	(ON)	985
	RENAUD, Monique M.	(ON)	1023
	ROLLAND-THOMAS, Paule	(PQ)	1051
	TESSIER, Richard	(PQ)	1233
Subject analysis & classification	CROWTHER, Carol	(CA)	262
Subject analysis & social sciences	WRIGHT, Sylvia H.	(NY)	1373
System analysis	STRIBLING, Lorraine R.	(CA)	1202
	CORTEZ, Edwin M.	(DC)	248
	DODSON, Whit	(VA)	308
System analysis & design	DIENER, Carol W.	(MD)	302
Systems analysis	BALES, F K.	(CA)	52
	EPSTEIN, Susan B.	(CA)	351
	HADLEY, Peter H.	(CA)	482
	HALL, Anthony	(CA)	487
	KAZLAUSKAS, Edward J.	(CA)	632
	GUERRIERO, Donald A.	(DC)	476
	LEWIS, Robert J.	(DC)	724
	PARMING, Marju R.	(DC)	943
	COVEY, William C.	(FL)	252
	LOGAN, Elisabeth L.	(FL)	737
	SHEPARD, Clayton A.	(IN)	1126
	MCKIRDY, Pamela R.	(MA)	812
	ASSOUAD, Carol S.	(MD)	37
	LABEAU, Dennis	(MI)	685
	KANAFANI, Kyung C.	(MO)	624
	STACK, Laurie A.	(MT)	1177
	FRANTS, Valery	(NJ)	398
	HEINEMAN, Stephanie R.	(NY)	522
	HSIAO, Shu Y.	(NY)	567
	LANDAU, Herbert B.	(NY)	692
	JOSEPH, Patricia A.	(PA)	617
	HUNN, Marvin T.	(TX)	574
	SWIGGER, Keith	(TX)	1216
	DEBARDELEBEN, Marian Z.	(VA)	284
	STEPHENSON, Mary S.	(BC)	1188
	FAWCETT, Patrick J.	(MB)	367
	DYSART, Jane I.	(ON)	331
	LA CHAPELLE, Jennifer R.	(ON)	686

ANALYSIS (Cont'd)

Systems analysis & design	STOVEL, Madeleine D. . .	(CA)	1199
	LISTON, David M.	(MD)	732
	CONNORS, William E. . .	(NY)	238
	WAGNER, Stephen K. . .	(NY)	1292
	REDMER, Paul C.	(VA)	1014
	BALON, Brett J.	(SK)	53
	ARTEAGA, Georgina . . .	(MEX)	35
Systems analysis & development	HILL, Helen K.	(OK)	540
Systems analysis & records management	SIEGERT, Lindy E.	(NS)	1136
Systems analysis, micro	COX, Bruce B.	(MO)	253
Systs analysis, microcomputer program	NEWCOMER, Susan N. .	(CA)	898
Systems analyst	ENGERRAND, Steven W.	(GA)	349
Training information analysts	HALL, Homer J.	(NJ)	488
Training research analysts	BERWICK, Mary C.	(PA)	91
Training systems design, analysis	SYPERT, Clyde F.	(CA)	1217
User requirements analysis	DIENER, Carol W.	(MD)	302
Water & air analysis	LEE, Diana W.	(AB)	709
Workflow analysis	LOWELL, Virginia L.	(OH)	744

ANATOMY

Anatomy, physiology, & microbiology	MANDERSCHEID, Dorothy H.	(MI)	765

ANCIENT (See also Antiquity, History)

Ancient & Renaissance manuscripts	WITTEN, Laurence	(CT)	1358
Ancient histories	ABNEY, Timothy A.	(CA)	2
Ancient studies	GILLUM, Gary P.	(UT)	436
Library research in ancient history	SEAVER, James E.	(KS)	1110
Religion & ancient history databases	FRAZER, Ruth F.	(FL)	399

ANESTHESIA

Anesthesia history	WRIGHT, Amos J.	(AL)	1370

ANGLICAN (See also Episcopal)

Anglican theology	KEARNEY, Robert D. . . .	(NY)	633

ANGLO-AFRICAN (See also British)

British, Australian, Anglo-African	HAWK, Susan P.	(FL)	513

ANGLO-SAXON

International & Anglo-Saxon collections	IOANID, Aurora S.	(NY)	583

ANIMALS (See also Veterinary, Zoology)

Alternatives to test animals	THURSTON, Ethel H. . . .	(NY)	1243
Animal welfare information	LARSON, Jean A.	(MD)	699
Animals in children's books	FREEDMAN, Barbara G. .	(NC)	400
Information foreign animal diseases	PERLMAN, Stephen E. . .	(NY)	959
Protection of animal environment	THURSTON, Ethel H. . . .	(NY)	1243

ANIMATION (See also Film)

Animation	BAZINET, Jeanne	(PQ)	68
	BROSSEAU, Lise	(PQ)	141
	DEMERS, Madeleine M. .	(PQ)	291
	HEON, Gerard	(PQ)	530
	KHOUZAM, Monique . . .	(PQ)	646
	LAMOUREUX, Michele . .	(PQ)	691
	LEMIEUX, Louise	(PQ)	715
	MARION, Luce	(PQ)	770
	ROY, Helene	(PQ)	1063
Cryonics & suspended animation	BRIDGE, Stephen W. . . .	(IN)	135
Film animation	GLABICKI, Paul	(PA)	439

ANNIVERSARY

Anniversary celebrations	CLAYTON, John M.	(DE)	220

ANTHROPOLOGY

Anthropological bibliography	WEEKS, John M.	(MN)	1315
Anthropological information systems	CLARK, Barton M.	(IL)	216
Anthropology	DEW, T R.	(CO)	297
	PRENDERGAST, Kathleen M.	(IL)	990
	O'CONNELL, Susan	(NY)	915
	REMECZKI, Paul W. . . .	(NY)	1022
	WALTZ, Mary A.	(NY)	1302
	KING, Eleanor M.	(PA)	650
Anthropology & archeology	TOOLE, Gregor K.	(FL)	1250
Anthropology & archaeology	KOBELKA, Carolynn L. . .	(NT)	666
Anthropology bibliography	FINNEGAN, Gregory A. .	(NH)	378
	OGBURN, Joyce L.	(PA)	918
Anthropology collection development	FAIRBANKS, Deborah M.	(FL)	361
	KIBBEE, Josephine Z. . . .	(IL)	646
	MITTEN, Lisa A.	(PA)	850
Anthropology reference	DAVIES, Mary K.	(DC)	277
Anthropology subjects	BARNWELL, Jane L. . . .	(OR)	58
Bibliographies & anthropology	KRAKAUER, Elizabeth . .	(CA)	675
Subject cataloging anthropology	CARNAHAN, Stephanie B.	(DC)	183
Visual anthropology	WILLIAMS, Carroll W. . .	(NM)	1342

ANTIQUARIAN (See also Early, Editions, Old, Out-of-Print, Rare)

Antiquarian art books	MCGILVERY, Laurence .	(CA)	806
Antiquarian books	LOWMAN, Matt P.	(CA)	744
	YAPLE, Henry M.	(WA)	1377
Antiquarian books collection management	GOGGIN, Margaret K. . .	(FL)	444
Antiquarian juvenile books	GOLEY, Elaine P.	(TX)	447
Antiquarian law books	LUTTRELL, Jordan D. . . .	(CA)	750
Antiquarian maps	BERGEN, Kathleen M. . .	(MI)	85
Antiquarian materials	SHARP, Linda C.	(OH)	1122
Antiquarian music dealer	MERZ, Lawrie H.	(PA)	827
Antiquarian periodicals	OKERSON, Ann L.	(NY)	920
Antiquarian theatre books sales	KAHAN, Gerald	(GA)	621
Antique cars	HESSELBEIN, Krista M. .	(OH)	534
Antique maps	CRESSWELL, Donald H. .	(PA)	258
Antique phonograph records archives	JACOBSEN, Arnold	(MI)	590
Art architecture & antiques	MCCONKEY, Jill T.	(PA)	797
Books on antiques & art	JOHNSON, Nancy E. . . .	(IA)	608
Buying antiquarian books	MONDLIN, Marvin	(NY)	854

ANTIQUITY (See also Ancient)

Classical antiquity, reference	AVDOYAN, Levon	(DC)	41

APL (See also Computers, Microcomputers, Programming)

APL programming	ETZI, Richard	(NY)	356

APPALACHIAN

Appalachian studies	OLSON, Eric J.	(NC)	922

APPELLATE

Appellate procedure	WRIGHT, Jacqueline S. .	(AR)	1371

APPLE (See also Computers, Microcomputers)

Apple & Macintosh computer software	TRAVILLIAN, Mary W. . .	(IA)	1254
Microcomputer library systems, Apple IIe	BOCHTE, Terrence C. . .	(WI)	109
Microcomputer support Apple Macintosh	DEEMER, Selden S. . . .	(GA)	286

APPLICATIONS

Application of info technology in libs	AMAN, Mohammed M. . .	(WI)	19
Application of videotext technology	BROWNRIDGE, James R.	(ON)	149
Applications design & implementation	HORACEK, Paula B. . . .	(CA)	558
Applications development	SJOGREN, Mack D.	(NY)	1145
Applications of information technology	CHARTRAND, Robert L.	(DC)	203
Applications of microcomputers	CAINE, William C.	(TX)	171
Applications programming	CANGANELLI, Patrick W.	(IN)	178
Artificial intelligence applications	FOX, Edward A.	(VA)	394
Audiovisual technology, computer appls	NOLAN, Joan	(PA)	907

APPLICATIONS (Cont'd)

Specialty	Name	State	Page
Automation & computer applications	POWELL, Mary E.	(TX)	988
Automation applications	LOKEN, Sarah F.	(WA)	738
Automation of business applications	BROWN, Maxine M.	(DC)	146
CAI application & implementation	CARDENAS, Mary E.	(SAF)	180
CD-ROM & CD-I applications	GALE, John C.	(VA)	413
CD-ROM applications	SCHIPMA, Peter B.	(IL)	1093
	GRAMINSKI, Denise M.	(NY)	457
	BILLS, Linda G.	(PA)	96
	WIEMAN, Jean M.	(WA)	1336
CD-ROM publishing applications	KNOERDEL, Joan E.	(MD)	665
Clinical applications	MENDELSON, Martin	(WA)	823
Computer applicability	PETERSON, Randall T.	(IL)	964
Computer application & data management	GREGORY, Melissa R.	(IL)	466
Computer application & management	COLDWELL, Charles P.	(WA)	230
Computer applications	VEENSTRA, Robert J.	(AL)	1281
	MARCHIANO, Marilyn C.	(CA)	768
	RUDOLPH, Anne L.	(CA)	1066
	HORRIGAN, John J.	(CT)	560
	MANUEL, Larry L.	(DE)	767
	BOULA, Lillian Y.	(FL)	119
	REZNICK, Evi P.	(GA)	1025
	MATHER, Becky R.	(IA)	783
	FENSKE, Ruth E.	(IL)	371
	GRUMBLING, Dennis K.	(IL)	474
	JOHNSTON, James R.	(IL)	610
	LI, Richard T.	(IL)	725
	ROTT, Richard A.	(IL)	1060
	SWANSON, Don R.	(IL)	1213
	TZE-CHUNG, Li	(IL)	1267
	WELCH, Eric C.	(IL)	1321
	DEANE, Paul D.	(IN)	284
	KASER, John A.	(IN)	628
	ROSENTHAL, Marylu C.	(MA)	1057
	PAPENFUSE, Edward C.	(MD)	939
	QUINN, Carol J.	(MD)	1000
	ANDERSON, Marjorie E.	(ME)	24
	BURESH, Reggie F.	(MN)	158
	GRAZIER, Dorothy W.	(NH)	460
	LEVINE, Riesa E.	(NJ)	721
	MAYNES, Kathleen R.	(NJ)	790
	TIEDRICH, Ellen K.	(NJ)	1244
	PRINZ, Jane A.	(NY)	993
	SMITH, Mark J.	(NY)	1158
	WISEMAN, Karin M.	(NY)	1357
	AMICONE, Janice L.	(PA)	20
	FORD, Sylverna V.	(PA)	390
	LYONS, Evelyn L.	(PA)	753
	EDELEN, Joseph R.	(SD)	335
	GAUDET, Susan E.	(TN)	422
	MILLER, Karl F.	(TX)	839
	WALKER, Tamara E.	(TX)	1296
	REHMS, Jane C.	(WA)	1017
	BURGIS, Grover C.	(ON)	159
	CRAVEN, Timothy C.	(ON)	256
	ALSANARRAI, Hafidh S.	(SDA)	17
Computer applications & automation	SHEPARD, Clayton A.	(IN)	1126
Computer applications & mgmt consulting	BOSSEAU, Don L.	(CA)	117
Computer applications & systems	KIRKWOOD, Francis T.	(ON)	655
Computer applications development	BROWN, Jeanne I.	(NJ)	145
Computer applications in banking	BOSMA, Elske M.	(ON)	117
Computer applications in libraries	WOLF, Nola M.	(CA)	1360
	HUPP, Sharon W.	(CT)	577
	GLUCK, Myke H.	(NC)	442
	MINEMIER, Betty M.	(NY)	845
	SMITH-GREENWOLD, Kathryn R.	(NY)	1162
	TOSTEVIN, Patricia A.	(WA)	1252
	MOON, Jeffrey D.	(ON)	857
Computer applications in schools	WEST, Marian S.	(MI)	1326
Computer applications to acquisitions	DELONG, Douglas A.	(IL)	290
Computer applications to instruction	TERWILLIGER, Gloria P.	(VA)	1232
Computer applications to libraries	KRANCH, Douglas A.	(IA)	676
	YARBROUGH, Joseph W.	(MI)	1378
Computer applications to writing	SCHWARTZ, James M.	(SD)	1104
Computer industry & applications	BJORNER, Susan N.	(MA)	100
Computer-based applications	PEPPER, David A.	(BC)	958
Computerized applications	MULLANE, William H.	(AZ)	877

APPLICATIONS (Cont'd)

Specialty	Name	State	Page
Database & automation applications	SAUTER, Sylvia E.	(WA)	1085
Database applications	DAVIS, Becky C.	(CA)	277
	FRANCIS, Diane S.	(DE)	396
	BOWEN, Louise E.	(GA)	120
	HUSSEY, Laurie L.	(MA)	578
	BALL, John L.	(ON)	52
Database applications programming	ROSENFELD, Jane D.	(NY)	1056
Database publishing applications	KNOERDEL, Joan E.	(MD)	665
Educational technology application	STARKEY, Richard E.	(MA)	1182
End-user marketing applications	MOYER, Barbara A.	(CA)	874
Financial databases & applications	CORVESE, Lisa A.	(NY)	248
Full-text applications	SMITH, David F.	(NY)	1154
Full-text database applications	ROACH, Eddie D.	(OK)	1037
Geological computer applications	STARK, Philip H.	(CO)	1182
Historic & archaeological applications	DRAKE, Robert E.	(MA)	318
Information technology applications	BISHOP, Sarah G.	(DC)	99
	MILEVSKI, Sandra N.	(DC)	835
Library applications of CD-ROM	MILLER, Davic C.	(CA)	836
Library computer applications	STUHLMAN, Daniel D.	(IL)	1205
	JAFFE, Lawrence J.	(PA)	591
	BOWLES, David M.	(SC)	121
	LANE, Steven P.	(WA)	694
Library, media computer applications	RENICK, Paul R.	(ND)	1023
Library micro applications	EVENSEN, Sharon L.	(ND)	358
Library microcomputer applications	MAIN, Annette Z.	(PA)	761
	STANLEY, Kerry G.	(PA)	1180
	JEWELL, Timothy D.	(WA)	600
	KELNER, Gregory H.	(BC)	638
Library optical disk applications	SWORA, Tamara	(DC)	1217
Lib systems, microcomputer applications	ONSI, Patricia W.	(NY)	924
Macintosh applications	KRAFT, Gwen L.	(AK)	675
Mainframe & minicomputer applications	BROWN, Maxine M.	(DC)	146
Management computer applications	COMEAU, Reginald A.	(NH)	234
Manual & automated technl applications	MERRITT, Betty A.	(CA)	827
Manufacturing processes & applications	GROEN, Paulette E.	(MI)	471
Manuscript & grant applications	PARR, John R.	(ON)	943
Media applications in education	TOWNSEND, Catherine M.	(SC)	1253
Medical computer applications	CLARKE, Elba C.	(GA)	218
Micro applications	AIROLDI, Melissa	(TX)	9
Micro-based applications	STACK, Laurie A.	(MT)	1177
Microcomputer & CD-ROM applications	DAVIDSON, Lloyd A.	(IL)	276
Microcomputer application in libraries	WRIGHT, Keith C.	(NC)	1372
	CORNEIL, Charlotte E.	(OK)	246
	WONG, Elizabeth M.	(WI)	1362
Microcomputer applications	MCCARTHY, Sherri L.	(AL)	794
	MCGARITY, Marysue	(AL)	805
	MEAD, Thomas L.	(AZ)	819
	ERTEL, Monica	(CA)	353
	FARMER, Lesley S.	(CA)	364
	HOFFMAN, William J.	(CA)	548
	MACEK, Rosanne M.	(CA)	755
	MAIN, Linda Y.	(CA)	761
	MOONEY, Margaret T.	(CA)	858
	NAUMER, Janet N.	(CA)	889
	NEWTON, Deborah A.	(CA)	900
	ROSENBERGER, Diane C.	(CA)	1056
	SKAPURA, Robert J.	(CA)	1145
	SLEETER, Ellen L.	(CA)	1148
	TASH, Steven J.	(CA)	1224
	WRIGHT, Kathleen J.	(CA)	1372
	FLAM, Floris	(DC)	383
	HO, James K.	(DC)	545
	LANE, Elizabeth S.	(DC)	694
	CONAWAY, Charles W.	(FL)	235
	ACKER, Robert L.	(IL)	3
	BARRETTE, Linda J.	(IL)	59
	GRISCOM, Richard W.	(IL)	471
	MCKENZIE, Duncan A.	(IL)	811
	VACCARO, William J.	(IL)	1270
	WESTON, E P.	(IL)	1327
	DOLAN, Robert T.	(IN)	309
	ERDMANN, Charlotte A.	(IN)	352
	SHEETS, Michael T.	(IN)	1125
	TUCKER, Dennis C.	(IN)	1261

APPLICATIONS (Cont'd)

Microcomputer applications

ZUCK, Gregory J.	(KS)	1391
KIRK, Thomas G.	(KY)	654
BOND, Marvin A.	(MD)	113
BRITTEN, William A.	(MD)	137
MARCHIONINI, Gary J.	(MD)	769
MASTROIANNI, Richard L.	(MD)	783
GOODWIN, Bryan D.	(ME)	450
MORROW, Blaine V.	(MI)	869
BIRMINGHAM, Frank R.	(MN)	98
HORTON, James T.	(NC)	561
RANCER, Susan P.	(NC)	1006
VAN HOY, Catherine S.	(NC)	1276
FELTON, John D.	(NE)	370
LANGSCHIELD, Linda S.	(NJ)	696
STEPIEN, Karen K.	(NJ)	1189
STURM, H P.	(NV)	1205
BARTENBACH, Martha A.	(NY)	60
BARTH, Joseph M.	(NY)	61
BARTLE, Susan M.	(NY)	61
BLOHM, Laura A.	(NY)	106
BRETSCHER, Susan M.	(NY)	134
CLARK, Philip M.	(NY)	218
HORNE, Dorice L.	(NY)	560
JOHNSON, Steven P.	(NY)	609
MCMORRAN, Charles E.	(NY)	815
MITTELGLUCK, Eugene L.	(NY)	850
ROHMANN, Gloria P.	(NY)	1050
SERCHUK, Barnett	(NY)	1116
ARNOLD, Judith M.	(OH)	33
HUNTER, James J.	(OH)	576
MARCOTTE, Frederick A.	(OH)	769
MILLER, John E.	(OH)	839
MOGREN, Diane A.	(OH)	852
PIETY, John S.	(OH)	972
SHAW, Debra S.	(OH)	1123
HUESMANN, James L.	(OK)	570
BALAS, Janet L.	(PA)	50
KING, Mimi	(PA)	652
LINGLE, Virginia A.	(PA)	730
PENNELL, Charles	(PA)	957
SMALL, Sally S.	(PA)	1151
MILLS, Debra D.	(TN)	844
CALDWELL, Marlene	(TX)	172
COCHRAN, Carolyn	(TX)	225
FOUDRAY, Rita C.	(TX)	393
HAMBLETON, James E.	(TX)	490
SAMSON, Robert C.	(TX)	1079
SKINNER, Robert G.	(TX)	1146
WILSON, Thomas C.	(TX)	1353
ENGLISH, Susan B.	(VA)	350
JOACHIM, Robert J.	(VA)	600
BREKKE, Elaine C.	(WA)	132
KETCHELL, Debra S.	(WA)	645
BARLOGA, Carolyn J.	(WI)	57
FLETCHER, Nancy S.	(WI)	384
GOSZ, Kathleen M.	(WI)	453
FAULKNER, Ronnie W.	(WV)	366
SIFTON, Patricia A.	(BC)	1137
FAIR, Linda A.	(UN)	361
MORTON, Robert E.	(ON)	870
WILBURN, Gene	(ON)	1338
WILBURN, Marion T.	(ON)	1338
ZHU, Xiaofeng	(CHI)	1387

Microcomputer applications & management

MCSPADDEN, Robert M.	(OH)	818

Microcomputer applications & support — WILLIAMS, David W. (NY) 1342

Microcomputer applications & training

MARSH, Elizabeth C.	(OH)	773
MARMION, Daniel K.	(TX)	772

Microcomputer applications development

NICKEL, Edgar B.	(CO)	902
KNAACK, Linda M.	(MA)	663

Microcomputer appls/electronic publshg — HULSEY, Richard A. (MI) 573

Microcomputer applications for libraries — CONVERSE, Wm R. (MB) 239

APPLICATIONS (Cont'd)

Microcomputer applications in libraries

KASALKO, Sally G.	(AR)	628
CHAFE, Douglas A.	(HI)	197
SCHMIDT, Kathy W.	(IN)	1095
BENSON, Peggy	(MI)	83
COAN, La V.	(MI)	224
BRIZUELA, B S.	(PA)	138
SVEINSSON, Joan L.	(TX)	1212
FONG, Wilfred W.	(WI)	388

Microcomputer applications in management — HOWARD, Ada M. (TX) 563

Microcomputer applications/programming — DALY, Jay (MA) 271

Microcomputer applications research — STRAHAN, Michael F. (ND) 1199

Microcomputer library applications — OPPENHEIM, Roberta A. (MA) 925

MCCULLEY, P M. (SC) 800

Microcomputer use, library applications — KENNEDY, Charlene F. (CA) 640

Microcomputer-based library applications — BEISER, Karl A. (ME) 75

Microcomputers & applications — CLINE, Sharon D. (CA) 222

ROMANIUK, Elena (BC) 1052

Microcomputers applications in libraries — LYNCH, Mollie S. (MI) 752

Microcomputers applications reference — MILLER, Susan E. (LA) 842

Microcomputers used for lib applications — MILLS, Elaine L. (KS) 844

Microcomputing applications — HARLAN, John B. (IN) 502

Microfiche applications — MILLER, Diane C. (IL) 837

Mini & microcomputer applications — SWEENEY, Urban J. (CA) 1215

Online computer applications — ROSENFELD, Joseph S. (OH) 1056

Online library applications — ALMQUIST, Deborah T. (MA) 17

Online microcomputer application — VIDMANIS, Visvaldis E. (MA) 1283

Online searching & computer applications — RANKIN, Carol A. (NY) 1007

Optical applications — CHEN, Ching S. (MA) 205

Optical card applications — GALE, John C. (VA) 413

Optical disk applications — WEBB, Duncan C. (CA) 1313

ROBERTSON, Michael A. (NY) 1042

PC applications — MADDOCK, Jerome T. (CO) 759

MCGINNIS, Joan M. (NH) 806

Personal computer applications

MITCHELL, Elaine M.	(DC)	848
BENNETT, Lee L.	(IL)	82
MUNTEAN, Deborah E.	(MN)	879
HANEY, Kevin M.	(NJ)	495
HOLLEY, James L.	(NY)	551
MASH, S D.	(NY)	780
ROACH, Linda	(PA)	1038

Personal computer applications in libs — PESCHEL, Susan M. (WI) 961

Personal computer software applications — SABATINI, Joseph D. (NM) 1072

Personal computers & applications — DOOLING, Marie (NY) 312

Planning & application of technology — DIDIER, Elaine K. (MI) 301

Programming applications — UCHIDA, Deborah K. (HI) 1267

Publishing technology applications info — KLEIMAN, Gerald S. (DC) 659

Regional computer applications — NELSON, James B. (NY) 894

SAS programming application — ROSTAMI, Janet (ON) 1059

Science, info applications, of computers — MITCHELL, Steve (CA) 849

Small computer applications — ELWELL, Pamela M. (OH) 347

Small library computer applications — MORRIS, R P (NC) 867

Software applications — FUKAI, Eiko (IL) 408

Software applications in libraries — STEWART, Douglas J. (AZ) 1192

Technical services computer applications — FRANCQ, Carole (IN) 396

Telefacsimile applications — BROWN, Steven A. (GA) 147

Television, library applications — RITZ, Mary E. (CA) 1037

Video applications — BIRMINGHAM, Frank R. (MN) 98

WORM applications — GALE, John C. (VA) 413

APPLIED

Applied arts research — FRANKLIN, Linda C. (NY) 398

Applied arts, writing & editing — FRANKLIN, Linda C. (NY) 398

Applied economics — LETNES, Louise M. (MN) 718

Biomedical & applied science databases — LETT, Rosalind K. (GA) 719

APPRAISAL (See also Assessment, Evaluation, Personnel, Valuation)

Appraisal	JONES, Thomas Q.	(IN)	615
	SANFORD, John D.	(MI)	1081
	WARNOW-BLEWETT, Joan N.	(NY)	1305
	BRYSON, Gary B.	(TX)	152
	WINFREE, Waverly K.	(VA)	1354
Appraisal & accessioning	WALLER, M C.	(KY)	1298
Appraisal & collection development	DELOACH, Lynda J.	(MN)	290
Appraisal & disposition	PACIFICO, Michele F.	(DC)	933
	PAUL, Karen D.	(DC)	949
Appraisal & records disposition	BRADSHER, James G.	(DC)	126
Appraisal archivist	BEAM, Christopher M.	(DC)	69
Appraisal, authentication of manuscripts	GORDON, Robert S.	(ON)	451
Appraisal of archival materials	BEST, Rickey D.	(AL)	92
Appraisal of military books	AIMONE, Alan C.	(NY)	8
Appraisal of theatre collections	KAHAN, Gerald	(GA)	621
Appraisal reporting	FELDER, Bruce B.	(OH)	369
Appraisals	LEAB, Katharine K.	(CT)	706
	CHANEY, Bev	(NY)	200
	LIEBERMAN, Ronald	(PA)	726
	PRESGRAVES, Jim	(VA)	991
	STROUD, John N.	(WV)	1203
Appraisals of medical collections	KLENK, Anne S.	(CO)	660
Appraisals of sound recordings	SMOLIAN, Steven J.	(MD)	1162
Appraising current market value	MONDLIN, Marvin	(NY)	854
Appraising government records	BENGE, Joy L.	(TX)	80
Appraising law firm collections	SCAMMAHORN, Lynne	(PA)	1087
Appraising record & phonograph cols	FABRIZIO, Timothy C.	(NY)	360
Archival appraisal	BRICHFORD, Maynard J.	(IL)	134
	CYPHERS, James E.	(MA)	268
	BRUEMMER, Bruce H.	(MN)	149
	RICHIUSO, John P.	(NY)	1030
	KLUMPENHOUWER, Richard	(AB)	662
Archival collections appraisals	RENDELL, Kenneth W.	(MA)	1023
Archives appraisal	HARWOOD, James L.	(DC)	510
Archives appraisal & cataloging	CORNELIUS, Charlene E.	(WI)	246
Book appraisal	LABUDDE, Kenneth J.	(MO)	686
Books & manuscripts appraisal	LEBO, Shirley B.	(DC)	708
Books & manuscripts appraisals	TWENEY, George H.	(WA)	1266
Editing & library appraisal	BROOKS, Jerrold L.	(NC)	140
Employee appraisals	BRANDWEIN, Larry	(NY)	128
Film & video consultant, appraiser	MACAULEY, C C.	(CA)	754
Health risk appraisal systems	ABRAMSON, Lawrence J.	(MI)	3
Managing & appraising rare books	MICHAELS, Carolyn L.	(SC)	831
Manuscript appraisals	RENDELL, Kenneth W.	(MA)	1023
Manuscripts appraisal	CRONENWETT, Philip N.	(NH)	260
Media appraisal & procurement	HOLSINGER, Katherine	(AZ)	554
Personnel admin, performance appraisal	VEANER, Allen B.	(ON)	1280
Rare book appraisal	MARSHALL, Mary G.	(IL)	774
	HEANEY, Howell J.	(PA)	518
Rare books appraisal	GLENN, Ardis L.	(MO)	441
	DU BOIS, Paul Z.	(NJ)	322
Rare record appraisal	ALLEN, Douglas R.	(FL)	14
Recorded media consultation, appraisal	MACAULEY, C C.	(CA)	754
Records appraisal	HONHART, Frederick L.	(MI)	556
	HAVENER, Ralph S.	(MO)	513
Records appraisal & scheduling	NASH, Cherie A.	(UT)	888
Special col management & appraisal	WEISS, Egon A.	(NY)	1320
Still photography consultant, appraiser	MACAULEY, C C.	(CA)	754

APPRECIATION

Children's literature appreciation	BROWN, Judith B.	(MD)	145
Literature guidance & appreciation	MCCLELLAND, Katherine L.	(GA)	796
Teaching literature appreciation	MERRILL, Barbara P.	(NY)	826
Youth literature appreciation	USHIRODA, Christine H.	(HI)	1270

APPROVAL (See also Acquisitions)

Approval plan development	HAMILTON, Marsha J.	(OH)	492
Approval plan management	WARZALA, Martin L.	(CT)	1307
	GRANTIER, John R.	(NY)	458

APPROVAL (Cont'd)

Approval plans	MARSHALL, David L.	(DC)	774
	HARDY, Eileen D.	(MA)	500
	DUCHIN, Douglas	(NH)	322
	KAPOOR, Jagdish C.	(NH)	626
	NARDINI, Robert F.	(NH)	888
Approval plans & continuations	JAGER, Conradus	(MA)	591
Approval programs	NAGEL, Lawrence D.	(CA)	886
Approval programs, continuations	SCHRIFT, Leonard B.	(NY)	1100
Monitoring approval plans for Hispanics	SALINERO, Amelia	(NY)	1076

AQUACULTURE

Aquaculture	KELLER, Susan E.	(BC)	636
Aquaculture information center	HANFMAN, Deborah A.	(MD)	495
Controlled environment aquaculture	LAKE, Mary S.	(AZ)	689

AQUATIC

Aquatic sciences	MORITZ, Thomas D.	(CA)	865
Aquatic sciences & fisheries information	SEARS, Jonathan R.	(MD)	1110

ARAB

Arabic & Hebrew cataloging	CHAMMOU, Eliezer	(CA)	198
Arabic cataloging	MYERS-HAYER, Patricia A.	(DC)	885
	HIRSCH, David G.	(NJ)	543
Arabic language	KHAN, Mohammed A.	(SDA)	646
Arabic script cataloging	WERYHO, Jan W.	(PQ)	1325
Early Arab numismatics	MOLINE, Judi A.	(MD)	853
French & Arabic education	YASSA, Lucie M.	(CA)	1378
French, Arabic, English translation	YASSA, Lucie M.	(CA)	1378

ARCHAEOLOGY

Anthropology & archeology	TOOLE, Gregor K.	(FL)	1250
Anthropology & archaeology	KOBELKA, Carolynn L.	(NT)	666
Archaeology	O'CONNELL, Susan	(NY)	915
	REMECZKI, Paul W.	(NY)	1022
Biblical archaeology	IBACH, Robert D.	(TX)	581
Historic & archaeological applications	DRAKE, Robert E.	(MA)	318
Historical research for archaeologist	STINE, Roy S.	(NC)	1194
History & archaeology	BROWN, William A.	(VA)	148

ARCHDIOCESAN (See also Catholic)

Archdiocesan school system libraries	DALY, Sally A.	(PA)	271

ARCHITECTURE (See also Building, Construction, Design, Interiors, Space)

American architecture slides	ROMEO, Sheryl R.	(DC)	1052
Architectural & interior design	WIEGMAN, John H.	(TX)	1336
Architectural & interiors firm libraries	TENNEY, Kimberly M.	(MA)	1231
Architectural archives	WITTHUS, Rutherford W.	(CO)	1358
	SCHROCK, Nancy C.	(MA)	1100
	WILSON, Michael E.	(TX)	1352
Architectural drawings	STERN, Teena B.	(CA)	1189
	LAVERTY, Bruce	(PA)	703
	DUNNIGAN, Mary C.	(VA)	327
	ENGEMAN, Richard H.	(WA)	349
Architectural, engineering archives	DRAKE, Robert E.	(MA)	318
Architectural history	BROWN, Steven A.	(GA)	147
Architectural information	BURROUGHS, Christine M.	(NY)	163
	PISCIOTTA, Henry A.	(PA)	976
Architectural records	LATHROP, Alan K.	(MN)	701
Architectural records & drawings	BRUNK, Thomas M.	(MI)	150
Architectural reference	GRANADOS, Rose A.	(CA)	457
Architectural research	BAERWALD, Susan M.	(MO)	45
Architectural special library materials	STEWARD, Martha J.	(CA)	1192
Architecture	CLINKSCALES, Joyce M.	(AR)	222
	CALDWELL, Kenneth R.	(CA)	172
	SNOW, Maryly A.	(CA)	1164
	HANSEN, Roland C.	(IL)	498
	HAIL, Christopher	(MA)	484
	SKLAR, Hinda F.	(MA)	1146

ARCHITECTURE (Cont'd)

Architecture
	SIMS, Sally R.	(MD) 1142
	LATHROP, Alan K.	(MN) 701
	AVELEYRA, Luz M.	(NC) 41
	CLARKE, D S.	(NY) 218
	GREENBERG, Roberta D.	(NY) 463
	KEAVENEY, Sydney S.	(NY) 633
	HAMILTON, Dennis O.	(OH) 492
	MAKELA, Helen M.	(OH) 762
	GRAY, Priscilla M.	(PA) 460
	MOSS, Roger W.	(PA) 872
Architecture & art	NORTON, Margaret W.	(IL) 910
Architecture & buildings	LUCKER, Jay K.	(MA) 746
Architecture & design resources	GRIGORIS, Lygia	(MA) 470
Architecture & library design	NIELSEN, Sonja M.	(MA) 903
Architecture books	ROMEO, Sheryl R.	(DC) 1052
Architecture cataloging	CHIBNIK, Katharine R.	(NY) 207
Architecture history	KIMBERLIN, Robert L.	(DC) 649
Architecture librarianship	BYRNE, Elizabeth D.	(CA) 169
	LOGAN-PETERS, Kay E.	(NE) 737
	REED, Barbara E.	(NH) 1014
Architecture libraries	ABRAMS, Leslie E.	(SC) 3
Architecture literature & information	HAVLIK, Robert J.	(IN) 513
Architecture practice	KIMBERLIN, Robert L.	(DC) 649
Architecture reference	AVERILL, Laurie J.	(RI) 41
Architecture research	GRETES, Frances C.	(NY) 467
	FLESHMAN, Nancy A.	(TX) 384
Architecture research & reference	WRIGHT, Sylvia H.	(NY) 1373
Architecture slide libraries	CINLAR, Anne	(NJ) 214
Architecture slides	STEWARD, Martha J.	(CA) 1192
Architecture specialization	VAN DYKE, Stephen H.	(NY) 1275
Archival architectural records	BAUS, J W.	(IN) 67
Art & architectural databases	ROBERTSON, Jack	(MD) 1042
Art & architectural documtn sources	ROBERTSON, Jack	(MD) 1042
Art & architectural history	FRIEDMAN, Richard E.	(AL) 404
	COIR, Mark A.	(MI) 229
	LABUDDE, Kenneth J.	(MO) 686
	BEETHAM, Donald W.	(NJ) 74
Art & architectural indexing	ROBERTSON, Jack	(MD) 1042
Art & architecture	THOMPSON, Neville M.	(DE) 1241
	GODLEWSKI, Susan G.	(IL) 442
	WITHEE, Jane S.	(IL) 1358
	WOO, Janice	(NY) 1363
Art & architecture bibliography	SHAW, Renata V.	(DC) 1123
Art & architecture collections devlpmnt	BEGLO, Jo N.	(ON) 74
Art & architecture databases	VAN DYKE, Stephen H.	(NY) 1275
Art & architecture librarianship	KUSNERZ, Peggy A.	(MI) 685
	CARMIN, James H.	(OR) 183
	KLOS, Sheila M.	(OR) 662
Art & architecture reference	KEMPE, Deborah A.	(NY) 639
Art & architecture specialization	TEAGUE, Edward H.	(FL) 1229
Art & architecture specialized ref	BEGLO, Jo N.	(ON) 74
Art architecture & antiques	MCCONKEY, Jill T.	(PA) 797
Art, architecture databases	GOODMAN, Edward C.	(NY) 449
Art library architecture	IRVINE, Betty J.	(IN) 584
Bibliographer, art & architecture	OLSON, Joann D.	(OH) 922
Cartographic & architectural archives	KIDD, Betty H.	(ON) 646
Cataloging architectural & engineering	SPAHR, Cheryl L.	(OH) 1170
Cataloging art & architecture slides	FOWLER, Michele R.	(OH) 394
Collection development, architecture	BRACKNEY, Kathryn S.	(GA) 125
Collection development in architecture	SCHUSTER, Adeline	(IL) 1103
Construction site, architect coolections	WRIGHT, Paul L.	(KY) 1372
Creating & organizing architectural libs	ROTHMAN, Marilyn R.	(CO) 1060
Energy efficient architecture	MARCIL, Louise	(PQ) 769
Fine arts & architecture bibliography	CEDERHOLM, Theresa D.	(MA) 196
Fine arts & architecture cataloging	MOHAMMED, Selima	(PQ) 852
Fine arts & architecture sources	SPENCER, Deirdre D.	(FL) 1173
History of architectural theory	ARNTZEN, Etta M.	(IL) 34
Information architecture	REED, Patricia A.	(DC) 1015
Landscape architecture	RAVENHALL, Mary	(IL) 1010
	HAIL, Christopher	(MA) 484
Languages, architecture & art	CULLARS, John M.	(IL) 263
Library architectural planning	ZAFREN, Herbert C.	(OH) 1385
Library architecture	KIRWAN, William J.	(NC) 656
	HECHT, James M.	(NJ) 519
	GREENE, Richard L.	(PQ) 464
Library architecture & design	BECK, Erla P.	(IN) 71

ARCHITECTURE (Cont'd)

Library architecture, interior design	COHEN, Aaron	(NY) 227
Library design & architecture	BRYANT, David S.	(NJ) 152
Ordering architectural, engrng books	SPAHR, Cheryl L.	(OH) 1170
Philadelphia architects	LAVERTY, Bruce	(PA) 703
Public library architecture	DEL SORDO, Jean S.	(MD) 290
Reference, art & architecture	OLSON, Joann D.	(OH) 922
Research architectural history	ROARK, Carol E.	(TX) 1038
Research in architecture	HUNT, Judy L.	(CA) 575
Special art & architecture librarianship	BEGLO, Jo N.	(ON) 74

ARCHIVES (See also Records)

Academic archives	SWEENEY, Shelley T.	(SK) 1215
Acquisitions, archival & law field	SHEPARD, E L.	(VA) 1126
Administering university archives	MATTHEW, Jeannette M.	(IN) 785
Administration in archives	WINN, Carolyn P.	(MA) 1355
Advocacy of archival administration	SANTORO, Corrado A.	(MB) 1082
American Indian archives	SPOTTED EAGLE, Joy	(MT) 1175
	THIEL, Mark G.	(WI) 1235
American musical theatre archives	ROSENBURG, Betsy R.	(CT) 1056
Antique phonograph records archives	JACOBSEN, Arnold	(MI) 590
Appraisal archivist	BEAM, Christopher M.	(DC) 69
Appraisal of archival materials	BEST, Rickey D.	(AL) 92
Architectural archives	WITTHUS, Rutherford W.	(CO) 1358
	SCHROCK, Nancy C.	(MA) 1100
	WILSON, Michael E.	(TX) 1352
Architectural, engineering archives	DRAKE, Robert E.	(MA) 318
Archival acquisition projects	MORRISSEY, Charles T.	(VT) 869
Archival administration	BRIDGES, Edwin C.	(AL) 135
	OETTING, Edward C.	(AZ) 917
	BONFIELD, Lynn A.	(CA) 114
	NEWHALL, Ann C.	(CT) 898
	BURKE, Frank G.	(DC) 160
	JACOBS, Richard A.	(DC) 590
	PINKETT, Harold T.	(DC) 974
	MAYER, Dale C.	(IA) 789
	STEWART, Virginia R.	(IL) 1193
	REDMON, Sherrill	(KY) 1014
	PAPENFUSE, Edward C.	(MD) 939
	DUVAL, Marjorie A.	(ME) 329
	COIR, Mark A.	(MI) 229
	HONHART, Frederick L.	(MI) 556
	JONES, Clifton H.	(MI) 612
	SHAFER, Steven I.	(MI) 1119
	DANIELS, Paul A.	(MN) 273
	YOUNG, Julia M.	(MS) 1382
	MEVERS, Frank C.	(NH) 829
	DENSMORE, Christopher	(NY) 293
	LACHATANERE, Diana	(NY) 686
	BAUMANN, Roland M.	(OH) 66
	CORNELL, Alice M.	(OH) 246
	GOERLER, Raimund E.	(OH) 443
	HILAND, Gerard P.	(OH) 538
	REILLY, Sara L.	(PA) 1020
	SUMNERS, Bill F.	(TN) 1209
	HOWINGTON, Tad C.	(TX) 566
	KENAMORE, Jane A.	(TX) 640
	SCHULTZ, Charles R.	(TX) 1101
	WILSON, Michael E.	(TX) 1352
	MANARIN, Louis H.	(VA) 764
	CLINE, Robert S.	(WA) 222
	EASTWOOD, Terence M.	(BC) 333
	WALSH, G M.	(ON) 1299
	WOLVSKY, Haya S.	(ISR) 1362
Archival & library activities	SEEBER, Frances M.	(NY) 1111
Archival & manuscript collections	SHOCKLEY, Ann A.	(TN) 1132
Archival & photographic administration	DENSKY, Lois R.	(NJ) 293
Archival & rare books	YUILLE, Willie K.	(MD) 1384
	ROSS, David J.	(NY) 1058
Archival appraisal	BRICHFORD, Maynard J.	(IL) 134
	CYPHERS, James E.	(MA) 268
	BRUEMMER, Bruce H.	(MN) 149
	RICHIUSO, John P.	(NY) 1030
	KLUMPENHOUWER, Richard	(AB) 662
Archival architectural records	BAUS, J W.	(IN) 67

ARCHIVES (Cont'd)

Archival arrangement & description	BEST, Rickey D. . . . . (AL)	92
	MAHER, William J. . . . . . (IL)	760
	PRIMER, Ben . . . . (MD)	993
	BARTKOWSKI, Patricia . (MI)	61
	SMITH, Michael O. . . . . . (MI)	1158
	OAKHILL, Harold W. . . . . (NY)	913
	RICHIUSO, John P. . . . . (NY)	1030
	CORNELL, Alice M. . . . . (OH)	246
	CLINE, Robert S. . . . . . . (WA)	222
	BEHRND-KLODT, Menzi L. (WI)	75
	KLUMPENHOUWER,	
	Richard . . . . (AB)	662
Archival automation	ELLISON, J T. . . . . (CO)	345
	BURKE, Frank G. . . . . . . (DC)	160
	CARSON, James G. . . . . (IL)	188
	GILDEMEISTER, Glen A. (IL)	434
	WEBER, Lisa B. . . . . (IL)	1314
	GILLILAND, Anne J. . . . . (OH)	436
Archival automation, cataloging	WEINBERG, David M. . . (PA)	1317
Archival cataloging	BAUMSTEIN, Paschal M. (NC)	66
	HARGIS-LYTLE, Betty L. (OK)	501
Archival collection development	CHRISTOPHER, Paul . . . (CA)	212
Archival collections	PETERSON, Scott W. . . . (IL)	964
Archival collections appraisals	RENDELL, Kenneth W. . . (MA)	1023
Archival conservation	ANDERSON, James C. . . (KY)	23
Archival conservation & preservation	MARRELLI, Nancy M. . . . (PQ)	773
Archival consulting	SCHUMACHER, Carolyn	
	S. . . . . (PA)	1102
	TOMAN, Jocelyn B. . . . . (PA)	1249
Archival control systems	MOTTRAM, Geoffrey . . . (IL)	873
Archival databases	DAWSON, Barbara J. . . . (DC)	282
Archival description	PURDY, Virginia C. . . . . . (DC)	998
	YOST, F D. . . . . (DC)	1381
	ENGERRAND, Steven W. (GA)	349
	FRENCH, Melodee J. . . . (GA)	402
Archival description & arrangement	CASSEDY, James G. . . . (DC)	193
Archival descriptive standards	MACDERMAID, Anne . . . (ON)	754
Archival education	BURNS, John F. . . . . (CA)	162
	PUGH, Mary J. . . . . (CA)	997
	JIMERSON, Randall C. . . (CT)	600
	QUINN, Patrick M. . . . . . (IL)	1000
	MORISON, William J. . . . (KY)	865
	DESNOYERS, Megan F. . (MA)	295
	SNIFFIN-MARINO, Megan	
	G. . . . . (MA)	1163
	BOLES, Frank . . . . (MI)	112
	PETTIT, Marilyn H. . . . . . (NY)	965
	BAUMANN, Roland M. . . (OH)	66
	HARRISON, Dennis I. . . . (OH)	506
	MILLER, Fredric M. . . . . (PA)	837
	STOUT, Leon J. . . . . (PA)	1198
	SCHULZ, Constance B. . (SC)	1102
	BEHRND-KLODT, Menzi L. (WI)	75
Archival evaluation	BOECKMAN, Frances B. . (MS)	109
Archival exhibits	WEST, Donald . . . . (MI)	1326
	HALLER, Douglas M. . . . (PA)	489
	SCHUMACHER, Carolyn	
	S. . . . . (PA)	1102
Archival facilities	LATHROP, Alan K. . . . . . (MN)	701
Archival field work	WEST, Donald . . . . (MI)	1326
Archival full-text databases	MARKERT, Patricia B. . . (NY)	771
Archival history	BRADSHER, James G. . . (DC)	126
Archival history & theory	BRICHFORD, Maynard J. (IL)	134
Archival implementation &		
management	DAWSON, Barbara J. . . . (DC)	282
Archival indexing systems	GORDON, Martin K. . . . . (VA)	451
Archival information systems	EASTWOOD, Terence M. (BC)	333
Archival inventory	COOVER, Robert W. . . . (CA)	244
Archival management	STEPHENSON, Shirley E. (CA)	1189
	ELLISON, J T. . . . . (CO)	345
	GAUSS, Nancy V. . . . . . (CO)	423
	PAUL, Karen D. . . . . (DC)	949
	DICKENS, Rosa L. . . . . . (GA)	300
	SOWINSKI, Carolyn M. . (IN)	1170
	CONSTANCE, Joseph W. (MA)	238
	FISHBEIN, Meyer H. . . . (MD)	380
	FOREMAN, Kenneth J. . . (NC)	390
	OLSON, David J. . . . . . . (NC)	922
	SARETZKY, Gary D. . . . (NJ)	1082

ARCHIVES (Cont'd)

Archival management		
	FRUSCIANO, Thomas J. (NY)	406
	HUNTER, Gregory S. . . . (NY)	576
	RICHIUSO, John P. . . . . (NY)	1030
	TAYLOR, Robert N. . . . . (NY)	1228
	NOLAN, Patrick B. . . . . . (OH)	907
	FILSON, Laurie . . . . (OR)	377
	KOHL, Michael F. . . . . . . (SC)	668
	CAMERON, Sam A. . . . . (TN)	175
	HOOKS, Michael Q. . . . . (TX)	556
	STIRLING, Dale A. . . . . . (WA)	1195
	TAYLOR, Hugh A. . . . . . (NS)	1227
Archival management & automation	SERBAN, William M. . . . (LA)	1116
Archival manuscripts collections	RICHMOND, Robert W. . . (KS)	1031
Archival manuscripts control MARC		
format	WEBER, Lisa B. . . . . (IL)	1314
Archival material automation	SMITH, William K. . . . . . (MI)	1161
Archival materials	GRIFFIN, Thomas E. . . . (CA)	469
	WATANABE, Ruth T. . . . (NY)	1308
	KIRKALI, Meral . . . . (WI)	654
Archival materials conservation	ELLISON, J T. . . . . (CO)	345
Archival methods & records		
management	CAIN, Charlene C. . . . . . (LA)	171
Archival microfilming	JONES, C L. . . . . (PA)	611
Archival needs evaluation	EDGERLY, Linda . . . . . . (MA)	336
Archival organization	HOFFBERG, Judith A. . . (CA)	547
	BAUMSTEIN, Paschal M. (NC)	66
	HOOKS, Michael Q. . . . . (TX)	556
Archival photographs	BAUS, J W. . . . . (IN)	67
Archival planning	JIMERSON, Randall C. . . (CT)	600
Archival practices	STONE, Ellen C. . . . . . . (CT)	1197
Archival preparation	COOKE, Anna L. . . . . . . (TN)	240
Archival preservation	CHRISTOPHER, Paul . . . (CA)	212
	MULDREY, Mary H. . . . . (LA)	876
	GRIFFIN, Marie E. . . . . . (NJ)	468
Archival preservation techniques	TAMMARO, James M. . . (NY)	1221
Archival printing	WAYLAND, Terry T. . . . . (TX)	1311
Archival processing	ODOM, Jane H. . . . . (DC)	917
	ELTZROTH, Elsbeth L. . . (GA)	346
	FRENCH, Melodee J. . . . (GA)	402
	BOECKMAN, Frances B. (MS)	109
	DISHON, Robert M. . . . . (NY)	305
	OAKHILL, Harold W. . . . . (NY)	913
	OVERTON, Julie M. . . . . (OH)	931
	LEVITT, Martin L. . . . . . . (PA)	721
	SNYDER, Theresa . . . . . (PA)	1165
Archival processing & description	SICILIANO, Peg P. . . . . . (MI)	1135
Archival publications consltng &		
editing	MARRELLI, Nancy M. . . . (PQ)	773
Archival reference	BAKER, Russell P. . . . . . (AR)	49
	MILLER, Leon C. . . . . . . (AR)	839
	CASSEDY, James G. . . . (DC)	193
	OAKHILL, Harold W. . . . (NY)	913
Archival research	KREPS, Lise E. . . . . (WA)	678
Archival science	DOWNS, Charles F. . . . . (DC)	317
Archival searching	RITTER, Helen . . . . (NY)	1036
Archival support	EDGERLY, Linda . . . . . . (MA)	336
Archival systems	BURNS, John F. . . . . (CA)	162
Archival techniques	SPEISMAN, Stephen A. . (ON)	1172
Archival theory	KIMBALL, Gregg D. . . . . (VA)	649
Archival training	JONES, Allen W. . . . . . . (AL)	610
	BARTKOWSKI, Patricia . (MI)	61
Archive & manuscript processing	THWEATT, John H. . . . . (TN)	1243
Archive automation	GILHEANY, Stephen J. . . (CA)	435
Archive contributing	EPPES, William D. . . . . . (NY)	351
Archive creation	GIBSON, Joanne . . . . . . (CA)	432
Archive establishment	KESSLER, Selma P. . . . . (NJ)	645
Archive management	VANDEGRIFT, Barbara P. (DC)	1273
	PILKINGTON, James P. . (TN)	973
Archive, museum, & library admin	WRIGHT, John C. . . . (HI)	1371
Archive organization	MAASS, Eleanor A. . . . . (PA)	753
Archive program	KERR, Kevin G. . . . . (IL)	644
Archives	NEWTON, Virginia A. . . . (AK)	900
	BENTLEY, Elna J. . . . . . (AL)	83
	ROBERTS, Eddie F. . . . . (AL)	1039
	HAYES, Franklin D. . . . . (AR)	515
	WALLS, Edwina . . . . (AR)	1298
	O'NEIL, Mary A. . . . . (AZ)	924
	AHOUSE, John B. . . . . . (CA)	8

ARCHIVES (Cont'd)
Archives

DOWNEY, Lynn A.	(CA)	316
ESCHER, Nancy	(CA)	354
GUNDERSON, Jeffery R.	(CA)	477
MCLOONE, Harriet V.	(CA)	814
PUGSLEY, Sharon G.	(CA)	997
SUNDSTRAND, Jacquelyn K.	(CA)	1210
SWAFFORD, William M.	(CA)	1212
DEW, T R.	(CO)	297
NEWMAN, John	(CO)	899
WOLFE, F M.	(CO)	1360
JASKEL, Mary A.	(CT)	595
MCDONALD, Lois E.	(CT)	803
MILLER, Irene K.	(CT)	838
PALMQUIST, David W.	(CT)	937
SAMUEL, Harold E.	(CT)	1079
ALDRICH, Michele L.	(DC)	11
BEDARD, Laura A.	(DC)	73
BOHANAN, Robert D.	(DC)	111
CHURCHVILLE, Lida H.	(DC)	213
DOWD, Mary J.	(DC)	315
FONT, Mary M.	(DC)	388
HARDING, Robert S.	(DC)	500
KOVACS, Katherine M.	(DC)	673
MCGUIRE, Brian	(DC)	808
NIELSEN, Elizabeth A.	(DC)	903
PETERSON, Trudy H.	(DC)	964
RUSSELL, John T.	(DC)	1069
RUSSELL, Marvin F.	(DC)	1069
TRYON, Roy H.	(DE)	1260
ABBOTT, Elizabeth L.	(FL)	1
DEBOLT, W D.	(FL)	284
DE VARONA, Esperanza B.	(FL)	297
JOHNSON, Susan J.	(FL)	609
JOLINSKI, Jenny R.	(FL)	610
BROCK, Kathy T.	(GA)	138
BURKHART, Sue W.	(GA)	161
GARFINKLE, Gail J.	(GA)	419
HOUGH, Leslie S.	(GA)	562
LANNING, E K.	(GA)	696
BECK, Marianne J.	(IA)	71
FENSTERMANN, Duane W.	(IA)	371
GIBSON, Michael D.	(IA)	432
MONTGOMERY, David E.	(IA)	856
ROGERS, Earl M.	(IA)	1049
WIESE, Glenda C.	(IA)	1337
BELAN, Judith A.	(IL)	75
BRIGGS, Martha T.	(IL)	135
CARSON, James G.	(IL)	188
GILDEMEISTER, Glen A.	(IL)	434
HANRATH, Linda C.	(IL)	497
HOLZENBERG, Eric J.	(IL)	555
KOCH, David V.	(IL)	667
MILLER, Janet	(IL)	838
MILLER, Robert	(IL)	841
NEAL, Donn C.	(IL)	890
OSBORN, Walter	(IL)	927
QUINN, Patrick M.	(IL)	1000
RYAN, Sheila	(IL)	1071
WITTMAN, Elisabeth C.	(IL)	1358
BISHOP, Barbara N.	(IN)	99
EIGEMAN, Laurence E.	(IN)	340
LYSY, Peter J.	(IN)	753
MCSHANE, Stephen G.	(IN)	818
BOGAN, Mary E.	(KS)	110
DONNELLY, Lela M.	(KS)	311
THOMPSON, Mary A.	(KS)	1240
ANDERSON, James C.	(KY)	23
BELL, Mary M.	(KY)	77
CREAMER, Mary M.	(KY)	257
FRENCH, Robert B.	(KY)	402
LEVSTIK, Frank R.	(KY)	721
ROBERTS, Gerald F.	(KY)	1040
STONE, Sue L.	(KY)	1197
THOMPSON, Ann B.	(KY)	1238
WHITE, Ernest M.	(KY)	1331

ARCHIVES (Cont'd)
Archives

DRAUGHON, Ralph B.	(LA)	318
BATES, Susie M.	(MA)	64
CHAPDELAINE, Susan A.	(MA)	201
COHEN, Christina M.	(MA)	228
KENDALL, John D.	(MA)	640
LANE, Margaret	(MA)	694
MACDONALD, Wayne D.	(MA)	754
MELNICK, Ralph	(MA)	823
SLY, Margery N.	(MA)	1150
SNIFFIN-MARINO, Megan G.	(MA)	1163
STICKNEY, Zephorene L.	(MA)	1193
WEBBER, Donna E.	(MA)	1313
WOODARD, Paul E.	(MA)	1366
YOUNT, Diana	(MA)	1384
HOGAN, Peter E.	(MD)	549
HOLLOWAK, Thomas L.	(MD)	552
LOWENS, Margery M.	(MD)	744
MERZ, Nancy M.	(MD)	827
SCHAAF, Elizabeth	(MD)	1088
SLEEMAN, William E.	(MD)	1148
TITCOMB, Anne S.	(MD)	1247
VIRTA, Alan K.	(MD)	1285
BOLES, Frank	(MI)	112
FRANTILLA, K A.	(MI)	398
GAYLOR, Robert G.	(MI)	423
HALL, Lawrence E.	(MI)	488
LARONGE, Philip V.	(MI)	698
NOWICKE, Carole E.	(MI)	911
NUCKOLLS, Karen A.	(MI)	912
PFLUG, Warner W.	(MI)	966
SPENCE, Theresa S.	(MI)	1173
WARNER, Robert M.	(MI)	1305
DECKER, John W.	(MN)	286
GREENE, Mark A.	(MN)	464
KLAASSEN, David J.	(MN)	657
NAUEN, Lindsay B.	(MN)	889
ANDERSON, Paul G.	(MO)	25
BAER, Eleanora A.	(MO)	45
DEKEN, Jean M.	(MO)	288
DEWAELSCHE, Thomas M.	(MO)	297
GLENN, Michael D.	(MO)	441
MASON, Laura L.	(MO)	781
OFSTAD, Odessa L.	(MO)	917
RILEY, Martha J.	(MO)	1034
STAUTER, Mark C.	(MO)	1183
WOHLRABE, John C.	(MO)	1359
BUSH, Mary E.	(NC)	165
JONES, H G.	(NC)	613
LENNON, Donald R.	(NC)	715
MILLER, Barry K.	(NC)	836
TOOMER, Clarence	(NC)	1251
BECKER, Ronald L.	(NJ)	72
BOWLING, Mary B.	(NJ)	121
COLLINS, Sarah F.	(NJ)	233
CROSS, Roberta A.	(NJ)	261
PALMISANO-DRUCKER, Elsalyn	(NJ)	937
THOMPSON, Janet A.	(NM)	1240
BLESSE, Robert E.	(NV)	105
AUBRY, John C.	(NY)	38
BRODY, Catherine T.	(NY)	139
CAMMACK, Bruce P.	(NY)	175
CIOLLI, Antoinette	(NY)	214
CLARK, Diane A.	(NY)	216
COLMAN, Gould P.	(NY)	233
CRYSTAL, Bernard R.	(NY)	262
DOE, Lynn M.	(NY)	308
EARLE, Marcia H.	(NY)	332
GELLER, Lawrence D.	(NY)	426
HIGGINS, Steven	(NY)	538
HOGAN, Matthew	(NY)	549
LAFEVER, C R.	(NY)	687
MILLER, Barbara K.	(NY)	835
PACKARD, Agnes K.	(NY)	933
PERKUS, Paul C.	(NY)	959
POMRENZE, Seymour J.	(NY)	982

ARCHIVES (Cont'd)
Archives

RACHOW, Louis A. . . . . (NY) 1001
ROSHON, Nina C. . . . . . (NY) 1057
ROWLAND, Eileen . . . . . (NY) 1062
RUSSO, Mary . . . . (NY) 1070
SETTANNI, Joseph A. . . (NY) 1117
SIEGEL, Steven W. . . . . (NY) 1136
STAPLETON, Darwin H. . (NY) 1181
TAYLOR, Gladys M. . . . . (NY) 1226
WILSTED, Thomas P. . . . (NY) 1353
WOLFE, Allis . . . . (NY) 1360
WOLOHAN, Juliet F. . . . (NY) 1362
WOSH, Peter J. . . . . . . (NY) 1369
ARNOLD, Gary J. . . . . . (OH) 33
BAIN, George W. . . . . . (OH) 47
BERG, Richard R. . . . . . (OH) 84
BERGDORF, Randolph S. . (OH) 85
BRANDT, Michael H. . . . (OH) 128
COHEN, Susan J. . . . . . (OH) 229
ENGEL, Carl T. . . . . . . (OH) 348
HARRISON, Dennis I. . . . (OH) 506
JENKINS, Glen P. . . . . . (OH) 597
SCHLICHTING, Catherine
    N. . . . . (OH) 1094
SMITH, Thomas A. . . . . . (OH) 1161
RELPH, Martha H. . . . . . (OK) 1022
TURNBAUGH, Roy C. . . (OR) 1264
BROWN, Charlotte B. . . (PA) 142
CHAFF, Sandra L. . . . . . (PA) 197
DAVIES, Grace A. . . . . . (PA) 277
FROMM, Roger W. . . . . . (PA) 405
HOLUB, Joseph C. . . . . . (PA) 555
HORROCKS, Thomas A. (PA) 561
LEIBOLD, Cheryl A. . . . . (PA) 713
MILLER, Fredric M. . . . . (PA) 837
MORRIS, Leslie A. . . . . . (PA) 867
O'NEILL, Philip M. . . . . (PA) 924
STALLARD, Kathryn E. . . (PA) 1179
TERRY, Terese M. . . . . . (PA) 1232
WEINBERG, David M. . . (PA) 1317
ZORICH, Phillip J. . . . . . (PA) 1390
CHERPAK, Evelyn M. . . (RI) 206
MASLYN, David C. . . . . . (RI) 780
WAGNER, Albin . . . . . . (RI) 1291
CHOPESIUK, Ronald J. . (SC) 210
JOHNSON, Minnie M. . . (SC) 607
LAWSON, James F. . . . . (SC) 705
THOMPSON, Harry F. . . (SD) 1239
ALDERFER, Jane B. . . . . (TN) 11
HARRISON, Richard H. . (TN) 507
HARWELL, Sara J. . . . . (TN) 509
HOOPER, James E. . . . . (TN) 557
HUGHES, Marylin B. . . . (TN) 572
RATKIN, Annette L. . . . . (TN) 1009
SHORT, William M. . . . . (TN) 1132
WOLFE, Marice . . . . (TN) 1361
ALLEN, Peggy G. . . . . . (TX) 15
ALLEN, Virginia M. . . . . (TX) 16
ATKINS, Winston . . . . . (TX) 38
CRIST, Lynda L. . . . . . . (TX) 259
DIVELY, Reddy . . . . . . (TX) 306
HIMMEL, Richard L. . . . (TX) 542
KLEPPER, Bobbie J. . . . (TX) 660
LETSON, Dawn E. . . . . . (TX) 719
PAYNE, John R. . . . . . . (TX) 951
ROBINSON, Kathleen M. (TX) 1044
SALL, Larry D. . . . . (TX) 1076
SCHAADT, Robert L. . . . (TX) 1088
WHITE, Elizabeth B. . . . (TX) 1331
EVANS, Max J. . . . . (UT) 357
HEFNER, Loretta L. . . . . (UT) 520
ROWLEY, Edward D. . . . (UT) 1063
COLLINS, Sara D. . . . . . (VA) 233
GRANT, Juanita G. . . . . (VA) 458
LINDEMANN, Richard H. (VA) 729
PINEL, Stephen L. . . . . . (VA) 974
SHEPARD, E L. . . . . . . (VA) 1126
THOMPSON, Anthony B. (VA) 1239
WALCH, Victoria I. . . . . . (VA) 1293

ARCHIVES (Cont'd)
Archives

                                        EBERT, John J. . . . . (WI) 334
                                        GROSKOPF, Amy L. . . . (WI) 472
                                        KINZER, Ferdinelle M. . . (WI) 653
                                        MISNER, Barbara . . . . . . (WI) 847
                                        PIETERS, Donald L. . . . . (WI) 972
                                        SHUTKIN, Sara A. . . . . . (WI) 1134
                                        STEINWALL, Susan D. . (WI) 1186
                                        ARMSTRONG, Fredrick H. (WV) 32
                                        OSTRYE, Anne T. . . . . . (WY) 929
                                        FYFE, Janet H. . . . . (ON) 411
                                        SEBANC, Mark F. . . . . . (ON) 1110
                                        BROCHU, Frederick . . . . (PQ) 138
                                        LUSSIER, Claudine . . . . (PQ) 749
Archives acquisition   SUMNERS, Bill F. . . . . . (TN) 1209
Archives administration   DABRISHUS, Michael J. . (AR) 269
                                        BUTLER, Randall R. . . . . (CA) 167
                                        OKEEFE, Julia C. . . . . . . (CA) 919
                                        BRADSHER, James G. . . (DC) 126
                                        CRAWFORD, Elva B. . . . (DC) 256
                                        HEISS, Harry G. . . . . (DC) 523
                                        SAHLI, Nancy A. . . . . . . (DC) 1075
                                        ELZY, Martin I. . . . . (GA) 347
                                        SCHEWE, Donald B. . . . (GA) 1092
                                        GAYNON, David B. . . . . (IL) 424
                                        CONNELLY, James T. . . (IN) 237
                                        HARING, Jacqueline K. . (MA) 501
                                        HOLDEN, Harley P. . . . . (MA) 550
                                        HORN, David E. . . . . (MA) 559
                                        MCLAIN, Guy A. . . . . . . (MA) 813
                                        O'TOOLE, James M. . . . (MA) 930
                                        BOEDER, Thelma B. . . . . (MN) 109
                                        JESSEE, W S. . . . . (MN) 600
                                        SHOPTAUGH, Terry L. . . (MN) 1132
                                        WURL, Joel F. . . . . (MN) 1374
                                        HAVENER, Ralph S. . . . . (MO) 513
                                        JONES, Martin J. . . . . . . (NY) 614
                                        SERBACKI, Mary . . . . . . (NY) 1116
                                        SVIBRUCK, Jonathan . . . (NY) 1212
                                        WHEELER, Elaine . . . . . (NY) 1328
                                        FLAHIVE, Mary E. . . . . . (OH) 383
                                        STOLT, Wilbur A. . . . . . . (OK) 1196
                                        THELEN, Richard L. . . . . (OR) 1234
                                        TURNBAUGH, Roy C. . . (OR) 1264
                                        ANDERSON, R J. . . . . . (PA) 25
                                        LYTLE, Richard H. . . . . . (PA) 753
                                        SPENCER, Catherine K. . (TX) 1173
                                        WACHTER-NELSON, Ruth
                                            M. . . . . (TX) 1290
                                        EDWARDS, Steven M. . . (WA) 338
                                        RHOADS, James B. . . . . (WA) 1026
                                        BEYEA, Marion L. . . . . . (NB) 93
                                        TAYLOR, Hugh A. . . . . . (NS) 1227
                                        CAYA, Marcel . . . . (PQ) 195
                                        ORTIZ MONASTERIO,
                                            Leonor . . . . (MEX) 927
Archives administration & operations   ROTHMAN, John . . . . . . (NY) 1060
Archives administration, land records   TEMPLE, Wayne C. . . . . (IL) 1230
Archives & historical manuscripts   WILLARD, Anne H. . . . . (CT) 1341
                                        GRIGG, Susan . . . . (MA) 470
Archives & indexing   SIARNY, William D. . . . . (IL) 1134
Archives & library automation   SYKES, Stephanie L. . . . (PQ) 1217
Archives & library management   SYKES, Stephanie L. . . . (PQ) 1217
Archives & manuscript collection
    mgmt   FRYE, Dorothy T. . . . . . . (MI) 407
Archives & manuscript collections   NODLER, Charles E. . . . (MO) 906
Archives & manuscripts   BRECK, Paul A. . . . . (AR) 131
                                        DAY, Deborah C. . . . . . . (CA) 282
                                        MCPHAIL, Martha E. . . . (CA) 817
                                        PUGH, Mary J. . . . . (CA) 997
                                        RICHARDSON, John V. . (CA) 1029
                                        VANSLYKE, Lisa M. . . . . (CA) 1277
                                        NOLEN, Anita L. . . . . (DC) 908
                                        SUNG, Carolyn H. . . . . . (DC) 1210
                                        BISHOP, Beverly D. . . . . (GA) 99
                                        KLINE, Laura S. . . . . (IA) 661
                                        HANSEN, Ralph W. . . . . (ID) 498
                                        WELLS, Merle W. . . . . . (ID) 1322
                                        EVANS, Linda J. . . . . (IL) 357

ARCHIVES (Cont'd)

Archives & manuscripts

	MOTLEY, Archie	(IL)	872
	SHUSTER, Robert D.	(IL)	1134
	WEBER, Lisa B.	(IL)	1314
	OTTO, Kathryn D.	(KS)	930
	MORISON, William J.	(KY)	865
	TURNER, I B.	(LA)	1264
	DOWLER, Lawrence E.	(MA)	315
	ELLIOTT, Clark A.	(MA)	343
	STUART, Karen A.	(MD)	1204
	TATE, Vernon D.	(MD)	1225
	YEAGER, Gerry	(MD)	1378
	KROSCH, Penelope S.	(MN)	680
	BURCKEL, Nicholas C.	(MO)	158
	BRABHAM, Robert F.	(NC)	124
	GRAY, David P.	(ND)	459
	JOYCE, William L.	(NJ)	618
	COX, Richard J.	(NY)	253
	DOYAL, Patricia A.	(NY)	317
	MENT, David M.	(NY)	824
	WARNOW-BLEWETT, Joan N.	(NY)	1305
	PIKE, Kermit J.	(OH)	972
	ANDRICK, Annita A.	(PA)	27
	WICKEY, Colleen	(PA)	1335
	ZABROSKY, Frank A.	(PA)	1385
	DUBIEL, Laura R.	(TX)	321
	HUMPHREY, David C.	(TX)	573
	JOHNSON, Jeffery O.	(UT)	606
	JACOB, Diane B.	(VA)	589
	JACOB, John N.	(VA)	589
	GALLAGHER, Connell B.	(VT)	413

Archives & manuscripts administration	PARHAM, Robert B.	(AK)	940
	LATOUR, Terry S.	(MS)	701
	KOVAN, Allan S.	(WI)	673
Archives & manuscripts automation	BROWN, Barbara J.	(VA)	142
Archives & manuscripts control	CARROLL-HORROCKS, Elizabeth	(PA)	187
Archives & manuscripts management	PINSON, Patricia A.	(WY)	975
Archives & manuscripts processing	BECK, Alison M.	(TX)	71
Archives & music rarities	WALKER, Elizabeth	(PA)	1295
Archives & preservation	COURSEY, W T.	(GA)	251
Archives & rare books	LARSGAARD, Mary L.	(CO)	698
	STEVENS, Marjorie	(MI)	1190
	TAYLOR, Carolyn L.	(MO)	1226
	HILL, Susan E.	(TX)	540
	EDMONDS, Susan M.	(WA)	336
	DESOMOGYI, Aileen A.	(ON)	295
Archives & record management	OSTERFIELD, George T.	(OH)	928
Archives & records	HOLDEN, Harley P.	(MA)	550
Archives & records center management	CAMPBELL, Margaret E.	(NS)	177
Archives & records management	NEWCOMER, Susan N.	(CA)	898
	CANTELON, Philip L.	(MD)	179
	STIELOW, Frederick J.	(MD)	1194
	BLOUIN, Francis X.	(MI)	107
	REHKOPF, Charles F.	(MO)	1017
	PRICE, William S.	(NC)	993
	ERLANDSSON, Alf M.	(NY)	353
	LAIST, Sharon B.	(NY)	688
	CLARK, Robert L.	(OK)	218
	MURRAY, Lucia M.	(OR)	882
	CEBRUN, Mary J.	(TX)	196
	GRACY, David B.	(TX)	455
	EULENBERG, Julia N.	(WA)	356
	ROBERTSON, Guy M.	(BC)	1041
	ARDERN, Christine M.	(ON)	31
	MURDOCH, Arthur W.	(ON)	879
Archives & records management teaching	WHALEN, Lucille	(NY)	1328
Archives & research	BRUNK, Thomas W.	(MI)	150
Archives & special collections	MCCRANK, Lawrence J.	(AL)	800
	CRAFT, Guy C.	(GA)	254
	MEADOR, Patricia L.	(LA)	819
	STEEL, Suzanne F.	(MS)	1183
	OSBORNE, Nancy S.	(NY)	927
	MCCALLUM, Brenda W.	(OH)	793
Archives & storage	PROCTOR, Dixie L.	(FL)	994
Archives appraisal	HARWOOD, James L.	(DC)	510

ARCHIVES (Cont'd)

Archives appraisal & cataloging	CORNELIUS, Charlene E.	(WI)	246
Archives arrangement & description	MYERS, Roger	(AZ)	885
	SERBACKI, Mary	(NY)	1116
Archives automated description	PENDLETON, Debbie D.	(AL)	956
Archives automation	BEARMAN, David A.	(PA)	69
	VAILLANCOURT, Alain	(PQ)	1270
Archives collection development	JESSEE, W S.	(MN)	600
Archives development	DUNGER, George A.	(SD)	326
	KLUMPENHOUWER, Richard	(AB)	662
Archives education	O'TOOLE, James M.	(MA)	930
Archives exhibits	KIRWAN, Kathleen	(NY)	656
Archives for small businesses	HOMMEL, Claudia	(NY)	555
Archives, historic building preservation	RABINS, Joan W.	(TX)	1001
Archives, history of medicine	VADEBONCOEUR, Elizabeth J.	(CA)	1270
Archives in gerontology	EDWARDS, Willie M.	(MI)	338
Archives, labor records	RABINS, Joan W.	(TX)	1001
Archives librarianship	MISRA, Jayasri T.	(GA)	847
Archives, library, museum services	SUELFLOW, August R.	(MO)	1206
Archives management	PICKARD, Mary A.	(AL)	970
	CALMES, Alan R.	(DC)	174
	MOSS, William W.	(DC)	872
	PACIFICO, Michele F.	(DC)	933
	VOGT-O'CONNOR, Diane L.	(DC)	1287
	ADAMS, Larry D.	(IA)	5
	HAY, Charles C.	(KY)	515
	BLATZ, Imogene	(MN)	104
	KELLY, Patricia J.	(MO)	638
	HAUPERT, Thomas J.	(NC)	512
	WAITE, William F.	(NJ)	1293
	ROCHA, Guy L.	(NV)	1045
	HESS, James W.	(NY)	534
	JOHNSON, Judith	(NY)	606
	MAURER, Eric	(NY)	787
	MOORE, Rue I.	(NY)	861
	NEAT, Charles M.	(NY)	891
	TEICHMAN, Raymond J.	(NY)	1230
	FALZON, Judith A.	(OR)	363
	HARDY, John L.	(ON)	500
	ST. PIERRE, Normand	(ON)	1075
	NEFSKY, Judith L.	(PQ)	892
	FAGERLUND, M L.	(SWZ)	361
Archives management & administration	DUNN, Lucia S.	(IL)	327
Archives, manuscript management	STOPKA, Christina K.	(WY)	1198
Archives, manuscripts	CARTLEDGE, Connie L.	(DC)	190
Archives, manuscripts collections	SMITH, Edith	(CA)	1154
Archives of computer industry	BRUEMMER, Bruce H.	(MN)	149
Archives organization & training	KEATS, Susan E.	(MA)	633
Archives processing	WOOD, Steven R.	(UT)	1365
Archives processing & reference	BLACK, J A.	(TX)	101
Archives, rare books	RAY, Joyce M.	(TX)	1011
Archives, records management education	RHOADS, James B.	(WA)	1026
Archives reference	BRILEY, Carol A.	(MO)	136
	KUCHERENKO, Eugenia	(OH)	682
Archives, religious	HAURY, David A.	(KS)	512
Archives studies	RISHEL, Joseph F.	(PA)	1035
Archives supervision	CURTIS, George H.	(MO)	267
Archives training	TOUCHETTE, Francois G.	(PQ)	1252
Archives, training & development	RABINS, Joan W.	(TX)	1001
Archiving	LEGER, Norissa	(CA)	712
Archiving art slides on video disks	SHARER, E J.	(CO)	1122
Archiving corporate records	LEMON, Nancy A.	(OH)	715
Archivist	JOHNSON, Georgina	(KS)	604
	KELLS, Laura J.	(MD)	637
	MARTIN, Janet L.	(NY)	776
	CRAWFORD, Miriam I.	(PA)	257
Archivist for hospital	KILPATRICK, Barbara A.	(TN)	648
Archivists training & development	SANTORO, Corrado A.	(MB)	1082
Association archives	GILTINAN, Celia E.	(MO)	437
Audio archives	SALY, Alan J.	(NY)	1078
Audio recording & archives	RUNYON, Steven C.	(CA)	1067
Audiovisual archives	BIRDWHISTELL, Terry L.	(KY)	98
	GOODRICH, Allan B.	(MA)	449
Automated archival description	PURDY, Virginia C.	(DC)	998

ARCHIVES (Cont'd)

Automated archival systems	SZARY, Richard V.	(DC)	1218
Automated systems for archives	HONHART, Frederick L.	(MI)	556
Automation, archival	SMITH, Michael O.	(MI)	1158
Automation in archives	BOHANAN, Robert D.	(DC)	111
	MORISON, William J.	(KY)	865
	STOUT, Leon J.	(PA)	1198
Automation of newspaper archives	ENNS, Carol F.	(NB)	350
Binarization of archival materials	GILHEANY, Stephen J.	(CA)	435
Books & manuscripts archives	GAMBLE, Mary J.	(CA)	416
Broadcasting archives	CNATTINGIUS, Claes M.	(SWE)	224
Business archives	YATES, Donald N.	(IN)	1378
	SARETZKY, Gary D.	(NJ)	1082
	GRACE, William M.	(PA)	455
Business archives administration	KING, Eleanor M.	(PA)	650
Canadian archival theory	COOK, Terry G.	(ON)	240
Cartographic & architectural archives	KIDD, Betty H.	(ON)	646
Cataloging & preserving archival mtrls	FALCONE, Elena C.	(NY)	362
Cataloging archival moving images	HARRISON, Harriet W.	(DC)	506
Cataloging archives & manuscripts	CARNES, Suzanne M.	(CA)	183
	CALKIN, Homer L.	(VA)	173
Catholic archives	CASLIN, Adele	(PA)	193
Catholic social action archives	RUNKEL, Phillip M.	(WI)	1067
Church archives	PINKARD, Ophelia T.	(DC)	974
	WIEDERAENDE, Robert C.	(IA)	1336
	NESBITT, John R.	(MO)	896
Classical music sound archives	MAROTH, Frederick J.	(CA)	772
College & university archives	REYNOLDS, Jon K.	(DC)	1025
	MAHER, William J.	(IL)	760
	BARTKOWSKI, Patricia	(MI)	61
	DUNLAP, Barbara J.	(NY)	326
	STOUT, Leon J.	(PA)	1198
College archives	KNAPP, Peter J.	(CT)	663
	THORSTENSSON, Edith J.	(MN)	1243
	VAN BENTHUYSEN, Robert F.	(NJ)	1272
	GORCHELS, Clarence C.	(OR)	451
	HUX, Roger K.	(SC)	579
	SCOBELL, Elizabeth H.	(WV)	1106
College, university archives	BERKELEY, Edmund	(VA)	87
Congressional projects in archives	HARWOOD, James L.	(DC)	510
Consulting on archival administration	BEHRND-KLODT, Menzi L.	(WI)	75
Corporate archives	EVANS, M R.	(CA)	357
	HEDLIN, Ethel W.	(DC)	520
	STEGH, Leslie J.	(IL)	1185
	VOLLMAR, William J.	(MO)	1288
	OLEARY, Martha H.	(NY)	920
Corporate archives & records center	PEGLER, Ross J.	(FL)	954
Corporate archives & records centers	CLAYTON, John M.	(DE)	220
Corporate archives, information services	DYER, Esther R.	(NY)	330
Corporate archives planning	EDGERLY, Linda	(MA)	336
Corporate records & archives	RUNYON, Judith A.	(CA)	1067
County records administration & archives	WEAVER, Clifton W.	(AL)	1312
Creating archival collections	METZLER, Valerie	(IL)	829
Creating university archives	MATTHEW, Jeannette M.	(IN)	785
Curriculum archives	WYBORNEY, Charles E.	(CA)	1374
Custom research, library & archives	TURNER, Ellis S.	(MD)	1264
Database archives design	DAWSON, Barbara J.	(DC)	282
Database archiving	PICKARD, Mary A.	(AL)	970
Description of archives	BUCKWALD, Joel	(NJ)	155
Disaster recovery of archival materials	MARRELLI, Nancy M.	(PQ)	773
Discographer, recording archivist	NOVITSKY, Edward G.	(NY)	911
Education archives & records	DEARSTYNE, Bruce W.	(NY)	284
Educational & non-profit archives	SCHUMACHER, Carolyn S.	(PA)	1102
Equity research archival database	MILLS, Andrew G.	(MA)	843
Ethnic & religious archives	GRACE, William M.	(PA)	455
Federal government archives	PFEIFFER, David A.	(DC)	966
Film & television archives	JOHNSON, Jane D.	(CA)	605
Film & video archiving	WEATHERFORD, Elizabeth	(NY)	1311
Film archives	YEAGER, Gerry	(MD)	1378
Financial archival arrangement	LAMBKIN, Anthony	(IRE)	690
Fiscal projects & reference in archives	HARWOOD, James L.	(DC)	510
Folk music archives	POST, Jennifer C.	(VT)	986
Frank Sinatra archivist	ROSS, Ric	(CA)	1058
French archival records & manuscripts	KOHN, Roger S.	(NY)	668

ARCHIVES (Cont'd)

General archives	UHL, M C.	(OK)	1268
Government archives	HEDLIN, Ethel W.	(DC)	520
	PROVINE, Dorothy S.	(DC)	996
Government archives & history	CHRISTNER, Deborah S.	(CA)	212
Government archives & records	HACKMAN, Larry J.	(NY)	481
Historic archives	WATIER-LALONDE, Chantal	(PQ)	1309
Historical & archival discography	GLASFORD, G R.	(NY)	440
Historical & archival research	MCGAUGHRAN, Roberta W.	(DC)	805
Historical archive recordings	BUCHSBAUM, Robert E.	(OH)	153
Historical collection archives	LEVIS, Gail A.	(IL)	721
Historical research & archives	HECKMAN, Marlin L.	(CA)	520
History, archives	HADDEN, Robert L.	(MD)	481
History of botany archives	STIEBER, Michael T.	(PA)	1193
History of medicine archives	GILHEANY, Rosary S.	(NJ)	434
Humanistic psychology archivist	GRAZIANO, Eugene	(CA)	460
Humanities & archives indexing	MOODY, Suzanna	(MN)	857
Jewish archives	KOHN, Roger S.	(NY)	668
Libraries & archives	MATTHEW, Jeannette M.	(IN)	785
Library & archival need assessments	FOURIE, Denise K.	(CA)	393
Library & archival systems	BARRY, Paul J.	(DC)	60
Library & archive administration	DOAK, Wesley A.	(OR)	306
Library & archive management	FINE, Deborah J.	(CA)	377
Library & archive planning	SWINBURNE, Ralph E.	(NY)	1216
Library & archive preservation	GARLICK, Karen	(DC)	419
Lib & archives conservation management	CUNHA, George M.	(KY)	265
Library & archives management	MOORE, Emily C.	(AL)	859
Library & archives relation	KOEL, Maria O.	(CT)	667
Library & archives systems	TONEY, Stephen R.	(MD)	1250
Library archives	KNOWLTON, John D.	(DC)	665
Library, museum & archives admin	HYATT, John D.	(TX)	580
Local archives	SCOTT, Sharon A.	(OH)	1108
Local government archives	BENGE, Joy L.	(TX)	80
Local history & archives	OTTOSEN, Charles F.	(AB)	930
	KEARNS, Linda J.	(ON)	633
Local history & university archives	WALKER, Mary J.	(NM)	1296
Lutheran Church history, archives	WITTMAN, Elisabeth C.	(IL)	1358
Maintaining province archives	STRECK, Helen T.	(KS)	1201
Management of archives	HANSEN, Peggy A.	(WA)	498
	GORDON, Robert S.	(ON)	451
Managing archives collection	PARKER, Peter J.	(PA)	942
Manuscript & archival description	HENSEN, Steven L.	(NC)	529
Manuscript & archive conservation	GARLICK, Karen	(DC)	419
Manuscript & archive management	JERDE, Curtis D.	(LA)	599
Manuscript librarianship, archives	WHEALAN, Ronald E.	(MA)	1328
Manuscripts & archival processing	WHITE, William T.	(MN)	1332
Manuscripts & archival reference	KAPLAN, Diane E.	(CT)	626
Manuscripts & archives	MCLACHLAN, Ross W.	(AZ)	812
	RULE, Amy E.	(AZ)	1067
	ZEIDBERG, David S.	(CA)	1387
	NEILON, Barbara L.	(CO)	892
	BROWN, William E.	(CT)	148
	WAIT, Gary E.	(CT)	1293
	BATTLE, Thomas C.	(DC)	65
	KNOWLTON, John D.	(DC)	665
	NYGREN, Deborah A.	(DC)	912
	RUDISELL, Carol A.	(DE)	1065
	PHILLIPS, Faye	(LA)	968
	EPPARD, Philip B.	(MA)	351
	LOSCALZO, Anita B.	(MA)	741
	MOSELEY, Eva S.	(MA)	870
	PERCY, Theresa R.	(MA)	958
	LOHF, Kenneth A.	(NY)	737
	DUCKETT, Kenneth W.	(OR)	322
	LLOYD, James B.	(TN)	735
	LARSEN, A D.	(UT)	698
	DIBIASE, Linda P.	(WA)	299
Manuscripts & archives administration	HARDWICK, Bonnie S.	(CA)	500
Manuscripts & archives collections	ASHFORD, Marguerite K.	(HI)	36
Manuscripts, archives processing	BOOTHE, Nancy L.	(TX)	116
Manuscripts, archives resrchr guidance	BOOTHE, Nancy L.	(TX)	116
Marketing archives & library services	SYKES, Stephanie L.	(PQ)	1217
Medical archives	GRACE, William M.	(PA)	455
Microcomputer use in archives	JACOB, Diane B.	(VA)	589
Motion picture & television archiving	FIELDING, Raymond E.	(TX)	376
Moving images archivist	DE ARMAN, Charles L.	(DC)	284

ARCHIVES (Cont'd)

Municipal archives	GRESSITT, Alexandra S.	(MS)	467
	BOCKMAN, Eugene J.	(NY)	109
Museum & archival cataloging, organz	DEE, Camille C.	(NY)	286
Museum archives	FINERMAN, Carol B.	(MI)	378
	WAGNER, Cherryl A.	(MI)	1291
	BELL, Mary F.	(NY)	77
	HOMMEL, Claudia	(NY)	555
	JOHNSON, Steven P.	(NY)	609
	HALLER, Douglas M.	(PA)	489
Music archives	BOWLING, Lance C.	(CA)	121
Music collections & archives	GREEN, Walter H.	(MO)	463
Music museums & archives	HASSE, John E.	(DC)	511
Natural resource archives	COOK, Terry G.	(ON)	240
Newspaper archive systems	ROACH, Eddie D.	(OK)	1037
Newspaper archives	JONES, Martin J.	(NY)	614
Newspaper photo archives	PARISOT, Beverly J.	(NE)	940
Optical disk information archiving	PASCHAL, John M.	(OK)	945
Organizational archives	KRAFT, Katherine G.	(MA)	675
Performing arts archives	WOODS, Alan L.	(OH)	1366
	PRITCHARD, Jane E.	(ENG)	994
Photo archives	FURR, Susan H.	(VA)	410
Photographic archives	BERGEN, Philip S.	(MA)	85
	COTTEN, Jerry W.	(NC)	250
	HALLER, Douglas M.	(PA)	489
	SCHULZ, Constance B.	(SC)	1102
	STONE, Gerald K.	(ON)	1197
	HANDE, D A.	(SK)	494
Photographic archives & research	SPINA, Marie C.	(NY)	1175
Photography archives	HENDERSON, Ellen B.	(CA)	526
Preservation of archival records	CALMES, Alan R.	(DC)	174
Presidential archives	SMITH, Nancy K.	(TX)	1158
Private jazz archivist	ROBINSON, David F.	(VA)	1043
Processing archival collections	HAWES, Grace M.	(CA)	513
	VIOL, Robert W.	(OH)	1285
Processing archival materials	SANDERS, Robert L.	(CA)	1080
	WADE, D J.	(MO)	1290
Processing archives & manuscripts	SIEBERS, Bruce L.	(MI)	1135
Processing manuscripts & archives	CHESTNUT, Paul I.	(DC)	207
Processing of archival materials	RABCHUK, Gordon K.	(PQ)	1001
Professional development of archivists	THOMAS, Evangeline M.	(KS)	1236
Public relations for archives	WALSH, G M.	(ON)	1299
Radio archives	JOHNSON, Jane D.	(CA)	605
Railroad archives	MUSICH, Gerald D.	(WI)	883
Rare books & archives	BEDARD, Laura A.	(DC)	73
	INGLES, Ernie B.	(SK)	582
Rare books, archives, & reference	KAPLAN, Sylvia Y.	(IL)	626
Rare books, college archives	GALLAGHER, Mary E.	(MA)	414
Rare books, manuscripts, & archives	FIELD, William N.	(NJ)	376
Rare sound recordings archives	MAWHINNEY, Paul C.	(PA)	787
Recorded sound archives	GAUNT, Sandra L.	(OH)	423
Records & archival management	SANTORO, Corrado A.	(MB)	1082
Records & archives management	CAN, Hung V.	(PQ)	177
Records management & archives	PEARLSTEIN, Toby	(MA)	952
	OGAWA, Chiyoko	(JAP)	918
Records management, archives	PRESTON, Deirdre R.	(WA)	991
Reference & archives	MACKENZIE, Alberta E.	(OH)	756
Reference archivist	LEMMON, Alfred E.	(LA)	715
Regional archives	MOORE, Karl R.	(IL)	860
Religious archives	BAKER, Russell P.	(AR)	49
	WHITE, Joyce L.	(CO)	1331
	JANSSEN, Gene R.	(MN)	594
	BODLING, Kurt A.	(MO)	109
	DEUTSCH, N E.	(MO)	297
	SULLIVAN, Majella M.	(NY)	1208
	YAKEL, Elizabeth	(NY)	1376
	CLAYTON, J G.	(SC)	220
	WILLIAMSON, Jane K.	(TN)	1347
	LOCH, Edward J.	(TX)	735
	BROCKMAN, Norbert C.	(KEN)	138
Religious archives administration	JOHNSON, Timothy J.	(IL)	609
Religious community archives	PATTERSON, Mary E.	(WA)	948
Religious denomination archives	WARNER, Wayne E.	(MO)	1305
Researching foreign archive institutions	OGAWA, Chiyoko	(JAP)	918
Science archives	GOODSTEIN, Judith R.	(CA)	450
Scientific tape film archives	SALY, Alan J.	(NY)	1078
Searching & retrieving archival sources	FALK, Candace S.	(CA)	362
Security for libraries & archives	WALCH, Timothy G.	(DC)	1293

ARCHIVES (Cont'd)

Setting up archives	ARNOLD, Judith M.	(OH)	33
Small archives	WEBBER, Steven L.	(CA)	1313
Social history archives	COOK, Terry G.	(ON)	240
Sound archives	ROTH, Stacy F.	(NJ)	1059
	BLUTH, John F.	(PA)	108
Sound archives, restoration	FRANK, Mortimer H.	(NY)	397
Sound archiving	SERCOMBE, Laurel	(WA)	1116
Spanish archivist	LEMMON, Alfred E.	(LA)	715
Special collections & archives	ABRAHAM, Terry	(ID)	3
	SPRANKLE, Anita T.	(PA)	1176
	TATUM, George W.	(VA)	1225
Special collections, archives	ROBBINS, Louise S.	(OK)	1039
Special collections including archives	HOLLAND, Mary M.	(TX)	551
Special collecticns, rare books, archive	NAINIS, Linda	(DC)	886
Special library & archives management	CLASPER, James W.	(OH)	219
State archives	BAKER, Russell P.	(AR)	49
	LOWELL, Howard P.	(OK)	744
	HELSLEY, Alexia J.	(SC)	525
Statewide archival development	HACKMAN, Larry J.	(NY)	481
Teaching archival management	YOUNKIN, C G.	(TX)	1383
Teaching archival start-up	CASLIN, Adele	(PA)	193
Technical support for archives	MURDOCH, Arthur W.	(ON)	879
Television archives	SCHREIBMAN, Fay C.	(NY)	1099
Television news film archives	WHITSON, Helene	(CA)	1334
Texas newspaper archives	MATHIS, Rama F.	(TX)	784
Theater archives	FRITZ, Donald D.	(MI)	405
	COLEMAN, Faith	(NY)	231
Toxicology archive administration	YOUNG, Carolyn K.	(KS)	1381
Transcribing archive recordings	PENGELLY, Joe	(ENG)	956
University archives	D'ANTONIO, Lynn M.	(AZ)	274
	WHITSON, Helene	(CA)	1334
	WITTHUS, Rutherford W.	(CO)	1358
	JIMERSON, Randall C.	(CT)	600
	BAMBERGER, Mary A.	(IL)	53
	GRAHAM, Robert W.	(IL)	456
	LEONARD, Kevin B.	(IL)	716
	MEYER, Daniel	(IL)	830
	TURNER, Nancy K.	(IN)	1265
	CRAWFORD, Anthony R.	(KS)	256
	BIRDWHISTELL, Terry L.	(KY)	98
	SCHMIDT, Jean M.	(LA)	1095
	BOLES, Frank	(MI)	112
	GRESSITT, Alexandra S.	(MS)	467
	SIMMONS, Ruth J.	(NJ)	1140
	SOLOMON, Geri E.	(NY)	1166
	STERN, Marc J.	(NY)	1189
	GALLAGHER, Dennis J.	(PA)	414
	LANDIS, Lawrence A.	(TX)	693
	DANIELS, Jerome P.	(WI)	273
	HARADA, Ryukichi	(JAP)	499
Video & oral history archives	JAGOE, Katherine P.	(TX)	591
Writer & history archives	NEWTON, Virginia A.	(AK)	900

ARCTIC (See also Polar)

Alaska & arctic information reference	SOKOLOV, Barbara J.	(AK)	1165
Arctic information	COOKE, Geraldine A.	(AB)	241
Arctic information referral	SOKOLOV, Barbara J.	(AK)	1165
Arctic regions	GOODWIN, C R.	(AB)	450

AREA

Area health education learning resources	JOHN, Stephanie C.	(MI)	601
Area studies	BEESON, Lone C.	(CA)	74
	ALBIN, Michael W.	(DC)	10
	EASTERBROOK, David L.	(IL)	333
	SINHA, Vaswati R.	(IL)	1143
Area studies, African studies	ELSASSER, Katharine K.	(DC)	346
Area studies librarianship	JOHNSON, Donald C.	(MN)	603
	STRALEY, Dona S.	(OH)	1200
Asian area studies	BURLINGHAM, Merry L.	(TX)	161
Environmental research areas	PRESBY, Richard A.	(CA)	990
Germanic area, central Europe	FRANK, Peter R.	(CA)	397
Germanic area studies	FELLER, Siegfried	(MA)	370
Ibero-American area studies	BROW, Ellen H.	(MA)	141
Latin American area studies	READ, Glenn F.	(IN)	1012

AREA (Cont'd)

Library local area network	MILLER, Richard A.	(VA)	841
Library technical areas	COHEN, Rochelle F.	(NY)	229
Local area computer networks	KEMPER, Marlyn J.	(FL)	639
Local area network research	PFUDERER, Helen A.	(TN)	966
Local area networking	ELAZAR, David H.	(ISR)	341
Local area networks	CARD, Sandra E.	(CA)	180
	MOORE, Richard K.	(CA)	861
	CHU, Ellen M.	(MD)	212
Louisville area history	REDMON, Sherrill	(KY)	1014
Middle East area studies	BEZIRGAN, Basima	(IL)	93
Organizing problem areas	BERG, David C.	(MN)	84
Planning area library services	BLASINGAME, Ralph	(NJ)	104
Public health areas	SONG, Seungja Y.	(WA)	1167
Scandinavian area studies	SPETLAND, Charles G.	(MN)	1174
Slavic area specialist	MOLLOY, Molly F.	(AZ)	853
South Asian area studies	NELSON, David N.	(ND)	893
UNIX local area network	ROSE, Phillip E.	(CO)	1055
Using local area network for catalogs	HUGHES, Carol A.	(OK)	571
Western European area studies	BROGAN, Martha L.	(MN)	139

ARID

Arid lands	JONES, Douglas E.	(AZ)	612
Arid lands information	HUSBAND, Susan M.	(AZ)	578

ARKANSAS

Arkansas historical information	FERGUSON, John L.	(AR)	372
Arkansas periodical index	MCKEE, Elizabeth C.	(AR)	810
Arkansas-related documents & books	FERGUSON, John L.	(AR)	372

ARMED FORCES (See also Air Force, Armor, Coast Guard, Militia, Navy)

Armed forces libraries	VANDERBURG, Mary A.	(FL)	1274
	GORDON, Diane M.	(IL)	451
	BANICKI, Cynthia A.	(NM)	54
Armed forces library management	WONG, Carol Y.	(CA)	1362

ARMENIAN

Armenian language	CAPRIELIAN, Arevig	(NY)	180
Armenology reference	AVDOYAN, Levon	(DC)	41

ARMOR (See also Armed Forces)

Armor & calvary history	HOLT, David A.	(KY)	554

ARMORED

Armored vehicles	HOLT, David A.	(KY)	554

ARMS (See also Defense, Ordnance)

Arms race curriculum	MEYER, Jimmy E.	(OH)	830
Arms race films databases	DOWLING, John	(PA)	316
Arms race materials & reference	MEYER, Jimmy E.	(OH)	830

ARRANGEMENT (See also Organization)

Archival arrangement & description	BEST, Rickey D.	(AL)	92
	MAHER, William J.	(IL)	760
	PRIMER, Ben	(MD)	993
	BARTKOWSKI, Patricia	(MI)	61
	SMITH, Michael O.	(MI)	1158
	OAKHILL, Harold W.	(NY)	913
	RICHIUSO, John P.	(NY)	1030
	CORNELL, Alice M.	(OH)	246
	CLINE, Robert S.	(WA)	222
	BEHRND-KLODT, Menzi L.	(WI)	75
	KLUMPENHOUWER, Richard	(AB)	662
Archival description & arrangement	CASSEDY, James G.	(DC)	193
Archives arrangement & description	MYERS, Roger	(AZ)	885
	SERBACKI, Mary	(NY)	1116
Arrangement & description	BREEDLOVE, Michael A.	(AL)	131
	CHEESEMAN, Bruce S.	(CT)	204
	NOLEN, Anita L.	(DC)	908
	WALLER, M C.	(KY)	1298

ARRANGEMENT (Cont'd)

Arrangement & description

	SHAFER, Steven I.	(MI)	1119
	WILLIAMS, Gene J.	(NC)	1343
	GRAY, David P.	(ND)	459
	BARTO, Stephen C.	(NY)	61
	TAYLOR, Dennis S.	(SC)	1226
	TISSING, Robert W.	(TX)	1247
	MOHOLT, Megan L.	(WA)	852
	MUTSCHLER, Charles V.	(WA)	883
	HALLBERG, Carl V.	(WY)	489
	TENER, Jean F.	(AB)	1231
Arrangement & description, manuscripts	PARHAM, Robert B.	(AK)	940
Arrangement of manuscript collections	MAYER, Dale C.	(IA)	789
Arranging, describing, indexing	BUSAM, Emma C.	(KY)	164
Description & arrangement	INGLE, Bernita W.	(GA)	582
Financial archival arrangement	LAMBKIN, Anthony	(IRE)	690
Interior arrangement & design	BELLIN, Bernard E.	(WI)	78
Interior arrangement & layout	STORCK, Bernadette R.	(FL)	1198
Manuscript arrangement & description	KENNICK, Sylvia B.	(NY)	642
	O'KEEFE, Laura K.	(NY)	919
Manuscripts arrangement & description	MYERS, Roger	(AZ)	885
	BOWEN, Laurel G.	(IL)	120
	MICHAELIS, Patricia A.	(KS)	831
Music arranging & orchestrating	NIGHTINGALE, Daniel	(PA)	904
Preservation & arrangement of records	YOUNKIN, C G.	(TX)	1383

ART (See also Arts, Drawings, Graphics, Iconography, Painting)

Afro-American literature & art	HUTSON, Jean B.	(NY)	579
American art	WEIDMAN, Jeffrey	(OH)	1316
	BUSHNELL, Marietta P.	(PA)	165
American art bibliography	WALKER, William B.	(NY)	1296
American art history	BRUNK, Thomas W.	(MI)	150
American art reference	FALK, Peter H.	(CT)	362
	LYNAGH, Patricia M.	(DC)	751
American art song	SHERIDAN, Margaret G.	(PA)	1127
Antiquarian art books	MCGILVERY, Laurence	(CA)	806
Architecture & art	NORTON, Margaret W.	(IL)	910
Archiving art slides on video disks	SHARER, E J.	(CO)	1122
Art	CLINKSCALES, Joyce M.	(AR)	222
	MCCOY, Evelyn G.	(AR)	799
	SORENSEN, Lee R.	(AZ)	1168
	YOUNG, Barbara N.	(FL)	1381
	HANSEN, Roland C.	(IL)	498
	MACE, Mary B.	(MA)	754
	FERGUSON, Russell	(NY)	372
	HAIMOVSKY, Kira A.	(NY)	484
	HILL, Thomas E.	(NY)	541
	KEAVENEY, Sydney S.	(NY)	633
	SCHENK, Kathryn L.	(NY)	1091
	ROUTH, Sheila J.	(OH)	1061
	WADDINGTON, Susan R.	(RI)	1290
	BRAGER, Beverly J.	(WI)	127
Art & architectural databases	ROBERTSON, Jack	(MD)	1042
Art & architectural documtn sources	ROBERTSON, Jack	(MD)	1042
Art & architectural history	FRIEDMAN, Richard E.	(AL)	404
	COIR, Mark A.	(MI)	229
	LABUDDE, Kenneth J.	(MO)	686
	BEETHAM, Donald W.	(NJ)	74
Art & architectural indexing	ROBERTSON, Jack	(MD)	1042
Art & architecture	THOMPSON, Neville M.	(DE)	1241
	GODLEWSKI, Susan G.	(IL)	442
	WITHEE, Jane S.	(IL)	1358
	WOO, Janice	(NY)	1363
Art & architecture bibliography	SHAW, Renata V.	(DC)	1123
Art & architecture collections devlpmnt	BEGLO, Jo N.	(ON)	74
Art & architecture databases	VAN DYKE, Stephen H.	(NY)	1275
Art & architecture librarianship	KUSNERZ, Peggy A.	(MI)	685
	CARMIN, James H.	(OR)	183
	KLOS, Sheila M.	(OR)	662
Art & architecture reference	KEMPE, Deborah A.	(NY)	639
Art & architecture specialization	TEAGUE, Edward H.	(FL)	1229
Art & architecture specialized ref	BEGLO, Jo N.	(ON)	74
Art & art history librarianship	QUIGLEY, Suzanne L.	(OH)	999
Art & historical photography	FALK, Peter H.	(CT)	362

ART (Cont'd)

Art & language rare books — COE, Miriam M. . . . . . . (LA) 226
Art & literature bibliography — MCCLEARY, William E. . (LA) 796
Art & literature reference — REID, Kendall M. . . . . . . (VA) 1018
Art & music — SUNDELL, Elizabeth B. . . (IL) 1210
— MELIK, Ella M. . . . . (OK) 822
Art & music reference — BARNETT, Jean D. . . . . (OR) 57
Art & reference publishing — MCGILVERY, Laurence . (CA) 806
Art & women studies — PUNIELLO, Francoise S. . (NJ) 997
Art & women's studies bibliography — ALLEN, Susan M. . . . . . . (CA) 16
Art & women's studies reference — ALLEN, Susan M. . . . . . . (CA) 16
Art & world symbolism — RONNBERG, Annmari . . (NY) 1053
Art architecture & antiques — MCCONKEY, Jill T. . . . (PA) 797
Art, architecture databases — GOODMAN, Edward C. . (NY) 449
Art bibliographies — DAVIS, L C. . . . . (CA) 280
— STARR, Daniel A. . . . . . (NY) 1182
Art bibliography — TEAGUE, Edward H. . . . . (FL) 1229
— FREITAG, Wolfgang M. . . (MA) 401
— STEPHENSON, Marilyn R. (NC) 1188
— DANE, William J. . . . . . . (NJ) 272
— OPATOW, Judith . . . . . . (NY) 925
— PHILLPOT, Clive J. . . . . (NY) 969
— ABID, Ann B. . . . . (OH) 2
— HUGHSTON, Milan R. . . (TX) 572
— JONES, Lois S. . . . . (TX) 613
— SHEAROUSE, Linda N. . . (TX) 1124
Art books acquisitions — RICE, Ralph A. . . . . (TX) 1027
Art books cataloging — SEVY, Barbara S. . . . . . . (PA) 1117
Art cataloging — CHIBNIK, Katharine R. . . (NY) 207
— STARR, Daniel A. . . . . . (NY) 1182
Art collection development — KORENIC, Lynette M. . . . (CA) 671
— CLAYTON, William R. . . (GA) 220
— MAJOR, Marla J. . . . . . . (MI) 762
— SIGALA, Stephanie C. . . (MO) 1137
— ROSENBERG-NUGENT, Nanci B. . . . . (NY) 1056
Art collections & museum administration — SOMMER, Ursula M. . . . (NJ) 1167
Art colleges — FOWLER, Michele R. . . . . (OH) 394
Art database searching — WISNIEWSKI, Julia L. . . (DC) 1357
Art databases — UPDIKE, Christina B. . . . (VA) 1269
Art deco — STACY, Betty A. . . . . . . (VA) 1178
Art documentation — WATIER-LALONDE, Chantal . . . . (PQ) 1309
Art documentation & cataloging — IBACH, Marilyn . . . . (DC) 581
Art films reference & programming — WARREN, Ann R. . . . . . . (NH) 1306
Art, fine arts, & music — COLDWELL, Charles P. . (WA) 230
Art gallery outreach learning centers — PATTERSON, Grace L. . (NY) 948
Art historical periodicals — ALLENTUCK, Marcia E. . (NY) 16
Art historical research — WYKLE, Helen H. . . . . . . (CA) 1375
— KNOWLES, Susan W. . . (TN) 665
Art history — SORENSEN, Lee R. . . . . (AZ) 1168
— FELACO, Maja K. . . . . . (DC) 369
— FAHNERT, Elizabeth K. . (FL) 361
— RITCHIE, Verna F. . . . . (IA) 1036
— HUNT, Janis E. . . . . . . (IL) 575
— TOPPAN, Muriel L. . . . . (MD) 1251
— REMECZKI, Paul W. . . . (NY) 1022
— LEWIS, Marjorie B. . . . . (PA) 724
— TRINKAUS, Tanya . . . . . (RI) 1256
— FECKO, Marybeth . . . . . (SC) 367
— JACOBY, Mary M. . . . . . (VA) 590
— CORBEIL, Lizette . . . . . . (PQ) 245
— STONE, Toby G. . . . . . . (FRN)1197
Art history acquisition — CICCONE, Amy N. . . . . . (VA) 214
Art history & aesthetics — MILLER, Jack E. . . . . . . (GA) 838
Art history & design — HORNBACH, Ruth M. . . (MI) 559
Art history bibliography — ROSS, Alexander D. . . . . (CA) 1057
Art history classification — UPDIKE, Christina B. . . . (VA) 1269
Art history collection development — SMITH, Beryl K. . . . . . . (NJ) 1153
Art history reference — SMITH, Beryl K. . . . . . . (NJ) 1153
Art history research — YARNALL, James L. . . . (DC) 1378
— TRINKOFF, Elaine . . . . (NY) 1257
— CICCONE, Amy N. . . . . (VA) 214
Art history slide organizing — GRAY, Shirley M. . . . . . (NY) 460
Art history slides — KRUPANSKI, Pamela M. . (MA) 680
Art information — POIRRIER, Sherry . . . . . (MA) 980
Art information systems — PETERSEN, Toni . . . . . (MA) 962
Art, law, humanities — KLEIN, Ilene R. . . . . . . (MD) 659
Art librarian — ANNETT, Susan E. . . . . . (CA) 28

ART (Cont'd)

Art librarianship — BYRNE, Elizabeth D. . . . (CA) 169
— VAN NIMMEN, Jane . . . (DC) 1276
— BLOOM, Stephen C. . . . . (IL) 106
— AUCHSTETTER, Rosann M. . . . . (IN) 38
— IRVINE, Betty J. . . . . . . (IN) 584
— WILLIAMS, Maudine . . . (IN) 1345
— CRAIG, Susan V. . . . . . . (KS) 254
— RUSHING, Darla H. . . . . (LA) 1068
— GIBSON, Sarah S. . . . . . (MA) 432
— SIDEN, Harriet F. . . . . . (MI) 1135
— BETH, Dana L. . . . . (MO) 92
— MACEWAN, Bonnie J. . . (MO) 755
— REED, Barbara E. . . . . . (NH) 1014
— CLARKE, D S. . . . . (NY) 218
— EKDAHL, Janis K. . . . . (NY) 341
— HORRELL, Jeffrey L. . . . (NY) 560
— KERR, Virginia M. . . . . . (NY) 644
— PHILLPOT, Clive J. . . . . (NY) 969
— ROZENE, Janette B. . . . . (NY) 1064
— SCOTT, Frances Y. . . . . (NY) 1107
— STAM, Deirdre C. . . . . . (NY) 1179
— SWIESZKOWSK, L S. . . (NY) 1216
— PROMOS, Marianne . . . . (PA) 995
— TERRY, Carol S. . . . . . . (RI) 1232
— BURT, Eugene C. . . . . . (TX) 164
— CABLE, Carole L. . . . . . (TX) 170
— DOWNING, Jeannette D. (TX) 316
— RICHARDS, Valerie . . . . (NZD)1028
Art libraries — ALLEN, Nancy S. . . . . . . (MA) 15
— LIGHTNER, Karen J. . . . (PA) 727
— SMITH, Mary M. . . . . . . (PA) 1158
— BRAUNSTEIN, Mark M. . (RI) 130
— ABRAMS, Leslie E. . . . . (SC) 3
— JONES, Lois S. . . . . (TX) 613
— WHITE, Lynda S. . . . . . (VA) 1331
Art libraries & fine art materials — GILBERT, Gail R. . . . . . (KY) 433
Art library administration — SCHMIDT, Mary M. . . . (NJ) 1095
Art library architecture — IRVINE, Betty J. . . . . . . (IN) 584
Art library management — ROSS, Alexander D. . . . . (CA) 1057
— VAN DYKE, Stehpen H. . (NY) 1275
Art material cataloging — HERMAN, Elizabeth . . . . (CA) 531
Art museum libraries — CHIN, Cecilia H. . . . . . . (DC) 208
Art museum library management — WALKER, William B. . . . (NY) 1296
— DOWNING, Jeannette D. (TX) 316
— SHEAROUSE, Linda N. . (TX) 1124
Art museums & schools — LEIBOLD, Cheryl A. . . . . (PA) 713
Art, music, & audiovisual librarianship — SECKELSON, Linda E. . . (NY) 1110
Art, music & drama — ALTER, Forrest H. . . . . . (MI) 18
Art, music & sports collection devlpmnt — BAKER, Paula J. . . . . . . (OH) 49
Art of fine arts — GRIFFISS, M K. . . . . . . (TN) 469
Art of paper conservation — MOORE, Harold H. . . . . (GA) 859
Art of the Pacific — TIMBERLAKE, Cynthia A. (HI) 1245
Art online searching — KORENIC, Lynette M. . . . (CA) 671
Art reference — CARSCH, Ruth E. . . . . . (CA) 187
— ROSS, Alexander D. . . . . (CA) 1057
— DOUMATO, Lamia . . . . . (DC) 314
— LYNAGH, Patricia M. . . . (DC) 751
— BIRNEY, Ann E. . . . . . . (KS) 98
— MANNING, Mary L. . . . . (MN) 766
— SIMPSON, Leslie T. . . . . (MO) 1142
— CLARK, Diane E. . . . . . (MS) 216
— MCARTHUR, Anne . . . . (NJ) 792
— REDLICH, Barry . . . . . . (NJ) 1014
— BRAUCH, Patricia O. . . . (NY) 129
— DEMARCO, Elizabeth A. . (NY) 291
— FREEMAN, Carla C. . . . (NY) 400
— WIERZBA, Christine . . . . (NY) 1337
— TOTH, Georgina G. . . . . (OH) 1252
— BISSELL, Joann S. . . . . (PA) 100
— TACK, A C. . . . . (PA) 1219
— AVERILL, Laurie J. . . . . (RI) 41
Art reference literature — WALKER, William B. . . . (NY) 1296
Art reference services — KORENIC, Lynette M. . . . (CA) 671
Art research — KLEIN, Kristine J. . . . . . (DC) 659
— COREY, Glenn M. . . . . . (MI) 246
Art research methodology — JONES, Lois S. . . . . (TX) 613
Art slide collections — BLAIR, Madeline S. . . . . (DC) 102

ART (Cont'd)

Topic	Name	State	Page
Art slide library systems	DULAN, Peter A.	(CO)	324
Art special collections	CASHMAN, Norine D.	(RI)	192
Art specialist	AYARI, Kaye W.	(SC)	42
Art subject	SMITH, Elizabeth J.	(PA)	1154
Bibliographer, art & architecture	OLSON, Joann D.	(OH)	922
Bibliography of American art	SMITH, Raymond W.	(CT)	1159
Bibliography of art history	ARNTZEN, Etta M.	(IL)	34
Books as art form	PASCAL, Barbara R.	(CA)	945
Books on antiques & art	JOHNSON, Nancy E.	(IA)	608
Canadian art & culture	GRODSKI, Renata	(ON)	471
Cataloging art & architecture slides	FOWLER, Michele R.	(OH)	394
Cataloging art & music	RICHARDSON, Emma G.	(NY)	1029
Cataloging art books	FORMAN, Camille L.	(CT)	390
Cataloging of art slides	BAILEY, Tuuli T.	(AZ)	47
Collection development for art	MCKEE, George D.	(NY)	810
Complete art library management	WAXMAN, Joanne	(ME)	1311
Contemporary art	BYRNE, Nadene M.	(IL)	169
	HOGAN, Matthew	(NY)	549
	MARTIN, Richard	(NY)	778
Contemporary art & video	HORIGAN, Evelyn A.	(CA)	559
Contemporary art history	FURTAK, Rosemary	(MN)	410
Copier art	NEADERLAND, Louise O.	(NY)	890
Corporate art collections	CLAYTON, John M.	(DE)	220
Crafts & folk art	BENEDETTI, Joan M.	(CA)	80
Creating video disks for art	SHARER, E J.	(CO)	1122
Decorative art	THOMPSON, Neville M.	(DE)	1241
Development of art bibliographies	KING, Carmen M.	(MI)	650
Fine art & handicraft specialization	MANNING, Mary J.	(IL)	766
History & art reference	PINSON, Patricia A.	(WY)	975
History, art reference	STOPKA, Christina K.	(WY)	1198
History of 18th century art	ARNTZEN, Etta M.	(IL)	34
Interactive art video disks	SHARER, E J.	(CO)	1122
Islamic art	MOLINE, Judi A.	(MD)	853
Jewish art	LEVY, Jane	(CA)	721
Languages, architecture & art	CULLARS, John M.	(IL)	263
Library art shows	NANCE, Betty L.	(TX)	887
Library graphic design & art	BRYAN, Carol L.	(WV)	151
Literature & art databases	HOFFMAN, Herbert H.	(CA)	548
Literature & art history books	ALLENTUCK, Marcia E.	(NY)	16
Literature of art history	REED, Marcia C.	(CA)	1015
Modern & contemporary art	CANDAU, Eugenie	(CA)	178
Modern art	BROOKE, Anna	(DC)	140
Modern Christian art & bibliography	RAMSEY, Robert D.	(CA)	1006
Museum, art libraries	HUMPHRY, James	(NY)	574
19th & 20th century art	SCHNEIDER, Karen	(DC)	1097
19th century & 20th century art	HATCHER, Nolan C.	(GA)	511
Organizing art exhibitions	FORMAN, Camille L.	(CT)	390
Personal univ-quality art collections	BLAIR, Madeline S.	(DC)	102
Precolumbian art	GRIFFISS, M K.	(TN)	469
Printing & graphics art	WEISER, Douglas E.	(MI)	1319
Prior art searches	ANTOS, Brian F.	(PA)	29
Public relations & art	NICHOLSON, Myreen M.	(VA)	902
Rare & out-of-print art books	DAVIS, L C.	(CA)	280
Rare art books	POCKROSE, Sheryl R.	(OH)	979
Reference, art & architecture	OLSON, Joann D.	(OH)	922
Reference for art	MCKEE, George D.	(NY)	810
Reference, music & art	BLUM, Fred	(MI)	107
Renaissance & Baroque art	OSTROW, Stephen E.	(DC)	929
Renaissance art	FURTAK, Rosemary	(MN)	410
Research, art nouveau, Victorian art	STACY, Betty A.	(VA)	1178
Research support for art	MCKEE, George D.	(NY)	810
Social sciences & art	BRADLEY, Jared W.	(LA)	126
Special art & architecture librarianship	BEGLO, Jo N.	(ON)	74
Special collections	NESBURG, Janet A.	(MI)	896
Supervising art slide library	LANTZ, Louise K.	(MD)	697
Training art educators & docents	GENSHAFT, Carole M.	(OH)	427
USSR, Asia, South American, Europe art	BLAIR, Madeline S.	(DC)	102
Victorian art	ROBERTS, Helene E.	(MA)	1040
Women's art history	FURTAK, Rosemary	(MN)	410

ARTIFACTS

Topic	Name	State	Page
Book & artifact cataloging	HALEY, Marguerite R.	(WA)	486
Rare books & artifacts	SPOTTED EAGLE, Joy	(MT)	1175

ARTIFICIAL (See also AI, CAI, Expert, Knowledge)

Topic	Name	State	Page
Artificial experience systems	KARR, Ronald D.	(MA)	628
Artificial intelligence	ROSE, Steven C.	(CA)	1055
	RADA, Roy F.	(MD)	1002
	FRISSE, Mark E.	(MO)	405
	MITCHELL, Joyce A.	(MO)	849
	BURGIN, Robert E.	(NC)	159
	FRANTS, Valery	(NJ)	398
	SUNDAY, Donald E.	(NJ)	1210
	METZLER, Douglas P.	(PA)	829
	TREMBLAY, Gerald F.	(SC)	1255
	TRAVIS, Irene L.	(VA)	1254
	BOOHER, Craig S.	(WI)	115
Artificial intelligence applications	FOX, Edward A.	(VA)	394
Artificial intelligence based retrieval	VLADUTZ, George E.	(PA)	1286
Artificial intelligence, expert systems	VEENKER, Linda J.	(CA)	1281
	DIEHL, Mark	(IL)	302
Artificial intelligence in medicine	MUSEN, Mark A.	(CA)	883
Expert systems & artificial intelligence	CHANG, Roy T.	(IL)	201
	MOTT, Thomas H.	(NJ)	872

ARTISTS

Topic	Name	State	Page
Artists' books	BYRNE, Nadene M.	(IL)	169
	ROM, Cristine C.	(OH)	1052
	VAN DER BELLEN, Liana	(ON)	1273
Artists' books & publications	HOFFBERG, Judith A.	(CA)	547
Artists' bookworks	MCNULTY, Karen	(CT)	817
Artists' resources	BYRNE, Nadene M.	(IL)	169
Biographical research for artists	BAILEY, Tuuli T.	(AZ)	47
Early recording artists, 1890-1930	RIGGS, Quentin V.	(CA)	1034
Research of artists & exhibitions	GENSHAFT, Carole M.	(OH)	427
Research on artists	SHERIDAN, Helen A.	(MI)	1127
Research on women artists	WASSERMAN, Krystyna	(DC)	1308
Vertical file on artists	MCNULTY, Karen	(CT)	817
Women artists	FALK, Peter H.	(CT)	362
	RITCHIE, Verna F.	(IA)	1036

ARTS (See also Art, Crafts, Culture, Folk, Graphics, Humanities)

Topic	Name	State	Page
African literature history & arts	HUTSON, Jean B.	(NY)	579
American decorative arts	LANTZ, Louise K.	(MD)	697
American folk arts	LIND, Judith Y.	(NJ)	728
Applied arts research	FRANKLIN, Linda C.	(NY)	398
Applied arts, writing & editing	FRANKLIN, Linda C.	(NY)	398
Art, fine arts, & music	COLDWELL, Charles P.	(WA)	230
Art of fine arts	GRIFFISS, M K.	(TN)	469
Arts	SELTH, Jefferson P.	(CA)	1114
Arts administration	MYERS, Maria P.	(NY)	884
	HECK, Thomas F.	(OH)	519
	LEWIS, Marjorie B.	(PA)	724
Arts advocacy	STRAWDER, Maxine S.	(TN)	1201
Arts & humanities	HOPKINS, Richard L.	(BC)	558
Arts & humanities adult programming	SMOTHERS, Joyce W.	(NJ)	1162
Arts & humanities collection development	MESSINEO, Leonard L.	(KS)	828
Arts & humanities database marketing	ZAJDEL, George J.	(PA)	1385
Arts & humanities programming	GANN, Daniel H.	(IN)	416
Arts & humanities reference	GRILIKHES, Sandra B.	(PA)	470
Arts & humanities research & development	PIERCE, Mildred L.	(NV)	971
Arts & sciences	KELLOGG, Rebecca B.	(AZ)	637
Arts automation	PISCIOTTA, Henry A.	(PA)	976
Arts collection development	VAN NIEL, Eloise S.	(HI)	1276
	ANDERSON, Gail	(AB)	23
Arts, humanities & social sciences	LOMBARDI, Mary L.	(CA)	738
Arts literature	PISCIOTTA, Henry A.	(PA)	976
Arts of the book	WALKER, Robin G.	(CT)	1296
Arts reference	DOLAN-HEITLINGER, Eileen	(IN)	309
	LIKNESS, Craig S.	(TX)	727
Audiovisual & graphic arts	GIBLON, Charles B.	(FL)	431
Book arts	KOTIN, David B.	(ON)	673
	VAN DER BELLEN, Liana	(ON)	1273
Book arts history	ALTERMAN, Deborah H.	(NJ)	18
Book arts journals	MONGOLD, Alice D.	(TX)	854
Cataloging fine arts, serials	MILLS, Rolland W.	(PR)	844
Cinema arts instruction	TALIT, Lynn	(CT)	1221
Collection development in arts	VAN WIEMOKLY, Jane G.	(NJ)	1277

ARTS (Cont'd)

Collection development, performing arts — DIMMICK, Mary L. . . . . . (PA) 304
Contemporary visual arts information — HOFFBERG, Judith A. . . (CA) 547
Cultural arts community development — TRASATTI, Margaret S. . (NV) 1254
Decorative arts — MOSS, Roger W. . . . . . . (PA) 872
Decorative arts & crafts — LIND, Judith Y. . . . . . . (NJ) 728
Fine & performing arts — HOFFMAN, Irene M. . . . . (CA) 548
Fine & performing arts bibliography — GROVES, Percilla E. . . . . (BC) 474
Fine arts — JEFFERY, Phyllis D. . . . . (AL) 596
KIRKING, Clayton C. . . . (AZ) 655
SMITH, Matilda M. . . . . . (GA) 1158
HUNT, Janis E. . . . . (IL) 575
MILLER, Janet . . . . (IL) 838
SCHAAF, Elizabeth . . . . (MD) 1088
SIMMONS, Rebecca A. . (NY) 1140
LORANTH, Alice N. . . . . (OH) 741
LEWIS, Marjorie B. . . . . . (PA) 724
DRUMMOND, Donald R. (TX) 321
EDMUNDSON, Margaret B. . . . . (UT) 336
BURDET, Michele C. . . . (SWZ) 158
Fine arts & architecture bibliography — CEDERHOLM, Theresa D. . (MA) 196
Fine arts & architecture cataloging — MOHAMMED, Selima . . (PQ) 852
Fine arts & architecture sources — SPENCER, Deirdre D. . . (FL) 1173
Fine arts bibliographic instruction — SCHERER, Herbert G. . . (MN) 1092
Fine arts bibliography — MORR, Lynell A. . . . . . . (FL) 866
EVENSEN, Robert L. . . . (MA) 358
HASWELL, Hollee . . . . . (NY) 511
Fine arts book illustration — BANTA, Gratia J. . . . . . . (OH) 55
Fine arts book selection — SCHERER, Herbert G. . . (MN) 1092
Fine arts books — RICE, Ralph A. . . . . (TX) 1027
Fine arts cataloging — WALTON, Carol G. . . . . (FL) 1301
Fine arts collection development — BOHRER, Karen M. . . . . (CT) 111
MOORE, Emily C. . . . . . (NC) 859
DOGU, Hikmet S. . . . . . . (UT) 309
PARR, Loraine E. . . . . . . (WA) 943
TOBIN, R J. . . . . (WI) 1247
Fine arts collections, books — RUSSELL, Marilyn L. . . . (KS) 1069
Fine arts databases — DOGU, Hikmet S. . . . . . . (UT) 309
Fine arts librarianship — GUNDERSON, Jeffery R. (CA) 477
KUNSELMAN, Joan D. . . (CA) 684
HEHMAN, Jennifer L. . . . (IN) 521
CABLE, Carole L. . . . . . (TX) 170
Fine arts library management — GAMER, May L. . . . . . . (MO) 416
Fine arts, local history collections — MCNULTY, Karen . . . . . (CT) 817
Fine arts museum — JACOBY, Mary M. . . . . . (VA) 590
Fine arts reference — DONIO, Dorothy . . . . (FL) 311
MORR, Lynell A. . . . . . . (FL) 866
SCHERER, Herbert G. . . (MN) 1092
DOGU, Hikmet S. . . . . . . (UT) 309
Fine arts reference services — MENDRO, Donna C. . . . . (TX) 824
Fine arts research — MILLER, Hester M. . . . . . (NM) 838
Fine arts researcher — HEHMAN, Jennifer L. . . . (IN) 521
Freelance performing arts research — BRAYTON, Roy S. . . . . (NY) 130
Galleries & arts programs — WILKINSON, Billy R. . . . (MD) 1340
Graphic arts — BARRINGER, George M. (DC) 59
WHITE, George R. . . . . . (KS) 1331
BARNHILL, Georgia B. . . (MA) 58
HAMMOND, Wayne G. . (MA) 494
DAVENPORT, Marilyn G. (NV) 275
BRODY, Catherine T. . . . (NY) 139
COHN, Alan M. . . . . (IL) 229
Humanities & fine arts reference — BLATT, Gloria T. . . . . . . (MI) 104
Language arts — BUBOLTZ, Dale D. . . . . . (CA) 152
Language arts & English education — SHAPIRO, Marian S. . . . (MO) 1121
Liberal arts — BECKER, Charlotte B. . . (VA) 72
Liberal arts cataloging — LUSK, Betty M. . . . . . . (SAF) 749
Liberal arts, religion, music cataloging — SERDZIAK, Edward J. . . (CA) 1116
Medical arts indexing — DAVIS, Joy V. . . . . (GA) 279
Music & fine arts reference — MAYER, George L. . . . . (NY) 789
Music & performing arts librarianship — WILKINS, Marilyn W. . . . (LA) 1340
Music, arts & recreation — LUBRANO, Judith A. . . . (MA) 745
Music, dance, theatre arts — HARDISH, Patrick M. . . . (NY) 500
Music performing arts reference — LEMMON, Alfred E. . . . . (LA) 715
Performing arts — VAN HOVEN, William D. (NC) 1276
CHACH, Maryann . . . . . (NY) 196
HIGGINS, Steven . . . . . (NY) 538
SOMMER, Susan T. . . . (NY) 1167
WOOD, Thor E. . . . . . . (NY) 1365

ARTS (Cont'd)

Performing arts — MCGLINN, Frank C. . . . . (PA) 806
Performing arts administration — BUCK, Richard M. . . . . . (NY) 154
Performing arts archives — WOODS, Alan L. . . . . . (OH) 1366
PRITCHARD, Jane E. . . . (ENG) 994
Performing arts librarianship — KUNSELMAN, Joan D. . . (CA) 684
DIDHAM, Reginald A. . . . (MA) 301
DUCLOW, Geradline . . . (PA) 322
Performing arts libraries, museums — GOLDING, Alfred S. . . . . (OH) 445
Performing arts publishing — PINE, Ralph . . . . (NY) 974
Performing arts reference — WISE, Matthew W. . . . . (NY) 1357
Performing arts reference, research — DEE, Camille C. . . . . . . (NY) 286
Performing arts reference work — VELEZ, Sara B. . . . . . . (NY) 1281
Performing arts research — MILLER, Hester M. . . . . . (NM) 838
Performing arts selection & bibliography — VAN NIEL, Eloise S. . . . . (HI) 1276
Performing arts, speech communication — KELLY, Richard J. . . . . . (MN) 638
Public, fine arts librarianship — MATYI, Stephen G. . . . . (OH) 786
Reference, arts & humanities — DIAL, Clarence M. . . . . . (AZ) 299
Reference, fine & performing arts — DOCTOROW, Erica . . . . (NY) 307
Secretarial arts — EDWARDS, Barnett A. . . (NY) 337
Subject specialist in fine arts — PIRON, Alice M. . . . . . . (IL) 975
Theatre arts — SNOW, Marina . . . . (CA) 1164
Visual arts — DEW, T R. . . . . (CO) 297
THISTLE, Dawn R. . . . . (MA) 1235
Visual arts reference — SHERIDAN, Helen A. . . . (MI) 1127
Visual arts resources — MCRAE, Linda . . . . (FL) 818

ASIA (See also Oriental)

Asia & South Pacific — WARPHEA, Rita C. . . . . (VA) 1306
Asia Pacific business collection — CHAN, Diana L. . . . . . . (BC) 199
Asian area studies — BURLINGHAM, Merry L. (TX) 161
Asian bibliography — WONG, William S. . . . . . (IL) 1363
Asian languages & literature cataloging — TIBBITS, Edith J. . . . . . (NE) 1243
Asian librarianship — FUNG, Margaret C. . . . . (MA) 409
Asian materials — RIEDY, Allen J. . . . . . . (HI) 1033
Asian materials acquisition — CHAN, Moses C. . . . . . . (NC) 199
Asian materials cataloging — CHAN, Moses C. . . . . . . (NC) 199
Asian studies — TAI, Henry H. . . . . (CA) 1220
HUBER, Kristina R. . . . . (MN) 569
LEE, Chui C. . . . . (NY) 709
PAK, Moo J. . . . . (OH) 935
Bibliography of Asian studies — SHULMAN, Frank J. . . . . (MD) 1133
Collection development in South Asia — SEN, Joyce H. . . . . . . (NY) 1115
East Asia — LEE, Thomas H. . . . . . . (IN) 711
East Asian collections — SIGGINS, Jack A. . . . . . (CT) 1137
East Asian languages — HSIEH, Cynthia C. . . . . (IL) 567
East Asian librarianship — WEI, Karen T. . . . . (IL.) 1316
SHULMAN, Frank J. . . . . (MD) 1133
East Asian library administration — KANEKO, Hideo . . . . . . (CT) 625
East Asian library automation — WEI, Karen T. . . . . (IL) 1316
East Asian library services — WU, Ai H. . . . . (AZ) 1373
East Asian materials — KLEIN, Kenneth D. . . . . (CA) 659
East Asian studies — KIM, Joy H. . . . . (CA) 649
History & East Asian studies bibl — BERGER, Kenneth W. . . (NC) 85
Printing & publishing in Asia — DIEHL, Katharine S. . . . . (TX) 302
Social sciences, South Asia — WOOD, Ann L. . . . . . . (MA) 1363
South & Southeast Asia — HARPER, Marie F. . . . . (AL) 503
South Asian area studies — NELSON, David N. . . . . (ND) 893
South Asian bibliography — NYE, James H. . . . . . . (IL) 912
South Asian bibliography & research — SEN, Joyce H. . . . . . . (NY) 1115
Southeast Asia — DUTTON, Lee S. . . . . . (IL) 329
MILLER, David A. . . . . . (OH) 836
Southeast Asian languages — HICKEY, John T. . . . . . (NY) 536
Southeast Asian reference services — ASHMUN, Lawrence F. . (NY) 36
Southeast Asian studies — KOH, Siew B. . . . . (IL) 668
ASHMUN, Lawrence F. . (NY) 36
BARNWELL, Jane L. . . . (OR) 58
Southeast Asian studies bibliography — GAMER, May L. . . . . . . (MO) 416
Southeast Asian technical services — ASHMUN, Lawrence F. . (NY) 36
USSR, Asia, South American, Europe art — BLAIR, Madeline S. . . . . (DC) 102

ASSEMBLY

Legislative assembly documents — O'KEEFE, Kevin T. . . . . . (NT) 919

ASSESSMENT (See also Appraisal, Evaluation)

Assessing corporate strategies	MCLANE, John F.	(CT)	813
Collection assessment	GOODMAN, Rhonna A.	(NY)	449
Collection assessment & development	CRAMER, Eugene C.	(AB)	255
Collection evaluation & assessment	SIGNORI, Donna L.	(BC)	1137
Community assessments	KENNEDY, Rose M.	(CA)	641
Community needs assessment	HEIL, Kathleen A.	(MD)	521
Competitive assessment	BROCK, Laurie N.	(CO)	138
Competitive assessment program	MOYNIHAN, Mary B.	(CT)	874
Consulting & needs assessment	WEISFIELD, Cynthia F.	(PA)	1319
Education media services assessment	COMEAU, Reginald A.	(NH)	234
Information systems needs assessment	ROBERTS, Lesley A.	(DC)	1040
Information technology assessment	DUCHESNE, Roderick M.	(ON)	322
Library & archival need assessments	FOURIE, Denise K.	(CA)	393
Library collection assessment	KELLY, Glen J.	(ON)	637
Needs assessment	HOLT, Raymond M.	(CA)	554
	SIGLER, Ronald F.	(CA)	1137
	TABACHNICK, Sharon	(TN)	1219
Needs assessment & evaluation	RUBIN, Rhea J.	(CA)	1064
Public library needs assessment	EVANS, Patricia D.	(AB)	357
Technology assessment	LAWRENCE, Gary S.	(CA)	704
	MOYER, Barbara A.	(CA)	874
	RATH, Charla M.	(DC)	1009
	HODGE, Gail M.	(PA)	546
User needs assessment	ROCQUE, Bernice L.	(NY)	1046

ASSISTANTS

Library technical assistants	HARWOOD, Judith A.	(IL)	510
Student assistant management	FREEMAN, Evangeline M.	(NC)	400
Student assistant training	MORRIS, Betty J.	(AL)	866
Supervising assistants	VANDERBECK, Maria	(CA)	1273
Training library assistants	SHEARIN, Cynthia E.	(NJ)	1124
Training of student assistants	GLADIEUX, Mary B.	(MO)	439

ASSOCIATIONS (See also Membership, Multiassociation)

American Library Association chapters	GESSNER, Marianne	(MI)	430
Association archives	GILTINAN, Celia E.	(MO)	437
Association executive	GREENFIELD, Robert E.	(MD)	464
Association leadership	BOSTLEY, Jean R.	(MA)	117
Association libraries	ZOOK, Ruth A.	(CO)	1390
Association management	HAMILTON-PENNELL, Christine	(CO)	492
	BATTAGLIA, Richard D.	(DC)	64
	BENDER, David R.	(DC)	79
	HITCHENS, Howard B.	(DE)	544
	BOURDON, Cathleen J.	(IL)	119
	JEPSON, William H.	(IL)	599
	LEE, Joel M.	(IL)	710
	MYERS, Margaret R.	(IL)	884
	NEAL, Donn C.	(IL)	890
	PALMER, Raymond A.	(IL)	936
	WEBSTER, Lois S.	(IL)	1314
	MARTELLO, Joyce M.	(IN)	775
	HARRIS, Patricia R.	(MD)	505
	MCCARTNEY, Jean A.	(MO)	794
	LIAN, Nancy W.	(NY)	725
	BAUER, Margaret D.	(PA)	65
	PHILLIPS, Janet C.	(PA)	968
	NANCE, Betty	(TN)	887
Association, management, & membership	SCARRY, Patricia A.	(IL)	1088
Association organization & operation	PARSONS, Augustine C.	(OH)	944
Associations	MOORE, Lawrence A.	(ON)	860
Bar association library	GHIDOTTI, Pauline A.	(AR)	430
District association annuals	YEISER, Doris B.	(KY)	1379
Library association management	PARRY, Pamela J.	(AZ)	944
	FERRELL, Mary S.	(CA)	373
Library associations	GESSNER, Marianne	(MI)	430
	BUSCH, B J.	(AB)	165
Management of libraries & associations	COONEY, Jane	(ON)	241
Organization & association leadership	BEDARD, Bernard J.	(PQ)	73
Professional association	DEARSTYNE, Bruce W.	(NY)	284
Professional association involvement	BEARD, Charles E.	(GA)	69
State associations	GESSNER, Marianne	(MI)	430
	DANNUNZIO, Rebecca T.	(WV)	274

ASSOCIATIONS (Cont'd)

State library association	SUTTON, Sandra K.	(AL)	1211
Theatre library association contributor	EPPES, William D.	(NY)	351
Trade association information management	HILL, Susan M.	(DC)	540

ASTRONOMY (See also Meteorological)

Astronomical catalogs & atlases	KNUDSEN, Helen Z.	(CA)	666
Astronomy	STERN, David	(IL)	1189
	POPLAWSKY, Diane M.	(WI)	983
Astronomy & astrophysics	BOUTON, Ellen N.	(VA)	119
Astronomy & astrophysics bibliography	STEVENS-RAYBURN, Sarah L.	(MD)	1191
Astronomy & astrophysics lit & databases	KNUDSEN, Helen Z.	(CA)	666
Astronomy literature	PRIMACK, Alice L.	(FL)	993
Literature of astronomy	VANATTA, Cathaleen E.	(AZ)	1272
Literature searching & astronomy	KNUDSEN, Helen Z.	(CA)	666
Physics & astronomy reference	SCHNOOR, Harriet E.	(IL)	1098
Solar system astronomy	CHAPMAN, Jennalyn W.	(AZ)	202

ASTROPHYSICS

Astronomy & astrophysics	BOUTON, Ellen N.	(VA)	119
Astronomy & astrophysics bibliography	STEVENS-RAYBURN, Sarah L.	(MD)	1191
Astronomy & astrophysics lit & databases	KNUDSEN, Helen Z.	(CA)	666

ATLASES (See also Maps)

Astronomical catalogs & atlases	KNUDSEN, Helen Z.	(CA)	666
Indexing cultural atlases	BLOZIS, Jolene M.	(DC)	107
Map & atlas collection development	RIVERA, Diana H.	(MI)	1037
Maps, aerial photos, atlases	EASTON, William W.	(IL)	333
Maps & atlases	STRICKLAND, Muriel	(CA)	1202
	ALLISON, Brent	(MN)	17

ATMOSPHERIC

Atmospheric sciences	SMITH, Shirley M.	(NV)	1161

ATTORNEYS (See also Law, Legal)

Attorney information systems consulting	STERN, Michael P.	(MD)	1189
Training attorneys on databases	DONNELLY, Kathleen	(OH)	311

AUCTION

Auction catalog reference services	TIEMAN, Robert S.	(CA)	1244

AUDIO (See also Audiovisual, Cassette, Media, Sound)

Audio	ROUTH, Sheila J.	(OH)	1061
Audio & video collection	BERGER, Brenda L.	(NJ)	85
Audio & video programs	LOCKE, William G.	(NY)	736
Audio archives	SALY, Alan J.	(NY)	1078
Audio book production	CYLKE, Frank K.	(DC)	268
Audio cassette collection management	TREMBLAY, Carolyn B.	(NH)	1255
Audio collection development	WARREN, Ann R.	(NH)	1306
Audio consulting	PATRYCH, Joseph	(NY)	947
Audio library production	MASSIS, Bruce E.	(NY)	782
Audio recording & archives	RUNYON, Steven C.	(CA)	1067
Audio recording & engineering	SUMMERHILL, Craig A.	(MI)	1209
Audio recordings	WARD, Shirlene A.	(IL)	1304
Audio services	BAKER, Paula J.	(OH)	49
Audio tapes, audio books	SANDY, Marjorie M.	(MI)	1081
Media services, audio & video	SLYHOFF, Merle J.	(PA)	1151
Supply video & audio tapes	GRAY, Lee H.	(NJ)	460
Video & audio services manager	EVANS, Mark S.	(FL)	357
Wholesaling of audio & video materials	JACOBS, Peter J.	(CA)	590

AUDIOLOGY

Allied health, audiology, hearing sci   MCFARLAND, Robert T.   (MO)   805

AUDIOVISUAL (See also Audio, Media)

Acquisitions, monographic & audiovisual	WILLIAMS, Charles M. . .	(IL)	1342
Art, music, & audiovisual librarianship	SECKELSON, Linda E. . . .	(NY)	1110
Audiovisual	GOTHBERG, Helen M. . .	(AZ)	453
	AROS, Andrew A.	(CA)	34
	LEE, William D.	(CA)	711
	MCLEAN, Janice A.	(CA)	814
	PETTAS, William A.	(CA)	965
	RECTOR, Wendell H. . . .	(CT)	1013
	GOODIER, Darlene P. . .	(FL)	448
	HISS, Sheila M.	(FL)	544
	LICHTENFELS, David D. .	(FL)	725
	STANBERY, Nancy M. . . .	(GA)	1179
	DAGLEY, Helen J.	(IA)	269
	FALK, Mark F.	(IA)	362
	MYRON, Victoria L.	(IA)	885
	HARRIS, Thomas J.	(IL)	506
	MIKOLYZK, Thomas A. . .	(IL)	834
	O'HEARON, Doris M. . . .	(IL)	919
	ROZANSKI, Barbara . . .	(IL)	1064
	SUNDELL, Elizabeth B. . .	(IL)	1210
	KASER, John A.	(IN)	628
	SCHAEFER, Patricia	(IN)	1089
	VOLLNOGLE, Leslie A. . .	(IN)	1288
	ZIMMER, Connie W. . . .	(KY)	1388
	TRIPLETT, Billy L.	(LA)	1257
	GROSSHANS, Maxine Z.	(MD)	473
	O'BRIEN, Lee A.	(MD)	914
	GUNN, Diane M.	(MI)	477
	MICHAUD, John C.	(MI)	832
	ALEY, Judy M.	(NJ)	12
	COHEN, Susan K.	(NJ)	229
	CONNICK, Kathleen D. . .	(NJ)	237
	STEEN, Carol N.	(NJ)	1184
	THOMAS, Carren A. . . .	(NJ)	1236
	BARNES, Robert W.	(NY)	57
	BOURKE, Thomas A. . . .	(NY)	119
	DAVIDSON, Steven I. . . .	(NY)	276
	GALLAGHER, Patricia E.	(NY)	414
	HOFFMAN, Barbara E. . .	(NY)	547
	JONES, Kevin R.	(NY)	613
	KEEFER, Ethel A.	(NY)	634
	NEUMEISTER, Susan M.	(NY)	897
	RICHTER, Kathleen A. . .	(NY)	1031
	COHEN, Steven J.	(OH)	229
	HAYS, George W.	(OH)	517
	MICHNAY, Susan E. . . .	(OH)	832
	RAY, Laura E.	(OH)	1011
	SLEEMAN, Linda E.	(OH)	1148
	WOOD, Ann F.	(OH)	1363
	THOMAS, Lynda H.	(PA)	1237
	TURNER, Sue E.	(PA)	1265
	YU, Lorraine L.	(PA)	1384
	DAVIS, Philip M.	(TX)	280
	DIXON, Donna S.	(TX)	306
	GROSS, Iva H.	(TX)	472
	LEATHERMAN, Donald G.	(TX)	707
	POWELL, Patricia K. . . .	(TX)	988
	EDMUNDSON, Margaret B.	(UT)	336
	DELONG, Edward J.	(VA)	290
	DEMARS, Patricia	(VA)	291
	SELF, James R.	(VA)	1113
	SIMPSON, W S.	(WI)	1142
	WASICK, Mary A.	(WI)	1308
	GUILBERT, N P.	(MB)	476
Audiovisual acquisition	WILCOX, Carolyn G. . . .	(CT)	1338
Audiovisual administration	CONOVER, Kathryn H. . .	(FL)	238
Audiovisual aids	KITTUR, Krishna N.	(IND)	657
Audiovisual & film reviewing	LOCKE, John W.	(IL)	736
Audiovisual & general reference	PIKUL, Diane M.	(CT)	973
Audiovisual & graphic arts	GIBLON, Charles B.	(FL)	431
Audiovisual & instructional design	PROVINCE, William R. . .	(IL)	996
Audiovisual & library science reference	RUSIEWSKI, Charles B. .	(IL)	1068

AUDIOVISUAL (Cont'd)

Audiovisual & machine-readable data file	RITCHIE, David G.	(NY)	1036
Audiovisual & media	MEYERS, Kathleen H. . .	(AZ)	831
Audiovisual & microcomputer software	DAVIS, Shelley E.	(GA)	281
Audiovisual & microform cataloging	BURCHELL, Patricia M. .	(ON)	158
Audiovisual & non-book media	HARRINGTON, Thomas R.	(DC)	504
Audiovisual & 16mm film & video	FISH, Marie	(CA)	380
Audiovisual & television	KUBIC, Joseph C.	(CA)	682
Audiovisual archives	BIRDWHISTELL, Terry L.	(KY)	98
	GOODRICH, Allan B. . . .	(MA)	449
Audiovisual cataloging	BASKIN, Jeffrey L.	(AR)	63
	HAWKINS, Nina L.	(CA)	514
	WURANGIAN, Nelia C. . .	(CA)	1374
	CARTER, Nancy F.	(CO)	189
	HARLOW, Aileen W. . . .	(CT)	502
	KELLY, Mark M.	(DC)	638
	GREESON-SCHARDL, Tamra J.	(GA)	465
	CORCORAN, Frances E.	(IL)	245
	POWELL, Martha C.	(KY)	988
	WINZER, Kathleen M. . .	(MD)	1356
	REGAN, Lesley E.	(MI)	1017
	MCCROSKEY, Marilyn J.	(MO)	800
	MYRICK, Judy C.	(MS)	885
	MASCIA, Regina B.	(NY)	780
	WEITZ, Jay N.	(OH)	1320
	SMITH, Terry M.	(OR)	1161
	GARRETT, Stuart	(TN)	420
	OWEN, Richard L.	(TN)	932
	CAINE, William C.	(TX)	171
	HOWE, Patricia A.	(VA)	565
	WHYTE, Sean	(VA)	1335
	GILCHRIST-DOBSON, Norma J.	(NS)	434
	FINLAY, Barbara J.	(PQ)	378
Audiovisual cataloging & acquisitions	SPIEGELMAN, Barbara M.	(PA)	1174
Audiovisual center management	GOLDBERGER, Virginia F.	(IL)	445
Audiovisual centers	BROWN, Janis F.	(CA)	144
Audiovisual collection	DAVIS, Bernice	(IN)	277
	LINN, Mott R.	(PA)	731
Audiovisual collection development	BASKIN, Jeffrey L.	(AR)	63
	RITTEN, Karla J.	(CO)	1036
	TAYLOR, Mary L.	(HI)	1227
	SIARNY, William D.	(IL)	1134
	STUCKWICH, Chris E. . .	(LA)	1204
	SALITA, Christine T.	(NY)	1076
	GARRETT, Melinda R. . .	(OH)	420
	FIDISHUN, Dolores	(PA)	375
	STAINBROOK, Lynn M. .	(WI)	1178
Audiovisual collection development, mgmt	GAUDET, Susan E.	(TN)	422
Audiovisual collections	GARDNER, W J.	(CO)	418
	GOLEY, Elaine P.	(TX)	447
	MCCOY, Judy I.	(TX)	799
	REID, Patricia M.	(AB)	1019
Audiovisual communications	SINK, Thomas R.	(OH)	1143
Audiovisual, computing in libraries	JAX, John J.	(WI)	595
Audiovisual consulting	SMITH, Richard J.	(LA)	1160
Audiovisual coordination	ARNOLD, Peggy	(MI)	34
	GAGNON, Ruth	(NH)	412
	EMERICK, John L.	(PA)	347
	GODWIN, Frances L. . . .	(TX)	443
Audiovisual curriculum alignment	NEBEL, Jean C.	(CA)	891
Audiovisual database	KELLEY, Dennis L.	(NY)	636
	YUSTER, Leigh C.	(NY)	1385
Audiovisual department head	WIRIG, Joan S.	(IL)	1356
Audiovisual distributor	HEMPEL, Gordon J.	(IL)	525
Audiovisual documentation	DUCHESNEAU, Pierre . .	(PQ)	322
Audiovisual education	BURESH, Reggie F.	(MN)	158
Audiovisual equipment	SEGOR, Phyllis L.	(FL)	1112
	COBB, Marilyn R.	(IL)	225
	SYFERT, Samuel R.	(IL)	1217
	WOLFE, Mary S.	(PA)	1361
Audiovisual equipment administration	WALTERS, Corky	(WY)	1301
Audiovisual equipment & materials	LEDOUX, Mary E.	(OH)	709
Audiovisual equipment & productions	BURMAN, Marilyn P. . . .	(WY)	161
Audiovisual equipment, materials	HERBERT, Barbara R. . .	(NJ)	530
Audiovisual equipment purchasing	SHARP, Betty L.	(TX)	1122

AUDIOVISUAL (Cont'd)

Audiovisual equipment services	SHARMA, Shirley K. ...	(KS)	1122
Audiovisual, film, video	ENGLE, Joyce C.	(NJ)	349
Audiovisual, films	SANDY, Marjorie M.	(MI)	1081
Audiovisual for young adults	CHARVAT, Catherine T. .	(OH)	203
Audiovisual genealogy	VIERGEVER, Dan W.	(KS)	1284
Audiovisual hardware	MYHRE, Char	(MN)	885
	GORMAN, Mary B.	(NY)	452
Audiovisual instruction & production	FALLON, Marianna L. ...	(IN)	362
Audiovisual instruction utilization	KERSTETTER, John ...	(OH)	644
Audiovisual librarian	ANNETT, Susan E.	(CA)	28
Audiovisual librarianship	SLAPSYS, Richard M. ..	(MA)	1148
	FRYER, Philip	(MD)	407
	WIRTANEN, James	(ND)	1356
Audiovisual librarianship & acquisitions	EARL, Susan R.	(NC)	332
Audiovisual library design	BASKIN, Jeffrey L.	(AR)	63
Audiovisual material	WILLIAMS, Helen E. ...	(KY)	1343
	HUDZIK, Robert T.	(OH)	570
Audiovisual material cataloging	TRAVILLIAN, Mary W. ..	(IA)	1254
	ESMAN, Michael D.	(MD)	354
	MCENTEE, Mary F.	(TX)	804
Audiovisual material selection	WOOD, Irene P.	(IL)	1364
Audiovisual materials	JEFFERY, Phyllis D.	(AL)	596
	BERCIK, Mary E.	(CA)	84
	CROSS, Claudette S. ...	(CA)	260
	BROGDEN, Stephen R. .	(IA)	139
	COBB, Marilyn R.	(IL)	225
	LUKASIK, Marion F.	(IL)	747
	TEO, Elizabeth A.	(IL)	1231
	VACCARO, William J. ..	(IL)	1270
	ANJIER, Jennifer S.	(LA)	28
	YOUNG, Ruth H.	(LA)	1383
	CLOHERTY, Lauretta M.	(MA)	223
	CASSARO, James P. ...	(NY)	193
	EDWARDS, Harriet M. ..	(NY)	337
	GURIEVITCH, Grania B. .	(NY)	478
	USES, Ann K.	(PA)	1270
	BELL, David B.	(SC)	76
	HAMLIN, Lisa K.	(TN)	493
	COOK, Anne S.	(TX)	239
	DUBIEL, Laura R.	(TX)	321
	HALL, Halbert W.	(TX)	487
	LEVINE, Harriet L.	(TX)	720
	BIDD, Donald W.	(PQ)	94
	SAVARD, Rejean	(PQ)	1085
	CHUO, Josephine Y.	(TAI)	213
Audiovisual materials & service	SHAW, Richard N.	(DE)	1124
Audiovisual materials & services	HURLEY, John	(NJ)	577
Audiovisual materials cataloging	CLEMENT, Patsy	(UT)	221
Audiovisual materials for schools	ELLIS, Caryl A.	(AZ)	344
Audiovisual materials organization	SHEFFO, Belinda M.	(PA)	1125
Audiovisual materials production	CARLISLE, Carol A.	(CT)	182
Audiovisual materials selection	SHEFFO, Belinda M. ...	(PA)	1125
Audiovisual media	DOWNEY, Christine D. ..	(CA)	316
	GIUNTA, Victoria J.	(FL)	439
	FLYNN, Barbara L.	(IL)	386
	FRADKIN, Bernard	(IL)	395
	THOMPSON, Anna M. ..	(IN)	1238
	BUCCO, Louise F.	(VA)	153
	SCHERDIN, Mary J.	(WI)	1092
	VERMA, Prem V.	(WV)	1282
	GOODELL, Paulette M. .	(AUS)	448
Audiovisual media & equipment	MITCHELL, George D. ..	(TX)	848
Audiovisual media cataloging	ZASLOW, Barry J.	(OH)	1386
Audiovisual media development	CHESHER, Joyce A. ...	(TX)	206
Audiovisual media facility management	GRAY, Shirley M.	(NY)	460
Audiovisual, media services	MCCARTHY, Germaine A.	(MA)	794
Audiovisual ordering	SPERRY, Linda S.	(OH)	1174
Audiovisual print specialist	PHEGAN, Dolores M. ...	(TX)	967
Audiovisual production	BEEBE, Richard J.	(CA)	74
	WESTBROOK, Patricia C.	(CT)	1326
	DEANS, Janice P.	(FL)	284
	BADGER, Barbara	(IL)	44
	TUGGLE, Ann M.	(IL)	1262
	NEWTON, Evah B.	(IN)	900
	O'LOUGHLIN, Marilyn L.	(MD)	921
	EDWARDS, Rosa C. ...	(NC)	338
	HAY, Mary K.	(WI)	515

AUDIOVISUAL (Cont'd)

Audiovisual production training	RUNYON, Steven C. ...	(CA)	1067
Audiovisual programs	SLONE, Eugenia F.	(CT)	1150
	LAY, Shirley	(MD)	705
Audiovisual records	STERN, Marc J.	(NY)	1189
Audiovisual reference	GARRETT, Melinda R. ..	(OH)	420
	KASOW, Harriet	(ISR)	629
Audiovisual resources	FORREST, Charles G. ..	(IL)	390
	ZOGOTT, Joyce	(PA)	1390
Audiovisual selection	TRIVISON, Margaret A. .	(CA)	1257
	DOWD, Frank B.	(MD)	315
Audiovisual selection & advisory	ORMOND, Sarah C.	(MI)	926
Audiovisual service	EASTMAN, Franklin R. ..	(CA)	333
Audiovisual service management	KERSTETTER, John ...	(OH)	644
Audiovisual services	WALCH, David B.	(CA)	1293
	WALTHER, Richard E. ...	(CA)	1301
	MULAWKA, Chet	(CT)	876
	ROLLIN, Marian B.	(CT)	1051
	STEMMER, Katherine R. .	(CT)	1186
	STRADER, Helen B.	(FL)	1199
	AHN, Hyonah K.	(IL)	8
	BADGER, Barbara	(IL)	44
	NUTTY, David J.	(IL)	912
	ROLSTAD, Gary O.	(IL)	1052
	MILLS, Richard E.	(IN)	844
	OSTROWSKI, Lawrence C.	(IN)	929
	GOLDBERG, Steven R. .	(MA)	444
	SIPPEN, Kathi H.	(NC)	1144
	THIBODEAU, Patricia L. .	(NC)	1235
	BLESH, Tamara E.	(NH)	105
	GARDINER, Judith R. ...	(NJ)	417
	PELLETIER, Karen E. ...	(NJ)	955
	BRANDEAU, John H. ...	(NY)	128
	CARLSON, Marie S. ...	(NY)	182
	CORRY, Emmett	(NY)	247
	LEVERING, Philip	(NY)	719
	MILLER, Michael D.	(NY)	841
	MORAN, Sylvia J.	(NY)	862
	MORRISON, J M.	(NY)	868
	NOVIK, Sandra P.	(NY)	911
	SIMCOE, Darryl D.	(NY)	1139
	WIENER, Paul B.	(NY)	1336
	HABINSKI, Carol A.	(OH)	481
	NOVAK, Mary S.	(OH)	911
	MAXWELL, James G. ...	(OR)	788
	JONES, Debra A.	(PA)	612
	MAYOVER, Steven J. ...	(PA)	791
	BYROM, Jeanne	(TX)	170
	GRAY, Paul W.	(TX)	460
	KRALISZ, Victor F.	(TX)	675
	WILSON, George N. ...	(TX)	1351
	BISCHOFF, Frances A. .	(VA)	99
	PEARSON, Marilyn R. ..	(VA)	953
	SCHMIDT, Raymond J. .	(AB)	1095
	BURTON, Donna M.	(ON)	164
	PHELAN, Daniel F.	(ON)	967
Audiovisual services administration	LATZKE, Henry R.	(IL)	702
Audiovisual services management	CYR, Helen W.	(MD)	268
Audiovisual skills	HSU, Peter T.	(ON)	567
Audiovisual software	REIMAN, Anthony C. ...	(NY)	1020
Audiovisual software & hardware	WARREN, Ann R.	(NH)	1306
Audiovisual software & services	DIAMOND, Shela W. ...	(KY)	299
Audiovisual software cataloging	DUHAMELL, Lynnette H.	(IN)	324
	HORAN, Meredith L.	(MD)	559
Audiovisual specialization	ROGINSKI, Donna J. ...	(IL)	1050
Audiovisual technology, computer appls	NOLAN, Joan	(PA)	907
Audiovisual training	HARLOW, Aileen W. ...	(CT)	502
Audiovisual training & development	STUCKWICH, Chris E. ..	(LA)	1204
	CLEMONS, Kenneth L. ..	(NC)	221
Audiovisual use	MEADOR, Cornie M. ...	(TX)	819
Audiovisual uses	VIDMANIS, Visvaldis E. .	(MA)	1283
Audiovisuals	LAING, Susan J.	(AL)	688
	MCMICHAEL, Sandra C.	(FL)	815
	DAVIS, Shelley E.	(GA)	281
	SMITH, Matilda M.	(GA)	1158
	HUSLIG, Dennis M.	(IL)	578
	MCGIVERIN, Rolland H. .	(IN)	806
	MOGLE, Dawn E.	(IN)	852

AUDIOVISUAL (Cont'd)

Audiovisuals

	FORTE, Joseph E.	(KS)	391
	CANTILLAS, Caroline M.	(LA)	179
	BOEHR, Diane L.	(MD)	109
	MASSEY, James E.	(MD)	782
	DUROCHER, Jeanne M.	(MI)	328
	MUETH, Elizabeth C.	(MO)	875
	CRITCHLOW, Therese E.	(NJ)	259
	SCHALK-GREENE, Katherine	(NJ)	1089
	SCHMITT, Judy	(NJ)	1096
	CARUSO, Janet A.	(NY)	190
	FRIEDMAN, Lydia	(NY)	404
	LA SORTE, Antonia J.	(NY)	700
	LIEBER, Ellen C.	(NY)	726
	LISZCZYNSKYJ, Halyna A.	(NY)	733
	NAPOLITANO, Joan A.	(NY)	887
	SEMKOW, Julie L.	(NY)	1115
	SHER, Deborah M.	(NY)	1127
	LUST, Jeanette M.	(OH)	749
	CARTULARO, Teresa C.	(PA)	190
	FIDISHUN, Dolores	(PA)	375
	VICK, Kathleen	(PA)	1283
	ROBERTSON, Sally A.	(TN)	1042
	CRAIG, Thomas B.	(TX)	254
	GUENTHER, Jody	(TX)	475
	ELLIS, Margaret D.	(VT)	345
	BRAGER, Beverly J.	(WI)	127
Audiovisuals & cataloging	EMAHISER, Joan A.	(MI)	347
Audiovisuals & media	HILTON, Beverly A.	(KY)	541
Audiovisuals & microcomputers	WU, Harry P.	(MI)	1373
Audiovisuals & video media	DIAL, Ron	(NY)	299
Audiovisuals cataloging	LOMEN, Nancy L.	(NY)	738
Audiovisuals, film & video	MINOR, Barbara G.	(MN)	846
Audiovisuals including computers	RYAN, Sharon K.	(OH)	1071
Audiovisuals, medical	VAN SCHAIK, Jo A.	(TX)	1277
Book & audiovisual media selection	YOUNG, Patricia S.	(TN)	1383
Book & audiovisual software reviewer	LEIBOLD, Cynthia K.	(OH)	713
Book selection, audiovisual services	DE CASTRO, Elinore H.	(PHP)	285
Books & audiovisual equipment selection	ANDIS, Norma B.	(TX)	26
Books & audiovisual materials selection	SCHILL, Julie G.	(PA)	1092
Cataloging audiovisual materials	URBANSKI, Verna P.	(FL)	1269
	HARTSOCK, Ralph M.	(PA)	508
Cataloging audiovisual media	KEARNEY, Jeanne E.	(NJ)	633
Cataloging audiovisuals, monographs	VAN STRATEN, Daniel G.	(WI)	1277
Cataloging books & audiovisual media	YOUNG, Patricia S.	(TN)	1383
Cataloging music & audiovisual materials	SLOMSKI, Monica J.	(CT)	1150
Copyright & audiovisuals	FRYER, Philip	(MD)	407
Creative use of audiovisual materials	DAY, Martha T.	(VT)	282
Distribution audiovisuals	SOLIN, Myron	(NY)	1166
Educational technology, audiovisual	SPENCER, Albert F.	(GA)	1173
Elementary use of audiovisual equipment	SLOAN, Mary J.	(GA)	1149
Exhibition & programming of AV materials	SCHREIBMAN, Fay C.	(NY)	1099
Exhibits, audiovisual presentations	SHIDELER, John C.	(WA)	1129
Global education audiovisuals	HUGHES, Rolanda L.	(IN)	572
Health sciences audiovisuals	MCLEAN, Martha L.	(TN)	814
Instructional design, audiovisual	PICHETTE, William H.	(TX)	970
Library & audiovisual management	SIMARD, Denis	(PQ)	1139
Local history, audiovisual, reference	WOOD, Lois R.	(IL)	1364
Maintaining audiovisual equipment	SUTHERLAND, Helen G.	(CA)	1211
Management & audiovisual	MOORE, Virginia B.	(DC)	861
Management & development of audiovisuals	AHN, Hyonah K.	(IL)	8
Media & audiovisual consulting	TARANKO, Walter J.	(ME)	1223
Media, audiovisual equipment, video	RUBIN, Ellen B.	(NY)	1064
Media, audiovisual market research	HOPE, Thomas W.	(NY)	557
Media, audiovisual services	MANDEL, Debra H.	(MA)	764
Medical audiovisuals	AGUILAR, Barbara S.	(MO)	8
Music & audiovisual cataloging	ALMQUIST, Sharon G.	(TX)	17
Music & audiovisual librarianship	SEAMAN, Sally G.	(IL)	1109
Music, audiovisual	AYRES, Edwin M.	(TX)	43
Non-print media & audiovisuals	CURTIS, James A.	(NY)	267
OCLC audiovisual format	TEMPLE, Harold L.	(IL)	1230

AUDIOVISUAL (Cont'd)

Print & audiovisual communications	NORTON, Alice	(CT)	910
Production audiovisuals	SOLIN, Myron	(NY)	1166
Reference & audiovisual service	PINE, Nancy M.	(FL)	974
Reviewing AV & computer software	MILLER, John E.	(OH)	839
Reviewing audiovisual materials	RYBARCZYK, Barclay S.	(NY)	1071
Reviewing children's books & audiovisual	SHERMAN, Louise L.	(NJ)	1128
Serials, AV materials, automation	SOPER, Mary E.	(WA)	1168
Statewide audiovisual distribution	NAUGLE, Gretchen R.	(NE)	889
Student audiovisual productions	PROCTOR, Deborah K.	(WY)	994
Supervise all audiovisual	MARVEL, Frances J.	(CA)	780
Teaching audiovisual education	WIRTANEN, James	(ND)	1356
Teaching, audiovisual production	POWELL, Patricia K.	(TX)	988
Teaching library, audiovisual skills	CONOVER, Kathryn H.	(FL)	238
Videocassettes & AV materials	SCHOLTZ, James C.	(IL)	1098
Written & audiovisual documentation	MARCHAND, Jacques	(PQ)	768
Young adult & audiovisual services	HULTZ, Karen W.	(NY)	573

AUDITING (See also Accounting)

Accounting & audit reference	MCDEVITT-PARKS, Kathryn B.	(CA)	802
Accounting & auditing	SHEERAN, Carole A.	(DC)	1125
Accounting & auditing literature	DOSER, Virginia A.	(CA)	313
Accounting & auditing research	VEASLEY, Mignon M.	(CA)	1280
	EMERSON, Beth A.	(TX)	347
Accounting, auditing & taxation ref	HETZLER, Jill K.	(WA)	534
Accounting auditing reference	SWANTEK, Kathleen M.	(IL)	1214
Auditing, accounting	MCCALLUM, Anita J.	(ON)	793
Information auditing	ANDEL, June	(PA)	21
IRM reviews & audits	HORTON, Forest W.	(DC)	561
Securities & commodities audits	JOHNSON, G V.	(IL)	604

AUSTEN

Jane Austen	MARSHALL, Mary G.	(IL)	774

AUSTRALIA

Australian bibliography	ROUTH, Spencer	(AUS)	1061
British, Australian, Anglo-African	HAWK, Susan P.	(FL)	513

AUTHENTICATION

Appraisal, authentication of manuscripts	GORDON, Robert S.	(ON)	451

AUTHORITY (See also Cataloging, Classification, Technical)

Authorities	DAVIS, Carol C.	(OH)	277
Authorities control	STEINHAGEN, Elizabeth N.	(ID)	1186
Authority & bibliographic relationships	CARNEY, Marillyn L.	(VA)	183
Authority control	FIEGEN, Ann M.	(AZ)	375
	ROCKE, Reve P.	(CA)	1046
	HIATT, Robert M.	(DC)	536
	LIGGETT, Suzanne L.	(DC)	726
	FRAZER, Ruth F.	(FL)	399
	HILL, Janet S.	(IL)	540
	HSIEH, Cynthia C.	(IL)	567
	STRAWN, Gary L.	(IL)	1201
	GOODWIN, Vania M.	(IN)	450
	MARTIN, Norma H.	(LA)	777
	HOSTAGE, John B.	(MA)	562
	LINSKY, Leonore K.	(MA)	731
	TAVARES, Cecelia M.	(MA)	1225
	KLAIR, Arlene F.	(MD)	657
	HERVEY, Norma J.	(MN)	533
	REISNER, Suzanne R.	(MN)	1021
	BERTCHUME, Gary	(NY)	90
	SMIRAGLIA, Richard P.	(NY)	1152
	STAM, Deirdre C.	(NY)	1179
	THOMAS, Catherine M.	(NY)	1236
	KIRKBRIDE, Amey L.	(OH)	654
	LUDY, Lorene E.	(OH)	747
	FULLER, Elizabeth E.	(PA)	408
	BROSS, Valerie	(TN)	141
	GRADY, Agnes M.	(TN)	455
	CRAIG, Marilyn J.	(TX)	254

AUTHORITY (Cont'd)
Authority control

	SADOWSKI, Frank E. . . .	(VA)	1074
	FRITZ, Richard J.	(ON)	405
	SAKAMOTO, Hiroshi . . .	(JAP)	1076
Authority control services	HANIFORD, K L.	(MO)	496
Authority control work	TURKALO, David M. . . .	(MA)	1263
Authority file maintenance	ASPER, Mary K.	(CO)	37
Authority files	DOBBIN, Geraldine F. . .	(BC)	307
Authority record conversion	STUBBS, Linda T.	(DC)	1204
Authority validation	BATTOE, Melanie K. . . .	(NY)	65
Authority work	ZUCKERMAN, Arline . . .	(CA)	1391
	IRGON, Deborah A. . . .	(NJ)	583
	NEWHOUSE, Brian G. . .	(NJ)	899
Authority work cataloging	FINLAY, Barbara J.	(PQ)	378
Automated authorities	THOMSON, Donna K. . .	(ON)	1241
Automated authority control	GRUTCHFIELD, Walter .	(NY)	475
	MILLER, Daniel J.	(OR)	836
Automated cataloging, authority control	GLASSMAN, Penny L. . .	(MA)	440
Automated linked authority control	BISOM, Diane B.	(CA)	99
Building & maintaining authority files	LESSER, Barbara	(VA)	718
Cataloging & authority control	TILLETT, Barbara B. . . .	(CA)	1245
	IDDINGS, Daniel H. . . .	(IL)	581
	WEE, Lily K.	(IL)	1315
	ENGLE, Constance B. . .	(MI)	349
Cataloging & name authorities	SCHUITEMA, Joan E. . .	(OH)	1101
Cataloging including automated authority	BULAONG, Grace F. . . .	(ON)	156
Creating automated name authorities	DAWE, Heather L.	(ON)	282
Implementing automated authority control	FISHER, Carl D.	(VA)	380
Monographic series, authority control	DECKER, Jean S.	(NY)	285
NACO name authority work	JONES, Edgar A.	(MA)	612
Name authorities	BILEYDI, Lois G.	(MN)	96
Name authority records	SCHMIDT, Holly H. . . .	(OR)	1095
Online authority control	BERRINGER, Virginia M. .	(OH)	90
	FRIEDLAND, Frances K. .	(ON)	403
Subject & name authority control	BADING, Kathryn E. . . .	(TX)	44
Subject authority	PAGELS, Helen H.	(NY)	934
Subject authority control	HURLBERT, Irene W. . . .	(CA)	577
Subject authority records	SCHMIDT, Holly H.	(OR)	1095
Visual resources authority control	MOST, Gregory P.	(TX)	872

AUTHORS (See also Writing)

Author	WALKER, Elinor	(MN)	1295
Author, children's textbooks	BISSETT, Donald J. . . .	(MI)	100
Author interviews & reviews	HOLTZE, Sally H.	(NY)	555
Author of books on theatre	WILMETH, Don B.	(RI)	1349
Author of children's biographies	MILLENDER, Dharathola .	(IN)	835
Author of library history	FRISBIE, Margery	(IL)	405
Bookmaking, children as authors	HERRICK, Johanna W. . .	(HI)	532
Books by Maine authors	LYONS, Dean E.	(ME)	753
Children's activity books author	HAAS, Carolyn B.	(IL)	480
Children's author	KERBY, Ramona A.	(TX)	643
Corp author name formation & database	KANE, Astor V.	(VA)	624
Developing librarian authors	FRANKLIN, Robert M. . .	(NC)	398
Indiana authors, bibliography	GILLIS, Ruth J.	(MN)	436
Organization of author conferences	HIRABAYASHI, Joanne .	(CA)	543
Story & author programs	LOPEZ, Silvia P.	(FL)	741

AUTOGRAPHS

Americana, famous American autographs	STRINGFELLOW, William T.	(NY)	1202
Autograph dealership	CADY, Richard H.	(IL)	170
Autograph manuscripts	CAHOON, Herbert	(NY)	171
Manuscript & autograph material	PETERSON, Scott W. . .	(IL)	964
Music autographs	MACNUTT, Richard P. . .	(ENG)	758

AUTOMATION (See also Bar (Coding), Computers)

Acquisitions & serials automation	MCCALLISTER, Myrna J.	(ME)	793
Acquisitions automation	LOWELL, Gerald R.	(CT)	744
	PRESLEY, Roger L.	(GA)	991
	CHAMBERLAIN, Carol E.	(PA)	197

AUTOMATION (Cont'd)

Archival automation	ELLISON, J T.	(CO)	345
	BURKE, Frank G.	(DC)	160
	CARSON, James G. . . .	(IL)	188
	GILDEMEISTER, Glen A.	(IL)	434
	WEBER, Lisa B.	(IL)	1314
	GILLILAND, Anne J. . . .	(OH)	436
Archival automation, cataloging	WEINBERG, David M. . .	(PA)	1317
Archival management & automation	SERBAN, William M. . . .	(LA)	1116
Archival material automation	SMITH, William K.	(MI)	1161
Archive automation	GILHEANY, Stephen J. . .	(CA)	435
Archives & library automation	SYKES, Stephanie L. . . .	(PQ)	1217
Archives & manuscripts automation	BROWN, Barbara J. . . .	(VA)	142
Archives automated description	PENDLETON, Debbie D. .	(AL)	956
Archives automation	BEARMAN, David A. . . .	(PA)	69
	VAILLANCOURT, Alain .	(PQ)	1270
Arts automation	PISCIOTTA, Henry A. . .	(PA)	976
Automated acquisitions	FRYMIRE, Jane K.	(MN)	407
Automated acquisitions control	DE LUISE, Alexandra . . .	(PQ)	290
Automated acquisitions systems	BARKER, Joseph W. . . .	(CA)	56
	TRIMINGHAM, Robert . .	(CA)	1256
	KAPOOR, Jagdish C. . . .	(NH)	626
	HUDSON, Gary A.	(SD)	569
Automated administrative systems	ARROWOOD, Donna J. .	(CA)	34
Automated & integrated library systems	GABRIEL, Linda	(NJ)	411
Automated archival description	PURDY, Virginia C.	(DC)	998
Automated archival systems	SZARY, Richard V.	(DC)	1218
Automated authorities	THOMSON, Donna K. . .	(ON)	1241
Automated authority control	GRUTCHFIELD, Walter .	(NY)	475
	MILLER, Daniel J.	(OR)	836
Automated automation	SOMERS, Sally W.	(GA)	1167
Automated bibliographic databases	CUMMINGS, Christopher H.	(UT)	264
Automated bibliographic maintenance	WEE, Lily K.	(IL)	1315
Automated bibliographic systems	SZARY, Richard V.	(DC)	1218
Automated bibliography production	CHERVENAK, Joseph F.	(CO)	206
Automated book exchange	FINK, Norman	(PQ)	378
Automated catalog	FRYMIRE, Jane K.	(MN)	407
Automated catalog maintenance	BRANDT, Janet E.	(MN)	128
Automated cataloging	CARSON, Susan A.	(CA)	188
	MILLER, Daniel J.	(OR)	836
	GREAVES, H P.	(ON)	461
Automated cataloging, authority control	GLASSMAN, Penny L. . .	(MA)	440
Automated catalogs	STOUT, Mary A.	(AZ)	1199
	RANSOM-BERGSTROM, Janette F.	(MI)	1008
Automated circulation	WATTS, Richard S.	(CA)	1310
	GLICK, Kenneth W.	(CT)	441
	MICHAUD, Noreen R. . . .	(CT)	832
	BERGER, Marianne C. . .	(IL)	85
	LAMB, Robert S.	(IN)	690
	SKIPTON, Iris E.	(MA)	1146
	COOPER, Judith C.	(MD)	243
	MARSHALL, Suzanne K.	(TX)	775
Automated circulation implementation	MORELAND, Rachel S. . .	(KS)	863
Automated circulation, public catalog	NIEMEYER, Karen K. . . .	(IN)	903
Automated circulation system	LANE, Linda A.	(GA)	694
	ELDREDGE, Jeffrey R. . .	(HI)	342
Automated circulation systems	CASTONGUAY, Russell .	(CA)	194
	EICHELBERGER, Susan .	(CA)	339
	PARKS, Amy N.	(CT)	943
	SHURMAN, Richard L. . .	(IL)	1134
	PHENIX, Katharine J. . . .	(LA)	967
	PURCELL, Kathleen V. . .	(MD)	998
	FARHAT, Elizabeth M. . .	(MI)	363
	HENRY, Peggy L.	(MO)	529
	ROSENBERG, Harlene Z.	(NJ)	1056
	MORRIS, Jennifer D. . . .	(NY)	866
	RIEBEL, Ellis F.	(PA)	1033
	IVES, Gary W.	(VA)	585
	ICE, Priscilla T.	(WA)	581
	HAYES, Janice E.	(ON)	516
Automated collection devlpmnt techniques	LAREW, Christian K. . . .	(NJ)	697
Automated community information service	MESSINEO, Leonard L. .	(KS)	828
Automated database coordination	ROSS, Carole L.	(CT)	1058
Automated databases	CRANOR, Alice T.	(DC)	255

AUTOMATION (Cont'd)

Automated databases & conversions — PHILLIPS, Clifford R. ... (CA) 968
Automated indexing — ZBORAY, Ronald J. ..... (CA) 1386
Automated indexing & retrieval — MATLOCK, Teresa A. ... (TX) 784
Automated information brokering — COLLARD, R M. ...... (CO) 232
Automated information retrieval — SANDERS, Robert L. ... (CA) 1080
Automated information retrieval systems — MACIAS-CHAPULA, Cesar A. .... (MEX) 755
Automated information systems — HUNE, Mary G. .... (OH) 574
— NORTON, Nancy P. ..... (TN) 910
Automated information systems management — WEINSTEIN, Lois ...... (NY) 1318
Automated integrated library network — EMAHISER, Joan A. ..... (MI) 347
Automated integrated library system — OBERC, Susanne F. ..... (OH) 913
Automated journal circulation — LEWIS, Martha S. ...... (IL) 724
Automated language processing — BORKO, Harold .... (CA) 116
Automated legal research — GOTT, Gary D. .... (ND) 453
— GREENBERG, Charles J. (NY) 463
Automated library circulation systems — ULRICH, Paul S. ...... (WGR) 268
Automated library control systems — YOUNG, Peter R. ...... (DC) 1383
Automated library, information systems — KANNEL, Ene .... (ON) 625
Automated library networks — HOUGH, Allen D. ...... (NY) 562
Automated Library of Congress cataloging — BENSON, Laurel D. ..... (MN) 83
Automated library services — ROSS, Gary M. .... (SC) 1058
Automated library system — MATTHEWS, Joseph R. . (CA) 785
— HUMMEL, Janice A. .... (MD) 573
Automated library systems — ODSEN, Elizabeth R. ... (AK) 917
— MUIR, Scott P. .... (AL) 876
— BLANK, Karen L. ...... (CA) 104
— BULLARD, Sharon W. .. (CA) 156
— LEE, Hee J. .... (CA) 710
— SOY, Susan K. .... (CA) 1170
— BATES, Charles E. ..... (CO) 63
— HAYNAM, Kenneth W. ... (CT) 516
— SKOP, Vera .... (CT) 1147
— MITCHELL, Phyllis R. ... (GA) 849
— OHRLUND, Bruce L. ... (IA) 919
— HAMMER, Donald P. .... (IL) 493
— HILDRETH, Charles R. ... (IL) 539
— YATES, Dudley V. ..... (KY) 1378
— KNAACK, Linda M. .... (MA) 663
— TAHIR, Mary M. .... (MD) 1220
— MARTIN, John E. ...... (MI) 776
— MOSEY, Jeanette ...... (MI) 871
— BECK, Susan E. .... (MO) 71
— RICKERSON, George T. . (MO) 1031
— DAVIDSON, Laura B. ... (NC) 276
— MOREHOUSE, Valerie J. (ND) 863
— ROCK, Sue W. .... (NJ) 1046
— O'DONNELL, Maryann T. (NY) 917
— SALAZAR, Pamela R. ... (NY) 1076
— MCMURRAY, Sallylou .. (OH) 815
— SHAW, Debra S. ...... (OH) 1123
— SHREWSBURY, Lynn D. (OH) 1133
— FULLER, Elizabeth E. ... (PA) 408
— LANDRUM, John H. ..... (SC) 693
— BEHRENS, Elizabeth A. . (TN) 75
— MILLS, Debra D. ...... (TN) 844
— UBALDINI, Michael W. .. (TN) 1267
— ALLEN, Virginia M. ..... (TX) 16
— CLARK, Jay B. .... (TX) 217
— MULLINS, James R. ..... (TX) 878
— PEDEN, Robert M. ..... (TX) 954
— KANE, Dorothea S. ..... (VA) 624
— SCOTT, Mona L. ...... (VA) 1107
— WEIST, Melody S. ..... (VA) 1320
— WILLIAMSON, Judy D. . (WV) 1347
— TAYYEB, Rashid ...... (NS) 1229
— PIGGOTT, Sylvia E. .... (PQ) 972
Automated library systems implementation — DUMONT, Paul E. ..... (TX) 325
Automated linked authority control — BISOM, Diane B. ..... (CA) 99
Automated magazine production — HAVENS, Shirley E. .... (NY) 513
Automated medical records — LONG, John M. .... (MN) 739
Automated microcomputer systems — ROSE, Pamela M. ...... (NY) 1055
Automated networks — SMITH, Randolph R. ..... (CO) 1159
— WREGE, Ann S. .... (CT) 1370

AUTOMATION (Cont'd)

Automated pageform catalogs — GRUTCHFIELD, Walter . (NY) 475
Automated public library systems — MEAGHER, Janet H. ... (MA) 819
Automated publishing support — GRIMES, Judith E. ...... (MD) 470
Automated reference service — JOHNSON, Carolynn K. . (WA) 603
Automated reference services — JOHNSON, Charlotte L. . (IL) 603
— MASSEY-BURZIO, Virginia (MA) 782
Automated reference systems — BECK, Susan E. .... (MO) 71
Automated reference work — GORDON, Martin K. ..... (VA) 451
Automated retrospective conversion — JOHNSON, Pat M. ...... (TX) 608
Automated searches — NORRIS, Loretta W. ..... (DC) 909
Automated serial control systems — FONG, Wilfred W. ...... (WI) 388
Automated serials & acquisitions — ROYLE, Maryanne ..... (IL) 1063
Automated serials control — TALLMAN, Karen D. ... (AZ) 1221
— KIRK, Darcy .... (MA) 654
Automated serials management — REID, Janine A. .... (VA) 1018
Automated serials management systems — CLAPPER, Mary E. .... (MA) 216
Automated services — WILLIAMS, Joan F. .... (CA) 1344
— WINANS, Diane D. .... (OH) 1354
Automated storage & retrieval — LEVINE, Emil H. .... (DC) 720
Automated system implementation — STAHL, Wilson M. ..... (NC) 1178
Automated system networking — MAINIERO, Elizabeth T. . (CT) 761
Automated systems — BRUMAN, Janet L. ..... (CA) 150
— PISANO, Vivian M. .... (CA) 975
— SZYNAKA, Edward M. ... (CA) 1219
— BOWERS, Sandra L. ... (CO) 121
— AUSTIN, Monique C. ... (DC) 40
— APPELQUIST, Donald L. (FL) 30
— MOUW, James R. ..... (IL) 874
— CIUCKI, Marcella A. ... (IN) 215
— FUTA, Debra D. .... (IN) 411
— MOORE, Thomas J. .... (IN) 861
— BADEN, Diane G. ...... (MA) 44
— BAILEY, Carol A. ...... (MD) 46
— BLEGEN, John C. ..... (MD) 105
— GALLAGHER, Charles F. (MD) 413
— O'BRIEN, Lee A. .... (MD) 914
— GOSLING, William A. ... (MI) 453
— ELFSTRAND, Stephen F. (MN) 342
— CONNORS, Theresa ... (MO) 238
— HAMMOND, John J. ..... (MO) 493
— MYERS, Carol B. ...... (NC) 884
— BLUMENTHAL, Sidney L. (NJ) 107
— STAVETSKI, Norma K. ... (NJ) 1183
— KLOPFER, Jerome J. ... (NM) 662
— BORRESS, Lewis R. ... (NY) 117
— DAVIS, Robert J. ...... (NY) 280
— HITT, Gail D. .... (NY) 544
— LOLLIS, Martha J. ...... (NY) 738
— SIVULICH, Kenneth G. .. (NY) 1145
— UCHTORFF, Barbara J. . (NY) 1267
— RASKIN, Rosa S. ...... (OH) 1009
— DAYO, Ayo .... (TX) 283
— SARGENT, Charles W. ... (TX) 1082
— WILSON, D K. .... (UT) 1350
— CALLAHAN, John J. .... (VA) 173
— UMBERGER, Sheila S. ... (VA) 1268
— WINTERS, Sharon A. ... (VA) 1356
— CONABLE, Irene H. .... (WA) 235
— BARUTH, Barbara P. ... (WI) 62
— JEFFCOTT, Janet B. ... (WI) 596
— TOOTH, John E. .... (MB) 1251
Automated systems & indexing — TAYLOR, James B. ... (WA) 1227
Automated systems for archives — HONHART, Frederick L. . (MI) 556
Automated systems for circulation — JOHNSON, Martha A. .. (VA) 607
Automated systems plng & implementation — PATTERSON, Robert H. . (OK) 948
Automated systems training & development — BOWRIN-MARSH, Donna M. .... (CA) 122
— LOCASCIO, Aline M. ... (NY) 735
Automated technical processing — TAYYEB, Rashid ...... (NS) 1229
Automated techniques — FISHBEIN, Meyer H. ..... (MD) 380
Automated text analyses — VON KEITZ, Wolfgang .. (WGR) 288
Automated union catalogs & indexes — JAGOE, Katherine P. ... (TX) 591
Automated visual resources — LUSKEY, Judith .... (DC) 749
Automatic document indexing — SPANGLER, Bruce ..... (CO) 1171
Automatic identification systems — PAVELY, Richard W. ... (NJ) 950

AUTOMATION (Cont'd)

Automatic indexing   GENUARDI, Michael T. . . (MD) 427
  DILLON, Martin . . . . (OH) 303
  VON KEITZ, Wolfgang . . (WGR)288
Automatic indexing & classification   RAGHAVAN, Vijay V. . . . (LA) 1003
Automatic indexing system   VLEDUTS-STOKOLOV,
    Natalia . . . . (PA) 1286
Automatic indexing, system design   VLADUTZ, George E. . . . (PA) 1286
Automatic text processing   SALTON, Gerard . . . . . . (NY) 1077
Automating law firm libraries   DILORETO, Ann M. . . . . (CA) 303
Automating libraries   SWITZER, Catherine M. . . (WI) 1216
Automating library catalog   AROKSAAR, Richard D. . . (WA) 34
Automating library systems   YALCINTAS, Rana . . . . . (TN) 1376
Automating school libraries   KRENTZ, Roger F. . . . . . (WI) 677
Automating special collections   WEAVER, Thomas M. . . (DC) 1312
Automation   LANCASTER III, Thomas
    A. . . . . (AL) 692
  SOUTER, Thomas A. . . . (AL) 1169
  MILLER, Larry A. . . . . . . (AZ) 839
  ARNOLD, Donna W. . . . (CA) 33
  BILYEU, David D. . . . . . . (CA) 97
  BOUCHE, Nicole L. . . . . (CA) 118
  BOWLES, Garrett H. . . . (CA) 121
  CARLSON, Alan C. . . . . (CA) 182
  CARPIO, Virginia A. . . . . (CA) 185
  CONNELL, William S. . . . (CA) 237
  DICKENS, Jan . . . . (CA) 300
  ENYINGI, Peter . . . . . . (CA) 351
  GILBERT, Carol L. . . . . . (CA) 433
  GREGORY, Timothy P. . . (CA) 466
  HADLEY, Peter H. . . . . . (CA) 482
  HERON, Susan J. . . . . . (CA) 532
  LAMONTAGNE, Therese (CA) 691
  LIU, Susanna J. . . . . . . (CA) 734
  MCELROY, Neil J. . . . . . (CA) 804
  MEGLIO, Delores D. . . . . (CA) 821
  MOKRZYCKI, Karen M. . (CA) 852
  REEDER, Norman L. . . . (CA) 1015
  REICH, Victoria A. . . . . . (CA) 1018
  RYAN, Frederick W. . . . . (CA) 1071
  SCHOLAND, Julia E. . . . (CA) 1098
  SERTIC, Kenneth J. . . . . (CA) 1116
  SILBERSTEIN, Stephen M. (CA) 1137
  SMITH, Marvin E. . . . . . (CA) 1158
  THOMAS, Mary C. . . . . (CA) 1237
  WERNER, Gloria . . . . . (CA) 1324
  EIDSON, Alreeta . . . . . (CO) 340
  SHELDON, L S. . . . . . . (CO) 1126
  FERRO, Frank J. . . . . . (CT) 374
  FLANAGAN, Leo N. . . . (CT) 383
  HILL, John R. . . . . (CT) 540
  LA FOGG, Mary C. . . . . (CT) 688
  LUSHINGTON, Nolan . . . (CT) 749
  STONE, Dennis J. . . . . . (CT) 1197
  SWIFT, Janet B. . . . . . . (CT) 1216
  YOUNG, Marianne F. . . . (CT) 1382
  AVERA, Victoria E. . . . . (DC) 41
  CIMERMANIS, Ilze V. . . . (DC) 214
  HOA, Quynh N. . . . . . . (DC) 545
  KECK, Bruce L. . . . . . . (DC) 633
  OAKLEY, Robert L. . . . . (DC) 913
  RATHER, Lucia J. . . . . . (DC) 1009
  REID, Judith P. . . . . . . (DC) 1018
  SULLIVAN, Robert C. . . . (DC) 1208
  ULRICH, Sue . . . . (DE) 1268
  BRIERTY, Carol A. . . . . . (FL) 135
  HOGUE, Margaret A. . . . (FL) 549
  LABRAKE, Orlyn B. . . . . (FL) 686
  MARTIN, James R. . . . . (FL) 776
  COHRS, Joyce S. . . . . . (GA) 229
  HOWARD, Mary R. . . . . (GA) 564
  JOHNSON, Jane G. . . . . (GA) 605
  LONG, Linda E. . . . . . . (GA) 739
  MCCLELLAND, Katherine
    L. . . . . (GA) 796
  ROBISON, Carolyn L. . . . (GA) 1045
  HASSLER, William B. . . . (HI) 511
  SNIDER, Jacqueline I. . . (IA) 1163
  BECKER, Jacquelyn B. . . (IL) 72
  BRUEMMER, Alice . . . . . (IL) 149

AUTOMATION (Cont'd)

Automation   CLELAND, Camille S. . . . (IL) 220
  CONWAY, Colleen M. . . . (IL) 239
  HUFFMAN, Carol P. . . . . (IL) 571
  KISTNER, Glen A. . . . . . (IL) 657
  KNUDTSON, Gail L. . . . . (IL) 666
  MCCARTNEY, Elizabeth J. (IL) 794
  OLSON, Rue E. . . . . . . (IL) 923
  RAST, Elaine K. . . . . . . (IL) 1009
  SHERRY, Diane H. . . . . . (IL) 1129
  STRAWN, Gary L. . . . . . (IL) 1201
  VONDRUSKA, Eloise M. . (IL) 1288
  MILLER, Robert C. . . . . . (IN) 841
  STUSSY, Susan A. . . . . (IN) 1205
  GRASS, Charlene G. . . . (KS) 458
  RATZLAFF, Marcella J. . . (KS) 1010
  WARREN, G G. . . . . . . (KS) 1306
  FOWLER, James W. . . . . (KY) 393
  NILES, Judith F. . . . . . . (KY) 904
  HALES, Margaret L. . . . . (MA) 486
  HAPIJ, Maria S. . . . . . . (MA) 499
  HERMAN, Douglas C. . . . (MA) 531
  HOLMBERG, Olga S. . . . (MA) 553
  INGERSOLL, Diane S. . . . (MA) 582
  MOULTON, Lynda W. . . (MA) 873
  SNYDER, David A. . . . . (MA) 1164
  TUCHMAN, Helene L. . . (MA) 1261
  BROADY, Jessie . . . . . . (MD) 138
  CHU, Ellen M. . . . . (MD) 212
  MCKEAN, Joan M. . . . . (MD) 810
  SUTTON, Sharan D. . . . . (MD) 1212
  WALLINGFORD, Karen T. (MD) 1298
  DOUBLESTEIN, Judith A. (MI) 313
  DRABENSTOTT, Jon D. . (MI) 317
  FLAHERTY, Kevin C. . . . (MI) 383
  MA, Helen Y. . . . . (MI) 753
  RAWLINSON, Pamela . . (MI) 1011
  SMITH, Nancy J. . . . . . . (MI) 1158
  SPYERS-DURAN, Peter . (MI) 1177
  STEPHENS, Karen L. . . . (MI) 1188
  WAGAR, Joanna M. . . . . (MI) 1291
  DAVIS, Emmett A. . . . . . (MN) 279
  SCHROEDER, Janet K. . (MN) 1100
  BEAGLE, Donald R. . . . . (NC) 68
  HORTON, James T. . . . . (NC) 561
  POWELL, Lucy A. . . . . . (NC) 988
  BIALAC, Verda H. . . . . . (NE) 93
  COOK, Anita I. . . . . (NE) 239
  SCHULZ, Stanley D. . . . . (NE) 1102
  WISE, Sally H. . . . . (NE) 1357
  BRYAN, Arthur L. . . . . . . (NH) 151
  BITTER, Jane L. . . . . . . (NJ) 100
  BOWERS, Alyce J. . . . . (NJ) 120
  FERRIBY, Peter G. . . . . . (NJ) 373
  MANTHEY, Carolyn M. . . (NJ) 767
  PRUETT, Nancy J. . . . . . (NM) 996
  FASANA, Paul J. . . . . . . (NY) 366
  GIBBARD, Judith R. . . . . (NY) 431
  GREENBERG, Linda . . . . (NY) 463
  JANIAK, Jane M. . . . . . . (NY) 593
  KINYATTI, Njoki W. . . . . (NY) 653
  LAPIER, Cynthia B. . . . . (NY) 697
  MATZEK, Richard A. . . . . (NY) 786
  MORRIS, Leslie R. . . . . . (NY) 867
  NAYLOR, Richard J. . . . . (NY) 890
  ORGREN, Sally C. . . . . . (NY) 925
  RICHARDSON, John A. . . (NY) 1029
  RYAN, Donald L. . . . . . . (NY) 1070
  SHAPIRO, June R. . . . . . (NY) 1121
  SHERWOOD, Nancy . . . (NY) 1129
  SMITH, Frederick E. . . . . (NY) 1155
  SMITH, Mark J. . . . . (NY) 1158
  VAN ZANTEN, Frank V. . (NY) 1278
  BRIELL, Robert D. . . . . . (OH) 135
  CHESKI, Richard M. . . . . (OH) 207
  GREEN, Gary A. . . . . . . (OH) 461
  KNOBLAUCH, Carol J. . . (OH) 665
  MCCOY, Betty J. . . . . . . (OH) 799
  O'CONNOR, Deborah F. . (OH) 916

AUTOMATION (Cont'd)

Automation

RADER, Hannelore B.	(OH)	1002
SCOLES, Clyde S.	(OH)	1106
JONES, Beverly A.	(OK)	611
RYLANDER, Carolyn S.	(OK)	1072
AMSBERRY, Dan F.	(OR)	20
BROOKS, Harry F.	(OR)	140
BROWNE, Joseph P.	(OR)	148
DOAK, Wesley A.	(OR)	306
ELLSON, Linda R.	(OR)	345
WEBB, John	(OR)	1313
BARREAU, Deborah K.	(PA)	58
KAMPER, Albert F.	(PA)	624
RICH, Denise A.	(PA)	1027
RYAN, Patricia M.	(PA)	1071
SCHWIND, Penelope	(PA)	1106
SHAPERA, Gladys S.	(PA)	1121
WHITTAKER, Edward L.	(PA)	1334
WILSON, Martin P.	(PA)	1352
COHEN, Barbara S.	(RI)	228
MEYER, Richard W.	(SC)	830
CRANMER, Donna C.	(SD)	255
DERTIEN, James L.	(SD)	294
EDELEN, Joseph R.	(SD)	335
CARLIN, Don	(TN)	182
DYER, Barbara M.	(TN)	330
JACKSON, Joseph A.	(TN)	587
JONES, Roger G.	(TN)	615
MENDINA, Guy T.	(TN)	824
SLOAN, Lynette S.	(TN)	1149
BAILEY, Alvin R.	(TX)	46
BALDWIN, Joe M.	(TX)	51
BANDELIN, Janis M.	(TX)	53
CAGE, Alvin C.	(TX)	170
CANALES, Herbert G.	(TX)	178
DIXON, Donna S.	(TX)	306
FREY, Emil F.	(TX)	402
INKS, Cordelia R.	(TX)	583
MCCANN, Debra W.	(TX)	794
RICKLEFS, Dale L.	(TX)	1032
TAYLOR, Nancy L.	(TX)	1228
TISSING, Robert W.	(TX)	1247
WALTON, Robert A.	(TX)	1301
ZABEL, Patricia L.	(TX)	1385
BLAKE, Mary K.	(VA)	103
GRIFFLER, Carl W.	(VA)	469
HUGHES, J M.	(VA)	571
LISZEWSKI, Edward H.	(VA)	733
MACLEOD, James M.	(VA)	757
NIGAM, Alok C.	(VA)	904
SELF, James R.	(VA)	1113
UMBERGER, Stan	(VA)	1268
WARD, Robert C.	(VT)	1304
ERICKSON, Randall D.	(WA)	352
HAGAN, Dalia L.	(WA)	482
MORGAN, Erma J.	(WA)	864
ZALESKI, Mary A.	(WA)	1385
HSIEH-YEE, Ingrid P.	(WI)	567
JAMBREK, William L.	(WI)	592
MORITZ, William D.	(WI)	865
PATANE, John R.	(WI)	946
BROWN, Thomas M.	(WV)	148
RULE, Judy K.	(WV)	1067
FELL, Anthony M.	(AB)	370
GEE, Sharon	(AB)	425
RICHARDS, Vincent P.	(AB)	1029
CARVALHO, Sarah V.	(ON)	191
CURTIS, Alison J.	(ON)	267
KRYGSMAN, Nancy T.	(ON)	681
DARBON, Ginette	(PQ)	274
DUVAL, Marc	(PQ)	329
TAMEEM, Jamal A.	(SDA)	1221

Automation administration	RAWLEY, Wayne	(IA)	1010
	BULAONG, Grace F.	(ON)	156
Automation & circulation	PARKHURST, Kathleen A.	(NY)	942
Automation & computer applications	POWELL, Mary E.	(TX)	988
Automation & computer services	FRADKIN, Bernard	(IL)	395
Automation & database development	DUNN, Jamie N.	(MN)	326
Automation & database searching	JACKA, David C.	(NE)	586

AUTOMATION (Cont'd)

Automation & information systems	SAHLI, Nancy A.	(DC)	1075
Automation & library systems	EZQUERRA, Isabel	(FL)	360
	FUN, Winnie W.	(VA)	409
Automation & networking	SIMPSON, Donald B.	(IL)	1141
	PATRICK, Ruth J.	(MT)	947
	BETCHER, Melissa A.	(OH)	92
Automation & new technologies	ROSSMAN, Muriel J.	(MN)	1059
Automation & new technology	ACCARDI, Joseph J.	(WI)	3
Automation & organizing libraries	HARRIS, Marie	(DC)	505
Automation & systems for libraries	WELCH, Donald A.	(TX)	1321
Automation & technical services	CLEVENGER, Judy B.	(AR)	221
Automation & work analysis	WEAVER-MEYERS, Pat L.	(OK)	1313
Automation applications	LOKEN, Sarah F.	(WA)	738
Automation, archival	SMITH, Michael O.	(MI)	1158
Automation book catalog, circulation	THOMAN, Nancy L.	(DE)	1236
Automation, book collection devlpmnt	SIMON, Bradley A.	(OK)	1140
Automation cataloging	CHEN, Helen M.	(TN)	205
Automation, computerization	GARA, Otto G.	(NY)	416
Automation consultation	QUEYROUZE, Mary E.	(TX)	999
Automation consulting	BUSCH, Barbara	(CA)	165
	EPSTEIN, Susan B.	(CA)	351
	SMITH, Richard J.	(LA)	1160
	ERLAND, Virginia K.	(NY)	353
	JUERGENS, Bonnie	(TX)	619
	RUDDY, Mary K.	(TX)	1065
	STANDIFER, Hugh A.	(TX)	1179
Automation conversion	BAKER, Narcissa L.	(OH)	49
Automation coordinating	OLSON, Anton J.	(IL)	922
Automation coordination	MISNER, Joyce V.	(MI)	847
	HODGES, Pauline R.	(OH)	546
Automation, databases, memorandum	FRY, Mary A.	(GA)	406
Automation development	MARSHALL, Kathryn E.	(IL)	774
Automation education	WILBURN, Marion T.	(ON)	1338
Automation implementation	KREYCHE, Michael R.	(OH)	678
Automation implementation & planning	WALSH, Joanna M.	(MA)	1299
Automation in archives	BOHANAN, Robert D.	(DC)	111
	MORISON, William J.	(KY)	865
	STOUT, Leon J.	(PA)	1198
Automation in elementary libraries	PASSARELLO, Nancy H.	(FL)	946
Automation in libraries	DIENER, Ronald E.	(OH)	302
	BILLINSKY, Christyn G.	(SC)	96
	DOUGLAS, Daphne R.	(JAM)	314
Automation in library services	WONG, Ming K.	(DC)	1363
Automation in multitype cooperatives	DAW, May B.	(CT)	282
Automation in school libraries	HAND, M D.	(TX)	494
Automation, microcomputers	THIBAULT, Jean	(ON)	1235
Automation networks	BROWN, Louise R.	(MA)	145
Automation of bibliographic control	BENGTSON, Betty G.	(TN)	80
Automation of bibliographic databases	BERNARD, Patrick S.	(DC)	88
Automation of bibliographies	MCNELLIS, Claudia H.	(DC)	817
Automation of business applications	BROWN, Maxine M.	(DC)	146
Automation of collection management	EVANS, Linda J.	(IL)	357
Automation of libraries	CARD, Sandra E.	(CA)	180
	MALINCONICO, S M.	(NY)	763
Automation of library functions	SARGENT, Phyllis M.	(OR)	1083
Automation of library systems	LAMANN, Amber N.	(NY)	689
Automation of medium & small libraries	BARRUS, Phyl	(TX)	60
Automation of newspaper archives	ENNS, Carol F.	(NB)	350
Automation of public services	ANDERSON, Kari D.	(VA)	24
Automation of records centers	SMITH, David F.	(NY)	1154
Automation of serials & acquisitions	WAN, William W.	(TX)	1302
Automation of slide collections	HENDERSON, Joyce C.	(AZ)	526
Automation of small libraries	DICENSO, Jacquelyn C.	(VT)	300
Automation of special collections	SMITH, David F.	(NY)	1154
	LLOYD, James B.	(TN)	735
Automation of technical services	MCDONALD, Michael L.	(DC)	803
	KLINK, Carol A.	(IL)	662
Automation, online retrieval services	BEACHELL, Doria M.	(DC)	68
Automation online systems	STEPHENS, Jerry W.	(AL)	1188
Automation planning	STANGL, Peter	(CA)	1221
	SNELSON, Pamela	(NJ)	1163
	SILVERMAN, Scott H.	(PA)	1138
	LANG, Elizabeth A.	(SD)	695
	WOOSTER, Linda I.	(WA)	1368
Automation planning, coordinating	DEMYANOVICH, Peter	(NJ)	291
Automation plng, multitype networking	DIENER, Margaret M.	(CA)	302
Automation procedure writing	PALMER, Marguerite C.	(WV)	936

AUTOMATION (Cont'd)

Automation project management	MILLSAP, Gina J.	(MO)	844
Automation projects	FIELD, Judith J.	(MI)	375
Automation records programs	BUTLER, Tyrone G.	(NY)	167
Automation selection & implementation	DONALDSON, Timothy P.	(OH)	311
Automation software	ERLAND, Virginia K.	(NY)	353
Automation, system implementation	NICHOLSON, Dianne L.	(BC)	902
Automation systems	CHU, Felix T.	(IL)	212
	EVANS, James M.	(LA)	357
Automation, systems analysis	STAMBOULIEH, Nora	(PQ)	1179
Automation systems & services	RUBENS, Charlotte C.	(CA)	1064
Automation, systems operations	SIMPSON, W S.	(WI)	1142
Bibliographic automated systems	BROWN, Rowland C.	(OH)	147
Bibliographic instruction automated syst	PALLARDY, Judy S.	(MO)	935
Cataloging & automated systems	SEXTON, Ebba J.	(KY)	1118
Cataloging, automation	LAKSHMAN, Malathi K.	(MD)	689
Cataloging including automated authority	BULAONG, Grace F.	(ON)	156
Cataloging on automated systems	WONG, Ming K.	(DC)	1363
Circulation, automation	GYESZLY, Suzanne D.	(TX)	479
Circulation system automation	NOBLE, Barbara N.	(MO)	906
CLSI automated circulation system	CALLANAN, Ellen M.	(NJ)	173
Collection development & automation	POWER, Colleen J.	(CA)	989
Collection development automation	MIDDLETON, Robert K.	(TX)	833
Comparative automated retrieval systems	O'CONNOR, Sandra L.	(NC)	916
Computer applications & automation	SHEPARD, Clayton A.	(IN)	1126
Computers & automation	JONES, Clifton H.	(MI)	612
	MCGRIFF, Ronald I.	(MN)	808
Computers automation	RICHMOND, Diane A.	(IL)	1030
Consulting & automation	HOGAN, Patricia M.	(IL)	549
Coordination of automated systems	THOMPSON, John W.	(IL)	1240
Creating automated name authorities	DAWE, Heather L.	(ON)	282
Database & automation applications	SAUTER, Sylvia E.	(WA)	1085
Database & automation management	STAINBROOK, Lynn M.	(WI)	1178
Database management, library automation	MAIN, Linda Y.	(CA)	761
Documents librarianship, automation	JAMISON, Carolyn C.	(PA)	593
East Asian library automation	WEI, Karen T.	(IL)	1316
Elementary school library automation	MULLER, Madeline A.	(OH)	877
Factory automation	LARSON, Anna M.	(ON)	699
Factory automation directory	LEE, Douglas E.	(NY)	709
French library automation	BAIRD, Lynn N.	(ID)	47
Hospital library automation	LECOMPTE, Louis L.	(PQ)	708
IBM automation system	ROBERSON, Janis L.	(TX)	1039
Impacts of library automation	CORY, Kenneth A.	(MI)	248
Implementation of automated systems	HAAK, John R.	(HI)	480
	SMITH, Robert S.	(OH)	1160
Implementing automated authority control	FISHER, Carl D.	(VA)	380
Industrial automation databases	FOWELLS, Fumi T.	(MI)	393
In-house automation	SMITH, Valerie M.	(OH)	1161
In-house systems automation	MOUNTFORD, Eve	(CT)	873
In-process control automation	WARZALA, Martin L.	(CT)	1307
Integrated & automated library systems	WORMINGTON, Peggie	(CA)	1369
Integrated automated library systems	LASETER, Shirley B.	(AL)	700
	SIDMAN, George C.	(CA)	1135
	MOORE, Barbara N.	(MN)	858
Integrated library automation	KIMZEY, Ann C.	(TX)	649
Integrated library automation systems	SHURMAN, Richard L.	(IL)	1134
Integrated library system automation	BREEDLOVE, Elizabeth A.	(NJ)	131
Integrated systems automation	BRIDGE, Frank R.	(TX)	135
Laboratory automation	KOSMAN, Joyce E.	(IL)	672
Law firm library automation	PETERSON, Christine E.	(WI)	963
Law library automation	FU, Paul S.	(OH)	407
Law office automation	GRIFFITH, Cary J.	(MN)	469
Law office, library automation	LEITER, Richard A.	(NE)	714
Library administration & automation	FUNG, Margaret C.	(MA)	409
Library & office automation	MOORE, Penelope F.	(VA)	861
Library automated systems	ALLEN, Linda G.	(FL)	15
	REDFEARN, Linda E.	(MA)	1014
	MURRAY, Diane E.	(MI)	881
	SHEVIAK, Jean K.	(NY)	1129
	NEAL, James G.	(PA)	890
	RAMBLER, Linda K.	(PA)	1005
	LINDBERG, Sandra	(VT)	728

AUTOMATION (Cont'd)

Library automation	WIGET, Laurence A.	(AK)	1337
	DAMICO, James A.	(AL)	271
	GREGORY, Vicki L.	(AL)	466
	KASKE, Neal K.	(AL)	628
	BALDWIN, Charlene M.	(AZ)	51
	BIERMAN, Kenneth J.	(AZ)	95
	BUXTON, David T.	(AZ)	168
	MOSLEY, Shelley E.	(AZ)	872
	POTTER, William G.	(AZ)	987
	ARIEL, Joan	(CA)	31
	BERGER, Michael G.	(CA)	85
	BISOM, Diane B.	(CA)	99
	BURTON, Hilary D.	(CA)	164
	CHAO, Yuan T.	(CA)	201
	CHWEH, Steven S.	(CA)	214
	CLIFFORD, Susan G.	(CA)	222
	CLINE, Cheryl L.	(CA)	222
	CRAWFORD, Walt	(CA)	257
	CREW-NOBLE, Sara M.	(CA)	258
	CUNNINGHAM, Jay L.	(CA)	265
	DAVIS, Douglas A.	(CA)	278
	DEMENT, Alice R.	(CA)	291
	GESCHKE, Nancy A.	(CA)	430
	GIFFORD, Becky J.	(CA)	433
	HALL, Anthony	(CA)	487
	HOLLAND, Mary	(CA)	551
	JOHNSON, Deanna L.	(CA)	603
	JOHNSON, Diane D.	(CA)	603
	JURIST, Susan	(CA)	620
	KAYE, Karen	(CA)	632
	KENSINGER, Colleen O.	(CA)	642
	LANDGRAF, Mary N.	(CA)	692
	LARSON, Ray R.	(CA)	699
	LIGHTBOWN, Parke P.	(CA)	726
	MORRIS, Jacquelyn M.	(CA)	866
	NICHOLS, Elizabeth D.	(CA)	901
	NOE, Christopher J.	(CA)	906
	PIERCE, Patricia J.	(CA)	971
	PRESTON, Cecilia M.	(CA)	991
	PRICE, Bennett J.	(CA)	992
	SALMON, Stephen R.	(CA)	1077
	SANDELL, Judy L.	(CA)	1079
	SAVAGE, Gretchen S.	(CA)	1085
	SESSIONS, Judith A.	(CA)	1117
	SKAPURA, Robert J.	(CA)	1145
	STOVEL, Madeleine D.	(CA)	1199
	TENNANT, Roy	(CA)	1231
	THOMPSON, James C.	(CA)	1240
	WALTHER, Richard E.	(CA)	1301
	WILLIAMS, Mary S.	(CA)	1345
	BURKE, Marianne D.	(CO)	160
	CAMPBELL, John D.	(CO)	176
	FULMER, Russell F.	(CO)	409
	GARZA, Rosario	(CO)	421
	HENSINGER, James S.	(CO)	529
	JANES, Nina	(CO)	593
	KENNEY, Brigitte L.	(CO)	641
	KOHL, David F.	(CO)	668
	NICKEL, Edgar B.	(CO)	902
	PHINNEY, Hartley K.	(CO)	969
	PRESTON, Lawrence N.	(CO)	991
	RICHMOND, Rick	(CO)	1030
	SMITH, Randolph R.	(CO)	1159
	AKEROYD, Richard G.	(CT)	9
	BALAY, Robert E.	(CT)	50
	BANKS, Mary E.	(CT)	54
	CAMPO, Lynn D.	(CT)	177
	JACOB, William	(CT)	589
	PIKUL, Diane M.	(CT)	973
	POUNDSTONE, Sally H.	(CT)	987
	SMITH, Lydia K.	(CT)	1157
	SORENSEN, Pamela	(CT)	1168
	STRAKA, Kathy M.	(CT)	1199
	SUPRYNOWICZ, Mary M.	(CT)	1210
	TRAINER, Karin A.	(CT)	1253
	TRIOLO, Victor A.	(CT)	1257
	AGENBROAD, James E.	(DC)	7
	BOSS, Richard W.	(DC)	117
	BRIMSEK, Tobi A.	(DC)	136

AUTOMATION (Cont'd)
Library automation

BUCK, Dayna E. . . . . (DC) 153
CHANG, Frances M. . . . . (DC) 200
CORTEZ, Edwin M. . . . . (DC) 248
DENHAM, Maryanne H. . . (DC) 292
DRUMMOND, Louis E. . . (DC) 321
GUERRIERO, Donald A. . . (DC) 476
LOO, Shirley . . . . (DC) 740
MCNELLIS, Claudia H. . . (DC) 817
PACIFICI, Sabrina I. . . . . (DC) 933
PRICE, Mary S. . . . . . . (DC) 992
REYNOLDS, Dennis J. . . (DC) 1025
SARANGAPANI, Chetluru (DC) 1082
SETTLER, Leo H. . . . . . (DC) 1117
SHEN, I Y. . . . . (DC) 1126
STARNER, James A. . . . (DC) 1182
TURTELL, Neal T. . . . . . (DC) 1265
VINCENT, Susan R. . . . . (DC) 1284
COREY, James F. . . . . . (FL) 246
DEWAR, Jo E. . . . . (FL) 298
DOERRER, David H. . . . (FL) 308
KEMPER, Marlyn J. . . . . (FL) 639
KETCHERSID, Arthur L. . (FL) 645
LOGAN, Elisabeth L. . . . (FL) 737
METCALF, Davinci C. . . (FL) 828
PRITCHARD, Teresa N. . (FL) 994
STONE, Alva T. . . . . . . (FL) 1196
TABOR, Curtis H. . . . . . (FL) 1219
WALTON, Terence M. . . (FL) 1302
AMMERMAN, Jackie W. . (GA) 20
BAKER, Gordon N. . . . . (GA) 48
LUKAS, Vicki A. . . . . . . (GA) 747
MOELLER, Edward R. . . (GA) 851
WALKER, Alice O. . . . . (GA) 1295
WILSON, Lesley P. . . . . (GA) 1351
LUNDEEN, Gerald W. . . . (HI) 748
SAKAI, Diane H. . . . . . . (HI) 1076
BUDREW, John . . . . (IA) 155
RICE, James G. . . . . . . (IA) 1027
ROBINSON, Caitlin M. . . (IA) 1043
SCHMIDT, Sandra L. . . . (IA) 1096
TRUCK, Lorna R. . . . . . (IA) 1259
FORCE, Ronald W. . . . . (ID) 389
FUNABIKI, Ruth P. . . . . . (ID) 409
WATSON, Peter G. . . . . (ID) 1310
BROWN, Doris R. . . . . . (IL) 143
BUCKLEY, Ja A. . . . . . . (IL) 154
CHANG, Roy T. . . . . . . (IL) 201
DESSOUKY, Ibtesam . . . (IL) 296
ELDER, Nancy J. . . . . . (IL) 342
ELL, Elizabeth L. . . . . . (IL) 343
EMBAR, Indrani M. . . . . (IL) 347
GORDON, Lewis A. . . . . (IL) 451
HARRIS, Thomas J. . . . . (IL) 506
HORNY, Karen L. . . . . . (IL) 560
KAUFFMAN, S B. . . . . . (IL) 631
LARISON, Brenda . . . . . (IL) 697
LI, Grace Y. . . . . (IL) 724
LONGMAN, Judith J. . . . (IL) 740
MARSHALL, Maggie L. . (IL) 774
MCCLINTOCK, Patrick J. (IL) 797
MCKENZIE, Duncan J. . . (IL) 811
MICKELBERRY, Mark B. (IL) 833
ONGLEY, David C. . . . . (IL) 924
RAO, Paladugu V. . . . . (IL) 1008
SCHULTHEISS, Louis A. (IL) 1101
SHACKLETON, Suzanne
    M. . . . . (IL) 1118
SHURMAN, Richard L. . . (IL) 1134
SMITH, Linda C. . . . . . . (IL) 1157
SPENCER, Joan M. . . . . (IL) 1173
SWORSKY, Felicia G. . . (IL) 1217
TOROK, Andrew G. . . . . (IL) 1251
WAITE, Ellen J. . . . . . . (IL) 1293
BAUMGARTNER, Kurt O. (IN) 66
KRULL, Jeffrey R. . . . . . (IN) 680
PIEPENBURG, Scott R. . (IN) 971
ROBSON, John M. . . . . (IN) 1045
SACZAWA, Rosemary . . (IN) 1073

AUTOMATION (Cont'd)
Library automation

SCHOONOVER, Phyllis J. (IN) 1098
SHIH, Philip C. . . . . (IN) 1130
STANLEY, Luana K. . . . . (IN) 1180
WALLACE, Danny P. . . . (IN) 1297
BRAND, Alice A. . . . . . . (KS) 127
CARROLL, James K. . . . (KS) 187
ENSIGN, David J. . . . . . (KS) 350
GATTIN, Leroy M. . . . . . (KS) 422
BING, Dorothy A. . . . . . (KY) 97
BOYARSKI, Jennie S. . . (KY) 122
FAUPEL, David W. . . . . (KY) 366
SCHULTZ, Lois E. . . . . . (KY) 1102
ARNY, Philip H. . . . . . . (LA) 34
KLEINER, Janellyn P. . . (LA) 660
BEGG, Karin E. . . . . . . (MA) 74
BELASTOCK, Tjalda N. . (MA) 76
BRIAND, Margaret M. . . (MA) 134
CHAMBERLAIN, Ruth B. (MA) 197
DAMICO, Nancy B. . . . . (MA) 272
DONOVAN, Paul . . . . . . (MA) 312
DUGAN, Robert E. . . . . (MA) 324
EDWARDS, Betty . . . . . (MA) 337
GLASSMAN, Penny L. . . (MA) 440
HATVANY, Bela R. . . . . (MA) 512
HAYES, Alison M. . . . . . (MA) 515
HONESS, Mary E. . . . . . (MA) 555
MAXANT, Vicary . . . . . . (MA) 787
MCKIRDY, Pamela R. . . (MA) 812
MOSKOWITZ, Michael A. (MA) 871
PAYNE, Douglass B. . . . (MA) 951
POSTLETHWAITE, Bonnie
    S. . . . . (MA) 986
SANTOSUOSSO, Joseph
    P. . . . . (MA) 1082
SCHWARTZ, Frederick E. (MA) 1104
ANDRE, Pamela Q. . . . . (MD) 26
BERGER, Patricia W. . . (MD) 86
BLUTE, Mary R. . . . . . . (MD) 107
BROWN, Carolyn P. . . . (MD) 142
CHEN, John H. . . . . (MD) 205
ELDER, Richard H. . . . . (MD) 342
HENDERSON, Susanne . (MD) 527
JOHNSON, Bruce C. . . . (MD) 602
KALTENBORN, Helen P. (MD) 623
MARTIN, Susan K. . . . . (MD) 778
MEYER, Alan H. . . . . . . (MD) 829
SCHWARTZ, Betsy J. . . (MD) 1104
SHOCKLEY, Cynthia W. . (MD) 1132
WILSEY, Charlotte A. . . (MD) 1349
WILT, Larry J. . . . . (MD) 1353
BEISER, Karl A. . . . . . . (ME) 75
NICHOLSON, Carol C. . . (ME) 902
WISMER, Donald . . . . . . (ME) 1357
DAVID, Indra M. . . . . . . (MI) 276
ENGELKE, Hans . . . . . . (MI) 349
FITZPATRICK, Nancy C. (MI) 383
FRY, James W. . . . . (MI) 406
HEMPHILL, Frank A. . . . (MI) 525
LANSDALE, Metta T. . . (MI) 696
LUKASIEWICZ, Barbara . (MI) 747
MARTIN, Patricia W. . . . (MI) 777
MORROW, Blaine V. . . . (MI) 869
OSTROM, Kriss T. . . . . . (MI) 929
PALMER, Catherine S. . . (MI) 936
PRETZER, Dale H. . . . . (MI) 992
SHUMAN, Bruce A. . . . . (MI) 1134
STANTON, Beth L. . . . . (MI) 1181
AXDAL, Joan L. . . . . . . (MN) 42
CARRISON, Dale K. . . . . (MN) 187
EPSTEIN, Rheda . . . . . . (MN) 351
FRYMIRE, Jane K. . . . . (MN) 407
KING, Jack B. . . . . (MN) 651
MAGNUSON, Norris A. . (MN) 759
METZ, T J. . . . . (MN) 828
RASMUSSEN, Mary L. . . (MN) 1009
VETH, Terry R. . . . . (MN) 1283
YOUNGHOLM, Philip . . . (MN) 1383
FUCHS, Curt R. . . . . . . (MO) 408

AUTOMATION (Cont'd)
Library automation

HANKS, Nancy C. . . . . . (MO) 496
HOHENSTEIN, Margaret L. (MO) 549
KEMP, Charles H. . . . . . (MO) 639
MEADOR, John M. . . . . . (MO) 819
MURPHY, Kathryn L. . . . (MO) 880
ONSAGER, Lawrence W. (MO) 924
PALLARDY, Judy S. . . . (MO) 935
PARKER, Ralph H. . . . . . (MO) 942
PLUTCHAK, T S. . . . . . (MO) 979
RAITHEL, Frederick J. . . (MO) 1004
WILKINSON, William A. . . (MO) 1340
ANDERSON, Sherry . . . . (NC)   25
BAILEY, Charles W. . . . . (NC)   46
BURGIN, Robert E. . . . . (NC) 159
CHUNG, Helen S. . . . . . (NC) 213
GREGORY, Roderick F. . (NC) 466
JARRELL, James R. . . . . (NC) 594
LOSEE, Robert M. . . . . . (NC) 742
MOORE, Patricia R. . . . . (NC) 860
NYE, Julie B. . . . . (NC) 912
PARKER, Lanny C. . . . . (NC) 942
PRITCHARD, John A. . . . (NC) 994
SPEER, Susan C. . . . . . (NC) 1172
SPELLER, Benjamin F. . . (NC) 1172
STIGLEMAN, Sue E. . . . (NC) 1194
STRAHAN, Michael F. . . (ND) 1199
FELTON, John D. . . . . . (NE) 370
BOGIS, Nana E. . . . . . . (NJ) 110
CANOSE, Joseph A. . . . (NJ) 179
CHU, Wendy N. . . . . . . (NJ) 213
CHUNG, Hai C. . . . . . . (NJ) 213
COHN, John M. . . . . . . (NJ) 229
EBELING, Elinor H. . . . . (NJ) 334
FALK, Howard . . . . (NJ) 362
KELSEY, Ann L. . . . . . . (NJ) 639
KING, Donald R. . . . . . . (NJ) 650
PAVELY, Richard W. . . . (NJ) 950
PLAZA, Joyce S. . . . . . (NJ) 978
ROUX, Yvonne R. . . . . . (NJ) 1062
SHAFER, Leona M. . . . . (NJ) 1119
SILVA, Nelly H. . . . . . . (NJ) 1138
STEPHEN, Ross G. . . . . (NJ) 1187
WANG, Hsi H. . . . . (NJ) 1303
WOLFORD, Larry E. . . . . (NJ) 1361
BANICKI, Cynthia A. . . . (NM)   54
HARRISON, Susan E. . . (NV) 507
ORTIZ, Cynthia . . . . (NV) 927
CASTRO, Julio E. . . . . . (NY) 194
CHIANG, Nancy . . . . . . (NY) 207
CURRAN, George L. . . . (NY) 266
CYPSER, Rudy J. . . . . . (NY) 268
FIEGAS, Barbara E. . . . . (NY) 375
FORCE, Stephen . . . . . . (NY) 389
GARLAND, Kathleen . . . (NY) 419
GRECO, Gloria T. . . . . . (NY) 461
GRUTCHFIELD, Walter . (NY) 475
LAWRENCE, Thomas A. (NY) 705
LEE, Chui C. . . . . (NY) 709
LEE, Sang C. . . . . (NY) 711
MANDEL, Carol A. . . . . (NY) 764
MARKER, Rhonda J. . . . (NY) 771
MATTA, Seoud M. . . . . . (NY) 785
MILLER, Betty . . . . (NY) 836
MOLHOLT, Pat . . . . (NY) 852
NICHOLS, Gerald D. . . . (NY) 901
NOLTE, James S. . . . . . (NY) 908
PARRIS, Angela P. . . . . (NY) 944
PAULSON, Peter J. . . . . (NY) 950
PERRY, Rodney B. . . . . . (NY) 961
REGAZZI, John J. . . . . . (NY) 1017
SAFFADY, William . . . . . (NY) 1074
STEFANI, Carolyn R. . . . (NY) 1185
YERKEY, A N. . . . . (NY) 1380
ANDERSON, Carl A. . . . (OH)   21
COTE, Susan J. . . . . . . (OH) 249
CUPP, Christian M. . . . . (OH) 265
DIAL, David E. . . . . (OH) 299
FENDER, Kimber L. . . . . (OH) 371

AUTOMATION (Cont'd)
Library automation

HAYNES, Kathleen J. . . . (OH) 516
HEARD, Jeffrey L. . . . . . (OH) 518
KARRE, David J. . . . . . . (OH) 628
KENT, Joel S. . . . . (OH) 642
KIE, Kathleen M. . . . . . . (OH) 646
LEE, Hwa W. . . . . (OH) 710
LOGAN, Susan J. . . . . . (OH) 737
MC CORMICK, Lisa L. . . (OH) 798
RUSH, James E. . . . . . . (OH) 1068
TROVER, Larry E. . . . . . (OH) 1258
TUROCI, Esther M. . . . . (OH) 1265
UNGER, Monica A. . . . . (OH) 1269
VENABLE, Andrew A. . . (OH) 1282
WILSON, Lucy . . . . (OH) 1351
DAVIS, Joyce N. . . . . . . (OK) 279
HILL, Helen K. . . . . (OK) 540
MADAUS, J R. . . . . (OK) 758
ROBINSON, Joel M. . . . . (OK) 1044
CLELAND, Mary V. . . . . (OR) 220
FERGUSON, Douglas K. . (OR) 372
PURCELL, V N. . . . . (OR) 998
SELLE, Donna M. . . . . . (OR) 1113
BELANGER, David L. . . . (PA)   75
BROADBENT, H E. . . . . (PA) 138
BRUSH, Cassandra . . . . (PA) 151
FITZGERALD, Patricia A. (PA) 382
HEAD, John W. . . . . (PA) 518
HELMS, Frank Q. . . . . . (PA) 525
OGLETREE, Elizabeth H. (PA) 918
RAC-FEDORIJCZUK,
  Karola C. . . . . (PA) 1001
SILVERMAN, Karen S. . . (PA) 1138
WILLIAMS, James G. . . . (PA) 1344
DELGADO-NUNEZ, Milton (PR) 289
GARCIA-RUIZ, Maritza L. (PR) 417
RODRIGUEZ, Ketty . . . . (PR) 1048
BUNDY, Annalee M. . . . . (RI) 157
LATHROP, Irene M. . . . . (RI) 701
MITLIN, Laurance R. . . . (SC) 850
WOOD, Richard J. . . . . . (SC) 1365
JENSEN, Mary B. . . . . . (SD) 599
RANEY, Leon . . . . (SD) 1007
SPRULES, Marcia L. . . . (SD) 1176
CO, Francisca . . . . (TN) 224
ELDRIDGE, Virginia L. . . (TN) 342
GAUDET, Susan E. . . . . (TN) 422
HUNTER, Joy W. . . . . . . (TN) 576
BEAN, Norma P. . . . . . . (TX)   69
BELL, Charise F. . . . . . . (TX)   76
CLAER, Joycelyn H. . . . . (TX) 215
CORBIN, John . . . . (TX) 245
DIXON, Catherine A. . . . (TX) 306
HANES, Fred W. . . . . . . (TX) 495
HELFER, Robert S. . . . . (TX) 523
KELLEY, Betty H. . . . . . (TX) 636
MARTIN, Jean K. . . . . . . (TX) 776
PELOQUIN, Margaret I. . (TX) 955
SAMSON, Robert C. . . . (TX) 1079
SKINNER, Vicki F. . . . . . (TX) 1146
SZARKA, Tamara J. . . . . (TX) 1218
VAUGHN, Frances A. . . . (TX) 1280
WEBB, Sue E. . . . . (TX) 1313
WETHERBEE, Louella V. (TX) 1327
WHITE, Douglas A. . . . . (TX) 1330
NOEL, Eileen V. . . . . . . (UT) 907
PETERSON, Douglas L. . (UT) 963
VAN ORDEN, Richard D. (UT) 1276
ARNESON, Rosemary H. (VA)   33
BONNETT, Mary B. . . . . (VA) 114
BRAUN, Mina H. . . . . . . (VA) 129
CARTER, Ann M. . . . . . (VA) 189
DUNCAN, Cynthia B. . . . (VA) 325
GAUDET, Jean A. . . . . . (VA) 422
GOLDBERG, Lisbeth S. . (VA) 444
HEYMAN, Berna L. . . . . (VA) 536
JOACHIM, Robert J. . . . (VA) 600
KRIZ, Harry M. . . . . (VA) 679
LIU, Albert C. . . . . (VA) 734

AUTOMATION (Cont'd)
Library automation

SPRENGER, Suzanne F.	(VA)	1176
TURNER, Robert L.	(VA)	1265
TYSINGER, Barbara R.	(VA)	1267
WEIST, Melody S.	(VA)	1320
EATON, Nancy L.	(VT)	334
BAKER, Robert K.	(WA)	49
DECOSTER, Barbara L.	(WA)	286
KOPP, James J.	(WA)	671
MAIOLI, Jerry R.	(WA)	762
MENANTEAUX, A R.	(WA)	823
NESSE, Mark A.	(WA)	896
SHERMAN-PETERSON, Ronald A.	(WA)	1128
SONG, Seungja Y.	(WA)	1167
VYHNANEK, Kay E.	(WA)	1290
WIRT, Michael J.	(WA)	1356
BOOHER, Craig S.	(WI)	115
DREW, Sally J.	(WI)	319
ENGELBERT, Alan M.	(WI)	348
HOUKOM, Susan L.	(WI)	563
LAMB, Cheryl M.	(WI)	689
MCALLISTER, Caryl K.	(WI)	792
PAUL, Patricia J.	(WI)	949
PAYSON, Evelyn H.	(WI)	951
PENNINGTON, Jerome G.	(WI)	957
SAGER, Donald J.	(WI)	1074
TORNQUIST, Kristi M.	(WI)	1251
WILSON, William J.	(WI)	1353
MCKEE, Jean A.	(WV)	810
MULLER, William A.	(WV)	877
BYERS, Edward W.	(WY)	168
STEWART, William L.	(WY)	1193
GUTTERIDGE, Paul	(BC)	479
HSIUNG, Lai Y.	(NS)	567
CHIU, Lily F.	(ON)	209
DYSART, Jane I.	(ON)	331
KRALIK, Jane M.	(ON)	675
LADD, Kenneth F.	(ON)	687
LEWIS, Leslie	(ON)	723
MCCALLUM, David L.	(ON)	793
MERILEES, Bobbie	(ON)	826
POWELL, Wyley L.	(ON)	989
SCHABAS, Ann H.	(ON)	1088
SLATER, Ronald J.	(ON)	1148
WELLS, Nancy E.	(ON)	1322
ASSUNCAO, Isabel	(PQ)	37
EDER, Sonya	(PQ)	336
GOLDEN, Helene	(PQ)	445
KO, Jean S.	(PQ)	666
LEFRANCOIS, Carol	(PQ)	712
PARADIS, Jacques	(PQ)	939
STAHL, Hella	(PQ)	1178
TREMBLAY, Levis	(PQ)	1255
FIELDEN, Janet	(SK)	376
KING, Karen P.	(SK)	651
ZHU, Xiaofeng	(CHI)	1387
MAHOUD ALY, Usama E.	(EGY)	761
GRATTAN, Robert	(FRN)	458
FABRE DE MORLHON, Christiane	(ITL)	360
TOGUCHI, Eiko	(JAP)	1248
ARTEAGA, Georgina	(MEX)	35
AJIBERO, Matthew I.	(NGR)	9
HUANG, Shih H.	(TAI)	568
LEE, Lucy T.	(TAI)	710

Library automation administration BRUNELL, David H. (CO) 150
Library automation & communications KOUNTZ, John C. (CA) 673
Library automation & databases CARRINGTON, David K. (DC) 186
Library automation & networking SLEETER, Ellen L. (CA) 1148

LAUGHLIN, Cheryl H.	(MS)	703
VARIEUR, Normand L.	(NJ)	1278

Library automation & systems MORROW, Deborah (MI) 869

LUCKER, Amy E.	(NY)	746
RAWLINS, Gordon W.	(PA)	1010

Library automation & systems
  analysis   MAURA-SARDO, Mariano
                      A. (PR) 787

AUTOMATION (Cont'd)

Library automation & technology MCQUEEN, Judith D. (MD) 817

WAGNER, Rod G.	(NE)	1292

Library automation &
  telecommunications   BALCOM, Karen S. (TX) 51
Library automation CD-ROM WHITE, Robert W. (NJ) 1332
Library automation consultation HAWKINS, Nina L. (CA) 514

LINSE, Mary M.	(MO)	731

Library automation consulting FALANGA, Rosemarie E. (CA) 361
Library automation cooperatives BISHOFF, Lizbeth J. (CA) 99
Library automation, data conversion KERSHNER, Lois M. (CA) 644
Library automation, database
  management   FINCH, Mildred E. (VA) 377
Library automation implementation BILLS, Linda G. (PA) 96
Lib automation implementation liaison RUDDY, Mary K. (TX) 1065
Library automation, Macintosh BUTLER, Rebekah O. (NY) 167
Library automation, microcomputers LEE, Sylvia (NY) 711
Library automation programs SIMON, Anne E. (NY) 1140
Library automation system WANG, Gary Y. (MA) 1302
Library automation system, Book Trak JACKSON, Nancy I. (FL) 588
Library automation systems BARKALOW, Pat A. (CA) 56

JOHNSON, Mary L.	(CA)	607
HENTZ, Margaret B.	(CT)	530
CANICK, Maureen L.	(DC)	178
TURNER, Susan A.	(DC)	1265
BROWN, Pamela P.	(IL)	146
HOWREY, Mary M.	(IL)	566
BUCKLAND, Lawrence F.	(MA)	154
STACK, Laurie A.	(MT)	1177
STICKEL, William R.	(NJ)	1193
KERSCHNER, Joan G.	(NV)	644
RAHN, Erwin P.	(NY)	1003
DAVIS, Linda M.	(OH)	280
CADY, Susan A.	(PA)	170
GOULD, Douglas A.	(UT)	454
ESPLEY, John L.	(VA)	354
DIXON, Edith M.	(WI)	306
DZIERZAK, Edward M.	(WV)	331

Library automation systems
  management   HOWE, Patricia A. (VA) 565
Library automation training MILLER, Randy S. (IL) 841
Library automation using
  microcomputers   TUCKER, Mary E. (NY) 1262
Library automation vending NASATIR, Marilyn (CA) 888
Library catalog automation WIWEL, Pamela S. (PA) 1359
Library consortium automation SMITH, Ann M. (MA) 1152
Library consulting, automated services COLLARD, R M. (CO) 232
Library holdings automation YOUNG, Carolyn K. (KS) 1381
Library networking & automation JACOB, Mary E. (OH) 589
Library office automation ROSE, Phillip E. (CO) 1055
Library systems analysis &
  automation   ALBERTUS, Donna M. (NY) 10
Library systems & automation BOSSEAU, Don L. (CA) 117

SUGRANES, Maria R.	(CA)	1207
PITKIN, Gary M.	(CO)	976
DONOHUE, Christine N.	(CT)	311
CRIST, Margaret L.	(MA)	259
MCDONALD, Stanley M.	(MA)	803
STEVENS, Michael L.	(MA)	1190
CHIANG, Ahushun	(MD)	207
FREIBURGER, Gary A.	(MD)	401
BUGG, Louise M.	(MI)	155
COHEN, Rosemary C.	(NY)	229
LISTOVITCH, Denise A.	(RI)	733
HUBBARD, William J.	(VA)	568
POPE, Nolan F.	(WI)	983
BEAUMONT, Jane	(ON)	70
PARKER, Arthur D.	(ON)	941
GONZALEZ, Paloma	(PQ)	448
RAITT, David I.	(NET)	1004

Library systems, automation ARNOLD, Donna W. (CA) 33

LEHMAN, Douglas K.	(FL)	712
MCGINN, Thomas P.	(IL)	806
MORRIS, Louis M.	(MD)	867
PAWSON, Robert D.	(NJ)	951
KOUTNIK, Charles J.	(VA)	673

Local system automation KOUTNIK, Charles J. (VA) 673
Maintaining automated databases ZYNJUK, Nila L. (MD) 1392
Management & office automation LEONARD, Lucinda E. (VA) 716
Managing library automation &
  technology   LEACH, Ronald G. (IN) 706

AUTOMATION (Cont'd)

Manual & automated catalog
  management KLAIR, Arlene F. ...... (MD) 657
Manual & automated reference MCGOWAN, Anna T. .... (DC) 807
Manual & automated technl
  applications MERRITT, Betty A. ..... (CA) 827
Manufacturing automation GROEN, Paulette E. ..... (MI) 471
Medical library automation FEINBERG, Linda J. ..... (IL) 368
 CARTER, Bobby R. ..... (TX) 189
Micro-based automation ANDERSON, Eric S. ..... (OH) 22
Micro-based library automation MATTINGLY, Debra B. ... (CO) 786
Microcomputer automation REYNOLDS, Jon K. ..... (DC) 1025
 MOORE, Scott L. ..... (NC) 861
Microcomputer library automation COSTA, Betty L. ...... (CO) 249
 TREVANION, Margaret U. (PA) 1255
Microcomputer-based automation LUCIANI, Ellie .... (ON) 746
Microcomputerization automation KAZLAUSKAS, Edward J. (CA) 632
Microcomputers & automation WIBLE, Joseph G. ..... (CA) 1335
 GIEBEL, Thomas W. ..... (WI) 432
Multi-library automation networks KERSHNER, Lois M. .... (CA) 644
 JONES-LITTEER, Corene
  A. .... (ID) 616
Network Library automation VIERGEVER, Dan W. .... (KS) 1284
Networking & automation JOHNSON, Herbert F. .. (GA) 605
Newspaper library automation ELLENBOGEN, Barbara R. (MI) 343
 HUNTER, James J. .... (OH) 576
 RHYDWEN, David A. ... (ON) 1026
Office automation CIRCIELLO, Jean M. ... (CA) 215
 COVEY, William C. ..... (FL) 252
 CHUNG, Alison L. ..... (IL) 213
 DESROCHES, Richard A. (MA) 295
 PRICE, Douglas S. ..... (MD) 992
 STIGLEMAN, Sue E. ... (NC) 1194
 D'ALLEYRAND, Marc R. (NY) 270
 MARTIN, Thomas H. .. (NY) 778
 MASYR, Caryl L. ...... (NY) 783
 PERSKY, Gail M. ...... (NY) 961
 GILLILAND, Anne J. .... (OH) 436
 JOSEPH, Patricia A. .... (PA) 617
 RAMBO, Neil H. ...... (TX) 1005
 BERGERON, Pierrette .. (PQ) 86
Office systems automation SYPERT, Clyde F. ..... (CA) 1217
Online searching & automation STERN, David .... (IL) 1189
 SIEGERT, Lindy E. ..... (NS) 1136
Online searching & library automation FU, Ting W. .... (HKG) 407
Periodical system automation REED, Virginia R. ...... (IL) 1015
Planning for automation & videodiscs VOGT-O'CONNOR, Diane
  L. .... (DC) 1287
Politics of library automation PHELAN, Mary C. ..... (MA) 967
Preparing for automation & new lib
  bldg INGIBERGSSON, Asgeir (AB) 582
Public libraries automated systems NEAL, Jan .... (CA) 890
Public library automated consortia O'BRIEN, Anne M. ..... (MA) 914
Public library automation SCHLESINGER, Deborah
  L. .... (MT) 1094
Reference & automated services O'HANLON, Nancyanne (OH) 919
Regional union catalog automation PARRAVANO, Ellen A. ... (NY) 944
RLIN automation SOLOMON, Geri E. .... (NY) 1166
School library automation HALL, Howard L. ...... (CA) 488
 HECKLINGER, Ellen L. .. (CA) 519
 KARON, Joyce E. ...... (IL) 627
 LYNN, Barbara A. ..... (KS) 752
 HOLLEY, Rebecca M. ... (LA) 551
 PRESTEBAK, Jane R. .. (MN) 991
 TUZINSKI, Jean H. .... (PA) 1266
 HUNT, Linda A. ...... (VA) 575
 SORENSEN, Richard J. . (WI) 1168
 GELINAS, Rene .... (PQ) 426
School library media center
  automation JOYCE, Robert A. ..... (NC) 618
Scientific information, automation MCGREGOR, M C. ..... (CT) 808
Serials, AV materials, automation SOPER, Mary E. ...... (WA) 1168
Serials automation STAYNER, Delsie A. .... (CA) 1183
 LOWELL, Gerald R. .... (CT) 744
 PRESLEY, Roger L. .... (GA) 991
 CHATTERTON, Leigh A. (MA) 204
 KING, Kenneth E. ..... (MI) 651
 HELMS, Mary E. ...... (MO) 525
 FINLAY, J A. .... (NH) 378
 HEPFER, Cynthia K. .... (NY) 530

AUTOMATION (Cont'd)

Serials automation SHEVIAK, Jean K. ..... (NY) 1129
 MOORE, Brian P. ..... (OH) 858
 WOODS, Janet R. ..... (WY) 1367
Shared automated systems MARTIN, Robert A. .... (FL) 778
Site preparation for automation GREGORY, Roderick F. . (NC) 466
Small business automation SEN, Joyce H. .... (NY) 1115
Small library automation LANGHORNE, Mary J. .. (IA) 696
 MARKUSON, Carolyn A. (MA) 772
 COOK, Nancy E. ...... (SD) 240
 PROVOST, Paul E. ..... (PQ) 996
Small library circulation automation STOUT, Chester B. .... (OH) 1198
Speaking, writing, automation JOHNSON, Pat M. ..... (TX) 608
Special libraries automation KALVINSKAS, Louanne A. (CA) 623
Special library automation HARTT, Richard W. ..... (VA) 509
Special projects research, automation RHYNAS, Don M. ...... (ON) 1026
Spine labels & automated production CHILDRESS, Eric R. .... (NC) 208
Statewide automation HOPKINS, Benjamin .... (MA) 557
System automation planning RHEIN, Jean F. .... (FL) 1025
Systems & automation LOWELL, Felice K. ..... (FL) 744
Systems automation FORSMAN, Rick B. .... (CO) 391
Systems automation consultant GRAMINSKI, Denise M. . (NY) 457
Technical services & automation SEBRIGHT, Terence F. .. (FL) 1110
Technical services automated
  systems BAIRD, Lynn N. .... (ID) 47
Technical services automation KELSEY, Mary J. ...... (CT) 639
 STARCK, William L. .... (DC) 1181
 FROSCHER, Jean L. ... (FL) 406
 STRYCK, B C. .... (IL) 1203
 INTNER, Sheila S. ..... (MA) 583
 DRUM, Eunice P. ...... (NC) 321
 JUDKINS, Timothy C. ... (OK) 619
 GRADY, Agnes M. ..... (TN) 455
 AIROLDI, Melissa .... (TX) 9
 FESSLER, Vera F. ..... (VA) 374
 DJEVALIKIAN, Sonia ... (PQ) 306
Technical services, library automation BIGLIN, Karen E. ...... (AZ) 96
Training for automation use JUERGENS, Bonnie .... (TX) 619
Training library automation software DOEHLERT, Irene C. ... (CA) 308
Training on automated systems WELCH, Grace D. ..... (ON) 1321
Turnkey automated information
  systems SIDMAN, George C. .... (CA) 1135
University library automation HAMMOND, Jane L. .... (NY) 493
User interface, automated systems SACKETT-WILK, Susan A. (TX) 1073
Workplace automation BERGERON, Pierrette .. (PQ) 86

AUTOMOTIVE (See also Cars)

Aerospace, automotive, engineering YOUNGEN, Gregory K. . (IN) 1383
Automobiles JOHNS, John E. .... (OH) 601
Automotive MONTGOMERY, Mary E. (MI) 856
 PERECMAN, Carol J. .... (MI) 958
Automotive engineering literature WARD, Maryanne ..... (WA) 1304
Automotive history WREN, James A. ...... (MI) 1370
Automotive industry research GIGLIO, Linda M. ...... (MI) 433
Automotive libraries BERGIN, Karen S. ..... (MI) 86
Automotive medicine BARTH, Nancy L. .... (CA) 61
Automotive patent & trademark
  research WREN, James A. ...... (MI) 1370
Automotive safety VAN ALLEN, Neil K. ..... (MI) 1271
Automotive technical innovations WREN, James A. ...... (MI) 1370
Special collections, automotive HELVERSON, Louis G. ... (PA) 525

AVIATION (See also Aeronautics)

Aviation MAYERS, Karen A. .... (CA) 789
Aviation & aerospace medicine ROGERS, Ruth T. ...... (FL) 1050
Aviation & avionics LEAVITT, Judith A. ..... (IA) 707
Avionics software FRIEDMAN, Sandra M. ... (CA) 404
Historic aviation literature PARKS, Dennis H. ..... (WI) 943
History of aviation HALPIN, Jerome H. .... (CA) 490

AWARDS (See also Medals)

Academy Awards research STOCKSTILL, Patrick E. . (CA) 1195
Award reference books SIEGMAN, Gita .... (MD) 1136

BAKING (See also Culinary)
Baking science & technology ... HORTIN, Judith K. ..... (KS) 561

BALLET
Ballet ... GUILMETTE, Pierre .... (PQ) 476
Ballets on videocassettes ... HEDLUND, Dennis M. ... (NJ) 520

BAND
Band music recordings research ... MITZIGA, Walter J. ..... (IL) 850
Cataloging band recordings ... MITZIGA, Walter J. ..... (IL) 850

BANKING (See also Finance, Thrift)
Banking ... GAINES, Irene A. ...... (NY) 412
Banking & agriculture reference ... PHILLIPS, Lena M. ..... (MD) 968
Banking & finance ... MORRISON, Patricia ... (CA) 868
... GERVINO, Joan .... (DC) 429
... CHAFE, Douglas A. .... (HI) 197
Banking & finance subject field ... GALLUP, Jane H. ...... (DC) 415
Banking & financial services ... ENGRAM, Sandra K. .... (IL) 350
Banking & management ... GORMAN, Judith F. ..... (AZ) 452
Banking, economics & business ... NAULTY, Deborah M. .... (PA) 889
Banking, finance & business
   reference ... MIRANDA, Esmeralda C. (MN) 847
Banking law ... VAN BEEK, Susan ..... (MA) 1272
... CONGDON, Rodney H. . (NY) 236
Banking reference ... MERBACH, Peggy O. .... (CA) 825
Banking research ... LASKOWITZ, Roberta G. (NY) 700
Banks & banking ... ANDERSON, Connie J. . (CA) 22
... ANDERSON, Connie J. . (CA) 22
... FUJII, Cynthia M. ...... (CO) 408
... FUJII, Cynthia M. ...... (CO) 408
Brief bank indexing & abstracting ... FRANKS, Janice ...... (AL) 398
Canadian banking ... ORLANDO, Richard P. .. (PQ) 926
Commercial banking ... GROSSMAN, Adrian J. .. (NY) 473
Computer applications in banking ... BOSMA, Elske M. ..... (ON) 117
Development banks ... GUILBERT, Manon M. .. (ON) 476
Electronic banking ... MESHINSKY, Jeff M. .... (MD) 827
Investment banking ... GOLDSTEIN, Bernard ... (NJ) 446
... BOWLES, Nancy J. ..... (NY) 121
... DAVID, Julia A. .... (NY) 276
Investment banking, debt & equity ... ABELES, Tom .... (MN) 2
Theology or banking reference ... JORDAN, Charles R. .... (IL) 616
Trademarks, banking, accounting
   services ... FLEMING, Jack C. ..... (ON) 384

BAPTIST
Baptist history ... COURSEY, W T. ...... (GA) 251
... DEBUSMAN, Paul M. ... (KY) 285
... GRENGA, Kathy A. .... (TN) 467
Cataloging, Baptist history, doctrine ... ROBINSON, Nancy D. ... (KY) 1044
North Carolina Baptists ... WOODARD, John R. ... (NC) 1365

BAR (See also Automation, Law)
Bar association library ... GHIDOTTI, Pauline A. .. (AR) 430
Bar code system design ... VOGT, Herwart C. ..... (NJ) 1287

BARGAINING (See also Negotiations)
Collective bargaining ... COOLMAN, Jacqueline .. (CA) 241
... CRANE, Hugh M. ...... (MA) 255
... MORRIS, Irving .... (NY) 866

BAROQUE
French Baroque ... VOLLEN, Gene E. ..... (KS) 1287
Renaissance & Baroque art ... OSTROW, Stephen E. .. (DC) 929

BARRIERS (See also Access)
Political barriers to information ... BIRNEY, Ann E. .... (KS) 98

BASALT
Basalt waste isolation project ... TRAUB, Teresa L. ..... (WA) 1254

BASEBALL
Baseball history ... GIETSCHIER, Steven P. . (MO) 433

BATTLE
Battle of books ... GREESON, Janet S. ..... (AR) 465
Battle of the books ... CRAVER, Susan J. ..... (IA) 256

BEERBOHM
Max Beerbohm bibliography ... LASNER, Mark S. ..... (DC) 700

BEHAVIOR
Behavior information users ... BOISSY, Robert W. ..... (NY) 111
Behavioral science ... AJIBERO, Matthew I. ... (NGR) 9
Behavioral sciences ... SEGAL, Judith .... (NY) 1112
Behavioral sciences & education
   research ... SWARTZ, Jon D. .... (TX) 1214
Behavioral sciences databases ... BAXTER, Pam M. ..... (IN) 67
Criminological & behavioral sciences ... BEAUDET, Normand ... (PQ) 70
Education & behavioral sciences ... WOMACK, Sharon K. ... (NE) 1362
Education, behavioral sciences ... O'BRIEN, Nancy P. ..... (IL) 915
End-user behavior ... SEWELL, Winifred ...... (MD) 1118
Information seeking behavior ... BATES, Marcia J. ...... (CA) 64
... BENIDIR, Samia .... (CA) 80
... KUHLTHAU, Carol C. .... (NJ) 682
... VONDRAN, Raymond F. . (TX) 1288
... KRIKELAS, James ..... (WI) 678
Management & organizational
   behavior ... DENIS, Laurent G. ..... (ON) 292
Online searching behavior ... FIDEL, Raya .... (WA) 374
Organizational behavior ... JOHNSON, Margaret A. . (MN) 607
... RUNYON, Robert S. .... (NE) 1067
Organizational behavior management ... COFFMAN, M H. .... (MA) 227
Psychology & behavioral sciences ... BAXTER, Pam M. ..... (IN) 67
Psychology, behavioral science
   databases ... KAUFFMAN, Inge S. ... (CA) 631
Social & behavioral sciences ... KNAPP, Sara D. .... (NY) 663

BENCHMARKING
Competitive tracking, benchmarking ... LEWARK, Kathryn W. .. (CA) 722

BENEFITS
Benefits analysis & evaluation ... DUFORE, Thomas H. .... (AZ) 324
Employee benefits ... COSTELLO, Robert C. .. (CA) 249
... MILLER, Herbert A. ..... (DC) 838
... REYNOLDS, Carol C. .... (GA) 1025
... PORTA, Catherine M. ... (NY) 984
... BIRSCHEL, Dee B. ...... (WI) 99
... CHOUDHURI, Kabita ... (ON) 211
Employee benefits, home resource
   mgmt ... JACQUES, Donna M. ... (MA) 591
Employee benefits research ... GRANDE, Paula G. ..... (NY) 457
Executive compensation & benefits ... KAZANJIAN, Donna S. . (NY) 632
Insurance & employee benefits ... KORMAN, Adrienne S. .. (MA) 671
Pay & benefit administration ... LEBRUN, Marlene M. ... (MD) 708

BERNOULLI
ZyIndex use with Bernoulli ... LINEWEAVER, Joe R. .. (MN) 730

BIBLE
Bible & theology collection
   development ... ZINK, Esther L. .... (ND) 1389
Biblical & religious studies ... WUNDERLICH, Clifford S. (MA) 1374
Biblical archaeology ... IBACH, Robert D. ...... (TX) 581
Biblical research ... KIRKESY, Oliver M. ..... (MI) 655
Biblical studies ... MERRILL, Arthur L. ..... (MN) 826
... PAKALA, Denise M. ..... (PA) 935
... PAKALA, James C. ..... (PA) 935
... RITTER, Ralph E. ...... (PA) 1037
French Bibles ... CHAMBERS, Bettye T. .. (DC) 198
Reference, biblical/religious studies ... GILNER, David J. ...... (OH) 437
Theology & biblical backgrounds ... ANDERSON, Norman E. . (MA) 24
Theology, biblical studies ... MUNDAY, Robert S. ..... (PA) 878

BIBLIO/POETRY
Biblio/poetry therapy   HYNES, Arleen M. . . . . . (MN) 580

BIBLIOFILE
Bibliofile database   ARMSTRONG, Ruth C. . . (NY) 32
OCLC, bibliofile   BISSETT, Claudia K. . . . (NH) 100

BIBLIOGRAPHER (See Bibliography)

BIBLIOGRAPHIC
Academic bibliographic instruction ENGLE, Michael O. . . . . (OR) 349
Acquisitions & bibliographic control LINDGREN, Arla M. . . . . (NY) 729
Admin, bibliographic instruction COSTELLO, Janice M. . . (WI) 249
Authority & bibliographic relationships CARNEY, Marillyn L. . . . (VA) 183
Automated bibliographic databases CUMMINGS, Christopher
    H. . . . . (UT) 264
Automated bibliographic maintenance WEE, Lily K. . . . . (IL) 1315
Automated bibliographic systems SZARY, Richard V. . . . . (DC) 1218
Automation of bibliographic control BENGTSON, Betty G. . . (TN) 80
Automation of bibliographic databases BERNARD, Patrick S. . . (DC) 88
Bibliographic ABBOTT, Randy L. . . . . (FL) 1
Bibliographic & information access DEL CERVO, Diane M. . . (CT) 289
Bibliographic & library instruction NAKANO, Kimberly L. . . (HI) 887
Bibliographic & resource sharing
  network REDDY, Sigrid R. . . . . . (MA) 1014
Bibliographic automated systems BROWN, Rowland C. . . . (OH) 147
Bibliographic citation systems BRANDT, Daryl S. . . . . . (IN) 128
Bibliographic compilation WITHERELL, Julian W. . . (DC) 1358
  RIDINGER, Robert B. . . . (IL) 1032
  SKINNER, Robert E. . . . (LA) 1146
  KULIBERT, Marie M. . . . (MI) 683
Bibliographic computer searching KNAPP, Sara D. . . . . . . (NY) 663
  NESBIT, Kathryn W. . . . . (NY) 896
Bibliographic control NEAVILL, Gordon B. . . . (AL) 891
  KIRKLAND, Janice J. . . . (CA) 655
  BALMER, Mary . . . . (CT) 53
  KOEL, Ake I. . . . . (CT) 667
  PRICE, Mary S. . . . . . . (DC) 992
  MEAD-DONALDSON,
    Susan L. . . . . (FL) 819
  LEVSTIK, Frank R. . . . . (KY) 721
  OMAR, Elizabeth A. . . . (MD) 923
  DAVIS, Anne C. . . . . . . (MI) 277
  MOSEY, Jeanette . . . . . (MI) 871
  MANDEL, Carol A. . . . . (NY) 764
  MIKSA, Francis L. . . . . . (TX) 834
  SHEETS, Shirley H. . . . (TX) 1125
  SKELLEY, Grant T. . . . (WA) 1145
  PAREDES-RUIZ, Eudoxio
    B. . . . . (SK) 940
Bibliographic control, non-print media TOTTEN, Herman L. . . . (TX) 1252
Bibliographic control of newspapers FIELD, Kenneth C. . . . . (BC) 375
Bibliographic control of serials KOMOROUS, Hana J. . . (BC) 670
Bibliographic control systems GUILES, Kay D. . . . . . . (DC) 476
Bibliographic data publishing TARR, Susan M. . . . . . . (DC) 1224
Bibliographic database design CHERVENAK, Joseph F. . (CO) 206
  GRIMES, Judith E. . . . . (MD) 470
  COMSTOCK, Daniel L. . . (NM) 235
  BREGMAN, Joan R. . . . . (NY) 131
Bibliographic database development NIXON, Judith M. . . . . . (IN) 906
  REILLY, Brian O. . . . . . . (ON) 1020
Bibliographic database maintenance VAN SICKLE, Mary L. . . (KS) 1277
Bibliographic database management MILLER, Dick R. . . . . . . (CA) 837
  COMSTOCK, Daniel L. . . (NM) 235
  HILLMANN, Diane I. . . . . (NY) 541
  MUTTER, Letitia N. . . . . (NY) 883
  SALVAGE, Barbara A. . . (NY) 1078
Bibliographic database products &
  srvs PAUL, Rameshwar N. . . . (MD) 949
Bibliographic database searches MORTON, Dorothy J. . . . (DE) 870
Bibliographic database searching CARRICABURU, Robert . (CA) 186
  CHAIKIN, Mary C. . . . . . (NJ) 197
Bibliographic databases BENIDIR, Samia . . . . . . (CA) 80
  MCCOY-LARSON, Sandra (DC) 799
  ECKERSON, Gale E. . . . (MA) 334
  MCCONE, Gary K. . . . . (MD) 797
  TALLY, Roy D. . . . . (MN) 1221

BIBLIOGRAPHIC (Cont'd)
Bibliographic databases
  MURDOCK, Douglas W. . (NE) 879
  PRAVER, Robin I. . . . . . (NY) 990
  WOODS, Lawrence J. . . (NY) 1367
  SAUVE, Deborah A. . . . . (VA) 1085
  DECOSTER, Barbara L. . (WA) 286
Bibliographic descriptions DAVIS, L C. . . . . (CA) 280
Bibliographic development BUCK, Patricia K. . . . . . (PA) 154
Bibliographic education BUCCO, Louise F. . . . . . (VA) 153
Bibliographic file conversion CHIU, Ida K. . . . . (TX) 209
Bibliographic guides AGEE, Victoria V. . . . . . (MD) 7
Bibliographic information systems LARSON, Ray R. . . . . . . (CA) 699
  ODOM, Jane H. . . . . . . (DC) 917
  WALL, Eugene . . . . (MD) 1297
  LI, Marjorie H. . . . . (NJ) 724
Bibliographic instruction BIGGS-WILLIAMS, Evelyn
    A. . . . . (AL) 95
  BLEILER, Richard J. . . . (AL) 105
  FRIEDMAN, Richard E. . . (AL) 404
  KENDRICK, Aubrey W. . (AL) 640
  KETCHAM, Lee C. . . . . (AL) 645
  LAUGHLIN, Steven G. . . (AL) 703
  MERRILL, Martha . . . . . (AL) 826
  PEARSON, Peter E. . . . (AL) 953
  SCALES, Diann R. . . . . (AL) 1087
  WILLIAMS, Pauline C. . . (AL) 1346
  BEARD, Craig W. . . . . . (AR) 69
  CLOUGHERTY, Leo P. . . (AR) 223
  DEW, Stephen H. . . . . . (AR) 297
  ESTES, Pamela J. . . . . . (AR) 355
  COLE, Mitzi M. . . . . (AZ) 231
  DAANE, Jeanette K. . . . (AZ) 269
  HAWBAKER, A C. . . . . . (AZ) 513
  REICHEL, Mary . . . . (AZ) 1018
  VATHIS, Alma C. . . . . . (AZ) 1279
  ABRAMSON, Jenifer S. . (CA) 3
  ARIARATNAM, Lakshmi V. (CA) 31
  BELL, Christina D. . . . . . (CA) 76
  BERGMAN, Emily A. . . . (CA) 86
  BOOKHEIM, Louis W. . . (CA) 115
  BOYER, Laura M. . . . . . (CA) 123
  BRIL, Patricia L. . . . . . . (CA) 136
  BROIDY, Ellen J. . . . . . . (CA) 139
  BRUNDAGE, Christina A. (CA) 150
  CARAVELLO, Patti S. . . (CA) 180
  CLARENCE, Judy . . . . . (CA) 216
  DOWELL, Connie V. . . . . (CA) 315
  DURAN, Karin J. . . . . . . (CA) 328
  ELNOR, Nancy G. . . . . . (CA) 346
  ENGELBRECHT, Mary E. (CA) 349
  FITZGERALD, Diana S. . (CA) 382
  FUSICH, Monica G. . . . . (CA) 410
  GALLOWAY, Sue . . . . . (CA) 415
  GLENDENNING, Barbara
    J. . . . . (CA) 441
  GLITZ, Beryl . . . . (CA) 441
  GORDON, Wendy R. . . . (CA) 452
  GUEDON, Mary S. . . . . . (CA) 475
  HAIKALIS, Peter D. . . . . (CA) 484
  HARMON, Robert B. . . . (CA) 502
  HILLMAN, Stephanie . . . (CA) 541
  HOGAN, Eddy . . . . (CA) 549
  HURLBERT, Irene W. . . . (CA) 577
  JOHNSON, Diane D. . . . (CA) 603
  JOHNSON, Peter A. . . . . (CA) 608
  KAUN, Thomas T. . . . . . (CA) 631
  KELLY, Myla S. . . . . (CA) 638
  KENYON, Sharmon H. . . (CA) 643
  KIRESEN, Evelyn M. . . . (CA) 654
  KNOWLES, Em C. . . . . . (CA) 665
  LESH, Jane G. . . . . (CA) 718
  LO, Henrietta W. . . . . . . (CA) 735
  MANTHEY, Teresa M. . . (CA) 767
  MARIE, Jacquelyn . . . . . (CA) 770
  MCGREEVY, Kathleen T. (CA) 808
  MELTZER, Ellen J. . . . . (CA) 823
  MORRIS, Jacquelyn M. . (CA) 866
  MULLEN, Cecilia P. . . . . (CA) 877

BIBLIOGRAPHIC (Cont'd)
Bibliographic instruction

NICKELSON-DEARIE,
   Tammy A. . . . . (CA) 902
PORTILLA, Teresa M. . . (CA) 985
POSEY, Vernell W. . . . . . (CA) 985
POSTER, Susan E. . . . . . (CA) 986
REYNOLDS, Judith L. . . (CA) 1025
SANTOS, Bob . . . . (CA) 1082
SHAWL, Janice H. . . . . . (CA) 1124
SHERLOCK, John A. . . . (CA) 1128
SHORT, Virginia . . . . (CA) 1132
SMALLEY, Topsy N. . . . (CA) 1151
SPRAIN, Mara L. . . . . . (CA) 1176
TASH, Steven J. . . . . . . (CA) 1224
TENNANT, Roy . . . . (CA) 1231
WHEELER, Helen R. . . . (CA) 1329
WOBBE, Jean . . . . (CA) 1359
WOLLTER, Patricia M. . . (CA) 1361
WOOD, Elizabeth H. . . . . (CA) 1364
ZYROFF, Ellen S. . . . . . (CA) 1392
ANTHES, Susan H. . . . . (CO) 28
KRISMANN, Carol H. . . . (CO) 678
BOLLIER, John A. . . . . . (CT) 112
COHEN, Morris L. . . . . . (CT) 228
COLLIER, Bonnie . . . . . . (CT) 232
HAAG, Nancy R. . . . . . (CT) 480
HUGHES, Frances M. . . . (CT) 571
JENSEN, Joan W. . . . . . (CT) 598
JOHNSON, Eric W. . . . . (CT) 604
KLINE, Nancy M. . . . . . (CT) 661
LAWRENCE, Scott W. . . (CT) 705
LYNCH, M W. . . . . (CT) 751
MCKINNEY, Linda R. . . . (CT) 812
NATALE, Barbara G. . . . (CT) 889
ROGERS, Mary E. . . . . (CT) 1050
SAVAGE, Judith G. . . . . (CT) 1085
STODDARD, Charles E. . . (CT) 1196
SWIFT, Janet B. . . . . . . (CT) 1216
BEACHELL, Doria M. . . . (DC) 68
RISHWORTH, Susan K. . . (DC) 1036
ROGERS, Sharon J. . . . . (DC) 1050
STEBELMAN, Scott D. . . . (DC) 1183
TOOHEY, Anne K. . . . . . (DC) 1250
VAN NIMMEN, Jane . . . (DC) 1276
AHMAD, Carol F. . . . . . . (FL) 8
APPELQUIST, Donald L. (FL) 30
ATKINS, Donna A. . . . . . (FL) 37
BATTISTE, Anita L. . . . . (FL) 65
BILAL, Dania M. . . . . . . (FL) 96
BLOODWORTH, Velda J. (FL) 106
BROWN, Pia T. . . . . . . (FL) 147
BYRD, Beverly P. . . . . . . (FL) 168
BYRD, Susan G. . . . . . . (FL) 169
CARILLO, Sherry J. . . . . (FL) 181
EVERETT, David D. . . . . (FL) 358
HARDESTY, Larry L. . . . (FL) 499
HUDSON, Phyllis J. . . . . (FL) 569
MALANCHUK, Iona R. . . . (FL) 762
MEAD-DONALDSON,
   Susan L. . . . . (FL) 819
PELLEN, Rita M. . . . . . . (FL) 955
PFARRER, Theodore R. . . (FL) 966
PINC, Nancy M. . . . . . . (FL) 974
SCHWENN, Janet M. . . . (FL) 1105
TOIFEL, Peggy W. . . . . . (FL) 1248
WILER, Linda L. . . . . . . (FL) 1339
WOOD, James F. . . . . . . (FL) 1364
BANJA, Judith A. . . . . . . (GA) 54
BUFFALOE, Catherine S. (GA) 155
COMPTON, Lawrence E. (GA) 235
FARMER, Nancy R. . . . . (GA) 364
HARRISON, James O. . . (GA) 506
JONES, Helen C. . . . . . (GA) 613
LARSEN, Mary T. . . . . . (GA) 698
MALCOLM, Carol L. . . . . (GA) 762
MCCLELLAND, Katherine
   L. . . . . (GA) 796
MORELAND, Virginia F. . (GA) 863
SELF, Sharon W. . . . . . . (GA) 1113

BIBLIOGRAPHIC (Cont'd)
Bibliographic instruction

THAXTON, Lyn . . . . (GA) 1234
WALD, Marlena M. . . . . (GA) 1294
WENDEROTH, Christine . (GA) 1323
WILLIAMS, Sara E. . . . . (GA) 1346
WRIGHT, Dianne H. . . . . (GA) 1371
TAKAHASHI, Annabelle T. (HI) 1220
KNEFEL, Mary A. . . . . . (IA) 664
REHMKE, Denise M. . . . (IA) 1017
SCHACHT, John N. . . . . (IA) 1088
SCHERUBEL, Melody . . . (IA) 1092
SHAW, James T. . . . . . (IA) 1123
ZORDELL, Pamela K. . . . (IA) 1390
BECK, Richard J. . . . . . . (ID) 71
ECKWRIGHT, Gail Z. . . . (ID) 335
TAYLOR, Adrien P. . . . . (ID) 1225
ANDERSON, Byron P. . . (IL) 21
BALL, Mary A. . . . . (IL) 52
BODI, Sonia E. . . . . (IL) 109
BOLT, Janice A. . . . . . . (IL) 113
BOPP, Richard E. . . . . . (IL) 116
CAMPANA, Deborah A. . (IL) 175
DUCHOW, Sally . . . . . . (IL) 322
DUNN, Lucia S. . . . . . . (IL) 327
FISHER, Marshall . . . . . (IL) 381
FRY, Roy H. . . . . (IL) 406
GRAVES, Karen J. . . . . . (IL) 459
HARWOOD, Judith A. . . (IL) 510
HIGGINBOTHAM, Richard
   C. . . . . (IL) 537
HOPKINS, Jane L. . . . . . (IL) 558
HOWREY, Mary M. . . . . (IL) 566
JEFFORDS, Rebecca J. . (IL) 596
KELLEY, Rhona S. . . . . . (IL) 636
KESSINGER, Pamela C. . (IL) 644
KISSINGER, Patricia A. . (IL) 656
MASON, Marjorie L. . . . . (IL) 781
MIKOLYZK, Thomas A. . . (IL) 834
MILLER, Marian I. . . . . . (IL) 840
MOCH, Mary I. . . . . (IL) 851
MOSBORG, Stella F. . . . (IL) 870
NIELSEN, Brian . . . . (IL) 903
ONGLEY, David C. . . . . . (IL) 924
PERSON, Roland C. . . . . (IL) 961
PORCELLA, Brewster . . . (IL) 984
RUDNIK, Mary C. . . . . . . (IL) 1065
SHAFER, Anne E. . . . . . (IL) 1119
SHEDLOCK, James . . . . (IL) 1124
TROY, Shannon M. . . . . (IL) 1258
WILSON, Lizabeth A. . . . (IL) 1351
WRIGHT, Joyce C. . . . . . (IL) 1372
BAXTER, Pam M. . . . . . (IN) 67
BONNER, Robert J. . . . . (IN) 114
DANIELS, Ann A. . . . . . . (IN) 273
FARBER, Evan I. . . . . . . (IN) 363
GREMMELS, Gillian S. . . (IN) 467
HOHL, Robert J. . . . . . . (IN) 550
KONDELIK, Marlene R. . . (IN) 670
MEEK, Janet E. . . . . . . (IN) 821
MEYER, Ellen R. . . . . . . (IN) 830
MILNE, Sally J. . . . . (IN) 845
PASK, Judith M. . . . . . . (IN) 946
RICHWINE, Margaret W. (IN) 1031
STOCKER, Randi L. . . . . (IN) 1195
FENLON, Mary P. . . . . . (KS) 371
GALLOWAY, Mary A. . . (KS) 415
GAYNOR, Kathy A. . . . . (KS) 424
KEMPF, Andrea C. . . . . . (KS) 639
RHODES, Saralinda A. . . (KS) 1026
WHITE, George R. . . . . . (KS) 1331
WILLIAMS, Brian W. . . . (KS) 1342
BIRCHFIELD, Martha J. . (KY) 98
BLACKBURN-FOSTER,
   Brenda . . . . (KY) 102
BRYSON, Kathleen C. . . (KY) 152
BUSER, Robin A. . . . . . . (KY) 165
COALTER, Milton J. . . . . (KY) 224
CONNOR, Lynn S. . . . . . (KY) 238
COSSEY, M E. . . . . (KY) 249

BIBLIOGRAPHIC (Cont'd)
Bibliographic instruction

CRABB, George W. .... (KY) 254
CUDD, John M. .... (KY) 263
HAWLEY, Mary B. ..... (KY) 514
KIRK, Thomas G. ...... (KY) 654
MOORE, Elaine E. ..... (KY) 859
PRIOR, Barbara Q. ..... (KY) 993
SCHLENE, Vickie J. .... (KY) 1094
TEN HOOR, Joan M. .... (KY) 1231
BRAZILE, Orella R. .... (LA) 130
CURTIS, Robert L. ..... (LA) 267
DANTIN, Doris B. ...... (LA) 274
DESSINO, Jacquelyn A. . (LA) 296
HASCHAK, Paul G. . ... (LA) 510
HOGAN, Sharon A. .... (LA) 549
JARRED, Ada D. ...... (LA) 594
KING, Anne M. .... (LA) 650
KLEINER, Janellyn P. ... (LA) 660
MAXSTADT, John M. .... (LA) 788
MAYEAUX, Thurlow M. . (LA) 789
MCFADDEN, Sue J. ..... (LA) 804
MOONEY, Sandra T. ... (LA) 858
SARKODIE-MENSAH,
    Kwasi .... (LA) 1083
SNOW, Maxine L. ..... (LA) 1164
STAFFORD, Cecilia D. .. (LA) 1178
ANDERSON, Wanda E. . (MA) 25
BEZERA, Elizabeth A. ... (MA) 93
CHANDRASEKHAR,
    Ratna .... (MA) 200
COOLIDGE, Christina L. . (MA) 241
DUTCHER, Henry D. ... (MA) 329
GELB, Linda .... (MA) 425
GONNEVILLE, Priscilla R. (MA) 447
KHAN, Syed M. .... (MA) 646
MERRIAM, Joyce ...... (MA) 826
MILLER, George M. .... (MA) 837
PARSON, Lethiel C. .... (MA) 944
ROBINSON, Phyllis A. . . (MA) 1044
SCHATZ, Cindy A. ..... (MA) 1090
SHERER, Elaine R. ..... (MA) 1127
SHIH, Jenny .... (MA) 1130
STOCKARD, Joan ..... (MA) 1195
TAUPIER, Andrea S. ... (MA) 1225
TU, Shu C. .... (MA) 1261
WURTZEL, Barbara S. .. (MA) 1374
ZIEPER, Linda R. ...... (MA) 1388
ARRINGTON, Susan J. . (MD) 34
CONNER, P Z. .... (MD) 237
CREST, Sarah E. ...... (MD) 258
HINEGARDNER, Patricia
    G. .... (MD) 542
JACKSON, Carleton .... (MD) 587
LABASH, Stephen P. ... (MD) 685
LARSEN, Lida L. ...... (MD) 698
MERIKANGAS, Robert J. (MD) 826
QUIST, Edwin A. ...... (MD) 1001
REPENNING, Julie A. ... (MD) 1023
RUSSELL, Rose M. ..... (MD) 1069
THOMAS, Fannette H. .. (MD) 1236
VAN CAMPEN, Rebecca
    J. .... (MD) 1272
WILLIAMS, Mary A. .... (MD) 1345
WILLIAMS, Pamela S. .. (MD) 1346
ARNDT, Arleen .... (MI) 33
BAKER, Jean S. .... (MI) 48
BEAUBIEN, Anne K. .... (MI) 70
BLACK, Shirley R. ..... (MI) 101
BROWN-MAY, Patricia A. (MI) 148
BURNS, David J. ...... (MI) 162
COURTOIS, Martin P. .. (MI) 251
DRISCOLL, Jacqueline .. (MI) 320
FORSYTH, Karen R. ... (MI) 391
HEGEDUS, Mary E. .... (MI) 521
HILDEBRAND, Linda L. . (MI) 538
LUKASIEWICZ, Barbara . (MI) 747
MEADOWS, Brenda L. .. (MI) 819
NICHOLS, Darlene P. .... (MI) 901

BIBLIOGRAPHIC (Cont'd)
Bibliographic instruction

SATTERTHWAITE, Diane
    A. .... (MI) 1084
SCHAAFSMA, Roberta A. (MI) 1088
SCHNEIDER, Janet M. .. (MI) 1097
SMITH, Paul M. .... (MI) 1159
STANGER, Keith J. .... (MI) 1180
VINT, Patricia A. ...... (MI) 1285
WESTBROOK, Jo L. ... (MI) 1326
WILDMAN, Linda ...... (MI) 1339
YEE, Sandra G. .... (MI) 1379
CHRISTENSEN, Beth E. . (MN) 211
ENRICI, Pamela L. ..... (MN) 350
FISHEL, Teresa A. ..... (MN) 380
FISTER, Barbara R. .... (MN) 382
GANGL, Susan D. ..... (MN) 416
HALES-MABRY, Celia E. (MN) 486
HAWTHORNE, Dorothy M. (MN) 514
HITT, Charles J. ...... (MN) 544
HUBER, Kristina R. ..... (MN) 569
JOHNSON, Donald C. .. (MN) 603
MARION, Donald J. .... (MN) 770
READY, Sandra K. ..... (MN) 1012
REIERSON, Pamela M. . (MN) 1019
SANFORD, Carolyn C. .. (MN) 1081
SINHA, Dorothy P. ..... (MN) 1143
TIBLIN, Mariann E. ..... (MN) 1244
TURNER, Patricia ...... (MN) 1265
WALDEN, Barbara L. ... (MN) 1294
BHULLAR, Pushpajit D. . (MO) 93
DEWEESE, June L. .... (MO) 298
ELLEBRACHT, Eleanor V. (MO) 343
ELS, Nancy T. .... (MO) 346
HOCHSTETLER, Donald
    D. .... (MO) 545
IGLAUER, Carol .... (MO) 581
JOSEPH, Miriam E. .... (MO) 617
LOCKHART, Carol A. ... (MO) 736
REIMAN, David A. ..... (MO) 1020
SINCLAIR, Regina A. ... (MO) 1143
STEWART, J A. .... (MO) 1192
VAN BLAIR, Betty A. ... (MO) 1272
BECK, Allisa L. .... (MS) 71
GRAVES, Gail T. ...... (MS) 459
HARPER, Laura G. ..... (MS) 503
OELZ, Erling R. .... (MT) 917
DICKERSON, Jimmy ... (NC) 300
DODGE, Michael R. .... (NC) 308
GARTRELL, Ellen G. ... (NC) 420
GETCHELL, Charles M. . (NC) 430
GLUCK, Myke H. ...... (NC) 442
LAVINE, Marcia M. ..... (NC) 703
MIDDLETON, Beverly D. (NC) 833
MOORE, Kathryn L. .... (NC) 860
OSEGUEDA, Laura M. .. (NC) 927
PETERSON, Cynthia L. . (NC) 963
PHILBECK, Jo S. ...... (NC) 967
SHEPHERD, Gay W. ... (NC) 1127
SINCLAIR, R F. .... (NC) 1142
SUMMERFORD, Steven L. (NC) 1209
TAYLOR, Christine M. .. (NC) 1226
YOUNG, Judith E. ..... (NC) 1382
BRATTON, Phyllis A. ... (ND) 129
GARD, Betty A. .... (ND) 417
NIENOW, Beth M. ..... (ND) 904
EGBERS, Gail L. ...... (NE) 339
LU, Janet C. .... (NE) 745
FITZPATRICK, Robert E. (NH) 383
GAGNON, Ruth .... (NH) 412
KIETZMAN, William D. .. (NH) 647
THOMAS, Jacquelyn H. . (NH) 1236
VINCENT, Charles P. ... (NH) 1284
AXEL-LUTE, Paul ..... (NJ) 42
BOLESTA, Linda ...... (NJ) 112
BOYLE, Jean E. .... (NJ) 124
BUTCHER, Patricia S. .. (NJ) 166
CASSEL, Jeris F. ...... (NJ) 193
HENNEMAN, John B. ... (NJ) 528
MARTINEZ, Jane A. ..... (NJ) 779

BIBLIOGRAPHIC (Cont'd)
Bibliographic instruction

NASH, Stanley D. . . . . . . (NJ) 888
RANDALL, Lynn E. . . . . (NJ) 1006
SCHUT, Grace W. . . . . . (NJ) 1103
TALAR, Anita . . . . (NJ) 1220
VLOYANETES, Jeanne M. (NJ) 1286
WILSON, Myoung C. . . . (NJ) 1352
WOODLEY, Robert H. . . (NJ) 1366
GROTHEY, Mina J. . . . . (NM) 473
HENDRICKSON, Linnea
    M. . . . . (NM) 527
MCBETH, Deborah E. . . . (NM) 792
RASSAM, Cynthia K. . . . (NM) 1009
CONWAY, Susan L. . . . . (NV) 239
BANKS-ISZARD, Kimberly
    K. . . . . (NY) 54
BAXTER, Paula A. . . . . . (NY) 67
BENSEN, Mary L. . . . . . (NY) 83
BERNSTEIN, Mark P. . . . (NY) 89
BLANDY, Susan G. . . . . (NY) 104
BURSTEIN, Rose A. . . . . (NY) 164
CAVINESS, Ann N. . . . . (NY) 195
COONS, William W. . . . . (NY) 242
COOPER, Catherine M. . . (NY) 242
DEDONATO, Ree . . . . . (NY) 286
DOEZEMA, Linda P. . . . . (NY) 308
DREW, Wilfred E. . . . . . (NY) 319
FRANCIS, Barbara B. . . . (NY) 396
FRANCO, Kathryn C. . . . (NY) 396
FRASER, Charlotte R. . . . (NY) 399
FREESE, Melanie L. . . . . (NY) 401
FREIDES, Thelma . . . . . (NY) 401
GRUNDT, Leonard . . . . . (NY) 475
HECKMAN, Lucy T. . . . . (NY) 519
HORNE, Dorice L. . . . . . (NY) 560
HORNICK-LOCKARD,
    Barbara A. . . . . (NY) 560
IRWIN, Iris . . . . (NY) 584
JUDD, Blanche E. . . . . . (NY) 618
KING, Christine E. . . . . . (NY) 650
KLAVANO, Ann M. . . . . (NY) 658
KLEIMAN, Rhoda E. . . . . (NY) 659
KONOVALOFF, Maria S. (NY) 670
KUGLER, Sharon . . . . . . (NY) 682
KUHNER, Robert A. . . . . (NY) 683
LARSEN, Joan A. . . . . . (NY) 698
LOWRY, Lina M. . . . . . . (NY) 745
LUTZKER, Marilyn L. . . . (NY) 750
MACOMBER, Nancy . . . (NY) 758
MAUL, Shirley A. . . . . . . (NY) 787
O'DONNELL, Mary A. . . (NY) 917
PAGEL, Scott B. . . . . . . (NY) 934
PODELL, Diane K. . . . . . (NY) 979
POWIS, Katherine E. . . . (NY) 989
REMUSAT, Suzanne L. . (NY) 1023
RICKER, Shirley E. . . . . (NY) 1031
ROBERTS, Anne F. . . . . (NY) 1039
RUBEY, Daniel R. . . . . . (NY) 1064
SCHMIDTMANN, Nancy
    K. . . . . (NY) 1096
SHAPIRO, Martin P. . . . . (NY) 1121
SLUSS, Sara B. . . . . . . (NY) 1150
SORGEN, Herbert J. . . . (NY) 1168
STEWART, Linda G. . . . (NY) 1192
TOTH, Gregory M. . . . . . (NY) 1252
VANDELINDER, Bonnie L. (NY) 1273
WAGNER, Janet S. . . . . (NY) 1291
WELLS, Margaret R. . . . (NY) 1322
WISHART, H L. . . . . (NY) 1357
WOLF, Carolyn M. . . . . . (NY) 1359
WORTZEL, Murray N. . . (NY) 1369
ALTAN, Susan B. . . . . . (OH) 18
ANDERSON, Janice L. . . (OH) 23
BOX, Krista J. . . . . (OH) 122
BRINK, David R. . . . . . . (OH) 136
CAIN, Linda B. . . . . (OH) 171
CARY, Mary K. . . . . (OH) 191
CURRIE, William W. . . . . (OH) 266
DUFFETT, Gorman L. . . . (OH) 323

BIBLIOGRAPHIC (Cont'd)
Bibliographic instruction

EMRICK, Nancy J. . . . . . (OH) 348
FACINELLI, Jaclyn R. . . . (OH) 360
FIDLER, Linda M. . . . . . (OH) 375
GATTEN, Jeffrey N. . . . . (OH) 422
GODWIN, Eva D. . . . . . (OH) 443
GREEN, Denise D. . . . . (OH) 461
GROHL, Arlene P. . . . . . (OH) 471
GUSTAFSON, Julia C. . . (OH) 478
HALIBEY-BILYK, Christine
    M. . . . . (OH) 486
HARDESTY, Vicki H. . . . (OH) 499
KIE, Kathleen M. . . . . . (OH) 646
LANTZ, Elizabeth A. . . . (OH) 697
LEIBOLD, Cynthia K. . . . (OH) 713
MILLER, William . . . . . . (OH) 843
O'HANLON, Nancyanne . (OH) 919
PORTER, Marlene A. . . . (OH) 985
PURSEL, Janet E. . . . . . (OH) 998
RADER, Hannelore B. . . . (OH) 1002
ROMARY, Michael P. . . . (OH) 1052
SANKOT, Janice M. . . . . (OH) 1081
SANTAVICCA, Edmund F. (OH) 1082
SCHIRMER, Robert W. . . (OH) 1093
SCHMALBERG, Aaron . . (OH) 1094
SWAIN, Richard H. . . . . (OH) 1212
SWEENY, Mary K. . . . . . (OH) 1215
TUCKER, Debbie B. . . . . (OH) 1261
WHITAKER, Constance C. (OH) 1329
BRICK, Sarah E. . . . . . . (OK) 134
CALLARD, Joanne C. . . (OK) 173
FLINNER, Beatrice E. . . . (OK) 385
FULK, Mary C. . . . . (OK) 408
HOVDE, David M. . . . . . (OK) 563
KENNEDY, James W. . . (OK) 641
MCCALL, Patricia . . . . . (OK) 793
NASH, Helen B. . . . . . . (OK) 888
WEISS, Catharine H. . . . (OK) 1320
HENDERSON, Carol G. . (OR) 526
LAWRENCE, Robert E. . (OR) 705
ADAMS, Mignon S. . . . . (PA) 5
ANDRILLI, Ene M. . . . . . (PA) 27
BURNS-DUFFY, Mary A. (PA) 163
CAMPION, Carol M. . . . . (PA) 177
CRAWFORD, Gregory A. (PA) 256
CRESCENT, Victoria L. . (PA) 258
DEEGAN, Rosemary L. . (PA) 286
DONOVAN, Judith G. . . (PA) 312
ERDICK, Joseph W. . . . . (PA) 352
EZELL, Johanna V. . . . . (PA) 360
FEDRICK, Mary A. . . . . (PA) 368
FILLER, Mary A. . . . . . . (PA) 377
FREEMAN, Michael S. . . (PA) 401
FUSELER-MCDOWELL,
    Elizabeth A. . . . . (PA) 410
HALL, Martha H. . . . . . . (PA) 488
HESP, Judith A. . . . . . . (PA) 534
JEAN, Lorraine A. . . . . . (PA) 596
JOHNSON, Joan E. . . . . (PA) 606
KREITZBURG, Marilyn J. (PA) 677
LARSON, Mary E. . . . . . (PA) 699
LEHMANN, Stephen R. . (PA) 713
LINGLE, Virginia A . . . . (PA) 730
LYNCH, Mary D. . . . . . . (PA) 752
MCCOY, James F. . . . . (PA) 799
MORGANTI, Deena J. . . (PA) 864
NOLF, Marsha L. . . . . . . (PA) 908
PAWLIK, Deborah A. . . . (PA) 951
RAINEY, Nancy B. . . . . . (PA) 1004
RIDGEWAY, Patricia M. . (PA) 1032
ROSENBERGER, Merry G. (PA) 1056
SENECAL, Kristin S. . . . (PA) 1115
THOMAS, Deborah A. . . (PA) 1236
ULINCY, Loretta D. . . . . (PA) 1268
VOROS, David S. . . . . . (PA) 1289
WEBER ROOCHVARG,
    Lynn E. . . . . (PA) 1314
WEIS, Aimee L. . . . . . . (PA) 1319
YOUNG, Dorothy E. . . . (PA) 1381

BIBLIOGRAPHIC (Cont'd)
Bibliographic instruction

ZABEL, Diane M. . . . . . . (PA) 1385
CONCEPCION, Luis . . . . (PR) 235
BRYAN, Susan M. . . . . . (RI) 152
CAMERON, Lucille W. . . (RI) 175
KEEFE, Margaret J. . . . . (RI) 634
KRAUSSE, Sylvia C. . . . (RI) 676
SHERIDAN, Jean . . . . . . (RI) 1127
SIEBURTH, Janice F. . . . (RI) 1135
YOUNG, Arthur P. . . . . . (RI) 1381
BAKER, Steven L. . . . . . (SC) 49
DRYDEN, Sherre H. . . . . (SC) 321
DUSENBERRY, Mary D. . (SC) 329
GOING, Susan C. . . . . . . (SC) 444
HOLLEY, E J. . . . . (SC) 551
LAFAYE, Cary D. . . . . . . (SC) 687
MICHAELS, Carolyn L. . . (SC) 831
MORGAN, Nancy T. . . . . (SC) 864
SCHMITT, John P. . . . . . (SC) 1096
SEAMAN, Sheila L. . . . . (SC) 1109
TAPLEY, Bridgette M. . . . (SC) 1223
VASSALLO, John A. . . . (SC) 1279
WEATHERS, Virginia W. (SC) 1312
SMITH, Rise L. . . . . (SD) 1160
HAMBERG, Cheryl J. . . . (TN) 490
HARRISON, Richard H. . (TN) 507
LAMBERT, Sarah E. . . . . (TN) 690
MANNING, Dale . . . . (TN) 766
MEREDITH, Don L. . . . . (TN) 825
MURGAI, Sarla R. . . . . . (TN) 880
NORRIS, Carol B. . . . . . (TN) 909
PHILLIPS, Linda L. . . . . . (TN) 968
RIDENOUR, Lisa R. . . . . (TN) 1032
ROMANS, Lawrence M. . (TN) 1052
ROTHACKER, John M. . (TN) 1059
RUDOLPH, N J. . . . . (TN) 1066
SHORT, William M. . . . . (TN) 1132
SMITH, Lori D. . . . . (TN) 1157
TABACHNICK, Sharon . . (TN) 1219
TURNER, Deborah M. . . (TN) 1264
WALLACE, Alan H. . . . . (TN) 1297
WARD, James E. . . . . . . (TN) 1304
WATTS, Adalyn . . . . (TN) 1310
BAILEY, William G. . . . . (TX) 47
BARRINGER, Sallie H. . . (TX) 60
CAMPBELL, Shirley A. . . (TX) 177
HAGLE, Claudette S. . . . (TX) 483
HARPER, Marsha W. . . . (TX) 503
HYMAN, Ferne B. . . . . . (TX) 580
JESER-SKAGGS, Sharlee
    A. . . . . (TX) 600
KELLOUGH, Jean L. . . . (TX) 637
KHADER, Majed J. . . . . (TX) 645
KUJOORY, Parvin . . . . . (TX) 683
LOWRY, Andretta G. . . . (TX) 745
MARLEY, Judith L. . . . . . (TX) 772
MILLER, Susan A. . . . . . (TX) 842
NOLAN, Christopher W. . (TX) 907
PEYTON, Janice L. . . . . (TX) 966
PHILLIPS, Robert L. . . . . (TX) 969
SHEETS, Janet E. . . . . . (TX) 1125
SPECHT, Alice W. . . . . . (TX) 1172
TAYLOR, Anne E. . . . . . (TX) 1226
TEVEBAUGH, Joyce E. . (TX) 1233
TOLBERT, Jean F. . . . . . (TX) 1248
TROST, Theresa K. . . . . (TX) 1258
WASSENICH, Red . . . . . (TX) 1308
WYGANT, Alice C. . . . . . (TX) 1375
WIGGINS, Marvin E. . . . (UT) 1337
ANDERSON, Kari D. . . . (VA) 24
BRAINARD, Blair . . . . . . (VA) 127
CASEY, Wayne T. . . . . . (VA) 192
CHISHOLM, Clarence E. (VA) 209
DIERCKS, Thelma C. . . . (VA) 302
EISENBERG, Phyllis B. . . (VA) 340
GREFE, Richard F. . . . . (VA) 465
HAUSMAN, Patricia R. . . (VA) 513
HILL, Nancy A. . . . . (VA) 540
HOLLY, Janet S. . . . . . . (VA) 552

BIBLIOGRAPHIC (Cont'd)
Bibliographic instruction

JENNERICH, Elaine Z. . . (VA) 598
JOHNSON, Martha A. . . (VA) 607
KILLEEN, Erlene B. . . . . (VA) 648
MYERS, Martha O. . . . . . (VA) 884
OBRIST, Cynthia W. . . . (VA) 915
PEARSON, Marilyn R. . . (VA) 953
DURFEE, Tamara . . . . . (VT) 328
LUZER, Nancy H. . . . . . (VT) 750
ALEXANDER, Malcolm D. (WA) 12
ALKIRE, Leland G. . . . . . (WA) 13
FRALEY, David B. . . . . . (WA) 395
GARRETSON, Laurie J. . (WA) 420
GILCHRIST, Debra L. . . . (WA) 434
JENNERICH, Edward J. . (WA) 598
NEWELL, Rick K. . . . . . . (WA) 898
PRINGLE, Robert M. . . . (WA) 993
RICIGLIANO, Lorraine M. (WA) 1031
RICKERSON, Carla . . . . (WA) 1031
SCHREINER, Suzanne M. (WA) 1100
WYNN, Debra D. . . . . . . (WA) 1375
CARR, Jo A. . . . . (WI) 185
ENGELDINGER, Eugene
    A. . . . . (WI) 349
FLIEGEL, Deborah A. . . . (WI) 385
FU, Tina C. . . . . (WI) 407
GERLACH, Donald E. . . . (WI) 429
JESUDASON, Melba . . . (WI) 600
MANDERNACK, Scott B. (WI) 765
MCCLEMENTS, Nancy A. (WI) 796
PIETERS, Donald L. . . . . (WI) 972
STRUPP, Sybil A. . . . . . (WI) 1203
THOMPSON, Glenn J. . . (WI) 1239
SCOBELL, Elizabeth H. . (WV) 1106
WATSON, Carolyn R. . . . (WV) 1309
MACK, Bonnie R. . . . . . . (WY) 756
DROESSLER, Judith B. . (AB) 320
NOGA, Dolores A. . . . . . (AB) 907
VINE, Rita F. . . . . (AB) 1285
WHITE, Donald J. . . . . . . (BC) 1330
MCNALLY, Brian D. . . . . (NB) 815
MACLENNAN, Oriel C. . . (NS) 757
NOWAKOWSKI, Frances
    C. . . . . (NS) 911
GILMORE, Carolyn . . . . . (PQ) 437
PETRYK, Louise O. . . . . (PQ) 965
AFFLECK, Delburt E. . . . (SK) 7
MACK, A Y. . . . . (SK) 756
FOX, Peter K. . . . . (IRE) 395
BOWEN, Dorothy N. . . . . (KEN) 120
BERNAT, Mary A. . . . . . (VEN) 88

Bibliographic instruction, admin | BAUNER, Ruth E. . . . . . . (IL) 67
Bibliographic instruction &
    development | WILLIAMS, Suzanne C. . (TX) 1346
Bibliographic instruction & online | BURR, Charlotte A. . . . . (WI) 163
Bibliographic instruction & reference | PATTERSON, Grace L. . (NY) 948
    | TORNQUIST, Kristi M. . . (WI) 1251
Bibliographic instruction automated
    syst | PALLARDY, Judy S. . . . (MO) 935
Bibliographic instruction for education | WILKE, Janet S. . . . . . . (KS) 1339
Bibliographic instruction for music | SILCOX, Tinsley E. . . . . . (TN) 1137
Bibliographic instruction librarianship | HUPP, Stephen L. . . . . . (MI) 577
Bibliographic instruction of online | WARD, Sandra N. . . . . . (CA) 1304
Bibliographic instruction programs | DEWAR, Jo E. . . . . (FL) 298
Bibliographic maintenance | COOPER, Jean L. . . . . . (VA) 243
Bibliographic networking | BILLINGS, Harold W. . . . (TX) 96
Bibliographic organization | CARPENTER, Michael A. (LA) 185
    | BOLL, John J. . . . . (WI) 112
Bibliographic organization control | HENDERSON, Kathryn L. (IL) 526
Bibliographic OSI protocol | ARBEZ, Gilbert J. . . . . . (ON) 30
Bibliographic preparation | BAXTER, Paula A. . . . . . (NY) 67
Bibliographic problem solving | JOHNSON, Everett J. . . . (DC) 604
Bibliographic problems | BROWN, Sharon D. . . . . (MD) 147
Bibliographic product analysis | FARINA, Robert A. . . . . (DC) 363
Bibliographic products | LAWALL, Marie . . . . (VA) 704
Bibliographic products & services | SEGEL, Bernard J. . . . . . (DC) 1112
    | SETTLER, Leo H. . . . . . (DC) 1117
    | PARENT, Ingrid T. . . . . . (ON) 940
Bibliographic reference service | YU, Priscilla C. . . . . (IL) 1384

BIBLIOGRAPHIC (Cont'd)

Bibliographic research	KRUKONIS, Perkunas P.	(MA)	680
	FORSYTH, Karen R.	(MI)	391
	SCHMIDT, Diana M.	(ON)	1095
	SAUCIER, Danielle	(PQ)	1084
Bibliographic retrieval	HALASZ, Marilynn J.	(IL)	484
Bibliographic science instruction	DERKSEN, Charlotte R.	(CA)	294
Bibliographic search	OLSON, Carol A.	(MN)	922
Bibliographic searching	LASETER, Shirley B.	(AL)	700
	DI MUCCIO, Mary J.	(CA)	304
	LAMBRECHT, Jay H.	(IL)	691
	LAMB, Robert S.	(IN)	690
	MANGIN, Julianne	(MD)	765
	FLOWERS, Janet L.	(NC)	386
	MEEHAN-BLACK, Elizabeth C.	(NC)	821
	SWANSON, Dorothy T.	(NY)	1213
	FUSELER-MCDOWELL, Elizabeth A.	(PA)	410
	COLE, Lorna P.	(ON)	231
Bibliographic searching & access	MARTIN, Noelene P.	(PA)	777
Bibliographic services	FORMAN, Jack	(CA)	390
	PALMORE, Sandra N.	(IL)	937
	HOLLAND, Helen K.	(WA)	550
Bibliographic standards	GLAZIER, Ed	(CA)	440
	ATTIG, John C.	(PA)	38
Bibliographic standards & systems	CARRINGTON, David K.	(DC)	186
Bibliographic systems	HENKE, Dan	(CA)	528
	TANTOCO, Dolores W.	(IN)	1223
	KILGOUR, Frederick G.	(OH)	648
Bibliographic tape processing	MCQUEEN, Judith D.	(MD)	817
Bibliographic utilities	SHIRASAWA, Sharon V.	(CA)	1131
	DUDLEY, Robyn A.	(MD)	323
	MORRIS, Jennifer D.	(NY)	866
	SLATER, Ronald J.	(ON)	1148
Bibliographic utility	PRESLAN, Bruce H.	(CA)	991
Bibliographic verification	NIELSON, Paula I.	(UT)	903
	ALLISON, Scott	(AB)	17
	HOBBS, Brian	(AB)	545
Bibliographical checking	VANCE, Mary L.	(MS)	1273
Bibliographical compilation	FRANKLIN, Linda C.	(NY)	398
	RAO, Rama K.	(PA)	1008
	HOWARD-HILL, Trevor	(SC)	564
Bibliographical control	DWORACZEK, Marian	(AB)	330
Bibliographical databases	ALSTON, Sandra	(ON)	18
Bibliographical instruction	HALES, David A.	(AK)	486
	OTTOSON, Robin D.	(CO)	930
	MEREDITH, Phyllis C.	(PA)	825
	ROSENSHIELD, Jill K.	(WI)	1057
Bibliographical instruction & research	FREITAG, Wolfgang M.	(MA)	401
Bibliographical research	DEUTSCH, James I.	(DC)	296
	FIGUEREDO, Danilo H.	(NY)	376
	NYQUIST, Corinne E.	(NY)	913
	BRETON, Lise	(PQ)	133
Bibliographical searching	MCTYRE, Ruthann B.	(TX)	818
Bibliographical studies	VALLEJO, Rosa M.	(PHP)	1271
Bibliographical theory	HOWARD-HILL, Trevor	(SC)	564
Bibliographics	HIRON, Barbara A.	(PQ)	543
Bibliography-biography of people	THOMPSON, Donald E.	(IN)	1239
Business bibliographic databases	POJE, Mary E.	(NY)	980
Canadiana bio-bibliographical research	DOWDING, Martin R.	(ON)	315
Chemistry bibliographic instruction	WIGGINS, Gary D.	(IN)	1337
Compiling bibliographic data	MCCRAY, Evelina W.	(LA)	800
Computer file bibliographic control	HERMAN, Elizabeth	(CA)	531
Computer-based bibliographic info systs	COCHRANE, Pauline A.	(NY)	226
Cooperative bibliographic instruction	RATZER, Mary B.	(NY)	1010
Editing bibliographical records	WANG, Ann C.	(DC)	1302
Fine arts bibliographic instruction	SCHERER, Herbert G.	(MN)	1092
Graduate level bibliographic instruction	ILACQUA, Anne K.	(MA)	581
Hybrid numeric bibliographic systems	SCULLY, Patrick F.	(CA)	1109
Indexing & bibliographic editing	DRAPER, Linda J.	(MO)	318
International bibliographic control	COOK, C D.	(ON)	239
Legal bibliographic instruction	CHERRY, Anna M.	(MN)	206
Legal bibliographical instruction	LANGSTON, Sally J.	(TX)	696

BIBLIOGRAPHIC (Cont'd)

Library & bibliographic instruction	LAKE, Gretchen L.	(AK)	688
	GAREY, Anita I.	(CA)	418
	ZIEGLER, Janet M.	(CA)	1388
	HUDSON, Donna T.	(NC)	569
	WORTMAN, William A.	(OH)	1369
	DAVIDSON, Nancy M.	(SC)	276
Library & bibliographical instruction	KIRKENDALL, Carolyn A.	(MI)	654
Library or bibliographic instruction	SWAINE, Cynthia W.	(VA)	1212
Machine-readable bibliographic format	SPAANS, David N.	(DC)	1170
Management bibliographic services	WALSH, James A.	(PA)	1299
Marketing bibliographic products	STEVENS, Roberta A.	(DC)	1191
Medical bibliographic instruction	ANDERSON, Gail C.	(GA)	23
Medical online bibliographic searching	HARMAN, Susan E.	(MD)	502
Music reference & bibliographic instrc	BOGNAR, Dorothy M.	(CT)	111
One-person libraries or biblgph instrc	KLEIN, Penny	(NY)	659
Online bibliographic control	HORNE, Ernest L.	(MI)	560
Online bibliographic database searching	SUBRAMANIAN, Jane M.	(NY)	1206
Online bibliographic databases	CALCAGNO, Philip M.	(IL)	172
Online bibliographic instruction	SPAANS, David N.	(DC)	1170
Online bibliographic retrieval	ROSS, Nina M.	(PA)	1058
Online bibliographic search	TU, Shu C.	(MA)	1261
Online bibliographic searching	WYBORNEY, Charles E.	(CA)	1374
	WESTON, E P.	(IL)	1327
	COLLINS, Mary E.	(IN)	233
	BEZERA, Elizabeth A.	(MA)	93
	LEE, Susan M.	(MT)	711
	NASE, Lois M.	(NJ)	888
	CURRY, Lenora Y.	(NY)	266
	HARDY, Gayle J.	(NY)	500
	PERRY, Claudia A.	(NY)	960
	TUCKER, Debbie B.	(OH)	1261
	JOHNSON, Jane W.	(VA)	605
Online bibliographic services	CANICK, Maureen L.	(DC)	178
	HARTZ, Mary K.	(DC)	509
	HILDITCH, Bonny M.	(MD)	539
	DESCHENE, Dorice	(OH)	294
Online bibliographic systems	MONTGOMERY, Michael S.	(NJ)	856
Online bibliographic training	PERRY, Claudia A.	(NY)	960
Online searching & biblgph retrieval	KING, Hannah M.	(DC)	651
Online srvs & bibliographic utilities	MORGAN, Ferrell	(CA)	864
Orientation & bibliographic instruction	ARMSTRONG, Mary L.	(AB)	32
	LAKHANPAL, Sarv K.	(SK)	689
Petroleum bibliographic info systs	HILL, Linda L.	(OK)	540
Reference & bibliographic instruction	PETERS, Marion C.	(CA)	962
	NORONHA, Marilyn S.	(CT)	909
	COHN, William L.	(FL)	229
	MALANCHUK, Peter P.	(FL)	762
	CANN, Sharon F.	(GA)	178
	GIAQUINTA, C J.	(IA)	431
	HUFFORD, Gordon L.	(IN)	571
	MCDONALD, Stanley M.	(MA)	803
	SIGALA, Stephanie C.	(MO)	1137
	FARRELL, Michele A.	(NY)	365
	HARDY, Gayle J.	(NY)	500
	LYONS, Evelyn L.	(PA)	753
	LEGET, Max	(SD)	712
	CONIGLIO, Jamie W.	(VA)	236
	HOWE, Patricia A.	(VA)	565
	EDMONDS, Michael	(WI)	336
	NECHKA, Ada M.	(AB)	891
	LEVESQUE, Nancy B.	(BC)	719
Reference & bibliographic works	NGUYEN, Vy K.	(PQ)	901
Reference, bibliographic	RUBY, Irple P.	(NE)	1065
Reference, bibliographic instruction	THOMAS, Mary C.	(CA)	1237
References & bibliographic instruction	KOK, Victoria T.	(VA)	669
Research methods & bibliographic instrc	TROUTMAN, Joseph E.	(GA)	1258
Science bibliographic instruction	CULOTTA, Wendy A.	(CA)	264
	STANKUS, Tony	(MA)	1180
Scientific bibliographic databases	PERRONE, Jeanne M.	(DC)	960
Selected annotated bibliographics	PARKER, John C.	(CA)	942
Serials bibliographic control & review	STEINHAGEN, Elizabeth N.	(ID)	1186
Social science bibliographic instruction	NESBITT, Renee D.	(CA)	896
Theatre bibliographic researching	ULRICH, Paul S.	(WGR)	268
Training, bibliographic instruction	WIBLE, Joseph G.	(CA)	1335

BIBLIOGRAPHIC (Cont'd)

Word processing, biblgph preparation	MANDEL, Douglas J. . . .	(IL)	765
Young adult bibliographic instruction	REIF, Lenore S.	(IL)	1019

BIBLIOGRAPHY (See also Cartobibliography)

Abstracting, indexing, bibliography	OREJANA, Rebecca D. . .	(PHP)	925
Accounting & business bibliography	NELOMS, Karen H. . . .	(NY)	893
Acquisitions bibliography	PINES, Doralynn	(NY)	974
African bibliography	KRAEHE, Mary A.	(VA)	674
African studies bibliography	KAGAN, Alfred	(CT)	621
	HOWELL, John B.	(IA)	565
Africana bibliography	FINNEGAN, Gregory A. .	(NH)	378
Afro-American bibliography	BULLOCK, Penelope L. .	(GA)	156
	SCOTT, Sharon E.	(IL)	1108
	GUNN, Arthur C.	(MI)	477
	WRAY, Wendell L.	(PA)	1370
Agricultural bibliography	STUBBAN, Vanessa L. . .	(KS)	1204
Agricultural sciences reference & bibl	MANNARINO, Elizabeth R.	(OR)	766
American & English lit bibliography	BAKY, John S.	(PA)	50
American art bibliography	WALKER, William B. . . .	(NY)	1296
American history bibliography	GETCHELL, Charles M. .	(NC)	430
American Indian bibliography	WEEKS, John M.	(MN)	1315
American music bibliography	CARNOVALE, A N.	(MS)	184
Analytical bibliography of music	BOORMAN, Stanley H. . .	(NY)	115
Annotated bibliographies	MANSINGH, Laxmi	(JAM)	767
Anthropological bibliography	WEEKS, John M.	(MN)	1315
Anthropology bibliography	FINNEGAN, Gregory A. .	(NH)	378
	OGBURN, Joyce L.	(PA)	918
Art & architecture bibliography	SHAW, Renata V.	(DC)	1123
Art & literature bibliography	MCCLEARY, William E. .	(LA)	796
Art & women's studies bibliography	ALLEN, Susan M.	(CA)	16
Art bibliographies	DAVIS, L C.	(CA)	280
	STARR, Daniel A.	(NY)	1182
Art bibliography	TEAGUE, Edward H. . . .	(FL)	1229
	FREITAG, Wolfgang M. .	(MA)	401
	STEPHENSON, Marilyn R.	(NC)	1188
	DANE, William J.	(NJ)	272
	OPATOW, Judith	(NY)	925
	PHILLPOT, Clive J.	(NY)	969
	ABID, Ann B.	(OH)	2
	HUGHSTON, Milan R. . .	(TX)	572
	JONES, Lois S.	(TX)	613
	SHEAROUSE, Linda N. .	(TX)	1124
Art history bibliography	ROSS, Alexander D.	(CA)	1057
Asian bibliography	WONG, William S.	(IL)	1363
Astronomy & astrophysics bibliography	STEVENS-RAYBURN, Sarah L.	(MD)	1191
Australian bibliography	ROUTH, Spencer	(AUS)	1061
Automated bibliography production	CHERVENAK, Joseph F. .	(CO)	206
Automation of bibliographies	MCNELLIS, Claudia H. . .	(DC)	817
Bibliographer	PAPADEMETRIOU, George C.	(MA)	938
	MERRILL, Arthur L.	(MN)	826
	BURGALASSI, Anthony J.	(NY)	159
	POPOVIC, Tanya V.	(NY)	983
	COHEN, Jane L.	(WA)	228
Bibliographer, art & architecture	OLSON, Joann D.	(OH)	922
Bibliographies	CAMPBELL, Dierdre A. .	(AZ)	176
	BROWN, Elizabeth E. . .	(CA)	143
	BASA, Eniko M.	(DC)	62
	CHAVES, Francisco M. . .	(FL)	204
	FORD, Marcia K.	(IN)	389
	STUHR-ROMMEREIM, Rebecca A.	(KS)	1205
	COURTOT, Marilyn E. . .	(MD)	251
	KNOBBE, Mary L.	(MD)	665
	JAEGER, Sally J.	(MI)	591
	BROCKMAN, William S. .	(NJ)	138
	NARDUCCI, Frances . . .	(NY)	888
	VOLAT-SHAPIRO, Helene M.	(NY)	1287
	WARNER, Susan B.	(OH)	1305
	JONES, Charles E.	(OK)	611
	ADAMS, Thomas R.	(RI)	6
	BROWN, Muriel W.	(TX)	146
	WESTBROOK, Brenda S.	(TX)	1326
	BARRICK, Susan O.	(VA)	59
	WHITE, William	(VA)	1332

BIBLIOGRAPHY (Cont'd)
Bibliographies

	GREENE, Victor R.	(WI)	464
	OZAKI, Hiroko	(ON)	932
Bibliographies & anthropology	KRAKAUER, Elizabeth . .	(CA)	675
Bibliographies & indexing	EVANS, Stephen P.	(OH)	358
Bibliographies for classroom units	WRIGHT, Carolyn R. . . .	(OK)	1370
Bibliographies of Acadian works	POTVIN, Claude	(NB)	987
Bibliography	WISE, Kenda C.	(AL)	1357
	DICKINSON, Donald C. .	(AZ)	300
	FAHY, Terry W.	(AZ)	361
	GOEBEL, Heather L. . . .	(AZ)	443
	GREGORY, Joan A.	(AZ)	466
	POWELL, Lawrence C. . .	(AZ)	988
	BRANDT, Steven R.	(CA)	128
	DURSO, Angeline M. . . .	(CA)	329
	EDELSTEIN, J M.	(CA)	335
	HAMILTON, David M. . . .	(CA)	491
	SHOUSE, Richard	(CA)	1133
	WRIGLEY, Elizabeth S. . .	(CA)	1373
	LI, Hong C.	(CT)	724
	SLOMSKI, Monica J. . . .	(CT)	1150
	BLANDAMER, Ann W. . .	(DC)	103
	DOUMATO, Lamia	(DC)	314
	HICKERSON, Joseph C. .	(DC)	536
	MYERS, R D.	(DC)	885
	SERVERINO, Roberto . .	(DC)	1116
	CATES, Jo A.	(FL)	194
	HO, Paul J.	(FL)	545
	PRATT, Darnell D.	(FL)	990
	ROVIROSA, Dolores F. . .	(FL)	1062
	SKALLERUP, Harry R. . .	(FL)	1145
	AGGARWAL, Narindar K.	(IL)	7
	CALDWELL, John	(IL)	172
	DOYLE, Francis R.	(IL)	317
	EBERHART, George M. .	(IL)	334
	EPP, Ronald H.	(IL)	351
	KRUMMEL, Donald W. . .	(IL)	680
	SKIDMORE, Gail	(IL)	1146
	WELLS, James M.	(IL)	1322
	FUDERER, Laura S.	(IN)	408
	DEGRUSON, Eugene H. .	(KS)	288
	VANDER VELDE, John J.	(KS)	1274
	WILDE, Lucy E.	(KS)	1338
	DESOTO, Randy A.	(LA)	295
	FLEURY, Bruce E.	(LA)	385
	CARPENTER, Kenneth E.	(MA)	185
	SCOTT, Alison M.	(MA)	1106
	STODDARD, Roger E. . .	(MA)	1196
	FILBY, P W.	(MD)	376
	FRYSER, Benjamin S. . .	(MD)	407
	QUINN, Sidney	(MD)	1000
	ARVIN, Charles S.	(MI)	35
	DRAPER, James P.	(MI)	318
	RZEPECKI, Arnold M. . .	(MI)	1072
	MILLES, James G.	(MO)	843
	KELLY, John M.	(MS)	638
	COTTER, Michael G. . . .	(NC)	250
	HARDIE, Karen R.	(NC)	499
	PEDERSON, Randy L. . . .	(ND)	954
	EDWARDS, Susan M. . .	(NJ)	338
	MARCO, Guy A.	(NJ)	769
	MINTZ, Donald M.	(NJ)	847
	SWARTZBURG, Susan G.	(NJ)	1214
	CORNETT, John L.	(NM)	247
	HENDRICKSON, Linnea M.	(NM)	527
	FOLTER, Roland	(NY)	388
	GUBERT, Betty K.	(NY)	475
	HAGSTROM, Jack W. . .	(NY)	483
	JUHL, M E.	(NY)	619
	MARGOLIES, Alan	(NY)	770
	MOONEY, James E.	(NY)	858
	ROSEN, Nathan A.	(NY)	1055
	SMITH, Nicholas N.	(NY)	1159
	SOMERS, Wayne F.	(NY)	1167
	BAILEY, Lois E.	(OH)	46
	CLARK, Harry	(OK)	217
	BAUER, Marilyn A.	(OR)	65
	BUSHMAN, James L. . . .	(OR)	165

BIBLIOGRAPHY (Cont'd)
Bibliography

AZZOLINA, David S. . . .	(PA)	43
BOYTINCK, Paul	(PA)	124
POST, Jeremiah B.	(PA)	986
WOO, Lisa C.	(PA)	1363
MONTEIRO, George . . .	(RI)	856
CHENEY, Frances N. . . .	(TN)	206
DIEHL, Katharine S.	(TX)	302
FRANKUM, Katherine H.	(TX)	398
GIROUARD, J L.	(TX)	438
GOODWIN, Willard	(TX)	450
HARTNESS, Ann	(TX)	508
KENDALL, Lyle H. . . .	(TX)	640
LAVENDER, Kenneth . . .	(TX)	703
LEWIS, John S.	(TX)	723
STONE, Marvin H.	(TX)	1197
CASADY, Richard L. . . .	(UT)	191
YANG, Basil P.	(UT)	1377
GAVER, Mary V.	(VA)	423
HABERLAND, Jody	(VA)	481
HIGBEE, Florence	(VA)	537
JOHNSON, Bryan R. . . .	(VA)	602
THOMAS, Mary E.	(VA)	1237
CARROLL, Barbara T. . .	(WI)	187
MARCUS, Terry C.	(WI)	769
STRATHERN, Gloria V. .	(AB)	1200
MILLER, Gordon	(BC)	838
DIVAY, Gabriele	(MB)	306
SIMUNDSSON, Elva D. .	(MB)	1142
LANDON, Richard G. . . .	(ON)	693
MORLEY, William F.	(ON)	865
WARREN, Peggy A.	(ON)	1306
ALAIN, Jean M.	(PQ)	9
ASTBURY, Effie C.	(PQ)	37
BOILARD, Gilberte	(PQ)	111
CHAGNON, Danielle G. .	(PQ)	197
PELLETIER, Rosaire	(PQ)	955
POWNALL, David E. . . .	(AUS)	989
WANG, Sing W.	(AUS)	1303
GARRETA, J C.	(FRN)	420
OGBAA, Clara K.	(NGR)	918
CHENG, Sheung O.	(TAI)	206
WANG, Sin C.	(TAI)	1303

Bibliography, abstracting, indexing	FALK, Joyce D.	(CA)	362
Bibliography & annotations	BAKISH, David J.	(NY)	50
Bibliography & collection development	COOVER, James B.	(NY)	244
Bibliography & indexing	STIRLING, Dale A.	(WA)	1195
Bibliography & publishing	WOLTER, John A.	(DC)	1362
Bibliography & reference	SEEGRABER, Frank J. . .	(MA)	1111
Bibliography & reference services	WANG, Chi	(DC)	1302
Bibliography & research	ETTER, Patricia A.	(AZ)	355
Bibliography & research guides	LITT, Dorothy E.	(NY)	733
Bibliography & textual	ROYTMAN, Serafima . . .	(NY)	1063
Bibliography & textual studies	BERGER, Sidney E.	(IL)	86
Bibliography, codicology	MATHIESEN, Thomas J. .	(UT)	784
Bibliography, compiling	DELZELL, William R. . . .	(MA)	290
Bibliography development	KINNELL, Susan K.	(CA)	653
	RAJPAR, Shamin H.	(PA)	1004
	NISENOFF, Sylvia	(VA)	905
Bibliography, European hist & religion	ROBERTS, Susanne F. . .	(CT)	1041
Bibliography, imprints	PROPER, David R.	(MA)	995
Bibliography in film & video field	CYR, Helen W.	(MD)	268
Bibliography indexing	BRIERE, Joan M.	(ON)	135
Bibliography, music	LOWENS, Margery M. . . .	(MD)	744
Bibliography of American art	SMITH, Raymond W. . . .	(CT)	1159
Bibliography of art history	ARNTZEN, Etta M.	(IL)	34
Bibliography of Asian studies	SHULMAN, Frank J.	(MD)	1133
Bibliography of doctoral dissertations	SHULMAN, Frank J.	(MD)	1133
Bibliography of English literature	PROPAS, Sharon W. . . .	(OH)	995
Bibliography of history	BOHANAN, Robert D. . . .	(DC)	111
	GRISSO, Karl M.	(IL)	471
	SHELDON, Ted P.	(MO)	1126
Bibliography of Japanese music	SIDDONS, James D. . . .	(VA)	1135
Bibliography of music	TANNO, John W.	(CA)	1223
Bibliography of photography	RULE, Amy E.	(AZ)	1067
Bibliography of psychometrics	JORDAN, Robert P.	(IA)	616
Bibliography of religious studies	STARKEY, Edward D. . . .	(IN)	1182
Bibliography preparation	JOY, Patricia L.	(CT)	618
	CLARK, Jane F.	(GA)	217

BIBLIOGRAPHY (Cont'd)

Bibliography, social scis & humanities	PARROTT, Margaret S. . .	(NC)	944
Bibliography teaching	SCHMITZ, Eugenia E. . .	(WI)	1096
Bibliography, translating, editing	KRAMER-GREENE, Judith	(NY)	675
Bibliography, women's studies	BJORKLUND, Edi	(WI)	100
Biological science bibliography	LUCHSINGER, Arlene E.	(GA)	746
Biological sciences reference & bibl	MANNARINO, Elizabeth R.	(OR)	766
Biology & agriculture bibliography	BLANCHARD, J R.	(CA)	103
Black studies bibliographies	THOMPSON, Karolyn S. .	(MS)	1240
Book selection & bibliography	WEISBAUM, Earl	(TX)	1319
Books, bibliography	GINN, Marjorie J.	(MN)	437
Botanical reference & bibliography	SCHALLERT, Ruth F. . . .	(DC)	1089
Boychoir history & bibliography	ROOT, Arlene V.	(KS)	1053
Business & legal bibliography	CRINION, Jacquelyn A. .	(TX)	259
Business bibliographies	DANIELLS, Lorna M. . . .	(MA)	273
Business bibliography	NEELY, Glenda S.	(KY)	892
	BEAL, Sarell W.	(MI)	68
Business management bibliographies	CHAN, Diana L.	(BC)	199
Business reference bibliography	BROWN, Charlotte D. . . .	(VA)	142
Calvin & Calvinism bibliography	DE KLERK, Peter	(MI)	288
Canadian business bibliography	BROWN, Barbara E. . . .	(ON)	142
Canadiana bibliography	RIDER, Lillian M.	(PQ)	1032
Caribbean bibliography	NANTON-COMISSIONG, Barbara L.	(TRN)	887
Catalan bibliographies	VELA, Leonor G.	(SPN)	1281
Cataloging, bibliographer	DERRICKSON, Margaret	(NY)	294
Chemical engineering bibliography	WEAVER, James B.	(FL)	1312
Chinese bibliography	CHERN, Jenn C.	(GA)	206
Chiropractic resources & bibliography	PETERSON, Dennis R. . . .	(IA)	963
Clinical medical reference bibliography	KINNAIRD, Cheryl D.	(IL)	653
Clinical science bibliography	LIMAYE, Asha A.	(IL)	727
Collection development & bibliography	GRAMENZ, Francis L. . .	(MA)	457
Compilation of bibliographies	PUCCIO, Joseph A.	(DC)	997
	SCHROEDER, Anne M. . .	(IL)	1100
Compiling computer science bibliography	WEINER, Carolynn N. . . .	(NY)	1318
Contemporary American music bibliography	HARTSOCK, Ralph M. . . .	(PA)	508
Criminal justice bibliography	LUNT, Ruth B.	(NY)	749
Current bibliographies	ROADS, Clarice D.	(OK)	1038
Dance bibliography	JACOB, Scott J.	(PA)	589
Descriptive bibliography	HANFF, Peter E.	(CA)	495
	PODESCHI, John B.	(IL)	979
	EPPARD, Philip B.	(MA)	351
	FERGUSON, Stephen . . .	(NJ)	372
	EDDY, Donald D.	(NY)	335
	O'DONNELL, Mary A. . . .	(NY)	917
	BAKY, John S.	(PA)	50
	KAISER, John R.	(PA)	622
	BREGMAN, Alvan M. . . .	(ON)	131
Development of art bibliographies	KING, Carmen M.	(MI)	650
Drug abuse bibliography	ANDREWS, Theodora A.	(IN)	27
Earth sciences bibliography	DERKSEN, Charlotte R. .	(CA)	294
Editing, proofreading, bibliographies	BRADWAY, Becky J.	(IL)	126
Education & psychology bibliography	BAUNER, Ruth E.	(IL)	67
Education bibliographer	CONNORS, Kathleen M.	(OR)	238
Education bibliography	FLOYD, Rebecca M. . . .	(NC)	386
	MCGOWAN, Kathleen M.	(NY)	807
	PILLAI, Karlye A.	(NY)	973
	WEINBERG, Wanda J. . .	(OH)	1318
	SCHWARTZ, Philip J. . .	(TX)	1105
	HINKLE, Mary R.	(VA)	542
Education bibliography, collection mgmt	BROWN, M S.	(FL)	145
Educational bibliography	CARTER, Nancy F.	(CO)	189
Egyptological bibliography	WERNER, Edward K. . . .	(NY)	1324
18th century bibliography	MCNAMARA, Charles B.	(NC)	816
English literature bibliography	THOMSON, Dorothy F. . .	(ON)	1241
Enumerative & textual bibliographies	ABOYADE, Beatrice O. .	(NGR)	2
Enumerative bibliography	COHN, Alan M.	(IL)	229
	WADSWORTH, Robert W.	(IL)	1290
	O'DONNELL, Mary A. . .	(NY)	917
	HARNER, James L.	(OH)	503
Fine & performing arts bibliography	GROVES, Percilla E.	(BC)	474
Fine arts & architecture bibliography	CEDERHOLM, Theresa D.	(MA)	196
Fine arts bibliography	MORR, Lynell A.	(FL)	866
	EVENSEN, Robert L. . . .	(MA)	358
	HASWELL, Hollee	(NY)	511
Foreign affairs bibliography	CARLSON, Julia F.	(DC)	182

BIBLIOGRAPHY (Cont'd)

Foreign law bibliography	SCHWERIN, Kurt	(IL)	1106
	TARNAWSKY, Marta	(PA)	1224
Francophonic African bibliography	SHAYNE, Mette H.	(IL)	1124
French bibliography	WOESTHOFF, Catherine F.	(NY)	1359
Geographical bibliography	BALDWIN, James A.	(IN)	51
George Moore bibliography	GILCHER, Edwin	(VT)	434
Gifted & talented bibliography	GRAVITZ, Ina A.	(NY)	459
High/low literacy bibliographer	KORNITSKY, Judith M.	(FL)	672
Hispanic & Latin American bibliography	ZUBATSKY, David S.	(PA)	1390
Hispanic bibliography	GRUENBECK, Laurie	(TX)	474
Historical bibliography	SMITH, Michael K.	(TX)	1158
	STOKES, Roy B.	(BC)	1196
	WISEMAN, John A.	(ON)	1357
Historical dance & bibliography	KELLER, Kate V.	(PA)	635
History & East Asian studies bibl	BERGER, Kenneth W.	(NC)	85
History bibliographer	CLARKE, Susan M.	(IL)	219
	MISTARAS, Evangeline	(IL)	848
History bibliographies	GEARY, James W.	(OH)	424
History bibliography	CRIDLAND, Nancy C.	(IN)	258
	STOLLER, Michael E.	(NY)	1196
	MYCUE, David J.	(TX)	884
History of bibliography	RAYWARD, W B.	(AUS)	1011
History of photography bibliography	HUGHSTON, Milan R.	(TX)	572
History of Russian, Soviet bibliography	WHITBY, Thomas J.	(CO)	1330
History, political science bibliography	THOMPSON, Ann M.	(OH)	1238
History reference & bibliography	CUDD, John M.	(KY)	263
Holocaust bibliographer	HEUMAN, Rabbi F.	(NY)	535
Humanities & philosophy bibliography	HANNAFORD, William E.	(PA)	496
Humanities & social science bibliography	ROTHACKER, John M.	(TN)	1059
Humanities & social scis bibliography	MCELROY, Neil J.	(CA)	804
	MENZEL, John P.	(NJ)	825
Humanities bibliography	GATES, Jean K.	(FL)	422
	COUTTS, Brian E.	(KY)	252
	MCCALLISTER, Myrna J.	(ME)	793
	GARGAN, William M.	(NY)	419
	HENRY, Mary K.	(NY)	529
Humanities reference & bibliography	BYRE, Calvin S.	(IL)	169
	CUDD, John M.	(KY)	263
	FISHER, Kim N.	(PA)	381
Humanities research & bibliography	DWOSKIN, Beth M.	(MI)	330
Index editing & bibliographies	PETERMAN, Claudia A.	(CA)	962
Indexer, researcher, bibliographer	BELCHER, Emily M.	(NJ)	76
Indexing & bibliographies	KANELY, Edna A.	(DC)	625
Indexing & bibliography	KALE, Shirley W.	(NM)	623
Indexing, bibliography & col devlpmnt	SANCHEZ, Sara M.	(FL)	1079
Indiana authors, bibliography	GILLIS, Ruth J.	(MN)	436
Instructor of music bibliography	MIXTER, Keith E.	(OH)	850
Insurance bibliography	JUSTIE, Julie H.	(IL)	620
Italian bibliography	QUARTELL, Robert J.	(NY)	999
Journal indexes & bibliographies	KAHN, Paul J.	(CA)	622
Judaica bibliography	BAKER, Zachary M.	(NY)	50
Latin American bibliography	MARSHALL, Thomas H.	(AZ)	775
	BRISCOE, Peter M.	(CA)	136
	BALLANTYNE, Lygia M.	(FL)	53
	HALLEWELL, Laurence	(MN)	489
	BETANCOURT, Ingrid T.	(NJ)	92
	SABLE, Martin H.	(WI)	1072
Latin American studies bibliography	GUTIERREZ, Margo	(TX)	479
Latvian bibliography & research	OZOLINS, Karl L.	(MN)	933
Law bibliography	WOOD, Elizabeth B.	(OH)	1364
Lecturing in ethnic & gen bibliography	FISHER, Edith M.	(CA)	380
Legal bibliographies	SURRENCY, Erwin C.	(GA)	1210
Legal bibliographies & databases	KAVASS, Igor I.	(TN)	631
Legal bibliography	BRIDGMAN, David L.	(CA)	135
	SULLIVAN, Martha J.	(CT)	1208
	GEHRINGER, Susanne E.	(DC)	425
	WOODARD, Joseph L.	(FL)	1365
	KLINK, Carol A.	(IL)	662
	ENSIGN, David J.	(KS)	350
	COOPER, Byron D.	(MI)	242
	BOMARC, M D.	(NC)	113
	GOTT, Gary D.	(ND)	453
	ANTHONY, Donald C.	(NY)	28
	HAMMOND, Jane L.	(NY)	493
	KLECKNER, Simone M.	(NY)	658

BIBLIOGRAPHY (Cont'd)

Legal bibliography	MOREHEAD, Joe	(NY)	863
	RICHERT, Paul	(OH)	1030
	GLOECKNER, Paul B.	(PA)	441
	KERCHOF, Kathryn K.	(PA)	643
	CROSS, Joseph R.	(SC)	260
	HOOD, Lawrence E.	(TX)	556
	TEMPLETON, Virginia E.	(TX)	1231
	WALTER, Raimund E.	(WGR)	1300
Legal bibliography, rare books	TRIFFIN, Nicholas	(NY)	1256
Legal bibliography reference	NELSON, Mary A.	(MO)	894
Legal research & bibliography	SCHANCK, Peter C.	(KS)	1090
Legal research, bibliography	DUNCAN, Rebecca	(CA)	325
Libraries, bibliography of Latin America	JACKSON, William V.	(TX)	588
Linguistics, bibliography, reference	KELLY, Richard J.	(MN)	638
Literary bibliography	ABBOTT, Craig S.	(IL)	1
Manual & online bibliography	KREITZBURG, Marilyn J.	(PA)	677
Manuscripts & records bibl control	KELLER, William B.	(DC)	636
Max Beerbohm bibliography	LASNER, Mark S.	(DC)	700
Medical bibliographies	MARTIN, Lyn M.	(NY)	777
Medical bibliography	KLINK, Carol A.	(IL)	662
	EDDY, Leonard M.	(KY)	335
	KOBAYASHI, Michiko	(MD)	666
	KRIVDA, Marita J.	(PA)	679
Medical databases bibliography	BLOKH, Basheva	(NY)	106
Mexican studies bibliographer	RIVERA, Diana H.	(MI)	1037
Mexican-American bibliography	TRUJILLO, Roberto G.	(CA)	1259
Mexican-American studies bibliography	GUTIERREZ, Margo	(TX)	479
Microcomputers in bibliography	LANCASTER, John	(MA)	692
Modern Christian art & bibliography	RAMSEY, Robert D.	(CA)	1006
Multisubject bibliographies compilation	HOTIMLANSKA, Leah D.	(IL)	562
Music bibliography	SMITH, Dorman H.	(AZ)	1154
	ADAMSON, Danette	(CA)	6
	COLBY, Edward E.	(CA)	230
	DUGGAN, Mary K.	(CA)	324
	ELLIOTT, Patricia G.	(CA)	344
	FRY, Stephen M.	(CA)	407
	MOULTON, Suzanne L.	(CO)	873
	KELLER, Michael A.	(CT)	635
	PRUETT, James W.	(DC)	996
	TEMPERLEY, Nicholas	(IL)	1230
	FLING, Robert M.	(IN)	385
	MCKNIGHT, Mark C.	(LA)	812
	EVENSEN, Robert L.	(MA)	358
	OCHS, Michael	(MA)	915
	SHEETS, Robin R.	(MD)	1125
	BLACK-SHIER, Mary L.	(MI)	102
	DRUESEDOW, John E.	(NC)	320
	WURSTEN, Richard B.	(NC)	1374
	DIAMOND, Harold J.	(NY)	299
	FOLTER, Siegrun H.	(NY)	388
	HILL, George R.	(NY)	539
	ELLIKER, Calvin	(PA)	343
	YOUNG, James B.	(PA)	1382
	BRENNAN, Patricia B.	(RI)	133
	PEAKE, Luise E.	(SC)	952
	REED, Marcia E.	(WA)	1015
	WENK, Arthur B.	(PQ)	1324
	SCHUURSMA, Ann B.	(NET)	1103
Music bibliography & cataloging	HARTIG, Linda	(WI)	508
Music bibliography & discography	MCCLELLAN, William M.	(IL)	796
Music bibliography & history	VILES, Elza A.	(TN)	1284
Music bibliography & publishing	BRYCE, Maria C.	(ON)	152
Music bibliography & reference	HAEFLIGER, Kathleen A.	(NY)	482
Music cataloging & bibliography	DURIS, Richard M.	(PA)	328
Mythology bibliography & research	GARDNER, Sue A.	(NJ)	418
National & historical bibliography	KEMP, Thomas J.	(CT)	639
National & trade bibliography	ROPER, Fred W.	(SC)	1054
Near East bibliography	WERYHO, Jan W.	(PQ)	1325
New Jersey bibliography	SINCLAIR, Donald A.	(NJ)	1142
New Orleans bibliography	JUMONVILLE, Florence M.	(LA)	619
Newspaper bibliography	HOVISH, Joseph J.	(IN)	563
Northern bibliography	KOBELKA, Carolynn L.	(NT)	666
Nuclear magnetic resonance bibliography	PARR, John R.	(ON)	943
Numismatic bibliography	CAMPBELL, Francis D.	(NY)	176
Nursing bibliography	ANDREWS, Theodora A.	(IN)	27

BIBLIOGRAPHY (Cont'd)

Pathfinders & bibliographies — MORGAN, Pamela S. . . . (NF) 864
Performing arts selection & bibliography — VAN NIEL, Eloise S. . . . . (HI) 1276
Pharmaceutical sciences bibliography — ANDREWS, Theodora A. (IN) 27
Pharmacy bibliography — ARTH, Janet M. . . . . (MN) 35
Pharmacy reference & bibliography — MANNARINO, Elizabeth R. (OR) 766
Philosophical bibliography — BYNAGLE, Hans E. . . . . (WA) 168
Physical sciences bibliography — SEILER, Susan L. . . . . . . (FL) 1112
Political science bibliography — WERTHEIMER, Marilyn L. (CO) 1325
Popular culture bibliography — SCOTT, Randall W. . . . . (MI) 1108
Popular music bibliography — COOPER, B L. . . . . (MI) 242
Psychology & education bibliography — JOHNSON, Linda B. . . . (CA) 607
Psychology bibliography — WHELAN, Julia S. . . . . . (MA) 1329
Psychology reference & bibliography — KAUFFMAN, Inge S. . . . (CA) 631
Quaker bibliography — DENSMORE, Christopher (NY) 293
Quebec legal bibliography — TANGUAY, Guy . . . . . . (PQ) 1222
Rare books & bibliography — CRESSWELL, Donald H. . (PA) 258
Rare books of bibliography — DOAK, Wesley A. . . . . . . (OR) 306
Reference & bibliography — JOHNSON, Elizabeth G. . (AL) 604
　　— RAMER, James D. . . . . . (AL) 1005
　　— WOLD, Shelley T. . . . . . (AR) 1359
　　— MAACK, Mary N. . . . . . (CA) 753
　　— RAFAEL, Ruth K. . . . . . (CA) 1003
　　— BARTHELL, Daniel W. . . (DC) 61
　　— CAHALANE, Edmond P. . (DC) 171
　　— TRUETT, Carol A. . . . . . (HI) 1259
　　— CUNNINGHAM, William D. (MD) 265
　　— SLAVENS, Thomas P. . . (MI) 1148
　　— CARROLL, C E. . . . . . . (MO) 187
　　— COLBY, Robert A. . . . . . (NY) 230
　　— STERN, Liselotte B. . . . . (NY) 1189
　　— SANTAVICCA, Edmund F. (OH) 1082
　　— BURNS, Richard K. . . . . (PA) 162
　　— CLARKSON, Mary C. . . . (TX) 219
　　— THORNE, Bonnie B. . . . . (TX) 1242
　　— CORBEIL, Lizette . . . . . . (PQ) 245
Reference & bibliography services — MUNDELL, Eric L. . . . . (IN) 878
Reference & bibliography work — LAMPRECHT, Sandra J. . (CA) 691
Reference & education bibliography — ROBERTS, Francis X. . . . (CO) 1040
Reference bibliography — ECKLUND, Kristin A. . . . (CA) 335
Ref, bibliography, humanities, soc scis — DAVIS, Donald G. . . . . . (TX) 278
Reference, humanities bibliography — KRAUSSE, Sylvia C. . . . (RI) 676
Reference, psychology bibliography — CROSBY-MUILENBURG, Corryn . . . . (CA) 260
Reference, research & bibliography — DICKSON, Katherine M. . (MD) 301
Reference work & bibliographies — EARL, Susan R. . . . . (NC) 332
Religion & philosophy bibliography — HIGGINBOTHAM, Richard C. . . . . (IL) 537
　　— ALTMANN, Thomas F. . . (WI) 18
Religion & theology bibliography — MCGARTY, Jean R. . . . . (MI) 805
Religious studies bibliography — CRIDLAND, Nancy C. . . (IN) 258
Research & bibliography — STEFANCIC, Jean A. . . . (CA) 1185
Researcher & bibliographer — LEONARD, Angela M. . . (DC) 716
Russian & East European bibliography — BEAVEN, Miranda J. . . . (MN) 71
Russian bibliography — POLANSKY, Patricia A. . (HI) 980
Scandinavian bibliography — THORSTENSSON, Edith J. (MN) 1243
Science & engineering bibliography — MALINOWSKY, H R. . . . (IL) 763
Science & history bibliography — LEE, J S. . . . . (NJ) 710
Science & technology bibliography — BAILEY, Martha J. . . . . (IN) 46
　　— GLUCK, Myke H. . . . . . . (NC) 442
　　— COHEN, Jackson B. . . . . (NY) 228
Science bibliography — LUDWIG, J D. . . . . (AK) 746
　　— CHAMPLIN, Peggy . . . . . (CA) 198
　　— FLICK, Frances J. . . . . . (IA) 385
　　— MARSHALL, Jessica A. . . (IA) 774
　　— PETERSON, Sally R. . . . (IA) 964
　　— MARION, Donald J. . . . . (MN) 770
　　— CLARK, Camille S. . . . . . (NV) 216
　　— KREIDER, Janice A. . . . . (BC) 677
Science bibliography & reference — DEGOLYER, Christine C. (NY) 288
Science, biology & nursing bibliography — COOPER, Rosemarie A. . (IL) 243
Science fiction bibliography — KRIEGER, Lee A. . . . . . (NC) 678
　　— DAWSON, Terry P. . . . . (WI) 282
Scientific bibliography — LAVKULICH, Joanne . . . (AB) 704
17th century French bibliography — CHAMBERS, Bettye T. . . (DC) 198
Sisters of Mercy bibliography & history — MULDREY, Mary H. . . . . (LA) 876

BIBLIOGRAPHY (Cont'd)

16th century French bibliography — CHAMBERS, Bettye T. . . (DC) 198
Slavic bibliography — ZALEWSKI, Wojciech . . . (CA) 1385
　　— DOBCZANSKY, Jurij W. . (DC) 307
　　— LORKOVIC, Tatjana B. . . (IA) 741
　　— STUART, Mary P. . . . . . . (IL) 1204
　　— GALIK, Barbara A. . . . . . (MI) 413
　　— CORRSIN, Stephen D. . . (NY) 247
　　— GOERNER, Tatiana . . . . (NY) 443
　　— RAINWATER, Jean M. . . (RI) 1004
Slavic bibliography & reference — TURCHYN, Andrew . . . . (IN) 1263
Social science bibliographies — DESSAINT, Alain Y. . . . . (VA) 295
Social science bibliography — MCNAMARA, Jay . . . . . (AL) 816
　　— SCHILLER, Anita R. . . . . (CA) 1093
　　— HALIBEY, Areta V. . . . . . (IL) 486
　　— GERACI, Diane . . . . (NY) 428
　　— LUNT, Ruth B. . . . . (NY) 749
　　— HOVDE, David M. . . . . . (OK) 563
Social sciences & history bibliography — BROWN, Philip L. . . . . . . (SD) 146
Social sciences bibliographer — MISTARAS, Evangeline . (IL) 848
　　— COHEN, Steven J. . . . . . (OH) 229
Social sciences bibliography — TSANG, Daniel C. . . . . . (CA) 1260
　　— MEDER, Marylouise D. . . (KS) 820
　　— COUTTS, Brian E. . . . . . (KY) 252
　　— BEAL, Sarell W. . . . . . . (MI) 68
　　— JOHNSON, Deborah S. . . (MN) 603
　　— SWINDLER, Luke . . . . . . (NC) 1216
　　— HAGERMAN, George F. . . (NY) 483
South Asian bibliography — NYE, James H. . . . . (IL) 912
South Asian bibliography & research — SEN, Joyce H. . . . . (NY) 1115
Southeast Asian studies bibliography — GAMER, May L. . . . . (MO) 416
Spanish & Latin American bibliography — MORENO, Rafael . . . . . . (PA) 863
Spanish bibliographies — CORREDOR, Javier . . . . (TX) 247
Special librarianship & bibliography — BRITT, Mary C. . . . . (AL) 137
Special music bibliographies — LYON, Bruce C. . . . . (FL) 752
State & regnl literature & history bibl — RAZER, Robert L. . . . . . (AR) 1012
Subject bibliographer — MARKSON, Eileen . . . . . (PA) 771
Subject bibliographies — MARSCHNER, Robyn J. . (CO) 773
　　— SPARKS, Martha E. . . . . (NC) 1171
Subject bibliography — OLSON, Lowell E. . . . . . (MN) 923
　　— MEYERS, Charles . . . . . (NY) 830
Subject bibliography for nursing — CHAN, Lillian L. . . . . . . (CA) 199
Subject bibliography for public health — CHAN, Lillian L. . . . . . . (CA) 199
Textual & enumerative bibliography — WHITE, D J. . . . . (MO) 1330
Theatre bibliography — RAKSHI, Sri R. . . . . (NY) 1004
　　— BALL, John L. . . . . (ON) 52
Theater history & bibliography — HECK, Thomas F. . . . . . (OH) 519
Theological bibliography — MILLER, William C. . . . . (MO) 843
　　— FERRIBY, Peter G. . . . . . (NJ) 373
　　— TAYLOR, Sharon A. . . . . (NJ) 1228
　　— WARTLUFT, David J. . . . (PA) 1307
　　— FRITZ, William R. . . . . . . (SC) 405
　　— HAYMES, Don . . . . (TN) 516
　　— IBACH, Robert D. . . . . . (TX) 581
Theological bibliography & research — OZOLINS, Karl L. . . . . . (MN) 933
Theological, bibl, collection devlpmnt — ERDEL, Timothy P. . . . . (JAM) 352
Toxicology bibliographies — HAUTH, Carol A. . . . . . . (CA) 513
US history bibliography — RHODES, Saralinda A. . . (KS) 1026
Urban planning bibliography — CHIBNIK, Katharine R. . . (NY) 207
Veterinary medicine bibliography — KERKER, Ann E. . . . . . . (IN) 643
Victorian literature & bibliography — LASNER, Mark S. . . . . . (DC) 700
World War II bibliography — ZIEGLER, Janet M. . . . . (CA) 1388

BIBLIOMETRICS

Bibliometric analyses — FETTERMAN, Nelma I. . . (AB) 374
Bibliometric studies — MOUREAU, Magdeleine . (FRN) 873
Bibliometric studies, col development — CLARK, Sharon E. . . . . . (IL) 218
Bibliometrics — COFFMAN, Joseph W. . . (GA) 227
　　— LANCASTER, Frederick W. . . . . (IL) 691
　　— DESTEFANO, Daniel A. . (MA) 296
　　— PAO, Miranda L. . . . . . . (MI) 938
　　— WITTIG, Glenn R. . . . . . (MS) 1358
　　— BURTON, Robert E. . . . . (NY) 164
　　— GRIFFITH, Belver C. . . . (PA) 469
　　— CHOI, Jin M. . . . . (SC) 210
　　— SCHRADER, Alvin M. . . . (AB) 1099
　　— YAMAZAKI, Shigeaki . . . (JAP) 1377

BIBLIOMETRICS (Cont'd)
Bibliometrics & citation studies — AVERSA, Elizabeth S. . . . (DC) 41
Bibliometrics & scientometrics — HURT, Charlie D. . . . . . . (AZ) 578

BIBLIOSERVICES
Multilingual biblioservices — MEUNIER, Pierre . . . . . . (PQ) 829

BIBLIOTHERAPY
Bibliotherapy — BROWN, Marie H. . . . . . (CA) 146
BROWN, Marie H. . . . . . (CA) 146
HELO, Martin . . . . (MA) 525
ROBINSON, Doris J. . . . . (OH) 1043
BURT, Lesta N. . . . . . . (TX) 164
NISBY, Dora R. . . . . . . (TX) 904
MERWINE, Glenda M. . . (WA) 827
MONROE, Margaret E. . . (WI) 855
BEATTIE, Kathleen M. . . (AUS) 70
ADENEY, Carol D. . . . . (WGR) 6
Bibliotherapy training — HYNES, Arleen M. . . . . . (MN) 580
Children & youth services,
   bibliotherapy — SMITH, Alice G. . . . . . . (FL) 1152

BILINGUAL (See also Multilingual)
Bilingual education — PEISER, Richard H. . . . . (IL) 955
DE CUENCA, Pilar A. . . . (NY) 286
Bilingual interpretation — CHANG, Joseph I. . . . . . (NJ) 200
Bilingual librarianship — MAYES, Susan E. . . . . . (NC) 789
Bilingual materials — DALE, Doris C. . . . . (IL) 270
Bilingual services — CASTRO, Rafaela G. . . . (CA) 194
Bilingual services in Spanish — DIAZ, Magna M. . . . . . . (PA) 299
Bilingual translation — CHANG, Joseph I. . . . . . (NJ) 200

BINDERS
Binders board manufacturing — BROOKS, Alfred C. . . . . (NJ) 140

BINDINGS (See also Repair)
Binding — ARMSTRONG, Ruth C. . . (FL) 32
SWANSON, Joe . . . . . . (GA) 1213
CALCAGNO, Philip M. . . (IL) 172
STAPLETON, Diana L. . . (KY) 1181
UNGER, Carol P. . . . . . (MD) 1269
Binding & book preservation — SNELL, Patricia P. . . . . . (CA) 1163
Binding & repair — WOODS, Janet R. . . . . . (WY) 1367
Binding preparation — GELENTER, Winifred H. . (MD) 426
Cataloging, binding — NESBITT, Olive K. . . . . . (PA) 896
Early illustrated books & bindings — WITTEN, Laurence . . . . . (CT) 1358
History of binding — NEEDHAM, Paul . . . . . . (NY) 891
Library binding — HENDERSON, William T. . (IL) 527
FAIRFIELD, John R. . . . (NC) 361
GRAUER, Sally M. . . . . (NY) 458
HEIDTMANN, Toby . . . . (OH) 521
Library binding services — HECKMAN, Stephen P. . . (IN) 520
Online computerized binding
   preparation — HECKMAN, Stephen P. . . (IN) 520
Preservation, binding, restoration — ALLEN, Doris L. . . . . . . (CA) 14
Serials binding & acquisitions — GOLIAN, Linda M. . . . . . (FL) 447

BIOCHEMISTRY
Biochemistry & electronics — MULDER, Marjorie M. . . . (OH) 876
Biochemistry & general sciences — ROMANIUK, Elena . . . . . (BC) 1052
Biochemistry, steroid hormone
   receptors — MCFARLAND, Robert T. . (MO) 805
Medicine, toxicology, & biochemistry — JOHNSON, Susan W. . . (MD) 609
Online biochemistry searching — SIESS, Judith A. . . . . . . (OH) 1136

BIOELECTROMAGNETIC
Bioelectromagnetic medicine — DIAL, Zona P. . . . . (AZ) 299

BIOENGINEERING
Bioengineering — FUENTES, Ismael . . . . . (SPN) 408

BIOETHICS
Bioethics — MOORE, Rue I. . . . . . . (NY) 861

BIOGRAPHY
American history & biography — HANKAMER, Roberta A. (MA) 496
Author of children's biographies — MILLENDER, Dharathola . (IN) 835
Biographic collection — MOFFETT, Martha L. . . . (FL) 852
Biographical information — MASON, Margaret E. . . . (IL) 781
Biographical research — BERGAN, Helen J. . . . . . (DC) 85
ARMEIT, Marilyn . . . . . (NY) 32
Biographical research for artists — BAILEY, Tuuli T. . . . . . . (AZ) 47
Biography — NASSO, Christine . . . . . (MI) 889
Biography reference — DOPP, Bonnie J. . . . . . . (DC) 312
History, biography & genealogy — MUTCH, Donald G. . . . . (ON) 883
Regional medical biography — REDMON, Sherrill . . . . . (KY) 1014
Science & technology biogph
   instruction — SABIN, Robert G. . . . . . . (AL) 1072
Theatre biographical indexing — ULRICH, Paul S. . . . . . . (WGR) 268

BIOLOGY (See also Microbiology)
Agriculture & biology online searching — GRAINGER, Bruce . . . . . (PQ) 457
Biological & agricultural databases — CACCESE, Vincent . . . . (CA) 170
JOHNSON, Deanna L. . . (CA) 603
SHAH, Syed M. . . . . . . (NY) 1119
Biological & agricultural journals — SHAH, Syed M. . . . . . . (NY) 1119
Biological & chemical databases — BORCK, Liba . . . . (ISR) 116
Biological & medical databases — ROBINSON, Michaele M. (CA) 1044
Biological database searching — FELDMAN, Laurence M. . (MA) 369
Biological databases — STOCKER, Randi L. . . . . (IN) 1195
EVANS, Sylvia D. . . . . . (MD) 358
ALLRED, Paula M. . . . . . (MI) 17
THOMAS, Katharine S. . . (NC) 1237
HOFFMAN, Helen B. . . . (NJ) 548
NOCKA, Jean A. . . . . . (NJ) 906
WILLIAMS, Doris C. . . . (NY) 1343
KELLY, Maureen C. . . . (PA) 638
KENNEDY, H E. . . . . . . (PA) 641
SEPP, Frederick C. . . . . (PA) 1115
SAMPLE, Charles R. . . . (WA) 1078
Biological libraries — SOLBRIG, Dorothy J. . . . (MA) 1166
Biological literature — DAVIS, Elisabeth B. . . . . (IL) 278
Biological literature instruction — WILLIAMS, Doris C. . . . . (NY) 1343
Biological science bibliography — LUCHSINGER, Arlene E. (GA) 746
Biological science medicine reference — CHASTAIN-WARHEIT,
   Christine C. . . . . (DE) 203
Biological science reference — MACLEAN, Jayne T. . . . (MD) 757
GAGE, Marilyn K. . . . . . (OK) 412
Biological sciences — BULLARD, Rita J. . . . . . (MI) 156
HAMMARSKJOLD,
   Carolyn A. . . . . (MI) 493
SCHMIDT, Jean M. . . . . (MN) 1095
BUSH, Renee B. . . . . . . (NY) 165
ZIPF, Elizabeth M. . . . . . (PA) 1389
LOPICCOLO, Cathy J. . . (TX) 741
BOISVENUE, Marie J. . . (ON) 111
Biological sciences cataloging — HAWVER, Nancy . . . . . (CA) 515
Biological sciences reference & bibl — MANNARINO, Elizabeth R. (OR) 766
Biology — DONOVAN, William A. . . (IL) 312
LEWIS, Ruth E. . . . . . . (MO) 724
KURZ, David B. . . . . . . (OH) 685
MCGEE, Yvonne M. . . . (PA) 806
MACLEAN, Eleanor A. . . (PQ) 757
Biology, agriculture & environment — LANE, David M. . . . . . . (NH) 694
Biology & agriculture bibliography — BLANCHARD, J R. . . . . (CA) 103
Biology & chemistry — ANDERSON, Ruby N. . . . (AL) 25
Biology & chemistry collection
   devlpmnt — DODSON, Snowdy D. . . . (CA) 308
Biology & marine science — BROWNLOW, Judith . . . (MA) 148
Biology, chemistry — KHAN, Mohammed A. . . . (SDA) 646
Biology databases — PETERSON, Gretchen N. (CA) 963
GRAY, Dorothy A. . . . . . (KY) 459
Biology libraries — DARLING, John B. . . . . . (NC) 275
Biology, psychology, geology — RONNERMANN, Gail . . . (NY) 1053
Biology reference — WILLIAMS, Doris C. . . . . (NY) 1343
Biology reference & selection — WINIARZ, Elizabeth . . . . (PQ) 1355
Chemical & biological databases — STODDARD, Charles E. . (CT) 1196
SUPEAU, Cynthia . . . . . (CT) 1210

BIOLOGY (Cont'd)

Chemical, biological & medical databases	LONGENECKER, William H.	(MD)	740
Chemical, biological, medical databases	FARREN, Ann L.	(PA)	365
Computer searching, biological sciences	CULOTTA, Wendy A.	(CA)	264
Information virology, molecular biology	PERLMAN, Stephen E.	(NY)	959
Marine biology	COLEMAN, David E.	(HI)	231
Marine biology information	BALDRIDGE, Alan	(CA)	51
Marine biology reference	MARKHAM, James W.	(CA)	771
Medical & biological databases	NEWAY, Julie M.	(CA)	898
Medical, biological, & business database	MANDEL, Douglas J.	(IL)	765
Molecular biology immunogenetics	BERWICK, Mary C.	(PA)	91
Online biology searching	CHEN, Flora F.	(SK)	205
Science, biology & nursing bibliography	COOPER, Rosemarie A.	(IL)	243

BIOMEDICAL

Biomedical	KEIZUR, Berta L.	(CA)	635
Biomedical & applied science databases	LETT, Rosalind K.	(GA)	719
Biomedical & bioscience	JENSEN, Marilyn A.	(CA)	599
Biomedical & health reference	MYER, Nancy E.	(NM)	884
Biomedical & medical socioeconomic info	BANKS, Jane L.	(DC)	54
Biomedical & scientific databases	CARRIGAN, John L.	(CA)	186
Biomedical communications	BADER, Shelley	(DC)	44
	HARRIS, John C.	(MA)	504
Biomedical comms & documents delivery	LETT, Rosalind K.	(GA)	719
Biomedical computerized lit searching	DORNER, Marian T.	(OH)	313
Biomedical computing	JAMES, Brent C.	(UT)	592
Biomedical data acquisitions	PEETERS, Marc D.	(BEL)	954
Biomedical database searching	KUSHINKA, Kerry L.	(NJ)	685
	BAKER, Carole A.	(OH)	48
Biomedical databases	BLITZ, Ruth R.	(CA)	105
	TAOKA, Wesley M.	(CA)	1223
	WEISS, Barbara M.	(CT)	1319
	FRANKLIN, Janice C.	(KS)	397
	GERMANN, Malcolm P.	(KS)	429
	LEIGHTON, Helene L.	(MA)	714
	COLAIANNI, Lois A.	(MD)	229
	HARRIMAN, Jenny F.	(MD)	503
	BAKER, Alison	(ME)	47
	SHIPLEY, Ruth M.	(MO)	1131
	PHILLIPS, Carol H.	(NJ)	967
	SZE, Melanie C.	(NJ)	1218
	WEGLARZ, Catherine R.	(NJ)	1316
	FALVEY, Genemary H.	(NY)	363
	WEIS, Ann M.	(NY)	1319
	BERWICK, Mary C.	(PA)	91
	GREEN, Patricia L.	(PA)	462
	KLEINSTEIN, Bruce H.	(PA)	660
	SEEDS, Robert S.	(PA)	1111
	WICKS, Pamela J.	(PA)	1335
	HANKS, Ellen T.	(TX)	496
	CLEMANS, Margaret H.	(VA)	220
	WILDER, Patricia A.	(WA)	1339
	MENITOVE, Symie D.	(WI)	824
	HAYWARD, Miriam C.	(PQ)	517
	NOZOE, Atsutake	(JAP)	911
Biomedical ethics databases & info	GROVER, Wilma S.	(FL)	474
Biomedical indexing & abstracting	JOHNSON, Hilary C.	(DE)	605
Biomedical information	HUNT, Richard K.	(CA)	575
	HAYWARD, Miriam C.	(PQ)	517
	NOZOE, Atsutake	(JAP)	911
Biomedical information resources	BROERING, Naomi C.	(DC)	139
Biomedical information services	KOLMAN, Roberta F.	(HI)	669
	SHIPLEY, Ruth M.	(MO)	1131
Biomedical librarianship	SCHEETZ, Kathy D.	(IA)	1091
Biomedical libraries	NEELEY, Kathleen L.	(KS)	892
	NOZOE, Atsutake	(JAP)	911
Biomedical literature research, indexing	COMPTON, Joan C.	(CA)	235
Biomedical literature searching	SMITH, Yvonne B.	(NJ)	1161
Biomedical online database searching	COAN, La V.	(MI)	224

BIOMEDICAL (Cont'd)

Biomedical polymers	STAVETSKI, Norma K.	(NJ)	1183
Biomedical reference	WEGLARZ, Catherine R.	(NJ)	1316
	KANESHIRO, Kellie N.	(TX)	625
	VAN REENEN, Johannes A.	(BC)	1277
Biomedical reference service	FURUMOTO, Viola G.	(HI)	410
Biomedical reference services	COSKEY, Rosemary B.	(MD)	248
Biomedical references	CONNOR, Elizabeth	(MD)	237
Biomedical research online & manual	LETT, Rosalind K.	(GA)	719
Biomedical science information	POWELL, James R.	(MI)	988
Bio-medical science reference	MOORE, John R.	(IL)	860
Biomedical sciences	DURSO, Angeline M.	(CA)	329
	HADDEN, Robert L.	(MD)	481
Biomedical sciences cataloging	WURANGIAN, Nelia C.	(CA)	1374
Biomedical searching	KENTON, Charlotte	(MD)	642
	CYGAN, Rose M.	(MI)	268
	MACKSEY, Julie A.	(MI)	757
Biomedical searching online	DOBBS, David L.	(OH)	307
Biomedical subjects	CRAIG, James L.	(MA)	254
Biomedical unit management	LEITH, Anna R.	(BC)	714
Chemical & biomedical information	RADER, Ronald A.	(DC)	1002
History of biomedicine	DAVIS, Elisabeth B.	(IL)	278
Online searching, biomedical literature	INGUI, Bettejean	(CO)	583
Scientific & biomedical database mktg	ZAJDEL, George J.	(PA)	1385

BIOSCIENCE

Biomedical & bioscience	JENSEN, Marilyn A.	(CA)	599
Bioscience	RAFATS, Jerome M.	(MD)	1003
Bio-sciences databases	CARUSO, Joy L.	(IL)	190

BIOTECHNOLOGY

Agricultural biotechnology	LARSON, Jean A.	(MD)	699
Biotechnology	RADER, Ronald A.	(DC)	1002
	HOFFMAN, Helen B.	(NJ)	548
	CAMBRIA, Roberto	(NY)	174
Biotechnology databases	LANG, Anita E.	(TX)	695
	SCHEPPER, Josee H.	(PQ)	1091
Biotechnology information	SAARI, David S.	(IN)	1072
	SCHEPPER, Josee H.	(PQ)	1091
Biotechnology information retrieval	SCHEPPER, Josee H.	(PQ)	1091
Biotechnology information services	NEWAY, Julie M.	(CA)	898
Biotechnology search analyst	FRANZELLO, Joseph J.	(TX)	398
Pharmaceutical & biotechnology info	DIXON, Michael D.	(VA)	306

BLACK (See also Afro-American)

American Black Catholic history	HOGAN, Peter E.	(MD)	549
Black American culture	SCOTT, Lydia E.	(PA)	1107
Black American history manuscripts	WEST, Donald	(MI)	1326
Black experience	CORBIN, Evelyn D.	(NY)	245
Black genealogy, Indian genealogy	DAVIS, Denyvetta	(OK)	278
Black history	OAKLANDER, Linda G.	(MI)	913
	MENINGALL, Evelyn L.	(NJ)	824
	GREEN, Jeffrey P.	(ENG)	462
Black history collection maintenance	PULLER, Maryam W.	(PA)	997
Black music	RICHARDSON, Deborra A.	(DC)	1029
Black music research	DE LERMA, Dominique R.	(MD)	289
	GRENDYSA, Peter A.	(WI)	467
Black studies	BULLOCK, Penelope L.	(GA)	156
	HORNE, Dorice L.	(NY)	560
Black studies bibliographies	THOMPSON, Karolyn S.	(MS)	1240
Black studies librarianship	RUDISELL, Carol A.	(DE)	1065
	KENDRICK, Curtis L.	(NY)	640
Black, women & management studies	JONES-TRENT, Bernice R.	(VA)	616
Retailer of Black literature	MILLENDER, Dharathola	(IN)	835

BLAIR

Blair County culture	SHERIDAN, Margaret G.	(PA)	1127

BLIND (See also Braille, Impaired, Large, Talking, Visually)

Blind & handicapped	KLAUBER, Julie B.	(NY)	658
Blind & physically handicapped	COLEMAN, James M.	(AL)	231
Blind library services, computers	ROATCH, Mary A.	(AZ)	1038
Blind reading services	MCCASLIN, Cheryl A.	(TX)	795
Handicaps & blindness information	WILSON, Barbara L.	(RI)	1350

BLIND (Cont'd)

Libraries for the blind	GORAL, Barbara J.	(CO)	451
	LIGHTNER, Karen J.	(PA)	727
	HERZ, Michael J.	(VI)	534
Services to the blind	FINNEY, Lance C.	(MD)	379
Training the blind	BEIMAN, Frances M.	(NJ)	75

BLOOD

Blood platelet function	LASSLO, Andrew	(TN)	700

BOARDS (See also Trusteeship)

Administration board relationships	MEADOWS, Donald F.	(BC)	819
Binders board manufacturing	BROOKS, Alfred C.	(NJ)	140
Board-operated resource centers	BERTRAND, Doreen M.	(ON)	91
County library board management	COLE, Jack W.	(MN)	230
Electronic bulletin boards	POLLY, Jean A.	(NY)	981
	SCHWARZ, Joy L.	(WI)	1105
Electronic mail & bulletin boards	O'NEILL, Sue	(MD)	924
Library boards, community relations	GIBSON, Barbara H.	(CT)	431
Library boards selection & training	LIPTON, Connie F.	(MI)	732
Library bulletin boards	MENINGALL, Evelyn L.	(NJ)	824
LSCA advisory board	STEVENSON, Marilyn E.	(CA)	1191
PC bulletin boards	ROSE, Phillip E.	(CO)	1055
Printed circuit boards	ZANG, Patricia J.	(VA)	1386
Public library trustee board	GRUHL, Andrea M.	(DC)	474
Staff, board training & development	GIBSON, Barbara H.	(CT)	431
Training of boards of trustees	STIEGEMEYER, Nancy H.	(MO)	1193

BOND (See also Elections, Finance, Investment, Securities, Stock)

Bond elections	KELLUM-ROSE, Nancy P.	(CA)	637
Bond issue & tax referendums	BECKER, Josephine M.	(FL)	72
Bond rating	ZOTTOLI, Danny A.	(NY)	1390
Domestic stock & bonds	LAWSON, George F.	(NY)	705
Stock & bond pricing	SOSTACK, Maura	(NY)	1169
Stock & bond quotations	PAYNE, Linda C.	(NY)	951

BOOK TRAK

Library automation system, Book Trak	JACKSON, Nancy I.	(FL)	588

BOOKBINDING

Book-binding	BROWN, G R.	(FL)	144
	PYATT, Timothy D.	(OR)	999
	THOMAS, Page A.	(TX)	1238
	VAN ESS, James E.	(WI)	1275
Bookbinding repair	LANE, David R.	(CA)	694
Book-binding, repair, conservation	AUSTIN, Kristi N.	(WA)	40
Bookbinding services	BOWEN, Theodora	(CA)	120
Hand bookbinding	MOORE, Harold H.	(GA)	859
Rare books & hand bookbinding	SMITH, Margit J.	(ENG)	1157

BOOKMAKING

Bookmaking, children as authors	HERRICK, Johanna W.	(HI)	532

BOOKMOBILES

Book selection, bookmobiles	MONTANA, Edward J.	(MA)	855
Bookmobile & outreach services	LEONARD, Gloria J.	(WA)	716
Bookmobile coordination	GRIMLEY, Susan M.	(SC)	470
Bookmobile extension	PHILIP, John J.	(OH)	967
Bookmobile funding	MARSHALL, Ruth T.	(GA)	775
Bookmobile library services	SWAIN, Lillian A.	(VA)	1212
Bookmobile management	ROH, Jae M.	(CA)	1050
Bookmobile operation	WIRICK, Terry L.	(PA)	1356
Bookmobile service	JESSUP, Carrie	(CA)	600
	BERRY, Diana M.	(OH)	90
Bookmobile services	LARSON, Larry	(AR)	699
	BERNARDI, John V.	(NE)	88
	SPEAR, Linda A.	(OH)	1172
	LAW, Aileen E.	(SC)	704
	RODERICK, Mary P.	(TX)	1047
	KEASCHUK, Michael J.	(SK)	633
Bookmobiles	SEIDL, James C.	(IL)	1112
	GRAHAM, Heather F.	(MB)	456

BOOKMOBILES (Cont'd)

Branch, bookmobile, outreach services	BEECH, Vivian W.	(NC)	74
Extension services, bookmobile	HOLMES, Nancy M.	(GA)	553
Outreach & bookmobile services, literacy	JONES, Charlotte W.	(WA)	611
Outreach, bookmobile	KELLEY, H N.	(IL)	636
Public library outreach & bookmobiles	HOLE, Carol C.	(FL)	550

BOOKS (See also Monographs)

Academic & research libraries book sales	SCHRIFT, Leonard B.	(NY)	1100
Academic library book jobber	NAGEL, Lawrence D.	(CA)	886
Acquisition of rare books	BUFF, Iva M.	(NY)	155
Acquisitions, books & serials	MIRANDA, Cecilia	(TX)	847
Acquisitions, bks, records, music scores	SILVER, Martin A.	(CA)	1138
Acquisitions of books & serials	WARD, Dorothy S.	(AL)	1303
Administering nursing book collection	DAUGHERTY, Carolyn M.	(MD)	275
Administration & book selection	SNYDER, Esther M.	(ISR)	1164
Adult & children's book selection	GENCO, Barbara A.	(NY)	426
Adult book selection	COFFEY, Dorothy A.	(MI)	227
Aeronautical history rare books	BARRETT, Donald J.	(CO)	59
Analyses of book industry	APPELBAUM, Judith P.	(PA)	29
Animals in children's books	FREEDMAN, Barbara G.	(NC)	400
Antiquarian art books	MCGILVERY, Laurence	(CA)	806
Antiquarian books	LOWMAN, Matt P.	(CA)	744
	YAPLE, Henry M.	(WA)	1377
Antiquarian books collection management	GOGGIN, Margaret K.	(FL)	444
Antiquarian juvenile books	GOLEY, Elaine P.	(TX)	447
Antiquarian law books	LUTTRELL, Jordan D.	(CA)	750
Antiquarian theatre books sales	KAHAN, Gerald	(GA)	621
Appraisal of military books	AIMONE, Alan C.	(NY)	8
Architecture books	ROMEO, Sheryl R.	(DC)	1052
Archival & rare books	YUILLE, Willie K.	(MD)	1384
	ROSS, David J.	(NY)	1058
Archives & rare books	LARSGAARD, Mary L.	(CO)	698
	STEVENS, Marjorie	(MI)	1190
	TAYLOR, Carolyn L.	(MO)	1226
	HILL, Susan E.	(TX)	540
	EDMONDS, Susan M.	(WA)	336
	DESOMOGYI, Aileen A.	(ON)	295
Archives, rare books	RAY, Joyce M.	(TX)	1011
Arkansas-related documents & books	FERGUSON, John L.	(AR)	372
Art & language rare books	COE, Miriam M.	(LA)	226
Art books acquisitions	RICE, Ralph A.	(TX)	1027
Art books cataloging	SEVY, Barbara S.	(PA)	1117
Artists' books	BYRNE, Nadene M.	(IL)	169
	ROM, Cristine C.	(OH)	1052
	VAN DER BELLEN, Liana	(ON)	1273
Artists' books & publications	HOFFBERG, Judith A.	(CA)	547
Arts of the book	WALKER, Robin G.	(CT)	1296
Audio book production	CYLKE, Frank K.	(DC)	268
Audio tapes, audio books	SANDY, Marjorie M.	(MI)	1081
Author of books on theatre	WILMETH, Don B.	(RI)	1349
Automated book exchange	FINK, Norman	(PQ)	378
Automation book catalog, circulation	THOMAN, Nancy L.	(DE)	1236
Automation, book collection devlpmnt	SIMON, Bradley A.	(OK)	1140
Award reference books	SIEGMAN, Gita	(MD)	1136
Battle of books	GREESON, Janet S.	(AR)	465
Battle of the books	CRAVER, Susan J.	(IA)	256
Binding & book preservation	SNELL, Patricia P.	(CA)	1163
Book acquisition	KRAMER, William J.	(DC)	675
	PATTERSON, Anne S.	(MD)	948
Book acquisitions	FARKAS, Charles R.	(NY)	364
	JOHNSON, Joan E.	(PA)	606
	LASATER, Mary C.	(TN)	700
Book & artifact cataloging	HALEY, Marguerite R.	(WA)	486
Book & audiovisual media selection	YOUNG, Patricia S.	(TN)	1383
Book & audiovisual software reviewer	LEIBOLD, Cynthia K.	(OH)	713
Book & directory publishing	CSENGE, Maragaret L.	(NY)	262
Book & journal acquisitions	GREGORY, Melissa R.	(IL)	466
Book & journal publishing	FAHERTY, Robert L.	(DC)	361
Book & journal selection	MAYRAND, Lise M.	(PQ)	791
Book & library history	KASER, David	(IN)	628
Book & magazine indexing	BRADWAY, Becky J.	(IL)	126
Book & media selection	HUBER, Donald L.	(OH)	569
	MC NAIR, Marian B.	(OH)	815

BOOKS (Cont'd)

Book & paper conservation	SUNDSTRAND, Jacquelyn K.	(CA)	1210
	HANTHORN, Ivan E.	(IA)	499
Book & periodical indexing	KOEHNLEIN, Bill	(NY)	667
Book & periodical publishing	MECKLER, Alan E.	(CT)	820
	WOOD, Richard T.	(MI)	1365
Book & serial collection	ELSTEIN, Rochelle S.	(IL)	346
Book & serial selection	VELEZ, Sara B.	(NY)	1281
Book appraisal	LABUDDE, Kenneth J.	(MO)	686
Book arts	KOTIN, David B.	(ON)	673
	VAN DER BELLEN, Liana	(ON)	1273
Book arts history	ALTERMAN, Deborah H.	(NJ)	18
Book arts journals	MONGOLD, Alice D.	(TX)	854
Book cataloging	SHANNON, Kathleen L.	(IL)	1120
Book collecting	DICKINSON, Donald C.	(AZ)	300
	CAMERON, Sam A.	(TN)	175
Book collection	HUDSON, Susan P.	(BC)	570
	VIIERANS, Mary E.	(BC)	1284
Book collection development	HABERLAND, Jody	(VA)	481
Book collection evaluation	NIXON, Arless B.	(AZ)	906
Book collections development	KIERANS, Mary E.	(BC)	647
Book compilation	KRUSE, Luanne M.	(TX)	681
Book conservation	MILEVSKI, Robert J.	(DC)	834
	SCHROCK, Nancy C.	(MA)	1100
Book discussion groups	ALLEN, Richard H.	(NE)	16
Book distribution	GERARD, James W.	(VT)	428
Book distribution systems	KOLTAY, Emery I.	(NY)	670
Book evaluation	HIRABAYASHI, Joanne	(CA)	543
	OSSEN, Virginia F.	(CA)	928
	CHANDRA, Jane H.	(NC)	200
Book examination programs	NICHTER, Alan	(FL)	902
Book exhibits	WISE, Leona L.	(CA)	1357
Book illustration techniques	DONAHUE, Katharine E.	(CA)	310
Book indexing	PORPA, Edythe C.	(CO)	984
	SCHROEDER, Anne M.	(IL)	1100
	ABEND, Jody U.	(NY)	2
	LINZER, Elliot	(NY)	732
Book knowledge	NYREN, Dorothy E.	(NY)	913
Book manufacturing	BROOKS, Alfred C.	(NJ)	140
Book marketing	GERARD, James W.	(VT)	428
Book ordering	BECKNER, Barbara J.	(FL)	73
	MCLENNA, D S.	(TX)	814
Book preparation	SULTANOF, Jeff B.	(NJ)	1208
Book processing	WEISER, Douglas E.	(MI)	1319
Book processing services	NAGEL, Lawrence D.	(CA)	886
Book production	FITZGERALD, Ardra F.	(CA)	382
	HUCHTING, Mary	(IL)	569
	KRAMER-GREENE, Judith	(NY)	675
Book promotion & publicity	BIANCO, David P.	(MI)	94
Book publishing	WALCH, Timothy G.	(DC)	1293
	ALLEN, Walter C.	(IL)	16
	KING, Kenneth	(MI)	651
	SHIDELER, John C.	(WA)	1129
	DITTMER, Luther A.	(WGR)	306
Book publishing, writing & editing	EASTMAN, Ann H.	(VA)	333
Book repair	KALLENBERG, Mary E.	(AK)	623
Book repair & reconstitution	GLEESON, Joyce M.	(IL)	441
Book research	FRANK, Peter R.	(CA)	397
	FELDMAN, Linda A.	(IL)	369
Book review	WALKER, Elinor	(MN)	1295
Book reviewer	HOFFMANN, Maurine L.	(IL)	548
	TASHJIAN, Virginia A.	(MA)	1224
Book reviewer & speaker	GLATT, Carol R.	(NJ)	440
Book reviewing	JANUS, Bridget M.	(IA)	594
	CALLAGHAN, Linda W.	(IL)	173
	DONOVAN, William A.	(IL)	312
	EPP, Ronald H.	(IL)	351
	MALLER, Mark P.	(IL)	763
	OTT, Bill	(IL)	930
	RETTIG, James R.	(IL)	1024
	WRIGHT, Helen K.	(IL)	1371
	BLANK, Annette C.	(MD)	104
	CIERZNIEWSKI, Robert J.	(MI)	214
	GREFRATH, Richard W.	(NV)	465
	BARTH, Joseph M.	(NY)	61
	JENNINGS, Vincent	(NY)	598
	SOUDERS, Marilyn N.	(NY)	1169
	HAGLOCH, Susan B.	(OH)	483
	MCKEE, Barbara J.	(OH)	810

BOOKS (Cont'd)

Book reviewing			
	WIEHE, Janet C.	(OH)	1336
	JENKINS, Georgann K.	(PA)	597
	MACK, Sara R.	(PA)	756
	DEILY, Carole C.	(TX)	288
	TWENEY, George H.	(WA)	1266
Book reviewing & editing	GUSHEE, Marion S.	(IL)	478
Book reviewing, children's	PAGOTTO, Sarah L.	(PA)	934
Book reviews	DONOVAN, Diane C.	(CA)	312
	WENDROFF, Catriona	(CA)	1323
	JOHNSON, Eric W.	(CT)	604
	CZARNECKI, Cary J.	(IL)	268
	ROBERTSON, Deborah G.	(IL)	1041
	LEVEL, M J.	(KS)	719
	POLACHECK, Demarest L.	(OH)	980
	WEEKS, Patsy L.	(TX)	1315
	CARROLL, Barbara T.	(WI)	187
Book selection	VOSS, Ruth A.	(AR)	1289
	CROWTHER, Carol	(CA)	262
	FRANK, Peter R.	(CA)	397
	STERLIN, Annette S.	(CA)	1189
	WINKLER, Jean J.	(CO)	1355
	ADAMS, Gustav C.	(FL)	4
	HENDERSON, Patricia A.	(FL)	526
	SKUBISH, Barbara E.	(FL)	1147
	GLISSON, Patricia A.	(GA)	441
	SUMNER, Ellen L.	(GA)	1209
	BRANDT, Garnet J.	(IA)	128
	CURRY, Jean K.	(IL)	266
	LEVIN, Joan E.	(IL)	720
	NELSON, Barbara L.	(IL)	893
	TIWANA, Nazar H.	(IL)	1247
	MILLER, Marsha A.	(IN)	840
	SHIPPS, Anthony W.	(IN)	1131
	SMYERS, Richard P.	(IN)	1162
	SCHEUERMAN, Luanne J.	(KS)	1092
	SMITH, Barbara J.	(ME)	1153
	CHAMBERS, E G.	(MI)	198
	GLIKIN, Ronda	(MI)	441
	KINGSTON, Jo A.	(MI)	652
	ORMOND, Sarah C.	(MI)	926
	VANDERLAAN, Robert J.	(MI)	1274
	WISCHMEYER, Carol A.	(MI)	1356
	BLANKENSHIP, Phyllis E.	(MO)	104
	LARSON, Josephine	(NC)	699
	ANDERSON, Janelle E.	(NJ)	23
	BERGER, Morey R.	(NJ)	86
	DOBRZYNSKI, Terenita	(NY)	307
	SALINERO, Amelia	(NY)	1076
	SZMUK, Szilvia E.	(NY)	1218
	BURKE, Ambrose L.	(OH)	160
	FREW, Martha G.	(OH)	402
	GORDON, Shirlee J.	(OH)	452
	LEWIS, Betty J.	(OH)	722
	PLUMMER, Karen A.	(OH)	978
	POLACHECK, Demarest L.	(OH)	980
	MADER, Marion C.	(PA)	759
	JACKSON, Harriett D.	(TN)	587
	YAPLE, Marilyn V.	(TX)	1378
	PETERSON, Francine	(UT)	963
	CHAMBERLAIN, M J.	(VA)	197
	POWERS, Linda J.	(VA)	989
	ZWICK, Susan G.	(VA)	1392
	POPECKI, Jeanne M.	(VT)	983
	SCOTT, John E.	(WV)	1107
	STAFFORD, Leva L.	(WY)	1178
	GOW, Susan P.	(BC)	454
	INSELBERG, Diana E.	(BC)	583
	MARTEN, Mary L.	(MB)	775
	WRIGHT, Patrick D.	(MB)	1372
	LAMBERT, Deborah B.	(ON)	690
	COUGHLIN, Violet L.	(PQ)	250
	FINNEMORE, Mary A.	(PQ)	378
	OUIMET, Yves	(PQ)	930
	ROY, Helene	(PQ)	1063
	STILMAN, Ruth	(PQ)	1194
Book selection & acquisition	LANGEVIN, Ann T.	(NV)	695
	GRAY, Patricia B.	(VA)	460
	MEHRAD, Jafar	(IRN)	821

BOOKS (Cont'd)

Book selection & acquisitions — HARRINGTON, Charles W. . . . . (LA) 504
Book selection & bibliography — WEISBAUM, Earl . . . . . . (TX) 1319
Book selection & cataloging — MILLER, Jean J. . . . . (CT) 838
Book selection & collection development — HOLSTINE, Lesa G. . . . . (FL) 554
Book selection & evaluation — PATRON, Susan H. . . . . (CA) 947
Book selection & purchase — GENSHAFT, Carole M. . . (OH) 427
Book selection & reviewing — WAGNER, Sharon L. . . . (CA) 1292
Book selection, audiovisual services — DE CASTRO, Elinore H. . (PHP) 285
Book selection, bookmobiles — MONTANA, Edward J. . . (MA) 855
Book selection catalog department — KING, Willard B. . . . . (NC) 652
Book selection, children's — LYTLE, Marian M. . . . . (NC) 753
Book selling — MARKS, Cicely P. . . . . . (MD) 771
Book storage & conservation — HERON, David W. . . . . . (CA) 532
Book supply — SCHMIEDL, Keith S. . . . (NY) 1096
Book trade — KAVANAGH, Susan E. . . (ON) 631
Book wholesaling — STEVENS, Sharon G. . . (NJ) 1191
Book writing — STUDWELL, William E. . (IL) 1204
Books — CHESHIER, Robert G. . (OH) 206
Books about books — BUSHMAN, James L. . . . (OR) 165
Books & audiovisual equipment selection — ANDIS, Norma B. . . . . . . (TX) 26
Books & audiovisual materials selection — SCHILL, Julie G. . . . . . . (PA) 1092
Books & manuscripts appraisal — LEBO, Shirley B. . . . . . . (DC) 708
Books & manuscripts appraisals — TWENEY, George H. . . . (WA) 1266
Books & manuscripts archives — GAMBLE, Mary J. . . . . . (CA) 416
Books & newsletters, non-profit groups — TAFT, James R. . . . . (DC) 1219
Books & non-book cataloging — WU, Harriet . . . . (CA) 1373
Books & printing history — LOWE, Mildred . . . . (NY) 744
Books & reading — RABBAN, Elana . . . . (NY) 1001
Books & serials acquisitions — OSIER, Donald V. . . . . . (SDA) 928
Books as art form — PASCAL, Barbara R. . . . (CA) 945
Books, bibliography — GINN, Marjorie J. . . . . . . (MN) 437
Books by Maine authors — LYONS, Dean E. . . . . . . (ME) 753
Books cataloging — WOODWARD, Lawrence W. . . . . (DC) 1368
Books for children — RUSS, Kennetta P. . . . . . (MD) 1068
Books for gifted children — HALSTED, Judith W. . . . (MI) 490
Books for schools & libraries — RARESHEID, Cynthia L. . (OH) 1008
Books, manuscripts, maps — JONES, Dora A. . . . . . . (SD) 612
Books marketing — KOBASA, Paul A. . . . . . (IL) 666
Books on antiques & art — JOHNSON, Nancy E. . . . (IA) 608
Books on collectibles & nostalgia — JOHNSON, Nancy E. . . . (IA) 608
Books sold through trade — GAUNT, James R. . . . . . (FL) 423
Booktalking, children's books — GREESON, Janet S. . . . . (AR) 465
Branch adult book selection — RODGER, Elizabeth A. . . (ON) 1047
Building book collection — KNOLL, Betty A. . . . . . . (WA) 665
Buying & selling of rare books — MARTIN, John W. . . . . . (IL) 776
Buying antiquarian books — MONDLIN, Marvin . . . . . (NY) 854
Caldecott medal books — HEINRICH, Lois M. . . . . . (MD) 522
Cataloging & book ordering — VIERGEVER, Dan W. . . . (KS) 1284
Cataloging & classifying books — MILTON, Ardyce A. . . . . (WI) 845
Cataloging & indexing books — GOLDBERG, Judy W. . . . (NY) 444
Cataloging art books — FORMAN, Camille L. . . . (CT) 390
Cataloging, book & non-book — COTTINGHAM, Elsie E. . . (IN) 250
Cataloging books — HEFZALLAH, Mona G. . . (CT) 521
Cataloging books & audiovisual media — YOUNG, Patricia S. . . . . (TN) 1383
Cataloging Italian & Spanish books — CHANG, Roselyne M. . . . (DC) 201
Cataloging North Carolina books — MCGLOHON, Leah L. . . . (NC) 807
Cataloging rare books — LAND, Barbara J. . . . . . (CA) 692
— SMIRENSKY, Helen K. . . (NY) 1152
Cataloging, rare books, reference — STUFF, Marjorie A. . . . . . (NE) 1205
Checking out books — HEYDUCK, Marilyn J. . . . (IL) 535
Children & young adult books — GILBERT, Ophelia R. . . . (MO) 434
— MCELDERRY, Margaret K. (NY) 804
Children's activity books author — HAAS, Carolyn B. . . . . . (IL) 480
Children's & foreign books — ROBIEN, Eleanor K. . . . . (IL) 1043
Children's & young adult books — JONES, Trevelyn E. . . . . (NY) 615
Children's book editing — VESTAL, Jeanne G. . . . . (NY) 1283
Children's book illustration — OLDERSHAW, Anne . . . (NY) 920
Children's book information service — RUSS, Kennetta P. . . . . . (MD) 1068
Children's book publishing — SUTHERLAND, Zena B. . (IL) 1211
— EPSTEIN, Connie C. . . . . (NY) 351
Children's book reviewer — NICHOLS, Margaret M. . (AZ) 901

BOOKS (Cont'd)

Children's book reviewing — WILSON, Phillis M. . . . . . (IL) 1352
— GILLIS, Ruth J. . . . . (MN) 436
— WILLIAMS, Deborah H. . . (NY) 1342
Children's book selection — WISOTZKI, Lila B. . . . . . (MD) 1358
— RAFAL, Marian D. . . . . . (MI) 1003
Children's book selection & programming — STEELE, Anitra T. . . . . . (MO) 1184
Children's books — GENDRON, Michele M. . (PA) 426
— SACHSE, Gladys M. . . . . (AR) 1073
— ELLEMAN, Barbara J. . . . (IL) 343
— MADAY, Geraldine . . . . . (IL) 758
— TURCHI, Marilyn L. . . . . (IL) 1263
— HOGAN, Margaret A. . . . (MA) 549
— SILVEY, Anita L. . . . . . . (MA) 1139
— MORGAN, Betty J. . . . . . (MD) 863
— COOPER, Ruth K. . . . . . (NC) 243
— FREEMAN, Patricia E. . . (NM) 401
— BREEN, Karen B. . . . . . (NY) 131
— GAUCH, Patricia L. . . . . (NY) 422
— HOLTZE, Sally H. . . . . . (NY) 555
— LAPIDUS, Lois E. . . . . . (NY) 697
— WHIPPLE, Judith R. . . . . (NY) 1329
— NANCE, Lena L. . . . . . . (OH) 887
— OVERHOLT, Maria B. . . . (OH) 931
— FIELD, Carolyn W. . . . . . (PA) 375
— YOUREE, Beverly B. . . . (TN) 1384
— TEDDER, Dorothy L. . . . . (TX) 1229
— REMICK, Katherine G. . . (VA) 1022
— MATHES, Miriam S. . . . . (WA) 783
— MEYER, Laura M. . . . . . (WA) 830
— ALLARD, Diane . . . . (PQ) 14
— LONDON, Eleanor . . . . . (PQ) 738
Children's books & literature — MOSES, Camelia T. . . . . (NY) 871
Children's books & programming — BADERTSCHER, Kimberlin H. . . . . (IN) 44
Children's books consulting — FEDERICI, Yolanda D. . . (IL) 368
Children's books, editing — BENEDUCE, Ann K. . . . . (NJ) 80
Children's books, publishing & libraries — BOTHAM, Jane . . . . (WI) 118
Children's rare books — SEDNEY, Frances V. . . . (MD) 1111
Children's trade books — RIBAROFF, Margaret F. . (CT) 1026
Children's work, book banners — DEVEREAUX, Amy E. . . (CA) 297
Chinese rare books — KECSKES, Lily C. . . . . . (DC) 633
Comic books, comic strips — SCOTT, Randall W. . . . . (MI) 1108
Compiling film reference books — TUDIVER, Lillian . . . . . (NY) 1262
Complete book acquisition service — ABRAMOFF, Lawrence J. (MA) 3
Computer book indexing — GARCIA, Kathleen J. . . . (NY) 417
Computer books & software — BLAKE, Harry W. . . . . . (CA) 103
Construction books — LUNSTEDT, Ralph A. . . . (CA) 749
Cooperative book depositories — STOCKTON, Gloria J. . . (CA) 1196
Current book acquisitions — DE LUISE, Alexandra . . . (PQ) 290
Database & book indexing — LYNCH, Jacqueline . . . . (MA) 751
Displaying books — SALPETER, Janice L. . . . (NY) 1077
Early illustrated books & bindings — WITTEN, Laurence . . . . (CT) 1358
Early printed books — NORTON, Margaret W. . . (IL) 910
Early printed books of 1450-1600 — WITTEN, Laurence . . . . (CT) 1358
Editing book reviews — ESTES, Sally C. . . . . . . (IL) 355
Editing library media books — TROJAN, Judith L. . . . . (NY) 1257
Editing professional books — FRANKLIN, Robert M. . . (NC) 398
Editing reference books — BRAUNSTEIN, Mark M. . (RI) 130
Education for rare books — BELANGER, Terry . . . . . (NY) 76
Educational books — BOWMAN, James K. . . . (NY) 121
Electronic medical books — FRISSE, Mark E. . . . . . (MO) 405
English & French book selection — TAGGART, William R. . . (BC) 1220
English & French books selection — DAVIS, Virginia K. . . . . (ON) 281
Ethnic studies & history of the book — WYNAR, Lubomyr R. . . . (OH) 1375
Evaluating children's book collections — EDMONDS, May H. . . . . (FL) 336
Evaluating teenage books — ESTES, Sally C. . . . . . . (IL) 355
Festival books — BOWLES, Edmund A. . . . (NY) 121
Fiction, books selection — SANDY, Marjorie M. . . . (MI) 1081
Fine arts book illustration — BANTA, Gratia J. . . . . . (OH) 55
Fine arts book selection — SCHERER, Herbert G. . . (MN) 1092
Fine arts books — RICE, Ralph A. . . . . (TX) 1027
Fine arts collections, books — RUSSELL, Marilyn L. . . . (KS) 1069
Foreign language books — MERKIN, David . . . . . . (NY) 826
Foreign law book acquisition — KREH, Fritz . . . . (WGR) 677
French books — BADGER, Carole . . . . . (PQ) 44
— DUHAMEL, Louis . . . . . (PQ) 324
Fundraising, book publishing & writing — GRAVES, Sid F. . . . . . . (MS) 459

BOOKS (Cont'd)

Fundraising for rare books	IVES, Sidney E.	(FL)	586
General books	DONOVAN, Diane C.	(CA)	312
Guiding children's book selection	SUTHERLAND, Helen G.	(CA)	1211
Hebrew manuscripts & rare books	KOHN, Roger S.	(NY)	668
Herbal books	CROTZ, D K.	(IL)	261
Historical children's books, research	GILBERT, Ophelia R.	(MO)	434
Historical libraries & rare books	MERRIAM, Louise A.	(WI)	826
History books & printing	COLBY, Robert A.	(NY)	230
History, books, libraries	ROTHACKER, John M.	(TN)	1059
History of books	COLE, John Y.	(DC)	231
	HALPORN, Barbara	(IN)	490
	GOULD, Karen K.	(TX)	454
History of books & libraries	TURNER, Frank L.	(TX)	1264
	MULVANEY, John P.	(VA)	878
	DE SCOSSA, Catriona	(AB)	295
	SIBAI, Mohamed M.	(SDA)	1134
History of books & manuscripts	CARNOVSKY, Ruth F.	(CA)	184
History of books & printing	KIRSHENBAUM, Sandra D.	(CA)	655
	THOMPSON, Susan O.	(NY)	1241
	JOHNSON, Bryan R.	(VA)	602
	BREGMAN, Alvan M.	(ON)	131
History of books & rare books	WINCKLER, Paul A.	(NY)	1354
History of medical literature, rare bks	MIMS, Dorothy H.	(GA)	845
History of the book	GONIWIECHA, Mark C.	(AK)	447
	NEAVILL, Gordon B.	(AL)	891
	MAXWELL, Margaret F.	(AZ)	788
	HARLAN, Robert D.	(CA)	502
	ROGERS, Brian D.	(CT)	1049
	HANSON, Norma S.	(OH)	498
	SUMMERS, George V.	(PA)	1209
	SKELLEY, Grant T.	(WA)	1145
	LANDON, Richard G.	(ON)	693
Horticulture books	CROTZ, D K.	(IL)	261
Indexing books	HEFZALLAH, Mona G.	(CT)	521
Indexing books & periodicals	O'LEARY, Mary E.	(MN)	920
Japanese language books	ASAWA, Edward E.	(CA)	35
Japanese rare books	SEWELL, Robert G.	(NY)	1117
Journal & book editing	PHILLIPS, Janet C.	(PA)	968
Juvenile books in Spanish	SCHON, Isabel	(AZ)	1098
Latin American book market	MARSHALL, David L.	(DC)	774
Law book acquisitions	WALSH, Sharon T.	(PA)	1300
Law book publishing	DANNE, William H.	(IL)	274
	MORSE, Alan L.	(NY)	869
	KUEHNLE, Emery C.	(OH)	682
	WALSH, Sharon T.	(PA)	1300
Law books	COX, Irvin E.	(MD)	253
	LOCKE, William G.	(NY)	736
	MAYL, Gene	(OH)	790
Legal & reserve book circulation	DINDAYAL, Joyce S.	(NY)	304
Legal bibliography, rare books	TRIFFIN, Nicholas	(NY)	1256
Library, book trade market	BUCENEC, Nancy L.	(NY)	153
Library books & supplies	AMIS, Terence K.	(NB)	20
Library school teaching of rare books	HEANEY, Howell J.	(PA)	518
Literature & art history books	ALLENTUCK, Marcia E.	(NY)	16
Local history, books, programs	JAMISON, Susan C.	(DE)	593
Mail-order children's books	RUSS, Kennetta P.	(MD)	1068
Managing & appraising rare books	MICHAELS, Carolyn L.	(SC)	831
Manuscripts & rare books	YOUNG, Noraleen A.	(IN)	1382
	ROUNDTREE, Lynn P.	(LA)	1061
Manuscripts & rare books literary resrch	REIMAN, Donald H.	(NY)	1020
Map & book cataloging	SHARP, Alice L.	(CO)	1122
Marketing books	TAYLOR, George A.	(DC)	1226
Material security & book theft	BAHR, Alice H.	(PA)	45
Medical & nursing books	CASSAR, Ann	(PA)	193
Medical & scientific books	FUGLE, Mary E.	(NY)	408
Medical book & journal indexing	GARCIA, Kathleen J.	(NY)	417
Medical book deselection	FARLEY, Alfred E.	(KS)	364
Medical book discounter	PUALWAN, Emily	(PA)	996
Medical book indexing	WEIR, Alexandra L.	(PA)	1319
Medical book publishing	FORD, Andrew E.	(NY)	389
Medical books & journals	AIDE, Kathryn S.	(AL)	8
	ZUNDEL, Karen M.	(PA)	1391
Medical rare books	POND, Frederick C.	(NY)	982
Medieval era book selection	HILL, Lawrence H.	(PA)	540
Miniature books	ADOMEIT, Ruth E.	(OH)	7
Monitoring book censorship attempts	KRUSE, Ginny M.	(WI)	681
Moving large book collections	PARRY, David R.	(CO)	944

BOOKS (Cont'd)

Multisubject book indexing	HOTIMLANSKA, Leah D.	(IL)	562
Music books	BAHR, Edward R.	(MS)	45
Mystery fiction books	O'BRIEN, Marlys H.	(MN)	915
Natural history, rare books	DONAHUE, Katharine E.	(CA)	310
New & used book trade	SORGENFREI, Robert K.	(CA)	1168
Newbery book club	DRZEWIECKI, Iris M.	(NY)	321
19th century US rare books	GARDNER, Ralph D.	(NY)	418
Nonfiction trade books	RIBAROFF, Margaret F.	(CT)	1026
North Carolina rare books	TOMLINSON, Charles E.	(NC)	1250
Nursing, allied health book discounter	PUALWAN, Emily	(PA)	996
Nursing book publishing	FORD, Andrew E.	(NY)	389
Nursing journals & books	KODER, Alma	(PA)	667
Old & rare books	O'BRIEN, Francis M.	(ME)	914
Ordering & catlgng books & non-book mtrl	SPIEGEL, Bertha	(NY)	1174
Ordering architectural, engrng books	SPAHR, Cheryl L.	(OH)	1170
Ordering books	GLASS, Gerald	(PQ)	440
Out-of-print books	MONIE, Willis J.	(NY)	855
	BRAUTIGAM, David K.	(PA)	130
	FOUTS, Judith F.	(TX)	393
Out-of-print scholarly books	SOMERS, Wayne F.	(NY)	1167
Overseeing Talking Book program	STEWART, Jeanne E.	(MS)	1192
Paper book preservation	MOLTKE-HANSEN, David	(SC)	853
Peer book writing instructor	KORNITSKY, Judith M.	(FL)	672
Periodical & book indexing	KEMP, Thomas J.	(CT)	639
	AGEE, Victoria V.	(MD)	7
	THICKITT, Lisa	(NC)	1235
Phonograph recordings & rare books	BROWNE, J P.	(CA)	148
Picture books	BUCKLEY, Virginia L.	(NY)	154
Picture books, early childhood	GREENE, Ellin P.	(NJ)	464
Political science book selection	YORK, Grace A.	(MI)	1381
Post-cataloging book handling	MARX, Patricia C.	(TX)	780
Preservation of books & paper	HUTTNER, Sidney F.	(OK)	579
Preservation of maps in books	KLIMLEY, Susan	(NY)	661
Preservation of rare books	HALEY, Marguerite R.	(WA)	486
Processing books for shelving	HEYDUCK, Marilyn J.	(IL)	535
Professional & reference books	BUCENEC, Nancy L.	(NY)	153
	TOPEL, Iris N.	(NY)	1251
Professional book publishing	KING, Timothy B.	(NY)	652
Professional, technical books	BOWMAN, James K.	(NY)	121
Promoting reference books	ROMIG, Thomas L.	(MI)	1053
Public library book selection	OTT, Bill	(IL)	930
Publication services, books, newsletters	MOLLO, Terry	(NY)	853
Publish high tech reference books	CONNORS, Martin G.	(MI)	238
Publishing & book distribution	GSTALDER, Herbert W.	(NY)	475
Publishing & book trade	STUART-STUBBS, Basil F.	(BC)	1204
Publishing & marketing children's books	MASON, H J.	(NY)	781
Publishing book development	THOMPSON, Anne E.	(AZ)	1238
Publishing music reference books	BALK, Leo F.	(NY)	52
Publishing professional books & journals	GRAYSON, Martin	(NY)	460
Publishing reference books	BRYFONSKI, Dedria A.	(MI)	152
Purchase & classification of books	LACAILLADE, Jacqueline	(PQ)	686
Purchasing medical books	POLLARD, Joan B.	(VA)	981
Rare & out-of-print art books	DAVIS, L C.	(CA)	280
Rare & out-of-print books	SMITH, Nolan E.	(CT)	1159
Rare & scholarly books	KIEFFER, Jay	(CA)	647
Rare art books	POCKROSE, Sheryl R.	(OH)	979
Rare book acquisition & cataloging	COX, Shelley M.	(IL)	253
Rare book appraisal	MARSHALL, Mary G.	(IL)	774
	HEANEY, Howell J.	(PA)	518
Rare book cataloging	ZALL, Elisabeth W.	(CA)	1386
	ROONEY, Eugene M.	(DC)	1053
	MARSHALL, Mary G.	(IL)	774
	MUELLER, Robert W.	(IL)	875
	RENSHAW, Marita	(IL)	1023
	SALAZAR, Pamela R.	(NY)	1076
	FRITZ, William R.	(SC)	405
	GISSENDANNER, Cassandra S.	(SC)	438
	HUMMEL, Ray O.	(VA)	573
	STAFFORD, Leva L.	(WY)	1178
Rare book collection	CAUSLEY, Monroe S.	(NJ)	195
Rare book collections	SMITH, Ledell B.	(LA)	1157
	MULVIHILL, Maureen E.	(NY)	878
Rare book curator	PINKHAM, Eleanor H.	(MI)	974

BOOKS (Cont'd)

Rare book dealer   TWENEY, George H. ... (WA) 1266
Rare book dealership   CADY, Richard H. ..... (IL) 170
Rare book librarianship   DUNLAP, Barbara J. ... (NY) 326
Rare book library administration   KNACHEL, Philip A. .... (DC) 663
Rare book library history   BELANGER, Terry ..... (NY) 76
Rare book photographic services   MCKENNEY, Kathryn K. .. (DE) 811
Rare book preservation   BEDARD, Laura A. .... (DC) 73
Rare book research   MONDLIN, Marvin ..... (NY) 854
Rare book sales   MUELLER, Robert W. ... (IL) 875
Rare books   BRITT, Mary C. .... (AL) 137
NELSON, Michael B. .... (AL) 894
PFAU, Julia G. .... (AL) 966
RAMER, James D. ..... (AL) 1005
ALSMEYER, Henry L. ... (AR) 18
HARRISON, John A. .... (AR) 506
MCNEIL, William K. .... (AR) 816
MCLACHLAN, Ross W. ... (AZ) 812
O'NEIL, Mary A. .... (AZ) 924
STUART, Gerard W. .... (AZ) 1204
AHLSTROM, Romaine .. (CA) 8
AHOUSE, John B. ...... (CA) 8
BARROW, Jerry .... (CA) 60
BENOIT, Gerald .... (CA) 82
BEVERAGE, Stephanie L. (CA) 93
BIDWELL, John .... (CA) 95
CARNES, Suzanne M. .. (CA) 183
DAVIS, James .... (CA) 279
DIMUNATION, Mark G. .. (CA) 304
DRAKE, Dorothy M. .... (CA) 318
EDELSTEIN, J M. ...... (CA) 335
ELLIOTT, C D. .... (CA) 343
EWEN, Eric P. .... (CA) 359
FAY, Evelyn V. .... (CA) 367
GOODSTEIN, Judith R. . (CA) 450
GRIFFIN, Thomas E. ... (CA) 469
HAMILTON, David M. ... (CA) 491
HARLAN, Robert D. .... (CA) 502
HAYES, Melinda K. .... (CA) 516
HOLLEMAN, Marian P. .. (CA) 551
HUNTER, David C. ..... (CA) 576
JORDAN, Joan A. ..... (CA) 616
KRAKAUER, Elizabeth .. (CA) 675
KUHNER, David A. ..... (CA) 683
LEVY, Jane .... (CA) 721
LOWMAN, Matt P. ..... (CA) 744
LUTTRELL, Jordan D. .. (CA) 750
MONTGOMERY, John W. (CA) 856
PARCHUCK, Jill A. .... (CA) 940
PERRY, Edward C. ..... (CA) 960
REED, Marcia C. ...... (CA) 1015
SHAFFER, Ellen .... (CA) 1119
SNYDER, Henry L. ..... (CA) 1164
STALKER, Laura A. .... (CA) 1178
THOMAS, Vivian ...... (CA) 1238
TREGGIARI, Arnaldo ... (CA) 1255
VOSPER, Robert ...... (CA) 1289
WHITSON, Helene ..... (CA) 1334
WREDEN, William P. ... (CA) 1370
WRIGLEY, Elizabeth S. .. (CA) 1373
YEUNG, Esther Y. ...... (CA) 1380
ZEIDBERG, David S. ... (CA) 1387
BOYD, Ruth E. .... (CO) 122
MASON, Ellsworth G. ... (CO) 781
NEILON, Barbara L. .... (CO) 892
QUINLAN, Nora J. ..... (CO) 1000
ASH, Lee M. .... (CT) 35
BENEDICT, Williston R. . (CT) 80
CROOKER, Cynthia L. .. (CT) 260
EMBARDO, Ellen E. .... (CT) 347
FRANKLIN, Ralph W. ... (CT) 398
HOLMER, Paul L. ..... (CT) 553
KAIMOWITZ, Jeffery H. . (CT) 622
LEAB, Katharine K. ..... (CT) 706
PELTIER, Karen V. ..... (CT) 955
RESTOUT, Denise T. ... (CT) 1024
SAMUEL, Harold E. .... (CT) 1079
SCHIMMELPFENG,
   Richard H. .... (CT) 1093
SILVERSTEIN, Louis H. . (CT) 1139

BOOKS (Cont'd)

Rare books
WAIT, Gary E. .... (CT) 1293
WEIMERSKIRCH, Philip J. (CT) 1317
BARRINGER, George M. (DC) 59
BARRY, Paul J. .... (DC) 60
BURNEY, Thomas D. ... (DC) 162
BYERS, Laura T. ...... (DC) 168
CRAWFORD, Elva B. ... (DC) 256
DOGGETT, Rachel H. ... (DC) 308
KALKUS, Stanley ...... (DC) 623
KRIVATSY, Nati H. ..... (DC) 679
LASNER, Mark S. ..... (DC) 700
MWALIMU, Charles .... (DC) 884
PORTER, Suzanne ..... (DC) 985
SERVERINO, Roberto .. (DC) 1116
TURTELL, Neal T. ..... (DC) 1265
VASLEF, Irene .... (DC) 1279
PUFFER, Nathaniel H. .. (DE) 997
SCHREYER, Alice D. .... (DE) 1100
BOLDRICK, Samuel J. ... (FL) 112
CLOPINE, John J. ..... (FL) 223
DEBOLT, W D. .... (FL) 284
DE VARONA, Esperanza
   B. .... (FL) 297
HOLLOWAY, David R. ... (FL) 552
HURTES, Reva .... (FL) 578
JACOBSON, June B. ... (FL) 590
MATHEWS, Richard B. . (FL) 784
HOUGH, Leslie S. ..... (GA) 562
JORDAN, Casper L. ..... (GA) 616
OVERBECK, James A. ... (GA) 931
EIMAS, Richard .... (IA) 340
BELAN, Judith A. ...... (IL) 75
BERGER, Sidney E. ..... (IL) 86
BOLEF, Doris .... (IL) 112
BURROWS, Thomas W. .. (IL) 163
CLOONAN, Michele V. ... (IL) 223
COBB, David A. .... (IL) 224
CROTZ, D K. .... (IL) 261
GILLFILLAN, Nancy M. . (IL) 435
GODLEWSKI, Susan G. .. (IL) 442
HALIBEY, Areta V. ..... (IL) 486
HEYMAN, Jerome S. .... (IL) 536
HOLZENBERG, Eric J. .. (IL) 555
HORST, Stanley E. ..... (IL) 561
KINGERY, Victor P. ..... (IL) 652
KLESTINSKI, Martha A. .. (IL) 661
KOCH, David V. .... (IL) 667
LANIER, Donald L. ..... (IL) 696
LOWMAN, Judith T. ..... (IL) 744
MATTHEWS, Elizabeth W. (IL) 785
MAYLONE, R R. .... (IL) 790
MOORE, Milton C. ..... (IL) 860
NASH, N F. .... (IL) 888
OWNES, Dorothy J. .... (IL) 932
PETERSON, Scott W. ... (IL) 964
PODESCHI, John B. ..... (IL) 979
POSNER, Frances A. .... (IL) 985
RENSHAW, Marita ..... (IL) 1023
RYAN, Diane M. .... (IL) 1070
WELLS, James M. ..... (IL) 1322
DARBEE, Leigh .... (IN) 274
RUDOLPH, L C. .... (IN) 1066
SILVER, Joel B. .... (IN) 1138
SPRINGER, Joe A. ..... (IN) 1176
TURNER, Nancy K. ..... (IN) 1265
VANCIL, David E. ...... (IN) 1273
DEGRUSON, Eugene H. . (KS) 288
HAURY, David A. ...... (KS) 512
JOHNSON, Georgina ... (KS) 604
MEDER, Marylouise D. .. (KS) 820
VANDER VELDE, John J. (KS) 1274
BUNDY, David D. ...... (KY) 157
HUFF, James E. .... (KY) 570
MARTIN, June H. ...... (KY) 777
MILLS, Constance A. ... (KY) 844
ROBERTS, Gerald F. ... (KY) 1040
WARTH, L T. .... (KY) 1307
COMBE, David A. ...... (LA) 234

BOOKS (Cont'd)
Rare books

DRAUGHON, Ralph B. . . . (LA) 318
FOX, Willard . . . . (LA) 395
HAMSA, Charles F. . . . . (LA) 494
JUMONVILLE, Florence M. (LA) 619
MARTIN, Robert S. . . . . (LA) 778
PERRAULT, Anna H. . . . (LA) 959
SHIFLETT, Orvin L. . . . . (LA) 1130
TURNER, I B. . . . . (LA) 1264
ASCHMANN, Althea . . . (MA) 35
CAYLOR, Lawrence M. . (MA) 195
FISCHER, Marge . . . . . . (MA) 380
HAMMOND, Wayne G. . (MA) 494
HANKAMER, Roberta A. (MA) 496
HAPIJ, Maria S. . . . . (MA) 499
HOPKINS, Benjamin . . . . (MA) 557
KENDALL, John D. . . . . . (MA) 640
LEWONTIN, Amy . . . . . . (MA) 724
LUBRANO, Judith A. . . . (MA) 745
MCGARRY, Marie L. . . . (MA) 805
MORTIMER, Ruth . . . . . (MA) 870
OLDHAM, Ellen M. . . . . . (MA) 920
RHINELANDER, Mary F. (MA) 1025
SCOTT, Alison M. . . . . . (MA) 1106
SEEGRABER, Frank J. . . (MA) 1111
SLAPSYS, Richard M. . . (MA) 1148
STICKNEY, Zephorene L. (MA) 1193
STRAND, Bethany . . . . . (MA) 1200
WALSH, James E. . . . . . (MA) 1299
WARRINGTON, David R. (MA) 1307
WASOWICZ, Laura E. . . (MA) 1308
CREIGHTON, Alice S. . . (MD) 258
FARREN, Donald . . . . . . (MD) 365
FILBY, P W. . . . . (MD) 376
FORSHAW, William S. . . (MD) 391
GIORDANO, Peter . . . . . (MD) 438
HIRTLE, Peter B. . . . . . . (MD) 544
JACKSON, Doris G. . . . . (MD) 587
KIM, Sunnie I. . . . . (MD) 649
SHAY, Donald E. . . . . . . (MD) 1124
TATE, Vernon D. . . . . . . (MD) 1225
TEIGEN, Philip M. . . . . . (MD) 1230
SAEGER, Edwin J. . . . . . (ME) 1074
BUTZ, Helen S. . . . . (MI) 168
CRAWFORD, David E. . . (MI) 256
DRAPER, James P. . . . . (MI) 318
FRANCIS, Gloria A. . . . . (MI) 396
GAYLOR, Robert G. . . . . (MI) 423
KOCH, Henry C. . . . . . . (MI) 667
KEY, Jack D. . . . . (MN) 645
KUKLA, Edward R. . . . . (MN) 683
OVERMIER, Judith A. . . . (MN) 931
RULON-MILLER, Robert . (MN) 1067
WENTE, Norman G. . . . . (MN) 1324
DEL CASTILLO, Mireya . (MO) 289
GLENN, Ardis L. . . . . . . (MO) 441
GULSTAD, Wilma B. . . . (MO) 477
HALL, Holly . . . . (MO) 487
HOWELL, Margaret A. . . (MO) 565
JENKINS, Harold R. . . . . (MO) 597
O'DELL, Charles A. . . . . (MO) 916
OFSTAD, Odessa L. . . . . (MO) 917
SHIRKY, Martha H. . . . . (MO) 1131
JONES, Dolores B. . . . . (MS) 612
KELLY, John M. . . . . (MS) 638
VERICH, Thomas M. . . . (MS) 1282
MILLS, Douglas E. . . . . . (MT) 844
BRABHAM, Robert F. . . . (NC) 124
CHENAULT, Elizabeth A. (NC) 205
MCNAMARA, Charles B. (NC) 816
SCOTT, Ralph L. . . . . . . (NC) 1108
SEVERANCE, Robert W. (NC) 1117
WILKINSON, Fleeta M. . (NC) 1340
MURDOCK, Douglas W. . (NE) 879
BROWN, Stanley W. . . . (NH) 147
BRODOWSKI, Joyce H. . (NJ) 139
CARLISLE, Scott G. . . . . (NJ) 182
COLLINS, Sarah F. . . . . (NJ) 233
FARRELL, Mark R. . . . . . (NJ) 365

BOOKS (Cont'd)
Rare books

FERGUSON, Stephen . . . (NJ) 372
GENNETT, Robert G. . . . (NJ) 427
HUDSON, Julie . . . . (NJ) 569
JONES, Arthur E. . . . . . . (NJ) 611
JOYCE, William L. . . . . . (NJ) 618
KOONTZ, John . . . . (NJ) 671
SINCLAIR, Donald A. . . . (NJ) 1142
WILINSKI, Grant W. . . . . (NJ) 1339
ZULEWSKI, Gerald J. . . . (NJ) 1391
CHEN, Laura F. . . . . (NM) 205
BLESSE, Robert E. . . . . (NV) 105
KADANS, Joseph M. . . . (NV) 621
BAGNALL, Whitney S. . . (NY) 45
BARR, Jeffrey A. . . . . . . (NY) 58
BERGMANN, Allison M. . (NY) 86
CAPRIELIAN, Arevig . . . (NY) 180
CHANEY, Bev . . . . (NY) 200
CIOLLI, Antoinette . . . . . (NY) 214
CLARK, Diane A. . . . . . . (NY) 216
COLE, Maud D. . . . . (NY) 231
CRYSTAL, Bernard R. . . (NY) 262
DOCTOROW, Erica . . . . (NY) 307
DOWD, Philip M. . . . . . . (NY) 315
EDDY, Donald D. . . . . . . (NY) 335
ELLENBOGEN, Rudolph S. (NY) 343
FOLTER, Roland . . . . . . (NY) 388
GADBOIS, Frank W. . . . (NY) 411
GAFFNEY, Ellen E. . . . . (NY) 412
GELLER, Lawrence D. . . (NY) 426
GLASER, June E. . . . . . (NY) 439
GRECH, Anthony P. . . . . (NY) 461
GRIFFITH, Sheryl . . . . . . (NY) 469
HEFNER, Xavier M. . . . . (NY) 520
JUNG, Norman O. . . . . . (NY) 620
JURIST, Janet . . . . (NY) 620
KASTEN, Seth E. . . . . . . (NY) 629
LESTER, Lillian . . . . (NY) 718
LOHF, Kenneth A. . . . . . (NY) 737
MACKECHNIE, Nancy S. (NY) 756
MAYO, Hope . . . . (NY) 790
MENT, David M. . . . . (NY) 824
MERKIN, David . . . . (NY) 826
MONIE, Willis J. . . . . (NY) 855
MOONEY, James E. . . . . (NY) 858
NEEDHAM, Paul . . . . . . (NY) 891
OSTWALD, Mark F. . . . . (NY) 929
PAULSON, Barbara A. . . (NY) 950
PEPPER, Jerold L. . . . . . (NY) 958
RAMER, Bruce J. . . . . . . (NY) 1005
SENTZ, Lilli . . . . (NY) 1115
SOMERS, Wayne F. . . . . (NY) 1167
STALKER, Dianne S. . . . (NY) 1178
THOMPSON, Susan O. . (NY) 1241
VESLEY, Roberta A. . . . . (NY) 1283
WALSH, Daniel P. . . . . . (NY) 1299
ADOMEIT, Ruth E. . . . . . (OH) 7
BAIN, George W. . . . . . . (OH) 47
BIRK, Nancy . . . . (OH) 98
EAST, Dennis . . . . (OH) 332
GILDZEN, Alex J. . . . . . . (OH) 434
IRWIN, James W. . . . . . . (OH) 584
JENKINS, Fred W. . . . . . (OH) 597
LORANTH, Alice N. . . . . (OH) 741
MACIUSZKO, Jerzy J. . . (OH) 755
PIKE, Kermit J. . . . . (OH) 972
SMITH, Thomas A. . . . . . (OH) 1161
VANBRIMMER, Barbara A. (OH) 1272
BENDER, Nathan E. . . . . (OK) 79
BLEDSOE, Kathleen E. . . (OK) 105
GOODMAN, Marcia M. . . (OK) 449
LARSEN, Nancy E. . . . . (OK) 698
BAUER, Marilyn A. . . . . . (OR) 65
INGRAHAM-SWETS,
    Leonoor . . . . (OR) 582
OTNES, Harold M. . . . . . (OR) 930
PYATT, Timothy D. . . . . (OR) 999
DAVIS, Samuel A. . . . . . (PA) 281
DEIBLER, Barbara E. . . . (PA) 288

BOOKS (Cont'd)
Rare books

GREEN, James N.	(PA)	462
HEANEY, Howell J.	(PA)	518
HEDRICK, David T.	(PA)	520
HORROCKS, Thomas A.	(PA)	561
JOHNSEN, Mary C.	(PA)	602
LEAHY, Mary S.	(PA)	707
LIEBERMAN, Ronald	(PA)	726
LUNDY, M W.	(PA)	748
MAASS, Eleanor A.	(PA)	753
MANN, Charles W.	(PA)	766
MCGLINN, Frank C.	(PA)	806
MERZ, Lawrie H.	(PA)	827
METZGER, Philip A.	(PA)	829
MORRIS, Leslie A.	(PA)	867
MORSE, Alfred W.	(PA)	869
NEGHERBON, Vincent R.	(PA)	892
NEITZ, Cordelia M.	(PA)	892
NELSON, Vernon H.	(PA)	895
PAKALA, Denise M.	(PA)	935
ROOT, Deane L.	(PA)	1054
RUGGERE, Christine A.	(PA)	1066
SWIGART, William E.	(PA)	1216
TRAISTER, Daniel H.	(PA)	1253
WOOLMER, J H.	(PA)	1368
YOLTON, Jean S.	(PA)	1380
ZORICH, Phillip J.	(PA)	1390
CASAS DE FAUNCE, Maria	(PR)	191
LANDIS, Dennis C.	(RI)	693
MASLYN, David C.	(RI)	780
PEARCE, Douglas A.	(RI)	952
CHOPESIUK, Ronald J.	(SC)	210
HAMILTON, Ben	(SC)	491
RIDGE, Davy J.	(SC)	1032
THOMPSON, Harry F.	(SD)	1239
BRANTIGAN-STOWELL, Martha J.	(TN)	129
HARWELL, Sara J.	(TN)	509
LLOYD, James B.	(TN)	735
BOOTHE, Nancy L.	(TX)	116
CABLE, Carole L.	(TX)	170
CONRAD, James H.	(TX)	238
CULP, Paul M.	(TX)	264
FARMER, David	(TX)	364
GARNER, Jane	(TX)	419
GOODWIN, Willard	(TX)	450
GOULD, Karen K.	(TX)	454
HOOD, Sandra D.	(TX)	556
KENDALL, Lyle H.	(TX)	640
LAVENDER, Kenneth	(TX)	703
LOYD, Roger L.	(TX)	745
MACDONALD, Hugh	(TX)	754
MERSKY, Roy M.	(TX)	827
PAYNE, John R.	(TX)	951
RASCHE, Richard R.	(TX)	1008
RICE, Ralph A.	(TX)	1027
SALL, Larry D.	(TX)	1076
STONE, Marvin H.	(TX)	1197
THOMAS, Page A.	(TX)	1238
WHITE, Elizabeth B.	(TX)	1331
FLAKE, Chad J.	(UT)	383
LARSEN, A D.	(UT)	698
BERWICK, Philip C.	(VA)	91
CHAMBERLAIN, William R.	(VA)	197
GORDON, Vesta L.	(VA)	452
JAFFE, John G.	(VA)	591
KARRER, Jonathan K.	(VA)	628
KELLY, Ardie L.	(VA)	637
PINEL, Stephen L.	(VA)	974
SARTAIN, Sara M.	(VA)	1083
THOMPSON, Anthony B.	(VA)	1239
TYSINGER, Barbara R.	(VA)	1267
SINGER, George C.	(VT)	1143
SWIFT, Esther M.	(VT)	1216
LANE, Steven P.	(WA)	694
LIPTON, Laura E.	(WA)	732
CORBLY, James E.	(WI)	245

BOOKS (Cont'd)
Rare books

EDMONDS, Michael	(WI)	336
HILL, Edwin L.	(WI)	539
SADLON, Ramona J.	(WI)	1074
BARNES, Jean S.	(WV)	57
CRESSWELL, Stephen	(WV)	258
NATHANSON, David	(WV)	889
STROUD, John N.	(WV)	1203
STOPKA, Christina K.	(WY)	1198
KUJANSUU, Asko J.	(AB)	683
LOVENBURG, Susan L.	(AB)	743
STEELE, Apollonia L.	(AB)	1184
ROBERTSON, Guy M.	(BC)	1041
ROSEVEAR, E C.	(NB)	1057
ETTLINGER, John R.	(NS)	356
ALSTON, Sandra	(ON)	18
HOFFMAN, Susan J.	(ON)	548
KOTIN, David B.	(ON)	673
LANDON, Richard G.	(ON)	693
MORLEY, William F.	(ON)	865
PULLEYBLANK, Mildred C.	(ON)	997
SEBANC, Mark F.	(ON)	1110
THOMSON, Dorothy F.	(ON)	1241
VAN DER BELLEN, Liana	(ON)	1273
WISEMAN, John A.	(ON)	1357
RATNER, Sabina T.	(PQ)	1010
GAGE, Laurie E.	(ENG)	412
MACNUTT, Richard P.	(ENG)	758
GARRETA, J C.	(FRN)	420
DE MACEDO, Maria L.	(PTG)	290
BARBEN, Tanya A.	(SAF)	55

Rare books administration

Rare books, Americana

Rare books & archives

KENAMORE, Jane A.	(TX)	640
REESE, William S.	(CT)	1016
BEDARD, Laura A.	(DC)	73
INGLES, Ernie B.	(SK)	582

Rare books & artifacts
Rare books & bibliography
Rare books & genealogy
Rare books & hand bookbinding
Rare books & literary manuscripts

SPOTTED EAGLE, Joy	(MT)	1175
CRESSWELL, Donald H.	(PA)	258
SABA, Bettye M.	(IN)	1072
SMITH, Margit J.	(ENG)	1157

Rare books & manuscripts

EBELING-KONING, Blanche T.	(MD)	334
ROBROCK, David P.	(AZ)	1045
ESCHER, Nancy	(CA)	354
HORWITZ, Steven F.	(CA)	561
LEERHOFF, Ruth E.	(CA)	712
SORGENFREI, Robert K.	(CA)	1168
WHITING, F B.	(CA)	1333
WOODWARD, Daniel	(CA)	1368
BOGENSCHNEIDER, Duane R.	(CT)	110
PARKS, Stephen	(CT)	943
SCHMIDT, Alesandra M.	(CT)	1095
WILKIE, Everett C.	(CT)	1340
BEDARD, Laura A.	(DC)	73
ADAMS, Barbara M.	(DE)	4
IVES, Sidney E.	(FL)	586
TIMBERLAKE, Cynthia A.	(HI)	1245
ADAMS, Larry D.	(IA)	5
CULLEN, Charles T.	(IL)	263
GERDES, Neil W.	(IL)	428
GUSHEE, Marion S.	(IL)	478
MCCOY, Ralph E.	(IL)	799
MASON, Alexandra	(KS)	780
MILLER, Robert H.	(KY)	842
ENGLISH, Cynthia J.	(MA)	350
LANCASTER, John	(MA)	692
LOMBARDO, Daniel J.	(MA)	738
MELNICK, Ralph	(MA)	823
STODDARD, Roger E.	(MA)	1196
GWYN, Ann S.	(MD)	479
ALLENTUCK, Marcia E.	(NY)	16
DUPONT, Inge	(NY)	327
RACHOW, Louis A.	(NY)	1001
WILSON, Fredric W.	(NY)	1351
HANSON, Norma S.	(OH)	498
MCCALLUM, Brenda W.	(OH)	793
BAKER, Sylva S.	(PA)	49
BAKY, John S.	(PA)	50

BOOKS (Cont'd)

Rare books & manuscripts
- KOREY, Marie E. . . . . . . (PA) 671
- WOLF, Edwin . . . . (PA) 1360
- COLEY, Betty A. . . . . . . (TX) 231
- HENDERSON, Cathy . . . (TX) 526
- KLEPPER, Bobbie J. . . . (TX) 660
- LEACH, Sally S. . . . . . . (TX) 706
- NOLAN, Edward W. . . . . (WA) 907

Rare books & modern manuscripts HUTTNER, Sidney F. . . . (OK) 579
Rare books & reference work HARADA, Ryukichi . . . . . (JAP) 499
Rare books & special collections WALCOTT, M A. . . . . . . (FL) 1294
- BROWN, Norman B. . . . (IL) 146
- TUCHMAN, Maurice S. . (MA) 1261
- GOLDSBERG, Elizabeth D. (MD) 446
- RAME, Mary E. . . . . . . (NY) 1005
- SZMUK, Szilvia E. . . . . . (NY) 1218
- ZAFREN, Herbert C. . . . . (OH) 1385
- POST, Jeremiah B. . . . . . (PA) 986
- RAINWATER, Jean M. . . (RI) 1004
- BJORKLUND, Edi . . . . . (WI) 100
- MILLER, Beth M. . . . . . . (ON) 836

Rare books appraisal GLENN, Ardis L. . . . . . . (MO) 441
- DU BOIS, Paul Z. . . . . . . (NJ) 322

Rare books, archives, & reference KAPLAN, Sylvia Y. . . . . . (IL) 626
Rare books cataloging REITH, Louis J. . . . . (DC) 1022
- HOUSE, Katherine L. . . . (KY) 563
- LANE, Mary J. . . . . (LA) 694
- KISTLER, Ellen D. . . . . . (MO) 656
- MYERS, Victor C. . . . . . (MO) 885
- CALLINAN, Mary H. . . . . (NY) 174
- GOERNER, Tatiana . . . . (NY) 443

Rare books, college archives GALLAGHER, Mary E. . . (MA) 414
Rare books, exhibits NICKERSON, Donna L. . . (NY) 902
Rare books for children MCNAMARA, Shelley G. . (ME) 816
Rare books, history of medicine FREY, Emil F. . . . . (TX) 402
Rare books in theology VANDEGRIFT, J R. . . . . (DC) 1273
Rare books, literature, music AUSTIN, Kristi N. . . . . . (WA) 40
Rare books, manuscripts ZINN, Nancy W. . . . . . . (CA) 1389
- HASWELL, Hollee . . . . . (NY) 511

Rare books, manuscripts, & archives FIELD, William N. . . . . . (NJ) 376
Rare books, medical JENKINS, Glen P. . . . . . (OH) 597
Rare books, music STRINGFELLOW, William
- T. . . . . (NY) 1202

Rare books of bibliography DOAK, Wesley A. . . . . . (OR) 306
Rare books, photographs, ephemerae HARDY, D C. . . . . (LA) 500
Rare books, printing history ALLEN, Susan M. . . . . . (CA) 16
Rare books purchase & sales MCKITTRICK, Bruce W. . (PA) 812
Rare books, special collections SPONDER, Dorothy R. . . (DC) 1175
- JONES, Christine S. . . . (TN) 611

Rare books subject collections WOLFE, Marice . . . . . . (TN) 1361
Rare books, West Americana DOBBERTEEN, Sara J. . (OK) 307
Rare books, West Virginia MARTIN, June R. . . . . . (WV) 777
Rare children's books COUGHLAN, Margaret N. (DC) 250
- SPIRT, Diana L. . . . . . . (NY) 1175
- BROWN, Muriel W. . . . . (TX) 146

Rare children's books in English JOHNSON, Carolyn E. . . (CA) 602
Rare juvenile books MATHER, Becky R. . . . . (IA) 783
Rare law books BOYER, Larry M. . . . . . (DC) 123
- REES, Warren D. . . . . . (MN) 1016

Rare medical books JENSEN, Joseph E. . . . . (MD) 599
- KEYS, Thomas F . . . . . (MN) 645
- WHITCOMB, Dorothy V. . (WI) 1330

Rare numismatic books CAMPBELL, Francis D. . (NY) 176
Rare Sisters of Mercy books MULDREY, Mary H. . . . . (LA) 876
Readers advisory book information IRGON, Deborah A. . . . . (NJ) 583
Reference & scholarly books SCHORR, Alan E. . . . . . (AK) 1099
Reference book design FRANKLIN, Robert M. . . (NC) 398
Reference book design & research KLINE, Victoria E. . . . . . (CA) 661
Reference book publications KNAPPMAN, Edward W. . (NY) 663
Reference book publishing MARLOW, Cecilia A. . . . (MI) 772
- YOUNG, Margaret L. . . . (MN) 1382

Reference book publishing &
marketing WHITELEY, Sandra M. . . (IL) 1333
Reference book reviewing JENSEN, Joan W. . . . . . (CT) 598
- MEYERS, Arthur S. . . . . (IN) 830

Reference book reviews HOGAN, Patricia M. . . . . (IL) 549

BOOKS (Cont'd)

Reference books
- WOOD, Raymund F. . . . . (CA) 1364
- WYNAR, Bohdan S. . . . . (CO) 1375
- HAYES, James L. . . . . . (CT) 515
- STEWART, Donald E. . . . (IL) 1192
- WRIGHT, Helen K. . . . . . (IL) 1371
- BREWER, Annie M. . . . . (MI) 134
- CROWLEY, Ellen T. . . . . (MI) 261
- MACFARLAND, Scott D. . (NY) 755
- SPIER, Margaret M. . . . . (NY) 1174
- HEINZKILL, J R. . . . . . . (OR) 522
- VELA, Leonor G. . . . . . . (SPN) 1281

Reference books evaluation MCSWEENEY, Josephine (NY) 818
Religious book selection SMITH, Newland F. . . . . (IL) 1159
- HILL, Lawrence H. . . . . . (PA) 540

Religious books DOLLEN, Charles J. . . . . (CA) 310
- MEDER, Stephen A. . . . . (MI) 820
- HEISER, W C. . . . . (MO) 523
- HEFNER, Xavier M. . . . . (NY) 520

Religious books, evangelism FERM, Lois R. . . . . (MN) 373
Reserve books NAMSICK, Lynn J. . . . . . (AZ) 887
Reviewer of children's books GOODRICH PETERSON,
- Marilyn . . . . (KS) 450

Reviewing children's books NIX, Kemie . . . . (GA) 905
- CRAIGHEAD, Alice A. . . (TX) 254
- POLISHUK, Bernard . . . . (WA) 980
- KRUSE, Ginny M. . . . . . (WI) 681

Reviewing children's books &
audiovisual SHERMAN, Louise L. . . . (NJ) 1128
Scholarly & reference book publishing BERKNER, Dimity S. . . . (NY) 87
Scholarly books ASH, Lee M. . . . . (CT) 35
- EDWARDS, David M. . . . (PA) 337

Scholarly law books LUTTRELL, Jordan D. . . (CA) 750
Science books for children JENSEN, Ann M. . . . . . . (CA) 598
Scientific books editing SKALLERUP, Amy G. . . . (FL) 1145
Scientific, technical & reference books PECK, Brian T. . . . . (FL) 953
Selecting & purchasing books JACKSON, Mildred E. . . (MN) 588
Selection of books ADRIAN, Donna J. . . . . . (PQ) 7
Selection of books & journals THOMAS, Yvonne . . . . . (CA) 1238
Selection of English books DJEVALIKIAN, Sonia . . . (PQ) 306
17th century English books SILVER, Joel B. . . . . . . (IN) 1138
17th century New England books BISHOP, John . . . . (MA) 99
Sound recordings books MAWHINNEY, Paul C. . . (PA) 787
Spanish language children's books ZWICK, Louise Y. . . . . . (TX) 1392
Special collections, rare books SAHAK, Judy H. . . . . . . (CA) 1075
- MENGES, Gary L. . . . . . (WA) 824

Special collections, rare books,
archive NAINIS, Linda . . . . (DC) 886
Spiritual book buying HLUHANY, Patricia . . . . (PA) 544
Stratemeyer series books THORNDILL, Christine M. (WA) 1242
Subject cataloging of law books KREH, Fritz . . . . (WGR) 667
Supervising all book orders DOYLE, Patricia A. . . . . (TX) 317
Talking books JENNINGS, Mary . . . . . . (AK) 598
- COLEMAN, James M. . . . (AL) 231
- WAZNIS, Betty . . . . (CA) 1311
- KELLEY, H N. . . . . (IL) 636
- PARK, T P. . . . . (NY) 941

Talking books service LADUE, Annette S. . . . . (NY) 687
Technical book reviewing KRUPP, Robert G. . . . . (NJ) 681
Text book indexing WEIR, Alexandra L. . . . . (PA) 1319
Textbook & technical book databases JACKRELL, Thomas L. . . (NJ) 586
Textiles databases & books DAVIS, Jeannette . . . . . (MA) 279
Theatre books & memorabilia BOWLEY, Craig . . . . . . (NY) 121
Theological books GAGE, Laurie H. . . . . . . (ENG) 412
Theological rare books KANSFIELD, Norman J. . (NY) 625
Trade books for beginning readers BAUER, Carolyn J. . . . . (OK) 65
Unique books PASCAL, Barbara R. . . . (CA) 945
Used law book sales BROWN, G R. . . . . (FL) 144
- KILLIAN, Mary C. . . . . . (MI) 648

Writing & editing professional books WEISBURG, Hilda K. . . . (NJ) 1319
Writing book reviews ESTES, Sally A. . . . . . . (IL) 355
Writing children's non-fiction books MARSTON, Hope I. . . . . (NY) 775
Young adult book club newsletter JACKSON, Nancy D. . . . (NY) 588
Young adult book selection MOORE, Richard K. . . . . (CA) 861
- WINSLOW, Carol M. . . . (IN) 1355
- WISOTZKI, Lila B. . . . . . (MD) 1358
- WRIGHT, Patricia Y. . . . (OK) 1372

Young adult book talks OSSOLINSKI, Lynn . . . . (NV) 928

BOOKS (Cont'd)

Young adult books	BURGESS, Eileen E. ...	(MD)	159
	HOLTZE, Sally H.	(NY)	555
	WARD, Peter K.	(NY)	1304
Young adult books, acquisition & editing	JACKSON, Nancy D.	(NY)	588
Young adult books & materials	WILLIAMS, Helen E. ...	(MD)	1343
Young adult books promotion & publicity	JACKSON, Nancy D.	(NY)	588
Young people's book selection	DAVIS, Inez W.	(TN)	279
Young teens book selection	RAPPELT, John F.	(NY)	1008

BOOKS-BY-MAIL

Books-by-mail	RYAN, Audrey H.	(FL)	1070
	SUVAK, Daniel S.	(OH)	1212
Books-by-mail service	SILVER, Gary L.	(MI)	1138

BOOKSELLING (See also Sales, Selling, Vendor)

Book sales	AXT, Randolph W.	(WI)	42
Book sales to libraries	FAST, Barry	(NY)	366
Bookseller	CRAWFORD, Miriam I. ..	(PA)	257
Booksellers	LINCOLN, Robert S.	(MB)	728
Bookselling & publishing	DOLE, Wanda V.	(PA)	309
International booksellers	GROSSMANN, Pierre ..	(BRA)	473
International scientific bookselling	OVEREYNDER, Rombout E.	(NET)	931

BOOKSTACKS (See also Stack)

| Bookstack maintenance | CORNWALL, Scot J. .... | (MA) | 247 |
| Manufacturing steel bookstacks | VAN PELT, Peter J. .... | (NY) | 1277 |

BOOKTALKING (See also Talking)

Book talks	DOMINESKE, Alice M. ...	(NJ)	310
	WEIDEMANN, Margaret A.	(NY)	1316
Booktalking	OVERMYER, Elizabeth C.	(CA)	931
	BODART-TALBOT, Joni .	(KS)	109
	LYNN, Barbara A.	(KS)	752
	GUILFORD, Diane E. ..	(VA)	476
Booktalking, children's books	GREESON, Janet S. ...	(AR)	465
Booktalks	BECKING, Mara S.	(IN)	73
	PAULIN, Mary A.	(MI)	950
	SELANDER, Lucy M. ...	(MN)	1113
Children & young adults booktalking	ROCHMAN, Hazel P. ...	(IL)	1046

BOOTH

| The Junius Brutus Booth family | ARCHER, Stephen M. ... | (MO) | 31 |

BOSTON

| Urban history, Boston | BERGEN, Philip S. ...... | (MA) | 85 |

BOTANY (See also Plants)

Botanical reference & bibliography	SCHALLERT, Ruth F.	(DC)	1089
Botanical systematics & taxonomy	CHANDLER, Jody A. ...	(UT)	200
Botany	GIGNAC, Solange G. ...	(CO)	433
	KURZ, David B.	(OH)	685
	OVERHOLT, Maria B. ...	(OH)	931
Botany & horticulture	LANE, David M.	(NH)	694
Botany libraries	DEFATO, Joan	(CA)	287
Botany reference	MARKHAM, James W. ..	(CA)	771
	TEETER, Enola J.	(PA)	1229
Catalog of portraits of botanists	STIEBER, Michael T. ...	(PA)	1193
History of botany archives	STIEBER, Michael T. ...	(PA)	1193

BOYCHOIR

| Boychoir history & bibliography | ROOT, Arlene V. ...... | (KS) | 1053 |

BRAILLE

| Braille production | CYLKE, Frank K. ...... | (DC) | 268 |
| Recorded & braille materials & sources | WILSON, Barbara L. ..... | (RI) | 1350 |

BRANCH (See also Community, Multibranch, Neighborhood, Outlets)

Academic branch libraries	SEAL, Robert A.	(TX)	1109
Administration, branch library	BRACKNEY, Kathryn S. .	(GA)	125
Administration of central & main branch	APPELBAUM, Sara B. ..	(FL)	29
Branch administration	BROCKMAN, B D.	(GA)	138
	RODERICK, Mary P. ...	(TX)	1047
	VIIERANS, Mary E.	(BC)	1284
Branch adminstrv & supervisory skills	SMITH-EPPS, E P.	(GA)	1161
Branch adult book selection	RODGER, Elizabeth A. ..	(ON)	1047
Branch & extension services	KINGSTON, Jo A.	(MI)	652
Branch & neighborhood services	SCHNEIDER, Francisca M.	(CA)	1097
Branch & regional library layouts	COBURN, Morton	(IL)	225
Branch, bookmobile, outreach services	BEECH, Vivian W.	(NC)	74
Branch coordination	GRIMLEY, Susan M. ...	(SC)	470
Branch development	KOZLOWSKI, Ronald S. .	(OH)	674
Branch development & management	LEITLE, Barbara K.	(MO)	714
Branch leadership	THOMAS, Louise V. ...	(MI)	1237
Branch librarianship	NEWHARD, Eleanor M. .	(CA)	899
	STANLEY, Sydney J.	(CA)	1180
	STENSTROM, Patricia F.	(IL)	1187
	MATYI, Stephen G.	(OH)	786
Branch libraries	CARNAHAN, Mabel A. ...	(FL)	183
	NETZ, David H.	(MI)	896
	FOSTER, Veo G.	(MN)	393
	LEWIS, Betty J.	(OH)	722
	KALTWASSER, Patricia F.	(PA)	623
	CRONEIS, Karen S.	(TX)	260
	FRENCH, Randy A.	(VA)	402
	LEHNERT, Sharon A. ...	(ON)	713
Branch libraries administration	RAWLES-HEISER, Carolyn	(IN)	1010
Branch library	WALKER, Terri L.	(GA)	1296
Branch library administration	CRAIG, Susan V.	(KS)	254
	SEABORN, Frances L. ..	(PA)	1109
	GOLDBERG, Rhoda L. ..	(TX)	444
	GREEN, Carol C.	(WA)	461
Branch library building	DAVIES, Jo	(WA)	277
Branch library buildings	RADOFF, Leonard I.	(TX)	1002
Branch library collection development	GENCO, Barbara A. ...	(NY)	426
Branch library consulting	PALMER, Marguerite C. .	(WV)	936
Branch library coordination	FRANKS, Janice	(AL)	398
Branch library layout	BUFKIN, Anne G.	(FL)	155
Branch library management	ANDREWS, Karen L. ...	(CA)	26
	BOYLLS, Virginia W. ...	(CA)	124
	GILDEN, Susanna C. ...	(CA)	434
	ROH, Jae M.	(CA)	1050
	WEISENBURGER, Patricia J.	(KS)	1319
	MATTESON, James S. ...	(MI)	785
	SICHEL, Beatrice	(MI)	1135
	FUNK, Nancy J.	(NY)	410
	MCKINNEY, Venora	(WI)	812
Branch library operations	TREJO-MEEHAN, Tamiye	(IL)	1255
Branch library service	SCHMIDT, Robert R. ...	(CA)	1096
	MARSHALL, Jane C. ...	(VA)	774
Branch library services	COBB, Karen B.	(CA)	225
	CROMER, Kenneth L. ...	(OH)	260
Branch library services & programs	ALSTON-REEDER, Lizzie A.	(NC)	18
Branch library systems	LANDGRAF, Mary N. ...	(CA)	692
Branch library work	SHERWOOD, Judith	(CA)	1129
Branch management	HAUSSMANN, Virginia D.	(CA)	513
	NICKERSON, Louann M.	(CA)	902
	NOGA, Michael M.	(CA)	907
	ROSASCHI, Jim P.	(CA)	1054
	BOSWELL, Peggy B. ...	(CO)	118
	BERBERICH, Patricia L. .	(CT)	84
	ROBINSON, Cathy A. ...	(DC)	1043
	BURKE, Donna J.	(FL)	160
	STEELE, Patricia A.	(IN)	1184
	WOODY, Jacqueline B. .	(MD)	1368
	STEWART, Jeanne E. ...	(MS)	1192
	PARR, Louise M.	(NJ)	943
	GENDRON, Michele M. .	(PA)	426
	BUZZELL, Bonnie G.	(RI)	168
	GRIFFLER, Carl W.	(VA)	469
	AUSTIN, Martha L.	(WA)	40
	JONES, Charlotte W. ...	(WA)	611
	SCOTT-MILLER, Gwen .	(WA)	1108

BRANCH (Cont'd)
Branch management
                                KIERANS, Mary E. . . . . . (BC)   647
                                MULLERBECK, Aino . . . (ON)   877
Branch management public libraries REILLY, Jane A. . . . . . . (IL) 1020
Branch operations   STORCK, Bernadette R. . (FL) 1198
                                PINDER, Jo A. . . . . (MD)   974
Branch planning & development   SMITH, Robert F. . . . . . (TN) 1160
Branch services   LOSEY, Doris C. . . . . . (FL)   742
                                TOMS, Merrill F. . . . . . . (MO) 1250
                                DUNAWAY, Charjean L. . (MS)   325
                                CARPENTER, Jennifer K. (NC)   184
                                BELVIN, Carolyn J. . . . . (NJ)   78
                                THOMPSON, Evan L. . . . (VT) 1239
                                MCKENZIE, Donald R. . . (PQ)   811
Branch supervising   PICHA, Charlotte G. . . . (IN)   970
Branch supervision   JOHNSON, Beth . . . . . . (GA)   602
Branches & long-range planning HOLT, Raymond M. . . . . (CA)   554
Central & branches   MOLTZAN, Janet R. . . . . (TX)   854
Community branch libraries   BARKLEY, Laura P. . . . . (CA)   57
Coordinating & administrating
  branches   ALGAZE, Selma B. . . . . (FL)   13
Coordinating branch services   WALSH, Mary A. . . . . . . (PQ) 1300
Library branch administration   FELTON, Barbara M. . . . (IN)   370
Library systems with branches   DAVIES, Jo . . . . (WA)   277
Public library branch administration MOLZ, Jean B. . . . . (MD)   854
                                PITTMAN, Dorothy E. . . . (MD)   976
Public library branch management BERGMANN, Sue A. . . . (GA)   87
                                BROWN, Merrikay E. . . . (NC)   146
Public library branch supervision DOWDLE, Glen L. . . . . . (TX)   315
Public library branch work   RUDER, Clarice M. . . . . (FL) 1065
Public library branches   MAGNUSSEN, Ruth A. . . (IL)   760
Rural branch libraries   MCCORMICK, Tamsie . . (IN)   799
Science, branch librarianship   CAMPBELL, Susan M. . . . (PA)   177
Supervising branch library system RADOFF, Leonard I. . . . . (TX) 1002

BRANDEIS
Louis D Brandeis records   HODGSON, Janet B. . . . (KY)   546

BRASS
Brass music   MARTIN, Jean F. . . . . . . (NY)   776

BRAZIL
Brazilian studies   NELSON, William N. . . . . (AL)   895

BREWING
Brewing industry history   VOLLMAR, William J. . . . (MO) 1288

BRITISH (See also Anglo-African, Anglo-Saxon, English)
British & Canadian documents   VOGEL, Jane G. . . . . . . (NC) 1286
British & Commonwealth govt
  publications   BEAN, Charles W. . . . . . (DC)   69
British, Australian, Anglo-African HAWK, Susan P. . . . . . . (FL)   513
British business & culture   JONES, Adrian . . . . (IL)   610
British collection development REES, Warren D. . . . . . . (MN) 1016
British history specialist   BRUGNOLOTTI, Phyllis T. (NY)   150
18th century British history & culture DEVINE, Marie E. . . . . . . (CT)   297
18th century British literature DEVINE, Marie E. . . . . . . (CT)   297
19th century British & American lit COLEY, Betty A. . . . . . . (TX)   231
19th century British theatre   DONOHUE, Joseph . . . . (MA)   312

BRITISH-AMERICAN
Chronology, British-American theater LONEY, Glenn M. . . . . . . (NY)   739
Modern British-American literature COX, Shelley M. . . . . (IL)   253

BROADCASTING (See also Cable, Radio, Television)
Broadcast history   RUNYON, Steven C. . . . (CA) 1067
                                HEINZ, Catharine F. . . . . (DC)   522
Broadcasting   HILL, Susan M. . . . . (DC)   540
                                CAMPBELL, R A. . . . . . . (HI)   177
                                VOLPATTI, Rechilde . . . (ON) 1288
Broadcasting & communications
  research   SLOCUM, Leslie E. . . . . (NY) 1150

BROADCASTING (Cont'd)
Broadcasting archives   CNATTINGIUS, Claes M. (SWE) 224
Broadcasting research   KATZ, Doris B. . . . . (NY)   630
Cable television & broadcast
  television   WALSH, Mark L. . . . . . . (CT) 1300
Canadian broadcasting   EARLS, M L. . . . . (ON)   332
Classical music broadcasting   FRANK, Mortimer H. . . . . (NY)   397
Data broadcasting on VBI   WILLIAMS, Fred . . . . . . (GA) 1343
History of broadcasting   BRAGG, William J. . . . . (TX)   127
Indexing film & broadcast trade
  journals   HOFFER, Thomas W. . . . (FL)   547
Mechanical music, broadcasting, film MUNSICK, Lee R. . . . . . (NJ)   879
Television broadcasting   KLEM, Marjorie R. . . . . (NC)   660

BROKERAGE
Automated information brokering COLLARD, R M. . . . . . . (CO)   232
Broker analysis research   HEFFRON, Betsy A. . . . . (NY)   520
Holdings & information brokering HAHN, Margaret M. . . . . (VA)   483
Information broker   DE ARMAN, Charles L. . . (DC)   284
Information broker & supplier   POND, Frederick C. . . . . (NY)   982
Information broker services   CARROLL, Hardy . . . . . . (MI)   187
Information brokerage   TEBO, Jay D. . . . . (CA) 1229
                                MCELHANEY, William E. . (CT)   804
                                HUTCHINS, Richard G. . . (IL)   579
                                EASLEY, Janet T. . . . . . . (WA)   332
                                DUPLESSIS, Daniel . . . . (PQ)   327
Information brokerage consulting KLEMENT, Susan P. . . . (ON)   660
Information brokering   CUEVAS, John R. . . . . . (CA)   263
                                REISMAN, Sydelle S. . . . (CT) 1021
                                LEIGHTON, Victoria C. . . (GA)   714
                                INGISH, Karen S. . . . . . . (IL)   582
                                MOORHEAD, John D. . . . (IL)   862
                                COPPOLA, Peter A. . . . . (MA)   245
                                BEAUBIEN, Anne K. . . . . (MI)   70
                                HALES-MABRY, Celia E. . (MN)   486
                                REHKOP, Barbara L. . . . . (MO) 1017
                                MCZORN, Bonita A. . . . . (NC)   819
                                DEFALCO, Joseph . . . . . (NY)   287
                                DENOTO, Dorothy E. . . . (NY)   293
                                GIGLIOTTI, Mary J. . . . . (NY)   433
                                DE STRICKER, Ulla . . . . (ON)   296
                                DIMITRESCU, Ioana . . . . (PQ)   304
                                DUBEAU, Pierre . . . . (PQ)   321
Information brokering & supplying ALDERSON, Karen A. . . . (IA)   11
Information brokering businesses BALL, Thomas W. . . . . . (DC)   52
Info brokering, supplying, consulting AXT, Randolph W. . . . . . (WI)   42
Information services brokering GOURLAY, Una M. . . . . . (TX)   454
Intrapreneuring & information
  brokering   BROWN, Ina A. . . . . (NJ)   144
Online searching, brokerage,
  insurance   ENGLISH, Christopher C. (NJ)   350
Research on information brokers WALLS, Francine E. . . . . (WA) 1299

BROOKLYNIANA
Brooklyniana   CIOLLI, Antoinette . . . . . (NY)   214
                                LESTER, Lillian . . . . (NY)   718

BROWNING
Robert & Elizabeth Barrett Browning COLEY, Betty A. . . . . . . (TX)   231

BRS
BRS databases   GELMAN-KMEC, Marsha (CA)   426
DIALOG & BRS   SMITH, Frances P. . . . . . (HI) 1155
End-user instruction, BRS after dark COONS, William W. . . . . (NY)   242
Online searching, NLM, DIALOG,
  BRS   NELSON, Iris N. . . . . (CA)   894

BUDGET (See also Accounting, Cost, Finance, Expenditure)
Academic library budgeting &
  planning   SMITH, Gordon W. . . . . . (CA) 1155
Accounting, budgeting   LLOYD, H R. . . . . (PA)   735
Acquisitions & budget   JARABEK, Leona T. . . . . (OH)   594
Acquisitions & budgeting   CHANG, Min M. . . . . . . (CA)   200
                                PARISI, Judith A. . . . . . . (CT)   940
Administering budget   ROGERS, William F. . . . . (OH) 1050

BUDGET (Cont'd)

Administration, budgeting	MEYERS, Duane H.	(OK)	830
Administration, personnel, budget	DAVID, Indra M.	(MI)	276
Administration, personnel, budget, space	ROSENFELD, Mary A.	(DC)	1056
All media budget & purchase	DU CARMONT, M C.	(LA)	322
Analyzing finances & budgeting	BENDER, Betty W.	(WA)	79
Budget	MORRIS, George H.	(CA)	866
	OYLER, David K.	(CA)	932
	BLACKBURN, Joy M.	(IL)	102
	JAMES, William	(KY)	592
	COGGINS, Timothy L.	(NC)	227
	DOBRZYNSKI, Terenita	(NY)	307
	WELLS, Gladysann	(NY)	1322
	ENGLISH, Raymond A.	(OH)	350
	REEVES, Marjorie A.	(OR)	1017
	SCHWIND, Penelope	(PA)	1106
Budget administration	PANZERA, Donald P.	(DC)	938
	KAUFFMAN, Betty G.	(NJ)	631
	BONAMICI, Andrew R.	(OR)	113
	ROY, Helene	(PQ)	1063
Budget & accounts payable	VOIT, Irene E.	(NV)	1287
Budget & administration	FRALEY, Ruth A.	(NY)	395
Budget & finance	APPEL, Anne M.	(CA)	29
	HAWLEY, Marsha S.	(IL)	514
	SUGDEN, Barbara L.	(IL)	1206
	DOMBOURIAN, Sona J.	(LA)	310
	LEBRUN, Marlene M.	(MD)	708
	HERNANDEZ, Ramon R.	(MI)	532
	DESCIORA, Susan O.	(NY)	294
	VAN RIPER, Joy C.	(NY)	1277
	SENG, Mary A.	(TX)	1115
Budget & fiscal management	CONNORS, William E.	(NY)	238
Budget & fund management	MARCINKO, Dorothy K.	(AL)	769
Budget & personnel administration	HEMPHILL, Jean F.	(CO)	525
Budget & personnel management	MORITZ, William D.	(WI)	865
Budget & planning	DYER, Charles R.	(CA)	330
	CHESLEY, Thea B.	(IL)	207
	POLACH, Frank	(NJ)	980
Budget & statistics	JENSEN, Charla J.	(UT)	598
Budget control	WU, Painan R.	(NY)	1373
Budget development	O'BRIEN, Patrick M.	(TX)	915
Budget management	DAY, Janeth N.	(AL)	282
Budget, personnel actions administration	CURTIS, George H.	(MO)	267
Budget, personnel, systems development	HARRIS, Linda S.	(DC)	505
Budget planning	SCHATZ, Natalie M.	(MA)	1090
Budget planning & control	CHRISTIANSON, Ellory J.	(MN)	212
Budget preparation	MITCHELL, Deborah S.	(MS)	848
	CARTER, Darline L.	(NY)	189
Budget priorities & preparation	NANCE, Betty L.	(TX)	887
Budget process	JOHNSON, Wayne H.	(WY)	609
Budget, reference, personnel	FARKAS, Charles R.	(NY)	364
Budgetary control	FROSCHER, Jean L.	(FL)	406
Budgeting	FELDER, Jimmie R.	(AL)	369
	DIENER, Margaret M.	(CA)	302
	GREGORY, Timothy P.	(CA)	466
	LEONARD, Barbara G.	(CA)	716
	SCHERREI, Rita A.	(CA)	1092
	CARROLL VIRGO, Julie	(IL)	187
	KUBIAK, Matthew C.	(IL)	682
	WILSON, W R.	(IL)	1353
	MCKAY, Eleanor	(MD)	809
	VINNES, Norman M.	(MN)	1285
	BRENNER, Saundra H.	(MO)	133
	MCKAY, Micheal W.	(MO)	810
	HESS, Jayne L.	(NJ)	534
	VELLUCCI, Sherry L.	(NJ)	1282
	FRIEDMAN, Barbara S.	(NY)	403
	ROSEN, Albert	(NY)	1055
	KEANE, John J.	(PA)	633
	MEARS, William F.	(TX)	820
	HASKELL, John D.	(VA)	510
	THOMAS, Lawrence E.	(WA)	1237
	BANNEN, Carol A.	(WI)	54
	MACINTOSH, Ian R.	(NS)	755
	VOHRA, Pran	(SK)	1287
Budgeting & administration	MACFARLANE, Judy A.	(PQ)	755
Budgeting & budget control	STIFFLEAR, Allan J.	(MA)	1194

BUDGET (Cont'd)

Budgeting & cost estimating	MILLER, Ellen L.	(NY)	837
Budgeting & cost recovery techniques	FOX, Marylou P.	(CA)	395
Budgeting & finance	BERRY, Louise P.	(CT)	90
	TUCKER, Florence R.	(MI)	1261
	LEVESQUE, Janet A.	(RI)	719
	SIEBERSMA, Dan	(WY)	1135
Budgeting & finances	COULTER, Cynthia M.	(OK)	251
Budgeting & financial management	MUNTEAN, Deborah E.	(MN)	879
Budgeting & fiscal administration	ALMONY, Robert A.	(MO)	17
Budgeting & fiscal control	KEHOE, Patrick E.	(DC)	634
Budgeting & management	BAILEY, Alvin R.	(TX)	46
Budgeting & planning	RILEY, Richard K.	(TX)	1034
Budgeting & program planning	HEINTZELMAN, Susan K.	(NY)	522
Budgeting & purchasing	ESPER, Elizabeth	(FL)	354
Budgeting & tax levying process	PLAISTED, Glen L.	(KS)	977
Budgeting, library materials	FROMMEYER, L R.	(OH)	405
Budgeting process	GOEHNER, Donna M.	(IL)	443
Budgeting systems	CANNON, Robert E.	(NC)	179
Budgets	GILROY, Rupert E.	(MA)	437
Budgets & specifications	MAY, Robert E.	(SC)	789
Budgets, cost controls	BAUMGARTNER, Robert M.	(OH)	66
Business & budgeting	LEVITT, Irene S.	(MA)	721
Business management, budgeting	WARNER, Alice S.	(MA)	1305
Coordinate library budget & expenditures	REID, Richard H.	(LA)	1019
Defense planning & budgeting	BROWN, George F.	(MA)	144
Library acquisitions & library budgeting	KELLY, Glen J.	(ON)	637
Library budget	MUELLER, Elizabeth	(IL)	875
Library budget administration	MURPHY, Joyce	(BC)	880
Library budgeting	MONTANELLI, Dale S.	(IL)	855
	LITTLETON, Isaac T.	(NC)	734
	SCHNEIDER, Lynette C.	(NJ)	1097
Library maintenance & budgets	BALKIN, Ruth G.	(NY)	52
Library planning & budgeting	RAMSEY, Inez L.	(VA)	1006
Library system budget funding	NETTLES, Jess	(MS)	896
Management & budgeting	LINDGREN, Arla M.	(NY)	729
Management & budgeting info technologies	LOWRY, Charles B.	(TX)	745
Management & budgets	JACKA, David C.	(NE)	586
Management budgeting	MILLER, Ronald F.	(CA)	842
Mgmt, planning, budgeting, supervising	ZAENGER, Kathleen L.	(MI)	1385
Operating & capital budgets	RAPHAEL, Mary E.	(DC)	1008
Personnel & budget management	WONG, Clark C.	(CA)	1362
Personnel & budgeting	MCCOOL, Donna L.	(WA)	798
Personnel & budgeting administrative	LETTIERI, Robin M.	(NY)	719
Personnel, planning & budgeting	BROOM, Susan E.	(FL)	141
Planning & budget, university libraries	DORR, Ralze W.	(KY)	313
Planning & budgeting	CLIFTON, Joe A.	(CA)	222
	NICKERSON, Susan L.	(CA)	902
	FORTIER, Jan M.	(MA)	391
	HOLMGREN, Edwin S.	(NY)	553
Planning & budgeting for library service	WINSON, Gail I.	(CA)	1355
Planning & budgeting systems	NERODA, Edward W.	(MT)	895
Planning, budgeting, & supervision	THAKER, Virbala M.	(CA)	1234
Public library administration, budget	NIEMI, Peter G.	(WI)	903
Public relations, publishing, budgeting	ARROWOOD, Donna J.	(CA)	34

BUILDING (See also Architecture, Construction, Design, Expansion, Facilities, Remodeling, Renovation, Site)

Academic library building planning	ELLSWORTH, Ralph E.	(CO)	345
	MCDONALD, John P.	(CT)	802
	GALVIN, Hoyt R.	(NC)	415
	PARK, Leland M.	(NC)	941
	ROUSE, Roscoe	(OK)	1061
	SIEGMANN, Starla C.	(WI)	1136
Academic library buildings	MIRSKY, Phyllis S.	(CA)	847
	KASER, David	(IN)	628
	PARKS, George R.	(ME)	943
	ENGELKE, Hans	(MI)	349
	CLEMMER, Joel G.	(MN)	221
	ESHELMAN, William R.	(OH)	354
Acquisitions, collection building	CADLE, Dean	(NC)	170
Administration & building consulting	KUHN, Warren B.	(IA)	682
Architecture & buildings	LUCKER, Jay K.	(MA)	746

BUILDING (Cont'd)

Archives, historic building preservation	RABINS, Joan W.	(TX)	1001
Branch library building	DAVIES, Jo	(WA)	277
Branch library buildings	RADOFF, Leonard I.	(TX)	1002
Building	BENNETT, Carson W.	(CA)	81
	SCHROEDER, Janet K.	(MN)	1100
	UMBERGER, Stan	(VA)	1268
Building & capital renovation	NYERGES, Michael S.	(NY)	912
Building & collections development	LIU, David T.	(TX)	734
Building & contracting	KRUZIC, Evelyn D.	(WA)	681
Building & equipment	MORITZ, William D.	(WI)	865
Building & maintaining authority files	LESSER, Barbara	(VA)	718
Building & planning	MEANS, Raymond B.	(NE)	820
Building & renovation	TOMPKINS, Philip	(CA)	1250
Building & space planning	CLARK, Alice S.	(CA)	216
	ROHLF, Robert H.	(MN)	1050
	WATERS, Richard L.	(TX)	1308
Building & staff administration	BALCOM, William T.	(IL)	51
Building book collection	KNOLL, Betty A.	(WA)	665
Building collection	SOURS, Katherine M.	(FL)	1169
Building construction management	SINTZ, Edward F.	(FL)	1144
Building construction plng & development	MARTIN, Mason G.	(MO)	777
Building consultant	COOK, Jeannine S.	(NY)	240
Building consulting	PLACE, Philip A.	(FL)	977
	WILSON, David C.	(GA)	1350
	JACKSON, Susan M.	(IL)	588
	SAKEY, Joseph G.	(MA)	1076
	MCFERRAN, Warren A.	(MI)	805
	ARD, Harold J.	(TX)	31
	WHITE, James W.	(WI)	1331
Building design	PINCOCK, Rulon D.	(CA)	974
	HENSON, Llewellyn L.	(FL)	529
	DOUGLAS, Alice W.	(MA)	314
	JACKSON, Patience K.	(NH)	588
	CONNORS, William E.	(NY)	238
	MITTELGLUCK, Eugene L.	(NY)	850
	WALDEN, Winston A.	(TN)	1294
	MOORE, Russell S.	(VT)	861
Building design & renovation	WU, Harry P.	(MI)	1373
	CADA, Elizabeth J.	(ON)	170
Building design for preservation	OGDEN, Barclay W.	(CA)	918
Building development	CURTIS, George H.	(MO)	267
Building expansion	EICHELBERGER, Marianne	(KS)	339
Building industry information	CLARK, Margery M.	(DC)	217
Building knowledge bases	HOROWITZ, Roberta S.	(CA)	560
Building layout & construction	NEAL, Robert L.	(MD)	890
Building libraries	PALMIERI, Lucien E.	(NY)	937
Building library collection	GREMONT, Joan C.	(TX)	467
Building local history collection	MILLER, Ida M.	(IN)	838
Building management	MUSSER, Egbert G.	(MA)	883
Building planning	DAVIDSON, Donald C.	(CA)	276
	GAY, Elizabeth K.	(CA)	423
	SPINKS, Paul	(CA)	1175
	TERRY, Josephine R.	(CA)	1232
	BARRETT, Donald J.	(CO)	59
	MAGRATH, Lynn L.	(CO)	760
	D'ALESSANDRO, Edward A.	(DC)	270
	BUSTETTER, Stanley R.	(FL)	166
	KETCHERSID, Arthur L.	(FL)	645
	SCHULTHEISS, Louis A.	(IL)	1101
	JOHNSON, Duane F.	(KS)	603
	DE BEAR, Richard S.	(MI)	284
	CARMACK, Mona	(MN)	183
	METZ, T J.	(MN)	828
	ORNE, Jerrold	(NC)	926
	BERNSTEIN, Judith R.	(NM)	89
	DE KLERK, Ann M.	(PA)	288
	TANIS, James R.	(PA)	1222
	BALDWIN, Joe M.	(TX)	51
	HENINGTON, David M.	(TX)	528
Building planning, academic libraries	DORR, Ralze W.	(KY)	313
Building planning & construction	STEWART, George R.	(AL)	1192
Building planning & renovation	BARRY, James W.	(PA)	60
Building planning & space allocation	RAWLEY, Wayne	(IA)	1010
Building plans	BRANDON, Alfred N.	(FL)	128
Building program	MAINIERO, Elizabeth T.	(CT)	761

BUILDING (Cont'd)

Building program devlpmnt & construction	MOODY, Marilyn D.	(PA)	857
Building program, planning	HUNSBERGER, Charles W.	(NV)	574
Building programming	MCADAMS, Nancy R.	(TX)	792
Building programs	COBURN, Morton	(IL)	225
	STOFFEL, Lester L.	(IL)	1196
	BOWLING, Carol L.	(SC)	121
Building programs & feasibility study	WRIGHT, Paul L.	(KY)	1372
Building programs & furnishings	POWELL, Mary E.	(TX)	988
Building programs & planning	PETERSON, Stephen L.	(CT)	964
Building programs & space utilization	PALMATIER, Susan M.	(NH)	936
Building projects	KINCHEN, Robert P.	(NY)	650
Building reference collection	COFFEY, Dorothy A.	(MI)	227
Building renovation	STAHL, Wilson M.	(NC)	1178
	SZILASSY, Sandor	(NJ)	1218
Building renovation & additions	JOHNSTON, James R.	(IL)	610
Building renovation supervision	BURNS, Mary F.	(IL)	162
Building renovations	TITUS, H M.	(DE)	1247
Building services	MC LAUGHLIN, Terry L.	(IL)	813
Building, space planning	MCKEE, Christopher	(IA)	810
	TELATNIK, George M.	(NY)	1230
Building, weeding pamphlet collection	ADAMS, Velma L.	(MS)	6
Buildings	MIELKE, Linda	(FL)	833
	BENOIT, Anthony H.	(LA)	82
	JENSEN, David P.	(MI)	598
	PERRY, Rodney B.	(NY)	961
	FINAN, Patrick E.	(OH)	377
	KNASIAK, Theresa J.	(OH)	663
	MAURER, Charles B.	(OH)	787
	PEREZ-LOPEZ, Rene	(VA)	958
	SHEPHERD, Murray C.	(ON)	1127
Buildings & designs	DRAPER, James D.	(GA)	318
Buildings & equipment	SANNWALD, William W.	(CA)	1081
	SEBRIGHT, Terence F.	(FL)	1110
Buildings & facilities	ARMSTRONG, Carole S.	(MI)	32
Buildings & facilities planning	HAKA, Clifford H.	(MI)	484
Buildings & furnishings	NELSON, James B.	(NY)	894
Buildings & space planning	SIGLER, Ronald F.	(CA)	1137
Buildings, financing plans	SANDSTEDT, Carl R.	(MO)	1081
Capital building program	HALL, Edward B.	(MD)	487
Chemical databases building	BAKER, Dale B.	(OH)	48
Chemical information database building	PLATAU, Gerard O.	(OH)	977
Collection & building consultation	DONAHUGH, Robert H.	(OH)	310
Collection building	MITCHELL, Jan E.	(FL)	848
	MATHER, Becky R.	(IA)	783
	MUNDELL, Eric L.	(IN)	878
	HUFF, James E.	(KY)	570
	LIVELY, Nancy J.	(MD)	734
	LANIER, Gene D.	(NC)	696
	VON BROCKDORFF, Eric	(NY)	1288
	SAWIN, Philip Q.	(WI)	1086
	SCHARFENBERG, George E.	(WI)	1090
Collection building in theology	ZIMPFER, William E.	(MA)	1389
Collection building resource	WATSON, Joyce N.	(ON)	1309
Collection development & building	FUNG, Margaret C.	(MA)	409
Database building	FREDERICK, Sidney C.	(IL)	399
	COPENHAVER, Ida L.	(OH)	244
Database conversion & buildup	MEDINA, Ildefonso M.	(NY)	820
Design & planning of library buildings	TRELEASE, Robert J.	(IL)	1255
Design of library buildings	BASSNETT, Peter J.	(ON)	63
Financing & construction building plng	KELLUM-ROSE, Nancy P.	(CA)	637
Florida building regulations	FOSTER, Helen M.	(FL)	392
Grantsmanship & buildings	CORBUS, Lawrence J.	(OH)	245
Hospital library building	LECOMPTE, Louis L.	(PQ)	708
Indexing, abstracting & thesaurus bldg	SUIDAN, Randa H.	(IL)	1207
Junior high building collections	LEWIS, Marjorie	(NY)	723
Library building	MORRILL, Walter D.	(IN)	866
	MCNIFF, Philip J.	(MA)	817
	KALDENBERG, Katherine A.	(NJ)	622
	LEE, Sul H.	(OK)	711
	BRIGGS, Geoffrey H.	(ON)	135
	HARE, Judith E.	(ON)	501
	LACROIX, Yvon A.	(PQ)	687
Library building additions consulting	RIBNICKY, Karen F.	(CT)	1026

BUILDING (Cont'd)

Library building & equipment	LEWIS, Thomas F.	(MA)	724
	WEISS, Egon A.	(NY)	1320
Library building & planning	LOOMIS, Barbara L.	(CA)	740
	MARSHALL, Ruth T.	(GA)	775
Library building construction	ZENKE, Mary H.	(IL)	1387
	DUNCAN, Cynthia B.	(VA)	325
Library building construction/renovation	VENABLE, Andrew A.	(OH)	1282
Library building consultant	SILVER, Cy H.	(CA)	1138
Library building consultation	MCCABE, Gerard B.	(PA)	792
Library building consulting	MASON, Ellsworth G.	(CO)	781
	MCNEAL, Archie L.	(FL)	816
	ROVELSTAD, Howard	(MD)	1062
	MCDONOUGH, Kathleen C.	(NH)	803
	TOOMBS, Kenneth E.	(SC)	1251
	MUTSCHLER, Herbert F.	(WA)	883
	JAX, John J.	(WI)	595
Library building design	BECKMAN, Margaret L.	(ON)	73
	HART, Thomas L.	(FL)	507
	PEARSON, Roger L.	(IL)	953
	SMITH, Lester K.	(IL)	1157
	KANSFIELD, Norman J.	(NY)	625
	LEE, Sang C.	(NY)	711
	WALTERS, Daniel L.	(WA)	1301
	ROBIN, Madeleine	(PQ)	1043
Library building design & planning	MCCABE, James P.	(PA)	793
Library building maintenance	LUEDER, Dianne B.	(IL)	747
Library building management	BURNS, Robert W.	(CO)	163
Library building planning	ANDERSON, Herschel V.	(AZ)	23
	DAVIS, Douglas A.	(CA)	278
	JONES, Wyman	(CA)	615
	NOVAK, Gloria J.	(CA)	910
	JONES, William G.	(IL)	615
	LEE, Sang C.	(NY)	711
	BRAWNER, Lee B.	(OK)	130
	BEAUMIER, Renald	(PQ)	70
Library building planning & design	SICKLES, Linda C.	(MI)	1135
Library building, planning, construction	BROWN, Louise M.	(MA)	145
Library building program writing	STEWART, John D.	(VA)	1192
Library building programs	MCPHERSON, Kenneth F.	(NJ)	817
Library building projects	BEDSOLE, Dan T.	(VA)	73
Library building supervision	MALOY, Frances	(NY)	764
Library buildings	DAMICO, James A.	(AL)	271
	SOUTER, Thomas A.	(AL)	1169
	LARSON, Larry	(AR)	699
	NELSON, Helen M.	(CA)	893
	SABSAY, David	(CA)	1073
	TANIS, Norman E.	(CA)	1222
	ANDERSON, Lemoyne W.	(CO)	24
	ADAMS, J R.	(CT)	5
	BEASLEY, Clarence W.	(FL)	69
	JENKINS, Althea H.	(FL)	597
	SESSA, Frank B.	(FL)	1116
	SCHEETZ, George H.	(IA)	1090
	ALLEN, Walter C.	(IL)	16
	COX, James C.	(IL)	253
	KISTNER, Glen A.	(IL)	657
	RUNKLE, Martin D.	(IL)	1067
	TITUS, Elizabeth M.	(IL)	1247
	UBEL, James A.	(IL)	1267
	BOZONE, Billie R.	(MA)	124
	HILTON, Robert C.	(MA)	541
	KISSNER, Arthur J.	(MA)	656
	PILLSBURY, Mary J.	(MA)	973
	KRENITSKY, Michael V.	(MI)	677
	MARQUIS, Rollin P.	(MI)	773
	WAGMAN, Frederick H.	(MI)	1291
	HOPP, Ralph H.	(MN)	558
	GOVAN, James F.	(NC)	454
	KIRWAN, William J.	(NC)	656
	ROBERTS, William H.	(NC)	1041
	THIELE, Barbara J.	(NJ)	1235
	BOBINSKI, Mary F.	(NY)	108
	DE GENNARO, Richard	(NY)	287
	KOSTER, Gregory E.	(NY)	673
	WILDER, David T.	(NY)	1338
	BUZZELL, Bonnie G.	(RI)	168
	CHAIT, William	(SC)	197

BUILDING (Cont'd)

Library buildings	DOVE, Herbert P.	(SC)	314
	ALLMAND, Linda F.	(TX)	17
	HEEZEN, Ronald R.	(TX)	520
	WROTENBERY, Carl R.	(TX)	1373
	ALBRECHT, Sterling J.	(UT)	10
	BOYLAN, Merle N.	(WA)	123
	DAHLGREN, Anders C.	(WI)	269
	GARDNER, William M.	(WI)	418
	BRUNDIN, Robert E.	(AB)	150
	DINEEN, Diane M.	(ON)	304
	SCHWENGER, Frances S.	(ON)	1105
	SALT, David P.	(SK)	1077
Library buildings & additions	WALSH, Robert R.	(NY)	1300
Library buildings & collection layout	BELGUM, Kathie G.	(IA)	76
Library buildings & equipment	BROADUS, Robert N.	(NC)	138
	MOYER, James M.	(NC)	874
	HANES, Fred W.	(TX)	495
Library buildings & furnishings	BROWN, Carol J.	(TX)	142
Library buildings & interior design	FOX, James R.	(PA)	394
Library buildings & interiors	ORR, Cynthia	(OH)	926
Library buildings & programming	YATES, Ella G.	(VA)	1378
Library buildings consultant, Japan, USA	GITLER, Robert L.	(CA)	438
Library financing & building programming	HELLUM-BERMAN, Bertha D.	(CA)	524
New & remodel buildings	COURTRIGHT, Harry R.	(PA)	252
New building planning	GARDNER, W J.	(CO)	418
New buildings & renovations planning	VANN, John D.	(PA)	1276
Physical building needs	ROGERS, William F.	(OH)	1050
Planning & construction of lib buildings	HEAD, Anita K.	(DC)	518
Planning & design of library buildings	BEWLEY, Lois M.	(BC)	93
Planning buildings	EVANS, Frank B.	(DC)	357
Planning library buildings	PALMER, David W.	(MI)	936
	BREEN, M F.	(NY)	131
	SNAPP, Elizabeth M.	(TX)	1162
	OROZCO-TENORIO, Jose M.	(MEX)	926
Preparing for automation & new lib bldg	INGIBERGSSON, Asgeir	(AB)	582
Programming buildings & plan review	HOLT, Raymond M.	(CA)	554
Public library building design	BARTON, Phillip K.	(NC)	62
	MURPHY, Richard W.	(VA)	881
Public library building planning	KEOUGH, Francis P.	(MA)	643
	GALVIN, Hoyt R.	(NC)	415
Public library building programs	SMITH, Elizabeth M.	(CA)	1154
	WELCH, John T.	(NC)	1321
Public library building projects	SMITH, David R.	(MN)	1154
Public library buildings	DEAKYNE, William J.	(CT)	283
	LUSHINGTON, Nolan	(CT)	749
	BECKER, Josephine M.	(FL)	72
	CHITWOOD, Julius R.	(IL)	209
	SCHABEL, Donald J.	(KY)	1088
	FINNEY, Lance C.	(MD)	379
	YOUNG, Jerry F.	(MN)	1382
	COUMBE, Robert E.	(NJ)	251
	HALL, Alan C.	(OH)	486
Public library planning & building	MCGRIFF, Ronald I.	(MN)	808
Reference building & service	ADAMS, Velma L.	(MS)	6
Science administration & buildings	SOMERVILLE, Arleen N.	(NY)	1167
Small academic building design	LUCAS, Linda L.	(CA)	746
Small & medium public library buildings	FARACE, Virginia K.	(FL)	363
Small libraries building planning	MILLIKEN, Ruth L.	(FL)	843
Small public library buildings	RASKA, Ginny	(TX)	1009
Team building	MUNGER, Freda R.	(OR)	879
Thesaurus building	FRIED, Suzanne C.	(NY)	403
Thesaurus buildup	PILLET, Sylvaine M.	(KEN)	973
Videocassette collection building	AROS, Andrew A.	(CA)	34
Writing building programs	DAHLGREN, Jean E.	(TX)	269

BULLETIN (See also Mail, Message)

Electronic bulletin boards	POLLY, Jean A.	(NY)	981
	SCHWARZ, Joy L.	(WI)	1105
Electronic mail & bulletin boards	O'NEILL, Sue	(MD)	924
Library bulletin boards	MENINGALL, Evelyn L.	(NJ)	824

BULLETIN (Cont'd)

PC bulletin boards ROSE, Phillip E. . . . . (CO) 1055

BUSINESS (See also Business Databases, Commerce, Companies, Corporate, Entrepreneurship, Firms, Industry, Mergers, Office, Trade)

Accounting & business BEHAR, Evelyn W. . . . . . (NY) 74
Accounting & business bibliography NELOMS, Karen H. . . . . (NY) 893
Advertising & business information MASTROIANNI, Richard L. (MD) 783
Analyze business opportunities KIESER, Scott P. . . . . . . (NY) 647
Archives for small businesses HOMMEL, Claudia . . . . . (NY) 555
Asia Pacific business collection CHAN, Diana L. . . . . . . (BC) 199
Automation of business applications BROWN, Maxine M. . . . . (DC) 146
Banking, economics & business NAULTY, Deborah M. . . . . (PA) 889
Banking, finance & business
  reference MIRANDA, Esmeralda C. (MN) 847
British business & culture JONES, Adrian . . . . (IL) 610
Business COSTELLO, Robert C. . . . (CA) 249
  DEGOOD, S K. . . . . (CA) 288
  KEIZUR, Berta L. . . . . . . (CA) 635
  KENYON, Sharmon H. . . . (CA) 643
  LEWIS, Gretchen S. . . . . (CA) 723
  LITTLEJOHN, Alice C. . . (CA) 734
  O'NEILL, Diane J. . . . . . (CA) 924
  PERKINS, Michael J. . . . (CA) 959
  POPA, Opritsa A. . . . . . . (CA) 983
  SWEENEY, Suzanne . . . (CA) 1215
  DOMINIANNI, Beth S. . . . (CT) 310
  FOWLER, Louise D. . . . (CT) 394
  ACKERMAN, F C. . . . . . (DC) 3
  MOULTON, David A. . . . (DC) 873
  BRUEMMER, Alice . . . . . (IL) 149
  JAMESON, Martha E. . . . (IL) 592
  LAM, Judy . . . . (IL) 689
  PRENDERGAST, Kathleen
    M. . . . . (IL) 990
  RADER, Jennette S. . . . . (IL) 1002
  RYAN, Betsey A. . . . . . . (KS) 1070
  BOYER, Janice S. . . . . . (NE) 123
  BRAUN, Carl F. . . . . . . (NY) 129
  HALPIN, James R. . . . . . (NY) 490
  RABER, Steven . . . . (NY) 1001
  SMITH, Melanie W. . . . . (NY) 1158
  VOGEL, Dorothy H. . . . . (NY) 1286
  WITSENHAUSEN, Helen
    A. . . . . (NY) 1358
  MAKELA, Helen M. . . . . (OH) 762
  BISHOP, Donna M. . . . . (OK) 99
  BLAIR, William W. . . . . . (PA) 103
  WESTERMAN, Melvin E. (PA) 1327
  CROWTHER, Karmen N. (TN) 262
  PATTERSON, Jennifer J. (TN) 948
  ARNOLD, Patricia K. . . . (TX) 34
  DEPETRO, Thomas G. . . (TX) 293
  SCHMELZIE, Joan C. . . . (TX) 1094
  CANNON, Ruth M. . . . . (VA) 179
  MAXWELL, Littleton M. . (VA) 788
  HAMMOND, Mary W. . . . (WA) 494
  AMAN, Mary J. . . . . (WI) 19
  JENKINS-PENDER,
    Maureen . . . . (AB) 597
  COURTEMANCHE, Pierre
    O. . . . . (PQ) 251
Business administration HICKS, Mary F. . . . . (CA) 537
  TEMPLETON, Mary E. . . (GA) 1231
  RUSIEWSKI, Charles B. . (IL) 1068
  FERRERE, Cathy M. . . . . (NY) 373
  SIMONIS, James J. . . . . (NY) 1141
Business, advertising & legal research FISHER, Daphne V. . . . . (PA) 380
Business analysis & forecasting BRINNER, Roger E. . . . . (MA) 136
Business & advertising reference BUSSEY, Holly J. . . . . . . (NY) 165
Business & budgeting LEVITT, Irene S. . . . . . . (MA) 721
Business & chemistry databases DAVIS, Sara . . . . (TX) 281
Business & computer information PETTEY, Brent . . . . (CA) 965
Business & computer information
  sources AHERN, Camille P. . . . . . (NH) 8
Business & consulting TICE, Kathleen A. . . . . . (CA) 1244
Business & corporate information STANGL-WALKER,
    Teresa L. . . . . (ON) 1180
Business & corporate research DENOTO, Dorothy E. . . . (NY) 293

BUSINESS (Cont'd)

Business & current events databases LOVE, Sandra R. . . . . . . (CA) 743
Business & economic development CASTLEBERRY, Crata L. (AR) 194
Business & economic information
  services CARROLL, Hardy . . . . . . (MI) 187
Business & economic materials MARKHAM, Scott C. . . . (MN) 771
Business & economic research DUFFY, Brenda F. . . . . . (DC) 324
Business & economics HUMPHREYS, Nancy K. (CA) 574
  VUGRINECZ, Anna E. . . (CA) 1289
  WOLFF, Stephen G. . . . . (DE) 1361
  GEROW, Sandra F. . . . . (IL) 429
  KLEIN, Regina D. . . . . . (MO) 659
  OTA, Leslie H. . . . . (NJ) 930
  RANSOM, Cynthia E. . . . (NY) 1007
  NASRALLAH, Wahib T. . (OH) 888
  JONES-TRENT, Bernice R. (VA) 616
Business & economics databases MCKAY, Peter Z. . . . . . . (FL) 810
Business & economics information GELINNE, Michael S. . . . (MO) 426
Business & economics librarianship LIM, Peck B. . . . . (IL) 727
Business & economics reference KRISTIE, William J. . . . . (CA) 679
  LARSEN, Lynda L. . . . . . (DC) 698
  WIZA, Judith M. . . . . (KY) 1359
  DODGE, Michael R. . . . . (NC) 308
Business & employment information HOLTZMAN, Douglas A. (CA) 555
Business & engineering databases LO, Maryanne H. . . . . . . (MN) 735
  HAWLEY, Laurie J. . . . . (TX) 514
Business & engineering information GRELL, Holly J. . . . . (GA) 467
Business & finance PROBST, Virginia M. . . . (IL) 994
  HARNDEN, Donna J. . . . (MN) 502
  BURNS, Violanda O. . . . (NY) 163
  ENGLER, Gretchen . . . . (NY) 349
  HERMAN, Marsha . . . . . (NY) 531
  HOUGHTON, Joan I. . . . (NY) 562
  STEWART, Elizabeth A. . (ON) 1192
Business & finance database
  research STOOPS, Louise . . . . . . (NY) 1198
Business & finance databases CROFT, Elizabeth G. . . . (NY) 260
  WALKER, Jeanette F. . . . (NY) 1295
Business & finance information OLSHEN, Toni . . . . (ON) 922
Business & finance libraries LONGMAN, Judith J. . . . (IL) 740
Business & finance reference NARCISO, Susan D. . . . . (NY) 888
Business & finance research ARMEIT, Marilyn . . . . . . (NY) 32
  CLOWE, Isabel B. . . . . . (NY) 223
  MAYOPOULOS, Karen L. (NY) 791
Business & finance statistics MEREDITH, Meri . . . . . . (IN) 825
Business & financial databases WARNER, Claudette S. . (IL) 1305
  BARRETT, Michael D. . . (NY) 59
  BERNTSEN, Robert M. . . (NY) 90
  DAVID, Julia A. . . . . (NY) 276
  ESPO, Hal . . . . (NY) 354
  JONES, Sarah C. . . . . . . (NY) 615
  MARSHALL, Patricia K. . (NY) 775
  SANTORO, Tesse F. . . . (NY) 1082
  VAZQUEZ, Edward . . . . (NY) 1280
Business & financial information MEARNS, Mary A. . . . . . (CA) 820
  BROWN, George F. . . . . (MA) 144
  COOPER, J P. . . . . (MA) 243
  GUHERIDGE, Allison A. . (ON) 476
Business & financial information spclst DARNOWSKI, Christina M. (NY) 275
Business & financial research SOROBAY, Roman T. . . . (NY) 1169
Business & general reference BOLL, Charles K. . . . . . . (NJ) 112
  CARR, Timothy B. . . . . . (VA) 186
Business & government affairs BALL, Thomas W. . . . . . (DC) 52
Business & government information MILLER, Carmen L. . . . . (WA) 836
Business & government publications IVES, Peter B. . . . . (NM) 586
Business & humanities reference GROVES, Helen G. . . . . (TX) 474
Business & industrial publishing SAFRAN, Scott A. . . . . . (NY) 1074
Business & industrial reference PFOHL, Theodore E. . . . (NY) 966
Business & industry LARSEN, Linda E. . . . . . (IL) 698
Business & industry databases CURRY, John A. . . . . . . (IL) 266
Business & industry reference &
  resrch LUXNER, Dick . . . . (NJ) 750
Business & industry research RATZABI, Arlene . . . . . . (NY) 1010
Business & information publishing HOLLY, James H. . . . . . (CA) 552
Business & insurance databases MACKINTOSH, Pamela J. (NJ) 757
Business & investment services KOLLAR, Mary E. . . . . . (OH) 669
Business & law databases KUMAR, C S. . . . . (NY) 684
Business & law reference PERELLA, Susanne B. . . (DC) 958
Business & legal bibliography CRINION, Jacquelyn A. . (TX) 259

BUSINESS (Cont'd)

Business & legal databases   ZYGMONT, Carolyn A. . . (CT) 1392
                                    RYAN, James J. . . . . (NY) 1071
Business & legal library consulting GIGANTE, Vickilyn M. . . (MD) 433
Business & legal online database
  srchng   NICOL, Margaret W. . . . (NY) 903
Business & legal research   WHITTLESEY, Jane M. . . (TX) 1334
Business & management   PENDRAK, Eileen . . . . . (TX) 956
Business & management databases   CLIFT, Crystal A. . . . . . (MN) 222
Business & management information TASHIMA, Marie . . . . . . (CA) 1224
Business & marketing databases   CRAWFORD, Marilyn L. . (CA) 257
Business & marketing information   FULLER, Kathleen B. . . . (OH) 408
Business & marketing info resources BARTL, Richard P. . . . . . (NY)   61
Business & marketing information
  sources   STEPIEN, Karen K. . . . . (NJ) 1189
Business & marketing libraries   TALCOTT, Ann W. . . . . . (NJ) 1221
Business & marketing reference   WHITT, Diane M. . . . . . . (IL) 1334
                                    CLIFT, Crystal A. . . . . . (MN) 222
Business & marketing research   TUCKERMAN, Susan . . . (NY) 1262
Business & marketing searching   BRANCHICK, Susan E. . . (OH) 127
Business & medical databases   LOKETS BEISCHROT,
                                      Dina . . . . (CT) 738
Business & medical intelligence   LOKETS BEISCHROT,
                                      Dina . . . . (CT) 738
Business & patent sources   GALBRAITH, Barry E. . . (NY) 413
Business & public affairs research COCHRAN, Catherine . . (MI) 225
Business & regulatory research   MERINGOLO, Joseph A. (MD) 826
Business & religious reference
  sources   FEW, John E. . . . . (CA) 374
Business & science databases   CALDWELL, Marlene . . . (TX) 172
Business & science reference   MEYERS, Kathleen H. . . (AZ) 831
Business & scientific databases   MITCHELL, Cynthia R. . . (TX) 848
Business & scientific information BUNCE, George D. . . . . (ENG) 157
Business & sci-tech databases   GALTON, Gwen . . . . (ON) 415
Business & social science   RUPPRECHT, Leslie P. . . (NJ) 1068
Business & social sciences databases KENYON, Sharmon H. . . (CA) 643
                                    SLOCUM, Hannah R. . . . (CA) 1150
Business & tax research   WATERS, Susan S. . . . . (DC) 1309
Business & technical databases   DONAHUE, Karin V. . . . . (IL) 310
                                    WEBER, Robert F. . . . . . (OR) 1314
                                    WHITEHURST, Dori A. . . (PA) 1333
                                    ARMSTRONG, Denise M. (SAF)   32
Business & technical engineering   GRIFFITTS, Joan K. . . . . (IN) 469
Business & technical information   RUTHERFORD, Frederick
                                      S. . . . . (ON) 1070
Business & technical reference   WILLIAMS, Constance H. (CO) 1342
                                    REILLY, Dayle A. . . . . . . (MA) 1020
Business & technology   BOSMA, Elske M. . . . . . (ON) 117
Business & technology research   SOVNER-RIBBLER, Judith (MA) 1170
                                    MENNELLA, Dona M. . . . (MD) 824
Business archives   YATES, Donald N. . . . . . (IN) 1378
                                    SARETZKY, Gary D. . . . . (NJ) 1082
                                    GRACE, William M. . . . . (PA) 455
Business archives administration   KING, Eleanor M. . . . . . (PA) 650
Business bibliographic databases   POJE, Mary E. . . . . (NY) 980
Business bibliographies   DANIELLS, Lorna M. . . . (MA) 273
Business bibliography   NEELY, Glenda S. . . . . . (KY) 892
                                    BEAL, Sarell W. . . . . (MI)   68
Business collection development   DANIELLS, Lorna M. . . . (MA) 273
                                    TERTELL, Susan M. . . . . (MN) 1232
                                    NOTARSTEFANO, Vincent
                                      C. . . . . (NY) 910
                                    ALLEN, Sarabeth . . . . . . (TX)   16
                                    DUFFUS, Sylvia J. . . . . . (AB) 323
Business communications
  management   SLOAN, Cheryl A. . . . . . (MD) 1149
Business communications services   MAYNARD, John C. . . . . (ON) 790
Business, competitive information NEWMAN, Robert M. . . . (TX) 899
Business conditions   MCKELVEY, Michael J. . . (DC) 811
Business consulting   GRANT, Mary M. . . . . . . (NY) 458
Business data   DONOHUE, Delaine R. . . (PA) 312
Business development   DAWSON, Debra A. . . . . (CA) 282
                                    GREENHOUSE, Lee R. . (NY) 464
                                    HALL, Alix M. . . . . (NY) 486
Business development, electronic
  publshg   GROSSMAN, Allen N. . . . (NJ) 473
Business development, mgmt &
  admin   PATRICIU, Florin S. . . . . (MD) 947
Business directories   KRAMER, Allan F. . . . . . (NY) 675
                                    JACKSON, Craig A. . . . . (ON) 587

BUSINESS (Cont'd)

Business, economic & mining
  reference   KIEFER, Karen N. . . . . . (CA) 647
Business, economic resources   ERWIN, Nancy S. . . . . . (OH) 353
Business, education, humanities   WILLIAMS, Robert C. . . . (AK) 1346
Business, engineering, & med
  databases   POLK, Diana B. . . . . (IL) 981
Business, finance & accounting
  databases   KILBERG, Jacqueline L. . (NY) 648
Business, financial databases   SAYWARD, Nick H. . . . . (NY) 1087
Business, health care, engrng
  databases   PLOTSKY, Andrea G. . . . (CA) 978
Business history   STEGH, Leslie J. . . . . . . (IL) 1185
Business, industry, accounting info WELLS, Nancy E. . . . . . (ON) 1322
Business information   SEEKAMP, Linda W. . . . . (CA) 1111
                                    WALTER, Virginia A. . . . (CA) 1300
                                    BERLIET, Nathalie B. . . . (CT)   87
                                    DIMATTIA, Susan S. . . . (CT) 304
                                    LANEY, Helen B. . . . . . . (DC) 695
                                    O'BRIEN, Kathleen . . . . . (DC) 914
                                    FEDECZKO, Joyce L. . . . (IL) 367
                                    LEE, Ann H. . . . . (IL) 709
                                    MURPHY, Therese B. . . . (IL) 881
                                    MUZZO, Steven E. . . . . . (IL) 883
                                    SENN, Mary S. . . . . (IL) 1115
                                    OKEY, Susan T. . . . . . . (IN) 920
                                    ARNOLD, Stephen E. . . . (KY)   34
                                    O'CONNOR, Jerry . . . . . (MA) 916
                                    BLASCHAK, Mary M. . . . (MI) 104
                                    ELLIS, Gloria B. . . . . . . (MI) 344
                                    WAGENVELD, Linda M. . (MI) 1291
                                    EVANS, June C. . . . . . . (NC) 357
                                    GENTNER, Claudia A. . . (NJ) 427
                                    MASILAMANI, Mary P. . . (NJ) 780
                                    TILLMAN, Hope N. . . . . (NJ) 1245
                                    WARD, Catherine J. . . . . (NJ) 1303
                                    BERNSTEIN, Judith R. . . (NM)   89
                                    BUTLER, Barbara E. . . . (NV) 166
                                    WELLS, David B. . . . . . . (NV) 1322
                                    GRANKA, Bernard D. . . . (NY) 457
                                    RIPIN, Laura G. . . . . (NY) 1035
                                    TICKER, Susan L. . . . . . (NY) 1244
                                    BUTCHER, Sharon L. . . . (OH) 166
                                    FELL, Sally B. . . . . (OH) 370
                                    RASKIN, Rosa S. . . . . . . (OH) 1009
                                    VARA, Margaret E. . . . . (OH) 1278
                                    GRAHAM, John . . . . (OK) 456
                                    SHAVER, Donna B. . . . . (OR) 1123
                                    COOPER, Linda . . . . (PA) 243
                                    HOSTETTER, Sandra F. . (PA) 562
                                    CAMP, Joyce H. . . . . . . (TX) 175
                                    SHEA, Kathleen . . . . (TX) 1124
                                    WILSON, Brenda J. . . . . (UT) 1350
                                    GILL, Gerald L. . . . . (VA) 435
                                    MAROTZ, Karen V. . . . . (BC) 772
                                    DE STRICKER, Ulla . . . . (ON) 296
                                    MONTY, Vivienne . . . . . . (ON) 857
Business information analysis   MILLS, Catherine H. . . . . (RI) 843
Business information & related
  services   STRYKER, Charles W. . . . (NJ) 1203
Business information & research   RUTKOWSKI, Hollace A. (PA) 1070
Business information database
  searching   ROSENBERGER,
                                      Constance G. . . . . . . (PA) 1056
Business information databases   MAH, Jeffery . . . . (CA) 760
                                    BOYD, Cheryl J. . . . . . . (MN) 122
Business information management   BAZAN, Lorraine R. . . . . (CA)   68
                                    SEASE, Sandra A. . . . . . (NY) 1110
Business information resources   MICKEY, Melissa B. . . . (IL) 833
Business information search   MIWA, Makiko . . . . (JAP) 850
Business information services   BAUER, Leslie L. . . . . . . (GA)   65
                                    MCZORN, Bonita A. . . . . (NC) 819
                                    HASSAN, Mohammad Z. (NY) 511
                                    VEGTER, Amy H. . . . . . . (NY) 1281
Business information sources   STANYON, Kelly . . . . . . (CT) 1181
                                    JACOBS, Leslie R. . . . . . (MA) 589
Business information sources &
  research   CVELJO, Katherine . . . . (TX) 268
Business information specialization SCOTT, Rupert N. . . . . . (GA) 1108

BUSINESS (Cont'd)

Business information system development	LITTLE, Dean K.	(OH)	733
Business information systems	SHAFFER, Richard P.	(NY)	1119
Business intelligence	CARR, Sallyann	(DC)	186
	CARR, Sallyann	(FL)	186
	RYANS, Kathryn J.	(ON)	1071
Business, jobs, & careers	ROUDEBUSH, Lawanda C.	(IA)	1061
Business law vocational education	DIAL, Ron	(NY)	299
Business librarianship	LAUGHLIN, Steven G.	(AL)	703
	STEEL, Virginia	(AZ)	1183
	MCNAMEE, Gilbert W.	(CA)	816
	THAU, Richard	(NJ)	1234
	HOWELL, Josephine T.	(NY)	565
	MELVILLE, Karen E.	(ON)	823
Business libraries	MURRAY, Marilyn R.	(IL)	882
	BERNSTEIN, Judith R.	(NM)	89
	SABOURIN, Agathe	(PQ)	1073
Business library instruction	BENSON-TALLEY, Lois I.	(CA)	83
Business library management	CANNING, Joan M.	(NY)	178
	MILLER, Ellen L.	(NY)	837
	CAMERON, Hazel M.	(BC)	175
	CHAN, Diana L.	(BC)	199
Business library organization, operation	RABER, Nevin W.	(IN)	1001
Business literature	GRAYSON, Virginia S.	(CT)	460
	ROSENTHAL, Andrea M.	(MA)	1057
	ERICKSON, Sandra E.	(NY)	352
Business management	BISSO, Arthur J.	(GA)	100
	FIDOTEN, Robert E.	(PA)	375
	SOWICZ, Eugenia V.	(PA)	1170
	RYANS, Kathryn J.	(ON)	1071
Business management & research	KIRSHBAUM, Priscilla J.	(CO)	655
Business management bibliographies	CHAN, Diana L.	(BC)	199
Business management, budgeting	WARNER, Alice S.	(MA)	1305
Business, management information	DUDLEY, Durand S.	(OH)	323
Business market research	DEHN, Lydia A.	(CA)	288
Business, marketing & advertising resrch	PIDALA, Veronica C.	(NY)	971
Business, marketing & technoeconomics	GUIDA, Pat	(NJ)	476
Business, marketing database	COMPTON, Erlinda R.	(TX)	235
Business, marketing databases	ECKLUND, Lynn M.	(CA)	335
Business, marketing research	LEWARK, Kathryn W.	(CA)	722
Business material	FOWLES, Alison C.	(PQ)	394
Business materials	PIERCE, Linda I.	(AK)	971
	HARRIS, Linda S.	(AL)	505
	HICKS, James M.	(MO)	537
Business materials reference	CANNING, Joan M.	(NY)	178
Business online databases	PHILLIPS, Sylvia E.	(TX)	969
Business online research	BURYLO, Michelle A.	(PA)	164
Business online searching	TERTELL, Susan M.	(MN)	1232
	POLLARD, Bobbie T.	(NY)	981
	TRICKEY, Katherine M.	(TX)	1256
Business operations	CLEMENS, Bonnie J.	(GA)	220
	HEATH, Henry H.	(MD)	519
	KEANE, John J.	(PA)	633
Business opportunities	MOUREY, Deborah A.	(NY)	874
Business periodical databases	MARKERT, Patricia B.	(NY)	771
Business periodicals	REGNER, Erlinda J.	(IL)	1017
	MARCACCIO, Kathleen Y.	(MI)	768
Business plan consulting	MOSLEY, Thomas E.	(OK)	872
Business plan development	MILLER, Ronald F.	(CA)	842
Business planning	JACOBUS, Nancy M.	(CA)	590
	HALL, Alix M.	(NY)	486
Business planning & development	BARTLETT, Jay P.	(NY)	61
Business publishing	KLAUS, Roger D.	(IL)	658
Business records disaster recovery	EULENBERG, Julia N.	(WA)	356
Business records storage	EIGEMAN, Laurence E.	(IN)	340
Business reference	ENGEBRETSON, Mary E.	(AL)	348
	KENDRICK, Aubrey W.	(AL)	640
	AWE, Susan C.	(AZ)	42
	HAWBAKER, A C.	(AZ)	513
	BENSON-TALLEY, Lois I.	(CA)	83
	BRONARS, Lori A.	(CA)	140
	CARSCH, Ruth E.	(CA)	187
	CLAEYS, Luisa T.	(CA)	215
	COSTELLO, M R.	(CA)	249
	DUFFY, Karen R.	(CA)	324
	EICHELBERGER, Susan	(CA)	339

BUSINESS (Cont'd)

Business reference

FROST, Michelle	(CA)	406
GERSTLE, Steven M.	(CA)	429
GORDON, Wendy R.	(CA)	452
HOFFMAN, Irene M.	(CA)	548
JACOBSEN, Lavonne	(CA)	590
KENNEDY, Charlene F.	(CA)	640
MOORE-EVANS, Angela	(CA)	862
STEELMAN, Lucille A.	(CA)	1184
STERNHEIM, Karen	(CA)	1189
WENDROFF, Catriona	(CA)	1323
WILKINSON, David W.	(CA)	1340
SANI, Martha J.	(CO)	1081
SHORE, Julia M.	(CT)	1132
UBYSZ, Priscilla M.	(CT)	1267
ZYGMONT, Carolyn A.	(CT)	1392
BLANDAMER, Ann W.	(DC)	103
CARDWELL, Diane O.	(DC)	181
POSNIAK, John R.	(DC)	985
STREHL, Susan J.	(DC)	1201
UPDEGROVE, Robert A.	(DC)	1269
WENGEL, Linda	(DC)	1324
LADNER, Sharyn J.	(FL)	687
MCKAY, Peter Z.	(FL)	810
MORRIS, Steve R.	(FL)	867
PFARRER, Theodore R.	(FL)	966
COONIN, Bryna R.	(GA)	242
MACK, Debora S.	(GA)	756
BRADLEY, Anne	(IL)	125
BURGH, Scott G.	(IL)	159
GARDNER, Margaret L.	(IL)	418
GIAMBRONE, Richard J.	(IL)	430
GROSCH, Mary F.	(IL)	472
HAMILTON, Dawn M.	(IL)	492
HILBURGER, Mary J.	(IL)	538
HUSFELDT, Jerry J.	(IL)	578
MADDEN, Michael J.	(IL)	758
MASON, Margaret E.	(IL)	781
MOULTON, James C.	(IL)	873
SWANTEK, Kathleen M.	(IL)	1214
WAGNER, Ralph D.	(IL)	1292
NEELY, Glenda S.	(KY)	892
BROWN, Sue S.	(LA)	147
HANKEL, Marilyn L.	(LA)	496
BENDER, Helen F.	(MA)	79
COLEMAN, James R.	(MA)	231
DANIELLS, Lorna M.	(MA)	273
EWING, Lydia M.	(MA)	359
FEIDLER, Anita J.	(MA)	368
MAGUIRE, Patricia V.	(MA)	760
JACKSON, Carleton	(MD)	587
HEGEDUS, Mary E.	(MI)	521
LEB, Joan P.	(MI)	707
RING, Donna M.	(MI)	1035
WHITE, Jane F.	(MI)	1331
ANDERSON, Rebekah E.	(MN)	25
CLARKE, Norman F.	(MN)	219
GADE, Rachel P.	(MN)	411
REYNEN, Richard G.	(MN)	1025
TERTELL, Susan M.	(MN)	1232
VAN WHY, Carol B.	(MN)	1277
HUND, Flower L.	(MO)	574
REINHOLD, Edna J.	(MO)	1021
HEBERT, Robert A.	(NC)	519
MILLER, Barry K.	(NC)	836
AU, Ka N.	(NJ)	38
BARZELATTO, Elba G.	(NJ)	62
CHANG, Bernadine A.	(NJ)	200
GREENBLATT, Ruth	(NJ)	463
LATINI, Samuel A.	(NJ)	701
OTT, Linda G.	(NJ)	930
SKYZINSKI, Susan E.	(NJ)	1147
TIPTON, Roberta L.	(NJ)	1247
ABBITT, Viola I.	(NY)	1
APPEL, Marsha C.	(NY)	29
BEALER, Jane A.	(NY)	68
BULSON, Christine	(NY)	156
CARLSON, Robert E.	(NY)	182
COONEY, Martha D.	(NY)	242

BUSINESS (Cont'd)

Business reference

DIMARTINO, Diane J. . .	(NY)	303
DREIFUSS, Richard A. . .	(NY)	319
HECKMAN, Lucy T.	(NY)	519
HRYVNIAK, Joseph T. . .	(NY)	567
JOHNSON, David J.	(NY)	603
MACLEAN, Paul	(NY)	757
NERBOSO, Donna L. . . .	(NY)	895
REID, Richard C.	(NY)	1019
ROSENFELD, Jane D. . .	(NY)	1056
ROWAN, Diane M.	(NY)	1062
RUBINO, Cynthia C. . . .	(NY)	1065
RYAN, James J.	(NY)	1071
SCIATTARA, Diane M. . .	(NY)	1106
SOUDERS, Marilyn N. . .	(NY)	1169
STERLING, Sheila	(NY)	1189
TIFFEAULT, Alice A. . . .	(NY)	1244
VENER, Lucille	(NY)	1282
CARY, Mary K.	(OH)	191
HELSER, Fred L.	(OH)	525
IRELAND, Clara R.	(OH)	583
KEATING, Michael F. . . .	(OH)	633
LINDSTROM, Elaine C. . .	(OH)	730
MAURER, Lewis R.	(OH)	787
POPOVICH, Charles J. . .	(OH)	984
CATTIE, Mary M.	(PA)	195
DEWANE, Kathleen M. . .	(PA)	298
GRIFFITH, Dorothy A. . .	(PA)	469
KALIN, Sarah G.	(PA)	623
KIRCHER, Linda M.	(PA)	654
THOMPSON, Dorothea M.	(PA)	1239
WRIGHT, Barbara C. . . .	(PA)	1370
CRAVEN, Trudy W.	(SC)	256
MCREE, John W.	(SC)	818
SILER, Freddie B.	(SC)	1137
SMITH, Stephen C.	(SC)	1161
DEAN, Leann F.	(SD)	283
MADER, Sharon B.	(TN)	759
DAVIS, Carolyn	(TX)	278
GAMEZ, Juanita L.	(TX)	416
GRIMES, Carolyn E.	(TX)	470
HOLMAN, Linda E.	(TX)	553
MORRIS, Pamela A.	(TX)	867
SPECHT, Alice W.	(TX)	1172
WEATHERS, Jerry D. . . .	(TX)	1312
WISE, Olga B.	(TX)	1357
CASH, Susan R.	(VA)	192
MERRIFIELD, Mark D. . . .	(VA)	826
REID, Kendall M.	(VA)	1018
TOSIANO, Barbara A. . . .	(VA)	1252
BURKE, Vivienne C.	(WA)	160
PASSARELLI, Anne B. . .	(WA)	946
BELL, Hope A.	(ON)	77
SEDGWICK, Dorothy L. .	(ON)	1111
DUPUIS, Marcel	(PQ)	327

Business reference & instruction BATISTA, Emily J. . . . . . (PA) 64
Business reference & legal research SEAMAN, Sally G. . . . . . (IL) 1109
Business reference & research MATTHEWSON, David S. (CT) 786

TEW, Robin L.	(FL)	1233
WASYLENKO, Lydia W. .	(NY)	1308
ETCHINGHAM, John B. . .	(RI)	355

Business reference bibliography BROWN, Charlotte D. . . . (VA) 142
Business reference databases LEE, Soon H. . . . . (IL) 711

DITMARS, Robert D. . . .	(NJ)	305

Business reference information PINSON, Mark . . . . (MA) 975
Business reference insurance ALDRICH, Linda W. . . . . (CA) 11
Business reference materials GORDON, Donna M. . . . . (AB) 451
Business reference publications DITMARS, Robert D. . . . (NJ) 305

SIMON, David H.	(NJ)	1140

Business reference resources SINWELL, Carol A. . . . . (VA) 1144
Business reference service MOORE, Sheryl R. . . . . . (TX) 861

TIRRELL, Brenda P.	(TX)	1247

Business reference services SLOCUM, Hannah R. . . . (CA) 1150

STRAUSS, Diane	(NC)	1201
SMITH, Sweetman R. . . .	(NY)	1161
MILLER, Clayton M.	(OH)	836
STANLEY, Jean B.	(OH)	1180
SEARS, Robert W.	(OK)	1110
COORSH, Katalin	(ON)	244

BUSINESS (Cont'd)

Business reference sources

EDWARDS, Betty	(MA)	337
CARMACK, Norma J. . . .	(TX)	183

Business reference specialist DICKSON, Laura K. . . . . (NE) 301
Business reference tools LANDOLFI, Lisa M. . . . . (NY) 693
Business research ADAMS, Linda L. . . . . . . (CA) 5

GERSH, Barbara S.	(CA)	429
GHAZARIAN, Salpi H. . .	(CA)	430
MILLER, Ralph D.	(CA)	841
BRUNER, Robert B.	(CO)	150
KRISMANN, Carol H. . . .	(CO)	678
SMART, Marriott W.	(CO)	1151
SOLOMON, Arnold D. . .	(DC)	1166
BRYANT, Nancy J.	(GA)	152
COOPER, Glenn	(GA)	243
BARNUM, Sally J.	(IL)	58
GROFT, Mary L.	(IL)	471
REED, Janet S.	(IL)	1015
HAYWARD, Sheila S. . . .	(MA)	517
KELLEY, Barbara C. . . .	(MI)	636
POQUETTE, Mary L. . . .	(MN)	984
BAERWALD, Susan M. .	(MO)	45
THOMPSON, Barbara F.	(NC)	1239
JONES, Deborah A.	(NJ)	612
LAUB, Barbara J.	(NJ)	702
COOPER, Catherine M. . .	(NY)	242
GROSS, Gretchen	(NY)	472
HUBBARD, Susan E. . . .	(NY)	568
KATZ, Doris B.	(NY)	630
MANN, Amy S.	(NY)	765
MINTZ, Anne P.	(NY)	847
ROSENFELD, Lillian E. . .	(NY)	1056
TYLER, David M.	(NY)	1266
BORUCKI, Jennifer A. . .	(OH)	117
BOWIE, Angela B.	(OH)	121
POPOVICH, Charles J. . .	(OH)	984
SKUTNIK, John S.	(OH)	1147
MOSLEY, Thomas E. . . .	(OK)	872
KASPERKO, Jean M. . . .	(PA)	629
WHITAKER, Cynthia D. .	(PA)	1329
QUINN, Joan M.	(TN)	1000
FELSTED, Carla M.	(TX)	370
MCCLURE, Margaret R. . .	(TX)	797
HARMALA, Amy A.	(WA)	502
WATERSTREET, Darlene E.	(WI)	1309
CARVALHO, Sarah V. . .	(ON)	191
CASEY, Victoria L.	(ON)	192
ELLERT, Barbara M.	(ON)	343
SEDGWICK, Dorothy L. .	(ON)	1111
DARLINGTON, Susan . .	(PQ)	275

Business resrch, acquisitions, & instrc CAMERON, Constance B. (RI) 174
Business research analysis JACKSON, Craig A. . . . . (ON) 587
Business research & databases MORRIS, Ann . . . . (IL) 866
Business research in databases HOPKINS, Terry F. . . . . . (TX) 558
Business research services ADAMO, Clare . . . . (CT) 4
Business resources EMBAR, Indrani M. . . . . . (IL) 347

BURYLO, Michelle A. . . .	(PA)	164
PAGELL, Ruth A.	(PA)	934
PIETZAK, Stephen D. . . .	(PA)	972
MIDGETT, Ann S.	(TX)	833

Business, science & industry SUGDEN, Martin D. . . . . (FL) 1206
Business science & technology database DIMITRESCU, Ioana . . . . (PQ) 304
Business, science, & technology ref REGNER, Erlinda J. . . . . (IL) 1017

RICHMOND, Diane A. . .	(IL)	1030

Business, science reference & research LEDBETTER, Sherry H. . . (MD) 708
Business searching WEHNER, Karen B. . . . . (TN) 1316
Business, securities FOWLIE, Linda K. . . . . . (DC) 394
Business services SAMUELS, David H. . . . . (FL) 1079

OSTROWSKI, Lawrence C.	(IN)	929
PAPAI, Beverly D.	(MI)	938
BRANCH, Susan	(OH)	127

Business, social sciences TAYLOR, Douglas M. . . . (AL) 1226
Business sources LOOMIS, Mary K. . . . . . . (CT) 740

MUTCH, Donald G.	(ON)	883

Business strategy ERES, Beth K. . . . . (ISR) 352

BUSINESS (Cont'd)

Business subjects	ENDRES, Maureen D. . .	(PA)	348
	BELL, Barbara	(BC)	76
Business/technical information research	MICHAEL, Ann B.	(IL)	831
Business-related collection development	PASSARELLI, Anne B. . .	(WA)	946
Canadian business bibliography	BROWN, Barbara E.	(ON)	142
Canadian business information	VARMA, Divakara K. . . .	(ON)	1278
Canadian business information sources	KING, Alan S.	(ME)	650
Chemical & business databases	MARTINO, Sharon C. . . .	(IN)	779
Chemical & business reference	WILLARD, Ann M.	(CA)	1341
Chemical business	LERITZ, M K.	(CT)	717
Chemical business information databases	REITANO, Maimie V. . . .	(NY)	1022
Chemical business, marketing	FOOS, Ferol A.	(LA)	388
Chemistry & business	ALSTADT, Nancy A. . . .	(PA)	18
Collection development, business, econ	BELANGER, Sandra E. . .	(CA)	75
Collection development for business	KENDRICK, Aubrey W. . .	(AL)	640
Developing new business opportunities	MCLANE, John F.	(CT)	813
Economics & business	CARRINGTON, Bessie M.	(NC)	186
Energy & business reference	WEBER, Robert F.	(OR)	1314
Engineering & business online searching	ARROWOOD, Nina R. . .	(NJ)	35
Engineering & business reference	KAUFENBERG, Jane M.	(MN)	630
Finance & business information research	SINGER, Susan A.	(NJ)	1143
Financial & business research	THAU, Richard	(NJ)	1234
Financial, business libraries	MCDAVID, Sara J.	(GA)	801
General & business reference	HAULE, Laura M.	(IL)	512
	KONOVALOFF, Maria S.	(NY)	670
	WEEKS, Gerald M.	(BC)	1315
General business	SCANLAN, Jean M.	(MA)	1087
	TALLEY, Pat L.	(TX)	1221
General business & corporate research	POJE, Mary E.	(NY)	980
General business information	WEINSTEIN, Daniel L. . .	(CT)	1318
	THIVIERGE, Lynda M. . .	(PQ)	1235
General business, marketing & humanities	BAUGH, L S.	(IL)	65
General business reference	MCGARVEY, Eileen B. . .	(NY)	805
General business research	KAZANJIAN, Donna S. . .	(NY)	632
	BELL, Steven J.	(PA)	77
General publishing business	JACHINO, Robert J.	(NY)	586
General reference & business	DOLMON, Barbara N. . . .	(IL)	310
Government & business databases	MOONEY, Margaret T. . .	(CA)	858
Government & business library services	MARVIN, Stephen G. . . .	(PA)	780
Hawaiian & Pacific business periodicals	SCHULTZ, Elaine V.	(HI)	1102
Health, science & business collections	ARMSTRONG, Mary L. . .	(AB)	32
Indexing of business periodicals	PEDALINO, M C.	(NY)	954
Info & research, business & technical	SPINA, Marie C.	(NY)	1175
Information brokering businesses	BALL, Thomas W.	(DC)	52
Insurance & business reference	GEE, Ka C.	(NY)	424
International business	WARD, Edith	(NY)	1303
International business & marketing	HERMAN, Marsha	(NY)	531
International business information	SIMON, David H.	(NJ)	1140
Japanese business & culture	JONES, Adrian	(IL)	610
Japanese business & management info	NOGUCHI, Sachie	(IL)	907
Law & business cataloging	CASSIDY, Joni L.	(NJ)	193
Law & business collection development	BURGESS, Rita N.	(PA)	159
Law & business library maintenance	HELBURN, Judith D. . . .	(TX)	523
Law & business library organization	HELBURN, Judith D. . . .	(TX)	523
Law & business writing & editing	HOYT, Henry M.	(NY)	566
Legal & business reference	GERIG, Reginald R.	(DC)	428
	ANES, Joy R.	(IL)	27
	HIBBELER, Sara J.	(MO)	536
Legal & business research	CAIN, Susan H.	(MA)	171
Legal, business & general reference	WAY, Kathy A.	(CA)	1311
Library business management	HUGGINS, Annelle R. . . .	(TN)	571
Library service for business	MCWILLIAM, Deborah A.	(OH)	818
Local Maine businesses	AIREY, Martha R.	(ME)	9
Machine-readable business information	AULD, Dennis B.	(KY)	39

BUSINESS (Cont'd)

Management & business information	SCHNEDEKER, Donald W.	(NY)	1096
Market analysis business reports	KASE-MCLAREN, Karen A.	(NY)	628
Market research, business intelligence	MIMNAUGH, Ellen N. . . .	(OH)	845
Medical & business	FIRTH, Margaret A.	(MA)	379
Medical & business online searching	BLACKBURN-FOSTER, Brenda	(KY)	102
Medical, business	GARCIA, Ceil K.	(NJ)	417
Military history, business reference	ROTHENBERG, Mark H.	(NY)	1060
Online business information	ROMERO, Georg L.	(CA)	1052
	CRIM, Elias F.	(IL)	258
Online business searching	STREHL, Susan J.	(DC)	1201
	BURKE, Vivienne C.	(WA)	160
Online databases, business & financial	GARMAN, Nancy J.	(KY)	419
Online indexing of business reports	SEASE, Sandra A.	(NY)	1110
Online information retrieval, business	OSTROW, Rona	(NY)	929
Online searching for business	LEIGHTON, Victoria C. . .	(GA)	714
Online searching for general business	ENGLISH, Christopher C.	(NJ)	350
Pharmaceutical, medical, business ref	MCMASTER, Deborah L.	(CT)	815
Political & business research	KAPNICK, Laura B.	(NY)	626
Reference, business & technical	POST, Linda C.	(CA)	986
Reference, business sources	MACKEY, Wendy W. . . .	(MA)	757
Reference in business college	SULLIVAN, Cecil G.	(NY)	1207
Science & business reference	EYLES, Heberle H.	(FL)	359
Services to business	MARSHALL, Deborah M.	(IL)	774
Small business automation	SEN, Joyce H.	(NY)	1115
Small business counseling	MESMER, Frank B.	(NH)	827
Small business information	ROWE, David G.	(PQ)	1062
	THIVIERGE, Lynda M. . .	(PQ)	1235
Small business start-up	MCWILLIAM, Deborah A.	(OH)	818
Small businesses	COORSH, Katalin	(ON)	244
	MCINTOSH, Julia E.	(PQ)	809
Social sciences & business	SAFLEY, Ellen D.	(TX)	1074
Social sciences & business reference	HATTENDORF, Lynn C. .	(IL)	512
Sources of business information	OSWALD, Edward E. . . .	(FL)	929
Specialized business reference	LEVINSON, Catherine K.	(NC)	721
Strategic business management services	CARTER, Daniel H.	(TX)	189
Subscription agency business management	CLASQUIN, Frank F. . . .	(MA)	219
Teaching, technical & business info	CHAMIS, Alice Y.	(OH)	198
Technical & business online searching	DIETRICH, Peter J.	(NY)	302
Technical & business reference	GABRIEL, Linda	(NJ)	411
US government documents, business	TAYLOR, William R.	(TN)	1229
Written business communication	SILVA, Mary E.	(WA)	1138

BUSINESS DATABASES (See also Business, Online)

Business database	ANDERSON, Rebekah E.	(MN)	25
	AVERILL, M S.	(NJ)	41
	ETTLINGER, Sandra E. .	(NY)	356
	KRAUSS, Susan E.	(NY)	676
Business database searching	STERNHEIM, Karen	(CA)	1189
	ST. GEORGE, Susan M. .	(CT)	1075
	MARANO, Nancy H.	(IL)	768
	OJALA, Marydee P.	(KS)	919
	ORENSTEIN, Ruth M. . .	(MA)	925
	SOSTACK, Maura	(NY)	1169
	FREY, Luanne C.	(WI)	402
Business databases	EGGLESTON, Phyllis A. .	(AK)	339
	MCCARTHY, Sherri L. . .	(AL)	794
	BAUM, Ester R.	(AZ)	66
	HAWBAKER, A C.	(AZ)	513
	LESHY, Dede	(AZ)	718
	ADAMS, Joyce A.	(CA)	5
	ALBRIGHT, Sue R.	(CA)	10
	ANNAND, Stewart S. . . .	(CA)	28
	BAZAN, Lorraine R.	(CA)	68
	BENSON-TALLEY, Lois I.	(CA)	83
	CUEVAS, John R.	(CA)	263
	CURTIS, Richard A.	(CA)	267
	FUSICH, Monica G.	(CA)	410
	GARDISER, Kathleen E. .	(CA)	417
	GOVAARS, Inga	(CA)	454
	HEDDEN, Judy A.	(CA)	520
	KAPLAN, Robin	(CA)	626
	KLEINER, Donna H.	(CA)	660
	KONG, Leslie M.	(CA)	670

BUSINESS DATABASES (Cont'd)
Business databases

LEE, Diane T.	(CA)	709
MEGLIO, Delores D.	(CA)	821
MILLER, Jean R.	(CA)	839
SHARP, Geoffrey H.	(CA)	1122
SIMONS, Maurice M.	(CA)	1141
WENDROFF, Catriona	(CA)	1323
WRIGHT, Betty A.	(CA)	1370
MARSCHNER, Robyn J.	(CO)	773
PRESTON, Lawrence N.	(CO)	991
COLUCCI, Mildred A.	(CT)	234
DVORIN, Nancy T.	(CT)	330
ESCARILLA, Jose G.	(CT)	354
LIU, Jessie	(CT)	734
LOOMIS, Mary K.	(CT)	740
STANKIEWICZ, Carol A.	(CT)	1180
DURAKO, Frances G.	(DC)	328
MECRAY, Freida S.	(DE)	820
MORRIS, Steve R.	(FL)	867
OSWALD, Edward E.	(FL)	929
CASSELL, Judy A.	(GA)	193
HICKMAN, Michael L.	(GA)	536
KENNEDY, Joanna C.	(GA)	641
KLOPPER, Susan M.	(GA)	662
ALTGILBERS, Cynthia J.	(IL)	18
COTILLAS, Therese G.	(IL)	250
EGAN, Elizabeth M.	(IL)	338
GARDNER, Margaret L.	(IL)	418
GAUMOND, Suzanne M.	(IL)	423
HAMILTON, Dawn J.	(IL)	492
JUSTIE, Julie H.	(IL)	620
KEELER, Janice S.	(IL)	634
MUNSON, Kathleen J.	(IL)	879
NICKELS, Judith L.	(IL)	902
PERMAN, Karen A.	(IL)	959
ROMANO, Katherine V.	(IL)	1052
TAYLOR, Terry S.	(IL)	1229
COPLER, Judith A.	(IN)	244
MASON, Dorothy L.	(IN)	781
JAMES, Bonnie B.	(KY)	592
JAMIOLKOWSKI, Nancy J.	(KY)	593
KENNEDY, Amy J.	(MA)	640
LAROSA, Sharon M.	(MA)	698
MACIVER, Linda B.	(MA)	756
PELLEGRINI, Deborah A.	(MA)	955
STEVENSON, Michael I.	(MA)	1191
CARR, Margaret M.	(MD)	186
ROBINSON, Mark L.	(MD)	1044
AMES, Kay L.	(MI)	20
BRACKETT, Norman S.	(MI)	124
HEILEMAN, Gene C.	(MI)	521
KELLEY, Barbara C.	(MI)	636
RING, Donna M.	(MI)	1035
ROCHLEN, Rita E.	(MI)	1046
SELBERG, Janice K.	(MI)	1113
BLUMENFELD, Judith K.	(MN)	107
DINGLEY, Doris A.	(MN)	305
HERTHER, Nancy K.	(MN)	533
HONEBRINK, Andrea C.	(MN)	555
PETERSON, Julia C.	(MN)	963
DEKEN, Jean M.	(MO)	288
SUTTER, Mary A.	(MO)	1211
HEBERT, Robert A.	(NC)	519
CLARK, Rick	(NJ)	218
CROSS, Roberta A.	(NJ)	261
JONES, Deborah A.	(NJ)	612
LINGELBACH, Lorene N.	(NJ)	730
LOGAN, Harold J.	(NJ)	737
MASILAMANI, Mary P.	(NJ)	780
MILLINGTON, Kathleen A.	(NJ)	843
PEABODY, Kenneth W.	(NJ)	951
RODEAWALD, Patricia M.	(NJ)	1047
SIMON, David H.	(NJ)	1140
STRYKER, Charles W.	(NJ)	1203
TIPTON, Roberta L.	(NJ)	1247
BARNETT, Philip	(NY)	58
BEALER, Jane A.	(NY)	68
BUDGE, William D.	(NY)	155

BUSINESS DATABASES (Cont'd)
Business databases

BUZZANGA, Heidi S.	(NY)	168
CARLSON, Robert E.	(NY)	182
FODY, Barbara A.	(NY)	387
KASE-MCLAREN, Karen A.	(NY)	628
KUCSMA, Susan P.	(NY)	682
LETTIS, Lucy B.	(NY)	719
LOWE, Ida B.	(NY)	743
MANN, Amy S.	(NY)	765
MONTALBANO, James J.	(NY)	855
PINGITORE, Patricia E.	(NY)	974
REID, Richard C.	(NY)	1019
RUBIN, Ellen R.	(NY)	1064
SAFRAN, Scott A.	(NY)	1074
SHELTON, Anita L.	(NY)	1126
ZIPPER, Masha	(NY)	1390
HECHT, Joseph A.	(OH)	519
LANDIS, Kay A.	(OH)	693
PATIENCE, Alice	(OH)	947
POPOVICH, Charles J.	(OH)	984
QUINN, Caroline E.	(OH)	1000
SEIK, Jo E.	(OH)	1112
CHEATHAM, Gary L.	(OK)	204
ABRAMS, Joan R.	(PA)	3
DINNIMAN, Margo P.	(PA)	305
DRIEHAUS, Rosemary H.	(PA)	320
FISHMAN, Lee H.	(PA)	381
HALPERIN, Michael	(PA)	489
KERCHOF, Kathryn K.	(PA)	643
NAULTY, Deborah M.	(PA)	889
GRAHAM, Sylvia R.	(TN)	456
QUINN, Joan M.	(TN)	1000
BARRETT, Carol A.	(TX)	59
BREWER, Stanley E.	(TX)	134
CARMACK, Norma J.	(TX)	183
DAVIS, Carolyn	(TX)	278
DOBSON, Christine B.	(TX)	307
GRIMES, Carolyn E.	(TX)	470
HULSE, Phyllis	(TX)	573
KOHRS, Charlotte A.	(TX)	669
BROWN, Charlotte D.	(VA)	142
VAN SICKLEN, Lindsay L.	(VA)	1277
WALDE, Norma J.	(VA)	1294
CARVER, Sue A.	(WA)	191
HALL, Deborah A.	(WI)	487
SAYRS, Judith A.	(WI)	1087
TERANIS, Mara	(WI)	1231
WEEKS, Gerald M.	(BC)	1315
ATHA, Shirley A.	(ON)	37
BREGAINT, Bernard J.	(ON)	131
CHAPMAN, Phyllis C.	(ON)	202
COONEY, Jane	(ON)	241
DARLINGTON, Susan	(PQ)	275
LAPLANTE, Carole	(PQ)	697
POGUE, Basil G.	(SK)	979
BORCK, Liba	(ISR)	116
KATAOKA, Yoko	(JAP)	629

Business databases & reference

Business databases online searching

SCOTT, Miranda D.	(NJ)	1107
MCDAVID, Michael W.	(GA)	801
CANNING, Joan M.	(NY)	178

Business databases searching

Health & business databases

FENTON, Patricia F.	(MN)	371
SEXTON, Sally V.	(OH)	1118

Japanese technical & business databases

Legal & business databases

QUINN, Ralph M.	(NJ)	1000
HOLLINGSWORTH, Dena M.	(CA)	552
BLUM, Elaine G.	(NY)	107
ROBERTS, Ann B.	(VA)	1039
MORRIS, Sandra M.	(ON)	867

Management & business databases

Marketing & business databases

CORNWELL, Douglas W.	(FL)	247
LEMON, Nancy A.	(OH)	715
VIXIE, Anne C.	(OR)	1286

Medical & business databases

Medical, biological, & business database

AIREY, Martha R.	(ME)	9
MANDEL, Douglas J.	(IL)	765

Medical, pharmaceutical & bus databases

DUDLEY, Debbra C.	(NJ)	323

BUSINESS DATABASES (Cont'd)

News & business databases	WALLAS, Philip R.	(MA)	1298
	KARCICH, Grant J.	(ON)	627
Online business databases	SAMUELS, Lois A.	(CT)	1079
	KANE, Nancy J.	(MA)	625
	MAKAREWICZ, Grace E.	(BC)	762
Online searching & business databases	MICKEY, Melissa B.	(IL)	833
Online searching business databases	BRADLEY, Anne	(IL)	125
	ROSTAMI, Janet	(ON)	1059
Online searching of business databases	MCDEVITT-PARKS, Kathryn B.	(CA)	802
Patent, chemical & business databases	TAYLOR, Donna I.	(NJ)	1226
Patents, science & business databases	TUNG, Sandra J.	(CA)	1263
Pharmaceutical, medical, bus databases	MCMASTER, Deborah L.	(CT)	815
Science & business databases	SHAW, Debra S.	(OH)	1123
Science, technology & business databases	TOSTEVIN, Patricia A.	(WA)	1252
Scientific & business databases	AUGHEY, Kathleen M.	(NJ)	39
Scientific, technical business databases	ALEXANDER, Mary B.	(TN)	12
Social sciences & business databases	ALLERTON, Ellen M.	(NY)	16

BUYING (See also Acquisitions, Approval, Orders, Procurement, Purchasing, Shopping)

Buyer & seller representation	PICKETT, Doyle C.	(NJ)	970
Buying & selling of American literature	MARTIN, John W.	(IL)	776
Buying & selling of English literature	MARTIN, John W.	(IL)	776
Buying & selling of rare books	MARTIN, John W.	(IL)	776
Buying & selling 78 & LP records	SMOLIAN, Steven J.	(MD)	1162
Buying antiquarian books	MONDLIN, Marvin	(NY)	854
CD-ROM buyer procurement support	MILLER, Davic C.	(CA)	836
Cooperative buying	SCHWELK, Jennifer C.	(OH)	1105
Music-related buying & cataloging	RUSTMAN, Mark M.	(KS)	1070
Spiritual book buying	HLUHANY, Patricia	(PA)	544

BUYOUTS

Leveraged buyouts	SLUSSER, W P.	(NY)	1150

BYLAWS (See also Constitution)

Bylaws of organizations	DUJSIK, Gerald	(IL)	324

BYZANTINE

Byzantine & medieval studies reference	AVDOYAN, Levon	(DC)	41

CABLE (See also Broadcasting, Television)

Cable television	CHAMBERLIN, Leslie A.	(CA)	198
	RITZ, Mary E.	(CA)	1037
	MILLER, Robert	(IL)	841
	SIVULICH, Sandra S.	(NY)	1145
Cable television & broadcast television	WALSH, Mark L.	(CT)	1300
Cable television public access	PEARSON, Roger L.	(IL)	953
Community cable television	PORMEN, Paul E.	(OH)	984
Municipal cable television programming	VARNES, Richard S.	(CO)	1279
Public access & local cable	BARNETT, Donald E.	(OR)	57
Video & cable services	DRESANG, Eliza T.	(WI)	319

CAD/CAM

CAD/CAM & AI research	POLK, Diana B.	(IL)	981

CAI (See also AI, Artificial, Intelligence)

CAI application & implementation	CARDENAS, Mary E.	(SAF)	180

CALDECOTT

Caldecott medal books	HEINRICH, Lois M.	(MD)	522

CALENDAR

Calendar systems	CHASE, William D.	(MI)	203

CALIFORNIA

California county records	WEBBER, Steven L.	(CA)	1313
California documents	PERITORE, Laura D.	(CA)	958
California geology	BRUNTON, Angela	(CA)	151
California historical research, poetry	MOORE, Richard K.	(CA)	861
California history	ELLISON, Bettye H.	(CA)	345
California law	AKEY, Sharon A.	(CA)	9
California legal legislative materials	GOMEZ, Cheryl J.	(CA)	447
California local history	DRUMMOND, Herbert	(CA)	321
Early California history	SANTOS, Bob	(CA)	1082
Federal & California law reference	CH'NG, Saw K.	(CA)	209
Historical records of California	HANEL, Mary A.	(CA)	495
Los Angeles & California history	STERN, Teena B.	(CA)	1189
Transportation history of California	HANEL, Mary A.	(CA)	495

CALVARY

Armor & calvary history	HOLT, David A.	(KY)	554

CALVINISM

Calvin & Calvinism bibliography	DE KLERK, Peter	(MI)	288

CAMPBELL-STONE

Campbell-Stone movement	MCWHIRTER, David I.	(TN)	818

CAMPUS (See also Academic, College, University)

Campus library services	EMMER, Barbara L.	(PA)	348
Extended campus library services	PICKETT, Mary J.	(IL)	970
	HERRON, Nancy L.	(PA)	533
	KEMP, Barbara E.	(WA)	639
Extended campus services	LABRAKE, Orlyn B.	(FL)	686

CANADA (See also Provincial and names of specific provinces)

British & Canadian documents	VOGEL, Jane G.	(NC)	1286
Canadian & US companies & industries	ORLANDO, Richard P.	(PQ)	926
Canadian & United States history	OTTOSEN, Charles F.	(AB)	930
Canadian archival theory	COOK, Terry G.	(ON)	240
Canadian art & culture	GRODSKI, Renata	(ON)	471
Canadian banking	ORLANDO, Richard P.	(PQ)	926
Canadian broadcasting	EARLS, M L.	(ON)	332
Canadian business bibliography	BROWN, Barbara E.	(ON)	142
Canadian business information	VARMA, Divakara K.	(ON)	1278
Canadian business information sources	KING, Alan S.	(ME)	650
Canadian children's literature	MARTINEZ, Helen	(NF)	779
	AUBREY, Irene E.	(ON)	38
	HAMBLETON, Alixe E.	(SK)	490
Canadian constitutional law	TANGUAY, Guy	(PQ)	1222
Canadian corporate documents	GRAY, Sandra A.	(ON)	460
Canadian federal government publications	ROSE, Frances E.	(BC)	1054
Canadian genealogy	GUTTERIDGE, Paul	(BC)	479
Canadian government information policy	ROSE, Frances E.	(BC)	1054
Canadian government publications	WIHBEY, Francis R.	(ME)	1337
	NIELSON, Paul F.	(MB)	903
Canadian governmental documents	RUSSELL, Moira	(ON)	1069
Canadian health care system	BOITE, Mary E.	(ON)	111
Canadian history	REID, Marianne E.	(SK)	1019
Canadian libraries & librarianship	ANDERSON, Beryl L.	(ON)	21
Canadian medical librarianship	WALUZYNIEC, Hanna	(PQ)	1302
Canadian monographs pre-1950	ALGAR, L E.	(ON)	13
Canadian public company information	BONIN, Denise R.	(BC)	114
Canadian studies	SHULER, John A.	(OR)	1133
Canadian studies & Canadiana	MILLER, Beth M.	(ON)	836
Canadian studies research	FOX, Rosalie	(ON)	395

CANADA (Cont'd)

Canadiana	BROOKING, Ruth P. . . .	(ON)	140
	MORLEY, William F.	(ON)	865
Canadiana & local history	LLOYD, Mary E.	(ON)	735
Canadiana bibliography	RIDER, Lillian M.	(PQ)	1032
Canadiana bio-bibliographical research	DOWDING, Martin R. . . .	(ON)	315
Canadiana cataloging	DAWE, Heather L.	(ON)	282
Cataloging Canadian government documents	TURNER, Sharon	(ON)	1265
French Canadian children's literature	POTVIN, Claude	(NB)	987
	AUBREY, Irene E.	(ON)	38
French Canadian literature education	GUERETTE, Charlotte M.	(PQ)	476
Musical Canadiana	KALLMANN, Helmut M. . .	(ON)	623
Reference, Canadian studies	WILLIAMSON, Michael W.	(ON)	1347
Reference, especially Canadian studies	EVANS, Gwynneth	(ON)	357
Ukrainian Canadians	VERYHA, Wasyl	(ON)	1283

CANCER

Cancer	BLOOMSTONE, Ajaye . .	(LA)	106
Cancer databases	DICKINSON, Patricia C. .	(MD)	301
	OSTROW, Dianne G. . . .	(MD)	929
Cancer information	O'DELL, Charles A.	(MO)	916
	NOBLE, David	(BC)	906
Cancer information collection	KAWASHIMA, Hiroko . . .	(JAP)	632
Cancer information systems	DICKINSON, Patricia C. .	(MD)	301
Cancer registries	TEUN, Rebecca L.	(TX)	1233

CANDIDATES

Preliminary screening of candidates	RATZABI, Arlene	(NY)	1010

CANTATA

Solo cantata	VOLLEN, Gene E.	(KS)	1287

CAPITAL

Building & capital renovation	NYERGES, Michael S. . .	(NY)	912
Capital building program	HALL, Edward B.	(MD)	487
Growth & capital formation	BRINNER, Roger E.	(MA)	136
Operating & capital budgets	RAPHAEL, Mary E.	(DC)	1008
Venture capital research	SOROBAY, Roman T. . .	(NY)	1169

CAPTIONED

Captioned media for the hearing impaired	MODICA, Mary L.	(SD)	851

CARD

Computerized card cataloging	KIEFER, Marilyn V.	(MI)	647
Credit cards	MESHINSKY, Jeff M.	(MD)	827
Historical card catalogs	WOOD, Sallie B.	(NY)	1365
Media center card cataloging	MITCHELL, Phyllis R. . . .	(GA)	849
Optical card applications	GALE, John C.	(VA)	413
Revising card catalog	WESTOVER, Mary L. . . .	(AL)	1327
Writing programs, online card catalog	JORDAN, Sharon L.	(WA)	617

CAREER (See also Employment, Job, Occupational, Vocational)

Alternative careers	SIMONE-HOHE, M J. . . .	(PA)	1141
Business, jobs, & careers	ROUDEBUSH, Lawanda C.	(IA)	1061
Career & education resources	WHITNEY, Howard F. . . .	(MA)	1334
Career & employment centers	MALLINGER, Stephen M.	(PA)	763
Career change for librarians	BERKNER, Dimity S.	(NY)	87
Career counseling	CONDREY, Barbara K. . .	(CA)	236
	PORTER-ROTH, Anne . .	(CA)	985
Career development	TIWANA, Nazar H.	(IL)	1247
	HEIM, Kathleen M.	(LA)	521
	EDWARDS, Guy P.	(NY)	337
	OCHS, Phyllis E.	(NY)	915
	BOUEY, Elaine F.	(AB)	119
Career development & placement	ANSELMO, Edith H.	(NJ)	28
Career education information advising	LYONS, A J.	(MO)	753
Career information	MOORHEAD, Kenneth E.	(CT)	862
	WEEG, Barbara E.	(IA)	1315
	HUSFELDT, Jerry J.	(IL)	578

CAREER (Cont'd)

Career information services	HEINEMAN, Stephanie R.	(NY)	522
Career path planning	SIMON, Ralph C.	(IN)	1141
Career planning & development	ARNOLD, Barbara J. . . .	(WI)	33
Career planning & placement	SCOTT, Melissa C.	(MI)	1107
Career resources	SCOTT, Melissa C.	(MI)	1107
Job & career education	GREEN, Vera A.	(PA)	462
Job & career information	LANE, Steven P.	(WA)	694
Library & information science careers	SCHERDIN, Mary J.	(WI)	1092
Reference career centers	HAWKE, Susan J.	(PQ)	513

CARIBBEAN

African & Caribbean music	RICHARDSON, Deborra A.	(DC)	1029
Caribbean bibliography	NANTON-COMISSIONG, Barbara L.	(TRN)	887
Caribbean Jewish history	CAHEN, Joel J.	(NET)	171
Caribbean studies	MCCLEAN, Vernon E. . . .	(NJ)	796
Latin American & Caribbean	MILLER, David A.	(OH)	836
Latin American & Caribbean studies	FINEMAN, Charles S. . . .	(IL)	377

CARPETING

Modular carpeting for libraries	KELLY, Patrick M.	(GA)	638

CARS (See also Automotive)

Antique cars	HESSELBEIN, Krista M. .	(OH)	534

CARTOBIBLIOGRAPHY

Cartobibliography	STEPHENSON, Richard W.	(DC)	1188

CARTOGRAPHY (See also Atlases, Cartobibliography, Maps)

Cartographic & architectural archives	KIDD, Betty H.	(ON)	646
Cartographic cataloging	ANDREW, Paige G.	(GA)	26
Cartographic information	STRICKLAND, Muriel . . .	(CA)	1202
Cartographic materials	SELMER, Marsha L.	(IL)	1114
	SELDIN, Daniel T.	(IN)	1113
	ALLISON, Brent	(MN)	17
	WALSTROM, Jon L.	(MN)	1300
	CRISSINGER, John D. . .	(TX)	259
	TESSIER, Yves	(PQ)	1233
Cartographic materials cataloging	COOMBS, James A. . . .	(MO)	241
Cartographic materials reference service	COOMBS, James A. . . .	(MO)	241
Cartographic mtrl collection development	WYMAN, Kathleen M. . .	(ON)	1375
Cartography	STEWART, James A.	(IL)	1192
	BERGEN, Kathleen M. . .	(MI)	85
	HUDSON, Alice C.	(NY)	569
	HEDRICK, David T.	(PA)	520
	MCQUILLAN, David C. . .	(SC)	817
Cartography history	STEPHENSON, Richard W.	(DC)	1188
Cartography materials librarianship	LARSGAARD, Mary L. . .	(CO)	698
Geography, cartography	EASTON, William W.	(IL)	333
Historical cartography	SUTHERLAND, Johnnie D.	(GA)	1211
History of cartography	RAY, Jean M.	(IL)	1011
	WALSTROM, Jon L. . . .	(MN)	1300
Maps & cartographic information	REX, Heather	(NM)	1024
Maps & cartography	WALTZ, Mary A.	(NY)	1302
Research on cartographic librarianship	STEVENS, Stanley D. . . .	(CA)	1191
Sources of cartographic materials	MINTON, James O.	(AZ)	846

CAS (See also Databases)

CAS online database searching	ROSS, Johanna C.	(CA)	1058
CAS online end-user training	ROSS, Johanna C.	(CA)	1058
CAS online searching	DESS, Howard M.	(NJ)	295

CASSATT

Mary Cassatt	LEAHY, Mary S.	(PA)	707

CASSETTE (See also Audio, Video)

Audio cassette collection management	TREMBLAY, Carolyn B. .	(NH)	1255
Cataloging cassettes & compact discs	SCHWANN, William J. . . .	(MA)	1104
Record & cassette selection	ANDERSON, Gail	(AB)	23
Record, cassette & score cataloging	DONIO, Dorothy	(FL)	311
Select music, records, cassettes	CAPPAERT, Lael R. . . .	(MI)	180
Video cassettes	SKUBISH, Barbara E. . . .	(FL)	1147
Walking tours on cassette	ECKRICH, Herman J. . . .	(CT)	335

CATALAN

Catalan bibliographies	VELA, Leonor G.	(SPN)	1281

CATALOGING (See also AMC, Authority, Conversion, Cross-Referencing, Description, Headings, MARC, NACO, OCLC, Subject, Tagging, Technical)

Abstracting, indexing & cataloging	HART, Patricia H.	(MI)	507
Acquisition & cataloging serials	CHANG, Min M.	(CA)	200
Acquisition, cataloging of record col	MECHTENBERG, Paul . .	(IL)	820
Acquisitions & cataloging	LAPOLT, Margaret B. . . .	(CT)	697
	LOOMIS, Barbara	(IL)	740
	SADLER, Shirley L.	(IL)	1073
	BROWN, Sandra S.	(IN)	147
	LUNG, Chan S.	(NY)	748
	TASNADI, Deborah L. . .	(WI)	1224
Acquisitions cataloging	OLMSTEAD, Nancy L. . . .	(CA)	921
	MIRANDA, Esmeralda C.	(MN)	847
	SULLIVAN, Stephen W. .	(NY)	1208
Acquisitions, cataloging, circulation	TODD, Hal W.	(FL)	1248
Administration, purchasing, cataloging	HEDGES, Bonnie L.	(VA)	520
Africa & Middle East cataloging	LEONARD, Louise F. . . .	(FL)	716
Africana cataloging	STAMM, Andrea L.	(IL)	1179
Arabic & Hebrew cataloging	CHAMMOU, Eliezer	(CA)	198
Arabic cataloging	MYERS-HAYER, Patricia A.	(DC)	885
	HIRSCH, David G.	(NJ)	543
Arabic script cataloging	WERYHO, Jan W.	(PQ)	1325
Architecture cataloging	CHIBNIK, Katharine R. . .	(NY)	207
Archival automation, cataloging	WEINBERG, David M. . .	(PA)	1317
Archival cataloging	BAUMSTEIN, Paschal M. .	(NC)	66
	HARGIS-LYTLE, Betty L. .	(OK)	501
Archives appraisal & cataloging	CORNELIUS, Charlene E.	(WI)	246
Art books cataloging	SEVY, Barbara S.	(PA)	1117
Art cataloging	CHIBNIK, Katharine R. . .	(NY)	207
	STARR, Daniel A.	(NY)	1182
Art documentation & cataloging	IBACH, Marilyn	(DC)	581
Art material cataloging	HERMAN, Elizabeth	(CA)	531
Asian languages & literature cataloging	TIBBITS, Edith J.	(NE)	1243
Asian materials cataloging	CHAN, Moses C.	(NC)	199
Audiovisual & microform cataloging	BURCHELL, Patricia M. .	(ON)	158
Audiovisual cataloging	BASKIN, Jeffrey L.	(AR)	63
	HAWKINS, Nina L.	(CA)	514
	WURANGIAN, Nelia C. .	(CA)	1374
	CARTER, Nancy F.	(CO)	189
	HARLOW, Aileen W. . . .	(CT)	502
	KELLY, Mark M.	(DC)	638
	GREESON-SCHARDL, Tamra J.	(GA)	465
	CORCORAN, Frances E.	(IL)	245
	POWELL, Martha C. . . .	(KY)	988
	WINZER, Kathleen M. . .	(MD)	1356
	REGAN, Lesley E.	(MI)	1017
	MCCROSKEY, Marilyn J.	(MO)	800
	MYRICK, Judy C.	(MS)	885
	MASCIA, Regina B.	(NY)	780
	WEITZ, Jay N.	(OH)	1320
	SMITH, Terry M.	(OR)	1161
	GARRETT, Stuart	(TN)	420
	OWEN, Richard L.	(TN)	932
	CAINE, William C.	(TX)	171
	HOWE, Patricia A.	(VA)	565
	WHYTE, Sean	(VA)	1335
	GILCHRIST-DOBSON, Norma J.	(NS)	434
	FINLAY, Barbara J.	(PQ)	378
Audiovisual cataloging & acquisitions	SPIEGELMAN, Barbara M.	(PA)	1174

CATALOGING (Cont'd)

Audiovisual material cataloging	TRAVILLIAN, Mary W. . .	(IA)	1254
	ESMAN, Michael D.	(MD)	354
	MCENTEE, Mary F.	(TX)	804
Audiovisual materials cataloging	CLEMENT, Patsy	(UT)	221
Audiovisual media cataloging	ZASLOW, Barry A.	(OH)	1386
Audiovisual software cataloging	DUHAMELL, Lynnette H. .	(IN)	324
	HORAN, Meredith L. . . .	(MD)	559
Audiovisuals & cataloging	EMAHISER, Joan A.	(MI)	347
Audiovisuals cataloging	LOMEN, Nancy L.	(NY)	738
Authority work cataloging	FINLAY, Barbara J.	(PQ)	378
Automated cataloging	CARSON, Susan A.	(CA)	188
	MILLER, Daniel J.	(OR)	836
	GREAVES, H P.	(ON)	461
Automated cataloging, authority control	GLASSMAN, Penny L. . .	(MA)	440
Automated Library of Congress cataloging	BENSON, Laurel D.	(MN)	83
Automation cataloging	CHEN, Helen M.	(TN)	205
Biological sciences cataloging	HAWVER, Nancy	(CA)	515
Biomedical sciences cataloging	WURANGIAN, Nelia C. .	(CA)	1374
Book & artifact cataloging	HALEY, Marguerite R. . .	(WA)	486
	SHANNON, Kathleen L. .	(IL)	1120
Book cataloging	MILLER, Jean J.	(CT)	838
Book selection & cataloging	WU, Harriet	(CA)	1373
Books & non-book cataloging	WOODWARD, Lawrence W.	(DC)	1368
Books cataloging	DAWE, Heather L.	(ON)	282
	ANDREW, Paige G.	(GA)	26
Canadiana cataloging	COOMBS, James A.	(MO)	241
Cartographic cataloging	BOEHMER, Elaine	(AK)	109
Cartographic materials cataloging	MUDD, Isabelle G.	(AK)	875
Cataloging	PUTZ, Paul D.	(AK)	998
	RICKS, Bonnie B.	(AK)	1032
	ROSS, Rosemary E. . . .	(AK)	1058
	ADAMS, Emily J.	(AL)	4
	BUCKNER, Rebecca S. . .	(AL)	154
	COLEMAN, L Z.	(AL)	231
	DUNMIRE, Raymond V. .	(AL)	326
	ELLIOTT, Riette B.	(AL)	344
	FELDER, Jimmie R.	(AL)	369
	FINLEY, Vera L.	(AL)	378
	GRAMKA, Billie J.	(AL)	457
	GRIFFITH, Ethel T.	(AL)	469
	JOHNSON, Elizabeth G. .	(AL)	604
	KING, Karen H.	(AL)	651
	LIAW, Barbara C.	(AL)	725
	MARTIN, John B.	(AL)	776
	MAYTON, Regina A. . . .	(AL)	791
	MCGARITY, Marysue . . .	(AL)	805
	MCKINLEY, Beebe M. . . .	(AL)	811
	MILLER, Hannelore A. . .	(AL)	838
	PARKS, Bernice Z.	(AL)	943
	PERESICH, Mary G.	(AL)	958
	PFAU, Julia G.	(AL)	966
	SPILLERS, Doris H.	(AL)	1174
	SUTTON, Sandra K.	(AL)	1211
	TAYLOR, Carol P.	(AL)	1226
	WILLIAMS, Delmus E. . .	(AL)	1342
	ASHCRAFT, Carolyn A. .	(AR)	35
	CALLAHAN, Patrick F. . .	(AR)	173
	CHICK, Catherine P. . . .	(AR)	208
	CHILDRESS, Schelley H. .	(AR)	208
	ESTES, Pamela J.	(AR)	355
	HAWKS, Mary S.	(AR)	514
	MCNEIL, William K.	(AR)	816
	MITCHAM, Janet C.	(AR)	848
	MOORE, Gay G.	(AR)	859
	PIERSON, Betty	(AR)	972
	PIRRERA, Aaron C.	(AR)	975
	ROSE, Donna K.	(AR)	1054
	STOWE, Jean E.	(AR)	1199
	WATSON, Ellen I.	(AR)	1309
	WILSON, Janora E.	(AR)	1351
	BRZOZOWSKI, Margery E.	(AZ)	152
	CHUNG, Catherine L. . . .	(AZ)	213
	EVANS, Iris I.	(AZ)	357
	FIEGEN, Ann M.	(AZ)	375
	FORE, Janet S.	(AZ)	390

CATALOGING (Cont'd)
Cataloging

FOX, Frances J. . . . . (AZ) 394
GRANADE, Victoria A. . . (AZ) 457
HOWARD, Pamela F. . . . (AZ) 564
KESSLER, Katheryn M. . (AZ) 645
KLATT, Dixie K. . . . . (AZ) 657
KLIMIADES, Mario N. . . . (AZ) 661
KNEPP, Kenneth B. . . . . (AZ) 664
MARSHALL, Thomas H. . (AZ) 775
MAXWELL, Margaret F. . (AZ) 788
MCBRIDE, Patricia A. . . . (AZ) 792
MCLACHLAN, Ross W. . (AZ) 812
MILLS, Victoria A. . . . . . (AZ) 844
MOORE, Susan M. . . . . . (AZ) 861
PATTEE, Alice P. . . . . . . (AZ) 947
RAWAN, Atifa R. . . . . . . (AZ) 1010
RIISE, Milton B. . . . . (AZ) 1034
ROBROCK, David P. . . . (AZ) 1045
ROTHLISBERG, Allen P. (AZ) 1060
SABOVIK, Pavel . . . . . . (AZ) 1073
STOUT, Mary A. . . . . . . (AZ) 1199
WU, Ai H. . . . . (AZ) 1373
ABRAMSON, Jenifer S. . (CA) 3
ALLEN, Doris L. . . . . (CA) 14
AMARA, Margaret F. . . . (CA) 19
ARNDAL, Robert E. . . . . (CA) 33
ASHLEY, Elizabeth . . . . . (CA) 36
AUGUSTINE, Rolf S. . . . (CA) 39
BAILEY, Rolene M. . . . . . (CA) 46
BALES, F K. . . . . (CA) 52
BARROW, Jerry . . . . (CA) 60
BATTAGLIA, Bonnie J. . . (CA) 64
BECKER, Carol J. . . . . . (CA) 72
BENNETT, Agnes H. . . . (CA) 81
BENOIT, Gerald . . . . (CA) 82
BERGMAN, Emily A. . . . (CA) 86
BERLOWITZ, Sara B. . . (CA) 88
BERNHART, Barbara M. (CA) 89
BIDWELL, Lynne H. . . . (CA) 95
BLUE, Margaret L. . . . . . (CA) 107
BOWMAN, Frances A. . . (CA) 121
BREWSAUGH, Susan J. (CA) 134
BRIDGMAN, Amy R. . . . (CA) 135
BRISCOE, Georgia K. . . (CA) 136
BRITTAIN, Cynthia E. . . . (CA) 137
BROWN, Barbara L. . . . . (CA) 142
BROWN, Elizabeth E. . . . (CA) 143
BRUNTON, Angela . . . . . (CA) 151
CAPPADONNA, Mary S. (CA) 180
CARNOVSKY, Ruth F. . . (CA) 184
CARRICABURU, Robert . (CA) 186
CELLE, Deborah A. . . . . (CA) 196
COLALILLO, Robert M. . (CA) 230
COLBY, Michael D. . . . . (CA) 230
CONDIT, Larry D. . . . . . . (CA) 235
COOVER, Robert W. . . . (CA) 244
CREELY, Kathryn L. . . . . (CA) 257
DERSHEM, Larry D. . . . (CA) 294
DICKINSON, Dan C. . . . (CA) 300
DIFFERDING, Jane B. . . (CA) 302
DOBB, Linda S. . . . . (CA) 307
DOLLEN, Charles J. . . . . (CA) 310
DOUGLAS, Carolyn T. . . (CA) 314
DOUGLAS, Nancy E. . . . (CA) 314
DRIVER, Linda A. . . . . . . (CA) 320
DUNKLEE, Joanna E. . . (CA) 326
DWYER, James R. . . . . . (CA) 330
EWEN, Eric P. . . . . (CA) 359
FELDMAN, Irwin . . . . (CA) 369
FISHER, Leslie R. . . . . . (CA) 381
FRANK, Anne E. . . . . . . (CA) 396
FRASHIER, Anne E. . . . . (CA) 399
FREUDENBERGER, Elsie
    L. . . . . (CA) 402
GARDNER, Laura L. . . . . (CA) 418
GINSBURG, Helen W. . . (CA) 438
GRAY, Tomysena F. . . . . (CA) 460
GRIFFIN, Thomas E. . . . (CA) 469
GULLION, Susan L. . . . . (CA) 477

CATALOGING (Cont'd)
Cataloging

HAAS, Florence A. . . . . . (CA) 480
HAGEN, Dennis D. . . . . . (CA) 483
HAMBRIDGE, Sally L. . . (CA) 491
HANSEN, Linda L. . . . . . (CA) 497
HANSEN, Phyllis J. . . . . (CA) 498
HARDIN, Betty N. . . . . . (CA) 500
HAYES, Melinda K. . . . . (CA) 516
HAZEKAMP, Phyllis W. . (CA) 517
HECKART, Ronald J. . . . (CA) 519
HELFER, Doris S. . . . . . (CA) 523
HERDMAN, Elena . . . . . (CA) 530
HERON, Susan J. . . . . . (CA) 532
HICKS, Mary F. . . . . (CA) 537
HIXON, Donald L. . . . . . (CA) 544
HOCKING, Theresa R. . . (CA) 546
HODSON, Sara S. . . . . . (CA) 546
HOFLAND, Freda B. . . . (CA) 548
HOLLAND, Rebecca J. . . (CA) 551
HUNT, Deborah S. . . . . . (CA) 575
HUNTER, David C. . . . . . (CA) 576
IVERSON, Diann S. . . . . (CA) 585
JOHNSON, Clifford R. . . (CA) 603
JOHNSON, Jane D. . . . . (CA) 605
JOHNSON, Mary E. . . . . (CA) 607
JORDAN, Joan A. . . . . . (CA) 616
JUNG, Soon J. . . . . (CA) 620
KACZOROWSKI, Monice
    M. . . . . (CA) 621
KATZ, Janet R. . . . . (CA) 630
KAUN, Thomas T. . . . . . (CA) 631
KAWAMOTO, Chizuko . . (CA) 632
KENSINGER, Colleen O. (CA) 642
KHATTAB, Hosneya M. . (CA) 646
KIM, Joy H. . . . . (CA) 649
KIRBY, Barbara L. . . . . . (CA) 653
LANE, David R. . . . . (CA) 694
LEE, Diane T. . . . . (CA) 709
LEE, Hee J. . . . . (CA) 710
LEGER, Norissa . . . . (CA) 712
LIM, Sue C. . . . . (CA) 727
LINDBERG, Susan J. . . . (CA) 729
LO, Grace C. . . . . (CA) 735
LOPEZ, Frank D. . . . . . . (CA) 741
MAHAFFEY, Susan M. . . (CA) 760
MANKE, Merrill E. . . . . . (CA) 765
MARCUS, Sharon F. . . . (CA) 769
MCGARRY, Dorothy . . . . (CA) 805
MICHAELS, Joan M. . . . (CA) 832
MINDEMAN, George A. . (CA) 845
MITTAN, Rhonda L. . . . . (CA) 850
MORENO, Catherine H. . (CA) 863
MORRISON, Deborah L. . (CA) 868
MOSER, Elizabeth C. . . . (CA) 870
MOSER, Judith E. . . . . . (CA) 871
MULE, Gabriel . . . . (CA) 876
MUSICK, Nancy W. . . . . (CA) 883
MYONG, Jae H. . . . . (CA) 885
NEELY, Jesse G. . . . . . . (CA) 892
NELSON, Iris N. . . . . (CA) 894
OKA, Susan Y. . . . . (CA) 919
OLSON, Sharon L. . . . . . (CA) 923
ORTOPAN, Leroy D. . . . (CA) 927
OSTROUMOV, Tatiana . . (CA) 929
PAI, Herman H. . . . . (CA) 934
PANSKI, Saul J. . . . . (CA) 938
PARCHUCK, Jill A. . . . . . (CA) 940
PAULS, Adonijah . . . . . . (CA) 950
PEASE, William J. . . . . . (CA) 953
PHILLIPS, Clifford R. . . . (CA) 968
PISANO, Vivian M. . . . . . (CA) 975
POLLACH, Karen F. . . . . (CA) 981
POSEY, Vernell W. . . . . . (CA) 985
PRESTON, Cecilia M. . . . (CA) 991
PRINTZ, Naomi J. . . . . . (CA) 993
REDFIELD, Elizabeth . . . (CA) 1014
REEDER, Ray A. . . . . . . (CA) 1015
REVEAL, Arlene H. . . . . (CA) 1024
RICHTER, Bertina . . . . . (CA) 1031

CATALOGING (Cont'd)
Cataloging

ROBINSON, Michaele M. (CA) 1044
ROCKE, Reve P. ...... (CA) 1046
RODRIGUEZ, Ronald ... (CA) 1048
ROLLING, George M. .... (CA) 1051
ROTTER, Virginia B. .... (CA) 1061
RYUS, Joseph E. ...... (CA) 1072
SANDFORD, Betsy R. .. (CA) 1080
SCHOTTLAENDER, Brian
    E. .... (CA) 1099
SCHRIEFER, Kent ..... (CA) 1100
SCLAR, Marta L. ...... (CA) 1106
SCRIBNER, Ruth B. .... (CA) 1108
SHAWL, Janice H. ..... (CA) 1124
SHERMAN, Roger S. .... (CA) 1128
SIEGEL, Jacquelin B. .... (CA) 1136
SIGLER, Lorraine ...... (CA) 1137
SLOAN, James W. ..... (CA) 1149
SMITH, Heather ...... (CA) 1155
SNYDER, Henry L. ..... (CA) 1164
SO, Henry K. .... (CA) 1165
SOUZA, Margaret A. .... (CA) 1170
SPIRO GREEN, Becky A. (CA) 1175
STALKER, Laura A. ..... (CA) 1178
STERLIN, Annette S. .... (CA) 1189
STEUBEN, Raymond L. . (CA) 1190
STOCKFLETH, Craig G. . (CA) 1195
SVENONIUS, Elaine .... (CA) 1212
SWANSON, Clara M. .... (CA) 1213
SWEENEY, Suzanne .... (CA) 1215
SZEGEDI, Laszlo ...... (CA) 1218
TAI, Henry H. .... (CA) 1220
TARCZY, Stephen I. ..... (CA) 1224
TAYLOR, Theodore R. ... (CA) 1229
THOMAS, Vivian ...... (CA) 1238
THOMAS, Yvonne ...... (CA) 1238
TING, Eunice T. .... (CA) 1246
TREGGIARI, Arnaldo ... (CA) 1255
TSAI, Sheh G. .... (CA) 1260
TSENG, Joan L. .... (CA) 1260
TSENG, Sally C. ...... (CA) 1260
TUOHY, Eileen M. ..... (CA) 1263
TYSON, Betty B. ...... (CA) 1267
UEBELE, Dorothy B. .... (CA) 1268
VANDERBECK, Maria ... (CA) 1273
VANDERBERG, Patricia S. (CA) 1273
VOTAW, Floyd M. ..... (CA) 1289
WALKER, James J. ..... (CA) 1295
WATSON, Benjamin .... (CA) 1309
WATTS, Richard S. .... (CA) 1310
WEINTRAUB, D K. .... (CA) 1318
WICKEY, Marjorie J. .... (CA) 1335
WIMMER, Ted .... (CA) 1354
WINEBURGH-FREED,
    Margaret .... (CA) 1354
WOO, Winnie H. ...... (CA) 1363
YEE, Martha M. .... (CA) 1379
YEUNG, Esther Y. ..... (CA) 1380
ZUCKERMAN, Arline .... (CA) 1391
BEUTHEL, Ellengail .... (CO) 93
BOYER, Carol C. ...... (CO) 123
BURKE, Marianne D. ... (CO) 160
ESKOZ, Patricia A. ... (CO) 354
FULMER, Russell F. .... (CO) 409
GARZA, Rosario ...... (CO) 421
GERMOVNIK, Francis I. . (CO) 429
HAMDY, Amira .... (CO) 491
HOFFMAN, Ann M. .... (CO) 547
KELVER, Ann E. ...... (CO) 639
LANGE, Holley R. ...... (CO) 695
LEITNER, Lavonne ..... (CO) 714
LINDGREN, William F. ... (CO) 729
MACARTHUR, Marit S. . (CO) 754
MOORE, Beverly B. .... (CO) 858
NEILON, Barbara L. .... (CO) 892
PATERSON, Judy L. ... (CO) 947
PROSSER, Judy A. .... (CO) 995
ROESCH, Gay E. ...... (CO) 1049
SUDOL, Barbara A. .... (CO) 1206

CATALOGING (Cont'd)
Cataloging

TREFZ, Robert O. ..... (CO) 1255
WITTHUS, Rutherford W. (CO) 1358
BAKER, Florence S. .... (CT) 48
BALDINI, Lois D. ...... (CT) 51
BENAMATI, Dennis C. ... (CT) 79
CROOKER, Cynthia L. ... (CT) 260
CUSTER, Deborah P. .... (CT) 267
DAW, May B. .... (CT) 282
FERNANDEZ, Nenita ... (CT) 373
FERRO, Frank J. ...... (CT) 374
FU, Theresa L. .... (CT) 407
GILLIES, Nancy H. ..... (CT) 436
HAHN, Boksoon ...... (CT) 483
HAMMOND, Harold A. ... (CT) 493
HILL, John R. .... (CT) 540
HUNENKO, Maria P. .... (CT) 574
ICHINOSE, Mitsuko .... (CT) 581
JARAMILLO, Ellen M. ... (CT) 594
KILLHEFFER, Robert E. . (CT) 648
KOLBIN, Ronda I. ...... (CT) 669
LANG, Norma F. ...... (CT) 695
MANDOUR, Cecile A. ... (CT) 765
MANNING, Beverley J. ... (CT) 766
MARTIN, Walter F. ..... (CT) 779
MCPHERSON, Mary A. . (CT) 817
MICHAUD, Noreen R. .... (CT) 832
MILLER, Irene K. ...... (CT) 838
MONTEE, Monty L. .... (CT) 856
PELTIER, Karen V. ..... (CT) 955
REILLY, Maureen E. ..... (CT) 1020
RESTOUT, Denise T. .... (CT) 1024
ROSS, Carole L. ...... (CT) 1058
SCHIMMELPFENG,
    Richard H. .... (CT) 1093
SCOTT, Joseph W. ..... (CT) 1107
SELVERSTONE, Harriet S. (CT) 1114
SHORE, Julia M. ...... (CT) 1132
SIROIS, Valerie M. ..... (CT) 1144
STEVENS, Hannah M. ... (CT) 1190
STONE, Ellen C. ...... (CT) 1197
STUEHRENBERG, Paul F. (CT) 1205
TRAVER, Julia M. ..... (CT) 1254
WAIT, Gary E. .... (CT) 1293
WARZALA, Allison B. .... (CT) 1307
YOUNG, Marianne F. .... (CT) 1382
AGENBROAD, James E. (DC) 7
ALEXANDER, Virginia A. (DC) 12
ALITO, Martha A. ...... (DC) 13
AVERA, Victoria E. ..... (DC) 41
AVRAM, Henriette D. ... (DC) 42
BASA, Eniko M. ...... (DC) 62
BENJAMIN, Marilyn .... (DC) 81
BERGQUIST, Christine F. (DC) 87
BERNARD, Patrick S. .... (DC) 88
BLIXRUD, Julia C. ..... (DC) 105
BOWMAN, James R. .... (DC) 122
BROWNE, Lynda S. .... (DC) 148
BYERS, Laura T. ...... (DC) 168
CASSEDY, Barbara S. ... (DC) 193
CHAPMAN, Susan E. .... (DC) 202
CIMERMANIS, Ilze V. .... (DC) 214
CRISTAN, Anita L. ..... (DC) 259
DANIELSON, Wilfred D. . (DC) 273
DEAN, Barbara C. ..... (DC) 283
DEARNBARGER, Dennis (DC) 284
DEHART, Odell .... (DC) 288
DENHAM, Maryanne H. . (DC) 292
DREWES, Arlene T. ... (DC) 319
DUVALL, John E. ...... (DC) 329
ELSASSER, Katharine K. (DC) 346
EWALD, Robert B. ..... (DC) 359
FELDMAN, Ellen S. .... (DC) 369
FILSTRUP, E C. ...... (DC) 377
FONT, Mary M. .... (DC) 388
FOX, Ann M. .... (DC) 394
GILLESPIE, Veronica M. . (DC) 435
GLASBY, Dorothy J. .... (DC) 439
GOREN, Morton S. ...... (DC) 452

CATALOGING (Cont'd)
Cataloging

GOUDREAU, Ronald A. . (DC) 454
GRUHL, Andrea M. . . . . (DC) 474
HANFORD, Sally . . . . . . (DC) 495
HIATT, Robert M. . . . . . (DC) 536
HIGBEE, Joan F. . . . . . (DC) 537
HOA, Quynh N. . . . . . . (DC) 545
HOPPER, Mildry S. . . . . (DC) 558
JOHANSON, Cynthia J. . (DC) 601
KECSKES, Lily C. . . . . . (DC) 633
KELLY, Mark M. . . . . . . (DC) 638
KESSINGER, Judith A. . . (DC) 644
KLEIN, Kristine J. . . . . . (DC) 659
KUTTY, Lalitha M. . . . . . (DC) 685
LEICH, Harold M. . . . . . (DC) 713
LEITCH, Karen E. . . . . . (DC) 714
LEONARD, Angela M. . . (DC) 716
LISOWSKI, Andrew H. . . (DC) 732
MANNING, Martin J. . . . (DC) 766
MCDONALD, Michael L. . (DC) 803
MCKINLEY, Sylvia J. . . . (DC) 811
MCLEMORE, Roberta T. . (DC) 814
MICHENER, David H. . . . (DC) 832
MOORE, Patsy H. . . . . . (DC) 861
MORRIS, Timothy J. . . . . (DC) 867
NAVE, Greer G. . . . . . . (DC) 890
NITZ, Andrew M. . . . . . (DC) 905
NYGREN, Deborah A. . . (DC) 912
PANITZ, Barbara R. . . . . (DC) 938
PFUND, Leona I. . . . . . . (DC) 966
RATESH, Ioana . . . . (DC) 1009
RATHER, Lucia J. . . . . . (DC) 1009
RUSH, Candace M. . . . . (DC) 1068
RUSHING, Naomi J. . . . . (DC) 1068
SANDIQUE-OWENS,
  Amelia A. . . . . (DC) 1080
SHEN, I Y. . . . . (DC) 1126
SHOREBIRD, Thomas S. (DC) 1132
SMITH, Elizabeth W. . . . (DC) 1154
STARCK, William L. . . . . (DC) 1181
STARNER, James A. . . . (DC) 1182
SYLVESTER, Carol . . . . (DC) 1217
TANSEY, Francis J. . . . . (DC) 1223
THOMPSON-JOYNER,
  Rita S. . . . . (DC) 1241
TOTH, George S. . . . . . (DC) 1252
TRACZEWSKI, Elizabeth
  P. . . . . (DC) 1253
TRIPP-MELBY, Pamela . (DC) 1257
UNVER, Amira V. . . . . . (DC) 1269
VANDEGRIFT, J R. . . . . (DC) 1273
VAN SYCKLE, Georgiana (DC) 1277
WANG, Ann C. . . . . (DC) 1302
WIENER, Theodore . . . . (DC) 1336
WIGGINS, Beacher J. . . (DC) 1337
WILLSON, Elizabeth . . . . (DC) 1349
WISNIEWSKI, Julia L. . . (DC) 1357
WOMELDORF, Jack H. . (DC) 1362
ZIMMERMANN, Carole R. (DC) 1389
CHOU, Vivian M. . . . . . . (DE) 210
COE, Gloria M. . . . . (DE) 226
PAUL, Jacqueline R. . . . (DE) 949
TRIBOLETTI, Kathleen . . (DE) 1256
TRUMBORE, Jean F. . . . (DE) 1259
ADAMS, Gustav C. . . . . (FL) 4
AHMAD, Saiyed A. . . . . (FL) 8
ANDREWS, Janet C. . . . (FL) 26
BENNETT, Renae M. . . . (FL) 82
BONFILI, Barbara J. . . . . (FL) 114
BROWN, Lyn S. . . . . . . (FL) 145
CHRISMAN, Larry G. . . . (FL) 211
CLARKSON, Jane S. . . . (FL) 219
COPELAND, Mildred A. . (FL) 244
CORNWELL, Douglas W. (FL) 247
DANIEL, Marianne M. . . . (FL) 272
FAHNERT, Elizabeth K. . (FL) 361
FOSTER, Helen M. . . . . (FL) 392
FRAZER, Ruth F. . . . . . (FL) 399
GEBET, Russell W. . . . . (FL) 424

CATALOGING (Cont'd)
Cataloging

GIBLON, Charles B. . . . . (FL) 431
HARKNESS, Mary L. . . . (FL) 501
HARRIS, Martha J. . . . . (FL) 505
HEMPHILL, Lia S. . . . . . (FL) 525
HERBSMAN, Yael . . . . . (FL) 530
HO, Paul J. . . . . (FL) 545
HOLT, Ethel F. . . . . (FL) 554
HOPE, Dorothy H. . . . . . (FL) 557
HUGHES, Joyce M. . . . . (FL) 572
HUNTER, Judith G. . . . . (FL) 576
JACOBSON, June B. . . . (FL) 590
JOHNSON, Betty D. . . . . (FL) 602
JOHNSON, Susan J. . . . (FL) 609
KANE, Joseph P. . . . . . . (FL) 624
KIEFER, Rosemary M. . . (FL) 647
LIANG, Diana F. . . . . . . (FL) 725
LINSLEY, Laurie S. . . . . (FL) 731
LOWELL, Felice K. . . . . (FL) 744
MCCLELLAN, Edna S. . . (FL) 796
MELLICAN, Nancy J. . . . (FL) 822
MERCADO, Marilyn J. . . (FL) 825
MESTRITS, Leila . . . . . . (FL) 828
MILLIKEN, Ruth L. . . . . . (FL) 843
MOJO, Anne Z. . . . . (FL) 852
MULLER, Charles W. . . . (FL) 877
NOL, Maryke E. . . . . (FL) 907
PINE, Nancy M. . . . . (FL) 974
PINGS, Joan G. . . . . (FL) 974
RABKIN, Judith R. . . . . . (FL) 1001
RANDTKE, Angela W. . . (FL) 1007
ROVIROSA, Dolores F. . . (FL) 1062
SCHWABEL, Lexie W. . . (FL) 1104
SHIAU, Ian L. . . . . (FL) 1129
SHINN, Allen E. . . . . (FL) 1130
SMITH, Linda L. . . . . . . (FL) 1157
SNYDER, Jean . . . . (FL) 1165
STONE, Alva T. . . . . (FL) 1196
STORCH, Barbara J. . . . (FL) 1198
TABOR, Curtis H. . . . . . (FL) 1219
TAYSOM, Daniel B. . . . . (FL) 1229
TERWILLEGAR, Jane C. (FL) 1232
VINSON, B J. . . . . (FL) 1285
ANDERSON, David G. . . (GA) 22
BAKER, Rowena E. . . . . (GA) 49
BALL, Ardella P. . . . . . . (GA) 52
BECHAM, Gerald C. . . . (GA) 71
BOZE, Lucy G. . . . . (GA) 124
BROWN, Lorene B. . . . . (GA) 145
BURKHART, Sue W. . . . (GA) 161
CHAMBERS, Shirley M. . (GA) 198
COLLINS, Eugenia A. . . . (GA) 232
DEES, Leslie M. . . . . . . (GA) 287
DOOLEY, Shelly Q. . . . . (GA) 312
DRAPER, James D. . . . . (GA) 318
FISTE, David A. . . . . . . (GA) 382
FLAVIN, Linda M. . . . . . (GA) 384
GLISSON, Patricia A. . . . (GA) 441
HARBER, Patty S. . . . . . (GA) 499
HARTZ, Frederic R. . . . . (GA) 509
HOWARD, Rachel L. . . . (GA) 564
HUGHES, Glenda J. . . . (GA) 571
HUGHES, Martha T. . . . (GA) 572
HUGHES, Neil R. . . . . . (GA) 572
LANDRAM, Christina L. . (GA) 693
MARONEY, Daryle M. . . (GA) 772
MASSEY, Katha D. . . . . (GA) 782
MCLAUGHLIN, Laverne L. (GA) 813
MISRA, Jayasri T. . . . . . (GA) 847
PASCHAL, Eloise R. . . . (GA) 945
ROBERTS, Lisa G. . . . . (GA) 1041
SCHEIN, Julia R. . . . . . . (GA) 1091
STANBERY, Nancy M. . . (GA) 1179
SWANSON, Joe . . . . . . (GA) 1213
TOOKES, Amos J. . . . . . (GA) 1250
VIDOR, Ann B. . . . . (GA) 1283
WILSON, Lesley P. . . . . (GA) 1351
AKAO, Pamela S. . . . . . (HI) 9
ENOMOTO, Wanda H. . . (HI) 350

CATALOGING (Cont'd)
Cataloging

FUKUDA, Jodel L.	(HI)	408
KOTO, Ann S.	(HI)	673
MATSUMORI, Donald M.	(HI)	784
RIEDY, Allen J.	(HI)	1033
ALDERSON, Karen A.	(IA)	11
BONATH, Gail J.	(IA)	113
BOWEN, Kay	(IA)	120
BROWN, Darmae J.	(IA)	143
CHAUDOIN, Sheila M.	(IA)	204
DICKES, Janis H.	(IA)	300
ELIZABETH, Martin A.	(IA)	343
GORMAN, Lawrence R.	(IA)	452
HARMON, Charles T.	(IA)	502
LARSON, Catherine A.	(IA)	699
LORKOVIC, Tatjana B.	(IA)	741
MADISON, Olivia M.	(IA)	759
MARTIN, Elizabeth A.	(IA)	776
OFFERMAN, Mary C.	(IA)	917
OHRLUND, Bruce L.	(IA)	919
OSMUS, Lori L.	(IA)	928
PARROTT, Lynn K.	(IA)	944
ROBINSON, Vera L.	(IA)	1045
SCHEETZ, Kathy D.	(IA)	1091
SCHMIDT, Sandra L.	(IA)	1096
SHIPE, Timothy R.	(IA)	1131
SORENSON, Debra J.	(IA)	1168
STUART, Kimberly A.	(IA)	1204
VINER, Mamie N.	(IA)	1285
WORK, Dawn E.	(IA)	1369
BOLLES, Charles A.	(ID)	112
CRANE, David E.	(ID)	255
CURL, Margo W.	(ID)	265
FUNABIKI, Ruth P.	(ID)	409
ROBERTSON, Naida	(ID)	1042
STEINHAGEN, Elizabeth N.	(ID)	1186
VERHOFF, Patricia A.	(ID)	1282
WILLIAMS, Brenda M.	(ID)	1342
WINWARD, Coleen C.	(ID)	1356
AGGARWAL, Narindar K.	(IL)	7
AISTARS, Aivars	(IL)	9
ALEXANDER, Lynetta L.	(IL)	12
ALLEN, Dorothy L.	(IL)	14
ATKINS, Stephen E.	(IL)	38
AULD, Lawrence W.	(IL)	40
BARNUM, Sally J.	(IL)	58
BAYER, Susan P.	(IL)	67
BOURKE, Jacqueline K.	(IL)	119
BROSK, Carol A.	(IL)	141
BROWN, Pamela P.	(IL)	146
BUCKLEY, Ja A.	(IL)	154
BURROWS, Thomas W.	(IL)	163
CALCAGNO, Philip M.	(IL)	172
CHANG, Roy T.	(IL)	201
CHANG, Sookang H.	(IL)	201
CHAPP, Debra R.	(IL)	202
CLELAND, Camille S.	(IL)	220
CLOONAN, Michele V.	(IL)	223
CLOUD, Patricia D.	(IL)	223
COATSWORTH, Patricia A.	(IL)	224
COBB, Marilyn R.	(IL)	225
CONROY, Margaret M.	(IL)	238
CONWAY, Colleen M.	(IL)	239
CRANE, Lilly E.	(IL)	255
DARLING, Elizabeth A.	(IL)	274
D'AVERSA, Concettina M.	(IL)	276
DELONG, Dianne S.	(IL)	290
DESSOUKY, Ibtesam	(IL)	296
ELL, Elizabeth L.	(IL)	343
FANG, Min L.	(IL)	363
FAYNZILBERG, Irina	(IL)	367
FEINBERG, Linda J.	(IL)	368
FIEG, Eugene C.	(IL)	375
FIELDING, Susan K.	(IL)	376
FITZGERALD, Adena H.	(IL)	382
FROST, Bruce Q.	(IL)	406
GALLAGHER, Eileen M.	(IL)	414

CATALOGING (Cont'd)
Cataloging

HAGEN, Loren R.	(IL)	483
HAMILTON, David A.	(IL)	491
HARRIS, Jane F.	(IL)	504
HASSERT, Rita M.	(IL)	511
HELGE, Brian L.	(IL)	524
HEYMAN, Jerome S.	(IL)	536
HILL, Janet S.	(IL)	540
HITCHCOCK, Gail A.	(IL)	544
HOOVER, Margaret R.	(IL)	557
HOTIMLANSKA, Leah D.	(IL)	562
HUETING, Gail P.	(IL)	570
JAGODZINSKI, Cecile M.	(IL)	591
JOHN, Nancy R.	(IL)	601
KARSTEN, Eileen S.	(IL)	628
KEISER, Mary P.	(IL)	635
KELLY, Raymond T.	(IL)	638
KELM, Carol R.	(IL)	638
KIENE, Andrea L.	(IL)	647
KINGERY, Victor P.	(IL)	652
KIRCHGRABER, Nancy B.	(IL)	654
KLESTINSKI, Martha A.	(IL)	661
KLOCKENGA, Gary R.	(IL)	662
KOH, Siew B.	(IL)	668
KREINBRING, Mary	(IL)	677
KRIIGEL, Barbara J.	(IL)	678
LAM, Judy	(IL)	689
LAMBRECHT, Jay H.	(IL)	691
LEONG, Carol L.	(IL)	717
LI, Grace Y.	(IL)	724
MAKINO, Yasuko	(IL)	762
MANSFIELD, Fred	(IL)	767
MATTHEWS, Elizabeth W.	(IL)	785
MCCOY, Patricia S.	(IL)	799
MCDOWELL, Myrnella J.	(IL)	804
MCGILL, Sara L.	(IL)	806
MCHENRY, Renee E.	(IL)	808
MEI, Angela L.	(IL)	821
MEYER, Beverly R.	(IL)	829
MILUTINOVIC, Eunhee C.	(IL)	845
MOCH, Mary I.	(IL)	851
MOORE, Milton C.	(IL)	860
MORRIS, Susan M.	(IL)	867
MORTON, Laura	(IL)	870
MOSS, Barbara J.	(IL)	872
MULLER, Karen	(IL)	877
MURRAY, Theresa A.	(IL)	882
NAGOLSKI, Donald J.	(IL)	886
NOGUCHI, Sachie	(IL)	907
OLSEN, Sarah G.	(IL)	922
OLSON, Anton J.	(IL)	922
OWNES, Dorothy J.	(IL)	932
PACETTI, Karen C.	(IL)	933
PAUSCH, Lois M.	(IL)	950
PEARSON, Karen L.	(IL)	952
PENDERGRASS, Margaret E.	(IL)	956
PEPLOW, Richard C.	(IL)	958
POLL, Diane R.	(IL)	981
POSNER, Frances A.	(IL)	985
POTEET, Susan S.	(IL)	986
PULVER, Emilie G.	(IL)	997
RANDALL, Sara L.	(IL)	1006
RAST, Elaine K.	(IL)	1009
RECKS, Dorcas E.	(IL)	1013
REIMER, Elizabeth A.	(IL)	1020
RICHARDSON, Vickie W.	(IL)	1030
RUDNIK, Mary C.	(IL)	1065
RYAN, Diane M.	(IL)	1070
SALTZMAN, Robbin R.	(IL)	1077
SCHROEDER, Anne M.	(IL)	1100
SHACKLETON, Suzanne M.	(IL)	1118
SHERMAN, William F.	(IL)	1128
SINHA, Vaswati R.	(IL)	1143
SINKUS, Raminta	(IL)	1144
SKIDMORE, Gail	(IL)	1146
SMITH, Newland F.	(IL)	1159
STAMM, Andrea L.	(IL)	1179

CATALOGING (Cont'd)
Cataloging

STEVENSON, Sheila M. .	(IL)	1191
STEWART, Richard A. . .	(IL)	1193
STONER, Ronald P.	(IL)	1198
STRAIT, Constance J. . .	(IL)	1199
STUDWELL, William E. .	(IL)	1204
SVED, Alexander	(IL)	1212
SYED, Mariam A.	(IL)	1217
TAYLOR, Terry S.	(IL)	1229
TEMPLE, Harold L.	(IL)	1230
THOMPSON, John W. . .	(IL)	1240
TIBBITS, George D. . . .	(IL)	1244
TODD, Margaret	(IL)	1248
UDDIN, Shantha C.	(IL)	1267
VANDER MEER, Gary L. .	(IL)	1274
VAN HOUTEN, Stephen .	(IL)	1275
VITOLINS, Ilga	(IL)	1286
WAGNER, Robin O.	(IL)	1292
WAJENBERG, Arnold S. .	(IL)	1293
WALLACE, Richard E. . .	(IL)	1298
WALTERS, Patsy M. . . .	(IL)	1301
WICKREMERATNE, Swarna	(IL)	1335
WILLIAMS, James W. . .	(IL)	1344
WINNER, Ronald	(IL)	1355
YOON, Choong N.	(IL)	1380
ZUIDERVELD, Sharon R.	(IL)	1391
AMSTUTZ, Mary	(IN)	21
ARNOLD, Joann M.	(IN)	33
ASHER, Richard E.	(IN)	36
BRETT, Lorraine E.	(IN)	134
BUSHING, Vera R.	(IN)	165
CONRADS, Douglas L. . .	(IN)	238
CORYA, William L.	(IN)	248
FRANCQ, Carole	(IN)	396
GOODWIN, Vania M. . . .	(IN)	450
HOLMAN, Mary J.	(IN)	553
JONES, Marjorie	(IN)	614
KASER, Jane	(IN)	628
KELLEY, Colleen L.	(IN)	636
KRAMER, Arlene H.	(IN)	675
KUO, Ming M.	(IN)	684
LAIR, Nancy C.	(IN)	688
LASHER, Esther L.	(IN)	700
LATSHAW, Ruth N.	(IN)	701
LEE, Thomas H.	(IN)	711
LE GUERN, Charles A. . .	(IN)	712
LITTLE, Robert D.	(IN)	733
MCCLOY, William B. . . .	(IN)	797
MCCUNE, Lois M.	(IN)	801
MILLER, Junelle	(IN)	839
MILLS, Richard E.	(IN)	844
MOON, Elizabeth A.	(IN)	857
NEVILLE, Ellen P.	(IN)	898
PEC, Jean A.	(IN)	953
PIEPENBURG, Scott R. . .	(IN)	971
REARDON, Ann L.	(IN)	1013
RILE, B B.	(IN)	1034
SACZAWA, Rosemary . .	(IN)	1073
SANER, Eileen K.	(IN)	1081
SELLBERG, Roxanne J. .	(IN)	1113
SMITH, Lary	(IN)	1156
SPRINGER, Joe A.	(IN)	1176
STEPHENSON, Doris F. .	(IN)	1188
SU, Julie C.	(IN)	1206
TANTOCO, Dolores W. .	(IN)	1223
THOMAS, Joseph W. . . .	(IN)	1237
WARREN, Lois B.	(IN)	1306
WENNER, Alexander W. .	(IN)	1324
WILLIS, Ione P.	(IN)	1348
WOLCOTT, Laurie J. . . .	(IN)	1359
CARSON, Doris L.	(KS)	188
COFFEE, Kathleen C. . . .	(KS)	226
COOKE, Bette L.	(KS)	241
CRANE, Lois F.	(KS)	255
FENLON, Mary P.	(KS)	371
GALLOWAY, Mary A. . . .	(KS)	415
GRASS, Charlene G. . . .	(KS)	458
JOHNSON, Georgina . . .	(KS)	604

CATALOGING (Cont'd)
Cataloging

JOHNSON, H J.	(KS)	605
KLOSTERMANN, Helen M.	(KS)	662
LEE, Earl W.	(KS)	709
MADSEN, Debora L. . . .	(KS)	759
MARSH, Martha M.	(KS)	773
MASON, Alexandra	(KS)	780
MELICK, Cal G.	(KS)	822
NEUGEBAUER, Rhonda L.	(KS)	897
PRENTICE, Margaret A. .	(KS)	990
TRONIER, Suzanne	(KS)	1258
VAN SICKLE, Mary L. . .	(KS)	1277
WILLIAMS, Ann E.	(KS)	1342
BENNETT, Donna S. . . .	(KY)	81
BRATCHER, Perry R. . . .	(KY)	129
BUTTERWORTH, Donald Q.	(KY)	167
COATES, Ann S.	(KY)	224
CZARSKI, Charles M. . .	(KY)	268
DAY, Mary M.	(KY)	283
DECKER, Charlotte J. . . .	(KY)	285
FRANCK, Ilona G.	(KY)	396
FRENCH, Robert B.	(KY)	402
HALL, Juanita J.	(KY)	488
HERRON, Darl H.	(KY)	533
HUFF, James E.	(KY)	570
LILLIE, Jean N.	(KY)	727
MCFARLING, Patricia G.	(KY)	805
SCHULTZ, Lois E.	(KY)	1102
SMITH, Lena D.	(KY)	1157
STROHECKER, Edwin C.	(KY)	1202
THOMAS, Carol J.	(KY)	1236
THOMPSON, Ann B. . . .	(KY)	1238
WARTH, L T.	(KY)	1307
WILLIAMSEN, Audrey M.	(KY)	1347
BROWNING, Sandra B. .	(LA)	148
CARPENTER, Michael A.	(LA)	185
COSPER, Mary F.	(LA)	249
EVANS, James M.	(LA)	357
FERGUSON, Anna S. . . .	(LA)	372
FLEURY, Mary E.	(LA)	385
GROSS, Mary D.	(LA)	472
HASCHAK, Paul G.	(LA)	510
JOHNS, Mary E.	(LA)	601
KELLY, Judy M.	(LA)	638
PATTERSON, Trudy J. . .	(LA)	948
PONG, Connie K.	(LA)	982
POUNCY, Mitchell L. . . .	(LA)	987
REPMAN, Denise C. . . .	(LA)	1023
RUSHING, Darla H.	(LA)	1068
SHULL, Janice K.	(LA)	1133
ALLEN, Joan C.	(MA)	15
ALTENBERGER, Alicja . .	(MA)	18
ANDREWS, Peter J.	(MA)	27
ARCHAMBAUL, Christine	(MA)	30
ASCHMANN, Althea . . .	(MA)	35
BADEN, Diane G.	(MA)	44
BAILEY, Leeta L.	(MA)	46
BATES, Susie M.	(MA)	64
BERNSTEIN, D S.	(MA)	89
BEST, Eleanor L.	(MA)	92
BETTENCOURT, Ronald J.	(MA)	92
BOEHME, Richard W. . . .	(MA)	109
BOLAND, Mary J.	(MA)	111
BOUCHARD-HALL, Robert W.	(MA)	118
CHILDERS, Martha P. . .	(MA)	208
CLARK, Elizabeth K.	(MA)	216
CLOUGH, Linda F.	(MA)	223
CODAIR, Frederick R. . . .	(MA)	226
CONNELLY, Ramona S. .	(MA)	237
CUNNINGHAM, Robert L.	(MA)	265
CURTIN-STEVENSON, Mary C.	(MA)	266
DAMICO, Nancy B.	(MA)	272
DAVIS, Barbara M.	(MA)	277
DESIMONE, Dorothy H. .	(MA)	295
DI BONA, Leslie F.	(MA)	299

CATALOGING (Cont'd)
Cataloging

DIDHAM, Reginald A. . . .	(MA)	301
DUFFEK, Elizabeth A. . . .	(MA)	323
DURANCEAU, Ellen F. . .	(MA)	328
EVANS, Sally	(MA)	358
FOX, Susan	(MA)	395
GAUDET, Dodie E.	(MA)	422
GILLIAM, Ellen M.	(MA)	436
GOLDBERG, Steven R. .	(MA)	444
GONNEVILLE, Priscilla R.	(MA)	447
GRIFFIN, Fredericia	(MA)	468
GUSTAFSON, Eleanor A.	(MA)	478
HAMMOND, Wayne G. .	(MA)	494
HARRISON, Sylvia E. . . .	(MA)	507
HARVEY, Paul W.	(MA)	509
HERMAN, Douglas C. . . .	(MA)	531
HORN, Joseph A.	(MA)	559
HOSTAGE, John B.	(MA)	562
HOVORKA, Marjorie J. . .	(MA)	563
HURD, Sandra H.	(MA)	577
KELLY, Patricia M.	(MA)	638
KOLCZYNSKI, Charlotte A.	(MA)	669
LADD, Dorothy P.	(MA)	687
LAPIERRE, Barbe	(MA)	697
LEASON, Jane	(MA)	707
LEIGHTON, Lee W.	(MA)	714
LINDHEIMER, Sandra K.	(MA)	729
MCGEE, Ruby T.	(MA)	805
MILLER, Kristen L.	(MA)	839
MOLTZ, Sandra S.	(MA)	854
MOULTON, Catherine A.	(MA)	873
NESS, Pamela M.	(MA)	896
NORMAN-CAMP, Melody	(MA)	909
NORTON, Linda N.	(MA)	910
PAISTE, Marsha S.	(MA)	935
PANAGOPOULOS, Beata D.	(MA)	937
PAPADEMETRIOU, Athanasia	(MA)	938
PARKS, P D.	(MA)	943
PETROFF, Loumona J. . .	(MA)	965
POLLARD, Russell O. . . .	(MA)	981
PORTSCH-SNOW, Joanne	(MA)	985
PRISTASH, Kenneth . . .	(MA)	993
PROPER, David R.	(MA)	995
PROUTY, Sharman E. . .	(MA)	996
RESSMEYER, Ellen H. . .	(MA)	1024
SBACCHI, Margareta E. .	(MA)	1087
SCHALOW, John M. . . .	(MA)	1089
SCOTT, Alison M.	(MA)	1106
SESKIN, Ann H.	(MA)	1116
SHARE, Donald S.	(MA)	1122
SKLAR, Hinda F.	(MA)	1146
SMITH, Barbara A.	(MA)	1152
SPROUL, Barbara A. . . .	(MA)	1176
STAACK, Katherine A. . .	(MA)	1177
STACK, May E.	(MA)	1177
STEVENS, Michael L. . . .	(MA)	1190
STRAND, Bethany	(MA)	1200
TSENG, Louisa	(MA)	1260
TURKALO, David M. . . .	(MA)	1263
WAKS, Jane B.	(MA)	1293
WALSH, James E.	(MA)	1299
WASOWICZ, Laura E. . .	(MA)	1308
WEISS, Bernice O.	(MA)	1320
AYER, Carol A.	(MD)	42
BOEHR, Diane L.	(MD)	109
BYERLY, Imogene J. . . .	(MD)	168
CAREY, John T.	(MD)	181
CARMAN, Carol A.	(MD)	183
COLLINS, Donna S.	(MD)	232
COSTABILE, Salvatore L.	(MD)	249
DURBIN, Ramona J.	(MD)	328
FRYSER, Benjamin S. . .	(MD)	407
GIBBONS, Katherine Y. .	(MD)	431
GIORDANO, Peter	(MD)	438
GOEL, Krishan S.	(MD)	443
HALE, Dawn L.	(MD)	485

CATALOGING (Cont'd)
Cataloging

JENG, Helene W.	(MD)	596
JOHNSON, Bruce C. . . .	(MD)	602
JOHNSON, Gary M.	(MD)	604
KIM, Chung S.	(MD)	648
KNICKERBOCKER, Wendy	(MD)	664
KOBAYASHI, Michiko . . .	(MD)	666
KOEHLER, Barbara M. . .	(MD)	667
KUAN, David A.	(MD)	681
KULP, William A.	(MD)	683
LAFFREY, Laurel W. . . .	(MD)	687
LASER, Debra L.	(MD)	700
MC HALE, Mary M.	(MD)	808
NIXON, Judith A.	(MD)	906
O'NEILL, Sue	(MD)	924
PHILLIPS, Gary B.	(MD)	968
PHILLIPS, Lena M.	(MD)	968
POSEY, Sussann F.	(MD)	985
POTTER, Andrea K.	(MD)	987
RAWSTHORNE, Grace C.	(MD)	1011
RICHTER, Mary L.	(MD)	1031
RICHWINE, Eleanor N. . .	(MD)	1031
SANDERS, Jacqueline C.	(MD)	1080
SHAMBARGER, Peter E.	(MD)	1120
SHORT, Eleanor P.	(MD)	1132
SMITH, Barbara G.	(MD)	1152
SMITH, Mary P.	(MD)	1158
SORENSON, Lynn K. . . .	(MD)	1168
SULLIVAN, Carol W. . . .	(MD)	1207
THAPAR, Shashi P.	(MD)	1234
THIES, Gail M.	(MD)	1235
YU, Pei	(MD)	1384
ALLEY, Katherine S. . . .	(ME)	16
MCKAY, Ann	(ME)	809
MILLIGAN, Patricia M. . .	(ME)	843
SAEGER, Edwin J.	(ME)	1074
STANTON, Linda J.	(ME)	1181
ADLER, Robert J.	(MI)	7
ARNDT, Arleen	(MI)	33
BERRY, Charlene	(MI)	90
BIELICH, Paul S.	(MI)	95
BORAM, Joan M.	(MI)	116
BREITENWISCHER, Rosalyn E.	(MI)	132
BRUNHUMER, Sondra K.	(MI)	150
BURNS, David J.	(MI)	162
BUTZ, Helen S.	(MI)	168
CARSON, Claudia A. . . .	(MI)	188
CLAYTOR, Jane B.	(MI)	220
CLULEY, Leonard E. . . .	(MI)	223
COOPER, Byron D.	(MI)	242
CUNNINGHAM, Tina Y. .	(MI)	265
DARGA, Carol M.	(MI)	274
DE BEAR, Estelle G. . . .	(MI)	284
DEY, Anita C.	(MI)	298
DWOSKIN, Beth M.	(MI)	330
DYKI, Judy	(MI)	331
GIFFORD, Paul M.	(MI)	433
GOLDSTEIN, Doris R. . .	(MI)	446
HART, David J.	(MI)	507
HEYMOSS, Jennifer M. .	(MI)	536
HOWLETT, Jacqueline L.	(MI)	566
IRWIN, Lawrence L.	(MI)	584
JERYAN, Christine B. . . .	(MI)	600
KILLIAN, Mary C.	(MI)	648
KLOSWICK, John	(MI)	662
KOSCHIK, Douglas R. . .	(MI)	672
LIGHT, Lin	(MI)	726
LILLEY, Barbara A.	(MI)	727
MARTIN, John E.	(MI)	776
MARTIN, Rose M.	(MI)	778
MOSHER, Robin A.	(MI)	871
NUCKOLLS, Karen A. . .	(MI)	912
PETERS, Stephen H. . . .	(MI)	962
PONOMARENKO, Ella . .	(MI)	982
ROENZWEIG, Merle	(MI)	1048
ROSEN, Barbara	(MI)	1055
ROSS, Mary E.	(MI)	1058

CATALOGING (Cont'd)
Cataloging

SCHONDELMAYER,
   Barbara B. . . . . (MI) 1098
SCOTT, Jane . . . . (MI) 1107
SIEGEL, Marilyn . . . . (MI) 1136
SMOLER, Shelly . . . . . . (MI) 1162
STEVENS, Sheryl R. . . . (MI) 1191
TATE, Carole A. . . . . (MI) 1225
THOMAS, Laverne J. . . . (MI) 1237
THUNELL, Allen E. . . . . . (MI) 1243
TODD, Suzanne L. . . . . . (MI) 1248
VANDERLAAN, Robert J. (MI) 1274
VIGES, R J. . . . . (MI) 1284
WALKER, Joe L. . . . . . . (MI) 1295
WEAVER, Clarence L. . . (MI) 1312
YAEK, Larry A. . . . . (MI) 1376
ANDERSON, Margaret J. (MN) 24
BERNDTSON, Janet L. . (MN) 88
BILEYDI, Lois G. . . . . . . (MN) 96
BLATZ, Imogene . . . . . . (MN) 104
BRANDT, Janet E. . . . . . (MN) 128
CARON, Theodore F. . . . (MN) 184
COLE, David H. . . . . (MN) 230
COVER, Teresa A. . . . . . (MN) 252
DAVIS, Emmett A. . . . . . (MN) 279
DESIREY, Janice M. . . . . (MN) 295
DITTMANN, Chrisma S. . (MN) 306
DODGE, Christopher N. . (MN) 308
ELFSTRAND, Stephen F. (MN) 342
ELLIOTT, Gwendolyn W. (MN) 344
FARNER, Susan G. . . . . (MN) 365
FERM, Lois R. . . . . (MN) 373
GALLIGAN, Sara A. . . . . (MN) 414
GRIGGS, Cynthia B. . . . . (MN) 470
HAMMARGREN, Betty L. (MN) 493
HEETER, Judith A. . . . . . (MN) 520
HILBER, Leocadia . . . . . (MN) 538
HILL, Constance L. . . . . (MN) 539
JOHNSON, Deborah S. . (MN) 603
LAPENSKY, Barbara A. . (MN) 697
LEACH, Sally A. . . . . (MN) 706
LINEWEAVER, Joe R. . . (MN) 730
LO, Maryanne H. . . . . . . (MN) 735
LUND, Bernard A. . . . . . (MN) 748
MANNING, Mary L. . . . . (MN) 766
MARION, Phyllis C. . . . . (MN) 770
MARKHAM, Scott C. . . . (MN) 771
MCCLASKEY, Marilyn H. (MN) 796
MOORE, Barbara N. . . . . (MN) 858
O'LEARY, Mary E. . . . . . (MN) 920
OSTAZEWSKI, Theodore (MN) 928
PALMER, Joy J. . . . . (MN) 936
PRETZER, Shari G. . . . . (MN) 992
REISNER, Suzanne R. . . (MN) 1021
RINE, Joseph L. . . . . (MN) 1035
SATZER, Patricia A. . . . . (MN) 1084
THORSTENSSON, Edith J. (MN) 1243
WEEKS, Diane M. . . . . . (MN) 1315
WELDON, Barbara J. . . . (MN) 1321
WOLF, Joy G. . . . . (MN) 1360
AMELUNG, Richard C. . . (MO) 19
BAER, Eleanora A. . . . . . (MO) 45
BICK, Barbara K. . . . . . . (MO) 94
BOETTCHER, Joel W. . . (MO) 110
CHUNG, Carolyn . . . . . . (MO) 213
CONNORS, Theresa . . . (MO) 238
CRAIG, Marian D. . . . . . (MO) 254
DEKEN, Jean M. . . . . . . (MO) 288
DEMUTH, Elizabeth J. . . (MO) 291
DOBRUNZ, Sally J. . . . . (MO) 307
FAIR, Norma J. . . . . (MO) 361
FEDDERS, Cynthia S. . . (MO) 367
FOX, Judith A. . . . . (MO) 395
HALLIER, Sara J. . . . . . . (MO) 489
HOHENSTEIN, Margaret L. (MO) 549
HOWELLS, Joyce W. . . . (MO) 565
HYDE, E C. . . . . (MO) 580
KOTAMRAJU, Sarada . . (MO) 673
LAURENSTEIN, Ann G. . (MO) 703

CATALOGING (Cont'd)
Cataloging

LAWS, Janet E. . . . . (MO) 705
MCKEE, Eugenia V. . . . . (MO) 810
MEIZNER, Karen L. . . . . (MO) 822
NYSTROM, Kathleen A. . (MO) 913
OAKES, Frank E. . . . . . . (MO) 913
SHIEH, Monica W. . . . . . (MO) 1129
SHIPLEY, Anne C. . . . . . (MO) 1131
SHIRKY, Martha H. . . . . (MO) 1131
SIMPSON, Leslie T. . . . . (MO) 1142
SLATTERY, Charles E. . . (MO) 1148
TIPSWORD, Thomas N. . (MO) 1246
TOLSON, Stephanie D. . . (MO) 1249
VERBECK, Alison F. . . . . (MO) 1282
VOSS, Kathryn J. . . . . . . (MO) 1289
WALKER, Stephen R. . . . (MO) 1296
CHRESSANTHIS, June D. (MS) 211
HART, Julie C. . . . . (MS) 507
JOHNSON, Max C. . . . . (MS) 607
MOMAN, Orthella P. . . . . (MS) 854
REID, Thomas G. . . . . . . (MS) 1019
RODICH, Nancy A. . . . . . (MS) 1048
SMITH, Rachel H. . . . . . (MS) 1159
WALL, Norma F. . . . . . . (MS) 1297
WHITE, Elaine R. . . . . . . (MS) 1331
WILSON, Ruth W. . . . . . (MS) 1352
BEKKEN, Helen L. . . . . . (MT) 75
FREEMAN, Lucile . . . . . (MT) 401
GRASMICK, Brenda . . . . (MT) 458
HARTMANN, M C. . . . . . (MT) 508
RITTER, Ann L. . . . . (MT) 1036
ABBOTT, Chien N. . . . . . (NC) 1
ABBOTT, Dorothy D. . . . (NC) 1
ABBOTT, Kent H. . . . . . . (NC) 1
ALDRICH, Willie L. . . . . . (NC) 11
ASPINALL, David L. . . . . (NC) 37
BACKMAN, Carroll H. . . (NC) 44
BROWN, Kathleen R. . . . (NC) 145
CADLE, Dean . . . . (NC) 170
CARSTENS, Timothy V. . (NC) 188
CHENG, Chao S. . . . . . . (NC) 206
CLAYTON, Sue N. . . . . . (NC) 220
CLEMONS, Kenneth L. . (NC) 221
FARRIS, Joyce L. . . . . . . (NC) 365
FLOYD, Rebecca M. . . . . (NC) 386
FRAZELLE, Betty . . . . . . (NC) 399
GEBBIE, Janet L. . . . . . . (NC) 424
GLEIM, David E. . . . . . . (NC) 441
GLEIM, Sharon S. . . . . . (NC) 441
GRANDAGE, Karen K. . . (NC) 457
HICKS, Michael . . . . (NC) 537
HIGH, Walter M. . . . . . . (NC) 538
HINSON, Doris M. . . . . . (NC) 543
HUTTON, Jean R. . . . . . (NC) 579
JOHNSTON, Rebecca M. (NC) 610
KAN, Irene E. . . . . (NC) 624
KLEM, Marjorie R. . . . . . (NC) 660
KLINE, Lawrence O. . . . . (NC) 661
LAWTON, Patrecia J. . . . (NC) 705
LEE, Charles D. . . . . (NC) 709
MAYES, Susan E. . . . . . (NC) 789
MCCONNELL, Judith J. . (NC) 797
MCGEACHY, John A. . . (NC) 805
MILLER, Gloria . . . . (NC) 838
MOORE, Maxine B. . . . . (NC) 860
MURCHISON, Margaret B. (NC) 879
SAYE, Terri O. . . . . (NC) 1086
SPENCER, Linda A. . . . . (NC) 1173
STETSON, Keith R. . . . . (NC) 1190
TABORY, Maxim . . . . . . (NC) 1219
TOMLINSON, Charles E. (NC) 1250
TRUMBULL, Jane . . . . . (NC) 1259
WOOD, Kelly S. . . . . (NC) 1364
BLUE, Margaret R. . . . . . (ND) 107
BRKIC, Beverly T. . . . . . (ND) 138
EVENSEN, Sharon L. . . . (ND) 358
NELSON, Colleen M. . . . (ND) 893
NELSON, David N. . . . . . (ND) 893
PEDERSEN, Lila . . . . . . (ND) 954

CATALOGING (Cont'd)
Cataloging

RENICK, Paul R. . . . . . . (ND) 1023
BARRICK, Judy H. . . . . . (NE) 59
BIALAC, Verda H. . . . . . (NE) 93
BOYER, Janice S. . . . . . (NE) 123
FAWCETT, Georgene E. . . (NE) 367
FREAUF, Louis E. . . . . . (NE) 399
GRABE, Lauralee F. . . . . (NE) 455
HERZINGER, Sandra S. . (NE) 534
MEIER, Marjorie A. . . . . . (NE) 821
MURDOCK, Douglas W. . . (NE) 879
OLTMANNS, Judith A. . . (NE) 923
RUBY, Irple P. . . . . (NE) 1065
SCHULZ, Stanley D. . . . (NE) 1102
VAN BAUCOM, Charles . (NE) 1272
BISSETT, Claudia K. . . . (NH) 100
DRUKE-STICKLER, Janet
A. . . . . (NH) 320
HAMILL, Martha L. . . . . (NH) 491
JACOBS, Gloria . . . . . . (NH) 589
KOZIKOWSKI, Derek M. (NH) 674
LE BLANC, Charles A. . . (NH) 708
LIZOTTE, Jeanette S. . . . (NH) 735
RICE, Gerald W. . . . . . . (NH) 1027
RYAN, Clare E. . . . . . . (NH) 1070
STEARNS, Melissa M. . . (NH) 1183
TIERNAN, Linda M. . . . . (NH) 1244
ACKROYD-KELLY, Elaine
S. . . . . (NJ) 4
AUSTIN, Fay A. . . . . . . (NJ) 40
BIELAWSKI, Marvin F. . . (NJ) 95
BULYA, Larissa . . . . . . (NJ) 157
CARLISLE, Scott G. . . . . (NJ) 182
CARNAHAN, Joan A. . . . (NJ) 183
CHAO, Gloria F. . . . . . . (NJ) 201
COE, D W. . . . . (NJ) 226
CONLEY, Gail D. . . . . . (NJ) 236
COPELAND, Alice T. . . . (NJ) 244
CORWIN, Dean W. . . . . (NJ) 248
CRAWFORD, Lynn D. . . (NJ) 257
DILLENSCHNEIDER,
Patricia A. . . . . (NJ) 303
DYKMAN, Elaine K. . . . . (NJ) 331
FARRELL, Mark R. . . . . . (NJ) 365
FERRIBY, Peter G. . . . . . (NJ) 373
GARNER, Linda J. . . . . . (NJ) 419
GARZILLO, Robert R. . . . (NJ) 421
GILLAN, Dennis P. . . . . . (NJ) 435
GODFREY, Florence L. . . (NJ) 442
GREEN, Donald T. . . . . . (NJ) 461
GREENBERG, Hinda F. . (NJ) 463
HALASZ, Etelka B. . . . . . (NJ) 484
HENKEL, Grace E. . . . . . (NJ) 528
HENRY, Mary B. . . . . . . (NJ) 529
HONTZ, M E. . . . . (NJ) 556
HSU, Hsiu H. . . . . (NJ) 567
HUGHES, Kathleen . . . . (NJ) 572
IRGON, Deborah A. . . . . (NJ) 583
IRVINE, James S. . . . . . (NJ) 584
JOB, Amy G. . . . . (NJ) 601
KRUSE, Theodore H. . . . (NJ) 681
LEVEROCK, Lisa A. . . . (NJ) 719
LUXNER, Ann F. . . . . . . (NJ) 750
MACKINTOSH, Pamela J. (NJ) 757
MALAKOFF, Diane L. . . . (NJ) 762
MEYERS, Elsa M. . . . . . (NJ) 831
MICHAL, Judith A. . . . . . (NJ) 832
MOONEY, Jennifer M. . . (NJ) 858
OGONEK, Donna L. . . . . (NJ) 918
PELLETIER, Karen E. . . . (NJ) 955
REINHARDT, Eileen . . . . (NJ) 1021
ROMANKO, Karen A. . . . (NJ) 1052
SANDERS, Mary C. . . . . (NJ) 1080
SANDLER, Gary D. . . . . (NJ) 1081
SCHUELER, Frances S. . (NJ) 1101
SKRAMOUSKY, Mary C. (NJ) 1147
STICKEL, William R. . . . (NJ) 1193
STOUFFER, Isabelle . . . . (NJ) 1198
SUTTON, Robert F. . . . . (NJ) 1211

CATALOGING (Cont'd)
Cataloging

TAORMINA, Anthony P. . . (NJ) 1223
TOMAR, Jeanne . . . . . . (NJ) 1249
TRAFTON, William M. . . (NJ) 1253
VELLUCCI, Sherry L. . . . (NJ) 1282
WANG, Hsi H. . . . . (NJ) 1303
WILEN, Rosamond L. . . . (NJ) 1339
ATKINS, Gene D. . . . . . (NM) 37
CHEN, Laura F. . . . . . . (NM) 205
HSU, Grace S. . . . . (NM) 567
HUMPHREY, Thomas W. (NM) 573
JOURDAIN, Janet M. . . . (NM) 618
KALE, Shirley W. . . . . . (NM) 623
KALER, Dorothy C. . . . . (NM) 623
KRUG, Ruth A. . . . . (NM) 680
LEON, Louise B. . . . . . . (NM) 716
MCGUIRE, Walter J. . . . (NM) 808
MOORER, Jenny R. . . . . (NM) 862
PIERSON, Robert M. . . . (NM) 972
RUCKMAN, Stanley N. . . (NM) 1065
SCHUBERT, Donald F. . . (NM) 1101
SUGNET, Christopher L. . (NM) 1206
DION, Kathleen L. . . . . . (NV) 305
OTERO-BOISVERT, Maria (NV) 930
POLSON, Billie M. . . . . . (NV) 982
AARON, Rina S. . . . . . . (NY) 1
ABLOVE, Gayle J. . . . . . (NY) 2
AKEY, Stephen . . . . (NY) 9
ANDERSON, Birgitta M. . (NY) 21
ARAYA, Rose M. . . . . . . (NY) 30
ARMSTRONG, Ruth C. . . (NY) 32
ARNOLD, Linda A. . . . . (NY) 34
ATKIN, Shifra . . . . (NY) 37
BAKER, Zachary M. . . . . (NY) 50
BARR, Jeffrey A. . . . . . . (NY) 58
BARRETT, John C. . . . . (NY) 59
BARTH, John E. . . . . . . (NY) 61
BERRYMAN, Karen L. . . (NY) 90
BLOHM, Laura A. . . . . . (NY) 106
BOREK, Mary A. . . . . . . (NY) 116
BORRESS, Lewis R. . . . (NY) 117
BOTKIN, Karen R. . . . . . (NY) 118
BRIGHAM, Jeffrey L. . . . (NY) 136
BRISTAH, Pamela J. . . . (NY) 137
BROUSE, Ann G. . . . . . (NY) 141
BURKETT, Donald E. . . : (NY) 161
CASE, Ann M. . . . . (NY) 191
CASSARO, James P. . . . (NY) 193
CHIANG, Nancy . . . . . . (NY) 207
CHITTAMPALLI, Padma S. (NY) 209
CHO-PARK, Jaung J. . . . (NY) 210
CHU, Sylvia . . . . (NY) 213
CHURCH, Virginia K. . . . (NY) 213
CLARE, Richard W. . . . . (NY) 216
CLARKE, D S. . . . . (NY) 218
CLAYPOOL, Richard D. . (NY) 220
COHEN, Hannah V. . . . . (NY) 228
COHEN, Renee G. . . . . . (NY) 229
COOMBS, Ronald L. . . . (NY) 241
CORDING, A C. . . . . . . (NY) 246
CORRSIN, Stephen D. . . (NY) 247
CORSON, Cornelia M. . . (NY) 248
CROFT, Elizabeth G. . . . (NY) 260
CULLEY, Paul T. . . . . . . (NY) 263
DAMON, Shirley J. . . . . (NY) 272
DEE, Camille C. . . . . . . (NY) 286
DEEBRAH, Grace J. . . . (NY) 286
DEMANDY, Claire . . . . . (NY) 291
DESSER, Darrilyn . . . . . (NY) 296
DEUSS, Jean . . . . (NY) 296
DI BIANCO, Phyllis R. . . (NY) 299
DIFEDE, Robert F. . . . . (NY) 302
DORN, Robert J. . . . . . . (NY) 313
DOUGLAS, Jacqueline A. (NY) 314
DOYLE, James J. . . . . . (NY) 317
DUNCAN, Elizabeth C. . . (NY) 325
DUTIKOW, Irene V. . . . . (NY) 329
ENTIN, Paula B. . . . . . . (NY) 351
ETHERIDGE, Virginia . . . (NY) 355

CATALOGING (Cont'd)
Cataloging

EVANS, Ruth A.	(NY)	358
FERNANDEZ, M L.	(NY)	373
FISHER, Maureen C.	(NY)	381
FOSTER, Selma V.	(NY)	392
FRANKLIN, Laurel F.	(NY)	398
GALGAN, Mary N.	(NY)	413
GARRETSON, Henry C.	(NY)	420
GARRETT, Margaret S.	(NY)	420
GAYNOR, Joann T.	(NY)	424
GEE, Ka C.	(NY)	424
GEIBEN, Rodney F.	(NY)	425
GIBBARD, Judith R.	(NY)	431
GICK, Julie	(NY)	432
GINES, Noriko	(NY)	437
GOLDSTEIN, Alicia P.	(NY)	446
GRAVES, Howard E.	(NY)	459
GUZMAN, Diane J.	(NY)	479
HAIMOVSKY, Kira A.	(NY)	484
HALL, Russell W.	(NY)	488
HEARN, Stephen S.	(NY)	518
HELLER, Jacqueline R.	(NY)	524
HICKEY, John T.	(NY)	536
HIGGINBOTHAM, Barbra B.	(NY)	537
HIGGINS, Michael J.	(NY)	538
HIGGINS, Virginia A.	(NY)	538
HILLEGAS, Ferne E.	(NY)	541
HOOGAKKER, David A.	(NY)	556
HSIAO, Shu Y.	(NY)	567
HSU, Karen M.	(NY)	567
HYMAN, Richard J.	(NY)	580
ICE, Diana C.	(NY)	581
IRONS, Florence E.	(NY)	584
JOHNSON, James G.	(NY)	605
JONES, Anne	(NY)	611
JOYCE, Therese	(NY)	618
KASSIN, Abby L.	(NY)	629
KASTNER, Arno A.	(NY)	629
KEEFER, Ethel A.	(NY)	634
KELLER, Katarina S.	(NY)	635
KELLOGG, Marya S.	(NY)	637
KEMPE, Deborah A.	(NY)	639
KERR, Virginia M.	(NY)	644
KETCHAM, Susan E.	(NY)	645
KIBBE, Lucena J.	(NY)	646
KIM, Chung N.	(NY)	648
KING, Esther	(NY)	651
KING, Maryde F.	(NY)	651
KINNEY, Daniel W.	(NY)	653
KLATT, Wilma F.	(NY)	658
KONOVALOFF, Maria S.	(NY)	670
KOROLIK, Margarita N.	(NY)	672
KOUO, Lily W.	(NY)	673
LA SORTE, Antonia J.	(NY)	700
LEW, Susan	(NY)	722
LEWIS, Gillian H.	(NY)	723
LIE, David W.	(NY)	725
LINCOLN, Betty W.	(NY)	728
LOLLIS, Martha J.	(NY)	738
LUCKER, Amy E.	(NY)	746
MACINICK, James W.	(NY)	755
MACK, Theodore D.	(NY)	756
MACKSEY, Susan A.	(NY)	757
MARGOLIES, Alan	(NY)	770
MARKER, Rhonda J.	(NY)	771
MARKOWITZ, Lois	(NY)	771
MARTIN, Lyn M.	(NY)	777
MASTRANGELO, Paul J.	(NY)	783
MAYER, Mary C.	(NY)	789
MAYO, Hope	(NY)	790
MCCOMBS, Gillian M.	(NY)	797
MCGRATH, Ellen T.	(NY)	807
MEYERS, Charles	(NY)	830
MOONEY, Martha T.	(NY)	858
MOTIHAR, Kamla	(NY)	872
MULIA, Gusti	(NY)	876
NARDUCCI, Frances	(NY)	888
NAVRATIL, Jean	(NY)	890

NELSON, Robert J.	(NY)	895
NELSON, Winifred S.	(NY)	895
NESTA, Frederick N.	(NY)	896
NEUMEISTER, Susan M.	(NY)	897
NICHOLS-RANDALL, Barbara L.	(NY)	902
NICKERSON, Donna L.	(NY)	902
O'DONNELL, Maryann T.	(NY)	917
ONSI, Patricia W.	(NY)	924
PAGELS, Helen H.	(NY)	934
PARRIS, Angela P.	(NY)	944
PASTERNACK, Marcia A.	(NY)	946
PENICH, Sonia S.	(NY)	956
PENNELL, Peggy P.	(NY)	957
PERONE, Karen L.	(NY)	959
PERRY, Paula J.	(NY)	960
PINSLEY, Lauren J.	(NY)	975
PIZER, Elizabeth F.	(NY)	977
PLATT, Mary L.	(NY)	977
POPOVIC, Tanya V.	(NY)	983
PRAGER, George A.	(NY)	989
QUINN, Sharon E.	(NY)	1000
RACHOW, Louis A.	(NY)	1001
RAHN, Suzanne M.	(NY)	1003
RAJEC, Elizabeth M.	(NY)	1004
RAME, Mary E.	(NY)	1005
RAPPELT, John F.	(NY)	1008
REEPMEYER, Marie C.	(NY)	1016
REID, Richard C.	(NY)	1019
REINSTEIN, Diana J.	(NY)	1021
RENTSCHLER, Cathy	(NY)	1023
RESCIGNO, Dolores S.	(NY)	1024
ROGERS, Jonathan B.	(NY)	1049
ROSIGNOLO, Beverly A.	(NY)	1057
ROUGEUX, Debora A.	(NY)	1061
ROY, Diptimoy	(NY)	1063
SALVAGE, Barbara A.	(NY)	1078
SCARANO, Lisa C.	(NY)	1087
SCOFIELD, Andrea	(NY)	1106
SENTZ, Lilli	(NY)	1115
SERCAN, Cecilia S.	(NY)	1116
SERCHUK, Barnett	(NY)	1116
SHAFFER, Kay L.	(NY)	1119
SHIH, Diana	(NY)	1130
SIMPSON, Charles W.	(NY)	1141
SJOGREN, Mack D.	(NY)	1145
SLOCUM, Robert B.	(NY)	1150
SMITH, Annie J.	(NY)	1152
SOKOLOWSKI, Denise G.	(NY)	1166
SPORE, Stuart	(NY)	1175
STAFFORD, Catherine H.	(NY)	1178
STALKER, Dianne S.	(NY)	1178
STEVENS, Jane E.	(NY)	1190
STRANC, Mary C.	(NY)	1200
SWETMAN, Barbara E.	(NY)	1216
SWORDS, Susan	(NY)	1217
TAN, Wendy W.	(NY)	1222
TISDALE, Barbara	(NY)	1247
TISHLER, Amnon	(NY)	1247
TRAVERS, Jane E.	(NY)	1254
TURIEL, David	(NY)	1263
VAN RIPER, Joy C.	(NY)	1277
VOLLONO, Millicent D.	(NY)	1288
WASYLENKO, Lydia W.	(NY)	1308
WAWRO, Wanda T.	(NY)	1311
WEAS, Andrea T.	(NY)	1311
WEINBERG, Valerie A.	(NY)	1318
WELLS, Phyllis L.	(NY)	1323
WERNER, Edward K.	(NY)	1324
WHITMAN, Ruth M.	(NY)	1333
WILD, Judith W.	(NY)	1338
WILLER, Kenneth H.	(NY)	1341
WILLIAMS, Richard C.	(NY)	1346
WILSON, Marijo S.	(NY)	1352
WING, Judith G.	(NY)	1354
WOLF, Marion	(NY)	1360
WOLOZIN, Sara	(NY)	1362
WULFING, Joyce	(NY)	1374

CATALOGING (Cont'd)
Cataloging

ABRAMS, Roger E. ..... (OH) 3
BAILEY, Lois E. .... (OH) 46
BAKER, Carol J. ...... (OH) 48
BAKER, Narcissa L. .... (OH) 49
BALCAS, Georgianne ... (OH) 50
BERG, Richard R. .... (OH) 84
BERRINGER, Virginia M. (OH) 90
BEYNEN, Gijsbertus K. ... (OH) 93
BITTER, Diane S. ...... (OH) 100
BRITTON, Constance J. . (OH) 137
BROWN, Stephen P. .... (OH) 147
BROWNELL, Barbara A. (OH) 148
CALL, J R. .... (OH) 173
CHANG, Tony H. ...... (OH) 201
COHEN, Steven J. ..... (OH) 229
CONNELL, Christopher J. (OH) 237
CONNERS, Margaret S. . (OH) 237
DAVIS, Carol C. .... (OH) 277
DISTEFANO, Marianne .. (OH) 305
DONNELLY, Kathleen ... (OH) 311
ENGLANDER, Marlene S. (OH) 349
ERNST, Gordon E. ..... (OH) 353
FOSTER, Julia A. ...... (OH) 392
GRABENSTATTER,
    Christine N. .... (OH) 455
HEARD, Jeffrey L. ..... (OH) 518
JENKINS, Fred W. ..... (OH) 597
JONES, Judykay ...... (OH) 613
JUNEJA, Derry C. ...... (OH) 620
KIE, Kathleen M. .... (OH) 646
KNASIAK, Theresa J. .... (OH) 663
KRAMER, Sally J. ..... (OH) 675
KRIEGER, Michael T. .... (OH) 678
KRUMM, Carol R. ...... (OH) 680
LANTZ, Elizabeth A. .... (OH) 697
LEE, Sooncha A. ...... (OH) 711
LONG, Melanie C. ..... (OH) 739
LOVELAND, Catherine R. (OH) 743
LUDY, Lorene E. ...... (OH) 747
LUTTRELL, Jeffrey R. .. (OH) 750
MCCROSKY, Janet E. ... (OH) 800
MILLER, David A. ...... (OH) 836
MOHLER, Dorothy C. .... (OH) 852
MOORE, Maxwell J. ..... (OH) 860
MURPHY, James L. ..... (OH) 880
NAM, Wonki K. .... (OH) 887
OBERC, Susanne F. ..... (OH) 913
OBERLE, Holly E. ...... (OH) 914
O'BRIEN, Betty A. ...... (OH) 914
OSTERFIELD, George T. (OH) 928
PATTON, Glenn E. ..... (OH) 949
PERRY, Rebecca A. .... (OH) 960
PETTY, Sue W. .... (OH) 965
POST, Phyllis C. .... (OH) 986
PRONEVITZ, Gregory .. (OH) 995
PURSCH, Lenore D. ..... (OH) 998
RHOADES, Nancy L. ... (OH) 1025
RICHARDSON, Katherine
    A. .... (OH) 1029
RICHMOND, Phyllis A. .. (OH) 1030
ROBSON, Timothy D. ... (OH) 1045
ROGERS, Sally A. ..... (OH) 1050
ROHMILLER, Thomas D. (OH) 1051
SALT, Elizabeth A. ..... (OH) 1077
SAMPLES, Judith L. .... (OH) 1078
SCHAEFGEN, Susan M. . (OH) 1089
SCHROEDER, Donna L. . (OH) 1100
SCOTT, Sharon A. ..... (OH) 1108
SEDLCOK, Barbara J. .. (OH) 1111
SHELLENBARGER, Linda
    K. .... (OH) 1126
SIMPSON, Alice H. .... (OH) 1141
SLOVASKY, Stephen ... (OH) 1150
STEVENS, Donna H. ... (OH) 1190
STRALEY, Dona S. .... (OH) 1200
TURNER, Freya A. ...... (CH) 1264
VIZINE-GOETZ, Diane .. (OH) 1286
WAGAR, Elsa A. .... (OH) 1290

CATALOGING (Cont'd)
Cataloging

WHITEHEAD, Beatrice A. (OH) 1332
BOOTENHOFF, Rebecca
    J. .... (OK) 116
CAROL, Barbara B. .... (OK) 184
COOPER, Sylvia J. ..... (OK) 243
FAW, Marc T. .... (OK) 366
HACKER, Connie J. .... (OK) 481
HUST, Carolyn R. ...... (OK) 578
JONES, Charles E. ..... (OK) 611
KIRKBRIDE, Rebecca M. (OK) 654
LARSEN, Nancy E. .... (OK) 698
NORTON, Paula T. .... (OK) 910
RELPH, Martha H. ..... (OK) 1022
ROBBINS, Louise S. ... (OK) 1039
RYLANDER, Carolyn S. . (OK) 1072
SANDERS, Melodie .... (OK) 1080
WRIGHT, Patricia Y. .... (OK) 1372
ALLEN, Alice J. .... (OR) 14
BENSON, Mary M. ..... (OR) 83
BOES, Rachel M. ..... (OR) 110
BROOKS, Harry F. ..... (OR) 140
BROWN, Patricia L. .... (OR) 146
BURKHOLDER, Sue A. . (OR) 161
BURNS, Carol J. ...... (OR) 162
CLELAND, Mary V. .... (OR) 220
DENOBLE, Augustine D. . (OR) 293
FARRIER, Kathy D. .... (OR) 365
GRIFFIN, Karen D. .... (OR) 468
HOTELLING, Katsuko T. . (OR) 562
PURCELL, V N. .... (OR) 998
ROBERTSON, Howard W. (OR) 1042
SARGENT, Phyllis M. ... (OR) 1083
SCHIWEK, Joseph A. ... (OR) 1093
SMITH, Terry M. ...... (OR) 1161
SPRAUER, Linda J. ..... (OR) 1176
TAMBLYN, Eldon W. ... (OR) 1221
WANG, Hsiao G. ...... (OR) 1303
WILLIAMS, Janet L. .... (OR) 1344
AL SADAT, Amira A. ... (PA) 17
ANDRICK, Annita A. ... (PA) 27
ANTOS, Brian F. ...... (PA) 29
ATTIG, John C. .... (PA) 38
BOYLAN, Lorena A. .... (PA) 123
BOYTINCK, Paul ...... (PA) 124
BRADLEY, James S. ... (PA) 126
BRUBAKER, Dale L. ... (PA) 149
BRUSH, Cassandra .... (PA) 151
BRYSON, Susan A. .... (PA) 152
BUCK, Patricia K. ..... (PA) 154
BURKHARD, Polly S. ... (PA) 161
CANTRALL, Rebecca J. . (PA) 179
CHANG, Shirley L. ..... (PA) 201
CULBERTSON, Judith D. (PA) 263
DAILY, Jay E. .... (PA) 270
DUCK, Patricia M. ..... (PA) 322
EMERICK, Kenneth F. .. (PA) 347
EMERICK, Michael J. ... (PA) 347
ENGLERT, Mary A. .... (PA) 350
ERDREICH, Gina B. .... (PA) 352
EVES, Judith A. ...... (PA) 359
FERRAINOLO, John J. ... (PA) 373
FOGAL, Annabel E. .... (PA) 387
FREEDMAN, Phyllis D. ... (PA) 400
FU, Clare S. .... (PA) 407
FULLER, Elizabeth E. ... (PA) 408
FUSCO, Marilyn A. ..... (PA) 410
GALLAGHER, Eileen W. . (PA) 414
GEORGE, Rachel ...... (PA) 428
GLASS, Catherine C. ... (PA) 440
GOLDSTAUB, Curt S. .. (PA) 446
GREENE, Nancy S. .... (PA) 464
GRIFFITHS, June B. ..... (PA) 469
GRZESIAK, Margaret M. (PA) 475
HINTON, Frances ...... (PA) 543
HLUHANY, Patricia .... (PA) 544
HODGE, Margaret T. ... (PA) 546
HOLSTON, Kim R. ..... (PA) 554
HOMICK, Elaine .... (PA) 555

CATALOGING (Cont'd)
Cataloging

HORN, Janice H.	(PA)	559
HURLEY, Doreen S.	(PA)	577
JABLONOWSKI, Mary D.	(PA)	586
JACOBY, Beth E.	(PA)	590
JAMISON, Carolyn C.	(PA)	593
JONES, Debra A.	(PA)	612
JONES, M C.	(PA)	614
KELLERMAN, Lydia S.	(PA)	636
KNEIL, Gertrude M.	(PA)	664
KOKOLUS, Cait C.	(PA)	669
KREDEL, Stephen F.	(PA)	677
KROLL, Anna L.	(PA)	679
LAZARUS, Karin	(PA)	706
LEIBOWITZ, Faye R.	(PA)	713
LIEM, Frieda	(PA)	726
LINDSAY, Ann M.	(PA)	729
LOTLIKAR, Sarojini D.	(PA)	742
LUNDY, M W.	(PA)	748
MACEY, John F.	(PA)	755
MARTIN, Shelby A.	(PA)	778
MAST, Joanne	(PA)	782
MCCAWLEY, Christina W.	(PA)	795
MCDONNELL, Janice M.	(PA)	803
MIKITA, Elizabeth G.	(PA)	834
MILLER, Marjorie M.	(PA)	840
MINES, Denise C.	(PA)	846
MONTOYA, Leopoldo	(PA)	856
MORSE, Alfred W.	(PA)	869
MOUNTS, Earl L.	(PA)	873
NEITZ, Cordelia M.	(PA)	892
NOLF, Marsha L.	(PA)	908
OSTRUM, Roxane M.	(PA)	929
PAKALA, Denise M.	(PA)	935
PEASE, Elaine K.	(PA)	953
PENNELL, Charles	(PA)	957
PHALAN, Mary A.	(PA)	967
PIECHNICK, Katarzyna M.	(PA)	971
POE, Terrence C.	(PA)	979
RAHKONEN, Carl J.	(PA)	1003
RICHARDSON, Joy A.	(PA)	1029
ROBBINS, Stephen L.	(PA)	1039
ROBERTSON, Robert B.	(PA)	1042
ROEDELL, Ray F.	(PA)	1048
ROGERS, Linda S.	(PA)	1049
ROHDY, Margaret A.	(PA)	1050
ROSE, Dianne E.	(PA)	1054
SALINGER, Florence A.	(PA)	1076
SAUNDERS, Allene W.	(PA)	1084
SHIVELY, Daniel C.	(PA)	1132
SHULENBERGER, Catherine T.	(PA)	1133
SPINNEY, Molly P.	(PA)	1175
STANLEY, Nancy M.	(PA)	1180
TEOLIS, Marilyn G.	(PA)	1231
TRUESDELL, Eugenia R.	(PA)	1259
TRUMPLER, Elisabeth	(PA)	1259
VAUGHAN-STERLING, Judith A.	(PA)	1280
WOO, Lisa C.	(PA)	1363
ZAGON, Eileen	(PA)	1385
ZEAGER, Lloyd	(PA)	1387
ALSTON, Jane C.	(PR)	18
BARRERAS, Dolly M.	(PR)	59
BERNAL-ROSA, Emilia	(PR)	88
CASAS DE FAUNCE, Maria	(PR)	191
CONCEPCION, Luis	(PR)	235
DE DEL VALLE, Heida C.	(PR)	286
DELGADO-NUNEZ, Milton	(PR)	289
GONZALEZ-VELEZ, Isaura	(PR)	448
LOPEZ, Elsa M.	(PR)	741
MARTINEZ-NAZARIO, Ronaldo	(PR)	779
MCCARTHY, Carmen H.	(PR)	794
MEJILL-VEGA, Gregorio	(PR)	822
PEREZ, Sarai	(PR)	958
RODRIGUEZ, Ketty	(PR)	1048
TORRES-TAPI, Manual A.	(PR)	1251

CATALOGING (Cont'd)
Cataloging

VALENTIN-MARTY, Jeannette	(PR)	1271
BELL, Judith H.	(RI)	77
BRYAN, Susan M.	(RI)	152
COULOMBE, Dominique C.	(RI)	250
GIEBLER, Albert C.	(RI)	432
HALL, Ann H.	(RI)	487
HRYCIW-WING, Carol A.	(RI)	566
LIGHT, Karen M.	(RI)	726
LISTOVITCH, Denise A.	(RI)	733
MEHR, Joseph O.	(RI)	821
SIBULKIN, Lucille	(RI)	1135
STONE, Howard P.	(RI)	1197
VOCINO, Michael C.	(RI)	1286
WATERS, Shirley V.	(RI)	1309
ALLEN, Debra C.	(SC)	14
BLAIR, Sharon K.	(SC)	103
BOONE, Shirley W.	(SC)	115
BOWLES, David M.	(SC)	121
CROSS, Mary R.	(SC)	260
ELLIS, Janet L.	(SC)	344
GEOGHEGAN, Doris J.	(SC)	427
GILBERT, Sybil M.	(SC)	434
GISSENDANNER, Cassandra S.	(SC)	438
GORDON, Clara B.	(SC)	451
HUYGEN, Eva	(SC)	580
LOWRIMORE, R T.	(SC)	745
MAZUR, Marjorie A.	(SC)	791
NEVILLE, Robert F.	(SC)	898
OLINGER, Elizabeth B.	(SC)	920
OSBALDISTON, Diana M.	(SC)	927
RUST, Roxy J.	(SC)	1070
SABINE, Davida M.	(SC)	1072
SLIFE, Joye D.	(SC)	1149
SMALLS, Mary L.	(SC)	1151
THOMAS, Julie L.	(SC)	1237
TOOMEY, Alice F.	(SC)	1251
CRANMER, Donna C.	(SD)	255
DAGANAAR, Mark L.	(SD)	269
DEAN, Leann F.	(SD)	283
EDELEN, Joseph R.	(SD)	335
HAGEMEIER, Deborah A.	(SD)	483
JONES, Dora A.	(SD)	612
LEGET, Max	(SD)	712
ABOUSHAMA, Mary F.	(TN)	2
BAKER, Bonnie U.	(TN)	48
BASKETT, D A.	(TN)	63
BEHRENS, Elizabeth A.	(TN)	75
BENGTSON, Betty G.	(TN)	80
BENNETT, Peg E.	(TN)	82
BEST, Reba A.	(TN)	92
BRANTIGAN-STOWELL, Martha J.	(TN)	129
BULL, Margaret J.	(TN)	156
BUNTING, Anne C.	(TN)	157
BURKHEART, Hilda S.	(TN)	161
CO, Francisca	(TN)	224
CONVERY, Sukhont K.	(TN)	239
COOKE, Anna L.	(TN)	240
DYER, Barbara M.	(TN)	330
FANSLOW, Malinda C.	(TN)	363
GLAUS, Roberta I.	(TN)	440
GRACE, Loranne J.	(TN)	455
GRADY, Agnes M.	(TN)	455
HALE, Relda D.	(TN)	485
HAMLIN, Lisa K.	(TN)	493
LASATER, Mary C.	(TN)	700
LEVINE, Fay E.	(TN)	720
MABBOTT, Deborah D.	(TN)	753
MCDONALD, Ethel Q.	(TN)	802
MCMAHAN, Elnor W.	(TN)	814
NOONAN, Patricia K.	(TN)	908
PENNINGTON, Melanie L.	(TN)	957
PERRY, Myrna G.	(TN)	960
PRESLAR, M G.	(TN)	991
RIEKE, Judith L.	(TN)	1033
ROBERTSON, Sally A.	(TN)	1042

CATALOGING (Cont'd)
Cataloging

SMITH, Philip M. . . . . . . (TN) 1159
STRICKLER, Candice S. . (TN) 1202
WANG, Hueychyi V. . . . . (TN) 1303
WUJCIK, Dennis S. . . . . (TN) 1374
ADDISON, Jane G. . . . . (TX) 6
ALEXANDER, Shirley B. . (TX) 12
ANDREWS, Virginia L. . . (TX) 27
AYRES, Edwin M. . . . . . (TX) 43
BABER, Elizabeth A. . . . . (TX) 43
BAKER, Nettie L. . . . . . . (TX) 49
BALSAM, Frances G. . . . (TX) 53
BLAYLOCK, James C. . . (TX) 105
BRADBERRY, Anna L. . . (TX) 125
BRAUTIGAM, Patsy R. . . (TX) 130
BREWSTER, Olive N. . . . (TX) 134
BURKS, Paula . . . . (TX) 161
BURLINGHAM, Merry L. (TX) 161
BYRNE, Jeanne M. . . . . (TX) 169
BYROM, Jeanne . . . . . . (TX) 170
CLAER, Joycelyn H. . . . . (TX) 215
CLEE, June E. . . . . (TX) 220
COKINOS, Elizabeth G. . (TX) 229
COOKSEY, Martha L. . . . (TX) 241
COPELAND, David R. . . (TX) 244
DAVIS, Mary F. . . . . (TX) 280
DAVIS, Sara . . . . . . (TX) 281
DUNCAN, Lucy E. . . . . . (TX) 325
EWALT, Rosalind H. . . . (TX) 359
FACKLER, Naomi P. . . . (TX) 360
FITE, Vicki A. . . . . (TX) 382
FORD, Margaret C. . . . . (TX) 389
FRANKSON, Marie S. . . (TX) 398
GONZALEZ, Sharon M. . (TX) 448
GROSS, Sally L. . . . . . . (TX) 472
HALL, John D. . . . . (TX) 488
HALVERSON, Jacquelyn
A. . . . . (TX) 490
HARLOW, Sally S. . . . . . (TX) 502
HELFER, Robert S. . . . . (TX) 523
HEMPEL, Ruth M. . . . . . (TX) 525
HICKEY, Lady J. . . . . . . (TX) 536
HOGAN, Sarah T. . . . . . (TX) 549
HOLLOWAY, Geraldine B. (TX) 552
HOOD, Elizabeth . . . . . . (TX) 556
HOOD, Sandra D. . . . . . (TX) 556
HOPKINS, Joyce A. . . . . (TX) 558
HOPPER, Lorraine E. . . . (TX) 558
HOWELL, Gladys M. . . . (TX) 565
HUSTON, Susan S. . . . . (TX) 578
INKS, Cordelia R. . . . . . (TX) 583
JOHANSEN, Priscilla P. . (TX) 601
KACENA, Carolyn . . . . . (TX) 621
KELLOUGH, Patrick H. . . (TX) 637
KENDRICK, Susan . . . . . (TX) 640
KIMZEY, Ann C. . . . . . . (TX) 649
KLEPPER, Bobbie J. . . . (TX) 660
LATTIMORE, Clare I. . . . (TX) 702
LEAHY, Sheila A. . . . . . (TX) 707
LUIKART, Nancy B. . . . . (TX) 747
LUTZ, Linda A. . . . . (TX) 750
MACBETH, Helen L. . . . (TX) 754
MASON, Timothy D. . . . . (TX) 781
MATHIS, Margaret H. . . . (TX) 784
MAULDIN, Lou A. . . . . . (TX) 787
MCLENNA, D S. . . . . . . (TX) 814
MIRANDA, Cecilia . . . . . (TX) 847
MOSS, Charmagne L. . . (TX) 872
MUCKLEROY, Sue A. . . (TX) 875
MURRAY, Kathleen R. . . (TX) 882
NOBLE, Ann A. . . . . (TX) 906
PAYNE, Leila M. . . . . . . (TX) 951
PETERS, Mary N. . . . . . (TX) 962
PROKESH, Jane . . . . . . (TX) 995
RAMSEY, Donna E. . . . . (TX) 1005
RANDALL, Laura H. . . . . (TX) 1006
RASCHE, Richard R. . . . (TX) 1008
RICKLEFS, Dale L. . . . . (TX) 1032
ROBERTS, Glenda S. . . (TX) 1040

CATALOGING (Cont'd)
Cataloging

RUSSELL, Barbara J. . . . (TX) 1068
SASSEN, Catherine J. . . (TX) 1083
SCHOOLFIELD, Dudley B. (TX) 1098
SIVARAM, Swaraj L. . . . (TX) 1144
SNODGRASS, Wilson D. (TX) 1163
SPARKMAN, Glenda K. . (TX) 1171
SPOEDE, Mary H. . . . . . (TX) 1175
SPRUG, Joseph W. . . . . (TX) 1176
STAMELOS, Ellen A. . . . (TX) 1179
STUBBLEFIELD, J G. . . (TX) 1204
SZARKA, Tamara J. . . . . (TX) 1218
TEOH, George M. . . . . . (TX) 1231
THOMAS, Page A. . . . . . (TX) 1238
THOMPSON, Christine E. (TX) 1239
TODD, Leslie N. . . . . . . (TX) 1248
TOURAINE, Linda S. . . . (TX) 1252
TURNER, Frank L. . . . . . (TX) 1264
UMOH, Linda K. . . . . . . (TX) 1268
WALDEN, Millicent F. . . . (TX) 1294
WALKER, Bonnie M. . . . (TX) 1295
WAYLAND, Sharon L. . . (TX) 1311
WHITE, Douglas A. . . . . (TX) 1330
WHITE, Lely K. . . . . (TX) 1331
WILBUR, Sharon F. . . . . (TX) 1338
WOLFE, Carl F. . . . . (TX) 1360
YOUNG, J A. . . . . (TX) 1382
YOUNG, Marjie D. . . . . . (TX) 1382
CASADY, Richard L. . . . (UT) 191
CLEMENT, Charles R. . . (UT) 221
DOWNEY REIDA, Linda K. (UT) 316
GOFORTH, Allene M. . . . (UT) 444
JOHNSON, Jeffery O. . . (UT) 606
NIELSON, Paula I. . . . . . (UT) 903
PATTERSON, Myron B. . (UT) 948
REED, Vernon M. . . . . . (UT) 1015
SHIELDS, Dorthy M. . . . (UT) 1130
SWENSEN, Dale S. . . . . (UT) 1215
WOOD, Steven R. . . . . . (UT) 1365
YANG, Basil P. . . . . (UT) 1377
BADERTSCHER, David A. (VA) 44
BAER, Eberhard A. . . . . (VA) 44
BECKER, Charlotte B. . . (VA) 72
BERGELT, Robert L. . . . (VA) 85
BERNE, Beth . . . . (VA) 88
BISSETT, John P. . . . . . (VA) 100
BLUE, Kathryn J. . . . . . . (VA) 107
BRAUN, Mina H. . . . . . . (VA) 129
BROWN, David C. . . . . . (VA) 143
BRUNER, Linda J. . . . . . (VA) 150
BUCCO, Louise F. . . . . . (VA) 153
CLAYMAN, Ida H. . . . . . (VA) 220
COLLINS, Mitzi L. . . . . . (VA) 233
COLTON, Norma W. . . . . (VA) 234
COMPARIN, Ida . . . . . . (VA) 235
COOK, Charlaine C. . . . . (VA) 239
COSGROVE-DAVIES, Lisa
A. . . . . (VA) 248
DANFORD, Robert E. . . . (VA) 272
DUKE, John K. . . . . (VA) 324
DUNAWAY, Carolyn D. . (VA) 325
EGERTSON, Yvonne L. . (VA) 339
GLENNON, Irene F. . . . . (VA) 441
HALL, Bonlyn G. . . . . . . (VA) 487
HANLON, Gloria L. . . . . . (VA) 496
HASKELL, Mary B. . . . . . (VA) 510
HILL, Nancy A. . . . . (VA) 540
KANE, Astor V. . . . . (VA) 624
KOUTNIK, Charles J. . . . (VA) 673
LAINE, Rebecca R. . . . . (VA) 688
LEE, Carl R. . . . . (VA) 709
LESSER, Barbara . . . . . (VA) 718
LINN, Cynthia S. . . . . . . (VA) 731
LIU, Albert C. . . . . (VA) 734
LUH, Lydia Y. . . . . (VA) 747
MACLEOD, James M. . . (VA) 757
MATTIS, George E. . . . . (VA) 786
MCLAUGHLIN, Elaine C. (VA) 813
MORGAN, Robert C. . . . (VA) 864

CATALOGING (Cont'd)
Cataloging

MORRISON, Jane B. . . . (VA) 868
NORSTEDT, Marilyn L. . . (VA) 909
OBRIST, Cynthia W. . . . (VA) 915
OWEN, Karen V. . . . . . . (VA) 931
POLLARD, Joan B. . . . . (VA) 981
SADOWSKI, Frank E. . . . (VA) 1074
SCHLAG, Gretchen A. . . (VA) 1093
SCHWARTZ, Marla J. . . (VA) 1105
SCOTT, Mona L. . . . . . . (VA) 1107
SEAMANS, Nancy H. . . . (VA) 1109
SLEEMAN, Allison M. . . . (VA) 1148
STURGIS, Marylee C. . . (VA) 1205
SUMMERS, Kathy B. . . . (VA) 1209
SWICEGOOD, Mary R. . . (VA) 1216
THOMASON, Dorothy G. (VA) 1238
THOMPSON, Connie B. . (VA) 1239
TYSINGER, Barbara R. . . (VA) 1267
WEEKS, Linda F. . . . . . . (VA) 1315
WHYTE, Sean . . . . (VA) 1335
WILLIAMS, Lila E. . . . . . (VA) 1344
WINFREE, Waverly K. . . (VA) 1354
WOODWARD, Elaine H. . . (VA) 1368
DICENSO, Jacquelyn C. . (VT) 300
ECKERT, Sharon S. . . . . (VT) 335
EVANS, Nancy I. . . . . . . (VT) 357
LINDBERG, Sandra . . . . (VT) 728
MCCULLOUGH, Doreen J. (VT) 801
POPECKI, Jeanne M. . . . (VT) 983
SHERMAN, Jacob R. . . . (VT) 1128
SWIFT, Esther M. . . . . . . (VT) 1216
ANDERSON, Christine M. (WA) 22
AROKSAAR, Richard D. . (WA) 34
BOSLEY, Dana L. . . . . . (WA) 117
CARR, Carol L. . . . . (WA) 185
CHADWICK, Leroy D. . . (WA) 197
DANIEL, Eunice L. . . . . (WA) 272
DEBUSE, Judith S. . . . . . (WA) 285
DECOSTER, Barbara L. . (WA) 286
GARRETSON, Laurie J. . (WA) 420
HAGAN, Dalia L. . . . . . . (WA) 482
HAMMOCK, Janice D. . . (WA) 493
HILDEBRANDT, Darlene
    M. . . . . (WA) 538
HOLLAND, Helen K. . . . . (WA) 550
KOPP, Carol S. . . . . (WA) 671
MAHONEY, Laura E. . . . (WA) 761
PAINTER, Agnes E. . . . . (WA) 935
SHERMAN-PETERSON,
    Ronald A. . . . . (WA) 1128
STORDAHL, Beth A. . . . (WA) 1198
SUGGS, John K. . . . . . . (WA) 1206
VAN MASON, Patricia M. (WA) 1276
WILSON, Anthony M. . . . (WA) 1349
WOOD-LIM, Eileen K. . . . (WA) 1366
WYNN, Debra D. . . . . . . (WA) 1375
YONGMAN, Zhang . . . . (WA) 1380
BOLL, John J. . . . . (WI) 112
BUGHER, Kathryn M. . . . (WI) 155
CLARK, Margaret E. . . . . (WI) 217
CORBLY, James E. . . . . (WI) 245
EVANS, Russel C. . . . . . (WI) 358
GENIN, M S. . . . . (WI) 427
HSIEH-YEE, Ingrid P. . . . (WI) 567
JOBELIUS, Nancy L. . . . (WI) 601
KALVONJIAN, Araxie . . . (WI) 623
KINZER, Ferdinelle M. . . (WI) 653
KIRKALI, Meral . . . . (WI) 654
KLAUSMEIER, Arno M. . (WI) 658
KRCHMAR, Sandra L. . . (WI) 677
KREINUS, Anthony A. . . (WI) 677
MILLER, Julia E. . . . . . . (WI) 839
PARSON, Karen L. . . . . . (WI) 944
PAUL, Patricia J. . . . . . . (WI) 949
PAYSON, Evelyn H. . . . . (WI) 951
PINGEL, Carol J. . . . . . . (WI) 974
POPESCU, Constantin C. (WI) 983
REEB, Richard C. . . . . . (WI) 1014
ROOZEN, Nancy L. . . . . (WI) 1054

CATALOGING (Cont'd)
Cataloging

SCHARFENBERG, George
    E. . . . . (WI) 1090
SCHMITT, Madelaine M. (WI) 1096
STRUPP, Sybil A. . . . . . (WI) 1203
THOMPSON, Glenn J. . . (WI) 1239
TIMMERS, Debra A. . . . . (WI) 1246
TURNER, Judith C. . . . . (WI) 1264
YOUNGER, Jennifer A. . . (WI) 1383
BARNES, Jean S. . . . . . (WV) 57
HUMPHRIES, Joy D. . . . (WV) 574
LANGER, Frank A. . . . . . (WV) 695
THACKER, Timothy M. . . (WV) 1233
CORS, Paul B. . . . . (WY) 248
EMERSON, Tamsen L. . . (WY) 347
HOFF, Vickie J. . . . . (WY) 547
KALABUS, Robert L. . . . (WY) 622
MENDOZA, Anthanett C. (WY) 824
BOULTBEE, Paul G. . . . . (AB) 119
BRUCE, Robert D. . . . . . (AB) 149
DEGINNUS, Roxie . . . . . (AB) 287
DWORACZEK, Marian . . (AB) 330
FELL, Anthony M. . . . . . (AB) 370
HAU, Edward T. . . . . (AB) 512
HOGAN, Kathleen M. . . . (AB) 549
HOWE, Ernest A. . . . . . . (AB) 565
JONES, Winstan M. . . . . (AB) 615
JORDAN, Peter A. . . . . . (AB) 616
KUJANSUU, Asko J. . . . (AB) 683
LASKOWSKI, Seno . . . . (AB) 700
LEESMENT, Helgi . . . . . (AB) 712
MATHEZER, Pauline B. . (AB) 784
OLSON, Hope A. . . . . . . (AB) 922
SMITHERS, Anne B. . . . (AB) 1162
STARR, Jane E. . . . . (AB) 1182
TRAICHEL, Rudolf D. . . . (AB) 1253
DEON, Judy S. . . . . (BC) 293
ELROD, J M. . . . . (BC) 346
FERJUC, Joan A. . . . . . . (BC) 372
FIELD, Kenneth C. . . . . . (BC) 375
MURPHY, Joyce . . . . . . (BC) 880
PLETT, Katherine . . . . . (BC) 978
SALMOND, Margaret A. . (BC) 1077
TROWSDALE, Robert G. (BC) 1258
DELONG, Linwood R. . . . (MB) 290
DIVAY, Gabriele . . . . (MB) 306
EMOND, Lucille I. . . . . . . (MB) 348
JONES, June D. . . . . (MB) 613
NICHOLLS, Pat . . . . (MB) 901
SMITH, John R. . . . . (MB) 1156
DIONNE, Charlotte A. . . . (NB) 305
GAUTHIER, Rose M. . . . (NB) 423
ROSEVEAR, E C. . . . . . (NB) 1057
RUSSELL, Sharon A. . . . (NB) 1069
DENNIS, Christopher J. . (NF) 292
MORGAN, Pamela S. . . . (NF) 864
GLENISTER, Peter . . . . . (NS) 441
HSIUNG, Lai Y. . . . . (NS) 567
SMITH, Arthur M. . . . . . . (NS) 1152
ABRAM, Persis R. . . . . . (ON) 3
ALBURGER, Thomas P. . (ON) 11
ALSTON, Sandra . . . . . . (ON) 18
ARMBRUST, Susan P. . . (ON) 31
ARONSON, Marcia L. . . . (ON) 34
BANFILL, Christine . . . . . (ON) 54
BELDAN, A C. . . . . (ON) 76
BELLAMY, Patricia C. . . (ON) 78
BENDIG, Regina . . . . . . (ON) 79
BISHOP, Heather F. . . . . (ON) 99
BLACK, Jane L. . . . . (ON) 101
BOWMAN, Robert J. . . . (ON) 122
BREGZIS, Ilze . . . . (ON) 131
BREZINA, Jennifer R. . . . (ON) 134
BROWN, Barbara E. . . . . (ON) 142
BROWN, Phyllis E. . . . . . (ON) 147
COOK, C D. . . . . (ON) 239
CZARNOTA, Les . . . . . . (ON) 268
DARBY, Janet M. . . . . . . (ON) 274
DAVIS, Wendy A. . . . . . (ON) 281

CATALOGING (Cont'd)
Cataloging

DELSEY, Thomas J.	(ON)	290
DESOMOGYI, Aileen A.	(ON)	295
DURANCE, Cynthia J.	(ON)	328
DUSSIAUME, Robert	(ON)	329
ELLERT, Barbara M.	(ON)	343
FRAUMENI, Michael A.	(ON)	399
GAZELEY, Joan E.	(ON)	424
GOODGER-HILL, Carol	(ON)	448
GOODMAN, Julia M.	(ON)	449
HICKS, Barbara A.	(ON)	536
IRELAND, Michael A.	(ON)	583
JARVIS, A W.	(ON)	595
JENSEN, L B.	(ON)	599
KAYE, Barbara J.	(ON)	632
KEYS, Sandra A.	(ON)	645
LATYSZEWSKYJ, Maria A.	(ON)	702
LEGAULT, Michel	(ON)	712
LOW, Mary	(ON)	743
LUCIANI, Ellie	(ON)	746
MARUNA, Oldrich Z.	(ON)	780
MASEN, Naunihal S.	(ON)	780
MAYRAND, Florian	(ON)	791
MEHTA, Subbash C.	(ON)	821
MILLS, Judy E.	(ON)	844
NEILSON, Ann	(ON)	892
NIXON, Audrey I.	(ON)	906
OKUDA, Sachiko E.	(ON)	920
OUIMET, Jacinthe	(ON)	930
OZAKI, Hiroko	(ON)	932
PORTEUS, Andrew C.	(ON)	985
RATSOY, Marye G.	(ON)	1010
RAY, Cathy J.	(ON)	1011
ROGERS, Dorothy S.	(ON)	1049
SABLJIC, John A.	(ON)	1072
SAVIC, Edward I.	(ON)	1086
SIMARD, Luc	(ON)	1139
SKELTON, Brooke	(ON)	1146
SLATER, Ronald J.	(ON)	1148
SMITH, Ruth P.	(ON)	1160
SOULES, Aline E.	(ON)	1169
SPARK, Catherine L.	(ON)	1171
TIPLER, Stephen B.	(ON)	1246
VANDOROS, Z	(ON)	1275
VEEKEN, Mary L.	(ON)	1280
VUKOV, Vesna	(ON)	1290
WEBB, Mary J.	(ON)	1313
WEIHS, Jean	(ON)	1317
WHALEN, George F.	(ON)	1328
WHALEY, E M.	(ON)	1328
ZVEJNIEKS, Laila R.	(ON)	1391
BEAUCLAIR, Rene	(PQ)	70
BERARDINUCCI, Heather R.	(PQ)	84
BISSON, Jacques	(PQ)	100
BUTLER, Patricia	(PQ)	167
DUSABLON-BOTTEGA, Nicole	(PQ)	329
FILIATRAULT, Sylvie	(PQ)	376
FINNEMORE, Mary A.	(PQ)	378
FORTIN, Jean	(PQ)	391
GAULIN, S D.	(PQ)	422
GILMORE, Carolyn	(PQ)	437
HOULE, Louis P.	(PQ)	563
JETTE, Monika E.	(PQ)	600
JUNEAU, Jocelyne B.	(PQ)	620
KAMICHAITIS, Penelope H.	(PQ)	624
KOBER, Gary L.	(PQ)	666
LAMBERT, Yvan	(PQ)	690
LAMONTAGNE, Jacqueline	(PQ)	691
LAPERRIERE, Celine	(PQ)	697
LAPLANTE, Carole	(PQ)	697
LAPOINTE, Louise	(PQ)	697
LEBEL, Clement	(PQ)	707
LESSARD, Josee	(PQ)	718
LUSSIER, Jean P.	(PQ)	749

CATALOGING (Cont'd)
Cataloging

	MAILLOUX, Jean Y.	(PQ)	761
	MARQUIS, Julien	(PQ)	773
	OUELLET, Louise M.	(PQ)	930
	PETRYK, Louise O.	(PQ)	965
	PLAMONDON, Yolande M.	(PQ)	977
	ROLLAND-THOMAS, Paule	(PQ)	1051
	ROWE, David G.	(PQ)	1062
	SHEERAN, Ruth J.	(PQ)	1125
	SMYTH, John	(PQ)	1162
	TESSIER, Richard	(PQ)	1233
	THACH, Phat V.	(PQ)	1233
	VONKA, Stephanie	(PQ)	1288
	BROWNE, Berks G.	(SK)	148
	CHEN, William Y.	(SK)	205
	FIELDEN, Stanley	(SK)	376
	PAREDES-RUIZ, Eudoxio B.	(SK)	940
	REID, Marianne E.	(SK)	1019
	NGUYEN, Michael V.	(AUS)	900
	MOSS, Loretta E.	(CSR)	872
	SMITH, Margit J.	(ENG)	1157
	CHU, Tat C.	(HKG)	213
	LEE, Betty W.	(HKG)	709
	COLLINS, William P.	(ISR)	233
	HADDAD, Aida N.	(ISR)	481
	MOULD, Edith L.	(ISR)	873
	KATO, Hisae	(JAP)	629
	SAKAMOTO, Hiroshi	(JAP)	1076
	TETSUYA, Inoue	(JAP)	1233
	AFOLAYAN, Matthew A.	(NGR)	7
	OKPARA, Ibiba M.	(NGR)	920
	COOK, Marjorie L.	(PHP)	240
	PICACHE, Ursula D.	(PHP)	970
	SEPTEMBER, Peter E.	(SAF)	1115
	ALI, Farooq M.	(SDA)	13
	BUTT, Abdul W.	(SDA)	167
	TAMEEM, Jamal A.	(SDA)	1221
	KIM, Soon C.	(SKO)	649
	CHOU, Nancy O.	(TAI)	210
	FRANK, Elizabeth W.	(TKY)	397
	ELLIOTT, Lirlyn J.	(TRN)	344
Cataloging, abstracting & indexing	CAN, Hung V.	(PQ)	177
Cataloging accessioned material	RHEAUME, Irene M.	(MD)	1025
Cataloging administration & teaching	AYRAULT, Margaret W.	(HI)	43
Cataloging administrative records	WHEELER, Elaine	(NY)	1328
Cataloging Africana materials	NIEKAMP, Dorothy R.	(IN)	903
Cataloging, all formats	SILVERMAN, Scott H.	(PA)	1138
Cataloging all medium types	ALGAR, L E.	(ON)	13
Cataloging & accessions	WEISS, Susan	(FL)	1320
Cataloging & acquisition	PHILLIPS, Patricia A.	(TN)	968
	FUN, Winnie W.	(VA)	409
Cataloging & acquisitions	HAYES, Linda J.	(CA)	516
	CHAPMAN, Elwynda K.	(DC)	202
	ELDER, Richard H.	(MD)	342
	LIU, David T.	(TX)	734
	RIEPMA, Helen J.	(TX)	1033
	PARKER, Charles G.	(PQ)	941
Cataloging & authority control	TILLETT, Barbara B.	(CA)	1245
	IDDINGS, Daniel H.	(IL)	581
	WEE, Lily K.	(IL)	1315
	ENGLE, Constance B.	(MI)	349
Cataloging & automated systems	SEXTON, Ebba J.	(KY)	1118
Cataloging & book ordering	VIERGEVER, Dan W.	(KS)	1284
Cataloging & cataloging systems	PAGE, Jacqueline M.	(MO)	934
Cataloging & church history	ROBINSON, Nancy D.	(KY)	1044
Cataloging & circulation	RUSIEWSKI, Charles B.	(IL)	1068
Cataloging & classification	BOWLES, Carol A.	(CA)	121
	WAY, Kathy A.	(CA)	1311
	FIELD, Oliver T.	(CO)	375
	JUKNIS, Ann M.	(CT)	619
	BARRY, Paul J.	(DC)	60
	CLACK, Doris H.	(FL)	215
	WALCOTT, M A.	(FL)	1294
	RIEMER, John J.	(GA)	1033
	HENDERSON, Kathryn L.	(IL)	526
	HOLZBERLEIN, Deanne B.	(IL)	555
	RICHARDSON, Susan C.	(KY)	1030

CATALOGING (Cont'd)

Cataloging & classification

	HORGAN, Laura A.	(MA)	559
	INTNER, Sheila S.	(MA)	583
	ST. AUBIN, Arleen K.	(MA)	1075
	PRATT, Laura C.	(MD)	990
	MIKA, Joseph J.	(MI)	834
	BETH, Dana L.	(MO)	92
	BOYD, William D.	(MS)	123
	VAN MELER, Vandelia L.	(MS)	1276
	SAYE, Jerry D.	(NC)	1086
	HASELWOOD, Eldon L.	(NE)	510
	GRIFFITH, Joan C.	(NH)	469
	KALIF, Alexander J.	(NJ)	623
	LINNAMAA, Mari M.	(NJ)	731
	LANCASTER, Kevin M.	(NM)	692
	BRADLEY, Carol J.	(NY)	125
	BRENNAN, Christopher P.	(NY)	132
	HOPKINS, Judith	(NY)	558
	MATTA, Seoud M.	(NY)	785
	SCHUTT, Dedre A.	(NY)	1103
	SMIRAGLIA, Richard P.	(NY)	1152
	WAGSCHAL, Sara G.	(NY)	1292
	GREBEY, Betty H.	(PA)	461
	BARNETT, Judith B.	(RI)	57
	EASTERLY, Ambrose	(TN)	333
	CALIMANO, Ivan E.	(TX)	173
	FERSTL, Kenneth L.	(TX)	374
	HERRING, Billie G.	(TX)	533
	MIKSA, Francis L.	(TX)	834
	THORNE, Bonnie B.	(TX)	1242
	WILLIAMS, Suzi	(TX)	1346
	HOLLEY, Robert P.	(UT)	551
	BILLERT, Julia A.	(VA)	96
	FINCH, Mildred E.	(VA)	377
	FISHER, Carl D.	(VA)	380
	RODRIGUEZ, Robert D.	(VA)	1048
	JORDAN, Sharon L.	(WA)	617
	DIETZ, Kathryn A.	(WI)	302
	LAM, Vinh T.	(ON)	689
	WILLIAMSON, Nancy J.	(ON)	1347
	DEMERS, Madeleine M.	(PQ)	291
	GARDNER, Richard K.	(PQ)	418
	KO, Jean S.	(PQ)	666
	GOODELL, John S.	(AUS)	448
	GOODELL, Paulette M.	(AUS)	448
	ADITIRTO, Irma U.	(IDN)	6
	DOUGLAS, Daphne R.	(JAM)	314
	SHAW, Shiow J.	(TAI)	1124
Cataloging & classification of slides	HENDERSON, Joyce C.	(AZ)	526
Cataloging & classifying books	MILTON, Ardyce A.	(WI)	845
Cataloging & classifying photographs	KOSHER, Helene J.	(CA)	672
Cataloging & classifying serials	WALKER, Elizabeth A.	(PQ)	1295
Cataloging & classifying slides	KOSHER, Helene J.	(CA)	672
Cataloging & clipping	DONNELLY, Lela M.	(KS)	311
Cataloging & collecting rare recordings	BROWNE, J P.	(CA)	148
Cataloging & collection development	BEDOR, Kathleen M.	(MN)	73
	FERRIGNO, Helen F.	(NH)	373
	SARTAIN, Sara M.	(VA)	1083
Cataloging & collection maintenance	WANG, Connie	(CA)	1302
Cataloging & conservation	WINROTH, Elizabeth C.	(OR)	1355
Cataloging & database management	CARTER, Ruth C.	(PA)	190
Cataloging & database searching	CHANG, Daphne Y.	(NY)	200
Cataloging & development	DENNIS, Mary R.	(IA)	292
Cataloging & finding aids	GUREWITSCH, Bonnie	(NY)	478
Cataloging & indexing	LENSCHAU, Jane A.	(CA)	715
	SPRUNG, Lori L.	(CA)	1176
	CARROON, Robert G.	(CT)	187
	DALLET, Jane L.	(FL)	270
	GILBERT, Mattana	(MD)	433
	THOMAS, Sarah E.	(MD)	1238
	ANGUS, Jacqueline A.	(MN)	28
	CHELARIU, Ana R.	(NJ)	204
	BEHAR, Evelyn W.	(NY)	74
	GRAVLEE, Diane D.	(NY)	459
	MCDANIELS, Patricia R.	(OR)	801
	LANG, Anita E.	(TX)	695
	LANE, Barbara K.	(AB)	694
	TREMBLAY, Levis	(PQ)	1255

CATALOGING (Cont'd)

Cataloging & indexing

	TREVICK, Selma D.	(PQ)	1255
Cataloging & indexing books	GOLDBERG, Judy W.	(NY)	444
Cataloging & indexing photographs	GRAUE, Luz B.	(CA)	458
Cataloging & information retrieval	CARROLL, Dewey E.	(TX)	187
Cataloging & manuscript processing	WESTERBERG, Kermit B.	(IL)	1326
Cataloging & name authorities	SCHUITEMA, Joan E.	(OH)	1101
Cataloging & NCIP	CLOUSTON, John S.	(ON)	223
Cataloging & online searching	GABBIANELLI, Patrice A.	(NJ)	411
Cataloging & ordering	CAMPBELL, Mary K.	(TX)	177
Cataloging & preserving archival mtrls	FALCONE, Elena C.	(NY)	362
Cataloging & processing	KOEL, Maria O.	(CT)	667
	ISHIMOTO, Carol F.	(MA)	585
	HESS, Marjorie A.	(PA)	534
Cataloging & processing manuscripts	WHITTINGTON, Erma P.	(NC)	1334
Cataloging & processing of materials	BIANCHI, Karen F.	(WA)	93
Cataloging & reclassification	HOOSE, Beverly D.	(CT)	557
	YEH, Thomas Y.	(WA)	1379
Cataloging & reference	DENNIS, Mary R.	(IA)	292
	RAMBO, Helen M.	(ID)	1005
	CHUNG, Hai C.	(NJ)	213
	CALDWELL, John M.	(PA)	172
Cataloging & reference services	ANTHONY, Paul L.	(IL)	29
Cataloging & retrospective conversion	ZIESELMAN, Paula M.	(NY)	1388
Cataloging & serials control	DRAPER, Linda J.	(MO)	318
Cataloging & subject analysis	TAYLOR, Arlene G.	(NY)	1226
Cataloging & supervision	UMBERGER, Sheila S.	(VA)	1268
Cataloging & technical services	SHAPIRO, Leonard P.	(CA)	1121
	LOPEZ, Deborah A.	(FL)	741
	LUNG, Mon Y.	(KS)	748
	LEONARD, Ruth S.	(MA)	717
	ANDERMAN, Lynea	(NJ)	21
	ENG, Mamie	(NY)	348
	MALINCONICO, S M.	(NY)	763
	ANDERSON, Elizabeth M.	(PA)	22
	ROCKWOOD, Susan M.	(PA)	1046
	MARTIN, Nannette	(SDA)	777
Cataloging & theology	LLOVIO, Kay M.	(CA)	735
	ROBINSON, Nancy D.	(KY)	1044
Cataloging architectural & engineering	SPAHR, Cheryl L.	(OH)	1170
Cataloging archival moving images	HARRISON, Harriet W.	(DC)	506
Cataloging archives & manuscripts	CARNES, Suzanne M.	(CA)	183
	CALKIN, Homer L.	(VA)	173
Cataloging art & architecture slides	FOWLER, Michele R.	(OH)	394
Cataloging art & music	RICHARDSON, Emma G.	(NY)	1029
Cataloging art books	FORMAN, Camille L.	(CT)	390
Cataloging audiovisual materials	URBANSKI, Verna P.	(FL)	1269
	HARTSOCK, Ralph M.	(PA)	508
Cataloging audiovisual media	KEARNEY, Jeanne E.	(NJ)	633
Cataloging audiovisuals, monographs	VAN STRATEN, Daniel G.	(WI)	1277
Cataloging, automation	LAKSHMAN, Malathi K.	(MD)	689
Cataloging band recordings	MITZIGA, Walter J.	(IL)	850
Cataloging, Baptist history, doctrine	ROBINSON, Nancy D.	(KY)	1044
Cataloging, bibliographer	DERRICKSON, Margaret	(NY)	294
Cataloging, binding	NESBITT, Olive K.	(PA)	896
Cataloging, book & non-book	COTTINGHAM, Elsie E.	(IN)	250
Cataloging books	HEFZALLAH, Mona G.	(CT)	521
Cataloging books & audiovisual media	YOUNG, Patricia S.	(TN)	1383
Cataloging Canadian government documents	TURNER, Sharon	(ON)	1265
Cataloging cassettes & compact discs	SCHWANN, William J.	(MA)	1104
Cataloging children's materials	WINKEL, Lois	(NC)	1355
Cataloging civil engineering materials	REINALDO DA SILVA, Joann T.	(MB)	1021
Cataloging classification	PORTER, Eva L.	(NJ)	984
	LIGHTHALL, Lynne I.	(BC)	727
Cataloging collections	AUTRY, Carolyn	(IN)	41
Cataloging conference proceedings	CARTER, Judith A.	(AZ)	189
Cataloging, conversion	WELLINGTON, Jean S.	(OH)	1322
Cataloging department management	LEBEL, Clement	(PQ)	707
Cataloging educational media	GRIFFIN, Kathryn A.	(IA)	468
Cataloging environmental engineering	CARROLL, Virginia L.	(MA)	187
Cataloging, especially of media	LAFEVER, Susan	(TN)	687
Cataloging European languages material	PHILLIPS, Richard F.	(NJ)	969
Cataloging fine arts, serials	MILLS, Rolland W.	(PR)	844
Cataloging for law libraries	DILORETO, Ann M.	(CA)	303
Cataloging foreign language material	INGIBERGSSON, Asgeir	(AB)	582
Cataloging foreign languages	KATZ, Solomon B.	(PQ)	630

CATALOGING (Cont'd)

Cataloging genealogy	FOLEY, Harriet E.	(OH)	387
Cataloging government documents	MILLER, Barbara K.	(NY)	835
	BLANKENBURG, Julie J.	(WI)	104
Cataloging history, philosophy, religion	YU, Priscilla C.	(IL)	1384
Cataloging in publication	PARENT, Ingrid T.	(ON)	940
	SIMARD, Luc	(ON)	1139
Cataloging in social science	HAN, Kenneth P.	(CA)	494
Cataloging including automated authority	BULAONG, Grace F.	(ON)	156
Cataloging, interlibrary loan	SUTTER, Mary A.	(MO)	1211
	SCHMIDT, Diana M.	(ON)	1095
Cataloging Italian & Spanish books	CHANG, Roselyne M.	(DC)	201
Cataloging, language & literature	MOORE, Anne C.	(AZ)	858
Cataloging law materials	KORKMAS, Carolyn C.	(TX)	671
Cataloging legal materials	MITTAN, Rhonda L.	(CA)	850
	GULSTAD, Wilma B.	(MO)	477
	MITTEN, Lisa A.	(PA)	850
	NASSERDEN, Marilyn D.	(AB)	889
Cataloging Lib of Congress, Dewey, Sears	RUSSELL, Richard A.	(WV)	1069
Cataloging, library systems	PERCELLI, Irene M.	(NY)	958
Cataloging local history collection	MILLER, Ida M.	(IN)	838
Cataloging LP records	SCHWANN, William J.	(MA)	1104
Cataloging, maintenance	NICHOLSON, Dianne L.	(BC)	902
Cataloging management	MARTIN, Norma H.	(LA)	777
	JIZBA, Laurel	(MI)	600
	JUNION, Gail J.	(NY)	620
	SLOVASKY, Stephen	(OH)	1150
Cataloging management & workflow	CLARK, Sharon E.	(IL)	218
Cataloging manuscript collections	OSTROFF, Harriet	(DC)	929
Cataloging manuscripts	MYERS, Roger	(AZ)	885
	BLUTH, John F.	(PA)	108
Cataloging manuscripts, using AMC format	CARTLEDGE, Connie L.	(DC)	190
Cataloging, MARC format	THIBAULT, Jean	(ON)	1235
Cataloging MARC formats	ROBINSON, Christie M.	(KY)	1043
Cataloging materials	SCHILL, Julie G.	(PA)	1092
	CHISUM, Emmett D.	(WY)	209
Cataloging media	WESTOVER, Mary L.	(AL)	1327
	HEFZALLAH, Mona G.	(CT)	521
Cataloging memorabilia	KESSLER, Selma P.	(NJ)	645
Cataloging Methodist-related materials	BERG, Richard R.	(OH)	84
Cataloging microcomputer software	CARTER, Judith A.	(AZ)	189
Cataloging Middle East materials	BEZIRGAN, Basima	(IL)	93
Cataloging monographs	FORMAN, Camille L.	(CT)	390
	MATTHEWS, Priscilla J.	(IL)	785
	BLEIL, Leslie A.	(MI)	105
Cataloging monographs & serials	NEVIN, Susanne	(MN)	898
Cataloging monographs, foreign languages	MIKLOSVARY, Jozsef	(CA)	834
Cataloging monographs, maps & documents	CAHILL, Colleen R.	(PA)	171
Cataloging music	CASEY, Carol A.	(TX)	192
	KATZ, Solomon B.	(PQ)	630
Cataloging music & audiovisual materials	SLOMSKI, Monica J.	(CT)	1150
Cataloging music & sound recordings	DORFMAN, Ethel L.	(NY)	312
	POWELL, Virginia L.	(PA)	989
Cataloging music manuscripts	PLAIN, Marilyn V.	(NY)	977
Cataloging music materials	PALKOVIC, Mark A.	(OH)	935
Cataloging musical loan collections	LYON, Bruce C.	(FL)	752
Cataloging New Jersey documents	HARDGROVE, David J.	(NJ)	499
Cataloging newspapers	GAIECK, Frederick W.	(OH)	412
	POLLARD, Margaret E.	(WI)	981
Cataloging non-book materials	BUSER, Robin A.	(KY)	165
	MEYER, Kenton T.	(PA)	830
Cataloging non-print materials	ADCOCK, Donald C.	(IL)	6
	GIBBS, Mary E.	(IL)	431
	WHYDE, John S.	(OH)	1335
Cataloging non-print media	MATTHEWS, Priscilla J.	(IL)	785
Cataloging North Carolina books	MCGLOHON, Leah L.	(NC)	807
Cataloging, OCLC	SALGAT, Anne M.	(PA)	1076
Cataloging of art slides	BAILEY, Tuuli V.	(AZ)	47
Cataloging of eductnl motion pictures	CHAVES, Francisco M.	(FL)	204
Cataloging of graphic materials	HOGAN, Kristine K.	(NY)	549
Cataloging of legal literature	ODSEN, Elizabeth R.	(AK)	917
Cataloging of legal materials	RUIZ-VALERA, Phoebe L.	(NY)	1067
Cataloguing of music materials	COLQUHOUN, Joan E.	(ON)	234
Cataloging of serials, journals, etc	WARD, Dorothy S.	(AL)	1303

CATALOGING (Cont'd)

Cataloging of Slavic materials	VERYHA, Wasyl	(ON)	1283
Cataloging of sound recordings	SCHUURSMA, Ann B.	(NET)	1103
Cataloging of technical reports	KLEIBER, Michael C.	(CA)	658
Cataloging of television news tapes	KEATING, Michael F.	(OH)	633
Cataloging old documents	BOECKMAN, Frances B.	(MS)	109
Cataloging on automated systems	WONG, Ming K.	(DC)	1363
Cataloging online	CAREY, Jane G.	(FL)	181
Cataloging, online searching, reference	PHILLIPS, Rosemary	(ON)	969
Cataloging, ordering, processing	GERMINDER, Robin L.	(NJ)	429
Cataloging, original & retrospective	SCHEITLE, Janet M.	(VA)	1091
Cataloging original materials	SCHUMANN, Iris T.	(TX)	1103
Cataloging photographs	CLARK, David L.	(CA)	216
	ZARCONE, Beth B.	(NY)	1386
	STONE, Gerald K.	(ON)	1197
Cataloging photographs & documents	FROST, Debra R.	(CO)	406
Cataloging photographs, collections mgmt	ROARK, Carol E.	(TX)	1038
Cataloging print & non-print	HSIEH, Cynthia C.	(IL)	567
Cataloging print media	KEARNEY, Jeanne E.	(NJ)	633
Cataloging, processing & annotating	BARNARD, Sandra K.	(CA)	57
Cataloging rare books	LAND, Barbara J.	(CA)	692
	SMIRENSKY, Helen K.	(NY)	1152
Cataloging, rare books, reference	STUFF, Marjorie A.	(NE)	1205
Cataloging reference	EARLY, Stephen T.	(WA)	332
	SIEMENS, Bessie M.	(MEX)	1136
Cataloging, reference, & circulation	MANDAL, Mina R.	(NY)	764
Cataloging reference, serials	VAN STRATEN, Daniel G.	(WI)	1277
Cataloging research	YEE, Martha M.	(CA)	1379
	VAJDA, Elizabeth A.	(NY)	1271
Cataloging retrospective conversion	ROBERTSON, Pamela S.	(ND)	1042
Cataloging, RLIN, OCLC experience	YU, Hsiao M.	(IA)	1384
Cataloging romance languages	KELLEY, Ann C.	(IA)	636
Cataloging rules	HU, Shih S.	(AB)	568
Cataloging school library media	SANDERS, Minda M.	(PA)	1080
Cataloging scores & sound recordings	MURRAY, Diane E.	(MI)	881
	WALLER, Elaine J.	(MI)	1298
Cataloging, selecting	ASLESEN, Rosalie V.	(SD)	36
Cataloging serials	WILLIAMS, Nancy F.	(FL)	1345
	ESMAN, Michael D.	(MD)	354
Cataloging serials, law, monographs	SPRANKLE, Vicki S.	(PA)	1176
Cataloging, Slavic language, non-book	JENKS, Zoya E.	(PA)	597
Cataloging Slavic monographs	SMIRENSKY, Helen K.	(NY)	1152
Cataloging small collections	KNOBBE, Mary L.	(MD)	665
Cataloging social sciences monographs	HARDGROVE, David J.	(NJ)	499
Cataloging sound recordings	BJORKE, Wallace S.	(MI)	100
Cataloging Spanish materials	LABODDA, Marsha J.	(TX)	686
Cataloging staff supervision	TAVARES, Cecelia M.	(MA)	1225
Cataloging standards	WEISS, Paul J.	(NY)	1320
Cataloging, subject analysis	SOPER, Mary E.	(WA)	1168
Cataloging supervision	SIMS, Phillip W.	(TX)	1142
Cataloging support	FINNI, John J.	(MA)	379
Cataloging systems	MANEY, Lana E.	(TX)	765
	ZIMMERMAN, Suzan E.	(ON)	1389
Cataloging teaching	SCHMITZ, Eugenia E.	(WI)	1096
Cataloging technical documents	PATTEN, Frederick W.	(CA)	947
Cataloging, technical services	MESNER, Lillian R.	(KY)	827
	BALDWIN, Betty J.	(NY)	51
	ROBICHAUD, Marcel J.	(NY)	1042
	TRINKAUS, Tanya	(RI)	1256
Cataloging theology & philosophy	ROONEY, Eugene M.	(DC)	1053
Cataloging theology & religion	WUNDERLICH, Clifford S.	(MA)	1374
Cataloging, training	STUHLMAN, Daniel D.	(IL)	1205
	WARTZOK, Susan G.	(IN)	1307
	COPELAND, Alice T.	(NJ)	244
Cataloging, training & development	KEATTS, Rowena W.	(TX)	633
Catlgng training, devlpmnt & instruction	JIZBA, Laurel	(MI)	600
Cataloging translations	NOWAK, Ildiko D.	(IL)	911
Cataloging unit management	NEILL, Sharon D.	(ON)	892
Cataloging utilities	BULLARD, Sharon W.	(CA)	156
Cataloging utilizing small computers	HOBBS, Henry C.	(MB)	545
Cataloging visual & sound materials	DRIESSEN, Karen C.	(MT)	320
Cataloging visual non-print materials	VISKOCHIL, Larry A.	(IL)	1285
Cataloging Western European monographs	SORURY, Kathryn L.	(IN)	1169
Cataloging with CATSS	ARSENAULT, Alban	(NB)	35

CATALOGING (Cont'd)

Cataloging with MARC AMC	BOYD, Sandra E.	(MS)	123
Children's cataloging	BAILEY, Darlene L.	(CA)	46
Chinese cataloging	KROMPART, Janet A.	(MI)	679
Church history & religion cataloging	MITCHELL, Annmarie D.	(CA)	848
Church library cataloging	WICHELMAN, Ruthann	(NJ)	1335
Classification & cataloging	RADEMACHER, Matthew J.	(MI)	1002
	RUSSELL, Elizabeth	(RI)	1068
	LEIDE, John E.	(PQ)	713
Classification, cataloging	MCKELVEY, Mary J.	(VA)	810
	SELING, Kathy A.	(WA)	1113
Classification, database cataloging	MCCONNIE, Mary	(TRN)	798
Collection development & cataloging	ROBINSON, Gayle N.	(AL)	1044
	ARTHUR, Donald B.	(TX)	35
Computer cataloging	GRAY, Shirley M.	(NY)	460
Computer database cataloging	VAN HORN, Neal F.	(OR)	1275
Computerized card cataloging	KIEFER, Marilyn V.	(MI)	647
Computerized music cataloging	GRIFFIN, Marie E.	(NJ)	468
	GOODWIN, Charles B.	(TX)	450
CONSER serials cataloging	JONES, Edgar A.	(MA)	612
Contract cataloging	KELLOUGH, Patrick H.	(TX)	637
Cooperative cataloging	LIGGETT, Suzanne L.	(DC)	726
Copy cataloging	ARAKAWA, Steven R.	(CT)	30
	O'NEIL, Rosanna M.	(OH)	924
	HALL, John D.	(TX)	488
Curriculum textbook cataloging	ONUFFER, Joachim	(PA)	924
Database cataloging	JIZBA, Laurel	(MI)	600
	FAWCETT-BRANDON, Pamela S.	(NJ)	367
	LIDSKY, Ella	(NY)	725
	BROWNELL, Barbara A.	(OH)	148
	SHELLENBARGER, Linda K.	(OH)	1126
	CRAIG, Marilyn J.	(TX)	254
	SHIH, Chia C.	(TX)	1130
Database cataloging & indexing	CHARBONNEAU, Ronald P.	(CA)	202
	DUMLAO, Mercedes G.	(CA)	325
	HAMILTON, D A.	(IL)	491
	ZIMMERMAN, Brenda M.	(IN)	1388
	SPURLING, Norman K.	(MD)	1177
	ROLONTZ, Linda	(MN)	1051
	FIELDING, Carol J.	(WA)	376
Database cataloging & searching	VELEZ, Sara B.	(NY)	1281
Database record guide cataloging	MCKNIGHT, Jesse H.	(FL)	812
Databases & cataloging	SIFTON, Patricia A.	(BC)	1137
Dental cataloging	RUBINSTEIN, Edith	(NY)	1065
Describing & cataloging records	SIEBERS, Bruce L.	(MI)	1135
Descriptive cataloging	CAHALANE, Edmond P.	(DC)	171
	GUILES, Kay D.	(DC)	476
	LIGGETT, Suzanne L.	(DC)	726
	WELLISCH, Hans H.	(MD)	1322
	BOYD, Alan D.	(OH)	122
	SELING, Kathy A.	(WA)	1113
	UHLMAN, Carol K.	(WA)	1268
	MANNING, Ralph W.	(ON)	767
Descriptive cataloging, legal materials	HAWKINS, Sandra J.	(DC)	514
Descriptive cataloging, monographs	HAWKINS, Sandra J.	(DC)	514
Descriptive cataloging, Slavic materials	MORGAN, Robert C.	(VA)	864
Document retrieval & cataloging	ELAM, Kim A.	(AK)	341
Documents cataloging	BLACK, Bernice B.	(MS)	101
Engineering cataloging	GRUBER, Linda R.	(PA)	474
Film cataloging & indexing	COVERT, Nadine	(NY)	252
Fine arts & architecture cataloging	MOHAMMED, Selima	(PQ)	852
Fine arts cataloging	WALTON, Carol G.	(FL)	1301
Fine print cataloging	REDLICH, Barry	(NJ)	1014
Foreign language cataloging	TSCHERNY, Alexander	(DC)	1260
	STEWART, Richard A.	(IL)	1193
	KIRKWOOD, Francis T.	(ON)	655
Foreign language reference & cataloging	MCCLAREY, Catherine A.	(IL)	796
Foreign languages cataloging	HALIBEY, Areta V.	(IL)	486
	FOLTER, Siegrun H.	(NY)	388
Genealogical cataloging	RANDALL, Gordon E.	(GA)	1006
General librarian reference cataloging	GOSDECK, David M.	(WI)	452
Government document cataloging	MCKOWEN, Dorothy K.	(IN)	812
Government documents cataloging	MARSHALL, Marion B.	(DC)	774
Health science cataloging	CAFFAREL, Agnes	(LA)	170

CATALOGING (Cont'd)

Health sciences cataloging	NEUFELD, Sue E.	(IA)	897
	COLSON, Elizabeth A.	(TX)	234
Hebraica & Judaica cataloging	WEINBERG, Bella H.	(NY)	1317
Hebrew cataloging	HIRSCH, David G.	(NJ)	543
History of medicine cataloging	GILLIAM, Susanne P.	(OH)	436
Implementing online cataloging system	FISHER, Carl D.	(VA)	380
Indexing & cataloging	BALABAN, Robin M.	(CA)	50
	KAPLAN, Tiby	(FL)	626
	VELARDI, Adrienne B.	(NY)	1281
	BOIVIN-OSTIGUY, Jocelyne	(PQ)	111
	DUMOULIN, Nicole L.	(PQ)	325
	PAPILLON, Yves	(PQ)	939
Indexing & cataloging for database	WEINBERG, Gail B.	(MN)	1317
Jazz record computer cataloging	WEAVER, James B.	(FL)	1312
Latin America cataloging	LEONARD, Louise F.	(FL)	716
Latin American cataloging	WALTON, Carol G.	(FL)	1301
Law & business cataloging	CASSIDY, Joni L.	(NJ)	193
Law cataloging	JOHNTING, Wendell E.	(IN)	610
	GEE, Ka C.	(NY)	424
	HARVEY, Suzanne	(WA)	509
Law cataloging & classification	STRIMAN, Brian D.	(NE)	1202
Law firm collections cataloging	SCAMMAHORN, Lynne	(PA)	1087
Law material cataloging	REID, Marianne E.	(SK)	1019
Learning center cataloging	KAWAGUCHI, Miyako	(VA)	632
Legal cataloging, monographs	WOODS, Frances B.	(CT)	1367
Legal material cataloging	HILLMANN, Diane I.	(NY)	541
Legal materials cataloging	IOANID, Aurora S.	(NY)	583
	ROSENFELD, Joseph S.	(OH)	1056
Legal serials cataloging	WOODS, Frances B.	(CT)	1367
Liberal arts cataloging	BECKER, Charlotte B.	(VA)	72
Liberal arts, religion, music cataloging	LUSK, Betty M.	(SAF)	749
Library of Congress cataloging	REYNOLDS, Dorsey	(PA)	1025
Lib of Congress cataloging conversion	DUNMIRE, Raymond V.	(AL)	326
Life sciences cataloging	PASTER, Amy L.	(PA)	946
Limited cataloging	CASWELL, Mary C.	(VA)	194
Machine-readable cataloging	QUEINNEC, Young H.	(ON)	999
Machine-readable cataloging distribution	TARR, Susan M.	(DC)	1224
Machine-readable data files cataloging	MYERS, Victor C.	(MO)	885
	WEITZ, Jay N.	(OH)	1320
Manual technical cataloging	WHITT, Diane M.	(IL)	1334
Manuscript cataloging	GILDZEN, Alex J.	(OH)	434
	MOLTKE-HANSEN, David	(SC)	853
	HANDE, D A.	(SK)	494
Manuscript cataloging online	CRONENWETT, Philip N.	(NH)	260
Manuscripts cataloging	MCLOONE, Harriet V.	(CA)	814
	ROUNDTREE, Lynn P.	(LA)	1061
	VIRTA, Alan K.	(MD)	1285
Manuscripts processing & cataloging	BOUCHE, Nicole L.	(CA)	118
Map & book cataloging	SHARP, Alice L.	(CO)	1122
Map cataloging	DIBLE, Joan B.	(CA)	299
	PETERSON, Charles B.	(DC)	963
	LEONARD, Louise F.	(FL)	716
	SCHREIBER, Robert E.	(IL)	1099
	SHIRLEY, David B.	(MI)	1131
	CORSARO, James	(NY)	248
	PERRY, Joanne M.	(OR)	960
	STONE, Howard P.	(RI)	1197
	PESCHEL, Susan M.	(WI)	961
Map cataloging & classification	GALNEDER, Mary H.	(WI)	415
Maps cataloging	WOODWARD, Lawrence W.	(DC)	1368
Materials cataloging & sourcing	LOWELL, Brian V.	(IL)	744
Materials selection & cataloging	KENT, Rose M.	(OH)	642
Media & education cataloging	FREESE, Melanie L.	(NY)	401
Media cataloging	PROSSER, Michael J.	(CA)	995
	SCHREIBER, Robert E.	(IL)	1099
	MICHAEL, Richard T.	(RI)	831
Media center card cataloging	MITCHELL, Phyllis R.	(GA)	849
Medical cataloging	MARSON, Joyce	(CA)	775
	RENNIE, Margaret C.	(LA)	1023
	WILLIS, Marilyn	(LA)	1348
	RAND, Pamela S.	(MD)	1006
	WINZER, Kathleen M.	(MD)	1356
	HANSON, Mary A.	(MI)	498
	GILLIAM, Susanne P.	(OH)	436

CATALOGING (Cont'd)

Medical cataloging

RISSINGER, Michael . . . (PA) 1036

Medical databases, reference, cataloging

MARK, Ronnie J. . . . . . . (NY) 770

Medical library cataloging

SIEBENMORGEN, Ruth . (CA) 1135
OSHEROFF, Shiela K. . . (OR) 928

Medical materials cataloging

SHRIER, Helene F. . . . . (NY) 1133

Microcomputer software cataloging

WEISS, Paul J. . . . . . . (NY) 1320

Microform cataloging

TSCHERNY, Alexander . (DC) 1260
MCKOWEN, Dorothy K. . (IN) 812
STONE, Howard P. . . . . (RI) 1197

Microforms acquisition & cataloging

HUGHES, Frances M. . . (CT) 571

Microforms cataloging

RENSHAW, Marita . . . . (IL) 1023

Middle East cataloging

CHAMMOU, Eliezer . . . . (CA) 198

Middle East languages cataloging

JAJKO, Edward A. . . . . (CA) 592

Minimal level cataloging

BRADY, Mary M. . . . . . (IL) 127

Monograph cataloging

DIBLE, Joan B. . . . . (CA) 299
ANDREW, Paige G. . . . . (GA) 26
BERG, Elizabeth R. . . . . (GA) 84
KONKEL, Mary S. . . . . (OH) 670

Monographic & serials cataloging

MORROW, Deborah . . . . (MI) 869

Monographic cataloging

NELSON, Michael B. . . . (AL) 894
KNIGHT, Rita C. . . . . . (AZ) 664
HARDIN, Barbara A. . . . (GA) 500
WATSON, Mark R. . . . . (OR) 1310
HALLOCK, Nancy L. . . . (PA) 489

Monographic cataloging unit training

DONAHUE, Janice E. . . . (FL) 310

Monographs & scores cataloging

SUDDUTH, William E. . . (MA) 1206

Monographs cataloging

ADAMSON, Danette . . . . (CA) 6
WANG, Margaret K. . . . . (DE) 1303
DEL CASTILLO, Mireya . (MO) 289
GOERNER, Tatiana . . . . (NY) 443

Museum & archival cataloging, organz

DEE, Camille C. . . . . . . (NY) 286

Museum cataloging

BIERBAUM, Esther G. . . (IA) 95

Music & audiovisual cataloging

ALMQUIST, Sharon G. . . (TX) 17

Music & sound recordings cataloging

SNODGRASS, Wilson D. . (TX) 1163

Music bibliography & cataloging

HARTIG, Linda . . . . (WI) 508

Music cataloging

FAIR, Kathy L. . . . . (AL) 361
EARNEST, Jeffrey D. . . . (AR) 332
EAGLESON, Laurie E. . . (AZ) 331
ADAMSON, Danette . . . . (CA) 6
BOCHIN, Janet S. . . . . . (CA) 108
ELLIOTT, Patricia G. . . . (CA) 344
CARTER, Nancy F. . . . . (CO) 189
SAVIG, Norman I. . . . . . (CO) 1086
DAVIS, Deta S. . . . . (DC) 278
PRICE, Harry H. . . . . . . (DC) 992
DAVIS, Joy V. . . . . (GA) 279
HUGHES, Neil R. . . . . . (GA) 572
BURBANK, Richard D. . . (IL) 158
GOUDY, Allie W. . . . . . . (IL) 454
GRISCOM, Richard W. . . (IL) 471
WARD, Shirlene A. . . . . . (IL) 1304
NELSON, Brenda . . . . . . (IN) 893
SCHOONOVER, Phyllis J. (IN) 1098
BRATCHER, Perry R. . . . (KY) 129
POWELL, Martha C. . . . . (KY) 988
PRITCHARD, Elsie T. . . . (KY) 994
RICHARDSON, Susan C. (KY) 1030
THOMPSON, Jeannette C. (LA) 1240
FELDT, Candice K. . . . . (MA) 369
SHEETS, Robin R. . . . . . (MD) 1125
PERRY-BOWDER, Libbie
E. . . . . (ME) 961
BLACK-SHIER, Mary L. . (MI) 102
BOWEN, Jennifer B. . . . . (MI) 120
HILDEBRAND, Linda L. . (MI) 538
CHRISTENSEN, Beth E. . (MN) 211
YOUNGHOLM, Philip . . . (MN) 1383
WURSTEN, Richard B. . . (NC) 1374
BRKIC, Beverly T. . . . . . (ND) 138
DOW, Carolyn E. . . . . . . (NE) 315
TIBBITS, Edith J. . . . . . . (NE) 1243
NEWHOUSE, Brian G. . . (NJ) 899
SKROBELA, Katherine C. (NJ) 1147
FLOERSHEIMER, Lee M. (NY) 385
FOLTER, Siegrun H. . . . . (NY) 388
HARDISH, Patrick M. . . . (NY) 500
RANSOM, Sarah B. . . . . (NY) 1007

CATALOGING (Cont'd)

Music cataloging

RORICK, William C. . . . . (NY) 1054
VAN BIEMA, Mary E. . . . (NY) 1272
WISE, Matthew W. . . . . . (NY) 1357
BALCAS, Georgianne . . . (OH) 50
HAMBLEY, Susan L. . . . (OH) 490
KNAPP, David . . . . (OH) 663
ROBSON, Timothy D. . . . (OH) 1045
WEITZ, Jay N. . . . . (OH) 1320
ZASLOW, Barry J. . . . . . (OH) 1386
RENFRO, Robert S. . . . . (OR) 1023
EISENBERG, Peter L. . . . (PA) 340
ELLIKER, Calvin . . . . (PA) 343
GERHART, Catherine A. . (PA) 428
STEPHENS, Norris L. . . . (PA) 1188
YOUNG, James B. . . . . . (PA) 1382
FAWVER, Darlene E. . . . (SC) 367
GARRETT, Stuart . . . . . . (TN) 420
CAINE, William C. . . . . . (TX) 171
CRAIG, Marilyn J. . . . . . (TX) 254
GEARY, Gregg S. . . . . . (TX) 424
POPE, Betty F. . . . . (TX) 983
BECKER, Charlotte B. . . (VA) 72
REED, Marcia E. . . . . . . (WA) 1015
LAVERTY, Corinne Y. . . (ON) 703
MOHAMMED, Selima . . . (PQ) 852

Music cataloging & bibliography

DURIS, Richard M. . . . . . (PA) 328

Music cataloging or Hebrew cataloging

FRIEDLAND, Frances K. . (ON) 403

Music material cataloging

GOODWIN, Charles B. . . (TX) 450

Music materials cataloging

ROSS, Mary E. . . . . (MI) 1058

Music materials, cataloging & processing

MEERVELD, Bert . . . . . . (ON) 821

Music reference & cataloging

MOORE, Emily C. . . . . . . (NC) 859

Music-related buying & cataloging

RUSTMAN, Mark M. . . . (KS) 1070

National Library of Medicine cataloging

WARD, Penny T. . . . . . . (CA) 1304
GILBERT, Carole M. . . . . (MI) 433
ELY, Betty L. . . . . (PA) 347
HIRSCH, David G. . . . . . (NJ) 543

Near East languages cataloging

MCGANN, Margot . . . . . (DC) 805

News & events cataloging

TRIVEDI, Harish S. . . . . (OH) 1257

News & information cataloging

DANKY, James P. . . . . . (WI) 274

Newspaper acquisition & cataloging

MCCARGAR, Susan E. . (TX) 794

Newspaper indexing & cataloging

PEARMAN, Sara J. . . . . (OH) 952

Non-book cataloging

KARON, Bernard L. . . . . (MN) 627

Non-book materials online cataloging

FAIR, Kathy L. . . . . (AL) 361

Non-print cataloging

WOOLDRIDGE, Steven M. (CA) 1368
KELLEY, Colleen L. . . . . (IN) 636
BRATCHER, Perry R. . . . (KY) 129
BADEN, Diane G. . . . . . . (MA) 44
BELL, Rebecca L. . . . . . . (TN) 77

Nursing science databases, cataloging

DIMATTEO, Lucy A. . . . . (NY) 304

OCLC cataloging

MITCHAM, Janet C. . . . . (AR) 848
O'BRIEN, Mary C. . . . . . (OR) 915
GOING, Susan C. . . . . . . (SC) 444
CASEY, Wayne T. . . . . . (VA) 192
MYERS, Victor C. . . . . . (MO) 885

OCLC cataloging systems

STORM, Jill . . . . (DC) 1198

OCLC map cataloging

GILLESPIE, Veronica M. . (DC) 435

Online cataloging

OSGOOD, James B. . . . . (IL) 928
WARTZOK, Susan G. . . . (IN) 1307
CLOUGH, Linda F. . . . . . (MA) 223
HORNE, Ernest M. . . . . . (MI) 560
ROZENE, Janette B. . . . . (NY) 1064
ZIPPER, Masha . . . . (NY) 1390
FELL, Sally B. . . . . (OH) 370
WALBRIDGE, Sharon L. . (OH) 1293
JAMES, Denise T. . . . . . (SC) 592
VAN ORDEN, Richard D. . (UT) 1276
HUANG, Paul T. . . . . (NS) 568
BOWEN, Tom G. . . . . . . (ON) 120
BURCHELL, Patricia M. . (ON) 158
THOMSON, Donna K. . . (ON) 1241
WISE, Eileen M. . . . . (ON) 1356
CHAUMONT, Elise . . . . . (PQ) 204
DANIS, Rolland J. . . . . . . (PQ) 273
RIOPEL, Jean M. . . . . . . (PQ) 1035

CATALOGING (Cont'd)

Topic	Name	State	Page
Online cataloging databases	LINSKY, Leonore K.	(MA)	731
Online cataloging, OCLC, RLIN	TURITZ, Mitch L.	(CA)	1263
Online cataloging system	RICHARD, Sheila A.	(VA)	1028
Online cataloging systems	FRIEDLAND, Frances K.	(ON)	403
Online microcomputer cataloging	BERNSTEIN, Elaine S.	(ON)	89
Online music cataloging	MASTRANGELO, Marjorie J.	(DC)	782
	OLMSTED, Elizabeth H.	(KY)	921
Ordering & catlgng books & non-book mtrl	SPIEGEL, Bertha	(NY)	1174
Organizing, cataloging church libraries	HAMMER, Louise K.	(IL)	493
Original cataloging	WILSON, Betty R.	(IL)	1350
	MAGUIRE, Shirley E.	(MI)	760
	SCOTT, Randall W.	(MI)	1108
	MANY, Florence L.	(NJ)	767
	PRITCHARD, Barbara	(PA)	994
	HAWLEY, Laurie J.	(TX)	514
	LACY, Yvonne M.	(TX)	687
Original cataloging romance languages	SALINERO, Amelia	(NY)	1076
Original cataloging, science	KARON, Bernard L.	(MN)	627
Original cataloging Slavic materials	KORT, Richard L.	(MA)	672
Original cataloging using computers	HANNAFORD, Claudia L.	(OH)	496
Original monograph cataloging	LINSKY, Leonore K.	(MA)	731
Periodicals cataloging	FLUK, Louise R.	(PQ)	386
Photograph reference & cataloging	STERN, Teena B.	(CA)	1189
Piano research & cataloging	YRIGOYEN, Robert P.	(NJ)	1384
Picture collection cataloging	NATHEWS, Ann	(AL)	889
Post-cataloging book handling	MARX, Patricia C.	(TX)	780
Preliminary cataloging	MASON, Pamela R.	(MD)	781
Preservation microfilm cataloging	JONES, Edgar A.	(MA)	612
Print & non-print cataloging	ROBERTS, Sallie H.	(OH)	1041
Print & non-print material cataloging	TIWANA, Shah J.	(IL)	1247
Print & non-print materials cataloging	BROWN, Biraj L.	(SDA)	142
Print cataloging	GREESON-SCHARDL, Tamra J.	(GA)	465
Printed & non-printed material catlgng	SZETO, Dorcas C.	(CA)	1218
Private records cataloging	BREEDLOVE, Michael A.	(AL)	131
Processing & cataloging manuscripts	ETTER, Patricia A.	(AZ)	355
Procurement & cataloging	JONES, Stephanie R.	(LA)	615
Psychology reference & cataloging	HUFFINE, Lucinda J.	(OR)	571
Purchased & gift item cataloging	DELZELL, William R.	(MA)	290
Purchasing & cataloging	MUNSEY, Joyce E.	(MD)	879
Rare book acquisition & cataloging	COX, Shelley M.	(IL)	253
Rare book cataloging	ZALL, Elisabeth W.	(CA)	1386
	ROONEY, Eugene M.	(DC)	1053
	MARSHALL, Mary G.	(IL)	774
	MUELLER, Robert W.	(IL)	875
	RENSHAW, Marita	(IL)	1023
	SALAZAR, Pamela R.	(NY)	1076
	FRITZ, William R.	(SC)	405
	GISSENDANNER, Cassandra S.	(SC)	438
	HUMMEL, Ray O.	(VA)	573
	STAFFORD, Leva L.	(WY)	1178
Rare books cataloging	REITH, Louis J.	(DC)	1022
	HOUSE, Katherine L.	(KY)	563
	LANE, Mary J.	(LA)	694
	KISTLER, Ellen D.	(MO)	656
	MYERS, Victor C.	(MO)	885
	CALLINAN, Mary H.	(NY)	174
	GOERNER, Tatiana	(NY)	443
Rare record cataloging	ALLEN, Douglas R.	(FL)	14
Record acquisition & cataloging	BARGAR, Arthur W.	(CT)	56
Record, cassette & score cataloging	DONIO, Dorothy	(FL)	311
Recorded sound cataloging	GAUNT, Sandra L.	(OH)	423
Reference & cataloging	NELSON, Mary L.	(IA)	894
	BROWN-MAY, Patricia A.	(MI)	148
	FACINELLI, Jaclyn R.	(OH)	360
	FILIATRAULT, Andre Y.	(PQ)	376
Reference, cataloging & acquisitions	KOPAN, Ellen K.	(CA)	671
Reference file development, cataloging	TYLER, Kim E.	(OR)	1266
Retrospective cataloging	OSGOOD, James B.	(IL)	928
Retrospective cataloging & editing	HUGGENS, Gary D.	(DC)	571
Romance language cataloging	CRISTAN, Anita L.	(DC)	259
	JAVONOVICH, Kenneth L.	(IL)	595
Science & engineering cataloging	BRUNNER, A M.	(TX)	151
Science & serials cataloging	DODSON, Snowdy D.	(CA)	308

CATALOGING (Cont'd)

Topic	Name	State	Page
Science & technology cataloging	WALLACE, Wendy L.	(NJ)	1298
	LANDIS, Kay A.	(OH)	693
Science cataloging	EDWARDS, Jennifer L.	(CA)	337
	MARKHAM, James W.	(CA)	771
Scientific & technical cataloging	ELSBREE, John J.	(VA)	346
Score & record cataloging	SEIBERT, Donald C.	(NY)	1112
Selection, admin, reference, cataloging	MALTBY, Florence H.	(MO)	764
Serial & microform cataloging	NADESKI, Karen L.	(PA)	886
Serial cataloging	SCOTT, Sharon K.	(AZ)	1108
	HERRICK, Judith M.	(DC)	532
	HUGGENS, Gary D.	(DC)	571
	BLEIL, Leslie A.	(MI)	105
	SWETMAN, Barbara E.	(NY)	1216
Serials acquisition & cataloging	GRIFFITH, Joan C.	(NH)	469
Serials & cataloging	SELMER, Sylvia L.	(KY)	1114
Serials & monographs cataloging	TAVARES, Cecelia M.	(MA)	1225
	CHALMERS, Lois M.	(MD)	197
	ROSENSHIELD, Jill K.	(WI)	1057
Serials cataloging	CALLAHAN, Patrick F.	(AR)	173
	RUSSELL, Carne	(AZ)	1068
	ANDERES, Susan M.	(CA)	21
	BULLARD, Sharon W.	(CA)	156
	CHURUKIAN, Araxie P.	(CA)	213
	FULSAAS, Esther M.	(CA)	409
	HSIA, Ting M.	(CA)	567
	TURITZ, Mitch L.	(CA)	1263
	WU, Harriet	(CA)	1373
	BARELA, Lori A.	(CO)	56
	GLASBY, Dorothy J.	(DC)	439
	HIRONS, Jean L.	(DC)	543
	WANG, Margaret K.	(DE)	1303
	DONAHUE, Janice E.	(FL)	310
	GOLIAN, Linda M.	(FL)	447
	HARDIN, Barbara A.	(GA)	500
	VIDOR, Ann B.	(GA)	1283
	VISK, Linda S.	(GA)	1285
	COLE, Jim E.	(IA)	230
	MELROY, Virginia A.	(IA)	823
	JONES, Ann L.	(IL)	611
	LEONG, Carol L.	(IL)	717
	TRIMMER, Keith R.	(IL)	1256
	MCKOWEN, Dorothy K.	(IN)	812
	MERING, Margaret V.	(LA)	826
	TIMBERLAKE, Phoebe W.	(LA)	1245
	PAYNE, Douglass B.	(MA)	951
	WILSON, Virginia G.	(MA)	1353
	KINGSTON, Mary L.	(MD)	652
	WINZER, Kathleen M.	(MD)	1356
	KING, Kenneth E.	(MI)	651
	VAN CLEVE, Nancy J.	(MN)	1273
	NIEMEYER, Mollie M.	(MO)	903
	NYSTROM, Kathleen A.	(MO)	913
	TUTTLE, Joseph C.	(NC)	1266
	LANE, Alice L.	(NE)	694
	STRIMAN, Brian D.	(NE)	1202
	WOOL, Gregory J.	(NE)	1368
	BARRETT, Beth R.	(NH)	59
	FINLAY, J A.	(NH)	378
	BORRIES, Michael S.	(NY)	117
	CHAPMAN, Renee D.	(NY)	202
	DECKER, Jean S.	(NY)	285
	ROSENBERG-NUGENT, Nanci B.	(NY)	1056
	SCHNEIDER, Judith A.	(NY)	1097
	THOMAS, Catherine M.	(NY)	1236
	ADREAN, Louis V.	(OH)	7
	O'NEIL, Rosanna M.	(OH)	924
	KANCHANAKPAN, Pongsak	(OK)	624
	TOOLEY, Katherine J.	(OK)	1250
	OSHEROFF, Shiela K.	(OR)	928
	WIWEL, Pamela S.	(PA)	1359
	YOLTON, Jean S.	(PA)	1380
	KELLEY, Gloria	(SC)	636
	THOMAS, Julie A.	(SC)	1237
	RICHARDS, Susan L.	(SD)	1028
	BROSS, Valerie	(TN)	141
	PERRY, Glenda L.	(TN)	960

CATALOGING (Cont'd)

Serials cataloging
- DOMA, Tshering .... (TX) 310
- LATTIMORE, Clare I. ... (TX) 702
- WAN, William W. ...... (TX) 1302
- LEWIS, Diane M. ...... (VA) 723
- SADOWSKI, Frank E. ... (VA) 1074
- SCHWARTZ, Marla J. .. (VA) 1105
- ROMANIUK, Elena .... (BC) 1052
- ANNETT, Adele M. ..... (ON) 28
- GOODMAN, Julia M. ... (ON) 449
- FINLAY, Barbara J. .... (PQ) 378
- KRISHAN, Kewal ...... (SK) 678
- HARKINS, Diane G. .... (ENG) 501

Serials cataloging & holdings — WANG, Anna M. ...... (OH) 1302
Serials cataloging & management — COLLINS, Susan H. ..... (NB) 233
Serials cataloging & union listing — MURRAY, Diane E. .... (MI) 881
Shared cataloging networking online — BROWN, Pauline .... (AUS) 146
Sheet music cataloging — HOUSE, Katherine L. ... (KY) 563

Slavic cataloging
- MOLLOY, Molly F. ..... (AZ) 853
- KELLY, Mark M. .... (DC) 638
- HOWE, Priscilla P. ..... (KS) 565

Slavic languages cataloging — CAPRIELIAN, Arevig ... (NY) 180
Slide classification & cataloging — MCRAE, Linda .... (FL) 818
Slide indexing & cataloging — WALD, Ingeborg ..... (NY) 1294
Social science subject cataloging — DEVERA, Rosalinda M. ... (NY) 297
Social sciences cataloging — NOTARSTEFANO, Vincent C. .... (NY) 910

Software cataloging
- DUMLAO, Mercedes G. .. (CA) 325
- FLUK, Louise R. .... (PQ) 386

Software for cataloging — LOWELL, Brian V. ...... (IL) 744
Sound recording cataloging & databases — KLINGER, William E. ... (OH) 661

Sound recordings cataloging
- NUZZO, Nancy B. ..... (NY) 912
- FOLLET, Robert E. ..... (TX) 388

Spanish language cataloging — JAVONOVICH, Kenneth L. (IL) 595
Special collection cataloging — LANE, Mary J. .... (LA) 694

Special collections cataloging
- HERMAN, Elizabeth .... (CA) 531
- PODESCHI, John B. .... (IL) 979
- CHAPERO, Alicia ...... (NY) 201

Special collections catlgng & retrieval — KELLY, John P. .... (NJ) 638
Special languages cataloging — MCCLOY, William B. .... (IN) 797
Special libraries cataloging — ELROD, J M. .... (BC) 346
Special library cataloging — PYKE, Carol J. .... (VA) 999
Special material cataloging — KROSCH, Penelope S. ... (MN) 680
Special subject education cataloging — VERMA, Prem V. ...... (WV) 1282
Specialized cataloging & indexing — DE WITT, Benjamin L. .. (NJ) 298

State document cataloging
- MITCHELL, Micheal L. .. (AK) 849
- MITCHAM, Janet C. ..... (AR) 848
- MORRISSETT, Elizabeth (AK) 868
- ENYINGI, Peter .... (CA) 351

Subject cataloging
- MILSTEAD, Jessica L. .. (CT) 845
- DOBCZANSKY, Jurij W. (DC) 307
- HORCHLER, Gabriel F. . (DC) 559
- PENKIUNAS, Ruta M. .. (DC) 956
- YASUMATSU, Janet R. . (DC) 1378
- CHAN, Lois M. .... (KY) 199
- MAILLET, Lucienne G. .. (NY) 761
- BALATTI, David R. ..... (ON) 50
- WANG, Sing W. .... (AUS)1303

Subject cataloging & classification — KIRKWOOD, Francis T. .. (ON) 655
Subject cataloging anthropology — CARNAHAN, Stephanie B. (DC) 183
Subject cataloging of law books — KREH, Fritz .... (WGR)677
Supervising copy cataloging — KNIGHT, Rita C. .... (AZ) 664
Supervision, training, cataloging — VAN STRATEN, Daniel G. (WI) 1277
Surgical cataloging — RUBINSTEIN, Edith .... (NY) 1065
Teaching beginning cataloging — ALSWORTH, Frances W. .. (OK) 18
Teaching cataloging — KATO, Hisae .... (JAP) 629
Teaching cataloging & classification — MILLER, Sarah J. ...... (NJ) 842
Technical cataloging — JADWIN, Rochelle J. .... (CA) 591
Technical cataloging & reference — SIMPSON, Alice H. ..... (OH) 1141
Technical processing & cataloging — WHITE, Ardeen L. ...... (VA) 1330
Technical services, acqs & cataloging — MAZZEI, Peter J. ..... (NJ) 791

Technical services & cataloging
- SPURRIER, Suzanne F. .. (AR) 1177
- MENDENHALL, Bethany R. .... (CA) 824
- ELLIOTT, Barbara J. .... (IN) 343
- THOMAS, Victoria K. ... (IN) 1238
- ECKERSON, Gale E. ... (MA) 334
- JACKSON, Nancy G. ... (VA) 588

CATALOGING (Cont'd)

Technical services cataloging
- HUSKEY, Janet S. ..... (FL) 578
- LORNE, Lorraine K. .... (MI) 741
- SUMMERS, Sheryl H. .... (MI) 1209
- HAMDY, Mohamed N. .. (KWT) 491

Test cataloging — JORDAN, Robert P. .... (IA) 616
Textbook & circulation cataloging — WILSON, Carole F. .... (CA) 1350
Theological materials cataloging — RZECZKOWSKI, Eugene M. .... (DC) 1072
Theology cataloging — BURKE, Ambrose L. .... (OH) 160
Training catalogers — WANG, Ann C. .... (DC) 1302
Training for catalogers — TRUMPLER, Elisabeth .. (PA) 1259
Training in cataloging — STEWART, Richard A. .. (IL) 1193
Training of catalogers — GRIFFIN, Karen D. .... (OR) 468
University library cataloging — BARKER, Victoria S. ... (CO) 56
Video cataloging, indexing & abstracting — LOFTHOUSE, Patricia A. (IL) 737
Water resources cataloging — TORNABENE, Charles .. (FL) 1251
Workflow & cataloging — HERVEY, Norma J. .... (MN) 533

CATALOGS (See also PAC)

All media catalog & circulation — DU CARMONT, M C. .... (LA) 322
Analytic catalog — HOFFMAN, Herbert H. .. (CA) 548
Astronomical catalogs & atlases — KNUDSEN, Helen Z. .... (CA) 666
Auction catalog reference services — TIEMAN, Robert S. ..... (CA) 1244
Automated catalog — FRYMIRE, Jane K. ..... (MN) 407
Automated catalog maintenance — BRANDT, Janet E. ..... (MN) 128

Automated catalogs
- STOUT, Mary A. ...... (AZ) 1199
- RANSOM-BERGSTROM, Janette F. .... (MI) 1008

Automated circulation, public catalog — NIEMEYER, Karen K. ... (IN) 903
Automated pageform catalogs — GRUTCHFIELD, Walter . (NY) 475
Automated union catalogs & indexes — JAGOE, Katherine P. ... (TX) 591
Automating library catalog — AROKSAAR, Richard D. . (WA) 34
Automation book catalog, circulation — THOMAN, Nancy L. .... (DE) 1236
Book selection catalog department — KING, Willard B. .... (NC) 652
Catalog — JONES, Annabel B. .... (PA) 611
Catalog activities — BERTCHUME, Gary .... (NY) 90
Catalog administration — MONTEE, Monty L. .... (CT) 856
Catalog & retrospective conversion — CHAN, Margy .... (ON) 199
Catalog department — REILLY, Violet M. .... (OH) 1020
Catalog district library materials — EMERICK, John L. ..... (PA) 347
Catalog editing — DODGE, Christopher N. . (MN) 308
Catalog editing & publication — HENDRICKSON, Norma K. (DC) 527
Catalog, index & directory production — BUCKLAND, Lawrence F. (MA) 154
Catalog information — CATTIE, Mary M. ...... (PA) 195

Catalog maintenance
- STEWART, Anna C. .... (CO) 1192
- HARRIS, Virginia B. .... (VA) 506
- TURLEY, Georgia P. ..... (WA) 1263
- POPESCU, Constantin C. (WI) 983

Catalog management
- SCHOTTLAENDER, Brian E. .... (CA) 1099
- PASTER, Luisa R. ..... (NJ) 946
- HUSTON, Susan S. .... (TX) 578

Catalog of music magazines — FITZNER, Robert N. ... (IL) 382
Catalog of portraits of botanists — STIEBER, Michael T. ... (PA) 1193
Catalog use studies — KRIKELAS, James ..... (WI) 678
Catalogs — LAZZARONI, Philip S. .. (MD) 706
CD-ROM catalog production — CUMMINGS, Christopher H. .... (UT) 264
CD-ROM union catalogs — BEISER, Karl A. ...... (ME) 75
Centralized processing union catalog — BENSON, Laurel D. .... (MN) 83
Classification systems & catalogs — GOLDBERG, Jolande E. . (DC) 444
Collection & catalog management — DAGANAAR, Mark L. ... (SD) 269
COM catalogs — BOWRIN-MARSH, Donna M. .... (CA) 122
Computer catalog instruction — HOCKEL, Kathleen N. .. (CA) 545
Computer catalogs — MOSS, Barbara J. ..... (IL) 872
Computerized catalogs & databases — VANDERBERG, Patricia S. (CA) 1273
Datatrek computer catalog, serials — GENTRY, Susan K. .... (CA) 427
Designing recordings catalogs — GLASFORD, G R. ..... (NY) 440
Exhibition catalogs — STARR, Daniel A. ..... (NY) 1182
Historical card catalogs — WOOD, Sallie B. ...... (NY) 1359
Library catalog automation — WIWEL, Pamela S. .... (PA) 1359
Library catalogs & databases — YANEZ, Elva K. .... (CA) 1377
Machine-readable catalog records — GUILES, Kay D. .... (DC) 476
Manual & automated catalog management — KLAIR, Arlene F. ...... (MD) 657
Music catalog — MCINTOSH, Nadia ..... (MA) 809

CATALOGS (Cont'd)

Non-print catalog development   REHMS, Jane C. . . . . . . (WA) 1017
Online catalog   KIRKLAND, Janice J. . . . (CA) 655
                                 MERCADO, Marilyn J. . . (FL) 825
                                 WILEY, Theresa K. . . . . . (KY) 1339
                                 CHU, Wendy N. . . . . (NJ) 213
Online catalog database   BOWLES, Carol A. . . . . . (CA) 121
Online catalog development   BERGER, Michael G. . . . (CA) 85
                                 CLAYTON, William R. . . . (GA) 220
                                 GLEIM, David E. . . . . . . (NC) 441
Online catalog development & use BAKER, Paula J. . . . . . . (OH) 49
Online catalog development
   evaluation   CLARK, Sharon E. . . . . . (IL) 218
Online catalog instruction   KIRESEN, Evelyn M. . . . (CA) 654
                                 KNOWLES, Em C. . . . . . (CA) 665
                                 ABBOTT, Randy L. . . . . (FL) 1
                                 BECK, Susan E. . . . . . . (MO) 71
                                 NOWAKOWSKI, Frances
                                    C. . . . . (NS) 911
Online catalog issues   RITCH, Alan W. . . . . . . (CA) 1036
Online catalog maintenance   KIRKBRIDE, Amey L. . . . (OH) 654
                                 BABER, Elizabeth A. . . . (TX) 43
Online catalog management   STUBBS, Linda T. . . . . . (DC) 1204
                                 SELLBERG, Roxanne J. . (IN) 1113
Online catalog systems   PERONE, Karen L. . . . . . (NY) 959
Online catalog training   NOLAN, Christopher W. . (TX) 907
Online catalogs   BARANOWSKI, George V. (CA) 55
                                 BROWNRIGG, Edwin B. . (CA) 149
                                 DWYER, James R. . . . . . (CA) 330
                                 MONTGOMERY, Teresa L. (CA) 856
                                 SASSE, Margo . . . . (CA) 1083
                                 WILLIAMS, Joan F. . . . . (CA) 1344
                                 PRITCHARD, Sarah M. . (DC) 994
                                 RATESH, Ioana . . . . . . (DC) 1009
                                 CAMPBELL, John L. . . . (GA) 176
                                 GORDON, Elaine H. . . . . (IL) 451
                                 VARNER, Carroll H. . . . . (IL) 1278
                                 READY, Sandra K. . . . . . (MN) 1012
                                 FOX, Judith A. . . . . (MO) 395
                                 DAVIS, Jinnie Y. . . . . . . (NC) 279
                                 BRKIC, Beverly T. . . . . . (ND) 138
                                 JUNION, Gail J. . . . . . . (NY) 620
                                 MORRIS, Jennifer D. . . . (NY) 866
                                 SHERBY, Louise S. . . . . (NY) 1127
                                 LOGAN, Susan J. . . . . . (OH) 737
                                 SLOVASKY, Stephen . . . (OH) 1150
                                 SOUCIE, Yan Y. . . . . . . (OR) 1169
                                 KALIN, Sarah G. . . . . . . (PA) 623
                                 SUTHERLAND, Carl T. . (SC) 1211
                                 COOPER, Jean L. . . . . . (VA) 243
                                 SALT, David P. . . . . (SK) 1077
Online catalogs & systems   FORKES, David . . . . . . (ON) 390
Online electronic catalog instruction HITT, Charles J. . . . . . . (MN) 544
Online library catalogs   HILDRETH, Charles R. . . (IL) 539
Online public access catalogs   BISOM, Diane B. . . . . . (CA) 99
                                 DRIVER, Linda A. . . . . . (CA) 320
                                 GLASSMAN, Penny L. . . (MA) 440
                                 STERLING, Judith K. . . . (MD) 1189
                                 FABIAN, William M. . . . . (MO) 360
                                 HOWE, Ernest A. . . . . . (AB) 565
Oral history catalog publication KENDRICK, Alice M. . . . (NY) 640
Order & catalog materials   JOHNSON, Elizabeth L. . (NE) 604
Organz & indexing of manufacturer
   catlgs   SCHUSTER, Adeline . . . (IL) 1103
Public access catalogs   SHAPTON, Gregory B. . . (CA) 1122
Public access online catalogs   PHENIX, Katharine J. . . . (LA) 967
Public online catalogs   KELLEY, Betty H. . . . . . (TX) 636
Recording catalogs   CAMPBELL, R A. . . . . . (HI) 177
Regional union catalog automation PARRAVANO, Ellen A. . . (NY) 944
Remote access online catalogs   KALIN, Sarah G. . . . . . (PA) 623
Revising card catalog   WESTOVER, Mary L. . . . (AL) 1327
Revising catalogs   MANOVILLE, Susanne . . (PE) 767
State online catalog department NAUGLE, Gretchen R. . . (NE) 889
Training users of ILS, online catalog PRESLAR, M G. . . . . . . (TN) 991
Union catalog production   TSUI, Josephine . . . . . . (ON) 1260
Union catalogues   MCQUEEN, Lorraine . . . (ON) 817
                                 ARORA, Ved P. . . . . . . (SK) 34
Using local area network for catalogs HUGHES, Carol A. . . . . (OK) 571
Writing programs, online card catalog JORDAN, Sharon L. . . . . (WA) 617

CATHOLIC (See also Archdiocesan)

American Black Catholic history HOGAN, Peter E. . . . . . (MD) 549
Catholic Americana   AMES, Charlotte A. . . . . (IN) 19
Catholic archives   CASLIN, Adele . . . . (PA) 193
Catholic Church   MACEY, John F. . . . . . . (PA) 755
Catholic Church history   HILAND, Gerard P. . . . . (OH) 538
Catholic historical collections WALCH, Timothy G. . . . (DC) 1293
Catholic literature   BELLAVANCE, Maria I. . (TX) 78
Catholic newspapers   AMES, Charlotte A. . . . . (IN) 19
Catholic social action archives RUNKEL, Phillip M. . . . . (WI) 1067
Consultation on American Catholic
   hist   THOMAS, Evangeline M. (KS) 1236

CATSS

Cataloging with CATSS   ARSENAULT, Alban . . . . (NB) 35

CD (See also Compact)

CD, LP, 45, 78 & Edison recordings BAHR, Edward R. . . . . . (MS) 45
Mastersearch of trademarks on CD NICKEL, R S. . . . . (PA) 902

CD-I

CD-ROM & CD-I applications   GALE, John C. . . . . . . (VA) 413
CD-ROM & CD-I prog design &
   production   DAVISSON, Darell D. . . . (CA) 281

CD-ROM

CD-ROM   MACHOVEC, George S. . (AZ) 755
                                 BELL, Christina D. . . . . . (CA) 76
                                 MCCAY, Lynne K. . . . . . (DC) 795
                                 HAMILTON, Fae K. . . . . (MA) 492
                                 URBACH, Peter F. . . . . . (MA) 1269
                                 WEINSCHENK, Andrea . (MA) 1318
                                 MAYDET, Steven I. . . . . (NJ) 789
                                 BROOKS, Martin . . . . . . (NY) 140
                                 LAPIER, Cynthia B. . . . . (NY) 697
                                 ROSE, Pamela M. . . . . . (NY) 1055
                                 CO, Francisca . . . . (TN) 224
                                 BLOECHLE, Marie K. . . . (TX) 106
                                 HELGERSON, Linda W. . (VA) 524
                                 PUZIAK, Kathleen M. . . . (WA) 998
                                 GAGNE, Frank . . . . (ON) 412
CD-ROM & CD-I applications   GALE, John C. . . . . . . (VA) 413
CD-ROM & CD-I prog design &
   production   DAVISSON, Darell D. . . . (CA) 281
CD-ROM & microcomputer   KNIGHT, Nancy H. . . . . (VA) 664
CD-ROM & new technology   CEBULA, Theodore R. . . (WI) 196
CD-ROM applications   SCHIPMA, Peter B. . . . (IL) 1093
                                 GRAMINSKI, Denise M. . (NY) 457
                                 BILLS, Linda G. . . . . . . (PA) 96
                                 WIEMAN, Jean M. . . . . . (WA) 1336
CD-ROM buyer procurement support MILLER, Davic C. . . . . . (CA) 836
CD-ROM catalog production   CUMMINGS, Christopher
                                    H. . . . . (UT) 264
CD-ROM consulting   RIETDYK, Ron J. . . . . . (MA) 1033
CD-ROM data preparation   BEFELER, Mike . . . . . . (CO) 74
CD-ROM database development   DIETLE, Craig I. . . . . . . (NY) 302
CD-ROM database preparation   CIUFFETTI, Peter D. . . . (MA) 215
                                 LOWRY, John D. . . . . . (ON) 745
CD-ROM database publishing   POOLEY, Christopher G. . (MA) 983
CD-ROM database services   LESLIE, Nathan . . . . . . (ON) 718
                                 LOWRY, Douglas B. . . . . (ON) 745
CD-ROM databases   BOWRIN-MARSH, Donna
                                    M. . . . . (CA) 122
                                 BUTLER, Matilda L. . . . . (CA) 167
                                 DUGGAN, Mary K. . . . . (CA) 324
                                 TSENG, Sally C. . . . . . . (CA) 1260
                                 RIETDYK, Ron J. . . . . . (MA) 1033
                                 ALBRIGHT, John B. . . . . (MD) 10
CD-ROM development   MACLEOD, Valerie R. . . (KY) 757
CD-ROM development & marketing ANDREWS, Chris C. . . . (CT) 26
                                 MAIOLI, Jerry R. . . . . . . (WA) 762
CD-ROM development & training   HORNIG-ROHAN, James
                                    E. . . . . (PA) 560
CD-ROM hardware integration   CIUFFETTI, Peter D. . . . (MA) 215
CD-ROM library reference information HATVANY, Bela R. . . . . (MA) 512
CD-ROM management   DUNN, Kathleen K. . . . . (CA) 327

CD-ROM (Cont'd)

CD-ROM marketing	OVEREYNDER, Rombout E.	(NET)	931
CD-ROM, optical information systems	DESMARAIS, Norman P.	(RI)	295
CD-ROM product design	MCCLELLAND, Bruce A.	(NY)	796
CD-ROM product development	SPENCER, John T.	(CA)	1173
CD-ROM product marketing	CORCHADO, Veronica A.	(CA)	245
CD-ROM production	BATOR, Eileen F.	(MD)	64
CD-ROM publications	MCSPADDEN, Robert M.	(OH)	818
CD-ROM publisher	CHRISTIANSEN, Eric G.	(OH)	211
CD-ROM publishing	MILLER, Davic C.	(CA)	836
	DICK, John H.	(IL)	300
	STEPHENSON, Jon R.	(PA)	1188
	LEDOUX, Marc A.	(PQ)	708
CD-ROM publishing applications	KNOERDEL, Joan E.	(MD)	665
CD-ROM reader distribution	LESLIE, Nathan	(ON)	718
	LOWRY, Douglas B.	(ON)	745
	LOWRY, John D.	(ON)	745
CD-ROM retrieval software	DITMARS, David W.	(OH)	305
CD-ROM services	RIETDYK, Ron J.	(MA)	1033
	ALLEN, Robert R.	(NY)	16
CD-ROM systems	BEFELER, Mike	(CO)	74
	PRATT, Allan D.	(CT)	989
	MOES, Robert T.	(NY)	852
CD-ROM systems development	GOOGINS, Jennifer J.	(NY)	450
CD-ROM systems integration	DAVISSON, Darell D.	(CA)	281
CD-ROM technology	WILSON, Wayne V.	(CA)	1353
	WATSON, Paula D.	(IL)	1310
	CROSS, Jennie B.	(MI)	260
	HURLEY, Geraldine C.	(OH)	577
CD-ROM technology management	PHILLIPS, J R.	(OK)	968
CD-ROM union catalogs	BEISER, Karl A.	(ME)	75
Educational online & CD-ROM searches	LIVELY, Nancy J.	(MD)	734
Federal regulations on CD-ROM	CHRISTIANSEN, Eric G.	(OH)	211
Laser disks, CD-ROMS	GARMAN, Nancy J.	(KY)	419
Library applications of CD-ROM	MILLER, Davic C.	(CA)	836
Library automation CD-ROM	WHITE, Robert W.	(NJ)	1332
Marketing CD-ROM & online products	HUDES, Nan	(NY)	569
Microcomputer & CD-ROM	WILBUR, Helen L.	(NY)	1338
Microcomputer & CD-ROM applications	DAVIDSON, Lloyd A.	(IL)	276
Microcomputers & CD-ROM	BUTHOD, J C.	(OK)	166
Online & CD-ROM searching	KACHALA, Bohdanna I.	(NY)	621
Online & CD-ROM systems	MAXWELL, Christine Y.	(CA)	788
Online CD-ROM database searching	GRABINSKY, Warren B.	(BC)	455
Online CD-ROM databases	SEARS, Jonathan R.	(MD)	1110
Online databases & CD-ROM	GERSH, Barbara S.	(CA)	429
Optical data products, CD-ROM	STEFFEY, Ramona J.	(TN)	1185
Optical disk & CD-ROM	ROSE, Steven C.	(CA)	1055
Optical disks & CD-ROM	TALLY, Roy D.	(MN)	1221
Publishing on CD-ROM	NICKEL, R S.	(PA)	902
Real estate CD-ROM product development	JENKINS, George A.	(FL)	597
Software, CD-ROM	EDWARDS, David M.	(PA)	337
Work with CD-ROM	CONNORS, Martin G.	(MI)	238

CELEBRATIONS

Anniversary celebrations	CLAYTON, John M.	(DE)	220
Corporate history celebration	TURNER, Ellis S.	(MD)	1264

CELTIC

Celtic language materials	MILNE, Dorothy J.	(NF)	845

CEMENT

Cement chemistry	SPIGELMAN, Cynthia A.	(IL)	1174
Keywording cement & concrete technology	SPIGELMAN, Cynthia A.	(IL)	1174

CENSORSHIP (See also Intellectual)

Censorship	KRUG, Judith F.	(IL)	680
	ALLAIN, Alexander P.	(LA)	13
	DAILY, Jay E.	(PA)	270
	BONNELL, Pamela G.	(TX)	114
Censorship & intellectual freedom	WOODS, L B.	(AR)	1367
	DELZELL, Robert F.	(MO)	290

CENSORSHIP (Cont'd)

Censorship in school libraries	SCHMUHL, Gayle B.	(OH)	1096
Intellectual freedom & censorship	SEREBNICK, Judith	(IN)	1116
	ANDERSON, A J.	(MA)	21
	MCDONALD, Frances B.	(MN)	802
	BRUWELHEIDE, Janis H.	(MT)	151
	KERESEY, Gayle	(NC)	643
Intellectual freedom, censorship	OSSOLINSKI, Lynn	(NV)	928
	COHEN, David	(NY)	228
Monitoring book censorship attempts	KRUSE, Ginny M.	(WI)	681
Speaker on censorships	HORN, Zoia	(CA)	559

CENSUS

Census data	YORK, Grace A.	(MI)	1381
Census information	VAN DE VOORDE, Philip E.	(IA)	1274
Census statistics	DICKMEYER, John N.	(IN)	301
Demographic & census files	RUBIN, David S.	(NY)	1064
Demographics & census	RUTTER, Nancy R.	(MA)	1070
US Bureau of Census materials	MACKEY, Wendy W.	(MA)	757
United States census maps	SCHULZE, Suzanne S.	(CO)	1102
United States historical census	SCHULZE, Suzanne S.	(CO)	1102

CENTERS

Administration of learning resource ctr	BOOK, Imogene I.	(SC)	115
Aquaculture information center	HANFMAN, Deborah A.	(MD)	495
Archives & records center management	CAMPBELL, Margaret E.	(NS)	177
Art gallery outreach learning centers	PATTERSON, Grace L.	(NY)	948
Audiovisual center management	GOLDBERGER, Virginia F.	(IL)	445
Audiovisual centers	BROWN, Janis F.	(CA)	144
Automation of records centers	SMITH, David F.	(NY)	1154
Board-operated resource centers	BERTRAND, Doreen M.	(ON)	91
Career & employment centers	MALLINGER, Stephen M.	(PA)	763
Clearinghouse & information center mgmt	BYRD, Harvey C.	(MD)	169
Community centers	KENT, Charles D.	(ON)	642
Computer center management	BROWNRIGG, Edwin B.	(CA)	149
Computer use in media center	CARTER, Ann M.	(VA)	189
Computers in media centers	KISER, Anita H.	(NC)	656
Corporate & government information ctr	PEGLER, Ross J.	(FL)	954
Corporate archives & records center	PEGLER, Ross J.	(FL)	954
Corporate archives & records centers	CLAYTON, John M.	(DE)	220
Corporate information center management	STURDIVANT, Clarence A.	(CO)	1205
Corporate information centers	SIMPSON, Evelyn L.	(CA)	1141
	MICKEY, Melissa B.	(IL)	833
Corporate library & information ctr mgmt	RUTKOWSKI, Hollace A.	(PA)	1070
Curriculum center	MOORHEAD, Kenneth E.	(CT)	862
Curriculum materials center	HUEBNER, Mary A.	(NY)	570
Curriculum materials centers	RUDIE, Helen M.	(MN)	1065
Development of historical center	DUNGER, George A.	(SD)	326
Directing library & media centers	HAYASHI, Chigusa	(NJ)	515
Directing media center	COVINGTON, Eddis E.	(ID)	252
Education curriculum center	NORDSTROM, Virginia	(NY)	908
Education resource center	BADGER, Barbara	(IL)	44
Elementary library media centers	FARRIS, Mary E.	(TN)	365
Elementary media center activities	VAN SOMEREN, Betty A.	(MN)	1277
Elementary school media centers	BURGOON, Roger S.	(GA)	159
Establishing resource centers	KUHL, Danuta	(VA)	682
Evaluation of film centers	RICHIE, Mark L.	(NJ)	1030
Fee-based information centers	JOSEPHINE, Helen B.	(AZ)	617
Handicapped center, public library	ROATCH, Mary A.	(AZ)	1038
High school libraries & media centers	PORTA, Mary D.	(PA)	984
High school media center	KLOZA, Paula P.	(NJ)	662
Information & documentation center mgmt	MOUREAU, Magdeleine	(FRN)	873
Information center administration	BONACORDA, James J.	(NY)	113
	BROOME, Diana M.	(BC)	141
	BELLEFONTAINE, Gillian	(ON)	78
Info center & special lib management	COOPER, Marianne	(NY)	243
Information center management	ANGLE, Joanne G.	(DC)	28
	ECKROADE, Carlene B.	(DE)	335
	SIMS, Edward N.	(KY)	1142
	EISENMANN, Laura M.	(MA)	341

CENTERS (Cont'd)

Information center management
STEIGER, Bettie A.	. . . .	(MD)	1185
HOWELL, M G.	. . . .	(NY)	565
MARSHALL, Patricia K.	. .	(NY)	775
RIGNEY, Shirley A.	. . . .	(NY)	1034
POLLIS, Angela R.	. . . . . .	(PA)	981
UBALDINI, Michael W.	. . .	(TN)	1267

Information center mgmt & organization — ALBERTUS, Donna M. . . . (NY) 10

Information center management systems — WEIL, Ben H. . . . . (NJ) 1317

Information centers
FRANK, Robyn C.	. . . . .	(MD)	397
BAKER, Carole A.	. . . . .	(OH)	48
LEVIN, Pauline G.	. . . .	(PA)	720
BIRKS, Grant F.	. . . . .	(ON)	98

Instructional materials center — JOHNSON, Scott R. . . . (MS) 609

Instructional materials centers
KIRKENDALL, Carolyn A.		(MI)	654
OLSON, Dennis H.	. . . . .	(WI)	922

Jewish media center — KATZ, Lawrence M. . . . . (OH) 630

Job information center — BRODERICK, Therese L. (NY) 139

Job information centers — DESCH, Carol A. . . . . . (NY) 294

Juvenile collection centers — DIRKS, Martha W. . . . . (KS) 305

Learning center cataloging — KAWAGUCHI, Miyako . . (VA) 632

Lrng resrch ctr mgmt & reorganization — MIAH, Abdul J. . . . . (VA) 831

Learning resource center administration — BOROWSKI, Joseph F. . (IL) 117

Learning resource center col standards — BOOK, Imogene I. . . . . . (SC) 115

Learning resource centers — CARR, Charles E. . . . . . . (AL) 185

Learning resources center — JOHNSON, Scott R. . . . . (MS) 609

Learning resources center management — CAROL, Barbara B. . . . . (OK) 184

Learning resources centers
FRIEDMAN, Arthur L. . . .		(NY)	403
ADAMS, Elaine P.	. . . . .	(TX)	4

Libraries as profit centers — LUPPINO, Julie B. . . . . . (SC) 749

Library & info center administration — CROSS, Jennie B. . . . . . (MI) 260

Library & info center establishment — FINGERMAN, Susan M. . (MA) 378

Library & information center management
CEPPOS, Karen F.	. . . . .	(CA)	196
LEWIS, Ralph W.	. . . . .	(CA)	724
MADDOCK, Jerome T.	. . .	(CO)	759
FINGERMAN, Susan M.	. .	(MA)	378
PARAS, Lucille P.	. . . . .	(NJ)	939

Library & media center — FAVORITE, Grealdine J. . (LA) 366

Library & reference center management — MISSAR, Charles D. . . . . (MD) 847

Library learning centers — FERRO-NYALKA, Ruth R. (IL) 374

Library media center — WALTER, Maria . . . . (NY) 1300

Library media center administration — BUCKINGHAM, Betty J. . . (IA) 154

Library media center facilities planning — FROST, Rebecca H. . . . . (PA) 406

Library media centers
HILL, Sue A.	. . . .	(LA)	540
BROOKS, Burton H.	. . . .	(MI)	140
THOMAS, Lucille C.	. . . .	(NY)	1237

Library resource center management — SMITH, Noralee W. . . . . (OH) 1159

Management, micro data center — ASU, Glynis V. . . . . (WI) 37

Management of media center
LINDGREN, Beverly P.	. . .	(IL)	729
PRILLAMAN, Susan M.	. .	(NC)	993

Media center — EPIL, Charlene M. . . . . . (HI) 351

Media center administration
CLAVER, M P.	. . . .	(AL)	219
KOEPP, Sara H.	. . . .	(IA)	668
HELLER, Dawn H.	. . . . .	(IL)	524
CLEAVER, Betty P.	. . . .	(OH)	220

Media center card cataloging — MITCHELL, Phyllis R. . . . (GA) 849

Media center design — DRECHSEL, Marcella J. . (NJ) 319

Media center development — TITCOMB, Anne S. . . . . (MD) 1247

Media center management
MITCHELL, Phyllis R.	. . .	(GA)	849
TALAB, Rosemary S.	. . .	(KS)	1220
TRIM, Kathryn	. . . .	(MI)	1256
KUTTEROFF, Ethel C.	. . .	(NJ)	685

Media center management & operation — BRAUER, Regina . . . . . . (NY) 129

Media center management & teaching — CLEAVER, Betty P. . . . . (OH) 220

Media center operation & administration — EGAN, Terence W. . . . . . . (AZ) 338

Media center organization — FOERTIN, Yves P. . . . . . . (PQ) 387

Media center programs — PAULEY, Charles W. . . . (MN) 950

CENTERS (Cont'd)

Media centers
MARCHAND, Janet H.	. .	(CT)	768
MARTHALER, Margaret K.		(MN)	775
CHANDLER, Devon	. . . .	(MT)	199
CARSTATER, Mary E.	. .	(NY)	188
GOODMAN, John E.	. . . .	(PA)	449
PHARES, Abner J.	. . . . . .	(VI)	967

Medical center library — GHALI, Raouf S. . . . . . . (NY) 430

Microcomputer center
MEARS, William F.	. . . . . .	(TX)	820
WYNNE, Joseph J.	. . . .	(VA)	1375

Microcomputer public access centers — LARSON, Teresa B. . . . . (IA) 700

Micros in libraries/information centers — TRUETT, Carol A. . . . . . (HI) 1259

Middle school library media center admin — GOZEMBA, Frances E. . . (MA) 455

Middle school media centers — EDWARDS, Barbara T. . (TN) 337

Planning library media centers — APPEL MOSESOF, Rhoda S. . . . . (NJ) 29

Planning two-year learning resource ctr — BOOK, Imogene I. . . . . . (SC) 115

Processing center supervision — WINTER, Bernadette G. . (IL) 1356

Puppet center — DUFF, Margaret K. . . . . . (CO) 323

Record center operations — EDWARDS, Steven M. . . (WA) 338

Record centers — MCCREARY, Gail A. . . . (MS) 800

Records center
BROWNE, Jeri A.	. . . . . .	(CA)	148
WAGNER, Albin	. . . . . .	(RI)	1291

Reference career centers — HAWKE, Susan J. . . . . . (PQ) 513

Regional educational media centers — FITZGERALD, Ruth F. . . (MI) 382

Resource center development — EVANS, Stephen P. . . . . (OH) 358

Resource center management — BECHOR, Malvina B. . . . (GA) 71

Resource centers — GREENBERG, Roberta D. (NY) 463

Running a job information center — BEIMAN, Frances M. . . . (NJ) 75

Satellite information ctrs establishment — LAVIN, Margaret A. . . . . (NJ) 703

School district media centers — MOHN, Kari . . . . (AK) 852

School learning resource ctr consulting — GOTHIA, Blanche . . . . . . (TX) 453

School librarianship, media centers — RYUS, Phyllis K. . . . . . . (CA) 1072

School libraries & media centers
CARR, Charles E.	. . . . . .	(AL)	185
PELOVSKY, Suzy A.	. . .	(CA)	955
WEICK, Robert J.	. . . . . .	(IN)	1316
HAWKINS, Marilyn J.	. . .	(MO)	514
MULLER, Madeline A.	. .	(OH)	877

School library & media center
HERRING, Billie G.	. . . . .	(TX)	533
JENKS, Arlene I.	. . . . . .	(AK)	597
LEFF, Barbara Y.	. . . . .	(CA)	712
FENWICK, Sara I.	. . . . .	(FL)	371
HIRSCH, Elizabeth		(MA)	543
COURTNEY, Marjorie S.	. .	(MO)	251
GARDNER, Janet K.	. . . .	(NC)	418
RILEY, Marie R.	. . . .	(NJ)	1034
RUSSELL, Paula V.	. . . .	(TX)	1069
WU, Jean	. . . .	(TX)	1373
AXT, Randolph W.	. . . . .	(WI)	42

School library & media center management
SNYDER, Denny L.	. . . .	(MD)	1164
STEVENS, Elizabeth B.	. .	(NY)	1190

School library & media centers
DIERCKS, Eileen K.	. . . .	(IL)	302
KIRZINGER, Denise C.	. .	(KY)	656
DALBOTTEN, Mary S.	. .	(MN)	270
WEISENFELS, Marjorie A.	(MO)	1319
HUNTER, Cecilia A.	. . . .	(TX)	576
MOELLENDICK, M J.	. . .	(WV)	851
KRATZ, Hans G.	. . . . . .	(AB)	676

School library media center
DOOLEY, Sally J.	. . . . .	(AZ)	312
DAY, Bettie B.	. . . .	(CA)	282
WHALEY, Janie B.	. . . . .	(IN)	1328
HOLLEY, Rebecca M.	. . .	(LA)	551
COLYER, Judith A.	. . . . .	(MI)	234
WALL, Marilyn M.	. . . . .	(MI)	1297
MCDONALD, Frances B.		(MN)	802
FIRSCHEIN, Sylvia H.	. .	(NJ)	379
DILLINGER, Mary A.	. . .	(TX)	303
VEENSTRA, Geraldine B.	(TX)	1281
HAUG, Pauline C.	. . . . .	(WI)	512
MCKILLIP, Rita J.	. . . . . .	(WI)	811
KOGA, Setsuko	. . . .	(JAP)	668

School library media center automation — JOYCE, Robert A. . . . . . (NC) 618

School library media center management
MILLER, John E.	. . . . . .	(OH)	839
STANTON, Vida C.	. . . .	(WI)	1181

CENTERS (Cont'd)

School library, media centers

	SACHSE, Gladys M.	(AR)	1073
	BOWMAN, Kathleen A.	(CA)	122
	NIEMEYER, Kay M.	(CA)	903
	HEMPSTEAD, John	(CO)	525
	LOERTSCHER, David V.	(CO)	737
	HALE, Robert G.	(CT)	485
	LAPOLT, Margaret B.	(CT)	697
	WHITE, Charles R.	(CT)	1330
	FOSTER, Candice L.	(FL)	392
	HOLMES, Gloria P.	(FL)	553
	JONES, Winona N.	(FL)	615
	RAMEY, Linda K.	(FL)	1005
	ELIZABETH, Martin A.	(IA)	343
	MARTIN, Elizabeth A.	(IA)	776
	BIBLO, Mary	(IL)	94
	BEILKE, Patricia F.	(IN)	75
	HUNT, Margaret M.	(IN)	575
	SOLDNER, Nancy C.	(KS)	1166
	LIVINGSTON, Sarah M.	(KY)	735
	CARSTENS, Jane E.	(LA)	188
	STANTON, Martha	(MA)	1181
	FITZGERALD, Ruth F.	(MI)	382
	NICKEL, Mildred L.	(MI)	902
	OLSON, Lowell E.	(MN)	923
	SCHULZETENBERG, Anthony C.	(MN)	1102
	LITTLE, Nina M.	(NE)	733
	KUHLTHAU, Carol C.	(NJ)	682
	SEVERINGHAUS, Ethel L.	(NY)	1117
	SPIRT, Diana L.	(NY)	1175
	STAINO, Rocco A.	(NY)	1178
	VELLEMAN, Ruth A.	(NY)	1281
	ARK, Connie E.	(OH)	31
	AVERY, Jacqueline R.	(OH)	41
	MELTON, Vivian B.	(OH)	823
	COWEN, Linda L.	(OK)	253
	MURPHY, Diana G.	(PA)	880
	CARPENTER, Dorothy B.	(TN)	184
	SCOTT, Willodene A.	(TN)	1108
	IMMROTH, Barbara F.	(TX)	582
	KAHLER, June	(TX)	621
	REIFEL, Louie E.	(TX)	1019
	MILLS, Fiolina B.	(VI)	844

School lib media ctrs staff development	SMITH, Jane B.	(AL)	1155
School library resource centers	BERTRAND, Doreen M.	(ON)	91
School media center	JENSEN, Kathryn E.	(MA)	599
School media center administration	ROTH, Alvin R.	(MN)	1059
	JOYCE, Robert A.	(NC)	618
	LATROBE, Kathy H.	(OK)	701
	LAUGHLIN, Mildred A.	(OK)	703
School media center design	LEVEILLEE, Louis R.	(RI)	719
School media center evaluation	SLYGH, Gyneth	(WI)	1151
School media center instruction	JOYCE, Robert A.	(NC)	618
School media center management	GARLAND, Kathleen	(NY)	419
School media center resources	RUDIE, Helen M.	(MN)	1065
School media centers	JOHNSEN, Ellen I.	(IL)	601
	KRAUSE, Roberta A.	(IL)	676
	ROBINSON, Phyllis A.	(MA)	1044
	BUIST, Elaine R.	(SC)	156
	ANDIS, Norma B.	(TX)	26
	LABODDA, Marsha J.	(TX)	686
	PRETLOW, Delores Z.	(VA)	992
	REINAGLE, Carol M.	(WI)	1021
Secondary school library media centers	MILLER, George M.	(MA)	837
Secondary school media centers	RAKE, Anthony I.	(IL)	1004
Special Dutch heritage center	SLIEKERS, Hendrik	(IL)	1149
Special libraries & information centers	STRABLE, Edward G.	(IL)	1199
Standards for school media centers	CAIN, Carolyn L.	(WI)	171
State records center program management	BITTLE, Christine M.	(OK)	100
Synagogue & center library	FIRSCHEIN, Sylvia H.	(NJ)	379
Teaching use of media center	DAVIES, Gordon D.	(MD)	277
Technical information center management	EYLES, Heberle H.	(FL)	359
	HALL, Deanna M.	(GA)	487
Technical information centers	PERELLA, Susanne B.	(DC)	958
Technical processing center admin	ENGELBERT, Alan M.	(WI)	348

CENTERS (Cont'd)

Women's center	ROBBINS, Diane D.	(NY)	1038

CENTRAL (See also Main, Public Library)

Administration of central & main branch	APPELBAUM, Sara B.	(FL)	29
Central & branches	MOLTZAN, Janet R.	(TX)	854
Germanic area, central Europe	FRANK, Peter R.	(CA)	397
Select weed central adult circulation	DOYLE, Patricia A.	(TX)	317

CERAMICS

Ceramic technology reference	CULLEY, Paul T.	(NY)	263
Glass & ceramics research	DREIFUSS, Richard A.	(NY)	319

CEREMONIAL

Social, folk, & ceremonial dances	KELLER, Kate V.	(PA)	635

CERTIFICATION

Certified financial planner	ROSS, Ric	(CA)	1058
Profession certification	KWAN, Julie K.	(CA)	685
School library media certification	SORENSEN, Richard J.	(WI)	1168
Standards & certification information	OVERMAN, Joanne R.	(MD)	931

CHAMBER

Chamber music	WALKER, Elizabeth	(PA)	1295

CHANGE

Career change for librarians	BERKNER, Dimity S.	(NY)	87
Change & loss in children's literature	ELAM, Barbara C.	(MA)	341
Change implementation	JOHNSON, Margaret A.	(MN)	607
Continuing education change agent	BRUCE, Robert K.	(MN)	149
Management of change	NERODA, Edward W.	(MT)	895
Monitoring corporate change intervals	BILES, Mark J.	(NJ)	96
Organization change	ROBINSON, Barbara M.	(MD)	1043
Organizational change	EHRHORN, Jean H.	(HI)	339
	SMALL, Sally S.	(PA)	1151
	BUSCH, B J.	(AB)	165

CHANT

Gregorian chant	WEBER, Jerome F.	(NY)	1314

CHAPTERS

American Library Association chapters	GESSNER, Marianne	(MI)	430

CHARACTER

Optical character recognition	MAYDET, Steven I.	(NJ)	789
	ERDT, Terrence	(PA)	352
	HARTT, Richard W.	(VA)	509

CHARTERED

Chartered accounting	PORTER, David E.	(ON)	984

CHEMISTRY (See also Biochemistry, CAS, Electrochemical, Petrochemicals, Toxicology)

Biological & chemical databases	BORCK, Liba	(ISR)	116
Biology & chemistry	ANDERSON, Ruby N.	(AL)	25
Biology & chemistry collection devlpmnt	DODSON, Snowdy D.	(CA)	308
Biology, chemistry	KHAN, Mohammed A.	(SDA)	646
Business & chemistry databases	DAVIS, Sara	(TX)	281
Cement chemistry	SPIGELMAN, Cynthia A.	(IL)	1174
Chemical abstracts searching	BOLEK, Ann D.	(OH)	112
Chemical & agriculture databases	CLARK, Wendolyn H.	(AL)	218
Chemical & agronomy research	GAMBRELL, Drucilla S.	(AL)	416
Chemical & biological databases	STODDARD, Charles E.	(CT)	1196
	SUPEAU, Cynthia	(CT)	1210
Chemical & biomedical information	RADER, Ronald A.	(DC)	1002
Chemical & business databases	MARTINO, Sharon C.	(IN)	779

CHEMISTRY (Cont'd)

Chemical & business reference	WILLARD, Ann M.	(CA)	1341
Chemical & coatings databases	KOZELKA, Catherine C.	(IL)	674
Chemical & engineering databases	SCHUTZBERG, Frances	(MA)	1103
Chemical & medical databases	CHATFIELD, Michele R.	(DC)	203
Chemical & metallurgical databases	BERGER, Lewis W.	(PA)	85
Chemical & physical scis database srchng	REDALJE, Susanne J.	(WA)	1013
Chemical & technical online searching	SPECTOR, Janice B.	(MI)	1172
Chemical & toxicological databases	COSMIDES, George J.	(MD)	249
Chemical & toxicology database searching	TAYLOR, Melissa P.	(CT)	1227
Chemical, biological & medical databases	LONGENECKER, William H.	(MD)	740
Chemical, biological, medical databases	FARREN, Ann L.	(PA)	365
Chemical business	LERITZ, M K.	(CT)	717
Chemical business information databases	REITANO, Maimie V.	(NY)	1022
Chemical business, marketing	FOOS, Ferol A.	(LA)	388
Chemical database	AUER, E E.	(NJ)	39
Chemical database development	CARSON, Bonnie L.	(MO)	188
Chemical database searching	REID, Angea S.	(MA)	1018
	FERRAINOLO, John J.	(PA)	373
	HESLIN, Catherine M.	(PA)	534
	WACASEY, Mary M.	(PQ)	1290
Chemical databases	CHADWICK, Sharon S.	(CA)	197
	HAUTH, Carol A.	(CA)	513
	LAI, Dennis	(CA)	688
	MOUNTFORD, Eve	(CT)	873
	KECK, Bruce L.	(DC)	633
	GAUMOND, Suzanne M.	(IL)	423
	STUNKARD, Gilbert L.	(IL)	1205
	CHANDIK, Barbara V.	(IN)	199
	FRANKLIN, Janice C.	(KS)	397
	COOPER WYMAN, Rosalind	(MA)	244
	EVANS, Sylvia D.	(MD)	358
	MARCHANT, Thomas O.	(MO)	768
	PORTER, Katherine R.	(NC)	985
	ALLISON, Kenneth J.	(NJ)	17
	CARNAHAN, Joan A.	(NJ)	183
	FEDORS, Maurica R.	(NJ)	368
	LEWIS, Dale E.	(NJ)	722
	NOCKA, Jean A.	(NJ)	906
	SKIDANOW, Helene	(NJ)	1146
	FALCONE, Elena C.	(NY)	362
	LANE, Sandra G.	(NY)	694
	WARDEN, Carolyn L.	(NY)	1304
	BUTCHER, Sharon L.	(OH)	166
	LANDIS, Kay A.	(OH)	693
	O'BRIEN, Mary C.	(OR)	915
	HANF, Elizabeth P.	(PA)	495
	STANLEY, Kerry G.	(PA)	1180
	BOWMAN, Laura M.	(TX)	122
	GRIMES, John F.	(TX)	470
	SAMPLE, Charles R.	(WA)	1078
	TIMMERS, Debra A.	(WI)	1246
	CHAPMAN, Phyllis C.	(ON)	202
	HOBBS, Kathleen M.	(ON)	545
	O'DONNELL, Rosemary F.	(ON)	917
	VUKOV, Vesna	(ON)	1290
Chemical databases & info retrieval	ROSENTHAL, Francine C.	(OH)	1057
Chemical databases & searching	LINEPENSEL, Kenneth C.	(IN)	730
Chemical databases & sources	GALBRAITH, Barry E.	(NY)	413
Chemical databases building	BAKER, Dale B.	(OH)	48
Chemical databases, science databases	COSGRIFF, John C.	(VA)	248
Chemical engineering	VOSS, Ingrid M.	(IL)	1289
	BIGGS, Barbara R.	(LA)	95
	GASPAR, Noel J.	(ON)	421
Chemical engineering bibliography	WEAVER, James B.	(FL)	1312
Chemical engineering indexing	WEAVER, James B.	(FL)	1312
Chemical engineering references	MONTGOMERY, Kimberly K.	(AL)	856
Chemical hazards databases	BRANSFORD, John S.	(TN)	129
Chemical indexing	PACETTI, Karen C.	(IL)	933
Chemical industry	KLEIN, Regina D.	(MO)	659

CHEMISTRY (Cont'd)

Chemical information	LOPEZ, Frank D.	(CA)	741
	ROTH, Dana L.	(CA)	1059
	TASHIMA, Marie	(CA)	1224
	HEARTY, John A.	(DC)	519
	DRUKKER, Alexander E.	(DE)	320
	O'NEILL, Patricia E.	(GA)	924
	KAMINECKI, Ronald M.	(IL)	624
	STOKES, Claire Z.	(MN)	1196
	DEDERT, Patricia L.	(NJ)	286
	KLEMM, Carol B.	(NJ)	660
	GILLEN, Bonnie J.	(PA)	435
	OWENS, Frederick H.	(PA)	932
	LYDEN, Edward W.	(TX)	750
	CLEMANS, Margaret H.	(VA)	220
	SOUTHWICK, Margaret A.	(VA)	1170
Chemical information database building	PLATAU, Gerard O.	(OH)	977
Chemical information instruction	SOMERVILLE, Arleen N.	(NY)	1167
Chemical information, lit searching	JOHNSON, David K.	(NJ)	603
Chemical information retrieval	SIMMONS, Edlyn S.	(OH)	1139
Chemical information searching	BUNTROCK, Robert E.	(IL)	157
Chemical information services	PORTER, Katherine R.	(NC)	985
Chemical information specialist	YANCEY, Marianne	(OH)	1377
Chemical information specialization	ROUSE, Kendall G.	(WI)	1061
Chemical information systems	BURCSU, James E.	(NC)	158
	LEWIS, Dale E.	(NJ)	722
	WAGNER, A B.	(NY)	1291
	DUANE, Carol A.	(OH)	321
	VLADUTZ, George E.	(PA)	1286
	ROSENBERG, Murray D.	(VA)	1056
Chemical literature	WILLHITE, Sherry	(CA)	1341
	MITCHELL, Martha M.	(IL)	849
	MAYER, June C.	(NJ)	789
Chemical literature & reference	YAGELLO, Virginia E.	(OH)	1376
Chemical literature search	CHU, Insoo L.	(CA)	212
Chemical literature searching	LAMBERT, Nancy	(CA)	690
	LERITZ, M K.	(CT)	717
	KASPERKO, Jean M.	(PA)	629
Chemical lit, substructure searching	SAARI, David S.	(IN)	1072
Chemical, medical databases	URKEN, Madeline	(NJ)	1270
Chemical nomenclature	JUTERBOCK, Deborah K.	(NJ)	620
	NOCKA, Jean A.	(NJ)	906
Chemical, patent databases	STAVETSKI, Norma K.	(NJ)	1183
Chemical patent searching	WEHNER, Karen B.	(TN)	1316
Chemical patents, literature databases	UMFLEET, Ruth A.	(TX)	1268
Chemical reactions information	DIXON, Michael D.	(VA)	306
Chemical reference	AVERY, May S.	(IL)	42
Chemical research	AUER, E E.	(NJ)	39
Chemical searches	FULLER, Kathleen B.	(OH)	408
Chemical searching	PACETTI, Karen C.	(IL)	933
	SKLADANOWSKI, Lawrence M.	(NC)	1146
	JUTERBOCK, Deborah K.	(NJ)	620
	LERITZ, M K.	(CT)	717
Chemical structure searching	SOUTHWICK, Margaret A.	(VA)	1170
Chemical structure software evaluation			
Chemical substance information retrieval	STOBAUGH, Robert E.	(OH)	1195
Chemical substructure searching	LEWIS, Dale E.	(NJ)	722
	DOBBS, David L.	(OH)	307
Chemical toxicology	NOWAK, Geraldine D.	(DC)	911
	MORRISON, Brian H.	(ON)	867
Chemicals & patents online searching	NEWMAN, Robert M.	(TX)	899
Chemistry	GROOT, Elizabeth N.	(CA)	472
	SAYLOR, Linda	(CA)	1086
	HALL, Deanna M.	(GA)	487
	GALOW, Donald G.	(IN)	415
	WEHLACZ, Joseph T.	(IN)	1316
	BIGGS, Barbara R.	(LA)	95
	JAZBINSCHEK, Jerri	(MI)	596
	GODT, Carol	(MO)	443
	SHAH, Syed M.	(NY)	1119
	MIMNAUGH, Ellen N.	(OH)	845
	SCHUTZ, Robert S.	(OH)	1103
	DONOVAN, Kathryn M.	(PA)	312
	SCHWARZ, Betty M.	(PA)	1105
	SCHWEITZER, Margaret C.	(PA)	1105
	GASPAR, Noel J.	(ON)	421

CHEMISTRY (Cont'd)

Chemistry & business	ALSTADT, Nancy A. ...	(PA)	18
Chemistry & engineering	THORP, Raymond G. ...	(ENG)	1242
Chemistry & engineering reference	BECK, Diane J.	(CA)	71
Chemistry & environmental databases	TYLER-WHITE, Patricia G.	(TX)	1266
Chemistry & geology reference	HOBBS, Kathleen M. ...	(ON)	545
Chemistry & industrial health	CASSAR, Ann	(PA)	193
Chemistry & physical sciences databases	BECK, Diane J.	(CA)	71
Chemistry & physics	ORCUTT, Roberta K. ...	(NV)	925
	HELWIG, Karen A.	(WI)	525
Chemistry & technology	GUIDA, Pat	(NJ)	476
Chemistry bibliographic instruction	WIGGINS, Gary D. ...	(IN)	1337
Chemistry databases	KLEINER, Donna H.	(CA)	660
	PETERSON, Gretchen N.	(CA)	963
	POKLAR, Mary J.	(CA)	980
	KLEMARCZYK, Laurice D.	(CT)	660
	CARUSO, Joy L.	(IL)	190
	OLIVER, James W.	(MI)	921
	DICKERSON, Jimmy ...	(NC)	300
	SMITH, Yvonne B.	(NJ)	1161
	MCGEE, Yvonne M.	(PA)	806
Chemistry databases & reference	MILLER, Dennis P.	(OH)	837
Chemistry, engineering	GARCIA, Ceil K.	(NJ)	417
Chemistry engineering & physics	SCHALIT, Michael	(CA)	1089
Chemistry including databases	MIRONENKO, Rimma ...	(CA)	847
Chemistry library management	DEGOLYER, Christine C.	(NY)	288
Chemistry, materials	SLOAN, Maureen G. ...	(OR)	1149
Chemistry, physics, soil science	VIERICH, Richard W. ...	(CA)	1284
Chemistry reference	HUBER, Charles F.	(CA)	568
	EVANS, Sylvia D.	(MD)	358
	DESS, Howard M.	(NJ)	295
Chemistry reference & online searching	STANLEY, Eileen H.	(LA)	1180
Chemistry searching	COHEN, Hannah V.	(NY)	228
	BRANCHICK, Susan E. .	(OH)	127
Chem structures & substructure searching	MACKSEY, Julie A.	(MI)	757
Chemistry subject specialization	DRUM, Carol A.	(FL)	320
Collection development, chemistry	BOWMAN, Laura M. ...	(TX)	122
Cosmetic & chemical information	DEXTER, Patrick J.	(MD)	298
Database searching, food sciences, chem	REED, Catherine A.	(NY)	1015
Database searching in chemistry & engrng	WEST, Deborah C.	(TX)	1326
Editing chemical & medical text	GRIFFITHS, Mary C. ...	(MD)	469
Encyclopedias, chemical & others	GRAYSON, Martin	(NY)	460
End-user instruction in chem databases	BECK, Diane J.	(CA)	71
Engineering physics & chemical databases	GENTRY, Susan K.	(CA)	427
Engineering, scintfc, chemical databases	PELLINI, Nancy M.	(MA)	955
	RILEY, Sarah A.	(MD)	1035
Flavor chemistry	NEMETH, Martha C.	(CA)	895
Food chemistry	RILEY, Sarah A.	(MD)	1035
Food science, chemistry & technology	HANF, Elizabeth P.	(PA)	495
Indexing chemical files	WENGER, Milton B.	(NY)	1324
Literature chemist	MEYER, Daniel E.	(PA)	830
Mainframe-based chemical info systems	STOBAUGH, Robert E. ...	(OH)	1195
Management chemical information research	LEICHTMAN, Anne B. ...	(NJ)	713
Medical & chemical databases	RATHGEBER, Jo F.	(NC)	1009
Medical & chemical searching	PAPROCKI, Mary E.	(NJ)	939
Medical chemical environmental databases	MOYNIHAN, Mary B.	(CT)	874
Medical pharmaceutical chemical database	LASSLO, Andrew	(TN)	700
Medicinal chemistry	MEYER, Daniel E.	(PA)	830
Microcomputer-based chemical info system	PETRY, Robyn E.	(IL)	965
Online chemical searching	CHEN, Flora F.	(SK)	205
Online chemistry searching	COGHLAN, Jill M.	(MA)	227
Organic chemistry searching	TAYLOR, Donna I.	(NJ)	1226
Patent, chemical & business databases	POOL, Madlyn K.	(VA)	982
Patents & chemistry	BONDAROVICH, Mary F.	(NJ)	113
Pharmaceutical chemistry	KAN, Halina S.	(NJ)	624
Physics & chemistry			

CHEMISTRY (Cont'd)

Reference, chemical & medical databases	WINGATE, Dawn A.	(CA)	1354
Research, chemistry & metallurgy	SCHLOTT, Florenceann .	(PA)	1094
Scientific & chemical indexing	BARNETT, Philip	(NY)	58
Scientific, chemical, medical databases	ANTOS, Brian F.	(PA)	29
Searching patent & chemical databases	MILES, Donald D.	(PA)	834
Software chemical, petroleum engineering	WILSON, John W.	(TX)	1351

CHEROKEE

Cherokee history	SUMNER, Delores T. ...	(OK)	1209

CHICANO (See also Hispanic, Mexican, Spanish)

Chicano studies	CHAVEZ, Linda	(CA)	204
	DURAN, Karin J.	(CA)	328
	PAUL, Jeff H.	(CA)	949

CHILDREN (See also Juvenile, Toddlers, Young, Youth)

Acquisitions, children's materials	CORLEE, Lisa	(OK)	246
Administration of children's department	GREENFIELD, Judith C. .	(NY)	464
Adult & children literacy	LENGES, Magdelene ...	(IN)	715
Adult & children reference	POTTER, Robert E.	(FL)	987
Adult & children's book selection	GENCO, Barbara A.	(NY)	426
Adult & children's programming	CHRISTNER, Terry A. ...	(KS)	212
	HILDEBRANT, Darrel D. .	(ND)	539
Adult & children's reference service	KAPUR, Geraldine P. ...	(MI)	626
Adult & children's services	ELGIN, Susan R.	(CA)	342
Afro-American children's literature	ELAM, Barbara C.	(MA)	341
All children's library services	KELLY, Anne V.	(FL)	637
Animals in children's books	FREEDMAN, Barbara G. .	(NC)	400
Author, children's textbooks	BISSETT, Donald J. ...	(MI)	100
Author of children's biographies	MILLENDER, Dharathola .	(IN)	835
Book reviewing, children's	PAGOTTO, Sarah L.	(PA)	934
Book selection, children's	LYTLE, Marian M.	(NC)	753
Bookmaking, children as authors	HERRICK, Johanna W. ...	(HI)	532
Books for children	RUSS, Kennetta P.	(MD)	1068
Books for gifted children	HALSTED, Judith W. ...	(MI)	490
Booktalking, children's books	GREESON, Janet S. ...	(AR)	465
Canadian children's literature	MARTINEZ, Helen	(NF)	779
	AUBREY, Irene E.	(ON)	38
	HAMBLETON, Alixe E. ...	(SK)	490
Cataloging children's materials	WINKEL, Lois	(NC)	1355
Change & loss in children's literature	ELAM, Barbara C.	(MA)	341
Child advocate, public relations	BANTA, Gratia J.	(OH)	55
Child growth & development	WALTHER, Richard E. ...	(CA)	1301
Child psychiatry	WALLER, Carolyn A.	(RI)	1298
Child-book interaction	WINKLER, Carol A.	(MO)	1355
Children	SALLSTROM, Marilee A.	(CA)	1077
	CHAPIN, Joan R.	(NJ)	201
	LOTZ, Marilyn R.	(NJ)	742
Children & adult reference & referral	DAYO, Ayo	(TX)	283
Children & storytelling	MOLLENKOPF, Carolyn M.	(MD)	853
Children & young adult books	GILBERT, Ophelia R. ...	(MO)	434
	MCELDERRY, Margaret K.	(NY)	804
Children & young adult library services	PARIS, Janelle A.	(TX)	940
Children & young adult literature	MARR, Charles A.	(CA)	773
	HATHAWAY, Milton G. .	(NC)	512
	BURT, Lesta N.	(TX)	164
Children & young adult reference	TUPPER, Bobbie	(HI)	1263
Children & young adult selection	MATECUN, Marilyn L. ...	(MI)	783
Children & young adult services	SRYGLEY, Sara K.	(FL)	1177
	BARRETT, John C.	(NY)	59
	PANCOE, Deborra S. ...	(PA)	937
	STATTON, Alison H.	(TX)	1183
	FLETCHER, Robert A. ..	(WA)	385
	SHELDEN, Lucinda D. ..	(WA)	1125
Children & young adults	PROVOST, Beverly A. ..	(NY)	996
Children & young adults booktalking	ROCHMAN, Hazel P. ...	(IL)	1046
Children & young people services	BARRON, Daniel B. ...	(SC)	60
Children & youth literature	OAKLEY, Adeline D. ...	(MA)	913
Children & youth services	CHURCH, Sonia J.	(CA)	213
	KAN, Katharine L.	(HI)	624

CHILDREN (Cont'd)

Children & youth services, bibliotherapy	SMITH, Alice G.	(FL)	1152
Children collection development	ADDY, Kathryn J.	(ON)	6
Children services	CZOPEK, Vanessa	(AZ)	269
	SLEEMAN, Linda E.	(OH)	1148
	HARKINS, Anna W.	(PA)	501
Children's activities	SCHULTZ, Christine K. . .	(MI)	1102
Children's activity books author	HAAS, Carolyn B.	(IL)	480
Children's & foreign books	ROBIEN, Eleanor K.	(IL)	1043
Children's & young adult books	JONES, Trevelyn E.	(NY)	615
Children's & young adult librarianship	TALBERT, Dorothy R. . .	(UT)	1220
Children's & young adult literature	ROSEN, Elizabeth M. . . .	(CA)	1055
	DAIGNEAULT, Audrey I.	(CT)	270
	FISHER, Margery M. . . .	(CT)	381
	SPENCER, Albert F.	(GA)	1173
	LOWE, Joy L.	(LA)	744
	EHRICH, Joan C.	(MA)	339
	WERNER, Laura L.	(MO)	1325
	O'BRYANT, Alice A. . . .	(MT)	915
	BUSBIN, O M.	(NC)	164
	HERBERT, Barbara R. . .	(NJ)	530
	VANDERGRIFT, Kay E. .	(NJ)	1274
	MASCIA, Regina B.	(NY)	780
	LATROBE, Kathy H.	(OK)	701
	LAUGHLIN, Mildred A. . .	(OK)	703
	ANTHONY, Rose M. . . .	(WI)	29
	DRESANG, Eliza T.	(WI)	319
	HOWARD, Elizabeth F. . .	(WV)	564
	SALTMAN, Judith M. . . .	(BC)	1077
	HAMBLETON, Alixe E. . .	(SK)	490
Children's & young adult mtrls selection	ROBERTS, Sallie H.	(OH)	1041
Children's & young adult programming	WALSH, Lynn R.	(FL)	1299
Children's & young adult programs	SOMERVILLE, Mary R. . .	(KY)	1167
	O'BRYANT, Alice A. . . .	(MT)	915
Children's & young adult services	CANTILLAS, Caroline M.	(LA)	179
	HOMAN, Frances M. . . .	(MD)	555
	GORMAN, Audrey J. . . .	(NJ)	452
	RAZZANO, Barbara W. .	(NJ)	1012
	CHEATHAM, Bertha M. .	(NY)	204
	LAUGHLIN, Mildred A. . .	(OK)	703
	BROADWAY, Marsha D. .	(UT)	138
	CHAUVETTE, Catherine A.	(VA)	204
	JONES, Norma L.	(WI)	614
Children's & young adult work	BARNARD, Sandra K. . .	(CA)	57
Children's & young people's literature	BRUNER, Katharine E. . .	(TN)	150
Children's & youth services	BOGGUS, Tamara K. . . .	(FL)	110
	KERESEY, Gayle	(NC)	643
Children's author	KERBY, Ramona A.	(TX)	643
Children's book editing	VESTAL, Jeanne G.	(NY)	1283
Children's book illustration	OLDERSHAW, Anne . . .	(NY)	920
Children's book information service	RUSS, Kennetta P.	(MD)	1068
Children's book publishing	SUTHERLAND, Zena B. .	(IL)	1211
	EPSTEIN, Connie C. . . .	(NY)	351
Children's book reviewer	NICHOLS, Margaret M. .	(AZ)	901
Children's book reviewing	WILSON, Phillis M.	(IL)	1352
	GILLIS, Ruth J.	(MN)	436
	WILLIAMS, Deborah H. .	(NY)	1342
Children's book selection	WISOTZKI, Lila B.	(MD)	1358
	RAFAL, Marian D.	(MI)	1003
	STEELE, Anitra T.	(MO)	1184
Children's book selection & programming	GENDRON, Michele M. . .	(PA)	426
Children's books	SACHSE, Gladys M.	(AR)	1073
	ELLEMAN, Barbara J. . .	(IL)	343
	MADAY, Geraldine	(IL)	758
	TURCHI, Marilyn L.	(IL)	1263
	HOGAN, Margaret A. . . .	(MA)	549
	SILVEY, Anita L.	(MA)	1139
	MORGAN, Betty J.	(MD)	863
	COOPER, Ruth K.	(NC)	243
	FREEMAN, Patricia E. . .	(NM)	401
	BREEN, Karen B.	(NY)	131
	GAUCH, Patricia L.	(NY)	422
	HOLTZE, Sally H.	(NY)	555
	LAPIDUS, Lois E.	(NY)	697
	WHIPPLE, Judith R.	(NY)	1329
	NANCE, Lena L.	(OH)	887

CHILDREN (Cont'd)

Children's books			
	OVERHOLT, Maria B. . . .	(OH)	931
	FIELD, Carolyn W.	(PA)	375
	YOUREE, Beverly B. . . .	(TN)	1384
	TEDDER, Dorothy L.	(TX)	1229
	REMICK, Katherine G. . .	(VA)	1022
	MATHES, Miriam S.	(WA)	783
	MEYER, Laura M.	(WA)	830
	ALLARD, Diane	(PQ)	14
	LONDON, Eleanor	(PQ)	738
Children's books & literature	MOSES, Camelia T.	(NY)	871
Children's books & programming	BADERTSCHER, Kimberlin H.	(IN)	44
Children's books consulting	FEDERICI, Yolanda D. . .	(IL)	368
Children's books, editing	BENEDUCE, Ann K.	(NJ)	80
Children's books, publishing & libraries	BOTHAM, Jane	(WI)	118
Children's cataloging	BAILEY, Darlene L.	(CA)	46
Children's circulation	CAPELLA, Jeanne M. . . .	(NJ)	179
Children's collection development	BECKER, Teresa J.	(AZ)	72
	KELLY, Anne V.	(FL)	637
	RASKIN, Susan R.	(MA)	1009
	MORRIS, Kim	(NY)	867
	BERNARD, Marie L.	(AB)	88
	MARION, Luce	(PQ)	770
	GAGNON, Andre	(SK)	412
Children's collections	WATERS, Bill F.	(MO)	1308
	STURM, Danna G.	(NV)	1205
Children's consultant	BAKULA, Patricia A.	(WI)	50
Children's consultant services	DOWNS, Jane B.	(IL)	317
Children's division	VAN HOORN, Audra G. . .	(IL)	1275
Children's education	HOLLAND, Deborah K. . .	(TX)	550
Children's English & French literature	WALSH, Mary A.	(PQ)	1300
Children's film production	DAVENPORT, Thomas R. ·	(VA)	276
Children's films & videotapes	GAFFNEY, Maureen	(NY)	412
Children's health care	ADENEY, Carol D.	(WGR)	6
Children's illustrators	RIFE, Mary C.	(MI)	1033
Children's librarian	HECKLINGER, Ellen L. . .	(CA)	519
	HEINTZMAN, Justina . . .	(KY)	522
	BECKER, Barbara S. . . .	(NE)	72
	BERRY, Mary A.	(TX)	90
	BAKULA, Patricia A.	(WI)	50
Children's librarian, elementary school	POBANZ, Becky L.	(MI)	979
Children's librarian, public library	POBANZ, Becky L.	(MI)	979
Children's librarian training	BREEN, Karen B.	(NY)	131
Children's libn training & development	BOTHAM, Jane	(WI)	118
Children's librarianship	JENKINS, Joyce K.	(AK)	597
	WRIGHT, Pauline W. . . .	(AR)	1372
	MURPHY, Patricia A. . . .	(CA)	881
	SPIRO GREEN, Becky A. .	(CA)	1175
	VAN ORDEN, Phyllis J. .	(FL)	1276
	SKELLIE, Karen S.	(GA)	1145
	STINCHCOMB, Maxine K.	(IL)	1194
	ALLEN, Janice K.	(IN)	15
	EIS, Myrna M.	(KS)	340
	FOSTER, Joan	(MA)	392
	MUNDY, Suzanne W. . . .	(MA)	879
	LIVELY, Nancy J.	(MD)	734
	PECK, Ann D.	(MD)	953
	BROWN, Merrikay E. . . .	(NC)	146
	DLUGOS, Carolyn M. . . .	(NJ)	306
	BAKER, Marie A.	(NY)	49
	BINA, Marcella A.	(OH)	97
	DRIESSEN, Diane	(OH)	320
	NOWAK, Leslie A.	(OH)	911
	WRIGHT, Catherine A. . .	(OR)	1370
	SULLIVAN, Kathryn A. . .	(PA)	1208
	BROOKS, Judy B. . . .	(TN)	140
	MCLENNA, D S.	(TX)	814
	WISECARVER, Betty A. .	(VA)	1357
	THOMPSON, Rosalind R.	(WA)	1241
	HUDSON, Susan P.	(BC)	570
	KISSICK, Barbara J. . . .	(NB)	656
	ISRAEL, Kathleen	(ON)	585
Children's libraries	GELEADI, Ruth H.	(FL)	425
	GRIFFIN, Fredericia	(MA)	468
	MC HALE, Mary M.	(MD)	808
	SCHAUB, Theresa F. . . .	(MI)	1090
	DE CUENCA, Pilar A. . . .	(NY)	286

CHILDREN (Cont'd)
Children's libraries

Children's library materials
Children's library service

Children's library services

Children's library work

Children's literature

KAPLAN, Lesly A. ...... (WA) 626
MCGREW, Mary L. .... (IA) 808
MORRIS, Effie L. ...... (CA) 866
BEAN, Bobby G. ...... (IL) 69
DOOLEY, Shelly Q. ..... (GA) 312
FAHERTY, Gladys W. .. (MD) 361
MORROW, Paula J. .... (MO) 869
ROSS, Shirley D. ...... (MO) 1059
CUTLER, Marsha L. .... (NV) 268
BUSH, Dianne .... (NY) 165
DENNEHY, Margaret ... (NY) 292
PELLOWSKI, Anne .... (NY) 955
VEENSTRA, Geraldine B. (TX) 1281
BENNE, Mae M. .... (WA) 81
BETZ-ZALL, Jonathan R. (WA) 92
NEAU, Philip F. .... (LA) 891
GUILER, Paula J. ..... (NY) 476
MCCLAIN, Harriet V. .... (AK) 795
CARR, Charles E. ...... (AL) 185
VISSCHER, Helga B. ... (AL) 1285
COLCLASURE, Marian S. (AR) 230
LANGSAM, Christine E. . (AR) 696
DOWNUM, Evelyn R. .... (AZ) 317
JANSON, Sherryl A. ..... (AZ) 594
NILSEN, Alleen P. ...... (AZ) 904
BAUER, Caroline F. .... (CA) 65
BOYLLS, Virginia W. .... (CA) 124
CONNOR, Anne C. ..... (CA) 237
DAY, Bettie B. .... (CA) 282
KING, Cynthia .... (CA) 650
MORRIS, Effie L. ...... (CA) 866
PRESSNALL, Patricia E. . (CA) 991
SIGMAN, Paula M. ..... (CA) 1137
VARKENTINE, Aganita .. (CA) 1278
WAGNER, Sharon L. ... (CA) 1292
WAKEFIELD, Jacqueline
    M. .... (CA) 1293
WEEDMAN, Judith ..... (CA) 1315
WINSTON, Gillian R. ... (CA) 1356
ZALE, Phyllis J. .... (CA) 1385
AKE, Mary W. .... (CO) 9
HUGHES, Sondra K. .... (CO) 572
VOLC, Judith G. .... (CO) 1287
EMBARDO, Ellen E. .... (CT) 347
FADER, Ellen G. .... (CT) 360
SCHULTZE, Salvatrice G. (CT) 1102
HAITH, Dorothy M. ..... (DC) 484
SALVADORE, Maria B. . (DC) 1078
YOUNG, Christina C. ... (DC) 1381
FIORE, Carole D. ...... (FL) 379
MILLER, Betty D. ...... (FL) 836
PATTISON, Joanne .... (FL) 948
STINES, Joe R. .... (FL) 1194
BENNETT, Priscilla B. .. (GA) 82
BRIGHTHARP, Wilma S. (GA) 136
KARP, Hazel B. .... (GA) 628
BURGESS, Barbara J. ... (IA) 159
CAMP, Emily E. .... (IA) 175
GRIFFIN, Kathryn A. .... (IA) 468
LETTOW, Lucille J. ..... (IA) 719
MEIER, Patricia L. ..... (IA) 821
TOVREA, Roxanna L. ... (IA) 1252
BOLT, Janice A. .... (IL) 113
BOURKE, Jacqueline K. . (IL) 119
CASE, Doris A. .... (IL) 191
GUNDERSEN, Shirley S. (IL) 477
HARRIS, Jane F. .... (IL) 504
REPTA, Vada L. .... (IL) 1024
RICHARDSON, Selma K. (IL) 1030
ROBERTSON, Ina N. ... (IL) 1042
SCHORMANN, Marguerite
    T. .... (IL) 1099
STRAWN, Aimee W. ... (IL) 1201
SUTHERLAND, Zena B. . (IL) 1211
VOTH, Mary S. .... (IL) 1289
WEISMAN, Kathryn M. ... (IL) 1319
ALLEN, Patricia J. ...... (IN) 15
BICKEL, Bernice M. .... (IN) 94

CHILDREN (Cont'd)
Children's literature

BRIDGE, Stephen W. .... (IN) 135
GLEASON, Ruth I. ...... (IN) 440
JACKSON, Susan M. .... (IN) 588
TEUBERT, Lola H. ...... (IN) 1233
TIMKO, Patricia A. ..... (IN) 1246
BARTLETT, Gwenell J. .. (KS) 61
BOGAN, Mary E. ...... (KS) 110
LEVEL, M J. .... (KS) 719
MCIRVIN, Jane P. ...... (KS) 809
MCKENZIE, Joe M. .... (KS) 811
MCLEOD, Debra A. .... (KS) 814
DOAN, Janice K. ...... (KY) 307
JACOBSON-BEYER,
    Harry E. .... (KY) 590
JAMES, Karen G. ...... (KY) 592
MILLER, Barbara S. .... (KY) 835
TURNER, Ray .... (KY) 1265
CARSTENS, Jane E. .... (LA) 188
KENNEDY, Frances C. .. (LA) 641
MOSLEY, Mattie J. ..... (LA) 871
STEWART, Mary E. ..... (LA) 1193
CAMPANELLA, Alice D. .. (MA) 175
GROSE, Rosemary F. ... (MA) 472
HEINS, Ethel L. .... (MA) 522
KELLMAN, Lillian S. .... (MA) 637
MCDONALD, Murray F. . (MA) 803
ROBINSON, Phyllis A. .. (MA) 1044
STAVIS, Ruth L. .... (MA) 1183
TASHJIAN, Virginia A. .. (MA) 1224
WEISCHEDEL, Elaine F. . (MA) 1319
DEAN, Frances C. ..... (MD) 283
PILZER, Cecily R. ..... (MD) 973
RUFF, Martha R. ...... (MD) 1066
BERRIE, Ellen T. ...... (ME) 90
BIELICH, Paul S. ...... (MI) 95
BLATT, Gloria T. ...... (MI) 104
BRAGLIA, Nancy L. ..... (MI) 127
BRANZBURG, Marian G. (MI) 129
CHAKLOSH, Cynthia L. . (MI) 197
MCCARTY, Linda A. ... (MI) 795
PEREZ-STABLE, Maria A. (MI) 958
STEPHENS, John H. .... (MI) 1188
STILLEY, Cynthia S. .... (MI) 1194
VOIGHT, Nancy R. ..... (MI) 1287
DIMENT, Elna N. ...... (MN) 304
GILLIS, Ruth J. .... (MN) 436
MONSON, Dianne L. .... (MN) 855
PIEHL, Kathleen K. ..... (MN) 971
SIBLEY, Carol H. ...... (MN) 1134
SIMMONS, Antoinette S. (MN) 1139
BELCHER, Nancy S. .... (MO) 76
ROSS, Shirley D. ...... (MO) 1059
SADLER, Philip A. ..... (MO) 1073
JONES, Dolores B. ..... (MS) 612
LAUGHLIN, Jeannine L. . (MS) 703
SUMRALL, Ada M. ..... (MS) 1210
DORNBERGER, Julie L. . (NC) 313
FISH, Barbara M. ...... (NC) 380
FREEDMAN, Barbara G. . (NC) 400
GOLDEN, Susan L. ..... (NC) 445
PENN, Lea M. .... (NC) 957
STRICKLAND, Mary L. .. (NC) 1202
WALKER, Judith A. .... (NC) 1295
KENT, Jeffrey A. ...... (NH) 642
SARLES, Christie V. .... (NH) 1083
TATE, Joanne D. ...... (NH) 1225
ANTCZAK, Janice ..... (NJ) 28
CONDIT, Martha O. .... (NJ) 235
FISHER, Scott L. ...... (NJ) 381
GOLDBERG, Barbara W. . (NJ) 444
SHERMAN, Louise L. ... (NJ) 1128
SKRAMOUSKY, Mary C. . (NJ) 1147
CARLSON, Kathleen A. . (NM) 182
HENDRICKSON, Linnea
    M. .... (NM) 527
MATTER, Kathy L. ..... (NM) 785
ODENHEIM, Claire E. ... (NM) 916
GROSSHANS, Merilyn P. (NV) 473

CHILDREN (Cont'd)
Children's literature

AMISON, Mary V. . . . . . (NY) 20
BEHRMANN, Christine A. . (NY) 75
BUTLER, Rebekah O. . . . (NY) 167
CANDE, Lorraine N. . . . . (NY) 178
CUMMINS, Julie A. . . . . (NY) 264
GAUCH, Patricia L. . . . . . (NY) 422
HATCH, Nancy W. . . . . . (NY) 511
HOPKINS, Lee B. . . . . . . (NY) 558
KLEINBURD, Freda . . . . (NY) 659
KULLESEID, Eleanor R. . (NY) 683
LENZ, Millicent A. . . . . . . (NY) 716
LONG, Joanna R. . . . . . . (NY) 739
LOPATIN, Edith K. . . . . . (NY) 740
MAGUDA, Joyce M. . . . . (NY) 760
NEVETT, Micki S. . . . . . . (NY) 897
PERSON, Diane G. . . . . . (NY) 961
PRUITT, Brenda F. . . . . . (NY) 996
SCHMIDTMANN, Nancy
   K. . . . . (NY) 1096
SIVULICH, Sandra S. . . . (NY) 1145
STRANC, Mary C. . . . . . (NY) 1200
TICE, Margaret E. . . . . . . (NY) 1244
WIGG, Ristiina M. . . . . . (NY) 1337
WITT, Susan T. . . . . (NY) 1358
BAKER, Carol J. . . . . . . (OH) 48
CLEM, Harriet M. . . . . . . (OH) 220
DRACH, Priscilla L. . . . . (OH) 318
KLAUS, Susan B. . . . . . . (OH) 658
MCDANIEL, Deanna J. . . (OH) 801
NOWAK, Leslie A. . . . . . (OH) 911
RODDA, Donna S. . . . . . (OH) 1047
SMITH, Noralee W. . . . . (OH) 1159
WARREN, Dorothea C. . . (OH) 1306
WILSON, Letitia A. . . . . . (OH) 1351
BAUER, Carolyn J. . . . . . (OK) 65
PARKER, Eleanor V. . . . (OK) 941
RABURN, Josephine R. . (OK) 1001
UNDERHILL, Jan . . . . . . (OK) 1268
FEUERHELM, Jill A. . . . . (OR) 374
MCCOY, Joanne . . . . . . (OR) 799
BAUMGARTNER, Barbara
   W. . . . . (PA) 66
CROWE, Virginia M. . . . . (PA) 261
DEFASSIO, Sharon L. . . (PA) 287
GEARHART, Carol A. . . . (PA) 424
GLASS, Catherine C. . . . (PA) 440
GRAHAM, Marilyn L. . . . (PA) 456
MARON-WOOD, Kathy M. (PA) 772
MILLER, Mary E. . . . . . . (PA) 840
NAISMITH, Patricia A. . . (PA) 887
SANDERS, Minda M. . . . (PA) 1080
WALSH, Carolyn C. . . . . (PA) 1299
WHEELER, Martha M. . . (PA) 1329
WOLFE, Mary S. . . . . . . (PA) 1361
MCKEE, Virginia W. . . . . (RI) 810
BRANTON, Mildred M. . . (SC) 129
JACOCKS, Marcia W. . . . (SC) 590
ESTES, Glenn E. . . . . . . (TN) 355
WRIGHT, David A. . . . . . (TN) 1371
BELL, Jo A. . . . . (TX) 77
CARTER, Betty B. . . . . . (TX) 189
DUFFY, Suzanne . . . . . . (TX) 324
EASON, Lisa H. . . . . (TX) 332
HOLLAND, Deborah K. . . (TX) 550
HOOVER, Gloria E. . . . . (TX) 557
IMMROTH, Barbara F. . . (TX) 582
MCBURNEY, Lynnea R. . (TX) 792
MCCASLIN, Cheryl A. . . (TX) 795
PARIS, Janelle A. . . . . . . (TX) 940
SCAMMAN, Carol J. . . . (TX) 1087
SILVERMAN, Barbara G. (TX) 1138
OLSEN, Katherine M. . . . (UT) 921
BIGELOW, Therese G. . . (VA) 95
BROWN, Dale W. . . . . . (VA) 143
GAVER, Mary V. . . . . . . (VA) 423
PAISLEY, Anna S. . . . . . (VA) 935
PEARL, Patricia D. . . . . . (VA) 952
RAMSEY, Inez L. . . . . . . (VA) 1006

CHILDREN (Cont'd)
Children's literature

WAMPLER, Dorris M. . . . (VA) 1302
GREENE, Grace W. . . . . (VT) 464
BENNE, Mae M. . . . . . . (WA) 81
BLUME, Scott . . . . (WA) 107
ERICKSON, Jane . . . . . . (WA) 352
HUTTON, Emily A. . . . . . (WA) 579
MACDONALD, Margaret
   R. . . . . (WA) 754
POLISHUK, Bernard . . . . (WA) 980
CZARNEZKI, Mary E. . . . (WI) 268
DEES DAUGHERTY,
   Kristin . . . . (WI) 287
DIETZ, Kathryn A. . . . . . (WI) 302
HERMAN, Gertrude B. . . (WI) 531
HUMPHRIES, Lajean . . . (WI) 574
MORROW, Kathryn M. . . (WI) 869
RETZER, Cathy E. . . . . . (WI) 1024
ROOZEN, Nancy L. . . . . (WI) 1054
WASSINK, Patricia L. . . . (WI) 1308
WILLETT, Holly G. . . . . . (WI) 1341
WISEMAN, Mary J. . . . . (WI) 1357
CRESSWELL, Stephen . . (WV) 258
CHATTON, Barbara A. . . (WY) 204
BROWN, David K. . . . . . (AB) 143
HERSCOVITCH, Pearl . . (AB) 533
KISSAU, Arlene M. . . . . . (AB) 656
LOVENBURG, Susan L. . (AB) 743
CHAN, Mary L. . . . . (BC) 199
FUNK, Grace E. . . . . . . (BC) 410
GIBB, Betty J. . . . . (BC) 431
EGAN, Bessie C. . . . . . . (MB) 338
BOUDREAU, Berthe . . . (NB) 118
RAUCH, Doris E. . . . . . . (NB) 1010
MEWS, Alison J. . . . . . . (NF) 829
CHURCHMAN, Alice M. . (ON) 213
CULLIS, Lois I. . . . . (ON) 263
FASICK, Adele M. . . . . . (ON) 366
KOSTIAK, Adele E. . . . . (ON) 673
LEMIEUX, Louise . . . . . . (PQ) 715
GAGNON, Andre . . . . . . (SK) 412

Children's literature & activities   PASSARELLO, Nancy H. (FL) 946
Children's literature & education   COLLINS, Mary E. . . . . . (IN) 233
Children's literature & library services   BUSH, Margaret A. . . . . . (MA) 165
Children's literature & materials   WILLIAMS, Helen E. . . . (MD) 1343
Children's literature & programming   NG, Carol S. . . . . (CA) 900
   HEITMAN, Lynn . . . . (IL) 523
   NOAH, Carolyn B. . . . . . (MA) 906
   REID, Margaret B. . . . . . (OH) 1018
Children's literature & programs   TOM, Chow L. . . . . (HI) 1249
Children's literature & service   BRETING, Elizabeth C. . . (MO) 133
Children's literature & services   PINNELL-STEPHENS,
   June A. . . . . (AK) 975
   ATKINSON, Joan L. . . . . (AL) 38
   VEITCH, Carol J. . . . . . . (NC) 1281
   COURTNEY, Aida N. . . . (NJ) 251
   FICHTELBERG, Susan . . (NJ) 374
   RAIVELY, Martha M. . . . (PA) 1004
Children's literature appreciation   BROWN, Judith B. . . . . . (MD) 145
Children's literature before 1900   BALDWIN, Ruth M. . . . . (FL) 52
Children's literature computer
  software   FEUERHELM, Jill A. . . . . (OR) 374
Children's literature criticism   LACY, Lyn E. . . . . (MN) 687
Children's literature, ethnic   AUSTIN, Mary C. . . . . . . (HI) 40
Children's literature for parents   WINKLER, Carol A. . . . . (MO) 1355
Children's literature for young children   BALDWIN, Ruth M. . . . . (FL) 52
Children's literature in education   MONSON, Dianne L. . . . (MN) 855
Children's literature in inner-city   NIX, Kemie . . . . (GA) 905
Children's literature, instruction   NELSON, Olga G. . . . . . (OH) 895
Children's literature lecturing   BATES, Barbara S. . . . . (PA) 63
Children's literature, library services   CORSARO, Julie A. . . . . (IL) 248
Children's literature, past & present   COUGHLAN, Margaret N. (DC) 250
Children's literature, preschool   WINFREE, Barbara S. . . (LA) 1354
Children's literature programs   FOERTIN, Yves P. . . . . . (PQ) 387
Children's literature, reading   MCGOWN, Sue W. . . . . (TX) 807
Children's literature reference   HURLEY, Doreen S. . . . . (PA) 577
Children's literature, software   HOFMANN, Susan M. . . (PA) 548
Children's literature specialist   ZEIGER, Hanna B. . . . . . (MA) 1387
Children's literature teaching   SCHMITZ, Eugenia E. . . (WI) 1096

CHILDREN (Cont'd)

Children's literature, 1900-1950	BALDWIN, Ruth M.	(FL)	52
Children's material special collections	DURSTON, Corinne L. . .	(BC)	329
Children's materials	GREESON-SCHARDL,		
	Tamra J.	(GA)	465
	BLANK, Annette C.	(MD)	104
	ROBERTS, Susan P.	(MD)	1041
	WINKEL, Lois	(NC)	1355
	PASHEL, Susan M.	(PA)	945
Children's materials & programming	MACRURY, Mary E.	(NS)	758
Children's materials & services	STANTON, Vida C.	(WI)	1181
Children's materials col development	HODGES, Lois F.	(NY)	546
	SMITH, Valerie M.	(OH)	1161
Children's media	HUNT, Mary A.	(FL)	575
	GAFFNEY, Maureen	(NY)	412
Children's media librarianship	ELLISOR, F L.	(TX)	345
Children's media programming	GAFFNEY, Maureen	(NY)	412
Children's media resources	WARNER, Wayne G. . . .	(GA)	1305
Children's museums	PATTISON, Joanne	(FL)	948
Children's outreach	HESS, M S.	(CA)	534
Children's outreach services	LYTLE, Marian M.	(NC)	753
Children's program	MORRIS, Kim	(NY)	867
Children's programming	STOWE, Jean E.	(AR)	1199
	BECKER, Teresa J.	(AZ)	72
	BAILEY, Darlene L.	(CA)	46
	WINKLER, Jean J.	(CO)	1355
	KELLY, Anne V.	(FL)	637
	SOVANSKI, Vincent G. . .	(IL)	1170
	BICKEL, Bernice M.	(IN)	94
	TIMKO, Patricia A.	(IN)	1246
	RASKIN, Susan R.	(MA)	1009
	ROBERTS, Susan P. . . .	(MD)	1041
	RAFAL, Marian D.	(MI)	1003
	VOIGHT, Nancy R.	(MI)	1287
	DORNBERGER, Julie L. . .	(NC)	313
	FARIAS, Elizabeth H. . . .	(NC)	363
	FREEDMAN, Barbara G. . .	(NC)	400
	LYTLE, Marian M.	(NC)	753
	HODGES, Lois F.	(NY)	546
	LOUISDHON-WALTER,		
	Marie L.	(NY)	742
	OLDERSHAW, Anne . . .	(NY)	920
	SIVULICH, Sandra S. . . .	(NY)	1145
	USTACH, Joanne B. . . .	(NY)	1270
	PAPA, Deborah M.	(OH)	938
	RUHL, Jodi S.	(OH)	1066
	STICHA, Denise S.	(PA)	1193
	DAVIS, Mary F.	(TX)	280
	MACFARLANE, Francis X.	(TX)	755
	MCCONNELL, Ruth M. .	(TX)	798
	PARNES, Daria M.	(VA)	943
	POWERS, Linda J.	(VA)	989
	SIPOLA, Debra L.	(WI)	1144
	LUTHY, Jean M.	(AB)	750
	MARSH, Mary L.	(NS)	773
	ADDY, Kathryn J.	(ON)	6
	GAGNON, Andre	(SK)	412
Children's programming & services	WOOLF, Amy K.	(KS)	1368
	MCLEAN, Paulette A. . . .	(ON)	814
Children's programming for preschoolers	BELCHEE, Nancy O. . . .	(NC)	76
Children's programming or services	KILLEEN, Erlene B.	(VA)	648
Children's programming, puppets	NORMAN, Nita V.	(AZ)	909
Children's programs	WILLIS, Jan L.	(MS)	1348
	ZINMAN, Sandra	(NY)	1389
	SAULSBURY, Margie M.	(TX)	1084
Children's public library programs	BOTHAM, Jane	(WI)	118
Children's public library services	WILLETT, Holly G.	(WI)	1341
Children's rare books	SEDNEY, Frances V. . . .	(MD)	1111
Children's reader services	THOMAS, Victoria K. . . .	(IN)	1238
Children's reading environment	TAKEUCHI, Satoru	(JAP)	1220
Children's reference	SMITH, Heather	(CA)	1155
	LAPOLT, Margaret B. . . .	(CT)	697
	REGNER, Erlinda J.	(IL)	1017
	ANDERSON, Valerie J. .	(VA)	25
	BROSSEAU, Lise	(PQ)	141
Children's reference & reader assistance	BECKER, Teresa J.	(AZ)	72
Children's reference materials	DRACH, Priscilla L.	(OH)	318
Children's religious literature	PEARL, Patricia D.	(VA)	952

CHILDREN (Cont'd)

Children's room programming	KIBREAH, Golam	(IN)	646
Children's selection & development	SIPOLA, Debra L.	(WI)	1144
Children's service	BRYAN, Michael G.	(FL)	151
	SNODGRASSE, Elaine . .	(FL)	1163
	BARZELAY, Mary S.	(VI)	62
	WASERMAN, Barbara . .	(ISR)	1307
Children's service consulting	SAGER, Lynn S.	(WI)	1074
Children's service, literature	RUBIN, Ellen B.	(NY)	1064
Children's services	JENKS, Arlene I.	(AK)	597
	ASHCRAFT, Carolyn A. .	(AR)	35
	CLEVENGER, Judy B. . . .	(AR)	221
	MARTIN, Rosemary S. . .	(AR)	778
	GILSON, Myral A.	(AZ)	437
	MURPHY, Ellen A.	(AZ)	880
	AMOS, Jeanne L.	(CA)	20
	BANGE, Stephanie D. . . .	(CA)	54
	BISHOP, Diane	(CA)	99
	BUTTERWORTH, Linda M.	(CA)	167
	CHESSMAN, Rebecca L.	(CA)	207
	COAKLEY, Dorothy J. . .	(CA)	224
	COLBY, Diana C.	(CA)	230
	COMSTOCK, Evelyn B. .	(CA)	235
	EAGER, Nancy A.	(CA)	331
	EASUN, M S.	(CA)	333
	FRANKEL, Kate M.	(CA)	397
	GIRARD, Valerie V. . . .	(CA)	438
	GRIFFITH, Virginia M. . . .	(CA)	469
	HOLM, Blair I.	(CA)	552
	JOHNSON, Carolyn E. . .	(CA)	602
	LAGIER, Jennifer B.	(CA)	688
	MARC-AURELE, Heidi L.	(CA)	768
	MATTHIES, Donna K. . . .	(CA)	786
	MCCORMACK, Carolyn .	(CA)	798
	MURTEN, Holly T.	(CA)	882
	NELSON, Helen M.	(CA)	893
	NYHAN, Catherine W. . .	(CA)	912
	OVERMYER, Elizabeth C.	(CA)	931
	PILLING, George P.	(CA)	973
	REGNER-HYATT, Anne L.	(CA)	1017
	RICHARDSON, Helen R. .	(CA)	1029
	SCHNEIDER, Marcia G. .	(CA)	1097
	TORKELSON, Jon A. . . .	(CA)	1251
	VANSONNENBERG,		
	Catherine	(CA)	1277
	WADE, Sherry A.	(CA)	1290
	WINSTON, Gillian R. . . .	(CA)	1356
	WONG, Maida L.	(CA)	1363
	YOUNG, Eleanor C.	(CA)	1381
	NICKEL, Robbie L.	(CO)	902
	BUSCH, Kathleen M. . . .	(CT)	165
	CARNAHAN, Anne D. . . .	(CT)	183
	FERRARI, Kathleen M. . .	(CT)	373
	ROCKMAN, Connie C. . .	(CT)	1046
	VAN DYKE, Aase S. . . .	(CT)	1275
	YARMAL, Ann	(CT)	1378
	BEAMER, Lisa M.	(DE)	69
	SIMMONS, Elizabeth M. .	(DE)	1139
	BROOM, Susan E.	(FL)	141
	GOODIER, Darlene P. . .	(FL)	448
	KINNEY, Molly S.	(FL)	653
	MILLER, Betty D.	(FL)	836
	O'CONNOR-LEVY, Linda		
	L.	(FL)	916
	PETERSON, Carolyn S. .	(FL)	963
	ROBINSON, Lois C.	(FL)	1044
	SMITH, Robyn H.	(FL)	1160
	STRADER, Helen B.	(FL)	1199
	PICKENS, Lynne R.	(GA)	970
	RHEAY, Mary L.	(GA)	1025
	TAYLOR, Prudence A. . .	(GA)	1228
	ELDREDGE, Jeffrey R. . .	(HI)	342
	FREITAS-OBREGON,		
	Brenda J.	(HI)	401
	DUTCHER, Terry R.	(IA)	329
	FOWLER, Linda J.	(IA)	394
	MURRAY, Rochelle A. . .	(IA)	882
	TALLEY, Loretta K.	(IA)	1221
	BABANOURY, Betty G. .	(IL)	43
	CALLAGHAN, Linda W. .	(IL)	173

CHILDREN (Cont'd)
Children's services

CAPANO, Laura M.	(IL)	179
DAVIS, Carol L.	(IL)	278
HACKETT, Nancy J.	(IL)	481
LAWSON, Mary L.	(IL)	705
LINTNER, Barbara J.	(IL)	731
MARABOTTI, Denise M. .	(IL)	768
MEYER, Barbara G.	(IL)	829
MORRIS, Susan M.	(IL)	867
PENDERGRASS, Margaret E.	(IL)	956
RICHARDSON, Selma K. .	(IL)	1030
RUMNEY, Leslie W.	(IL)	1067
SCHULTZ, Lois B.	(IL)	1102
SOVANSKI, Vincent G. .	(IL)	1170
TUTEUR, Civia M.	(IL)	1265
VETTER, Jean A.	(IL)	1283
WAGNER, Robin O.	(IL)	1292
FORD, Marcia K.	(IN)	389
MCNAIR, James	(IN)	815
PENROD, Saundra K.	(IN)	957
PICHA, Charlotte G.	(IN)	970
THOMAS, Victoria K.	(IN)	1238
VOORS, Mary R.	(IN)	1289
YAMAMOTO, M C.	(IN)	1377
COSPER, Mary F.	(LA)	249
LAROSE, Louise K.	(LA)	698
MIGUEZ, Betsy B.	(LA)	833
RAMBO, Gloria P.	(LA)	1005
SOTO, Donna G.	(LA)	1169
FRIEDMAN, Terri L.	(MA)	404
GILLIES, Irene B.	(MA)	436
HALES, Margaret L.	(MA)	486
MASSUCCO, Georgia A. .	(MA)	782
WEISCHEDEL, Elaine F. .	(MA)	1319
FISHER, Eleanor W.	(MD)	381
GIBBS, Beatrice E.	(MD)	431
JOHNSON, Jerry D.	(MD)	606
MCCARTY, Emily H.	(MD)	795
MONTGOMERY, Paula K.	(MD)	856
NITZBERG, Dale B.	(MD)	905
SEDNEY, Frances V.	(MD)	1111
SHAUCK, Stephanie M. .	(MD)	1123
THOMAS, Fannette H. ..	(MD)	1236
MOY, Agnes U.	(ME)	874
NICHOLSON, Carol C. ...	(ME)	902
FORD, Gale I.	(MI)	389
GREGORY, Helen B.	(MI)	466
HUNTER, Dorothea A. ..	(MI)	576
NIETHAMMER, Leslee ..	(MI)	904
REASONER, Mary B.	(MI)	1013
ROSE, Anne	(MI)	1054
HOSLETT, Andrea E.	(MN)	561
WEISS, Kay M.	(MN)	1320
WRONKA, Gretchen M. .	(MN)	1373
FRANKLIN, Jill S.	(MO)	397
GLEASON, Virginia L. ..	(MO)	440
LEITLE, Barbara K.	(MO)	714
RADGINSKI, Martha E. ...	(MO)	1002
READING, Barbara A. ...	(MO)	1012
STEELE, Anita T.	(MO)	1184
HART, Julie C.	(MS)	507
SANFORD, Janice R.	(MS)	1081
WYNNE, Tia J.	(MT)	1375
CAMERON, Mary T.	(NC)	175
HUGHES, Donna J.	(NC)	571
PENN, Lea M.	(NC)	957
SANDERS, Elizabeth S. .	(NC)	1080
LESSER, Charlotte B.	(NH)	718
BELVIN, Carolyn J.	(NJ)	78
BRYANT, Judith W.	(NJ)	152
BUTLER, Patricia M.	(NJ)	167
CARLSON, Dudley B. ..	(NJ)	182
DEL GUIDICE, M R.	(NJ)	289
GARDINER, Judith R.	(NJ)	417
GROSSBERG, Aileen D.	(NJ)	473
LATHAM, Candace	(NJ)	701
OLSON, Marilyn A.	(NJ)	923
ONELLI, Patricia M.	(NJ)	924

CHILDREN (Cont'd)
Children's services

RILEY, Marie R.	(NJ)	1034
SCARPELLINO, Rebecca A.	(NJ)	1088
SERPICO, Margaret A. ..	(NJ)	1116
THONER, Jane T.	(NJ)	1242
WILSON, Carol A.	(NJ)	1350
ANDERSEN-PUSEY, Vavene J.	(NM)	21
KRAEMER, Mary P.	(NM)	674
MATTER, Kathy L.	(NM)	785
BISSESSAR, Carmen T. .	(NY)	100
CAMPAGNA, Roxane R. .	(NY)	175
CUMMINS, Julie A.	(NY)	264
DEMALLIE, Marjorie W. .	(NY)	291
DENNIN, June A.	(NY)	292
DESCIORA, Susan O. ..	(NY)	294
DOW, Sally R.	(NY)	315
FUNK, Nancy J.	(NY)	410
GERHARDT, Lillian N. ..	(NY)	428
GINSBERG, Barbara ...	(NY)	438
HAMILTON, Reatha B. ..	(NY)	492
KARGE, James R.	(NY)	627
KIMMONS, Anita L.	(NY)	649
LEVIN, Peggy S.	(NY)	720
PILLA, Marianne L.	(NY)	973
PIRODSKY, Nancy E.	(NY)	975
RICKETSON, Karen F. ..	(NY)	1032
ROMANELLI, Catherine A.	(NY)	1052
SHEFFER, Karen M.	(NY)	1125
SPAIN, Frances L.	(NY)	1170
STARK, Li S.	(NY)	1181
TICE, Margaret E.	(NY)	1244
ZEIGLER, Susan A.	(NY)	1387
ALEXA, Cynthia M.	(OH)	12
BLAHA, Linda N.	(OH)	102
BRAUTIGAM, Faith J. ..	(OH)	130
CLARK, Marilyn L.	(OH)	217
DRACH, Priscilla L.	(OH)	318
EASTERLY-POTTER, Anne P.	(OH)	333
EVERETT, Janet J.	(OH)	358
FLOWER, Eileen D.	(OH)	386
HORVATH, Camilla K. ..	(OH)	561
JANKY, Donna L.	(OH)	593
LOVELAND, Catherine R.	(OH)	743
MC CLEAF-NESPECA, Sue E.	(OH)	796
NELSON, Olga G.	(OH)	895
PRYSZLAK, Lydia M.	(OH)	996
REED, Elizabeth M.	(OH)	1015
ROBINSON, Doris J.	(OH)	1043
SILVER, Linda R.	(OH)	1138
SPEAR, Linda A.	(OH)	1172
TAYLOR, Patricia L.	(OH)	1228
TUCKER, Mary C.	(OH)	1262
WAGNER, Evelyn M. ...	(OH)	1291
WEST, Loretta G.	(OH)	1326
JENNINGS, Kathryn L. ..	(OK)	598
STURDIVANT, Nan J. ..	(OK)	1205
GORDON, Patricia H. ...	(OR)	451
MCCOY, Joanne	(OR)	799
THOMPSON, Paulette ..	(OR)	1241
BURSK, Mary A.	(PA)	163
DOW, Sally C.	(PA)	315
FIELD, Carolyn W.	(PA)	375
FOY, Lorraine M.	(PA)	395
GALLIVAN, Marion F. ...	(PA)	414
GILMOUR, Marianne S. .	(PA)	437
GRAHAM, Anne M.	(PA)	456
KONOPKA, Amelia S. ..	(PA)	670
LICHTENBERG, Elsa R. .	(PA)	725
MAXWELL, Barbara A. ..	(PA)	788
MULLEN, Helen M.	(PA)	877
PECK, Marian B.	(PA)	953
SCHWALB, Ann W.	(PA)	1104
SHONTZ, Marilyn L.	(PA)	1132
SMITH, Mary M.	(PA)	1158
THOMPSON, Marian A. .	(PA)	1240

CHILDREN (Cont'd)
Children's services

WRIGHT, Irene R. . . . . . (PA) 1371
BIERDEN, Margaret W. . (RI) 95
LAMOUREUX, Jacquelyn
W. . . . . (RI) 691
ODEAN, Kathleen F. . . . . (RI) 916
MCGREGOR, Jane A. . . . (SC) 808
CARD, Judy . . . . (TN) 180
KARRENBROCK, Marilyn
H. . . . . (TN) 628
LOCKWOOD, Bonnie J. . . (TN) 736
ALFORD, Mary A. . . . . . (TX) 13
BLAIR, Elaine K. . . . . . . (TX) 102
DAVIS, Joyce . . . . (TX) 279
DILLINGER, Mary A. . . . (TX) 303
FISCHER, Beverly J. . . . (TX) 379
JOHNSTON, L J. . . . . . . (TX) 610
LACY, Yvonne M. . . . . . (TX) 687
LARSON, Jeanette C. . . (TX) 699
MCIVER, Lynne A. . . . . . (TX) 809
MILLER, Carol A. . . . . . . (TX) 836
SMITH, Lorraine K. . . . . (TX) 1157
SPRADLING, Nancy L. . . (TX) 1175
ZWICK, Louise Y. . . . . . (TX) 1392
GIACOMA, Pete J. . . . . . (UT) 430
PETERSON, Douglas L. . (UT) 963
SHIELDS, Dorthy M. . . . (UT) 1130
ANDERSON, Valerie J. . . (VA) 25
BREEN, Catherine H. . . . (VA) 131
BRITTO, Mary M. . . . . . (VA) 137
EFFRON, Barbara L. . . . (VA) 338
GARBELMAN, Alicia D. . . (VA) 417
GEORGE, Melba R. . . . . (VA) 427
HINDMAN, Pamela J. . . . (VA) 542
SWAIN, Lillian A. . . . . . . (VA) 1212
GREENE, Grace W. . . . . (VT) 464
HAY, Linda A. . . . . (VT) 515
ARBUCKLE, Marybeth M. (WA) 30
BUCKINGHAM, Rebecca
M. . . . . (WA) 154
CARLSON, Sandra L. . . . (WA) 182
FOWLER, Ellen T. . . . . . (WA) 393
GREGGS, Elizabeth M. . . (WA) 465
MYERS, Antoinette B. . . . (WA) 884
NELSON, Judy T. . . . . . . (WA) 894
PETTIT, Donna K. . . . . . (WA) 965
PUDERBAUGH, Velma E. (WA) 997
ABLEIDINGER, Rose A. . . (WI) 2
CZARNEZKI, Mary E. . . . (WI) 268
DAY, Pamela A. . . . . (WI) 283
HANAMAN, Nancy J. . . . (WI) 494
LOCH-WOUTERS, Marge (WI) 736
PAULI, David N. . . . . (WI) 950
PETERSON, Diane S. . . . (WI) 963
RETZER, Cathy E. . . . . . (WI) 1024
SANCHEZ, Alexander J. . (WI) 1079
SCHULLER, Susan M. . . (WI) 1101
THOMSON, Kathleen R. . (WI) 1241
UTZINGER, Orchard L. . . (WI) 1270
WAITY, Gloria J. . . . . . . (WI) 1293
RHYNES, H B. . . . . (AB) 1026
DUNCAN, Deborah J. . . . (BC) 325
GARRAWAY, Babs L. . . (BC) 420
GOW, Susan P. . . . . (BC) 454
SALTMAN, Judith M. . . . (BC) 1077
EGAN, Bessie C. . . . . . . (MB) 338
AMEY, Lorne J. . . . . (NS) 20
COX, Sharon P. . . . . (ON) 253
DETERVILLE, Linda C. . . (ON) 296
LAITMAN, Sheila . . . . . . (ON) 688
MULLERBECK, Aino . . . (ON) 877
READ-STARK, Marilyn A. (ON) 1012
BADGER, Carole . . . . . . (PQ) 44
RABY, Eva F. . . . . (PQ) 1001
CALEF, Daniel C. . . . . . . (SK) 172
DIAMANT, Betsy . . . . . . (ISR) 299
BERNAT, Mary A. . . . . . (VEN) 88
Children's services administration
GUTHRIE, Chab C. . . . . (OH) 479
FASICK, Adele M. . . . . . (ON) 366

CHILDREN (Cont'd)
Children's services & education
Children's services & literature

Children's services & media
Children's services & programming

Children's services & space needs
Children's services, collection
devlpmnt
Children's services, education
Children's services, librarianship
Children's services programming
Children's services, storytelling
Children's srvs, teaching, acquisitions
Children's social sciences reviewing
Children's trade books
Children's work

Children's work, age 3-14
Children's work, book banners
Collection development, children's
Computer programs for children
Consulting libs, children's programs
Coordinator of children's services
Developing country libraries, children
Early childhood & parenting
Early childhood children's services
Early childhood education

Early childhood learning
Early childhood literature
Early childhood program services
Early childhood programming
Early childhood resources
Education & curriculum of chlds
services
Education of gifted children
Educational instruction of children
Ethnic materials for children
Evaluating children's book collections
French Canadian children's literature

Guiding children's book selection
Historical children's books, research
Historical children's literature
History of children's literature

Hospital outreach services to children
International children's literature

Introducing children's literature
Lecturing on children's literature
Lib materials & services for children
Library materials for children
Library programming for children
Library service to children

Library services for children

LAWRENCE, Virginia W. (NC) 705
JOHNSON, Beth . . . . . . (GA) 602
EDMONDS, M L. . . . . . . (IL) 336
ROMAN, Susan . . . . (IL) 1052
MEIZNER, Kathie L. . . . . (MD) 822
ROSS, Kathleen A. . . . . . (NY) 1058
FENWICK, Sara I. . . . . . (FL) 371
WARREN, Catherine S. . (MS) 1306
HARTUNG, Nancy F. . . . (TN) 509
WARGO, Peggy M. . . . . . (CT) 1305

CORDUKES, Laura L. . . (ON) 246
TACKETT, Janet S. . . . . (KY) 1219
ABRAMSON, Jenifer S. . (CA) 3
HUNTER, Julie A. . . . . . (NC) 576
STRATTON, Martha G. . . (IN) 1200
BACHAND, Alice J. . . . . (KS) 43
WOLL, Christina B. . . . . . (TX) 1361
RIBAROFF, Margaret F. . (CT) 1026
MOORE, Patricia S. . . . . (AL) 861
EVANS, Iris I. . . . . (AZ) 357
MAAS, Dorothy W. . . . . . (CA) 753
TESTA, Barbara E. . . . . . (CA) 1233
YOON, Sandra G. . . . . . (CA) 1380
DUFF, Margaret K. . . . . . (CO) 323
RIFE, Mary C. . . . . (MI) 1033
KALKHOFF, Ann L. . . . . (NY) 623
SMITH, Maureen M. . . . . (OH) 1158
WOOD, Ann F. . . . . (OH) 1363
BARR, Marilyn P. . . . . . . (PA) 58
HANSEN, Paula J. . . . . . (PA) 498
HOFFMAN, Elizabeth P. . (PA) 547
BODKIN, Sharon C. . . . . (WA) 109
SCHLAFF, Donna G. . . . (MA) 1093
DEVEREAUX, Amy E. . . (CA) 297
STURDIVANT, Nan J. . . (OK) 1205
VOORS, Mary R. . . . . . . (IN) 1289
WALDEN, Katherine G. . (CT) 1294
COLE, Gayle . . . . (CA) 230
PELLOWSKI, Anne . . . . (NY) 955
SCHWARZLOSE, Sally F. (IL) 1105
LINVILLE, Marcia L. . . . . (HI) 731
HAWLEY, Marsha S. . . . (IL) 514
HAMMOND, Mary W. . . . (WA) 494
WRIGHT-HESS, Anne H. (NY) 1373
KOEPP, Sara H. . . . . . . (IA) 668
SCHWABACHER, Sara A. (NY) 1104
CLARK, Janet L. . . . . . . (NV) 217
HERSCOVITCH, Pearl . . (AB) 533

LOPEZ, Loretta K. . . . . . (WA) 741
LINDSLEY, Barbara N. . . (NY) 730
HANSON, Kathy H. . . . . (GA) 498
BEILKE, Patricia F. . . . . (IN) 75
EDMONDS, May H. . . . . (FL) 336
POTVIN, Claude . . . . (NB) 987
AUBREY, Irene E. . . . . . (ON) 38
SUTHERLAND, Helen G. (CA) 1211
GILBERT, Ophelia R. . . . (MO) 434
BROWN, June E. . . . . . . (NY) 145
MAXWELL, Margaret F. . (AZ) 788
CARSTENS, Jane E. . . . (LA) 188
POND, Patricia B. . . . . . (OR) 982
WALSH, Mary A. . . . . . . (PQ) 1300
POARCH, Margaret E. . . (CA) 979
WONG, Patricia M. . . . . (CA) 1363
STARRETT, Mildred J. . . (AZ) 1182
VOLC, Judith G. . . . . . . (CO) 1287
COUGHLIN, Violet L. . . . (PQ) 250
NOONAN, Eileen F. . . . . (IL) 908
GRAHAM, Marilyn L. . . . (PA) 456
NICHOLS, Margaret M. . (AZ) 901
GREENE, Ellin P. . . . . . . (NJ) 464
BEDNAR, Sheila . . . . . . (NY) 73
WILSON, Letitia A. . . . . . (OH) 1351
BAUMGARTNER, Barbara
W. . . . . (PA) 66
PATTISON, Joanne . . . . (FL) 948
HERMAN, Gertrude B. . . (WI) 531

CHILDREN (Cont'd)

Library services to children .... NEVETT, Micki S. .... (NY) 897
WIGG, Ristiina M. ...... (NY) 1337
ESTES, Glenn E. ...... (TN) 355
FASICK, Adele M. ...... (ON) 366
Library skills for children .... MCDANIEL, Deanna J. .. (OH) 801
Library systems & children's services .. POARCH, Margaret E. .. (CA) 979
Library work with children .... WARNER, Joyce E. ...... (HI) 1305
CARSON, Sheila M. ..... (PA) 188
LIGGETT, Julie A. ...... (PA) 726
BAKER, Augusta .... (SC) 47
Literature & programs children's srvs .. HUDDLESTON, Marsha E. (IL) 569
Literature for children .... SPIRT, Diana L. .... (NY) 1175
KIMMEL, Margaret M. .... (PA) 649
Literature for children & young adults .. FISHER, Joan W. ...... (MD) 381
Mail-order children's books .... RUSS, Kennetta P. ..... (MD) 1068
Materials & services for children ...... BARD, Therese B. ...... (HI) 56
MILLER, Marilyn L. ..... (NC) 840
Media for children .... ORSBURN, Elizabeth C. . (PA) 927
Media for exceptional children .... TAFFEL, Bobbe H. ..... (FL) 1219
Picture books, early childhood .... GREENE, Ellin P. ...... (NJ) 464
Preschool & early childhood programs . REZNICK, Evi P. .... (GA) 1025
Primary school children's libraries .... CARPENTER, Janella A. . (NC) 184
Programming for children .... SCHLANSER, Deborah B. (CA) 1093
FORD, Gale I. .... (MI) 389
Programming for children & youth ..... MANCALL, Jacqueline C. (PA) 764
Programming for children in libraries ... POLISHUK, Bernard .... (WA) 980
Programming for young children .... FADER, Ellen G. .... (CT) 360
Public library children's services ..... KASPER, Barbara ...... (CT) 629
STEMME, Virginia L. ... (ND) 1186
BANTA, Gratia J. ...... (OH) 55
Public service to children .... SENN, Sharon L. ...... (WA) 1115
Publishing & marketing children's
    books .... MASON, H J. .... (NY) 781
Rare books for children .... MCNAMARA, Shelley G. . (ME) 816
Rare children's books .... COUGHLAN, Margaret N. (DC) 250
SPIRT, Diana L. .... (NY) 1175
BROWN, Muriel W. .... (TX) 146
Rare children's books in English ..... JOHNSON, Carolyn E. .. (CA) 602
Reading guidance & children's
    literature .... KONNEKER, Rachel C. . (NC) 670
Reading motivation, children .... TRAINER, Leslie F. .... (PAK)1253
Reference & programs for children .... HACHMEISTER, Helen M. (WI) 481
Research in children's literature ..... BISSETT, Donald J. .... (MI) 100
MONSON, Dianne L. ... (MN) 855
Reviewer of children's books .... GOODRICH PETERSON,
    Marilyn .... (KS) 450
Reviewing children's books .... NIX, Kemie .... (GA) 905
CRAIGHEAD, Alice A. .. (TX) 254
POLISHUK, Bernard .... (WA) 980
KRUSE, Ginny M. ..... (WI) 681
Reviewing children's books &
    audiovisual .... SHERMAN, Louise L. .... (NJ) 1128
School & children's librarian .... LANE, Margaret .... (MA) 694
School & children's libraries .... LANE, Margaret .... (MA) 694
School & children's library .... BLACKSHEAR, Martha J. (AL) 102
School libraries, children's literature .. TERRY, Virginia W. .... (MO) 1232
School media children's services ..... AMISON, Mary V. ..... (NY) 20
Science books for children .... JENSEN, Ann M. ...... (CA) 598
Selection of children's materials ..... FORD, Marcia K. ...... (IN) 389
Service for elementary children ...... KORPELA, Betty L. ..... (OR) 672
Service to gifted children .... SWANTON, Susan I. ... (NY) 1214
Services for children .... MCKEE, Virginia W. .... (RI) 810
Services for children & young adults .. KIMMEL, Margaret M. ... (PA) 649
Serving children & the elderly .... WRIGHT, Linda D. ..... (NC) 1372
Spanish language children's books .... ZWICK, Louise Y. ..... (TX) 1392
Storytelling to children .... KNOTT, Joan Y. .... (MI) 665
Study of children's literature .... POVSIC, Frances F. .... (OH) 987
Teaching children & adolescent lit .... SANDERS, John B. .... (MO) 1080
Teaching children's literature .... WALDEN, Katherine G. . (CT) 1294
NIX, Kemie .... (GA) 905
ADCOCK, Betty L. ..... (IL) 6
Training children's services volunteers OVERMYER, Elizabeth C. (CA) 931
Work with children .... BOYE, Inger .... (CA) 123
WILL, Marie C. .... (IL) 1341
TROWELL, Amy U. .... (SC) 1258
Working with children .... BARAGONA, Lynn C. .. (MS) 55
Working with children & adolescents .. POLOMSKI, Linda ..... (CT) 982
Writing children's non-fiction books ... MARSTON, Hope I. .... (NY) 775
Writing for children .... WHITEHEAD, Jane .... (TN) 1332

CHILDREN (Cont'd)

Young adult & children's materials .... STURGEON, Mary C. .... (AR) 1205
Yng adult & children's print &
    non-print .... WOODS, Selina J. ..... (MA) 1367
Young adult & children's services .... POMERLEAU, Suzanne M. (FL) 982
SVEINSSON, Joan L. ... (TX) 1212
CURRIE, Bertha B. ..... (NS) 266
Young adults & children's services .... WASHINGTON, Idella A. (LA) 1307
Youth, childhood, social sciences .... WOODBURY, Marda ... (CA) 1366

CHINA

Chinese bibliography .... CHERN, Jenn C. ...... (GA) 206
Chinese cataloging .... KROMPART, Janet A. ... (MI) 679
Chinese collections .... CHENG, Sheung O. .... (TAI) 206
WANG, Sin C. .... (TAI) 1303
Chinese history .... WANG, Sing W. ...... (AUS)1303
Chinese law .... ROBERT, Berring C. ... (CA) 1039
Chinese librarianship .... WILSON, Amy S. ..... (MI) 1349
Chinese library history .... TING, Lee H. .... (IL) 1246
Chinese rare books .... KECSKES, Lily C. ..... (DC) 633
Chinese studies .... WOO, Lisa C. .... (PA) 1363
English material on Chinese law ..... LUNG, Mon Y. .... (KS) 748
Library science in China .... WEI, Karen T. .... (IL) 1316

CHIROPRACTIC

Chiropractic resources & bibliography PETERSON, Dennis R. ... (IA) 963

CHORAL (See also Boychoir)

Choral music literature .... SHARP, Avery T. ...... (TX) 1122
Choral speaking direction .... ANTHONY, Rose M. .... (WI) 29

CHRISTIAN

Christian holocaust scholar .... CARGAS, Harry J. ..... (MO) 181
Modern Christian art & bibliography .. RAMSEY, Robert D. .... (CA) 1006

CHRONOLOGY

Chronology .... CHASE, William D. ..... (MI) 203
Chronology, British-American theater .. LONEY, Glenn M. ...... (NY) 739

CHURCH (See also Archdiocesan, Clergy, Denomination, Ecclesiastical, Ministry, Parish, Synagogue and names of specific denominations)

Cataloging & church history .... ROBINSON, Nancy D. .. (KY) 1044
Catholic Church .... MACEY, John F. ...... (PA) 755
Catholic Church history .... HILAND, Gerard P. .... (OH) 538
Church & denominational records ..... WOODARD, John R. ... (NC) 1365
Church & parish libraries .... WHITE, Joyce L. ...... (CO) 1331
Church & synagogue library
    consulting .... KARON, Bernard L. .... (MN) 627
Church archives .... PINKARD, Ophelia T. ... (DC) 974
WIEDERAENDE, Robert C. (IA) 1336
NESBITT, John R. ..... (MO) 896
Church history .... STELLING, Dwight D. ... (IL) 1186
IZBICKI, Thomas M. .... (KS) 586
YEISER, Doris B. ...... (KY) 1379
MCNAMARA, Robert F. . (NY) 816
Church history & religion cataloging .. MITCHELL, Annmarie D. (CA) 848
Church history, theology resources ... SUELFLOW, August R. . (MO) 1206
Church librarianship .... GUINN, Patricia L. ..... (NY) 477
HOUSTON, Barbara B. .. (TX) 563
Church libraries .... BOSWELL, Peggy B. ... (CO) 118
GULLETTE, Irene ...... (FL) 477
SEVERINGHAUS, Ethel L. (NY) 1117
KRUMM, Carol R. ..... (OH) 680
GEARHART, Carol A. ... (PA) 424
MORRISON, Annette T. . (TN) 867
BELLAVANCE, Maria I. . (TX) 78
REIFEL, Louie E. ...... (TX) 1019
RUSSELL, Paula V. .... (TX) 1069
Church libraries training &
    development .... RODDA, Dorothy J. .... (PA) 1047
Church library .... CROWN, Faith W. ..... (PA) 262
Church library cataloging .... WICHELMAN, Ruthann . (NJ) 1335
Church library development .... JENSEN, Wilma M. .... (MN) 599
Church library service .... SINCLAIR, Rose P. ..... (TX) 1143

CHURCH (Cont'd)

Church library setup & management	OVERTON, Margaret C. .	(TN)	931
Church music	ROEPKE, David E.	(OH)	1048
Church of Scientology	LITTLER, June D.	(FL)	734
Church record & manuscripts	HILAND, Gerard P.	(OH)	538
Lutheran Church history, archives	WITTMAN, Elisabeth C. . .	(IL)	1358
Organ & church music	KENT, Frederick J.	(PA)	642
Organizing, cataloging church libraries	HAMMER, Louise K.	(IL)	493
Protestant & Episcopal Church clergy	HYDE, E C.	(MO)	580
Special collection for church groups	VANDEGRIFT, J R.	(DC)	1273
Training for church librarians	JENSEN, Wilma M.	(MN)	599

CINEMA (See also Film)

Cinema & television	THOMPSON, Don K. . . .	(CA)	1239
Cinema arts instruction	TALIT, Lynn	(CT)	1221
Cinema materials	O'CONNELL, Brian E. . .	(NY)	915
Cinema studies	CHESTER, Claudia J. . . .	(CA)	207
	SINGER, Phyllis Z.	(NY)	1143
Reference in cinema	BEAUCLAIR, Rene	(PQ)	70

CINEMATOGRAPHY

Cinematography & photography	ISOBE, Darron T.	(UT)	585

CIRCUIT

Circuit librarian programs	ANTES, E J.	(PA)	28
Circuit librarianship	PIFALO, Victoria	(DE)	972
	ENGLANDER, Marlene S.	(OH)	349
Circuit libraries	SIBLEY, Shawn C.	(NC)	1135
Circuit library program	LEVINE, Lillian S.	(OH)	720
Contract & circuit services	CREELAN, Marilee M. . .	(OH)	257
Printed circuit boards	ZANG, Patricia J.	(VA)	1386

CIRCULATION (See also Lending, Loan, Reserves)

Acquisitions, cataloging, circulation	TODD, Hal W.	(FL)	1248
Acquisitions, circulation, print media	GOODWYN, Betty R. . . .	(AL)	450
Administer circulation, processing	STAINBROOK, Lynn M. . .	(WI)	1178
All media catalog & circulation	DU CARMONT, M C. . . .	(LA)	322
Automated circulation	WATTS, Richard S.	(CA)	1310
	GLICK, Kenneth W.	(CT)	441
	MICHAUD, Noreen R. . . .	(CT)	832
	BERGER, Marianne C. . .	(IL)	85
	LAMB, Robert S.	(IN)	690
	SKIPTON, Iris E.	(MA)	1146
	COOPER, Judith C.	(MD)	243
	MARSHALL, Suzanne K.	(TX)	775
Automated circulation implementation	MORELAND, Rachel S. .	(KS)	863
Automated circulation, public catalog	NIEMEYER, Karen K. . . .	(IN)	903
Automated circulation system	LANE, Linda A.	(GA)	694
	ELDREDGE, Jeffrey R. . .	(HI)	342
Automated circulation systems	CASTONGUAY, Russell .	(CA)	194
	EICHELBERGER, Susan .	(CA)	339
	PARKS, Amy N.	(CT)	943
	SHURMAN, Richard L. . .	(IL)	1134
	PHENIX, Katharine J. . .	(LA)	967
	PURCELL, Kathleen V. . .	(MD)	998
	FARHAT, Elizabeth M. . .	(MI)	363
	HENRY, Peggy L.	(MO)	529
	ROSENBERG, Harlene Z.	(NJ)	1056
	MORRIS, Jennifer D. . . .	(NY)	866
	RIEBEL, Ellis F.	(PA)	1033
	IVES, Gary W.	(VA)	585
	ICE, Priscilla T.	(WA)	581
	HAYES, Janice E.	(ON)	516
Automated journal circulation	LEWIS, Martha S.	(IL)	724
Automated library circulation systems	ULRICH, Paul S.	(WGR)	1268
Automated systems for circulation	JOHNSON, Martha A. . .	(VA)	607
Automation & circulation	PARKHURST, Kathleen A.	(NY)	942
Automation book catalog, circulation	THOMAN, Nancy L.	(DE)	1236
Cataloging & circulation	RUSIEWSKI, Charles B. .	(IL)	1068
Cataloging, reference, & circulation	MANDAL, Mina R.	(NY)	764
Children's circulation	CAPELLA, Jeanne M. . . .	(NJ)	179
Circulating software collections	POLLY, Jean A.	(NY)	981
Circulation	SPILLERS, Doris H.	(AL)	1174
	RICK, Jean A.	(AR)	1031
	POSSNER, Roger D. . . .	(AZ)	986
	WHITE, Edward H.	(AZ)	1330

CIRCULATION (Cont'd)

Circulation

BRISCOE, Georgia K. . . .	(CA)	136
CROCKETT, Darla J. . . .	(CA)	259
CROSS, Mabel L.	(CA)	260
EICHELBERGER, Susan .	(CA)	339
FRIEDRICH, Barbara J. .	(CA)	404
KRASNER, Joan K.	(CA)	676
MYERS, Nancy J.	(CA)	884
NOE, Christopher J.	(CA)	906
WEINER, Carole B.	(CA)	1318
WILSON, Carole F.	(CA)	1350
WILSON, Karen A.	(CA)	1351
WONG, Maida L.	(CA)	1363
NEWMYER, Joann C. . . .	(CT)	900
SKOP, Vera	(CT)	1147
LEITCH, Karen E.	(DC)	714
SMITH, Thomas E.	(DC)	1161
BAIN, Janice W.	(FL)	47
BENNETT, Richard F. . . .	(FL)	82
CONKLIN, Candace V. . .	(FL)	236
JONES, Robert P.	(FL)	614
MITTLEMAN, Marilyn . . .	(FL)	850
PIKE, Nancy M.	(FL)	973
POTTER, Robert E.	(FL)	987
ROBARTS, Phyllis G. . . .	(FL)	1038
ELAM, Joice B.	(GA)	341
MULCAHY, Bryan L.	(GA)	876
HESS, Sandra K.	(IA)	534
HIEBER, Douglas M.	(IA)	537
STOUT, Robert J.	(IA)	1199
ZORDELL, Pamela K. . . .	(IA)	1390
AUSTIN, John R.	(IL)	40
ISOM, Bill V.	(IL)	585
JOHN, Nancy R.	(IL)	601
KAUTZ-WARTH, Linda S. .	(IL)	631
KINNERSLEY, Ruth T. . . .	(IL)	653
KISTNER, Glen A.	(IL)	657
MASON, Marjorie L.	(IL)	781
MCCARTNEY, Elizabeth J.	(IL)	794
MCKEARN, Anne B.	(IL)	810
FALLON, Marianna L. . . .	(IN)	362
SCHMIDT, Steven J. . . .	(IN)	1096
SMITH, Lary	(IN)	1156
DIEMER, Irvin T.	(KY)	302
GERON, Cary A.	(KY)	429
MILLER, Norma B.	(KY)	841
BINGHAM, Elizabeth E. .	(LA)	97
BYERS, Cora M.	(LA)	168
CARTEE, Lewis D.	(LA)	188
MARCKS, Carol J.	(LA)	769
BEARDEN, Eithne C. . . .	(MA)	69
DUTCHER, Henry D. . . .	(MA)	329
PEARCE, Jean K.	(MA)	952
HEUTTE, Frederic A. . . .	(MD)	535
PANDA, Rosamond E. . . .	(MD)	937
WOODS, Catharine C. . . .	(MD)	1366
KOBEL, Rose A.	(MI)	666
PALMER, Catherine S. . .	(MI)	936
SOPER, Marley H.	(MI)	1168
MOORE, Barbara N.	(MN)	858
BECK, Sara R.	(MO)	71
MURPHY, Kathryn L. . . .	(MO)	880
STEVENSON, Marsha J. .	(MO)	1191
BUTLER, James C.	(MS)	166
RAINWATER, Mark T. . . .	(MS)	1004
ABBOTT, Chien N.	(NC)	1
PALO, Eric E.	(NC)	937
BOYLE, Jeanne E.	(NJ)	124
CIMBALA, Diane J.	(NJ)	214
DEMYANOVICH, Peter . .	(NJ)	291
ENGLE, Joyce C.	(NJ)	349
GARRABRANT, William A.	(NJ)	420
MAMAN, Marie	(NJ)	764
MANTHEY, Carolyn M. . .	(NJ)	767
BERRY, Gayle C.	(NY)	90
LOLLIS, Martha J.	(NY)	738
METZ, Ray E.	(NY)	828
GOULD, Allison L.	(OH)	454
JAMISON, Martin P.	(OH)	593

CIRCULATION (Cont'd)

Circulation

JONES, Judykay	(OH)	613
PRESNELL, Jenny L.	(OH)	991
BRADLEY, James S.	(PA)	126
CADY, Susan A.	(PA)	170
FRANCOS, Alexis	(PA)	396
SWARTHOUT, Judy L.	(PA)	1214
SWINTON, Cordelia W.	(PA)	1216
RIVERA-ALVAREZ, Miguel A.	(PR)	1037
BUZZELL, Bonnie G.	(RI)	168
OLSON, Joann M.	(SC)	922
BRONSON, Mark C.	(SD)	140
CHEN, Helen M.	(TN)	205
MURGAI, Sarla R.	(TN)	880
SMITH, Lori D.	(TN)	1157
BAKER, Linda L.	(TX)	49
CAGE, Willa F.	(TX)	171
CLARKSON, Mary C.	(TX)	219
COOK, C C.	(TX)	239
HOWELL, Gladys M.	(TX)	565
JONES, Daniel H.	(TX)	612
THOMAS, Donald L.	(TX)	1236
JONES, Ruth J.	(UT)	615
DENGROVE, Richard A.	(VA)	292
DUKE, John K.	(VA)	324
GRANITZ, Adrienne D.	(VA)	457
MALMQUIST, Katherine E.	(VA)	763
SCHNEIDER, Holle E.	(VA)	1097
WINTERS, Sharon A.	(VA)	1356
VYHNANEK, Kay E.	(WA)	1290
YONGMAN, Zhang	(WA)	1380
HANAMAN, Nancy J.	(WI)	494
SIMPSON, W S.	(WI)	1142
WATSON, Carolyn R.	(WV)	1309
RAO, Dittakavi N.	(WY)	1008
LANOUETTE, Marie	(ON)	696
MANOVILLE, Susanne	(PE)	767
DEROODE, Clifford H.	(FRN)	294

Circulation, access services	EDWARDS, Dana S.	(IL)	337
Circulation & acquisitions	ROSS, Theodosia B.	(GA)	1059
Circulation & faculty reserves	HARER, John B.	(MD)	501
Circulation & interlibrary loan	STEWART, Jamie K.	(IL)	1192
Circulation & interlibrary loans	BULLARD, Rita J.	(MI)	156
Circulation & media services	RIEPMA, Helen J.	(TX)	1033
Circulation & reference	RINE, Joseph L.	(MN)	1035
Circulation & reference services	WATTERSON, Jane L.	(CO)	1310
Circulation & reserve	RASMUSSEN, Gordon E.	(IL)	1009
	DEBRECZENY, Gillian M.	(NC)	285
	THOMAS, Barbara C.	(TX)	1236
Circulation & reserve services	LACKS, Bernice K.	(NY)	686
	NECHKA, Ada M.	(AB)	891
Circulation & reserve systems & services	HENSHAW, Rod	(PA)	529
Circulation & reserves	HILL, Ann M.	(WA)	539
Circulation & stack management	PARKER, Susan E.	(MA)	942
Circulation & technical services	BENGSTON, Carl E.	(CA)	80
Circulation, automation	GYESZLY, Suzanne D.	(TX)	479
Circulation control	COHEN, Barbara S.	(RI)	228
Circulation control systems	DODGE, Christopher N.	(MN)	308
Circulation, database searching	ROBICHAUD, Marcel J.	(NY)	1042
Circulation department	ARNOLD, Donna W.	(CA)	33
	FEHRENBACH, Laurie A.	(OK)	368
Circulation desk	MAYHEW, Eileen G.	(DC)	790
Circulation development	THOMAS, Louise V.	(MI)	1237
Circulation duties	CASWELL, Mary C.	(VA)	194
Circulation, interlibrary loan	EDMONDS, Michael	(WI)	336
Circulation inventory control	GOULD, Douglas A.	(UT)	454
Circulation librarianship	DAUGHERTY, Robert A.	(IL)	275
	MITCHELL, W B.	(NC)	849
Circulation management	SPURRIER, Suzanne F.	(AR)	1177
	HOOVER, Clara G.	(NE)	557
	TRAMDACK, Philip J.	(OH)	1254
Circulation policies & procedures	COOK, Anita I.	(NE)	239
Circulation policy	BULERIN-LUGO, Josefina	(PR)	156
Circulation procedures	PORTER, Eva L.	(NJ)	984
Circulation, public services	FLIEGEL, Deborah A.	(WI)	385
Circulation, reader services	ADAMS, Velma L.	(MS)	6

CIRCULATION (Cont'd)

Circulation, reserve, interlibrary loan	MEAD-DONALDSON, Susan L.	(FL)	819
Circulation services	GOLDSMITH, Jan E.	(CA)	446
	SLINGER, Michael J.	(IN)	1149
	DALY, Kathleen E.	(MI)	271
	OSTROM, Kriss T.	(MI)	929
	PROFETA, Patricia C.	(NJ)	995
	ANDERSON, Carol L.	(NY)	22
	FISCHER, Beverly J.	(TX)	379
	SPARKMAN, Mickey M.	(TX)	1171
	PEARSON, Marilyn R.	(VA)	953
Circulation supervision	STAHL, Ramona J.	(CA)	1178
	ESTES, Elizabeth W.	(NC)	355
Circulation supervisor	REINBOLD, Janice K.	(OK)	1021
Circulation system automation	NOBLE, Barbara N.	(MO)	906
Circulation systems	FROHMBERG, Katherine A.	(CA)	405
	HESSLER, Nancy R.	(IL)	534
	DOELLMAN, Michael A.	(IN)	308
	DOVE, Samuel	(MD)	315
	FARK, Ronald K.	(RI)	364
	MILLER, G D.	(WA)	837
	CAPES, Judy L.	(BC)	179
	HAYTON, E E.	(ON)	517
	MAHARAJ, Diana J.	(PQ)	760
Circulation, theology	BULLOCK, Frances E.	(NY)	156
CLSI automated circulation system	CALLANAN, Ellen M.	(NJ)	173
Collection management & circulation	DAVIS, Douglas A.	(CA)	278
Computer circulation systems	WAGNER, Robin O.	(IL)	1292
Computerized circulation	SONDALLE, Barbara J.	(IL)	1167
	KIEFER, Marilyn V.	(MI)	647
	JACOBS, Mildred H.	(MO)	589
Computerized circulation systems	HANRATH, Richard A.	(IL)	497
	UNDERHILL, Jan	(OK)	1268
	EMERICK, Michael J.	(PA)	347
Custom circulation desk design	RIBNICKY, Karen F.	(CT)	1026
General public service, circulation	HOLMES, Nancy M.	(GA)	553
Head of circulation	BUCHWALD, Donald M.	(TX)	153
Information circulation & management	KAPLAN, Tiby	(FL)	626
Integrated circulation systems	CRISCO, Mary E.	(MD)	259
Interlibrary & circulation services	POSES, June A.	(PA)	985
Legal & reserve book circulation	DINDAYAL, Joyce S.	(NY)	304
Lending & circulation	LEFEBVRE, Veronica A.	(MD)	712
Library circulation control	RAHN, Erwin P.	(NY)	1003
Management of circulation systems	TREMBLAY, Carolyn B.	(NH)	1255
Online circulation system	BONNET, Janice M.	(CA)	114
Online circulation systems	EDWARDS, Dana S.	(IL)	337
	FOLEY, Mary D.	(KY)	387
Public circulation & access services	DREW, Wilfred E.	(NY)	319
Reference & circulation	OVERTON, Margaret C.	(TN)	931
	HARPER, Marsha W.	(TX)	503
	CASEY, Wayne T.	(VA)	192
Select weed central adult circulation	DOYLE, Patricia A.	(TX)	317
Small library circulation automation	STOUT, Chester B.	(OH)	1198
Technical services, circulation	CLAER, Joycelyn H.	(TX)	215
Textbook & circulation cataloging	WILSON, Carole F.	(CA)	1350
Training & supervising circulation staff	MANOVILLE, Susanne	(PE)	767
Videotape purchasing & circulation	BARGAR, Arthur W.	(CT)	56

CITATION

Bibliographic citation systems	BRANDT, Daryl S.	(IN)	128
Bibliometrics & citation studies	AVERSA, Elizabeth S.	(DC)	41
Legal citation form	NISSENBAUM, Robert J.	(OH)	905
Verifying citations & ordering	WILLIS, Joan K.	(CA)	1348

CITRUS

Citrus literature	RUSS, Pamela K.	(FL)	1068

CITY (See also Metropolitan, Urban)

Children's literature in inner-city	NIX, Kemie	(GA)	905
City & urban planning	SLOCUM, Charlotte A.	(NC)	1150
City government relations	WEST, Shirley L.	(NJ)	1326
City law libraries	COX, Irvin E.	(MD)	253
City planning librarianship	BYRNE, Elizabeth D.	(CA)	169
Programs for inner-city libraries	O'BRIEN, Anne M.	(MA)	914
Services to inner-city residents	NORMAN, Nita V.	(AZ)	909

CIVIL

Cataloging civil engineering materials	REINALDO DA SILVA, Joann T.	(MB)	1021
Civil & common law	NARANJO-BOSCH, Antonio A.	(IL)	888
Civil & environmental engineering	UZZO, Beatrice C.	(NY)	1270
Civil & mechanical engineering	AMRON, Irving	(NJ)	20
Civil & structural engineering	SPIGELMAN, Cynthia A.	(IL)	1174
Civil engineering	REICHARDT, Randall P.	(AB)	1018
Civil engineering, pavements, structures	MOBLEY, Arthur B.	(DC)	851
Civil law	SEADER, Jane M.	(NJ)	1109
	CORNEIL, Charlotte E.	(OK)	246
Civil, military, space databases	GAZZOLA, Kenneth E.	(DC)	424
Civil service testbooks	LUNSTEDT, Ralph A.	(CA)	749
Civil War	TEMPLE, Wayne C.	(IL)	1230
Civil War historical collections	JORDAN, Ervin L.	(VA)	616
Civil War history	BERENT, Irwin M.	(VA)	84
Civil War, North Carolina sources, units	WOODARD, John R.	(NC)	1365
Environmental & civil engineering libs	SPURLOCK, Pauline	(CA)	1177
United States Civil War history	CAHILL, Colleen R.	(PA)	171

CLASSICS

Classical antiquity, reference	AVDOYAN, Levon	(DC)	41
Classical Greek & Latin reference	CRITTENDEN, Robert R.	(CA)	259
Classical languages & literature	BYRE, Calvin S.	(IL)	169
Classical music broadcasting	FRANK, Mortimer H.	(NY)	397
Classical music criticism	LAMBERT, John W.	(NC)	690
Classical music sound archives	MAROTH, Frederick J.	(CA)	772
Classical music sound recordings	HALSEY, Richard S.	(NY)	490
Classics	TRAICHEL, Rudolf D.	(AB)	1253
English, linguistics & classics	RICKER, Shirley E.	(NY)	1031
Foreign languages & classics	PEDERSOLI, Heleni M.	(AL)	954
Opera & classical discography	COLLINS, William J.	(CA)	233
Philosophy, classics, music	CULLARS, John M.	(IL)	263
Rare classical recordings	CAMPBELL, R A.	(HI)	177

CLASSIFICATION (See also Authority, Cataloging, Declassification, Reclassification)

Art history classification	UPDIKE, Christina B.	(VA)	1269
Automatic indexing & classification	RAGHAVAN, Vijay V.	(LA)	1003
Cataloging & classification	BOWLES, Carol A.	(CA)	121
	WAY, Kathy A.	(CA)	1311
	FIELD, Oliver T.	(CO)	375
	JUKNIS, Ann M.	(CT)	619
	BARRY, Paul J.	(DC)	60
	CLACK, Doris H.	(FL)	215
	WALCOTT, M A.	(FL)	1294
	RIEMER, John J.	(GA)	1033
	HENDERSON, Kathryn L.	(IL)	526
	HOLZBERLEIN, Deanne B.	(IL)	555
	RICHARDSON, Susan C.	(KY)	1030
	HORGAN, Laura A.	(MA)	559
	INTNER, Sheila S.	(MA)	583
	ST. AUBIN, Arleen K.	(MA)	1075
	PRATT, Laura C.	(MD)	990
	MIKA, Joseph J.	(MI)	834
	BETH, Dana L.	(MO)	92
	BOYD, William D.	(MS)	123
	VAN MELER, Vandelia L.	(MS)	1276
	SAYE, Jerry D.	(NC)	1086
	HASELWOOD, Eldon L.	(NE)	510
	GRIFFITH, Joan C.	(NH)	469
	KALIF, Alexander J.	(NJ)	623
	LINNAMAA, Mari M.	(NJ)	731
	LANCASTER, Kevin M.	(NM)	692
	BRADLEY, Carol J.	(NY)	125
	BRENNAN, Christopher P.	(NY)	132
	HOPKINS, Judith	(NY)	558
	MATTA, Seoud M.	(NY)	785
	SCHUTT, Dedre A.	(NY)	1103
	SMIRAGLIA, Richard P.	(NY)	1152
	WAGSCHAL, Sara G.	(NY)	1292
	GREBEY, Betty H.	(PA)	461
	BARNETT, Judith B.	(RI)	57
	EASTERLY, Ambrose	(TN)	333
	CALIMANO, Ivan E.	(TX)	173

CLASSIFICATION (Cont'd)

Cataloging & classification	FERSTL, Kenneth L.	(TX)	374
	HERRING, Billie G.	(TX)	533
	MIKSA, Francis L.	(TX)	834
	THORNE, Bonnie B.	(TX)	1242
	WILLIAMS, Suzi	(TX)	1346
	HOLLEY, Robert P.	(UT)	551
	BILLERT, Julia A.	(VA)	96
	FINCH, Mildred E.	(VA)	377
	FISHER, Carl D.	(VA)	380
	RODRIGUEZ, Robert D.	(VA)	1048
	JORDAN, Sharon J.	(WA)	617
	DIETZ, Kathryn A.	(WI)	302
	LAM, Vinh T.	(ON)	689
	WILLIAMSON, Nancy J.	(ON)	1347
	DEMERS, Madeleine M.	(PQ)	291
	GARDNER, Richard K.	(PQ)	418
	KO, Jean S.	(PQ)	666
	GOODELL, John S.	(AUS)	448
	GOODELL, Paulette M.	(AUS)	448
	ADITIRTO, Irma U.	(IDN)	6
	DOUGLAS, Daphne R.	(JAM)	314
	SHAW, Shiow J.	(TAI)	1124
Cataloging & classification of slides	HENDERSON, Joyce C.	(AZ)	526
Cataloging & classifying books	MILTON, Ardyce A.	(WI)	845
Cataloging & classifying photographs	KOSHER, Helene J.	(CA)	672
Cataloging & classifying serials	WALKER, Elizabeth A.	(PQ)	1295
Cataloging & classifying slides	KOSHER, Helene J.	(CA)	672
Cataloging classification	PORTER, Eva L.	(NJ)	984
	LIGHTHALL, Lynne I.	(BC)	727
Classification	TSAI, Sheh G.	(CA)	1260
	BEALL, Julianne	(DC)	69
	ELSASSER, Katharine K.	(DC)	346
	KURT, Edgar	(IA)	684
	LATSHAW, Ruth N.	(IN)	701
	CHAN, Lois M.	(KY)	199
	MARCY, Henry O.	(MA)	769
	BREWER, Christina A.	(MD)	134
	POLSON, Billie M.	(NV)	982
	HYMAN, Richard J.	(NY)	580
	SLOCUM, Robert B.	(NY)	1150
	VIZINE-GOETZ, Diane	(OH)	1286
	WUJCIK, Dennis S.	(TN)	1374
	ELROD, J M.	(BC)	346
	BUTLER, Patricia	(PQ)	167
	CHAUMONT, Elise	(PQ)	204
	GAULIN, S D.	(PQ)	422
	LAFRENIERE, Myriam	(PQ)	688
	LALIBERTE, Madeleine A.	(PQ)	689
	LAPOINTE, Louise	(PQ)	697
	MAILLOUX, Jean Y.	(PQ)	761
	PELLETIER, Rosaire	(PQ)	955
	ROLLAND-THOMAS, Paule	(PQ)	1051
Classification & cataloging	RADEMACHER, Matthew J.	(MI)	1002
	RUSSELL, Elizabeth	(RI)	1068
	LEIDE, John E.	(PQ)	713
Classification & indexing	SVENONIUS, Elaine	(CA)	1212
Classification & subject analysis	DYKSTRA, Mary E.	(NS)	331
Classification, cataloging	MCKELVEY, Mary J.	(VA)	810
	SELING, Kathy A.	(WA)	1113
Classification, database cataloging	MCCONNIE, Mary	(TRN)	798
Classification education	BREGZIS, Ilze	(ON)	131
Classification research	RICHMOND, Phyllis A.	(OH)	1030
Classification schedules publishing	DERSHEM, Larry D.	(CA)	294
Classification scheme & systems devlpmnt	ELLIS, Kathy M.	(BC)	344
Classification system development	NEW, Gregory R.	(DC)	898
Classification systems	PAULSON, Peter J.	(NY)	950
Classification systems & catalogs	GOLDBERG, Jolande E.	(DC)	444
Classifying	JACKSON, Mildred E.	(MN)	588
Classifying information	ALBAIR, Catherine M.	(FL)	9
Classifying information about music	STRATELAK, Nadia A.	(MI)	1200
Decimal classification	RENAUD, Monique M.	(ON)	1023
Dewey decimal classification	DANIS, Rolland J.	(PQ)	273
Indexing & classification	RICHARDSON, Katherine A.	(OH)	1029
Indexing & classifying	HUBBARD, Susan E.	(NY)	568

CLASSIFICATION (Cont'd)

Law cataloging & classification	STRIMAN, Brian D.	(NE)	1202
Law classification	HU, Shih S.	(AB)	568
Library classification	SATYANARAYANA, Vadhri V.	(IND)	1084
Library of Congress classification	GLENISTER, Peter	(NS)	441
	PARADIS, Jacques	(PQ)	939
Library of Congress classification syst	SAVAGE, Helen	(MI)	1085
Library personnel classification	HEARTH, Fred E.	(CA)	519
Map cataloging & classification	GALNEDER, Mary H. . . .	(WI)	415
Non-book materials classification	HAMDY, Mohamed N. . . .	(KWT)	491
Organization & subject classification	HAYNES, Kathleen J. . . .	(OH)	516
Promoting Dewey decimal classification	KRAMER-GREENE, Judith	(NY)	675
Purchase & classification of books	LACAILLADE, Jacqueline	(PQ)	686
Science classification	CANTIN, Gemma	(PQ)	179
Slide classification	HAWKOS, Lise J.	(AZ)	514
Slide classification & cataloging	MCRAE, Linda	(FL)	818
Subject analysis & classification	CROWTHER, Carol	(CA)	262
Subject cataloging & classification	KIRKWOOD, Francis T. . .	(ON)	655
Subject classification	NEW, Gregory R.	(DC)	898
	LOVELL, Bonnie A.	(TX)	743
Teaching cataloging & classification	MILLER, Sarah J.	(NJ)	842
Thesaurus & classification construction	BATTY, Charles D.	(MD)	65
Training indexing & classification	LOMBARDI, Mary L. . . .	(CA)	738
Visual resources classification	FREEMAN, Carla C.	(NY)	400

CLEARANCE (See also Copyright)

Publication clearance	SEAGER, Janice R.	(NJ)	1109
Script clearances	PLUMB, Carolyn G.	(CA)	978

CLEARINGHOUSE

Clearinghouse & information center mgmt	BYRD, Harvey C.	(MD)	169
Clearinghouse management	BATES, Ruthann I.	(MD)	64
	BERUL, Lawrence H. . . .	(MD)	91
Health information clearinghouses	LUNIN, Lois F.	(VA)	749
Information clearinghouse	SHELBURNE, Elizabeth C.	(DC)	1125
Information clearinghouse methods	LIPETZ, Ben A.	(NY)	732

CLERGY (See also Ministry, Pastoral)

Protestant & Episcopal Church clergy	HYDE, E C.	(MO)	580

CLIENTS (See also Consumer, Customer, Patients, Patrons, User)

Client record maintenance	EMMONS, Mary E.	(AK)	348
Client services	RODGER, Stephen J. . . .	(ON)	1047
Commercial client relations	VALANDRA, Kent T. . . .	(NY)	1271
Corporate clients	BAKES, Floy L.	(NJ)	50
Public relations between firm & clients	BARNUM, Deborah C. . .	(CT)	58

CLINICAL

Clinical applications	MENDELSON, Martin . . .	(WA)	823
Clinical decision making	COOK, Galen B.	(SC)	240
Clinical epidemiology	HAYNES, Robert B.	(ON)	517
Clinical health care profiles	CHERNIN, David A.	(MA)	206
Clinical laboratory computing	FRIEDMAN, Bruce A. . . .	(MI)	403
Clinical librarianship	GUTH, Karen K.	(CO)	478
	HANSON, Elana L.	(CO)	498
	FREY, Barbara J.	(CT)	402
	WETMORE, Judith M. . .	(CT)	1328
	DOHERTY, Mary C.	(NY)	309
	MILLER, Naomi	(PA)	841
	STESIS, Karen R.	(PA)	1189
	BELLAMY, Lois M.	(TN)	77
	HAMBERG, Cheryl J. . . .	(TN)	490
	PEDERSEN, Wayne A. . .	(TX)	954
	ANGIER, Jennifer J.	(UT)	27
Clinical librarianship program	TRAVERS, Jane E.	(NY)	1254
Clinical libraries	MORSI, Pamela A.	(SC)	869
Clinical literature retrieval, databases	KINNAIRD, Cheryl D. . . .	(IL)	653
Clinical medical librarianship	DALE, Nancy	(IL)	270
	VUGRIN, Margaret Y. . . .	(TX)	1289
Clinical medical libraries	WATTS, Adalyn	(TN)	1310

CLINICAL (Cont'd)

Clinical medical reference bibliography	KINNAIRD, Cheryl D. . . .	(IL)	653
Clinical medicine	MONROE, Donald H. . . .	(IN)	855
	STRUB, Jeane E.	(NM)	1203
	LIN, Louise	(ON)	727
Clinical medicine & nursing	SMITH, Brian D.	(NY)	1153
	TREVANION, Margaret U.	(PA)	1255
Clinical medicine reference	ECKERT, Daniel L.	(WI)	335
Clinical medicine research	BRUCE, Marianne E. . . .	(AB)	149
Clinical oncology	BLOOMSTONE, Ajaye . .	(LA)	106
Clinical research	OWENS, Clayton S.	(AZ)	932
Clinical science bibliography	LIMAYE, Asha A.	(IL)	727
Clinical support & reference	MOORE, Sara L.	(DC)	861
Clinical systems	BOLLINGER, Robert O. . .	(MI)	112
Clinical teaching	RAMAKRISHNAN, T . . .	(LA)	1004
Hospital & clinical management subjects	BELT, Jane	(WA)	78
Medical & clinical	BRENNER, Lawrence . . .	(MA)	133
Medical clinical librarianship	GRAVES, Karen J.	(IL)	459

CLIPPINGS

Cataloging & clipping	DONNELLY, Lela M. . . .	(KS)	311
Clip files	BRITTON, Pilaivan H. . . .	(WA)	137
Clipping libraries	WESOLOWSKI, Paul G. .	(PA)	1325
Clippings files	EVANS, Stephen P.	(OH)	358
Indexing newspaper clips & photos	RICE, Margaret R.	(TX)	1027
News clip editing	CANT, Elaine N.	(CA)	179
Newspaper clip files	CROCKETT, Mary S. . . .	(SC)	259
Newspaper clipping & indexing	WALSH, Barclay	(DC)	1299
Newspaper clipping files	VANCE, Carolyn J.	(IL)	1272
Newspaper clipping systems	KANE, Angelika R.	(PA)	624
Newspaper clippings	HEARN, Geraldine B. . . .	(IL)	518
	KATZUNG, Judith	(MN)	630
	PARISOT, Beverly J. . . .	(NE)	940
	SPINA, Nan H.	(NV)	1175
Newspaper clippings & photos	CHANCE, Peggy J.	(PA)	199
Newspaper clippings services	STILES, William G.	(ON)	1194
Newspaper clips	MOFFETT, Martha L. . . .	(FL)	852
	PUSTAY, Marilyn J.	(MS)	998
Newspaper library clipping	CLARK, Audrey M.	(UT)	216
Organizing, clippings pamphlets reports	HORN, Zoia	(CA)	559

CLOTHING (See also Costumes, Fashion, Textiles)

Clothing & textiles literature	FETTERMAN, Nelma I. . .	(AB)	374

CLSI

CLSI	MOZGA, John P.	(IL)	874
	SHACKLETON, Suzanne M.	(IL)	1118
CLSI automated circulation system	CALLANAN, Ellen M. . . .	(NJ)	173
CLSI operations	LIGHT, Karen M.	(RI)	726

COALBED

Coalbed methane databases	WATSON, Linda S.	(AL)	1309

COAST GUARD (See also Armed Forces)

United States Coast Guard	SHERMAN, William F. . .	(DC)	1128

COATINGS

Chemical & coatings databases	KOZELKA, Catherine C. .	(IL)	674
Coatings	HSU, Helena S.	(OH)	567

COBOL

Programming COBOL	ZYNJUK, Nila L.	(MD)	1392

CODES

Bar code system design	VOGT, Herwart C.	(NJ)	1287
Bibliography, codicology	MATHIESEN, Thomas J. .	(UT)	784
Codes & standards	SANDVIKEN, Gordon L. .	(CA)	1081
	BONGARD, Nancy D. . . .	(ON)	114

CODES (Cont'd)

Codes of ordinances	HENDERSON, Laurel E. . .	(GA)	526
Codicology	CRONENWETT, Philip N.	(NH)	260
Document analysis & generic coding	KNOERDEL, Joan E. . . .	(MD)	665
Engineering codes & standards	BERNSTEIN, Anna L. . . .	(DC)	89
Filing source code documentation	BOZE, Lucy G.	(GA)	124
Filing source code listings	BOZE, Lucy G.	(GA)	124
Generic coding	FOSTER, Anne	(ON)	392
Standard nomenclature & code for medcn	CASIRAGHI, Edoardo . . .	(ITL)	192

COGNITION

Cognitive rehabilitation & computers	SHANEFIELD, Irene D. . . .	(PQ)	1120
Expert systems & human cognition	HARMON, Glynn	(TX)	502
Research on cognitive learning	KOCHEN, Manfred	(MI)	667

COLLECTIBLES

Books on collectibles & nostalgia	JOHNSON, Nancy E. . . .	(IA)	608
Collectible records 1950s, 1960s	MENNIE, Don	(NJ)	824

COLLECTING

Book collecting	DICKINSON, Donald C. .	(AZ)	300
	CAMERON, Sam A.	(TN)	175
Cataloging & collecting rare recordings	BROWNE, J P.	(CA)	148
Collect specific regulatory documents	HARDY, Kenneth J. . . .	(AB)	501
Collecting	HAGSTROM, Jack W. . .	(NY)	483
Collecting college records	VARGA, Nicholas	(MD)	1278
Collecting state religious history	ROLLER, Twila J.	(NM)	1051
Collectors & collecting	TOTH, Georgina G. . . .	(OH)	1252
Indexing & collecting pamphlets	RHYNAS, Don M.	(ON)	1026
Manuscript processing & collecting	HULL, Mary M.	(TX)	572
Sheet music collector	SETON, Charles B.	(NY)	1117

COLLECTIONS (See also Acquisitions, Deselection, Materials, Resources, Selection, Sources, Weeding)

Academic library collection development	MURRAY, Lucia M.	(OR)	882
Acquisition, cataloging of record col	MECHTENBERG, Paul . .	(IL)	820
Acquisitions & collection development	POTTER, William G. . . .	(AZ)	987
	WINTER, Eugenia B. . . .	(CA)	1356
	KASCUS, Marie A.	(CT)	628
	WOLFE, Susan J.	(DC)	1361
	DANNECKER, Joyce H. .	(FL)	274
	LOCKE, John W.	(IL)	736
	SOTO, Donna G.	(LA)	1169
	TATELMAN, Susan D. . .	(MA)	1225
	BEARSS, Daniel H.	(MD)	69
	TURKOS, Joseph A.	(MD)	1263
	ARNDT, Arleen	(MI)	33
	IRVING, Ophelia M.	(NC)	584
	JARRELL, James R.	(NC)	594
	GRABE, Lauralee F.	(NE)	455
	MCADOO, Jannifer C. . .	(NJ)	792
	THORSON, Connie C. . .	(NM)	1242
	BIDDEN, Julia E.	(NY)	94
	DESSER, Darrilyn	(NY)	296
	DEUTSCH, Karen A. . . .	(NY)	296
	O'BRIEN, Elmer J.	(OH)	914
	GRILIKHES, Sandra B. . .	(PA)	470
	RIEKE, Judith L.	(TN)	1033
	CARROLL, Dewey E. . . .	(TX)	187
	HOLLOWAY, Geraldine B.	(TX)	552
	DIERCKS, Thelma C. . . .	(VA)	302
	KALABUS, Robert L. . . .	(WY)	622
	ENGLESAKIS, Marina F. .	(AB)	350
	SNYDER, Lisa A.	(MAL)	1165
Acquisitions & collection management	KNAUFF, Elisabeth S. . . .	(DC)	663
Acquisitions, collection building	CADLE, Dean	(NC)	170
Acquisitions, collection development	WALSH, Lynn R.	(FL)	1299
	CHANG, Robert H.	(TX)	201
	UMBERGER, Sheila S. . .	(VA)	1268
Administering local history collection	CARTER, Susan M.	(IN)	190
Administering nursing book collection	DAUGHERTY, Carolyn M.	(MD)	275

COLLECTIONS (Cont'd)

Admin & collection development	LEISTER, Jack	(CA)	714
	NAIRN, Charles E.	(MI)	886
	PICQUET, D C.	(TN)	971
Administration & personal manuscript col	CUMMINGS, Hilary A. . .	(OR)	264
Administration, collection & development	RAFAEL, Ruth K.	(CA)	1003
Administration, collection development	BAREFOOT, Gary F. . . .	(NC)	56
Administration of periodicals collection	SMITH, Cynthia A.	(OH)	1153
Administration of visual collections	SHAW, Renata V.	(DC)	1123
Adult & young adult collection devlpmnt	STEVENSON, Sheila M. .	(IL)	1191
Adult collection development	AMESTOY, Helen M. . . .	(CA)	20
	BJORKLUND, Katharine B.	(NM)	100
Adult services & collection development	TYNES, Jacqueline K. . .	(NY)	1267
Afro-American collection development	MARSHALL, Albert P. . .	(MI)	773
	WRIGHT, Catherine A. . .	(OR)	1370
Afro-American collections	HAZEL, Debora E.	(NC)	517
	SHOCKLEY, Ann A.	(TN)	1132
Agriculture collection development	MILLER, Susan E.	(LA)	842
	HARPER, Judy A.	(MB)	503
Alaska collection development project	INNES-TAYLOR, Catherine E.	(AK)	583
American ethnic collections	SUTTON, David H.	(PA)	1211
American history collection development	VYHNANEK, Louis	(WA)	1290
Americana collection administration	JACKSON, Richard H. . .	(NY)	588
Anthropology collection development	FAIRBANKS, Deborah M.	(FL)	361
	KIBBEE, Josephine Z. . . .	(IL)	646
	MITTEN, Lisa A.	(PA)	850
Antiquarian books collection management	GOGGIN, Margaret K. . .	(FL)	444
Appraisal & collection development	DELOACH, Lynda J.	(MN)	290
Appraisal of theatre collections	KAHAN, Gerald	(GA)	621
Appraisals of medical collections	KLENK, Anne S.	(CO)	660
Appraising law firm collections	SCAMMAHORN, Lynne .	(PA)	1087
Appraising record & phonograph cols	FABRIZIO, Timothy C. . .	(NY)	360
Archival & manuscript collections	SHOCKLEY, Ann A.	(TN)	1132
Archival collection development	CHRISTOPHER, Paul . . .	(CA)	212
Archival collections	PETERSON, Scott W. . . .	(IL)	964
Archival collections appraisals	RENDELL, Kenneth W. . .	(MA)	1023
Archival manuscripts collections	RICHMOND, Robert W. .	(KS)	1031
Archives & manuscript collection mgmt	FRYE, Dorothy T.	(MI)	407
Archives & manuscript collections	NODLER, Charles E.	(MO)	906
Archives collection development	JESSEE, W S.	(MN)	600
Archives, manuscripts collections	SMITH, Edith	(CA)	1154
Arrangement of manuscript collections	MAYER, Dale C.	(IA)	789
Art & architecture collections devlpmnt	BEGLO, Jo N.	(ON)	74
Art collection development	KORENIC, Lynette M. . . .	(CA)	671
	CLAYTON, William R. . .	(GA)	220
	MAJOR, Marla J.	(MI)	762
	SIGALA, Stephanie C. . .	(MO)	1137
	ROSENBERG-NUGENT, Nanci B.	(NY)	1056
Art collections & museum administration	SOMMER, Ursula M. . . .	(NJ)	1167
Art history collection development	SMITH, Beryl K.	(NJ)	1153
Art, music & sports collection devlpmnt	BAKER, Paula J.	(OH)	49
Art slide collections	BLAIR, Madeline S.	(DC)	102
Arts & humanities collection development	MESSINEO, Leonard L. .	(KS)	828
Arts collection development	VAN NIEL, Eloise S.	(HI)	1276
	ANDERSON, Gail	(AB)	23
Asia Pacific business collection	CHAN, Diana L.	(BC)	199
Audio & video collection	BERGER, Brenda L.	(NJ)	85
Audio cassette collection management	TREMBLAY, Carolyn B. .	(NH)	1255
Audio collection development	WARREN, Ann R.	(NH)	1306
Audiovisual collection	DAVIS, Bernice	(IN)	277
	LINN, Mott R.	(PA)	731
Audiovisual collection development	BASKIN, Jeffrey L.	(AR)	63
	RITTEN, Karla J.	(CO)	1036
	TAYLOR, Mary L.	(HI)	1227
	SIARNY, William D.	(IL)	1134
	STUCKWICH, Chris E. . .	(LA)	1204

COLLECTIONS (Cont'd)

Audiovisual collection development

SALITA, Christine T. . . . . (NY) 1076
GARRETT, Melinda R. . . (OH) 420
FIDISHUN, Dolores . . . . . (PA) 375
STAINBROOK, Lynn M. . (WI) 1178

Audiovisual collection development, mgmt
GAUDET, Susan E. . . . . (TN) 422

Audiovisual collections
GARDNER, W J. . . . . . . (CO) 418
GOLEY, Elaine P. . . . . . . (TX) 447
MCCOY, Judy I. . . . . (TX) 799
REID, Patricia M. . . . . . . (AB) 1019

Automated collection devlpmnt techniques
LAREW, Christian K. . . . (NJ) 697

Automation, book collection devlpmnt SIMON, Bradley A. . . . . . (OK) 1140
Automation of collection management EVANS, Linda J. . . . . . . (IL) 357
Automation of slide collections HENDERSON, Joyce C. . (AZ) 526

Bible & theology collection development
ZINK, Esther L. . . . . (ND) 1389

Bibliography & collection development COOVER, James B. . . . . (NY) 244
Bibliometric studies, col development CLARK, Sharon E. . . . . . (IL) 218
Biographic collection MOFFETT, Martha L. . . . (FL) 852

Biology & chemistry collection devlpmnt
DODSON, Snowdy D. . . . (CA) 308

Black history collection maintenance PULLER, Maryam W. . . . (PA) 997
Book & serial collection ELSTEIN, Rochelle S. . . . (IL) 346
Book collection HUDSON, Susan P. . . . . (BC) 570
VIIERANS, Mary E. . . . . (BC) 1284

Book collection development HABERLAND, Jody . . . . (VA) 481
Book collection evaluation NIXON, Arless B. . . . . . . (AZ) 906
Book collections development KIERANS, Mary E. . . . . . (BC) 647

Book selection & collection development
HOLSTINE, Lesa G. . . . . (FL) 554

Branch library collection development GENCO, Barbara A. . . . . (NY) 426
British collection development REES, Warren D. . . . . . . (MN) 1016
Building & collections development LIU, David T. . . . . (TX) 734
Building book collection KNOLL, Betty A. . . . . . . (WA) 665
Building collection SOURS, Katherine M. . . (FL) 1169
Building library collection GREMONT, Joan C. . . . . (TX) 467
Building local history collection MILLER, Ida M. . . . . (IN) 838
Building reference collection COFFEY, Dorothy A. . . . (MI) 227
Building, weeding pamphlet collection ADAMS, Velma L. . . . . . (MS) 6
Business collection development DANIELLS, Lorna M. . . . (MA) 273
TERTELL, Susan M. . . . . (MN) 1232
NOTARSTEFANO, Vincent
C. . . . . (NY) 910
ALLEN, Sarabeth . . . . . . (TX) 16
DUFFUS, Sylvia J. . . . . . (AB) 323

Business-related collection development
PASSARELLI, Anne B. . . (WA) 946

Cancer information collection KAWASHIMA, Hiroko . . . (JAP) 632

Cartographic mtrl collection development
WYMAN, Kathleen M. . . (ON) 1375

Cataloging & collection development BEDOR, Kathleen M. . . . (MN) 73
FERRIGNO, Helen F. . . . (NH) 373
SARTAIN, Sara M. . . . . . (VA) 1083

Cataloging & collection maintenance WANG, Connie . . . . (CA) 1302
Cataloging collections AUTRY, Carolyn . . . . (IN) 41
Cataloging local history collection MILLER, Ida M. . . . . (IN) 838
Cataloging manuscript collections OSTROFF, Harriet . . . . . (DC) 929
Cataloging musical loan collections LYON, Bruce C. . . . . (FL) 752

Cataloging photographs, collections mgmt
ROARK, Carol E. . . . . . . (TX) 1038

Cataloging small collections KNOBBE, Mary L. . . . . . (MD) 665
Catholic historical collections WALCH, Timothy G. . . . . (DC) 1293
Children collection development ADDY, Kathryn J. . . . . . (ON) 6
Children's collection development BECKER, Teresa J. . . . . (AZ) 72
KELLY, Anne V. . . . . (FL) 637
RASKIN, Susan R. . . . . . (MA) 1009
MORRIS, Kim . . . . (NY) 867
BERNARD, Marie L. . . . . (AB) 88
MARION, Luce . . . . (PQ) 770
GAGNON, Andre . . . . . . (SK) 412

Children's collections WATERS, Bill F. . . . . (MO) 1308
STURM, Danna G. . . . . . (NV) 1205

Children's materials col development HODGES, Lois F. . . . . . . (NY) 546
SMITH, Valerie M. . . . . . (OH) 1161

Children's services, collection devlpmnt
CORDUKES, Laura L. . . (ON) 246

COLLECTIONS (Cont'd)

Chinese collections CHENG, Sheung O. . . . . (TAI) 206
WANG, Sin C. . . . . (TAI) 1303

Circulating software collections POLLY, Jean A. . . . . (NY) 981
Civil War historical collections JORDAN, Ervin L. . . . . . (VA) 616
Collection MILLER, Virginia L. . . . . (NJ) 843
GILLETTE, Meredith . . . . (WI) 435

Collection access & networks JOHNSON, Carolynn K. . (WA) 603
Collection analysis KRABBE, Natalie . . . . . . (OR) 674
ROUSSEAU, Denis . . . . (PQ) 1061

Collection analysis & development RINGER, Sarah A. . . . . . (AR) 1035
MACNEILL, Daniel S. . . . (MS) 758

Collection & building consultation DONAHUGH, Robert H. . (OH) 310
Collection & catalog management DAGANAAR, Mark L. . . . (SD) 269
Collection & development MENZIES, Pamela C. . . . (IL) 825
PHILLIPS, Faye . . . . (LA) 968

Collection & library development MIDGETT, Ann S. . . . . . (TX) 833
Collection & service development BUHR, Rosemary E. . . . . (MO) 156
Collection & space management DUNN, Jamie N. . . . . . . (MN) 326
Collection assessment GOODMAN, Rhonna A. . (NY) 449
Collection assessment & development CRAMER, Eugene C. . . . (AB) 255
Collection building MITCHELL, Jan E. . . . . . (FL) 848
MATHER, Becky R. . . . . (IA) 783
MUNDELL, Eric L. . . . . . (IN) 878
HUFF, James E. . . . . (KY) 570
LIVELY, Nancy J. . . . . . . (MD) 734
LANIER, Gene D. . . . . . . (NC) 696
VON BROCKDORFF, Eric (NY) 1288
SAWIN, Philip Q. . . . . . . (WI) 1086
SCHARFENBERG, George
E. . . . . (WI) 1090

Collection building in theology ZIMPFER, William E. . . . (MA) 1389
Collection building resource WATSON, Joyce N. . . . . (ON) 1309
Collection care & handling resources MOON, Myra J. . . . . (CO) 857
Collection consultation JOHNSON, Paul A. . . . . (CA) 608
Collection development BOEHMER, Elaine . . . . . (AK) 109
JENKINS, Joyce K. . . . . (AK) 597
MACLEAN, Barbara A. . . (AK) 757
NICOLSON, Mary C. . . . (AK) 903
SHELTON, Kathryn H. . . (AK) 1126
WIGET, Laurence A. . . . (AK) 1337
BATTISTELLA, Maureen
S. . . . . (AL) 65
CLARK, Wendolyn H. . . . (AL) 218
COOPER, Regina G. . . . (AL) 243
ELLIOTT, Riette B. . . . . . (AL) 344
GIBBS, Robert C. . . . . . (AL) 431
KETCHAM, Lee C. . . . . . (AL) 645
O'NEAL, Kenneth W. . . . (AL) 924
PARSLEY, Brantley H. . . (AL) 944
PRUITT, Paul M. . . . . . . (AL) 996
RUSSELL, Lisa R. . . . . . (AL) 1069
SELLEN, Mary K. . . . . . (AL) 1114
SMITH, Julia L. . . . . (AL) 1156
SPENCE, Paul H. . . . . . (AL) 1173
STEPHENS, Annabel K. . (AL) 1187
VISSCHER, Helga B. . . . (AL) 1285
WILLIAMS, Delmus E. . . (AL) 1342
ZLATOS, Christy L. . . . . (AL) 1390
BLAND, Janet A. . . . . . . (AR) 103
DUDEK, Robert J. . . . . . (AR) 323
GREEN, Douglas A. . . . . (AR) 461
HAMBY, Tracy A. . . . . . (AR) 491
HOUGHTON, Sally L. . . (AR) 563
PITTS, Cynthia F. . . . . . (AR) 976
ALABASTER, Carol . . . . (AZ) 9
ALTMAN, Ellen . . . . (AZ) 18
EVANS, Iris I. . . . . (AZ) 357
FAHY, Terry W. . . . . (AZ) 361
HEITSHU, Sara C. . . . . . (AZ) 523
HIEB, Louis A. . . . . (AZ) 537
JOHNSON, Robert K. . . . (AZ) 608
JONES, Douglas E. . . . . (AZ) 612
MAUTNER, Robert W. . . (AZ) 787
MINTON, James O. . . . . (AZ) 846
ROBROCK, David P. . . . (AZ) 1045
SHACKELFORD, Eileen R. (AZ) 1118
TEVIS, Raymond H. . . . . (AZ) 1233
WOLFSON, Catherine L. (AZ) 1361
WU, Ai H. . . . . (AZ) 1373

COLLECTIONS (Cont'd)
Collection development

AHLSTROM, Romaine . . (CA) 8
BASART, Ann P. . . . . . . (CA) 62
BILYEU, David D. . . . . . . (CA) 97
BIRCH, Tobeylynn . . . . . (CA) 98
BOORKMAN, Jo A. . . . . (CA) 115
BRIL, Patricia L. . . . . (CA) 136
BRISCOE, Peter M. . . . . (CA) 136
BROIDY, Ellen J. . . . . . . (CA) 139
BROWN, Carol G. . . . . . (CA) 142
BROWN, Paula D. . . . . . (CA) 146
BRUEGGEMAN, Peter L. (CA) 149
CHOUDHURY, Lori B. . . (CA) 211
CLARKE, Tobin D. . . . . . (CA) 219
CONDON, Erika M. . . . . (CA) 236
CONDRA, Darrel A. . . . . (CA) 236
CONNOR, Billie M. . . . . (CA) 237
DUNKLEE, Joanna E. . . . (CA) 326
ELLIOTT, C D. . . . . (CA) 343
ERVITI, Debra L. . . . . . . (CA) 353
EVANS, G E. . . . . (CA) 357
EVANS, M R. . . . . (CA) 357
FINE, Deborah J. . . . . . . (CA) 377
FORBES, Fred R. . . . . . . (CA) 389
FUSICH, Monica G. . . . . (CA) 410
GELFAND, Julia M. . . . . (CA) 426
GILDEN, Susanna C. . . . (CA) 434
GILMAN, Lelde B. . . . . . (CA) 436
GOODWATER, Leanna K. (CA) 450
GRASSIAN, Esther S. . . (CA) 458
GREGORY, Timothy P. . . (CA) 466
GRIEDER, Elmer M. . . . . (CA) 467
HALL, Anthony . . . . (CA) 487
HAYDEN, Ronald L. . . . . (CA) 515
HIXON, Donald L. . . . . . . (CA) 544
JESTES, Edward C. . . . . (CA) 600
JOHNSON, Clifford R. . . (CA) 603
KANTER, Elliot J. . . . . . . (CA) 625
KLEIBER, Michael C. . . . (CA) 658
KLUGMAN, Simone . . . . (CA) 662
LAWRENCE, John R. . . . (CA) 704
LEE, Mildred C. . . . . (CA) 711
LOMAX, Ronald C. . . . . . (CA) 738
LUCAS, Linda L. . . . . . . (CA) 746
LUST, Vernon G. . . . . . . (CA) 750
MALMGREN, Terri L. . . . (CA) 763
MARTIN, Rebecca R. . . . (CA) 778
MCCRACKEN, John R. . . (CA) 799
MCPHERON, William . . . (CA) 817
MILO, Albert J. . . . . (CA) 845
MINICK, Donna J. . . . . . . (CA) 846
MOORE, Phyllis C. . . . . . (CA) 861
MORSE, David H. . . . . . . (CA) 869
MULL, Richard G. . . . . . . (CA) 876
NAUMER, Janet N. . . . . (CA) 889
NEWMAN, Mark J. . . . . . (CA) 899
NISSLEY, Meta J. . . . . . (CA) 905
NOGA, Michael M. . . . . . (CA) 907
PANSKI, Saul J. . . . . (CA) 938
PAQUETTE, Judith . . . . . (CA) 939
PEASE, William J. . . . . . (CA) 953
PEATTIE, Noel . . . . (CA) 953
PERITORE, Laura D. . . . (CA) 958
PERKINS, David L. . . . . . (CA) 959
PETTAS, William A. . . . . (CA) 965
ROSS, Johanna C. . . . . . (CA) 1058
ROSS, Ruth K. . . . . (CA) 1058
SAHAK, Judy H. . . . . (CA) 1075
SANTOS, Bob . . . . (CA) 1082
SELTH, Jefferson P. . . . . (CA) 1114
SERTIC, Kenneth J. . . . . (CA) 1116
SHARROW, Marilyn J. . . (CA) 1122
SHERLOCK, John A. . . . (CA) 1128
SIBIA, Tejinder S. . . . . . . (CA) 1134
SINCLAIR, Lorelei P. . . . (CA) 1142
SMALLEY, Topsy N. . . . (CA) 1151
SMITH, Phillip A. . . . . . . (CA) 1159
SOETE, George J. . . . . . (CA) 1165
SONIN, Hille . . . . (CA) 1167

COLLECTIONS (Cont'd)
Collection development

STANGL, Peter . . . . (CA) 1180
STEELMAN, Lucille A. . . (CA) 1184
SULLIVAN, Kathleen A. . (CA) 1207
TAI, Henry H. . . . . (CA) 1220
TANIS, Norman E. . . . . . (CA) 1222
TAYLOR, Marion E. . . . . (CA) 1227
THOMAS, Mary C. . . . . . (CA) 1237
TING, Eunice T. . . . . (CA) 1246
VADEBONCOEUR,
    Elizabeth J. . . . . (CA) 1270
VANDEGRIFT, Glennda E. (CA) 1273
WALTERS, Mary D. . . . . (CA) 1301
WEBB, Gayle E. . . . . (CA) 1313
WELLS, Dorothy V. . . . . (CA) 1322
WERNER, O J. . . . . (CA) 1325
WHITE, Cecil R. . . . . (CA) 1330
WHITSON, William L. . . . (CA) 1334
WILSON, Barbara A. . . . (CA) 1350
WIMMER, Ted . . . . (CA) 1354
WINTER, Michael F. . . . . (CA) 1356
WUERTZ, Eva L. . . . . . . (CA) 1373
ZALEWSKI, Wojciech . . . (CA) 1385
ZEBROWSKI, Cheryl K. . (CA) 1387
CONNOR, Evelyn . . . . . . (CO) 238
CUMMING, Linda L. . . . . (CO) 264
GARRALDA, John C. . . . (CO) 420
HENSLEY, Charlotta C. . (CO) 529
JARAMILLO, George R. . (CO) 594
JOHNSON, K S. . . . . . . (CO) 606
SCHAFER, Jay G. . . . . . (CO) 1089
SITTER, Clara M. . . . . . . (CO) 1144
WATTERSON, Jane L. . . (CO) 1310
WYNNE, Allen . . . . (CO) 1375
ADAMO, Clare . . . . (CT) 4
ANDRONIK, Catherine M. (CT) 27
CAMPBELL, Barbara A. . (CT) 176
COSTA, Shirley W. . . . . . (CT) 249
CUSTER, Deborah P. . . . (CT) 267
DEAKYNE, William J. . . . (CT) 283
GOLOMB, Katherine A. . (CT) 447
JUKNIS, Ann M. . . . . (CT) 619
REISMAN, Sydelle S. . . . (CT) 1021
SCURA, Georgia A. . . . . (CT) 1109
SHOLTZ, Katherine J. . . (CT) 1132
VANDERLYKE, Barbara A. (CT) 1274
WALTER, Kenneth G. . . . (CT) 1300
WARGO, Peggy M. . . . . (CT) 1305
WILCOX, Carolyn G. . . . (CT) 1338
WILLIAMS, Judy R. . . . . (CT) 1344
YARMAL, Ann . . . . (CT) 1378
BARBEE, Norman N. . . . (DC) 55
BERGQUIST, Christine F. (DC) 87
DOGGETT, Rachel H. . . . (DC) 308
HARRIS, Marie . . . . (DC) 505
JOHNSON, Elaine B. . . . (DC) 604
KECSKES, Lily C. . . . . . (DC) 633
KUBAL, Gene J. . . . . (DC) 681
MCGOWAN, Anna T. . . . (DC) 807
PLETZKE, Linda . . . . (DC) 978
PORTER, Suzanne . . . . . (DC) 985
PUGH, Thurman A. . . . . . (DC) 997
RILEY, Eileen V. . . . . (DC) 1034
RISHWORTH, Susan K. . (DC) 1036
ROSENBERG, Jane A. . . (DC) 1056
SANCHEZ, Jose L. . . . . . (DC) 1079
SCHNEIDER, Karen . . . . (DC) 1097
SMITH, Martin A. . . . . . . (DC) 1158
STANN, Patsy H. . . . . . . (DC) 1180
STEBELMAN, Scott D. . . (DC) 1183
TOOHEY, Anne K. . . . . . (DC) 1250
WANG, Chi . . . . (DC) 1302
WASSERMAN, Krystyna (DC) 1308
WELCH, Thomas L. . . . . (DC) 1321
BEACH, Rose M. . . . . . . (DE) 68
BROWN, Sarah C. . . . . . (DE) 147
HALL, Alice W. . . . . (DE) 486
PUFFER, Nathaniel H. . . (DE) 997
TRUMBORE, Jean F. . . . (DE) 1259

COLLECTIONS (Cont'd)
Collection development

BROWN, Lyn S.	(FL)	145
CARR, Mary L.	(FL)	186
CESANEK, Sylvia B.	(FL)	196
COHEN, Kathleen F.	(FL)	228
CUBBERLEY, Carol W.	(FL)	263
DE MEO, Mary A.	(FL)	291
DRAKE, Grady	(FL)	318
ESPER, Elizabeth	(FL)	354
GUNN, Thomas H.	(FL)	477
HARRER, Gustave A.	(FL)	503
HARRIS, Martha J.	(FL)	505
HOLLOWAY, David R.	(FL)	552
HOLT, Ethel F.	(FL)	554
HOMEYARD, Marjorie A.	(FL)	555
JOHNSON, Betty D.	(FL)	602
JOHNSON, Theresa P.	(FL)	609
JULIEN, Dorothy C.	(FL)	619
LIANG, Diana F.	(FL)	725
MALANCHUK, Peter P.	(FL)	762
MARTIN, John H.	(FL)	776
MCKAY, Peter Z.	(FL)	810
MELLICAN, Nancy J.	(FL)	822
MIRANDA, Salvador	(FL)	847
MOJO, Anne Z.	(FL)	852
MOON, Eric	(FL)	857
NOAH, Julia T.	(FL)	906
PINTOZZI, Chestalene	(FL)	975
PRATT, Darnell D.	(FL)	990
RITZ, Paul S.	(FL)	1037
SCHWABEL, Lexie W.	(FL)	1104
SINTZ, Edward F.	(FL)	1144
SMITH, Alice G.	(FL)	1152
SMITH, Margaret N.	(FL)	1157
STAMPFL, Barbara A.	(FL)	1179
TIPPLE, Roberta L.	(FL)	1246
VAN ORDEN, Phyllis J.	(FL)	1276
WILLETT, Charles	(FL)	1341
ALLEN, William R.	(GA)	16
BRADLEY, Gail P.	(GA)	125
BUDLONG, Thomas F.	(GA)	155
CANN, Sharon F.	(GA)	178
CLEMENTS, Betty H.	(GA)	221
COURSEY, W T.	(GA)	251
DENNISON, Jacquelyn H.	(GA)	292
DOUGLASS, Charlene K.	(GA)	314
ELLIS, Marie C.	(GA)	345
HAAR, John M.	(GA)	480
HAMMOND, Elizabeth D.	(GA)	493
HANSON, Kathy H.	(GA)	498
HARRISON, James O.	(GA)	506
HARTZ, Frederic R.	(GA)	509
HOWINGTON, Lee R.	(GA)	566
JOBSON, Betty S.	(GA)	601
KUHLMAN, James R.	(GA)	682
MENEELY, William E.	(GA)	824
MOSLEY, Mary M.	(GA)	871
NITSCHKE, Eric R.	(GA)	905
NITSCHKE, Marie M.	(GA)	905
PATON, John C.	(GA)	947
PIERCE, Sydney J.	(GA)	972
RUSSELL, Ralph E.	(GA)	1069
SOUTHWICK, Mary L.	(GA)	1170
STRAUTMAN, Randolph B.	(GA)	1201
THAXTON, Lyn	(GA)	1234
TUTTLE, Jane S.	(GA)	1265
WILLIAMS, Nancy F.	(GA)	1345
WOODLEE, Rick G.	(GA)	1366
BUDREW, John	(IA)	155
CRAVER, Susan J.	(IA)	256
DOBSON, Cynthia	(IA)	307
DUNLAP, Leslie W.	(IA)	326
FLETCHALL, Josephine V.	(IA)	384
GALEJS, John E.	(IA)	413
GORMAN, Lawrence R.	(IA)	452
HARMON, Charles T.	(IA)	502
JOHNSON, Anne C.	(IA)	602
KENAGY, Charles R.	(IA)	640

COLLECTIONS (Cont'd)
Collection development

MARQUARDT, Larry D.	(IA)	772
MCKEE, Christopher	(IA)	810
OHRLUND, Ava L.	(IA)	919
SHIPE, Timothy R.	(IA)	1131
TRUCK, Lorna R.	(IA)	1259
TYCKOSON, David A.	(IA)	1266
DOWNEY, Howard R.	(ID)	316
FORD, Karin E.	(ID)	389
OSTRANDER, Gloria J.	(ID)	929
TAYLOR, Adrien P.	(ID)	1225
ABBOTT, John C.	(IL)	1
AGGARWAL, Narindar K.	(IL)	7
ANDERSON, Byron P.	(IL)	21
ATKINS, Stephen E.	(IL)	38
BALCOM, William T.	(IL)	51
BENNETT, Lee L.	(IL)	82
BERGER, Sidney E.	(IL)	86
BOAST, Carol	(IL)	108
BOELKE, Joanne H.	(IL)	110
BOUGHTON, Ruth E.	(IL)	119
BROWN, Diana M.	(IL)	143
BROWN, Mary J.	(IL)	146
BRYAN, Mila	(IL)	152
CLAYTON, Nina A.	(IL)	220
COOPER, Susan C.	(IL)	243
COX, James C.	(IL)	253
DI MAURO, Paul	(IL)	304
DORST, Thomas J.	(IL)	313
DUTTON, Lee S.	(IL)	329
EASTERBROOK, David L.	(IL)	333
FAIRCHILD, Constance A.	(IL)	361
FINEMAN, Charles S.	(IL)	377
GERDES, Neil W.	(IL)	428
GRAFTON, Mona R.	(IL)	456
GRIEGER, Sharon L.	(IL)	468
HALE, Charles E.	(IL)	485
HATTENDORF, Lynn C.	(IL)	512
HAULE, Laura M.	(IL)	512
HORST, Stanley E.	(IL)	561
JACOB, Merle L.	(IL)	589
JOHNSON, Judith M.	(IL)	606
KAPLAN, Paul M.	(IL)	626
KIM, Chung S.	(IL)	648
KISSINGER, Patricia A.	(IL)	656
KLINGBERG, Susan	(IL)	661
KRAMER, Pamela K.	(IL)	675
MALLER, Mark P.	(IL)	763
MCCLELLAN, William M.	(IL)	796
MCCOY, Ralph E.	(IL)	799
MEYER, Beverly R.	(IL)	829
MOORE, Annie M.	(IL)	858
MOULTON, James C.	(IL)	873
O'BRIEN, Nancy P.	(IL)	915
OSORIO, Nestor L.	(IL)	928
POOLE, Connie	(IL)	983
SADLER, Shirley L.	(IL)	1073
SANDERS, Charlene R.	(IL)	1079
SCHOR, Abby R.	(IL)	1099
SHAW, Joyce M.	(IL)	1123
SMITH, Lester K.	(IL)	1157
SODOWSKY, Kay M.	(IL)	1165
SWANSON, Patricia K.	(IL)	1213
TEO, Elizabeth A.	(IL)	1231
THAKORE, Manhar	(IL)	1234
THORNHILL, Robert E.	(IL)	1242
WENZEL, Duane E.	(IL)	1324
WILLSON, Richard E.	(IL)	1349
WRIGHT, Deborah L.	(IL)	1371
WRIGHT, Donald E.	(IL)	1371
YU, Priscilla C.	(IL)	1384
ALLEN, Joyce S.	(IN)	15
BAILEY, Martha J.	(IN)	46
BALDWIN, James A.	(IN)	51
BECK, Erla P.	(IN)	71
BERTRAM, Lee A.	(IN)	91
DURKIN, Virginia M.	(IN)	328
EISEN, David J.	(IN)	340
FUDERER, Laura S.	(IN)	408

COLLECTIONS (Cont'd)
Collection development

FUNKHOUSER, Richard L. (IN) 410
GALBRAITH, Leslie R. . . (IN) 413
GLEASON, Maureen L. . (IN) 440
HARLAND, Phyllis A. . . . (IN) 502
HODGE, Stanley P. . . . . (IN) 546
HOLMAN, Mary J. . . . . . (IN) 553
KONDELIK, John P. . . . . (IN) 670
KUDRYK, Oleg . . . . (IN) 682
KUO, Ming M. . . . . (IN) 684
LAIR, Nancy C. . . . . . . (IN) 688
LAW, Gordon T. . . . . . . (IN) 704
MCGINNIS, Mildred M. . . (IN) 806
MILLER, Junelle . . . . . . (IN) 839
MILLER, Robert C. . . . . (IN) 841
MITCHELL, Cynthia E. . . (IN) 848
MUELLER, Jeanne G. . . . (IN) 875
NIXON, Judith M. . . . . . (IN) 906
NORMAN, Orval G. . . . . (IN) 909
READ, Glenn F. . . . . . . (IN) 1012
STEPHENS, Gretchen . . (IN) 1188
THOMPSON, Susan J. . . (IN) 1241
VANCIL, David E. . . . . . (IN) 1273
WIGGINS, Gary D. . . . . (IN) 1337
YOUNG, Philip H. . . . . . (IN) 1383
CRAIG, Susan V. . . . . . (KS) 254
GATTIN, Leroy M. . . . . . (KS) 422
HOWARD, Clinton N. . . . (KS) 564
LEE, Earl W. . . . . (KS) 709
MASON, Alexandra . . . . (KS) 780
MCLEOD, Debra A. . . . . (KS) 814
MYERS, Marilyn . . . . . . (KS) 884
NEELEY, James D. . . . . (KS) 891
SCHAD, Jasper G. . . . . (KS) 1088
WILLIAMS, Brian W. . . . (KS) 1342
WILLIAMS, Sara R. . . . . (KS) 1346
WITMER, Tonya C. . . . . (KS) 1358
BARKSDALE, Milton K. . . (KY) 57
BIRCHFIELD, Martha J. . . (KY) 98
BROWN, Lucinda A. . . . . (KY) 145
COALTER, Milton J. . . . . (KY) 224
COSSEY, M E. . . . . (KY) 249
COUTTS, Brian E. . . . . . (KY) 252
CULPEPPER, Jetta C. . . (KY) 264
DARE, Philip N. . . . . . . (KY) 274
DAY, Mary M. . . . . (KY) 283
FAUPEL, David W. . . . . . (KY) 366
FRANCK, Ilona G. . . . . . (KY) 396
KRESSE, Kerry L. . . . . . (KY) 678
MAZUK, Melody . . . . . . (KY) 791
MESNER, Lillian R. . . . . (KY) 827
MOORE, Elaine E. . . . . . (KY) 859
RINEY, Judith N. . . . . . . (KY) 1035
ROBY, B D. . . . . (KY) 1045
WILLIAMS, Danby O. . . . (KY) 1342
BUCHANAN, William C. . . (LA) 153
COSPER, Mary F. . . . . . (LA) 249
GOLDSTEIN, Cynthia H. . (LA) 446
HAGEDORN, Dorothy L. . (LA) 482
HALFORD, Mary B. . . . . (LA) 486
HAMAKER, Charles A. . . (LA) 490
HAMSA, Charles F. . . . . (LA) 494
HEBERT, Madeline . . . . . (LA) 519
JARRED, Ada D. . . . . . . (LA) 594
KONTROVITZ, Eileen R. . (LA) 671
LANDRY, Abbie V. . . . . . (LA) 693
PASKOFF, Beth M. . . . . (LA) 946
PERRAULT, Anna H. . . . (LA) 959
REEDY, Ruth C. . . . . . . (LA) 1015
SHAUGHNESSY, Megan (LA) 1123
TURNER, I B. . . . . (LA) 1264
WICKER, W W. . . . . (LA) 1335
WILKINS, Marilyn W. . . . (LA) 1340
WOOD, Julienne L. . . . . (LA) 1364
YOUNG, Amanda M. . . . (LA) 1381
ABRAHAM, Deborah V. . (MA) 2
ALCORN, Cynthia W. . . . (MA) 11
ANDERSON, Wanda E. . . (MA) 25
BAKER, Elizabeth A. . . . (MA) 48

COLLECTIONS (Cont'd)
Collection development

BROW, Ellen H. . . . . . . (MA) 141
CAYLOR, Lawrence M. . . (MA) 195
COGHLAN, Jill M. . . . . . (MA) 227
CRAIG, James L. . . . . . (MA) 254
CURLEY, Arthur . . . . . . (MA) 265
DAVIS, Charles R. . . . . . (MA) 278
DESJARDINS, Andrea C. (MA) 295
DUNKLY, James W. . . . . (MA) 326
DVORAK, Robert . . . . . . (MA) 330
ERICKSON, Alan E. . . . . (MA) 352
EVENSEN, Robert L. . . . (MA) 358
FELLER, Siegfried . . . . . (MA) 370
FENG, Yen T. . . . . (MA) 371
HAPIJ, Maria S. . . . . . . (MA) 499
HARDY, Eileen D. . . . . . (MA) 500
HARZBECKER, Joseph J. (MA) 510
HILTON, Robert C. . . . . (MA) 541
HOLMBERG, Olga S. . . . (MA) 553
JONES, Frederick S. . . . (MA) 613
JUDD, Eleanor M. . . . . . (MA) 618
KOCSIS, Jeanne . . . . . . (MA) 667
KOVED, Ruth B. . . . . . . (MA) 674
KRIER, Mary M. . . . . . . (MA) 678
LEAHY, Lynda C. . . . . . (MA) 706
LINDHEIMER, Sandra K. (MA) 729
MCNIFF, Philip J. . . . . . (MA) 817
MICHAUD, Charles A. . . (MA) 832
MOREN, Harold M. . . . . (MA) 863
MUISE, Anita M. . . . . . . (MA) 876
O'NEAL, Ellis E. . . . . . . (MA) 923
PARSON, Lethiel C. . . . . (MA) 944
PECK, Ruth M. . . . . (MA) 953
PERCY, Theresa R. . . . . (MA) 958
PICCININO, Rocco . . . . . (MA) 970
PILLSBURY, Mary J. . . . (MA) 973
SCHATZ, Natalie M. . . . (MA) 1090
STAVIS, Ruth L. . . . . . . (MA) 1183
STEINFELD, Michael . . . (MA) 1186
STIFFLEAR, Allan J. . . . (MA) 1194
STUEART, Robert D. . . . (MA) 1205
SWANN, Thomas E. . . . . (MA) 1213
TUCHMAN, Maurice S. . (MA) 1261
VON KRIES, Beverley A. (MA) 1288
WOOD, Ann L. . . . . (MA) 1363
WURTZEL, Barbara S. . . (MA) 1374
BURGESS, Eileen E. . . . (MD) 159
CLARK, David S. . . . . . . (MD) 216
COSTABILE, Salvatore L. (MD) 249
COUPE, Jill M. . . . . (MD) 251
DADSON, Theresa E. . . . (MD) 269
DRACH, Marian C. . . . . (MD) 317
DYSART, Marcia J. . . . . (MD) 331
FREEDMAN, Lynn P. . . . (MD) 400
GILBERT, Mattana . . . . . (MD) 433
HEIL, Kathleen A. . . . . . (MD) 521
KINZER, Kathryn . . . . . . (MD) 653
KUNZ, Margarett N. . . . . (MD) 684
LEDBETTER, Sherry H. . (MD) 708
LEV, Yvonne T. . . . . (MD) 719
LORENZ, John G. . . . . . (MD) 741
MCADAM, Paul E. . . . . . (MD) 791
MCKEAN, Joan M. . . . . . (MD) 810
MOLTER, Maureen M. . . (MD) 853
NEIKIRK, Harold D. . . . . (MD) 892
PECK, Shirley S. . . . . . . (MD) 953
RAY, John G. . . . . (MD) 1011
RUFF, Martha R. . . . . . . (MD) 1066
STREIN, Barbara M. . . . . (MD) 1201
TRELEVEN, Richard L. . . (MD) 1255
WILSON, William G. . . . (MD) 1353
WOLF, Dorothy L. . . . . . (MD) 1360
BILODEAU, Judith M. . . . (ME) 97
CROSBY, Barbara A. . . . (ME) 260
KNOWLTON, Suzanne L. (ME) 666
THOR, Angela M. . . . . . (ME) 1242
WOODWARD, Robert C. (ME) 1368
BRANZBURG, Marian G. (MI) 129
BURINSKI, Walter W. . . . (MI) 160

COLLECTIONS (Cont'd)
Collection development

CHEN, Catherine W.	(MI)	205
D'ELIA, Joseph G.	(MI)	289
DOUBLESTEIN, Judith A.	(MI)	313
DRABENSTOTT, Jon D.	(MI)	317
DYKI, Judy	(MI)	331
EL MOUCHI, Joan S.	(MI)	346
GALIK, Barbara A.	(MI)	413
HERBST, Linda R.	(MI)	530
HOUGH, Carolyn A.	(MI)	562
JASPER, Richard P.	(MI)	595
JENSEN, David P.	(MI)	598
JOSE, Phyllis A.	(MI)	617
KINGSTON, Jo A.	(MI)	652
KNOCH, Daniel L.	(MI)	665
KOCH, Henry C.	(MI)	667
KROMPART, Janet A.	(MI)	679
LEARY, Margaret R.	(MI)	707
LIGHT, Lin	(MI)	726
LUFT, William	(MI)	747
MASLOW, Linda S.	(MI)	780
MISNER, Joyce V.	(MI)	847
MLODZIANOWSKI, Mary L.	(MI)	850
OLIVER, James W.	(MI)	921
PALMER, David W.	(MI)	936
RACZ, Twyla M.	(MI)	1001
RADEMACHER, Matthew J.	(MI)	1002
RZEPECKI, Arnold M.	(MI)	1072
SCHOLFIELD, Caroline A.	(MI)	1098
SHAPIRO, Beth J.	(MI)	1121
STEVENS, Sheryl R.	(MI)	1191
STUCK, Judy K.	(MI)	1204
TAYLOR, Margaret T.	(MI)	1227
WAGAR, Joanna M.	(MI)	1291
WAGMAN, Frederick H.	(MI)	1291
WHEATON, Julie A.	(MI)	1328
WIEMERS, Eugene L.	(MI)	1336
YAEK, Larry A.	(MI)	1376
BARBOUR-TALLEY, Donna L.	(MN)	55
BRANIN, Joseph J.	(MN)	128
BROGAN, Martha L.	(MN)	139
CARLSON, Stan W.	(MN)	182
FAGERLIE, Joan M.	(MN)	361
GALLIGAN, Sara A.	(MN)	414
GELINAS, Jeanne L.	(MN)	426
HARWOOD, Karen L.	(MN)	510
HAYS, Robert M.	(MN)	517
HEETER, Judith A.	(MN)	520
IMMLER, Frank	(MN)	582
ISMAIL, Noha S.	(MN)	585
MAGNUSON, Norris A.	(MN)	759
MARION, Donald J.	(MN)	770
NILES, Ann A.	(MN)	904
OVERMIER, Judith A.	(MN)	931
REHNBERG, Marilyn J.	(MN)	1017
SCOTT, Thomas L.	(MN)	1108
TABAR, Margaret E.	(MN)	1219
WALDEN, Barbara L.	(MN)	1294
WEEKS, John M.	(MN)	1315
WEISS, Kay M.	(MN)	1320
WURL, Joel F.	(MN)	1374
ABERNATHY, William F.	(MO)	2
BECK, Sara R.	(MO)	71
BRADBURY, Daniel J.	(MO)	125
BUIS; Edmund L.	(MO)	156
BURCKEL, Nicholas C.	(MO)	158
DEWEESE, June L.	(MO)	298
GILTINAN, Celia E.	(MO)	437
HESS, Stanley W.	(MO)	534
KIEL, Becky	(MO)	647
MACEWAN, Bonnie J.	(MO)	755
MILLER, William C.	(MO)	843
NELSON, Mary A.	(MO)	894
NORTH, Daniel L.	(MO)	909
POWELL, Ronald R.	(MO)	988
PRESTON, Jenny	(MO)	991

COLLECTIONS (Cont'd)
Collection development

SMITH, Harold F.	(MO)	1155
SMITH, Nancy M.	(MO)	1159
BOYD, William D.	(MS)	123
GRAVES, Gail T.	(MS)	459
HARPER, Laura G.	(MS)	503
KELLY, John M.	(MS)	638
REID, Thomas G.	(MS)	1019
ALLDREDGE, Noreen S.	(MT)	14
MILLS, Douglas E.	(MT)	844
PARKER, Sara A.	(MT)	942
SCHUSTER, Bonnie H.	(MT)	1103
ABBOTT, Dorothy D.	(NC)	1
ALSTON-REEDER, Lizzie A.	(NC)	18
BROADUS, Robert N.	(NC)	138
BYRD, Robert L.	(NC)	169
CLARK, Marie L.	(NC)	217
DUNN, Elizabeth B.	(NC)	326
FRANK, Linda V.	(NC)	397
GOLDEN, Susan L.	(NC)	445
HEWITT, Joe A.	(NC)	535
KARES, Artemis C.	(NC)	627
MANN, Sallie E.	(NC)	766
MCLEOD, Herbert E.	(NC)	814
POWELL, Lucy A.	(NC)	988
STETSON, Keith R.	(NC)	1190
SWINDLER, Luke	(NC)	1216
TAYLOR, Christine M.	(NC)	1226
WISE, Mintron S.	(NC)	1357
WRIGHT, Barbara A.	(NC)	1370
BOONE, Jon A.	(ND)	115
BRATTON, Phyllis A.	(ND)	129
NIENOW, Beth M.	(ND)	904
PEDERSEN, Lila	(ND)	954
BARRICK, Judy H.	(NE)	59
HOOVER, Clara G.	(NE)	557
REIDELBACH, John H.	(NE)	1019
SARTORI, Eva M.	(NE)	1083
WOMACK, Sharon K.	(NE)	1362
GAGNON, Ruth	(NH)	412
GAVRISH, Diane L.	(NH)	423
GRISWOLD, Esther A.	(NH)	471
JACOBS, Gloria	(NH)	589
MORAN, William S.	(NH)	862
RYAN, Clare E.	(NH)	1070
SHERWOOD, Janet R.	(NH)	1129
TATE, Joanne D.	(NH)	1225
ARROWOOD, Nina R.	(NJ)	35
BEEDE, Benjamin R.	(NJ)	74
BOLL, Charles K.	(NJ)	112
BRODOWSKI, Joyce H.	(NJ)	139
BRUNNER, Karen B.	(NJ)	151
CARLSON, Dudley B.	(NJ)	182
CHAMBERLIN, Cynthia C.	(NJ)	198
COE, D W.	(NJ)	226
CONNORS, Linda E.	(NJ)	238
CRESCENZI, Jean D.	(NJ)	258
DENSKY, Lois R.	(NJ)	293
DUTKA, Jeanne L.	(NJ)	329
FIELD, Jack	(NJ)	375
GARZILLO, Robert R.	(NJ)	421
GOLDSMITH, Maxine K.	(NJ)	446
HENNEMAN, John B.	(NJ)	528
HODGE, Patricia A.	(NJ)	546
HOELLE, Dolores M.	(NJ)	547
HOOKER, Joan M.	(NJ)	556
KALIF, Alexander J.	(NJ)	623
KAUFFMAN, Betty G.	(NJ)	631
LEE, Minja P.	(NJ)	711
LIOU, Pearl S.	(NJ)	732
LITTLE, Rosemary A.	(NJ)	734
MARCHOK, Catherine W.	(NJ)	769
MCCOY, W K.	(NJ)	799
NASE, Lois M.	(NJ)	888
PISKORIK, Elizabeth	(NJ)	976
POVILAITIS, Leanna J.	(NJ)	987
PUNIELLO, Francoise S.	(NJ)	997
RANIERI, Bernice A.	(NJ)	1007

COLLECTIONS (Cont'd)
Collection development

RICE, Anna C. . . . . (NJ) 1026
ROMANASKY, Marcia C. (NJ) 1052
SAWYER, Miriam . . . . . . (NJ) 1086
SCOTT, Mellouise J. . . . (NJ) 1107
SIMPSON, Barbara T. . . . (NJ) 1141
SKYZINSKI, Susan E. . . . (NJ) 1147
STEEN, Carol N. . . . . . . (NJ) 1184
STOCK, Norman . . . . . . (NJ) 1195
STUDDIFORD, Abigail M. (NJ) 1204
SZILASSY, Sandor . . . . (NJ) 1218
TAYLOR, Sharon A. . . . . (NJ) 1228
TIPTON, Roberta L. . . . . (NJ) 1247
TOMAR, Jeanne . . . . . . (NJ) 1249
TOMPKINS, Louise . . . . (NJ) 1250
ZIMMERMAN, Elisabeth K. (NJ) 1388
ELDREDGE, Jonathan D. (NM) 342
IVES, Peter B. . . . . (NM) 586
LEWIS, Linda K. . . . . . . (NM) 723
RICHARD, Harris M. . . . (NM) 1027
SOHN, Jeanne G. . . . . . (NM) 1165
TUBESING, Richard L. . . (NM) 1261
CURLEY, Elmer F. . . . . . (NV) 265
OTERO-BOISVERT, Maria (NV) 930
BONE, Larry E. . . . . (NY) 113
BREEN, Karen B. . . . . . (NY) 131
BUFF, Iva M. . . . . (NY) 155
BURNETTE, Michaelyn . . (NY) 162
CASSELL, Kay A. . . . . . (NY) 193
CHAMBERLAIN, Erna B. (NY) 197
CHO-PARK, Jaung J. . . . (NY) 210
CLUNE, John R. . . . . . . (NY) 223
COAN, Mary L. . . . . (NY) 224
COHEN, Ann E. . . . . . . (NY) 227
COLLANTES, Lourdes Y. (NY) 232
CROWLEY, John V. . . . . (NY) 261
DAVIS, Deborah G. . . . . (NY) 278
DEMAS, Samuel G. . . . . (NY) 291
DENNIN, June A. . . . . . . (NY) 292
DOE, Lynn M. . . . . (NY) 308
DOWNING, Elaine L. . . . (NY) 316
EARLY, Caroline L. . . . . (NY) 332
EVANS, Ruth A. . . . . . . (NY) 358
FARRELL, Michele A. . . . (NY) 365
FERNANDEZ, M L. . . . . (NY) 373
FIGUEREDO, Danilo H. . . (NY) 376
FINCH, C H. . . . . (NY) 377
GAFFNEY, Ellen E. . . . . (NY) 412
GATNER, Elliott S. . . . . (NY) 422
GAWLER, Ann C. . . . . . (NY) 423
GUY, Wendell A. . . . . . . (NY) 479
HARDISH, Patrick M. . . . (NY) 500
HARDY, Gayle J. . . . . . . (NY) 500
HARRIS, Carolyn L. . . . . (NY) 504
HEINTZELMAN, Susan K. (NY) 522
HENRY, Mary K. . . . . . . (NY) 529
HIGGINS, Judith H. . . . . (NY) 538
HODGSON, Elizabeth A. . (NY) 546
HOGAN, Matthew . . . . . (NY) 549
HORRELL, Jeffrey L. . . . (NY) 560
HOWELL, M G. . . . . (NY) 565
HULBERT, Linda A. . . . . (NY) 572
JUCHIMEK, Dianne M. . . (NY) 618
KARKHANIS, Sharad . . . (NY) 627
KATZ, William A. . . . . . . (NY) 630
KELLY, Donald V. . . . . . (NY) 637
KLECKNER, Simone M. . (NY) 658
KOLATA, Judith . . . . (NY) 669
KONDZELA, Jeanette M. (NY) 670
KROBER, Alfred C. . . . . (NY) 679
KUGLER, Sharon . . . . . (NY) 682
KUPFERBERG, Natalie . . (NY) 684
KUUSKMAE, Mati . . . . . (NY) 685
LANTZY, M L. . . . . (NY) 697
LESNIK, Pauline . . . . . . (NY) 718
LEWIS, Margaret S. . . . (NY) 723
LINDGREN, Arla M. . . . . (NY) 729
LINDNER, Charlotte K. . . (NY) 729
LOCKETT, Barbara A. . . (NY) 736

COLLECTIONS (Cont'd)
Collection development

MACK, Phyllis G. . . . . . (NY) 756
MALOY, Frances . . . . . . (NY) 764
MANNING, Jo A. . . . . . . (NY) 766
MARTINEZ-RIVERA, Ivette (NY) 779
MIHRAM, Danielle . . . . . (NY) 834
MULDOON, Jane K. . . . . (NY) 876
NAYLOR, David L. . . . . . (NY) 890
NEESE, Janet A. . . . . . . (NY) 892
NOLTE, James S. . . . . . (NY) 908
PATRICK, Patricia M. . . . (NY) 947
QUICK, Richard C. . . . . (NY) 999
RAY, Donald L. . . . . (NY) 1011
ROMANELLI, Catherine A. (NY) 1052
ROSSWURM, K M. . . . . (NY) 1059
RUBEY, Daniel R. . . . . . (NY) 1064
SCHEIN, Lorraine S. . . . (NY) 1091
SCHUMAN, Patricia G. . . (NY) 1103
SEGAL, Judith . . . . (NY) 1112
SELVAR, Jane C. . . . . . (NY) 1114
SEWELL, Robert G. . . . . (NY) 1117
SHAFFER, Kay L. . . . . . (NY) 1119
SMITH, Marian J. . . . . . (NY) 1157
STANTON, Lee W. . . . . . (NY) 1181
STIEVATER, Susan M. . . (NY) 1194
STOLLER, Michael E. . . . (NY) 1196
SUTHERLAND-NEHRING,
    Laurie A. . . . . (NY) 1211
SWERDLOVE, Dorothy L. (NY) 1215
TELATNIK, George M. . . (NY) 1230
TODOSOW, Helen K. . . . (NY) 1248
TOTH, Gregory M. . . . . . (NY) 1252
USTACH, Joanne B. . . . (NY) 1270
VAJDA, Elizabeth A. . . . (NY) 1271
VAUGHN, Susan J. . . . . (NY) 1280
VOLAT-SHAPIRO, Helene
    M. . . . . (NY) 1287
WALCOTT, Rosalind . . . (NY) 1294
WEATHERFORD,
    Elizabeth . . . . (NY) 1311
WILLOUGHBY, Nona C. . (NY) 1349
WOLFE, Barbara M. . . . . (NY) 1360
ZUBROW, Marcia L. . . . (NY) 1391
BERLIN, Susan T. . . . . . (OH) 87
BLOUGH, Keith A. . . . . . (OH) 106
BRINK, David R. . . . . . . (OH) 136
CARPENTER, Eric J. . . . (OH) 184
CHEEK, Fern M. . . . . . . (OH) 204
CURRIE, William W. . . . . (OH) 266
DEAN, Winifred F. . . . . . (OH) 284
DESCHENE, Dorice . . . . (OH) 294
DRONE, Jeanette M. . . . (OH) 320
EAGLEN, Audrey B. . . . . (OH) 331
GEARY, James W. . . . . . (OH) 424
GORDON, Shirlee J. . . . . (OH) 452
HAMBLEY, Susan L. . . . (OH) 490
HUGHES, Marcelle E. . . . (OH) 572
JENKINS, Fred W. . . . . . (OH) 597
MCCALLUM, Brenda W. (OH) 793
MCNEER, Elizabeth J. . . (OH) 816
MONGAN, Janet . . . . . . (OH) 854
NICHOLS, James T. . . . . (OH) 901
OBERLE, Holly E. . . . . . (OH) 914
O'HANLON, Nancyanne . (OH) 919
ORR, Cynthia . . . . (OH) 926
PAPA, Deborah M. . . . . (OH) 938
PARR, Virginia H. . . . . . (OH) 944
PROPAS, Sharon W. . . . (OH) 995
QUAY, Richard H. . . . . . (OH) 999
QUINTEN, Rebecca G. . . (OH) 1000
RUSSO, Stephen A. . . . . (OH) 1070
RYAN, Mary E. . . . . (OH) 1071
SANDERS, Nancy P. . . . (OH) 1080
SANTAVICCA, Edmund F. (OH) 1082
SCHMUHL, Gayle B. . . . (OH) 1096
SMITH, Thomas A. . . . . (OH) 1161
STRALEY, Dona S. . . . . (OH) 1200
SWINEHART, Katharine J. (OH) 1216
TIPKA, Donald A. . . . . . (OH) 1246

COLLECTIONS (Cont'd)
Collection development

TOLZMANN, Don H.	(OH)	1249
VARMA, Valsamani	(OH)	1278
VOIGT, Kathleen J.	(OH)	1287
WALDEN, Graham R.	(OH)	1294
WALDER, Antoinette L.	(OH)	1294
WALL, Carol	(OH)	1297
WANSER, Jeffery C.	(OH)	1303
WEST, Loretta G.	(OH)	1326
WORTMAN, William A.	(OH)	1369
YAGELLO, Virginia E.	(OH)	1376
ZAFREN, Herbert C.	(OH)	1385
ZAGER, Daniel A.	(OH)	1385
COULTER, Cynthia M.	(OK)	251
HACKER, Connie J.	(OK)	481
HILKER, Emerson W.	(OK)	539
HOLMES, Jill M.	(OK)	553
MURPHY, Peggy A.	(OK)	881
PATTERSON, Lotsee	(OK)	948
PELLEY, Shirley N.	(OK)	955
SARK, Sue	(OK)	1083
SMITH, Donald R.	(OK)	1154
BENSON, Mary M.	(OR)	83
BYRNE, Helen E.	(OR)	169
CRUMB, Lawrence N.	(OR)	262
HADDERMAN, Margaret	(OR)	482
HALGREN, Joanne V.	(OR)	486
KRUPP, Robert A.	(OR)	681
METZENBACHER, Gary W.	(OR)	828
ROBERTSON, Howard W.	(OR)	1042
SCHENCK, William Z.	(OR)	1091
TEICH, Steven	(OR)	1230
ARMISTEAD, Henry T.	(PA)	32
BAKER, Judith M.	(PA)	48
BARD, Nelson P.	(PA)	56
BARRY, James W.	(PA)	60
BECK, William L.	(PA)	72
BRAUTIGAM, David K.	(PA)	130
BRAVARD, Robert S.	(PA)	130
CAMPION, Carol M.	(PA)	177
COHEN, Laurie J.	(PA)	228
DOLE, Wanda V.	(PA)	309
FISHER, Kim N.	(PA)	381
GALLIVAN, Marion F.	(PA)	414
GLOVER, Peggy D.	(PA)	442
GREBEY, Betty H.	(PA)	461
HANNAFORD, William E.	(PA)	496
HELICHER, Karl W.	(PA)	524
HERRON, Nancy L.	(PA)	533
HOCKER, Justine L.	(PA)	545
HOLSTON, Kim R.	(PA)	554
HOMICK, Elaine	(PA)	555
HORN, Roger G.	(PA)	559
HOWLEY, Deborah H.	(PA)	566
JAFFE, Lawrence J.	(PA)	591
JARVIS, William E.	(PA)	595
JEAN, Lorraine A.	(PA)	596
JENKS, George M.	(PA)	597
KAISER, John R.	(PA)	622
KIRBY, Martha Z.	(PA)	654
KROAH, Larry A.	(PA)	679
KRZYS, Richard A.	(PA)	681
LEE, Janis M.	(PA)	710
LEHMANN, Stephen R.	(PA)	713
MACK, Sara R.	(PA)	756
MANCALL, Jacqueline C.	(PA)	764
MARCHETTI, Honey B.	(PA)	768
MARKSON, Eileen	(PA)	771
MARNET, Carole M.	(PA)	772
MCKOWN, Cornelius J.	(PA)	812
MONTOYA, Leopoldo	(PA)	856
MUNDAY, Robert S.	(PA)	878
PAUSTIAN, P R.	(PA)	950
RAJPAR, Shamin H.	(PA)	1004
SAUER, James L.	(PA)	1084
SEEDS, Robert S.	(PA)	1111
SEPP, Frederick C.	(PA)	1115
TEOLIS, Marilyn G.	(PA)	1231

COLLECTIONS (Cont'd)
Collection development

TERRY, Joseph D.	(PA)	1232
THOMPSON, Sandra K.	(PA)	1241
VANN, John D.	(PA)	1276
WESTERMAN, Melvin E.	(PA)	1327
WHITTINGTON, Christine A.	(PA)	1334
WILES-HAFFNER, Meredith L.	(PA)	1339
WRAY, Wendell L.	(PA)	1370
ZABEL, Diane M.	(PA)	1385
AYALA-ORTIZ, Orietta	(PR)	42
BULERIN-LUGO, Josefina	(PR)	156
CASAS DE FAUNCE, Maria	(PR)	191
MOMBILLE, Pedro	(PR)	854
AYLWARD, James F.	(RI)	42
DESJARLAIS-LUETH, Christine	(RI)	295
DEVIN, Robin B.	(RI)	297
FUTAS, Elizabeth	(RI)	411
BOWLING, Carol L.	(SC)	121
DAVIDSON, Nancy M.	(SC)	276
DRYDEN, Sherre H.	(SC)	321
JAMES, Denise T.	(SC)	592
MCGREGOR, Jane A.	(SC)	808
MILTON, Brenda R.	(SC)	845
RAINES, Thomas A.	(SC)	1004
ROSS, Gary M.	(SC)	1058
STRAUCH, Katina P.	(SC)	1200
VASSALLO, John A.	(SC)	1279
WASHINGTON, Nancy H.	(SC)	1307
DAGANAAR, Mark L.	(SD)	269
HULKONEN, David A.	(SD)	572
COOPER, Ellen R.	(TN)	242
DENTON, Ann L.	(TN)	293
EKKEBUS, Allen E.	(TN)	341
GRAHAM, Sylvia R.	(TN)	456
HAMLIN, Lisa K.	(TN)	493
HAYMES, Don	(TN)	516
HERRING, Mark Y.	(TN)	533
HUDSON, Earline H.	(TN)	569
JONES, Roger G.	(TN)	615
KARL, Roger M.	(TN)	627
LAMBERT, Sarah E.	(TN)	690
LYNCH, Frances H.	(TN)	751
MARSHALL, John D.	(TN)	774
MEREDITH, Don L.	(TN)	825
MITCHELL, Aubrey H.	(TN)	848
NICOL, Jessie T.	(TN)	902
PARKS, Dorothy R.	(TN)	943
PERRY, Glenda L.	(TN)	960
ROBERTS, Marica L.	(TN)	1041
ROBINSON, William C.	(TN)	1045
SCOTT, Margaret W.	(TN)	1107
TERRY, Carol D.	(TN)	1232
THWEATT, John H.	(TN)	1243
TURNER, Deborah M.	(TN)	1264
WALDEN, Winston A.	(TN)	1294
WALKER, Mary E.	(TN)	1296
WORLEY, Joan H.	(TN)	1369
ALESSI, Dana L.	(TX)	11
ANDERSON, Eliane G.	(TX)	22
ARD, Harold J.	(TX)	31
BAILEY, William G.	(TX)	47
BARRINGER, Sallie H.	(TX)	60
BAXTER, Barbara A.	(TX)	67
BEDARD, Evelyn M.	(TX)	73
BOOHER, Harold H.	(TX)	115
BREWSTER, Olive N.	(TX)	134
BROWN, Steven L.	(TX)	147
BROWN, Susan W.	(TX)	147
BUCKNALL, Carolyn F.	(TX)	154
BURLINGHAM, Merry L.	(TX)	161
CASE, Bonnie N.	(TX)	191
CHUANG, Felicia S.	(TX)	213
CLEMENTS, Cynthia L.	(TX)	221
COCHRAN, Carolyn	(TX)	225
CORREDOR, Javier	(TX)	247

COLLECTIONS (Cont'd)
Collection development

CRINION, Jacquelyn A. . .	(TX)	259
DAVIS, Donald G.	(TX)	278
DEILY, Carole C.	(TX)	288
DOWNING, Jeannette D.	(TX)	316
ELAM, Craig S.	(TX)	341
ENDELMAN, Sharon B. .	(TX)	348
FARMER, David	(TX)	364
FORD, Mary R.	(TX)	389
GIROUARD, J L.	(TX)	438
GOODMAN, Helen C. . . .	(TX)	449
GROVES, Helen G.	(TX)	474
HARVILL, Melba S.	(TX)	509
HEEZEN, Ronald R.	(TX)	520
HEMPEL, Ruth M.	(TX)	525
HILLMAN, Kathy R.	(TX)	541
HOLLEMAN, Curt	(TX)	551
HOPPER, Lorraine E. . . .	(TX)	558
JOITY, Donna M.	(TX)	610
JORDAN, Travis E.	(TX)	617
KARGES, Joann	(TX)	627
KINGSBERY, Evelyn B. .	(TX)	652
LARSON, Jeanette C. . .	(TX)	699
LAVENDER, Kenneth . . .	(TX)	703
LEE, Frank	(TX)	709
LIKNESS, Craig S.	(TX)	727
LOCKETT, Iva	(TX)	736
LOPICCOLO, Cathy J. . .	(TX)	741
LOYD, Roger L.	(TX)	745
MAGNER, Mary F.	(TX)	759
MAGRILL, Rose M.	(TX)	760
MCCANN, Charlotte P. . .	(TX)	793
MCCONNELL, Ruth M. . .	(TX)	798
MENDRO, Donna C.	(TX)	824
METIVIER, Donna M. . . .	(TX)	828
MIRANDA, Cecilia	(TX)	847
MURRAY, Margaret A. . .	(TX)	882
NISONGER, Thomas E. . .	(TX)	905
ORAM, Robert W.	(TX)	925
PEYTON, Janice L.	(TX)	966
PICHETTE, William H. . .	(TX)	970
POTIER, Gwendolyn J. . .	(TX)	986
SCHWARTZ, Charles A.	(TX)	1104
SHABOWICH, Stanley A.	(TX)	1118
SHARP, Betty L.	(TX)	1122
SPEARS, Norman L. . . .	(TX)	1172
WALKER, Constance M. .	(TX)	1295
WEEKS, Patsy L.	(TX)	1315
WERKING, Richard H. . .	(TX)	1324
WILSON, Craig A.	(TX)	1350
WOHLSCHLAG, Sarah A.	(TX)	1359
GILLUM, Gary P.	(UT)	436
HALL, Blaine H.	(UT)	487
HOLLEY, Robert P.	(UT)	551
LAMB, Connie	(UT)	689
LARSEN, A D.	(UT)	698
OLSEN, Randy J.	(UT)	921
PARTRIDGE, Cathleen F.	(UT)	945
REDDICK, Mary J.	(UT)	1013
ROWLEY, Edward D. . . .	(UT)	1063
SPERRY, Kip	(UT)	1174
AUSTON, Ione	(VA)	40
BARRICK, Susan O.	(VA)	59
BENKE, Robin P.	(VA)	81
BROWN, David C.	(VA)	143
BULLEY, Joan S.	(VA)	156
CASH, Susan R.	(VA)	192
CHISHOLM, Clarence E.	(VA)	209
CHRISTOLON, Blair B. . .	(VA)	212
DECAMPS, Alice L.	(VA)	285
ERICKSON, Lynda L. . . .	(VA)	352
FOX, Barbara S.	(VA)	394
GLENN, Lucy D.	(VA)	441
GOLDBERG, Lisbeth S. .	(VA)	444
GROVE, Pearce S.	(VA)	473
GUILFORD, Diane E. . . .	(VA)	476
GWIN, James E.	(VA)	479
HIGBEE, Florence	(VA)	537
HINDMAN, Pamela J. . . .	(VA)	542

COLLECTIONS (Cont'd)
Collection development

JAFFE, John G.	(VA)	591
KINGSLEY, Marcia S. . .	(VA)	652
KOK, Victoria T.	(VA)	669
LEVY, Sharon J.	(VA)	722
LISZEWSKI, Edward H. .	(VA)	733
LOHMAN, Toni A.	(VA)	737
MATTIS, George E.	(VA)	786
METZ, Paul D.	(VA)	828
MOSER, Emily F.	(VA)	870
MULVANEY, John P. . . .	(VA)	878
OSIA, Ruby R.	(VA)	928
PARHAM, Sandra H. . . .	(VA)	940
PARNES, Daria M.	(VA)	943
PEREZ-LOPEZ, Rene . . .	(VA)	958
RASMUSSEN, Lane D. .	(VA)	1009
ROYAL, Linda G.	(VA)	1063
STEINBERG, David L. . .	(VA)	1185
TATUM, George M.	(VA)	1225
TROTTI, John B.	(VA)	1258
ZWICK, Susan G.	(VA)	1392
SWIFT, Esther M.	(VT)	1216
YERBURGH, Mark R. . . .	(VT)	1379
BACON, Carey H.	(WA)	44
BOSLEY, Dana L.	(WA)	117
CHEN, Yvonne	(WA)	205
CHISMAN, Janet K.	(WA)	209
COHEN, Jane L.	(WA)	228
DIBIASE, Linda P.	(WA)	299
DOI, Makiko	(WA)	309
KREIMEYER, Vicki R. . . .	(WA)	677
PACKER, Donna E.	(WA)	933
REDALJE, Susanne J. . .	(WA)	1013
TAYLOR, James B. . . .	(WA)	1227
THOMAS, Lawrence E. . .	(WA)	1237
TRUHLER, Judith A.	(WA)	1259
WIERUM, Ann R.	(WA)	1337
YAPLE, Henry M.	(WA)	1377
AHL, Ruth E.	(WI)	8
CEBULA, Theodore R. . .	(WI)	196
GRUEL, Janice L.	(WI)	474
LINDSAY, Jane A.	(WI)	729
MARCUS, Terry C.	(WI)	769
PROCES, Stephen L. . . .	(WI)	994
SCHMITT, Madelaine M.	(WI)	1096
SEARING, Susan E.	(WI)	1109
TORNQUIST, Kristi M. . .	(WI)	1251
TURNER, Judith C.	(WI)	1264
WELSCH, Erwin K.	(WI)	1323
WILLIAMSON, William L.	(WI)	1348
FIDLER, Leah J.	(WV)	375
MARTIN, June R.	(WV)	777
WRIGHT, Linda G.	(WV)	1372
BYERS, Edward W.	(WY)	168
CORS, Paul B.	(WY)	248
MEALEY, Catherine E. . .	(WY)	820
RAO, Dittakavi N.	(WY)	1008
VANARSDALE, William O.	(WY)	1272
WALTERS, Corky	(WY)	1301
BOULTBEE, Paul G.	(AB)	119
DEBRUIJN, Deborah I. . .	(AB)	285
HOBBS, Brian	(AB)	545
JARVIS, Marylea	(AB)	595
LUTHY, Jean M.	(AB)	750
MCLAUGHLIN, W K. . . .	(AB)	813
RICHARDS, Vincent P. . .	(AB)	1029
ROBINS, Nora D.	(AB)	1043
STEVELMAN, Sharon R.	(AB)	1190
DEVAKOS, Elizabeth R. .	(BC)	297
MANSBRIDGE, John . . .	(BC)	767
WEESE, Dwain W.	(BC)	1316
MACLOWICK, Frederick B.	(MB)	757
TULLY, Sharon I.	(MB)	1262
EADIE, Tom	(NB)	331
LEBLANC, Amedee	(NB)	708
NADEAU, Sylvie	(NB)	886
RAUCH, Doris E.	(NB)	1010
CAMERON, H C.	(NF)	174
ELLIS, Richard H.	(NF)	345

COLLECTIONS (Cont'd)
Collection development

TILLOTSON, Joy G.	(NF)	1245
ETTLINGER, John R.	(NS)	356
GURAYA, Harinder	(NS)	478
MARSH, Mary L.	(NS)	773
ALBURGER, Thomas P.	(ON)	11
ASHTON, Margaret A.	(ON)	36
BLACK, Jane L.	(ON)	101
BOJIN, Minda A.	(ON)	111
CAMPBELL, Laurie G.	(ON)	177
CHAN, Bruce A.	(ON)	199
CORMAN, Linda W.	(ON)	246
DAVIS, Virginia K.	(ON)	281
FLEMING, Anne	(ON)	384
FYFE, Janet H.	(ON)	411
GARLOCK, Gayle N.	(ON)	419
ISRAEL, Kathleen	(ON)	585
JARVI, Edith T.	(ON)	594
JOHNSON, James R.	(ON)	605
KORNUTA, Helen	(ON)	672
LAWLESS, Ruthmary G.	(ON)	704
LEBLANC, Jean J.	(ON)	708
LIN, Louise	(ON)	727
LINTON, Linda J.	(ON)	731
NORRGARD, Don K.	(ON)	909
PARKKARI, John	(ON)	943
PICARD, Albert	(ON)	970
SCHRYER, Michel J.	(ON)	1100
SCHULTE-ALBERT, Hans G.	(ON)	1101
SPARK, Catherine L.	(ON)	1171
THOMSON, Dorothy F.	(ON)	1241
TSAI, Shaopan	(ON)	1260
VARMA, Divakara K.	(ON)	1278
WISEMAN, John A.	(ON)	1357
BAILLARGEON, Daniele	(PQ)	47
BAZINET, Jeanne	(PQ)	68
BERGERON, Gilles I.	(PQ)	86
BOIVIN-OSTIGUY, Jocelyne	(PQ)	111
BOUDREAU, Gerald E.	(PQ)	118
CYR, Solange	(PQ)	268
EVANS, Calvin D.	(PQ)	356
FORTIN, Jean L.	(PQ)	391
GAMEIRO, Maria H.	(PQ)	416
GARDNER, Richard K.	(PQ)	418
GELINAS, Michel R.	(PQ)	426
HERLINGER, Peggy	(PQ)	531
HETU, Sylvie	(PQ)	534
HOBBINS, Alan J.	(PQ)	545
KO, Jean S.	(PQ)	666
LAPLANTE, Carole	(PQ)	697
MARCOTTE, Marcel	(PQ)	769
MOLLER, Hans	(PQ)	853
ORMSBY, Eric	(PQ)	926
ROBIN, Madeleine	(PQ)	1043
ROY, Christine	(PQ)	1063
TAILLON, Yolande A.	(PQ)	1220
CANEVARI DE PAREDES, Donna A.	(SK)	178
MACK, A Y.	(SK)	756
VANDER LAAN, Lubbert	(SK)	1274
POWNALL, David E.	(AUS)	989
ROUTH, Spencer	(AUS)	1061
STEELE, Colin R.	(AUS)	1184
ABDEL-MOTEY, Yaser Y.	(KWT)	2
TARPLEY, Margaret J.	(NGR)	1224
COOK, Marjorie L.	(PHP)	240
KHAN, Mohammed A.	(SDA)	646

Collection development, acquisitions LEICH, Harold M. (DC) 713
Collection development, administration ANTHONY, Paul L. (IL) 29
Collection development, Afro-American BELCHER, Emily M. (NJ) 76
Collection development, agriculture NIPP, Deanna (NJ) 904
Collection development & acquisition DILUCIA, Samuel J. (HI) 303
Collection development & acquisitioning HAYES, Bonaventure F. (NY) 515

COLLECTIONS (Cont'd)

Collection development & acquisitions	WILSON, Jacqueline B.	(CA)	1351
	MEIKAMP, Kathie D.	(DC)	822
	NICHTER, Alan	(FL)	902
	TERNAK, Armand T.	(FL)	1232
	COVER, Teresa A.	(MN)	252
	MASON, Michael L.	(NJ)	781
	GILLESPIE, Gerald V.	(NY)	435
	KASPAR, Eileen	(NY)	629
	BLOMQUIST, Laura G.	(OH)	106
	HOLLOWAY, Johnna H.	(VA)	552
	KRAEHE, Mary A.	(VA)	674
Collection development & automation	POWER, Colleen J.	(CA)	989
Collection development & bibliography	GRAMENZ, Francis L.	(MA)	457
Collection development & building	FUNG, Margaret C.	(MA)	409
Collection development & cataloging	ROBINSON, Gayle N.	(AL)	1044
	ARTHUR, Donald B.	(TX)	35
Collection development & curation	MOORE, Emily C.	(AL)	859
Collection development & curriculum	PRIESING, Patricia L.	(NJ)	993
Collection development & evaluation	LO, Henrietta W.	(CA)	735
	ORTOPAN, Leroy D.	(CA)	927
	WRIGHT, Arthuree M.	(DC)	1370
	CASSERLY, Mary F.	(ME)	193
	OBERG, Larry R.	(MI)	914
	WINKEL, Lois	(NC)	1355
	CARLSON, Kathleen A.	(NM)	182
	LIN, Susan T.	(NY)	728
	RICHARDS, Daniel T.	(NY)	1028
	DAVIS, Yvonne M.	(OH)	281
	GARCIA, Lana C.	(TX)	417
	WAYLAND, Terry T.	(TX)	1311
	PURDY, Victor W.	(UT)	998
	HABAN, Mary F.	(VA)	480
	LIN, John T.	(VA)	727
	SCHNEIDER, Frank A.	(WA)	1097
	MILNE, Dorothy J.	(NF)	845
	BESSETTE, Madeleine	(PQ)	91
Collection development & faculty liaison	RAMBLER, Linda K.	(PA)	1005
Collection development & legal info	TOMCHYSHYN, Theresa M.	(SK)	1249
Collection development & maintenance	WAKS, Jane B.	(MA)	1293
	POJMAN, Paul E.	(OH)	980
	AUSTIN, Martha L.	(WA)	40
Collection development & management	STEPHENS, Dennis J.	(AK)	1187
	PEDERSOLI, Heleni M.	(AL)	954
	GREGORY, Joan A.	(AZ)	466
	TRUJILLO, Roberto G.	(CA)	1259
	ROBERTS, Susanne F.	(CT)	1041
	DE PEW, John N.	(FL)	293
	JONES, Linda L.	(FL)	613
	WALTON, Terence M.	(FL)	1302
	EGGERS, Lolly P.	(IA)	339
	KRIEGER, Alan D.	(IN)	678
	LEE, Thomas H.	(IN)	711
	CHIANG, Ahushun	(MD)	207
	COOPER, David J.	(MD)	242
	WETZBARGER, Cecilia G.	(MD)	1328
	YOCUM, Patricia B.	(MI)	1380
	PANKAKE, Marcia J.	(MN)	938
	TIBLIN, Mariann E.	(MN)	1244
	BENEDICT, Marjorie A.	(NY)	80
	EVANS, Robert W.	(NY)	358
	BOBICK, James E.	(OH)	108
	WEIDMAN, Jeffrey	(OH)	1316
	SAUNDERS, William B.	(PA)	1085
	ZUBATSKY, David S.	(PA)	1390
	BRENNAN, Mary H.	(TX)	132
	WEATHERS, Barbara H.	(TX)	1312
	CHADWICK, Leroy D.	(WA)	197
	SHORES, Sandra J.	(AB)	1132
	SIGNORI, Donna L.	(BC)	1137
	UTSUNOMIYA, Leslie D.	(BC)	1270
	CHOMENKO, Tamara L.	(MB)	210
Collection development & publicity	HAMMER, Louise K.	(IL)	493
Collection development & serials	ROGERS, Nancy H.	(AL)	1050
Collection development & serials control	BECHOR, Malvina B.	(GA)	71

COLLECTIONS (Cont'd)

Collection development, architecture	BRACKNEY, Kathryn S.	(GA)	125
Collection development automation	MIDDLETON, Robert K.	(TX)	833
Collection development, business, econ	BELANGER, Sandra E.	(CA)	75
Collection development, chemistry	BOWMAN, Laura M.	(TX)	122
Collection development, children's	STURDIVANT, Nan J.	(OK)	1205
Collection development, English	JOSEPH, Margaret A.	(TX)	617
Collection development, ethnic studies	FISHER, Edith M.	(CA)	380
Collection development, evaluation	DAVIES, Gordon D.	(MD)	277
Collection development, faculty liaison	TAYLOR, Anne E.	(TX)	1226
Collection development, foods, nutrition	NIPP, Deanna	(NJ)	904
Collection development for art	MCKEE, George D.	(NY)	810
Collection development for business	KENDRICK, Aubrey W.	(AL)	640
Collection development for curriculum	WILLIAMS, S J.	(MI)	1346
Collection development for education	WILKE, Janet S.	(KS)	1339
Collection development for humanities	CULLARS, John M.	(IL)	263
Collection devlpmnt for lrng disabled	KEYS, Marshall	(MA)	645
Collection development for medicine	HANKS, Ellen T.	(TX)	496
Collection devlpmnt, foundation grants	LEE, J S.	(NJ)	710
Collection development health sciences	WARD, Penny T.	(CA)	1304
Collection development, history	MCCOY, Patricia S.	(IL)	799
Collection development in architecture	SCHUSTER, Adeline	(IL)	1103
Collection development in arts	VAN WIEMOKLY, Jane G.	(NJ)	1277
Collection development in history	LAUBE, Lois R.	(IN)	702
	ZIEPER, Linda R.	(MA)	1388
	BUDNICK, Carol	(MB)	155
Collection development in large libs	EDWARDS, Ralph M.	(AZ)	337
Collection development in life sciences	SOWELL, Steven L.	(IN)	1170
Collection development in medicine	KATZ, Jacqueline E.	(NY)	630
Collection development in religion	PETERSON, Stephen L.	(CT)	964
Collection development in schools	MARTINEZ, Helen	(NF)	779
Collection development in science	WARD, Sandra N.	(CA)	1304
	WINN, Carolyn P.	(MA)	1355
	SUDENGA, Sara A.	(TX)	1206
Collection development in South Asia	SEN, Joyce H.	(NY)	1115
Collection development in intl affairs	HEWITT, Vivian D.	(NY)	535
Collection development, language lit	WARREN, Peggy A.	(ON)	1306
Collection development, legal	MOYER, Holley M.	(NJ)	874
Collection development, library science	VIA, Barbara J.	(NY)	1283
Collection development, local government	BALLENTINE, Rebecca S.	(NC)	53
Collection development, management	BROWN, Donald R.	(PA)	143
Collection development, performing arts	DIMMICK, Mary L.	(PA)	304
Col development, philosophy & religion	STEWART, Douglas J.	(AZ)	1192
Collection development policies	CASSERLY, Mary F.	(ME)	193
	DESJARLAIS-LUETH, Christine	(RI)	295
Collection development procedures	AUER, Margaret E.	(MI)	39
Collection development, public library	SILVER, Diane L.	(PA)	1138
Collection development, public relations	KNIGHT, Shirley D.	(NJ)	664
Collection development research	ST. CLAIR, Gloriana S.	(OR)	1075
Collection development, resource sharing	FISCHLER, Barbara B.	(IN)	380
	HEANEY, Henry J.	(SCT)	518
	KENNEY, Ann J.	(OR)	641
Collection development, school			
Collection development, school libraries	CORNWELL, Linda L.	(IN)	247
Collection development, science & tech	GREENE, Cathy C.	(MA)	463
Collection development, theology	KENDALL, Charles T.	(IN)	640
Col devlpmnt, theology, scriptures	MAINELLI, Helen K.	(CA)	761
Collection devlpmnt, Western Americana	CLARK, Robert M.	(MT)	218
Collection development zoology	CACCESE, Vincent	(CA)	170
Collection evaluation	MILLER, Edward P.	(AZ)	837
	COOPER, David J.	(MD)	242
	DRONE, Jeanette M.	(OH)	320
	LOPEZ, Elsa M.	(PR)	741
	MAGRILL, Rose M.	(TX)	760
	SHERMAN-PETERSON, Ronald A.	(WA)	1128
	DUPRE, Monique	(ON)	327

COLLECTIONS (Cont'd)

Collection evaluation			
	FAIRLEY, Craig R.	(ON)	361
Collection evaluation & assessment	SIGNORI, Donna L.	(BC)	1137
Collection evaluation & description	HIGBEE, Joan F.	(DC)	537
Collection evaluation & development	FOURIE, Denise K.	(CA)	393
Collection maintenance	FOLEY, Georgiana	(CO)	387
	LOMAX, Denise W.	(DC)	738
	STILLWATER, Rebecca S.	(GA)	1194
	HARMON, Charles T.	(IA)	502
	HANNA, Hildur W.	(MI)	496
	BELL, Carole R.	(RI)	76
	DESJARLAIS-LUETH, Christine	(RI)	295
	MALMQUIST, Katherine E.	(VA)	763
	HOOGKAMER, Dawne	(ON)	556
	HORNE, Bonnie L.	(ON)	560
Collection maintenance & development	BARTZ, Stephanie	(NJ)	62
	HOOTKIN, Neil M.	(WI)	557
Collection management	OSBURN, Charles B.	(AL)	927
	CHAN, Carl C.	(CA)	199
	HAIKALIS, Peter D.	(CA)	484
	JOHNSON, Peter A.	(CA)	608
	LUST, Vernon G.	(CA)	750
	OLSON, Sharon L.	(CA)	923
	PETERS, Marion C.	(CA)	962
	SOETE, George J.	(CA)	1165
	SOUTHARD, Sarah T.	(CT)	1169
	CHIN, Cecilia H.	(DC)	208
	GARDNER, Jeffrey J.	(DC)	418
	JOHANSON, Cynthia J.	(DC)	601
	KENYON, Kay A.	(DC)	643
	NAINIS, Linda	(DC)	886
	REED-SCOTT, Jutta R.	(DC)	1015
	TAYLOR, Joan R.	(DC)	1227
	AHMAD, Carol F.	(FL)	8
	ORSER, Frank W.	(FL)	927
	LEE, Lauren K.	(GA)	710
	SELF, Sharon W.	(GA)	1113
	MARSHALL, Jessica A.	(IA)	774
	BENNETT, Scott B.	(IL)	82
	BJORNCRANTZ, Leslie B.	(IL)	100
	GRISSO, Karl M.	(IL)	471
	MCBRIDE, Ruth B.	(IL)	792
	MICHAELSON, Robert C.	(IL)	832
	SHERMAN, Sarah	(IL)	1128
	WIBERLEY, Stephen E.	(IL)	1335
	MURPHY, Marcy	(IN)	881
	CHANNING, Rhoda K.	(MA)	201
	DRAKE, Robert E.	(MA)	318
	HOVORKA, Marjorie J.	(MA)	563
	JACKSON, Arlyne A.	(MA)	586
	MARTIN, Murray S.	(MA)	777
	FLORANCE, Valerie	(MD)	385
	WILT, Larry J.	(MD)	1353
	HULSEY, Richard A.	(MI)	573
	SLATTERY, Charles E.	(MO)	1148
	HUNT, Margaret R.	(NC)	575
	LACROIX, Michael J.	(NC)	686
	NUTTER, Susan K.	(NC)	912
	RODNEY, Mae L.	(NC)	1048
	KENNEDY, Kathleen A.	(NJ)	641
	MENZEL, John P.	(NJ)	825
	WHITING, Elaine M.	(NJ)	1333
	BARTO, Stephen C.	(NY)	61
	KOUO, Lily W.	(NY)	673
	BELL, Gladys S.	(OH)	77
	BENTLEY, Stella	(OH)	83
	BOLEK, Ann D.	(OH)	112
	HEIDTMANN, Toby	(OH)	521
	THOMPSON, Ann M.	(OH)	1238
	DEFASSIO, Sharon L.	(PA)	287
	FREEMAN, Larry S.	(SC)	401
	HOLLEMAN, Curt	(TX)	551
	HYMAN, Ferne B.	(TX)	580
	SCHLESSINGER, Bernard S.	(TX)	1094
	CALLAHAN, John J.	(VA)	173
	CAMPBELL, James M.	(VA)	176

COLLECTIONS (Cont'd)

Collection management
CAYWOOD, Carolyn A. . . (VA) 195
JOHNSON, Jane W. . . . (VA) 605
MILLER, Nancy M. . . . . . (VA) 841
WHALEY, John H. . . . . . (VA) 1328
GELLATLY, Peter . . . . . . (WA) 426
LOKEN, Sarah F. . . . . . (WA) 738
TOLLIVER, Barbara J. . . (WA) 1248
ADAM, Anthony J. . . . . . (WI) 4
SWEETLAND, James H. . (WI) 1215
GUTTERIDGE, Paul . . . . (BC) 479
AMEY, Lorne J. . . . . (NS) 20
LANOUETTE, Marie . . . . (ON) 696
MCLEAN-LOWE, Dallas . (ON) 814
WILLIAMSON, Michael W. (ON) 1347
NELSON, Ian C. . . . . . . (SK) 893
Collection management & circulation DAVIS, Douglas A. . . . . . (CA) 278
Collection management &
  development
ALLISON, Terry L. . . . . . (CA) 17
CARPENTER, Kathryn H. (IL) 185
FARRELL, David . . . . . . (IN) 365
SEREBNICK, Judith . . . . (IN) 1116
BEAVEN, Miranda J. . . . (MN) 71
GIORDANO, Frederick S. (NY) 438
WEAVER, Alice O. . . . . . (OH) 1312
MANNING, Dale . . . . . . (TN) 766
DILLON, John B. . . . . . . (WI) 303
Collection management development SHELDON, Ted P. . . . . . (MO) 1126
Collection of marketing research
  reports   COVIENSKY, Lana . . . . . (ON) 252
Collection organization   JANKOWSKI, Susan H. . . (WI) 593
Collection organizing   SUGGS, John K. . . . . . . (WA) 1206
Collection planning   GAREY, Anita I. . . . . . . (CA) 418
Collection policy & development WARTLUFT, David J. . . . (PA) 1307
Collection preservation   SAGE-GAGNE, Waneta . . (FL) 1074
Collection processing   MATTHEOU, Antonia . . . (NY) 785
                              VANDOREN, Sandra S. . . (PA) 1275
Collection selection & development LANKFORD, Mary D. . . . (TX) 696
Collection solicitation   INGERSOL, Robert S. . . (MO) 582
Collection supervision & maintenance CAMPBELL, Mary K. . . . (TX) 177
Collection utilization   DANIEL, Marianne M. . . . (FL) 272
Collections   DRESSLER, Alta L. . . . . (KS) 319
                              BIRD, Nora J. . . . . (MA) 98
                              BANFILL, Christine . . . . . (ON) 54
                              GROEN, Frances K. . . . . (PQ) 471
Collections development   MALINOWSKY, H R. . . . (IL) 763
                              VALAUSKAS, Edward J. . (IL) 1271
                              KRENITSKY, Michael V. . (MI) 677
                              OKERSON, Ann L. . . . . . (NY) 920
                              ZABROSKY, Frank A. . . (PA) 1385
                              BOAZ, Ruth L. . . . . (TN) 108
                              COLSON, Judith K. . . . . (NB) 234
                              POPE, Andrew T. . . . . . (NB) 983
                              BIANCHINI, Lucian . . . . . (NS) 94
                              RIPLEY, Victoria E. . . . . (ON) 1035
                              SMITH, Louise . . . . (ON) 1157
                              WARD, William D. . . . . . (ON) 1304
                              MACLEAN, Eleanor A. . . (PQ) 757
                              RESCH, Peter T. . . . . . . (SK) 1024
Collections development, law BLAKE, Timothy J. . . . . (LA) 103
Collections evaluation   MACDONALD, Patricia A. (ON) 754
Collections inventory   JOHNSON, Everett J. . . (DC) 604
Collections management   GALSWORTHY, Peter R. (ON) 415
Collections management &
  development   JONES, David L. . . . . . . (AB) 612
Collections management & NCIP CLOUSTON, John S. . . . (ON) 223
Collections processing   HEISS, Harry C. . . . . . . (DC) 523
                              MEVERS, Frank C. . . . . (NH) 829
College library collection development SIMMONS, Randall C. . . (ID) 1140
Complete collections of Adlerian jnls KAHN, Paul J. . . . . (CA) 622
Computer management of collections QUIGLEY, Suzanne L. . . (OH) 999
Computer science collection
  development   ENSOR, Pat L. . . . . (IN) 350
                              TINSLEY, Geraldine L. . . (PA) 1246
Computerizing collection   WEISLAK, Susan L. . . . . (TX) 1319
Congressional collections   BOCCACCIO, Mary A. . . (NC) 108
Consumer medical collections DIAL, Carolyn E. . . . . . . (FL) 299

COLLECTIONS (Cont'd)

Cooperative collection development STEPHENS, Dennis J. . . (AK) 1187
                              BATES, Henry E. . . . . . . (CA) 64
                              MEACHEN, Edward W. . (IL) 819
                              SMITH, Newland F. . . . . (IL) 1159
                              FARRELL, David . . . . . . (IN) 365
                              KENNEDY BRIGHT,
                                Sandra   (NY) 641
                              KLIMLEY, Susan . . . . . . (NY) 661
                              KRUEGER, Karen J. . . . (WI) 680
Corporate art collections   CLAYTON, John M. . . . . (DE) 220
Creating archival collections METZLER, Valerie . . . . . (IL) 829
Data collection & editing   TEUN, Rebecca L. . . . . (TX) 1233
Data collection & management VAN ORDER, Mary J. . . (ON) 1276
Deafness information & collections RITTER, Audrey L. . . . . (NY) 1036
Developing & maintaining collections GABBIANELLI, Patrice A. (NJ) 411
Developing the collections   FRANTZ, Ray W. . . . . . . (VA) 398
Developing video collections PURCELL, Marcia L. . . . (NY) 998
Director of pictorial resrch collection GORDON, Thelma S. . . . (CT) 452
East Asian collections   SIGGINS, Jack A. . . . . . (CT) 1137
Education bibliography, collection
  mgmt   BROWN, M S. . . . . (FL) 145
Education, collection development ANDREWS, Loretta K. . . (MD) 26
Education collections   KENNEDY, Kathleen A. . (NJ) 641
Education ref collection development DAVIS, Maryellen K. . . (IL) 280
Elementary, secondary col devlpmnt KUTTEROFF, Ethel C. . . (NJ) 685
Engineering collection development WILLIS, Glee M. . . . . . . (CA) 1348
                              LONG, Caroline C. . . . . (DC) 739
                              MYERS, Charles J. . . . . (PA) 884
                              WARD, Suzanne M. . . . (TN) 1304
Ethnic collections   DAVIS, Natalia G. . . . . . (NY) 280
Ethnic studies collection development KNOWLES, Em C. . . . . (CA) 665
Evaluating children's book collections EDMONDS, May H. . . . (FL) 336
Fashion & costume collections HALE, Kaycee . . . . (CA) 485
Fiction collection development VOSS, Joyce M. . . . . . . (IL) 1289
                              HIRSCH, Dorothy K. . . . (MD) 543
Fiction collections   MCILROY, William D. . . . (NJ) 809
Field work in manuscript collections KRASEAN, Thomas K. . . (IN) 676
Film & video collection   HANFT, Margie E. . . . . . (CA) 495
Film & video collection coordination NEBEL, Jean C. . . . . . . (CA) 891
Film & video collection development MOORE, Emily C. . . . . . (NC) 859
Film & video collections   FLYNN, Barbara L. . . . . (IL) 386
                              TUGGLE, Pamela C. . . . (VA) 1262
Fine arts collection development BOHRER, Karen M. . . . . (CT) 111
                              MOORE, Emily C. . . . . . (NC) 859
                              DOGU, Hikmet S. . . . . . (UT) 309
                              PARR, Loraine E. . . . . . (WA) 943
                              TOBIN, R J. . . . . (WI) 1247
Fine arts collections, books RUSSELL, Marilyn L. . . . (KS) 1069
Fine arts, local history collections MCNULTY, Karen . . . . . (CT) 817
Food & nutrition collection
  development   SZILARD, Paula . . . . (HI) 1218
Foreign & intl law collection devlpmnt TARNAWSKY, Marta . . . (PA) 1224
Foreign language collection
  development   HERNANDEZ, Hector R. . (IL) 531
                              MCELWAIN, William . . . (IL) 804
                              ALICEA, Ismael . . . . (NY) 13
Foreign language collections PUTZ, Paul D. . . . . (AK) 998
                              TSUNEISHI, Warren M. . (DC) 1260
Foreign language collections
  development   KRIEGER, Lee A. . . . . . (NC) 678
Foreign-language collection
  development   BELL, Irena L. . . . . (ON) 77
Foundation collection searches FRASER, Elizabeth L. . . (WV) 399
French collection development SPRY, Patricia . . . . (ON) 1176
French collections   MACLENNAN, Oriel C. . . (NS) 757
Gambling collection   GARDNER, Jack I. . . . . . (NV) 418
General collections   RICE, Joyce I. . . . . (MS) 1027
Geography collection development
  work   LAMPRECHT, Sandra J. . (CA) 691
Geologic map collection   GALKOWSKI, Patricia E. . (RI) 413
Geoscience collections &
  administration   WICK, Constance S. . . . (MA) 1335
German history collection
  development   BAER, Eberhard A. . . . . (VA) 44
Gerontology collections   MILANICH, Melanie M. . . (ON) 834
Government documents collection
  mgmt   MCSWEENEY, Josephine (NY) 818
Government publications collections MILLER, Mary E. . . . . . (PA) 840
Grade school collection development DRECHSEL, Marcella J. . (NJ) 319

COLLECTIONS (Cont'd)

Graduate school collections	SIMMONS, Hal	(GA)	1140
Health, science & business collections	ARMSTRONG, Mary L.	(AB)	32
Health sciences collection development	BRANDON, Alfred N.	(FL)	128
	NEUFELD, Sue E.	(IA)	897
Historic manuscript collections	RHINELANDER, Mary F.	(MA)	1025
Historical collection archives	LEVIS, Gail A.	(IL)	721
Historical collections	DOWNEY, Lynn A.	(CA)	316
	STUART, Karen A.	(MD)	1204
	EVANS, Max J.	(UT)	357
History & collection development	MONROE, William S.	(NY)	855
Hospital design & collection development	TOMLIN, Marsha A.	(OH)	1250
Humanities & social sciences cols	EDWARDS, Willie M.	(MI)	338
Humanities collection development	MILLER, Randy S.	(IL)	841
	NEWMAN, Gerald L.	(IL)	899
	HARNER, James L.	(OH)	503
	HEINZKILL, J R.	(OR)	522
	TOBIN, R J.	(WI)	1247
	MACDONALD, Patricia A.	(ON)	754
Humanities ref, collection development	NOURIE, Alan R.	(IL)	910
Indexing, bibliography & col devlpmnt	SANCHEZ, Sara M.	(FL)	1079
Information collection	NICHOLSON, Jill A.	(ON)	902
Instructional software collection	OSTROM, Kriss T.	(MI)	929
International & Anglo-Saxon collections	IOANID, Aurora S.	(NY)	583
International law collection development	VON PFEIL, Helena P.	(DC)	1288
James Thurber collection	BRANSCOMB, Lewis C.	(OH)	129
Japanese collection development	KANEKO, Hideo	(CT)	625
Japanese material collection development	GONNAMI, Tsuneharu	(BC)	447
Journal collection	WILLIAMS, Alma	(CO)	1341
Judaica collection development	GILNER, David J.	(OH)	437
Judaica collections	SIEGEL, Steven W.	(NY)	1136
Junior high building collections	LEWIS, Marjorie	(NY)	723
Juvenile & young adult col development	GOLEY, Elaine P.	(TX)	447
Juvenile collection centers	DIRKS, Martha W.	(KS)	305
Korean language collection	ROH, Jae M.	(CA)	1050
K-12 collection development	MATSUNAGA, Fay L.	(CO)	785
K-6 & English collection development	MCGLOHON, Leah L.	(NC)	807
Latin American collection development	GROTHEY, Mina J.	(NM)	473
Law & business collection development	BURGESS, Rita N.	(PA)	159
Law collection	KEARNEY, Jeanne E.	(NJ)	633
Law collection development	WALTERS, Roberta J.	(CA)	1301
Law firm collections cataloging	SCAMMAHORN, Lynne	(PA)	1087
Law library collection development	ADAN, Adrienne	(CA)	6
Learning resource center col standards	BOOK, Imogene I.	(SC)	115
Library administration, col development	BROWN, Biraj L.	(SDA)	142
Library buildings & collection layout	BELGUM, Kathie G.	(IA)	76
Library collection assessment	KELLY, Glen J.	(ON)	637
Library collection evaluation	LYNN-NELSON, Gayle	(NJ)	752
Library collection movement management	KURKUL, Donna L.	(MA)	684
Library collections	DANIEL, Marianne M.	(FL)	272
Library collections policies	TAGGART, William R.	(BC)	1220
Library management & collection devlpmnt	DOUVILLE, Judith A.	(CT)	314
Library science collection development	DAVIS, Sally A.	(WI)	281
Life sciences collection development	KELLAND, John L.	(RI)	635
Literature collections development	SWEEDLER, Ulla S.	(CA)	1214
Local history & photograph collections	BABBITT, Dennis L.	(IN)	43
Local history collection	SINGH, Rosemary A.	(WI)	1143
Local history collection development	DARR, William E.	(IN)	275
	ENG, Mamie	(NY)	348
Local history collections	BROCK, Kathy T.	(GA)	138
	VLOYANETES, Jeanne M.	(NJ)	1286
	HALL, Alan C.	(OH)	486
	COLLINS, Sara D.	(VA)	233
	RICKERSON, Carla	(WA)	1031
Local history manuscript collections	PACKARD, Agnes K.	(NY)	933
Management of microform collections	IANNUZZI, Patricia A.	(CT)	581

COLLECTIONS (Cont'd)

Management of slide collections	HENDERSON, Joyce C.	(AZ)	526
Managing archives collection	PARKER, Peter J.	(PA)	942
Manuscript collections	SLY, Margery N.	(MA)	1150
	PENNINGER, Randy	(NC)	957
	GARNER, Jane	(TX)	419
	BOONE, Edward J.	(VA)	115
Manuscripts & archives collections	ASHFORD, Marguerite K.	(HI)	36
Manuscripts collection	BERKELEY, Edmund	(VA)	87
Manuscripts collections	WIKANDER, Lawrence E.	(MA)	1338
Map & air photo collections	SUTHERLAND, Johnnie D.	(GA)	1211
Map & atlas collection development	RIVERA, Diana H.	(MI)	1037
Map & geography collections	SHARP, Linda C.	(OH)	1122
Map collection	ROBAR, Terri J.	(FL)	1038
Map collections	MILLER, Rosanna	(AZ)	842
	BURNS, Mary F.	(IL)	162
Marimba, xylophone collection	GERHARDT, Edwin L.	(MD)	428
Marine science collections development	SUTHERLAND, J E.	(NS)	1211
Maritime collections	KENNICK, Sylvia B.	(NY)	642
Marketing information collections	BURROWS, Shirley	(NY)	163
Materials selection, collection devlpmnt	THOMPSON, Elizabeth M.	(DC)	1239
Media collection development	LARSON, Teresa B.	(IA)	700
Media collection management	REIT, Janet W.	(VT)	1022
Media collections	STRANGE, Elizabeth B.	(DE)	1200
Media collections & services	CLAYTON, William R.	(GA)	220
Media materials, collections development	STEVENS, Roberta A.	(DC)	1191
Medical & academic collection devlpmnt	INGRAHAM-SWETS, Leonoor	(OR)	582
Medical & special library collections	SMITH-GREENWOLD, Kathryn R.	(NY)	1162
Medical collection	DUROCHER, Jeanne M.	(MI)	328
Medical collection acquisitions	PHILLIPS, Donna M.	(IA)	968
Medical collection development	KINNAIRD, Cheryl D.	(IL)	653
	WILSON, Susan W.	(MD)	1353
	HESSLEIN, Shirley B.	(NY)	534
	SAINT, Barbara J.	(BC)	1075
Medical journal collection management	HALLERBERG, Gretchen A.	(OH)	489
Medical libraries & their collections	SKICA, Janice K.	(NJ)	1146
Medical library collection development	BERK, Nancy G.	(AZ)	87
	RUDOLPH, Anne L.	(CA)	1066
Medical science collection development	DIMATTEO, Lucy A.	(NY)	304
Mental health collections	EPSTEIN, Barbara A.	(PA)	351
Mental health databases & collections	WIGGINS, Theresa S.	(PA)	1337
Microcomputer software collection mgmt	BEHNKE, Charles	(WI)	75
Microform collections	STRAITON, T H.	(AL)	1199
Microforms collection & equipment	KURKUL, Donna L.	(MA)	684
Microforms, collection development	KAUL, Kanhya L.	(MI)	631
Microforms collection management	JOHNS, Jean B.	(OH)	601
Middle East collections	JAJKO, Edward A.	(CA)	592
Middle East collections development	JAJKO, Edward A.	(CA)	592
Middle Eastern lit collection devlpmnt	BUNDY, David D.	(KY)	157
Military collections	BOONE, Edward J.	(VA)	115
Monastic collections	PIRRERA, Aaron C.	(AR)	975
Moving a library collection	SUTTON, Sandra K.	(AL)	1211
Moving collections	WALL, Carol	(OH)	1297
Moving large book collections	PARRY, David R.	(CO)	944
Moving library collections	RICHARDS, James H.	(NM)	1028
	MILLER, Scott W.	(NY)	842
	SVIBRUCK, Jonathan	(NY)	1212
	HINDMAN, Pamela J.	(VA)	542
Multilingual collections	HAABNIIT, Ene	(BC)	480
	ZIELINSKA, Marie F.	(ON)	1388
Multilingual library collections	SCHNEIDER, Francisca M.	(CA)	1097
Museum collections	BRENNER, M D.	(AK)	133
Music collection development	BOGNAR, Dorothy M.	(CT)	111
	FLING, Robert M.	(IN)	385
	RORICK, William C.	(NY)	1054
	WATANABE, Ruth T.	(NY)	1308
	PATTERSON, Myron B.	(UT)	948
	BRYCE, Maria C.	(ON)	152
Music collections	JAROSLOW, Sylvia W.	(NJ)	594
	DENNIS, Christopher J.	(NF)	292

COLLECTIONS (Cont'd)

Music collections & archives	GREEN, Walter H.	(MO)	463
Music history collections	SIMMONS, Hal	(GA)	1140
Music library & collection development	SUYEMATSU, Kiyo	(MN)	1212
Music library collection development	FISKEN, Patricia B.	(NH)	382
Music scores collection development	BERMAN, Marsha	(CA)	88
Mystery collection	HOOKER, Joan M.	(NJ)	556
Native American collection	CULL, Roberta	(AZ)	263
Native Americans collections	MITTEN, Lisa A.	(PA)	850
Neuropsychiatric collection	BURTON, Mary L.	(PA)	164
Neurosciences databases & collections	WIGGINS, Theresa S.	(PA)	1337
New library collections	DENOBLE, Augustine D.	(OR)	293
Newspaper & photo collections	SWARTZ, Patrice B.	(PA)	1214
Newspaper collections	BURROWS, Sandra	(ON)	163
Nonfiction collection development	CANTWELL, Mary L.	(OH)	179
Non-print collection development	NUTTY, David J.	(IL)	912
	CHAPLOCK, Sharon K.	(WI)	201
Non-print materials collections	JOHNSON, Carolynn K.	(WA)	603
Oklahoma collection	THORNE, Larry R.	(OK)	1242
Oklahoma State University collection	BLEDSOE, Kathleen E.	(OK)	105
Olympic games collection development	GHENT, Gretchen K.	(AB)	430
Opening day collections	LEE, Lauren K.	(GA)	710
Optical disk collection development	QUIGLEY, Suzanne L.	(OH)	999
Oral history collections	GRELE, Ronald J.	(NY)	467
Organization of library collections	HORTON, Kathy L.	(IL)	561
Organizing collections	JACOBS, Mildred H.	(MO)	589
Organizing existing library collections	KOPAN, Ellen K.	(CA)	671
Organizing reference collections	HAZEL, Debora E.	(NC)	517
Pediatrics collection development	ALLOCCO, Claudia	(NJ)	17
Performance & collection evaluation	JENSEN, L B.	(ON)	599
Periodical collection & ordering	PELZER, Adolf	(MI)	955
Personal univ-quality art collections	BLAIR, Madeline S.	(DC)	102
Petroleum related collections	GASHUS, Karin C.	(AB)	421
Phonograph record collections	EVANS, David H.	(TN)	356
Photo collection development	FRANKLIN, Alyce B.	(KY)	397
Photo collections	LARZELERE, David W.	(MI)	700
	NEU, Margaret J.	(TX)	896
Photograph collection	THOMPSON, Mary A.	(KS)	1240
	SUMNERS, Bill F.	(TN)	1209
Photograph collection administration	OKEEFE, Julia C.	(CA)	919
Photograph collection management	PINSON, Patricia A.	(WY)	975
Photograph collections	REIFMAN, Deborah S.	(CA)	1019
	O'DONOGHUE, Patrice	(TX)	917
	WILSON, Michael E.	(TX)	1352
	MOHOLT, Megan L.	(WA)	852
Photographic collection	LINN, Mott R.	(PA)	731
Photographic collection management	OETTING, Edward C.	(AZ)	917
Photographic collection organization	VOGT-O'CONNOR, Diane L.	(DC)	1287
Photographic collections	MUNOFF, Gerald J.	(IL)	879
	POIRRIER, Sherry	(MA)	980
	KIRWAN, Kathleen	(NY)	656
Photographs collections management	STONE, Gerald K.	(ON)	1197
Physical sciences & collection devlpmnt	MACEWEN, Virginia B.	(DC)	755
Physical sciences collection development	DESS, Howard M.	(NJ)	295
Physics collection development	WOELL, Yvette N.	(IL)	1359
Pictorial collections	OSTROW, Stephen E.	(DC)	929
Picture collection cataloging	NATHEWS, Ann	(AL)	889
Picture collection control	REDDINGTON, Mary E.	(OH)	1013
Picture collection management	ANDERSON, James C.	(KY)	23
Picture collections	EARLS, M L.	(ON)	332
Plays collection development	CENTING, Richard R.	(OH)	196
Poetry collection development	CENTING, Richard R.	(OH)	196
Polish collection development	MITCHELL, Annmarie D.	(CA)	848
Political sci & psychology col devlpmnt	SOUTH, Ruth E.	(OR)	1169
Political science collection development	TURNER, Patricia	(MN)	1265
Processing & organization of collections	AUTRY, Carolyn	(IN)	41
Processing archival collections	HAWES, Grace M.	(CA)	513
	VIOL, Robert W.	(OH)	1285
Processing manuscript collections	BOYD, Sandra E.	(MS)	123
	TEICHMAN, Raymond J.	(NY)	1230

COLLECTIONS (Cont'd)

Processing papers & records collections	ERICKSEN, Paul A.	(IL)	352
Processing private manuscript cols	GILSON, Barbara J.	(NY)	437
Professional collection education	CORCORAN, Frances E.	(IL)	245
Professional education collection	HABER, Elinor L.	(NY)	480
Program & collection development	JAFFARIAN, Sara	(MA)	591
Psychiatry collection development	ASBELL, Mildred S.	(CT)	35
Psychological collection development	LUNDGREN, Janan L.	(IL)	748
Public library collection development	THOMPSON, Betsy J.	(IA)	1229
	MOLZ, Jean B.	(MD)	854
	FOGAL, Annabel E.	(PA)	387
Public library media collections	FLYNN, Barbara L.	(IL)	386
Public school library collections	SPAULDING, Nancy J.	(TX)	1172
Rare & special collection	PERSHE, Frank F.	(MO)	961
Rare book collection	CAUSLEY, Monroe S.	(NJ)	195
Rare book collections	SMITH, Ledell B.	(LA)	1157
	MULVIHILL, Maureen E.	(NY)	878
Rare books subject collections	WOLFE, Marice	(TN)	1361
Record & tape collection	GORDON, Thelma S.	(CT)	452
Record collection	MARTUCCI, Louis U.	(CA)	779
Record collection development	MILLER, Charles W.	(NJ)	836
Recorded sound collections	STEEL, Suzanne F.	(MS)	1183
Records & collection management	WALKER, Heather C.	(DC)	1295
Reference & collection development	NING, Mary J.	(CA)	904
	SIBLEY, Elizabeth A.	(CA)	1135
	POINTON, Louis R.	(IL)	980
	STALZER, Rita M.	(IL)	1179
	TRINKAUS-RANDALL, Gregor	(MA)	1257
	NDENGA, Viola W.	(MI)	890
	CASTO, Lisa A.	(TX)	194
	BERNIER, Gaston	(PQ)	89
Reference & collection maintenance	WILES-HAFFNER, Meredith L.	(PA)	1339
Reference & collection management	BRUCE, Robert K.	(MN)	149
Reference & Virginiana collection	EHLKE, Nancy K.	(VA)	339
Reference collection development	MARIE, Jacquelyn	(CA)	770
	PORTILLA, Teresa M.	(CA)	985
	WATERS, Marie B.	(CA)	1308
	BROWN, Pia T.	(FL)	147
	MIDDLETON, Beverly D.	(NC)	833
	MOORE, Kathryn L.	(NC)	860
	REIK, Constance	(NH)	1020
	COMER, Cynthia H.	(OH)	234
	SCHMITT, John P.	(SC)	1096
	DANIEL, Mary H.	(VA)	272
	SKELTON, W M.	(ON)	1146
	BARLOW, Elizabeth A.	(SK)	57
Reference collections	SMITH, Phillip A.	(CA)	1159
	SAMMATARO, John A.	(MA)	1078
	MCCRACKEN, Ronald W.	(ON)	799
Reference service & collection devlmnt	WILCOX, Patricia F.	(WI)	1338
Reference service, collection management	WILLIAMS, Calvin	(MI)	1342
Reference services & collections	NEUBAUER, Richard A.	(MA)	896
	SAMMATARO, Linda J.	(TN)	1078
Rehabilitation collection development	COUCH, Susan H.	(PA)	250
Religious collections	LAMBREV, Garrett I.	(CA)	691
Reorganization of collections	GORMAN, Audrey J.	(NJ)	452
Report collections	LATYSZEWSKYJ, Maria A.	(ON)	702
Research collection development	KRUMMEL, Donald W.	(IL)	680
Research library collection development	KELLER, Michael A.	(CT)	635
Russian collection development	BAER, Eberhard A.	(VA)	44
School collection development	HULLUM, Cheri J.	(GA)	573
School library & media collections	TERWILLEGAR, Jane C.	(FL)	1232
School library collection & development	BERK, Nancy G.	(AZ)	87
School library services & collections	DAIGNEAULT, Audrey I.	(CT)	270
Schools, collection development	DEVEREAUX, Amy E.	(CA)	297
Science & medical collection development	HUNTER, John H.	(TX)	576
Science & medicine collection devlpmnt	MICHAELS, Debbie D.	(NJ)	832
Science & technical collection devlpmnt	PASTERCZYK, Catherine E.	(NM)	946

COLLECTIONS (Cont'd)

Science & technology collection
devlpmnt SABIN, Robert G. . . . . . . (AL) 1072
ANDREWS, Karen L. . . . (CA) 26
ROHMANN, Gloria P. . . . (NY) 1050
Science collection development WALTERS, Roberta J. . . (CA) 1301
KHAN, Syed M. . . . . (MA) 646
WILT, Charles F. . . . . . (OH) 1353
STIRLING, Isabel A. . . . . (OR) 1195
SMITH, Charles R. . . . . . (TX) 1153
Sciences collection development RICKER, Alison S. . . . . . (OH) 1031
Secondary school collections RIFFEY, Robin S. . . . . . (OH) 1033
Selection & collection development WHEELER, Helen R. . . . (CA) 1329
CUMLET, Harolyn S. . . . (LA) 264
STURCKEN, Rodney A. . . (LA) 1205
Serial collection devlpmnt &
management CONWAY, Susan L. . . . . (NV) 239
Serial control & collection
development MANDAL, Mina R. . . . . . (NY) 764
Serials collection development CENTING, Richard R. . . . (OH) 196
BOCHTE, Terrence C. . . (WI) 109
Shaker collection ADAMS, Barbara M. . . . . (DE) 4
Shifting & interfiling collections MILLER, Scott W. . . . . . . (NY) 842
Slavic collection development URBANIC, Allan J. . . . . (CA) 1269
CANEVARI DE PAREDES,
Donna A. . . . . (SK) 178
Slavic collections ALTENBERGER, Alicja . . (MA) 18
Slavic studies collection development WAWRO, Wanda T. . . . . (NY) 1311
Slide collection KLEEBERGER, Patricia L. (MD) 658
Slide collection development GANGL, Susan D. . . . . . (MN) 416
Slide collection evaluation PRINS, Johanna W. . . . . (NY) 993
Slide collection organization &
devlpmnt PRINS, Johanna W. . . . . (NY) 993
Slide collections ABRAMS, Leslie E. . . . . (SC) 3
WHITE, Lynda S. . . . . . . (VA) 1331
Small high school collections SHEPHERD, Rex L. . . . . (IA) 1127
Small public library collections RASKA, Ginny . . . . (TX) 1009
Social sci & humanities col
development DUPRE, Monique . . . . . . (ON) 327
Social science collection development NESBITT, Renee D. . . . . (CA) 896
GROVE, Shari T. . . . . . . (MA) 474
MAJOR, Marla J. . . . . . . (MI) 762
Social sciences collection
development MYERS, Robert C. . . . . . (KS) 885
ROMANS, Lawrence M. . (TN) 1052
Software collection development CHIANG, Katherine S. . . (NY) 207
Software engineering collection SOUCIE, Yan Y. . . . . (OR) 1169
Sound recording collection
development SAUNDERS, Sharon K. . (PA) 1084
Sound recordings collection ROSENBURG, Betsy R. . (CT) 1056
Sound recordings collection
development EARNEST, Jeffrey D. . . . (AR) 332
FOLLET, Robert E. . . . . . (TX) 388
ERICSON, Margaret D. . . (NY) 353
Sound recordings collections MILLER, Bryan M. . . . . . (NM) 836
Southwest collections BARZELATTO, Elba G. . . (NJ) 62
Spanish & Latin American collections PAREDES-RUIZ, Eudoxio
Spanish collection development B. . . . . (SK) 940
CARDENAS, Mary E. . . . (SAF) 180
CHAVEZ, Linda . . . . (CA) 204
Spanish language collection
Spanish language collection
development SIMAS, Therese C. . . . . (CA) 1139
BETANCOURT, Ingrid T. (NJ) 92
Spanish language collections CADY, Steven R. . . . . . . (CA) 170
Special art collections NESBURG, Janet A. . . . . (MI) 896
Special col management & appraisal WEISS, Egon A. . . . . . . (NY) 1320
Spcl cols exploitation internationally HEANEY, Henry J. . . . . . (SCT) 518
Special government collection KOCH, Patricia J. . . . . . (MT) 667
Special libraries & collections WATSON, Linda S. . . . . (AL) 1309
Special library collection development POST, Linda C. . . . . (CA) 986
State collections JONES, H G. . . . . (NC) 613
Storytelling, collection development HOUSEWARD, Bernice A. (MI) 563
Swedish-Americana collection
development WESTERBERG, Kermit B. (IL) 1326
Tax collection SCHIELACK, Tricia J. . . (TX) 1092
Teaching collection development TRYON, Jonathan S. . . . (RI) 1259
Teaching collection devlpmnt,
publishing HUMPHRY, James . . . . . (NY) 574
Technical collection development SAKAI, Diane H. . . . . . . (HI) 1076

COLLECTIONS (Cont'd)

Technical services & collection
devlpmnt FEINER, Arlene M. . . . . . (IL) 369
Technology collection development SMITH, Charles R. . . . . . (TX) 1153
Test collection development JORDAN, Robert P. . . . . (IA) 616
Test collections WHEELER, Claudia J. . . (IL) 1328
MANDEL, Debra H. . . . . (MA) 764
Theatre collection MCCABE, James P. . . . . (PA) 793
Theatre collections development KAHAN, Gerald . . . . (GA) 621
Theatrical collection development CURTIN-STEVENSON,
Mary C. . . . . (MA) 266
Theological, bibl, collection devlpmnt ERDEL, Timothy P. . . . . . (JAM) 352
Theological collection development BURDICK, Oscar C. . . . . (CA) 158
MINDEMAN, George A. . . (CA) 845
HADIDIAN, Dikran Y. . . . (PA) 482
SALGAT, Anne M. . . . . . (PA) 1076
OLSEN, Robert A. . . . . . (TX) 921
Theological collections HAIR, William B. . . . . (TN) 484
STROUD, John N. . . . . . (WV) 1203
Theology & religion collection
devlpmnt CAMP, Thomas E. . . . . . (TN) 175
ROONEY, Eugene M. . . . (DC) 1053
Theology collection development BUNDY, David D. . . . . . (KY) 157
SIVIGNY, Robert J. . . . . (VA) 1144
Training & collection development DAVIS, Denise . . . . (MD) 278
SALEY, Stacey . . . . (NY) 1076
20th century political collections VOGT, Sheryl B. . . . . . . (GA) 1287
Video & film collection development GORSEGNER, Betty D. . (WI) 452
Video collection NEWMARK-KRUGER,
Barbara . . . . (NJ) 900
WITT, Susan T. . . . . (NY) 1358
Video collection consultant REID, Margaret L. . . . . . (IL) 1019
Video collection development WISE, Ronnie W. . . . . . . (MS) 1357
CANTWELL, Mary L. . . . (OH) 179
Video collections MILLER, Michael D. . . . . (NY) 841
Videocassette collection building AROS, Andrew A. . . . . . (CA) 34
Visual resource collection AUCHSTETTER, Rosann
M. . . . . (IN) 38
Vocational collection development SAKAI, Diane H. . . . . . . (HI) 1076
Weeding collections MARTIN, Jess A. . . . . . . (TN) 776
Western European collection
development HUETING, Gail P. . . . . . . (IL) 570
Women's collection LOWMAN, Judith T. . . . . (IL) 744
Women's collections CHAFF, Sandra L. . . . . . (PA) 197
Women's studies collection BRANT, Susan L. . . . . . . (WI) 129
Women's studies collection
development REDFERN, Bernice I. . . . (CA) 1014
CANEVARI DE PAREDES,
Donna A. . . . . (SK) 178
Young adult collection development MEYERS, Kathleen H. . . (AZ) 831
RUBINSTEIN, Roslyn . . . (NY) 1065

COLLECTIVE (See also Negotiations)

Collective bargaining COOLMAN, Jacqueline . . (CA) 241
CRANE, Hugh M. . . . . . . (MA) 255
MORRIS, Irving . . . . (NY) 866

COLLEGE (See also Academic, Campus, Graduate, Higher, Off-Campus, Two-Year, Undergraduate, University)

Administration, community college libs HELLER, Nancy M. . . . . (NY) 524
Administration of college libraries MCKEE, Christopher . . . . (IA) 810
Administration of college library MCVEY, Susan C. . . . . . (OK) 818
Art colleges FOWLER, Michele R. . . . (OH) 394
Collecting college records VARGA, Nicholas . . . . . . (MD) 1278
College & library administration VEIT, Fritz . . . . (IL) 1281
College & research libraries TURNER, Frank L. . . . . . (TX) 1264
College & school accreditation FITZPATRICK, Kelly . . . (MD) 383
College & school library administration BROWN, Thomas M. . . . (WV) 148
College & university archives REYNOLDS, Jon K. . . . . (DC) 1025
MAHER, William J. . . . . . (IL) 760
BARTKOWSKI, Patricia . (MI) 61
DUNLAP, Barbara J. . . . (NY) 326
STOUT, Leon J. . . . . (PA) 1198
College & university libraries BERRY, John W. . . . . . . (IL) 90
WILLIAMSON, William L. (WI) 1348

COLLEGE (Cont'd)

College & university library admin	GITLER, Robert L.	(CA)	438
	KONDELIK, John P.	(IN)	670
	YOUNG, Tommie M.	(NC)	1383
	ALEXANDER, Shirley B.	(TX)	12
College & university teaching	GUENTHER, Charles J.	(MO)	475
College archives	KNAPP, Peter J.	(CT)	663
	THORSTENSSON, Edith J.	(MN)	1243
	VAN BENTHUYSEN, Robert F.	(NJ)	1272
	GORCHELS, Clarence C.	(OR)	451
	HUX, Roger K.	(SC)	579
	SCOBELL, Elizabeth H.	(WV)	1106
College history	GREENSLADE, Thomas B.	(OH)	465
College level library instruction	OAKLEY, Adeline D.	(MA)	913
College librarianship	SHERIDAN, John B.	(CO)	1127
	BOURDON, Cathleen J.	(IL)	119
	HANNAFORD, William E.	(PA)	496
	BYNAGLE, Hans E.	(WA)	168
College libraries	PANDOLFO, Steven P.	(CA)	937
	SULLIVAN, Mary A.	(GA)	1208
	CALDWELL, John	(IL)	172
	MILLER, Arthur H.	(IL)	835
	FRYE, Larry J.	(IN)	407
	SINGH, Swarn L.	(KS)	1143
	WELSH, Harry E.	(NY)	1323
College library administration	ROSS, Rosemary E.	(AK)	1058
	BOUSFIELD, Humphrey G.	(FL)	119
	HARDESTY, Larry L.	(FL)	499
	SIMMONS, Randall C.	(ID)	1140
	FARBER, Evan I.	(IN)	363
	MORRILL, Walter D.	(IN)	866
	DAVIS, Mavis W.	(MD)	280
	PARKS, James F.	(MS)	943
	JONES, Plummer A.	(NC)	614
	KROBER, Alfred C.	(NY)	679
	MCGOWAN, Sarah M.	(WI)	807
College library advisement	MCCULLOUGH, Jack W.	(NJ)	801
College library collection development	SIMMONS, Randall C.	(ID)	1140
College library directorship	SCARBOROUGH, Ruth E.	(NJ)	1087
College library instruction	SIMMONS, Randall C.	(ID)	1140
College library management	BESEMER, Susan P.	(NY)	91
	BURTON, Robert E.	(NY)	164
	MCDONALD, Joseph A.	(PA)	802
College library service research	MICIKAS, Lynda L.	(PA)	832
College public services	LANDMAN, Lillian L.	(NY)	693
College software publishing	NEEDHAM, Michael V.	(CA)	891
College textbook publisher	THORNTON, Jack N.	(CA)	1242
College textbook publishing	NEEDHAM, Michael V.	(CA)	891
College textbooks	BARCOMB, Wayne A.	(MA)	55
College, university archives	BERKELEY, Edmund	(VA)	87
Community & junior colleges	COHN, John M.	(NJ)	229
Community college	BISHOP, Diane	(CA)	99
Community college administration	MCCRACKEN, Barbara L.	(TX)	799
Community college education	JOHNSON, B L.	(CA)	602
Community college learning resources	KELLER, Jan K.	(CA)	635
	PERSON, Ruth J.	(PA)	961
Community college librarianship	FERRELL, Mary S.	(CA)	373
	REEVES, Cathy L.	(KS)	1016
	HILL, Suzanne P.	(MD)	541
	BOYCE, Emily S.	(NC)	122
	IVERSON, Deborah P.	(WY)	585
Community college libraries	DOLVEN, Mary	(CA)	310
	HOFFMAN, William J.	(CA)	548
	DALE, Doris C.	(IL)	270
	HISLE, W L.	(TX)	544
	BLACKABY, Sandra L.	(WA)	102
Community college library management	GARDNER, W J.	(CO)	418
	RICHARD, Harris M.	(NM)	1027
	HICKEY, Kate D.	(PA)	536
Community college library systems	HISLE, W L.	(TX)	544
Community college, public service	MILES, Ruby A.	(TX)	834
Community college resources	PARADISE, Don M.	(PA)	939
Community colleges	MARRIOTT, Lois I.	(CA)	773
	STEPHENS, Diana C.	(HI)	1188
	BARRETTE, Linda J.	(IL)	59
	HENDERSON, Rosemary	(KS)	527
Community, junior colleges	HUMPHRIES, Beverly H.	(IL)	574
Junior colleges	SLICK, Myrna H.	(PA)	1149

COLLEGE (Cont'd)

Library management, college, school	CORRIGAN, John T.	(PA)	247
Music acquisitions for college libraries	SMILEY, Marilynn J.	(NY)	1151
Online searching in community colleges	BERNHARDT, Frances	(VA)	89
Rare books, college archives	GALLAGHER, Mary E.	(MA)	414
Records research, college history	NELSON, Robert J.	(NY)	895
Reference in business college	SULLIVAN, Cecil G.	(NY)	1207
Research on college faculty	HARDESTY, Larry L.	(FL)	499
Schools, community colleges	SLICK, Myrna H.	(PA)	1149
Small college library administration	OLSEN, Rowena J.	(KS)	921
	SPICER, Orlin C.	(MO)	1174
	GARRETSON, Henry C.	(NY)	420
Small college library cooperation	OLSEN, Rowena J.	(KS)	921
Small college library management	OFFERMANN, Glenn W.	(MN)	917
	PAWLIK, Deborah A.	(PA)	951
	CORMAN, Linda W.	(ON)	246
Two-year college standards	WALLACE, James O.	(TX)	1297

COLONIAL

Colonial history	DALY, John E.	(IL)	271
Colonial records	STEPHENS, Alonzo T.	(TN)	1187

COLORADO

Colorado territorial records	KETELSEN, Terry	(CO)	645

COM

COM catalogs	BOWRIN-MARSH, Donna M.	(CA)	122

COMBUSTION

Combustion science	KITCHENS, Philips H.	(AL)	657

COMEDY

Comedy	TARANOW, Gerda	(CT)	1223

COMIC

Comic books, comic strips	SCOTT, Randall W.	(MI)	1108

COMMERCE (See also Business, Corporate, Industry, Trade)

Commerce & construction industry	MCCONNIE, Mary	(TRN)	798
Commercial & legislative database srchng	SCHOLFIELD, Caroline A.	(MI)	1098
Commercial banking	GROSSMAN, Adrian J.	(NY)	473
Commercial client relations	VALANDRA, Kent T.	(NY)	1271
Commercial databases	PAUL, Nora M.	(FL)	949
Commercial technical services	JACOBS, Peter J.	(CA)	590
Commercial use of special collections	KANE, Katherine	(CO)	625
Technical & tech commercial research	CRABTREE, Sandra A.	(CA)	254
Television commercial databases	LOFTHOUSE, Patricia A.	(IL)	737

COMMODITIES

Securities & commodities audits	JOHNSON, G V.	(IL)	604
Securities & commodities regulatory	JOHNSON, G V.	(IL)	604
Securities & commodities taxes	JOHNSON, G V.	(IL)	604

COMMON

Civil & common law	NARANJO-BOSCH, Antonio A.	(IL)	888
Common market law	ESSIEN, Victor K.	(NY)	354

COMMUNICATION (See also Telecommunication and other headings beginning with TELE)

Administrative & communications systems	MEADOWS, Donald F.	(BC)	819
Audiovisual communications	SINK, Thomas R.	(OH)	1143
Biomedical communications	BADER, Shelley	(DC)	44
	HARRIS, John C.	(MA)	504

COMMUNICATION (Cont'd)

Topic	Name		Page
Biomedical comms & documents delivery	LETT, Rosalind K.	(GA)	719
Broadcasting & communications research	SLOCUM, Leslie E.	(NY)	1150
Business communications management	SLOAN, Cheryl A.	(MD)	1149
Business communications services	MAYNARD, John C.	(ON)	790
Communication	WEEDMAN, Judith	(CA)	1315
	BRACKEN, James K.	(IN)	124
	BERLING, John G.	(MN)	88
Communication among scientists	WALKER, Richard D.	(WI)	1296
Communication & information retrieval	NADEAU, Johan	(PQ)	885
Communication & research	DALRYMPLE, Prudence W.	(IL)	271
Communication design	DAVENPORT, Marilyn G.	(NV)	275
Communication disorders	ZAHARKO, Nancy W.	(MD)	1385
Communication, info, lib relationships	VOIGT, Melvin J.	(CA)	1287
Communication law	PACE, Thomas	(NJ)	933
Communication of information	BERNHARD, Paulette	(PQ)	89
Communication research	CASE, Donald O.	(CA)	191
	PULVER, Thomas B.	(DC)	997
Communication satellites	LIU, Rosa	(DC)	734
Communication skills	OHLEMACHER, Janet H.	(WI)	919
Communication study	ASHEIM, Lester E.	(NC)	35
Communication systems	TILSON, Koleta B.	(TN)	1245
Communication technology in libraries	SHANK, Russell	(CA)	1120
Communications	ITNYRE, Jacqueline H.	(CA)	585
	FRAULINO, Philip S.	(DC)	399
	BRADLEY, Johanna	(IN)	126
	MONACO, James	(NY)	854
	PETTOLINA, Anthony M.	(NY)	965
	QUINN, David J.	(NY)	1000
	ROE, Eunice M.	(PA)	1048
	YOUNT, Natalie W.	(WA)	1384
	THOM, Pat A.	(WI)	1235
	CHALIFOUX, Jean P.	(PQ)	197
Communications & networking software	THOMAS, Hilary B.	(NY)	1236
Communications industry market research	LEIGHTON, Victoria C.	(GA)	714
Communications management	COFFMAN, M H.	(MA)	227
Communications networks	THORSTEINSON, William A.	(NS)	1243
Communications software marketing	CORCHADO, Veronica A.	(CA)	245
Communications sources	ARNESON, Rosemary H.	(VA)	33
Communications systems	ZOROWITZ, Richard D.	(IL)	1390
Communications systems design	BLISS, David H.	(IA)	105
Communications technology	THOMA, George R.	(MD)	1235
Communications, writing, editing	EATENSON, Ervin T.	(TX)	333
Computer & communications in libraries	DUCHESNE, Roderick M.	(ON)	322
Computer communications	RICE, Ronald E.	(CA)	1027
	HAMPTON, Sylvia S.	(RI)	494
	SILVA, Mary E.	(WA)	1138
	KEYS, Sandra A.	(ON)	645
	OHLMAN, Herbert	(SWZ)	919
Corporate communications	KANE, Jean B.	(MA)	624
Corporate communications consulting	MULVIHILL, Maureen E.	(NY)	878
Data communication network management	GETZ, Malcolm	(TN)	430
Data communications	HASSAN, Abe H.	(CA)	511
	BENNETT, Harry D.	(MD)	81
	STELZLE, James J.	(NY)	1186
	HAHN, Susan H.	(PA)	484
	ADAMS, Judith A.	(VA)	5
	WALDE, Norma J.	(VA)	1294
Data communications planning	BARNETT, Becky L.	(GA)	57
Database networking & communications	PASCHAL, John M.	(OK)	945
Electronic communication systems	VAN VELZER, Verna J.	(CA)	1277
Electronic communications	HAYWARD, Edith C.	(AB)	517
Emerging communication media technology	HOPE, Thomas W.	(NY)	557
Engineering & data communications	WIEHN, John F.	(CT)	1336
History of communications	BRAGG, William J.	(TX)	127
Human-computer communications	MEADOW, Charles T.	(ON)	819
Information & communication systems	RUBEN, Brent D.	(NJ)	1064
Information communication	WORTHEN, Dennis B.	(NY)	1369
Internal & external communication	GOODRICH, Nita K.	(AZ)	449

COMMUNICATION (Cont'd)

Topic	Name		Page
Internal communication	REAGAN, Bob	(CA)	1012
Interpersonal communication	ANDERSON, Dorothy J.	(CA)	22
Interpersonal comm & group processes	FLOOD, Barbara J.	(PA)	385
Interpersonal communication training	RUBEN, Brent D.	(NJ)	1064
Interpersonal communications	SHIELDS, Gerald R.	(NY)	1130
Interpersonal communications training	KOSHER, Helene J.	(CA)	672
Interpersonnel communication	HASKELL, Peter C.	(TX)	510
Intra-organization communication	LIBBEY, Miles A.	(NJ)	725
Library automation & communications	KOUNTZ, John C.	(CA)	673
Library communications systems	PLOTKIN, Nathan	(CA)	978
Marketing communications	OJALA, Marydee P.	(KS)	919
	KANE, Jean B.	(MA)	624
	SEITZ, Robert J.	(NY)	1113
Marketing communications, strategic plng	WASERSTEIN, Gina S.	(PA)	1307
Microcomputer communications	CLANCY, Stephen L.	(CA)	215
Oral & written communication	EBERHARD, Neysa C.	(KS)	334
Oral communication	HAYES, L S.	(FL)	516
Organz devlpmnt & communication systems	HUNT, Suellyn	(NY)	575
Organizational communication training	RUBEN, Brent D.	(NJ)	1064
Organizational dynamics & communication	CRETH, Sheila D.	(IA)	258
Organizational planning & communications	LOWRY, Charles B.	(TX)	745
OSI communication protocols	MACLELLAND, Margaret A.	(ON)	757
Patron-staff library communications	BROWN, Carol J.	(TX)	142
PC communications	DENNETT, Stephen C.	(CA)	292
Performing arts, speech communication	KELLY, Richard J.	(MN)	638
Personnel communications	ELDREDGE, Jonathan D.	(NM)	342
Print & audiovisual communications	NORTON, Alice	(CT)	910
Promotional communications	LAMBERT, Shirley A.	(CO)	690
Public relations & communication	GOTHBERG, Helen M.	(AZ)	453
Public relations & communications	TOMLIN, Marsha A.	(OH)	1250
Publications & communications	MOORE, Grace G.	(LA)	859
Satellite communications	SCHABERT, Daniel R.	(NY)	1088
Scholarly & scientific communication	EDELMAN, Hendrik	(NJ)	335
Scholarly communication	OSBURN, Charles B.	(AL)	927
	STIEG, Margaret F.	(AL)	1193
	GEORGE, Mary W.	(NJ)	427
	RICHARDS, Pamela S.	(NJ)	1028
	PURDY, Victor W.	(UT)	998
Scholarly communication for info tech	DOUGHERTY, Richard M.	(MI)	314
Scholarly communications	BRANIN, Joseph J.	(MN)	128
Science information communication	FRY, Bernard M.	(IN)	406
Scientific communication	SIEGEL, Elliot R.	(MD)	1136
	GRIFFITH, Belver C.	(PA)	469
	KRONICK, David A.	(TX)	679
	NADZIEJKA, David E.	(WI)	886
Technical communications	CASTO, Lisa A.	(TX)	194
Telecommunications & data communications	POTEAT, James B.	(NY)	986
Television industry & communication	WERSIG, Gernot	(WGR)	325
Visual communication	AINES, Andrew A.	(MD)	8
Writing history, federal communication	SILVA, Mary E.	(WA)	1138
Written business communication	ROBINSON, Jolene A.	(NY)	1044
Written communication			

COMMUNITY (See also Branch, Extension, Junior, Neighborhood, Two-Year)

Topic	Name		Page
Administration, community college libs	HELLER, Nancy M.	(NY)	524
Administration community library service	WECHTLER, Stephen R.	(NJ)	1315
Automated community information service	MESSINEO, Leonard L.	(KS)	828
Community affairs	THENELL, Janice C.	(OR)	1234
Community analysis	MILLER, Edward P.	(AZ)	837
	STINES, Joe R.	(FL)	1194
	LUEDER, Dianne B.	(IL)	747
	HALE, Martha L.	(KS)	485
	SUMLER, Claudia B.	(MD)	1209
	SMITHEE, Jeannette P.	(NY)	1161
	VERBESEY, J R.	(NY)	1282
	SAULMON, Sharon A.	(OK)	1084
Community & junior colleges	COHN, John M.	(NJ)	229
Community & library liaison	SHANK, Beverly C.	(MA)	1120

COMMUNITY (Cont'd)

Community & library services	PETRIE, Mildred M.	(FL)	965
Community assessments	KENNEDY, Rose M.	(CA)	641
Community branch libraries	BARKLEY, Laura P.	(CA)	57
Community cable television	PORMEN, Paul E.	(OH)	984
Community centers	KENT, Charles D.	(ON)	642
Community college	BISHOP, Diane	(CA)	99
Community college administration	MCCRACKEN, Barbara L.	(TX)	799
Community college education	JOHNSON, B L.	(CA)	602
Community college learning resources	KELLER, Jan K.	(CA)	635
	PERSON, Ruth J.	(PA)	961
Community college librarianship	FERRELL, Mary S.	(CA)	373
	REEVES, Cathy L.	(KS)	1016
	HILL, Suzanne P.	(MD)	541
	BOYCE, Emily S.	(NC)	122
	IVERSON, Deborah P.	(WY)	585
Community college libraries	DOLVEN, Mary	(CA)	310
	HOFFMAN, William J.	(CA)	548
	DALE, Doris C.	(IL)	270
	HISLE, W L.	(TX)	544
	BLACKABY, Sandra L.	(WA)	102
Community college library management	GARDNER, W J.	(CO)	418
	RICHARD, Harris M.	(NM)	1027
	HICKEY, Kate D.	(PA)	536
Community college library systems	HISLE, W L.	(TX)	544
Community college, public service	MILES, Ruby A.	(TX)	834
Community college resources	PARADISE, Don M.	(PA)	939
Community colleges	MARRIOTT, Lois I.	(CA)	773
	STEPHENS, Diana C.	(HI)	1188
	BARRETTE, Linda J.	(IL)	59
	HENDERSON, Rosemary	(KS)	527
Community education & development	GUTHRIE, Virginia G.	(AL)	479
Community group relations	SMOTHERS, Joyce W.	(NJ)	1162
Community health	THOMASSON, George O.	(CO)	1238
	FIORE, Francine	(PQ)	379
Community health information	KNIGHT, Dorothy H.	(IL)	664
Community history, Orange County	FRANK, Anne E.	(CA)	396
Community information	ANTHONY, Carolyn A.	(IL)	28
	BLANKENSHIP, Phyllis E.	(MO)	104
	JOHNSON, Patrelle E.	(NY)	608
	KRAMER, Mollie W.	(NY)	675
	WIERUCKI, Karen A.	(ON)	1337
Community information & referral	FERDUN, Georgenne M.	(CA)	372
	MATZKE, Ellen S.	(MI)	786
	SEKELY, Maryann	(NY)	1113
Community information & referral service	LIGHT, Jane E.	(CA)	726
Community information resources	DAVIS, Natalia G.	(NY)	280
Community information services	BEEBE, Richard J.	(CA)	74
	DAVIES, Jo	(WA)	277
Community information systems	REMINGTON, David G.	(WA)	1022
Community information transfer	SHIRK, John C.	(MN)	1131
Community interaction	CURTIS, Jean E.	(MI)	267
Community, junior colleges	HUMPHRIES, Beverly H.	(IL)	574
Community library service	SPENCER, Caroline P.	(HI)	1173
Community literacy councils	HALEY, Anne E.	(WA)	486
Community needs assessment	HEIL, Kathleen A.	(MD)	521
Community networking	BREDESON, Peggy Z.	(WI)	131
Community newspaper publication	COMPRI, Jeannine L.	(AB)	235
Community outreach	COOPER, Ginnie	(CA)	242
	SCLAR, Marta L.	(CA)	1106
	MEISSNER, Edie A.	(MN)	822
	BRETING, Elizabeth C.	(MO)	133
	OCHS, Phyllis E.	(NY)	915
	GUMPPER, Mary F.	(OH)	477
	BURNETT, Wayne C.	(ON)	162
	DE RONDE, Paula D.	(ON)	294
Community outreach & marketing	WALTER, Virginia A.	(CA)	1300
Community outreach services	PALMORE, Sandra N.	(IL)	937
	HARVELL, Valeria G.	(NJ)	509
Community programming	GRAYBIEL, Luisa	(SK)	460
Community relations	ARMITAGE, Constance	(CO)	32
	O'SHEA, Cornelius M.	(IL)	928
	WOODY, Jacqueline B.	(MD)	1368
	MAXWELL, Martha A.	(MO)	788
	ROBERTS, Jean A.	(MO)	1040
	FONTAINE, Sue	(NY)	388
	BRUCE, Dennis L.	(SC)	149
Community relations & services	WHITNEY, Howard F.	(MA)	1334

COMMUNITY (Cont'd)

Community resource development	MARKEY, Penny S.	(CA)	771
Community service	KERN, Stella V.	(NJ)	643
Community services	BURDASH, David H.	(DE)	158
	RICKERT, Carol A.	(IL)	1032
	TUCHMAN, Helene L.	(MA)	1261
	NEWMAN, Marianne L.	(OH)	899
	STEPHANOFF, Kathryn	(PA)	1187
Cooperative community programs	MAINIERO, Elizabeth T.	(CT)	761
Cultural arts community development	TRASATTI, Margaret S.	(NV)	1254
Developing community support programs	NATHAN, Frances E.	(NY)	889
Library & community liaison	REID, Richard H.	(LA)	1019
Library & community relations	HEFFINGTON, Carl O.	(GA)	520
Library & community relations networking	POSEL, Nancy R.	(PA)	985
Library & info community cooperation	BARTLEY, Linda K.	(DC)	61
Library boards, community relations	GIBSON, Barbara H.	(CT)	431
Nursing, nutrition, community health	FOX, Lynne M.	(CO)	395
Online searching in community colleges	BERNHARDT, Frances	(VA)	89
Outreach services, community services	LONG, Judith N.	(IL)	739
Outreach services to the community	MARTIN, Brian G.	(NY)	775
Programming & community relations	TANG, Grace L.	(NY)	1222
Public & community relations	DRESP, Donald F.	(NM)	319
	O'NEIL, Margaret M.	(NY)	924
Public relations, community involvement	BEATTIE, Brian	(KS)	70
Publicity, public & community relations	PIANE, Mimi	(IN)	969
Religious community archives	PATTERSON, Mary E.	(WA)	948
School library community relations	HASBROUCK, Clara H.	(TN)	510
Schools, community colleges	SLICK, Myrna H.	(PA)	1149
Services to ethnocultural communities	ZIELINSKA, Marie F.	(ON)	1388
Two-person community hospital library	WILLOUGHBY, Nona C.	(NY)	1349

COMPACT (See also CD, CD-I, CD-ROM, Recordings)

Cataloging cassettes & compact discs	SCHWANN, William J.	(MA)	1104
Compact disc	HELGERSON, Linda W.	(VA)	524
Compact disc interactive	GALL, Bert A.	(TN)	413
Compact discs	MOGLE, Dawn E.	(IN)	852
	CAPPAERT, Lael R.	(MI)	180
	KNIESNER, John T.	(OH)	664

COMPANIES (See also Business, Firms, Industry, Mergers)

Acquisitions of information companies	KEON, Edward F.	(NJ)	643
Canadian & US companies & industries	ORLANDO, Richard P.	(PQ)	926
Canadian public company information	BONIN, Denise R.	(BC)	114
Company & industry research	THAU, Richard	(NJ)	1234
Company databases	CORNELIUS, Peter K.	(LUX)	246
Company/industry competitive analysis	WARNER, Claudette S.	(IL)	1305
Company information	GINSBURG, Carol L.	(NY)	438
	WARD, Edith	(NY)	1303
	ZOTTOLI, Danny A.	(NY)	1390
Company information databases	BOYD, Cheryl J.	(MN)	122
Company intelligence	LIU, Jessie	(CT)	734
Company management function	FAST, Louise	(ON)	366
Company, product, & industry data	DLOTT, Nancy B.	(MA)	306
Company research	BELL, Steven J.	(PA)	77
Editing company news brief	WHITE, Jane F.	(MI)	1331
Indexing company documents	PETRY, Robyn E.	(IL)	965
Oil & gas company	WRIGHT, Craig W.	(TX)	1371
Reference, company information	BOODIS, Maxine S.	(PA)	115

COMPARATIVE (See also International)

Comparative automated retrieval systems	O'CONNOR, Sandra L.	(NC)	916
Comparative law	ESSIEN, Victor K.	(NY)	354
	PRATTER, Jonathan	(TX)	990
Comparative librarianship	TING, Lee H.	(IL)	1246
	ASHEIM, Lester E.	(NC)	35
	JOSEY, E J.	(PA)	618
	TAKEUCHI, Satoru	(JAP)	1220

COMPARATIVE (Cont'd)

Comparative library information systems — CARPENTER, Raymond L. (NC) 185
Comparative literature — KELLY, Richard J. (MN) 638
Comparative religion research — SMITH, Robert E. (IN) 1160
Foreign & comparative law — ZOLLER, R T. (WI) 1390
Foreign, international & comparative law — LYMAN, Lovisa (UT) 751
International & comparative libnshp — MAACK, Mary N. (CA) 753
VOSPER, Robert (CA) 1289
PATEL, Jashu (IL) 947
SPILLERS, Roger E. (MN) 1174
HORROCKS, Norman (NJ) 561
DUFFETT, Gorman L. (OH) 323
International comparative librarianship — DANTON, J P. (CA) 274
VEIT, Fritz (IL) 1281
RUFSVOLD, Margaret I. (IN) 1066
CVELJO, Katherine (TX) 268
WILLIAMSON, William L. (WI) 1348
COURRIER, Yves G. (FRN) 251

COMPENSATION (See also Benefits, Pay, Salary)

Compensation — MILLER, Herbert A. (DC) 838
Executive compensation & benefits — KAZANJIAN, Donna S. (NY) 632
Salary & compensation analysis — FRETWELL, Gordon E. (MA) 402

COMPETITIVE

Academic competition — CORNWELL, Linda L. (IN) 247
Business, competitive information — NEWMAN, Robert M. (TX) 899
Company/industry competitive analysis — WARNER, Claudette S. (IL) 1305
Competitive analysis — MILLER, Ralph D. (CA) 841
CARR, Sallyann (DC) 186
MCDANIEL, Sara H. (GA) 801
BRAIMON, Margie S. (NJ) 127
MOUREY, Deborah A. (NY) 874
BORUCKI, Jennifer A. (OH) 117
Competitive assessment — BROCK, Laurie N. (CO) 138
Competitive assessment program — MOYNIHAN, Mary B. (CT) 874
Competitive databases — KENDRIC, Marisa A. (NY) 640
Competitive information — BIRKS, Grant F. (ON) 98
Competitive intelligence — BIRKHOLD, Martha S. (IL) 98
MACIVER, Linda B. (MA) 756
SOLSETH, Gwenn M. (MN) 1166
CHANG, Bernadine A. (NJ) 200
RONDELLI, Marilyn H. (NJ) 1053
LETTIS, Lucy B. (NY) 719
O'GRADY, Jean P. (NY) 918
SEIK, Jo E. (OH) 1112
THOMAS, Sandra L. (OR) 1238
Competitive intelligence systems — MOBLEY, Kathleen S. (KS) 851
Competitive research, analyses — SOUDER, Edith I. (PA) 1169
Competitive tracking, benchmarking — LEWARK, Kathryn W. (CA) 722
Competitor analysis & evaluation — PICKETT, Doyle C. (NJ) 970
Competitor intelligence — MEYER, Andrea P. (CO) 829
GAGNE, Susan P. (CT) 412
HARRIS, Jeanne G. (IL) 504
LANDRY, Ronald (IL) 694
MURPHY, Therese B. (IL) 881
STANAT, Ruth E. (NY) 1179
RYDESKY, Mary M. (TX) 1071
Competitor intelligence systems — SEASE, Sandra A. (NY) 1110
Competitor tracking — CURTIS, Richard A. (CA) 267

COMPUTERS (See also Automation, Mainframe, Microcomputers, Minicomputer, Online, Personal Computers, Turnkey and commercial names of specific computers & computer systems)

Academic computing — CLINE, Nancy M. (PA) 222
Apple & Macintosh computer software — TRAVILLIAN, Mary W. (IA) 1254
Archives of computer industry — BRUEMMER, Bruce H. (MN) 149
Audiovisual, computing in libraries — JAX, John J. (WI) 595
Audiovisual technology, computer appls — NOLAN, Joan (PA) 907
Audiovisuals including computers — RYAN, Sharon K. (OH) 1071
Automation & computer applications — POWELL, Mary E. (TX) 988
Automation & computer services — FRADKIN, Bernard (IL) 395
Automation, computerization — GARA, Otto G. (NY) 416

COMPUTERS (Cont'd)

Bibliographic computer searching — KNAPP, Sara D. (NY) 663
NESBIT, Kathryn W. (NY) 896
Biomedical computerized lit searching — DORNER, Marian T. (OH) 313
Biomedical computing — JAMES, Brent C. (UT) 592
Blind library services, computers — ROATCH, Mary A. (AZ) 1038
Business & computer information — PETTEY, Brent (CA) 965
Business & computer information sources — AHERN, Camille P. (NH) 8
Cataloging utilizing small computers — HOBBS, Henry C. (MB) 545
Children's literature computer software — FEUERHELM, Jill A. (OR) 374
Clinical laboratory computing — FRIEDMAN, Bruce A. (MI) 403
Cognitive rehabilitation & computers — SHANEFIELD, Irene D. (PQ) 1120
Compiling computer science bibliography — WEINER, Carolynn N. (NY) 1318
Computer & communications in libraries — DUCHESNE, Roderick M. (ON) 322
Computer & software technology — AMMERMAN, Jackie W. (GA) 20
Computer & technical liaison — EVANS, Mark S. (FL) 357
Computer & telecommunications technology — BAILEY, Charles W. (NC) 46
Computer & video based instruction — BUTLER, David W. (CA) 166
Computer & video education — KRAUSE, Roberta A. (IL) 676
Computer applicability — PETERSON, Randall T. (IL) 964
Computer application & data management — GREGORY, Melissa R. (IL) 466
Computer application & management — COLDWELL, Charles P. (WA) 230
Computer applications — VEENSTRA, Robert J. (AL) 1281
MARCHIANO, Marilyn C. (CA) 768
RUDOLPH, Anne L. (CA) 1066
HORRIGAN, John J. (CT) 560
MANUEL, Larry L. (DE) 767
BOULA, Lillian Y. (FL) 119
REZNICK, Evi P. (GA) 1025
MATHER, Becky R. (IA) 783
FENSKE, Ruth E. (IL) 371
GRUMBLING, Dennis K. (IL) 474
JOHNSTON, James R. (IL) 610
LI, Richard T. (IL) 725
ROTT, Richard A. (IL) 1060
SWANSON, Don R. (IL) 1213
TZE-CHUNG, Li (IL) 1267
WELCH, Eric C. (IL) 1321
DEANE, Paul D. (IN) 284
KASER, John A. (IN) 628
ROSENTHAL, Marylu C. (MA) 1057
PAPENFUSE, Edward C. (MD) 939
QUINN, Carol J. (MD) 1000
ANDERSON, Marjorie E. (ME) 24
BURESH, Reggie F. (MN) 158
GRAZIER, Dorothy W. (NH) 460
LEVINE, Riesa E. (NJ) 721
MAYNES, Kathleen R. (NJ) 790
TIEDRICH, Ellen K. (NJ) 1244
PRINZ, Jane A. (NY) 993
SMITH, Mark J. (NY) 1158
WISEMAN, Karin M. (NY) 1357
AMICONE, Janice L. (PA) 20
FORD, Sylverna V. (PA) 390
LYONS, Evelyn L. (PA) 753
EDELEN, Joseph R. (SD) 335
GAUDET, Susan E. (TN) 422
MILLER, Karl F. (TX) 839
WALKER, Tamara E. (TX) 1296
REHMS, Jane C. (WA) 1017
BURGIS, Grover C. (ON) 159
CRAVEN, Timothy C. (ON) 256
ALSANARRAI, Hafidh S. (SDA) 17
Computer applications & automation — SHEPARD, Clayton A. (IN) 1126
Computer applications & mgmt consulting — BOSSEAU, Don L. (CA) 117
Computer applications & systems — KIRKWOOD, Francis T. (ON) 655
Computer applications development — BROWN, Jeanne I. (NJ) 145
Computer applications in banking — BOSMA, Elske M. (ON) 117
Computer applications in libraries — WOLF, Nola M. (CA) 1360
HUPP, Sharon W. (CT) 577
GLUCK, Myke H. (NC) 442
MINEMIER, Betty M. (NY) 845

COMPUTERS (Cont'd)

Computer applications in libraries

SMITH-GREENWOLD,
    Kathryn R. . . . . (NY) 1162
TOSTEVIN, Patricia A. . . (WA) 1252
MOON, Jeffrey D. . . . . . . (ON) 857

Computer applications in schools   WEST, Marian S. . . . . . . (MI) 1326
Computer applications to acquisitions   DELONG, Douglas A. . . . (IL) 290
Computer applications to instruction   TERWILLIGER, Gloria P. (VA) 1232
Computer applications to libraries   KRANCH, Douglas A. . . . (IA) 676
    YARBROUGH, Joseph W. (MI) 1378
Computer applications to writing   SCHWARTZ, James M. . . (SD) 1104
Computer assistance   ROBINSON, David A. . . . (OH) 1043
Computer assistance to students   BLAIR, Sharon K. . . . . . . (SC) 103
Computer book indexing   GARCIA, Kathleen J. . . . (NY) 417
Computer books & software   BLAKE, Harry W. . . . . . . (CA) 103
Computer catalog instruction   HOCKEL, Kathleen N. . . (CA) 545
Computer cataloging   GRAY, Shirley M. . . . . . . (NY) 460
Computer catalogs   MOSS, Barbara J. . . . . . (IL) 872
Computer center management   BROWNRIGG, Edwin B. . (CA) 149
Computer circulation systems   WAGNER, Robin O. . . . . (IL) 1292
Computer communications   RICE, Ronald E. . . . . . . (CA) 1027
    HAMPTON, Sylvia S. . . . (RI) 494
    SILVA, Mary E. . . . . (WA) 1138
    KEYS, Sandra A. . . . . . . (ON) 645
    OHLMAN, Herbert . . . . . (SWZ) 919
Computer conferencing   GRIEVE, Shelley . . . . . . (OH) 468
Computer conversions   LANE, Elizabeth J. . . . . (NY) 694
Computer coordinating   DAVIS, Judy R. . . . . (NC) 279
Computer coordination   HOERGER, Helen L. . . . (MI) 547
Computer curriculum development   BIHLER, Charles H. . . . . (CT) 96
Computer data entry   MURRAY, Theresa A. . . (IL) 882
Computer database   CLARK, David L. . . . . . . (CA) 216
Computer database cataloging   VAN HORN, Neal F. . . . (OR) 1275
Computer database development   HARWELL, Trudy J. . . . . (AZ) 509
Computer database indexing   LEE, Lydia H. . . . . (CA) 710
Computer database searching   NICHOLS, Amy S. . . . . . (AL) 901
    ADAMO, Clare . . . . (CT) 4
    ECKWRIGHT, Gail Z. . . . (ID) 335
    ANES, Joy R. . . . . (IL) 27
    HATTENDORF, Lynn C. . (IL) 512
    KINNERSLEY, Ruth T. . . (IL) 653
    WORRELL, Diane F. . . . (NC) 1369
    HABER, Mark N. . . . . . . (NY) 481
    MANDERNACK, Scott B. (WI) 765
    MILTON, Ardyce A. . . . . (WI) 845
Computer database structure   MARTINEZ, Jane A. . . . (NJ) 779
Computer databases   LAZINGER, Susan S. . . . (CT) 706
    JONES, David E. . . . . . . (NJ) 612
    O'DONNELL, Maureen D. (NY) 917
    BAKER, Carol J. . . . . . . (OH) 48
    THOMAS, Barbara C. . . . (TX) 1236
    VAN SICKLEN, Lindsay L. (VA) 1277
    WARD, Carol T. . . . . (VA) 1303
    BURSON, Scott F. . . . . . (WA) 163
    BOSMA, Elske M. . . . . . (ON) 117
Computer desktop publishing   MOLLO, Terry . . . . (NY) 853
Computer documentation   SAUNDERS, Vinette A. . (DC) 1085
    RIDER, Philip R. . . . . . . (IL) 1032
    MCGEE, Ruby T. . . . . . . (MA) 805
Computer education   MIDDLESWART, Patricia
    A. . . . . (IA) 833
    TROUTNER, Joanne J. . (IN) 1258
    GARDNER, Laura L. . . . (MO) 418
Computer engineering databases   WOJCIKIEWICZ, Carol A. (MI) 1359
Computer file bibliographic control   HERMAN, Elizabeth . . . . (CA) 531
Computer graphics   TYLER, Sharon R. . . . . . (CA) 1266
    ROBB, Thomas W. . . . . (DC) 1038
    VAUGHAN, John . . . . . . (NY) 1279
Computer hardware & software   GRIFFIN, Hillis L. . . . . . . (CA) 468
    FALK, Howard . . . . (NJ) 362
    FERRIN, Eric G. . . . . (PA) 373
    BELL, David B. . . . . (SC) 76
Computer hardware & software
    manuals   CASSAR, Ann . . . . (PA) 193
Computer hardware & software
    reference   ROBSON, Amy K. . . . . . (IL) 1045
Computer health ergonomics issues   MILLER, R B. . . . . (CA) 841
Computer high tech databases   CHICHESTER, Gerald C. (CT) 208
Computer implementation   CHICCO, Giuliano . . . . . (NY) 208

COMPUTERS (Cont'd)

Computer indexing data management   SCHLICHTING, Catherine
    N. . . . . (OH) 1094
Computer indexing systems   SEMONCHE, Barbara P. (NC) 1115
Computer industry   JAMESON, Martha E. . . . (IL) 592
    KORBER, Nancy . . . . . . (NH) 671
    LAUB, Barbara J. . . . . . . (NJ) 702
Computer industry & applications   BJORNER, Susan N. . . . (MA) 100
Computer industry databases   MASTERS, Kathy B. . . . (CT) 782
    CLIFT, Crystal A. . . . . . . (MN) 222
Computer industry research   KRUSE, Luanne M. . . . . (TX) 681
Computer industry resources   LAPENSKY, Barbara A. . (MN) 697
Computer information   AUSTIN, Rhea C. . . . . . . (MD) 40
Computer information srvs
    environment   SCHWALLER, Marian C. (MA) 1104
Computer info sources, end-user
    systems   GODT, Carol . . . . (MO) 443
Computer input & training   THACKER, Timothy M. . . (WV) 1233
Computer inservice   WALKER, Patricia A. . . . (MO) 1296
Computer instruction   COOPER, William E. . . . (CA) 244
    WAGNER, A C. . . . . (NY) 1291
    LINDSEY, Nancy L. . . . . (TN) 730
Computer laboratories   ARNY, Philip H. . . . . (LA) 34
Computer laboratory coordination   WIRTANEN, James . . . . (ND) 1356
Computer laboratory coordinator   TRIM, Kathryn . . . . (MI) 1256
Computer laboratory design   LEVEILLEE, Louis R. . . . (RI) 719
Computer law   WARRICK, Thomas S. . . (DC) 1307
Computer library-oriented programs   O'BRIEN, Doris J. . . . . . (CT) 914
Computer literacy   HALLBERG, Sharon P. . . (CA) 489
    BADER, Shelley . . . . (DC) 44
    BURGESS, Barbara J. . . (IA) 159
    BARTLETT, Gwenell J. . . (KS) 61
Computer literacy for students   HUNTER, Cecilia A. . . . . (TX) 576
Computer literacy skills   VALLAR, Cynthia L. . . . . (MD) 1271
Computer literacy software   ROSEN, Elizabeth M. . . . (CA) 1055
Computer literacy training   NEWHARD, Eleanor M. . (CA) 899
    ARNY, Philip H. . . . . (LA) 34
Computer literature searching   BELANGER, Sandra E. . . (CA) 75
    GLENDENNING, Barbara
    J. . . . . (CA) 441
    MONTAG, Diane . . . . . . (CO) 855
    MACKEY, Wendy W. . . . (MA) 757
    LAUTENSCHLAG,
    Elisabeth C. . . . . (PA) 703
    KERSTETTER, Virginia M. (VA) 644
    NOFSINGER, Mary M. . . (WA) 907
Computer management   ALDRICH, Michele L. . . . (DC) 11
    HACKNEY, Judith G. . . . (TX) 481
    STANDIFER, Hugh A. . . (TX) 1179
    ADRIAN, Donna J. . . . . . (PQ) 7
Computer management of collections   QUIGLEY, Suzanne L. . . (OH) 999
Computer management systems   GILLETTE, Robert S. . . . (TX) 435
Computer manipulation of information   KERNS, John T. . . . . (CA) 644
Computer manuals   PRITCHARD, Barbara . . (PA) 994
Computer music   DAVIS, Deta S. . . . . (DC) 278
Computer networking   RANKIN, Jocelyn A. . . . . (GA) 1007
    DONOVAN, Paul . . . . . . (MA) 312
    O'NEILL, Sue . . . . (MD) 924
Computer newspaper indexing   SEMONCHE, Barbara P. (NC) 1115
Computer online searching   WAI, Lily C. . . . . (ID) 1292
    TRICKEY, Katherine M. . (TX) 1256
Computer operating   GAMBLE, Marian L. . . . . (MI) 416
Computer operation   PROSSER, Judith M. . . . (WV) 995
Computer performance   DIENER, Ronald E. . . . . (OH) 302
Computer programming   ZHANG, Foster J. . . . . . (CA) 1387
    SMITH, Randolph R. . . . . (CO) 1159
    HEINRITZ, Fred J. . . . . . (CT) 522
    DREWETT, William O. . . (IL) 319
    SLACH, June E. . . . . (MI) 1147
    KANAFANI, Kyung C. . . (MO) 624
    MCGLOHON, Charlotte L. (NC) 807
    YERKEY, A N. . . . . (NY) 1380
    SCHEEREN, Judith A. . . (PA) 1090
    MINAIKIT, Nonglak . . . . . (THA) 845
Computer programming for libraries   ANDERSEN, Eileen . . . . (WA) 21
Computer programming in BASIC   BRETT, Lorraine E. . . . . (IN) 134
Computer programs for children   VOORS, Mary R. . . . . . . (IN) 1289
Computer reference service
    coordination   KONG, Leslie M. . . . . . . (CA) 670
Computer reference service, scientific   WANAT, Camille A. . . . . (CA) 1302

COMPUTERS (Cont'd)

Computer reference services — HOGAN, Eddy .... (CA) 549
TAYLOR, Anne E. ..... (TX) 1226
Computer research & retrieval — WOLFE, Bardie C. ..... (FL) 1360
Computer resources — MONTGOMERY, Kimberly K. .... (AL) 856
Computer resources for teachers — COLEMAN, Barbara K. ... (OH) 231
Computer scholarship matching service — SHAW, Ben B. .... (TX) 1123
Computer science — GUST, Kathleen D. ..... (CA) 478
VARNER, James H. .... (CO) 1279
COPPOLA, H P. .... (MA) 245
MATTHEWS, Charles E. . (MA) 785
BEDDES, Marianne T. .. (NJ) 73
HOUGHTON, Joan I. ... (NY) 562
HAHN, Susan H. ...... (PA) 484
MYERS, Charles J. ..... (PA) 884
BELL, Charise F. ...... (TX) 76
GOODWIN, C R. .... (AB) 450
FUENTES, Ismael ...... (SPN) 408
Computer science & math — TIMBERS, Jill G. ...... (MI) 1245
Computer science collection development — ENSOR, Pat L. .... (IN) 350
TINSLEY, Geraldine L. .. (PA) 1246
Computer science education — FOX, Edward A. .... (VA) 394
Computer science, high tech industry — SLOAN, Maureen G. ... (OR) 1149
Computer science library — SUBLETTE, Doris L. .... (CA) 1206
Computer science literature — MCDANIEL, Sara H. .... (GA) 801
Computer science resources — CARNES, Mary J. ...... (NE) 183
Computer science, start-up libraries — FUCHS, Karola M. ..... (PA) 408
Computer searches — KALRA, Bhupinder S. .... (IL) 623
KOLLIN, Richard P. ..... (PA) 669
HOFFMAN, Sandra D. ... (PQ) 548
Computer searching — COOPER, William E. ..... (CA) 244
GIBBONS, Carolbeth ... (CA) 431
SCHWENN, Janet M. .... (FL) 1105
SCHACHT, John N. ..... (IA) 1088
SNYDER, Fritz .... (KS) 1164
ADAMS, Deborah L. ..... (MI) 4
SARTORI, Eva M. ...... (NE) 1083
MAMAN, Marie .... (NJ) 764
BUTLER, Barbara E. ..... (NV) 166
BATTOE, Melanie K. .... (NY) 65
BENEDICT, Marjorie A. . (NY) 80
BUSH, Joyce .... (NY) 165
PURSCH, Lenore D. ..... (OH) 998
STARRETT, Patricia L. ... (OH) 1182
VOIGT, Kathleen J. .... (OH) 1287
CONNORS, Kathleen M. . (OR) 238
SAYRE, Samuel R. ...... (OR) 1087
TENOR, Randell B. ..... (PA) 1231
BAILEY, William G. .... (TX) 47
CHISHOLM, Clarence E. (VA) 209
DELONG, Kathleen M. ... (AB) 290
TULLY, Sharon I. ...... (MB) 1262
Computer searching, biological sciences — CULOTTA, Wendy A. .... (CA) 264
Computer searching medical databases — TAPPANA, Kathy A. ..... (OK) 1223
CAMPBELL, Shirley A. ... (TX) 177
ARMSTRONG, Jennifer E. (ON) 32
Computer srchng, online info retrieval — SOUTH, Ruth E. .... (OR) 1169
Computer services — MINICK, Donna J. ..... (CA) 846
ARCARI, Ralph D. ..... (CT) 30
LISI, Susan C. .... (GA) 732
KATZ, William A. ...... (NY) 630
RICHTER, Kathleen A. .. (NY) 1031
Computer skills instruction — JACOBS, Lois S. ...... (MA) 589
Computer software — CROSS, Claudette S. .... (CA) 260
DAVENPORT, Constance B. .... (CA) 275
SANDELL, Judy L. ..... (CA) 1079
JONES, David E. ...... (NJ) 612
STROZIER, Sandra L. .. (OH) 1203
Computer software database — CHICHESTER, Gerald C. (CT) 208
Computer software databases — KOOLISH, Ruth K. ..... (CA) 671
Computer software evaluation — KELLY, Patricia M. .... (MA) 638
Computer software hardware — SHENASSA, Daryoosh .. (IL) 1126
Computer specialist — MARGOLIS, Suzanne M. . (MI) 770
Computer stock market research — HEFFRON, Betsy A. ..... (NY) 520

COMPUTERS (Cont'd)

Computer storage & retrieval — MERRYWEATHER, J M. ... (ON) 827
Computer system administration — PETERSON, Barbara E. .. (PA) 962
Computer system integration — WANG, Gary Y. .... (MA) 1302
Computer system management — GIANGRANDE, Mark G. . (IL) 430
HANAFEE, Valerie ..... (MI) 494
Computer system research & development — DIEHL, Mark .... (IL) 302
Computer systems — HALPIN, Peter .... (DC) 490
AAGAARD, James S. ... (IL) 1
GRIES, James P. .... (IL) 468
BERNARD, Bobbi ...... (MA) 88
BENNETT, Harry D. .... (MD) 81
KOSCHIK, Douglas R. ... (MI) 672
WALKER, M G. .... (NY) 1296
KOOPMAN, Frances A. . (TX) 671
MCCORD, Stanley J. ... (TX) 798
SY, Karen J. .... (WA) 1217
VAILLANCOURT, Alain . (PQ) 1270
GOMEZ, Michael J. .. (WGR) 447
Computer systems analysis — CHRISTY, Ann K. ..... (DC) 212
Computer systems & databases — SPARKS, Marie C. ..... (IN) 1171
Computer systems & online research — REED, Carol A. .... (HI) 1014
Computer systems & software — BURTON, Mary L. ...... (PA) 164
Computer systems design — WHITEHEAD, James M. . (GA) 1332
Computer systems development — POLLARD, Louise ..... (UT) 981
Computer systems for libraries — ELLIOTT, Riette B. ..... (AL) 344
Computer systems in health — BENNETT, David M. .... (AUS) 81
Computer systems integration — SPYKERMAN, Bryan R. .. (UT) 1177
Computer systems management — MITCHELL, Betty J. .... (CA) 848
Computer systems training — ROBAR, Terri J. .... (FL) 1038
Computer technology — JARAMILLO, George R. .. (CO) 594
SHAPIRO, Barbara G. .. (NY) 1121
TEPE, Ann S. .... (OH) 1231
DRIEHAUS, Rosemary H. (PA) 320
Computer technology directory — LEE, Douglas E. .... (NY) 709
Computer technology for high sch libs — TOLMAN, Bonnie B. .... (MI) 1249
Computer training — FERDUN, Georgenne M. . (CA) 372
FISHER, Georgeann .... (MO) 381
RAPPAPORT, Susan E. .. (NY) 1008
STOCK, Carole G. ..... (WA) 1195
Computer training & development — TABORN, Kym M. ..... (CA) 1219
Computer training & programming — NEUWILLER, Charlene .. (WGR) 897
Computer training staff & students — DUHAMELL, Lynnette H. (IN) 324
Computer tutorials database searching — CARUSO, Nicholas C. .. (PA) 190
Computer typesetting & interfacing — MEDINA, Ildefonso M. .. (NY) 820
Computer usage training — BERG, David C. .... (MN) 84
Computer use — BENDER, Nancy W. ..... (MA) 79
JONES, John W. ...... (NC) 613
HABAN, Mary F. ...... (VA) 480
Computer use & programming — CLAPP, David F. .... (IL) 215
Computer use in libraries — MOLLER, Steffen A. .... (WA) 853
Computer use in media center — CARTER, Ann M. ...... (VA) 189
Computer use in school libraries — WHITNEY, Karen A. .... (AZ) 1334
Computer utilities for education — COLCLASURE, Marian S. . (AR) 230
Computer utilization — DAVIS, Bernice .... (IN) 277
WATERS, Bill F. .... (MO) 1308
Computer utilization in libraries — HILAND, Leah F. .... (IA) 538
Computer word processing — COUP, William A. ...... (FL) 251
Computer-aided indexing — AGEE, Victoria V. ...... (MD) 7
BUCHAN, Ronald L. .... (MD) 153
SILVESTER, June P. ... (MD) 1139
Computer-aided indexing for records — FROST, Debra R. ...... (CO) 406
Computer-aided simulation — ALSANARRAI, Hafidh S. . (SDA) 17
Computer-assisted indexing — POFELSKI, David ...... (IL) 979
SCHROEDER, Sandra J. . (IL) 1100
QUINN, Sidney .... (MD) 1000
LINZER, Elliot .... (NY) 732
JOSLYN, Camille ...... (VA) 618
Computer-assisted instruction — CATER, Judy J. .... (CA) 194
SHAMS, Kamruddin .... (CA) 1120
WILLIAMS, Valencia ... (CA) 1347
PROVINCE, William R. .. (IL) 996
TEO, Elizabeth A. ...... (IL) 1231
DOLAK, Frank J. ...... (IN) 309
GERRITY, Marline R. ... (MO) 429
NIPP, Deanna .... (NJ) 904
FITZGERALD, Patricia A. (PA) 382
LARSON, Mary E. ..... (PA) 699

COMPUTERS (Cont'd)

Computer-assisted instruction

	ANDERSON, Kari D. . . . (VA)	24

Computer-assisted instruction lib syst | DICARLO, Michael A. . . . (LA) | 300
Computer-assisted learning | OLIVE, J F. . . . . (AL) | 921
Computer-assisted legal research | DOHERTY, Walter E. . . . (AZ) | 309
| | WIEBELHAUS, Richard J. . (AZ) | 1336
| | CASTETTER, Karla M. . . (CA) | 194
| | GRIGST, Denise J. . . . . . (CA) | 470
| | JONES, Michael D. . . . . . (CA) | 614
| | MOORE, Gregory B. . . . . (CA) | 859
| | WERNER, O J. . . . . (CA) | 1325
| | WATERS, Sally G. . . . . . (FL) | 1308
| | GRIFFITH, Cary J. . . . . . (MN) | 469
| | ELAM, Kristy L. . . . . . . (MO) | 341
| | COCHRAN, J W. . . . . . (MS) | 225
| | O'CONNOR, Sandra L. . . (NC) | 916
| | DESMOND, Andrew R. . . (NY) | 295
| | D'AMORE, Denice M. . . (OH) | 272
| | HARVAN, Christine C. . . (PA) | 509
| | SHAW, Ben B. . . . . (TX) | 1123

Computer-assisted management | PRETLOW, Delores Z. . . . (VA) | 992
Computer-assisted nursing instruction | GUENTHER, Jody . . . . . (TX) | 475
Computer-assisted reference | SCHOLAND, Julia E. . . . (CA) | 1098
| | TALALAY, Kathryn M. . . (IN) | 1220
| | RICCI, Patricia L. . . . . . (MN) | 1026
Computer-assisted reference service | BALDWIN, Charlene M. . (AZ) | 51
Computer-assisted reference services | WILKINSON, David W. . . (CA) | 1340
Computer-assisted research | JOHNSRUD, Thomas E. . (CA) | 609
| | SHELAR, James W. . . . . (DC) | 1125
| | HINSON, Karen C. . . . . (MD) | 543
| | MCKENZIE, Elizabeth M. (MO) | 811
| | CARRINGTON, Bessie M. (NC) | 186
| | BEJNAR, Thaddeus P. . . (NM) | 75
| | MCGOEY, Richard P. . . . (NM) | 807
| | GLOECKNER, Donna S. . (NY) | 441
Computer-assisted text retrieval | PRICKETT, Dan S. . . . . (OH) | 993
Computer-associated legal research | MOYER, Holley M. . . . . (NJ) | 874
Computer-based applications | PEPPER, David A. . . . . (BC) | 958
Computer-based bibliographic info syst | COCHRANE, Pauline A. . (NY) | 226
Computer-based education | SIEGEL, Martin A. . . . . (IL) | 1136
Computer-based indexing | FARLEY, Alfred E. . . . . (KS) | 364
| | COLON, Carlos W. . . . . (LA) | 234
| | LUDGIN, Donald H. . . . (ME) | 746
Computer-based information management | WACHTER, Margery C. . . (FRN) | 1290
Computer-based information services | FRIEND, Gary I. . . . . . . (DC) | 404
| | BYRN, William H. . . . . . (MA) | 169
Computer-based information systems | SAWYER, Edmond J. . . . (DC) | 1086
| | PARK, Margaret K. . . . . (GA) | 941
| | RUSH, James E. . . . . . . (OH) | 1068
Computer-based interactive video | HAUSMAN, Julie . . . . . (IA) | 513
Computer-based legal reference | HARBISON, John H. . . . (DC) | 499
Computer-based library management | SIMS, Joyce W. . . . . . . (AL) | 1142
Computer-based reference | LIDSKY, Ella . . . . (NY) | 725
| | FOWLER, Margaret A. . . (MB) | 394
Computer-based reference service | COSTELLO, M R. . . . . . (CA) | 249
| | SPURLOCK, Pauline . . . (CA) | 1177
| | BOROSON, Sarah . . . . . (NY) | 116
| | REINALDO DA SILVA, Joann T. . . . . (MB) | 1021
| | JUOZAPAVICIUS, Danguole T. . . . . (ON) | 620
| | PAPOUTSIS, Fotoula . . . (ON) | 939
| | KELLY, Claire B. . . . . . (PQ) | 637
Computer-based reference services | BEARD, Craig W. . . . . . (AR) | 69
| | NEELY, Jesse G. . . . . . (CA) | 892
| | STEELE, Noreen O. . . . (CT) | 1184
| | MCNAMARA, Emma J. . (DC) | 816
| | PACIFICI, Sabrina I. . . . (DC) | 933
| | DEWBERRY, Claire D. . . (GA) | 298
| | LOTZ, Marsha A. . . . . . (IL) | 742
| | ROMANO, Katherine V. . (IL) | 1052
| | WONG, Mabel K. . . . . . (IL) | 1363
| | MAYEAUX, Thurlow M. . (LA) | 789
| | WOJCIKIEWICZ, Carol A. (MI) | 1359
| | WOODARD, Beth E. . . . (MI) | 1365
| | BEST-NICHOLS, Barbara J. . . . . (NC) | 92

COMPUTERS (Cont'd)

Computer-based reference services

	BUSH, Renee B. . . . . . . (NY)	165

| | DREZEN, Richard . . . . . (NY) | 319
| | HEWITT, Mary L. . . . . . (NY) | 535
| | PIENITZ, Eleanor . . . . . (NY) | 971
| | RICE, Cecelia E. . . . . . . (NY) | 1027
| | SHADE, Ronald H. . . . . (NY) | 1118
| | GATTEN, Jeffrey N. . . . (OH) | 422
| | LUST, Jeanette M. . . . . (OH) | 749
| | BAKER, Judith M. . . . . (PA) | 48
| | KATUCKI, June P. . . . . (PA) | 630
| | PIERCE, Miriam D. . . . . (PA) | 971
| | SCHWARZ, Betty P. . . . (PA) | 1105
| | JOHNSON, Johanna H. . (TX) | 606
| | MCCONNELL, Karen S. . (TX) | 797
| | NOREM, Monica R. . . . (TX) | 908
| | SHIH, Chia C. . . . . (TX) | 1130
| | LARMOUR, Rosamond E. (VA) | 698
| | CRANDALL, Michael D. . (WA) | 255
| | MOFJELD, Pamela A. . . (WA) | 852
| | PASSARELLI, Anne B. . . (WA) | 946
| | EKLAND, Patricia A. . . . (BC) | 341
| | JESKE, Margo . . . . (ON) | 600
| | BONNELLY, Claude . . . (PQ) | 114
| | FIORE, Francine . . . . . . (PQ) | 379
| | KITTUR, Krishna N. . . . (IND) | 657
| | LEE, Lucy T. . . . . (TAI) | 710
Computer-based research | SKRUKRUD, Nora L. . . . (CA) | 1147
Computer-based search services | COOPER, Jean L. . . . . . (VA) | 243
Computer-based text editing | LUDGIN, Donald H. . . . (ME) | 746
Computer-generated newspaper indexing | BOLDRICK, Samuel J. . . (FL) | 112
Computer-human interface design | SIEGEL, Martin A. . . . . (IL) | 1136
Computerization | SMITH, Julie L. . . . . . . (CA) | 1156
| | LAMB, Gertrude . . . . . (CT) | 690
| | CLEGG, Michael B. . . . (IN) | 220
| | SNYDER, David A. . . . . (MA) | 1164
| | MACPHAIL, Jessica . . . (NC) | 758
| | SPANGLER, William N. . (NJ) | 1171
| | BARTLE, Matthew W. . . (NY) | 61
| | LEVIS, Joel . . . . (ON) | 721
| | COLLINS, William P. . . . (ISR) | 233
Computerization in library systems | LEE, Sulan I. . . . . (AL) | 711
Computerization of legal information | HOLOCH, S A. . . . . . . (OH) | 553
Computerization of technical services | PICCOLI, Roberta A. . . . (IL) | 970
Computerization of the library | SOKOLOWSKI, Denise G. (NY) | 1166
Computerization, technical services, ref | HEISE, George F. . . . . . (NJ) | 522
Computerized acquisitions | BOYCE, Harold W. . . . . (IN) | 122
Computerized applications | MULLANE, William H. . . (AZ) | 877
Computerized card cataloging | KIEFER, Marilyn V. . . . . (MI) | 647
Computerized catalogs & databases | VANDERBERG, Patricia S. (CA) | 1273
Computerized circulation | SONDALLE, Barbara J. . . (IL) | 1167
| | KIEFER, Marilyn V. . . . . (MI) | 647
| | JACOBS, Mildred H. . . . (MO) | 589
Computerized circulation systems | HANRATH, Richard A. . . (IL) | 497
| | UNDERHILL, Jan . . . . . (OK) | 1268
| | EMERICK, Michael J. . . . (PA) | 347
Computerized database creation | PASQUARIELLA, Susan K. . . . . (NY) | 946
Computerized database management | HANAFEE, Valerie . . . . . (MI) | 494
Computerized database retrieval | WHITE, Chandlee . . . . . (MA) | 1330
Computerized database searching | HUMPHRIES, Anne W. . (MD) | 574
| | GOURLAY, Una M. . . . . (TX) | 454
Computerized databases | KOTO, Ann S. . . . . (HI) | 673
Computerized documentation | ALLEN, Nancy S. . . . . . (MA) | 15
Computerized files & library materials | BENNETT, Laura B. . . . . (IL) | 82
Computerized indexing | GAUSE, George R. . . . . (TX) | 423
Computerized information | MILLER, Constance R. . . (IN) | 836
Computerized information retrieval | CARRIGAN, John L. . . . (CA) | 186
| | LEE, William D. . . . . . . (CA) | 711
| | WILDE, Daniel U. . . . . . (CT) | 1338
| | MARCUS, Richard S. . . . (MA) | 769
Computerized information services | FOX, Rosalie . . . . (ON) | 395
Computerized information systems | DAY, Melvin S. . . . . . . (VA) | 283
Computerized instructional systems | FROST, Rebecca H. . . . . (PA) | 406
Computerized learning resources | STANKE, Judith U. . . . . (MN) | 1180

COMPUTERS (Cont'd)

Computerized legal research	ANDREWS, Sylvia L. . . .	(IN)	27
	HANLEY, Thomas L. . . .	(OH)	496
	SIMON, Dale	(OR)	1140
Computerized legal research instruction	STOPPEL, Ellen K.	(IA)	1198
Computerized library	SHINER, Sharon L.	(NJ)	1130
Computerized library information system	OMARA, Marie T.	(MD)	923
Computerized library operation	SHIAU, Ian L.	(FL)	1129
Computerized library services	WOOD, Barbara G.	(PA)	1363
Computerized library systems	GRIFFIN, Hillis L.	(CA)	468
	MITCHELL, Joyce P. . . .	(IL)	849
	DRUKE-STICKLER, Janet A.	(NH)	320
	CARTER, Jackson H. . . .	(NM)	189
	SKIDMORE, Kerry F. . . .	(UT)	1146
Computerized literature	WONG, Anita	(ON)	1362
Computerized literature searching	HENTZ, Margaret B. . . .	(CT)	530
	NESBIT, Angus B.	(IL)	896
	JONES, Deborah A.	(IN)	612
	DLOTT, Nancy B.	(MA)	306
	HALL, Robert G.	(MA)	488
Computerized literature training	WONG, Ming K.	(DC)	1363
Computerized local newspaper indexing	KAGANN, Laurie K.	(IL)	621
Computerized management systems	FROST, Rebecca H.	(PA)	406
Computerized medical databases	WALES, Patricia L.	(CT)	1294
Computerized medical records	STEAD, William W.	(NC)	1183
Computerized music cataloging	GRIFFIN, Marie E.	(NJ)	468
	GOODWIN, Charles B. . .	(TX)	450
Computerized processing	TABAR, Margaret E.	(MN)	1219
Computerized psychological databases	WALES, Patricia L.	(CT)	1294
Computerized reference service	MIDDLETON, Robert K. . .	(TX)	833
Computerized reference services	LA BORDE, Charlotte A. .	(CA)	686
	BILLY, George J.	(NY)	97
	BROMLEY, Alice V.	(NY)	140
	GOLDSTEIN, Cynthia N. .	(WA)	446
Computerized research	REDDY, Michael B.	(IL)	1013
Computerized retrieval system	OSTROW, Dianne G. . . .	(MD)	929
Computerized searching	DAVIS, Anne C.	(MI)	277
Computerized system design	JOHNSON, Jane S.	(IL)	605
Computerized system in libraries	TILLETT, Barbara B.	(CA)	1245
Computerized systems	OLIVARES, Jose A.	(CA)	920
Computerized typesetting	GRIES, James P.	(IL)	468
Computerizing collection	WEISLAK, Susan L.	(TX)	1319
Computerizing libraries	KAST, Gloria E.	(CA)	629
Computerizing print & non-print mtrls	BIANCHINO, Cecelia . . .	(IN)	94
Computer-managed programs	BROWN, Anita P.	(NJ)	142
Computer-mediated conferencing	BOND, George	(NH)	113
Computer-readable statistical databases	HENSON, Jane E.	(IN)	529
Computer-related market studies	GOOGINS, Jennifer J. . .	(NY)	450
Computers	SILBERSTEIN, Stephen M.	(CA)	1137
	BELZER, Jack	(FL)	78
	LAGRUTTA, Charles J. . .	(IL)	688
	PROVINCE, William R. . .	(IL)	996
	TURCHI, Marilyn L.	(IL)	1263
	ASHLEY, Roger S.	(MI)	36
	DOBRUNZ, Sally J.	(MO)	307
	VORBEAU, Barbara E. . .	(NH)	1289
	ODERWALD, Sara M. . .	(NJ)	916
	PAWSON, Robert D. . . .	(NJ)	951
	MADSEN, Carol	(NV)	759
	DAVIDSON, Steven J. . .	(NY)	276
	GALLAGHER, Patricia E. .	(NY)	414
	HOFFMAN, Barbara E. . .	(NY)	547
	FEUERHELM, Jill A.	(OR)	374
	EVEY, Patricia G.	(PA)	359
	FIDISHUN, Dolores	(PA)	375
	GAEBLER, Ralph F.	(PA)	411
	SCHEEREN, William O. .	(PA)	1090
	CORBLY, James E.	(WI)	245
	GREEN, Thomas A.	(WI)	462
	WASSINK, Patricia L. . . .	(WI)	1308
Computers & automation	JONES, Clifton H.	(MI)	612
	MCGRIFF, Ronald I.	(MN)	808
Computers & computer repair	RADER, H J.	(WV)	1002
Computers & information systems	HORGAN, Laura A.	(MA)	559

COMPUTERS (Cont'd)

Computers & libraries	RESCH, Peter T.	(SK)	1024
Computers & microcomputers	BOWERS, Alyce J.	(NJ)	120
Computers & psychiatry	LESAGE, Jacques	(PQ)	717
Computers & public access	HERMAN, Felicia G.	(CT)	531
Computers & public libraries	BASSNETT, Peter J. . . .	(ON)	63
Computers & software	MAIN, Isabelle G.	(AZ)	761
Computers & teaching	BRODMAN, Estelle	(NJ)	139
Computers automation	RICHMOND, Diane A. . . .	(IL)	1030
Computers for administrative purposes	FOLEY, Mary D.	(KY)	387
Computers for the disabled	MCHARG, Kathleen M. . .	(OR)	808
Computers in education	GRIFFIN, Kathryn A.	(IA)	468
	LANGHORNE, Mary J. . .	(IA)	696
	NEWTON, Evah B.	(IN)	900
	MATECUN, Marilyn L. . .	(MI)	783
	SORELL, Janice G.	(MN)	1168
	SMITH, Sara B.	(SC)	1160
Computers in health care	COVVEY, H D.	(MB)	252
Computers in instruction	HALE, Robert G.	(CT)	485
	SOLDNER, Nancy C. . . .	(KS)	1166
Computers in law libraries	EICHER, Thomas E.	(IA)	339
Computers in libraries	HU, Robert T.	(IL)	568
	SCHMIDT, Steven J.	(IN)	1096
	GILLMORE, Salley G. . . .	(OH)	436
Computers in media centers	KISER, Anita H.	(NC)	656
Computers in religion	ANDERSON, Norman E. .	(MA)	24
Computers in school libraries	PORMEN, Paul E.	(OH)	984
Computers in schools	MCDANIEL, Deanna J. . .	(OH)	801
Computers in small libraries	HENDRICKS, Thom	(ND)	527
Computers in the library	OGDEN, William S.	(TX)	918
Computers, management systems	CULL, Roberta	(AZ)	263
Computers resource specialist	CAMPANELLA, Alice D. .	(MA)	175
Computers, telematics	KRATZ, Hans G.	(AB)	676
Computing literature	HILDEBRANDT, Darlene M.	(WA)	538
Computing science	BUCHANAN, Zoe A. . . .	(ON)	153
Consulting, computer databases	CHAMIS, Alice Y.	(OH)	198
Custom computer programming	GILLETTE, Robert S. . . .	(TX)	435
Data processing & computers	MCBRIDE, Jessica W. . .	(NY)	792
Database computer searching	KING, Anne M.	(LA)	650
Database management systems on computers	RAEDER, Aggi W.	(CA)	1003
Database searching by computer	CESARD, Mary A.	(NJ)	196
Datatrek computer catalog, serials	GENTRY, Susan K.	(CA)	427
Distribution in computer industry	MONOSSON, Adolf S. . .	(MA)	855
Editing computer science magazines	WEINER, Carolynn N. . . .	(NY)	1318
Educational & library computing	BENDER, Evelyn	(PA)	79
Educational computers	GRIFFIN, Cheryl J.	(NY)	468
Educational computing	PHILBRICK, Marcia	(KS)	967
	BAKER, Shirley K.	(MA)	49
	WESTNEAT, Helen C. . .	(OH)	1327
Educational computing & media	DIERCKS, Eileen K.	(IL)	302
Educational use of computers	STEINBERG, Marilyn H. .	(MA)	1185
Electronic messaging & comp conferencing	BLACK, John B.	(ON)	101
Electronics & computing research	CRABTREE, Sandra A. . .	(CA)	254
Elementary computer curriculum	FARRIS, Mary E.	(TN)	365
Elementary computer education	DOAN, Janice K.	(KY)	307
End-user training for MEDLINE computer	POND, Frederick C.	(NY)	982
Federal computer & telecom procurement	DODSON, Whit	(VA)	308
Genealogical computing & research	O'BRIEN, Doris J.	(CT)	914
Geological computer applications	STARK, Philip H.	(CO)	1182
Health sciences computer software	MCLEAN, Martha L.	(TN)	814
History of modern computing	BRUEMMER, Bruce H. . .	(MN)	149
Human factors in computer systems	CHERRY, Joan M.	(ON)	206
Human interaction with computers	MARTIN, Thomas H. . . .	(NY)	778
Humanities computing	ERDT, Terrence	(PA)	352
Information reference computers	MAJOR, Marla J.	(MI)	762
Information science & computer tech	NEWMAN, Wilda B.	(MD)	900
Information searches, manual & computer	SHALLEY, Doris P.	(PA)	1119
In-house computer databases	NELSON, Dwayne L. . . .	(IL)	893
In-house computer literacy	KRONE, Judith P.	(GA)	679
Instructional computer coordination	PENDLETON, Kim B. . . .	(AK)	956
Instructional computing	MERCHANT, Cheryl N. . .	(TX)	825
Instructional uses of computers	DONHAM, Jean O.	(IA)	311
Intelligent computer-assisted instrc	PARROTT, James R. . . .	(ON)	944

COMPUTERS (Cont'd)

Interlibrary loans, computer searching	SARGENT, Phyllis M. . . .	(OR)	1083
Jazz record computer cataloging	WEAVER, James B.	(FL)	1312
Large computers & small libraries	STEVENS-RAYBURN, Sarah L.	(MD)	1191
Library & computer instruction	SACHS, Kathie B.	(PA)	1073
Library computer applications	STUHLMAN, Daniel D. . .	(IL)	1205
	JAFFE, Lawrence J.	(PA)	591
	BOWLES, David M.	(SC)	121
	LANE, Steven P.	(WA)	694
Library computer services	MOORE, Maxwell L.	(OK)	860
Library computer systems	SEGEL, Bernard J.	(DC)	1112
	STELZLE, James J.	(NY)	1186
	YAVARKOVSKY, Jerome	(NY)	1378
	PIPER, Larry W.	(OR)	975
	WOODS, Richard F.	(FIJ)	1367
Library computerization	SINHA, Pramod K.	(IND)	1143
Library computerization on MacIntosh	FORD, Marjorie F.	(CA)	389
Library computerization, systems	MILLER, Suzanne M. . . .	(CA)	842
Library computerized management	PARKER, Eleanor V. . . .	(OK)	941
Library computers & systems	SINK, Thomas R.	(OH)	1143
Library, media computer applications	RENICK, Paul R.	(ND)	1023
Local area computer networks	KEMPER, Marlyn J.	(FL)	639
Macintosh computer	CISLER, Stephen A.	(CA)	215
Manage computer databases	KROEHLER, Beth A.	(IN)	679
Management computer applications	COMEAU, Reginald A. . .	(NH)	234
Managing large library computers	FORTH, Stuart	(PA)	391
Marcon Plus computer usage	MATTHEOU, Antonia . . .	(NY)	785
Math & computer science databases	DAVIDOFF, Gary N.	(IL)	276
Mathematics, statistics, computer sci	PIERCE, Miriam D.	(PA)	971
Medical computer applications	CLARKE, Elba C.	(GA)	218
Medical computer training & development	HORNIG-ROHAN, James E.	(PA)	560
Music & computer indexing	KELLER, Kate V.	(PA)	635
National language computing	SEDELOW, Walter A. . . .	(AR)	1110
Natural language computing	SEDELOW, Sally Y.	(AR)	1110
Online computer	BAZE, Mary P.	(WA)	68
Online computer applications	ROSENFELD, Joseph S.	(OH)	1056
Online computerized binding preparation	HECKMAN, Stephen P. .	(IN)	520
Online searching & computer applications	RANKIN, Carol A.	(NY)	1007
Online searching, computers	STRAKA, Kathy M.	(CT)	1199
Original cataloging using computers	HANNAFORD, Claudia L.	(OH)	496
Patron computer services	WEBER, Julie A.	(IL)	1314
Performing online & computer searches	DUCHARME, Judith C. . .	(NM)	322
Personnel computing	ENGER, Kathy B.	(IA)	349
Pharmacy computer systems	FASSETT, William E. . . .	(WA)	366
Print & computerized reference	MCDONALD, Michael L. .	(DC)	803
Public access computers	MCCOY, Judy I.	(TX)	799
	BLUME, Scott	(WA)	107
Reference & computer information search	MOORHEAD, Kenneth E.	(CT)	862
Reference & computer services	POSES, June A.	(PA)	985
Regional computer applications	NELSON, James B.	(NY)	894
Reviewing AV & computer software	MILLER, John E.	(OH)	839
S/38 computer software	TODD, Hal W.	(FL)	1248
School library computer systems	SLYGH, Gyneth	(WI)	1151
School library computers	MCANALLY, Charlotte L.	(TN)	792
School library media computerization	LITTLE, Nina M.	(NE)	733
School-wide computer coordination	LINDSEY, Nancy L.	(TN)	730
Science & computer science	MATTHEWS, Priscilla J. .	(IL)	785
Science & technology computer searching	CHADWICK, Alena F. . . .	(MA)	196
Science, info applications, of computers	MITCHELL, Steve	(CA)	849
Small computer applications	ELWELL, Pamela M. . . .	(OH)	347
Small computers	BOND, George	(NH)	113
Small library computer applications	MORRIS, R P.	(NC)	867
Small library computing	STARK, Ted	(IA)	1182
Social science & computer indexing	LINDHEIMER, Elinor	(CA)	729
Social sciences, humanities & computers	WOGGON, Michele	(CA)	1359
Soil science & computers	HANDROW, Margaret M.	(TX)	495
Staff & public computer training	MCMURRAY, Sallylou . .	(OH)	815
Statistical computing	JAMES, Brent C.	(UT)	592
Supercomputing, computational science	MAISEL, Merry W.	(CA)	762

COMPUTERS (Cont'd)

Symphony computer programs	BURNS, Robert W.	(CO)	163
Teacher, computer science	EFFERTZ, Rose	(IL)	338
Teaching library skills & computers	YOUNG, Patricia S.	(TN)	1383
Technical services computer applications	FRANCQ, Carole	(IN)	396
Telecommunications, computers	KISHEL, Deane A.	(MN)	656
Television, computers, & other tech	EGAN, Mary J.	(NY)	338
Traditional & computer reference	AUSTIN, Martha L.	(WA)	40
Training of computer searchers	SOPELAK, Mary J.	(NY)	1168
Trends in computer systems	BILES, Mark J.	(NJ)	96
Usability of computer systems	CHERRY, Joan M.	(ON)	206
Utilization of computer software	CLEMENTS, Cynthia L. .	(TX)	221
Very basic computer programming	EIS, Myrna M.	(KS)	340
Westlaw computer-based research	SMITH, Susan A.	(CA)	1161
Workshops on computers	YARBROUGH, Joseph W.	(MI)	1378

CONCERT

Concert reviews	LAMBERT, John W.	(NC)	690
Live music concert coordination	RUSTMAN, Mark M. . . .	(KS)	1070
20th century concert music	PIZER, Charles R.	(NY)	977
	PIZER, Elizabeth F.	(NY)	977

CONCHOLOGY

Conchology, malacology	STONE, Joyce L.	(CO)	1197

CONCRETE

Keywording cement & concrete technology	SPIGELMAN, Cynthia A.	(IL)	1174

CONFERENCES (See also Convention, Meetings, Teleconferences)

Cataloging conference proceedings	CARTER, Judith A.	(AZ)	189
Computer conferencing	GRIEVE, Shelley	(OH)	468
Computer-mediated conferencing	BOND, George	(NH)	113
Conference & workshop planning	MOON, Ilse	(FL)	857
Conference coordination	BARR, Arlene E.	(CO)	58
	HOWARD, Ada M.	(TX)	563
Conference management	BOZOIAN, Paula	(MA)	124
	TRICARICO, Mary A. . . .	(MA)	1256
	RUPERT, Mary A.	(NH)	1068
	PHILLIPS, Janet C.	(PA)	968
Conference organizing	HOGAN, Thomas H.	(NJ)	549
Conference planning	MCCARTNEY, Jean A. . .	(MO)	794
Conference session highlights	THOMAS, Dorothy	(NY)	1236
Conference testing, resrch & development	ARBEZ, Gilbert J.	(ON)	30
Conferences	NELSON, Nancy M.	(NY)	894
Conferencing & public relations	WILLIAMS, Susan S. . . .	(MI)	1346
Convention & conference management	AUCOIN, Sharilynn A. . .	(LA)	38
Electronic messaging & comp conferencing	BLACK, John B.	(ON)	101
Library conference planning	SUTHERLAND, Thomas A.	(KY)	1211
Organization of author conferences	HIRABAYASHI, Joanne . .	(CA)	543
STM conference management	YAMAKAWA, Takashi . .	(JAP)	1376
Training & conference management	HUFFER, Mary A.	(MD)	570
White House conferences	MILEVSKI, Sandra N. . . .	(DC)	835

CONFLICT

Conflict resolution	PEISCHL, Thomas P. . . .	(MN)	955
Docket, conflict administration	KERN, Sharon P.	(IA)	643

CONGREGATIONAL

Establishment of congregational libs	BURSON, Lorraine E. . . .	(OR)	163
Organization of congregational libraries	HANNAFORD, Claudia L.	(OH)	496

CONGRESS

Congress reference	JONES, Catherine A. . . .	(DC)	611
Congressional & legislative research	CARR, Timothy B.	(VA)	186
Congressional collections	BOCCACCIO, Mary A. . .	(NC)	108
Congressional document retrieval	MILLER, William S.	(DC)	843
Congressional projects in archives	HARWOOD, James L. . .	(DC)	510

CONGRESS (Cont'd)

Congressional publications	SEELE, Ronald E.	(DC)	1111
Congressional records	ODOM, Jane H.	(DC)	917
Congressional research	SEELE, Ronald E.	(DC)	1111
Federal govt & congressional info srvs	ROTHBART, Linda S.	(VA)	1060
International congress organization	WALCKIERS, Marc A.	(BEL)	1293
Legal & congressional databases	PULVER, Thomas B.	(DC)	997

CONNECTICUT

Connecticut history & culture	SCHMIDT, Alesandra M.	(CT)	1095
Connecticut state documents	ENSEL, Ellen H.	(CT)	350

CONSER

CONSER	HERRICK, Judith M.	(DC)	532
CONSER serials cataloging	JONES, Edgar A.	(MA)	612

CONSERVATION (See also Reconstitution, Repair, Paper, Preservation)

Archival conservation	ANDERSON, James C.	(KY)	23
Archival conservation & preservation	MARRELLI, Nancy M.	(PQ)	773
Archival materials conservation	ELLISON, J T.	(CO)	345
Art of paper conservation	MOORE, Harold H.	(GA)	859
Book & paper conservation	SUNDSTRAND, Jacquelyn K.	(CA)	1210
	HANTHORN, Ivan E.	(IA)	499
Book conservation	MILEVSKI, Robert J.	(DC)	834
	SCHROCK, Nancy C.	(MA)	1100
Book storage & conservation	HERON, David W.	(CA)	532
Book-binding, repair, conservation	AUSTIN, Kristi N.	(WA)	40
Cataloging & conservation	WINROTH, Elizabeth C.	(OR)	1355
Conservation	BOUCHE, Nicole L.	(CA)	118
	DONAHUE, Katharine E.	(CA)	310
	GRANGER, Dorothy J.	(CA)	457
	CHEESEMAN, Bruce S.	(CT)	204
	HOLMER, Paul L.	(CT)	553
	BEDARD, Laura A.	(DC)	73
	ABBOTT, Elizabeth L.	(FL)	1
	CULLEN, Charles T.	(IL)	263
	MAYLONE, R R.	(IL)	790
	BRYSON, Kathleen C.	(KY)	152
	BURKETT, Nancy H.	(MA)	161
	CORNWALL, Scot J.	(MA)	247
	SHAFER, Steven I.	(MI)	1119
	NODLER, Charles E.	(MO)	906
	BOCCACCIO, Mary A.	(NC)	108
	WALLIN, Cornelia B.	(NH)	1298
	BURT, Leah	(NJ)	164
	GELLER, Lawrence D.	(NY)	426
	NYERGES, Michael S.	(NY)	912
	GRIFFITHS, June B.	(PA)	469
	ZORICH, Phillip J.	(PA)	1390
	MCCOY, Gail	(SC)	799
	NEAL, James H.	(TN)	890
	BRYSON, Gary B.	(TX)	152
	GRACY, David B.	(TX)	455
	MARX, Patricia C.	(TX)	780
	BEYEA, Marion L.	(NB)	93
	SPEISMAN, Stephen A.	(ON)	1172
	MACLEAN, Eleanor A.	(PQ)	757
Conservation administration	BAKER, John P.	(NY)	48
	HOGAN, Kristine K.	(NY)	549
Conservation & preservation	BUTLER, Randall R.	(CA)	167
	CARROON, Robert G.	(CT)	187
	DE PEW, John N.	(FL)	293
	NAKANO, Kimberly L.	(HI)	887
	KLEEBERGER, Patricia L.	(MD)	658
	LATOUR, Terry S.	(MS)	701
	ALTERMAN, Deborah H.	(NJ)	18
	GRAUER, Sally M.	(NY)	458
	O'CONNELL, Brian E.	(NY)	915
	PEPPER, Jerold L.	(NY)	958
	BAUER, Barbara B.	(PA)	65
	REPP, Robert M.	(PA)	1024
	RUGGERE, Christine A.	(PA)	1066
Conservation & preservation services	HECKMAN, Stephen P.	(IN)	520
Conservation & preservation techniques	HOLT, David A.	(KY)	554
Conservation education	WRIGHT, John C.	(HI)	1371

CONSERVATION (Cont'd)

Conservation of library materials	LUNDEEN, Gerald W.	(HI)	748
	FERGUSON, Bonnie E.	(IL)	372
	HENDERSON, William T.	(IL)	527
	SMITH, Richard D.	(IL)	1159
	DARLING, Pamela W.	(NY)	275
	SCOTT, Sharon A.	(OH)	1108
	COLLISTER, Edward A.	(PQ)	233
Conservation of library resources	DEVENISH-CASSEL, Ann W.	(NY)	297
Conservation of paper	GRAUE, Luz B.	(CA)	458
Conservation of print materials	COUPER, Richard W.	(NJ)	251
Conservation policy	FOX, Peter K.	(IRE)	395
Conservation services	FAIRFIELD, John R.	(NC)	361
Conservation training specialist	MILEVSKI, Robert J.	(DC)	834
Conservatorial consultation	JONSON, Laurence F.	(IA)	616
Energy conservation	MARCIL, Louise	(PQ)	769
Forestry, conservation	PERSHE, Frank F.	(MO)	961
Lib & archives conservation management	CUNHA, George M.	(KY)	265
Library conservation	MCCOLGIN, Michael A.	(AZ)	797
	DUPLAIX, Sally T.	(RI)	327
	CALDWELL, Richard C.	(WA)	172
Library consulting, paper conservation	MUELLER, Jane L.	(CA)	875
Library material conservation	MERKLEY, John P.	(CA)	826
Manuscript & archive conservation	GARLICK, Karen	(DC)	419
Manuscript conservation	KENNICK, Sylvia B.	(NY)	642
Manuscripts conservation & microfilming	BOWEN, Laurel G.	(IL)	120
	KIDD, Betty H.	(ON)	646
Map conservation	BUMGARNER, John L.	(NC)	157
Paper & photographic conservation	GARLICK, Karen	(DC)	419
Paper conservation	METZLER, Valerie	(IL)	829
	LOMBARDO, Daniel J.	(MA)	738
	MOORE, Harold H.	(GA)	859
Paper document conservation	MATTESON, Murray M.	(IL)	785
Photographic conservation	SARETZKY, Gary D.	(NJ)	1082
Preservation & conservation	HAYES, Melinda K.	(CA)	516
	MAINELLI, Helen K.	(CA)	761
	MILLBROOKE, Anne	(CT)	835
	PIZER, Irwin H.	(IL)	977
	WITHEE, Jane S.	(IL)	1358
	GIETSCHIER, Steven P.	(MO)	433
	BELL, Mary F.	(NY)	77
	SEEMANN, Ann M.	(NY)	1111
	STERN, Marc J.	(NY)	1189
	SUNDT, Christine L.	(OR)	1210
	GYESZLY, Suzanne D.	(TX)	479
	MASON, Timothy D.	(TX)	781
	KARRER, Jonathan K.	(VA)	628
	MOLLER, Hans	(PQ)	853
	DE MACEDO, Maria L.	(PTG)	290
Preservation & conservation literature	HUEMER, Christina G.	(ITL)	570
Promoting conservation	REINSTEIN, Julia B.	(NY)	1021
Repair & conservation of documents	JORDAN, Ervin L.	(VA)	616
Resource conservation	PLOCKELMAN, Cynthia H.	(FL)	978
Science, nature, & conservation science	PFOHL, Theodore E.	(NY)	966

CONSORTIA (See also Networks)

Consortia	LEMKE, Darrell H.	(DC)	715
	KLINE, Eve P.	(PA)	661
	PLASO, Kathy A.	(PA)	977
Consortia or networks	VICK, Kathleen	(PA)	1283
Consortium	GRISHAM, Frank P.	(GA)	471
	BREWER, Karen L.	(OH)	134
Consortium activities	SEARLS, Eileen R.	(MO)	1110
Consortium development	RUSSELL, Lisa R.	(AL)	1069
	DALY, Jay	(MA)	271
	WILLIS, Dorothy B.	(NE)	1348
	MCCORD, Stanley J.	(TX)	798
Consortium management	ADAMS, J R.	(CT)	5
Cooperative strategies, consortia	OFFERMANN, Glenn W.	(MN)	917
Interlibrary cooperation consortia	BROWN, Thomas M.	(WV)	148
Interlibrary loan, consortia	ROEDELL, Ray F.	(PA)	1048
Library consortia	CAMACHO, Nancy S.	(TX)	174
Library consortium automation	SMITH, Ann M.	(MA)	1152
Network & consortium administration	NEUFELD, Judith B.	(NY)	897
Network & consortium governance	MITCHELL, Joan M.	(PA)	849

CONSORTIA (Cont'd)
Networking & consortia .... BAUGHMAN, Steven A. .. (GA)   66
Networks & consortia .... VANVUREN, Darcy D. ... (CA) 1277
                                       RAITHEL, Frederick J. ... (MO) 1004
Public library automated consortia ... O'BRIEN, Anne M. ...... (MA) 914

CONSTITUTION (See also Bylaws)
Canadian constitutional law .... TANGUAY, Guy .... (PQ) 1222
Constitution rights .... JUERGENSMEYER, John
                                         E. .... (IL)   619

CONSTRUCTION (See also Architecture, Building, Design, Facilities, Site, Space)
Academic library construction .... RICHARDS, James H. ... (NM) 1028
Building construction management ..... SINTZ, Edward F. ...... (FL) 1144
Building construction plng &
  development .... MARTIN, Mason G. .... (MO) 777
Building layout & construction .... NEAL, Robert L. .... (MD) 890
Building planning & construction ..... STEWART, George R. ... (AL) 1192
Building program devlpmnt &
  construction .... MOODY, Marilyn D. .... (PA) 857
Commerce & construction industry ..... MCCONNIE, Mary ...... (TRN) 798
Construction .... KNUP, Marie S. .... (PA) 666
Construction books .... LUNSTEDT, Ralph A. ... (CA) 749
Construction finance .... LEWIS, Thomas F. ..... (MA) 724
Construction management .... GRANADOS, Rose A. ... (CA) 457
Construction of facilities .... HAMMOND, John J. .... (MO) 493
Construction planning .... SHAPIRO, June R. ..... (NY) 1121
Construction project administration .. WALTERS, Daniel L. ... (WA) 1301
Construction site, architect selections WRIGHT, Paul L. .... (KY) 1372
Database construction .... WILDE, Daniel U. ...... (CT) 1338
                                       DEHART, Odell .... (DC) 288
                                       OMAR, Elizabeth A. ... (MD) 923
Database construction & creation ..... MENNELLA, Dona M. ... (MD) 824
Database construction & maintenance .. BRITTON, Jeffrey W. ... (NJ) 137
Database design & construction .... DENTON, Francesca L. . (MA) 293
                                       HLAVA, Marjorie M. .... (NM) 544
                                       HALE, Linda L. .... (BC) 485
Design & construction of new facilities PAPENFUSE, Edward C. . (MD) 939
Engineering & construction databases . HARBERT, Cathy E. .... (MD) 499
Engineering database construction .... PIERCE, Anne L. ...... (CT) 971
Financing & construction building plng KELLUM-ROSE, Nancy P. (CA) 637
Fundraising, construction .... MINERVA, Jane R. ..... (NY) 846
Indexing database construction .... JACKRELL, Thomas L. .. (NJ) 586
Informational database construction .. BERGMANN, Allison M. . (NY)   86
In-house database construction .... ROFF, Jill R. .... (MA) 1049
Library building construction .... ZENKE, Mary H. .... (IL) 1387
                                       DUNCAN, Cynthia B. .... (VA) 325
Library building, planning, construction BROWN, Louise R. ..... (MA) 145
Library construction .... RHEIN, Jean F. .... (FL) 1025
                                       STRAUTMAN, Randolph
                                         B. .... (GA) 1201
                                       MULLINS, James L. ..... (IN) 878
                                       LEWIS, David D. ...... (MA) 722
                                       MAYESKI, John K. ..... (NE) 790
                                       WOLFORD, Larry E. .... (NJ) 1361
                                       DRESP, Donald F. ..... (NM) 319
                                       NICHOLS, Gerald D. ... (NY) 901
                                       CUPP, Christian M. ..... (OH) 265
                                       WOODRUM, Patricia A. . (OK) 1366
                                       MULLEN, Francis X. .... (PA) 877
                                       COSTA, Robert N. ..... (VA) 249
                                       NADEAU, Leonard ..... (PQ) 886
Library construction & design .... PRITCHARD, John A. .. (NC) 994
Library construction, planning .... SIMON, Bradley A. ..... (OK) 1140
Library planning & construction ...... ROBINSON, Joel M. .... (OK) 1044
Library renovation, construction ..... WILLIAMS, Edwin E. ... (CT) 1343
Library space planning, construction . NEIKIRK, Harold D. .... (MD) 892
New facilities construction .... STEELE, Leah J. .... (IL) 1184
Online database construction &
  searching .... CHAMIS, Alice Y. ...... (OH) 198
Planning & construction of lib
  buildings .... HEAD, Anita K. .... (DC) 518
Public library construction .... MULKEY, Jack C. ...... (AR) 876
                                       FORK, Donald J. ...... (DC) 390
                                       FORSEE, Joe B. .... (GA) 391
                                       COLLIER, Virginia S. ... (TN) 232
Public library planning & construction BROWNLEE, Jerry W. .. (FL) 148

CONSTRUCTION (Cont'd)
Rural library construction .... MCCORMICK, Tamsie .. (IN) 799
Specialized database construction .... LIVNY, Efrat .... (WI) 735
Thesauri construction .... HEWINS, Elizabeth H. .. (TX) 535
Thesaurus & classification
  construction .... BATTY, Charles D. ..... (MD)   65
Thesaurus construction .... SPRUNG, Lori L. ...... (CA) 1176
                                       SVENONIUS, Elaine .... (CA) 1212
                                       LYNCH, Jacqueline .... (MA) 751
                                       PETERSEN, Toni ...... (MA) 962
                                       AMATRUDA, William T. . (MD)   19
                                       LASER, Debra L. ...... (MD) 700
                                       SOERGEL, Dagobert ... (MD) 1165
                                       BRENNER, Everett H. ... (NY) 133
                                       MOLHOLT, Pat .... (NY) 852
                                       PHILLIPS, Sylvia E. .... (TX) 969
                                       LECOMPTE, Louis L. ... (PQ) 708
                                       VAN SLYPE, Georges ... (BEL) 1277
Thesaurus construction &
  maintenance .... KLEIMAN, Helen M. .... (DC) 659
Thesaurus construction &
  management .... VAN HALM, Johan ..... (NET) 1275
Thesaurus construction, technical .... GENUARDI, Michael T. . (MD) 427
Vocabulary & thesaurus construction .. SAVAGE, Gretchen S. .. (CA) 1085

CONSTRUCTION/RENOVATION
Library building
  construction/renovation .... VENABLE, Andrew A. .. (OH) 1282

CONSULTING (See also Advising, Advisory, Counseling, Guidance)
Academic libraries consulting .... MCDONOUGH, Kathleen
                                         C. .... (NH) 803
Accounting & management consulting ... WONG, Mabel K. ...... (IL) 1363
Administration & building consulting . KUHN, Warren B. ...... (IA) 682
Administration & consulting .... KASPER, Barbara ..... (CT) 629
Advertising, public relations consulting FRISBIE, Richard ...... (IL) 405
American history consulting .... SCHEIPS, Paul J. ...... (MD) 1091
Archival consulting .... SCHUMACHER, Carolyn
                                         S. .... (PA) 1102
                                       TOMAN, Jocelyn B. .... (PA) 1249
Archival publications conslntg &
  editing .... MARRELLI, Nancy M. .. (PQ) 773
Attorney information systems
  consulting .... STERN, Michael P. ..... (MD) 1189
Audio consulting .... PATRYCH, Joseph ..... (NY) 947
Audiovisual consulting .... SMITH, Richard J. ..... (LA) 1160
Automation consultation .... QUEYROUZE, Mary E. ... (TX) 999
Automation consulting .... BUSCH, Barbara ...... (CA) 165
                                       EPSTEIN, Susan B. .... (CA) 351
                                       SMITH, Richard J. ..... (LA) 1160
                                       ERLAND, Virginia K. .... (NY) 353
                                       JUERGENS, Bonnie .... (TX) 619
                                       RUDDY, Mary K. ...... (TX) 1065
                                       STANDIFER, Hugh A. ... (TX) 1179
Branch library consulting .... PALMER, Marguerite C. . (WV) 936
Building consultant .... COOK, Jeannine S. .... (NY) 240
Building consulting .... PLACE, Philip A. ...... (FL) 977
                                       WILSON, David C. ..... (GA) 1350
                                       JACKSON, Susan M. .... (IL) 588
                                       SAKEY, Joseph G. ..... (MA) 1076
                                       MCFERRAN, Warren A. .. (MI) 805
                                       ARD, Harold J. .... (TX)   31
                                       WHITE, James W. ...... (WI) 1331
Business & consulting .... TICE, Kathleen A. ...... (CA) 1244
Business & legal library consulting .. GIGANTE, Vickilyn M. .. (MD) 433
Business consulting .... GRANT, Mary M. ...... (NY) 458
Business plan consulting .... MOSLEY, Thomas E. .... (OK) 872
CD-ROM consulting .... RIETDYK, Ron J. ...... (MA) 1033
Children's books consulting .... FEDERICI, Yolanda D. .. (IL) 368
Children's consultant .... BAKULA, Patricia A. .... (WI)   50
Children's consultant services .... DOWNS, Jane B. .... (IL) 317
Children's service consulting .... SAGER, Lynn S. .... (WI) 1074
Church & synagogue library
  consulting .... KARON, Bernard L. .... (MN) 627
Collection & building consultation ... DONAHUGH, Robert H. . (OH) 310
Collection consultation .... JOHNSON, Paul A. ..... (CA) 608
Computer applications & mgmt
  consulting .... BOSSEAU, Don L. ...... (CA) 117

CONSULTING (Cont'd)

Conservatorial consultation	JONSON, Laurence F.	(IA)	616
Consultancy services	BARTEN, Sharon S.	(NY)	60
Consultant	MUSSEHL, Allan A.	(DC)	883
	ALBSMEYER, Betty J.	(IL)	11
	HENDERSON, Deborah A.	(ON)	526
Consultant, film & video production	HEMPEL, Gordon J.	(IL)	525
Consultant, public, special libraries	WILLIAMS, Edwin E.	(CT)	1343
Consultant services	FANCHER, Evelyn P.	(TN)	363
Consultant to public libraries	HINDMARSH, Douglas P.	(UT)	542
Consultant to schools & libraries	HAAS, Carolyn B.	(IL)	480
Consultation & training	BRZUSTOWICZ, Richard J.	(WA)	152
Consultation on American Catholic hist	THOMAS, Evangeline M.	(KS)	1236
Consultation on setup, systems	RICHARDS, Stella	(PQ)	1028
Consultation, public relations	HARRIS, Linda S.	(DC)	505
Consulting	OAKES, Patricia A.	(AK)	913
	BARKEY, Patrick T.	(CA)	56
	WELLS, H L.	(CA)	1322
	X, Laura	(CA)	1376
	REISMAN, Sydelle S.	(CT)	1021
	BORYS, Cynthia A.	(DC)	117
	PETERSON, Carolyn S.	(FL)	963
	ENSLEY, Robert F.	(IL)	350
	HAMMER, Donald P.	(IL)	493
	HUTCHINS, Mary J.	(IL)	579
	MIFFLIN, Michael J.	(IL)	833
	MORRIS, Susan M.	(IL)	867
	GIULIANO, Lillian C.	(MA)	439
	PLUNKET, Linda	(MA)	979
	RENKIEWICZ, Frank A.	(MI)	1023
	HAMMARGREN, Betty L.	(MN)	493
	HANKS, Gardner C.	(MN)	496
	SIBLEY, Shawn C.	(NC)	1135
	CUNNIFFE, Charlene M.	(NH)	265
	MURO, Ernest A.	(NJ)	880
	NELSON, Nancy M.	(NY)	894
	BAYER, Bernard I.	(OH)	67
	PARSONS, Augustine C.	(OH)	944
	MORRISON, Perry D.	(OR)	868
	CAMPION, Carol M.	(PA)	177
	OSTRUM, Roxane M.	(PA)	929
	LEE, Regina H.	(TX)	711
	WELLS, Mary K.	(TX)	1322
	MCCLYMONT, Karen A.	(ON)	797
	DAUNAIS, Marie J.	(PQ)	275
	WADE, C A.	(PQ)	1290
	STONE, Clarence W.	(IDN)	1197
	HANHAN, Leila M.	(LEB)	495
	RODRIGUEZ, Serafin L.	(MEX)	1048
Consulting & automation	HOGAN, Patricia M.	(IL)	549
Consulting & continuing education	SEIDENBERG, Edward	(TX)	1112
Consulting & evaluation	HENDERSON, Rosemary	(KS)	527
Consulting & managing one-person libs	DALY, Eudice	(CA)	271
Consulting & move planning	MILLER, Scott W.	(NY)	842
Consulting & needs assessment	WEISFIELD, Cynthia F.	(PA)	1319
Consulting & planning	SIZEMORE, William C.	(WV)	1145
Consulting & research	DANTON, J P.	(CA)	274
Consulting & seminars	ACKERMAN, Katherine K.	(MI)	4
Consulting, computer databases	CHAMIS, Alice Y.	(OH)	198
Consulting firms	GOZDZ, Wanda E.	(FL)	455
Consulting for small & medium libraries	LEAMON, David L.	(MI)	707
Consulting foreign language libraries	VALENTINE, Patrick M.	(NC)	1271
Consulting in information organizations	PRUSAK, Laurence	(MA)	996
Consulting in public libraries	CLARK, Jay B.	(TX)	217
Consulting information, publishing	CHICOREL, Marietta S.	(AZ)	208
Consulting large & small libraries	WEST, L P.	(IL)	1326
Consulting libs, children's programs	WALDEN, Katherine G.	(CT)	1294
Consulting, library management	SCHWARZ, Shirlee	(CT)	1105
Consulting, library space planning	SCHWARZ, Shirlee	(CT)	1105
Consulting on administrative issues	RICH, Marcia A.	(MA)	1027
Consulting on archival administration	BEHRND-KLODT, Menzi L.	(WI)	75
Consulting, public libraries	CRANE, Karen R.	(AK)	255
Consulting service	BRANDT, Garnet J.	(IA)	128
Consulting services	SOY, Susan K.	(CA)	1170
	MILLER, Richard T.	(MO)	841

CONSULTING (Cont'd)

Consulting services to schools	LEVEL, M J.	(KS)	719
Consulting to educational publishers	MOSELEY, Cameron S.	(NY)	870
Consulting to financial institutions	PHILLIPS, Steven G.	(MA)	969
Consulting to public libraries	VANDERLYKE, Barbara A.	(CT)	1274
Corporate communications consulting	MULVIHILL, Maureen E.	(NY)	878
Corporate library consulting	MITCHE, Cynthia R.	(TX)	848
	MITCHELL, Cynthia R.	(TX)	848
Cultural agency consultation	WRIGHT, John C.	(HI)	1371
Curriculum consultant	REILLY, Maureen E.	(CT)	1020
	BROWN, Gerald R.	(MB)	144
Data entry consulting	HLAVA, Marjorie M.	(NM)	544
Database & systems consultant	CHAPMAN, Kathleen A.	(WA)	202
Database consultation	MLYNAR, Mary	(OH)	850
Database DBA & consulting	SYVERSON, Kathleen A.	(IL)	1217
Database development consultant	GROTE, Janet H.	(NY)	473
Databases & software consulting	GIGANTE, Vickilyn M.	(MD)	433
Developing country library consultancy	LEE, Amy C.	(DC)	709
Editorial consultation	ALKIRE, Leland G.	(WA)	13
Electronic publishing consulting	BERUL, Lawrence H.	(MD)	91
End-user training & consultation	INGUI, Bettejean	(CO)	583
Environmental topics consulting	IRELAND, Laverne H.	(CA)	583
Evaluation consultation	BEDARD, Evelyn M.	(TX)	73
Facility consulting	DAVIS, Glenn G.	(IL)	279
Film & video consultant, appraiser	MACAULEY, C C.	(CA)	754
Financial consulting	LINDSEY, Susan B.	(PA)	730
Fundraising consulting	BERGAN, Helen J.	(DC)	85
General consultant	MIAH, Abdul J.	(VA)	831
General consulting	KNEPEL, Nancy	(CO)	664
	PLUEMER, Bonnie J.	(IA)	978
	WOZNY, Jay	(IL)	1370
General law library consulting	MARKE, Julius J.	(NY)	771
General library consultant	HAWKINS, Paul J.	(KS)	514
General library consulting	MAPP, Erwin E.	(FL)	768
	MOORMAN, John A.	(IL)	862
	ANGLIN, Richard V.	(NY)	28
General library consulting, liaison	OMARA, Marie T.	(MD)	923
General library consulting overseas	BERGQUIST, Christine F.	(DC)	87
General library, information consulting	ALLEN, Richard H.	(NE)	16
	THOMPSON, Debra J.	(NH)	1239
	PROVOST, Beverly A.	(NY)	996
General public library consulting	WUNDERLICH, Nina M.	(IL)	1374
	LAW, Aileen E.	(SC)	704
Health library consulting	GREENWOOD, Jan	(ON)	465
High technology consulting	JAGIELLOWICZ, Jadzia	(ON)	591
High tech research & devlpmnt consulting	HERTHER, Nancy K.	(MN)	533
Historical agency consultation	DU BOIS, Paul Z.	(NJ)	322
Historical research consultation	ESALA, Lillian H.	(MN)	354
Hospital & medical library consulting	BLADEN, Marguerite	(CA)	102
Hospital consultation	SZCZCPANIAK, Adam S.	(MD)	1218
Hospital consulting	KETCHELL, Debra S.	(WA)	645
Hospital libraries consulting	POLAND, Ursula H.	(NY)	980
Hospital library consultation	DALTON, Richard R.	(MO)	271
	BUTSON, Linda C.	(NC)	167
Hospital library consulting	BENELISHA, Eleanor	(CA)	80
	AMBROSE, Karen S.	(IL)	19
	O'BRIEN, Marjorie S.	(MA)	914
	GREATHOUSE, Brenda J.	(WV)	461
Independent consulting	SARRIS, Shirley C.	(NY)	1083
Information brokerage consulting	KLEMENT, Susan P.	(ON)	660
Info brokering, supplying, consulting	AXT, Randolph W.	(WI)	42
Information consulting	CRAWFORD, Marilyn L.	(CA)	257
	ADDISON, Paul H.	(IN)	6
	OJALA, Marydee P.	(KS)	919
	LANDMAN, Lillian L.	(NY)	693
	OWENS, Irene E.	(PA)	932
	LALONDE, Diane	(PQ)	689
Information, library services consulting	PARMING, Marju R.	(DC)	943
Information management consulting	HORTON, Forest W.	(DC)	561
Information management srvs consulting	GROCKI, Daniel J.	(MD)	471
Information processing consulting	ETZI, Richard	(NY)	356
Information systems consultant	SHAMS, Kamruddin	(CA)	1120
Information systems planning, consulting	GROTE, Janet H.	(NY)	473
Internal consulting	SELLERS, Alexander G.	(ON)	1114
International development consultant	SMITH, Jessie C.	(MD)	1156
Jazz consulting, movie studios	COLLINS, Richard H.	(CA)	233

CONSULTING (Cont'd)

Latin American school library consulting — CARDENAS, Mary E. . . . (SAF) 180
Law & tax library consulting — EVERLOVE, Nora J. . . . . (FL) 359
Law firm consulting — DAVIS, Becky C. . . . . . (CA) 277
EARHART, Marilyn N. . . (CA) 332
Law library consultant — BROSK, Carol A. . . . . . (IL) 141
Law library consulting — FOX, Elyse H. . . . . (MA) 394
Library & information consultant — MOON, Fletcher F. . . . . (TN) 857
Library & information systems consulting — MADDOCK, Jerome T. . . (CO) 759
Library & records management consulting — GAGNON, Donna M. . . . (CA) 412
Library automation consultation — HAWKINS, Nina L. . . . . . (CA) 514
LINSE, Mary M. . . . . . (MO) 731
Library automation consulting — FALANGA, Rosemarie E. . (CA) 361
Library building additions consulting — RIBNICKY, Karen F. . . . . (CT) 1026
Library building consultant — SILVER, Cy H. . . . . (CA) 1138
Library building consultation — MCCABE, Gerard B. . . . (PA) 792
Library building consulting — MASON, Ellsworth G. . . (CO) 781
MCNEAL, Archie L. . . . (FL) 816
ROVELSTAD, Howard . . (MD) 1062
MCDONOUGH, Kathleen C. . . . . (NH) 803
TOOMBS, Kenneth E. . . . (SC) 1251
MUTSCHLER, Herbert F. . (WA) 883
JAX, John J. . . . . (WI) 595
BECKMAN, Margaret L. . (ON) 73
Library buildings consultant, Japan, USA — GITLER, Robert L. . . . . . (CA) 438
Library consultancy — NANTON-COMISSIONG, Barbara L. . . . . (TRN) 887
Library consultant — KUHNER, David A. . . . . . (CA) 683
LOHRER, Alice . . . . (IL) 737
ROGGENKAMP, Alice M. (NY) 1050
Library consultation — LEVINE, Marion H. . . . . (CT) 720
FITZPATRICK, Kelly . . . (MD) 383
RICHARDSON, Beverly S. (NC) 1029
NATHANSON, David . . . (WV) 889
WARREN, Lois M. . . . . . (BC) 1306
Library consulting — KOLB, Audrey P. . . . . . . (AK) 669
DAY, Bettie B. . . . . (CA) 282
MCCAUGHTRY, Dorothy H. . . . . (CT) 795
COFFEE, E G. . . . . (KS) 226
WOLPERT, Ann J. . . . . . (MA) 1362
CHEN, John H. . . . . . . (MD) 205
MENNELLA, Dona M. . . . (MD) 824
CATES, Sheila A. . . . . . (MT) 195
GREENAWAY, Emerson . (NH) 463
THOMPSON, Debra J. . . (NH) 1239
DENNIS, Anne R. . . . . . (NY) 292
HARRISON, Karen A. . . . (ON) 507
Library consulting, automated services — COLLARD, R M. . . . . . . (CO) 232
Library consulting, paper conservation — MUELLER, Jane L. . . . . . (CA) 875
Library conversion consulting — PHILLIPS, Ray S. . . . . . (TX) 969
Library education consultation — SULLIVAN, Peggy A. . . . (IL) 1208
Library fundraising consulting — KUHN, Warren B. . . . . . (IA) 682
Library, information mgmt consulting — GOSSAGE, Wayne . . . . (NY) 453
Library management consulting — ACCARDI, Joseph J. . . . (WI) 3
Library planning & layout consulting — WEINZIMMER, William A. (NY) 1318
Library system consulting — LEWIS, Alan D. . . . . . . (MN) 722
Library systems & database consulting — DILORETO, Ann M. . . . . (CA) 303
Library systems consultation — GISHLER, John R. . . . . . (AB) 438
Library systems consulting — FEINER, Arlene M. . . . . . (IL) 369
BECKMAN, Margaret L. . (ON) 73
Library telecommunications consulting — BOWDEN, Philip L. . . . . . (IL) 120
Literary research consultation — MASON, Michael L. . . . (NJ) 781
Local history consulting — KRASEAN, Thomas K. . . (IN) 676
Magazine & editorial consulting — LIPTON, Howard . . . . . . (MI) 732
Management consulting — EPSTEIN, Susan B. . . . . (CA) 351
JUROW, Susan R. . . . . . (DC) 620
LARSEN, Linda E. . . . . . (IL) 698
VIRGO, Julie A. . . . . . . (IL) 1285
FISHER, Jean K. . . . . . . (MA) 381
MCDONALD, Dennis D. . (MD) 802
BERGFELD, C D. . . . . . (NY) 86
MILLER-KUMMERFELD, Elizabeth . . . . (NY) 843

CONSULTING (Cont'd)

Management consulting — TREFRY, Mary G. . . . . . (NY) 1255
JUERGENS, Bonnie . . . (TX) 619
SCHIELACK, Tricia J. . . (TX) 1092
STANDIFER, Hugh A. . . (TX) 1179
MCCALLUM, Anita J. . . . (ON) 793
Management, consulting & research — RUDD, Janet K. . . . . . . (CA) 1065
Management consulting reference — FLEISHMAN, Lauren Z. . (NY) 384
Management information consulting — CARTELLI, Alessandra J. (PA) 188
PLEFKA, Cathleen S. . . . (PA) 978
Management training & consulting — SCEPANSKI, Jordan M. . (CA) 1088
Managerial library consulting — PHILLIPS, Ray S. . . . . . (TX) 969
Market research consulting — STILLMAN, Stanley W. . . (NY) 1194
Marketing consulting — HITCHENS, Howard B. . . (DE) 544
Marketing database consultant services — CHAPMAN, Kathleen A. . (WA) 202
Media & audiovisual consulting — TARANKO, Walter J. . . . (ME) 1223
Media consulting — BERKLUND, Nancy D. . . . (MI) 87
GURIEVITCH, Grania B. . (NY) 478
Medical library consultation — CREERON, Carolyn E. . . (FL) 257
KELLY, Kay . . . . (MI) 638
CARTER, Bobby R. . . . . (TX) 189
Medical library consulting — HARRIS, Vallena D. . . . . (CA) 506
KYKER, Penelope R. . . . (IN) 685
ARNN, Judith A. . . . . . . (TX) 33
Medical risk management consulting — THOMASSON, George O. (CO) 1238
Minority library services consulting — EWUNES, Ernest L. . . . . (TX) 359
Miscellaneous consulting — HOLAB-ABELMAN, Robin S. . . . . (TX) 550
Movies & radio formats consultation — SMITH, Walter H. . . . . . (VA) 1161
Multitype lib cooperation consultation — VOSS, Anne E. . . . . . . (NJ) 1289
Music consulting & discography — PATRYCH, Joseph . . . . . (NY) 947
Networking & consulting — WAGNER, Rod G. . . . . . (NE) 1292
New product potential consulting — HOPE, Thomas W. . . . . . (NY) 557
Newspaper library consulting — IPPOLITO, Andrew V. . . . (NY) 583
Online database consultation — LAMB, Connie . . . . (UT) 689
Online search service consulting — KLINGLER, Thomas E. . . (OH) 662
Online searching & consulting — CUEVAS, John R. . . . . . (CA) 263
Oral history consulting — GRELE, Ronald J. . . . . . (NY) 467
MORRISSEY, Charles T. . (VT) 869
Organizational consulting — GARDNER, Jeffrey J. . . . (DC) 418
Overseas consulting — CANDELMO, Emily . . . . (NY) 178
Personnel management consulting — SMITH, Catherine . . . . . (NC) 1153
Piano music & consulting — PATRYCH, Joseph . . . . . (NY) 947
Planning consultation — MCCRACKEN, Ronald W. (ON) 799
Preservation consulting — MILEVSKI, Robert J. . . . (DC) 834
Print & non-print teacher consulting — CARLISLE, Carol A. . . . . (CT) 182
Private law firm consulting — PLUNKET, Joy H. . . . . . (MA) 978
Program consultant — BROWN, Gerald R. . . . . (MB) 144
Program consulting — CLAVER, M P. . . . . (AL) 219
Public & institutions libs consulting — MADDEN, Doreitha R. . . . (NJ) 758
Public libraries consulting — CASSELL, Kay A. . . . . . (NY) 193
Public library consultant — PHILLIPS, Clifford R. . . . (CA) 968
JOHNSON, Jean G. . . . . (NH) 605
Public library consultation — BECKERMAN, Edwin P. . (NJ) 72
WAGGONER, Susan M. . (PA) 1291
Public library consulting — GOLDBERG, Susan S. . . (AZ) 445
MERRILL, Mary G. . . . . (CT) 827
LOCKE, John W. . . . . . . (IL) 736
MOORMAN, John A. . . . (IL) 862
HELLARD, Ellen G. . . . . (KY) 524
KLEE, Edward L. . . . . . (KY) 658
PERRY, Emma B. . . . . . (MA) 960
SCHLESINGER, Deborah L. . . . . (MT) 1094
FREEMAN, Larry S. . . . . (SC) 401
NOLTE, Alice I. . . . . (SC) 908
GUBBIN, Barbara A. . . . (TX) 475
DOWNEY REIDA, Linda K. (UT) 316
MORRISON, Meris E. . . . (VT) 868
SAGER, Lynn S. . . . . . . (WI) 1074
Public library development consulting — FUNK, Elizabeth A. . . . . (PA) 410
Publishing & consulting — DUMONT, Monique . . . . (PQ) 325
Publishing consulting — FRISBIE, Richard . . . . . (IL) 405
Reading, writing, literacy consulting — MCDONOUGH, Timothy M. . . . . (CA) 803
Recorded media consultation, appraisal — MACAULEY, C C. . . . . . (CA) 754
Records management consulting — FREEMAN, Carla . . . . . (DC) 400

CONSULTING (Cont'd)

Reference & consultation	DUBOIS, Henry J.	(CA)	322
Reference & consultation services	SINCLAIR, Lorelei P.	(CA)	1142
Reference services & consultation	WONG, Anita	(ON)	1362
Research & consultation sales	MIDDLETON, Carl H.	(DC)	833
Research consulting	MIDDLETON, Carl H.	(DC)	833
	SANCHEZ, Jose L.	(DC)	1079
	ROWLAND, Lucy M.	(GA)	1062
Researcher, consultant, & analyst	KNIGHTLY, John J.	(TN)	664
Rural library consulting	HAYNES, Jean	(NY)	516
Sales consulting	IVAK, Patricia A.	(PA)	585
School district consulting	HIRABAYASHI, Joanne	(CA)	543
School learning resource ctr consulting	GOTHIA, Blanche	(TX)	453
School library consulting	HARADA, Violet H.	(HI)	499
	VAUGHN, Robert V.	(VI)	1280
School library media consultation	DOWNES, Valerie	(IL)	316
School, regional services consulting	BUCKINGHAM, Betty J.	(IA)	154
Science & technology library consulting	PHINNEY, Hartley K.	(CO)	969
Sheet music consultant	SETON, Charles B.	(NY)	1117
Slide library consulting	DULAN, Peter A.	(CO)	324
Small library consulting	DAVIDOFF, Marcia	(FL)	276
	BACKMAN, Carroll H.	(NC)	44
	BULLEY, Joan S.	(VA)	156
Small special libraries consulting	HAMILTON, Patricia J.	(SD)	492
Social work library consulting	BUTLER, Evelyn	(PA)	166
Software consultation	FARAONE, Maria B.	(NY)	363
Speaking & consulting	REID, Judith P.	(DC)	1018
Special libraries consultant	HUSBAND, Susan M.	(AZ)	578
Special libraries consulting	MCDONOUGH, Kathleen C.	(NH)	803
Special library consulting	GOLDMAN, Ava R.	(FL)	445
	BARRISH, Alan S.	(KY)	60
	THOMAS, Margaret J.	(MI)	1237
	QUINTEN, Rebecca G.	(OH)	1000
	CARVER, Sue A.	(WA)	191
Special library design consulting	MAIN, Annette Z.	(PA)	761
Special library services consulting	FUNK, Elizabeth A.	(PA)	410
State, special & public lib consulting	PHILLIPS, Ray S.	(TX)	969
Statewide library program consulting	LEWIS, Alan D.	(MN)	722
Statistical consulting	JAIN, Nem C.	(MA)	592
Still photography consultant, appraiser	MACAULEY, C C.	(CA)	754
Systems automation consultant	GRAMINSKI, Denise M.	(NY)	457
Taxation research, management consulting	VEASLEY, Mignon M.	(CA)	1280
Teacher consultation	GERRING, Cheryl B.	(MD)	429
Teacher resource consultant	REESE, Virginia D.	(KY)	1016
Training & consulting	STRONG, Sunny A.	(WA)	1203
	MIWA, Makiko	(JAP)	850
Trustee consulting	SWAN, James A.	(KS)	1213
Trustee education consulting	LYNCH, Minnie L.	(LA)	752
University libraries consulting	SHAPIRO, S R.	(NY)	1121
Vendor consulting for libraries	MURO, Ernest A.	(NJ)	880
Veterinary medical libraries consulting	KERKER, Ann E.	(IN)	643
Video collection consultant	REID, Margaret L.	(IL)	1019
Videocassette consulting	REID, Peg L.	(IL)	1019

CONSUMER (See also Clients, Customer, End-User, Patients, Patrons, User)

Consumer & patient health information	LINDNER, Katherine L.	(NJ)	729
Consumer database	VALANDRA, Kent T.	(NY)	1271
Consumer electronics	HASSAN, Abe H.	(CA)	511
Consumer health	BEATTIE, Barbara C.	(NC)	70
	ADAMS, Bruce A.	(NY)	4
Consumer health information	MCCARTHY, Sherri L.	(AL)	794
	RICHETELLE, Alberta L.	(CT)	1030
	MAYO, Kathleen O.	(FL)	790
	WHITED, Diane D.	(LA)	1332
	MCKAY, Ann	(ME)	809
	LANSDALE, Metta T.	(MI)	696
	SERLING, Kitty	(MO)	1116
	CARABATEAS, Clarissa D.	(NY)	180
	ROBBINS, Diane D.	(NY)	1038
	JANES, Jodith	(OH)	593
	JENNINGS, Kathryn L.	(OK)	598
Consumer health information services	TAYLOR, Margaret P.	(ON)	1227

CONSUMER (Cont'd)

Consumer health selection, reference	TAPPANA, Kathy A.	(OK)	1223
Consumer, legal, & medical information	LEBRUN, Anne	(ON)	708
Consumer marketing	UBYSZ, Priscilla M.	(CT)	1267
	GROSVENOR, Philip G.	(OH)	473
Consumer medical collections	DIAL, Carolyn E.	(FL)	299
Consumer products, health care	SILVERMAN, Susanne	(CT)	1139
Consumer products markets	COMPTON, Erlinda R.	(TX)	235
Consumer products, personal care	SILVERMAN, Susanne	(CT)	1139
Consumer protection law	ENGLISH, Susan B.	(VA)	350
Health information for consumers	HESSLEIN, Shirley B.	(NY)	534
Patient & consumer subjects	CESARD, Mary A.	(NJ)	196
Technical editing, consumer electronics	MENNIE, Don	(NJ)	824

CONTINUATIONS (See also Acquisitions)

Approval plans & continuations	JAGER, Conradus	(MA)	591
Approval programs, continuations	SCHRIFT, Leonard B.	(NY)	1100
Continuations & standing orders	BACON, Lois C.	(MA)	44
Direct marketing & continuities	KING, Timothy B.	(NY)	652
Standing orders, continuations	BEN-SIMON, Julie E.	(WA)	83

CONTINUING (See also Adults, Lifelong, Professional, Staff)

Adult basic & continuing education	WASSERMAN, Ricki F.	(NY)	1308
Consulting & continuing education	SEIDENBERG, Edward	(TX)	1112
Continuing education	LAWSON, Martha G.	(AR)	705
	ALIX, Cleta M.	(CA)	13
	HUTCHESON, Don S.	(CA)	578
	KRUGLET, Jo A.	(CO)	680
	CARRINGTON, Virginia F.	(CT)	186
	BEATON, Barbara E.	(DC)	70
	STONE, Elizabeth W.	(DC)	1197
	WYCHE, Louise E.	(DE)	1374
	BROWN, Eva R.	(IL)	143
	HICKS, Frederick M.	(IL)	537
	SNYDER, Sherrie E.	(IL)	1165
	WINNER, Ronald	(IL)	1355
	FARLEY, Janice S.	(IN)	364
	STRATTON, Martha G.	(IN)	1200
	HENEGHAN, Mary A.	(MA)	528
	RICH, Marcia A.	(MA)	1027
	EZELL, Charlaine L.	(MI)	360
	HAWTHORNE, Dorothy M.	(MN)	514
	MAHMOODI, Suzanne H.	(MN)	760
	SELTZER, Ada M.	(MS)	1114
	PATRICK, Ruth J.	(MT)	947
	WILLIAMS, M J.	(NC)	1345
	MOREHOUSE, Valerie J.	(ND)	863
	MEANS, Raymond B.	(NE)	820
	STUDDIFORD, Abigail M.	(NJ)	1204
	GOODMAN, Rhonna A.	(NY)	449
	HANSON, Jan E.	(NY)	498
	LAWRENCE, Thomas A.	(NY)	705
	PACKARD, Joan L.	(NY)	933
	SIMON, Patricia B.	(NY)	1140
	FRY, Mildred C.	(OH)	406
	ROADS, Clarice D.	(OK)	1038
	WOLFE, Gary D.	(PA)	1360
	WOLL, Christina B.	(TX)	1361
	DOWNEY REIDA, Linda K.	(UT)	316
	BELT, Jane	(WA)	78
	TOLLIVER, Barbara J.	(WA)	1248
	CAIN, Carolyn L.	(WI)	171
	LAMB, Donald K.	(WI)	689
	MATTHEWS, Geraldine M.	(WI)	785
	ROBBERS, Sandra M.	(WI)	1038
	WAITY, Gloria J.	(WI)	1293
	CRAIG, Wendy E.	(ON)	254
	KENT, Charles D.	(ON)	642
	WALCKIERS, Marc A.	(BEL)	1293
Continuing educ & professional devlpmnt	BRIDGE, Frank R.	(TX)	135
Continuing education & staff development	TYER, Travis E.	(IL)	1266
Continuing education & training	HOWARD, Mary R.	(GA)	564
	CHOBOT, Mary C.	(VA)	210
Continuing education change agent	BRUCE, Robert K.	(MN)	149

CONTINUING (Cont'd)

Continuing education coordination	SNOWDEN, Deanna	(IN)	1164
Continuing education for librarians	SWATOS, Priscilla L.	(IL)	1214
Continuing education for librarianship	WALTERS, Corky	(WY)	1301
Continuing education, inservice	TASSIA, Margaret R.	(PA)	1224
Continuing education instruction	BURNETT, James H.	(CO)	161
Continuing education programming	TREBBY, Janis G.	(WI)	1255
Continuing education, resource sharing	SHELDON, Brooke E.	(TX)	1125
Continuing education seminars	RUSH, James E.	(OH)	1068
Continuing educ, training & development	WELLS, Mary K.	(TX)	1322
Continuing library education	BLOESCH, Ethel B.	(IA)	106
Continuing medical education	MANNING, Phil R.	(CA)	767
	SIMPSON, Evelyn L.	(CA)	1141
	STLUKA, Thomas H.	(IL)	1195
	KELLY, Kay	(MI)	638
	KELLER, Marlo L.	(OH)	635
Continuing medical education programming	BEDARD, Martha A.	(MA)	73
Continuing professional education	VARLEJS, Jana	(NJ)	1278
Library & continuing education	TOM, Chow L.	(HI)	1249
Library continuing education	TARANKO, Walter J.	(ME)	1223
	DAHLSTROM, Joe F.	(TX)	269
Library education & continuing education	MCCROSSAN, John A.	(FL)	800
Medical librarian continuing education	EZQUERRA, Isabel	(FL)	360
Professional continuing education	WILFORD, Valerie J.	(IL)	1339
Providing continuing education	KRUSE, Ginny M.	(WI)	681
Staff development & continuing education	HIATT, Peter	(WA)	536
Training & continuing education	DREWETT, William O.	(IL)	319
	HYMAN, Karen D.	(NJ)	580

CONTRACTS

Building & contracting	KRUZIC, Evelyn D.	(WA)	681
Contract administration	SLOCA, Sue E.	(DC)	1150
	BOGGESS, John J.	(MD)	110
Contract & circuit services	CREELAN, Marilee M.	(OH)	257
Contract cataloging	KELLOUGH, Patrick H.	(TX)	637
Contract law	POOLEY, Beverly J.	(MI)	983
Contract libraries	GENAWAY, David C.	(OH)	426
Contract library management	RAPETTI, Vincent A.	(FL)	1008
Contract library services	GARVEY, Nancy G.	(NJ)	421
Contract negotiation	GROSSMAN, Allen N.	(NJ)	473
Electronic publishing contracting	BROWN-SPRUILL, Debra K.	(NY)	149
Federal libraries contracting	STALLINGS, Elizabeth A.	(DC)	1179
Government contracting	FATTIBENE, James F.	(DC)	366
Government contracts	FOWLIE, Linda K.	(DC)	394
Government documents, contract mgmt	LAKSHMAN, Malathi K.	(MD)	689
Grant & contract databases	OSTROW, Dianne G.	(MD)	929
Library contract management	CHIESA, Adele M.	(MD)	208
Library service contracts	WALTERS, Daniel L.	(WA)	1301
Managing grants & contracts	SCULL, Roberta A.	(LA)	1108
Managing library contracts	STALLINGS, Elizabeth A.	(DC)	1179
Service contracts	HYMAN, Karen D.	(NJ)	580

CONTROL

Acquisitions & bibliographic control	LINDGREN, Arla M.	(NY)	729
Archival control systems	MOTTRAM, Geoffrey	(IL)	873
Archival manuscripts control MARC format	WEBER, Lisa B.	(IL)	1314
Archives & manuscripts control	CARROLL-HORROCKS, Elizabeth	(PA)	187
Authorities control	STEINHAGEN, Elizabeth N.	(ID)	1186
Authority control	FIEGEN, Ann M.	(AZ)	375
	ROCKE, Reve P.	(CA)	1046
	HIATT, Robert M.	(DC)	536
	LIGGETT, Suzanne L.	(DC)	726
	FRAZER, Ruth F.	(FL)	399
	HILL, Janet S.	(IL)	540
	HSIEH, Cynthia C.	(IL)	567
	STRAWN, Gary L.	(IL)	1201
	GOODWIN, Vania M.	(IN)	450
	MARTIN, Norma H.	(LA)	777

CONTROL (Cont'd)

Authority control	HOSTAGE, John B.	(MA)	562
	LINSKY, Leonore K.	(MA)	731
	TAVARES, Cecelia M.	(MA)	1225
	KLAIR, Arlene F.	(MD)	657
	HERVEY, Norma J.	(MN)	533
	REISNER, Suzanne R.	(MN)	1021
	BERTCHUME, Gary	(NY)	90
	SMIRAGLIA, Richard P.	(NY)	1152
	STAM, Deirdre C.	(NY)	1179
	THOMAS, Catherine M.	(NY)	1236
	KIRKBRIDE, Amey L.	(OH)	654
	LUDY, Lorene E.	(OH)	747
	FULLER, Elizabeth E.	(PA)	408
	BROSS, Valerie	(TN)	141
	GRADY, Agnes M.	(TN)	455
	CRAIG, Marilyn J.	(TX)	254
	SADOWSKI, Frank E.	(VA)	1074
	FRITZ, Richard J.	(ON)	405
	SAKAMOTO, Hiroshi	(JAP)	1076
Authority control services	HANIFORD, K L.	(MO)	496
Authority control work	TURKALO, David M.	(MA)	1263
Automated acquisitions control	DE LUISE, Alexandra	(PQ)	290
Automated authority control	GRUTCHFIELD, Walter	(NY)	475
	MILLER, Daniel J.	(OR)	836
Automated cataloging, authority control	GLASSMAN, Penny L.	(MA)	440
Automated library control systems	YOUNG, Peter R.	(DC)	1383
Automated linked authority control	BISOM, Diane B.	(CA)	99
Automated serial control systems	FONG, Wilfred W.	(WI)	388
Automated serials control	TALLMAN, Karen D.	(AZ)	1221
	KIRK, Darcy	(MA)	654
Automation of bibliographic control	BENGTSON, Betty G.	(TN)	80
Bibliographic control	NEAVILL, Gordon B.	(AL)	891
	KIRKLAND, Janice J.	(CA)	655
	BALMER, Mary	(CT)	53
	KOEL, Ake I.	(CT)	667
	PRICE, Mary S.	(DC)	992
	MEAD-DONALDSON, Susan L.	(FL)	819
	LEVSTIK, Frank R.	(KY)	721
	OMAR, Elizabeth A.	(MD)	923
	DAVIS, Anne C.	(MI)	277
	MOSEY, Jeanette	(MI)	871
	MANDEL, Carol A.	(NY)	764
	MIKSA, Francis L.	(TX)	834
	SHEETS, Shirley H.	(TX)	1125
	SKELLEY, Grant T.	(WA)	1145
	PAREDES-RUIZ, Eudoxio B.	(SK)	940
Bibliographic control, non-print media	TOTTEN, Herman L.	(TX)	1252
Bibliographic control of newspapers	FIELD, Kenneth C.	(BC)	375
Bibliographic control of serials	KOMOROUS, Hana J.	(BC)	670
Bibliographic control systems	GUILES, Kay D.	(DC)	476
Bibliographic organization control	HENDERSON, Kathryn L.	(IL)	526
Bibliographical control	DWORACZEK, Marian	(AB)	330
	WU, Painan R.	(NY)	1373
Budget control	CHRISTIANSON, Ellory J.	(MN)	212
Budget planning & control	FROSCHER, Jean L.	(FL)	406
Budgetary control	STIFFLEAR, Allan J.	(MA)	1194
Budgeting & budget control	KEHOE, Patrick E.	(DC)	634
Budgets, cost controls	BAUMGARTNER, Robert M.	(OH)	66
Cataloging & authority control	TILLETT, Barbara B.	(CA)	1245
	IDDINGS, Daniel H.	(IL)	581
	WEE, Lily K.	(IL)	1315
	ENGLE, Constance B.	(MI)	349
Cataloging & serials control	DRAPER, Linda J.	(MO)	318
Circulation control	COHEN, Barbara S.	(RI)	228
Circulation control systems	DODGE, Christopher N.	(MN)	308
Circulation inventory control	GOULD, Douglas A.	(UT)	454
Collection development & serials control	BECHOR, Malvina B.	(GA)	71
Computer file bibliographic control	HERMAN, Elizabeth	(CA)	531
Curriculum materials control	CLARK, Alice S.	(CA)	216
Database design & quality control	VEGTER, Amy H.	(NY)	1281
Database management & quality control	HOMAN, J M.	(MI)	555
Database quality control	KOLMAN, Roberta F.	(HI)	669

CONTROL (Cont'd)

Device control systems	ZOROWITZ, Richard D. .	(IL)	1390
Document control database	ZBORAY, Ronald J.	(CA)	1386
Document distribution & control	SANDERS, Mary C.	(NJ)	1080
Implementing automated authority control	FISHER, Carl D.	(VA)	380
Information processing & control	SPATH, Charles E.	(TN)	1171
In-process control automation	WARZALA, Martin L. . . .	(CT)	1307
International bibliographic control	COOK, C D.	(ON)	239
Inventory control, vendor management	MCGRAW, Scott C.	(IL)	807
Library circulation control	RAHN, Erwin P.	(NY)	1003
Library systems, serials control	WANG, Anna M.	(OH)	1302
Loss control in libraries & universities	MORRIS, John	(CA)	866
Manuscripts & records bibl control	KELLER, William B. . . .	(DC)	636
Medical serials acquisitions & control	WOODBURN, Judy I. . . .	(NC)	1366
Monographic series, authority control	DECKER, Jean S.	(NY)	285
Online authority control	BERRINGER, Virginia M.	(OH)	90
	FRIEDLAND, Frances K. .	(ON)	403
	HORNE, Ernest L.	(MI)	560
Online bibliographic control	RAHN, Erwin P.	(NY)	1003
Patron & inventory control	KRAMER, Helen A.	(CA)	675
Periodical control	REDDINGTON, Mary E. .	(OH)	1013
Picture collection control	MORALES, Milton F. . . .	(MO)	862
Policy & control of library systems	AMELUNG, Richard C. . .	(MO)	19
Quality control	DAVIS, Carol C.	(OH)	277
Quality control & training	NADZIEJKA, David E. . .	(WI)	886
Records management & control	REID, Angea S.	(MA)	1018
Serial control & collection development	MANDAL, Mina R.	(NY)	764
Serials acquisition & control	KHOURY, Nancy L.	(LA)	646
Serials acquisitions & control	SCHWARTZ, Marla J. . .	(VA)	1105
Serials bibliographic control & review	STEINHAGEN, Elizabeth N.	(ID)	1186
Serials check-in & control	GERLOTT, Eleanor L. . . .	(PA)	429
Serials control	WHITE, Larry R.	(CA)	1331
	WILLARD, Ann M.	(CA)	1341
	CARNEGLIA, Anna L. . .	(CT)	183
	HOLLYFIELD, Diane S. .	(DC)	552
	PUGH, Thurman A.	(DC)	997
	VISK, Linda S.	(GA)	1285
	DARLING, Elizabeth A. . .	(IL)	274
	EILERS, Marsha J.	(IN)	340
	VIGEANT, Robert J.	(IN)	1284
	FORFIA, Linda S.	(KS)	390
	GASKINS, Betty	(KY)	421
	SCULLIN, Janice J.	(MA)	1109
	MOLTER, Maureen M. . .	(MD)	853
	LARONGE, Philip V.	(MI)	698
	MOSHER, Robin A.	(MI)	871
	WHEATON, Julie A.	(MI)	1328
	MOONEY, Jennifer M. . .	(NJ)	858
	CARLSON, Robert E. . . .	(NY)	182
	DECKER, Jean S.	(NY)	285
	FINCH, Frances	(NY)	377
	FOSTER, Selma V.	(NY)	392
	PERCELLI, Irene M.	(NY)	958
	RESCIGNO, Dolores S. .	(NY)	1024
	RUIZ-VALERA, Phoebe L.	(NY)	1067
	GRABENSTATTER, Christine N.	(OH)	455
	LEE, Sooncha A.	(OH)	711
	MOORE, Maxwell J.	(OH)	860
	TANNFHILL, Robert S. . .	(OH)	1222
	WELLS, Catherine A. . . .	(OH)	1322
	FACKLER, Naomi P.	(TX)	360
	KIMZEY, Ann C.	(TX)	649
	SWEARINGEN, Wilba S.	(TX)	1214
	ANDERSON, Janet A. . .	(UT)	23
	MERRYMAN, Margaret M.	(VA)	827
	MURDEN, Steven H. . . .	(VA)	879
	CHRISTMAN, Inese R. . .	(WI)	212
	CRAWFORD, Josephine .	(WI)	256
	MILLER, Julia E.	(WI)	839
	FU, Ting W.	(HKG)	407
Serials control & online databases	CHAPMAN, Elwynda K. .	(DC)	202
Serials control systems	LONG, Roger J.	(IL)	739
Serials records control	CLASQUIN, Frank F. . . .	(MA)	219
Serials selection & control	KRIER, Mary M.	(MA)	678

CONTROL (Cont'd)

Software system quality control	KOLMAN, Roberta F. . . .	(HI)	669
	VEGTER, Amy H.	(NY)	1281
Subject & name authority control	BADING, Kathryn E.	(TX)	44
Subject authority control	HURLBERT, Irene W. . . .	(CA)	577
Visual resources authority control	MOST, Gregory P.	(TX)	872

CONTROLLED

Controlled environment agriculture	LAKE, Mary S.	(AZ)	689
Controlled environment aquaculture	LAKE, Mary S.	(AZ)	689
Controlled vocabularies	NADZIEJKA, David E. . .	(WI)	886
Controlled vocabulary development	WALL, Eugene	(MD)	1297
Controlled vocabulary indexing	LINDER, Elliott	(NY)	729

CONVENTION (See also Conferences)

Annual convention	YEISER, Doris B.	(KY)	1379
Convention & conference management	AUCOIN, Sharilynn A. . .	(LA)	38

CONVERSION (See also Reclassification, Reconversion, Retrospective)

Authority record conversion	STUBBS, Linda T.	(DC)	1204
Automated databases & conversions	PHILLIPS, Clifford R. . . .	(CA)	968
Automated retrospective conversion	JOHNSON, Pat M.	(TX)	608
Automation conversion	BAKER, Narcissa L.	(OH)	49
Bibliographic file conversion	CHIU, Ida K.	(TX)	209
Catalog & retrospective conversion	CHAN, Margy	(ON)	199
Cataloging & retrospective conversion	ZIESELMAN, Paula M. . .	(NY)	1388
Cataloging, conversion	WELLINGTON, Jean S. .	(OH)	1322
Cataloging retrospective conversion	ROBERTSON, Pamela S.	(ND)	1042
Computer conversions	LANE, Elizabeth J.	(NY)	694
Conversion & database maintenance	SHEAFFER, Marc L.	(PA)	1124
Data conversion	HARRIS, Michael A.	(CO)	505
Data entry & conversion	MEDINA, Ildefonso M. . .	(NY)	820
Database conversion	HIATT, Robert M.	(DC)	536
	JANK, David A.	(MA)	593
	KREYCHE, Michael R. . .	(OH)	678
Database conversion & buildup	MEDINA, Ildefonso M. . .	(NY)	820
Database conversion projects	DIXON, Edith M.	(WI)	306
Database retrospective conversion	MORGAN, Ferrell	(CA)	864
Inventory retrospective conversion	SCHMIDT, Mary A.	(TX)	1095
Library automation, data conversion	KERSHNER, Lois M. . . .	(CA)	644
Library conversion consulting	PHILLIPS, Ray S.	(TX)	969
Lib of Congress cataloging conversion	DUNMIRE, Raymond V. .	(AL)	326
Machine-readable shelflist conversion	NOBLE, Barbara N.	(MO)	906
Optical disk conversion	BARRETT, Darryl D.	(MN)	59
Retrospective conversion	MOORE, Anne C.	(AZ)	858
	DRIVER, Linda A.	(CA)	320
	MAINELLI, Helen K.	(CA)	761
	NEAL, Jan	(CA)	890
	SASSE, Margo	(CA)	1083
	SCHOTTLAENDER, Brian E.	(CA)	1099
	SWEENEY, Suzanne . . .	(CA)	1215
	THELIN, Sonya R.	(CA)	1234
	WILLIAMS, Mary S.	(CA)	1345
	HILL, John R.	(CT)	540
	LISOWSKI, Andrew H. . .	(DC)	732
	REED-SCOTT, Jutta R. .	(DC)	1015
	SANDIQUE-OWENS, Amelia A.	(DC)	1080
	PINGS, Joan G.	(FL)	974
	WILLIAMS, Nancy L. . . .	(FL)	1345
	WILSON, Lesley P.	(GA)	1351
	CURL, Margo W.	(ID)	265
	OSTRANDER, Gloria J. .	(ID)	929
	IDDINGS, Daniel H.	(IL)	581
	JAGODZINSKI, Cecile M.	(IL)	591
	OWNES, Dorothy J.	(IL)	932
	WILLIAMS, Charles M. . .	(IL)	1342
	EBERSHOFF-COLES, Susan V.	(IN)	334
	PEC, Jean A.	(IN)	953
	WARTZOK, Susan G. . . .	(IN)	1307
	DEARUJO, Georgia R. . .	(KY)	284
	KUKLINSKI, Joan L.	(MA)	683
	SMITH, Barbara G.	(MD)	1152
	SMITH, Mary P.	(MD)	1158

CONVERSION (Cont'd)

Retrospective conversion

	BRUNHUMER, Sondra K.	(MI)	150
	DOMBROWSKI, Mark A.	(MI)	310
	ENGLE, Constance B.	(MI)	349
	GERLACH, William P.	(MI)	429
	MA, Helen Y.	(MI)	753
	CHAN, Jeanny T.	(MO)	199
	MYRICK, Judy C.	(MS)	885
	MAYES, Susan E.	(NC)	789
	GARZILLO, Robert R.	(NJ)	421
	LI, Marjorie H.	(NJ)	724
	WILEN, Rosamond L.	(NJ)	1339
	BANICKI, Cynthia A.	(NM)	54
	SAUNDERS, Laverna M.	(NV)	1084
	ANDERSON, Birgitta M.	(NY)	21
	BERTUCA, David J.	(NY)	91
	CHAPMAN, Renee D.	(NY)	202
	ERLAND, Virginia K.	(NY)	353
	GALGAN, Mary N.	(NY)	413
	KIM, Chung N.	(NY)	648
	LOW, Frederick E.	(NY)	743
	LUCKER, Amy E.	(NY)	746
	NICHOLS-RANDALL, Barbara L.	(NY)	902
	SALVAGE, Barbara A.	(NY)	1078
	STALKER, Dianne S.	(NY)	1178
	WERNER, Edward K.	(NY)	1324
	CALL, J R.	(OH)	173
	DAVIS, Linda M.	(OH)	280
	SAMPLES, Judith L.	(OH)	1078
	LOWRIMORE, R T.	(SC)	745
	THOMAS, Julie A.	(SC)	1237
	WALTON, Robert A.	(TX)	1301
	YEH, Helen S.	(TX)	1379
	NOEL, Eileen V.	(UT)	907
	SMITH, John R.	(MB)	1156
Retrospective conversion coordination	WALSH, Joanna M.	(MA)	1299
Retrospective conversion of serials	TUTTLE, Joseph C.	(NC)	1266
	POST, Phyllis C.	(OH)	986
Retrospective conversion projects	PAYNE, Leila M.	(TX)	951
Retrospective conversion services	HANIFORD, K L.	(MO)	496
Serials processing, holdings conversion	RONEN, Naomi	(MA)	1053
Serials retrospective conversion	KING, Kenneth E.	(MI)	651
Text conversion	BEATTY, Samuel B.	(MD)	70

COOLIDGE

Calvin Coolidge history	WIKANDER, Lawrence E.	(MA)	1338

COOLING

Passive solar cooling techniques	LAKE, Mary S.	(AZ)	689

COOPERATION (See also Partnerships, Sharing)

Academic library cooperation	LEMKE, Darrell H.	(DC)	715
Cooperation	FRITZ, Linda	(SK)	405
Cooperation for resource sharing	BESEMER, Susan P.	(NY)	91
Departmental cooperation	SOURS, Katherine M.	(FL)	1169
Development of regional cooperation	CANAVAN, Roberta N.	(NJ)	178
Inter-institutional cooperation	NEAL, Donn C.	(IL)	890
Interlibrary cooperation	THOMAS, Margie J.	(AK)	1237
	RICHMOND, Elizabeth B.	(CO)	1030
	BRYAN, Barbara D.	(CT)	151
	HOLLOWAY, Patricia W.	(CT)	552
	MILLER, Laurence A.	(FL)	839
	MOUNCE, Marvin W.	(FL)	873
	MURPHEY, Barbara A.	(FL)	880
	NEUHOFE, M D.	(FL)	897
	FORSEE, Joe B.	(GA)	391
	CRISPEN, Joanne	(IL)	259
	LAMONT, Bridget L.	(IL)	691
	MEACHEN, Edward W.	(IL)	819
	ROSENFELD, Joel C.	(IL)	1056
	WANK, Paul G.	(LA)	1303
	STEINFELD, Michael	(MA)	1186
	GELINAS, Jeanne L.	(MN)	426
	ALEXANDER, Susanna	(MO)	12

COOPERATION (Cont'd)

Interlibrary cooperation

	HAWLEY, George S.	(NJ)	514
	CALLAHAM, Betty E.	(SC)	173
	CAMACHO, Nancy S.	(TX)	174
	KRENTZ, Roger F.	(WI)	677
	JOHNSON, Wayne H.	(WY)	609
Interlibrary cooperation & networking	WILKINS, Barratt	(FL)	1340
Interlibrary cooperation consortia	BROWN, Thomas M.	(WV)	148
International cooperation	POLAND, Ursula H.	(NY)	980
	DE LIAMCHIN, Lana	(PQ)	289
International liaison & cooperation	RICHER, Suzanne	(ON)	1030
International library cooperation	BALL, Alice D.	(DC)	52
Intertype library cooperation	TUTTLE, Walter A.	(NC)	1266
	CONDON, John J.	(WI)	236
Intralibrary cooperation	ARN, Nancy L.	(AR)	33
Librarian-teacher cooperation	RASSAM, Cynthia K.	(NM)	1009
Library & info community cooperation	BARTLEY, Linda K.	(DC)	61
Library cooperation	SHACKELFORD, Eileen R.	(AZ)	1118
	GALLOWAY, R D.	(CA)	415
	SALMON, Stephen R.	(CA)	1077
	ANDERSON, Lemoyne W.	(CO)	24
	CAMPBELL, John D.	(CO)	176
	SARGENT, Dency C.	(CT)	1083
	URICCHIO, William J.	(CT)	1269
	HORNEY, Joyce C.	(IL)	560
	MCCLARREN, Robert R.	(IL)	796
	SIMPSON, Donald B.	(IL)	1141
	STRATTON, Martha G.	(IN)	1200
	SWEEN, Roger	(MN)	1214
	HIEBING, Dottie	(NJ)	537
	EVANS, Robert W.	(NY)	358
	ALBRECHT, Cheryl C.	(OH)	10
	WAREHAM, Nancy L.	(OH)	1304
	HUGHES, Carol A.	(OK)	571
	SAUER, James L.	(PA)	1084
	HASBROUCK, Clara H.	(TN)	510
	LINDENFELD, Joseph F.	(TN)	729
	BILLINGS, Harold W.	(TX)	96
Library cooperation & networking	NYQUIST, Corinne E.	(NY)	913
	MONTAG, John	(OH)	855
	BUNGE, Charles A.	(WI)	157
Library systems & cooperation	WILDER, David T.	(NY)	1338
Multi-library cooperation	ROYCE, Carolyn S.	(NJ)	1063
Multitype cooperation	ECKERT, Daniel L.	(WI)	335
Multi-type library cooperation	FALSONE, Anne M.	(CO)	363
	BURGER, Leslie B.	(CT)	159
	HUPP, Sharon W.	(CT)	577
	POUNDSTONE, Sally H.	(CT)	987
	BROWN, Eva R.	(IL)	143
	OLSEN, Rowena J.	(KS)	921
	DEJOHN, William T.	(MN)	288
	LOWRY, Lucy J.	(MN)	745
	PARKER, Sara A.	(MT)	942
	PERRY, Douglas F.	(NC)	960
	NEUMANN, Joan	(NY)	897
	WASHBURN, Keith E.	(NY)	1307
	WAREHAM, Nancy L.	(OH)	1304
	TREBBY, Janis G.	(WI)	1255
Multitype lib cooperation consultation	VOSS, Anne E.	(NJ)	1289
Multitype library systems, cooperation	KNEPEL, Nancy	(CO)	664
National & international cooperation	LINTON, William D.	(NIR)	731
Networking & cooperation	KATZ, Ruth M.	(NC)	630
	WILLEMSE, John	(SAF)	1341
Public & school library cooperation	LEITLE, Barbara K.	(MO)	714
Public library cooperation	SONDALLE, Barbara J.	(IL)	1167
Public library, school cooperation	LONG, Judith N.	(IL)	739
Regional library cooperation	JENNINGS, Martha F.	(MI)	598
School & public library cooperation	BRAINARD, Elsie K.	(MA)	127
Small college library cooperation	OLSEN, Rowena J.	(KS)	921
University library cooperation	DUPUIS, Onil	(PQ)	327
University, school & library cooperation	BERLING, John G.	(MN)	88

COOPERATIVE (See also Systems)

Automation in multitype cooperatives	DAW, May B.	(CT)	282
Cooperative bibliographic instruction	RATZER, Mary B.	(NY)	1010
Cooperative book depositories	STOCKTON, Gloria J.	(CA)	1196
Cooperative buying	SCHWELK, Jennifer C.	(OH)	1105

COOPERATIVE (Cont'd)

Cooperative cataloging	LIGGETT, Suzanne L. . . .	(DC)	726
Cooperative collection development	STEPHENS, Dennis J. . . .	(AK)	1187
	BATES, Henry E.	(CA)	64
	MEACHEN, Edward W. .	(IL)	819
	SMITH, Newland F.	(IL)	1159
	FARRELL, David	(IN)	365
	KENNEDY BRIGHT, Sandra	(NY)	641
	KLIMLEY, Susan	(NY)	661
	KRUEGER, Karen J. . . .	(WI)	680
Cooperative community programs	MAINIERO, Elizabeth T. .	(CT)	761
Cooperative library agreements	MARTIN, Robert A.	(FL)	778
Cooperative library development	WHITE, Robert W.	(NJ)	1332
Cooperative library projects	SPECHT, Joe W.	(TX)	1172
Cooperative library service	DALTON, Phyllis I.	(NV)	271
Cooperative library services	ROBLEE, Martha A.	(IN)	1045
Cooperative library systems	PIKE, Lee E.	(AL)	973
	KNUTSON, Linda J. . . .	(IL)	666
	MCCULLY, William C. . .	(IL)	801
	BUFFINGTON, Karyl L. .	(KS)	155
	PATRICK, Patricia M. . . .	(NY)	947
	VERDIBELLO, Muriel F. .	(NY)	1282
	WELLS, Mary K.	(TX)	1322
Cooperative medical library systems	JOHN, Stephanie C.	(MI)	601
Cooperative multitype library systems	JAGOE, Katherine P. . . .	(TX)	591
Cooperative networking	REYNOLDS, Dennis J. . . .	(DC)	1025
Cooperative networks	HAHN, Ellen	(DC)	483
Cooperative planning	MICHAELIS, Kathryn S. .	(WI)	831
Cooperative planning & teaching	SCOTT, William H.	(BC)	1108
Cooperative planning teaching	MACRAE, Lorne G.	(AB)	758
Cooperative programs for libraries	JURIST, Susan	(CA)	620
Cooperative purchase	LAUGHLIN, Beverly E. . . .	(LA)	702
Cooperative reference	ROOSE, Tina	(IL)	1053
Cooperative reference services	GIBBS, Margareth	(IL)	431
Cooperative serials agreements	ROBERTS, Elizabeth P. .	(WA)	1039
Cooperative serials projects	UPHAM, Lois N.	(SC)	1269
Cooperative services	BENN, James R.	(CT)	81
Cooperative strategies, consortia	OFFERMANN, Glenn W. .	(MN)	917
Cooperative systems	MAXWELL, James G. . .	(OR)	788
	GOLDEN, Helene	(PQ)	445
Cooperative teaching	WILLIAMS, Eve A.	(NB)	1343
Cooperative theological lib development	WARTLUFT, David J. . . .	(PA)	1307
Cooperatives	HUDSON, Rosetta A. . . .	(MO)	570
Library automation cooperatives	BISHOFF, Lizbeth J. . . .	(CA)	99
Library cooperatives	CUNNINGHAM, Tina Y. .	(MI)	265
	SALVAYON, Connie	(PA)	1078
Library cooperatives, networking	CHAPMAN, Mary A. . . .	(MI)	202
	MASSEY, Eleanor N. . . .	(NJ)	782
Multitype cooperative projects	DORST, Thomas J.	(IL)	313
Multitype cooperatives	DAW, May B.	(CT)	282
Multitype library cooperative	ROSENBERG, Gail L. . . .	(NJ)	1056
Reference, cooperative	GOULDING, Mary A. . . .	(IL)	454
Regional cooperative library systems	HURREY, Katharine C. . .	(MD)	577
Teacher/librarian cooperatives	ANDRIST, Shirley A. . . .	(SK)	27

COORDINATION (See also Management)

Access review & coordination	GRAF, Thomas H.	(DC)	456
Audiovisual coordination	ARNOLD, Peggy	(MI)	34
	GAGNON, Ruth	(NH)	412
	EMERICK, John L.	(PA)	347
	GODWIN, Frances L. . . .	(TX)	443
Automated database coordination	ROSS, Carole L.	(CT)	1058
Automation coordinating	OLSON, Anton J.	(IL)	922
Automation coordination	MISNER, Joyce V.	(MI)	847
	HODGES, Pauline R. . . .	(OH)	546
Automation planning, coordinating	DEMYANOVICH, Peter . .	(NJ)	291
Bookmobile coordination	GRIMLEY, Susan M. . . .	(SC)	470
Branch coordination	GRIMLEY, Susan M. . . .	(SC)	470
Branch library coordination	FRANKS, Janice	(AL)	398
Computer coordinating	DAVIS, Judy R.	(NC)	279
Computer coordination	HOERGER, Helen L.	(MI)	547
Computer laboratory coordination	WIRTANEN, James	(ND)	1356
Computer laboratory coordinator	TRIM, Kathryn	(MI)	1256
Computer reference service coordination	KONG, Leslie M.	(CA)	670
Conference coordination	BARR, Arlene E.	(CO)	58
	HOWARD, Ada M.	(TX)	563

COORDINATION (Cont'd)

Continuing education coordination	SNOWDEN, Deanna . . .	(IN)	1164
Coordinate library budget & expenditures	REID, Richard H.	(LA)	1019
Coordinating & administrating branches	ALGAZE, Selma B.	(FL)	13
Coordinating branch services	WALSH, Mary A.	(PQ)	1300
Coordinating indexing services	BLOZIS, Jolene M.	(DC)	107
Coordinating K-12 library programs	CHAPMAN, Peggy H. . . .	(NC)	202
Coordinating materials selection	ZIEGLER, Fred	(AB)	1388
Coordinating public services	TITUS, Barbara K.	(DE)	1247
Coordinating with curriculum	IMONDI, Lenore R.	(RI)	582
Coordination	DEYOUNG, Gail O.	(MI)	298
Coordination of automated systems	THOMPSON, John W. . . .	(IL)	1240
Coordination of library services	WALCH, David B.	(CA)	1293
Coordination of literary programs	CALLAHAN, Helen H. . . .	(CT)	173
Coordinator, library technology program	DAANE, Jeanette K.	(AZ)	269
Coordinator of children's services	COLE, Gayle	(CA)	230
County law library coordination	CRAWFORD, Nola N. . . .	(NJ)	257
Curriculum coordination	KONNEKER, Rachel C. .	(NC)	670
	DAVIS, Joan C.	(TX)	279
Database coordinating	PERDUE, Robert W.	(FL)	958
Database coordination	KEMPF, Jody L.	(NM)	639
Database searching coordination	DURNIAK, Barbara A. . . .	(NY)	328
District-wide coordination, supervision	VAUGHAN, Janet E.	(MN)	1279
Division level library coordination	MCLEOD, Karen E.	(SK)	814
Documentation analysis & coordination	HACKMAN, Larry J.	(NY)	481
Elementary school library coordination	HERRON, Bettie J.	(AZ)	533
Exhibit coordination	NELSON, Norma	(NY)	894
Exhibition coordination	YOUNG, Barbara N.	(FL)	1381
Film & video collection coordination	NEBEL, Jean C.	(CA)	891
Friends coordination & development	CASELLA, Roberta L. . . .	(TX)	192
Grants coordination	SUMMERS, Lorraine S. . .	(FL)	1209
IBM-PC/XT network coordination	LYDEN, Edward W.	(TX)	750
Information services coordination	SHORT, William M.	(TN)	1132
Instructional computer coordination	PENDLETON, Kim B. . . .	(AK)	956
Liaison coordinating	YAEK, Larry A.	(MI)	1376
Library coordination	DUPUIS, Onil	(PQ)	327
Library coordinator supervision	FRIEDMAN, Tevia L. . . .	(TX)	404
Library system coordination	EBERSHOFF-COLES, Susan V.	(IN)	334
Library technician program coordination	MCDONALD, Marilyn M.	(CA)	803
Literacy coordinator	KROEHLER, Beth A. . . .	(IN)	679
Literacy program coordination	STEWART, Jeanne E. . .	(MS)	1192
Live music concert coordination	RUSTMAN, Mark M. . . .	(KS)	1070
LSCA coordination	CATES, Sheila A.	(MT)	195
Media coordinating	DAVIS, Judy R.	(NC)	279
Media coordination	ZACHARY, Patricia A. . . .	(OK)	1385
Microcomputer coordination	DYKHUIS, Randy	(MI)	331
Network coordination	FELLA, Sarah C.	(OR)	370
	DANIEL, Eileen	(ON)	272
	JANIK, Sophie	(PQ)	593
Online coordination	BREMER, Thomas A. . . .	(MT)	132
Online coordination & searching	TAYLOR, Douglas M. . . .	(AL)	1226
Online search coordination	PATTON, Linda L.	(FL)	949
Online searching & search coordination	ROBERTS, Sally M.	(IL)	1041
Online searching coordinator	WILKINSON, David W. . .	(CA)	1340
Pamphlet file coordination	ROBINSON, David A. . . .	(OH)	1043
Periodicals coordinating	ZIRBES, Colette M.	(WI)	1390
Planning & coordinating training	TOWNSEND, Carolyn J. .	(PA)	1253
Planning & coordination	KERSCHNER, Joan G. . .	(NV)	644
Practicum & internship coordination	COLEMAN, J G.	(AL)	231
Program coordination	MANBECK, Virginia B. . .	(NY)	764
	LOCKETT, Iva	(TX)	736
Project management & coordination	BAADE, Harley D.	(TX)	43
Public programming coordination	ATCHISON, Fres D.	(KS)	37
Public relations & program coordination	MOORE, Virginia B.	(DC)	861
Reference services coordinating	QUEEN, Margaret E. . . .	(CA)	999
Regional coordination	WEITKEMPER, Larry D. .	(MO)	1320
Research & curriculum coordination	BANKHEAD, Elizabeth M.	(CO)	54
Resource coordination	BRICK, Sarah E.	(OK)	134
Retrospective conversion coordination	WALSH, Joanna M.	(MA)	1299
School & public library coordination	MORROW, Blaine V. . . .	(MI)	869
School district coordinator	GILBERT, Betty H.	(AZ)	433
School region lib, media coordination	RIVERA, Antonio	(NY)	1037

COORDINATION (Cont'd)

School-wide computer coordination	LINDSEY, Nancy L.	(TN)	730
Serials coordinating	MOORE, Sheryl R.	(TX)	861
Staff duty coordination	BULLOCK, Jessie M.	(PA)	156
Technical services coordination	ALLEN, Joan W.	(TX)	15
	MATHIS, Margaret H. . . .	(TX)	784
Union list coordination	ARNN, Judith A.	(TX)	33
User education coordination	FREY, Barbara J.	(CT)	402
Video program coordination	SIEBL, Linda M.	(NY)	1135
Voluntary coordination	MOORE, Sheryl R.	(TX)	861
Volunteer coordination	ALLEN, Stephanie O. . . .	(AZ)	16
	SPAZIANI, Carol	(IA)	1172
Volunteer program coordinator	SALVATORE, Gayle E. .	(LA)	1078
Workshop design & coordination	WEBSTER, Linda	(TX)	1314

COPY

Copier art	NEADERLAND, Louise O.	(NY)	890
Copier services	GREGORY, Carla L.	(VA)	466
Copier vend systems	SCHULTZ, Michael W. . . .	(AZ)	1102
Copier vending systems	MERKERT, Robert J. . . .	(NJ)	826
Copy cataloging	ARAKAWA, Steven R. . . .	(CT)	30
	O'NEIL, Rosanna M.	(OH)	924
	HALL, John D.	(TX)	488
Copy editing	KLEIN, Barbara L.	(WY)	659
Copy services, security	ALMONY, Robert A.	(MO)	17
Journal copying, interlibrary loan	BROWN, Elizabeth E. . . .	(CA)	143
Listing notices, label copy	WOOD, Sallie B.	(NY)	1365
Photographic copy work	DESJARDINS, Andrea C.	(MA)	295
Supervising copy cataloging	KNIGHT, Rita C.	(AZ)	664

COPYRIGHT (See also Clearance, Permissions, Property)

Copyright	SINOFSKY, Esther R. . . .	(CA)	1144
	MCKINLEY, Sylvia J. . . .	(DC)	811
	RISHER, Carol A.	(DC)	1036
	TABB, Winston	(DC)	1219
	KAZLAUSKAS, Diane W.	(FL)	632
	RYSTROM, Barbara B. . .	(GA)	1072
	SURRENCY, Erwin C. . .	(GA)	1210
	HALE, Charles E.	(IL)	485
	JOHNSON, Ellen S.	(KS)	604
	TALAB, Rosemary S. . . .	(KS)	1220
	DITXLER, Carol J.	(MD)	306
	ARMSTRONG, Joanne D.	(NY)	32
	LERNER, Rita G.	(NY)	717
	PAULSON, Peter J.	(NY)	950
	JACKSON, Mary E.	(PA)	588
	MARSHALL, Nancy H. . .	(VA)	775
	TSAI, Shaopan	(ON)	1260
Copyright & audiovisuals	FRYER, Philip	(MD)	407
Copyright & intellectual property	JENSEN, Mary B.	(SD)	599
Copyright & legal issues in management	NASRI, William Z.	(PA)	888
Copyright compliance systems	WEIL, Ben H.	(NJ)	1317
Copyright information	MASTRANGELO, Marjorie J.	(DC)	782
Copyright issues	RADER, Joe C.	(TN)	1002
Copyright law	CREWS, Kenneth D. . . .	(CA)	258
	HELLER, James S.	(ID)	524
	ANDERSON, Patricia E. .	(KY)	25
	BRUWELHEIDE, Janis H.	(MT)	151
	GASAWAY, Laura N. . . .	(NC)	421
	MILLER, Jerome K.	(WA)	839
	GORSEGNER, Betty D. .	(WI)	452
Copyright law for educators	DAY, Martha T.	(VT)	282
Copyright laws & regulations	KATZ, Bernard M.	(ON)	630
Copyright, non-print media	THOMAS, Fred	(MD)	1236
Copyright permissions	IFFLAND, Carol D.	(IL)	583
Copyright research	MISSAR, Margaret M. . . .	(DC)	847
Copyright, school library issues	WEBSTER, Patricia B. . .	(NY)	1315
Copyright, trademark	MESMER, Frank B.	(NH)	827
Copyrights	INNES-TAYLOR, Catherine E.	(AK)	583
	TAPHORN, Joseph B. . .	(NY)	1223
Library copyright issues	ENSIGN, David J.	(KS)	350
Scientific & technical info copyright	WOOD, Julienne L.	(LA)	1364

COPYWRITING (See also Writing)

Advertising copywriter	MITZIGA, Walter J.	(IL)	850
Copywriting	BIANCO, David P.	(MI)	94
Design, layout, copywriting	LAMBERT, Shirley A. . . .	(CO)	690

CORPORATE (See also Business, Industry, Takeover)

Administration of non-profit corporation	TREBBY, Janis G.	(WI)	1255
Archiving corporate records	LEMON, Nancy A.	(OH)	715
Assessing corporate strategies	MCLANE, John F.	(CT)	813
Business & corporate information	STANGL-WALKER, Teresa L.	(ON)	1180
Business & corporate research	DENOTO, Dorothy E. . . .	(NY)	293
Canadian corporate documents	GRAY, Sandra A.	(ON)	460
Corporate	LASTRES, Steven A. . . .	(NY)	701
Corporate acquisitions	HYLAND, Barbara	(ON)	580
Corporate administration support	HOOTKIN, Neil M.	(WI)	557
Corporate & government information ctr	PEGLER, Ross J.	(FL)	954
Corporate & industrial libraries	MATARAZZO, James M.	(MA)	783
Corporate & legal databases	HUNE, Mary G.	(OH)	574
Corporate & legal library development	WALSH, Joanna M.	(MA)	1299
Corporate & securities	PATTERSON, Patricia A.	(IL)	948
Corporate archives	EVANS, M R.	(CA)	357
	HEDLIN, Ethel W.	(DC)	520
	STEGH, Leslie J.	(IL)	1185
	VOLLMAR, William J. . . .	(MO)	1288
	OLEARY, Martha H.	(NY)	920
Corporate archives & records center	PEGLER, Ross J.	(FL)	954
Corporate archives & records centers	CLAYTON, John M.	(DE)	220
Corporate archives, information services	DYER, Esther R.	(NY)	330
Corporate archives planning	EDGERLY, Linda	(MA)	336
Corporate art collections	CLAYTON, John M.	(DE)	220
Corporate clients	BAKES, Floy L.	(NJ)	50
Corporate communications	KANE, Jean B.	(MA)	624
Corporate communications consulting	MULVIHILL, Maureen E. .	(NY)	878
Corporate databases	WOLF, Noel C.	(AZ)	1360
Corporate development	ANDERSEN, Robert J. . .	(NY)	21
Corporate documents	POJE, Mary E.	(NY)	980
Corporate documents & reference	NOVICK, Ruth	(NY)	911
Corporate electronic publishing systems	PETERSON, George B. .	(MD)	963
Corporate fact finding	OLSEN, Stephen	(MN)	922
Corporate financial databases	HAMBRIC, Donna R. . . .	(CO)	491
Corporate financial information	HENDERSON, Joanne L.	(DE)	526
Corporate giving research	KLETZIEN, S D.	(PA)	661
Corporate historian	SOLSETH, Gwenn M. . . .	(MN)	1166
Corporate history	MATTHEWS, Darwin C. .	(MI)	785
Corporate history celebration	TURNER, Ellis S.	(MD)	1264
Corporate information	TICKER, Susan L.	(NY)	1244
	IRWIN, James W.	(OH)	584
	HELLER, Patricia A.	(PA)	524
Corporate information & library services	WAGNER, Stephen K. . .	(NY)	1292
Corporate information center management	STURDIVANT, Clarence A.	(CO)	1205
Corporate information centers	SIMPSON, Evelyn L. . . .	(CA)	1141
	MICKEY, Melissa B.	(IL)	833
Corporate information service	WOLPERT, Ann J.	(MA)	1362
Corporate information services	ROSHON, Nina C.	(NY)	1057
Corporate information sources	JACKSON, Craig A.	(ON)	587
Corporate intelligence	ADAMS, Joyce A.	(CA)	5
	BAUMGARTNER, Kurt O.	(IN)	66
Corporate intelligence research	DETWILER, Susan M. . .	(IN)	296
Corporate law	HENDLEY, David D.	(PA)	527
Corporate legal research databases	MORRIS, Ann	(IL)	866
Corporate libraries	RUNYON, Judith A.	(CA)	1067
	DORSETT, Anita W.	(TX)	313
Corporate library & information ctr mgmt	RUTKOWSKI, Hollace A.	(PA)	1070
Corporate library consulting	MITCHE, Cynthia R.	(TX)	848
	MITCHELL, Cynthia R. . .	(TX)	848
Corporate library management	STANLEY, Kerry G.	(PA)	1180
Corporate library network management	LAMB, Cheryl M.	(WI)	689
Corporate library organz & development	NIELSEN, Sonja M.	(MA)	903

CORPORATE (Cont'd)

Corporate library services | ROBERTSON, Guy M. . . | (BC) | 1041
Corporate materials | MERKIN, David . . . . | (NY) | 826
Corporate planning | MACDONALD, Christine S. | (ON) | 754
Corporate planning & strategy | MARKS, Larry . . . . | (CA) | 771
Corporate printing & publishing | ARNSDORF, Dennis A. . | (DC) | 34
Corporate records & archives | RUNYON, Judith A. . . . | (CA) | 1067
Corporate records management | SALMON, Robin R. . . . . | (SC) | 1077
Corporate reference | ADAMO, Marilyn H. . . . . | (NY) | 4
 | JOHNSON, John E. . . . . | (ON) | 606
Corporate research | CALLAHAN, Joan . . . . . | (MA) | 173
 | GOETZ, Helen L. . . . . . . | (NY) | 443
 | KRAMER, Allan F. . . . . | (NY) | 675
 | THOM, Janice E. . . . . . . | (NY) | 1235
Corporate research & devlpmnt info systs | BURCSU, James E. . . . . | (NC) | 158
Corporate sources | GRAY, Sandra A. . . . . . . | (ON) | 460
Corporate travel | HERNDON, Stan J. . . . . | (VT) | 532
Corp author name formation & database | KANE, Astor V. . . . . . . | (VA) | 624
Corp information system implementation | GRENIER, Serge . . . . . . | (PQ) | 467
Digital equipment corporation | MONOSSON, Adolf S. . . . | (MA) | 855
Establishing corporate libraries | STAHL, Wilson M. . . . . . | (NC) | 1178
General business & corporate research | POJE, Mary E. . . . . | (NY) | 980
General legal, corporate & tax reference | RAUCH, Anne . . . . | (NY) | 1010
Information services for corporations | LAW, Gordon T. . . . . . . | (IN) | 704
Internal corporate databases | RUBIN, Lenard H. . . . . . | (TX) | 1064
Legal, medical, corporate printer | SCULLIN, Frank E. . . . . . | (PA) | 1109
Long-term corporate research | SOSTACK, Maura . . . . . | (NY) | 1169
Monitoring corporate change intervals | BILES, Mark J. . . . . | (NJ) | 96
Planning small corporate libraries | MONTAG, Diane . . . . . . | (CO) | 855
SDI in corporate research & development | MONDSCHEIN, Lawrence G. . . . . | (NJ) | 854
Strategic corporate information analysis | BEICHMAN, John C. . . . | (MI) | 75
Supervise corporate technical library | CARPENTER, Dale . . . . | (NY) | 184
Technical corporate libraries | BERGIN, Karen S. . . . . . | (MI) | 86

CORRECTIONAL (See also Prison)

Correctional institution librarianship | NOZICK, Sandy B. . . . . . | (CA) | 911
Correctional institution library service | BATSON, Darrell L. . . . . | (NV) | 64
Correctional institution outreach | PETIT, J M. . . . . | (OH) | 965
Correctional law libraries | WELCH, Steven J. . . . . . | (IL) | 1321
Correctional librarianship | MORGAN, James E. . . . | (NV) | 864
Correctional libraries | BEQUETTE, V L. . . . . . . | (MO) | 84
 | MALLINGER, Stephen M. | (PA) | 763
Services for correctional facilities | MARKARIAN, Rita J. . . . | (NY) | 771

CORRESPONDENCE

Correspondence education | CURL, Margo W. . . . . . . | (ID) | 265
Correspondence, ephemerae, etc | GAMBLE, Mary J. . . . . . | (CA) | 416
Medical correspondence | KOELLE, Joyce G. . . . . . | (NJ) | 667

COSMETICS

Cosmetic & chemical information | DEXTER, Patrick J. . . . . | (MD) | 298
Medicine, cosmetics & hair | CLAGGETT, Laura K. . . . | (IL) | 215

COST (See also Accounting, Budget, Pricing)

Budgeting & cost estimating | MILLER, Ellen L. . . . . . . | (NY) | 837
Budgeting & cost recovery techniques | FOX, Marylou P. . . . . . . | (CA) | 395
Budgets, cost controls | BAUMGARTNER, Robert M. . . . . | (OH) | 66
Cost accounting | REDRICK, Miriam J. . . . . | (NJ) | 1014
Cost analysis, library administration | ANDERSON, Sherry . . . . | (NC) | 25
Cost finding | MIELKE, Linda . . . . | (FL) | 833
Cost recovery policies | BYRD, Harvey C. . . . . . . | (MD) | 169
Cost-benefit analysis | GOODFELLOW, Marjorie E. . . . . | (PQ) | 448
Costing & management data | WEAVER-MEYERS, Pat L. | (OK) | 1313
Library cost analysis | SAYRE, Edward C. . . . . | (NM) | 1087
Library cost analysis studies | FRANKLIN, Brinley R. . . | (DC) | 397
Library indirect cost allocations | FRANKLIN, Brinley R. . . | (DC) | 397

COST (Cont'd)

Management & cost accounting | FRANKLIN, Brinley R. . . | (DC) | 397
Research methods & cost analysis | WEBRECK, Susan J. . . . | (PA) | 1314

COSTUMES (See also Clothing, Fashion)

Costume design & history | STOWELL, Donald C. . . . | (GA) | 1199
Costumes | MARTIN, Richard . . . . . . | (NY) | 778
Fashion & costume collections | HALE, Kaycee . . . . | (CA) | 485
Fashion & costume video | HALE, Kaycee . . . . | (CA) | 485
Writing, Hollywood costumes | NELSON-HARB, Sally R. | (CA) | 895

COUNSELING (See also Advising, Advisory, Consulting)

Career counseling | CONDREY, Barbara K. . . | (CA) | 236
 | PORTER-ROTH, Anne . . | (CA) | 985
Counseling psychology | GERITY, Louise P. . . . . . | (OR) | 428
Information counseling | DEBONS, Anthony . . . . | (PA) | 285
 | MAURA-SARDO, Mariano A. . . . . | (PR) | 787
Small business counseling | MESMER, Frank B. . . . . | (NH) | 827

COUNTRY

Country music | PRUETT, Barbara J. . . . . | (DC) | 996
Country music historian | MARTUCCI, Louis U. . . . | (CA) | 779
Country music history | SEEMANN, Charles H. . . | (TN) | 1111
Libraries in foreign countries | TSUNEISHI, Warren M. . | (DC) | 1260

COUNTY

Blair County culture | SHERIDAN, Margaret G. | (PA) | 1127
California county records | WEBBER, Steven L. . . . | (CA) | 1313
County law library coordination | CRAWFORD, Nola N. . . | (NJ) | 257
County libraries | STORCK, John N. . . . . . | (OH) | 1198
County library administration | TRAVER, Dorothy A. . . . | (CA) | 1254
 | HALL, Edward B. . . . . . . | (MD) | 487
County library board management | COLE, Jack W. . . . . | (MN) | 230
County library systems | SMITH, David R. . . . . . . | (MN) | 1154
 | HARPER, Marjory B. . . . | (TN) | 503
County museums volunteer librarianship | HOWE, Mary T. . . . . . . | (IL) | 565
County network library services | MARSHALL, Ruth T. . . . | (GA) | 775
County records administration & archives | WEAVER, Clifton W. . . . | (AL) | 1312
County systems | SHIRTS, Russell B. . . . . | (UT) | 1131
Municipal & county government | STRICKLAND, Ann T. . . | (AZ) | 1202
Pennsylvania county records | STAYER, Jonathan R. . . | (PA) | 1183
Town, township, county history | CARTER, Susan M. . . . . | (IN) | 190
Working with county library system | WINGLE, Rita M. . . . . . . | (PA) | 1355

COURSES (See also Education, Instruction, Instructional, Teaching)

Basic library science courses | SANDERS, John B. . . . . | (MO) | 1080
Course-integrated instruction | MORRIS, Karen T. . . . . . | (OK) | 867
Course-related instruction | WHITTINGTON, Christine A. . . . . | (PA) | 1334
Courseware evaluation | BARALOTO, R A. . . . . . | (MD) | 55
Library instruction, credit courses | OSTROW, Rona . . . . . . | (NY) | 929
Library teaching assistance courses | STRANC, Mary C. . . . . . | (NY) | 1200
Microcomputer courseware | BROWN, David K. . . . . . | (AB) | 143
Organization of meetings & courses | ROBERTS, Kenneth H. . . | (FRN) | 1040
Social sciences reference courses | LI, Richard T. . . . . | (IL) | 725
Teaching folklore course | MICHNAY, Susan E. . . . | (OH) | 832
Teaching graduate public libs course | VALENTINE, Patrick M. . | (NC) | 1271
Teaching library science courses | MATHES, Miriam S. . . . . | (WA) | 783
 | RUSSELL, Richard A. . . . | (WV) | 1069
Teaching religion courses | BOISCLAIR, Regina A. . . | (PA) | 111
Teaching undergraduate courses | FREEMAN, C L. . . . . . . | (MO) | 400
Training & teaching library courses | KUJOORY, Parvin . . . . . | (TX) | 683
Video courses | HARLOW, Aileen W. . . . | (CT) | 502

COURTS (See also Justice)

Court libraries | FESSENDEN, Ann T. . . . | (MO) | 374
 | ROONEY, Mary T. . . . . . | (NY) | 1053
Criminal & family court libraries | ROONEY, Mary T. . . . . . | (NY) | 1053
Facilitate legal procedures to court | SIENDA, Madeline M. . . | (WA) | 1136
Law library administration for courts | WELKER, Kathy J. . . . . . | (OH) | 1321
Public & court records management | COATES, Paul F. . . . . . | (KY) | 224

CRAFTS (See also Arts, Folk, Handicrafts, Quilt)
Contemporary American crafts   POLSTER, Joanne . . . . .   (NY)   982
Craft programming   EDGREN, Gale R. . . . . .   (IL)   336
Crafts & folk art   BENEDETTI, Joan M. . . .   (CA)   80
Decorative arts & crafts   LIND, Judith Y. . . . . (NJ)   728

CREATION
Archive creation   GIBSON, Joanne . . . . . . (CA)   432
Computerized database creation   PASQUARIELLA, Susan
                                       K. . . . . (NY)   946
Creating & organizing architectural
  libs   ROTHMAN, Marilyn R. . .   (CO) 1060
Creating & organizing private libraries ROTHMAN, Marilyn R. . .   (CO) 1060
Creating archival collections   METZLER, Valerie . . . . . (IL)   829
Creating automated name authorities DAWE, Heather L. . . . . . (ON)   282
Creating or redesigning libraries   BELTON, Jennifer H. . . . . (DC)   78
Creating relational database   PEGLER, Ross J. . . . . .   (FL)   954
Creating university archives   MATTHEW, Jeannette M. . . (IN)   785
Creating video disks for art   SHARER, E J. . . . .   (CO) 1122
Database construction & creation   MENNELLA, Dona M. . . . . (MD)   824
Database creation   TALBOT, Dawn E. . . . . .   (CA) 1220
                                     WRIGHT, Joseph F. . . . .   (FL) 1372
                                     STUHLMAN, Daniel D. . . .   (IL) 1205
                                     GORDON, Helen A. . . . . . (IN)   451
                                     PREVE, Roberta J. . . . . . (MA)   992
                                     FREEDMAN, Lynn P. . . . .   (MD)   400
                                     COTY, Patricia A. . . . . . . (NY)   250
                                     OLSEN, Wallace C. . . . . . (NY)   922
                                     MARTINEZ, Linda W. . . . . (WA)   779
                                     MILLS, Judy E. . . . . (ON)   844
Database creation & management   LAMANN, Amber N. . . . .   (NY)   689
Database creation & marketing   HAWKINS, John W. . . . . . (IN)   514
Database management & creation   HAWK, Susan A. . . . . . . (MD)   513
Database software creation   GARMAN, Nancy J. . . . . . (KY)   419
Direct marketing, creation   HUBBARD, Roy . . . . (NY)   568
Management & policy creation   WILLIAMSON, Michael W.   (ON) 1347
New library creation   YURO, David A. . . . . (NY) 1384
Reference & internal database
  creation   IRONS, Carol A. . . . . (IL)   584

CREDIT
Credit cards   MESHINSKY, Jeff M. . . . . (MD)   827
Credit unions   ZYSKOWSKI, Dianne D.   (MI) 1392
Library instruction, credit courses OSTROW, Rona . . . . . .   (NY)   929

CRIME (See also Theft)
Criminal & family court libraries   ROONEY, Mary T. . . . . .   (NY) 1053
Criminal justice   ZIMMERMAN, Donna K. . .   (IN) 1388
                                     LUTZKER, Marilyn L. . . . . (NY)   750
                                     STORMS, Kate . . . .   (NY) 1198
                                     CENTER, Sue L. . . . . . .   (WI)   196
Criminal justice & justice studies   FERRALL, J E. . . . . (AZ)   373
Criminal justice bibliography   LUNT, Ruth B. . . . . (NY)   749
Criminal justice databases   SMITH, Ellen A. . . . . (OH) 1154
Criminal justice information
  management   BYRD, Harvey C. . . . . . . (MD)   169
Criminal justice publications   KUEHNLE, Emery C. . . . . (OH)   682
Criminal law   LYNES, Tezeta G. . . . . . . (KY)   752
Criminological & behavioral sciences BEAUDET, Normand . . . . (PQ)   70
Law & criminal justice   DRAGOVICH, Pamela M. . . (DC)   318
Victims of violent crime   ARBELBIDE, Cindy L. . .   (TX)   30

CRITICAL
Critical care systems   PORTER, William R. . . . . (TN)   985
Critical reviews of literature   HENDERSON, Madeline
                                       M. . . . . (MD)   526
Critical thinking   SENATOR, Rochelle B. . .   (CT) 1115
Critical viewing & thinking   BRAUN, Robert L. . . . . . (NY)   130
Critical viewing skills   NEWMAN, Eileen M. . . . .   (NY)   899

CRITICISM (See also Evaluation, Reviewing)
Children's literature criticism   LACY, Lyn E. . . . . (MN)   687
Classical music criticism   LAMBERT, John W. . . . .   (NC)   690
Criticism of professional literature SHAPIRO, Lillian L. . . . . (NY) 1121
Editorial & textual criticism   REIMAN, Donald H. . . . . . (NY) 1020

CRITICISM (Cont'd)
Film criticism & journalism   CROWDUS, Gary A. . . . .   (NY)   261
Music, literary criticism   FRANK, Mortimer H. . . . . (NY)   397
Russian criticism   ROYTMAN, Serafima . . .   (NY) 1063

CROPS (See also Agricultural, Farm, Food, Grain)
Crops   STRANSKY, Maria . . . . .   (MD) 1200

CROSS-REFERENCING (See also Cataloging, Indexing)
Cross-referencing   HARGIS-LYTLE, Betty L.   (OK)   501

CRYONICS
Cryonics & suspended animation   BRIDGE, Stephen W. . . .   (IN)   135

CUBAN
Cuban political prisoners   PEREZ, Maria L. . . . . . . (FL)   958

CULINARY (See also Baking)
Hospitality industry culinary research JOHNSON, Sheila A. . . . (NY)   609

CULTURE (See also Arts, Multicultural)
American cultural history   MOSS, Roger W. . . . . . . (PA)   872
American culture   WILLIAMS, Martin T. . . .   (DC) 1345
Black American culture   SCOTT, Lydia E. . . . . . . (PA) 1107
Blair County culture   SHERIDAN, Margaret G.   (PA) 1127
British business & culture   JONES, Adrian . . . . (IL)   610
Canadian art & culture   GRODSKI, Renata . . . . .   (ON)   471
Connecticut history & culture   SCHMIDT, Alesandra M.   (CT) 1095
Cross-cultural education   PEISER, Richard H. . . . .   (IL)   955
Cultural agency consultation   WRIGHT, John C. . . . . . . (HI) 1371
Cultural arts community development TRASATTI, Margaret S. .   (NV) 1254
Cultural information databases   SZARY, Richard V. . . . . . (DC) 1218
Cultural programs on videocassettes HEDLUND, Dennis M. . . . (NJ)   520
Early American history & culture   MONTGOMERY, Michael
                                       S. . . . . (NJ)   856
18th century British history & culture DEVINE, Marie E. . . . . . (CT)   297
Foreign languages & cultures   COMPRI, Jeannine L. . . .   (AB)   235
Hispanic culture & history   CULP, Paul M. . . . . (TX)   264
Indexing cultural atlases   BLOZIS, Jolene M. . . . . . (DC)   107
International info & cultural exchange STEERE, Paul J. . . . . . . (DC) 1184
Jamaican history & culture   REGNER-HYATT, Anne L.   (CA) 1017
Japanese business & culture   JONES, Adrian . . . . (IL)   610
Japanese culture   WEIGEL, James S. . . . . .   (CT) 1316
Managing cultural programming   BRODERICK, John C. . . .   (DC)   138
Maritime material culture   BUMGARNER, John L. . . .   (NC)   157
Mexican culture   NOLAND, Jon . . . .   (CA)   908
Popular culture   DEUTSCH, James I. . . . . . (DC)   296
                                     EZELL, Johanna V. . . . . . (PA)   360
Popular culture bibliography   SCOTT, Randall W. . . . .   (MI) 1108
Public & cultural programming   BLANDY, Susan G. . . . . . (NY)   104
Tribal history & culture   HENDRICKS, Thom . . . .   (ND)   527

CURATORSHIP
Collection development & curation   MOORE, Emily C. . . . . . . (AL)   859
Curating   LENTHALL, Franklyn . . .   (ME)   715
Curator   COATES, Ann S. . . . . . .   (KY)   224
Manuscripts curating   CHOPESIUK, Ronald J. .   (SC)   210
Manuscripts curatorship   ROBINSON, Kathleen M.   (TX) 1044
Map curatorship   DEVERA, Rosalinda M. . .   (NY)   297
                                     KIDD, Betty H. . . . . (ON)   646
Museum curating   KELM, Carol R. . . . . (IL)   638
Museum curator   WHEELER, Elaine . . . . . . (NY) 1328
Photograph curator   BECK, Alison M. . . . . (TX)   71
Rare book curator   PINKHAM, Eleanor H. . . . . (MI)   974
Slide curatorship   GUNN, Diane M. . . . . . .   (MI)   477
Visual resources curator   WYKLE, Helen H. . . . . . . (CA) 1375

CURRENT
Abstracting current medical literature SHIPLEY, Ruth M. . . . . . (MO) 1131
Appraising current market value   MONDLIN, Marvin . . . . .   (NY)   854
Business & current events databases LOVE, Sandra R. . . . . .   (CA)   743
Current affairs   EARLS, M L. . . . . (ON)   332

CURRENT (Cont'd)

Current affairs & journalism research	BEAUDET, Normand . . .	(PQ)	70
Current affairs databases	LESHY, Dede	(AZ)	718
Current affairs, general research	ROBINSON, Betty J. . . .	(CA)	1043
Current & historical theatre	BUCK, Richard M.	(NY)	154
Current awareness	HADLEY, Alice E.	(CA)	482
	PETERSON, Julia C. . . .	(MN)	963
	REITANO, Maimie V. . . .	(NY)	1022
	MITTAG, Erika	(TX)	850
	PARKER, David F.	(TX)	941
	SHARP, Charlotte J.	(TX)	1122
	DENGROVE, Richard A. .	(VA)	292
Current awareness of lit for routing	FOSTER, Helen M.	(FL)	392
Current awareness publications	CURTIS, Richard A.	(CA)	267
Current awareness resource materials	SEXTON, Spencer K. . . .	(NC)	1118
Current awareness service	DUELTGEN, Ronald R. . .	(MN)	323
	SCHAEFFER, Judith E. . .	(PA)	1089
Current awareness services	NOVACK, Dona A.	(CA)	910
	OBERG, Judy M.	(CO)	914
	KLEINMUNTZ, Dalia S. .	(IL)	660
	GURAYA, Harinder	(NS)	478
	STILES, William G.	(ON)	1194
Current bibliographies	ROADS, Clarice D.	(OK)	1038
Current book acquisitions	DE LUISE, Alexandra . . .	(PQ)	290
Current events	REIFMAN, Deborah S. . .	(CA)	1019
Current events databases	CONGER, Lucinda D. . . .	(DC)	236
Current events reference	VANDEGRIFT, Barbara P. .	(DC)	1273
Current information databases	HILL, Fay G.	(IA)	539
Current information selection	CYPSER, Rudy J.	(NY)	268
Current news & information databases	JOBE, Shirley A.	(MA)	601
Current periodicals management	JOHNS, Jean B.	(OH)	601
Faculty current awareness service	BATISTA, Emily J.	(PA)	64
Media research of current events	BROWN, Phyllis J.	(TN)	147
Online & current awareness reference	LOGAN, Nancy L.	(ON)	737
Preparing current awareness publications	MILTON, Ardyce A.	(WI)	845
Public & current affairs	MCFARLANE, Agnes . . .	(PQ)	805
Research on current awareness services	MONDSCHEIN, Lawrence G.	(NJ)	854
SDI, current awareness	BUNTROCK, Robert E. . .	(IL)	157

CURRICULUM (See also Education, Instructional, Lessons)

Arms race curriculum	MEYER, Jimmy E.	(OH)	830
Audiovisual curriculum alignment	NEBEL, Jean C.	(CA)	891
Collection development & curriculum	PRIESING, Patricia L. . . .	(NJ)	993
Collection development for curriculum	WILLIAMS, S J.	(MI)	1346
Computer curriculum development	BIHLER, Charles H.	(CT)	96
Coordinating with curriculum	IMONDI, Lenore R.	(RI)	582
Curricula development	ANDERSON, Marcia M. .	(VA)	24
Curriculum	ORGREN, Sally C.	(NY)	925
	SHIVERDECKER, Darlene J.	(OH)	1132
Curriculum advising	DOUGLASS, Charlene K. .	(GA)	314
Curriculum & instruction	DIRKSEN, Phyllis A.	(CO)	305
Curriculum & integrated instruction	RATZER, Mary B.	(NY)	1010
Curriculum & research skills	PITLUK, Paula K.	(CA)	976
Curriculum & school libraries	EGAN, Mary J.	(NY)	338
Curriculum & teacher assistance	MILLER, Marian A.	(OH)	840
Curriculum archives	WYBORNEY, Charles E. .	(CA)	1374
Curriculum center	MOORHEAD, Kenneth E. .	(CT)	862
Curriculum consultant	REILLY, Maureen E.	(CT)	1020
	BROWN, Gerald R.	(MB)	144
Curriculum coordination	KONNEKER, Rachel C. . .	(NC)	670
	DAVIS, Joan C.	(TX)	279
Curriculum development	JONES, Wanda F.	(AR)	615
	MCKINNEY, Barbara J. . .	(AR)	812
	KAUN, Thomas T.	(CA)	631
	MCDONOUGH, Timothy M.	(CA)	803
	MARCHAND, Janet H. . .	(CT)	768
	SERGEL, Carol K.	(CT)	1116
	MITCHELL, Jan E.	(FL)	848
	DANIELSON, Connie S. .	(IA)	273
	PARK, Dona F.	(IA)	941
	YOUNG, Nancy J.	(IL)	1382
	JOHNSON, Jean L.	(MA)	606
	BARTH, Edward W.	(MD)	61
	PARR, Michael P.	(MI)	944

CURRICULUM (Cont'd)

Curriculum development	ST. AMAND, Norma P. . . .	(MI)	1075
	TOLMAN, Bonnie B.	(MI)	1249
	CASEY, Mary A.	(NJ)	192
	HOROWITZ, Marjorie B. . .	(NJ)	560
	LOPEZ, Kathryn P.	(NM)	741
	BERGER, Pam P.	(NY)	86
	NEWMAN, Eileen M.	(NY)	899
	WEBSTER, Patricia B. . .	(NY)	1315
	WOLF, Catharine D.	(NY)	1360
	MAYER, Mary C.	(OH)	789
	MEESE, Jane E.	(OH)	821
	KOSTIS, Leigh W.	(PA)	673
	TASSIA, Margaret R.	(PA)	1224
	WALKER, Sue A.	(PA)	1296
	ALDRICH, Linda S.	(RI)	11
	CAPUTO, Anne S.	(VA)	180
	GAUDET, Jean A.	(VA)	422
	BRADLEY, Harold K. . . .	(AB)	126
Curriculum development & design	MOORE, Lawrence A. . . .	(ON)	860
Curriculum development K-8	BENDER, Nancy W.	(MA)	79
Curriculum education	FOWLER, Louise D.	(CT)	394
Curriculum enrichment	PARADISE, Don M.	(PA)	939
Curriculum innovation	FISHER, Georgeann	(MO)	381
Curriculum integration	SALLE, Ellen M.	(CO)	1076
	UNDERHILL, Jan	(OK)	1268
Curriculum involvement	REHMKE, Denise M. . . .	(IA)	1017
Curriculum laboratory	RAMBO, Helen M.	(ID)	1005
Curriculum libraries	DIRKS, Martha W.	(KS)	305
	UPPGARD, Jeannine . . .	(MA)	1269
Curriculum library	SCHLATTER, M W.	(GA)	1093
	JOHNSON, Scott R.	(MS)	609
	LUGER, Mary J.	(SD)	747
Curriculum materials	DURAN, Karin J.	(CA)	328
	STAVIS, Ruth L.	(MA)	1183
	CLEAVER, Betty P.	(OH)	220
	POVSIC, Frances F.	(OH)	987
	BROWN, David K.	(AB)	143
	HERSCOVITCH, Pearl . . .	(AB)	533
Curriculum materials & media	JARRELL, James R.	(NC)	594
Curriculum materials center	HUEBNER, Mary A.	(NY)	570
Curriculum materials centers	RUDIE, Helen M.	(MN)	1065
Curriculum materials control	CLARK, Alice S.	(CA)	216
Curriculum materials K-12	KING, Kathryn L.	(MI)	651
	HERBERT, Barbara R. . . .	(NJ)	530
Curriculum planning	HAMEL, Eleanor C.	(PR)	491
Curriculum services	ROSE, David L.	(CA)	1054
Curriculum support	YELVERTON, Mildred G.	(AL)	1379
	GUNDERSEN, Shirley S.	(IL)	477
	SCHAACK, Wilma J. . . .	(IL)	1088
Curriculum support for faculty	DAVIS, Deanna S.	(IA)	278
Curriculum teaching materials	FISHER, Joan W.	(MD)	381
Curriculum textbook cataloging	ONUFFER, Joachim	(PA)	924
Curriculum textbooks	MEWS, Alison J.	(NF)	829
Curriculum use of media	SPEIRS, Gilmary	(PA)	1172
Curriculum writing	JENKINS, Lydia E.	(DC)	597
Curriculum-based library skills	GOODRICH PETERSON, Marilyn	(KS)	450
Curriculum-related material purchasing	SKELLY, Laurie J.	(MN)	1146
Development of library curriculum	HOSKINS, Sylvia H.	(VA)	561
Education & curriculum of chlds services	LOPEZ, Loretta K.	(WA)	741
Education curriculum center	NORDSTROM, Virginia . .	(NY)	908
Educational curriculum	HAGGARD, Lynn	(TX)	483
	POLLOCK, Ethel L.	(VA)	981
Educational resources, curriculum	SACK, Jean C.	(MD)	1073
Elementary computer curriculum	FARRIS, Mary E.	(TN)	365
Elementary curriculum	HUNT, Margaret M.	(IN)	575
Elementary library media curriculum	PROCTOR, Deborah K. . .	(WY)	994
Evaluation research, curriculum software	HERB, Elizabeth D.	(OH)	530
High school curriculum development	MAIN, Isabelle G.	(AZ)	761
	KAPLAN, Lois J.	(OH)	626
High school curriculum implementation	MEANS, E P.	(KS)	820
High school curriculum support	DAVIS, Inez W.	(TN)	279
Information science education curriculum	MOLL, Joy K.	(NJ)	853

CURRICULUM (Cont'd)

Info skills & curriculum correlation   JONES, Wanda F. . . . . .   (AR)   615
                                       MCKINNEY, Barbara J. . .   (AR)   812
Information skills curriculum   COWEN, Linda L. . . . . . .   (OK)   253
Information skills in curriculum   HAYCOCK, Kenneth R. . .   (BC)   515
Integrated curriculum   SNYDER, Denny L. . . . .   (MD)   1164
Integrating curriculum   HEINRICH, Lois M. . . . .   (MD)   522
Integration, library skills, curriculum   HOROWITZ, Marjorie B. . .   (NJ)   560
Integration of media to curriculum   MURRAY, William A. . . .   (CO)   882
Legal research curriculum   COYLE, Christopher B. . .   (OH)   253
Library, classroom curriculum
  devlpmnt   MURPHY, Diana G. . . . .   (PA)   880
Library curriculum guide development   NOBLE, Barbara N. . . . .   (MO)   906
Library media skills curriculum   MURTO, Kathleen A. . . . .   (WI)   883
Library science curriculum   SWIGGER, Keith . . . . . .   (TX)   1216
Library science curriculum
  development   SPILLERS, Roger E. . . . .   (MN)   1174
Library skills curriculum   KAHLER, June . . . .   (TX)   621
Library within the curriculum   TALLMAN, Julie I. . . . . .   (NY)   1221
Media & curriculum   HENDRICKSON, Charles
                                         R. . . . .   (CO)   527
Media selection for curriculum   HILLER, Catherine C. . . .   (CT)   541
Microcomputer use in curriculum   CHAMPLIN, Constance J.   (IN)   198
                                       KESTER, Diane D. . . . . .   (NC)   645
Microcomputers in curriculum   WHALEY, Janie B. . . . . .   (IN)   1328
Non-print curriculum materials   FISHER, Carolyn H. . . . .   (NY)   380
Research & curriculum coordination   BANKHEAD, Elizabeth M.   (CO)   54
School curriculum planning   HUSTED, Ruth E. . . . . . .   (OK)   578
School curriculum programs   WEISLAK, Susan L. . . . .   (TX)   1319
School library curricula   PALMER, Julia R. . . . . .   (NY)   936
School library curriculum   KARON, Joyce E. . . . . . .   (IL)   627
                                       MIZIK, Judy G. . . . .   (PA)   850
School library curriculum integration   ZEIGER, Hanna B. . . . . .   (MA)   1387
School library curriculum involvement   FREEMAN, Evangeline M.   (NC)   400
School library media curriculum   LITTLE, Nina M. . . . . . .   (NE)   733
                                       ROSCELLO, Frances R. . .   (NY)   1054
Secondary curriculum, database
  searching   WILSON, M L. . . . .   (CO)   1352
Secondary curriculum, satellite use   WILSON, M L. . . . .   (CO)   1352
Secondary education curriculum
  materials   LAURITO, Gerard P. . . . .   (PA)   703
Secondary library curriculum   MERRELL, Sheila J. . . . .   (MO)   826
Social studies curriculum   HIGGINS, Judith H. . . . .   (NY)   538
Supporting curriculum Grades K-4   MEINEL, Nancy T. . . . . .   (LA)   822
Technology integration with
  curriculum   TROUTNER, Joanne J. . .   (IN)   1258
Training & curriculum development   HARADA, Violet H. . . . . .   (HI)   499
Writing library & literature curriculum   JACKSON, Gloria D. . . .   (CA)   587
Writing library curriculum skills   SWITZER, Catherine M. . .   (WI)   1216

CUSTOM

Custom circulation desk design   RIBNICKY, Karen F. . . . .   (CT)   1026
Custom computer programming   GILLETTE, Robert S. . . .   (TX)   435
Custom data products   LA MARCHE, David L. . .   (ON)   689
Custom microcomputer programming   MARSH, Elizabeth C. . . .   (OH)   773
Custom research   MOORHEAD, John D. . . .   (IL)   862
Custom research, library & archives   TURNER, Ellis S. . . . . . .   (MD)   1264
Customized databases   RUBINSTEIN, Ed . . . . . .   (NY)   1065
High technology custom research
  services   JAGIELLOWICZ, Jadzia .   (ON)   591
Software customization   SOUDER, Edith I. . . . . .   (PA)   1169

CUSTOMER (See also Clients, Consumer, End-User, Patients, Patrons, User)

Assisting customers   GLASS, Gerald . . . .   (PQ)   440
Customer & technical services   LEE, Doreen H. . . . .   (CA)   709
Customer financial information
  requests   GAYNOR, Joann T. . . . .   (NY)   424
Customer relations   HUGHES, Marilyn A. . . . .   (PA)   572
Customer service   HASHEM, Judy A. . . . . .   (IN)   510
Customer service support   ROMERO, Georg L. . . . .   (CA)   1052
Customer services   WINIARSKI, Marilee E. . .   (VA)   1355
Customer services, training   HECHT, Joseph A. . . . . .   (OH)   519
Customer support   LOCASCIO, Aline M. . . .   (NY)   735
                                       FOSTER, Anne . . . .   (ON)   392
Customer technical support   PIKE, Christine M. . . . . .   (NJ)   972
Marketing sales & customer service   KINLEY, Jo H. . . . .   (DC)   652
Training & customer services   CHAMPANY, Barry W. . . .   (CA)   198

CUSTOMS

Customs   PARSONAGE, Dianne L.   (ON)   944
Customs, folklore, etiquette, holidays   HAWK, Susan P. . . . . . .   (FL)   513
Folklore, mythology & customs   MCCANN, Judith B. . . . .   (ON)   794
US Customs law research   MATTERA, Joseph J. . . .   (NY)   785
United States Customs Service   SHERMAN, William F. . . .   (DC)   1128

CYBERNETIC

Cybernetic concepts   BISHOP, John . . . .   (MA)   99

DAKOTAS

Dakotas history   MC CAULEY, Philip F. . . .   (SD)   795

DANCE (See also Ballet)

Dance   WOOD, Linda L. . . . .   (PA)   1364
                                       GUILMETTE, Pierre . . . .   (PQ)   476
Dance bibliography   JACOB, Scott J. . . . . . .   (PA)   589
Dance research   JEROME, Michael S. . . .   (CA)   599
Early music & dance   COLDWELL, Charles P. . .   (WA)   230
Historical dance & bibliography   KELLER, Kate V. . . . . . .   (PA)   635
Jazz & hot dance music   LOTZ, Rainer E. . . . .   (WGR)   742
Music & dance librarianship   HECK, Thomas F. . . . . .   (OH)   519
Music & dance reference   HEUTTE, Frederic A. . . .   (MD)   535
Music, dance, theatre arts   LUBRANO, Judith A. . . . .   (MA)   745
Physical education & dance   MAYRAND, Lise M. . . . .   (PQ)   791
Social, folk, & ceremonial dances   KELLER, Kate V. . . . . . .   (PA)   635
Traditional dance   ANDERSON, Janet A. . . .   (UT)   23

DATA (See also Computers, EDP, Microcomputers)

Abstracting & indexing technical data   HOWARD, Susanna J. . . .   (NC)   564
Audiovisual & machine-readable data
  file   RITCHIE, David G. . . . . .   (NY)   1036
Bibliographic data publishing   TARR, Susan M. . . . . . .   (DC)   1224
Biomedical data acquisitions   PEETERS, Marc D. . . . .   (BEL)   954
Business data   DONOHUE, Delaine R. . .   (PA)   312
CD-ROM data preparation   BEFELER, Mike . . . .   (CO)   74
Census data   YORK, Grace A. . . . .   (MI)   1381
Company, product, & industry data   DLOTT, Nancy B. . . . . . .   (MA)   306
Compiling bibliographic data   MCCRAY, Evelina W. . . . .   (LA)   800
Computer application & data
  management   GREGORY, Melissa R. . . .   (IL)   466
Computer data entry   MURRAY, Theresa A. . . .   (IL)   882
Computer indexing data management   SCHLICHTING, Catherine
                                         N. . . . .   (OH)   1094
Costing & management data   WEAVER-MEYERS, Pat L.   (OK)   1313
Custom data products   LA MARCHE, David L. . .   (ON)   689
Data administration   DENNISON, Lynn C. . . . .   (CA)   292
                                       REED, Patricia A. . . . . . .   (DC)   1015
                                       BREWER, Christina A. . . .   (MD)   134
                                       MCDONALD, David R. . . .   (MI)   802
Data analysis & retrieval   YACOUBY, Ray S. . . . . .   (MA)   1376
Data & voice networking   VEDDER, Harvey B. . . . .   (PA)   1280
Data broadcasting on VBI   WILLIAMS, Fred . . . . . .   (GA)   1343
Data capture & management   BRUTON, Robert T. . . . .   (MN)   151
Data collection & editing   TEUN, Rebecca L. . . . . .   (TX)   1233
Data collection & management   VAN ORDER, Mary J. . . .   (ON)   1276
Data communication network
  management   GETZ, Malcolm . . . .   (TN)   430
Data communications   HASSAN, Abe H. . . . . . .   (CA)   511
                                       BENNETT, Harry D. . . . .   (MD)   81
                                       STELZLE, James J. . . . . .   (NY)   1186
                                       HAHN, Susan H. . . . .   (PA)   484
                                       ADAMS, Judith A. . . . . . .   (VA)   5
                                       WALDE, Norma J. . . . . . .   (VA)   1294
Data communications planning   BARNETT, Becky L. . . . .   (GA)   57
Data conversion   HARRIS, Michael A. . . . .   (CO)   505
Data design   KOENIG, Michael E. . . . .   (NY)   668
Data element standardization   BREWER, Christina A. . . .   (MD)   134
Data entry & conversion   MEDINA, Ildefonso M. . . .   (NY)   820
Data entry consulting   HLAVA, Marjorie M. . . . .   (NM)   544
Data management   MEYER, Garry S. . . . . . .   (NY)   830
                                       PIPER, Paula . . . .   (PA)   975
Data management, databases   SAGAR, Mary B. . . . . . .   (MI)   1074
Data modeling   REED, Patricia A. . . . . . .   (DC)   1015
Data preparation electronic publishing   KERR, Robert C. . . . . . .   (CO)   644

DATA (Cont'd)

Data processing	PEMPE, Ruta	(DC)	956
	BREEN, Joanell C.	(IL)	131
	CHUNG, Alison L.	(IL)	213
	MYLES, Bobbie	(MA)	885
	CLARK, William E.	(MI)	218
	VETH, Terry R.	(MN)	1283
	SHAFFER, Richard P.	(NY)	1119
	WILSON, Fredric W.	(NY)	1351
	HYNUM, Jill A.	(WI)	580
Data processing & computers	MCBRIDE, Jessica W.	(NY)	792
Data processing & production	BORKENSTEIN, Donald M.	(NY)	116
Data processing hardware & software	KOOLISH, Ruth K.	(CA)	671
Data processing management	CANGANELLI, Patrick W.	(IN)	178
Data processing research	REIST, Paul A.	(CA)	1022
	SMITH, Lydia K.	(CT)	1157
Data processing systems	CLASQUIN, Frank F.	(MA)	219
Data quality	PIKE, Christine M.	(NJ)	972
Data resource management	VALENTINE, Scott	(ON)	1271
Data specialist	MCZORN, Bonita A.	(NC)	819
Data standards	LEVINE, Emil H.	(DC)	720
Data, text input	FISHER, Douglas A.	(PA)	380
Data tracking	BISHOP, John	(MA)	99
Databases & data dictionaries	PULLEYBLANK, Mildred C.	(ON)	997
Defense data	ROBINSON, David F.	(VA)	1043
Discography, gathering & tabulating data	BLACKER, George A.	(CT)	102
Dissemination of digital data	WILTSHIRE, Denise A.	(VA)	1354
Electronic data processing systems	MOUNIR, Khalil A.	(NY)	873
Engineering & data communications	WIEHN, John F.	(CT)	1336
Engineering, data processing	FLEMING, Jack C.	(ON)	384
English language text data	SCHULTZ, Arnold J.	(MN)	1101
Environmental information & data policy	SNODGRASS, Rex J.	(NC)	1163
Geological, geophysical data systems	AULBACH, Louis F.	(TX)	39
Hazardous material data	KAZIMIR, Edward O.	(NJ)	632
Historical & present financial data	PAYNE, Linda C.	(NY)	951
Historical data	HEFNER, Xavier M.	(NY)	520
Information management & data search	ZIAIAN, Monir	(CA)	1387
Institutional documents & data	GOODMAN, L D.	(CA)	449
Internal data organization	MORROW, Ellen B.	(PA)	869
Legal deposition, evidentiary data	SCHULTZ, Arnold J.	(MN)	1101
Library & data records administration	HURT, Nancy S.	(TX)	578
Library automation, data conversion	KERSHNER, Lois M.	(CA)	644
Machine-readable data	STRAUSS, Diane	(NC)	1201
Machine-readable data files	GERKEN, Ann E.	(CA)	429
	KUHLMAN, James R.	(GA)	682
	KING, Ebba K.	(NC)	650
Machine-readable data files cataloging	MYERS, Victor C.	(MO)	885
	WEITZ, Jay N.	(OH)	1320
Management, micro data center	ASU, Glynis V.	(WI)	37
Management of medical & research data	COLLINS, Kenneth A.	(MD)	233
MARC data processing	SEGEL, Bernard J.	(DC)	1112
Marketing data systems	SEULOWITZ, Lois	(NY)	1117
Microcomputer data management	MORGAN, James J.	(IN)	864
Microfilming data for resrch purposes	FROST, Debra R.	(CO)	406
Non-Roman alphabet data processing	AGENBROAD, James E.	(DC)	7
Numeric data files	TSANG, Daniel C.	(CA)	1260
Online search, data manipulation	FOURNIER, Susan K.	(MD)	393
Optical data products, CD-ROM	STEFFEY, Ramona J.	(TN)	1185
Patron data entry	WALKER, Laura L.	(IL)	1295
Proprietary data retrieval	ROBERTSON, Betty M.	(NY)	1041
Retailing statistical data	PALMER, Shirley	(CT)	937
Stock data	PAYNE, Linda C.	(NY)	951
Stock/options trading data	ELASIK, Ronald G.	(MD)	341
Telecommunications & data communications	CASTO, Lisa A.	(TX)	194

DATABANKS (See also Databases)

Hazardous substances databanks	COSMIDES, George J.	(MD)	249

DATABASE SEARCHING (See also Data, Databases, Computers, Online)

Agricultural database searching	BARBER, Helen M.	(NM)	55
All phases of database searching	WEATHERS, Jerry D.	(TX)	1312
Art database searching	WISNIEWSKI, Julia L.	(DC)	1357
Automation & database searching	JACKA, David C.	(NE)	586
Bibliographic database searches	MORTON, Dorothy J.	(DE)	870
Bibliographic database searching	CARRICABURU, Robert	(CA)	186
	CHAIKIN, Mary C.	(NJ)	197
	FELDMAN, Laurence M.	(MA)	369
Biological database searching	KUSHINKA, Kerry L.	(NJ)	685
Biomedical database searching	BAKER, Carole A.	(OH)	48
Business information database searching	ROSENBERGER, Constance G.	(PA)	1056
Cataloging & database searching	CHANG, Daphne Y.	(NY)	200
Chemical & physical scis database srchng	REDALJE, Susanne J.	(WA)	1013
Chemical & toxicology database searching	TAYLOR, Melissa P.	(CT)	1227
Chemical database searching	REID, Angea S.	(MA)	1018
	FERRAINOLO, John J.	(PA)	373
	HESLIN, Catherine M.	(PA)	534
	WACASEY, Mary M.	(PQ)	1290
Circulation, database searching	ROBICHAUD, Marcel J.	(NY)	1042
Commercial & legislative database srchng	SCHOLFIELD, Caroline A.	(MI)	1098
Computer database searching	NICHOLS, Amy S.	(AL)	901
	ADAMO, Clare	(CT)	4
	ECKWRIGHT, Gail Z.	(ID)	335
	ANES, Joy R.	(IL)	27
	HATTENDORF, Lynn C.	(IL)	512
	KINNERSLEY, Ruth T.	(IL)	653
	WORRELL, Diane F.	(NC)	1369
	HABER, Mark N.	(NY)	481
	MANDERNACK, Scott B.	(WI)	765
	MILTON, Ardyce A.	(WI)	845
Computer tutorials database searching	CARUSO, Nicholas C.	(PA)	190
Computerized database searching	HUMPHRIES, Anne W.	(MD)	574
	GOURLAY, Una M.	(TX)	454
Database search service, trainer	CARR, Caryn J.	(PA)	185
Database search systems	MEADOW, Charles T.	(ON)	819
Database searcher	LUDWIG, J D.	(AK)	746
	VARGHA, Rebecca B.	(NC)	1278
	PARAS, Lucille P.	(NJ)	939
Database searches	PEPPER, Alice A.	(MI)	958
	ERBE, Evalina S.	(NJ)	352
	DAVIS, Cynthia V.	(TX)	278
	TIME, Ming M.	(TX)	1245
Database searching	AIDE, Kathryn S.	(AL)	8
	HALL, Patricia N.	(AL)	488
	HARRIS, Linda S.	(AL)	505
	STEWART, Sharon L.	(AL)	1193
	WILLIAMS, Pauline C.	(AL)	1346
	HALL, Deborah N.	(AR)	487
	EDGINGTON, Linda A.	(AZ)	336
	AMARA, Margaret F.	(CA)	19
	BOYER, Laura M.	(CA)	123
	CASTAGNOZZI, Carol A.	(CA)	194
	CHARBONNEAU, Ronald P.	(CA)	202
	DEGOOD, S K.	(CA)	288
	DOWNS, Sandra P.	(CA)	317
	FARMAR, Donna M.	(CA)	364
	FLOWERS, Pat	(CA)	386
	GALLEGO, Bert H.	(CA)	414
	GELFAND, Julia M.	(CA)	426
	HANDMAN, Gary P.	(CA)	495
	KLUGMAN, Simone	(CA)	662
	KOBZINA, Norma G.	(CA)	666
	NOGA, Michael M.	(CA)	907
	SCHMIDT, Ford C.	(CA)	1095
	SEGAL, Naomi R.	(CA)	1112
	STANLEY, Dale R.	(CA)	1180
	VEENKER, Linda J.	(CA)	1281
	WEBB, Ty	(CA)	1313
	WILLIS, Joan K.	(CA)	1348
	WUERTZ, Eva L.	(CA)	1373
	NORBIE, Dorothy E.	(CO)	908

DATABASE SEARCHING (Cont'd)
Database searching

ROESCH, Gay E.	(CO)	1049
SHIELDS, Caryl L.	(CO)	1129
BOHRER, Karen M.	(CT)	111
BUNKER, Patricia J.	(CT)	157
CAMPO, Lynn D.	(CT)	177
SCURA, Georgia A.	(CT)	1109
UBYSZ, Priscilla M.	(CT)	1267
DOERNBERG, David G.	(DC)	308
FARKAS, Susan A.	(DC)	364
HENEKS, Julia A.	(DC)	528
HUDGINS, Peggy	(DC)	569
LATOUR, Catherine M.	(DC)	701
NELSON, Marilyn L.	(DC)	894
NEVIN, Barbara B.	(DC)	898
ROBINSON, Robert C.	(DC)	1044
SANCHEZ, Jose L.	(DC)	1079
BROWN, Pia T.	(FL)	147
TOIFEL, Peggy W.	(FL)	1248
HENNER, Terry A.	(GA)	528
WILLIAMS, Sara E.	(GA)	1346
KNEFEL, Mary A.	(IA)	664
OHRLUND, Bruce L.	(IA)	919
PETERSON, Dennis R.	(IA)	963
SCHEETZ, Kathy D.	(IA)	1091
AUSTIN, John R.	(IL)	40
COOPER, Rosemarie A.	(IL)	243
O'BRIEN, Barbara E.	(IL)	914
ROCHE, Richard G.	(IL)	1046
STENGER, Brenda E.	(IL)	1187
STEVENS, Michael	(IL)	1190
TROY, Shannon M.	(IL)	1258
WALSH, Susan E.	(IL)	1300
WATSON, Robert E.	(IL)	1310
WRIGHT, Deborah L.	(IL)	1371
NORMAN, Orval G.	(IN)	909
SPULBER, Pauline	(IN)	1176
FORFIA, Linda S.	(KS)	390
CRABB, George W.	(KY)	254
TEN HOOR, Joan M.	(KY)	1231
DESSINO, Jacquelyn A.	(LA)	296
SHAUGHNESSY, Megan	(LA)	1123
SKINNER, Robert E.	(LA)	1146
SNOW, Maxine L.	(LA)	1164
GEVIRTZMAN, Joyce L.	(MA)	430
GRAHAM, Katherine I.	(MA)	456
KELLY, Patricia M.	(MA)	638
TAUPIER, Andrea S.	(MA)	1225
WAKS, Jane B.	(MA)	1293
LAFFREY, Laurel W.	(MD)	687
LEDBETTER, Sherry H.	(MD)	708
MASTROIANNI, Richard L.	(MD)	783
MOLLENKOPF, Carolyn M.	(MD)	853
POTTER, Andrea K.	(MD)	987
SULLIVAN, Carol W.	(MD)	1207
VAN BRUNT, Virginia	(MD)	1272
VAN CAMPEN, Rebecca J.	(MD)	1272
WILLIAMS, Pamela S.	(MD)	1346
WILSON, Susan W.	(MD)	1353
BALOK, Becki	(MI)	53
BENSON, Peggy	(MI)	83
BLASCHAK, Mary M.	(MI)	104
BRENNAN, Jean M.	(MI)	132
CARUSO, Genevieve O.	(MI)	190
COCHRAN, Catherine	(MI)	225
COREY, Marjorie	(MI)	246
COURTOIS, Martin P.	(MI)	251
DAVIDSEN, Susanna L.	(MI)	276
FEDER, Carol S.	(MI)	367
KING, Kathryn L.	(MI)	651
KONDAK, Ann	(MI)	670
KORMELINK, Barbara A.	(MI)	671
NUFFER, Roy A.	(MI)	912
PEREZ-STABLE, Maria A.	(MI)	958
RANSOM-BERGSTROM, Janette F.	(MI)	1008
SCHUCKEL, Sally B.	(MI)	1101
SMITH, Peter A.	(MI)	1159

DATABASE SEARCHING (Cont'd)
Database searching

STANGER, Keith J.	(MI)	1180
STREETER, Linda D.	(MI)	1201
STUCK, Judy K.	(MI)	1204
TODD, Suzanne L.	(MI)	1248
VERGE, Colleen R.	(MI)	1282
YETMAN, Nancy J.	(MI)	1380
DOLAN, Mary M.	(MN)	309
FOREMAN, Gertrude E.	(MN)	390
MCINERNEY, Claire R.	(MN)	809
MICHEL, William D.	(MN)	832
VAN WHY, Carol B.	(MN)	1277
WELDON, Barbara J.	(MN)	1321
CANN, Cheryle J.	(MO)	178
IGLAUER, Carol	(MO)	581
TOLSON, Stephanie D.	(MO)	1249
BECK, Allisa L.	(MS)	71
BRELAND, June M.	(MS)	132
BUCHANAN, William E.	(NC)	153
STEPHENSON, Marilyn R.	(NC)	1188
WALDERA, Katherine A.	(ND)	1294
OYER, Kenneth E.	(NE)	932
SLOAN, Patricia K.	(NE)	1149
TOLLMAN, Thomas A.	(NE)	1249
WOMACK, Sharon K.	(NE)	1362
MADDEN, Robert J.	(NH)	758
GABRIEL, Linda	(NJ)	411
KAPLAN, Susan J.	(NJ)	626
NEWMAN, Lisa A.	(NJ)	899
OTT, Linda G.	(NJ)	930
RONDELLI, Marilyn H.	(NJ)	1053
ROTHENBERG, Patricia	(NJ)	1060
SWARTZ, Betty J.	(NJ)	1214
BONACORDA, James J.	(NY)	113
BOTKIN, Karen R.	(NY)	118
BRESLIN, Ellen R.	(NY)	133
BURKEY, Lynne	(NY)	161
CAGAN, Penny M.	(NY)	170
CLOWE, Isabel B.	(NY)	223
CRAWFORD-OPPENHIE-MER, Christine	(NY)	257
DAWSON, Victoria A.	(NY)	282
DENNIS, Anne R.	(NY)	292
DI BIANCO, Phyllis R.	(NY)	299
DIMARTINO, Diane J.	(NY)	303
GINSBURG, Carol L.	(NY)	438
GOLD, Hilary G.	(NY)	444
GOLLOP, Sandra G.	(NY)	447
HECKMAN, Lucy T.	(NY)	519
JAROSEK, Joan E.	(NY)	594
KING, Christine E.	(NY)	650
KOLATA, Judith	(NY)	669
KUPFERBERG, Natalie	(NY)	684
LEVINE, Linda A.	(NY)	720
MAILLET, Lucienne G.	(NY)	761
MCLAUGHLIN, Pamela W.	(NY)	813
MIHRAM, Danielle	(NY)	834
MINTZ, Anne P.	(NY)	847
NEUFELD, Judith B.	(NY)	897
PINEDA, Conchita J.	(NY)	974
PLUMER, F I.	(NY)	978
POWIS, Katherine E.	(NY)	989
ROSEN, Wendy L.	(NY)	1055
ROUGEUX, Debora A.	(NY)	1061
SALBER, Peter J.	(NY)	1076
SCHNEIDER, Helen S.	(NY)	1097
SCIATTARA, Diane M.	(NY)	1106
SHAPIRO, Martin P.	(NY)	1121
STEVENSON, Mata	(NY)	1191
TAN, Wendy W.	(NY)	1222
TIFFEAULT, Alice A.	(NY)	1244
YUCHT, Donald J.	(NY)	1384
ANDERSON, Janice L.	(OH)	23
BAKER, Martha A.	(OH)	49
BELL, Gladys S.	(OH)	77
ENGLANDER, Marlene S.	(OH)	349
HELSER, Fred L.	(OH)	525
KEOGH, Jeanne M.	(OH)	643
NOVAK, Mary S.	(OH)	911

DATABASE SEARCHING (Cont'd)

Database searching

SUVAK, Daniel S. . . . . . (OH) 1212
TERHUNE, R S. . . . . (OH) 1231
VOELKER, James R. . . . (OH) 1286
WAGNER, Judith O. . . . . (OH) 1292
WEHMEYER, Jeffrey M. . . (OH) 1316
GRAHAM, John . . . . (OK) 456
REINBOLD, Janice K. . . . (OK) 1021
ROBIN, Annabeth . . . . . . (OK) 1043
JUDKINS, Dolores Z. . . . (OR) 619
ALSTADT, Nancy A. . . . (PA) 18
BOLGER, Dorita F. . . . . . (PA) 112
COHEN, Laurie J. . . . . . . (PA) 228
DIMMICK, Mary L. . . . . . (PA) 304
DUVALLY, Charlotte F. . . (PA) 330
ERDICK, Joseph W. . . . . (PA) 352
HOWLEY, Deborah H. . . (PA) 566
MCCREARY, Diane M. . . . (PA) 800
MESSICK, Karen J. . . . . . (PA) 828
MOUNTS, Earl L. . . . . . . (PA) 873
PAUL, Suzanne . . . . (PA) 949
POE, Terrence C. . . . . . . (PA) 979
ROEDELL, Ray F. . . . . . (PA) 1048
SPIVACK, Amy D. . . . . . (PA) 1175
STEFANACCI, Michal A. (PA) 1185
CAMERON, Lucille W. . . (RI) 175
WALTON, Linda J. . . . . . (RI) 1301
ANDERSON, Marcia . . . (SC) 24
HAGEMEIER, Deborah A. (SD) 483
SMITH, Rise L. . . . . (SD) 1160
SPRULES, Marcia L. . . . (SD) 1176
CLELAND, Nancy D. . . . (TN) 220
CROWTHER, Karmen N. (TN) 262
LEACH, Sandra S. . . . . . (TN) 706
MOON, Fletcher F. . . . . . (TN) 857
SAMMATARO, Linda J. . (TN) 1078
SELF, George A. . . . . . . (TN) 1113
VIERA, Ann R. . . . . (TN) 1284
WALLACE, Alan H. . . . . (TN) 1297
BARRUS, Phyl . . . . (TX) 60
BROWN, Susan W. . . . . (TX) 147
BUTKOVICH, Nancy J. . . (TX) 166
CLEE, June E. . . . . (TX) 220
HEWINS, Elizabeth H. . . (TX) 535
KANESHIRO, Kellie N. . . (TX) 625
KIRTNER, R R. . . . . (TX) 655
MOORE, Guusje Z. . . . . . (TX) 859
O'DONOGHUE, Patrice (TX) 917
OGDEN, Suzanne M. . . . (TX) 918
TINSMAN, William A. . . . (TX) 1246
TROMBLEY, Patricia A. . (TX) 1258
WORCHEL, Harris M. . . . (TX) 1368
WYGANT, Alice C. . . . . (TX) 1375
ELLEFSEN, David . . . . . (UT) 343
HAGGERTY, Maxine R. . (UT) 483
CAPUTO, Richard P. . . . (VA) 180
CHUNG, Catherine A. . . . (VA) 213
MCCULLEY, Lucretia . . . (VA) 800
MONTGOMERY, Suzanne
L. . . . . (VA) 856
MORRIS, Karen L. . . . . . (VA) 867
SINNOTT, Gertrude M. . . (VA) 1144
TOSIANO, Barbara A. . . . (VA) 1252
DICENSO, Jacquelyn C. . (VT) 300
LAMSON, Maria W. . . . . (VT) 691
LAPIDOW, Amy R. . . . . (VT) 697
DELAUCHE, Jean E. . . . (WI) 289
LINTNER, Mary K. . . . . (WI) 731
ODDAN, Linda . . . . (WI) 916
ROUSE, Kendall G. . . . . (WI) 1061
SCHMITT, Madelaine M. (WI) 1096
WESTON, Karen A. . . . (WI) 1327
MCKEE, Jean A. . . . . . . (WV) 810
FRAUMENI, Michael A. . (ON) 399
LOVE, Barbara . . . . (ON) 743
SNYDER, Esther M. . . . . (ISR) 1164

Database searching & acquisitions HERMAN, Marsha . . . . . (NY) 531
Database searching & development WALSH, Kathryn A. . . . . (CT) 1299

DATABASE SEARCHING (Cont'd)

Database searching & medical databases KARASICK, Alice W. . . . (CA) 627
Database searching & reviews NITECKI, Danuta A. . . . . . (MD) 905
Database searching & social sciences FISHEL, Teresa A. . . . . . (MN) 380
Database searching & systems WILLIAMS, Calvin . . . . . (MI) 1342
Database searching by computer CESARD, Mary A. . . . . . (NJ) 196
Database searching coordination DURNIAK, Barbara A. . . (NY) 328
Database searching, DIALOG HAGE, Christine C. . . . . . (MI) 482
LAPAS, Martha E. . . . . . (NC) 697
MOSS, Charmagne L. . . . (TX) 872
Database searching, education GOLDSMITH, Maxine K. . (NJ) 446
Database searching, financial databases CONNER, Norma . . . . . . (NY) 237
Database searching, food sciences, chem REED, Catherine A. . . . . (NY) 1015
Database searching in chemistry & engrng WEST, Deborah C. . . . . . (TX) 1326
Database searching in education ZLATOS, Christy L. . . . . (AL) 1390
Database searching, medical databases HUDSON, Donna T. . . . . (NC) 569
Database searching on DIALOG MOXNESS, Mary J. . . . . (MN) 874
Database searching, research, reference BEDOR, Kathleen M. . . . (MN) 73
Database searching, toxicology & medical LEMMON, Anne B. . . . . . (LA) 715
Databases searching FRANCK, Ilona G. . . . . . (KY) 396
WILLIAMS, Guynell . . . . (SC) 1343
DIALOG database searching HUGHES, Frances M. . . (CT) 571
MAGUIRE, Shirley E. . . . (MI) 760
MILLER, Carmen L. . . . (WA) 836
Diversified database searching SMART, Marriott W. . . . . (CO) 1151
DTIC database searching MAGUIRE, Shirley E. . . . (MI) 760
Education database searching VISSCHER, Helga B. . . . (AL) 1285
Electronic database searching LIRA, Judith A. . . . . (CO) 732
BROWNE, Scott M. . . . . (NY) 148
Engineering databases searching THIBAUDEAU, Louise . . (PQ) 1235
Environmental database searching CIVITARESE, Kathleen A. (FL) 215
Journalism database searching ALLCORN, Mary E. . . . . (MO) 14
Legal & general database searching DUMAINE, Paul R. . . . . (RI) 325
Legal research & database searching ELAM, Joice B. . . . . (GA) 341
Marine science database searching HALE, Kay K. . . . . (FL) 485
Medical & other database searching POTTER, Laurene . . . . . (CA) 987
Medical databases, database searching DONOVAN, Judith G. . . . (PA) 312
MEDLARS database searching ALLOCCO, Claudia . . . . (NJ) 17
MYER, Nancy E. . . . . . . (NM) 884
Microcomputer training database searches KENNEDY, James W. . . (OK) 641
OCLC database searching ROBERTS, Lisa G. . . . . . (GA) 1041
Online bibliographic database searching SUBRAMANIAN, Jane M. (NY) 1206
Online CD-ROM database searching GRABINSKY, Warren B. (BC) 455
On-line database searching PALMA, Nancy C. . . . . . (PA) 935
Online searching, database searching HURYCH, Jitka M. . . . . . (IL) 578
Proposal writing & database searching KUHL, Danuta . . . . (VA) 682
Psychological database searching LINTON, Helen W. . . . . . (MA) 731
Reference & database searching SHELTON, Kathryn H. . . (AK) 1126
ALITO, Martha A. . . . . . . (DC) 13
THOMPSON, Susan J. . . (IN) 1241
MATHAI, Aleyamma . . . . (NJ) 783
BATES, Ellen . . . . (NY) 63
FRASENE, Joanne R. . . . (NY) 399
KATZ, Jacqueline E. . . . . (NY) 630
MURRAY, Elizabeth F. . . (NY) 881
JENSEN, Mary B. . . . . . (SD) 599
HELWIG, Karen A. . . . . . (WI) 525
Reference database searching HALL, Alice W. . . . . (DE) 486
MASON, Marjorie L. . . . . (IL) 781
FLEURY, Bruce E. . . . . . (LA) 385
OSBORNE, Nancy S. . . . (NY) 927
BANNEN, Carol A. . . . . . (WI) 54
Reference work & database searching DIBARTOLO, Amy L. . . . (NY) 299
Science & technology database searching SENKUS, Linda J. . . . . . (CT) 1115
SMISEK, Thomas P. . . . (MN) 1152
HASELBAUER, Kathleen
J. . . . . (WA) 510
SCHARMER, Roger C. . . (WI) 1090

DATABASE SEARCHING (Cont'd)

Science database searcher	PERDUE, Robert W.	(FL)	958
Science database searching	HART, David J.	(MI)	507
	DANFORD, Robert E.	(VA)	272
Scientific database search	BAIR, Alice E.	(IL)	47
Scientific database searching	BANKS, Mary E.	(CT)	54
	VELLIKY, Mary M.	(MI)	1281
	FREY, Luanne C.	(WI)	402
Secondary curriculum, database searching	WILSON, M L.	(CO)	1352
Social science database searching	GETCHELL, Charles M.	(NC)	430
Social sciences database searching	GOODWIN, Bryan D.	(ME)	450
	MILLER, Mary E.	(PA)	840
	RICHARDSON, Linda B.	(VA)	1029
SOLINET database searching	ROBERTS, Lisa G.	(GA)	1041
Toxicological database searching	MCDONELL, W E.	(TN)	803
Westlaw database searching	SHEINWALD, Franette	(NY)	1125

DATABASES (See also Full-Text and names of specific databases, e.g. BRS, ERIC, LEXIS, OCLC, etc.)

Abstracting & indexing databases	GOLDENBERG, Joan M.	(VA)	445
Academic databases	KAHN, Martin F.	(NY)	622
Access review databases	GRAF, Thomas H.	(DC)	456
Accounting databases	ROSENFELD, Lillian E.	(NY)	1056
Advertising & marketing databases	ZILAVY, Julie A.	(NY)	1388
Advertising database	KELLEY, Dennis L.	(NY)	636
Advertising databases	GOODSELL, Joan W.	(NY)	450
Advertising databases & publishing	LITTLE, Dean K.	(OH)	733
Aerospace & engineering databases	ANTHONY, Paul L.	(IL)	29
Aerospace information & databases	SMALLWOOD, James R.	(CT)	1151
Agricultural & scientific databases	PORTA, Maria A.	(IL)	984
Agricultural database	SPARKS, Richard M.	(DC)	1171
Agricultural databases	RUSS, Pamela K.	(FL)	1068
	CRAWFORD, Sherrida J.	(GA)	257
	LEDFORD, Carole L.	(GA)	708
	MATHEWS, Eleanor R.	(IA)	784
	THOMPSON, Michael E.	(MD)	1240
	BLUMENFELD, Judith K.	(MN)	107
	PETERSON, Julia C.	(MN)	963
	GIBSON, Marianne	(MO)	432
	LAVOY, Constance J.	(NC)	704
	BRITTON, Constance J.	(OH)	137
	NOGA, Dolores A.	(AB)	907
	COOK, Elaine	(ENG)	239
	JOLING, Carole G.	(ITL)	610
Agricultural engineering databases	MCNAUGHT, Hugh W.	(ON)	816
Agricultural veterinary databases	NEELEY, Dana M.	(TX)	891
Agriculture databases	CURTIS, Susan C.	(GA)	267
	ADAM, Anthony J.	(WI)	4
Alaska environmental databases	SOKOLOV, Barbara J.	(AK)	1165
Archival databases	DAWSON, Barbara J.	(DC)	282
Archival full-text databases	MARKERT, Patricia B.	(NY)	771
Arms race films databases	DOWLING, John	(PA)	316
Art & architectural databases	ROBERTSON, Jack	(MD)	1042
Art & architecture databases	VAN DYKE, Stephen H.	(NY)	1275
Art, architecture databases	GOODMAN, Edward C.	(NY)	449
Art databases	UPDIKE, Christina B.	(VA)	1269
Arts & humanities database marketing	ZAJDEL, George J.	(PA)	1385
Astronomy & astrophysics lit & databases	KNUDSEN, Helen Z.	(CA)	666
Audiovisual database	KELLEY, Dennis L.	(NY)	636
	YUSTER, Leigh C.	(NY)	1385
Automated bibliographic databases	CUMMINGS, Christopher H.	(UT)	264
Automated database coordination	ROSS, Carole L.	(CT)	1058
Automated databases	CRANOR, Alice T.	(DC)	255
Automated databases & conversions	PHILLIPS, Clifford R.	(CA)	968
Automation & database development	DUNN, Jamie N.	(MN)	326
Automation, databases, memorandum	FRY, Mary A.	(GA)	406
Automation of bibliographic databases	BERNARD, Patrick S.	(DC)	88
Behavioral sciences databases	BAXTER, Pam M.	(IN)	67
Bibliofile database	ARMSTRONG, Ruth C.	(NY)	32
Bibliographic database design	CHERVENAK, Joseph F.	(CO)	206
	GRIMES, Judith E.	(MD)	470
	COMSTOCK, Daniel L.	(NM)	235
	BREGMAN, Joan R.	(NY)	131
Bibliographic database development	NIXON, Judith M.	(IN)	906
	REILLY, Brian O.	(ON)	1020
Bibliographic database maintenance	VAN SICKLE, Mary L.	(KS)	1277

DATABASES (Cont'd)

Bibliographic database management	MILLER, Dick R.	(CA)	837
	COMSTOCK, Daniel L.	(NM)	235
	HILLMANN, Diane I.	(NY)	541
	MUTTER, Letitia N.	(NY)	883
	SALVAGE, Barbara A.	(NY)	1078
Bibliographic database products & srvs	PAUL, Rameshwar N.	(MD)	949
Bibliographic databases	BENIDIR, Samia	(CA)	80
	MCCOY-LARSON, Sandra	(DC)	799
	ECKERSON, Gale E.	(MA)	334
	MCCONE, Gary K.	(MD)	797
	TALLY, Roy D.	(MN)	1221
	MURDOCK, Douglas W.	(NE)	879
	PRAVER, Robin I.	(NY)	990
	WOODS, Lawrence J.	(NY)	1367
	SAUVE, Deborah A.	(VA)	1085
	DECOSTER, Barbara L.	(WA)	286
Bibliographical databases	ALSTON, Sandra	(ON)	18
Biological & agricultural databases	CACCESE, Vincent	(CA)	170
	JOHNSON, Deanna L.	(CA)	603
	SHAH, Syed M.	(NY)	1119
Biological & chemical databases	BORCK, Liba	(ISR)	116
Biological databases	STOCKER, Randi L.	(IN)	1195
	EVANS, Sylvia D.	(MD)	358
	ALLRED, Paula M.	(MI)	17
	THOMAS, Katharine S.	(NC)	1237
	HOFFMAN, Helen B.	(NJ)	548
	NOCKA, Jean A.	(NJ)	906
	WILLIAMS, Doris C.	(NY)	1343
	KELLY, Maureen C.	(PA)	638
	KENNEDY, H E.	(PA)	641
	SEPP, Frederick C.	(PA)	1115
	SAMPLE, Charles R.	(WA)	1078
Biology databases	PETERSON, Gretchen N.	(CA)	963
	GRAY, Dorothy A.	(KY)	459
Biomedical & applied science databases	LETT, Rosalind K.	(GA)	719
Biomedical & scientific databases	CARRIGAN, John L.	(CA)	186
Biomedical databases	BLITZ, Ruth R.	(CA)	105
	TAOKA, Wesley M.	(CA)	1223
	WEISS, Barbara M.	(CT)	1319
	FRANKLIN, Janice C.	(KS)	397
	GERMANN, Malcolm P.	(KS)	429
	LEIGHTON, Helene L.	(MA)	714
	COLAIANNI, Lois A.	(MD)	229
	HARRIMAN, Jenny F.	(MD)	503
	BAKER, Alison	(ME)	47
	SHIPLEY, Ruth M.	(MO)	1131
	PHILLIPS, Carol H.	(NJ)	967
	SZE, Melanie C.	(NJ)	1218
	WEGLARZ, Catherine R.	(NJ)	1316
	FALVEY, Genemary H.	(NY)	363
	WEIS, Ann M.	(NY)	1319
	BERWICK, Mary C.	(PA)	91
	GREEN, Patricia L.	(PA)	462
	KLEINSTEIN, Bruce H.	(PA)	660
	SEEDS, Robert S.	(PA)	1111
	WICKS, Pamela J.	(PA)	1335
	HANKS, Ellen T.	(TX)	496
	CLEMANS, Margaret H.	(VA)	220
	WILDER, Patricia A.	(WA)	1339
	MENITOVE, Symie D.	(WI)	824
	HAYWARD, Miriam C.	(PQ)	517
Biomedical ethics databases & info	NOZOE, Atsutake	(JAP)	911
Bio-sciences databases	GROVER, Wilma S.	(FL)	474
Biotechnology databases	CARUSO, Joy L.	(IL)	190
	LANG, Anita E.	(TX)	695
BRS databases	SCHEPPER, Josee H.	(PQ)	1091
Business & chemistry databases	GELMAN-KMEC, Marsha	(CA)	426
Business & current events databases	DAVIS, Sara	(TX)	281
Business & economics databases	LOVE, Sandra R.	(CA)	743
Business & engineering databases	MCKAY, Peter Z.	(FL)	810
	LO, Maryanne H.	(MN)	735
	HAWLEY, Laurie J.	(TX)	514
Business & finance database research	STOOPS, Louise	(NY)	1198
Business & finance databases	CROFT, Elizabeth G.	(NY)	260
	WALKER, Jeanette F.	(NY)	1295

DATABASES (Cont'd)

Business & financial databases   WARNER, Claudette S. . . (IL) 1305
BARRETT, Michael D. . . (NY) 59
BERNTSEN, Robert M. . . (NY) 90
DAVID, Julia A. . . . . . . (NY) 276
ESPO, Hal . . . . (NY) 354
JONES, Sarah C. . . . . . (NY) 615
MARSHALL, Patricia K. . (NY) 775
SANTORO, Tesse F. . . . (NY) 1082
VAZQUEZ, Edward . . . . (NY) 1280
Business & industry databases   CURRY, John A. . . . . . . (IL) 266
Business & insurance databases   MACKINTOSH, Pamela J. (NJ) 757
Business & management databases   CLIFT, Crystal A. . . . . . (MN) 222
Business & marketing databases   CRAWFORD, Marilyn L. . (CA) 257
Business & science databases   CALDWELL, Marlene . . . (TX) 172
Business & scientific databases   MITCHELL, Cynthia R. . . (TX) 848
Business & sci-tech databases   GALTON, Gwen . . . . (ON) 415
Business & social sciences databases   KENYON, Sharmon H. . . (CA) 643
SLOCUM, Hannah R. . . (CA) 1150
Business & technical databases   DONAHUE, Karin V. . . . . (IL) 310
WEBER, Robert F. . . . . . (OR) 1314
WHITEHURST, Dori A. . . (PA) 1333
ARMSTRONG, Denise M. (SAF) 32
Business bibliographic databases   POJE, Mary E. . . . . (NY) 980
Business, finance & accounting
  databases   KILBERG, Jacqueline L. . (NY) 648
Business, financial databases   SAYWARD, Nick H. . . . . (NY) 1087
Business, health care, engrng
  databases   PLOTSKY, Andrea G. . . . (CA) 978
MAH, Jeffery . . . . (CA) 760
Business information databases   BOYD, Cheryl J. . . . . . . (MN) 122
COMPTON, Erlinda R. . . (TX) 235
Business, marketing database   ECKLUND, Lynn M. . . . . (CA) 335
Business, marketing databases   MARKERT, Patricia B. . . (NY) 771
Business periodical databases   LEE, Soon H. . . . . (IL) 711
Business reference databases   DITMARS, Robert D. . . . (NJ) 305
MORRIS, Ann . . . . (IL) 866
Business research & databases   HOPKINS, Terry F. . . . . . (TX) 558
Business research in databases
Business science & technology
  database   DIMITRESCU, Ioana . . . . (PQ) 304
Cancer databases   DICKINSON, Patricia C. . (MD) 301
OSTROW, Dianne G. . . . (MD) 929
Cataloging & database management   CARTER, Ruth C. . . . . . (PA) 190
CD-ROM database development   DIETLE, Craig I. . . . . . . (NY) 302
CD-ROM database preparation   CIUFFETTI, Peter D. . . . (MA) 215
LOWRY, John D. . . . . . . (ON) 745
CD-ROM database publishing   POOLEY, Christopher G. (MA) 983
CD-ROM database services   LESLIE, Nathan . . . . (ON) 718
LOWRY, Douglas B. . . . . (ON) 745
CD-ROM databases   BOWRIN-MARSH, Donna
  M. . . . . (CA) 122
BUTLER, Matilda L. . . . . (CA) 167
DUGGAN, Mary K. . . . . . (CA) 324
TSENG, Sally C. . . . . . . (CA) 1260
RIETDYK, Ron J. . . . . . . (MA) 1033
ALBRIGHT, John B. . . . . (MD) 10
Chemical & agriculture databases   CLARK, Wendolyn H. . . (AL) 218
Chemical & biological databases   STODDARD, Charles E. . (CT) 1196
SUPEAU, Cynthia . . . . . (CT) 1210
Chemical & business databases   MARTINO, Sharon C. . . . (IN) 779
Chemical & coatings databases   KOZELKA, Catherine C. . (IL) 674
Chemical & engineering databases   SCHUTZBERG, Frances . (MA) 1103
Chemical & metallurgical databases   BERGER, Lewis W. . . . . (PA) 85
Chemical & toxicological databases   COSMIDES, George J. . . (MD) 249
Chemical business Information
  databases   REITANO, Maimie V. . . . (NY) 1022
Chemical database   AUER, E E. . . . . (NJ) 39
Chemical database development   CARSON, Bonnie L. . . . . (MO) 188
Chemical databases   CHADWICK, Sharon S. . (CA) 197
HAUTH, Carol A. . . . . . . (CA) 513
LAI, Dennis . . . . (CA) 688
MOUNTFORD, Eve . . . . (CT) 873
KECK, Bruce L. . . . . (DC) 633
GAUMOND, Suzanne M. (IL) 423
STUNKARD, Gilbert L. . . (IL) 1205
CHANDIK, Barbara V. . . (IN) 199
FRANKLIN, Janice C. . . (KS) 397
COOPER WYMAN,
  Rosalind . . . . (MA) 244
EVANS, Sylvia D. . . . . . . (MD) 358

DATABASES (Cont'd)

Chemical databases   MARCHANT, Thomas O. (MO) 768
PORTER, Katherine R. . . (NC) 985
ALLISON, Kenneth J. . . . (NJ) 17
CARNAHAN, Joan A. . . . (NJ) 183
FEDORS, Maurica R. . . . (NJ) 368
LEWIS, Dale E. . . . . (NJ) 722
NOCKA, Jean A. . . . . . . (NJ) 906
SKIDANOW, Helene . . . . (NJ) 1146
FALCONE, Elena C. . . . . (NY) 362
LANE, Sandra G. . . . . . . (NY) 694
WARDEN, Carolyn L. . . . (NY) 1304
BUTCHER, Sharon L. . . . (OH) 166
LANDIS, Kay A. . . . . (OH) 693
O'BRIEN, Mary C. . . . . . (OR) 915
HANF, Elizabeth P. . . . . . (PA) 495
STANLEY, Kerry G. . . . . (PA) 1180
BOWMAN, Laura M. . . . (TX) 122
GRIMES, John F. . . . . . . (TX) 470
SAMPLE, Charles R. . . . (WA) 1078
TIMMERS, Debra A. . . . . (WI) 1246
CHAPMAN, Phyllis C. . . (ON) 202
HOBBS, Kathleen M. . . . (ON) 545
O'DONNELL, Rosemary F. (ON) 917
VUKOV, Vesna . . . . (ON) 1290
Chemical databases & info retrieval   ROSENTHAL, Francine C. (OH) 1057
Chemical databases & searching   LINEPENSEL, Kenneth C. (IN) 730
Chemical databases & sources   GALBRAITH, Barry E. . . (NY) 413
Chemical databases building   BAKER, Dale B. . . . . (OH) 48
Chemical databases, science
  databases   COSGRIFF, John C. . . . . (VA) 248
Chemical hazards databases   BRANSFORD, John S. . . (TN) 129
Chemical information database
  building   PLATAU, Gerard O. . . . . (OH) 977
Chemical, patent databases   STAVETSKI, Norma K. . . (NJ) 1183
Chemical patents, literature databases   UMFLEET, Ruth A. . . . . . (TX) 1268
Chemistry & environmental databases   TYLER-WHITE, Patricia G. (TX) 1266
Chemistry & physical sciences
  databases   BECK, Diane J. . . . . (CA) 71
Chemistry databases   KLEINER, Donna H. . . . . (CA) 660
PETERSON, Gretchen N. (CA) 963
POKLAR, Mary J. . . . . . . (CA) 980
KLEMARCZYK, Laurice D. (CT) 660
CARUSO, Joy L. . . . . . . (IL) 190
OLIVER, James W. . . . . . (MI) 921
DICKERSON, Jimmy . . . (NC) 300
SMITH, Yvonne B. . . . . . (NJ) 1161
MCGEE, Yvonne M. . . . . (PA) 806
MILLER, Dennis P. . . . . . (OH) 837
MIRONENKO, Rimma . . . (CA) 847
Chemistry databases & reference
Chemistry including databases   GAZZOLA, Kenneth E. . . (DC) 424
Civil, military, space databases   MCCONNIE, Mary . . . . . (TRN) 798
Classification, database cataloging   KINNAIRD, Cheryl D. . . . (IL) 653
Clinical literature retrieval, databases   WATSON, Linda S. . . . . (AL) 1309
Coalbed methane databases   PAUL, Nora M. . . . . (FL) 949
Commercial databases   CORNELIUS, Peter K. . . (LUX) 246
Company databases   BOYD, Cheryl J. . . . . . . (MN) 122
Company information databases   KENDRIC, Marisa A. . . . (NY) 640
Competitive databases   CLARK, David L. . . . . . . (CA) 216
Computer database   VAN HORN, Neal F. . . . . (OR) 1275
Computer database cataloging   HARWELL, Trudy J. . . . . (AZ) 509
Computer database development   LEE, Lydia H. . . . . (CA) 710
Computer database indexing   MARTINEZ, Jane A. . . . . (NJ) 779
Computer database structure   LAZINGER, Susan S. . . . (CT) 706
Computer databases   JONES, David E. . . . . . . (NJ) 612
O'DONNELL, Maureen D. (NY) 917
BAKER, Carol J. . . . . . . (OH) 48
THOMAS, Barbara C. . . . (TX) 1236
VAN SICKLEN, Lindsay L. (VA) 1277
WARD, Carol T. . . . . (VA) 1303
BURSON, Scott F. . . . . . (WA) 163
BOSMA, Elske M. . . . . . (ON) 117
Computer engineering databases   WOJCIKIEWICZ, Carol A. (MI) 1359
Computer high tech databases   CHICHESTER, Gerald C. (CT) 208
Computer industry databases   MASTERS, Kathy B. . . . (CT) 782
CLIFT, Crystal A. . . . . . . (MN) 222
CHICHESTER, Gerald C. (CT) 208
Computer software database   KOOLISH, Ruth K. . . . . . (CA) 671
Computer software databases
Computer systems & databases   SPARKS, Marie C. . . . . . (IN) 1171

DATABASES (Cont'd)

Computerized catalogs & databases	VANDERBERG, Patricia S.	(CA)	1273
Computerized database creation	PASQUARIELLA, Susan K.	(NY)	946
Computerized database management	HANAFEE, Valerie	(MI)	494
Computerized database retrieval	WHITE, Chandlee	(MA)	1330
Computerized database	KOTO, Ann S.	(HI)	673
Computerized psychological databases	WALES, Patricia L.	(CT)	1294
Computer-readable statistical databases	HENSON, Jane E.	(IN)	529
Consulting, computer databases	CHAMIS, Alice Y.	(OH)	198
Consumer database	VALANDRA, Kent T.	(NY)	1271
Conversion & database maintenance	SHEAFFER, Marc L.	(PA)	1124
Corporate databases	WOLF, Noel C.	(AZ)	1360
Corporate financial databases	HAMBRIC, Donna R.	(CO)	491
Corporate legal research databases	MORRIS, Ann	(IL)	866
Corp author name formation & database	KANE, Astor V.	(VA)	624
Creating relational database	PEGLER, Ross J.	(FL)	954
Criminal justice databases	SMITH, Ellen A.	(OH)	1154
Cultural information databases	SZARY, Richard V.	(DC)	1218
Current affairs databases	LESHY, Dede	(AZ)	718
Current events databases	CONGER, Lucinda D.	(DC)	236
Current information databases	HILL, Fay G.	(IA)	539
Current news & information databases	JOBE, Shirley A.	(MA)	601
Customized databases	RUBINSTEIN, Ed	(NY)	1065
Data management, databases	SAGAR, Mary B.	(MI)	1074
Database	CANTER, Judy A.	(CA)	179
	GRATE, Jon F.	(CO)	458
	LOVAS, Paula M.	(DC)	743
	BAUM, Nathan	(NY)	66
	BACON, Agnes K.	(OH)	44
Database administration	TRIMBLE, Kathy W.	(CA)	1256
	CURRAN, George L.	(NY)	266
	MCCLURE, Margaret R.	(TX)	797
	MOONEY, Shirley E.	(BC)	858
	LEWIS, Leslie	(ON)	723
Database analysis	DE ARMAN, Charles L.	(DC)	284
	WHITMAN, Jean A.	(MD)	1333
	GARCIA, Joseph E.	(MI)	417
	HARDIN, Nancy E.	(TN)	500
Database analysis & design	TAYLOR, Alice J.	(CA)	1226
Database & automation applications	SAUTER, Sylvia E.	(WA)	1085
Database & automation management	STAINBROOK, Lynn M.	(WI)	1178
Database & book indexing	LYNCH, Jacqueline	(MA)	751
Database & information system design	BATTY, Charles D.	(MD)	65
Database & system design	VANCE, Julia M.	(MD)	1273
Database & systems administration	KINLEY, Jo H.	(DC)	652
Database & systems analysis	ROCHELEAU, Kathleen D.	(MA)	1046
Database & systems consultant	CHAPMAN, Kathleen A.	(WA)	202
Database & systems design	CUTRONA, Cheryl	(PA)	268
Database applications	DAVIS, Becky C.	(CA)	277
	FRANCIS, Diane S.	(DE)	396
	BOWEN, Louise E.	(GA)	120
	HUSSEY, Laurie L.	(MA)	578
	BALL, John L.	(ON)	52
Database applications programming	ROSENFELD, Jane D.	(NY)	1056
Database archives design	DAWSON, Barbara J.	(DC)	282
Database archiving	PICKARD, Mary A.	(AL)	970
Database building	FREDERICK, Sidney C.	(IL)	399
	COPENHAVER, Ida L.	(OH)	244
Database cataloging	JIZBA, Laurel	(MI)	600
	FAWCETT-BRANDON, Pamela S.	(NJ)	367
	LIDSKY, Ella	(NY)	725
	BROWNELL, Barbara A.	(OH)	148
	SHELLENBARGER, Linda K.	(OH)	1126
	CRAIG, Marilyn J.	(TX)	254
	SHIH, Chia C.	(TX)	1130
Database cataloging & indexing	CHARBONNEAU, Ronald P.	(CA)	202
	DUMLAO, Mercedes G.	(CA)	325
	HAMILTON, D A.	(IL)	491
	ZIMMERMAN, Brenda M.	(IN)	1388
	SPURLING, Norman K.	(MD)	1177
	ROLONTZ, Linda	(MN)	1051
	FIELDING, Carol J.	(WA)	376

DATABASES (Cont'd)

Database cataloging & searching	VELEZ, Sara B.	(NY)	1281
Database computer searching	KING, Anne M.	(LA)	650
Database construction	WILDE, Daniel U.	(CT)	1338
	DEHART, Odell	(DC)	288
	OMAR, Elizabeth A.	(MD)	923
Database construction & creation	MENNELLA, Dona M.	(MD)	824
Database construction & maintenance	BRITTON, Jeffrey W.	(NJ)	137
Database consultation	MLYNAR, Mary	(OH)	850
Database conversion	HIATT, Robert M.	(DC)	536
	JANK, David A.	(MA)	593
	KREYCHE, Michael R.	(OH)	678
Database conversion & buildup	MEDINA, Ildefonso M.	(NY)	820
Database conversion projects	DIXON, Edith M.	(WI)	306
Database coordinating	PERDUE, Robert W.	(FL)	958
Database coordination	KEMPF, Jody L.	(NM)	639
Database creation	TALBOT, Dawn E.	(CA)	1220
	WRIGHT, Joseph F.	(FL)	1372
	STUHLMAN, Daniel D.	(IL)	1205
	GORDON, Helen A.	(IN)	451
	PREVE, Roberta J.	(MA)	992
	FREEDMAN, Lynn P.	(MD)	400
	COTY, Patricia A.	(NY)	250
	OLSEN, Wallace C.	(NY)	922
	MARTINEZ, Linda W.	(WA)	779
	MILLS, Judy E.	(ON)	844
Database creation & management	LAMANN, Amber N.	(NY)	689
Database creation & marketing	HAWKINS, John W.	(IN)	514
Database DBA & consulting	SYVERSON, Kathleen A.	(IL)	1217
Database demonstration	GUILLEMARD DE COLON, Teresita	(PR)	476
Database demonstrations & training	FRYER, Regina K.	(CT)	407
Database demos & training	WRIGHT, Larry L.	(NC)	1372
	MOON, Fletcher F.	(TN)	857
Database design	CREW-NOBLE, Sara M.	(CA)	258
	DONLEY, Leigh M.	(CA)	311
	HORACEK, Paula B.	(CA)	558
	HOROWITZ, Roberta S.	(CA)	560
	KALVINSKAS, Louanne A.	(CA)	623
	MCCARTHY, John L.	(CA)	794
	PAPERMASTER, Cynthia L.	(CA)	939
	STANLEY, Dale R.	(CA)	1180
	STRIBLING, Lorraine R.	(CA)	1202
	WITTMANN, Cecelia V.	(CA)	1358
	TRIOLO, Victor A.	(CT)	1257
	MODLIN, Marilyn J.	(DC)	851
	ROAN, Tattie W.	(GA)	1038
	SCHNICK, Robert M.	(GA)	1097
	CIBULSKIS, Elizabeth R.	(IL)	214
	CLARK, Gerald L.	(IL)	217
	GROSSMAN, David G.	(IL)	473
	JACOBSON, William R.	(IL)	590
	KOSMAN, Joyce E.	(IL)	672
	MILLER, Thomas R.	(IL)	843
	PERLMAN, Michael S.	(IL)	959
	SHAW, Debora	(IL)	1123
	SUIDAN, Randa H.	(IL)	1207
	WILLIAMS, Martha E.	(IL)	1345
	HASHEM, Judy A.	(IN)	510
	HAMILTON, Fae K.	(MA)	492
	LYNCH, Jacqueline	(MA)	751
	BLUTE, Mary R.	(MD)	107
	CHESLOCK, Rosalind P.	(MD)	207
	VONDERHAAR, Mark N.	(MD)	1288
	WETZBARGER, Cecilia G.	(MD)	1328
	SCHMITTROTH, John	(MI)	1096
	BURCSU, James E.	(NC)	158
	KISER, Anita H.	(NC)	656
	ANDERSON, James D.	(NJ)	23
	BILBOUL, Roger R.	(NJ)	96
	GEORGE, Muriel S.	(NJ)	428
	RILEY, Robert H.	(NJ)	1034
	WALLMARK, John S.	(NJ)	1298
	BERGER, Mary C.	(NY)	85
	BROWN-SPRUILL, Debra K.	(NY)	149
	GREENGRASS, Alan R.	(NY)	464
	MACKESY, Eileen M.	(NY)	756
	PISCITELLI, Rosalie A.	(NY)	976

DATABASES (Cont'd)

Database design

	RAKSHI, Sri R.	(NY)	1004
	MAXWELL, Marjo V.	(OH)	788
	RIFFLE, Linda	(OH)	1034
	PASCHAL, Linda P.	(OK)	945
	BOWDEN, Gail L.	(PA)	120
	HODGE, Gail M.	(PA)	546
	WILLIAMS, James G.	(PA)	1344
	GOVE, N B.	(TN)	454
	HEWINS, Elizabeth H.	(TX)	535
	O'DONOGHUE, Patrice	(TX)	917
	PEDEN, Robert K.	(TX)	954
	WORCHEL, Harris M.	(TX)	1368
	CUMMINGS, Christopher H.	(UT)	264
	DEBARDELEBEN, Marian Z.	(VA)	284
	ROSENBERG, Murray D.	(VA)	1056
	CRANDALL, Michael D.	(WA)	255
	FIDEL, Raya	(WA)	374
	KLAVER, Timothy J.	(WI)	658
	LANK, Dannette H.	(WI)	696
	PARKS, Dennis H.	(WI)	943
	SCHARMER, Roger C.	(WI)	1090
	NICHOL, Kathleen M.	(BC)	901
	STEPHENSON, Mary S.	(BC)	1188
	SABLJIC, John A.	(ON)	1072
	MIRABELLI, Gerardo	(CSR)	847
	YAMAZAKI, Hisamichi	(JAP)	1377
Database design & administration	JONES, Anne	(NY)	611
Database design & construction	DENTON, Francesca L.	(MA)	293
	HLAVA, Marjorie M.	(NM)	544
	HALE, Linda L.	(BC)	485
Database design & development	HOLLOWAY, Dona W.	(CA)	552
	HUNT, Richard K.	(CA)	575
	LA BORDE, Charlotte A.	(CA)	686
	MARKWORTH, Lawrence L.	(CA)	772
	MORITZ, Thomas D.	(CA)	865
	SPRUNG, Lori L.	(CA)	1176
	STAN, Gail A.	(CA)	1179
	WOLF, Nola M.	(CA)	1360
	ROARK, Robin D.	(DC)	1038
	SAWYER, Edmond J.	(DC)	1086
	STOCKTON, Ken R.	(DC)	1196
	TURNER, Susan A.	(DC)	1265
	HUSSEY, Laurie L.	(MA)	578
	LAROSA, Sharon M.	(MA)	698
	BOBKA, Marlene S.	(MD)	108
	PUGH, W J.	(MD)	997
	BELLI, Frank G.	(NY)	78
	WEINSTEIN, Lois	(NY)	1318
	GUBIOTTI, Ross A.	(OH)	475
	JOSEPH, Patricia A.	(PA)	617
	NATHANSON, Esther M.	(PA)	889
	LYDEN, Edward W.	(TX)	750
	MOORE, Penelope F.	(VA)	861
	SAUVE, Deborah A.	(VA)	1085
	WILTSHIRE, Denise A.	(VA)	1354
	YODER, William M.	(VA)	1380
	POPE, Nolan F.	(WI)	983
	MCCLYMONT, Karen A.	(ON)	797
	LEDOUX, Marc A.	(PQ)	708
	FUENTES, Ismael	(SPN)	408
Database design & documentation	MACLEOD, Valerie R.	(KY)	757
Database design & implementation	DAMOTH, Douglas L.	(NY)	272
	GOODWIN, C R.	(AB)	450
Database design & indexing	FORKES, David	(ON)	390
Database design & maintenance	WEIDA, William A.	(OH)	1316
	ROSENBERG, Kenyon C.	(VA)	1056
	FRITZ, Richard J.	(ON)	405
Database design & management	ANDRADE, Rebecca	(CA)	26
	BURNS, Nancy R.	(CA)	162
	PEPETONE, Diane S.	(IA)	957
	MACKEY, Denise R.	(IL)	756
	SLAWNIAK, Patricia M.	(IL)	1148
	NATOLI, Dorothy L.	(MA)	889
	ADLER, Robert J.	(MI)	7
	EARLE, Marcia H.	(NY)	332

DATABASES (Cont'd)

Database design & management

	MANES, Estelle L.	(OK)	765
	RAMBO, Neil H.	(TX)	1005
	FOSTER, Anne	(ON)	392
	SOKOV, Asta M.	(PQ)	1166
	NEUWILLER, Charlene	(WGR)	897
Database design & production	BATES, Ruthann I.	(MD)	64
	BRUNELLE, Bette S.	(NY)	150
	LAM, Vinh T.	(ON)	689
Database design & quality control	VEGTER, Amy H.	(NY)	1281
Database design & search	SCHWALLER, Marian C.	(MA)	1104
Database design & use	KASKE, Neal K.	(AL)	628
	MACIUSZKO, Kathleen L.	(OH)	755
Database design, development, management	SHELLENBARGER, Linda K.	(OH)	1126
	FURR, Susan H.	(VA)	410
	BEHNKE, Charles	(WI)	75
Database design for materials	LOWELL, Brian V.	(IL)	744
Database design, management	UMFLEET, Ruth A.	(TX)	1268
Database designer	LABEAU, Dennis	(MI)	685
Database designs	LI, Marjorie H.	(NJ)	724
Database development	HAWKOS, Lise A.	(AZ)	514
	BOEHM, Ronald J.	(CA)	109
	COYLE, Karen E.	(CA)	253
	DEHN, Lydia A.	(CA)	288
	GIFFORD, Becky J.	(CA)	433
	HAY, Wayne M.	(CA)	515
	HENKE, Dan	(CA)	528
	HOLLAND, Mary	(CA)	551
	HUNT, Judy L.	(CA)	575
	KATTLOVE, Rose W.	(CA)	630
	OLIVARES, Jose A.	(CA)	920
	PRESTON, Cecilia M.	(CA)	991
	RAZE, Nasus B.	(CA)	1012
	SALM, Kay E.	(CA)	1077
	VRATNY-WATTS, Janet M.	(CA)	1289
	MALYSHEV, Nina A.	(CO)	764
	ORRICO, James T.	(CT)	926
	WILLSON, Katherine H.	(CT)	1349
	ANGLE, Joanne G.	(DC)	28
	BLIXRUD, Julia C.	(DC)	105
	DOENGES, John C.	(DC)	308
	DOERNBERG, David G.	(DC)	308
	BRETON, Ernest J.	(DE)	133
	UCHIDA, Deborah K.	(HI)	1267
	HURD, Albert E.	(IL)	577
	RUSSELL, Janet	(IL)	1069
	WAY, Harold E.	(KS)	1311
	DONOHUE, Joseph	(MA)	312
	FEIDLER, Anita J.	(MA)	368
	ISAACS, Cynthia W.	(MA)	584
	SPROUL, Barbara A.	(MA)	1176
	BEATTY, Samuel B.	(MD)	70
	BRANCH, Katherine A.	(MD)	127
	CHAPUT, Linda J.	(MD)	202
	FLORANCE, Valerie	(MD)	385
	FREIBURGER, Gary A.	(MD)	401
	JONES, Gerry U.	(MD)	613
	SPURLING, Norman K.	(MD)	1177
	KELLER, Karen A.	(MI)	635
	MAXWELL, Bonnie J.	(MI)	788
	HALLSTROM, Curtis H.	(MN)	489
	LINEWEAVER, Joe R.	(MN)	730
	RALPH, Randy D.	(NC)	1004
	THOMPSON, Reubin C.	(NC)	1241
	CONLEY, Gail D.	(NJ)	236
	HANEY, Kevin M.	(NJ)	495
	RODEAWALD, Patricia M.	(NJ)	1047
	SHAFER, Leona M.	(NJ)	1119
	BROWN-SPRUILL, Debra K.	(NY)	149
	FREIFELD, Roberta I.	(NY)	401
	GREENFIELD, Stanley R.	(NY)	464
	HERNANDEZ, Tamsen M.	(NY)	532
	JENSEN, Dennis F.	(NY)	598
	STELZLE, James J.	(NY)	1186
	VAN BRUNT, Amy S.	(NY)	1272

DATABASES (Cont'd)
Database development

ZIRPOLO, Frank	(NY)	1390
BAUMGARTNER, Robert M.	(OH)	66
JANKOWSKI, Dorothy A.	(OH)	593
MARSH, Elizabeth C. . .	(OH)	773
ELSTON, Andrew S. . . .	(PA)	346
LOCKETT, Cheryl L. . . .	(PA)	736
MARLOW, Kathryn E. . . .	(PA)	772
RUTKOWSKI, Hollace A.	(PA)	1070
SCHREIBER-COIA, Barbara J.	(PA)	1099
BORRELLI, Barbara A. . .	(TN)	117
JONES, Kendra A.	(TN)	613
BIRD, H C.	(TX)	98
TYLER-WHITE, Patricia G.	(TX)	1266
LEONARD, Lucinda E. . .	(VA)	716
WILLS, Luella G.	(VA)	1349
EIPERT, Susan L.	(WA)	340
GREATHOUSE, Brenda J.	(WV)	461
BROOME, Diana M.	(BC)	141
ENNS, Carol F.	(NB)	350
LARSON, Anna M.	(ON)	699
MILLER, Katherine J. . . .	(ON)	839
HOFFMANN, Eliahu W. . .	(ISR)	548
HUEMER, Christina G. . .	(ITL)	570
CORNELIUS, Peter K. . .	(LUX)	246

Database development & design

KENNY-SLOAN, Linda . .	(CA)	642
YODER, Susan M.	(CA)	1380

Database development & documentation

GRIPPO, Christopher F. .	(WA)	471

Database development & maintenance

HALPERN, Marilyn	(NJ)	489

Database development & management

GREENWAY, Helen B. . .	(CT)	465
MCNAMARA, Emma J. . .	(DC)	816
GATTIS, R G.	(MI)	422
AKS, Gloria	(NY)	9
KOLTAY, Emery I.	(NY)	670

Database development & marketing

TOWNLEY, Richard L. . .	(NY)	1253

Database development & retrieval

SAUNDERS, Leslie E. . .	(MA)	1084

Database development consultant

GROTE, Janet H.	(NY)	473

Database development, indexing, reviews

WOODARD, Beth E.	(MI)	1365

Database development project management

TELFER, Margaret E. . . .	(NC)	1230

Database directories

BUCENEC, Nancy L. . . .	(NY)	153
TOPEL, Iris N.	(NY)	1251

Database distribution

SPALA, Jeanne L.	(CA)	1170

Database documentation & promotion ideas

MILLER, Carmen L.	(WA)	836

Database documentation chapter writing

MARANGONI, Eugene G.	(CA)	768

Database documentation design

PUGH, W J.	(MD)	997

Database end-user services

ECKLUND, Kristin A. . . .	(CA)	335

Database evaluation & searching

HEWISON, Nancy S. . . .	(IN)	535

Database evaluations

CYGAN, Rose M.	(MI)	268

Database full-text systems

PHILLIPS, J R.	(OK)	968

Database generation

JANSSON, John F.	(IL)	594

Database indexing

PICKARD, Mary A.	(AL)	970
STEVENS, Michael	(IL)	1190
WISE, Matthew W.	(NY)	1357
SHUPAK, Harris J.	(PA)	1134

Database indexing & maintenance

NEUWILLER, Charlene . .	(WGR)	897

Database information

WARD, Catherine J. . . .	(NJ)	1303

Database information publishing

RICCOBONO, Joseph V.	(CT)	1026

Database information retrieval

MAGNER, Mary F.	(TX)	759

Database installation & use

RUDA, Donna R.	(NY)	1065

Database instruction & training

WILCOX, Patricia F. . . .	(WI)	1338

Database lib srvs, plng & implementing

MADDEN, Doreitha R. . .	(NJ)	758

Database maintenance

BROWN, Barbara L. . . .	(CA)	142
GARDNER, Laura L. . . .	(CA)	418
MOOMEY, Margaret M. .	(CO)	857
BROWN, Jeanette L. . . .	(FL)	144
FORFIA, Linda S.	(KS)	390
MARTIN, Norma H. . . .	(LA)	777
CRAWFORD, Lynn D. . .	(NJ)	257
MCCOMBS, Gillian M. . .	(NY)	797

DATABASES (Cont'd)
Database maintenance

SANDERS, Melodie	(OK)	1080
PUKL, Joseph M.	(SC)	997

Database maintenance & management
Database maintenance, batch mode
Database management

YUSTER, Leigh C.	(NY)	1385
BADING, Kathryn E. . . .	(TX)	44
EMMONS, Mary E.	(AK)	348
PUTZ, Paul D.	(AK)	998
MONTGOMERY, Kimberly K.	(AL)	856
RICHMOND, John W. . .	(AZ)	1030
GEIGER, Richard G. . . .	(CA)	425
MIELKE, Marsha K. . . .	(CA)	833
SULLIVAN, Edward A. . .	(CA)	1207
LAMPREY, Patricia M. . .	(CO)	691
GONZALEZ, Suzanna S.	(CT)	448
HARBISON, John H. . . .	(DC)	499
THURONYI, Geza T. . . .	(DC)	1243
ALZOFON, Sammy R. . .	(FL)	19
BEVERIDGE, Mary I. . . .	(IA)	93
ENGER, Kathy B.	(IA)	349
STUART, Kimberly A. . . .	(IA)	1204
STUNKARD, Gilbert L. . .	(IL)	1205
ASHER, Richard E. . . .	(IN)	36
GOLOVIN, Naomi E. . . .	(IN)	447
SHARMA, Shirley K. . . .	(KS)	1122
FOWLER, James W. . . .	(KY)	393
BOZOIAN, Paula	(MA)	124
MACDONALD, Wayne D.	(MA)	754
BRANDHORST, Wesley T.	(MD)	128
FLORANCE, Valerie	(MD)	385
MCCUTCHEON, Dianne E.	(MD)	801
TAHIR, Mary M.	(MD)	1220
UNGER, Carol P.	(MD)	1269
WOODS, Catharine C. . .	(MD)	1366
CUNNINGHAM, Tina Y. . .	(MI)	265
REGAN, Lesley E.	(MI)	1017
BALDWIN, Jerome C. . .	(MN)	51
CHAN, Jeanny T.	(MO)	199
MUETH, Elizabeth C. . . .	(MO)	875
BRUCE, Nancy G.	(NC)	149
DAVIS, Jinnie Y.	(NC)	279
RALPH, Randy D.	(NC)	1004
STEARNS, Melissa M. . .	(NH)	1183
BREEDLOVE, Elizabeth A.	(NJ)	131
DOUGLASS, Leslie A. . .	(NJ)	314
JOHNSON, Minnie L. . . .	(NJ)	607
KELLY, John P.	(NJ)	638
PAPROCKI, Mary E.	(NJ)	939
PASTER, Luisa R.	(NJ)	946
RIHACEK, Karen S.	(NJ)	1034
WALLMARK, John S. . . .	(NJ)	1298
BENSON, James A.	(NY)	83
CASTRO, Julio E.	(NY)	194
COVERT, Nadine	(NY)	252
FRUSCIANO, Thomas J.	(NY)	406
GOLDBERG, Judy W. . .	(NY)	444
HUDAK, Barbara M. . . .	(NY)	569
KLINE, Harriet	(NY)	661
VELARDI, Adrienne B. . .	(NY)	1281
WILSON, Marijo S.	(NY)	1352
KNOBLAUCH, Carol J. . .	(OH)	665
FORCIER, Peggy C. . . .	(OR)	389
DUSENBERRY, Mary D. .	(SC)	329
LOWRIMORE, R T.	(SC)	745
BELLAMY, Lois M.	(TN)	77
RUSHING, Jessie W. . . .	(TN)	1068
BICHTELER, Julie H. . . .	(TX)	94
HENDERSON, Lennijo P.	(TX)	526
SZARKA, Tamara J.	(TX)	1218
LIU, Kitty P.	(UT)	734
BERGMAN, Rita F.	(VA)	86
HARVEY, Suzanne	(WA)	509
VAN DYKE, Ruth L. . . .	(WA)	1275
ALLEN, Christina Y. . . .	(WI)	14
DWORACZEK, Marian . .	(AB)	330
FOSTER, Margaret A. . . .	(ON)	392
GRIMES, Deirdre E. . . .	(ON)	470
NELSON, Michael J.	(ON)	894

DATABASES (Cont'd)

Database management

MALEK, Stanislaw A. .... (PQ) 763

Database management &
  administration   SLEETER, Ellen L. ..... (CA) 1148
Database management & creation HAWK, Susan A. ...... (MD) 513
Database management & design VARAT, Nancy L. ...... (CA) 1278
                          BROWN, Maxine M. ..... (DC) 146
                          KRANCH, Douglas A. .... (IA) 676
                          ANDREWS, Sylvia L. .... (IN) 27
                          JOHNSON, Judith ...... (NY) 606
                          PUKL, Joseph M. ...... (SC) 997

Database management &
  development   REDFIELD, Elizabeth ... (CA) 1014
                          INGLE, Bernita W. ..... (GA) 582
                          CANNATA, Arleen ..... (NY) 178
                          EDWARDS, Melanie G. ... (NY) 337
Database management & distribution SIMON, Ralph C. ...... (IN) 1141
Database management &
  implementation   MCGREGOR, M C. ..... (CT) 808
Database management & quality
  control   HOMAN, J M. .... (MI) 555
Database management in humanities CRAWFORD, David E. ... (MI) 256
Database management, library
  automation   MAIN, Linda Y. .... (CA) 761
Database management, reprint files MENZUL, Faina .... (NJ) 825
Database management software YAU, Linda S. .... (CA) 1378
Database management system ROBB, Thomas W. ..... (DC) 1038
                          NASU, Yukio .... (JAP) 889
Database management systems ANDERSON, Clifford D. . (CA) 22
                          CUADRA, Carlos A. .... (CA) 262
                          SHARP, Geoffrey H. .... (CA) 1122
                          WEISS, William B. ..... (CA) 1320
                          CARR, Sallyann .... (DC) 186
                          CARR, Sallyann .... (FL) 186
                          WRIGHT, John H. ..... (FL) 1371
                          VAN BRUNT, Virginia ... (MD) 1272
                          COX, Bruce B. .... (MO) 253
                          STEAD, William W. .... (NC) 1183
                          MOTT, Thomas H. ..... (NJ) 872
                          FROEHLICH, Thomas J. . (NY) 405
                          GUBIOTTI, Ross A. .... (OH) 475
                          EASTMAN, Caroline M. . (SC) 333
                          SNYDER, Cathrine E. ... (TN) 1164
                          FASSETT, William E. ... (WA) 366
                          SCHUELLER, Janette H. . (WA) 1101
                          COLE, Lorna P. .... (ON) 231

Database management·systems
  development   ROSENTHAL, Marylu C. . (MA) 1057
Database management systems on
  computers   RAEDER, Aggi W. ..... (CA) 1003
Database market research MAYERS, Henry L. ..... (MI) 789
Database marketing   GABOR, John M. ...... (NY) 411
                          ELSTON, Andrew S. .... (PA) 346
                          GOSLING, Carolyn ..... (VA) 453
                          SULLIVAN, Michael M. .. (VA) 1208
                          BILLINGSLEY, Andrew G. (ON) 96
Database marketing & development GAGNE, Frank .... (ON) 412
Database marketing & sales PAPPALARDO, Marcia J. (IL) 939
Database mergers   WATKINS, Dorothy .... (NY) 1309
Database networking &
  communications   PASCHAL, John M. ..... (OK) 945
Database online searching SINGER, Susan A. ..... (NJ) 1143
Database organization   DENIGER, Constant .... (PQ) 292
Database processing   ALLEN, Norene F. ..... (KS) 15
Database producer services ZIRPOLO, Frank .... (NY) 1390
Database product development ROSEN, Theresa H. .... (PA) 1055
                          TRUBKIN, Loene ...... (BC) 1259

Database production   LUEVANE, Marsha A. ... (CO) 747
                          GOERS, Willona G. .... (IA) 443
                          DEPKE, Robert W. ..... (IL) 293
                          REMEIKIS, Lois A. ..... (IL) 1022
                          ROTT, Richard A. ...... (IL) 1060
                          JAMES, Bonnie B. ..... (KY) 592
                          WEINBERG, Gail B. .... (MN) 1317
                          ROLETT, Virginia V. .... (NH) 1051
                          BARTENBACH, Wilhelm
                            K. .... (NY) 60
                          GORDON, Marjorie ..... (NY) 451
                          LAWRENCE, Barbara ... (NY) 704

DATABASES (Cont'd)

Database production
                          LEWICKY, George I. .... (NY) 722
                          MOLINE, Gloria .... (NY) 853
                          MOONEY, Martha T. ... (NY) 858
                          SHAPIRO, Barbara G. .. (NY) 1121
                          KELLY, Maureen C. .... (PA) 638
                          CARROLL, Bonnie C. .... (TN) 187
                          OLIVETTI, L J. .... (VA) 921
                          FAST, Louise .... (ON) 366
                          OLMSTEAD, Marcia E. .. (ON) 921
                          KLOK, Buddhi .... (PQ) 662
                          AITCHISON, Thomas M. (ENG) 9
Database production & design CORNICK, Ron .... (IL) 247
Database production & development BROWNRIDGE, James R. (ON) 149
Database production & indexing SPENCER, John T. .... (CA) 1173
Database production & maintenance STEVENS, Paula F. .... (AZ) 1190
Database programming   MICHELS, Fredrick A. .. (MI) 832
                          RUBIN, Myra P. .... (NY) 1064
Database programs   EARLEY, Dorothy A. .... (NE) 332
Database promotion & support CRAUMER, Patricia A. .. (PA) 255
Database publishing   HOLLY, James H. ...... (CA) 552
                          SCLAR, Herbert .... (CA) 1106
                          ATKIN, Michael I. ..... (DC) 37
                          TRIGAUX, Robert ...... (DC) 1256
                          URBACH, Peter F. ..... (MA) 1269
                          MCRAE, Alexander D. .. (MD) 818
                          HART, Patricia H. ..... (MI) 507
                          WERLING, Anita L. .... (MI) 1324
                          ALLAN, John .... (NY) 14
                          BURKE, Edward .... (NY) 160
                          FINCH, Brian .... (NY) 377
                          FREY, Ned .... (NY) 402
                          HENDERSON, Brad .... (NY) 526
                          KRAUS, James .... (NY) 676
                          MACFARLAND, Scott D. (NY) 755
                          MALKIN, Peter .... (NY) 763
                          NOVEMBER, Robert S. . (NY) 911
                          REDEL, Judy A. .... (NY) 1014
                          RUSLING, Con A. ...... (NY) 1068
                          SIMON, Peter E. ...... (NY) 1140
                          TYSON, David .... (NY) 1267
                          VELLA, Carl .... (NY) 1281
                          ZIMMERMAN, William .. (NY) 1389
Database publishing & development PRICKETT, Dan S. ..... (OH) 993
Database publishing applications KNOERDEL, Joan E. .... (MD) 665
Database quality control KOLMAN, Roberta F. ... (HI) 669
Database record guide cataloging MCKNIGHT, Jesse H. .. (FL) 812
Database reference services LUNG, Chan S. .... (NY) 748
Database research   LARSON, Donald A. ..... (CA) 699
                          VILLERE, Dawn N. ..... (CA) 1284
                          ALBAIR, Catherine M. .. (FL) 9
                          GIANNINI, Evelyn L. .... (IL) 431
                          EDER, Sonya .... (PQ) 336
                          FORRESTER, John H. .. (ITL) 391
Database research, high schools WARAKSA, Raymond P. . (CT) 1303
Database researching   AARON, Rina S. ...... (NY) 1
Database retrieval   MEYER, Garry S. ...... (NY) 830
                          BONIN, Denise R. ..... (BC) 114
                          WARREN, Lois M. ..... (BC) 1306
Database retrieval & online searching ROTHSCHILD, M C. .... (VA) 1060
Database retrieval systems ODHO, Marc .... (ON) 917
Database retrospective conversion MORGAN, Ferrell ...... (CA) 864
Database sales   SINE, George H. .... (IL) 1143
                          GABOR, John M. ...... (NY) 411
Database search strategy assistance MARANGONI, Eugene G. (CA) 768
Database searching   TRIMBLE, Kathleen L. .. (DC) 1256
                          WILLIAMS, Eddie A. .... (MS) 1343
                          JACQUES, Eunice L. .... (NC) 591
Database searching, financial
  databases   CONNER, Norma ...... (NY) 237
Database services   GAUJARD, Pierre G. .... (MD) 422
                          PAPAI, Beverly D. ..... (MI) 938
                          HEATON, Shelley J. ..... (NV) 519
                          WILES-HAFFNER,
                            Meredith L. .... (PA) 1339
Database software   EDDISON, Elizabeth B. .. (MA) 335
                          LUCAS, Jean M. ...... (OH) 746
Database software creation GARMAN, Nancy J. .... (KY) 419
Database storage & retrieval KANTOR, Paul B. ...... (OH) 626

DATABASES (Cont'd)

Category	Name	State	Page
Database support & service	SOUDER, Edith I.	(PA)	1169
Database system development	ROWBERG, Alan H.	(WA)	1062
Database systems	HALPIN, Peter	(DC)	490
	EMBAR, Indrani M.	(IL)	347
	FITZPATRICK, Nancy C.	(MI)	383
	MITCHELL, Joyce A.	(MO)	849
	LEONARD, Teresa G.	(NC)	717
	KOPPELMAN, William H.	(NY)	671
	LEINBACH, Anne E.	(PA)	714
	WESSEL, Charles B.	(PA)	1325
	SACKETT-WILK, Susan A.	(TX)	1073
	NIGAM, Alok C.	(VA)	904
	ERICKSON, Randall D.	(WA)	352
Database systems & management	SIEGERT, Lindy E.	(NS)	1136
Database systems design	SHAPTON, Gregory B.	(CA)	1122
	KOSTINKO, Gail A.	(DC)	673
Database systems design & analysis	KAVANAGH, Janette R.	(CO)	631
Database systems design & development	SCHWARTZ, Betsy J.	(MD)	1104
Database systems development	ALBERTUS, Donna M.	(NY)	10
	AULBACH, Louis F.	(TX)	39
	JOHNSON, Pat M.	(TX)	608
Database systems, library indexing	FUNK, Carla J.	(IL)	409
Database systems production	BRENNER, Everett H.	(NY)	133
Database technology	DEBUSE, Raymond	(WA)	285
Database thesaurus preparation	KENTON, Charlotte	(MD)	642
Database training	JUDY, Joseph R.	(CA)	619
	ROSS, Margery M.	(DC)	1058
	ALZOFON, Sammy R.	(FL)	19
	PAPPALARDO, Marcia J.	(IL)	939
	EARLEY, Dorothy A.	(NE)	332
	ARTHUR, Christine	(NY)	35
	HOWARD, Joyce M.	(NY)	564
	RAUCH, Anne	(NY)	1010
	GOSLING, Carolyn	(VA)	453
Database training & demonstration	SANDULEAK, Barbara	(OH)	1081
Database training & development	PASCHAL, Linda P.	(OK)	945
	NEAL, James H.	(TN)	890
Database training & documentation	ACKERMAN, Katherine K.	(MI)	4
Database utilization	WILSON, Anthony M.	(WA)	1349
Database vendor	EWING, Alison L.	(AZ)	359
	HYLAND, Barbara	(ON)	580
Databases	SMITH, Catherine M.	(CA)	1153
	SNYDER, Henry L.	(CA)	1164
	PEMBERTON, Jeffery K.	(CT)	956
	GERIG, Reginald R.	(DC)	428
	MAGRO, Emanuel P.	(DC)	760
	PHILLIPS, Donald J.	(FL)	968
	PARK, Margaret K.	(GA)	941
	SCHIPMA, Peter B.	(IL)	1093
	SINHA, Vaswati R.	(IL)	1143
	BEAUBIEN, Anne K.	(MI)	70
	MENDELL, Stefanie	(NC)	823
	AHERN, Camille P.	(NH)	8
	HAWKINS, Donald T.	(NJ)	514
	HSU, Grace S.	(NM)	567
	BROOKS, Martin	(NY)	140
	CHEN, Barbara A.	(NY)	205
	HOFFMAN, David M.	(NY)	547
	MEHL, Cathy A.	(NY)	821
	WALD, Ingeborg	(NY)	1294
	HAUGH, Amy J.	(PA)	512
	RAHKONEN, Carl J.	(PA)	1003
	BUSSMANN, Steve	(VA)	166
	EDWARDS, Wilmoth O.	(VA)	338
	FILIPPONE, Anne	(VA)	377
	KELLER, Jay	(VA)	635
	LITTLE, William	(VA)	734
	LOVETT, Bruce	(VA)	743
	LOY, Dennis C.	(VA)	745
	MAJOR, Skip	(VA)	762
	NEWLAND, Barbara	(VA)	899
	RINALDI, Roberta	(VA)	1035
	RYAN, Maureen	(VA)	1071
	STRATT, Randy	(VA)	1200
	KRUZIC, Evelyn D.	(WA)	681
	DETWILER, Eve N.	(WI)	296
	MORGAN, Pamela S.	(NF)	864
	LEFRANCOIS, Carol	(PQ)	712

DATABASES (Cont'd)

Category	Name	State	Page
Databases	TREMBLAY, Levis	(PQ)	1255
	NOERR, Kathleen T.	(ENG)	907
Databases & cataloging	SIFTON, Patricia A.	(BC)	1137
Databases & data dictionaries	PULLEYBLANK, Mildred C.	(ON)	997
Databases & expert systems	MOLINE, Judi A.	(MD)	853
Databases & software consulting	GIGANTE, Vickilyn M.	(MD)	433
Databases & statistics	HSU, Elizabeth L.	(NY)	567
Databases & systems	OLSON, Rue E.	(IL)	923
Databases for serials, journals, etc	WARD, Dorothy S.	(AL)	1303
Databases in CAT	CONNOR, Evelyn	(CO)	238
Databases in social science & humanities	PRICE, Susan W.	(NY)	992
Databases, library systems	QUEYROUZE, Mary E.	(TX)	999
Databases, occupational health & safety	MCLAUGHLIN, W K.	(AB)	813
Databases, user producing	WELLS, Christine	(VA)	1322
Defense databases	IRWIN, Ruth A.	(MD)	584
Demographic databases	GRIMES, A R.	(DC)	470
Designing mainframe databases	MURRAY, Elizabeth F.	(NY)	881
Designing microcomputer databases	MURRAY, Elizabeth F.	(NY)	881
Development of internal databases	GOETZ, Helen L.	(NY)	443
DiALOG databases	HELBERS, Catherine A.	(NY)	523
DIALOG, log-on databases	STRICKLAND, Ann T.	(AZ)	1202
Digital image database	SHOREBIRD, Thomas S.	(DC)	1132
Dissertation database	WILSON, Amy S.	(MI)	1349
Document control database	ZBORAY, Ronald J.	(CA)	1386
DROLS database management	GALLERY, M C.	(CA)	414
Drug databases	HANES, Alice H.	(MD)	495
Earth science databases	WEST, Barbara F.	(TX)	1326
Economic & financial databases	WYSS, David A.	(MA)	1376
	ZURBRIGG, Lyn E.	(ON)	1391
Economic database & forecasts	BECK, Douglas J.	(DC)	71
Economic databases	GRIMES, A R.	(DC)	470
	ALMAN, Richard D.	(NY)	17
	STEIN, Pamela H.	(NY)	1185
Economics & international databases	HARTMAN, David G.	(MA)	508
Education & humanities databases	MCKEE, Elizabeth C.	(AR)	810
Education & legal databases	MCLANE, Kathleen	(VA)	813
Education & library databases	FOLKE, Carolyn W.	(WI)	387
Education & psychology databases	LEUNG, Terry S.	(CA)	719
Education & social sciences databases	GERKE, Ray	(MA)	428
Education databases	BROWN, M S.	(FL)	145
	HOLLOWAY, Dona W.	(CA)	552
	RENTER, Lois I.	(IA)	1023
	ALTENBERGER, Alicja	(MA)	18
	VANDER MEER, Patricia F.	(MI)	1274
	WISE, Mintron S.	(NC)	1357
	ELY, Donald P.	(NY)	347
	HOLMES, Jill M.	(OK)	553
	CAPUTO, Anne S.	(VA)	180
	ADAM, Anthony J.	(WI)	4
	THAUBERGER, Marianne T.	(SK)	1234
Educational & psychological databases	TU, Shu C.	(MA)	1261
Educational database	OLSON, Lucie M.	(NJ)	923
Educational databases	VATHIS, Alma C.	(AZ)	1279
	NOYES, Nicholas	(ME)	911
	DOYLE, James M.	(MI)	317
	BOWMAN, Gloria M.	(NC)	121
	PINGITORE, Patricia E.	(NY)	974
	BREGAINT, Bernard J.	(ON)	131
	PAPOUTSIS, Fotoula	(ON)	939
Electric power databases	JUDY, Joseph R.	(CA)	619
Electronic components databases	D'ADOLF, Steven P.	(CA)	269
Electronic database & distribution	CHICHESTER, Gerald C.	(CT)	208
Electronic databases	GRIMSLEY, Judy L.	(FL)	470
	PAUSLEY, Barbara H.	(OH)	950
Electronic databases for libraries	ZOELLICK, Bill	(CO)	1390
Electronics & physics databases	WOLF, Noel C.	(AZ)	1360
Electronics databases	LEAVITT, Judith A.	(IA)	707
End-user instruction in chem databases	BECK, Diane J.	(CA)	71
Energy & environment databases	MCDONALD, Ethel Q.	(TN)	802
Energy & technical databases	LOOP, Jacqueline N.	(ID)	740

DATABASES (Cont'd)

Subject	Name		Page
Energy database	JACKSON, Ella J.	(NV)	587
Energy databases	CORNWELL, Douglas W.	(FL)	247
	TUCKER, Clark F.	(MD)	1261
	SOLSETH, Gwenn M.	(MN)	1166
	SAMPLE, Charles R.	(WA)	1078
Engineering & construction databases	HARBERT, Cathy E.	(MD)	499
Engineering & environmental databases	CREW-NOBLE, Sara M.	(CA)	258
Engineering & related databases	HUNT, Deborah S.	(CA)	575
Engineering & technical databases	POZO, Frank J.	(NC)	989
	VIXIE, Anne C.	(OR)	1286
	MIDGETT, Ann S.	(TX)	833
Engineering database construction	PIERCE, Anne L.	(CT)	971
Engineering databases	ATKINSON, Calberta O.	(AL)	38
	FELLER, Amy I.	(CA)	370
	MARKWORTH, Lawrence L.	(CA)	772
	JOHNSON, Doris E.	(CT)	603
	MOON, Mary G.	(CT)	857
	STEELE, Noreen O.	(CT)	1184
	BERNSTEIN, Anna L.	(DC)	89
	HAMILTON, D A.	(IL)	491
	ERDMANN, Charlotte A.	(IN)	352
	BERNARD, Bobbi	(MA)	88
	MUISE, Anita M.	(MA)	876
	LAWSON, James R.	(ME)	705
	BRACKETT, Norman S.	(MI)	124
	BARRETT, Joyce C.	(NJ)	59
	BULYA, Larissa	(NJ)	157
	PEABODY, Kenneth W.	(NJ)	951
	BERGER, Mary C.	(NY)	85
	PINGITORE, Patricia E.	(NY)	974
	LIPPERT, Margret G.	(OH)	732
	MOGREN, Diane A.	(OH)	852
	O'BRIEN, Mary C.	(OR)	915
	CONKLING, Thomas W.	(PA)	236
	COTTER, Stacy L.	(TX)	250
	KANE, Deborah A.	(TX)	624
	ZANG, Patricia J.	(VA)	1386
	SMART, Doris M.	(WA)	1151
	D'AMBOISE, Marion J.	(ON)	271
	SANO, Hikomaro	(JAP)	1081
Engineering databases online searching	SCHNEIDER, Tatiana	(ON)	1097
Engineering physics & chemical databases	GENTRY, Susan K.	(CA)	427
Engineering research, databases	EVANS, M R.	(CA)	357
Engineering, scintfc, chemical databases	PELLINI, Nancy M.	(MA)	955
Environmental databases	MCNAMARA, Emma J.	(DC)	816
	CICHON, Marilyn T.	(IL)	214
	BRANSFORD, John S.	(TN)	129
	FIELDING, Carol J.	(WA)	376
	MARSHALL, Kenneth E.	(MB)	774
Environmental engineering databases	CARROLL, Virginia L.	(MA)	187
Environmental health databases	MOORE, Catherine I.	(MA)	859
Environmental information databases	MILUTINOVIC, Eunhee C.	(IL)	845
Environmental sci & engineering database	DONG, Tina	(MA)	311
Environmental sources & databases	HOTZ, Sharon M.	(CA)	562
Epidemiologic research databases	HOLMES, John H.	(PA)	553
Equity research archival database	MILLS, Andrew G.	(MA)	843
ERIC database online	MISSAR, Charles D.	(MD)	847
ERIC educational database	HENSON, Jane E.	(IN)	529
Ethnomusicology databases	SERCOMBE, Laurel	(WA)	1116
Expert systems & databases	SOERGEL, Dagobert	(MD)	1165
Film & television database retrieval	SALZ, Kay	(NY)	1078
Financial databases	BECK, Douglas J.	(DC)	71
	KEELER, Janice S.	(IL)	634
	REITER, Richard R.	(IL)	1022
	PHILLIPS, Steven G.	(MA)	969
	ALMAN, Richard D.	(NY)	17
	BING, Robert H.	(NY)	97
	BRAGG, Sanford B.	(NY)	127
	ESSMAN, Tallaine G.	(NY)	355
	LANDES, J C.	(NY)	692
	MEYER, Garry S.	(NY)	830
	O'CONOR, William C.	(NY)	916
	SOLOMON, Samuel H.	(NY)	1166

DATABASES (Cont'd)

Subject	Name		Page
Financial databases	TAPIERO, Judith	(NY)	1223
	BAILEY, Linda S.	(TX)	46
	GIBSON, Timothy T.	(TX)	432
	ODHO, Marc	(ON)	917
Financial databases & applications	CORVESE, Lisa A.	(NY)	248
Financial information databases	JONES, Frank	(VA)	613
Fine arts databases	DOGU, Hikmet S.	(UT)	309
Food industry database production	INGISH, Karen S.	(IL)	582
Food processing technology databases	MCNAUGHT, Hugh W.	(ON)	816
Full-text database applications	ROACH, Eddie D.	(OK)	1037
Full-text database design	GROCKI, Daniel J.	(MD)	471
Full-text databases	KRUSS, Daniel M.	(IL)	681
	LUCIER, Richard E.	(MD)	746
	RODEAWALD, Patricia M.	(NJ)	1047
	WILLCOX, M C.	(PA)	1341
	WILLMANN, Donna S.	(PA)	1348
	KLAVER, Timothy J.	(WI)	658
	HANDY, Mary J.	(ON)	495
Gas Net industry database management	DORNER, Steven J.	(VA)	313
Genealogical databases	MAYFIELD, David M.	(UT)	790
General databases	EGAN, Elizabeth M.	(IL)	338
Geological & geographic databases	FELDMAN, Laurence M.	(MA)	369
Geology databases	DIRLAM, Dona M.	(CA)	305
Geosciences databases	DERKSEN, Charlotte R.	(CA)	294
Geotechnical & engineering databases	JEROME, Susanne M.	(AZ)	599
Gerontological database	RAFFERTY, Eve	(DC)	1003
Government & business databases	MOONEY, Margaret T.	(CA)	858
Government & social science databases	BASEFSKY, Stuart M.	(NC)	62
Government databases	CALHOUN, Ellen	(NJ)	172
	MILLER, Katherine J.	(ON)	839
Government documents database	FELDMAN, Eleanor C.	(MD)	369
Government publications & databases	OSTROW, Dianne G.	(MD)	929
Grant & contract databases	TUCKER, Clark F.	(MD)	1261
Hazardous materials databases	RICHARDSON, Alice W.	(PA)	1029
Health administration databases	ROBINSON, Elizabeth A.	(OH)	1044
Health care databases	KINGSLEY, Marcia S.	(VA)	652
	PANTON, Linda A.	(ON)	938
Health care reference & databases	LEE, Soon H.	(IL)	711
Health databases	NG, Pauline	(IL)	900
Health information databases	KISH, Veronica R.	(PA)	656
	PRINGLE, Robert M.	(WA)	993
Health science databases	LEVY, Judith B.	(CA)	721
	HORAK, Ellen B.	(CT)	558
Health sciences database searching	NEUFELD, Sue E.	(IA)	897
Health sciences databases	BELL, R E.	(CA)	77
	KLEINMUNTZ, Dalia S.	(IL)	660
	KANNEL, Selma	(WA)	625
High tech databases	PRONIN, Monica	(NY)	995
	JAGIELLOWICZ, Jadzia	(ON)	591
History databases	KINNELL, Susan K.	(CA)	653
	BERGER, Kenneth W.	(NC)	85
Hospital administration databases	MAHOVLIC, Leanne M.	(OH)	761
Humanities & social science databases	TAKAHASHI, Annabelle T.	(HI)	1220
Humanities & social sciences databases	STORM, Jill	(DC)	1198
Humanities databases	BLEILER, Richard J.	(AL)	105
	BARRETT, Darryl D.	(MN)	59
	WIENER, Alissa L.	(MN)	1336
	CROSS, Roberta A.	(NJ)	261
	GARDNER, Sue A.	(NJ)	418
	DEDONATO, Ree	(NY)	286
	MACKESY, Eileen M.	(NY)	756
	BIANCHINI, Lucian	(NS)	94
Indexing & cataloging for database	WEINBERG, Gail B.	(MN)	1317
Indexing & database design	THOMAS, Dorothy	(NY)	1236
Indexing & database development	LUXNER, Dick	(NJ)	750
Indexing, database analysis	MOOMEY, Margaret M.	(CO)	857
Indexing database construction	JACKRELL, Thomas L.	(NJ)	586
Indexing, databases	JACOBS, Horace	(CA)	589
Indexing databases, journal articles	SCHOLFIELD, Caroline A.	(MI)	1098
Industrial automation databases	FOWELLS, Fumi T.	(MI)	393
Industry databases	FELMY, John C.	(DC)	370
Information database systems	RILEY, Sarah A.	(MD)	1035

DATABASES (Cont'd)

Information databases & networks	WOODS, Richard F.	(FIJ)	1367
Information systems, database design	FOURNIER, Susan K.	(MD)	393
Informational database construction	BERGMANN, Allison M.	(NY)	86
In-house computer databases	NELSON, Dwayne L.	(IL)	893
In-house database	MATTMILLER, C F.	(LA)	786
	SEIK, Jo E.	(OH)	1112
In-house database construction	ROFF, Jill R.	(MA)	1049
In-house database design	KARCHER, Tracey L.	(CA)	627
In-house database design & development	BECKER, Linda C.	(PA)	72
In-house database development	HAM, Beverly V.	(MN)	490
	LAMMERT, Diana P.	(PA)	691
In-house database management	TREVICK, Selma D.	(PQ)	1255
In-house databases	DUNCAN, Rebecca	(CA)	325
	GOODY, Cheryl S.	(HI)	450
	CIARAMELLA, Mary A.	(NJ)	214
	FRIHART, Anne R.	(NJ)	404
	LUSTIG, Joanne	(NJ)	750
	WRIGHT, Nancy M.	(PA)	1372
	TWEEDALE, Dellene M.	(NZD)	1266
Integrated medical financial databases	RUBIN, David S.	(NY)	1064
Integrated medical geographic databases	RUBIN, David S.	(NY)	1064
Internal corporate databases	RUBIN, Lenard H.	(TX)	1064
Internal database administration	LUNAS, Leslie K.	(NJ)	748
International affairs databases	FRIED, Suzanne C.	(NY)	403
International database development	MILGRIM, Martin S.	(NJ)	835
International trade database	PFLEIDERER, Stephen D.	(DC)	966
International trade databases	BECK, Douglas J.	(DC)	71
Inventory databases	VERNON, James R.	(TX)	1283
Investment databases	HAMBRIC, Donna R.	(CO)	491
	LEASON, Jane	(MA)	707
Lane databases	MASEN, Naunihal S.	(ON)	780
Large mainframe databases	TEUN, Rebecca L.	(TX)	1233
Law databases	LEE, Soon H.	(IL)	711
	WILLIAMSON, Carol L.	(NJ)	1347
	OBERLA, Janet L.	(WI)	914
Law databases, LEXIS	SMITH, Eugene J.	(PA)	1155
Law libraries, legal databases	WOLFE, Charles B.	(MI)	1360
Legal & congressional databases	PULVER, Thomas B.	(DC)	997
Legal & legislative databases	BARRETT, Lizabeth A.	(NY)	59
Legal & non-legal databases	ASMUTH, Gretchen W.	(DC)	36
	BURKHART, Sue W.	(GA)	161
	RODAWALT, Valarie J.	(TX)	1046
Legal bibliographies & databases	KAVASS, Igor I.	(TN)	631
Legal databases	ALFONSI-GIN, Mary A.	(IL)	13
Legal information databases	WEGMANN, Pamela A.	(TX)	1316
Legal, legislative & regulatory database	JOHNSON, Jacqueline B.	(DC)	605
Legal, medical & financial databases	LEVEROCK, Lisa A.	(NJ)	719
Legal publishing & databases	COLBORN, Robert J.	(MD)	230
Legal references & databases	FOSKO, Maureen E.	(NJ)	392
Legal research & databases	HEINEN, Margaret A.	(MI)	522
	EDMONDS, Edmund P.	(VA)	336
Legislative database development	GEISAR, Barbara J.	(WI)	425
Legislative databases	OVERTON, Kathryn R.	(DC)	931
	VEATCH, Laurie L.	(DC)	1280
LEXIS databases	HARRINGTON, Margaret V.	(IL)	504
Library & expert witnesses databases	MAULSBY, Tommie L.	(TX)	787
Library & information science databases	HOLLOWAY, Dona W.	(CA)	552
Library automation & databases	CARRINGTON, David K.	(DC)	186
Library automation, database management	FINCH, Mildred E.	(VA)	377
Library catalogs & databases	YANEZ, Elva K.	(CA)	1377
Library database development	SAUTER, Lyn F.	(WA)	1085
Library databases	LOPEZ, Frank D.	(CA)	741
	ESSLINGER, Guenter W.	(MN)	355
	STANAT, Ruth E.	(NY)	1179
Library systems & database consulting	DILORETO, Ann M.	(CA)	303
Library systems & database management	HUFFER, Mary A.	(MD)	570
Library systems & databases	HARTLEY, Gloria R.	(PA)	508
Library systems & RLIN database	LEE, Doreen H.	(CA)	709
Library uses, Tandy databases	TUGGLE, Pamela C.	(VA)	1262

DATABASES (Cont'd)

Life science databases	MITCHELL, Steve	(CA)	849
	WALSH, James A.	(PA)	1299
	YERGER, George A.	(PA)	1379
Life sciences databases	POWER, Colleen J.	(CA)	989
	HEWISON, Nancy S.	(IN)	535
	SAFFER-MARCHAND, Melinda	(MA)	1074
Life sciences databases online	DAVIDSON, Lloyd A.	(IL)	276
Linguistic databases	SERDZIAK, Edward J.	(CA)	1116
Literary manuscript databases	MACDERMAID, Anne	(ON)	754
Literature & art databases	HOFFMAN, Herbert H.	(CA)	548
Litigation support databases	LANK, Dannette H.	(WI)	696
Local database development	HUMPHRIES, Joy D.	(WV)	574
Local databases	FINNEGAN, Gregory A.	(NH)	378
Local distribution of database systems	NASATIR, Marilyn	(CA)	888
Local government databases	PICKETT, Olivia K.	(DC)	971
	LEHMAN, Tom	(MN)	713
	HEWLETT, Carol C.	(TN)	535
Maccs/Dataccs database management	SKIDANOW, Helene	(NJ)	1146
Mainframe evaluation database management	BARALOTO, R A.	(MD)	55
Maintaining automated databases	ZYNJUK, Nila L.	(MD)	1392
Manage computer databases	KROEHLER, Beth A.	(IN)	679
Management databases	VONSEGEN, Ann M.	(OR)	1288
Management of in-house database systems	LEMMON, Anne B.	(LA)	715
Managing various databases	CANTWELL, Mickey A.	(NY)	179
Manpower databases	BURN, Harry T.	(TN)	161
Manufacturing database systems	SINE, George H.	(IL)	1143
MARC databases	DAMICO, Nancy B.	(MA)	272
	JOHNSON, Bruce C.	(MD)	602
	SHEPHARD, Frank C.	(MA)	1127
Marine science databases	KAGAN, Ilse E.	(NY)	621
Maritime databases	BOYD, Cheryl J.	(MN)	122
Market information databases	UMFLEET, Ruth A.	(TX)	1268
Market research databases	BUSSEY, Holly J.	(NY)	165
Marketing & advertising databases	CHAPMAN, Kathleen A.	(WA)	202
Marketing database consultant services	MASON, Dorothy L.	(IN)	781
Marketing databases	GEER, Elizabeth F.	(MA)	425
	ROSEN, Theresa H.	(PA)	1055
Marketing databases & searching	LINEPENSEL, Kenneth C.	(IN)	730
Marketing support databases	POWELL, Timothy W.	(NY)	989
Materials sciences databases	VAUGHAN, Ruth M.	(IL)	1280
Math & computer science databases	DAVIDOFF, Gary N.	(IL)	276
Math databases online searching	CARTER, Jackson H.	(IN)	189
Medicaid databases	PETTOLINA, Anthony M.	(NY)	965
Medical & biological databases	NEWAY, Julie M.	(CA)	898
Medical & chemical databases	LEICHTMAN, Anne B.	(NJ)	713
Medical & dental databases	GLASER, June E.	(NY)	439
Medical & health care databases	MARIX, Mary L.	(LA)	770
Medical & health science databases	AIRTH, Elizabeth M.	(TX)	9
Medical & health-related databases	VONSEGEN, Ann M.	(OR)	1288
Medical & music databases	CHASE, Judith H.	(OR)	203
Medical & nursing databases	JENNINGS, Patricia S.	(FL)	598
	LIPPMAN, Anne F.	(MA)	732
Medical & psychological databases	KNOBLOCH, Shirley S.	(DC)	665
	DAVIS, Anne C.	(MI)	277
	PLASO, Kathy A.	(PA)	977
	STILMAN, Ruth	(PQ)	1194
Medical & reference databases	BINAU, Myra I.	(MD)	97
Medical & related databases	MAHONY, Doris D.	(MI)	761
Medical & science databases	ROBINSON, Betty J.	(CA)	1043
	HUNTER, John H.	(TX)	576
	BOULANGER, Mary E.	(WI)	119
Medical & scientific databases	VEENSTRA, Robert J.	(AL)	1281
	GOUVEIA, Sara C.	(CA)	454
	MALMGREN, Terri L.	(CA)	763
	BERNSTEIN, Lee S.	(DC)	89
	TAN, Elizabeth L.	(IL)	1222
	HAWTHORNE, Dorothy M.	(MN)	514
	AUSTON, Ione	(VA)	40
Medical & toxicology databases	MORRISON, Brian H.	(ON)	867
Medical chemical environmental databases	PAPROCKI, Mary E.	(NJ)	939
Medical databases	BRICE, Heather W.	(PA)	134
	BERNARD, Molly S.	(WA)	88

DATABASES (Cont'd)

Subject	Name	State	Page
Medical databases, engineering databases	GODT, Carol	(MO)	443
Medical documents & databases	NAGY, Cecile	(PQ)	886
Medical education & databases	WAYLAND, Marilyn T.	(MI)	1311
Medical education databases	GERRITY, Marline R.	(MO)	429
Medical informatics & databases	CASTAGNO, Lucio A.	(BRA)	194
Medical literature & databases	GIORDANO, Joan	(NY)	438
Medical, nursing database	HINKEL, Jeannine M.	(MD)	542
Medical nursing databases	SEXTON, Sally V.	(OH)	1118
Medical pharmaceutical chemical database	MOYNIHAN, Mary B.	(CT)	874
Med, psychological, educational database	KLINE, Eve P.	(PA)	661
Medical psychology databases	BLADEN, Marguerite	(CA)	102
Medical reference databases	FRYER, Regina K.	(CT)	407
	MARSHAK, Bonnie L.	(NY)	773
	MACK, Bonnie R.	(WY)	756
Medical, toxicological databases	CONNER, Shirley D.	(CT)	237
Membership databases	STLUKA, Thomas H.	(IL)	1195
Mental health databases	BRAND, Alice A.	(KS)	127
Mental health databases & collections	WIGGINS, Theresa S.	(PA)	1337
Microbiology databases	SHAY, Donald E.	(MD)	1124
Microcomputer database design	MOLL, Joy K.	(NJ)	853
	NEELAND, Margaret A.	(NY)	891
	SANDFELDER, Paula M.	(HKG)	1080
Microcomputer database development	MANGION, Barbara E.	(MA)	765
	MIDDLETON, Marcia S.	(NY)	833
Microcomputer database management	KENNEDY, Joanne	(CA)	641
Microcomputer databases	SUNDT, Christine L.	(OR)	1210
	HEATON, Gwynneth T.	(ON)	519
Microcomputerized database management	AU, Ka N.	(NJ)	38
Microcomputers database design	BURCH, David R.	(TX)	158
Microcomputing & database training	KATZ, Jacqueline E.	(NY)	630
Microelectronics technologies databases	WOLF, Noel C.	(AZ)	1360
Museum database systems	YARNALL, James L.	(DC)	1378
Music databases	CNATTINGIUS, Claes M.	(SWE)	224
Music indexing & database preparation	HILL, George R.	(NY)	539
Music industry databases	BLUME, August G.	(CA)	107
Music sales databases	VERNON, James R.	(TX)	1283
Musical databases	WESTERN, Eric D.	(WI)	1327
NASA, Dept of Defense, & DIALOG database	BOYD, Effie W.	(TN)	122
National Library of Medicine databases	HELBERS, Catherine A.	(NY)	523
	ELY, Betty L.	(PA)	347
	TREVANION, Margaret U.	(PA)	1255
	ASPRI, Jo A.	(RI)	37
Neurosciences databases & collections	WIGGINS, Theresa S.	(PA)	1337
News & media databases	MCCOY-LARSON, Sandra	(DC)	799
News databases	BEVERIDGE, David C.	(DC)	93
	DONOVAN, Elizabeth L.	(FL)	312
	VAZQUEZ, Edward	(NY)	1280
	GRANT, Roberta L.	(ON)	458
	LUSSIER, Richard	(PQ)	749
News media databases	WALSH, Barclay	(DC)	1299
Newspaper & publisher database systems	PASCHAL, John M.	(OK)	945
Newspaper database	VANCE, Sandra L.	(IL)	1273
	PARISOT, Beverly J.	(NE)	940
Newspaper databases	KIBBEE, Sally	(CA)	646
	PAUL, Nora M.	(FL)	949
	PAPPALARDO, Marcia J.	(IL)	939
	TANNER, Allan B.	(KS)	1222
	SMITH, Linda L.	(KY)	1157
	GREENGRASS, Alan R.	(NY)	464
	PASCHAL, Linda P.	(OK)	945
	WILLMANN, Donna S.	(PA)	1348
	LOVELL, Bonnie A.	(TX)	743
	METCALF, Judith A.	(TX)	828
	WORCHEL, Harris M.	(TX)	1368
Newspaper library databases	ROCKALL, Diane M.	(MI)	1046
Non-book databases	PEARMAN, Sara J.	(OH)	952
Non-legal databases	LONG, Clare S.	(OH)	739
NUC database	JACKSON, Nancy G.	(VA)	588
Nuclear fiction database	LENZ, Millicent A.	(NY)	716

DATABASES (Cont'd)

Subject	Name	State	Page
Numeric & statistical databases	MOON, Jeffrey D.	(ON)	857
Numeric databases	GERKEN, Ann E.	(CA)	429
Nursing, allied health databases	PRIME, Eugenie E.	(CA)	993
Nursing databases	DAUGHERTY, Carolyn M.	(MD)	275
	KATZER, Sylvia U.	(ON)	630
Nursing science databases, cataloging	DIMATTEO, Lucy A.	(NY)	304
Obstetrical databases	ANDERSEN, H F.	(MI)	21
OCLC database	ARMSTRONG, Ruth C.	(NY)	32
Oil & gas databases	PARKINSON, Susan L.	(AB)	943
On-disk databases	SMILLIE, Pauline A.	(MI)	1151
Online & database	REINKE, Carol R.	(MI)	1021
Online bibliographic databases	CALCAGNO, Philip M.	(IL)	172
Online catalog database	BOWLES, Carol A.	(CA)	121
Online cataloging databases	LINSKY, Leonore K.	(MA)	731
Online CD-ROM databases	SEARS, Jonathan R.	(MD)	1110
Online database	RAQUET, Jacqueline R.	(GA)	1008
	RUSSELL, Barbara J.	(TX)	1068
Online database access	LOGAN, Elisabeth L.	(FL)	737
Online database & medical databases	FRANK, Agnes T.	(NY)	396
Online database construction & searching	CHAMIS, Alice Y.	(OH)	198
Online database consultation	LAMB, Connie	(UT)	689
Online database design	LEMASTERS, Joann T.	(OH)	715
Online database development	KISSMAN, Henry M.	(MD)	656
	POQUETTE, Mary L.	(MN)	984
	DIETLE, Craig I.	(NY)	302
	CLASPER, James W.	(OH)	219
	SYEN, Sarah	(PA)	1217
Online database industry	CUADRA, Carlos A.	(CA)	262
	KNOPPERS, Jake V.	(ON)	665
Online database instruction	PARKER, Joan M.	(CA)	942
Online database maintenance	ISGANITIS, Jamie C.	(NY)	585
Online database management	CSENGE, Maragaret L.	(NY)	262
	TOWNLEY, Richard L.	(NY)	1253
Online database reference	BEAVERS, Janet W.	(ISR)	71
Online database research	NIXON, Judith A.	(MD)	906
Online information retrieval, databases	RAITT, David I.	(NET)	1004
Online mainframe databases	RICHARDS, Stella	(PQ)	1028
Online medical & scientific databases	REITANO, Maimie V.	(NY)	1022
Online news database	MCFARLANE, Agnes	(PQ)	805
Online scientific databases	SAMUELS, Lois A.	(CT)	1079
Online searching & databases	COCHRANE, Maryjane S.	(VA)	226
Online searching & psychology databases	GOSLING, Carolyn	(VA)	453
Online searching & technical database	LEREW, Ann A.	(CO)	717
Online searching databases	KIRBY, Diana G.	(MD)	654
Online searching, engineering databases	LYLE, Martha E.	(SC)	751
Online searching, MEDLARS databases	SZILARD, Paula	(HI)	1218
Online searching of databases	CHAPMAN, Ruby M.	(IL)	202
	MCDERMOTT, Margaret H.	(MO)	802
Online searching of scientific databases	WERT, Lucille M.	(IL)	1325
Online searching science databases	WHITE, Larry R.	(CA)	1331
	COONS, William W.	(NY)	242
Online searching science, tech databases	RAEDER, Aggi W.	(CA)	1003
Online searching, scientific databases	MORRIS, Sharon D.	(MD)	867
Online searching, technical databases	PRESTON, Deirdre R.	(WA)	991
Online statistical database	CHANG, Joseph I.	(NJ)	200
Online statistical database	MATTHEWS, Elizabeth W.	(IL)	785
Optical disk database system	BENGE, Bruce	(OK)	80
Patent & trademark databases	HU, Robert T.	(IL)	568
	HAYWARD, Diane J.	(NY)	517
Patent database & information retrieval	ROSENTHAL, Francine C.	(OH)	1057
Patent databases	NOVACK, Dona A.	(CA)	910
	MOUNTFORD, Eve	(CT)	873
	SAARI, David S.	(IN)	1072
	ALLISON, Kenneth J.	(NJ)	17
	GARNER, Linda J.	(NJ)	419
	SKIDANOW, Helene	(NJ)	1146
	WARDEN, Carolyn L.	(NY)	1304
	HANF, Elizabeth P.	(PA)	495
	ERWIN, Mary J.	(TN)	353

DATABASES (Cont'd)

Patent databases
WEI, Carl K. . . . . (ON) 1316
CORNELIUS, Peter K. . . (LUX) 246
Patent databases & searching   LINEPENSEL, Kenneth C. (IN)   730
Patent information databases   PLATAU, Gerard O. . . . . (OH)   977
Patent research & database   ENNIS, Mary J. . . . . . . (OH)   350
Periodical database   HAGOOD, Patricia C. . . (NY)   483
Personal computer database, sales   NASON, Stanley J. . . . . . (NY)   888
Personal computer database training   MULLINS, James R. . . . . (TX)   878
Personal computer databases   ROBSON, Amy K. . . . . . (IL) 1045
SULLIVAN, Michael M. . . (VA) 1208
Petroleum & energy database
 indexing   SHERRILL, Jocelyn T. . . (NY) 1129
Petroleum databases   STARK, Philip H. . . . . . . (CO) 1182
Pharmaceutical databases   DUTKA, Jeanne L. . . . . . (NJ)   329
MILLINGTON, Kathleen A. (NJ)   843
Pharmacological databases   WEIS, Ann M. . . . . (NY) 1319
Philanthropic databases   TAFT, James R. . . . . (DC) 1219
KLETZIEN, S D. . . . . (PA)   661
Physical sciences databases   HILDITCH, Bonny M. . . . (MD)   539
THAYER, Martha B. . . . . (WA) 1234
Physical scis databases online
 searching   CARTER, Jackson H. . . . (NM)   189
Physics databases   DAVIDOFF, Gary N. . . . . (IL)   276
BRACKETT, Norman S. . . (MI)   124
LERNER, Rita G. . . . . . . (NY)   717
Physics databases & reference   WOELL, Yvette N. . . . . . (IL) 1359
Polar databases   GOMEZ, Michael J. . . . . (WGR) 447
Political & sociological databases   BOILARD, Gilberte . . . . . (PQ)   111
Preservation database development   ZIMMERMANN, Carole R. (DC) 1389
Printing databases   LAMMERT, Diana P. . . . (PA)   691
Producing translations database   NOWAK, Ildiko D. . . . . . . (IL)   911
Product databases   WINDSOR, Donald A. . . . (NY) 1354
Proprietary database design   WAITE, William F. . . . . . (NJ) 1293
Psychiatric & psychological databases   KINZIE, Lenora A. . . . . . (KS)   653
WIGGINS, Theresa S. . . (PA) 1337
Psychiatric database   LESAGE, Jacques . . . . . (PQ)   717
Psychological databases   LUNDGREN, Janan L. . . (IL)   748
VAN CAMP, Ann J. . . . . (IN) 1272
Psychology, behavioral science
 databases   KAUFFMAN, Inge S. . . . (CA)   631
Psychology databases   BANKS-ISZARD, Kimberly
 K. . . . . (NY)   54
Public health databases   MOORE, Catherine I. . . . (MA)   859
Public library database   ABRAM, Persis R. . . . . . (ON)   3
Public policy databases   PILGRIM, Auriel J. . . . . . (DC)   973
Publishing database editing & design   THOMPSON, Anne E. . . (AZ) 1238
Pulp & paper databases   STAHL, Hella . . . . (PQ) 1178
Purchased materials databases   SINE, George H. . . . . . . (IL) 1143
QL database   KHAN, Asma S. . . . . (ON)   646
Real estate & legislative databases   KITZMILLER, Virginia G. . (DC)   657
Real estate databases   BRUTON, Robert T. . . . . (MN)   151
Reference & internal database
 creation   IRONS, Carol A. . . . . (IL)   584
Reference & research databases   JONES, Stephanie R. . . . (LA)   615
Reference databases   HAYDEN, Ronald L. . . . . (CA)   515
BRISTOW, Ann . . . . (IN)   137
Reference including databases   LARISON, Brenda . . . . . (IL)   697
Regional databases   FELMY, John C. . . . . (DC)   370
MARBAN, Ricio . . . . . . (GUA) 768
Relational database design   CAMOZZI-EKBERG,
 Patricia L. . . . . (WA)   175
WARD, Maryanne . . . . . (WA) 1304
Relational databases design & use   ROBINSON, David F. . . . (VA) 1043
Religion & ancient history databases   FRAZER, Ruth F. . . . . . . (FL)   399
Religion & humanities databases   HILGERT, Elvire R. . . . . . (IL)   539
Religion databases   OLSON, Ray A. . . . . (MN)   923
Religious databases   OTTOSON, Robin D. . . . (CO)   930
Research & engineering databases   DE TONNANCOUR, P R. (TX)   296
Research databases   ALSOP, Robyn J. . . . . . . (CO)   18
Research on databases   BELANGER, Sylvie . . . . (PQ)   76
Resource database development   SCHUELLER, Janette H. . (WA) 1101
RLIN/AMC Database   BROWN, William E. . . . . (CT)   148
RLIN database   KAPLAN, Diane E. . . . . . (CT)   626
Safety, toxicology databases   WEISS, Barbara M. . . . . (CT) 1319
Scholarly databases   BEARMAN, David A. . . . (PA)   69

DATABASES (Cont'd)

Science & engineering databases
BAUM, Ester B. . . . . (AZ)   66
WYLIE, Nethery A. . . . . . (CO) 1375
SAUER, David A. . . . . . . (MA) 1084
POWELL, Jill H. . . . . (NY)   988
HOLLIS, William F. . . . . . (OH)   552
LANG, Anita E. . . . . (TX)   695
Science & technical databases   PASTERCZYK, Catherine
 E. . . . . (NM)   946
Science & technological databases   TALBOT, Dawn E. . . . . . (CA) 1220
Science & technology databases   BARRETT, Carol A. . . . . (TX)   59
BROWN, Diane M. . . . . . (CA)   143
ECKLUND, Lynn M. . . . . (CA)   335
GRENIER, Myra T. . . . . . (CA)   467
LOVE, Sandra R. . . . . . . (CA)   743
MAH, Jeffery . . . . (CA)   760
SMITH, Sallye W. . . . . . . (CO) 1160
LONG, Caroline C. . . . . . (DC)   739
KENNEDY, Joanna C. . . (GA)   641
MARECEK, Robert J. . . . (IL)   770
VAUGHAN, Ruth M. . . . . (IL) 1280
ERDMANN, Charlotte A. . (IN)   352
COLBY, Beverly . . . . (MA)   230
SEELEY, Catherine R. . . (ME) 1111
HEILEMAN, Gene C. . . . (MI)   521
DUELTGEN, Ronald R. . . (MN)   323
KAN, Halina S. . . . . (NJ)   624
MCLAUGHLIN, Dorothy M. (NJ)   813
MAUTER, George A. . . . (NY)   787
MONTALBANO, James J. (NY)   855
QUINN, Caroline E. . . . . (OH) 1000
HILKER, Emerson W. . . . (OK)   539
DALLAS, Larayne J. . . . . (TX)   270
WONG, Lusi . . . . (ON) 1363
Science databases   BRUEGGEMAN, Peter L. (CA)   149
KENNY-SLOAN, Linda . . (CA)   642
STANLEY, Eileen H. . . . . (LA) 1180
ELLSBURY, Susan H. . . (MS)   345
DICKERSON, Jimmy . . . (NC)   300
OSEGUEDA, Laura M. . . (NC)   927
KEMPF, Jody L. . . . . (NM)   639
WILLIAMS, Esther L. . . . (NY) 1343
HOUDEK, G R. . . . . (OH)   562
DANIEL, Mary H. . . . . . . (VA)   272
BLASE, Nancy G. . . . . . . (WA)   104
CHISMAN, Janet K. . . . . (WA)   209
Sci databases, training &
 development   HOELLE, Dolores M. . . . . (NJ)   547
Science technical literature &
 databases   ROE, Eunice M. . . . . (PA) 1048
Science, technology engineering
 database   TODOSOW, Helen K. . . . (NY) 1248
Scientific & biomedical database mktg   ZAJDEL, George J. . . . . . (PA) 1385
Scientific & engineering databases   LANDAU, Herbert B. . . . (NY)   692
Scientific & pharmaceutical databases   BARNETT, Philip . . . . . . (NY)   58
Scientific & statistical databases   MCCARTHY, John L. . . . (CA)   794
Scientific & technical databases   LEVIN, Amy E. . . . . (DC)   720
ENRICI, Pamela L. . . . . . (MN)   350
CIARAMELLA, Mary A. . . (NJ)   214
ORTIZ, Cynthia . . . . (NV)   927
LETTIS, Lucy B. . . . . (NY)   719
LEMON, Nancy A. . . . . . (OH)   715
ELSBREE, John J. . . . . . (VA)   346
HOLLY, Janet S. . . . . . . (VA)   552
JOACHIM, Robert J. . . . . (VA)   600
Scientific & technical lit databases   MOBLEY, Emily R. . . . . . (IN)   851
Scientific bibliographic databases   PERRONE, Jeanne M. . . (DC)   960
Scientific databases   FELLER, Amy I. . . . . (CA)   370
ROTH, Dana L. . . . . (CA) 1059
SEHR, Dena P. . . . . (CA) 1112
MOON, Mary G. . . . . . . (CT)   857
SARANGAPANI, Chetluru (DC) 1082
KINNA, Dorothy H. . . . . (MD)   652
CORRADO, Margaret M. . (NJ)   247
KNEE, Michael . . . . (NY)   663
KRAMER, Sally J. . . . . . (OH)   675
EDWARDS, David M. . . . (PA)   337
ATHA, Shirley A. . . . . . . (ON)   37
THORP, Raymond G. . . (ENG) 1242
Scientific information databases   ZIAIAN, Monir . . . . (CA) 1387

DATABASES (Cont'd)

Scientific patent databases	POKLAR, Mary J.	(CA)	980
Scientific, technology databases	MACKSEY, Susan A.	(NY)	757
Sci-tech databases	EGGLESTON, Phyllis A.	(AK)	339
	WONG, Carol Y.	(CA)	1362
	REILLY, Francis S.	(DC)	1020
	SZE, Melanie C.	(NJ)	1218
	OBERLANDER, Deborah K.	(OH)	914
	GROSS, Margaret B.	(PQ)	472
	HETU, Sylvie	(PQ)	534
Searching databases	BROWN, Helen A.	(NE)	144
	WELCH, Donald A.	(TX)	1321
Searching patent & chemical databases	MILES, Donald D.	(PA)	834
Searching, social science databases	WEIMER, Sally W.	(CA)	1317
SEC databases	RUBIN, Ellen R.	(NY)	1064
Section filing databases	WRIGHT, John H.	(FL)	1371
Serials database	YUSTER, Leigh C.	(NY)	1385
Serials databases	HELMS, Mary E.	(MO)	525
Service & technical databases	DUFF, Ann M.	(ON)	323
Sex education databases	CAMPBELL, Patricia J.	(CA)	177
Small database design	FOWELLS, Fumi T.	(MI)	393
Small database development	ENGLISH, Bernard L.	(NJ)	350
Social science database	DICKSTEIN, Ruth H.	(AZ)	301
	THIES, Gail M.	(MD)	1235
Social science database marketing	ZAJDEL, George J.	(PA)	1385
Social science databases	ECKMAN, Charles D.	(CA)	335
	NESBITT, Renee D.	(CA)	896
	NEWMARK, Laura C.	(CA)	900
	SHOUSE, Richard	(CA)	1133
	FRANCIS, Barbara W.	(FL)	396
	BURNS, Marie T.	(IL)	162
	WISE, Mintron S.	(NC)	1357
	GERACI, Diane	(NY)	428
	REINSTEIN, Diana J.	(NY)	1021
	PARR, Virginia H.	(OH)	944
	ELSHAMI, Ahmed M.	(PA)	346
	ROSS, Nina M.	(PA)	1058
	DESSAINT, Alain Y.	(VA)	295
	MCCLEMENTS, Nancy A.	(WI)	796
	LANGERMAN, Shoshana P.	(ISR)	695
	KATAOKA, Yoko	(JAP)	629
Social sciences & humanities databases	COCHRANE, Kerry L.	(IL)	225
Social sciences databases	ILACQUA, Anne K.	(MA)	581
	BIGGS, Debra R.	(MI)	95
	VANDER MEER, Patricia F.	(MI)	1274
	HARDING, Mary H.	(NY)	500
	GUSS, Margaret B.	(OH)	478
	HAAG, Enid E.	(WA)	480
	COURNOYER, Joanne	(ON)	251
	REILLY, Francis S.	(DC)	1020
Socioeconomic databases			
Socioeconomic, LEXIS & NEXIS databases	MILUTINOVIC, Eunhee C.	(IL)	845
Sound recording cataloging & databases	KLINGER, William E.	(OH)	661
Sound recordings databases	MAWHINNEY, Paul C.	(PA)	787
Special focus database trainers	CARUSO, Nicholas C.	(PA)	190
Special index databases	TSUI, Josephine	(ON)	1260
Specialized database administration	BILES, Mark J.	(NJ)	96
Specialized database construction	LIVNY, Efrat	(WI)	735
Sports information & databases	GHENT, Gretchen K.	(AB)	430
Statistical financial databases	PRAVER, Robin I.	(NY)	990
Student records databases	THOMPSON, Jane K.	(VT)	1240
Subject index database	KENEFICK, Mary L.	(CA)	640
Submarine medicine databases	OMARA, Marie T.	(MD)	923
Systems & database development	HOWELL, M G.	(NY)	565
Tax databases	GIBSON, Timothy T.	(TX)	432
Tax-accounting databases	BARRETT, Carol A.	(TX)	59
Technical & engineering databases	ALBRIGHT, Sue R.	(CA)	10
Technical database development	D'ADOLF, Steven P.	(CA)	269
Technical databases	LEE, Dora T.	(CA)	709
	WRIGHT, Betty A.	(CA)	1370
	HARRIS, Michael A.	(CO)	505
	PRESTON, Lawrence N.	(CO)	991
	LADNER, Sharyn J.	(FL)	687
	CARTER, Ida	(IL)	189

DATABASES (Cont'd)

Technical databases	MASON, Dorothy L.	(IN)	781
	WILSON, Sharon L.	(OH)	1353
	DINNIMAN, Margo P.	(PA)	305
	KLEIN, Joanne S.	(PA)	659
	ERWIN, Mary J.	(TN)	353
	HULSE, Phyllis	(TX)	573
	BEHR, Alice S.	(WV)	75
	KAMICHAITIS, Penelope H.	(PQ)	624
	POGUE, Basil G.	(SK)	979
Technical databases, engineering	FINGERMAN, Susan M.	(MA)	378
Technology databases	CURRY, John A.	(IL)	266
	HECHT, Joseph A.	(OH)	519
Telecom database	HAMPTON, Sylvia S.	(RI)	494
Telecommunications database	TERRELL, Jane A.	(VA)	1232
Telecommunications databases	MASTERS, Kathy B.	(CT)	782
	BATES, Mary E.	(DC)	64
Television commercial databases	LOFTHOUSE, Patricia A.	(IL)	737
Text database design & development	CHU, John S.	(PA)	212
Text database development	BRIMSEK, Tobi A.	(DC)	136
	BOYLE, Stephen	(IL)	124
	LAFRANCHISE, David	(ON)	688
Text databases	HENDERSON, Ronald L.	(MD)	527
Textbases & databases	KRUSS, Daniel M.	(IL)	681
Textbook & technical book databases	JACKRELL, Thomas L.	(NJ)	586
Textile databases	BEST-NICHOLS, Barbara J.	(NC)	92
Textiles databases & books	DAVIS, Jeannette	(MA)	279
Textual database management	SCHWARTZ, James M.	(SD)	1104
Theatre database	MCCULLOUGH, Jack W.	(NJ)	801
Theological databases	DARR, William E.	(IN)	275
Thesaurus & terminological databases	MOUREAU, Magdeleine	(FRN)	873
Toxicology databases	BURSON, Sherrie L.	(CA)	164
	KLEMARCZYK, Laurice D.	(CT)	660
	SMITH, Yvonne B.	(NJ)	1161
	LIBERTINI, Arleen J.	(OR)	725
	WICKS, Pamela J.	(PA)	1335
Toxicology information, databases	DEXTER, Patrick J.	(MD)	298
Trademarks database	SIEGEL, Marilyn	(MI)	1136
Training attorneys on databases	DONNELLY, Kathleen	(OH)	311
Translations databases	SAMSON, Mary	(ON)	1079
Transportation databases	BROWN-WEBB, Deborah D.	(TX)	149
	WARREN, Lois M.	(BC)	1306
Transportation reference & databases	CORNELL, Pamela J.	(MN)	246
Travel industry databases	OGREN, Mark S.	(IL)	918
Typesetting from databases	LABEAU, Dennis	(MI)	685
Use of databases	MICHAUD, Noreen R.	(CT)	832
User interfaces & database frontends	CURRAN, George L.	(NY)	266
Veterinary medicine databases	DE WALERSTEIN, Linda S.	(MEX)	297
Visual resources database design	ELTZROTH, Elsbeth L.	(GA)	346
Visual resources databases	SCHAFFER, D J.	(NY)	1089
Water resources databases	JENSEN, Raymond A.	(VA)	599

DATATREK

Datatrek computer catalog, serials	GENTRY, Susan K.	(CA)	427

DAY CARE

Licensed day care information	TOHAL, Kate J.	(MN)	1248

DBASE

dBASE III programming	SULLIVAN, Robert G.	(NY)	1208

DBMS (See also Databases)

DBMS	PAPALAMBROS, Rita G.	(MA)	939
DBMS software	HASKINS, Dawn A.	(OH)	510

DEAFNESS (See also Hearing)

Deaf education	KLEINMAN, Elsa C.	(CA)	660
Deaf library services	ROATCH, Mary A.	(AZ)	1038
Deaf services	STROUSE, Roger L.	(IL)	1203
	MCCARTY, Emily H. . . .	(MD)	795
	STONE, Jason R.	(NJ)	1197
Deafness	DAY, John M.	(DC)	282
	HARRINGTON, Thomas R.	(DC)	504
Deafness & deaf people	HAGEMEYER, Alice L. . . .	(DC)	483
Deafness information & collections	RITTER, Audrey L.	(NY)	1036
Information on deafness	HURLEY, Faith P.	(DC)	577
Libraries for the Deaf	MYERS, Victoria B.	(DE)	885
Special programs of services for deaf	STEELE, Leah J.	(IL)	1184

DEALERSHIP

Antiquarian music dealer	MERZ, Lawrie H.	(PA)	827
Autograph dealership	CADY, Richard H.	(IL)	170
Rare book dealer	TWENEY, George H. . . .	(WA)	1266
Rare book dealership	CADY, Richard H.	(IL)	170

DEATH

Death penalty	LYNES, Tezeta G.	(KY)	752

DEBATES

Hansard debates	O'KEEFE, Kevin T.	(NT)	919

DEBT

Investment banking, debt & equity	ABELES, Tom	(MN)	2

DECIMAL

Decimal classification	RENAUD, Monique M. . .	(ON)	1023
Dewey decimal classification	DANIS, Rolland J.	(PQ)	273
Promoting Dewey decimal classification	KRAMER-GREENE, Judith	(NY)	675

DECISION

Clinical decision making	COOK, Galen B.	(SC)	240
Decision, management science	KANTOR, Paul B.	(OH)	626
Decision support systems	RANDOLPH, Kevin H. . .	(CA)	1007
	SMITH, Peggy C.	(OK)	1159
	LATHROP, Irene M.	(RI)	701
Department supervision & decisions	EARL, Susan R.	(NC)	332
Information systems & decision support	BERGFELD, C D.	(NY)	86
Strategic & decision software	BUNCE, George D.	(ENG)	157

DECLASSIFICATION

Government document declassification	GATLING, James L.	(AL)	422
Mandatory review declassification	BRILEY, Carol A.	(MO)	136
Records declassification	HUMPHREY, David C. . .	(TX)	573

DECOMMISSIONING

Decommissioning	NISH, Susan J.	(PQ)	905

DEFENSE (See also Arms, Ordnance)

Aerospace & defense	DEWBERRY, Claire D. . .	(GA)	298
Aerospace defense	DELTANO, Pauline T. . . .	(MA)	290
Defense & aerospace info resources	BARTL, Richard P.	(NY)	61
Defense & foreign affairs	COLSON, Harold G.	(AL)	234
Defense & security	BARON, Herman	(PA)	58
Defense data	ROBINSON, David F. . . .	(VA)	1043
Defense databases	IRWIN, Ruth A.	(MD)	584
Defense industry	GESCHKE, Nancy A. . . .	(CA)	430
Defense marketing information systems	MAUTER, George A. . . .	(NY)	787
Defense planning & budgeting	BROWN, George F.	(MA)	144
Defense technical information	HALL, Robert G.	(MA)	488
Department of Defense & AFR reports	BURDEN, John	(NY)	158
Intellectual freedom defense	MADDEN, Susan B.	(WA)	758

DEFENSE (Cont'd)

NASA & Defense technical reports	BOYD, Effie W.	(TN)	122
NASA, Dept of Defense, & DIALOG database	BOYD, Effie W.	(TN)	122
Online aerospace & defense searching	RICH, Denise A.	(PA)	1027
Science & technology defense	JOHNSON, Mary E.	(CA)	607
Takeover defense	SLUSSER, W P.	(NY)	1150

DELIVERY (See also Services)

Biomedical comms & documents delivery	LETT, Rosalind K.	(GA)	719
Delivery of information services	JOHNSON, Emily P.	(MD)	604
Document delivery	JOSEPHINE, Helen B. . .	(AZ)	617
	CARRIGAN, John L. . . .	(CA)	186
	LEVY, Judith B.	(CA)	721
	WEBB, Ty	(CA)	1313
	CHANAUD, Jo P.	(CO)	199
	GREALY, Deborah J. . . .	(CO)	461
	HOFFMAN, Ann M.	(CO)	547
	HARGRAVE, Charles W.	(DC)	501
	REYNOLDS, Dennis J. . .	(DC)	1025
	TAYLOR, Joan R.	(DC)	1227
	STOLZ, Marty R.	(ID)	1196
	FARRELL, Patricia H. . . .	(IL)	365
	GREGORY, Melissa R. . .	(IL)	466
	MCHENRY, Renee E. . . .	(IL)	808
	LISTON, Karen A.	(IN)	733
	BESANT, Larry X.	(KY)	91
	GASKINS, Betty	(KY)	421
	PARKER, Susan E.	(MA)	942
	BOBKA, Marlene S.	(MD)	108
	MANGIN, Julianne	(MD)	765
	BRYANT, Barton B.	(MI)	152
	REHKOP, Barbara L. . . .	(MO)	1017
	NEAL, Michelle H.	(NC)	890
	PALO, Eric E.	(NC)	937
	CUNNIFFE, Charlene M. .	(NH)	265
	ROSENSTEIN, Susan J. .	(NJ)	1057
	BERGER, Mary C.	(NY)	85
	BURKEY, Lynne	(NY)	161
	FARAONE, Maria B.	(NY)	363
	NOGA, Susan D.	(NY)	907
	STRIFE, Mary L.	(NY)	1202
	BALDWIN, Eleanor M. . .	(OH)	51
	GRAHAM, John	(OK)	456
	CARLIN, Don	(TN)	182
	HURD, Douglas P.	(VA)	577
	WOLF, Richard E.	(VA)	1360
	WOLFE, Martha K.	(ON)	1361
	WADE, C A.	(PQ)	1290
Document delivery & editorial	MAXWELL, Christine Y. .	(CA)	788
Document delivery & interlibrary loan	MEAHL, D D.	(MI)	819
	COURNOYER, Joanne . .	(ON)	251
Document delivery, interlibrary loan	ROLLINS, Stephen J. . . .	(NM)	1051
Document delivery service	BUSTAMANTE, Corazon R.	(NY)	166
	HAAS, Elaine H.	(NY)	480
Document delivery services	IVES, Gary W.	(VA)	585
Documents delivery	GIEBEL, Thomas W.	(WI)	432
Electronic delivery of information	TIBBETTS, David W. . . .	(NY)	1243
Electronic information delivery	HEARTY, John A.	(DC)	519
Electronic information delivery systems	PENNIMAN, W D.	(NJ)	957
Information delivery	WENGEL, Linda	(DC)	1324
Information delivery systems & analysis	GRIMES, A R.	(DC)	470
Interlibrary loan & document delivery	STATOM, Susan T.	(GA)	1183
	DITXLER, Carol J.	(MD)	306
	REID, Valerie L.	(MI)	1019
Interlibrary loan document delivery	MCFARLAND, Mary A. . .	(IL)	805
	MORRISON, Carol J. . . .	(IL)	868
International document delivery	GROSSMANN, Pierre . .	(BRA)	473
Library delivery systems & services	STOCKTON, Gloria J. . . .	(CA)	1196
Multipoint delivery networks	MAYNARD, John C.	(ON)	790
Online information delivery	HERNANDEZ, Tamsen M.	(NY)	532
Organization delivery	SMITH, William K.	(MI)	1161
Public library service delivery	O'BRIEN, Patrick M.	(TX)	915
Reference services delivery	EILERS, Marsha J.	(IN)	340

DELIVERY (Cont'd)
Young adult services delivery   TYSON, Christy . . . .   (WA) 1267

DEMAND
On demand publishing   SCLAR, Herbert . . . .   (CA) 1106
On-demand publishing   FITZSIMMONS, Joseph J.   (MI)   383
Research on-demand   MACCALLUM, Barbara B.   (NY)   754

DEMOGRAPHY
Demographic & census files   RUBIN, David S. . . . . . .   (NY) 1064
Demographic databases   GRIMES, A R. . . . .   (DC)   470
Demographic research   MARSCHNER, Robyn J.   (CO)   773
Demographic statistics   COMPTON, Erlinda R. . .   (TX)   235
Demographics & census   RUTTER, Nancy R. . . . .   (MA) 1070
Demography   WINTERS, Wilma E. . . . .   (MA) 1356
                                       ZIMMERMAN, Hugh N. . .   (NY) 1389
Marketing & demographic   MCWILLIAM, Deborah A.   (OH)   818

DEMONSTRATION
Database demonstration   GUILLEMARD DE
                                          COLON, Teresita . . . .   (PR)   476
Database demonstrations & training   FRYER, Regina K. . . . . .   (CT)   407
Database demos & training   WRIGHT, Larry L. . . . . .   (NC) 1372
                                       MOON, Fletcher F. . . . . .   (TN)   857
Database training & demonstration   SANDULEAK, Barbara . .   (OH) 1081
Demonstrating online systems   SOPELAK, Mary J. . . . . .   (NY) 1168
Library research & demonstration   STEVENS, Frank A. . . . .   (DC) 1190

DENOMINATION (See also Church)
Church & denominational records   WOODARD, John R. . . . .   (NC) 1365
Religious denomination archives   WARNER, Wayne E. . . . .   (MO) 1305

DENTAL
Dental cataloging   RUBINSTEIN, Edith . . . .   (NY) 1065
Dental education management   CHERNIN, David A. . . . . .   (MA)   206
Dental information systems   DIEHL, Mark . . . .   (IL)   302
Dental literature reference   WILLIAMS, Ann T. . . . . .   (TX) 1342
Dental reference   STROTHER, Elizabeth A.   (LA) 1203
Dental research   LYNN, Kenneth C. . . . . .   (MD)   752
Dentistry   MAROUSEK, Kathy A. . .   (NJ)   772
Medical & dental databases   GLASER, June E. . . . . . .   (NY)   439
Medical, dental information   PRATT, Gregory F. . . . . .   (IL)   990

DEPARTMENT (See also Division)
Academic departmental libraries   DARLING, John B. . . . . .   (NC)   275
Academic periodical department   KEIST, Sandra H. . . . . . .   (NM)   635
Acquisitions department management   LEBEL, Clement . . . .   (PQ)   707
Administration of children's
   department   GREENFIELD, Judith C. . .   (NY)   464
Administration of departmental library SHANKLAND, Anne H. .   (ME) 1120
Audiovisual department head   WIRIG, Joan S. . . . .   (IL) 1356
Book selection catalog department   KING, Willard B. . . . . . .   (NC)   652
Catalog department   REILLY, Violet M. . . . . . .   (OH) 1020
Cataloging department management   LEBEL, Clement . . . .   (PQ)   707
Circulation department   ARNOLD, Donna W. . . . .   (CA)   33
                                       FEHRENBACH, Laurie A.   (OK)   368
Department director   GUTH, Karen K. . . . .   (CO)   478
Department head   FRAZIER, Nancy E. . . . .   (MA)   399
Department management   WULFING, Joyce . . . . . .   (NY) 1374
Department of Defense & AFR
   reports   BURDEN, John . . . .   (NY)   158
Department supervision   WOLF, Dorothy L. . . . . .   (MD) 1360
Department supervision & decisions   EARL, Susan R. . . . .   (NC)   332
Department supervisor   PAPA, Deborah M. . . . . .   (OH)   938
Departmental administration   BENDER, Cynthia F. . . . .   (MD)   79
Departmental cooperation   SOURS, Katherine M. . . .   (FL) 1169
Departmental information managing   EKSTRAND, Nancy L. . .   (NC)   341
Departmental libraries   CLARK, Barton M. . . . . .   (IL)   216
Departmental management &
   administration   BOELKE, Joanne H. . . . .   (IL)   110
Editorial department management   BRAM, Leon L. . . . .   (NJ)   127
Information & library service
   department   ROE, Georgeanne T. . . .   (MA) 1048
Interlibrary loan department   RICHARDSON, Emma G.   (NY) 1029

DEPARTMENT (Cont'd)
Interlibrary loan department
   management   CARVER, Jane W. . . . . . .   (KS)   191
Managing department activities   SOURS, Katherine M. . . .   (FL) 1169
Media departments   DUGGAN, James E. . . . .   (LA)   324
Music departments   GERSTENBERGER,
                                          Martha F. . . . .   (IA)   429
NASA, Dept of Defense, & DIALOG
   database   BOYD, Effie W. . . . .   (TN)   122
Preparation of departmental
   newsletters   CHAMBERS, E G. . . . . .   (MI)   198
Reference department   ANDREWS, Margaret . . .   (MA)   27
                                       BOWEN, Ethel B. . . . . . .   (MS)   120
                                       MARYNOWYCH, Roman
                                          V. . . . .   (NJ)   780
Reference department management   DUCKETT, Joan . . . .   (MA)   322
Serial department   MOORE, Mildred M. . . . .   (LA)   860
Serials department   BOWEN, Ethel B. . . . . . .   (MS)   120
Special library department
   management   RYAN, Jenny L. . . . .   (NY) 1071
State online catalog department   NAUGLE, Gretchen R. . .   (NE)   889
Supervision department library   YAGELLO, Virginia E. . . .   (OH) 1376
Treasury Department fiscal records   SHERMAN, William F. . .   (DC) 1128

DEPOSITION
Legal deposition, evidentiary data   SCHULTZ, Arnold J. . . .   (MN) 1101

DEPOSITORY
Cooperative book depositories   STOCKTON, Gloria J. . .   (CA) 1196
Depository library history   MILLER, Sarah J. . . . . . .   (NJ)   842
Federal & depository publications   FOSTER, Leslie A. . . . . .   (WI)   392
Federal documents depository   MCGINNESS, Mary B. . . .   (PA)   806

DESCRIPTION (See also Cataloging)
Archival arrangement & description   BEST, Rickey D. . . . . . .   (AL)   92
                                       MAHER, William J. . . . . .   (IL)   760
                                       PRIMER, Ben . . . .   (MD)   993
                                       BARTKOWSKI, Patricia . .   (MI)   61
                                       SMITH, Michael O. . . . . .   (MI) 1158
                                       OAKHILL, Harold W. . . . .   (NY)   913
                                       RICHIUSO, John P. . . . . .   (NY) 1030
                                       CORNELL, Alice M. . . . . .   (OH)   246
                                       CLINE, Robert S. . . . . . .   (WA)   222
                                       BEHRND-KLODT, Menzi L. (WI)   75
                                       KLUMPENHOUWER,
                                          Richard . . . .   (AB)   662
Archival description   PURDY, Virginia C. . . . . .   (DC)   998
                                       YOST, F D. . . . .   (DC) 1381
                                       ENGERRAND, Steven W.   (GA)   349
                                       FRENCH, Melodee J. . . .   (GA)   402
Archival description & arrangement   CASSEDY, James G. . . . .   (DC)   193
Archival descriptive standards   MACDERMAID, Anne . . .   (ON)   754
Archival processing & description   SICILIANO, Peg P. . . . . .   (MI) 1135
Archives arrangement & description   MYERS, Roger . . . .   (AZ)   885
                                       SERBACKI, Mary . . . . . .   (NY) 1116
Archives automated description   PENDLETON, Debbie D. . .   (AL)   956
Arrangement & description   BREEDLOVE, Michael A.   (AL)   131
                                       CHEESEMAN, Bruce S. .   (CT)   204
                                       NOLEN, Anita L. . . . .   (DC)   908
                                       WALLER, M C. . . . .   (KY) 1298
                                       SHAFER, Steven I. . . . . .   (MI) 1119
                                       WILLIAMS, Gene J. . . . . .   (NC) 1343
                                       GRAY, David P. . . . .   (ND)   459
                                       BARTO, Stephen C. . . . . .   (NY)   61
                                       TAYLOR, Dennis S. . . . . .   (SC) 1226
                                       TISSING, Robert W. . . . . .   (TX) 1247
                                       MOHOLT, Megan L. . . . . .   (WA)   852
                                       MUTSCHLER, Charles V.   (WA)   883
                                       HALLBERG, Carl V. . . . . .   (WY)   489
                                       TENER, Jean F. . . . .   (AB) 1231
Arrangement & description,
   manuscripts   PARHAM, Robert B. . . . .   (AK)   940
Arranging, describing, indexing   BUSAM, Emma C. . . . . . .   (KY)   164
Automated archival description   PURDY, Virginia C. . . . . .   (DC)   998
Bibliographic descriptions   DAVIS, L C. . . . .   (CA)   280
Collection evaluation & description   HIGBEE, Joan F. . . . . . .   (DC)   537
Describing & cataloging records   SIEBERS, Bruce L. . . . . .   (MI) 1135

DESCRIPTION (Cont'd)

Description & arrangement	INGLE, Bernita W.	(GA)	582
Description of archives	BUCKWALD, Joel	(NJ)	155
Description of legislative records	EFIRD, Frank K.	(IL)	338
Description, organization of information	BIERBAUM, Esther G.	(IA)	95
Descriptive bibliography	HANFF, Peter E.	(CA)	495
	PODESCHI, John B.	(IL)	979
	EPPARD, Philip B.	(MA)	351
	FERGUSON, Stephen	(NJ)	372
	EDDY, Donald D.	(NY)	335
	O'DONNELL, Mary A.	(NY)	917
	BAKY, John S.	(PA)	50
	KAISER, John R.	(PA)	622
	BREGMAN, Alvan M.	(ON)	131
Descriptive cataloging	CAHALANE, Edmond P.	(DC)	171
	GUILES, Kay D.	(DC)	476
	LIGGETT, Suzanne L.	(DC)	726
	WELLISCH, Hans H.	(MD)	1322
	BOYD, Alan D.	(OH)	122
	SELING, Kathy A.	(WA)	1113
	UHLMAN, Carol K.	(WA)	1268
	MANNING, Ralph W.	(ON)	767
Descriptive cataloging, legal materials	HAWKINS, Sandra J.	(DC)	514
Descriptive cataloging, monographs	HAWKINS, Sandra J.	(DC)	514
Descriptive cataloging, Slavic materials	MORGAN, Robert C.	(VA)	864
Descriptive systems	BURKE, Frank G.	(DC)	160
Manuscript & archival description	HENSEN, Steven L.	(NC)	529
Manuscript arrangement & description	KENNICK, Sylvia B.	(NY)	642
	O'KEEFE, Laura K.	(NY)	919
Manuscript organization & description	ONN, Shirley A.	(AB)	924
Manuscript processing & description	KAPLAN, Diane E.	(CT)	626
Manuscripts arrangement & description	MYERS, Roger	(AZ)	885
	BOWEN, Laurel G.	(IL)	120
	MICHAELIS, Patricia A.	(KS)	831
Records description	DOWD, Mary J.	(DC)	315

DESELECTION (See also Collections, Selection, Weeding)

Medical book deselection	FARLEY, Alfred E.	(KS)	364

DESIGN (See also Architecture, Building, Construction, Facilities, Interiors, Layout, Redesigning)

Academic science library design	STANKUS, Tony	(MA)	1180
Administration & library design	LISZEWSKI, Edward H.	(VA)	733
Administrative system design	CLARKE, Elba C.	(GA)	218
Analysis design information systems	DEBONS, Anthony	(PA)	285
Applications design & implementation	HORACEK, Paula B.	(CA)	558
Architectural & interior design	WIEGMAN, John H.	(TX)	1336
Architecture & design resources	GRIGORIS, Lygia	(MA)	470
Architecture & library design	NIELSEN, Sonja M.	(MA)	903
Art history & design	HORNBACH, Ruth M.	(MI)	559
Audiovisual & instructional design	PROVINCE, William R.	(IL)	996
Audiovisual library design	BASKIN, Jeffrey L.	(AR)	63
Automatic indexing, system design	VLADUTZ, George E.	(PA)	1286
Bar code system design	VOGT, Herwart C.	(NJ)	1287
Bibliographic database design	CHERVENAK, Joseph F.	(CO)	206
	GRIMES, Judith E.	(MD)	470
	COMSTOCK, Daniel L.	(NM)	235
	BREGMAN, Joan R.	(NY)	131
Building design	PINCOCK, Rulon D.	(CA)	974
	HENSON, Llewellyn L.	(FL)	529
	DOUGLAS, Alice W.	(MA)	314
	JACKSON, Patience K.	(NH)	588
	CONNORS, William E.	(NY)	238
	MITTELGLUCK, Eugene L.	(NY)	850
	WALDEN, Winston A.	(TN)	1294
	MOORE, Russell S.	(VT)	861
Building design & renovation	WU, Harry P.	(MI)	1373
	CADA, Elizabeth J.	(ON)	170
Building design for preservation	OGDEN, Barclay W.	(CA)	918
Buildings & designs	DRAPER, James D.	(GA)	318
CD-ROM & CD-I prog design & production	DAVISSON, Darell D.	(CA)	281
CD-ROM product design	MCCLELLAND, Bruce A.	(NY)	796
Communication design	DAVENPORT, Marilyn G.	(NV)	275
Communications systems design	BLISS, David H.	(IA)	105

DESIGN (Cont'd)

Computer laboratory design	LEVEILLEE, Louis R.	(RI)	719
Computer systems design	WHITEHEAD, James M.	(GA)	1332
Computer-human interface design	SIEGEL, Martin A.	(IL)	1136
Computerized system design	JOHNSON, Jane S.	(IL)	605
Costume design & history	STOWELL, Donald C.	(GA)	1199
Curriculum development & design	MOORE, Lawrence A.	(ON)	860
Custom circulation desk design	RIBNICKY, Karen F.	(CT)	1026
Data design	KOENIG, Michael E.	(NY)	668
Database analysis & design	TAYLOR, Alice J.	(CA)	1226
Database & information system design	BATTY, Charles D.	(MD)	65
Database & system design	VANCE, Julia M.	(MD)	1273
Database & systems design	CUTRONA, Cheryl	(PA)	268
Database archives design	DAWSON, Barbara J.	(DC)	282
Database design	CREW-NOBLE, Sara M.	(CA)	258
	DONLEY, Leigh M.	(CA)	311
	HORACEK, Paula B.	(CA)	558
	HOROWITZ, Roberta S.	(CA)	560
	KALVINSKAS, Louanne A.	(CA)	623
	MCCARTHY, John L.	(CA)	794
	PAPERMASTER, Cynthia L.	(CA)	939
	STANLEY, Dale R.	(CA)	1180
	STRIBLING, Lorraine R.	(CA)	1202
	WITTMANN, Cecelia V.	(CA)	1358
	TRIOLO, Victor A.	(CT)	1257
	MODLIN, Marilyn J.	(DC)	851
	ROAN, Tattie W.	(GA)	1038
	SCHNICK, Robert M.	(GA)	1097
	CIBULSKIS, Elizabeth R.	(IL)	214
	CLARK, Gerald L.	(IL)	217
	GROSSMAN, David G.	(IL)	473
	JACOBSON, William R.	(IL)	590
	KOSMAN, Joyce E.	(IL)	672
	MILLER, Thomas R.	(IL)	843
	PERLMAN, Michael S.	(IL)	959
	SHAW, Debora	(IL)	1123
	SUIDAN, Randa H.	(IL)	1207
	WILLIAMS, Martha E.	(IL)	1345
	HASHEM, Judy A.	(IN)	510
	HAMILTON, Fae K.	(MA)	492
	LYNCH, Jacqueline	(MA)	751
	BLUTE, Mary R.	(MD)	107
	CHESLOCK, Rosalind P.	(MD)	207
	VONDERHAAR, Mark N.	(MD)	1288
	WETZBARGER, Cecilia G.	(MD)	1328
	SCHMITTROTH, John	(MI)	1096
	BURCSU, James E.	(NC)	158
	KISER, Anita H.	(NC)	656
	ANDERSON, James D.	(NJ)	23
	BILBOUL, Roger R.	(NJ)	96
	GEORGE, Muriel S.	(NJ)	428
	RILEY, Robert H.	(NJ)	1034
	WALLMARK, John S.	(NJ)	1298
	BERGER, Mary C.	(NY)	85
	BROWN-SPRUILL, Debra K.	(NY)	149
	GREENGRASS, Alan R.	(NY)	464
	MACKESY, Eileen M.	(NY)	756
	PISCITELLI, Rosalie A.	(NY)	976
	RAKSHI, Sri R.	(NY)	1004
	MAXWELL, Marjo V.	(OH)	788
	RIFFLE, Linda	(OH)	1034
	PASCHAL, Linda P.	(OK)	945
	BOWDEN, Gail L.	(PA)	120
	HODGE, Gail M.	(PA)	546
	WILLIAMS, James G.	(PA)	1344
	GOVE, N B.	(TN)	454
	HEWINS, Elizabeth H.	(TX)	535
	O'DONOGHUE, Patrice	(TX)	917
	PEDEN, Robert M.	(TX)	954
	WORCHEL, Harris M.	(TX)	1368
	CUMMINGS, Christopher H.	(UT)	264
	DEBARDELEBEN, Marian Z.	(VA)	284
	ROSENBERG, Murray D.	(VA)	1056
	CRANDALL, Michael D.	(WA)	255
	FIDEL, Raya	(WA)	374

DESIGN (Cont'd)

Database design

KLAVER, Timothy J. . . . . (WI) 658
LANK, Dannette H. . . . . . (WI) 696
PARKS, Dennis H. . . . . . (WI) 943
SCHARMER, Roger C. . . (WI) 1090
NICHOL, Kathleen M. . . . (BC) 901
STEPHENSON, Mary S. . . (BC) 1188
SABLJIC, John A. . . . . (ON) 1072
MIRABELLI, Gerardo . . . (CSR) 847
YAMAZAKI, Hisamichi . . (JAP) 1377

Database design & administration JONES, Anne . . . . (NY) 611
Database design & construction DENTON, Francesca L. . (MA) 293
HLAVA, Marjorie M. . . . (NM) 544
HALE, Linda L. . . . . . . (BC) 485
Database design & development HOLLOWAY, Dona W. . . (CA) 552
HUNT, Richard K. . . . . . (CA) 575
LA BORDE, Charlotte A. . (CA) 686
MARKWORTH, Lawrence
L. . . . . (CA) 772
MORITZ, Thomas D. . . . (CA) 865
SPRUNG, Lori L. . . . . . (CA) 1176
STAN, Gail A. . . . . (CA) 1179
WOLF, Nola M. . . . . . . (CA) 1360
ROARK, Robin D. . . . . . (DC) 1038
SAWYER, Edmond J. . . (DC) 1086
STOCKTON, Ken R. . . . (DC) 1196
TURNER, Susan A. . . . . (DC) 1265
HUSSEY, Laurie L. . . . . (MA) 578
LAROSA, Sharon M. . . . (MA) 698
BOBKA, Marlene S. . . . (MD) 108
PUGH, W J. . . . . (MD) 997
BELLI, Frank G. . . . . . . (NY) 78
WEINSTEIN, Lois . . . . . (NY) 1318
GUBIOTTI, Ross A. . . . . (OH) 475
JOSEPH, Patricia A. . . . (PA) 617
NATHANSON, Esther M. . (PA) 889
LYDEN, Edward W. . . . (TX) 750
MOORE, Penelope F. . . (VA) 861
SAUVE, Deborah A. . . . (VA) 1085
WILTSHIRE, Denise A. . . (VA) 1354
YODER, William M. . . . (VA) 1380
POPE, Nolan F. . . . . . . (WI) 983
MCCLYMONT, Karen A. . (ON) 797
LEDOUX, Marc A. . . . . (PQ) 708
FUENTES, Ismael . . . . (SPN) 408
Database design & documentation MACLEOD, Valerie R. . . (KY) 757
Database design & implementation DAMOTH, Douglas L. . . (NY) 272
GOODWIN, C R. . . . . . (AB) 450
Database design & indexing FORKES, David . . . . . . (ON) 390
Database design & maintenance WEIDA, William A. . . . . (OH) 1316
ROSENBERG, Kenyon C. (VA) 1056
FRITZ, Richard J. . . . . . (ON) 405
Database design & management ANDRADE, Rebecca . . . (CA) 26
BURNS, Nancy R. . . . . (CA) 162
PEPETONE, Diane S. . . (IA) 957
MACKEY, Denise R. . . . (IL) 756
SLAWNIAK, Patricia M. . (IL) 1148
NATOLI, Dorothy L. . . . (MA) 889
ADLER, Robert J. . . . . (MI) 7
EARLE, Marcia H. . . . . (NY) 332
MANES, Estelle L. . . . . (OK) 765
RAMBO, Neil H. . . . . . (TX) 1005
FOSTER, Anne . . . . . . (ON) 392
SOKOV, Asta M. . . . . . (PQ) 1166
NEUWILLER, Charlene . . (WGR) 897
Database design & production BATES, Ruthann I. . . . . (MD) 64
BRUNELLE, Bette S. . . (NY) 150
LAM, Vinh T. . . . . (ON) 689
Database design & quality control VEGTER, Amy H. . . . . . (NY) 1281
Database design & search SCHWALLER, Marian C. . (MA) 1104
Database design & use KASKE, Neal K. . . . . . (AL) 628
MACIUSZKO, Kathleen L. (OH) 755
Database design, development,
management SHELLENBARGER, Linda
K. . . . . (OH) 1126
FURR, Susan H. . . . . . (VA) 410
BEHNKE, Charles . . . . (WI) 75
Database design for materials LOWELL, Brian V. . . . . (IL) 744
Database design, management UMFLEET, Ruth A. . . . . (TX) 1268

DESIGN (Cont'd)

Database designer LABEAU, Dennis . . . . . (MI) 685
Database designs LI, Marjorie H. . . . . . . (NJ) 724
Database development & design KENNY-SLOAN, Linda . . (CA) 642
YODER, Susan M. . . . . (CA) 1380
Database documentation design PUGH, W J. . . . . (MD) 997
Database management & design VARAT, Nancy L. . . . . . (CA) 1278
BROWN, Maxine M. . . . (DC) 146
KRANCH, Douglas A. . . (IA) 676
ANDREWS, Sylvia L. . . (IN) 27
JOHNSON, Judith . . . . (NY) 606
PUKL, Joseph M. . . . . . (SC) 997
Database production & design CORNICK, Ron . . . . . . (IL) 247
Database systems design SHAPTON, Gregory B. . . (CA) 1122
KOSTINKO, Gail A. . . . (DC) 673
Database systems design & analysis KAVANAGH, Janette R. . (CO) 631
Database systems design &
development SCHWARTZ, Betsy J. . . (MD) 1104
Design DIRKSEN, Phyllis A. . . . (CO) 305
Design & construction of new facilities PAPENFUSE, Edward C. (MD) 939
Design & development REMKIEWICZ, Frank L. . (CA) 1022
Design & eval of info systs & lib srvs COCHRANE, Pauline A. . (NY) 226
Design & planning of library buildings TRELEASE, Robert J. . . (IL) 1255
Design, layout, copywriting LAMBERT, Shirley A. . . . (CO) 690
Design of library buildings BASSNETT, Peter J. . . . (ON) 63
Design of shelving systems BAYLIS, Ted . . . . (MA) 67
Designing & editing newsletters ENSEL, Ellen H. . . . . . . (CT) 350
Designing & manufacturing lib
equipment KINGSLEY, Eleanor V. . . (CA) 652
Designing mainframe databases MURRAY, Elizabeth F. . . (NY) 881
Designing media programs COOK, Sybilla A. . . . . . (OR) 240
Designing medical information
systems LAZAROW-STETTEN,
Jane K. . . . . (MD) 706
Designing microcomputer databases MURRAY, Elizabeth F. . . (NY) 881
Designing online systems BELTON, Jennifer H. . . . (DC) 78
Designing recordings catalogs GLASFORD, G R. . . . . . (NY) 440
Designing records management
systems BOWKER, Scott W. . . . . (NY) 121
Designing special library systems HAUSRATH, Donald C. . (NY) 513
Develop & design accounting systems CHRISTIANSON, Ellory J. (MN) 212
Editing & designing publications SHUMAN, Marilyn J. . . . (IL) 1134
Editing, writing & design MOLLO, Terry . . . . (NY) 853
Educational materials design WALD, Marlena M. . . . . (GA) 1294
Electronic design & manufacturing KLINGER, William E. . . . (OH) 661
End-user online product design LIPPERT, Margret G. . . . (OH) 732
Ergonomics in system design FONG, Wilfred W. . . . . (WI) 388
Facilities design & planning HOWLAND, Margaret E. . (MA) 566
Facilities planning & design BANNERMAN-WILLIAMS,
Cheryl F. . . . . (TN) 54
Facility design CALLISON, Daniel J. . . . (IN) 174
JEFFCOTT, Janet B. . . . (WI) 596
File systems design HUFF, Patricia M. . . . . . (VA) 570
Filing system design QUINN, Sidney . . . . (MD) 1000
Full-text database design GROCKI, Daniel J. . . . . (MD) 471
Graphic design FRISCH, Corrine A. . . . . (IL) 405
JONES, Sally L. . . . . . . (WA) 615
Graphics & magazine design WISE, Eileen M. . . . . . (ON) 1356
History & aesthetics stage design STOWELL, Donald C. . . . (GA) 1199
Hospital design & collection
development TOMLIN, Marsha A. . . . (OH) 1250
Index design & development BOOTH, Barbara A. . . . (CA) 116
MORSE, June E. . . . . . (VA) 869
Indexing & database design THOMAS, Dorothy . . . . (NY) 1236
Indexing systems design ANDERSON, James D. . (NJ) 23
Information product design &
development DAY, Melvin S. . . . . . . (VA) 283
Information product design &
maintenance PISCITELLI, Rosalie A. . . (NY) 976
Information retrieval design system KORNFELD, Carol E. . . . (NJ) 672
Information retrieval software design BRUNELLE, Bette S. . . . (NY) 150
Information retrieval system design MEYER, Alan H. . . . . . (MD) 829
MCCLELLAND, Bruce A. (NY) 796
Information retrieval systems design ANDERSON, James D. . (NJ) 23
Information services design BURNS, Christopher . . . . (MA) 162
Information system design KOPP, Kurt W. . . . . . . (MO) 671
RUSHING, Jessie W. . . (TN) 1068
MEADOW, Charles T. . . (ON) 819
VAN SLYPE, Georges . . (BEL) 1277

DESIGN (Cont'd)

Information system design & management	FREEDMAN, Bernadette .	(PA)	400
	LAZAR, Peter	(HUN)	706
Information systems analysis & design	BORKO, Harold	(CA)	116
	WILLIAMS, James G. . . .	(PA)	1344
Information systems, database design	FOURNIER, Susan K. . . .	(MD)	393
Information systems design	MICHEL, Dee A.	(CA)	832
	TUNG, Sandra J.	(CA)	1263
	KENNEY, Brigitte L.	(CO)	641
	RADER, Ronald A.	(DC)	1002
	SOERGEL, Dagobert . . .	(MD)	1165
	KELLER, Karen A.	(MI)	635
	WAGNER, A B.	(NY)	1291
	WARD, Edith	(NY)	1303
	HOLMES, John H.	(PA)	553
	LEONARD, Lucinda E. . . .	(VA)	716
	BOOHER, Craig S.	(WI)	115
Information systems design, analysis	SYPERT, Clyde F.	(CA)	1217
Information systems design & development	WHITE, Suellen S.	(CO)	1332
	CLARK, Rick	(NJ)	218
Information systems design & evaluation	LEVITAN, Karen B.	(MD)	721
Information systems design & integration	CHU, John S.	(PA)	212
In-house database design	KARCHER, Tracey L. . . .	(CA)	627
In-house database design & development	BECKER, Linda C.	(PA)	72
Instruction design & development	TREGLOAN, Donald C. . .	(MI)	1255
Instructional design	BUTLER, David W.	(CA)	166
	ROSE, David L.	(CA)	1054
	SINOFSKY, Esther R. . . .	(CA)	1144
	HAUSMAN, Julie	(IA)	513
	DAVIS, H S.	(IN)	279
	SMINK, Anna R.	(MD)	1152
	HAMMITT, Margaret R. . .	(NE)	493
	WEAVER-MEYERS, Pat L.	(OK)	1313
Instructional design & library skills	EFFERTZ, Rose	(IL)	338
Instructional design, audiovisual	PICHETTE, William H. . .	(TX)	970
Instructional implementation & design	JENKINS, Lydia E.	(DC)	597
Instructional involvement, design	CORNWELL, Linda L. . .	(IN)	247
Instructional media design	CHAPLOCK, Sharon K. .	(WI)	201
Interface design	BRUNELLE, Bette S. . . .	(NY)	150
	DILLON, Martin	(OH)	303
Interior arrangement & design	BELLIN, Bernard E.	(WI)	78
Interior design	CALDWELL, Kenneth R. .	(CA)	172
	YOUNG, Nancy J.	(IL)	1382
Interior design for libraries	NOVAK, Gloria J.	(CA)	910
Interior planning & design	DE BEAR, Richard S. . . .	(MI)	284
	MICHAELS, David L. . . .	(VA)	832
Knowledge software design	GRENIER, Serge	(PQ)	467
Law library design	EVERLOVE, Nora J.	(FL)	359
Law library planning & design	KREMER, Jill L.	(PA)	677
Law library systems design	RAUM, Tamar	(NY)	1010
Library architecture & design	BECK, Erla P.	(IN)	71
Library architecture, interior design	COHEN, Aaron	(NY)	227
Library building design	HART, Thomas L.	(FL)	507
	PEARSON, Roger L. . . .	(IL)	953
	SMITH, Lester K.	(IL)	1157
	KANSFIELD, Norman J. .	(NY)	625
	LEE, Sang C.	(NY)	711
	WALTERS, Daniel L. . . .	(WA)	1301
	ROBIN, Madeleine	(PQ)	1043
Library building design & planning	MCCABE, James P.	(PA)	793
Library building planning & design	SICKLES, Linda C.	(MI)	1135
Library buildings & interior design	FOX, James R.	(PA)	394
Library construction & design	PRITCHARD, John A. . .	(NC)	994
Library design	SCHULTZ, Ute M.	(CA)	1102
	CRAIG, James P.	(FL)	254
	RABER, Nevin W.	(IN)	1001
	PHIPPS, Bert L.	(ME)	969
	BLUMENTHAL, Sidney L.	(NJ)	107
	BUCK, Anne M.	(NJ)	153
	KRUPP, Robert G.	(NJ)	681
	IOBST, Barbara J.	(PA)	583
	DAVIS, Joan C.	(TX)	279
	MURPHY, Robert D. . . .	(VA)	881
	GISHLER, John R.	(AB)	438
	RYAN, Noel	(ON)	1071

DESIGN (Cont'd)

Library design & architecture	BRYANT, David S.	(NJ)	152
Library design & moving projects	SCHUBACK COHN, Judith	(NJ)	1101
Library design & renovation	BIHLER, Charles H.	(CT)	96
Library design & space planning	DAVIS, Glenn G.	(IL)	279
Library design & systems planning	KAPNICK, Laura B.	(NY)	626
Library display systems design	RIBNICKY, Karen F.	(CT)	1026
Library facilities design	HAAS, Eva L.	(NY)	480
Library graphic design & art	BRYAN, Carol L.	(WV)	151
Library interior planning & design	MICHAELS, Andrea A. . .	(VA)	831
Library layout & design	MCPHERSON, Kenneth F.	(NJ)	817
Library planning & design	OGLETREE, Elizabeth H.	(PA)	918
Library space design	D'ANGELO, Paul P.	(NY)	272
Library system analysis & design	MORGAN, Ferrell	(CA)	864
Library systems & design	HENDERSON, Deborah A.	(ON)	526
Library systems design	GABBERT, Gretchen W. .	(CA)	411
	WHITEHEAD, James M. .	(GA)	1332
	O'NEIL, Rosanna M.	(OH)	924
	MCDONALD, Joseph A. .	(PA)	918
	MAGALONI, Ana M.	(MEX)	759
Library systems design & layout	AKS, Gloria	(NY)	9
Manual systems design	PISCITELLI, Rosalie A. . .	(NY)	976
Media center design	DRECHSEL, Marcella J. .	(NJ)	319
Media design & instruction	ALBUM, Bernie	(CA)	11
Media design, production & utilization	LIGGAN, Mary K.	(VA)	726
Medical database design	TINGLEY, Dianne E.	(MD)	1246
Medical info system analysis & design	HENDRICKSON, Maria F.	(NY)	527
Microcomputer database design	MOLL, Joy K.	(NJ)	853
	NEELAND, Margaret A. .	(NY)	891
	SANDFELDER, Paula M.	(HKG)	1080
Microcomputer design	SHENASSA, Daryoosh . .	(IL)	1126
Microcomputers & software design	KARR, Ronald D.	(MA)	628
Microcomputers database design	BURCH, David R.	(TX)	158
National library networks design	MAGALONI, Ana M.	(MEX)	759
Office design	CALDWELL, John M. . . .	(PA)	172
Online database design	LEMASTERS, Joann T. .	(OH)	715
Online product design development	ODHO, Marc	(ON)	917
Online systems design	MCLAREN, M B.	(NM)	813
	NORMORE, Lorraine F. .	(OH)	909
Oral history program design	KENDRICK, Alice M. . . .	(NY)	640
Photo morgue design & implementation	DAMOTH, Douglas L. . .	(NY)	272
Planning & design of library buildings	BEWLEY, Lois M.	(BC)	93
Printing, design & production	NAGLE, Ann	(NY)	886
Production system design	HODGE, Gail M.	(PA)	546
Program design	WILLIAMSON, Phyllis B. .	(MT)	1348
Proprietary database design	WAITE, William F.	(NJ)	1293
Public library building design	BARTON, Phillip K.	(NC)	62
	MURPHY, Richard W. . . .	(VA)	881
Publications design & development	STEPHENSON, Judy A. .	(KY)	1188
Publishing database editing & design	THOMPSON, Anne E. . .	(AZ)	1238
Reference book design	FRANKLIN, Robert M. . .	(NC)	398
Reference book design & research	KLINE, Victoria E.	(CA)	661
Reference publication design	STONE, Nancy Y.	(MI)	1197
Relational database design	CAMOZZI-EKBERG, Patricia L.	(WA)	175
	WARD, Maryanne	(WA)	1304
Relational databases design & use	ROBINSON, David F. . . .	(VA)	1043
Research design	TAGUE, Jean M.	(ON)	1220
Research design & analysis	CHOBOT, Mary C.	(VA)	210
	LUECHT, Richard M. . . .	(WI)	747
Retrieval systems design	HOWARD, Susanna J. . .	(NC)	564
School media center design	LEVEILLEE, Louis R. . . .	(RI)	719
Scientific information systems design	DIESING, Arthur C.	(KY)	302
Slides & picture files design	KEAVENEY, Sydney S. .	(NY)	633
Small academic building design	LUCAS, Linda L.	(CA)	746
Small database design	FOWELLS, Fumi T.	(MI)	393
Software design	MULVANY, Nancy	(CA)	878
Software design & development	RICKERSON, George T. .	(MO)	1031
Space planning & design	TEICH, Steven	(OR)	1230
Special library design consulting	MAIN, Annette Z.	(PA)	761
Special library organization & design	BURNS, Marie T.	(IL)	162
Storage & retrieval system design	TRAVIS, Irene L.	(VA)	1254
System analysis & design	DIENER, Carol W.	(MD)	302
System design	SARGENT, Charles W. .	(TX)	1082
	CARNEY, Marillyn L. . . .	(VA)	183
	LUNIN, Lois F.	(VA)	749
	BLOCH, Uri	(ISR)	105
System design & development	HALPIN, Peter	(DC)	490
System design & programming	LARSON, Ray R.	(CA)	699

DESIGN (Cont'd)

Systems analysis & design	STOVEL, Madeleine D. . .	(CA)	1199
	LISTON, David M.	(MD)	732
	CONNORS, William E. . .	(NY)	238
	WAGNER, Stephen K. . .	(NY)	1292
	REDMER, Paul C.	(VA)	1014
	BALON, Brett J.	(SK)	53
	ARTEAGA, Georgina . . .	(MEX)	35
Systems design	ELLIS, Ruth M.	(CA)	345
	WHITE, Cecil R.	(CA)	1330
	WEST, L P.	(IL)	1326
	MORGAN, James J.	(IN)	864
	GOLDSCHMIDT, Peter G.	(MD)	446
	WEISFIELD, Cynthia F. .	(PA)	1319
	YODER, William M. . . .	(VA)	1380
	MCCUBBIN, George M. .	(ON)	800
Systems design & programming	RAO, Paladugu V.	(IL)	1008
Systems designing	BORBELY, Jack	(NY)	116
Systems planning & design	STANLEY, Dale R.	(CA)	1180
Text database design & development	CHU, John S.	(PA)	212
Thesaurus design & maintenance	LINDER, Elliott	(NY)	729
Thesaurus design & preparation	FEINBERG, Hilda W. . . .	(GA)	368
Training systems design, analysis	SYPERT, Clyde F.	(CA)	1217
Type design & typography	KIRSHENBAUM, Sandra D.	(CA)	655
Typesetting & graphic design	MILLER, Thomas R. . . .	(IL)	843
User interface design	HURLEY, Geraldine C. . .	(OH)	577
Video disk instructional design	CONNELL, William S. . .	(CA)	237
Videodisc design & productions	HAUSMAN, Julie	(IA)	513
Visual resources database design	ELTZROTH, Elsbeth L. .	(GA)	346
Workshop design & coordination	WEBSTER, Linda	(TX)	1314
Writer, designer, technology	SEITZ, Robert J.	(NY)	1113

DESKTOP

Computer desktop publishing	MOLLO, Terry	(NY)	853
Desktop information management systems	HARTT, Richard W. . . .	(VA)	509
Desktop publishing	CISLER, Stephen A. . . .	(CA)	215
	COYLE, Leslie P.	(CA)	253
	ELLIOT, Hugh	(DC)	343
	DICK, John H.	(IL)	300
	MCKENZIE, Duncan J. . .	(IL)	811
	VACCARO, William J. . .	(IL)	1270
	BOZOIAN, Paula	(MA)	124
	PAPALAMBROS, Rita G.	(MA)	939
	BRUTON, Robert T. . . .	(MN)	151
	KEIM, Robert	(MN)	635
	BROWN, Stanley W. . . .	(NH)	147
	ANDERSON, Eric S. . . .	(OH)	22
	PITCHON, Cindy A. . . .	(PA)	976
	KRUSE, Luanne M. . . .	(TX)	681
	LIVNY, Efrat	(WI)	735
	WESTERN, Eric D.	(WI)	1327
Personal computer desktop publishing	BALCOM, Karen S. . . .	(TX)	51
Public relations, desktop publishing	WEIDEMANN, Margaret A.	(NY)	1316

DETECTIVE (See also Mystery)

Detective fiction	YOUNG, Juana R.	(AR)	1382
Gothic tradition, detective fiction	FISHER, Benjamin F. . . .	(MS)	380

DEVELOPING COUNTRIES (See also Third World)

Developing countries	HARRIS, Susan C.	(CA)	506
	WOODWARD, Anthony M.	(ENG)	1367
	PILLET, Sylvaine M. . . .	(KEN)	973
Developing countries & information	LAU, Jesus G.	(MEX)	702
Developing countries reference	BOYLE, James E.	(DC)	123
Developing country libraries, children	PELLOWSKI, Anne	(NY)	955
Developing country library consultancy	LEE, Amy C.	(DC)	709
Libraries in developing countries	WETHERBEE, Louella V.	(TX)	1327
Microcomputers in developing countries	DAVIES, Carol A.	(NY)	277

DEVELOPMENTALLY (See also Special)

Developmentally disabled lib services	DUX-IDEUS, Sherrie L. . .	(NE)	330

DEVICE

Device control systems	ZOROWITZ, Richard D. . .	(IL)	1390
Medical devices	SNELL, Charles E.	(CA)	1163

DEWEY

Cataloging Lib of Congress, Dewey, Sears	RUSSELL, Richard A. . . .	(WV)	1069
Dewey decimal classification	DANIS, Rolland J.	(PQ)	273
Promoting Dewey decimal classification	KRAMER-GREENE, Judith	(NY)	675

DIALOG

Database searching, DIALOG	HAGE, Christine C.	(MI)	482
	LAPAS, Martha E.	(NC)	697
	MOSS, Charmagne L. . . .	(TX)	872
Database searching on DIALOG	MOXNESS, Mary J.	(MN)	874
DIALOG & BRS	SMITH, Frances P.	(HI)	1155
DIALOG database searching	HUGHES, Frances M. . . .	(CT)	571
	MAGUIRE, Shirley E. . . .	(MI)	760
	MILLER, Carmen L.	(WA)	836
DiALOG databases	HELBERS, Catherine A. . .	(NY)	523
DIALOG, log-on databases	STRICKLAND, Ann T. . .	(AZ)	1202
DIALOG searches	MARCHANT, Cathy	(UT)	768
DIALOG searching	ASTIFIDIS, Maria	(NY)	37
	TOMLIN, Celia K.	(UT)	1250
	CARR, Carol L.	(WA)	185
DIALOG service	VALENTIN-MARTY, Jeannette	(PR)	1271
Managing DIALOG	SUMMIT, Roger K.	(CA)	1209
NASA, Dept of Defense, & DIALOG database	BOYD, Effie W.	(TN)	122
Online searching, DIALOG	GROVES, Helen G.	(TX)	474
Online searching, DIALOG, STN	O'NEILL, Patricia E. . . .	(GA)	924
Online searching, NLM, DIALOG, BRS	NELSON, Iris N.	(CA)	894

DICKINSON

Emily Dickinson & Robert Frost	LOMBARDO, Daniel J. . .	(MA)	738
Emily Dickinson, poet, info	MOREY, Frederick L. . . .	(MD)	863

DICTIONARIES (See also Lexicography, Thesaurus)

Databases & data dictionaries	PULLEYBLANK, Mildred C.	(ON)	997
Dictionaries, encyclopedias	BREWER, Annie M.	(MI)	134
Dictionary publishing	NAULT, William H.	(IL)	889
Online thesauri, dictionary research	LIBBEY, Miles A.	(NJ)	725

DIFFUSION

Diffusion of innovations	RICE, Ronald E.	(CA)	1027
Diffusion of medical innovations	ANDERSON, Marilyn M. .	(IN)	24
Forecasting new media diffusion	KLOPFENSTEIN, Bruce C.	(OH)	662

DIGITAL

Digital equipment corporation	MONOSSON, Adolf S. . .	(MA)	855
Digital image database	SHOREBIRD, Thomas S.	(DC)	1132
Digitize image manipulation software	BENGE, Bruce	(OK)	80
Dissemination of digital data	WILTSHIRE, Denise A. . .	(VA)	1354
Image digitization	BESSER, Howard A. . . .	(CA)	91
Integrated services digital network	GILHEANY, Stephen J. . .	(CA)	435
Microimagery & digitizing standards	BAGG, Thomas C.	(MD)	45

DILIGENCE

Due diligence investigation	MOSLEY, Thomas E. . . .	(OK)	872

DIPLOMACY

American diplomatic history	MCDONALD, Ellen J. . . .	(MA)	802
Public affairs & diplomacy	STEERE, Paul J.	(DC)	1184
20th century diplomatic records	PFEIFFER, David A. . . .	(DC)	966

DIRECT

Direct mail marketing	PHILLIPS, Angela B. . . .	(NY)	967
	WORTON, Geoffrey P. . .	(NY)	1369
Direct mail markets	MELKIN, Audrey D.	(NY)	822
Direct mail promotion management	OGREN, Mark S.	(IL)	918
Direct marketing	WALSH, Mark L.	(CT)	1300
Direct marketing & continuities	KING, Timothy B.	(NY)	652
Direct marketing & sales management	JOHNSON, Richard K. . .	(MD)	608
Direct marketing, creation	HUBBARD, Roy	(NY)	568
Marketing & direct mail	DYER, Carolyn A.	(CT)	330

DIRECTING

Choral speaking direction	ANTHONY, Rose M. . . .	(WI)	29
College library directorship	SCARBOROUGH, Ruth E.	(NJ)	1087
Department director	GUTH, Karen K.	(CO)	478
Directing a public library	VALENTINE, Patrick M. .	(NC)	1271
Directing & managing museum & library	PARKER, Peter J.	(PA)	942
Directing library & media centers	HAYASHI, Chigusa	(NJ)	515
Directing library skills instruction	HACKMAN, Mary H. . . .	(MD)	481
Directing media center	COVINGTON, Eddis E. . .	(ID)	252
Directing public libraries	CANAVAN, Roberta N. . .	(NJ)	178
	KING, Dennis W.	(NY)	650
Director	SANBORN, Dorothy C. . .	(CA)	1079
	MUSSEHL, Allan A.	(DC)	883
	GROTH, Robert E.	(IA)	473
Director & actor	NIEHAUS, Barbara J. . . .	(IL)	903
Director of pictorial resrch collection	GORDON, Thelma S. . . .	(CT)	452
Directorship	HUEBNER, Mary A.	(NY)	570
Grimm tales production & direction	DAVENPORT, Thomas R. .	(VA)	276
Language of play direction	TRAPIDO, Joel	(HI)	1254
Library direction	OBERLY, Beverly R.	(KS)	914
	LODATO, James J.	(NY)	736
Library director	BOCKMAN, Glenda C. . .	(IN)	109
	CRANE, Gerri G.	(KS)	255
	EVANS, Nancy I.	(VT)	357
Library directorship	MORR, Lynell A.	(FL)	866
Library services direction	WOFSE, Joy G.	(NY)	1359
Library systems direction	SAYRE, Edward C.	(NM)	1087
Non-print media director	DINNESEN, Peter H.	(OH)	305
Producing & directing	GURIEVITCH, Grania B. .	(NY)	478
Professional & special library direction	ROTHMAN, Marilyn R. . .	(CO)	1060
Public library direction	NICHOLS, Joyce N.	(NY)	901
Research director	SMITH, Cynthia M.	(ON)	1153
School library direction	APEL, Catherine D.	(WV)	29
Strategic direction	CHANDLER, James	(CA)	200
Writing & directing educational films	HARTLEY, Elda E.	(CT)	508

DIRECTORIES

Book & directory publishing	CSENGE, Maragaret L. . .	(NY)	262
Business directories	KRAMER, Allan F.	(NY)	675
	JACKSON, Craig A.	(ON)	587
Catalog, index & directory production	BUCKLAND, Lawrence F.	(MA)	154
Compiling directories	GILBERT, Mattana	(MD)	433
Computer technology directory	LEE, Douglas E.	(NY)	709
Database directories	BUCENEC, Nancy L. . . .	(NY)	153
	TOPEL, Iris N.	(NY)	1251
Directories	YOUNG, Dorothy B.	(NY)	1381
Directories research	REDEL, Judy A.	(NY)	1014
Directory compilation & publishing	SCARBOROUGH, Katharine T.	(CA)	1087
Directory publishing	D'ADOLF, Steven P.	(CA)	269
	KIMMEL, Mark R.	(MD)	649
	MARLOW, Cecilia A. . . .	(MI)	772
	SCHMITTROTH, John . .	(MI)	1096
	GREENFIELD, Stanley R.	(NY)	464
	DARLINGTON, Susan . .	(PQ)	275
Electronic network directories	MACLELLAND, Margaret A.	(ON)	757
Factory automation directory	LEE, Douglas E.	(NY)	709
Fundraising directories	TAFT, James R.	(DC)	1219
Newsletters, directory	GAZZOLA, Kenneth E. . .	(DC)	424
Periodical directories	HAGOOD, Patricia C. . . .	(NY)	483
Trade magazines & directories	DALY, Charles P.	(NJ)	271
Travel directory publications	BUZAN, Norma J.	(MI)	168

DISABLED (See also Impaired, Handicapped, Retardation)

Collection devlpmnt for lrng disabled	KEYS, Marshall	(MA)	645
Computers for the disabled	MCHARG, Kathleen M. . .	(OR)	808
Development disabilities	HOWIE, Maryann	(NY)	566
Developmentally disabled lib services	DUX-IDEUS, Sherrie L. . .	(NE)	330
Disability	BROWN, Dale S.	(DC)	143
Disability & rehabilitation evaluation	SMITH, Kathleen A.	(MD)	1156
Disabled	STONE, Elizabeth W. . . .	(DC)	1197
Disabled, older adults	DUPERREAULT, Marilyn J.	(SK)	327
Disabled services	MAYO, Kathleen O.	(FL)	790
	SCHWENGER, Frances S.	(ON)	1105
Independent living for disabled	ELLIS, Kathy M.	(BC)	344
Learning disabled library projects	WILLIAMS, Eve A.	(NB)	1343
Library service for disabled persons	DALTON, Phyllis I.	(NV)	271
Library services for the disabled	CAGLE, Robert B.	(LA)	171
	SMITH, Audrey J.	(NY)	1152
Public services learning for disabled	KEYS, Marshall	(MA)	645
Reading disabilities literature	SPARKS, Martha E.	(NC)	1171
Service to disabled persons	LUCAS, Linda S.	(SC)	746
Service to disabled youth	HARRIS, Karen H.	(LA)	505
Service to the disabled	KEMPF, Andrea C.	(KS)	639
	KLEIMAN, Allan M.	(NY)	658
Services for disabled	MCCLASKEY, Marilyn H.	(MN)	796
Services for disabled persons	CHAN, Arlene S.	(ON)	199
Services to disabled patrons	LEVERING, Mary B.	(DC)	719
Services to disabled persons	WRIGHT, Keith C.	(NC)	1372
	LOVEJOY, Eunice G. . . .	(OH)	743
	MCCHESNEY, Kathryn M.	(OH)	795
	HAYES, Janice E.	(ON)	516
	RIDLER, Elizabeth A. . . .	(SK)	1032
Services to persons with disabilities	SORENSON, Liene S. . . .	(IL)	1168
Services to the disabled	MCCARTY, Emily H.	(MD)	795
	FOGLESONG, Marilee . .	(NY)	387
Work with disabled	WILSON, Betty R.	(IL)	1350

DISADVANTAGED

Service to rural disadvantaged	POWELL, Anice C.	(MS)	988

DISASTER

Business records disaster recovery	EULENBERG, Julia N. . .	(WA)	356
Disaster planning	PEPPER, Jerold L.	(NY)	958
	FU, Paul S.	(OH)	407
	BALON, Brett J.	(SK)	53
Disaster planning & preservation	TOOLEY, Katherine J. . .	(OK)	1250
Disaster planning for recovery	MOON, Myra J.	(CO)	857
Disaster preparedness	MCGREGOR, James W. .	(IL)	808
	KROAH, Larry A.	(PA)	679
Disaster recovery of archival materials	MARRELLI, Nancy M. . . .	(PQ)	773
Disaster recovery planning	EULENBERG, Julia N. . .	(WA)	356
Preservation & lib disaster prevention	DITXLER, Carol J.	(MD)	306

DISC (See Disk)

DISCOGRAPHY (See also Phonodisc, Phonograph)

Discographer, recording archivist	NOVITSKY, Edward G. . .	(NY)	911
Discography	BOWLING, Lance C.	(CA)	121
	GRAY, Michael H.	(DC)	460
	JELLINEK, George	(NY)	596
	WEBER, Jerome F.	(NY)	1314
	VILES, Elza A.	(TN)	1284
	LEWIS, John S.	(TX)	723
	GRENDYSA, Peter A. . .	(WI)	467
	PUSATERI, Liborio	(ITL)	998
	ELSTE, R O.	(WGR)	346
	LOTZ, Rainer E.	(WGR)	742
Discography, gathering & tabulating data	BLACKER, George A. . . .	(CT)	102
Discography, writing	MORAN, William R.	(CA)	862
Editing, discography, prose	SHAPIRO, Burton J.	(MD)	1121
Historical & archival discography	GLASFORD, G R.	(NY)	440
Music bibliography & discography	MCCLELLAN, William M.	(IL)	796
Music consulting & discography	PATRYCH, Joseph	(NY)	947
Opera & classical discography	COLLINS, William J.	(CA)	233
Piano discographies	YRIGOYEN, Robert P. . .	(NJ)	1384
Popular music discography	COOPER, B L.	(MI)	242

DISCOUNT

Medical book discounter	PUALWAN, Emily	(PA)	996
Nursing, allied health book discounter	PUALWAN, Emily	(PA)	996

DISCUSSION

Book discussion groups	ALLEN, Richard H.	(NE)	16
Great Books discussion leader	GINSBURG, Coralie S.	(IL)	438
Questioning techniques, lit discussions	SENATOR, Rochelle B.	(CT)	1115

DISEASES (See also Epidemiology, Virology and names of specific diseases)

Information foreign animal diseases	PERLMAN, Stephen E.	(NY)	959

DISK (See also Recordings)

Analogue disc preservation	WAYLAND, Terry T.	(TX)	1311
Archiving art slides on video disks	SHARER, E J.	(CO)	1122
Cataloging cassettes & compact discs	SCHWANN, William J.	(MA)	1104
Compact disc	HELGERSON, Linda W.	(VA)	524
Compact disc interactive	GALL, Bert A.	(TN)	413
Compact discs	MOGLE, Dawn E.	(IN)	852
	CAPPAERT, Lael R.	(MI)	180
	KNIESNER, John T.	(OH)	664
Creating video disks for art	SHARER, E J.	(CO)	1122
Disc transcriptions	GERBER, Warren C.	(NJ)	428
Interactive art video disks	SHARER, E J.	(CO)	1122
Interactive video disk development	HORNIG-ROHAN, James E.	(PA)	560
Key trainer for the optical disk	BEAN, Charles W.	(DC)	69
Laser disks, CD-ROMS	GARMAN, Nancy J.	(KY)	419
Library optical disk applications	SWORA, Tamara	(DC)	1217
On-disk databases	SMILLIE, Pauline A.	(MI)	1151
Optical disc products	SPALA, Jeanne L.	(CA)	1170
Optical disk	VONDERHAAR, Mark N.	(MD)	1288
	BETCHER, Melissa A.	(OH)	92
Optical disk & CD-ROM	ROSE, Steven C.	(CA)	1055
Optical disk applications	WEBB, Duncan C.	(CA)	1313
	ROBERTSON, Michael A.	(NY)	1042
Optical disk collection development	QUIGLEY, Suzanne L.	(OH)	999
Optical disk conversion	BARRETT, Darryl D.	(MN)	59
Optical disk database system	BENGE, Bruce	(OK)	80
Optical disk information archiving	PASCHAL, John M.	(OK)	945
Optical disk publishing	ZOELLICK, Bill	(CO)	1390
Optical disk storage & retrieval	ELMAN, Stanley A.	(CA)	345
Optical disk systems	ABBOTT, George L.	(NY)	1
	HODGSON, Cynthia A.	(PA)	546
Optical disk technology	BOSS, Richard W.	(DC)	117
	PRICE, Joseph W.	(DC)	992
	REGAZZI, John J.	(NY)	1017
	ARJONA, Sandra K.	(PA)	31
	ALI, Syed N.	(BRN)	13
Optical disks & CD-ROM	TALLY, Roy D.	(MN)	1221
Optical disks, gateways	MARSHALL, Mary E.	(OH)	774
Optical disks in libraries	RASMUSSEN, Mary L.	(MN)	1009
Optical laser disk products	HANIFORD, K L.	(MO)	496
Optical video disk	GALL, Bert A.	(TN)	413
Video disk instructional design	CONNELL, William S.	(CA)	237

DISNEY

Disney history	SIGMAN, Paula M.	(CA)	1137

DISORDERS

Communication disorders	ZAHARKO, Nancy W.	(MD)	1385
Information on genetic disorders	HOLT, Suzy	(MT)	554

DISPLAYS (See also Exhibits)

Display & programming	MCCAFFERY, Laurabelle	(IN)	793
Displaying books	SALPETER, Janice L.	(NY)	1077
Displays	SHEPHERD, Gay W.	(NC)	1127
Displays & exhibitions	HUTCHINSON, Beck	(FL)	579
Displays & exhibits	KEMP, Henrietta J.	(IA)	639
	THOMPSON, Jane K.	(VT)	1240
Displays & public relations	COONEY, Mata M.	(NV)	242
Displays for humanities	CLOHESSY, Antoinette M.	(CO)	223
Exhibit displays	RUSSELL, Marilyn L.	(KS)	1069

DISPLAYS (Cont'd)

Library display systems design	RIBNICKY, Karen F.	(CT)	1026
Public relations, exhibits, displays	DAANE, Jeanette K.	(AZ)	269
Publicity & displays	PIKE, Nancy M.	(FL)	973
Writing & display publicity	BOYD, Ruth E.	(CO)	122

DISPOSITION

Appraisal & disposition	PACIFICO, Michele F.	(DC)	933
	PAUL, Karen D.	(DC)	949
Appraisal & records disposition	BRADSHER, James G.	(DC)	126
Records disposition	GORDON, Martin K.	(VA)	451

DISSEMINATION

Agricultural information dissemination	SINHA, Pramod K.	(IND)	1143
Dissemination of digital data	WILTSHIRE, Denise A.	(VA)	1354
Dissemination of federal information	BISHOP, Sarah G.	(DC)	99
Dissemination of information	MARTIN, Sandra D.	(KY)	778
	MINOR, Barbara A.	(NY)	846
Dissemination systems	SIMS, Edward N.	(KY)	1142
Gathering & disseminating statistics	CANTWELL, Mickey A.	(NY)	179
Gifted resources dissemination	WARNER, Wayne G.	(GA)	1305
Information dissemination	YU, Hsiao M.	(IA)	1384
	FISH, Paula H.	(NC)	380
Information dissemination, routing	SHALLEY, Doris P.	(PA)	1119
Selective dissemination of information	KRAFT, Gwen L.	(AK)	675
	MORTON, Dorothy J.	(DE)	870
	TINGLEY, Dianne E.	(MD)	1246
	SHILL, Harold B.	(WV)	1130
	MACIAS-CHAPULA, Cesar A.	(MEX)	755

DISSERTATIONS

Bibliography of doctoral dissertations	SHULMAN, Frank J.	(MD)	1133
Dissertation database	WILSON, Amy S.	(MI)	1349

DISTANCE

Distance education	KOLB, Audrey P.	(AK)	669
	MING, Marilyn	(AB)	846
	VOLPATTI, Rechilde	(ON)	1288
	GALLER, Anne M.	(PQ)	414
Distance education library services	SLADE, Alexander L.	(BC)	1147
	AFFLECK, Delburt E.	(SK)	7
Distance learning	BIRMINGHAM, Frank R.	(MN)	98
Library services to distance education	BUDNICK, Carol	(MB)	155
Telecommunications, distance learning	SCHABERT, Daniel R.	(NY)	1088

DISTRIBUTION

Audiovisual distributor	HEMPEL, Gordon J.	(IL)	525
Book distribution	GERARD, James W.	(VT)	428
Book distribution systems	KOLTAY, Emery I.	(NY)	670
CD-ROM reader distribution	LESLIE, Nathan	(ON)	718
	LOWRY, Douglas B.	(ON)	745
	LOWRY, John D.	(ON)	745
Database distribution	SPALA, Jeanne L.	(CA)	1170
Database management & distribution	SIMON, Ralph C.	(IN)	1141
Distributed information systems	DEERWESTER, Scott C.	(IL)	287
Distributing educational films	KONICEK, Karen B.	(MA)	670
Distribution audiovisuals	SOLIN, Myron	(NY)	1166
Distribution in computer industry	MONOSSON, Adolf S.	(MA)	855
Distribution of educational films	HARTLEY, Elda E.	(CT)	508
Distribution of public domain software	SHAW, Ben B.	(TX)	1123
Distributor	YANNOTTA, Peter J.	(NJ)	1377
Document distribution & control	SANDERS, Mary C.	(NJ)	1080
Electronic database & distribution	CHICHESTER, Gerald C.	(CT)	208
Film & television distribution	KLUGHERZ, Dan	(NY)	662
Film & video distribution	BLANK, Les	(CA)	104
	WHITE, Matthew H.	(IL)	1331
	CABEZAS, Sue A.	(MA)	170
Film distribution	MONDELL, Cynthia B.	(TX)	854
Information distribution	SMITH, Denis J.	(IL)	1154
	KEON, Edward F.	(NJ)	643
International distribution	SMITH, Richard A.	(CA)	1159
Laser printing distribution	CONTESSA, William B.	(NY)	239
Local distribution of database systems	NASATIR, Marilyn	(CA)	888

DISTRIBUTION (Cont'd)

Machine-readable cataloging distribution	TARR, Susan M.	(DC)	1224
Overseas online distributors	YAMAKAWA, Takashi	(JAP)	1376
Poetry video production & distribution	LESNIAK, Rose	(NY)	718
Publications distribution management	LEONARD, Lawrence E.	(DC)	716
Publishing & book distribution	GSTALDER, Herbert W.	(NY)	475
Researching film distributors	SHABERLY, Leanna J.	(AZ)	1118
Selective distribution of information	BARTLETT, Vernell W.	(MN)	61
Small press distribution	LEISNER, Anthony B.	(IL)	714
Software manual distribution	BYERS, Cathy L.	(ON)	168
Standards organization & distribution	RICE, Gerald W.	(NH)	1027
State document distribution	MITCHELL, Micheal L.	(AK)	849
Statewide audiovisual distribution	NAUGLE, Gretchen R.	(NE)	889
Television production & distribution	WILSON, George N.	(TX)	1351

DISTRICT

Catalog district library materials	EMERICK, John L.	(PA)	347
District association annuals	YEISER, Doris B.	(KY)	1379
District libraries	ANDERSON, Karen T.	(IL)	23
	FEATHER, Pamela P.	(IL)	367
District library organz & supervision	DICK, Norma P.	(CA)	300
District media management	POOLE, Rebecca S.	(CO)	983
District media services	WURBS, Sue A.	(WY)	1374
District school library administration	CURRIE, Bertha B.	(NS)	266
District, school library evaluation	LEVEILLEE, Louis R.	(RI)	719
District-wide coordination, supervision	VAUGHAN, Janet E.	(MN)	1279
Public relations, school district	NIEMEYER, Karen K.	(IN)	903
School district consulting	HIRABAYASHI, Joanne	(CA)	543
School district coordinator	GILBERT, Betty H.	(AZ)	433
School district information systems	SLYGH, Gyneth	(WI)	1151
School district libraries	SZEMRAJ, Edward R.	(NY)	1218
School district library administration	APPEL MOSESOF, Rhoda S.	(NJ)	29
School district library services	BAGAN, Beverly S.	(VA)	45
School district library supervision	BURGESON, Clair D.	(NY)	159
School district media centers	MOHN, Kari	(AK)	852
School district media services	STAAS, Gretchen L.	(TX)	1177

DIVISION (See also Department)

Children's division	VAN HOORN, Audra G.	(IL)	1275
Division level library coordination	MCLEOD, Karen E.	(SK)	814
Divisional administration	TAGGART, William R.	(BC)	1220

DOBIS

Library systems DOBIS	DEEMER, Selden S.	(GA)	286
Working online on DOBIS	DAWE, Heather L.	(ON)	282

DOCENTS

Training art educators & docents	GENSHAFT, Carole M.	(OH)	427

DOCKET

Docket, conflict administration	KERN, Sharon P.	(IA)	643

DOCTORAL

Bibliography of doctoral dissertations	SHULMAN, Frank J.	(MD)	1133

DOCUMENTARY

Documentary editing	ZBORAY, Ronald J.	(CA)	1386
	DOWD, Mary J.	(DC)	315
	EPPARD, Philip B.	(MA)	351
	FRYE, Dorothy T.	(MI)	407
	VAN HORNE, John C.	(PA)	1275
	MONTEIRO, George	(RI)	856
	CRIST, Lynda L.	(TX)	259
Documentary films	SPEARS, Ross	(TN)	1172
Documentary films & videotapes	RICHTER, Robert	(NY)	1031
Documentary languages	JANIK, Sophie	(PQ)	593
Documentary production training	WILLIAMS, Carroll W.	(NM)	1342
Historical documentary editing	SCHULZ, Constance B.	(SC)	1102
Preservation of documentary materials	YOUNG, Julia M.	(MS)	1382

DOCUMENTATION

Art & architectural documtn sources	ROBERTSON, Jack	(MD)	1042
Art documentation	WATIER-LALONDE, Chantal	(PQ)	1309
Art documentation & cataloging	IBACH, Marilyn	(DC)	581
Audiovisual documentation	DUCHESNEAU, Pierre	(PQ)	322
Computer documentation	SAUNDERS, Vinette A.	(DC)	1085
	RIDER, Philip R.	(IL)	1032
	MCGEE, Ruby T.	(MA)	805
Computerized documentation	ALLEN, Nancy S.	(MA)	15
Database design & documentation	MACLEOD, Valerie R.	(KY)	757
Database development & documentation	GRIPPO, Christopher F.	(WA)	471
Database documentation & promotion ideas	MILLER, Carmen L.	(WA)	836
Database documentation chapter writing	MARANGONI, Eugene G.	(CA)	768
Database documentation design	PUGH, W J.	(MD)	997
Database training & documentation	ACKERMAN, Katherine K.	(MI)	4
Documentation	KATZ, Jeffrey P.	(CA)	630
	LONGO, Margaret K.	(CA)	740
	MORISSEAU, Anne L.	(MD)	865
	CARSON, M S.	(PA)	188
	FREIVALDS, Dace I.	(PA)	402
	MORGAN, Bradford A.	(SD)	863
	MCCANN, Charlotte P.	(TX)	793
	TETSUYA, Inoue	(JAP)	1233
Documentation acquisition	ARROWOOD, Nina R.	(NJ)	35
Documentation analysis & coordination	HACKMAN, Larry J.	(NY)	481
Documentation & research	LEFFALL, Dolores C.	(DC)	712
Documentation maintenance	JADWIN, Rochelle J.	(CA)	591
Documentation of online systems	SOPELAK, Mary J.	(NY)	1168
Documentation production	FITZGERALD, Ardra F.	(CA)	382
Documentation writer	EPPES, William D.	(NY)	351
Filing source code documentation	BOZE, Lucy G.	(GA)	124
Genealogical research & documentation	PARKER, Mary A.	(SC)	942
Historical documentation	BAUMSTEIN, Paschal M.	(NC)	66
IBM Documentation of SLSS	KEALEY, Catherine M.	(ON)	632
Information & documentation center mgmt	MOUREAU, Magdeleine	(FRN)	873
Internal documentation	MCGEE, Ruby T.	(MA)	805
Intl govt organizations' documentation	WILLIAMSON, Linda E.	(IL)	1347
Library documentation	MAYFIELD, Betty L.	(BC)	790
Military documentation	KUHL, Danuta	(VA)	682
Navy documentation	MCCLAIN, Deborah C.	(VA)	795
Online documentation	RADUAZO, Dorothy M.	(DC)	1002
Online software documentation	GIRILL, T R.	(CA)	438
Patent documentation	JONES, Michael W.	(VA)	614
Personal documentation	YAMAZAKI, Hisamichi	(JAP)	1377
Quilt research & documentation, indexing	PARKER, Mary A.	(SC)	942
Records & documentation management	GRITZKA, Gerda M.	(PQ)	471
Records & info development & documtn	GRAHAM, Su D.	(CO)	456
Records documentation systems	HAMILTON, Meredith L.	(IL)	492
Social economics documentation	VAN GARSSE, Yvan	(BEL)	1275
Software documentation	CONNELL, Christopher J.	(OH)	237
System documentation	PETTOLINA, Anthony M.	(NY)	965
Technical documentation	SPINKS, Paul	(CA)	1175
	QUINN, Candy L.	(CO)	1000
	SCOTT, Mona L.	(VA)	1107
	REILLY, Brian O.	(ON)	1020
Technical writing, software documtn	GREENE, Nancy S.	(PA)	464
Terminological documentation	RICHER, Suzanne	(ON)	1030
Training & documentation	ANDREWS, Chris C.	(CT)	26
	ANDERSON, Thomas G.	(GA)	25
	ECKERSON, Gale E.	(MA)	334
	SARAIDARIDIS, Susan B.	(MA)	1082
	WUNDERLICH, Clifford S.	(MA)	1374
	BOBKA, Marlene S.	(MD)	108
	CHAPMAN, Janet L.	(NJ)	202
	MLYNAR, Mary	(OH)	850
Training & user documentation	DIXON, Edith M.	(WI)	306
Training, development, & documentation	KAPLAN, Robin	(CA)	626
Training documentation	HIRONS, Jean L.	(DC)	543
	GAROOGIAN, Rhoda	(NY)	420

DOCUMENTATION (Cont'd)

Urban history documentation	KELLER, William B.	(DC)	636
User documentation & training	DIENER, Carol W.	(MD)	302
User training & documentation	GREEN-MALONEY, Nancy	(CA)	465
Writing documentation	ROTH, Alison C.	(CT)	1059
Writing of user documentation	WHITMAN, Mary L.	(PA)	1333
Written & audiovisual documentation	MARCHAND, Jacques	(PQ)	768

DOCUMENTS (See also Records)

Arkansas-related documents & books	FERGUSON, John L.	(AR)	372
Automatic document indexing	SPANGLER, Bruce	(CO)	1171
Biomedical comms & documents delivery	LETT, Rosalind K.	(GA)	719
British & Canadian documents	VOGEL, Jane G.	(NC)	1286
California documents	PERITORE, Laura D.	(CA)	958
Canadian corporate documents	GRAY, Sandra A.	(ON)	460
Canadian governmental documents	RUSSELL, Moira	(ON)	1069
Cataloging Canadian government documents	TURNER, Sharon	(ON)	1265
Cataloging government documents	MILLER, Barbara K.	(NY)	835
	BLANKENBURG, Julie J.	(WI)	104
Cataloging monographs, maps & documents	CAHILL, Colleen R.	(PA)	171
Cataloging New Jersey documents	HARDGROVE, David J.	(NJ)	499
Cataloging old documents	BOECKMAN, Frances B.	(MS)	109
Cataloging photographs & documents	FROST, Debra R.	(CO)	406
Cataloging technical documents	PATTEN, Frederick W.	(CA)	947
Collect specific regulatory documents	HARDY, Kenneth J.	(AB)	501
Congressional document retrieval	MILLER, William S.	(DC)	843
Connecticut state documents	ENSEL, Ellen H.	(CT)	350
Corporate documents	POJE, Mary E.	(NY)	980
Corporate documents & reference	NOVICK, Ruth	(NY)	911
Document acquisitions	STEVENS, Marjorie	(MI)	1190
Document analysis	THACH, Phat V.	(PQ)	1233
Document analysis & generic coding	KNOERDEL, Joan E.	(MD)	665
Document control database	ZBORAY, Ronald J.	(CA)	1386
Document delivery	JOSEPHINE, Helen B.	(AZ)	617
	CARRIGAN, John L.	(CA)	186
	LEVY, Judith B.	(CA)	721
	WEBB, Ty	(CA)	1313
	CHANAUD, Jo P.	(CO)	199
	GREALY, Deborah J.	(CO)	461
	HOFFMAN, Ann M.	(CO)	547
	HARGRAVE, Charles W.	(DC)	501
	REYNOLDS, Dennis J.	(DC)	1025
	TAYLOR, Joan R.	(DC)	1227
	STOLZ, Marty R.	(ID)	1196
	FARRELL, Patricia H.	(IL)	365
	GREGORY, Melissa R.	(IL)	466
	MCHENRY, Renee E.	(IL)	808
	LISTON, Karen A.	(IN)	733
	BESANT, Larry X.	(KY)	91
	GASKINS, Betty	(KY)	421
	PARKER, Susan E.	(MA)	942
	BOBKA, Marlene S.	(MD)	108
	MANGIN, Julianne	(MD)	765
	BRYANT, Barton B.	(MI)	152
	REHKOP, Barbara L.	(MO)	1017
	NEAL, Michelle H.	(NC)	890
	PALO, Eric E.	(NC)	937
	CUNNIFFE, Charlene M.	(NH)	265
	ROSENSTEIN, Susan J.	(NJ)	1057
	BERGER, Mary C.	(NY)	85
	BURKEY, Lynne	(NY)	161
	FARAONE, Maria B.	(NY)	363
	NOGA, Susan D.	(NY)	907
	STRIFE, Mary L.	(NY)	1202
	BALDWIN, Eleanor M.	(OH)	51
	GRAHAM, John	(OK)	456
	CARLIN, Don	(TN)	182
	HURD, Douglas P.	(VA)	577
	WOLF, Richard E.	(VA)	1360
	WOLFE, Martha K.	(ON)	1361
	WADE, C A.	(PQ)	1290
Document delivery & editorial	MAXWELL, Christine Y.	(CA)	788
Document delivery & interlibrary loan	MEAHL, D D.	(MI)	819
	COURNOYER, Joanne	(ON)	251
Document delivery, interlibrary loan	ROLLINS, Stephen J.	(NM)	1051

DOCUMENTS (Cont'd)

Document delivery service	BUSTAMANTE, Corazon R.	(NY)	166
	HAAS, Elaine H.	(NY)	480
Document delivery services	IVES, Gary W.	(VA)	585
Document distribution & control	SANDERS, Mary C.	(NJ)	1080
Document handling & preparation	SWORA, Tamara	(DC)	1217
Document indexing	ROSENTHAL, Marylu C.	(MA)	1057
	GRIMM, Ann C.	(MI)	470
Document preparation for microfilming	CHACE, Myron B.	(DC)	196
Document preservation	PICKENS, Nancy C.	(KY)	970
Document production	DENNETT, Stephen C.	(CA)	292
Document, reprint, photocopy supply	KOSTENBAUDER, Scott	(NY)	673
Document retrieval	CHAMPANY, Barry W.	(CA)	198
	BOGART, Betty B.	(MA)	110
	CAIN, Susan H.	(MA)	171
	DLOTT, Nancy B.	(MA)	306
	RAUM, Tamar	(NY)	1010
	FELL, Sally B.	(OH)	370
	GOURLAY, Una M.	(TX)	454
	SCHRAEDER, Diana C.	(TX)	1099
Document retrieval & cataloging	ELAM, Kim A.	(AK)	341
Document retrieval & federal agencies	TURNER, Ellis S.	(MD)	1264
Document retrieval & interlibrary loan	FELDMAN, Eleanor C.	(MD)	369
Document retrieval systems	WRIGHT, John H.	(FL)	1371
Document searching	GRAF, Thomas H.	(DC)	456
Document selection	LAHR, Thomas F.	(VA)	688
Document storage & retrieval systems	BAGG, Thomas C.	(MD)	45
Documents	CROWE, Gloria J.	(AZ)	261
	WILLIAMS, Pamela D.	(FL)	1345
	CORRELL, Emily N.	(GA)	247
	LITTLEWOOD, John M.	(IL)	734
	WHICKER, Gene A.	(KY)	1329
	SCHLESINGER, Frances C.	(MA)	1094
	SIEGEL, Bette L.	(MA)	1136
	LOUP, Jean L.	(MI)	742
	MOODY, Carol L.	(MO)	857
	HUYGEN, Michaele L.	(MT)	580
	HUFFORD, Jon R.	(NY)	571
	BURNS-DUFFY, Mary A.	(PA)	163
	SMITH, Diane H.	(PA)	1154
	ALBRIGHT, Susie K.	(TX)	10
	CHANG, Robert H.	(TX)	201
	SCHWERBEL, Jeannette E.	(TX)	1105
	WEISS, Stephen C.	(UT)	1320
	COLLIER, Carol A.	(WY)	232
Documents & serials	AIDE, Kathryn S.	(AL)	8
Documents cataloging	BLACK, Bernice B.	(MS)	101
Documents delivery	GIEBEL, Thomas W.	(WI)	432
Documents librarian	RICHTER, John H.	(MI)	1031
Documents librarianship, automation	JAMISON, Carolyn C.	(PA)	593
Documents management	LAI, Dennis	(CA)	688
Documents reference	SHAABAN, Marian F.	(IN)	1118
	PARHAM, Kay B.	(OK)	940
Documents services management	WATSON, Paula D.	(IL)	1310
Documents specialist	CAGLE, Robert B.	(LA)	171
Electronic document handling systems	SPANGLER, Bruce	(CO)	1171
Engineering documents	BARRETT, Joyce C.	(NJ)	59
Federal & international state documents	BASEFSKY, Stuart M.	(NC)	62
Federal documents	KONOP, Bonnie M.	(FL)	670
	SHELDEN, Patricia R.	(HI)	1125
	NASON, Jennifer L.	(MA)	888
	HAUSMAN, Lisa M.	(MI)	513
	WATSON, Janice D.	(MO)	1309
	GARD, Betty A.	(ND)	417
	HAWLEY, George S.	(NJ)	514
	RAILSBACK, Beverly D.	(NJ)	1003
	HARRIS, Maureen	(SC)	505
	RUHLIN, Michele T.	(UT)	1066
	BROWN, David C.	(VA)	143
	LEASURE, Lois A.	(WV)	707
Federal documents depository	MCGINNESS, Mary B.	(PA)	806
Federal government documents	ADAMS, Leonard R.	(MA)	5
	FISCHER, Catherine S.	(MN)	379
Federal government documents reference	LINDSEY, Thomas K.	(TX)	730
Federal governments documents	CORCORAN, Nancy L.	(MN)	246

DOCUMENTS (Cont'd)

Foreign Documents

WESTFALL, Gloria D. . . (IN) 1327

General & government documents
reference

BALSARA, Aspi . . . . (NF) 53

Government & federal documents

MACK, Debora S. . . . . . . (GA) 756

Government document cataloging

MCKOWEN, Dorothy K. . (IN) 812

Government document
declassification

GATLING, James L. . . . . (AL) 422

Government document processing

HARTMAN, Anne M. . . . (NY) 508

Government document publications

DOUGLAS-BONNELL,
   Eileen . . . . (PQ) 314

Government documents

PIERCE, Linda I. . . . . . . (AK) 971
MCNAMARA, Jay . . . . . (AL) 816
PEARSON, Peter E. . . . . (AL) 953
WATSON, Linda S. . . . . (AL) 1309
WATTERS, Annette J. . . (AL) 1310
MORRISON, Margaret L. . (AR) 868
WOLD, Shelley T. . . . . . (AR) 1359
BRZOZOWSKI, Margery
   E. . . . . (AZ) 152
RAWAN, Atifa R. . . . . . . (AZ) 1010
VATHIS, Alma C. . . . . . . (AZ) 1279
DOBB, Linda S. . . . . (CA) 307
JACOBSEN, Lavonne . . . (CA) 590
JOHNSON, Linda B. . . . (CA) 607
JOHNSRUD, Thomas E. . (CA) 609
LEWANDOWSKI, Joseph
   J. . . . . (CA) 722
MARTINEZ, Barbara A. . (CA) 779
MAZUR, Victoria P. . . . . (CA) 791
MILFORD, Charles C. . . . (CA) 835
MOSER, Maxine M. . . . . (CA) 871
NELSON, Alice R. . . . . . (CA) 893
NICHOLS, Gail M. . . . . . (CA) 901
SEBO, Lorraine M. . . . . (CA) 1110
SHARP, Linda F. . . . . . . (CA) 1122
SPENCER, Patricia O. . . (CA) 1173
STEELMAN, Lucille A. . . (CA) 1184
TING, Eunice T. . . . . . . (CA) 1246
WELLS, Dorothy V. . . . . (CA) 1322
WILLIAMS, Leonette M. . (CA) 1344
FIELD, Oliver T. . . . . (CO) 375
JONES-EDDY, Julie . . . . (CO) 615
SCHMIDT, Fred C. . . . . . (CO) 1095
BARNES, Denise M. . . . . (CT) 57
SPURGEON, Kathy R. . . (CT) 1176
BEALL, Barbara A. . . . . . (DC) 68
CHURCHVILLE, Lida H. . (DC) 213
CROCKETT, Martha L. . . (DC) 259
FARINA, Robert A. . . . . . (DC) 363
JEMIOLA, Nancy E. . . . . (DC) 596
OAKS, Robert K. . . . . . . (DC) 913
UPDEGROVE, Robert A. (DC) 1269
ZICH, Joanne A. . . . . . . (DC) 1388
KNIGHT, Rebecca C. . . . (DE) 664
YOUNG, Kathryn A. . . . . (DE) 1382
HARRIS, Frank D. . . . . . (FL) 504
LITTON, Sally C. . . . . . . (FL) 734
CHRISTIAN, Gayle R. . . (GA) 211
MALCOLM, Carol L. . . . . (GA) 762
MCCANN, Jett C. . . . . . (GA) 794
WHEELER, Carol L. . . . . (GA) 1328
BUDREW, John . . . . (IA) 155
EMDE, Susan J. . . . . . . (IA) 347
GIAQUINTA, C J. . . . . . . (IA) 431
HUNTING, Susan K. . . . . (IA) 576
AUFDENKAMP, Joann . . (IL) 39
BENGTSON, Marjorie C. . (IL) 80
BURGH, Scott G. . . . . . . (IL) 159
CHEN, Robert P. . . . . . . (IL) 205
FRY, Roy H. . . . . (IL) 406
KLOCKENGA, Gary R. . . (IL) 662
LI, Dorothy W. . . . . (IL) 724
MULHERIN, William S. . . (IL) 876
NYBERG, Cheryl R. . . . . (IL) 912
ROYLE, Maryanne . . . . . (IL) 1063
SHERMAN, Sarah . . . . . (IL) 1128
YOUNG, Peter W. . . . . . (IL) 1383
CONRADS, Douglas L. . . (IN) 238
DICKMEYER, John N. . . (IN) 301

DOCUMENTS (Cont'd)

Government documents

GREMMELS, Gillian S. . . (IN) 467
HOLTERHOFF, Sarah G. (IN) 555
LYLE, Jack W. . . . . (IN) 751
MURDOCK, J L. . . . . . . (IN) 879
STAPLES, James A. . . . (IN) 1181
LUNG, Mon Y. . . . . (KS) 748
STEWART, Henry R. . . . (KS) 1192
MCFARLING, Patricia G. (KY) 805
SHEPHERD-SHLECHTER,
   Rae . . . . (KY) 1127
BALL, Dannie J. . . . . . . (LA) 52
BRADLEY, Jared W. . . . (LA) 126
FULLING, Richard W. . . . (LA) 409
HANKEL, Marilyn L. . . . . (LA) 496
HIMEL, Sandra M. . . . . . (LA) 542
KELLY, Judy M. . . . . . . (LA) 638
MAYEAUX, Thurlow M. . (LA) 789
NACHOD, Katherine B. . . (LA) 885
ROCHE, Alvin A. . . . . . . (LA) 1045
SHIFLETT, Orvin L. . . . . (LA) 1130
SHULL, Janice K. . . . . . (LA) 1133
ARCHAMBAUL, Christine (MA) 30
DRESLEY, Susan C. . . . (MA) 319
RANDALL, Kristie C. . . . (MA) 1006
RUTTER, Nancy R. . . . . (MA) 1070
ST. AUBIN, Kendra J. . . (MA) 1075
VAN BEEK, Susan . . . . (MA) 1272
JOHNSON, Richard K. . . (MD) 608
LEV, Yvonne T. . . . . (MD) 719
QUINN, Carol J. . . . . . . (MD) 1000
SULLIVAN, Carol W. . . . (MD) 1207
BOURGEOIS, Ann M. . . . (MI) 119
BROW, Judith A. . . . . . . (MI) 141
BUCKLEY, Francis J. . . . (MI) 154
BURINSKI, Walter W. . . . (MI) 160
BUXBAUM, Sharolyn . . . (MI) 168
CROSS, Jennie B. . . . . . (MI) 260
EVANS, Kathy J. . . . . . . (MI) 357
HEGEDUS, Mary E. . . . . (MI) 521
JERYAN, Christine B. . . . (MI) 600
MOUZON, Margaret W. . (MI) 874
SHIRLEY, David B. . . . . (MI) 1131
YERMAN, Roslyn F. . . . . (MI) 1380
YORK, Grace A. . . . . . . (MI) 1381
ANDERSON, E A. . . . . . (MN) 22
BAUM, Marsha L. . . . . . (MN) 66
JACOB, Rosamond T. . . (MN) 589
SANFORD, Carolyn C. . . (MN) 1081
BARNES, Everett W. . . . (MO) 57
COURT, Patricia . . . . . . (MO) 251
GELINNE, Michael S. . . . (MO) 426
HICKS, James M. . . . . . (MO) 537
HOCHSTETLER, Donald
   D. . . . . (MO) 545
MCKENZIE, Elizabeth M. (MO) 811
SCHRAMM, Betty V. . . . (MO) 1099
STEWART, Byron . . . . . (MO) 1192
WATTS, Anne . . . . (MO) 1310
GRASMICK, Brenda . . . . (MT) 458
ALLEN, Regina L. . . . . . (NC) 15
BOMARC, M D. . . . . . . (NC) 113
BUCHANAN, William E. . (NC) 153
CLARK, Marie L. . . . . . . (NC) 217
COHEN, Edward S. . . . . (NC) 228
COTTER, Michael G. . . . (NC) 250
DALTON, Lisa K. . . . . . . (NC) 271
MCGEACHY, John A. . . . (NC) 805
OSER, Anita K. . . . . (NC) 928
ROWLAND, Janet M. . . . (NC) 1062
SCOTT, Ralph L. . . . . . . (NC) 1108
WEBSTER, Deborah K. . (NC) 1314
WILLIAMS, Wiley J. . . . . (NC) 1347
BOONE, Nila J. . . . . (ND) 115
MUNDELL, Jacqueline L. (NE) 878
BERTHIAUME, Dennis A. (NH) 90
CHUNG, Hai C. . . . . (NJ) 213
GUSTAFSON, Ruth . . . . (NJ) 478
LATINI, Samuel A. . . . . . (NJ) 701

DOCUMENTS (Cont'd)
Government documents

MASILAMANI, Mary P. . (NJ) 780
MILLER, Mary A. ...... (NJ) 840
MILLER, Sarah J. ...... (NJ) 842
OTA, Leslie H. .... (NJ) 930
RAFFERTY, Stephen P. . (NJ) 1003
SWARTZ, Betty J. ..... (NJ) 1214
TUTWILER, Dorothea F. . (NJ) 1266
WANGGAARD, Janice H. (NJ) 1303
WILSON, Myoung C. .... (NJ) 1352
ADAMS, Dena R. ...... (NM) 4
MOUJAES, Sylva S. ..... (NV) 873
AXTMANN, Margaret M. (NY) 42
BURNETTE, Michaelyn .. (NY) 162
CHRISTENSON, Janet S. (NY) 211
CROWLEY, John V. ..... (NY) 261
DONG, Alvin L. .... (NY) 311
D'ONOFRIO, Erminio ... (NY) 311
EIDELMAN, Diane L. ... (NY) 340
FREIDES, Thelma ...... (NY) 401
GADBOIS, Frank W. .... (NY) 411
GUINN, Patricia L. .... (NY) 477
JENNINGS, Vincent .... (NY) 598
JUDD, Blanche E. ...... (NY) 618
KELLER, Katarina S. ... (NY) 635
LOWE, Mildred .... (NY) 744
MACOMBER, Nancy .... (NY) 758
MAY, Jonathan B. ..... (NY) 788
MULLEN, Marion L. .... (NY) 877
O'HARA, Frederic J. .... (NY) 919
SHIROMA, Susan G. ... (NY) 1131
SMITH, Barbara E. ..... (NY) 1152
SMITH, Karen F. ...... (NY) 1156
WILLET, Ruth J. ...... (NY) 1341
WOLFE, Theresa L. .... (NY) 1361
ADAMS, Liese A. ...... (OH) 5
BALDWIN, Julia F. ..... (OH) 51
BLOCK, Bernard A. .... (OH) 106
GOULD, Allison L. ..... (OH) 454
HORDUSKY, Clyde W. .. (OH) 559
JONES, Alice W. ...... (OH) 610
KRAMER, Sally J. ..... (OH) 675
WANSER, Jeffery C. .... (OH) 1303
WEILANT, Edward ..... (OH) 1317
KANE, Kathy .... (OK) 625
NASH, Helen B. .... (OK) 888
ROBBINS, Louise S. ... (OK) 1039
ROBERTSON, Retha M. . (OK) 1042
CHASE, Judith H. ..... (OR) 203
FISCHER, Karen ...... (OR) 379
GERITY, Louise P. ..... (OR) 428
HORAN, Patricia F. .... (OR) 559
RASH, David W. ...... (OR) 1009
COURTNEY, June M. ... (PA) 251
DUSZAK, Thomas J. .... (PA) 329
GARNER, Diane L. ..... (PA) 419
JACOBS, Mark D. ..... (PA) 589
MARVIN, Stephen G. ... (PA) 780
REGUEIRO, Judith E. ... (PA) 1017
SAXMAN, Susan E. .... (PA) 1086
ALEXANDER, Jacqueline
   P. .... (RI) 12
CHENICK, Michael J. ... (RI) 206
KINTNER, Susan B. .... (SC) 653
SMITH, Stephen C. ..... (SC) 1161
PICQUET, D C. ..... (TN) 971
ROMANS, Lawrence M. . (TN) 1052
SELF, George A. ...... (TN) 1113
WILLIAMS, Saundra W. . (TN) 1346
ALLEN, Virginia M. .... (TX) 16
BUCHWALD, Donald M. . (TX) 153
CARMACK, Norma J. .. (TX) 183
FORD, Barbara J. ...... (TX) 389
HENRICKS, Duane E. ... (TX) 529
HOLLAND, Mary M. .... (TX) 551
KENDRICK, Susan .... (TX) 640
MCDONALD, Brenda D. . (TX) 802
SAFLEY, Ellen D. ...... (TX) 1074
SCHMELZIE, Joan C. .... (TX) 1094

DOCUMENTS (Cont'd)
Government documents

TROST, Theresa K. .... (TX) 1258
LYMAN, Lovisa .... (UT) 751
CIPRIANI, Debra A. .... (VA) 215
COLLINS, Mitzi L. ..... (VA) 233
DECAMPS, Alice L. .... (VA) 285
LONG, Elizabeth T. ...... (VA) 739
MCGINN, Ellen T. ...... (VA) 806
OWEN, Karen V. ...... (VA) 931
PALMER, Forrest C. ..... (VA) 936
THOMPSON, Connie B. . (VA) 1239
WOODWARD, Elaine H. . (VA) 1368
CHANG, Henry C. ..... (VI) 200
RAUM, Hans L. .... (VT) 1010
BURSON, Scott F. ..... (WA) 163
VILLAR, Susanne P. ..... (WA) 1284
VYHNANEK, Louis ..... (WA) 1290
YEH, Thomas Y. .... (WA) 1379
BOLL, John J. .... (WI) 112
JOHNSON, Denise J. .... (WI) 603
KRUEGER, Gerald J. .... (WI) 680
MCGOWAN, Sarah M. .. (WI) 807
RINGER, Susan G. ..... (WI) 1035
SECHREST, Sandra L. .. (WI) 1110
WESTON, Karen A. ..... (WI) 1327
COOPER, Candace S. . . (WV) 242
EMERSON, Tamsen L. .. (WY) 347
KELNER, Gregory H. ... (BC) 638
COLSON, Judith K. ..... (NB) 234
MCNALLY, Brian D. ..... (NB) 815
COLBORNE, Michael B. . (NS) 230
DUHAMEL, Marie .... (ON) 324
GILLHAM, Virginia A. ... (ON) 436
GOLTZ, Eileen A. ...... (ON) 447
JARVI, Edith T. .... (ON) 594
MOON, Jeffrey D. ...... (ON) 857
O'NEILL, Louise N. ...... (ON) 924
QUIXLEY, James V. .... (ON) 1001
ROURKE, Lorna E. ..... (ON) 1061
VAN GARSSE, Yvan ... (BEL) 1275

Government documents acquisitions — MARSHALL, Marion B. ... (DC) 774
Government documents & maps — SHANNON, Michael O. .. (NY) 1120
Government documents & maps reference — WALKER, Barbara J. ... (GA) 1295
Government documents & patents — GREALY, Deborah J. ... (CO) 461
Government documents & publications —
    SINGH, Swarn L. ...... (KS) 1143
    HENSON, Stephen ...... (LA) 530
    WALSH, Jim ..... (MA) 1299
Government documents cataloging — MARSHALL, Marion B. ... (DC) 774
Government documents collection mgmt — MCSWEENEY, Josephine (NY) 818
Government documents, contract mgmt — LAKSHMAN, Malathi K. . (MD) 689
Government documents database — MILLER, Katherine J. .... (ON) 839
Government documents, federal — JOHNSON, Dorothy A. .. (MA) 603
Government documents librarian — KOEPP, Donna P. ..... (KS) 668
Government documents librarianship — MILLER, Veronica E. .... (VI) 843
Government documents management — PONNAPPA, Biddanda P. (TN) 982
Government documents, publications, info — WILLIAMSON, Linda E. . (IL) 1347
Government documents reference —
    WEATHERLY, Cynthia D. (AL) 1312
    COONIN, Bryna R. ...... (GA) 242
    CAIN, Charlene C. ..... (LA) 171
    SUDDUTH, William E. .. (MA) 1206
Governmental documents — THAKER, Virbala M. .... (CA) 1234
Governments documents —
    BRENNER, Willis F. .... (AR) 133
    GOLDMAN, Ava R. ..... (FL) 445
Indexing company documents — PETRY, Robyn E. ...... (IL) 965
Institutional documents & data — GOODMAN, L D. ...... (CA) 449
Intergovernmental organization documents — WESTFALL, Gloria D. ... (IN) 1327
Interlibrary loan & document delivery —
    STATOM, Susan T. ..... (GA) 1183
    DITXLER, Carol J. ..... (MD) 306
    REID, Valerie L. .... (MI) 1019
Interlibrary loan document delivery —
    MCFARLAND, Mary A. .. (IL) 805
    MORRISON, Carol J. ... (IL) 868
International & foreign documents — KAGAN, Alfred .... (CT) 621
International document delivery — GROSSMANN, Pierre .. (BRA) 473

DOCUMENTS (Cont'd)

International documents	SCHAAF, Robert W. . . .	(DC)	1088
	KOHLER, Carolyn W. . . .	(IA)	668
International government documents	FETZER, Mary K.	(NJ)	374
Intl intergovernmental documents	MOREHEAD, Joe	(NY)	863
International organization documents	SHAABAN, Marian F. . . .	(IN)	1118
Law reference, government documents	KAUL, Kanhya L.	(MI)	631
Legislative assembly documents	O'KEEFE, Kevin T.	(NT)	919
Legislative documents	STALLARD, Thomas W. .	(CA)	1179
Library & administrative documents	MEUNIER, Pierre	(PQ)	829
Local documents	HILBURGER, Mary J. . . .	(IL)	538
Local government documents	CASTONGUAY, Russell .	(CA)	194
	CORCORAN, Nancy L. . .	(MN)	246
Louisiana state documents	MARSHALL, Susan O. . .	(LA)	775
Manuscripts & holographic documents	LEVITT, Martin L.	(PA)	721
Maps & government documents	SCHORR, Alan E.	(AK)	1099
Maps, documents & microforms	DONLEY, Leigh M.	(CA)	311
Medical documents & databases	NAGY, Cecile	(PQ)	886
Medical government documents	WHITE, Anne E.	(IL)	1330
Military documents	KING, Elizabeth	(FL)	650
	PIENITZ, Eleanor	(NY)	971
Moving image documents	O'CONNOR, Brian C. . . .	(CA)	915
Municipal document management	SCHLIPF, Frederick A. . .	(IL)	1094
Municipal documents	KRITEMEYER, Ann C. . . .	(CT)	679
	BENIGNO, Linda J.	(IL)	80
	BRENNAN, Ellen	(PA)	132
National & international document supply	LINE, Maurice B.	(ENG)	730
New York state & local documents	PANDIT, Jyoti P.	(NY)	937
New York state documents	ESPOSITO, Michael A. . .	(NY)	354
Official documents	MURRAY-LACHAPELLE, Rosemary F.	(ON)	882
Ohio documents	RYAN, Richard A.	(OH)	1071
Paper document conservation	MOORE, Harold H.	(GA)	859
Pennsylvania state documents	SWAN, Christine H.	(PA)	1213
Photographs as historical documents	CHRISTOPHER, Paul . . .	(CA)	212
Proprietary documents organization	LAVIN, Margaret A.	(NJ)	703
Public documents	PARROTT, Margaret S. . .	(NC)	944
Reference & documents	CRETINI, Blanche M. . . .	(LA)	258
Repair & conservation of documents	JORDAN, Ervin L.	(VA)	616
Science agency government documents	CURTIS, Susan C.	(GA)	267
Scientific documents	GIBSON, Joanne	(CA)	432
Serials & government documents	PANDA, Rosamond E. . .	(MD)	937
Spanish documents	DRIVER, Marjorie G.	(GU)	320
State & federal documents	HOM, Sharon L.	(TN)	555
State & local documents	LUNDQUIST, David A. . .	(CA)	748
	SWAFFORD, William M. .	(CA)	1212
	ESKOZ, Patricia A.	(CO)	354
	LEVY, Suzanne S.	(VA)	722
State & local government documents	HAMMOND, Louise H. . .	(IL)	494
State document cataloging	MITCHELL, Micheal L. . .	(AK)	849
	MITCHAM, Janet C.	(AR)	848
State document distribution	MITCHELL, Micheal L. . .	(AK)	849
State documents	RIESBERG, Eunice L. . . .	(IA)	1033
	SWANSON, Byron E. . . .	(IN)	1213
	YOUNG, Noraleen A. . . .	(IN)	1382
	MOORE, Grace G.	(LA)	859
	NASON, Jennifer L.	(MA)	888
	SANDERS, Lou H.	(MS)	1080
	QUINN, Karen H.	(RI)	1000
	WILLIAMS, Saundra W. .	(TN)	1346
	KELLOUGH, Jean L.	(TX)	637
	FOSTER, Leslie A.	(WI)	392
State government documents	ADAMS, Leonard R.	(MA)	5
State of Florida documents	KONOP, Bonnie M.	(FL)	670
Storage & retrieval of records & docums	RAC-FEDORIJCZUK, Karola C.	(PA)	1001
Technical & engineering documents	SCHULTZ, Arnold J.	(MN)	1101
Technical processing, govt documents	ADAMS, Leonard R.	(MA)	5
Technical report document retrieval	WHITE, Chandlee	(MA)	1330
United Nations documents	SHELDEN, Patricia R. . . .	(HI)	1125
	BOYCE, Barbara S.	(MA)	122
	MCDONALD, Ellen J. . . .	(MA)	802
	PANDIT, Jyoti P.	(NY)	937
United States & international documents	ELAM, Joice B.	(GA)	341

DOCUMENTS (Cont'd)

US documents	SACHSE, Gladys M.	(AR)	1073
	FINLEY, Mary M.	(CA)	378
	WESTFALL, Gloria D. . . .	(IN)	1327
	HANSSEN, Nancy E. . . .	(MA)	499
	COBB, Sylvia R.	(OK)	225
United States documents reference	SPAHR, Janet E.	(VA)	1170
United States federal documents	HAUSE, Aaron H.	(MT)	512
United States government & documents	MORENO, Rafael	(PA)	863
US government documents	IRBY, Geraldine A.	(AL)	583
	COSTELLO, M R.	(CA)	249
	SANSOBRINO, Jean C. .	(CA)	1081
	HURLEY, Trudy M.	(CT)	577
	MELNICOVE, Annette R. .	(FL)	823
	COLLINS, Patrick	(GA)	233
	WAI, Lily C.	(ID)	1292
	BECK, Mary C.	(MI)	71
	ESSLINGER, Guenter W.	(MN)	355
	LAUGHLIN, Cheryl H. . . .	(MS)	703
	KENDRA, William E.	(NE)	640
	BEAUDRIE, Ronald A. . .	(NY)	70
	FELLER, Judith M.	(PA)	370
	WRIGHT, Barbara C.	(PA)	1370
	TINSMAN, William A. . . .	(TX)	1246
	DAVIS, Wylma P.	(VA)	281
	HAYS, Peggy W.	(VA)	517
US government documents, business	TAYLOR, William R.	(TN)	1229
University of Florida documents	KONOP, Bonnie M.	(FL)	670

DOMINICAN

Dominican literature	NITZ, Andrew M.	(DC)	905

DONOR

Donor prospect research	ANDERSON, Clifford D. .	(CA)	22

DOOLITTLE

Hilda Doolittle	SILVERSTEIN, Louis H. .	(CT)	1139

DRAMA (See also Theater)

Art, music, & drama	ALTER, Forrest H.	(MI)	18
Contemporary American drama	DACE, Tish	(MA)	269
Contemporary English drama	DACE, Tish	(MA)	269
Drama	MCCOY, Evelyn G.	(AR)	799
Drama & film	CIOPPA, Lawrence	(NY)	214
Dramatic literature	OGDEN, Dunbar H.	(CA)	918
Language of dramatic production	TRAPIDO, Joel	(HI)	1254
Storytelling & drama	ROSS, Theodosia B.	(GA)	1059
Theatre & drama	SHAPIRO, Barbara S. . . .	(NY)	1121

DRAWINGS

Architectural drawings	STERN, Teena B.	(CA)	1189
	LAVERTY, Bruce	(PA)	703
	DUNNIGAN, Mary C. . . .	(VA)	327
	ENGEMAN, Richard H. . .	(WA)	349
Architectural records & drawings	BRUNK, Thomas W.	(MI)	150
Manuscripts & drawings	HAIL, Christopher	(MA)	484
Paintings, drawings, water colors	MELTON, Howard E. . . .	(OK)	823

DROLS

DROLS database management	GALLERY, M C.	(CA)	414

DRUGS (See also Alcohol, Pharmaceutical, Substance)

Alcohol & drug abuse	KING, Karen P.	(SK)	651
Alcohol & drug use & abuse	MITCHELL, Andrea L. . .	(CA)	848
Alcohol & drugs	REIMER, Bette J.	(AB)	1020
Drug abuse	MITCHELL, Andrea L. . .	(CA)	848
Drug abuse bibliography	ANDREWS, Theodora A. .	(IN)	27
Drug abuse training projects	CNATTINGIUS, Claes M.	(SWE)	224
Drug databases	HANES, Alice H.	(MD)	495

DRUGS (Cont'd)

Drug information   WALSH, Kathryn A. . . . . (CT) 1299

CARPENTER, Vincent P. (NC) 185

LUSTIG, Joanne . . . . (NJ) 750

SCARFIA, Angela M. . . . (NY) 1087

STARR, Lea K. . . . . (AB) 1182

Drug information interchange standards   FASSETT, William E. . . . (WA) 366

Drug information sources   SEWELL, Winifred . . . . . (MD) 1118

Drug research   SUPEAU, Cynthia . . . . . . (CT) 1210

Sex, drugs, & teenagers   LONG, Gary . . . . (LA) 739

DTIC

DTIC database searching   MAGUIRE, Shirley E. . . . (MI) 760

DTIC liaison   GALLERY, M C. . . . . (CA) 414

NASA & DTIC online databases   GENTRY, Susan K. . . . . (CA) 427

DUTCH

Dutch Jewish history   CAHEN, Joel J. . . . . (NET) 171

Dutch studies   SPOHRER, James H. . . . (CA) 1175

Special Dutch heritage center   SLIEKERS, Hendrik . . . . (IL) 1149

DYNAMICS

Group dynamics in libraries   SMITH, Ann M. . . . . (MA) 1152

Information dynamics   ONONOGBO, Raphael U. (NGR) 924

Organizational dynamics & communication   CRETH, Sheila D. . . . . . (IA) 258

DYSLEXIC

Dyslexic adult students   THOMPSON, Jane K. . . . (VT) 1240

EARLY (See also Antiquarian, Incunabula, Old, Out-of-Print, Preschool, Rare, Toddlers)

Early American history & culture   MONTGOMERY, Michael S. . . . . (NJ) 856

Early American history 1492-1800 ADAMS, Thomas R. . . . . (RI) 6

Early Arab numismatics   MOLINE, Judi A. . . . . . . (MD) 853

Early California history   SANTOS, Bob . . . . (CA) 1082

Early childhood & parenting   SCHWARZLOSE, Sally F. (IL) 1105

Early childhood children's services LINVILLE, Marcia L. . . . . (HI) 731

Early childhood education   HAWLEY, Marsha S. . . . (IL) 514

HAMMOND, Mary W. . . . (WA) 494

Early childhood learning   WRIGHT-HESS, Anne H. (NY) 1373

Early childhood literature   KOEPP, Sara H. . . . . . . (IA) 668

Early childhood program services SCHWABACHER, Sara A. (NY) 1104

Early childhood programming   CLARK, Janet L. . . . . . . (NV) 217

Early childhood resources   HERSCOVITCH, Pearl . . (AB) 533

Early illustrated books & bindings WITTEN, Laurence . . . . . (CT) 1358

Early maps   COLE, Maud D. . . . . (NY) 231

Early music & dance   COLDWELL, Charles P. . (WA) 230

Early phonograph recordings, 1890-1930   RIGGS, Quentin T. . . . . . (CA) 1034

Early popular songs   RIGGS, Quentin T. . . . . . (CA) 1034

Early printed books   NORTON, Margaret W. . (IL) 910

Early printed books of 1450-1600 WITTEN, Laurence . . . . . (CT) 1358

Early printing & publishing   GONIWIECHA, Mark C. . (AK) 447

Early public library development   MCNAMARA, Shelley G. (ME) 816

Early recording artists, 1890-1930 RIGGS, Quentin T. . . . . . (CA) 1034

Early training for online searching MINEMIER, Betty M. . . . (NY) 845

Jazz, early to late 1940's   BROWNE, J P. . . . . (CA) 148

Picture books, early childhood   GREENE, Ellin P. . . . . . (NJ) 464

Preschool & early childhood programs REZNICK, Evi P. . . . . . . (GA) 1025

Scientific & technical early periodicals KRONICK, David A. . . . . (TX) 679

EARTH (See also Geology)

Earth & environmental sciences   RUDD, Janet K. . . . . (CA) 1065

Earth science   NEWMAN, Linda P. . . . . (NV) 899

Earth science databases   WEST, Barbara F. . . . . . (TX) 1326

Earth science, geology & petroleum DEPETRO, Thomas G. . . (TX) 293

Earth science information   ALBRIGHT, Donald A. . . (NT) 10

Earth science reference   MURRAY, James T. . . . . (OK) 882

EARTH (Cont'd)

Earth sciences   KRICK, Mary . . . . (IL) 678

HEISER, Lois . . . . (IN) 523

MERRYMAN, Margaret M. (VA) 827

HAU, Edward T. . . . . (AB) 512

Earth sciences bibliography   DERKSEN, Charlotte R. . (CA) 294

Earth sciences reference & research SORROUGH, Gail L. . . . (CA) 1169

Physical sciences, earth sciences VIERICH, Richard W. . . . (CA) 1284

EARTHQUAKE

Earthquake engineering   WEBSTER, James K. . . . (NY) 1314

Earthquake engineering reference service   SVIHRA, S J. . . . . (CA) 1212

EAST

East Asia   LEE, Thomas H. . . . . . . (IN) 711

East Asian collections   SIGGINS, Jack A. . . . . . (CT) 1137

East Asian languages   HSIEH, Cynthia C. . . . . . (IL) 567

East Asian librarianship   WEI, Karen T. . . . . (IL) 1316

SHULMAN, Frank J. . . . . (MD) 1133

East Asian library administration   KANEKO, Hideo . . . . . . (CT) 625

East Asian library automation   WEI, Karen T. . . . . (IL) 1316

East Asian library services   WU, Ai H. . . . . (AZ) 1373

East Asian materials   KLEIN, Kenneth D. . . . . (CA) 659

East Asian studies   KIM, Joy H. . . . . (CA) 649

East Europe & Middle East studies PINSON, Mark . . . . (MA) 975

East European studies   POVSIC, Frances F. . . . . (OH) 987

ARTHUR, Donald B. . . . . (TX) 35

Eastern Europe & Soviet Union   TOTH, George S. . . . . . (DC) 1252

Eastern European languages   KRUKONIS, Perkunas P. (MA) 680

History & East Asian studies bibl   BERGER, Kenneth W. . . (NC) 85

Research on East Germany   HUETING, Gail P. . . . . . (IL) 570

Russian & East European bibliography   BEAVEN, Miranda J. . . . (MN) 71

Russian & East European studies ROBERTSON, Howard W. (OR) 1042

Slavic & East European   CHOLDIN, Marianna T. . . (IL) 210

Slavic & East European librarianship LEICH, Harold M. . . . . . . (DC) 713

ECCLESIASTICAL (See also Church)

Ecclesiastical law   HORWITZ, Steven F. . . . (CA) 561

ECOLOGY (See also Environment, Radioecology)

Ecological research   PRESBY, Richard A. . . . . (CA) 990

Ecology   HAMMARSKJOLD, Carolyn A. . . . . (MI) 493

Geolinguistic ecology   SHEARER, Kenneth D. . . (NC) 1124

Home economics & human ecology MACKEY, Neosha A. . . . (MO) 756

ECONOMETRICS (See also Economics)

Econometric modeling   O'REILLY, Daniel F. . . . . (MA) 925

Econometrics teaching   JAIN, Nem C. . . . . (MA) 592

Economics & econometrics   BROWN, George F. . . . . (MA) 144

ECONOMICS (See also Econometrics, Income, Market, Socioeconomic, Technoeconomics)

Agricultural economics   CASEMENT, Susan D. . . (CA) 192

SCHULTZ, Susan . . . . . . (IL) 1102

LETNES, Louise M. . . . . (MN) 718

Agricultural economics reference   PERMAN, Karen A. . . . . (IL) 959

REEDMAN, M R. . . . . (MB) 1015

Applied economics   LETNES, Louise M. . . . . (MN) 718

Banking, economics & business   NAULTY, Deborah M. . . . (PA) 889

Business & economic development CASTLEBERRY, Crata L. (AR) 194

Business & economic information services   CARROLL, Hardy . . . . . . (MI) 187

Business & economic materials   MARKHAM, Scott C. . . . (MN) 771

Business & economic research   DUFFY, Brenda F. . . . . . (DC) 324

Business & economics   HUMPHREYS, Nancy K. (CA) 574

VUGRINECZ, Anna E. . . (CA) 1289

WOLFF, Stephen G. . . . . (DE) 1361

GEROW, Sandra F. . . . . (IL) 429

KLEIN, Regina D. . . . . . . (MO) 659

OTA, Leslie H. . . . . (NJ) 930

RANSOM, Cynthia E. . . . (NY) 1007

ECONOMICS (Cont'd)

Business & economics

	NASRALLAH, Wahib T. .	(OH)	888
	JONES-TRENT, Bernice R.	(VA)	616
Business & economics databases	MCKAY, Peter Z.	(FL)	810
Business & economics information	GELINNE, Michael S.	(MO)	426
Business & economics librarianship	LIM, Peck B.	(IL)	727
Business & economics reference	KRISTIE, William J.	(CA)	679
	LARSEN, Lynda L.	(DC)	698
	WIZA, Judith M.	(KY)	1359
	DODGE, Michael R.	(NC)	308
Business, economic & mining reference	KIEFER, Karen N.	(CA)	647
Business, economic resources	ERWIN, Nancy S.	(OH)	353
Collection development, business, econ	BELANGER, Sandra E.	(CA)	75
Development economics	ZIMMERMAN, Hugh N.	(NY)	1389
Economic & financial databases	WYSS, David A.	(MA)	1376
	ZURBRIGG, Lyn E.	(ON)	1391
Economic & financial forecasting srvs	ZURBRIGG, Lyn E.	(ON)	1391
Economic & industrial development	LANDRY, Ronald	(IL)	694
Economic & industry analysis	FELDMAN, Stanley J.	(MA)	369
Economic & information development	LAU, Jesus G.	(MEX)	702
Economic & labor research	KIBILDIS, Melba	(MI)	646
Economic database & forecasts	BECK, Douglas J.	(DC)	71
Economic databases	GRIMES, A R.	(DC)	470
	ALMAN, Richard D.	(NY)	17
	STEIN, Pamela H.	(NY)	1185
Economic development	CURRY, John A.	(IL)	266
Economic forecasting	MCKELVEY, Michael J.	(DC)	811
	CARTER, Walter F.	(MA)	190
	CATON, Christopher N.	(MA)	195
Economic information	MUZZO, Steven E.	(IL)	883
	WILSON, Brenda J.	(UT)	1350
Economic outlook publications	HARTMAN, David G.	(MA)	508
Economic research	BRUNER, Robert B.	(CO)	150
Economic research & analysis	COOPER, J P.	(MA)	243
Economic, statistical & quantitative std	KING, Donald W.	(MD)	650
Economic statistics reference	RANDOLPH, Susan E.	(DC)	1007
Economics	ANDERSON, Connie J.	(CA)	22
	POPA, Opritsa A.	(CA)	983
	HUDGINS, Peggy	(DC)	569
	RADER, Jennette S.	(IL)	1002
	SMITH, Judy E.	(IL)	1156
	DAVY, Edgar W.	(MA)	281
	TOMPKINS, Louise	(NJ)	1250
	BRAUN, Carl F.	(NY)	129
	GETZ, Malcolm	(TN)	430
	CANNON, Ruth M.	(VA)	179
	MAXWELL, Littleton M.	(VA)	788
	MCNAIR, Alison T.	(NS)	815
	BUCHANAN, Zoe A.	(ON)	153
Economics & business	CARRINGTON, Bessie M.	(NC)	186
Economics & econometrics	BROWN, George F.	(MA)	144
Economics & finance	BURDET, Michele C.	(SWZ)	158
Economics & finance acquisitions	MAYNARD, Elizabeth	(OH)	790
Economics & finance reference	MAYNARD, Elizabeth	(OH)	790
Economics & international databases	HARTMAN, David G.	(MA)	508
Economics & psychological acquisitions	RICHARDSON, Linda B.	(VA)	1029
Economics & social sciences	TOTH, George S.	(DC)	1252
Economics & sociology	FIELD, Louise P.	(NY)	375
Economics of information	BRAUNSTEIN, Yale M.	(CA)	130
	VAN HOUSE, Nancy A.	(CA)	1275
	KANTOR, Paul B.	(OH)	626
Economics of libraries	MEYER, Richard W.	(SC)	830
Economics reference	GROSCH, Mary F.	(IL)	472
Economics research	MALEK, Stanislaw A.	(PQ)	763
Energy & the economy	YANCHAR, Joyce M.	(MA)	1377
Home economics	RONNERMANN, Gail	(NY)	1053
Home economics & human ecology	MACKEY, Neosha A.	(MO)	756
Home economics reference	GAGE, Marilyn K.	(OK)	412
Home economics subject specialization	SANDERS, Nancy P.	(OH)	1080
Home economy	MILLER, Sylvia G.	(NC)	843
Industrial & economic development info	GRELL, Holly J.	(GA)	467
Information economics	LAMBERTON, Donald M.	(AUS)	690
Information economics & marketing	YOUNG, Peter R.	(DC)	1383
Information industry economics	BURNS, Christopher	(MA)	162

ECONOMICS (Cont'd)

Information technology economics	MCSPADDEN, Robert M.	(OH)	818
International economics	MCKELVEY, Michael J.	(DC)	811
Labor economics	WEINRICH, Gloria	(NY)	1318
Library economics	SKRZESZEWSKI, Stan E.	(ON)	1147
Management & economics	DI MEGLEO, Arthur J.	(NY)	304
Medical economics	GALLAGHER, Philip J.	(NJ)	414
Social economics documentation	VAN GARSSE, Yvan	(BEL)	1275
World economic outlook publications	HARTMAN, David G.	(MA)	508

EDISON

CD, LP, 45, 78 & Edison recordings	BAHR, Edward R.	(MS)	45
Thomas A Edison	MUNSICK, Lee R.	(NJ)	879

EDITING (See also Editorial, Proofreading)

Abstracting & abstract editing	HOFFMAN, Allen	(NY)	547
Abstracting, editing, translation	REITH, Louis J.	(DC)	1022
Abstracting, indexing, editing	HYSLOP, Marjorie R.	(OH)	580
Acquisitions & editing	BATES, Barbara S.	(PA)	63
Applied arts, writing & editing	FRANKLIN, Linda C.	(NY)	398
Archival publications consltng & editing	MARRELLI, Nancy M.	(PQ)	773
Bibliography, translating, editing	KRAMER-GREENE, Judith	(NY)	675
Book publishing, writing & editing	EASTMAN, Ann H.	(VA)	333
Book reviewing & editing	GUSHEE, Marion S.	(IL)	478
Catalog editing	DODGE, Christopher N.	(MN)	308
Catalog editing & publication	HENDRICKSON, Norma K.	(DC)	527
Children's book editing	VESTAL, Jeanne G.	(NY)	1283
Children's books, editing	BENEDUCE, Ann K.	(NJ)	80
Communications, writing, editing	EATENSON, Ervin T.	(TX)	333
Computer-based text editing	LUDGIN, Donald H.	(ME)	746
Copy editing	KLEIN, Barbara L.	(WY)	659
Data collection & editing	TEUN, Rebecca L.	(TX)	1233
Designing & editing newsletters	ENSEL, Ellen H.	(CT)	350
Documentary editing	ZBORAY, Ronald J.	(CA)	1386
	DOWD, Mary J.	(DC)	315
	EPPARD, Philip B.	(MA)	351
	FRYE, Dorothy T.	(MI)	407
	VAN HORNE, John C.	(PA)	1275
	MONTEIRO, George	(RI)	856
	CRIST, Lynda L.	(TX)	259
Editing	GOODMAN, Anita S.	(AL)	449
	JOHNSON, Harlan R.	(AZ)	605
	LEE, Judith C.	(CA)	710
	FERRO, Frank J.	(CT)	374
	BLUMER, Thomas J.	(DC)	107
	JONES, Elin D.	(DC)	612
	IVES, Sidney E.	(FL)	586
	BOSTIAN, Irma R.	(IL)	117
	CAMP, John F.	(IL)	175
	EPP, Ronald H.	(IL)	351
	HUCHTING, Mary	(IL)	569
	WADSWORTH, Robert W.	(IL)	1290
	WINGER, Howard W.	(IL)	1355
	EMOND, Kathleen A.	(MA)	348
	LANCASTER, John	(MA)	692
	PRINDLE, Paul E.	(MA)	993
	TAUBER, Stephen J.	(MA)	1225
	TATE, Elizabeth L.	(MD)	1225
	CARLEN, Claudia	(MI)	181
	DOUGHERTY, Ann P.	(MI)	313
	MARLOW, Cecilia A.	(MI)	772
	RUNCHOCK, Rita M.	(MI)	1067
	WEAVER, Clarence L.	(MI)	1312
	EZZELL, Joline E.	(NC)	360
	HEROLD, Virginia L.	(NC)	532
	WHITTINGTON, Erma P.	(NC)	1334
	BECKER, Ronald L.	(NJ)	72
	SCHEPP, Brad J.	(NJ)	1091
	CARRICK, Bruce R.	(NY)	186
	HESS, James W.	(NY)	534
	KARNEZIS, Kristine C.	(NY)	627
	LANE, Elizabeth L.	(NY)	694
	LAWRENCE, Arthur P.	(NY)	704
	MARGOLIES, Alan	(NY)	770
	MARK, Linda R.	(NY)	770
	MEAGHER, Anne E.	(NY)	819
	MOONEY, Martha T.	(NY)	858

EDITING (Cont'd)

Editing

	NAGLE, Ann	(NY)	886
	NYREN, Dorothy E.	(NY)	913
	SCHNEIDER, Adele	(NY)	1096
	SCOFIELD, Andrea	(NY)	1106
	WULKER, Clare	(OH)	1374
	MCCABE, Gerard B.	(PA)	792
	CLELAND, Nancy D.	(TN)	220
	WHITEHEAD, Jane	(TN)	1332
	FELSTED, Carla M.	(TX)	370
	MATHIESEN, Thomas J.	(UT)	784
	LOY, Dennis C.	(VA)	745
	MURPHY, Mary	(VA)	881
	WHITE, William	(VA)	1332
	GRAF, David L.	(WI)	455
	JORDAHL, Ronald I.	(AB)	616
	HART, Elizabeth	(BC)	507
	CHOUINARD, Germain	(PQ)	211
	FLUK, Louise R.	(PQ)	386
	KISHIMOTO, Hiroko	(JAP)	656
Editing & abstracting	TAKACS, Sharon N.	(IL)	1220
Editing & designing publications	SHUMAN, Marilyn J.	(IL)	1134
Editing & library appraisal	BROOKS, Jerrold L.	(NC)	140
Editing & manuscript evaluation	MOON, Eric	(FL)	857
Editing & proofreading	KNICKERBOCKER, Wendy	(MD)	664
	BAKISH, David J.	(NY)	50
Editing & publishing	ALLEY, Brian	(IL)	16
	EBERHART, George M.	(IL)	334
	RICHMOND, Robert W.	(KS)	1031
	GATTIS, R G.	(MI)	422
	READE, Judith G.	(NS)	1012
Editing & reviewing	RAZER, Robert L.	(AR)	1012
	BALLARD, Robert M.	(NC)	53
Editing & writing	FILES, Patricia T.	(CA)	376
	WISMER, Donald	(ME)	1357
	BLUMBERG-MCKEE, Hazel	(MN)	107
	TANNER, Anne B.	(PA)	1222
	TAYLOR, Nancy L.	(TX)	1228
	CHAGNON, Danielle G.	(PQ)	197
Editing bibliographical records	WANG, Ann C.	(DC)	1302
Editing book reviews	ESTES, Sally C.	(IL)	355
Editing chemical & medical text	GRIFFITHS, Mary C.	(MD)	469
Editing company news brief	WHITE, Jane F.	(MI)	1331
Editing completed indexes	BERNAL, Rose M.	(NY)	88
Editing computer science magazines	WEINER, Carolynn N.	(NY)	1318
Editing, discography, prose	SHAPIRO, Burton J.	(MD)	1121
Editing indexes	BLOZIS, Jolene M.	(DC)	107
	ASTON, Jennefer	(IRE)	37
Editing information news stories	LYONS, Ivan	(NY)	753
Editing in-house publications	MINOR, Barbara B.	(NY)	846
Editing law review articles	STEFANCIC, Jean A.	(CA)	1185
Editing library media books	TROJAN, Judith L.	(NY)	1257
Editing library media magazines	TROJAN, Judith L.	(NY)	1257
Editing library newsletter	KULIBERT, Marie M.	(MI)	683
Editing medical & pharmacological texts	HAMILTON, Gloria R.	(PA)	492
Editing music & music literature	PRUETT, James W.	(DC)	996
Editing newsletter	ROTH, Alison C.	(CT)	1059
Editing of reference works	HARNER, James L.	(OH)	503
Editing of technical materials	WOODLOCK, Stephanie	(PA)	1366
Editing professional books	FRANKLIN, Robert M.	(NC)	398
Editing professional publications	SCHEETZ, Mary D.	(PA)	1091
Editing, proofreading, bibliographies	BRADWAY, Becky J.	(IL)	126
Editing publications	WOLFSON, Catherine L.	(AZ)	1361
Editing reference books	BRAUNSTEIN, Mark M.	(RI)	130
Editing, reviewing, young adult lib srvs	CAMPBELL, Patricia J.	(CA)	177
Editing short research topics	MCCRAY, Evelina W.	(LA)	800
Editing, writing	GOTTLIEB, Robert A.	(ME)	453
Editing, writing & design	MOLLO, Terry	(NY)	853
Editing, writing, public relations	WEISENBURGER, Patricia J.	(KS)	1319
Editing, writing, researching	MANNING, Jo A.	(NY)	766
Editor & writer	NIEHAUS, Barbara J.	(IL)	903
Editor of legal translations	SCHLACKS, Charles	(CA)	1093
Editor, writer	GROTE, Janet H.	(NY)	473
Encyclopedia manuscript editing	LAGIES, Meinhart J.	(CA)	688
Freelance editing	OTT, Bill	(IL)	930

EDITING (Cont'd)

Grant & other writing & editing	WRIGHT-HESS, Anne H.	(NY)	1373
Historical documentary editing	SCHULZ, Constance B.	(SC)	1102
Historical editing	GRABOWSKI, John J.	(OH)	455
Index editing & bibliographies	PETERMAN, Claudia A.	(CA)	962
Indexing, abstracting & editing	DOUVILLE, Judith A.	(CT)	314
Indexing & bibliographic editing	DRAPER, Linda J.	(MO)	318
Indexing & editing music information	STRATELAK, Nadia A.	(MI)	1200
Inventory editing	INGERSOL, Robert S.	(MO)	582
Journal & book editing	PHILLIPS, Janet C.	(PA)	968
Journal editing	BALL, Dannie J.	(LA)	52
	DAVISH, William	(MD)	281
	LAMBERTON, Donald M.	(AUS)	690
Journal editor	CRAWFORD, Susan Y.	(MO)	257
Law & business writing & editing	HOYT, Henry M.	(NY)	566
Library, information science editing	SCHAEFER, Mary E.	(VA)	1089
Library science editing & publishing	CASINI, Barbara P.	(PA)	192
Magazine publishing & editing	LEHURAY, Stephen D.	(MD)	713
Manuscript editing	HURTES, Reva	(FL)	578
	EDELSON, Ken	(NJ)	335
Medical editing	CARVER, Mary	(NY)	191
	ZIMMERMANN, Albert J.	(WI)	1389
Medical writing & editing	CLEMENTS, Betty H.	(GA)	221
	SPARKS, Martha E.	(NC)	1171
Music editing	BLOTNER, Linda S.	(MA)	106
	BROUDE, Ronald	(NY)	141
Music editing & proofreading	NIGHTINGALE, Daniel	(PA)	904
Music research, writing, editing	GLASFORD, G R.	(NY)	440
News clip editing	CANT, Elaine N.	(CA)	179
Newsletter editing	BASART, Ann P.	(CA)	62
	CROCKETT, Darla J.	(CA)	259
	WELLSMAN, Jennifer A.	(NJ)	1323
Newsletter publishing & editing	TAYLOR, David C.	(NC)	1226
Online editing	GOLDBERG, Judy W.	(NY)	444
Proofreading, writing, editing, indexing	GAGNON, Donna M.	(CA)	412
Publications editing & writing	SHIRES, Nancy P.	(NC)	1131
Publishing database editing & design	THOMPSON, Anne E.	(AZ)	1238
Publishing editing	THOMPSON, Anne E.	(AZ)	1238
Reference editing	REGAN, Lesley E.	(MI)	1017
Report editing, management systems	KEE, Walter A.	(NC)	634
Research & editing	ROBINSON, Michaele M.	(CA)	1044
	CUTHBERT, John A.	(WV)	267
Research, writing & editing	CHRISTIANSON, Elin B.	(IN)	212
Retrospective cataloging & editing	HUGGENS, Gary D.	(DC)	571
Review writing & editing	SILVER, Gary L.	(MI)	1138
Reviewing, editing, writing	ARK, Connie E.	(OH)	31
Reviews of editing & writing	GORDON, Ruth I.	(CA)	452
Reviews, writing, editing	VAN NIEL, Eloise S.	(HI)	1276
Scientific books editing	SKALLERUP, Amy G.	(FL)	1145
Teaching writing & editing	BLUMER, Thomas J.	(DC)	107
Technical & general editing	JOSLYN, Camille	(VA)	618
Technical editing	DAVIS, Marianne W.	(CA)	280
	RIDER, Philip R.	(IL)	1032
	BARRETT, Joyce C.	(NJ)	59
	CASSELL, Gerald S.	(TN)	193
	HACKNEY, Judith G.	(TX)	481
Technical editing, consumer electronics	MENNIE, Don	(NJ)	824
Technical editor	HINTON, N E.	(KS)	543
Technical writing & editing	GIRILL, T R.	(CA)	438
	JACOBS, Horace	(CA)	589
	WEIL, Ben H.	(NJ)	1317
Technical writing, editing	URKEN, Madeline	(NJ)	1270
Telecommunications newsletter editing	IMPERIALE, Karen P.	(NJ)	582
Textual editing	YEANDLE, Laetitia	(DC)	1378
	BIRK, Nancy	(OH)	98
Writing & editing	COYLE, Leslie P.	(CA)	253
	DOWNEY, Lynn A.	(CA)	316
	MACKINTOSH, Mary L.	(CA)	757
	MILLER, Ralph D.	(CA)	841
	SCARBOROUGH, Katharine T.	(CA)	1087
	MEYER, Andrea P.	(CO)	829
	GRAY, Dorothy L.	(DC)	459
	KENDRICK, Brent L.	(DC)	640
	KIEFER, Rosemary M.	(FL)	647
	KNOBLAUCH, Mark G.	(IL)	665
	PEARSON, Lois R.	(IL)	952
	HOOK-SHELTON, Sara A.	(IN)	556

EDITING (Cont'd)
Writing & editing

ROTH, Sally . . . . (KS) 1059
STEVENSON, Michael I. . (MA) 1191
HEISER, Nancy E. . . . . . (ME) 523
MAGNUSON, Norris A. . (MN) 759
DECANDIDO, Graceanne
A. . . . . (NY) 285
WRIGHT, Sylvia H. . . . . . (NY) 1373
FRY, Mildred C. . . . . . . (OH) 406
MILLER, William . . . . . . (OH) 843
RATLIFF, Priscilla . . . . . . (OH) 1009
SULLIVAN, Frances L. . . (OH) 1207
LARSON, Signe E. . . . . . (OR) 700
BLEIER, Carol S. . . . . . (PA) 105
CUTRONA, Cheryl . . . . . (PA) 268
ZIPF, Elizabeth M. . . . . . (PA) 1389
BAKER, Bonnie U. . . . . . (TN) 48
GEARY, Kathleen A. . . . . (TX) 424
BELLAMY, Patricia C. . . (ON) 78

Writing & editing news & features   CHEATHAM, Bertha M. . . (NY) 204
Writing & editing pictorial histories   LUSKEY, Judith . . . . (DC) 749
Writing & editing policy manuals   COURSON, M S. . . . . . . (MD) 251
Writing & editing professional books   WEISBURG, Hilda K. . . . (NJ) 1319
Writing & editing scientific reports   LAUTENSCHLAG,
Elisabeth C. . . . . (PA) 703
Writing, editing   HUNTER, Joy W. . . . . . (TN) 576
Writing, editing & indexing   PALMER, Marguerite C. . (WV) 936
Writing, editing & publishing   JOHNSON, Richard D. . . (NY) 608
Writing, editing, & training   SYMES, Dal S. . . . . (WA) 1217
Writing reviews & editing   MATHES, Miriam S. . . . . (WA) 783
Young adult books, acquisition &
editing   JACKSON, Nancy D. . . . (NY) 588

EDITIONS (See also Antiquarian, Rare)
Fine printing, limited editions   KIRSHENBAUM, Sandra
D. . . . . (CA) 655
First edition   LOWMAN, Matt P. . . . . . (CA) 744
First editions & manuscripts of music   STRINGFELLOW, William
T. . . . . (NY) 1202
First editions, 19th century music   BRODY, Elaine . . . . (NY) 139
Intl publishing, student editions   HARMON, James R. . . . (NY) 502
Modern first editions   CHANEY, Bev . . . . (NY) 200
KENDALL, Lyle H. . . . . . (TX) 640
Publishing new music editions   BALK, Leo F. . . . . (NY) 52

EDITORIAL (See also Editing, Newspapers)
Document delivery & editorial   MAXWELL, Christine Y. . (CA) 788
Editorial   FOREMAN, Kenneth J. . . (NC) 390
NELSON, Nancy M. . . . (NY) 894
ROBERTS, Gloria A. . . . (NY) 1040
FOSTER, Margaret A. . . . (ON) 392
Editorial & microform operations   DEL CERVO, Diane M. . . (CT) 289
Editorial & textual criticism   REIMAN, Donald H. . . . (NY) 1020
Editorial assistance   TEAGUE, Edward H. . . . (FL) 1229
Editorial consultation   ALKIRE, Leland G. . . . . . (WA) 13
Editorial department management   BRAM, Leon L. . . . . (NJ) 127
Editorial, journals   BURNS, Richard K. . . . . (PA) 162
Editorial librarian   JANSSEN, Gene R. . . . . (MN) 594
Editorial libraries   PAUL, Thomas A. . . . . . . (MI) 949
Editorial management   SABOSIK, Patricia E. . . (CT) 1073
Editorial processing   ARJONA, Sandra K. . . . . (PA) 31
Editorial publishing   PLOTNIK, Arthur . . . . . . (IL) 978
PEDOLSKY, Andrea D. . (NY) 954
Editorial research & development   SOKOLOFF, Michele . . . (PA) 1165
Editorial services   STEWART, Donald E. . . (IL) 1192
GOLD, Renee L. . . . . . . (NY) 444
Editorial work   HOYT, Beryl E. . . . . (TX) 566
Editorials & publishing   STEVENS, Stanley D. . . (CA) 1191
Magazine & editorial consulting   LIPTON, Howard . . . . . . (MI) 732
Music publications, editorial   MAYER, George L. . . . . (NY) 789
Supervision of editorial staff   STRATELAK, Nadia A. . . (MI) 1200

EDP (See also Data, Processing)
EDP librarianship   FLEISHMAN, Lauren Z. . (NY) 384

EDUCATION (See also Courses, Curriculum, Instruction, Learning, Teaching, Training, Skills)
Acquisition of eductnl motion pictures   CHAVES, Francisco M. . . (FL) 204
Administration, medical education   KERR, Audrey M. . . . . . (MB) 644
Adult basic & continuing education   WASSERMAN, Ricki F. . (NY) 1308
Adult basic education   MARTIN, Brian G. . . . . . (NY) 775
Adult education   GUARINO, John P. . . . . (CA) 475
STEVENSON, Grace T. . (CA) 1191
CANAVAN, Roberta N. . . (NJ) 178
PULLER, Maryam W. . . . (PA) 997
WEBER ROOCHVARG,
Lynn E. . . . . (PA) 1314
Adult education, lifelong learning   GANN, Daniel H. . . . . . (IN) 416
Archival education   BURNS, John F. . . . . . . (CA) 162
PUGH, Mary J. . . . . (CA) 997
JIMERSON, Randall C. . . (CT) 600
QUINN, Patrick M. . . . . (IL) 1000
MORISON, William J. . . (KY) 865
DESNOYERS, Megan F. . (MA) 295
SNIFFIN-MARINO, Megan
G. . . . . (MA) 1163
BOLES, Frank . . . . (MI) 112
PETTIT, Marilyn H. . . . . (NY) 965
BAUMANN, Roland M. . . (OH) 66
HARRISON, Dennis I. . . (OH) 506
MILLER, Fredric M. . . . . (PA) 837
STOUT, Leon J. . . . . . . (PA) 1198
SCHULZ, Constance B. . (SC) 1102
BEHRND-KLODT, Menzi L. (WI) 75
Archives education   O'TOOLE, James M. . . . (MA) 930
Archives, records management
education   RHOADS, James B. . . . (WA) 1026
Area health education learning
resources   JOHN, Stephanie C. . . . (MI) 601
Audiovisual education   BURESH, Reggie F. . . . . (MN) 158
Automation education   WILBURN, Marion T. . . . (ON) 1338
Behavioral sciences & education
research   SWARTZ, Jon D. . . . . . (TX) 1214
Bibliographic education   BUCCO, Louise F. . . . . (VA) 153
Bibliographic instruction for education   WILKE, Janet S. . . . . . (KS) 1339
Bilingual education   PEISER, Richard H. . . . . (IL) 955
DE CUENCA, Pilar A. . . (NY) 286
Business, education, humanities   WILLIAMS, Robert C. . . (AK) 1346
Business law vocational education   DIAL, Ron . . . . (NY) 299
Career & education resources   WHITNEY, Howard F. . . (MA) 1334
Career education information advising   LYONS, A J. . . . . (MO) 753
Cataloging educational media   GRIFFIN, Kathryn A. . . . (IA) 468
Cataloging of eductnl motion pictures   CHAVES, Francisco M. . . (FL) 204
Children's education   HOLLAND, Deborah K. . . (TX) 550
Children's literature & education   COLLINS, Mary E. . . . . (IN) 233
Children's literature in education   MONSON, Dianne L. . . . (MN) 855
Children's services & education   LAWRENCE, Virginia W. (NC) 705
Children's services, education   TACKETT, Janet S. . . . . (KY) 1219
Classification education   BREGZIS, Ilze . . . . (ON) 131
Collection development for education   WILKE, Janet S. . . . . . . (KS) 1339
Community college education   JOHNSON, B L. . . . . . . (CA) 602
Community education & development   GUTHRIE, Virginia G. . . (AL) 479
Computer & video education   KRAUSE, Roberta A. . . . (IL) 676
Computer education   MIDDLESWART, Patricia
A. . . . . (IA) 833
TROUTNER, Joanne J. . (IN) 1258
GARDNER, Laura L. . . . (MO) 418
Computer science education   FOX, Edward A. . . . . . . (VA) 394
Computer utilities for education   COLCLASURE, Marian S. (AR) 230
Computer-based education   SIEGEL, Martin A. . . . . (IL) 1136
Computers in education   GRIFFIN, Kathryn A. . . . (IA) 468
LANGHORNE, Mary J. . . (IA) 696
NEWTON, Evah B. . . . . (IN) 900
MATECUN, Marilyn L. . . (MI) 783
SORELL, Janice G. . . . . (MN) 1168
SMITH, Sara B. . . . . . . (SC) 1160
WRIGHT, John C. . . . . . (HI) 1371
Conservation education   SEIDENBERG, Edward . . (TX) 1112
Consulting & continuing education   MOSELEY, Cameron S. . (NY) 870
Consulting to educational publishers   LAWSON, Martha G. . . . (AR) 705
Continuing education   ALIX, Cleta M. . . . . (CA) 13
HUTCHESON, Don S. . . (CA) 578
KRUGLET, Jo A. . . . . . (CO) 680
CARRINGTON, Virginia F. (CT) 186
BEATON, Barbara E. . . . (DC) 70

EDUCATION (Cont'd)

Continuing education

STONE, Elizabeth W.	(DC)	1197
WYCHE, Louise E.	(DE)	1374
BROWN, Eva R.	(IL)	143
HICKS, Frederick M.	(IL)	537
SNYDER, Sherrie E.	(IL)	1165
WINNER, Ronald	(IL)	1355
FARLEY, Janice S.	(IN)	364
STRATTON, Martha G.	(IN)	1200
HENEGHAN, Mary A.	(MA)	528
RICH, Marcia A.	(MA)	1027
EZELL, Charlaine L.	(MI)	360
HAWTHORNE, Dorothy M.	(MN)	514
MAHMOODI, Suzanne H.	(MN)	760
SELTZER, Ada M.	(MS)	1114
PATRICK, Ruth J.	(MT)	947
WILLIAMS, M J.	(NC)	1345
MOREHOUSE, Valerie J.	(ND)	863
MEANS, Raymond B.	(NE)	820
STUDDIFORD, Abigail M.	(NJ)	1204
GOODMAN, Rhonna A.	(NY)	449
HANSON, Jan E.	(NY)	498
LAWRENCE, Thomas A.	(NY)	705
PACKARD, Joan L.	(NY)	933
SIMON, Patricia B.	(NY)	1140
FRY, Mildred C.	(OH)	406
ROADS, Clarice D.	(OK)	1038
WOLFE, Gary D.	(PA)	1360
WOLL, Christina B.	(TX)	1361
DOWNEY REIDA, Linda K.	(UT)	316
BELT, Jane	(WA)	78
TOLLIVER, Barbara J.	(WA)	1248
CAIN, Carolyn L.	(WI)	171
LAMB, Donald K.	(WI)	689
MATTHEWS, Geraldine M.	(WI)	785
ROBBERS, Sandra M.	(WI)	1038
WAITY, Gloria J.	(WI)	1293
CRAIG, Wendy E.	(ON)	254
KENT, Charles D.	(ON)	642
WALCKIERS, Marc A.	(BEL)	1293

Continuing educ & professional
  devlpmnt — BRIDGE, Frank R. (TX) 135
Continuing education & staff
  development — TYER, Travis E. (IL) 1266
Continuing education & training — HOWARD, Mary R. (GA) 564
  CHOBOT, Mary C. (VA) 210
Continuing education change agent — BRUCE, Robert K. (MN) 149
Continuing education coordination — SNOWDEN, Deanna (IN) 1164
Continuing education for librarians — SWATOS, Priscilla L. (IL) 1214
Continuing education for librarianship — WALTERS, Corky (WY) 1301
Continuing education, inservice — TASSIA, Margaret R. (PA) 1224
Continuing education instruction — BURNETT, James H. (CO) 161
Continuing education programming — TREBBY, Janis G. (WI) 1255
Continuing education, resource
  sharing — SHELDON, Brooke E. (TX) 1125
Continuing education seminars — RUSH, James E. (OH) 1068
Continuing educ, training &
  development — WELLS, Mary K. (TX) 1322
Continuing library education — BLOESCH, Ethel B. (IA) 106
Continuing medical education — MANNING, Phil R. (CA) 767
  SIMPSON, Evelyn L. (CA) 1141
  STLUKA, Thomas H. (IL) 1195
  KELLY, Kay (MI) 638
  KELLER, Marlo L. (OH) 635
Continuing medical education
  programming — BEDARD, Martha A. (MA) 73
Continuing professional education — VARLEJS, Jana (NJ) 1278
Copyright law for educators — DAY, Martha T. (VT) 282
Correspondence education — CURL, Margo W. (ID) 265
Cross-cultural education — PEISER, Richard H. (IL) 955
Curriculum education — FOWLER, Louise D. (CT) 394
Database searching, education — GOLDSMITH, Maxine K. (NJ) 446
Database searching in education — ZLATOS, Christy L. (AL) 1390
Deaf education — KLEINMAN, Elsa C. (CA) 660
Dental education management — CHERNIN, David A. (MA) 206
Development of educational materials — MOSELEY, Cameron S. (NY) 870

EDUCATION (Cont'd)

Distance education — KOLB, Audrey P. (AK) 669
  MING, Marilyn (AB) 846
  VOLPATTI, Rechilde (ON) 1288
  GALLER, Anne M. (PQ) 414
Distance education library services — SLADE, Alexander L. (BC) 1147
  AFFLECK, Delburt E. (SK) 7
Distributing educational films — KONICEK, Karen B. (MA) 670
Distribution of educational films — HARTLEY, Elda E. (CT) 508
Early childhood education — HAWLEY, Marsha S. (IL) 514
  HAMMOND, Mary W. (WA) 494
Educating information users — KUHLTHAU, Carol C. (NJ) 682
Educating staff — INGERSOLL, Lyn L. (DC) 582
Education — MAJOR, Caryl M. (AZ) 762
  WHORTON, Pamela J. (AZ) 1334
  BOURNE, Charles P. (CA) 119
  FINLEY, Mary M. (CA) 378
  HUCKINS, Barbara W. (CA) 569
  SLATER, Barbara M. (CA) 1148
  LAMB, Gertrude (CT) 690
  AUSTIN, Monique C. (DC) 40
  JONES, Milbrey L. (DC) 614
  SCUKA, Aletta N. (DC) 1108
  COONS, Daniel E. (DE) 242
  TORRENTE, Kathryn J. (GA) 1251
  COOK, Margaret K. (IL) 240
  GRUNDKE, Patricia J. (IL) 475
  VILARO, Annette B. (IL) 1284
  BAVER, Cynthia M. (IN) 67
  BROTON, Cecilianne S. (IN) 141
  MCGIVERIN, Rolland H. (IN) 806
  BRUMM, Gordon L. (MA) 150
  PALMER, Richard J. (MI) 936
  PAO, Miranda L. (MI) 938
  HELMICK, Aileen B. (MO) 525
  LYONS, A J. (MO) 753
  SHAPIRO, Marian S. (MO) 1121
  BERGERON, Cheri Y. (MT) 86
  YLINIEMI, Hazel A. (ND) 1380
  BUTCHER, Patricia S. (NJ) 166
  GOLLA, Viola K. (NJ) 447
  BJORKQUIST, Donna M. (NY) 100
  FEINBERG, Renee (NY) 369
  HEWITT, Mary L. (NY) 535
  HUEBNER, Mary A. (NY) 570
  VANNORTWICK, Barbara
    L. (NY) 1276
  MORRIS, Trisha A. (OH) 867
  OVERHOLT, Maria B. (OH) 931
  JONES, Annabel B. (PA) 611
  USES, Ann K. (PA) 1270
  WETHERBY, Ivor L. (SC) 1328
  CLARKSON, Mary C. (TX) 219
  MCCULLEY, Lois P. (TX) 800
  SPENCER, Barbara L. (TX) 1173
  THORNE, Bonnie B. (TX) 1242
  DRYE, Jerry L. (VA) 321
  GRIEVE, Karen R. (VA) 468
  KIRKALI, Meral (WI) 654
  MARKOWETZ, Marianna
    C. (WI) 771
  COTTAM, Keith M. (WY) 250
  HAMILTON, Donald E. (BC) 492
  HAYCOCK, Carol A. (BC) 515
  CHURCHMAN, Alice M. (ON) 213
  BERGERON, Gilles I. (PQ) 86
Education & Africa — WISE, Kenda C. (AL) 1357
Education & behavioral sciences — WOMACK, Sharon K. (NE) 1362
Education & curriculum of chlds
  services — LOPEZ, Loretta K. (WA) 741
Education & humanities databases — MCKEE, Elizabeth C. (AR) 810
Education & industry learning material — LESURE, Alan B. (NY) 718
Education & job information services — WASSERMAN, Ricki F. (NY) 1308
Education & legal databases — MCLANE, Kathleen (VA) 813
Education & library databases — FOLKE, Carolyn W. (WI) 387
Education & professional development — MCCRANK, Lawrence J. (AL) 800
Education & psychology bibliography — BAUNER, Ruth E. (IL) 67
Education & psychology databases — LEUNG, Terry S. (CA) 719
  GERKE, Ray (MA) 428
Education & psychology reference — MULVIHILL, Joann (AZ) 878

EDUCATION (Cont'd)

Education & psychology research | LEUNG, Terry S. | (CA) | 719
Education & social sciences databases | BROWN, M S. | (FL) | 145
Education & the social sciences | WEST, Loretta G. | (OH) | 1326
Education & training | BELLARDO, Trudi | (DC) | 78
 | BLOUIN, Francis X. | (MI) | 107
 | COVVEY, H D. | (MB) | 252
 | ELLIOTT, Pirkko E. | (ENG) | 344
 | POON, Paul W. | (HKG) | 983
 | LAZAR, Peter | (HUN) | 706
 | KIM, Soon C. | (SKO) | 649
 | CHOU, Nancy O. | (TAI) | 210
Education & training library technicians | ANASTASIOU, Joan D. | (BC) | 21
Education archives & records | DEARSTYNE, Bruce W. | (NY) | 284
Education, behavioral sciences | O'BRIEN, Nancy P. | (IL) | 915
Education bibliographer | CONNORS, Kathleen M. | (OR) | 238
Education bibliography | FLOYD, Rebecca M. | (NC) | 386
 | MCGOWAN, Kathleen M. | (NY) | 807
 | PILLAI, Karlye A. | (NY) | 973
 | WEINBERG, Wanda J. | (OH) | 1318
 | SCHWARTZ, Philip J. | (TX) | 1105
 | HINKLE, Mary R. | (VA) | 542
Education bibliography, collection mgmt | BROWN, M S. | (FL) | 145
Education, collection development | ANDREWS, Loretta K. | (MD) | 26
Education collections | KENNEDY, Kathleen A. | (NJ) | 641
Education curriculum center | NORDSTROM, Virginia | (NY) | 908
Education database searching | VISSCHER, Helga B. | (AL) | 1285
Education databases | HOLLOWAY, Dona W. | (CA) | 552
 | RENTER, Lois I. | (IA) | 1023
 | ALTENBERGER, Alicja | (MA) | 18
 | VANDER MEER, Patricia F. | (MI) | 1274
 | WISE, Mintron S. | (NC) | 1357
 | ELY, Donald P. | (NY) | 347
 | HOLMES, Jill M. | (OK) | 553
 | CAPUTO, Anne S. | (VA) | 180
 | ADAM, Anthony J. | (WI) | 4
 | THAUBERGER, Marianne T. | (SK) | 1234
Education for information management | FOSKETT, Antony C. | (AUS) | 392
Education for K-12 | TOOTH, John E. | (MB) | 1251
Education for librarianship | REAGAN, Agnes L. | (AR) | 1012
 | LAWSON, A V. | (GA) | 705
 | LAWSON, Venable A. | (GA) | 705
 | AULD, Lawrence W. | (IL) | 40
 | TING, Lee H. | (IL) | 1246
 | RUFSVOLD, Margaret I. | (IN) | 1066
 | OCHS, Michael | (MA) | 915
 | DUTCHER, Gale A. | (MD) | 329
 | CHURCHWELL, Charles | (MI) | 213
 | CORY, Kenneth A. | (MI) | 248
 | ASHEIM, Lester E. | (NC) | 35
 | SHEARER, Kenneth D. | (NC) | 1124
 | KARETZKY, Stephen | (NJ) | 627
 | DALTON, Jack | (NY) | 271
 | JACKSON, William V. | (TX) | 588
 | ROBBINS, Jane B. | (WI) | 1038
 | STOKES, Roy B. | (BC) | 1196
 | COUGHLIN, Violet L. | (PQ) | 250
 | LEIDE, John E. | (PQ) | 713
 | TAKEUCHI, Satoru | (JAP) | 1220
 | ABDEL-MOTEY, Yaser Y. | (KWT) | 2
 | PICACHE, Ursula D. | (PHP) | 970
 | SENG, Harris B. | (TAI) | 1115
Education for library & information sci | WYLLYS, Ronald E. | (TX) | 1375
Education for music librarianship | BRADLEY, Carol J. | (NY) | 125
Education for rare books | BELANGER, Terry | (NY) | 76
Education for reference | DINGLE, Susan | (PA) | 304
Education for school librarianship | HAYCOCK, Kenneth R. | (BC) | 515
 | WHALEN, George F. | (ON) | 1328
Education generalism | BABER, Eric R. | (KS) | 43
Education, information science | ERDT, Terrence | (PA) | 352
Education, instructional resources | STAVROLAKIS, Rachel G. | (GA) | 1183
Education K-12 | HOOVER, Jonnette L. | (MO) | 557
Education librarianship | DENDY, Adele S. | (VA) | 291
 | POPE, Andrew T. | (NB) | 983

EDUCATION (Cont'd)

Education libraries | HINDS, Vira C. | (NY) | 542
 | BOUDREAU, Berthe | (NB) | 118
Education library | LINK, Margaret A. | (NC) | 730
Education library & information science | KASPER, Barbara | (CT) | 629
 | TIBBO, Helen R. | (MD) | 1244
Education library services | KRATZ, Abby R. | (TX) | 676
Education materials | SIBLEY, Carol H. | (MN) | 1134
 | ST. AMANT, Robert | (ON) | 1075
Education media | BERNHART, Barbara M. | (CA) | 89
Education media services assessment | COMEAU, Reginald A. | (NH) | 234
Education, medical databases | MCNALLY, Ruth C. | (CA) | 816
Education of gifted children | LINDSLEY, Barbara N. | (NY) | 730
Education of information professionals | HALSEY, Richard S. | (NY) | 490
Education of science librarians | ALEXANDER, Carol G. | (VA) | 12
Education of teacher librarians | BROWN, Jean I. | (NF) | 144
Education, psychology, human development | HENEBRY, Carolyn L. | (TX) | 528
Education reference | TISE, Barbara L. | (CA) | 1247
 | ALTHAGE, Celia J. | (IL) | 18
 | BROWN, Sue S. | (LA) | 147
 | TYLER, Carolyn S. | (SC) | 1266
Education reference & instruction | HINKLE, Mary R. | (VA) | 542
Education ref collection development | DAVIS, Maryellen K. | (IL) | 280
Education reference service | MCKEE, Elizabeth C. | (AR) | 810
Education research | COLLINS, John W. | (MA) | 232
 | PERKUS, Paul C. | (NY) | 959
Education resource center | BADGER, Barbara | (IL) | 44
Education resources | SCHROEDER, Eileen E. | (NY) | 1100
Education, social science reference | ROBERTSON, Ina N. | (IL) | 1042
Education specialized reference services | BROWN, M S. | (FL) | 145
Education technology | HINDS, Vira C. | (NY) | 542
Education training & development | WILSON, Jacqueline B. | (CA) | 1351
Educ, training & professional devlpmnt | AMAN, Mohammed M. | (WI) | 19
Education, young adults | SCHULTZ, Cathern J. | (WI) | 1101
Educational administration | BOISSE, Joseph A. | (CA) | 111
 | BRAUDE, Robert M. | (NY) | 129
 | SCHERDIN, Mary J. | (WI) | 1092
Educational & historical research | KLEIN, Victor C. | (LA) | 659
Educational & library computing | BENDER, Evelyn | (PA) | 79
Educational & non-profit archives | SCHUMACHER, Carolyn S. | (PA) | 1102
Educational & psychological databases | TU, Shu C. | (MA) | 1261
Educational bibliography | CARTER, Nancy F. | (CO) | 189
Educational books | BOWMAN, James K. | (NY) | 121
Educational computers | GRIFFIN, Cheryl J. | (NY) | 468
Educational computing | PHILBRICK, Marcia | (KS) | 967
 | BAKER, Shirley K. | (MA) | 49
Educational computing & media | WESTNEAT, Helen C. | (OH) | 1327
Educational curriculum | HAGGARD, Lynn | (TX) | 483
 | POLLOCK, Ethel L. | (VA) | 981
Educational database | OLSON, Lucie M. | (NJ) | 923
Educational databases | VATHIS, Alma C. | (AZ) | 1279
 | NOYES, Nicholas | (ME) | 911
 | DOYLE, James M. | (MI) | 317
 | BOWMAN, Gloria M. | (NC) | 121
 | PINGITORE, Patricia E. | (NY) | 974
 | BREGAINT, Bernard J. | (ON) | 131
 | PAPOUTSIS, Fotoula | (ON) | 939
Educational development | LEAHY, Michael D. | (CT) | 707
Educational film | MACINTYRE, Ronald R. | (NY) | 755
Educational film & video evaluation | MODICA, Mary L. | (SD) | 851
Educational film & video selection | MODICA, Mary L. | (SD) | 851
Educational films | WIENER, Paul B. | (NY) | 1336
Educational films & videotapes | FISHER, Carolyn H. | (NY) | 380
Educational films on aging | YAHNKE, Robert E. | (MN) | 1376
Educational guidance | BURSON, Lorraine E. | (OR) | 163
Educational information libraries | EUSTACE, Susan J. | (MD) | 356
Educational instruction of children | HANSON, Kathy H. | (GA) | 498
Educational librarianship | RIDER, Lillian M. | (PQ) | 1032
Educational mailing list development | MOSELEY, Cameron S. | (NY) | 870
Educational materials | CARR, Jo A. | (WI) | 185
 | BALDWIN, David A. | (WY) | 51
Educational materials design | WALD, Marlena M. | (GA) | 1294
Educational materials for teachers | MAY, Frank C. | (CA) | 788

EDUCATION (Cont'd)

Educational media
EBY, James F. . . . . (CA) 334
MACY, Edwin L. . . . . (CO) 758
DOUGLASS, Charlene K. (GA) 314
DAVIS, H S. . . . . (IN) 279
EVANS, James M. . . . . . . (LA) 357
BRAINARD, Elsie K. . . . . (MA) 127
PENSYL, Ornella L. . . . . (MA) 957
BUSBIN, O M. . . . . (NC) 164
HATHAWAY, Milton G. . (NC) 512
MAZURKIEWICZ, Helen L. (NJ) 791
KEIST, Sandra H. . . . . . (NM) 635
COLEMAN, Barbara K. . . (OH) 231
RODDA, Donna S. . . . . . (OH) 1047
SCHEEREN, William O. . (PA) 1090
Educational media & technology GASTON, Judith A. . . . . (MN) 421
BENDER, Evelyn . . . . . . (PA) 79
Educational media management SIMCOE, Darryl D. . . . . (NY) 1139
MAXWELL, James G. . . . (OR) 788
CHANG, Robert H. . . . . . (TX) 201
Educational media services RUFSVOLD, Margaret I. . (IN) 1066
Educational microcomputing FITZGERALD, Ruth F. . . (MI) 382
Educational online & CD-ROM
searches LIVELY, Nancy J. . . . . . . (MD) 734
Educational politics FLOWERS, Helen F. . . . (NY) 386
Educational program development MACKAMAN, Frank H. . . (IL) 756
Educational programming PHELPS, Thomas C. . . . (DC) 967
Educational programs CLARY, Rochelle L. . . . . (CA) 219
Educational reference, research FARRIS, Loretta . . . . . . (PA) 365
Educational reference services MISSAR, Charles D. . . . (MD) 847
Educational research JACKSON, Gloria D. . . . (CA) 587
STOCKTON, Ken R. . . . (DC) 1196
KAYAIAN, Mary S. . . . . . (IL) 632
VAN BUSKIRK, Elisabeth
L. . . . . (NJ) 1272
HITT, Gail D. . . . . (NY) 544
Educational resources, curriculum SACK, Jean C. . . . . (MD) 1073
Educational resources management &
ref ILACQUA, Anne K. . . . . (MA) 581
Educational services THOMSON, Diane G. . . . (NY) 1241
Educational software LATHROP, Ann . . . . (CA) 701
BOLSTER, Kathryn . . . . . (CT) 113
Educational sources STURM, Rebecca R. . . . (KY) 1205
Educational specifications SMINK, Anna R. . . . . . . (MD) 1152
Educational technology BERG, Charlene J. . . . . . (CA) 84
LUDWIG, Deborah M. . . (CO) 746
PORTER, Kathryn W. . . . (CT) 985
WHITE, Charles R. . . . . (CT) 1330
BADER, Shelley . . . . . . (DC) 44
KLASING, Jane P. . . . . . (FL) 657
STABLER, William H. . . . (FL) 1177
WILLARD, Gayle K. . . . . (KS) 1341
ALLAN, David W. . . . . . . (MN) 14
WALKER, Judith A. . . . . (NC) 1295
SJURSON, Gail M. . . . . . (NE) 1145
ELY, Donald P. . . . . (NY) 347
WAGNER, A C. . . . . (NY) 1291
DEMARS, Patricia . . . . . (VA) 291
BOLDUC, Yves . . . . (PQ) 112
Educational technology & media KRANCH, Douglas A. . . . (IA) 676
Educational technology application STARKEY, Richard E. . . (MA) 1182
Educational technology, audiovisual SPENCER, Albert F. . . . (GA) 1173
Educational television VOLPATTI, Rechilde . . . (ON) 1288
Educational use of computers DIERCKS, Eileen K. . . . . (IL) 302
Educational uses of microcomputers CARTER, Betty D. . . . . . (TX) 189
Educational video MACINTYRE, Ronald R. . (NY) 755
Elementary & secondary education MCDOWELL, Judith H. . . (OH) 804
DOAN, Janice K. . . . . . (KY) 307
Elementary computer education MCGREW, Linda L. . . . . (IA) 808
Elementary education MURRAY, Bruce C. . . . . (MD) 881
ROSAR, Virginia W. . . . . (NY) 1054
HARPER, Marjory B. . . . (TN) 503
SPENCER, Barbara L. . . (TX) 1173
WORTHY, Annie B. . . . . (TX) 1369
Elementary media education LACY, Lyn E. . . . . (MN) 687
PAULEY, Charles W. . . . (MN) 950
Elementary, secondary library
education CARTER, Yvonne B. . . . (DC) 190
MUELLER, Julie M. . . . . (IL) 875
End-user education RILEY, Ruth A. . . . . (MO) 1034

EDUCATION (Cont'd)

End-user searching & education GLASGOW, Vicki L. . . . . (MN) 440
English education DONNELLY, Lela M. . . . (KS) 311
Environmental education ALASTI, Aryt . . . . (MA) 9
ERIC educational database HENSON, Jane E. . . . . . (IN) 529
Family medicine education MENDELSON, Martin . . . (WA) 823
French & Arabic education YASSA, Lucie M. . . . . . (CA) 1378
French Canadian literature education GUERETTE, Charlotte M. (PQ) 476
French educational software GELINAS, Rene . . . . (PQ) 426
French literature education GUERETTE, Charlotte M. (PQ) 476
General education YAHNKE, Robert E. . . . (MN) 1376
Gifted & talented education ABILOCK, Debbie . . . . . (CA) 2
Global education audiovisuals HUGHES, Rolanda L. . . . (IN) 572
Health education RICHETELLE, Alberta L. . (CT) 1030
KRONENFELD, Michael R. (SC) 679
Health education & evaluation WAYLAND, Marilyn T. . . (MI) 1311
Health science library educ, research LOVE, Erika . . . . (NM) 743
Higher education TESTA, Elizabeth M. . . . . (CA) 1233
RESNIK, Linda I. . . . . . . (DC) 1024
AUGUST, Sidney . . . . . (PA) 39
REENSTJERNA, Frederick
R. . . . . (WV) 1016
Higher education administration FUSTUKJIAN, Samuel Y. (FL) 410
KATZ, Ruth M. . . . . (NC) 630
PERSON, Ruth J. . . . . . (PA) 961
Higher education, library interfacing BREIVIK, Patricia S. . . . (CO) 132
Higher education planning JORDAN, Robert T. . . . . (DC) 617
History of education MENT, David M. . . . . . . (NY) 824
History of higher education BRABHAM, Robert F. . . . (NC) 124
Holocaust education KLEINBURD, Freda . . . . (NY) 659
Information education CROWLEY, John D. . . . . (CT) 261
Information management education HORAK, Ellen B. . . . . . . (CT) 558
MARTIN, Elaine R. . . . . . (DC) 776
MCGOWAN, Anna T. . . . (DC) 807
TOOEY, Mary J. . . . . . . (MD) 1250
WILSON, Barbara A. . . . (TX) 1349
Information science education CONAWAY, Charles W. . (FL) 235
SYWAK, Myron . . . . (NY) 1217
YERKEY, A N. . . . . (NY) 1380
LEE, Lucy T. . . . . (TAI) 710
Information science education
curriculum MOLL, Joy K. . . . . (NJ) 853
Information technologies education BOONE, Morell D. . . . . . (MI) 115
Instructional materials, teacher educ PRILLAMAN, Susan M. . (NC) 993
International education KIRKESY, Oliver M. . . . . (MI) 655
Job & career education GREEN, Vera A. . . . . . . (PA) 462
K-12 education SEADER, Jane M. . . . . . (NJ) 1109
K-12 educational materials GOWDY, Laura E. . . . . . (IL) 455
K-12 visual education LACY, Lyn E. . . . . (MN) 687
Language arts & English education BUBOLTZ, Dale D. . . . . (CA) 152
Law schools, legal education COYLE, Christopher B. . . (OH) 253
Legal education PETERSON, Randall T. . . (IL) 964
HOLOCH, S A. . . . . (OH) 553
Legal information retrieval education BARBEN, Tanya A. . . . . (SAF) 55
Librarianship education BLOESCH, Ethel B. . . . . (IA) 106
HILL, Janet S. . . . . (IL) 540
WHITBECK, George W. . (IN) 1329
ASTBURY, Effie C. . . . . . (PQ) 37
Libraries in teacher education SAVAGE, Daniel A. . . . . (ON) 1085
Library adult education programs REILLY, Jane A. . . . . . . (IL) 1020
Library & continuing education TOM, Chow L. . . . . (HI) 1249
Library & information education MAHOUD ALY, Usama E. (EGY) 761
Library & information profession educ GALVIN, Thomas J. . . . (IL) 415
Library & information science
education DEQUIN, Henry C. . . . . (IL) 293
HURD, Julie M. . . . . (IL) 577
SINEATH, Timothy W. . . (KY) 1143
SLAVENS, Thomas P. . . (MI) 1148
MALINCONICO, S M. . . (NY) 763
POND, Patricia B. . . . . . (OR) 982
HANSON, Eugene R. . . . (PA) 498
CHISHOLM, Margaret . . . (WA) 209
HIATT, Peter . . . . (WA) 536
GARDNER, Richard K. . . (PQ) 418
Library & information user education EL-DUWEINI, Aadel K. . . (EGY) 342
Library continuing education TARANKO, Walter J. . . . (ME) 1223
DAHLSTROM, Joe F. . . . (TX) 269

EDUCATION (Cont'd)
Library education

CLAVER, M P.	(AL)	219
STURGEON, Mary C.	(AR)	1205
HURT, Charlie D.	(AZ)	578
ROTHLISBERG, Allen P.	(AZ)	1060
DANTON, J P.	(CA)	274
GRAVES, Frances M.	(CA)	459
POARCH, Margaret E.	(CA)	979
BAYLES, Carmen L.	(CT)	67
BRADBERRY, Richard P.	(CT)	125
KUSACK, James M.	(CT)	685
PIKUL, Diane M.	(CT)	973
AVERSA, Elizabeth S.	(DC)	41
BATTAGLIA, Richard D.	(DC)	64
HAITH, Dorothy M.	(DC)	484
MARCUM, Deanna B.	(DC)	769
STEVENS, Frank A.	(DC)	1190
FARKAS, Andrew	(FL)	364
SRYGLEY, Sara K.	(FL)	1177
JAMES, Stephen E.	(GA)	592
JONES, Helen C.	(GA)	613
BOLLES, Charles A.	(ID)	112
BERK, Robert A.	(IL)	87
DALRYMPLE, Prudence W.	(IL)	271
ELINOR, Yungmeyer	(IL)	342
ESTABROOK, Leigh S.	(IL)	355
LANIER, Donald L.	(IL)	696
MYERS, Margaret R.	(IL)	884
STENSTROM, Patricia F.	(IL)	1187
VEIT, Fritz	(IL)	1281
LITTLE, Robert D.	(IN)	733
STEELE, Patricia A.	(IN)	1184
WHITE, Herbert S.	(IN)	1331
STROHECKER, Edwin C.	(KY)	1202
ZIMMER, Connie W.	(KY)	1388
GIBSON, Sarah S.	(MA)	432
DENMAN-WEST, Margaret W.	(MD)	292
BIDLACK, Russell E.	(MI)	95
DAUB, Peggy E.	(MI)	275
GROTZINGER, Laurel A.	(MI)	473
MOSEY, Jeanette	(MI)	871
WARNER, Robert M.	(MI)	1305
HARWOOD, Karen L.	(MN)	510
MASON, Laura L.	(MO)	781
SHAUGHNESSY, Thomas W.	(MO)	1123
HAUTH, Allan C.	(MS)	513
BALLARD, Robert M.	(NC)	53
COLLINS, Donald E.	(NC)	232
FEEHAN, Patricia E.	(NC)	368
HOLLEY, Edward G.	(NC)	551
YOUNG, Tommie M.	(NC)	1383
KARAIM, Betty J.	(ND)	627
COUGHLIN, Caroline M.	(NJ)	250
HORROCKS, Norman	(NJ)	561
MARCO, Guy A.	(NJ)	769
REELING, Patricia G.	(NJ)	1016
PIERSON, Robert M.	(NM)	972
BARR, Janet L.	(NY)	58
BOBINSKI, George S.	(NY)	108
GAFFNEY, Denis C.	(NY)	412
HARRIS, Martha	(NY)	505
HARVEY, John F.	(NY)	509
JOHNSON, Nancy B.	(NY)	608
KULLESEID, Eleanor R.	(NY)	683
PARR, Mary Y.	(NY)	944
PODELL, Diane K.	(NY)	979
SLATE, Ted	(NY)	1148
SYWAK, Myron	(NY)	1217
DU MONT, Rosemary R.	(OH)	325
OLSZEWSKI, Lawrence J.	(OH)	923
LAU, Ray D.	(OK)	702
DETLEFSEN, Ellen G.	(PA)	296
LOCKE, Jill L.	(PA)	736
NOLAN, Joan	(PA)	907
NOLF, Marsha L.	(PA)	908
RICE, Patricia O.	(PA)	1027
TRAISTER, Daniel H.	(PA)	1253

EDUCATION (Cont'd)
Library education

	YOUNG, James B.	(PA)	1382
	FUTAS, Elizabeth	(RI)	411
	CARPENTER, Dorothy B.	(TN)	184
	FANCHER, Evelyn P.	(TN)	363
	GLEAVES, Edwin S.	(TN)	441
	YOUREE, Beverly B.	(TN)	1384
	COOK, Anne S.	(TX)	239
	BENKE, Robin P.	(VA)	81
	GAVER, Mary V.	(VA)	423
	MULVANEY, John P.	(VA)	878
	CARMACK, Bob	(WI)	183
	JONES, Norma L.	(WI)	614
	JONES, Richard E.	(WI)	614
	STRUPP, Sybil A.	(WI)	1203
	WIEGAND, Wayne A.	(WI)	1336
	ZWEIZIG, Douglas L.	(WI)	1392
	WRIGHT, John G.	(AB)	1371
	BOWMAN, Robert J.	(ON)	122
	BREGMAN, Alvan M.	(ON)	131
	LAND, Reginald B.	(ON)	692
	SCHULTE-ALBERT, Hans G.	(ON)	1101
	WHITE, Janette H.	(ON)	1331
	TAILLON, Yolande A.	(PQ)	1220
	RAYWARD, W B.	(AUS)	1011
	DOUGLAS, Daphne R.	(JAM)	314
	TOGUCHI, Eiko	(JAP)	1248
	HAMDY, Mohamed N.	(KWT)	491
	LAU, Jesus G.	(MEX)	702
	HU, James S.	(TAI)	567
Library education & administration	BOMAR, Cora P.	(NC)	113
Library education & continuing education	MCCROSSAN, John A.	(FL)	800
Library education & school librarians	LYDERS, Josette A.	(TX)	750
Library education consultation	SULLIVAN, Peggy A.	(IL)	1208
Library education instruction	GROSS, Richard F.	(ME)	472
Library education reference instruction	JOHNSON, Denise J.	(WI)	603
Lib education teaching & administration	SULLIVAN, Peggy A.	(IL)	1208
Library education, training & devlpmnt	EGAN, Terence W.	(AZ)	338
Library exhibitions & public education	WOODWARD, Daniel	(CA)	1368
Library, information education	BEARMAN, Toni C.	(PA)	69
Library, information science education	OLSON, Lowell E.	(MN)	923
Library instruction & user education	LIPPINCOTT, Joan K.	(NY)	732
Library media education	SCHULZETENBERG, Anthony C.	(MN)	1102
	HUPP, Mary A.	(WV)	577
Library media specialist education	MCNAMARA, Marie F.	(NY)	816
Library school education	ALLEN, Nancy S.	(MA)	15
	MORGAN, Lynn K.	(NY)	864
Library school education, music	COOVER, James B.	(NY)	244
Library science education	RICKS, Bonnie B.	(AK)	1032
	WOLD, Shelley T.	(AR)	1359
	BURICH, Nancy J.	(KS)	160
	YATES, Dudley V.	(KY)	1378
	PALMER, Forrest C.	(VA)	936
Library science education administration	FOOS, Donald D.	(FL)	388
Library services to distance education	BUDNICK, Carol	(MB)	155
Library skill education for K-12	LAU, Ray D.	(OK)	702
Library skills & research education	YOUNG, Marjie D.	(TX)	1382
Library skills education	WOLFE, Barbara M.	(NY)	1360
Library technician education	WILSON, Lucy	(OH)	1351
Library training & education	MILLER, Beth M.	(ON)	836
Library trustee education	PANZ, Richard	(NY)	938
Library trusteeship, educ & development	WILLIAMS, Lorraine O.	(ON)	1344
Library use education	ALSTON, Jane C.	(PR)	18
Library user education	HENNER, Terry A.	(GA)	528
	PALMER, Virginia E.	(OH)	937
	CHISMAN, Janet K.	(WA)	209
	FRICK, Elizabeth A.	(NS)	403
Literacy education	VAUGHAN, Elinor F.	(GA)	1279
	ROLSTAD, Gary O.	(IL)	1052
Literature of education	GREEY, Kathleen M.	(OR)	465
	WHALEN, George F.	(ON)	1328
Literature of higher education	QUAY, Richard H.	(OH)	999
Management education	ODERWALD, Sara M.	(NJ)	916

EDUCATION (Cont'd)

Manuscripts educational uses	MICHAELIS, Patricia A. .	(KS)	831
Media & education cataloging	FREESE, Melanie L.	(NY)	401
Media applications in education	TOWNSEND, Catherine M.	(SC)	1253
Media education training & development	FORTIN, Clifford C.	(WI)	391
Medical education	BOLLINGER, Robert O. .	(MI)	112
	BREWER, Karen L.	(OH)	134
Medical education & databases	WAYLAND, Marilyn T. . .	(MI)	1311
Medical education databases	GERRITY, Marline R. . . .	(MO)	429
Medical education library services	SNYDER, Elizabeth A. . .	(ENG)	1164
Medical librarian continuing education	EZQUERRA, Isabel	(FL)	360
Med, psychological, educational database	KLINE, Eve P.	(PA)	661
Medical school education	MORGAN, Lynn K.	(NY)	864
Microcomputer in education	WALKER, Judith A.	(NC)	1295
Microcomputers in education	PRILLAMAN, Susan M. . .	(NC)	993
Modernizing education	COE, Miriam M.	(LA)	226
Music education	THOMPSON, Anna M. . .	(IN)	1238
Native people's education	FINN, Julia P.	(PQ)	378
Nursing education	ECHOLS, Susan P.	(NE)	334
Nursing education & research	SOME, Barbara K.	(NJ)	1166
Nursing research & education	KELLEY, John F.	(PA)	636
Nutrition education & training	KREBS-SMITH, James J. .	(MD)	677
Online searching & education	SCHROEDER, Eileen E. .	(NY)	1100
Online searching education	GOWDY, Laura E.	(IL)	455
	CONWAY, Michael J. . . .	(MI)	239
Parent education	PETERSON, Carolyn S. .	(FL)	963
	NEVETT, Micki S.	(NY)	897
Patient education	PROTTSMAN, Mary F. . .	(AL)	995
	ELSESSER, Lionelle H. .	(MO)	346
	SERLING, Kitty	(MO)	1116
	WISEMAN, Karin M.	(NY)	1357
	JONES, Ruth A.	(WA)	615
Patron education	ANDERSON, Marcia . . .	(SC)	24
Peace research & education	KOCSIS, Jeanne	(MA)	667
Physical education & dance	MAYRAND, Lise M.	(PQ)	791
Preservation education	JONES, Maraiyn	(CA)	614
	HANTHORN, Ivan E. . . .	(IA)	499
Preservation education & training	OGDEN, Barclay W.	(CA)	918
Primary education	CROTTS, Carolyn D. . . .	(KS)	261
Prison education	GALLER, Anne M.	(PQ)	414
Professional collection education	CORCORAN, Frances E. .	(IL)	245
Professional continuing education	WILFORD, Valerie J. . . .	(IL)	1339
Professional education	MILLER, Sylvia G.	(NC)	843
Professional education & training progs	ROBERTS, Kenneth H. . .	(FRN)	1040
Professional education at Master's level	MATARAZZO, James M. .	(MA)	783
Professional education collection	HABER, Elinor L.	(NY)	480
Professional library education	SIBAI, Mohamed M.	(SDA)	1134
Providing continuing education	KRUSE, Ginny M.	(WI)	681
Psychology & education bibliography	JOHNSON, Linda B.	(CA)	607
Public & private music education	MILLER, Charles W.	(NJ)	836
Public education	TOWNSEND, Catherine M.	(SC)	1253
Public legal education	HEBDITCH, Suzan A. . . .	(AB)	519
Public legal information & education	TOMCHYSHYN, Theresa M.	(SK)	1249
Public library, adult education	BROWN, Freddiemae E. .	(TX)	144
Public library user education	HANSON, Jan E.	(NY)	498
Public relations & education	ROBERTS, Anne F.	(NY)	1039
Reference & education	LESSARD, Elizabeth B. .	(NH)	718
Reference & education bibliography	ROBERTS, Francis X. . .	(CO)	1040
Reference & literature education	NORRIS, Carol R.	(TN)	909
Reference & user education	KIBBEE, Josephine Z. . .	(IL)	646
Reference for education	WILKE, Janet S.	(KS)	1339
Reference in education	DICKSTEIN, Ruth H. . . .	(AZ)	301
	BEUTHEL, Ellengail . . .	(CO)	93
	GIRARD, Luc	(PQ)	438
Reference work in education	BEIMAN, Frances M. . . .	(NJ)	75
Regional educational media centers	FITZGERALD, Ruth F. . .	(MI)	382
Religion & education reference	GRIMES, Timothy P. . . .	(MI)	470
Religious education	PARSLEY, Brantley H. . .	(AL)	944
	HIBLER, James P.	(MI)	536
	OFFERMANN, Glenn W.	(MN)	917
Research & education	CULLEN, Charles T.	(IL)	263
	WEST, Richard T.	(MD)	1326
	BRISFJORD, Inez S. . . .	(NY)	136
Research skills education	BERGEN, Dessa C.	(NY)	85

EDUCATION (Cont'd)

School librarian education	ALSWORTH, Frances W.	(OK)	18
	HAMMEL, Philip J.	(SK)	493
School librarianship & education	BERNHARD, Paulette . . .	(PQ)	89
School librarianship education	BUTLER, Christina	(OH)	166
	MERRIAM, Doris E.	(PA)	826
	BLANKENBURG, Judith B.	(VA)	104
School library & media specialists educ	PATTERSON, Lotsee . . .	(OK)	948
School library education	SIGRIST, Staci E.	(OH)	1137
	FUNK, Grace E.	(BC)	410
	GRAZIER, Margaret H. . .	(MI)	461
School library media education	BUBOLTZ, Dale D.	(CA)	152
Science education	SHAPIRO, Lillian L.	(NY)	1121
Secondary education			
Secondary education curriculum materials	LAURITO, Gerard P.	(PA)	703
Serials education	ROGERS, Nancy H.	(AL)	1050
Sex education databases	CAMPBELL, Patricia J. . .	(CA)	177
Sexuality education resources	FORREST, Phyllis E. . . .	(DC)	391
Social science, history, education	NELSON, Michael L. . . .	(WY)	894
Social sciences & education	ATCHISON, Fres D.	(KS)	37
Social sciences education	AMAN, Mary J.	(WI)	19
Sociology of professional education	PAGE, Jacqueline M. . . .	(MO)	934
Special education	HAYNES, Douglas E. . . .	(NM)	516
Special education & rehabilitation	VELLEMAN, Ruth A. . . .	(NY)	1281
Special education classes	TEEGARDEN, Maude B. .	(KY)	1229
Special education libraries	DINNESEN, Peter H. . . .	(OH)	305
Special education personnel development	RUDDOCK, Velda I.	(CA)	1065
Special physical education	GRIFFITH, Joan C.	(NH)	469
Special subject education cataloging	VERMA, Prem V.	(WV)	1282
Staff development & continuing education	HIATT, Peter	(WA)	536
Teacher education	GILLAN, Dennis P.	(NJ)	435
	BROWN, Jean I.	(NF)	144
Teacher education, reading specialist	AUSTIN, Mary C.	(HI)	40
Teaching audiovisual education	WIRTANEN, James	(ND)	1356
Technical education	RICE, Joyce I.	(MS)	1027
Training & continuing education	DREWETT, William O. . .	(IL)	319
	HYMAN, Karen D.	(NJ)	580
Training & education	KAGER, Jeffrey F.	(PA)	621
	CORBEIL, Lizette	(PQ)	245
	KOGA, Setsuko	(JAP)	668
	BASCOM, James F.	(SDA)	62
Training & user education	SEELEY, Catherine R. . .	(ME)	1111
Training art educators & docents	GENSHAFT, Carole M. . .	(OH)	427
Trustee education	SWAN, James A.	(KS)	1213
Trustee education consulting	LYNCH, Minnie L.	(LA)	752
Trustee educator	YOUNG, Virginia G.	(MO)	1383
Trustee training & education	STEVENSON, Marilyn E.	(CA)	1191
Undergraduate library education	BUTLER, Christina	(OH)	166
User & information management education	BERNARD, Molly S.	(WA)	88
User education	MORRISON, Margaret L.	(AR)	868
	CARAVELLO, Patti S. . .	(CA)	180
	CASTAGNOZZI, Carol A.	(CA)	194
	FRY, Thomas K.	(CA)	407
	MCMASTER, Deborah L.	(CT)	815
	APOSTLE, Lynne M. . . .	(DC)	29
	WILLIAMS, Mitsuko	(IL)	1345
	HARZBECKER, Joseph J.	(MA)	510
	BRANCH, Katherine A. . .	(MD)	127
	HUMPHRIES, Anne W. . .	(MD)	574
	SIMS, Sally R.	(MD)	1142
	SCHWARTZ, Diane G. . .	(MI)	1104
	STOFFLE, Carla J.	(MI)	1196
	VAN TOLL, Faith	(MI)	1277
	POLLARD, Bobbie T. . . .	(NY)	981
	MULARSKI, Carol A. . . .	(OH)	876
	MILLER, Naomi	(PA)	841
	SEEDS, Robert S.	(PA)	1111
	WARNER, Elizabeth R. . .	(PA)	1305
	THOMPSON, Annie F. . .	(PR)	1239
	WELCH, C B.	(TX)	1321
	BADER, Susan G.	(VA)	44
	MCCULLEY, Lucretia . . .	(VA)	800
	NOFSINGER, Mary M. . .	(WA)	907
	STRUBE, Kathleen	(WI)	1203
	WU, Edith Y.	(HKG)	1373

EDUCATION (Cont'd)

User education & information transfer   BOROVANSKY, Vladimir T. . . . . (AZ)   117
User education & orientation   PATTERSON, Charlean P. (PA)   948
User education coordination   FREY, Barbara J. . . . . . . (CT)   402
User education, library orientation   SEARCY HOWARD, Linda M. . . . . (BC)   1109
Vocational education   DAY, Virginia M. . . . . (MA)   283
Writing & directing educational films   HARTLEY, Elda E. . . . . . (CT)   508
Young adult education   MCKEE, Barbara J. . . . . (OH)   810
Youth library use education   USHIRODA, Christine H. . (HI)   1270

EFFECTIVENESS (See also Measurement)

Effective media utilization   LANKFORD, Mary D. . . . . (TX)   696
Effective presentations & slide shows   SANKER, Paul N. . . . . . . (NY)   1081
Info service effectiveness measures   TIFFT, Jeanne D. . . . . . . (DC)   1244
Library effectiveness   WILLEMSE, John . . . . . . (SAF)   1341
Mgmt & organizational effectiveness   RIZZO, John R. . . . . (MI)   1037
Organization effectiveness   SEARS, Carlton A. . . . . . (NY)   1110

EGYPTOLOGICAL

Egyptological bibliography   WERNER, Edward K. . . . (NY)   1324

EIGHTEENTH CENTURY

18th century American history   GROVE, Pearce S. . . . . . (VA)   473
18th century bibliography   MCNAMARA, Charles B. (NC)   816
18th century British history & culture   DEVINE, Marie E. . . . . . . (CT)   297
18th century British literature   DEVINE, Marie E. . . . . . . (CT)   297
18th century Williamsburg imprints   BERG, Susan . . . . (VA)   85
History of 18th century art   ARNTZEN, Etta M. . . . . . (IL)   34

ELDERLY (See also Aging, Geriatrics, Gerontology, Older, Senior)

Elderly   NICKELSBURG, Marilyn M. . . . . (IA)   902
Elderly & handicapped   RING, Anne M. . . . . (IL)   1035
Impaired elderly   RYAN, Audrey H. . . . . . . (FL)   1070
Programming for elderly   RING, Anne M. . . . . (IL)   1035
Researching material for the elderly   MCCRAY, Evelina W. . . . (LA)   800
Services to aging, elderly   NEALE, Marilee . . . . (TX)   891
Services to elderly   LOVEJOY, Eunice G. . . . (OH)   743
Serving children & the elderly   WRIGHT, Linda D. . . . . . (NC)   1372

ELECTIONS (See also Bond, Referendums)

Bond elections   KELLUM-ROSE, Nancy P. (CA)   637
Library tax elections & referendums   AVANT, Julia K. . . . . (LA)   41
Newsletters, elections   THORSEN, Jeanne M. . . (WA)   1242
Tax elections   BENOIT, Anthony H. . . . . (LA)   82

ELECTRICITY

Electric power databases   JUDY, Joseph R. . . . . . . (CA)   619
Electric utilities   JOHNSON, Doris E. . . . . (CT)   603
   STANLEY, Nelda J. . . . . (LA)   1180
   BALL, Susan C. . . . . (WA)   52
Electric utilities & energy   FARKAS, Susan A. . . . . (DC)   364
Electric utility   FELDMAN, Rosalie M. . . (CO)   369
Electric utility engineering   WEBER, Robert F. . . . . . (OR)   1314
Electric utility research   HORAH, Richard H. . . . . (GA)   558
Electrical & computer engineering   STEINBERG, Marilyn H. . (MA)   1185
Electrical & electronic engineering   BEDDES, Marianne T. . . (NJ)   73
   THODY, Susan I. . . . . . . (ON)   1235
Electrical engineering   VARNER, James H. . . . . (CO)   1279
   THOMA, George R. . . . . (MD)   1235
   SUNDAY, Donald E. . . . . (NJ)   1210
   HAHN, Susan H. . . . . . . (PA)   484
   FENKER, John A. . . . . . . (WA)   371
Energy, electric utility industry   MUIR, Scott P. . . . . (AL)   876
Natural gas, petroleum & electricity   LOOS, Carolyn F. . . . . . (TX)   740

ELECTROCHEMICAL

Electrochemical information organization   LANGKAU, Claire M. . . . (OH)   696
Electrochemical information retrieval   LANGKAU, Claire M. . . . (OH)   696

ELECTROGRAPHIC

Electrographic printmaking   NEADERLAND, Louise O. (NY)   890

ELECTRONIC (See also Bioelectromagnetic, Bulletin, Computers, Microcomputers)

Biochemistry & electronics   MULDER, Marjorie M. . . . (OH)   876
Business development, electronic publshg   GROSSMAN, Allen N. . . (NJ)   473
Consumer electronics   HASSAN, Abe H. . . . . . . (CA)   511
Corporate electronic publishing systems   PETERSON, George B. . (MD)   963
Data preparation electronic publishing   KERR, Robert C. . . . . . . (CO)   644
Electrical & electronic engineering   BEDDES, Marianne T. . . (NJ)   73
   THODY, Susan I. . . . . . . (ON)   1235
Electronic advertising   PODWOL, Sharon L. . . . (NY)   979
Electronic banking   MESHINSKY, Jeff M. . . . (MD)   827
Electronic bulletin boards   POLLY, Jean A. . . . . (NY)   981
   SCHWARZ, Joy L. . . . . . (WI)   1105
Electronic communication systems   VAN VELZER, Verna J. . (CA)   1277
Electronic communications   HAYWARD, Edith C. . . . (AB)   517
Electronic components databases   D'ADOLF, Steven P. . . . (CA)   269
Electronic data processing systems   MOUNIR, Khalil A. . . . . (NY)   873
Electronic database & distribution   CHICHESTER, Gerald C. (CT)   208
Electronic database searching   LIRA, Judith A. . . . . (CO)   732
   BROWNE, Scott M. . . . . (NY)   148
Electronic databases   GRIMSLEY, Judy L. . . . . (FL)   470
   PAUSLEY, Barbara H. . . (OH)   950
Electronic databases for libraries   ZOELLICK, Bill . . . . (CO)   1390
Electronic delivery of information   TIBBETTS, David W. . . . (NY)   1243
Electronic design & manufacturing   KLINGER, William E. . . . (OH)   661
Electronic document handling systems   SPANGLER, Bruce . . . . (CO)   1171
Electronic engineering & geography   RICHARD, Marie F. . . . . (PQ)   1028
Electronic information   GAPEN, D K. . . . . (WI)   416
Electronic information delivery   HEARTY, John A. . . . . . (DC)   519
Electronic information delivery systems   PENNIMAN, W D. . . . . . (NJ)   957
Electronic information services   STILLMAN, Stanley W. . . (NY)   1194
Electronic information systems   WOOD, Richard T. . . . . . (MI)   1365
Electronic libraries   RAITT, David I. . . . . . . (NET)   1004
Electronic library   MCCANLESS, Christel L. . (AL)   793
Electronic mail   LEE, Joel M. . . . . (IL)   710
   SPARKS, Joanne L. . . . . (IL)   1171
   GRIEVE, Shelley . . . . . . (OH)   468
   TYLER, Kim E. . . . . (OR)   1266
   BUSSMANN, Steve . . . . (VA)   166
   EDWARDS, Wilmoth O. . (VA)   338
   FILIPPONE, Anne . . . . . . (VA)   377
   KELLER, Jay . . . . (VA)   635
   LOVETT, Bruce . . . . (VA)   743
   MAJOR, Skip . . . . (VA)   762
   NEWLAND, Barbara . . . . (VA)   899
   RINALDI, Roberta . . . . . . (VA)   1035
   RYAN, Maureen . . . . (VA)   1071
   STRATT, Randy . . . . (VA)   1200
Electronic mail administration   BEDARD, Bernard J. . . . (PQ)   73
Electronic mail & bulletin boards   O'NEILL, Sue . . . . (MD)   924
Electronic mail news services   STILLMAN, Stanley W. . . (NY)   1194
Electronic mail system management   WAGNER, Judith O. . . . (OH)   1292
Electronic media   CHANDLER, James . . . . (CA)   200
   KING, Ebba K. . . . . (NC)   650
Electronic media reference   HATVANY, Bela R. . . . . (MA)   512
Electronic media-specialized market srvs   SIECK, Steven K. . . . . . (NY)   1135
Electronic medical books   FRISSE, Mark E. . . . . . . (MO)   405
Electronic messaging   PICKETT, Olivia K. . . . . (DC)   971
   GENNARO, John L. . . . . (VA)   427
Electronic messaging & comp conferencing   BLACK, John B. . . . . . . (ON)   101
Electronic network directories   MACLELLAND, Margaret A. . . . . (ON)   757
Electronic prepress publishing systems   BRAWLEY, Paul H. . . . . (IL)   130
Electronic printing & publishing   GRIMES, Judith E. . . . . (MD)   470
Electronic product development   BING, Robert H. . . . . . . (NY)   97
Electronic products   MCGILL, Thomas J. . . . . (NJ)   806
Electronic publishing   BUTLER, Matilda L. . . . . (CA)   167
   CARSON, Susan A. . . . . (CA)   188
   LIGHTBOWN, Parke P. . . (CA)   726
   PAISLEY, William J. . . . . (CA)   935

ELECTRONIC (Cont'd)

Electronic publishing

SPIGAI, Fran	(CA)	1174
ZOELLICK, Bill	(CO)	1390
SABOSIK, Patricia E.	(CT)	1073
LEE, Joel M.	(IL)	710
MANDEL, Douglas J.	(IL)	765
REEDY, Martha J.	(MA)	1015
BEATTY, Samuel B.	(MD)	70
MCRAE, Alexander D.	(MD)	818
MEYER, Alan H.	(MD)	829
PATRICIU, Florin S.	(MD)	947
STEIGER, Bettie A.	(MD)	1185
ADLER, Robert J.	(MI)	7
SMILLIE, Pauline A.	(MI)	1151
KEIM, Robert	(MN)	635
DEMAS, Samuel G.	(NY)	291
PAUL, Sandra K.	(NY)	949
REGAZZI, John J.	(NY)	1017
SIMON, Peter E.	(NY)	1140
MAYNARD, John C.	(ON)	790
OLSHEN, Toni	(ON)	922
CUSWORTH, George R.	(ENG)	267

Electronic publishing & merchandising	MOFFITT, Michael D.	(MA)	852
Electronic publishing consulting	BERUL, Lawrence H.	(MD)	91
Electronic publishing contracting	BROWN-SPRUILL, Debra K.	(NY)	149
Electronic publishing service	CONTESSA, William B.	(NY)	239
Electronic reference services	FLEMMING, Tom	(ON)	384
Electronic rural libraries	HOLT, Suzy	(MT)	554
Electronic services	GAUJARD, Pierre G.	(MD)	422
	GROVER, Iva S.	(WA)	474
Electronic tax research	SPEYER, Thomas W.	(NY)	1174
Electronic technology	ZUCK, Gregory J.	(KS)	1391
Electronic warfare	VAN VELZER, Verna J.	(CA)	1277
Electronic-mail	LITTLE, William	(VA)	734
Electronics	KONISHI, Sue S.	(IL)	670
Electronics & computing research	CRABTREE, Sandra A.	(CA)	254
Electronics & engineering	LUNSTEDT, Ralph A.	(CA)	749
Electronics & physics databases	WOLF, Noel C.	(AZ)	1360
Electronics databases	LEAVITT, Judith A.	(IA)	707
Electronics engineering	WALDE, Norma J.	(VA)	1294
Electronics industry information	THOMAS, Sandra L.	(OR)	1238
Electronics information specialist	COOK, Kathleen M.	(CA)	240
Electronics literature	MCGORRAY, John J.	(AZ)	807
Electronics searching	COGHLAN, Jill M.	(MA)	227
Electronics training	GRIEVE, Shelley	(OH)	468
Home electronics literature	FETTERMAN, Nelma I.	(AB)	374
Imaging systems, electronic	GOUDELOCK, Carol V.	(CA)	454
Installation of electronic libraries	BOWDEN, Gail L.	(PA)	120
Marketing electronic information	ARNOLD, Stephen E.	(KY)	34
Microcomputers & electronic mail	MELTON, Emily I.	(IL)	823
Online database, electronic publishing	HERRICK, Carol L.	(OH)	532
Online electronic catalog instruction	HITT, Charles J.	(MN)	544
Online electronic information services	HARRISON, Burgess A.	(CT)	506
Professional networks, electronic mail	LEHMAN, Tom	(MN)	713
Publisher of electronic services	HYLAND, Barbara	(ON)	580
Technical editing, consumer electronics	MENNIE, Don	(NJ)	824
Teletext electronic publishing	WILLIAMS, Fred	(GA)	1343

ELEMENTARY (See also Grade, Grammar, Kindergarten, School)

Automation in elementary libraries	PASSARELLO, Nancy H.	(FL)	946
Children's librarian, elementary school	POBANZ, Decky L.	(MI)	979
Development of elementary libraries	TAYLOR, Joie L.	(NE)	1227
Elementary & high school libraries	SULLIVAN, Mary A.	(GA)	1208
Elementary & middle school	ROONEY, Merilyn H.	(IN)	1053
Elementary & secondary education	MCDOWELL, Judith H.	(OH)	804
Elementary computer curriculum	FARRIS, Mary E.	(TN)	365
Elementary computer education	DOAN, Janice K.	(KY)	307
Elementary curriculum	HUNT, Margaret M.	(IN)	575
Elementary education	MCGREW, Linda L.	(IA)	808
	MURRAY, Bruce C.	(MD)	881
	ROSAR, Virginia W.	(NY)	1054
	HARPER, Marjory B.	(TN)	503
	SPENCER, Barbara L.	(TX)	1173
	WORTHY, Annie B.	(TX)	1369
Elementary, junior & senior high schools	ABBOTT, Ruth J.	(TX)	1

ELEMENTARY (Cont'd)

Elementary, junior high library services	DOMESCIK, Carol J.	(IL)	310
Elementary librarianship	HERRICK, Johanna W.	(HI)	532
	KOCH, Fran C.	(NY)	667
	SPRENGER, Suzanne F.	(VA)	1176
Elementary library media	CAMPA, Josephine	(MD)	175
Elementary library media centers	FARRIS, Mary E.	(TN)	365
Elementary library media curriculum	PROCTOR, Deborah K.	(WY)	994
Elementary library programming	ZACHARY, Patricia A.	(OK)	1385
Elementary media	STAHLMAN, Cherry S.	(FL)	1178
	CARPENTER, Charlotte L.	(TX)	184
Elementary media center activities	VAN SOMEREN, Betty A.	(MN)	1277
Elementary media education	LACY, Lyn E.	(MN)	687
	PAULEY, Charles W.	(MN)	950
Elementary medial specialization	SMITH, Judy B.	(GA)	1156
Elementary school librarian	FITZGERALD, M A.	(MD)	382
	SCHULTE, Teresa M.	(WI)	1101
Elementary school librarianship	TRIDLE, Jeanne A.	(AK)	1256
	SULLIVAN, Geraldine M.	(IL)	1207
	TEEGARDEN, Maude B.	(KY)	1229
	FORD, Delores C.	(TX)	389
Elementary school libraries	ELLIS, Caryl A.	(AZ)	344
	SKEHAN, Patricia A.	(CA)	1145
	MORIARTY, Ann	(DC)	865
	GRANTHAM, Ann V.	(GA)	458
	BAKER, Ethelyn J.	(IL)	48
	HUNT, Margaret M.	(IN)	575
	LONG, Marilyn B.	(LA)	739
	NOLAN, Peggy H.	(LA)	907
	NOLES, Judy H.	(LA)	908
	MASSEY, Eleanor N.	(NJ)	782
	TUNISON, Janice A.	(NY)	1263
	CHERESNOWSKI, Linda M.	(PA)	206
	PASHEL, Susan M.	(PA)	945
	SACHS, Kathie B.	(PA)	1073
	MCGOWN, Sue W.	(TX)	807
Elementary school libraries admin	ZUCKER, Blanche M.	(NV)	1391
Elementary school library	SCHAEFER, Elizabeth K.	(IL)	1088
	BRUNO, Frances J.	(NY)	151
Elementary school library automation	MULLER, Madeline A.	(OH)	877
Elementary school library coordination	HERRON, Bettie J.	(AZ)	533
Elementary school library instruction	SHABERLY, Leanna J.	(AZ)	1118
Elementary school library skills	CANDE, Lorraine N.	(NY)	178
Elementary school library systems	BERRIE, Ellen T.	(ME)	90
Elementary school media	GREENWOOD, Anna S.	(DC)	465
	KILPATRICK, Marguerite C.	(GA)	648
	NEWTON, Evah B.	(IN)	900
	SCHEU, Jean W.	(MN)	1092
Elementary school media centers	BURGOON, Roger S.	(GA)	159
Elementary school media services	HARTMAN, Linda C.	(MO)	508
Elementary schools	DEES DAUGHERTY, Kristin	(WI)	287
Elementary, secondary col devlpmnt	KUTTEROFF, Ethel C.	(NJ)	685
Elementary, secondary library education	CARTER, Yvonne B.	(DC)	190
Elementary, secondary school materials	PIEHL, Kathleen K.	(MN)	971
Elementary teaching	SKEHAN, Patricia A.	(CA)	1145
Elementary use of audiovisual equipment	SLOAN, Mary J.	(GA)	1149
High school & elementary libraries	STUBBLEFIELD, J G.	(TX)	1204
Management elementary school libraries	CRAIGHEAD, Alice A.	(TX)	254
Managing elementary school libraries	HOWELL, Wanda H.	(FL)	565
Service for elementary children	KORPELA, Betty L.	(OR)	672
Teaching elementary library skills	HEINRICH, Lois M.	(MD)	522
	TOWNSEND, Rita M.	(PA)	1253
Teaching elementary media skills	SULLI, Gerard C.	(CT)	1207
Training elementary library volunteers	HLUHANY, Patricia	(PA)	544

EMPLOYEE (See also Benefits, Hiring, Interviewing, Labor, Paraprofessionals, Part-Time, Professional, Technician, Temporary)

Employee appraisals	BRANDWEIN, Larry	(NY)	128
Employee assistance plans	BELLEFONTAINE, Arnold G.	(DC)	78

EMPLOYEE (Cont'd)

Employee benefits	COSTELLO, Robert C. . .	(CA)	249
	MILLER, Herbert A.	(DC)	838
	REYNOLDS, Carol C. . . .	(GA)	1025
	PORTA, Catherine M. . . .	(NY)	984
	BIRSCHEL, Dee B.	(WI)	99
	CHOUDHURI, Kabita . . .	(ON)	211
Employee benefits, home resource mgmt	JACQUES, Donna M. . . .	(MA)	591
Employee benefits research	GRANDE, Paula G.	(NY)	457
Employee involvement	HILDEBRAND, Carol I. . .	(OR)	538
Employee motivation & evaluation	BOYER, Calvin J.	(CA)	123
Employee relations	LIBBEY, George H.	(GA)	725
	WEATHERFORD, John W.	(MI)	1311
	GOODINGS, Sally A. . . .	(ON)	449
Insurance & employee benefits	KORMAN, Adrienne S. . .	(MA)	671
Supervision & training of employees	MCIVER, Stephanie P. . .	(GA)	809
Workstudy employee supervision	FOX, Lynne M.	(CO)	395

EMPLOYMENT (See also Career, Job, Manpower, Occupational, Outplacement, Placement)

Business & employment information	HOLTZMAN, Douglas A.	(CA)	555
Career & employment centers	MALLINGER, Stephen M.	(PA)	763
Employment management	KURKUL, Donna L.	(MA)	684
Employment services	DINERMAN, Gloria	(NJ)	304

ENCYCLOPEDIAS

Dictionaries, encyclopedias	BREWER, Annie M.	(MI)	134
Encyclopedia development	NAULT, William H.	(IL)	889
Encyclopedia manuscript editing	LAGIES, Meinhart J.	(CA)	688
Encyclopedia publishing	GOSDEN, George	(NY)	452
Encyclopedias	HAYES, James L.	(CT)	515
Encyclopedias, chemical & others	GRAYSON, Martin	(NY)	460
Indexing encyclopedia articles	BERNAL, Rose M.	(NY)	88

ENDOWMENT (See also Funding)

Endowment & grant funding	DEYOUNG, Charles D. . .	(IN)	298
Fundraising & endowment	CADDELL, Claude W. . .	(IN)	170

END-USER (See also User)

CAS online end-user training	ROSS, Johanna C.	(CA)	1058
Computer info sources, end-user systems	GODT, Carol	(MO)	443
Database end-user services	ECKLUND, Kristin A. . . .	(CA)	335
End-user access	LEVY, Louise R.	(NJ)	721
End-user behavior	SEWELL, Winifred	(MD)	1118
End-user education	MUELLER, Julie M.	(IL)	875
	RILEY, Ruth A.	(MO)	1034
End-user equipment	PRICE, Bennett J.	(CA)	992
End-user instruction, BRS after dark	COONS, William W.	(NY)	242
End-user instruction in chem databases	BECK, Diane J.	(CA)	71
End-user managing	PERINO, Elaine S.	(MA)	958
End-user marketing applications	MOYER, Barbara A.	(CA)	874
End-user needs analysis	SHELBURNE, Elizabeth C.	(DC)	1125
End-user online product design	LIPPERT, Margret G. . . .	(OH)	732
End-user online searching	WHITLEY, Katherine M. .	(AZ)	1333
End-user online training	HARBERT, Cathy E.	(MD)	499
	MACKSEY, Julie A.	(MI)	757
End-user search instruction	LIEBER, Ellen C.	(NY)	726
	CAMPBELL, Sandra M. .	(AB)	177
End-user search systems	CHAPMAN, Janet L. . . .	(NJ)	202
End-user searching	HOGAN, Eddy	(CA)	549
	LITTLEJOHN, Alice C. . .	(CA)	734
	DAVIDSON, Lloyd A. . . .	(IL)	276
	HURYCH, Jitka M.	(IL)	578
	GREENE, Cathy C.	(MA)	463
	TEITELBAUM, Sandra D.	(MD)	1230
	NASH, Stanley D.	(NJ)	888
	LIPPINCOTT, Joan K. . .	(NY)	732
	HALPERIN, Michael	(PA)	489
	BADER, Susan G.	(VA)	44
	STARR, Lea K.	(AB)	1182
	MARSHALL, Joanne G. .	(ON)	774
	ST. JACQUES, Suzanne L.	(ON)	1075
End-user searching & education	GLASGOW, Vicki L.	(MN)	440

END-USER (Cont'd)

End-user searching & training	BATISTA, Emily J.	(PA)	64
End-user searching training	NESBIT, Kathryn W.	(NY)	896
	KONDRASKE, Linda N. .	(TX)	670
End-user services & training	BRUNDAGE, Christina A.	(CA)	150
End-user systems	NICHOLS, Amy S.	(AL)	901
	MENEELY, William E. . . .	(GA)	824
	SPARKS, Joanne L.	(IL)	1171
End-user training	DAVIS, Rebecca A.	(CA)	280
	DEENEY, Kay E.	(CA)	286
	MANTHEY, Teresa M. . .	(CA)	767
	MIELKE, Marsha K.	(CA)	833
	PETERS, Marion C.	(CA)	962
	SHERMAN, Judith E. . . .	(CA)	1128
	SIMON, Nancy L.	(CO)	1140
	BANKS, Jane L.	(DC)	54
	JOHNSON, Hilary C. . . .	(DE)	605
	HSU, Pi Y.	(FL)	567
	BEVERIDGE, Mary I. . . .	(IA)	93
	BUNTROCK, Robert E. . .	(IL)	157
	BUTTON, Katherine H. . .	(MA)	167
	LOSCALZO, Anita B. . . .	(MA)	741
	OPPENHEIM, Roberta A.	(MA)	925
	HERIN, Nancy J.	(MD)	531
	OSEGUEDA, Laura M. . .	(NC)	927
	AUGHEY, Kathleen M. . .	(NJ)	39
	GREENBERG, Charles J.	(NY)	463
	SAFRAN, Scott A.	(NY)	1074
	SOLLENBERGER, Julia F.	(NY)	1166
	SEXTON, Sally V.	(OH)	1118
	MADER, Sharon B.	(TN)	759
	LEE, Donna K.	(VT)	709
End-user training & consultation	INGUI, Bettejean	(CO)	583
End-user training & development	STRAHAN, Michael F. . .	(ND)	1199
End-user training for MEDLINE computer	POND, Frederick C.	(NY)	982
End-user training, staff training	MEREDITH, Meri	(IN)	825
Medical end-user systems	TURMAN, Lynne U.	(VA)	1264
Online searching & end-users	SCHATZ, Cindy A.	(MA)	1090
Online searching, end-user training	KASALKO, Sally G.	(AR)	628
Online services & end-user services	SATTERTHWAITE, Rebecca K.	(MD)	1084
Reference end-user service	EDWARDS, Willie M. . . .	(MI)	338
Technology & end-users	RUSSELL, Keith W.	(MD)	1069
Training end-users	REID, Valerie L.	(MI)	1019
	ETTL, Lorraine R.	(ND)	356
Training end-users searching	BROWN, Carolyn M. . . .	(GA)	142

ENERGY (See also Power, Solar)

Alternate forms of energy	JESKE, Margo	(ON)	600
Electric utilities & energy	FARKAS, Susan A.	(DC)	364
Energy	RADEMACHER, Kurt A. .	(CA)	1002
	TOCH, Terryann	(DC)	1248
	WINQUIST, Elaine W. . .	(MA)	1355
	SPARER, Saretta	(NY)	1171
	KNUP, Marie S.	(PA)	666
	ALEXANDER, Ginger H. .	(WA)	12
	GASPAR, Noel J.	(ON)	421
Energy & business reference	WEBER, Robert F.	(OR)	1314
Energy & environment databases	MCDONALD, Ethel Q. . .	(TN)	802
Energy & environment research	STANLEY, Eileen H. . . .	(LA)	1180
Energy & environmental science	CLARK, Peter W.	(WI)	217
Energy & mineral resources information	HARDY, Kenneth J.	(AB)	501
Energy & technical databases	LOOP, Jacqueline N. . . .	(ID)	740
Energy & the economy	YANCHAR, Joyce M. . . .	(MA)	1377
Energy conservation	MARCIL, Louise	(PQ)	769
Energy database	JACKSON, Ella J.	(NV)	587
Energy databases	CORNWELL, Douglas W.	(FL)	247
	TUCKER, Clark F.	(MD)	1261
	SOLSETH, Gwenn M. . . .	(MN)	1166
	SAMPLE, Charles R. . . .	(WA)	1078
Energy disciplines	SMITH, Catherine A. . . .	(MI)	1153
Energy efficient architecture	MARCIL, Louise	(PQ)	769
Energy efficient portable library	POWELL, Anice C.	(MS)	988
Energy, electric utility industry	MUIR, Scott P.	(AL)	876
Energy industry	KERWIN, Camillus A. . . .	(TX)	644
Energy information resources	RIX, Dolores M.	(IL)	1037
Energy information services	FEINBERG, Beryl L.	(DC)	368

ENERGY (Cont'd)

Energy medicine	DIAL, Zona P.	(AZ)	299
Energy reference & library management	BLANDAMER, Ann W.	(DC)	103
Energy reference & natural gas	MARSHALL, Alexandra P.	(ON)	773
Energy regulatory matters	PARK, Nancy R.	(ON)	941
Energy statistics	BAILEY, Linda S.	(TX)	46
Energy technology	MARCIL, Louise	(PQ)	769
Engineering, energy, environmental	AKS, Gloria	(NY)	9
Hazardous waste, energy & environment	HASTINGS, Constance M.	(TN)	511
Magnetic fusion energy	KNAACK, Linda M.	(MA)	663
Nuclear energy	KEIZUR, Berta L.	(CA)	635
Petroleum & energy database indexing	SHERRILL, Jocelyn T.	(NY)	1129
Petroleum & energy law	DUDLEY, Durand S.	(OH)	323

ENFORCEMENT

Law enforcement	DILUCIA, Samuel J.	(HI)	303
	CORDONI, Earl C.	(IL)	246
Law enforcement, one-person library	ZIMMERMAN, Donna K.	(IN)	1388
Police & law enforcement	RAMM, Dorothy V.	(IL)	1005
Police training & law enforcement	MERRYWEATHER, J M.	(ON)	827

ENGINEERING (See also Bioengineering)

Aeronautical engineering information	AUSTIN, Rhea C.	(MD)	40
Aerospace & engineering databases	ANTHONY, Paul L.	(IL)	29
Aerospace, automotive, engineering	YOUNGEN, Gregory K.	(IN)	1383
Agricultural engineering databases	MCNAUGHT, Hugh W.	(ON)	816
Architectural, engineering archives	DRAKE, Robert E.	(MA)	318
Audio recording & engineering	SUMMERHILL, Craig A.	(MI)	1209
Automotive engineering literature	WARD, Maryanne	(WA)	1304
Business & engineering databases	LO, Maryanne H.	(MN)	735
	HAWLEY, Laurie J.	(TX)	514
Business & engineering information	GRELL, Holly J.	(GA)	467
Business & technical engineering	GRIFFITTS, Joan K.	(IN)	469
Business, engineering, & med databases	POLK, Diana B.	(IL)	981
Business, health care, engrng databases	PLOTSKY, Andrea G.	(CA)	978
Cataloging architectural & engineering	SPAHR, Cheryl L.	(OH)	1170
Cataloging civil engineering materials	REINALDO DA SILVA, Joann T.	(MB)	1021
Cataloging environmental engineering	CARROLL, Virginia L.	(MA)	187
Chemical & engineering databases	SCHUTZBERG, Frances	(MA)	1103
Chemical engineering	VOSS, Ingrid M.	(IL)	1289
	BIGGS, Barbara R.	(LA)	95
	GASPAR, Noel J.	(ON)	421
Chemical engineering bibliography	WEAVER, James B.	(FL)	1312
Chemical engineering indexing	WEAVER, James B.	(FL)	1312
Chemical engineering references	MONTGOMERY, Kimberly K.	(AL)	856
Chemistry & engineering	THORP, Raymond G.	(ENG)	1242
Chemistry & engineering reference	BECK, Diane J.	(CA)	71
Chemistry, engineering	GARCIA, Ceil K.	(NJ)	417
Chemistry engineering & physics	SCHALIT, Michael	(CA)	1089
Civil & environmental engineering	UZZO, Beatrice C.	(NY)	1270
Civil & mechanical engineering	AMRON, Irving	(NJ)	20
Civil & structural engineering	SPIGELMAN, Cynthia A.	(IL)	1174
Civil engineering	REICHARDT, Randall P.	(AB)	1018
Civil engineering, pavements, structures	MOBLEY, Arthur B.	(DC)	851
Computer engineering databases	WOJCIKIEWICZ, Carol A.	(MI)	1359
Database searching in chemistry & engrng	WEST, Deborah C.	(TX)	1326
Earthquake engineering	WEBSTER, James K.	(NY)	1314
Earthquake engineering reference service	SVIHRA, S J.	(CA)	1212
Electric utility engineering	WEBER, Robert F.	(OR)	1314
Electrical & computer engineering	STEINBERG, Marilyn H.	(MA)	1185
Electrical & electronic engineering	BEDDES, Marianne T.	(NJ)	73
	THODY, Susan I.	(ON)	1235
Electrical engineering	VARNER, James H.	(CO)	1279
	THOMA, George R.	(MD)	1235
	SUNDAY, Donald E.	(NJ)	1210
	HAHN, Susan H.	(PA)	484
	FENKER, John A.	(WA)	371
Electronic engineering & geography	RICHARD, Marie F.	(PQ)	1028

ENGINEERING (Cont'd)

Electronics & engineering	LUNSTEDT, Ralph A.	(CA)	749
Electronics engineering	WALDE, Norma J.	(VA)	1294
Engineering	FINEMAN, Michael	(CA)	377
	GESCHKE, Nancy A.	(CA)	430
	GUST, Kathleen D.	(CA)	478
	HUTCHESON, Don S.	(CA)	578
	MIRONENKO, Rimma	(CA)	847
	SANDVIKEN, Gordon L.	(CA)	1081
	WETTS, Hazel H.	(CA)	1328
	ZACHER, Elaine F.	(CA)	1385
	MATTINGLY, Debra B.	(CO)	786
	SCHINDLER, Jo A.	(HI)	1093
	CARTER, Ida	(IL)	189
	RYAN, Betsey A.	(KS)	1070
	GIBBS, Paige	(MA)	431
	MASON, Hayden	(MA)	781
	SILVERBERG, Mary E.	(MA)	1138
	NELSON, Catherine G.	(MN)	893
	SCHMIDT, Jean M.	(MN)	1095
	SMISEK, Thomas P.	(MN)	1152
	KAPLAN, Isabel C.	(NY)	626
	HAMILTON, Dennis O.	(OH)	492
	MAKELA, Helen H.	(OH)	762
	KNUP, Marie S.	(PA)	666
	MYERS, Charles J.	(PA)	884
	HASTINGS, Constance M.	(TN)	511
	ARNOLD, Patricia K.	(TX)	34
	BELL, Charise F.	(TX)	76
	BLOECHLE, Marie K.	(TX)	106
	DAVIS, Sara	(TX)	281
	DOYLE, Frances M.	(VA)	317
	LORD, Charles R.	(WA)	741
	SLIVKA, Enid M.	(WA)	1149
	CIBOCH, Lorraine A.	(WI)	214
	JOBELIUS, Nancy L.	(WI)	601
	BUISMAN, Maria J.	(ON)	156
	CROXFORD, Agnes M.	(ON)	262
	SENNETT, Judith A.	(ON)	1115
Engineering & business online searching	ARROWOOD, Nina R.	(NJ)	35
Engineering & business reference	KAUFENBERG, Jane M.	(MN)	630
Engineering & construction databases	HARBERT, Cathy E.	(MD)	499
Engineering & data communications	WIEHN, John F.	(CT)	1336
Engineering & environmental databases	CREW-NOBLE, Sara M.	(CA)	258
Engineering & manufacturing reference	NESBITT, Olive K.	(PA)	896
Engineering & materials reference	WOODLOCK, Stephanie	(PA)	1366
Engineering & medical databases	MOUZON, Margaret W.	(MI)	874
Engineering & medical research	SARAIDARIDIS, Susan B.	(MA)	1082
Engineering & related databases	HUNT, Deborah S.	(CA)	575
Engineering & science information	LUCKER, Jay K.	(MA)	746
Engineering & science reference	MULLEN, Cecilia P.	(CA)	877
	TINSLEY, Geraldine L.	(PA)	1246
Engineering & science research	SOKOV, Asta M.	(PQ)	1166
Engineering & technical databases	POZO, Frank J.	(NC)	989
	VIXIE, Anne C.	(OR)	1286
	MIDGETT, Ann S.	(TX)	833
Engineering & technical library	MCDANIELS, Patricia R.	(OR)	801
Engineering cataloging	GRUBER, Linda R.	(PA)	474
Engineering codes & standards	BERNSTEIN, Anna L.	(DC)	89
Engineering collection development	WILLIS, Glee M.	(CA)	1348
	LONG, Caroline C.	(DC)	739
	MYERS, Charles J.	(PA)	884
	WARD, Suzanne M.	(TN)	1304
Engineering, data processing	FLEMING, Jack C.	(ON)	384
Engineering database construction	PIERCE, Anne L.	(CT)	971
Engineering databases	ATKINSON, Calberta O.	(AL)	38
	FELLER, Amy I.	(CA)	370
	MARKWORTH, Lawrence L.	(CA)	772
	JOHNSON, Doris E.	(CT)	603
	MOON, Mary G.	(CT)	857
	STEELE, Noreen O.	(CT)	1184
	BERNSTEIN, Anna L.	(DC)	89
	HAMILTON, D A.	(IL)	491
	ERDMANN, Charlotte A.	(IN)	352
	BERNARD, Bobbi	(MA)	88
	MUISE, Anita M.	(MA)	876

ENGINEERING (Cont'd)

Engineering databases

LAWSON, James R.	(ME)	705
BRACKETT, Norman S.	(MI)	124
BARRETT, Joyce C.	(NJ)	59
BULYA, Larissa	(NJ)	157
PEABODY, Kenneth W.	(NJ)	951
BERGER, Mary C.	(NY)	85
PINGITORE, Patricia E.	(NY)	974
LIPPERT, Margret G.	(OH)	732
MOGREN, Diane A.	(OH)	852
O'BRIEN, Mary C.	(OR)	915
CONKLING, Thomas W.	(PA)	236
COTTER, Stacy L.	(TX)	250
KANE, Deborah A.	(TX)	624
ZANG, Patricia J.	(VA)	1386
SMART, Doris M.	(WA)	1151
D'AMBOISE, Marion J.	(ON)	271
SANO, Hikomaro	(JAP)	1081

Engineering databases online searching — SCHNEIDER, Tatiana (ON) 1097
Engineering databases searching — THIBAUDEAU, Louise (PQ) 1235
Engineering documents — BARRETT, Joyce C. (NJ) 59
Engineering, energy, environmental — AKS, Gloria (NY) 9
Engineering information

OBERG, Judy M.	(CO)	914
SLOAN, Carol L.	(NY)	1149
O'GORMAN, Jack	(OH)	918
POLAND, Jean A.	(OK)	980
CONKLING, Thomas W.	(PA)	236
SLOAN, Stephen M.	(AB)	1150

Engineering information & reference — SCHEIN, Lorraine S. (NY) 1091
Engineering information provider — AUSTIN, Ralph A. (NY) 40
Engineering information retrieval — CHANG, Frances M. (DC) 200
Engineering information sources — PATIENCE, Alice (OH) 947
Engineering librarianship — DALLAS, Larayne J. (TX) 270
Engineering libraries — BAGBY, Felicia R. (CA) 45
Engineering library personnel — LOOMIS, Barbara (IL) 740
Engineering library resources management — PFANN, Mary L. (NJ) 966
Engineering literature

GRAYSON, Virginia S.	(CT)	460
CANDELMO, Emily	(NY)	178
ERICKSON, Sandra E.	(NY)	352
WEBSTER, James K.	(NY)	1314
ROUTLEDGE, Patricia A.	(MB)	1062

Engineering literature & information — HAVLIK, Robert J. (IN) 513
Engineering material information — SHINER, Sharon L. (NJ) 1130
Engineering materials — COLLISHAW, Jackie J. (NJ) 233
Engineering periodicals — PIENITZ, Eleanor (NY) 971
Engineering physics & chemical databases — GENTRY, Susan K. (CA) 427
Engineering reference

ANDREWS, Karen L.	(CA)	26
GRANADOS, Rose A.	(CA)	457
LARUSSA, Carol J.	(CA)	700
RANCATORE, Celeste L.	(CA)	1006
BLAKE, Martha A.	(IL)	103
SCHRAMM, Mary T.	(IL)	1099
BARRY, Richard A.	(NY)	60
MURRAY, James T.	(OK)	882
WARD, Suzanne M.	(TN)	1304
LINDSEY, Thomas K.	(TX)	730

Engineering reference information — ST. AUBIN, Kendra J. (MA) 1075
Engineering research

SHAFER, Leona M.	(NJ)	1119
BLAUERT, Mary A.	(PA)	105
SMART, Doris M.	(WA)	1151

Engineering research, databases — EVANS, M R. (CA) 357
Engineering, scintfc, chemical databases — PELLINI, Nancy M. (MA) 955
Engineering standards — RICCI, Patricia L. (MN) 1026
Engineering standards reference — MOORE, John R. (IL) 860
Engineering subjects — SPARER, Saretta (NY) 1171
Engineering technologies — HARE, William J. (NH) 501
Environmental & civil engineering libs — SPURLOCK, Pauline (CA) 1177
Environmental engineering

SANSOBRINO, Jean C.	(CA)	1081
KAYES, Mary J.	(WI)	632

Environmental engineering databases — CARROLL, Virginia L. (MA) 187
Environmental engineering information — TUCKER, Mary E. (NC) 1262
Environmental sci & engineering database — DONG, Tina (MA) 311
Genetic engineering — SAFFER-MARCHAND, Melinda (MA) 1074

ENGINEERING (Cont'd)

Geotechnical & engineering databases — JEROME, Susanne M. (AZ) 599
Information modeling & engineering — MAXWELL, Marjo V. (OH) 788
Information systems engineering — LISTON, David M. (MD) 732
Knowledge engineering — VLEDUTS-STOKOLOV, Natalia (PA) 1286

GLAMM, Amy E.	(VA)	439

Literature of engineering — MAYLES, William F. (IN) 790
Marine engineering — JOBA, Judith C. (PQ) 601
Medical databases, engineering databases — GODT, Carol (MO) 443
Medicine, engineering reference — COSGRIFF, John C. (VA) 248
Metallurgical & engineered materials — BALDWIN, Eleanor M. (OH) 51
Metals, metallurgical sci, engineering — HYSLOP, Marjorie R. (OH) 580
Military engineering — KOCH, Kathy R. (CA) 667
Nuclear engineering

SHERMAN, Dottie	(CT)	1128
DOENGES, John C.	(DC)	308
NISH, Susan J.	(PQ)	905

Nuclear engineering sciences — MAYER, Erich J. (NY) 789
Nuclear safety & nuclear engineering — TODOSOW, Helen K. (NY) 1248
Nuclear science & engineering — WEBSTER, Lois S. (IL) 1314
Online searching, engineering — SHLIONSKY, Anatoly (PQ) 1132
Online searching, engineering databases — LYLE, Martha E. (SC) 751
Online searching, science & engineering — WILLS, Luella G. (VA) 1349
Ordering architectural, engrng books — SPAHR, Cheryl L. (OH) 1170
Physical, life scis & engrng reference — MURPHY, Joan F. (CA) 880
Physical sciences & engineering — HADDEN, Robert L. (MD) 481
Power engineering — SEABERG, Eileen J. (IL) 1109
Process engineering

GOLBITZ, Peter	(ME)	444
KINGMA, Sharyn L.	(ME)	652

Reference engineering subjects — PERTELL, Grace M. (IL) 961
Reference, physical sci & engineering — SIEBURTH, Janice F. (RI) 1135
Reference services, engineering — OMAR, Elizabeth A. (MD) 923
Reference services in engineering — MORRIS, Louis M. (MD) 867
Research & engineering databases — DE TONNANCOUR, P R. (TX) 296
Safety engineering research — HANSEN, Cheryl A. (IL) 497
Science & engineering

SMITH, Martin A.	(DC)	1158
FARAH, Barbara D.	(MA)	363
BALACHANDRAN, Sarojini	(MO)	50
FREEDMAN, Jack A.	(MS)	400
HECHT, Judith N.	(OH)	519
ZEIDNER, Christine M.	(UT)	1387

Science & engineering bibliography — MALINOWSKY, H R. (IL) 763
Science & engineering cataloging — BRUNNER, A M. (TX) 151
Science & engineering databases

BAUM, Ester B.	(AZ)	66
WYLIE, Nethery A.	(CO)	1375
SAUER, David A.	(MA)	1084
POWELL, Jill H.	(NY)	988
HOLLIS, William F.	(OH)	552
LANG, Anita E.	(TX)	695

Science & engineering literature

MCGORRAY, John J.	(AZ)	807
BUNTZEN, Joan L.	(CA)	157
SASS, Samuel	(MA)	1083

Science & engineering online searching — BRUNNER, A M. (TX) 151
Science & engineering reference

HODGSON, Elizabeth A.	(NY)	546
PANCAKE, Edwina	(VA)	937
FISHER, Rita C.	(WA)	381

Science & engineering reference service — BALDWIN, Charlene M. (AZ) 51
Science & engineering reference services — TABACHNICK, Sharon (TN) 1219
Science, engineering — VARNER, James H. (CO) 1279
Science, engineering & medical databases — ARIARATNAM, Lakshmi V. (CA) 31
Science, engineering, & technology — GNAT, Jean M. (IN) 442
Science, technology engineering database — TODOSOW, Helen K. (NY) 1248
Scientific & engineering databases — LANDAU, Herbert B. (NY) 692
Software chemical, petroleum engineering — WILSON, John W. (TX) 1351
Software engineering

BAILEY, Charles W.	(NC)	46
THOMAS, James M.	(OH)	1237

Software engineering collection — SOUCIE, Yan Y. (OR) 1169
Systems engineering — LISTON, David M. (MD) 732
Technical & engineering databases — ALBRIGHT, Sue R. (CA) 10

ENGINEERING (Cont'd)
Technical & engineering documents — SCHULTZ, Arnold J. . . . (MN) 1101
Technical & engineering information — HARTLEY, Gloria R. . . . . (PA) 508
Technical databases, engineering — FINGERMAN, Susan M. . (MA) 378
Traffic engineering — HATHAWAY, Kay E. . . . (VA) 512
Water & wastewater engineering — SANSOBRINO, Jean C. . (CA) 1081
Working with engineers — LAVIN, Margaret A. . . . . (NJ) 703

ENGLISH (See also Anglo-African, Anglo-Saxon, British)
American & English literature — ELDREDGE, Mary . . . . . (CA) 342
DAVIS, Sandra B. . . . . . (IL) 281
American & English lit bibliography — BAKY, John S. . . . . (PA) 50
Bibliography of English literature — PROPAS, Sharon W. . . . . (OH) 995
Buying & selling of English literature — MARTIN, John W. . . . . . (IL) 776
Children's English & French literature — WALSH, Mary A. . . . . (PQ) 1300
Collection development, English — JOSEPH, Margaret A. . . . (TX) 617
Contemporary English drama — DACE, Tish . . . . (MA) 269
English — MCDOWELL, Judith H. . . (OH) 804
English & American literature — MCPHERON, William . . (CA) 817
KING, Judith D. . . . . . . (CT) 651
STEBELMAN, Scott D. . . (DC) 1183
ELLIS, Marie C. . . . . . . (GA) 345
NAIMAN, Sandra M. . . . . (IL) 886
BRACKEN, James K. . . . (IN) 124
IMMLER, Frank . . . . . (MN) 582
BROCKMAN, William S. . . (NJ) 138
JONES, Arthur E. . . . . . (NJ) 611
FRALEY, David B. . . . . (WA) 395
English & continental material — ZALL, Elisabeth W. . . . . (CA) 1386
English & French book selection — TAGGART, William R. . . (BC) 1220
English & French books selection — DAVIS, Virginia K. . . . . (ON) 281
English as a second language — PEISER, Richard H. . . . . (IL) 955
English education — DONNELLY, Lela M. . . . (KS) 311
English history — STAM, David H. . . . . . . (NY) 1179
English language text data — SCHULTZ, Arnold J. . . . (MN) 1101
English, linguistics & classics — RICKER, Shirley E. . . . . (NY) 1031
English literature — MEEKER, Robert B. . . . . (IL) 821
FUDERER, Laura S. . . . . (IN) 408
DICKSON, Katherine M. . (MD) 301
GAUCH, Patricia L. . . . . . (NY) 422
LINDSAY, Jean S. . . . . . (NY) 729
MARTIN, Lyn M. . . . . . . (NY) 777
MCGLINCHEE, Claire . . . (NY) 806
WIERUM, Ann R. . . . . . (WA) 1337
O'NEILL, Louise N. . . . . . (ON) 924
English literature bibliography — THOMSON, Dorothy F. . . (ON) 1241
English literature, romantic — STAM, David H. . . . . . . (NY) 1179
English literature selector — THORSON, Connie C. . . (NM) 1242
English material on Chinese law — LUNG, Mon Y. . . . . (KS) 748
English renaissance manuscripts — YEANDLE, Laetitia . . . . . (DC) 1378
English social sciences — STURGIS, Marylee C. . . (VA) 1205
French, Arabic, English translation — YASSA, Lucie M. . . . . . . (CA) 1378
Information science, english literature — JONES-TRENT, Bernice R. (VA) 616
K-6 & English collection development — MCGLOHON, Leah L. . . (NC) 807
Language arts & English education — BUBOLTZ, Dale D. . . . . . (CA) 152
Literacy & English classes — GRUENBECK, Laurie . . . (TX) 474
Modern English poetry — KAISER, John R. . . . . . (PA) 622
Rare children's books in English — JOHNSON, Carolyn E. . . (CA) 602
Selection of English books — DJEVALIKIAN, Sonia . . . (PQ) 306
17th century English books — SILVER, Joel B. . . . . . . (IN) 1138
Subject, English literature — SILVER, Diane L. . . . . . (PA) 1138
Translation Spanish to English — DRIVER, Marjorie G. . . . . (GU) 320
Turkish literature, English translations — BILEYDI, Lois G. . . . . . . (MN) 96
Tutoring English as a foreign
    language — NORRIS, Loretta W. . . . . (DC) 909

ENRICHMENT
Curriculum enrichment — PARADISE, Don M. . . . . (PA) 939
Enrichment — LESUEUR, Joan K. . . . . . (NC) 718

ENROLLMENT
Declining enrollment & school
    closings — FLOWERS, Helen F. . . . (NY) 386

ENTERTAINMENT (See also Games)
American popular entertainments — LOMONACO, Martha S. . . (NY) 738
Entertainment research — PLUMB, Carolyn G. . . . . (CA) 978
PRUETT, Barbara J. . . . . (DC) 996
Sports & entertainment law — EDMONDS, Edmund P. . . (VA) 336

ENTOMOLOGY
Entomology — JACOBSON, June B. . . . (FL) 590

ENTREPRENEURSHIP
Entrepreneur resources — SKONIECZNY, Jill . . . . . (MI) 1147
Entrepreneuring — WARNER, Alice S. . . . . . (MA) 1305
Information entrepreneurship — BOYER, Calvin J. . . . . . . (CA) 123

ENUMERATIVE
Enumerative & textual bibliographies — ABOYADE, Beatrice O. . (NGR) 2
Enumerative bibliography — COHN, Alan M. . . . . (IL) 229
WADSWORTH, Robert W. (IL) 1290
O'DONNELL, Mary A. . . (NY) 917
HARNER, James L. . . . . (OH) 503
Textual & enumerative bibliography — WHITE, D J. . . . . (MO) 1330

ENVIRONMENT (See also Air, Ecology, Hazards, Rain, Waste)
Alaska environmental databases — SOKOLOV, Barbara J. . . (AK) 1165
Biology, agriculture & environment — LANE, David M. . . . . . . (NH) 694
Cataloging environmental engineering — CARROLL, Virginia L. . . (MA) 187
Chemistry & environmental databases — TYLER-WHITE, Patricia G. (TX) 1266
Children's reading environment — TAKEUCHI, Satoru . . . . (JAP) 1220
Civil & environmental engineering — UZZO, Beatrice C. . . . . . (NY) 1270
Computer information srvs
    environment — SCHWALLER, Marian C. (MA) 1104
Controlled environment agriculture — LAKE, Mary S. . . . . (AZ) 689
Controlled environment aquaculture — LAKE, Mary S. . . . . (AZ) 689
Earth & environmental sciences — RUDD, Janet K. . . . . . . (CA) 1065
Energy & environment databases — MCDONALD, Ethel Q. . . (TN) 802
Energy & environment research — STANLEY, Eileen H. . . . . (LA) 1180
Energy & environmental science — CLARK, Peter W. . . . . . (WI) 217
Engineering & environmental
    databases — CREW-NOBLE, Sara M. . (CA) 258
Engineering, energy, environmental — AKS, Gloria . . . . (NY) 9
Environment research — WEISENBURGER, Patricia
    J. . . . . (KS) 1319
Environmental — PRUHS, Sharon . . . . . . (CA) 996
STANLEY, Nelda J. . . . . (LA) 1180
Environmental & civil engineering libs — SPURLOCK, Pauline . . . (CA) 1177
Environmental & health regulations — LE BLANC, Judith E. . . . (OH) 708
Environmental database searching — CIVITARESE, Kathleen A. (FL) 215
Environmental databases — MCNAMARA, Emma J. . (DC) 816
CICHON, Marilyn T. . . . . (IL) 214
BRANSFORD, John S. . . (TN) 129
FIELDING, Carol J. . . . . . (WA) 376
MARSHALL, Kenneth E. . (MB) 774
Environmental education — ALASTI, Aryt . . . . (MA) 9
Environmental engineering — SANSOBRINO, Jean C. . (CA) 1081
KAYES, Mary J. . . . . . (WI) 632
Environmental engineering databases — CARROLL, Virginia L. . . (MA) 187
Environmental engineering information — TUCKER, Mary E. . . . . . (NC) 1262
Environmental health — NOWAK, Geraldine D. . . (DC) 911
Environmental health databases — MOORE, Catherine I. . . . (MA) 859
Environmental history — BAIRD, Dennis W. . . . . . (ID) 47
Environmental information — SCHEIBEL, Susan . . . . . (CA) 1091
EDDY, Dolores D. . . . . . (CO) 335
YOUNGEN, Gregory K. . (IN) 1383
WHELAN, Julia S. . . . . . (MA) 1329
MCCAULEY, Betty P. . . . (OR) 795
STERLING, Alida B. . . . . (PA) 1189
LOVENBURG, Susan L. . (AB) 743
Environmental information & data
    policy — SNODGRASS, Rex J. . . (NC) 1163
Environmental information databases — MILUTINOVIC, Eunhee C. (IL) 845
Environmental information
    management — SNODGRASS, Rex J. . . (NC) 1163
Environmental information resources — STOSS, Frederick W. . . . (NY) 1198
Environmental law — ERTZ, Ginger E. . . . . . . (PA) 353
Environmental laws & regulations — KAYES, Mary J. . . . . . . (WI) 632

ENVIRONMENT (Cont'd)

Environmental protection	WOLFE, Theresa L.	(NY)	1361
	BELLEFONTAINE, Gillian	(ON)	78
Environmental reference	RODES, Barbara K.	(DC)	1047
	BARATTA, Maria	(NJ)	55
Environmental reference & research	JOHNSON, Mary E.	(CA)	607
Environmental research	LARASON, Larry	(LA)	697
	LANK, Dannette H.	(WI)	696
Environmental research & info service	FELICETTI, Barbara W. .	(MA)	370
Environmental research areas	PRESBY, Richard A. . . .	(CA)	990
Environmental sci & engineering database	DONG, Tina	(MA)	311
Environmental sciences	CARRICABURU, Robert .	(CA)	186
	BROOKES, Barbara	(NY)	140
Environmental sources	VAN BRUNT, Amy S. . . .	(NY)	1272
Environmental sources & databases	HOTZ, Sharon M.	(CA)	562
Environmental topics consulting	IRELAND, Laverne H. . . .	(CA)	583
Government regulations on environment	GROOT, Elizabeth N. . . .	(CA)	472
Hazardous waste, energy & environment	HASTINGS, Constance M.	(TN)	511
Health & environment	HOFFMAN, Allen	(NY)	547
Medical chemical environmental databases	PAPROCKI, Mary E. . . .	(NJ)	939
Natural resources & environment ref	LARSEN, Lynda L.	(DC)	698
Protection of animal environment	THURSTON, Ethel H. . . .	(NY)	1243

EPHEMERAE (See also Memorabilia)

Correspondence, ephemerae, etc	GAMBLE, Mary J.	(CA)	416
Ephemera	VANSLYKE, Lisa M.	(CA)	1277
	MONIE, Willis J.	(NY)	855
Ephemeral materials	PEREZ, Maria L.	(FL)	958
Maps, printed ephemera	SILVER, Marcy L.	(MD)	1138
Rare books, photographs, ephemerae	HARDY, D C.	(LA)	500
Theatre ephemera	WOODS, Alan L.	(OH)	1366
Underground writing & ephemera	BJORKLUND, Edi	(WI)	100

EPIDEMIOLOGY (See also Diseases)

Clinical epidemiology	HAYNES, Robert B.	(ON)	517
Epidemiologic research databases	HOLMES, John H.	(PA)	553
Epidemiology	EPSTEIN, Robert S.	(MD)	351
	CAREL, Rafael S.	(ISR)	181

EPISCOPAL (See also Anglican)

Protestant & Episcopal Church clergy	HYDE, E C.	(MO)	580

EPISTEMOLOGY

Social epistemology	FROEHLICH, Thomas J. .	(NY)	405

EQUIPMENT (See also Bookstacks, Furniture, Hardware, Shelving)

Audiovisual equipment	SEGOR, Phyllis L.	(FL)	1112
	COBB, Marilyn R.	(IL)	225
	SYFERT, Samuel R.	(IL)	1217
	WOLFE, Mary S.	(PA)	1361
Audiovisual equipment administration	WALTERS, Corky	(WY)	1301
Audiovisual equipment & materials	LEDOUX, Mary E.	(OH)	709
Audiovisual equipment & productions	BURMAN, Marilyn P. . . .	(WY)	161
Audiovisual equipment, materials	HERBERT, Barbara R. . .	(NJ)	530
Audiovisual equipment purchasing	SHARP, Betty L.	(TX)	1122
Audiovisual equipment services	SHARMA, Shirley K.	(KS)	1122
Audiovisual media & equipment	MITCHELL, George D. . .	(TX)	848
Books & audiovisual equipment selection	ANDIS, Norma B.	(TX)	26
Building & equipment	MORITZ, William D.	(WI)	865
Buildings & equipment	SANNWALD, William W. .	(CA)	1081
	SEBRIGHT, Terence F. .	(FL)	1110
Designing & manufacturing lib equipment	KINGSLEY, Eleanor V. . .	(CA)	652
Digital equipment corporation	MONOSSON, Adolf S. . .	(MA)	855
Elementary use of audiovisual equipment	SLOAN, Mary J.	(GA)	1149
End-user equipment	PRICE, Bennett J.	(CA)	992
Equipment maintenance, replacement plng	CHRISTIANSON, Ellory J.	(MN)	212
Equipment sales	MAY, Robert E.	(SC)	789

EQUIPMENT (Cont'd)

Library building & equipment	LEWIS, Thomas F.	(MA)	724
	WEISS, Egon A.	(NY)	1320
Library buildings & equipment	BROADUS, Robert N. . . .	(NC)	138
	MOYER, James M.	(NC)	874
	HANES, Fred W.	(TX)	495
Library furniture & equipment	VAN ORSDEL, Darrell E. .	(WI)	1276
Library shelving & equipment	DAVIS, Glenn G.	(IL)	279
Maintaining audiovisual equipment	SUTHERLAND, Helen G. .	(CA)	1211
Materials & equipment evaluation	OSIER, Donald V.	(SDA)	928
Media, audiovisual equipment, video	RUBIN, Ellen B.	(NY)	1064
Media materials & equipment	LINK, Margaret A.	(NC)	730
Microforms collection & equipment	KURKUL, Donna L.	(MA)	684
Microforms, equipment, photocopy	GREEN, Walter H.	(MO)	463
Semiconductor equipment & materials	SHERMAN, Roger S. . . .	(CA)	1128
Shelving technical equipment	DE BEAR, Richard S. . . .	(MI)	284
Video media & equipment	MITCHELL, George D. . .	(TX)	848

EQUITY

Equity research archival database	MILLS, Andrew G.	(MA)	843
Equity research news service	MILLS, Andrew G.	(MA)	843
Investment banking, debt & equity	ABELES, Tom	(MN)	2
Pay equity	GALLOWAY, Sue	(CA)	415
	DOWELL, David R.	(IL)	315
	RAY, Jean M.	(IL)	1011
	FEYE-STUKAS, Janice . .	(MN)	374
Personnel pay & equity	JOHANSON, Cynthia J. .	(DC)	601

ERGONOMICS

Computer health ergonomics issues	MILLER, R B.	(CA)	841
Ergonomics	PRICE, Bennett J.	(CA)	992
	CAMPBELL, Brian G. . . .	(BC)	176
Ergonomics in system design	FONG, Wilfred W.	(WI)	388
Human factors, ergonomics	TOROK, Andrew G.	(IL)	1251

ERIC

ERIC & social sciences	MEEKER, Robert B.	(IL)	821
ERIC database online	MISSAR, Charles D.	(MD)	847
ERIC educational database	HENSON, Jane E.	(IN)	529
ERIC searching	SCHWARTZ, Philip J. . . .	(TX)	1105
	MCCART, Vernon A.	(VA)	794

ESSAYS

General exposition essays & reviews	HUMEZ, Nicholas D.	(ME)	573

ESTABLISHING

Archive establishment	KESSLER, Selma P.	(NJ)	645
Establishing corporate libraries	STAHL, Wilson M.	(NC)	1178
Establishing hospital libraries	CARLSON, Stan W.	(MN)	182
Establishing integrated library services	BELTON, Jennifer H. . . .	(DC)	78
Establishing lib & information systems	LEFFALL, Dolores C. . . .	(DC)	712
Establishing new libraries	SMITH, Kathleen S.	(DC)	1156
Establishing new school libraries	GOODMAN, Helen C. . . .	(TX)	449
Establishing resource centers	KUHL, Danuta	(VA)	682
Establishing school libraries	KRENTZ, Roger F.	(WI)	677
Establishing special libraries	WITMER, Tonya C.	(KS)	1358
Establishment of congregational libs	BURSON, Lorraine E. . . .	(OR)	163
Law firm library establishment	ROCKWOOD, Susan M. .	(PA)	1046
Library & info center establishment	FINGERMAN, Susan M. .	(MA)	378
Library establishment	DOLL, Harriet A.	(PA)	309
	VONKA, Stephanie	(PQ)	1288
Planning & establishing library systems	STANKIEWICZ, Carol A.	(CT)	1180
Satellite information ctrs establishment	LAVIN, Margaret A.	(NJ)	703
Small library establishment	STEFANACCI, Michal A.	(PA)	1185
Special lib establishment & development	LOKETS BEISCHROT, Dina	(CT)	738

ESTATE

Estate planning	MESMER, Frank B.	(NH)	827

ETHICS (See also Bioethics)

Biomedical ethics databases & info	GROVER, Wilma S.	(FL)	474
Ethics for information professionals	HORN, David E.	(MA)	559
Ethics research	MOLINARI, Joseph G. . .	(NY)	853
Hospital ethics	FINNERTY, James L. . . .	(IL)	379
Professional ethics	ARDEN, Caroline	(VA)	31
Sports ethics	CARGAS, Harry J.	(MO)	181
Theology & ethics	DAVISH, William	(MD)	281
Values & professional ethics	HALL, Homer J.	(NJ)	488

ETHNIC (See also names of specific ethnic groups, e.g. Black, Chicano, Polish, etc.)

American ethnic collections	SUTTON, David H.	(PA)	1211
Children's literature, ethnic	AUSTIN, Mary C.	(HI)	40
Collection development, ethnic studies	FISHER, Edith M.	(CA)	380
Ethnic & religious archives	GRACE, William M.	(PA)	455
Ethnic collections	DAVIS, Natalia G.	(NY)	280
Ethnic history & folklore	PENTI, Marsha E.	(MI)	957
Ethnic library service	KLEIMAN, Allan M.	(NY)	658
Ethnic library services	GALLEGO, Bert H.	(CA)	414
	SMITH, Elizabeth M.	(CA)	1154
Ethnic materials for children	BEILKE, Patricia F.	(IN)	75
Ethnic services	NAVARRO, Frank A.	(CA)	889
	WHITE, Lelia C.	(CA)	1331
Ethnic studies	WERTSMAN, Vladimir F. .	(NY)	1325
	ANDERSON, R J	(PA)	25
Ethnic studies & history of the book	WYNAR, Lubomyr R. . . .	(OH)	1375
Ethnic studies collection development	KNOWLES, Em C.	(CA)	665
Ethnicity & librarianship	COHEN, David	(NY)	228
Hispanic & Ethnic materials	AYALA, John L.	(CA)	42
Lecturing in ethnic & gen bibliography	FISHER, Edith M.	(CA)	380
Outreach to ethnic minorities	BETANCOURT, Ingrid T. .	(NJ)	92
Reference, American ethnic studies	RENKIEWICZ, Frank A. .	(MI)	1023
Reference in women's & ethnic studies	MARIE, Jacquelyn	(CA)	770
Reference services, ethnic & general	FISHER, Edith M.	(CA)	380
Services to ethnocultural communities	ZIELINSKA, Marie F. . . .	(ON)	1388

ETHNOMUSICOLOGY

Ethnomusicology	HICKERSON, Joseph C. .	(DC)	536
	NELSON, Brenda	(IN)	893
	RAHKONEN, Carl J.	(PA)	1003
	POST, Jennifer C.	(VT)	986
Ethnomusicology databases	SERCOMBE, Laurel	(WA)	1116
Musicology, ethnomusicology, romanticism	HAEFLIGER, Kathleen A.	(NY)	482
Subject access to ethnomusicology	SCHUURSMA, Ann B. . .	(NET)	1103

ETIQUETTE

Customs, folklore, etiquette, holidays	HAWK, Susan P.	(FL)	513

EUROPEAN

American & European history	GRIPPO, Christopher F. .	(WA)	471
Bibliography, European hist & religion	ROBERTS, Susanne F. . .	(CT)	1041
Cataloging European languages material	PHILLIPS, Richard F. . . .	(NJ)	969
Cataloging Western European monographs	SORURY, Kathryn L. . . .	(IN)	1169
East Europe & Middle East studies	PINSON, Mark	(MA)	975
East European studies	POVSIC, Frances F.	(OH)	987
	ARTHUR, Donald B. . . . ,	(TX)	35
Eastern Europe & Soviet Union	TOTH, George S.	(DC)	1252
Eastern European languages	KRUKONIS, Perkunas P. .	(MA)	680
European & American history	THOMPSON, Janet A. . . .	(NM)	1240
European history	HENNEMAN, John B. . . .	(NJ)	528
	NASH, Stanley D.	(NJ)	888
	BLACK, J A	(TX)	101
	WELSCH, Erwin K.	(WI)	1323
	VERYHA, Wasyl	(ON)	1283
European history major	BRUGNOLOTTI, Phyllis T.	(NY)	150
European languages & literature	KUJANSUU, Asko J.	(AB)	683
European literature	SIGNORI, Donna L.	(BC)	1137
European studies	CAMPBELL, James M. . .	(VA)	176
	STONE, Toby G.	(FRN)	1197
Foreign languages, European complex	PERSHE, Frank F.	(MO)	961
Germanic area, central Europe	FRANK, Peter R.	(CA)	397

EUROPEAN (Cont'd)

Government, US & European history	HERTZ, Sylvia	(MI)	533
Modern European history	O'CONNOR, Thomas F. .	(CA)	916
Modern European languages & literature	POLIT, Carlos E.	(IN)	980
Russian & East European bibliography	BEAVEN, Miranda J. . . .	(MN)	71
Russian & East European studies	ROBERTSON, Howard W. .	(OR)	1042
SDI European information	BERLIET, Nathalie B. . . .	(CT)	87
Slavic & East European	CHOLDIN, Marianna T. . .	(IL)	210
Slavic & East European librarianship	LEICH, Harold M.	(DC)	713
USSR, Asia, South American, Europe art	BLAIR, Madeline S.	(DC)	102
West European academic monographs	JAGER, Conradus	(MA)	591
West European studies	FINEMAN, Charles S. . . .	(IL)	377
West European subscription agencies	JAGER, Conradus	(MA)	591
Western European area studies	BROGAN, Martha L.	(MN)	139
Western European collection development	HUETING, Gail P.	(IL)	570
Western European humanities	DILLON, John B.	(WI)	303
Western European language materials	NEVIN, Susanne	(MN)	898
Western European languages & literature	BYRE, Calvin S.	(IL)	169

EVALUATION (See also Appraisal, Assessment, Criticism, Examination, Measurement)

Academic library evaluation	NEUHOFE, M D.	(FL)	897
	WILLIAMS-JENKINS, Barbara J.	(SC)	1347
Accreditation & program evaluation	MITCHELL, Joan M.	(PA)	849
Acquisition & evaluation of rare records	WAXMAN, Jack	(FL)	1311
Administrative planning & evaluation	TERNAK, Armand T.	(FL)	1232
Archival evaluation	BOECKMAN, Frances B. .	(MS)	109
Archival needs evaluation	EDGERLY, Linda	(MA)	336
Benefits analysis & evaluation	DUFORE, Thomas H. . . .	(AZ)	324
Book collection evaluation	NIXON, Arless B.	(AZ)	906
Book evaluation	HIRABAYASHI, Joanne .	(CA)	543
	OSSEN, Virginia F.	(CA)	928
	CHANDRA, Jane H.	(NC)	200
Book selection & evaluation	PATRON, Susan H.	(CA)	947
Chemical structure software evaluation	SOUTHWICK, Margaret A.	(VA)	1170
Collection development & evaluation	LO, Henrietta W.	(CA)	735
	ORTOPAN, Leroy D.	(CA)	927
	WRIGHT, Arthuree M. . . .	(DC)	1370
	CASSERLY, Mary F. . . .	(ME)	193
	OBERG, Larry R.	(MI)	914
	WINKEL, Lois	(NC)	1355
	CARLSON, Kathleen A. . .	(NM)	182
	LIN, Susan T.	(NY)	728
	RICHARDS, Daniel T. . . .	(NY)	1028
	DAVIS, Yvonne M.	(OH)	281
	GARCIA, Lana C.	(TX)	417
	WAYLAND, Terry T. . . .	(TX)	1311
	PURDY, Victor W.	(UT)	998
	HABAN, Mary F.	(VA)	480
	LIN, John T.	(VA)	727
	SCHNEIDER, Frank A. . .	(WA)	1097
	MILNE, Dorothy J.	(NF)	845
	BESSETTE, Madeleine . .	(PQ)	91
Collection development, evaluation	DAVIES, Gordon B.	(MD)	277
Collection evaluation	MILLER, Edward P.	(AZ)	837
	COOPER, David J.	(MD)	242
	DRONE, Jeanette M. . . .	(OH)	320
	LOPEZ, Elsa M.	(PR)	741
	MAGRILL, Rose M.	(TX)	760
	SHERMAN-PETERSON, Ronald A.	(WA)	1128
	DUPRE, Monique	(ON)	327
	FAIRLEY, Craig R.	(ON)	361
Collection evaluation & assessment	SIGNORI, Donna L.	(BC)	1137
Collection evaluation & description	HIGBEE, Joan F.	(DC)	537
Collection evaluation & development	FOURIE, Denise K.	(CA)	393

EVALUATION (Cont'd)

Topic	Name	State	Page
Collections evaluation	MACDONALD, Patricia A.	(ON)	754
Competitor analysis & evaluation	PICKETT, Doyle C.	(NJ)	970
Computer software evaluation	KELLY, Patricia M.	(MA)	638
Consulting & evaluation	HENDERSON, Rosemary	(KS)	527
Courseware evaluation	BARALOTO, R A.	(MD)	55
Database evaluation & searching	HEWISON, Nancy S.	(IN)	535
Database evaluations	CYGAN, Rose M.	(MI)	268
Disability & rehabilitation evaluation	SMITH, Kathleen A.	(MD)	1156
District, school library evaluation	LEVEILLEE, Louis R.	(RI)	719
Editing & manuscript evaluation	MOON, Eric	(FL)	857
Educational film & video evaluation	MODICA, Mary L.	(SD)	851
Employee motivation & evaluation	BOYER, Calvin J.	(CA)	123
Evaluating children's book collections	EDMONDS, May H.	(FL)	336
Evaluating federal library programs	KIRSCHENBAUM. Arthur S.	(DC)	655
Evaluating teenage books	ESTES, Sally C.	(IL)	355
Evaluation	SALVATORE, Gayle E.	(LA)	1078
	GRIFFITHS, Jose M.	(MD)	469
	DURRANCE, Joan C.	(MI)	328
	ADAMS, Mignon S.	(PA)	5
	MERCHANT, Cheryl N.	(TX)	825
	CHOBOT, Mary C.	(VA)	210
Evaluation & accreditation	GORCHELS, Clarence C.	(OR)	451
Evaluation & planning	RODERER, Nancy K.	(NY)	1047
	MOMBILLE, Pedro	(PR)	854
Evaluation & selection of library media	PETERSON, Miriam E.	(IL)	964
Evaluation consultation	BEDARD, Evelyn M.	(TX)	73
Evaluation of film centers	RICHIE, Mark L.	(NJ)	1030
Evaluation of information services	MCLAUGHLIN, W K.	(AB)	813
Evaluation of libraries & info services	KING, Donald W.	(MD)	650
Evaluation of library materials	MILLER, Margaret S.	(CA)	840
Evaluation of library services	LANCASTER, Frederick W.	(IL)	691
	GOODWIN, Jane G.	(VA)	450
Evaluation of library software	SAVAGE, Gretchen S.	(CA)	1085
Evaluation of records	MOSES, Julian M.	(NY)	871
Evaluation of reference services	BUNGE, Charles A.	(WI)	157
Evaluation of school librarians	OLSEN, Katherine M.	(UT)	921
Evaluation of school library programs	HUNT, Linda A.	(VA)	575
Evaluation of school library services	BOMAR, Cora P.	(NC)	113
Evaluation of services	MCGRIFF, Ronald I.	(MN)	808
Evaluation of technical information	HALL, Homer J.	(NJ)	488
Evaluation of vendor performance	ANDERSON, E A.	(MN)	22
Evaluation research	LUND, Patricia A.	(WI)	748
Evaluation research, curriculum software	HERB, Elizabeth D.	(OH)	530
Evaluation research, information systems	SIEGEL, Elliot R.	(MD)	1136
Evaluation school libraries	CRAIGHEAD, Alice A.	(TX)	254
Evaluation selection	MACRAE, Lorne G.	(AB)	758
Evaluative & developmental research	LIPETZ, Ben A.	(NY)	732
Faculty development & evaluation	BEDSOLE, Dan T.	(VA)	73
Grant program evaluations	EATENSON, Ervin T.	(TX)	333
Health education & evaluation	WAYLAND, Marilyn T.	(MI)	1311
Historical & evaluation research	DU MONT, Rosemary R.	(OH)	325
Information needs evaluations & analysis	HOLDEN, Douglas H.	(ND)	550
Info services measurement evaluation	WERT, Lucille M.	(IL)	1325
Information system evaluation	GRIFFITH, Belver C.	(PA)	469
	VAN SLYPE, Georges	(BEL)	1277
Information systems design & evaluation	LEVITAN, Karen B.	(MD)	721
Job analysis & evaluation	DUFORE, Thomas H.	(AZ)	324
Job evaluation	KIRKPATRICK, Jane E.	(ON)	655
Library collection evaluation	LYNN-NELSON, Gayle	(NJ)	752
Library evaluation	FRICK, Elizabeth A.	(NS)	403
Library evaluation & research	MULLINER, Kent	(OH)	878
Library evaluations	RUNYON, Robert S.	(NE)	1067
Library management & evaluation	ETTER, Constance L.	(IL)	355
Library measurement & evaluation	RODGER, Eleanor J.	(IL)	1047
Library planning & evaluation	JENKINS, Darrell L.	(IL)	597
	ROBINSON, Charles W.	(MD)	1043
	BRAWNER, Lee B.	(OK)	130
Library program evaluations	EATENSON, Ervin T.	(TX)	333
Library self-study & evaluation	KANIA, Antoinette M.	(NY)	625
Library services evaluation	SUIDAN, Randa H.	(IL)	1207
Library systems evaluation	GOODELL, John S.	(AUS)	448
Literacy prog development & evaluation	MADDEN, Doreitha R.	(NJ)	758

EVALUATION (Cont'd)

Topic	Name	State	Page
Mainframe evaluation database management	BARALOTO, R A.	(MD)	55
Materials & equipment evaluation	OSIER, Donald V.	(SDA)	928
Materials evaluation & selection	HOWLAND, Margaret E.	(MA)	566
Measurement & evaluation	ANTHONY, Carolyn A.	(IL)	28
	EDMONDS, M L.	(IL)	336
	EISENBERG, Michael B.	(NY)	340
	ROY, Loriene	(TX)	1063
Media evaluation	OHLMAN, Herbert	(SWZ)	919
Media production & evaluation	BELT, Jane	(WA)	78
Media selection & evaluation	CHEEKS, Cellestine	(MD)	204
Microcomputer software evaluation	MAY, Frank C.	(CA)	788
	MICHELS, Fredrick A.	(MI)	832
Needs assessment & evaluation	RUBIN, Rhea J.	(CA)	1064
Needs evaluation	ASSUNCAO, Isabel	(PQ)	37
Online catalog development evaluation	CLARK, Sharon E.	(IL)	218
Online systems evaluation	WOODSMALL, Rose M.	(MD)	1367
Performance & collection evaluation	JENSEN, L B.	(ON)	599
Performance & program evaluation	MARRIOTT, Lois I.	(CA)	773
Personnel evaluation & development	YUEH, Norma N.	(NJ)	1384
	ROBERTSON, Billy O.	(TN)	1041
Personnel evaluation system	VIELE, George B.	(NC)	1283
Personnel evaluations	GREESON, Judy G.	(TN)	465
Personnel hiring, evaluating, objectives	NOLAN, Deborah A.	(MD)	907
Personnel training & evaluation	EYLES, Heberle H.	(FL)	359
Planning & evaluation	DESSY, Blane K.	(AL)	296
	VAN HOUSE, Nancy A.	(CA)	1275
	BOLT, Nancy M.	(CO)	113
	WYCHE, Louise E.	(DE)	1374
	BALCOM, Kathleen M.	(IL)	51
	SLATER, Susan B.	(MD)	1148
	SMITH, Catherine	(NC)	1153
	ROBERTSON, Retha M.	(OK)	1042
	FELIX, Sally T.	(PA)	370
Planning & evaluation of info srvs	MCCLURE, Charles R.	(NY)	797
Planning, evaluation & management	SHELDON, Brooke E.	(TX)	1125
Preview, evaluate & purchase films	NEBEL, Jean C.	(CA)	891
Program development & evaluation	WALLACE, Michael T.	(DC)	1298
Program evaluation	MEDINA, Sue O.	(AL)	820
	PENNINGTON, Walter W.	(AL)	957
	WILLIAMS, Delmus E.	(AL)	1342
	CHELTON, Mary K.	(MD)	204
	HARER, John B.	(MD)	501
	WAYLAND, Marilyn T.	(MI)	1311
	MULLER, Claudya B.	(NY)	877
Program planning & foundation evaluation	JONES, C L.	(PA)	611
Programming, planning & evaluating	PEISCHL, Thomas P.	(MN)	955
Project evaluation	SPYKERMAN, Bryan R.	(UT)	1177
Public library planning & evaluation	SMITH, David R.	(MN)	1154
Purchase evaluation	MINNICH, Conrad H.	(OH)	846
Reference books evaluation	MCSWEENEY, Josephine	(NY)	818
Reference evaluation	BENHAM, Frances	(AL)	80
Reference, teaching & evaluation	CROWLEY, Terence	(CA)	262
Research & evaluation	LOERTSCHER, David V.	(CO)	737
	HERNON, Peter	(MA)	532
	ROBBINS, Jane B.	(WI)	1038
School library evaluation	RANDAZZO, Corinne O.	(MS)	1006
	ANDERSON, Pauline H.	(NY)	25
School library organization & evaluation	BAGAN, Beverly S.	(VA)	45
School media center evaluation	SLYGH, Gyneth	(WI)	1151
Selection & evaluation of non-print mtrl	AHN, Hyonah K.	(IL)	8
Slide collection evaluation	PRINS, Johanna W.	(NY)	993
Software evaluation	LATHROP, Ann	(CA)	701
	GROSCH, Audrey N.	(MN)	472
	WILTSHIRE, Denise A.	(VA)	1354
	ATTINGER, Monique L.	(ON)	38
Software evaluation for libraries	ASSUNCAO, Isabel	(PQ)	37
Special library services evaluation	BERLIN, Arthur E.	(NH)	87
Staff evaluation	BLACKABY, Sandra L.	(WA)	102
Staff evaluation & development	SCHNEIDER, Frank A.	(WA)	1097
Staff training & evaluation	LEE, Janis M.	(PA)	710
	TONGATE, John T.	(TX)	1250
Standards & evaluation	WALL, H D.	(PA)	1297
Surveys & evaluations	VELLUCCI, Matthew J.	(MD)	1282

EVALUATION (Cont'd)

Teacher evaluation policys	KRATZ, Hans G.	(AB)	676
Toxicological evaluation	MUNRO, Nancy B.	(TN)	879
Train, supervise & evaluate staff	DAYO, Ayo	(TX)	283

EVANGELICALISM

Evangelicalism	MINDEMAN, George A. .	(CA)	845

EVANGELISM

Religious books, evangelism	FERM, Lois R.	(MN)	373

EVENTS (See also News)

Business & current events databases	LOVE, Sandra R.	(CA)	743
Current events	REIFMAN, Deborah S. . .	(CA)	1019
Current events databases	CONGER, Lucinda D. . . .	(DC)	236
Current events reference	VANDEGRIFT, Barbara P.*	(DC)	1273
Fundraising events	TITUS, Barbara K.	(DE)	1247
Media research of current events	BROWN, Phyllis J.	(TN)	147
News & events cataloging	MCGANN, Margot	(DC)	805
News & events reference	MCGANN, Margot	(DC)	805
Public events management	EZELL, Charlaine L.	(MI)	360
Special events	BRENNAN, Deborah B. .	(RI)	132
Special events, fairs, & festivals	CHASE, William D.	(MI)	203
Special events promotion	GOODRICH, Nita K.	(AZ)	449

EXAMINATION (See also Evaluation)

Book examination programs	NICHTER, Alan	(FL)	902

EXCEPTIONAL (See also Special)

Media for exceptional children	TAFFEL, Bobbe H.	(FL)	1219

EXCHANGE (See also Acquisitions)

Acquisitions, gifts & exchanges	EASTERLY, Ambrose . . .	(TN)	333
Automated book exchange	FINK, Norman	(PQ)	378
Exchange	BELLO, Susan E.	(MA)	78
Exchange activities	TAYLOR, Carolyn L.	(MO)	1226
Exchange serials	BALL, Alice D.	(DC)	52
Gift & exchange acquisitions	DECKER, Leola M.	(MD)	286
Gift & exchanges management	DUPRE, Monique	(ON)	327
Gifts & exchange	WISE, Leona L.	(CA)	1357
	FAIRBANKS, Deborah M.	(FL)	361
	HOUGH, Carolyn A.	(MI)	562
Gifts & exchanges	BARKER, Joseph W. . . .	(CA)	56
	ROUSEK, Marie B.	(NJ)	1061
	LESNIK, Pauline	(NY)	718
	WEAVER, Alice O.	(OH)	1312
	ROBERTS, Marica L. . . .	(TN)	1041
	LAKHANPAL, Sarv K. . .	(SK)	689
	OSIER, Donald V.	(SDA)	928
Gifts, exchanges	MARX, Patricia C.	(TX)	780
International exchange of librarians	WILLIAMSON, Linda E. .	(IL)	1347
International info & cultural exchange	STEERE, Paul J.	(DC)	1184
International library exchanging	ALLEN, Christina Y.	(WI)	14
International relations & exchange	MCCOOL, Donna L.	(WA)	798
Private information exchange networks	BUSSMANN, Steve	(VA)	166
	EDWARDS, Wilmoth O. .	(VA)	338
	FILIPPONE, Anne	(VA)	377
	KELLER, Jay	(VA)	635
	LITTLE, William	(VA)	734
	LOVETT, Bruce	(VA)	743
	MAJOR, Skip	(VA)	762
	NEWLAND, Barbara	(VA)	899
	RINALDI, Roberta	(VA)	1035
	RYAN, Maureen	(VA)	1071
	STRATT, Randy	(VA)	1200
Securities & Exchange Commission	BARRETT, Michael D. . .	(NY)	59
Securities & Exchange Commission filings	GELINNE, Michael S. . . .	(MO)	426
Slavic exchange	HOWE, Priscilla P.	(KS)	565
Worldwide exchange agreements	SNIDER, Elizabeth M. . . .	(OH)	1163

EXECUTIVE (See also Administration, Directing, Management)

Association executive	GREENFIELD, Robert E. .	(MD)	464
Executive compensation & benefits	KAZANJIAN, Donna S. . .	(NY)	632
Executive information systems	HARRIS, Jeanne G.	(IL)	504
Executive leadership	MCKENZIE, Harry	(CA)	811
Executive level management	ASHTON, Rick J.	(CO)	36
Executive management	AULD, Dennis B.	(KY)	39
Executive recruiting	GAMBER, Deborah D. . .	(CT)	416
	FELDMAN, Linda A.	(IL)	369
Executive search	JONG, Jennifer L.	(NY)	616
Executive search & recruitment	BRYANT, Nancy J.	(GA)	152
Executive search firms	MARSHALL, Deborah M. .	(IL)	774
Library, information exec recruitment	GOSSAGE, Wayne	(NY)	453
Presidential & executive papers	NESBITT, John R.	(MO)	896

EXERCISE

Exercise science	WINIARZ, Elizabeth	(PQ)	1355

EXHIBITS (See also Displays)

Archival exhibits	WEST, Donald	(MI)	1326
	HALLER, Douglas M. . . .	(PA)	489
	SCHUMACHER, Carolyn S.	(PA)	1102
Archives exhibits	KIRWAN, Kathleen	(NY)	656
Book exhibits	WISE, Leona L.	(CA)	1357
Displays & exhibitions	HUTCHINSON, Beck . . .	(FL)	579
Displays & exhibits	KEMP, Henrietta J.	(IA)	639
	THOMPSON, Jane K. . . .	(VT)	1240
Exhibit coordination	NELSON, Norma	(NY)	894
Exhibit development	ERICKSEN, Paul A.	(IL)	352
Exhibit displays	RUSSELL, Marilyn L. . . .	(KS)	1069
Exhibit program	HIEBER, Douglas M.	(IA)	537
Exhibition & programming of AV materials	SCHREIBMAN, Fay C. . .	(NY)	1099
Exhibition catalogs	STARR, Daniel A.	(NY)	1182
Exhibition coordination	YOUNG, Barbara N.	(FL)	1381
Exhibition development	STEWART, Virginia R. . .	(IL)	1193
Exhibitions	DAVIS, James	(CA)	279
	VIOLA, Herman J.	(DC)	1285
	DOCTOROW, Erica	(NY)	307
	LACHATANERE, Diana .	(NY)	686
Exhibitions & friends programs	STODDARD, Roger E. . .	(MA)	1196
Exhibits	BROWN, Marie H.	(CA)	146
	DIMUNATION, Mark G. . .	(CA)	304
	SMITH, Rebecca A.	(FL)	1159
	RYAN, Sheila	(IL)	1071
	SORENSEN, Mark W. . . .	(IL)	1168
	KENT, Caroline M.	(MA)	642
	SEEGRABER, Frank J. . .	(MA)	1111
	SHEAR, Joan A.	(MA)	1124
	DOWNING, Elaine L. . . .	(NY)	316
	WOLFE, Allis	(NY)	1360
	WOO, Janice	(NY)	1363
Exhibits & public programming	MESSINEO, Leonard L. .	(KS)	828
Exhibits & publicity	COPLAN, Kate M.	(MD)	244
Exhibits, audiovisual presentations	SHIDELER, John C.	(WA)	1129
Library exhibitions & public education	WOODWARD, Daniel . . .	(CA)	1368
Major exhibitions	LEAHY, Mary S.	(PA)	707
Organizing art exhibitions	FORMAN, Camille L. . . .	(CT)	390
Programming & exhibits	ROTH, Claire J.	(NY)	1059
Public relations, exhibits, displays	DAANE, Jeanette K. . . .	(AZ)	269
Rare books, exhibits	NICKERSON, Donna L. .	(NY)	902
Research for exhibition development	SHERIDAN, Helen A. . . .	(MI)	1127
Research of artists & exhibitions	GENSHAFT, Carole M. . .	(OH)	427

EXPANSION (See also Building, Facilities)

Building expansion	EICHELBERGER, Marianne	(KS)	339
Development & expansion	GUBITS, Helen S.	(NY)	475
Library expansion	REED, Sally G.	(VT)	1015
Public school library expansion	SPAULDING, Nancy J. . .	(TX)	1172
Renovation & expansion planning	KELSH, Virginia J.	(CA)	639

EXPENDITURE (See also Accounting, Budget)

Coordinate library budget & expenditures — REID, Richard H. ...... (LA) 1019
Overseeing expenditure of federal funds — MACLEAN, Ellen G. .... (VI) 757

EXPERIMENTAL

Experimental film — GLABICKI, Paul .... (PA) 439
Experimental methodology — DOWNS, Sandra P. .... (CA) 317
Experimental theatre — DACE, Tish .... (MA) 269

EXPERT (See also AI, Artificial, CAI, Knowledge)

AI expert systems — SIEGEL, Elliot R. ...... (MD) 1136
Artificial intelligence, expert systems — VEENKER, Linda J. ..... (CA) 1281
　 — DIEHL, Mark .... (IL) 302
Databases & expert systems — MOLINE, Judi A. ...... (MD) 853
Expert & optical information systems — SCHNEIDER, Karl R. .... (MD) 1097
Expert medical systems — RAMAKRISHNAN, T .... (LA) 1004
Expert retrieval assistance systems — MARCUS, Richard S. .... (MA) 769
Expert system development — LINDER, Elliott .... (NY) 729
Expert system in reference — MICCO, Helen M. .... (PA) 831
Expert systems — FOX, Ann M. .... (DC) 394
　 — PARK, Margaret K. ..... (GA) 941
　 — SAVAGE, Allan G. ..... (MD) 1085
　 — WATERS, Samuel T. ... (MD) 1309
　 — METZLER, Douglas P. .. (PA) 829
　 — MEYER, Daniel E. ...... (PA) 830
　 — WILBURN, Clouse R. ... (TN) 1338
　 — PARROTT, James R. .... (ON) 944
Expert systems & AI — PITT, William B. .... (MD) 976
Expert systems & artificial intelligence — CHANG, Roy T. .... (IL) 201
　 — MOTT, Thomas M. ...... (NJ) 872
Expert systems & databases — SOERGEL, Dagobert .... (MD) 1165
Expert systems & human cognition — HARMON, Glynn .... (TX) 502
Expert systems for reference service — RICHARDSON, John V. . (CA) 1029
Expert systems in medical databases — LONG, John M. .... (MN) 739
Expert systems in reference — EKLAND, Patricia A. ..... (BC) 341
Knowledge acquisition for expert systems — MUSEN, Mark A. ...... (CA) 883
Library & expert witnesses databases — MAULSBY, Tommie L. ... (TX) 787
Nursing expert systems — HENDRICKSON, Maria F. (NY) 527

EXPLOITATION

Spcl cols exploitation internationally — HEANEY, Henry J. ...... (SCT) 518

EXPLORATION

Exploration records management — MOORE, Guusje Z. ...... (TX) 859
Oil & gas exploration — DURIE, Debbie L. .... (AB) 328
Petroleum exploration & production — ANDERSON, Margaret .. (TX) 24

EXPORT (See also Tariff)

Export information — PFLEIDERER, Stephen D. (DC) 966
Export marketing management — OVEREYNDER, Rombout E. .... (NET) 931

EXPOSITION

General exposition essays & reviews — HUMEZ, Nicholas D. ..... (ME) 573

EXTENSION (See also Bookmobiles, Books-By-Mail, Community, Outreach)

Bookmobile extension — PHILIP, John J. .... (OH) 967
Branch & extension services — KINGSTON, Jo A. ..... (MI) 652
Extended campus library services — PICKETT, Mary J. ..... (IL) 970
　 — HERRON, Nancy L. .... (PA) 533
　 — KEMP, Barbara E. ..... (WA) 639
Extended campus services — LABRAKE, Orlyn B. .... (FL) 686
Extension — CLOUGHERTY, Leo P. .. (AR) 223
　 — GLASS, Nellie L. ...... (FL) 440
Extension agency management, supervision — GRAY, Patricia B. ...... (VA) 460
Extension & outreach — ENGELBERT, Alan M. .. (WI) 348
Extension & outreach services — MEIZNER, Kathie L. .... (MD) 822
Extension library services — SLADE, Alexander L. ... (BC) 1147

EXTENSION (Cont'd)

Extension services — STANBERY, Nancy M. .. (GA) 1179
　 — TRUCK, Lorna R. .... (IA) 1259
　 — CARY, Jan E. .... (IL) 191
　 — CHENOWETH, Rose M. . (IL) 206
　 — DECKER, Judy J. ...... (IL) 286
　 — RICKERT, Carol A. ..... (IL) 1032
　 — GUNNELLS, Danny C. .. (IN) 477
　 — BEECH, Vivian W. ..... (NC) 74
　 — WILSON, Memory A. ... (OH) 1352
　 — GRIMLEY, Susan M. ... (SC) 470
　 — DOWDLE, Glen L. ..... (TX) 315
Extension services, bookmobile — HOLMES, Nancy M. .... (GA) 553
Outreach & extension services — ALLEN, Debra C. ...... (SC) 14

EXTRASENSORY (See also Parapsychology)

Extrasensory perception — NORMAN, Wayne R. ... (NY) 909

FACILITIES (See also Architecture, Building, Design, Expansion, Remodeling, Renovation)

Archival facilities — LATHROP, Alan K. ...... (MN) 701
Audiovisual media facility management — GRAY, Shirley M. ...... (NY) 460
Buildings & facilities — ARMSTRONG, Carole S. (MI) 32
Buildings & facilities planning — HAKA, Clifford H. ...... (MI) 484
Construction of facilities — HAMMOND, John J. .... (MO) 493
Design & construction of new facilities — PAPENFUSE, Edward C. (MD) 939
Developing new media facilities — SCHREIBMAN, Fay C. .. (NY) 1099
Development of new facilities — ROYCE, Carolyn S. ..... (NJ) 1063
Facilities — KECK, Bruce L. .... (DC) 633
　 — VINNES, Norman M. ... (MN) 1285
Facilities design & planning — HOWLAND, Margaret E. . (MA) 566
Facilities for school programs — HOLTER, Charlotte S. ... (MD) 554
Facilities management — MONTANELLI, Dale S. .. (IL) 855
　 — PAIETTA, Ann C. ...... (IL) 935
　 — ROSSOFF, Judith H. ... (NY) 1059
Facilities planning — SIMON, William H. ..... (CT) 1141
　 — BOSS, Richard W. ...... (DC) 117
　 — GRANT, George C. ..... (FL) 458
　 — CURLEY, Arthur .... (MA) 265
　 — DALY, Kathleen E. ..... (MI) 271
　 — STONE, Jason R. ...... (NJ) 1197
　 — SCHLOMAN, Barbara F. (OH) 1094
　 — HABER, Walter H. ..... (PA) 481
　 — PIERCE, William S. ..... (PA) 972
　 — PHILLIPS, Luouida V. ... (TX) 968
　 — SENG, Mary A. .... (TX) 1115
Facilities planning & design — BANNERMAN-WILLIAMS, Cheryl F. .... (TN) 54
Facilities planning & remodeling — BUCKINGHAM, Betty J. . (IA) 154
Facilities programming & planning — MERRIFIELD, Thomas C. (CA) 826
Facility consulting — DAVIS, Glenn G. .... (IL) 279
Facility design — CALLISON, Daniel J. .... (IN) 174
　 — JEFFCOTT, Janet B. .... (WI) 596
Facility layout & planning — MURDOCH, Arthur W. .. (ON) 879
Facility planning — HAMILTON, Rita .... (AZ) 492
　 — BECKER, Joseph ...... (CA) 72
　 — WARREN, Charles D. .... (SC) 1306
Facility planning school media — COMEAU, Reginald A. ... (NH) 234
Facility remodeling — KRABBE, Natalie ...... (OR) 674
Law library facilities planning — MERRIFIELD, Thomas C. (CA) 826
Library facilities — THORNTON, Alice J. .... (DE) 1242
　 — BUCHANAN, William C. . (LA) 153
　 — LIEBERFELD, Lawrence . (NY) 726
Library facilities design — HAAS, Eva L. .... (NY) 480
Library facilities planning — MERRIFIELD, Thomas C. (CA) 826
　 — SPURLOCK, Sandra E. .. (NM) 1177
　 — MCADAMS, Nancy R. .. (TX) 792
Library facility planning — MOSLEY, Shelley E. ..... (AZ) 872
　 — COHEN, Aaron .... (NY) 227
Library media center facilities planning — FROST, Rebecca H. ..... (PA) 406
Maintenance & remodeling facilities — EVANS, Constance L. ... (KS) 356
Management & planning facilities — NEUBAUER, Richard A. . (MA) 896
New facilities construction — STEELE, Leah J. ...... (IL) 1184
Organization & facilities — STROUGAL, Patricia G. . (GA) 1203
Organization of new facilities — SCHUSTER, Adeline .... (IL) 1103
Physical facilities — GILROY, Rupert E. ..... (MA) 437
Physical facilities management — WEBB, Gisela M. .... (TX) 1313

FACILITIES (Cont'd)

Planning pub lib services & facilities	CURTIS, Jean E.	(MI)	267
Public library facilities	THRASHER, Jerry A.	(NC)	1243
Public library facility planning	HARRIS, Patricia L.	(ND)	505
Research facilities management	LANOUETTE, Marie	(ON)	696
School library facilities	MARKUSON, Carolyn A.	(MA)	772
	ANDERSON, Pauline H.	(NY)	25
	KAHLER, June	(TX)	621
School library media facilities	PATRICK, Retta B.	(AR)	947
	SHUMAN, Susan E.	(NY)	1134
	EHRHARDT, Margaret W.	(SC)	339
Secondary research facilities	CROTTS, Carolyn D.	(KS)	261
Services for correctional facilities	MARKARIAN, Rita J.	(NY)	771
Small high school facilities	SHEPHERD, Rex L.	(IA)	1127
Space planning facilities	FRALEY, Ruth A.	(NY)	395

FACSIMILES (See Reprints)

Publishing music reprints, facsimiles	BALK, Leo F.	(NY)	52

FACTORY (See also Manufacturing)

Factory automation	LARSON, Anna M.	(ON)	699
Factory automation directory	LEE, Douglas E.	(NY)	709

FACULTY

Circulation & faculty reserves	HARER, John B.	(MD)	501
Collection development & faculty liaison	RAMBLER, Linda K.	(PA)	1005
Collection development, faculty liaison	TAYLOR, Anne E.	(TX)	1226
Curriculum support for faculty	DAVIS, Deanna S.	(IA)	278
Faculty & library liaison	TAPLEY, Bridgette M.	(SC)	1223
Faculty current awareness service	BATISTA, Emily J.	(PA)	64
Faculty development	JORDAN, Travis E.	(TX)	617
Faculty development & evaluation	BEDSOLE, Dan T.	(VA)	73
Faculty development assistance	ROBINSON, Gayle N.	(AL)	1044
Faculty governance & status	THORSON, Connie C.	(NM)	1242
Faculty liaison	JONES, Frederick S.	(MA)	613
Faculty research support	BRENNAN, Edward P.	(MD)	132
Faculty services	HAMEL, Eleanor C.	(PR)	491
Faculty status for librarians	GALLOWAY, R D.	(CA)	415
	SCEPANSKI, Jordan M.	(CA)	1088
	MITCHELL, W B.	(NC)	849
Library, faculty relationship	FARBER, Evan I.	(IN)	363
Professional outreach to faculty	RIDINGER, Robert B.	(IL)	1032
Research on college faculty	HARDESTY, Larry L.	(FL)	499
Secondary faculty research	MERRELL, Sheila J.	(MO)	826
Service to faculty	OLSEN, Sarah G.	(IL)	922
Student & faculty services	MORRISSETT, Elizabeth	(AK)	868
Supervise library faculty & staff	REID, Richard H.	(LA)	1019
Working with students & faculty	SOUTHARD, Sarah T.	(CT)	1169

FAIRS

Special events, fairs, & festivals	CHASE, William D.	(MI)	203

FAMILY (See also Parent)

Criminal & family court libraries	ROONEY, Mary T.	(NY)	1053
Family & local history research	WILLIAMS, Janet L.	(OR)	1344
Family history	CARTER, Janet K.	(TX)	189
	CLEMENT, Charles R.	(UT)	221
Family law	CENTER, Sue L.	(WI)	196
Family medicine	THOMASSON, George O.	(CO)	1238
	CRANDALL, Elisabeth G.	(NC)	255
Family medicine education	MENDELSON, Martin	(WA)	823
Family planning	WINTERS, Wilma E.	(MA)	1356
	ZIMMERMAN, Hugh N.	(NY)	1389
Family planning, population, soc mktg	WILLSON, Katherine H.	(CT)	1349
Family research	HORNUNG, Susan D.	(WI)	560
Family studies	KNIGHT, Rebecca C.	(DE)	664
Genealogy, family history	THOMAS, Cornel W.	(AR)	1236
Instructor, genealogy & family history	SPERRY, Kip	(UT)	1174
Kennedy family photographs	GOODRICH, Allan B.	(MA)	449
Knowledge of family planning	ROBERTS, Gloria A.	(NY)	1040
Local & family history	HAMILTON, Patricia A.	(IL)	492
Military families & women	HARPER, Marie F.	(AL)	503
Population & family planning	BARROWS, William D.	(NC)	60
The Junius Brutus Booth family	ARCHER, Stephen M.	(MO)	31

FANTASY (See also Fiction)

Fantasy & science fiction	BRIDGE, Stephen W.	(IN)	135
Science fiction & fantasy research	PELZ, Bruce E.	(CA)	955
Science fiction, fantasy research	KAN, Katharine L.	(HI)	624

FANZINES

Amateur journals & fanzines	PELZ, Bruce E.	(CA)	955

FARM (See also Agricultural, Crops)

Farm crisis information	TOHAL, Kate J.	(MN)	1248
Farming	GALLENTINE, Richard J.	(IA)	414

FASHION (See also Costumes)

Fashion & costume collections	HALE, Kaycee	(CA)	485
Fashion & costume video	HALE, Kaycee	(CA)	485

FEDERAL (See also Congress, Documents, Government, United States)

Advising, federal & state government	CASEY, Daniel W.	(DC)	192
Canadian federal government publications	ROSE, Frances E.	(BC)	1054
Dissemination of federal information	BISHOP, Sarah G.	(DC)	99
Document retrieval & federal agencies	TURNER, Ellis S.	(MD)	1264
Evaluating federal library programs	KIRSCHENBAUM, Arthur S.	(DC)	655
Federal acquisition regulations	SMITH, David A.	(VA)	1153
Federal & California law reference	CH'NG, Saw K.	(CA)	209
Federal & depository publications	FOSTER, Leslie A.	(WI)	392
Federal & international state documents	BASEFSKY, Stuart M.	(NC)	62
Federal & state government publications	BROWN, Philip L.	(SD)	146
Federal & state law	SCHUTT, Cheryl M.	(CT)	1103
Federal & state law research	VARGA, William R.	(DC)	1278
Federal & state legislative materials	CAMMARATA, Paul J.	(KY)	175
Federal & state library legislation	HICKS, Frederick M.	(IL)	537
Federal computer & telecom procurement	DODSON, Whit	(VA)	308
Federal documents	KONOP, Bonnie M.	(FL)	670
	SHELDEN, Patricia R.	(HI)	1125
	NASON, Jennifer L.	(MA)	888
	HAUSMAN, Lisa M.	(MI)	513
	WATSON, Janice D.	(MO)	1309
	GARD, Betty A.	(ND)	417
	HAWLEY, George S.	(NJ)	514
	RAILSBACK, Beverly D.	(NJ)	1003
	HARRIS, Maureen	(SC)	505
	RUHLIN, Michele T.	(UT)	1066
	BROWN, David C.	(VA)	143
	LEASURE, Lois A.	(WV)	707
Federal documents depository	MCGINNESS, Mary B.	(PA)	806
Federal government	RUBIN, Lenard H.	(TX)	1064
	WEATHERHEAD, Barbara A.	(ON)	1312
Federal govt & congressional info srvs	ROTHBART, Linda S.	(VA)	1060
Federal government archives	PFEIFFER, David A.	(DC)	966
Federal government documents	ADAMS, Leonard R.	(MA)	5
	FISCHER, Catherine S.	(MN)	379
Federal government documents reference	LINDSEY, Thomas K.	(TX)	730
Federal government organization	DOWNS, Charles F.	(DC)	317
Federal government publications	STRAITON, T H.	(AL)	1199
	CALDWELL, George H.	(DC)	172
	EWING, Jerry L.	(MO)	359
	PANDIT, Jyoti P.	(NY)	937
Federal governments documents	CORCORAN, Nancy L.	(MN)	246
Federal grants management	KLASSEN, Robert L.	(DC)	657
Federal information policy	HARPER, Lucy B.	(OH)	503
	MASON, Marilyn G.	(OH)	781
Federal legal material	MOSS, Karen M.	(MA)	872
Federal legal materials	EWING, Florence E.	(CA)	359
Federal legislation regarding libraries	COOKE, Eileen D.	(DC)	241
Federal legislative reference	COCHRAN, Catherine	(MI)	225
Federal libraries	SCULLY, Mark F.	(DC)	1109
	SMITH, David A.	(VA)	1153
Federal libraries contracting	STALLINGS, Elizabeth A.	(DC)	1179

FEDERAL (Cont'd)

Federal library policy	HEANUE, Anne A.	(DC)	518
	KLASSEN, Robert L.	(DC)	657
Federal library programs	WELCH, John T.	(NC)	1321
Federal procurement support	SLOAN, Cheryl A.	(MD)	1149
Federal program administration	CROCKETT, Martha L.	(DC)	259
Federal publications	SCULLY, Mark F.	(DC)	1109
	PARSONS, Kathy A.	(IA)	945
	KECK, Kerry A.	(TX)	633
Federal Register publications	BYRNE, John E.	(DC)	169
Federal regulations	NOWAK, Geraldine D.	(DC)	911
Federal regulations on CD-ROM	CHRISTIANSEN, Eric G.	(OH)	211
Federal relations	HEANUE, Anne A.	(DC)	518
Federal, state, & government research	KIRSHBAUM, Priscilla J.	(CO)	655
Federal, state, local govt publications	NAKATA, Yuri	(OR)	887
Federal statistics	WILKINSON, Patrick J.	(IA)	1340
Government & federal documents	MACK, Debora S.	(GA)	756
Government documents, federal	JOHNSON, Dorothy A.	(MA)	603
Overseeing expenditure of federal funds	MACLEAN, Ellen G.	(VI)	757
Reference services to federal agencies	CHO, Sung Y.	(DC)	209
Research in federal Indian law	HARRAGARRA WATERS, Deana J.	(CO)	503
State & federal documents	HOM, Sharon L.	(TN)	555
United States federal documents	HAUSE, Aaron H.	(MT)	512
United States federal publications	SLOAN, Tom W.	(AL)	1150
	MCCLEARY, William E.	(LA)	796
Writing history, federal communication	AINES, Andrew A.	(MD)	8

FEE-BASED

Fee-based information centers	JOSEPHINE, Helen B.	(AZ)	617
Fee-based information services	TOMAJKO, Kathy L.	(GA)	1249
	REMEIKIS, Lois A.	(IL)	1022
	FELICETTI, Barbara W.	(MA)	370
Fee-based library services	ROLLINS, Stephen J.	(NM)	1051
	MARVIN, Stephen G.	(PA)	780
Fee-based service	RUBENS, Donna J.	(MN)	1064
Fee-based services	WYLIE, Nethery A.	(CO)	1375
	WILLIAMS, Thomas L.	(FL)	1347
	RUTHERFORD, Virginia L.	(GA)	1070
	WARNER, Alice S.	(MA)	1305
	WOLFE, N J.	(NY)	1361
Research projects, fee-based	HARRIS, Virginia B.	(VA)	506

FEMINISM (See also Women)

Feminism & librarianship	ENGLE, Michael O.	(OR)	349
Feminist theory	MCDERMOTT, Patrice	(IL)	802

FERMENTATION

Reference in fermentation technology	BOND, Mary J.	(CO)	113

FESTIVALS

Festival books	BOWLES, Edmund A.	(NY)	121
Special events, fairs, & festivals	CHASE, William D.	(MI)	203

FICTION (See also Detective, Fantasy, Literature, Mystery, Novels)

Adolescent fiction	SHANNON, Jerry B.	(TX)	1120
Adult fiction	ALLENBACH, Norma A.	(NY)	16
	LEGO, Jane B.	(VA)	712
Adult genre fiction	PENN, Lea M.	(NC)	957
Contemporary literature, poetry, fiction	HUDZIK, Robert T.	(OH)	570
Detective fiction	YOUNG, Juana R.	(AR)	1382
Fantasy & science fiction	BRIDGE, Stephen W.	(IN)	135
Fiction	FISH, Marie	(CA)	380
	WIEHE, Janet C.	(OH)	1336
	PALMER, Judith L.	(TX)	936
	HABERLAND, Jody	(VA)	481
Fiction & literature	JORDAN, Linda K.	(OK)	616
Fiction & mysteries	COFFEY, Dorothy A.	(MI)	227
Fiction & nonfiction	RARESHEID, Cynthia L.	(OH)	1008
Fiction, books selection	SANDY, Marjorie M.	(MI)	1081
Fiction collection development	VOSS, Joyce M.	(IL)	1289
	HIRSCH, Dorothy K.	(MD)	543

FICTION (Cont'd)

Fiction collections	MCILROY, William D.	(NJ)	809
Fiction, history	SALLSTROM, Marilee A.	(CA)	1077
Fiction, literature	HUNT, Janis E.	(IL)	575
Fiction reviewing	SMITH, Maureen M.	(OH)	1158
Fiction selection	SIMONS, Maurice M.	(CA)	1141
French fiction	BOUCHARD, Martin	(PQ)	118
Genre & general fiction	HAWK, Susan P.	(FL)	513
Gothic tradition, detective fiction	FISHER, Benjamin F.	(MS)	380
Middle grade fiction & nonfiction acqs	BUCKLEY, Virginia L.	(NY)	154
Mystery fiction	MAIO, Kathleen L.	(MA)	762
Mystery fiction books	O'BRIEN, Marlys H.	(MN)	915
Nonfiction & fiction writing	BRADWAY, Becky J.	(IL)	126
Nuclear fiction database	LENZ, Millicent A.	(NY)	716
Popular fiction & nonfiction	GANYARD, Margaret E.	(MO)	416
Reference & fiction training	BARKER, Lillian H.	(MD)	56
Science fiction	HALL, Halbert W.	(TX)	487
	MACFARLANE, Francis X.	(TX)	755
	ESPLEY, John L.	(VA)	354
Science fiction alternative histories	COLLINS, William J.	(CA)	233
Science fiction & fantasy research	PELZ, Bruce E.	(CA)	955
Science fiction bibliography	KRIEGER, Lee A.	(NC)	678
	DAWSON, Terry P.	(WI)	282
Science fiction, fantasy research	KAN, Katharine L.	(HI)	624
Science fiction history	COLLINS, William J.	(CA)	233
Victorian literature, fiction, poetry	FISHER, Benjamin F.	(MS)	380
Young adult fiction	BRADBURN, Frances B.	(NC)	125
Young adult fiction & nonfiction acqs	BUCKLEY, Virginia L.	(NY)	154
Young adult fiction selection	TYSON, Edith S.	(OH)	1267
Young adult nonfiction & fiction	CROSS, Claudette S.	(CA)	260

FILES

Audiovisual & machine-readable data file	RITCHIE, David G.	(NY)	1036
Authority file maintenance	ASPER, Mary K.	(CO)	37
Authority files	DOBBIN, Geraldine F.	(BC)	307
Bibliographic file conversion	CHIU, Ida K.	(TX)	209
Building & maintaining authority files	LESSER, Barbara	(VA)	718
Clip files	BRITTON, Pilaivan H.	(WA)	137
Clippings files	EVANS, Stephen P.	(OH)	358
Computer file bibliographic control	HERMAN, Elizabeth	(CA)	531
Computerized files & library materials	BENNETT, Laura B.	(IL)	82
Database management, reprint files	MENZUL, Faina	(NJ)	825
Demographic & census files	RUBIN, David S.	(NY)	1064
File maintenance	GEBBIE, Janet L.	(NC)	424
File room personnel supervision	DICKERSON, Mary J.	(TX)	300
File systems design	HUFF, Patricia M.	(VA)	570
Filing	WESTOVER, Mary L.	(AL)	1327
	LATSHAW, Ruth N.	(IN)	701
Filing & indexing	MCKAY, Alberta S.	(NC)	809
Filing & maintenance	SMOTHERS, Alyce A.	(LA)	1162
Filing source code documentation	BOZE, Lucy G.	(GA)	124
Filing source code listings	BOZE, Lucy G.	(GA)	124
Filing supervision & training	ABRAMS, Roger E.	(OH)	3
Filing system design	QUINN, Sidney	(MD)	1000
Filing systems	MCCREARY, Gail A.	(MS)	800
Form file systems	GRIGST, Denise J.	(CA)	470
Indexing chemical files	HANF, Elizabeth P.	(PA)	495
InMagic software file management system	HOUSTON, Louise B.	(ON)	563
Legal filing	O'BRIEN, Doris J.	(CT)	914
Looseleaf filing	MCGRAW, Scott C.	(IL)	807
Machine file processing	MARTIN, Robert A.	(FL)	778
Machine-readable data files	GERKEN, Ann E.	(CA)	429
	KUHLMAN, James R.	(GA)	682
	KING, Ebba K.	(NC)	650
Machine-readable data files cataloging	MYERS, Victor C.	(MO)	885
	WEITZ, Jay N.	(OH)	1320
Maintain library & information file	RATZABI, Arlene	(NY)	1010
Newspaper clip files	CROCKETT, Mary S.	(SC)	259
Newspaper clipping files	VANCE, Carolyn J.	(IL)	1272
Non-bibliographic information files	CHIANG, Katherine S.	(NY)	207
Numeric data files	TSANG, Daniel C.	(CA)	1260
Pamphlet file	TURNER, Sue E.	(PA)	1265
Pamphlet file coordination	ROBINSON, David A.	(OH)	1043
Pamphlet file development	LINDSTROM, Elaine C.	(OH)	730
Pamphlet file maintenance	LAROSA, Thomas J.	(NY)	698
Patient index file maintenance	PARR, John R.	(ON)	943

FILES (Cont'd)

Photo filing systems	SCARANO, Lisa C.	(NY)	1087
Picture file	MACIUSZKO, Kathleen L.	(OH)	755
Records & information filing & retrieval	GRAHAM, Su D.	(CO)	456
Reference file development, cataloging	TYLER, Kim E.	(OR)	1266
Section filing databases	WRIGHT, John H.	(FL)	1371
Slides & picture files design	KEAVENEY, Sydney S.	(NY)	633
Subject files	BENDES, Adele N.	(NY)	79
University filing systems	SWEENEY, Shelley T.	(SK)	1215
Vertical file	GOLDMACHER, Sheila L.	(CA)	445
	STEWART, Anna C.	(CO)	1192
	TODD, Suzanne L.	(MI)	1248
	MALLORY, Elizabeth J.	(TX)	763
Vertical file on artists	MCNULTY, Karen	(CT)	817
Vertical files	CHESTER, Claudia J.	(CA)	207
	WATT, Richard S.	(NC)	1310
Vertical files organization, maintenance	GODFREY, Florence L.	(NJ)	442

FILM (See also Animation, Audiovisual, Cinema, Cinematography, Documentary, Footage, Hollywood, Media, Motion, Movies, Slides, Video)

Administrator, film & video library	MORRISON, George J.	(NY)	868
Arms race films databases	DOWLING, John	(PA)	316
Art films reference & programming	WARREN, Ann R.	(NH)	1306
Audiovisual & film reviewing	LOCKE, John W.	(IL)	736
Audiovisual & 16mm film & video	FISH, Marie	(CA)	380
Audiovisual, film, video	ENGLE, Joyce C.	(NJ)	349
Audiovisual, films	SANDY, Marjorie M.	(MI)	1081
Audiovisuals, film & video	MINOR, Barbara G.	(MN)	846
Bibliography in film & video field	CYR, Helen W.	(MD)	268
Children's film production	DAVENPORT, Thomas R.	(VA)	276
Children's films & videotapes	GAFFNEY, Maureen	(NY)	412
Compiling film reference books	TUDIVER, Lillian	(NY)	1262
Consultant, film & video production	HEMPEL, Gordon J.	(IL)	525
Distributing educational films	KONICEK, Karen B.	(MA)	670
Distribution of educational films	HARTLEY, Elda E.	(CT)	508
Documentary films	SPEARS, Ross	(TN)	1172
Documentary films & videotapes	RICHTER, Robert	(NY)	1031
Drama & film	CIOPPA, Lawrence	(NY)	214
Educational film	MACINTYRE, Ronald R.	(NY)	755
Educational film & video evaluation	MODICA, Mary L.	(SD)	851
Educational film & video selection	MODICA, Mary L.	(SD)	851
Educational films	WIENER, Paul B.	(NY)	1336
Educational films & videotapes	FISHER, Carolyn H.	(NY)	380
Educational films on aging	YAHNKE, Robert E.	(MN)	1376
Evaluation of film centers	RICHIE, Mark L.	(NJ)	1030
Experimental film	GLABICKI, Paul	(PA)	439
Film	HISS, Sheila M.	(FL)	544
	MILLER, Lynn F.	(NJ)	840
	NIGRIN, Albert G.	(NJ)	904
	CHACH, Maryann	(NY)	196
	SLOAN, William J.	(NY)	1150
Film & photograph research	GOTTFRIED, Erika D.	(NY)	453
Film & television archives	JOHNSON, Jane D.	(CA)	605
Film & television database retrieval	SALZ, Kay	(NY)	1078
Film & television distribution	KLUGHERZ, Dan	(NY)	662
Film & television media	MONACO, James	(NY)	854
Film & television preservation	SALZ, Kay	(NY)	1078
Film & television production	COHEN, Frederick	(NY)	228
	KLUGHERZ, Dan	(NY)	662
Film & television research	MICHAELS, Joan M.	(CA)	832
	GLADSTONE, Mark A.	(NJ)	439
Film & theater memorabilia	WESOLOWSKI, Paul G.	(PA)	1325
Film & TV information	ALLEN, Nancy H.	(MI)	15
Film & video	POOLE, Rebecca S.	(CO)	983
	GASTON, Judith A.	(MN)	421
	HADDOCK, Mable	(OH)	482
Film & video acquisition	HUGHES, Rolanda L.	(IN)	572
	HAYNES, Jean	(NY)	516
Film & video archiving	WEATHERFORD, Elizabeth	(NY)	1311
Film & video collection	HANFT, Margie E.	(CA)	495
Film & video collection coordination	NEBEL, Jean C.	(CA)	891
Film & video collection development	MOORE, Emily C.	(NC)	859
Film & video collections	FLYNN, Barbara L.	(IL)	386
	TUGGLE, Pamela C.	(VA)	1262

FILM (Cont'd)

Film & video consultant, appraiser	MACAULEY, C C.	(CA)	754
Film & video distribution	BLANK, Les	(CA)	104
	WHITE, Matthew H.	(IL)	1331
	CABEZAS, Sue A.	(MA)	170
Film & video for schools	MAY, Frank C.	(CA)	788
Film & video librarianship	AYARI, Kaye W.	(SC)	42
Film & video libraries	BARNES, Robert W.	(NY)	57
Film & video library	WEISER, Douglas E.	(MI)	1319
	LINK, Margaret A.	(NC)	730
	SOUTHARD, Ruth K.	(TX)	1169
Film & video library administration	THOMAS, Fred	(MD)	1236
Film & video library management	HOLSINGER, Katherine	(AZ)	554
Film & video media	JENNINGS, Mary	(AK)	598
Film & video production	WHITE, Matthew H.	(IL)	1331
	CABEZAS, Sue A.	(MA)	170
Film & video programming	THOMPSON, Elizabeth M.	(DC)	1239
	CANTWELL, Mary L.	(OH)	179
Film & video recordings	OLIVER, Scot	(KY)	921
Film & video resources	ALLAN, David W.	(MN)	14
Film & video reviewing & programming	BRAUN, Robert L.	(NY)	130
Film & video services	DEAN, Martha L.	(CA)	283
Film & video stock footage	SUMMERS, Robert A.	(NJ)	1209
Film & video writing & production	TALIT, Lynn	(CT)	1221
Film animation	GLABICKI, Paul	(PA)	439
Film archives	YEAGER, Gerry	(MD)	1378
Film cataloging & indexing	COVERT, Nadine	(NY)	252
Film criticism & journalism	CROWDUS, Gary A.	(NY)	261
Film distribution	MONDELL, Cynthia B.	(TX)	854
Film history	STOCKSTILL, Patrick E.	(CA)	1195
	MARTIN, Vernon E.	(CT)	778
	DRUMMOND, Donald R.	(TX)	321
Film information	COVERT, Nadine	(NY)	252
Film instruction	NIGRIN, Albert G.	(NJ)	904
Film lending libraries	WILLIAMS, Helen E.	(KY)	1343
Film library & video library	GORDON, Thelma S.	(CT)	452
Film library management	RICHIE, Mark L.	(NJ)	1030
Film music	ANDERSON, Gillian B.	(DC)	23
	WRIGHT, H S.	(IL)	1371
Film production	BORUZKOWSKI, Lilly A.	(IL)	117
	CEDERHOLM, Theresa D.	(MA)	196
	MONDELL, Cynthia B.	(TX)	854
Film programming & research	VOURVOULIAS, Sabrina M.	(NY)	1289
Film programming for adults	JEFFERY, Phyllis D.	(AL)	596
Film reference	GOLDMAN, Nancy L.	(CA)	445
Film research	SUMMERS, Robert A.	(NJ)	1209
	MONTGOMERY, Patrick	(NY)	856
	DUCLOW, Geradline	(PA)	322
Film research, television production	LIMBACHER, James L.	(MI)	727
Film reviewer	SECKELSON, Linda E.	(NY)	1110
Film studies	DOSER, Virginia A.	(CA)	313
Film, television & radio	YEE, Martha M.	(CA)	1379
	DAVIDSON, Steven I.	(NY)	276
Film, theatre, television	KARATNYTSKY, Christine A.	(NY)	627
Film, video selection & programming	BUCHANAN, Gerald	(MS)	153
Film, video selection development	SHAPIRO, Leila C.	(MD)	1121
Films	LIE, David W.	(NY)	725
	GRIFFISS, M K.	(TN)	469
Films, publications & teaching aids	FORREST, Phyllis E.	(DC)	391
Genre films	FREEMAN, John P.	(TX)	401
Graduate film study	FREEMAN, John P.	(TX)	401
History of silent film	ALTOMARA, Rita E.	(NJ)	18
Independent filmmaking	DAVENPORT, Thomas R.	(VA)	276
Indexing film & broadcast trade journals	HOFFER, Thomas W.	(FL)	547
Interactive software & films	FORD, Andrew E.	(NY)	389
John F Kennedy film & photographs	GOODRICH, Allan B.	(MA)	449
Managing film & video libraries	HAYNES, Jean	(NY)	516
Mechanical music, broadcasting, film	MUNSICK, Lee R.	(NJ)	879
Movies & film	WITT, Kenneth W.	(MN)	1358
Non-theatrical film	MACINTYRE, Ronald R.	(NY)	755
Non-theatrical films	GURN, Robert M.	(NY)	478
Personal film, theatre library	TUDIVER, Lillian	(NY)	1262
Preview, evaluate & purchase films	NEBEL, Jean C.	(CA)	891
Producing informational films	HOFFER, Thomas W.	(FL)	547
Production, film & video	BEATTY, R M.	(IN)	70

FILM (Cont'd)

Rare jazz records, films & photographs	BRADLEY, Jack	(MA)	126
Reference film & television	TODD, Rose A.	(PQ)	1248
Reference related to film	DIAMANT, Betsy	(ISR)	299
Regional film library	HOFSTAD, Alice M.	(MN)	548
Researching film distributors	SHABERLY, Leanna J.	(AZ)	1118
Researching historic photos & film	LUSKEY, Judith	(DC)	749
Reviewing film, video & media	TROJAN, Judith L.	(NY)	1257
Reviewing nuclear issues films	DOWLING, John	(PA)	316
Reviewing physics films	DOWLING, John	(PA)	316
Scientific tape film archives	SALY, Alan J.	(NY)	1078
16mm film	KREAMER, Jean T.	(LA)	677
16mm film & video	GOTTLIEB, Delia	(NY)	453
16mm film selection	ANDERSON, Gail	(AB)	23
16mm film selection & reference	LOCKE-GAGNON, Rebecca A.	(OH)	736
16mm film usage	BARGAR, Arthur W.	(CT)	56
16mm films, slides, & videocassettes	CRITCHLOW, Therese E.	(NJ)	259
Soviet film history	DAY, Martha T.	(VT)	282
Story & visual research for films	FINE, Deborah J.	(CA)	377
Telecommunications & film reference	GRILIKHES, Sandra B.	(PA)	470
Television news film archives	WHITSON, Helene	(CA)	1334
Video & film collection development	GORSEGNER, Betty D.	(WI)	452
Video & film purchasing	RICHIE, Mark L.	(NJ)	1030
Writer for film & video	BEATTY, R M.	(IN)	70
Writing & directing educational films	HARTLEY, Elda E.	(CT)	508

FINANCE (See also Accounting, Banking, Bond, Economics, Funding, Fundraising, Grants)

Administration & finance	BRYAN, Arthur L.	(NH)	151
Analyzing finances & budgeting	BENDER, Betty W.	(WA)	79
Banking & finance	MORRISON, Patricia	(CA)	868
	GERVINO, Joan	(DC)	429
	CHAFE, Douglas A.	(HI)	197
Banking & finance subject field	GALLUP, Jane H.	(DC)	415
Banking & financial services	ENGRAM, Sandra K.	(IL)	350
Banking, finance & business reference	MIRANDA, Esmeralda C.	(MN)	847
Budget & finance	APPEL, Anne M.	(CA)	29
	HAWLEY, Marsha S.	(IL)	514
	SUGDEN, Barbara L.	(IL)	1206
	DOMBOURIAN, Sona J.	(LA)	310
	LEBRUN, Marlene M.	(MD)	708
	HERNANDEZ, Ramon R.	(MI)	532
	DESCIORA, Susan O.	(NY)	294
	VAN RIPER, Joy C.	(NY)	1277
	SENG, Mary A.	(TX)	1115
Budget & fiscal management	CONNORS, William E.	(NY)	238
Budgeting & finance	BERRY, Louise P.	(CT)	90
	TUCKER, Florence R.	(MI)	1261
	LEVESQUE, Janet A.	(RI)	719
	SIEBERSMA, Dan	(WY)	1135
Budgeting & finances	COULTER, Cynthia M.	(OK)	251
Budgeting & financial management	MUNTEAN, Deborah E.	(MN)	879
Budgeting & fiscal administration	ALMONY, Robert A.	(MO)	17
Budgeting & fiscal control	KEHOE, Patrick E.	(DC)	634
Buildings, financing plans	SANDSTEDT, Carl R.	(MO)	1081
Business & finance	PROBST, Virginia M.	(IL)	994
	HARNDEN, Donna J.	(MN)	502
	BURNS, Violanda O.	(NY)	163
	ENGLER, Gretchen	(NY)	349
	HERMAN, Marsha	(NY)	531
	HOUGHTON, Joan I.	(NY)	562
	STEWART, Elizabeth A.	(ON)	1192
Business & finance database research	STOOPS, Louise	(NY)	1198
Business & finance databases	CROFT, Elizabeth G.	(NY)	260
	WALKER, Jeanette F.	(NY)	1295
Business & finance information	OLSHEN, Toni	(ON)	922
Business & finance libraries	LONGMAN, Judith J.	(IL)	740
Business & finance reference	NARCISO, Susan D.	(NY)	888
Business & finance research	ARMEIT, Marilyn	(NY)	32
	CLOWE, Isabel B.	(NY)	223
	MAYOPOULOS, Karen L.	(NY)	791
Business & finance statistics	MEREDITH, Meri	(IN)	825

FINANCE (Cont'd)

Business & financial databases	WARNER, Claudette S.	(IL)	1305
	BARRETT, Michael D.	(NY)	59
	BERNTSEN, Robert M.	(NY)	90
	DAVID, Julia A.	(NY)	276
	ESPO, Hal	(NY)	354
	JONES, Sarah C.	(NY)	615
	MARSHALL, Patricia K.	(NY)	775
	SANTORO, Tesse F.	(NY)	1082
	VAZQUEZ, Edward	(NY)	1280
Business & financial information	MEARNS, Mary A.	(CA)	820
	BROWN, George F.	(MA)	144
	COOPER, J P.	(MA)	243
	GUHERIDGE, Allison A.	(ON)	476
Business & financial information spclst	DARNOWSKI, Christina M.	(NY)	275
Business & financial research	SOROBAY, Roman T.	(NY)	1169
Business, finance & accounting databases	KILBERG, Jacqueline L.	(NY)	648
Business, financial databases	SAYWARD, Nick H.	(NY)	1087
Certified financial planner	ROSS, Ric	(CA)	1058
Construction finance	LEWIS, Thomas F.	(MA)	724
Consulting to financial institutions	PHILLIPS, Steven G.	(MA)	969
Corporate financial databases	HAMBRIC, Donna R.	(CO)	491
Corporate financial information	HENDERSON, Joanne L.	(DE)	526
Customer financial information requests	GAYNOR, Joann T.	(NY)	424
Database searching, financial databases	CONNER, Norma	(NY)	237
Domestic reference fiscal policy	ANDERSON, John M.	(DC)	23
Economic & financial databases	WYSS, David A.	(MA)	1376
	ZURBRIGG, Lyn E.	(ON)	1391
Economic & financial forecasting srvs	ZURBRIGG, Lyn E.	(ON)	1391
Economics & finance	BURDET, Michele C.	(SWZ)	158
Economics & finance acquisitions	MAYNARD, Elizabeth	(OH)	790
Economics & finance reference	MAYNARD, Elizabeth	(OH)	790
Finance	DRAKE, Miriam A.	(GA)	318
	ALTGILBERS, Cynthia J.	(IL)	18
	MCKAY, Micheal W.	(MO)	810
	SANDSTEDT, Carl R.	(MO)	1081
	DI MEGLEO, Arthur J.	(NY)	304
	LERNER, Arthur	(NY)	717
	SCHUMAN, Patricia G.	(NY)	1103
	SILVER, Linda R.	(OH)	1138
	BISHOP, Donna M.	(OK)	99
	PATTERSON, Jennifer J.	(TN)	948
	PRENTICE, Ann E.	(TN)	990
	CANALES, Herbert G.	(TX)	178
	OGDEN, Howard A.	(VA)	918
Finance & administration	WASCHLER, Merl E.	(AZ)	1307
	COTE, Susan J.	(OH)	249
Finance & business information research	SINGER, Susan A.	(NJ)	1143
Finance & investment	HERBERT, Annette F.	(NY)	530
Finance & personnel	PERRY, Rodney B.	(NY)	961
Finances & financial planning	TABORN, Kym M.	(CA)	1219
Financial administration	EIDSON, Alreeta	(CO)	340
	THOMPSON, Mary A.	(DC)	1240
	GALLOWAY, Margaret E.	(TX)	415
	SKELTON, W M.	(ON)	1146
Financial analysis	JONES, Jennifer R.	(NY)	613
Financial analysis research	HEFFRON, Betsy A.	(NY)	520
Financial & business research	THAU, Richard	(NJ)	1234
Financial & industry information	GINSBURG, Carol L.	(NY)	438
Financial & investment information	WEINSTEIN, Daniel L.	(CT)	1318
Financial & thrift industry	CALLINAN, Mary H.	(NY)	174
Financial archival arrangement	LAMBKIN, Anthony	(IRE)	690
Financial, business libraries	MCDAVID, Sara J.	(GA)	801
Financial consulting	LINDSEY, Susan B.	(PA)	730
Financial databases	BECK, Douglas J.	(DC)	71
	KEELER, Janice S.	(IL)	634
	REITER, Richard R.	(IL)	1022
	PHILLIPS, Steven G.	(MA)	969
	ALMAN, Richard D.	(NY)	17
	BING, Robert H.	(NY)	97
	BRAGG, Sanford B.	(NY)	127
	ESSMAN, Tallaine G.	(NY)	355
	LANDES, J C.	(NY)	692
	MEYER, Garry S.	(NY)	830
	O'CONOR, William C.	(NY)	916
	SOLOMON, Samuel H.	(NY)	1166

FINANCE (Cont'd)

Financial databases
    TAPIERO, Judith ...... (NY) 1223
    BAILEY, Linda S. ...... (TX) 46
    GIBSON, Timothy T. .... (TX) 432
    ODHO, Marc .... (ON) 917
Financial databases & applications CORVESE, Lisa A. ...... (NY) 248
Financial forecasting WYSS, David A. .... (MA) 1376
Financial industry information HALL, Robert C. ...... (NY) 488
Financial industry trading systems HALL, Robert C. .... (NY) 488
Financial information STANTON, Beth L. .... (MI) 1181
    ZOTTOLI, Danny A. .... (NY) 1390
    FAIR, Linda A. .... (ON) 361
Financial information & transaction RANDOLPH, Kevin H. .. (CA) 1007
Financial information databases JONES, Frank .... (VA) 613
Financial information products TIERNEY, Richard H. ... (NY) 1244
Financial information services LANDES, J C. .... (NY) 692
Financial information surveying JONES, Frank .... (VA) 613
Financial information systems DEFALCO, Joseph ..... (NY) 287
Financial institutions DATTALO, Elmo F. ..... (DC) 275
    LEAMEN, Nancy J. .... (ON) 707
Financial institutions & services FEATHERS, John E. ..... (WA) 367
Financial management LYNCH, Hugh J. ...... (IL) 751
    VIRGO, Julie A. .... (IL) 1285
    KIRBY, Frederick J. .... (MI) 654
    HAMMOND, John J. .... (MO) 493
    BARTH, Joseph M. ...... (NY) 61
    MEYER, Andrew W. .... (NY) 829
    DEWBERRY, Betty B. ... (TX) 298
    BYERS, Edward W. .... (WY) 168
    DUFFIN, Elizabeth A. ... (IRE) 323
Financial market analysis PHILLIPS, Steven G. ... (MA) 969
Financial models WYSS, David A. .... (MA) 1376
Financial news & publishing CASEY, Robert W. ..... (NY) 192
Financial planning MARTIN, Murray S. ..... (MA) 777
    SUDALL, Arthur D. ..... (NJ) 1206
Financial planning & reporting SELLGREN, James A. ... (MI) 1114
Financial printing & publishing ARNSDORF, Dennis A. .. (DC) 34
Financial publishing TIERNEY, Richard H. ... (NY) 1244
Financial records VANCE, Mary L. ...... (MS) 1273
Financial reference VAZQUEZ, Edward ..... (NY) 1280
Financial reference sources STONER, Ronald P. ..... (IL) 1198
Financial reporting reference JOHNSON, John E. ..... (ON) 606
Financial research SAYRS, Judith A. ...... (WI) 1087
Financial research & modeling COOPER, J P. .... (MA) 243
Financial services GAINES, Irene A. ...... (NY) 412
    GREENHOUSE, Lee R. . (NY) 464
    NOBLE, James K. ...... (NY) 906
    TALLEY, Pat L. .... (TX) 1221
    CITROEN, Julie M. ..... (ON) 215
Financial services industry CARTLEDGE, Ellen G. .. (CT) 190
    REMEIKIS, Lois A. ..... (IL) 1022
Financial services industry information WARNER, Claudette S. .. (IL) 1305
Financial services information TRIGAUX, Robert ...... (DC) 1256
    ALLAN, John .... (NY) 14
    BURKE, Edward .... (NY) 160
    FINCH, Brian .... (NY) 377
    FREY, Ned .... (NY) 402
    HENDERSON, Brad .... (NY) 526
    KRAUS, James .... (NY) 676
    MALKIN, Peter .... (NY) 763
    NOVEMBER, Robert S. . (NY) 911
    RUSLING, Con A. ..... (NY) 1068
    TYSON, David .... (NY) 1267
    VELLA, Carl .... (NY) 1281
    ZIMMERMAN, William .. (NY) 1389
Financial services online searching JORDAN, Charles R. .... (IL) 616
    STENGER, Brenda E. ... (IL) 1187
Financing & construction building plng KELLUM-ROSE, Nancy P. (CA) 637
Fiscal affairs BARKSDALE, Milton K. . (KY) 57
Fiscal & monetary policy BRINNER, Roger E. .... (MA) 136
Fiscal management HAMILTON, Rita ...... (AZ) 492
    ALLMAND, Linda F. .... (TX) 17
Fiscal matters FLOWER, Kenneth E. ... (MD) 386
Fiscal projects & reference in archives HARWOOD, James L. .. (DC) 510
Fiscal responsibility KELVER, Ann E. ...... (CO) 639
Fiscal services SEISER, Virginia .... (NM) 1113
Fundraising & financial development FLOWER, Kenneth E. ... (MD) 386
Health care financing AHRENSFELD, Jan .... (IL) 8
Historical & present financial data PAYNE, Linda C. ...... (NY) 951

FINANCE (Cont'd)

Integrated medical financial databases RUBIN, David S. ...... (NY) 1064
Legal, medical & financial databases LEVEROCK, Lisa A. .... (NJ) 719
Library administration & finance HOWINGTON, Lee R. .. (GA) 566
Library finance SONDHEIM, John W. .... (MD) 1167
Library finance & administration EVERINGHAM, Neil G. ... (VA) 358
Library finances CLEM, Harriet M. ...... (OH) 220
    DICKERSON, Lon R. .... (WA) 300
Library financing & building programming HELLUM-BERMAN, Bertha D. .... (CA) 524
Library management & finance STUDER, William J. .... (OH) 1204
Local government finance BEVERLEY, Barbara S. . (NY) 93
Management & finance DAVY, Edgar W. ...... (MA) 281
Market & financial information services HASSAN, Mohammad Z. (NY) 511
MIS & finance PATRICIU, Florin S. .... (MD) 947
Mortgage finance MCKEE, Margaret J. .... (WI) 810
Online databases, business & financial GARMAN, Nancy J. ..... (KY) 419
Public finance SHIH, Philip C. .... (IN) 1130
Public finance research MARSHALL, Marion B. ... (DC) 774
Real-time financial information REEDY, Martha L. ..... (MA) 1015
Retail financial technologies RATH, Charla M. ...... (DC) 1009
Statistical financial databases PRAVER, Robin I. ...... (NY) 990
Treasury Department fiscal records SHERMAN, William F. ... (DC) 1128

FINDING

Cataloging & finding aids GUREWITSCH, Bonnie . (NY) 478
Corporate fact finding OLSEN, Stephen ...... (MN) 922
Cost finding MIELKE, Linda .... (FL) 833
Finding aid preparation WADE, D J. .... (MO) 1290
Finding aids TURNBAUGH, Roy C. .. (OR) 1264
Information finding BERKMAN, Robert I. ... (NY) 87
Production of find-aids RABCHUK, Gordon K. .. (PQ) 1001

FINE

Art, fine arts, & music COLDWELL, Charles P. . (WA) 230
Art libraries & fine art materials GILBERT, Gail R. ...... (KY) 433
Art of fine arts GRIFFISS, M K. .... (TN) 469
Cataloging fine arts, serials MILLS, Rolland W. ..... (PR) 844
Fine & performing arts HOFFMAN, Irene M. .... (CA) 548
Fine & performing arts bibliography GROVES, Percilla E. .... (BC) 474
Fine art & handicraft specialization MANNING, Mary J. .... (IL) 766
Fine arts JEFFERY, Phyllis D. .... (AL) 596
    KIRKING, Clayton C. ... (AZ) 655
    SMITH, Matilda M. ..... (GA) 1158
    HUNT, Janis E. .... (IL) 575
    MILLER, Janet .... (IL) 838
    SCHAAF, Elizabeth ..... (MD) 1088
    SIMMONS, Rebecca A. . (NY) 1140
    LORANTH, Alice N. .... (OH) 741
    LEWIS, Marjorie B. .... (PA) 724
    DRUMMOND, Donald R. (TX) 321
    EDMUNDSON, Margaret B. .... (UT) 336
Fine arts & architecture bibliography BURDET, Michele C. ... (SWZ) 158
Fine arts & architecture cataloging CEDERHOLM, Theresa D. (MA) 196
Fine arts & architecture sources MOHAMMED, Selima ... (PQ) 852
Fine arts bibliographic instruction SPENCER, Deirdre D. .. (FL) 1173
Fine arts bibliography SCHERER, Herbert G. .. (MN) 1092
    MORR, Lynell A. ...... (FL) 866
    EVENSEN, Robert L. ... (MA) 358
    HASWELL, Hollee ..... (NY) 511
Fine arts book illustration BANTA, Gratia J. ...... (OH) 55
Fine arts book selection SCHERER, Herbert G. .. (MN) 1092
Fine arts books RICE, Ralph A. .... (TX) 1027
Fine arts cataloging WALTON, Carol G. ..... (FL) 1301
Fine arts collection development BOHRER, Karen M. .... (CT) 111
    MOORE, Emily C. ...... (NC) 859
    DOGU, Hikmet S. ...... (UT) 309
    PARR, Loraine E. ...... (WA) 943
    TOBIN, R J. .... (WI) 1247
Fine arts collections, books RUSSELL, Marilyn L. ... (KS) 1069
Fine arts databases DOGU, Hikmet S. ...... (UT) 309

FINE (Cont'd)

Fine arts librarianship	GUNDERSON, Jeffery R.	(CA)	477
	KUNSELMAN, Joan D.	(CA)	684
	HEHMAN, Jennifer L.	(IN)	521
	CABLE, Carole L.	(TX)	170
Fine arts library management	GAMER, May L.	(MO)	416
Fine arts, local history collections	MCNULTY, Karen	(CT)	817
Fine arts museum	JACOBY, Mary M.	(VA)	590
Fine arts reference	DONIO, Dorothy	(FL)	311
	MORR, Lynell A.	(FL)	866
	SCHERER, Herbert G.	(MN)	1092
	DOGU, Hikmet S.	(UT)	309
Fine arts reference services	MENDRO, Donna C.	(TX)	824
Fine arts research	MILLER, Hester M.	(NM)	838
Fine arts researcher	HEHMAN, Jennifer L.	(IN)	521
Fine press	PASCAL, Barbara R.	(CA)	945
Fine press publisher	ALTERMAN, Deborah H.	(NJ)	18
Fine print cataloging	REDLICH, Barry	(NJ)	1014
Fine printing & incunabula	MENTHE, Melissa	(NJ)	825
Fine printing, limited editions	KIRSHENBAUM, Sandra D.	(CA)	655
Fine printing, private presses	MATHEWS, Richard B.	(FL)	784
Fine prints	OSTROW, Stephen E.	(DC)	929
	DANE, William J.	(NJ)	272
History of fine printing	DANE, William J.	(NJ)	272
Humanities & fine arts reference	COHN, Alan M.	(IL)	229
Modern fine printing	COLE, Maud D.	(NY)	231
Music & fine arts reference	DAVIS, Joy V.	(GA)	279
Public, fine arts librarianship	MATYI, Stephen G.	(OH)	786
Reference, fine & performing arts	DOCTOROW, Erica	(NY)	307
Subject specialist in fine arts	PIRON, Alice M.	(IL)	975

FIRE

Fire protection in libraries & museums	MORRIS, John	(CA)	866
Fire research	JASON, Nora H.	(MD)	595
Fire science research	SALY, Alan J.	(NY)	1078
Fire sciences & technology	GOLD, Sandra	(ON)	444

FIRMS (See also Business, Companies, Industry, Mergers)

Accounting firm libraries	MURRAY, Marilyn R.	(IL)	882
Administration of law firm library	D'AMORE, Denice M.	(OH)	272
Appraising law firm collections	SCAMMAHORN, Lynne	(PA)	1087
Architectural & interiors firm libraries	TENNEY, Kimberly M.	(MA)	1231
Automating law firm libraries	DILORETO, Ann M.	(CA)	303
Consulting firms	GOZDZ, Wanda E.	(FL)	455
Executive search firms	MARSHALL, Deborah M.	(IL)	774
Law firm acquisitions	SNYDER, Elizabeth A.	(ENG)	1164
Law firm collections cataloging	SCAMMAHORN, Lynne	(PA)	1087
Law firm consulting	DAVIS, Becky C.	(CA)	277
	EARHART, Marilyn N.	(CA)	332
Law firm, information systems	EWING, Alison L.	(AZ)	359
Law firm libraries	CROSS, Joseph R.	(SC)	260
Law firm library administration	YALLER, Loretta O.	(DE)	1376
	VARGAS, Gwen S.	(PA)	1278
Law firm library automation	PETERSON, Christine E.	(WI)	963
Law firm library establishment	ROCKWOOD, Susan M.	(PA)	1046
Law firm library management	MATTHEWSON, David S.	(CT)	786
	HARRIS, Helen Y.	(MD)	504
	JULIAN, Julie L.	(TN)	619
Private law firm administration	SCHIPPER, Joan A.	(CA)	1093
	KLEBBA, Lisa A.	(MO)	658
Private law firm consulting	PLUNKET, Joy H.	(MA)	978
Private law firms	GOLDMAN, Teri B.	(MO)	446
Public relations between firm & clients	BARNUM, Deborah C.	(CT)	58
Reorganizing law firm libraries	BYRNE, Jeanne M.	(TX)	169
Setting up library systems in law firms	BYRNE, Jeanne M.	(TX)	169
Small law firms	WEZELMAN, Joy L.	(ND)	1328

FISCAL (See Financial)

FISHERIES

Aquatic sciences & fisheries information	SEARS, Jonathan R.	(MD)	1110

FISHING

Hunting & fishing	FOERSTER, Trey	(WI)	387

FLAVOR

Flavor chemistry	RILEY, Sarah A.	(MD)	1035

FLORIDA

Florida building regulations	FOSTER, Helen M.	(FL)	392
Florida information	BYRD, Beverly P.	(FL)	168
Florida public health history	HALL, M C.	(FL)	488
State of Florida documents	KONOP, Bonnie M.	(FL)	670
University of Florida documents	KONOP, Bonnie M.	(FL)	670

FLOW

Information flow in industries	JACKSON, Eugene B.	(TX)	587
Information flow in organizations	DANIEL, Evelyn H.	(NC)	272

FOLK (See also Arts, Crafts, Mythology, Tales)

American folk arts	LIND, Judith Y.	(NJ)	728
American folklife indexing	OLSON, Eric J.	(NC)	922
Crafts & folk art	BENEDETTI, Joan M.	(CA)	80
Customs, folklore, etiquette, holidays	HAWK, Susan P.	(FL)	513
Ethnic history & folklore	PENTI, Marsha E.	(MI)	957
Folk music	VUKAS, Rachel R.	(KS)	1290
Folk music archives	POST, Jennifer C.	(VT)	986
Folklife studies	SEEMANN, Charles H.	(TN)	1111
Folklore	HICKERSON, Joseph C.	(DC)	536
	LORANTH, Alice N.	(OH)	741
	AZZOLINA, David S.	(PA)	43
	ODEAN, Kathleen F.	(RI)	916
	MCCONNELL, Ruth M.	(TX)	798
Folklore & folklife	ANDERSON, Janet A.	(UT)	23
Folklore & mythology	SLATTERY, Carole C.	(MA)	1148
Folklore & storytelling	HARDESTY, Vicki H.	(OH)	499
Folklore, mythology & customs	MCCANN, Judith B.	(ON)	794
Folklore unit	DRZEWIECKI, Iris M.	(NY)	321
Folksong	ROTH, Stacy F.	(NJ)	1059
Lecturing about folklore	MACDONALD, Margaret R.	(WA)	754
Music & folklore research	MCCULLOH, Judith M.	(IL)	801
Polish folklore storytelling	MAZUREK, Adam P.	(MD)	791
Social, folk, & ceremonial dances	KELLER, Kate V.	(PA)	635
Storytelling & folklore	BOLT, Janice A.	(IL)	113
	HERMAN, Gertrude B.	(WI)	531
Teaching folklore course	MICHNAY, Susan E.	(OH)	832

FOOD (See also Citrus, Crops, Grain, Meat, Nutrition, Soyfoods)

Agriculture & food	BATEMAN, Robert A.	(AB)	63
Collection development, foods, nutrition	NIPP, Deanna	(NJ)	904
Database searching, food sciences, chem	REED, Catherine A.	(NY)	1015
Food	GALT, Judith A.	(MN)	415
Food, agriculture, nutrition information	JOHNSON, Sheila A.	(NY)	609
Food & nutrition	HUNT, Jennie P.	(MD)	575
Food & nutrition collection development	SZILARD, Paula	(HI)	1218
Food & nutrition literature	CULBERTSON, Diana L.	(IL)	263
Food & nutrition reference	SZILARD, Paula	(HI)	1218
Food chemistry	NEMETH, Martha C.	(CA)	895
Food consumption	KREBS-SMITH, James J.	(MD)	677
Food industry	CARTER, Steva L.	(MO)	190
	WILTON, Greg J.	(MB)	1353
Food industry database production	INGISH, Karen S.	(IL)	582
Food industry reference	DEPKE, Robert W.	(IL)	293
Food industry research & development	WILTON, Greg J.	(MB)	1353
Food marketing	MARTIN, Irmgarde D.	(TX)	776
Food marketing & research	SWANSON, Mary A.	(NY)	1213
Food processing technology databases	MCNAUGHT, Hugh W.	(ON)	816
Food safety information systems	CHATFIELD, Michele R.	(DC)	203
Food science	ARNOLD, Patricia K.	(TX)	34
	MUNDSTOCK, Aileen M.	(WI)	879
Food science & medical databases	FALCONE, Elena C.	(NY)	362

FOOD (Cont'd)

Food science & technology	WHITEMARSH, Thomas R.	(WI)	1333
Food science & textiles	MANDERSCHEID, Dorothy H.	(MI)	765
Food science, chemistry & technology	RILEY, Sarah A.	(MD)	1035
Food science reference	PERMAN, Karen A.	(IL)	959
Food science, technology	MARTIN, Irmgarde D.	(TX)	776
Food service	SMALLEY, Ann W.	(DC)	1151
Food service industry	SMYTH, Mary B.	(CA)	1162
Food service research	DEPKE, Robert W.	(IL)	293
Food technology	WRIGHT, Nancy M.	(PA)	1372
Food technology online searching	LAMANNA, Joan M.	(CA)	689
Foods & nutrition selection	LAMONTAGNE, Therese	(CA)	691
Research in hlth, socty, music, foods	STARKEY, Bonnie F.	(WV)	1182

FOOTAGE

Film & video stock footage	SUMMERS, Robert A.	(NJ)	1209
Stock footage libraries	MONTGOMERY, Patrick	(NY)	856

FORECASTING

Business analysis & forecasting	BRINNER, Roger E.	(MA)	136
Economic & financial forecasting srvs	ZURBRIGG, Lyn E.	(ON)	1391
Economic database & forecasts	BECK, Douglas J.	(DC)	71
Economic forecasting	MCKELVEY, Michael J.	(DC)	811
	CARTER, Walter F.	(MA)	190
	CATON, Christopher N.	(MA)	195
Financial forecasting	WYSS, David A.	(MA)	1376
Forecasting new media diffusion	KLOPFENSTEIN, Bruce C.	(OH)	662
Forecasting services	FELMY, John C.	(DC)	370
Industry forecasts	BAILEY, Linda S.	(TX)	46

FOREIGN (See also Global, International, Overseas, World)

American & foreign language literature	SHIRES, Nancy P.	(NC)	1131
Cataloging foreign language material	INGIBERGSSON, Asgeir	(AR)	582
Cataloging foreign languages	KATZ, Solomon B.	(PQ)	630
Cataloging monographs, foreign languages	MIKLOSVARY, Jozsef	(CA)	834
Children's & foreign books	ROBIEN, Eleanor K.	(IL)	1043
Consulting foreign language libraries	VALENTINE, Patrick M.	(NC)	1271
Defense & foreign affairs	COLSON, Harold G.	(AL)	234
Foreign affairs bibliography	CARLSON, Julia F.	(DC)	182
Foreign affairs indexing	CARLSON, Julia F.	(DC)	182
Foreign & comparative law	ZOLLER, R T.	(WI)	1390
Foreign & domestic periodicals	LONG, Roger J.	(IL)	739
Foreign & international law	BERKEY, Irene	(IL)	87
	YACKLE, Jeanette F.	(MA)	1376
	DIEFENBACH, Dale A.	(NY)	301
Foreign & intl law collection devlpmnt	TARNAWSKY, Marta	(PA)	1224
Foreign & international law reference	TARNAWSKY, Marta	(PA)	1224
	WEISBAUM, Earl	(TX)	1319
Foreign & international law research	GOLDBERG, Jolande E.	(DC)	444
Foreign & international legal research	ARANDA-COODOU, Patricio	(DC)	30
Foreign & international standards	OVERMAN, Joanne R.	(MD)	931
Foreign Documents	WESTFALL, Gloria D.	(IN)	1327
Foreign government publications	MAACK, David J.	(WA)	753
Foreign, international & comparative law	LYMAN, Lovisa	(UT)	751
Foreign, international law	GERMAIN, Claire M.	(NC)	429
Foreign language acquisitions	MCELWAIN, William	(IL)	804
Foreign language books	MERKIN, David	(NY)	826
Foreign language cataloging	TSCHERNY, Alexander	(DC)	1260
	STEWART, Richard A.	(IL)	1193
	KIRKWOOD, Francis T.	(ON)	655
Foreign language collection development	HERNANDEZ, Hector R.	(IL)	531
	MCELWAIN, William	(IL)	804
	ALICEA, Ismael	(NY)	13
Foreign language collections	PUTZ, Paul D.	(AK)	998
	TSUNEISHI, Warren M.	(DC)	1260
Foreign language collections development	KRIEGER, Lee A.	(NC)	678
Foreign language instruction	LERNER, Esther T.	(OH)	717
Foreign language interpreting	HOMNACK, Mark	(CA)	555
Foreign language libraries	CLOHESSY, Antoinette M.	(CO)	223

FOREIGN (Cont'd)

Foreign language literature selection	DOLAN-HEITLINGER, Eileen	(IN)	309
Foreign language materials	NAVARRO, Frank A.	(CA)	889
	LANDIS, Dennis C.	(RI)	693
	KAYE, Barbara J.	(ON)	632
Foreign language non-book materials	MCELWAIN, William	(IL)	804
Foreign language reference & cataloging	MCCLAREY, Catherine A.	(IL)	796
Foreign language scientific literature	SAMSON, Mary	(ON)	1079
Foreign language teaching	HSU, Patrick K.	(TX)	567
Foreign language translating	HOMNACK, Mark	(CA)	555
Foreign language translation	SICILIANO, Peg P.	(MI)	1135
Foreign language typesetting	HOMNACK, Mark	(CA)	555
Foreign languages	KHATTAB, Hosneya M.	(CA)	646
	BIRO, Juliane	(NY)	99
	WERTSMAN, Vladimir F.	(NY)	1325
	CLARK, Peter W.	(WI)	217
Foreign languages & classics	PEDERSOLI, Heleni M.	(AL)	954
Foreign languages & cultures	COMPRI, Jeannine L.	(AB)	235
Foreign languages & literatures	TIMBERS, Jill G.	(MI)	1245
Foreign languages cataloging	HALIBEY, Areta V.	(IL)	486
	FOLTER, Siegrun H.	(NY)	388
Foreign languages, European complex	PERSHE, Frank F.	(MO)	961
Foreign law	PRATTER, Jonathan	(TX)	990
Foreign law bibliography	SCHWERIN, Kurt	(IL)	1106
	TARNAWSKY, Marta	(PA)	1224
Foreign law book acquisition	KREH, Fritz	(WGR)	677
Foreign law research	KAVASS, Igor I.	(TN)	631
Foreign legal materials	RAUCH, Anne	(NY)	1010
Foreign libraries for youth	JACKSON, Clara O.	(OH)	587
Foreign literature	GLIKIN, Ronda	(MI)	441
Foreign literatures	MACIUSZKO, Jerzy J.	(OH)	755
Foreign official publications	MARLEAU, Gilles	(ON)	772
Foreign relations research	QUARTELL, Robert J.	(NY)	999
Foreign scientific technical literature	BROPHY, Charles A.	(OH)	141
Foreign students & libraries	SARKODIE-MENSAH, Kwasi	(LA)	1083
Foreign title acquisitions	SIEVERS, Arlene M.	(IN)	1136
Foreign trade, political science	LERNER, Arthur	(NY)	717
Foreign trade statistics	MORTON, Dorothy J.	(DE)	870
Foreign-language acquisitions	BELL, Irena L.	(ON)	77
Foreign-language collection development	BELL, Irena L.	(ON)	77
Information foreign animal diseases	PERLMAN, Stephen E.	(NY)	959
International & foreign documents	KAGAN, Alfred	(CT)	621
International & foreign law	NARANJO-BOSCH, Antonio A.	(IL)	888
International & foreign legal literature	HEAD, Anita K.	(DC)	518
Libraries in foreign countries	TSUNEISHI, Warren M.	(DC)	1260
Market entry foreign publishers	PICKETT, Doyle C.	(NJ)	970
Online information, US & foreign	PINSON, Mark	(MA)	975
Researching foreign archive institutions	OGAWA, Chiyoko	(JAP)	918
Services to the foreign-born	SCHNEIDER, Francisca M.	(CA)	1097
Tutoring English as a foreign language	NORRIS, Loretta W.	(DC)	909
Upgrading foreign academic libraries	SIEMENS, Bessie M.	(MEX)	1136

FORENSIC

Forensic psychiatry	STARESINA, Lois J.	(MI)	1181

FORESTRY

Forestry	WALKER, Luise E.	(OR)	1295
	CLOSE, Elizabeth G.	(UT)	223
	LORD, Charles R.	(WA)	741
Forestry, conservation	PERSHE, Frank F.	(MO)	961
Forestry reference	KINCH, Michael P.	(OR)	649
Pulp, paper & forestry information	MARTINEZ, Linda W.	(WA)	779

FORMS

Alternate forms of energy	JESKE, Margo	(ON)	600
Forms & procedures management	GENESEN, Judith L.	(IL)	427
Forms generation software	CONTESSA, William B.	(NY)	239
Personal computer software, legal forms	KUEHNLE, Emery C.	(OH)	682

FOUNDATIONS

Collection devlpmnt, foundation grants	LEE, J S.	(NJ)	710
Foundation administration	THOMPSON, Mary A.	(DC)	1240
Foundation collection searches	FRASER, Elizabeth L.	(WV)	399
Foundation of information science	SKOVIRA, Robert J.	(PA)	1147
Foundation research	DICK, Ellen A.	(IL)	300
	KLETZIEN, S D.	(PA)	661
Foundation sources	JOHNSEN-HARRIS, Amy	(RI)	602
Foundations & grantsmanship	WILLIAMS, Guynell	(SC)	1343
Foundations information science	BOISSY, Robert W.	(NY)	111
Foundations of information science	FROEHLICH, Thomas J.	(NY)	405
Foundations of librarianship	GATES, Jean K.	(FL)	422
Grants & foundations	FERRALL, J E.	(AZ)	373
	NOLAN, Patrick B.	(OH)	907
Program planning & foundation evaluation	JONES, C L.	(PA)	611
Researching foundations	DUCKWORTH, Paul M.	(MO)	322

FOURTH

Fourth generation language	STOCKTON, Ken R.	(DC)	1196

FRANCOPHONIC

Francophonic African bibliography	SHAYNE, Mette H.	(IL)	1124

FRAUD

Health fraud & quackery	SERLING, Kitty	(MO)	1116

FREEDOM

Censorship & intellectual freedom	WOODS, L B.	(AR)	1367
	DELZELL, Robert F.	(MO)	290
Freedom of information	NIELSON, Paul F.	(MB)	903
Freedom of information processing	DOLAN, Maura E.	(DC)	309
Intellectual freedom	PINNELL-STEPHENS, June A.	(AK)	975
	TALLMAN, Karen D.	(AZ)	1221
	FLETCHER, Homer L.	(CA)	384
	FLUM, Judith G.	(CA)	386
	SESSIONS, Judith A.	(CA)	1117
	KNEPEL, Nancy	(CO)	664
	MURRAY, William A.	(CO)	882
	MILLER, Laurence A.	(FL)	839
	BUDLONG, Thomas F.	(GA)	155
	MCGREW, Mary L.	(IA)	808
	KRUG, Judith F.	(IL)	680
	MCDERMOTT, Patrice	(IL)	802
	GUNNELLS, Danny C.	(IN)	477
	ALLAIN, Alexander P.	(LA)	13
	DAVIS, Denise	(MD)	278
	DEAN, Frances C.	(MD)	283
	FRYER, Philip	(MD)	407
	RICHWINE, Eleanor N.	(MD)	1031
	LANIER, Gene D.	(NC)	696
	GOULD, Martha B.	(NV)	454
	CUSEO, Allan A.	(NY)	267
	LIU, Carol F.	(NY)	734
	RABBAN, Elana	(NY)	1001
	SHIELDS, Gerald R.	(NY)	1130
	HARDESTY, Vicki H.	(OH)	499
	WRIGHT, Janet K.	(OR)	1371
	BRAVARD, Robert S.	(PA)	130
	DAY, J D.	(UT)	282
	CAYWOOD, Carolyn A.	(VA)	195
	WISECARVER, Betty A.	(VA)	1357
	CONABLE, Gordon M.	(WA)	235
	BRANT, Susan L.	(WI)	129
	HOPKINS, Dianne M.	(WI)	557
	WILSON, William J.	(WI)	1353
	CORS, Paul B.	(WY)	248
	SCHRADER, Alvin M.	(AB)	1099
Intellectual freedom & censorship	SEREBNICK, Judith	(IN)	1116
	ANDERSON, A J.	(MA)	21
	MCDONALD, Frances B.	(MN)	802
	BRUWELHEIDE, Janis H.	(MT)	151
	KERESEY, Gayle	(NC)	643
Intellectual freedom, censorship	OSSOLINSKI, Lynn	(NV)	928
	COHEN, David	(NY)	228

FREEDOM (Cont'd)

Intellectual freedom committees	KRANZ, Ralph	(UT)	676
Intellectual freedom defense	MADDEN, Susan B.	(WA)	758
Intellectual freedom issues	BUCK, Richard M.	(NY)	154
Intellectual freedom teaching	EISENBACH, Elizabeth R.	(CA)	340
School libraries & intellectual freedom	BLANKENBURG, Judith B.	(VA)	104
Teaching intellectual freedom	TRYON, Jonathan S.	(RI)	1259

FREELANCE (See also Independent)

Freelance editing	OTT, Bill	(IL)	930
Freelance librarian	GOLDMAN, Teri B.	(MO)	446
Freelance performing arts research	BRAYTON, Roy S.	(NY)	130
Freelance research	HEISER, Nancy E.	(ME)	523
	GRIFFITH, Dorothy A.	(PA)	469
Freelance writing	RUGG, John D.	(OH)	1066
Freelancing	MARTIN, Teresa B.	(KS)	778
	LEESMENT, Helgi	(AB)	712

FREEMASONRY

Freemasonry & related subjects	HANKAMER, Roberta A.	(MA)	496

FRENCH (See also Francophonic)

Children's English & French literature	WALSH, Mary A.	(PQ)	1300
English & French book selection	TAGGART, William R.	(BC)	1220
English & French books selection	DAVIS, Virginia K.	(ON)	281
French	GORMAN, Lawrence R.	(IA)	452
French & Arabic education	YASSA, Lucie M.	(CA)	1378
French & theater	NELSON, Ian C.	(SK)	893
French, Arabic, English translation	YASSA, Lucie M.	(CA)	1378
French archival records & manuscripts	KOHN, Roger S.	(NY)	668
French Baroque	VOLLEN, Gene E.	(KS)	1287
French Bibles	CHAMBERS, Bettye T.	(DC)	198
French bibliography	WOESTHOFF, Catherine F.	(NY)	1359
French books	BADGER, Carole	(PQ)	44
	DUHAMEL, Louis	(PQ)	324
French Canadian children's literature	POTVIN, Claude	(NB)	987
	AUBREY, Irene E.	(ON)	38
French Canadian literature education	GUERETTE, Charlotte M.	(PQ)	476
French collection development	SPRY, Patricia	(ON)	1176
French collections	MACLENNAN, Oriel C.	(NS)	757
French educational software	GELINAS, Rene	(PQ)	426
French fiction	BOUCHARD, Martin	(PQ)	118
French language & literature	DEON, Judy S.	(BC)	293
French language library services	NICHOLSON, Jill A.	(ON)	902
French language publication	BERNARD, Marie L.	(AB)	88
French librarianship	CARRINGTON, Samuel M.	(TX)	186
French library automation	BAIRD, Lynn N.	(ID)	47
French literature	WIERUM, Ann R.	(WA)	1337
French literature & history	MCNAMARA, Charles B.	(NC)	816
French literature education	GUERETTE, Charlotte M.	(PQ)	476
French poetry	CARRINGTON, Samuel M.	(TX)	186
French solo vocal music	VOLLEN, Gene E.	(KS)	1287
Reference in French studies	GIRARD, Luc	(PQ)	438
17th century French bibliography	CHAMBERS, Bettye T.	(DC)	198
16th century French bibliography	CHAMBERS, Bettye T.	(DC)	198

FRIENDS

Exhibitions & friends programs	STODDARD, Roger E.	(MA)	1196
Friends	RICE, Dorothy F.	(NV)	1027
Friends & citizen organizing	FADDEN, Donald M.	(PA)	360
Friends & trustees groups	WINSLOW, Carol M.	(IN)	1355
Friends & volunteers	PALMATIER, Susan M.	(NH)	936
Friends coordination & development	CASELLA, Roberta L.	(TX)	192
Friends groups	HARRINGTON, Charles W.	(LA)	504
	GWYN, Ann S.	(MD)	479
Friends of academic libraries	ORAM, Robert W.	(TX)	925
Friends of libraries organization	MARSHALL, John D.	(TN)	774
Friends of libs organizing & developing	DOLNICK, Sandy F.	(IL)	310
Friends of library groups	DEMPSEY, Frank J.	(IL)	291
Friends of public libraries	PHELAN, Mary C.	(MA)	967
Friends of the libraries	DRESP, Donald F.	(NM)	319

FRIENDS (Cont'd)

Friends of the library	NIXON, Arless B.	(AZ)	906
	BROWN, Marie H.	(CA)	146
	EZZELL, Joline R.	(NC)	360
	PENNINGTON, Melanie L.	(TN)	957
	MCCONNELL, Shirley M.	(WI)	798
Friends of the library program	HERRING, Mark Y.	(TN)	533
Friends organizations	STRAUTMAN, Randolph B.	(GA)	1201
Library friends groups	ELLIOTT, C D.	(CA)	343
Personnel & friends of the library	ALMONY, Robert A.	(MO)	17
Public library friends group	KOCHOFF, Stephen T. . .	(NY)	667
Trustees & friends	CRABB, Elizabeth A.	(TX)	254

FRONT-END

Front-end software	KING, Joseph T.	(CA)	651
Frontends & gateways	LEVY, Louise R.	(NJ)	721
Search system software: front-end	WOODSMALL, Rose M. .	(MD)	1367
User interfaces & database frontends	CURRAN, George L. . . .	(NY)	266

FROST

Emily Dickinson & Robert Frost	LOMBARDO, Daniel J. . .	(MA)	738

FULL-TEXT

Archival full-text databases	MARKERT, Patricia B. . .	(NY)	771
Database full-text systems	PHILLIPS, J R.	(OK)	968
Full-text applications	SMITH, David F.	(NY)	1154
Full-text database applications	ROACH, Eddie D.	(OK)	1037
Full-text database design	GROCKI, Daniel J.	(MD)	471
Full-text databases	KRUSS, Daniel M.	(IL)	681
	LUCIER, Richard E. . . .	(MD)	746
	RODEAWALD, Patricia M.	(NJ)	1047
	WILLCOX, M C.	(PA)	1341
	WILLMANN, Donna S. . .	(PA)	1348
	KLAVER, Timothy J. . . .	(WI)	658
	HANDY, Mary J.	(ON)	495
Full-text newspaper library systems	DONCEVIC, Lois A. . . .	(PA)	311
Full-text retrieval	LEVINE, Emil H.	(DC)	720
Full-text retrieval software	BENGE, Bruce	(OK)	80
Online full-text retrieval	WHITMAN, Mary L. . . .	(PA)	1333
Online searching, especially full-text	REIFSNYDER, Betsy S. .	(DC)	1020

FUMIGATION

Fumigation	HANTHORN, Ivan E. . . .	(IA)	499

FUNDING (See also Accounting, Budget, Endowment, Finance, Gifts)

Attracting outside funding	SCULL, Roberta A.	(LA)	1108
Bookmobile funding	MARSHALL, Ruth T. . . .	(GA)	775
Budget & fund management	MARCINKO, Dorothy K. .	(AL)	769
Development & funding proposals	BAKER, Sylva S.	(PA)	49
Endowment & grant funding	DEYOUNG, Charles D. . .	(IN)	298
Formula funding of academic libraries	SMITH, Gordon W.	(CA)	1155
Fund accounting systems	FRIEDMAN, Barbara S. .	(NY)	403
Funding	HARRIS, Patricia L. . . .	(ND)	505
Funding research	HERFURTH, Sharon M. .	(TX)	530
Grant & fund development	KLIMEK, Chester R. . . .	(NY)	661
Grant writing & external funding	FELLA, Sarah C.	(OR)	370
Grants & external funding	TOMLIN, Marsha A.	(OH)	1250
Legislation & funding	RAPHAEL, Mary E.	(DC)	1008
Library funding	HANSON, Roger K.	(UT)	498
Library system budget funding	NETTLES, Jess	(MS)	896
Overseeing expenditure of federal funds	MACLEAN, Ellen G. . . .	(VI)	757
Public library funding	HUNSBERGER, Charles W.	(NV)	574
	LAMB, Donald K.	(WI)	689
Researcher for private funding sources	ROBERTSON, Ina N. . .	(IL)	1042
State library legislation & funding	PECK, Ruth M.	(MA)	953
Statewide library funding services	YATES, Ella G.	(VA)	1378

FUNDRAISING (See also Finance)

Administration & fundraising	HEINZ, Catharine F.	(DC)	522
Development & fundraising	FUSTUKJIAN, Samuel Y. .	(FL)	410
	LEE, Geoffrey J.	(TN)	710
Fundraising	MEDINA, Sue O.	(AL)	820
	COAKLEY, Dorothy J. . .	(CA)	224
	ESQUEVIN, Christian R. .	(CA)	354
	MORAN, Irene E.	(CA)	862
	SCHRIBER, James E. . . .	(CA)	1100
	SZYNAKA, Edward M. . .	(CA)	1219
	WALTERS, Suzanne . . .	(CO)	1301
	GIBSON, Barbara H. . . .	(CT)	431
	BOHLEN, Jeanne L.	(DC)	111
	PUFFER, Nathaniel H. . .	(DE)	997
	GRUBMAN, Donna Y. . .	(FL)	474
	CHANIN, Leah F.	(GA)	201
	CLOW, Faye E.	(IA)	223
	EGGERS, Lolly P.	(IA)	339
	DOLNICK, Sandy F.	(IL)	310
	MACKAMAN, Frank H. . .	(IL)	756
	MCGOWAN, John P. . . .	(IL)	807
	BAKER, Donald E.	(IN)	48
	CEDERHOLM, Theresa D.	(MA)	196
	MCKAY, Eleanor	(MD)	809
	PAPAI, Beverly D.	(MI)	938
	SCHERBA, Sandra A. . . .	(MI)	1092
	HAEUSER, Michael J. . .	(MN)	482
	HAGE, Elizabeth A.	(MN)	482
	MEISSNER, Edie A.	(MN)	822
	KAUP, Jermain A.	(ND)	631
	ROSS, Robert D.	(NJ)	1058
	TUBESING, Richard L. . .	(NM)	1261
	TRASATTI, Margaret S. .	(NV)	1254
	EVELAND, Ruth A.	(NY)	358
	GLASER, Gloria T.	(NY)	439
	JAHR, Joanne B.	(NY)	591
	BURLINGAME, Dwight F. .	(OH)	161
	FRY, Mildred C.	(OH)	406
	MOFFETT, William A. . . .	(OH)	852
	PARSONS, Augustine C.	(OH)	944
	PASQUAL, Patricia E. . .	(OH)	946
	FERGUSON, Douglas K. .	(OR)	372
	GORCHELS, Clarence C.	(OR)	451
	COURTRIGHT, Harry R. .	(PA)	252
	SMITH, Barbara J.	(PA)	1153
	STEPHANOFF, Kathryn .	(PA)	1187
	BAILEY, Alvin R.	(TX)	46
	BONNELL, Pamela G. . . .	(TX)	114
	HEEZEN, Ronald R.	(TX)	520
	WOLFE, Lisa A.	(WA)	1361
	CUTHBERT, John A.	(WV)	267
	SIZEMORE, William C. . .	(WV)	1145
	HORNE, Alan J.	(ON)	560
	SHIRINIAN, George N. . .	(ON)	1131
	SIEMENS, Bessie M. . . .	(MEX)	1136
Fundraising & development	STANLEY, Sydney J. . . .	(CA)	1180
	BRADBURY, Daniel J. . .	(MO)	125
	CAMPBELL, Jerry D. . . .	(NC)	176
	EZZELL, Joline R.	(NC)	360
	KARMAZIN, Sharon M. .	(NJ)	627
	GODWIN, Mary J.	(NY)	443
Fundraising & development research	EVERETT, Amy E.	(DE)	358
Fundraising & endowment	CADDELL, Claude W. . .	(IN)	170
Fundraising & financial development	FLOWER, Kenneth E. . . .	(MD)	300
Fundraising & grantsmanship	WILLIAMS, Lisa B.	(CA)	1344
	BROWN, Louise R.	(MA)	145
Fundraising & public relations	TERNAK, Armand T. . . .	(FL)	1232
Fundraising, book publishing & writing	GRAVES, Sid F.	(MS)	459
Fundraising, construction	MINERVA, Jane R.	(NY)	846
Fundraising consulting	BERGAN, Helen J.	(DC)	85
Fundraising development	CHANNING, Rhoda K. . .	(MA)	201
Fundraising directories	TAFT, James R.	(DC)	1219
Fundraising events	TITUS, Barbara K.	(DE)	1247
Fundraising for libraries	WELCH, Theodore F. . . .	(IL)	1321
Fundraising for rare books	IVES, Sidney D.	(FL)	586
Fundraising for research projects	THOMAS, Evangeline M. .	(KS)	1236
Fundraising, grantsmanship	THOMPSON, Ronelle K. .	(SD)	1241
Fundraising information support	EVERETT, Amy E.	(DE)	358
Fundraising, public relations	FISCHLER, Barbara B. . .	(IN)	380
Fundraising reference	ABBITT, Viola I.	(NY)	1

FUNDRAISING (Cont'd)

Grant writing & fundraising	DUPLAIX, Sally T.	(RI)	327
Library development & fundraising	MCDONALD, John P.	(CT)	802
Library fundraising	CHUPP, Linda D.	(GA)	213
	LORENZ, John G.	(MD)	741
	BUNDY, Annalee M.	(RI)	157
	TAYLOR, Merrily E.	(RI)	1227
	CLARK, Charlene K.	(TX)	216
Library fundraising consulting	KUHN, Warren B.	(IA)	682
Library research & fundraising	MOLLER, Hans	(PQ)	853
Local fundraising	BEATTIE, Brian	(KS)	70
Program development, fundraising	PIKE, Kermit J.	(OH)	972
Proposal writing & fundraising	GOLDBERG, Susan S.	(AZ)	445
Public library fundraising	THRASHER, Jerry A.	(NC)	1243
Public relations & fundraising	ROCHELEAU, Kathleen D.	(MA)	1046
	STICHA, Denise S.	(PA)	1193

FURNITURE (See also Equipment)

Building programs & furnishings	POWELL, Mary E.	(TX)	988
Buildings & furnishings	NELSON, James B.	(NY)	894
Furniture, shelving, space planning	WATSON, Joyce N.	(ON)	1309
Library buildings & furnishings	BROWN, Carol J.	(TX)	142
Library furniture & equipment	VAN ORSDEL, Darrell E.	(WI)	1276
Library furniture & space planning	GRANT, Robert S.	(MI)	458
Library furniture, space planning	TUCKER, Richard B.	(NH)	1262
Library shelving & furniture	WEINZIMMER, William A.	(NY)	1318
Manufacturing lib technical furniture	VAN PELT, Peter J.	(NY)	1277
Manufacturing wood library furniture	VAN PELT, Peter J.	(NY)	1277
Remodeling, renovation, furniture layout	WALSH, Robert R.	(NY)	1300
Writing furniture specifications	DAHLGREN, Jean E.	(TX)	269

FUSION

Magnetic fusion energy	KNAACK, Linda M.	(MA)	663

FUTURE

Future libraries	SURPRENANT, Thomas T.	(NY)	1210
Future of university libraries	CLUFF, E D.	(TX)	223
Future planning	JONES, C L.	(PA)	611
Future trends in libraries	SMALLS, Mary L.	(SC)	1151
Library future	GRIFFEN, Agnes M.	(MD)	468

FUZZY

Fuzzy set theory	KRAFT, Donald H.	(LA)	674

GALLERIES (See also Museums)

Art gallery outreach learning centers	PATTERSON, Grace L.	(NY)	948
Galleries & arts programs	WILKINSON, Billy R.	(MD)	1340

GAMBLING

Gambling collection	GARDNER, Jack I.	(NV)	418

GAMES

Games development & manufacture	FORSHAW, William S.	(MD)	391
Olympic games collection development	GHENT, Gretchen K.	(AB)	430

GAS

Energy reference & natural gas	MARSHALL, Alexandra P.	(ON)	773
Gas industry regulation	DORNER, Steven J.	(VA)	313
Gas Net industry database management	DORNER, Steven J.	(VA)	313
Natural gas industry	DORNER, Steven J.	(VA)	313
Natural gas, petroleum & electricity	LOOS, Carolyn F.	(TX)	740
Oil & gas	CAMBRIA, Roberto	(NY)	174
	POWELL, Alan D.	(TX)	987
Oil & gas company	WRIGHT, Craig W.	(TX)	1371
Oil & gas databases	PARKINSON, Susan L.	(AB)	943
Oil & gas exploration	DURIE, Debbie L.	(AB)	328
Oil & gas reference	DILLARD, Lois A.	(TX)	303

GATEWAYS

Frontends & gateways	LEVY, Louise R.	(NJ)	721
Gateway management	LOGAN, Harold J.	(NJ)	737
Gateway project management	MALONEY, James J.	(CA)	764
Gateway sales & marketing	GROSSMAN, Allen N.	(NJ)	473
Online searching gateways	HORWITZ, Seth	(PA)	561
Optical disks, gateways	MARSHALL, Mary E.	(OH)	774
Technology gatekeeper	BLISS, David H.	(IA)	105

GAY

Gay & lesbian studies	RIDINGER, Robert B.	(IL)	1032

GEAC

GEAC training & development	WERT, Alice L.	(IN)	1325

GEMOLOGY (See also Jewelry)

Gemology information	DIRLAM, Dona M.	(CA)	305

GENEALOGY (See also Heritage)

Audiovisual genealogy	VIERGEVER, Dan W.	(KS)	1284
Black genealogy, Indian genealogy	DAVIS, Denyvetta	(OK)	278
Canadian genealogy	GUTTERIDGE, Paul	(BC)	479
Cataloging genealogy	FOLEY, Harriet E.	(OH)	387
Genealogical cataloging	RANDALL, Gordon E.	(GA)	1006
Genealogical computing & research	O'BRIEN, Doris J.	(CT)	914
Genealogical databases	MAYFIELD, David M.	(UT)	790
Genealogical reference	DECKER, John W.	(MN)	286
	OVERTON, Julie M.	(OH)	931
	SPERRY, Kip	(UT)	1174
Genealogical reference service	PARKER, John C.	(CA)	942
Genealogical research	LEVIS, Gail A.	(IL)	721
	WILLSON, Richard E.	(IL)	1349
	ESALA, Lillian H.	(MN)	354
	SUELFLOW, August R.	(MO)	1206
	RUGG, John D.	(OH)	1066
	LAMAR, Christine L.	(RI)	689
	GOODFELLOW, Marjorie E.	(PQ)	448
Genealogical research & documentation	PARKER, Mary A.	(SC)	942
Genealogical research & reference	CARTER, Janet K.	(TX)	189
Genealogical services	HANDE, D A.	(SK)	494
Genealogy	ABNEY, Timothy A.	(CA)	2
	GLOVER, Frank J.	(CA)	442
	LARSON, Donald A.	(CA)	699
	STREETER, David	(CA)	1201
	BOYER, Carol C.	(CO)	123
	MULCAHY, Bryan L.	(GA)	876
	WALKER, Alice O.	(GA)	1295
	BURGH, Scott G.	(IL)	159
	CAROTHERS, Diane F.	(IL)	184
	EDSTROM, James A.	(IL)	337
	CLEGG, Michael B.	(IN)	220
	ELLIOTT, Joan M.	(IN)	344
	HEIM, Keith M.	(KY)	521
	KING, Charles D.	(KY)	650
	CALLARD, Carole	(MI)	173
	KULL, Christine L.	(MI)	683
	LARSON, Catherine A.	(MI)	699
	POBANZ, Becky L.	(MI)	979
	NAUEN, Lindsay B.	(MN)	889
	GULSTAD, Wilma B.	(MO)	477
	KARNS, Kermit B.	(MO)	627
	MEYERS, Martha L.	(MO)	831
	O'DELL, Charles A.	(MO)	916
	DRAKE, Betty S.	(MS)	318
	WISE, Ronnie W.	(MS)	1357
	BROOKES, Barbara	(NY)	140
	MOUSTAFA, Theresa A.	(NY)	874
	PACKARD, Agnes K.	(NY)	933
	POHL, Gunther E.	(NY)	979
	MCCROSKY, Janet E.	(OH)	800
	WYLLIE, Stanley C.	(OH)	1375
	SEARS, Robert W.	(OK)	1110
	THORNE, Larry R.	(OK)	1242
	VARNER, Joyce	(OK)	1279

GENEALOGY (Cont'd)
Genealogy

LIVENGOOD, Candice C. (PA) 734
NEITZ, Cordelia M. (PA) 892
WEIHERER, Patricia D. (PA) 1317
SILVA, Phyllis C. (RI) 1138
COTHAM, James S. (TN) 249
HUGHES, Marylin B. (TN) 572
BOCKSTRUCK, Lloyd D. (TX) 109
CARTER, Janet K. (TX) 189
GAUSE, George R. (TX) 423
KLEHN, Victoria L. (TX) 658
MYLER, Josephine P. (TX) 885
PALMER, Judith L. (TX) 936
TOURAINE, Linda S. (TX) 1252
CLEMENT, Charles R. (UT) 221
LEVY, Suzanne S. (VA) 722
MORRIS, Karen L. (VA) 867
REESE, Gary F. (WA) 1016
TURNER, Kathleen G. (WA) 1264
GROSKOPF, Amy L. (WI) 472
HELWIG, Karen A. (WI) 525
RYAN, Carol E. (WI) 1070
OUIMET, Yves (PQ) 930
Genealogy & heraldry — FILBY, P W. (MD) 376
Genealogy & law libraries — BURCHILL, Mary D. (KS) 158
Genealogy & local history — KEMP, Thomas J. (CT) 639
DAY, Thomas L. (IN) 283
MUTH, Thomas J. (KS) 883
PAYNE, David L. (MS) 951
JONES, Plummer A. (NC) 614
ESWORTHY, Lori L. (NY) 355
JANOWSKY, Cara A. (NY) 593
ENGEL, Carl T. (OH) 348
LUST, Jeanette M. (OH) 749
HARPER, Sarah H. (TX) 503
STEINBERG, David L. (VA) 1185
Genealogy, family history — THOMAS, Cornel W. (AR) 1236
Genealogy libraries — LE DORR, Lillian E. (CA) 708
Genealogy library — ROYAL, Henrietta (GA) 1063
Genealogy, local history — STEPHENS, Doris G. (NC) 1188
MONCLA, Carolyn S. (TX) 854
Genealogy methodology — WITCHER, Curt B. (IN) 1358
Genealogy reference — CRITTENDEN, Robert R. (CA) 259
CLARK, Diane E. (MS) 216
BAKER, Zachary M. (NY) 50
TURNER, Robert L. (VA) 1265
Genealogy research — MAPP, Erwin E. (FL) 768
FREEMAN, Patricia E. (NM) 401
GRAVLEE, Diane D. (NY) 459
Genealogy subject specialization — HAMILTON, Darlene E. (WA) 491
Heritage sociology & genealogy — SCHLOTT, Florenceann (PA) 1094
Historical & genealogical research — HELSLEY, Alexia J. (SC) 525
Historical genealogy — WITCHER, Curt B. (IN) 1358
History & genealogy — ASHTON, Rick J. (CO) 36
COUP, William A. (FL) 251
History, biography & genealogy — MUTCH, Donald G. (ON) 883
Instructor, genealogy & family history — SPERRY, Kip (UT) 1174
Interlibrary loan of genealogical resrcs — MEYERS, Martha L. (MO) 831
Jewish genealogy — BERENT, Irwin M. (VA) 84
Local history & genealogy — GOFF, Linda J. (CA) 443
KOEL, Maria O. (CT) 667
KANELY, Edna A. (DC) 625
REID, Judith P. (DC) 1018
BAKER, Donald E. (IN) 48
MILLS, Helen L. (TX) 844
Local history & genealogy reference — WIENER, Alissa L. (MN) 1336
Local history, genealogy, preservation — BROWN, Donald R. (PA) 143
Native American genealogy — AUTRY, Brick (TX) 41
Pennsylvania genealogy — STAYER, Jonathan R. (PA) 1183
Rare books & genealogy — SABA, Bettye M. (IN) 1072
Regional history, genealogy — PROPER, David R. (MA) 995
Reviewing genealogical materials — CRAWFORD, Carolyn (CA) 256
Texas history & genealogy — SMITH, Michael K. (TX) 1158

GENERALISM
Education generalism — BABER, Eric R. (KS) 43
Generalism — SCHADE, Barbara L. (MO) 1088
Generalist — HEISER, Lois (IN) 523
FRIEND, Ann S. (MA) 404
JONES, Sandra K. (NJ) 615
HALE, Carolyn R. (PA) 485
Generalist - public schools — YOUNG, Barbara A. (FL) 1381
Generalities — PETRAK, Janet C. (PA) 965
Generalization — MITCHELL, Mary H. (ON) 849
Public library, generalist — HANSEN, Paula J. (PA) 498

GENERATIVE
Generative grammars — WENK, Arthur B. (PQ) 1324

GENERIC
Document analysis & generic coding — KNOERDEL, Joan E. (MD) 665
Generic coding — FOSTER, Anne (ON) 392

GENETICS (See also Immunogenetics)
Genetic engineering — SAFFER-MARCHAND, Melinda (MA) 1074
Genetics — RICCARDI, Vincent M. (TX) 1026
Genetics information — GREEN, Patricia L. (PA) 462
Information on genetic disorders — HOLT, Suzy (MT) 554

GENRE
Adult genre fiction — PENN, Lea M. (NC) 957
Genre & general fiction — HAWK, Susan P. (FL) 513
Genre films — FREEMAN, John P. (TX) 401

GEOGRAPHY (See also Maps)
Electronic engineering & geography — RICHARD, Marie F. (PQ) 1028
Geographic information — REX, Heather (NM) 1024
Geographic information systems — CHAMMOU, Eliezer (CA) 198
SUTHERLAND, Johnnie D. (GA) 1211
BOURGEOIS, Ann M. (MI) 119
REINHARD, Christine M. (WI) 1021
Geographical bibliography — BALDWIN, James A. (IN) 51
Geographical librarianship — FREEDMAN, Jack A. (MS) 400
Geographical reference — PESCHEL, Susan M. (WI) 961
Geography — PETERSON, Charles B. (DC) 963
SELDIN, Daniel T. (IN) 1113
ARNETT, Stanley K. (MI) 33
ALLISON, Brent (MN) 17
WALTZ, Mary A. (NY) 1302
MCQUILLAN, David C. (SC) 817
Geography & map specialist — MULAWKA, Chet (CT) 876
Geography & maps — NIELSEN, Elizabeth A. (DC) 903
HANDROW, Margaret M. (TX) 495
Geography, cartography — EASTON, William W. (IL) 333
Geography collection development work — LAMPRECHT, Sandra J. (CA) 691
Geography subjects — MILLER, Rosanna (AZ) 842
Geological & geographic databases — FELDMAN, Laurence M. (MA) 369
Integrated medical geographic databases — RUBIN, David S. (NY) 1064
Map & geography collections — SHARP, Linda C. (OH) 1122
Map & geography librarianship — FLATNESS, James A. (DC) 384
Map & geography reference — PERRY, Joanne M. (OR) 960
Map librarianship & geography — EUKEY, Jim O. (WI) 356
Maps & geographic information — IVES, Peter B. (NM) 586
Maps & geography — WEDIG, Eric M. (TN) 1315

GEOLINGUISTIC
Geolinguistic ecology — SHEARER, Kenneth D. (NC) 1124

GEOLOGY (See also Earth, Hydrogeology)
Biology, psychology, geology — RONNERMANN, Gail (NY) 1053
California geology — BRUNTON, Angela (CA) 151
Chemistry & geology reference — HOBBS, Kathleen M. (ON) 545
Earth science, geology & petroleum — DEPETRO, Thomas G. (TX) 293
Geologic map collection — GALKOWSKI, Patricia E. (RI) 413

GEOLOGY (Cont'd)
Geologic maps   SELLIN, Jon B. . . . .   (VA) 1114
Geological & geographic databases   FELDMAN, Laurence M. . .   (MA)   369
Geological & geophysical records   MATLOCK, Teresa A. . .   (TX)   784
Geological computer applications   STARK, Philip H. . . . . . .   (CO) 1182
Geological, geophysical data systems   AULBACH, Louis F. . . . .   (TX)   39
Geological information   SINNOTT, Gertrude M. . .   (VA) 1144
Geological references   DAVIS, Connie J. . . . . . .   (TX)   278
Geological technical info management   DICKERSON, Mary J. . . .   (TX)   300
Geology   WETTS, Hazel H. . . . . . .   (CA) 1328
                                           EASTON, William W. . . .   (IL)   333
                                           WHEELER, Marjorie W. . .   (TX) 1329
Geology databases   DIRLAM, Dona M. . . . . .   (CA)   305
Geology literature & information   KLIMLEY, Susan . . . . . .   (NY)   661
Geotechnical & geological research   JEROME, Susanne M. . .   (AZ)   599
Mining & geology research   STRACHAN, Pamela H. .   (ON) 1199
North American geology   WEST, Barbara F. . . . . .   (TX) 1326
Online searching, geology   METIVIER, Donna M. . . .   (TX)   828
Petroleum geology   SHANKS, Katherine N. . .   (OK) 1120
Serials, geology   BOYER, Ann T. . . . .   (WI)   123

GEOPHYSICAL
Geological & geophysical records   MATLOCK, Teresa A. . .   (TX)   784
Geological, geophysical data systems   AULBACH, Louis F. . . . .   (TX)   39

GEOPOLITICS
Information geopolitics & policy   AINES, Andrew A. . . . . .   (MD)   8

GEOSCIENCE
Geoscience collections &
  administration   WICK, Constance S. . . . .   (MA) 1335
Geoscience information   MOUNT, Jack D. . . . . . .   (AZ)   873
                                           COPPIN, Ann S. . . . . . .   (CA)   245
                                           BIER, Robert A. . . . .   (CO)   95
                                           WICK, Constance S. . . . .   (MA) 1335
                                           PRUETT, Nancy J. . . . . .   (NM)   996
                                           STEPP, Dena F. . . . .   (OH) 1189
                                           CHAPPELL, Barbara A. .   (VA)   202
Geoscience information, processing
  mgmt   BICHTELER, Julie H. . . .   (TX)   94
Geoscience information retrieval   WICK, Constance S. . . . .   (MA) 1335
Geoscience reference   MESSICK, Carol H. . . . .   (VA)   828
Geosciences databases   DERKSEN, Charlotte R. .   (CA)   294

GEOTECHNICAL
Geotechnical & engineering
  databases   JEROME, Susanne M. . .   (AZ)   599
Geotechnical & geological research   JEROME, Susanne M. . .   (AZ)   599

GERIATRICS (See also Aging, Elderly)
Geriatric information & research   BENSING, Karen M. . . . .   (OH)   83
Geriatric information resources   STEPHENSON, Judy A. . .   (KY) 1188
Geriatric medicine   KERN, Donald C. . . . . . .   (MA)   643
Geriatrics   BURHANS, Barbara C. . .   (MI)   159
                                           JUNEAU, Jocelyne B. . . .   (PQ)   620
Geriatrics & gerontology   CORCORAN, Virginia H. .   (CT)   246
                                           COLLAZO, Maria L. . . . .   (PR)   232
                                           YANCHINSKI, Roma N. .   (ON) 1377
Gerontology & geriatrics literature   POST, Joyce A. . . . .   (PA)   986

GERMAN
German handwriting   NELSON, Vernon H. . . . .   (PA)   895
German history   VINCENT, Charles P. . . .   (NH) 1284
German history collection
  development   BAER, Eberhard A. . . . . .   (VA)   44
German language & literature   STUHR-ROMMEREIM,
                                             Rebecca A. . . . .   (KS) 1205
                                           MCKILLIP, Rita J. . . . . . .   (WI)   811
                                           TRAICHEL, Rudolf D. . . .   (AB) 1253
German language services   BLUMBERG-MCKEE,
                                             Hazel . . . .   (MN)   107
German language specialist   LUTZ, Linda J. . . . .   (ON)   750
German legal sources   MENZEL, William H. . . . .   (NY)   825

GERMAN (Cont'd)
German literature   WISE, Leona L. . . . .   (CA) 1357
                                           THYM, Jurgen . . . .   (NY) 1243
German selection   COULOMBE, Dominique C.   (RI)   250
German studies   SPOHRER, James H. . . .   (CA) 1175
                                           TOLZMANN, Don H. . . .   (OH) 1249
                                           CAMPBELL, James M. . .   (VA)   176
Germanic area, central Europe   FRANK, Peter R. . . . . . .   (CA)   397
Germanic area studies   FELLER, Siegfried . . . . .   (MA)   370
Medieval German literature   SPOHRER, James H. . . .   (CA) 1175
Modern German history   BAZILLION, Richard J. . .   (ON)   68
Research on East Germany   HUETING, Gail P. . . . . . .   (IL)   570

GERONTOLOGY
Archives in gerontology   EDWARDS, Willie M. . . .   (MI)   338
Geriatrics & gerontology   CORCORAN, Virginia H.   (CT)   246
                                           COLLAZO, Maria L. . . . .   (PR)   232
                                           YANCHINSKI, Roma N. .   (ON) 1377
Gerontological database   RAFFERTY, Eve . . . . . .   (DC) 1003
Gerontological reference services   HARTZ, Mary K. . . . . . .   (DC)   509
Gerontology   LOVAS, Paula M. . . . . . .   (DC)   743
                                           EPSTEIN, Robert S. . . . .   (MD)   351
Gerontology & geriatrics literature   POST, Joyce A. . . . .   (PA)   986
Gerontology collections   MILANICH, Melanie M. . .   (ON)   834
Handicapped & gerontology   LEATHERMAN, Donald G.   (TX)   707
Humanities & gerontology   YAHNKE, Robert E. . . . .   (MN) 1376

GIFTED (See also Special)
Books for gifted children   HALSTED, Judith W. . . . .   (MI)   490
Education of gifted children   LINDSLEY, Barbara N. . .   (NY)   730
Gifted & talented bibliography   GRAVITZ, Ina A. . . . . . .   (NY)   459
Gifted & talented education   ABILOCK, Debbie . . . . .   (CA)   2
Gifted & talented services   TALLEY, Loretta K. . . . .   (IA) 1221
Gifted resources dissemination   WARNER, Wayne G. . . . .   (GA) 1305
Media for gifted   HAMMITT, Margaret R. . .   (NE)   493
Media for gifted students   FITZPATRICK, Janis M. . .   (OH)   383
Service to gifted children   SWANTON, Susan I. . . . .   (NY) 1214
Service to gifted youth   HARRIS, Karen H. . . . . . .   (LA)   505

GIFTS (See also Acquisitions, Philanthropy)
Acquisitions, gifts & exchanges   EASTERLY, Ambrose . . .   (TN)   333
Corporate giving research   KLETZIEN, S D. . . . .   (PA)   661
Gift acquisitions   COOMBS, Elisabeth G. . .   (CT)   241
Gift & exchange acquisitions   DECKER, Leola M. . . . . .   (MD)   286
Gift & exchanges management   DUPRE, Monique . . . . . .   (ON)   327
Gift materials   HILLMAN, Kathy R. . . . . .   (TX)   541
Gifts   RINGER, Sarah A. . . . . . .   (AR) 1035
                                           BELLO, Susan E. . . . . . .   (MA)   78
                                           SUTTON, Robert F. . . . . .   (NJ) 1211
                                           RICE, Dorothy F. . . . . . .   (NV) 1027
                                           MONGAN, Janet . . . .   (OH)   854
                                           TUCKER, Cornelia A. . . . .   (PA) 1261
                                           BELL, Carole R. . . . .   (RI)   76
Gifts & exchange   WISE, Leona L. . . . .   (CA) 1357
                                           FAIRBANKS, Deborah M. .   (FL)   361
                                           HOUGH, Carolyn A. . . . .   (MI)   562
Gifts & exchanges   BARKER, Joseph W. . . . .   (CA)   56
                                           ROUSEK, Marie B. . . . . .   (NJ) 1061
                                           LESNIK, Pauline . . . .   (NY)   718
                                           WEAVER, Alice O. . . . . .   (OH) 1312
                                           ROBERTS, Marica L. . . . .   (TN) 1041
                                           LAKHANPAL, Sarv K. . . .   (SK)   689
                                           OSIER, Donald V. . . . . . .   (SDA) 928
Gifts, exchanges   MARX, Patricia C. . . . . . .   (TX)   780
Non-rare gifts   RUDOLPH, Ellen T. . . . . .   (IN) 1066
Processing gifts   TAYLOR, Carolyn L. . . . .   (MO) 1226
Purchased & gift item cataloging   DELZELL, William R. . . .   (MA)   290

GLASS
Glass & ceramics research   DREIFUSS, Richard A. . .   (NY)   319

GLOBAL (See also International, World)
Global education audiovisuals   HUGHES, Rolanda L. . . .   (IN)   572

GOALS (See also Objectives)

Goals & objectives	MACDONALD, Christine S.	(ON)	754
Planning system goals & objectives	COURSON, M S.	(MD)	251
Setting goals & objectives	MARTIN, Ron G.	(IN)	778

GOTHIC

Gothic tradition, detective fiction	FISHER, Benjamin F.	(MS)	380

GOVERNANCE

Faculty governance & status	THORSON, Connie C.	(NM)	1242
Governance	NOLAN, Deborah A.	(MD)	907
Librarians in university governance	COLLINS, Evron S.	(OH)	232
Network & consortium governance	MITCHELL, Joan M.	(PA)	849
Public library governance	SHANNON, Marcia A.	(MA)	1120
Trusteeship in governance	BAUGHMAN, James C.	(MA)	66

GOVERNMENT (See also City, Congress, County, Courts, Diplomacy, Federal, Intergovernmental, Legislative, Parliamentary, Supreme Court, Town, Treasury, United States)

Administration of government records	WALCH, Victoria I.	(VA)	1293
Advising, federal & state government	CASEY, Daniel W.	(DC)	192
American government	CHANCE, Truett L.	(TX)	199
Appraising government records	BENGE, Joy L.	(TX)	80
British & Commonwealth govt publications	BEAN, Charles W.	(DC)	69
Business & government affairs	BALL, Thomas W.	(DC)	52
Business & government information	MILLER, Carmen L.	(WA)	836
Business & government publications	IVES, Peter B.	(NM)	586
Canadian federal government publications	ROSE, Frances E.	(BC)	1054
Canadian government information policy	ROSE, Frances E.	(BC)	1054
Canadian government publications	WIHBEY, Francis R.	(ME)	1337
	NIELSON, Paul F.	(MB)	903
Canadian governmental documents	RUSSELL, Moira	(ON)	1069
Cataloging Canadian government documents	TURNER, Sharon	(ON)	1265
Cataloging government documents	MILLER, Barbara K.	(NY)	835
	BLANKENBURG, Julie J.	(WI)	104
City government relations	WEST, Shirley L.	(NJ)	1326
Collection development, local government	BALLENTINE, Rebecca S.	(NC)	53
Corporate & government information ctr	PEGLER, Ross J.	(FL)	954
Federal & state government publications	BROWN, Philip L.	(SD)	146
Federal government	RUBIN, Lenard H.	(TX)	1064
	WEATHERHEAD, Barbara A.	(ON)	1312
Federal govt & congressional info srvs	ROTHBART, Linda S.	(VA)	1060
Federal government archives	PFEIFFER, David A.	(DC)	966
Federal government documents	ADAMS, Leonard R.	(MA)	5
	FISCHER, Catherine S.	(MN)	379
Federal government documents reference	LINDSEY, Thomas K.	(TX)	730
Federal government organization	DOWNS, Charles F.	(DC)	317
Federal government publications	STRAITON, T H.	(AL)	1199
	CALDWELL, George H.	(DC)	172
	EWING, Jerry L.	(MO)	359
	PANDIT, Jyoti P.	(NY)	937
Federal governments documents	CORCORAN, Nancy L.	(MN)	246
Federal, state, & government research	KIRSHBAUM, Priscilla J.	(CO)	655
Federal, state, local govt publications	NAKATA, Yuri	(OR)	887
Foreign government publications	MAACK, David J.	(WA)	753
General & government documents reference	BALSARA, Aspi	(NF)	53
Government	WILLIAMSON, Carol L.	(NJ)	1347
Government & business databases	MOONEY, Margaret T.	(CA)	858
Government & business library services	MARVIN, Stephen G.	(PA)	780
Government & federal documents	MACK, Debora S.	(GA)	756
Government & industry liaison	FATTIBENE, James F.	(DC)	366
Government & legal database development	YODER, Susan M.	(CA)	1380
Government & legal information	JACOBS, Leslie R.	(MA)	589
Government & parliamentary libraries	PARE, Richard	(ON)	940

GOVERNMENT (Cont'd)

Government & social science databases	BASEFSKY, Stuart M.	(NC)	62
Government archives	HEDLIN, Ethel W.	(DC)	520
	PROVINE, Dorothy S.	(DC)	996
Government archives & history	CHRISTNER, Deborah S.	(CA)	212
Government archives & records	HACKMAN, Larry J.	(NY)	481
Government contracting	FATTIBENE, James F.	(DC)	366
Government contracts	FOWLIE, Linda K.	(DC)	394
Government databases	CALHOUN, Ellen	(NJ)	172
Government document cataloging	MCKOWEN, Dorothy K.	(IN)	812
Government document declassification	GATLING, James L.	(AL)	422
Government document processing	HARTMAN, Anne M.	(NY)	508
Government document publications	DOUGLAS-BONNELL, Eileen	(PQ)	314
Government documents	PIERCE, Linda I.	(AK)	971
	MCNAMARA, Jay	(AL)	816
	PEARSON, Peter E.	(AL)	953
	WATSON, Linda S.	(AL)	1309
	WATTERS, Annette J.	(AL)	1310
	MORRISON, Margaret L.	(AR)	868
	WOLD, Shelley T.	(AR)	1359
	BRZOZOWSKI, Margery E.	(AZ)	152
	RAWAN, Atifa R.	(AZ)	1010
	VATHIS, Alma C.	(AZ)	1279
	DOBB, Linda S.	(CA)	307
	JACOBSEN, Lavonne	(CA)	590
	JOHNSON, Linda B.	(CA)	607
	JOHNSRUD, Thomas E.	(CA)	609
	LEWANDOWSKI, Joseph J.	(CA)	722
	MARTINEZ, Barbara A.	(CA)	779
	MAZUR, Victoria P.	(CA)	791
	MILFORD, Charles C.	(CA)	835
	MOSER, Maxine M.	(CA)	871
	NELSON, Alice R.	(CA)	893
	NICHOLS, Gail M.	(CA)	901
	SEBO, Lorraine M.	(CA)	1110
	SHARP, Linda F.	(CA)	1122
	SPENCER, Patricia O.	(CA)	1173
	STEELMAN, Lucille A.	(CA)	1184
	TING, Eunice T.	(CA)	1246
	WELLS, Dorothy V.	(CA)	1322
	WILLIAMS, Leonette M.	(CA)	1344
	FIELD, Oliver L.	(CO)	375
	JONES-EDDY, Julie	(CO)	615
	SCHMIDT, Fred C.	(CO)	1095
	BARNES, Denise M.	(CT)	57
	SPURGEON, Kathy R.	(CT)	1176
	BEALL, Barbara A.	(DC)	68
	CHURCHVILLE, Lida H.	(DC)	213
	CROCKETT, Martha L.	(DC)	259
	FARINA, Robert A.	(DC)	363
	JEMIOLA, Nancy E.	(DC)	596
	OAKS, Robert K.	(DC)	913
	UPDEGROVE, Robert A.	(DC)	1269
	ZICH, Joanne A.	(DC)	1388
	KNIGHT, Rebecca C.	(DE)	664
	YOUNG, Kathryn A.	(DE)	1382
	HARRIS, Frank D.	(FL)	504
	LITTON, Sally C.	(FL)	734
	CHRISTIAN, Gayle R.	(GA)	211
	MALCOLM, Carol L.	(GA)	762
	MCCANN, Jett C.	(GA)	794
	WHEELER, Carol L.	(GA)	1328
	BUDREW, John	(IA)	155
	EMDE, Susan J.	(IA)	347
	GIAQUINTA, C J.	(IA)	431
	HUNTING, Susan K.	(IA)	576
	AUFDENKAMP, Joann	(IL)	39
	BENGTSON, Marjorie C.	(IL)	80
	BURGH, Scott G.	(IL)	159
	CHEN, Robert P.	(IL)	205
	FRY, Roy H.	(IL)	406
	KLOCKENGA, Gary R.	(IL)	662
	LI, Dorothy W.	(IL)	724
	MULHERIN, William S.	(IL)	876
	NYBERG, Cheryl R.	(IL)	912

GOVERNMENT (Cont'd)
Government documents

ROYLE, Maryanne . . . . . (IL) 1063
SHERMAN, Sarah . . . . . (IL) 1128
YOUNG, Peter W. . . . . . (IL) 1383
CONRADS, Douglas L. . . (IN) 238
DICKMEYER, John N. . . (IN) 301
GREMMELS, Gillian S. . . (IN) 467
HOLTERHOFF, Sarah G. (IN) 555
LYLE, Jack W. . . . . (IN) 751
MURDOCK, J L. . . . . . . (IN) 879
STAPLES, James A. . . . (IN) 1181
LUNG, Mon Y. . . . (KS) 748
STEWART, Henry R. . . . (KS) 1192
MCFARLING, Patricia G. (KY) 805
SHEPHERD-SHLECHTER,
   Rae . . . . (KY) 1127
BALL, Dannie J. . . . . . . (LA) 52
BRADLEY, Jared W. . . . (LA) 126
FULLING, Richard W. . . . (LA) 409
HANKEL, Marilyn L. . . . . (LA) 496
HIMEL, Sandra M. . . . . . (LA) 542
KELLY, Judy M. . . . . (LA) 638
MAYEAUX, Thurlow M. . . (LA) 789
NACHOD, Katherine B. . . (LA) 885
ROCHE, Alvin A. . . . . . . (LA) 1045
SHIFLETT, Orvin L. . . . . (LA) 1130
SHULL, Janice K. . . . . . . (LA) 1133
ARCHAMBAUL, Christine (MA) 30
DRESLEY, Susan C. . . . (MA) 319
RANDALL, Kristie C. . . . (MA) 1006
RUTTER, Nancy R. . . . . (MA) 1070
ST. AUBIN, Kendra J. . . (MA) 1075
VAN BEEK, Susan . . . . . (MA) 1272
JOHNSON, Richard K. . . (MD) 608
LEV, Yvonne T. . . . . (MD) 719
QUINN, Carol J. . . . . . . (MD) 1000
SULLIVAN, Carol W. . . . (MD) 1207
BOURGEOIS, Ann M. . . . (MI) 119
BROW, Judith A. . . . . . . (MI) 141
BUCKLEY, Francis J. . . . (MI) 154
BURINSKI, Walter W. . . . (MI) 160
BUXBAUM, Sharolyn . . . (MI) 168
CROSS, Jennie B. . . . . . (MI) 260
EVANS, Kathy J. . . . . . . (MI) 357
HEGEDUS, Mary E. . . . . (MI) 521
JERYAN, Christine B. . . . (MI) 600
MOUZON, Margaret W. . (MI) 874
SHIRLEY, David B. . . . . . (MI) 1131
YERMAN, Roslyn F. . . . . (MI) 1380
YORK, Grace A. . . . . (MI) 1381
ANDERSON, E A. . . . . . (MN) 22
BAUM, Marsha L. . . . . . . (MN) 66
JACOB, Rosamond T. . . (MN) 589
SANFORD, Carolyn C. . . (MN) 1081
BARNES, Everett W. . . . (MO) 57
COURT, Patricia . . . . (MO) 251
GELINNE, Michael S. . . . (MO) 426
HICKS, James M. . . . . . . (MO) 537
HOCHSTETLER, Donald
   D. . . . . (MO) 545
MCKENZIE, Elizabeth M. (MO) 811
SCHRAMM, Betty V. . . . (MO) 1099
STEWART, Byron . . . . . (MO) 1192
WATTS, Anne . . . . (MO) 1310
GRASMICK, Brenda . . . . (MT) 458
ALLEN, Regina L. . . . . . . (NC) 15
BOMARC, M D. . . . . (NC) 113
BUCHANAN, William E. . (NC) 153
CLARK, Marie L. . . . . . . (NC) 217
COHEN, Edward S. . . . . (NC) 228
COTTER, Michael G. . . . (NC) 250
DALTON, Lisa K. . . . . . . (NC) 271
MCGEACHY, John A. . . (NC) 805
OSER, Anita K. . . . . (NC) 928
ROWLAND, Janet M. . . . (NC) 1062
SCOTT, Ralph L. . . . . . . (NC) 1108
WEBSTER, Deborah K. . (NC) 1314
WILLIAMS, Wiley J. . . . . (NC) 1347
BOONE, Nila J. . . . . (ND) 115

GOVERNMENT (Cont'd)
Government documents

MUNDELL, Jacqueline L. (NE) 878
BERTHIAUME, Dennis A. (NH) 90
CHUNG, Hai C. . . . . (NJ) 213
GUSTAFSON, Ruth . . . . (NJ) 478
LATINI, Samuel A. . . . . . (NJ) 701
MASILAMANI, Mary P. . . (NJ) 780
MILLER, Mary A. . . . . . . (NJ) 840
MILLER, Sarah J. . . . . . . (NJ) 842
OTA, Leslie H. . . . . (NJ) 930
RAFFERTY, Stephen P. . (NJ) 1003
SWARTZ, Betty J. . . . . . (NJ) 1214
TUTWILER, Dorothea F. . (NJ) 1266
WANGGAARD, Janice H. (NJ) 1303
WILSON, Myoung C. . . . (NJ) 1352
ADAMS, Dena R. . . . . . . (NM) 4
MOUJAES. Sylva S. . . . . (NV) 873
AXTMANN, Margaret M. . (NY) 42
BURNETTE, Michaelyn . . (NY) 162
CHRISTENSON, Janet S. (NY) 211
CROWLEY, John V. . . . . (NY) 261
DONG, Alvin L. . . . . (NY) 311
D'ONOFRIO, Erminio . . . (NY) 311
EIDELMAN, Diane L. . . . (NY) 340
FREIDES, Thelma . . . . . (NY) 401
GADBOIS, Frank W. . . . (NY) 411
GUINN, Patricia L. . . . . . (NY) 477
JENNINGS, Vincent . . . . (NY) 598
JUDD, Blanche E. . . . . . (NY) 618
KELLER, Katarina S. . . . (NY) 635
LOWE, Mildred . . . . (NY) 744
MACOMBER, Nancy . . . (NY) 758
MAY, Jonathan B. . . . . . (NY) 788
MULLEN, Marion L. . . . . (NY) 877
O'HARA, Frederic J. . . . (NY) 919
SHIROMA, Susan G. . . . (NY) 1131
SMITH, Barbara E. . . . . . (NY) 1152
SMITH, Karen F. . . . . . . (NY) 1156
WILLET, Ruth J. . . . . (NY) 1341
WOLFE, Theresa L. . . . . (NY) 1361
ADAMS, Liese A. . . . . . . (OH) 5
BALDWIN, Julia F. . . . . . (OH) 51
BLOCK, Bernard A. . . . . (OH) 106
GOULD, Allison L. . . . . . (OH) 454
HORDUSKY, Clyde W. . . (OH) 559
JONES, Alice W. . . . . . . (OH) 610
KRAMER, Sally J. . . . . . (OH) 675
WANSER, Jeffery C. . . . (OH) 1303
WEILANT, Edward . . . . . (OH) 1317
KANE, Kathy . . . . (OK) 625
NASH, Helen B. . . . . (OK) 888
ROBBINS, Louise S. . . . (OK) 1039
ROBERTSON, Retha M. . (OK) 1042
CHASE, Judith H. . . . . . . (OR) 203
FISCHER, Karen . . . . . . (OR) 379
GERITY, Louise P. . . . . . (OR) 428
HORAN, Patricia F. . . . . (OR) 559
RASH, David W. . . . . . . (OR) 1009
COURTNEY, June M. . . . (PA) 251
DUSZAK, Thomas J. . . . (PA) 329
GARNER, Diane L. . . . . (PA) 419
JACOBS, Mark D. . . . . . (PA) 589
MARVIN, Stephen G. . . . (PA) 780
REGUEIRO, Judith E. . . (PA) 1017
SAXMAN, Susan E. . . . . (PA) 1086
ALEXANDER, Jacqueline
   P. . . . . (RI) 12
CHENICK, Michael J. . . . (RI) 206
KINTNER, Susan B. . . . . (SC) 653
SMITH, Stephen C. . . . . (SC) 1161
PICQUET, D C. . . . . (TN) 971
ROMANS, Lawrence M. . (TN) 1052
SELF, George A. . . . . . . (TN) 1113
WILLIAMS, Saundra W. . (TN) 1346
ALLEN, Virginia M. . . . . . (TX) 16
BUCHWALD, Donald M. . (TX) 153
CARMACK, Norma J. . . . (TX) 183
FORD, Barbara J. . . . . . . (TX) 389
HENRICKS, Duane E. . . (TX) 529

GOVERNMENT (Cont'd)
Government documents

	HOLLAND, Mary M.	(TX)	551
	KENDRICK, Susan	(TX)	640
	MCDONALD, Brenda D.	(TX)	802
	SAFLEY, Ellen D.	(TX)	1074
	SCHMELZIE, Joan C.	(TX)	1094
	TROST, Theresa K.	(TX)	1258
	LYMAN, Lovisa	(UT)	751
	CIPRIANI, Debra A.	(VA)	215
	COLLINS, Mitzi L.	(VA)	233
	DECAMPS, Alice L.	(VA)	285
	LONG, Elizabeth T.	(VA)	739
	MCGINN, Ellen T.	(VA)	806
	OWEN, Karen V.	(VA)	931
	PALMER, Forrest C.	(VA)	936
	THOMPSON, Connie B.	(VA)	1239
	WOODWARD, Elaine H.	(VA)	1368
	CHANG, Henry C.	(VI)	200
	RAUM, Hans L.	(VT)	1010
	BURSON, Scott F.	(WA)	163
	VILLAR, Susanne P.	(WA)	1284
	VYHNANEK, Louis	(WA)	1290
	YEH, Thomas Y.	(WA)	1379
	BOLL, John J.	(WI)	112
	JOHNSON, Denise J.	(WI)	603
	KRUEGER, Gerald J.	(WI)	680
	MCGOWAN, Sarah M.	(WI)	807
	RINGER, Susan G.	(WI)	1035
	SECHREST, Sandra L.	(WI)	1110
	WESTON, Karen A.	(WI)	1327
	COOPER, Candace S.	(WV)	242
	EMERSON, Tamsen L.	(WY)	347
	KELNER, Gregory H.	(BC)	638
	COLSON, Judith K.	(NB)	234
	MCNALLY, Brian D.	(NB)	815
	COLBORNE, Michael B.	(NS)	230
	DUHAMEL, Marie	(ON)	324
	GILLHAM, Virginia A.	(ON)	436
	GOLTZ, Eileen A.	(ON)	447
	JARVI, Edith T.	(ON)	594
	MOON, Jeffrey D.	(ON)	857
	O'NEILL, Louise N.	(ON)	924
	QUIXLEY, James V.	(ON)	1001
	ROURKE, Lorna E.	(ON)	1061
	VAN GARSSE, Yvan	(BEL)	1275
Government documents acquisitions	MARSHALL, Marion B.	(DC)	774
Government documents & maps	SHANNON, Michael O.	(NY)	1120
Government documents & maps reference	WALKER, Barbara J.	(GA)	1295
Government documents & patents	GREALY, Deborah J.	(CO)	461
Government documents & publications	SINGH, Swarn L.	(KS)	1143
	HENSON, Stephen	(LA)	530
	WALSH, Jim	(MA)	1299
Government documents cataloging	MARSHALL, Marion B.	(DC)	774
Government documents collection mgmt	MCSWEENEY, Josephine	(NY)	818
Government documents, contract mgmt	LAKSHMAN, Malathi K.	(MD)	689
Government documents database	MILLER, Katherine J.	(ON)	839
Government documents, federal	JOHNSON, Dorothy A.	(MA)	603
Government documents librarian	KOEPP, Donna P.	(KS)	668
Government documents librarianship	MILLER, Veronica E.	(VI)	843
Government documents management	PONNAPPA, Biddanda P.	(TN)	982
Government documents, publications, info	WILLIAMSON, Linda E.	(IL)	1347
Government documents reference	WEATHERLY, Cynthia D.	(AL)	1312
	COONIN, Bryna R.	(GA)	242
	CAIN, Charlene C.	(LA)	171
	SUDDUTH, William E.	(MA)	1206
Government information	RICHARDSON, John V.	(CA)	1029
	PETERSON, Sandra K.	(CT)	964
	BARRETT, G J.	(DC)	59
	BECKERMAN, George	(DC)	72
	HEANUE, Anne A.	(DC)	518
	HERNON, Peter	(MA)	532
	TAYLOR, Marcia E.	(MD)	1227
	DURRANCE, Joan C.	(MI)	328
	MORTON, Bruce	(MT)	870

GOVERNMENT (Cont'd)
Government information

	ISACCO, Jeanne M.	(NC)	584
	REELING, Patricia G.	(NJ)	1016
	ZINK, Steven D.	(NV)	1389
	BARRETT, Michael D.	(NY)	59
	MCCLURE, Charles R.	(NY)	797
	MOREHEAD, Joe	(NY)	863
	SHULER, John A.	(OR)	1133
	ROE, Eunice M.	(PA)	1048
	EISENBEIS, Kathleen M.	(TX)	340
	NIELSON, Paul F.	(MB)	903
	BRIERE, Jean M.	(ON)	135
	HUBBERTZ, Andrew P.	(SK)	568
Government information access	JOHNSON, Veronica A.	(MI)	609
Government info index & retrieval	MASSA, Paul P.	(MD)	781
Government information policies	ARDEN, Caroline	(VA)	31
Government information policy	SERBAN, William M.	(LA)	1116
Government information, publications	HINZ, Julianne P.	(UT)	543
Government information services	PINELLI, Thomas E.	(VA)	974
Government information sources	CROWLEY, Terence	(CA)	262
Government, libraries liaison	JOHNSON, Veronica A.	(MI)	609
Government library management	RICHER, Suzanne	(ON)	1030
Government library material acquisitions	BLACKBURN, Clayton E.	(NY)	102
Government Printing Office publications	MAST, Joanne	(PA)	782
Government procurement	AVERY, Galen V.	(OH)	41
Government publication	WHITBECK, George W.	(IN)	1329
Government publications	HOGAN, Catherine R.	(AL)	549
	REAGAN, Agnes L.	(AR)	1012
	ANDERSEN, Thomas K.	(CA)	21
	DINTRONE, Charles V.	(CA)	305
	HAGEN, Dennis D.	(CA)	483
	HORN, Judy K.	(CA)	559
	LINVILLE, Herbert	(CA)	731
	MITTAN, Rhonda L.	(CA)	850
	MOONEY, Margaret T.	(CA)	858
	BYRNE, Timothy L.	(CO)	169
	SCHULZE, Suzanne S.	(CO)	1102
	KONERDING, Erhard F.	(CT)	670
	DANIELSON, Wilfred D.	(DC)	273
	PUCCIO, Joseph A.	(DC)	997
	MECRAY, Freida S.	(DE)	820
	ROEHLING, Steven R.	(GA)	1048
	STEVENS, Robert D.	(HI)	1190
	KOHLER, Carolyn W.	(IA)	668
	MOODY, Marilyn K.	(IA)	857
	VAN DE VOORDE, Philip E.	(IA)	1274
	WILKINSON, Patrick J.	(IA)	1340
	MANCUYAS, Natividad D.	(IL)	764
	NOLLEN, Sheila H.	(IL)	908
	STEWART, James A.	(IL)	1192
	STRANGE, Michele M.	(IL)	1200
	WEECH, Terry L.	(IL)	1315
	DAVISON, Ruth M.	(IN)	281
	FRY, Bernard M.	(IN)	406
	HAYES, Stephen M.	(IN)	516
	SCHMIDT, Kathy W.	(IN)	1095
	VIOLETTE, Judith L.	(IN)	1285
	KLOSTERMANN, Helen M.	(KS)	662
	CAMMARATA, Paul J.	(KY)	175
	MCANINCH, Sandra L.	(KY)	792
	BURG, Barbara A.	(MA)	159
	PARKER, Susan E.	(MA)	942
	BEHLES, Patricia A.	(MD)	74
	SCHWARZKOPF, Leroy C.	(MD)	1105
	GUNN, Arthur C.	(MI)	477
	ELLIOTT, Gwendolyn W.	(MN)	344
	LA BISSONIERE, William R.	(MN)	686
	KESSLER, Ridley R.	(NC)	645
	FETZER, Mary K.	(NJ)	374
	PROFETA, Patricia C.	(NJ)	995
	BROWN, Eulalie W.	(NM)	143
	MCGUIRE, Laura H.	(NM)	808
	HERMAN, Edward	(NY)	531

GOVERNMENT (Cont'd)

Government publications

LARSEN, Joan A.	(NY)	698
WELSH, Harry E.	(NY)	1323
YUKAWA, Masako	(NY)	1384
HARPER, Lucy B.	(OH)	503
SALT, Elizabeth A.	(OH)	1077
BAHR, Alice H.	(PA)	45
BARON, Herman	(PA)	58
FERYOK, Joseph A.	(PA)	374
MORPHET, Norman D.	(PA)	865
SCHNEIDER, Stewart P.	(RI)	1097
VOCINO, Michael C.	(RI)	1286
ROBINSON, William C.	(TN)	1045
WEDIG, Eric M.	(TN)	1315
JOHNSON, Johanna H.	(TX)	606
LEE, Frank	(TX)	709
MORRIS, Pamela A.	(TX)	867
MORRISON, David L.	(UT)	868
SMITH, Ruth S.	(VA)	1160
FUGATE, Cynthia S.	(WA)	408
MAACK, David J.	(WA)	753
SY, Karen J.	(WA)	1217
GERLACH, Donald E.	(WI)	429
HEBDITCH, Suzan A.	(AB)	519
DODSON, Suzanne C.	(BC)	308
FOOTE, Martha L.	(ON)	388
HAJNAL, Peter I.	(ON)	484
LAND, Reginald B.	(ON)	692
MONTY, Vivienne	(ON)	857
RHYNAS, Don M.	(ON)	1026

Government publications, access to info	WHITAKER, Constance C.	(OH)	1329
Government publications & databases	FELDMAN, Eleanor C.	(MD)	369
Government publications collections	MILLER, Mary E.	(PA)	840
Government publications reference srv	CALHOUN, Ellen	(NJ)	172
Government purchasing & marketing	KEATING, Michael F.	(OH)	633
Government records	SAYED, Joyce P.	(CA)	1086
	RUSSELL, Marvin F.	(DC)	1069
	CHAPDELAINE, Susan A.	(MA)	201
	NEWBORG, Gerald G.	(ND)	898
	NEAL, James H.	(TN)	890
Government records administration	OLSON, David J.	(NC)	922
Government records management	BOCKMAN, Eugene J.	(NY)	109
Government reference	BELL, Hope A.	(ON)	77
Government regulations	DUFFY, Brenda F.	(DC)	324
Government regulations on environment	GROOT, Elizabeth N.	(CA)	472
Government relations	WOOD, Linda M.	(CA)	1364
	MCDONOUGH, Roger H.	(NJ)	803
	THENELL, Janice C.	(OR)	1234
	SHELKROT, Elliot L.	(PA)	1126
Government research	MISSAR, Margaret M.	(DC)	847
	RABER, Steven	(NY)	1001
Government specifications & standards	AUSTIN, Stephen	(CA)	40
Government, US & European history	HERTZ, Sylvia	(MI)	533
Governmental affairs	COCHRAN, William M.	(IA)	225
Governmental documents	THAKER, Virbala M.	(CA)	1234
Governmental information services	ROUMFORT, Susan B.	(NJ)	1061
Governmental procurement procedures	HAAS, Eva L.	(NY)	480
Governmental relations	KINCHEN, Robert P.	(NY)	650
	BRUCE, Dennis L.	(SC)	149
Governmental relations & lobbying	GODWIN, Mary J.	(NY)	443
Governments documents	BRENNER, Willis F.	(AR)	133
	GOLDMAN, Ava R.	(FL)	445
History & government	WILLET, Ruth J.	(NY)	1341
International government documents	FETZER, Mary K.	(NJ)	374
Intl govt organizations' documentation	WILLIAMSON, Linda E.	(IL)	1347
International government publications	ALEXANDER, Liz C.	(IL)	12
	MAACK, David J.	(WA)	753
Intl Governmental Organizations Pubns	RUHLIN, Michele T.	(UT)	1066
Law reference, government documents	KAUL, Kanhya L.	(MI)	631
Legislative & governmental services	FOWLER, Louise D.	(CT)	394
Library government & organization	SABSAY, David	(CA)	1073
Local government	DUBEAU, Pierre	(PQ)	321

GOVERNMENT (Cont'd)

Local government archives	BENGE, Joy L.	(TX)	80
Local government databases	PICKETT, Olivia K.	(DC)	971
	LEHMAN, Tom	(MN)	713
	HEWLETT, Carol C.	(TN)	535
Local government documents	CASTONGUAY, Russell	(CA)	194
	CORCORAN, Nancy L.	(MN)	246
Local government finance	BEVERLEY, Barbara S.	(NY)	93
Local government information	STRICKLAND, Ann T.	(AZ)	1202
Local government information network	AHLIN, Nancy	(FL)	8
Local government publications & records	HEWLETT, Carol C.	(TN)	535
Local government records	WEBBER, Steven L.	(CA)	1313
	MOORE, Karl R.	(IL)	860
	HOLLAND, Michael E.	(TX)	551
	SCHAADT, Robert L.	(TX)	1088
Local government reference	FREEDMAN, Phyllis D.	(PA)	400
Maps & government documents	SCHORR, Alan E.	(AK)	1099
Medical government documents	WHITE, Anne E.	(IL)	1330
Municipal & county government	STRICKLAND, Ann T.	(AZ)	1202
Municipal government information srvs	HENDERSON, Harriet	(VA)	526
Municipal government reference	BRADDOCK, Virginia O.	(CO)	125
Municipal government reference services	TAYLOR, Patricia A.	(NY)	1228
Politics & government	LOWENTHAL, Jane E.	(DC)	744
Providing research & government info	CASO, Gasper	(MA)	193
Provincial & municipal government	WEATHERHEAD, Barbara A.	(ON)	1312
Provincial government publications	ROSE, Frances E.	(BC)	1054
Science agency government documents	CURTIS, Susan C.	(GA)	267
Serials & government documents	PANDA, Rosamond E.	(MD)	937
Serials, government publications	ZIMMERMAN, Martha B.	(MD)	1389
Special government collection	KOCH, Patricia J.	(MT)	667
State & local government documents	HAMMOND, Louise H.	(IL)	494
State & local government publications	SULZER, John H.	(PA)	1209
State & local government records	DEARSTYNE, Bruce W.	(NY)	284
State government documents	ADAMS, Leonard R.	(MA)	5
State government reference	REES, Pamela C.	(IA)	1016
Technical processing, govt documents	ADAMS, Leonard R.	(MA)	5
United States government & documents	MORENO, Rafael	(PA)	863
US government documents	IRBY, Geraldine A.	(AL)	583
	COSTELLO, M R.	(CA)	249
	SANSOBRINO, Jean C.	(CA)	1081
	HURLEY, Trudy M.	(CT)	577
	MELNICOVE, Annette R.	(FL)	823
	COLLINS, Patrick	(GA)	233
	WAI, Lily C.	(ID)	1292
	BECK, Mary C.	(MI)	71
	ESSLINGER, Guenter W.	(MN)	355
	LAUGHLIN, Cheryl H.	(MS)	703
	KENDRA, William E.	(NE)	640
	BEAUDRIE, Ronald A.	(NY)	70
	FELLER, Judith M.	(PA)	370
	WRIGHT, Barbara C.	(PA)	1370
	TINSMAN, William A.	(TX)	1246
	DAVIS, Wylma P.	(VA)	281
	HAYS, Peggy W.	(VA)	517
US government documents, business	TAYLOR, William R.	(TN)	1229
United States government publications	DOWNS, Charles F.	(DC)	317
	TRAUTMAN, Maryellen	(DC)	1254
	WOODWARD, Lawrence W.	(DC)	1368
	WIHBEY, Francis R.	(ME)	1337
	FROBOM, Jerome B.	(NE)	405
	POWELL, Margaret S.	(OH)	988
	BELEU, Steve	(OK)	76
	BERWIND, Anne M.	(TN)	91
	BRADLEY, C D.	(TX)	125

GRADE (See also Elementary, School)

Grade school collection development	DRECHSEL, Marcella J.	(NJ)	319
K-8 grades	TEEGARDEN, Maude B.	(KY)	1229
Middle grade fiction & nonfiction acqs	BUCKLEY, Virginia L.	(NY)	154
Preschool to grade nine	CHAPIN, Joan R.	(NJ)	201
Primary through third grade libraries	BURKE, Mary E.	(TN)	160

GRADE (Cont'd)

Storyhours for toddlers through grade 2	SALUZZO, Mary S.	(NY)	1078
Supporting curriculum Grades K-4	MEINEL, Nancy T.	(LA)	822

GRADUATE (See also College, University)

Graduate film study	FREEMAN, John P.	(TX)	401
Graduate instruction	ZIMPFER, William E.	(MA)	1389
Graduate level bibliographic instruction	ILACQUA, Anne K.	(MA)	581
Graduate libraries	GAINES, James E.	(VA)	412
Graduate library training resource	HOLSINGER, Katherine	(AZ)	554
Graduate media programs	TEMPLE, Leroy E.	(CT)	1230
Graduate placement	MATARAZZO, James M.	(MA)	783
Graduate program services	NETZ, David H.	(MI)	896
Graduate reference	STRAUSS, Diane	(NC)	1201
Graduate school collections	SIMMONS, Hal	(GA)	1140
Graduate school teaching	MANES, Estelle L.	(OK)	765
Tape recording graduate textbooks	BULLOCK, Frances E.	(NY)	156
Teaching graduate public libs course	VALENTINE, Patrick M.	(NC)	1271

GRAIN (See also Crops)

Grain trade	EMOND, Lucille I.	(MB)	348
	REEDMAN, M R.	(MB)	1015

GRAMMAR (See also Elementary)

Grammar school libraries	LANE, Mary K.	(NY)	694

GRAMMARS

Generative grammars	WENK, Arthur B.	(PQ)	1324

GRANTS (See also Finance, Funding, Proposals)

Administration including grant writing	LYNCH, Mary D.	(PA)	752
Collection devlpmnt, foundation grants	LEE, J S.	(NJ)	710
Development of grant proposals	WALCH, Victoria I.	(VA)	1293
Endowment & grant funding	DEYOUNG, Charles D.	(IN)	298
Federal grants management	KLASSEN, Robert L.	(DC)	657
Foundations & grantsmanship	WILLIAMS, Guynell	(SC)	1343
Fundraising & grantsmanship	WILLIAMS, Lisa B.	(CA)	1344
	BROWN, Louise R.	(MA)	145
Fundraising, grantsmanship	THOMPSON, Ronelle K.	(SD)	1241
Grant accounting systems	FRIEDMAN, Barbara S.	(NY)	403
Grant administration	THOMPSON, Mary A.	(DC)	1240
	DAHLEN, Roger W.	(MD)	269
Grant & contract databases	OSTROW, Dianne G.	(MD)	929
Grant & fund development	KLIMEK, Chester R.	(NY)	661
Grant & other writing & editing	WRIGHT-HESS, Anne H.	(NY)	1373
Grant management	SCARBOROUGH, Katharine T.	(CA)	1087
Grant program administration	LEWIS, Alan D.	(MN)	722
Grant program evaluations	EATENSON, Ervin T.	(TX)	333
Grant proposal writing	MORAN, Irene E.	(CA)	862
Grant proposals	TARAN, Nadia P.	(MD)	1223
Grant proposals & administration	CABEZAS, Sue A.	(MA)	170
Grant seeking	LESLIE, Camille J.	(OH)	718
Grant supervision	MOSES, Lynn M.	(PA)	871
Grant writing	MCWHORTER, Jimmie M.	(AL)	818
	MARTZ, David J.	(DC)	779
	KIEFFER, Marian L.	(IA)	647
	ROBISON, Diana E.	(IL)	1045
	SOMERVILLE, Mary R.	(KY)	1167
	HELO, Martin	(MA)	525
	TRICARICO, Mary A.	(MA)	1256
	DEL SORDO, Jean S.	(MD)	290
	MORROW, Paula J.	(MO)	869
	CLARK, Robert M.	(MT)	218
	LINDSLEY, Barbara N.	(NY)	730
	FINAN, Patrick E.	(OH)	377
	LONG, Sarah A.	(OR)	740
	BRICE, Heather W.	(PA)	134
	EVERHART, Nancy L.	(PA)	358
	MITCHELL, Joan M.	(PA)	849
	YATES, Diane G.	(PA)	1378
Grant writing, administration	SARLES, Christie V.	(NH)	1083
Grant writing & external funding	FELLA, Sarah C.	(OR)	370

GRANTS (Cont'd)

Grant writing & fundraising	DUPLAIX, Sally T.	(RI)	327
Grant writing & implementation	BRENNAN, Deborah B.	(RI)	132
Grants	GRENDLER, Marcella	(NC)	467
	BOWERS, Alyce J.	(NJ)	120
	WEST, Shirley L.	(NJ)	1326
Grants administration	SMITH, George V.	(AK)	1155
	LINSLEY, Priscilla M.	(CO)	731
	JACOBS, Richard A.	(DC)	590
	SAHLI, Nancy A.	(DC)	1075
	MOUNCE, Marvin W.	(FL)	873
	BRONSON, Diane A.	(GA)	140
Grants administration & program devlpmnt	WRIGHT, Paul L.	(KY)	1372
Grants analysis	HEDLIN, Ethel W.	(DC)	520
Grants & external funding	TOMLIN, Marsha A.	(OH)	1250
Grants & foundations	FERRALL, J E.	(AZ)	373
	NOLAN, Patrick B.	(OH)	907
Grants coordination	SUMMERS, Lorraine S.	(FL)	1209
Grants development	VARNER, Carroll H.	(IL)	1278
Grants information	BEY, Leon S.	(OH)	93
Grants, research & proposal writing	SECKELSON, Linda E.	(NY)	1110
Grantsmanship	MCGOVERN, Gail J.	(CA)	807
	HENEHAN, Alva D.	(FL)	528
	GODLEWSKI, Susan G.	(IL)	442
	JOHNSON, Frances E.	(MD)	604
	THRESHER, Jacquelyn E.	(NJ)	1243
	HUGE, Sharon A.	(OH)	571
	MACDERMAID, Anne	(ON)	754
Grantsmanship & buildings	CORBUS, Lawrence J.	(OH)	245
Grantsmanship for libraries	CORRY, Emmett	(NY)	247
Grantsmanship writing & reviewing	KELLEY, John F.	(PA)	636
Library development, research, grants	COLLARD, R M.	(CO)	232
Management & grants	BARNETT, Jean D.	(OR)	57
Management, public relations, grants	KISER, Mary D.	(FL)	656
Managing grants & contracts	SCULL, Roberta A.	(LA)	1108
Manuscript & grant applications	PARR, John R.	(ON)	943
Planning & grant review	SCHUTT, Cheryl M.	(CT)	1103
Prepare, implement grants	SHEA, Margaret	(RI)	1124
Writing & monitoring grants	TRIVISON, Margaret A.	(CA)	1257

GRAPHICS (See also Art, Arts)

Audiovisual & graphic arts	GIBLON, Charles B.	(FL)	431
Cataloging of graphic materials	HOGAN, Kristine K.	(NY)	549
Computer graphics	TYLER, Sharon R.	(CA)	1266
	ROBB, Thomas W.	(DC)	1038
	VAUGHAN, John	(NY)	1279
Graphic arts	BARRINGER, George M.	(DC)	59
	WHITE, George R.	(KS)	1331
	BARNHILL, Georgia B.	(MA)	58
	HAMMOND, Wayne G.	(MA)	494
	DAVENPORT, Marilyn G.	(NV)	275
	BRODY, Catherine T.	(NY)	139
Graphic design	FRISCH, Corrine A.	(IL)	413
	JONES, Sally L.	(WA)	615
Graphic information analysis	PECK, Brian T.	(FL)	953
Graphics	HALE, Janice L.	(MA)	485
Graphics & magazine design	WISE, Eileen M.	(ON)	1356
Graphics libraries	GEIGER, Richard G.	(CA)	425
Graphics production	HART, Thomas L.	(FL)	507
Instructional graphics	WILSON, George N.	(TX)	1351
Library graphic design & art	BRYAN, Carol L.	(WV)	151
Medical graphics	ROSSOUW, Steve F.	(SAF)	1059
Printing & graphics art	WEISER, Douglas E.	(MI)	1319
Typesetting & graphic design	MILLER, Thomas R.	(IL)	843

GREAT BOOKS

Great Books discussion leader	GINSBURG, Coralie S.	(IL)	438

GREEK

Classical Greek & Latin reference	CRITTENDEN, Robert R.	(CA)	259
Greek & Latin literature	CARNOVSKY, Ruth F.	(CA)	184
Greek paleography	MATHIESEN, Thomas J.	(UT)	784

GREGORIAN

Gregorian chant	WEBER, Jerome F.	(NY)	1314

GRIMM

Grimm tales production & direction — DAVENPORT, Thomas R. (VA) 276

GROUPS

Book discussion groups — ALLEN, Richard H. (NE) 16
Books & newsletters, non-profit groups — TAFT, James R. (DC) 1219
Community group relations — SMOTHERS, Joyce W. (NJ) 1162
Facilitation of group planning — TONEY, Stephen R. (MD) 1250
Friends & trustees groups — WINSLOW, Carol M. (IN) 1355
Friends groups — HARRINGTON, Charles W. (LA) 504
GWYN, Ann S. (MD) 479
Friends of library groups — DEMPSEY, Frank J. (IL) 291
Group dynamics in libraries — SMITH, Ann M. (MA) 1152
Group training & development — BURGER, Leslie B. (CT) 159
Interpersonal comm & group processes — FLOOD, Barbara J. (PA) 385
Library friends groups — ELLIOTT, C D. (CA) 343
Library school student groups — COLEMAN, J G. (AL) 231
Library users groups — BRANDT, Daryl S. (IN) 128
Outreach services to special groups — HAABNIIT, Ene (BC) 480
Parent groups, development of reading — WALDEN, Katherine G. (CT) 1294
Public library friends group — KOCHOFF, Stephen T. (NY) 667
Service to minority groups — COHEN, David (NY) 228
Service to special groups — VIGNOVICH, Ray L. (WI) 1284
Services to special groups teaching — WHALEN, Lucille (NY) 1328
Small group training — FORD, Marjorie F. (CA) 389
Special collection for church groups — VANDEGRIFT, J R. (DC) 1273
Support group liaison — SCHWARTZ, Virginia C. (WI) 1105

GROWTH

Child growth & development — WALTHER, Richard E. (CA) 1301
Growth & capital formation — BRINNER, Roger E. (MA) 136

GUARD

Militia & National Guard history — WEAVER, Thomas M. (DC) 1312

GUIDANCE (See also Advising, Advisory, Consulting)

Educational guidance — BURSON, Lorraine E. (OR) 163
Guidance for adult learners — O'HARA, Frederic J. (NY) 919
Guiding children's book selection — SUTHERLAND, Helen G. (CA) 1211
Literature guidance & appreciation — MCCLELLAND, Katherine L. (GA) 796
Literature instruction & guidance — WOBBE, Jean (CA) 1359
Manuscripts, archives resrchr guidance — BOOTHE, Nancy L. (TX) 116
Reader guidance — SCALES, Pat R. (SC) 1087
Readers guidance — BAKER, Sharon L. (IA) 49
Reader's guidance & reference — SHEARIN, Cynthia E. (NJ) 1124
Reading guidance — MCCARTHY, Carrol B. (DE) 794
CRAVER, Susan J. (IA) 256
PARK, Dona F. (IA) 941
MOSKOWITZ, May K. (MI) 871
WIENER, Sylvia B. (NY) 1336
KENT, Rose M. (OH) 642
NORRIS, Gale K. (SC) 909
FORTIN, Clifford C. (WI) 391
Reading guidance & children's literature — KONNEKER, Rachel C. (NC) 670
Reading, listening & viewing guidance — RING, Constance B. (NY) 1035
Reference, reader guidance — WEICK, Robert J. (IN) 1316
Young adult reading guidance — MALTBY, Florence H. (MO) 764

GUIDELINES

Guidelines development — LINDHEIMER, Sandra K. (MA) 729
Procedure & guideline writing — STRONG, Sunny A. (WA) 1203

GUIDES (See also Handbooks)

Bibliographic guides — AGEE, Victoria V. (MD) 7
Bibliography & research guides — LITT, Dorothy E. (NY) 733
Compiling annotated guides — SATER, Analya (CA) 1083
Database record guide cataloging — MCKNIGHT, Jesse H. (FL) 812

GUIDES (Cont'd)

Library curriculum guide development — NOBLE, Barbara N. (MO) 906
Personal computer user guide composition — MILLER, Ann M. (ON) 835
Writing manuscript guide entries — HULL, Mary M. (TX) 572

GUTENBERG

Gutenberg studies — SONNE, Niels H. (NJ) 1167

HABITS

Reading habits research — LANGERMAN, Shoshana P. (ISR) 695

HAIR

Medicine, cosmetics & hair — CLAGGETT, Laura K. (IL) 215

HALF-LIFE

Information half-life studies — ASIS, Moises (CUB) 36

HANDBOOKS (See also Guides, Manuals)

Development handbooks — NAPOLITANO, Wanda M. (NY) 887
Handbook preparation — WAGNER, Sharon L. (CA) 1292

HANDICAPPED (See also Disabled, Impaired, Retardation)

Blind & handicapped — KLAUBER, Julie B. (NY) 658
Blind & physically handicapped — COLEMAN, James M. (AL) 231
Elderly & handicapped — RING, Anne M. (IL) 1035
Handicapped — HOWIE, Maryann (NY) 566
Handicapped access to libraries — SMITH, Ann M. (MA) 1152
Handicapped & gerontology — LEATHERMAN, Donald G. (TX) 707
Handicapped center, public library — ROATCH, Mary A. (AZ) 1038
Handicapped patrons — BURKE, Saretta K. (OH) 160
Handicapped services — HUANG, Samuel T. (IL) 568
JONES, Dorothy E. (IL) 612
CRAM, Mary E. (OH) 255
RADER, Joe C. (TN) 1002
Handicapped services & materials — THOMAS, James L. (TX) 1237
Handicaps & blindness information — WILSON, Barbara L. (RI) 1350
Home services for the handicapped — UTSUNOMIYA, Leslie D. (BC) 1270
Job access for handicapped — SOMERS, Betty J. (NY) 1166
Libraries for print handicapped — MINOR, Dorothy C. (FL) 846
Library service to handicapped — HAVENS, Shirley E. (NY) 513
SOMERS, Betty J. (NY) 1166
BARKALOW, Irene M. (VA) 56
Organizing library for handicapped — BULLOCK, Frances E. (NY) 156
Outreach for handicapped & homebound — BRYANT, Judith W. (NJ) 152
Physical handicapped services — BIVINS, Hulen E. (AL) 100
Physical handicaps — HAYNES, Douglas E. (NM) 516
Physically handicapped reading services — MCCASLIN, Cheryl A. (TX) 795
Publications about handicapped persons — HOLT, June C. (MA) 554
Service to the handicapped — CARR, Charles E. (NJ) 185
Services to the handicapped — SNAIR, Dale S. (VA) 1162
ADAMS, Karen G. (SK) 5
Travel for the handicapped — SHANEFIELD, Irene D. (PQ) 1120

HANDICRAFT (See also Crafts)

Fine art & handicraft specialization — MANNING, Mary J. (IL) 766

HANDWRITING

German handwriting — NELSON, Vernon H. (PA) 895

HANFORD

Hanford site — TRAUB, Teresa L. (WA) 1254

HANSARD

Hansard debates — O'KEEFE, Kevin T. (NT) 919

HARDWARE (See also Equipment)
Audiovisual hardware .... MYHRE, Char .... (MN) 885
.... GORMAN, Mary B. ..... (NY) 452
Audiovisual software & hardware .. WARREN, Ann R. ...... (NH) 1306
CD-ROM hardware integration ..... CIUFFETTI, Peter D. ... (MA) 215
Computer hardware & software .... GRIFFIN, Hillis L. ...... (CA) 468
.... FALK, Howard .... (NJ) 362
.... FERRIN, Eric G. ...... (PA) 373
.... BELL, David B. .... (SC) 76
Computer hardware & software
   manuals .... CASSAR, Ann .... (PA) 193
Computer hardware & software
   reference .... ROBSON, Amy K. ...... (IL) 1045
Computer software hardware ...... SHENASSA, Daryoosh .. (IL) 1126
Data processing hardware & software KOOLISH, Ruth K. ...... (CA) 671
Microcomputers, hardware & software ZABEL, Patricia L. ..... (TX) 1385
Personal computer hardware &
   software .... MILLER, Ann M. .... (ON) 835

HAWAII
Hawaii .... CHAFE, Douglas A. .... (HI) 197
Hawaii & the Pacific reference ... ASHFORD, Marguerite K. (HI) 36
Hawaii, Pacific .... HORIE, Ruth H. .... (HI) 559
Hawaiian & Pacific business
   periodicals .... SCHULTZ, Elaine V. .... (HI) 1102
Hawaiian & Pacific history ...... TIMBERLAKE, Cynthia A. (HI) 1245

HAZARDS (See also Toxicology)
Chemical hazards databases ...... BRANSFORD, John S. ... (TN) 129
Hazardous material data .... KAZIMIR, Edward O. ... (NJ) 632
Hazardous materials .... WEBSTER, James K. ... (NY) 1314
Hazardous materials databases ... TUCKER, Clark F. ..... (MD) 1261
Hazardous substances databanks .. COSMIDES, George J. .. (MD) 249
Hazardous waste .... LAWSON, James R. ... (ME) 705
.... WOLFE, Theresa L. .... (NY) 1361
Hazardous waste, energy &
   environment .... HASTINGS, Constance M. (TN) 511
Hazardous wastes .... BUISMAN, Maria J. .... (ON) 156
.... CROXFORD, Agnes M. .. (ON) 262
Research on risks & hazards ..... KASPERSON, Jeanne X. (MA) 629
Solid, hazardous waste management KAYES, Mary J. .... (WI) 632

HEAD
Audiovisual department head ..... WIRIG, Joan S. .... (IL) 1356
Department head .... FRAZIER, Nancy E. .... (MA) 399
Head librarian .... MARVEL, Frances J. ... (CA) 780
Head librarianship .... EIKEN, Mary A. ...... (MO) 340
Head of circulation .... BUCHWALD, Donald M. . (TX) 153
Head of library .... WARD, Brenda H. ..... (VA) 1303
Head of technical services ...... ROCK, Sue W. .... (NJ) 1046
Head, technical services .... SOUZA, Margaret A. ... (CA) 1170
K-12 head librarian .... LYONS, Dean E. ...... (ME) 753
Otolaryngology, head & neck surgery JOHNSTON, Bruce A. .. (PA) 610

HEADINGS
Lib of Congress music subject
   headings .... PRICE, Harry H. ...... (DC) 992
Music uniform headings .... MC HALE, Mary M. .... (MD) 808
Politics of subject headings ..... MICHEL, Dee A. .... (CA) 832
Subject headings .... GOUDREAU, Ronald A. . (DC) 454
.... WRIGHT, Joseph F. .... (FL) 1372
.... POLSON, Billie M. ..... (NV) 982

HEALTH (See also Hygiene, Illness, Medical)
Allied health .... BERRY, Mary W. ...... (NC) 90
.... LEINHEISER, Diane R. .. (PA) 714
.... WETHERBY, Ivor L. .... (SC) 1328
Allied health, audiology, hearing sci MCFARLAND, Robert T. (MO) 805
Area health education learning
   resources .... JOHN, Stephanie C. .... (MI) 601
Biomedical & health reference .... MYER, Nancy E. ...... (NM) 884
Business, health care, engrng
   databases .... PLOTSKY, Andrea G. .. (CA) 978
Canadian health care system ..... BOITE, Mary E. .... (ON) 111
Chemistry & industrial health .... CASSAR, Ann .... (PA) 193

HEALTH (Cont'd)
Children's health care .... ADENEY, Carol D. ..... (WGR) 6
Clinical health care profiles .... CHERNIN, David A. .... (MA) 206
Collection development health
   sciences .... WARD, Penny T. ...... (CA) 1304
Community health .... THOMASSON, George O. (CO) 1238
.... FIORE, Francine ...... (PQ) 379
Community health information .... KNIGHT, Dorothy H. ... (IL) 664
Computer health ergonomics issues MILLER, R B. .... (CA) 841
Computer systems in health ...... BENNETT, David M. .... (AUS) 81
Computers in health care .... COVVEY, H D. .... (MB) 252
Consumer & patient health
   information .... LINDNER, Katherine L. .. (NJ) 729
Consumer health .... BEATTIE, Barbara C. ... (NC) 70
.... ADAMS, Bruce A. ..... (NY) 4
Consumer health information ..... MCCARTHY, Sherri L. .. (AL) 794
.... RICHETELLE, Alberta L. . (CT) 1030
.... MAYO, Kathleen O. .... (FL) 790
.... WHITED, Diane D. ..... (LA) 1332
.... MCKAY, Ann .... (ME) 809
.... LANSDALE, Metta T. ... (MI) 696
.... SERLING, Kitty .... (MO) 1116
.... CARABATEAS, Clarissa
                                        D. .... (NY) 180
.... ROBBINS, Diane D. .... (NY) 1038
.... JANES, Jodith .... (OH) 593
.... JENNINGS, Kathryn L. .. (OK) 598
Consumer health information services TAYLOR, Margaret P. .. (ON) 1227
Consumer health selection, reference TAPPANA, Kathy A. .... (OK) 1223
Consumer products, health care .. SILVERMAN, Susanne .. (CT) 1139
Databases, occupational health &
   safety .... MCLAUGHLIN, W K. ... (AB) 813
Environmental & health regulations LE BLANC, Judith E. ... (OH) 708
Environmental health .... NOWAK, Geraldine D. .. (DC) 911
Environmental health databases .. MOORE, Catherine I. ... (MA) 859
Florida public health history .... HALL, M C. .... (FL) 488
Health .... SCHINDLER, Jo A. .... (HI) 1093
.... MACKLER, Leslie G. ... (NC) 757
Health administration .... PINKOWSKI, Patricia E. . (IL) 975
.... SAHYOUN, Naim K. .... (MI) 1075
Health administration databases .. RICHARDSON, Alice W. (PA) 1029
Health administration literature .. POOLE, Connie .... (IL) 983
.... SCHWARTZ, Dorothy D. (NY) 1104
Health & business databases ..... SEXTON, Sally V. ..... (OH) 1118
Health & environment .... HOFFMAN, Allen ...... (NY) 547
Health & human services .... MAZUR, Ronald M. .... (MA) 791
Health & humanities sciences
   reference .... CHASE, Judith H. ..... (OR) 203
Health & safety .... BELLEFONTAINE, Gillian (ON) 78
Health & safety at work .... MERCIER, Diane ...... (PQ) 825
Health & safety research .... GAMBRELL, Drucilla S. . (AL) 416
Health care .... DAVITT, Theresa B. .... (MA) 281
.... ABRAMS, Joan R. ..... (PA) 3
.... RYDESKY, Mary M. .... (TX) 1071
Health care administration &
   management .... PATTERSON, Jennifer J. (TN) 948
Health care administration reference
   srv .... HAMILTON, Elizabeth J. . (VA) 492
Health care & hospitals online
   searching .... CLINTON, Janet C. ..... (PA) 222
Health care databases .... ROBINSON, Elizabeth A. (OH) 1044
.... KINGSLEY, Marcia S. .. (VA) 652
.... PANTON, Linda A. ..... (ON) 938
Health care financing .... AHRENSFELD, Jan ..... (IL) 8
Health care industry .... DETWILER, Susan M. .. (IN) 296
Health care information sources .. MESSERLE, Judith R. ... (MO) 828
Health care information systems .. JACOBSEN, Teresa T. .. (IL) 590
Health care issues .... HAWKES, Warren G. ... (NY) 513
Health care library management .. LINTON, William D. .... (NIR) 731
Health care management research . BELL, Steven J. .... (PA) 77
Health care reference .... NANSTIEL, Barbara L. .. (PA) 887
Health care reference & databases LEE, Soon H. .... (IL) 711
Health care services .... GALLAGHER, Philip J. .. (NJ) 414
Health databases .... NG, Pauline .... (IL) 900
Health education .... RICHETELLE, Alberta L. . (CT) 1030
.... KRONENFELD, Michael R. (SC) 679
Health education & evaluation .... WAYLAND, Marilyn T. .. (MI) 1311
Health effects research writing ... MUNRO, Nancy B. ..... (TN) 879
Health fraud & quackery .... SERLING, Kitty .... (MO) 1116
Health informatics .... COVVEY, H D. .... (MB) 252

HEALTH (Cont'd)

Health information	MARA, Ruth M.	(DC)	768
	VICK, Kathleen	(PA)	1283
Health information clearinghouses	LUNIN, Lois F.	(VA)	749
Health information databases	KISH, Veronica R.	(PA)	656
	PRINGLE, Robert M.	(WA)	993
Health information for consumers	HESSLEIN, Shirley B.	(NY)	534
Health information management	BYRD, Gary D.	(NC)	168
Health information resources planning	BYRD, Gary D.	(NC)	168
Health information science	MOEHR, Jochen R.	(BC)	851
Health information sciences	ALPERT, Hillel R.	(MA)	17
Health information systems	JENKIN, Michael A.	(FL)	596
	POST, Joyce A.	(PA)	986
Health insurance	COX, Joyce M.	(IL)	253
Health library consulting	GREENWOOD, Jan	(ON)	465
Health library management	SHIFF, Linda S.	(ON)	1130
Health library networks	PANTON, Linda A.	(ON)	938
Health physics	SHERMAN, Dottie	(CT)	1128
Health planning research	FLETCHER, Nancy S.	(WI)	384
Health policy research	JENSEN, Joseph E.	(MD)	599
Health professionals & training	BISCHOFF, Frances A.	(VA)	99
Health promotion	RICHETELLE, Alberta L.	(CT)	1030
Health reference services	TURNER, Ray	(KY)	1265
Health risk analysis research	MUNRO, Nancy B.	(TN)	879
Health risk appraisal systems	ABRAMSON, Lawrence J.	(MI)	3
Health, science & business collections	ARMSTRONG, Mary L.	(AB)	32
Health science cataloging	CAFFAREL, Agnes	(LA)	170
Health science databases	LEVY, Judith B.	(CA)	721
	HORAK, Ellen B.	(CT)	558
Health science information	NEVEU, Wilma B.	(LA)	897
	LONG, Susan S.	(MT)	740
Health science information services	SWATOS, Priscilla L.	(IL)	1214
Health science library administration	FULLER, Sherrilynne S.	(MN)	409
Health science library educ. research	LOVE, Erika	(NM)	743
Health science library networks	WILLIS, Dorothy B.	(NE)	1348
Health science literature	GREEN, Deidre E.	(ON)	461
Health science reference	LIPPMAN, Anne F.	(MA)	732
	ARTH, Janet M.	(MN)	35
	PATTERSON, Charlean P.	(PA)	948
Health sciences	FOLLICK, Edwin D.	(CA)	388
	HALL, Forest A.	(DC)	487
	HURYCH, Jitka M.	(IL)	578
	LANDWIRTH, Trudy K.	(IL)	694
	HILL, Elizabeth C.	(KY)	539
	LEWIS, Ruth E.	(MO)	724
	HARE, William J.	(NH)	501
	BAIN, Christine A.	(NY)	47
	BOROCK, Freddie	(NY)	116
	ROSEN, Wendy L.	(NY)	1055
	STERN, Marilyn	(NY)	1189
	JUDKINS, Dolores Z.	(OR)	619
	BRANDRETH, Elizabeth A.	(PA)	128
	KELLERMAN, Frank R.	(RI)	636
	LLOYD, Lynn A.	(RI)	735
	PUHEK, Esther L.	(WI)	997
	SCHLUGE, Vicki L.	(WI)	1094
	ARMSTRONG, Jennifer E.	(ON)	32
Health sciences acquisitions	GRIMES, Maxyne M.	(FL)	470
Health sciences audiovisuals	MCLEAN, Martha L.	(TN)	814
Health sciences cataloging	NEUFELD, Sue E.	(IA)	897
	COLSON, Elizabeth A.	(TX)	234
Health sciences collection development	BRANDON, Alfred N.	(FL)	128
	NEUFELD, Sue E.	(IA)	897
Health sciences computer software	MCLEAN, Martha L.	(TN)	814
Health sciences database searching	NEUFELD, Sue E.	(IA)	897
Health sciences databases	BELL, R E.	(CA)	77
	KLEINMUNTZ, Dalia S.	(IL)	660
	KANNEL, Selma	(WA)	625
Health sciences including alternative	WOODBURY, Marda	(CA)	1366
Health sciences information resources	ALMQUIST, Deborah T.	(MA)	17
Health sciences information services	MATER, Dee A.	(NC)	783
Health sciences liaison	GIOVENALE, Sharon	(RI)	438
Health sciences librarianship	BERK, Robert A.	(IL)	87
	FENSKE, Ruth E.	(IL)	371
	WEST, Richard T.	(MD)	1326
	MCKININ, Emma J.	(MO)	811
	BRADIGAN, Pamela S.	(OH)	125
	EMPEY, Verla	(ON)	348
	SMITHIES, Roger	(ON)	1162

HEALTH (Cont'd)

Health sciences librarianship	CRAWFORD, David S.	(PQ)	256
	WILSON, Concepcion S.	(AUS)	1350
Health sciences libraries	GRAHAM, Elaine	(CA)	456
	BINGHAM, James L.	(KS)	97
	DRAYSON, Pamela K.	(MO)	318
Health sciences library administration	EATON, Elizabeth K.	(MA)	333
	ANDERSON, Rachael K.	(NY)	25
	RICHARDS, Daniel T.	(NY)	1028
Health sciences library management	KAFES, Frederick W.	(NJ)	621
Health sciences library services	FLOWER, M A.	(ON)	386
Health sciences literature	ROPER, Fred W.	(SC)	1054
Health sciences literature access	FLEMMING, Tom	(ON)	384
Health sciences medical online searching	STANKE, Judith U.	(MN)	1180
Health sciences online searching	MATER, Dee A.	(NC)	783
Health sciences reference	BELL, R E.	(CA)	77
	KAMENOFF, Lovisa	(MA)	623
	SULLIVAN, Joanne L.	(MD)	1207
	WENGER, Milton B.	(NY)	1324
	GIOVENALE, Sharon	(RI)	438
Health sciences selection	GIOVENALE, Sharon	(RI)	438
Health sciences specialization	KAYA, Kathryn A.	(MT)	632
Health services administration	ACKERMAN, F C.	(DC)	3
Health services administration research	PLOTSKY, Andrea G.	(CA)	978
Health services research	ANDERSON, Marilyn M.	(IN)	24
	KERN, Donald C.	(MA)	643
Health-related libraries	RANSOM, Christina R.	(NY)	1007
History of health sciences	ZINN, Nancy W.	(CA)	1389
History of the health sciences	BRITT, Mary C.	(AL)	137
	EDDY, Leonard M.	(KY)	335
Hospital & health care law	MULCAHY, Brian J.	(NY)	876
Hospital & health science libraries	CAMACHO, Nancy S.	(TX)	174
Institutional services, mental health	BOLIN, Nancy C.	(MD)	112
Life & health insurance	SLOAN, Virgene K.	(NE)	1150
Life & health insurance research	HILL, Judith L.	(PA)	540
Medical & health	RONNERMANN, Gail	(NY)	1053
Medical & health care databases	MARIX, Mary L.	(LA)	770
Medical & health literature	WORTZEL, Murray N.	(NY)	1369
Medical & health science databases	AIRTH, Elizabeth J.	(TX)	9
Medical & health sciences reference	STANKE, Judith U.	(MN)	1180
Medical & health-related databases	VONSEGEN, Ann M.	(OR)	1288
Medical databases, HMO	KNARZER, Arlene	(IL)	663
Medicine & allied health reference	NEELAND, Ellen L.	(TX)	891
Medicine, nursing, allied health	KARCH, Linda S.	(NY)	627
	COHEN, Nancy E.	(OH)	228
Medicine, nursing & allied health	BOROCK, Freddie	(NY)	116
Mental health	KRUK, Pauline A.	(CT)	680
	LABREE, Rosanne	(MA)	686
	AEBLI, Carol L.	(MI)	7
	DAVIDSON, Silvia	(NY)	276
	STERN, Deborah S.	(NY)	1189
	OLSON-URLIE, Carolyn T.	(OR)	923
	SOULTOUKIS, Donna Z.	(PA)	1169
Mental health advocacy	COOPER, Joanne S.	(PA)	243
Mental health collections	EPSTEIN, Barbara A.	(PA)	351
Mental health databases	BRAND, Alice A.	(KS)	127
Mental health databases & collections	WIGGINS, Theresa S.	(PA)	1337
Mental health field reference	KIMBLE, Valerie F.	(OK)	649
Mental health indexing	ROUP, Carol E.	(ON)	1061
Mental health information service	MERRILL, Susan S.	(MD)	827
Mental health information services	DANIELS, Pam	(NY)	273
Mental health libraries	VIGORITO, Patricia M.	(RI)	1284
Mental health literature	COHAN, Lois	(NY)	227
	SORG, Elizabeth A.	(PA)	1168
Mental health material	GROSS, Elinor L.	(NY)	472
Mental health reference	VAN DER VOORN, Neal P.	(WA)	1274
	ROUP, Carol E.	(ON)	1061
Mental health research	EVANS, Josephine K.	(FL)	357
Nursing, allied health book discounter	PUALWAN, Emily	(PA)	996
Nursing, allied health databases	PRIME, Eugenie E.	(CA)	993
Nursing, allied health services	DORNER, Marian T.	(OH)	313
Nursing & allied health	BALCERZAK, Judy A.	(ID)	50
Nursing & allied health resources	MCCULLOCH, Elizabeth A.	(PA)	801
	PRINGLE, Robert M.	(WA)	993
Nursing & health sciences	AIRTH, Elizabeth J.	(TX)	9
Nursing, nutrition, community health	FOX, Lynne M.	(CO)	395

HEALTH (Cont'd)

Occupational health	CHANDLER, Constance P.	(CO)	199
Occupational health & safety	LE BLANC, Judith E.	(OH)	708
	MORRISON, Brian H.	(ON)	867
	GREGOIRE, Fleurette	(PQ)	466
Occupational health & safety information	TUCKER, Mary E.	(NC)	1262
	ZUBA, Elizabeth J.	(AB)	1390
Patient & health information	POMERANTZ, Karyn L.	(MD)	982
Patient health information	DEWEY, Marjorie C.	(MA)	298
Psychiatry & mental health	FREDENBURG, Anne M.	(MD)	399
Psychiatry, psychology, mental health	WARD, Nancy E.	(MI)	1304
Psychology & mental health	LARMOUR, Rosamond E.	(VA)	698
Public health	PRUHS, Sharon	(CA)	996
	ALECCIA, Janet A.	(IL)	11
	FRANKLIN, Annette E.	(IL)	397
	GALLAGHER, Philip J.	(NJ)	414
	KRONENFELD, Michael R.	(SC)	679
Public health administration	HORAK, Ellen B.	(CT)	558
Public health areas	SONG, Seungja Y.	(WA)	1167
Public health databases	MOORE, Catherine I.	(MA)	859
Public health literature	MUNSEY, Joyce E.	(MD)	879
Public services in health sciences	BLACK, Lawrence	(NY)	101
Research in hlth, socty, music, foods	STARKEY, Bonnie F.	(WV)	1182
Rural health	TOVREA, Roxanna L.	(IA)	1252
	KATZER, Sylvia U.	(ON)	630
Rural health information transfer	BOISSY, Robert W.	(NY)	111
Sciences & health sciences	WILSON, Jacqueline B.	(CA)	1351
Social sciences, mental health	HORNUNG, Susan D.	(WI)	560
Subject bibliography for public health	CHAN, Lillian L.	(CA)	199
Women's health	VANHINE, Pamela M.	(DC)	1275

HEARING (See also Deafness)

Allied health, audiology, hearing sci	MCFARLAND, Robert T.	(MO)	805
Captioned media for the hearing impaired	MODICA, Mary L.	(SD)	851
Hearing sciences	CHARBONNEAU, Ronald P.	(CA)	202

HEBREW (See also Jewish, Judaica)

Arabic & Hebrew cataloging	CHAMMOU, Eliezer	(CA)	198
Hebraica & Judaica cataloging	WEINBERG, Bella H.	(NY)	1317
Hebrew cataloging	HIRSCH, David G.	(NJ)	543
Hebrew manuscripts & rare books	KOHN, Roger S.	(NY)	668
Judaica, Hebrew day schools	HERTZ, Cynthia L.	(NY)	533
Music cataloging or Hebrew cataloging	FRIEDLAND, Frances K.	(ON)	403

HEMINGWAY

Ernest Hemingway personal papers	DESNOYERS, Megan F.	(MA)	295

HERALDRY

Genealogy & heraldry	FILBY, P W.	(MD)	376
Heraldry	BOCKSTRUCK, Lloyd D.	(TX)	109

HERBAL

Herbal & horticultural information	CHADWICK, Alena F.	(MA)	196
Herbal books	CROTZ, D K.	(IL)	261

HERITAGE (See also Ehtnic, Genealogy)

Heritage sociology & genealogy	SCHLOTT, Florenceann	(PA)	1094
Irish-American heritage	REID, Peg L.	(IL)	1019
Multiculturalism & heritage	GRODSKI, Renata	(ON)	471
Special Dutch heritage center	SLIEKERS, Hendrik	(IL)	1149

HIGH (See also School)

Academic, junior & senior highs	COLLINS, Judith A.	(CA)	232
Computer high tech databases	CHICHESTER, Gerald C.	(CT)	208
Computer science, high tech industry	SLOAN, Maureen G.	(OR)	1149
Computer technology for high sch libs	TOLMAN, Bonnie B.	(MI)	1249
Database research, high schools	WARAKSA, Raymond P.	(CT)	1303
Elementary & high school libraries	SULLIVAN, Mary A.	(GA)	1208

HIGH (Cont'd)

Elementary, junior & senior high schools	ABBOTT, Ruth J.	(TX)	1
Elementary, junior high library services	DOMESCIK, Carol J.	(IL)	310
General reference high quality	TURNER, Kathleen G.	(WA)	1264
High school administration	BOULA, Lillian Y.	(FL)	119
High school & elementary libraries	STUBBLEFIELD, J G.	(TX)	1204
High school curriculum development	MAIN, Isabelle G.	(AZ)	761
	KAPLAN, Lois J.	(OH)	626
High school curriculum implementation	MEANS, E P.	(KS)	820
High school curriculum support	DAVIS, Inez W.	(TN)	279
High school, junior high	JENSEN, Kathryn E.	(MA)	599
High school librarianship	LATIMER, Mary A.	(CA)	701
	SLANGA, Joanne	(MD)	1147
	CLUM, Audna T.	(NY)	223
	GODWIN, Frances L.	(TX)	443
	WILLIAMSON, Judy D.	(WV)	1347
High school libraries	HEINTZ, Mary L.	(AZ)	522
	WOLFF, Mary K.	(CA)	1361
	BEUTHEL, Ellengail	(CO)	93
	FALK, Louise G.	(IA)	362
	RODDY, Ruth	(MD)	1047
	ZANARINI, Linda S.	(NE)	1386
	BROWN, Anita P.	(NJ)	142
	WEISBURG, Hilda K.	(NJ)	1319
	CARSTATER, Mary E.	(NY)	188
	LANE, Mary K.	(NY)	694
	MCCANN, Kathleen	(NY)	794
	SUSSMAN, Valerie J.	(NY)	1210
	SZEMRAJ, Edward R.	(NY)	1218
	CHERESNOWSKI, Linda M.	(PA)	206
	MILLS, Wanda R.	(TN)	844
	GOTHIA, Blanche	(TX)	453
	HAY, Mary K.	(WI)	515
	MIDDLETON, Dorothy J.	(WY)	833
High school libraries & media centers	PORTA, Mary D.	(PA)	984
High school library	HAZLETT, Florence E.	(AZ)	517
	WALTER, Maria	(NY)	1300
	MILLER, Marian A.	(OH)	840
High school library administration	GOZEMBA, Frances E.	(MA)	455
High school library management	OSTHUS, Mary J.	(SD)	928
High school library operations	CHANDRA, Jane H.	(NC)	200
High school library service	TOLMAN, Bonnie B.	(MI)	1249
High school library system	KING, Willard B.	(NC)	652
High school library teaching	JEFFORDS, Margaret C.	(NY)	596
High school media	GRADY, Alida J.	(FL)	455
High school media center	KLOZA, Paula P.	(NJ)	662
High school media programs	KIRK, Mary L.	(IA)	654
High school media specialist	THOMPSON, Myra D.	(OH)	1240
High school reference	HOLBROCK, Mary A.	(IL)	550
	KAPLAN, Lois J.	(OH)	626
High school student services	WONSEVER, Eithne C.	(NY)	1363
High school students	PESTUN, Aloysius J.	(CA)	961
High schools	BAIRD, Patricia M.	(MI)	47
	PARTHUM, John W.	(MI)	945
High technology	VUGRINECZ, Anna E.	(CA)	1289
	PEERS, Charles T.	(MA)	954
	CAMBRIA, Roberto	(NY)	174
High technology consulting	JAGIELLOWICZ, Jadzia	(ON)	591
High technology custom research services	JAGIELLOWICZ, Jadzia	(ON)	591
High tech databases	PRONIN, Monica	(NY)	995
	JAGIELLOWICZ, Jadzia	(ON)	591
High technology industries	LEWIS, Gretchen S.	(CA)	723
High technology information	ROARK, Robin D.	(DC)	1038
High technology reference	CARSCH, Ruth E.	(CA)	187
High tech research & devlpmnt consulting	HERTHER, Nancy K.	(MN)	533
Junior & senior high schools	DANIEL, Donna M.	(OH)	272
Junior high building collections	LEWIS, Marjorie	(NY)	723
Junior high library skills	LEWIS, Marjorie	(NY)	723
Junior high, middle school	HAUG, Pauline C.	(WI)	512
Junior high reading encouragement	LEWIS, Marjorie	(NY)	723
Junior high reference	SHEPARD, Jon R.	(OH)	1127
Junior High school librarianship	COOK, Anne S.	(TX)	239
Junior high services	BAZE, Mary P.	(WA)	68

HIGH (Cont'd)

Large high school library
  administration .... SPICER, Orlin C. ...... (MO) 1174
Library skills, high schools ...... WARAKSA, Raymond P. (CT) 1303
Nuclear high level waste .... KING, Betty J. .... (WA) 650
Online high school instruction .... GARDNER, Laura L. .... (MO) 418
Public services high quality ...... TURNER, Kathleen G. ... (WA) 1264
Publish high tech reference books CONNORS, Martin G. ... (MI) 238
Small high school collections ..... SHEPHERD, Rex L. .... (IA) 1127
Small high school facilities ...... SHEPHERD, Rex L. .... (IA) 1127

HIGHER (See also College, University)

Higher education .... TESTA, Elizabeth M. .... (CA) 1233
                                   RESNIK, Linda I. ...... (DC) 1024
                                   AUGUST, Sidney .... (PA)   39
                                   REENSTJERNA, Frederick
                                     R. .... (WV) 1016
Higher education administration .. FUSTUKJIAN, Samuel Y. (FL) 410
                                   KATZ, Ruth M. .... (NC) 630
                                   PERSON, Ruth J. ...... (PA) 961
Higher education, library interfacing BREIVIK, Patricia S. .... (CO) 132
Higher education planning .... JORDAN, Robert T. .... (DC) 617
History of higher education ...... BRABHAM, Robert F. ... (NC) 124
Institutions of higher learning ... WOLVSKY, Haya S. ..... (ISR) 1362
Literature of higher education ... QUAY, Richard H. ...... (OH) 999

HIGHWAY (See also Traffic)

Highway research transportation info MOBLEY, Arthur B. .... (DC) 851

HIRING

Interviewing & hiring .... DEDAS, Madelyn W. ... (WA) 286
Personnel hiring, evaluating,
  objectives .... NOLAN, Deborah A. .... (MD) 907

HISPANIC (See also Chicano, Mexican, Spanish)

Hispanic & Ethnic materials ...... AYALA, John L. .... (CA) 42
Hispanic & Latin American
  bibliography .... ZUBATSKY, David S. .... (PA) 1390
Hispanic bibliography .... GRUENBECK, Laurie ... (TX) 474
Hispanic culture & history .... CULP, Paul M. .... (TX) 264
Hispanic outreach .... SIMAS, Therese C. .... (CA) 1139
Hispanic studies reference library HOOPES, Maria S. ..... (AZ) 557
Hispanics in the United States ... PEREZ-LOPEZ, Rene ... (VA) 958
Library service to Hispanics ..... RAMIREZ, William L. ... (CA) 1005
Library services to Hispanics .... HERNANDEZ, Hector R. .. (IL) 531
Monitoring approval plans for
  Hispanics .... SALINERO, Amelia ..... (NY) 1076

HISTORICAL (See also History)

Archives & historical manuscripts WILLARD, Anne H. .... (CT) 1341
                                   GRIGG, Susan .... (MA) 470
Archives, historic building
  preservation .... RABINS, Joan W. ..... (TX) 1001
Arkansas historical information ... FERGUSON, John L. ... (AR) 372
Art & historical photography ..... FALK, Peter H. .... (CT) 362
Art historical periodicals .... ALLENTUCK, Marcia E. .. (NY) 16
Art historical research .... WYKLE, Helen H. ...... (CA) 1375
                                   KNOWLES, Susan W. ... (TN) 665
California historical research, poetry MOORE, Richard K. .... (CA) 861
Catholic historical collections ... WALCH, Timothy G. .... (DC) 1293
Civil War historical collections .. JORDAN, Ervin L. ..... (VA) 616
Current & historical theatre ..... BUCK, Richard M. ..... (NY) 154
Development of historical center .. DUNGER, George A. .... (SD) 326
Educational & historical research . KLEIN, Victor C. .... (LA) 659
Historic & archaeological applications DRAKE, Robert E. ..... (MA) 318
Historic archives .... WATIER-LALONDE,
                                     Chantal .... (PQ) 1309
Historic aviation literature ...... PARKS, Dennis H. ..... (WI) 943
Historic libraries .... MENARD, Michael J. ... (WY) 823
Historic manuscript collections ... RHINELANDER, Mary F. . (MA) 1025
Historic manuscripts .... LANDIS, Lawrence A. ... (TX) 693
Historic photographs .... LANDIS, Lawrence A. ... (TX) 693
                                   JACOB, Diane B. ...... (VA) 589
Historic preservation .... SIMS, Sally R. .... (MD) 1142
                                   MORGAN, Anne E. .... (BC) 863

HISTORICAL (Cont'd)

Historic recordings preservation . PETRIE, Mildred M. .... (FL) 965
Historic theaters & preservation . LONEY, Glenn M. ..... (NY) 739
Historical agency consultation ... DU BOIS, Paul Z. ...... (NJ) 322
Historical & archival discography GLASFORD, G R. ...... (NY) 440
Historical & archival research ... MCGAUGHRAN, Roberta
                                     W. .... (DC) 805
Historical & evaluation research .. DU MONT, Rosemary R. . (OH) 325
Historical & genealogical research HELSLEY, Alexia J. .... (SC) 525
Historical & literary manuscripts . DUNLAP, Leslie W. .... (IA) 326
                                   THOMPSON, Harry F. .. (SD) 1239
Historical & present financial data PAYNE, Linda C. ...... (NY) 951
Historical archive recordings ..... BUCHSBAUM, Robert E. . (OH) 153
Historical bibliography .... SMITH, Michael K. ..... (TX) 1158
                                   STOKES, Roy B. ...... (BC) 1196
                                   WISEMAN, John A. .... (ON) 1357
Historical card catalogs .... WOOD, Sallie B. ...... (NY) 1365
Historical cartography .... SUTHERLAND, Johnnie D. (GA) 1211
Historical children's books, research GILBERT, Ophelia R. ... (MO) 434
Historical children's literature ... BROWN, June E. ...... (NY) 145
Historical collection archives .... LEVIS, Gail A. .... (IL) 721
Historical collections .... DOWNEY, Lynn A. ..... (CA) 316
                                   STUART, Karen A. ..... (MD) 1204
                                   EVANS, Max J. .... (UT) 357
Historical dance & bibliography ... KELLER, Kate V. ...... (PA) 635
Historical data .... HEFNER, Xavier M. ..... (NY) 520
Historical documentary editing ... SCHULZ, Constance B. . (SC) 1102
Historical documentation .... BAUMSTEIN, Paschal M. (NC) 66
Historical editing .... GRABOWSKI, John J. ... (OH) 455
Historical genealogy .... WITCHER, Curt R. ..... (IN) 1358
Historical interpretations in museums BATTLE, Thomas C. .... (DC) 65
Historical libraries & rare books . MERRIAM, Louise A. ... (WI) 826
Historical manuscripts .... STAUTER, Mark C. .... (MO) 1183
                                   WOLOHAN, Juliet F. ... (NY) 1362
                                   MILLER, Fredric M. .... (PA) 837
                                   WEINBERG, David M. .. (PA) 1317
                                   HILL, Edwin L. .... (WI) 539
Historical materials .... MCGUIRE, Brian ...... (DC) 808
Historical papers .... ROTH, Stacy F. .... (NJ) 1059
Historical phonograph records ... BRYAN, Martin F. ...... (VT) 151
Historical photographs .... BRENNER, M D. ...... (AK) 133
                                   D'ANTONIO, Lynn M. ... (AZ) 274
                                   ABRAHAM, Terry ...... (ID)   3
                                   CALDWELL, Richard C. . (WA) 172
                                   ENGEMAN, Richard H. .. (WA) 349
                                   HILL, Edwin L. .... (WI) 539
Historical photos .... ARONER, Miriam D. ... (CA) 34
Historical prints .... CRESSWELL, Donald H. . (PA) 258
Historical recording ledgers ..... WOOD, Sallie B. ...... (NY) 1365
Historical records .... MILLBROOKE, Anne ... (CT) 835
                                   GIAQUINTA, C J. ...... (IA) 431
                                   EAST, Dennis .... (OH) 332
                                   BROCHU, Frederick .... (PQ) 138
                                   ORTIZ MONASTERIO,
                                     Leonor .... (MEX) 927
Historical records of California ... HANEL, Mary A. ...... (CA) 495
Historical records, phonographs .. STRONG, Darrell G. .... (PA) 1203
Historical reference .... BENTLEY, Elna J. ..... (AL) 83
                                   BERGEN, Philip S. .... (MA) 85
Historical research .... CLARK, David L. ...... (CA) 216
                                   JOHNSON, Paul A. .... (CA) 608
                                   MASON, Ellsworth G. .. (CO) 781
                                   WOLFE, F M. .... (CO) 1360
                                   ALDRICH, Michele L. ... (DC) 11
                                   PINKETT, Harold T. .... (DC) 974
                                   BOPP, Richard E. ..... (IL) 116
                                   LEVIS, Gail A. .... (IL) 721
                                   METZLER, Valerie ..... (IL) 829
                                   SNOKE, Elizabeth R. ... (KS) 1163
                                   KELLS, Laura J. ...... (MD) 637
                                   MCNAMARA, Shelley G. (ME) 816
                                   FRYE, Dorothy T. ..... (MI) 407
                                   SMITH, Michael O. .... (MI) 1158
                                   SULTANOF, Jeff B. .... (NJ) 1208
                                   ROCHA, Guy L. .... (NV) 1045
                                   ROBINSON, Mitchell L. . (NY) 1044
                                   BAGBY, Ross F. ...... (OH) 45
                                   RUGG, John D. .... (OH) 1066
                                   GIMPL, Caroline A. .... (OR) 437
                                   LAMAR, Christine L. ... (RI) 689

HISTORICAL (Cont'd)

Historical research

	SILVA, Phyllis C.	(RI)	1138
	CRIST, Lynda L.	(TX)	259
	GOLTZ, Eileen A.	(ON)	447
	CHANDLER, George	(ENG)	200
Historical research & archives	HECKMAN, Marlin L.	(CA)	520
Historical research & development	JONSON, Laurence F.	(IA)	616
Historical research & writing	BROOKS, Jerrold L.	(NC)	140
	HESS, James W.	(NY)	534
	MORRISSEY, Charles T.	(VT)	869
	DIBIASE, Linda P.	(WA)	299
Historical research consultation	ESALA, Lillian H.	(MN)	354
Historical research for archaeologist	STINE, Roy S.	(NC)	1194
Historical research, indexing & writing	DENNIS, Mary R.	(IA)	292
Historical research, report preparation	STINE, Roy S.	(NC)	1194
Historical researching	SNYDER, Theresa	(PA)	1165
Historical resources	KOBELKA, Carolynn L.	(NT)	666
Historical society	COLLINS, Sarah F.	(NJ)	233
Historical society libraries	BOWERS, Rhoda E.	(MD)	120
Historical society, library admin	MILLER, Irene K.	(CT)	838
Historical writing	CHRISTENSEN, Erin S.	(CO)	211
	PINKETT, Harold T.	(DC)	974
	FRIDLEY, Russell W.	(ME)	403
Historico-legal studies	GOLDBERG, Jolande E.	(DC)	444
Historico-theological research	CAMILLI, E M.	(PA)	175
Local historical reference	DECKER, John W.	(MN)	286
National & historical bibliography	KEMP, Thomas J.	(CT)	639
New Orleans historical sources	HARDY, D C.	(LA)	500
Phonodisc historical research	GRENDYSA, Peter A.	(WI)	467
Photographs as historical documents	CHRISTOPHER, Paul	(CA)	212
Public historical research	CHRISTENSEN, Erin S.	(CO)	211
Rare or historical recordings	FABRIZIO, Timothy C.	(NY)	360
Researching historic photos & film	LUSKEY, Judith	(DC)	749
Researching historical material	HAZEL, Debora E.	(NC)	517
State & local historical research	CHRISTENSEN, Erin S.	(CO)	211
United States historical census	SCHULZE, Suzanne S.	(CO)	1102
Use of historical records	DENSMORE, Christopher	(NY)	293

HISTORY (See also Ancient, Antiquity, Historical and centuries such as Eighteenth Century and periods such as Colonial & Renaissance)

Administering local history collection	CARTER, Susan M.	(IN)	190
Aeronautical history	FOX, Howard A.	(WA)	394
Aeronautical history rare books	BARRETT, Donald J.	(CO)	59
African literature history & arts	HUTSON, Jean B.	(NY)	579
Afro-American history	KNOX, Jo E.	(MD)	666
	MACK, Phyllis G.	(NY)	756
	LOTZ, Rainer E.	(WGR)	742
American & European history	GRIPPO, Christopher F.	(WA)	471
American & local history	LEERHOFF, Ruth E.	(CA)	712
American art history	BRUNK, Thomas W.	(MI)	150
American Black Catholic history	HOGAN, Peter E.	(MD)	549
American cultural history	MOSS, Roger W.	(PA)	872
American diplomatic history	MCDONALD, Ellen J.	(MA)	802
American history	ALLAN, Nancy P.	(IL)	14
	BRIGGS, Martha T.	(IL)	135
	O'TOOLE, James M.	(MA)	930
	PETTIT, Marilyn H.	(NY)	965
	VAN HORNE, John C.	(PA)	1275
	BLACK, J A.	(TX)	101
American history & biography	HANKAMER, Roberta A.	(MA)	496
American history bibliography	GETCHELL, Charles M.	(NC)	430
American history collection development	VYHNANEK, Louis	(WA)	1290
American history consulting	SCHEIPS, Paul J.	(MD)	1091
American Jewish history	CLINE, Robert S.	(WA)	222
American library history	HOLLEY, Edward G.	(NC)	551
American literacy history	ABBOTT, Craig S.	(IL)	1
American presidency history	ELZY, Martin I.	(GA)	347
American social history	ANDERSON, R J.	(PA)	25
American theatre history	ARCHER, Stephen M.	(MO)	31
Anabaptist history	MARNET, Carole M.	(PA)	772
Ancient histories	ABNEY, Timothy A.	(CA)	2
Anesthesia history	WRIGHT, Amos J.	(AL)	1370
Architectural history	BROWN, Steven A.	(GA)	147
Architecture history	KIMBERLIN, Robert L.	(DC)	649
Archival history	BRADSHER, James G.	(DC)	126
Archival history & theory	BRICHFORD, Maynard J.	(IL)	134

HISTORY (Cont'd)

Archives, history of medicine	VADEBONCOEUR, Elizabeth J.	(CA)	1270
Armor & calvary history	HOLT, David A.	(KY)	554
Art & architectural history	FRIEDMAN, Richard E.	(AL)	404
	COIR, Mark A.	(MI)	229
	LABUDDE, Kenneth J.	(MO)	686
	BEETHAM, Donald W.	(NJ)	74
Art & art history librarianship	QUIGLEY, Suzanne L.	(OH)	999
Art history	SORENSEN, Lee R.	(AZ)	1168
	FELACO, Maja K.	(DC)	369
	FAHNERT, Elizabeth K.	(FL)	361
	RITCHIE, Verna F.	(IA)	1036
	HUNT, Janis E.	(IL)	575
	TOPPAN, Muriel L.	(MD)	1251
	REMECZKI, Paul W.	(NY)	1022
	LEWIS, Marjorie B.	(PA)	724
	TRINKAUS, Tanya	(RI)	1256
	FECKO, Marybeth	(SC)	367
	JACOBY, Mary M.	(VA)	590
	CORBEIL, Lizette	(PQ)	245
	STONE, Toby G.	(FRN)	1197
Art history acquisition	CICCONE, Amy N.	(VA)	214
Art history & aesthetics	MILLER, Jack E.	(GA)	838
Art history & design	HORNBACH, Ruth M.	(MI)	559
Art history bibliography	ROSS, Alexander D.	(CA)	1057
Art history classification	UPDIKE, Christina B.	(VA)	1269
Art history collection development	SMITH, Beryl K.	(NJ)	1153
Art history reference	SMITH, Beryl K.	(NJ)	1153
Art history research	YARNALL, James L.	(DC)	1378
	TRINKOFF, Elaine	(NY)	1257
	CICCONE, Amy N.	(VA)	214
Art history slide organizing	GRAY, Shirley M.	(NY)	460
Art history slides	KRUPANSKI, Pamela M.	(MA)	680
Author of library history	FRISBIE, Margery	(IL)	405
Automotive history	WREN, James A.	(MI)	1370
Baptist history	COURSEY, W T.	(GA)	251
	DEBUSMAN, Paul M.	(KY)	285
	GRENGA, Kathy A.	(TN)	467
Baseball history	GIETSCHIER, Steven P.	(MO)	433
Bibliography, European hist & religion	ROBERTS, Susanne F.	(CT)	1041
Bibliography of art history	ARNTZEN, Etta E.	(IL)	34
Bibliography of history	BOHANAN, Robert D.	(DC)	111
	GRISSO, Karl M.	(IL)	471
	SHELDON, Ted P.	(MO)	1126
Black American history manuscripts	WEST, Donald	(MI)	1326
Black history	OAKLANDER, Linda G.	(MI)	913
	MENINGALL, Evelyn L.	(NJ)	824
	GREEN, Jeffrey P.	(ENG)	462
Black history collection maintenance	PULLER, Maryam W.	(PA)	997
Book & library history	KASER, David	(IN)	628
Book arts history	ALTERMAN, Deborah H.	(NJ)	18
Books & printing history	LOWE, Mildred	(NY)	744
Boychoir history & bibliography	ROOT, Arlene V.	(KS)	1053
Brewing industry history	VOLLMAR, William J.	(MO)	1288
British history specialist	BRUGNOLOTTI, Phyllis T.	(NY)	150
Broadcast history	RUNYON, Steven C.	(CA)	1067
	HEINZ, Catharine F.	(DC)	522
Building local history collection	MILLER, Ida M.	(IN)	838
Business history	STEGH, Leslie J.	(IL)	1185
California history	ELLISON, Bettye H.	(CA)	345
California local history	DRUMMOND, Herbert	(CA)	321
Calvin Coolidge history	WIKANDER, Lawrence E.	(MA)	1338
Canadian & United States history	OTTOSEN, Charles F.	(AB)	930
Canadian history	REID, Marianne E.	(SK)	1019
Canadiana & local history	LLOYD, Mary E.	(ON)	735
Caribbean Jewish history	CAHEN, Joel J.	(NET)	171
Cartography history	STEPHENSON, Richard W.	(DC)	1188
Cataloging & church history	ROBINSON, Nancy D.	(KY)	1044
Cataloging, Baptist history, doctrine	ROBINSON, Nancy D.	(KY)	1044
Cataloging history, philosophy, religion	YU, Priscilla C.	(IL)	1384
Cataloging local history collection	MILLER, Ida M.	(IN)	838
Catholic Church history	HILAND, Gerard P.	(OH)	538
Cherokee history	SUMNER, Delores T.	(OK)	1209
Chinese history	WANG, Sing W.	(AUS)	1303
Chinese library history	TING, Lee H.	(IL)	1246

HISTORY (Cont'd)

Subject	Name	State	Page
Church history	STELLING, Dwight D.	(IL)	1186
	IZBICKI, Thomas M.	(KS)	586
	YEISER, Doris B.	(KY)	1379
	MCNAMARA, Robert F.	(NY)	816
Church history & religion cataloging	MITCHELL, Annmarie D.	(CA)	848
Church history, theology resources	SUELFLOW, August R.	(MO)	1206
Civil War history	BERENT, Irwin M.	(VA)	84
Collecting state religious history	ROLLER, Twila J.	(NM)	1051
Collection development, history	MCCOY, Patricia S.	(IL)	799
Collection development in history	LAUBE, Lois R.	(IN)	702
	ZIEPER, Linda R.	(MA)	1388
	BUDNICK, Carol	(MB)	155
College history	GREENSLADE, Thomas B.	(OH)	465
Colonial history	DALY, John E.	(IL)	271
Community history, Orange County	FRANK, Anne E.	(CA)	396
Compiling legislative histories	DULEY, Kay E.	(LA)	324
Connecticut history & culture	SCHMIDT, Alesandra M.	(CT)	1095
Consultation on American Catholic hist	THOMAS, Evangeline M.	(KS)	1236
Contemporary art history	FURTAK, Rosemary	(MN)	410
Corporate historian	SOLSETH, Gwenn M.	(MN)	1166
Corporate history	MATTHEWS, Darwin C.	(MI)	785
Corporate history celebration	TURNER, Ellis S.	(MD)	1264
Costume design & history	STOWELL, Donald C.	(GA)	1199
Country music historian	MARTUCCI, Louis U.	(CA)	779
Country music history	SEEMANN, Charles H.	(TN)	1111
Dakotas history	MC CAULEY, Philip F.	(SD)	795
Depository library history	MILLER, Sarah J.	(NJ)	842
Disney history	SIGMAN, Paula M.	(CA)	1137
Dutch Jewish history	CAHEN, Joel J.	(NET)	171
Early American history & culture	MONTGOMERY, Michael S.	(NJ)	856
Early American history 1492-1800	ADAMS, Thomas R.	(RI)	6
Early California history	SANTOS, Bob	(CA)	1082
18th century American history	GROVE, Pearce S.	(VA)	473
18th century British history & culture	DEVINE, Marie E.	(CT)	297
English history	STAM, David H.	(NY)	1179
Environmental history	BAIRD, Dennis W.	(ID)	47
Ethnic history & folklore	PENTI, Marsha E.	(MI)	957
Ethnic studies & history of the book	WYNAR, Lubomyr R.	(OH)	1375
European & American history	THOMPSON, Janet A.	(NM)	1240
European history	HENNEMAN, John B.	(NJ)	528
	NASH, Stanley D.	(NJ)	888
	BLACK, J A.	(TX)	101
	WELSCH, Erwin K.	(WI)	1323
	VERYHA, Wasyl	(ON)	1283
European history major	BRUGNOLOTTI, Phyllis T.	(NY)	150
Family & local history research	WILLIAMS, Janet L.	(OR)	1344
Family history	CARTER, Janet K.	(TX)	189
	CLEMENT, Charles R.	(UT)	221
Fiction, history	SALLSTROM, Marilee A.	(CA)	1077
Film history	STOCKSTILL, Patrick E.	(CA)	1195
	MARTIN, Vernon E.	(CT)	778
	DRUMMOND, Donald R.	(TX)	321
Fine arts, local history collections	MCNULTY, Karen	(CT)	817
Florida public health history	HALL, M C.	(FL)	488
French literature & history	MCNAMARA, Charles B.	(NC)	816
Genealogy & local history	KEMP, Thomas J.	(CT)	639
	DAY, Thomas L.	(IN)	283
	MUTH, Thomas J.	(KS)	883
	PAYNE, David L.	(MS)	951
	JONES, Plummer A.	(NC)	614
	ESWORTHY, Lori L.	(NY)	355
	JANOWSKY, Cara A.	(NY)	593
	ENGEL, Carl T.	(OH)	348
	LUST, Jeanette M.	(OH)	749
	HARPER, Sarah H.	(TX)	503
	STEINBERG, David L.	(VA)	1185
Genealogy, family history	THOMAS, Cornel W.	(AR)	1236
Genealogy, local history	STEPHENS, Doris G.	(NC)	1188
	MONCLA, Carolyn S.	(TX)	854
General history	WITT, Kenneth W.	(MN)	1358
General history of Pittsburgh	KURTIK, Frank J.	(PA)	685
German history	VINCENT, Charles P.	(NH)	1284
German history collection development	BAER, Eberhard A.	(VA)	44
Government archives & history	CHRISTNER, Deborah S.	(CA)	212
Government, US & European history	HERTZ, Sylvia	(MI)	533
Hawaiian & Pacific history	TIMBERLAKE, Cynthia A.	(HI)	1245

HISTORY (Cont'd)

Subject	Name	State	Page
Helping researchers, Methodist history	ROLLER, Twila J.	(NM)	1051
Hispanic culture & history	CULP, Paul M.	(TX)	264
Historian	FOREMAN, Kenneth J.	(NC)	390
	HAYMOND, Jay M.	(UT)	516
Historiography of mental illness	EVANS, Josephine K.	(FL)	357
History	BRIDGES, Edwin C.	(AL)	135
	DEW, Stephen H.	(AR)	297
	WOOD, Raymund F.	(CA)	1364
	GEHRES, Eleanor M.	(CO)	425
	BOORSTIN, Daniel J.	(DC)	115
	HARDING, Robert S.	(DC)	500
	LEHMAN, Douglas K.	(FL)	712
	WOOD, James F.	(FL)	1364
	MARTIN, Clarece	(GA)	775
	BOYLE, Lawrence C.	(IL)	124
	SHUSTER, Robert D.	(IL)	1134
	STEWART, James A.	(IL)	1192
	WITTMAN, Elisabeth C.	(IL)	1358
	SEAGLE, Janet M.	(NJ)	1109
	ZINK, Steven D.	(NV)	1389
	HALPIN, James R.	(NY)	490
	COHEN, Susan J.	(OH)	229
	PLUMMER, Karen A.	(OH)	978
	BAUER, Barbara B.	(PA)	65
	SILVERMAN, Scott H.	(PA)	1138
	BRADY, Josiah B.	(TN)	126
	JOYCE, Donald F.	(TN)	618
	BOGIE, Thomas M.	(TX)	110
	RICHARD, Marc	(PQ)	1028
History, American West	EMERSON, Tamsen L.	(WY)	347
History & aesthetics stage design	STOWELL, Donald C.	(GA)	1199
History & archaeology	BROWN, William A.	(VA)	148
History & art reference	PINSON, Patricia A.	(WY)	975
History & collection development	MONROE, William S.	(NY)	855
History & East Asian studies bibl	BERGER, Kenneth W.	(NC)	85
History & genealogy	ASHTON, Rick J.	(CO)	36
	COUP, William A.	(FL)	251
History & general reference	HOUSE, Katherine L.	(KY)	563
History & government	WILLET, Ruth J.	(NY)	1341
History & humanities	BLOUIN, Francis X.	(MI)	107
History & law	CAMPBELL, Laurie G.	(ON)	177
History & literature	LAMBREV, Garrett I.	(CA)	691
History & philosophy of librarianship	STIELOW, Frederick J.	(MD)	1194
History & political science	AULD, Hampton M.	(NC)	39
History & politics	TAYLOR, Marion E.	(CA)	1227
History & public policy	PREER, Jean L.	(DC)	990
History, archives	HADDEN, Robert L.	(MD)	481
History, art reference	STOPKA, Christina K.	(WY)	1198
History bibliographer	CLARKE, Susan M.	(IL)	219
	MISTARAS, Evangeline	(IL)	848
History bibliographies	GEARY, James W.	(OH)	424
History bibliography	CRIDLAND, Nancy C.	(IN)	258
	STOLLER, Michael E.	(NY)	1196
	MYCUE, David J.	(TX)	884
History, biography & genealogy	MUTCH, Donald G.	(ON)	883
History books & printing	COLBY, Robert A.	(NY)	230
History, books, libraries	ROTHACKER, John M.	(TN)	1059
History databases	KINNELL, Susan K.	(CA)	653
	BERGER, Kenneth W.	(NC)	85
History, humanities, women's studies	FALK, Joyce D.	(CA)	362
History kitchenware & jewelry	LANTZ, Louise K.	(MD)	697
History Micronesia	DRIVER, Marjorie G.	(GU)	320
History of American libraries	MCMULLEN, Charles H.	(VA)	815
History of American printing	MCCORISON, Marcus A.	(MA)	798
History of architectural theory	ARNTZEN, Etta M.	(IL)	34
History of aviation	HALPIN, Jerome H.	(CA)	490
History of bibliography	RAYWARD, W B.	(AUS)	1011
History of binding	NEEDHAM, Paul	(NY)	891
History of biomedicine	DAVIS, Elisabeth B.	(IL)	278
History of books	COLE, John Y.	(DC)	231
	HALPORN, Barbara	(IN)	490
	GOULD, Karen K.	(TX)	454
History of books & libraries	TURNER, Frank L.	(TX)	1264
	MULVANEY, John P.	(VA)	878
	DE SCOSSA, Catriona	(AB)	295
	SIBAI, Mohamed M.	(SDA)	1134
History of books & manuscripts	CARNOVSKY, Ruth F.	(CA)	184

HISTORY (Cont'd)

History of books & printing	KIRSHENBAUM, Sandra D.	(CA)	655
	THOMPSON, Susan O.	(NY)	1241
	JOHNSON, Bryan R.	(VA)	602
	BREGMAN, Alvan M.	(ON)	131
History of books & rare books	WINCKLER, Paul A.	(NY)	1354
History of botany archives	STIEBER, Michael T.	(PA)	1193
History of broadcasting	BRAGG, William J.	(TX)	127
History of cartography	RAY, Jean M.	(IL)	1011
	WALSTROM, Jon L.	(MN)	1300
History of children's literature	MAXWELL, Margaret F.	(AZ)	788
	CARSTENS, Jane E.	(LA)	188
	POND, Patricia B.	(OR)	982
History of communications	BRAGG, William J.	(TX)	127
History of education	MENT, David M.	(NY)	824
History of 18th century art	ARNTZEN, Etta M.	(IL)	34
History of fine printing	DANE, William J.	(NJ)	272
History of health sciences	ZINN, Nancy W.	(CA)	1389
History of higher education	BRABHAM, Robert F.	(NC)	124
History of information science	KENT, Allen	(PA)	642
History of librarianship	BERGEN, Daniel P.	(NY)	85
History of libraries	WINGER, Howard W.	(IL)	1355
	HALPORN, Barbara	(IN)	490
	SLAVENS, Thomas P.	(MI)	1148
	BOYD, William D.	(MS)	123
History of libraries & librarianship	MEISELS, Henry R.	(IL)	822
	DAIN, Phyllis	(NJ)	270
History of medical literature, rare bks	MIMS, Dorothy H.	(GA)	845
History of medicine	WALLS, Edwina	(AR)	1298
	WOOD, Elizabeth H.	(CA)	1364
	ARCARI, Ralph D.	(CT)	30
	HIRTLE, Peter B.	(MD)	544
	JENSEN, Joseph E.	(MD)	599
	PARASCANDOLA, John L.	(MD)	939
	ANDERSON, Paul G.	(MO)	25
	BRODMAN, Estelle	(NJ)	139
	IRWIN, Barbara S.	(NJ)	584
	MOORE, Rue I.	(NY)	861
	RAMER, Bruce J.	(NY)	1005
	METZGER, Philip A.	(PA)	829
	SAWYER, Warren A.	(SC)	1086
	RAY, Joyce M.	(TX)	1011
	WYGANT, Larry J.	(TX)	1375
	GROEN, Frances K.	(PQ)	471
History of medicine archives	GILHEANY, Rosary S.	(NJ)	434
History of medicine cataloging	GILLIAM, Susanne P.	(OH)	436
History of medicine, reference	JENKINS, Glen P.	(OH)	597
History of modern computing	BRUEMMER, Bruce H.	(MN)	149
History of papermaking	BIDWELL, John	(CA)	95
History of periodicals	NOURIE, Alan R.	(IL)	910
History of photography	RULE, Amy E.	(AZ)	1067
	MENTHE, Melissa	(NJ)	825
History of photography bibliography	HUGHSTON, Milan R.	(TX)	572
History of printing	WELLS, James M.	(IL)	1322
	WINGER, Howard W.	(IL)	1355
	HALPORN, Barbara	(IN)	490
	BRODY, Catherine T.	(NY)	139
	TICHENOR, Irene	(NY)	1244
	FLAKE, Chad J.	(UT)	383
	ETTLINGER, John R.	(NS)	356
History of printing & publishing	DUGGAN, Mary K.	(CA)	324
History of psychology	POPPLESTONE, John A.	(OH)	984
History of recorded sound	FABRIZIO, Timothy C.	(NY)	360
History of research libraries	BELANGER, Terry	(NY)	76
History of Russian, Soviet bibliography	WHITBY, Thomas J.	(CO)	1330
History of science	CHAMPLIN, Peggy	(CA)	198
	ELLIOTT, Clark A.	(MA)	343
	RAMER, Bruce J.	(NY)	1005
	WARNOW-BLEWETT, Joan N.	(NY)	1305
	GOODMAN, Marcia M.	(OK)	449
History of science & technology	ANDERSON, Marjorie E.	(ME)	24
	STAPLETON, Darwin H.	(NY)	1181
History of silent film	ALTOMARA, Rita E.	(NJ)	18
History of technology	HARDING, Robert S.	(DC)	500
History of telephony	SWINBURNE, Ralph E.	(NY)	1216

HISTORY (Cont'd)

History of the book	GONIWIECHA, Mark C.	(AK)	447
	NEAVILL, Gordon B.	(AL)	891
	MAXWELL, Margaret F.	(AZ)	788
	HARLAN, Robert D.	(CA)	502
	ROGERS, Brian D.	(CT)	1049
	HANSON, Norma S.	(OH)	498
	SUMMERS, George V.	(PA)	1209
	SKELLEY, Grant T.	(WA)	1145
	LANDON, Richard G.	(ON)	693
History of the health sciences	BRITT, Mary C.	(AL)	137
	EDDY, Leonard M.	(KY)	335
History of the institution & medicine	MIMS, Dorothy H.	(GA)	845
History of the theatre	TARANOW, Gerda	(CT)	1223
History, political science bibliography	THOMPSON, Ann M.	(OH)	1238
History reference	MONROE, William S.	(NY)	855
History reference & bibliography	CUDD, John M.	(KY)	263
History, reference librarian	EMMICK, Nancy J.	(CA)	348
History research & writing	SHIDELER, John C.	(WA)	1129
History selection & orientation	APPLEBY, Judith A.	(PQ)	30
Humanities & history	HOLT, Lisa A.	(NY)	554
Immigrant history	ASHKENAS, Bruce F.	(VA)	36
Instructor, genealogy & family history	SPERRY, Kip	(UT)	1174
Jamaican history & culture	REGNER-HYATT, Anne L.	(CA)	1017
Jazz history reference	JERDE, Curtis D.	(LA)	599
Jewelry history	DIRLAM, Dona M.	(CA)	305
Jewish history	CAHEN, Joel J.	(NET)	171
Jewish history & life	ARONER, Miriam D.	(CA)	34
Judaism & Jewish history	WIENER, Theodore	(DC)	1336
Kentucky history	STONE, Sue L.	(KY)	1197
Labor history	SWANSON, Dorothy T.	(NY)	1213
Latter Day Saint history	HALLIER, Sara J.	(MO)	489
Law history	KREH, Fritz	(WGR)	677
Legal history	COOPER, Byron D.	(MI)	242
	BAGNALL, Whitney S.	(NY)	45
Legislative histories	SCHUTT, Cheryl M.	(CT)	1103
	BOYER, Larry M.	(DC)	123
	CILIBERTI, Nancy A.	(DC)	214
	SEELE, Ronald E.	(DC)	1111
	WOODWARD, Elaine H.	(VA)	1368
Legislative history	BONYNGE, Jeanne R.	(DC)	115
	BRAVY, Gary J.	(DC)	130
	LOCKWOOD, David J.	(DC)	736
	LASKOWITZ, Roberta G.	(NY)	700
	STORMS, Kate	(NY)	1198
	GARDNER, Linda	(TX)	418
Legislative history compilation	RUGE, Audrey L.	(DC)	1066
Legislative history research	GORDON, Kaye B.	(NJ)	451
Library history	STIEG, Margaret F.	(AL)	1193
	EDELSTEIN, J M.	(CA)	335
	MAACK, Mary N.	(CA)	753
	O'CONNOR, Thomas F.	(CA)	916
	COLLIER, Bonnie	(CT)	232
	KNOWLTON, John D.	(DC)	665
	SESSA, Frank B.	(FL)	1116
	PETERSON, Kenneth G.	(IL)	964
	WAGNER, Ralph D.	(IL)	1292
	BAILEY, Joanne P.	(IN)	46
	SHIFLETT, Orvin L.	(LA)	1130
	FISCHER, Marge	(MA)	380
	BUCHANAN, William E.	(NC)	153
	JONES, Plummer A.	(NC)	614
	KEENE, Roberta E.	(NV)	634
	BOBINSKI, George S.	(NY)	108
	HIGGINBOTHAM, Barbra B.	(NY)	537
	BETCHER, Melissa A.	(OH)	92
	JAMISON, Martin P.	(OH)	593
	MCCHESNEY, Kathryn M.	(OH)	795
	OTNES, Harold M.	(OR)	930
	MAIN, Annette Z.	(PA)	761
	DAVIS, Donald G.	(TX)	278
	JULIAN, Charles A.	(WV)	619
	ROTHSTEIN, Samuel	(BC)	1060
	FYFE, Janet H.	(ON)	411
	SEPTEMBER, Peter E.	(SAF)	1115
Library history, libraries in society	KUSNERZ, Peggy A.	(MI)	685
Library history, women	GROTZINGER, Laurel A.	(MI)	473
Library history writing	MCCRIMMON, Barbara S.	(FL)	800
Library information science history	MIKSA, Francis L.	(TX)	834

HISTORY (Cont'd)

Library of Congress history	COLE, John Y.	(DC)	231
Library research in ancient history	SEAVER, James E.	(KS)	1110
Library research in Jewish history	SEAVER, James E.	(KS)	1110
Library research in medieval history	SEAVER, James E.	(KS)	1110
Literature & art history books	ALLENTUCK, Marcia E.	(NY)	16
Literature & history reference	BARNETT, Jean D.	(OR)	57
Literature of art history	REED, Marcia C.	(CA)	1015
Local & family history	HAMILTON, Patricia A.	(IL)	492
Local & regional history interpretation	LEAHY, M J.	(AK)	706
Local history	GARNER, Carolyn L.	(CA)	419
	HELLING, Madelyn	(CA)	524
	STREETER, David	(CA)	1201
	PALMQUIST, David W.	(CT)	937
	REITER, Elizabeth A.	(CT)	1022
	DEANE, Roxanna	(DC)	284
	RAY, Kathryn C.	(DC)	1011
	BOLDRICK, Samuel J.	(FL)	112
	CONOVER, Kathryn H.	(FL)	238
	WALKER, Alice O.	(GA)	1295
	COCHRAN, William M.	(IA)	225
	CRAWFORD, Daniel R.	(IA)	256
	HUNTING, Susan K.	(IA)	576
	ALLAN, Nancy P.	(IL)	14
	EDSTROM, James A.	(IL)	337
	MUNDELL, Eric L.	(IN)	878
	TURNER, Nancy K.	(IN)	1265
	HEIM, Keith M.	(KY)	521
	KING, Charles D.	(KY)	650
	ABRAHAM, Deborah V.	(MA)	2
	FISCHER, Marge	(MA)	380
	MCLAIN, Guy A.	(MA)	813
	MINTON, Alix M.	(MA)	846
	SLEEMAN, William E.	(MD)	1148
	TURNER, David E.	(MD)	1264
	CALLARD, Carole	(MI)	173
	FEDEROWSKI, Marjorie S.	(MI)	368
	LARSON, Catherine A.	(MI)	699
	REASONER, Mary B.	(MI)	1013
	GLENN, Michael D.	(MO)	441
	MEYERS, Martha L.	(MO)	831
	MAXWELL, Daisy D.	(NC)	788
	YORK, Maurice C.	(NC)	1381
	CUMMINGS, Charles F.	(NJ)	264
	MONROE-SECHREST, Nancy H.	(NJ)	855
	VAN BENTHUYSEN, Robert F.	(NJ)	1272
	CARLSON, Marie S.	(NY)	182
	DISHON, Robert M.	(NY)	305
	JEANNENEY, Mary L.	(NY)	596
	WELLS, Phyllis L.	(NY)	1323
	WILLET, Ruth J.	(NY)	1341
	BERGDORF, Randolph S.	(OH)	85
	FARRELL, Maureen C.	(OH)	365
	SEARS, Robert W.	(OK)	1110
	FULCHER, Jane M.	(PA)	408
	LIVENGOOD, Candice C.	(PA)	734
	WEIHERER, Patricia D.	(PA)	1317
	HEARNE, Mary G.	(TN)	518
	BOCKSTRUCK, Lloyd D.	(TX)	109
	ENDELMAN, Sharon B.	(TX)	348
	GRAY, Wayne D.	(TX)	460
	MYLER, Josephine P.	(TX)	885
	LEVY, Suzanne S.	(VA)	722
	WILLBERG, Carolyn S.	(WA)	1341
	GROSKOPF, Amy L.	(WI)	472
	HOFFMAN, Susan J.	(ON)	548
	MEHTA, Subbash C.	(ON)	821
	MOLSON, Gerda A.	(ON)	853
Local history & affairs	VIGNOVICH, Ray L.	(WI)	1284
Local history & archives	OTTOSEN, Charles F.	(AB)	930
	KEARNS, Linda J.	(ON)	633
Local history & genealogy	GOFF, Linda J.	(CA)	443
	KOEL, Maria O.	(CT)	667
	KANELY, Edna A.	(DC)	625
	REID, Judith P.	(DC)	1018
	BAKER, Donald E.	(IN)	48
	MILLS, Helen L.	(TX)	844
Local history & genealogy reference	WIENER, Alissa L.	(MN)	1336

HISTORY (Cont'd)

Local history & oral history	MUELLER, Jane L.	(CA)	875
Local history & photograph collections	BABBITT, Dennis L.	(IN)	43
Local history & university archives	WALKER, Mary J.	(NM)	1296
Local history, audiovisual, reference	WOOD, Lois R.	(IL)	1364
Local history, books, programs	JAMISON, Susan C.	(DE)	593
Local history collection	SINGH, Rosemary A.	(WI)	1143
Local history collection development	DARR, William E.	(IN)	275
	ENG, Mamie	(NY)	348
Local history collections	BROCK, Kathy T.	(GA)	138
	VLOYANETES, Jeanne M.	(NJ)	1286
	HALL, Alan C.	(OH)	486
	COLLINS, Sara D.	(VA)	233
	RICKERSON, Carla	(WA)	1031
Local history consulting	KRASEAN, Thomas K.	(IN)	676
Local history field agent	MILLER, Ida M.	(IN)	838
Local history, genealogy, preservation	BROWN, Donald R.	(PA)	143
Local history manuscript collections	PACKARD, Agnes K.	(NY)	933
Local history microfilming	BAUS, J W.	(IN)	67
Local history of upstate New York	KABELAC, Karl S.	(NY)	620
Local history research	MATTIS, George E.	(VA)	786
Local history research projects	WOLFE, Barbara M.	(NY)	1360
Local history sources	GRABOWSKI, John J.	(OH)	455
Local medical history	GOLDSTEIN, Cynthia H.	(LA)	446
Los Angeles & California history	STERN, Teena B.	(CA)	1189
Louisiana history	JUMONVILLE, Florence M.	(LA)	619
Louisville area history	REDMON, Sherrill	(KY)	1014
Lutheran Church history, archives	WITTMAN, Elisabeth C.	(IL)	1358
Lutheran history & reference	WOHLRABE, John C.	(MO)	1359
Maritime & naval history	KNAPP, Peter J.	(CT)	663
Maritime history	ADAMS, Thomas R.	(RI)	6
Medical history	WRIGHT, Amos J.	(AL)	1370
	EIMAS, Richard	(IA)	340
	BEATTY, William K.	(IL)	70
	BRENNER, Lawrence	(MA)	133
	KEYS, Thomas E.	(MN)	645
	SENTZ, Lilli	(NY)	1115
	KRONICK, David A.	(TX)	679
	WEINSTOCK, Joanna S.	(VT)	1318
Medical history reference	RUGGERE, Christine A.	(PA)	1066
Medieval history	IZBICKI, Thomas M.	(KS)	586
Michigan history	KULL, Christine L.	(MI)	683
	MULLIGAN, William H.	(MI)	877
Military & naval history	SHERIDAN, Robert N.	(NY)	1128
Military history	BARON, Herman	(PA)	58
	WHITE-WILLIAMS, Patricia	(VA)	1333
Military history, business reference	ROTHENBERG, Mark H.	(NY)	1060
Military science & military history	DOYLE, Frances M.	(VA)	317
Militia & National Guard history	WEAVER, Thomas M.	(DC)	1312
Milwaukee history	COONEY, Charles W.	(WI)	241
Missouri history	PARKES, Darla J.	(MO)	942
Missouri library history	TUCKER, Phillip H.	(MO)	1262
Modern European history	O'CONNOR, Thomas F.	(CA)	916
Modern German history	BAZILLION, Richard J.	(ON)	68
Montana history	MORROW, Delores J.	(MT)	869
Music bibliography & history	VILES, Elza A.	(TN)	1284
Music history	MARTIN, Vernon E.	(CT)	778
	JELLINEK, George	(NY)	596
	LINDAHL, Charles E.	(NY)	728
	NOVITSKY, Edward G.	(NY)	911
	PEAKE, Luise E.	(SC)	952
Music history & literature	DONALDSON, Anna L.	(TX)	311
Music, history & women's studies	LOMBARDI, Mary L.	(CA)	738
Music history collections	SIMMONS, Hal	(GA)	1140
Music printing history	BOORMAN, Stanley H.	(NY)	115
Musical historiography	GRAMENZ, Francis L.	(MA)	457
Musical theater history & production	LONEY, Glenn M.	(NY)	739
Natural history	SHIH, Diana	(NY)	1130
	SPAWN, Carol M.	(PA)	1172
Natural history & natural sciences	MORITZ, Thomas D.	(CA)	865
Natural history media	ALASTI, Aryt	(MA)	9
Natural history, rare books	DONAHUE, Katharine E.	(CA)	310
Natural history reference	JERYAN, Christine B.	(MI)	600
New England local history	SKILLIN, Glenn B.	(PA)	1146
New Jersey history	IRWIN, Barbara S.	(NJ)	584
New Orleans history	HARDY, D C.	(LA)	500
19th century Oregon history	EMMENS, Thomas A.	(OR)	348
19th century Pacific Northwest history	EMMENS, Thomas A.	(OR)	348
Northern Kentucky history	AVERDICK, Michael R.	(KY)	41

HISTORY (Cont'd)

Specialty	Name	State	No.
Nursing history	LINEBACH, Laura M.	(MO)	730
Oklahoma history	SUMNER, Delores T.	(OK)	1209
Opera history	MOSES, Julian M.	(NY)	871
Opera singers & operatic history	FARKAS, Andrew	(FL)	364
Oral histories	CHERPAK, Evelyn M.	(RI)	206
Oral history	BENNETT, Celestine C.	(CA)	81
	BURNS, John F.	(CA)	162
	GOODSTEIN, Judith R.	(CA)	450
	DEANE, Roxanna	(DC)	284
	MOSS, William W.	(DC)	872
	ROSS, Rodney A.	(DC)	1058
	LESLIE, Elizabeth J.	(GA)	718
	ERICKSEN, Paul A.	(IL)	352
	KRASEAN, Thomas K.	(IN)	676
	MCSHANE, Stephen G.	(IN)	818
	BIRDWHISTELL, Terry L.	(KY)	98
	NOWICKE, Carole E.	(MI)	911
	WAGNER, Cherryl A.	(MI)	1291
	BAKER, Tracey I.	(MN)	50
	BRILEY, Carol A.	(MO)	136
	WARNER, Wayne E.	(MO)	1305
	MCCULLOUGH, Jack W.	(NJ)	801
	SOMMER, Ursula M.	(NJ)	1167
	COLMAN, Gould P.	(NY)	233
	DISHON, Robert M.	(NY)	305
	GUREWITSCH, Bonnie	(NY)	478
	LACHATANERE, Diana	(NY)	686
	GOERLER, Raimund E.	(OH)	443
	BLUTH, John F.	(PA)	108
	WRAY, Wendell L.	(PA)	1370
	CONRAD, James H.	(TX)	238
	DRUMMOND, Donald R.	(TX)	321
	COLLINS, Sara D.	(VA)	233
	PENGELLY, Joe	(ENG)	956
Oral history catalog publication	KENDRICK, Alice M.	(NY)	640
Oral history collections	GRELE, Ronald J.	(NY)	467
Oral history consulting	GRELE, Ronald J.	(NY)	467
	MORRISSEY, Charles T.	(VT)	869
Oral history interview training	KENDRICK, Alice M.	(NY)	640
Oral history interviewing	CAMERON, Sam A.	(TN)	175
Oral history interviewing techniques	STEPHENSON, Shirley E.	(CA)	1189
Oral history program design	KENDRICK, Alice M.	(NY)	640
Oral history projects	JONES, Martin J.	(NY)	614
Oral history teaching	GRELE, Ronald J.	(NY)	467
Pacific islands history	SHELDEN, Patricia R.	(HI)	1125
Pacific Northwest history	CALDWELL, Richard C.	(WA)	172
Pacific Northwest regional local history	EMMENS, Thomas A.	(OR)	348
Parish histories	AMES, Charlotte A.	(IN)	19
Parliamentary history	DIONNE, Guy	(PQ)	305
Performance historian	LOMONACO, Martha S.	(NY)	738
Philadelphia, general history	LAVERTY, Bruce	(PA)	703
Philadelphia history	WOLF, Edwin	(PA)	1360
Photographic history	VISKOCHIL, Larry A.	(IL)	1285
Photography & urban history	GRAY, Priscilla M.	(PA)	460
Polish music history	WILK, Wanda	(CA)	1339
Political history	PAPAZIAN, Pierre	(NJ)	939
President McKinley history	STOUT, Chester B.	(OH)	1198
Printing & publishing history	BIDWELL, John	(CA)	95
Printing history	SILVER, Joel B.	(IN)	1138
Promoting regional American history	REINSTEIN, Julia B.	(NY)	1021
Province history, articles & lectures	STRECK, Helen T.	(KS)	1201
Public history	SCHEIPS, Paul J.	(MD)	1091
Public history administration	PRICE, William S.	(NC)	993
Publishing & printing histories	BUSHMAN, James L.	(OR)	165
Publishing history	CLARK, Harry	(OK)	217
	GREEN, James N.	(PA)	462
	METZGER, Philip A.	(PA)	829
Railroad history	MUTSCHLER, Charles V.	(WA)	883
Rare book library history	BELANGER, Terry	(NY)	76
Rare books, history of medicine	FREY, Emil F.	(TX)	402
Rare books, printing history	ALLEN, Susan M.	(CA)	16
Recent American history	ELZY, Martin I.	(GA)	347
Records research, college history	NELSON, Robert J.	(NY)	895
Reference local history	GOLDENKOFF, Isabel M.	(NY)	445
Regional history	GRAHAM, Robert W.	(IL)	456
	MUTSCHLER, Charles V.	(WA)	883
Regional history, genealogy	PROPER, David R.	(MA)	995
Religion & ancient history databases	FRAZER, Ruth F.	(FL)	399

HISTORY (Cont'd)

Specialty	Name	State	No.
Renaissance & Reformation history	REITH, Louis J.	(DC)	1022
Research & writing American history	SCHEIPS, Paul J.	(MD)	1091
Research architectural history	ROARK, Carol E.	(TX)	1038
Research in local history	CREAMER, Mary M.	(KY)	257
Research in theatre history	DONOHUE, Joseph	(MA)	312
Researching history of recording	PENGELLY, Joe	(ENG)	956
Researching piano history & technology	RICHARDS, James H.	(TX)	1028
Researching reed organ history	RICHARDS, James H.	(TX)	1028
Russian history	YERBURGH, Mark R.	(VT)	1379
Russian history, revolutionary period	ST. AUBIN, Arleen K.	(MA)	1075
Russian library history	STUART, Mary P.	(IL)	1204
St Paul history	HLAVSA, Larry B.	(MN)	544
Science & history bibliography	LEE, J S.	(NJ)	710
Science fiction alternative histories	COLLINS, William J.	(CA)	233
Science fiction history	COLLINS, William J.	(CA)	233
Selection in history & political science	WRIGHT, Joanna S.	(IL)	1371
Shaker history	CHRISTENSON, Donald E.	(OH)	211
Sisters of Mercy bibliography & history	MULDREY, Mary H.	(LA)	876
Social history archives	COOK, Terry G.	(ON)	240
Social science, history, education	NELSON, Michael L.	(WY)	894
Social sciences & history bibliography	BROWN, Philip L.	(SD)	146
Social work & history	CAGLE, Robert B.	(LA)	171
Sound recording history & technology	KLINGER, William E.	(OH)	661
South Carolina history	SALMON, Robin R.	(SC)	1077
South Texas history	MITTELSTAEDT, Gerard E.	(TX)	850
Southern library history	CARMICHAEL, James V.	(NC)	183
Southern Lutheran history	FRITZ, William R.	(SC)	405
Southwest history reference services	D'ANTONIO, Lynn M.	(AZ)	274
Soviet film history	DAY, Martha T.	(VT)	282
Speaking on local history	NELSON, Maggie E.	(IL)	894
Sports history	GIETSCHIER, Steven P.	(MO)	433
State & local history	SCHMIDT, Jean M.	(LA)	1095
	CURTIS, Peter H.	(MD)	267
State & local history research	OAKES, Patricia A.	(AK)	913
State & regnl literature & history bibl	RAZER, Robert L.	(AR)	1012
Steam history & technology	ARNOLD, Nancy K.	(PA)	34
Swedish-American history	JOHNSON, Timothy J.	(IL)	609
Teaching music history	SMILEY, Marilynn J.	(NY)	1151
Tennessee history	COTHAM, James S.	(TN)	249
Texas & Northeastern Mexico history	GAUSE, George R.	(TX)	423
Texas history & genealogy	SMITH, Michael K.	(TX)	1158
Theatre history	OGDEN, Dunbar H.	(CA)	918
	LENTHALL, Franklyn	(ME)	715
	WALLIN, Cornelia B.	(NH)	1298
	MYERS, Maria P.	(NY)	884
	TAYLOR, Robert N.	(NY)	1228
	WILMETH, Don B.	(RI)	1349
Theater history & bibliography	HECK, Thomas F.	(OH)	519
Town, township, county history	CARTER, Susan M.	(IN)	190
Transportation history of California	HANEL, Mary A.	(CA)	495
Tribal history & culture	HENDRICKS, Thom	(ND)	527
20th century American history	BARTHELL, Daniel W.	(DC)	61
United States & women's history	GALLOWAY, Sue	(CA)	415
United States Civil War history	CAHILL, Colleen R.	(PA)	171
US history	DALY, John E.	(IL)	271
	KENDALL, John D.	(MA)	640
	POHL, Gunther E.	(NY)	979
	SMITH, Michael K.	(TX)	1158
	SHERMAN, Madeline R.	(VT)	1128
US history bibliography	RHODES, Saralinda A.	(KS)	1026
US public library history	HECK-RABI, Louise E.	(MI)	520
United States Western mining history	MC CAULEY, Philip F.	(SD)	795
United States women's history	MOSELEY, Eva S.	(MA)	870
Urban history	DALY, John E.	(IL)	271
Urban history, Boston	BERGEN, Philip S.	(MA)	85
Urban history documentation	KELLER, William B.	(DC)	636
Video & oral history archives	JAGOE, Katherine P.	(TX)	591
Western American Jewish history	ARONER, Miriam D.	(CA)	34
Western Jewish history	ABRAMS, Jeanne E.	(CO)	3
Western United States history	MC CAULEY, Philip F.	(SD)	795
Women's art history	FURTAK, Rosemary	(MN)	410
Women's history	MILLER, Janet	(IL)	838
	KRAFT, Katherine G.	(MA)	675
Women's history & nursing	PALMISANO-DRUCKER, Elsalyn	(NJ)	937
World history	OSWALT, Paul K.	(TX)	929

HISTORY (Cont'd)

Writer & history archives   NEWTON, Virginia A. . . .   (AK)   900
Writing & editing pictorial histories   LUSKEY, Judith . . . . (DC)   749
Writing history, federal communication AINES, Andrew A. . . . . .   (MD)   8
Writing institutional histories   CANTELON, Philip L. . . .   (MD)   179
Writing province history   STRECK, Helen T. . . . . .   (KS) 1201
Writing United Methodist history   ROLLER, Twila J. . . . . . . (NM) 1051
Wyoming history   CHISUM, Emmett D. . . . . . (WY)   209

HOLIDAYS

Customs, folklore, etiquette, holidays HAWK, Susan P. . . . . . .   (FL)   513
Storytelling, poetry, holiday themes   BAUER, Caroline F. . . . .   (CA)   65

HOLISTIC

Holistic libraries   HEISTER, Carla G. . . . . . (IL)   523

HOLLYWOOD

Writing, Hollywood costumes   NELSON-HARB, Sally R.   (CA)   895

HOLMES

Sherlock Holmes   AKE, Mary W. . . . . (CO)   9

HOLOCAUST

Christian holocaust scholar   CARGAS, Harry J. . . . . .   (MO)   181
Holocaust   STEINBERG, Eileen . . . .   (PA) 1185
Holocaust bibliographer   HEUMAN, Rabbi F. . . . .   (NY)   535
Holocaust education   KLEINBURD, Freda . . . .   (NY)   659
Holocaust studies   GUREWITSCH, Bonnie . (NY)   478

HOLOGRAPHIC

Manuscripts & holographic documents LEVITT, Martin L. . . . . . . (PA)   721

HOME (See also Shut-Ins)

Employee benefits, home resource
  mgmt   JACQUES, Donna M. . . .   (MA)   591
Home economics   RONNERMANN, Gail . . .   (NY) 1053
Home economics & human ecology   MACKEY, Neosha A. . . .   (MO)   756
Home economics reference   GAGE, Marilyn K. . . . . .   (OK)   412
Home economics subject
  specialization   SANDERS, Nancy P. . . .   (OH) 1080
Home economy   MILLER, Sylvia G. . . . . . (NC)   843
Home electronics literature   FETTERMAN, Nelma I. . .   (AB)   374
Home services for the handicapped   UTSUNOMIYA, Leslie D.   (BC) 1270
Home video retailing   WHITE, Matthew H. . . . .   (IL) 1331
Homebound services   WRIGHT, Linda D. . . . . .   (NC) 1372
Nursing home library   RING, Anne M. . . . . (IL) 1035
Outreach for handicapped &
  homebound   BRYANT, Judith W. . . . .   (NJ)   152
Services to homebound   RYAN, Audrey H. . . . . . . (FL) 1070

HORMONE

Biochemistry, steroid hormone
  receptors   MCFARLAND, Robert T.   (MO)   805

HOROLOGY

Horology   SUMMAR, Donald J. . . .   (PA) 1209

HORTICULTURE (See also Plants)

Botany & horticulture   LANE, David M. . . . . . .   (NH)   694
Herbal & horticultural information   CHADWICK, Alena F. . .   (MA)   196
Horticultural information   LAND, Barbara J. . . . . . . (CA)   692
Horticultural reference   TEETER, Enola J. . . . . .   (PA) 1229
Horticulture   GIGNAC, Solange G. . . .   (CO)   433
                                        MILLER, Heather S. . . . .   (NY)   838
Horticulture books   CROTZ, D K. . . . .   (IL)   261
Horticulture libraries   DEFATO, Joan . . . . (CA)   287
Medicine & horticulture indexing   LINDHEIMER, Elinor . . . . (CA)   729

HOSPITAL (See also Institutions, Medical)

Administration in hospital libraries   MALMGREN, Terri L. . . .   (CA)   763
Archivist for hospital   KILPATRICK, Barbara A.   (TN)   648
Establishing hospital libraries   CARLSON, Stan W. . . . .   (MN)   182
Health care & hospitals online
  searching   CLINTON, Janet C. . . . .   (PA)   222
Hospital administration   TOVREA, Roxanna L. . . .   (IA) 1252
                                        LARKIN, Virgil C. . . . . . (NY)   698
                                        CREELAN, Marilee M. . .   (OH)   257
                                        PIPER, Paula . . . . (PA)   975
                                        KAKOSCHKE, Mona S. .   (ON)   622
Hospital administration databases   MAHOVLIC, Leanne M. .   (OH)   761
Hospital administration reference   SCHULTZ, Therese A. . . .   (IL) 1102
Hospital administration resources   BRETSCHER, Susan M. .   (NY)   134
Hospital & clinical management
  subjects   BELT, Jane . . . . (WA)   78
Hospital & health care law   MULCAHY, Brian J. . . . .   (NY)   876
Hospital & health science libraries   CAMACHO, Nancy S. . . .   (TX)   174
Hospital & medical library consulting   BLADEN, Marguerite . . . . (CA)   102
Hospital & medical school   LANDWIRTH, Trudy K. .   (IL)   694
Hospital consultation   SZCZCPANIAK, Adam S.   (MD) 1218
Hospital consulting   KETCHELL, Debra S. . . .   (WA)   645
Hospital design & collection
  development   TOMLIN, Marsha A. . . . .   (OH) 1250
Hospital ethics   FINNERTY, James L. . . . .   (IL)   379
Hospital information system   HOYT, Lester H. . . . . . .   (IN)   566
Hospital information systems   ANDERSON, Marilyn M. .   (IN)   24
                                        BUCHANAN, Holly S. . . . .   (KY)   153
                                        LATHROP, Irene M. . . . . .   (RI)   701
Hospital librarianship   JAJKO, Pamela J. . . . . . . (CA)   592
                                        ZAREMSKA, Maryann . . . .   (CA) 1386
                                        AMBROSE, Karen S. . . . .   (IL)   19
                                        DALE, Nancy . . . . (IL)   270
                                        KALUZSA, Karen L. . . . .   (IL)   623
                                        SWATOS, Priscilla L. . . . . (IL) 1214
                                        SLOCUM, Ann L. . . . . . .   (NY) 1150
                                        BENISHEK, Kristine K. . .   (OH)   81
                                        ROBINSON, Elizabeth A.   (OH) 1044
                                        TESMER, Nancy . . . . . .   (OH) 1233
                                        DONOVAN, James M. . .   (OK)   312
Hospital libraries   COOK, Mickey . . . . (DC)   240
                                        RANKIN, Jocelyn A. . . . .   (GA) 1007
                                        GRAVES, Karen J. . . . . . . (IL)   459
                                        BRADLEY, Johanna . . . .   (IN)   126
                                        SALTZMAN, E J. . . . . . .   (IN) 1077
                                        MARIX, Mary L. . . . . (LA)   770
                                        WARD, Nancy E. . . . . . .   (MI) 1304
                                        CRABTREE, Anna B. . . . .   (MO)   254
                                        COBB, Margaret L. . . . . .   (NC)   225
                                        SIBLEY, Shawn C. . . . . .   (NC) 1135
                                        TIERNAN, Linda M. . . . . .   (NH) 1244
                                        CONNICK, Kathleen D. . .   (NJ)   237
                                        SHELSTAD, Kirsten R. . .   (NM) 1126
                                        PACKARD, Joan L. . . . . .   (NY)   933
                                        RANSOM, Christina R. . .   (NY) 1007
                                        TAYLOR, Rosemarie K. . .   (PA) 1228
                                        GILDEA, Ruthann . . . . . .   (RI)   434
                                        ODDAN, Linda . . . . (WI)   916
                                        WALUZYNIEC, Hanna . . . .   (PQ) 1302
                                        CHUO, Josephine Y. . . . .   (TAI)   213
Hospital libraries administration   O'CONNOR, Elizabeth W.   (NJ)   916
Hospital libraries consulting   POLAND, Ursula H. . . . . . (NY)   980
Hospital library   WRIGLEY, Kathryn J. . . . . (IL) 1373
                                        MACKO, Lucinda M. . . . .   (IN)   757
Hospital library administration   STRUB, Jeane E. . . . . . . (NM) 1203
                                        WALLER, Carolyn A. . . . .   (RI) 1298
                                        TAYLOR, Margaret P. . . . . (ON) 1227
Hospital library administration & mgmt WALES, Patricia L. . . . . . (CT) 1294
Hospital library automation   LECOMPTE, Louis L. . . . .   (PQ)   708
Hospital library building   LECOMPTE, Louis L. . . . .   (PQ)   708
Hospital library consultation   DALTON, Richard R. . . . .   (MO)   271
                                        BUTSON, Linda C. . . . . .   (NC)   167
Hospital library consulting   BENELISHA, Eleanor . . . .   (CA)   80
                                        AMBROSE, Karen S. . . . .   (IL)   19
                                        O'BRIEN, Marjorie S. . . . . (MA)   914
                                        GREATHOUSE, Brenda J.   (WV)   461
Hospital library development   CRAIG, James P. . . . . . .   (FL)   254
                                        BARTEN, Sharon S. . . . .   (NY)   60
                                        WILSON, Fred L. . . . . (PA) 1351
                                        WARD, Deborah H. . . . . .   (TX) 1303

HOSPITAL (Cont'd)

Hospital library functions	SOBKOWIAK, Emily J. . .	(IL)	1165
Hospital library management	BENELISHA, Eleanor . . .	(CA)	80
	KELLY, Janice E.	(IL)	637
	BUCHANAN, Holly S. . . .	(KY)	153
	CAFFAREL, Agnes	(LA)	170
	HIGGINBOTHAM, Cecelia B.	(LA)	537
	FREDENBURG, Anne M.	(MD)	399
	LONG, Susan S.	(MT)	740
	MILLER, Nancy H.	(NC)	841
	BABISH, Jo A.	(PA)	43
	SCARPATO, Loann C. . .	(PA)	1088
	JARVIS, Mary E.	(TX)	595
	LEE, Regina H.	(TX)	711
	CAMPBELL, Mary E. . . .	(WA)	177
Hospital literature	MONROE, Donald H. . . .	(IN)	855
	GALVIN, Jeanne D.	(NY)	415
Hospital outreach	SCHNEIDER, Marcia G. .	(CA)	1097
Hospital outreach services to children	WALSH, Mary A.	(PQ)	1300
Hospital patient librarianship	MC LAIN, Swan M.	(GA)	813
Hospital reference	NESBITT, Olive K.	(PA)	896
Hospital statistics	RICHARDSON, Alice W. .	(PA)	1029
Managing small hospital libraries	KRATZ, Gale G.	(CA)	676
Medical & hospital libraries	STEPHENS, Diana C. . .	(HI)	1188
	SPIEGEL, Nancy C. . . .	(ME)	1174
	MUDLOFF, Cherrie M. . .	(MI)	875
Medical, hospital libraries	PETIT, J M.	(OH)	965
Medical, hospital reference	STRAUSS, Carol D.	(IL)	1201
One-person hospital medical libraries	SHELDON, Marie A. . . .	(NY)	1126
Special library hospital settings	GROSS, Elinor L.	(NY)	472
Substitute hospital librarian	ROBINSON, Betty J. . . .	(CA)	1043
Two-person community hospital library	WILLOUGHBY, Nona C. .	(NY)	1349

HOSPITALITY

Hospitality industry	SMYTH, Mary B.	(CA)	1162
Hospitality industry culinary research	JOHNSON, Sheila A. . . .	(NY)	609
Hospitality industry information	LAURENCE, Katherine S.	(NY)	703

HOUSING

Housing	MARTINEZ, Barbara A. .	(CA)	779

HUMAN (See also Interpersonal)

Education, psychology, human development	HENEBRY, Carolyn L. . .	(TX)	528
Expert systems & human cognition	HARMON, Glynn	(TX)	502
Health & human services	MAZUR, Ronald M.	(MA)	791
Home economics & human ecology	MACKEY, Neosha A. . . .	(MO)	756
Human factors	NORMORE, Lorraine F. .	(OH)	909
	DEBONS, Anthony	(PA)	285
Human factors, ergonomics	TOROK, Andrew G.	(IL)	1251
Human factors in computer systems	CHERRY, Joan M.	(ON)	206
Human factors user interface	MCALLISTER, Caryl K. .	(WI)	792
Human interaction with computers	MARTIN, Thomas H. . . .	(NY)	778
Human relations	MISSAVAGE, Leonard . .	(FL)	848
	SUMMERFORD, Steven L.	(NC)	1209
Human relations skill development	LENOX, Mary F.	(MO)	715
Human resource development	CARROLL VIRGO, Julie .	(IL)	187
	BLASINGAME, Ralph . . .	(NJ)	104
Human resource management	SWEENEY, June D.	(DC)	1215
	RIDDLE, Raymond E. . . .	(KS)	1032
	PINDER, Jo A.	(MD)	974
	WEBB, Gisela M.	(TX)	1313
	WILKINSON, John P. . . .	(ON)	1340
Human resources	BOSTON, Mary T.	(CO)	118
	BRYANT, Nancy J.	(GA)	152
	CRANE, John G.	(NH)	255
	FULMER, Dina J.	(PA)	409
Human resources & labor relations	HARE, Judith E.	(ON)	501
Human resources development	SHERMAN, Mary A. . . .	(OK)	1128
Human resources in library services	SAVARD, Rejean	(PQ)	1085
Human resources management	COFFMAN, M H.	(MA)	227
	MEADOWS, Donald F. . .	(BC)	819
Human resources research	BRUNER, Robert B.	(CO)	150
Human rights implementation	KLOK, Buddhi	(PQ)	662
Human sexuality	WHITBY, Thomas J.	(CO)	1330

HUMAN (Cont'd)

Human system language interface	WEI, Yin M.	(OH)	1316
Humanistic psychology archivist	GRAZIANO, Eugene	(CA)	460
Information for world peace & humanity	KIANG, C K.	(IN)	646
International human rights law	PERKINS, Steven C. . . .	(CA)	959
Reference, veterinary & human medicine	VEENSTRA, Robert J. . .	(AL)	1281
Staff development & human relations	MIAH, Abdul J.	(VA)	831
Staff development, human relationships	SMITH, Robert F.	(TN)	1160

HUMAN-COMPUTER

Human-computer communications	MEADOW, Charles T. . .	(ON)	819
Human-computer interaction	KASKE, Neal K.	(AL)	628
	CHERRY, Joan M.	(ON)	206
Human-computer interface	DITO, William R.	(CA)	305
	ROMALEWSKI, Robert S.	(LA)	1052

HUMANITIES (See also Arts)

Art, law, humanities	KLEIN, Ilene R.	(MD)	659
Arts & humanities	HOPKINS, Richard L. . .	(BC)	558
Arts & humanities adult programming	SMOTHERS, Joyce W. . .	(NJ)	1162
Arts & humanities collection development	MESSINEO, Leonard L. .	(KS)	828
Arts & humanities database marketing	ZAJDEL, George J.	(PA)	1385
Arts & humanities programming	GANN, Daniel H.	(IN)	416
Arts & humanities reference	GRILIKHES, Sandra B. . .	(PA)	470
Arts & humanities research & development	PIERCE, Mildred L.	(NV)	971
Arts, humanities & social sciences	LOMBARDI, Mary L. . . .	(CA)	738
Back-of-book humanities indexes	HUMEZ, Nicholas D. . . .	(ME)	573
Bibliography, social scis & humanities	PARROTT, Margaret S. .	(NC)	944
Bookman, humanities	LANDINGHAM, Alpha M.	(TX)	692
Business & humanities reference	GROVES, Helen G.	(TX)	474
Business, education, humanities	WILLIAMS, Robert C. . . .	(AK)	1346
Collection development for humanities	CULLARS, John M.	(IL)	263
Database management in humanities	CRAWFORD, David E. . .	(MI)	256
Databases in social science & humanities	PRICE, Susan W.	(NY)	992
Displays for humanities	CLOHESSY, Antoinette M.	(CO)	223
Education & humanities databases	MCKEE, Elizabeth C. . . .	(AR)	810
General & humanities reference	SANDERS, Lou H.	(MS)	1080
	DEDONATO, Ree	(NY)	286
General business, marketing & humanities	BAUGH, L S.	(IL)	65
Health & humanities sciences reference	CHASE, Judith H.	(OR)	203
History & humanities	BLOUIN, Francis X.	(MI)	107
History, humanities, women's studies	FALK, Joyce D.	(CA)	362
Humanities	ADAMS, Judith A.	(AL)	5
	SELTH, Jefferson P.	(CA)	1114
	BERGER, Marianne C. . .	(IL)	85
	DAVIS, Sandra B.	(IL)	281
	LARSEN, John C.	(IL)	698
	WIBERLEY, Stephen E. .	(IL)	1335
	MOON, Elizabeth A.	(IN)	857
	BRUMM, Gordon L.	(MA)	150
	ISAACSON, David K. . . .	(MI)	584
	IMMLER, Frank	(MN)	582
	LEVINE, Cynthia R.	(NC)	720
	PERLUNGHER, Richard A.	(NH)	959
	O'NEILL, Philip M.	(PA)	924
	MARSH, Corrie V.	(RI)	773
	GOODWIN, Willard	(TX)	450
	HARNSBERGER, R S. . .	(TX)	503
	SCAMMAN, Carol J. . . .	(TX)	1087
	ZUK, Donna R.	(AB)	1391
Humanities acquisition	HOWARD-HILL, Trevor .	(SC)	564
Humanities & archives indexing	MOODY, Suzanna	(MN)	857
Humanities & fine arts reference	COHN, Alan M.	(IL)	229
Humanities & general reference	COSSEY, M E.	(KY)	249
Humanities & gerontology	YAHNKE, Robert E. . . .	(MN)	1376
Humanities & history	HOLT, Lisa A.	(NY)	554
Humanities & philosophy bibliography	HANNAFORD, William E.	(PA)	496
Humanities & social science bibliography	ROTHACKER, John M. .	(TN)	1059

HUMANITIES (Cont'd)

Humanities & social science databases	TAKAHASHI, Annabelle T.	(HI)	1220
Humanities & social science reference	LO, Henrietta W.	(CA)	735
	TAKAHASHI, Annabelle T.	(HI)	1220
	HOLLEY, E J.	(SC)	551
	MACLENNAN, Oriel C.	(NS)	757
Humanities & social scis bibliography	MCELROY, Neil J.	(CA)	804
	MENZEL, John P.	(NJ)	825
Humanities & social sciences cols	EDWARDS, Willie M.	(MI)	338
Humanities & social sciences databases	STORM, Jill	(DC)	1198
Humanities & social sciences reference	JOHNSON, Diane D.	(CA)	603
	ECKWRIGHT, Gail Z.	(ID)	335
Humanities bibliography	GATES, Jean K.	(FL)	422
	COUTTS, Brian E.	(KY)	252
	MCCALLISTER, Myrna J.	(ME)	793
	GARGAN, William M.	(NY)	419
	HENRY, Mary K.	(NY)	529
Humanities collection development	MILLER, Randy S.	(IL)	841
	NEWMAN, Gerald L.	(IL)	899
	HARNER, James L.	(OH)	503
	HEINZKILL, J R.	(OR)	522
	TOBIN, R J.	(WI)	1247
	MACDONALD, Patricia A.	(ON)	754
Humanities computing	ERDT, Terrence	(PA)	352
Humanities databases	BLEILER, Richard J.	(AL)	105
	BARRETT, Darryl D.	(MN)	59
	WIENER, Alissa L.	(MN)	1336
	CROSS, Roberta A.	(NJ)	261
	GARDNER, Sue A.	(NJ)	418
	DEDONATO, Ree	(NY)	286
	MACKESY, Eileen M.	(NY)	756
	BIANCHINI, Lucian	(NS)	94
Humanities development	COOPER, David J.	(MD)	242
Humanities literature	BROADUS, Robert N.	(NC)	138
Humanities materials	ROSENBERG, Melvin H.	(CA)	1056
Humanities online databases	MACEWAN, Bonnie J.	(MO)	755
	LEWIS, Linda K.	(NM)	723
Humanities programming	PALMER, Virginia E.	(OH)	937
	BENDER, Evelyn	(PA)	79
Humanities reference	BLEILER, Richard J.	(AL)	105
	CURRY, Janette M.	(AL)	266
	OLSRUD, Lois C.	(AZ)	923
	HERZIG, Stella J.	(CA)	534
	COLLIER, Bonnie	(CT)	232
	MILLER, Margaret R.	(FL)	840
	PALMER, Carole L.	(IL)	936
	TUCKER, John M.	(IN)	1261
	LANDRY, Francis R.	(MA)	693
	KAHN, Leslie A.	(NJ)	622
	MONTGOMERY, Michael S.	(NJ)	856
	DUNLAP, Barbara J.	(NY)	326
	WALL, Richard L.	(NY)	1297
	BRYANT, James M.	(TX)	152
	LIKNESS, Craig S.	(TX)	727
	SMITH, Charles R.	(TX)	1153
	ONN, Shirley A.	(AB)	924
Humanities reference & bibliography	BYRE, Calvin S.	(IL)	169
	CUDD, John M.	(KY)	263
	FISHER, Kim N.	(PA)	381
Humanities ref, collection development	NOURIE, Alan R.	(IL)	910
Humanities reference librarian	POLIT, Carlos E.	(IN)	980
Humanities research	JOY, Patricia L.	(CT)	618
	STIELOW, Frederick J.	(MD)	1194
Humanities research & bibliography	DWOSKIN, Beth M.	(MI)	330
Humanities research, literature	TIBBO, Helen R.	(MD)	1244
Humanities resources	MARCHAND, Janet H.	(CT)	768
Humanities selection	VOLAT-SHAPIRO, Helene M.	(NY)	1287
Humanities, social science reference	REIK, Constance	(NH)	1020
Humanities sources & services	WINCKLER, Paul A.	(NY)	1354
Literature of the humanities	LAIR, Nancy C.	(IN)	688
	OAKLEY, Adeline D.	(MA)	913
	THOMPSON, Susan O.	(NY)	1241
	DE SCOSSA, Catriona	(AB)	295
Microcomputers in the humanities	GARDNER, Sue A.	(NJ)	418

HUMANITIES (Cont'd)

Reference & humanities	PEDERSOLI, Heleni M.	(AL)	954
Reference, arts & humanities	DIAL, Clarence M.	(AZ)	299
Ref, bibliography, humanities, soc scis	DAVIS, Donald G.	(TX)	278
Reference, general humanities	OLSON, Joann D.	(OH)	922
Reference, humanities	BLUM, Fred	(MI)	107
Reference, humanities & social sciences	ROUTH, Spencer	(AUS)	1061
Reference, humanities bibliography	KRAUSSE, Sylvia C.	(RI)	676
Reference, social science & humanities	WIZA, Judith M.	(KY)	1359
Reference, social sciences & humanities	MCCLEARY, William E.	(LA)	796
Religion & humanities databases	HILGERT, Elvire R.	(IL)	539
Research methods in humanities	COHN, Alan M.	(IL)	229
Social sci & humanities col development	DUPRE, Monique	(ON)	327
Social science & humanities librarians	HUPP, Stephen L.	(MI)	577
Social science & humanities reference	BILAL, Dania M.	(FL)	96
	PATTON, Linda L.	(FL)	949
	WESTON, E P.	(IL)	1327
Social sciences & humanities	WINTER, Michael F.	(CA)	1356
	OTA, Leslie H.	(NJ)	930
	PENCHANSKY, Mimi B.	(NY)	956
	ANDERSON, Madeleine J.	(TX)	24
Social sciences & humanities databases	COCHRANE, Kerry L.	(IL)	225
Social sciences & humanities reference	COCHRANE, Kerry L.	(IL)	225
	TURLEY, Harriet M.	(NY)	1264
	TOLBERT, Jean F.	(TX)	1248
	ST. JACQUES, Suzanne L.	(ON)	1075
Social sciences, humanities & computers	WOGGON, Michele	(CA)	1359
Western European humanities	DILLON, John B.	(WI)	303

HUMOR

Humor	GINSBURG, Joanne R.	(NY)	438
Library humor	STEVENS, Norman D.	(CT)	1190
	HOLE, Carol C.	(FL)	550

HUNGER

Research on world hunger	KASPERSON, Jeanne X.	(MA)	629

HUNTING

Hunting & fishing	FOERSTER, Trey	(WI)	387

HYDROGEOLOGY

Hydrogeology	GRIFFITTS, Joan K.	(IN)	469

HYDROLOGY

Water resources & hydrology	HANSON, Donna M.	(ID)	498

HYGIENE (See also Health)

Alcoholism, Mental hygiene	GILSON, Robert	(NY)	437
Industrial hygiene	WEINRICH, Gloria	(NY)	1318
Industrial hygiene information	TUCKER, Mary E.	(NC)	1262

HYMN

Hymn tune indexing	TEMPERLEY, Nicholas	(IL)	1230
Hymnology	ZEAGER, Lloyd	(PA)	1387

IAIMS

IAIMS	BUTTER, Karen A.	(MD)	167
	LUCIER, Richard E.	(MD)	746

IBERIA

Ibero-American area studies	BROW, Ellen H.	(MA)	141
Latin America & Iberia	KAHLER, Mary E.	(DC)	622

IBM
IBM automation system	ROBERSON, Janis L.	(TX)	1039
IBM Documentation of SLSS	KEALEY, Catherine M.	(ON)	632
IBM-PC microcomputers & software	COLE, David H.	(MN)	230
IBM-PC/XT network coordination	LYDEN, Edward W.	(TX)	750
Microcomputer support IBM PC	DEEMER, Selden S.	(GA)	286

ICONOGRAPHY
Iconography	JORDAN, Louis E.	(IN)	616
Musical iconography	BOWLES, Edmund A.	(NY)	121

IDENTIFICATION
Automatic identification systems	PAVELY, Richard W.	(NJ)	950
Information identification	BELZER, Jack	(FL)	78
Market identification	LAMBERT, Shirley A.	(CO)	690
Translations identification	HIMMELSBACH, Carl J.	(MA)	542

ILLITERATES (See also Literacy)
Services to illiterates	ABOYADE, Beatrice O.	(NGR)	2

ILLNESS (See also Health)
Historiography of mental illness	EVANS, Josephine K.	(FL)	357
Mentally ill library programming	VAN DER VOORN, Neal P.	(WA)	1274

ILLUSTRATION
Book illustration techniques	DONAHUE, Katharine E.	(CA)	310
Children's book illustration	OLDERSHAW, Anne	(NY)	920
Children's illustrators	RIFE, Mary C.	(MI)	1033
Early illustrated books & bindings	WITTEN, Laurence	(CT)	1358
Fine arts book illustration	BANTA, Gratia J.	(OH)	55
Illustration	DAVENPORT, Marilyn G.	(NV)	275

ILS
Training users of ILS, online catalog	PRESLAR, M G.	(TN)	991

IMAGES
Cataloging archival moving images	HARRISON, Harriet W.	(DC)	506
Digital image database	SHOREBIRD, Thomas S.	(DC)	1132
Digitize image manipulation software	BENGE, Bruce	(OK)	80
Image digitization	BESSER, Howard A.	(CA)	91
Image management	COATES, Paul F.	(KY)	224
Image processing	CALMES, Alan R.	(DC)	174
	THOMA, George R.	(MD)	1235
Image processing software	DAVISSON, Darell D.	(CA)	281
Imaging systems, electronic	GOUDELOCK, Carol V.	(CA)	454
Imaging technology	HILL, Kristin E.	(CA)	540
Information & image management	YODER, William M.	(VA)	1380
Micrographics & image quality	BAGG, Thomas C.	(MD)	45
Moving image documents	O'CONNOR, Brian C.	(CA)	915
Moving images archivist	DE ARMAN, Charles L.	(DC)	284

IMMIGRATION
Immigrant history	ASHKENAS, Bruce F.	(VA)	36
Immigration	RUBENS, Jane C.	(NY)	1064

IMMUNOGENETICS
Molecular biology immunogenetics	BERWICK, Mary C.	(PA)	91

IMMUNOLOGY
Information microbiology, immunology	PERLMAN, Stephen E.	(NY)	959

IMPAIRED (See also Blind, Disabled, Dyslexic, Handicapped)
Captioned media for the hearing impaired	MODICA, Mary L.	(SD)	851
Impaired elderly	RYAN, Audrey H.	(FL)	1070
Impaired older adult services	LEONARD, Gloria J.	(WA)	716
Service to visually impaired	POPP, Mary F.	(IN)	984

IMPRINTS (See also Publications)
Bibliography, imprints	PROPER, David R.	(MA)	995
18th century Williamsburg imprints	BERG, Susan	(VA)	85
Imprints	POWELL, Margaret S.	(OH)	988
Maine imprints to 1820	SKILLIN, Glenn B.	(PA)	1146

INCOME
Low income, minority services	PALMER, Julia R.	(NY)	936
Real-time fixed income research	MILLS, Andrew G.	(MA)	843

INCUNABULA
Fine printing & incunabula	MENTHE, Melissa	(NJ)	825
Incunabula, watermarks	KRAKAUER, Elizabeth	(CA)	675

INDEPENDENT (See also Freelance)
Adult independent learners	MCGRIFF, Mary E.	(NC)	808
Independent consulting	SARRIS, Shirley C.	(NY)	1083
Independent filmmaking	DAVENPORT, Thomas R.	(VA)	276
Independent living for disabled	ELLIS, Kathy M.	(BC)	344
Independent school librarianship	SANDERS, Jacqueline C.	(MD)	1080
Independent school libraries	SANTINGA, Reda A.	(MI)	1082
	MATTHEWS, Stephen L.	(VA)	786
Independent secondary school librarian	REARDON, Elizabeth M.	(TN)	1013
Independent telephone operations	KAPLAN, Rosalyn L.	(IL)	626
Mgmt of independent research libraries	MCCORISON, Marcus A.	(MA)	798

INDEXES
Automated union catalogs & indexes	JAGOE, Katherine P.	(TX)	591
Back-of-book humanities indexes	HUMEZ, Nicholas D.	(ME)	573
Back-of-the-book indexes	HALLER, Robin M.	(CO)	489
Cumulating psychoanalytic indexes	KLUMPNER, George H.	(IL)	663
Developing psychoanalytic indexes	KLUMPNER, George H.	(IL)	663
Editing completed indexes	BERNAL, Rose M.	(NY)	88
Editing indexes	BLOZIS, Jolene M.	(DC)	107
	ASTON, Jennefer	(IRE)	37
Indexes	BAUGH, L S.	(IL)	65
	KOLLIN, Richard P.	(PA)	669
	PIETZAK, Stephen D.	(PA)	972
Journal indexes & bibliographies	KAHN, Paul J.	(CA)	622
Medical indexes	TOPP, Marvalyn G.	(IL)	1251
Newspaper indexes	BURROWS, Sandra	(ON)	163
Newspapers, indexes	DAZE, Colleen J.	(NY)	283
Preparing indexes & legal reference	HOYT, Henry M.	(NY)	566
Publication, quarterly & annual indexes	SIVE, Mary R.	(CT)	1144
Publishing indexes	FAST, Louise	(ON)	366
Typecoding of indexes	GARCIA, Kathleen J.	(NY)	417

INDEXING (See also Cross-Referencing, Keywording)
Abstract & indexing services	WERLING, Anita L.	(MI)	1324
Abstracting & indexing	GATLING, James L.	(AL)	422
	SPIGAI, Fran	(CA)	1174
	ALSOP, Robyn J.	(CO)	18
	LUEVANE, Marsha A.	(CO)	747
	KASCUS, Marie A.	(CT)	628
	FRAULINO, Philip S.	(DC)	399
	THURONYI, Geza T.	(DC)	1243
	HALASZ, Marilynn J.	(IL)	484
	VALAUSKAS, Edward J.	(IL)	1271
	HENSON, Jane E.	(IN)	529
	JAMES, Bonnie B.	(KY)	592
	BOYCE, Bert R.	(LA)	122
	TETTEH, Joseph A.	(LA)	1233
	BATES, Ruthann I.	(MD)	64
	GENUARDI, Michael T.	(MD)	427
	WALL, Eugene	(MD)	1297
	MAXWELL, Bonnie J.	(MI)	788
	SMITH, Catherine A.	(MI)	1153
	AMIRZAFARI, Jamileh A.	(NJ)	20
	HOGAN, Thomas H.	(NJ)	549
	MANY, Florence L.	(NJ)	767
	OLSON, Lucie M.	(NJ)	923
	HLAVA, Marjorie M.	(NM)	544

INDEXING (Cont'd)

Abstracting & indexing

BIDDEN, Julia E.	(NY)	94
BRISFJORD, Inez S.	(NY)	136
COCHRANE, Pauline A.	(NY)	226
GOODSELL, Joan W.	(NY)	450
MINOR, Barbara B.	(NY)	846
MUTTER, Letitia N.	(NY)	883
PISTILLI, Susan A.	(NY)	976
SPERR BRISFJORD, Inez L.	(NY)	1173
WINDSOR, Donald A.	(NY)	1354
WOODS, Lawrence J.	(NY)	1367
COPENHAVER, Ida L.	(OH)	244
SHELLENBERGER, Dawn M.	(PA)	1126
CHOI, Jin M.	(SC)	210
BURT, Eugene C.	(TX)	164
BRZUSTOWICZ, Richard J.	(WA)	152
BERTRAND-GASTALDY, Suzanne	(PQ)	91
GAULIN, S D.	(PQ)	422
LUSSIER, Richard	(PQ)	749
PELLETIER, Rosaire	(PQ)	955
SATYANARAYANA, Vadhri V.	(IND)	1084
AFOLAYAN, Matthew A.	(NGR)	7

Abstracting & indexing databases	GOLDENBERG, Joan M.	(VA)	445
Abstracting & indexing service	LAWRENCE, Philip D.	(VA)	704
Abstracting & indexing services	MARCACCIO, Kathleen Y.	(MI)	768
	DENIGER, Constant	(PQ)	292
	AGRAWAL, Surendra P.	(IND)	7
Abstracting & indexing technical data	HOWARD, Susanna J.	(NC)	564
Abstracting, indexing	HALPERN, Marilyn	(NJ)	489
Abstracting, indexing & cataloging	HART, Patricia H.	(MI)	507
Abstracting, indexing, bibliography	OREJANA, Rebecca D.	(PHP)	925
Abstracting, indexing, editing	HYSLOP, Marjorie R.	(OH)	580
Aeronautical indexing	LEVIN, Amy E.	(DC)	720
Alcohol studies indexing	WEGLARZ, Catherine R.	(NJ)	1316
American folklife indexing	OLSON, Eric J.	(NC)	922
Archival indexing systems	GORDON, Martin K.	(VA)	451
Archives & indexing	SIARNY, William D.	(IL)	1134
Arkansas periodical index	MCKEE, Elizabeth C.	(AR)	810
Arranging, describing, indexing	BUSAM, Emma C.	(KY)	164
Art & architectural indexing	ROBERTSON, Jack	(MD)	1042
Automated indexing	ZBORAY, Ronald J.	(CA)	1386
Automated indexing & retrieval	MATLOCK, Teresa A.	(TX)	784
Automated systems & indexing	TAYLOR, James B.	(WA)	1227
Automatic document indexing	SPANGLER, Bruce	(CO)	1171
Automatic indexing	GENUARDI, Michael T.	(MD)	427
	DILLON, Martin	(OH)	303
	VON KEITZ, Wolfgang	(WGR)	288
Automatic indexing & classification	RAGHAVAN, Vijay V.	(LA)	1003
Automatic indexing system	VLEDUTS-STOKOLOV, Natalia	(PA)	1286
Automatic indexing, system design	VLADUTZ, George E.	(PA)	1286
Back-of-book indexing	NEUMANN, Mary G.	(IN)	897
	WIDLUND, Harriet L.	(PA)	1336
Back-of-the-book indexing	PANGALLO, Karen L.	(MA)	938
	DUREN, Norman	(TX)	328
Bibliographies & indexing	EVANS, Stephen P.	(OH)	358
Bibliography, abstracting, indexing	FALK, Joyce D.	(CA)	362
Bibliography & indexing	STIRLING, Dale A.	(WA)	1195
Bibliography indexing	BRIERE, Jean M.	(ON)	135
Biomedical indexing & abstracting	JOHNSON, Hilary C.	(DE)	605
Biomedical literature research, indexing	COMPTON, Joan C.	(CA)	235
Book & magazine indexing	BRADWAY, Becky J.	(IL)	126
Book & periodical indexing	KOEHNLEIN, Bill	(NY)	667
Book indexing	PORPA, Edythe C.	(CO)	984
	SCHROEDER, Anne M.	(IL)	1100
	ABEND, Jody U.	(NY)	2
	LINZER, Elliot	(NY)	732
Brief bank indexing & abstracting	FRANKS, Janice	(AL)	398
Catalog, index & directory production	BUCKLAND, Lawrence F.	(MA)	154
Cataloging, abstracting & indexing	CAN, Hung V.	(PQ)	177

INDEXING (Cont'd)

Cataloging & indexing	LENSCHAU, Jane A.	(CA)	715
	SPRUNG, Lori L.	(CA)	1176
	CARROON, Robert G.	(CT)	187
	DALLET, Jane L.	(FL)	270
	GILBERT, Mattana	(MD)	433
	THOMAS, Sarah E.	(MD)	1238
	ANGUS, Jacqueline A.	(MN)	28
	CHELARIU, Ana R.	(NJ)	204
	BEHAR, Evelyn W.	(NY)	74
	GRAVLEE, Diane D.	(NY)	459
	MCDANIELS, Patricia R.	(OR)	801
	LANG, Anita E.	(TX)	695
	LANE, Barbara K.	(AB)	694
	TREMBLAY, Levis	(PQ)	1255
	TREVICK, Selma D.	(PQ)	1255
Cataloging & indexing books	GOLDBERG, Judy W.	(NY)	444
Cataloging & indexing photographs	GRAUE, Luz B.	(CA)	458
Chemical engineering indexing	WEAVER, James B.	(FL)	1312
Chemical indexing	PACETTI, Karen C.	(IL)	933
Classification & indexing	SVENONIUS, Elaine	(CA)	1212
Computer book indexing	GARCIA, Kathleen J.	(NY)	417
Computer database indexing	LEE, Lydia H.	(CA)	710
Computer indexing data management	SCHLICHTING, Catherine N.	(OH)	1094
Computer indexing systems	SEMONCHE, Barbara P.	(NC)	1115
Computer newspaper indexing	SEMONCHE, Barbara P.	(NC)	1115
Computer-aided indexing	AGEE, Victoria V.	(MD)	7
	BUCHAN, Ronald L.	(MD)	153
	SILVESTER, June P.	(MD)	1139
Computer-aided indexing for records	FROST, Debra R.	(CO)	406
Computer-assisted indexing	POFELSKI, David	(IL)	979
	SCHROEDER, Sandra J.	(IL)	1100
	QUINN, Sidney	(MD)	1000
	LINZER, Elliot	(NY)	732
	JOSLYN, Camille	(VA)	618
Computer-based indexing	FARLEY, Alfred E.	(KS)	364
	COLON, Carlos W.	(LA)	234
	LUDGIN, Donald H.	(ME)	746
Computer-generated newspaper indexing	BOLDRICK, Samuel J.	(FL)	112
Computerized indexing	GAUSE, George R.	(TX)	423
Computerized local newspaper indexing	KAGANN, Laurie K.	(IL)	621
Controlled vocabulary indexing	LINDER, Elliott	(NY)	729
Coordinating indexing services	BLOZIS, Jolene M.	(DC)	107
Database & book indexing	LYNCH, Jacqueline	(MA)	751
Database cataloging & indexing	CHARBONNEAU, Ronald P.	(CA)	202
	DUMLAO, Mercedes G.	(CA)	325
	HAMILTON, D A.	(IL)	491
	ZIMMERMAN, Brenda M.	(IN)	1388
	SPURLING, Norman K.	(MD)	1177
	ROLONTZ, Linda	(MN)	1051
	FIELDING, Carol J.	(WA)	376
Database design & indexing	FORKES, David	(ON)	390
Database development, indexing, reviews	WOODARD, Beth E.	(MI)	1365
Database indexing	PICKARD, Mary A.	(AL)	970
	STEVENS, Michael	(IL)	1190
	WISE, Matthew W.	(NY)	1357
	SHUPAK, Harris J.	(PA)	1134
Database indexing & maintenance	NEUWILLER, Charlene	(WGR)	897
Database production & indexing	SPENCER, John T.	(CA)	1173
Database systems, library indexing	FUNK, Carla J.	(IL)	409
Document indexing	ROSENTHAL, Marylu C.	(MA)	1057
	GRIMM, Ann C.	(MI)	470
Filing & indexing	MCKAY, Alberta S.	(NC)	809
Film cataloging & indexing	COVERT, Nadine	(NY)	252
Foreign affairs indexing	CARLSON, Julia F.	(DC)	182
General subject indexing	LINDHEIMER, Elinor	(CA)	729
Government info index & retrieval	MASSA, Paul P.	(MD)	781
Historical research, indexing & writing	DENNIS, Mary R.	(IA)	292
Humanities & archives indexing	MOODY, Suzanna	(MN)	857
Hymn tune indexing	TEMPERLEY, Nicholas	(IL)	1230
Index & abstract technical reports	CIBULSKIS, Elizabeth R.	(IL)	214
Index design & development	BOOTH, Barbara A.	(CA)	116
	MORSE, June E.	(VA)	869
Index development	DYER, Carolyn A.	(CT)	330
	LOCKETT, Cheryl L.	(PA)	736

INDEXING (Cont'd)

Index editing & bibliographies
Index memoranda
Index publications
Index systems
Indexer
Indexer, researcher, bibliographer
Indexing

PETERMAN, Claudia A. . . (CA) 962
CASSIDY, Joni L. . . . . . . (NJ) 193
LEINBACH, Anne E. . . . . (PA) 714
CLIFT, Scott B. . . . . . . (MA) 222
DAVIS, Margo . . . . (LA) 280
BELCHER, Emily M. . . . . (NJ) 76
GOODMAN, Anita S. . . . (AL) 449
SHANE, Charlotte J. . . . . (AR) 1120
CAMPBELL, Dierdre A. . (AZ) 176
CASE, Patricia J. . . . . . . (CA) 191
GRIFFIN, Michael D. . . . . (CA) 468
HAMBRIDGE, Sally L. . . (CA) 491
HORN, Judy K. . . . . (CA) 559
HOROWITZ, Roberta S. . (CA) 560
HUMPHREYS, Nancy K. . (CA) 574
JUNG, Soon J. . . . . (CA) 620
LEACH, Elizabeth A. . . . . (CA) 706
MICHAELS, Joan M. . . . . (CA) 832
MULVANY, Nancy . . . . . (CA) 878
NEWCOMBE, Barbara T. (CA) 898
PARKER, John C. . . . . . (CA) 942
ROOS, Barbara J. . . . . . (CA) 1053
TEBO, Jay D. . . . . (CA) 1229
TROTTA, Victoria K. . . . . (CA) 1258
INGUI, Bettejean . . . . (CO) 583
SZABO, Kathleen S. . . . . (CO) 1218
KRITEMEYER, Ann C. . . (CT) 679
KUHR, Patricia S. . . . . . (CT) 683
MCKULA, Kathleen S. . . (CT) 812
MILSTEAD, Jessica L. . . (CT) 845
STANYON, Kelly . . . . . . (CT) 1181
CLARK, Margery M. . . . . (DC) 217
KLEIMAN, Helen M. . . . . (DC) 659
KOSLOSKE, Verleah B. . (DC) 672
NEWTON, Robert C. . . . (DC) 900
OSTROFF, Harriet . . . . . (DC) 929
PICKETT, Olivia K. . . . . . (DC) 971
REIFSNYDER, Betsy S. . (DC) 1020
SWANBERG, Lisa A. . . . (DC) 1213
WENGEL, Linda . . . . (DC) 1324
TABOR, Curtis H. . . . . . . (FL) 1219
BROWN, Lorene B. . . . . (GA) 145
FEINBERG, Hilda W. . . . (GA) 368
GIBSON, Ricky S. . . . . . (GA) 432
HENDERSON, Laurel E. . (GA) 526
HULLUM, Cheri J. . . . . . (GA) 573
MCDAVID, Michael W. . . (GA) 801
MONTGOMERY, Denise L. (GA) 856
SOUTHWICK, Mary L. . . (GA) 1170
KAN, Katharine L. . . . . . (HI) 624
SCHULTZ, Elaine V. . . . . (HI) 1102
CLARK, Maeve K. . . . . . (IA) 217
CRAWFORD, Daniel R. . . (IA) 256
KURT, Edgar . . . . (IA) 684
LARSON, Catherine A. . . (IA) 699
GREEN, Carol A. . . . . . . (ID) 461
CARUSO, Joy L. . . . . . . (IL) 190
DICK, Ellen A. . . . . (IL) 300
FEDERICI, Yolanda D. . . (IL) 368
KELM, Carol R. . . . . (IL) 638
PERLMAN, Michael S. . . (IL) 959
PILARSKI, James P. . . . (IL) 973
PINKOWSKI, Patricia E. . (IL) 975
RAMM, Dorothy V . . . (IL) 1005
TREESH, Erica . . . . (IL) 1255
WICKREMERATNE,
    Swarna . . . . (IL) 1335
BUDD, Anne D. . . . . . . (IN) 155
BURCHILL, Mary D. . . . . (KS) 158
VANDER VELDE, John J. (KS) 1274
PICKENS, Nancy C. . . . . (KY) 970
FERGUSON, Anna S. . . . (LA) 372
HIMEL, Sandra M. . . . . . (LA) 542
WILLIS, Marilyn . . . . (LA) 1348
ANDREWS, Peter J. . . . . (MA) 27
LAPIERRE, Barbe . . . . . (MA) 697
LEASON, Jane . . . . (MA) 707
NATOLI, Dorothy L. . . . . (MA) 889
O'NEAL, Ellis E. . . . . . . (MA) 923

INDEXING (Cont'd)

Indexing

REID, Angea S. . . . . (MA) 1018
SPROUL, Barbara A. . . . (MA) 1176
WELLINGTON, Carol S. . (MA) 1321
AMATRUDA, William T. . (MD) 19
BATTY, Charles D. . . . . (MD) 65
DADSON, Theresa E. . . . (MD) 269
EDWARDS, Shirley J. . . (MD) 338
HOLLOWAK, Thomas L. . (MD) 552
HOOD, Martha W. . . . . . (MD) 556
KIGER, Anne F. . . . . . . (MD) 647
LABASH, Stephen P. . . . (MD) 685
SHORT, Eleanor P. . . . . (MD) 1132
STRANSKY, Maria . . . . . (MD) 1200
VIRTA, Alan K. . . . . (MD) 1285
WALLINGFORD, Karen T. (MD) 1298
CARLEN, Claudia . . . . . . (MI) 181
DAVIDSEN, Susanna L. . (MI) 276
ELLENBOGEN, Barbara R. (MI) 343
RUNCHOCK, Rita M. . . . (MI) 1067
RZEPECKI, Arnold M. . . (MI) 1072
WEAVER, Clarence L. . . (MI) 1312
BLUMBERG-MCKEE,
    Hazel . . . . (MN) 107
WELYGAN, Sylvia M. . . . (MN) 1323
SUMMERS, Janice K. . . (MO) 1209
RITTER, Ann L. . . . . (MT) 1036
HARDIE, Karen R. . . . . . (NC) 499
SAYE, Jerry D. . . . . (NC) 1086
WALTON, Carol G. . . . . (NC) 1301
EVENSEN, Sharon L. . . . (ND) 358
DANIELS, Sherrill F. . . . (NE) 273
CUMMINGS, Charles F. . (NJ) 264
ELIASON, Elisabetha S. . (NJ) 342
KUSHINKA, Kerry L. . . . (NJ) 685
MENZUL, Faina . . . . . . (NJ) 825
O'CONNOR, Christine T. (NJ) 916
SCHRIMPE, Janice E. . . (NJ) 1100
SEAGER, Janice R. . . . . (NJ) 1109
VAN BUSKIRK, Elisabeth
    L. . . . . (NJ) 1272
MILLER, Hester M. . . . . (NM) 838
BATTOE, Melanie K. . . . (NY) 65
BOTKIN, Karen R. . . . . . (NY) 118
BOWEN, Christopher E. . (NY) 120
BROWNE, Scott M. . . . . (NY) 148
CASE, Ann M. . . . . (NY) 191
CHEN, Barbara A. . . . . . (NY) 205
CORSON, Cornelia M. . . (NY) 248
DAWSON, Victoria A. . . . (NY) 282
DAY, Ross . . . . (NY) 283
DEEBRAH, Grace J. . . . (NY) 286
DIBARTOLO, Amy L. . . . (NY) 299
FIORILLO, Barbara A. . . (NY) 379
FISHER, Maureen C. . . . (NY) 381
FLANZRAICH, Gerri . . . . (NY) 384
GIGLIOTTI, Mary J. . . . . (NY) 433
GOODMAN, Edward C. . (NY) 449
GUILER, Paula J. . . . . . (NY) 476
HEWITT, Mary L. . . . . . (NY) 535
HOWARD, Joyce M. . . . (NY) 564
HYMAN, Richard J. . . . . (NY) 580
KEMPE, Deborah A. . . . . (NY) 639
KERR, Virginia M. . . . . . (NY) 644
KING, Trina E. . . . . (NY) 652
KNEE, Michael . . . . (NY) 663
LILLY, Elise M. . . . . (NY) 727
LISS, Gail . . . . (NY) 732
MACKESY, Eileen M. . . . (NY) 756
MARTINEZ-RIVERA, Ivette (NY) 779
MELITO, Joyce A. . . . . . (NY) 822
NELOMS, Karen H. . . . . (NY) 893
PATTERSON, Kathleen J. (NY) 948
PATTISON, Frederick W. (NY) 948
PEHE, Jana . . . . (NY) 954
PRESCHEL, Barbara M. . (NY) 991
RENTSCHLER, Cathy . . (NY) 1023
ROSHON, Nina C. . . . . . (NY) 1057
ROSIGNOLO, Beverly A. (NY) 1057

INDEXING (Cont'd)
Indexing

ROY, Diptimoy	(NY)	1063
SCOFIELD, Andrea	(NY)	1106
SEKELY, Maryann	(NY)	1113
STEVENS, Jane E.	(NY)	1190
SULLIVAN, Robert G.	(NY)	1208
SULOUFF, Patricia T.	(NY)	1208
TANNENBAUM, Robin L.	(NY)	1222
UTTS, Janet R.	(NY)	1270
WHITMAN, Ruth M.	(NY)	1333
ARNOLD, Judith M.	(OH)	33
HSU, Helena S.	(OH)	567
O'BRIEN, Betty A.	(OH)	914
O'BRIEN, Elmer J.	(OH)	914
RYERSON, George D.	(OH)	1071
TIPKA, Donald A.	(OH)	1246
WULKER, Clare	(OH)	1374
CHEATHAM, Gary L.	(OK)	204
MATHIS, Barbara B.	(OK)	784
NORTON, Paula T.	(OK)	910
KAWABATA, Julie	(OR)	632
MOBERG, F A.	(OR)	851
TAMBLYN, Eldon W.	(OR)	1221
BULLOCK, Jessie M.	(PA)	156
CORNOG, Martha	(PA)	247
DISANTE, Linda B.	(PA)	305
GUENTHER, Nancy A.	(PA)	476
MORGAN, Dorothy H.	(PA)	863
RICH, Denise A.	(PA)	1027
SALINGER, Florence A.	(PA)	1076
SCHREIBER-COIA, Barbara J.	(PA)	1099
SWARTZ, Patrice B.	(PA)	1214
WEBER, A C.	(PA)	1313
WICKS, Pamela J.	(PA)	1335
BERNAL-ROSA, Emilia	(PR)	88
FERNANDEZ, Josefina L.	(PR)	373
MCCARTHY, Carmen H.	(PR)	794
RODRIGUEZ, Vidalina	(PR)	1048
MILTON, Brenda R.	(SC)	845
MYERS, Nancy L.	(SD)	884
CASSELL, Gerald S.	(TN)	193
WHITEHEAD, Jane	(TN)	1332
DIVELY, Reddy	(TX)	306
FOUDRAY, Rita C.	(TX)	393
HARPER, Marsha W.	(TX)	503
MORTON, Diane E.	(TX)	870
SPRUG, Joseph W.	(TX)	1176
WEBSTER, Linda	(TX)	1314
FUJIMOTO, Jan D.	(UT)	408
DUNAWAY, Carolyn D.	(VA)	325
FIENCKE, Elaine L.	(VA)	376
GLAMM, Amy E.	(VA)	439
GLENNON, Irene F.	(VA)	441
HAUCK, Janice B.	(VA)	512
LARMOUR, Rosamond E.	(VA)	698
BAUMANN, Charles H.	(WA)	66
FIDEL, Raya	(WA)	374
KOPP, James J.	(WA)	671
REED, Marcia E.	(WA)	1015
SPEARMAN, Marie A.	(WA)	1172
JOBELIUS, Nancy L.	(WI)	601
KLAVER, Timothy J.	(WI)	658
OLSON, Dennis H.	(WI)	922
PARKS, Dennis H.	(WI)	943
RISTIC, Jovanka	(WI)	1036
SHAFTMAN, Sarah	(WI)	1119
WATERSTREET, Darlene E.	(WI)	1309
KLEIN, Barbara L.	(WY)	659
COOKE, Geraldine A.	(AB)	241
HARVEY, Carl G.	(AB)	509
PLETT, Katherine	(BC)	978
TRIP, Barbara M.	(BC)	1257
DIONNE, Charlotte A.	(NB)	305
ARONSON, Marcia L.	(ON)	34
CHIU, Lily F.	(ON)	209
CRAVEN, Timothy C.	(ON)	256
LEWIS, Leslie	(ON)	723

INDEXING (Cont'd)
Indexing

LUCIANI, Ellie	(ON)	746
MORRISON, Carol A.	(ON)	868
ROBINSON, W D.	(ON)	1045
SABLJIC, John A.	(ON)	1072
SMITH, Anne C.	(ON)	1152
STEWART, Elizabeth A.	(ON)	1192
TEMPLIN, Dorothy	(ON)	1231
ALAIN, Jean M.	(PQ)	9
AMNOTTE, Celine	(PQ)	20
BERARDINUCCI, Heather R.	(PQ)	84
BISSON, Jacques	(PQ)	100
FIORE, Francine	(PQ)	379
GAUDREAU, Louis	(PQ)	422
JULIEN, Guy	(PQ)	619
LAFRENIERE, Myriam	(PQ)	688
LATOUR, Pierre	(PQ)	701
MARION, Guylaine	(PQ)	770
NAGY, Cecile	(PQ)	886
TEES, Miriam H.	(PQ)	1229
CHU, Tat C.	(HKG)	213
BEAVERS, Janet W.	(ISR)	71
MANSINGH, Laxmi	(JAM)	767
MACIAS-CHAPULA, Cesar A.	(MEX)	755
OGBAA, Clara K.	(NGR)	918
LUMANDE, Edward	(ZAM)	748

Indexing, abstracting & editing

DOUVILLE, Judith A.	(CT)	314

Indexing, abstracting & retrieval

JOHNSON, David K.	(NJ)	603

Indexing, abstracting & thesaurus bldg

SUIDAN, Randa H.	(IL)	1207

Indexing & abstracting

KACZOROWSKI, Monice M.	(CA)	621
WHITBY, Thomas J.	(CO)	1330
JOY, Patricia L.	(CT)	618
SENKUS, Linda J.	(CT)	1115
DEARNBARGER, Dennis	(DC)	284
PICCIANO, Laura	(DC)	970
MISRA, Jayasri T.	(GA)	847
BEATTY, William K.	(IL)	70
DAVIS, Richard A.	(IL)	280
HURD, Albert E.	(IL)	577
KIENE, Andrea L.	(IL)	647
KOWITZ, Aletha A.	(IL)	674
PERTELL, Grace M.	(IL)	961
STEVENSON, Katherine	(IL)	1191
EISENMANN, Laura M.	(MA)	341
GIBSON, Sarah S.	(MA)	432
KING, Laurie L.	(MA)	651
SCHWARTZ, Candy S.	(MA)	1104
KNICKERBOCKER, Wendy	(MD)	664
SAGAR, Mary B.	(MI)	1074
VAN ALLEN, Neil K.	(MI)	1271
JOB, Rose A.	(MO)	601
FERRIGNO, Helen F.	(NH)	373
AMRON, Irving	(NJ)	20
CONLEY, Gail D.	(NJ)	236
ESKA, Dorothy I.	(NJ)	354
GLADSTONE, Mark A.	(NJ)	439
THIRD, Bettie J.	(NJ)	1235
ASTIFIDIS, Maria	(NY)	37
BELLI, Frank G.	(NY)	78
BRENNER, Everett H.	(NY)	133
FRIED, Suzanne C.	(NY)	403
GAMAL, Sandra H.	(NY)	416
GREENGRASS, Alan R.	(NY)	464
HOLMES, Harvey L.	(NY)	553
ISGANITIS, Jamie C.	(NY)	585
LEWICKY, George I.	(NY)	722
LIPETZ, Ben A.	(NY)	732
MATTA, Seoud M.	(NY)	785
MEAGHER, Anne E.	(NY)	819
POLAND, Jean A.	(OK)	980
LARSON, Signe E.	(OR)	700
CUTRONA, Cheryl	(PA)	268
PILKINGTON, James P.	(TN)	973
BAGHAL-KAR, Vali E.	(TX)	45
GRACY, David B.	(TX)	455

INDEXING (Cont'd)

Indexing & abstracting
JACKSON, Eugene B. . . (TX) 587
JACKSON, Ruth L. . . . . (TX) 588
SCHLESSINGER, Bernard S. . . . . (TX) 1094
SELWYN, Laurie . . . . . . (TX) 1114
WILLIAMS, Suzi . . . . (TX) 1346
RODRIGUEZ, Robert D. . (VA) 1048
DYKSTRA, Mary E. . . . (NS) 331
BOJIN, Minda A. . . . . . (ON) 111
SCHABAS, Ann H. . . . . (ON) 1088
DUMONT, Monique . . . . (PQ) 325
GOODELL, Paulette M. . (AUS) 448
HUEMER, Christina G. . . (ITL) 570

Indexing & abstracting analysis TAN, Elizabeth L. . . . . (IL) 1222
Indexing & bibliographic editing DRAPER, Linda J. . . . . (MO) 318
Indexing & bibliographies KANELY, Edna A. . . . . (DC) 625
Indexing & bibliography KALE, Shirley W. . . . (NM) 623
Indexing & cataloging BALABAN, Robin M. . . . (CA) 50
KAPLAN, Tiby . . . . . (FL) 626
VELARDI, Adrienne B. . (NY) 1281
BOIVIN-OSTIGUY, Jocelyne . . . . (PQ) 111
DUMOULIN, Nicole L. . . . (PQ) 325
PAPILLON, Yves . . . . . (PQ) 939
Indexing & cataloging for database WEINBERG, Gail B. . . . . (MN) 1317
Indexing & classification RICHARDSON, Katherine A. . . . . (OH) 1029
Indexing & classifying HUBBARD, Susan E. . . (NY) 568
Indexing & collecting pamphlets RHYNAS, Don M. . . . . (ON) 1026
Indexing & database design THOMAS, Dorothy . . . . (NY) 1236
Indexing & database development LUXNER, Dick . . . . . (NJ) 750
Indexing & editing music information STRATELAK, Nadia A. . . (MI) 1200
Indexing & information systems MCCRANK, Lawrence J. (AL) 800
Indexing & ISAR PITT, William B. . . . . . . (MD) 976
Indexing & retrieval HARRIS, Michael A. . . . . (CO) 505
Indexing & thesaurus development LAFRANCHISE, David . . (ON) 688
Indexing, bibliography & col devlpmnt SANCHEZ, Sara M. . . . (FL) 1079
Indexing books HEFZALLAH, Mona G. . . (CT) 521
Indexing books & periodicals O'LEARY, Mary E. . . . (MN) 920
Indexing chemical files HANF, Elizabeth P. . . . . (PA) 495
Indexing company documents PETRY, Robyn E. . . . . . (IL) 965
Indexing cultural atlases BLOZIS, Jolene M. . . . . (DC) 107
Indexing, database analysis MOOMEY, Margaret M. . (CO) 857
Indexing database construction JACKRELL, Thomas L. . . (NJ) 586
Indexing, databases JACOBS, Horace . . . . (CA) 589
Indexing databases, journal articles SCHOLFIELD, Caroline A. (MI) 1098
Indexing encyclopedia articles BERNAL, Rose M. . . . . (NY) 88
Indexing film & broadcast trade journals HOFFER, Thomas W. . . . (FL) 547
Indexing general ZOLNERZAK, Robert . . . (NY) 1390
Indexing, in-house precedents/opinions EDER, Sonya . . . . (PQ) 336
Indexing internal information AVERY, May S. . . . . . . (IL) 42
Indexing journals, serial publications POST, Joyce A. . . . . . . (PA) 986
Indexing languages TRAVIS, Irene L. . . . . (VA) 1254
Indexing languages & thesauri PAUL, Rameshwar N. . . (MD) 949
Indexing legislative resolutions GEISAR, Barbara J. . . . (WI) 425
Indexing local newspapers BROOKES, Barbara . . (NY) 140
VAN DE CASTLE, Raymond M. . . . . (PA) 1273
Indexing medical & pharmacological texts HAMILTON, Gloria R. . . . (PA) 492
Indexing monographs SUGNET, Christopher L. . (NM) 1206
Indexing news stories SINCLAIR, John M. . . . (AB) 1142
Indexing newspaper articles KHAN, Asma S. . . . . (ON) 646
Indexing newspaper clips & photos RICE, Margaret R. . . . . (TX) 1027
Indexing newspaper photographs BASNIGHT, Clara P. . . (VA) 63
Indexing of business periodicals PEDALINO, M C. . . . . . (NY) 954
Indexing of petroleum-related material TERLIZZI, Joseph M. . . (NY) 1232
Indexing periodical articles BRISTOW, Barbara A. . . (NY) 137
Indexing periodical literature VARKENTINE, Aganita . . (CA) 1278
Indexing photographs SINCLAIR, John M. . . . . (AB) 1142
Indexing representations WOOD, Judith B. . . . . . (NC) 1364
Indexing research & teaching WEINBERG, Bella H. . . . (NY) 1317
Indexing science journals DOWNEN, Kathleen Z. . . (NY) 316
Indexing scientific materials GHOSH, Subhra . . . . . (NY) 430

INDEXING (Cont'd)

Indexing services
Indexing system development
Indexing systems
Indexing systems design
Indexing Thai law
Indexing, theology
Information retrieval & indexing
International treaty indexing
Latin American indexing
Law indexing
Legal indexing
Legal publishing & indexing
Legislative indexing
Library indexing systems
Local newspaper indexing
Manual indexing
Medical abstracting & indexing
Medical arts indexing
Medical book & journal indexing
Medical book indexing
Medical indexing
Medical literature indexing
Medicine & horticulture indexing
Mental health indexing
Microcomputer index systems
Microcomputer indexing
Multisubject book indexing
Music & computer indexing
Music indexing
Music indexing & database preparation
Music thematic indexing
Newspaper clipping & indexing
Newspaper indexing
Newspaper indexing & cataloging
Online & indexing services
Online indexing of business reports
Online legal indexing compilation
Online systems & indexing
Organz & indexing of manufacturer catlgs
Organization & microfilm pubn with index
Patient index file maintenance
Periodical & book indexing
Periodical indexing
Periodical literature indexing
Periodicals, abstracting & indexing
Petroleum & energy database indexing
Photo indexing

BURNHAM-KIDWELL, Debbie . . . . (AZ) 162
JULIANELLE, Shelley M. (VT) 619
KLEMENT, Susan P. . . . (ON) 660
SAUNDERS, Vinette A. . (DC) 1085
FLOOD, Barbara J. . . . . (PA) 385
COTE, Jean P. . . . . . . (PQ) 249
ANDERSON, James D. . . (NJ) 23
RUNGSANG, Rebecca J. (THA) 1067
LALIBERTE, Madeleine A. (PQ) 689
HUMPHREY, Susanne M. (MD) 573
KAVASS, Igor I. . . . . . . (TN) 631
SATER, Analya . . . . . . (CA) 1083
THOMAS, Dorothy . . . . (NY) 1236
RODICH, Lorraine E. . . . (CA) 1047
THOMPSON, Johanna W. (DC) 1240
DAVIS, Yvonne M. . . . (OH) 281
SHERRILL, Jocelyn T. . . (NY) 1129
OVERTON, Kathryn R. . . (DC) 931
MAJURE, William D. . . . (MS) 762
ALLING, M P. . . . . (IA) 16
LINZER, Elliot . . . . (NY) 732
CARVER, Mary . . . . . (NY) 191
SERDZIAK, Edward J. . . (CA) 1116
GARCIA, Kathleen J. . . (NY) 417
WEIR, Alexandra L. . . . (PA) 1319
GERRITY, Marline R. . . . (MO) 429
FLANZRAICH, Gerri . . . . (NY) 384
ZOLNERZAK, Robert . . . (NY) 1390
WEAVER, Nancy B. . . . (MO) 1312
LINDHEIMER, Elinor . . . . (CA) 729
ROUP, Carol E. . . . . . . (ON) 1061
FISLER, Charlotte D. . . . (PA) 382
KEARNS, Linda J. . . . . (ON) 633
HOTIMLANSKA, Leah D. . (IL) 562
KELLER, Kate V. . . . . (PA) 635
RUSHING, Darla H. . . . . (LA) 1068
BLOTNER, Linda S. . . . . (MA) 106
HILL, George R. . . . . . (NY) 539
LINCOLN, Harry B. . . . . (NY) 728
WALSH, Barclay . . . . . (DC) 1299
HINTZMAN, Bonnie . . . . (AZ) 543
HOCKEL, Kathleen N. . . (CA) 545
WELLS, Merle W. . . . . . (ID) 1322
STEPHENS, Janet A. . . (IL) 1188
HAENICKE, Carol A. . . . (MI) 482
LARZELERE, David W. . . (MI) 700
PEPPER, Alice A. . . . . . (MI) 958
STEVENS, Robert R. . . . (MO) 1191
KARES, Artemis C. . . . (NC) 627
GARDNER, Jack I. . . . . (NV) 418
SCHLAERTH, Sally G. . . (NY) 1093
FRIEDMAN, Amy G. . . . . (SC) 403
MORRISON, Annette T. . (TN) 867
NEU, Margaret J. . . . . . (TX) 896
VAUGHN, Robert V. . . . (VI) 1280
BRITTON, Pilaivan H. . . . (WA) 137
MCCARGAR, Susan E. . . (TX) 794
STILES, William G. . . . (ON) 1194
SEASE, Sandra A. . . . (NY) 1110
WONG, Patricia M. . . . (CA) 1363
MALCOLM, J P. . . . . . . (MI) 762
SCHUSTER, Adeline . . . (IL) 1103
FALK, Candace S. . . . . (CA) 362
PARR, John R. . . . . . . (ON) 943
KEMP, Thomas J. . . . . . (CT) 639
AGEE, Victoria V. . . . . (MD) 7
THICKITT, Lisa . . . . . . (NC) 1235
CRAVENS, Vickie L. . . . (MO) 256
TERHUNE, R S. . . . . . . (OH) 1231
HALLMAN, Clark N. . . . (SD) 489
FOX, Elyse H. . . . . . . (MA) 394
RICHARD, Marie F. . . . (PQ) 1028
SHERRILL, Jocelyn T. . . (NY) 1129
LYONS, Valerie S. . . . . (GA) 753

INDEXING (Cont'd)

Photo research & indexing	FRANKLIN, Alyce B.	(KY)	397
Physical science indexing	SERDZIAK, Edward J.	(CA)	1116
Private legal database indexing	LEVINTON, Juliette	(NY)	721
Proofreading, writing, editing, indexing	GAGNON, Donna M.	(CA)	412
Quilt research & documentation, indexing	PARKER, Mary A.	(SC)	942
Reference & indexing	MEVERS, Frank C.	(NH)	829
	MORRIS, Trisha A.	(OH)	867
Research & indexing	LE DORR, Lillian E.	(CA)	708
Science indexing	CANTIN, Gemma	(PQ)	179
Scientific & chemical indexing	BARNETT, Philip	(NY)	58
Scientific & medical indexing	TRIMBLE, Kathy W.	(CA)	1256
Scientific indexing	ZOLNERZAK, Robert	(NY)	1390
Searching & indexing online databases	KREPS, Lise E.	(WA)	678
Serials indexing	SHUPAK, Harris J.	(PA)	1134
Slide indexing & cataloging	WALD, Ingeborg	(NY)	1294
Social science & computer indexing	LINDHEIMER, Elinor	(CA)	729
Social science indexing	FLANZRAICH, Gerri	(NY)	384
	LANGERMAN, Shoshana P.	(ISR)	695
Sound recording indexing	CALDWELL, John M.	(PA)	172
Special index databases	TSUI, Josephine	(ON)	1260
Specialized cataloging & indexing	DE WITT, Benjamin L.	(NJ)	298
Standards indexing	SHUPAK, Harris J.	(PA)	1134
Subject index database	KENEFICK, Mary L.	(CA)	640
Subject indexing	MOOERS, Calvin N.	(MA)	857
	WELLISCH, Hans H.	(MD)	1322
	CIARAMELLA, Mary A.	(NJ)	214
Technical indexing	BAIR, Alice E.	(IL)	47
Technical indexing & abstracting	WILLS, Luella G.	(VA)	1349
Technical information indexing	BRETON, Ernest J.	(DE)	133
Technical services, indexing	HALES, David A.	(AK)	486
Text book indexing	WEIR, Alexandra L.	(PA)	1319
Theatre biographical indexing	ULRICH, Paul S.	(WGR)	1268
Thesaurus elaboration & indexing	BRETON, Lise	(PQ)	133
Topical indexing	OVERTON, Julie M.	(OH)	931
Training, abstracting & indexing	AUSTON, Ione	(VA)	40
Training indexers	BERNAL, Rose M.	(NY)	88
Training indexing & classification	LOMBARDI, Mary L.	(CA)	738
United States voluntary standards index	OVERMAN, Joanne R.	(MD)	931
Video cataloging, indexing & abstracting	LOFTHOUSE, Patricia A.	(IL)	737
Writing & indexing	VAILLANCOURT, Pauline M.	(NY)	1271
Writing, editing & indexing	PALMER, Marguerite C.	(WV)	936

INDIAN (See also Cherokee)

American Indian archives	SPOTTED EAGLE, Joy	(MT)	1175
	THIEL, Mark G.	(WI)	1235
American Indian bibliography	WEEKS, John M.	(MN)	1315
American Indian special collections	THIEL, Mark G.	(WI)	1235
American Indians	DAVIS, Mary B.	(NY)	280
Black genealogy, Indian genealogy	DAVIS, Denyvetta	(OK)	278
Development of tribal & Indian libraries	PATTERSON, Lotsee	(OK)	948
Indian records	SCHMIDT HACKER, Margaret H.	(TX)	1096
Research, American Indian studies	BLUMER, Thomas J.	(DC)	107
Research in federal Indian law	HARRAGARRA WATERS, Deana J.	(CO)	503

INDIANA

Indiana authors, bibliography	GILLIS, Ruth J.	(MN)	436

INDIVIDUAL

Individual & self-development	NOBLE, Valerie	(MI)	906

INDUSTRIAL (See also Commerce)

Business & industrial publishing	SAFRAN, Scott A.	(NY)	1074
Business & industrial reference	PFOHL, Theodore E.	(NY)	966
Chemistry & industrial health	CASSAR, Ann	(PA)	193
Corporate & industrial libraries	MATARAZZO, James M.	(MA)	783
Economic & industrial development	LANDRY, Ronald	(IL)	694

INDUSTRIAL (Cont'd)

Industrial advertising	WISE, Eileen M.	(ON)	1356
Industrial & economic development info	GRELL, Holly J.	(GA)	467
Industrial & organizational psychology	FULMER, Dina J.	(PA)	409
Industrial automation databases	FOWELLS, Fumi T.	(MI)	393
Industrial hygiene	WEINRICH, Gloria	(NY)	1318
Industrial hygiene information	TUCKER, Mary E.	(NC)	1262
Industrial labor relations	FRASER, Charlotte R.	(NY)	399
Industrial materials	VENNE, Louise	(PQ)	1282
Industrial products	YANCHAR, Joyce M.	(MA)	1377
Industrial relations	CHAPLAN, Margaret A.	(IL)	201
	WATSON, Marjorie O.	(NJ)	1310
	LA MARCHE, David L.	(ON)	689
Layout of industrial libraries	RANDALL, Gordon E.	(GA)	1006
Toxicology, industrial medicine	SELZER, Nancy S.	(DE)	1114

INDUSTRY (See also Business, Commerce, Companies, Firms, Industrial, Trade)

Aerospace industry research	BELL, Karen L.	(GA)	77
Analyses of book industry	APPELBAUM, Judith P.	(PA)	29
Archives of computer industry	BRUEMMER, Bruce H.	(MN)	149
Automotive industry research	GIGLIO, Linda M.	(MI)	433
Brewing industry history	VOLLMAR, William J.	(MO)	1288
Building industry information	CLARK, Margery M.	(DC)	217
Business & industry	LARSEN, Linda E.	(IL)	698
Business & industry databases	CURRY, John A.	(IL)	266
Business & industry reference & resrch	LUXNER, Dick	(NJ)	750
Business & industry research	RATZABI, Arlene	(NY)	1010
Business, industry, accounting info	WELLS, Nancy E.	(ON)	1322
Business, science & industry	SUGDEN, Martin D.	(FL)	1206
Canadian & US companies & industries	ORLANDO, Richard P.	(PQ)	926
Chemical industry	KLEIN, Regina D.	(MO)	659
Commerce & construction industry	MCCONNIE, Mary	(TRN)	798
Communications industry market research	LEIGHTON, Victoria C.	(GA)	714
Company & industry research	THAU, Richard	(NJ)	1234
Company, product, & industry data	DLOTT, Nancy B.	(MA)	306
Computer industry	JAMESON, Martha E.	(IL)	592
	KORBER, Nancy	(NH)	671
	LAUB, Barbara J.	(NJ)	702
Computer industry & applications	BJORNER, Susan N.	(MA)	100
Computer industry databases	MASTERS, Kathy B.	(CT)	782
	CLIFT, Crystal A.	(MN)	222
Computer industry research	KRUSE, Luanne M.	(TX)	681
Computer industry resources	LAPENSKY, Barbara A.	(MN)	697
Computer science, high tech industry	SLOAN, Maureen G.	(OR)	1149
Defense industry	GESCHKE, Nancy A.	(CA)	430
Distribution in computer industry	MONOSSON, Adolf S.	(MA)	855
Economic & industry analysis	FELDMAN, Stanley J.	(MA)	369
Education & industry learning material	LESURE, Alan B.	(NY)	718
Electronics industry information	THOMAS, Sandra L.	(OR)	1238
Energy, electric utility industry	MUIR, Scott P.	(AL)	876
Energy industry	KERWIN, Camillus A.	(TX)	644
Financial & industry information	GINSBURG, Carol L.	(NY)	438
Financial & thrift industry	CALLINAN, Mary H.	(NY)	174
Financial industry information	HALL, Robert C.	(NY)	488
Financial industry trading systems	HALL, Robert C.	(NY)	488
Financial services industry	CARTLEDGE, Ellen G.	(CT)	190
	REMEIKIS, Lois A.	(IL)	1022
Financial services industry information	WARNER, Claudette S.	(IL)	1305
Food industry	CARTER, Steva L.	(MO)	190
	WILTON, Greg J.	(MB)	1353
Food industry database production	INGISH, Karen S.	(IL)	582
Food industry reference	DEPKE, Robert W.	(IL)	293
Food industry research & development	WILTON, Greg J.	(MB)	1353
Food service industry	SMYTH, Mary B.	(CA)	1162
Gas industry regulation	DORNER, Steven J.	(VA)	313
Gas Net industry database management	DORNER, Steven J.	(VA)	313
Government & industry liaison	FATTIBENE, James F.	(DC)	366
Health care industry	DETWILER, Susan M.	(IN)	296
High technology industries	LEWIS, Gretchen S.	(CA)	723
Hospitality industry	SMYTH, Mary B.	(CA)	1162
Hospitality industry culinary research	JOHNSON, Sheila A.	(NY)	609
Hospitality industry information	LAURENCE, Katherine S.	(NY)	703

INDUSTRY (Cont'd)

Industry analysis	BAKST, Shelley D.	(MA)	50
	HUSSEY, Laurie L.	(MA)	578
Industry databases	FELMY, John C.	(DC)	370
Industry forecasts	BAILEY, Linda S.	(TX)	46
Industry information	TICKER, Susan L.	(NY)	1244
Industry reports	HENDERSON, Joanne L.	(DE)	526
Industry research	O'BRIEN, Barbara E.	(IL)	914
	NOBLE, James K.	(NY)	906
Industry standards	AUSTIN, Stephen	(CA)	40
	RANSOM-BERGSTROM, Janette F.	(MI)	1008
	HAMPTON, Sylvia S.	(RI)	494
	HOLAB-ABELMAN, Robin S.	(TX)	550
Information flow in industries	JACKSON, Eugene B.	(TX)	587
Information industry	QUINT, Barbara E.	(CA)	1000
	ATKIN, Michael I.	(DC)	37
	RUBIN, Lenard H.	(TX)	1064
Info industry & technology tracking	SIECK, Steven K.	(NY)	1135
Information industry economics	BURNS, Christopher	(MA)	162
Insurance industry	CARICONE, Paul	(NY)	181
Lending industry	FELDER, Bruce B.	(OH)	369
Library, information industry interface	MACDONALD, Alan H.	(AB)	754
Lodging industry	SMYTH, Mary B.	(CA)	1162
Market & industry research	LANDRY, Ronald	(IL)	694
Market research for the info industry	SOVNER-RIBBLER, Judith	(MA)	1170
Microcomputer software industry	SLAVIN, Vicky J.	(MA)	1148
Music industry databases	BLUME, August G.	(CA)	107
Natural gas industry	DORNER, Steven J.	(VA)	313
Nuclear power industry	SPARER, Saretta	(NY)	1171
Online database industry	CUADRA, Carlos A.	(CA)	262
	KNOPPERS, Jake V.	(ON)	665
Online industry	GORDON, Helen A.	(IN)	451
Packaging industry	TRUE, Jacqueline J.	(IL)	1259
Petroleum industry information	ROBERTSON, Betty M.	(NY)	1041
Pharmaceutical industry	KOZAK, Marlene G.	(IL)	674
Plastics industry information sources	KANE, Nancy J.	(MA)	625
Research retail & wholesale industries	LAMBE, Michael	(NY)	690
Securities industry	GROSSMAN, Adrian J.	(NY)	473
Software industry	PUGH, Ann E.	(MA)	997
Television industry & communication	POTEAT, James B.	(NY)	986
Travel industry databases	OGREN, Mark S.	(IL)	918

INFORMATICS

Health informatics	COVVEY, H D.	(MB)	252
Medical informatics	MANNING, Phil R.	(CA)	767
	KERN, Donald C.	(MA)	643
	HSIEH, Richard K.	(MD)	567
	FRISSE, Mark E.	(MO)	405
	SPEER, Susan C.	(NC)	1172
	STEAD, William W.	(NC)	1183
	DETLEFSEN, Ellen G.	(PA)	296
	TREMBLAY, Gerald F.	(SC)	1255
	ARMES, Patti	(TX)	32
	LUECHT, Richard M.	(WI)	747
	MOEHR, Jochen R.	(BC)	851
	CASIRAGHI, Edoardo	(ITL)	192
Medical informatics & databases	CASTAGNO, Lucio A.	(BRA)	194
Research in medical informatics	FULLER, Sherrilynne S.	(MN)	409

INFORMATION (See also MIS, Reference, SDI)

Academic information systems	JENKIN, Michael A.	(FL)	596
	WILSON, Marjorie P.	(MD)	1352
Access to information	WEBRECK, Susan J.	(PA)	1314
Acquisitions & information retrieval	MOORE, Virginia B.	(DC)	861
Acquisitions of information companies	KEON, Edward F.	(NJ)	643
Administration of information agencies	SHANK, Russell	(CA)	1120
Administration of library & info srvs	RODAWALT, Valarie J.	(TX)	1046
Advanced info telecommunication tech	GOODMAN, Henry J.	(AB)	449
Advertising & business information	MASTROIANNI, Richard L.	(MD)	783
Advertising information	HUBBARD, Susan E.	(NY)	568
Aeronautical engineering information	AUSTIN, Rhea C.	(MD)	40
Aerospace information	KENNY-SLOAN, Linda	(CA)	642
	HALL, Robert G.	(MA)	488
Aerospace information & databases	SMALLWOOD, James R.	(CT)	1151
Aerospace information resources	KITCHENS, Philips H.	(AL)	657

INFORMATION (Cont'd)

Agricultural information	HARRIS, Susan C.	(CA)	506
	KENNEDY, Amy J.	(MA)	640
	IRURIA, Daniel M.	(KEN)	584
Agricultural information abstracting	ASIS, Moises	(CUB)	36
Agricultural information dissemination	SINHA, Pramod K.	(IND)	1143
Agricultural information systems	BURTON, Hilary D.	(CA)	164
	OLSEN, Wallace C.	(NY)	922
	LUMANDE, Edward	(ZAM)	748
Agricultural, plant science information	MITCHELL, Steve	(CA)	849
Alaska & arctic information reference	SOKOLOV, Barbara J.	(AK)	1165
Alcohol information online	MITCHELL, Andrea L.	(CA)	848
Analysis design information systems	DEBONS, Anthony	(PA)	285
Analysis of information needs	HOSONO, Kimio	(JAP)	562
Analysis of medical information	LAMPORT, Bernard	(NY)	691
Animal welfare information	LARSON, Jean A.	(MD)	699
Anthropological information systems	CLARK, Barton M.	(IL)	216
Application of info technology in libs	AMAN, Mohammed M.	(WI)	19
Applications of information technology	CHARTRAND, Robert L.	(DC)	203
Aquaculture information center	HANFMAN, Deborah A.	(MD)	495
Aquatic sciences & fisheries information	SEARS, Jonathan R.	(MD)	1110
Architectural information	BURROUGHS, Christine M.	(NY)	163
	PISCIOTTA, Henry A.	(PA)	976
Architecture literature & information	HAVLIK, Robert J.	(IN)	513
Archival information systems	EASTWOOD, Terence M.	(BC)	333
Arctic information	COOKE, Geraldine A.	(AB)	241
Arctic information referral	SOKOLOV, Barbara J.	(AK)	1165
Arid lands information	HUSBAND, Susan M.	(AZ)	578
Arkansas historical information	FERGUSON, John L.	(AR)	372
Art information	POIRRIER, Sherry	(MA)	980
Art information systems	PETERSEN, Toni	(MA)	962
Attorney information systems consulting	STERN, Michael P.	(MD)	1189
Automated community information service	MESSINEO, Leonard L.	(KS)	828
Automated information brokering	COLLARD, R M.	(CO)	232
Automated information retrieval	SANDERS, Robert L.	(CA)	1080
Automated information retrieval systems	MACIAS-CHAPULA, Cesar A.	(MEX)	755
Automated information systems	HUNE, Mary G.	(OH)	574
	NORTON, Nancy P.	(TN)	910
Automated information systems management	WEINSTEIN, Lois	(NY)	1318
Automated library, information systems	KANNEL, Ene	(ON)	625
Automation & information systems	SAHLI, Nancy A.	(DC)	1075
Background information	EVANS, Deborah L.	(CA)	356
Behavior information users	BOISSY, Robert W.	(NY)	111
Bibliographic & information access	DEL CERVO, Diane M.	(CT)	289
Bibliographic information systems	LARSON, Ray R.	(CA)	699
	ODOM, Jane H.	(DC)	917
	WALL, Eugene	(MD)	1297
	LI, Marjorie H.	(NJ)	724
Biographical information	MASON, Margaret E.	(IL)	781
Biomedical & medical socioeconomic info	BANKS, Jane L.	(DC)	54
Biomedical ethics databases & info	GROVER, Wilma S.	(FL)	474
Biomedical information	HUNT, Richard K.	(CA)	575
	HAYWARD, Miriam C.	(PQ)	517
	NOZOE, Atsutake	(JAP)	911
Biomedical information resources	BROERING, Naomi C.	(DC)	139
Biomedical science information	POWELL, James R.	(MI)	988
Biotechnology information	SAARI, David S.	(IN)	1072
	SCHEPPER, Josee H.	(PQ)	1091
Biotechnology information retrieval	SCHEPPER, Josee H.	(PQ)	1091
Building industry information	CLARK, Margery M.	(DC)	217
Business & computer information	PETTEY, Brent	(CA)	965
Business & computer information sources	AHERN, Camille P.	(NH)	8
Business & corporate information	STANGL-WALKER, Teresa L.	(ON)	1180
Business & economic information services	CARROLL, Hardy	(MI)	187
Business & economics information	GELINNE, Michael S.	(MO)	426
Business & employment information	HOLTZMAN, Douglas A.	(CA)	555
Business & engineering information	GRELL, Holly J.	(GA)	467
Business & finance information	OLSHEN, Toni	(ON)	922

INFORMATION (Cont'd)

Business & financial information	MEARNS, Mary A.	(CA)	820
	BROWN, George F.	(MA)	144
	COOPER, J P.	(MA)	243
	GUHERIDGE, Allison A.	(ON)	476
Business & financial information spclst	DARNOWSKI, Christina M.	(NY)	275
Business & government information	MILLER, Carmen L.	(WA)	836
Business & information publishing	HOLLY, James H.	(CA)	552
Business & management information	TASHIMA, Marie	(CA)	1224
Business & marketing information	FULLER, Kathleen B.	(OH)	408
Business & marketing info resources	BARTL, Richard P.	(NY)	61
Business & marketing information sources	STEPIEN, Karen K.	(NJ)	1189
Business & scientific information	BUNCE, George D.	(ENG)	157
Business & technical information	RUTHERFORD, Frederick S.	(ON)	1070
Business, competitive information	NEWMAN, Robert M.	(TX)	899
Business, industry, accounting info	WELLS, Nancy E.	(ON)	1322
Business information	SEEKAMP, Linda W.	(CA)	1111
	WALTER, Virginia A.	(CA)	1300
	BERLIET, Nathalie B.	(CT)	87
	DIMATTIA, Susan S.	(CT)	304
	LANEY, Helen B.	(DC)	695
	O'BRIEN, Kathleen	(DC)	914
	FEDECZKO, Joyce L.	(IL)	367
	LEE, Ann H.	(IL)	709
	MURPHY, Therese B.	(IL)	881
	MUZZO, Steven E.	(IL)	883
	SENN, Mary S.	(IL)	1115
	OKEY, Susan T.	(IN)	920
	ARNOLD, Stephen E.	(KY)	34
	O'CONNOR, Jerry	(MA)	916
	BLASCHAK, Mary M.	(MI)	104
	ELLIS, Gloria B.	(MI)	344
	WAGENVELD, Linda M.	(MI)	1291
	EVANS, June C.	(NC)	357
	GENTNER, Claudia A.	(NJ)	427
	MASILAMANI, Mary P.	(NJ)	780
	TILLMAN, Hope N.	(NJ)	1245
	WARD, Catherine J.	(NJ)	1303
	BERNSTEIN, Judith R.	(NM)	89
	BUTLER, Barbara E.	(NV)	166
	WELLS, David B.	(NV)	1322
	GRANKA, Bernard D.	(NY)	457
	RIPIN, Laura G.	(NY)	1035
	TICKER, Susan L.	(NY)	1244
	BUTCHER, Sharon L.	(OH)	166
	FELL, Sally B.	(OH)	370
	RASKIN, Rosa S.	(OH)	1009
	VARA, Margaret E.	(OH)	1278
	GRAHAM, John	(OK)	456
	SHAVER, Donna B.	(OR)	1123
	COOPER, Linda	(PA)	243
	HOSTETTER, Sandra F.	(PA)	562
	CAMP, Joyce H.	(TX)	175
	SHEA, Kathleen	(TX)	1124
	WILSON, Brenda J.	(UT)	1350
	GILL, Gerald L.	(VA)	435
	MAROTZ, Karen V.	(BC)	772
	DE STRICKER, Ulla	(ON)	296
	MONTY, Vivienne	(ON)	857
Business information analysis	MILLS, Catherine H.	(RI)	843
Business information & related services	STRYKER, Charles W.	(NJ)	1203
Business information & research	RUTKOWSKI, Hollace A.	(PA)	1070
Business information database searching	ROSENBERGER, Constance G.	(PA)	1056
Business information databases	MAH, Jeffery	(CA)	760
	BOYD, Cheryl J.	(MN)	122
Business information management	BAZAN, Lorraine R.	(CA)	68
	SEASE, Sandra A.	(NY)	1110
Business information resources	MICKEY, Melissa B.	(IL)	833
Business information search	MIWA, Makiko	(JAP)	850
Business information services	BAUER, Leslie L.	(GA)	65
	MCZORN, Bonita A.	(NC)	819
	VEGTER, Amy H.	(NY)	1281
Business information sources	STANYON, Kelly	(CT)	1181
	JACOBS, Leslie R.	(MA)	589

INFORMATION (Cont'd)

Business information sources & research	CVELJO, Katherine	(TX)	268
Business information specialization	SCOTT, Rupert N.	(GA)	1108
Business information system development	LITTLE, Dean K.	(OH)	733
Business information systems	SHAFFER, Richard P.	(NY)	1119
Business, management information	DUDLEY, Durand S.	(OH)	323
Business reference information	PINSON, Mark	(MA)	975
Business/technical information research	MICHAEL, Ann B.	(IL)	831
Canadian business information	VARMA, Divakara K.	(ON)	1278
Canadian business information sources	KING, Alan S.	(ME)	650
Canadian government information policy	ROSE, Frances E.	(BC)	1054
Canadian public company information	BONIN, Denise R.	(BC)	114
Cancer information	O'DELL, Charles A.	(MO)	916
	NOBLE, David	(BC)	906
Cancer information collection	KAWASHIMA, Hiroko	(JAP)	632
Cancer information systems	DICKINSON, Patricia C.	(MD)	301
Career education information advising	LYONS, A J.	(MO)	753
Career information	MOORHEAD, Kenneth E.	(CT)	862
	WEEG, Barbara E.	(IA)	1315
	HUSFELDT, Jerry J.	(IL)	578
Cartographic information	STRICKLAND, Muriel	(CA)	1202
Catalog information	CATTIE, Mary M.	(PA)	195
Cataloging & information retrieval	CARROLL, Dewey E.	(TX)	187
CD-ROM library reference information	HATVANY, Bela R.	(MA)	512
CD-ROM, optical information systems	DESMARAIS, Norman P.	(RI)	295
Census information	VAN DE VOORDE, Philip E.	(IA)	1274
Chemical & biomedical information	RADER, Ronald A.	(DC)	1002
Chemical business information databases	REITANO, Maimie V.	(NY)	1022
Chemical databases & info retrieval	ROSENTHAL, Francine C.	(OH)	1057
Chemical information	LOPEZ, Frank D.	(CA)	741
	ROTH, Dana L.	(CA)	1059
	TASHIMA, Marie	(CA)	1224
	HEARTY, John A.	(DC)	519
	DRUKKER, Alexander E.	(DE)	320
	O'NEILL, Patricia E.	(GA)	924
	KAMINECKI, Ronald M.	(IL)	624
	STOKES, Claire Z.	(MN)	1196
	DEDERT, Patricia L.	(NJ)	286
	KLEMM, Carol B.	(NJ)	660
	GILLEN, Bonnie J.	(PA)	435
	OWENS, Frederick H.	(PA)	932
	LYDEN, Edward W.	(TX)	750
	CLEMANS, Margaret H.	(VA)	220
	SOUTHWICK, Margaret A.	(VA)	1170
Chemical information database building	PLATAU, Gerard O.	(OH)	977
Chemical information instruction	SOMERVILLE, Arleen N.	(NY)	1167
Chemical information, lit searching	JOHNSON, David K.	(NJ)	603
Chemical information retrieval	SIMMONS, Edlyn S.	(OH)	1139
Chemical information searching	BUNTROCK, Robert E.	(IL)	157
Chemical information specialist	YANCEY, Marianne	(OH)	1377
Chemical information specialization	ROUSE, Kendall G.	(WI)	1061
Chemical information systems	BURCSU, James E.	(NC)	158
	LEWIS, Dale E.	(NJ)	722
	WAGNER, A B.	(NY)	1291
	DUANE, Carol A.	(OH)	321
	VLADUTZ, George E.	(PA)	1286
	ROSENBERG, Murray D.	(VA)	1056
Chemical reactions information	DIXON, Michael D.	(VA)	306
Chemical substance information retrieval	STOBAUGH, Robert E.	(OH)	1195
Children's book information service	RUSS, Kennetta P.	(MD)	1068
Classifying information	ALBAIR, Catherine M.	(FL)	9
Classifying information about music	STRATELAK, Nadia A.	(MI)	1200
Clearinghouse & information center mgmt	BYRD, Harvey C.	(MD)	169
Collection development & legal info	TOMCHYSHYN, Theresa M.	(SK)	1249
Communication & information retrieval	NADEAU, Johan	(PQ)	885
Communication, info, lib relationships	VOIGT, Melvin J.	(CA)	1287
Communication of information	BERNHARD, Paulette	(PQ)	89
Community health information	KNIGHT, Dorothy H.	(IL)	664

INFORMATION (Cont'd)

Community information	ANTHONY, Carolyn A. . .	(IL)	28
	BLANKENSHIP, Phyllis E.	(MO)	104
	JOHNSON, Patrelle E. . .	(NY)	608
	KRAMER, Mollie W.	(NY)	675
	WIERUCKI, Karen A. . . .	(ON)	1337
Community information & referral	FERDUN, Georgenne M. .	(CA)	372
	MATZKE, Ellen S.	(MI)	786
	SEKELY, Maryann	(NY)	1113
Community information & referral service	LIGHT, Jane E.	(CA)	726
Community information resources	DAVIS, Natalia G.	(NY)	280
Community information systems	REMINGTON, David G. . .	(WA)	1022
Community information transfer	SHIRK, John C.	(MN)	1131
Company information	GINSBURG, Carol L. . . .	(NY)	438
	WARD, Edith	(NY)	1303
	ZOTTOLI, Danny A.	(NY)	1390
Company information databases	BOYD, Cheryl J.	(MN)	122
Comparative library information systems	CARPENTER, Raymond L.	(NC)	185
Competitive information	BIRKS, Grant F.	(ON)	98
Computer information	AUSTIN, Rhea C.	(MD)	40
Computer information srvs environment	SCHWALLER, Marian C.	(MA)	1104
Computer info sources, end-user systems	GODT, Carol	(MO)	443
Computer manipulation of information	KERNS, John T.	(CA)	644
Computer srchng, online info retrieval	SOUTH, Ruth E.	(OR)	1169
Computer-based bibliographic info systs	COCHRANE, Pauline A. .	(NY)	226
Computer-based information management	WACHTER, Margery C. .	(FRN)	1290
Computer-based information services	FRIEND, Gary I.	(DC)	404
	BYRN, William H.	(MA)	169
Computer-based information systems	SAWYER, Edmond J. . . .	(DC)	1086
	PARK, Margaret K.	(GA)	941
	RUSH, James E.	(OH)	1068
Computerization of legal information	HOLOCH, S A.	(OH)	553
Computerized information	MILLER, Constance R. . .	(IN)	836
Computerized information retrieval	CARRIGAN, John L. . . .	(CA)	186
	LEE, William D.	(CA)	711
	WILDE, Daniel U. . .	(CT)	1338
	MARCUS, Richard S. . . .	(MA)	769
Computerized information systems	DAY, Melvin S.	(VA)	283
Computerized library information system	OMARA, Marie T.	(MD)	923
Computers & information systems	HORGAN, Laura A.	(MA)	559
Consulting in information organizations	PRUSAK, Laurence	(MA)	996
Consulting information, publishing	CHICOREL, Marietta S. .	(AZ)	208
Consumer & patient health information	LINDNER, Katherine L. . .	(NJ)	729
Consumer health information	MCCARTHY, Sherri L. . .	(AL)	794
	RICHETELLE, Alberta L. .	(CT)	1030
	MAYO, Kathleen O.	(FL)	790
	WHITED, Diane D.	(LA)	1332
	MCKAY, Ann	(ME)	809
	LANSDALE, Metta T. . . .	(MI)	696
	SERLING, Kitty	(MO)	1116
	CARABATEAS, Clarissa D.	(NY)	180
	ROBBINS, Diane D.	(NY)	1038
	JANES, Jodith	(OH)	593
	JENNINGS, Kathryn L. . .	(OK)	598
Consumer, legal, & medical information	LEBRUN, Anne	(ON)	708
Contemporary visual arts information	HOFFBERG, Judith A. . .	(CA)	547
Copyright information	MASTRANGELO, Marjorie J.	(DC)	782
Corporate & government information ctr	PEGLER, Ross J.	(FL)	954
Corporate financial information	HENDERSON, Joanne L.	(DE)	526
Corporate information	TICKER, Susan L.	(NY)	1244
	IRWIN, James W.	(OH)	584
	HELLER, Patricia A. . . .	(PA)	524
Corporate information & library services	WAGNER, Stephen K. . .	(NY)	1292
Corporate information center management	STURDIVANT, Clarence A.	(CO)	1205

INFORMATION (Cont'd)

Corporate information centers	SIMPSON, Evelyn L. . . .	(CA)	1141
	MICKEY, Melissa B. . . .	(IL)	833
Corporate information sources	JACKSON, Craig A.	(ON)	587
Corporate library & information ctr mgmt	RUTKOWSKI, Hollace A.	(PA)	1070
Corporate research & devlpmnt info systs	BURCSU, James E.	(NC)	158
Corp information system implementation	GRENIER, Serge	(PQ)	467
Cosmetic & chemical information	DEXTER, Patrick J.	(MD)	298
Criminal justice information management	BYRD, Harvey C.	(MD)	169
Cultural information databases	SZARY, Richard V.	(DC)	1218
Current information databases	HILL, Fay G.	(IA)	539
Current information selection	CYPSER, Rudy J.	(NY)	268
Current news & information databases	JOBE, Shirley A.	(MA)	601
Customer financial information requests	GAYNOR, Joann T.	(NY)	424
Database & information system design	BATTY, Charles D.	(MD)	65
Database information	WARD, Catherine J.	(NJ)	1303
Database information publishing	RICCOBONO, Joseph V. .	(CT)	1026
Database information retrieval	MAGNER, Mary F.	(TX)	759
Deafness information & collections	RITTER, Audrey L.	(NY)	1036
Defense & aerospace info resources	BARTL, Richard P.	(NY)	61
Defense marketing information systems	MAUTER, George A. . . .	(NY)	787
Defense technical information	HALL, Robert G.	(MA)	488
Dental information systems	DIEHL, Mark	(IL)	302
Departmental information managing	EKSTRAND, Nancy L. . .	(NC)	341
Description, organization of information	BIERBAUM, Esther G. . .	(IA)	95
Design & eval of info systs & lib srvs	COCHRANE, Pauline A. .	(NY)	226
Designing medical information systems	LAZAROW-STETTEN, Jane K.	(MD)	706
Desktop information management systems	HARTT, Richard W.	(VA)	509
Developing countries & information	LAU, Jesus G.	(MEX)	702
Developing nations, information systems	JETT, Don W.	(TN)	600
Development information	MARA, Ruth M.	(DC)	768
Dissemination of federal information	BISHOP, Sarah G.	(DC)	99
Dissemination of information	MARTIN, Sandra D.	(KY)	778
	MINOR, Barbara B.	(NY)	846
Distributed information systems	DEERWESTER, Scott C. .	(IL)	287
Drug information	WALSH, Kathryn A.	(CT)	1299
	CARPENTER, Vincent P.	(NC)	185
	LUSTIG, Joanne	(NJ)	750
	SCARFIA, Angela M. . . .	(NY)	1087
	STARR, Lea K.	(AB)	1182
Drug information interchange standards	FASSETT, William E. . . .	(WA)	366
Drug information sources	SEWELL, Winifred	(MD)	1118
Earth science information	ALBRIGHT, Donald A. . .	(NT)	10
Economic & information development	LAU, Jesus G.	(MEX)	702
Economic information	MUZZO, Steven E.	(IL)	883
	WILSON, Brenda J.	(UT)	1350
Economics of information	BRAUNSTEIN, Yale M. .	(CA)	130
	VAN HOUSE, Nancy A. .	(CA)	1275
	KANTOR, Paul B.	(OH)	626
Editing information news stories	LYONS, Ivan	(NY)	753
Educating information users	KUHLTHAU, Carol C. . . .	(NJ)	682
Education for information management	FOSKETT, Antony C. . . .	(AUS)	392
Education of information professionals	HALSEY, Richard S. . . .	(NY)	490
Educational information libraries	EUSTACE, Susan J.	(MD)	356
Electrochemical information organization	LANGKAU, Claire M. . . .	(OH)	696
Electrochemical information retrieval	LANGKAU, Claire M. . . .	(OH)	696
Electronic delivery of information	TIBBETTS, David W. . . .	(NY)	1243
Electronic information	GAPEN, D K.	(WI)	416
Electronic information delivery	HEARTY, John A.	(DC)	519
Electronic information delivery systems	PENNIMAN, W D.	(NJ)	957
Electronic information services	STILLMAN, Stanley W. . .	(NY)	1194
Electronic information systems	WOOD, Richard T.	(MI)	1365
Electronics industry information	THOMAS, Sandra L. . . .	(OR)	1238
Electronics information specialist	COOK, Kathleen M.	(CA)	240

INFORMATION (Cont'd)

Emily Dickinson, poet, info	MOREY, Frederick L. . . .	(MD)	863
Energy & mineral resources information	HARDY, Kenneth J.	(AB)	501
Energy information resources	RIX, Dolores M.	(IL)	1037
Engineering & science information	LUCKER, Jay K.	(MA)	746
Engineering information	OBERG, Judy M.	(CO)	914
	SLOAN, Carol L.	(NY)	1149
	O'GORMAN, Jack	(OH)	918
	POLAND, Jean A.	(OK)	980
	CONKLING, Thomas W. .	(PA)	236
	SLOAN, Stephen M. . . .	(AB)	1150
Engineering information & reference	SCHEIN, Lorraine S.	(NY)	1091
Engineering information provider	AUSTIN, Ralph A.	(NY)	40
Engineering information retrieval	CHANG, Frances M.	(DC)	200
Engineering information sources	PATIENCE, Alice	(OH)	947
Engineering literature & information	HAVLIK, Robert J.	(IN)	513
Engineering material information	SHINER, Sharon L.	(NJ)	1130
Engineering reference information	ST. AUBIN, Kendra J. . .	(MA)	1075
Environmental engineering information	TUCKER, Mary E.	(NC)	1262
Environmental information	SCHEIBEL, Susan	(CA)	1091
	EDDY, Dolores D.	(CO)	335
	YOUNGEN, Gregory K. . .	(IN)	1383
	WHELAN, Julia S.	(MA)	1329
	MCCAULEY, Betty P. . . .	(OR)	795
	STERLING, Alida B.	(PA)	1189
	LOVENBURG, Susan L. .	(AB)	743
Environmental information & data policy	SNODGRASS, Rex J. . .	(NC)	1163
Environmental information databases	MILUTINOVIC, Eunhee C.	(IL)	845
Environmental information management	SNODGRASS, Rex J. . .	(NC)	1163
Environmental information resources	STOSS, Frederick W. . . .	(NY)	1198
Establishing lib & information systems	LEFFALL, Dolores C. . . .	(DC)	712
Ethics for information professionals	HORN, David E.	(MA)	559
Evaluation of technical information	HALL, Homer J.	(NJ)	488
Evaluation research, information systems	SIEGEL, Elliot R.	(MD)	1136
Executive information systems	HARRIS, Jeanne G.	(IL)	504
Expert & optical information systems	SCHNEIDER, Karl R. . . .	(MD)	1097
Export information	PFLEIDERER, Stephen D.	(DC)	966
Farm crisis information	TOHAL, Kate J.	(MN)	1248
Federal information policy	HARPER, Lucy B.	(OH)	503
	MASON, Marilyn G.	(OH)	781
Fee-based information centers	JOSEPHINE, Helen B. . .	(AZ)	617
Film & TV information	ALLEN, Nancy H.	(MI)	15
Film information	COVERT, Nadine	(NY)	252
Finance & business information research	SINGER, Susan A.	(NJ)	1143
Financial & industry information	GINSBURG, Carol L. . . .	(NY)	438
Financial & investment information	WEINSTEIN, Daniel L. . .	(CT)	1318
Financial industry information	HALL, Robert C.	(NY)	488
Financial information	STANTON, Beth L.	(MI)	1181
	ZOTTOLI, Danny A.	(NY)	1390
	FAIR, Linda A.	(ON)	361
Financial information & transaction	RANDOLPH, Kevin H. . .	(CA)	1007
Financial information databases	JONES, Frank	(VA)	613
Financial information products	TIERNEY, Richard H. . . .	(NY)	1244
Financial information surveying	JONES, Frank	(VA)	613
Financial information systems	DEFALCO, Joseph	(NY)	287
Financial services industry information	WARNER, Claudette S. .	(IL)	1305
Financial services information	TRIGAUX, Robert	(DC)	1256
	ALLAN, John	(NY)	14
	BURKE, Edward	(NY)	160
	FINCH, Brian	(NY)	377
	FREY, Ned	(NY)	402
	HENDERSON, Brad	(NY)	526
	KRAUS, James	(NY)	676
	MALKIN, Peter	(NY)	763
	NOVEMBER, Robert S. .	(NY)	911
	RUSLING, Con A.	(NY)	1068
	TYSON, David	(NY)	1267
	VELLA, Carl	(NY)	1281
	ZIMMERMAN, William . .	(NY)	1389
Flexable packaging information analysis	MILLS, Catherine H.	(RI)	843
Florida information	BYRD, Beverly P.	(FL)	168
Food, agriculture, nutrition information	JOHNSON, Sheila A. . . .	(NY)	609
Food safety information systems	CHATFIELD, Michele R. .	(DC)	203
Freedom of information	NIELSON, Paul F.	(MB)	903

INFORMATION (Cont'd)

Freedom of information processing	DOLAN, Maura E.	(DC)	309
Fundraising information support	EVERETT, Amy E.	(DE)	358
Gemology information	DIRLAM, Dona M.	(CA)	305
General business information	WEINSTEIN, Daniel L. . .	(CT)	1318
	THIVIERGE, Lynda M. . .	(PQ)	1235
General information	HARRIS, Jay	(AL)	504
	SALEY, Stacey	(NY)	1076
General library information	EPIL, Charlene M.	(HI)	351
	TANNER, Linda L.	(WI)	1223
General library, information consulting	ALLEN, Richard H.	(NE)	16
	THOMPSON, Debra J. . .	(NH)	1239
	PROVOST, Beverly A. . .	(NY)	996
General reference & information	BUSH, Rhoda H.	(MD)	165
	LINDSAY, Jean S.	(NY)	729
Genetics information	GREEN, Patricia L.	(PA)	462
Geographic information	REX, Heather	(NM)	1024
Geographic information systems	CHAMMOU, Eliezer	(CA)	198
	SUTHERLAND, Johnnie D.	(GA)	1211
	BOURGEOIS, Ann M. . . .	(MI)	119
	REINHARD, Christine M.	(WI)	1021
Geological information	SINNOTT, Gertrude M. . .	(VA)	1144
Geological technical info management	DICKERSON, Mary J. . .	(TX)	300
Geology literature & information	KLIMLEY, Susan	(NY)	661
Geoscience information	MOUNT, Jack D.	(AZ)	873
	COPPIN, Ann S.	(CA)	245
	BIER, Robert A.	(CO)	95
	WICK, Constance S. . . .	(MA)	1335
	PRUETT, Nancy J.	(NM)	996
	STEPP, Dena F.	(OH)	1189
	CHAPPELL, Barbara A. .	(VA)	202
Geoscience information, processing mgmt	BICHTELER, Julie H. . . .	(TX)	94
Geoscience information retrieval	WICK, Constance S.	(MA)	1335
Geriatric information & research	BENSING, Karen M.	(OH)	83
Geriatric information resources	STEPHENSON, Judy A. .	(KY)	1188
Government & legal information	JACOBS, Leslie R.	(MA)	589
Government documents, publications, info	WILLIAMSON, Linda E. .	(IL)	1347
Government information	RICHARDSON, John V. .	(CA)	1029
	PETERSON, Sandra K. . .	(CT)	964
	BARRETT, G J.	(DC)	59
	BECKERMAN, George . .	(DC)	72
	HEANUE, Anne A.	(DC)	518
	HERNON, Peter	(MA)	532
	TAYLOR, Marcia E.	(MD)	1227
	DURRANCE, Joan C. . . .	(MI)	328
	MORTON, Bruce	(MT)	870
	ISACCO, Jeanne M.	(NC)	584
	REELING, Patricia G. . . .	(NJ)	1016
	ZINK, Steven D.	(NV)	1389
	BARRETT, Michael D. . .	(NY)	59
	MCCLURE, Charles R. . .	(NY)	797
	MOREHEAD, Joe	(NY)	863
	SHULER, John A.	(OR)	1133
	ROE, Eunice M.	(PA)	1048
	EISENBEIS, Kathleen M.	(TX)	340
	NIELSON, Paul F.	(MB)	903
	BRIERE, Jean M.	(ON)	135
	HUBBERTZ, Andrew P. .	(SK)	568
Government information access	JOHNSON, Veronica A. .	(MI)	609
Government info index & retrieval	MASSA, Paul P.	(MD)	781
Government information policies	ARDEN, Caroline	(VA)	31
Government information policy	SERBAN, William M. . . .	(LA)	1116
Government information, publications	HINZ, Julianne P.	(UT)	543
Government information sources	CROWLEY, Terence . . .	(CA)	262
Government publications, access to info	WHITAKER, Constance C.	(OH)	1329
Grants information	BEY, Leon S.	(OH)	93
Graphic information analysis	PECK, Brian T.	(FL)	953
Handicaps & blindness information	WILSON, Barbara L. . . .	(RI)	1350
Health care information sources	MESSERLE, Judith R. . .	(MO)	828
Health care information systems	JACOBSEN, Teresa T. . .	(IL)	590
Health information	MARA, Ruth M.	(DC)	768
	VICK, Kathleen	(PA)	1283
Health information clearinghouses	LUNIN, Lois F.	(VA)	749
Health information databases	KISH, Veronica R.	(PA)	656
	PRINGLE, Robert M. . . .	(WA)	993
Health information for consumers	HESSLEIN, Shirley B. . . .	(NY)	534
Health information management	BYRD, Gary D.	(NC)	168

INFORMATION (Cont'd)

Health information resources planning	BYRD, Gary D.	(NC)	168
Health information systems	JENKIN, Michael A.	(FL)	596
	POST, Joyce A.	(PA)	986
Health science information	NEVEU, Wilma B.	(LA)	897
	LONG, Susan S.	(MT)	740
Health sciences information resources	ALMQUIST, Deborah T.	(MA)	17
Herbal & horticultural information	CHADWICK, Alena F.	(MA)	196
High technology information	ROARK, Robin D.	(DC)	1038
Highway research transportation info	MOBLEY, Arthur B.	(DC)	851
Holdings & information brokering	HAHN, Margaret M.	(VA)	483
Horticultural information	LAND, Barbara J.	(CA)	692
Hospital information system	HOYT, Lester H.	(IN)	566
Hospital information systems	ANDERSON, Marilyn M.	(IN)	24
	BUCHANAN, Holly S.	(KY)	153
	LATHROP, Irene M.	(RI)	701
Hospitality industry information	LAURENCE, Katherine S.	(NY)	703
Impact of information technologies	DIENER, Richard A.	(MD)	302
Impact of info technologies on society	FISHER, H L.	(CA)	381
Indexing & editing music information	STRATELAK, Nadia A.	(MI)	1200
Indexing & information systems	MCCRANK, Lawrence J.	(AL)	800
Indexing internal information	AVERY, May S.	(IL)	42
Industrial & economic development info	GRELL, Holly J.	(GA)	467
Industrial hygiene information	TUCKER, Mary E.	(NC)	1262
Industry information	TICKER, Susan L.	(NY)	1244
Information	KISER, Mary D.	(FL)	656
	BOWMAN, Gloria M.	(NC)	121
	HAYNES, Patricia	(NY)	516
	MONACO, James	(NY)	854
	SUDDUTH, Susan F.	(OR)	1206
	WILBURN, Clouse R.	(TN)	1338
Information access	RUBY, Carmela M.	(CA)	1065
Information access & reference	LARY, Marilyn S.	(GA)	700
Information access instruction	GROVER, Iva S.	(WA)	474
Information accumulation	HOGAN, Peter E.	(MD)	549
Information acquisition & analysis	CARSON, Bonnie L.	(MO)	188
Information analysis	PAUSLEY, Barbara H.	(OH)	950
Information & communication systems	RUBEN, Brent D.	(NJ)	1064
Information & documentation center mgmt	MOUREAU, Magdeleine	(FRN)	873
Information & image management	YODER, William M.	(VA)	1380
Information & library service department	ROE, Georgeanne T.	(MA)	1048
Information & library systems	OREJANA, Rebecca D.	(PHP)	925
Information & material acquisitions	CARPENTER, Dale	(NY)	184
Information & productivity research	KOENIG, Michael E.	(NY)	668
Information & public services	CAREN, Loretta	(NY)	181
Information & records management	KATTLOVE, Rose W.	(CA)	630
	OPEM, John D.	(IL)	925
	VAN BRUNT, Virginia	(MD)	1272
Information & records retrieval	LEE, William D.	(CA)	711
Information & reference	WERNE, Kenneth L.	(CO)	1324
	MOTIHAR, Kamla	(NY)	872
Information & reference services	MURTEN, Holly T.	(CA)	882
	GRAHAM, Sylvia R.	(TN)	456
Information & referral	CROWLEY, Terence	(CA)	262
	FISHER, Alice J.	(CA)	380
	NICKERSON, Louann M.	(CA)	902
	TSCHERNY, Elena	(DC)	1260
	JOSEPH, Eleanor C.	(LA)	617
	HEIL, Kathleen A.	(MD)	521
	ZARYCZNY, Wlodzimierz A.	(MI)	1386
	VALANCE, Marsha J.	(MN)	1271
	BEAGLE, Donald R.	(NC)	68
	PARRISH, Nancy B.	(NC)	944
	REILLY, Carol H.	(NC)	1020
	WALDERA, Katherine A.	(ND)	1294
	ELENAUSKY, Edward V.	(NJ)	342
	CRONEBERGER, Robert B.	(PA)	260
	GIBLIN, Carol C.	(PA)	431
	NEWPORT, Dorothea D.	(PA)	900
	BREDESON, Peggy Z.	(WI)	131
	MATTHEWS, Geraldine M.	(WI)	785
	WIERUCKI, Karen A.	(ON)	1337
Information & referral service	CARRINGTON, Ruth	(NY)	186
	ELLIS, Kathy M.	(BC)	344

INFORMATION (Cont'd)

Information & referral services	PAQUETTE, John F.	(CA)	939
	COLON, Carlos W.	(LA)	234
	HSU, Elizabeth L.	(NY)	567
Info & research, business & technical	SPINA, Marie C.	(NY)	1175
Information & retrieval systems	ANDRADE, Rebecca	(CA)	26
Information architecture	REED, Patricia A.	(DC)	1015
Information auditing	ANDEL, June	(PA)	21
Information broker	DE ARMAN, Charles L.	(DC)	284
Information broker & supplier	POND, Frederick C.	(NY)	982
Information broker services	CARROLL, Hardy	(MI)	187
Information brokerage	TEBO, Jay D.	(CA)	1229
	MCELHANEY, William E.	(CT)	804
	HUTCHINS, Richard G.	(IL)	579
	EASLEY, Janet T.	(WA)	332
	DUPLESSIS, Daniel	(PQ)	327
Information brokerage consulting	KLEMENT, Susan P.	(ON)	660
Information brokering	CUEVAS, John R.	(CA)	263
	REISMAN, Sydelle S.	(CT)	1021
	LEIGHTON, Victoria C.	(GA)	714
	INGISH, Karen S.	(IL)	582
	MOORHEAD, John D.	(IL)	862
	COPPOLA, Peter A.	(MA)	245
	BEAUBIEN, Anne K.	(MI)	70
	HALES-MABRY, Celia E.	(MN)	486
	REHKOP, Barbara L.	(MO)	1017
	MCZORN, Bonita A.	(NC)	819
	DEFALCO, Joseph	(NY)	287
	DENOTO, Dorothy E.	(NY)	293
	GIGLIOTTI, Mary J.	(NY)	433
	DE STRICKER, Ulla	(ON)	296
	DIMITRESCU, Ioana	(PQ)	304
	DUBEAU, Pierre	(PQ)	321
Information brokering & supplying	ALDERSON, Karen A.	(IA)	11
Information brokering businesses	BALL, Thomas W.	(DC)	52
Info brokering, supplying, consulting	AXT, Randolph W.	(WI)	42
Information center administration	BONACORDA, James J.	(NY)	113
	BROOME, Diana M.	(BC)	141
	BELLEFONTAINE, Gillian	(ON)	78
Info center & special lib management	COOPER, Marianne	(NY)	243
Information center management	ANGLE, Joanne G.	(DC)	28
	ECKROADE, Carlene B.	(DE)	335
	SIMS, Edward N.	(KY)	1142
	EISENMANN, Laura M.	(MA)	341
	STEIGER, Bettie A.	(MD)	1185
	HOWELL, M G.	(NY)	565
	MARSHALL, Patricia K.	(NY)	775
	RIGNEY, Shirley A.	(NY)	1034
	POLLIS, Angela R.	(PA)	981
	UBALDINI, Michael W.	(TN)	1267
Information center mgmt & organization	ALBERTUS, Donna M.	(NY)	10
Information center management systems	WEIL, Ben H.	(NJ)	1317
Information centers	FRANK, Robyn C.	(MD)	397
	BAKER, Carole A.	(OH)	48
	LEVIN, Pauline G.	(PA)	720
	BIRKS, Grant F.	(ON)	98
Information circulation & management	KAPLAN, Tiby	(FL)	626
Information clearinghouse	SHELBURNE, Elizabeth C.	(DC)	1125
Information clearinghouse methods	LIPETZ, Ben A.	(NY)	732
Information collection	NICHOLSON, Jill A.	(ON)	902
Information communication	WORTHEN, Dennis B.	(NY)	1369
Information compilation	CARSON, Bonnie L.	(MO)	188
Information consulting	CRAWFORD, Marilyn L.	(CA)	257
	ADDISON, Paul H.	(IN)	6
	OJALA, Marydee P.	(KS)	919
	LANDMAN, Lillian L.	(NY)	693
	OWENS, Irene E.	(PA)	932
	LALONDE, Diane	(PQ)	689
Information counseling	DEBONS, Anthony	(PA)	285
	MAURA-SARDO, Mariano A.	(PR)	787
Information database systems	RILEY, Sarah A.	(MD)	1035
Information databases & networks	WOODS, Richard F.	(FIJ)	1367
Information delivery	WENGEL, Linda	(DC)	1324
Information delivery systems & analysis	GRIMES, A R.	(DC)	470
Information desk	WOODARD, Beth S.	(IL)	1365
Information desk & public service	PAWLEY, Carolyn P.	(ON)	951

INFORMATION (Cont'd)

Information dissemination	YU, Hsiao M.	(IA)	1384
	FISH, Paula H.	(NC)	380
Information dissemination, routing	SHALLEY, Doris P.	(PA)	1119
Information distribution	SMITH, Denis J.	(IL)	1154
	KEON, Edward F.	(NJ)	643
Information dynamics	ONONOGBO, Raphael U.	(NGR)	924
Information economics	LAMBERTON, Donald M.	(AUS)	690
Information economics & marketing	YOUNG, Peter R.	(DC)	1383
Information education	CROWLEY, John D.	(CT)	261
Information entrepreneurship	BOYER, Calvin J.	(CA)	123
Information finding	BERKMAN, Robert I.	(NY)	87
Information flow in industries	JACKSON, Eugene B.	(TX)	587
Information flow in organizations	DANIEL, Evelyn H.	(NC)	272
Information for managers & organization	KATZER, Jeffrey	(NY)	630
Information for strategic planning	HANSEN, Kathelen L.	(MN)	497
Information for world peace & humanity	KIANG, C K.	(IN)	646
Information foreign animal diseases	PERLMAN, Stephen E.	(NY)	959
Information gathering	PAUSLEY, Barbara H.	(OH)	950
Information gathering seminars	BERKMAN, Robert I.	(NY)	87
Information geopolitics & policy	AINES, Andrew A.	(MD)	8
Information half-life studies	ASIS, Moises	(CUB)	36
Information identification	BELZER, Jack	(FL)	78
Information industry	QUINT, Barbara E.	(CA)	1000
	ATKIN, Michael I.	(DC)	37
	RUBIN, Lenard H.	(TX)	1064
Info industry & technology tracking	SIECK, Steven K.	(NY)	1135
Information industry economics	BURNS, Christopher	(MA)	162
Information integration	HANSEN, Kathelen L.	(MN)	497
Information law	MARX, Peter	(MA)	780
Information, library services consulting	PARMING, Marju R.	(DC)	943
Information linguistics research	WEINBERG, Bella H.	(NY)	1317
Information literacy	SALLE, Ellen M.	(CO)	1076
Information management	BRAUNSTEIN, Yale M.	(CA)	130
	KAPLAN, Robin	(CA)	626
	KWAN, Julie K.	(CA)	685
	MARLOR, Hugh T.	(CA)	772
	WIERZBA, Heidemarie B.	(CA)	1337
	HUGHES, Brad R.	(CO)	571
	MASTERS, Fred N.	(CT)	782
	STEELE, Noreen O.	(CT)	1184
	FRAULINO, Philip S.	(DC)	399
	KOSTINKO, Gail A.	(DC)	673
	AHLIN, Nancy	(FL)	8
	ROAN, Tattie W.	(GA)	1038
	BECKER, Jacquelyn B.	(IL)	72
	BERGER, Carol A.	(IL)	85
	BRICHFORD, Maynard J.	(IL)	134
	REED, Janet S.	(IL)	1015
	SHEDLOCK, James	(IL)	1124
	STRABLE, Edward G.	(IL)	1199
	HALE, Martha L.	(KS)	485
	CHEN, Ching C.	(MA)	205
	JACQUES, Donna M.	(MA)	591
	MOFFITT, Michael D.	(MA)	852
	CHESLOCK, Rosalind P.	(MD)	207
	DIENER, Richard A.	(MD)	302
	FISHBEIN, Meyer H.	(MD)	380
	JASON, Nora H.	(MD)	595
	POQUETTE, Mary L.	(MN)	984
	BONDAROVICH, Mary F.	(NJ)	113
	DEDERT, Patricia L.	(NJ)	286
	JOHNSON, Minnie L.	(NJ)	607
	MENZUL, Faina	(NJ)	825
	SPAULDING, Frank H.	(NJ)	1172
	BADERTSCHER, David G.	(NY)	44
	BLAKE-O'HOGAN, Kathleen E.	(NY)	103
	CROCKETT, Denise J.	(NY)	259
	EARLE, Marcia H.	(NY)	332
	TAYLOR, Robert S.	(NY)	1228
	WILLNER, Richard A.	(NY)	1349
	BACON, Agnes K.	(OH)	44
	JANKOWSKI, Dorothy A.	(OH)	593
	PETERSON, Barbara E.	(PA)	962
	MASON, Florence M.	(TX)	781
	MIDDLETON, Robert K.	(TX)	833
	PHILLIPS, Toni M.	(TX)	969

INFORMATION (Cont'd)

Information management			
	CAPUTO, Richard P.	(VA)	180
	KUNEY, Joseph H.	(VA)	684
	ROSENBERG, Murray D.	(VA)	1056
	SCHUTTE, Raymond R.	(WA)	1103
	DYSART, Jane I.	(ON)	331
	NOKES, Jane E.	(ON)	907
	NASU, Yukio	(JAP)	889
	WERSIG, Gernot	(WGR)	1325
Information management analysis	BUSSEY, Holly J.	(NY)	165
Information management & data search	ZIAIAN, Monir	(CA)	1387
Information management & marketing	HARMON, Glynn	(TX)	502
Information management & organization	KADEC, Sarah T.	(MD)	621
Information management & planning	JENKINS, Ann A.	(CA)	597
Information management & retention	CHRISTNER, Deborah S.	(CA)	212
Information management consulting	HORTON, Forest W.	(DC)	561
Information management education	HORAK, Ellen B.	(CT)	558
	MARTIN, Elaine R.	(DC)	776
	MCGOWAN, Anna T.	(DC)	807
	TOOEY, Mary J.	(MD)	1250
	WILSON, Barbara A.	(TX)	1349
Information management, library devlpmnt	CONDREY, Barbara K.	(CA)	236
Information management, plng, & systs	KOZAK, Marlene G.	(IL)	674
Information management procedures	HENDERSON, Madeline M.	(MD)	526
Information management resources	STEIGER, Bettie A.	(MD)	1185
Information management srvs consulting	GROCKI, Daniel J.	(MD)	471
Information management software	HASKINS, Dawn A.	(OH)	510
Information management systems	WITTMANN, Cecelia V.	(CA)	1358
	WEST, Richard T.	(MD)	1326
	BAADE, Harley D.	(TX)	43
	KLEIN, Mindy F.	(TX)	659
Information management training	STARK, Philip H.	(CO)	1182
Information marketing	HANEY, Kevin M.	(NJ)	495
Information marketing projects	VAN HALM, Johan	(NET)	1275
Information media research	SETTANNI, Joseph A.	(NY)	1117
Information microbiology, immunology	PERLMAN, Stephen E.	(NY)	959
Information modeling	DENNISON, Lynn C.	(CA)	292
Information modeling & engineering	MAXWELL, Marjo V.	(OH)	788
Information needs & uses	CASE, Donald O.	(CA)	191
	WALDHART, Thomas J.	(KY)	1294
	KIM, Soon C.	(SKO)	649
Information needs evaluations & analysis	HOLDEN, Douglas H.	(ND)	550
Information needs of politicians	TILLOTSON, Greig S.	(AUS)	1245
Information needs, user studies	DURRANCE, Joan C.	(MI)	328
Information network, resource sharing	AGRAWAL, Surendra P.	(IND)	7
Information networks	TUROCK, Betty J.	(NJ)	1265
Information of international relations	RIGNEY, Janet M.	(NY)	1034
Information on deafness	HURLEY, Faith P.	(DC)	577
Information on genetic disorders	HOLT, Suzy	(MT)	554
Information organization	NYBERG, Lelia J.	(CA)	912
Information policies	BERGER, Patricia W.	(MD)	86
	JACOB, Mary E.	(OH)	589
	MACDONALD, Alan H.	(AB)	754
Information policy	SCHILLER, Anita R.	(CA)	1093
	BARRETT, G J.	(DC)	59
	MILEVSKI, Sandra N.	(DC)	835
	PEYTON, David	(DC)	966
	RATH, Charla M.	(DC)	1009
	ENGLER, June L.	(GA)	350
	MCDERMOTT, Patrice	(IL)	802
	HEIM, Kathleen M.	(LA)	521
	DANIEL, Evelyn H.	(NC)	272
	KLEMPNER, Irving M.	(NY)	660
	BEARMAN, Toni C.	(PA)	69
	SY, Karen J.	(WA)	1217
	HOWARD, Helen A.	(PQ)	564
Information policy administration	DE TONNANCOUR, P R.	(TX)	296
Information policy & planning	JACKSON, Miles M.	(HI)	588
Information policy & security	KNOPPERS, Jake V.	(ON)	665
Information policy development	SPATH, Charles E.	(TN)	1171
Information policy issues	CHARTRAND, Robert L.	(DC)	203

INFORMATION (Cont'd)

Information processing

	CRIM, Dewey H.	(GA)	258
	ROTHMAN, John	(NY)	1060
	SCHUTT, Dedre A.	(NY)	1103
	CARNEY, Marillyn L.	(VA)	183
Information processing & control	SPATH, Charles E.	(TN)	1171
Information processing consulting	ETZI, Richard	(NY)	356
Information processing technology	SAFFADY, William	(NY)	1074
Information product design & development	DAY, Melvin S.	(VA)	283
Information product design & maintenance	PISCITELLI, Rosalie A.	(NY)	976
Information product development	HART, Patricia H.	(MI)	507
	BARTLETT, Jay P.	(NY)	61
Information product development mgmt	BRAM, Leon L.	(NJ)	127
Information product management	LEHMANN, Edward J.	(VA)	713
Information product market development	SAYER, John S.	(MD)	1086
Information products	MUZZO, Steven E.	(IL)	883
Information products development	ABLES, Timothy D.	(MS)	2
Information program development	FRIERSON, Eleanor G.	(DC)	404
Information publishing	GREENWAY, Helen B.	(CT)	465
	SEVERTSON, Susan M.	(VA)	1117
Information publishing, professionals	RICCOBONO, Joseph V.	(CT)	1026
Information, reference & referral	GUSS, Emily R.	(IL)	478
Information reference computers	MAJOR, Marla J.	(MI)	762
Information, reference services	MARTIN, Elaine R.	(DC)	776
Information research	PECK, Brian T.	(FL)	953
Information resource management	DENNISON, Lynn C.	(CA)	292
	MCCARTHY, John L.	(CA)	794
	STAN, Gail A.	(CA)	1179
	BEICHMAN, John C.	(MI)	75
	DANIEL, Evelyn H.	(NC)	272
	KOENIG, Michael E.	(NY)	668
	HODGSON, Cynthia A.	(PA)	546
	LYTLE, Richard H.	(PA)	753
	BURNS, Barrie A.	(ON)	162
Information resource systems	THOMAS, Margaret J.	(MI)	1237
Information resources	ROBBINS, Gordon D.	(TN)	1038
Information resources management	POEHLMAN, Dorothy J.	(DC)	979
	EVERETT, Amy E.	(DE)	358
	BROWN, Patricia L.	(IL)	146
	REITER, Richard R.	(IL)	1022
	MOBLEY, Kathleen S.	(KS)	851
	LEVITAN, Karen B.	(MD)	721
	NEWMAN, Wilda B.	(MD)	900
	PRICE, Douglas S.	(MD)	992
	HAMLIN, Eileen M.	(NY)	493
	MARCHAND, Donald A.	(NY)	768
	MARTIN, Thomas H.	(NY)	778
	RODERER, Nancy K.	(NY)	1047
	MOORE, Penelope F.	(VA)	861
Information retention & disposal	ROFES, William L.	(NY)	1049
Information retrieval	NEMCHEK, Lee R.	(CA)	895
	NEWMAN, Mark J.	(CA)	899
	SHANMAN, Roberta	(CA)	1120
	SHARP, Geoffrey H.	(CA)	1122
	CHANAUD, Jo P.	(CO)	199
	CONRAD, Celia B.	(CT)	238
	SUPEAU, Cynthia	(CT)	1210
	BELLARDO, Trudi	(DC)	78
	EDWARDS, Andrea Y.	(DC)	337
	LUNDEEN, Gerald W.	(HI)	748
	ANTON, Tess	(IL)	29
	BIRKHOLD, Martha S.	(IL)	98
	CAREY, Kevin J.	(IL)	181
	DEERWESTER, Scott C.	(IL)	287
	HILDRETH, Charles R.	(IL)	539
	JOHNSON, Anita D.	(IL)	602
	LANCASTER, Frederick W.	(IL)	691
	SMITH, Linda C.	(IL)	1157
	SWANSON, Don R.	(IL)	1213
	HARTER, Stephen P.	(IN)	508
	HICKLING, Jeanne	(IN)	536
	MARKEE, Katherine M.	(IN)	771
	BOYCE, Bert R.	(LA)	122
	KRAFT, Donald H.	(LA)	674
	RAGHAVAN, Vijay V.	(LA)	1003

INFORMATION (Cont'd)

Information retrieval

	BOGART, Betty B.	(MA)	110
	DENTON, Francesca L.	(MA)	293
	DRESLEY, Susan C.	(MA)	319
	BRANDHORST, Wesley T.	(MD)	128
	BUCHAN, Ronald L.	(MD)	153
	CARR, Margaret M.	(MD)	186
	BALOK, Becki	(MI)	53
	EVERITT, Janet M.	(MI)	359
	ASPNES, Grieg G.	(MN)	37
	BURGIN, Robert E.	(NC)	159
	KISER, Anita H.	(NC)	656
	LOSEE, Robert M.	(NC)	742
	DATUS, Marie B.	(NE)	275
	AMIRZAFARI, Jamileh A.	(NJ)	20
	SARACEVIC, Tefko	(NJ)	1082
	BERRY, Gayle C.	(NY)	90
	CARICONE, Paul	(NY)	181
	CULLEN, Martin J.	(NY)	263
	CYPSER, Rudy J.	(NY)	268
	ETTLINGER, Sandra E.	(NY)	356
	KATZER, Jeffrey	(NY)	630
	KRONISH, Priscilla T.	(NY)	680
	PEARCE, Karla J.	(NY)	952
	SALTON, Gerard	(NY)	1077
	SCHAFFER, Rita K.	(NY)	1089
	BROWN, Rowland C.	(OH)	147
	HARTNER, Elizabeth P.	(PA)	508
	MICCO, Helen M.	(PA)	831
	PAUL, Thompson	(PA)	949
	CARLIN, Don	(TN)	182
	MCDONALD, Ethel Q.	(TN)	802
	ECHT, Sandy A.	(TX)	334
	HELFER, Robert S.	(TX)	523
	MOORE, Guusje Z.	(TX)	859
	WALKER, Constance M.	(TX)	1295
	LIU, Kitty P.	(UT)	734
	PITERNICK, Anne B.	(BC)	976
	NELSON, Michael J.	(ON)	894
	RIDLEY, A M.	(ON)	1033
	TAGUE, Jean M.	(ON)	1220
	THACH, Phat V.	(PQ)	1233
	WALKER, Elizabeth A.	(PQ)	1295
	BEATTIE, Kathleen M.	(AUS)	70
	CLEVERDON, Cyril W.	(ENG)	221
	BLOCH, Uri	(ISR)	105
	ELAZAR, David H.	(ISR)	341
	NASU, Yukio	(JAP)	889
	YAMAZAKI, Hisamichi	(JAP)	1377
Information retrieval & analysis	OWEN, Beth C.	(MA)	931
Information retrieval & indexing	HUMPHREY, Susanne M.	(MD)	573
Information retrieval & reference	DONNELLY, Kathleen	(OH)	311
Information retrieval & services	COFFEE, E G.	(KS)	226
Information retrieval design system	KORNFELD, Carol E.	(NJ)	672
Information retrieval in Latin America	GREEN-MALONEY, Nancy	(CA)	465
Information retrieval research	COOPER, William S.	(CA)	244
	HUESTIS, Jeffrey C.	(MO)	570
	FOX, Edward A.	(VA)	394
Information retrieval service	BOURNE, Charles P.	(CA)	119
Information retrieval services	WILLMANN, Donna S.	(PA)	1348
Information retrieval software	RALBOVSKY, Edward A.	(NY)	1004
	NICHOL, Kathleen M.	(BC)	901
Information retrieval software design	BRUNELLE, Bette S.	(NY)	150
Information retrieval software	LEDOUX, Marc A.	(PQ)	708
Information retrieval system	SANO, Hikomaro	(JAP)	1081
Information retrieval system design	MEYER, Alan H.	(MD)	829
	MCCLELLAND, Bruce A.	(NY)	796
Information retrieval systems	CUADRA, Carlos A.	(CA)	262
	GABBERT, Gretchen W.	(CA)	411
	SHELBURNE, Elizabeth C.	(DC)	1125
	SCHIPMA, Peter B.	(IL)	1093
	EISENMANN, Laura M.	(MA)	341
	BONDAROVICH, Mary F.	(NJ)	113
	CHAPMAN, Janet L.	(NJ)	202
	FRANTS, Valery	(NJ)	398
	GLAMM, Amy E.	(VA)	439
	SAUVE, Deborah A.	(VA)	1085
	REILLY, Brian O.	(ON)	1020
	ZHU, Xiaofeng	(CHI)	1387

INFORMATION (Cont'd)
Information retrieval systems

ROBERTSON, Stephen E. (ENG)1042
CHAUMIER, Jacques . . . (FRN) 204
Information retrieval systems design ANDERSON, James D. . (NJ) 23
Information retrieval technologies HOLMES, Lyndon S. . . . (MA) 553
Information retrieval theories HOSONO, Kimio . . . . . . (JAP) 562
Information retrieval thesaurus ASIS, Moises . . . . (CUB) 36
Information sales & marketing BARTLETT, Jay P. . . . . . (NY) 61
Information searches SPAHR, Cheryl L. . . . . . (OH) 1170
Information searches, manual &
  computer SHALLEY, Doris P. . . . . . (PA) 1119
Information searching VAUGHN, Robert V. . . . . (VI) 1280
Information security ROFES, William L. . . . . . (NY) 1049
Information seeking behavior BATES, Marcia J. . . . . . . (CA) 64
  BENIDIR, Samia . . . . (CA) 80
  KUHLTHAU, Carol C. . . . (NJ) 682
  VONDRAN, Raymond F. . . (TX) 1288
  KRIKELAS, James . . . . . (WI) 678
Information seeking strategies MARCHIONINI, Gary J. . (MD) 769
Info service effectiveness measures TIFFT, Jeanne D. . . . . . . (DC) 1244
Info services, acq diversification REEDY, Martha J. . . . . . (MA) 1015
Info services measurement evaluation WERT, Lucille M. . . . . . . (IL) 1325
Info skills & curriculum correlation JONES, Wanda F. . . . . . (AR) 615
  MCKINNEY, Barbara J. . . (AR) 812
Information skills curriculum COWEN, Linda L. . . . . . . (OK) 253
Information skills in curriculum HAYCOCK, Kenneth R. . (BC) 515
Information sources & services PIERCE, Sydney J. . . . . . (GA) 972
  TAYLOR, Margaret T. . . . (MI) 1227
  ESTES, Glenn E. . . . . . . (TN) 355
Information sources & utilization VOIGT, Melvin J. . . . . . . (CA) 1287
Information specialist TRZICKY, Richard F. . . . (AZ) 1260
  BERGEN, Dessa C. . . . . (NY) 85
  GILLESBY, John D. . . . . (WI) 435
Information specialization ROOSHAN, Gertrude I. . . (CA) 1053
  LEREW, Ann A. . . . . (CO) 717
  RAND, Pamela S. . . . . . . (MD) 1006
Information standards KELLY, Maureen C. . . . . (PA) 638
Information storage & retrieval KENDRICK, Brent L. . . . (DC) 640
  CARR, Sallyann . . . . (FL) 186
  CHERN, Jenn C. . . . . . . (GA) 206
  GOODY, Cheryl S. . . . . . (HI) 450
  BOOKSTEIN, Abraham . . (IL) 115
  SHAW, Debora . . . . (IL) 1123
  WALDHART, Thomas J. . (KY) 1294
  BRIAND, Margaret M. . . . (MA) 134
  GEORGE, Muriel S. . . . . (NJ) 428
  AUSTIN, Ralph A. . . . . . (NY) 40
  GREENBERG, Linda . . . . (NY) 463
  WYLLYS, Ronald E. . . . . (TX) 1375
  MORRISON, David L. . . . . (UT) 868
  BONNETT, Mary B. . . . . . (VA) 114
  SCHABAS, Ann H. . . . . . (ON) 1088
  WILSON, Concepcion S. . (AUS)1350
Information storage & retrieval theory WILSON, Patrick . . . . . . (CA) 1352
Information strategic planning JACOBSEN, Teresa T. . . (IL) 590
Information studies GARSON, Kenneth W. . . (PA) 420
Information supply MAHAFFEY, Susan M. . . (CA) 760
  GRANT, Mary M. . . . . . . (NY) 458
Information support for researchers JONES, Kendra A. . . . . . (TN) 613
Information system & services
  planning KITTUR, Krishna N. . . . . (IND) 657
Information system design KOPP, Kurt W. . . . . (MO) 671
  RUSHING, Jessie W. . . . (TN) 1068
  MEADOW, Charles T. . . (ON) 819
  VAN SLYPE, Georges . . (BEL)1277
Information system design &
  management FREEDMAN, Bernadette . (PA) 400
  LAZAR, Peter . . . . (HUN) 706
Information system development JONES, Gerry U. . . . . . . (MD) 613
  KOPP, Kurt W. . . . . (MO) 671
  GUBIOTTI, Ross A. . . . . (OH) 475
Information system evaluation GRIFFITH, Belver C. . . . (PA) 469
  VAN SLYPE, Georges . . (BEL)1277
Information systems SEDELOW, Sally Y. . . . . (AR) 1110
  SEDELOW, Walter A. . . . (AR) 1110
  HOTZ, Sharon M. . . . . . . (CA) 562
  LEWIS, Gretchen S. . . . . (CA) 723
  PALLONE, Kitty J. . . . . . (CA) 935
  PETERMAN, Claudia A. . (CA) 962

INFORMATION (Cont'd)
Information systems

VARAT, Nancy L. . . . . . . (CA) 1278
SHAW, Ward . . . . (CO) 1124
ORRICO, James T. . . . . (CT) 926
FOX, Ann M. . . . . (DC) 394
FRANCIS, Diane S. . . . . (DE) 396
GRIES, James P. . . . . . . (IL) 468
COPLER, Judith A. . . . . . (IN) 244
FRY, Bernard M. . . . . . . (IN) 406
ROMALEWSKI, Robert S. (LA) 1052
DOWLER, Lawrence E. . (MA) 315
FERGUSON, Roberta J. . (MA) 372
KANG, Wen . . . . (MA) 625
O'REILLY, Daniel F. . . . . (MA) 925
YACOUBY, Ray S. . . . . . (MA) 1376
ANDERSON, John E. . . . (MD) 23
JOHNSON, Susan W. . . (MD) 609
PAUL, Thomas A. . . . . . (MI) 949
ABLES, Timothy D. . . . . . (MS) 2
SNODGRASS, Rex J. . . . (NC) 1163
KELSEY, Ann L. . . . . (NJ) 639
PENNIMAN, W D. . . . . . (NJ) 957
HARRISON, Susan E. . . (NV) 507
EISENBERG, Debra . . . . (NY) 340
SCHARF, Davida . . . . . . (NY) 1090
SIMONIS, James J. . . . . (NY) 1141
KILGOUR, Frederick G. . (OH) 648
KISER, Betsy N. . . . . (OH) 656
MCCONNELL, Pamela J. . (OH) 798
ROMANOS, Vasso A. . . (OH) 1052
TRIVISON, Donna . . . . . (OH) 1257
PETERSON, Barbara E. . (PA) 962
TOMASOVIC, Evelyn . . . (PA) 1249
TILSON, Koleta B. . . . . . (TN) 1245
ANDERSON, Madeleine J. (TX) 24
VONDRAN, Raymond F. . . (TX) 1288
LAHR, Thomas F. . . . . . . (VA) 688
MORSE, June E. . . . . . . (VA) 869
TATALIAS, Jean A. . . . . (VA) 1225
MCCORMICK, Jack M. . . (WA) 798
DYKSTRA, Mary E. . . . . (NS) 331
BIRKS, Grant F. . . . . (ON) 98
SIMARD, Denis . . . . (PQ) 1139
NEAME, Roderick L. . . . (AUS) 891
IRURIA, Daniel M. . . . . . (KEN) 584
LIM, Hucktee E. . . . . (MLY) 727
Information systems analysis & design BORKO, Harold . . . . (CA) 116
  WILLIAMS, James G. . . . (PA) 1344
Information systems & decision
  support BERGFELD, C D. . . . . . . (NY) 86
Information systems & technologies FRIERSON, Eleanor G. . . (DC) 404
Information systems consultant SHAMS, Kamruddin . . . . (CA) 1120
Information systems, database design FOURNIER, Susan K. . . . (MD) 393
Information systems design MICHEL, Dee A. . . . . (CA) 832
  TUNG, Sandra J. . . . . . . (CA) 1263
  KENNEY, Brigitte L. . . . . (CO) 641
  RADER, Ronald A. . . . . . (DC) 1002
  SOERGEL, Dagobert . . . (MD) 1165
  KELLER, Karen A. . . . . . (MI) 635
  WAGNER, A B. . . . . (NY) 1291
  WARD, Edith . . . . (NY) 1303
  HOLMES, John H. . . . . . (PA) 553
  LEONARD, Lucinda E. . . (VA) 716
  BOOHER, Craig S. . . . . . (WI) 115
Information systems design, analysis SYPERT, Clyde F. . . . . . (CA) 1217
Information systems design &
  development WHITE, Suellen S. . . . . . (CO) 1332
  CLARK, Rick . . . . (NJ) 218
Information systems design &
  evaluation LEVITAN, Karen B. . . . . (MD) 721
Information systems design &
  integration CHU, John S. . . . . (PA) 212
Information systems development PARSONS, John W. . . . . (DC) 945
  KOSMAN, Joyce E. . . . . (IL) 672
  HOLMES, Lyndon S. . . . (MA) 553
  ETZI, Richard . . . . (NY) 356
  BERGMAN, Rita F. . . . . . (VA) 86
  COTTER, Gladys A. . . . . (VA) 250
  HOWARD, Theresa M. . . (ENG) 564

INFORMATION (Cont'd)

Information systems engineering	LISTON, David M.	(MD)	732
Information systems management	TETTEH, Joseph A.	(LA)	1233
	MENOU, Michel J.	(ITL)	824
Information systems, microcomputers	ANDERSON, Axel R.	(WI)	21
Information systems needs assessment	ROBERTS, Lesley A.	(DC)	1040
Information systems planning	PARMING, Marju R.	(DC)	943
	ABLES, Timothy D.	(MS)	2
	FABRE DE MORLHON, Christiane	(ITL)	360
Information systems planning, consulting	GROTE, Janet H.	(NY)	473
Information systems research	SNYDER, Cathrine E.	(TN)	1164
Information systems research & devlpmnt	TONKERY, Thomas D.	(NY)	1250
Information systems strategic planning	PEETERS, Marc D.	(BEL)	954
Information technologies	MASON, Marilyn G.	(OH)	781
	WERSIG, Gernot	(WGR)	1325
Information technologies & services	CARTER, Daniel H.	(TX)	189
Information technologies education	BOONE, Morell D.	(MI)	115
Information technology	BUTLER, Matilda L.	(CA)	167
	CASE, Donald O.	(CA)	191
	HELFER, Doris S.	(CA)	523
	PAISLEY, William J.	(CA)	935
	WALTER, Virginia A.	(CA)	1300
	DREWES, Arlene T.	(DC)	319
	PRICE, Joseph W.	(DC)	992
	DRAKE, Miriam A.	(GA)	318
	DOWELL, David R.	(IL)	315
	PARK, Chung I.	(IL)	940
	WATERS, Samuel T.	(MD)	1309
	D'ALLEYRAND, Marc R.	(NY)	270
	SWEENEY, Richard T.	(NY)	1215
	PRICKETT, Dan S.	(OH)	993
	ERES, Beth K.	(ISR)	352
	MINAIKIT, Nonglak	(THA)	845
Information technology & management	FIDOTEN, Robert E.	(PA)	375
Information technology applications	BISHOP, Sarah G.	(DC)	99
	MILEVSKI, Sandra N.	(DC)	835
Information technology assessment	DUCHESNE, Roderick M.	(ON)	322
Information technology economics	MCSPADDEN, Robert M.	(OH)	818
Information technology management	MCKIRDY, Pamela R.	(MA)	812
	BECKMAN, Margaret L.	(ON)	73
Information technology planning	BURNS, Christopher	(MA)	162
	TAUBER, Stephen J.	(MA)	1225
Info tools & implementation development	MARTINEZ-GOLDMAN, Aline	(MD)	779
Information training	CHICOREL, Marietta S.	(AZ)	208
	ADDISON, Paul H.	(IN)	6
Information transfer	JASON, Nora H.	(MD)	595
Information use & users	WILKINSON, John P.	(ON)	1340
Information, user interface	HUTTON, Emily A.	(WA)	579
Information uses	TAYLOR, Robert S.	(NY)	1228
Information utilities	MORGAN, Bradford A.	(SD)	863
Information virology, molecular biology	PERLMAN, Stephen E.	(NY)	959
Information work	MEDER, Marylouise D.	(KS)	820
Informational database construction	BERGMANN, Allison M.	(NY)	86
Informational skills instruction	LOPEZ, Kathryn P.	(NM)	741
Information-products produced harmlessly	THURSTON, Ethel H.	(NY)	1243
Information-seeking skills instruction	MICIKAS, Lynda L.	(PA)	832
Instruction in information skills	COOK, Sybilla A.	(OR)	240
Insurance information	STRAZDON, Maureen E.	(NY)	1201
Integrated info resources management	KNOPPERS, Jake V.	(ON)	665
Integrated information systems	RAGHAVAN, Vijay V.	(LA)	1003
	CHIANG, Katherine S.	(NY)	207
Integrated service for info resources	BERGERON, Pierrette	(PQ)	86
Internal information	FEDORS, Maurica R.	(NJ)	368
International business information	SIMON, David H.	(NJ)	1140
International information	MARA, Ruth M.	(DC)	768
International info & cultural exchange	STEERE, Paul J.	(DC)	1184
International information issues	TIFFT, Jeanne D.	(DC)	1244
	EL-HADIDY, Bahaa	(FL)	342
International information planning	CAMPBELL, Harry	(ON)	176
International information sources	WILLIAMS, Robert V.	(SC)	1346
International information standards	KOLTAY, Emery I.	(NY)	670

INFORMATION (Cont'd)

International information transfer	GREENFIELD, Stanley R.	(NY)	464
International library & information prog	GRAY, Dorothy L.	(DC)	459
Intl library & information systems	GOODMAN, Henry J.	(AB)	449
Intrapreneuring & information brokering	BROWN, Ina A.	(NJ)	144
Investing information	WARD, Catherine J.	(NJ)	1303
Investment information systems	CAHILL, Jack F.	(MA)	171
Japanese business & management info	NOGUCHI, Sachie	(IL)	907
Japanese information	TUCKER, Laura R.	(NY)	1262
Japanese life sciences information	WILLIAMS, Mitsuko	(IL)	1345
Japanese science & tech information	SHERMAN, Roger S.	(CA)	1128
	QUINN, Ralph M.	(NJ)	1000
Japanese science technology information	TALBOT, Dawn E.	(CA)	1220
Job & career information	LANE, Steven P.	(WA)	694
Job information	WERTSMAN, Vladimir F.	(NY)	1325
Job information center	BRODERICK, Therese L.	(NY)	139
Job information centers	DESCH, Carol A.	(NY)	294
Knowledge-based information system	WEI, Yin M.	(OH)	1316
Land use information	HURLBERT, Roger W.	(CA)	577
Large-scale information systems	SAYER, John S.	(MD)	1086
Law firm, information systems	EWING, Alison L.	(AZ)	359
Law information processing	ARAJ, Houda	(PQ)	30
Legal information	KANJI, Zainab J.	(CA)	625
	JOHNSON, John R.	(OH)	606
	ANDERSON, Axel R.	(WI)	21
Legal information & reference work	OREJANA, Rebecca D.	(PHP)	925
Legal information databases	WEGMANN, Pamela A.	(TX)	1316
Legal information management	COMSTOCK, Daniel L.	(NM)	235
Legal information marketing	HALL, Brian H.	(CO)	487
Legal information publishing	HALL, Brian H.	(CO)	487
Legal information retrieval education	BARBEN, Tanya A.	(SAF)	55
Legal information systems	STERN, Michael P.	(MD)	1189
Legislative & regulatory information	JOHNSON, Jacqueline B.	(DC)	605
Leveraging information technologies	MCLANE, John F.	(CT)	813
Library & info center administration	CROSS, Jennie B.	(MI)	260
Library & info center establishment	FINGERMAN, Susan M.	(MA)	378
Library & information center management	CEPPOS, Karen F.	(CA)	196
	LEWIS, Ralph W.	(CA)	724
	MADDOCK, Jerome T.	(CO)	759
	FINGERMAN, Susan M.	(MA)	378
	PARAS, Lucille P.	(NJ)	939
Library & info community cooperation	BARTLEY, Linda K.	(DC)	61
Library & information consultant	MOON, Fletcher F.	(TN)	857
Library & information education	MAHOUD ALY, Usama E.	(EGY)	761
Library & information instruction	FEW, John E.	(CA)	374
Library & information law	HAMMERLY, Hernan D.	(ARG)	493
Library & information magazines	GOLD, Renee L.	(NY)	444
Library & information management	BENDER, David R.	(DC)	79
	BOYLE, Stephen	(IL)	124
	BROWN, Ina A.	(NJ)	144
Library & information networks	ENGLER, June L.	(GA)	350
	STUART-STUBBS, Basil F.	(BC)	1204
	MINAIKIT, Nonglak	(THA)	845
Library & information policy	MOORE, Bessie B.	(DC)	858
Library & information profession educ	GALVIN, Thomas J.	(IL)	415
Library & information publishing	GOLD, Renee L.	(NY)	444
Library & information resource systems	NELSON, James A.	(KY)	894
Library & info science placement	WELSH, Barbara W.	(PA)	1323
Library & information skills	TALLMAN, Julie I.	(NY)	1221
Library & information skills instruction	RATZER, Mary B.	(NY)	1010
Library & information studies	LEAHY, Michael D.	(CT)	707
	DE SCOSSA, Catriona	(AB)	295
Library & information systems	DEBUSE, Raymond	(WA)	285
	WARD, Maryanne	(WA)	1304
	CHANDLER, George	(ENG)	200
Library & information systems & tech	GRIFFITHS, Jose M.	(MD)	469
Library & information systems consulting	MADDOCK, Jerome T.	(CO)	759
Library & info technology standards	MANNING, Ralph W.	(ON)	767
Library & information user education	EL-DUWEINI, Aadel K.	(EGY)	342
Library information & reference services	STUART, Gerard W.	(AZ)	1204
Library, information education	BEARMAN, Toni C.	(PA)	69
Library, information exec recruitment	GOSSAGE, Wayne	(NY)	453

INFORMATION (Cont'd)

Library, information industry interface	MACDONALD, Alan H. . .	(AB)	754
Library information management	SMART, Marriott W.	(CO)	1151
Library, information mgmt consulting	GOSSAGE, Wayne	(NY)	453
Library information management systems	SMITH, Jessie C.	(MD)	1156
Library information networks	RAWLINS, Gordon W. . .	(PA)	1010
Library, information personnel services	GOSSAGE, Wayne	(NY)	453
Library information science history	MIKSA, Francis L.	(TX)	834
Library information system	ZHANG, Foster J.	(CA)	1387
Library information systems	KERR, Robert C.	(CO)	644
	HERNANDEZ, Hector R. .	(IL)	531
	LUDWIG, Logan T.	(IL)	747
	VAN HOUTEN, Stephen .	(IL)	1275
	ASSOUAD, Carol S.	(MD)	37
	PAUL, Rameshwar N. . . .	(MD)	949
	JENSEN, Charla J.	(UT)	598
Library management & information	MILLER, Merna B.	(FL)	841
Licensed day care information	TOHAL, Kate J.	(MN)	1248
Life sciences information	SEARS, Jonathan R. . . .	(MD)	1110
Local government information	STRICKLAND, Ann T. . . .	(AZ)	1202
Local government information network	AHLIN, Nancy	(FL)	8
Machine-readable business information	AULD, Dennis B.	(KY)	39
Mainframe-based chemical info systems	MEYER, Daniel E.	(PA)	830
Maintain library & information file	RATZABI, Arlene	(NY)	1010
Management & budgeting info technologies	LOWRY, Charles B.	(TX)	745
Management & business information	SCHNEDEKER, Donald W.	(NY)	1096
Management chemical information research	STOBAUGH, Robert E. . .	(OH)	1195
Management information	VASSALLO, Paul	(NM)	1279
	MONTY, Vivienne	(ON)	857
Management information consulting	CARTELLI, Alessandra J.	(PA)	188
	PLEFKA, Cathleen S. . . .	(PA)	978
Management information systems	SCHERREI, Rita A.	(CA)	1092
	TRIOLO, Victor A.	(CT)	1257
	SHENASSA, Daryoosh . .	(IL)	1126
	RADEMACHER, Richard J.	(KS)	1002
	ANDERSON, John E. . . .	(MD)	23
	MOTT, Thomas H.	(NJ)	872
	LITTLE, Paul L.	(OK)	733
	SKOVIRA, Robert J.	(PA)	1147
	BONNELLY, Claude	(PQ)	114
Management information systems for libs	SCHUELLER, Janette H.	(WA)	1101
Management of information, records	WELCH, Donald A.	(TX)	1321
Management of information services	MANCALL, Jacqueline C.	(PA)	764
Management of information systems	MOSER, Jane W.	(CA)	870
Managing information in systems	ARDERN, Christine M. . .	(ON)	31
Managing pharmaceutical information	DRUKKER, Alexander E. .	(DE)	320
Manufacturing information resources	KELLER, Karen A.	(MI)	635
Manufacturing information systems	BEICHMAN, John C. . . .	(MI)	75
Map information	REINHARD, Christine M.	(WI)	1021
Maps & cartographic information	REX, Heather	(NM)	1024
Maps & geographic information	IVES, Peter B.	(NM)	586
Marine & land-based information	CAMPBELL, Margaret E.	(NS)	177
Marine biology information	BALDRIDGE, Alan	(CA)	51
Marine sciences information	BALDRIDGE, Alan	(CA)	51
Maritime information	SHIPMAN, Natalie W. . .	(TX)	1131
Maritime science information	SHIPMAN, Natalie W. . .	(TX)	1131
Market information	GARDNER, Catherine P.	(MA)	417
	THOMAS, Sandra L. . . .	(OR)	1238
	GILLEN, Bonnie J.	(PA)	435
Market information databases	BOYD, Cheryl J.	(MN)	122
Market research for the info industry	SOVNER-RIBBLER, Judith	(MA)	1170
Marketing electronic information	ARNOLD, Stephen E. . . .	(KY)	34
Marketing information	RANDOLPH, Kevin H. . .	(CA)	1007
	BERLIET, Nathalie B. . . .	(CT)	87
	PALMER, Shirley	(CT)	937
	MURPHY, Therese B. . . .	(IL)	881
	OKEY, Susan T.	(IN)	920
	MCDONALD, Dennis D. .	(MD)	802
	CHANG, Bernadine A. . .	(NJ)	200
	MOLITERNO, Daniel A. .	(NY)	853
Marketing information & library service	ALIX, Cleta M.	(CA)	13
Marketing information collections	BURROWS, Shirley	(NY)	163

INFORMATION (Cont'd)

Marketing information products	GERSH, Barbara S.	(CA)	429
Marketing of information	KEON, Edward F.	(NJ)	643
Mass media information	ALLEN, Nancy H.	(MI)	15
Mass transit information	KANE, Deborah A.	(TX)	624
Mechanized information retrieval	KENT, Allen	(PA)	642
Medical care information & reference	CAHALAN, Thomas H. . .	(MA)	171
Medical, dental information	PRATT, Gregory F.	(IL)	990
Medical information	MARSON, Joyce	(CA)	775
	ROWLAND, Lucy M. . . .	(GA)	1062
	FEDECZKO, Joyce L. . . .	(IL)	367
	JOHNSON, Anita D.	(IL)	602
	BRYANT, Barton B.	(MI)	152
	TOHAL, Kate J.	(MN)	1248
	CRANDALL, Elisabeth G.	(NC)	255
	TIEDRICH, Ellen K.	(NJ)	1244
	THOMSON, Diane G. . . .	(NY)	1241
	HAYNES, Robert B.	(ON)	517
	VEEKEN, Mary L.	(ON)	1280
	HANHAN, Leila M.	(LEB)	495
Medical information & librarianship	EL-MASRY, Mohammed .	(EGY)	345
Medical information & research	SMITH, Sharon	(CSR)	1160
Medical information research	WHITESIDE, Lee A.	(FL)	1333
Medical information retrieval	WAKEFIELD, Jacqueline M.	(CA)	1293
Medical information sources	TEITELBAUM, Sandra D.	(MD)	1230
Medical info system analysis & design	HENDRICKSON, Maria F.	(NY)	527
Medical information systems	JENKIN, Michael A.	(FL)	596
	BAKER, Benjamin R. . . .	(MD)	48
	HUMPHREYS, Betsy L. .	(MD)	573
	JACOBS, Patt	(OR)	590
	PORTER, William R.	(TN)	985
	URATA, Kazuo	(JAP)	1269
Medical information transfer	SEWELL, Winifred	(MD)	1118
Medical psychology information research	BLADEN, Marguerite . . .	(CA)	102
Microcomputer information	SPIGAI, Fran	(CA)	1174
Microcomputer information retrieval	WOODWARD, Anthony M.	(ENG)	1367
Microcomputer information sources	MAYER, Erich J.	(NY)	789
Microcomputer-based chemical info system	MEYER, Daniel E.	(PA)	830
Microcomputer-based information systems	JOHNSON, Jane S.	(IL)	605
Motivational & informational speaker	LYNCH, Minnie L.	(LA)	752
Municipal information systems	BOCKMAN, Eugene J. . .	(NY)	109
Museum information systems	BEARMAN, David A. . . .	(PA)	69
National information networks	BLOCH, Uri	(ISR)	105
National information planning	CAMPBELL, Harry	(ON)	176
National information policies	MENOU, Michel J.	(ITL)	824
National security information	RUSSELL, Marvin F. . . .	(DC)	1069
Natural language information processing	HAYDEN, Richard F. . . .	(CA)	515
New information product development	CARTER, Daniel H.	(TX)	189
New information technology	CHEN, Ching C.	(MA)	205
News & information cataloging	TRIVEDI, Harish S.	(OH)	1257
News & information storage & retrieval	TRIVEDI, Harish S.	(OH)	1257
Non-bibliographic information files	CHIANG, Katherine S. . .	(NY)	207
Nuclear waste information	LANE, Sandra G.	(NY)	694
Nursing information	WATKINS, Elizabeth A. .	(NJ)	1309
	GUENTHER, Jody	(TX)	475
Nursing information & reference	BERG, Rebecca M.	(CO)	84
Nursing information resources	ALLEN, Margaret A.	(WI)	15
Occupational health & safety information	TUCKER, Mary E.	(NC)	1262
	ZUBA, Elizabeth J.	(AB)	1390
Office & information technology	VASILAKIS, Mary	(PA)	1279
Oncology information	LEBRUN, Anne	(ON)	708
Online business information	ROMERO, Georg L.	(CA)	1052
	CRIM, Elias F.	(IL)	258
Online information delivery	HERNANDEZ, Tamsen M.	(NY)	532
Online information marketing	ROACH, Eddie D.	(OK)	1037
Online information research	ROYAL, Linda G.	(VA)	1063
Online information retrieval	ANDERSON, Clifford D. .	(CA)	22
	GRENIER, Myra T.	(CA)	467
	FINE, Sandra R.	(DC)	377
	KOVITZ, Nancy R.	(IL)	674
	JACK, Robert F.	(MD)	586
	HAM, Beverly V.	(MN)	490
	MULTER, Ell P.	(MO)	878

INFORMATION (Cont'd)

Online information retrieval

CALLANAN, Ellen M. . . . . (NJ) 173
HSIAO, Shu Y. . . . . (NY) 567
LOWE, Ida B. . . . . (NY) 743
MARTINEZ-NAZARIO,
  Ronaldo . . . . (PR) 779
MILLS, Catherine H. . . . . (RI) 843
DOBSON, Christine B. . . . (TX) 307
ACCARDI, Joseph J. . . . (WI) 3
SWEETLAND, James H. . . (WI) 1215
MACKENZIE, Shirley A. . (ON) 756
Online information retrieval & storage WILLIAMS, Martha E. . . . (IL) 1345
Online information retrieval, business OSTROW, Rona . . . . . . (NY) 929
Online information retrieval, databases RAITT, David I. . . . . (NET)1004
Online information systems SULLIVAN, Edward A. . . (CA) 1207
SWEENEY, Urban J. . . . (CA) 1215
HEARTY, John A. . . . . . (DC) 519
WILSON, Lizabeth A. . . . (IL) 1351
SMITH, Jo T. . . . . (NJ) 1156
HILL, Linda L. . . . . (OK) 540
BILLINSKY, Christyn G. . (SC) 96
GENNARO, John L. . . . . (VA) 427
YAMANAKA, Tai . . . . . . (JAP)1377
Online information, US & foreign PINSON, Mark . . . . (MA) 975
Optical disk information archiving PASCHAL, John M. . . . . (OK) 945
Optical information system HEIDENREICH, Fred L. . . (AZ) 521
Optical information systems ANDRE, Pamela Q. . . . . (MD) 26
MARMION, Daniel K. . . . (TX) 772
DEBUSE, Raymond . . . . (WA) 285
REMINGTON, David G. . (WA) 1022
Organization of information BERRING, Robert C. . . . (CA) 90
BRITE, Agnes . . . . (MA) 137
WATERSTREET, Darlene
  E. . . . . (WI) 1309
Patent & trademark information DI MUCCIO, Mary J. . . . (CA) 304
CROCKETT, Martha L. . . (DC) 259
Patent database & information
  retrieval ROSENTHAL, Francine C. (OH) 1057
Patent information JACOBS, Leslie R. . . . . . (MA) 589
WAGNER, Louis F. . . . . (OH) 1292
DONOVAN, Kathryn M. . (PA) 312
DIXON, Michael D. . . . . (VA) 306
MEREK, Charles J. . . . . (VA) 825
Patent information databases PLATAU, Gerard O. . . . . (OH) 977
Patent information retrieval SIMMONS, Edlyn S. . . . . (OH) 1139
Patent & health information POMERANTZ, Karyn L. . (MD) 982
Patient care information requirements JACOBSEN, Teresa T. . . (IL) 590
Patient health information DEWEY, Marjorie C. . . . . (MA) 298
Personal information systems BURTON, Hilary D. . . . . (CA) 164
Pesticides information SPURLING, Norman K. . . (MD) 1177
Petroleum bibliographic info systs HILL, Linda L. . . . . (OK) 540
Petroleum industry information ROBERTSON, Betty M. . (NY) 1041
Petroleum information BREWER, Stanley E. . . . (TX) 134
Pharmaceutical & biotechnology info DIXON, Michael D. . . . . . (VA) 306
Pharmaceutical & medical information LAUTENSCHLAG,
  Elisabeth C. . . . . (PA) 703
Pharmaceutical information HULL, Peggy F. . . . . (NC) 573
CLEMANS, Margaret H. . (VA) 220
WACASEY, Mary M. . . . (PQ) 1290
Pharmaceutical information scientist THOMPSON, Reubin C. . (NC) 1241
Pharmaceutical research info systems PEETERS, Marc D. . . . . (BEL) 954
Photography resources information HOFFKNECHT, Carmen L. (CA) 547
Planning & evaluation of info srvs MCCLURE, Charles R. . . (NY) 797
Planning national information systems MENOU, Michel J. . . , . , (ITL) 824
Plastics industry information sources KANE, Nancy J. . . . . (MA) 625
Political barriers to information BIRNEY, Ann E. . . . . (KS) 98
Polymer information KLEMM, Carol B. . . . . . (NJ) 660
Private information exchange
  networks BUSSMANN, Steve . . . . (VA) 166
EDWARDS, Wilmoth O. . (VA) 338
FILIPPONE, Anne . . . . . (VA) 377
KELLER, Jay . . . . (VA) 635
LITTLE, William . . . . (VA) 734
LOVETT, Bruce . . . . (VA) 743
MAJOR, Skip . . . . (VA) 762
NEWLAND, Barbara . . . . (VA) 899
RINALDI, Roberta . . . . . (VA) 1035
RYAN, Maureen . . . . . . (VA) 1071
STRATT, Randy . . . . (VA) 1200

INFORMATION (Cont'd)

Producing informational films HOFFER, Thomas W. . . . . (FL) 547
Professional information NISENOFF, Sylvia . . . . . (VA) 905
Providing information from references JOHNSON, Elaine B. . . . (DC) 604
Providing research & government info CASO, Gasper . . . . (MA) 193
Psychology of information use BODART-TALBOT, Joni . (KS) 109
Public access to information HALLINAN, Patricia R. . . (NY) 489
Public affairs information CATHCART, Marilyn S. . . (MN) 195
Public information PEDAK-KARI, Maria . . . . (MD) 954
ROBINSON, Jolene A. . . (NY) 1044
HORNAK, Anna F. . . . . . (TX) 559
HENDERSON, Harriet . . . (VA) 526
Public information & relations WELLS, Gladysann . . . . (NY) 1322
Public information programs PAISLEY, William J. . . . . (CA) 935
Public information strategies CROWTHER, Warren W. . (CSR) 262
Public information systems SMITH, Peggy C. . . . . . . (OK) 1159
Public information video production RANCER, Susan P. . . . . (NC) 1006
Public legal information & education TOMCHYSHYN, Theresa
  M. . . . . (SK) 1249
Public library information & referral GUMPPER, Mary F. . . . . (OH) 477
Public library information services MOLZ, Jean B. . . . . (MD) 854
Public management information
  systems CROWTHER, Warren W. . (CSR) 262
Public relations & public information KUSZMAUL, Marcia J. . . (IL) 685
Public relations information EBERHARD, Neysa C. . . (KS) 334
Public service information desk SPENSLEY, Malcolm C. . (NY) 1173
Public services information MURRAY, Bruce C. . . . . (MD) 881
Public services reference &
  information GRAY, Patricia B. . . . . . . (VA) 460
Public utility information BOBAN, Carol A. . . . . . . (IL) 108
Publishing information newsletters LYONS, Ivan . . . . (NY) 753
Publishing policy development info KLEIMAN, Gerald S. . . . (DC) 659
Publishing program management info KLEIMAN, Gerald S. . . . (DC) 659
Publishing technology applications
  info KLEIMAN, Gerald S. . . . (DC) 659
Pulp, paper & forestry information MARTINEZ, Linda W. . . . (WA) 779
Radiology information EKSTRAND, Nancy L. . . (NC) 341
Readers advisory book information IRGON, Deborah A. . . . . (NJ) 583
Real-time financial information REEDY, Martha J. . . . . . (MA) 1015
Records & info development &
  documtn GRAHAM, Su D. . . . . . . (CO) 456
Records & information filing &
  retrieval GRAHAM, Su D. . . . . . . (CO) 456
Records & information management PHILLIPS, Donna M. . . . (IA) 968
MUNTEAN, Deborah E. . (MN) 879
ROFES, William L. . . . . . (NY) 1049
MANARIN, Louis H. . . . . (VA) 764
STIRLING, Dale A. . . . . . (WA) 1195
Reference & computer information
  search MOORHEAD, Kenneth E. (CT) 862
Reference & information GOEBEL, Heather L. . . . . (AZ) 443
JOHMANN, Nancy . . . . . (CT) 601
RAILSBACK, Patsy S. . . (IA) 1003
CORNETT, John L. . . . . (NM) 247
KUJOORY, Parvin . . . . . (TX) 683
WILSON, Brenda J. . . . . (UT) 1350
TOMCHYSHYN, Theresa
  M. . . . . (SK) 1249
BARBERENA, Elsa . . . . (MEX) 55
Reference & information management LAWSON, Venable A. . . (GA) 705
Reference & information research THOMPSON, Myra D. . . (OH) 1240
Reference & information retrieval HEINZ, Catharine F. . . . (DC) 522
MOORE, Patricia R. . . . . (NC) 860
RICE, Anna C. . . . . (NJ) 1026
BEAUDRIE, Ronald A. . . (NY) 70
STOAN, Stephen K. . . . . (TX) 1195
Reference & info retrieval systems MASON, Michael L. . . . . (NJ) 781
Reference & information specialist MISTARAS, Evangeline . (IL) 848
Reference & online info retrieval YOUNGEN, Gregory K. . (IN) 1383
Reference & research information MCCARTNEY, Margaret
  M. . . . . (NY) 794
Reference, company information BOODIS, Maxine S. . . . . (PA) 115
Reference information EVANS, June C. . . . . (NC) 357
MINNICH, Conrad H. . . . (OH) 846
KING, Olive E. . . . . (ON) 652
Reference, information & referral HOPPER, Lorraine E. . . . (TX) 558
Reference, information management MULCAHY, Bryan L. . . . (GA) 876
Reference information retrieval STEPANICK, John R. . . . (FL) 1187
Regional information library OAKES, Patricia A. . . . . (AK) 913
Regulatory information RATHGEBER, Jo F. . . . . (NC) 1009

INFORMATION (Cont'd)

Regulatory information access — MCRAE, Alexander D. — (MD) 818
Rehabilitation information — COUCH, Susan H. — (PA) 250
Research & information — DALY, Eudice — (CA) 271
Research & information retrieval — ROE, Georgeanne T. — (MA) 1048
— HACKNEY, Judith G. — (TX) 481
Research for slide information — BAILEY, Tuuli T. — (AZ) 47
Research information — LOCH, Edward J. — (TX) 735
— CHISUM, Emmett D. — (WY) 209
Research information for reporters — RICE, Margaret R. — (TX) 1027
Research on information brokers — WALLS, Francine E. — (WA) 1299
Researching unavailable information — TERZIAN, Shohig S. — (CA) 1232
Resource recovery information — COLLISHAW, Jackie J. — (NJ) 233
Retrieving information for students — LONNING, Roger D. — (MN) 740
Retrieving technical information — HALLSTROM, Curtis H. — (MN) 489
Running a job information center — BEIMAN, Frances M. — (NJ) 75
Rural health information transfer — BOISSY, Robert W. — (NY) 111
Satellite information ctrs establishment — LAVIN, Margaret A. — (NJ) 703
Scholarly communication for info tech — DOUGHERTY, Richard M. — (MI) 314
School district information systems — SLYGH, Gyneth — (WI) 1151
Science & information policy — ROSENBERG, Kenyon C. — (VA) 1056
Science & technology information — CULLEY, Paul T. — (NY) 263
— SALT, David P. — (SK) 1077
— ALI, Syed N. — (BRN) 13
Science information — HURD, Julie M. — (IL) 577
— CLANCY, Ron — (BC) 215
Science, info applications, of computers — MITCHELL, Steve — (CA) 849
Science information communication — FRY, Bernard M. — (IN) 406
Science information retrieval — BROWN, Cynthia D. — (NY) 142
Science information services — SOMERVILLE, Arleen N. — (NY) 1167
Science information sources — WOOD, Judith B. — (NC) 1364
Scientific & technical information — DOUVILLE, Judith A. — (CT) 314
— WALDHART, Thomas J. — (KY) 1294
— AINES, Andrew A. — (MD) 8
— SMITH, Robert B. — (PA) 1160
— WALKER, Richard D. — (WI) 1296
Scientific & technical info copyright — WOOD, Julienne L. — (LA) 1364
Scientific & technical info management — CARROLL, Bonnie C. — (TN) 187
— SPATH, Charles E. — (TN) 1171
Scientific & technical info retrieval — HOWARD, Theresa M. — (ENG) 564
Scientific information — HOPP, Ralph H. — (MN) 558
— O'GORMAN, Jack — (OH) 918
— OWENS, Frederick H. — (PA) 932
Scientific information, automation — MCGREGOR, M C. — (CT) 808
Scientific information databases — ZIAIAN, Monir — (CA) 1387
Scientific information systems design — DIESING, Arthur C. — (KY) 302
Sci-tech information — LAUB, Barbara J. — (NJ) 702
— MAASS, Eleanor A. — (PA) 753
SDI European information — BERLIET, Nathalie B. — (CT) 87
Secondary information — ARTHUR, Christine — (NY) 35
Selective dissemination of information — KRAFT, Gwen L. — (AK) 675
— MORTON, Dorothy J. — (DE) 870
— TINGLEY, Dianne E. — (MD) 1246
— SHILL, Harold B. — (WV) 1130
— MACIAS-CHAPULA, Cesar A. — (MEX) 755
Selective distribution of information — BARTLETT, Vernell W. — (MN) 61
Small business information — ROWE, David G. — (PQ) 1062
— THIVIERGE, Lynda M. — (PQ) 1235
Social science information — SERBAN, William M. — (LA) 1116
— TAMURA, Shunsaku — (JAP) 1221
Social science information resources — SHIELDS, Gerald R. — (NY) 1130
Social sciences information sources — CONGER, Lucinda D. — (DC) 236
Social studies in information — WILSON, Patrick — (CA) 1352
Social studies of information — CEPPOS, Karen F. — (CA) 196
Sources of business information — OSWALD, Edward E. — (FL) 929
Special libraries & information centers — STRABLE, Edward G. — (IL) 1199
Sports information & databases — GHENT, Gretchen K. — (AB) 430
Standards & certification information — OVERMAN, Joanne R. — (MD) 931
Standards in information systems — HENDERSON, Madeline M. — (MD) 526
State information resource management — EVANS, Max J. — (UT) 357
Strategic corporate information analysis — BEICHMAN, John C. — (MI) 75
Strategic information planning — HORTON, Forest W. — (DC) 561
Strategic use of information technology — MARCHAND, Donald A. — (NY) 768

INFORMATION (Cont'd)

Study & information skills — BRAUER, Regina — (NY) 129
Subject access to information — COLLINS, William P. — (ISR) 233
Subject approach to information — WILLIAMSON, Nancy J. — (ON) 1347
— FOSKETT, Antony C. — (AUS) 392
Supplying information — LONG, Brideen — (WI) 739
Tax-related information — ENSEL, Ellen H. — (CT) 350
Teach information retrieval skills — SMITH, Margie G. — (CA) 1157
Teaching information science — FLOOD, Barbara J. — (PA) 385
Teaching, technical & business info — CHAMIS, Alice Y. — (OH) 198
Technical & engineering information — HARTLEY, Gloria R. — (PA) 508
Technical information — JENKINS, Ann A. — (CA) 597
— OKEY, Susan T. — (IN) 920
— MATTHEWS, Charles E. — (MA) 785
— YUILLE, Willie K. — (MD) 1384
— KEOGH, Jeanne M. — (OH) 643
— LANGKAU, Claire M. — (OH) 696
— BERGER, Lewis W. — (PA) 85
— DRAKE, James B. — (ON) 318
— FAIRLEY, Craig R. — (ON) 361
Technical information acquisition — RICE, Gerald W. — (NH) 1027
Technical information acquisitions — MONTGOMERY, Suzanne L. — (VA) 856
Technical information center management — EYLES, Heberle H. — (FL) 359
— HALL, Deanna M. — (GA) 487
Technical information centers — PERELLA, Susanne B. — (DC) 958
Technical information indexing — BRETON, Ernest J. — (DE) 133
Technical information management — SAYLOR, Linda — (CA) 1086
— MAYER, June C. — (NJ) 789
— DE TONNANCOUR, P R. — (TX) 296
Technical information research — LAHR, Thomas F. — (VA) 688
Technical information resources — BARTL, Richard P. — (NY) 61
Technical information retrieval — NELSON, Alice R. — (CA) 893
— SCHALIT, Michael — (CA) 1089
— LAZARUS, Josephine G. — (CO) 706
Technical information searching — FISLER, Charlotte D. — (PA) 382
Technical information specialist — COOK, Kathleen M. — (CA) 240
Technical petroleum information — STURDIVANT, Clarence A. — (CO) 1205
Technical, scientific information — ISGANITIS, Jamie C. — (NY) 585
Technology & information transfer — HATTERY, Lowell H. — (MD) 512
Technology information — WALKER, Patricia A. — (MO) 1296
Telecom regulatory information — MASON-WARD, Lesley — (ON) 781
Telecommunications & information policy — RIPLEY, Joseph M. — (KY) 1035
Telecommunications & info transfer — RESNIK, Linda I. — (DC) 1024
Telecommunications information — COOPER, Linda — (PA) 243
Telephone information — BRADY, Mary T. — (NY) 127
Textile information storage & retrieval — LAWRENCE, Philip D. — (VA) 704
Theory of information retrieval — MOOERS, Calvin N. — (MA) 857
— ROBERTSON, Stephen E. — (ENG) 1042
Third World information — HOWELL, John B. — (IA) 565
Tobacco information — DEBARDELEBEN, Marian Z. — (VA) 284
Top-down information systems planning — TELFER, Margaret E. — (NC) 1230
Toxic substances information — MULTER, Ell P. — (MO) 878
Toxicological information — EVERITT, Janet M. — (MI) 359
Toxicology information — KERNS, John T. — (CA) 644
— WEHLACZ, Joseph T. — (IN) 1316
Toxicology information & literature — EICKENHORST, Joanna W. — (CT) 339
Toxicology information, databases — DEXTER, Patrick J. — (MD) 298
Trade association information management — HILL, Susan M. — (DC) 540
Trade information — MAROTZ, Karen V. — (BC) 772
— JONES, Roger A. — (SWZ) 615
Training & public information — GILLIGAN, Julie — (NY) 436
Training information analysts — HALL, Homer J. — (NJ) 488
Training information desk personnel — DUCHARME, Judith C. — (NM) 322
Training information specialists & users — COURRIER, Yves G. — (FRN) 251
Transportation information — REILLY, Francis S. — (DC) 1020
— KANE, Deborah A. — (TX) 624
Transportation information & research — ARMEIT, Marilyn — (NY) 32
Travel & tourism information systems — MOLL, Joy K. — (NJ) 853
Troubleshooting information bottlenecks — SAUTER, Sylvia E. — (WA) 1085

INFORMATION (Cont'd)

Turnkey automated information
  systems   SIDMAN, George C. . . . . (CA) 1135
US information policy   JUERGENSMEYER, John
                                  E. . . . . (IL)   619
Use of information   BEARMAN, Toni C. . . . . (PA)   69
User & information management
  education   BERNARD, Molly S. . . . . (WA)   88
User education & information transfer BOROVANSKY, Vladimir
                                  T. . . . . (AZ) 117
User information   FRANCOS, Alexis . . . . . (PA) 396
Utility information sources   KING, Alan S. . . . . (ME) 650
Veterinary medicine information   COOK, Elaine . . . . (ENG) 239
Women's information services   NERBOSO, Donna L. . . . (NY) 895
Women's studies information   HICKS, Barbara A. . . . . . (ON) 536

INFORMATION SCIENCE (See also Reference)

Education for library & information sci WYLLYS, Ronald E. . . . . (TX) 1375
Education, information science   ERDT, Terrence . . . . (PA) 352
Education library & information
  science   KASPER, Barbara . . . . . (CT) 629
                                  TIBBO, Helen R. . . . . . . (MD) 1244
Foundation of information science SKOVIRA, Robert J. . . . . (PA) 1147
Foundations of information science BOISSY, Robert W. . . . . (NY) 111
Foundations of information science FROEHLICH, Thomas J. . . (NY) 405
Health information science   MOEHR, Jochen R. . . . . (BC) 851
Health information sciences   ALPERT, Hillel R. . . . . . . (MA)   17
History of information science   KENT, Allen . . . . (PA) 642
Information science   BORKO, Harold . . . . (CA) 116
                                  BOURNE, Charles P. . . . (CA) 119
                                  COOPER, William S. . . . (CA) 244
                                  MAGRO, Emanuel P. . . . (DC) 760
                                  HOLZBERLEIN, Deanne B. (IL) 555
                                  TOROK, Andrew G. . . . . (IL) 1251
                                  PIEPENBURG, Scott R. . . (IN) 971
                                  SHEPARD, Clayton A. . . . (IN) 1126
                                  WALLACE, Danny P. . . . (IN) 1297
                                  BOYCE, Bert R. . . . . (LA) 122
                                  MASYS, Daniel R. . . . . . (MD) 783
                                  SHUMAN, Bruce A. . . . . (MI) 1134
                                  MITCHELL, Joyce A. . . . . (MO) 849
                                  PARKER, Ralph H. . . . . . (MO) 942
                                  WITTIG, Glenn R. . . . . . (MS) 1358
                                  LOSEE, Robert M. . . . . . (NC) 742
                                  SARACEVIC, Tefko . . . . (NJ) 1082
                                  BENSON, James A. . . . . (NY)   83
                                  BILLY, George J. . . . . . . (NY)   97
                                  COOPER, Marianne . . . . (NY) 243
                                  GARLAND, Kathleen . . . (NY) 419
                                  NARBY, Ann E. . . . . (NY) 888
                                  TAYLOR, Robert S. . . . . (NY) 1228
                                  RICHMOND, Phyllis A. . . (OH) 1030
                                  FAIBISOFF, Sylvia G. . . . (OK) 361
                                  HEAD, John W. . . . . (PA) 518
                                  JENGAJI-EL, Taifa . . . . . (PA) 596
                                  SIITONEN, Leena M. . . . (RI) 1137
                                  CHOI, Jin M. . . . . (SC) 210
                                  JENSEN, Raymond A. . . (VA) 599
                                  KIEWITT, Eva L. . . . . . . (VA) 647
                                  JONES, Norma L. . . . . . (WI) 614
                                  POPE, Nolan F. . . . . (WI) 983
                                  DESCHATELETS, Gilles H. (PQ) 294
                                  COURRIER, Yves G. . . . (FRN) 251
                                  HUANG, Shih H. . . . . . . (TAI) 568
Information science & computer tech NEWMAN, Wilda B. . . . . (MD) 900
Information science & technology HARMON, Glynn . . . . . . (TX) 502
Information science education   CONAWAY, Charles W. . . (FL) 235
                                  SYWAK, Myron . . . . (NY) 1217
                                  YERKEY, A N. . . . . (NY) 1380
                                  LEE, Lucy T. . . . . (TAI) 710
Information science education
  curriculum   MOLL, Joy K. . . . . (NJ) 853
Information science, english literature JONES-TRENT, Bernice R. (VA) 616
Information science instruction   WILSON, Anthony M. . . . (WA) 1349
Information science, publishing
  research   DINGLE, Susan . . . . (PA) 304
Information science research   MARCUS, Richard S. . . . (MA) 769
                                  MARSHALL, Joanne G. . . (ON) 774

INFORMATION SCIENCE (Cont'd)

Information science systems   HAMMER, Donald P. . . . (IL) 493
                                  CANNATA, Arleen . . . . . (NY) 178
Information science, technology
  systems   JOHNSON, David K. . . . (NJ) 603
Instruction in information science EMMICK, Nancy J. . . . . . (CA) 348
Library & information science   SEDELOW, Walter A. . . . (AR) 1110
                                  GITLER, Robert L. . . . . . (CA) 438
                                  MELTON, Emily I. . . . . . . (IL) 823
                                  DELLA-CAVA, Olha . . . . (NY) 289
                                  ELY, Donald P. . . . . (NY) 347
                                  CHILDERS, Thomas A. . . (PA) 208
                                  JONES, B E. . . . . (ON) 611
Library & information science careers SCHERDIN, Mary J. . . . . (WI) 1092
Library & information science
  databases   HOLLOWAY, Dona W. . . (CA) 552
Library & information science
  education   DEQUIN, Henry C. . . . . . (IL) 293
                                  HURD, Julie M. . . . . (IL) 577
                                  SINEATH, Timothy W. . . (KY) 1143
                                  SLAVENS, Thomas P. . . . (MI) 1148
                                  MALINCONICO, S M. . . . (NY) 763
                                  POND, Patricia B. . . . . . . (OR) 982
                                  HANSON, Eugene R. . . . (PA) 498
                                  CHISHOLM, Margaret . . . (WA) 209
                                  HIATT, Peter . . . . (WA) 536
                                  GARDNER, Richard K. . . (PQ) 418
Library & information science
  research   PRABHA, Chandra G. . . . (OH) 989
                                  BOWERS, Paul A. . . . . . (PA) 120
                                  ELLIOTT, Pirkko E. . . . . . (ENG) 344
Library, information science editing SCHAEFER, Mary E. . . . (VA) 1089
Library, information science education OLSON, Lowell E. . . . . . (MN) 923
Library information sciences   GREEN, Joyce M. . . . . . (PA) 462
Reference & information science   EASTMAN, Franklin R. . . (CA) 333
                                  BRANDEL, Pamela A. . . (WI) 128
                                  NEILL, Sam D. . . . . (ON) 892

INFORMATION SERVICES (See also Information, Reference)

Abstracts & information services
  admin   PLATAU, Gerard O. . . . . (OH) 977
Administration of information services RUTHERFORD, Virginia L. (GA) 1070
Agricultural information services MLYNAR, Mary . . . . (OH) 850
                                  WOODWARD, Anthony M. (ENG)1367
Biomedical information services   KOLMAN, Roberta F. . . . (HI) 669
                                  SHIPLEY, Ruth M. . . . . . (MO) 1131
Biotechnology information services NEWAY, Julie M. . . . . . . (CA) 898
Business information services   HASSAN, Mohammad Z. . (NY) 511
Career information services   HEINEMAN, Stephanie R. (NY) 522
Chemical information services   PORTER, Katherine R. . . (NC) 985
Community information services   BEEBE, Richard J. . . . . . (CA)   74
                                  DAVIES, Jo . . . . (WA) 277
Computerized information services FOX, Rosalie . . . . (ON) 395
Consumer health information services TAYLOR, Margaret P. . . . (ON) 1227
Corporate archives, information
  services   DYER, Esther R. . . . . . . (NY) 330
Corporate information service   WOLPERT, Ann J. . . . . . (MA) 1362
Corporate information services   ROSHON, Nina C. . . . . . (NY) 1057
Delivery of information services JOHNSON, Emily P. . . . . (MD) 604
Development of information services BLASINGAME, Ralph . . . (NJ) 104
                                  MCGILL, Nancy A. . . . . . (WI) 806
Education & job information services WASSERMAN, Ricki F. . . (NY)* 1308
Energy information services   FEINBERG, Beryl L. . . . . (DC) 368
Environmental research & info service FELICETTI, Barbara W. . . (MA) 370
Evaluation of information services MCLAUGHLIN, W K. . . . (AB) 813
Evaluation of libraries & info services KING, Donald W. . . . . . . (MD) 650
Federal govt & congressional info srvs ROTHBART, Linda S. . . . (VA) 1060
Fee-based information services   TOMAJKO, Kathy L. . . . . (GA) 1249
                                  REMEIKIS, Lois A. . . . . . (IL) 1022
                                  FELICETTI, Barbara W. . . (MA) 370
Financial information services   LANDES, J C. . . . . (NY) 692
Government information services   PINELLI, Thomas E. . . . . (VA) 974
Governmental information services ROUMFORT, Susan B. . . (NJ) 1061
Health science information services SWATOS, Priscilla L. . . . (IL) 1214
Health sciences information services MATER, Dee A. . . . . (NC) 783
Information service   PUFFER, Yvonne L. . . . . (DE) 997
                                  BARKLEY, Carolyn L. . . . (VA)   56
Information service management   STANTON, Robert O. . . . (NJ) 1181
                                  LAWRENCE, Barbara . . . (NY) 704

INFORMATION SERVICES (Cont'd)

Specialty	Name	State	Page
Information service marketing	WEAVER, Maggie	(ON)	1312
Information services	CLINTWORTH, William A.	(CA)	222
	ELLIS, Ruth M.	(CA)	345
	FILES, Patricia T.	(CA)	376
	WIERZBA, Heidemarie B.	(CA)	1337
	SILVERSTEIN, Jeffrey S.	(CT)	1139
	SMITH, Nolan E.	(CT)	1159
	FONT, Mary M.	(DC)	388
	SMALLEY, Ann W.	(DC)	1151
	CARR, Mary L.	(FL)	186
	HSU, Pi Y.	(FL)	567
	MOON, Ilse	(FL)	857
	DREAZEN, Elizabeth P.	(IL)	318
	JONES, Dorothy E.	(IL)	612
	OPEM, John D.	(IL)	925
	MCFADDEN, Sue J.	(LA)	804
	PATTERSON, Charles D.	(LA)	948
	WHITNEY, Howard F.	(MA)	1334
	BUTTER, Karen A.	(MD)	167
	FRANK, Robyn C.	(MD)	397
	BOSE, Deborah L.	(MI)	117
	SCHUMACHER, Patricia C.	(MN)	1103
	MORTON, Bruce	(MT)	870
	DEVITO, Robert M.	(NC)	297
	ELLIS, Kem B.	(NC)	345
	METZGER, Eva C.	(NC)	829
	MOXLEY, Melody A.	(NC)	874
	ROLETT, Virginia V.	(NH)	1051
	HENRY, Mary B.	(NJ)	529
	SHINER, Sharon L.	(NJ)	1130
	GRECO, Gloria T.	(NY)	461
	OCKENE, David L.	(NY)	915
	POMRENZE, Seymour J.	(NY)	982
	WEATHERFORD, Elizabeth	(NY)	1311
	LITTLE, Dean K.	(OH)	733
	SIMONS, Linda K.	(OH)	1141
	WEBER, A C.	(PA)	1313
	BARRON, Daniel D.	(SC)	60
	KINTNER, Susan B.	(SC)	653
	GEARY, Kathleen A.	(TX)	424
	JONES, Sue P.	(VA)	615
	DANIEL, Eunice L.	(WA)	272
	FREDRICKSON, Dennis C.	(WA)	400
	HILDEBRANDT, Darlene M.	(WA)	538
	KREIMEYER, Vicki R.	(WA)	677
	BRUNDIN, Robert E.	(AB)	150
	KENNEDY, Marcia G.	(AB)	641
	MATHEZER, Pauline B.	(AB)	784
	KIERANS, Mary E.	(BC)	647
	READE, Judith G.	(NS)	1012
	DANCE, Barbara L.	(ON)	272
	JARVI, Edith T.	(ON)	594
	TEMPLIN, Dorothy	(ON)	1231
	BARLOW, Elizabeth A.	(SK)	57
	VANDER LAAN, Lubbert	(SK)	1274
	POON, Paul W.	(HKG)	983
Information services & reference	TOWNSEND, Silas H.	(PA)	1253
	CAMPBELL, Laurie G.	(ON)	177
Information services brokering	GOURLAY, Una M.	(TX)	454
Information services coordination	SHORT, William M.	(TN)	1132
Information services design	BURNS, Christopher	(MA)	162
Information services for corporations	LAW, Gordon T.	(IN)	704
Information services law	PACE, Thomas	(NJ)	933
Information services management	BALDWIN, Jerome C.	(MN)	51
	BATTIN, Patricia	(NY)	64
	PEARCE, Karla J.	(NY)	952
	WEINSTEIN, Lois	(NY)	1318
	BAKER, Dale B.	(OH)	48
	JUDGE, Joseph M.	(PA)	619
	VASILAKIS, Mary	(PA)	1279
	CLOSE, Elizabeth G.	(UT)	223
Information services marketing	TRAUTMAN, Maryellen	(DC)	1254
	BINGHAM, Kathleen S.	(NY)	97
	MITTERMEYER, Diane	(PQ)	850
Information services planning	PRENTICE, Ann E.	(TN)	990
Information services reference	MOORE, Jean B.	(NJ)	860

INFORMATION SERVICES (Cont'd)

Specialty	Name	State	Page
Information services, school	KENNEY, Ann J.	(OR)	641
Information services to public	KLAUSMEIER, Arno M.	(WI)	658
International library & info services	NASRI, William Z.	(PA)	888
Legal information services	CARROLL, Hardy	(MI)	187
	ASTON, Jennefer	(IRE)	37
Legislative information services	CALLINAN, Ellen M.	(DC)	173
Library & information services mgmt	FITZGERALD, Diana S.	(CA)	382
Management of information services	HONEBRINK, Andrea C.	(MN)	555
	MARBAN, Ricio	(GUA)	768
Management of library & info services	NASRI, William Z.	(PA)	888
	SIITONEN, Leena M.	(RI)	1137
Managing information services	BROWN, Paula D.	(CA)	146
	BUCK, Anne M.	(NJ)	153
Managing information services & systems	HALLSTROM, Curtis H.	(MN)	489
Market & financial information services	HASSAN, Mohammad Z.	(NY)	511
Marketing information services	BALL, Thomas W.	(DC)	52
	TAYLOR, George A.	(DC)	1226
	CROCKER, Susan O.	(NY)	259
	TUCKER, Laura R.	(NY)	1262
	DUBEAU, Pierre	(PQ)	321
	ARMSTRONG, Denise M.	(SAF)	32
Marketing information services & systems	LAROSA, Sharon M.	(MA)	698
Marketing information services, systems	EL-DUWEINI, Aadel K.	(EGY)	342
Marketing of information services	FERNALD, Anne C.	(MA)	373
Medical & nursing information services	JENNINGS, Patricia S.	(FL)	598
Medical information service	KELLY, Kay	(MI)	638
Medical information services	SCHULMAN, Jacque L.	(MD)	1101
Medical information services development	REID, Carolyn A.	(NY)	1018
Medical reference & information services	MAHONY, Doris D.	(MI)	761
Mental health information service	MERRILL, Susan S.	(MD)	827
Mental health information services	DANIELS, Pam	(NY)	273
Municipal government information srvs	HENDERSON, Harriet	(VA)	526
News information services	DORSETT, Anita W.	(TX)	313
Online & manual information services	GALBRAITH, Barry E.	(NY)	413
Online electronic information services	HARRISON, Burgess A.	(CT)	506
Online information services	EL-HADIDY, Bahaa	(FL)	342
	PEAKE, Sharon K.	(OH)	952
	GRAY, Paul W.	(TX)	460
Packaging of information services	TIBBETTS, David W.	(NY)	1243
Planning of new information services	SIECK, Steven K.	(NY)	1135
Reference & information service	PINTOZZI, Chestalene	(FL)	975
	KIM, Chung S.	(IL)	648
	TAYLOR, Rebecca A.	(LA)	1228
	ANDREWS, Mark J.	(MO)	27
	SMITH, Nancy M.	(MO)	1159
	ROBINSON, W D.	(ON)	1045
Reference & information services	HERON, David W.	(CA)	532
	SHORT, Virginia	(CA)	1132
	JAY, Hilda L.	(CT)	596
	DANNECKER, Joyce H.	(FL)	274
	BARD, Therese B.	(HI)	56
	RICE, James G.	(IA)	1027
	KLEKOWSKI, Lynn M.	(IL)	660
	JACKSON, Arlyne A.	(MA)	586
	MOORE, Craig P.	(MD)	859
	PITTMAN, Dorothy E.	(MD)	976
	FISCHER, Catherine S.	(MN)	379
	OBERMAN, Cerise G.	(MN)	914
	ROSSMAN, Muriel J.	(MN)	1059
	SPICER, Orlin C.	(MO)	1174
	BRUCE, Nancy G.	(NC)	149
	PARROTT, Margaret S.	(NC)	944
	STEPHENS, Ann E.	(NE)	1187
	MCDERMOTT, Ellen	(NJ)	801
	GRAY, Robert G.	(NV)	460
	DOYAL, Patricia A.	(NY)	317
	ORR, Coleridge W.	(NY)	926
	WELLS, Margaret R.	(NY)	1322
	NEAL, James G.	(PA)	890
	SCHNEIDER, Stewart P.	(RI)	1097
	KRATZ, Abby R.	(TX)	676

INFORMATION SERVICES (Cont'd)

Reference & information services

BROADWAY, Marsha D.	(UT)	138
VANDERBERG, E S.	(VA)	1273
SHERMAN, Jacob R.	(VT)	1128
KEMP, Barbara E.	(WA)	639
DAWSON, Terry P.	(WI)	282
PARSONS, Patricia S.	(WI)	945
SEARCY HOWARD, Linda M.	(BC)	1109
BUDNICK, Carol	(MB)	155
KEARNS, Linda J.	(ON)	633
SCOTT, Judith W.	(ON)	1107
PROVOST, Paul E.	(PQ)	996

Reference information service — CHRISTOLON, Blair B. (VA) 212

Reference information services
ALLENSWORTH, James H.	(CA)	16
WHITE, Lucinda M.	(ME)	1331
SHIP, Martin I.	(ON)	1131

Reference or information service — HOFFMAN, Frank W. (TX) 548

Research & information services — ROTHMAN, John (NY) 1060

Scientific & technical information srvs — MOSER, Jane W. (CA) 870

Technical information services
LERNER, Frederick A.	(NH)	717
HASSAN, Mohammad Z.	(NY)	511
STAIR, Fred	(OK)	1178

Toxicology information services — KISSMAN, Henry M. (MD) 656

INJURY

Personal injury law — KOEING, Sherman (FL) 667

INMAGIC

InMagic software file management system — HOUSTON, Louise B. (ON) 563

INMATE (See also Correctional, Prison)

Inmate law libraries	ROMALIS, Carl	(NY)	1052
Inmate legal library maintenance	SIENDA, Madeline M.	(WA)	1136
Inmate services	WALSH, Donamarie F.	(CA)	1299
Service to prison inmates	REHNBERG, Marilyn J.	(MN)	1017

INNOPAC

Innovacq & Innopac systems — TEMPLE, Harold L. (IL) 1230

INNOVACQ

Innovacq & Innopac systems — TEMPLE, Harold L. (IL) 1230

INSERVICE (See also Instruction, Training)

Computer inservice	WALKER, Patricia A.	(MO)	1296
Continuing education, inservice	TASSIA, Margaret R.	(PA)	1224
Development of inservices	HOLDREN, Ann E.	(TX)	550
Inservice	EVERHART, Nancy L.	(PA)	358
Inservice for librarians	MC NAIR, Marian B.	(OH)	815
Inservice training	PATRICK, Patricia M.	(NY)	947
	VANDERGRIFF, Kathleen E.	(TN)	1274
	BURKS, C J.	(UT)	161
Staff inservice	SORELL, Janice G.	(MN)	1168
Teacher, inservice in technology	HOFSTAD, Alice M.	(MN)	548

INSTITUTES (See also Workshops)

Workshops & institutes — LYNCH, Mary D. (PA) 752

INSTITUTIONS (See also Correctional, Hospital, Prison)

Consulting to financial institutions	PHILLIPS, Steven G.	(MA)	969
Correctional institution librarianship	NOZICK, Sandy B.	(CA)	911
Correctional institution library service	BATSON, Darrell L.	(NV)	64
Correctional institution outreach	PETIT, J M.	(OH)	965
Financial institutions	DATTALO, Elmo F.	(DC)	275
	LEAMEN, Nancy J.	(ON)	707
Financial institutions & services	FEATHERS, John E.	(WA)	367
History of the institution & medicine	MIMS, Dorothy H.	(GA)	845
Institution libraries	LEFFERS, Mary J.	(CA)	712

INSTITUTIONS (Cont'd)

Institution library services	RUBIN, Rhea J.	(CA)	1064
Institution or special libraries	HOFFMAN, Frank W.	(TX)	548
Institutional documents & data	GOODMAN, L D.	(CA)	449
Institutional librarianship	MAYO, Kathleen O.	(FL)	790
	OVERSTREET, Allen J.	(FL)	931
	HOM, Sharon L.	(TN)	555
Institutional libraries	EATON, Barbara F.	(CO)	333
Institutional library operation	ELLIOTT, Kay M.	(IA)	344
Institutional library services	PARTRIDGE, James C.	(MD)	945
Institutional planning	KARL, Roger M.	(TN)	627
Institutional public relations	FRISBIE, Margery	(IL)	405
	CLARK, Charlene K.	(TX)	216
Institutional publications	GOODMAN, L D.	(CA)	449
Institutional records	TENER, Jean F.	(AB)	1231
Institutional research	STILLMAN, Mary E.	(PA)	1194
Institutional services	MC LAUGHLIN, Terry L.	(IL)	813
	SNAIR, Dale S.	(VA)	1162
Institutional services, mental health	BOLIN, Nancy C.	(MD)	112
Institutions	MOORE, Mary L.	(CA)	860
	ALEY, Judy M.	(NJ)	12
Institutions library services	VAN DER VOORN, Neal P.	(WA)	1274
Institutions of higher learning	WOLVSKY, Haya S.	(ISR)	1362
Inter-institutional cooperation	NEAL, Donn C.	(IL)	890
Marketing photos to public institutions	HENDERSON, Ellen B.	(CA)	526
Medieval institutions	HORWITZ, Steven F.	(CA)	561
Public & institutions libs consulting	MADDEN, Doreitha R.	(NJ)	758
Researching foreign archive institutions	OGAWA, Chiyoko	(JAP)	918
Service to institutionalized persons	LUCAS, Linda S.	(SC)	746
Services for institutionalized	SHEPHERD, Antoinette	(TX)	1127
Special & institutional libraries	GRAY, Karen S.	(IL)	460
State & institution libraries	CASEY, Genevieve M.	(MI)	192
Writing institutional histories	CANTELON, Philip L.	(MD)	179

INSTRUCTION (See also Courses, Education, Inservice, Orientation, Skills, Teaching, Tutoring)

Academic bibliographic instruction	ENGLE, Michael O.	(OR)	349
Admin, bibliographic instruction	COSTELLO, Janice M.	(WI)	249
Administration, management & instruction	QUIRING, Virginia M.	(KS)	1000
Adult programming & instruction	UTSUNOMIYA, Leslie D.	(BC)	1270
Audiovisual instruction & production	FALLON, Marianna L.	(IN)	362
Audiovisual instruction utilization	KERSTETTER, John	(OH)	644
Bibliographic & library instruction	NAKANO, Kimberly L.	(HI)	887
Bibliographic instruction	BIGGS-WILLIAMS, Evelyn A.	(AL)	95
	BLEILER, Richard J.	(AL)	105
	FRIEDMAN, Richard E.	(AL)	404
	KENDRICK, Aubrey W.	(AL)	640
	KETCHAM, Lee C.	(AL)	645
	LAUGHLIN, Steven G.	(AL)	703
	MERRILL, Martha	(AL)	826
	PEARSON, Peter E.	(AL)	953
	SCALES, Diann R.	(AL)	1087
	WILLIAMS, Pauline C.	(AL)	1346
	BEARD, Craig W.	(AR)	69
	CLOUGHERTY, Leo P.	(AR)	223
	DEW, Stephen H.	(AR)	297
	ESTES, Pamela J.	(AR)	355
	COLE, Mitzi M.	(AZ)	231
	DAANE, Jeanette K.	(AZ)	269
	HAWBAKER, A C.	(AZ)	513
	REICHEL, Mary	(AZ)	1018
	VATHIS, Alma C.	(AZ)	1279
	ABRAMSON, Jenifer S.	(CA)	3
	ARIARATNAM, Lakshmi V.	(CA)	31
	BELL, Christina D.	(CA)	76
	BERGMAN, Emily A.	(CA)	86
	BOOKHEIM, Louis W.	(CA)	115
	BOYER, Laura M.	(CA)	123
	BRIL, Patricia L.	(CA)	136
	BROIDY, Ellen J.	(CA)	139
	BRUNDAGE, Christina A.	(CA)	150
	CARAVELLO, Patti S.	(CA)	180
	CLARENCE, Judy	(CA)	216
	DOWELL, Connie V.	(CA)	315
	DURAN, Karin J.	(CA)	328

INSTRUCTION (Cont'd)
Bibliographic instruction

ELNOR, Nancy G. . . . . . (CA) 346
ENGELBRECHT, Mary E. . (CA) 349
FITZGERALD, Diana S. . . (CA) 382
FUSICH, Monica G. . . . . (CA) 410
GALLOWAY, Sue . . . . . (CA) 415
GLENDENNING, Barbara
    J. . . . . (CA) 441
GLITZ, Beryl . . . . (CA) 441
GORDON, Wendy R. . . . (CA) 452
GUEDON, Mary S. . . . . . (CA) 475
HAIKALIS, Peter D. . . . . (CA) 484
HARMON, Robert B. . . . . (CA) 502
HILLMAN, Stephanie . . . (CA) 541
HOGAN, Eddy . . . . (CA) 549
HURLBERT, Irene W. . . . (CA) 577
JOHNSON, Diane D. . . . . (CA) 603
JOHNSON, Peter A. . . . . (CA) 608
KAUN, Thomas T. . . . . . (CA) 631
KELLY, Myla S. . . . . (CA) 638
KENYON, Sharmon H. . . (CA) 643
KIRESEN, Evelyn M. . . . (CA) 654
KNOWLES, Em C. . . . . . (CA) 665
LESH, Jane G. . . . . (CA) 718
LO, Henrietta W. . . . . . . (CA) 735
MANTHEY, Teresa M. . . (CA) 767
MARIE, Jacquelyn . . . . . (CA) 770
MCGREEVY, Kathleen T. (CA) 808
MELTZER, Ellen J. . . . . . (CA) 823
MORRIS, Jacquelyn M. . (CA) 866
MULLEN, Cecilia P. . . . . (CA) 877
NICKELSON-DEARIE,
    Tammy A. . . . . (CA) 902
PORTILLA, Teresa M. . . (CA) 985
POSEY, Vernell W. . . . . . (CA) 985
POSTER, Susan E. . . . . . (CA) 986
REYNOLDS, Judith L. . . (CA) 1025
SANTOS, Bob . . . . (CA) 1082
SHAWL, Janice H. . . . . . (CA) 1124
SHERLOCK, John A. . . . (CA) 1128
SHORT, Virginia . . . . (CA) 1132
SMALLEY, Topsy N. . . . (CA) 1151
SPRAIN, Mara L. . . . . . . (CA) 1176
TASH, Steven J. . . . . . . (CA) 1224
TENNANT, Roy . . . . (CA) 1231
WHEELER, Helen R. . . . (CA) 1329
WOBBE, Jean . . . . (CA) 1359
WOLLTER, Patricia M. . . (CA) 1361
WOOD, Elizabeth H. . . . . (CA) 1364
ZYROFF, Ellen S. . . . . . (CA) 1392
ANTHES, Susan H. . . . . (CO) 28
KRISMANN, Carol H. . . . (CO) 678
BOLLIER, John A. . . . . . (CT) 112
COHEN, Morris L. . . . . . (CT) 228
COLLIER, Bonnie . . . . . . (CT) 232
HAAG, Nancy R. . . . . . . (CT) 480
HUGHES, Frances M. . . . (CT) 571
JENSEN, Joan W. . . . . . (CT) 598
JOHNSON, Eric W. . . . . (CT) 604
KLINE, Nancy M. . . . . . . (CT) 661
LAWRENCE, Scott W. . . (CT) 705
LYNCH, M W. . . . . (CT) 751
MCKINNEY, Linda R. . . . (CT) 812
NATALE, Barbara G. . . . (CT) 889
ROGERS, Mary E. . . . . . (CT) 1050
SAVAGE, Judith G. . . . . (CT) 1085
STODDARD, Charles E. . . (CT) 1196
SWIFT, Janet B. . . . . (CT) 1216
BEACHELL, Doria M. . . . (DC) 68
RISHWORTH, Susan K. . . (DC) 1036
ROGERS, Sharon J. . . . . (DC) 1050
STEBELMAN, Scott D. . . (DC) 1183
TOOHEY, Anne K. . . . . . (DC) 1250
VAN NIMMEN, Jane . . . (DC) 1276
AHMAD, Carol F. . . . . . . (FL) 8
APPELQUIST, Donald L. . (FL) 30
ATKINS, Donna A. . . . . . (FL) 37
BATTISTE, Anita L. . . . . (FL) 65
BILAL, Dania M. . . . . (FL) 96

INSTRUCTION (Cont'd)
Bibliographic instruction

BLOODWORTH, Velda J. (FL) 106
BROWN, Pia T. . . . . (FL) 147
BYRD, Beverly P. . . . . . . (FL) 168
BYRD, Susan G. . . . . . . (FL) 169
CARILLO, Sherry J. . . . . (FL) 181
EVERETT, David D. . . . . (FL) 358
HARDESTY, Larry L. . . . (FL) 499
HUDSON, Phyllis J. . . . . (FL) 569
MALANCHUK, Iona R. . . (FL) 762
MEAD-DONALDSON,
    Susan L. . . . . (FL) 819
PELLEN, Rita M. . . . . . . (FL) 955
PFARRER, Theodore R. . . (FL) 966
PINE, Nancy M. . . . . (FL) 974
SCHWENN, Janet M. . . . (FL) 1105
TOIFEL, Peggy W. . . . . . (FL) 1248
WILER, Linda L. . . . . (FL) 1339
WOOD, James F. . . . . . . (FL) 1364
BANJA, Judith A. . . . . . . (GA) 54
BUFFALOE, Catherine S. (GA) 155
COMPTON, Lawrence E. (GA) 235
FARMER, Nancy R. . . . . (GA) 364
HARRISON, James O. . . (GA) 506
JONES, Helen C. . . . . . . (GA) 613
LARSEN, Mary T. . . . . . (GA) 698
MALCOLM, Carol L. . . . . (GA) 762
MCCLELLAND, Katherine
    L. . . . . (GA) 796
MORELAND, Virginia F. . (GA) 863
SELF, Sharon W. . . . . . . (GA) 1113
THAXTON, Lyn . . . . (GA) 1234
WALD, Marlena M. . . . . . (GA) 1294
WENDEROTH, Christine . (GA) 1323
WILLIAMS, Sara E. . . . . (GA) 1346
WRIGHT, Dianne H. . . . . (GA) 1371
TAKAHASHI, Annabelle T. (HI) 1220
KNEFEL, Mary A. . . . . . . (IA) 664
REHMKE, Denise M. . . . (IA) 1017
SCHACHT, John N. . . . . (IA) 1088
SCHERUBEL, Melody . . . (IA) 1092
SHAW, James T. . . . . . . (IA) 1123
ZORDELL, Pamela K. . . . (IA) 1390
BECK, Richard J. . . . . . . (ID) 71
ECKWRIGHT, Gail Z. . . . (ID) 335
TAYLOR, Adrien P. . . . . (ID) 1225
ANDERSON, Byron P. . . (IL) 21
BALL, Mary A. . . . . (IL) 52
BODI, Sonia E. . . . . (IL) 109
BOLT, Janice A. . . . . (IL) 113
BOPP, Richard E. . . . . . (IL) 116
CAMPANA, Deborah A. . (IL) 175
DUCHOW, Sally . . . . (IL) 322
DUNN, Lucia S. . . . . (IL) 327
FISHER, Marshall . . . . . . (IL) 381
FRY, Roy H. . . . . (IL) 406
GRAVES, Karen J. . . . . . (IL) 459
HARWOOD, Judith A. . . (IL) 510
HIGGINBOTHAM, Richard
    C. . . . . (IL) 537
HOPKINS, Jane L. . . . . . (IL) 558
HOWREY, Mary M. . . . . (IL) 566
JEFFORDS, Rebecca J. . (IL) 596
KELLEY, Rhona S. . . . . . (IL) 636
KESSINGER, Pamela C. . (IL) 644
KISSINGER, Patricia A. . (IL) 656
MASON, Marjorie L. . . . . (IL) 781
MIKOLYZK, Thomas A. . . (IL) 834
MILLER, Marian I. . . . . . . (IL) 840
MOCH, Mary I. . . . . (IL) 851
MOSBORG, Stella F. . . . (IL) 870
NIELSEN, Brian . . . . (IL) 903
ONGLEY, David C. . . . . . (IL) 924
PERSON, Roland C. . . . . (IL) 961
PORCELLA, Brewster . . . (IL) 984
RUDNIK, Mary C. . . . . . . (IL) 1065
SHAFER, Anne E. . . . . . (IL) 1119
SHEDLOCK, James . . . . (IL) 1124
TROY, Shannon M. . . . . (IL) 1258

INSTRUCTION (Cont'd)
Bibliographic instruction

WILSON, Lizabeth A. . . . (IL) 1351
WRIGHT, Joyce C. . . . . . (IL) 1372
BAXTER, Pam M. . . . . . (IN) 67
BONNER, Robert J. . . . . (IN) 114
DANIELS, Ann A. . . . . . . (IN) 273
FARBER, Evan I. . . . . . . (IN) 363
GREMMELS, Gillian S. . . . (IN) 467
HOHL, Robert J. . . . . (IN) 550
KONDELIK, Marlene R. . (IN) 670
MEEK, Janet E. . . . . (IN) 821
MEYER, Ellen R. . . . . . . (IN) 830
MILNE, Sally J. . . . . (IN) 845
PASK, Judith M. . . . . (IN) 946
RICHWINE, Margaret W. (IN) 1031
STOCKER, Randi L. . . . . (IN) 1195
FENLON, Mary P. . . . . . (KS) 371
GALLOWAY, Mary A. . . (KS) 415
GAYNOR, Kathy A. . . . . (KS) 424
KEMPF, Andrea C. . . . . . (KS) 639
RHODES, Saralinda A. . . (KS) 1026
WHITE, George R. . . . . . (KS) 1331
WILLIAMS, Brian W. . . . . (KS) 1342
BIRCHFIELD, Martha J. . (KY) 98
BLACKBURN-FOSTER,
    Brenda . . . . (KY) 102
BRYSON, Kathleen C. . . (KY) 152
BUSER, Robin A. . . . . . . (KY) 165
COALTER, Milton J. . . . . (KY) 224
CONNOR, Lynn S. . . . . . (KY) 238
COSSEY, M E. . . . . (KY) 249
CRABB, George W. . . . . (KY) 254
CUDD, John M. . . . . (KY) 263
HAWLEY, Mary B. . . . . . (KY) 514
KIRK, Thomas G. . . . . . . (KY) 654
MOORE, Elaine E. . . . . . (KY) 859
PRIOR, Barbara Q. . . . . . (KY) 993
SCHLENE, Vickie J. . . . . (KY) 1094
TEN HOOR, Joan M. . . . (KY) 1231
BRAZILE, Orella R. . . . . (LA) 130
CURTIS, Robert L. . . . . . (LA) 267
DANTIN, Doris B. . . . . . . (LA) 274
DESSINO, Jacquelyn A. . (LA) 296
HASCHAK, Paul G. . . . . (LA) 510
HOGAN, Sharon A. . . . . (LA) 549
JARRED, Ada D. . . . . . . (LA) 594
KING, Anne M. . . . . (LA) 650
KLEINER, Janellyn P. . . . (LA) 660
MAXSTADT, John M. . . . (LA) 788
MAYEAUX, Thurlow M. . (LA) 789
MCFADDEN, Sue J. . . . . (LA) 804
MOONEY, Sandra T. . . . (LA) 858
SARKODIE-MENSAH,
    Kwasi . . . . (LA) 1083
SNOW, Maxine L. . . . . . (LA) 1164
STAFFORD, Cecilia D. . . (LA) 1178
ANDERSON, Wanda E. . (MA) 25
BEZERA, Elizabeth A. . . . (MA) 93
CHANDRASEKHAR,
    Ratna . . . . (MA) 200
COOLIDGE, Christina L. . (MA) 241
DUTCHER, Henry D. . . . (MA) 329
GELB, Linda . . . . (MA) 425
GONNEVILLE, Priscilla R. (MA) 447
KHAN, Syed M. . . . . (MA) 646
MERRIAM, Joyce . . . . . . (MA) 826
MILLER, George M. . . . . (MA) 837
PARSON, Lethiel C. . . . . (MA) 944
ROBINSON, Phyllis A. . . (MA) 1044
SCHATZ, Cindy A. . . . . . (MA) 1090
SHERER, Elaine R. . . . . . (MA) 1127
SHIH, Jenny . . . . (MA) 1130
STOCKARD, Joan . . . . . (MA) 1195
TAUPIER, Andrea S. . . . (MA) 1225
TU, Shu C. . . . . (MA) 1261
WURTZEL, Barbara S. . . (MA) 1374
ZIEPER, Linda R. . . . . . . (MA) 1388
ARRINGTON, Susan J. . (MD) 34
CONNER, P Z. . . . . (MD) 237

INSTRUCTION (Cont'd)
Bibliographic instruction

CREST, Sarah E. . . . . . . (MD) 258
HINEGARDNER, Patricia
    G. . . . . (MD) 542
JACKSON, Carleton . . . . (MD) 587
LABASH, Stephen P. . . . (MD) 685
LARSEN, Lida L. . . . . . . (MD) 698
MERIKANGAS, Robert J. (MD) 826
QUIST, Edwin A. . . . . . . (MD) 1001
REPENNING, Julie A. . . . (MD) 1023
RUSSELL, Rose M. . . . . (MD) 1069
THOMAS, Fannette H. . . (MD) 1236
VAN CAMPEN, Rebecca
    J. . . . . (MD) 1272
WILLIAMS, Mary A. . . . . (MD) 1345
WILLIAMS, Pamela S. . . (MD) 1346
ARNDT, Arleen . . . . (MI) 33
BAKER, Jean S. . . . . (MI) 48
BEAUBIEN, Anne K. . . . . (MI) 70
BLACK, Shirley R. . . . . . (MI) 101
BROWN-MAY, Patricia A. (MI) 148
BURNS, David J. . . . . . . (MI) 162
COURTOIS, Martin P. . . (MI) 251
DRISCOLL, Jacqueline . . (MI) 320
FORSYTH, Karen R. . . . (MI) 391
HEGEDUS, Mary E. . . . . (MI) 521
HILDEBRAND, Linda L. . (MI) 538
LUKASIEWICZ, Barbara . (MI) 747
MEADOWS, Brenda L. . . (MI) 819
NICHOLS, Darlene P. . . . (MI) 901
SATTERTHWAITE, Diane
    A. . . . . (MI) 1084
SCHAAFSMA, Roberta A. (MI) 1088
SCHNEIDER, Janet M. . . (MI) 1097
SMITH, Paul M. . . . . (MI) 1159
STANGER, Keith J. . . . . (MI) 1180
VINT, Patricia A. . . . . . . (MI) 1285
WESTBROOK, Jo L. . . . (MI) 1326
WILDMAN, Linda . . . . . . (MI) 1339
YEE, Sandra G. . . . . (MI) 1379
CHRISTENSEN, Beth E. . (MN) 211
ENRICI, Pamela L. . . . . . (MN) 350
FISHEL, Teresa A. . . . . . (MN) 380
FISTER, Barbara R. . . . . (MN) 382
GANGL, Susan D. . . . . . (MN) 416
HALES-MABRY, Celia E. (MN) 486
HAWTHORNE, Dorothy M. (MN) 514
HITT, Charles J. . . . . (MN) 544
HUBER, Kristina R. . . . . (MN) 569
JOHNSON, Donald C. . . (MN) 603
MARION, Donald J. . . . . (MN) 770
READY, Sandra K. . . . . . (MN) 1012
REIERSON, Pamela M. . (MN) 1019
SANFORD, Carolyn C. . . (MN) 1081
SINHA, Dorothy P. . . . . . (MN) 1143
TIBLIN, Mariann E. . . . . (MN) 1244
TURNER, Patricia . . . . . . (MN) 1265
WALDEN, Barbara L. . . . (MN) 1294
BHULLAR, Pushpajit D. . (MO) 93
DEWEESE, June L. . . . . (MO) 298
ELLEBRACHT, Eleanor V. (MO) 343
ELS, Nancy T. . . . . (MO) 346
HOCHSTETLER, Donald
    D. . . . . (MO) 545
IGLAUER, Carol . . . . (MO) 581
JOSEPH, Miriam E. . . . . (MO) 617
LOCKHART, Carol A. . . . (MO) 736
REIMAN, David A. . . . . . (MO) 1020
SINCLAIR, Regina A. . . . (MO) 1143
STEWART, J A. . . . . (MO) 1192
VAN BLAIR, Betty A. . . . (MO) 1272
BECK, Allisa L. . . . . (MS) 71
GRAVES, Gail T. . . . . . . (MS) 459
HARPER, Laura G. . . . . . (MS) 503
OELZ, Erling R. . . . . (MT) 917
DICKERSON, Jimmy . . . (NC) 300
DODGE, Michael R. . . . . (NC) 308
GARTRELL, Ellen G. . . . (NC) 420
GETCHELL, Charles M. . (NC) 430

INSTRUCTION (Cont'd)
Bibliographic instruction

GLUCK, Myke H. . . . . . . (NC) 442
LAVINE, Marcia M. . . . . . (NC) 703
MIDDLETON, Beverly D. (NC) 833
MOORE, Kathryn L. . . . . (NC) 860
OSEGUEDA, Laura M. . . (NC) 927
PETERSON, Cynthia L. . (NC) 963
PHILBECK, Jo S. . . . . . . (NC) 967
SHEPHERD, Gay W. . . . (NC) 1127
SINCLAIR, R F. . . . . (NC) 1142
SUMMERFORD, Steven L. (NC) 1209
TAYLOR, Christine M. . . (NC) 1226
YOUNG, Judith E. . . . . . (NC) 1382
BRATTON, Phyllis A. . . . (ND) 129
GARD, Betty A. . . . . (ND) 417
NIENOW, Beth M. . . . . . (ND) 904
EGBERS, Gail L. . . . . . . (NE) 339
LU, Janet C. . . . . (NE) 745
FITZPATRICK, Robert E. (NH) 383
GAGNON, Ruth . . . . (NH) 412
KIETZMAN, William D. . . (NH) 647
THOMAS, Jacquelyn H. . (NH) 1236
VINCENT, Charles P. . . . (NH) 1284
AXEL-LUTE, Paul . . . . . . (NJ) 42
BOLESTA, Linda . . . . . . (NJ) 112
BOYLE, Jean E. . . . . . . (NJ) 124
BUTCHER, Patricia S. . . (NJ) 166
CASSEL, Jeris F. . . . . . . (NJ) 193
HENNEMAN, John B. . . . (NJ) 528
MARTINEZ, Jane A. . . . . (NJ) 779
NASH, Stanley D. . . . . . (NJ) 888
RANDALL, Lynn E. . . . . (NJ) 1006
SCHUT, Grace W. . . . . . (NJ) 1103
TALAR, Anita . . . . (NJ) 1220
VLOYANETES, Jeanne M. (NJ) 1286
WILSON, Myoung C. . . . (NJ) 1352
WOODLEY, Robert H. . . (NJ) 1366
GROTHEY, Mina J. . . . . (NM) 473
HENDRICKSON, Linnea
    M. . . . . (NM) 527
MCBETH, Deborah E. . . . (NM) 792
RASSAM, Cynthia K. . . . (NM) 1009
CONWAY, Susan L. . . . . (NV) 239
BANKS-ISZARD, Kimberly
    K. . . . . (NY) 54
BAXTER, Paula A. . . . . . (NY) 67
BENSEN, Mary L. . . . . . (NY) 83
BERNSTEIN, Mark P. . . . (NY) 89
BLANDY, Susan G. . . . . (NY) 104
BURSTEIN, Rose A. . . . . (NY) 164
CAVINESS, Ann N. . . . . (NY) 195
COONS, William W. . . . . (NY) 242
COOPER, Catherine M. . (NY) 242
DEDONATO, Ree . . . . . . (NY) 286
DOEZEMA, Linda P. . . . . (NY) 308
DREW, Wilfred E. . . . . . . (NY) 319
FRANCIS, Barbara B. . . . (NY) 396
FRANCO, Kathryn C. . . . (NY) 396
FRASER, Charlotte R. . . (NY) 399
FREESE, Melanie L. . . . . (NY) 401
FREIDES, Thelma . . . . . . (NY) 401
GRUNDT, Leonard . . . . . (NY) 475
HECKMAN, Lucy T. . . . . (NY) 519
HORNE, Dorice L. . . . . . (NY) 560
HORNICK-LOCKARD,
    Barbara A. . . . . (NY) 560
IRWIN, Iris . . . . (NY) 584
JUDD, Blanche E. . . . . . (NY) 618
KING, Christine E. . . . . . (NY) 650
KLAVANO, Ann M. . . . . (NY) 658
KLEIMAN, Rhoda E. . . . . (NY) 659
KONOVALOFF, Maria S. (NY) 670
KUGLER, Sharon . . . . . . (NY) 682
KUHNER, Robert A. . . . . (NY) 683
LARSEN, Joan A. . . . . . (NY) 698
LOWRY, Lina M. . . . . . . (NY) 745
LUTZKER, Marilyn L. . . . (NY) 750
MACOMBER, Nancy . . . (NY) 758
MAUL, Shirley A. . . . . . . (NY) 787

INSTRUCTION (Cont'd)
Bibliographic instruction

O'DONNELL, Mary A. . . (NY) 917
PAGEL, Scott B. . . . . . . (NY) 934
PODELL, Diane K. . . . . . (NY) 979
POWIS, Katherine E. . . . (NY) 989
REMUSAT, Suzanne L. . (NY) 1023
RICKER, Shirley E. . . . . (NY) 1031
ROBERTS, Anne F. . . . . (NY) 1039
RUBEY, Daniel R. . . . . . (NY) 1064
SCHMIDTMANN, Nancy
    K. . . . . (NY) 1096
SHAPIRO, Martin P. . . . . (NY) 1121
SLUSS, Sara B. . . . . (NY) 1150
SORGEN, Herbert J. . . . (NY) 1168
STEWART, Linda G. . . . (NY) 1192
TOTH, Gregory M. . . . . . (NY) 1252
VANDELINDER, Bonnie L. (NY) 1273
WAGNER, Janet S. . . . . (NY) 1291
WELLS, Margaret R. . . . (NY) 1322
WISHART, H L. . . . . (NY) 1357
WOLF, Carolyn M. . . . . . (NY) 1359
WORTZEL, Murray N. . . (NY) 1369
ALTAN, Susan B. . . . . . . (OH) 18
ANDERSON, Janice L. . . (OH) 23
BOX, Krista J. . . . . (OH) 122
BRINK, David R. . . . . . . (OH) 136
CAIN, Linda B. . . . . (OH) 171
CARY, Mary K. . . . . (OH) 191
CURRIE, William W. . . . . (OH) 266
DUFFETT, Gorman L. . . . (OH) 323
EMRICK, Nancy J. . . . . . (OH) 348
FACINELLI, Jaclyn R. . . . (OH) 360
FIDLER, Linda M. . . . . . . (OH) 375
GATTEN, Jeffrey N. . . . . (OH) 422
GODWIN, Eva D. . . . . . . (OH) 443
GREEN, Denise D. . . . . . (OH) 461
GROHL, Arlene P. . . . . . (OH) 471
GUSTAFSON, Julia C. . . (OH) 478
HALIBEY-BILYK, Christine
    M. . . . . (OH) 486
HARDESTY, Vicki H. . . . (OH) 499
KIE, Kathleen M. . . . . . . (OH) 646
LANTZ, Elizabeth A. . . . . (OH) 697
LEIBOLD, Cynthia K. . . . (OH) 713
MILLER, William . . . . . . (OH) 843
O'HANLON, Nancyanne . (OH) 919
PORTER, Marlene A. . . . (OH) 985
PURSEL, Janet E. . . . . . (OH) 998
RADER, Hannelore B. . . (OH) 1002
ROMARY, Michael P. . . . (OH) 1052
SANKOT, Janice M. . . . . (OH) 1081
SANTAVICCA, Edmund F. (OH) 1082
SCHIRMER, Robert W. . . (OH) 1093
SCHMALBERG, Aaron . . (OH) 1094
SWAIN, Richard H. . . . . (OH) 1212
SWEENY, Mary K. . . . . . (OH) 1215
TUCKER, Debbie B. . . . . (OH) 1261
WHITAKER, Constance C. (OH) 1329
BRICK, Sarah E. . . . . . . (OK) 134
CALLARD, Joanne C. . . (OK) 173
FLINNER, Beatrice E. . . . (OK) 385
FULK, Mary C. . . . . (OK) 408
HOVDE, David M. . . . . . (OK) 563
KENNEDY, James W. . . (OK) 641
MCCALL, Patricia . . . . . . (OK) 793
NASH, Helen B. . . . . (OK) 888
WEISS, Catharine H. . . . (OK) 1320
HENDERSON, Carol G. . (OR) 526
LAWRENCE, Robert E. . (OR) 705
ADAMS, Mignon S. . . . . (PA) 5
ANDRILLI, Ene M. . . . . . (PA) 27
BURNS-DUFFY, Mary A. (PA) 163
CAMPION, Carol M. . . . (PA) 177
CRAWFORD, Gregory A. (PA) 256
CRESCENT, Victoria L. . (PA) 258
DEEGAN, Rosemary L. . . (PA) 286
DONOVAN, Judith G. . . . (PA) 312
ERDICK, Joseph W. . . . . (PA) 352
EZELL, Johanna V. . . . . . (PA) 360

INSTRUCTION (Cont'd)
Bibliographic instruction

FEDRICK, Mary A. . . . . . (PA) 368
FILLER, Mary A. . . . . . . (PA) 377
FREEMAN, Michael S. . . (PA) 401
FUSELER-MCDOWELL,
   Elizabeth A. . . . . (PA) 410
HALL, Martha H. . . . . . . (PA) 488
HESP, Judith A. . . . . . . (PA) 534
JEAN, Lorraine A. . . . . . (PA) 596
JOHNSON, Joan E. . . . . (PA) 606
KREITZBURG, Marilyn J. (PA) 677
LARSON, Mary E. . . . . . (PA) 699
LEHMANN, Stephen R. . (PA) 713
LINGLE, Virginia A. . . . (PA) 730
LYNCH, Mary D. . . . . . . (PA) 752
MCCOY, James F. . . . . . (PA) 799
MORGANTI, Deena J. . . (PA) 864
NOLF, Marsha L. . . . . . . (PA) 908
PAWLIK, Deborah A. . . . (PA) 951
RAINEY, Nancy B. . . . . (PA) 1004
RIDGEWAY, Patricia M. . (PA) 1032
ROSENBERGER, Merry G. (PA) 1056
SENECAL, Kristin S. . . . (PA) 1115
THOMAS, Deborah A. . . (PA) 1236
ULINCY, Loretta D. . . . . (PA) 1268
VOROS, David S. . . . . . (PA) 1289
WEBER ROOCHVARG,
   Lynn E. . . . . (PA) 1314
WEIS, Aimee L. . . . . . . (PA) 1319
YOUNG, Dorothy E. . . . (PA) 1381
ZABEL, Diane M. . . . . . (PA) 1385
CONCEPCION, Luis . . . . (PR) 235
BRYAN, Susan M. . . . . . (RI) 152
CAMERON, Lucille W. . . (RI) 175
KEEFE, Margaret J. . . . (RI) 634
KRAUSSE, Sylvia C. . . . (RI) 676
SHERIDAN, Jean . . . . . . (RI) 1127
SIEBURTH, Janice F. . . . (RI) 1135
YOUNG, Arthur P. . . . . . (RI) 1381
BAKER, Steven L. . . . . . (SC)   49
DRYDEN, Sherre H. . . . . (SC) 321
DUSENBERRY, Mary D. . (SC) 329
GOING, Susan C. . . . . . (SC) 444
HOLLEY, E J. . . . . (SC) 551
LAFAYE, Cary D. . . . . . (SC) 687
MICHAELS, Carolyn L. . . (SC) 831
MORGAN, Nancy T. . . . . (SC) 864
SCHMITT, John P. . . . . . (SC) 1096
SEAMAN, Sheila L. . . . . (SC) 1109
TAPLEY, Bridgette M. . . . (SC) 1223
VASSALLO, John A. . . . (SC) 1279
WEATHERS, Virginia W. (SC) 1312
SMITH, Rise L. . . . . (SD) 1160
HAMBERG, Cheryl J. . . . (TN) 490
HARRISON, Richard H. . (TN) 507
LAMBERT, Sarah E. . . . . (TN) 690
MANNING, Dale . . . . (TN) 766
MEREDITH, Don L. . . . . (TN) 825
MURGAI, Sarla R. . . . . . (TN) 880
NORRIS, Carol B. . . . . . (TN) 909
PHILLIPS, Linda L. . . . . (TN) 968
RIDENOUR, Lisa R. . . . . (TN) 1032
ROMANS, Lawrence M. . (TN) 1052
ROTHACKER, John M. . (TN) 1059
RUDOLPH, N J. . . . . (TN) 1066
SHORT, William M. . . . . (TN) 1132
SMITH, Lori D. . . . . (TN) 1157
TABACHNICK, Sharon . . (TN) 1219
TURNER, Deborah M. . . (TN) 1264
WALLACE, Alan H. . . . . (TN) 1297
WARD, James E. . . . . . . (TN) 1304
WATTS, Adalyn . . . . (TN) 1310
BAILEY, William G. . . . . (TX)   47
BARRINGER, Sallie H. . . (TX)   60
CAMPBELL, Shirley A. . . (TX) 177
HAGLE, Claudette S. . . . (TX) 483
HARPER, Marsha W. . . . (TX) 503
HYMAN, Ferne B. . . . . . (TX) 580

INSTRUCTION (Cont'd)
Bibliographic instruction

JESER-SKAGGS, Sharlee
   A. . . . . (TX) 600
KELLOUGH, Jean L. . . . (TX) 637
KHADER, Majed J. . . . . (TX) 645
KUJOORY, Parvin . . . . . (TX) 683
LOWRY, Andretta G. . . . (TX) 745
MARLEY, Judith L. . . . . (TX) 772
MILLER, Susan A. . . . . . (TX) 842
NOLAN, Christopher W. . (TX) 907
PEYTON, Janice L. . . . . (TX) 966
PHILLIPS, Robert L. . . . . (TX) 969
SHEETS, Janet E. . . . . . (TX) 1125
SPECHT, Alice W. . . . . . (TX) 1172
TAYLOR, Anne E. . . . . . (TX) 1226
TEVEBAUGH, Joyce E. . (TX) 1233
TOLBERT, Jean F. . . . . . (TX) 1248
TROST, Theresa K. . . . . (TX) 1258
WASSENICH, Red . . . . . (TX) 1308
WYGANT, Alice C. . . . . . (TX) 1375
WIGGINS, Marvin E. . . . (UT) 1337
ANDERSON, Kari D. . . . (VA)   24
BRAINARD, Blair . . . . . . (VA) 127
CASEY, Wayne T. . . . . . (VA) 192
CHISHOLM, Clarence E. (VA) 209
DIERCKS, Thelma C. . . . (VA) 302
EISENBERG, Phyllis B. . (VA) 340
GREFE, Richard F. . . . . (VA) 465
HAUSMAN, Patricia R. . . (VA) 513
HILL, Nancy A. . . . . (VA) 540
HOLLY, Janet S. . . . . . . (VA) 552
JENNERICH, Elaine Z. . . (VA) 598
JOHNSON, Martha A. . . (VA) 607
KILLEEN, Erlene B. . . . . (VA) 648
MYERS, Martha O. . . . . (VA) 884
OBRIST, Cynthia W. . . . (VA) 915
PEARSON, Marilyn R. . . (VA) 953
DURFEE, Tamara . . . . . . (VT) 328
LUZER, Nancy H. . . . . . (VT) 750
ALEXANDER, Malcolm D. (WA)   12
ALKIRE, Leland G. . . . . (WA)   13
FRALEY, David B. . . . . . (WA) 395
GARRETSON, Laurie J. . (WA) 420
GILCHRIST, Debra L. . . . (WA) 434
JENNERICH, Edward J. . (WA) 598
NEWELL, Rick K. . . . . . (WA) 898
PRINGLE, Robert M. . . . (WA) 993
RICIGLIANO, Lorraine M. (WA) 1031
RICKERSON, Carla . . . . (WA) 1031
SCHREINER, Suzanne M. (WA) 1100
WYNN, Debra D. . . . . . . (WA) 1375
CARR, Jo A. . . . . (WI) 185
ENGELDINGER, Eugene
   A. . . . . (WI) 349
FLIEGEL, Deborah A. . . . (WI) 385
FU, Tina C. . . . . (WI) 407
GERLACH, Donald E. . . . (WI) 429
JESUDASON, Melba . . . (WI) 600
MANDERNACK, Scott B. (WI) 765
MCCLEMENTS, Nancy A. (WI) 796
PIETERS, Donald L. . . . . (WI) 972
STRUPP, Sybil A. . . . . . (WI) 1203
THOMPSON, Glenn J. . . (WI) 1239
SCOBELL, Elizabeth H. . (WV) 1106
WATSON, Carolyn R. . . . (WV) 1309
MACK, Bonnie R. . . . . . (WY) 756
DROESSLER, Judith B. . (AB) 320
NOGA, Dolores A. . . . . . (AB) 907
VINE, Rita F. . . . . (AB) 1285
WHITE, Donald J. . . . . . (BC) 1330
MCNALLY, Brian D. . . . . (NB) 815
MACLENNAN, Oriel C. . . (NS) 757
NOWAKOWSKI, Frances
   C. . . . . (NS) 911
GILMORE, Carolyn . . . . . (PQ) 437
PETRYK, Louise O. . . . . (PQ) 965
AFFLECK, Delburt E. . . . (SK)   7
MACK, A Y. . . . . (SK) 756
FOX, Peter K. . . . . (IRE) 395

INSTRUCTION (Cont'd)

Bibliographic instruction

BOWEN, Dorothy N. . . . . (KEN) 120
BERNAT, Mary A. . . . . . (VEN) 88
Bibliographic instruction, admin BAUNER, Ruth E. . . . . . . (IL) 67
Bibliographic instruction &
development WILLIAMS, Suzanne C. . (TX) 1346
Bibliographic instruction & online BURR, Charlotte A. . . . . . (WI) 163
Bibliographic instruction & reference PATTERSON, Grace L. . (NY) 948
TORNQUIST, Kristi M. . . (WI) 1251
Bibliographic instruction automated
syst PALLARDY, Judy S. . . . (MO) 935
Bibliographic instruction for education WILKE, Janet S. . . . . . . (KS) 1339
Bibliographic instruction for music SILCOX, Tinsley E. . . . . (TN) 1137
Bibliographic instruction librarianship HUPP, Stephen L. . . . . . (MI) 577
Bibliographic instruction of online WARD, Sandra N. . . . . . (CA) 1304
Bibliographic instruction programs DEWAR, Jo E. . . . . (FL) 298
Bibliographic science instruction DERKSEN, Charlotte R. . (CA) 294
Bibliographical instruction HALES, David A. . . . . . (AK) 486
OTTOSON, Robin D. . . . (CO) 930
MEREDITH, Phyllis C. . . (PA) 825
ROSENSHIELD, Jill K. . . (WI) 1057
Bibliographical instruction & research FREITAG, Wolfgang M. . (MA) 401
Biological literature instruction WILLIAMS, Doris C. . . . (NY) 1343
Business library instruction BENSON-TALLEY, Lois I. (CA) 83
Business reference & instruction BATISTA, Emily J. . . . . . (PA) 64
Business resrch, acquisitions, & instrc CAMERON, Constance B. (RI) 174
Catlgng training, devlpmnt &
instruction JIZBA, Laurel . . . . (MI) 600
Chemical information instruction SOMERVILLE, Arleen N. (NY) 1167
Chemistry bibliographic instruction WIGGINS, Gary D. . . . . (IN) 1337
Children's literature, instruction NELSON, Olga G. . . . . . (OH) 895
Cinema arts instruction TALIT, Lynn . . . . (CT) 1221
Classroom instruction LIRA, Judith A. . . . . . . (CO) 732
Classroom library instruction ROBBINS, Lora A. . . . . (MI) 1039
College level library instruction OAKLEY, Adeline D. . . . (MA) 913
College library instruction SIMMONS, Randall C. . . (ID) 1140
Computer & video based instruction BUTLER, David W. . . . . (CA) 166
Computer applications to instruction TERWILLIGER, Gloria P. (VA) 1232
Computer catalog instruction HOCKEL, Kathleen N. . . (CA) 545
Computer instruction COOPER, William E. . . . (CA) 244
WAGNER, A C. . . . . . . (NY) 1291
LINDSEY, Nancy L. . . . . (TN) 730
Computer skills instruction JACOBS, Lois S. . . . . . . (MA) 589
Computer-assisted instruction CATER, Judy J. . . . . . . (CA) 194
SHAMS, Kamruddin . . . . (CA) 1120
WILLIAMS, Valencia . . . (CA) 1347
PROVINCE, William R. . . (IL) 996
TEO, Elizabeth A. . . . . . (IL) 1231
DOLAK, Frank J. . . . . . (IN) 309
GERRITY, Marline R. . . . (MO) 429
NIPP, Deanna . . . . (NJ) 904
FITZGERALD, Patricia A. (PA) 382
LARSON, Mary E. . . . . . (PA) 699
ANDERSON, Kari D. . . . (VA) 24
Computer-assisted instruction lib syst DICARLO, Michael A. . . . (LA) 300
Computer-assisted nursing instruction GUENTHER, Jody . . . . . (TX) 475
Computerized legal research
instruction STOPPEL, Ellen K. . . . . . (IA) 1198
Computers in instruction HALE, Robert G. . . . . . . (CT) 485
SOLDNER, Nancy C. . . . (KS) 1166
Continuing education instruction BURNETT, James H. . . . (CO) 161
Cooperative bibliographic instruction RATZER, Mary B. . . . . . (NY) 1010
Course-integrated instruction MORRIS, Karen T. . . . . . (OK) 867
Course-related instruction WHITTINGTON, Christine
A. . . . . (PA) 1334
Curriculum & instruction DIRKSEN, Phyllis A. . . . (CO) 305
Curriculum & integrated instruction RATZER, Mary B. . . . . . (NY) 1010
Database instruction & training WILCOX, Patricia F. . . . (WI) 1338
Directing library skills instruction HACKMAN, Mary H. . . . (MD) 481
Education reference & instruction HINKLE, Mary R. . . . . . (VA) 542
Educational instruction of children HANSON, Kathy H. . . . . (GA) 498
Elementary school library instruction SHABERLY, Leanna J. . . (AZ) 1118
End-user instruction, BRS after dark COONS, William W. . . . (NY) 242
End-user instruction in chem
databases BECK, Diane J. . . . . . . (CA) 71
End-user search instruction LIEBER, Ellen C. . . . . . (NY) 726
CAMPBELL, Sandra M. . (AB) 177
Film instruction NIGRIN, Albert G. . . . . . (NJ) 904
Fine arts bibliographic instruction SCHERER, Herbert G. . . (MN) 1092

INSTRUCTION (Cont'd)

Foreign language instruction LERNER, Esther T. . . . . . (OH) 717
General library instruction MCCART, Vernon A. . . . (VA) 794
Graduate instruction ZIMPFER, William E. . . . (MA) 1389
Graduate level bibliographic
instruction ILACQUA, Anne K. . . . . (MA) 581
Information access instruction GROVER, Iva S. . . . . . . (WA) 474
Information science instruction WILSON, Anthony M. . . . (WA) 1349
Informational skills instruction LOPEZ, Kathryn P. . . . . (NM) 741
Information-seeking skills instruction MICIKAS, Lynda L. . . . . (PA) 832
Instruction WYLIE, Nethery A. . . . . (CO) 1375
WILLIAMS, Judy R. . . . . (CT) 1344
BRIERTY, Carol A. . . . . (FL) 135
FLETCHALL, Josephine V. (IA) 384
KELLY, Raymond T. . . . . (IL) 638
KINNEY, M R. . . . . (IL) 653
WITTKOPF, Barbara J. . . (LA) 1358
PRINZ, Jane A. . . . . . . (NY) 993
LYNESS, Ann L. . . . . . (PA) 752
POOL, Jeraldine B. . . . . (TX) 982
GRANITZ, Adrienne D. . . (VA) 457
CONABLE, Irene H. . . . (WA) 235
Instruction design & development TREGLOAN, Donald C. . (MI) 1255
Instruction in information science EMMICK, Nancy J. . . . . (CA) 348
Instruction in information skills COOK, Sybilla A. . . . . . (OR) 240
Instruction in library skills HILLER, Catherine C. . . (CT) 541
Instruction in library usage GOODWYN, Betty R. . . . (AL) 450
Instruction in library use SHIP, Martin I. . . . . (ON) 1131
DOUGLAS-BONNELL,
Eileen . . . . (PQ) 314
Instruction in research methods TROTTI, John B. . . . . . (VA) 1258
Instruction of media skills KOEPP, Sara H. . . . . . . (IA) 668
Instruction of online database
searching LOVELAND, Catherine R. (OH) 743
Instruction services ECKLUND, Kristin A. . . . (CA) 335
Instruction, teaching CARUSO, Genevieve O. . (MI) 190
Instruction using media & technology TREGLOAN, Donald C. . (MI) 1255
Instructor, genealogy & family history SPERRY, Kip . . . . (UT) 1174
Instructor of music bibliography MIXTER, Keith E. . . . . . (OH) 850
Integrated library skills instruction HUSTED, Ruth E. . . . . . (OK) 578
Intelligent computer-assisted instrc PARROTT, James R. . . . (ON) 944
Interdisciplinary research & instruction STONE, Nancy Y. . . . . . (MI) 1197
K-12 library instruction MATSUNAGA, Fay L. . . . (CO) 785
Legal bibliographic instruction CHERRY, Anna M. . . . . (MN) 206
Legal bibliographical instruction LANGSTON, Sally J. . . . (TX) 696
Legal database instruction CHERRY, Anna M. . . . . (MN) 206
HILL, Ruth J. . . . . (TN) 540
Legal database instruction &
searching ESKRIDGE, Virginia C. . . (WV) 354
Legal instruction HUGHES, John M. . . . . (CT) 571
Legal research instruction CASTETTER, Karla M. . . (CA) 194
STREIKER, Susan L. . . . (CA) 1201
BRENNAN, Edward P. . . (MD) 132
BAUM, Marsha L. . . . . . (MN) 66
LEITER, Richard A. . . . . (NE) 714
KENNEDY, Bruce M. . . . (NY) 640
KOSTER, Gregory E. . . . (NY) 673
ZUBROW, Marcia L. . . . (NY) 1391
Library & bibliographic instruction LAKE, Gretchen L. . . . . (AK) 688
GAREY, Anita I. . . . . . . (CA) 418
ZIEGLER, Janet M. . . . . (CA) 1388
HUDSON, Donna T. . . . . (NC) 569
WORTMAN, William A. . . (OH) 1369
DAVIDSON, Nancy M. . . (SC) 276
Library & bibliographical instruction KIRKENDALL, Carolyn A. (MI) 654
Library & computer instruction SACHS, Kathie B. . . . . . (PA) 1073
Library & information instruction FEW, John E. . . . . (CA) 374
Library & information skills instruction RATZER, Mary B. . . . . . (NY) 1010
Library & media skill instruction GOODMAN, Roslyn L. . . (AK) 449
Library education instruction GROSS, Richard F. . . . . (ME) 472
Library education reference instruction JOHNSON, Denise J. . . . (WI) 603
Library instruction GONIWIECHA, Mark C. . (AK) 447
SMITH, Jane B. . . . . . . (AL) 1155
STEWART, Sharon L. . . (AL) 1193
MILLER, Larry A. . . . . . (AZ) 839
PHIPPS, Shelley E. . . . . (AZ) 969
RICE, Virginia E. . . . . . (AZ) 1027
WILLIAMS, Karen B. . . . (AZ) 1344
BIBEL, Barbara M. . . . . (CA) 94
BRITTON, Helen H. . . . . (CA) 137

INSTRUCTION (Cont'd)
Library instruction

BROOKS, Mary A. . . . . . (CA) 140
BROWN, Diane M. . . . . . (CA) 143
DEBOER, Kee K. . . . . . (CA) 284
DICKENS, Jan . . . . (CA) 300
DINTRONE, Charles V. . . (CA) 305
DOLVEN, Mary . . . . (CA) 310
GEBHARD, Patricia . . . . (CA) 424
GIBBONS, Carolbeth . . . (CA) 431
GOFF, Linda J. . . . . (CA) 443
GRASSIAN, Esther S. . . (CA) 458
HOFFMAN, Irene M. . . . (CA) 548
KOBZINA, Norma G. . . . (CA) 666
KONG, Leslie M. . . . . . (CA) 670
KRISTIE, William J. . . . (CA) 679
LEVINE, Beryl . . . . (CA) 720
LUCAS, Linda L. . . . . . (CA) 746
MCCORMICK, Mona . . . (CA) 798
SIBLEY, Elizabeth A. . . . (CA) 1135
SKAPURA, Robert J. . . . (CA) 1145
VANDERBERG, Patricia S. (CA) 1273
WHITSON, William L. . . . (CA) 1334
BREIVIK, Patricia S. . . . . (CO) 132
FINK, Deborah . . . . (CO) 378
ROBERTS, Francis X. . . (CO) 1040
SITTER, Clara M. . . . . . (CO) 1144
ANDRONIK, Catherine M. (CT) 27
FRYER, Regina K. . . . . . (CT) 407
GIUNTA, Victoria J. . . . (FL) 439
STILLMAN, June S. . . . (FL) 1194
OWINGS, Priscilla A. . . . (GA) 932
WILSON, Janice E. . . . . (GA) 1351
HERRICK, Johanna W. . . (HI) 532
HERRICK, Kenneth R. . . (HI) 532
NAHL-JAKOBOVITS,
   Diane . . . . (HI) 886
PETERSON, Lorna . . . . (IA) 964
BERGER, Marianne C. . . (IL) 85
BURRUSS, Marsha A. . . (IL) 163
FULTON, Tara L. . . . . . (IL) 409
GALLAGHER, Eileen M. . (IL) 414
GIBBS, Mary E. . . . . . . (IL) 431
GORDON, Elaine H. . . . (IL) 451
MILLER, Doris A. . . . . . (IL) 837
OSORIO, Nestor L. . . . . (IL) 928
SHERMAN, William F. . . (IL) 1128
VANCURA, Joyce B. . . . (IL) 1273
DAVIS, H S. . . . . (IN) 279
JONES, Deborah A. . . . (IN) 612
MILLER, Marsha A. . . . . (IN) 840
POPP, Mary F. . . . . . . (IN) 984
ROBSON, John M. . . . . (IN) 1045
SANER, Eileen K. . . . . . (IN) 1081
STUSSY, Susan A. . . . . (IN) 1205
TRUESDELL, Cheryl B. . (IN) 1259
VIOLETTE, Judith L. . . . (IN) 1285
BROWN, Mary A. . . . . . (KS) 146
GERMANN, Malcolm P. . (KS) 429
DEERING, Ronald F. . . . (KY) 287
DU CARMONT, M C. . . . (LA) 322
MIDDLETON, Francine K. (LA) 833
COHEN, Christina M. . . . (MA) 228
DACHS, Jerald K. . . . . (MA) 269
HUDSON, Robert E. . . . (MA) 570
MAIO, Kathleen L. . . . . (MA) 762
MASSEY-BURZIO, Virginia (MA) 782
REPENNING, Julie A. . . (MD) 1023
NUFFER, Roy A. . . . . . (MI) 912
VANDERLAAN, Sharon J. (MI) 1274
MUELLER, Mary G. . . . (MN) 875
OBERMAN, Cerise G. . . (MN) 914
PANKAKE, Marcia J. . . . (MN) 938
SPETLAND, Charles G. . (MN) 1174
DELIVUK, John A. . . . . (MO) 289
KNAUSS, Bonnie S. . . . (MO) 663
MCDERMOTT, Margaret
   H. . . . . (MO) 802
BRELAND, June M. . . . . (MS) 132
ELLSBURY, Susan H. . . (MS) 345

GENTRY, Etherlene H. . . . (MS) 427
SANDERS, Lou H. . . . . . (MS) 1080
KAYA, Kathryn A. . . . . . (MT) 632
DUNN, Elizabeth B. . . . . (NC) 326
KING, Ebba K. . . . . (NC) 650
MEEHAN-BLACK,
   Elizabeth C. . . . . (NC) 821
TOLLMAN, Thomas A. . . . (NE) 1249
CASEY, Mary A. . . . . . . (NJ) 192
FRIEDMAN, Ruth . . . . . . (NJ) 404
GEORGE, Mary W. . . . . (NJ) 427
JOB, Amy G. . . . . (NJ) 601
SCOTT, Mellouise J. . . . (NJ) 1107
TILLMAN, Hope N. . . . . (NJ) 1245
CROCKER, Judith A. . . . (NM) 259
MASTALIR, Janet K. . . . (NV) 782
BAUM, Nathan . . . . (NY) 66
BREEN, M F. . . . . (NY) 131
BULSON, Christine . . . . (NY) 156
CHICKERING, F W. . . . . (NY) 208
CLINE, Herman H. . . . . . (NY) 222
ESPOSITO, Michael A. . . (NY) 354
FEAGLEY, Ethel M. . . . . (NY) 367
HASKO, John J. . . . . . . (NY) 510
MOSLANDER, Charlotte D. (NY) 871
O'DONNELL, Michael J. . (NY) 917
PEELE, Marla N. . . . . . (NY) 954
POLLARD, Bobbie T. . . . (NY) 981
DEAN, Winifred F. . . . . (OH) 284
GEORGE, Linda H. . . . . (OH) 427
KRUMM, Carol R. . . . . . (OH) 680
NICHOLS, James T. . . . . (OH) 901
QUAY, Richard H. . . . . . (OH) 999
SMITH, Timothy D. . . . . (OH) 1161
BATT, Fred . . . . (OK) 64
BARNWELL, Jane L. . . . (OR) 58
FRANTZ, Paul A. . . . . . (OR) 398
BARD, Nelson P. . . . . . (PA) 56
BARR, Marilyn P. . . . . . (PA) 58
BURLINGAME, Connie . . (PA) 161
ENDRES, Maureen D. . . (PA) 348
FROST, William J. . . . . (PA) 406
PALMA, Nancy C. . . . . (PA) 935
PARSONS, Muriel W. . . . (PA) 945
QUINTILIANO, Barbara . (PA) 1000
THOMPSON, Dorothea M. (PA) 1239
WELLE, Jacob P. . . . . . (PA) 1321
WHITMORE, Marilyn P. . (PA) 1333
JARAMILLO, Juana S. . . (PR) 594
THOELKE, Elisabeth A. . . (SD) 1235
HENDRIX, Wilma P. . . . . (TN) 528
CAMERON, Dee B. . . . . (TX) 174
DUNCAN, Donna P. . . . . (TX) 325
HOWARD, Elizabeth A. . (TX) 564
KOOPMAN, Frances A. . (TX) 671
OLSSON, Margaret G. . . (TX) 923
PIETTE, Mary I. . . . . . . (UT) 972
SANDERS, William D. . . (UT) 1080
ENGELBRECHT, Pamela
   N. . . . . (VA) 349
JORDAN, Katherine H. . . (VA) 616
KENNEY, Donald J. . . . (VA) 641
REAM, Daniel L. . . . . . (VA) 1012
SOLES, Elizabeth S. . . . (VA) 1166
HENSLEY, Randall B. . . (WA) 529
BENDIX, Linda A. . . . . . (WI) 79
MCKINNEY, Venora . . . (WI) 812
OLSON, Dennis H. . . . . (WI) 922
VAN ESS, James E. . . . (WI) 1275
CAMPBELL, Sandra M. . (AB) 177
DELONG, Kathleen M. . . (AB) 290
JARVIS, Marylea . . . . . (AB) 595
STEVELMAN, Sharon R. (AB) 1190
DEVAKOS, Elizabeth R. . (BC) 297
WEEKS, Gerald M. . . . . (BC) 1315
HAUCK, Danuta . . . . . . (ON) 512
JOHNSON, James R. . . (ON) 605
LOVE, Barbara . . . . . . (ON) 743

INSTRUCTION (Cont'd)

Library instruction

	SINGLETON, Cynthia B. .	(ON) 1143
	KIELLY, Marion J.	(PE) 647
	BOLDUC, Yves	(PQ) 112
	GRAINGER, Bruce	(PQ) 457
	BRILL, Kathryn R.	(ENG) 136
	GUNN, Shirley A.	(NGR) 477
Library instruction & orientation	MACKENZIE, Shirley A. .	(ON) 756
Library instruction & reader's advisory	LINDGREN, Beverly P. . .	(IL) 729
Library instruction & reference	BECK, Erla P.	(IN) 71
	HADDERMAN, Margaret .	(OR) 482
Library instruction & user education	LIPPINCOTT, Joan K. . .	(NY) 732
Library instruction, credit courses	OSTROW, Rona	(NY) 929
Library instruction, social sciences	WEIMER, Sally W.	(CA) 1317
Library instruction, women's studies	OSBORNE, Nancy S. . . .	(NY) 927
Library media instruction	SWEET, Sally K.	(CO) 1215
	DIRKS, Martha W.	(KS) 305
	CLARK, Elizabeth K.	(MA) 216
Library media skill instruction	RAMSEY, Inez L.	(VA) 1006
Library media skills instruction	EHRICH, Joan C.	(MA) 339
	TASSIA, Margaret R. . . .	(PA) 1224
Library or bibliographic instruction	SWAINE, Cynthia W. . . .	(VA) 1212
Library orientation & instruction	CLARK, Wendolyn H. . . .	(AL) 218
	MORRIS, Karen T.	(OK) 867
Library research instruction	LODER, Michael W. . . .	(PA) 736
Library research skills instruction	ROSENBERG, Harlene Z. .	(NJ) 1056
Library research strategies instruction	KUNSELMAN, Joan D. . .	(CA) 684
Library school instruction	HARRIS, Margaret J. . . .	(OH) 505
Library science instruction	MCNALLY, Ruth C.	(CA) 816
	GLEESON, Joyce M. . . .	(IL) 441
	BAER, Eleanora A.	(MO) 45
	LAINE, Rebecca R.	(VA) 688
Library science instructor	JOHNSON, Jean G.	(NH) 605
Library sciences instruction	KUTTEROFF, Ethel C. . .	(NJ) 685
	WYLLIE, Stanley F.	(OH) 1375
Library services instruction	ROBERTS, Scott J.	(MI) 1041
Library skills instruction	PENDLETON, Kim B. . . .	(AK) 956
	CHESSMAN, Rebecca L.	(CA) 207
	AKE, Mary W.	(CO) 9
	DEANS, Janice P.	(FL) 284
	JACKSON, Nancy I.	(FL) 588
	KRAMER, Pamela K. . . .	(IL) 675
	SHANNON, Kathleen L. .	(IL) 1120
	KELLY, Sarah A.	(KY) 638
	PECK, Ruth M.	(MA) 953
	FITZGERALD, M A.	(MD) 382
	MONTGOMERY, Paula K.	(MD) 856
	RUFF, Martha R.	(MD) 1066
	WILLIAMS, J L.	(MD) 1343
	SKELLY, Laurie J.	(MN) 1146
	FABIAN, William M. . . .	(MO) 360
	DRUKE-STICKLER, Janet A.	(NH) 320
	DOMINESKE, Alice M. . .	(NJ) 310
	AVERY, Linda S.	(NM) 42
	BRAMLETT, Suzanne M. .	(NM) 127
	DI BIANCO, Phyllis R. . .	(NY) 299
	MCCOY, Joanne	(OR) 799
	EMERICK, Michael J. . . .	(PA) 347
	KOSTIS, Leigh W.	(PA) 673
	SMITH, Sara B.	(SC) 1160
	BANNERMAN-WILLIAMS, Cheryl F.	(TN) 54
	PONTIUS, Louise	(TX) 982
	SMITH, Dorothy B.	(TX) 1154
	OWENS, Martha A.	(VA) 932
	YOUNGER, Melinda M. . .	(VA) 1383
	BACON, Carey H.	(WA) 44
	PITEL, Vonna J.	(WI) 976
Library use instruction	COE, Gloria M.	(DE) 226
	RICE, James G.	(IA) 1027
	MCLEAN, Paulette A. . . .	(ON) 814
Literature instruction & guidance	WOBBE, Jean	(CA) 1359
Management training, instruction	KLEIN, Victor C.	(LA) 659
Mathematics & science instruction	STRAWN, Aimee W. . . .	(IL) 1201
Media & instruction support	YEE, Sandra G.	(MI) 1379
Media design & instruction	ALBUM, Bernie	(CA) 11
Media instruction	MERWINE, Glenda M. . .	(WA) 827

INSTRUCTION (Cont'd)

Media skills instruction	CHAPMAN-SIMPSON, Alisa M.	(IA) 202
	KONNEKER, Rachel C. .	(NC) 670
	SOUTHERLAND, Carol A.	(NC) 1169
Medial skill instruction	SMITH, Judy B.	(GA) 1156
Medical bibliographic instruction	ANDERSON, Gail C. . . .	(GA) 23
Microcomputer programming & instruction	CARROLL, James K. . . .	(KS) 187
Microcomputer use instruction	NICHOLS, Darlene P. . . .	(MI) 901
Music reference & bibliographic instrc	BOGNAR, Dorothy M. . .	(CT) 111
One-person libraries or biblgph instrc	KLEIN, Penny	(NY) 659
Online bibliographic instruction	SPAANS, David N.	(DC) 1170
Online catalog instruction	KIRESEN, Evelyn M. . . .	(CA) 654
	KNOWLES, Em C.	(CA) 665
	ABBOTT, Randy L.	(FL) 1
	BECK, Susan E.	(MO) 71
	NOWAKOWSKI, Frances C.	(NS) 911
Online database instruction	PARKER, Joan M.	(CA) 942
Online electronic catalog instruction	HITT, Charles J.	(MN) 544
Online high school instruction	GARDNER, Laura L. . . .	(MO) 418
Online instruction	FEINGLOS, Susan J. . . .	(NC) 369
	SNOW, Bonnie	(PA) 1164
Orientation & bibliographic instruction	ARMSTRONG, Mary L. .	(AB) 32
	LAKHANPAL, Sarv K. . .	(SK) 689
Orientation & instruction	KAYE, Karen	(CA) 632
Paralegal instruction	ALCORN, Marianne S. . .	(AZ) 11
Peer book writing instructor	KORNITSKY, Judith M. .	(FL) 672
Public school library instruction	SPAULDING, Nancy J. . .	(TX) 1172
Public service & instruction	JAFFE, Lee D.	(CA) 591
Reference & bibliographic instruction	PETERS, Marion C.	(CA) 962
	NORONHA, Marilyn S. . .	(CT) 909
	COHN, William L.	(FL) 229
	MALANCHUK, Peter P. .	(FL) 762
	CANN, Sharon F.	(GA) 178
	GIAQUINTA, C J.	(IA) 431
	HUFFORD, Gordon L. . . .	(IN) 571
	MCDONALD, Stanley M. .	(MA) 803
	SIGALA, Stephanie C. . .	(MO) 1137
	FARRELL, Michele A. . . .	(NY) 365
	HARDY, Gayle J.	(NY) 500
	LYONS, Evelyn L.	(PA) 753
	LEGET, Max	(SD) 712
	CONIGLIO, Jamie W. . . .	(VA) 236
	HOWE, Patricia A.	(VA) 565
	EDMONDS, Michael	(WI) 336
	NECHKA, Ada M.	(AB) 891
	LEVESQUE, Nancy B. . .	(BC) 719
Reference & instruction	ROCKMAN, Ilene F. . . .	(CA) 1046
	WILDE, Lucy E.	(KS) 1338
	BAILEY, Madeleine J. . . .	(AB) 46
Reference & instruction academic support	VERNON, Christie D. . . .	(VA) 1283
Reference & library instruction	STARKEY, Edward D. . .	(IN) 1182
Reference, bibliographic instruction	THOMAS, Mary C.	(CA) 1237
Reference instruction	ROBINS, Nora D.	(AB) 1043
Reference services & instruction	KENT, Rose M.	(OH) 642
References & bibliographic instruction	KOK, Victoria T.	(VA) 669
Research methods & bibliographic instrc	TROUTMAN, Joseph E. .	(GA) 1258
Research skill instruction	BROWN, Judith B.	(MD) 145
Research skills instruction	MAIN, Isabelle G.	(AZ) 761
School library instruction	MIZIK, Judy G.	(PA) 850
School library media instruction	RING, Constance B. . . .	(NY) 1035
School media center instruction	JOYCE, Robert A.	(NC) 618
Science & technology biogph instruction	SABIN, Robert G.	(AL) 1072
Science bibliographic instruction	CULOTTA, Wendy A. . . .	(CA) 264
	STANKUS, Tony	(MA) 1180
Science database searching, instruction	STIRLING, Isabel A. . . .	(OR) 1195
Self-paced instruction	CODER, Ann	(CA) 226
Skill instruction	GERRING, Cheryl B. . . .	(MD) 429
Social science bibliographic instruction	NESBITT, Renee D. . . .	(CA) 896
Storytelling instruction	NELSON, Olga G.	(OH) 895
Study skills instruction	CARPENTER, Carole H. .	(DE) 184
Training & instruction	CARTER-LOVEJOY, Steven H.	(VA) 190

INSTRUCTION (Cont'd)

Training, bibliographic instruction	WIBLE, Joseph G.	(CA)	1335
Undergraduate science instruction	MICIKAS, Lynda L.	(PA)	832
Unit method of library instruction	GOODRICH PETERSON, Marilyn	(KS)	450
Workbook instruction	RAJPAR, Shamin H.	(PA)	1004
Young adult bibliographic instruction	REIF, Lenore S.	(IL)	1019

INSTRUCTIONAL

Audiovisual & instructional design	PROVINCE, William R.	(IL)	996
Co-design instructional units	SMITH, Margie G.	(CA)	1157
Computerized instructional systems	FROST, Rebecca H.	(PA)	406
Education, instructional resources	STAVROLAKIS, Rachel G.	(GA)	1183
Instructional computer coordination	PENDLETON, Kim B.	(AK)	956
Instructional computing	MERCHANT, Cheryl N.	(TX)	825
Instructional design	BUTLER, David W.	(CA)	166
	ROSE, David L.	(CA)	1054
	SINOFSKY, Esther R.	(CA)	1144
	HAUSMAN, Julie	(IA)	513
	DAVIS, H S.	(IN)	279
	SMINK, Anna R.	(MD)	1152
	HAMMITT, Margaret R.	(NE)	493
	WEAVER-MEYERS, Pat L.	(OK)	1313
Instructional design & library skills	EFFERTZ, Rose	(IL)	338
Instructional design, audiovisual	PICHETTE, William H.	(TX)	970
Instructional development	BEDIENT, Douglas	(IL)	73
	ANDERSON, Della L.	(MD)	22
	CHEEKS, Cellestine	(MD)	204
	HOOFNAGLE, Bettea J.	(MD)	556
	RABURN, Josephine R.	(OK)	1001
Instructional graphics	WILSON, George N.	(TX)	1351
Instructional implementation & design	JENKINS, Lydia E.	(DC)	597
Instructional involvement, design	CORNWELL, Linda L.	(IN)	247
Instructional materials	BOULA, Lillian Y.	(FL)	119
	GROSS, Iva H.	(TX)	472
Instructional materials center	JOHNSON, Scott R.	(MS)	609
Instructional materials centers	KIRKENDALL, Carolyn A.	(MI)	654
	OLSON, Dennis H.	(WI)	922
Instructional materials selection	WOBBE, Jean	(CA)	1359
Instructional materials, teacher educ	PRILLAMAN, Susan M.	(NC)	993
Instructional media	PROSSER, Michael J.	(CA)	995
	HORRIGAN, John J.	(CT)	560
	TEMPLE, Leroy E.	(CT)	1230
	MARSH, Paul W.	(NE)	773
	MAYNES, Kathleen R.	(NJ)	790
	TOWNSEND, Catherine M.	(SC)	1253
	CARPENTER, Dorothy B.	(TN)	184
	ROBERTSON, Billy O.	(TN)	1041
Instructional media & technology	GOFF, Linda J.	(CA)	443
	LEAHY, Michael D.	(CT)	707
	VAN MELER, Vandelia L.	(MS)	1276
Instructional media design	CHAPLOCK, Sharon K.	(WI)	201
Instructional media, microcomputers	MARTIN, Elaine R.	(DC)	776
Instructional media production	POWELL, Patricia K.	(TX)	988
	REHMS, Jane C.	(WA)	1017
Instructional media resources	ALLAN, David W.	(MN)	14
Instructional media services	WAGNER, A C.	(NY)	1291
Instructional media specialist	SCHEU, Susan P.	(NY)	1092
Instructional media utilization	CONLIFFE, Bobbi L.	(OH)	236
Instructional resources	DAVILA, Daniel	(NY)	277
	NOVIK, Sandra P.	(NY)	911
Instructional services	FORMAN, Jack	(CA)	390
	GREENBERG, Charles J.	(NY)	463
Instructional services management	JORDAN, Travis E.	(TX)	617
Instructional software	FOLKE, Carolyn W.	(WI)	387
Instructional software collection	OSTROM, Kriss T.	(MI)	929
Instructional specialist	TRZICKY, Richard F.	(AZ)	1260
Instructional systems technology	BERMAN, Arthur	(AR)	88
Instructional technology	ROYAL, Selvin W.	(AR)	1063
	ALBUM, Bernie	(CA)	11
	KELLY, Myla S.	(CA)	638
	HALE, Robert G.	(CT)	485
	RECTOR, Wendell H.	(CT)	1013
	TEMPLE, Leroy E.	(CT)	1230
	FORK, Donald J.	(DC)	390
	CAMPA, Josephine	(MD)	175
	CHANDLER, Devon	(MT)	199
	MARTIN, Richard T.	(NC)	778
	SURPRENANT, Thomas T.	(NY)	1210

INSTRUCTIONAL (Cont'd)

Instructional technology	BROWN, Dale W.	(VA)	143
Instructional technology specialist	MCGHEE, Patricia L.	(WI)	806
Instructional television	BURGESS, Barbara J.	(IA)	159
Instructional uses of computers	DONHAM, Jean O.	(IA)	311
Instructional video/ITV	BOYNTON, John W.	(ME)	124
Library instructional skills	LAMBERTH, Linda E.	(TX)	690
Reference & instructional services	HINCKLEY, Ann T.	(CA)	542
	NESBIT, Angus B.	(IL)	896
School librarian's instructional role	MINEMIER, Betty M.	(NY)	845
Training & instructional development	JASSAL, Raghbir S.	(NM)	595
Video disk instructional design	CONNELL, William S.	(CA)	237

INSTRUMENTS (See also names of specific instruments, e.g. Marimba, Piano)

Musical instruments	ELSTE, R O.	(WGR)	346
Researching keyboard instruments	RICHARDS, James H.	(TX)	1028
Surgical instrument development	MCGREGOR, Walter	(NJ)	808

INSURANCE (See also Medicaid)

Business & insurance databases	MACKINTOSH, Pamela J.	(NJ)	757
Business reference insurance	ALDRICH, Linda W.	(CA)	11
Health insurance	COX, Joyce M.	(IL)	253
Insurance	DOMINIANNI, Beth S.	(CT)	310
	REYNOLDS, Carol C.	(GA)	1025
	CALLAHAN, Joan	(MA)	173
	ZYSKOWSKI, Dianne D.	(MI)	1392
	GINDRA, Janice J.	(MO)	437
	AARON, Rina S.	(NY)	1
	GAINES, Irene A.	(NY)	412
	ROSIGNOLO, Beverly A.	(NY)	1057
	BELLOWS, Leslie A.	(WI)	78
	BIRSCHEL, Dee B.	(WI)	99
	CHOUDHURI, Kabita	(ON)	211
	GIBSON, Elizabeth A.	(ON)	432
Insurance & business reference	GEE, Ka C.	(NY)	424
Insurance & employee benefits	KORMAN, Adrienne S.	(MA)	671
Insurance bibliography	JUSTIE, Julie H.	(IL)	620
Insurance industry	CARICONE, Paul	(NY)	181
Insurance information	STRAZDON, Maureen E.	(NY)	1201
Insurance law	WOODS, Marcia G.	(CA)	1367
Insurance reference	COOK, Pamela D.	(NY)	240
	IVES, Jean E.	(OH)	586
	NUERNBURG, Donna S.	(WI)	912
Insurance research	FIELD, Connie N.	(IL)	375
Insurance sources	KUCSMA, Susan P.	(NY)	682
Life & health insurance	SLOAN, Virgene K.	(NE)	1150
Life & health insurance research	HILL, Judith L.	(PA)	540
Life insurance	COX, Joyce M.	(IL)	253
	CITROEN, Julie M.	(ON)	215
Mortgage insurance	MCKEE, Margaret J.	(WI)	810
Online searching, brokerage, insurance	ENGLISH, Christopher C.	(NJ)	350

INTEGRATION

Automated & integrated library systems	GABRIEL, Linda	(NJ)	411
Automated integrated library network	EMAHISER, Joan A.	(MI)	347
Automated integrated library system	OBERC, Susanne F.	(OH)	913
CD-ROM hardware integration	CIUFFETTI, Peter D.	(MA)	215
CD-ROM systems integration	DAVISSON, Darell D.	(CA)	281
Computer system integration	WANG, Gary Y.	(MA)	1302
Computer systems integration	SPYKERMAN, Bryan R.	(UT)	1177
Curriculum & integrated instruction	RATZER, Mary B.	(NY)	1010
Curriculum integration	SALLE, Ellen M.	(CO)	1076
	UNDERHILL, Jan	(OK)	1268
Establishing integrated library services	BELTON, Jennifer H.	(DC)	78
Information integration	HANSEN, Kathelen L.	(MN)	497
Information systems design & integration	CHU, John S.	(PA)	212
Integrated & automated library systems	WORMINGTON, Peggie	(CA)	1369
Integrated automated library systems	LASETER, Shirley B.	(AL)	700
	SIDMAN, George C.	(CA)	1135
	MOORE, Barbara N.	(MN)	858
Integrated circulation systems	CRISCO, Mary E.	(MD)	259

INTEGRATION (Cont'd)

Integrated curriculum	SNYDER, Denny L.	(MD)	1164
Integrated info resources management	KNOPPERS, Jake V.	(ON)	665
Integrated information systems	RAGHAVAN, Vijay V.	(LA)	1003
	CHIANG, Katherine S.	(NY)	207
Integrated library automation	KIMZEY, Ann C.	(TX)	649
Integrated library automation systems	SHURMAN, Richard L.	(IL)	1134
Integrated library media skills	WALKER, Sue A.	(PA)	1296
Integrated library skills instruction	HUSTED, Ruth E.	(OK)	578
Integrated library software	MOSER, Maxine M.	(CA)	871
Integrated library system automation	BREEDLOVE, Elizabeth A.	(NJ)	131
Integrated library systems	ELMAN, Stanley A.	(CA)	345
	NASATIR, Marilyn	(CA)	888
	SWEENEY, Urban J.	(CA)	1215
	WOLF, Nola M.	(CA)	1360
	TODD, Hal W.	(FL)	1248
	BALL, Mary A.	(IL)	52
	DREWETT, William O.	(IL)	319
	BOND, Marvin A.	(MD)	113
	HENDERSON, Susanne	(MD)	527
	MENEGAUX, Edmond A.	(MD)	824
	STERLING, Judith K.	(MD)	1189
	EPSTEIN, Rheda	(MN)	351
	KAN, Halina S.	(NJ)	624
	CHAPMAN, Renee D.	(NY)	202
	HOPKINS, Judith	(NY)	558
	FERRIN, Eric G.	(PA)	373
	RITTENHOUSE, Robert J.	(PA)	1036
	AIROLDI, Melissa	(TX)	9
	GALTON, Gwen	(ON)	415
Integrated medical financial databases	RUBIN, David S.	(NY)	1064
Integrated medical geographic databases	RUBIN, David S.	(NY)	1064
Integrated online library systems	WEISS, William B.	(CA)	1320
	MARQUARDT, Steve R.	(WI)	772
Integrated service for info resources	BERGERON, Pierrette	(PQ)	86
Integrated services digital network	GILHEANY, Stephen J.	(CA)	435
Integrated systems	SHERIDAN, John B.	(CO)	1127
	LAKSHMAN, Malathi K.	(MD)	689
	HEMPEL, Ruth M.	(TX)	525
Integrated systems automation	BRIDGE, Frank R.	(TX)	135
Integrating curriculum	HEINRICH, Lois M.	(MD)	522
Integrating library skills	RICHARDSON, Constance H.	(NY)	1029
Integration, library skills, curriculum	HOROWITZ, Marjorie B.	(NJ)	560
Integration of media & technology	TREGLOAN, Donald C.	(MI)	1255
Integration of media to curriculum	MURRAY, William A.	(CO)	882
Library online integrated systems	KING, Maryde F.	(NY)	651
Microcomputer-based integrated systems	MEIKAMP, Kathie D.	(DC)	822
School library curriculum integration	ZEIGER, Hanna B.	(MA)	1387
Serials & integrated systems	CLINE, Sharon D.	(CA)	222
Technology integration with curriculum	TROUTNER, Joanne J.	(IN)	1258

INTELLECTUAL (See also Censorship)

Censorship & intellectual freedom	WOODS, L B.	(AR)	1367
	DELZELL, Robert F.	(MO)	290
Copyright & intellectual property	JENSEN, Mary B.	(SD)	599
Intellectual freedom	PINNELL-STEPHENS, June A.	(AK)	975
	TALLMAN, Karen D.	(AZ)	1221
	FLETCHER, Homer L.	(CA)	384
	FLUM, Judith G.	(CA)	386
	SESSIONS, Judith A.	(CA)	1117
	KNEPEL, Nancy	(CO)	664
	MURRAY, William A.	(CO)	882
	MILLER, Laurence A.	(FL)	839
	BUDLONG, Thomas F.	(GA)	155
	MCGREW, Mary L.	(IA)	808
	KRUG, Judith F.	(IL)	680
	MCDERMOTT, Patrice	(IL)	802
	GUNNELLS, Danny C.	(IN)	477
	ALLAIN, Alexander P.	(LA)	13
	DAVIS, Denise	(MD)	278
	DEAN, Frances C.	(MD)	283
	FRYER, Philip	(MD)	407
	RICHWINE, Eleanor N.	(MD)	1031

INTELLECTUAL (Cont'd)

Intellectual freedom	LANIER, Gene D.	(NC)	696
	GOULD, Martha B.	(NV)	454
	CUSEO, Allan A.	(NY)	267
	LIU, Carol F.	(NY)	734
	RABBAN, Elana	(NY)	1001
	SHIELDS, Gerald R.	(NY)	1130
	HARDESTY, Vicki H.	(OH)	499
	WRIGHT, Janet K.	(OR)	1371
	BRAVARD, Robert S.	(PA)	130
	DAY, J D.	(UT)	282
	CAYWOOD, Carolyn A.	(VA)	195
	WISECARVER, Betty A.	(VA)	1357
	CONABLE, Gordon M.	(WA)	235
	BRANT, Susan L.	(WI)	129
	HOPKINS, Dianne M.	(WI)	557
	WILSON, William J.	(WI)	1353
	CORS, Paul B.	(WY)	248
	SCHRADER, Alvin M.	(AB)	1099
Intellectual freedom & censorship	SEREBNICK, Judith	(IN)	1116
	ANDERSON, A J.	(MA)	21
	MCDONALD, Frances B.	(MN)	802
	BRUWELHEIDE, Janis H.	(MT)	151
	KERESEY, Gayle	(NC)	643
Intellectual freedom, censorship	OSSOLINSKI, Lynn	(NV)	928
	COHEN, David	(NY)	228
Intellectual freedom committees	KRANZ, Ralph	(UT)	676
Intellectual freedom defense	MADDEN, Susan B.	(WA)	758
Intellectual freedom issues	BUCK, Richard M.	(NY)	154
Intellectual freedom teaching	EISENBACH, Elizabeth R.	(CA)	340
Intellectual property	CONNOR, Billie M.	(CA)	237
Management of intellectual enterprises	BOYER, Calvin J.	(CA)	123
School libraries & intellectual freedom	BLANKENBURG, Judith B.	(VA)	104
Teaching intellectual freedom	TRYON, Jonathan S.	(RI)	1259

INTELLIGENCE

Aerospace intelligence	MAUTER, George A.	(NY)	787
Artificial intelligence	ROSE, Steven C.	(CA)	1055
	RADA, Roy F.	(MD)	1002
	FRISSE, Mark E.	(MO)	405
	MITCHELL, Joyce A.	(MO)	849
	BURGIN, Robert E.	(NC)	159
	FRANTS, Valery	(NJ)	398
	SUNDAY, Donald E.	(NJ)	1210
	METZLER, Douglas P.	(PA)	829
	TREMBLAY, Gerald F.	(SC)	1255
	TRAVIS, Irene L.	(VA)	1254
	BOOHER, Craig S.	(WI)	115
Artificial intelligence applications	FOX, Edward A.	(VA)	394
Artificial intelligence based retrieval	VLADUTZ, George E.	(PA)	1286
Artificial intelligence, expert systems	VEENKER, Linda J.	(CA)	1281
	DIEHL, Mark	(IL)	302
Artificial intelligence in medicine	MUSEN, Mark A.	(CA)	883
Business & medical intelligence	LOKETS BEISCHROT, Dina	(CT)	738
Business intelligence	CARR, Sallyann	(DC)	186
	CARR, Sallyann	(FL)	186
	RYANS, Kathryn J.	(ON)	1071
Company intelligence	LIU, Jessie	(CT)	734
Competitive intelligence	BIRKHOLD, Martha S.	(IL)	98
	MACIVER, Linda B.	(MA)	756
	SOLSETH, Gwenn M.	(MN)	1166
	CHANG, Bernadine A.	(NJ)	200
	RONDELLI, Marilyn H.	(NJ)	1053
	LETTIS, Lucy B.	(NY)	719
	O'GRADY, Jean P.	(NY)	918
	SEIK, Jo E.	(OH)	1112
	THOMAS, Sandra L.	(OR)	1238
Competitive intelligence systems	MOBLEY, Kathleen S.	(KS)	851
Competitor intelligence	MEYER, Andrea P.	(CO)	829
	GAGNE, Susan P.	(CT)	412
	HARRIS, Jeanne G.	(IL)	504
	LANDRY, Ronald	(IL)	694
	MURPHY, Therese B.	(IL)	881
	STANAT, Ruth E.	(NY)	1179
	RYDESKY, Mary M.	(TX)	1071
Competitor intelligence systems	SEASE, Sandra A.	(NY)	1110

INTELLIGENCE (Cont'd)

Corporate intelligence	ADAMS, Joyce A.	(CA)	5
	BAUMGARTNER, Kurt O.	(IN)	66
Corporate intelligence research	DETWILER, Susan M.	(IN)	296
Expert systems & artificial intelligence	CHANG, Roy T.	(IL)	201
	MOTT, Thomas H.	(NJ)	872
Intelligent computer-assisted instrc	PARROTT, James R.	(ON)	944
Market research, business intelligence	MIMNAUGH, Ellen N.	(OH)	845
Military intelligence	BURNS, Dean A.	(DC)	162
Research on management intelligence syst	KOCHEN, Manfred	(MI)	667
Scientific & technical intelligence	CRANOR, Alice T.	(DC)	255

INTERACTION (See also Interfaces)

Child-book interaction	WINKLER, Carol A.	(MO)	1355
Community interaction	CURTIS, Jean E.	(MI)	267
Human interaction with computers	MARTIN, Thomas H.	(NY)	778
Human-computer interaction	KASKE, Neal K.	(AL)	628
	CHERRY, Joan M.	(ON)	206
Online interaction	SARACEVIC, Tefko	(NJ)	1082

INTERACTIVE

Compact disc interactive	GALL, Bert A.	(TN)	413
Computer-based interactive video	HAUSMAN, Julie	(IA)	513
Easy-to-use interactive services	THOMAS, Hilary B.	(NY)	1236
Interactive art video disks	SHARER, E J.	(CO)	1122
Interactive media	VAUGHAN, John	(NY)	1279
Interactive online databases	PODWOL, Sharon L.	(NY)	979
Interactive software & films	FORD, Andrew E.	(NY)	389
Interactive video	TROUTNER, Joanne J.	(IN)	1258
Interactive video disk development	HORNIG-ROHAN, James E.	(PA)	560
Interactive videodisc	CHAPLOCK, Sharon K.	(WI)	201
Interactive videodisc programs	STEELE, Tom M.	(NC)	1184
On-site interactive video	PODWOL, Sharon L.	(NY)	979

INTERDISCIPLINARY

Interdisciplinary methodology	SWIGGER, Keith	(TX)	1216
Interdisciplinary research	BAUGHMAN, James C.	(MA)	66
Interdisciplinary research & instruction	STONE, Nancy Y.	(MI)	1197
Interdisciplinary technology	ADAMS, Judith A.	(AL)	5

INTERFACES (See also Interaction)

Computer typesetting & interfacing	MEDINA, Ildefonso M.	(NY)	820
Computer-human interface design	SIEGEL, Martin A.	(IL)	1136
Higher education, library interfacing	BREIVIK, Patricia S.	(CO)	132
Human factors user interface	MCALLISTER, Caryl K.	(WI)	792
Human system language interface	WEI, Yin M.	(OH)	1316
Human-computer interface	DITO, William R.	(CA)	305
	ROMALEWSKI, Robert S.	(LA)	1052
Information, user interface	HUTTON, Emily A.	(WA)	579
Interface design	BRUNELLE, Bette S.	(NY)	150
	DILLON, Martin	(OH)	303
Interface with management	SAUSEDO, Ann E.	(CA)	1085
Interfaces	SANTOSUOSSO, Joseph P.	(MA)	1082
Library, information industry interface	MACDONALD, Alan H.	(AB)	754
Library systems interfaces	CLAPPER, Mary E.	(MA)	216
	LAREW, Christian K.	(NJ)	697
Online subject access interfaces	BATES, Marcia J.	(CA)	64
User interface	VAUGHAN, John	(NY)	1279
User interface, automated systems	SACKETT-WILK, Susan A.	(TX)	1073
User interface design	HURLEY, Geraldine C.	(OH)	577
User interface development	VEATCH, Laurie L.	(DC)	1280
User interfaces	EASTMAN, Caroline M.	(SC)	333
User interfaces & database frontends	CURRAN, George L.	(NY)	266
Video-database interfaces	KRUSS, Daniel M.	(IL)	681

INTER-FAITH

Inter-faith dialogue	BERENT, Irwin M.	(VA)	84

INTERGOVERNMENTAL

Intergovernmental organization documents	WESTFALL, Gloria D.	(IN)	1327
Intl intergovernmental documents	MOREHEAD, Joe	(NY)	863
Urban & intergovernmental affairs	ORTIZ, Diane	(NV)	927

INTERIORS (See also Architecture, Design, Layout, Lighting, Space)

Architectural & interior design	WIEGMAN, John H.	(TX)	1336
Architectural & interiors firm libraries	TENNEY, Kimberly M.	(MA)	1231
Interior arrangement & design	BELLIN, Bernard E.	(WI)	78
Interior arrangement & layout	STORCK, Bernadette R.	(FL)	1198
Interior design	CALDWELL, Kenneth R.	(CA)	172
	YOUNG, Nancy J.	(IL)	1382
Interior design for libraries	NOVAK, Gloria J.	(CA)	910
Interior planning & design	DE BEAR, Richard S.	(MI)	284
	MICHAELS, David L.	(VA)	832
Library architecture, interior design	COHEN, Aaron	(NY)	227
Library buildings & interior design	FOX, James R.	(PA)	394
Library buildings & interiors	ORR, Cynthia	(OH)	926
Library interior planning & design	MICHAELS, Andrea A.	(VA)	831
Library interior space planning	STEWART, John D.	(VA)	1192
Library interiors	FINNEY, Lance C.	(MD)	379

INTERLENDING

Interlending	CLEMENT, Hope E.	(ON)	221

INTERLIBRARY (See also ILS, Interlending, Interloans)

Acquisitions & interlibrary loan	TERRY, Susan N.	(DC)	1232
	RUST, Roxy J.	(SC)	1070
Acquisitions, interlibrary loan	NEILL, Sharon E.	(ON)	892
Cataloging, interlibrary loan	SUTTER, Mary A.	(MO)	1211
	SCHMIDT, Diana M.	(ON)	1095
Circulation & interlibrary loan	STEWART, Jamie K.	(IL)	1192
Circulation & interlibrary loans	BULLARD, Rita J.	(MI)	156
Circulation, interlibrary loan	EDMONDS, Michael	(WI)	336
Circulation, reserve, interlibrary loan	MEAD-DONALDSON, Susan L.	(FL)	819
Document delivery & interlibrary loan	MEAHL, D D.	(MI)	819
	COURNOYER, Joanne	(ON)	251
Document delivery, interlibrary loan	ROLLINS, Stephen J.	(NM)	1051
Document retrieval & interlibrary loan	FELDMAN, Eleanor C.	(MD)	369
Interlibrary & circulation services	POSES, June A.	(PA)	985
Interlibrary cooperation	THOMAS, Margie J.	(AK)	1237
	RICHMOND, Elizabeth B.	(CO)	1030
	BRYAN, Barbara D.	(CT)	151
	HOLLOWAY, Patricia W.	(CT)	552
	MILLER, Laurence A.	(FL)	839
	MOUNCE, Marvin W.	(FL)	873
	MURPHEY, Barbara A.	(FL)	880
	NEUHOFE, M D.	(FL)	897
	FORSEE, Joe B.	(GA)	391
	CRISPEN, Joanne	(IL)	259
	LAMONT, Bridget L.	(IL)	691
	MEACHEN, Edward W.	(IL)	819
	ROSENFELD, Joel C.	(IL)	1056
	WANK, Paul G.	(LA)	1303
	STEINFELD, Michael	(MA)	1186
	GELINAS, Jeanne L.	(MN)	426
	ALEXANDER, Susanna	(MO)	12
	HAWLEY, George S.	(NJ)	514
	CALLAHAM, Betty E.	(SC)	173
	CAMACHO, Nancy S.	(TX)	174
	KRENTZ, Roger F.	(WI)	677
	JOHNSON, Wayne H.	(WY)	609
Interlibrary cooperation & networking	WILKINS, Barratt	(FL)	1340
Interlibrary cooperation consortia	BROWN, Thomas M.	(WV)	148
Interlibrary lending & borrowing	ENGEL, Kevin R.	(IA)	348
Interlibrary loan	LEE, Sulan I.	(AL)	711
	LIAW, Barbara C.	(AL)	725
	WILLIAMS, Nelle T.	(AL)	1345
	STEEL, Virginia	(AZ)	1183
	BROOKS, Mary A.	(CA)	140
	ELLIOTT, Valerie E.	(CA)	344
	FRANCISCO, Marylynn	(CA)	396
	GOLDSMITH, Jan E.	(CA)	446
	GUARINO, John P.	(CA)	475
	HERZIG, Stella J.	(CA)	534

INTERLIBRARY (Cont'd)
Interlibrary loan

JORGENSEN, Venita	(CA)	617
LAWRENCE, John R.	(CA)	704
LEE, Don A.	(CA)	709
MCNALLY, Ruth C.	(CA)	816
REDFIELD, Dale E.	(CA)	1014
TIENHAARA, Kaarina I.	(CA)	1244
BOUCHER, Virginia P.	(CO)	118
DOBBS, Ann R.	(CO)	307
GRATE, Jon F.	(CO)	458
HAMDY, Amira	(CO)	491
SHIELDS, Caryl L.	(CO)	1129
VERCIO, Roseanne	(CO)	1282
BUNKER, Patricia J.	(CT)	157
EBINGER, Meada G.	(CT)	334
HOLMER, Paul L.	(CT)	553
LOW, Jocelyn L.	(CT)	743
NEWMYER, Joann C.	(CT)	900
PENN, Elinor K.	(CT)	957
SIROIS, Valerie M.	(CT)	1144
BEATON, Barbara E.	(DC)	70
JOHNSON, Jacqueline B.	(DC)	605
LEONE, Rosemarie G.	(DC)	717
MEIKAMP, Kathie D.	(DC)	822
JOHNSON, Theresa P.	(FL)	609
MAHAN, Cheryl A.	(FL)	760
MOORE, Dahrl E.	(FL)	859
TIBBS, Jo A.	(FL)	1244
BOYD, Ruth V.	(GA)	123
LARSEN, Mary T.	(GA)	698
PATON, John C.	(GA)	947
RYSTROM, Barbara B.	(GA)	1072
TOMAJKO, Kathy L.	(GA)	1249
WHITE, Carol A.	(GA)	1330
MOODY, Marilyn K.	(IA)	857
RAILSBACK, Patsy S.	(IA)	1003
RIESBERG, Eunice L.	(IA)	1033
SWANSON, P A.	(IA)	1213
BURRUSS, Marsha A.	(IL)	163
GINSBURG, Coralie S.	(IL)	438
HORNEY, Joyce C.	(IL)	560
KEENAN, Mary T.	(IL)	634
KELLY, Janice E.	(IL)	637
LEWIS, Martha S.	(IL)	724
MCCARTNEY, Elizabeth J.	(IL)	794
MCCLAREY, Catherine A.	(IL)	796
NEWMAN, Lorna R.	(IL)	899
OSBORN, Walter	(IL)	927
PICKETT, Mary J.	(IL)	970
ROMANACE, Gisele R.	(IL)	1052
SACHS, Iris P.	(IL)	1073
STUTZ, Patricia A.	(IL)	1206
TODD, Margaret	(IL)	1248
TROFIMUK, Janette A.	(IL)	1257
WALKER, Laura L.	(IL)	1295
WALSH, Susan E.	(IL)	1300
WOELL, Yvette N.	(IL)	1359
BAVER, Cynthia M.	(IN)	67
DAY, Thomas L.	(IN)	283
EILERS, Marsha J.	(IN)	340
LISTON, Karen A.	(IN)	733
SCHMIDT, Steven J.	(IN)	1096
TRIBBLE, Judith E.	(IN)	1256
TRUESDELL, Cheryl B.	(IN)	1259
GAYNOR, Kathy A.	(KS)	424
MAY, Cecilia J.	(KS)	788
REIMER, Sylvia D.	(KS)	1021
FLAHERTY, Margaret P.	(KY)	383
GERON, Cary A.	(KY)	429
SCHLENE, Vickie J.	(KY)	1094
TURNER, Rebecca M.	(KY)	1265
CRETINI, Blanche M.	(LA)	258
HUSSEY, Sandra R.	(LA)	578
NUCKLES, Nancy E.	(LA)	912
ANDREWS, Margaret	(MA)	27
BAKER, Shirley K.	(MA)	49
BEARDEN, Eithne C.	(MA)	69
COOLIDGE, Christina L.	(MA)	241
DAMES, Barbara B.	(MA)	271

INTERLIBRARY (Cont'd)
Interlibrary loan

ENGLISH, Cynthia J.	(MA)	350
HOLM, Edla K.	(MA)	552
KELEHER, Carolyn P.	(MA)	635
TURKALO, David M.	(MA)	1263
BOURKOFF, Vivienne R.	(MD)	119
CARMAN, Carol A.	(MD)	183
COOPER, Judith C.	(MD)	243
GLOCK, Martha H.	(MD)	441
LEFEBVRE, Veronica A.	(MD)	712
MALLERY, Mary S.	(MD)	763
MANGIN, Julianne	(MD)	765
MORRIS, Sharon D.	(MD)	867
STEINHOFF, Cynthia K.	(MD)	1186
BAKER, Jean S.	(MI)	48
CHAPMAN, Mary A.	(MI)	202
HAGE, Christine C.	(MI)	482
MEADOWS, Brenda L.	(MI)	819
MORGAN, Patricia L.	(MI)	864
PALMER, Catherine S.	(MI)	936
SCHUCKEL, Sally B.	(MI)	1101
JONES, Mary A.	(MN)	614
KAUFENBERG, Jane M.	(MN)	630
LORING, Christopher B.	(MN)	741
PRETZER, Shari G.	(MN)	992
WIENER, Alissa L.	(MN)	1336
BICK, Barbara K.	(MO)	94
FREEMAN, C L.	(MO)	400
GREGORY, Kirk	(MO)	466
KIEL, Becky	(MO)	647
LUH, Ming	(MO)	747
PARKES, Darla J.	(MO)	942
STEVENSON, Marsha J.	(MO)	1191
WATTS, Anne	(MO)	1310
TUCKER, Ellis E.	(MS)	1261
KOCH, Patricia J.	(MT)	667
LEE, Susan M.	(MT)	711
ADAMS, Elizabeth L.	(NC)	4
CARPENTER, Jennifer K.	(NC)	184
EVANS, June C.	(NC)	357
HULL, Laurence O.	(NC)	572
NEAL, Michelle H.	(NC)	890
VARGHA, Rebecca B.	(NC)	1278
BERNARDI, John V.	(NE)	88
MUNDELL, Jacqueline L.	(NE)	878
ACKROYD-KELLY, Elaine S.	(NJ)	4
GARRABRANT, William A.	(NJ)	420
LIN, Fumei C.	(NJ)	727
REISLER, Reina	(NJ)	1021
SCHWARTZ, Lawrence C.	(NJ)	1104
TALAR, Anita	(NJ)	1220
SAMPSON, Ellanie S.	(NM)	1078
COONEY, Mata M.	(NV)	242
STURM, Danna G.	(NV)	1205
BARNELLO, Inga H.	(NY)	57
BUSTAMANTE, Corazon R.	(NY)	166
CARSON, Anne R.	(NY)	188
CONEY, Kim C.	(NY)	236
CRAWFORD-OPPENHIE-MER, Christine	(NY)	257
DUNN, Mary B.	(NY)	327
FRANKE, Gail E.	(NY)	397
FRASENE, Joanne R.	(NY)	399
GERBERG, Andrea F.	(NY)	428
HALL, Russell W.	(NY)	488
HANE, Paula J.	(NY)	495
HOLLIDAY, Geneva R.	(NY)	552
KARKHANIS, Sharad	(NY)	627
KLEIN, Penny	(NY)	659
LEWANDOWSKI, Virginia M.	(NY)	722
MAUL, Shirley A.	(NY)	787
NOLAN, John A.	(NY)	907
PARKHURST, Kathleen A.	(NY)	942
PARRAVANO, Ellen A.	(NY)	944
PLUMER, F I.	(NY)	978
REMUSAT, Suzanne L.	(NY)	1023

INTERLIBRARY (Cont'd)
Interlibrary loan

ROGERS, Elizabeth S. . . (NY) 1049
ROOT, Christine . . . . (NY) 1053
ROTHSTEIN, Pauline M. . (NY) 1060
SHRIER, Helene F. . . . . . (NY) 1133
TAN, Wendy W. . . . . (NY) 1222
TANNER, Ellen B. . . . . . (NY) 1222
TOMLIN, Anne C. . . . . . (NY) 1250
TUCKER, Laura R. . . . . . (NY) 1262
VERDIBELLO, Muriel F. . (NY) 1282
WAGNER, Janet S. . . . . (NY) 1291
WENGER, Milton B. . . . . (NY) 1324
ZIESELMAN, Paula M. . . (NY) 1388
BALCON, William J. . . . . (OH) 51
DICKINSON, Luren E. . . (OH) 301
GODWIN, Eva D. . . . . . . (OH) 443
HALIBEY-BILYK, Christine
M. . . . . (OH) 486
ROHMILLER, Ellen L. . . . (OH) 1051
ROMARY, Michael P. . . . (OH) 1052
SANKOT, Janice M. . . . . (OH) 1081
WILLIAMS, Karen J. . . . (OH) 1344
WILSON, Memory A. . . . (OH) 1352
VARNER, Joyce . . . . (OK) 1279
WOLFF, Cynthia J. . . . . . (OK) 1361
BROOKS, Harry F. . . . . . (OR) 140
HALGREN, Joanne V. . . (OR) 486
SAYRE, Samuel R. . . . . . (OR) 1087
BOLGER, Dorita F. . . . . (PA) 112
BRIZUELA, B S. . . . . . . (PA) 138
BURSTEIN, Karen . . . . . (PA) 164
CARRIER, Esther J. . . . . (PA) 186
CLINTON, Janet C. . . . . (PA) 222
COURTNEY, June M. . . . (PA) 251
CRESCENT, Victoria L. . (PA) 258
FUSCO, Marilyn A. . . . . . (PA) 410
HENSHAW, Rod . . . . . . (PA) 529
JACKSON, Mary E. . . . . (PA) 588
MALCOM, Dorothy L. . . . (PA) 763
MARCHETTI, Honey B. . . (PA) 768
MARTIN, Noelene P. . . . (PA) 777
MOREY, Carol M. . . . . . (PA) 863
NISTA, Ann S. . . . . (PA) 905
REILLY, Rebecca S. . . . . (PA) 1020
WESSEL, Charles B. . . . (PA) 1325
COHEN, Barbara S. . . . . (RI) 228
HUX, Roger K. . . . . (SC) 579
WILLIAMS, Betty H. . . . . (SC) 1342
HAGEMEIER, Deborah A. (SD) 483
HILMOE, Deann D. . . . . (SD) 541
RITTER, Linda B. . . . . . (SD) 1036
GIVENS, Mary K. . . . . . (TN) 439
MYERS, William F. . . . . (TN) 885
RIDENOUR, Lisa R. . . . (TN) 1032
SELF, George A. . . . . . . (TN) 1113
CLEE, June E. . . . . (TX) 220
HAGGARD, Lynn . . . . . (TX) 483
JARVIS, Mary E. . . . . . . (TX) 595
KIRTNER, R R. . . . . . . (TX) 655
KOOPMAN, Frances A. . (TX) 671
METIVIER, Donna M. . . . (TX) 828
METZGER, Oscar F. . . . (TX) 829
MUCK, Bruce E. . . . . . . (TX) 874
MYCUE, David J. . . . . . (TX) 884
PHILLIPS, Robert L. . . . (TX) 969
PROKESH, Jane . . . . . . (TX) 995
SELLIN, Linda M. . . . . . (TX) 1114
WILLIAMS, Ann T. . . . . (TX) 1342
WOLFE, Carl F. . . . . . . (TX) 1360
JONES, Ruth J. . . . . . . (UT) 615
CASWELL, Mary C. . . . . (VA) 194
COCHRANE, Lynn S. . . . (VA) 225
COOPER, Nancy C. . . . (VA) 243
HURD, Douglas P. . . . . (VA) 577
MALMQUIST, Katherine E. (VA) 763
MCGINN, Ellen T. . . . . . (VA) 806
MERRIFIELD, Mark D. . . (VA) 826
LUZER, Nancy H. . . . . . (VT) 750
BOSLEY, Dana L. . . . . . (WA) 117

INTERLIBRARY (Cont'd)
Interlibrary loan

BRADY, Eileen E. . . . . . (WA) 126
HILL, Ann M. . . . . (WA) 539
PUZIAK, Kathleen M. . . . (WA) 998
DREW, Sally J. . . . . (WI) 319
MERCHANT, Thomas L. . (WI) 825
MICHAELIS, Kathryn S. . (WI) 831
PARSON, Karen L. . . . . (WI) 944
SCHWARZ, Joy L. . . . . (WI) 1105
SCOFIELD, Constance V. (WI) 1106
FRASER, Elizabeth L. . . (WV) 399
CAMERON, H C. . . . . . (NF) 174
MORASH, Claire E. . . . . (NS) 862
ARONSON, Marcia L. . . (ON) 34
FLEMING, Anne . . . . . . (ON) 384
HAYTON, E E. . . . . (ON) 517
IRELAND, Michael A. . . . (ON) 583
SMALE, Carol . . . . (ON) 1151
WOLFE, Martha K. . . . . (ON) 1361
GRITZKA, Gerda M. . . . (PQ) 471
ARORA, Ved P. . . . . . . (SK) 34
WU, Edith Y. . . . . (HKG)1373

Interlibrary loan & document delivery
STATOM, Susan T. . . . . (GA) 1183
DITXLER, Carol J. . . . . . (MD) 306
REID, Valerie L. . . . . . . (MI) 1019

Interlibrary loan & serial management
WILLIAMS, Calvin . . . . . (MI) 1342
Interlibrary loan, consortia
ROEDELL, Ray F. . . . . . (PA) 1048
Interlibrary loan department
RICHARDSON, Emma G. (NY) 1029
Interlibrary loan department
  management
CARVER, Jane W. . . . . . (KS) 191
Interlibrary loan document delivery
MCFARLAND, Mary A. . (IL) 805
MORRISON, Carol J. . . . (IL) 868
Interlibrary loan networking
GIBBS, Margareth . . . . . (IL) 431
ICKES, Barbara J. . . . . (PA) 581
Interlibrary loan networks
KNUTSON, Linda J. . . . . (IL) 666
BOAZ, Ruth L. . . . . (TN) 108
SEIDENBERG, Edward . . (TX) 1112
Interlibrary loan of genealogical resrcs
MEYERS, Martha L. . . . (MO) 831
Interlibrary loan on OCLC
RISHWORTH, Susan K. . (DC) 1036
Interlibrary loan, resource sharing
THOMPSON, Dorothea M. (PA) 1239
Interlibrary loan services
COBB, Jean L. . . . . (CA) 224
SHEPHERD-SHLECHTER,
  Rae . . . . (KY) 1127
DEBROWER, Amy M. . . (MD) 285
REED, Catherine A. . . . (NY) 1015
Interlibrary loan, subject requests
LLOYD, H R. . . . . (PA) 735
Interlibrary loan subsystem
THOMPSON, Karolyn S. . (MS) 1240
Interlibrary loan workshops
SCHWEERS, Lucy . . . . (CO) 1105
Interlibrary loans
CARAVELLO, Patti S. . . (CA) 180
GUPTA, Ann D. . . . . . . (CA) 478
HAYES, Linda J. . . . . . (CA) 516
MAHAFFEY, Susan M. . . (CA) 760
BERG, Rebecca M. . . . . (CO) 84
WATERS, W R. . . . . . . (CO) 1309
ROBBINS, Rachel H. . . . (DE) 1039
TAYLOR, Rose M. . . . . (FL) 1228
FARMER, Nancy R. . . . . (GA) 364
MONTGOMERY, Denise L. (GA) 856
MAZZOLA, Patricia R. . . (HI) 791
MOORE, Annie M. . . . . (IL) 858
POULTNEY, Judy R. . . . (IL) 987
RASMUSSEN, Gordon E. (IL) 1009
SEVIER, Susan G. . . . . (KS) 1117
LAUGHLIN, Beverly E. . . (LA) 702
PRITCHARD, Robert W. . (MA) 994
SARAVIS, Judith A. . . . (MA) 1082
FEDER, Carol S. . . . . . (MI) 367
ANGUS, Jacqueline A. . . (MN) 28
BARBOUR-TALLEY,
  Donna L. . . . . (MN) 55
HUGHES, Joan L. . . . . (MO) 571
DENSON, Janeen J. . . . (NC) 293
KOZIKOWSKI, Derek M. (NH) 674
KALIF, Alexander J. . . . (NJ) 623
HINKSON, Colin S. . . . . (NY) 542
KAIN, Joan P. . . . . (NY) 622
NOLTE, James S. . . . . (NY) 908
TURNER, Freya A. . . . . (OH) 1264
FLINNER, Beatrice E. . . (OK) 385

INTERLIBRARY (Cont'd)
Interlibrary loans

	WEIS, Aimee L.	(PA)	1319
	MCREE, John W.	(SC)	818
	DEAN, Leann F.	(SD)	283
	ARMONTROUT, Brian A.	(TN)	32
	GRENGA, Kathy A.	(TN)	467
	MILLS, Debra D.	(TN)	844
	ROBERTSON, Sally A.	(TN)	1042
	DAVIS, Cynthia V.	(TX)	278
	PARHAM, Sandra H.	(VA)	940
	WHITE, Ardeen L.	(VA)	1330
	MIDDLETON, Dale R.	(WA)	833
	VYHNANEK, Kay E.	(WA)	1290
	GIBB, Betty J.	(BC)	431
	LEONARDO, Joan M.	(ON)	717
	PAWLEY, Carolyn P.	(ON)	951
	WALDRON, Nerine R.	(ON)	1294
Interlibrary loans, computer searching	SARGENT, Phyllis M.	(OR)	1083
Interlibrary loans online	TURLEY, Georgia P.	(WA)	1263
Interlibrary loans, reference	KOLBIN, Ronda I.	(CT)	669
Interlibrary services	NITECKI, Danuta A.	(MD)	905
	TURLEY, Harriet M.	(NY)	1264
	BAGHAL-KAR, Vali E.	(TX)	45
	HALVERSON, Jacquelyn A.	(TX)	490
Interloans	REID, Bette C.	(MI)	1018
Journal & interlibrary loan systems	ROBERTS, Linda L.	(OK)	1041
Journal copying, interlibrary loan	BROWN, Elizabeth E.	(CA)	143
Library systems, interlibrary loans	CLAYTOR, Jane B.	(MI)	220
Management of interlibrary loans	IANNUZZI, Patricia A.	(CT)	581
Multitype & interloan	LUND, Patricia A.	(WI)	748
Networking, interlibrary loan	SCHUBACK COHN, Judith	(NJ)	1101
	WOLFE, Gary D.	(PA)	1360
Novice level interlibrary loans	WEBER, Julie A.	(IL)	1314
OCLC interlibrary loan	RONDESTVEDT, Helen F.	(TN)	1053
Orientations & interlib loan reference	BAYER, Susan P.	(IL)	67
Reference & interlibrary loan	ROUDEBUSH, Lawanda C.	(IA)	1061
	LACROIX, Eve M.	(MD)	686
	NAIRN, Charles E.	(MI)	886
	CARR, Charles E.	(NJ)	185
Reference & interlibrary loans	HUTCHINS, Mary J.	(IL)	579
	GENTRY, Etherlene H.	(MS)	427
	LIN, Susan T.	(NY)	728
Reference work, interlibrary loans	LEHWALDT, Marliese	(ON)	713
Reserves & interlibrary loan	PARK, T P.	(NY)	941
Reserves, interlibrary loan	MILLSAP, Gina J.	(MO)	844
Statewide interlibrary loan networks	ROBERTSON, Linda L.	(IA)	1042
Supervision of interlibrary loan	WRIGHT, Joanna S.	(IL)	1371

INTERNAL

Development of internal databases	GOETZ, Helen L.	(NY)	443
Indexing internal information	AVERY, May S.	(IL)	42
Internal & external communication	GOODRICH, Nita K.	(AZ)	449
Internal communication	REAGAN, Bob	(CA)	1012
Internal consulting	SELLERS, Alexander G.	(ON)	1114
Internal corporate databases	RUBIN, Lenard H.	(TX)	1064
Internal data organization	MORROW, Ellen B.	(PA)	869
Internal database administration	LUNAS, Leslie K.	(NJ)	748
Internal documentation	MCGEE, Ruby T.	(MA)	805
Internal information	FEDORS, Maurica R.	(NJ)	368
Internal specification maintenance	GRUEL, Janice L.	(WI)	474
Reference & internal database creation	IRONS, Carol A.	(IL)	584
Reorganization of internal policies	LOMEN, Nancy L.	(NY)	738

INTERNATIONAL (See also Foreign, Global, Comparative, World)

Collection development, intl affairs	HEWITT, Vivian D.	(NY)	535
Domestic & international marketing	SABOSIK, Patricia E.	(CT)	1073
Economics & international databases	HARTMAN, David G.	(MA)	508
Federal & international state documents	BASEFSKY, Stuart M.	(NC)	62
Foreign & international law	BERKEY, Irene	(IL)	87
	YACKLE, Jeanette F.	(MA)	1376
	DIEFENBACH, Dale A.	(NY)	301
Foreign & intl law collection devlpmnt	TARNAWSKY, Marta	(PA)	1224
Foreign & international law reference	TARNAWSKY, Marta	(PA)	1224
	WEISBAUM, Earl	(TX)	1319

INTERNATIONAL (Cont'd)

Foreign & international law research	GOLDBERG, Jolande E.	(DC)	444
Foreign & international legal research	ARANDA-COODOU, Patricio	(DC)	30
Foreign & international standards	OVERMAN, Joanne R.	(MD)	931
Foreign, international & comparative law	LYMAN, Lovisa	(UT)	751
Foreign, international law	GERMAIN, Claire M.	(NC)	429
Information of international relations	RIGNEY, Janet M.	(NY)	1034
International	FLEMING, Thomas B.	(DC)	384
	HSIEH, Richard K.	(MD)	567
International affairs	PAPAZIAN, Pierre	(NJ)	939
	FENTON, Heike	(NY)	371
International affairs databases	FRIED, Suzanne C.	(NY)	403
International & Anglo-Saxon collections	IOANID, Aurora S.	(NY)	583
International & comparative libnshp	MAACK, Mary N.	(CA)	753
	VOSPER, Robert	(CA)	1289
	PATEL, Jashu	(IL)	947
	SPILLERS, Roger E.	(MN)	1174
	HORROCKS, Norman	(NJ)	561
	DUFFETT, Gorman L.	(OH)	323
International & domestic library search	FALK, Candace S.	(CA)	362
International & foreign documents	KAGAN, Alfred	(CT)	621
International & foreign law	NARANJO-BOSCH, Antonio A.	(IL)	888
International & foreign legal literature	HEAD, Anita K.	(DC)	518
International & Latin American studies	SANCHEZ, Sara M.	(FL)	1079
International aspects of librarianship	CONAWAY, Charles W.	(FL)	235
International bibliographic control	COOK, C D.	(ON)	239
International booksellers	GROSSMANN, Pierre	(BRA)	473
International business	WARD, Edith	(NY)	1303
International business & marketing	HERMAN, Marsha	(NY)	531
International business information	SIMON, David H.	(NJ)	1140
International children's literature	POARCH, Margaret E.	(CA)	979
	WONG, Patricia M.	(CA)	1363
International comparative librarianship	DANTON, J P.	(CA)	274
	VEIT, Fritz	(IL)	1281
	RUFSVOLD, Margaret I.	(IN)	1066
	CVELJO, Katherine	(TX)	268
	WILLIAMSON, William L.	(WI)	1348
	COURRIER, Yves G.	(FRN)	251
International congress organization	WALCKIERS, Marc A.	(BEL)	1293
International cooperation	POLAND, Ursula H.	(NY)	980
	DE LIAMCHIN, Lana	(PQ)	289
International database development	MILGRIM, Martin S.	(NJ)	835
International development	BETTS, Ardith M.	(DC)	92
	BREKKE, Elaine C.	(WA)	132
	FISHER, Rita C.	(WA)	381
	ST. AMANT, Robert	(ON)	1075
International development consultant	SMITH, Jessie C.	(MD)	1156
International distribution	SMITH, Richard A.	(CA)	1159
International document delivery	GROSSMANN, Pierre	(BRA)	473
International documents	SCHAAF, Robert W.	(DC)	1088
	KOHLER, Carolyn W.	(IA)	668
International economics	MCKELVEY, Michael J.	(DC)	811
International education	KIRKESY, Oliver M.	(MI)	655
International exchange of librarians	WILLIAMSON, Linda E.	(IL)	1347
International government documents	FETZER, Mary K.	(NJ)	374
Intl govt organizations' documentation	WILLIAMSON, Linda E.	(IL)	1347
International government publications	ALEXANDER, Liz C.	(IL)	12
	MAACK, David J.	(WA)	753
Intl Governmental Organizations Pubns	RUHLIN, Michele T.	(UT)	1066
International human rights law	PERKINS, Steven C.	(CA)	959
International information	MARA, Ruth M.	(DC)	768
International info & cultural exchange	STEERE, Paul J.	(DC)	1184
International information issues	TIFFT, Jeanne D.	(DC)	1244
	EL-HADIDY, Bahaa	(FL)	342
International information planning	CAMPBELL, Harry	(ON)	176
International information sources	WILLIAMS, Robert V.	(SC)	1346
International information standards	KOLTAY, Emery I.	(NY)	670
International information transfer	GREENFIELD, Stanley R.	(NY)	464
Intl intergovernmental documents	MOREHEAD, Joe	(NY)	863
International law	PERKINS, Steven C.	(CA)	959
	WARRICK, Thomas S.	(DC)	1307
	BOYCE, Barbara S.	(MA)	122
	ESSIEN, Victor K.	(NY)	354
	FENTON, Heike	(NY)	371
	LEWIS, Anne	(NY)	722

INTERNATIONAL (Cont'd)

International law
PRATTER, Jonathan ... (TX) 990
International law & treaties MCDONALD, Ellen J. ... (MA) 802
International law collection
development VON PFEIL, Helena P. ... (DC) 1288
International law librarianship STRZYNSKI, John C. . (IL) 1204
International law libraries FLYNN, Lauri R. ...... (OR) 387
International law research TRIFFIN, Nicholas ..... (NY) 1256
FOX, James R. .... (PA) 394
International liaison & cooperation RICHER, Suzanne ..... (ON) 1030
International librarianship BOONE, Mary L. ...... (CA) 115
BEAN, Charles W. ..... (DC) 69
BORYS, Cynthia A. .... (DC) 117
ROVELSTAD, Mathilde V. (DC) 1062
LOHRER, Alice .... (IL) 737
PIZER, Irwin H. .... (IL) 977
QUERY, Lance D. ..... (IL) 999
HOVISH, Joseph J. ..... (IN) 563
KASER, David .... (IN) 628
SNYDER, Carolyn A. ... (IN) 1164
TANTOCO, Dolores W. . (IN) 1223
STUEART, Robert D. ... (MA) 1205
GAURI, Kul B. .... (MI) 423
LOWRIE, Jean E. ...... (MI) 744
DYER, Esther R. .... (NY) 330
GITNER, Fred J. .... (NY) 439
HARVEY, John F. ...... (NY) 509
NYQUIST, Corinne E. ... (NY) 913
BIRK, Nancy .... (OH) 98
LEE, Hwa W. .... (OH) 710
SIITONEN, Leena M. ... (RI) 1137
GLEAVES, Edwin S. .... (TN) 441
CRAWFORD, David S. .. (PQ) 256
JONES, Roger A. ...... (SWZ) 615
SENG, Harris B. .... (TAI) 1115
International library & information prog GRAY, Dorothy L. ...... (DC) 459
International library & info services NASRI, William Z. ..... (PA) 888
Intl library & information systems GOODMAN, Henry J. ... (AB) 449
International library cooperation BALL, Alice D. .... (DC) 52
International library development GALVIN, Thomas J. .... (IL) 415
HAUSRATH, Donald C. . (NY) 513
LIEBERMAN, Ronald ... (PA) 726
International library exchanging ALLEN, Christina Y. .... (WI) 14
International library relations HUTCHINSON, Beck ... (FL) 579
MASSIS, Bruce E. ..... (NY) 782
International library relationships TSUNEISHI, Warren M. . (DC) 1260
International market research HANSEN, Kathelen L. ... (MN) 497
SHELTON, Anita L. ..... (NY) 1126
International marketing SMITH, Richard A. ..... (CA) 1159
WORTON, Geoffrey P. .. (NY) 1369
TAYLOR, William R. .... (TN) 1229
International marketing research TAYLOR, Alice J. ...... (CA) 1226
International monographs CHANDLER, George ... (ENG) 200
International networking BAKER, Dale B. .... (OH) 48
BROWN, Rowland C. ... (OH) 147
International official publications MARLEAU, Gilles ...... (ON) 772
International organization documents SHAABAN, Marian F. ... (IN) 1118
International organization publications RYAN, Richard A. ..... (OH) 1071
International organizations CLARIE, Thomas C. .... (CT) 216
GUILBERT, Manon M. .. (ON) 476
HAJNAL, Peter I. ...... (ON) 484
International profsnl & academic
publshg SMITH, Richard A. ..... (CA) 1159
Intl publishing, student editions HARMON, James R. ... (NY) 502
International relations BEESON, Lone C. ..... (CA) 74
DIMATTIA, Ernest A. ... (CT) 304
LOWENTHAL, Jane E. .. (DC) 744
PANOFSKY, Hans E. ... (IL) 938
International relations & exchange MCCOOL, Donna L. .... (WA) 798
International schools GAMAL, Sandra H. .... (NY) 416
International schools librarianship SERVENTE, Marcia M. .. (ENG) 1116
International scientific bookselling OVEREYNDER, Rombout
E. .... (NET) 931
International serials pricing HAMAKER, Charles A. .. (LA) 490
International telecommunication LIU, Rosa .... (DC) 734
International telecommunications CANNATA, Arleen ..... (NY) 178
International television programming PAEN, Alexander L. .... (CA) 934
International theatre BURDICK, Elizabeth B. .. (NY) 158
International trade PRUETT, Barbara J. .... (DC) 996

INTERNATIONAL (Cont'd)

International trade database PFLEIDERER, Stephen D. (DC) 966
International trade databases BECK, Douglas J. ...... (DC) 71
International trade research MATTERA, Joseph J. .... (NY) 785
International treaty indexing KAVASS, Igor I. .... (TN) 631
Legal research in international law KLECKNER, Simone M. . (NY) 658
National & international cooperation LINTON, William D. .... (NIR) 731
National & international document
supply LINE, Maurice B. ...... (ENG) 730
National & international standards ORNE, Jerrold .... (NC) 926
Research managing, international
team CLARK, Joan .... (NJ) 217
Spcl cols exploitation internationally HEANEY, Henry J. ..... (SCT) 518
United States & international
documents ELAM, Joice B. .... (GA) 341
US & international marketing MIELE, Madeline F. .... (MA) 833

INTERNSHIP (See also Student)

Internship programs EISENBACH, Elizabeth R. (CA) 340
Internships NYHAN, Constance W. . (CA) 912
Practicum & internship coordination COLEMAN, J G. ...... (AL) 231

INTERPERSONAL (See also Human)

Interpersonal communication ANDERSON, Dorothy J. . (CA) 22
Interpersonal comm & group
processes FLOOD, Barbara J. ..... (PA) 385
Interpersonal communication training RUBEN, Brent D. ...... (NJ) 1064
Interpersonal communications SHIELDS, Gerald R. .... (NY) 1130
Interpersonal communications training KOSHER, Helene J. .... (CA) 672
Interpersonal relations SMITH, Nathan M. ..... (UT) 1159
Interpersonal skills training &
devlpmnt KNIGHT, Shirley D. .... (NJ) 664

INTERPRETATION

Bilingual interpretation CHANG, Joseph I. ..... (NJ) 200
Foreign language interpreting HOMNACK, Mark ...... (CA) 555
Historical interpretations in museums BATTLE, Thomas C. ... (DC) 65
Local & regional history interpretation LEAHY, M J. .... (AK) 706
Oral interpretation ZALESKI, Mary A. ..... (WA) 1385

INTERSYSTEMS

Intersystems linking SANTOSUOSSO, Joseph
P. .... (MA) 1082

INTERTYPE (See also Multitype)

Intertype library cooperation TUTTLE, Walter A. ..... (NC) 1266
CONDON, John J. ..... (WI) 236

INTERVIEWING

Author interviews & reviews HOLTZE, Sally H. ...... (NY) 555
Interviewing & hiring DEDAS, Madelyn W. ... (WA) 286
Interviewing musicians SEIBERT, Donald C. .... (NY) 1112
Oral history interview training KENDRICK, Alice M. ... (NY) 640
Oral history interviewing CAMERON, Sam A. .... (TN) 175
Oral history interviewing techniques STEPHENSON, Shirley E. (CA) 1189
Patient interview systems COOK, Galen B. .... (SC) 240
Staff interviewing, placement &
devlpmnt MOODY, Marilyn D. .... (PA) 857

INTERWAR

Interwar period ASHKENAS, Bruce F. .. (VA) 36

INTRALIBRARY

Intralibrary cooperation ARN, Nancy L. .... (AR) 33

INTRA-ORGANIZATION

Intra-organization communication LIBBEY, Miles A. ...... (NJ) 725

INTRAPRENEURING

Intrapreneuring & information brokering	BROWN, Ina A.	(NJ)	144

INVENTORY

Archival inventory	COOVER, Robert W.	(CA)	244
Circulation inventory control	GOULD, Douglas A.	(UT)	454
Collections inventory	JOHNSON, Everett J.	(DC)	604
Inventory & weeding	TURLEY, Georgia P.	(WA)	1263
Inventory control, vendor management	MCGRAW, Scott C.	(IL)	807
Inventory databases	VERNON, James R.	(TX)	1283
Inventory editing	INGERSOL, Robert S.	(MO)	582
Inventory retrospective conversion	SCHMIDT, Mary A.	(TX)	1095
Patron & inventory control	RAHN, Erwin P.	(NY)	1003
Records inventory	DELOACH, Lynda J.	(MN)	290
Records surveys & inventories	FOURIE, Denise K.	(CA)	393
Shelf & shelflist inventory	BADING, Kathryn E.	(TX)	44

INVESTMENT (See also Bond, Securities, Stock)

Business & investment services	KOLLAR, Mary E.	(OH)	669
Finance & investment	HERBERT, Annette F.	(NY)	530
Financial & investment information	WEINSTEIN, Daniel L.	(CT)	1318
Investing information	WARD, Catherine J.	(NJ)	1303
Investment advice	NOBLE, James K.	(NY)	906
Investment banking	GOLDSTEIN, Bernard	(NJ)	446
	BOWLES, Nancy J.	(NY)	121
	DAVID, Julia A.	(NY)	276
Investment banking, debt & equity	ABELES, Tom	(MN)	2
Investment databases	HAMBRIC, Donna R.	(CO)	491
	LEASON, Jane	(MA)	707
Investment information systems	CAHILL, Jack F.	(MA)	171
Investment research	AVITABILE, Susan L.	(MA)	42
	RUBIN, Ellen R.	(NY)	1064
Investments	ANDERSON, Connie J.	(CA)	22
	WOODWORTH, Bonnie J.	(CT)	1368
	SUSMAN, Beatrice	(NY)	1210

INVOICE

Invoice processing	BURKHARD, Polly S.	(PA)	161

IOLS

IOLS library systems	BENTE, June E.	(NJ)	83

IRISH-AMERICAN

Irish-American heritage	REID, Peg L.	(IL)	1019

IRM

IRM reviews & audits	HORTON, Forest W.	(DC)	561

IRON RANGE

Iron Range Minnesota research	ESALA, Lillian H.	(MN)	354

ISAR

Indexing & ISAR	PITT, William B.	(MD)	976
Photo ISAR	TIFFT, Jeanne D.	(DC)	1244

ISLAMIC

Islamic art	MOLINE, Judi A.	(MD)	853
Islamic studies	FERAHIAN, Salwa	(PQ)	371

ISLANDS

Pacific islands history	SHELDEN, Patricia R.	(HI)	1125

ISRAEL (See also Hebrew)

Israel, Zionism	BEN-ZVI, Hava	(CA)	84

ISSUES

Computer health ergonomics issues	MILLER, R B.	(CA)	841
Consulting on administrative issues	RICH, Marcia A.	(MA)	1027
Contemporary American Jewish issues	HOROWITZ, Cyma M.	(NY)	560
Copyright & legal issues in management	NASRI, William Z.	(PA)	888
Copyright issues	RADER, Joe C.	(TN)	1002
Copyright, school library issues	WEBSTER, Patricia B.	(NY)	1315
Development issues, African affairs	KOSTINKO, Gail A.	(DC)	673
Health care issues	HAWKES, Warren G.	(NY)	513
Information policy issues	CHARTRAND, Robert L.	(DC)	203
Intellectual freedom issues	BUCK, Richard M.	(NY)	154
International information issues	TIFFT, Jeanne D.	(DC)	1244
	EL-HADIDY, Bahaa	(FL)	342
Issues development	SWEEN, Roger	(MN)	1214
Issues management	DORSETT, Anita W.	(TX)	313
Library copyright issues	ENSIGN, David J.	(KS)	350
Library personnel issues	GAUGHAN, Thomas M.	(NC)	422
Medico-legal issues	ROSEN, Gloria K.	(PA)	1055
Online catalog issues	RITCH, Alan W.	(CA)	1036
Personnel issues	BIGGS, Debra R.	(MI)	95
Professional trends & issues	PHELPS, Thomas C.	(DC)	967
Reference & aging issues	TABER, Sally A.	(DC)	1219
Regulatory issues	GOLDSMITH, Carol C.	(NJ)	446
Research & management issues	FORD, Gary E.	(MO)	389
Reviewing nuclear issues films	DOWLING, John	(PA)	316
Sexuality & religion issues	MAZUR, Ronald M.	(MA)	791
Small public library issues	HAYES, Richard E.	(MA)	516
Special library issues & management	MORRISON, Patricia	(CA)	868
Strategies for salary issues	SHANNON, Marcia A.	(MA)	1120
Women's issues	KONDELIK, Marlene R.	(IN)	670

ITALIAN

Cataloging Italian & Spanish books	CHANG, Roselyne M.	(DC)	201
Italian bibliography	QUARTELL, Robert J.	(NY)	999
Selection, Italian literature	WACHEL, Kathleen B.	(IA)	1290

ITALIAN-AMERICAN

Italian-American literature	GREEN, Rose B.	(PA)	462

ITV

ITV	MILLER, Robert H.	(MN)	842

JAMAICAN

Jamaican history & culture	REGNER-HYATT, Anne L.	(CA)	1017

JAPAN

Acquisition of materials on Japan	MAKINO, Yasuko	(IL)	762
Bibliography of Japanese music	SIDDONS, James D.	(VA)	1135
Japan	STEIN, Pamela H.	(NY)	1185
	DOI, Makiko	(WA)	309
Japan studies	HOTELLING, Katsuko T.	(OR)	562
Japanese & Korean law research	CHO, Sung Y.	(DC)	209
Japanese business & culture	JONES, Adrian	(IL)	610
Japanese business & management info	NOGUCHI, Sachie	(IL)	907
Japanese collection development	KANEKO, Hideo	(CT)	625
Japanese culture	WEIGEL, James S.	(CT)	1316
Japanese information	TUCKER, Laura R.	(NY)	1262
Japanese language books	ASAWA, Edward E.	(CA)	35
Japanese librarianship	NOGUCHI, Sachie	(IL)	907
Japanese library materials	KANEKO, Hideo	(CT)	625
Japanese life sciences information	WILLIAMS, Mitsuko	(IL)	1345
Japanese material collection development	GONNAMI, Tsuneharu	(BC)	447
Japanese rare books	SEWELL, Robert G.	(NY)	1117
Japanese science & tech information	SHERMAN, Roger S.	(CA)	1128
	QUINN, Ralph M.	(NJ)	1000
Japanese science technology information	TALBOT, Dawn E.	(CA)	1220
Japanese studies & reference	MAKINO, Yasuko	(IL)	762
Japanese subjects reference services	GONNAMI, Tsuneharu	(BC)	447
Japanese technical & business databases	QUINN, Ralph M.	(NJ)	1000

JAPAN (Cont'd)

Japanese technl literature abstracting	FOWELLS, Fumi T.	(MI)	393
Japanese technical translations	QUINN, Ralph M.	(NJ)	1000
Libraries in Japan	WELCH, Theodore F.	(IL)	1321
Library buildings consultant, Japan, USA	GITLER, Robert L.	(CA)	438
SCAP-occupied Japan	DIMKOFF, Diane L.	(MD)	304

JAPANESE-AMERICAN

Japanese-American experience	YAMAMOTO, Conrad S.	(CA)	1376

JAZZ

Jazz & hot dance music	LOTZ, Rainer E.	(WGR)	742
Jazz & other music	WILLIAMS, Martin T.	(DC)	1345
Jazz consulting, movie studios	COLLINS, Richard H.	(CA)	233
Jazz, early to late 1940's	BROWNE, J P.	(CA)	148
Jazz history reference	JERDE, Curtis D.	(LA)	599
Jazz publications	COHEN, Frederick S.	(NY)	228
Jazz record computer cataloging	WEAVER, James B.	(FL)	1312
Jazz recordings & musicians	COHEN, Frederick S.	(NY)	228
Private jazz archivist	ROBINSON, David F.	(VA)	1043
Rare jazz records, films & photographs	BRADLEY, Jack	(MA)	126

JEWELRY (See also Genology)

History kitchenware & jewelry	LANTZ, Louise K.	(MD)	697
Jewelry history	DIRLAM, Dona M.	(CA)	305

JEWISH (See also Hebrew, Judaica, Judaism)

American Jewish history	CLINE, Robert S.	(WA)	222
Caribbean Jewish history	CAHEN, Joel J.	(NET)	171
Contemporary American Jewish issues	HOROWITZ, Cyma M.	(NY)	560
Dutch Jewish history	CAHEN, Joel J.	(NET)	171
Jewish archives	KOHN, Roger S.	(NY)	668
Jewish art	LEVY, Jane	(CA)	721
Jewish genealogy	BERENT, Irwin M.	(VA)	84
Jewish history	CAHEN, Joel J.	(NET)	171
Jewish history & life	ARONER, Miriam D.	(CA)	34
Jewish libraries	RATKIN, Annette L.	(TN)	1009
Jewish library resources	SHEPARD, Jon R.	(OH)	1127
Jewish life & thought	BEN-ZVI, Hava	(CA)	84
Jewish literature	WIENER, Theodore	(DC)	1336
Jewish media center	KATZ, Lawrence M.	(OH)	630
Judaism & Jewish history	WIENER, Theodore	(DC)	1336
Latin American Jewish studies	SATER, Analya	(CA)	1083
Library research in Jewish history	SEAVER, James E.	(KS)	1110
Western American Jewish history	ARONER, Miriam D.	(CA)	34
Western Jewish history	ABRAMS, Jeanne E.	(CO)	3

JOB (See also Career, Employment, Occupational, Vocational)

Business, jobs, & careers	ROUDEBUSH, Lawanda C.	(IA)	1061
Education & job information services	WASSERMAN, Ricki F.	(NY)	1308
Job access for handicapped	SOMERS, Betty J.	(NY)	1166
Job analysis & evaluation	DUFORE, Thomas H.	(AZ)	324
Job & career education	GREEN, Vera A.	(PA)	462
Job & career information	LANE, Steven P.	(WA)	694
Job evaluation	KIRKPATRICK, Jane E.	(ON)	655
Job information	WERTSMAN, Vladimir F.	(NY)	1325
Job information center	BRODERICK, Therese L.	(NY)	139
Job information centers	DESCH, Carol A.	(NY)	294
Running a job information center	BEIMAN, Frances M.	(NJ)	75

JOBBERS

Academic library book jobber	NAGEL, Lawrence D.	(CA)	886
Academic library jobbers & acquisitions	BERKNER, Dimity S.	(NY)	87
Library jobber	PUALWAN, Emily	(PA)	996

JOURNALISM

Current affairs & journalism research	BEAUDET, Normand	(PQ)	70
Film criticism & journalism	CROWDUS, Gary A.	(NY)	261
Journalism	DOWELL, Connie V.	(CA)	315
	WALDOW, Mitch	(CA)	1294
	KANE, Jean B.	(MA)	624
	TUDOR, Dean F.	(ON)	1262
Journalism database searching	ALLCORN, Mary E.	(MO)	14
Journalism, radio & television	CAROTHERS, Diane F.	(IL)	184
Journalism reference & research	CATES, Jo A.	(FL)	194
Library journalism	FLAGG, Gordon E.	(IL)	383
	PLOTNIK, Arthur	(IL)	978
School library journalism	WILLIAMS, Eve A.	(NB)	1343
Video journalism	PLOTNIK, Arthur	(IL)	978

JOURNALS (See also Periodicals, Serials)

Amateur journals & fanzines	PELZ, Bruce E.	(CA)	955
Automated journal circulation	LEWIS, Martha S.	(IL)	724
Biological & agricultural journals	SHAH, Syed M.	(NY)	1119
Book & journal acquisitions	GREGORY, Melissa R.	(IL)	466
Book & journal publishing	FAHERTY, Robert L.	(DC)	361
Book & journal selection	MAYRAND, Lise M.	(PQ)	791
Book arts journals	MONGOLD, Alice D.	(TX)	854
Cataloging of serials, journals, etc	WARD, Dorothy S.	(AL)	1303
Complete collections of Adlerian jnls	KAHN, Paul J.	(CA)	622
Databases for serials, journals, etc	WARD, Dorothy S.	(AL)	1303
Editorial, journals	BURNS, Richard K.	(PA)	162
Indexing databases, journal articles	SCHOLFIELD, Caroline A.	(MI)	1098
Indexing film & broadcast trade journals	HOFFER, Thomas W.	(FL)	547
Indexing journals, serial publications	POST, Joyce A.	(PA)	986
Indexing science journals	DOWNEN, Kathleen Z.	(NY)	316
Journal abstracting	PANGALLO, Karen L.	(MA)	938
Journal acquisitions	PRITCHARD, Robert W.	(MA)	994
Journal & book editing	PHILLIPS, Janet C.	(PA)	968
Journal & interlibrary loan systems	ROBERTS, Linda L.	(OK)	1041
Journal & magazine publishing	BRAWLEY, Paul H.	(IL)	130
Journal collection	WILLIAMS, Alma	(CO)	1341
Journal copying, interlibrary loan	BROWN, Elizabeth E.	(CA)	143
Journal development	PATTERSON, Anne S.	(MD)	948
Journal editing	BALL, Dannie J.	(LA)	52
	DAVISH, William	(MD)	281
	LAMBERTON, Donald M.	(AUS)	690
Journal editor	CRAWFORD, Susan Y.	(MO)	257
Journal indexes & bibliographies	KAHN, Paul J.	(CA)	622
Journal management	WASSON, Patricia G.	(IL)	1308
Journal selection	RADA, Roy F.	(MD)	1002
Journals	POLLARD, Joan B.	(VA)	981
Journals publishing	COHEN, Bill	(NY)	228
	HUNTER, Karen A.	(NY)	576
	KING, Timothy B.	(NY)	652
Journals, technical publications	FINDLING, Carol A.	(NE)	377
Medical & scientific journals	FUGLE, Mary E.	(NY)	408
Medical book & journal indexing	GARCIA, Kathleen J.	(NY)	417
Medical books & journals	AIDE, Kathryn S.	(AL)	8
	ZUNDEL, Karen M.	(PA)	1391
Medical journal collection management	HALLERBERG, Gretchen A.	(OH)	489
Nursing journals & books	KODER, Alma	(PA)	667
Periodicals & journals	LAFAYE, Cary D.	(SC)	687
Publishing professional books & journals	GRAYSON, Martin	(NY)	460
Scholarly journal coverage	WALSH, James A.	(PA)	1299
Scientific journals	YAMAZAKI, Shigeaki	(JAP)	1377
Selection of books & journals	THOMAS, Yvonne	(CA)	1238
Theology journals	MONGOLD, Alice D.	(TX)	854
Writing for professional journals	EAGLEN, Audrey B.	(OH)	331

JUDAICA (See also Hebrew, Jewish, Judaism)

Hebraica & Judaica cataloging	WEINBERG, Bella H.	(NY)	1317
Judaic librarianship	DWOSKIN, Beth M.	(MI)	330
Judaica	KURLAND, Roslyn S.	(FL)	684
	BRICKER, Naomi S.	(NY)	135
	HONOR, Naomi G.	(NY)	556
	KUPERMAN, Aaron W.	(NY)	684
	OSTWALD, Mark F.	(NY)	929
	MALLINGER, Stephen M.	(PA)	763

JUDAICA (Cont'd)
Judaica bibliography   BAKER, Zachary M. . . . . (NY)   50
Judaica collection development   GILNER, David J. . . . . . . (OH)   437
Judaica collections   SIEGEL, Steven W. . . . . (NY) 1136
Judaica, Hebrew day schools   HERTZ, Cynthia L. . . . . . (NY)   533
Judaica librarianship   LEFF, Barbara Y. . . . . . . (CA)   712
                                 GREENBLATT, Ruth . . . . . (NJ)   463
Judaica libraries   HERBSMAN, Yael . . . . . (FL)   530
Judaica reference   SALTZMAN, Robbin R. . (IL) 1077
Judaica studies   FRIEDMAN, Sylvia . . . . . (FL)   404
                                 ROBARTS, Phyllis G. . . . (FL) 1038

JUDAISM (See also Judaica, Jewish)
Judaism & Jewish history   WIENER, Theodore . . . . (DC) 1336

JUNIOR (See also Community, Two-Year)
Academic, junior & senior highs COLLINS, Judith A. . . . . (CA)   232
Community & junior colleges   COHN, John M. . . . . . . (NJ)   229
Community, junior colleges   HUMPHRIES, Beverly H. (IL)   574
Elementary, junior & senior high
  schools   ABBOTT, Ruth J. . . . . . . (TX)   1
Elementary, junior high library
  services   DOMESCIK, Carol J. . . . (IL)   310
High school, junior high   JENSEN, Kathryn E. . . . . (MA)   599
Junior & senior high schools   DANIEL, Donna M. . . . . . (OH)   272
Junior colleges   SLICK, Myrna H. . . . . . . (PA) 1149
Junior high building collections LEWIS, Marjorie . . . . (NY)   723
Junior high library skills   LEWIS, Marjorie . . . . (NY)   723
Junior high, middle school   HAUG, Pauline C. . . . . . (WI)   512
Junior high reading encouragement LEWIS, Marjorie . . . . (NY)   723
Junior high reference   SHEPARD, Jon R. . . . . . (OH) 1127
Junior High school librarianship COOK, Anne S. . . . . (TX)   239
Junior high services   BAZE, Mary P. . . . . (WA)   68

JUSTICE (See also Courts, Law)
Criminal justice   ZIMMERMAN, Donna K. . . (IN) 1388
                                 LUTZKER, Marilyn L. . . . . (NY)   750
                                 STORMS, Kate . . . . (NY) 1198
                                 CENTER, Sue L. . . . . . . (WI)   196
Criminal justice & justice studies FERRALL, J E. . . . . (AZ)   373
Criminal justice bibliography   LUNT, Ruth B. . . . . (NY)   749
Criminal justice databases   SMITH, Ellen A. . . . . . . (OH) 1154
Criminal justice information
  management   BYRD, Harvey C. . . . . . . (MD)   169
                                 KUEHNLE, Emery C. . . . (OH)   682
Law & criminal justice   DRAGOVICH, Pamela M. (DC)   318
Law & justice   KEENON, Una H. . . . . . . (OH)   634
Peace & social justice   KLINE, Victoria E. . . . . . . (CA)   661

JUVENILE (See also Children)
Adult & juvenile storytelling   MACFARLANE, Francis X. (TX)   755
Antiquarian juvenile books   GOLEY, Elaine P. . . . . . . (TX)   447
Juvenile & young adult col
  development   GOLEY, Elaine P. . . . . . . (TX)   447
Juvenile & young adult literature HOUSEWARD, Bernice A. (MI)   563
Juvenile & young adult programming HOUSEWARD, Bernice A. (MI)   563
Juvenile books in Spanish   SCHON, Isabel . . . . (AZ) 1098
Juvenile collection centers   DIRKS, Martha W. . . . . . (KS)   305
Juvenile literature   PATRON, Susan H. . . . . . (CA)   947
                                 CRACE, Sallye C. . . . . . (KY)   254
                                 CHEW, Susan M. . . . . . . (LA)   207
                                 MELLON, Constance A. . (NC)   822
                                 RYLANDER, Carolyn S. . (OK) 1072
Juvenile materials   VANKE, Judith P. . . . . . . (OH) 1276
Juvenile services   VANKE, Judith P. . . . . . . (OH) 1276
Rare juvenile books   MATHER, Becky R. . . . . (IA)   783

KENNEDY
John F Kennedy film & photographs GOODRICH, Allan B. . . . (MA)   449
Kennedy family photographs   GOODRICH, Allan B. . . . (MA)   449

KENTUCKY (See also Louisville)
Kentuckiana   MILLS, Constance A. . . . (KY)   844
Kentucky history   STONE, Sue L. . . . . (KY) 1197
Northern Kentucky history   AVERDICK, Michael R. . . (KY)   41

KEYBOARD
Researching keyboard instruments RICHARDS, James H. . . . (TX) 1028

KEYWORDING (See also Indexing)
Keywording cement & concrete
  technology   SPIGELMAN, Cynthia A. (IL) 1174

KINDERGARTEN
Kindergarten use of library   SLOAN, Mary J. . . . . (GA) 1149

KITCHENWARE
History kitchenware & jewelry   LANTZ, Louise K. . . . . . . (MD)   697

KNOWLEDGE (See also AI, Artificial, CAI, Expert)
Book knowledge   NYREN, Dorothy E. . . . . . (NY)   913
Building knowledge bases   HOROWITZ, Roberta S. . (CA)   560
Knowledge acquisition for expert
  systems   MUSEN, Mark A. . . . . . . (CA)   883
Knowledge engineering   VLEDUTS-STOKOLOV,
                                   Natalia . . . . (PA) 1286
                                 GLAMM, Amy E. . . . . . . (VA)   439
Knowledge of family planning   ROBERTS, Gloria A. . . . . (NY) 1040
Knowledge representation   DIENER, Richard A. . . . . (MD)   302
                                 WEI, Yin M. . . . . (OH) 1316
Knowledge software design   GRENIER, Serge . . . . . . (PQ)   467
Knowledge systems   GOLDSCHMIDT, Peter G. (MD)   446
Knowledge-based information system WEI, Yin M. . . . . (OH) 1316
Knowledge-based systems   HUMPHREY, Susanne M. (MD)   573
Organization of recorded knowledge HALSEY, Richard S. . . . . (NY)   490
Sociology of knowledge   PIERCE, Sydney J. . . . . . (GA)   972

KOREA
Japanese & Korean law research   CHO, Sung Y. . . . . (DC)   209
Korean language collection   ROH, Jae M. . . . . (CA) 1050

K-12
Coordinating K-12 library programs CHAPMAN, Peggy H. . . . . (NC)   202
Curriculum development K-8   BENDER, Nancy W. . . . . . (MA)   79
Curriculum materials K-12   KING, Kathryn L. . . . . . . (MI)   651
                                 HERBERT, Barbara R. . . . (NJ)   530
Education for K-12   TOOTH, John E. . . . . (MB) 1251
Education K-12   HOOVER, Jonnette L. . . . . (MO)   557
K-12 collection development   MATSUNAGA, Fay L. . . . (CO)   785
K-12 education   SEADER, Jane M. . . . . . . (NJ) 1109
K-12 educational materials   GOWDY, Laura E. . . . . . . (IL)   455
K-12 head librarian   LYONS, Dean E. . . . . (ME)   753
K-12 library instruction   MATSUNAGA, Fay L. . . . (CO)   785
K-12 library skills   VELTEMA, John H. . . . . . (MI) 1282
K-12 library systems   JOHNSON, Elizabeth L. . (NE)   604
K-12 school administration   REMKIEWICZ, Frank L. . . (CA) 1022
K-12 school libraries   GAMAL, Sandra H. . . . . . (NY)   416
K-12 school media   LUKASIK, Marion F. . . . . (IL)   747
K-12 visual education   LACY, Lyn E. . . . . (MN)   687
K-6 & English collection development MCGLOHON, Leah L. . . . (NC)   807
K-8 grades   TEEGARDEN, Maude B. . . (KY) 1229
Library skill education for K-12 LAU, Ray D. . . . . (OK)   702
Public school librarian, K-12   KOHRT, Ruth D. . . . . (IA)   669
School libraries K-12   BARTZ, Alice P. . . . . (PA)   62
School library, K-5   GOODRICH, Carolyn B. . (NY)   449
School library services for K-6 ROTSAERT, Stefanie C. . (NJ) 1060
Supporting curriculum Grades K-4 MEINEL, Nancy T. . . . . . (LA)   822

LABOR (See also Employee, Unions)
Administration, especially labor unions LANDRY, Mary E. . . . . . (MD)   693
Archives, labor records   RABINS, Joan W. . . . . . . (TX) 1001
Economic & labor research   KIBILDIS, Melba . . . . (MI)   646
Human resources & labor relations HARE, Judith D. . . . . . . (ON)   501
Industrial labor relations   FRASER, Charlotte R. . . . (NY)   399
Labor   PANOFSKY, Hans E. . . . . (IL)   938
Labor economics   WEINRICH, Gloria . . . . . . (NY) 1318
Labor history   SWANSON, Dorothy T. . . (NY) 1213
Labor law   KUMAR, C S. . . . . (NY)   684
Labor negotiations   MORRIS, Irving . . . . (NY)   866

LABOR (Cont'd)

Labor relations BOISSE, Joseph A. .... (CA) 111
MCINDOO, Larry R. .... (CA) 809
TAUSKY, Janice ...... (MA) 1225
STUDDIFORD, Abigail M. (NJ) 1204
BUCK, Jeremy R. ...... (OH) 153
SMITH, Ellen A. .... (OH) 1154
FARK, Ronald K. ...... (RI) 364
LEATHER, Deborah J. .. (VA) 707
Labor research MOLINARI, Joseph G. .. (NY) 853
Labor studies MILLER, Everett G. ..... (MD) 837
Librarians & labor unions POTTER, Janet L. ...... (NY) 987
Online analysis of labor ANDERSEN, H F. .... (MI) 21
Personnel & labor relations APPEL, Anne M. .... (CA) 29
Personnel management & labor
relations FRANCIS, Derek R. ..... (BC) 396
Public library labor relations BRANDWEIN, Larry .... (NY) 128

LABORATORIES

Clinical laboratory computing FRIEDMAN, Bruce A. .... (MI) 403
Computer laboratories ARNY, Philip H. .... (LA) 34
Computer laboratory coordination WIRTANEN, James .... (ND) 1356
Computer laboratory coordinator TRIM, Kathryn .... (MI) 1256
Computer laboratory design LEVEILLEE, Louis R. ... (RI) 719
Curriculum laboratory RAMBO, Helen M. ..... (ID) 1005
Laboratory automation KOSMAN, Joyce E. ..... (IL) 672
Management of microcomputer labs PLAZA, Joyce S. ...... (NJ) 978
Medical laboratory sciences STANDING, Doris A. ... (ON) 1179
Microcomputer laboratories YEE, Sandra G. .... (MI) 1379
Personal computer lab BRENNAN, Edward P. ... (MD) 132

LAND

Archives administration, land records TEMPLE, Wayne C. .... (IL) 1230
Arid lands JONES, Douglas E. .... (AZ) 612
Arid lands information HUSBAND, Susan M. .... (AZ) 578
Land use information HURLBERT, Roger W. .. (CA) 577
Land use planning HANDROW, Margaret M. (TX) 495
Marine & land-based information CAMPBELL, Margaret E. (NS) 177
Public lands BAIRD, Dennis W. ..... (ID) 47
Special library land use & planning MARTINEZ, Barbara A. . (CA) 779

LANDMARKS

Restoration of national landmarks MCDONALD, Lois E. .... (CT) 803

LANDSCAPE

Landscape architecture RAVENHALL, Mary .... (IL) 1010
HAIL, Christopher ...... (MA) 484

LANE

Lane databases MASEN, Naunihal S. ... (ON) 780

LANGUAGE (See also Linguistics, Multilingual and names of specific languages)

American & foreign language
literature SHIRES, Nancy P. ..... (NC) 1131
Arabic language KHAN, Mohammed A. .. (SDA) 646
Armenian language CAPRIELIAN, Arevig ... (NY) 180
Art & language rare books COE, Miriam M. .... (LA) 226
Asian languages & literature
cataloging TIBBITS, Edith J. ...... (NE) 1243
Automated language processing BORKO, Harold .... (CA) 116
Cataloging European languages
material PHILLIPS, Richard F. ... (NJ) 969
Cataloging foreign language material INGIBERGSSON, Asgeir (AB) 582
Cataloging foreign languages KATZ, Solomon B. ..... (PQ) 630
Cataloging, language & literature MOORE, Anne C. ...... (AZ) 858
Cataloging monographs, foreign
languages MIKLOSVARY, Jozsef .. (CA) 834
Cataloging romance languages KELLEY, Ann C. ...... (IA) 636
Cataloging, Slavic language,
non-book JENKS, Zoya E. .... (PA) 597
Celtic language materials MILNE, Dorothy J. ..... (NF) 845
Classical languages & literature BYRE, Calvin S. .... (IL) 169
Collection development, language lit WARREN, Peggy A. .... (ON) 1306

LANGUAGE (Cont'd)

Consulting foreign language libraries VALENTINE, Patrick M. . (NC) 1271
Documentary languages JANIK, Sophie .... (PQ) 593
East Asian languages HSIEH, Cynthia C. ..... (IL) 567
Eastern European languages KRUKONIS, Perkunas P. (MA) 680
English as a second language PEISER, Richard H. .... (IL) 955
English language text data SCHULTZ, Arnold J. ... (MN) 1101
European languages & literature KUJANSUU, Asko J. ... (AB) 683
Foreign language acquisitions MCELWAIN, William ... (IL) 804
Foreign language books MERKIN, David .... (NY) 826
Foreign language cataloging TSCHERNY, Alexander . (DC) 1260
STEWART, Richard A. ... (IL) 1193
KIRKWOOD, Francis T. . (ON) 655
Foreign language collection
development HERNANDEZ, Hector R. . (IL) 531
MCELWAIN, William .. (IL) 804
ALICEA, Ismael .... (NY) 13
Foreign language collections PUTZ, Paul D. .... (AK) 998
TSUNEISHI, Warren M. . (DC) 1260
Foreign language collections
development KRIEGER, Lee A. ...... (NC) 678
Foreign language instruction LERNER, Esther T. ..... (OH) 717
Foreign language interpreting HOMNACK, Mark ...... (CA) 555
Foreign language libraries CLOHESSY, Antoinette M. (CO) 223
Foreign language literature selection DOLAN-HEITLINGER,
Eileen .... (IN) 309
Foreign language materials NAVARRO, Frank A. ... (CA) 889
LANDIS, Dennis C. .... (RI) 693
KAYE, Barbara J. ...... (ON) 632
Foreign language non-book materials MCELWAIN, William ... (IL) 804
Foreign language reference &
cataloging MCCLAREY, Catherine A. (IL) 796
Foreign language scientific literature SAMSON, Mary .... (ON) 1079
Foreign language teaching HSU, Patrick K. .... (TX) 567
Foreign language translating HOMNACK, Mark ...... (CA) 555
Foreign language translation SICILIANO, Peg P. ..... (MI) 1135
Foreign language typesetting HOMNACK, Mark ...... (CA) 555
Foreign languages KHATTAB, Hosneya M. . (CA) 646
BIRO, Juliane .... (NY) 99
WERTSMAN, Vladimir F. (NY) 1325
CLARK, Peter W. ...... (WI) 217
Foreign languages & classics PEDERSOLI, Heleni M. .. (AL) 954
Foreign languages & cultures COMPRI, Jeannine L. .... (AB) 235
Foreign languages & literatures TIMBERS, Jill G. ...... (MI) 1245
Foreign languages cataloging HALIBEY, Areta V. ..... (IL) 486
FOLTER, Siegrun H. .... (NY) 388
Foreign languages, European complex PERSHE, Frank F. ...... (MO) 961
Fourth generation language STOCKTON, Ken R. ... (DC) 1196
French language & literature DEON, Judy S. .... (BC) 293
French language library services NICHOLSON, Jill A. .... (ON) 902
French language publication BERNARD, Marie L. .... (AB) 88
German language & literature STUHR-ROMMEREIM,
Rebecca A. .... (KS) 1205
MCKILLIP, Rita J. ...... (WI) 811
TRAICHEL, Rudolf D. .... (AB) 1253
German language services BLUMBERG-MCKEE,
Hazel .... (MN) 107
German language specialist LUTZ, Linda J. .... (ON) 750
Human system language interface WEI, Yin M. .... (OH) 1316
Indexing languages TRAVIS, Irene L. ...... (VA) 1254
Indexing languages & thesauri PAUL, Rameshwar N. ... (MD) 949
Japanese language books ASAWA, Edward E. .... (CA) 35
Korean language collection ROH, Jae M. .... (CA) 1050
Language arts BLATT, Gloria T. ...... (MI) 104
Language arts & English education BUBOLTZ, Dale D. ..... (CA) 152
Language of dramatic production TRAPIDO, Joel .... (HI) 1254
Language of play direction TRAPIDO, Joel .... (HI) 1254
Languages SPULBER, Pauline ..... (IN) 1176
Languages, architecture & art CULLARS, John M. ..... (IL) 263
Literature & language reference THEWS, Dorothy D. .... (MN) 1234
Middle East languages cataloging JAJKO, Edward A. ..... (CA) 592
Modern European languages &
literature POLIT, Carlos E. ...... (IN) 980
Modern languages MELIK, Ella M. .... (OK) 822
National language computing SEDELOW, Walter A. ... (AR) 1110
Natural language computing SEDELOW, Sally Y. .... (AR) 1110
Natural language information
processing HAYDEN, Richard F. ... (CA) 515

LANGUAGE (Cont'd)

Natural language processing	TRIVISON, Donna	(OH)	1257
	VLEDUTS-STOKOLOV, Natalia	(PA)	1286
Natural language search strategy	HAYDEN, Richard F.	(CA)	515
Natural languages processing	METZLER, Douglas P.	(PA)	829
Near East languages cataloging	HIRSCH, David G.	(NJ)	543
Oriental language terminal	WANG, Gary Y.	(MA)	1302
Original cataloging romance languages	SALINERO, Amelia	(NY)	1076
Programming languages	SKOVIRA, Robert J.	(PA)	1147
	EASTMAN, Caroline M.	(SC)	333
Reference languages & literature	WARREN, Peggy A.	(ON)	1306
Romance language cataloging	CRISTAN, Anita L.	(DC)	259
	JAVONOVICH, Kenneth L.	(IL)	595
Romance languages	CANTRELL, Clyde H.	(AL)	179
	SMITH, Mary P.	(MD)	1158
	SHIRKY, Martha H.	(MO)	1131
Romance languages & literature	POLIT, Carlos E.	(IN)	980
Slavic languages	SABOVIK, Pavel	(AZ)	1073
	ESMAN, Michael D.	(MD)	354
	FORBES, John B.	(MD)	389
Slavic languages cataloging	CAPRIELIAN, Arevig	(NY)	180
Slavic reference, Russian language	PRICE, Susan W.	(NY)	992
Southeast Asian languages	HICKEY, John T.	(NY)	536
Spanish & Portuguese languages	NEUGEBAUER, Rhonda L.	(KS)	897
Spanish language acquisitions	PETERSON, Anita R.	(CA)	962
Spanish language & literature	COLLAZO, Maria L.	(PR)	232
Spanish language cataloging	JAVONOVICH, Kenneth L.	(IL)	595
Spanish language children's books	ZWICK, Louise Y.	(TX)	1392
Spanish language collection	CHAVEZ, Linda	(CA)	204
Spanish language collection development	SIMAS, Therese C.	(CA)	1139
	BETANCOURT, Ingrid T.	(NJ)	92
Spanish language collections	CADY, Steven R.	(CA)	170
Spanish language materials	NAVARRO, Frank A.	(CA)	889
	ANDERSON, Mark	(TX)	24
Spanish language services	PISANO, Vivian M.	(CA)	975
Special languages cataloging	MCCLOY, William B.	(IN)	797
Theatre language	TRAPIDO, Joel	(HI)	1254
Tibetan language materials	SCHOENING, Jeffrey D.	(MA)	1098
Tutoring English as a foreign language	NORRIS, Loretta W.	(DC)	909
Western European language materials	NEVIN, Susanne	(MN)	898
Western European languages & literature	BYRE, Calvin S.	(IL)	169

LANKES

Letters of J J Lankes	LANKES, J B.	(VA)	696
Paintings of J J Lankes	LANKES, J B.	(VA)	696
Woodcuts of J J Lankes	LANKES, J B.	(VA)	696

LARGE

Collection development in large libs	EDWARDS, Ralph M.	(AZ)	337
Consulting large & small libraries	WEST, L P.	(IL)	1326
Large computers & small libraries	STEVENS-RAYBURN, Sarah L.	(MD)	1191
Large high school library administration	SPICER, Orlin C.	(MO)	1174
Large mainframe databases	TEUN, Rebecca L.	(TX)	1233
Large print	MASSIS, Bruce E.	(NY)	782
	BORCHERT, Catherine G.	(OH)	116
Large-scale information systems	SAYER, John S.	(MD)	1086
Literacy & large print	LEGO, Jane B.	(VA)	712
Managing large library computers	FORTH, Stuart	(PA)	391
Moving large book collections	PARRY, David R.	(CO)	944

LASER

Laser disks, CD-ROMS	GARMAN, Nancy J.	(KY)	419
Laser optic publishing services	ALCOCK, Anthony J.	(CA)	11
Laser optical technology	KERR, Robert C.	(CO)	644
Laser printing	DICK, John H.	(IL)	300
Laser printing distribution	CONTESSA, William B.	(NY)	239
Optical laser disk products	HANIFORD, K L.	(MO)	496

LATIN

Classical Greek & Latin reference	CRITTENDEN, Robert R.	(CA)	259
Greek & Latin literature	CARNOVSKY, Ruth F.	(CA)	184

LATIN AMERICA (See also Caribbean)

Hispanic & Latin American bibliography	ZUBATSKY, David S.	(PA)	1390
Information retrieval in Latin America	GREEN-MALONEY, Nancy	(CA)	465
International & Latin American studies	SANCHEZ, Sara M.	(FL)	1079
Latin America	COLSON, Harold G.	(AL)	234
	NEUGEBAUER, Rhonda L.	(KS)	897
Latin America & Africa	WARPHEA, Rita C.	(VA)	1306
Latin America & Iberia	KAHLER, Mary E.	(DC)	622
Latin America cataloging	LEONARD, Louise F.	(FL)	716
Latin America research	FIGUEREDO, Danilo H.	(NY)	376
Latin American acquisitions	MAKUCH, Andrew L.	(AZ)	762
Latin American & Caribbean	MILLER, David A.	(OH)	836
Latin American & Caribbean studies	FINEMAN, Charles S.	(IL)	377
Latin American & general reference	GROTHEY, Mina J.	(NM)	473
Latin American area studies	READ, Glenn F.	(IN)	1012
Latin American bibliography	MARSHALL, Thomas H.	(AZ)	775
	BRISCOE, Peter M.	(CA)	136
	BALLANTYNE, Lygia M.	(FL)	53
	HALLEWELL, Laurence	(MN)	489
	BETANCOURT, Ingrid T.	(NJ)	92
	SABLE, Martin H.	(WI)	1072
Latin American book market	MARSHALL, David L.	(DC)	774
Latin American cataloging	WALTON, Carol G.	(FL)	1301
Latin American collection development	GROTHEY, Mina J.	(NM)	473
Latin American indexing	SATER, Analya	(CA)	1083
Latin American Jewish studies	SATER, Analya	(CA)	1083
Latin American law	GONZALEZ, Armando E.	(DC)	448
Latin American libraries	MCGINN, Thomas P.	(IL)	806
Latin American library development	BRESIE, Mayellen	(TX)	133
Latin American materials acquisitions	BALLANTYNE, Lygia M.	(FL)	53
Latin American school library consulting	CARDENAS, Mary E.	(SAF)	180
Latin American selection	CLINE, Herman W.	(NY)	222
Latin American studies	NELSON, William N.	(AL)	895
	HOWARD, Pamela F.	(AZ)	564
	JARAMILLO, Ellen M.	(CT)	594
	WELCH, Thomas L.	(DC)	1321
	WIEMERS, Eugene L.	(MI)	1336
	GARNER, Jane	(TX)	419
Latin American studies bibliography	GUTIERREZ, Margo	(TX)	479
Latin American studies selection	KELLEY, Ann C.	(IA)	636
Latin American studies specialist	HARRINGTON, Charles W.	(LA)	504
Latin American subjects	CARRENO, Angela M.	(NY)	186
Latin Americana	HENRY, Mary K.	(NY)	529
Libraries, bibliography of Latin America	JACKSON, William V.	(TX)	588
Spanish & Latin American bibliography	MORENO, Rafael	(PA)	863
Spanish & Latin American collections	BARZELATTO, Elba G.	(NJ)	62

LATTER DAY SAINT (See also Mormonism)

Latter Day Saint history	HALLIER, Sara J.	(MO)	489

LATVIAN

Latvian bibliography & research	OZOLINS, Karl L.	(MN)	933
Latvian materials	BUNDZA, Maira	(MI)	157

LAUBACH

Laubach tutor training	TEUBERT, Lola H.	(IN)	1233

LAW (See also Attorneys, Bar, Justice, Legislation, Litigation, Ordinances, Police, Statute, Witnesses and headings beginning with LEGAL)

Acquisitions, archival & law field	SHEPARD, E L.	(VA)	1126
Administer law library	CONNORS, Jean M.	(OR)	238
Administration, law library	GIANNATTASI, Gerard E.	(NY)	430
Administration of law firm library	D'AMORE, Denice M.	(OH)	272
Admiralty & maritime law	COMBE, David A.	(LA)	234

LAW (Cont'd)

Admiralty law	RABER, Steven	(NY)	1001
Air & space law	FOX, James R.	(PA)	394
American law	RIEMANN, Frederick A.	(TX)	1033
Antiquarian law books	LUTTRELL, Jordan D.	(CA)	750
Appraising law firm collections	SCAMMAHORN, Lynne	(PA)	1087
Art, law, humanities	KLEIN, Ilene R.	(MD)	659
Automating law firm libraries	DILORETO, Ann M.	(CA)	303
Banking law	VAN BEEK, Susan	(MA)	1272
	CONGDON, Rodney H.	(NY)	236
Business & law reference	PERELLA, Susanne B.	(DC)	958
Business law vocational education	DIAL, Ron	(NY)	299
California law	AKEY, Sharon A.	(CA)	9
Canadian constitutional law	TANGUAY, Guy	(PQ)	1222
Cataloging for law libraries	DILORETO, Ann M.	(CA)	303
Cataloging law materials	KORKMAS, Carolyn C.	(TX)	671
Cataloging serials, law, monographs	SPRANKLE, Vicki S.	(PA)	1176
Chinese law	ROBERT, Berring C.	(CA)	1039
City law libraries	COX, Irvin E.	(MD)	253
Civil & common law	NARANJO-BOSCH, Antonio A.	(IL)	888
Civil law	SEADER, Jane M.	(NJ)	1109
	CORNEIL, Charlotte E.	(OK)	246
Collections development, law	BLAKE, Timothy J.	(LA)	103
Common market law	ESSIEN, Victor K.	(NY)	354
Communication law	PACE, Thomas	(NJ)	933
Comparative law	ESSIEN, Victor K.	(NY)	354
	PRATTER, Jonathan	(TX)	990
Computer law	WARRICK, Thomas S.	(DC)	1307
Computers in law libraries	EICHER, Thomas E.	(IA)	339
Consumer protection law	ENGLISH, Susan B.	(VA)	350
Contract law	POOLEY, Beverly J.	(MI)	983
Copyright law	CREWS, Kenneth D.	(CA)	258
	HELLER, James S.	(ID)	524
	ANDERSON, Patricia E.	(KY)	25
	BRUWELHEIDE, Janis H.	(MT)	151
	GASAWAY, Laura N.	(NC)	421
	MILLER, Jerome K.	(WA)	839
	GORSEGNER, Betty D.	(WI)	452
Copyright law for educators	DAY, Martha T.	(VT)	282
Copyright laws & regulations	KATZ, Bernard M.	(ON)	630
Corporate law	HENDLEY, David D.	(PA)	527
Correctional law libraries	WELCH, Steven J.	(IL)	1321
County law library coordination	CRAWFORD, Nola N.	(NJ)	257
Criminal law	LYNES, Tezeta G.	(KY)	752
Ecclesiastical law	HORWITZ, Steven F.	(CA)	561
Editing law review articles	STEFANCIC, Jean A.	(CA)	1185
English material on Chinese law	LUNG, Mon Y.	(KS)	748
Environmental law	ERTZ, Ginger E.	(PA)	353
Environmental laws & regulations	KAYES, Mary J.	(WI)	632
Family law	CENTER, Sue L.	(WI)	196
Federal & California law reference	CH'NG, Saw K.	(CA)	209
Federal & state law	SCHUTT, Cheryl M.	(CT)	1103
Federal & state law research	VARGA, William R.	(DC)	1278
Foreign & comparative law	ZOLLER, R T.	(WI)	1390
Foreign & international law	BERKEY, Irene	(IL)	87
	YACKLE, Jeanette F.	(MA)	1376
	DIEFENBACH, Dale A.	(NY)	301
Foreign & intl law collection devlpmnt	TARNAWSKY, Marta	(PA)	1224
Foreign & international law reference	TARNAWSKY, Marta	(PA)	1224
	WEISBAUM, Earl	(TX)	1319
Foreign & international law research	GOLDBERG, Jolande E.	(DC)	444
Foreign, international & comparative law	LYMAN, Lovisa	(UT)	751
Foreign, international law	GERMAIN, Claire M.	(NC)	429
Foreign law	PRATTER, Jonathan	(TX)	990
Foreign law bibliography	SCHWERIN, Kurt	(IL)	1106
	TARNAWSKY, Marta	(PA)	1224
Foreign law book acquisition	KREH, Fritz	(WGR)	677
Foreign law research	KAVASS, Igor I.	(TN)	631
Genealogy & law libraries	BURCHILL, Mary D.	(KS)	158
General law library consulting	MARKE, Julius J.	(NY)	771
General law reference	WOOD, Elizabeth B.	(OH)	1364
History & law	CAMPBELL, Laurie G.	(ON)	177
Hospital & health care law	MULCAHY, Brian J.	(NY)	876
Indexing Thai law	RUNGSANG, Rebecca J.	(THA)	1067
Information law	MARX, Peter	(MA)	780
Information services law	PACE, Thomas	(NJ)	933
Inmate law libraries	ROMALIS, Carl	(NY)	1052
Insurance law	WOODS, Marcia G.	(CA)	1367

LAW (Cont'd)

International & foreign law	NARANJO-BOSCH, Antonio A.	(IL)	888
International human rights law	PERKINS, Steven C.	(CA)	959
International law	PERKINS, Steven C.	(CA)	959
	WARRICK, Thomas S.	(DC)	1307
	BOYCE, Barbara S.	(MA)	122
	ESSIEN, Victor K.	(NY)	354
	FENTON, Heike	(NY)	371
	LEWIS, Anne	(NY)	722
	PRATTER, Jonathan	(TX)	990
International law & treaties	MCDONALD, Ellen J.	(MA)	802
International law collection development	VON PFEIL, Helena P.	(DC)	1288
International law librarianship	STRZYNSKI, John C.	(IL)	1204
International law libraries	FLYNN, Lauri R.	(OR)	387
International law research	TRIFFIN, Nicholas	(NY)	1256
	FOX, James R.	(PA)	394
Japanese & Korean law research	CHO, Sung Y.	(DC)	209
Labor law	KUMAR, C S.	(NY)	684
Latin American law	GONZALEZ, Armando E.	(DC)	448
Law	FOLLICK, Edwin D.	(CA)	388
	HOFSTADTER, Marc E.	(CA)	549
	RAFFALOW, Janet W.	(CA)	1003
	SIMONS, Robert A.	(CA)	1141
	STROMME, Gary L.	(CA)	1203
	BILLINGS, Edward S.	(DC)	96
	BOYER, Larry M.	(DC)	123
	MARTIN, Kathleen S.	(DC)	777
	SHELAR, James W.	(DC)	1125
	WINSTEAD, Jean D.	(DE)	1356
	MILLER, Jewell J.	(FL)	839
	PETIT, Michael J.	(FL)	965
	BRUEMMER, Alice	(IL)	149
	COX, Joyce M.	(IL)	253
	HARRINGTON, Margaret V.	(IL)	504
	LAM, Judy	(IL)	689
	SMITH, Judy E.	(IL)	1156
	YOUNG, Peter W.	(IL)	1383
	BOOHER, William V.	(IN)	115
	DICKMEYER, John N.	(IN)	301
	ENGLE, Madge	(IN)	349
	SLINGER, Michael J.	(IN)	1149
	WHICKER, Gene A.	(KY)	1329
	FRANZEK, Karyn	(MA)	398
	FREEHLING, Dan J.	(MA)	400
	GIBBS, Paige	(MA)	431
	HILL, Byron C.	(MA)	539
	LEONARD, Sharen C.	(MA)	717
	MATIS, Lynn	(MA)	784
	MOLONEY, Kevin F.	(MA)	853
	GONTRUM, Barbara S.	(MD)	448
	RASCHKA, Katherine E.	(MD)	1008
	SIMISON, Joan B.	(MD)	1139
	SLEEMAN, William E.	(MD)	1148
	CLARK, Georgia A.	(MI)	217
	WISE, Virginia J.	(MI)	1357
	GRANDE, Anne W.	(MN)	457
	COURT, Patricia	(MO)	251
	REAMS, Bernard D.	(MO)	1013
	BOERINGER, Margaret J.	(NC)	110
	HALL, Frances H.	(NC)	487
	MATZEN, Constance M.	(NC)	786
	WASHBURN, Anne C.	(NC)	1307
	BRUNNER, Karen B.	(NJ)	151
	ELIASON, Elisabetha S.	(NJ)	342
	WATSON, Marjorie O.	(NJ)	1310
	ANTHONY, Mary M.	(NY)	28
	DUNN, Mary B.	(NY)	327
	KARNEZIS, Kristine C.	(NY)	627
	OSTWALD, Mark F.	(NY)	929
	PILLAI, Karlye A.	(NY)	973
	ROBBINS, Sara E.	(NY)	1039
	SCOTT, Bettie H.	(NY)	1106
	SHANNON, Michael O.	(NY)	1120
	STORMS, Kate	(NY)	1198
	TRACY, Janet R.	(NY)	1253
	SHEW, Anita K.	(OH)	1129
	BLAIR, William W.	(PA)	103

LAW (Cont'd)
Law
   CHAMBERLIN, Richard R. (PA) 198
   GARNER, Diane L. (PA) 419
   NANES, Evelyn M. (PA) 887
   SMITH, Eugene J. (PA) 1155
   ZANAN, Arthur S. (PA) 1386
   ALBRIGHT, Susie K. (TX) 10
   BOGIE, Thomas M. (TX) 110
   EICHSTADT, John R. (TX) 339
   HOLLAND, Jane D. (TX) 550
   MCDONALD, Brenda D. (TX) 802
   MUCK, Bruce E. (TX) 874
   PALMER, Forrest C. (VA) 936
   HOLT, Barbara C. (WA) 554
   ZIKE, Ruth D. (WA) 1388
Law acquisitions GARCIA, Mary E. (CA) 417
Law administration MAZZA, Joanne C. (CA) 791
Law & business cataloging CASSIDY, Joni L. (NJ) 193
Law & business collection
   development BURGESS, Rita N. (PA) 159
Law & business library maintenance HELBURN, Judith D. (TX) 523
Law & business library organization HELBURN, Judith D. (TX) 523
Law & business writing & editing HOYT, Henry M. (NY) 566
Law & criminal justice DRAGOVICH, Pamela M. (DC) 318
Law & justice KEENON, Una H. (OH) 634
Law & legal databases SHOSTROM, Marian L. (CA) 1133
   STEARNS, Barry T. (MA) 1183
Law & legislation reference ROCHE, Richard G. (IL) 1046
Law & legislative reference RINDEN, Constance T. (NH) 1035
Law & literature BANDER, Edward J. (MA) 54
Law & social sciences ESPOSITO, Michael A. (NY) 354
Law & tax libraries TAYLOR, Kathryn E. (CA) 1227
   BALKIN, Ruth G. (NY) 52
Law & tax library consulting EVERLOVE, Nora J. (FL) 359
Law bibliography WOOD, Elizabeth B. (OH) 1364
Law book acquisitions WALSH, Sharon T. (PA) 1300
Law book publishing DANNE, William H. (IL) 274
   MORSE, Alan L. (NY) 869
   KUEHNLE, Emery C. (OH) 682
   WALSH, Sharon T. (PA) 1300
Law books COX, Irvin E. (MD) 253
   LOCKE, William G. (NY) 736
   MAYL, Gene (OH) 790
Law cataloging JOHNTING, Wendell E. (IN) 610
   GEE, Ka C. (NY) 424
   HARVEY, Suzanne (WA) 509
Law cataloging & classification STRIMAN, Brian D. (NE) 1202
Law classification HU, Shih S. (AB) 568
Law collection KEARNEY, Jeanne E. (NJ) 633
Law collection development WALTERS, Roberta J. (CA) 1301
Law databases LEE, Soon H. (IL) 711
   WILLIAMSON, Carol L. (NJ) 1347
   OBERLA, Janet L. (WI) 914
Law databases, LEXIS SMITH, Eugene J. (PA) 1155
Law enforcement DILUCIA, Samuel J. (HI) 303
   CORDONI, Earl C. (IL) 246
Law enforcement, one-person library ZIMMERMAN, Donna K. (IN) 1388
Law firm acquisitions SNYDER, Elizabeth A. (ENG) 1164
Law firm collections cataloging SCAMMAHORN, Lynne (PA) 1087
Law firm consulting DAVIS, Becky C. (CA) 277
   EARHART, Marilyn N. (CA) 332
Law firm, information systems EWING, Alison L. (AZ) 359
Law firm libraries CROSS, Joseph R. (SC) 260
Law firm library administration YALLER, Loretta O. (DE) 1376
   VARGAS, Gwen S. (PA) 1278
Law firm library automation PETERSON, Christine E. (WI) 963
Law firm library establishment ROCKWOOD, Susan M. (PA) 1046
Law firm library management MATTHEWSON, David S. (CT) 786
   HARRIS, Helen Y. (MD) 504
   JULIAN, Julie L. (TN) 619
Law history KREH, Fritz (WGR) 677
Law indexing THOMAS, Dorothy (NY) 1236
Law information processing ARAJ, Houda (PQ) 30
Law/legal reference LATEGOLO, Meldie A. (DC) 701
Law librarian BURGALASSI, Anthony J. (NY) 159
Law librarianship FEENKER, Cherie D. (AL) 368
   NEWMAN, Sharon K. (AL) 900
   WIEBELHAUS, Richard J. (AZ) 1336
   CARTER, Nancy C. (CA) 189

LAW (Cont'd)
Law librarianship
   CONLEY, Linda A. (CA) 236
   CREWS, Kenneth D. (CA) 258
   MCKENZIE, Alice M. (CA) 811
   SCHMIDT, Robert R. (CA) 1096
   CALVERT, Lois M. (CO) 174
   COCO, Al (CO) 226
   GONZALEZ, Armando E. (DC) 448
   KELMAN, Rosalind S. (DC) 638
   KOVER, Steven J. (DC) 674
   OAKLEY, Robert L. (DC) 913
   GIBBS, Rosalyn D. (FL) 431
   KERN, Sharon P. (IA) 643
   HELLER, James S. (ID) 524
   HOUDEK, Frank G. (IL) 562
   MOEN, Art J. (IL) 851
   ENGELBERT, Peter J. (IN) 348
   PIASECKI, Patricia S. (IN) 970
   WILLIS, Paul A. (KY) 1348
   HOAGLAND, E L. (MA) 545
   GREEN, Katherine A. (MI) 462
   HEINEN, Margaret A. (MI) 522
   HOLSTEN, Terri L. (MO) 554
   GENNETT, Robert G. (NJ) 427
   GRECH, Anthony P. (NY) 461
   YIRKA, Carl A. (NY) 1380
   NOVAK, Mary S. (OH) 911
   HAAS, Carol C. (PA) 480
   METZ, Betty A. (PA) 828
   SVENGALIS, Kendall F. (RI) 1212
   HOOD, Lawrence E. (TX) 556
   NORWOOD, Deborah A. (WA) 910
   DENTON, Vivienne K. (ON) 293
   FORTIN, Jean L. (PQ) 391
   YOUNG, Patricia M. (PQ) 1383
Law libraries MEERIANS, Patti L. (AZ) 821
   HARMON, Marlene K. (CA) 502
   MACARTHUR, Marit S. (CO) 754
   HORRIGAN, John J. (CT) 560
   MCCAUGHTRY, Dorothy
   H. (CT) 795
   FLEMING, Thomas B. (DC) 384
   FENTON, Elaine P. (GA) 371
   JANES, Virginia (IL) 593
   SCHWERIN, Kurt (IL) 1106
   WRIGHT, Judith M. (IL) 1372
   LUCAS, Ann (MI) 745
   FESSENDEN, Ann T. (MO) 374
   BLUM, Elaine G. (NY) 107
   GARA, Otto G. (NY) 416
   ALLEN, Cameron (OH) 14
   GAEBLER, Ralph F. (PA) 411
   PROCTOR, David J. (PA) 994
   SCHLUETER, Kay (TX) 1094
   HUMMEL, Patricia A. (UT) 573
   HUMPHRIES, Lajean (WI) 574
   KOSLOV, Marcia J. (WI) 672
   SCOTT, Marianne F. (ON) 1107
   CHAREST, Ronald (PQ) 203
Law libraries administration MARKE, Julius J. (NY) 771
Law libraries, legal databases WOLFE, Charles B. (MI) 1360
Law library DENGEL, Bette S. (PA) 292
Law library acquisitions EICHER, Thomas E. (IA) 339
Law library administration CLAPP, Laurel R. (AL) 216
   ADAN, Adrienne (CA) 6
   CASTETTER, Karla M. (CA) 194
   HAYTHORN, Joseph D. (CA) 517
   NEMCHEK, Lee R. (CA) 895
   MCGUIRL, Marlene C. (DC) 808
   PREBLE, Leverett L. (DC) 990
   DANIELS, Westwell R. (FL) 273
   EFRON, Muriel C. (FL) 338
   WOODARD, Joseph L. (FL) 1365
   JACOBS, Roger F. (IN) 590
   FISHER, Collette J. (LA) 380
   DUNN, Donald J. (MA) 326
   MATZ, Ruth G. (MA) 786
   MURRAY, Lynn T. (MA) 882
   TRUBEY, Cornelia (MA) 1258

LAW (Cont'd)

Law library administration

Specialty	Name	State	Page
Law library administration	POOLEY, Beverly J.	(MI)	983
	SEARLS, Eileen H.	(MO)	1110
	GASAWAY, Laura N.	(NC)	421
	WILLIAMS, Lisa W.	(NC)	1344
	GIANNATTASI, Gerard E.	(NY)	430
	HAMMOND, Jane L.	(NY)	493
	PAGEL, Scott B.	(NY)	934
	NISSENBAUM, Robert J.	(OH)	905
	FLYNN, Lauri R.	(OR)	387
	BEYER, Robyn L.	(PA)	93
	SMITH, Linda D.	(PA)	1157
	CHAMPION, Walter T.	(TX)	198
	EDMONDS, Edmund P.	(VA)	336
	RAE, E A.	(ON)	1002
Law library administration for courts	WELKER, Kathy J.	(OH)	1321
Law library automation	FU, Paul S.	(OH)	407
Law library collection development	ADAN, Adrienne	(CA)	6
Law library consultant	BROSK, Carol A.	(IL)	141
Law library consulting	FOX, Elyse H.	(MA)	394
Law library design	EVERLOVE, Nora J.	(FL)	359
Law library development	PIERCE, Ann E.	(ME)	971
Law library facilities planning	MERRIFIELD, Thomas C.	(CA)	826
Law library management	BALABAN, Robin M.	(CA)	50
	DATTALO, Elmo F.	(DC)	275
	SMITH, Mary D.	(FL)	1158
	HUTCHINS, Richard G.	(IL)	579
	ANDREWS, Sylvia L.	(IN)	27
	LAMBERT, Lyn D.	(MA)	690
	KILLIAN, Mary C.	(MI)	648
	DIGIOVANNA, Josephine A.	(NY)	303
	FRALEY, Ruth A.	(NY)	395
	KAIN, Joan P.	(NY)	622
	HANLEY, Thomas L.	(OH)	496
	BURGESS, Rita N.	(PA)	159
	MACBETH, Eileen M.	(PA)	754
	BALCOMBE, Judith A.	(TX)	51
	GARCIA, Lana C.	(TX)	417
	HOUSTON, Barbara B.	(TX)	563
	MOORE, Dianne T.	(VA)	859
	MURPHY, Robert D.	(VA)	881
	YEN, David S.	(HKG)	1379
Law library management administration	HERNANDEZ, Marilyn J.	(MB)	531
Law library management & planning	ARANDA-COODOU, Patricio	(DC)	30
Law library, medical library	SUMMERS, Sheryl H.	(MI)	1209
Law library organization	SMITH, Susan A.	(CA)	1161
Law library planning & design	KREMER, Jill L.	(PA)	677
Law library reference services	MATZ, Ruth E.	(MA)	786
Law library space planning	CHICK, Cynthia L.	(CA)	208
	RAE, E A.	(ON)	1002
Law library supervision	COX, Irvin E.	(MD)	253
	BEQUETTE, V L.	(MO)	84
Law library systems	BUTTS, Willie D.	(MD)	168
	BROWN, Vicki L.	(OH)	148
Law library systems design	RAUM, Tamar	(NY)	1010
Law library technical services	ADAN, Adrienne	(CA)	6
	PIPER, Patricia L.	(CA)	975
	NASSERDEN, Marilyn D.	(AB)	889
Law library upkeep & organization	RIGGS, Judith M.	(SK)	1034
Law material cataloging	REID, Marianne E.	(SK)	1019
Law materials reference	TENOR, Randell B.	(PA)	1231
Law office automation	GRIFFITH, Cary J.	(MN)	469
Law office, library automation	LEITER, Richard A.	(NE)	714
Law publishing	HALE, William B.	(NY)	486
	GATES, Robert G.	(OH)	422
Law reference	HEATHER, Joleen	(CA)	519
	SCHIPPER, Joan A.	(CA)	1093
	GAULT, Robin R.	(FL)	423
	HEMPHILL, Lia S.	(FL)	525
	ENGELBERT, Peter J.	(IN)	348
	JOHNSON, David J.	(NY)	603
	KUMAR, C S.	(NY)	684
	SMITH, Diane H.	(PA)	1154
	BRAUTIGAM, Patsy R.	(TX)	130
	MORRIS, Pamela A.	(TX)	867
	ORLANDO, Karen T.	(WV)	926

LAW (Cont'd)

Specialty	Name	State	Page
Law reference, government documents	KAUL, Kanhya L.	(MI)	631
Law reference services	BLAKE, Timothy J.	(LA)	103
Law school libraries	LUCAS, Ann	(MI)	745
Law school library	GHIDOTTI, Pauline A.	(AR)	430
Law school professor	DYER, Charles R.	(CA)	330
Law schools	LONG, Clare S.	(OH)	739
Law schools, legal education	COYLE, Christopher B.	(OH)	253
Law serials	ROYLE, Maryanne	(IL)	1063
Legal research in international law	KLECKNER, Simone M.	(NY)	658
Library & information law	HAMMERLY, Hernan D.	(ARG)	493
Library law	JUERGENSMEYER, John E.	(IL)	619
	MCCLARREN, Robert R.	(IL)	796
	DUKELOW, Ruth H.	(MI)	324
Library law & legislation	LADENSON, Alex	(IL)	687
Managing small to medium law libraries	SCAMMAHORN, Lynne	(PA)	1087
Maritime law & technology	COMEAU, Amy R.	(NY)	234
Matrimonial law	BROWN, Ronald L.	(NY)	147
Medical & law online searching	BERK, Nancy G.	(AZ)	87
New Jersey school law	VAN BUSKIRK, Elisabeth L.	(NJ)	1272
New York law	WESTHUIS, Judith A.	(NY)	1327
Oregon library law	GINNANE, Mary J.	(OR)	437
Pennsylvania law	SMITH, Eugene J.	(PA)	1155
Personal injury law	KOEING, Sherman	(FL)	667
Petroleum & energy law	DUDLEY, Durand S.	(OH)	323
Planning & moving of law libraries	PLUNKET, Joy H.	(MA)	978
Police & law enforcement	RAMM, Dorothy V.	(IL)	1005
Police training & law enforcement	MERRYWEATHER, J M.	(ON)	827
Population law	HEACOCK, Pamela P.	(MA)	518
Prison law libraries	BOTTA, Jean C.	(NY)	118
Prisoner's access law	WARNER, Marnie M.	(MA)	1305
Private law firm administration	SCHIPPER, Joan A.	(CA)	1093
	KLEBBA, Lisa A.	(MO)	658
Private law firm consulting	PLUNKET, Joy H.	(MA)	978
Private law firms	GOLDMAN, Teri B.	(MO)	446
Private law libraries	WALLACE, Marie G.	(CA)	1297
Private law library	ROLLINS, James H.	(CA)	1051
	KOSLOSKE, Verleah B.	(DC)	672
Private law library management	KISSANE, Mary K.	(MO)	656
Professional reference law publications	HALPIN, Gerard B.	(ON)	490
Public access law	WARNER, Marnie M.	(MA)	1305
Public access to law	DUNN, Mary B.	(NY)	327
Public or private law	STAYNER, Delsie A.	(CA)	1183
Public services, law	BLAKE, Timothy J.	(LA)	103
Rare law books	BOYER, Larry M.	(DC)	123
	REES, Warren D.	(MN)	1016
Reference, law	KRIKORIAN, Rosanne	(CA)	678
	HEITZ, Kathleen R.	(GA)	523
Reference law librarian	BURGALASSI, Anthony J.	(NY)	159
Reorganizing law firm libraries	BYRNE, Jeanne M.	(TX)	169
Research in federal Indian law	HARRAGARRA WATERS, Deana J.	(CO)	503
Research in law	LAEUCHLI, Ann J.	(CT)	687
Scholarly law books	LUTTRELL, Jordan D.	(CA)	750
Setting up library systems in law firms	BYRNE, Jeanne M.	(TX)	169
Small law firms	WEZELMAN, Joy L.	(ND)	1328
Space planning of law libraries	WELKER, Kathy J.	(OH)	1321
Spanish law	GONZALEZ, Armando E.	(DC)	448
Sports & entertainment law	EDMONDS, Edmund P.	(VA)	336
Sports law	CHAMPION, Walter T.	(TX)	198
State agency law libraries	BOTTA, Jean C.	(NY)	118
Subject cataloging of law books	KREH, Fritz	(WGR)	677
Tax & securities law	DOWLING, Shelley L.	(DC)	316
Tax law	FISHER, Jean K.	(MA)	381
	HOWE, Paula E.	(TX)	565
Tax law reference	REID, Pauline	(NY)	1019
Tax law research	MAXON, William N.	(DC)	787
Technical services, law	LINNANE, Mary L.	(IL)	731
US Customs law research	MATTERA, Joseph J.	(NY)	785
United States law	WESTHUIS, Judith A.	(NY)	1327
Used law book sales	BROWN, G R.	(FL)	144
	KILLIAN, Mary C.	(MI)	648
Wisconsin law	BEMIS, Michael F.	(WI)	79
	PAUL, Sara J.	(WI)	949
Wisconsin library law	BAKER, Douglas	(WI)	48

LAYOUT (See also Design, Interiors, Remodeling, Renovation, Space)

Branch & regional library layouts	COBURN, Morton	(IL)	225
Branch library layout	BUFKIN, Anne G.	(FL)	155
Building layout & construction	NEAL, Robert L.	(MD)	890
Design, layout, copywriting	LAMBERT, Shirley A.	(CO)	690
Facility layout & planning	MURDOCH, Arthur W.	(ON)	879
Interior arrangement & layout	STORCK, Bernadette R.	(FL)	1198
Layout & planning	BAYLIS, Ted	(MA)	67
Layout of industrial libraries	RANDALL, Gordon E.	(GA)	1006
Library buildings & collection layout	BELGUM, Kathie G.	(IA)	76
Library layout & design	MCPHERSON, Kenneth F.	(NJ)	817
Library planning & layout consulting	WEINZIMMER, William A.	(NY)	1318
Library systems design & layout	AKS, Gloria	(NY)	9
Remodeling, renovation, furniture layout	WALSH, Robert R.	(NY)	1300

LEADERSHIP (See also Administration, Management)

Administrative leadership	GOULD, Douglas A.	(UT)	454
Association leadership	BOSTLEY, Jean R.	(MA)	117
Branch leadership	THOMAS, Louise V.	(MI)	1237
Executive leadership	MCKENZIE, Harry	(CA)	811
Leadership	HERSBERGER, Rodney M.	(CA)	533
Leadership & management	RIGGS, Donald E.	(AZ)	1034
Leadership development	SHERMAN, Mary A.	(OK)	1128
Leadership research	WALLS, Francine E.	(WA)	1299
Leadership training	SKELLEY, Cornelia A.	(WA)	1145
Organization & association leadership	BEDARD, Bernard J.	(PQ)	73

LEARNING (See also Education, Instructional, Library, Media)

Administration of learning resource ctr	BOOK, Imogene I.	(SC)	115
Adult education, lifelong learning	GANN, Daniel H.	(IN)	416
Adult independent learners	MCGRIFF, Mary E.	(NC)	808
Area health education learning resources	JOHN, Stephanie C.	(MI)	601
Art gallery outreach learning centers	PATTERSON, Grace L.	(NY)	948
Collection devlpmnt for lrng disabled	KEYS, Marshall	(MA)	645
Community college learning resources	KELLER, Jan K.	(CA)	635
	PERSON, Ruth J.	(PA)	961
Computer-assisted learning	OLIVE, J F.	(AL)	921
Computerized learning resources	STANKE, Judith U.	(MN)	1180
Distance learning	BIRMINGHAM, Frank R.	(MN)	98
Early childhood learning	WRIGHT-HESS, Anne H.	(NY)	1373
Education & industry learning material	LESURE, Alan B.	(NY)	718
Guidance for adult learners	O'HARA, Frederic J.	(NY)	919
Institutions of higher learning	WOLVSKY, Haya S.	(ISR)	1362
Learning center cataloging	KAWAGUCHI, Miyako	(VA)	632
Learning disabled library projects	WILLIAMS, Eve A.	(NB)	1343
Lrng resrch ctr mgmt & reorganization	MIAH, Abdul J.	(VA)	831
Learning resource center administration	BOROWSKI, Joseph F.	(IL)	117
Learning resource center col standards	BOOK, Imogene I.	(SC)	115
Learning resource centers	CARR, Charles E.	(AL)	185
Learning resource programs	CLARKE, Tobin D.	(CA)	219
Learning resource services	HISLE, W L.	(TX)	544
Learning resources	CODER, Ann	(CA)	226
	RONEY, Raymond G.	(CA)	1053
	SCHLATTER, M W.	(GA)	1093
	SORELL, Janice G.	(MN)	1168
	HAMMITT, Margaret R.	(NE)	493
	PONTIUS, Louise	(TX)	982
	SULLIVAN, Janice L.	(TX)	1207
	POLLOCK, Ethel L.	(VA)	981
Learning resources administration	BOONE, Morell D.	(MI)	115
	JASSAL, Raghbir S.	(NM)	595
Learning resources center	JOHNSON, Scott R.	(MS)	609
Learning resources center management	CAROL, Barbara B.	(OK)	184
Learning resources centers	FRIEDMAN, Arthur L.	(NY)	403
	ADAMS, Elaine P.	(TX)	4
Learning resources management	BERLING, John G.	(MN)	88
Learning resources programs	HUNSUCKER, David L.	(NC)	575
Library learning centers	FERRO-NYALKA, Ruth R.	(IL)	374
Lifelong learning	HEISER, Jane C.	(MD)	523
	SHIRK, John C.	(MN)	1131
Planning two-year learning resource ctr	BOOK, Imogene I.	(SC)	115
Public services learning for disabled	KEYS, Marshall	(MA)	645

LEARNING (Cont'd)

Research on cognitive learning	KOCHEN, Manfred	(MI)	667
School learning resource ctr consulting	GOTHIA, Blanche	(TX)	453
Telecommunications, distance learning	SCHABERT, Daniel R.	(NY)	1088

LECTURING (See also Speaking, Teaching)

Children's literature lecturing	BATES, Barbara S.	(PA)	63
Guest lecturer on various topics	SALVATORE, Gayle E.	(LA)	1078
Lecturer, school library service	MARSH, Martha M.	(KS)	773
Lecturing	WATERS, Marie B.	(CA)	1308
	ELLIOTT, Pirkko E.	(ENG)	344
Lecturing about folklore	MACDONALD, Margaret R.	(WA)	754
Lecturing & teaching	ROMAN, Susan	(IL)	1052
Lecturing in ethnic & gen bibliography	FISHER, Edith M.	(CA)	380
Lecturing on children's literature	VOLC, Judith G.	(CO)	1287
Province history, articles & lectures	STRECK, Helen T.	(KS)	1201
Teaching & lecturing library admin	GRIFFEN, Agnes M.	(MD)	468
Travel photography & lectures	PETERSON, Mildred O.	(IL)	964

LEDGERS

Historical recording ledgers	WOOD, Sallie B.	(NY)	1365

LEGAL (See also Law, Paralegal)

Acquisitions of legal materials	STOPPEL, Ellen K.	(IA)	1198
Advanced legal research	NISSENBAUM, Robert J.	(OH)	905
Automated legal research	GOTT, Gary D.	(ND)	453
	GREENBERG, Charles J.	(NY)	463
Business, advertising & legal research	FISHER, Daphne V.	(PA)	380
Business & legal bibliography	CRINION, Jacquelyn A.	(TX)	259
Business & legal library consulting	GIGANTE, Vickilyn M.	(MD)	433
Business & legal online database srchng	NICOL, Margaret W.	(NY)	903
Business & legal research	WHITTLESEY, Jane M.	(TX)	1334
Business reference & legal research	SEAMAN, Sally G.	(IL)	1109
California legal legislative materials	GOMEZ, Cheryl J.	(CA)	447
Cataloging legal materials	MITTAN, Rhonda L.	(CA)	850
	GULSTAD, Wilma B.	(MO)	477
	MITTEN, Lisa A.	(PA)	850
	NASSERDEN, Marilyn D.	(AB)	889
Cataloging of legal literature	ODSEN, Elizabeth R.	(AK)	917
Cataloging of legal materials	RUIZ-VALERA, Phoebe L.	(NY)	1067
Collection development & legal info	TOMCHYSHYN, Theresa M.	(SK)	1249
Collection development, legal	MOYER, Holley M.	(NJ)	874
Computer-assisted legal research	DOHERTY, Walter E.	(AZ)	309
	WIEBELHAUS, Richard J.	(AZ)	1336
	CASTETTER, Karla M.	(CA)	194
	GRIGST, Denise J.	(CA)	470
	JONES, Michael D.	(CA)	614
	MOORE, Gregory B.	(CA)	859
	WERNER, O J.	(CA)	1325
	WATERS, Sally G.	(FL)	1308
	GRIFFITH, Cary J.	(MN)	469
	ELAM, Kristy L.	(MO)	341
	COCHRAN, J W.	(MS)	225
	O'CONNOR, Sandra L.	(NC)	916
	DESMOND, Andrew R.	(NY)	295
	D'AMORE, Denice M.	(OH)	272
	HARVAN, Christine C.	(PA)	509
	SHAW, Ben B.	(TX)	1123
Computer-associated legal research	MOYER, Holley M.	(NJ)	874
Computer-based legal reference	HARBISON, John H.	(DC)	499
Computerization of legal information	HOLOCH, S A.	(OH)	553
Computerized legal research	ANDREWS, Sylvia L.	(IN)	27
	HANLEY, Thomas L.	(OH)	496
	SIMON, Dale	(OR)	1140
Computerized legal research instruction	STOPPEL, Ellen K.	(IA)	1198
Consumer, legal, & medical information	LEBRUN, Anne	(ON)	708
Copyright & legal issues in management	NASRI, William Z.	(PA)	888
Corporate & legal library development	WALSH, Joanna M.	(MA)	1299
Corporate legal research databases	MORRIS, Ann	(IL)	866

LEGAL (Cont'd)

Specialty	Name	State	Page
Descriptive cataloging, legal materials	HAWKINS, Sandra J.	(DC)	514
Editor of legal translations	SCHLACKS, Charles	(CA)	1093
Education & legal databases	MCLANE, Kathleen	(VA)	813
Facilitate legal procedures to court	SIENDA, Madeline M.	(WA)	1136
Federal legal material	MOSS, Karen M.	(MA)	872
Federal legal materials	EWING, Florence E.	(CA)	359
Foreign & international legal research	ARANDA-COODOU, Patricio	(DC)	30
Foreign legal materials	RAUCH, Anne	(NY)	1010
General & legal research	GIANNINI, Evelyn L.	(IL)	431
General legal, corporate & tax reference	RAUCH, Anne	(NY)	1010
General legal reference	REID, Pauline	(NY)	1019
German legal sources	MENZEL, William H.	(NY)	825
Government & legal information	JACOBS, Leslie R.	(MA)	589
Inmate legal library maintenance	SIENDA, Madeline M.	(WA)	1136
International & foreign legal literature	HEAD, Anita K.	(DC)	518
Law libraries, legal databases	WOLFE, Charles B.	(MI)	1360
Law schools, legal education	COYLE, Christopher B.	(OH)	253
Legal	SCHRIBER, James E.	(CA)	1100
	GIANGRANDE, Mark G.	(IL)	430
	GINDRA, Janice J.	(MO)	437
	DOKS, Vija	(NY)	309
Legal access litigation	WELCH, Steven J.	(IL)	1321
Legal administrative support systems	CROCKETT, Denise J.	(NY)	259
Legal affairs	INKELLIS, Barbara G.	(MD)	583
Legal aid	RYDEN, John	(IL)	1071
Legal & accounting library services	SMOTHERS, Alyce A.	(LA)	1162
Legal & accounting reference	ROESCH, Gay E.	(CO)	1049
Legal & business databases	HOLLINGSWORTH, Dena M.	(CA)	552
	BLUM, Elaine G.	(NY)	107
	ROBERTS, Ann B.	(VA)	1039
	MORRIS, Sandra M.	(ON)	867
Legal & business reference	GERIG, Reginald R.	(DC)	428
	ANES, Joy R.	(IL)	27
	HIBBELER, Sara J.	(MO)	536
Legal & business research	CAIN, Susan H.	(MA)	171
Legal & congressional databases	PULVER, Thomas B.	(DC)	997
Legal & general database searching	DUMAINE, Paul R.	(RI)	325
Legal & general reference	BRANN, Andrew R.	(OH)	128
Legal & general research	DUMAINE, Paul R.	(RI)	325
Legal & legislative databases	BARRETT, Lizabeth A.	(NY)	59
Legal & medical databases	HENRY, Nancy J.	(IL)	529
	ENGLE, Madge	(IN)	349
Legal & non-legal databases	ASMUTH, Gretchen W.	(DC)	36
	BURKHART, Sue W.	(GA)	161
	RODAWALT, Valarie J.	(TX)	1046
Legal & non-legal research & reference	BENNIN, Cheryl S.	(NY)	82
Legal & political studies	NGUYEN, Vy K.	(PQ)	901
Legal & reserve book circulation	DINDAYAL, Joyce S.	(NY)	304
Legal & tax publications	FLEMING, Jack C.	(ON)	384
Legal assistance	WEISBAUM, Earl	(TX)	1319
Legal bibliographic instruction	CHERRY, Anna M.	(MN)	206
Legal bibliographical instruction	LANGSTON, Sally J.	(TX)	696
Legal bibliographies	SURRENCY, Erwin C.	(GA)	1210
Legal bibliographies & databases	KAVASS, Igor I.	(TN)	631
Legal bibliography	BRIDGMAN, David L.	(CA)	135
	SULLIVAN, Martha J.	(CT)	1208
	GEHRINGER, Susanne E.	(DC)	425
	WOODARD, Joseph L.	(FL)	1365
	KLINK, Carol A.	(IL)	662
	ENSIGN, David J.	(KS)	350
	COOPER, Byron D.	(MI)	242
	BOMARC, M D.	(NC)	113
	GOTT, Gary D.	(ND)	453
	ANTHONY, Donald C.	(NY)	28
	HAMMOND, Jane L.	(NY)	493
	KLECKNER, Simone M.	(NY)	658
	MOREHEAD, Joe	(NY)	863
	RICHERT, Paul	(OH)	1030
	GLOECKNER, Paul B.	(PA)	441
	KERCHOF, Kathryn K.	(PA)	643
	CROSS, Joseph R.	(SC)	260
	HOOD, Lawrence E.	(TX)	556
	TEMPLETON, Virginia E.	(TX)	1231
	WALTER, Raimund E.	(WGR)	1300
Legal bibliography, rare books	TRIFFIN, Nicholas	(NY)	1256

LEGAL (Cont'd)

Specialty	Name	State	Page
Legal bibliography reference	NELSON, Mary A.	(MO)	894
Legal, business & general reference	WAY, Kathy A.	(CA)	1311
Legal cataloging, monographs	WOODS, Frances B.	(CT)	1367
Legal citation form	NISSENBAUM, Robert J.	(OH)	905
Legal databases	ALFONSI-GIN, Mary A.	(IL)	13
Legal deposition, evidentiary data	SCHULTZ, Arnold J.	(MN)	1101
Legal education	PETERSON, Randall T.	(IL)	964
	HOLOCH, S A.	(OH)	553
Legal filing	O'BRIEN, Doris J.	(CT)	914
Legal history	COOPER, Byron D.	(MI)	242
	BAGNALL, Whitney S.	(NY)	45
Legal indexing	RODICH, Lorraine E.	(CA)	1047
	THOMPSON, Johanna W.	(DC)	1240
	DAVIS, Yvonne M.	(OH)	281
Legal information	KANJI, Zainab J.	(CA)	625
	JOHNSON, John R.	(OH)	606
	ANDERSON, Axel R.	(WI)	21
Legal information & reference work	OREJANA, Rebecca D.	(PHP)	925
Legal information databases	WEGMANN, Pamela A.	(TX)	1316
Legal information management	COMSTOCK, Daniel L.	(NM)	235
Legal information marketing	HALL, Brian H.	(CO)	487
Legal information publishing	HALL, Brian H.	(CO)	487
Legal information retrieval education	BARBEN, Tanya A.	(SAF)	55
Legal information services	CARROLL, Hardy	(MI)	187
	ASTON, Jennefer	(IRE)	37
Legal information systems	STERN, Michael P.	(MD)	1189
Legal instruction	HUGHES, John M.	(CT)	571
Legal, legislative & regulatory database	JOHNSON, Jacqueline B.	(DC)	605
Legal legislative research	BRESLIN, Ellen R.	(NY)	133
Legal librarianship	BESTE, Ian R.	(CA)	92
	CAMPAGNA, Roxane R.	(NY)	175
Legal library management administration	HERNANDEZ, Marilyn J.	(MB)	531
Legal literature	ROFF, Jill R.	(MA)	1049
	GOLDMAN, Martha A.	(NY)	445
	ROJAS, Alexandra A.	(NY)	1051
Legal material cataloging	HILLMANN, Diane I.	(NY)	541
Legal materials	WANG, Connie	(CA)	1302
	DOWLER, John W.	(FL)	315
	FISHER, Scott L.	(NJ)	381
	CHUNG, Catherine A.	(VA)	213
	DUFFUS, Sylvia J.	(AB)	323
Legal materials cataloging	IOANID, Aurora S.	(NY)	583
	ROSENFELD, Joseph S.	(OH)	1056
Legal materials selection	TENOR, Randell B.	(PA)	1231
Legal, medical & financial databases	LEVEROCK, Lisa A.	(NJ)	719
Legal, medical, corporate printer	SCULLIN, Frank E.	(PA)	1109
Legal methods	BOMARC, M D.	(NC)	113
Legal periodicals	CRAWFORD, Nola N.	(NJ)	257
Legal printing & publishing	ARNSDORF, Dennis A.	(DC)	34
Legal publishing	DEGLER, Stanley E.	(DC)	287
	KLAUS, Roger D.	(IL)	658
	DESMOND, Andrew R.	(NY)	295
	CUSWORTH, George R.	(ENG)	267
Legal publishing & databases	COLBORN, Robert J.	(MD)	230
Legal publishing & indexing	SHERRILL, Jocelyn T.	(NY)	1129
Legal records	MCREYNOLDS, R M.	(DC)	818
Legal records systems	KANE, Dorothea S.	(VA)	624
Legal reference	LEWIS, Timothy A.	(AL)	724
	MAYS, Allison P.	(AR)	791
	FRIEDMAN, Zena K.	(AZ)	404
	OLEARY, Jennie L.	(AZ)	920
	SCHNEIDER, Elizabeth K.	(AZ)	1097
	CHICK, Cynthia L.	(CA)	208
	FRIEDRICH, Barbara J.	(CA)	404
	JEROME, Michael S.	(CA)	599
	KARR, Linda	(CA)	628
	KAWAMOTO, Chizuko	(CA)	632
	KUCZMA, Michelle	(CA)	682
	LAMARTINE, Elisabeth A.	(CA)	689
	OPPENHEIM, Michael R.	(CA)	925
	PALMER, Catherine C.	(CA)	936
	PAPERMASTER, Cynthia L.	(CA)	939
	PERITORE, Laura D.	(CA)	958
	SHOSTROM, Marian L.	(CA)	1133
	STAHL, Ramona J.	(CA)	1178
	STREIKER, Susan L.	(CA)	1201

LEGAL (Cont'd)
Legal reference

WHISMAN, Linda A. ... (CA) 1329
BINTLIFF, Barbara A. ... (CO)   97
FAAS, Caroline .... (CT) 360
JERNIGAN, Denise D. .. (CT) 599
SATTERLUND, Lisa L. ... (CT) 1084
BAXTER, Janet G. ..... (DC)   67
CAREY, Marsha C. ..... (DC) 181
CILIBERTI, Nancy A. ... (DC) 214
DOWLING, Shelley L. ... (DC) 316
ERICSON, Richard J. ... (DC) 353
KAHN, Victoria .... (DC) 622
LARSEN, Lynda L. ..... (DC) 698
LOCKWOOD, David J. ... (DC) 736
MAXON, William N. ..... (DC) 787
RUGE, Audrey L. ...... (DC) 1066
SMITH, Clara M. ...... (DC) 1153
DANIELS, Westwell R. .. (FL) 273
GEBET, Russell W. .... (FL) 424
MELNICOVE, Annette R.   (FL) 823
MORRIS, Steve R. ..... (FL) 867
SMITH, Mary D. .... (FL) 1158
WATERS, Sally G. ..... (FL) 1308
CAMBELL, Miriam A. ... (GA) 174
TUTTLE, Jane S. ...... (GA) 1265
WONG, Irene K. .... (HI) 1362
BAUMANN, Walter R. .. (IL)   66
COLLINS, Janet .... (IL) 232
EMRE, Serpil A. ...... (IL) 348
HOUDEK, Frank G. ..... (IL) 562
LEWIS, Sherman L. .... (IL) 724
WLEKLINSKI, William A.   (IL) 1359
MATTS, Constance .... (IN) 786
WATTS, Tim J. .... (IN) 1310
BREDEMEYER, Carol ... (KY) 131
DUGGAN, James E. .... (LA) 324
TOWLES, Anne S. ..... (LA) 1252
CLOUGH, Linda F. ..... (MA) 223
RANDALL, Kristie C. ... (MA) 1006
RONEN, Naomi .... (MA) 1053
AMATRUDA, William T. . (MD)   19
DULL, Karen A. .... (MD) 324
HOLDEN, Nancy K. .... (MD) 550
SPIVEY, Lynne G. ..... (MD) 1175
BRAITHWAITE, Heather J. (MI) 127
REES, Warren D. ...... (MN) 1016
ELAM, Kristy L. .... (MO) 341
GREGORY, Kirk .... (MO) 466
MILLES, James G. ..... (MO) 843
COHEN, Edward S. .... (NC) 228
DUVAL, Barbara C. .... (NC) 329
WILLIAMS, Lisa W. .... (NC) 1344
FORSMAN, Avis B. .... (NE) 391
GENDLER, Carol J. .... (NE) 426
CRAWFORD, Nola N. ... (NJ) 257
LITTLE, Rosemary A. ... (NJ) 734
SCHRIEK, Robert W. ... (NJ) 1100
SEADER, Jane M. ..... (NJ) 1109
MORLEY, Sarah K. .... (NM) 865
SOUTHWICK, Susan A. . (NV) 1170
ADAMO, Marilyn H. .... (NY)   4
ALIFANO, Alison F. .... (NY)   13
ARMSTRONG, Joanne D. (NY)   32
BARRETT, Lizabeth A. ... (NY)   59
BERGER, Paula E. ..... (NY)   86
BRILL, Krista C. .... (NY) 136
COOPER, Jo E. .... (NY) 243
DONG, Alvin L. .... (NY) 311
JAROSEK, Joan E. .... (NY) 594
KASPAR, Eileen .... (NY) 629
KJOLSTAD-ERLANDSSO-
   N, Britt S. .... (NY) 657
SAHLEM, James R. .... (NY) 1075
WIERZBA, Christine .... (NY) 1337
WILLIAMS, David W. ... (NY) 1342
FISHER, Jo A. .... (OH) 381
GREEN, Lynda C. ..... (OH) 462
VOELKER, James R. ... (OH) 1286
KANE, Kathy .... (OK) 625

LEGAL (Cont'd)
Legal reference

PIPER, Larry W. .... (OR) 975
ARMSTRONG, Nancy A. . (PA)   32
BERGER, Joellen ...... (PA)   85
MAST, Joanne .... (PA) 782
SCHAEFER, John A. ... (PA) 1089
SPIVACK, Amy D. ..... (PA) 1175
STEWART, Barbara R. ... (PA) 1192
SWARTHOUT, Judy L. ... (PA) 1214
VARGAS, Gwen S. ..... (PA) 1278
WEINGRAM, Ida ...... (PA) 1318
TORRES-TAPI, Manual A.   (PR) 1251
ALEXANDER, Jacqueline
   P. .... (RI)   12
GATES, Diane E. ...... (TX) 421
GRUBEN, Karl T. ...... (TX) 474
LANGSTON, Sally J. ... (TX) 696
TEMPLETON, Virginia E.   (TX) 1231
TRAFFORD, Susan M. .. (TX) 1253
BISSETT, John P. ..... (VA) 100
LIEBERMAN, Sharon A. . (VA) 726
SAUR, Cindy S. .... (VA) 1085
HARBOLD, Mary J. ..... (WA) 499
KOSLOV, Marcia J. .... (WI) 672

Legal reference & management
Legal reference & research

HARBISON, John H. ... (DC) 499
LEVINE, Patricia M. ..... (AL) 720
NORBIE, Dorothy E. .... (CO) 908
BARNUM, Deborah C. ... (CT)   58
BROQUE, Suzanne .... (CT) 141
LUBIN, Joan S. .... (CT) 745
MATTHEWSON, David S. (CT) 786
HOTCHKISS, Mary A. ... (DC) 562
AUSTIN, John R. ...... (IL)   40
NYBERG, Cheryl R. .... (IL) 912
MAZZEI, Peter J. ...... (NJ) 791
JACKSON, George R. .. (OH) 587

Legal reference service
COLOKATHIS, Jane ... (MN) 234
VIGLIATURO, Kristy .... (MO) 1284

Legal reference services
KING, Kamla J. .... (DC) 651
SHEINWALD, Franette .. (NY) 1125
WEILANT, Edward ..... (OH) 1317
COTE, Carolee T. ...... (TX) 249
WARREN, Gail .... (VA) 1306

Legal references & databases
FOSKO, Maureen E. .... (NJ) 392
Legal research
ALCORN, Marianne S. ... (AZ)   11
WHITE, Edward H. ..... (AZ) 1330
BERRING, Robert C. ... (CA)   90
BIRNIE, Elizabeth B. ..... (CA)   98
BRAZIL, Lynne E. ...... (CA) 130
GINSBURG, Helen W. .. (CA) 438
GRIGST, Denise J. ..... (CA) 470
HENKE, Dan .... (CA) 528
HOLLINGSWORTH, Dena
   M. .... (CA) 552
HUSTON, Esther L. .... (CA) 578
LEWIS, Alfred J. .... (CA) 722
LEWIS, Cookie A. ..... (CA) 722
MACLEOD, June F. .... (CA) 757
OPPEDAL, Teresa A. .. (CA) 925
ROBERT, Berring C. .... (CA) 1039
RODICH, Lorraine E. ... (CA) 1047
ROLLINS, James H. .... (CA) 1051
RUNYON, Judith A. .... (CA) 1067
SMITH, Catherine M. ... (CA) 1153
SMITH, Susan A. ...... (CA) 1161
STROMME, Gary L. .... (CA) 1203
TAYLOR, Susan E. .... (CA) 1228
TRIVISON, Margaret A. . (CA) 1257
WEBB, Gayle E. .... (CA) 1313
WINSON, Gail I. .... (CA) 1355
CALVERT, Lois M. ..... (CO) 174
COCO, Al .... (CO) 226
BURKE, Jane D. ...... (CT) 160
COHEN, Morris L. ..... (CT) 228
MARIANI, Carolyn A. ... (CT) 770
DURAKO, Frances G. ... (DC) 328
GEHRINGER, Susanne E. (DC) 425
MCDERMOTT, Patricia M. (DC) 802
NEVIN, Barbara B. ..... (DC) 898

LEGAL (Cont'd)
Legal research

NORRIS, Loretta W.	(DC)	909
PACIFICI, Sabrina I.	(DC)	933
STOCKTON, Sue T.	(DC)	1196
THOMPSON, Johanna W.	(DC)	1240
WOLFE, Susan J.	(DC)	1361
EFRON, Muriel C.	(FL)	338
OVERSTREET, Allen J. .	(FL)	931
TAYLOR, Betty W.	(FL)	1226
WOLFE, Bardie C.	(FL)	1360
BAUSCH, Donna K.	(GA)	67
COOPER, Glenn	(GA)	243
GROOVER, Marion D. . .	(GA)	472
GUERIN, Roberta T.	(GA)	476
WEINGARTH, Darlene . .	(GU)	1318
REED, Carol R.	(HI)	1014
DONAHUE, Karin V.	(IL)	310
DOYLE, Francis R.	(IL)	317
FREY, Roxanne C.	(IL)	403
HUTCHINS, Richard G. .	(IL)	579
MARTIN, Bennie E.	(IL)	775
PERSYN, Mary G.	(IN)	961
CONNOR, Lynn S.	(KY)	238
GILMER, Wesley	(KY)	437
DULEY, Kay E.	(LA)	324
FISHER, Collette J.	(LA)	380
DUCKETT, Joan	(MA)	322
HAYES, Alison M.	(MA)	515
LAMBERT, Lyn D.	(MA)	690
MCLELLAN, Mary T. . . .	(MA)	814
CAMILLO, Janet H.	(MD)	175
BONGE, Barbara M.	(MI)	114
KONDAK, Ann	(MI)	670
TURNER, Ann S.	(MN)	1264
GIBSON, Helen R.	(MO)	432
HUNT, Lori A.	(MO)	575
KLEBBA, Lisa A.	(MO)	658
MCKENZIE, Elizabeth M.	(MO)	811
SCHELL, Rosalie F.	(MO)	1091
STRAUSE, Robert C. . . .	(MO)	1200
TEANEY, Carol R.	(MO)	1229
WHITE, Cheryl L.	(MO)	1330
WEST, Carol C.	(MS)	1326
GASAWAY, Laura N. . . .	(NC)	421
HANNUM-MCPHERSON,		
Melissa A.	(NC)	497
MURPHY, Malinda M. . . .	(NC)	881
WEZELMAN, Joy L.	(ND)	1328
LOMAX, Anne M.	(NE)	738
ERBE, Evalina S.	(NJ)	352
GORDON, Kaye B.	(NJ)	451
BEJNAR, Thaddeus P. . .	(NM)	75
MCGOEY, Richard P. . . .	(NM)	807
MORGAN, James E.	(NV)	864
BERNSTEIN, Mark P. . . .	(NY)	89
CARTAFALSA, Joan C. . .	(NY)	188
CHICCO, Giuliano	(NY)	208
COLE, Charles D.	(NY)	230
CURCI, Lucy	(NY)	265
DAVENPORT, Margaret J.	(NY)	275
DIGIOVANNA, Josephine		
A.	(NY)	303
GRECH, Anthony P.	(NY)	461
HAYWARD, Diane J.	(NY)	517
KUPERMAN, Aaron W. . .	(NY)	684
LASKOWITZ, Roberta G. .	(NY)	700
LILLY, Elise M.	(NY)	727
LOCKE, William G.	(NY)	736
MANN, Amy S.	(NY)	765
NEWMAN, Marie S.	(NY)	899
O'GRADY, Jean P.	(NY)	918
PAGEL, Scott B.	(NY)	934
PINSLEY, Lauren J.	(NY)	975
RAUM, Tamar	(NY)	1010
VAJDA, Carolyn M.	(NY)	1271
CHRISTY, Patricia A. . . .	(OH)	212
GILL, Judith L.	(OH)	435
HOLOCH, S A.	(OH)	553
LEONARD, James	(OH)	716

LEGAL (Cont'd)
Legal research

MCFARLAND, Anne S. . .	(OH)	804
ORLANDO, Jacqueline M.	(OH)	926
SPOHR, Cynthia L.	(OH)	1175
WERNERSBACH,		
Geraldine S.	(OH)	1325
CORNEIL, Charlotte E. . .	(OK)	246
DUCEY, Richard E.	(OK)	322
BAUER, Marilyn A.	(OR)	65
DAVID, Kay O.	(OR)	276
ARMSTRONG, Nancy A. .	(PA)	32
BEYER, Robyn L.	(PA)	93
HORVATH, Patricia M. . .	(PA)	561
REGUEIRO, Judith E. . . .	(PA)	1017
SILVERMAN, Marc B. . . .	(PA)	1138
SULZER, John H.	(PA)	1209
SABATER-SOLA, Rigel .	(PR)	1072
LABEDZ, Elizabeth K. . . .	(RI)	686
BARKAN, Steven M.	(TX)	56
BLACK, Elizabeth A.	(TX)	101
CHAMPION, Walter T. . . .	(TX)	198
CORBIN, John	(TX)	245
GARDNER, Linda	(TX)	418
GILBERT, Barry	(TX)	433
HAMBLETON, James E. .	(TX)	490
HOUSTON, Barbara B. . .	(TX)	563
MAGNER, Mary F.	(TX)	759
OLM, Jane G.	(TX)	921
PARKER, David F.	(TX)	941
TRANFAGLIA, Twyla L. .	(TX)	1254
CALHOUN, Clayne M. . . .	(VA)	172
SCHAEFER, Mary E. . . .	(VA)	1089
TOSIANO, Barbara A. . . .	(VA)	1252
ABAZARNIA, Diane B. . .	(VT)	1
LAWSON, Annetta	(WA)	705
PERLSON, Beverly J. . . .	(WI)	959
ESKRIDGE, Virginia C. . .	(WV)	354
DEYOUNG, Marie	(NS)	298
HEARDER-MOAN, Wendy		
P.	(ON)	518
ARAJ, Houda	(PQ)	30
TANGUAY, Guy	(PQ)	1222
SAKAMOTO, Hiroshi . . .	(JAP)	1076
RUNGSANG, Rebecca J.	(THA)	1067

Legal research & bibliography

SCHANCK, Peter C. . . .	(KS)	1090

Legal research & compliance

KNARZER, Arlene	(IL)	663

Legal research & database searching

ELAM, Joice B.	(GA)	341

Legal research & databases

HEINEN, Margaret A. . . .	(MI)	522
EDMONDS, Edmund P. .	(VA)	336

Legal research & material

FOWLES, Alison C.	(PQ)	394

Legal research & reference

MAYERS, Karen A.	(CA)	789
VEGA, Carolyn L.	(CA)	1281
HUGHES, John M.	(CT)	571
NEWTON, Stephanne K.	(DC)	900
EICHER, Thomas E.	(IA)	339
SHAPIRO, Fred R.	(NY)	1121
TRIFFIN, Nicholas	(NY)	1256
SUHRE, Carol A.	(OH)	1207
PARTIN, Gail A.	(PA)	945
BULERIN-LUGO, Josefina	(PR)	156

Legal research & resources management

Legal research & teaching

Legal research & writing

DEMPSEY, Pamela M. . .	(NM)	291
PIERCE, Ann E.	(ME)	971
BRIDGMAN, David L. . . .	(CA)	135
KRIKORIAN, Rosanne . .	(CA)	678
EDWARDS, John D.	(IA)	337
POINTON, Louis R.	(IL)	980
COCHRAN, J W.	(MS)	225
COGGINS, Timothy L. . .	(NC)	227
GIANNATTASI, Gerard E.	(NY)	430
HANLEY, Thomas L. . . .	(OH)	496

Legal research & writing teaching

MURRAY, James M. . . .	(WA)	882

Legal research assistance

GERLOTT, Eleanor L. . . .	(PA)	429

Legal research, bibliography

DUNCAN, Rebecca	(CA)	325

Legal research curriculum

COYLE, Christopher B. . .	(OH)	253

Legal research in international law

KLECKNER, Simone M. .	(NY)	658

LEGAL (Cont'd)

Legal research instruction	CASTETTER, Karla M. . .	(CA)	194
	STREIKER, Susan L. . . .	(CA)	1201
	BRENNAN, Edward P. . .	(MD)	132
	BAUM, Marsha L.	(MN)	66
	LEITER, Richard A.	(NE)	714
	KENNEDY, Bruce M. . . .	(NY)	640
	KOSTER, Gregory E. . . .	(NY)	673
	ZUBROW, Marcia L. . . .	(NY)	1391
Legal research, LEXIS	PATTELA, Rao R.	(PA)	947
Legal research reference	REYNOLDS, Diane C. . .	(CA)	1025
Legal research, reference & writing	KISSANE, Mary K.	(MO)	656
Legal research reference online manual	VON PFEIL, Helena P. . .	(DC)	1288
Legal research retrieval systems	EVERLOVE, Nora J. . . .	(FL)	359
Legal research teaching	PREBLE, Leverett L.	(DC)	990
Legal research training	SHEAR, Joan A.	(MA)	1124
Legal research training & development	COYLE, Christopher B. . .	(OH)	253
Legal resources for non-lawyers	EWING, Florence E. . . .	(CA)	359
Legal serials cataloging	WOODS, Frances B. . . .	(CT)	1367
Legal serials management	GOLIAN, Linda M.	(FL)	447
Legal services	CREWS, Kenneth D. . . .	(CA)	258
	KEENON, Una H.	(OH)	634
Legal software	GRIFFITH, Cary J.	(MN)	469
Legal training & development	STEELE, Tom M.	(NC)	1184
Legal writing	WEST, Carol C.	(MS)	1326
	LEONARD, James	(OH)	716
	MCFARLAND, Anne S. . .	(OH)	804
Legislative & legal reference	BROWNE, Lynda S.	(DC)	148
	QUINN, Karen H.	(RI)	1000
Medical & legal research	BEDARD, Evelyn M.	(TX)	73
New Hampshire legal materials	RINDEN, Constance T. . .	(NH)	1035
New York legal research	MOLINARI, Joseph G. . .	(NY)	853
Online legal indexing compilation	WONG, Patricia M.	(CA)	1363
Online legal research	SKRUKRUD, Nora L. . . .	(CA)	1147
	CALVERT, Lois M.	(CO)	174
	ROSS, Margery M.	(DC)	1058
Online legal research services	WEBSTER, Deborah K. . .	(NC)	1314
Online medical & legal systems	MORRIS, Timothy J.	(DC)	867
Online searching legal	WELSH, Eric L.	(VA)	1323
Personal computer software, legal forms	KUEHNLE, Emery C. . . .	(OH)	682
Preparing indexes & legal reference	HOYT, Henry M.	(NY)	566
Public legal education	HEBDITCH, Suzan A. . . .	(AB)	519
Public legal information & education	TOMCHYSHYN, Theresa M.	(SK)	1249
Publisher of legal translations	SCHLACKS, Charles . . .	(CA)	1093
Quebec legal bibliography	TANGUAY, Guy	(PQ)	1222
Reference & legal research	TATELMAN, Susan D. . .	(MA)	1225
	HAASE, Gretchen E. . . .	(MN)	480
Researcher of legal translations	SCHLACKS, Charles . . .	(CA)	1093
Space planning, legal	MOYER, Holley M.	(NJ)	874
Teaching legal research	FOSTER, Lynn	(AR)	392
Teaching legal research skills	WHISMAN, Linda A. . . .	(CA)	1329
	WELKER, Kathy J.	(OH)	1321
Training & development, legal research	MCGUIRL, Marlene C. . .	(DC)	808
United States legal research	ARANDA-COODOU, Patricio	(DC)	30

LEGAL DATABASES (See also Law, LEXIS)

Business & law databases	KUMAR, C S.	(NY)	684
Business & legal databases	ZYGMONT, Carolyn A. . .	(CT)	1392
	RYAN, James J.	(NY)	1071
Corporate & legal databases	HUNE, Mary G.	(OH)	574
Government & legal database development	YODER, Susan M.	(CA)	1380
Law & legal databases	SHOSTROM, Marian L. .	(CA)	1133
	STEARNS, Barry T.	(MA)	1183
Legal database	THOMPSON, James A. . .	(CA)	1239
	TAYLOR, Terry S.	(IL)	1229
Legal database instruction	CHERRY, Anna M.	(MN)	206
	HILL, Ruth J.	(TN)	540
Legal database instruction & searching	ESKRIDGE, Virginia C. . .	(WV)	354
Legal database publishing	STERN, Michael P.	(MD)	1189
Legal database research	CINQUE, Douglas V. . . .	(NY)	214
	ROCKWOOD, Susan M. .	(PA)	1046

LEGAL DATABASES (Cont'd)

Legal database researcher	WOODRUFF, Brenda B. . .	(OH)	1366
Legal database searches	TUTTLE, Jane S.	(GA)	1265
Legal database searching	RODICH, Lorraine E. . . .	(CA)	1047
	RUGE, Audrey L.	(DC)	1066
	DULEY, Kay E.	(LA)	324
	CHERRY, Anna M.	(MN)	206
	KENNEDY, Bruce M. . . .	(NY)	640
	WYNNE, Joseph J.	(VA)	1375
Legal database searching & training	KAUL, Kanhya L.	(MI)	631
Legal database set up	AMNOTTE, Celine	(PQ)	20
Legal databases	LEWIS, Timothy A.	(AL)	724
	LOWE, David	(AL)	743
	ALCORN, Marianne S. . .	(AZ)	11
	ANNAND, Stewart S. . . .	(CA)	28
	BOOTH, Barbara A.	(CA)	116
	BRIDGMAN, David L. . . .	(CA)	135
	HOOD, Mary D.	(CA)	556
	JEROME, Michael S. . . .	(CA)	599
	LEWIS, Alfred J.	(CA)	722
	SARRAINO, Kathleen A. .	(CA)	1083
	TAYLOR, Susan E.	(CA)	1228
	WALLACE, Marie G.	(CA)	1297
	WEBB, Duncan C.	(CA)	1313
	BINTLIFF, Barbara A. . . .	(CO)	97
	ESTES, Mark E.	(CO)	355
	LUBIN, Joan S.	(CT)	745
	DURAKO, Frances G. . . .	(DC)	328
	LATEGOLO, Meldie A. . .	(DC)	701
	MOTEN, Derryn E.	(DC)	872
	NEWTON, Stephanne K. .	(DC)	900
	QUINN, Susan	(DC)	1000
	DANIELS, Westwell R. . .	(FL)	273
	EFRON, Muriel C.	(FL)	338
	PRITCHARD, Teresa N. . .	(FL)	994
	HEITZ, Kathleen R.	(GA)	523
	WEINGARTH, Darlene . .	(GU)	1318
	EDWARDS, John D.	(IA)	337
	DRAKE, Francis L.	(IL)	318
	FINNER, Susan L.	(IL)	378
	HARRINGTON, Margaret V.	(IL)	504
	HUXSAW, Charles F. . . .	(IL)	580
	JUSTIE, Julie H.	(IL)	620
	KAUFFMAN, S B.	(IL)	631
	KRUPKA, Karen K.	(IL)	680
	LEWIS, Sherman L.	(IL)	724
	PATTERSON, Patricia A. .	(IL)	948
	OVERSHINER, Barbara A.	(IN)	931
	RIES, Steven T.	(IN)	1033
	SCHMIDT, Paula O.	(IN)	1095
	ANDERSON, Patricia E. .	(KY)	25
	BREDEMEYER, Carol . .	(KY)	131
	FOGLE, Dianna L.	(KY)	387
	SELMER, Sylvia A.	(KY)	1114
	DUGGAN, James E.	(LA)	324
	SHULL, Janice K.	(LA)	1133
	HAYES, Alison M.	(MA)	515
	HILL, Byron C.	(MA)	539
	SHEAR, Joan A.	(MA)	1124
	SWANN, Thomas E.	(MA)	1213
	WALLAS, Philip R.	(MA)	1298
	HARRIS, Helen Y.	(MD)	504
	BRAITHWAITE, Heather J.	(MI)	127
	MASLOW, Linda S.	(MI)	780
	SELBERG, Janice K. . . .	(MI)	1113
	ANDERSON, Anita M. . .	(MN)	21
	MINOR, Barbara G.	(MN)	846
	TURNER, Ann S.	(MN)	1264
	COURT, Patricia	(MO)	251
	KLEBBA, Lisa A.	(MO)	658
	MILLES, James O.	(MO)	843
	VIGLIATURO, Kristy	(MO)	1284
	AHLERS, Glen P.	(NC)	8
	STEELE, Tom M.	(NC)	1184
	LOMAX, Anne M.	(NE)	738
	BERNSTEIN, Mark P. . . .	(NY)	89
	DESMOND, Andrew R. . .	(NY)	295
	LASTRES, Steven A. . . .	(NY)	701
	LEWIS, Anne	(NY)	722

LEGAL DATABASES (Cont'd)
Legal databases

MENZEL, William H.	(NY)	825
NEWMAN, Marie S.	(NY)	899
OHMAN, Elisabeth T.	(NY)	919
SHAPIRO, Fred R.	(NY)	1121
CHRISTIAN, Patricia A.	(OH)	211
JACKSON, George R.	(OH)	587
LONG, Clare S.	(OH)	739
SCOTT, Melvia A.	(OH)	1107
CLAYTON, Mary E.	(OR)	220
DAVID, Kay O.	(OR)	276
DRIEHAUS, Rosemary H.	(PA)	320
HORVATH, Patricia M.	(PA)	561
ORSAG, Ann	(PA)	927
PARTIN, Gail A.	(PA)	945
SCHAEFER, John A.	(PA)	1089
STEWART, Barbara R.	(PA)	1192
SWARTHOUT, Judy L.	(PA)	1214
VARGAS, Gwen S.	(PA)	1278
WEINGRAM, Ida	(PA)	1318
LABEDZ, Elizabeth K.	(RI)	686
GILBERT, Barry	(TX)	433
GRIMES, Carolyn E.	(TX)	470
GRIMES, John F.	(TX)	470
JETER, Ann H.	(TX)	600
KORKMAS, Carolyn C.	(TX)	671
LANGSTON, Sally J.	(TX)	696
MCDONALD, Brenda D.	(TX)	802
O'MARA, Joan	(TX)	923
TRAFFORD, Susan M.	(TX)	1253
HUMMEL, Patricia A.	(UT)	573
MURPHY, Robert D.	(VA)	881
SAUR, Cindy S.	(VA)	1085
ABAZARNIA, Diane B.	(VT)	1
HAZELTON, Penelope A.	(WA)	517
MENANTEAUX, A R.	(WA)	823
JANKOWSKI, Susan H.	(WI)	593
PAUL, Nancy A.	(WI)	949
PETERSON, Christine E.	(WI)	963
BURMAN, Marilyn P.	(WY)	161
ARAJ, Houda	(PQ)	30
DENIGER, Constant	(PQ)	292
HAGOPIAN, Shake	(PQ)	483

Legal databases, LEXIS & Westlaw	MURPHY, Malinda M.	(NC)	881
Legal databases training	STREIKER, Susan L.	(CA)	1201
Legal databases, Westlaw, LEXIS	SWAN, Christine H.	(PA)	1213
Medical & legal databases	MARTIN, Laquita V.	(TN)	777
Online legal database	KERN, Sharon P.	(IA)	643
Online legal databases	HASKO, John J.	(NY)	510
Private legal database indexing	LEVINTON, Juliette	(NY)	721
Reference & legal databases	BONADIA, Roseann	(NY)	113
Reference, legal databases	BLOUGH, Keith A.	(OH)	106
Research legal databases	WOOD, Elizabeth B.	(OH)	1364

LEGISLATION (See also Law, Legislative, Parliamentary)

Advocate library legislation	BEARD, Charles E.	(GA)	69
Federal & state library legislation	HICKS, Frederick M.	(IL)	537
Federal legislation regarding libraries	COOKE, Eileen D.	(DC)	241
Law & legislation reference	ROCHE, Richard G.	(IL)	1046
Legislation	DUFFY, Brenda F.	(DC)	324
	FLEMING, Thomas B.	(DC)	384
	BUSTETTER, Stanley R.	(FL)	166
	BOLEF, Doris	(IL)	112
	BROWN, Eva R.	(IL)	143
	MCENANY, Arthur E.	(LA)	804
	SABATINI, Joseph D.	(NM)	1072
	SCOLES, Clyde S.	(OH)	1106
	BURGESS, Dean	(VA)	159
	SHILL, Harold B.	(WV)	1130
Legislation & funding	RAPHAEL, Mary E.	(DC)	1008
Legislation & lobbying	BENN, James R.	(CT)	81
Legislature	SELLERS, Wayne C.	(TX)	1114
Library law & legislation	LADENSON, Alex	(IL)	687
Library legislation	HELLUM-BERMAN, Bertha D.	(CA)	524
	FORSEE, Joe B.	(GA)	391
	MILLER, Melanie A.	(KS)	841
	MARGOLIS, Bernard A.	(MI)	770

LEGISLATION (Cont'd)
Library legislation

	ASP, William G.	(MN)	37
	SHUBERT, Joseph F.	(NY)	1133
	COLEMAN, Judith	(OH)	231
	CASINI, Barbara P.	(PA)	192
	GIACOMA, Pete J.	(UT)	430
	BEWLEY, Lois M.	(BC)	93
	SKRZESZEWSKI, Stan E.	(ON)	1147
	VANDERELST, Wil	(ON)	1274
Library legislation & advocacy	LARSON, Phyllis S.	(PA)	699
Library legislation liaison	GRAMINSKI, Denise M.	(NY)	457
Library legislation lobbying	KRETTEK, Josephine G.	(IA)	678
Library related legislation	BARRETT, G J.	(DC)	59
Politics, legislation & libraries	VERNON, Christie D.	(VA)	1283
Social welfare legislation	AUSTIN, Monique C.	(DC)	40
State legislation	O'BRIEN, Anne M.	(MA)	914
	HALEY, Anne E.	(WA)	486
State legislature & library development	NIXON, Arless B.	(AZ)	906
State library legislation	HUBBS, Ronald B.	(CT)	568
State library legislation & funding	PECK, Ruth M.	(MA)	953
Washington affairs & legislation	MILLENSON, Roy H.	(MD)	835

LEGISLATIVE (See also Government, Law, Legislation, Lobbying)

California legal legislative materials	GOMEZ, Cheryl J.	(CA)	447
Commercial & legislative database srchng	SCHOLFIELD, Caroline A.	(MI)	1098
Compiling legislative histories	DULEY, Kay E.	(LA)	324
Congressional & legislative research	CARR, Timothy B.	(VA)	186
Description of legislative records	EFIRD, Frank K.	(IL)	338
Federal & state legislative materials	CAMMARATA, Paul J.	(KY)	175
Federal legislative reference	COCHRAN, Catherine	(MI)	225
Indexing legislative resolutions	GEISAR, Barbara J.	(WI)	425
Law & legislative reference	RINDEN, Constance T.	(NH)	1035
Legal & legislative databases	BARRETT, Lizabeth A.	(NY)	59
Legal, legislative & regulatory database	JOHNSON, Jacqueline B.	(DC)	605
Legal legislative research	BRESLIN, Ellen R.	(NY)	133
Legislative abstracting	OVERTON, Kathryn R.	(DC)	931
Legislative action	ARRIVEE, Sally D.	(MI)	34
Legislative activities	HELICHER, Karl W.	(PA)	524
	HENINGER, Irene C.	(WA)	528
Legislative analysis	COAKLEY, Dorothy J.	(CA)	224
Legislative & governmental services	FOWLER, Louise D.	(CT)	394
Legislative & legal reference	BROWNE, Lynda S.	(DC)	148
	QUINN, Karen H.	(RI)	1000
Legislative & regulatory information	JOHNSON, Jacqueline B.	(DC)	605
Legislative assembly documents	O'KEEFE, Kevin T.	(NT)	919
Legislative database development	GEISAR, Barbara J.	(WI)	425
Legislative databases	OVERTON, Kathryn R.	(DC)	931
	VEATCH, Laurie L.	(DC)	1280
Legislative development	GIBBS, Nancy J.	(AL)	431
Legislative documents	STALLARD, Thomas W.	(CA)	1179
Legislative histories	SCHUTT, Cheryl M.	(CT)	1103
	BOYER, Larry M.	(DC)	123
	CILIBERTI, Nancy A.	(DC)	214
	SEELE, Ronald E.	(DC)	1111
	WOODWARD, Elaine H.	(VA)	1368
Legislative history	BONYNGE, Jeanne R.	(DC)	115
	BRAVY, Gary J.	(DC)	130
	LOCKWOOD, David J.	(DC)	736
	LASKOWITZ, Roberta G.	(NY)	700
	STORMS, Kate	(NY)	1198
	GARDNER, Linda	(TX)	418
Legislative history compilation	RUGE, Audrey L.	(DC)	1066
Legislative history research	GORDON, Kaye B.	(NJ)	451
Legislative indexing	OVERTON, Kathryn R.	(DC)	931
Legislative information services	CALLINAN, Ellen M.	(DC)	173
Legislative lobbying	LINVILLE, Marcia L.	(HI)	731
	GOULD, Martha B.	(NV)	454
Legislative monitoring	MILLER, William S.	(DC)	843
Legislative record technique	MERINGOLO, Joseph A.	(MD)	826
Legislative reference	JERNIGAN, Denise D.	(CT)	599
	BEALL, Barbara A.	(DC)	68
	KENNEDY, Lynne	(DC)	641
	DULL, Karen A.	(MD)	324
	BALLENTINE, Rebecca S.	(NC)	53
	HALPEREN, Vivian P.	(NC)	489

LEGISLATIVE (Cont'd)
Legislative reference

	MCVEY, Susan C.	(OK)	818
	BAXA, Jay W.	(VA)	67
Legislative reference & research	GRAY, Kevin P.	(NY)	460
Legislative relations	FONTAINE, Sue	(NY)	388
Legislative research	LATEGOLO, Meldie A.	(DC)	701
	MILLER, William S.	(DC)	843
	OAKS, Robert K.	(DC)	913
	KELLERSTRASS, Amy L.	(IL)	636
	LARISON, Brenda	(IL)	697
	MCLELLAN, Mary T.	(MA)	814
	GORDON, Kaye B.	(NJ)	451
	CAHN, Mary Z.	(NY)	171
	CHENICK, Michael J.	(RI)	206
	GEISAR, Barbara J.	(WI)	425
	DEYOUNG, Marie	(NS)	298
Legislative specialist	SIKKEMA, Fern C.	(DC)	1137
Preservation of legislative records	EFIRD, Frank K.	(IL)	338
Real estate & legislative databases	KITZMILLER, Virginia G.	(DC)	657

LEISURE
Sports, recreation & leisure	GRODSKI, Renata	(ON)	471

LENDING (See also Circulation, Loan)
Film lending libraries	WILLIAMS, Helen E.	(KY)	1343
Interlibrary lending & borrowing	ENGEL, Kevin R.	(IA)	348
Lending & circulation	LEFEBVRE, Veronica A.	(MD)	712
Lending industry	FELDER, Bruce B.	(OH)	369
Lending services	THOMPSON, Michael E.	(MD)	1240
Software lending	SHIRINIAN, George N.	(ON)	1131

LESBIAN
Gay & lesbian studies	RIDINGER, Robert B.	(IL)	1032

LESSONS
Acquisitions & lesson plans	JORDAN, Sharon L.	(WA)	617
Library orientation lessons	KEENE, Roberta E.	(NV)	634
Media lessons development	MULLINS, Carolyn J.	(CA)	878

LETTERPRESS
Letterpress printing	JOHNSON, Bryan R.	(VA)	602

LEVERAGING
Leveraged buyouts	SLUSSER, W P.	(NY)	1150
Leveraging information technologies	MCLANE, John F.	(CT)	813

LEVYING
Budgeting & tax levying process	PLAISTED, Glen L.	(KS)	977

LEXICOGRAPHY (See also Dictionaries)
Lexicography	SAWYER, Edmond J.	(DC)	1086
	WADSWORTH, Robert W.	(IL)	1290
	NESS, Arthur J.	(MA)	896
	BUCHAN, Ronald L.	(MD)	153

LEXIS (See also Legal Databases)
Law databases, LEXIS	SMITH, Eugene J.	(PA)	1155
Legal databases, LEXIS & Westlaw	MURPHY, Malinda M.	(NC)	881
Legal databases, Westlaw, LEXIS	SWAN, Christine H.	(PA)	1213
Legal research, LEXIS	PATTELA, Rao R.	(PA)	947
LEXIS & NEXIS	KANJI, Zainab J.	(CA)	625
LEXIS & Westlaw	GOTT, Gary D.	(ND)	453
LEXIS & Westlaw searching	BUTLER, Marguerite L.	(TX)	166
LEXIS & Westlaw training	WINSON, Gail I.	(CA)	1355
LEXIS databases	HARRINGTON, Margaret V.	(IL)	504
Socioeconomic, LEXIS & NEXIS databases	MILUTINOVIC, Eunhee C.	(IL)	845
Westlaw & LEXIS training	DOWLING, Shelley L.	(DC)	316

LIABILITY
Literature search product liability	KENNEDY, Joanna C.	(GA)	641
Product safety & liability research	MOUZON, Margaret W.	(MI)	874
Products liability	PATTELA, Rao R.	(PA)	947

LIAISON
Collection development & faculty liaison	RAMBLER, Linda K.	(PA)	1005
Collection development, faculty liaison	TAYLOR, Anne E.	(TX)	1226
Community & library liaison	SHANK, Beverly C.	(MA)	1120
Computer & technical liaison	EVANS, Mark S.	(FL)	357
DTIC liaison	GALLERY, M C.	(CA)	414
Faculty & library liaison	TAPLEY, Bridgette M.	(SC)	1223
Faculty liaison	JONES, Frederick S.	(MA)	613
General library consulting, liaison	OMARA, Marie T.	(MD)	923
Government & industry liaison	FATTIBENE, James F.	(DC)	366
Government, libraries liaison	JOHNSON, Veronica A.	(MI)	609
Health sciences liaison	GIOVENALE, Sharon	(RI)	438
International liaison & cooperation	RICHER, Suzanne	(ON)	1030
Liaison coordinating	YAEK, Larry A.	(MI)	1376
Liaison with non-public schools	MACLEAN, Ellen G.	(VI)	757
Liaison with state library	MOSES, Lynn M.	(PA)	871
Library & community liaison	REID, Richard H.	(LA)	1019
Lib automation implementation liaison	RUDDY, Mary K.	(TX)	1065
Library legislation liaison	GRAMINSKI, Denise M.	(NY)	457
Marketing, technical liaison	ZIRPOLO, Frank	(NY)	1390
NACO liaison	COLLINS, Donna S.	(MD)	232
Political liaison	MULLER, William A.	(WV)	877
Support group liaison	SCHWARTZ, Virginia C.	(WI)	1105
Technical liaison	ANDEL, June	(PA)	21
Youth service organization liaisonship	WRONKA, Gretchen M.	(MN)	1373

LIBERAL
Liberal arts	SHAPIRO, Marian S.	(MO)	1121
Liberal arts cataloging	BECKER, Charlotte B.	(VA)	72
Liberal arts, religion, music cataloging	LUSK, Betty M.	(SAF)	749

LIBRARIANSHIP
Academic librarian status	KELLOGG, Rebecca B.	(AZ)	637
	HOSEL, Harold V.	(CA)	561
Academic librarianship	KELLOGG, Rebecca B.	(AZ)	637
	WEISS, William B.	(CA)	1320
	UYEHARA, Harry Y.	(GU)	1270
	WHITELEY, Sandra M.	(IL)	1333
	CLARK, Georgia A.	(MI)	217
	REELING, Patricia G.	(NJ)	1016
	VASSALLO, Paul	(NM)	1279
	HELLING, James T.	(OH)	524
	BELL, Carole R.	(RI)	76
	VOCINO, Michael C.	(RI)	1286
	WILKINSON, Eoin H.	(AUS)	1340
Academic librarianship, administration	POLLARD, Frances M.	(IL)	981
Academic librarianship & administration	DE PEW, John N.	(FL)	293
Academic librarianship & reference	SINGH, Swarn L.	(KS)	1143
Academic science librarianship	WANAT, Camille A.	(CA)	1302
Adult librarianship	TSAI, Fu M.	(MI)	1260
	SMITH, Judy S.	(MS)	1156
All phases of general librarianship	FINCH, Lynette	(NC)	377
Architecture librarianship	BYRNE, Elizabeth D.	(CA)	169
	LOGAN-PETERS, Kay E.	(NE)	737
	REED, Barbara E.	(NH)	1014
Archives librarianship	MISRA, Jayasri T.	(GA)	847
Area studies librarianship	JOHNSON, Donald C.	(MN)	603
	STRALEY, Dona S.	(OH)	1200
Art & architecture librarianship	KUSNERZ, Peggy A.	(MI)	685
	CARMIN, James H.	(OR)	183
	KLOS, Sheila M.	(OR)	662
	QUIGLEY, Suzanne L.	(OH)	999
Art & art history librarianship	ANNETT, Susan E.	(CA)	28
Art librarian	BYRNE, Elizabeth D.	(CA)	169
Art librarianship	VAN NIMMEN, Jane	(DC)	1276
	BLOOM, Stephen C.	(IL)	106
	AUCHSTETTER, Rosann M.	(IN)	38
	IRVINE, Betty J.	(IN)	584
	WILLIAMS, Maudine	(IN)	1345

LIBRARIANSHIP (Cont'd)

Art librarianship

	CRAIG, Susan V.	(KS)	254
	RUSHING, Darla H.	(LA)	1068
	GIBSON, Sarah S.	(MA)	432
	SIDEN, Harriet F.	(MI)	1135
	BETH, Dana L.	(MO)	92
	MACEWAN, Bonnie J.	(MO)	755
	REED, Barbara E.	(NH)	1014
	CLARKE, D S.	(NY)	218
	EKDAHL, Janis K.	(NY)	341
	HORRELL, Jeffrey L.	(NY)	560
	KERR, Virginia M.	(NY)	644
	PHILLPOT, Clive J.	(NY)	969
	ROZENE, Janette B.	(NY)	1064
	SCOTT, Frances Y.	(NY)	1107
	STAM, Deirdre C.	(NY)	1179
	SWIESZKOWSK, L S.	(NY)	1216
	PROMOS, Marianne	(PA)	995
	TERRY, Carol S.	(RI)	1232
	BURT, Eugene C.	(TX)	164
	CABLE, Carole L.	(TX)	170
	DOWNING, Jeannette D.	(TX)	316
	RICHARDS, Valerie	(NZD)	1028
Art, music, & audiovisual librarianship	SECKELSON, Linda E.	(NY)	1110
Asian librarianship	FUNG, Margaret C.	(MA)	409
Audiovisual librarian	ANNETT, Susan E.	(CA)	28
Audiovisual librarianship	SLAPSYS, Richard M.	(MA)	1148
	FRYER, Philip	(MD)	407
	WIRTANEN, James	(ND)	1356
Audiovisual librarianship & acquisitions	EARL, Susan R.	(NC)	332
Bibliographic instruction librarianship	HUPP, Stephen L.	(MI)	577
Bilingual librarianship	MAYES, Susan E.	(NC)	789
Biomedical librarianship	SCHEETZ, Kathy D.	(IA)	1091
Black studies librarianship	RUDISELL, Carol A.	(DE)	1065
	KENDRICK, Curtis L.	(NY)	640
Branch librarianship	NEWHARD, Eleanor M.	(CA)	899
	STANLEY, Sydney J.	(CA)	1180
	STENSTROM, Patricia F.	(IL)	1187
	MATYI, Stephen G.	(OH)	786
Business & economics librarianship	LIM, Peck B.	(IL)	727
Business librarianship	LAUGHLIN, Steven G.	(AL)	703
	STEEL, Virginia	(AZ)	1183
	MCNAMEE, Gilbert W.	(CA)	816
	THAU, Richard	(NJ)	1234
	HOWELL, Josephine T.	(NY)	565
	MELVILLE, Karen E.	(ON)	823
Canadian libraries & librarianship	ANDERSON, Beryl L.	(ON)	21
Canadian medical librarianship	WALUZYNIEC, Hanna	(PQ)	1302
Career change for librarians	BERKNER, Dimity S.	(NY)	87
Cartography materials librarianship	LARSGAARD, Mary L.	(CO)	698
Children's & young adult librarianship	TALBERT, Dorothy R.	(UT)	1220
Children's librarian	HECKLINGER, Ellen L.	(CA)	519
	HEINTZMAN, Justina	(KY)	522
	BECKER, Barbara S.	(NE)	72
	BERRY, Mary A.	(TX)	90
	BAKULA, Patricia A.	(WI)	50
Children's librarian, elementary school	POBANZ, Becky L.	(MI)	979
Children's librarian, public library	POBANZ, Becky L.	(MI)	979
Children's librarian training	BREEN, Karen B.	(NY)	131
Children's libn training & development	BOTHAM, Jane	(WI)	118
Children's librarianship	JENKINS, Joyce K.	(AK)	597
	WRIGHT, Pauline W.	(AR)	1372
	MURPHY, Patricia A.	(CA)	881
	SPIRO GREEN, Becky A.	(CA)	1175
	VAN ORDEN, Phyllis J.	(FL)	1276
	SKELLIE, Karen S.	(GA)	1145
	STINCHCOMB, Maxine K.	(IL)	1194
	ALLEN, Janice K.	(IN)	15
	EIS, Myrna M.	(KS)	340
	FOSTER, Joan	(MA)	392
	MUNDY, Suzanne W.	(MA)	879
	LIVELY, Nancy J.	(MD)	734
	PECK, Ann D.	(MD)	953
	BROWN, Merrikay E.	(NC)	146
	DLUGOS, Carolyn M.	(NJ)	306
	BAKER, Marie A.	(NY)	49
	BINA, Marcella A.	(OH)	97
	DRIESSEN, Diane	(OH)	320

LIBRARIANSHIP (Cont'd)

Children's librarianship

	NOWAK, Leslie A.	(OH)	911
	WRIGHT, Catherine A.	(OR)	1370
	SULLIVAN, Kathryn A.	(PA)	1208
	BROOKS, Judy B.	(TN)	140
	MCLENNA, D S.	(TX)	814
	WISECARVER, Betty A.	(VA)	1357
	THOMPSON, Rosalind R.	(WA)	1241
	HUDSON, Susan P.	(BC)	570
	KISSICK, Barbara J.	(NB)	656
	ISRAEL, Kathleen	(ON)	585
Children's media librarianship	ELLISOR, F L.	(TX)	345
Children's services, librarianship	ABRAMSON, Jenifer S.	(CA)	3
Chinese librarianship	WILSON, Amy S.	(MI)	1349
Church librarianship	GUINN, Patricia L.	(NY)	477
	HOUSTON, Barbara B.	(TX)	563
Circuit librarian programs	ANTES, E J.	(PA)	28
Circuit librarianship	PIFALO, Victoria	(DE)	972
	ENGLANDER, Marlene S.	(OH)	349
Circulation librarianship	DAUGHERTY, Robert A.	(IL)	275
	MITCHELL, W B.	(NC)	849
City planning librarianship	BYRNE, Elizabeth D.	(CA)	169
Clinical librarianship	GUTH, Karen K.	(CO)	478
	HANSON, Elana L.	(CO)	498
	FREY, Barbara J.	(CT)	402
	WETMORE, Judith M.	(CT)	1328
	DOHERTY, Mary C.	(NY)	309
	MILLER, Naomi	(PA)	841
	STESIS, Karen R.	(PA)	1189
	BELLAMY, Lois M.	(TN)	77
	HAMBERG, Cheryl J.	(TN)	490
	PEDERSEN, Wayne A.	(TX)	954
	ANGIER, Jennifer J.	(UT)	27
Clinical librarianship program	TRAVERS, Jane E.	(NY)	1254
Clinical medical librarianship	DALE, Nancy	(IL)	270
	VUGRIN, Margaret Y.	(TX)	1289
College librarianship	SHERIDAN, John B.	(CO)	1127
	BOURDON, Cathleen J.	(IL)	119
	HANNAFORD, William E.	(PA)	496
	BYNAGLE, Hans E.	(WA)	168
Community college librarianship	FERRELL, Mary S.	(CA)	373
	REEVES, Cathy L.	(KS)	1016
	HILL, Suzanne P.	(MD)	541
	BOYCE, Emily S.	(NC)	122
	IVERSON, Deborah P.	(WY)	585
Comparative librarianship	TING, Lee H.	(IL)	1246
	ASHEIM, Lester E.	(NC)	35
	JOSEY, E J.	(PA)	618
	TAKEUCHI, Satoru	(JAP)	1220
Continuing education for librarians	SWATOS, Priscilla L.	(IL)	1214
Continuing education for librarianship	WALTERS, Corky	(WY)	1301
Correctional institution librarianship	NOZICK, Sandy B.	(CA)	911
Correctional librarianship	MORGAN, James E.	(NV)	864
County museums volunteer librarianship	HOWE, Mary T.	(IL)	565
Developing librarian authors	FRANKLIN, Robert M.	(NC)	398
Documents librarian	RICHTER, John H.	(MI)	1031
Documents librarianship, automation	JAMISON, Carolyn C.	(PA)	593
East Asian librarianship	WEI, Karen T.	(IL)	1316
	SHULMAN, Frank J.	(MD)	1133
Editorial librarian	JANSSEN, Gene R.	(MN)	594
EDP librarianship	FLEISHMAN, Lauren Z.	(NY)	384
Education for librarianship	REAGAN, Agnes L.	(AR)	1012
	LAWSON, A V.	(GA)	705
	LAWSON, Venable A.	(GA)	705
	AULD, Lawrence W.	(IL)	40
	TING, Lee H.	(IL)	1246
	RUFSVOLD, Margaret I.	(IN)	1066
	OCHS, Michael	(MA)	915
	DUTCHER, Gale A.	(MD)	329
	CHURCHWELL, Charles	(MI)	213
	CORY, Kenneth A.	(MI)	248
	ASHEIM, Lester E.	(NC)	35
	SHEARER, Kenneth D.	(NC)	1124
	KARETZKY, Stephen	(NJ)	627
	DALTON, Jack	(NY)	271
	JACKSON, William V.	(TX)	588
	ROBBINS, Jane B.	(WI)	1038
	STOKES, Roy B.	(BC)	1196

LIBRARIANSHIP (Cont'd)

Education for librarianship
COUGHLIN, Violet L. . . . (PQ) 250
LEIDE, John E. . . . . (PQ) 713
TAKEUCHI, Satoru . . . . . (JAP) 1220
ABDEL-MOTEY, Yaser Y. (KWT) 2
PICACHE, Ursula D. . . . (PHP) 970
SENG, Harris B. . . . . . . (TAI) 1115

Education for music librarianship
BRADLEY, Carol J. . . . . (NY) 125

Education for school librarianship
HAYCOCK, Kenneth R. . . (BC) 515
WHALEN, George F. . . . (ON) 1328

Education librarianship
DENDY, Adele S. . . . . . (VA) 291
POPE, Andrew T. . . . . . (NB) 983

Education of science librarians
ALEXANDER, Carol G. . . (VA) 12

Education of teacher librarians
BROWN, Jean I. . . . . . . (NF) 144

Educational librarianship
RIDER, Lillian M. . . . . . (PQ) 1032

Elementary librarianship
HERRICK, Johanna W. . . (HI) 532
KOCH, Fran C. . . . . (NY) 667
SPRENGER, Suzanne F. (VA) 1176

Elementary school librarian
FITZGERALD, M A. . . . . (MD) 382
SCHULTE, Teresa M. . . . (WI) 1101

Elementary school librarianship
TRIDLE, Jeanne A. . . . . (AK) 1256
SULLIVAN, Geraldine M. (IL) 1207
TEEGARDEN, Maude B. . (KY) 1229
FORD, Delores C. . . . . . (TX) 389
DALLAS, Larayne J. . . . (TX) 270

Engineering librarianship
COHEN, David . . . . (NY) 228

Ethnicity & librarianship
Evaluation of school librarians
OLSEN, Katherine M. . . (UT) 921

Faculty status for librarians
GALLOWAY, R D. . . . . . (CA) 415
SCEPANSKI, Jordan M. . (CA) 1088
MITCHELL, W B. . . . . . (NC) 849

Feminism & librarianship
ENGLE, Michael O. . . . . (OR) 349

Film & video librarianship
AYARI, Kaye W. . . . . . . (SC) 42

Fine arts librarianship
GUNDERSON, Jeffery R. (CA) 477
KUNSELMAN, Joan D. . . (CA) 684
HEHMAN, Jennifer L. . . . (IN) 521
CABLE, Carole L. . . . . . (TX) 170

Foundations of librarianship
GATES, Jean K. . . . . . . (FL) 422

Freelance librarian
GOLDMAN, Teri B. . . . . (MO) 446

French librarianship
CARRINGTON, Samuel M. (TX) 186

General librarian reference cataloging
GOSDECK, David M. . . . (WI) 452

General librarianship
MILLER, Stella M. . . . . (IL) 842
GLADIEUX, Mary B. . . . . (MO) 439
HAY, Gerald M. . . . . . . (NC) 515
LADUE, Annette S. . . . . (NY) 687

Geographical librarianship
FREEDMAN, Jack A. . . . (MS) 400

Government documents librarian
KOEPP, Donna P. . . . . . (KS) 668

Government documents librarianship
MILLER, Veronica E. . . . (VI) 843

Head librarian
MARVEL, Frances J. . . . (CA) 780

Head librarianship
EIKEN, Mary A. . . . . . . (MO) 340

Health sciences librarianship
BERK, Robert A. . . . . . . (IL) 87
FENSKE, Ruth E. . . . . . (IL) 371
WEST, Richard T. . . . . . (MD) 1326
MCKININ, Emma J. . . . . (MO) 811
BRADIGAN, Pamela S. . . (OH) 125
EMPEY, Verla . . . . (ON) 348
SMITHIES, Roger . . . . . (ON) 1162
CRAWFORD, David S. . . (PQ) 256
WILSON, Concepcion S. (AUS)1350

High school librarianship
LATIMER, Mary A. . . . . (CA) 701
SLANGA, Joanne . . . . . (MD) 1147
CLUM, Audna T. . . . . . . (NY) 223
GODWIN, Frances L. . . . (TX) 443
WILLIAMSON, Judy D. . . (WV) 1347

History & philosophy of librarianship
STIELOW, Frederick J. . . (MD) 1194

History of librarianship
BERGEN, Daniel P. . . . . (NY) 85

History of libraries & librarianship
MEISELS, Henry R. . . . . (IL) 822
DAIN, Phyllis . . . . (NJ) 270

History, reference librarian
EMMICK, Nancy J. . . . . (CA) 348

Hospital librarianship
JAJKO, Pamela J. . . . . . (CA) 592
ZAREMSKA, Maryann . . (CA) 1386
AMBROSE, Karen S. . . . (IL) 19
DALE, Nancy . . . . (IL) 270
KALUZSA, Karen L. . . . . (IL) 623
SWATOS, Priscilla L. . . . (IL) 1214
SLOCUM, Ann L. . . . . . . (NY) 1150
BENISHEK, Kristine K. . . (OH) 81
ROBINSON, Elizabeth A. (OH) 1044
TESMER, Nancy . . . . . . (OH) 1233
DONOVAN, James M. . . (OK) 312

LIBRARIANSHIP (Cont'd)

Hospital patient librarianship
MC LAIN, Swan M. . . . . (GA) 813

Humanities reference librarian
POLIT, Carlos E. . . . . . . (IN) 980

Independent school librarianship
SANDERS, Jacqueline C. (MD) 1080

Independent secondary school librarian
REARDON, Elizabeth M. . (TN) 1013

Inservice for librarians
MC NAIR, Marian B. . . . . (OH) 815

Institutional librarianship
MAYO, Kathleen O. . . . . (FL) 790
OVERSTREET, Allen J. . (FL) 931
HOM, Sharon L. . . . . . . (TN) 555

International & comparative libnshp
MAACK, Mary N. . . . . . (CA) 753
VOSPER, Robert . . . . . . (CA) 1289
PATEL, Jashu . . . . (IL) 947
SPILLERS, Roger E. . . . . (MN) 1174
HORROCKS, Norman . . (NJ) 561
DUFFETT, Gorman L. . . (OH) 323

International aspects of librarianship
CONAWAY, Charles W. . (FL) 235

International comparative librarianship
DANTON, J P. . . . . (CA) 274
VEIT, Fritz . . . . (IL) 1281
RUFSVOLD, Margaret I. . (IN) 1066
CVELJO, Katherine . . . . (TX) 268
WILLIAMSON, William L. (WI) 1348
COURRIER, Yves G. . . . (FRN) 251

International exchange of librarians
WILLIAMSON, Linda E. . (IL) 1347

International law librarianship
STRZYNSKI, John C. . . . (IL) 1204

International librarianship
BOONE, Mary L. . . . . . . (CA) 115
BEAN, Charles W. . . . . . (DC) 69
BORYS, Cynthia A. . . . . (DC) 117
ROVELSTAD, Mathilde V. (DC) 1062
LOHRER, Alice . . . . (IL) 737
PIZER, Irwin H. . . . . (IL) 977
QUERY, Lance D. . . . . . (IL) 999
HOVISH, Joseph J. . . . . (IN) 563
KASER, David . . . . (IN) 628
SNYDER, Carolyn A. . . . (IN) 1164
TANTOCO, Dolores W. . (IN) 1223
STUEART, Robert D. . . . (MA) 1205
GAURI, Kul B. . . . . (MI) 423
LOWRIE, Jean E. . . . . . (MI) 744
DYER, Esther R. . . . . . . (NY) 330
GITNER, Fred J. . . . . . . (NY) 439
HARVEY, John F. . . . . . (NY) 509
NYQUIST, Corinne E. . . . (NY) 913
BIRK, Nancy . . . . (OH) 98
LEE, Hwa W. . . . . (OH) 710
SIITONEN, Leena M. . . . (RI) 1137
GLEAVES, Edwin S. . . . (TN) 441
CRAWFORD, David S. . . (PQ) 256
JONES, Roger A. . . . . . (SWZ) 615
SENG, Harris B. . . . . . . (TAI) 1115

International schools librarianship
SERVENTE, Marcia M. . (ENG)1116

Japanese librarianship
NOGUCHI, Sachie . . . . . (IL) 907

Judaic librarianship
DWOSKIN, Beth M. . . . . (MI) 330

Judaica librarianship
LEFF, Barbara Y. . . . . . (CA) 712
GREENBLATT, Ruth . . . (NJ) 463

Junior High school librarianship
COOK, Anne S. . . . . . . (TX) 239

K-12 head librarian
LYONS, Dean E. . . . . . . (ME) 753

Law librarian
BURGALASSI, Anthony J. (NY) 159

Law librarianship
FEENKER, Cherie D. . . . (AL) 368
NEWMAN, Sharon K. . . . (AL) 900
WIEBELHAUS, Richard J. (AZ) 1336
CARTER, Nancy C. . . . . (CA) 189
CONLEY, Linda A. . . . . . (CA) 236
CREWS, Kenneth D. . . . (CA) 258
MCKENZIE, Alice M. . . . (CA) 811
SCHMIDT, Robert R. . . . (CA) 1096
CALVERT, Lois M. . . . . . (CO) 174
COCO, Al . . . . (CO) 226
GONZALEZ, Armando E. (DC) 448
KELMAN, Rosalind S. . . (DC) 638
KOVER, Steven J. . . . . . (DC) 674
OAKLEY, Robert L. . . . . (DC) 913
GIBBS, Rosalyn D. . . . . (FL) 431
KERN, Sharon P. . . . . . (IA) 643
HELLER, James S. . . . . (ID) 524
HOUDEK, Frank G. . . . . (IL) 562
MOEN, Art J. . . . . (IL) 851
ENGELBERT, Peter J. . . (IN) 348
PIASECKI, Patricia S. . . (IN) 970
WILLIS, Paul A. . . . . . . (KY) 1348

LIBRARIANSHIP (Cont'd)

Law librarianship	HOAGLAND, E L.	(MA)	545
	GREEN, Katherine A.	(MI)	462
	HEINEN, Margaret A.	(MI)	522
	HOLSTEN, Terri L.	(MO)	554
	GENNETT, Robert G.	(NJ)	427
	GRECH, Anthony P.	(NY)	461
	YIRKA, Carl A.	(NY)	1380
	NOVAK, Mary S.	(OH)	911
	HAAS, Carol C.	(PA)	480
	METZ, Betty A.	(PA)	828
	SVENGALIS, Kendall F.	(RI)	1212
	HOOD, Lawrence E.	(TX)	556
	NORWOOD, Deborah A.	(WA)	910
	DENTON, Vivienne K.	(ON)	293
	FORTIN, Jean L.	(PQ)	391
	YOUNG, Patricia M.	(PQ)	1383
Legal librarianship	BESTE, Ian R.	(CA)	92
	CAMPAGNA, Roxane R.	(NY)	175
Librarian	MARTIN, Janet L.	(NY)	776
Librarian & teacher teams	LESH, Jane G.	(CA)	718
Librarian & technician supervision	DEYOUNG, Gail O.	(MI)	298
Librarian training	WALTER, Raimund E.	(WGR)	300
Librarians & labor unions	POTTER, Janet L.	(NY)	987
Librarians & public speaking	MCPEAK, James J.	(OH)	817
Librarians in university governance	COLLINS, Evron S.	(OH)	232
Librarians training & development	BARTZ, Alice P.	(PA)	62
Librarianship	LEONARD, Barbara G.	(CA)	716
	STEVENS, Norman D.	(CT)	1190
	KOEING, Sherman	(FL)	667
	HORTIN, Judith K.	(KS)	561
	STEWART, Vicki	(OK)	1193
	JACOB, John N.	(VA)	589
Librarianship, administration	PETERSON, Randall T.	(IL)	964
Librarianship education	BLOESCH, Ethel B.	(IA)	106
	HILL, Janet S.	(IL)	540
	WHITBECK, George W.	(IN)	1329
	ASTBURY, Effie C.	(PQ)	37
Librarian-teacher cooperation	RASSAM, Cynthia K.	(NM)	1009
Library education & school librarians	LYDERS, Josette A.	(TX)	750
Library science librarian	WEINSTEIN, Ellen B.	(NY)	1318
Management aspects of librarianship	WILLIAMS, Gayle A.	(MI)	1343
Manuscript librarianship, archives	WHEALAN, Ronald E.	(MA)	1328
Manuscripts librarianship	LINDEMANN, Richard H.	(VA)	729
Map & geography librarianship	FLATNESS, James A.	(DC)	384
Map librarian	KOEPP, Donna P.	(KS)	668
Map librarianship	HOEHN, Philip	(CA)	547
	LUNDQUIST, David A.	(CA)	748
	STEVENS, Stanley D.	(CA)	1191
	ANTHES, Susan H.	(CO)	28
	CARRINGTON, David K.	(DC)	186
	STEPHENSON, Richard W.	(DC)	1188
	WOLTER, John A.	(DC)	1362
	COBB, David A.	(IL)	224
	KOH, Siew B.	(IL)	668
	RAY, Jean M.	(IL)	1011
	CURTIS, Peter H.	(MD)	267
	BOURGEOIS, Ann M.	(MI)	119
	HANSEN, Joanne J.	(MI)	497
	HUDSON, Alice C.	(NY)	569
	OTNES, Harold M.	(OR)	930
	STARK, Peter L.	(OR)	1181
	BOARDMAN, Richard C.	(PA)	108
	POST, Jeremiah B.	(PA)	986
	ROBERTSON, Robert B.	(PA)	1042
	SPRANKLE, Anita T.	(PA)	1176
	JOHANSEN, Priscilla P.	(TX)	601
	MURPHY, Mary	(VA)	881
	GALNEDER, Mary H.	(WI)	415
	RISTIC, Jovanka	(WI)	1036
	WOOD, Alberta A.	(NF)	1363
	WELCH, Grace D.	(ON)	1321
	TESSIER, Yves	(PQ)	1233
Map librarianship & geography	EUKEY, Jim O.	(WI)	356
Maps librarianship	KRISTIE, William J.	(CA)	679
	DONNELL, Marianne	(FL)	311
Marketing for librarians	ROGERS, Nancy H.	(AL)	1050
Media librarians	DENDY, Adele S.	(VA)	291

LIBRARIANSHIP (Cont'd)

Media librarianship	ELLISON, John W.	(NY)	345
	FRIEDMAN, Arthur L.	(NY)	403
Medical & science librarianship	EBRO, Diane C.	(MN)	334
Medical & scientific librarianship	ANDERSON, Christine	(CA)	22
Medical clinical librarianship	GRAVES, Karen J.	(IL)	459
Medical information & librarianship	EL-MASRY, Mohammed	(EGY)	345
Medical librarian	ALLARD, Andre	(PQ)	14
Medical librarian continuing education	EZQUERRA, Isabel	(FL)	360
Medical librarian teaching	SUGA, Toshinobu	(JAP)	1206
Medical librarianship	FITZGERALD, Diana S.	(CA)	382
	MIRSKY, Phyllis S.	(CA)	847
	RYAN, Ann	(CA)	1070
	VANVUREN, Darcy D.	(CA)	1277
	NELSON, Marie L.	(CO)	894
	DAVIDOFF, Marcia	(FL)	276
	DIAL, Carolyn E.	(FL)	299
	HOLLOWAY, David R.	(FL)	552
	REAM, Diane F.	(FL)	1013
	MC LAIN, Swan M.	(GA)	813
	MILLER, Jeanne L.	(IN)	839
	ISON, Betty S.	(KY)	585
	KELLER, Nancy H.	(LA)	635
	CLEVESY, Sandra R.	(MA)	222
	DESTEFANO, Daniel A.	(MA)	296
	RIVARD, Timothy D.	(MA)	1037
	WEINSCHENK, Andrea	(MA)	1318
	SMITH, Victoria A.	(MI)	1161
	REPETTO, Ann M.	(MO)	1023
	BREMER, Thomas A.	(MT)	132
	EDWARDS, Rosa C.	(NC)	338
	GLATT, Carol R.	(NJ)	440
	PACHMAN, Frederic C.	(NJ)	933
	HELBERS, Catherine A.	(NY)	523
	MAILLET, Lucienne G.	(NY)	761
	WAHLERT, George A.	(NY)	1292
	WEINSTEIN, Judith K.	(NY)	1318
	BRADIGAN, Pamela S.	(OH)	125
	HOLCZER, Lolita B.	(OH)	550
	CARR, Caryn J.	(PA)	185
	HO, Carol T.	(PA)	545
	SHERRARD, Mary A.	(VA)	1129
	MATCHINSKI, William L.	(WY)	783
	REID, Elizabeth A.	(ON)	1018
Microform librarianship	DODSON, Suzanne C.	(BC)	308
Middle East librarianship	HAMILTON, Marsha J.	(OH)	492
Military librarianship	SIEBENMORGEN, Ruth	(CA)	1135
	SMITH, David A.	(VA)	1153
Minority librarianship & resources	HARVELL, Valeria G.	(NJ)	509
Multicultural librarianship	SCHULTE-ALBERT, Hans G.	(ON)	1101
Multilingual librarianship	MANEY, Lana E.	(TX)	765
Museum librarianship	LENTHALL, Franklyn	(ME)	715
Music & audiovisual librarianship	SEAMAN, Sally G.	(IL)	1109
Music & dance librarianship	HECK, Thomas F.	(OH)	519
Music & performing arts librarianship	MAYER, George L.	(NY)	789
Music librarianship	SMITH, Dorman H.	(AZ)	1154
	BERMAN, Marsha	(CA)	88
	BOWLES, Garrett H.	(CA)	121
	COLBY, Michael D.	(CA)	230
	FRY, Stephen M.	(CA)	407
	HERSH, Daniel	(CA)	533
	HUNTER, David C.	(CA)	576
	KRAMLICH, Raymonde S.	(CA)	676
	ROBERTS, John H	(CA)	1040
	TANNO, John W.	(CA)	1223
	WILLIAMS, Valencia	(CA)	1347
	MOULTON, Suzanne L.	(CO)	873
	JOHNSON, Carolyn A.	(CT)	602
	GUNN, Thomas H.	(FL)	477
	SCHERUBEL, Melody	(IA)	1092
	WORK, Dawn E.	(IA)	1369
	ADKINS, Marjorie R.	(IL)	6
	GOUDY, Allie W.	(IL)	454
	ROBERTS, Donald L.	(IL)	1039
	WILLIAMS, Nyal Z.	(IN)	1345
	KORDA, Marion	(KY)	671
	CURTIS, Robert L.	(LA)	267
	DANKNER, Laura R.	(LA)	273
	KEENAN, Elizabeth L.	(MA)	634

LIBRARIANSHIP (Cont'd)

Music librarianship

OCHS, Michael	(MA)	915
SLAPSYS, Richard M.	(MA)	1148
HALE, Dawn L.	(MD)	485
QUIST, Edwin A.	(MD)	1001
RAND, Pamela S.	(MD)	1006
BOWEN, Jennifer B.	(MI)	120
WURSTEN, Richard B.	(NC)	1374
MORGAN, Paula M.	(NJ)	864
BRISTAH, Pamela J.	(NY)	137
CASSARO, James P.	(NY)	193
CORAL, Lenore	(NY)	245
ERICSON, Margaret D.	(NY)	353
GOTTLIEB, Jane E.	(NY)	453
HAEFLIGER, Kathleen A.	(NY)	482
KAUFMAN, Judith L.	(NY)	631
KINNEY, Daniel W.	(NY)	653
RANSOM, Sarah B.	(NY)	1007
SHUMAN, Kristen K.	(NY)	1134
SMIRAGLIA, Richard P.	(NY)	1152
SOMMER, Susan T.	(NY)	1167
DRONE, Jeanette M.	(OH)	320
MCMAHON, Melody L.	(OH)	814
PALKOVIC, Mark A.	(OH)	935
ROBSON, Timothy D.	(OH)	1045
VAN DER SCHALIE, Eric J.	(OH)	1274
ZAGER, Daniel A.	(OH)	1385
DILWORTH, Kirby D.	(PA)	303
MERZ, Lawrie H.	(PA)	827
THOMPSON, Annie F.	(PR)	1239
HERFURTH, Sharon M.	(TX)	530
MARLEY, Judith L.	(TX)	772
SIMS, Phillip W.	(TX)	1142
HALL, Bonlyn G.	(VA)	487
SONNEMANN, Gail J.	(VA)	1167
WALKER, Diane P.	(VA)	1295
REHBACH, Jeffrey R.	(VT)	1017
KREPS, Lise E.	(WA)	678
JONES, Richard E.	(WI)	614
VINE, Rita F.	(AB)	1285
COLQUHOUN, Joan E.	(ON)	234

Music librarianship & teaching — BLACK, Dorothy M. (PA) 101

Music librarianship & theology — PARKER, Charles G. (PQ) 941

Music librarianship, reference — KOLCZYNSKI, Charlotte A. (MA) 669

Navy, technical librarianship — DAVIDOFF, Marcia (FL) 276

New librarian training & development — BUSH, Joyce (NY) 165

News librarianship — HENDERSON, Linda L. (RI) 526

News media librarianship — FURR, Susan H. (VA) 410

Newspaper librarian — PARE, Gilles G. (PQ) 940

Newspaper librarianship — BEVERIDGE, David C. (DC) 93

SHERR, Merrill F. (NY) 1129

Non-print media librarianship — WHYTE, Sean (VA) 1335

Nursing school librarianship — BENISHEK, Kristine K. (OH) 81

One-person librarian — DUX-IDEUS, Sherrie L. (NE) 330

One-person librarianship — BELLIS, Gloria K. (TX) 78

THOM, Pat A. (WI) 1235

SLINEY, Marjory T. (IRE) 1149

Online services librarian — MAGEE, Patricia A. (NY) 759

Orchestra librarianship — GROSSMAN, Robert M. (PA) 473

Parliamentary librarianship — SPICER, Erik J. (ON) 1174

TILLOTSON, Greig S. (AUS) 1245

Performing arts librarianship — KUNSELMAN, Joan D. (CA) 684

DIDHAM, Reginald A. (MA) 301

DUCLOW, Geradline (PA) 322

Philosophy of librarianship — BERGEN, Daniel P. (NY) 85

SORGEN, Herbert J. (NY) 1168

ENGLE, Michael O. (OR) 349

NEILL, Sam D. (ON) 892

Planning librarian — MATTY, Paul D. (AZ) 786

Poetry & librarianship — MOFFEIT, Tony A. (CO) 852

Politics of public librarianship — SHAVIT, David (IL) 1123

Prison librarianship — HARTZ, Frederic R. (GA) 509

LONG, Gary (LA) 739

PEARSON, Barbara F. (WA) 952

Professional development of librarians — EDWARDS, Ralph M. (AZ) 337

Public, fine arts librarianship — MATYI, Stephen G. (OH) 786

Public, music librarianship — MATYI, Stephen G. (OH) 786

LIBRARIANSHIP (Cont'd)

Public school librarian, K-12 — KOHRT, Ruth D. (IA) 669

Public school librarianship — STURGEON, Mary C. (AR) 1205

WILLIAMSON, Lanelle S. (TX) 1347

Public service librarianship — GREEN, Carol C. (WA) 461

Publishing for librarians — ESHELMAN, William R. (OH) 354

Rare book librarianship — DUNLAP, Barbara J. (NY) 326

Records management & librarianship — ORTIZ, Diane (NV) 927

Recruitment of librarians — DEWEY, Barbara I. (IA) 298

Reference, acquisitions librarianship — ENGLAND, Ellen M. (VA) 349

Reference law librarian — BURGALASSI, Anthony J. (NY) 159

Reference librarian — ANNETT, Susan E. (CA) 28

SARAVIS, Judith A. (MA) 1082

Reference librarianship — WATERS, Marie B. (CA) 1308

PERDUE, Robert W. (FL) 958

SCOTT, Rupert N. (GA) 1108

ADKINS, Marjorie R. (IL) 6

HEMENWAY, Patti J. (IL) 525

HUCHTING, Mary (IL) 569

KRAMER, Ruth M. (IL) 675

MARKHAM, Robert P. (IL) 771

ENSOR, Pat L. (IN) 350

ARNOLD, Peggy (MI) 34

COREY, Marjorie (MI) 246

HUPP, Stephen L. (MI) 577

KEYSER, Sue C. (VA) 645

GERLACH, Donald E. (WI) 429

GRANATSTEIN, M E. (ON) 457

RIDER, Lillian M. (PQ) 1032

TILLOTSON, Greig S. (AUS) 1245

Research in librarianship — BENNION, Bruce C. (CA) 82

MCCROSSAN, John A. (FL) 800

VALLEJO, Rosa M. (PHP) 1271

Research librarianship — AMAN, Ann L. (CO) 19

CRESCENT, Victoria L. (PA) 258

Research on cartographic librarianship — STEVENS, Stanley D. (CA) 1191

Reserve & Afro-American librarianship — GENTRY, Etherlene H. (MS) 427

Resume assistance for librarians — KLEMENT, Susan P. (ON) 660

Role of academic librarians — EKLAND, Patricia A. (BC) 341

Rural librarianship — KRUGLET, Jo A. (CO) 680

HANKS, Gardner C. (MN) 496

HENDRICKS, Thom (ND) 527

School & children's librarian — LANE, Margaret (MA) 694

School librarian — PRESSNALL, Patricia E. (CA) 991

RECHNITZ, Harriet L. (DE) 1013

VITELLO, Susan (FL) 1286

STEBEN, Florence E. (LA) 1183

FRIEND, Ann S. (MA) 404

School librarian education — ALSWORTH, Frances W. (OK) 18

HAMMEL, Philip J. (SK) 493

School librarian media specialist — COACHMAN, Dorothea L. (NY) 224

School librarian's instructional role — MINEMIER, Betty M. (NY) 845

School librarianship — MCCLAIN, Harriet V. (AK) 795

ROYAL, Selvin W. (AR) 1063

EASUN, M S. (CA) 333

GRAVES, Frances M. (CA) 459

DUBEAU, Marsha (CT) 321

POLOMSKI, Linda (CT) 982

MYERS, Victoria B. (DE) 885

VAN ORDEN, Phyllis J. (FL) 1276

TOM, Chow L. (HI) 1249

HANNON, Bobbie A. (IL) 497

SCHORMANN, Marguerite T. (IL) 1099

STINCHCOMB, Maxine K. (IL) 1194

REEVES, Cathy L. (KS) 1016

WILLIAMS, Helen E. (MD) 1343

BERTRAND, Beverly P. (MI) 91

HOERGER, Helen L. (MI) 547

BROOKS, S B. (MN) 141

BREIMEIER, Lois (MO) 132

FABIAN, William M. (MO) 360

SMITH, Sharon M. (MO) 1160

BOYCE, Emily S. (NC) 122

BUSBIN, O M. (NC) 164

DICKINSON, Gail K. (NC) 301

FISH, Barbara M. (NC) 380

WILKINSON, Fleeta M. (NC) 1340

LIBRARIANSHIP (Cont'd)

School librarianship

	HASELWOOD, Eldon L. .	(NE)	510
	GILLESPIE, John T.	(NY)	435
	HENDRICKS, Elaine M. .	(NY)	527
	KLEINBURD, Freda	(NY)	659
	MERRILL, Barbara P. . . .	(NY)	826
	MEYER, Albert	(NY)	829
	SCHEU, Susan P.	(NY)	1092
	TALLMAN, Julie I.	(NY)	1221
	DRIESSEN, Diane	(OH)	320
	GILLMORE, Salley G. . . .	(OH)	436
	POJMAN, Paul E.	(OH)	980
	COCHENOUR, Donnice K.	(OK)	225
	GEARHART, Carol A. . . .	(PA)	424
	RUPERT, Elizabeth A. . .	(PA)	1068
	SHAW, Doris G.	(PA)	1123
	SCALES, Pat R.	(SC)	1087
	WATSON, Gail H.	(TN)	1309
	BASS, Martha L.	(TX)	63
	GONZALEZ, Sharon M. .	(TX)	448
	SMITH, Lorraine K.	(TX)	1157
	SHIELDS, Dorthy M.	(UT)	1130
	GREENAWALT, Ruth A. . .	(VA)	463
	PYKE, Carol J.	(VA)	999
	WAMPLER, Dorris M. . . .	(VA)	1302
	SHELDEN, Lucinda D. . .	(WA)	1125
	TERESINSKI, Sally S. . .	(WI)	1231
	HOWARD, Elizabeth F. . .	(WV)	564
	OBERG, Dianne	(AB)	913
	WRIGHT, John G.	(AB)	1371
	HAMILTON, Donald E. . .	(BC)	492
	HAYCOCK, Carol A. . . .	(BC)	515
	WRIGHT, Jonathan C. . .	(ON)	1371
	GALLER, Anne M.	(PQ)	414
	PHILLIPS, Yvonne A. . . .	(PQ)	969
	SLINEY, Marjory T.	(IRE)	1149
	PICACHE, Ursula D.	(PHP)	970
School librarianship & education	BERNHARD, Paulette . . .	(PQ)	89
School librarianship education	BUTLER, Christina	(OH)	166
	MERRIAM, Doris E.	(PA)	826
	BLANKENBURG, Judith B.	(VA)	104
School librarianship, media centers	RYUS, Phyllis K.	(CA)	1072
Science & technology librarianship	SMITH, Eric J.	(NC)	1155
Science, branch librarianship	CAMPBELL, Susan M. . .	(PA)	177
Science librarianship	PARKER, Joan M.	(CA)	942
	BROWN, Steven A.	(GA)	147
	BLACK, George W.	(IL)	101
	OLSON, James	(IL)	922
	SWANSON, Patricia K. .	(IL)	1213
	GARRABRANT, William A.	(NJ)	420
	WALCOTT, Rosalind . . .	(NY)	1294
	TIMMERS, Debra A.	(WI)	1246
	MILNE, Dorothy J.	(NF)	845
	WALLACE, Kathryn M. . .	(ON)	1297
Science librarianship & management	STIRLING, Isabel A.	(OR)	1195
Secondary school librarianship	KLEINMAN, Elsa C.	(CA)	660
	AUFSES, Harriet W.	(NY)	39
	KENT, Candace D.	(TN)	642
	SHANNON, Theresa M. .	(VA)	1121
	KITTS, T J.	(ON)	657
Serials librarianship	BAUMGARDNER, Sandra A.	(DC)	66
	POSTLETHWAITE, Bonnie S.	(MA)	986
	CIPOLLA, Wilma H.	(NY)	215
	OKERSON, Ann L.	(NY)	920
	NICOL, Jessie T.	(TN)	902
	BROWN, Pauline	(AUS)	146
Slavic & East European librarianship	LEICH, Harold M.	(DC)	713
Slavic librarianship	ZALEWSKI, Wojciech . . .	(CA)	1385
	BEYNEN, Gijsbertus K. . .	(OH)	93
	SWENSEN, Dale S.	(UT)	1215
	MORGAN, Robert C. . . .	(VA)	864
Slide librarianship	KING, Carmen M.	(MI)	650
Social science & humanities librarians	HUPP, Stephen L.	(MI)	577
Social science librarianship	BERGEN, Daniel P.	(NY)	85
Special art & architecture librarianship	BEGLO, Jo N.	(ON)	74
Staff development for school librarians	WHITE, Ann T.	(SC)	1330
State librarianship	OWEN, Amy	(UT)	931

LIBRARIANSHIP (Cont'd)

Substitute hospital librarian	ROBINSON, Betty J. . . .	(CA)	1043
Supervise & training librarians	EMERICK, John L.	(PA)	347
Supervision of reference librarians	MUTCH, Donald G.	(ON)	883
Supervision of school librarians	VANDERGRIFF, Kathleen E.	(TN)	1274
Taxonomy of librarianship	JORDAN, Robert T.	(DC)	617
Teacher librarian	CADY, Ruth A.	(CA)	170
Teacher librarianship	LINDSAY, Jane A.	(WI)	729
Teaching, reference librarian	TRIM, Kathryn	(MI)	1256
Theatre librarianship	WALL, Richard L.	(NY)	1297
Theological librarianship	WENDEROTH, Christine .	(GA)	1323
	GRUMBLING, Dennis K. .	(IL)	474
	THOMPSON, John W. . . .	(IL)	1240
	DEERING, Ronald F. . . .	(KY)	287
	MCLEOD, Herbert E. . . .	(NC)	814
	KASTEN, Seth E.	(NY)	629
	MAURER, Eric	(NY)	787
	SAYRE, John L.	(OK)	1087
	KRUPP, Robert A.	(OR)	681
	CAMILLI, E M.	(PA)	175
	DERRICK, Mitzi J.	(SC)	294
	BAKER, Bonnie U.	(TN)	48
	LOYD, Roger L.	(TX)	745
	MANEY, James W.	(TX)	765
	PAYSON, Evelyn H.	(WI)	951
	CORMAN, Linda W.	(ON)	246
Training for church librarians	JENSEN, Wilma M.	(MN)	599
Training school librarians	GAUDET, Jean A.	(VA)	422
Undergraduate librarianship	FERGUSON, Chris D. . . .	(CA)	372
	FLOWERS, Pat	(CA)	386
Upgrading status of librarians	NANCE, Betty L.	(TX)	887
Veterinary medical librarianship	STEPHENS, Gretchen . .	(IN)	1188
Videotape librarianship	BOGIS, Nana E.	(NJ)	110
Women in librarianship	MOSLANDER, Charlotte D.	(NY)	871
Women's studies librarianship	RUDISELL, Carol A.	(DE)	1065
	COMER, Cynthia H.	(OH)	234
World librarianship	KRZYS, Richard A.	(PA)	681
Young adult librarianship	CLARK, Patricia A.	(CA)	217
	GERARD, Sandra C. . . .	(CA)	428
	MANOR, Lawanda	(DC)	767
	HEMENWAY, Patti J. . . .	(IL)	525
	MUNDY, Suzanne W. . . .	(MA)	879
	HABINSKI, Carol A.	(OH)	481
Youth librarianship	LOCKE, Jill L.	(PA)	736

LIBRARIES (See names of specific types of libraries)

LIBRARIES/INFORMATION

Micros in libraries/information centers	TRUETT, Carol A.	(HI)	1259

LIBRARY DEVELOPMENT (See also LSCA)

African library development assistance	PASQUARIELLA, Susan K.	(NY)	946
Church library development	JENSEN, Wilma M.	(MN)	599
Collection & library development	MIDGETT, Ann S.	(TX)	833
Cooperative library development	WHITE, Robert W.	(NJ)	1332
Cooperative theological lib development	WARTLUFT, David J. . . .	(PA)	1307
Corporate & legal library development	WALSH, Joanna M.	(MA)	1299
Hospital library development	CRAIG, James P.	(FL)	254
	BARTEN, Sharon S.	(NY)	60
	WILSON, Fred L.	(PA)	1351
	WARD, Deborah H.	(TX)	1303
Information management, library devlpmnt	CONDREY, Barbara K. . .	(CA)	236
International library development	GALVIN, Thomas J.	(IL)	415
	HAUSRATH, Donald C. .	(NY)	513
	LIEBERMAN, Ronald . . .	(PA)	726
Latin American library development	BRESIE, Mayellen	(TX)	133
Law library development	PIERCE, Ann E.	(ME)	971
Library development	SMITH, George V.	(AK)	1155
	CUMMINGS, Mozelle B. .	(AL)	264
	DESSY, Blane K.	(AL)	296
	RICHARDSON, Gail	(CA)	1029
	BETTS, Ardith M.	(DC)	92

LIBRARY DEVELOPMENT (Cont'd)
Library development

WILKINS, Barratt	(FL)	1340
HEFFINGTON, Carl O.	(GA)	520
DOELLMAN, Michael A.	(IN)	308
DUGAN, Robert E.	(MA)	324
SACK, Jean C.	(MD)	1073
BOYNTON, John W.	(ME)	124
PARKER, Sara A.	(MT)	942
WILLIAMS, M J.	(NC)	1345
MOREHOUSE, Valerie J.	(ND)	863
HIEBING, Dottie	(NJ)	537
JASSIN, Raymond M.	(NY)	595
SHUBERT, Joseph F.	(NY)	1133
WILDER, David T.	(NY)	1338
RICHARDSON, Katherine A.	(OH)	1029
SKVARLA, Donna J.	(OK)	1147
BYRNE, Helen E.	(OR)	169
FORCIER, Peggy C.	(OR)	389
DANIELS, Bruce E.	(RI)	273
OWEN, Amy	(UT)	931
BULLEY, Joan S.	(VA)	156
ZUSSY, Nancy L.	(WA)	1391

Library development & fundraising	MCDONALD, John P.	(CT)	802
Library development & implementation	PARR, Loraine E.	(WA)	943
Library development & maintenance	FALK, Diane M.	(DC)	362
Library development & management	WARPHEA, Rita C.	(VA)	1306
Library development & organization	NIEMI, Peter G.	(WI)	903
Library development & placement	MUELLER, Elizabeth	(IL)	875
Library development from scratch	DEWBERRY, Claire D.	(GA)	298
Library development management	STANLEY, Nelda J.	(LA)	1180
Library development, research, grants	COLLARD, R M.	(CO)	232
Medical library development	AVERILL, M S.	(NJ)	41
Multitype library development & service	KOYAMA, Janice T.	(CA)	674
New library development	KELVER, Ann E.	(CO)	639
Newspaper libraries development	DONCEVIC, Lois A.	(PA)	311
Non-print library development	BARRIE, John L.	(NY)	59
Planning library development activities	ROBERTS, Kenneth H.	(FRN)	1040
Public & state library development	LASETER, Ernest P.	(AL)	700
	SHELDON, Brooke E.	(TX)	1125
Regional library development	LANDRUM, Margaret C.	(CO)	693
	LOPEZ, Deborah A.	(FL)	741
	NELSON, James B.	(NY)	894
	RAY, Gordon L.	(BC)	1011
Rural library development	PACEY, Brenda M.	(IL)	933
	LANGEVIN, Ann T.	(NV)	695
	GINNANE, Mary J.	(OR)	437
	KNIEVEL, Helen A.	(OR)	664
Rural library development & training	WILLIAMS, Susan S.	(MI)	1346
School library development	TARANKO, Walter J.	(ME)	1223
	GUILBERT, N P.	(MB)	476
	FINN, Julia P.	(PQ)	378
School library development & management	BERKLUND, Nancy J.	(MI)	87
Small library development	NOTARSTEFANO, Vincent C.	(NY)	910
	GINNANE, Mary J.	(OR)	437
	KNIEVEL, Helen A.	(OR)	664
Small lib development & administration	HILL, Susan E.	(TX)	540
State legislature & library development	NIXON, Arless B.	(AZ)	906
Technical library development	WHITMAN, Jean A.	(MD)	1333
Technology library development	HARMON, Jacqueline B.	(TX)	502

LIBRARY EDUCATION (See Education)

LIBRARY OF CONGRESS

Automated Library of Congress cataloging	BENSON, Laurel D.	(MN)	83
Cataloging Lib of Congress, Dewey, Sears	RUSSELL, Richard A.	(WV)	1069
Library of Congress cataloging	REYNOLDS, Dorsey	(PA)	1025
Lib of Congress cataloging conversion	DUNMIRE, Raymond V.	(AL)	326
Library of Congress classification	GLENISTER, Peter	(NS)	441
	PARADIS, Jacques	(PQ)	939

LIBRARY OF CONGRESS (Cont'd)

Library of Congress classification syst	SAVAGE, Helen	(MI)	1085
Library of Congress history	COLE, John Y.	(DC)	231
Lib of Congress music subject headings	PRICE, Harry H.	(DC)	992
Music at the Library of Congress	ANDERSON, Gillian B.	(DC)	23

LIBRARY SCIENCE (See Science, Information Science)

LIBRARY SERVICES (See also Adults, Bookmobiles, Children, Community, Delivery, Outreach, Programming, Public Services, Special, Young)

Administering library services	BROWN, Atlanta T.	(DE)	142
Administration community library service	WECHTLER, Stephen R.	(NJ)	1315
Administration of library service	LYDERS, Josette A.	(TX)	750
Administration of library services	NEWTON, Stephanne K.	(DC)	900
	JOHNSON, Stephen C.	(OH)	609
All children's library services	KELLY, Anne V.	(FL)	637
Automated library services	ROSS, Gary M.	(SC)	1058
Automation in library services	WONG, Ming K.	(DC)	1363
Blind library services, computers	ROATCH, Mary A.	(AZ)	1038
Bookmobile library services	SWAIN, Lillian A.	(VA)	1212
Branch library service	SCHMIDT, Robert R.	(CA)	1096
	MARSHALL, Jane C.	(VA)	774
Branch library services	COBB, Karen B.	(CA)	225
	CROMER, Kenneth L.	(OH)	260
Branch library services & programs	ALSTON-REEDER, Lizzie A.	(NC)	18
Campus library services	EMMER, Barbara L.	(PA)	348
Children's library service	MORRIS, Effie L.	(CA)	866
	BEAN, Bobby G.	(IL)	69
Children's library services	DOOLEY, Shelly A.	(GA)	312
	FAHERTY, Gladys W.	(MD)	361
	MORROW, Paula J.	(MO)	869
	ROSS, Shirley D.	(MO)	1059
	CUTLER, Marsha L.	(NV)	268
	BUSH, Dianne	(NY)	165
	DENNEHY, Margaret	(NY)	292
	PELLOWSKI, Anne	(NY)	955
	VEENSTRA, Geraldine B.	(TX)	1281
	BENNE, Mae M.	(WA)	81
	BETZ-ZALL, Jonathan R.	(WA)	92
Children's literature & library services	BUSH, Margaret A.	(MA)	165
Children's literature, library services	CORSARO, Julie A.	(IL)	248
Church library service	SINCLAIR, Rose P.	(TX)	1143
College library service research	MICIKAS, Lynda L.	(PA)	832
Community & library services	PETRIE, Mildred M.	(FL)	965
Computerized library services	WOOD, Barbara G.	(PA)	1363
Contract library services	GARVEY, Nancy G.	(NJ)	421
Cooperative library service	DALTON, Phyllis I.	(NV)	271
Cooperative library services	ROBLEE, Martha A.	(IN)	1045
Coordination of library services	WALCH, David B.	(CA)	1293
Corporate information & library services	WAGNER, Stephen K.	(NY)	1292
Corporate library services	ROBERTSON, Guy M.	(BC)	1041
Correctional institution library service	BATSON, Darrell L.	(NV)	64
County network library services	MARSHALL, Ruth T.	(GA)	775
Database lib srvs, plng & implementing	MADDEN, Doreitha R.	(NJ)	758
Deaf library services	ROATCH, Mary A.	(AZ)	1038
Development of library service	FOUST, Judith M.	(PA)	393
Development of library services	MCCULLY, William C.	(IL)	801
Developmentally disabled lib services	DUX-IDEUS, Sherrie L.	(NE)	330
Distance education library services	SLADE, Alexander L.	(BC)	1147
	AFFLECK, Delburt E.	(SK)	7
East Asian library services	WU, Ai H.	(AZ)	1373
Education library services	KRATZ, Abby R.	(TX)	676
Elementary, junior high library services	DOMESCIK, Carol J.	(IL)	310
Establishing integrated library services	BELTON, Jennifer H.	(DC)	78
Ethnic library service	KLEIMAN, Allan M.	(NY)	658
Ethnic library services	GALLEGO, Bert H.	(CA)	414
	SMITH, Elizabeth M.	(CA)	1154
Evaluation of library services	LANCASTER, Frederick W.	(IL)	691
	GOODWIN, Jane G.	(VA)	450
Evaluation of school library services	BOMAR, Cora P.	(NC)	113

LIBRARY SERVICES (Cont'd)

Extended campus library services	PICKETT, Mary J.	(IL)	970
	HERRON, Nancy L.	(PA)	533
	KEMP, Barbara E.	(WA)	639
Extension library services	SLADE, Alexander L.	(BC)	1147
Fee-based library services	ROLLINS, Stephen J.	(NM)	1051
	MARVIN, Stephen G.	(PA)	780
French language library services	NICHOLSON, Jill A.	(ON)	902
General library service	TENCATE, Sri P.	(HI)	1231
General library services	HARPER, Nancy L.	(MI)	503
	HULL, Catherine C.	(RI)	572
	DUHAMEL, Louis	(PQ)	324
Government & business library services	MARVIN, Stephen G.	(PA)	780
High school library service	TOLMAN, Bonnie B.	(MI)	1249
Human resources in library services	SAVARD, Rejean	(PQ)	1085
Information & library service department	ROE, Georgeanne T.	(MA)	1048
Information, library services consulting	PARMING, Marju R.	(DC)	943
Institution library services	RUBIN, Rhea J.	(CA)	1064
Institutional library services	PARTRIDGE, James C.	(MD)	945
Institutions library services	VAN DER VOORN, Neal P.	(WA)	1274
Lecturer, school library service	MARSH, Martha M.	(KS)	773
Legal & accounting library services	SMOTHERS, Alyce A.	(LA)	1162
Library service	JOHNSON, Joanne D.	(IL)	606
	DAUB, Albert W.	(NJ)	275
	BURSON, Lorraine E.	(OR)	163
	ELAM, Barbara J.	(OR)	341
Library service contracts	WALTERS, Daniel L.	(WA)	1301
Library service for business	MCWILLIAM, Deborah A.	(OH)	818
Library service for disabled persons	DALTON, Phyllis I.	(NV)	271
Library service for special populations	DALTON, Phyllis I.	(NV)	271
Library service for youth	LONG, Joanna R.	(NY)	739
Library service in prisons	GROSSHANS, Merilyn P.	(NV)	473
Library service programs	MCPHERSON, Kenneth F.	(NJ)	817
Library service to aging	PETERSON, Vivian A.	(NE)	964
	MONROE, Margaret E.	(WI)	855
Library service to children	NICHOLS, Margaret M.	(AZ)	901
	GREENE, Ellin P.	(NJ)	464
	BEDNAR, Sheila	(NY)	73
	WILSON, Letitia A.	(OH)	1351
	BAUMGARTNER, Barbara W.	(PA)	66
Library service to handicapped	HAVENS, Shirley E.	(NY)	513
	SOMERS, Betty J.	(NY)	1166
	BARKALOW, Irene M.	(VA)	56
Library service to Hispanics	RAMIREZ, William L.	(CA)	1005
Library service to special populations	KIRSCHENBAUM, Arthur S.	(DC)	655
Library service to young adults	BEDNAR, Sheila	(NY)	73
Library services	LEWIS, Ralph W.	(CA)	724
	CHAMBERS, Joan L.	(CO)	198
	SMITH, Nolan E.	(CT)	1159
	FREEMAN, Carla	(DC)	400
	PLADERA, Lucretia	(HI)	977
	BROOKS, Carolyn B.	(KY)	140
	WALKER, Patricia A.	(MO)	1296
	DAVILA, Daniel	(NY)	277
	KELLER, Marlo L.	(OH)	635
	MADER, Marion C.	(PA)	759
Library services & management	GENESEN, Judith L.	(IL)	427
	CHIANG, Ahushun	(MD)	207
Library services & personnel	FLEMING, Anne	(ON)	384
Library services development	SCULL, Roberta A.	(LA)	1108
Library services direction	WOFSE, Joy G.	(NY)	1359
Library services evaluation	SUIDAN, Randa H.	(IL)	1207
Library services for children	PATTISON, Joanne	(FL)	948
	HERMAN, Gertrude B.	(WI)	531
Library services for the disabled	CAGLE, Robert B.	(LA)	171
	SMITH, Audrey J.	(NY)	1152
Library services instruction	ROBERTS, Scott J.	(MI)	1041
Library services management	JONES, Adrian	(IL)	610
	PICARD, Albert	(ON)	970
Library services marketing	WOOD, Richard C.	(TX)	1365
Library services planning, development	NIEMI, Peter G.	(WI)	903
Library services to adults	HANSEN, Andrew M.	(IL)	497

LIBRARY SERVICES (Cont'd)

Library services to children	NEVETT, Micki S.	(NY)	897
	WIGG, Ristiina M.	(NY)	1337
	ESTES, Glenn E.	(TN)	355
	FASICK, Adele M.	(ON)	366
Library services to distance education	BUDNICK, Carol	(MB)	155
Library services to Hispanics	HERNANDEZ, Hector R.	(IL)	531
Library services to prisoners	CHESLEY, Thea B.	(IL)	207
Library services to the aging	FERSTL, Kenneth L.	(TX)	374
Library services to the Spanish speaking	TSCHERNY, Elena	(DC)	1260
Library services to youth	JACKSON, Clara O.	(OH)	587
Managing library services	SPRAGUE, Karol S.	(MI)	1176
Marketing archives & library services	SYKES, Stephanie L.	(PQ)	1217
Marketing information & library service	ALIX, Cleta M.	(CA)	13
Marketing library services	HARRIS, Susan C.	(CA)	506
	KUSZMAUL, Marcia J.	(IL)	685
	DEL SORDO, Jean S.	(MD)	290
	MARSHALL, Mary E.	(OH)	774
	SOUCIE, Yan Y.	(OR)	1169
	INGRAHAM, Alice L.	(PA)	582
	LAVKULICH, Joanne	(AB)	704
Marketing of library services	JOHNSON, Stephen C.	(OH)	609
	SAVARD, Rejean	(PQ)	1085
Measuring library services	CLARK, Philip M.	(NY)	218
Medical education library services	SNYDER, Elizabeth A.	(ENG)	1164
Metropolitan library services	SIVULICH, Kenneth G.	(NY)	1145
Minority library services consulting	EWUNES, Ernest L.	(TX)	359
Multicultural library services	BURNETT, Wayne C.	(ON)	162
Off-campus library services	HEARTH, Fred E.	(CA)	519
	BURICH, Nancy J.	(KS)	160
	SLADE, Alexander L.	(BC)	1147
	NORMAN, Nita V.	(AZ)	909
Outreach library services	BATSON, Darrell L.	(NV)	64
Planning & budgeting for library service	WINSON, Gail I.	(CA)	1355
Planning area library services	BLASINGAME, Ralph	(NJ)	104
Planning library services	DURBIN, Roger	(OH)	328
	RIVERA-ALVAREZ, Miguel A.	(PR)	1037
Prison library service	MOSIER, Eric M.	(CA)	871
Professional library services	DEAN, Martha L.	(CA)	283
Promotion of library services	SPIEGELMAN, Barbara M.	(PA)	1174
Psychiatric patient library services	MERRILL, Susan S.	(MD)	827
Reference library service	ARMONTROUT, Brian A.	(TN)	32
Regional library service system	OWEN, Mary J.	(CO)	932
Rural library service	LAWSON, Martha G.	(AR)	705
	UBEL, James A.	(IL)	1267
	SPILLERS, Roger E.	(MN)	1174
	JOHNSON, Corinne E.	(OH)	603
	REID, Margaret B.	(OH)	1018
	WASH, Melba W.	(TN)	1307
	LABUIK, Karen L.	(SK)	686
Rural library services	MCCORMICK, Tamsie	(IN)	799
	BOESE, Robert A.	(MN)	110
	DEGRUYTER, M L.	(TX)	288
School district library services	BAGAN, Beverly S.	(VA)	45
School library service	SHELTON, Elease B.	(GA)	1126
	BOMAR, Cora P.	(NC)	113
	POND, Patricia B.	(OR)	982
	SINCLAIR, Rose P.	(TX)	1143
School library services	DEAN, Martha L.	(CA)	283
	SERIS, Eileen J.	(CO)	1116
	SCARBROUGH, S J.	(MI)	1087
	GERHARDT, Lillian N.	(NY)	428
	KENNEDY BRIGHT, Sandra	(NY)	641
	FRENCH, Janet D.	(PA)	402
	LINDSEY, Nancy L.	(TN)	730
School library services & collections	DAIGNEAULT, Audrey I.	(CT)	270
School library services for K-6	ROTSAERT, Stefanie C.	(NJ)	1060
Small library services	DEGRUYTER, M L.	(TX)	288
Small, rural library service	MILLER, Pearl F.	(IA)	841
Speaking on library services	NELSON, Maggie E.	(IL)	894
Special & outreach library services	PARTRIDGE, James C.	(MD)	945
State library service & networks	JOSEY, E J.	(PA)	618
Statewide library services	STEVENSON, Marilyn E.	(CA)	1191
	ROBLEE, Martha A.	(IN)	1045
Statewide planning library services	DREW, Sally J.	(WI)	319

LIBRARY SERVICES (Cont'd)
Teaching academic library services   TRYON, Jonathan S. . . .   (RI)   1259
Theological library services   CHEATHAM, Gary L. . . .   (OK)   204
Young people's library services   FAHERTY, Gladys W. . .   (MD)   361
Youth library services   DENNEHY, Margaret . . .   (NY)   292

LICENSING
Licenses   TAPHORN, Joseph B. . .   (NY)   1223
Permissions & licensing rights   MARKERT, Patricia B. . .   (NY)   771

LIFE
Collection development in life
  sciences   SOWELL, Steven L. . . . .   (IN)   1170
Japanese life sciences information   WILLIAMS, Mitsuko . . . .   (IL)   1345
Jewish history & life   ARONER, Miriam D. . . . .   (CA)   34
Jewish life & thought   BEN-ZVI, Hava . . . .   (CA)   84
Life & health insurance   SLOAN, Virgene K. . . . .   (NE)   1150
Life & health insurance research   HILL, Judith L. . . . .   (PA)   540
Life insurance   COX, Joyce M. . . . .   (IL)   253
   CITROEN, Julie M. . . . . .   (ON)   215
Life science databases   MITCHELL, Steve . . . . .   (CA)   849
   WALSH, James A. . . . . .   (PA)   1299
   YERGER, George A. . . . .   (PA)   1379
Life science online searching   WILLIAMS, Mitsuko . . . .   (IL)   1345
Life science reference   CURTIS, Susan C. . . . . .   (GA)   267
Life sciences   LUDWIG, J D. . . . .   (AK)   746
   FINEMAN, Michael . . . . .   (CA)   377
   PARKER, Joan M. . . . . .   (CA)   942
   WALKER, Luise E. . . . . .   (OR)   1295
   ELDER, Nancy I. . . . . . .   (TX)   342
Life sciences & physical sciences   WILLIAMS, Robert C. . . .   (AK)   1346
Life sciences cataloging   PASTER, Amy L. . . . . . .   (PA)   946
Life sciences collection development   KELLAND, John L. . . . . .   (RI)   635
Life sciences databases   POWER, Colleen J. . . . .   (CA)   989
   HEWISON, Nancy S. . . .   (IN)   535
   SAFFER-MARCHAND,
     Melinda . . . .   (MA)   1074
Life sciences databases online   DAVIDSON, Lloyd A. . . .   (IL)   276
Life sciences information   SEARS, Jonathan R. . . .   (MD)   1110
Life sciences literature   FLEURY, Bruce E. . . . . .   (LA)   385
   DODSON, Carolyn . . . . .   (NM)   308
Life sciences, medical databases   BAUGH, L S. . . . .   (IL)   65
Life sciences reference   TALBERT, David M. . . . .   (NC)   1220
   PASTER, Amy L. . . . . . .   (PA)   946
   KELLAND, John L. . . . . .   (RI)   635
Medicine & life sciences   GUIDA, Pat . . . .   (NJ)   476
Physical, life scis & engrng reference   MURPHY, Joan F. . . . . .   (CA)   880
Physics & life sciences   COHEN, Rosemary C. . .   (NY)   229
Reference services in life sciences   SOWELL, Steven L. . . . .   (IN)   1170
Research, Eugene O'Neill life works   MCDONALD, Lois E. . . .   (CT)   803

LIFELONG (See also Adults, Continuing)
Adult education, lifelong learning   GANN, Daniel H. . . . . . .   (IN)   416
Lifelong learning   HEISER, Jane C. . . . . . .   (MD)   523
   SHIRK, John C. . . . .   (MN)   1131

LIGHTING
Lighting for libraries   NOVAK, Gloria J. . . . . . .   (CA)   910

LIMNOLOGY
Limnology   POPLAWSKY, Diane M. . .   (WI)   983

LINCOLN
Abraham Lincoln   TEMPLE, Wayne C. . . . .   (IL)   1230

LINGUISTICS (See also Geolinguistics, Language)
English, linguistics & classics   RICKER, Shirley E. . . . . .   (NY)   1031
Information linguistics research   WEINBERG, Bella H. . . .   (NY)   1317
Linguistic databases   SERDZIAK, Edward J. . .   (CA)   1116
Linguistics   HARRIS, Mary J. . . . . . .   (AZ)   505
   ARTHUR, Donald B. . . . .   (TX)   35
Linguistics & library science   WEISS, Paul J. . . . .   (NY)   1320
Linguistics, bibliography, reference   KELLY, Richard J. . . . . .   (MN)   638

LINGUISTICS (Cont'd)
Teaching linguistics   WILLIAMSON, Susan G.   (PA)   1348

LINKED (See also Multilink)
Automated linked authority control   BISOM, Diane B. . . . . . .   (CA)   99
Intersystems linking   SANTOSUOSSO, Joseph
     P. . . . .   (MA)   1082
Linked systems   BESSER, Howard A. . . .   (CA)   91
   VEDDER, Harvey B. . . . .   (PA)   1280
Linked systems project   GLAZIER, Ed . . . .   (CA)   440
   SCHUITEMA, Joan E. . .   (OH)   1101
Online records linking   HARRIS, Virginia B. . . . .   (VA)   506

LIST
Educational mailing list development   MOSELEY, Cameron S. . .   (NY)   870
Filing source code listings   BOZE, Lucy G. . . . .   (GA)   124
Library listings   CORWIN, Betty L. . . . . .   (NY)   248
Listing notices, label copy   WOOD, Sallie B. . . . . . .   (NY)   1365
Mailing lists   POWELL, Timothy W. . .   (NY)   989
Online union serial listing   PARRAVANO, Ellen A. . . .   (NY)   944
Publishing monthly sales lists   SMITH, Walter H. . . . . . .   (VA)   1161
Serials & union listing   HICKEY, John T. . . . . . .   (NY)   536
Serials cataloging & union listing   MURRAY, Diane E. . . . . .   (MI)   881
Serials union listing   MANEY, Lana E. . . . . . .   (TX)   765
Serials union listings   CRAWFORD-OPPENHIE-
     MER, Christine . . . . .   (NY)   257
Serials union lists   BOUCHARD-HALL, Robert
     W. . . . .   (MA)   118
Union list   TRACY, Joan I. . . . .   (WA)   1253
Union list coordination   ARNN, Judith A. . . . .   (TX)   33
Union list of serials   PIKE, Lee E. . . . .   (AL)   973
   HAGGARD, Lynn . . . . . .   (TX)   483
   CHENG, Sheung O. . . . .   (TAI)   206
   WANG, Sin C. . . . .   (TAI)   1303
Union list serials   HIGGINS, Flora T. . . . . .   (NJ)   537
Union listing   CHANG, Sookang H. . . .   (IL)   201
   CHATTERTON, Leigh A.   (MA)   204
   KINGSTON, Mary L. . . . .   (MD)   652
   HARTMAN, Anne M. . . .   (NY)   508
   MOORE, Brian P. . . . . . .   (OH)   858
   WARREN, Karen T. . . . .   (SC)   1306
   WALKER, Bonnie M. . . .   (TX)   1295
   POLLARD, Margaret E. . .   (WI)   981
Union listing, serials   MONTGOMERY, Teresa L.   (CA)   856
Union listings   O'DONOVAN, Patricia A.   (OR)   917
   CHIU, Ida K. . . . .   (TX)   209
Union lists   HAAS, Florence A. . . . . .   (CA)   480
   MCCUTCHEON, Dianne E.   (MD)   801
   MCQUEEN, Lorraine . . . .   (ON)   817
Union lists of serials   NEUFELD, Judith B. . . . .   (NY)   897
   ADREAN, Louis V. . . . . .   (OH)   7

LISTENING
Reading, listening & viewing guidance   RING, Constance B. . . . .   (NY)   1035

LITERACY (See also Illiterates)
Adult & children literacy   LENGES, Magdelene . . .   (IN)   715
Adult literacy   THOMAS, Vivian . . . . . .   (CA)   1238
   MCCAFFERY, Laurabelle   (IN)   793
   ARMITAGE, Katherine Y.   (NC)   32
   ROMISHER, Sivya S. . . .   (NJ)   1053
   LYMAN, Helen H. . . . . . .   (NY)   751
   BERLIN, Susan T. . . . . .   (OH)   87
   GREESON, Judy G. . . . .   (TN)   465
   STRAWDER, Maxine S. .   (TN)   1201
Adult literacy materials   GOLDBERG, Rhoda L. . .   (TX)   444
Adult literacy tutor trainer   KORNITSKY, Judith M. .   (FL)   672
American literacy history   ABBOTT, Craig S. . . . . .   (IL)   1
Community literacy councils   HALEY, Anne E. . . . . . .   (WA)   486
Computer literacy   HALLBERG, Sharon P. . .   (CA)   489
   BADER, Shelley . . . .   (DC)   44
   BURGESS, Barbara J. . .   (IA)   159
   BARTLETT, Gwenell J. . .   (KS)   61
Computer literacy for students   HUNTER, Cecilia A. . . . .   (TX)   576
Computer literacy skills   VALLAR, Cynthia L. . . . .   (MD)   1271
Computer literacy software   ROSEN, Elizabeth M. . . .   (CA)   1055

LITERACY (Cont'd)

Subject	Name	State	Page
Computer literacy training	NEWHARD, Eleanor M.	(CA)	899
	ARNY, Philip H.	(LA)	34
High/low literacy bibliographer	KORNITSKY, Judith M.	(FL)	672
Information literacy	SALLE, Ellen M.	(CO)	1076
In-house computer literacy	KRONE, Judith P.	(GA)	679
Libraries & literacy	FISCHER, Anna M.	(PA)	379
	LOCKETT, Sandra B.	(WI)	736
Library literacy programs	LAW, Aileen E.	(SC)	704
Library literacy services	STRONG, Gary E.	(CA)	1203
Literacy	LINSLEY, Priscilla M.	(CO)	731
	JONES, Douglas M.	(FL)	612
	NICKELSBURG, Marilyn M.	(IA)	902
	KIRK, Sherwood	(IL)	654
	HOLT, Vickie L.	(IN)	554
	PIANE, Mimi	(IN)	969
	PICHA, Charlotte G.	(IN)	970
	WELLS, Stewart L.	(MD)	1323
	LANGEVIN, Ann T.	(NV)	695
	OSSOLINSKI, Lynn	(NV)	928
	MARKARIAN, Rita J.	(NY)	771
	MARTIN, Brian G.	(NY)	775
	MILLER, Roy D.	(NY)	842
	PALMER, Julia R.	(NY)	936
	RYAN, Jenny L.	(NY)	1071
	SCHWABACHER, Sara A.	(NY)	1104
	BELL, Ellen	(OH)	76
	VESELY, Marilyn L.	(OK)	1283
	SHUEY, Andrea L.	(TX)	1133
	BURNETT, Wayne C.	(ON)	162
Literacy & English classes	GRUENBECK, Laurie	(TX)	474
Literacy & large print	LEGO, Jane B.	(VA)	712
Literacy & reading comprehension	SIEGEL, Martin A.	(IL)	1136
Literacy & reading promotion	ALLEN, Richard H.	(NE)	16
Literacy beyond mere comprehension	WINKLER, Carol A.	(MO)	1355
Literacy coordinator	KROEHLER, Beth A.	(IN)	679
Literacy education	VAUGHAN, Elinor F.	(GA)	1279
	ROLSTAD, Gary O.	(IL)	1052
Literacy efforts	MCCORMICK, Sheila P.	(MA)	799
Literacy program	POWELL, Anice C.	(MS)	988
	MCCONNELL, Lorelei C.	(NJ)	797
	STEWART, Jeanne E.	(MS)	1192
Literacy program coordination			
Literacy prog development & evaluation	MADDEN, Doreitha R.	(NJ)	758
Literacy programs	BRONSON, Diane A.	(GA)	140
	LINTNER, Barbara J.	(IL)	731
	WESTNEAT, Helen C.	(OH)	1327
	RADOFF, Leonard I.	(TX)	1002
Literacy programs in libraries	PARK, Janice R.	(MI)	941
Literacy programs in public libraries	CARD, Judy	(TN)	180
Literacy volunteerism	DIRKSEN, Jean	(SK)	305
Outreach & bookmobile services, literacy	JONES, Charlotte W.	(WA)	611
Promoting literacy projects	KRETTEK, Josephine G.	(IA)	678
Reading, writing, literacy consulting	MCDONOUGH, Timothy M.	(CA)	803
Services to the underserved, literacy	RUBY, Carmela M.	(CA)	1065
Volunteer literacy programs	TATE, Elizabeth L.	(MD)	1225

LITERATURE (See also Fiction, Nonfiction, Philological, Poetry, Prose)

Subject	Name	State	Page
Abstracting current medical literature	SHIPLEY, Ruth M.	(MO)	1131
Accounting & auditing literature	DOSER, Virginia A.	(CA)	313
Adolescent literature	KIRK, Mary L.	(IA)	654
	LANGHORNE, Mary J.	(IA)	696
	GROSE, Rosemary F.	(MA)	472
	GIBSON, Robert S.	(VA)	432
	JONES, Sally L.	(WA)	615
Advertising & promotional literature	LONGO, Margaret K.	(CA)	740
Aerospace literature	SCOTT, Catherine D.	(DC)	1107
Aerospace technical literature	BOYD, Effie W.	(TN)	122
African literature history & arts	HUTSON, Jean B.	(NY)	579
Afro-American, American lit resrch	BAKISH, David J.	(NY)	50
Afro-American children's literature	ELAM, Barbara C.	(MA)	341
Afro-American literature & art	HUTSON, Jean B.	(NY)	579
American & English literature	ELDREDGE, Mary	(CA)	342
	DAVIS, Sandra B.	(IL)	281
American & English lit bibliography	BAKY, John S.	(PA)	50

LITERATURE (Cont'd)

Subject	Name	State	Page
American & foreign language literature	SHIRES, Nancy P.	(NC)	1131
American literature	DOSER, Virginia A.	(CA)	313
	FLYNN, Richard M.	(DC)	387
	MORTON, Bruce	(MT)	870
	WHITTINGTON, Erma P.	(NC)	1334
	BROWAR, Lisa M.	(NY)	141
	DAVIS, Inez W.	(TN)	279
American literature, romanticism	FISHER, Benjamin F.	(MS)	380
Anglo-American literature	WIENER, Paul B.	(NY)	1336
Architecture literature & information	HAVLIK, Robert J.	(IN)	513
Art & literature bibliography	MCCLEARY, William E.	(LA)	796
Art & literature reference	REID, Kendall M.	(VA)	1018
Arts literature	WALKER, William B.	(NY)	1296
	PISCIOTTA, Henry A.	(PA)	976
Asian languages & literature cataloging	TIBBITS, Edith J.	(NE)	1243
Astronomy & astrophysics lit & databases	KNUDSEN, Helen Z.	(CA)	666
Astronomy literature	PRIMACK, Alice L.	(FL)	993
Automotive engineering literature	WARD, Maryanne	(WA)	1304
Bibliography of English literature	PROPAS, Sharon W.	(OH)	995
Biological literature	DAVIS, Elisabeth B.	(IL)	278
Biological literature instruction	WILLIAMS, Doris C.	(NY)	1343
Biomedical computerized lit searching	DORNER, Marian T.	(OH)	313
Biomedical literature research, indexing	COMPTON, Joan C.	(CA)	235
Biomedical literature searching	SMITH, Yvonne B.	(NJ)	1161
Business literature	GRAYSON, Virginia S.	(CT)	460
	ROSENTHAL, Andrea M.	(MA)	1057
	ERICKSON, Sandra E.	(NY)	352
Buying & selling of American literature	MARTIN, John W.	(IL)	776
Buying & selling of English literature	MARTIN, John W.	(IL)	776
Canadian children's literature	MARTINEZ, Helen	(NF)	779
	AUBREY, Irene E.	(ON)	38
	HAMBLETON, Alixe E.	(SK)	490
Cataloging, language & literature	MOORE, Anne C.	(AZ)	858
Cataloging of legal literature	ODSEN, Elizabeth R.	(AK)	917
Catholic literature	BELLAVANCE, Maria I.	(TX)	78
Change & loss in children's literature	ELAM, Barbara C.	(MA)	341
Chemical information, lit searching	JOHNSON, David K.	(NJ)	603
Chemical literature	WILLHITE, Sherry	(CA)	1341
	MITCHELL, Martha M.	(IL)	849
	MAYER, June C.	(NJ)	789
Chemical literature & reference	YAGELLO, Virginia E.	(OH)	1376
Chemical literature search	CHU, Insoo L.	(CA)	212
Chemical literature searching	LAMBERT, Nancy	(CA)	690
	LERITZ, M K.	(CT)	717
	KASPERKO, Jean M.	(PA)	629
Chemical lit, substructure searching	SAARI, David S.	(IN)	1072
Chemical patents, literature databases	UMFLEET, Ruth A.	(TX)	1268
Children & young adult literature	MARR, Charles A.	(CA)	773
	HATHAWAY, Milton G.	(NC)	512
	BURT, Lesta N.	(TX)	164
Children & youth literature	OAKLEY, Adeline D.	(MA)	913
Children's & young adult literature	ROSEN, Elizabeth M.	(CA)	1055
	DAIGNEAULT, Audrey I.	(CT)	270
	FISHER, Margery M.	(CT)	381
	SPENCER, Albert F.	(GA)	1173
	LOWE, Joy L.	(LA)	744
	EHRICH, Joan C.	(MA)	339
	WERNER, Laura L.	(MO)	1325
	O'BRYANT, Alice A.	(MT)	915
	BUSBIN, O M.	(NC)	164
	HERBERT, Barbara R.	(NJ)	530
	VANDERGRIFT, Kay E.	(NJ)	1274
	MASCIA, Regina B.	(NY)	780
	LATROBE, Kathy H.	(OK)	701
	LAUGHLIN, Mildred A.	(OK)	703
	ANTHONY, Rose M.	(WI)	29
	DRESANG, Eliza T.	(WI)	319
	HOWARD, Elizabeth F.	(WV)	564
	SALTMAN, Judith M.	(BC)	1077
	HAMBLETON, Alixe E.	(SK)	490
Children's & young people's literature	BRUNER, Katharine E.	(TN)	150
Children's books & literature	MOSES, Camelia T.	(NY)	871
Children's English & French literature	WALSH, Mary A.	(PQ)	1300

LITERATURE (Cont'd)
Children's literature

MCCLAIN, Harriet V.	(AK)	795
CARR, Charles E.	(AL)	185
VISSCHER, Helga B.	(AL)	1285
COLCLASURE, Marian S.	(AR)	230
LANGSAM, Christine E.	(AR)	696
DOWNUM, Evelyn R.	(AZ)	317
JANSON, Sherryl A.	(AZ)	594
NILSEN, Alleen P.	(AZ)	904
BAUER, Caroline F.	(CA)	65
BOYLLS, Virginia W.	(CA)	124
CONNOR, Anne C.	(CA)	237
DAY, Bettie B.	(CA)	282
KING, Cynthia	(CA)	650
MORRIS, Effie L.	(CA)	866
PRESSNALL, Patricia E.	(CA)	991
SIGMAN, Paula M.	(CA)	1137
VARKENTINE, Aganita	(CA)	1278
WAGNER, Sharon L.	(CA)	1292
WAKEFIELD, Jacqueline M.	(CA)	1293
WEEDMAN, Judith	(CA)	1315
WINSTON, Gillian R.	(CA)	1356
ZALE, Phyllis J.	(CA)	1385
AKE, Mary W.	(CO)	9
HUGHES, Sondra K.	(CO)	572
VOLC, Judith G.	(CO)	1287
EMBARDO, Ellen E.	(CT)	347
FADER, Ellen G.	(CT)	360
SCHULTZE, Salvatrice G.	(CT)	1102
HAITH, Dorothy M.	(DC)	484
SALVADORE, Maria B.	(DC)	1078
YOUNG, Christina C.	(DC)	1381
FIORE, Carole D.	(FL)	379
MILLER, Betty D.	(FL)	836
PATTISON, Joanne	(FL)	948
STINES, Joe R.	(FL)	1194
BENNETT, Priscilla B.	(GA)	82
BRIGHTHARP, Wilma S.	(GA)	136
KARP, Hazel B.	(GA)	628
BURGESS, Barbara J.	(IA)	159
CAMP, Emily E.	(IA)	175
GRIFFIN, Kathryn A.	(IA)	468
LETTOW, Lucille J.	(IA)	719
MEIER, Patricia L.	(IA)	821
TOVREA, Roxanna L.	(IA)	1252
BOLT, Janice A.	(IL)	113
BOURKE, Jacqueline K.	(IL)	119
CASE, Doris A.	(IL)	191
GUNDERSEN, Shirley S.	(IL)	477
HARRIS, Jane F.	(IL)	504
REPTA, Vada L.	(IL)	1024
RICHARDSON, Selma K.	(IL)	1030
ROBERTSON, Ina N.	(IL)	1042
SCHORMANN, Marguerite T.	(IL)	1099
STRAWN, Aimee W.	(IL)	1201
SUTHERLAND, Zena B.	(IL)	1211
VOTH, Mary S.	(IL)	1289
WEISMAN, Kathryn M.	(IL)	1319
ALLEN, Patricia J.	(IN)	15
BICKEL, Bernice M.	(IN)	94
BRIDGE, Stephen W.	(IN)	135
GLEASON, Ruth I.	(IN)	440
JACKSON, Susan M.	(IN)	588
TEUBERT, Lola H.	(IN)	1233
TIMKO, Patricia A.	(IN)	1246
BARTLETT, Gwenell J.	(KS)	61
BOGAN, Mary E.	(KS)	110
LEVEL, M J.	(KS)	719
MCIRVIN, Jane P.	(KS)	809
MCKENZIE, Joe M.	(KS)	811
MCLEOD, Debra A.	(KS)	814
DOAN, Janice K.	(KY)	307
JACOBSON-BEYER, Harry E.	(KY)	590
JAMES, Karen G.	(KY)	592
MILLER, Barbara S.	(KY)	835
TURNER, Ray	(KY)	1265
CARSTENS, Jane E.	(LA)	188

LITERATURE (Cont'd)
Children's literature

KENNEDY, Frances C.	(LA)	641
MOSLEY, Mattie J.	(LA)	871
STEWART, Mary E.	(LA)	1193
CAMPANELLA, Alice D.	(MA)	175
GROSE, Rosemary F.	(MA)	472
HEINS, Ethel L.	(MA)	522
KELLMAN, Lillian S.	(MA)	637
MCDONALD, Murray F.	(MA)	803
ROBINSON, Phyllis A.	(MA)	1044
STAVIS, Ruth L.	(MA)	1183
TASHJIAN, Virginia A.	(MA)	1224
WEISCHEDEL, Elaine F.	(MA)	1319
DEAN, Frances C.	(MD)	283
PILZER, Cecily R.	(MD)	973
RUFF, Martha R.	(MD)	1066
BERRIE, Ellen T.	(ME)	90
BIELICH, Paul S.	(MI)	95
BLATT, Gloria T.	(MI)	104
BRAGLIA, Nancy L.	(MI)	127
BRANZBURG, Marian G.	(MI)	129
CHAKLOSH, Cynthia L.	(MI)	197
MCCARTY, Linda A.	(MI)	795
PEREZ-STABLE, Maria A.	(MI)	958
STEPHENS, John H.	(MI)	1188
STILLEY, Cynthia S.	(MI)	1194
VOIGHT, Nancy R.	(MI)	1287
DIMENT, Elna N.	(MN)	304
GILLIS, Ruth J.	(MN)	436
MONSON, Dianne L.	(MN)	855
PIEHL, Kathleen K.	(MN)	971
SIBLEY, Carol H.	(MN)	1134
SIMMONS, Antoinette S.	(MN)	1139
BELCHER, Nancy S.	(MO)	76
ROSS, Shirley D.	(MO)	1059
SADLER, Philip A.	(MO)	1073
JONES, Dolores B.	(MS)	612
LAUGHLIN, Jeannine L.	(MS)	703
SUMRALL, Ada M.	(MS)	1210
DORNBERGER, Julie L.	(NC)	313
FISH, Barbara M.	(NC)	380
FREEDMAN, Barbara G.	(NC)	400
GOLDEN, Susan L.	(NC)	445
PENN, Lea M.	(NC)	957
STRICKLAND, Mary L.	(NC)	1202
WALKER, Judith A.	(NC)	1295
KENT, Jeffrey A.	(NH)	642
SARLES, Christie V.	(NH)	1083
TATE, Joanne D.	(NH)	1225
ANTCZAK, Janice	(NJ)	28
CONDIT, Martha O.	(NJ)	235
FISHER, Scott L.	(NJ)	381
GOLDBERG, Barbara W.	(NJ)	444
SHERMAN, Louise L.	(NJ)	1128
SKRAMOUSKY, Mary C.	(NJ)	1147
CARLSON, Kathleen A.	(NM)	182
HENDRICKSON, Linnea M.	(NM)	527
MATTER, Kathy L.	(NM)	785
ODENHEIM, Claire E.	(NM)	916
GROSSHANS, Merilyn P.	(NV)	473
AMISON, Mary V.	(NY)	20
BEHRMANN, Christine A.	(NY)	75
BUTLER, Rebekah O.	(NY)	167
CANDE, Lorraine N.	(NY)	178
CUMMINS, Julie A.	(NY)	264
GAUCH, Patricia L.	(NY)	422
HATCH, Nancy W.	(NY)	511
HOPKINS, Lee B.	(NY)	558
KLEINBURD, Freda	(NY)	659
KULLESEID, Eleanor R.	(NY)	683
LENZ, Millicent A.	(NY)	716
LONG, Joanna R.	(NY)	739
LOPATIN, Edith K.	(NY)	740
MAGUDA, Joyce M.	(NY)	760
NEVETT, Micki S.	(NY)	897
PERSON, Diane G.	(NY)	961
PRUITT, Brenda F.	(NY)	996

LITERATURE (Cont'd)
Children's literature

SCHMIDTMANN, Nancy
  K. . . . . (NY) 1096
SIVULICH, Sandra S. . . . (NY) 1145
STRANC, Mary C. . . . . . (NY) 1200
TICE, Margaret E. . . . . . . (NY) 1244
WIGG, Ristiina M. . . . . . . (NY) 1337
WITT, Susan T. . . . . (NY) 1358
BAKER, Carol J. . . . . . . (OH) 48
CLEM, Harriet M. . . . . . . (OH) 220
DRACH, Priscilla L. . . . . (OH) 318
KLAUS, Susan B. . . . . . . (OH) 658
MCDANIEL, Deanna J. . . (OH) 801
NOWAK, Leslie A. . . . . . (OH) 911
RODDA, Donna S. . . . . . (OH) 1047
SMITH, Noralee W. . . . . (OH) 1159
WARREN, Dorothea C. . . (OH) 1306
WILSON, Letitia A. . . . . . (OH) 1351
BAUER, Carolyn J. . . . . . (OK) 65
PARKER, Eleanor V. . . . . (OK) 941
RABURN, Josephine R. . . (OK) 1001
UNDERHILL, Jan . . . . . . (OK) 1268
FEUERHELM, Jill A. . . . . (OR) 374
MCCOY, Joanne . . . . . (OR) 799
BAUMGARTNER, Barbara
  W. . . . . (PA) 66
CROWE, Virginia M. . . . . (PA) 261
DEFASSIO, Sharon L. . . (PA) 287
GEARHART, Carol A. . . . (PA) 424
GLASS, Catherine C. . . . (PA) 440
GRAHAM, Marilyn L. . . . (PA) 456
MARON-WOOD, Kathy M. (PA) 772
MILLER, Mary E. . . . . . . (PA) 840
NAISMITH, Patricia A. . . (PA) 887
SANDERS, Minda M. . . . (PA) 1080
WALSH, Carolyn C. . . . . (PA) 1299
WHEELER, Martha M. . . (PA) 1329
WOLFE, Mary S. . . . . . . (PA) 1361
MCKEE, Virginia W. . . . . (RI) 810
BRANTON, Mildred M. . . (SC) 129
JACOCKS, Marcia W. . . . (SC) 590
ESTES, Glenn E. . . . . . (TN) 355
WRIGHT, David A. . . . . . (TN) 1371
BELL, Jo A. . . . . (TX) 77
CARTER, Betty B. . . . . . (TX) 189
DUFFY, Suzanne . . . . . . (TX) 324
EASON, Lisa H. . . . . . . (TX) 332
HOLLAND, Deborah K. . . (TX) 550
HOOVER, Gloria E. . . . . (TX) 557
IMMROTH, Barbara F. . . (TX) 582
MCBURNEY, Lynnea R. . . (TX) 792
MCCASLIN, Cheryl A. . . (TX) 795
PARIS, Janelle A. . . . . . . (TX) 940
SCAMMAN, Carol J. . . . (TX) 1087
SILVERMAN, Barbara G. (TX) 1138
OLSEN, Katherine M. . . . (UT) 921
BIGELOW, Therese G. . . (VA) 95
BROWN, Dale W. . . . . . (VA) 143
GAVER, Mary V. . . . . . . (VA) 423
PAISLEY, Anna S. . . . . . (VA) 935
PEARL, Patricia D. . . . . . (VA) 952
RAMSEY, Inez L. . . . . . . (VA) 1006
WAMPLER, Dorris M. . . . (VA) 1302
GREENE, Grace W. . . . . (VT) 464
BENNE, Mae M. . . . . . . (WA) 81
BLUME, Scott . . . . (WA) 107
ERICKSON, Jane . . . . . . (WA) 352
HUTTON, Emily A. . . . . . (WA) 579
MACDONALD, Margaret
  R. . . . . (WA) 754
POLISHUK, Bernard . . . . (WA) 980
CZARNEZKI, Mary E. . . . (WI) 268
DEES DAUGHERTY,
  Kristin . . . . (WI) 287
DIETZ, Kathryn A. . . . . . (WI) 302
HERMAN, Gertrude B. . . (WI) 531
HUMPHRIES, Lajean . . . (WI) 574
MORROW, Kathryn M. . . (WI) 869
RETZER, Cathy E. . . . . . (WI) 1024

LITERATURE (Cont'd)
Children's literature

ROOZEN, Nancy L. . . . . (WI) 1054
WASSINK, Patricia L. . . . (WI) 1308
WILLETT, Holly G. . . . . . (WI) 1341
WISEMAN, Mary J. . . . . (WI) 1357
CRESSWELL, Stephen . . (WV) 258
CHATTON, Barbara A. . . (WY) 204
BROWN, David K. . . (AB) 143
HERSCOVITCH, Pearl . . (AB) 533
KISSAU, Arlene M. . . . . . (AB) 656
LOVENBURG, Susan L. . . (AB) 743
CHAN, Mary L. . . . . (BC) 199
FUNK, Grace E. . . . . (BC) 410
GIBB, Betty J. . . . . (BC) 431
EGAN, Bessie C. . . . . . . (MB) 338
BOUDREAU, Berthe . . . . (NB) 118
RAUCH, Doris E. . . . . . . (NB) 1010
MEWS, Alison J. . . . . . . (NF) 829
CHURCHMAN, Alice M. . (ON) 213
CULLIS, Lois I. . . . . (ON) 263
FASICK, Adele M. . . . . . (ON) 366
KOSTIAK, Adele E. . . . . (ON) 673
LEMIEUX, Louise . . . . . . (PQ) 715
GAGNON, Andre . . . . . . (SK) 412

Children's literature & activities PASSARELLO, Nancy H. (FL) 946
Children's literature & education COLLINS, Mary E. . . . . . (IN) 233
Children's literature & library services BUSH, Margaret A. . . . . . (MA) 165
Children's literature & materials WILLIAMS, Helen E. . . . (MD) 1343
Children's literature & programming NG, Carol S. . . . . (CA) 900
  HEITMAN, Lynn . . . . (IL) 523
  NOAH, Carolyn B. . . . . . (MA) 906
  REID, Margaret B. . . . . . (OH) 1018
Children's literature & programs TOM, Chow L. . . . . (HI) 1249
Children's literature & service BRETING, Elizabeth C. . . (MO) 133
Children's literature & services PINNELL-STEPHENS,
  June A. . . . . (AK) 975
  ATKINSON, Joan L. . . . . (AL) 38
  VEITCH, Carol J. . . . . . . (NC) 1281
  COURTNEY, Aida N. . . . (NJ) 251
  FICHTELBERG, Susan . . (NJ) 374
  RAIVELY, Martha M. . . . (PA) 1004
Children's literature appreciation BROWN, Judith B. . . . . . (MD) 145
Children's literature before 1900 BALDWIN, Ruth M. . . . . (FL) 52
Children's literature computer
  software FEUERHELM, Jill A. . . . . (OR) 374
Children's literature criticism LACY, Lyn E. . . . . (MN) 687
Children's literature, ethnic AUSTIN, Mary C. . . . . . . (HI) 40
Children's literature for parents WINKLER, Carol A. . . . . (MO) 1355
Children's literature for young children BALDWIN, Ruth M. . . . . (FL) 52
Children's literature in education MONSON, Dianne L. . . . (MN) 855
Children's literature in inner-city NIX, Kemie . . . . (GA) 905
Children's literature, instruction NELSON, Olga G. . . . . . (OH) 895
Children's literature lecturing BATES, Barbara S. . . . . (PA) 63
Children's literature, library services CORSARO, Julie A. . . . . (IL) 248
Children's literature, past & present COUGHLAN, Margaret N. (DC) 250
Children's literature, preschool WINFREE, Barbara S. . . (LA) 1354
Children's literature programs FOERTIN, Yves P. . . . . . (PQ) 387
Children's literature, reading MCGOWN, Sue W. . . . . (TX) 807
Children's literature reference HURLEY, Doreen S. . . . . (PA) 577
Children's literature, software HOFMANN, Susan M. . . (PA) 548
Children's literature specialist ZEIGER, Hanna B. . . . . . (MA) 1387
Children's literature teaching SCHMITZ, Eugenia E. . . (WI) 1096
Children's literature, 1900-1950 BALDWIN, Ruth M. . . . . (FL) 52
Children's religious literature PEARL, Patricia D. . . . . . (VA) 952
Children's service, literature RUBIN, Ellen B. . . . . (NY) 1064
Children's services & literature JOHNSON, Beth . . . . . . (GA) 602
  EDMONDS, M L. . . . . . . (IL) 336
  ROMAN, Susan . . . . (IL) 1052
  MEIZNER, Kathie L. . . . . (MD) 822
  ROSS, Kathleen A. . . . . . (NY) 1058
Choral music literature SHARP, Avery T. . . . . . . (TX) 1122
Citrus literature RUSS, Pamela K. . . . . . . (FL) 1068
Classical languages & literature BYRE, Calvin S. . . . . . . (IL) 169
Clinical literature retrieval, databases KINNAIRD, Cheryl D. . . (IL) 653
Clothing & textiles literature FETTERMAN, Nelma I. . . (AB) 374
Collection development, language lit WARREN, Peggy A. . . . . (ON) 1306
Comparative literature KELLY, Richard J. . . . . . (MN) 638

LITERATURE (Cont'd)

Subject	Name	State	Page
Computer literature searching	BELANGER, Sandra E.	(CA)	75
	GLENDENNING, Barbara J.	(CA)	441
	MONTAG, Diane	(CO)	855
	MACKEY, Wendy W.	(MA)	757
	LAUTENSCHLAG, Elisabeth C.	(PA)	703
	KERSTETTER, Virginia M.	(VA)	644
	NOFSINGER, Mary M.	(WA)	907
Computer science literature	MCDANIEL, Sara H.	(GA)	801
Computerized literature	WONG, Anita	(ON)	1362
Computerized literature searching	HENTZ, Margaret B.	(CT)	530
	NESBIT, Angus B.	(IL)	896
	JONES, Deborah A.	(IN)	612
	DLOTT, Nancy B.	(MA)	306
	HALL, Robert G.	(MA)	488
Computerized literature training	WONG, Ming K.	(DC)	1363
Computing literature	HILDEBRANDT, Darlene M.	(WA)	538
Contemporary literature, poetry, fiction	HUDZIK, Robert T.	(OH)	570
Coordination of literary programs	CALLAHAN, Helen H.	(CT)	173
Critical reviews of literature	HENDERSON, Madeline M.	(MD)	526
Criticism of professional literature	SHAPIRO, Lillian L.	(NY)	1121
Current awareness of lit for routing	FOSTER, Helen M.	(FL)	392
Dental literature reference	WILLIAMS, Ann T.	(TX)	1342
Development literature	HOWELL, John B.	(IA)	565
Dominican literature	NITZ, Andrew M.	(DC)	905
Dramatic literature	OGDEN, Dunbar H.	(CA)	918
Early childhood literature	KOEPP, Sara H.	(IA)	668
Editing music & music literature	PRUETT, James W.	(DC)	996
18th century British literature	DEVINE, Marie E.	(CT)	297
Electronics literature	MCGORRAY, John J.	(AZ)	807
Engineering literature	GRAYSON, Virginia S.	(CT)	460
	CANDELMO, Emily	(NY)	178
	ERICKSON, Sandra E.	(NY)	352
	WEBSTER, James K.	(NY)	1314
	ROUTLEDGE, Patricia A.	(MB)	1062
Engineering literature & information	HAVLIK, Robert J.	(IN)	513
English & American literature	MCPHERON, William	(CA)	817
	KING, Judith D.	(CT)	651
	STEBELMAN, Scott D.	(DC)	1183
	ELLIS, Marie C.	(GA)	345
	NAIMAN, Sandra M.	(IL)	886
	BRACKEN, James K.	(IN)	124
	IMMLER, Frank	(MN)	582
	BROCKMAN, William S.	(NJ)	138
	JONES, Arthur E.	(NJ)	611
	FRALEY, David B.	(WA)	395
English literature	MEEKER, Robert B.	(IL)	821
	FUDERER, Laura S.	(IN)	408
	DICKSON, Katherine M.	(MD)	301
	GAUCH, Patricia L.	(NY)	422
	LINDSAY, Jean S.	(NY)	729
	MARTIN, Lyn M.	(NY)	777
	MCGLINCHEE, Claire	(NY)	806
	WIERUM, Ann R.	(WA)	1337
	O'NEILL, Louise N.	(ON)	924
English literature bibliography	THOMSON, Dorothy F.	(ON)	1241
English literature, romantic	STAM, David H.	(NY)	1179
English literature selector	THORSON, Connie C.	(NM)	1242
European languages & literature	KUJANSUU, Asko J.	(AB)	683
European literature	SIGNORI, Donna L.	(BC)	1137
Fiction & literature	JORDAN, Linda K.	(OK)	616
Fiction, literature	HUNT, Janis E.	(IL)	575
Food & nutrition literature	CULBERTSON, Diana L.	(IL)	263
Foreign language literature selection	DOLAN-HEITLINGER, Eileen	(IN)	309
Foreign language scientific literature	SAMSON, Mary	(ON)	1079
Foreign languages & literatures	TIMBERS, Jill G.	(MI)	1245
Foreign literature	GLIKIN, Ronda	(MI)	441
Foreign literatures	MACIUSZKO, Jerzy J.	(OH)	755
Foreign scientific technical literature	BROPHY, Charles A.	(OH)	141
French Canadian children's literature	POTVIN, Claude	(NB)	987
	AUBREY, Irene E.	(ON)	38
French Canadian literature education	GUERETTE, Charlotte M.	(PQ)	476
French language & literature	DEON, Judy S.	(BC)	293
French literature	WIERUM, Ann R.	(WA)	1337
French literature & history	MCNAMARA, Charles B.	(NC)	816

LITERATURE (Cont'd)

Subject	Name	State	Page
French literature education	GUERETTE, Charlotte M.	(PQ)	476
Geology literature & information	KLIMLEY, Susan	(NY)	661
German language & literature	STUHR-ROMMEREIM, Rebecca A.	(KS)	1205
	MCKILLIP, Rita J.	(WI)	811
	TRAICHEL, Rudolf D.	(AB)	1253
German literature	WISE, Leona L.	(CA)	1357
	THYM, Jurgen	(NY)	1243
Gerontology & geriatrics literature	POST, Joyce A.	(PA)	986
Greek & Latin literature	CARNOVSKY, Ruth F.	(CA)	184
Health administration literature	POOLE, Connie	(IL)	983
	SCHWARTZ, Dorothy D.	(NY)	1104
Health science literature	GREEN, Deidre E.	(ON)	461
Health sciences literature	ROPER, Fred W.	(SC)	1054
Health sciences literature access	FLEMMING, Tom	(ON)	384
Historic aviation literature	PARKS, Dennis H.	(WI)	943
Historical & literary manuscripts	DUNLAP, Leslie W.	(IA)	326
	THOMPSON, Harry F.	(SD)	1239
Historical children's literature	BROWN, June E.	(NY)	145
History & literature	LAMBREV, Garrett I.	(CA)	691
History of children's literature	MAXWELL, Margaret F.	(AZ)	788
	CARSTENS, Jane E.	(LA)	188
	POND, Patricia B.	(OR)	982
History of medical literature, rare bks	MIMS, Dorothy H.	(GA)	845
Home electronics literature	FETTERMAN, Nelma I.	(AB)	374
Hospital literature	MONROE, Donald H.	(IN)	855
	GALVIN, Jeanne D.	(NY)	415
Humanities literature	BROADUS, Robert N.	(NC)	138
Humanities research, literature	TIBBO, Helen R.	(MD)	1244
Indexing periodical literature	VARKENTINE, Aganita	(CA)	1278
Information science, english literature	JONES-TRENT, Bernice R.	(VA)	616
International & foreign legal literature	HEAD, Anita K.	(DC)	518
International children's literature	POARCH, Margaret E.	(CA)	979
	WONG, Patricia M.	(CA)	1363
Introducing children's literature	STARRETT, Mildred J.	(AZ)	1182
Italian-American literature	GREEN, Rose B.	(PA)	462
Japanese technl literature abstracting	FOWELLS, Fumi T.	(MI)	393
Jewish literature	WIENER, Theodore	(DC)	1336
Juvenile & young adult literature	HOUSEWARD, Bernice A.	(MI)	563
Juvenile literature	PATRON, Susan H.	(CA)	947
	CRACE, Sallye C.	(KY)	254
	CHEW, Susan M.	(LA)	207
	MELLON, Constance A.	(NC)	822
Latgalian literature	BRISKA, Boniface	(NY)	137
Law & literature	BANDER, Edward J.	(MA)	54
Lecturing on children's literature	VOLC, Judith G.	(CO)	1287
Legal literature	ROFF, Jill R.	(MA)	1049
	GOLDMAN, Martha A.	(NY)	445
	ROJAS, Alexandra A.	(NY)	1051
Library literature	STENSTROM, Patricia F.	(IL)	1187
Library professional literature	WYNAR, Bohdan S.	(CO)	1375
Library science literature	STEELE, Patricia A.	(IN)	1184
Life sciences literature	FLEURY, Bruce E.	(LA)	385
	DODSON, Carolyn	(NM)	308
Literary agent	ROBLING, John S.	(MI)	1045
Literary bibliography	ABBOTT, Craig S.	(IL)	1
Literary magazines	CASSELL, Kay A.	(NY)	193
Literary manuscript databases	MACDERMAID, Anne	(ON)	754
Literary manuscripts	BROWAR, Lisa M.	(NY)	141
Literary quotations	SHIPPS, Anthony W.	(IN)	1131
Literary research	HO, Paul J.	(FL)	545
Literary research consultation	MASON, Michael L.	(NJ)	781
Literary scholarship	LEWIS, John S.	(TX)	723
Literary videos	LESNIAK, Rose	(NY)	718
Literature	NASSO, Christine	(MI)	889
	SHAPIRO, Marian S.	(MO)	1121
	STOCK, Norman	(NJ)	1195
	NICHOLSON, Myreen M.	(VA)	902
Literature & art databases	HOFFMAN, Herbert H.	(CA)	548
Literature & art history books	ALLENTUCK, Marcia E.	(NY)	16
Literature & history reference	BARNETT, Jean D.	(OR)	57
Literature & language reference	THEWS, Dorothy D.	(MN)	1234
Literature & programs children's srvs	HUDDLESTON, Marsha E.	(IL)	569
Literature & social sciences	NEVIN, Susanne	(MN)	898
Literature chemist	WENGER, Milton B.	(NY)	1324
Literature collections development	SWEEDLER, Ulla S.	(CA)	1214
Literature for adolescents	SADLER, Philip A.	(MO)	1073
Literature for children	SPIRT, Diana L.	(NY)	1175
	KIMMEL, Margaret M.	(PA)	649

LITERATURE (Cont'd)

Subject	Name	State	Page
Literature for children & young adults	FISHER, Joan W.	(MD)	381
Literature for youth	JACKSON, Clara O.	(OH)	587
Literature guidance & appreciation	MCCLELLAND, Katherine L.	(GA)	796
Literature instruction & guidance	WOBBE, Jean	(CA)	1359
Literature of American Southwest	BROGDEN, Stephen R.	(IA)	139
Literature of art history	REED, Marcia C.	(CA)	1015
Literature of astronomy	VANATTA, Cathaleen E.	(AZ)	1272
Literature of education	GREEY, Kathleen M.	(OR)	465
	WHALEN, George F.	(ON)	1328
Literature of engineering	MAYLES, William F.	(IN)	790
Literature of higher education	QUAY, Richard H.	(OH)	999
Literature of Mormonism	PURDY, Victor W.	(UT)	998
Literature of science	MAYLES, William F.	(IN)	790
Literature of science & technology	PINELLI, Thomas E.	(VA)	974
Literature of social sciences	SHAW, Shiow J.	(TAI)	1124
Literature of the humanities	LAIR, Nancy C.	(IN)	688
	OAKLEY, Adeline D.	(MA)	913
	THOMPSON, Susan O.	(NY)	1241
	DE SCOSSA, Catriona	(AB)	295
Literature, poetry	KARATNYTSKY, Christine A.	(NY)	627
Literature procurement	GALLAGHER, Eileen W.	(PA)	414
Literature research	CONRAD, Celia B.	(CT)	238
Literature search	EVES, Judith A.	(PA)	359
Literature search product liability	KENNEDY, Joanna C.	(GA)	641
Literature search supervision	CYGAN, Rose M.	(MI)	268
Literature searches	HAYES, Linda J.	(CA)	516
	HURTES, Reva	(FL)	578
	SUMMERS, Kathy B.	(VA)	1209
	MENDOZA, Anthanett C.	(WY)	824
Literature searching	BREWSAUGH, Susan J.	(CA)	134
	KATTLOVE, Rose W.	(CA)	630
	MURPHY, Joan F.	(CA)	880
	PETERSON, Gretchen N.	(CA)	963
	KELLY, Karon M.	(CO)	638
	LUEVANE, Marsha A.	(CO)	747
	WILLIAMS, Alexander	(FL)	1341
	MANGION, Barbara E.	(MA)	765
	REDFEARN, Linda E.	(MA)	1014
	OLIVER, James W.	(MI)	921
	METZGER, Eva C.	(NC)	829
	HOLDEN, Douglas H.	(ND)	550
	CHU, Wendy N.	(NJ)	213
	HAAS, Elaine H.	(NY)	480
	HOOD, Katherine T.	(NY)	556
	MUELLER, Leta A.	(NY)	875
	MOORE, Susan J.	(OH)	861
	ZAPOROZHETZ, Laurene E.	(OH)	1386
	HOWARD, Dianne D.	(PA)	564
	SCHWARZ, Betty P.	(PA)	1105
	MANNING, Helen M.	(TX)	766
Literature searching & astronomy	KNUDSEN, Helen Z.	(CA)	666
Literature searching & reference	HOMAN, J M.	(MI)	555
Literature searching & research	SPARK, Catherine L.	(ON)	1171
Literature sharing	CROCKER, Judith A.	(NM)	259
Manual literature searching	WELCH, Carol J.	(PA)	1321
Manuscripts & rare books literary resrch	REIMAN, Donald H.	(NY)	1020
Marine science literature	PERRONE, Jeanne M.	(DC)	960
Medical & health literature	WORTZEL, Murray N.	(NY)	1369
Medical & nursing literature	KAISLER, Dolores H.	(MD)	622
Medical & pharmaceutical literature	TANEN, Lee J.	(NJ)	1222
Medical literature	TOPP, Marvalyn G.	(IL)	1251
	WALKER, Luise E.	(OR)	1295
	HOUKE, Billy P.	(TX)	563
Medical literature & databases	GIORDANO, Joan	(NY)	438
Medical literature & searching	KATES, Jacqueline R.	(MA)	629
Medical literature indexing	WEAVER, Nancy B.	(MO)	1312
Medical literature searches	SIKORSKI, Charlene S.	(NY)	1137
Medical literature searching	RAINEY, Kathleen O.	(NJ)	1004
Medical reference & literature	NOYES, Suzanne N.	(MA)	911
Medieval & Renaissance literature	WHITE, D J.	(MO)	1330
Medieval German literature	SPOHRER, James H.	(CA)	1175
Mental health literature	COHAN, Lois	(NY)	227
	SORG, Elizabeth A.	(PA)	1168
Methods of literary research	ABBOTT, Craig S.	(IL)	1
Middle Eastern lit collection devlpmnt	BUNDY, David D.	(KY)	157

LITERATURE (Cont'd)

Subject	Name	State	Page
Middle school & young adult literature	MILLER, Ellen L.	(VA)	837
Military & naval literature	AIMONE, Alan C.	(NY)	8
Mining literature	GRAYSON, Virginia S.	(CT)	460
Modern British-American literature	COX, Shelley M.	(IL)	253
Modern European languages & literature	POLIT, Carlos E.	(IN)	980
Modern literary manuscripts	HALL, Holly	(MO)	487
Modern literature	HARRISON, John A.	(AR)	506
Music history & literature	DONALDSON, Anna L.	(TX)	311
Music, literary criticism	FRANK, Mortimer H.	(NY)	397
Music literature abstracting	HOLMES, John H.	(PA)	553
Natural resources literature searching	WAGNER, Barbara L.	(CO)	1291
19th century & 20th century Engl lit	HATCHER, Nolan C.	(GA)	511
19th century British & American lit	COLEY, Betty A.	(TX)	231
19th century literature	FECKO, Marybeth	(SC)	367
Nursing literature	SMITH, Julie L.	(CA)	1156
	GIBSON, Patricia M.	(IL)	432
	STEVENS, Sheryl R.	(MI)	1191
	GEARY, Linda L.	(OH)	424
	COOK, Peggy M.	(OK)	240
Nursing literature research	AUFIERO, Joan I.	(BC)	39
OCLC & literature searching	REILLY, Dayle A.	(MA)	1020
Online literature, sci & tech searching	WALLACE, Wendy L.	(NJ)	1298
Online literature search	CHUNG, Helen S.	(NC)	213
Online literature searching	CRUM, Norman J.	(CA)	262
	GLYNN, Jeannette E.	(CA)	442
	HUNT, Richard K.	(CA)	575
	BODI, Sonia E.	(IL)	109
	BRINKMAN, Carol S.	(KY)	136
	KRESSE, Kerry L.	(KY)	678
	SHEPARD, Margaret E.	(MI)	1127
	OBERC, Susanne F.	(OH)	913
	ROHMILLER, Ellen L.	(OH)	1051
	BERGER, Lewis W.	(PA)	85
	FU, Clare S.	(PA)	407
	KELLAND, John L.	(RI)	635
	WORLEY, Merry P.	(TX)	1369
	PARHAM, Sandra H.	(VA)	940
	LAMB, Cheryl M.	(WI)	689
Online medical literature search	ABRAMSON, Lawrence J.	(MI)	3
Online searching, biomedical literature	INGUI, Bettejean	(CO)	583
Patent literature	COX, Bruce B.	(MO)	253
	ADAMS, Dena R.	(NM)	4
	RIFFLE, Linda	(OH)	1034
Periodical literature indexing	FOX, Elyse H.	(MA)	394
Physics literature	WANAT, Camille A.	(CA)	1302
	PRIMACK, Alice L.	(FL)	993
Place name literature	POWELL, Margaret S.	(OH)	988
Popular literature	SCHLIPF, Frederick A.	(IL)	1094
Preservation & conservation literature	HUEMER, Christina G.	(ITL)	570
Product literature	SATTLER, Pauline	(MI)	1084
	KOELLE, Joyce G.	(NJ)	667
Psychiatric literature	COHAN, Lois	(NY)	227
	TOMASULO, Patricia A.	(NY)	1249
Psychological literature	PORTER, Suzanne	(DC)	985
Public health literature	MUNSEY, Joyce E.	(MD)	879
Publishing & popular literature	TAYLOR, Margaret T.	(MI)	1227
Pulp & paper literature	GAGNON, Vernon N.	(OR)	412
Questioning techniques, lit discussions	SENATOR, Rochelle B.	(CT)	1115
Rare books & literary manuscripts	EBELING-KONING, Blanche T.	(MD)	334
Rare books, literature, music	AUSTIN, Kristi N.	(WA)	40
Reading disabilities literature	SPARKS, Martha F.	(NC)	1171
Reading guidance & children's literature	KONNEKER, Rachel C.	(NC)	670
Reference & literature education	NORRIS, Carol B.	(TN)	909
Reference languages & literature	WARREN, Peggy A.	(ON)	1306
Reference literature	ULINCY, Loretta D.	(PA)	1268
Reference online literature searching	DUNKEL, Lisa M.	(CA)	326
Report literature	HECHT, Judith N.	(OH)	519
Research in American literature	BRODERICK, John C.	(DC)	138
Research in children's literature	BISSETT, Donald J.	(MI)	100
	MONSON, Dianne L.	(MN)	855
Research in the study of literature	MILLER, Robert H.	(KY)	842
Retailer of Black literature	MILLENDER, Dharathola	(IN)	835
Romance languages & literature	POLIT, Carlos E.	(IN)	980
Scandinavian literature	MOLLER, Hans	(PQ)	853
School libraries, children's literature	TERRY, Virginia W.	(MO)	1232

LITERATURE (Cont'd)

Science & engineering literature	MCGORRAY, John J.	(AZ)	807
	BUNTZEN, Joan L.	(CA)	157
	SASS, Samuel	(MA)	1083
Science & medical literature	MOSER, Emily F.	(VA)	870
Science & technology literature	HEINRITZ, Fred J.	(CT)	522
	HOWARD, Helen A.	(PQ)	564
Science literature	ALURI, Rao	(AZ)	19
	HOWARD, Joyce M.	(NY)	564
	WILSON, Concepcion S.	(AUS)	1350
Science technical literature & databases	ROE, Eunice M.	(PA)	1048
Scientific & med literature searching	TRIMBLE, Kathy W.	(CA)	1256
Scientific & technical literature	FOREMAN, Anne P.	(AL)	390
	SNYDER, Richard L.	(PA)	1165
	GARNETT, Joyce C.	(PQ)	419
	JOBA, Judith C.	(PQ)	601
Scientific & technical lit databases	MOBLEY, Emily R.	(IN)	851
Scientific literature	ECKROADE, Carlene B.	(DE)	335
Scientific literature research	HAMILTON, Beth A.	(IL)	491
Scientific medical literature searches	DAVEY, Dorothy M.	(ON)	276
Selection, Italian literature	WACHEL, Kathleen B.	(IA)	1290
Slavic literature	BRISKA, Boniface	(NY)	137
Slavic literatures & oral poetry	POPOVIC, Tanya V.	(NY)	983
Social science literature	WHITBECK, George W.	(IN)	1329
Social sciences literature	WYNAR, Lubomyr R.	(OH)	1375
South American literature	WELCH, Thomas L.	(DC)	1321
Southwestern literature	POWELL, Lawrence C.	(AZ)	988
Spanish language & literature	COLLAZO, Maria L.	(PR)	232
Spanish literature	CHU, Felix T.	(IL)	212
State & regnl literature & history bibl	RAZER, Robert L.	(AR)	1012
Study of children's literature	POVSIC, Frances F.	(OH)	987
Subject, English literature	SILVER, Diane L.	(PA)	1138
Substance abuse literature	GANGLOFF, Tory W.	(OH)	416
Teaching Afro-American literature	PERRY, Margaret	(IN)	960
Teaching children & adolescent lit	SANDERS, John B.	(MO)	1080
Teaching children's literature	WALDEN, Katherine G.	(CT)	1294
	NIX, Kemie	(GA)	905
	ADCOCK, Betty L.	(IL)	6
Teaching literature appreciation	MERRILL, Barbara P.	(NY)	826
Technical literature	KORNFELD, Carol E.	(NJ)	672
	SWINBURNE, Ralph E.	(NY)	1216
Technical literature search	MIWA, Makiko	(JAP)	850
Technical literature searches	BARTLETT, Vernell W.	(MN)	61
Technical literature searching	WHITT, Diane M.	(IL)	1334
	YANCEY, Marianne	(OH)	1377
Technological literature	TANEN, Lee J.	(NJ)	1222
Teenage literature	STEINBERG, Eileen	(PA)	1185
Theological literature	HART, Elizabeth	(BC)	507
Toxicology information & literature	EICKENHORST, Joanna W.	(CT)	339
Turkish literature, English translations	BILEYDI, Lois G.	(MN)	96
20th century literature	CAMMACK, Bruce P.	(NY)	175
	ROYTMAN, Serafima	(NY)	1063
	FECKO, Marybeth	(SC)	367
Underground literature	PEREZ, Maria L.	(FL)	958
Unorthodox medical literature	KIRCHFELD, Friedhelm	(OR)	654
Utopian literature	YAMAMOTO, Conrad S.	(CA)	1376
Victorian literature & bibliography	LASNER, Mark S.	(DC)	700
Victorian literature, fiction, poetry	FISHER, Benjamin F.	(MS)	380
Western European languages & literature	BYRE, Calvin S.	(IL)	169
Writing about Afro-American literature	PERRY, Margaret	(IN)	960
Writing library & literature curriculum	JACKSON, Gloria D.	(CA)	587
Young adult literature	NILSEN, Alleen P.	(AZ)	904
	CAMPBELL, Patricia J.	(CA)	177
	JAIN, Celeste C.	(CA)	591
	WILKINSON, Evalyn S.	(GA)	1340
	KOLLASCH, Matthew A.	(IA)	669
	HOLBROCK, Mary A.	(IL)	550
	JACKSON, Susan M.	(IN)	588
	DRUSE, Judith A.	(KS)	321
	LYNN, Barbara A.	(KS)	752
	JACOBSON-BEYER, Harry E.	(KY)	590
	MOSLEY, Mattie J.	(LA)	871
	GALLAGHER, Mary E.	(MA)	414
	LEVINE, Susan H.	(MD)	721
	BIELICH, Paul S.	(MI)	95
	ROBERTS, Scott J.	(MI)	1041

LITERATURE (Cont'd)

Young adult literature	SIBLEY, Carol H.	(MN)	1134
	BELCHER, Nancy S.	(MO)	76
	RANCER, Susan P.	(NC)	1006
	RENICK, Paul R.	(ND)	1023
	GRAZIER, Dorothy W.	(NH)	460
	FICHTELBERG, Susan	(NJ)	374
	GROSSHANS, Merilyn P.	(NV)	473
	CUSEO, Allan A.	(NY)	267
	FLOWERS, Helen F.	(NY)	386
	HIGGINS, Judith H.	(NY)	538
	HOPKINS, Lee B.	(NY)	558
	LENZ, Millicent A.	(NY)	716
	LONG, Joanna R.	(NY)	739
	RYBARCZYK, Barclay S.	(NY)	1071
	RIFFEY, Robin S.	(OH)	1033
	SCHWELK, Jennifer C.	(OH)	1105
	WYNN, Vivian R.	(OH)	1375
	ALSWORTH, Frances W.	(OK)	18
	COWEN, Linda L.	(OK)	253
	HALE, Carolyn R.	(PA)	485
	MILLER, Mary E.	(PA)	840
	YOUREE, Beverly B.	(TN)	1384
	CARTER, Betty B.	(TX)	189
	HOLLAND, Deborah K.	(TX)	550
	WIDENER, Sarah A.	(TX)	1335
	BIGELOW, Therese G.	(VA)	95
	KNAPP, Marilyn S.	(VA)	663
	ANDERSEN, Eileen	(WA)	21
	CHATTON, Barbara A.	(WY)	204
	OBERG, Dianne	(AB)	913
	KOSTIAK, Adele E.	(ON)	673
Young adult literature & services	BUSH, Margaret A.	(MA)	165
	VEITCH, Carol J.	(NC)	1281
Young adult literature reviewing	TUZINSKI, Jean H.	(PA)	1266
Young adult religious literature	PEARL, Patricia D.	(VA)	952
Young adult services & literature	EDMONDS, M L.	(IL)	336
Young adult services, literature	RUBIN, Ellen B.	(NY)	1064
Young people's literature	MILLER, Barbara S.	(KY)	835
	MCGARRY, Marie L.	(MA)	805
	SCHOLTEN, Frances	(MD)	1098
Youth literature & services	BODART-TALBOT, Joni	(KS)	109
Youth literature appreciation	USHIRODA, Christine H.	(HI)	1270

LITIGATION

Legal access litigation	WELCH, Steven J.	(IL)	1321
Litigation & regulatory support	SCULLY, Patrick F.	(CA)	1109
Litigation support	EVANS, Deborah L.	(CA)	356
	SMITH, Catherine C.	(CO)	1153
	KRONE, Judith P.	(GA)	679
	BERUL, Lawrence H.	(MD)	91
Litigation support databases	LANK, Dannette H.	(WI)	696

LITTLE

| Little magazines | ROM, Cristine C. | (OH) | 1052 |
| Little magazines, special collections | FOX, Willard | (LA) | 395 |

LOAN (See also Circulation, Lending)

Acquisitions & interlibrary loan	TERRY, Susan N.	(DC)	1232
	RUST, Roxy J.	(SC)	1070
Acquisitions, interlibrary loan	NEILL, Sharon E.	(ON)	892
Cataloging, interlibrary loan	SUTTER, Mary A.	(MO)	1211
	SCHMIDT, Diana M.	(ON)	1095
Cataloging musical loan collections	LYON, Bruce C.	(FL)	752
Circulation & interlibrary loan	STEWART, Jamie K.	(IL)	1192
Circulation & interlibrary loans	BULLARD, Rita J.	(MI)	156
Circulation, interlibrary loan	EDMONDS, Michael	(WI)	336
Circulation, reserve, interlibrary loan	MEAD-DONALDSON, Susan L.	(FL)	819
Document delivery & interlibrary loan	MEAHL, D D.	(MI)	819
	COURNOYER, Joanne	(ON)	251
Document delivery, interlibrary loan	ROLLINS, Stephen J.	(NM)	1051
Document retrieval & interlibrary loan	FELDMAN, Eleanor C.	(MD)	369

LOAN (Cont'd)
Interlibrary loan

LEE, Sulan I. . . . . (AL) 711
LIAW, Barbara C. . . . . . (AL) 725
WILLIAMS, Nelle T. . . . . (AL) 1345
STEEL, Virginia . . . . (AZ) 1183
BROOKS, Mary A. . . . . . (CA) 140
ELLIOTT, Valerie E. . . . . (CA) 344
FRANCISCO, Marylynn . (CA) 396
GOLDSMITH, Jan E. . . . (CA) 446
GUARINO, John P. . . . . (CA) 475
HERZIG, Stella J. . . . . . . (CA) 534
JORGENSEN, Venita . . . (CA) 617
LAWRENCE, John R. . . . (CA) 704
LEE, Don A. . . . . (CA) 709
MCNALLY, Ruth C. . . . . (CA) 816
REDFIELD, Dale E. . . . . (CA) 1014
TIENHAARA, Kaarina I. . (CA) 1244
BOUCHER, Virginia P. . . (CO) 118
DOBBS, Ann R. . . . . . . (CO) 307
GRATE, Jon F. . . . . (CO) 458
HAMDY, Amira . . . . (CO) 491
SHIELDS, Caryl L. . . . . (CO) 1129
VERCIO, Roseanne . . . . (CO) 1282
BUNKER, Patricia J. . . . (CT) 157
EBINGER, Meada G. . . . (CT) 334
HOLMER, Paul L. . . . . . (CT) 553
LOW, Jocelyn L. . . . . . . (CT) 743
NEWMYER, Joann C. . . (CT) 900
PENN, Elinor K. . . . . (CT) 957
SIROIS, Valerie M. . . . . (CT) 1144
BEATON, Barbara E. . . . (DC) 70
JOHNSON, Jacqueline B. (DC) 605
LEONE, Rosemarie G. . . (DC) 717
MEIKAMP, Kathie D. . . . (DC) 822
JOHNSON, Theresa P. . . (FL) 609
MAHAN, Cheryl A. . . . . . (FL) 760
MOORE, Dahrl E. . . . . . (FL) 859
TIBBS, Jo A. . . . . (FL) 1244
BOYD, Ruth V. . . . . (GA) 123
LARSEN, Mary T. . . . . . (GA) 698
PATON, John C. . . . . . . (GA) 947
RYSTROM, Barbara B. . . (GA) 1072
TOMAJKO, Kathy L. . . . . (GA) 1249
WHITE, Carol A. . . . . . . (GA) 1310
MOODY, Marilyn K. . . . . (IA) 857
RAILSBACK, Patsy S. . . (IA) 1003
RIESBERG, Eunice L. . . . (IA) 1033
SWANSON, P A. . . . . . . (IA) 1213
BURRUSS, Marsha A. . . (IL) 163
GINSBURG, Coralie S. . . (IL) 438
HORNEY, Joyce C. . . . . (IL) 560
KEENAN, Mary T. . . . . . (IL) 634
KELLY, Janice E. . . . . . . (IL) 637
LEWIS, Martha S. . . . . . (IL) 724
MCCARTNEY, Elizabeth J. (IL) 794
MCCLAREY, Catherine A. (IL) 796
NEWMAN, Lorna R. . . . . (IL) 899
OSBORN, Walter . . . . . . (IL) 927
PICKETT, Mary J. . . . . . (IL) 970
ROMANACE, Gisele R. . (IL) 1052
SACHS, Iris P. . . . . (IL) 1073
STUTZ, Patricia A. . . . . (IL) 1206
TODD, Margaret . . . . . . (IL) 1248
TROFIMUK, Janette A. . . (IL) 1257
WALKER, Laura L. . . . . . (IL) 1295
WALSH, Susan E. . . . . . (IL) 1300
WOELL, Yvette N. . . . . . (IL) 1359
BAVER, Cynthia M. . . . . (IN) 67
DAY, Thomas L. . . . . . . (IN) 283
EILERS, Marsha J. . . . . (IN) 340
LISTON, Karen A. . . . . . (IN) 733
SCHMIDT, Steven J. . . . (IN) 1096
TRIBBLE, Judith E. . . . . (IN) 1256
TRUESDELL, Cheryl B. . (IN) 1259
GAYNOR, Kathy A. . . . . (KS) 424
MAY, Cecilia J. . . . . (KS) 788
REIMER, Sylvia D. . . . . . (KS) 1021
FLAHERTY, Margaret P. . (KY) 383
GERON, Cary A. . . . . . . (KY) 429
SCHLENE, Vickie J. . . . . (KY) 1094

LOAN (Cont'd)
Interlibrary loan

TURNER, Rebecca M. . . (KY) 1265
CRETINI, Blanche M. . . . (LA) 258
HUSSEY, Sandra R. . . . (LA) 578
NUCKLES, Nancy E. . . . (LA) 912
ANDREWS, Margaret . . . (MA) 27
BAKER, Shirley K. . . . . . (MA) 49
BEARDEN, Eithne C. . . . (MA) 69
COOLIDGE, Christina L. . (MA) 241
DAMES, Barbara B. . . . . (MA) 271
ENGLISH, Cynthia J. . . . (MA) 350
HOLM, Edla K. . . . . (MA) 552
KELEHER, Carolyn P. . . (MA) 635
TURKALO, David M. . . . (MA) 1263
BOURKOFF, Vivienne R. . (MD) 119
CARMAN, Carol A. . . . . (MD) 183
COOPER, Judith C. . . . . (MD) 243
GLOCK, Martha H. . . . . (MD) 441
LEFEBVRE, Veronica A. . (MD) 712
MALLERY, Mary S. . . . . (MD) 763
MANGIN, Julianne . . . . . (MD) 765
MORRIS, Sharon D. . . . . (MD) 867
STEINHOFF, Cynthia K. . (MD) 1186
BAKER, Jean S. . . . . . . (MI) 48
CHAPMAN, Mary A. . . . (MI) 202
HAGE, Christine C. . . . . (MI) 482
MEADOWS, Brenda L. . . (MI) 819
MORGAN, Patricia L. . . . (MI) 864
PALMER, Catherine S. . . (MI) 936
SCHUCKEL, Sally B. . . . (MI) 1101
JONES, Mary A. . . . . . . (MN) 614
KAUFENBERG, Jane M. . (MN) 630
LORING, Christopher B. . (MN) 741
PRETZER, Shari G. . . . . (MN) 992
WIENER, Alissa L. . . . . . (MN) 1336
BICK, Barbara K. . . . . . . (MO) 94
FREEMAN, C L. . . . . . . (MO) 400
GREGORY, Kirk . . . . (MO) 466
KIEL, Becky . . . . (MO) 647
LUH, Ming . . . . (MO) 747
PARKES, Darla J. . . . . . (MO) 942
STEVENSON, Marsha J. . (MO) 1191
WATTS, Anne . . . . (MO) 1310
TUCKER, Ellis E. . . . . . (MS) 1261
KOCH, Patricia J. . . . . . (MT) 667
LEE, Susan M. . . . . (MT) 711
ADAMS, Elizabeth L. . . . (NC) 4
CARPENTER, Jennifer K. (NC) 184
EVANS, June C. . . . . . . (NC) 357
HULL, Laurence O. . . . . (NC) 572
NEAL, Michelle H. . . . . . (NC) 890
VARGHA, Rebecca B. . . (NC) 1278
BERNARDI, John V. . . . . (NE) 88
MUNDELL, Jacqueline L. (NE) 878
ACKROYD-KELLY, Elaine
  S. . . . . (NJ) 4
GARRABRANT, William A. (NJ) 420
LIN, Fumei C. . . . . (NJ) 727
REISLER, Reina . . . . . . (NJ) 1021
SCHWARTZ, Lawrence C. (NJ) 1104
TALAR, Anita . . . . (NJ) 1220
SAMPSON, Ellanie S. . . (NM) 1078
COONEY, Mata M. . . . . (NV) 242
STURM, Danna G. . . . . . (NV) 1205
BARNELLO, Inga H. . . . . (NY) 57
BUSTAMANTE, Corazon
  R. . . . . (NY) 166
CARSON, Anne R. . . . . (NY) 188
CONEY, Kim C. . . . . (NY) 236
CRAWFORD-OPPENHIE-
  MER, Christine . . . . . (NY) 257
DUNN, Mary B. . . . . (NY) 327
FRANKE, Gail E. . . . . . . (NY) 397
FRASENE, Joanne R. . . (NY) 399
GERBERG, Andrea F. . . (NY) 428
HALL, Russell W. . . . . . (NY) 488
HANE, Paula J. . . . . (NY) 495
HOLLIDAY, Geneva R. . . (NY) 552
KARKHANIS, Sharad . . . (NY) 627

LOAN (Cont'd)
Interlibrary loan

KLEIN, Penny . . . . (NY) 659
LEWANDOWSKI, Virginia
  M. . . . . (NY) 722
MAUL, Shirley A. . . . . . . (NY) 787
NOLAN, John A. . . . . . . (NY) 907
PARKHURST, Kathleen A. (NY) 942
PARRAVANO, Ellen A. . . (NY) 944
PLUMER, F I. . . . . (NY) 978
REMUSAT, Suzanne L. . (NY) 1023
ROGERS, Elizabeth S. . . (NY) 1049
ROOT, Christine . . . . (NY) 1053
ROTHSTEIN, Pauline M. . (NY) 1060
SHRIER, Helene F. . . . . . (NY) 1133
TAN, Wendy W. . . . . (NY) 1222
TANNER, Ellen B. . . . . . (NY) 1222
TOMLIN, Anne C. . . . . . (NY) 1250
TUCKER, Laura R. . . . . . (NY) 1262
VERDIBELLO, Muriel F. . (NY) 1282
WAGNER, Janet S. . . . . (NY) 1291
WENGER, Milton B. . . . . (NY) 1324
ZIESELMAN, Paula M. . . (NY) 1388
BALCON, William J. . . . . (OH)   51
DICKINSON, Luren E. . . (OH) 301
GODWIN, Eva D. . . . . . . (OH) 443
HALIBEY-BILYK, Christine
  M. . . . . (OH) 486
ROHMILLER, Ellen L. . . (OH) 1051
ROMARY, Michael P. . . . (OH) 1052
SANKOT, Janice M. . . . . (OH) 1081
WILLIAMS, Karen J. . . . (OH) 1344
WILSON, Memory A. . . . (OH) 1352
VARNER, Joyce . . . . (OK) 1279
WOLFF, Cynthia J. . . . . . (OK) 1361
BROOKS, Harry F. . . . . . (OR) 140
HALGREN, Joanne V. . . (OR) 486
SAYRE, Samuel R. . . . . . (OR) 1087
BOLGER, Dorita F. . . . . . (PA) 112
BRIZUELA, B S. . . . . . . (PA) 138
BURSTEIN, Karen . . . . . (PA) 164
CARRIER, Esther J. . . . . (PA) 186
CLINTON, Janet C. . . . . (PA) 222
COURTNEY, June M. . . . (PA) 251
CRESCENT, Victoria L. . (PA) 258
FUSCO, Marilyn A. . . . . (PA) 410
HENSHAW, Rod . . . . . . (PA) 529
JACKSON, Mary E. . . . . (PA) 588
MALCOM, Dorothy L. . . . (PA) 763
MARCHETTI, Honey B. . . (PA) 768
MARTIN, Noelene P. . . . (PA) 777
MOREY, Carol M. . . . . . (PA) 863
NISTA, Ann S. . . . . (PA) 905
REILLY, Rebecca S. . . . . (PA) 1020
WESSEL, Charles B. . . . (PA) 1325
COHEN, Barbara S. . . . . (RI) 228
HUX, Roger K. . . . . (SC) 579
WILLIAMS, Betty H. . . . . (SC) 1342
HAGEMEIER, Deborah A. (SD) 483
HILMOE, Deann D. . . . . (SD) 541
RITTER, Linda B. . . . . . . (SD) 1036
GIVENS, Mary K. . . . . . . (TN) 439
MYERS, William F. . . . . (TN) 885
RIDENOUR, Lisa R. . . . . (TN) 1032
SELF, George A. . . . . . . (TN) 1113
CLEE, June E. . . . . (TX) 220
HAGGARD, Lynn . . . . . . (TX) 483
JARVIS, Mary E. . . . . . . (TX) 595
KIRTNER, R R. . . . . (TX) 655
KOOPMAN, Frances A. . (TX) 671
METIVIER, Donna M. . . . (TX) 828
METZGER, Oscar F. . . . (TX) 829
MUCK, Bruce E. . . . . . . (TX) 874
MYCUE, David J. . . . . . . (TX) 884
PHILLIPS, Robert L. . . . . (TX) 969
PROKESH, Jane . . . . . . (TX) 995
SELLIN, Linda M. . . . . . . (TX) 1114
WILLIAMS, Ann T. . . . . . (TX) 1342
WOLFE, Carl F. . . . . (TX) 1360
JONES, Ruth J. . . . . (UT) 615

LOAN (Cont'd)
Interlibrary loan

CASWELL, Mary C. . . . . (VA) 194
COCHRANE, Lynn S. . . . (VA) 225
COOPER, Nancy C. . . . . (VA) 243
HURD, Douglas P. . . . . . (VA) 577
MALMQUIST, Katherine E. (VA) 763
MCGINN, Ellen T. . . . . . (VA) 806
MERRIFIELD, Mark D. . . (VA) 826
LUZER, Nancy H. . . . . . (VT) 750
BOSLEY, Dana L. . . . . . (WA) 117
BRADY, Eileen E. . . . . . (WA) 126
HILL, Ann M. . . . . (WA) 539
PUZIAK, Kathleen M. . . . (WA) 998
DREW, Sally J. . . . . (WI) 319
MERCHANT, Thomas L. . (WI) 825
MICHAELIS, Kathryn S. . (WI) 831
PARSON, Karen L. . . . . (WI) 944
SCHWARZ, Joy L. . . . . . (WI) 1105
SCOFIELD, Constance V. (WI) 1106
FRASER, Elizabeth L. . . (WV) 399
CAMERON, H C. . . . . . . (NF) 174
MORASH, Claire E. . . . . (NS) 862
ARONSON, Marcia L. . . (ON)   34
FLEMING, Anne . . . . . . (ON) 384
HAYTON, E E. . . . . (ON) 517
IRELAND, Michael A. . . . (ON) 583
SMALE, Carol . . . . (ON) 1151
WOLFE, Martha K. . . . . . (ON) 1361
GRITZKA, Gerda M. . . . . (PQ) 471
ARORA, Ved P. . . . . (SK)   34
WU, Edith Y. . . . . (HKG)1373

Interlibrary loan & document delivery STATOM, Susan T. . . . . (GA) 1183
                                        DITXLER, Carol J. . . . . . (MD) 306
                                        REID, Valerie L. . . . . (MI) 1019
Interlibrary loan & serial management   WILLIAMS, Calvin . . . . . (MI) 1342
Interlibrary loan, consortia   ROEDELL, Ray F. . . . . . (PA) 1048
Interlibrary loan department   RICHARDSON, Emma G. (NY) 1029
Interlibrary loan department
    management
Interlibrary loan document delivery   CARVER, Jane W. . . . . . (KS) 191
                                        MCFARLAND, Mary A. . . (IL) 805
                                        MORRISON, Carol J. . . . (IL) 868
Interlibrary loan networking   GIBBS, Margareth . . . . . (IL) 431
                                        ICKES, Barbara J. . . . . . (PA) 581
Interlibrary loan networks   KNUTSON, Linda J. . . . . (IL) 666
                                        BOAZ, Ruth L. . . . . (TN) 108
                                        SEIDENBERG, Edward . . (TX) 1112
Interlibrary loan of genealogical resrcs MEYERS, Martha L. . . . . (MO) 831
Interlibrary loan on OCLC   RISHWORTH, Susan K. . (DC) 1036
Interlibrary loan, resource sharing   THOMPSON, Dorothea M. (PA) 1239
Interlibrary loan services   COBB, Jean L. . . . . (CA) 224
                                        SHEPHERD-SHLECHTER,
                                          Rae . . . . (KY) 1127
                                        DEBROWER, Amy M. . . (MD) 285
                                        REED, Catherine A. . . . . (NY) 1015
Interlibrary loan, subject requests   LLOYD, H R. . . . . (PA) 735
Interlibrary loan subsystem   THOMPSON, Karolyn S. . (MS) 1240
Interlibrary loan workshops   SCHWEERS, Lucy . . . . . (CO) 1105
Interlibrary loans   CARAVELLO, Patti S. . . (CA) 180
                                        GUPTA, Ann D. . . . . (CA) 478
                                        HAYES, Linda J. . . . . . . (CA) 516
                                        MAHAFFEY, Susan M. . . (CA) 760
                                        BERG, Rebecca M. . . . . (CO)   84
                                        WATERS, W R. . . . . (CO) 1309
                                        ROBBINS, Rachel H. . . . (DE) 1039
                                        TAYLOR, Rose M. . . . . . (FL) 1228
                                        FARMER, Nancy R. . . . . (GA) 364
                                        MONTGOMERY, Denise L. (GA) 856
                                        MAZZOLA, Patricia R. . . (HI) 791
                                        MOORE, Annie M. . . . . . (IL) 858
                                        POULTNEY, Judy R. . . . (IL) 987
                                        RASMUSSEN, Gordon E. (IL) 1009
                                        SEVIER, Susan G. . . . . . (KS) 1117
                                        LAUGHLIN, Beverly E. . . (LA) 702
                                        PRITCHARD, Robert W. . (MA) 994
                                        SARAVIS, Judith A. . . . . (MA) 1082
                                        FEDER, Carol S. . . . . . . (MI) 367
                                        ANGUS, Jacqueline A. . . (MN)   28
                                        BARBOUR-TALLEY,
                                          Donna L. . . . . (MN)   55

LOAN (Cont'd)
Interlibrary loans

	HUGHES, Joan L.	(MO)	571
	DENSON, Janeen J.	(NC)	293
	KOZIKOWSKI, Derek M.	(NH)	674
	KALIF, Alexander J.	(NJ)	623
	HINKSON, Colin S.	(NY)	542
	KAIN, Joan P.	(NY)	622
	NOLTE, James S.	(NY)	908
	TURNER, Freya A.	(OH)	1264
	FLINNER, Beatrice E.	(OK)	385
	WEIS, Aimee L.	(PA)	1319
	MCREE, John W.	(SC)	818
	DEAN, Leann F.	(SD)	283
	ARMONTROUT, Brian A.	(TN)	32
	GRENGA, Kathy A.	(TN)	467
	MILLS, Debra D.	(TN)	844
	ROBERTSON, Sally A.	(TN)	1042
	DAVIS, Cynthia V.	(TX)	278
	PARHAM, Sandra H.	(VA)	940
	WHITE, Ardeen L.	(VA)	1330
	MIDDLETON, Dale R.	(WA)	833
	VYHNANEK, Kay E.	(WA)	1290
	GIBB, Betty J.	(BC)	431
	LEONARDO, Joan M.	(ON)	717
	PAWLEY, Carolyn P.	(ON)	951
	WALDRON, Nerine R.	(ON)	1294
Interlibrary loans, computer searching	SARGENT, Phyllis M.	(OR)	1083
Interlibrary loans online	TURLEY, Georgia P.	(WA)	1263
Interlibrary loans, reference	KOLBIN, Ronda I.	(CT)	669
Journal & interlibrary loan systems	ROBERTS, Linda L.	(OK)	1041
Journal copying, interlibrary loan	BROWN, Elizabeth E.	(CA)	143
Library systems, interlibrary loans	CLAYTOR, Jane B.	(MI)	220
Management of interlibrary loans	IANNUZZI, Patricia A.	(CT)	581
Networking, interlibrary loan	SCHUBACK COHN, Judith	(NJ)	1101
	WOLFE, Gary D.	(PA)	1360
Novice level interlibrary loans	WEBER, Julie A.	(IL)	1314
OCLC interlibrary loan	RONDESTVEDT, Helen F.	(TN)	1053
Orientations & interlib loan reference	BAYER, Susan P.	(IL)	67
Reference & interlibrary loan	ROUDEBUSH, Lawanda C.	(IA)	1061
	LACROIX, Eve M.	(MD)	686
	NAIRN, Charles E.	(MI)	886
	CARR, Charles E.	(NJ)	185
Reference & interlibrary loans	HUTCHINS, Mary J.	(IL)	579
	GENTRY, Etherlene H.	(MS)	427
	LIN, Susan T.	(NY)	728
Reference work, interlibrary loans	LEHWALDT, Marliese	(ON)	713
Reserves & interlibrary loan	PARK, T P.	(NY)	941
Reserves, interlibrary loan	MILLSAP, Gina J.	(MO)	844
Statewide interlibrary loan networks	ROBERTSON, Linda L.	(IA)	1042
Supervision of interlibrary loan	WRIGHT, Joanna S.	(IL)	1371

LOBBYING (See also Advocacy, Legislative)

Advocacy & lobbying	FADDEN, Donald M.	(PA)	360
Governmental relations & lobbying	GODWIN, Mary J.	(NY)	443
Legislation & lobbying	BENN, James R.	(CT)	81
Legislative lobbying	LINVILLE, Marcia L.	(HI)	731
	GOULD, Martha B.	(NV)	454
Library legislation lobbying	KRETTEK, Josephine G.	(IA)	678
Lobbying	PEYTON, David	(DC)	966
	MILLER, Roy D.	(NY)	842
Lobbying & political action	WARD, Robert C.	(VT)	1304
Lobbying for libraries	MILLER, Deborah	(IL)	837
Political lobbying	HALL, Edward B.	(MD)	487
Political lobbying for libraries	KIEFFER, Marian L.	(IA)	647
Public relations, lobbying, training	SANKER, Paul N.	(NY)	1081
Registered lobbyist	NATHAN, Frances E.	(NY)	889

LOCAL

Administering local history collection	CARTER, Susan M.	(IN)	190
American & local history	LEERHOFF, Ruth E.	(CA)	712
Building local history collection	MILLER, Ida M.	(IN)	838
California local history	DRUMMOND, Herbert	(CA)	321
Canadiana & local history	LLOYD, Mary E.	(ON)	735
Cataloging local history collection	MILLER, Ida M.	(IN)	838
Collection development, local government	BALLENTINE, Rebecca S.	(NC)	53

LOCAL (Cont'd)

Computerized local newspaper indexing	KAGANN, Laurie K.	(IL)	621
Family & local history research	WILLIAMS, Janet L.	(OR)	1344
Federal, state, local govt publications	NAKATA, Yuri	(OR)	887
Fine arts, local history collections	MCNULTY, Karen	(CT)	817
Genealogy & local history	KEMP, Thomas J.	(CT)	639
	DAY, Thomas L.	(IN)	283
	MUTH, Thomas J.	(KS)	883
	PAYNE, David L.	(MS)	951
	JONES, Plummer A.	(NC)	614
	ESWORTHY, Lori L.	(NY)	355
	JANOWSKY, Cara A.	(NY)	593
	ENGEL, Carl T.	(OH)	348
	LUST, Jeanette M.	(OH)	749
	HARPER, Sarah H.	(TX)	503
	STEINBERG, David L.	(VA)	1185
Genealogy, local history	STEPHENS, Doris G.	(NC)	1188
	MONCLA, Carolyn S.	(TX)	854
Indexing local newspapers	BROOKES, Barbara	(NY)	140
	VAN DE CASTLE, Raymond M.	(PA)	1273
Library local area network	MILLER, Richard A.	(VA)	841
Local & family history	HAMILTON, Patricia A.	(IL)	492
Local & regional history interpretation	LEAHY, M J.	(AK)	706
Local archives	SCOTT, Sharon A.	(OH)	1108
Local area computer networks	KEMPER, Marlyn J.	(FL)	639
Local area network research	PFUDERER, Helen A.	(TN)	966
Local area networking	ELAZAR, David H.	(ISR)	341
Local area networks	CARD, Sandra E.	(CA)	180
	MOORE, Richard K.	(CA)	861
	CHU, Ellen M.	(MD)	212
Local database development	HUMPHRIES, Joy D.	(WV)	574
Local databases	FINNEGAN, Gregory A.	(NH)	378
Local distribution of database systems	NASATIR, Marilyn	(CA)	888
Local documents	HILBURGER, Mary J.	(IL)	538
Local fundraising	BEATTIE, Brian	(KS)	70
Local government	DUBEAU, Pierre	(PQ)	321
Local government archives	BENGE, Joy L.	(TX)	80
Local government databases	PICKETT, Olivia K.	(DC)	971
	LEHMAN, Tom	(MN)	713
	HEWLETT, Carol C.	(TN)	535
Local government documents	CASTONGUAY, Russell	(CA)	194
	CORCORAN, Nancy L.	(MN)	246
Local government finance	BEVERLEY, Barbara S.	(NY)	93
Local government information	STRICKLAND, Ann T.	(AZ)	1202
Local government information network	AHLIN, Nancy	(FL)	8
Local government publications & records	HEWLETT, Carol C.	(TN)	535
Local government records	WEBBER, Steven L.	(CA)	1313
	MOORE, Karl R.	(IL)	860
	HOLLAND, Michael E.	(TX)	551
	SCHAADT, Robert L.	(TX)	1088
Local government reference	FREEDMAN, Phyllis D.	(PA)	400
Local historical reference	DECKER, John W.	(MN)	286
Local history	GARNER, Carolyn L.	(CA)	419
	HELLING, Madelyn	(CA)	524
	STREETER, David	(CA)	1201
	PALMQUIST, David W.	(CT)	937
	REITER, Elizabeth A.	(CT)	1022
	DEANE, Roxanna	(DC)	284
	RAY, Kathryn C.	(DC)	1011
	BOLDRICK, Samuel J.	(FL)	112
	CONOVER, Kathryn H.	(FL)	238
	WALKER, Alice O.	(GA)	1295
	COCHRAN, William M.	(IA)	225
	CRAWFORD, Daniel R.	(IA)	256
	HUNTING, Susan K.	(IA)	576
	ALLAN, Nancy P.	(IL)	14
	EDSTROM, James A.	(IL)	337
	MUNDELL, Eric L.	(IN)	878
	TURNER, Nancy K.	(IN)	1265
	HEIM, Keith M.	(KY)	521
	KING, Charles D.	(KY)	650
	ABRAHAM, Deborah V.	(MA)	2
	FISCHER, Marge	(MA)	380
	MCLAIN, Guy A.	(MA)	813
	MINTON, Alix M.	(MA)	846
	SLEEMAN, William E.	(MD)	1148
	TURNER, David E.	(MD)	1264

LOCAL (Cont'd)

Local history		
	CALLARD, Carole	(MI) 173
	FEDEROWSKI, Marjorie S.	(MI) 368
	LARSON, Catherine A. ...	(MI) 699
	REASONER, Mary B.	(MI) 1013
	GLENN, Michael D.	(MO) 441
	MEYERS, Martha L.	(MO) 831
	MAXWELL, Daisy D.	(NC) 788
	YORK, Maurice C.	(NC) 1381
	CUMMINGS, Charles F. .	(NJ) 264
	MONROE-SECHREST, Nancy H.	(NJ) 855
	VAN BENTHUYSEN, Robert F.	(NJ) 1272
	CARLSON, Marie S.	(NY) 182
	DISHON, Robert M.	(NY) 305
	JEANNENEY, Mary L. ..	(NY) 596
	WELLS, Phyllis L.	(NY) 1323
	WILLET, Ruth J.	(NY) 1341
	BERGDORF, Randolph S.	(OH) 85
	FARRELL, Maureen C. ...	(OH) 365
	SEARS, Robert W.	(OK) 1110
	FULCHER, Jane M.	(PA) 408
	LIVENGOOD, Candice C.	(PA) 734
	WEIHERER, Patricia D. .	(PA) 1317
	HEARNE, Mary G.	(TN) 518
	BOCKSTRUCK, Lloyd D.	(TX) 109
	ENDELMAN, Sharon B. .	(TX) 348
	GRAY, Wayne D.	(TX) 460
	MYLER, Josephine P. ...	(TX) 885
	LEVY, Suzanne S.	(VA) 722
	WILLBERG, Carolyn S. .	(WA) 1341
	GROSKOPF, Amy L. ...	(WI) 472
	HOFFMAN, Susan J.	(ON) 548
	MEHTA, Subbash C. ...	(ON) 821
	MOLSON, Gerda A.	(ON) 853
Local history & affairs	VIGNOVICH, Ray L.	(WI) 1284
Local history & archives	OTTOSEN, Charles F. ..	(AB) 930
	KEARNS, Linda J.	(ON) 633
Local history & genealogy	GOFF, Linda J.	(CA) 443
	KOEL, Maria O.	(CT) 667
	KANELY, Edna A.	(DC) 625
	REID, Judith P.	(DC) 1018
	BAKER, Donald E.	(IN) 48
	MILLS, Helen L.	(TX) 844
Local history & genealogy reference	WIENER, Alissa L.	(MN) 1336
Local history & oral history	MUELLER, Jane L.	(CA) 875
Local history & photograph collections	BABBITT, Dennis L.	(IN) 43
Local history & university archives	WALKER, Mary J.	(NM) 1296
Local history, audiovisual, reference	WOOD, Lois R.	(IL) 1364
Local history, books, programs	JAMISON, Susan C. ...	(DE) 593
Local history collection	SINGH, Rosemary A. ...	(WI) 1143
Local history collection development	DARR, William E.	(IN) 275
	ENG, Mamie	(NY) 348
Local history collections	BROCK, Kathy T.	(GA) 138
	VLOYANETES, Jeanne M.	(NJ) 1286
	HALL, Alan C.	(OH) 486
	COLLINS, Sara D.	(VA) 233
	RICKERSON, Carla	(WA) 1031
Local history consulting	KRASEAN, Thomas K. ..	(IN) 676
Local history field agent	MILLER, Ida M.	(IN) 838
Local history, genealogy, preservation	BROWN, Donald R.	(PA) 143
Local history manuscript collections	PACKARD, Agnes K. ...	(NY) 933
Local history microfilming	BAUS, J W.	(IN) 67
Local history of upstate New York	KABELAC, Karl S.	(NY) 620
Local history research	MATTIS, George E.	(VA) 786
Local history research projects	WOLFE, Barbara M.	(NY) 1360
Local history sources	GRABOWSKI, John J. ...	(OH) 455
Local library systems	SEVIER, Susan G.	(KS) 1117
	SMITH, Barbara G.	(MD) 1152
	THOMAS, James M.	(OH) 1237
Local Maine businesses	AIREY, Martha R.	(ME) 9
Local medical history	GOLDSTEIN, Cynthia H. .	(LA) 446
Local networks & systems	STEFFEY, Ramona J. ..	(TN) 1185
Local news	VANCE, Carolyn J.	(IL) 1272
Local newspaper indexing	ALLING, M P.	(IA) 16
Local Records	LEVSTIK, Frank R.	(KY) 721
Local system automation	KOUTNIK, Charles J. ...	(VA) 673
Local systems	CURTIS, Alison J.	(ON) 267

LOCAL (Cont'd)

Local systems planning	HILLMANN, Diane I.	(NY) 541
Local systems training	BERRINGER, Virginia M. .	(OH) 90
New England local history	SKILLIN, Glenn B.	(PA) 1146
New York state & local documents	PANDIT, Jyoti P.	(NY) 937
Pacific Northwest regional local history	EMMENS, Thomas A.	(OR) 348
Public access & local cable	BARNETT, Donald E. ...	(OR) 57
Reference local history	GOLDENKOFF, Isabel M. .	(NY) 445
Research in local history	CREAMER, Mary M. ...	(KY) 257
Speaking on local history	NELSON, Maggie E.	(IL) 894
State & local documents	LUNDQUIST, David A. ...	(CA) 748
	SWAFFORD, William M. .	(CA) 1212
	ESKOZ, Patricia A.	(CO) 354
	LEVY, Suzanne S.	(VA) 722
State & local government documents	HAMMOND, Louise H. ...	(IL) 494
State & local government publications	SULZER, John H.	(PA) 1209
State & local government records	DEARSTYNE, Bruce W. .	(NY) 284
State & local historical research	CHRISTENSEN, Erin S. .	(CO) 211
State & local history	SCHMIDT, Jean M.	(LA) 1095
	CURTIS, Peter H.	(MD) 267
State & local history research	OAKES, Patricia A.	(AK) 913
State & local records	WAGGENER, Jean B. ...	(TN) 1291
UNIX local area network	ROSE, Phillip E.	(CO) 1055
Using local area network for catalogs	HUGHES, Carol A.	(OK) 571

LODGING

Lodging industry	SMYTH, Mary B.	(CA) 1162

LOGISTICS

Logistics	GRAY, Elisabeth M.	(OH) 459
Logistics management	ROBINSON, Mitchell L. .	(NY) 1044
Workshop logistics	SPARKMAN, Mickey M. .	(TX) 1171

LONG-RANGE

Branches & long-range planning	HOLT, Raymond M.	(CA) 554
Library strategic, long-range planning	MANN, Thomas	(CA) 766
Long-range & strategic planning	BETTENCOURT, Nancy J.	(CO) 92
	VELLUCCI, Matthew J. ...	(MD) 1282
	BAUER, Margaret D. ...	(PA) 65
Long-range library planning	SAGER, Donald J.	(WI) 1074
Long-range planning	MARRIOTT, Lois I.	(CA) 773
	MANCINI, Donna D.	(GA) 764
	ANTHONY, Carolyn A. ...	(IL) 28
	HAWLEY, Marsha S.	(IL) 514
	WILFORD, Valerie J.	(IL) 1339
	WOODARD, Marcia S. ...	(IL) 1366
	RADEMACHER, Richard J.	(KS) 1002
	STEPHAN, Sandra S.	(MD) 1187
	NOBLE, Valerie	(MI) 906
	SWEEN, Roger	(MN) 1214
	WEISS, Kay M.	(MN) 1320
	ANDERSEN, Robert J. ...	(NY) 21
	MULLER, Claudya B.	(NY) 877
	JOHNSON, Corinne E. ...	(OH) 603
	KOZLOWSKI, Ronald S. .	(OH) 674
	SALMON, Kay H.	(OR) 1077
	ALBRECHT, Lois K.	(PA) 10
	BROWN, David E.	(PA) 143
	HEDRICK, David T.	(PA) 520
	MANNING, Helen M. ...	(TX) 766
Long-range planning & implementation	DIEHL, Carol L.	(WI) 301
Long-range planning programs	CHAMBERLAIN, Ruth B.	(MA) 197
Long-range plans	FINAN, Patrick E.	(OH) 377
Long-range strategic planning	NEEDHAM, George M. ...	(OH) 891

LONG-TERM

Long-term corporate research	SOSTACK, Maura	(NY) 1169

LOS ANGELES

Los Angeles & California history	STERN, Teena B.	(CA) 1189

LOSS
Change & loss in children's literature	ELAM, Barbara C.	(MA)	341
Loss control in libraries & universities	MORRIS, John	(CA)	866

LOUISIANA (See also New Orleans)
Louisiana history	JUMONVILLE, Florence M.	(LA)	619
Louisiana reference	MARSHALL, Susan O.	(LA)	775
Louisiana state documents	MARSHALL, Susan O.	(LA)	775

LOUISVILLE
Louisville area history	REDMON, Sherrill	(KY)	1014

LSCA
LSCA advisory board	STEVENSON, Marilyn E.	(CA)	1191
LSCA coordination	CATES, Sheila A.	(MT)	195
LSCA criteria & planning	CLARK, Robert L.	(OK)	218

LUTE
Lute prints & manuscripts	NESS, Arthur J.	(MA)	896

LUTHERAN
Lutheran Church history, archives	WITTMAN, Elisabeth C.	(IL)	1358
Lutheran history & reference	WOHLRABE, John C.	(MO)	1359
Lutheran pastoral ministry	SMITH, Robert E.	(IN)	1160
Southern Lutheran history	FRITZ, William R.	(SC)	405

MACCS/DATACCS
Maccs/Dataccs database management	SKIDANOW, Helene	(NJ)	1146

MACHINE-READABLE
Audiovisual & machine-readable data file	RITCHIE, David G.	(NY)	1036
Machine file processing	MARTIN, Robert A.	(FL)	778
Machine-readable bibliographic format	SPAANS, David N.	(DC)	1170
Machine-readable business information	AULD, Dennis B.	(KY)	39
Machine-readable catalog records	GUILES, Kay D.	(DC)	476
Machine-readable cataloging	QUEINNEC, Young H.	(ON)	999
Machine-readable cataloging distribution	TARR, Susan M.	(DC)	1224
Machine-readable data	STRAUSS, Diane	(NC)	1201
Machine-readable data files	GERKEN, Ann E.	(CA)	429
	KUHLMAN, James R.	(GA)	682
	KING, Ebba K.	(NC)	650
Machine-readable data files cataloging	MYERS, Victor C.	(MO)	885
	WEITZ, Jay N.	(OH)	1320
Machine-readable shelflist conversion	NOBLE, Barbara N.	(MO)	906

MACINTOSH
Apple & Macintosh computer software	TRAVILLIAN, Mary W.	(IA)	1254
Library automation, Macintosh	BUTLER, Rebekah O.	(NY)	167
Library computerization on Macintosh	FORD, Marjorie F.	(CA)	389
Macintosh applications	KRAFT, Gwen L.	(AK)	675
Macintosh computer	CISLER, Stephen A.	(CA)	215
Macintosh microcomputers	WOOLDRIDGE, Steven M.	(CA)	1308
Microcomputer support Apple Macintosh	DEEMER, Selden S.	(GA)	286

MAGAZINES (See also Fanzines, Periodicals)
Automated magazine production	HAVENS, Shirley E.	(NY)	513
Book & magazine indexing	BRADWAY, Becky J.	(IL)	126
Catalog of music magazines	FITZNER, Robert N.	(IL)	382
Editing computer science magazines	WEINER, Carolynn N.	(NY)	1318
Editing library media magazines	TROJAN, Judith L.	(NY)	1257
Graphics & magazine design	WISE, Eileen M.	(ON)	1356
Journal & magazine publishing	BRAWLEY, Paul H.	(IL)	130
Library & information magazines	GOLD, Renee L.	(NY)	444
Literary magazines	CASSELL, Kay A.	(NY)	193
Little magazines	ROM, Cristine C.	(OH)	1052

MAGAZINES (Cont'd)
Little magazines, special collections	FOX, Willard	(LA)	395
Magazine & editorial consulting	LIPTON, Howard	(MI)	732
Magazine contributions	SMALLWOOD, Carol A.	(MI)	1151
Magazine publishing	MACIUSZKO, Kathleen L.	(OH)	755
	BROWN, Kent L.	(PA)	145
Magazine publishing & editing	LEHURAY, Stephen D.	(MD)	713
Music magazines	BAHR, Edward R.	(MS)	45
Trade magazine research	DAMOTH, Douglas L.	(NY)	272
Trade magazines & directories	DALY, Charles P.	(NJ)	271

MAGNETIC
Magnetic fusion energy	KNAACK, Linda M.	(MA)	663
Nuclear magnetic resonance bibliography	PARR, John R.	(ON)	943

MAIL (See also Bulletin, Message, Postal)
Direct mail marketing	PHILLIPS, Angela B.	(NY)	967
	WORTON, Geoffrey P.	(NY)	1369
Direct mail markets	MELKIN, Audrey D.	(NY)	822
Direct mail promotion management	OGREN, Mark S.	(IL)	918
Educational mailing list development	MOSELEY, Cameron S.	(NY)	870
Electronic mail	LEE, Joel M.	(IL)	710
	SPARKS, Joanne L.	(IL)	1171
	GRIEVE, Shelley	(OH)	468
	TYLER, Kim E.	(OR)	1266
	BUSSMANN, Steve	(VA)	166
	EDWARDS, Wilmoth O.	(VA)	338
	FILIPPONE, Anne	(VA)	377
	KELLER, Jay	(VA)	635
	LOVETT, Bruce	(VA)	743
	MAJOR, Skip	(VA)	762
	NEWLAND, Barbara	(VA)	899
	RINALDI, Roberta	(VA)	1035
	RYAN, Maureen	(VA)	1071
	STRATT, Randy	(VA)	1200
Electronic mail administration	BEDARD, Bernard J.	(PQ)	73
Electronic mail & bulletin boards	O'NEILL, Sue	(MD)	924
Electronic mail news services	STILLMAN, Stanley W.	(NY)	1194
Electronic mail system management	WAGNER, Judith O.	(OH)	1292
Mail order	PAGE, Dennis N.	(ND)	934
Mailing lists	POWELL, Timothy W.	(NY)	989
Mail-order children's books	RUSS, Kennetta P.	(MD)	1068
Marketing & direct mail	DYER, Carolyn A.	(CT)	330
Microcomputers & electronic mail	MELTON, Emily I.	(IL)	823
Professional networks, electronic mail	LEHMAN, Tom	(MN)	713
Publishing & mail order	HAAS, Carolyn B.	(IL)	480

MAIN (See also Central, Public Library)
Administration of central & main branch	APPELBAUM, Sara B.	(FL)	29
Urban main library	PRESSING, Kirk L.	(IL)	991

MAINE
Books by Maine authors	LYONS, Dean E.	(ME)	753
Local Maine businesses	AIREY, Martha R.	(ME)	9
Maine imprints to 1820	SKILLIN, Glenn B.	(PA)	1146
State of Maine	CAMPO, Charles A.	(ME)	177

MAINFRAME (See also Computers)
Designing mainframe databases	MURRAY, Elizabeth F.	(NY)	881
Large mainframe databases	TEUN, Rebecca L.	(TX)	1233
Mainframe & minicomputer applications	BROWN, Maxine M.	(DC)	146
Mainframe & personal computer software	POLLARD, Louise	(UT)	981
Mainframe evaluation database management	BARALOTO, R A.	(MD)	55
Mainframe-based chemical info systems	MEYER, Daniel E.	(PA)	830
Micro & mainframe library software	SPENCER, John T.	(CA)	1173
Micro & mainframe programming	BRITTON, Jeffrey W.	(NJ)	137
Online mainframe databases	RICHARDS, Stella	(PQ)	1028

MAINTENANCE

Acquisition & maintenance	DATUS, Marie B.	(NE)	275
Acquisitions, serials maintenance	PICQUET, D C.	(TN)	971
Authority file maintenance	ASPER, Mary K.	(CO)	37
Automated bibliographic maintenance	WEE, Lily K.	(IL)	1315
Automated catalog maintenance	BRANDT, Janet E.	(MN)	128
Bibliographic database maintenance	VAN SICKLE, Mary L.	(KS)	1277
Bibliographic maintenance	COOPER, Jean L.	(VA)	243
Black history collection maintenance	PULLER, Maryam W.	(PA)	997
Bookstack maintenance	CORNWALL, Scot J.	(MA)	247
Building & maintaining authority files	LESSER, Barbara	(VA)	718
Catalog maintenance	STEWART, Anna C.	(CO)	1192
	HARRIS, Virginia B.	(VA)	506
	TURLEY, Georgia P.	(WA)	1263
	POPESCU, Constantin C.	(WI)	983
Cataloging & collection maintenance	WANG, Connie	(CA)	1302
Cataloging, maintenance	NICHOLSON, Dianne L.	(BC)	902
Client record maintenance	EMMONS, Mary E.	(AK)	348
Collection development & maintenance	WAKS, Jane B.	(MA)	1293
	POJMAN, Paul E.	(OH)	980
	AUSTIN, Martha L.	(WA)	40
Collection maintenance	FOLEY, Georgiana	(CO)	387
	LOMAX, Denise W.	(DC)	738
	STILLWATER, Rebecca S.	(GA)	1194
	HARMON, Charles T.	(IA)	502
	HANNA, Hildur W.	(MI)	496
	BELL, Carole R.	(RI)	76
	DESJARLAIS-LUETH, Christine	(RI)	295
	MALMQUIST, Katherine E.	(VA)	763
	HOOGKAMER, Dawne	(ON)	556
	HORNE, Bonnie L.	(ON)	560
Collection maintenance & development	BARTZ, Stephanie	(NJ)	62
	HOOTKIN, Neil M.	(WI)	557
Collection supervision & maintenance	CAMPBELL, Mary K.	(TX)	177
Conversion & database maintenance	SHEAFFER, Marc L.	(PA)	1124
Database construction & maintenance	BRITTON, Jeffrey W.	(NJ)	137
Database design & maintenance	WEIDA, William A.	(OH)	1316
	ROSENBERG, Kenyon C.	(VA)	1056
	FRITZ, Richard J.	(ON)	405
Database development & maintenance	HALPERN, Marilyn	(NJ)	489
Database indexing & maintenance	NEUWILLER, Charlene	(WGR)	897
Database maintenance	BROWN, Barbara L.	(CA)	142
	GARDNER, Laura L.	(CA)	418
	MOOMEY, Margaret M.	(CO)	857
	BROWN, Jeanette L.	(FL)	144
	FORFIA, Linda S.	(KS)	390
	MARTIN, Norma H.	(LA)	777
	CRAWFORD, Lynn D.	(NJ)	257
	MCCOMBS, Gillian M.	(NY)	797
	SANDERS, Melodie	(OK)	1080
	PUKL, Joseph M.	(SC)	997
Database maintenance & management	YUSTER, Leigh C.	(NY)	1385
Database maintenance, batch mode	BADING, Kathryn E.	(TX)	44
Database production & maintenance	STEVENS, Paula F.	(AZ)	1190
Developing & maintaining collections	GABBIANELLI, Patrice A.	(NJ)	411
Documentation maintenance	JADWIN, Rochelle J.	(CA)	591
Equipment maintenance, replacement plng	CHRISTIANSON, Ellory J.	(MN)	212
File maintenance	GEBBIE, Janet L.	(NC)	424
Filing & maintenance	SMOTHERS, Alyce A.	(LA)	1162
Information product design & maintenance	PISCITELLI, Rosalie A.	(NY)	976
Inmate legal library maintenance	SIENDA, Madeline M.	(WA)	1136
Internal specification maintenance	GRUEL, Janice L.	(WI)	474
Law & business library maintenance	HELBURN, Judith D.	(TX)	523
Library building maintenance	LUEDER, Dianne B.	(IL)	747
Library development & maintenance	FALK, Diane M.	(DC)	362
Library maintenance	MARTIN, Laquita V.	(TN)	777
Library maintenance & budgets	BALKIN, Ruth G.	(NY)	52
Library maintenance services	GOZDZ, Wanda E.	(FL)	455
Library organization & maintenance	HAM, Beverly V.	(MN)	490
Maintain library & information file	RATZABI, Arlene	(NY)	1010
Maintaining audiovisual equipment	SUTHERLAND, Helen G.	(CA)	1211
Maintaining automated databases	ZYNJUK, Nila L.	(MD)	1392
Maintaining province archives	STRECK, Helen T.	(KS)	1201

MAINTENANCE (Cont'd)

Maintenance	TERRY, Joseph D.	(PA)	1232
	SKELTON, W M.	(ON)	1146
Maintenance & remodeling facilities	EVANS, Constance L.	(KS)	356
Maintenance of records	LONG, Brideen	(WI)	739
Museum maintenance	STELLING, Dwight D.	(IL)	1186
Office maintenance	DUNN, Susan M.	(IA)	327
Online catalog maintenance	KIRKBRIDE, Amey L.	(OH)	654
	BABER, Elizabeth A.	(TX)	43
Online database maintenance	ISGANITIS, Jamie C.	(NY)	585
Pamphlet file maintenance	LAROSA, Thomas J.	(NY)	698
Patient index file maintenance	PARR, John R.	(ON)	943
Reference & collection maintenance	WILES-HAFFNER, Meredith L.	(PA)	1339
	WILSON, Karen A.	(CA)	1351
Stack maintenance	SWINTON, Cordelia W.	(PA)	1216
Thesaurus construction & maintenance	KLEIMAN, Helen M.	(DC)	659
Thesaurus design & maintenance	LINDER, Elliott	(NY)	729
Thesaurus maintenance	MUTTER, Letitia N.	(NY)	883
Vertical files organization, maintenance	GODFREY, Florence L.	(NJ)	442

MALACOLOGY

| Conchology, malacology | STONE, Joyce L. | (CO) | 1197 |

MANAGEMENT (See also Administration, Change, Coordination, Directing, Executive, Head, Leadership, MIS, Organization, Reorganization, Supervision, Team)

Academic & special library management	PHINNEY, Hartley K.	(CO)	969
Academic library admin & management	VEANER, Allen B.	(ON)	1280
Academic library management	RENEKER, Maxine H.	(AZ)	1023
	HOSEL, Harold V.	(CA)	561
	KOYAMA, Janice T.	(CA)	674
	WEBER, David C.	(CA)	1314
	MCDONALD, John P.	(CT)	802
	LEE, Hwa W.	(OH)	710
	WATSON, Tom G.	(TN)	1310
	JENNERICH, Elaine Z.	(VA)	598
	SWEETLAND, James H.	(WI)	1215
	FRANCIS, Derek R.	(BC)	396
	BONNELLY, Claude	(PQ)	114
Account management	BROWN, Sandra S.	(IN)	147
Accounting & management consulting	WONG, Mabel K.	(IL)	1363
Acquisitions & collection management	KNAUFF, Elisabeth S.	(DC)	663
Acquisitions department management	LEBEL, Clement	(PQ)	707
Acquisitions management	GREGORY, Joan A.	(AZ)	466
Administration & management	FRANK, Donald G.	(AZ)	396
	HIEB, Louis A.	(AZ)	537
	APPEL, Anne M.	(CA)	29
	ELLSWORTH, Dianne J.	(CA)	345
	KIRBY, Barbara L.	(CA)	653
	MONROE, Shula H.	(CA)	855
	NICKERSON, Susan L.	(CA)	902
	OLMSTEAD, Nancy L.	(CA)	921
	ROSE, Melissa M.	(CA)	1055
	SCHWARZMANN, Diane D.	(CA)	1105
	SMITH, Elizabeth M.	(CA)	1154
	WOOD, Linda M.	(CA)	1364
	MOBLEY, Arthur B.	(DC)	851
	WEIHER, Claudine J.	(DC)	1316
	BOWER, Beverly L.	(FL)	120
	BRANDON, Alfred N.	(FL)	128
	MILLER, Charles E.	(FL)	836
	LARY, Marilyn S.	(GA)	700
	TYLER, Audrey Q.	(GA)	1266
	WOODLEE, Rick G.	(GA)	1366
	DUJSIK, Gerald	(IL)	324
	HORST, Stanley E.	(IL)	561
	KLINGBERG, Susan	(IL)	661
	MACKAMAN, Frank H.	(IL)	756
	PARENT, Roger H.	(IL)	940
	SHAW, Joyce M.	(IL)	1123
	SIMON, Ralph C.	(IN)	1141
	MOORE, Grace G.	(LA)	859

MANAGEMENT (Cont'd)

Administration & management

MUSSER, Egbert G.	(MA)	883
POLLARD, Russell O.	(MA)	981
FLOWER, Kenneth E.	(MD)	386
HUMPHREYS, Betsy L.	(MD)	573
JOHNSON, Emily P.	(MD)	604
SANDS, George A.	(MD)	1081
CLARK, Georgia A.	(MI)	217
HERNANDEZ, Ramon R.	(MI)	532
LEE, Lucy W.	(MI)	710
PORTER, Jean F.	(MI)	984
SMITH, Nancy J.	(MI)	1158
ZARYCZNY, Wlodzimierz A.	(MI)	1386
BROGAN, Martha L.	(MN)	139
ROHLF, Robert H.	(MN)	1050
CAMPBELL, Jerry D.	(NC)	176
HANSEL, Patsy J.	(NC)	497
ISACCO, Jeanne M.	(NC)	584
WAGNER, Rod G.	(NE)	1292
PERLUNGHER, Jane R.	(NH)	959
HESS, Jayne L.	(NJ)	534
KELSEY, Ann L.	(NJ)	639
LYNN-NELSON, Gayle	(NJ)	752
STRONG, Moira O.	(NJ)	1203
KRAEMER, Mary P.	(NM)	674
BATES, Ellen	(NY)	63
CADE, Roberta G.	(NY)	170
KASPAR, Eileen	(NY)	629
NEWMAN, Jerald C.	(NY)	899
REID, Carolyn A.	(NY)	1018
ALBRECHT, Cheryl C.	(OH)	10
BLACK, Larry D.	(OH)	101
BREWER, Karen L.	(OH)	134
DUANE, Carol A.	(OH)	321
DU MONT, Rosemary R.	(OH)	325
GARDNER, John R.	(OH)	418
NEWCOMBE, Jack A.	(PA)	898
POSES, June A.	(PA)	985
VANN, John D.	(PA)	1276
TOWELL, Fay J.	(SC)	1252
HEYMAN, Berna L.	(VA)	536
SCHEITLE, Janet M.	(VA)	1091
KEMP, Barbara E.	(WA)	639
BANNEN, Carol A.	(WI)	54
BEHR, Alice S.	(WV)	75
OSBORN, Lucie P.	(WY)	927
WURBS, Sue A.	(WY)	1374
VAN REENEN, Johannes A.	(BC)	1277
BASSNETT, Peter J.	(ON)	63
KENDALL, Sandra A.	(ON)	640
BARLOW, Elizabeth A.	(SK)	57

Administration & personnel management

HAGLE, Claudette S.	(TX)	483

Administration, management

SULLIVAN, Suzanne E.	(CA)	1208
CHATFIELD, Michele R.	(DC)	203
LOVE, Erika	(NM)	743
KROAH, Larry A.	(PA)	679
CURRAN, William M.	(PQ)	266

Administration, management & instruction

QUIRING, Virginia M.	(KS)	1000

Administration management techniques

BENOIT, Anthony H.	(LA)	82

Administration, middle management

TONGATE, John T.	(TX)	1250

Administration, personnel management

MCCARTHY, Germaine A.	(MA)	794

Administration training & staff mgmt

NANTON-COMISSIONG, Barbara L.	(TRN)	887

Administrative management

FREEDMAN, Jack A.	(MS)	400

Administrative services & library mgmt

LEVIN, Marc A.	(CA)	720

Adult services management

BRYAN, Mila	(IL)	152

Advertising sales management

KOBASA, Paul A.	(IL)	666

Aerospace library management

PAUL, Donald C.	(CA)	949

Antiquarian books collection management

GOGGIN, Margaret K.	(FL)	444

Approval plan management

WARZALA, Martin L.	(CT)	1307
GRANTIER, John R.	(NY)	458

MANAGEMENT (Cont'd)

Archival implementation & management

Archival management

DAWSON, Barbara J.	(DC)	282
STEPHENSON, Shirley E.	(CA)	1189
ELLISON, J T.	(CO)	345
GAUSS, Nancy V.	(CO)	423
PAUL, Karen D.	(DC)	949
DICKENS, Rosa L.	(GA)	300
SOWINSKI, Carolyn M.	(IN)	1170
CONSTANCE, Joseph W.	(MA)	238
FISHBEIN, Meyer H.	(MD)	380
FOREMAN, Kenneth J.	(NC)	390
OLSON, David J.	(NC)	922
SARETZKY, Gary D.	(NJ)	1082
FRUSCIANO, Thomas J.	(NY)	406
HUNTER, Gregory S.	(NY)	576
RICHIUSO, John P.	(NY)	1030
TAYLOR, Robert N.	(NY)	1228
NOLAN, Patrick B.	(OH)	907
FILSON, Laurie	(OR)	377
KOHL, Michael F.	(SC)	668
CAMERON, Sam A.	(TN)	175
HOOKS, Michael Q.	(TX)	556
STIRLING, Dale A.	(WA)	1195
TAYLOR, Hugh A.	(NS)	1227

Archival management & automation

SERBAN, William M.	(LA)	1116

Archival methods & records management

Archive management

CAIN, Charlene C.	(LA)	171
VANDEGRIFT, Barbara P.	(DC)	1273
PILKINGTON, James P.	(TN)	973

Archives & library management

SYKES, Stephanie L.	(PQ)	1217

Archives & manuscript collection mgmt

FRYE, Dorothy T.	(MI)	407

Archives & manuscripts management

PINSON, Patricia A.	(WY)	975

Archives & record management

OSTERFIELD, George T.	(OH)	928

Archives & records center management

CAMPBELL, Margaret E.	(NS)	177

Archives & records management

NEWCOMER, Susan N.	(CA)	898
CANTELON, Philip L.	(MD)	179
STIELOW, Frederick J.	(MD)	1194
BLOUIN, Francis X.	(MI)	107
REHKOPF, Charles F.	(MO)	1017
PRICE, William S.	(NC)	993
ERLANDSSON, Alf M.	(NY)	353
LAIST, Sharon B.	(NY)	688
CLARK, Robert L.	(OK)	218
MURRAY, Lucia M.	(OR)	882
CEBRUN, Mary J.	(TX)	196
GRACY, David B.	(TX)	455
EULENBERG, Julia N.	(WA)	356
ROBERTSON, Guy M.	(BC)	1041
ARDERN, Christine M.	(ON)	31
MURDOCH, Arthur W.	(ON)	879

Archives & records management teaching

Archives management

WHALEN, Lucille	(NY)	1328
PICKARD, Mary A.	(AL)	970
CALMES, Alan R.	(DC)	174
MOSS, William W.	(DC)	872
PACIFICO, Michele F.	(DC)	933
VOGT-O'CONNOR, Diane L.	(DC)	1287
ADAMS, Larry D.	(IA)	5
HAY, Charles C.	(KY)	515
BLATZ, Imogene	(MN)	104
KELLY, Patricia J.	(MO)	638
HAUPERT, Thomas J.	(NC)	512
WAITE, William F.	(NJ)	1293
ROCHA, Guy L.	(NV)	1045
HESS, James W.	(NY)	534
JOHNSON, Judith	(NY)	606
MAURER, Eric	(NY)	787
MOORE, Rue I.	(NY)	861
NEAT, Charles M.	(NY)	891
TEICHMAN, Raymond J.	(NY)	1230
FALZON, Judith A.	(OR)	363
HARDY, John L.	(ON)	500
ST. PIERRE, Normand	(ON)	1075
NEFSKY, Judith L.	(PQ)	892
FAGERLUND, M L.	(SWZ)	361

MANAGEMENT (Cont'd)

Archives management &
administration — DUNN, Lucia S. . . . . (IL) 327
Archives, manuscript management — STOPKA, Christina K. . . . . (WY) 1198
Archives, records management
education — RHOADS, James B. . . . . . (WA) 1026
Armed forces library management — WONG, Carol Y. . . . . (CA) 1362
Art library management — ROSS, Alexander D. . . . . . (CA) 1057
VAN DYKE, Stehpen H. . . (NY) 1275
Art museum library management — WALKER, William B. . . . (NY) 1296
DOWNING, Jeannette D. . (TX) 316
SHEAROUSE, Linda N. . . (TX) 1124
Association management — HAMILTON-PENNELL,
Christine . . . . (CO) 492
BATTAGLIA, Richard D. . (DC) 64
BENDER, David R. . . . . . (DC) 79
HITCHENS, Howard B. . . (DE) 544
BOURDON, Cathleen J. . . (IL) 119
JEPSON, William H. . . . . (IL) 599
LEE, Joel M. . . . . (IL) 710
MYERS, Margaret R. . . . (IL) 884
NEAL, Donn C. . . . . (IL) 890
PALMER, Raymond A. . . (IL) 936
WEBSTER, Lois S. . . . . . (IL) 1314
MARTELLO, Joyce M. . . (IN) 775
HARRIS, Patricia R. . . . . (MD) 505
MCCARTNEY, Jean A. . (MO) 794
LIAN, Nancy W. . . . . (NY) 725
BAUER, Margaret D. . . . (PA) 65
PHILLIPS, Janet C. . . . . (PA) 968
NANCE, Betty . . . . (TN) 887
Association, management, &
membership — SCARRY, Patricia A. . . . (IL) 1088
Audio cassette collection
management — TREMBLAY, Carolyn B. . (NH) 1255
Audiovisual center management — GOLDBERGER, Virginia F. (IL) 445
Audiovisual collection development,
mgmt — GAUDET, Susan E. . . . . (TN) 422
Audiovisual media facility
management — GRAY, Shirley M. . . . . . . (NY) 460
Audiovisual service management — KERSTETTER, John . . . (OH) 644
Audiovisual services management — CYR, Helen W. . . . . (MD) 268
Automated information systems
management — WEINSTEIN, Lois . . . . . . (NY) 1318
Automated serials management — REID, Janine A. . . . . (VA) 1018
Automated serials management
systems — CLAPPER, Mary E. . . . (MA) 216
Automation of collection management — EVANS, Linda J. . . . . . . (IL) 357
Automation project management — MILLSAP, Gina J. . . . . . (MO) 844
Banking & management — GORMAN, Judith F. . . . (AZ) 452
Bibliographic database management — MILLER, Dick R. . . . . . (CA) 837
COMSTOCK, Daniel L. . . (NM) 235
HILLMANN, Diane I. . . . . (NY) 541
MUTTER, Letitia N. . . . . (NY) 883
SALVAGE, Barbara A. . . (NY) 1078
Biomedical unit management — LEITH, Anna R. . . . . (BC) 714
Black, women & management studies — JONES-TRENT, Bernice R. (VA) 616
Bookmobile management — ROH, Jae M. . . . . (CA) 1050
Branch development & management — LEITLE, Barbara K. . . . . . (MO) 714
Branch library management — ANDREWS, Karen L. . . . (CA) 26
BOYLLS, Virginia W. . . . (CA) 124
GILDEN, Susanna C. . . . (CA) 434
ROH, Jae M. . . . . (CA) 1050
WEISENBURGER, Patricia
J. . . . . (KS) 1319
MATTESON, James S. . . (MI) 785
SICHEL, Beatrice . . . . . . (MI) 1135
FUNK, Nancy J. . . . . (NY) 410
MCKINNEY, Venora . . . . (WI) 812
Branch management — HAUSSMANN, Virginia D. (CA) 513
NICKERSON, Louann M. . (CA) 902
NOGA, Michael M. . . . . . (CA) 907
ROSASCHI, Jim P. . . . . (CA) 1054
BOSWELL, Peggy B. . . . (CO) 118
BERBERICH, Patricia L. . (CT) 84
ROBINSON, Cathy A. . . (DC) 1043
BURKE, Donna J. . . . . . (FL) 160
STEELE, Patricia A. . . . . (IN) 1184
WOODY, Jacqueline B. . (MD) 1368
STEWART, Jeanne E. . . (MS) 1192

MANAGEMENT (Cont'd)

Branch management — PARR, Louise M. . . . . . (NJ) 943
GENDRON, Michele M. . (PA) 426
BUZZELL, Bonnie G. . . . (RI) 168
GRIFFLER, Carl W. . . . . (VA) 469
AUSTIN, Martha L. . . . . . (WA) 40
JONES, Charlotte W. . . . (WA) 611
SCOTT-MILLER, Gwen . (WA) 1108
KIERANS, Mary E. . . . . . (BC) 647
MULLERBECK, Aino . . . (ON) 877
Branch management public libraries — REILLY, Jane A. . . . . . . (IL) 1020
Budget & fiscal management — CONNORS, William E. . . (NY) 238
Budget & fund management — MARCINKO, Dorothy K. . (AL) 769
Budget & personnel management — MORITZ, William D. . . . . (WI) 865
Budget management — DAY, Janeth N. . . . . (AL) 282
Budgeting & financial management — MUNTEAN, Deborah E. . (MN) 879
Budgeting & management — BAILEY, Alvin R. . . . . . . (TX) 46
Building construction management — SINTZ, Edward F. . . . . . (FL) 1144
Building management — MUSSER, Egbert G. . . . . (MA) 883
Business & management — PENDRAK, Eileen . . . . . (TX) 956
Business & management databases — CLIFT, Crystal A. . . . . . (MN) 222
Business & management information — TASHIMA, Marie . . . . . . (CA) 1224
Business communications
management — SLOAN, Cheryl A. . . . . . (MD) 1149
Business development, mgmt &
admin — PATRICIU, Florin S. . . . . (MD) 947
Business information management — BAZAN, Lorraine R. . . . . (CA) 68
SEASE, Sandra A. . . . . . (NY) 1110
Business library management — CANNING, Joan M. . . . . (NY) 178
MILLER, Ellen L. . . . . . . (NY) 837
CAMERON, Hazel M. . . . (BC) 175
CHAN, Diana L. . . . . (BC) 199
Business management — BISSO, Arthur J. . . . . . . (GA) 100
FIDOTEN, Robert E. . . . (PA) 375
SOWICZ, Eugenia V. . . . (PA) 1170
RYANS, Kathryn J. . . . . . (ON) 1071
Business management & research — KIRSHBAUM, Priscilla J. (CO) 655
Business management bibliographies — CHAN, Diana L. . . . . . . (BC) 199
Business management, budgeting — WARNER, Alice S. . . . . (MA) 1305
Business, management information — DUDLEY, Durand S. . . . (OH) 323
Catalog management — SCHOTTLAENDER, Brian
E. . . . . (CA) 1099
PASTER, Luisa R. . . . . . (NJ) 946
HUSTON, Susan S. . . . . (TX) 578
Cataloging & database management — CARTER, Ruth C. . . . . . (PA) 190
Cataloging department management — LEBEL, Clement . . . . . . (PQ) 707
Cataloging management — MARTIN, Norma H. . . . . (LA) 777
JIZBA, Laurel . . . . (MI) 600
JUNION, Gail J. . . . . (NY) 620
SLOVASKY, Stephen . . . (OH) 1150
Cataloging management & workflow — CLARK, Sharon E. . . . . (IL) 218
Cataloging photographs, collections
mgmt — ROARK, Carol E. . . . . . (TX) 1038
Cataloging unit management — NEILL, Sharon E. . . . . . (ON) 892
CD-ROM management — DUNN, Kathleen K. . . . . (CA) 327
CD-ROM technology management — PHILLIPS, J R. . . . . (OK) 968
Chemistry library management — DEGOLYER, Christine C. (NY) 288
Church library setup & management — OVERTON, Margaret C. . (TN) 931
Circulation & stack management — PARKER, Susan E. . . . . (MA) 942
Circulation management — SPURRIER, Suzanne F. . (AR) 1177
HOOVER, Clara G. . . . . (NE) 557
TRAMDACK, Philip J. . . . (OH) 1254
Clearinghouse & information center
mgmt — BYRD, Harvey C. . . . . . (MD) 169
Clearinghouse management — BATES, Ruthann I. . . . . . (MD) 64
BERUL, Lawrence H. . . . (MD) 91
Collection & catalog management — DAGANAAR, Mark L. . . . (SD) 269
Collection & space management — DUNN, Jamie N. . . . . . . (MN) 326
Collection development &
management — STEPHENS, Dennis J. . . (AK) 1187
PEDERSOLI, Heleni M. . . (AL) 954
GREGORY, Joan A. . . . . (AZ) 466
TRUJILLO, Roberto G. . . (CA) 1259
ROBERTS, Susanne F. . . (CT) 1041
DE PEW, John N. . . . . . (FL) 293
JONES, Linda L. . . . . . . (FL) 613
WALTON, Terence M. . . (FL) 1302
EGGERS, Lolly P. . . . . . (IA) 339
KRIEGER, Alan D. . . . . . (IN) 678

MANAGEMENT (Cont'd)

Collection development & management

LEE, Thomas H.	(IN)	711
CHIANG, Ahushun	(MD)	207
COOPER, David J.	(MD)	242
WETZBARGER, Cecilia G.	(MD)	1328
YOCUM, Patricia B.	(MI)	1380
PANKAKE, Marcia J.	(MN)	938
TIBLIN, Mariann E.	(MN)	1244
BENEDICT, Marjorie A.	(NY)	80
EVANS, Robert W.	(NY)	358
BOBICK, James E.	(OH)	108
WEIDMAN, Jeffrey	(OH)	1316
SAUNDERS, William B.	(PA)	1085
ZUBATSKY, David S.	(PA)	1390
BRENNAN, Mary H.	(TX)	132
WEATHERS, Barbara H.	(TX)	1312
CHADWICK, Leroy D.	(WA)	197
SHORES, Sandra J.	(AB)	1132
SIGNORI, Donna L.	(BC)	1137
UTSUNOMIYA, Leslie D.	(BC)	1270
CHOMENKO, Tamara L.	(MB)	210

Collection development, management
Collection management

BROWN, Donald R.	(PA)	143
OSBURN, Charles B.	(AL)	927
CHAN, Carl C.	(CA)	199
HAIKALIS, Peter D.	(CA)	484
JOHNSON, Peter A.	(CA)	608
LUST, Vernon G.	(CA)	750
OLSON, Sharon L.	(CA)	923
PETERS, Marion C.	(CA)	962
SOETE, George J.	(CA)	1165
SOUTHARD, Sarah T.	(CT)	1169
CHIN, Cecilia H.	(DC)	208
GARDNER, Jeffrey J.	(DC)	418
JOHANSON, Cynthia J.	(DC)	601
KENYON, Kay A.	(DC)	643
NAINIS, Linda	(DC)	886
REED-SCOTT, Jutta R.	(DC)	1015
TAYLOR, Joan R.	(DC)	1227
AHMAD, Carol F.	(FL)	8
ORSER, Frank W.	(FL)	927
LEE, Lauren K.	(GA)	710
SELF, Sharon W.	(GA)	1113
MARSHALL, Jessica A.	(IA)	774
BENNETT, Scott B.	(IL)	82
BJORNCRANTZ, Leslie B.	(IL)	100
GRISSO, Karl M.	(IL)	471
MCBRIDE, Ruth B.	(IL)	792
MICHAELSON, Robert C.	(IL)	832
SHERMAN, Sarah	(IL)	1128
WIBERLEY, Stephen E.	(IL)	1335
MURPHY, Marcy	(IN)	881
CHANNING, Rhoda K.	(MA)	201
DRAKE, Robert E.	(MA)	318
HOVORKA, Marjorie J.	(MA)	563
JACKSON, Arlyne A.	(MA)	586
MARTIN, Murray S.	(MA)	777
FLORANCE, Valerie	(MD)	385
WILT, Larry J.	(MD)	1353
HULSEY, Richard A.	(MI)	573
SLATTERY, Charles E.	(MO)	1148
HUNT, Margaret R.	(NC)	575
LACROIX, Michael J.	(NC)	686
NUTTER, Susan K.	(NC)	912
RODNEY, Mae L.	(NC)	1048
KENNEDY, Kathleen A.	(NJ)	641
MENZEL, John P.	(NJ)	825
WHITING, Elaine M.	(NJ)	1333
BARTO, Stephen C.	(NY)	61
KOUO, Lily W.	(NY)	673
BELL, Gladys S.	(OH)	77
BENTLEY, Stella	(OH)	83
BOLEK, Ann D.	(OH)	112
HEIDTMANN, Toby	(OH)	521
THOMPSON, Ann M.	(OH)	1238
DEFASSIO, Sharon L.	(PA)	287
FREEMAN, Larry S.	(SC)	401
HOLLEMAN, Curt	(TX)	551
HYMAN, Ferne B.	(TX)	580

MANAGEMENT (Cont'd)

Collection management

SCHLESSINGER, Bernard S.	(TX)	1094
CALLAHAN, John J.	(VA)	173
CAMPBELL, James M.	(VA)	176
CAYWOOD, Carolyn A.	(VA)	195
JOHNSON, Jane W.	(VA)	605
MILLER, Nancy M.	(VA)	841
WHALEY, John H.	(VA)	1328
GELLATLY, Peter	(WA)	426
LOKEN, Sarah F.	(WA)	738
TOLLIVER, Barbara J.	(WA)	1248
ADAM, Anthony J.	(WI)	4
SWEETLAND, James H.	(WI)	1215
GUTTERIDGE, Paul	(BC)	479
AMEY, Lorne J.	(NS)	20
LANOUETTE, Marie	(ON)	696
MCLEAN-LOWE, Dallas	(ON)	814
WILLIAMSON, Michael W.	(ON)	1347
NELSON, Ian C.	(SK)	893

Collection management & circulation	DAVIS, Douglas A.	(CA)	278
Collection management & development	ALLISON, Terry L.	(CA)	17
	CARPENTER, Kathryn H.	(IL)	185
	FARRELL, David	(IN)	365
	SEREBNICK, Judith	(IN)	1116
	BEAVEN, Miranda J.	(MN)	71
	GIORDANO, Frederick S.	(NY)	438
	WEAVER, Alice O.	(OH)	1312
	MANNING, Dale	(TN)	766
	DILLON, John B.	(WI)	303
Collection management development	SHELDON, Ted P.	(MO)	1126
Collections management	GALSWORTHY, Peter R.	(ON)	415
Collections management & development	JONES, David L.	(AB)	612
Collections management & NCIP	CLOUSTON, John S.	(ON)	223
College library management	BESEMER, Susan P.	(NY)	91
	BURTON, Robert E.	(NY)	164
	MCDONALD, Joseph A.	(PA)	802
Communications management	COFFMAN, M H.	(MA)	227
Community college library management	GARDNER, W J.	(CO)	418
	RICHARD, Harris M.	(NM)	1027
	HICKEY, Kate D.	(PA)	536
Company management function	FAST, Louise	(ON)	366
Complete art library management	WAXMAN, Joanne	(ME)	1311
Computer application & data management	GREGORY, Melissa R.	(IL)	466
Computer application & management	COLDWELL, Charles P.	(WA)	230
Computer applications & mgmt consulting	BOSSEAU, Don L.	(CA)	117
Computer center management	BROWNRIGG, Edwin B.	(CA)	149
Computer indexing data management	SCHLICHTING, Catherine N.	(OH)	1094
Computer management	ALDRICH, Michele L.	(DC)	11
	HACKNEY, Judith G.	(TX)	481
	STANDIFER, Hugh A.	(TX)	1179
	ADRIAN, Donna J.	(PQ)	7
Computer management of collections	QUIGLEY, Suzanne L.	(OH)	999
Computer management systems	GILLETTE, Robert S.	(TX)	435
Computer system management	GIANGRANDE, Mark G.	(IL)	430
	HANAFEE, Valerie	(MI)	494
Computer systems management	MITCHELL, Betty J.	(CA)	848
Computer-assisted management	PRETLOW, Delores Z.	(VA)	992
Computer-based information management	WACHTER, Margery C.	(FRN)	1290
Computer-based library management	SIMS, Joyce W.	(AL)	1142
Computerized database management	HANAFEE, Valerie	(MI)	494
Computerized management systems	FROST, Rebecca H.	(PA)	406
Computers, management systems	CULL, Roberta	(AZ)	263
Conference management	BOZOIAN, Paula	(MA)	124
	TRICARICO, Mary A.	(MA)	1256
	RUPERT, Mary A.	(NH)	1068
	PHILLIPS, Janet C.	(PA)	968
Configuration management	FRIEDMAN, Sandra M.	(CA)	404
Consortium management	ADAMS, J R.	(CT)	5
Construction management	GRANADOS, Rose A.	(CA)	457
Consulting & managing one-person libs	DALY, Eudice	(CA)	271

MANAGEMENT (Cont'd)

Specialty	Name	State	Page
Consulting, library management	SCHWARZ, Shirlee	(CT)	1105
Contract library management	RAPETTI, Vincent A.	(FL)	1008
Convention & conference management	AUCOIN, Sharilynn A.	(LA)	38
Copyright & legal issues in management	NASRI, William Z.	(PA)	888
Corporate information center management	STURDIVANT, Clarence A.	(CO)	1205
Corporate library & information ctr mgmt	RUTKOWSKI, Hollace A.	(PA)	1070
Corporate library management	STANLEY, Kerry G.	(PA)	1180
Corporate library network management	LAMB, Cheryl M.	(WI)	689
Corporate records management	SALMON, Robin R.	(SC)	1077
Costing & management data	WEAVER-MEYERS, Pat L.	(OK)	1313
County library board management	COLE, Jack W.	(MN)	230
Criminal justice information management	BYRD, Harvey C.	(MD)	169
Current periodicals management	JOHNS, Jean B.	(OH)	601
Cutback management	O'BRIEN, Patrick M.	(TX)	915
Data capture & management	BRUTON, Robert T.	(MN)	151
Data collection & management	VAN ORDER, Mary J.	(ON)	1276
Data communication network management	GETZ, Malcolm	(TN)	430
Data management	MEYER, Garry S.	(NY)	830
	PIPER, Paula	(PA)	975
Data management, databases	SAGAR, Mary B.	(MI)	1074
Data processing management	CANGANELLI, Patrick W.	(IN)	178
Data resource management	VALENTINE, Scott	(ON)	1271
Database & automation management	STAINBROOK, Lynn M.	(WI)	1178
Database creation & management	LAMANN, Amber N.	(NY)	689
Database design & management	ANDRADE, Rebecca	(CA)	26
	BURNS, Nancy R.	(CA)	162
	PEPETONE, Diane S.	(IA)	957
	MACKEY, Denise R.	(IL)	756
	SLAWNIAK, Patricia M.	(IL)	1148
	NATOLI, Dorothy L.	(MA)	889
	ADLER, Robert J.	(MI)	7
	EARLE, Marcia H.	(NY)	332
	MANES, Estelle L.	(OK)	765
	RAMBO, Neil H.	(TX)	1005
	FOSTER, Anne	(ON)	392
	SOKOV, Asta M.	(PQ)	1166
	NEUWILLER, Charlene	(WGR)	897
Database design, development, management	SHELLENBARGER, Linda K.	(OH)	1126
	FURR, Susan H.	(VA)	410
	BEHNKE, Charles	(WI)	75
Database design, management	UMFLEET, Ruth A.	(TX)	1268
Database development & management	GREENWAY, Helen B.	(CT)	465
	MCNAMARA, Emma J.	(DC)	816
	GATTIS, R G.	(MI)	422
	AKS, Gloria	(NY)	9
	KOLTAY, Emery I.	(NY)	670
Database development project management	TELFER, Margaret E.	(NC)	1230
Database maintenance & management	YUSTER, Leigh C.	(NY)	1385
Database management	EMMONS, Mary E.	(AK)	348
	PUTZ, Paul D.	(AK)	998
	MONTGOMERY, Kimberly K.	(AL)	856
	RICHMOND, John W.	(AZ)	1030
	GEIGER, Richard G.	(CA)	425
	MIELKE, Marsha K.	(CA)	833
	SULLIVAN, Edward A.	(CA)	1207
	LAMPREY, Patricia M.	(CO)	691
	GONZALEZ, Suzanna S.	(CT)	448
	HARBISON, John H.	(DC)	499
	THURONYI, Geza T.	(DC)	1243
	ALZOFON, Sammy R.	(FL)	19
	BEVERIDGE, Mary I.	(IA)	93
	ENGER, Kathy B.	(IA)	349
	STUART, Kimberly A.	(IA)	1204
	STUNKARD, Gilbert L.	(IL)	1205
	ASHER, Richard E.	(IN)	36

MANAGEMENT (Cont'd)

Specialty	Name	State	Page
Database management	GOLOVIN, Naomi E.	(IN)	447
	SHARMA, Shirley K.	(KS)	1122
	FOWLER, James W.	(KY)	393
	BOZOIAN, Paula	(MA)	124
	MACDONALD, Wayne D.	(MA)	754
	BRANDHORST, Wesley T.	(MD)	128
	FLORANCE, Valerie	(MD)	385
	MCCUTCHEON, Dianne E.	(MD)	801
	TAHIR, Mary M.	(MD)	1220
	UNGER, Carol P.	(MD)	1269
	WOODS, Catharine C.	(MD)	1366
	CUNNINGHAM, Tina Y.	(MI)	265
	REGAN, Lesley E.	(MI)	1017
	BALDWIN, Jerome C.	(MN)	51
	CHAN, Jeanny T.	(MO)	199
	MUETH, Elizabeth C.	(MO)	875
	BRUCE, Nancy G.	(NC)	149
	DAVIS, Jinnie Y.	(NC)	279
	RALPH, Randy D.	(NC)	1004
	STEARNS, Melissa M.	(NH)	1183
	BREEDLOVE, Elizabeth A.	(NJ)	131
	DOUGLASS, Leslie A.	(NJ)	314
	JOHNSON, Minnie L.	(NJ)	607
	KELLY, John P.	(NJ)	638
	PAPROCKI, Mary E.	(NJ)	939
	PASTER, Luisa R.	(NJ)	946
	RIHACEK, Karen S.	(NJ)	1034
	WALLMARK, John S.	(NJ)	1298
	BENSON, James A.	(NY)	83
	CASTRO, Julio E.	(NY)	194
	COVERT, Nadine	(NY)	252
	FRUSCIANO, Thomas J.	(NY)	406
	GOLDBERG, Judy W.	(NY)	444
	HUDAK, Barbara M.	(NY)	569
	KLINE, Harriet	(NY)	661
	VELARDI, Adrienne B.	(NY)	1281
	WILSON, Marijo S.	(NY)	1352
	KNOBLAUCH, Carol J.	(OH)	665
	FORCIER, Peggy C.	(OR)	389
	DUSENBERRY, Mary D.	(SC)	329
	LOWRIMORE, R T.	(SC)	745
	BELLAMY, Lois M.	(TN)	77
	RUSHING, Jessie W.	(TN)	1068
	BICHTELER, Julie H.	(TX)	94
	HENDERSON, Lennijo P.	(TX)	526
	SZARKA, Tamara J.	(TX)	1218
	LIU, Kitty P.	(UT)	734
	BERGMAN, Rita F.	(VA)	86
	HARVEY, Suzanne	(WA)	509
	VAN DYKE, Ruth L.	(WA)	1275
	ALLEN, Christina Y.	(WI)	14
	DWORACZEK, Marian	(AB)	330
	FOSTER, Margaret A.	(ON)	392
	GRIMES, Deirdre E.	(ON)	470
	NELSON, Michael J.	(ON)	894
	MALEK, Stanislaw A.	(PQ)	763
Database management & administration	SLEETER, Ellen L.	(CA)	1148
Database management & creation	HAWK, Susan A.	(MD)	513
Database management & design	VARAT, Nancy L.	(CA)	1278
	BROWN, Maxine M.	(DC)	146
	KRANCH, Douglas A.	(IA)	676
	ANDREWS, Sylvia L.	(IN)	27
	JOHNSON, Judith	(NY)	606
	PUKL, Joseph M.	(SC)	997
Database management & development	REDFIELD, Elizabeth	(CA)	1014
	INGLE, Bernita W.	(GA)	582
	CANNATA, Arleen	(NY)	178
	EDWARDS, Melanie G.	(NY)	337
Database management & distribution	SIMON, Ralph C.	(IN)	1141
Database management & implementation	MCGREGOR, M C.	(CT)	808
Database management & quality control	HOMAN, J M.	(MI)	555
Database management in humanities	CRAWFORD, David E.	(MI)	256
Database management, library automation	MAIN, Linda Y.	(CA)	761

MANAGEMENT (Cont'd)

Database management, reprint files	MENZUL, Faina	(NJ)	825
Database management software	YAU, Linda S.	(CA)	1378
Database management system	ROBB, Thomas W.	(DC)	1038
	NASU, Yukio	(JAP)	889
Database management systems	ANDERSON, Clifford D.	(CA)	22
	CUADRA, Carlos A.	(CA)	262
	SHARP, Geoffrey H.	(CA)	1122
	WEISS, William B.	(CA)	1320
	CARR, Sallyann	(DC)	186
	CARR, Sallyann	(FL)	186
	WRIGHT, John H.	(FL)	1371
	VAN BRUNT, Virginia	(MD)	1272
	COX, Bruce B.	(MO)	253
	STEAD, William W.	(NC)	1183
	MOTT, Thomas H.	(NJ)	872
	FROEHLICH, Thomas J.	(NY)	405
	GUBIOTTI, Ross A.	(OH)	475
	EASTMAN, Caroline M.	(SC)	333
	SNYDER, Cathrine E.	(TN)	1164
	FASSETT, William E.	(WA)	366
	SCHUELLER, Janette H.	(WA)	1101
	COLE, Lorna P.	(ON)	231
Database management systems development	ROSENTHAL, Marylu C.	(MA)	1057
Database management systems on computers	RAEDER, Aggi W.	(CA)	1003
Database systems & management	SIEGERT, Lindy E.	(NS)	1136
Decision, management science	KANTOR, Paul B.	(OH)	626
Dental education management	CHERNIN, David A.	(MA)	206
Department management	WULFING, Joyce	(NY)	1374
Departmental information managing	EKSTRAND, Nancy L.	(NC)	341
Departmental management & administration	BOELKE, Joanne H.	(IL)	110
Designing records management systems	BOWKER, Scott W.	(NY)	121
Desktop information management systems	HARTT, Richard W.	(VA)	509
Direct mail promotion management	OGREN, Mark S.	(IL)	918
Direct marketing & sales management	JOHNSON, Richard K.	(MD)	608
Directing & managing museum & library	PARKER, Peter J.	(PA)	942
District media management	POOLE, Rebecca S.	(CO)	983
Documents management	LAI, Dennis	(CA)	688
Documents services management	WATSON, Paula D.	(IL)	1310
DROLS database management	GALLERY, M C.	(CA)	414
Editorial department management	BRAM, Leon L.	(NJ)	127
Editorial management	SABOSIK, Patricia E.	(CT)	1073
Education bibliography, collection mgmt	BROWN, M S.	(FL)	145
Education for information management	FOSKETT, Antony C.	(AUS)	392
Educational media management	SIMCOE, Darryl D.	(NY)	1139
	MAXWELL, James G.	(OR)	788
	CHANG, Robert H.	(TX)	201
Educational resources management & ref	ILACQUA, Anne K.	(MA)	581
Electronic mail system management	WAGNER, Judith O.	(OH)	1292
Employee benefits, home resource mgmt	JACQUES, Donna M.	(MA)	591
Employment management	KURKUL, Donna L.	(MA)	684
End-user managing	PERINO, Elaine S.	(MA)	958
Energy reference & library management	BLANDAMER, Ann W.	(DC)	103
Engineering library resources management	PFANN, Mary L.	(NJ)	966
Environmental information management	SNODGRASS, Rex J.	(NC)	1163
Executive level management	ASHTON, Rick J.	(CO)	36
Executive management	AULD, Dennis B.	(KY)	39
Exploration records management	MOORE, Guusje Z.	(TX)	859
Export marketing management	OVEREYNDER, Rombout E.	(NET)	931
Extension agency management, supervision	GRAY, Patricia B.	(VA)	460
Facilities management	MONTANELLI, Dale S.	(IL)	855
	PAIETTA, Ann C.	(IL)	935
	ROSSOFF, Judith H.	(NY)	1059
Federal grants management	KLASSEN, Robert L.	(DC)	657
Film & video library management	HOLSINGER, Katherine	(AZ)	554

MANAGEMENT (Cont'd)

Film library management	RICHIE, Mark L.	(NJ)	1030
Financial management	LYNCH, Hugh J.	(IL)	751
	VIRGO, Julie A.	(IL)	1285
	KIRBY, Frederick J.	(MI)	654
	HAMMOND, John J.	(MO)	493
	BARTH, Joseph M.	(NY)	61
	MEYER, Andrew W.	(NY)	829
	DEWBERRY, Betty B.	(TX)	298
	BYERS, Edward W.	(WY)	168
	DUFFIN, Elizabeth A.	(IRE)	323
Fine arts library management	GAMER, May L.	(MO)	416
Fiscal management	HAMILTON, Rita	(AZ)	492
	ALLMAND, Linda F.	(TX)	17
Forms & procedures management	GENESEN, Judith L.	(IL)	427
Full-service library management	HUNSUCKER, Alice E.	(CA)	574
Gas Net industry database management	DORNER, Steven J.	(VA)	313
Gateway management	LOGAN, Harold J.	(NJ)	737
Gateway project management	MALONEY, James J.	(CA)	764
General administration & management	EASTMAN, Ann H.	(VA)	333
General library management	NORBIE, Dorothy E.	(CO)	908
	DAWSON, Victoria A.	(NY)	282
General library management, admin	DOLAN, Mary M.	(MN)	309
General management	MCENTIRE, James E.	(CO)	804
	SMITH, Stephen S.	(CO)	1161
	KRAMER, Sheldon I.	(CT)	675
	LUQUIRE, Wilson	(IL)	749
	NELSON, James A.	(KY)	894
	PECON, Sally N.	(NJ)	953
	GROSSMAN, Adrian J.	(NY)	473
	TORRONE, Joan M.	(NY)	1251
General management & administration	FREEDMAN, Bernadette	(PA)	400
General management, small special lib	GALLUP, Jane H.	(DC)	415
General medical library management	FETKOVICH, Malinda M.	(PA)	374
Geological technical info management	DICKERSON, Mary J.	(TX)	300
Geoscience information, processing mgmt	BICHTELER, Julie H.	(TX)	94
Gift & exchanges management	DUPRE, Monique	(ON)	327
Government documents collection mgmt	MCSWEENEY, Josephine	(NY)	818
Government documents, contract mgmt	LAKSHMAN, Malathi K.	(MD)	689
Government documents management	PONNAPPA, Biddanda P.	(TN)	982
Government library management	RICHER, Suzanne	(ON)	1030
Government records management	BOCKMAN, Eugene J.	(NY)	109
Grant management	SCARBOROUGH, Katharine T.	(CA)	1087
Health care administration & management	PATTERSON, Jennifer J.	(TN)	948
Health care library management	LINTON, William D.	(NIR)	731
Health care management research	BELL, Steven J.	(PA)	77
Health information management	BYRD, Gary D.	(NC)	168
Health library management	SHIFF, Linda S.	(ON)	1130
Health sciences library management	KAFES, Frederick W.	(NJ)	621
High school library management	OSTHUS, Mary J.	(SD)	928
Hospital & clinical management subjects	BELT, Jane	(WA)	78
Hospital library administration & mgmt	WALES, Patricia L.	(CT)	1294
Hospital library management	BENELISHA, Eleanor	(CA)	80
	KELLY, Janice E.	(IL)	637
	BUCHANAN, Holly S.	(KY)	153
	CAFFAREL, Agnes	(LA)	170
	HIGGINBOTHAM, Cecelia B.	(LA)	537
	FREDENBURG, Anne M.	(MD)	399
	LONG, Susan S.	(MT)	740
	MILLER, Nancy H.	(NC)	841
	BABISH, Jo A.	(PA)	43
	SCARPATO, Loann C.	(PA)	1088
	JARVIS, Mary E.	(TX)	595
	LEE, Regina H.	(TX)	711
	CAMPBELL, Mary E.	(WA)	177
Human resource management	SWEENEY, June D.	(DC)	1215
	RIDDLE, Raymond E.	(KS)	1032
	PINDER, Jo A.	(MD)	974
	WEBB, Gisela M.	(TX)	1313
	WILKINSON, John P.	(ON)	1340

MANAGEMENT (Cont'd)

Human resources management — COFFMAN, M H. . . . . . (MA) 227
MEADOWS, Donald F. . . (BC) 819
Image management — COATES, Paul F. . . . . . . (KY) 224
Inactive records management — RYAN, Betsey A. . . . . . . (KS) 1070
Information & documentation center mgmt — MOUREAU, Magdeleine . (FRN) 873
Information & image management — YODER, William M. . . . . (VA) 1380
Information & records management — KATTLOVE, Rose W. . . . . (CA) 630
OPEM, John D. . . . . (IL) 925
VAN BRUNT, Virginia . . . (MD) 1272
Info center & special lib management — COOPER, Marianne . . . (NY) 243
Information center management — ANGLE, Joanne G. . . . . . (DC) 28
ECKROADE, Carlene B. . (DE) 335
SIMS, Edward N. . . . . . (KY) 1142
EISENMANN, Laura M. . (MA) 341
STEIGER, Bettie A. . . . . (MD) 1185
HOWELL, M G. . . . . . . (NY) 565
MARSHALL, Patricia K. . . (NY) 775
RIGNEY, Shirley A. . . . . (NY) 1034
POLLIS, Angela R. . . . . . (PA) 981
UBALDINI, Michael W. . . (TN) 1267
Information center mgmt & organization — ALBERTUS, Donna M. . . (NY) 10
Information center management systems — WEIL, Ben H. . . . . (NJ) 1317
Information circulation & management — KAPLAN, Tiby . . . . (FL) 626
Information for managers & organization — KATZER, Jeffrey . . . . . . (NY) 630
Information management — BRAUNSTEIN, Yale M. . (CA) 130
KAPLAN, Robin . . . . (CA) 626
KWAN, Julie K. . . . . (CA) 685
MARLOR, Hugh T. . . . . (CA) 772
WIERZBA, Heidemarie B. (CA) 1337
HUGHES, Brad R. . . . . (CO) 571
MASTERS, Fred N. . . . . (CT) 782
STEELE, Noreen O. . . . . (CT) 1184
FRAULINO, Philip S. . . . (DC) 399
KOSTINKO, Gail A. . . . . (DC) 673
AHLIN, Nancy . . . . (FL) 8
ROAN, Tattie W. . . . . . . (GA) 1038
BECKER, Jacquelyn B. . . (IL) 72
BERGER, Carol A. . . . . . (IL) 85
BRICHFORD, Maynard J. . (IL) 134
REED, Janet S. . . . . (IL) 1015
SHEDLOCK, James . . . . (IL) 1124
STRABLE, Edward G. . . . (IL) 1199
HALE, Martha L. . . . . . . (KS) 485
CHEN, Ching C. . . . . . . (MA) 205
JACQUES, Donna M. . . . (MA) 591
MOFFITT, Michael D. . . . (MA) 852
CHESLOCK, Rosalind P. . (MD) 207
DIENER, Richard A. . . . . (MD) 302
FISHBEIN, Meyer H. . . . . (MD) 380
JASON, Nora H. . . . . . . (MD) 595
POQUETTE, Mary L. . . . (MN) 984
BONDAROVICH, Mary F. (NJ) 113
DEDERT, Patricia L. . . . . (NJ) 286
JOHNSON, Minnie L. . . . (NJ) 607
MENZUL, Faina . . . . (NJ) 825
SPAULDING, Frank H. . . (NJ) 1172
BADERTSCHER, David G. (NY) 44
BLAKE-O'HOGAN, Kathleen E. . . . . (NY) 103
CROCKETT, Denise J. . . (NY) 259
EARLE, Marcia H. . . . . . (NY) 332
TAYLOR, Robert S. . . . . (NY) 1228
WILLNER, Richard A. . . . (NY) 1349
BACON, Agnes K. . . . . . (OH) 44
JANKOWSKI, Dorothy A. (OH) 593
PETERSON, Barbara E. . (PA) 962
MASON, Florence M. . . . (TX) 781
MIDDLETON, Robert K. . (TX) 833
PHILLIPS, Toni M. . . . . . (TX) 969
CAPUTO, Richard P. . . . (VA) 180
KUNEY, Joseph H. . . . . (VA) 684
ROSENBERG, Murray D. (VA) 1056
SCHUTTE, Raymond R. . (WA) 1103
DYSART, Jane I. . . . . . . (ON) 331
NOKES, Jane E. . . . . . . (ON) 907

MANAGEMENT (Cont'd)

Information management — NASU, Yukio . . . . (JAP) 889
WERSIG, Gernot . . . . . . (WGR) 325
Information management analysis — BUSSEY, Holly J. . . . . . (NY) 165
Information management & data search — ZIAIAN, Monir . . . . (CA) 1387
Information management & marketing — HARMON, Glynn . . . . . . (TX) 502
Information management & organization — KADEC, Sarah T. . . . . . (MD) 621
Information management & planning — JENKINS, Ann A. . . . . . (CA) 597
Information management & retention — CHRISTNER, Deborah S. (CA) 212
Information management consulting — HORTON, Forest W. . . . (DC) 561
Information management education — HORAK, Ellen B. . . . . . (CT) 558
MARTIN, Elaine R. . . . . . (DC) 776
MCGOWAN, Anna T. . . . (DC) 807
TOOEY, Mary J. . . . . . . (MD) 1250
WILSON, Barbara A. . . . (TX) 1349
Information management, library devlpmnt — CONDREY, Barbara K. . . (CA) 236
Information management, plng, & systs — KOZAK, Marlene G. . . . (IL) 674
Information management procedures — HENDERSON, Madeline M. . . . . (MD) 526
Information management resources — STEIGER, Bettie A. . . . . (MD) 1185
Information management srvs consulting — GROCKI, Daniel J. . . . . . (MD) 471
Information management software — HASKINS, Dawn A. . . . . (OH) 510
Information management systems — WITTMANN, Cecelia V. . (CA) 1358
WEST, Richard T. . . . . . (MD) 1326
BAADE, Harley D. . . . . . (TX) 43
KLEIN, Mindy F. . . . . . . (TX) 659
STARK, Philip H. . . . . . . (CO) 1182
Information management training —
Information product development mgmt — BRAM, Leon L. . . . . . . (NJ) 127
Information product management — LEHMANN, Edward J. . . (VA) 713
Information resource management — DENNISON, Lynn C. . . . (CA) 292
MCCARTHY, John L. . . . (CA) 794
STAN, Gail A. . . . . (CA) 1179
BEICHMAN, John C. . . . (MI) 75
DANIEL, Evelyn H. . . . . . (NC) 272
KOENIG, Michael E. . . . (NY) 668
HODGSON, Cynthia A. . . (PA) 546
LYTLE, Richard H. . . . . . (PA) 753
BURNS, Barrie A. . . . . . (ON) 162
Information resources management — POEHLMAN, Dorothy J. . (DC) 979
EVERETT, Amy E. . . . . . (DE) 358
BROWN, Patricia L. . . . . (IL) 146
REITER, Richard R. . . . . (IL) 1022
MOBLEY, Kathleen S. . . (KS) 851
LEVITAN, Karen B. . . . . (MD) 721
NEWMAN, Wilda B. . . . . (MD) 900
PRICE, Douglas S. . . . . . (MD) 992
HAMLIN, Eileen M. . . . . (NY) 493
MARCHAND, Donald A. . (NY) 768
MARTIN, Thomas H. . . . (NY) 778
RODERER, Nancy K. . . . (NY) 1047
MOORE, Penelope F. . . . (VA) 861
Information service management — STANTON, Robert O. . . . (NJ) 1181
LAWRENCE, Barbara . . . (NY) 704
Information services management — BALDWIN, Jerome C. . . . (MN) 51
BATTIN, Patricia . . . . . . (NY) 64
PEARCE, Karla J. . . . . . (NY) 952
WEINSTEIN, Lois . . . . . . (NY) 1318
BAKER, Dale B. . . . . . . (OH) 48
JUDGE, Joseph M. . . . . (PA) 619
VASILAKIS, Mary . . . . . (PA) 1279
CLOSE, Elizabeth G. . . . (UT) 223
Information system design & management — FREEDMAN, Bernadette . (PA) 400
LAZAR, Peter . . . . (HUN) 706
Information systems management — TETTEH, Joseph A. . . . . (LA) 1233
MENOU, Michel J. . . . . . (ITL) 824
Information technology & management — FIDOTEN, Robert E. . . . (PA) 375
Information technology management — MCKIRDY, Pamela R. . . . (MA) 812
BECKMAN, Margaret L. . (ON) 73
In-house database management — TREVICK, Selma D. . . . . (PQ) 1255
InMagic software file management system — HOUSTON, Louise B. . . . (ON) 563

MANAGEMENT (Cont'd)

Instructional services management	JORDAN, Travis E.	(TX)	617
Integrated info resources management	KNOPPERS, Jake V.	(ON)	665
Interface with management	SAUSEDO, Ann E.	(CA)	1085
Interlibrary loan & serial management	WILLIAMS, Calvin	(MI)	1342
Interlibrary loan department management	CARVER, Jane W.	(KS)	191
Inventory control, vendor management	MCGRAW, Scott C.	(IL)	807
Issues management	DORSETT, Anita W.	(TX)	313
Japanese business & management info	NOGUCHI, Sachie	(IL)	907
Journal management	WASSON, Patricia G.	(IL)	1308
Law firm library management	MATTHEWSON, David S.	(CT)	786
	HARRIS, Helen Y.	(MD)	504
	JULIAN, Julie L.	(TN)	619
Law library management	BALABAN, Robin M.	(CA)	50
	DATTALO, Elmo F.	(DC)	275
	SMITH, Mary D.	(FL)	1158
	HUTCHINS, Richard G.	(IL)	579
	ANDREWS, Sylvia L.	(IN)	27
	LAMBERT, Lyn D.	(MA)	690
	KILLIAN, Mary C.	(MI)	648
	DIGIOVANNA, Josephine A.	(NY)	303
	FRALEY, Ruth A.	(NY)	395
	KAIN, Joan P.	(NY)	622
	HANLEY, Thomas L.	(OH)	496
	BURGESS, Rita N.	(PA)	159
	MACBETH, Eileen M.	(PA)	754
	BALCOMBE, Judith A.	(TX)	51
	GARCIA, Lana C.	(TX)	417
	HOUSTON, Barbara B.	(TX)	563
	MOORE, Dianne T.	(VA)	859
	MURPHY, Robert D.	(VA)	881
	YEN, David S.	(HKG)	1379
Law library management administration	HERNANDEZ, Marilyn J.	(MB)	531
Law library management & planning	ARANDA-COODOU, Patricio	(DC)	30
Leadership & management	RIGGS, Donald E.	(AZ)	1034
Lrng resrch ctr mgmt & reorganization	MIAH, Abdul J.	(VA)	831
Learning resources center management	CAROL, Barbara B.	(OK)	184
Learning resources management	BERLING, John G.	(MN)	88
Legal information management	COMSTOCK, Daniel L.	(NM)	235
Legal library management administration	HERNANDEZ, Marilyn J.	(MB)	531
Legal reference & management	HARBISON, John H.	(DC)	499
Legal research & resources management	DEMPSEY, Pamela M.	(NM)	291
Legal serials management	GOLIAN, Linda M.	(FL)	447
Library administration & management	ANDERSON, Herschel V.	(AZ)	23
	BENGSTON, Carl E.	(CA)	80
	BOSSEAU, Don L.	(CA)	117
	MINUDRI, Regina U.	(CA)	847
	WALCH, David B.	(CA)	1293
	STEERE, Paul J.	(DC)	1184
	SIROIS, Julie J.	(HI)	1144
	BERRY, John W.	(IL)	90
	SPARKS, Marie C.	(IN)	1171
	REDDY, Sigrid R.	(MA)	1014
	KOSMIN, Linda J.	(MD)	672
	NEWMAN, Wilda B.	(MD)	900
	DIDIER, Elaine K.	(MI)	301
	ENGELKE, Hans	(MI)	349
	COGSWELL, James A.	(MN)	227
	ALBRITTON, Rosie L.	(MO)	10
	RICKERSON, George T.	(MO)	1031
	HUTCHINSON, Barbara J.	(NJ)	579
	CHANG, Daphne Y.	(NY)	200
	BURRIER, Donald H.	(OH)	163
	MASON, Marilyn G.	(OH)	781
	WOOD, Richard J.	(SC)	1365
	LOWRY, Charles B.	(TX)	745
Library & archive management	FINE, Deborah J.	(CA)	377
Lib & archives conservation management	CUNHA, George M.	(KY)	265
Library & archives management	MOORE, Emily C.	(AL)	859

MANAGEMENT (Cont'd)

Library & audiovisual management	SIMARD, Denis	(PQ)	1139
Library & information center management	CEPPOS, Karen F.	(CA)	196
	LEWIS, Ralph W.	(CA)	724
	MADDOCK, Jerome T.	(CO)	759
	FINGERMAN, Susan M.	(MA)	378
	PARAS, Lucille P.	(NJ)	939
Library & information management	BENDER, David R.	(DC)	79
	BOYLE, Stephen	(IL)	124
	BROWN, Ina A.	(NJ)	144
Library & information services mgmt	FITZGERALD, Diana S.	(CA)	382
Library & management systems	BLACKBURN, Joy M.	(IL)	102
Library & media management	SOLES, Elizabeth S.	(VA)	1166
Library & records management	BLUM, Linda C.	(CA)	107
	CONNER, Norma	(NY)	237
Library & records management consulting	GAGNON, Donna M.	(CA)	412
Library & reference center management	MISSAR, Charles D.	(MD)	847
Library association management	PARRY, Pamela J.	(AZ)	944
	FERRELL, Mary S.	(CA)	373
Library automation, database management	FINCH, Mildred E.	(VA)	377
Library automation systems management	HOWE, Patricia A.	(VA)	565
Library building management	BURNS, Robert W.	(CO)	163
Library business management	HUGGINS, Annelle R.	(TN)	571
Library collection movement management	KURKUL, Donna L.	(MA)	684
Library computerized management	PARKER, Eleanor V.	(OK)	941
Library contract management	CHIESA, Adele M.	(MD)	208
Library development & management	WARPHEA, Rita C.	(VA)	1306
Library development management	STANLEY, Nelda J.	(LA)	1180
Library function management	DICKERSON, Mary J.	(TX)	300
Library information management	SMART, Marriott W.	(CO)	1151
Library, information mgmt consulting	GOSSAGE, Wayne	(NY)	453
Library information management systems	SMITH, Jessie C.	(MD)	1156
Library management	GREGORY, Vicki L.	(AL)	466
	HURTT, Betty D.	(AL)	578
	LANE, Robert B.	(AL)	694
	ASHCRAFT, Carolyn A.	(AR)	35
	LANEY-SHEEHAN, Susan	(AR)	695
	GOTHBERG, Helen M.	(AZ)	453
	KLATT, Dixie K.	(AZ)	657
	PILLOW, William H.	(AZ)	973
	WELLIK, Kay E.	(AZ)	1321
	ATKINS, Gregg T.	(CA)	38
	CHAMPANY, Barry W.	(CA)	198
	CHESSMAN, Rebecca L.	(CA)	207
	CODER, Ann	(CA)	226
	CRAWFORD, Marilyn L.	(CA)	257
	CROSBY-MUILENBURG, Corryn	(CA)	260
	DAVENPORT, Constance B.	(CA)	275
	DESOIER, Jacqueline J.	(CA)	295
	DUNN, Kathleen K.	(CA)	327
	DYSON, Allan J.	(CA)	331
	EASTMAN, Franklin R.	(CA)	333
	ESQUEVIN, Christian R.	(CA)	354
	EVANS, G E.	(CA)	357
	FLETCHER, Homer L.	(CA)	384
	GOVAARS, Inga	(CA)	454
	GREGOR, Dorothy D.	(CA)	466
	HEINES, Rodney M.	(CA)	522
	HERSBERGER, Rodney M.	(CA)	533
	KALVINSKAS, Louanne A.	(CA)	623
	KLEIBER, Michael C.	(CA)	658
	LA BORDE, Charlotte A.	(CA)	686
	LEE, Dora T.	(CA)	709
	LEWIS, Cookie A.	(CA)	722
	LINDEN, Margaret J.	(CA)	729
	LOMAX, Ronald C.	(CA)	738
	MACKINTOSH, Mary L.	(CA)	757
	MCDONALD, Marilyn M.	(CA)	803
	MCGREEVY, Kathleen T.	(CA)	808
	MURPHY, Joan F.	(CA)	880
	OSSEN, Virginia F.	(CA)	928

MANAGEMENT (Cont'd)
Library management

PAIK, Nan H.	(CA)	935
PAPERMASTER, Cynthia L.	(CA)	939
PARKS, Mary L.	(CA)	943
PORTER-ROTH, Anne	(CA)	985
POST, William E.	(CA)	986
RUBENS, Charlotte C.	(CA)	1064
SCEPANSKI, Jordan M.	(CA)	1088
SEVIER, Jeffrey A.	(CA)	1117
SMOKEY, Sheila C.	(CA)	1162
SOETE, George J.	(CA)	1165
STANEK, Suzanne	(CA)	1179
SZYNAKA, Edward M.	(CA)	1219
VAN HOUSE, Nancy A.	(CA)	1275
VILLERE, Dawn N.	(CA)	1284
WAWRZONEK, Mary S.	(CA)	1311
WHITE, Cecil R.	(CA)	1330
WHITE, Lelia C.	(CA)	1331
YANEZ, Elva K.	(CA)	1377
COSTA, Betty L.	(CO)	249
KELLY, Karon M.	(CO)	638
KOHL, David F.	(CO)	668
MANNING, Leslie A.	(CO)	766
MOORE, Beverly B.	(CO)	858
PITKIN, Gary M.	(CO)	976
REITER, Ellie W.	(CO)	1022
WAGNER, Barbara L.	(CO)	1291
CAMPO, Lynn D.	(CT)	177
LOOMIS, Mary K.	(CT)	740
NEUFELD, Irving H.	(CT)	897
PORTER, Kathryn W.	(CT)	985
SILVERMAN, Susanne	(CT)	1139
BATES, Mary E.	(DC)	64
GERVINO, Joan	(DC)	429
GUERRIERO, Donald A.	(DC)	476
HO, James K.	(DC)	545
LEONARD, Lawrence E.	(DC)	716
LEVERING, Mary B.	(DC)	719
MOTTA, Camille A.	(DC)	872
NAVE, Greer G.	(DC)	890
PERRONE, Jeanne M.	(DC)	960
POEHLMAN, Dorothy J.	(DC)	979
RATNER, Rhoda S.	(DC)	1010
RENNINGER, Karen	(DC)	1023
THOMAS, Patricia A.	(DC)	1238
UPDEGROVE, Robert A.	(DC)	1269
VANDEGRIFT, Barbara P.	(DC)	1273
WASHINGTON, Sigrid M.	(DC)	1308
ZELINKA, Mary A.	(DC)	1387
BAIN, Janice W.	(FL)	47
HENEHAN, Alva D.	(FL)	528
MALANCHUK, Iona R.	(FL)	762
MALANCHUK, Peter P.	(FL)	762
MARTIN, John H.	(FL)	776
MILLER, Laurence A.	(FL)	839
PINGS, Vern M.	(FL)	974
RAPETTI, Vincent A.	(FL)	1008
BIBBY, Elizabeth A.	(GA)	94
CLEMONS, John E.	(GA)	221
JOHNSON, Herbert F.	(GA)	605
MCDAVID, Michael W.	(GA)	801
MCIVER, Stephanie P.	(GA)	809
REZNICK, Evi P.	(GA)	1025
RHEAY, Mary L.	(GA)	1025
WAVERCHAK, Gail A.	(GA)	1311
SMITH, Frances P.	(HI)	1155
URAGO, Gail M.	(HI)	1269
BAKER, Sharon L.	(IA)	49
GEORGE, Shirley H.	(IA)	428
HIRST, Donna L.	(IA)	543
LAWSON, George T.	(IA)	705
LORKOVIC, Tatjana B.	(IA)	741
JONES-LITTEER, Corene A.	(ID)	616
SPICKELMIER, Pamela S.	(ID)	1174
WATSON, Peter G.	(ID)	1310
BLOSS, Marjorie E.	(IL)	106
DREAZEN, Elizabeth P.	(IL)	318

MANAGEMENT (Cont'd)
Library management

FINNERTY, James L.	(IL)	379
FURLONG, Robert E.	(IL)	410
GUY, Jeniece N.	(IL)	479
HAGBERG, Betty S.	(IL)	482
HOGAN, Louise G.	(IL)	549
KNOBLAUCH, Mark G.	(IL)	665
MARSHALL, Maggie L.	(IL)	774
MCBRIDE, Ruth B.	(IL)	792
MUNOFF, Gerald J.	(IL)	879
MURRAY, Marilyn R.	(IL)	882
OLSON, Rue E.	(IL)	923
PROBST, Virginia M.	(IL)	994
RODGER, Eleanor J.	(IL)	1047
SCHULTZ, Therese A.	(IL)	1102
WERNETTE, Janice J.	(IL)	1325
WILSON, Charlotte A.	(IL)	1350
ALLEN, Joyce S.	(IN)	15
BERG, Rita J.	(IN)	85
BONHOMME, Mary S.	(IN)	114
DOELLMAN, Michael A.	(IN)	308
FUNKHOUSER, Richard L.	(IN)	410
GALOW, Donald G.	(IN)	415
LAW, Gordon T.	(IN)	704
LEACH, Ronald G.	(IN)	706
MOORE, Thomas J.	(IN)	861
POOR, William E.	(IN)	983
PUNGITORE, Verna L.	(IN)	997
SOWELL, Steven L.	(IN)	1170
ZEUGNER, Lorenzo A.	(IN)	1387
FORTE, Joseph E.	(KS)	391
LAUFFER, Donna J.	(KS)	702
NEELEY, James D.	(KS)	891
STEWART, Henry R.	(KS)	1192
WILLARD, Gayle K.	(KS)	1341
DOUTHITT, Rita C.	(KY)	314
MARTIN, June H.	(KY)	777
YATES, Dudley V.	(KY)	1378
AVANT, Julia K.	(LA)	41
GREAVES, F L.	(LA)	461
HOGAN, Sharon A.	(LA)	549
LEE, Lynda M.	(LA)	710
MCKANN, Michael R.	(LA)	809
BAUGHMAN, James C.	(MA)	66
DRESLEY, Susan C.	(MA)	319
FRYDRYK, Teresa E.	(MA)	407
HANSSEN, Nancy E.	(MA)	499
KEYS, Marshall	(MA)	645
KING, Laurie L.	(MA)	651
MARCY, Henry O.	(MA)	769
MAXANT, Vicary	(MA)	787
MAZURANIC, Joseph R.	(MA)	791
MCNIFF, Philip J.	(MA)	817
PEARLSTEIN, Toby	(MA)	952
ROFF, Jill R.	(MA)	1049
SCHWALLER, Marian C.	(MA)	1104
SEIDMAN, Ruth K.	(MA)	1112
SIMEONE, Therese A.	(MA)	1139
STUEART, Robert D.	(MA)	1205
VON KRIES, Beverley A.	(MA)	1288
WOLPERT, Ann J.	(MA)	1362
APPLEBAUM, Edmond L.	(MD)	30
BAILEY, Carol A.	(MD)	46
BERGER, Patricia W.	(MD)	86
BLUTE, Mary R.	(MD)	107
HAMMETT, Marcia G.	(MD)	493
HINSON, Karen C.	(MD)	543
HSIEH, Rebecca T.	(MD)	567
JOHNSON, Carol A.	(MD)	602
KOBAYASHI, Michiko	(MD)	666
MASSEY, James E.	(MD)	782
SHAPIRO, Leila C.	(MD)	1121
SMITH, Kathleen A.	(MD)	1156
THAPAR, Shashi P.	(MD)	1234
GREENLAW, Evelyn A.	(ME)	465
NICHOLSON, Carol C.	(ME)	902
CHEN, Catherine W.	(MI)	205
DOUGHERTY, Richard M.	(MI)	314
EL MOUCHI, Joan S.	(MI)	346

MANAGEMENT (Cont'd)
Library management

ESTRY, Donna S.	(MI)	355
FEDEROWSKI, Marjorie S.	(MI)	368
HALL, Jo A.	(MI)	488
NETZ, David H.	(MI)	896
ROOP, Donna K.	(MI)	1053
SPECTOR, Janice B.	(MI)	1172
YOCUM, Patricia B.	(MI)	1380
ZYSKOWSKI, Douglas A.	(MI)	1392
BARBOUR-TALLEY, Donna L.	(MN)	55
D'ELIA, George P.	(MN)	289
FABIO, Janet L.	(MN)	360
STEINKE, Cynthia A.	(MN)	1186
TAYLOR, Judith K.	(MN)	1227
CRAVENS, Vickie L.	(MO)	256
DRAYSON, Pamela K.	(MO)	318
GAFFEY, Mary V.	(MO)	411
JENKINS, Harold R.	(MO)	597
MECHANIC, Margaret A.	(MO)	820
ONSAGER, Lawrence W.	(MO)	924
PLUTCHAK, T S.	(MO)	979
SHELDON, Ted P.	(MO)	1126
BLACK, Bernice B.	(MS)	101
BUCHANAN, Gerald	(MS)	153
WALL, Norma F.	(MS)	1297
WILTSE, Elaine E.	(MS)	1353
BEATTIE, Barbara C.	(NC)	70
KEE, Walter A.	(NC)	634
KIRWAN, William J.	(NC)	656
LANEY, Elizabeth J.	(NC)	695
LANIER, Gene D.	(NC)	696
LUBANS, John	(NC)	745
RALPH, Randy D.	(NC)	1004
SEMONCHE, Barbara P.	(NC)	1115
SPELLER, Benjamin F.	(NC)	1172
WILLIAMS, M J.	(NC)	1345
WILLIAMS, Mildred J.	(NC)	1345
WILLIAMS, Wiley J.	(NC)	1347
VYZRALEK, Dolores E.	(ND)	1290
BOYLE, Thomas E.	(NE)	124
HENDRICKSON, Kent H.	(NE)	527
MARSH, Paul W.	(NE)	773
BERLIN, Arthur E.	(NH)	87
MCCANN, Susan F.	(NH)	794
AUER, E E.	(NJ)	39
BOSS, Catherine M.	(NJ)	117
CANOSE, Joseph A.	(NJ)	179
COURTNEY, Aida N.	(NJ)	251
ENGLISH, Bernard L.	(NJ)	350
GONZALES, Victoria E.	(NJ)	448
HENRY, Mary B.	(NJ)	529
HUNT, Florine E.	(NJ)	575
JONES, Dorothy S.	(NJ)	612
KELLY, John P.	(NJ)	638
KRANIS, Janet C.	(NJ)	676
LINGELBACH, Lorene N.	(NJ)	730
LUSTIG, Joanne	(NJ)	750
MARCHOK, Catherine W.	(NJ)	769
MCDERMOTT, Ellen	(NJ)	801
PACHMAN, Frederic C.	(NJ)	933
PANDELAKIS, Helene S.	(NJ)	937
ROBERTS, Leila J.	(NJ)	1040
ROUMFORT, Susan B.	(NJ)	1061
SCHNEIDER, Lynette C.	(NJ)	1097
SILVA, Nelly H.	(NJ)	1138
SOBIN, Maryann D.	(NJ)	1165
STANTON, Robert O.	(NJ)	1181
TALCOTT, Ann W.	(NJ)	1221
WILLIAMS, Janet L.	(NJ)	1344
COVINGTON, Robert D.	(NV)	252
DEACON, Mary D.	(NV)	283
ORTIZ, Cynthia	(NV)	927
BADERTSCHER, David G.	(NY)	44
BARRETT, Lizabeth A.	(NY)	59
BATTIN, Patricia	(NY)	64
BAUM, Christina D.	(NY)	66
BERNER, Andrew J.	(NY)	88
BOROSON, Sarah	(NY)	116

MANAGEMENT (Cont'd)
Library management

CHICARELLA, Joseph T.	(NY)	207
CLARK, Philip M.	(NY)	218
COOKE, Constance B.	(NY)	241
DE GENNARO, Richard	(NY)	287
DUMONT, Normand E.	(NY)	325
FRANK, Agnes T.	(NY)	396
GLEASON, Robert W.	(NY)	440
GREEN, Joseph H.	(NY)	462
HAAS, Eva L.	(NY)	480
HASWELL, Hollee	(NY)	511
HUDAK, Barbara M.	(NY)	569
JASSIN, Raymond M.	(NY)	595
JENSEN, Dennis F.	(NY)	598
LAMBKIN, Claire A.	(NY)	691
MELTON RSM, Marie F.	(NY)	823
MILLER, J G.	(NY)	838
NELOMS, Karen H.	(NY)	893
O'DELL, Lorraine I.	(NY)	916
PALMER, Robert B.	(NY)	936
PARKER, Margaret S.	(NY)	942
PETERS, Jean R.	(NY)	962
PINEDA, Conchita J.	(NY)	974
PRINZ, Jane A.	(NY)	993
RABBAN, Elana	(NY)	1001
RECORD, William J.	(NY)	1013
RUDA, Donna R.	(NY)	1065
ST. CLAIR, Guy	(NY)	1075
SANTORO, Tesse F.	(NY)	1082
SHER, Deborah M.	(NY)	1127
SHERWIG, Mary J.	(NY)	1129
STERLING, Sheila	(NY)	1189
YAVARKOVSKY, Jerome	(NY)	1378
ZIPPER, Masha	(NY)	1390
BLOUGH, Keith A.	(OH)	106
BUTTLAR, Lois J.	(OH)	167
CLEM, Harriet M.	(OH)	220
DESCHENE, Dorice	(OH)	294
KEOGH, Jeanne M.	(OH)	643
KERBOW, Sandra C.	(OH)	643
KONKEL, Mary S.	(OH)	670
LUCAS, Jean M.	(OH)	746
MACIUSZKO, Jerzy J.	(OH)	755
MARCOTTE, Frederick A.	(OH)	769
RODGERS, Judith P.	(OH)	1047
TEPE, Ann S.	(OH)	1231
VENABLE, Andrew A.	(OH)	1282
YANCURA, Ann J.	(OH)	1377
HUGHES, Carol A.	(OK)	571
JOHNSON, Edward R.	(OK)	604
ROBERTS, Linda L.	(OK)	1041
STAIR, Fred	(OK)	1178
JENSEN, Gary D.	(OR)	598
WRIGHT, Catherine A.	(OR)	1370
ADAMS, Mignon S.	(PA)	5
DIXON, Rebecca D.	(PA)	306
FELIX, Sally T.	(PA)	370
FITZGERALD, Patricia A.	(PA)	382
FOUST, Judith M.	(PA)	393
FUSELER-MCDOWELL, Elizabeth A.	(PA)	410
KNAPP, Mabel J.	(PA)	663
KREMER, Jill L.	(PA)	677
MAXIN, Jacqueline A.	(PA)	787
MCCREARY, Diane M.	(PA)	800
MEREDITH, Phyllis C.	(PA)	825
OWENS, Frederick H.	(PA)	932
PARSONS, Muriel W.	(PA)	945
SAUER, James L.	(PA)	1084
SCHILL, Julie G.	(PA)	1092
STEVENS, Marian A.	(PA)	1190
STRIEDIECK, Suzanne S.	(PA)	1202
TANIS, James R.	(PA)	1222
ZUBATSKY, David S.	(PA)	1390
BALDWIN, Mark F.	(RI)	52
PEARCE, Douglas A.	(RI)	952
YOUNG, Arthur P.	(RI)	1381
BRUCE, Dennis L.	(SC)	149
EDEN, David E.	(SC)	336

MANAGEMENT (Cont'd)
Library management

WARREN, Charles D.	(SC)	1306
BULL, Margaret J.	(TN)	156
CRAIG, James D.	(TN)	254
EKKEBUS, Allen E.	(TN)	341
UBALDINI, Michael W.	(TN)	1267
WATSON, Tom G.	(TN)	1310
ADAMS, Elaine P.	(TX)	4
BROWN, Freddiemae E.	(TX)	144
DUNCAN, Donna P.	(TX)	325
EWUNES, Ernest L.	(TX)	359
JACKSON, Sara J.	(TX)	588
LANDINGHAM, Alpha M.	(TX)	692
MCCANN, Charlotte P.	(TX)	793
METCALF, Judith A.	(TX)	828
NEELEY, Dana M.	(TX)	891
PARRIS, Lou B.	(TX)	944
PEDERSEN, Wayne A.	(TX)	954
PHILLIPS, Sylvia E.	(TX)	969
RAMBO, Neil H.	(TX)	1005
STOAN, Stephen K.	(TX)	1195
TOTTEN, Herman L.	(TX)	1252
ELLEFSEN, David	(UT)	343
NIELSEN, Steven P.	(UT)	903
BARKALOW, Irene M.	(VA)	56
BROOKS, Terri A.	(VA)	141
GREENAWALT, Ruth A.	(VA)	463
POLLOK, Karen E.	(VA)	981
STROHL, Leroy S.	(VA)	1202
STUBBS, Kendon L.	(VA)	1204
TATALIAS, Jean A.	(VA)	1225
TEAL, Erika U.	(VA)	1229
TYSON, John C.	(VA)	1267
ELLIS, Margaret D.	(VT)	345
MORRISON, Meris E.	(VT)	868
YERBURGH, Mark R.	(VT)	1379
CONABLE, Gordon M.	(WA)	235
MARTINEZ, Linda W.	(WA)	779
MOORE, Mary Y.	(WA)	860
PRIVAT, Jeannette M.	(WA)	994
ZUSSY, Nancy L.	(WA)	1391
BAYORGEON, Mary M.	(WI)	68
LINDSAY, Jane A.	(WI)	729
MCGILL, Nancy A.	(WI)	806
REENSTJERNA, Frederick R.	(WV)	1016
BAILEY, Madeleine J.	(AB)	46
BRUCE, Robert D.	(AB)	149
FRALICK, Deborah L.	(AB)	395
KAVANAGH, Elizabeth G.	(AB)	631
LASKOWSKI, Seno	(AB)	700
REIMER, Bette J.	(AB)	1020
SINCLAIR, John M.	(AB)	1142
STRATHERN, Gloria V.	(AB)	1200
APPLETON, Brenda F.	(BC)	30
CARTER, Charles R.	(BC)	189
BANFIELD, Eilzabeth S.	(NS)	54
SUTHERLAND, J E.	(NS)	1211
BAYNE, Jennifer M.	(ON)	67
BICE, Lee A.	(ON)	94
BRODIE, Nancy E.	(ON)	139
CALBICK, Ian M.	(ON)	172
CLEMENT, Hope E.	(ON)	221
FAIR, Linda A.	(ON)	361
GALTON, Gwen	(ON)	415
LOUET, Sandra	(ON)	742
MORTON, Margaret L.	(ON)	870
PARK, Nancy R.	(ON)	941
ST. PIERRE, Normand	(ON)	1075
BELANGER, Sylvie	(PQ)	76
CARTIER, Celine	(PQ)	190
FLORIAN, Trudel	(PQ)	385
GROSS, Margaret B.	(PQ)	472
OUIMET, Yves	(PQ)	930
YOUNG, Patricia M.	(PQ)	1383
ADAMS, Karen G.	(SK)	5
DIRKSEN, Jean	(SK)	305
GOODELL, John S.	(AUS)	448
DUFFIN, Elizabeth A.	(IRE)	323

MANAGEMENT (Cont'd)
Library management

	FOX, Peter K.	(IRE)	395
	DIAMANT, Betsy	(ISR)	299
	KATAOKA, Yoko	(JAP)	629
	ARTEAGA, Georgina	(MEX)	35
	WILLEMSE, John	(SAF)	1341
	HEANEY, Henry J.	(SCT)	518
Library management & administration	LEUNG, Shirley W.	(CA)	719
	LOOMIS, Barbara L.	(CA)	740
	STRONG, Gary E.	(CA)	1203
	SITTER, Clara M.	(CO)	1144
	SUNG, Carolyn H.	(DC)	1210
	DEYOUNG, Charles D.	(IN)	298
	FLAHERTY, Barbara A.	(MA)	383
	KERSHNER, Stephen A.	(MI)	644
	WILSON, Patricia L.	(MI)	1352
	BRANIN, Joseph J.	(MN)	128
	EUSTER, Joanne R.	(NJ)	356
	SHELSTAD, Kirsten R.	(NM)	1126
	GREEN, Judith G.	(NY)	462
	KARRE, David J.	(OH)	628
	CLINE, Nancy M.	(PA)	222
	HELMS, Frank Q.	(PA)	525
	TODD, Fred W.	(TX)	1248
	DUNCAN, Cynthia B.	(VA)	325
	RODGER, Jane	(ON)	1047
Library management & collection devlpmnt	DOUVILLE, Judith A.	(CT)	314
Library management & development	CLIFFORD, Susan G.	(CA)	222
	DOE, Lynn M.	(NY)	308
Library management & evaluation	ETTER, Constance L.	(IL)	355
Library management & finance	STUDER, William J.	(OH)	1204
Library management & information	MILLER, Merna B.	(FL)	841
Library management & operation	CROCKER, Judith A.	(NM)	259
Library management & organization	CREAGHE, Norma S.	(CA)	257
	SHERMAN, Mary A.	(OK)	1128
Library management & planning	LUSTER, Arlene L.	(HI)	750
	HORTON, Kathy L.	(IL)	561
	BAKER, Sylva S.	(PA)	49
	COCHRANE, Thomas G.	(AUS)	226
Library management & serials orders	VON PFEIL, Helena P.	(DC)	1288
Library management & statewide devlpmnt	KLINCK, Patricia E.	(VT)	661
Library management & supervision	HARRAGARRA WATERS, Deana J.	(CO)	503
	CASTRO, Maritza	(PR)	194
	EISENBERG, Phyllis B.	(VA)	340
Library management, college, school	CORRIGAN, John T.	(PA)	247
Library management consulting	ACCARDI, Joseph J.	(WI)	3
Library management experience	CALHOUN, Margie B.	(AL)	172
Library management, public	WILSON, William J.	(WI)	1353
Library management, public services	HENDRIX, Wilma P.	(TN)	528
Library management, regional young adult	CHARVAT, Catherine T.	(OH)	203
Library management, staff development	DE KLERK, Ann M.	(PA)	288
	MCLEAN-LOWE, Dallas	(ON)	814
Library management, training, devlpmnt	WILLIAMS, Edwin E.	(CT)	1343
Library management with microcomputer	KESTER, Diane D.	(NC)	645
Library middle management	DRUM, Carol A.	(FL)	320
Library operations, management	MANN, Thomas	(CA)	766
	BARNUM, Deborah C.	(CT)	58
Library organization & management	BEASLEY, Clarence W.	(FL)	69
	MURPHY, Marcy	(IN)	881
	LORENZ, John G.	(MD)	741
	ASP, William G.	(MN)	37
	SANDERS, John B.	(MO)	1080
	TUROCK, Betty J.	(NJ)	1265
	SHERIDAN, Robert N.	(NY)	1128
	HAMILTON, Elizabeth J.	(VA)	492
Library personnel management	GUY, Jeniece N.	(IL)	479
	TROVER, Larry E.	(OH)	1258
	PERSON, Ruth J.	(PA)	961
Library planning & management	KAWAMOTO, Chizuko	(CA)	632
Library records management	EVERINGHAM, Neil G.	(VA)	358
Library resource center management	SMITH, Noralee W.	(OH)	1159
Library risk management	SCHMIDT, Theodore A.	(MT)	1096

MANAGEMENT (Cont'd)

Library services & management	GENESEN, Judith L.	(IL)	427
	CHIANG, Ahushun	(MD)	207
Library services management	JONES, Adrian	(IL)	610
	PICARD, Albert	(ON)	970
Library setup & management	BALABAN, Robin M.	(CA)	50
Library supervision & management	GERLOTT, Eleanor L.	(PA)	429
Library system management	COBLE, Gerald M.	(FL)	225
Library systems & database management	HUFFER, Mary A.	(MD)	570
Library systems & management	SCHRIFT, Leonard B.	(NY)	1100
Library systems management	PRINTZ, Naomi J.	(CA)	993
	AVERSA, Elizabeth S.	(DC)	41
	RUSH, Candace M.	(DC)	1068
	BRESLAUER, Lester M.	(FL)	133
	STONE, Nancy Y.	(MI)	1197
	CAVINESS, Ann N.	(NY)	195
	DURBIN, Roger	(OH)	328
	DYE, Luella I.	(WV)	330
Library systems, management & promotion	CHAN, Margy	(ON)	199
Lib systems organization & management	CHITWOOD, Julius R.	(IL)	209
Logistics management	ROBINSON, Mitchell L.	(NY)	1044
Maccs/Dataccs database management	SKIDANOW, Helene	(NJ)	1146
Mainframe evaluation database management	BARALOTO, R A.	(MD)	55
Manage	TERRY, Carol D.	(TN)	1232
Manage computer databases	KROEHLER, Beth A.	(IN)	679
Manage online databases	CONNORS, Martin G.	(MI)	238
Management	BUSH, Nancy W.	(AL)	165
	MOORE, Patricia S.	(AL)	861
	MORRIS, Betty J.	(AL)	866
	NICHOLS, Shirley G.	(AL)	901
	ALTMAN, Ellen	(AZ)	18
	HOLLEMAN, Margaret	(AZ)	551
	PHIPPS, Shelley E.	(AZ)	969
	BARKALOW, Pat A.	(CA)	56
	BROPHY, Mary J.	(CA)	141
	CATER, Judy J.	(CA)	194
	CHAMBERLIN, Leslie A.	(CA)	198
	CIRCIELLO, Jean M.	(CA)	215
	CLIFTON, Joe A.	(CA)	222
	CRANFORD, Theodore N.	(CA)	255
	CURZON, Susan C.	(CA)	267
	DICKENS, Jan	(CA)	300
	DOBB, Linda S.	(CA)	307
	DONINI, Elizabeth A.	(CA)	311
	DUFFY, Karen R.	(CA)	324
	GLYNN, Jeannette E.	(CA)	442
	GREEN, Ellen W.	(CA)	461
	HALBROOK, Anne M.	(CA)	485
	HAZEKAMP, Phyllis W.	(CA)	517
	HOFFMAN, William J.	(CA)	548
	HOLLAND, Mary	(CA)	551
	HOLLEMAN, Marian P.	(CA)	551
	HOWLAND, Joan S.	(CA)	566
	JAMES, Olive C.	(CA)	592
	KILLIAN, Sandra L.	(CA)	648
	KISLITZIN, Elizabeth H.	(CA)	656
	KRASNER, Joan K.	(CA)	676
	LAMONTAGNE, Therese	(CA)	691
	LEONARD, Barbara G.	(CA)	716
	LONDON, Glenn S.	(CA)	738
	MOSER, Maxine M.	(CA)	871
	MULL, Richard G.	(CA)	876
	O'HEARN, Sarah A.	(CA)	919
	OROSZ, Barbara J.	(CA)	926
	OYLER, David K.	(CA)	932
	RAMSEY, Jack	(CA)	1006
	REICH, Victoria A.	(CA)	1018
	RHEE, Susan F.	(CA)	1025
	RYAN, Frederick W.	(CA)	1071
	SANNWALD, William W.	(CA)	1081
	STANGL, Peter	(CA)	1180
	STOCKS, Lee P.	(CA)	1195
	STRATFORD, Vaughn M.	(CA)	1200
	SUGRANES, Maria R.	(CA)	1207
	SZABO, Carolyn J.	(CA)	1218

MANAGEMENT (Cont'd)

Management

UEBELE, Dorothy B.	(CA)	1268
VEENKER, Linda J.	(CA)	1281
VIERICH, Richard W.	(CA)	1284
WHITLATCH, Jo B.	(CA)	1333
WOODS, Lawrence A.	(CA)	1367
BIER, Robert A.	(CO)	95
EIDSON, Alreeta	(CO)	340
LIRA, Judith A.	(CO)	732
MAGRATH, Lynn L.	(CO)	760
VOLZ, Edward J.	(CO)	1288
BRANCIFORTE, Eileen G.	(CT)	127
CARTLEDGE, Ellen G.	(CT)	190
DIMATTIA, Susan S.	(CT)	304
DOMINIANNI, Beth S.	(CT)	310
LANG, Norma F.	(CT)	695
LYNCH, M W.	(CT)	751
POUNDSTONE, Sally H.	(CT)	987
PROSTANO, Emanuel T.	(CT)	995
SAMUELS, Lois A.	(CT)	1079
SKOP, Vera	(CT)	1147
STONE, Dennis J.	(CT)	1197
BELLEFONTAINE, Arnold G.	(DC)	78
CHAPMAN, Susan E.	(DC)	202
CLEMMER, Dan O.	(DC)	221
COOK, Marilyn M.	(DC)	240
COOK, Mickey	(DC)	240
CUMMING, Leighton H.	(DC)	264
DAY, John M.	(DC)	282
HERMAN, Steven J.	(DC)	531
JEFFERSON, Karen L.	(DC)	596
LEWIS, Robert J.	(DC)	724
MARCUM, Deanna B.	(DC)	769
MCCAY, Lynne K.	(DC)	795
PERELLA, Susanne B.	(DC)	958
PLETZKE, Linda	(DC)	978
RANDOLPH, Susan E.	(DC)	1007
STANHOPE, Charles V.	(DC)	1180
STANN, Patsy H.	(DC)	1180
TANSEY, Francis J.	(DC)	1223
WARD, Victoria M.	(DC)	1304
YOUNG, Peter R.	(DC)	1383
BROWN, Sarah C.	(DE)	147
ALLEN, Linda G.	(FL)	15
BALLANTYNE, Lygia M.	(FL)	53
BENNETT, Renae M.	(FL)	82
FLEMING, Lois D.	(FL)	384
GALLAHAR, Christine M.	(FL)	414
HAYES, L S.	(FL)	516
KANE, Joseph P.	(FL)	624
LIANG, Diana F.	(FL)	725
MARTIN, James R.	(FL)	776
METCALF, Davinci C.	(FL)	828
MOSLEY, Madison M.	(FL)	871
POTTER, Robert E.	(FL)	987
PRITCHARD, Teresa N.	(FL)	994
SMITH, Linda L.	(FL)	1157
CHANIN, Leah F.	(GA)	201
DRAKE, Miriam A.	(GA)	318
KUHLMAN, James R.	(GA)	682
MASSEY, Katha D.	(GA)	782
MOYE, Edna B.	(GA)	874
ROBISON, Carolyn L.	(GA)	1045
TOOKES, Amos J.	(GA)	1250
FUJINO, Amy H.	(HI)	408
BELGUM, Kathie G.	(IA)	76
CLAYBURN, Marginell P.	(IA)	220
CLOW, Faye E.	(IA)	223
KENAGY, Charles R.	(IA)	640
MORRIS, Dilys E.	(IA)	866
OHRLUND, Ava L.	(IA)	919
RUNGE, Kay K.	(IA)	1067
SHELTON, Diane E.	(IA)	1126
VINER, Mamie N.	(IA)	1285
BEN-SHIR, Rya H.	(IL)	83
BREEN, Joanell C.	(IL)	131
CARPENTER, Kathryn H.	(IL)	185
CARROLL VIRGO, Julie	(IL)	187

MANAGEMENT (Cont'd)
Management

ESTABROOK, Leigh S.	(IL)	355
FROST, Bruce Q.	(IL)	406
GAUMOND, Suzanne M.	(IL)	423
GLANZ, Lenore M.	(IL)	439
GRAFTON, Mona R.	(IL)	456
GRIFFITHS, Suzanne N.	(IL)	469
KELLERSTRASS, Amy L.	(IL)	636
KUBIAK, Matthew C.	(IL)	682
LANDWIRTH, Trudy K.	(IL)	694
MARANO, Nancy H.	(IL)	768
MORRISON, Samuel F.	(IL)	868
RAST, Elaine K.	(IL)	1009
REDINGTON, Deirdre E.	(IL)	1014
ROBISON, Diana E.	(IL)	1045
SEGAL, Joan S.	(IL)	1111
SHERRY, Diane H.	(IL)	1129
SLIEKERS, Hendrik	(IL)	1149
SNYDER, Sherrie E.	(IL)	1165
STRAIT, Constance J.	(IL)	1199
STROYAN, Susan E.	(IL)	1203
VARNET, Harvey	(IL)	1279
WALLACE, Richard E.	(IL)	1298
WALTERS, Patsy M.	(IL)	1301
WHITEHEAD, Joyce E.	(IL)	1332
WILSON, W R.	(IL)	1353
ALFRED, Judith C.	(IN)	13
BEATTY, R M.	(IN)	70
BOYCE, Harold W.	(IN)	122
HARLAN, John B.	(IN)	502
HENN, Barbara J.	(IN)	528
HOLLENHORST, Bernice M.	(IN)	551
HOLT, Vickie L.	(IN)	554
HUFFORD, Gordon L.	(IN)	571
KELLEY, Colleen L.	(IN)	636
MORAN, Robert F.	(IN)	862
OVERSHINER, Barbara A.	(IN)	931
SNOWDEN, Deanna	(IN)	1164
WITTORF, Robert H.	(IN)	1359
YOUNG, Philip H.	(IN)	1383
MARVIN, James C.	(KS)	780
MCKENZIE, Joe M.	(KS)	811
NEELEY, Kathleen L.	(KS)	892
WAY, Harold E.	(KS)	1311
ZUCK, Gregory J.	(KS)	1391
GRIDER, Patty B.	(KY)	467
SCHULTZ, Lois E.	(KY)	1102
SINEATH, Timothy W.	(KY)	1143
TEITELBAUM, Gene W.	(KY)	1230
WILEY, Theresa K.	(KY)	1339
BINGHAM, Elizabeth E.	(LA)	97
CARPENTER, Michael A.	(LA)	185
DESOTO, Randy A.	(LA)	295
HEIM, Kathleen M.	(LA)	521
STROTHER, Garland	(LA)	1203
WITTKOPF, Barbara J.	(LA)	1358
ALCORN, Cynthia W.	(MA)	11
ANDERSON, A J.	(MA)	21
BEGG, Karin E.	(MA)	74
BENDER, Elizabeth H.	(MA)	79
DOUGLAS, Alice W.	(MA)	314
FENG, Yen T.	(MA)	371
HALES, Margaret L.	(MA)	486
JACKSON, Arlyne A.	(MA)	586
JACOBSON, Nancy C.	(MA)	590
MORNER, Claudia J.	(MA)	865
MOSKOWITZ, Michael A.	(MA)	871
PENSYL, Ornella L.	(MA)	957
PORTSCH-SNOW, Joanne	(MA)	985
STACK, May E.	(MA)	1177
SUTTON, Joyce A.	(MA)	1211
WESTLING, Ellen R.	(MA)	1327
ASSOUAD, Carol S.	(MD)	37
BROWN, Judith B.	(MD)	145
HAIRE, Jennifer C.	(MD)	484
WALLER, Madalyn M.	(MD)	1298
ARMSTRONG, Carole S.	(MI)	32
KOBEL, Rose A.	(MI)	666

MANAGEMENT (Cont'd)
Management

KORMELINK, Barbara A.	(MI)	671
MCDONALD, David R.	(MI)	802
NOBLE, Valerie	(MI)	906
REINKE, Carol R.	(MI)	1021
SKONIECZNY, Jill	(MI)	1147
SOPER, Marley H.	(MI)	1168
STEVENS, Marjorie	(MI)	1190
WEATHERFORD, John W.	(MI)	1311
WOODROW, Carolyn M.	(MI)	1366
CARMACK, Mona	(MN)	183
FEMAL, Mary B.	(MN)	370
HELTSLEY, Mary K.	(MN)	525
KEY, Jack D.	(MN)	645
FOWLER, Linda F.	(MO)	393
HOOVER, Jonnette L.	(MO)	557
MESSERLE, Judith R.	(MO)	828
SMITH, Jewell	(MO)	1156
BURKS, Alvin L.	(MS)	161
BYRD, Robert L.	(NC)	169
DORNBERGER, Julie L.	(NC)	313
FERGUSSON, David G.	(NC)	372
HUTTON, Jean R.	(NC)	579
KLEM, Marjorie R.	(NC)	660
LESUEUR, Joan K.	(NC)	718
MCGINN, Howard F.	(NC)	806
MILLER, Gloria	(NC)	838
MORAN, Barbara B.	(NC)	862
ROLLINS, Marilyn H.	(NC)	1051
TROMBITAS, Ildiko D.	(NC)	1258
WINDHAM, Shirley L.	(NC)	1354
BOONE, Jon A.	(ND)	115
NEWBORG, Gerald G.	(ND)	898
PAGE, Dennis N.	(ND)	934
YLINIEMI, Hazel A.	(ND)	1380
BUNDY, John F.	(NH)	157
GRISWOLD, Esther A.	(NH)	471
BENTE, June E.	(NJ)	83
CAPOOR, Asha	(NJ)	180
ELENAUSKY, Edward V.	(NJ)	342
HALPERN, Marilyn	(NJ)	489
JONES, Anita M.	(NJ)	610
ANDERSEN-PUSEY, Vavene J.	(NM)	21
FREED, J A.	(NM)	400
KRUG, Ruth A.	(NM)	680
RUCKMAN, Stanley N.	(NM)	1065
APPEL, Marsha C.	(NY)	29
BORBELY, Jack	(NY)	116
CLANCY, Kathy	(NY)	215
COOK, Jeannine S.	(NY)	240
COPLEN, Ron	(NY)	244
CRAWFORD, Carter	(NY)	256
DEUSS, Jean	(NY)	296
DEVERS, Charlotte M.	(NY)	297
DOOLING, Marie	(NY)	312
ELLISON, John W.	(NY)	345
FODY, Barbara A.	(NY)	387
GIBBARD, Judith R.	(NY)	431
GOODHARTZ, Gerald	(NY)	448
GREGORIAN, Vartan	(NY)	466
GSTALDER, Herbert W.	(NY)	475
HEWITT, Julia F.	(NY)	535
JUDD, J V.	(NY)	619
LOCKETT, Barbara A.	(NY)	736
MCCLURE, Charles R.	(NY)	797
MCCOMBS, Gillian M.	(NY)	797
MEISELES, Linda	(NY)	822
MINTZ, Anne P.	(NY)	847
MULDOON, Jane K.	(NY)	876
RAY, Donald L.	(NY)	1011
SACCO, Gail A.	(NY)	1073
SALEY, Stacey	(NY)	1076
SIKORSKI, Charlene S.	(NY)	1137
SIVULICH, Kenneth G.	(NY)	1145
SOMERS, Betty J.	(NY)	1166
TONKERY, Thomas D.	(NY)	1250
TOYAMA, Ryoko	(NY)	1253
WOODS, Lawrence J.	(NY)	1367

MANAGEMENT (Cont'd)
Management

BAYER, Bernard I.	(OH)	67
CARTER, James W.	(OH)	189
CHESHIER, Robert G.	(OH)	206
CHESKI, Richard M.	(OH)	207
CORBUS, Lawrence J.	(OH)	245
DICKINSON, Luren E.	(OH)	301
ERWIN, Nancy S.	(OH)	353
FELTES, Carol A.	(OH)	370
HEISHMAN, Eleanor L.	(OH)	523
JACOBER, Sheryl A.	(OH)	589
KNASIAK, Theresa J.	(OH)	663
MAURER, Lewis R.	(OH)	787
NANCE, Lena L.	(OH)	887
SCOTT, Melvia A.	(OH)	1107
SEELY, Edward	(OH)	1111
ALDRIDGE, Betsy B.	(OK)	11
COOPER, Sylvia J.	(OK)	243
MURPHY, Peggy A.	(OK)	881
PARHAM, Kay B.	(OK)	940
PHILLIPS, J R.	(OK)	968
RABURN, Josephine R.	(OK)	1001
WOODRUM, Patricia A.	(OK)	1366
FISCHER, Karen	(OR)	379
CHILDERS, Thomas A.	(PA)	208
CRONEBERGER, Robert B.	(PA)	260
DONOVAN, Kathryn M.	(PA)	312
GRIFFIN, Mary A.	(PA)	468
MORROW, Ellen B.	(PA)	869
PAUSTIAN, P R.	(PA)	950
REIFF, Harry B.	(PA)	1019
ROSE, Dianne E.	(PA)	1054
STEPHANOFF, Kathryn	(PA)	1187
TAYLOR, Larry D.	(PA)	1227
TOMAN, Jocelyn B.	(PA)	1249
TUCCI, Valerie K.	(PA)	1261
WOOD, Barbara G.	(PA)	1363
RODRIGUEZ, Vidalina	(PR)	1048
BELL, Judith H.	(RI)	77
DENNIS, Everett J.	(SC)	292
MORSI, Pamela A.	(SC)	869
HAMILTON, Patricia J.	(SD)	492
CASSELL, Gerald S.	(TN)	193
HERRING, Mark Y.	(TN)	533
OWEN, Richard L.	(TN)	932
POURCIAU, Lester J.	(TN)	987
PRENTICE, Ann E.	(TN)	990
ROBBINS, Gordon D.	(TN)	1038
VEACH, Lynn H.	(TN)	1280
BANDELIN, Janis M.	(TX)	53
BRYAN, Carla W.	(TX)	151
BRYSON, Gary B.	(TX)	152
BURT, Eugene C.	(TX)	164
CAGE, Alvin C.	(TX)	170
CLARK, Jay B.	(TX)	217
CORBIN, John	(TX)	245
CROUCH, Vivian E.	(TX)	261
FRAMEL, Phyllis M.	(TX)	395
LEE, Frank	(TX)	709
MCCLURE, Margaret R.	(TX)	797
MURRAY, Kathleen R.	(TX)	882
PELOQUIN, Margaret I.	(TX)	955
POTIER, Gwendolyn J.	(TX)	986
SPOEDE, Mary H.	(TX)	1175
THOMPSON, Christine E.	(TX)	1239
DAY, J D.	(UT)	282
LAYTON, A J.	(UT)	705
STECKER, Alexander T.	(UT)	1183
BARKLEY, Carolyn L.	(VA)	56
BURGESS, Dean	(VA)	159
CANNON, Ruth M.	(VA)	179
DELONG, Edward J.	(VA)	290
DRYE, Jerry L.	(VA)	321
HUGHES, J M.	(VA)	571
LEHMAN, James O.	(VA)	712
PLITT, Jeanne G.	(VA)	978
REDMER, Paul C.	(VA)	1014
ROSENBERG, Kenyon C.	(VA)	1056

MANAGEMENT (Cont'd)
Management

ROTHBART, Linda S.	(VA)	1060
SCHLAG, Gretchen A.	(VA)	1093
SIMS, Martha J.	(VA)	1142
SMITH, Ruth S.	(VA)	1160
SWICEGOOD, Mary R.	(VA)	1216
TROTTI, John B.	(VA)	1258
UMBERGER, Stan	(VA)	1268
WELLS, Christine	(VA)	1322
YATES, Ella G.	(VA)	1378
CONABLE, Irene H.	(WA)	235
MCCORMICK, Jack M.	(WA)	798
PARR, Loraine E.	(WA)	943
TRACY, Joan I.	(WA)	1253
WARNER, Gail P.	(WA)	1305
ZALESKI, Mary A.	(WA)	1385
DAVIS, Sally A.	(WI)	281
JAMBREK, William L.	(WI)	592
REITMAN, Jo	(WI)	1022
ROBBINS, Jane B.	(WI)	1038
SIEGMANN, Starla C.	(WI)	1136
MULLER, William A.	(WV)	877
ORLANDO, Karen T.	(WV)	926
SIEBERSMA, Dan	(WY)	1135
BOUEY, Elaine F.	(AB)	119
GEE, Sharon	(AB)	425
MANSON, Bill B.	(AB)	767
ROBINS, Nora D.	(AB)	1043
ASHCROFT, Susan M.	(BC)	35
BELL, Barbara	(BC)	76
MILLER, Gordon	(BC)	838
STUART-STUBBS, Basil F.	(BC)	1204
WHITELEY, Catherine M.	(BC)	1333
BROWN, Gerald R.	(MB)	144
HERNANDEZ, Marilyn J.	(MB)	531
NADEAU, Sylvie	(NB)	886
MACINTOSH, Ian R.	(NS)	755
BERCOVITCH, Sari	(ON)	84
BONAVERO, Leonard C.	(ON)	113
BROWN, Mabel	(ON)	145
BUCHANAN, Zoe A.	(ON)	153
DANIEL, Eileen	(ON)	272
DAVIDSON-ARNOTT, Frances E.	(ON)	277
DELSEY, Thomas J.	(ON)	290
DUNN, Mary J.	(ON)	327
FLOWER, M A.	(ON)	386
FOSTER, Margaret A.	(ON)	392
GRANATSTEIN, M E.	(ON)	457
HAYES, Janice E.	(ON)	516
HEATON, Gwynneth T.	(ON)	519
LUNAU, Carrol D.	(ON)	748
MCBURNEY, Margot B.	(ON)	792
MOORE, Heather J.	(ON)	859
MULLEN, Gail C.	(ON)	877
SELLERS, Alexander G.	(ON)	1114
SHEPHERD, Murray C.	(ON)	1127
SMITH, Ruth P.	(ON)	1160
WEATHERHEAD, Barbara A.	(ON)	1312
WILSON, Valerie E.	(ON)	1353
WOOD, Ronald P.	(ON)	1365
BERNIER, Gaston	(PQ)	89
BOUDREAU, Gerald E.	(PQ)	118
CHAREST, Ronald	(PQ)	203
COTE, Jean P.	(PQ)	249
COURTEMANCHE, Pierre O.	(PQ)	251
DUBOIS, Florian	(PQ)	322
DUHAMEL, Louis	(PQ)	324
FILIATRAULT, Sylvie	(PQ)	376
HERLINGER, Peggy	(PQ)	531
HOWARD, Helen A.	(PQ)	564
LUSSIER, Jean P.	(PQ)	749
MARCOTTE, Marcel	(PQ)	769
PETRYK, Louise O.	(PQ)	965
STAHL, Hella	(PQ)	1178
TEES, Miriam H.	(PQ)	1229

MANAGEMENT (Cont'd)

Management

	JENSEN, Ken	(SK)	599
	STONE, Toby G.	(FRN)	1197
	WASERMAN, Barbara	(ISR)	1307
	TETSUYA, Inoue	(JAP)	1233
	LIM, Hucktee E.	(MLY)	727
	ARMSTRONG, Denise M.	(SAF)	32
	SEPTEMBER, Peter E.	(SAF)	1115
Management accounting	REDRICK, Miriam J.	(NJ)	1014
Management administration	EATON, Elizabeth K.	(MA)	333
	SHAUGHNESSY, Thomas W.	(MO)	1123
	CAMPBELL, Joylene E.	(SK)	177
Management, administration, programs	LEHMAN, Tom	(MN)	713
Management, administration, supervisory	MARSHALL, Kathryn E.	(IL)	774
Management analysis	ORTIZ, Diane	(NV)	927
Management & administration	HARDIN, Willie	(AR)	500
	FELDMAN, Irwin	(CA)	369
	LUSHINGTON, Nolan	(CT)	749
	WILLSON, Katherine H.	(CT)	1349
	DICKSON, Constance P.	(DC)	301
	FEINBERG, Beryl L.	(DC)	368
	HEAD, Anita K.	(DC)	518
	HOWARD, Mary R.	(GA)	564
	HUNTER, Julie V.	(GA)	576
	TRAINOR, Donna J.	(GA)	1253
	COATSWORTH, Patricia A.	(IL)	224
	HANKES, Janice R.	(IL)	496
	FARLEY, Janice S.	(IN)	364
	SCHAD, Jasper G.	(KS)	1088
	BROGDON, Jennie L.	(MD)	139
	HOMAN, J M.	(MI)	555
	SCHROEDER, Janet K.	(MN)	1100
	CRAIG, Marian D.	(MO)	254
	SUTTON, Judith K.	(NC)	1211
	STEPHENS, Ann E.	(NE)	1187
	ANSELMO, Edith H.	(NJ)	28
	STEEN, Carol N.	(NJ)	1184
	THRESHER, Jacquelyn E.	(NJ)	1243
	FRIEDMAN, Judy B.	(NY)	404
	NEWMAN, George C.	(NY)	899
	PRONIN, Monica	(NY)	995
	SEARS, Carlton A.	(NY)	1110
	BLACK, Frances P.	(OH)	101
	COPENHAVER, Ida L.	(OH)	244
	AXAM, John A.	(PA)	42
	DILLEN, Judith A.	(PA)	303
	GUTHRIE, Melinda L.	(TX)	479
	HOADLEY, Irene B.	(TX)	545
	DRESANG, Eliza T.	(WI)	319
	NECHKA, Ada M.	(AB)	891
	PREMONT, Jacques	(PQ)	990
	ROY, Lucille Y.	(PQ)	1063
Management & administrative activities	LAWRENCE, Thomas A.	(NY)	705
Management & adult public services	SZETO, Dorcas C.	(CA)	1218
Management & audiovisual	MOORE, Virginia B.	(DC)	861
Management & budgeting	LINDGREN, Arla M.	(NY)	729
Management & budgeting info technologies	LOWRY, Charles B.	(TX)	745
Management & budgets	JACKA, David C.	(NE)	586
Management & business databases	CORNWELL, Douglas W.	(FL)	247
Management & business information	SCHNEDEKER, Donald W.	(NY)	1096
Management & cost accounting	FRANKLIN, Brinley R.	(DC)	397
Management & development of audiovisuals	AHN, Hyonah K.	(IL)	8
Management & economics	DI MEGLEO, Arthur J.	(NY)	304
Management & finance	DAVY, Edgar W.	(MA)	281
Management & grants	BARNETT, Jean D.	(OR)	57
Management & office automation	LEONARD, Lucinda E.	(VA)	716
Management & organization	DIMATTIA, Ernest A.	(CT)	304
	MARKUSON, Carolyn A.	(MA)	772
	MEAHL, D D.	(MI)	819
	WRIGHT, Linda G.	(WV)	1372
Management & organizational behavior	DENIS, Laurent G.	(ON)	292

MANAGEMENT (Cont'd)

Mgmt & organizational effectiveness	RIZZO, John R.	(MI)	1037
Management & personnel	KUPERMAN, Agota M.	(DC)	684
Management & personnel administration	JONES, Anne	(NY)	611
Management & planning	NING, Mary J.	(CA)	904
	WISMER, Donald	(ME)	1357
	LANDAU, Herbert B.	(NY)	692
Management & planning facilities	NEUBAUER, Richard A.	(MA)	896
Management & planning studies	KING, Donald W.	(MD)	650
Management & policy creation	WILLIAMSON, Michael W.	(ON)	1347
Management & programming	CUMMINS, Julie A.	(NY)	264
Management & public relations	HUFFER, Mary A.	(MD)	570
Management & public services	COOK, Anita I.	(NE)	239
Management & strategic planning	MALCOLM, J P.	(MI)	762
Management & supervision	CROCKETT, Darla J.	(CA)	259
	MACEK, Rosanne M.	(CA)	755
	VETTER, Jean A.	(IL)	1283
	PICCININO, Rocco	(MA)	970
	DAVIS, Denise	(MD)	278
	KELLOGG, Joanne T.	(ME)	637
	FARHAT, Elizabeth M.	(MI)	363
	TSAI, Fu M.	(MI)	1260
	WILROY, Joann	(MS)	1349
	AULD, Hampton M.	(NC)	39
	MATHAI, Aleyamma	(NJ)	783
	ROYSTER, Peggy K.	(OK)	1063
	MAYNARD, James E.	(SC)	790
	LEONARD, Gloria J.	(WA)	716
	WEBER, Joan L.	(WA)	1314
	BELLOWS, Leslie A.	(WI)	78
Management & supervision of lib programs	PETERSON, Miriam E.	(IL)	964
Management & supervisory training	PARSONS, Jerry L.	(CA)	945
Management & systems	CRAWFORD, Geraldine H.	(MI)	256
Management & training	MILLS, Victoria A.	(AZ)	844
	WRIGHT, Joseph F.	(FL)	1372
Management aspects of librarianship	WILLIAMS, Gayle A.	(MI)	1343
Management assistance	MOCKOVAK, Holly E.	(MA)	851
Management bibliographic services	WALSH, James A.	(PA)	1299
Management budgeting	MILLER, Ronald F.	(CA)	842
Management chemical information research	STOBAUGH, Robert E.	(OH)	1195
Management computer applications	COMEAU, Reginald A.	(NH)	234
Management consulting	EPSTEIN, Susan B.	(CA)	351
	JUROW, Susan R.	(DC)	620
	LARSEN, Linda E.	(IL)	698
	VIRGO, Julie A.	(IL)	1285
	FISHER, Jean K.	(MA)	381
	MCDONALD, Dennis D.	(MD)	802
	BERGFELD, C D.	(NY)	86
	MILLER-KUMMERFELD, Elizabeth	(NY)	843
	TREFRY, Mary G.	(NY)	1255
	JUERGENS, Bonnie	(TX)	619
	SCHIELACK, Tricia J.	(TX)	1092
	STANDIFER, Hugh A.	(TX)	1179
	MCCALLUM, Anita J.	(ON)	793
Management, consulting & research	RUDD, Janet K.	(CA)	1065
Management consulting reference	FLEISHMAN, Lauren Z.	(NY)	384
Management databases	VONSEGEN, Ann M.	(OR)	1288
Management development	YEH, Irene K.	(CA)	1379
	VERBESEY, J R.	(NY)	1282
	PARKER, Arthur D.	(ON)	941
Management development seminars	SULLIVAN, Daniel M.	(NY)	1207
Management education	ODERWALD, Sara M.	(NJ)	916
Management elementary school libraries	CRAIGHEAD, Alice A.	(TX)	254
Management in academic libraries	LEONHARDT, Thomas W.	(CA)	717
Management information	VASSALLO, Paul	(NM)	1279
	MONTY, Vivienne	(ON)	857
Management information consulting	CARTELLI, Alessandra J.	(PA)	188
	PLEFKA, Cathleen S.	(PA)	978
Management information systems	SCHERREI, Rita A.	(CA)	1092
	TRIOLO, Victor A.	(CT)	1257
	SHENASSA, Daryoosh	(IL)	1126
	RADEMACHER, Richard J.	(KS)	1002
	ANDERSON, John E.	(MD)	23
	MOTT, Thomas H.	(NJ)	872
	LITTLE, Paul L.	(OK)	733

MANAGEMENT (Cont'd)

Management information systems

SKOVIRA, Robert J. . . . . (PA) 1147
BONNELLY, Claude . . . . (PQ) 114

Management information systems for libs

SCHUELLER, Janette H. (WA) 1101
Management, micro data center — ASU, Glynis V. . . . . (WI) 37
Management of access services — DEVLIN, Margaret K. . . . (PA) 297
Management of archives — HANSEN, Peggy A. . . . . (WA) 498
GORDON, Robert S. . . . (ON) 451
Management of change — NERODA, Edward W. . . . (MT) 895
Management of circulation systems — TREMBLAY, Carolyn B. . (NH) 1255
Mgmt of independent research libraries

MCCORISON, Marcus A. (MA) 798
Management of information, records — WELCH, Donald A. . . . . (TX) 1321
Management of information services — HONEBRINK, Andrea C. (MN) 555
MANCALL, Jacqueline C. (PA) 764
MARBAN, Ricio . . . . (GUA) 768
Management of information systems — MOSER, Jane W. . . . . . (CA) 870
Management of in-house database systems

LEMMON, Anne B. . . . . (LA) 715
Management of intellectual enterprises

BOYER, Calvin J. . . . . . (CA) 123
Management of interlibrary loans — IANNUZZI, Patricia A. . . (CT) 581
Management of libraries — ANDERSON, Dorothy J. . (CA) 22
HILL, Malcolm K. . . . . . (NY) 540
MACDONALD, Alan H. . . (AB) 754
Management of libraries & associations

COONEY, Jane . . . . (ON) 241
Management of library — JONES, Milbrey L. . . . . . (DC) 614
SUTHERLAND-NEHRING, Laurie A. . . . . (NY) 1211
Management of library & info services — NASRI, William Z. . . . . . (PA) 888
SIITONEN, Leena M. . . . (RI) 1137
Management of library systems — FORGET, Louis J. . . . . . (ON) 390
Management of media center — LINDGREN, Beverly P. . . (IL) 729
PRILLAMAN, Susan M. . (NC) 993
Management of medical & research data

COLLINS, Kenneth A. . . (MD) 233
Management of microcomputer labs — PLAZA, Joyce S. . . . . . (NJ) 978
Management of microform collections — IANNUZZI, Patricia A. . . (CT) 581
Management of nuclear records — WOODLEY, Victoria B. . . (MI) 1366
Management of online searching — KOGA, James S. . . . . . (CA) 668
Management of online services — GOODWIN, Jane G. . . . . (VA) 450
Management of public libraries — MOORE, Thomas L. . . . . (NC) 861
Management of public library — JONKE, Grace M. . . . . . (MD) 616
Management of public services — MARTIN, Ron G. . . . . . . (IN) 778
HANNA, Hildur W. . . . . . (MI) 496
DALRYMPLE, Tamsen . . (OH) 271
Management of publishing operations — BOYD, Joseph W. . . . . . (IL) 122
Management of research activity — RUSSELL, John T. . . . . . (DC) 1069
Management of science libraries — ALEXANDER, Carol G. . . (VA) 12
Management of serials organization — DONAHUE, Janice E. . . . (FL) 310
Management of slide collections — HENDERSON, Joyce C. . (AZ) 526
Management of small libraries — BERK, Robert A. . . . . . . (IL) 87
STEINBERG, David L. . . (VA) 1185
Management of special libraries — WINQUIST, Elaine W. . . (MA) 1355
Management of special library — PALMISANO-DRUCKER, Elsalyn . . . . (NJ) 937
Management of technical services — SLOCA, Sue E. . . . . (DC) 1150
STEVENS, Roberta A. . . (DC) 1191
BETH, Dana L. . . . . (MO) 92
KAWAGUCHI, Miyako . . (VA) 632
Management personnel — SCHABEL, Donald J. . . . (KY) 1088
WASIELEWSKI, Eleanor B. . . . . (MD) 1308
Mgmt, planning, budgeting, supervising

ZAENGER, Kathleen L. . . (MI) 1385
Management, planning, systems — FLOERSHEIMER, Lee M. (NY) 385
Management, public relations, grants — KISER, Mary D. . . . . . . (FL) 656
Management records administration — AUSTIN, Ralph A. . . . . . (NY) 40
Management, reference — BAILEY, George M. . . . . (CA) 46
Management reviews — STEELE, Colin R. . . . . . . (AUS) 1184
Management science — HSIEH, Richard K. . . . . (MD) 567
HOUGHTON, Joan I. . . . (NY) 562
Management services — SOY, Susan K. . . . . (CA) 1170
Management simulation training — WRIGHT, Keith C. . . . . . (NC) 1372
Management skills — ROMAN, Susan . . . . (IL) 1052
Management statistics — TANNEHILL, Robert S. . . (OH) 1222
Management studies — VELLUCCI, Matthew J. . . (MD) 1282

MANAGEMENT (Cont'd)

Management studies & surveys — D'ALESSANDRO, Edward A. . . . . (DC) 270
Management, supervising — MCDONOUGH, Douglas M. . . . . (RI) 803
Management, supervision & training — BOWLES, Carol A. . . . . . (CA) 121
Management systems — PRICE, Douglas S. . . . . (MD) 992
Management techniques — SCHUBERT, Donald F. . . (NM) 1101
Management, theological library — HICKS, Barbara A. . . . . (ON) 536
Management training — BOBAN, Carol A. . . . . . (IL) 108
FORRESTER, John H. . . (ITL) 391
Management training & consulting — SCEPANSKI, Jordan M. . (CA) 1088
Management, training & development — SLOCUM, Hannah R. . . . (CA) 1150
PERRY, Emma B. . . . . . (MA) 960
RIZZO, John R. . . . . . . (MI) 1037
Management training, instruction — KLEIN, Victor C. . . . . . . (LA) 659
Manager — MURPHY, Patricia A. . . . (CA) 881
HALE, Carolyn R. . . . . (PA) 485
Manager & administrator of library — BERGEN, Dessa C. . . . (NY) 85
Managerial — AHL, Ruth E. . . . . (WI) 8
Managerial library consulting — PHILLIPS, Ray S. . . . . . (TX) 969
Managing — CONWAY, Colleen M. . . (IL) 239
PERRY, Guest . . . . (MA) 960
BUHR, Rosemary E. . . . (MO) 156
MIYAUCHI, Phyllis J. . . (NY) 850
TURNER, Margaret A. . . (ON) 1264
COOK, Marjorie L. . . . . (PHP) 240
Managing a one-person library — SPONDER, Dorothy R. . . (DC) 1175
KATES, Jacqueline R. . . (MA) 629
MCVICAR, Ann L. . . . . (TX) 818
Managing a scientific, technical library — GIBSON, Gladys N. . . . . (MB) 432
Managing, administration — MCCALLUM, Anita J. . . . (ON) 793
Managing & administering personnel — ROUDEBUSH, Lawanda C. (IA) 1061
Managing & appraising rare books — MICHAELS, Carolyn L. . . (SC) 831
Managing archives collection — PARKER, Peter J. . . . . . (PA) 942
Managing cultural programming — BRODERICK, John C. . . . (DC) 138
Managing department activities — SOURS, Katherine M. . . . (FL) 1169
Managing DIALOG — SUMMIT, Roger K. . . . . (CA) 1209
Managing elementary school libraries — HOWELL, Wanda H. . . . (FL) 565
Managing film & video libraries — HAYNES, Jean . . . . . . (NY) 516
Managing grants & contracts — SCULL, Roberta A. . . . . (LA) 1108
Managing information in systems — ARDERN, Christine M. . . (ON) 31
Managing information services — BROWN, Paula D. . . . . (CA) 146
BUCK, Anne M. . . . . . . (NJ) 153
Managing information services & systems

HALLSTROM, Curtis H. . . (MN) 489
Managing large library computers — FORTH, Stuart . . . . (PA) 391
Managing libraries — SANCHEZ, Eliana P. . . . (NY) 1079
BENDER, Betty W. . . . . (WA) 79
Managing library automation & technology

LEACH, Ronald G. . . . . (IN) 706
Managing library contracts — STALLINGS, Elizabeth A. (DC) 1179
Managing library services — SPRAGUE, Karol S. . . . . (MI) 1176
Managing pharmaceutical information — DRUKKER, Alexander E. . (DE) 320
Managing reference & research studies

BRODERICK, John C. . . (DC) 138
Managing research libraries — MILES, Donald D. . . . . . (PA) 834
Managing school libraries — WHITE, Ann T. . . . . (SC) 1330
Managing school library & media — JANTZ, Helen N. . . . . . (KS) 594
Managing school library programs — HACKMAN, Mary H. . . . (MD) 481
Managing several sections — ROGERS, Dean C. . . . . (VA) 1049
Managing small hospital libraries — KRATZ, Gale G. . . . . . . (CA) 676
Managing small libraries — INGERSOLL, Lyn L. . . . . (DC) 582
LAURENSTEIN, Ann G. . . (MO) 703
Managing small special libraries — KAMICHAITIS, Penelope H. . . . . (PQ) 624
Managing small to medium law libraries

SCAMMAHORN, Lynne . (PA) 1087
Managing student workers — KEMP, Henrietta J. . . . . (IA) 639
Managing systems development — PEMPE, Ruta . . . . (DC) 956
Managing technical services — DJEVALIKIAN, Sonia . . . (PQ) 306
Managing various databases — CANTWELL, Mickey A. . . (NY) 179
Manual & automated catalog management

KLAIR, Arlene F. . . . . . (MD) 657
Manuscript & archive management — JERDE, Curtis D. . . . . . (LA) 599
Marketing research resources management

SEULOWITZ, Lois . . . . (NY) 1117

MANAGEMENT (Cont'd)

Media center management	MITCHELL, Phyllis R.	(GA)	849
	TALAB, Rosemary S.	(KS)	1220
	TRIM, Kathryn	(MI)	1256
	KUTTEROFF, Ethel C.	(NJ)	685
Media center management & operation	BRAUER, Regina	(NY)	129
Media center management & teaching	CLEAVER, Betty P.	(OH)	220
Media collection management	REIT, Janet W.	(VT)	1022
Media management	GILBERT, Betty H.	(AZ)	433
Medical journal collection management	HALLERBERG, Gretchen A.	(OH)	489
Medical libraries management	REYES, Helen M.	(CA)	1024
Medical library management	BREINICH, John A.	(HI)	132
	O'BRIEN, Elizabeth J.	(MA)	914
	WEITKEMPER, Larry D.	(MO)	1320
	REGENBERG, Patricia B.	(NJ)	1017
	HUANG, C K.	(NY)	568
	MINNERATH, Janet E.	(OK)	846
	GROEN, Frances K.	(PQ)	471
Medical risk management consulting	THOMASSON, George O.	(CO)	1238
Meeting planning, management	ZOOK, Ruth A.	(CO)	1390
Membership management	AUCOIN, Sharilynn A.	(LA)	38
Mending office management	DURNIAK, Barbara A.	(NY)	328
Microcomputer applications & management	MCSPADDEN, Robert M.	(OH)	818
Microcomputer applications in management	HOWARD, Ada M.	(TX)	563
Microcomputer data management	MORGAN, James J.	(IN)	864
Microcomputer database management	KENNEDY, Joanne	(CA)	641
Microcomputer library management	TRAVILLIAN, Mary W.	(IA)	1254
Microcomputer management	REHMKE, Denise M.	(IA)	1017
Microcomputer management of libraries	BANKHEAD, Elizabeth M.	(CO)	54
Microcomputer management of library	SHARMA, Shirley K.	(KS)	1122
Microcomputer software collection mgmt	BEHNKE, Charles	(WI)	75
Microcomputerized database management	AU, Ka N.	(NJ)	38
Microcomputers for library management	MCCANN, Susan F.	(NH)	794
Microfilming & records management	KNARZER, Arlene	(IL)	663
Microforms collection management	JOHNS, Jean B.	(OH)	601
Microforms management	PONNAPPA, Biddanda P.	(TN)	982
Middle management	RAZER, Robert L.	(AR)	1012
	BROWN, Pamela P.	(IL)	146
	ALLEN, Patricia J.	(IN)	15
	RUHL, Jodi S.	(OH)	1066
	MEADOR, Joan S.	(OK)	819
	LAFEVER, Susan	(TN)	687
Middle management & supervision	BAILEY, Martha J.	(IN)	46
	HENRY, Peggy L.	(MO)	529
MIS library management	ROBSON, Amy K.	(IL)	1045
Motivation personnel management	STEPHENS, Jerry W.	(AL)	1188
Multiassociation management	UNDERWOOD, Mary S.	(KY)	1269
Multimedia management	ENGLESAKIS, Marina F.	(AB)	350
Multiple-library management	KLAUS, Susan B.	(OH)	658
Municipal document management	SCHLIPF, Frederick A.	(IL)	1094
Museum management	MOORE, Emily C.	(AL)	859
	ADAMS, Larry D.	(IA)	5
	CAYA, Marcel	(PQ)	195
Music library administration & mgmt	BOGNAR, Dorothy M.	(CT)	111
Network management	KUKLINSKI, Joan L.	(MA)	683
	SPYKERMAN, Bryan R.	(UT)	1177
Newspaper library management	HARDNETT, Carolyn J.	(MD)	500
	BULLOCK, Jessie M.	(PA)	156
Non-book material management	WEIHS, Jean	(ON)	1317
Nuclear waste management	NISH, Susan J.	(PQ)	905
Nursing library management	SHIFF, Linda S.	(ON)	1130
Office management	INGERSOL, Robert S.	(MO)	582
	VOIT, Irene E.	(NV)	1287
One-person library management	KENNEDY, Joanne	(CA)	641
	MILLIGAN, Jane M.	(MA)	843
	COTE-THIBODEAU, Donna E.	(ME)	249
	RUDA, Donna R.	(NY)	1065
	LUPPINO, Julie B.	(SC)	749
	PETERS, Mary N.	(TX)	962
	WEST, Deborah C.	(TX)	1326

MANAGEMENT (Cont'd)

One-professional library management	TURK, Sally	(CA)	1263
Online catalog management	STUBBS, Linda T.	(DC)	1204
	SELLBERG, Roxanne J.	(IN)	1113
Online database management	CSENGE, Maragaret L.	(NY)	262
	TOWNLEY, Richard L.	(NY)	1253
Online management & training	KIBBEE, Josephine Z.	(IL)	646
Online searching & management	STANLEY, Jean B.	(OH)	1180
Online searching & management thereof	FISHER, H L.	(CA)	381
Online services management	FARAH, Barbara D.	(MA)	363
Online system management	REINBOLD, Janice K.	(OK)	1021
Online training & management	SINGLETON, Cynthia B.	(ON)	1143
Operation & management	JEFFCOAT, Phyllis C.	(AR)	596
Operations management	WALKER, Patricia A.	(CA)	1296
	FULLER, Ruth V.	(GA)	409
	BACON, Lois C.	(MA)	44
	ATRI, Pushkala V.	(TX)	38
Organization & management	FRADKIN, Bernard	(IL)	395
	POWNALL, David E.	(AUS)	989
Organizational behavior management	COFFMAN, M H.	(MA)	227
Organizational management	BAKER, Gordon N.	(GA)	48
Overall administration & management	SHAW, Elizabeth L.	(OR)	1123
Periodicals management	BEAVERS, Janet W.	(ISR)	71
Personal computer system management	ROSENFELD, Jane D.	(NY)	1056
Personal management	AUGER, Bernard	(PQ)	39
Personnel & budget management	WONG, Clark C.	(CA)	1362
Personnel development & management	CLEMONS, John E.	(GA)	221
Personnel management	LANE, Robert B.	(AL)	694
	HILLMAN, Stephanie	(CA)	541
	MOFFEIT, Tony A.	(CO)	852
	SULLIVAN, Maureen	(CT)	1208
	HEISS, Harry G.	(DC)	523
	BADGER, Lynn C.	(FL)	44
	MARSHALL, Maggie L.	(IL)	774
	RUBIN, Richard E.	(IL)	1065
	VARNET, Harvey	(IL)	1279
	GALBRAITH, Leslie R.	(IN)	413
	TUCKER, John M.	(IN)	1261
	KONESKI-WHITE, Bonnie L.	(MA)	670
	SUDDUTH, William E.	(MA)	1206
	AUER, Margaret E.	(MI)	39
	HAENICKE, Carol A.	(MI)	482
	KIRBY, Frederick J.	(MI)	654
	MOSS, Josievet	(MI)	872
	WOODFORD, Arthur M.	(MI)	1366
	KING, Jack B.	(MN)	651
	ANDERSON, James F.	(MS)	23
	BARTON, Phillip K.	(NC)	62
	KAUP, Jermain A.	(ND)	631
	DAVIS, Hiram L.	(NM)	279
	WU, Painan R.	(NY)	1373
	CALL, J R.	(OH)	173
	COLEMAN, Judith	(OH)	231
	HILDEBRAND, Carol I.	(OR)	538
	SHAW, Elizabeth L.	(OR)	1123
	HESS, Marjorie A.	(PA)	534
	WEBRECK, Susan J.	(PA)	1314
	KELLEY, Gloria	(SC)	636
	WARREN, Charles D.	(SC)	1306
	ALLMAND, Linda F.	(TX)	17
	CARGILL, Jennifer S.	(TX)	181
	GAMEZ, Juanita L.	(TX)	416
	ICE, Priscilla T.	(WA)	581
	SHAFFER, Maryann	(WA)	1119
	COGSWELL, Howard L.	(NB)	227
	LEVIS, Joel	(ON)	721
	SKEITH, Mary E.	(ON)	1145
	GLASS, Gerald	(PQ)	440
Personnel management & administration	SCOTT, Thomas L.	(MN)	1108
	GIORDANO, Frederick S.	(NY)	438
Personnel management & labor relations	FRANCIS, Derek R.	(BC)	396
Personnel management & staff development	PARENT, Roger H.	(IL)	940
Personnel management & training	DEMPSEY, Pamela M.	(NM)	291

MANAGEMENT (Cont'd)

Personnel management consulting	SMITH, Catherine	(NC)	1153
Personnel management, public libraries	HAGLOCH, Susan B.	(OH)	483
Photograph collection management	PINSON, Patricia A.	(WY)	975
Photographic collection management	OETTING, Edward C.	(AZ)	917
Photographs collections management	STONE, Gerald K.	(ON)	1197
Physical facilities management	WEBB, Gisela M.	(TX)	1313
Picture collection management	ANDERSON, James C.	(KY)	23
Planning & management	MILLER, Edward P.	(AZ)	837
	SIGLER, Ronald F.	(CA)	1137
Planning & strategic management	BRADBURY, Daniel J.	(MO)	125
Planning, evaluation & management	SHELDON, Brooke E.	(TX)	1125
Preservation management	MAHER, William J.	(IL)	760
	SEWELL, Robert G.	(NY)	1117
Prison library management	ROMALIS, Carl	(NY)	1052
Private law library management	KISSANE, Mary K.	(MO)	656
Processing management	STEVENS, Michael L.	(MA)	1190
Product development & management	FOUSER, Jane G.	(IL)	393
Product management	BARNETT, Becky L.	(GA)	57
	KIESER, Scott P.	(NY)	647
Product management & development	RYAN, R P.	(VA)	1071
Productivity management	NEWBERG, Ellen J.	(MT)	898
Program development & management	WASSERMAN, Ricki F.	(NY)	1308
	PETERSON, Denise D.	(OK)	963
Program management	CRANOR, Alice T.	(DC)	255
	TESMER, Nancy	(OH)	1233
Program management for libraries	HARRIS, Linda S.	(DC)	505
Project management	MOYER, Barbara A.	(CA)	874
	ENGERRAND, Steven W.	(GA)	349
	JANSSON, John F.	(IL)	594
	MILLER, Thomas R.	(IL)	843
	RUSSELL, Janet	(IL)	1069
	BATOR, Eileen F.	(MD)	64
	FIELD, Judith J.	(MI)	375
	DINERMAN, Gloria	(NJ)	304
	FISHER, Douglas A.	(PA)	380
	HOFFMAN, David R.	(PA)	547
	MENDINA, Guy T.	(TN)	824
	MOORE, Mary Y.	(WA)	860
	BROOME, Diana M.	(BC)	141
	HALE, Linda L.	(BC)	485
	CAMPBELL, Bonnie	(ON)	176
	FOX, Rosalie	(ON)	395
	LEUNG, Frank F.	(ON)	719
Project management & administration	MANBECK, Virginia B.	(NY)	764
Project management & coordination	BAADE, Harley D.	(TX)	43
Project management & development	DEL CERVO, Diane M.	(CT)	289
Projects management	ST. AMANT, Robert	(ON)	1075
Prospect & library management	AMAN, Ann L.	(CO)	19
Psychiatry library management	STRICKLAND, F J.	(PA)	1202
Psychoanalytic library management	STRICKLAND, F J.	(PA)	1202
Public & court records management	COATES, Paul F.	(KY)	224
Public events management	EZELL, Charlaine L.	(MI)	360
Public library branch management	BERGMANN, Sue A.	(GA)	87
	BROWN, Merrikay E.	(NC)	146
Public library management	MARTIN, Rosemary S.	(AR)	778
	PACK, Nancy C.	(AR)	933
	COOPER, Ginnie	(CA)	242
	JOHNSON, Carolyn E.	(CA)	602
	TURNER, Anne M.	(CA)	1264
	DOWLIN, Kenneth E.	(CO)	316
	ARNOLD, Arleen B.	(CT)	33
	BALCOM, Kathleen M.	(IL)	51
	STEELE, Leah J.	(IL)	1184
	WARREN, Janet B.	(KS)	1306
	SCHABEL, Donald J.	(KY)	1088
	STEENSLAND, Ronald P.	(KY)	1184
	COADY, Reginald P.	(LA)	224
	CHAMBERLAIN, Ruth B.	(MA)	197
	FLANNERY, Susan M.	(MA)	383
	KELLSTEDT, Jenny	(MA)	637
	PURCELL, Kathleen V.	(MD)	998
	TRELEVEN, Richard L.	(MD)	1255
	RAZ, Robert E.	(MI)	1012
	BYRNE, Roseanne	(MN)	169
	VINNES, Norman M.	(MN)	1285
	SANDERS, Jan W.	(MO)	1080
	MOXLEY, Melody A.	(NC)	874
	SAYRE, Edward C.	(NM)	1087

MANAGEMENT (Cont'd)

Public library management			
	FRANZ, David A.	(NY)	398
	HOLLEY, James L.	(NY)	551
	LIU, Carol F.	(NY)	734
	PHILLIPS, Ruth M.	(NY)	969
	RANSOM, Stanley A.	(NY)	1007
	COLEMAN, Judith	(OH)	231
	HALL, Alan C.	(OH)	486
	HARRIS, Margaret J.	(OH)	505
	WALDER, Antoinette L.	(OH)	1294
	LONG, Sarah A.	(OR)	740
	BAUER, Margaret D.	(PA)	65
	GARRISON, Guy G.	(PA)	420
	CHAIT, William	(SC)	197
	NESSE, Mark A.	(WA)	896
	GATES, Mary D.	(WI)	422
Public library management & organization	TREZZA, Alphonse F.	(FL)	1256
Public library management service	MITCHELL, Joyce L.	(NC)	849
Public library organizing & managing	AUSTIN, Neal F.	(NC)	40
Public library systems management	DILLARD, Thomas W.	(NC)	303
Public management information systems	CROWTHER, Warren W.	(CSR)	262
	FONTAINE, Sue	(NY)	388
Public relations management	GILREATH, Charles L.	(AZ)	437
Public service management	FOREMAN, Gertrude E.	(MN)	390
Public services management	NITECKI, Danuta A.	(MD)	905
	DEYOUNG, Gail O.	(MI)	298
	MALOY, Frances	(NY)	764
	CONIGLIO, Jamie W.	(VA)	236
	LEGERE, Monique E.	(ON)	712
Public utility management	ERTZ, Ginger E.	(PA)	353
Publications distribution management	LEONARD, Lawrence E.	(DC)	716
Publications management	MORSE, June E.	(VA)	869
Publishing management	LEE, Judith C.	(CA)	710
Publishing program management info	KLEIMAN, Gerald S.	(DC)	659
Purchasing & management	BERGER, Brenda L.	(NJ)	85
Radioactive waste management	CURRY, Lenora Y.	(NY)	266
	TRAUB, Teresa L.	(WA)	1254
Real estate rentals management	COMPRI, Jeannine L.	(AB)	235
Record management	STEVENSON, Katherine	(IL)	1191
Records & archival management	SANTORO, Corrado A.	(MB)	1082
Records & archives management	CAN, Hung V.	(PQ)	177
Records & collection management	WALKER, Heather C.	(DC)	1295
Records & documentation management	GRITZKA, Gerda M.	(PQ)	471
Records & information management	PHILLIPS, Donna M.	(IA)	968
	MUNTEAN, Deborah E.	(MN)	879
	ROFES, William L.	(NY)	1049
	MANARIN, Louis H.	(VA)	764
	STIRLING, Dale A.	(WA)	1195
Records & library management	SHANNON, Norma M.	(OR)	1120
Records & micrographics management	GENESEN, Judith L.	(IL)	427
Records management	NEWTON, Virginia A.	(AK)	900
	BRIDGES, Edwin C.	(AL)	135
	JONES, Allen W.	(AL)	610
	OETTING, Edward C.	(AZ)	917
	BROWNE, Jeri A.	(CA)	148
	BURSON, Sherrie L.	(CA)	164
	GABBERT, Gretchen W.	(CA)	411
	GOUDELOCK, Carol V.	(CA)	454
	HUNT, Judy L.	(CA)	575
	JENSEN, Marilyn A.	(CA)	599
	LARSON, Donald A.	(CA)	699
	MASTERS, Robin J.	(CA)	782
	MUSICK, Nancy W.	(CA)	883
	NEMCHEK, Lee R.	(CA)	895
	NYBERG, Lelia J.	(CA)	912
	PLATE, Kenneth H.	(CA)	977
	WITTMANN, Cecelia V.	(CA)	1358
	FELDMAN, Rosalie M.	(CO)	369
	GAUSS, Nancy V.	(CO)	423
	MACARTHUR, Marit S.	(CO)	754
	NEWMAN, John	(CO)	899
	WOLFE, F M.	(CO)	1360
	MCGREGOR, M C.	(CT)	808
	PALMQUIST, David W.	(CT)	937
	SIMON, William H.	(CT)	1141

MANAGEMENT (Cont'd)
Records management

CARTLEDGE, Connie L. . (DC) 190
CASSEDY, James G. . . . (DC) 193
NEWTON, Robert C. . . . (DC) 900
O'BRIEN, Kathleen . . . . . (DC) 914
PACIFICO, Michele F. . . (DC) 933
PAUL, Karen D. . . . . . . (DC) 949
PROVINE, Dorothy S. . . . (DC) 996
SHOREBIRD, Thomas S. (DC) 1132
YOST, F D. . . . . (DC) 1381
FRANCIS, Diane S. . . . . (DE) 396
THOMAN, Nancy L. . . . . (DE) 1236
TRYON, Roy H. . . . . . . (DE) 1260
LANNING, E K. . . . . . . (GA) 696
LONG, Linda E. . . . . . . (GA) 739
ALDERSON, Karen A. . . (IA) 11
WELLS, Merle W. . . . . . (ID) 1322
BURNS, Marie T. . . . . . (IL) 162
CULBERTSON, Diana L. . (IL) 263
FARRELL, Patricia H. . . . (IL) 365
GAYNON, David B. . . . . (IL) 424
HANRATH, Linda C. . . . . (IL) 497
KERR, Kevin G. . . . . . . (IL) 644
MACKEY, Denise R. . . . . (IL) 756
SORENSEN, Mark W. . . (IL) 1168
STEGH, Leslie J. . . . . . (IL) 1185
SYVERSON, Kathleen A. (IL) 1217
BISHOP, Barbara N. . . . . (IN) 99
SOWINSKI, Carolyn M. . . (IN) 1170
YATES, Donald N. . . . . . (IN) 1378
BELL, Mary M. . . . . (KY) 77
FOGLE, Dianna L. . . . . . (KY) 387
HAY, Charles C. . . . . . . (KY) 515
CHAPDELAINE, Susan A. (MA) 201
CYPHERS, James E. . . . (MA) 268
EMOND, Kathleen A. . . . (MA) 348
HORN, David E. . . . . . . (MA) 559
HUENNEKE, Judith A. . . (MA) 570
HUGGINS, Dean A. . . . . (MA) 571
MCLAIN, Guy A. . . . . . . (MA) 813
SCHWARTZ, Candy S. . . (MA) 1104
STICKNEY, Zephorene L. (MA) 1193
HOLLOWAK, Thomas L. . (MD) 552
KADEC, Sarah T. . . . . . (MD) 621
MERZ, Nancy M. . . . . . . (MD) 827
PFLUG, Warner W. . . . . (MI) 966
DEWAELSCHE, Thomas
  M. . . . . (MO) 297
MCCREARY, Gail A. . . . (MS) 800
OLSON, David J. . . . . . . (NC) 922
SAYE, Jerry D. . . . . (NC) 1086
GRAY, David P. . . . . . . (ND) 459
BROWN, Jeanne I. . . . . . (NJ) 145
KAUFFMAN, Betty G. . . . (NJ) 631
MAZZEI, Peter J. . . . . . . (NJ) 791
MOSS, Susan K. . . . . . . (NJ) 872
PARAS, Lucille P. . . . . . (NJ) 939
SIMMONS, Ruth J. . . . . . (NJ) 1140
VOGT, Herwart C. . . . . . (NJ) 1287
BEJNAR, Thaddeus P. . . (NM) 75
MILLER, Bryan M. . . . . . (NM) 836
ROCHA, Guy L. . . . . . . (NV) 1045
AUBRY, John C. . . . . . . (NY) 38
BERNTSEN, Robert M. . . (NY) 90
BONACORDA, James J. . (NY) 113
BOROSON, Sarah . . . . . (NY) 116
BUTLER, Tyrone G. . . . . (NY) 167
CROCKETT, Denise J. . . (NY) 259
D'ALLEYRAND, Marc R. (NY) 270
FREIFELD, Roberta I. . . . (NY) 401
GRANKA, Bernard D. . . . (NY) 457
HERBERT, Annette F. . . (NY) 530
HOMMEL, Claudia . . . . . (NY) 555
HUDAK, Barbara M. . . . . (NY) 569
HUNTER, Gregory S. . . . (NY) 576
JONES, Sarah C. . . . . . . (NY) 615
KLINE, Harriet . . . . (NY) 661
LAFEVER, C R. . . . . . . (NY) 687
MASYR, Caryl L. . . . . . . (NY) 783

MANAGEMENT (Cont'd)
Records management

PARRIS, Angela P. . . . . . (NY) 944
POMRENZE, Seymour J. (NY) 982
ROBERTSON, Betty M. . (NY) 1041
SAFFADY, William . . . . . (NY) 1074
SEEBER, Frances M. . . . (NY) 1111
SETTANNI, Joseph A. . . (NY) 1117
TAMMARO, James M. . . (NY) 1221
TAYLOR, Patricia A. . . . . (NY) 1228
UZZO, Beatrice C. . . . . . (NY) 1270
WILSTED, Thomas P. . . . (NY) 1353
GARTEN, Edward D. . . . (OH) 420
GILLILAND, Anne J. . . . . (OH) 436
GOERLER, Raimund E. . (OH) 443
SULLIVAN, Frances L. . . (OH) 1207
LOWELL, Howard P. . . . (OK) 744
FILSON, Laurie . . . . (OR) 377
THELEN, Richard L. . . . . (OR) 1234
ANDEL, June . . . . (PA) 21
KIRCHER, Linda M. . . . . (PA) 654
VANDOREN, Sandra S. . (PA) 1275
WAGNER, Albin . . . . (RI) 1291
EZELL, Margaret M. . . . . (SC) 360
KINTNER, Susan B. . . . . (SC) 653
KOHL, Michael F. . . . . . . (SC) 668
MCCOY, Gail . . . . (SC) 799
SUTHERLAND, Carl T. . . (SC) 1211
WILLIAMS, Robert V. . . . (SC) 1346
NORTON, Nancy P. . . . . (TN) 910
PEMBERTON, J M. . . . . (TN) 956
THWEATT, John H. . . . . (TN) 1243
ANDERSON, Margaret . . (TX) 24
AULBACH, Louis F. . . . . (TX) 39
BENGE, Joy L. . . . . (TX) 80
DAVIS, Connie J. . . . . . . (TX) 278
DILLARD, Lois A. . . . . . . (TX) 303
DUMONT, Paul E. . . . . . (TX) 325
HIMMEL, Richard L. . . . . (TX) 542
HOLLAND, Michael E. . . (TX) 551
HOOTON, Virginia A. . . . (TX) 557
KESHISHIAN, Maria L. . . (TX) 644
KLEIN, Mindy F. . . . . (TX) 659
MATLOCK, Teresa A. . . (TX) 784
MCCANN, Debra W. . . . (TX) 794
PHILLIPS, Toni M. . . . . . (TX) 969
SCHAADT, Robert L. . . . (TX) 1088
SCOTT, Paul R. . . . . (TX) 1108
BAILEY, Clint R. . . . . . . (UT) 46
HEFNER, Loretta L. . . . . (UT) 520
SCOTT, Patricia L. . . . . . (UT) 1107
FIENCKE, Elaine L. . . . . (VA) 376
GOLDBERG, Lisbeth S. . (VA) 444
HUFF, Patricia M. . . . . . (VA) 570
KANE, Dorothea S. . . . . (VA) 624
TATALIAS, Jean A. . . . . (VA) 1225
HERNDON, Stan J. . . . . (VT) 532
EDWARDS, Steven M. . . (WA) 338
RHOADS, James B. . . . (WA) 1026
SCHUTTE, Raymond R. . (WA) 1103
BLUE, Richard I. . . . . . . (WI) 107
CONDON, John J. . . . . . (WI) 236
HYNUM, Jill A. . . . . (WI) 580
KOVAN, Allan S. . . . . . . (WI) 673
RYAN, Carol E. . . . . (WI) 1070
SHUTKIN, Sara A. . . . . . (WI) 1134
GISHLER, John R. . . . . . (AB) 438
BEYEA, Marion L. . . . . . (NB) 93
CHAN, Margy . . . . (ON) 199
HARDY, John L. . . . . . . (ON) 500
LAFRANCHISE, David . . (ON) 688
SERMAT-HARDING, Kaili
  I. . . . . (ON) 1116
WILLIAMSON, Nancy J. . (ON) 1347
BROCHU, Frederick . . . . (PQ) 138
CAYA, Marcel . . . . (PQ) 195
PAPILLON, Yves . . . . . . (PQ) 939
TESSIER, Mario C. . . . . (PQ) 1233
VAILLANCOURT, Alain . (PQ) 1270

MANAGEMENT (Cont'd)

Records management

ORTIZ MONASTERIO,
Leonor . . . . (MEX) 927
FAGERLUND, M L. . . . . (SWZ) 361

Records management & archives PEARLSTEIN, Toby . . . . (MA) 952
OGAWA, Chiyoko . . . . . (JAP) 918
Records management & control REID, Angea S. . . . . . . (MA) 1018
Records management & librarianship ORTIZ, Diane . . . . (NV) 927
Records management &
micrographics WALSH, G M. . . . . (ON) 1299
Records management &
micrographics syst BRIMSEK, Tobi A. . . . . . (DC) 136
Records management & online
searching IRONS, Carol A. . . . . . . (IL) 584
Records management & services HOWINGTON, Tad C. . . (TX) 566
Records management, archives PRESTON, Deirdre R. . . (WA) 991
Records management consulting FREEMAN, Carla . . . . . . (DC) 400
Records management in academia SCHULTZ, Charles R. . . (TX) 1101
Records management programs SAYED, Joyce P. . . . . . . (CA) 1086
Records management, retention
scheduling NEWHALL, Ann C. . . . . . (CT) 898
Records management systems HENDERSON, Deborah A. (ON) 526
Records management systems
analysis BALON, Brett J. . . . . (SK) 53
MOORE, Gwen A. . . . . . (UT) 859
Records management training NASH, Cherie A. . . . . . . (UT) 888
Records managing RITTER, Helen . . . . (NY) 1036
Reference & collection management BRUCE, Robert K. . . . . . (MN) 149
Reference & information management LAWSON, Venable A. . . (GA) 705
Reference & research in management CHOUDHURY, Lori B. . . (CA) 211
Reference department management DUCKETT, Joan . . . . . . (MA) 322
Reference, information management MULCAHY, Bryan L. . . . (GA) 876
Reference management MYERS, R D. . . . . (DC) 885
QUINLAN, Judy B. . . . . . (GA) 1000
DUCKWORTH, Paul M. . (MO) 322
WOOD, M S. . . . . (PA) 1364
MACDONALD, Hugh . . . (TX) 754
SHEETS, Janet E. . . . . . (TX) 1125
THOMPSON, Jean T. . . . (WI) 1240
Reference product & publishing mgmt BRAM, Leon L. . . . . (NJ) 127
Reference service, collection
management WILLIAMS, Calvin . . . . . (MI) 1342
Reference service management SCHWARTZ, Virginia C. . (WI) 1105
Reference services & management
skills THOMAS, Fannette H. . . (MD) 1236
Reference services management CROOKS, Joyce M. . . . . (CA) 260
POEHLMAN, Dorothy J. . (DC) 979
WATSON, Paula D. . . . . (IL) 1310
Report editing, management systems KEE, Walter A. . . . . (NC) 634
Research & management issues FORD, Gary E. . . . . (MO) 389
Research facilities management LANOUETTE, Marie . . . . (ON) 696
Research libraries management DOWLER, Lawrence E. . . (MA) 315
Research library management LUCKER, Jay K. . . . . . . (MA) 746
EDELMAN, Hendrik . . . . (NJ) 335
Research management JOHNSON, Minnie L. . . . (NJ) 607
FIDOTEN, Robert E. . . . (PA) 375
Research managing, international
team CLARK, Joan . . . . (NJ) 217
Research on management intelligence
syst KOCHEN, Manfred . . . . . (MI) 667
Resource center management BECHOR, Malvina B. . . . (GA) 71
Resource management KRIZ, Harry M. . . . . . . (VA) 679
Response management system POWELL, Timothy W. . . (NY) 989
Risk management REYNOLDS, Carol C. . . . (GA) 1025
Risk management & preservation SEAL, Robert A. . . . . . . (TX) 1109
Rural library management BREIT, Anitra D. . . . . . . (WA) 132
School & public library management MILLER, Marilyn L. . . . . (NC) 840
School library & media center
management SNYDER, Denny L. . . . . (MD) 1164
STEVENS, Elizabeth B. . (NY) 1190
School library development &
management BERKLUND, Nancy J. . . (MI) 87
School library management HILLIS, Patricia K. . . . . (CA) 541
DANIELSON, Connie S. . (IA) 273
MASON, John A. . . . . . (IL) 781
ROBIEN, Eleanor K. . . . (IL) 1043
SHAW, Louis P. . . . . . . (IL) 1123
CALLISON, Daniel J. . . . (IN) 174
O'BRIEN, John F. . . . . . (MA) 914

MANAGEMENT (Cont'd)

School library management

LATHAM, Candace . . . . (NJ) 701
SCOTT, Mellouise J. . . . (NJ) 1107
MCCAULEY, Elfrieda B. . (NM) 795
BURGESON, Clair D. . . (NY) 159
ALTAN, Susan B. . . . . . . (OH) 18
WOLFORD, Betty K. . . . (OH) 1361
BARRON, Daniel D. . . . . (SC) 60
HASBROUCK, Clara H. . (TN) 510
VAN ORSDEL, Darrell E. (WI) 1276
ALTURKAIT, Adela A. . . (KWT) 19
School library media center
management MILLER, John E. . . . . . . (OH) 839
STANTON, Vida C. . . . . (WI) 1181
School library media management GREGORY, Mary L. . . . . (WA) 466
School media center management GARLAND, Kathleen . . . (NY) 419
School system library media
management KAUFMAN, Polly W. . . . (MA) 631
Science librarianship & management STIRLING, Isabel A. . . . . (OR) 1195
Science library management RICKER, Alison S. . . . . . (OH) 1031
Scientific & technical info
management CARROLL, Bonnie C. . . . (TN) 187
SPATH, Charles E. . . . . . (TN) 1171
WONG, Carol Y. . . . . . . (CA) 1362
Sci-tech library management
Serial collection devlpmnt &
management CONWAY, Susan L. . . . . (NV) 239
Serial management NOGA, Susan D. . . . . . . (NY) 907
Serials cataloging & management COLLINS, Susan H. . . . . (NB) 233
Serials management ODSEN, Elizabeth R. . . . (AK) 917
BATTISTELLA, Maureen
S. . . . . (AL) 65
ANDERES, Susan M. . . . (CA) 21
LIU, Susanna J. . . . . . . (CA) 734
PALM, Miriam W. . . . . . (CA) 935
WONG, Cecilia . . . . (CA) 1362
BARELA, Lori A. . . . . . . (CO) 56
GLASBY, Dorothy J. . . . (DC) 439
PRICE, Mary S. . . . . . . (DC) 992
SMITH, Thomas E. . . . . (DC) 1161
CARR, Mary L. . . . . (FL) 186
PEARSON, Karen L. . . . . (IL) 952
JOHNTING, Wendell E. . (IN) 610
SIEVERS, Arlene M. . . . . (IN) 1136
HAMAKER, Charles A. . . (LA) 490
TIMBERLAKE, Phoebe W. (LA) 1245
WOJKOWSKI, Suhad K. . (LA) 1359
BACON, Lois C. . . . . . . (MA) 44
DI BONA, Leslie F. . . . . (MA) 299
BROWN-MAY, Patricia A. (MI) 148
MORELAND, Patricia L. . (MI) 863
SMOLER, Shelly . . . . . . (MI) 1162
WILDMAN, Linda . . . . . (MI) 1339
TUTTLE, Marcia L. . . . . (NC) 1266
SCHOTT, Mark E. . . . . . (NM) 1099
HARTMAN, Anne M. . . . (NY) 508
NICHOLS-RANDALL,
Barbara L. . . . . (NY) 902
PRAGER, George A. . . . (NY) 989
SCHNEIDER, Helen S. . . (NY) 1097
SCHUTT, Dedre A. . . . . (NY) 1103
TUOHEY, Jeanne D. . . . (NY) 1263
HARRINGTON, Sue A. . . (OK) 504
SHROUT, Sally J. . . . . . (OK) 1133
CHAMBERLAIN, Carol E. (PA) 197
RICHARDS, Susan L. . . . (SD) 1028
ANDERSON, Madeleine J. (TX) 24
MURPHY, Pency G. . . . . (TX) 881
DEBUSE, Judith S. . . . . (WA) 285
GELLATLY, Peter . . . . . . (WA) 426
KOMOROUS, Hana J. . . (BC) 670
MILANICH, Melanie M. . . (ON) 834
DARIS, Claude . . . . (BEL) 274
Serials systems & management VANDERPOORTEN, Mary
B. . . . . (AL) 1274
Services & materials management EDWARDS, Andrea Y. . . (DC) 337
Services management JOHNSON, Thomas L. . . (CA) 609
Set up & management of a thesaurus AMNOTTE, Celine . . . . . (PQ) 20
Shared resources management MILLER, Charles E. . . . . (FL) 836
Slide library management MCKENNEY, Kathryn K. . (DE) 811

MANAGEMENT (Cont'd)

Small academic library management	DALY, Simeon	(IN)	271
Small college library management	OFFERMANN, Glenn W.	(MN)	917
	PAWLIK, Deborah A.	(PA)	951
	CORMAN, Linda W.	(ON)	246
Small library management	DAVIS, Becky C.	(CA)	277
	MORRISON, M C.	(DC)	868
	OGDEN, Nina M.	(ID)	918
	SIEVING, Pamela C.	(MI)	1136
	BARROWS, William D.	(NC)	60
	SHAPIRO, Ruth T.	(PA)	1121
	MCGOWAN, Anne W.	(WY)	807
Small public library management	LAPIERRE, France	(PQ)	697
Social sciences & management	GREEN, Kathleen A.	(MA)	462
Software configuration management	DURHAM, Mary J.	(MA)	328
Solid, hazardous waste management	KAYES, Mary J.	(WI)	632
Space management	D'ALESSANDRO, Edward A.	(DC)	270
Space planning, management	KENDRICK, Curtis L.	(NY)	640
Special col management & appraisal	WEISS, Egon A.	(NY)	1320
Special libraries management	SPURLOCK, Pauline	(CA)	1177
	ST. AUBIN, Kendra J.	(MA)	1075
	WILKINSON, William A.	(MO)	1340
	KING, Maryde F.	(NY)	651
	WILT, Charles F.	(OH)	1353
	VASILAKIS, Mary	(PA)	1279
	WILLIAMS, Robert V.	(SC)	1346
	OLIVETTI, L J.	(VA)	921
	STARR, Marian U.	(VA)	1182
Special library & archives management	CLASPER, James W.	(OH)	219
Special library department management	RYAN, Jenny L.	(NY)	1071
Special library issues & management	MORRISON, Patricia	(CA)	868
Special library management	ATKINSON, Calberta O.	(AL)	38
	CAMPBELL, Bill W.	(CA)	176
	COPPIN, Ann S.	(CA)	245
	HALEY, Roger K.	(DC)	486
	KNAUFF, Elisabeth S.	(DC)	663
	GOLDMAN, Ava R.	(FL)	445
	WHITESIDE, Lee A.	(FL)	1333
	MCDAVID, Sara J.	(GA)	801
	BERGER, Carol A.	(IL)	85
	FUKAI, Eiko	(IL)	408
	MICHAEL, Ann B.	(IL)	831
	SCHRAMM, Mary T.	(IL)	1099
	VELLIKY, Mary M.	(MI)	1281
	PRESTON, Jenny	(MO)	991
	CONNOLLY, Bruce E.	(NY)	237
	ERICKSON, Sandra E.	(NY)	352
	RATLIFF, Priscilla	(OH)	1009
	SPOHR, Cynthia L.	(OH)	1175
	HILL, Linda L.	(OK)	540
	PYKE, Carol J.	(VA)	999
	CAMPBELL, Corinne A.	(WA)	176
	CAMPBELL, Harry	(ON)	176
Special library organization, management	COOKE, Geraldine A.	(AB)	241
Special projects management	FARLEY, Alfred E.	(KS)	364
Stack management & remote storage	HENSHAW, Rod	(PA)	529
Staff management	COOPER, Jacquelyn B.	(RI)	243
	KRATZ, Abby R.	(TX)	676
	WAUGH, Alan L.	(AB)	1310
Staff management & development	FLEMMING, Tom	(ON)	384
Standing order selection & management	ROMANASKY, Marcia C.	(NJ)	1052
State & public library management	WALTERS, Clarence R.	(OH)	1301
State information resource management	EVANS, Max J.	(UT)	357
State records center program management	BITTLE, Christine M.	(OK)	100
STM conference management	YAMAKAWA, Takashi	(JAP)	1376
Strategic business management services	CARTER, Daniel H.	(TX)	189
Student assistant management	FREEMAN, Evangeline M.	(NC)	400
Subscription agency business management	CLASQUIN, Frank F.	(MA)	219
Subscriptions sales management	KOBASA, Paul A.	(IL)	666
Supervising school library management	BROWN, Atlanta T.	(DE)	142

MANAGEMENT (Cont'd)

Supervision & management	BENZ, Lieselotte	(NY)	84
	LAMBERT, Sarah E.	(TN)	690
Supervisory & management training	GARDNER, Jeffrey J.	(DC)	418
System library management	DOCKINS, Glenn	(IL)	307
System management	HOMEYARD, Marjorie A.	(FL)	555
Systems analysis & records management	SIEGERT, Lindy E.	(NS)	1136
Systems management	COVILL, Bruce	(NJ)	252
	WILBURN, Gene	(ON)	1338
Taxation research, management consulting	VEASLEY, Mignon M.	(CA)	1280
Teaching archival management	YOUNKIN, C G.	(TX)	1383
Team management	LUTHER, M J.	(GA)	750
Technical & research libraries mgmt	CRENSHAW, Tena L.	(FL)	258
Technical information center management	EYLES, Heberle H.	(FL)	359
	HALL, Deanna M.	(GA)	487
Technical information management	SAYLOR, Linda	(CA)	1086
	MAYER, June C.	(NJ)	789
	DE TONNANCOUR, P R.	(TX)	296
Technical library management	REITER, Martha B.	(CT)	1022
	FILLER, Mary A.	(PA)	377
Technical management	GAGNON, Donna M.	(CA)	412
	BLISS, David H.	(IA)	105
Technical report management	CONKLING, Thomas W.	(PA)	236
Technical services & management	FENSTERMANN, Duane W.	(IA)	371
Technical services management	LESH, Nancy L.	(AK)	718
	BISHOFF, Lizbeth J.	(CA)	99
	JOHNSON, Thomas L.	(CA)	609
	MILLER, Dick R.	(CA)	837
	LEONARD, Lawrence E.	(DC)	716
	HELGE, Brian L.	(IL)	524
	PETERSEN, Karla D.	(IL)	962
	FRANZEK, Karyn	(MA)	398
	HEWITT, Joe A.	(NC)	535
	MYERS, Carol B.	(NC)	884
	SAUNDERS, Laverna M.	(NV)	1084
	DUNCAN, Elizabeth C.	(NY)	325
	JUNION, Gail J.	(NY)	620
	TRAMDACK, Philip J.	(OH)	1254
	CORBIN, John	(TX)	245
	PAYNE, Leila M.	(TX)	951
	NICHOLSON, Dianne L.	(BC)	902
Telemarketing management	OGREN, Mark S.	(IL)	918
Text management & retrieval systems	LOWENSTEIN, Richard A.	(CT)	744
Textual database management	SCHWARTZ, James M.	(SD)	1104
Thesaurus construction & management	VAN HALM, Johan	(NET)	1275
Time management	MCGOVERN, Gail J.	(CA)	807
	SMITH-EPPS, E P.	(GA)	1161
Trade association information management	HILL, Susan M.	(DC)	540
Training & conference management	HUFFER, Mary A.	(MD)	570
Training & development management	HOCKER, Justine L.	(PA)	545
Training & development records mgmt	CORNELIUS, Charlene E.	(WI)	246
Training in records management	ARDERN, Christine M.	(ON)	31
Unit management	LOUP, Jean L.	(MI)	742
University library management	BERGER, Michael G.	(CA)	85
Urban public library management	ICKES, Barbara J.	(PA)	581
User & information management education	BERNARD, Molly S.	(WA)	88
Video & audio services manager	EVANS, Mark S.	(FL)	357
Visual resource management	HOGAN, Kristine K.	(NY)	549
	FOWLER, Michele R.	(OH)	394
Visual resources management, development	PRINS, Johanna W.	(NY)	993
Vital records management	MONTGOMERY, Suzanne L.	(VA)	856
Volunteer management	HAUSSMANN, Virginia D.	(CA)	513
Volunteers management	KLAUS, Susan B.	(OH)	658
Water management, reference service	PLOCKELMAN, Cynthia H.	(FL)	978
Water utility management	ERTZ, Ginger E.	(PA)	353
Word processing, record management systs	KEE, Walter A.	(NC)	634

MANIPULATION
Computer manipulation of information	KERNS, John T.	(CA)	644
Digitize image manipulation software	BENGE, Bruce	(OK)	80
Online search, data manipulation	FOURNIER, Susan K.	(MD)	393
Text manipulation	HENDERSON, Ronald L.	(MD)	527

MANPOWER (See also Employment)
Manpower databases	BURN, Harry T.	(TN)	161
Manpower planning	HUNT, Suellyn	(NY)	575

MANUAL
Biomedical research online & manual	LETT, Rosalind K.	(GA)	719
Information searches, manual & computer	SHALLEY, Doris P.	(PA)	1119
Legal research reference online manual	VON PFEIL, Helena P.	(DC)	1288
Manual & automated catalog management	KLAIR, Arlene F.	(MD)	657
Manual & automated reference	MCGOWAN, Anna T.	(DC)	807
Manual & automated technl applications	MERRITT, Betty A.	(CA)	827
Manual & online bibliography	KREITZBURG, Marilyn J.	(PA)	677
Manual & online searching	HOLDEN, Douglas H.	(ND)	550
Manual indexing	LINZER, Elliot	(NY)	732
Manual library research	SPEARMAN, Marie A.	(WA)	1172
Manual literature searching	WELCH, Carol J.	(PA)	1321
Manual medical reference	VAIL, Evelyn J.	(IL)	1270
Manual online reference services	GINSLER, Mindy F.	(ON)	438
Manual searching	SCHRAEDER, Diana C.	(TX)	1099
Manual systems design	PISCITELLI, Rosalie A.	(NY)	976
Manual technical cataloging	WHITT, Diane M.	(IL)	1334
Manual writing	NEW, Gregory R.	(DC)	898
Market research, online & manual	MAXWELL, Christine Y.	(CA)	788
Online & manual information services	GALBRAITH, Barry E.	(NY)	413
Online & manual searching	BOGART, Betty B.	(MA)	110
Online, manual search strategy	BATES, Marcia J.	(CA)	64
Procedure manual development	KOSTIS, Leigh W.	(PA)	673
Software manual distribution	BYERS, Cathy L.	(ON)	168

MANUALS (See also Handbooks, Manual)
Computer hardware & software manuals	CASSAR, Ann	(PA)	193
Computer manuals	PRITCHARD, Barbara	(PA)	994
Policy manuals	NAVRATIL, Jean	(NY)	890
Procedure manuals	PLOTSKY, Andrea G.	(CA)	978
Training aids & manuals	CORNICK, Ron	(IL)	247
Writing & editing policy manuals	COURSON, M S.	(MD)	251
Writing of manuals	SCOTT, Patricia L.	(UT)	1107
Writing procedures manuals	ZYNJUK, Nila L.	(MD)	1392

MANUFACTURING (See also Factory)
Binders board manufacturing	BROOKS, Alfred C.	(NJ)	140
Book manufacturing	BROOKS, Alfred C.	(NJ)	140
Designing & manufacturing lib equipment	KINGSLEY, Eleanor V.	(CA)	652
Electronic design & manufacturing	KLINGER, William E.	(OH)	661
Engineering & manufacturing reference	NESBITT, Olive K.	(PA)	896
Games development & manufacture	FORSHAW, William S.	(MD)	391
Manufacture of shelving systems	BAYLIS, Ted	(MA)	67
Manufacturing automation	GROEN, Paulette E.	(MI)	471
Manufacturing database systems	SINE, George H.	(IL)	1143
Manufacturing information resources	KELLER, Karen A.	(MI)	635
Manufacturing information systems	BEICHMAN, John C.	(MI)	75
Manufacturing lib technical furniture	VAN PELT, Peter J.	(NY)	1277
Manufacturing processes & applications	GROEN, Paulette E.	(MI)	471
Manufacturing statistics	LANEY, Helen B.	(DC)	695
Manufacturing steel bookstacks	VAN PELT, Peter J.	(NY)	1277
Manufacturing technology acquisition	STEVENS, Michael	(IL)	1190
Manufacturing wood library furniture	VAN PELT, Peter J.	(NY)	1277
Organz & indexing of manufacturer catlgs	SCHUSTER, Adeline	(IL)	1103

MANUSCRIPTS (See also Autographs, Paper, Rare)
Acquisition of manuscripts	HODSON, Sara S.	(CA)	546
	GORDON, Robert S.	(ON)	451
Administration & personal manuscript col	CUMMINGS, Hilary A.	(OR)	264
AMC & MARC format manuscripts	ROBINSON, Christie M.	(KY)	1043
Ancient & Renaissance manuscripts	WITTEN, Laurence	(CT)	1358
Appraisal, authentication of manuscripts	GORDON, Robert S.	(ON)	451
Archival & manuscript collections	SHOCKLEY, Ann A.	(TN)	1132
Archival manuscripts collections	RICHMOND, Robert W.	(KS)	1031
Archival manuscripts control MARC format	WEBER, Lisa B.	(IL)	1314
Archive & manuscript processing	THWEATT, John H.	(TN)	1243
Archives & historical manuscripts	WILLARD, Anne H.	(CT)	1341
Archives & manuscript collection mgmt	GRIGG, Susan	(MA)	470
Archives & manuscript collections	FRYE, Dorothy T.	(MI)	407
Archives & manuscripts	NODLER, Charles E.	(MO)	906
	BRECK, Paul A.	(AR)	131
	DAY, Deborah C.	(CA)	282
	MCPHAIL, Martha E.	(CA)	817
	PUGH, Mary J.	(CA)	997
	RICHARDSON, John V.	(CA)	1029
	VANSLYKE, Lisa M.	(CA)	1277
	NOLEN, Anita L.	(DC)	908
	SUNG, Carolyn H.	(DC)	1210
	BISHOP, Beverly D.	(GA)	99
	KLINE, Laura S.	(IA)	661
	HANSEN, Ralph W.	(ID)	498
	WELLS, Merle W.	(ID)	1322
	EVANS, Linda J.	(IL)	357
	MOTLEY, Archie	(IL)	872
	SHUSTER, Robert D.	(IL)	1134
	WEBER, Lisa B.	(IL)	1314
	OTTO, Kathryn D.	(KS)	930
	MORISON, William J.	(KY)	865
	TURNER, I B.	(LA)	1264
	DOWLER, Lawrence E.	(MA)	315
	ELLIOTT, Clark A.	(MA)	343
	STUART, Karen A.	(MD)	1204
	TATE, Vernon D.	(MD)	1225
	YEAGER, Gerry	(MD)	1378
	KROSCH, Penelope S.	(MN)	680
	BURCKEL, Nicholas C.	(MO)	158
	BRABHAM, Robert F.	(NC)	124
	GRAY, David P.	(ND)	459
	JOYCE, William L.	(NJ)	618
	COX, Richard J.	(NY)	253
	DOYAL, Patricia A.	(NY)	317
	MENT, David M.	(NY)	824
	WARNOW-BLEWETT, Joan N.	(NY)	1305
	PIKE, Kermit J.	(OH)	972
	ANDRICK, Annita A.	(PA)	27
	WICKEY, Colleen	(PA)	1335
	ZABROSKY, Frank A.	(PA)	1385
	DUBIEL, Laura R.	(TX)	321
	HUMPHREY, David C.	(TX)	573
	JOHNSON, Jeffery O.	(UT)	606
	JACOB, Diane B.	(VA)	589
	JACOB, John N.	(VA)	589
	GALLAGHER, Connell B.	(VT)	413
Archives & manuscripts administration	PARHAM, Robert B.	(AK)	940
	LATOUR, Terry S.	(MS)	701
	KOVAN, Allan S.	(WI)	673
Archives & manuscripts automation	BROWN, Barbara J.	(VA)	142
Archives & manuscripts control	CARROLL-HORROCKS, Elizabeth	(PA)	187
Archives & manuscripts management	PINSON, Patricia A.	(WY)	975
Archives & manuscripts processing	BECK, Alison M.	(TX)	71
Archives, manuscript management	STOPKA, Christina K.	(WY)	1198
Archives, manuscripts	CARTLEDGE, Connie L.	(DC)	190
Archives, manuscripts collections	SMITH, Edith	(CA)	1154
Arrangement & description, manuscripts	PARHAM, Robert B.	(AK)	940
Arrangement of manuscript collections	MAYER, Dale C.	(IA)	789
Autograph manuscripts	CAHOON, Herbert	(NY)	171
Black American history manuscripts	WEST, Donald	(MI)	1326
Books & manuscripts appraisal	LEBO, Shirley B.	(DC)	708

MANUSCRIPTS (Cont'd)

Books & manuscripts appraisals	TWENEY, George H.	(WA)	1266
Books & manuscripts archives	GAMBLE, Mary J.	(CA)	416
Books, manuscripts, maps	JONES, Dora A.	(SD)	612
Cataloging & manuscript processing	WESTERBERG, Kermit B.	(IL)	1326
Cataloging & processing manuscripts	WHITTINGTON, Erma P.	(NC)	1334
Cataloging archives & manuscripts	CARNES, Suzanne M.	(CA)	183
	CALKIN, Homer L.	(VA)	173
Cataloging manuscript collections	OSTROFF, Harriet	(DC)	929
Cataloging manuscripts	MYERS, Roger	(AZ)	885
	BLUTH, John F.	(PA)	108
Cataloging manuscripts, using AMC format	CARTLEDGE, Connie L.	(DC)	190
Cataloging music manuscripts	PLAIN, Marilyn V.	(NY)	977
Church record & manuscripts	HILAND, Gerard P.	(OH)	538
Editing & manuscript evaluation	MOON, Eric	(FL)	857
Encyclopedia manuscript editing	LAGIES, Meinhart J.	(CA)	688
English renaissance manuscripts	YEANDLE, Laetitia	(DC)	1378
Field work in manuscript collections	KRASEAN, Thomas K.	(IN)	676
First editions & manuscripts of music	STRINGFELLOW, William T.	(NY)	1202
French archival records & manuscripts	KOHN, Roger S.	(NY)	668
Hebrew manuscripts & rare books	KOHN, Roger S.	(NY)	668
Historic manuscript collections	RHINELANDER, Mary F.	(MA)	1025
Historic manuscripts	LANDIS, Lawrence A.	(TX)	693
Historical & literary manuscripts	DUNLAP, Leslie W.	(IA)	326
	THOMPSON, Harry F.	(SD)	1239
Historical manuscripts	STAUTER, Mark C.	(MO)	1183
	WOLOHAN, Juliet F.	(NY)	1362
	MILLER, Fredric M.	(PA)	837
	WEINBERG, David M.	(PA)	1317
	HILL, Edwin L.	(WI)	539
History of books & manuscripts	CARNOVSKY, Ruth F.	(CA)	184
Literary manuscript databases	MACDERMAID, Anne	(ON)	754
Literary manuscripts	BROWAR, Lisa M.	(NY)	141
Local history manuscript collections	PACKARD, Agnes K.	(NY)	933
Lute prints & manuscripts	NESS, Arthur J.	(MA)	896
Manuscript acquisitions	MCCULLOH, Judith M.	(IL)	801
Manuscript administration	LENNON, Donald R.	(NC)	715
Manuscript & archival description	HENSEN, Steven L.	(NC)	529
Manuscript & archive conservation	GARLICK, Karen	(DC)	419
Manuscript & archive management	JERDE, Curtis D.	(LA)	599
Manuscript & autograph material	PETERSON, Scott W.	(IL)	964
Manuscript & grant applications	PARR, John R.	(ON)	943
Manuscript appraisals	RENDELL, Kenneth W.	(MA)	1023
Manuscript arrangement & description	KENNICK, Sylvia B.	(NY)	642
	O'KEEFE, Laura K.	(NY)	919
Manuscript cataloging	GILDZEN, Alex J.	(OH)	434
	MOLTKE-HANSEN, David	(SC)	853
	HANDE, D A.	(SK)	494
Manuscript cataloging online	CRONENWETT, Philip N.	(NH)	260
Manuscript collections	SLY, Margery N.	(MA)	1150
	PENNINGER, Randy	(NC)	957
	GARNER, Jane	(TX)	419
	BOONE, Edward J.	(VA)	115
Manuscript conservation	KENNICK, Sylvia B.	(NY)	642
Manuscript editing	HURTES, Reva	(FL)	578
	EDELSON, Ken	(NJ)	335
Manuscript librarianship, archives	WHEALAN, Ronald E.	(MA)	1328
Manuscript organization & description	ONN, Shirley A.	(AB)	924
Manuscript processing	MILLER, Leon C.	(AR)	839
	SHARP, Alice L.	(CO)	1122
	NEWHALL, Ann C.	(CT)	898
	HODGSON, Janet B.	(KY)	546
	GIFFORD, Paul M.	(MI)	433
	JESSEE, W S.	(MN)	600
	TRASK, Benjamin H.	(VA)	1254
	WEBER, Anita M.	(VA)	1313
Manuscript processing & collecting	HULL, Mary M.	(TX)	572
Manuscript processing & description	KAPLAN, Diane E.	(CT)	626
Manuscript studies	JORDAN, Louis E.	(IN)	616
Manuscripts	HODSON, Sara S.	(CA)	546
	PUGSLEY, Sharon G.	(CA)	997
	KAIMOWITZ, Jeffery H.	(CT)	622
	PELTIER, Karen V.	(CT)	955
	BARRINGER, George M.	(DC)	59
	CHESTNUT, Paul I.	(DC)	207
	CRAWFORD, Elva B.	(DC)	256
	JEFFERSON, Karen L.	(DC)	596

MANUSCRIPTS (Cont'd)

Manuscripts

	MCGUIRE, Brian	(DC)	808
	SERVERINO, Roberto	(DC)	1116
	SCHREYER, Alice D.	(DE)	1100
	SMITH, Rebecca A.	(FL)	1159
	DEES, Anthony R.	(GA)	287
	GULLEY, J L.	(GA)	477
	BAMBERGER, Mary A.	(IL)	53
	BRIGGS, Martha T.	(IL)	135
	GILDEMEISTER, Glen A.	(IL)	434
	HOLLI, Melvin G.	(IL)	552
	KOCH, David V.	(IL)	667
	QUINN, Patrick M.	(IL)	1000
	ROBISON, Carley R.	(IL)	1045
	RYAN, Sheila	(IL)	1071
	ELLIOTT, Joan M.	(IN)	344
	MCSHANE, Stephen G.	(IN)	818
	CRAWFORD, Anthony R.	(KS)	256
	BELL, Mary M.	(KY)	77
	HAY, Charles C.	(KY)	515
	STONE, Sue L.	(KY)	1197
	DRAUGHON, Ralph B.	(LA)	318
	MARTIN, Robert S.	(LA)	778
	ENGELHART, Anne D.	(MA)	349
	HOLDEN, Harley P.	(MA)	550
	TRINKAUS-RANDALL, Gregor	(MA)	1257
	WARRINGTON, David R.	(MA)	1307
	YOUNT, Diana	(MA)	1384
	CREIGHTON, Alice S.	(MD)	258
	HIRTLE, Peter B.	(MD)	544
	HENNEN, Earl M.	(MS)	528
	BYRD, Robert L.	(NC)	169
	GARTRELL, Ellen G.	(NC)	420
	MOORE, Scott L.	(NC)	861
	BECKER, Ronald L.	(NJ)	72
	BOWLING, Mary B.	(NJ)	121
	JONES, Arthur E.	(NJ)	611
	SINCLAIR, Donald A.	(NJ)	1142
	THOMPSON, Janet A.	(NM)	1240
	BLESSE, Robert E.	(NV)	105
	BARTO, Stephen C.	(NY)	61
	CRYSTAL, Bernard R.	(NY)	262
	KABELAC, Karl S.	(NY)	620
	LINDSAY, Jean S.	(NY)	729
	MACKECHNIE, Nancy S.	(NY)	756
	MAYO, Hope	(NY)	790
	PAULSON, Barbara A.	(NY)	950
	EAST, Dennis	(OH)	332
	HARRISON, Dennis I.	(OH)	506
	HORROCKS, Thomas A.	(PA)	561
	MORRIS, Leslie A.	(PA)	867
	NELSON, Vernon H.	(PA)	895
	CHERPAK, Evelyn M.	(RI)	206
	GEOGHEGAN, Doris J.	(SC)	427
	LAWSON, James F.	(SC)	705
	HARWELL, Sara J.	(TN)	509
	HUGHES, Marylin B.	(TN)	572
	WAGGENER, Jean B.	(TN)	1291
	WOLFE, Marice	(TN)	1361
	CONRAD, James H.	(TX)	238
	CULP, Paul M.	(TX)	264
	LETSON, Dawn E.	(TX)	719
	ROWLEY, Edward D.	(UT)	1063
	GORDON, Vesta L.	(VA)	452
	KIMBALL, Gregg D.	(VA)	649
	THOMPSON, Anthony B.	(VA)	1239
	ARMSTRONG, Fredrick H.	(WV)	32
	MENARD, Michael J.	(WY)	823
	STEELE, Apollonia L.	(AB)	1184
Manuscripts & archival processing	WHITE, William T.	(MN)	1332
Manuscripts & archival reference	KAPLAN, Diane E.	(CT)	626
Manuscripts & archives	MCLACHLAN, Ross W.	(AZ)	812
	RULE, Amy E.	(AZ)	1067
	ZEIDBERG, David S.	(CA)	1387
	NEILON, Barbara L.	(CO)	892
	BROWN, William E.	(CT)	148
	WAIT, Gary E.	(CT)	1293
	BATTLE, Thomas C.	(DC)	65

MANUSCRIPTS (Cont'd)

Manuscripts & archives

KNOWLTON, John D.	(DC)	665
NYGREN, Deborah A.	(DC)	912
RUDISELL, Carol A.	(DE)	1065
PHILLIPS, Faye	(LA)	968
EPPARD, Philip B.	(MA)	351
LOSCALZO, Anita B.	(MA)	741
MOSELEY, Eva S.	(MA)	870
PERCY, Theresa R.	(MA)	958
LOHF, Kenneth A.	(NY)	737
DUCKETT, Kenneth W.	(OR)	322
LLOYD, James B.	(TN)	735
LARSEN, A D.	(UT)	698
DIBIASE, Linda P.	(WA)	299

Manuscripts & archives administration	HARDWICK, Bonnie S.	(CA)	500
Manuscripts & archives collections	ASHFORD, Marguerite K.	(HI)	36
Manuscripts & drawings	HAIL, Christopher	(MA)	484
Manuscripts & holographic documents	LEVITT, Martin L.	(PA)	721
Manuscripts & publications acquisitions	VIOL, Robert W.	(OH)	1285
Manuscripts & rare books	YOUNG, Noraleen A.	(IN)	1382
	ROUNDTREE, Lynn P.	(LA)	1061
Manuscripts & rare books literary resrch	REIMAN, Donald H.	(NY)	1020
Manuscripts & records bibl control	KELLER, William B.	(DC)	636
Manuscripts & special collections	SNIFFIN-MARINO, Megan G.	(MA)	1163
	CORSARO, James	(NY)	248
Manuscripts appraisal	CRONENWETT, Philip N.	(NH)	260
Manuscripts, archives processing	BOOTHE, Nancy L.	(TX)	116
Manuscripts, archives resrchr guidance	BOOTHE, Nancy L.	(TX)	116
Manuscripts arrangement & description	MYERS, Roger	(AZ)	885
	BOWEN, Laurel G.	(IL)	120
	MICHAELIS, Patricia A.	(KS)	831
Manuscripts cataloging	MCLOONE, Harriet V.	(CA)	814
	ROUNDTREE, Lynn P.	(LA)	1061
	VIRTA, Alan K.	(MD)	1285
Manuscripts collection	BERKELEY, Edmund	(VA)	87
Manuscripts collections	WIKANDER, Lawrence E.	(MA)	1338
Manuscripts conservation & microfilming	BOWEN, Laurel G.	(IL)	120
Manuscripts curating	CHOPESIUK, Ronald J.	(SC)	210
Manuscripts curatorship	ROBINSON, Kathleen M.	(TX)	1044
Manuscripts educational uses	MICHAELIS, Patricia A.	(KS)	831
Manuscripts general preservation	MICHAELIS, Patricia A.	(KS)	831
Manuscripts librarianship	LINDEMANN, Richard H.	(VA)	729
Manuscripts processing	PAUL, Andrea I.	(NE)	949
Manuscripts processing & cataloging	BOUCHE, Nicole L.	(CA)	118
Manuscripts processing & reference	WELLS, Anne S.	(MS)	1322
Manuscripts reference	BOWEN, Laurel G.	(IL)	120
Manuscripts solicitation & processing	GRABOWSKI, John J.	(OH)	455
Medieval & modern manuscripts	PRESTON, Jean F.	(NJ)	991
	IZBICKI, Thomas M.	(KS)	586
Medieval manuscripts	FOLTER, Roland	(NY)	388
	HALL, Holly	(MO)	487
Modern literary manuscripts	MEYER, Daniel	(IL)	830
Modern manuscripts	ORMSBY, Eric	(PQ)	926
Near Eastern manuscripts	RATNER, Sabina T.	(PQ)	1010
19th century manuscripts	MASLYN, David C.	(RI)	780
Personal papers, manuscripts	GRAHAM, Robert W.	(IL)	456
Private manuscripts & records	ETTER, Patricia A.	(AZ)	355
Processing & cataloging manuscripts	SIEBERS, Bruce I.	(MI)	1135
Processing archives & manuscripts	BOYD, Sandra E.	(MS)	123
Processing manuscript collections	TEICHMAN, Raymond J.	(NY)	1230
	CHESTNUT, Paul I.	(DC)	207
Processing manuscripts & archives	GILSON, Barbara J.	(NY)	437
Processing private manuscript cols	EBELING-KONING, Blanche T.	(MD)	334
Rare books & literary manuscripts	ROBROCK, David P.	(AZ)	1045
	ESCHER, Nancy	(CA)	354
	HORWITZ, Steven F.	(CA)	561
	LEERHOFF, Ruth E.	(CA)	712
	SORGENFREI, Robert K.	(CA)	1168
	WHITING, F B.	(CA)	1333
	WOODWARD, Daniel	(CA)	1368
Rare books & manuscripts	BOGENSCHNEIDER, Duane R.	(CT)	110

MANUSCRIPTS (Cont'd)

Rare books & manuscripts

PARKS, Stephen	(CT)	943
SCHMIDT, Alesandra M.	(CT)	1095
WILKIE, Everett C.	(CT)	1340
BEDARD, Laura A.	(DC)	73
ADAMS, Barbara M.	(DE)	4
IVES, Sidney E.	(FL)	586
TIMBERLAKE, Cynthia A.	(HI)	1245
ADAMS, Larry D.	(IA)	5
CULLEN, Charles T.	(IL)	263
GERDES, Neil W.	(IL)	428
GUSHEE, Marion S.	(IL)	478
MCCOY, Ralph E.	(IL)	799
MASON, Alexandra	(KS)	780
MILLER, Robert H.	(KY)	842
ENGLISH, Cynthia J.	(MA)	350
LANCASTER, John	(MA)	692
LOMBARDO, Daniel J.	(MA)	738
MELNICK, Ralph	(MA)	823
STODDARD, Roger E.	(MA)	1196
GWYN, Ann S.	(MD)	479
ALLENTUCK, Marcia E.	(NY)	16
DUPONT, Inge	(NY)	327
RACHOW, Louis A.	(NY)	1001
WILSON, Fredric W.	(NY)	1351
HANSON, Norma S.	(OH)	498
MCCALLUM, Brenda W.	(OH)	793
BAKER, Sylva S.	(PA)	49
BAKY, John S.	(PA)	50
KOREY, Marie E.	(PA)	671
WOLF, Edwin	(PA)	1360
COLEY, Betty A.	(TX)	231
HENDERSON, Cathy	(TX)	526
KLEPPER, Bobbie J.	(TX)	660
LEACH, Sally S.	(TX)	706
NOLAN, Edward W.	(WA)	907

Rare books & modern manuscripts	HUTTNER, Sidney F.	(OK)	579
Rare books, manuscripts	ZINN, Nancy W.	(CA)	1389
	HASWELL, Hollee	(NY)	511
Rare books, manuscripts, & archives	FIELD, William N.	(NJ)	376
Scripts, manuscripts	KARATNYTSKY, Christine A.	(NY)	627
Writing manuscript guide entries	HULL, Mary M.	(TX)	572

MAPS (See also Atlases, Cartobibliography, Cartography, Geography)

Antiquarian maps	BERGEN, Kathleen M.	(MI)	85
Antique maps	CRESSWELL, Donald H.	(PA)	258
Books, manuscripts, maps	JONES, Dora A.	(SD)	612
Cataloging monographs, maps & documents	CAHILL, Colleen R.	(PA)	171
Early maps	COLE, Maud D.	(NY)	231
Geography & map specialist	MULAWKA, Chet	(CT)	876
Geography & maps	NIELSEN, Elizabeth A.	(DC)	903
	HANDROW, Margaret M.	(TX)	495
	GALKOWSKI, Patricia E.	(RI)	413
Geologic map collection	SELLIN, Jon B.	(VA)	1114
Geologic maps	SHANNON, Michael O.	(NY)	1120
Government documents & maps			
Government documents & maps reference	WALKER, Barbara J.	(GA)	1295
Map acquisitions	GALNEDER, Mary H.	(WI)	415
Map & air photo collections	SUTHERLAND, Johnnie D.	(GA)	1211
Map & atlas collection development	RIVERA, Diana H.	(MI)	1037
Map & book cataloging	SHARP, Alice L.	(CO)	1122
Map & geography collections	SHARP, Linda C.	(OH)	1122
Map & geography librarianship	FLATNESS, James A.	(DC)	384
Map & geography reference	PERRY, Joanne M.	(OR)	960
Map cataloging	DIBLE, Joan B.	(CA)	299
	PETERSON, Charles B.	(DC)	963
	LEONARD, Louise F.	(FL)	716
	SCHREIBER, Robert E.	(IL)	1099
	SHIRLEY, David B.	(MI)	1131
	CORSARO, James	(NY)	248
	PERRY, Joanne M.	(OR)	960
	STONE, Howard P.	(RI)	1197
	PESCHEL, Susan M.	(WI)	961
Map cataloging & classification	GALNEDER, Mary H.	(WI)	415
Map collection	ROBAR, Terri J.	(FL)	1038

MAPS (Cont'd)

Map collections

Map conservation
Map curatorship

Map information
Map librarian
Map librarianship

MILLER, Rosanna . . . . . . (AZ) 842
BURNS, Mary F. . . . . . . (IL) 162
KIDD, Betty H. . . . . . . (ON) 646
DEVERA, Rosalinda M. . (NY) 297
KIDD, Betty H. . . . . . . (ON) 646
REINHARD, Christine M. (WI) 1021
KOEPP, Donna P. . . . . (KS) 668
HOEHN, Philip . . . . (CA) 547
LUNDQUIST, David A. . (CA) 748
STEVENS, Stanley D. . . (CA) 1191
ANTHES, Susan H. . . . (CO) 28
CARRINGTON, David K. (DC) 186
STEPHENSON, Richard
W. . . . . (DC) 1188
WOLTER, John A. . . . . (DC) 1362
COBB, David A. . . . . . (IL) 224
KOH, Siew B. . . . . (IL) 668
RAY, Jean M. . . . . (IL) 1011
CURTIS, Peter H. . . . . (MD) 267
BOURGEOIS, Ann M. . . (MI) 119
HANSEN, Joanne J. . . . (MI) 497
HUDSON, Alice C. . . . . (NY) 569
OTNES, Harold M. . . . . (OR) 930
STARK, Peter L. . . . . . (OR) 1181
BOARDMAN, Richard C. (PA) 108
POST, Jeremiah B. . . . (PA) 986
ROBERTSON, Robert B. (PA) 1042
SPRANKLE, Anita T. . . (PA) 1176
JOHANSEN, Priscilla P. (TX) 601
MURPHY, Mary . . . . . . (VA) 881
GALNEDER, Mary H. . . (WI) 415
RISTIC, Jovanka . . . . . (WI) 1036
WOOD, Alberta A. . . . . (NF) 1363
WELCH, Grace D. . . . . (ON) 1321
TESSIER, Yves . . . . . . (PQ) 1233

Map librarianship & geography
Map libraries

Map library administration
Map reference
Mapping, technical libraries
Maps

EUKEY, Jim O. . . . . . . (WI) 356
CROWE, Gloria J. . . . . (AZ) 261
PERRY, Joanne M. . . . . (OR) 960
COOMBS, James A. . . . (MO) 241
WYMAN, Kathleen M. . . (ON) 1375
RUDD, Janet K. . . . . . . (CA) 1065
SLOAN, Tom W. . . . . . (AL) 1150
JACOBSEN, Lavonne . . (CA) 590
GREALY, Deborah J. . . (CO) 461
RAY, Kathryn C. . . . . . (DC) 1011
YOUNG, Kathryn A. . . . (DE) 1382
CHRISTIAN, Gayle R. . . (GA) 211
HUGHES, Glenda J. . . . (GA) 571
WILKINSON, Patrick J. . (IA) 1340
BAIRD, Dennis W. . . . . (ID) 47
NORTON, Margaret W. . (IL) 910
SELMER, Marsha L. . . . (IL) 1114
SHERWOOD, Arlyn K. . (IL) 1129
DARBEE, Leigh . . . . . . (IN) 274
MURDOCK, J L. . . . . . (IN) 879
SELDIN, Daniel T. . . . . (IN) 1113
OTTO, Kathryn D. . . . . (KS) 930
HENSON, Stephen . . . . (LA) 530
WALSH, Jim . . . . (MA) 1299
BERGEN, Kathleen M. . (MI) 85
BASEFSKY, Stuart M. . (NC) 62
DALTON, Lisa K. . . . . . (NC) 271
MILLER, Lewis R. . . . . (NC) 840
OSER, Anita K. . . . . . . (NC) 928
NEWMAN, Linda P. . . . (NV) 899
ICE, Diana C. . . . . (NY) 581
JENNINGS, Vincent . . . (NY) 598
COLLINS, Evron S. . . . (OH) 232
FARRELL, Maureen C. . (OH) 365
WINROTH, Elizabeth C. (OR) 1355
BOARDMAN, Richard C. (PA) 108
BURNS-DUFFY, Mary A. (PA) 163
HARRIS, Maureen . . . . (SC) 505
MCQUILLAN, David C. . (SC) 817
RHOLES, Julia M. . . . . (TX) 1026
HILLER, Steven Z. . . . . (WA) 541
VILLAR, Susanne P. . . . (WA) 1284
MUSICH, Gerald D. . . . (WI) 883
COLLIER, Carol A. . . . . (WY) 232

MAPS (Cont'd)

Maps, aerial photos, atlases
Maps & atlases

Maps & cartographic information
Maps & cartography
Maps & geographic information
Maps & geography
Maps & government documents
Maps cataloging

Maps, documents & microforms
Maps librarianship

Maps, printed ephemera
OCLC map cataloging
Preservation of maps in books
Rare maps

United States census maps

EASTON, William W. . . (IL) 333
STRICKLAND, Muriel . . . (CA) 1202
ALLISON, Brent . . . . . . (MN) 17
REX, Heather . . . . (NM) 1024
WALTZ, Mary A. . . . . . (NY) 1302
IVES, Peter B. . . . . . . (NM) 586
WEDIG, Eric M. . . . . . (TN) 1315
SCHORR, Alan E. . . . . (AK) 1099
WOODWARD, Lawrence
W. . . . . (DC) 1368
DONLEY, Leigh M. . . . . (CA) 311
KRISTIE, William J. . . . (CA) 679
DONNELL, Marianne . . . (FL) 311
SILVER, Marcy L. . . . . (MD) 1138
STORM, Jill . . . . (DC) 1198
KLIMLEY, Susan . . . . . (NY) 661
WALSTROM, Jon L. . . . (MN) 1300
HUDSON, Alice C. . . . . (NY) 569
SCHULZE, Suzanne S. . . (CO) 1102

MARC (See also Cataloging)

AMC & MARC format manuscripts
Archival manuscripts control MARC
format
Cataloging, MARC format
Cataloging MARC formats
Cataloging with MARC AMC
MARC

MARC data processing
MARC databases

MARC format

MARC format for music
MARC formats

MARC record formats
MARC record upgrade
MARC tape processing
MARC training & development
MARC-based systems
MARC-compatible systems
OCLC, MARC tagging
Serials holdings, MARC format
US MARC formats

ROBINSON, Christie M. . (KY) 1043

WEBER, Lisa B. . . . . . . (IL) 1314
THIBAULT, Jean . . . . . (ON) 1235
ROBINSON, Christie M. . (KY) 1043
BOYD, Sandra E. . . . . . (MS) 123
FREDERICK, Sidney C. . (IL) 399
MOSS, Barbara J. . . . . (IL) 872
SEGEL, Bernard J. . . . . (DC) 1112
DAMICO, Nancy B. . . . . (MA) 272
JOHNSON, Bruce C. . . . (MD) 602
BLUE, Margaret R. . . . . (ND) 107
SKROBELA, Katherine C. (NJ) 1147
SCHMIDT, Holly H. . . . . (OR) 1095
GRISCOM, Richard W. . . (IL) 471
COYLE, Karen E. . . . . . (CA) 253
GLAZIER, Ed . . . . (CA) 440
BARTLEY, Linda K. . . . . (DC) 61
GILLESPIE, Veronica M. . (DC) 435
GOUDREAU, Ronald A. . (DC) 454
DALEHITE, Michele I. . . . (FL) 270
CLARE, Richard W. . . . . (NY) 216
PERSKY, Gail M. . . . . . (NY) 961
PATTON, Glenn E. . . . . (OH) 949
ATTIG, John C. . . . . . . (PA) 38
KOMOROUS, Hana J. . . (BC) 670
QUEINNEC, Young H. . . (ON) 999
ESPLEY, John L. . . . . . (VA) 354
CHIU, Ida K. . . . . (TX) 209
HAMILTON, Fae K. . . . . (MA) 492
HENSEN, Steven L. . . . (NC) 529
EVANS, Linda J. . . . . . (IL) 357
MOTTRAM, Geoffrey . . . (IL) 873
LEONG, Carol L. . . . . . (IL) 717
VISK, Linda S. . . . . (GA) 1285
JANK, David A. . . . . . . (MA) 593
CARSON, M S. . . . . . . (PA) 188

MARCON

Marcon Plus computer usage

MATTHEOU, Antonia . . . (NY) 785

MARIMBA

Marimba, xylophone collection

GERHARDT, Edwin L. . . (MD) 428

MARINE (See also Oceanography)

Biology & marine science
Marine affairs, research & reference
Marine & land-based information
Marine biology
Marine biology information
Marine biology reference
Marine engineering
Marine science

BROWNLOW, Judith . . . (MA) 148
ETCHINGHAM, John B. . (RI) 355
CAMPBELL, Margaret E. (NS) 177
COLEMAN, David E. . . . (HI) 231
BALDRIDGE, Alan . . . . . (CA) 51
MARKHAM, James W. . . (CA) 771
JOBA, Judith C. . . . . . . (PQ) 601
KROST, Mary G. . . . . . (MD) 680
BARNETT, Judith B. . . . (RI) 57

MARINE (Cont'd)

Marine science collections development	SUTHERLAND, J E.	(NS)	1211
Marine science database searching	HALE, Kay K.	(FL)	485
Marine science databases	SHEPHARD, Frank C.	(MA)	1127
Marine science literature	PERRONE, Jeanne M.	(DC)	960
Marine science reference	HALE, Kay K.	(FL)	485
Marine sciences information	BALDRIDGE, Alan	(CA)	51
Marine studies, oceanography	HALL, Alice W.	(DE)	486
Medical & marine science libraries	TRUMBULL, Jane	(NC)	1259

MARITIME (See also Admiralty, Naval, Ship)

Admiralty & maritime law	COMBE, David A.	(LA)	234
Maritime & naval history	KNAPP, Peter J.	(CT)	663
Maritime collections	KENNICK, Sylvia B.	(NY)	642
Maritime databases	KAGAN, Ilse E.	(NY)	621
Maritime history	ADAMS, Thomas R.	(RI)	6
Maritime information	SHIPMAN, Natalie W.	(TX)	1131
Maritime law & technology	COMEAU, Amy R.	(NY)	234
Maritime material culture	BUMGARNER, John L.	(NC)	157
Maritime science information	SHIPMAN, Natalie W.	(TX)	1131
North Carolina maritime activities	BUMGARNER, John L.	(NC)	157

MARKET (See also Economics, Marketing)

Appraising current market value	MONDLIN, Marvin	(NY)	854
Business market research	DEHN, Lydia A.	(CA)	288
Common market law	ESSIEN, Victor K.	(NY)	354
Communications industry market research	LEIGHTON, Victoria C.	(GA)	714
Computer stock market research	HEFFRON, Betsy A.	(NY)	520
Computer-related market studies	GOOGINS, Jennifer J.	(NY)	450
Consumer products markets	COMPTON, Erlinda R.	(TX)	235
Database market research	MAYERS, Henry L.	(MI)	789
Direct mail markets	MELKIN, Audrey D.	(NY)	822
Electronic media-specialized market srvs	SIECK, Steven K.	(NY)	1135
Financial market analysis	PHILLIPS, Steven G.	(MA)	969
Information product market development	SAYER, John S.	(MD)	1086
International market research	HANSEN, Kathelen L.	(MN)	497
	SHELTON, Anita L.	(NY)	1126
Latin American book market	MARSHALL, David L.	(DC)	774
Library, book trade market	BUCENEC, Nancy L.	(NY)	153
Library market	TOPEL, Iris N.	(NY)	1251
Market analysis business reports	KASE-MCLAREN, Karen A.	(NY)	628
Market & financial information services	HASSAN, Mohammad Z.	(NY)	511
Market & industry research	LANDRY, Ronald	(IL)	694
Market & marketing research	OLSEN, Stephen	(MN)	922
Market development	MITCHEM, M T.	(PA)	849
Market entry foreign publishers	PICKETT, Doyle C.	(NJ)	970
Market identification	LAMBERT, Shirley A.	(CO)	690
Market information	GARDNER, Catherine P.	(MA)	417
	THOMAS, Sandra L.	(OR)	1238
	GILLEN, Bonnie J.	(PA)	435
	BOYD, Cheryl J.	(MN)	122
Market information databases			
Market planning, segmentation, research	HERRICK, Carol L.	(OH)	532
Market research	EVANS, Deborah L.	(CA)	356
	WARNOCK, Patric F.	(CA)	1305
	BROCK, Laurie N.	(CO)	138
	HALL, Brian H.	(CO)	487
	WHITE, Suellen S.	(CO)	1332
	STAHL, D G.	(GA)	1178
	KOVITZ, Nancy R.	(IL)	674
	DELTANO, Pauline T.	(MA)	290
	GEER, Elizabeth F.	(MA)	425
	ISAACS, Cynthia W.	(MA)	584
	SAUNDERS, Leslie E.	(MA)	1084
	FRYSER, Benjamin S.	(MD)	407
	KORBER, Nancy	(NH)	671
	FRIHART, Anne R.	(NJ)	404
	PAVELY, Richard W.	(NJ)	950
	RILEY, Robert H.	(NJ)	1034
	GOETZ, Helen L.	(NY)	443
	GRETES, Frances C.	(NY)	467
	HALL, Alix M.	(NY)	486

MARKET (Cont'd)

Market research	KRAMER, Allan F.	(NY)	675
	GROSVENOR, Philip G.	(OH)	473
	SHAPLEY, Ellen M.	(TX)	1122
	PETRUGA, Patricia L.	(ON)	965
Market research & analysis	ROE, Georgeanne T.	(MA)	1048
Market research & planning	PERRON, Michelle M.	(NH)	960
Market research & product	CUTLER, Judith	(PA)	268
Market research, business intelligence	MIMNAUGH, Ellen N.	(OH)	845
Market research consulting	STILLMAN, Stanley W.	(NY)	1194
Market research databases	UMFLEET, Ruth A.	(TX)	1268
Market research for the info industry	SOVNER-RIBBLER, Judith	(MA)	1170
Market research, online & manual	MAXWELL, Christine Y.	(CA)	788
Market research, planning & development	LINDAHL, Ann L.	(CA)	728
Market research, product development	LEVITAN, Karen B.	(MD)	721
Market research reports	NAPOLITANO, Wanda M.	(NY)	887
	SULLIVAN, Daniel M.	(NY)	1207
	MASON-WARD, Lesley	(ON)	781
Market support	LAUER, Marjorie A.	(ON)	702
Market trends	BRAIMON, Margie S.	(NJ)	127
Media, audiovisual market research	HOPE, Thomas W.	(NY)	557
New media market analysis	KLOPFENSTEIN, Bruce C.	(OH)	662
Soyfoods market research	GOLBITZ, Peter	(ME)	444
	KINGMA, Sharyn L.	(ME)	652
Strategic market planning	TELFER, Margaret E.	(NC)	1230
Transactions network markets	WRIGHT, Bernell	(NY)	1370

MARKETING (See also Advertising, Consumer, Market, Merchandising, Niche, Outreach, Promotion, Public Relations, Sales, Telemarketing)

Advertising & marketing	DELANEY, Jerry	(IL)	289
	GATES, Carol M.	(IL)	421
	ROSENBERG, Barbra E.	(MA)	1055
	PERECMAN, Carol J.	(MI)	958
	HARNDEN, Donna J.	(MN)	502
	COHEN, Marsha C.	(NY)	228
	FENTON, Joan T.	(NY)	371
	MORRIS, Margaret J.	(NY)	867
	SANTORO, Tesse F.	(NY)	1082
	SCHACHTER, Bert	(NY)	1088
	SWANSON, Mary A.	(NY)	1213
	POWERS, Sally J.	(TX)	989
Advertising & marketing databases	ZILAVY, Julie A.	(NY)	1388
Advertising & marketing research	STEINMANN, Lois S.	(CA)	1186
	MACIVER, Linda B.	(MA)	756
	ROCHLEN, Rita E.	(MI)	1046
	GESKE, Aina S.	(NY)	430
Advertising & marketing services	BROMLEY, Alice V.	(NY)	140
Advertising marketing reference service	OWENS, Tina M.	(IL)	932
Arts & humanities database marketing	ZAJDEL, George J.	(PA)	1385
Book marketing	GERARD, James W.	(VT)	428
Books marketing	KOBASA, Paul A.	(IL)	666
Business & marketing databases	CRAWFORD, Marilyn L.	(CA)	257
Business & marketing information	FULLER, Kathleen B.	(OH)	408
Business & marketing info resources	BARTL, Richard P.	(NY)	61
Business & marketing information sources	STEPIEN, Karen K.	(NJ)	1189
Business & marketing libraries	TALCOTT, Ann W.	(NJ)	1221
Business & marketing reference	WHITT, Diane M.	(IL)	1334
	CLIFT, Crystal A.	(MN)	222
Business & marketing research	TUCKERMAN, Susan	(NY)	1262
Business & marketing searching	BRANCHICK, Susan E.	(OH)	127
Business, marketing & advertising resrch	PIDALA, Veronica C.	(NY)	971
Business, marketing & technoeconomics	GUIDA, Pat	(NJ)	476
Business, marketing database	COMPTON, Erlinda R.	(TX)	235
Business, marketing databases	ECKLUND, Lynn M.	(CA)	335
Business, marketing research	LEWARK, Kathryn W.	(CA)	722
CD ROM development & marketing	ANDREWS, Chris C.	(CT)	26
	MAIOLI, Jerry R.	(WA)	762
CD-ROM marketing	OVEREYNDER, Rombout E.	(NET)	931
CD-ROM product marketing	CORCHADO, Veronica A.	(CA)	245
Chemical business, marketing	FOOS, Ferol A.	(LA)	388

MARKETING (Cont'd)

Collection of marketing research
  reports — COVIENSKY, Lana . . . . . (ON) 252
Communications software marketing — CORCHADO, Veronica A. (CA) 245
Community outreach & marketing — WALTER, Virginia A. . . . (CA) 1300
Consumer marketing — UBYSZ, Priscilla M. . . . . (CT) 1267
  GROSVENOR, Philip G. . . (OH) 473
Database creation & marketing — HAWKINS, John W. . . . . (IN) 514
Database development & marketing — TOWNLEY, Richard L. . . (NY) 1253
Database marketing — GABOR, John M. . . . . . (NY) 411
  ELSTON, Andrew S. . . . . (PA) 346
  GOSLING, Carolyn . . . . . (VA) 453
  SULLIVAN, Michael M. . . (VA) 1208
  BILLINGSLEY, Andrew G. . (ON) 96
Database marketing & development — GAGNE, Frank . . . . (ON) 412
Database marketing & sales — PAPPALARDO, Marcia J. (IL) 939
Defense marketing information
  systems — MAUTER, George A. . . . (NY) 787
Direct mail marketing — PHILLIPS, Angela B. . . . (NY) 967
  WORTON, Geoffrey P. . . (NY) 1369
Direct marketing — WALSH, Mark L. . . . . . . (CT) 1300
Direct marketing & continuities — KING, Timothy B. . . . . . (NY) 652
Direct marketing & sales management — JOHNSON, Richard K. . . (MD) 608
Direct marketing, creation — HUBBARD, Roy . . . . . . (NY) 568
Domestic & international marketing — SABOSIK, Patricia E. . . (CT) 1073
End-user marketing applications — MOYER, Barbara A. . . . . (CA) 874
Export marketing management — OVEREYNDER, Rombout
  E. . . . . (NET) 931
Family planning, population, soc mktg — WILLSON, Katherine H. . (CT) 1349
Food marketing — MARTIN, Irmgarde D. . . . (TX) 776
Food marketing & research — SWANSON, Mary A. . . . (NY) 1213
Gateway sales & marketing — GROSSMAN, Allen N. . . . (NJ) 473
General business, marketing &
  humanities — BAUGH, L S. . . . . (IL) 65
Government purchasing & marketing — KEATING, Michael F. . . . (OH) 633
Information economics & marketing — YOUNG, Peter R. . . . . . (DC) 1383
Information management & marketing — HARMON, Glynn . . . . . (TX) 502
Information marketing — HANEY, Kevin M. . . . . . (NJ) 495
Information marketing projects — VAN HALM, Johan . . . . . (NET)1275
Information sales & marketing — BARTLETT, Jay P. . . . . . (NY) 61
Information service marketing — WEAVER, Maggie . . . . . (ON) 1312
Information services marketing — TRAUTMAN, Maryellen . (DC) 1254
  BINGHAM, Kathleen S. . (NY) 97
  MITTERMEYER, Diane . . (PQ) 850
International business & marketing — HERMAN, Marsha . . . . . (NY) 531
International marketing — SMITH, Richard A. . . . . (CA) 1159
  WORTON, Geoffrey P. . . (NY) 1369
  TAYLOR, William R. . . . . (TN) 1229
International marketing research — TAYLOR, Alice J. . . . . . . (CA) 1226
Legal information marketing — HALL, Brian H. . . . . . . (CO) 487
Library marketing — MARKEY, Penny S. . . . . (CA) 771
  RAZE, Nasus B. . . . . . . (CA) 1012
  DONOHUE, Christine N. . (CT) 311
  WILSON, Charlotte A. . . (IL) 1350
  KING, Alan S. . . . . (ME) 650
  ANDERSON, Rebekah E. . (MN) 25
  ROMANASKY, Marcia C. (NJ) 1052
  ST. CLAIR, Guy . . . . . . (NY) 1075
  TOSTEVIN, Patricia A. . . (WA) 1252
Library marketing & promotion — SIMPSON, F T. . . . . . . (IA) 1141
Library promotion & marketing — EASTMAN, Ann H. . . . . . (VA) 333
Library services marketing — WOOD, Richard C. . . . . (TX) 1365
LRC marketing — MCLAREN, M B. . . . . . (NM) 813
Market & marketing research — OLSEN, Stephen . . . . . (MN) 922
Marketing — CORCHADO, Veronica A. (CA) 245
  HEDDEN, Judy A. . . . . . (CA) 520
  SANNWALD, William W. (CA) 1081
  SCHRIBER, James E. . . . (CA) 1100
  TARTER, Blodwen . . . . (CA) 1224
  VUGRINECZ, Anna E. . . (CA) 1289
  WOODS, Lawrence A. . . (CA) 1367
  ARMITAGE, Constance . (CO) 32
  WALTERS, Suzanne . . . (CO) 1301
  STONE, Dennis J. . . . . . (CT) 1197
  BATTAGLIA, Richard D. . (DC) 64
  RESNIK, Linda I. . . . . . (DC) 1024
  BURROWS, Suzetta C. . (FL) 163
  HARDT, James R. . . . . . (FL) 500
  BREEN, Joanell C. . . . . (IL) 131
  MULLER, Karen . . . . . . (IL) 877

MARKETING (Cont'd)

Marketing — TAKACS, Sharon N. . . . . (IL) 1220
  GILL, John H. . . . . (IN) 435
  ISCA, Joseph J. . . . . . . (IN) 585
  LEVINSON, Gail . . . . . . (MA) 721
  PERRY, Guest . . . . (MA) 960
  DUDLEY, Robyn A. . . . . (MD) 323
  FRANK, Robyn C. . . . . . (MD) 397
  GOTTLIEB, Robert A. . . . (ME) 453
  MARTIN, Patricia W. . . . (MI) 777
  LESLIE, Donald S. . . . . (MN) 718
  MEISSNER, Edie A. . . . . (MN) 822
  OLSON, Chris D. . . . . . (MN) 922
  MCGINN, Howard F. . . . (NC) 806
  CLARK, Joan . . . . (NJ) 217
  LEVY, Louise R. . . . . . . (NJ) 721
  LOGAN, Harold J. . . . . . (NJ) 737
  PIKE, Christine M. . . . . (NJ) 972
  COVINGTON, Robert D. . (NV) 252
  BOWMAN, James K. . . . (NY) 121
  BURKE, J L. . . . . (NY) 160
  FEUERSTEIN, Robin . . . (NY) 374
  HOWITT, Jeff . . . . (NY) 566
  KACHALA, Bohdanna I. . (NY) 621
  OLEARY, Martha H. . . . . (NY) 920
  VITART, Jane A. . . . . . . (NY) 1286
  WILLNER, Richard A. . . . (NY) 1349
  CHRISTOU, Corilee S. . . (OH) 212
  DAVIS, Denyvetta . . . . . (OK) 278
  GRAHAM, Deborah L. . . (OR) 456
  SUDDUTH, Susan F. . . . (OR) 1206
  ELIAS, Arthur W. . . . . . (PA) 342
  SCHWEITZER, Margaret
  C. . . . . (PA) 1105
  CARROLL, Bonnie C. . . . (TN) 187
  LEHMANN, Edward J. . . (VA) 713
  MCLANE, Kathleen . . . . (VA) 813
  ROTHSCHILD, M C. . . . (VA) 1060
  RYAN, R P. . . . . (VA) 1071
  OAKE, Rhena E. . . . . . . (AB) 913
  GUHERIDGE, Allison A. . (ON) 476
Marketing, advertising & sales — CORNICK, Ron . . . . (IL) 247
Marketing, advertising, public relations — BETTENCOURT, Nancy J. (CO) 92
Marketing & advertising — SHIRASAWA, Sharon V. . (CA) 1131
Marketing & advertising databases — BUSSEY, Holly J. . . . . . (NY) 165
Marketing & business databases — LEMON, Nancy A. . . . . (OH) 715
  VIXIE, Anne C. . . . . (OR) 1286
Marketing & demographic — MCWILLIAM, Deborah A. (OH) 818
Marketing & direct mail — DYER, Carolyn A. . . . . . (CT) 330
Marketing & marketing research — FRIEND, Gary I. . . . . . . (DC) 404
  AHERN, Camille P. . . . . (NH) 8
Marketing & merchandising — COUSINS, Gloria D. . . . . (NC) 252
Marketing & planning — WEINGAND, Darlene E. . (WI) 1318
Marketing & public relations — FEINBERG, Beryl L. . . . . (DC) 368
  KIES, Cosette N. . . . . . (IL) 647
  LEWIS, Thomas F. . . . . (MA) 724
  PECK, Shirley S. . . . . . . (MD) 953
  MUETH, Elizabeth C. . . . (MO) 875
  WALTERS, Carol G. . . . (NC) 1301
  SWEENEY, Richard T. . . (NY) 1215
  CRAUMER, Patricia A. . . (PA) 255
  BROWN, Carol J. . . . . . (TX) 142
  MAIOLI, Jerry R. . . . . . . (WA) 762
  LACROIX, Yvon A. . . . . . (PQ) 687
Marketing & publicity — ASU, Glynis V. . . . . (WI) 37
Marketing & sales — MALCOLM, J P. . . . . . . (MI) 762
  JAMIESON, Peter V. . . . (NY) 593
  KOCHOFF, Stephen T. . . (NY) 667
  MILLER, Frank W. . . . . . (NY) 837
  REED, Buzz . . . . (OH) 1014
Marketing & strategic planning — VANCE, Julia M. . . . . . . (MD) 1273
Marketing archives & library services — SYKES, Stephanie L. . . . (PQ) 1217
Marketing bibliographic products — STEVENS, Roberta A. . . (DC) 1191
Marketing books — TAYLOR, George A. . . . (DC) 1226
Marketing CD-ROM & online products — HUDES, Nan . . . . (NY) 569
Marketing communications — OJALA, Marydee P. . . . . (KS) 919
  KANE, Jean B. . . . . (MA) 624
  SEITZ, Robert J. . . . . . . (NY) 1113

MARKETING (Cont'd)

Entry	Name	State	Page
Marketing communications, strategic plng	WASERSTEIN, Gina S.	(PA)	1307
Marketing consulting	HITCHENS, Howard B.	(DE)	544
Marketing data systems	SEULOWITZ, Lois	(NY)	1117
Marketing database consultant services	CHAPMAN, Kathleen A.	(WA)	202
Marketing databases	MASON, Dorothy L.	(IN)	781
	GEER, Elizabeth F.	(MA)	425
	ROSEN, Theresa H.	(PA)	1055
Marketing databases & searching	LINEPENSEL, Kenneth C.	(IN)	730
Marketing electronic information	ARNOLD, Stephen E.	(KY)	34
Marketing for librarians	ROGERS, Nancy H.	(AL)	1050
Marketing for libraries	FAYNZILBERG, Irina	(IL)	367
Marketing for public libraries	LUEDER, Dianne B.	(IL)	747
	EISNER, Joseph	(NY)	341
	CORBUS, Lawrence J.	(OH)	245
Marketing in private practice	CLARKE, Elba C.	(GA)	218
Marketing information	RANDOLPH, Kevin H.	(CA)	1007
	BERLIET, Nathalie B.	(CT)	87
	PALMER, Shirley	(CT)	937
	MURPHY, Therese B.	(IL)	881
	OKEY, Susan T.	(IN)	920
	MCDONALD, Dennis D.	(MD)	802
	CHANG, Bernadine A.	(NJ)	200
	MOLITERNO, Daniel A.	(NY)	853
Marketing information & library service	ALIX, Cleta M.	(CA)	13
Marketing information collections	BURROWS, Shirley	(NY)	163
Marketing information products	GERSH, Barbara S.	(CA)	429
Marketing information services	BALL, Thomas W.	(DC)	52
	TAYLOR, George A.	(DC)	1226
	CROCKER, Susan O.	(NY)	259
	TUCKER, Laura R.	(NY)	1262
	DUBEAU, Pierre	(PQ)	321
	ARMSTRONG, Denise M.	(SAF)	32
Marketing information services & systems	LAROSA, Sharon M.	(MA)	698
Marketing information services, systems	EL-DUWEINI, Aadel K.	(EGY)	342
Marketing library products & services	ELLSWORTH, Dianne J.	(CA)	345
Marketing library services	HARRIS, Susan C.	(CA)	506
	KUSZMAUL, Marcia J.	(IL)	685
	DEL SORDO, Jean S.	(MD)	290
	MARSHALL, Mary E.	(OH)	774
	SOUCIE, Yan Y.	(OR)	1169
	INGRAHAM, Alice L.	(PA)	582
	LAVKULICH, Joanne	(AB)	704
Marketing non-profit agencies	RASSAM, Cynthia K.	(NM)	1009
Marketing non-profit services	LEISNER, Anthony B.	(IL)	714
Marketing of information	KEON, Edward F.	(NJ)	643
Marketing of information services	FERNALD, Anne C.	(MA)	373
Marketing of library services	JOHNSON, Stephen C.	(OH)	609
	SAVARD, Rejean	(PQ)	1085
Marketing of services, presentations	CURRAN, William M.	(PQ)	266
Marketing online database systems	POOL, Madlyn K.	(VA)	982
Marketing online services	JONES, Michael W.	(VA)	614
Marketing photos to public institutions	HENDERSON, Ellen B.	(CA)	526
Marketing professional services	FROST, Roxanna	(WA)	406
Marketing programs	LUTHER, M J.	(GA)	750
Marketing promotion	GAREN, Robert J.	(MI)	418
Marketing public libraries	MOORE, Thomas L.	(NC)	861
Marketing, public relations	SPIEGELMAN, Barbara M.	(PA)	1174
Marketing research	MARKS, Larry	(CA)	771
	GASKINS, Stephen D.	(GA)	421
	CHAPMAN, Ruby M.	(IL)	202
	KILBERG, Jacqueline L.	(NY)	648
	WASERSTEIN, Gina S.	(PA)	1307
	BALDWIN, Mark F.	(RI)	52
	FLESHMAN, Nancy A.	(TX)	384
Marketing research & analysis	EVANS, Shirley A.	(OH)	358
Marketing research resources management	SEULOWITZ, Lois	(NY)	1117
Marketing sales & customer service	KINLEY, Jo H.	(DC)	652
Marketing searching	RATHGEBER, Jo F.	(NC)	1009
Marketing services	BIBBY, Elizabeth A.	(GA)	94
Marketing special libraries	LUPPINO, Julie B.	(SC)	749
Marketing support databases	POWELL, Timothy W.	(NY)	989
Marketing systems	BAUMGARTNER, Robert M.	(OH)	66

MARKETING (Cont'd)

Entry	Name	State	Page
Marketing, technical liaison	ZIRPOLO, Frank	(NY)	1390
Marketing technical periodicals	FERRERE, Cathy M.	(NY)	373
Marketing the library	KAPLAN, Paul M.	(IL)	626
Marketing the public library	CAMERON, Bruce	(SK)	174
Marketing the small library	GARRISON, Michael G.	(OH)	420
Marketing to libraries	BIANCO, David P.	(MI)	94
Non-ferrous metal marketing	GOODINGS, Sally A.	(ON)	449
Online databases marketing	DAWSON, Debra A.	(CA)	282
Online development & marketing	ANDREWS, Chris C.	(CT)	26
Online information marketing	ROACH, Eddie D.	(OK)	1037
Online systems marketing	GABOR, John M.	(NY)	411
Online training & marketing	HOCK, Randolph E.	(MA)	545
Product development & marketing	JOHNSON, Emily P.	(MD)	604
Product marketing	JAIN, Nem C.	(MA)	592
Product rollouts & marketing	CORVESE, Lisa A.	(NY)	248
Public relations & marketing	CARTLEDGE, Ellen G.	(CT)	190
	JOHNSON, Veronica A.	(MI)	609
	ELDREDGE, Jonathan D.	(NM)	342
Public relations, marketing	SAULMON, Sharon A.	(OK)	1084
Publishing & marketing children's books	MASON, H J.	(NY)	781
Real estate online database marketing	JENKINS, George A.	(FL)	597
Reference book publishing & marketing	WHITELEY, Sandra M.	(IL)	1333
Reference library marketing	LEINBACH, Anne E.	(PA)	714
Reference, technical & marketing	GARVEY, Nancy G.	(NJ)	421
Sales & marketing	BARKALOW, Pat A.	(CA)	56
	POOLEY, Christopher G.	(MA)	983
	ARTHUR, Christine	(NY)	35
	BAILEY, Joe A.	(NY)	46
	MELKIN, Audrey D.	(NY)	822
	SOLOMON, Samuel H.	(NY)	1166
Sales & marketing online services	CLARK, Rick	(NJ)	218
Sales, marketing & publishing	BECK, Arthur R.	(CT)	71
Sales, marketing, product development	ALESSI, Dana L.	(TX)	11
Scientific & biomedical database mktg	ZAJDEL, George J.	(PA)	1385
Social science database marketing	ZAJDEL, George J.	(PA)	1385
Soybean production, mktg, & utilization	GIBSON, Marianne	(MO)	432
Strategic planning & marketing	OLSON, Christine A.	(MD)	922
	BERGFELD, C D.	(NY)	86
	PARKER, Arthur D.	(ON)	941
US & international marketing	MIELE, Madeline F.	(MA)	833

MASS

Entry	Name	State	Page
Mass media information	ALLEN, Nancy H.	(MI)	15
Mass transit information	KANE, Deborah A.	(TX)	624

MASTER'S

Entry	Name	State	Page
Master degree program	WILLIAMS, Carroll W.	(NM)	1342
Professional education at Master's level	MATARAZZO, James M.	(MA)	783

MATERIALS (See also Audiovisual, Books, Collections, Ephemerae, Film, Manuscripts, Media, Memorabilia, Monographs, Non-Book, Non-Print, Print, Recordings, Video)

Entry	Name	State	Page
Acquisition of library materials	BRADFORD, Daniel	(DC)	125
Acquisition of materials on Japan	MAKINO, Yasuko	(IL)	762
Acquisitions & materials processing	LESNIK, Pauline	(NY)	718
Acquisitions, children's materials	CORLEE, Lisa	(OK)	246
Acquisitions of legal materials	STOPPEL, Ellen K.	(IA)	1198
Acquisitions of materials	ZULA, Floyd M.	(LA)	1391
Acquisitions, young adult materials	CORLEE, Lisa	(OK)	246
Adolescent materials	MCDONALD, Frances B.	(MN)	802
Adult literacy materials	GOLDBERG, Rhoda L.	(TX)	444
Adult materials selection	NICHTER, Alan	(FL)	902
Adult new reader materials	MCGRIFF, Mary E.	(NC)	808
Adult reading interests & materials	FERSTL, Kenneth L.	(TX)	374
Antiquarian materials	SHARP, Linda C.	(OH)	1122
Appraisal of archival materials	BEST, Rickey D.	(AL)	92
Architectural special library materials	STEWARD, Martha J.	(CA)	1192
Archival material automation	SMITH, William K.	(MI)	1161
Archival materials	GRIFFIN, Thomas E.	(CA)	469
	WATANABE, Ruth T.	(NY)	1308
	KIRKALI, Meral	(WI)	654

MATERIALS (Cont'd)

Subject	Name	State	Page
Archival materials conservation	ELLISON, J T.	(CO)	345
Arms race materials & reference	MEYER, Jimmy E.	(OH)	830
Art libraries & fine art materials	GILBERT, Gail R.	(KY)	433
Art material cataloging	HERMAN, Elizabeth	(CA)	531
Asian materials	RIEDY, Allen J.	(HI)	1033
Asian materials acquisition	CHAN, Moses C.	(NC)	199
Asian materials cataloging	CHAN, Moses C.	(NC)	199
Audiovisual equipment & materials	LEDOUX, Mary E.	(OH)	709
Audiovisual equipment, materials	HERBERT, Barbara R.	(NJ)	530
Audiovisual material	WILLIAMS, Helen E.	(KY)	1343
	HUDZIK, Robert T.	(OH)	570
Audiovisual material cataloging	TRAVILLIAN, Mary W.	(IA)	1254
	ESMAN, Michael D.	(MD)	354
	MCENTEE, Mary F.	(TX)	804
Audiovisual material selection	WOOD, Irene P.	(IL)	1364
Audiovisual materials	JEFFERY, Phyllis D.	(AL)	596
	BERCIK, Mary E.	(CA)	84
	CROSS, Claudette S.	(CA)	260
	BROGDEN, Stephen R.	(IA)	139
	COBB, Marilyn R.	(IL)	225
	LUKASIK, Marion F.	(IL)	747
	TEO, Elizabeth A.	(IL)	1231
	VACCARO, William J.	(IL)	1270
	ANJIER, Jennifer S.	(LA)	28
	YOUNG, Ruth H.	(LA)	1383
	CLOHERTY, Lauretta M.	(MA)	223
	CASSARO, James P.	(NY)	193
	EDWARDS, Harriet M.	(NY)	337
	GURIEVITCH, Grania B.	(NY)	478
	USES, Ann K.	(PA)	1270
	BELL, David B.	(SC)	76
	HAMLIN, Lisa K.	(TN)	493
	COOK, Anne S.	(TX)	239
	DUBIEL, Laura R.	(TX)	321
	HALL, Halbert W.	(TX)	487
	LEVINE, Harriet L.	(TX)	720
	BIDD, Donald W.	(PQ)	94
	SAVARD, Rejean	(PQ)	1085
	CHUO, Josephine Y.	(TAI)	213
Audiovisual materials & service	SHAW, Richard N.	(DE)	1124
Audiovisual materials & services	HURLEY, John	(NJ)	577
Audiovisual materials cataloging	CLEMENT, Patsy	(UT)	221
Audiovisual materials for schools	ELLIS, Caryl A.	(AZ)	344
Audiovisual materials organization	SHEFFO, Belinda M.	(PA)	1125
Audiovisual materials production	CARLISLE, Carol A.	(CT)	182
Audiovisual materials selection	SHEFFO, Belinda M.	(PA)	1125
Bilingual materials	DALE, Doris C.	(IL)	270
Binarization of archival materials	GILHEANY, Stephen J.	(CA)	435
Books & audiovisual materials selection	SCHILL, Julie G.	(PA)	1092
Budgeting, library materials	FROMMEYER, L R.	(OH)	405
Business & economic materials	MARKHAM, Scott C.	(MN)	771
Business material	FOWLES, Alison C.	(PQ)	394
Business materials	PIERCE, Linda I.	(AK)	971
	HARRIS, Linda S.	(AL)	505
	HICKS, James M.	(MO)	537
Business materials reference	CANNING, Joan M.	(NY)	178
Business reference materials	GORDON, Donna M.	(AB)	451
California legal legislative materials	GOMEZ, Cheryl J.	(CA)	447
Cartographic materials	SELMER, Marsha L.	(IL)	1114
	SELDIN, Daniel T.	(IN)	1113
	ALLISON, Brent	(MN)	17
	WALSTROM, Jon L.	(MN)	1300
	CRISSINGER, John D.	(TX)	259
	TESSIER, Yves	(PQ)	1233
Cartographic materials cataloging	COOMBS, James A.	(MO)	241
Cartographic materials reference service	COOMBS, James A.	(MO)	241
Cartographic mtrl collection development	WYMAN, Kathleen M.	(ON)	1375
Cartography materials librarianship	LARSGAARD, Mary L.	(CO)	698
Catalog district library materials	EMERICK, John L.	(PA)	347
Cataloging accessioned material	RHEAUME, John L.	(MD)	1025
Cataloging Africana materials	NIEKAMP, Dorothy R.	(IN)	903
Cataloging & preserving archival mtrls	FALCONE, Elena C.	(NY)	362
Cataloging & processing of materials	BIANCHI, Karen F.	(WA)	93
Cataloging audiovisual materials	URBANSKI, Verna P.	(FL)	1269
	HARTSOCK, Ralph M.	(PA)	508
Cataloging children's materials	WINKEL, Lois	(NC)	1355

MATERIALS (Cont'd)

Subject	Name	State	Page
Cataloging civil engineering materials	REINALDO DA SILVA, Joann T.	(MB)	1021
Cataloging European languages material	PHILLIPS, Richard F.	(NJ)	969
Cataloging foreign language material	INGIBERGSSON, Asgeir	(AB)	582
Cataloging law materials	KORKMAS, Carolyn C.	(TX)	671
Cataloging legal materials	MITTAN, Rhonda L.	(CA)	850
	GULSTAD, Wilma B.	(MO)	477
	MITTEN, Lisa A.	(PA)	850
	NASSERDEN, Marilyn D.	(AB)	889
Cataloging materials	SCHILL, Julie G.	(PA)	1092
	CHISUM, Emmett D.	(WY)	209
Cataloging Methodist-related materials	BERG, Richard R.	(OH)	84
Cataloging Middle East materials	BEZIRGAN, Basima	(IL)	93
Cataloging music & audiovisual materials	SLOMSKI, Monica J.	(CT)	1150
Cataloging music materials	PALKOVIC, Mark A.	(OH)	935
Cataloging non-book materials	BUSER, Robin B.	(KY)	165
	MEYER, Kenton T.	(PA)	830
Cataloging non-print materials	ADCOCK, Donald C.	(IL)	6
	GIBBS, Mary E.	(IL)	431
	WHYDE, John S.	(OH)	1335
Cataloging of graphic materials	HOGAN, Kristine K.	(NY)	549
Cataloging of legal materials	RUIZ-VALERA, Phoebe L.	(NY)	1067
Cataloguing of music materials	COLQUHOUN, Joan E.	(ON)	234
Cataloging of Slavic materials	VERYHA, Wasyl	(ON)	1283
Cataloging original materials	SCHUMANN, Iris T.	(TX)	1103
Cataloging Spanish materials	LABODDA, Marsha J.	(TX)	686
Cataloging visual & sound materials	DRIESSEN, Karen C.	(MT)	320
Cataloging visual non-print materials	VISKOCHIL, Larry A.	(IL)	1285
Celtic language materials	MILNE, Dorothy J.	(NF)	845
Chemistry, materials	SLOAN, Maureen G.	(OR)	1149
Children's & young adult mtrls selection	ROBERTS, Sallie H.	(OH)	1041
Children's library materials	MCGREW, Mary L.	(IA)	808
Children's literature & materials	WILLIAMS, Helen E.	(MD)	1343
Children's material special collections	DURSTON, Corinne L.	(BC)	329
Children's materials	GREESON-SCHARDL, Tamra J.	(GA)	465
	BLANK, Annette C.	(MD)	104
	ROBERTS, Susan P.	(MD)	1041
	WINKEL, Lois	(NC)	1355
	PASHEL, Susan M.	(PA)	945
Children's materials & programming	MACRURY, Mary E.	(NS)	758
Children's materials & services	STANTON, Vida C.	(WI)	1181
Children's materials col development	HODGES, Lois F.	(NY)	546
	SMITH, Valerie M.	(OH)	1161
Children's reference materials	DRACH, Priscilla L.	(OH)	318
Cinema materials	O'CONNELL, Brian E.	(NY)	915
Computerized files & library materials	BENNETT, Laura B.	(IL)	82
Computerizing print & non-print mtrls	BIANCHINO, Cecelia	(IN)	94
Conservation of library materials	LUNDEEN, Gerald W.	(HI)	748
	FERGUSON, Bonnie E.	(IL)	372
	HENDERSON, William T.	(IL)	527
	SMITH, Richard D.	(IL)	1159
	DARLING, Pamela W.	(NY)	275
	SCOTT, Sharon A.	(OH)	1108
	COLLISTER, Edward A.	(PQ)	233
Conservation of print materials	COUPER, Richard W.	(NJ)	251
Coordinating materials selection	ZIEGLER, Fred	(AB)	1388
Corporate materials	MERKIN, David	(NY)	826
Creative use of audiovisual materials	DAY, Martha T.	(VT)	282
Current awareness resource materials	SEXTON, Spencer K.	(NC)	1118
Curriculum materials	DURAN, Karin J.	(CA)	328
	STAVIS, Ruth L.	(MA)	1183
	CLEAVER, Betty P.	(OH)	220
	POVSIC, Frances F.	(OH)	987
	BROWN, David K.	(AB)	143
	HERSCOVITCH, Pearl	(AB)	533
Curriculum materials & media	JARRELL, James R.	(NC)	594
Curriculum materials center	HUEBNER, Mary A.	(NY)	570
Curriculum materials centers	RUDIE, Helen M.	(MN)	1065
Curriculum materials control	CLARK, Alice S.	(CA)	216
Curriculum materials K-12	KING, Kathryn L.	(MI)	651
	HERBERT, Barbara R.	(NJ)	530
Curriculum teaching materials	FISHER, Joan W.	(MD)	381
Curriculum-related material purchasing	SKELLY, Laurie J.	(MN)	1146
Database design for materials	LOWELL, Brian V.	(IL)	744

MATERIALS (Cont'd)

Descriptive cataloging, legal materials HAWKINS, Sandra J. . . . . (DC) 514
Descriptive cataloging, Slavic
  materials MORGAN, Robert C. . . . (VA) 864
Development of educational materials MOSELEY, Cameron S. . (NY) 870
Disaster recovery of archival materials MARRELLI, Nancy M. . . (PQ) 773
East Asian materials KLEIN, Kenneth D. . . . . . (CA) 659
Editing of technical materials WOODLOCK, Stephanie . (PA) 1366
Education & industry learning material LESURE, Alan B. . . . . . . (NY) 718
Education materials SIBLEY, Carol H. . . . . . . (MN) 1134
   ST. AMANT, Robert . . . . (ON) 1075
Educational materials CARR, Jo A. . . . . (WI) 185
   BALDWIN, David A. . . . (WY) 51
Educational materials design WALD, Marlena M. . . . . . (GA) 1294
Educational materials for teachers MAY, Frank C. . . . . (CA) 788
Elementary, secondary school
  materials PIEHL, Kathleen K. . . . . . (MN) 971
Engineering & materials reference WOODLOCK, Stephanie . (PA) 1366
Engineering material information SHINER, Sharon L. . . . . . (NJ) 1130
Engineering materials COLLISHAW, Jackie J. . (NJ) 233
English & continental material ZALL, Elisabeth W. . . . . . (CA) 1386
English material on Chinese law LUNG, Mon Y. . . . . (KS) 748
Ephemeral materials PEREZ, Maria L. . . . . . . (FL) 958
Ethnic materials for children BEILKE, Patricia F. . . . . (IN) 75
Evaluation of library materials MILLER, Margaret S. . . . (CA) 840
Exhibition & programming of AV
  materials SCHREIBMAN, Fay C. . . (NY) 1099
Federal & state legislative materials CAMMARATA, Paul J. . . (KY) 175
Federal legal material MOSS, Karen M. . . . . . (MA) 872
Federal legal materials EWING, Florence E. . . . . (CA) 359
Foreign language materials NAVARRO, Frank A. . . . (CA) 889
   LANDIS, Dennis C. . . . . (RI) 693
   KAYE, Barbara J. . . . . . . (ON) 632
Foreign language non-book materials MCELWAIN, William . . . (IL) 804
Foreign legal materials RAUCH, Anne . . . . (NY) 1010
Gift materials HILLMAN, Kathy R. . . . . (TX) 541
Government library material
  acquisitions BLACKBURN, Clayton E. (NY) 102
Handicapped services & materials THOMAS, James L. . . . . (TX) 1237
Hazardous material data KAZIMIR, Edward O. . . (NJ) 632
Hazardous materials WEBSTER, James K. . . . (NY) 1314
Hazardous materials databases TUCKER, Clark F. . . . . . (MD) 1261
Hispanic & Ethnic materials AYALA, John L. . . . . (CA) 42
Historical materials MCGUIRE, Brian . . . . . (DC) 808
Humanities materials ROSENBERG, Melvin H. . (CA) 1056
Indexing of petroleum-related material TERLIZZI, Joseph M. . . (NY) 1232
Indexing scientific materials GHOSH, Subhra . . . . (NY) 430
Industrial materials VENNE, Louise . . . . (PQ) 1282
Information & material acquisitions CARPENTER, Dale . . . . (NY) 184
Instructional materials BOULA, Lillian Y. . . . . . . (FL) 119
   GROSS, Iva H. . . . . (TX) 472
Instructional materials center JOHNSON, Scott R. . . . . (MS) 609
Instructional materials centers KIRKENDALL, Carolyn A. (MI) 654
   OLSON, Dennis H. . . . . . (WI) 922
Instructional materials selection WOBBE, Jean . . . . (CA) 1359
Instructional materials, teacher educ PRILLAMAN, Susan M. . (NC) 993
Japanese library materials KANEKO, Hideo . . . . (CT) 625
Japanese material collection
  development GONNAMI, Tsuneharu . . (BC) 447
Juvenile materials RYLANDER, Carolyn S. . (OK) 1072
K-12 educational materials GOWDY, Laura E. . . . . . . (IL) 455
Latin American materials acquisitions BALLANTYNE, Lygia M. . (FL) 53
Latvian materials BUNDZA, Maira . . . . (MI) 157
Law material cataloging REID, Marianne E. . . . . . (SK) 1019
Law materials reference TENOR, Randell B. . . . . . (PA) 1231
Legal material cataloging HILLMANN, Diane I. . . . . (NY) 541
Legal materials WANG, Connie . . . . (CA) 1302
   DOWLER, John W. . . . . (FL) 315
   FISHER, Scott L. . . . . . . (NJ) 381
   CHUNG, Catherine A. . . . (VA) 213
   DUFFUS, Sylvia J. . . . . . (AB) 323
Legal materials cataloging IOANID, Aurora S. . . . . . (NY) 583
   ROSENFELD, Joseph S. . (OH) 1056
Legal materials selection TENOR, Randell B. . . . . . (PA) 1231
Legal research & material FOWLES, Alison C. . . . . (PQ) 394
Lib material, acquisition, preservation KALRA, Bhupinder S. . . . (IL) 623
Library material conservation MERKLEY, John P. . . . . (CA) 826
Library materials acquisition SHABOWICH, Stanley A. (TX) 1118
Lib materials & services for children COUGHLIN, Violet L. . . . (PQ) 250
Library materials for children NOONAN, Eileen F. . . . . (IL) 908

MATERIALS (Cont'd)

Library materials for young adults NOONAN, Eileen F. . . . . (IL) 908
Library materials preservation HAVENS, Shirley E. . . . . (NY) 513
Library materials prices LYNDEN, Frederick C. . . (RI) 752
Manuscript & autograph material PETERSON, Scott W. . . (IL) 964
Maritime material culture BUMGARNER, John L. . . (NC) 157
Material retrieval CUNNINGHAM, Mary A. . (NY) 265
Material security & book theft BAHR, Alice H. . . . . (PA) 45
Material selection BONE, Larry E. . . . . (NY) 113
   BEDDOES, Thomas P. . . (PA) 73
   LINDENFELD, Joseph F. . (TN) 729
Material selection & programming BRUNTON, Marilyn H. . . (MN) 151
Material tracking & processing KILLHEFFER, Robert E. . (CT) 648
Materials acquisition FELDER, Jimmie R. . . . . (AL) 369
   KAUFENBERG, Jane M. (MN) 630
   RUSSELL, Sharon A. . . . (NB) 1069
Materials & equipment evaluation OSIER, Donald V. . . . . . (SDA) 928
Materials & services for children BARD, Therese B. . . . . . (HI) 56
   MILLER, Marilyn L. . . . . . (NC) 840
Materials & services for young adults BARD, Therese B. . . . . . (HI) 56
   MILLER, Marilyn L. . . . . . (NC) 840
Materials cataloging & sourcing LOWELL, Brian V. . . . . . (IL) 744
Materials evaluation & selection HOWLAND, Margaret E. . (MA) 566
Materials preparation POUNCY, Mitchell L. . . . (LA) 987
Materials science COOK, Sherry M. . . . . . . (CA) 240
   BONHOMME, Mary S. . . (IN) 114
   LANE, Sandra G. . . . . . . (NY) 694
Materials sciences databases VAUGHAN, Ruth M. . . . (IL) 1280
Materials selection GOEBEL, Heather L. . . . (AZ) 443
   CROOKS, Joyce M. . . . . (CA) 260
   HUND, Flower L. . . . . . . (MO) 574
   BERLIN, Susan T. . . . . . (OH) 87
   HERSTAND, Joellen . . . . (OK) 533
   LATROBE, Kathy H. . . . . (OK) 701
   HOFFMAN, Elizabeth P. . (PA) 547
   TRIPP, Audrey J. . . . . . . (PA) 1257
   COOPER, Jacquelyn B. . (RI) 243
   FOUTS, Judith F. . . . . . . (TX) 393
   PENNER, Elaine C. . . . . (TX) 957
   LAM, Letitia E. . . . . (VA) 689
   WOODALL, Nancy C. . . (VA) 1365
   FUNK, Grace E. . . . . (BC) 410
Materials selection, all media CLARK, Elizabeth K. . . . (MA) 216
Materials selection & cataloging KENT, Rose M. . . . . (OH) 642
Materials selection & reader services TANG, Grace L. . . . . . . (NY) 1222
Materials selection, collection
  devlpmnt THOMPSON, Elizabeth M. (DC) 1239
Materials selection, public libraries LEE, Lauren K. . . . . (GA) 710
Media materials & equipment LINK, Margaret A. . . . . . (NC) 730
Media materials, collections
  development STEVENS, Roberta A. . . (DC) 1191
Medical library materials organization DOLL, Harriet A. . . . . . . (PA) 309
Medical materials WALLEN, Jody H. . . . . . (CA) 1298
   BOEHR, Diane I. . . . . . . (MD) 109
Medical materials cataloging SHRIER, Helene F. . . . . (NY) 1133
Mental health material GROSS, Elinor L. . . . . . (NY) 472
Metallurgical & engineered materials BALDWIN, Eleanor M. . . (OH) 51
Microtext materials RIEBEL, Ellis F. . . . . (PA) 1033
Music material cataloging GOODWIN, Charles B. . . (TX) 450
Music materials MARTIN, John B. . . . . . . (AL) 776
   HOFFMAN, Christine A. . (NY) 547
Music materials acquisitions FALCONER, Joan O. . . . (IA) 362
Music materials & recordings GOODWIN, Charles B. . . (TX) 450
Music materials cataloging ROSS, Mary E. . . . . (MI) 1058
Music materials, cataloging &
  processing MEERVELD, Bert . . . . . . (ON) 821
Music performance materials WELIVER, E D. . . . . (MI) 1321
New Hampshire legal materials RINDEN, Constance T. . . (NH) 1035
Non-book library materials BIVINS, Hulen E. . . . . . . (AL) 100
Non-book material management WEIHS, Jean . . . . (ON) 1317
Non-book materials CHESTER, Claudia J. . . . (CA) 207
   RODICH, Nancy A. . . . . (MS) 1048
   ANGEL, Kenneth E. . . . . (NY) 27
   KLEMPNER, Irving M. . . (NY) 660
   READ, Jean B. . . . . (NY) 1012
   HERRING, Billie G. . . . . (TX) 533
   LIGHTHALL, Lynne I. . . . (BC) 727
   ELLIOTT, Lirlyn J. . . . . . (TRN) 344
Non-book mtrls & microcomputer
  software INTNER, Sheila S. . . . . . (MA) 583

MATERIALS (Cont'd)

Non-book materials classification	HAMDY, Mohamed N. . .	(KWT) 491
Non-book materials online cataloging	KARON, Bernard L.	(MN) 627
Non-print curriculum materials	FISHER, Carolyn H.	(NY) 380
Non-print materials	POIRRIER, Sherry	(MA) 980
	JONES, David E.	(NJ) 612
	SPANGLER, William N. . .	(NJ) 1171
	WILDER, Nancy S.	(TX) 1339
	NORRGARD, Don K. . . .	(ON) 909
Non-print materials collections	JOHNSON, Carolynn K. .	(WA) 603
Northern or polar materials	ALBRIGHT, Donald A. . . .	(NT) 10
Nursing materials	KAMENOFF, Lovisa	(MA) 623
Order & catalog materials	JOHNSON, Elizabeth L. .	(NE) 604
Ordering & catlgng books & non-book mtrl	SPIEGEL, Bertha	(NY) 1174
Organization of library materials	DESSER, Darrilyn	(NY) 296
Organization of materials	YOUNG, Dorothy E.	(PA) 1381
Organizing materials since 1870	DOUET, Madeleine J. . . .	(NY) 313
Organizing miscellaneous materials	JONES, Dora A.	(SD) 612
Original cataloging Slavic materials	KORT, Richard L.	(MA) 672
Out-of-print material	GAGE, Laurie E.	(ENG) 412
Peace materials & reference	MEYER, Jimmy E.	(OH) 830
Popular materials in libraries	MCMULLEN, Charles H. .	(VA) 815
Preservation of documentary materials	YOUNG, Julia M.	(MS) 1382
Preservation of library materials	MERRILL-OLDHAM, Jan	(CT) 827
	CLOONAN, Michele V. . .	(IL) 223
	HENDERSON, William T. .	(IL) 527
	MCNEILL, Janice M.	(IL) 816
	DARLING, Pamela W. . . .	(NY) 275
	PYATT, Timothy D.	(OR) 999
	SAMET, Janet S.	(PA) 1078
	LANDRUM, John H.	(SC) 693
	DAVIS, Susan W.	(TN) 281
	POLLARD, Margaret E. . .	(WI) 981
	WHITCOMB, Dorothy V. .	(WI) 1330
Preservation of materials	SMITH, Ledell B.	(LA) 1157
Preservation of non-book material	ELLISON, John W.	(NY) 345
Preservation of research materials	ROGERS, Rutherford D. .	(CT) 1050
Print & non-print material cataloging	TIWANA, Shah J.	(IL) 1247
Print & non-print materials cataloging	BROWN, Biraj L.	(SDA) 142
Printed & non-printed material catlgng	SZETO, Dorcas C.	(CA) 1218
Processing accessioned material	RHEAUME, Irene M.	(MD) 1025
Processing archival materials	SANDERS, Robert L. . . .	(CA) 1080
	WADE, D J.	(MO) 1290
Processing materials	LONNING, Roger D.	(MN) 740
Processing of archival materials	RABCHUK, Gordon K. . .	(PQ) 1001
Professional materials	LAMBERTH, Linda E. . . .	(TX) 690
Public materials of Philadelphia	BRENNAN, Ellen	(PA) 132
Purchase of nonfiction material	LAMBERT, Sandra L. . . .	(IL) 690
Purchased materials databases	SINE, George H.	(IL) 1143
Purchasing research materials	KELLER, Dorothy B.	(CA) 635
Recorded & braille materials & sources	WILSON, Barbara L. . . .	(RI) 1350
Reference & adult materials	FELTON, Barbara M. . . .	(IN) 370
Reference & research materials	TUDOR, Dean F.	(ON) 1262
Reference materials	MECRAY, Freida S.	(DE) 820
	SKRAMOUSKY, Mary C.	(NJ) 1147
	SCHMALBERG, Aaron . .	(OH) 1094
	SKELLEY, Grant T.	(WA) 1145
Reference materials, teaching, services	STWODAH, M I.	(VA) 1206
Reference services & materials	BUNGE, Charles A.	(WI) 157
Related structural materials	HYSLOP, Marjorie R. . . .	(OH) 580
Research material	CLARK, Audrey M.	(UT) 216
Researching historical material	HAZEL, Debora E.	(NC) 517
Researching material for the elderly	MCCRAY, Evelina W. . . .	(LA) 800
Resource materials on women	SNAPP, Elizabeth M. . . .	(TX) 1162
Reviewing audiovisual materials	RYBARCZYK, Barclay S. .	(NY) 1071
Reviewing genealogical materials	CRAWFORD, Carolyn . .	(CA) 256
Reviewing materials, print & non-print	SELWYN, Laurie	(TX) 1114
Secondary education curriculum materials	LAURITO, Gerard P.	(PA) 703
Secondary library materials selection	MERRELL, Sheila J.	(MO) 826
Selecting materials in sciences	KRONISH, Priscilla T. . .	(NY) 680
Selecting popular materials	CROW, Rebecca N.	(TX) 261
Selection & acquisition of library mtrls	SMITH, Cynthia A.	(OH) 1153
Selection & acquisitions of materials	MORRIS, Trisha A.	(OH) 867
Selection & evaluation of non-print mtrl	AHN, Hyonah K.	(IL) 8

MATERIALS (Cont'd)

Selection of acquisition materials	BIANCHI, Karen F.	(WA) 93
Selection of children's materials	FORD, Marcia K.	(IN) 389
Selection of library materials	PANKAKE, Marcia J. . . .	(MN) 938
Selection of materials	PLOWDEN, Martha W. . .	(GA) 978
	GEORGE, Linda H.	(OH) 427
Selection of materials for schools	POOLE, Rebecca S.	(CO) 983
Selection of print & non-print material	GREENFIELD, Judith C. .	(NY) 464
Selection of science materials	REED, Virginia R.	(IL) 1015
Selection school library materials	HAMMEL, Philip J.	(SK) 493
Semiconductor equipment & materials	SHERMAN, Roger S. . . .	(CA) 1128
Serials, AV materials, automation	SOPER, Mary E.	(WA) 1168
Services & materials management	EDWARDS, Andrea Y. . .	(DC) 337
Sexism in school materials	NILSEN, Alleen P.	(AZ) 904
Slavic materials	PRONEVITZ, Gregory . .	(OH) 995
Sources of cartographic materials	MINTON, James O.	(AZ) 846
Spanish language materials	NAVARRO, Frank A. . . .	(CA) 889
	ANDERSON, Mark	(TX) 24
Spanish materials	CALIMANO, Ivan E.	(TX) 173
Special material cataloging	KROSCH, Penelope S. . .	(MN) 680
Supplementary materials for classroom	WRIGHT, Carolyn R. . . .	(OK) 1370
Teaching materials	ANDERSON, Virginia L. .	(IN) 25
Technical material selection	WILLIAMS, Alexander . .	(FL) 1341
Theatre materials	O'CONNELL, Brian E. . .	(NY) 915
Theological materials cataloging	RZECZKOWSKI, Eugene M.	(DC) 1072
Tibetan language materials	SCHOENING, Jeffrey D. .	(MA) 1098
Training & training materials	MARBAN, Ricio	(GUA) 768
US Bureau of Census materials	MACKEY, Wendy W. . . .	(MA) 757
Videocassettes & AV materials	SCHOLTZ, James C. . . .	(IL) 1098
Visual & sound material acquisition	DRIESSEN, Karen C. . . .	(MT) 320
Visual & sound material reference	DRIESSEN, Karen C. . . .	(MT) 320
Visual materials	RYAN, Diane M.	(IL) 1070
Vocational materials	AYALA, John L.	(CA) 42
Vocational materials development	WHITE, Charles R.	(CT) 1330
Western European language materials	NEVIN, Susanne	(MN) 898
Wholesaling of audio & video materials	JACOBS, Peter J.	(CA) 590
Young adult & children's materials	STURGEON, Mary C. . . .	(AR) 1205
Young adult books & materials	WILLIAMS, Helen E. . . .	(MD) 1343
Young adult materials	ROSENBERG, Melvin H. .	(CA) 1056
	DEQUIN, Henry C.	(IL) 293
	ZVIRIN, Stephanie H. . . .	(IL) 1392
	WHITLOW, Cherrill M. . .	(NM) 1333
	PASHEL, Susan M.	(PA) 945
	TYSON, Christy	(WA) 1267
Young adult materials & services	MITCHELL, Carolyn	(CO) 848
	ROGERS, Joann V.	(KY) 1049
	WRIGHT, John G.	(AB) 1371
Young adult services & materials	SHAEVEL, Evelyn F. . . .	(IL) 1118

MATHEMATICS (See also Statistics)

Computer science & math	TIMBERS, Jill G.	(MI) 1245
Mathematical analysis	ROBB, Thomas W.	(DC) 1038
Mathematical statistics	SEILER, Susan L.	(FL) 1112
	PAUSCH, Lois M.	(IL) 950
Mathematics	GRIFFIN, Michael D. . . .	(CA) 468
	VEITH, Charles R.	(OK) 1281
	ZEIDNER, Christine M. . .	(UT) 1387
	MURDOCH, Martha T. . .	(WA) 879
Math & computer science databases	DAVIDOFF, Gary N.	(IL) 276
Mathematics & science instruction	STRAWN, Aimee W.	(IL) 1201
Math databases online searching	CARTER, Jackson H. . . .	(NM) 189
Mathematics, physics, statistics	CZIFFRA, Peter	(NJ) 269
Mathematics reference	SCHNOOR, Harriet E. . .	(IL) 1098
	FUNKHOUSER, Richard L.	(IN) 410
Mathematics, statistics, computer sci	PIERCE, Miriam D.	(PA) 971
Mathematics subject specialist	ANDERSON, Nancy D. . .	(IL) 24
Physical sciences & mathematics	CRONEIS, Karen S.	(TX) 260
Physics & math reference	DAVIDOFF, Gary N.	(IL) 276
Reference in mathematics & statistics	MERCADO, Heidi	(OH) 825
Science, physics, mathematics	HOOKER, Ruth H.	(CA) 556

MATRIMONIAL

Matrimonial law	BROWN, Ronald L.	(NY) 147

MCKINLEY

President McKinley history	STOUT, Chester B.	(OH)	1198

MEASUREMENT (See also Appraisal, Assessment, Bibliometrics, Effectiveness, Evaluation, Productivity, Psychometrics, Scientometrics, Standards, Testing)

Info service effectiveness measures	TIFFT, Jeanne D.	(DC)	1244
Info services measurement evaluation	WERT, Lucille M.	(IL)	1325
Library measurement & evaluation	RODGER, Eleanor J.	(IL)	1047
Library performance measures	KANIA, Antoinette M.	(NY)	625
Measurement & evaluation	ANTHONY, Carolyn A.	(IL)	28
	EDMONDS, M L.	(IL)	336
	EISENBERG, Michael B.	(NY)	340
	ROY, Loriene	(TX)	1063
Measurement of services	BAKER, Elizabeth A.	(MA)	48
Measuring library services	CLARK, Philip M.	(NY)	218
Output measures	SHELKROT, Elliot L.	(PA)	1126
Performance measurement	BORCHUCK, Fred P.	(TN)	116
Planning & performance measurement	SKIDMORE, Stephen C.	(OK)	1146
Standards & service measures	WARGO, Peggy M.	(CT)	1305
Test & measurements reference	KAUFFMAN, Inge S.	(CA)	631

MEAT

Meat science & technology	WHITEMARSH, Thomas R.	(WI)	1333

MECHANICAL

Civil & mechanical engineering	AMRON, Irving	(NJ)	20
Mechanical music, broadcasting, film	MUNSICK, Lee R.	(NJ)	879
Mechanized information retrieval	KENT, Allen	(PA)	642

MEDALS (See also Awards)

Caldecott medal books	HEINRICH, Lois M.	(MD)	522
Commemorative medals	DREW, Frances K.	(GA)	319

MEDIA (See also Audio, Audiovisual, Books, Ephemerae, Film, Learning, Manuscripts, Multimedia, Non-Book, Non-Print, Print, Slides, Software, Sound, Video, Visual)

Academic library & media administration	PARKS, Gary D.	(MO)	943
Acquisition non-print media	SPEIRS, Gilmary	(PA)	1172
Acquisitions, circulation, print media	GOODWYN, Betty R.	(AL)	450
Administration of school lib media progs	KLASING, Jane P.	(FL)	657
All media budget & purchase	DU CARMONT, M C.	(LA)	322
All media catalog & circulation	DU CARMONT, M C.	(LA)	322
Answering of media inquiries	GIGLIO, Linda M.	(MI)	433
Audiovisual & media	MEYERS, Kathleen H.	(AZ)	831
Audiovisual & non-book media	HARRINGTON, Thomas R.	(DC)	504
Audiovisual media	DOWNEY, Christine D.	(CA)	316
	GIUNTA, Victoria J.	(FL)	439
	FLYNN, Barbara L.	(IL)	386
	FRADKIN, Bernard	(IL)	395
	THOMPSON, Anna M.	(IN)	1238
	BUCCO, Louise F.	(VA)	153
	SCHERDIN, Mary J.	(WI)	1092
	VERMA, Prem V.	(WV)	1282
	GOODELL, Paulette M.	(AUS)	448
Audiovisual media & equipment	MITCHELL, George D.	(TX)	848
Audiovisual media cataloging	ZASLOW, Barry J.	(OH)	1386
Audiovisual media development	CHESHER, Joyce A.	(TX)	206
Audiovisual media facility management	GRAY, Shirley M.	(NY)	460
Audiovisual, media services	MCCARTHY, Germaine A.	(MA)	794
Audiovisuals & media	HILTON, Beverly A.	(KY)	541
Audiovisuals & video media	DIAL, Ron	(NY)	299
Bibliographic control, non-print media	TOTTEN, Herman L.	(TX)	1252
Book & audiovisual media selection	YOUNG, Patricia S.	(TN)	1383
Book & media selection	HUBER, Donald L.	(OH)	569
	MC NAIR, Marian B.	(OH)	815
Captioned media for the hearing impaired	MODICA, Mary L.	(SD)	851
Cataloging audiovisual media	KEARNEY, Jeanne E.	(NJ)	633
Cataloging books & audiovisual media	YOUNG, Patricia S.	(TN)	1383

MEDIA (Cont'd)

Cataloging educational media	GRIFFIN, Kathryn A.	(IA)	468
Cataloging, especially of media	LAFEVER, Susan	(TN)	687
Cataloging media	WESTOVER, Mary L.	(AL)	1327
	HEFZALLAH, Mona G.	(CT)	521
Cataloging non-print media	MATTHEWS, Priscilla J.	(IL)	785
Cataloging print media	KEARNEY, Jeanne E.	(NJ)	633
Cataloging school library media	SANDERS, Minda M.	(PA)	1080
Centralized media services, schools	BERTRAND, Doreen M.	(ON)	91
Children's media	HUNT, Mary A.	(FL)	575
	GAFFNEY, Maureen	(NY)	412
Children's media librarianship	ELLISOR, F L.	(TX)	345
Children's media programming	GAFFNEY, Maureen	(NY)	412
Children's media resources	WARNER, Wayne G.	(GA)	1305
Children's services & media	FENWICK, Sara I.	(FL)	371
Circulation & media services	RIEPMA, Helen J.	(TX)	1033
Computer use in media center	CARTER, Ann M.	(VA)	189
Computers in media centers	KISER, Anita H.	(NC)	656
Copyright, non-print media	THOMAS, Fred	(MD)	1236
Curriculum materials & media	JARRELL, James R.	(NC)	594
Curriculum use of media	SPEIRS, Gilmary	(PA)	1172
Designing media programs	COOK, Sybilla A.	(OR)	240
Developing new media facilities	SCHREIBMAN, Fay C.	(NY)	1099
Directing library & media centers	HAYASHI, Chigusa	(NJ)	515
Directing media center	COVINGTON, Eddis E.	(ID)	252
District media management	POOLE, Rebecca S.	(CO)	983
District media services	WURBS, Sue A.	(WY)	1374
Editing library media books	TROJAN, Judith L.	(NY)	1257
Editing library media magazines	TROJAN, Judith L.	(NY)	1257
Education media	BERNHART, Barbara M.	(CA)	89
Education media services assessment	COMEAU, Reginald A.	(NH)	234
Educational computing & media	WESTNEAT, Helen C.	(OH)	1327
Educational media	EBY, James F.	(CA)	334
	MACY, Edwin L.	(CO)	758
	DOUGLASS, Charlene K.	(GA)	314
	DAVIS, H S.	(IN)	279
	EVANS, James M.	(LA)	357
	BRAINARD, Elsie K.	(MA)	127
	PENSYL, Ornella L.	(MA)	957
	BUSBIN, O M.	(NC)	164
	HATHAWAY, Milton G.	(NC)	512
	MAZURKIEWICZ, Helen L.	(NJ)	791
	KEIST, Sandra H.	(NM)	635
	COLEMAN, Barbara K.	(OH)	231
	RODDA, Donna S.	(OH)	1047
	SCHEEREN, William O.	(PA)	1090
Educational media & technology	GASTON, Judith A.	(MN)	421
	BENDER, Evelyn	(PA)	79
Educational media management	SIMCOE, Darryl D.	(NY)	1139
	MAXWELL, James G.	(OR)	788
	CHANG, Robert H.	(TX)	201
Educational media services	RUFSVOLD, Margaret I.	(IN)	1066
Educational technology & media	KRANCH, Douglas A.	(IA)	676
Effective media utilization	LANKFORD, Mary D.	(TX)	696
Electronic media	CHANDLER, James	(CA)	200
	KING, Ebba K.	(NC)	650
Electronic media reference	HATVANY, Bela R.	(MA)	512
Electronic media-specialized market srvs	SIECK, Steven K.	(NY)	1135
Elementary library media	CAMPA, Josephine	(MD)	175
Elementary library media centers	FARRIS, Mary E.	(TN)	365
Elementary library media curriculum	PROCTOR, Deborah K.	(WY)	994
Elementary media	STAHLMAN, Cherry S.	(FL)	1178
	CARPENTER, Charlotte L.	(TX)	184
Elementary media center activities	VAN SOMEREN, Betty A.	(MN)	1277
Elementary media education	LACY, Lyn E.	(MN)	687
	PAULEY, Charles W.	(MN)	950
Elementary medial specialization	SMITH, Judy B.	(GA)	1156
Elementary school media	GREENWOOD, Anna S.	(DC)	465
	KILPATRICK, Marguerite C.	(GA)	648
	NEWTON, Evah B.	(IN)	900
	SCHEU, Jean W.	(MN)	1092
Elementary school media centers	BURGOON, Roger S.	(GA)	159
Elementary school media services	HARTMAN, Linda C.	(MO)	508
Emerging communication media technology	HOPE, Thomas W.	(NY)	557
Evaluation & selection of library media	PETERSON, Miriam E.	(IL)	964
Facility planning school media	COMEAU, Reginald A.	(NH)	234
Film & television media	MONACO, James	(NY)	854

MEDIA (Cont'd)

Film & video media	JENNINGS, Mary	(AK)	598
Forecasting new media diffusion	KLOPFENSTEIN, Bruce C.	(OH)	662
General school media	WESTFALL, Martha L.	(IN)	1327
Graduate media programs	TEMPLE, Leroy E.	(CT)	1230
High school libraries & media centers	PORTA, Mary D.	(PA)	984
High school media	GRADY, Alida J.	(FL)	455
High school media center	KLOZA, Paula P.	(NJ)	662
High school media programs	KIRK, Mary L.	(IA)	654
High school media specialist	THOMPSON, Myra D.	(OH)	1240
Information media research	SETTANNI, Joseph A.	(NY)	1117
Instruction of media skills	KOEPP, Sara H.	(IA)	668
Instruction using media & technology	TREGLOAN, Donald C.	(MI)	1255
Instructional media	PROSSER, Michael J.	(CA)	995
	HORRIGAN, John J.	(CT)	560
	TEMPLE, Leroy E.	(CT)	1230
	MARSH, Paul W.	(NE)	773
	MAYNES, Kathleen R.	(NJ)	790
	TOWNSEND, Catherine M.	(SC)	1253
	CARPENTER, Dorothy B.	(TN)	184
	ROBERTSON, Billy O.	(TN)	1041
Instructional media & technology	GOFF, Linda J.	(CA)	443
	LEAHY, Michael D.	(CT)	707
	VAN MELER, Vandelia L.	(MS)	1276
Instructional media design	CHAPLOCK, Sharon K.	(WI)	201
Instructional media, microcomputers	MARTIN, Elaine R.	(DC)	776
Instructional media production	POWELL, Patricia K.	(TX)	988
	REHMS, Jane C.	(WA)	1017
Instructional media resources	ALLAN, David W.	(MN)	14
Instructional media services	WAGNER, A C.	(NY)	1291
Instructional media specialist	SCHEU, Susan P.	(NY)	1092
Instructional media utilization	CONLIFFE, Bobbi L.	(OH)	236
Integrated library media skills	WALKER, Sue A.	(PA)	1296
Integration of media & technology	TREGLOAN, Donald C.	(MI)	1255
Integration of media to curriculum	MURRAY, William A.	(CO)	882
Interactive media	VAUGHAN, John	(NY)	1279
Jewish media center	KATZ, Lawrence M.	(OH)	630
K-12 school media	LUKASIK, Marion F.	(IL)	747
Library & media	MOELLENDICK, M J.	(WV)	851
Library & media administration	RONEY, Raymond G.	(CA)	1053
	BLESH, Tamara E.	(NH)	105
Library & media center	FAVORITE, Grealdine J.	(LA)	366
Library & media management	SOLES, Elizabeth S.	(VA)	1166
Library & media services	HERMENS, Dorothy M.	(OR)	531
Library & media skill instruction	GOODMAN, Roslyn L.	(AK)	449
Library & media skills programs	MC NAIR, Marian B.	(OH)	815
Library media	ABBOTT, Kathleen A.	(CT)	1
	WARAKSA, Raymond P.	(CT)	1303
	FONTES, Patricia J.	(MA)	388
	KEMP, Charles H.	(MO)	639
	FOLEY, Harriet E.	(OH)	387
	HAY, Mary K.	(WI)	515
Library media administration	WONG, Clark C.	(CA)	1362
	ANDERSON, Della L.	(MD)	22
Library media center	WALTER, Maria	(NY)	1300
Library media center administration	BUCKINGHAM, Betty J.	(IA)	154
Library media center facilities planning	FROST, Rebecca H.	(PA)	406
Library media centers	HILL, Sue A.	(LA)	540
	BROOKS, Burton H.	(MI)	140
	THOMAS, Lucille C.	(NY)	1237
Library, media computer applications	RENICK, Paul R.	(ND)	1023
Library media education	SCHULZETENBERG, Anthony C.	(MN)	1102
	HUPP, Mary A.	(WV)	577
Library media instruction	SWEET, Sally K.	(CO)	1215
	DIRKS, Martha W.	(KS)	305
	CLARK, Elizabeth K.	(MA)	216
Library media program development	HOBBS, Henry C.	(MB)	545
Library media programs & services	WURBS, Sue A.	(WY)	1374
Library media resources	HUNT, Mary A.	(FL)	575
Library media services	BERNSTEIN, D S.	(MA)	89
	BROOKS, Burton H.	(MI)	140
	BYNON, George E.	(OR)	168
Library media skill instruction	RAMSEY, Inez L.	(VA)	1006
Library media skills	MEIER, Patricia L.	(IA)	821
	SULLIVAN, Jennifer B.	(PA)	1207
Library media skills curriculum	MURTO, Kathleen A.	(WI)	883
Library media skills instruction	EHRICH, Joan C.	(MA)	339
	TASSIA, Margaret R.	(PA)	1224
Library media specialist	CHANG, Isabelle E.	(MA)	200

MEDIA (Cont'd)

Library media specialist education	MCNAMARA, Marie F.	(NY)	816
Library media specialization	MILLER, Sylvia G.	(NC)	843
Management of media center	LINDGREN, Beverly P.	(IL)	729
	PRILLAMAN, Susan M.	(NC)	993
Managing school library & media	JANTZ, Helen N.	(KS)	594
Mass media information	ALLEN, Nancy H.	(MI)	15
Materials selection, all media	CLARK, Elizabeth K.	(MA)	216
Media	BIGGS-WILLIAMS, Evelyn A.	(AL)	95
	MAJOR, Caryl M.	(AZ)	762
	CADY, Ruth A.	(CA)	170
	CARROLL, Lois E.	(CA)	187
	BRAVY, Gary J.	(DC)	130
	NIBLEY, Elizabeth B.	(DC)	901
	BLOCK, Sandra S.	(FL)	106
	GOODIER, Darlene P.	(FL)	448
	KAZLAUSKAS, Diane W.	(FL)	632
	CHERN, Jenn C.	(GA)	206
	WILLIAMS, Anita	(GA)	1342
	DECKER, Charlotte J.	(KY)	285
	REEDY, Ruth C.	(LA)	1015
	LANGE, Clare M.	(MA)	695
	SLANGA, Joanne	(MD)	1147
	BROOKS, S B.	(MN)	141
	SCHEU, Jean W.	(MN)	1092
	FUCHS, Curt R.	(MO)	408
	BENDA, Constance M.	(NE)	79
	NIGRIN, Albert G.	(NJ)	904
	RICHARDSON, Robert J.	(NJ)	1030
	SAWYCKY, Roman A.	(NJ)	1086
	AFROMSKY, Ellen S.	(NY)	7
	BJORKQUIST, Donna M.	(NY)	100
	BURKE, J L.	(NY)	160
	FRANCO, Kathryn C.	(NY)	396
	KAHN, Laura	(NY)	622
	MCCONNELL, Robert D.	(PA)	798
	IRBY, Patricia P.	(TN)	583
	DUNCAN, Donna P.	(TX)	325
	MILLER, Karl F.	(TX)	839
	THEISS, Diane M.	(TX)	1234
	MILLER, Veronica E.	(VI)	843
	EDMONDS, Susan M.	(WA)	336
	BALDWIN, David A.	(WY)	51
Media acquisitions	SCHREFFLER, Lynne W.	(PA)	1099
Media administration	MATHAI, Aleyamma	(NJ)	783
	MICHAEL, Douglas O.	(NY)	831
Media & audiovisual consulting	TARANKO, Walter J.	(ME)	1223
Media & curriculum	HENDRICKSON, Charles R.	(CO)	527
Media & education cataloging	FREESE, Melanie L.	(NY)	401
Media & instruction support	YEE, Sandra G.	(MI)	1379
Media & library administration	NEILL, Laquita B.	(MS)	892
Media & technology in libraries	CHISHOLM, Margaret	(WA)	209
Media & technology services	BRUMBACK, Elsie	(NC)	150
Media & theatrical production	GOODMAN, John E.	(PA)	449
Media applications in education	TOWNSEND, Catherine M.	(SC)	1253
Media appraisal & procurement	HOLSINGER, Katherine	(AZ)	554
Media assistance	BLAIR, Sharon K.	(SC)	103
Media, audiovisual equipment, video	RUBIN, Ellen B.	(NY)	1064
Media, audiovisual market research	HOPE, Thomas W.	(NY)	557
Media, audiovisual services	MANDEL, Debra H.	(MA)	764
Media cataloging	PROSSER, Michael J.	(CA)	995
	SCHREIBER, Robert E.	(IL)	1099
	MICHAEL, Richard T.	(RI)	831
Media center	EPIL, Charlene M.	(HI)	351
Media center administration	CLAVER, M P.	(AL)	219
	KOEPP, Sara H.	(IA)	668
	HELLER, Dawn H.	(IL)	524
	CLEAVER, Betty P.	(OH)	220
Media center card cataloging	MITCHELL, Phyllis R.	(GA)	849
Media center design	DRECHSEL, Marcella J.	(NJ)	319
Media center development	TITCOMB, Anne S.	(MD)	1247
Media center management	MITCHELL, Phyllis R.	(GA)	849
	TALAB, Rosemary S.	(KS)	1220
	TRIM, Kathryn	(MI)	1256
	KUTTEROFF, Ethel C.	(NJ)	685
Media center management & operation	BRAUER, Regina	(NY)	129
Media center management & teaching	CLEAVER, Betty P.	(OH)	220

MEDIA (Cont'd)

Media center operation & administration	EGAN, Terence W.	(AZ)	338
Media center organization	FOERTIN, Yves P.	(PQ)	387
Media center programs	PAULEY, Charles W.	(MN)	950
Media centers	MARCHAND, Janet H.	(CT)	768
	MARTHALER, Margaret K.	(MN)	775
	CHANDLER, Devon	(MT)	199
	CARSTATER, Mary E.	(NY)	188
	GOODMAN, John E.	(PA)	449
	PHARES, Abner J.	(VI)	967
Media collection development	LARSON, Teresa B.	(IA)	700
Media collection management	REIT, Janet W.	(VT)	1022
Media collections	STRANGE, Elizabeth B.	(DE)	1200
Media collections & services	CLAYTON, William R.	(GA)	220
Media consulting	BERKLUND, Nancy J.	(MI)	87
	GURIEVITCH, Grania B.	(NY)	478
Media coordinating	DAVIS, Judy R.	(NC)	279
Media coordination	ZACHARY, Patricia A.	(OK)	1385
Media departments	DUGGAN, James E.	(LA)	324
Media design & instruction	ALBUM, Bernie	(CA)	11
Media design, production & utilization	LIGGAN, Mary K.	(VA)	726
Media development	WEST, Marian S.	(MI)	1326
	MARTIN, Richard T.	(NC)	778
	DAVILA, Daniel	(NY)	277
Media education training & development	FORTIN, Clifford C.	(WI)	391
Media evaluation	OHLMAN, Herbert	(SWZ)	919
Media for children	ORSBURN, Elizabeth C.	(PA)	927
Media for exceptional children	TAFFEL, Bobbe H.	(FL)	1219
Media for gifted	HAMMITT, Margaret R.	(NE)	493
Media for gifted students	FITZPATRICK, Janis M.	(OH)	383
Media in nursing & medicine selection	REIT, Janet W.	(VT)	1022
Media instruction	MERWINE, Glenda M.	(WA)	827
Media lessons development	MULLINS, Carolyn J.	(CA)	878
Media librarians	DENDY, Adele S.	(VA)	291
Media librarianship	ELLISON, John W.	(NY)	345
	FRIEDMAN, Arthur L.	(NY)	403
Media library	SOUTHARD, Ruth K.	(TX)	1169
Media, library administration	STRANGE, Elizabeth B.	(DE)	1200
Media management	GILBERT, Betty H.	(AZ)	433
Media materials & equipment	LINK, Margaret A.	(NC)	730
Media materials, collections development	STEVENS, Roberta A.	(DC)	1191
Media production	SMITH, Margie G.	(CA)	1157
	TAWYEA, Edward W.	(IL)	1225
	GERRING, Cheryl B.	(MD)	429
	HRYVNIAK, Joseph T.	(NY)	567
	YANOFF, Marcy S.	(NY)	1377
	LOCKETT, Iva	(TX)	736
Media production & evaluation	BELT, Jane	(WA)	78
Media relations	REAGAN, Bob	(CA)	1012
Media research of current events	BROWN, Phyllis J.	(TN)	147
Media reviewer	CHAKLOSH, Cynthia L.	(MI)	197
Media selection & evaluation	CHEEKS, Cellestine	(MD)	204
Media selection for curriculum	HILLER, Catherine C.	(CT)	541
Media services	HAMILTON, Ann H.	(AL)	491
	PAUL, Jeff H.	(CA)	949
	ROCKMAN, Ilene F.	(CA)	1046
	HEMPSTEAD, John	(CO)	525
	MEUCCI, Victoria F.	(CT)	829
	DONAHOE, Patricia A.	(IL)	310
	NUTTY, David J.	(IL)	912
	CHEW, Susan M.	(LA)	207
	DACHS, Jerald K.	(MA)	269
	HSIEH, Rebecca T.	(MD)	567
	FRITZ, Donald D.	(MI)	405
	HULSEY, Richard A.	(MI)	573
	JAROSLOW, Sylvia W.	(NJ)	594
	MALLALIEU, Robert K.	(NJ)	763
	ABBOTT, George L.	(NY)	1
	TASHJIAN, Sharon A.	(OR)	1224
	HUNTER, Joy W.	(TN)	576
	CONIGLIO, Jamie W.	(VA)	236
	MATTHEWS, Stephen L.	(VA)	786
	MCCULLOUGH, Doreen J.	(VT)	801
	GREGGS, Elizabeth M.	(WA)	465
Media services, audio & video	SLYHOFF, Merle J.	(PA)	1151
Media services program	PHILLIPS, Luouida V.	(TX)	968
Media skills	BOWEN, Louise E.	(GA)	120

MEDIA (Cont'd)

Media skills instruction	CHAPMAN-SIMPSON, Alisa M.	(IA)	202
	KONNEKER, Rachel C.	(NC)	670
	SOUTHERLAND, Carol A.	(NC)	1169
Media specialist	RECHNITZ, Harriet L.	(DE)	1013
	POLITIS, John V.	(PA)	981
	LAESSIG, Joan M.	(WI)	687
Media specialists training & development	RIVERA, Antonio	(NY)	1037
Media specialization	MILLER, Marian A.	(OH)	840
Media studies	WILSON, Mary S.	(MS)	1352
Media support services	MICHAEL, Richard T.	(RI)	831
Media technologies	AJIBERO, Matthew I.	(NGR)	9
Media use in schools	JOSEPH, Elizabeth T.	(PA)	617
Media utilization	GORMAN, Audrey J.	(NJ)	452
Medial skill instruction	SMITH, Judy B.	(GA)	1156
Medical media	LUDWIG, Logan T.	(IL)	747
	KAGER, Jeffrey F.	(PA)	621
Middle school library media center admin	GOZEMBA, Frances E.	(MA)	455
Middle school media centers	EDWARDS, Barbara T.	(TN)	337
Music media	HAMMARGREN, Betty L.	(MN)	493
Natural history media	ALASTI, Aryt	(MA)	9
New media market analysis	KLOPFENSTEIN, Bruce C.	(OH)	662
New media usage studies	KLOPFENSTEIN, Bruce C.	(OH)	662
News & media databases	MCCOY-LARSON, Sandra	(DC)	799
News media	SUMMERS, Janice K.	(MO)	1209
	STEIN, Pamela H.	(NY)	1185
News media databases	WALSH, Barclay	(DC)	1299
News media librarianship	FURR, Susan H.	(VA)	410
News media libraries	NEWCOMBE, Barbara T.	(CA)	898
News media research	LEVINSON, Debra J.	(NY)	721
News medias	CHALIFOUX, Jean P.	(PQ)	197
Non-book media	SNOW, Maryly A.	(CA)	1164
Non-print media	BESSER, Howard A.	(CA)	91
	DUBOIS, Henry J.	(CA)	322
	ERVITI, Debra L.	(CA)	353
	HANDMAN, Gary P.	(CA)	495
	WOOLDRIDGE, Steven M.	(CA)	1368
	HAMRELL, Larry G.	(FL)	494
	HOUGH, Leslie S.	(GA)	562
	COOPER, Susan C.	(IL)	243
	SOMMER, Ursula M.	(NJ)	1167
	KENSELAAR, Robert	(NY)	642
	RIVERA, Gregorio	(NY)	1037
	SCHABERT, Daniel R.	(NY)	1088
	BARNETT, Donald E.	(OR)	57
	VIGNOVICH, Ray L.	(WI)	1284
	GOODMAN, Henry J.	(AB)	449
Non-print media & audiovisuals	CURTIS, James A.	(NY)	267
Non-print media director	DINNESEN, Peter H.	(OH)	305
Non-print media librarianship	WHYTE, Sean	(VA)	1335
Non-print media services	VARNES, Richard S.	(CO)	1279
Non-print media utilization	THOMPSON, Elizabeth M.	(DC)	1239
	TOTTEN, Herman L.	(TX)	1252
Optical media	CARSON, Susan A.	(CA)	188
Optical media in libraries	DUCHESNE, Roderick M.	(ON)	322
Optical storage media technology	GALL, Bert A.	(TN)	413
Original media slide programs	OWENS, Martha A.	(VA)	932
Planning library media centers	APPEL MOSESOF, Rhoda S.	(NJ)	29
Processing media	BRANDT, Garnet J.	(IA)	128
Public library media collections	FLYNN, Barbara L.	(IL)	386
Public school library media	HAMILTON, Betty D.	(TX)	491
Racism, sexism in media	ADAMS, Elaine P.	(TX)	4
Recorded media consultation, appraisal	MACAULEY, C C.	(CA)	754
Reference & media	WILLER, Kenneth H.	(NY)	1341
Regional educational media centers	FITZGERALD, Ruth F.	(MI)	382
Research for media personnel	BROWN, Phyllis J.	(TN)	147
Reviewing film, video & media	TROJAN, Judith L.	(NY)	1257
Role of library media specialist	SCOTT, Willodene A.	(TN)	1108
School & library media	UTTS, Janet R.	(NY)	1270
School district media centers	MOHN, Kari	(AK)	852
School district media services	STAAS, Gretchen L.	(TX)	1177
School librarian media specialist	COACHMAN, Dorothea L.	(NY)	224
School librarianship, media centers	RYUS, Phyllis K.	(CA)	1072

MEDIA (Cont'd)

School libraries & media centers
CARR, Charles E. . . . . . . (AL) 185
PELOVSKY, Suzy A. . . . (CA) 955
WEICK, Robert J. . . . . . . (IN) 1316
HAWKINS, Marilyn J. . . . (MO) 514
MULLER, Madeline A. . . (OH) 877
HERRING, Billie G. . . . . . (TX) 533

School library & media
STRICKLAND, Mary L. . . (NC) 1202
BRADLEY, Patricia L. . . . (SC) 126

School library & media administration
JOSEPH, Elizabeth T. . . . (PA) 617
SKELLEY, Cornelia A. . . (WA) 1145

School library & media center
JENKS, Arlene I. . . . . . . (AK) 597
LEFF, Barbara Y. . . . . . . (CA) 712
FENWICK, Sara I. . . . . . (FL) 371
HIRSCH, Elizabeth . . . . (MA) 543
COURTNEY, Marjorie S. . (MO) 251
GARDNER, Janet K. . . . (NC) 418
RILEY, Marie R. . . . . . . (NJ) 1034
RUSSELL, Paula V. . . . (TX) 1069
WU, Jean . . . . (TX) 1373
AXT, Randolph W. . . . . . (WI) 42

School library & media center management
SNYDER, Denny L. . . . . (MD) 1164
STEVENS, Elizabeth B. . . (NY) 1190

School library & media centers
DIERCKS, Eileen K. . . . (IL) 302
KIRZINGER, Denise C. . . (KY) 656
DALBOTTEN, Mary S. . . (MN) 270
WEISENFELS, Marjorie A. (MO) 1319
HUNTER, Cecilia A. . . . . (TX) 576
MOELLENDICK, M J. . . . (WV) 851
KRATZ, Hans G. . . . . . . (AB) 676

School library & media collections
TERWILLEGAR, Jane C. . (FL) 1232

School library & media services
RUSK, Alice C. . . . . (MD) 1068

School library & media specialists educ
PATTERSON, Lotsee . . . (OK) 948

School library media
MCKISSICK, Mabel F. . . (CT) 812
SRYGLEY, Sara K. . . . . (FL) 1177
PASCHAL, Eloise R. . . . (GA) 945
SPENCE, Rethia C. . . . . (GA) 1173
TOLMAN, Lorraine E. . . . (MA) 1249
DAVIS, Mavis W. . . . . . (MD) 280
HELMICK, Aileen B. . . . . (MO) 525
STEMME, Virginia L. . . . (ND) 1186
CONDIT, Martha O. . . . . (NJ) 235
BANICK, Albert N. . . . . . (NY) 54
HARRIS, Martha . . . . . . (NY) 505
HERTZ, Cynthia L. . . . . . (NY) 533
BACK, Andrew W. . . . . . (PA) 43
COX, Carol A. . . . . (PA) 253
DALY, Sally A. . . . . (PA) 271
CALDWELL, Rossie B. . . (SC) 172
CASEY, Jean M. . . . . . . (WI) 192

School library media administration
CARTER, Yvonne B. . . . (DC) 190
YOUNG, Christina C. . . . (DC) 1381
NOONAN, Eileen F. . . . . (IL) 908
MEANS, E P. . . . . (KS) 820
KULLESEID, Eleanor R. . (NY) 683
CHISHOLM, Margaret . . . (WA) 209

School library media center
DOOLEY, Sally J. . . . . . (AZ) 312
DAY, Bettie B. . . . . (CA) 282
WHALEY, Janie B. . . . . . (IN) 1328
HOLLEY, Rebecca M. . . . (LA) 551
COLYER, Judith A. . . . . (MI) 234
WALL, Marilyn M. . . . . . (MI) 1297
MCDONALD, Frances B. . (MN) 802
FIRSCHEIN, Sylvia H. . . (NJ) 379
DILLINGER, Mary A. . . . (TX) 303
VEENSTRA, Geraldine B. (TX) 1281
HAUG, Pauline C. . . . . . (WI) 512
MCKILLIP, Rita J. . . . . . (WI) 811
KOGA, Setsuko . . . . . . (JAP) 668

School library media center automation
JOYCE, Robert A. . . . . . (NC) 618

School library media center management
MILLER, John E. . . . . . (OH) 839
STANTON, Vida C. . . . . (WI) 1181

School library, media centers
SACHSE, Gladys M. . . . (AR) 1073
BOWMAN, Kathleen A. . . (CA) 122
NIEMEYER, Kay M. . . . . (CA) 903
HEMPSTEAD, John . . . . (CO) 525

MEDIA (Cont'd)

School library, media centers
LOERTSCHER, David V. . (CO) 737
HALE, Robert G. . . . . . . (CT) 485
LAPOLT, Margaret B. . . . (CT) 697
WHITE, Charles R. . . . . (CT) 1330
FOSTER, Candice L. . . . (FL) 392
HOLMES, Gloria P. . . . . (FL) 553
JONES, Winona N. . . . . (FL) 615
RAMEY, Linda K. . . . . . (FL) 1005
ELIZABETH, Martin A. . . (IA) 343
MARTIN, Elizabeth A. . . . (IA) 776
BIBLO, Mary . . . . (IL) 94
BEILKE, Patricia F. . . . . (IN) 75
HUNT, Margaret M. . . . . (IN) 575
SOLDNER, Nancy C. . . . (KS) 1166
LIVINGSTON, Sarah M. . (KY) 735
CARSTENS, Jane E. . . . (LA) 188
STANTON, Martha . . . . (MA) 1181
FITZGERALD, Ruth F. . . (MI) 382
NICKEL, Mildred L. . . . . (MI) 902
OLSON, Lowell E. . . . . . (MN) 923
SCHULZETENBERG, Anthony C. . . . . (MN) 1102
LITTLE, Nina M. . . . . . . (NE) 733
KUHLTHAU, Carol C. . . (NJ) 682
SEVERINGHAUS, Ethel L. (NY) 1117
SPIRT, Diana L. . . . . . . (NY) 1175
STAINO, Rocco A. . . . . (NY) 1178
VELLEMAN, Ruth A. . . . (NY) 1281
ARK, Connie E. . . . . . . (OH) 31
AVERY, Jacqueline R. . . (OH) 41
MELTON, Vivian B. . . . . (OH) 823
COWEN, Linda L. . . . . . (OK) 253
MURPHY, Diana G. . . . . (PA) 880
CARPENTER, Dorothy B. (TN) 184
SCOTT, Willodene A. . . . (TN) 1108
IMMROTH, Barbara F. . . (TX) 582
KAHLER, June . . . . (TX) 621
REIFEL, Louie E. . . . . . (TX) 1019
MILLS, Fiolina B. . . . . . . (VI) 844

School lib media ctrs staff development
SMITH, Jane B. . . . . . . (AL) 1155

School library media certification
SORENSEN, Richard J. . (WI) 1168

School library media computerization
LITTLE, Nina M. . . . . . . (NE) 733

School library media consultation
DOWNES, Valerie . . . . (IL) 316

School library media curriculum
LITTLE, Nina M. . . . . . . (NE) 733
ROSCELLO, Frances R. . (NY) 1054

School library media development
LUDWIG, Deborah M. . . (CO) 746
DOWNES, Valerie . . . . . (IL) 316
VOSS, Anne E. . . . . . . (NJ) 1289

School library media education
GRAZIER, Margaret H. . . (MI) 461

School library media facilities
PATRICK, Retta B. . . . . (AR) 947
SHUMAN, Susan E. . . . (NY) 1134
EHRHARDT, Margaret W. (SC) 339

School library media improvement
MORRIS, Irving . . . . . . (NY) 866

School library media instruction
RING, Constance B. . . . (NY) 1035

School library media management
GREGORY, Mary L. . . . (WA) 466

School library media program
PATRICK, Retta B. . . . . (AR) 947

School library media programs
DEWEESE, Don B. . . . . (AR) 298
WHITNEY, Karen A. . . . (AZ) 1334
GREENBERG, Marilyn W. (CA) 463
WEIGEL, James S. . . . . (CT) 1316
HART, Thomas L. . . . . . (FL) 507
BROCK, Kathy T. . . . . . (GA) 138
HOLTER, Charlotte S. . . (MD) 554
SMINK, Anna R. . . . . . . (MD) 1152
MATECUN, Marilyn L. . . (MI) 783
MILLER, Robert H. . . . . (MN) 842
APPEL MOSESOF, Rhoda S. . . . . (NJ) 29
BARRON, Robert E. . . . . (NY) 60
RICHARDSON, Constance H. . . . . (NY) 1029
ROSCELLO, Frances R. . (NY) 1054
EHRHARDT, Margaret W. (SC) 339
EISENSTEIN, Jill M. . . . (TN) 341
LANKFORD, Mary D. . . . (TX) 696
WIEMAN, Jean M. . . . . (WA) 1336
FOLKE, Carolyn W. . . . . (WI) 387

MEDIA (Cont'd)

Specialty	Name	State	Page
School library media programs	HOPKINS, Dianne M.	(WI)	557
School library media public relations	BALL, Diane A.	(OH)	52
School library media services	GILBERT, Betty H.	(AZ)	433
	ROSE, David L.	(CA)	1054
	SKINNER, L M.	(FL)	1146
	DURAND, Joyce J.	(GA)	328
	UYEHARA, Harry Y.	(GU)	1270
	DEQUIN, Henry C.	(IL)	293
	TUGGLE, Ann M.	(IL)	1262
	MCNALLY, Crystal E.	(KS)	815
	COOPER, Judy L.	(KY)	243
	SMITH, Zelda G.	(MA)	1161
	MONTGOMERY, Paula K.	(MD)	856
	KERESEY, Gayle	(NC)	643
	VANDERGRIFT, Kay E.	(NJ)	1274
	EISENBERG, Michael B.	(NY)	340
	SHONTZ, Marilyn L.	(PA)	1132
	BROADWAY, Marsha D.	(UT)	138
	BROWN, Dale W.	(VA)	143
	JONES, Sally L.	(WA)	615
School library media skills	BUGHER, Kathryn M.	(WI)	155
School library, media specialist	CAZZULINO, Clara P.	(NY)	195
	GRIFFIN, Cheryl J.	(NY)	468
	DURHAM, Wanda J.	(TN)	328
	REARDON, Elizabeth M.	(TN)	1013
School library media specialization	ARKHURST, Joyce C.	(NY)	31
School library media supervision	JAFFARIAN, Sara	(MA)	591
School media	PENDLETON, Kim B.	(AK)	956
	JAIN, Celeste C.	(CA)	591
	HILL, Marian W.	(FL)	540
	MOORE, Vivian L.	(FL)	861
	DENNY, Mary C.	(ID)	293
	NEAL, Nancy J.	(IL)	890
	MATHEWS, Mary P.	(MD)	784
	SCHULTZ, Christine K.	(MI)	1102
	WEST, Marian S.	(MI)	1326
	GORDON, Muriel C.	(NJ)	451
School media administration	BURKE, Grace W.	(GA)	160
	WILSON, Mary S.	(MS)	1352
School media center	JENSEN, Kathryn E.	(MA)	599
School media center administration	ROTH, Alvin R.	(MN)	1059
	JOYCE, Robert A.	(NC)	618
	LATROBE, Kathy H.	(OK)	701
	LAUGHLIN, Mildred A.	(OK)	703
School media center design	LEVEILLEE, Louis R.	(RI)	719
School media center evaluation	SLYGH, Gyneth	(WI)	1151
School media center instruction	JOYCE, Robert A.	(NC)	618
School media center management	GARLAND, Kathleen	(NY)	419
School media center resources	RUDIE, Helen M.	(MN)	1065
School media centers	JOHNSEN, Ellen I.	(IL)	601
	KRAUSE, Roberta A.	(IL)	676
	ROBINSON, Phyllis A.	(MA)	1044
	BUIST, Elaine R.	(SC)	156
	ANDIS, Norma B.	(TX)	26
	LABODDA, Marsha J.	(TX)	686
	PRETLOW, Delores Z.	(VA)	992
	REINAGLE, Carol M.	(WI)	1021
School media children's services	AMISON, Mary V.	(NY)	20
School media libraries	MACLEAN, Ellen G.	(VI)	757
School media policy development	ADAMS, Helen R.	(WI)	5
School media programs	TUGWELL, Helen M.	(NC)	1262
School media services	BERG, Charlene J.	(CA)	84
	SYFERT, Samuel R.	(IL)	1217
	ZAPPONE, William F.	(NY)	1386
	KARRENBROCK, Marilyn H.	(TN)	628
	ZIMMERMAN, Nancy P.	(VA)	1389
School media specialist	RACZYNSKI, Mary K.	(IL)	1002
	BRUMIT, Nancy T.	(OH)	150
	HARDIN, Sue H.	(SC)	500
School media specialization	SMITH, Noralee W.	(OH)	1159
	DAY, Pamela A.	(WI)	283
School region lib, media coordination	RIVERA, Antonio	(NY)	1037
School system library media management	KAUFMAN, Polly W.	(MA)	631
Secondary library media	CAMPA, Josephine	(MD)	175
Secondary school library media centers	MILLER, George M.	(MA)	837

MEDIA (Cont'd)

Specialty	Name	State	Page
Secondary school media centers	RAKE, Anthony I.	(IL)	1004
Staff development, media personnel	BURKE, Grace W.	(GA)	160
Standards for school media centers	CAIN, Carolyn L.	(WI)	171
Student media production	JONES, Wanda F.	(AR)	615
	MCKINNEY, Barbara J.	(AR)	812
Supervise all media	MARVEL, Frances J.	(CA)	780
Supervising school library media progs	KLASING, Jane P.	(FL)	657
Teaching elementary media skills	SULLI, Gerard C.	(CT)	1207
Teaching media skills	HUNT, Susan O.	(FL)	576
	WINSLOW, Carol M.	(IN)	1355
	CUNNINGHAM, Mary A.	(NY)	265
Teaching use of media center	DAVIES, Gordon D.	(MD)	277
Telecommunications & media	WEINGAND, Darlene E.	(WI)	1318
Video media & equipment	MITCHELL, George D.	(TX)	848
Young adult media	HUNT, Mary A.	(FL)	575

MEDICAID

Specialty	Name	State	Page
Medicaid databases	PETTOLINA, Anthony M.	(NY)	965

MEDICAL (See also Biomedical, Clinical, Health, Hospital, Medicine)

Specialty	Name	State	Page
Abstracting current medical literature	SHIPLEY, Ruth M.	(MO)	1131
Administration, medical education	KERR, Audrey M.	(MB)	644
Analysis of medical information	LAMPORT, Bernard	(NY)	691
Appraisals of medical collections	KLENK, Anne S.	(CO)	660
Audiovisuals, medical	VAN SCHAIK, Jo A.	(TX)	1277
Automated medical records	LONG, John M.	(MN)	739
Biomedical & medical socioeconomic info	BANKS, Jane L.	(DC)	54
Business & medical intelligence	LOKETS BEISCHROT, Dina	(CT)	738
Canadian medical librarianship	WALUZYNIEC, Hanna	(PQ)	1302
Clinical medical librarianship	DALE, Nancy	(IL)	270
	VUGRIN, Margaret Y.	(TX)	1289
Clinical medical reference bibliography	KINNAIRD, Cheryl D.	(IL)	653
Computerized medical records	STEAD, William W.	(NC)	1183
Consumer, legal, & medical information	LEBRUN, Anne	(ON)	708
Consumer medical collections	DIAL, Carolyn E.	(FL)	299
Continuing medical education	MANNING, Phil R.	(CA)	767
	SIMPSON, Evelyn L.	(CA)	1141
	STLUKA, Thomas H.	(IL)	1195
	KELLY, Kay	(MI)	638
	KELLER, Marlo L.	(OH)	635
Continuing medical education programming	BEDARD, Martha A.	(MA)	73
Database searching, toxicology & medical	LEMMON, Anne B.	(LA)	715
Designing medical information systems	LAZAROW-STETTEN, Jane K.	(MD)	706
Develop medical record systems	KISH, Veronica R.	(PA)	656
Diffusion of medical innovations	ANDERSON, Marilyn M.	(IN)	24
Editing chemical & medical text	GRIFFITHS, Mary C.	(MD)	469
Editing medical & pharmacological texts	HAMILTON, Gloria R.	(PA)	492
Electronic medical books	FRISSE, Mark E.	(MO)	405
Engineering & medical research	SARAIDARIDIS, Susan B.	(MA)	1082
Expert medical systems	RAMAKRISHNAN, T	(LA)	1004
General & medical reference	SMITH, Thomas E.	(DC)	1161
	CRABTREE, Anna B.	(MO)	254
	MICHAELS, Debbie D.	(NJ)	832
	THOMAS, Mary E.	(VA)	1237
General medical searching	LATTA, Barbara K.	(MN)	702
Health sciences medical online searching	STANKE, Judith U.	(MN)	1180
History of medical literature, rare bks	MIMS, Dorothy H.	(GA)	845
Hospital & medical school	LANDWIRTH, Trudy K.	(IL)	694
Indexing medical & pharmacological texts	HAMILTON, Gloria R.	(PA)	492
Integrated medical financial databases	RUBIN, David S.	(NY)	1064
Integrated medical geographic databases	RUBIN, David S.	(NY)	1064
Legal, medical & financial databases	LEVEROCK, Lisa A.	(NJ)	719
Legal, medical, corporate printer	SCULLIN, Frank E.	(PA)	1109
Local medical history	GOLDSTEIN, Cynthia H.	(LA)	446

MEDICAL (Cont'd)

Subject	Name	State	Page
Management of medical & research data	COLLINS, Kenneth A.	(MD)	233
Manual medical reference	VAIL, Evelyn J.	(IL)	1270
Medical	PRUHS, Sharon	(CA)	996
	REINHARDT, Alice L.	(CA)	1021
	RALSTON, Anne C.	(MD)	1004
	GREVEN, Maryanne L.	(ME)	467
	SAHYOUN, Naim K.	(MI)	1075
	MACKLER, Leslie G.	(NC)	757
	NOFTLE, Dorothy B.	(NH)	907
Medical abstracting & indexing	CARVER, Mary	(NY)	191
Medical acquisitions	WAKEFORD, Paul J.	(CA)	1293
	RENNIE, Margaret C.	(LA)	1023
Medical & academic collection devlpmnt	INGRAHAM-SWETS, Leonoor	(OR)	582
Medical & biological databases	NEWAY, Julie M.	(CA)	898
Medical & business	FIRTH, Margaret A.	(MA)	379
Medical & business databases	AIREY, Martha R.	(ME)	9
Medical & business online searching	BLACKBURN-FOSTER, Brenda	(KY)	102
Medical & chemical databases	LEICHTMAN, Anne B.	(NJ)	713
Medical & chemical searching	RATHGEBER, Jo F.	(NC)	1009
Medical & clinical	BRENNER, Lawrence	(MA)	133
Medical & dental databases	GLASER, June E.	(NY)	439
Medical & health	RONNERMANN, Gail	(NY)	1053
Medical & health care databases	MARIX, Mary L.	(LA)	770
Medical & health literature	WORTZEL, Murray N.	(NY)	1369
Medical & health science databases	AIRTH, Elizabeth J.	(TX)	9
Medical & health sciences reference	STANKE, Judith U.	(MN)	1180
Medical & health-related databases	VONSEGEN, Ann M.	(OR)	1288
Medical & hospital libraries	STEPHENS, Diana C.	(HI)	1188
	SPIEGEL, Nancy C.	(ME)	1174
	MUDLOFF, Cherrie M.	(MI)	875
Medical & law online searching	BERK, Nancy G.	(AZ)	87
Medical & legal databases	MARTIN, Laquita V.	(TN)	777
Medical & legal research	BEDARD, Evelyn M.	(TX)	73
Medical & marine science libraries	TRUMBULL, Jane	(NC)	1259
Medical & music databases	CHASE, Judith H.	(OR)	203
Medical & nursing	VANNORTWICK, Barbara L.	(NY)	1276
Medical & nursing books	CASSAR, Ann	(PA)	193
Medical & nursing databases	JENNINGS, Patricia S.	(FL)	598
	LIPPMAN, Anne F.	(MA)	732
Medical & nursing information services	JENNINGS, Patricia S.	(FL)	598
Medical & nursing literature	KAISLER, Dolores H.	(MD)	622
Medical & nursing reference	SCHULTZ, Therese A.	(IL)	1102
Medical & nursing resources	BRETSCHER, Susan M.	(NY)	134
Medical & other database searching	POTTER, Laurene	(CA)	987
Medical & pharmaceutical literature	TANEN, Lee J.	(NJ)	1222
Medical & psychological databases	KNOBLOCH, Shirley S.	(DC)	665
	DAVIS, Anne C.	(MI)	277
	PLASO, Kathy A.	(PA)	977
	STILMAN, Ruth	(PQ)	1194
Medical & reference databases	BINAU, Myra I.	(MD)	97
Medical & related databases	MAHONY, Doris D.	(MI)	761
Medical & science databases	ROBINSON, Betty J.	(CA)	1043
	HUNTER, John H.	(TX)	576
	BOULANGER, Mary E.	(WI)	119
Medical & science librarianship	EBRO, Diane C.	(MN)	334
Medical & science online searching	RANSOM, Christina R.	(NY)	1007
Medical & scientific books	FUGLE, Mary E.	(NY)	408
Medical & scientific databases	VEENSTRA, Robert J.	(AL)	1281
	GOUVEIA, Sara C.	(CA)	454
	MALMGREN, Terri L.	(CA)	763
	BERNSTEIN, Lee S.	(DC)	89
	TAN, Elizabeth L.	(IL)	1222
	HAWTHORNE, Dorothy M.	(MN)	514
	AUSTON, Ione	(VA)	40
Medical & scientific journals	FUGLE, Mary E.	(NY)	408
Medical & scientific librarianship	ANDERSON, Christine	(CA)	22
Medical & special libraries	CVELJO, Katherine	(TX)	268
Medical & special library collections	SMITH-GREENWOLD, Kathryn R.	(NY)	1162
Medical & toxicology databases	MORRISON, Brian H.	(ON)	867
Medical archives	GRACE, William M.	(PA)	455
Medical arts indexing	SERDZIAK, Edward J.	(CA)	1116
Medical audiovisuals	AGUILAR, Barbara S.	(MO)	8

MEDICAL (Cont'd)

Subject	Name	State	Page
Medical bibliographic instruction	ANDERSON, Gail C.	(GA)	23
Medical bibliographies	MARTIN, Lyn M.	(NY)	777
Medical bibliography	KLINK, Carol A.	(IL)	662
	EDDY, Leonard M.	(KY)	335
	KOBAYASHI, Michiko	(MD)	666
	KRIVDA, Marita J.	(PA)	679
Medical, biological, & business database	MANDEL, Douglas J.	(IL)	765
Medical book & journal indexing	GARCIA, Kathleen J.	(NY)	417
Medical book deselection	FARLEY, Alfred E.	(KS)	364
Medical book discounter	PUALWAN, Emily	(PA)	996
Medical book indexing	WEIR, Alexandra L.	(PA)	1319
Medical book publishing	FORD, Andrew E.	(NY)	389
Medical books & journals	AIDE, Kathryn S.	(AL)	8
	ZUNDEL, Karen M.	(PA)	1391
Medical, business	GARCIA, Ceil K.	(NJ)	417
Medical care information & reference	CAHALAN, Thomas H.	(MA)	171
Medical care reference	SKIDMORE, Kerry F.	(UT)	1146
Medical cataloging	MARSON, Joyce	(CA)	775
	RENNIE, Margaret C.	(LA)	1023
	WILLIS, Marilyn	(LA)	1348
	RAND, Pamela S.	(MD)	1006
	WINZER, Kathleen M.	(MD)	1356
	HANSON, Mary A.	(MI)	498
	GILLIAM, Susanne P.	(OH)	436
	RISSINGER, Michael	(PA)	1036
Medical center library	GHALI, Raouf S.	(NY)	430
Medical chemical environmental databases	PAPROCKI, Mary E.	(NJ)	939
Medical clinical librarianship	GRAVES, Karen J.	(IL)	459
Medical collection	DUROCHER, Jeanne M.	(MI)	328
Medical collection acquisitions	PHILLIPS, Donna M.	(IA)	968
Medical collection development	KINNAIRD, Cheryl D.	(IL)	653
	WILSON, Susan W.	(MD)	1353
	HESSLEIN, Shirley B.	(NY)	534
	SAINT, Barbara J.	(BC)	1075
Medical computer applications	CLARKE, Elba C.	(GA)	218
Medical computer training & development	HORNIG-ROHAN, James E.	(PA)	560
Medical correspondence	KOELLE, Joyce G.	(NJ)	667
Medical databases	BRICE, Heather W.	(PA)	134
	BERNARD, Molly S.	(WA)	88
Medical, dental information	PRATT, Gregory F.	(IL)	990
Medical devices	SNELL, Charles E.	(CA)	1163
Medical documents & databases	NAGY, Cecile	(PQ)	886
Medical economics	GALLAGHER, Philip J.	(NJ)	414
Medical editing	CARVER, Mary	(NY)	191
	ZIMMERMANN, Albert J.	(WI)	1389
Medical education	BOLLINGER, Robert O.	(MI)	112
	BREWER, Karen L.	(OH)	134
Medical education & databases	WAYLAND, Marilyn T.	(MI)	1311
Medical education databases	GERRITY, Marline R.	(MO)	429
Medical education library services	SNYDER, Elizabeth A.	(ENG)	1164
Medical end-user systems	TURMAN, Lynne U.	(VA)	1264
Medical government documents	WHITE, Anne E.	(IL)	1330
Medical graphics	ROSSOUW, Steve F.	(SAF)	1059
Medical history	WRIGHT, Amos J.	(AL)	1370
	EIMAS, Richard	(IA)	340
	BEATTY, William K.	(IL)	70
	BRENNER, Lawrence	(MA)	133
	KEYS, Thomas E.	(MN)	645
	SENTZ, Lilli	(NY)	1115
	KRONICK, David A.	(TX)	679
	WEINSTOCK, Joanna S.	(VT)	1318
Medical history reference	RUGGERE, Christine A.	(PA)	1066
Medical, hospital libraries	PETIT, J M.	(OH)	965
Medical, hospital reference	STRAUSS, Carol D.	(IL)	1201
Medical indexes	TOPP, Marvalyn G.	(IL)	1251
Medical indexing	GERRITY, Marline R.	(MO)	429
	FLANZRAICH, Gerri	(NY)	384
	ZOLNERZAK, Robert	(NY)	1390
Medical informatics	MANNING, Phil R.	(CA)	767
	KERN, Donald C.	(MA)	643
	HSIEH, Richard K.	(MD)	567
	FRISSE, Mark E.	(MO)	405
	SPEER, Susan C.	(NC)	1172
	STEAD, William W.	(NC)	1183
	DETLEFSEN, Ellen G.	(PA)	296

MEDICAL (Cont'd)

Medical informatics

TREMBLAY, Gerald F. . . .	(SC)	1255
ARMES, Patti	(TX)	32
LUECHT, Richard M. . . .	(WI)	747
MOEHR, Jochen R.	(BC)	851
CASIRAGHI, Edoardo . . .	(ITL)	192

Medical informatics & databases	CASTAGNO, Lucio A. . .	(BRA)	194
Medical information	MARSON, Joyce	(CA)	775
	ROWLAND, Lucy M. . . .	(GA)	1062
	FEDECZKO, Joyce L. . . .	(IL)	367
	JOHNSON, Anita D.	(IL)	602
	BRYANT, Barton B.	(MI)	152
	TOHAL, Kate J.	(MN)	1248
	CRANDALL, Elisabeth G.	(NC)	255
	TIEDRICH, Ellen K.	(NJ)	1244
	THOMSON, Diane G. . . .	(NY)	1241
	HAYNES, Robert B.	(ON)	517
	VEEKEN, Mary L.	(ON)	1280
	HANHAN, Leila M.	(LEB)	495
Medical information & librarianship	EL-MASRY, Mohammed .	(EGY)	345
Medical information & research	SMITH, Sharon	(CSR)	1160
Medical information research	WHITESIDE, Lee A.	(FL)	1333
Medical information retrieval	WAKEFIELD, Jacqueline M.	(CA)	1293
Medical information service	KELLY, Kay	(MI)	638
Medical information services	SCHULMAN, Jacque L. .	(MD)	1101
Medical information services development	REID, Carolyn A.	(NY)	1018
Medical information sources	TEITELBAUM, Sandra D.	(MD)	1230
Medical info system analysis & design	HENDRICKSON, Maria F.	(NY)	527
Medical information systems	JENKIN, Michael A.	(FL)	596
	BAKER, Benjamin R. . . .	(MD)	48
	HUMPHREYS, Betsy L. . .	(MD)	573
	JACOBS, Patt	(OR)	590
	PORTER, William R. . . .	(TN)	985
	URATA, Kazuo	(JAP)	1269
Medical information transfer	SEWELL, Winifred	(MD)	1118
Medical journal collection management	HALLERBERG, Gretchen A.	(OH)	489
Medical laboratory sciences	STANDING, Doris A. . . .	(ON)	1179
Medical librarian	ALLARD, Andre	(PQ)	14
Medical librarian continuing education	EZQUERRA, Isabel	(FL)	360
Medical librarian teaching	SUGA, Toshinobu	(JAP)	1206
Medical librarianship	FITZGERALD, Diana S. .	(CA)	382
	MIRSKY, Phyllis S.	(CA)	847
	RYAN, Ann	(CA)	1070
	VANVUREN, Darcy D. . .	(CA)	1277
	NELSON, Marie L.	(CO)	894
	DAVIDOFF, Marcia	(FL)	276
	DIAL, Carolyn E.	(FL)	299
	HOLLOWAY, David R. . . .	(FL)	552
	REAM, Diane F.	(FL)	1013
	MC LAIN, Swan M.	(GA)	813
	MILLER, Jeanne L.	(IN)	839
	ISON, Betty S.	(KY)	585
	KELLER, Nancy H.	(LA)	635
	CLEVESY, Sandra R. . . .	(MA)	222
	DESTEFANO, Daniel A. .	(MA)	296
	RIVARD, Timothy D.	(MA)	1037
	WEINSCHENK, Andrea .	(MA)	1318
	SMITH, Victoria A.	(MI)	1161
	REPETTO, Ann M.	(MO)	1023
	BREMER, Thomas A. . . .	(MT)	132
	EDWARDS, Rosa C. . . .	(NC)	338
	GLATT, Carol R.	(NJ)	440
	PACHMAN, Frederic C. .	(NJ)	933
	HELBERS, Catherine A. .	(NY)	523
	MAILLET, Lucienne G. . .	(NY)	761
	WAHLERT, George A. . .	(NY)	1292
	WEINSTEIN, Judith K. . .	(NY)	1318
	BRADIGAN, Pamela S. .	(OH)	125
	HOLCZER, Lolita B.	(OH)	550
	CARR, Caryn J.	(PA)	185
	HO, Carol T.	(PA)	545
	SHERRARD, Mary A. . . .	(VA)	1129
	MATCHINSKI, William L. .	(WY)	783
	REID, Elizabeth A.	(ON)	1018
Medical library development	AVERILL, M S.	(NJ)	41

MEDICAL (Cont'd)

Medical library networking	MIDDLETON, Dale R. . . .	(WA)	833
Medical literature	TOPP, Marvalyn G.	(IL)	1251
	WALKER, Luise E.	(OR)	1295
	HOUKE, Billy P.	(TX)	563
Medical literature & databases	GIORDANO, Joan	(NY)	438
Medical literature & searching	KATES, Jacqueline R. . .	(MA)	629
Medical literature indexing	WEAVER, Nancy B.	(MO)	1312
Medical literature searches	SIKORSKI, Charlene S. . .	(NY)	1137
Medical literature searching	RAINEY, Kathleen O. . . .	(NJ)	1004
Medical materials	WALLEN, Jody H.	(CA)	1298
	BOEHR, Diane L.	(MD)	109
Medical materials cataloging	SHRIER, Helene F.	(NY)	1133
Medical media	LUDWIG, Logan T.	(IL)	747
	KAGER, Jeffrey F.	(PA)	621
Medical, nursing database	HINKEL, Jeannine M. . . .	(MD)	542
Medical nursing databases	SEXTON, Sally V.	(OH)	1118
Medical online bibliographic searching	HARMAN, Susan E.	(MD)	502
Medical online databases	NELSON, Norma	(NY)	894
Medical online searching	JONES, Dixie A.	(LA)	612
	WARNER, Elizabeth R. . .	(PA)	1305
	TRICKEY, Katherine M. . .	(TX)	1256
Medical periodicals	MCGILL, Thomas J.	(NJ)	806
Medical, pharmaceutical & bus databases	DUDLEY, Debbra C.	(NJ)	323
Medical pharmaceutical chemical database	MOYNIHAN, Mary B. . . .	(CT)	874
Medical, pharmaceutical writing	CARVER, Mary	(NY)	191
Med, psychological, educational database	KLINE, Eve P.	(PA)	661
Medical psychology databases	BLADEN, Marguerite . . .	(CA)	102
Medical psychology information research	BLADEN, Marguerite . . .	(CA)	102
Medical public policy	SCUKA, Aletta N.	(DC)	1108
Medical publishing	TAKACS, Sharon N.	(IL)	1220
	PATTERSON, Anne S. . .	(MD)	948
Medical rare books	POND, Frederick C.	(NY)	982
Medical record systems	KISH, Veronica R.	(PA)	656
Medical records	SPOTTED EAGLE, Joy .	(MT)	1175
	MENDELSON, Martin . . .	(WA)	823
Medical records & oncology	BRENNER, Lawrence . . .	(MA)	133
Medical reference	CLEMMONS, Nancy W. . .	(AL)	221
	HARRIS, Jay	(AL)	504
	SHEARER, Barbara S. . .	(AL)	1124
	WILLIAMS, Nelle T.	(AL)	1345
	CLOUGHERTY, Leo P. . .	(AR)	223
	CONNOR, Paul L.	(CA)	238
	CONTINI, Janice L.	(CA)	239
	CRUMP, Joyce A.	(CA)	262
	POTTER, Laurene	(CA)	987
	TISE, Barbara L.	(CA)	1247
	SIMON, Nancy L.	(CO)	1140
	EBINGER, Meada G. . . .	(CT)	334
	LEVINE, Marion H.	(CT)	720
	PENN, Elinor K.	(CT)	957
	SCURA, Georgia A.	(CT)	1109
	APOSTLE, Lynne M. . . .	(DC)	29
	ANDERSON, Gail C. . . .	(GA)	23
	BELL, Mamie J.	(GA)	77
	DENNISON, Jacquelyn H.	(GA)	292
	SCHNICK, Robert M. . . .	(GA)	1097
	KRAUS, Marilyn J.	(IA)	676
	BALCERZAK, Judy A. . .	(ID)	50
	AMBROSE, Karen S. . . .	(IL)	19
	BEAN, Janet R.	(IL)	69
	EGGERS, Thomas D. . . .	(IL)	339
	IWAMI, Russell A.	(IL)	586
	SCHNOOR, Harriet E. . .	(IL)	1098
	WHITE, Anne E.	(IL)	1330
	BRAHMI, Frances A. . . .	(IN)	127
	CORBETT, Ann L.	(IN)	245
	ELLSWORTH, Marlene A.	(IN)	345
	RICHWINE, Margaret W.	(IN)	1031
	CARVER, Jane W.	(KS)	191
	YOUNG, Stephanie O. . .	(KY)	1383
	JONES, Dixie A.	(LA)	612
	NOLAN-MITCHELL, Patricia	(LA)	908
	BEDARD, Martha A.	(MA)	73
	GELLER, Miriam R.	(MA)	426

MEDICAL (Cont'd)
Medical reference

HARRIS, John C.	(MA)	504
BACKUS, Joyce E.	(MD)	44
BRANCH, Katherine A.	(MD)	127
GOLDSTEIN, Helene B.	(MD)	446
HARRIMAN, Jenny F.	(MD)	503
HUNT, Jennie P.	(MD)	575
KRUSE, Kathryn W.	(MD)	681
SATTERTHWAITE, Rebecca K.	(MD)	1084
BRISTOR, Patricia R.	(MI)	137
BURHANS, Barbara C.	(MI)	159
ROBBINS, Lora A.	(MI)	1039
WILLIAMS, Gayle A.	(MI)	1343
GLASGOW, Vicki L.	(MN)	440
MUELLER, Mary G.	(MN)	875
SINHA, Dorothy P.	(MN)	1143
IGLAUER, Carol	(MO)	581
JOHNSON, E D.	(MO)	604
SMITH, Valerie K.	(MO)	1161
BARROWS, William D.	(NC)	60
FEINGLOS, Susan J.	(NC)	369
TALBERT, David M.	(NC)	1220
REINGOLD, Judith S.	(NH)	1021
CONNICK, Kathleen D.	(NJ)	237
NAGELE, Nancy C.	(NJ)	886
REGENBERG, Patricia B.	(NJ)	1017
SPRUNG, George	(NJ)	1176
CURTIS, James A.	(NY)	267
HESSLEIN, Shirley B.	(NY)	534
NELSON, Norma	(NY)	894
POONITHARA, Pradee P.	(NY)	983
ROWELL, Regina A.	(NY)	1062
SOLLENBERGER, Julia F.	(NY)	1166
UVA, Peter A.	(NY)	1270
WESTERMANN, Mary L.	(NY)	1327
CONNERS, Margaret S.	(OH)	237
GALLANT, Jennifer J.	(OH)	414
MULARSKI, Carol A.	(OH)	876
ROSENTHAL, Barbara G.	(OH)	1057
JORDAN, Cathryn M.	(OR)	616
ANTES, E J.	(PA)	28
FARNY, Diane M.	(PA)	365
GILLILAND, Lee P.	(PA)	436
GRIFFITH, Dorothy A.	(PA)	469
LEINHEISER, Diane R.	(PA)	714
MCNABB, Corrine R.	(PA)	815
MOWERY, Susan G.	(PA)	874
NANSTIEL, Barbara L.	(PA)	887
NEUMANN, Pamela A.	(PA)	897
RAINEY, Nancy B.	(PA)	1004
SCHANER, Marian E.	(PA)	1090
STESIS, Karen R.	(PA)	1189
GABLE, Sarah H.	(SC)	411
HIPPS, Gary M.	(SC)	543
WARREN, Karen T.	(SC)	1306
SELIG, Susan A.	(TN)	1113
FRIDLEY, Bonnie J.	(TX)	403
KNOTT, Teresa L.	(TX)	665
PEDERSEN, Judy K.	(TX)	954
WARD, Deborah H.	(TX)	1303
WILSON, Barbara A.	(TX)	1349
WISE, Olga B.	(TX)	1357
WORLEY, Merry P.	(TX)	1369
TURMAN, Lynne U.	(VA)	1264
SEKERAK, Robert J.	(VT)	1113
WEINSTOCK, Joanna S.	(VT)	1318
HARBOLD, Mary J.	(WA)	499
MILES, Pamela W.	(WA)	834
STOCK, Carole G.	(WA)	1195
HOLST, Ruth M.	(WI)	554
MADSEN, Joyce	(WI)	759
NUERNBURG, Donna S.	(WI)	912
WHITCOMB, Dorothy V.	(WI)	1330
AUBIN, Robert	(PQ)	38
WALUZYNIEC, Hanna	(PQ)	1302
SMITH, Marilynn C.	(SDA)	1157

Medical reference administration

HEIDENREICH, Fred L.	(AZ)	521

MEDICAL (Cont'd)

Medical reference & information services	MAHONY, Doris D.	(MI)	761
Medical reference & literature	NOYES, Suzanne N.	(MA)	911
Medical reference & online databases	HARBERT, Cathy E.	(MD)	499
Medical reference & research	KIEFER, Rosemary M.	(FL)	647
	SNYDER, Lisa A.	(MAL)	1165
Medical reference databases	FRYER, Regina K.	(CT)	407
	MARSHAK, Bonnie L.	(NY)	773
	MACK, Bonnie R.	(WY)	756
Medical reference service	ANTONIEWICZ, Carol M.	(WI)	29
Medical reference services	MOON, Peter S.	(CT)	858
	STEPHENS, Gretchen	(IN)	1188
	WELSCH, Melissa W.	(LA)	1323
	LAMBREMONT, Jane A.	(NC)	691
	BREGMAN, Joan R.	(NY)	131
	DORNER, Marian T.	(OH)	313
	KERSTETTER, Virginia M.	(VA)	644
	SINGER, Eleanore M.	(ON)	1143
Medical reference sources	HANKS, Ellen T.	(TX)	496
Medical references	OBLOY, Elaine C.	(OH)	914
	HESZ, Bianka M.	(PA)	534
	MAYO, Helen G.	(TX)	790
	LIN, Louise	(ON)	727
Medical research	HEMINGWAY, Beverly L.	(CA)	525
	SNELL, Charles E.	(CA)	1163
	ROYSTER, Jane G.	(KY)	1063
	HUMPHRIES, Anne W.	(MD)	574
	TORDOFF, Brian G.	(MO)	1251
	KIRSCH, Anne S.	(NY)	655
	MIYAUCHI, Phyllis J.	(NY)	850
	HARMALA, Amy A.	(WA)	502
	LIBRO, Teresa M.	(WI)	725
	HEUER, Jane T.	(WY)	535
Medical risk management consulting	THOMASSON, George O.	(CO)	1238
Medical school administration	WILSON, Marjorie P.	(MD)	1352
Medical school education	MORGAN, Lynn K.	(NY)	864
Medical school libraries	RANKIN, Jocelyn A.	(GA)	1007
Medical science collection development	DIMATTEO, Lucy A.	(NY)	304
Medical sciences	CONNOLLY, Betty F.	(CA)	237
	GREEN, Ellen W.	(CA)	461
	BULLARD, Rita J.	(MI)	156
Medical, scientific, technical reference	TIFFEAULT, Alice A.	(NY)	1244
Medical searches	NICKELS, Anita B.	(CO)	902
Medical serials	EGGERS, Thomas D.	(IL)	339
	BROWN, Sharon D.	(MD)	147
	WARREN, Karen T.	(SC)	1306
Medical serials acquisitions & control	WOODBURN, Judy I.	(NC)	1366
Medical software	RUMSEY, Eric T.	(IA)	1067
Medical special librarianship	SPARKS, Marie C.	(IN)	1171
Medical subject specialist	WORTHINGTON, A P.	(CA)	1369
Medical technical services	LAWRENCE, Carol A.	(CT)	704
Medical technology	COLEMAN, David E.	(HI)	231
Medical texts	MCGILL, Thomas J.	(NJ)	806
Medical, toxicological databases	CONNER, Shirley D.	(CT)	237
Medical writing	BEATTY, William K.	(IL)	70
Medical writing & editing	CLEMENTS, Betty H.	(GA)	221
	SPARKS, Martha E.	(NC)	1171
Medically-related reference	SHRIER, Helene F.	(NY)	1133
Medico-legal issues	ROSEN, Gloria K.	(PA)	1055
Medico-legal research	BENNETT, Laura B.	(IL)	82
Nursing, medical selection, reference	TAPPANA, Kathy A.	(OK)	1223
One-person hospital medical libraries	SHELDON, Marie A.	(NY)	1126
Online medical & legal systems	MORRIS, Timothy J.	(DC)	867
Online medical & scientific databases	REITANO, Maimie V.	(NY)	1022
Online medical literature search	ABRAMSON, Lawrence J.	(MI)	3
Online medical searches	ROWBERG, Alan H.	(WA)	1062
Online medical searching	POSTLEWAIT, Cheryl A.	(KS)	986
Pharmaceutical & medical information	LAUTENSCHLAG, Elisabeth C.	(PA)	703
Pharmaceutical, medical, bus databases	MCMASTER, Deborah L.	(CT)	815
Pharmaceutical, medical, business ref	MCMASTER, Deborah L.	(CT)	815
Purchasing medical books	POLLARD, Joan B.	(VA)	981
Rare books, medical	JENKINS, Glen P.	(OH)	597
Rare medical books	JENSEN, Joseph E.	(MD)	599
	KEYS, Thomas E.	(MN)	645
	WHITCOMB, Dorothy V.	(WI)	1330
Regional medical biography	REDMON, Sherrill	(KY)	1014

MEDICAL (Cont'd)

Research in medical informatics	FULLER, Sherrilynne S. .	(MN)	409
Rewriting medical & pharmacological text	HAMILTON, Gloria R. . . .	(PA)	492
School medical	KILPATRICK, Barbara A.	(TN)	648
Science & medical collection development	HUNTER, John H.	(TX)	576
Science & medical literature	MOSER, Emily F.	(VA)	870
Science & medical online searching	LAMANN, Amber N.	(NY)	689
Science & medical reference	LACY, Yvonne M.	(TX)	687
Scientific & medical indexing	TRIMBLE, Kathy W.	(CA)	1256
Scientific & med literature searching	TRIMBLE, Kathy W.	(CA)	1256
Scientific & medical reference	LANEY-SHEEHAN, Susan	(AR)	695
Scientific medical literature searches	DAVEY, Dorothy M.	(ON)	276
Scientific technical medical	KRIEGER, Robert E. . . .	(FL)	678
Training of medical students	LANDAU, Lucille	(OH)	692
Unorthodox medical literature	KIRCHFELD, Friedhelm .	(OR)	654
Veterinary medical librarianship	STEPHENS, Gretchen . .	(IN)	1188

MEDICAL DATABASES (See also MEDLARS, MEDLINE)

Biological & medical databases	ROBINSON, Michaele M. .	(CA)	1044
Business & medical databases	LOKETS BEISCHROT, Dina	(CT)	738
Business, engineering, & med databases	POLK, Diana B.	(IL)	981
Chemical & medical databases	CHATFIELD, Michele R. .	(DC)	203
Chemical, biological & medical databases	LONGENECKER, William H.	(MD)	740
Chemical, biological, medical databases	FARREN, Ann L.	(PA)	365
Chemical, medical databases	URKEN, Madeline	(NJ)	1270
Computer searching medical databases	TAPPANA, Kathy A.	(OK)	1223
	CAMPBELL, Shirley A. . .	(TX)	177
	ARMSTRONG, Jennifer E.	(ON)	32
Computerized medical databases	WALES, Patricia L.	(CT)	1294
Database searching & medical databases	KARASICK, Alice W. . . .	(CA)	627
Database searching, medical databases	HUDSON, Donna T.	(NC)	569
Education, medical databases	MCNALLY, Ruth C.	(CA)	816
Engineering & medical databases	MOUZON, Margaret W. .	(MI)	874
Expert systems in medical databases	LONG, John M.	(MN)	739
Food science & medical databases	FALCONE, Elena C.	(NY)	362
Legal & medical databases	HENRY, Nancy J.	(IL)	529
	ENGLE, Madge	(IN)	349
Life sciences, medical databases	BAUGH, L S.	(IL)	65
Medical database	SLATER, Barbara M. . . .	(CA)	1148
	BLAKE, Michael R.	(MA)	103
	MCFARLAND, Robert T.	(MO)	805
	BOOM, Ramon A.	(MEX)	115
Medical database design	TINGLEY, Dianne E.	(MD)	1246
Medical database online searching	HEETER, Judith A.	(MN)	520
	VUGRIN, Margaret Y. . . .	(TX)	1289
Medical database production	TINGLEY, Dianne E.	(MD)	1246
Medical database searching	CLEMMONS, Nancy W. .	(AL)	221
	SHEARER, Barbara S. . .	(AL)	1124
	COLALILLO, Robert M. .	(CA)	230
	WAKEFIELD, Jacqueline M.	(CA)	1293
	HELENIUS, Majlen	(CT) .	523
	MOON, Peter S.	(CT)	858
	WETMORE, Judith M. . .	(CT)	1328
	APOSTLE, Lynne M. . . .	(DC)	29
	ANDERSON, Gail C. . . .	(GA)	23
	BROWN, Carolyn M. . . .	(GA)	142
	BALCERZAK, Judy A. . .	(ID)	50
	KELLEY, Rhona S.	(IL)	636
	SWANSON, Ruth M. . . .	(IL)	1213
	RICHWINE, Margaret W.	(IN)	1031
	WEHLACZ, Joseph T. . .	(IN)	1316
	KRUSE, Kathryn W. . . .	(MD)	681
	MORISSEAU, Anne L. . .	(MD)	865
	BRISTOR, Patricia R. . . .	(MI)	137
	VAN TOLL, Faith	(MI)	1277
	ARTH, Janet M.	(MN)	35
	TORDOFF, Brian G.	(MO)	1251
	BELL, Cecelia L.	(MS)	76

MEDICAL DATABASES (Cont'd)

Medical database searching	GRANDAGE, Karen K. . .	(NC)	457
	REISLER, Reina	(NJ)	1021
	ABLOVE, Gayle J.	(NY)	2
	EDSALL, Shirley A.	(NY)	336
	KELLER, Sharon A.	(NY)	635
	LIEBER, Ellen C.	(NY)	726
	UVA, Peter A.	(NY)	1270
	WESTERMANN, Mary L.	(NY)	1327
	BENSING, Karen M.	(OH)	83
	GIROUARD, J L.	(TX)	438
	HASELBAUER, Kathleen J.	(WA)	510
	WOOD-LIM, Eileen K. . . .	(WA)	1366
	SCHELL, Catherine L. . .	(WY)	1091
	BRUCE, Marianne E. . . .	(AB)	149
	SMITH, Marilynn C.	(SDA)	1157
Medical databases	ANDRESS, Loretta M. . .	(AK)	26
	BUCKNER, Rebecca S. .	(AL)	154
	HALL, Patricia N.	(AL)	488
	PROTTSMAN, Mary F. . .	(AL)	995
	SIMS, Joyce W.	(AL)	1142
	WILLIAMS, Nelle T.	(AL)	1345
	WRIGHT, Amos J.	(AL)	1370
	BAUM, Ester B.	(AZ)	66
	HEIDENREICH, Fred L. .	(AZ)	521
	KING, Christee	(AZ)	650
	LEI, Polin P.	(AZ)	713
	LESHY, Dede	(AZ)	718
	MEAD, Thomas L.	(AZ)	819
	ALBRIGHT, Sue R.	(CA)	10
	ANDERSON, Christine . .	(CA)	22
	ATTARIAN, Lorraine B. .	(CA)	38
	BALOGH, Leeni I.	(CA)	53
	BENELISHA, Eleanor . . .	(CA)	80
	BENNETT, Michael W. . .	(CA)	82
	CARR, Richard D.	(CA)	186
	CHADWICK, Sharon S. .	(CA)	197
	CHU, Sally C.	(CA)	212
	CLANCY, Stephen L. . . .	(CA)	215
	CLARY, Rochelle L.	(CA)	219
	CONNOR, Paul L.	(CA)	238
	CONTINI, Janice L.	(CA)	239
	DAVIS, Marianne W. . . .	(CA)	280
	DITO, William R.	(CA)	305
	DURSO, Angeline M. . . .	(CA)	329
	FIEDLER, Albert E.	(CA)	375
	GELMAN-KMEC, Marsha	(CA)	426
	GLITZ, Beryl	(CA)	441
	GUPTA, Ann D.	(CA)	478
	HABETLER, Anna M. . . .	(CA)	481
	HARRIS, Vallena D.	(CA)	506
	HAUTH, Carol A.	(CA)	513
	HOUGHTON, Barbara H.	(CA)	562
	ITNYRE, Jacqueline H. . .	(CA)	585
	JACOBUS, Nancy M. . . .	(CA)	590
	JAJKO, Pamela J.	(CA)	592
	KACZOROWSKI, Monice M.	(CA)	621
	KENNEDY, Joanne	(CA)	641
	KING, Joseph T.	(CA)	651
	KWAN, Julie K.	(CA)	685
	LEVINE, Warren D.	(CA)	721
	LUEBKE, Margaret F. . . .	(CA)	747
	MANTHEY, Teresa M. . .	(CA)	767
	MILLER, Jean R.	(CA)	839
	MUSEN, Mark A.	(CA)	883
	NEWMARK, Laura C. . . .	(CA)	900
	NOUROK, Marlene E. . . .	(CA)	910
	NOVACK, Dona A.	(CA)	910
	PERLMAN-STITES, Janice	(CA)	959
	PHILLIPS, Jordan M. . . .	(CA)	968
	PINCKNEY, Cathey L. . .	(CA)	974
	POKLAR, Mary J.	(CA)	980
	RUDOLPH, Anne L.	(CA)	1066
	RYAN, Ann	(CA)	1070
	SAWYER, Anne R.	(CA)	1086
	SCHULTZ, Ute M.	(CA)	1102
	SCHULZ, Judith H.	(CA)	1102

MEDICAL DATABASES (Cont'd)
Medical databases

SEHR, Dena P. . . . . . . (CA) 1112
SHAMS, Kamruddin . . . . (CA) 1120
SHAPIRO, Leonard P. . . (CA) 1121
SHERMAN, Judith E. . . . (CA) 1128
SHEW, Anne L. . . . . . . (CA) 1129
SIMS, Sidney B. . . . . . . (CA) 1142
SMITH, Julie L. . . . . . . (CA) 1156
TREISTER, Cyril C. . . . (CA) 1255
WARD, Penny T. . . . . . (CA) 1304
WILSON, Barbara A. . . . (CA) 1350
WOOD, Elizabeth H. . . . . (CA) 1364
WORTHINGTON, A P. . . (CA) 1369
ZAREMSKA, Maryann . . (CA) 1386
ZEIND, Samir M. . . . . . (CA) 1387
BRAGDON, Lynn . . . . . . (CO) 127
BRITAIN, Karla K. . . . . (CO) 137
CHANDLER, Constance P. (CO) 199
GILBERT, Ruth E. . . . . . (CO) 434
GUTH, Karen K. . . . . . . (CO) 478
JANES, Nina . . . . (CO) 593
KLENK, Anne S. . . . . . . (CO) 660
SIMON, Nancy L. . . . . . (CO) 1140
SMITH, Catherine C. . . . (CO) 1153
VERCIO, Roseanne . . . . (CO) 1282
WILLIAMS, Alma . . . . . . (CO) 1341
ASBELL, Mildred S. . . . . (CT) 35
BRECK, Evelyn M. . . . . . (CT) 131
EICKENHORST, Joanna
    W. . . . . (CT) 339
FARADAY, Joanna . . . . . (CT) 363
FINNUCAN, Louise A. . . (CT) 379
FREY, Barbara J. . . . . . (CT) 402
STEMMER, Katherine R. (CT) 1186
TRAVER, Julia M. . . . . . (CT) 1254
WILCOX, Carolyn G. . . . (CT) 1338
BROERING, Naomi C. . . (DC) 139
BROWN, Dale S. . . . . . . (DC) 143
ELLIOT, Hugh . . . . (DC) 343
KUTTY, Lalitha M. . . . . . (DC) 685
LEVIN, Amy E. . . . . (DC) 720
MASSAY, Mary K. . . . . . (DC) 782
MCCRAY, Maceo E. . . . . (DC) 800
PATEL, Patricia C. . . . . . (DC) 947
SCHUERMANN, Lois J. . (DC) 1101
CHASTAIN-WARHEIT,
    Christine C. . . . . (DE) 203
ELLIOTT, Gwendolyn T. . (DE) 344
COSCULLUELA, Marta . (FL) 248
FRANCIS, Barbara W. . . (FL) 396
GROVER, Wilma S. . . . . (FL) 474
HSU, Pi Y. . . . . (FL) 567
JOHNSTON, Judy F. . . . (FL) 610
LADNER, Sharyn J. . . . . (FL) 687
SCHMID, Cynthia M. . . . (FL) 1094
STEINBERG, Celia L. . . . (FL) 1185
WALTERS, Gwen E. . . . . (FL) 1301
WHITESIDE, Lee A. . . . . (FL) 1333
BENEVICH, Lauren A. . . (GA) 80
CRAWFORD, Sherrida J. (GA) 257
HENDRIX, Linda S. . . . . (GA) 527
MARKWELL, Linda G. . . (GA) 772
OWINGS, Priscilla A. . . . (GA) 932
PAYNE-BUTTON, Linda . (GA) 951
SCHNICK, Robert M. . . . (GA) 1097
STANSELL, Janet S. . . . (GA) 1181
TORRENTE, Kathryn J. . (GA) 1251
WAVERCHAK, Gail A. . . (GA) 1311
FETTES, Virginia M. . . . (HI) 374
FURUMOTO, Viola G. . . (HI) 410
GOVERNS, Molly K. . . . . (HI) 454
MAZZOLA, Patricia R. . . (HI) 791
SMITH, Frances P. . . . . (HI) 1155
KROMMINGA, Patricia G. (IA) 679
NELSON, Donald A. . . . . (IA) 893
PHILLIPS, Donna M. . . . (IA) 968
RUMSEY, Eric T. . . . . . (IA) 1067
NELSON, Kathy J. . . . . . (ID) 894
SPICKELMIER, Pamela S. (ID) 1174

MEDICAL DATABASES (Cont'd)
Medical databases

WINWARD, Coleen C. . . (ID) 1356
BROWN, Patricia B. . . . . (IL) 146
FEINBERG, Linda J. . . . . (IL) 368
FINNERTY, James L. . . . (IL) 379
FOLEY, Donna H. . . . . . (IL) 387
GRUNDKE, Patricia J. . . (IL) 475
HAYES, Hazel I. . . . . . . (IL) 515
IWAMI, Russell A. . . . . . (IL) 586
KALUZSA, Karen L. . . . . (IL) 623
KEENAN, Mary T. . . . . . (IL) 634
KELLY, Janice E. . . . . . . (IL) 637
KRUPKA, Karen K. . . . . (IL) 680
LIANG, Ching C. . . . . . . (IL) 725
MIFFLIN, Michael J. . . . . (IL) 833
MORRIS, Lynne D. . . . . . (IL) 867
MUELLER, Julie M. . . . . (IL) 875
NAGOLSKI, Donald J. . . (IL) 886
NG, Pauline . . . . (IL) 900
PAIETTA, Ann C. . . . . . . (IL) 935
PILARSKI, James P. . . . (IL) 973
PINKOWSKI, Patricia E. . (IL) 975
ROGINSKI, Donna J. . . . (IL) 1050
ROMANACE, Gisele R. . (IL) 1052
STLUKA, Thomas H. . . . (IL) 1195
STROYAN, Susan E. . . . (IL) 1203
TOPP, Marvalyn G. . . . . (IL) 1251
TROFIMUK, Janette A. . . (IL) 1257
TYLMAN, Wieslawa T. . . (IL) 1266
VAN DYKE, Mary C. . . . (IL) 1275
WALTERS, Patsy M. . . . (IL) 1301
WARD, Meg . . . . (IL) 1304
WELCH, Eric C. . . . . . . (IL) 1321
WILLIAMSON, Harriet . . (IL) 1347
WIMMER, Katherine P. . . (IL) 1354
AVEN, Lauralee . . . . (IN) 41
BRAHMI, Frances A. . . . (IN) 127
DURKIN, Virginia M. . . . . (IN) 328
ELLSWORTH, Marlene A. (IN) 345
HOOK-SHELTON, Sara A. (IN) 556
KYKER, Penelope R. . . . (IN) 685
MARTINO, Sharon C. . . . (IN) 779
MONROE, Donald H. . . . (IN) 855
VAN CAMP, Ann J. . . . . (IN) 1272
BRADEN, Jan . . . . (KS) 125
GOTTSHALL, Judith L. . . (KS) 454
KINZIE, Lenora A. . . . . . (KS) 653
TANNER, Jane E. . . . . . (KS) 1223
JOHNSON, Garry B. . . . (KY) 604
YOUNG, Stephanie O. . . (KY) 1383
BLOOMSTONE, Ajaye . . (LA) 106
CAFFAREL, Agnes . . . . . (LA) 170
COPELAND, Patricia S. . (LA) 244
HAMORI, Annemarie R. . (LA) 494
HIGGINBOTHAM, Cecelia
    B. . . . . (LA) 537
KELLER, Nancy H. . . . . . (LA) 635
LOUBIERE, Sue . . . . . . (LA) 742
NEVEU, Wilma B. . . . . . (LA) 897
NOLAN-MITCHELL,
    Patricia . . . . (LA) 908
RAMAKRISHNAN, T . . . (LA) 1004
STROTHER, Elizabeth A. (LA) 1203
TETTEH, Joseph A. . . . . (LA) 1233
WELSCH, Melissa W. . . . (LA) 1323
WILLIS, Marilyn . . . . (LA) 1348
BRAUN, Robin E. . . . . . (MA) 130
BUTTON, Katherine H. . . (MA) 167
CAREY, Charlene E. . . . (MA) 181
CHRISTOPHER, Irene . . (MA) 212
DAVITT, Theresa B. . . . . (MA) 281
DEWEY, Marjorie C. . . . . (MA) 298
DUDA, Heidi E. . . . . (MA) 323
FRAZIER, Nancy E. . . . . (MA) 399
HOLMES, Lyndon S. . . . (MA) 553
HUNTER, Isabel . . . . . . (MA) 576
KAMENOFF, Lovisa . . . . (MA) 623
KANG, Wen . . . . (MA) 625
LOSCALZO, Anita B. . . . (MA) 741

MEDICAL DATABASES (Cont'd)
Medical databases

O'BRIEN, Elizabeth J. . . . (MA) 914
O'BRIEN, Marjorie S. . . . (MA) 914
OPPENHEIM, Roberta A. (MA) 925
PERINO, Elaine S. . . . . . (MA) 958
SIMEONE, Therese A. . . (MA) 1139
BACKUS, Joyce E. . . . . . (MD) 44
BUCHAN, Patricia C. . . . (MD) 153
BUTTER, Karen A. . . . . . (MD) 167
CONNER, P Z. . . . . (MD) 237
CONNOR, Elizabeth . . . . (MD) 237
COSKEY, Rosemary B. . (MD) 248
DICKINSON, Patricia C. . (MD) 301
EPSTEIN, Robert S. . . . . (MD) 351
GALLAGHER, Elizabeth M. (MD) 414
GOEL, Krishan S. . . . . . . (MD) 443
GOLDSCHMIDT, Peter G. (MD) 446
GOLDSTEIN, Helene B. . (MD) 446
HERIN, Nancy J. . . . . . . (MD) 531
HUMPHREY, Susanne M. (MD) 573
IRWIN, Ruth A. . . . . (MD) 584
JOHNSON, Gary M. . . . . (MD) 604
KIGER, Anne F. . . . . (MD) 647
KIM, Chung S. . . . . (MD) 648
KINNA, Dorothy H. . . . . . (MD) 652
KOTZIN, Sheldon . . . . . . (MD) 673
LAY, Shirley . . . . (MD) 705
LAZAROW-STETTEN,
    Jane K. . . . . (MD) 706
LYNN, Kenneth C. . . . . . (MD) 752
MARTINEZ-GOLDMAN,
    Aline . . . . (MD) 779
MASYS, Daniel R. . . . . . (MD) 783
MATHESON, Nina W. . . . (MD) 783
MUNSEY, Joyce E. . . . . (MD) 879
OGLE, Mary H. . . . . (MD) 918
POMERANTZ, Karyn L. . (MD) 982
SAVAGE, Allan G. . . . . . (MD) 1085
SCHOLTEN, Frances . . . (MD) 1098
SCHULTZ, Barbara A. . . (MD) 1101
SMITH, Karen G. . . . . . . (MD) 1156
SMITH, Kathleen A. . . . . (MD) 1156
SULLIVAN, Joanne L. . . . (MD) 1207
WALLINGFORD, Karen T. (MD) 1298
WILLIAMS, Mary A. . . . . (MD) 1345
WOLLAM, Martha A. . . . . (MD) 1361
YORKS, Melissa L. . . . . . (MD) 1381
YU, Pei . . . . (MD) 1384
ZAHARKO, Nancy W. . . . (MD) 1385
ZIMMERMAN, Martha B. (MD) 1389
DAMON, Cora M. . . . . . . (ME) 272
GREENLAW, Evelyn A. . (ME) 465
JAGELS, Suellen T. . . . . (ME) 591
SPIEGEL, Nancy C. . . . . (ME) 1174
ABRAMSON, Lawrence J. (MI) 3
ALLRED, Paula M. . . . . . (MI) 17
BINONIEMI, Amanda M. . (MI) 97
BOLLINGER, Robert O. . (MI) 112
CLAYTOR, Jane B. . . . . . (MI) 220
HEINLEN, Bethany A. . . . (MI) 522
KLEIN, Michele S. . . . . . (MI) 659
LEE, Lucy W. . . . . (MI) 710
MARSHALL, Betty J. . . . (MI) 773
MATHIS, Yvonne L. . . . . (MI) 784
MORELAND, Patricia L. . (MI) 863
MOSHER, Robin A. . . . . (MI) 871
O'DONNELL, Ellen E. . . . (MI) 917
ROBBINS, Lora A. . . . . . (MI) 1039
ROENZWEIG, Merle . . . . (MI) 1048
SKOGLUND, Susan E. . . (MI) 1147
SKONIECZNY, Jill . . . . . (MI) 1147
SMITH, Victoria A. . . . . . (MI) 1161
WARD, Nancy E. . . . . . . (MI) 1304
WILLIAMS, Gayle A. . . . (MI) 1343
ERWIN, Patricia J. . . . . . (MN) 353
FEMAL, Mary B. . . . . (MN) 370
LATTA, Barbara K. . . . . . (MN) 702
LO, Maryanne H. . . . . . . (MN) 735
LONG, John M. . . . . (MN) 739

MEDICAL DATABASES (Cont'd)
Medical databases

MUELLER, Mary G. . . . . (MN) 875
MYHRE, Char . . . . (MN) 885
SANDNESS, John G. . . . (MN) 1081
BRENNER, Saundra H. . . (MO) 133
CRABTREE, Anna B. . . . (MO) 254
DALTON, Richard R. . . . (MO) 271
DEMUTH, Elizabeth J. . . (MO) 291
GALLAGHER, Kathy E. . (MO) 414
GIBSON, Patricia A. . . . . (MO) 432
HUGHES, Joan L. . . . . . (MO) 571
JOHNSON, E D. . . . . . . (MO) 604
LUH, Ming . . . . (MO) 747
MARCHANT, Thomas O. (MO) 768
MCKININ, Emma J. . . . . (MO) 811
RIKLI, Arthur E. . . . . (MO) 1034
RUBY, Carolyn M. . . . . . (MO) 1065
SHIEH, Monica W. . . . . . (MO) 1129
SULLIVAN, Marilyn G. . . (MO) 1208
SUTTER, Mary A. . . . . . (MO) 1211
SELTZER, Ada M. . . . . . (MS) 1114
HOLT, Suzy . . . . (MT) 554
LONG, Susan S. . . . . . . (MT) 740
BUTSON, Linda C. . . . . . (NC) 167
COBB, Margaret L. . . . . . (NC) 225
CRANDALL, Elisabeth G. (NC) 255
EKSTRAND, Nancy L. . . (NC) 341
LAVINE, Marcia M. . . . . (NC) 703
NYE, Julie B. . . . . (NC) 912
RICHARDSON, Beverly S. (NC) 1029
THIBODEAU, Patricia L. . (NC) 1235
WALTON, Carol G. . . . . . (NC) 1301
ETTL, Lorraine R. . . . . . . (ND) 356
EARLEY, Dorothy A. . . . (NE) 332
BUNDY, John F. . . . . (NH) 157
MCGINNIS, Joan M. . . . (NH) 806
REED, Alice . . . . (NH) 1014
REINGOLD, Judith S. . . . (NH) 1021
BOSS, Catherine M. . . . . (NJ) 117
CORRADO, Margaret M. (NJ) 247
DUTKA, Jeanne L. . . . . . (NJ) 329
GARNER, Linda J. . . . . . (NJ) 419
GLASSER, Anne . . . . . . (NJ) 440
GUSTAFSON, Ruth . . . . (NJ) 478
HOFFMAN, Helen B. . . . (NJ) 548
HOVER, Leila M. . . . . . . (NJ) 563
LINGELBACH, Lorene N. (NJ) 730
LITTLE, Karen M. . . . . . . (NJ) 733
MARCHOK, Catherine W. (NJ) 769
MICHAELS, Debbie D. . . (NJ) 832
MILLINGTON, Kathleen A. (NJ) 843
MOELLER, Kathleen A. . (NJ) 851
O'CONNOR, Christine T. (NJ) 916
O'CONNOR, Elizabeth W. (NJ) 916
PANDELAKIS, Helene S. (NJ) 937
PIERMATTI, Patricia A. . (NJ) 972
RAINEY, Kathleen O. . . . (NJ) 1004
REGENBERG, Patricia B. (NJ) 1017
RYAN, Mary E. . . . . (NJ) 1071
SIEGEL, Robin D. . . . . . (NJ) 1136
SKICA, Janice K. . . . . . . (NJ) 1146
SPRUNG, George . . . . . (NJ) 1176
MORLEY, Sarah K. . . . . (NM) 865
STRUB, Jeane E. . . . . . . (NM) 1203
PRATT, Kathleen L. . . . . (NV) 990
STURM, H P. . . . . (NV) 1205
ABDULLAH, Bilquis . . . . (NY) 2
ARAYA, Rose M. . . . . . . (NY) 30
BANKS-ISZARD, Kimberly
    K. . . . . (NY) 54
BARTEN, Sharon S. . . . . (NY) 60
CALVANO, Margaret . . . (NY) 174
CHITTAMPALLI, Padma S. (NY) 209
COAN, Mary L. . . . . (NY) 224
DANSKER, Shirley E. . . . (NY) 274
DOHERTY, Mary C. . . . . (NY) 309
GAFFNEY, Denis C. . . . . (NY) 412
GRANT, Mary A. . . . . . . (NY) 458
HALL, Russell W. . . . . . . (NY) 488

MEDICAL DATABASES (Cont'd)
Medical databases

HELLER, Jacqueline R. . . . (NY) 524
HENDRICKSON, Maria F. . (NY) 527
HOLLIDAY, Geneva R. . . . (NY) 552
HUTCHINSON, Ann P. . . . (NY) 579
KAHN, Martin F. . . . . (NY) 622
KENEFICK, Colleen M. . . . (NY) 640
KLEIN, Penny . . . . (NY) 659
LEE, Judy A. . . . . (NY) 710
LISZCZYNSKYJ, Halyna
A. . . . . (NY) 733
MAURER, Eric . . . . (NY) 787
MIYAUCHI, Phyllis J. . . . (NY) 850
MOUNIR, Khalil A. . . . . . (NY) 873
MULCAHY, Brian J. . . . . (NY) 876
NAPOLITANO, Joan A. . . (NY) 887
NARDUCCI, Frances . . . (NY) 888
POONITHARA, Pradee P. . (NY) 983
REID, Carol L. . . . . (NY) 1018
REINSTEIN, Diana J. . . . (NY) 1021
RUBINSTEIN, Edith . . . . (NY) 1065
SHELANDER, Frances R. . (NY) 1125
SHER, Deborah M. . . . . . (NY) 1127
SMITH, Annie J. . . . . (NY) 1152
SMITH, Brian D. . . . . (NY) 1153
SOLLENBERGER, Julia F. (NY) 1166
STRAUSMAN, Jeanne . . (NY) 1201
TANNER, Ellen B. . . . . . . (NY) 1222
TOMASULO, Patricia A. . (NY) 1249
TOMLIN, Anne C. . . . . . (NY) 1250
TRAVERS, Jane E. . . . . (NY) 1254
WEINSTEIN, Judith K. . . (NY) 1318
WESTERFIELD, Marjorie
C. . . . . (NY) 1327
WISEMAN, Karin M. . . . . (NY) 1357
YUCHT, Donald J. . . . . . (NY) 1384
BRADIGAN, Pamela S. . (OH) 125
CHEEK, Fern H. . . . . (OH) 204
COHEN, Nancy E. . . . . . (OH) 228
CREELAN, Marilee M. . . (OH) 257
DAVIS, Linda M. . . . . . . (OH) 280
DZIEDZINA, Christine A. . (OH) 331
ELWELL, Pamela M. . . . (OH) 347
EMANI, Nirupama . . . . . . (OH) 347
GALLANT, Jennifer J. . . (OH) 414
GEARY, Linda L. . . . . . . (OH) 424
HALIBEY-BILYK, Christine
M. . . . . (OH) 486
HALLERBERG, Gretchen
A. . . . . (OH) 489
IBEN, Glenn A. . . . . (OH) 581
JANES, Jodith . . . . (OH) 593
JOHNSON, Debbie L. . . . (OH) 603
KERBOW, Sandra C. . . . (OH) 643
LANDAU, Lucille . . . . . . (OH) 692
LYNAM, Nancy J. . . . . . (OH) 751
MAHOVLIC, Leanne M. . (OH) 761
MALUCHNIK, Kathryn K. (OH) 764
MAXWELL, Marjo V. . . . (OH) 788
MC CORMICK, Lisa L. . . (OH) 798
MULARSKI, Carol A. . . . (OH) 876
OBLOY, Elaine C. . . . . . (OH) 914
OLIVER, Shirley . . . . (OH) 921
PHILLIPS, Judith Z. . . . . (OH) 968
PORTER, Marlene A. . . . (OH) 985
RASKIN, Rosa S. . . . . . . (OH) 1009
ROBINSON, Elizabeth A. (OH) 1044
ROSENTHAL, Barbara G. (OH) 1057
STANLEY, Jean B. . . . . . (OH) 1180
STROZIER, Sandra L. . . (OH) 1203
TILLMAN, Linda M. . . . . (OH) 1245
UNGER, Monica A. . . . . (OH) 1269
WARNER, Susan B. . . . . (OH) 1305
COOK, Peggy M. . . . . . . (OK) 240
MCKNIGHT, Michelynn . . (OK) 812
JORDAN, Cathryn M. . . . (OR) 616
LIBERTINI, Arleen J. . . . (OR) 725
OLSON-URLIE, Carolyn T. (OR) 923
TYLER, Kim E. . . . . (OR) 1266

MEDICAL DATABASES (Cont'd)
Medical databases

ARJONA, Sandra K. . . . . . (PA) 31
BABISH, Jo A. . . . . (PA) 43
BAKER, Judith M. . . . . . (PA) 48
BANDEMER, June E. . . . (PA) 54
BEACH, Linda M. . . . . . . (PA) 68
BURTON, Mary L. . . . . . (PA) 164
CAPITANI, Cheryl A. . . . (PA) 180
CLEVELAND, Susan E. . . (PA) 221
COGHLAN, Patricia M. . . (PA) 227
EVITTS, Beth A. . . . . (PA) 359
FALGER, David E. . . . . . (PA) 362
HARKE, Toby H. . . . . . . (PA) 501
HOMICK, Elaine . . . . (PA) 555
IOBST, Barbara J. . . . . . (PA) 583
IZZO, Kathleen A. . . . . . (PA) 586
JOHNSTON, Bruce A. . . (PA) 610
KATUCKI, June P. . . . . . (PA) 630
KELLEY, John F. . . . . . . (PA) 636
KERCHOF, Kathryn K. . . (PA) 643
KREULEN, Thomas . . . . (PA) 678
MAXIN, Jacqueline A. . . . (PA) 787
MCGEE, Yvonne M. . . . . (PA) 806
MILLER, Naomi . . . . (PA) 841
MOREY, Carol M. . . . . . (PA) 863
MOWERY, Susan G. . . . (PA) 874
NEUMANN, Pamela A. . . (PA) 897
NIPPERT, Carolyn C. . . . (PA) 904
RAINEY, Nancy B. . . . . . (PA) 1004
SCHEETZ, Mary D. . . . . (PA) 1091
SHULTZ, Suzanne M. . . . (PA) 1133
SNOW, Bonnie . . . . (PA) 1164
TAYLOR, Rosemarie K. . (PA) 1228
TEOLIS, Marilyn G. . . . . (PA) 1231
ULINCY, Loretta D. . . . . . (PA) 1268
WESSEL, Charles B. . . . (PA) 1325
WOOD, M S. . . . . (PA) 1364
ZUNDEL, Karen M. . . . . (PA) 1391
GARCIA-RUIZ, Maritza L. (PR) 417
ASPRI, Jo A. . . . . (RI) 37
CAMP, Mary A. . . . . (SC) 175
COOK, Galen B. . . . . (SC) 240
DAVIS, Patsy M. . . . . . . (SC) 280
GABLE, Sarah H. . . . . . . (SC) 411
POYER, Robert K. . . . . . (SC) 989
TOWELL, Fay J. . . . . (SC) 1252
HAMILTON, Patricia J. . . (SD) 492
HILMOE, Deann D. . . . . . (SD) 541
HULKONEN, David A. . . (SD) 572
BELLAMY, Lois M. . . . . . (TN) 77
BRANSFORD, John S. . . (TN) 129
COOPER, Ellen R. . . . . . (TN) 242
EUBANKS, Marie . . . . . . (TN) 356
FORBES, Evelyn H. . . . . (TN) 388
GIVENS, Mary K. . . . . . . (TN) 439
HALE, Relda D. . . . . (TN) 485
HAMBERG, Cheryl J. . . . (TN) 490
HARALSON, Robert H. . . (TN) 499
IRBY, Patricia P. . . . . . . (TN) 583
LEWIS, Carol E. . . . . . . (TN) 722
OWEN, Richard L. . . . . . (TN) 932
SELIG, Susan A. . . . . . . (TN) 1113
WATTS, Adalyn . . . . (TN) 1310
YALCINTAS, Rana . . . . . (TN) 1376
ARNN, Judith A. . . . . (TX) 33
BROOKS, Ruth H. . . . . . (TX) 140
CALDWELL, Marlene . . . (TX) 172
ECHT, Sandy A. . . . . (TX) 334
FRIDLEY, Bonnie J. . . . . (TX) 403
GALBRAITH, Paula L. . . (TX) 413
KNOTT, Teresa L. . . . . . (TX) 665
MAYO, Helen G. . . . . . . (TX) 790
NEELEY, Dana M. . . . . . (TX) 891
PEDERSEN, Judy K. . . . (TX) 954
PHILLIPS, Carol B. . . . . (TX) 967
RICCARDI, Vincent M. . . (TX) 1026
ROBERTS, Ernest J. . . . (TX) 1040
THOMAS, Donald L. . . . (TX) 1236
TRANFAGLIA, Twyla L. . (TX) 1254

MEDICAL DATABASES (Cont'd)
Medical databases

WILKERSON, Judith C. . .	(TX)	1339
WOOD, Richard C.	(TX)	1365
ANGIER, Jennifer J.	(UT)	27
JAMES, Brent C.	(UT)	592
STODDART, Joan M.	(UT)	1196
GENNARO, John L.	(VA)	427
HAMILTON, Elizabeth J. . .	(VA)	492
KOK, Victoria T.	(VA)	669
LUNIN, Lois F.	(VA)	749
RICHARD, Sheila A.	(VA)	1028
SEAMANS, Nancy H. . . .	(VA)	1109
CURTIS, Monica R.	(VT)	267
DURFEE, Tamara	(VT)	328
STANLEY, Donald E. . . .	(VT)	1180
WEINSTOCK, Joanna S. .	(VT)	1318
CARVER, Sue A.	(WA)	191
KANNEL, Selma	(WA)	625
PRESS, Nancy O.	(WA)	991
ROBERTSON, Ann	(WA)	1041
ROWBERG, Alan H.	(WA)	1062
SONG, Seungja Y.	(WA)	1167
SPEARMAN, Marie A. . .	(WA)	1172
STOCK, Carole G.	(WA)	1195
TURNER, Tamara A. . . .	(WA)	1265
ANTONIEWICZ, Carol M.	(WI)	29
BARLOGA, Carolyn J. . .	(WI)	57
BAYORGEON, Mary M. . .	(WI)	68
BLACKWELDER, Mary B. .	(WI)	102
ECKERT, Daniel L.	(WI)	335
GEBHARDT, Sharon E. . .	(WI)	424
HALL, Deborah A.	(WI)	487
MURPHY, Virginia A. . . .	(WI)	881
SHAIKH, Sunja L.	(WI)	1119
STRUBE, Kathleen	(WI)	1203
TERANIS, Mara	(WI)	1231
WILCOX, Patricia F.	(WI)	1338
WONG, Elizabeth M. . . .	(WI)	1362
ZIMMERMANN, Albert J. .	(WI)	1389
DZIERZAK, Edward M. . .	(WV)	331
GREATHOUSE, Brenda J.	(WV)	461
HEUER, Jane T.	(WY)	535
JACKSON, Sue H.	(WY)	588
SEEBAUM, Carol J.	(WY)	1111
STARR, Lea K.	(AB)	1182
AUFIERO, Joan I.	(BC)	39
SAINT, Barbara J.	(BC)	1075
VAN REENEN, Johannes A.	(BC)	1277
EAGLETON, Kathleen M.	(MB)	331
HEINO, Dan R.	(NF)	522
LOGAN, Penelope A. . . .	(NS)	737
BERNSTEIN, Elaine S. . .	(ON)	89
BREGAINT, Bernard J. . .	(ON)	131
GOLD, Sandra	(ON)	444
GOSS, Alison M.	(ON)	453
HAYNES, Robert B.	(ON)	517
HOARE, Colin G.	(ON)	545
KATZER, Sylvia U.	(ON)	630
LADD, Kenneth F.	(ON)	687
LAMBERT, Deborah B. . .	(ON)	690
LEBRUN, Anne	(ON)	708
MARSHALL, Joanne G. .	(ON)	774
MORRISON, Carol A. . . .	(ON)	868
VAN ORDER, Mary J. . . .	(ON)	1276
BEDARD, Bernard J. . . .	(PQ)	73
BOISVERT, Diane	(PQ)	111
BOLSVERT, Diane B. . . .	(PQ)	113
DUCHESNEAU, Pierre . .	(PQ)	322
KELLY, Claire B.	(PQ)	637
KOBER, Gary L.	(PQ)	666
LAMBROU, Angella	(PQ)	691
COBOLET, Guy P.	(FRN)	225
ROSSOUW, Steve F. . . .	(SAF)	1059
BASCOM, James F.	(SDA)	62
BUTT, Abdul W.	(SDA)	167

Medical databases & reference

HUTCHINSON, Beck . . .	(FL)	579
REES, Pamela C.	(IA)	1016
DUNCAN, Bettye M.	(MS)	325

MEDICAL DATABASES (Cont'd)

Medical databases & searching	GLASGOW, Vicki L.	(MN)	440
Medical databases & systems	SATTERTHWAITE, Rebecca K.	(MD)	1084
Medical databases bibliography	BLOKH, Basheva	(NY)	106
Medical databases, database searching	DONOVAN, Judith G. . . .	(PA)	312
Medical databases, engineering databases	GODT, Carol	(MO)	443
Medical databases, HMO	KNARZER, Arlene	(IL)	663
Medical databases online	SCHWARTZ, Dorothy D.	(NY)	1104
Medical databases, online searching	FEINGLOS, Susan J. . . .	(NC)	369
	CLINTON, Janet C.	(PA)	222
Medical databases, reference, cataloging	MARK, Ronnie J.	(NY)	770
Medical databases searching	KLECKER, Anita N.	(CA)	658
	WHITE, Anne E.	(IL)	1330
	GILBERT, Carole M. . . .	(MI)	433
	HESLIN, Catherine M. . .	(PA)	534
Medical databases training	REID, Carolyn A.	(NY)	1018
Online database & medical databases	FRANK, Agnes T.	(NY)	396
Online medical database searching	TIBBS, Jo A.	(FL)	1244
Online medical databases	CUTTS, William B.	(CO)	268
	REAM, Diane F.	(FL)	1013
	GOLDMAN, Richard	(PA)	446
Online searching & medical databases	MARTIN, Patricia W. . . .	(MI)	777
Online searching for medical databases	HILL, Barbarie F.	(OH)	539
Online searching in medical databases	SHEDLOCK, James	(IL)	1124
Online searching, medical databases	CRUMP, Joyce A.	(CA)	262
	CESANEK, Sylvia B. . . .	(FL)	196
	QUAIN, Julie R.	(NY)	999
	KRIVDA, Marita J.	(PA)	679
	ROSEN, Gloria K.	(PA)	1055
	FORD, Mary R.	(TX)	389
	KIELLY, Marion J.	(PE)	647
Pharmaceutical & medical databases	ROSENTHAL, Francine C.	(OH)	1057
Reference, chemical & medical databases	WINGATE, Dawn A.	(CA)	1354
Reference, medical databases	WRIGHT, Barbara A. . . .	(NC)	1370
Reference services, medical databases	BROWN, Biraj L.	(SDA)	142
Reference work & medical databases	FRATIES, Marie L.	(MI)	399
Science & medical databases	OSTROFF, Cynthia R. . .	(CT)	929
	MAYER, Erich J.	(NY)	789
Science, engineering & medical databases	ARIARATNAM, Lakshmi V.	(CA)	31
Scientific & medical databases	LANEY-SHEEHAN, Susan	(AR)	695
Scientific, chemical, medical databases	ANTOS, Brian F.	(PA)	29
Scientific medical databases	DAVEY, Dorothy M.	(ON)	276
Searching medical databases	SCARFIA, Angela M. . . .	(NY)	1087
	TANNENBAUM, Robin L.	(NY)	1222
	MILES, Donald D.	(PA)	834

MEDICAL LIBRARIES

Clinical medical libraries	WATTS, Adalyn	(TN)	1310
Cooperative medical library systems	JOHN, Stephanie C. . . .	(MI)	601
General medical library management	FETKOVICH, Malinda M.	(PA)	374
Hospital & medical library consulting	BLADEN, Marguerite . . .	(CA)	102
Law library, medical library	SUMMERS, Sheryl H. . . .	(MI)	1209
Medical libraries	RINGER, Sarah A.	(AR)	1035
	MCCRAY, Jeanette C. . .	(AZ)	800
	GILMAN, Nelson J.	(CA)	436
	DEE, Cheryl R.	(FL)	286
	BINGHAM, James L. . . .	(KS)	97
	WESTLING, Ellen R. . . .	(MA)	1327
	DRAYSON, Pamela K. . .	(MO)	318
	LAUGHLIN, Cheryl H. . . .	(MS)	703
	COBB, Margaret L.	(NC)	225
	LAMBREMONT, Jane A.	(NC)	691
	SPURLOCK, Sandra E. .	(NM)	1177
	JOHNSON, Millard F. . . .	(OR)	607
	TASHJIAN, Sharon A. . .	(OR)	1224
	COOK, Nedra J.	(TN)	240
	HELGUERA, Byrd S. . . .	(TN)	524
	ODDAN, Linda	(WI)	916

MEDICAL LIBRARIES (Cont'd)

Medical libraries
GELINAS, Gratien ..... (PQ) 426
Medical libraries & their collections   SKICA, Janice K. ...... (NJ) 1146
Medical libraries management   REYES, Helen M. ...... (CA) 1024
Medical library   BENNETT, Michael W. ... (CA) 82
MYONG, Jae H. .... (CA) 885
PERLES, Paul ...... (IL) 959
BERRY, Mary W. ...... (NC) 90
PRATT, Kathleen L. .... (NV) 990
Medical library administration   WALTERS, Gwen E. ... (FL) 1301
DALRYMPLE, Prudence
W. .... (IL) 271
GOLUB, Andrew J. ..... (ME) 447
ROSENSTEIN, Philip ... (NJ) 1057
ZUCKER, Blanche M. ... (NV) 1391
ANDERSON, Rachael K. (NY) 25
KIRSCH, Anne S. ...... (NY) 655
TANNER, Ellen B. ..... (NY) 1222
GALLANT, Jennifer J. .. (OH) 414
HALLERBERG, Gretchen
A. .... (OH) 489
BOWLBY, Raynna M. ... (RI) 121
FISHER, Janet S. ...... (TN) 381
KNOTT, Teresa L. ..... (TX) 665
MILLER, Jean K. ...... (TX) 838
ROBERTSON, Ann .... (WA) 1041
KIRKWOOD, Brenda S. . (SDA) 655
Medical library automation   FEINBERG, Linda J. .... (IL) 368
CARTER, Bobby R. ..... (TX) 189
Medical library cataloging   SIEBENMORGEN, Ruth . (CA) 1135
OSHEROFF, Shiela K. .. (OR) 928
Medical library collection development   BERK, Nancy G. ...... (AZ) 87
RUDOLPH, Anne L. .... (CA) 1066
Medical library consultation   CREERON, Carolyn E. .. (FL) 257
KELLY, Kay .... (MI) 638
CARTER, Bobby R. .... (TX) 189
Medical library consulting   HARRIS, Vallena D. .... (CA) 506
KYKER, Penelope R. ... (IN) 685
ARNN, Judith A. .... (TX) 33
Medical library fostering   OSERMAN, Stuart ..... (IL) 928
Medical library management   BREINICH, John A. .... (HI) 132
O'BRIEN, Elizabeth J. ... (MA) 914
WEITKEMPER, Larry D. . (MO) 1320
REGENBERG, Patricia B. (NJ) 1017
HUANG, C K. .... (NY) 568
MINNERATH, Janet E. .. (OK) 846
GROEN, Frances K. .... (PQ) 471
Medical library materials organization   DOLL, Harriet A. .... (PA) 309
Medical library networks   MAY, Ruby S. .... (IL) 789
Medical library service   MOSIER, Eric M. ...... (CA) 871
Medical library technical services   WOODBURN, Judy I. .... (NC) 1366
Veterinary medical libraries consulting   KERKER, Ann E. ...... (IN) 643

MEDICINE (See also Diseases, Epidemiology, Medical, National Library of Medicine, Nursing, Patients, Physicians and specific medical fields)

Agriculture & medicine online
searching   STUBBAN, Vanessa L. ... (KS) 1204
Archives, history of medicine   VADEBONCOEUR,
Elizabeth J. .... (CA) 1270
Artificial intelligence in medicine   MUSEN, Mark A. ...... (CA) 883
Automotive medicine   BARTH, Nancy L. ...... (CA) 61
Aviation & aerospace medicine   ROGERS, Ruth T. ...... (FL) 1050
Bioelectromagnetic medicine   DIAL, Zona P. .... (AZ) 299
Biological science medicine reference   CHASTAIN-WARHEIT,
Christine C. .... (DE) 203
Clinical medicine   MONROE, Donald H. ... (IN) 855
STRUB, Jeane E. ...... (NM) 1203
LIN, Louise .... (ON) 727
Clinical medicine & nursing   SMITH, Brian D. ...... (NY) 1153
TREVANION, Margaret U. (PA) 1255
Clinical medicine reference   ECKERT, Daniel L. ..... (WI) 335
Clinical medicine research   BRUCE, Marianne E. .... (AB) 149
Collection development for medicine   HANKS, Ellen T. .... (TX) 496
Collection development in medicine   KATZ, Jacqueline E. .... (NY) 630
Energy medicine   DIAL, Zona P. .... (AZ) 299
Family medicine   THOMASSON, George O. (CO) 1238
CRANDALL, Elisabeth G. (NC) 255
Family medicine education   MENDELSON, Martin ... (WA) 823

MEDICINE (Cont'd)

Geriatric medicine   KERN, Donald C. ...... (MA) 643
History of medicine   WALLS, Edwina .... (AR) 1298
WOOD, Elizabeth H. .... (CA) 1364
ARCARI, Ralph D. ..... (CT) 30
HIRTLE, Peter B. ...... (MD) 544
JENSEN, Joseph E. .... (MD) 599
PARASCANDOLA, John
L. .... (MD) 939
ANDERSON, Paul G. ... (MO) 25
BRODMAN, Estelle ..... (NJ) 139
IRWIN, Barbara S. ..... (NJ) 584
MOORE, Rue I. .... (NY) 861
RAMER, Bruce J. ...... (NY) 1005
METZGER, Philip A. .... (PA) 829
SAWYER, Warren A. ... (SC) 1086
RAY, Joyce M. .... (TX) 1011
WYGANT, Larry J. ..... (TX) 1375
GROEN, Frances K. .... (PQ) 471
History of medicine archives   GILHEANY, Rosary S. .. (NJ) 434
History of medicine cataloging   GILLIAM, Susanne P. ... (OH) 436
History of medicine, reference   JENKINS, Glen P. ..... (OH) 597
History of the institution & medicine   MIMS, Dorothy H. ..... (GA) 845
Media in nursing & medicine selection   REIT, Janet W. .... (VT) 1022
Medicinal chemistry   LASSLO, Andrew ...... (TN) 700
Medicine   BROWN, Jeanine B. .... (IA) 144
WHITESIDE, Phyllis J. .. (KS) 1333
MAROUSEK, Kathy A. ... (NJ) 772
LARKIN, Virgil C. ...... (NY) 698
LLOYD, Lynn A. .... (RI) 735
BELL, Joy A. .... (TX) 77
DOYLE, Frances M. .... (VA) 317
SAURIOL, Guy L. ...... (ON) 1085
STANGL-WALKER,
Teresa L. .... (ON) 1180
Medicine & allied health reference   NEELAND, Ellen L. .... (TX) 891
Medicine & horticulture indexing   LINDHEIMER, Elinor .... (CA) 729
Medicine & life sciences   GUIDA, Pat .... (NJ) 476
Medicine & nursing   REID, Carol L. .... (NY) 1018
Medicine, cosmetics & hair   CLAGGETT, Laura K. ... (IL) 215
Medicine, engineering reference   COSGRIFF, John C. .... (VA) 248
Medicine, nursing   KAKOSCHKE, Mona S. .. (ON) 622
Medicine, nursing, allied health   KARCH, Linda S. ...... (NY) 627
COHEN, Nancy E. ..... (OH) 228
Medicine, nursing & allied health   BOROCK, Freddie ..... (NY) 116
Medicine, toxicology   SCHATZ, Cindy A. ..... (MA) 1090
Medicine, toxicology, & biochemistry   JOHNSON, Susan W. ... (MD) 609
Online searching in medicine   TAYLOR, Margaret P. ... (ON) 1227
Orthopedics & sports medicine   CLEMENTS, Betty H. ... (GA) 221
Pediatric medicine   GREEN, Deidre E. ..... (ON) 461
Physical medicine & rehabilitation   SHANEFIELD, Irene D. .. (PQ) 1120
Rare books, history of medicine   FREY, Emil F. .... (TX) 402
Reference, veterinary & human
medicine   VEENSTRA, Robert J. ... (AL) 1281
References in medicine   HIGGINBOTHAM, Cecelia
B. .... (LA) 537
Rehabilitation medicine   KALUZSA, Karen L. ..... (IL) 623
Science & medicine collection
devlpmnt   MICHAELS, Debbie D. .. (NJ) 832
Science, technology, medicine   WOLF, Richard E. ..... (VA) 1360
Standard nomenclature & code for
medcn   CASIRAGHI, Edoardo ... (ITL) 192
Submarine medicine databases   OMARA, Marie T. ...... (MD) 923
Systematized nomenclature of
medicine   NITZ, Andrew M. ...... (DC) 905
Toxicology, industrial medicine   SELZER, Nancy S. ..... (DE) 1114
Veterinary medicine   WILLARD, Gayle K. .... (KS) 1341
LOUBIERE, Sue .... (LA) 742
SAFFER-MARCHAND,
Melinda .... (MA) 1074
CARLSON, Livija I. ..... (MN) 182
WILSON, Marijo S. .... (NY) 1352
SESSIONS, Robert ..... (WI) 1117
Veterinary medicine bibliography   KERKER, Ann E. ...... (IN) 643
Veterinary medicine databases   DE WALERSTEIN, Linda
S. .... (MEX) 297
Veterinary medicine information   COOK, Elaine .... (ENG) 239

MEDIEVAL

Byzantine & medieval studies reference	AVDOYAN, Levon	(DC)	41
Library research in medieval history	SEAVER, James E.	(KS)	1110
Medieval & modern manuscripts	PRESTON, Jean F.	(NJ)	991
Medieval & Renaissance literature	WHITE, D J.	(MO)	1330
Medieval & Renaissance studies	DILLON, John B.	(WI)	303
Medieval era book selection	HILL, Lawrence H.	(PA)	540
Medieval German literature	SPOHRER, James H.	(CA)	1175
Medieval history	IZBICKI, Thomas M.	(KS)	586
Medieval institutions	HORWITZ, Steven F.	(CA)	561
Medieval manuscripts	IZBICKI, Thomas M.	(KS)	586
	FOLTER, Roland	(NY)	388

MEDIUM

Automation of medium & small libraries	BARRUS, Phyl	(TX)	60
Cataloging all medium types	ALGAR, L E.	(ON)	13
Consulting for small & medium libraries	LEAMON, David L.	(MI)	707
Managing small to medium law libraries	SCAMMAHORN, Lynne	(PA)	1087
Medium-sized library administration	NEEDHAM, George M.	(OH)	891
	HALEY, Anne E.	(WA)	486
Public libraries, medium-sized	WILLIAMS, Ann W.	(FL)	1342
Small & medium, public	HOFFMANN, Maurine L.	(IL)	548
Small & medium public library buildings	FARACE, Virginia K.	(FL)	363

MEDLARS

MEDLARS database searching	ALLOCCO, Claudia	(NJ)	17
	MYER, Nancy E.	(NM)	884
MEDLARS training	VEEKEN, Mary L.	(ON)	1280
National Library of Medicine MEDLARS	KAKOSCHKE, Mona S.	(ON)	622
Online searching, MEDLARS databases	SZILARD, Paula	(HI)	1218

MEDLINE

End-user training for MEDLINE computer	POND, Frederick C.	(NY)	982
MEDLINE	KIRBY, Martha Z.	(PA)	654
MEDLINE dialogue	PINCKNEY, Cathey L.	(CA)	974
MEDLINE search training	KYKER, Penelope R.	(IN)	685
MEDLINE searches	NGUYEN, Michael V.	(AUS)	900
MEDLINE searching	HANSON, Elana L.	(CO)	498
	LINDNER, Katherine L.	(NJ)	729
	JUDKINS, Timothy C.	(OK)	619
MEDLINE training	HARRIMAN, Jenny F.	(MD)	503
	KINNA, Dorothy H.	(MD)	652
Online searching, MEDLINE	SNIDER, Jacqueline I.	(IA)	1163
Searching, MEDLINE	THOMAS, Yvonne	(CA)	1238

MEETINGS (See also Conferences, Convention)

Meeting planning	CORNOG, Martha	(PA)	247
Meeting planning, management	ZOOK, Ruth A.	(CO)	1390
Organization of meetings & courses	ROBERTS, Kenneth H.	(FRN)	1040

MEMBERSHIP

Association, management, & membership	SCARRY, Patricia A.	(IL)	1088
Membership databases	STLUKA, Thomas H.	(IL)	1195
Membership development	HAMILTON-PENNELL, Christine	(CO)	492
Membership management	AUCOIN, Sharilynn A.	(LA)	38
Outreach & membership	LEVINE, Lillian S.	(OH)	720

MEMORABILIA (See also Ephemerae)

Cataloging memorabilia	KESSLER, Selma P.	(NJ)	645
Film & theater memorabilia	WESOLOWSKI, Paul G.	(PA)	1325
Preserving memorabilia	KESSLER, Selma P.	(NJ)	645
Theatre books & memorabilia	BOWLEY, Craig	(NY)	121

MENNONITE

Mennonite studies	ENNS-REMPEL, Kevin M.	(CA)	350

MENTAL (See also Psychology)

Alcoholism, Mental hygiene	GILSON, Robert	(NY)	437
Historiography of mental illness	EVANS, Josephine K.	(FL)	357
Institutional services, mental health	BOLIN, Nancy C.	(MD)	112
Mental health	KRUK, Pauline A.	(CT)	680
	LABREE, Rosanne	(MA)	686
	AEBLI, Carol L.	(MI)	7
	DAVIDSON, Silvia	(NY)	276
	STERN, Deborah S.	(NY)	1189
	OLSON-URLIE, Carolyn T.	(OR)	923
	SOULTOUKIS, Donna Z.	(PA)	1169
Mental health advocacy	COOPER, Joanne S.	(PA)	243
Mental health collections	EPSTEIN, Barbara A.	(PA)	351
Mental health databases	BRAND, Alice A.	(KS)	127
Mental health databases & collections	WIGGINS, Theresa S.	(PA)	1337
Mental health field reference	KIMBLE, Valerie F.	(OK)	649
Mental health indexing	ROUP, Carol E.	(ON)	1061
Mental health information service	MERRILL, Susan S.	(MD)	827
Mental health information services	DANIELS, Pam	(NY)	273
Mental health libraries	VIGORITO, Patricia M.	(RI)	1284
Mental health literature	COHAN, Lois	(NY)	227
	SORG, Elizabeth A.	(PA)	1168
Mental health material	GROSS, Elinor L.	(NY)	472
Mental health reference	VAN DER VOORN, Neal P.	(WA)	1274
	ROUP, Carol E.	(ON)	1061
Mental health research	EVANS, Josephine K.	(FL)	357
Mental retardation	HAYNES, Douglas E.	(NM)	516
	GILSON, Robert	(NY)	437
	HOWIE, Maryann	(NY)	566
	LEONARD, Peter C.	(PA)	716
Mentally ill library programming	VAN DER VOORN, Neal P.	(WA)	1274
Psychiatry & mental health	FREDENBURG, Anne M.	(MD)	399
Psychiatry, psychology, mental health	WARD, Nancy E.	(MI)	1304
Psychology & mental health	LARMOUR, Rosamond E.	(VA)	698
Services to mentally retarded	HOMAN, Frances M.	(MD)	555
Social sciences, mental health	HORNUNG, Susan D.	(WI)	560

MERCHANDISING (See also Marketing)

Electronic publishing & merchandising	MOFFITT, Michael D.	(MA)	852
Marketing & merchandising	COUSINS, Gloria D.	(NC)	252
Merchandising	EICKHOFF, Jane S.	(MD)	339
Public relations & merchandising	FLUM, Judith G.	(CA)	386

MERGERS

Database mergers	WATKINS, Dorothy	(NY)	1309
Merger & acquisition reference	ANTONETZ, Dolores	(NY)	29
Merger & acquisition reporting	GREEN, Randall N.	(DC)	462
Mergers & acquisitions	GOLDSTEIN, Bernard	(NJ)	446
	SLUSSER, W P.	(NY)	1150
Mergers & acquisitions in publishing	BODDORF, James E.	(NY)	109
	DRONZEK, Ronald	(NY)	320
	HADLEY, J M.	(NY)	482
	HALE, Paul E.	(NY)	485
	HUNNEWELL, Walter	(NY)	574
	LAMB, David C.	(NY)	689
	SCHULTE, Anthony M.	(NY)	1101
	SHAPIRO, Marvin L.	(NY)	1121
	STEVENSON, Jeffery T.	(NY)	1191
	SUHLER, John S.	(NY)	1207
	VERONIS, John J.	(NY)	1283
Merging & moving libraries	LYNCH, Mollie S.	(MI)	752
Public, school library mergers	BROWN, Freddiemae E.	(TX)	144

MESSAGE (See also Bulletin, Mail)

Electronic messaging	PICKETT, Olivia K.	(DC)	971
	GENNARO, John L.	(VA)	427
Electronic messaging & comp conferencing	BLACK, John B.	(ON)	101
Niche targeting & message development	GREEN, Randall N.	(DC)	462

METAL
Chemical & metallurgical databases	BERGER, Lewis W.	(PA)	85
Metal & general statistics	GOODINGS, Sally A. . . .	(ON)	449
Metallurgical & engineered materials	BALDWIN, Eleanor M. . .	(OH)	51
Metallurgy	WOOLARD, Kathryn A. . .	(OH)	1368
Metals, metallurgical sci, engineering	HYSLOP, Marjorie R. . . .	(OH)	580
Non-ferrous metal marketing	GOODINGS, Sally A. . . .	(ON)	449
Research, chemistry & metallurgy	SCHLOTT, Florenceann .	(PA)	1094

METAPHYSICS
Metaphysics	BURDET, Michele C. . . .	(SWZ)	158

METEOROLOGICAL
Meteorological research	MEACHAM, Mary	(OK)	819

METHANE
Coalbed methane databases	WATSON, Linda S.	(AL)	1309

METHODIST
Cataloging Methodist-related materials	BERG, Richard R.	(OH)	84
Helping researchers, Methodist history	ROLLER, Twila J.	(NM)	1051
Writing United Methodist history	ROLLER, Twila J.	(NM)	1051

METHODS
Archival methods & records management	CAIN, Charlene C.	(LA)	171
Art research methodology	JONES, Lois S.	(TX)	613
CJK generating methods	ZHANG, Foster J.	(CA)	1387
Experimental methodology	DOWNS, Sandra P.	(CA)	317
Genealogy methodology	WITCHER, Curt B.	(IN)	1358
Information clearinghouse methods	LIPETZ, Ben A.	(NY)	732
Instruction in research methods	TROTTI, John B.	(VA)	1258
Interdisciplinary methodology	SWIGGER, Keith	(TX)	1216
Legal methods	BOMARC, M D.	(NC)	113
Library research methods	SMITH, Nathan M.	(UT)	1159
	CHANG, Henry C.	(VI)	200
Library research, statistical method	HITT, Charles J.	(MN)	544
Methodology	TOTH, Georgina G.	(OH)	1252
Methods of literary research	ABBOTT, Craig S.	(IL)	1
Qualitative research methods	MELLON, Constance A. .	(NC)	822
Quantitative methods	TAGUE, Jean M.	(ON)	1220
Research methodology	MAYES, Elizabeth A. . . .	(CA)	789
	GROTZINGER, Laurel A.	(MI)	473
Research methodology & statistics	KATZER, Jeffrey	(NY)	630
Research methods	CHRISMAN, Larry G. . . .	(FL)	211
	AULD, Lawrence W.	(IL)	40
	BOOKSTEIN, Abraham . .	(IL)	115
	PATEL, Jashu	(IL)	947
	WERT, Lucille M.	(IL)	1325
	HARTER, Stephen P. . . .	(IN)	508
	POWELL, Ronald R.	(MO)	988
	DAIN, Phyllis	(NJ)	270
	WYNAR, Lubomyr R. . . .	(OH)	1375
	HEAD, John W.	(PA)	518
	ROBINSON, William C. .	(TN)	1045
	MARCHANT, Maurice P. .	(UT)	768
	STEPHENSON, Mary S. .	(BC)	1188
	HU, James S.	(TAI)	567
Research methods & bibliographic instrc	TROUTMAN, Joseph E. .	(GA)	1258
Research methods & cost analysis	WEBRECK, Susan J. . . .	(PA)	1314
Research methods & systems analysis	FENSKE, Ruth E.	(IL)	371
Research methods in humanities	COHN, Alan M.	(IL)	229
Statistics & research methods	D'ELIA, George P.	(MN)	289
Theological research methodology	TROUTMAN, Joseph E. .	(GA)	1258
Theological research methods	ERDEL, Timothy P.	(JAM)	352
Unit method of library instruction	GOODRICH PETERSON, Marilyn	(KS)	450

METROPOLITAN (See also City, Municipal)
Metropolitan library services	SIVULICH, Kenneth G. . .	(NY)	1145

MEXICAN (See also Chicano, Hispanic, Spanish)
Contemporary Mexican painting	KIRKING, Clayton C. . . .	(AZ)	655
Mexican culture	NOLAND, Jon	(CA)	908
Mexican periodicals	OROZCO-TENORIO, Jose M.	(MEX)	926
Mexican studies bibliographer	RIVERA, Diana H.	(MI)	1037
Mexican-American bibliography	TRUJILLO, Roberto G. . .	(CA)	1259
Mexican-American studies bibliography	GUTIERREZ, Margo	(TX)	479
Services to Mexican Americans	NEALE, Marilee	(TX)	891
Texas & Northeastern Mexico history	GAUSE, George R.	(TX)	423

MICHIGAN
Michigan history	KULL, Christine L.	(MI)	683
	MULLIGAN, William H. . .	(MI)	877
Michigan reference	CALLARD, Carole	(MI)	173

MICROBASIS
MicroBASIS retrieval software	DITMARS, David W. . . .	(OH)	305

MICROBIOLOGY
Anatomy, physiology, & microbiology	MANDERSCHEID, Dorothy H.	(MI)	765
Information microbiology, immunology	PERLMAN, Stephen E. . .	(NY)	959
Microbiology	MUNDSTOCK, Aileen M.	(WI)	879
Microbiology databases	SHAY, Donald E.	(MD)	1124

MICROCOMPUTERS (See also Computers, Data, Personal Computers, Programming and names of specific computers, e.g. IBM)
Acquisitions on microcomputer	MILLS, Elaine L.	(KS)	844
Applications of microcomputers	CAINE, William C.	(TX)	171
Audiovisual & microcomputer software	DAVIS, Shelley E.	(GA)	281
Audiovisuals & microcomputers	WU, Harry P.	(MI)	1373
Automated microcomputer systems	ROSE, Pamela M.	(NY)	1055
Automation, microcomputers	THIBAULT, Jean	(ON)	1235
Cataloging microcomputer software	CARTER, Judith A.	(AZ)	189
CD-ROM & microcomputer	KNIGHT, Nancy H.	(VA)	664
Computers & microcomputers	BOWERS, Alyce J.	(NJ)	120
Custom microcomputer programming	MARSH, Elizabeth C. . . .	(OH)	773
Designing microcomputer databases	MURRAY, Elizabeth F. . .	(NY)	881
Educational microcomputing	FITZGERALD, Ruth F. . .	(MI)	382
Educational uses of microcomputers	CARTER, Betty B.	(TX)	189
IBM-PC microcomputers & software	COLE, David H.	(MN)	230
Information systems, microcomputers	ANDERSON, Axel R. . . .	(WI)	21
Instructional media, microcomputers	MARTIN, Elaine R.	(DC)	776
Library automation, microcomputers	LEE, Sylvia	(NY)	711
Library automation using microcomputers	TUCKER, Mary E.	(NY)	1262
Library management with microcomputer	KESTER, Diane D.	(NC)	645
Library micro applications	EVENSEN, Sharon L. . . .	(ND)	358
Library microcomputer applications	MAIN, Annette Z.	(PA)	761
	STANLEY, Kerry G.	(PA)	1180
	JEWELL, Timothy D. . . .	(WA)	600
	KELNER, Gregory H. . . .	(BC)	638
Library microcomputer systems	BAZILLION, Richard J. . .	(ON)	68
Library systems, library microcomputers	JAFFE, John G.	(VA)	591
Lib systems, microcomputer applications	ONSI, Patricia W.	(NY)	924
Library systems on microcomputers	TESSIER, Yves	(PQ)	1233
Macintosh microcomputers	WOOLDRIDGE, Steven M.	(CA)	1368
Management, micro data center	ASU, Glynis V.	(WI)	37
Management of microcomputer labs	PLAZA, Joyce S.	(NJ)	978
Micro & mainframe library software	SPENCER, John T.	(CA)	1173
Micro & mainframe programming	BRITTON, Jeffrey W. . . .	(NJ)	137
Micro applications	AIROLDI, Melissa	(TX)	9
Micro-based applications	STACK, Laurie A.	(MT)	1177
Micro-based automation	ANDERSON, Eric S.	(OH)	22
Micro-based library automation	MATTINGLY, Debra B. . .	(CO)	786
Microcomputer	MILLER, Robert	(IL)	841
	NELSON, Ian C.	(SK)	893
Microcomputer & CD-ROM	WILBUR, Helen L.	(NY)	1338
Microcomputer & CD-ROM applications	DAVIDSON, Lloyd A. . . .	(IL)	276

MICROCOMPUTERS (Cont'd)

Microcomputer application in libraries

WRIGHT, Keith C.	(NC)	1372
CORNEIL, Charlotte E.	(OK)	246
WONG, Elizabeth M.	(WI)	1362

Microcomputer applications

MCCARTHY, Sherri L.	(AL)	794
MCGARITY, Marysue	(AL)	805
MEAD, Thomas L.	(AZ)	819
ERTEL, Monica	(CA)	353
FARMER, Lesley S.	(CA)	364
HOFFMAN, William J.	(CA)	548
MACEK, Rosanne M.	(CA)	755
MAIN, Linda Y.	(CA)	761
MOONEY, Margaret T.	(CA)	858
NAUMER, Janet N.	(CA)	889
NEWTON, Deborah A.	(CA)	900
ROSENBERGER, Diane C.	(CA)	1056
SKAPURA, Robert J.	(CA)	1145
SLEETER, Ellen L.	(CA)	1148
TASH, Steven J.	(CA)	1224
WRIGHT, Kathleen J.	(CA)	1372
FLAM, Floris	(DC)	383
HO, James K.	(DC)	545
LANE, Elizabeth S.	(DC)	694
CONAWAY, Charles W.	(FL)	235
ACKER, Robert L.	(IL)	3
BARRETTE, Linda J.	(IL)	59
GRISCOM, Richard W.	(IL)	471
MCKENZIE, Duncan J.	(IL)	811
VACCARO, William J.	(IL)	1270
WESTON, E P.	(IL)	1327
DOLAN, Robert T.	(IN)	309
ERDMANN, Charlotte A.	(IN)	352
SHEETS, Michael T.	(IN)	1125
TUCKER, Dennis C.	(IN)	1261
ZUCK, Gregory J.	(KS)	1391
KIRK, Thomas G.	(KY)	654
BOND, Marvin A.	(MD)	113
BRITTEN, William A.	(MD)	137
MARCHIONINI, Gary J.	(MD)	769
MASTROIANNI, Richard L.	(MD)	783
GOODWIN, Bryan D.	(ME)	450
MORROW, Blaine V.	(MI)	869
BIRMINGHAM, Frank R.	(MN)	98
HORTON, James T.	(NC)	561
RANCER, Susan P.	(NC)	1006
VAN HOY, Catherine S.	(NC)	1276
FELTON, John D.	(NE)	370
LANGSCHIELD, Linda S.	(NJ)	696
STEPIEN, Karen K.	(NJ)	1189
STURM, H P.	(NV)	1205
BARTENBACH, Martha A.	(NY)	60
BARTH, Joseph M.	(NY)	61
BARTLE, Susan M.	(NY)	61
BLOHM, Laura A.	(NY)	106
BRETSCHER, Susan M.	(NY)	134
CLARK, Philip M.	(NY)	218
HORNE, Dorice L.	(NY)	560
JOHNSON, Steven P.	(NY)	609
MCMORRAN, Charles E.	(NY)	815
MITTELGLUCK, Eugene L.	(NY)	850
ROHMANN, Gloria P.	(NY)	1050
SERCHUK, Barnett	(NY)	1116
ARNOLD, Judith M.	(OH)	33
HUNTER, James J.	(OH)	576
MARCOTTE, Frederick A.	(OH)	769
MILLER, John E.	(OH)	839
MOGREN, Diane A.	(OH)	852
PIETY, John S.	(OH)	972
SHAW, Debra S.	(OH)	1123
HUESMANN, James L.	(OK)	570
BALAS, Janet L.	(PA)	50
KING, Mimi	(PA)	652
LINGLE, Virginia A.	(PA)	730
PENNELL, Charles	(PA)	957
SMALL, Sally S.	(PA)	1151
MILLS, Debra D.	(TN)	844
CALDWELL, Marlene	(TX)	172
COCHRAN, Carolyn	(TX)	225
FOUDRAY, Rita C.	(TX)	393
HAMBLETON, James E.	(TX)	490

MICROCOMPUTERS (Cont'd)

Microcomputer applications

SAMSON, Robert C.	(TX)	1079
SKINNER, Robert G.	(TX)	1146
WILSON, Thomas C.	(TX)	1353
ENGLISH, Susan B.	(VA)	350
JOACHIM, Robert J.	(VA)	600
BREKKE, Elaine C.	(WA)	132
KETCHELL, Debra S.	(WA)	645
BARLOGA, Carolyn J.	(WI)	57
FLETCHER, Nancy S.	(WI)	384
GOSZ, Kathleen M.	(WI)	453
FAULKNER, Ronnie W.	(WV)	366
SIFTON, Patricia A.	(BC)	1137
FAIR, Linda A.	(ON)	361
MORTON, Robert E.	(ON)	870
WILBURN, Gene	(ON)	1338
WILBURN, Marion T.	(ON)	1338
ZHU, Xiaofeng	(CHI)	1387

Microcomputer applications & management	MCSPADDEN, Robert M.	(OH)	818
Microcomputer applications & support	WILLIAMS, David W.	(NY)	1342
Microcomputer applications & training	MARSH, Elizabeth C.	(OH)	773
	MARMION, Daniel K.	(TX)	772
Microcomputer applications development	NICKEL, Edgar B.	(CO)	902
	KNAACK, Linda M.	(MA)	663
Microcomputer appls/electronic publshg	HULSEY, Richard A.	(MI)	573
Microcomputer applications for libraries	CONVERSE, Wm R.	(MB)	239
Microcomputer applications in libraries	KASALKO, Sally G.	(AR)	628
	CHAFE, Douglas A.	(HI)	197
	SCHMIDT, Kathy W.	(IN)	1095
	BENSON, Peggy	(MI)	83
	COAN, La V.	(MI)	224
	BRIZUELA, B S.	(PA)	138
	SVEINSSON, Joan L.	(TX)	1212
	FONG, Wilfred W.	(WI)	388
Microcomputer applications in management	HOWARD, Ada M.	(TX)	563
Microcomputer applications/programming	DALY, Jay	(MA)	271
Microcomputer applications research	STRAHAN, Michael F.	(ND)	1199
Microcomputer automation	REYNOLDS, Jon K.	(DC)	1025
	MOORE, Scott L.	(NC)	861
Microcomputer center	MEARS, William F.	(TX)	820
	WYNNE, Joseph J.	(VA)	1375
Microcomputer communications	CLANCY, Stephen L.	(CA)	215
Microcomputer coordination	DYKHUIS, Randy	(MI)	331
Microcomputer courseware	BROWN, David K.	(AB)	143
Microcomputer data management	MORGAN, James J.	(IN)	864
Microcomputer database design	MOLL, Joy K.	(NJ)	853
	NEELAND, Margaret A.	(NY)	891
	SANDFELDER, Paula M.	(HKG)	1080
Microcomputer database development	MANGION, Barbara E.	(MA)	765
	MIDDLETON, Marcia S.	(NY)	833
Microcomputer database management	KENNEDY, Joanne	(CA)	641
Microcomputer databases	SUNDT, Christine L.	(OR)	1210
	HEATON, Gwynneth T.	(ON)	519
Microcomputer design	SHENASSA, Daryoosh	(IL)	1126
Microcomputer development	BURNS, David J.	(MI)	162
	LEE, Donna K.	(VT)	709
Microcomputer in education	WALKER, Judith A.	(NC)	1295
Microcomputer index systems	FISLER, Charlotte D.	(PA)	382
Microcomputer indexing	KEARNS, Linda J.	(ON)	633
Microcomputer information	SPIGAI, Fran	(CA)	1174
Microcomputer information retrieval	WOODWARD, Anthony M.	(ENG)	1367
Microcomputer information sources	MAYER, Erich J.	(NY)	789
Microcomputer laboratories	YEE, Sandra G.	(MI)	1379
Microcomputer library applications	OPPENHEIM, Roberta A.	(MA)	925
	MCCULLEY, P M.	(SC)	800
Microcomputer library automation	COSTA, Betty L.	(CO)	249
	TREVANION, Margaret U.	(PA)	1255
Microcomputer library management	TRAVILLIAN, Mary W.	(IA)	1254
Microcomputer library systems	CURTIS, Alison J.	(ON)	267
Microcomputer library systems, Apple IIe	BOCHTE, Terrence C.	(WI)	109
Microcomputer management	REHMKE, Denise M.	(IA)	1017

MICROCOMPUTERS (Cont'd)

Microcomputer management of libraries	BANKHEAD, Elizabeth M.	(CO)	54
Microcomputer management of library	SHARMA, Shirley K.	(KS)	1122
Microcomputer network	KEASCHUK, Michael J.	(SK)	633
Microcomputer operation	YAU, Linda S.	(CA)	1378
Microcomputer programming & instruction	CARROLL, James K.	(KS)	187
Microcomputer programming & training	ANDREWS, Mark J.	(MO)	27
Microcomputer public access centers	LARSON, Teresa B.	(IA)	700
Microcomputer reference	SMITH, Karen F.	(NY)	1156
Microcomputer services	DOWNEY, Christine D.	(CA)	316
	SCHLATTER, M W.	(GA)	1093
	STRAUSS, Richard F.	(PA)	1201
Microcomputer software	BENIDIR, Samia	(CA)	80
	CLANCY, Stephen L.	(CA)	215
	SILVERSTEIN, Jeffrey S.	(CT)	1139
	DOLAK, Frank J.	(IN)	309
	HANE, Paula J.	(NY)	495
	HERB, Elizabeth D.	(OH)	530
	MITCHELL, George D.	(TX)	848
	YOUNT, Natalie W.	(WA)	1384
	JONES, B E.	(ON)	611
Microcomputer software cataloging	WEISS, Paul J.	(NY)	1320
Microcomputer software collection mgmt	BEHNKE, Charles	(WI)	75
Microcomputer software development	EVERSBERG, Bernhard	(WGR)	359
Microcomputer software evaluation	MAY, Frank C.	(CA)	788
	MICHELS, Fredrick A.	(MI)	832
Microcomputer software for libraries	YEH, Helen S.	(TX)	1379
Microcomputer software industry	SLAVIN, Vicky J.	(MA)	1148
Microcomputer software, new technologies	VEANER, Allen B.	(ON)	1280
Microcomputer software reviews	MANN, Carol A.	(TX)	765
Microcomputer support Apple Macintosh	DEEMER, Selden S.	(GA)	286
Microcomputer support IBM PC	DEEMER, Selden S.	(GA)	286
Microcomputer system configuration	COVEY, William C.	(FL)	252
Microcomputer system implementation	OYER, Kenneth E.	(NE)	932
Microcomputer systems	MILLER, Leon C.	(AR)	839
	RUMSEY, Eric T.	(IA)	1067
	CANGANELLI, Patrick W.	(IN)	178
	FOGLE, Dianna L.	(KY)	387
	ANGLIN, Richard V.	(NY)	28
	DOBSON, Christine B.	(TX)	307
	PUZIAK, Kathleen M.	(WA)	998
Microcomputer systems & networks	TALLY, Roy D.	(MN)	1221
Microcomputer systems in libraries	PRATT, Allan D.	(CT)	989
Microcomputer systems online searching	ROTHSTEIN, Pauline M.	(NY)	1060
Microcomputer teaching	MANN, Sallie E.	(NC)	766
Microcomputer technology	RUBIN, Myra P.	(NY)	1064
	PICHETTE, William H.	(TX)	970
Microcomputer training	ALURI, Rao	(AZ)	19
	JAJKO, Pamela J.	(CA)	592
	KARCHER, Tracey L.	(CA)	627
	CARLSON, Robert P.	(IL)	182
	FOURNIER, Susan K.	(MD)	393
	CONWAY, Michael J.	(MI)	239
	STOUT, Chester B.	(OH)	1198
	BRADLEY, John	(PA)	126
	FISLER, Charlotte D.	(PA)	382
	ZOGOTT, Joyce	(PA)	1390
	QUEYROUZE, Mary E.	(TX)	999
Microcomputer training & development	ELAM, Kristy L.	(MO)	341
	CHAPMAN, Kathleen A.	(WA)	202
	GRAF, David L.	(WI)	455
Microcomputer training database searches	KENNEDY, James W.	(OK)	641
Microcomputer training support	STIGLEMAN, Sue E.	(NC)	1194
Microcomputer usage	PRITCHARD, Jackie L.	(WA)	994
Microcomputer use	SWARTZ, Betty J.	(NJ)	1214
	RICHARDS, Barbara G.	(PA)	1028
	LEAHY, Sheila A.	(TX)	707
	BONIN, Denise R.	(BC)	114
Microcomputer use & training	NELSON, Margaret R.	(MA)	894
Microcomputer use in archives	JACOB, Diane B.	(VA)	589

MICROCOMPUTERS (Cont'd)

Microcomputer use in curriculum	CHAMPLIN, Constance J.	(IN)	198
	KESTER, Diane D.	(NC)	645
Microcomputer use in libraries	BELDAN, A C.	(ON)	76
Microcomputer use in school libraries	SCHMUHL, Gayle B.	(OH)	1096
Microcomputer use instruction	NICHOLS, Darlene P.	(MI)	901
Microcomputer use, library applications	KENNEDY, Charlene F.	(CA)	640
Microcomputer user support	OWEN, Willy	(NC)	932
Microcomputer uses in libraries	LODER, Michael W.	(PA)	736
Microcomputer utilization	PLANTON, Stanley P.	(OH)	977
Microcomputer-based automation	LUCIANI, Eliie	(ON)	746
Microcomputer-based chemical info system	MEYER, Daniel E.	(PA)	830
Microcomputer-based information systems	JOHNSON, Jane S.	(IL)	605
Microcomputer-based integrated systems	MEIKAMP, Kathie D.	(DC)	822
Microcomputer-based library applications	BEISER, Karl A.	(ME)	75
Microcomputer-based library systems	MILLER, Randy S.	(IL)	841
Microcomputerization & automation	KAZLAUSKAS, Edward J.	(CA)	632
Microcomputerized database management	AU, Ka N.	(NJ)	38
Microcomputers	GALBRAITH, William B.	(AK)	413
	MUIR, Scott P.	(AL)	876
	WEATHERLY, Cynthia D.	(AL)	1312
	VAN ARSDALE, Dennis G.	(AR)	1272
	HERSH, Daniel	(CA)	533
	HOLTZMAN, Douglas A.	(CA)	555
	INGEBRETSEN, Dorothy L.	(CA)	582
	LAI, Dennis	(CA)	688
	LOW, Kathleen	(CA)	743
	QUINT, Barbara E.	(CA)	1000
	RYUS, Joseph E.	(CA)	1072
	SIEGEL, Jacquelin B.	(CA)	1136
	HENSINGER, James S.	(CO)	529
	ANDREWS, Janet C.	(FL)	26
	GIBLON, Charles B.	(FL)	431
	MCKENNA, Gerald M.	(FL)	811
	PETIT, Michael J.	(FL)	965
	BASLER, Thomas G.	(GA)	63
	FORCE, Ronald W.	(ID)	389
	BYRNE, Janice M.	(IL)	169
	DUJSIK, Gerald	(IL)	324
	RAO, Paladugu V.	(IL)	1008
	RUSSELL, Janet	(IL)	1069
	SCHULTHEISS, Louis A.	(IL)	1101
	TAWYEA, Edward W.	(IL)	1225
	VALAUSKAS, Edward J.	(IL)	1271
	WEISMAN, Kathryn M.	(IL)	1319
	HUNSBERGER, Willard D.	(IN)	574
	OSTROWSKI, Lawrence C.	(IN)	929
	BUMBALOUGH, Bruce L.	(KS)	157
	ROUNDTREE, Lynn P.	(LA)	1061
	CONSTANCE, Joseph W.	(MA)	238
	MOSKOWITZ, Michael A.	(MA)	871
	BACKUS, Joyce E.	(MD)	44
	SMITH, Peter A.	(MI)	1159
	BALDWIN, Jerome C.	(MN)	51
	GROSCH, Audrey N.	(MN)	472
	HELMICK, Aileen B.	(MO)	525
	RAITHEL, Frederick J.	(MO)	1004
	BALLARD, Thomas H.	(MS)	53
	RICE, Joyce I.	(MS)	1027
	SNELSON, Pamela	(NJ)	1163
	BERTUCA, David J.	(NY)	91
	CURTIS, James A.	(NY)	267
	GALASSO, Nancy	(NY)	412
	GURN, Robert M.	(NY)	478
	KNEE, Michael	(NY)	663
	LEE, Sylvia	(NY)	711
	LIU, Carol F.	(NY)	734
	MACLEAN, Paul	(NY)	757
	NUZZO, David J.	(NY)	912
	SALAZAR, Pamela R.	(NY)	1076
	SLOAN, Carol L.	(NY)	1149
	SULLIVAN, Robert G.	(NY)	1208
	YOCHYM, Cynthia M.	(NY)	1380

MICROCOMPUTERS (Cont'd)

Microcomputers

BELVIN, Robert J.	(OH)	78
HILL, Barbarie F.	(OH)	539
MULLINER, Kent	(OH)	878
NEWMAN, Linda D.	(OH)	899
WALDER, Antoinette L.	(OH)	1294
COCHENOUR, Donnice K.	(OK)	225
CURTIS, Ronald A.	(OK)	267
KAWABATA, Julie	(OR)	632
BELANGER, David L.	(PA)	75
DOW, Elizabeth H.	(PA)	315
ELSHAMI, Ahmed M.	(PA)	346
NEWCOMBE, Jack A.	(PA)	898
WOODRUFF, William M.	(PA)	1366
SMITH, Philip M.	(TN)	1159
WILLIAMS, Marsha D.	(TN)	1345
HALL, Halbert W.	(TX)	487
HAYNIE, Altie V.	(TX)	517
KRANZ, Ralph	(UT)	676
WINTERS, Sharon A.	(VA)	1356
JOHNSON, Dana E.	(WA)	603
SESSIONS, Robert	(WI)	1117
TRUPIANO, Rose M.	(WI)	1259
WELSCH, Erwin K.	(WI)	1323
KING, Marjorie H.	(AB)	651
SLOAN, Stephen M.	(AB)	1150
HEINO, Dan R.	(NF)	522
BARCLAY, Susan L.	(ON)	55
BEAUMONT, Jane	(ON)	70
HSU, Peter T.	(ON)	567
NORTH, John A.	(ON)	909
SHIRINIAN, George N.	(ON)	1131
WEIR, Leslie	(ON)	1319
CHOUINARD, Germain	(PQ)	211
MAHARAJ, Diana J.	(PQ)	760

Microcomputers & applications — CLINE, Sharon D. (CA) 222; ROMANIUK, Elena (BC) 1052

Microcomputers & automation — WIBLE, Joseph G. (CA) 1335; GIEBEL, Thomas W. (WI) 432

Microcomputers & CD-ROM — BUTHOD, J C. (OK) 166

Microcomputers & electronic mail — MELTON, Emily I. (IL) 823

Microcomputers & library administration — RAPPAPORT, Susan E. (NY) 1008

Microcomputers & microcomputing — SHAW, Richard N. (DE) 1124

Microcomputers & new technology — ORR, Cynthia (OH) 926

Microcomputers & personal computers — YOUNT, Natalie W. (WA) 1384

Microcomputers & picocomputers — TIERNAN, Linda M. (NH) 1244

Microcomputers & public access — RAPPAPORT, Susan E. (NY) 1008

Microcomputers & software — STANLEY, Nancy M. (PA) 1180

Microcomputers & software design — KARR, Ronald D. (MA) 628

Microcomputers & technical services — JOHNSON, Gary M. (MD) 604

Microcomputers & telecommunications — LEWONTIN, Amy (MA) 724

Microcomputers applications in libraries — LYNCH, Mollie S. (MI) 752

Microcomputers applications reference — MILLER, Susan E. (LA) 842

Microcomputers database design — BURCH, David R. (TX) 158

Microcomputers for library management — MCCANN, Susan F. (NH) 794

Microcomputers, hardware & software — ZABEL, Patricia L. (TX) 1385

Microcomputers in bibliography — LANCASTER, John (MA) 692

Microcomputers in curriculum — WHALEY, Janie B. (IN) 1328

Microcomputers in developing countries — DAVIES, Carol A. (NY) 277

Microcomputers in education — PRILLAMAN, Susan M. (NC) 993

Microcomputers in libraries

RICHMOND, John W.	(AZ)	1030
WHITLEY, Katherine M.	(AZ)	1333
FALANGA, Rosemarie E.	(CA)	361
JAFFE, Lee D.	(CA)	591
TURITZ, Mitch L.	(CA)	1263
LOERTSCHER, David V.	(CO)	737
HELMINSKI, James C.	(DC)	525
HERRICK, Kenneth R.	(HI)	532
ANDERSON, Charles R.	(IL)	22
TALAB, Rosemary S.	(KS)	1220
WALL, Celia J.	(KY)	1297
RAMSAY, John E.	(MA)	1005

MICROCOMPUTERS (Cont'd)

Microcomputers in libraries

DEXTER, Patrick J.	(MD)	298
TAYLOR, Arthur R.	(MO)	1226
LE BLANC, Charles A.	(NH)	708
NEWMARK-KRUGER, Barbara	(NJ)	900
LAPIER, Cynthia B.	(NY)	697
MILLER, Betty	(NY)	836
MILLER, Michael D.	(NY)	841
LEWIS, Gwen C.	(OH)	723
FALGER, David E.	(PA)	362
VOROS, David S.	(PA)	1289
GOLDSTEIN, Cynthia N.	(WA)	446
KRIKELAS, James	(WI)	678

Microcomputers in library administration — HOFFACKER, Antoinette C. (PA) 547

Microcomputers in library offices — INGRAHAM, Alice L. (PA) 582

Microcomputers in public services — MARTIN, Ron G. (IN) 778

Microcomputers in school libraries — GREESON, Janet S. (AR) 465; LOWE, Joy L. (LA) 744; GROSE, Rosemary F. (MA) 472

Microcomputers in special libraries — HALL, Elizabeth L. (WI) 487

Microcomputers in technical services — RODICH, Nancy A. (MS) 1048

Microcomputers in the humanities — GARDNER, Sue A. (NJ) 418

Microcomputers, online searching — GUSTAFSON, Ruth (NJ) 478

Microcomputers used for lib applications — MILLS, Elaine L. (KS) 844

Microcomputing

DAY, Janeth N.	(AL)	282
HANDMAN, Gary P.	(CA)	495
SEMKOW, Julie L.	(NY)	1115
TAYYEB, Rashid	(NS)	1229
PROVOST, Paul E.	(PQ)	996

Microcomputing & database training — KATZ, Jacqueline E. (NY) 630

Microcomputing & libraries — ESTERMANN-WISKOTT, Yolande (SWZ) 355

Microcomputing applications — HARLAN, John B. (IN) 502

Microcomputing technologies — TOOEY, Mary J. (MD) 1250

Microelectronics technologies databases — WOLF, Noel C. (AZ) 1360

Micros in libraries/information centers — TRUETT, Carol A. (HI) 1259

Mini & microcomputer applications — SWEENEY, Urban J. (CA) 1215

Mini & microcomputer software — COLEMAN, James R. (MA) 231

Non-book mtrls & microcomputer software — INTNER, Sheila S. (MA) 583

Online microcomputer application — VIDMANIS, Visvaldis E. (MA) 1283

Online microcomputer cataloging — BERNSTEIN, Elaine S. (ON) 89

Personal & microcomputers — GARCIA, Joseph E. (MI) 417

Public access microcomputer services — BROWN, Janis F. (CA) 144

Public access microcomputers

MUDD, Isabelle G.	(AK)	875
LEWIS, Jean R.	(AZ)	723
HARRIS, Roger L.	(CA)	506
FORREST, Charles G.	(IL)	390
MILLS, Elaine L.	(KS)	844
UPPGARD, Jeannine	(MA)	1269
MCCANN, Susan F.	(NH)	794
POLLY, Jean A.	(NY)	981
RIVERA, Gregorio	(NY)	1037
HOFFACKER, Antoinette C.	(PA)	547
PIELE, Linda J.	(WI)	971

Public & staff library microcomputing — ROBERTSON, Michael A. (NY) 1042

Public microcomputer access — SMITH, Valerie M. (OH) 1161

Public use microcomputers — FERGUSON, Chris D. (CA) 372

Special library, microelectronics — HARMON, Jacqueline B. (TX) 502

Systems analysis, micro — COX, Bruce B. (MO) 253

Systs analysis, microcomputer program — NEWCOMER, Susan N. (CA) 898

Technical services & microcomputers — NIEMEYER, Karen K. (IN) 903

Telecommunications, microcomputers — OHLMAN, Herbert (SWZ) 919

Training in microcomputer use — ANGLIN, Richard V. (NY) 28; DYER, Barbara M. (TN) 330

Training in microcomputers — PLAZA, Joyce S. (NJ) 978

Training on micros & software — KANNEL, Ene (ON) 625

MICROFICHE

Microfiche	SCLAR, Herbert	(CA)	1106
Microfiche applications	MILLER, Diane C.	(IL)	837
Microfiche preservation	COOPER, Carol D.	(NY)	242

MICROFILM

Archival microfilming	JONES, C L.	(PA)	611
Document preparation for microfilming	CHACE, Myron B.	(DC)	196
In-house microfilming	CAMPO, Charles A.	(ME)	177
Local history microfilming	BAUS, J W.	(IN)	67
Manuscripts conservation & microfilming	BOWEN, Laurel G.	(IL)	120
Microfilm	WIEDERAENDE, Robert C.	(IA)	1336
	LYSY, Peter J.	(IN)	753
Microfilm service bureau	RUOCCHIO, James P.	(PA)	1068
Microfilm services	HOLLINGS, Marie F.	(SC)	552
Microfilm technologies	HOWINGTON, Tad C.	(TX)	566
Microfilming	GIBSON, Ricky S.	(GA)	432
	SCHRAMM, Mary T.	(IL)	1099
	BARBEE, Lisa M.	(NC)	55
	WARD, Christine W.	(NY)	1303
Microfilming & records management	KNARZER, Arlene	(IL)	663
Microfilming data for resrch purposes	FROST, Debra R.	(CO)	406
Microfilming preservation	MARKHAM, Robert P.	(IL)	771
Organization & microfilm pubn with index	FALK, Candace S.	(CA)	362
Preservation microfilm cataloging	JONES, Edgar A.	(MA)	612
Preservation microfilming	CHACE, Myron B.	(DC)	196
	FERRARESE, Mary A.	(DC)	373
	SWORA, Tamara	(DC)	1217
	UNGER, Carol P.	(MD)	1269
	BAKER, John P.	(NY)	48
	SWARTZELL, Ann G.	(NY)	1214
	BOOMGAARDEN, Wesley L.	(OH)	115

MICROFORM

Audiovisual & microform cataloging	BURCHELL, Patricia M.	(ON)	158
Editorial & microform operations	DEL CERVO, Diane M.	(CT)	289
Management of microform collections	IANNUZZI, Patricia A.	(CT)	581
Maps, documents & microforms	DONLEY, Leigh M.	(CA)	311
Microform	BREITENWISCHER, Rosalyn E.	(MI)	132
Microform cataloging	TSCHERNY, Alexander	(DC)	1260
	MCKOWEN, Dorothy K.	(IN)	812
	STONE, Howard P.	(RI)	1197
Microform collections	STRAITON, T H.	(AL)	1199
Microform librarianship	DODSON, Suzanne C.	(BC)	308
Microform publishing	DUPONT, A J.	(HI)	327
	SEVERTSON, Susan M.	(VA)	1117
Microform storage & retrieval systems	SKARR, Robert J.	(DC)	1145
Microforms	FREDERIKSEN, Patience A.	(AK)	400
	HORN, Judy K.	(CA)	559
	JOHNSRUD, Thomas E.	(CA)	609
	SHAW, Richard N.	(DE)	1124
	MCGIVERIN, Rolland H.	(IN)	806
	COMBE, David A.	(LA)	234
	MIDDLETON, Francine K.	(LA)	833
	NACHOD, Katherine B.	(LA)	885
	HUDSON, Robert E.	(MA)	570
	RONEN, Naomi	(MA)	1053
	SCHLESINGER, Frances C.	(MA)	1094
	TATE, Vernon D.	(MD)	1225
	NILES, Ann A.	(MN)	904
	HOWELL, Margaret A.	(MO)	565
	SUTTON, Ellen D.	(NC)	1211
	CAPARROS, Ilona S.	(NJ)	179
	HEGG, Judith L.	(NJ)	521
	BOURKE, Thomas A.	(NY)	119
	DIBARTOLO, Amy L.	(NY)	299
	FOLCARELLI, Ralph J.	(NY)	387
	HUFFORD, Jon R.	(NY)	571
	OHLE, William P.	(NY)	919
	JONES, Alice W.	(OH)	610
	LUTTRELL, Jeffrey R.	(OH)	750
	WEBB, John	(OR)	1313

MICROFORM (Cont'd)

Microforms	APOSTOLOS, Margaret M.	(PA)	29
	EVEY, Patricia G.	(PA)	359
	LAURITO, Gerard P.	(PA)	703
	SLYHOFF, Merle J.	(PA)	1151
	TRIBIT, Donald K.	(PA)	1256
	HOOD, Lawrence E.	(TX)	556
	RHOLES, Julia M.	(TX)	1026
	EDMONDS, Susan M.	(WA)	336
	YEH, Thomas Y.	(WA)	1379
	COLLIER, Carol A.	(WY)	232
	MOFFAT, N L.	(AB)	852
	SALMOND, Margaret A.	(BC)	1077
	DUHAMEL, Marie	(ON)	324
	GUILBERT, Manon M.	(ON)	476
Microforms acquisition & cataloging	HUGHES, Frances M.	(CT)	571
Microforms cataloging	RENSHAW, Marita	(IL)	1023
Microforms collection & equipment	KURKUL, Donna L.	(MA)	684
Microforms, collection development	KAUL, Kanhya L.	(MI)	631
Microforms collection management	JOHNS, Jean B.	(OH)	601
Microforms, equipment, photocopy	GREEN, Walter H.	(MO)	463
Microforms management	PONNAPPA, Biddanda P.	(TN)	982
Microforms technology	WIHBEY, Francis R.	(ME)	1337
Serial & microform cataloging	NADESKI, Karen L.	(PA)	886
Serials & microforms	IRBY, Geraldine A.	(AL)	583

MICROFORMATS

Microformats	NITECKI, Joseph Z.	(NY)	905
Reprographics, microformatting	WARD, Christine W.	(NY)	1303

MICROGRAPHICS (See also Microfiche, Microfilm, Microform, Microformats)

Micrographic standards	SHAFFER, Norman J.	(DC)	1119
Micrographic systems	PAVLAKIS, Christopher	(NY)	950
	KESHISHIAN, Maria L.	(TX)	644
Micrographics	GOUDELOCK, Carol V.	(CA)	454
	BRAVY, Gary J.	(DC)	130
	SCOTT, Catherine D.	(DC)	1107
	SHAFFER, Norman J.	(DC)	1119
	TRYON, Roy H.	(DE)	1260
	GAYNON, David B.	(IL)	424
	MATTENSON, Murray M.	(IL)	785
	COATES, Paul F.	(KY)	224
	WOOD, Richard T.	(MI)	1365
	CARROLL, C E.	(MO)	187
	VOGT, Herwart C.	(NJ)	1287
	HUNTER, Gregory S.	(NY)	576
	YAKEL, Elizabeth	(NY)	1376
	FILSON, Laurie	(OR)	377
	PEMBERTON, J M.	(TN)	956
	BOCK, Thomas A.	(VT)	109
Micrographics & image quality	BAGG, Thomas C.	(MD)	45
Micrographics systems	TAMMARO, James M.	(NY)	1221
Micrographs	ZICH, Joanne A.	(DC)	1388
Records & micrographics management	GENESEN, Judith L.	(IL)	427
Records management & micrographics	WALSH, G M.	(ON)	1299
Records management & micrographics systs	BRIMSEK, Tobi A.	(DC)	136
Reference services & micrographics	EISEN, David J.	(IN)	340
Training & development micrographic syst	CORNELIUS, Charlene E.	(WI)	246

MICROIMAGERY

Microimagery & digitizing standards	BAGG, Thomas C.	(MD)	45

MICRONESIA

History Micronesia	DRIVER, Marjorie G.	(GU)	320

MICROPUBLISHING
Micropublication   SAMMATARO, John A. . (MA) 1078
Micropublishing   BOGENSCHNEIDER,
                            Duane R. . . . . (CT) 110
                          GREENWAY, Helen B. . . . (CT) 465
                          KRAMER, Sheldon I. . . . (CT) 675
                          FITZSIMMONS, Joseph J. (MI) 383
                          JENSEN, Dennis F. . . . . (NY) 598
                          LARSEN, Nancy E. . . . . (OK) 698
                          RUOCCHIO, James P. . . (PA) 1068
                          OLMSTEAD, Marcia E. . . (ON) 921
Scholarly micropublishing JOHNSON, Richard K. . . . (MD) 608

MICROSOFTWARE
General purpose microsoftware   CARLSON, Robert P. . . . (IL) 182

MICROTEXT
Microtext & newspapers   SCANNELL, Henry F. . . . (MA) 1087
Microtext materials   RIEBEL, Ellis F. . . . . . . (PA) 1033

MIDDLE
Administration, middle management   TONGATE, John T. . . . . (TX) 1250
Administration, middle school library GERLACH, Gretchen J. . (IL) 429
Elementary & middle school   ROONEY, Merilyn H. . . . (IN) 1053
Junior high, middle school   HAUG, Pauline C. . . . . . (WI) 512
Library middle management   DRUM, Carol A. . . . . . . (FL) 320
Middle grade fiction & nonfiction acqs BUCKLEY, Virginia L. . . (NY) 154
Middle management   RAZER, Robert L. . . . . . (AR) 1012
                             BROWN, Pamela P. . . . . (IL) 146
                             ALLEN, Patricia J. . . . . . (IN)   15
                             RUHL, Jodi S. . . . . (OH) 1066
                             MEADOR, Joan S. . . . . . (OK) 819
                             LAFEVER, Susan . . . . . . (TN) 687
Middle management & supervision BAILEY, Martha J. . . . . (IN)   46
                             HENRY, Peggy L. . . . . . . (MO) 529
Middle school & young adult literature MILLER, Ellen L. . . . . . . (VA) 837
Middle school library media center
 admin   GOZEMBA, Frances E. . . . (MA) 455
Middle school media centers EDWARDS, Barbara T. . (TN) 337
Middle schools   PITLUK, Paula K. . . . . . . (CA) 976

MIDDLE EAST
Africa & Middle East cataloging   LEONARD, Louise F. . . . (FL) 716
African & Middle Eastern research WITHERELL, Julian W. . (DC) 1358
Cataloging Middle East materials BEZIRGAN, Basima . . . . (IL)   93
East Europe & Middle East studies PINSON, Mark . . . . (MA) 975
Middle East area studies   BEZIRGAN, Basima . . . . (IL)   93
Middle East cataloging   CHAMMOU, Eliezer . . . . (CA) 198
Middle East collections   JAJKO, Edward A. . . . . . (CA) 592
Middle East collections development JAJKO, Edward A. . . . . . (CA) 592
Middle East languages cataloging JAJKO, Edward A. . . . . . (CA) 592
Middle East librarianship   HAMILTON, Marsha J. . . (OH) 492
Middle East libraries   HONOR, Naomi G. . . . . . (NY) 556
Middle East 19th century photography THOMAS, Ritchie D. . . . . (OH) 1238
Middle East studies   CHURUKIAN, Araxie P. . (CA) 213
Middle Eastern affairs   THEWS, Dorothy D. . . . . (MN) 1234
Middle Eastern lit collection devlpmnt BUNDY, David D. . . . . . . (KY) 157
Serials & Middle East studies NIELSON, Paula I. . . . . . (UT) 903
Women's studies, Middle East BEZIRGAN, Basima . . . . (IL)   93

MILITARY (See also Armed Forces, Defense)
Appraisal of military books   AIMONE, Alan C. . . . . . . (NY)   8
Civil, military, space databases GAZZOLA, Kenneth E. . . (DC) 424
Military affairs   WHITE-WILLIAMS,
                              Patricia . . . . (VA) 1333
Military & aeronautics reference KYSELY, Elizabeth C. . . . (CO) 685
Military & naval history   SHERIDAN, Robert N. . . . (NY) 1128
Military & naval literature AIMONE, Alan C. . . . . . . (NY)   8
Military & naval service   NICULA, J G. . . . . (VA) 903
Military collections   BOONE, Edward J. . . . . . (VA) 115
Military documentation   KUHL, Danuta . . . . (VA) 682
Military documents   KING, Elizabeth . . . . (FL) 650
                             PIENITZ, Eleanor . . . . . . (NY) 971
Military engineering   KOCH, Kathy R. . . . . (CA) 667
Military families & women   HARPER, Marie F. . . . . . (AL) 503

MILITARY (Cont'd)
Military history   BARON, Herman . . . . . . (PA)   58
                             WHITE-WILLIAMS,
                              Patricia . . . . (VA) 1333
Military history, business reference ROTHENBERG, Mark H. . . (NY) 1060
Military intelligence   BURNS, Dean A. . . . . . . (DC) 162
Military librarianship   SIEBENMORGEN, Ruth . (CA) 1135
                             SMITH, David A. . . . . . . (VA) 1153
Military libraries   JONES, Kevin R. . . . . . . (NY) 613
Military science & military history DOYLE, Frances M. . . . . . (VA) 317
Military specifications & standards BARNES, Denise M. . . . . . (CT)   57
Military studies   FELLER, Siegfried . . . . . (MA) 370
Rare military affairs items AIMONE, Alan C. . . . . . . (NY)   8
20th century military records PFEIFFER, David A. . . . . (DC) 966

MILITIA
Militia & National Guard history WEAVER, Thomas M. . . (DC) 1312

MILWAUKEE
Milwaukee history   COONEY, Charles W. . . (WI) 241

MINERAL (See also Mining)
Energy & mineral resources
 information   HARDY, Kenneth J. . . . . (AB) 501

MINIATURE
Miniature books   ADOMEIT, Ruth E. . . . . . (OH)   7

MINICOMPUTER (See also Computers)
Mainframe & minicomputer
 applications   BROWN, Maxine M. . . . . (DC) 146
Mini & microcomputer applications SWEENEY, Urban J. . . . (CA) 1215
Mini & microcomputer software COLEMAN, James R. . . . (MA) 231
Minicomputer programming   JACKSON, Charles G. . . (NY) 587

MINING (See also Mineral and names of specific minerals, e.g. Coal, Oil, etc.)
Business, economic & mining
 reference   KIEFER, Karen N. . . . . . . (CA) 647
Mining & geology research   STRACHAN, Pamela H. . (ON) 1199
Mining literature   GRAYSON, Virginia S. . . (CT) 460
Surface mining   LE BLANC, Judith E. . . . (OH) 708
United States Western mining history MC CAULEY, Philip F. . . (SD) 795

MINISTRY (See also Clergy, Pastoral)
Lutheran pastoral ministry   SMITH, Robert E. . . . . . (IN) 1160
Pastoral ministry   O'LEARY, Teresa M. . . . (NJ) 920

MINNESOTA (See also St Paul)
Iron Range Minnesota research ESALA, Lillian H. . . . . . . (MN) 354
Minnesota reference   CLARKE, Norman F. . . . (MN) 219

MINORITY
Low income, minority services PALMER, Julia R. . . . . . (NY) 936
Minorities & women in science JOHNSON, Sheila A. . . . (NY) 609
Minority   ALSTON-REEDER, Lizzie
                              A. . . . . (NC)   18
Minority librarianship & resources HARVELL, Valeria G. . . . (NJ) 509
Minority library services consulting EWUNES, Ernest L. . . . . (TX) 359
Minority publications   DANKY, James P. . . . . . (WI) 274
Minority service programs   GOMEZ, Martin J. . . . . . (IL) 447
Minority services   NAUMER, Janet N. . . . . . (CA) 889
Minority services researching ALLEN, Christina Y. . . . . (WI)   14
Outreach to ethnic minorities BETANCOURT, Ingrid T. . (NJ)   92
Service to minority groups   COHEN, David . . . . (NY) 228
Social reforms, minorities   MOREY, Frederick L. . . . (MD) 863

MIS

MIS & finance	PATRICIU, Florin S.	(MD)	947
MIS implementation	JACOBS, Patt	(OR)	590
MIS library management	ROBSON, Amy K.	(IL)	1045
MIS training	JACOBS, Patt	(OR)	590

MISSOURI

Missouri history	PARKES, Darla J.	(MO)	942
Missouri library history	TUCKER, Phillip H.	(MO)	1262

MODELING

Data modeling	REED, Patricia A.	(DC)	1015
Econometric modeling	O'REILLY, Daniel F.	(MA)	925
Financial models	WYSS, David A.	(MA)	1376
Financial research & modeling	COOPER, J P.	(MA)	243
Information modeling	DENNISON, Lynn C.	(CA)	292
Information modeling & engineering	MAXWELL, Marjo V.	(OH)	788
Modelling	NIGAM, Alok C.	(VA)	904
Probabilistic models	ROBERTSON, Stephen E.	(ENG)	1042
Statistical modelling	KOUNTZ, John C.	(CA)	673
US model development	YANCHAR, Joyce M.	(MA)	1377

MOLECULAR

Information virology, molecular biology	PERLMAN, Stephen E.	(NY)	959
Molecular biology immunogenetics	BERWICK, Mary C.	(PA)	91

MONASTIC

Monastic collections	PIRRERA, Aaron C.	(AR)	975
Monastic libraries	MCMANAMON, Mary J.	(MA)	814

MONETARY (See Financial)

Fiscal & monetary policy	BRINNER, Roger E.	(MA)	136

MONOGRAPHS

Acquisitions, monographic & audiovisual	WILLIAMS, Charles M.	(IL)	1342
Acquisitions, monographic & serials	BENNETT, Lee L.	(IL)	82
Acquisitions, monographs & serials	WACHEL, Kathleen B.	(IA)	1290
Acquisitions, monographs, serials	BARKER, Joseph W.	(CA)	56
Acquisitions of monographic notes	MAGLADRY, George C.	(CA)	759
Canadian monographs pre-1950	ALGAR, L E.	(ON)	13
Cataloging audiovisuals, monographs	VAN STRATEN, Daniel G.	(WI)	1277
Cataloging monographs	FORMAN, Camille L.	(CT)	390
	MATTHEWS, Priscilla J.	(IL)	785
	BLEIL, Leslie A.	(MI)	105
Cataloging monographs & serials	NEVIN, Susanne	(MN)	898
Cataloging monographs, foreign languages	MIKLOSVARY, Jozsef	(CA)	834
Cataloging monographs, maps & documents	CAHILL, Colleen R.	(PA)	171
Cataloging serials, law, monographs	SPRANKLE, Vicki S.	(PA)	1176
Cataloging Slavic monographs	SMIRENSKY, Helen K.	(NY)	1152
Cataloging social sciences monographs	HARDGROVE, David J.	(NJ)	499
Cataloging Western European monographs	SORURY, Kathryn L.	(IN)	1169
Descriptive cataloging, monographs	HAWKINS, Sandra J.	(DC)	514
Indexing monographs	SUGNET, Christopher L.	(NM)	1206
International monographs	CHANDLER, George	(ENG)	200
Legal cataloging, monographs	WOODS, Frances B.	(CT)	1367
Monograph acquisitions	BILYEU, David D.	(CA)	97
	SCHUSTER, Bonnie H.	(MT)	1103
	HAMILTON, Marsha J.	(OH)	492
Monograph cataloging	DIBLE, Joan B.	(CA)	299
	ANDREW, Paige G.	(GA)	26
	BERG, Elizabeth R.	(GA)	84
	KONKEL, Mary S.	(OH)	670
Monographic acquisition	ERICKSON, Lynda L.	(VA)	352
Monographic acquisitions	ORR, Margaret H.	(IA)	926
	DELONG, Douglas A.	(IL)	290
	STIFFLEAR, Allan J.	(MA)	1194
	COOK, Kay A.	(MI)	240
	JASPER, Richard P.	(MI)	595
	FLOWERS, Janet L.	(NC)	386

MONOGRAPHS (Cont'd)

Monographic acquisitions	STETSON, Keith R.	(NC)	1190
	RITCHIE, David G.	(NY)	1036
	D'ANDRAIA, Dana D.	(OR)	272
	HUDSON, Gary A.	(SD)	569
Monographic & serials acquisitions	PERRYMAN, Wayne R.	(TX)	961
	WAN, William W.	(TX)	1302
Monographic & serials cataloging	MORROW, Deborah	(MI)	869
Monographic cataloging	NELSON, Michael B.	(AL)	894
	KNIGHT, Rita C.	(AZ)	664
	HARDIN, Barbara A.	(GA)	500
	WATSON, Mark R.	(OR)	1310
	HALLOCK, Nancy L.	(PA)	489
Monographic cataloging unit training	DONAHUE, Janice E.	(FL)	310
Monographic series, authority control	DECKER, Jean S.	(NY)	285
Monographs acquisition	MARCINKO, Dorothy K.	(AL)	769
	GEMPELER, Constance M.	(AZ)	426
Monographs & scores cataloging	SUDDUTH, William E.	(MA)	1206
Monographs cataloging	ADAMSON, Danette	(CA)	6
	WANG, Margaret K.	(DE)	1303
	DEL CASTILLO, Mireya	(MO)	289
	GOERNER, Tatiana	(NY)	443
Original monograph cataloging	LINSKY, Leonore K.	(MA)	731
Serial & monograph acquisitions	WETZBARGER, Cecilia G.	(MD)	1328
Serials & monographs cataloging	TAVARES, Cecelia M.	(MA)	1225
	CHALMERS, Lois M.	(MD)	197
	ROSENSHIELD, Jill K.	(WI)	1057
West European academic monographs	JAGER, Conradus	(MA)	591

MONTANA

Montana history	MORROW, Delores J.	(MT)	869

MOORE

George Moore bibliography	GILCHER, Edwin	(VT)	434

MORBIDITY

Mortality & morbidity statistics	MURPHY, Virginia A.	(WI)	881

MORGUE

Photo morgue design & implementation	DAMOTH, Douglas L.	(NY)	272

MORMONISM (See also Latter Day Saint)

Literature of Mormonism	PURDY, Victor W.	(UT)	998

MOROCCO

Library systems of Morocco	OUELLET, Louise M.	(PQ)	930

MORTALITY

Mortality & morbidity statistics	MURPHY, Virginia A.	(WI)	881

MORTGAGE

Mortgage finance	MCKEE, Margaret J.	(WI)	810
Mortgage insurance	MCKEE, Margaret J.	(WI)	810

MOTION (See also Film)

Acquisition of eductnl motion pictures	CHAVES, Francisco M.	(FL)	204
Acquisition of motion pictures & videos	TALIT, Lynn	(CT)	1221
Cataloging of eductnl motion pictures	CHAVES, Francisco M.	(FL)	204
Motion picture & television archiving	FIELDING, Raymond E.	(TX)	376
Motion picture & television research	BRADY, Eileen E.	(WA)	126
Motion picture production research	PLUMB, Carolyn G.	(CA)	978
Motion picture research	NAZARIAN, Anahid	(CA)	890
Motion pictures	DEUTSCH, James I.	(DC)	296
Motion pictures & television	SCHLOSSER, Anne G.	(CA)	1094
Research for motion picture, television	NELSON-HARB, Sally R.	(CA)	895

MOTIVATION

Employee motivation & evaluation	BOYER, Calvin J.	(CA)	123
Motivation personnel management	STEPHENS, Jerry W.	(AL)	1188
Motivational & informational speaker	LYNCH, Minnie L.	(LA)	752
Reading motivation	PAULIN, Mary A.	(MI)	950
Reading motivation, children	TRAINER, Leslie F.	(PAK)	1253
Staff development & motivation	AUSTIN, Neal F.	(NC)	40
Student motivation	SKELLY, Laurie J.	(MN)	1146

MOTORCYCLE

Motorcycle safety	DAWSON, Lawrence	(WI)	282

MOVIES

Jazz consulting, movie studios	COLLINS, Richard H.	(CA)	233
Movies & film	WITT, Kenneth W.	(MN)	1358
Movies & radio formats consultation	SMITH, Walter H.	(VA)	1161

MOVING

Cataloging archival moving images	HARRISON, Harriet W.	(DC)	506
Consulting & move planning	MILLER, Scott W.	(NY)	842
Library design & moving projects	SCHUBACK COHN, Judith	(NJ)	1101
Library moves	HEISHMAN, Eleanor L.	(OH)	523
Library planning & moving	LINDEN, Margaret J.	(CA)	729
Merging & moving libraries	LYNCH, Mollie S.	(MI)	752
Moving a library	JANKOWSKI, Susan H.	(WI)	593
Moving a library collection	SUTTON, Sandra K.	(AL)	1211
Moving & space planning	BALKIN, Ruth G.	(NY)	52
	GOLDMAN, Martha A.	(NY)	445
Moving collections	WALL, Carol	(OH)	1297
Moving image documents	O'CONNOR, Brian C.	(CA)	915
Moving images archivist	DE ARMAN, Charles L.	(DC)	284
Moving large book collections	PARRY, David R.	(CO)	944
Moving libraries	WORSTER, Carol L.	(IL)	1369
	TUCKER, Dennis C.	(IN)	1261
	SIEGMANN, Starla C.	(WI)	1136
Moving library collections	RICHARDS, James H.	(NM)	1028
	MILLER, Scott W.	(NY)	842
	SVIBRUCK, Jonathan	(NY)	1212
	HINDMAN, Pamela J.	(VA)	542
Planning & moving libraries	CARDENAS, Martha L.	(TX)	180
Planning & moving of law libraries	PLUNKET, Joy H.	(MA)	978
Space planning & moving libraries	FOX, Marylou P.	(CA)	395

MULTIASSOCIATION

Multiassociation management	UNDERWOOD, Mary S.	(KY)	1269

MULTIBRANCH

Multibranch libraries	FRANKLIN, Jill S.	(MO)	397

MULTICULTURAL

Multicultural & multilingual	DUPERREAULT, Marilyn J.	(SK)	327
Multicultural & multilingual lib srvs	GUNDARA, Jaswinder	(ON)	477
Multicultural librarianship	SCHULTE-ALBERT, Hans G.	(ON)	1101
Multicultural library services	BURNETT, Wayne C.	(ON)	162
Multicultural service	IVANOCHKO, Robert W.	(SK)	585
Multicultural services	LORENTOWICZ, Genia	(ON)	741
Multiculturalism & heritage	GRODSKI, Renata	(ON)	471

MULTI-IMAGE

Multi-image production	ISOBE, Darron T.	(UT)	585

MULTILINGUAL (See also Bilingual)

Multicultural & multilingual	DUPERREAULT, Marilyn J.	(SK)	327
Multicultural & multilingual lib srvs	GUNDARA, Jaswinder	(ON)	477
Multilingual biblioservices	MEUNIER, Pierre	(PQ)	829
Multilingual collections	HAABNIIT, Ene	(BC)	480
	ZIELINSKA, Marie F.	(ON)	1388
Multilingual librarianship	MANEY, Lana E.	(TX)	765
Multilingual library collections	SCHNEIDER, Francisca M.	(CA)	1097
Multilingual text processing	DEERWESTER, Scott C.	(IL)	287
Public library multilingual services	BELL, Irena L.	(ON)	77

MULTILINK

Multilink systems	BRANDEAU, John H.	(NY)	128

MULTIMEDIA

Multimedia management	ENGLESAKIS, Marina F.	(AB)	350
Multimedia programming	GAREN, Robert J.	(MI)	418
Multimedia services	CHICKERING, F W.	(NY)	208
Public school multimedia	METTLING, Cora E.	(KS)	828

MULTIPHASIC

Multiphasic screening	CAREL, Rafael S.	(ISR)	181

MULTIPLE-LIBRARY (See also Multitype)

Multi-library automation networks	KERSHNER, Lois M.	(CA)	644
	JONES-LITTEER, Corene A.	(ID)	616
Multi-library cooperation	ROYCE, Carolyn S.	(NJ)	1063
Multi-library network	HAYES, Richard E.	(MA)	516
Multi-library networking	SENNER, Rachel	(SD)	1115
Multiple-library management	KLAUS, Susan B.	(OH)	658

MULTIPOINT

Multipoint delivery networks	MAYNARD, John C.	(ON)	790

MULTISUBJECT

Multisubject bibliographies compilation	HOTIMLANSKA, Leah D.	(IL)	562
Multisubject book indexing	HOTIMLANSKA, Leah D.	(IL)	562

MULTITYPE (See also Intertype, Multiple-Library)

Automation in multitype cooperatives	DAW, May B.	(CT)	282
Automation plng, multitype networking	DIENER, Margaret M.	(CA)	302
Cooperative multitype library systems	JAGOE, Katherine P.	(TX)	591
Multitype & interloan	LUND, Patricia A.	(WI)	748
Multitype cooperation	ECKERT, Daniel L.	(WI)	335
Multitype cooperative projects	DORST, Thomas J.	(IL)	313
Multitype cooperatives	DAW, May B.	(CT)	282
Multi-type library cooperation	FALSONE, Anne M.	(CO)	363
	BURGER, Leslie B.	(CT)	159
	HUPP, Sharon W.	(CT)	577
	POUNDSTONE, Sally H.	(CT)	987
	BROWN, Eva R.	(IL)	143
	OLSEN, Rowena J.	(KS)	921
	DEJOHN, William T.	(MN)	288
	LOWRY, Lucy J.	(MN)	745
	PARKER, Sara A.	(MT)	942
	PERRY, Douglas F.	(NC)	960
	NEUMANN, Joan	(NY)	897
	WASHBURN, Keith E.	(NY)	1307
	WAREHAM, Nancy L.	(OH)	1304
	TREBBY, Janis G.	(WI)	1255
Multitype lib cooperation consultation	VOSS, Anne E.	(NJ)	1289
Multitype library cooperative	ROSENBERG, Gail L.	(NJ)	1056
Multitype library development & service	KOYAMA, Janice T.	(CA)	674
Multitype library network development	JOHNSON, Duane F.	(KS)	603
Multitype library network facilitation	SNOWDEN, Deanna	(IN)	1164
Multitype library networking	STEINER, Janet E.	(NY)	1186
Multitype library organizations	MORRISON, Carol J.	(IL)	868
Multitype library system	PACEY, Brenda M.	(IL)	933
Multitype library systems	WRIGHT, Kathryn D.	(AL)	1372
	HARRIET, Conklin W.	(IL)	503
	ROOSE, Tina	(IL)	1053
	TYER, Travis E.	(IL)	1266
	ELDRED, Heather A.	(WI)	342
Multitype library systems, cooperation	KNEPEL, Nancy	(CO)	664
Multitype networks	MARTHEY, Rebecca J.	(IN)	775
	IMMROTH, Barbara F.	(TX)	582
Multitype resource sharing	MICHAELIS, Kathryn S.	(WI)	831
Public library, multitype systems	WELCH, Steven J.	(WI)	1321
Regional multitype library systems	BERNER, Karen J.	(NE)	88

MUNICIPAL (See also City, Metropolitan)

Municipal & county government — STRICKLAND, Ann T. . . (AZ) 1202
Municipal archives — GRESSITT, Alexandra S. (MS) 467
— BOCKMAN, Eugene J. . . (NY) 109
Municipal cable television
  programming — VARNES, Richard S. . . . (CO) 1279
Municipal document management — SCHLIPF, Frederick A. . . (IL) 1094
Municipal documents — KRITEMEYER, Ann C. . . (CT) 679
— BENIGNO, Linda J. . . . . (IL) 80
— BRENNAN, Ellen . . . . . . (PA) 132
Municipal government information
  srvs — HENDERSON, Harriet . . . (VA) 526
Municipal government reference — BRADDOCK, Virginia O. . (CO) 125
Municipal government reference
  services — TAYLOR, Patricia A. . . . . (NY) 1228
Municipal information systems — BOCKMAN, Eugene J. . . (NY) 109
Municipal libraries — BERNARDIN, Luce . . . . . (PQ) 88
Municipal library administration — PERRY, Edward C. . . . . . (CA) 960
Municipal records — LA CHAPELLE, Jennifer R. (ON) 686
Municipal reference — NORDBY, Leslie L. . . . . . (CA) 908
— MARTINES, Karen E. . . (OH) 779
— HERFURTH, Sharon M. . (TX) 530
Municipal reference & services — FOREHAND, Margaret P. . (VA) 390
Provincial & municipal government — WEATHERHEAD, Barbara
  A. . . . . (ON) 1312
Records retention, municipal — BROWNE, Jeri A. . . . . . . (CA) 148

MUSEOLOGY (See also Museums)

Museology — SCOTT, Catherine D. . . . (DC) 1107
— SEEMANN, Charles H. . . (TN) 1111

MUSEUMS (See also Galleries, Museology)

Archive, museum, & library admin — WRIGHT, John C. . . . . . (HI) 1371
Archives, library, museum services — SUELFLOW, August R. . (MO) 1206
Art collections & museum
  administration — SOMMER, Ursula M. . . . (NJ) 1167
Art museum libraries — CHIN, Cecilia H. . . . . . . (DC) 208
Art museum library management — WALKER, William B. . . . (NY) 1296
— DOWNING, Jeannette D. (TX) 316
— SHEAROUSE, Linda N. . (TX) 1124
Art museums & schools — LEIBOLD, Cheryl A. . . . . (PA) 713
Children's museums — PATTISON, Joanne . . . . (FL) 948
County museums volunteer
  librarianship — HOWE, Mary T. . . . . (IL) 565
Development of museum — DUNGER, George A. . . . (SD) 326
Directing & managing museum &
  library — PARKER, Peter J. . . . . . (PA) 942
Fine arts museum — JACOBY, Mary M. . . . . . (VA) 590
Fire protection in libraries & museums — MORRIS, John . . . . (CA) 866
Historical interpretations in museums — BATTLE, Thomas C. . . . (DC) 65
Library, museum & archives admin — HYATT, John D. . . . . . . (TX) 580
Museum — STOCKDALE, Kay L. . . . (NC) 1195
Museum administration — SCHEWE, Donald B. . . . (GA) 1092
— STEWART, Virginia R. . . (IL) 1193
— KENAMORE, Jane A. . . (TX) 640
— JOHNSON, Kenneth P. . . (VA) 606
Museum & archival cataloging, organz — DEE, Camille C. . . . . . . (NY) 286
Museum archives — FINERMAN, Carol B. . . . (MI) 378
— WAGNER, Cherryl A. . . . (MI) 1291
— BELL, Mary F. . . . . (NY) 77
— HOMMEL, Claudia . . . . . (NY) 555
— JOHNSON, Steven P. . . (NY) 609
— HALLER, Douglas M. . . (PA) 489
Museum, art libraries — HUMPHRY, James . . . . . (NY) 574
Museum cataloging — BIERBAUM, Esther G. . . (IA) 95
Museum collections — BRENNER, M D. . . . . (AK) 133
Museum curating — KELM, Carol R. . . . . (IL) 638
Museum curator — WHEELER, Elaine . . . . (NY) 1328
Museum database systems — YARNALL, James L. . . . (DC) 1378
Museum development — KEATS, Susan E. . . . . . . (MA) 633
Museum information systems — BEARMAN, David A. . . . (PA) 69
Museum librarianship — LENTHALL, Franklyn . . . (ME) 715
Museum libraries — GREEN, Nancy W. . . . . . (CO) 462
— KANE, Katherine . . . . . (CO) 625
— WILT, Charles F. . . . . . . (OH) 1353
Museum maintenance — STELLING, Dwight D. . . . (IL) 1186

MUSEUMS (Cont'd)

Museum management — MOORE, Emily C. . . . . . (AL) 859
— ADAMS, Larry D. . . . . . (IA) 5
— CAYA, Marcel . . . . (PQ) 195
Museum objects — HERIOT, Ruthanne . . . . (WV) 531
Music museums & archives — HASSE, John E. . . . . . . (DC) 511
Performing arts libraries, museums — GOLDING, Alfred S. . . . (OH) 445
Small museum libraries — BENEDETTI, Joan M. . . (CA) 80

MUSIC (See also Band, Cantata, Concert, Gregorian, Hymn, Instruments, Jazz, Musicology, Opera, Orchestra, Scores, Songs, Tune)

Acquisitions, bks, records, music
  scores — SILVER, Martin A. . . . . . (CA) 1138
African & Caribbean music — RICHARDSON, Deborra A. (DC) 1029
Afro-American music — RICHARDSON, Deborra A. (DC) 1029
American music — ANDERSON, Gillian B. . . (DC) 23
— BARNHILL, Georgia B. . . (MA) 58
— COOLIDGE, Arlan R. . . . (RI) 241
American music bibliography — CARNOVALE, A N. . . . . (MS) 184
American music development — JERDE, Curtis D. . . . . . . (LA) 599
American music reference — JACKSON, Richard H. . . (NY) 588
American musical theatre archives — ROSENBURG, Betsy R. . . (CT) 1056
American popular music — WELLS, Paul F. . . . . (TN) 1323
Analytical bibliography of music — BOORMAN, Stanley H. . . (NY) 115
Antiquarian music dealer — MERZ, Lawrie H. . . . . . . (PA) 827
Archives & music rarities — WALKER, Elizabeth . . . . (PA) 1295
Art & music — SUNDELL, Elizabeth B. . . (IL) 1210
— MELIK, Ella M. . . . . (OK) 822
Art & music reference — BARNETT, Jean D. . . . . . (OR) 57
Art, fine arts, & music — COLDWELL, Charles P. . . (WA) 230
Art, music, & audiovisual librarianship — SECKELSON, Linda E. . . (NY) 1110
Art, music, & drama — ALTER, Forrest H. . . . . . (MI) 18
Art, music & sports collection
  devlpmnt — BAKER, Paula J. . . . . . . (OH) 49
Band music recordings research — MITZIGA, Walter J. . . . . (IL) 850
Bibliographic instruction for music — SILCOX, Tinsley E. . . . . (TN) 1137
Bibliography, music — LOWENS, Margery M. . . (MD) 744
Bibliography of Japanese music — SIDDONS, James D. . . . (VA) 1135
Bibliography of music — TANNO, John W. . . . . . . (CA) 1223
Black music — RICHARDSON, Deborra A. (DC) 1029
Black music research — DE LERMA, Dominique R. (MD) 289
— GRENDYSA, Peter A. . . (WI) 467
Brass music — MARTIN, Jean F. . . . . . (NY) 776
Catalog of music magazines — FITZNER, Robert N. . . . (IL) 382
Cataloging art & music — RICHARDSON, Emma G. (NY) 1029
Cataloging music — CASEY, Carol A. . . . . . (TX) 192
— KATZ, Solomon B. . . . . (PQ) 630
Cataloging music & audiovisual
  materials — SLOMSKI, Monica J. . . . (CT) 1150
Cataloging music & sound recordings — DORFMAN, Ethel L. . . . (NY) 312
— POWELL, Virginia L. . . . (PA) 989
Cataloging music manuscripts — PLAIN, Marilyn V. . . . . . (NY) 977
Cataloging music materials — PALKOVIC, Mark A. . . . (OH) 935
Cataloging musical loan collections — LYON, Bruce C. . . . . . . (FL) 752
Cataloguing of music materials — COLQUHOUN, Joan E. . . (ON) 234
Chamber music — WALKER, Elizabeth . . . . (PA) 1295
Choral music literature — SHARP, Avery T. . . . . . (TX) 1122
Church music — ROEPKE, David E. . . . . (OH) 1048
Classical music broadcasting — FRANK, Mortimer H. . . . (NY) 397
Classical music criticism — LAMBERT, John W. . . . . (NC) 690
Classical music sound archives — MAROTH, Frederick J. . . (CA) 772
Classical music sound recordings — HALSEY, Richard S. . . . (NY) 490
Classifying information about music — STRATELAK, Nadia A. . . (MI) 1200
Computer music — DAVIS, Deta S. . . . . . . (DC) 278
Computerized music cataloging — GRIFFIN, Marie E. . . . . (NJ) 468
— GOODWIN, Charles B. . . (TX) 450
Contemporary American music — BOZIWICK, George E. . . (NY) 124
Contemporary American music
  bibliography — HARTSOCK, Ralph M. . . (PA) 508
Contemporary music — MARTIN, Vernon E. . . . . (CT) 778
Country music — PRUETT, Barbara J. . . . . (DC) 996
Country music historian — MARTUCCI, Louis U. . . . (CA) 779
Country music history — SEEMANN, Charles H. . . (TN) 1111
Developing new music libraries — FLOERSHEIMER, Lee M. (NY) 385
Early music & dance — COLDWELL, Charles P. . . (WA) 230
Editing music & music literature — PRUETT, James W. . . . . (DC) 996
Education for music librarianship — BRADLEY, Carol J. . . . . (NY) 125
Film music — ANDERSON, Gillian B. . . (DC) 23
— WRIGHT, H S. . . . . (IL) 1371

MUSIC (Cont'd)

First editions & manuscripts of music

First editions, 19th century music
Folk music
Folk music archives
French solo vocal music
Indexing & editing music information
Instructor of music bibliography
Interviewing musicians
Jazz & hot dance music
Jazz & other music
Jazz recordings & musicians
Liberal arts, religion, music cataloging
Lib of Congress music subject
  headings
Library school education, music
Live music concert coordination
MARC format for music
Mechanical music, broadcasting, film
Medical & music databases
Music

STRINGFELLOW, William
  T. . . . . (NY) 1202
BRODY, Elaine . . . . (NY) 139
VUKAS, Rachel R. . . . . . (KS) 1290
POST, Jennifer C. . . . . . (VT) 986
VOLLEN, Gene E. . . . . . (KS) 1287
STRATELAK, Nadia A. . . (MI) 1200
MIXTER, Keith E. . . . . . (OH) 850
SEIBERT, Donald C. . . . . (NY) 1112
LOTZ, Rainer E. . . . . . . (WGR) 742
WILLIAMS, Martin T. . . . (DC) 1345
COHEN, Frederick S. . . . (NY) 228
LUSK, Betty M. . . . . . . (SAF) 749

PRICE, Harry H. . . . . . . (DC) 992
COOVER, James B. . . . . (NY) 244
RUSTMAN, Mark M. . . . . (KS) 1070
GRISCOM, Richard W. . . (IL) 471
MUNSICK, Lee R. . . . . . (NJ) 879
CHASE, Judith H. . . . . . (OR) 203
CLINKSCALES, Joyce M. (AR) 222
ANDERSEN, Leslie N. . . (CA)   21
GRIFFIN, Michael D. . . . . (CA) 468
RUHL, Taylor D. . . . . . . (CA) 1066
TAYLOR, Marion E. . . . . (CA) 1227
FARRINGTON, James . . (CT) 365
SAMUEL, Harold E. . . . . (CT) 1079
SCOTT, Joseph W. . . . . (CT) 1107
OSTROVE, Geraldine E. . (DC) 929
KOBIALKA, Nancy C. . . . (FL) 666
COSCARELLI, William F. (GA) 248
HUGHES, Neil R. . . . . . (GA) 572
MILLER, Anthony G. . . . (GA) 835
LITTLE, Margaret C. . . . . (IA) 733
RITCHIE, Verna F. . . . . (IA) 1036
ACKER, Robert L. . . . . . (IL)   3
EPSTEIN, Dena J. . . . . . (IL) 351
HANSEN, Eleanore E. . . (IL) 497
SCHWEGEL, Richard C. . (IL) 1105
DOLAK, Frank J. . . . . . . (IN) 309
ENGLE, Madge . . . . (IN) 349
HITCHENS, Susan H. . . . (KS) 544
KORDA, Marion . . . . (KY) 671
JUENGLING, Pamela K. . (MA) 619
PRISTASH, Kenneth . . . (MA) 993
ROGAN, Michael J. . . . . (MA) 1049
THISTLE, Dawn R. . . . . . (MA) 1235
WOOD, Ross . . . . (MA) 1365
BERRY, Charlene . . . . . . (MI)   90
WILDMAN, Linda . . . . . . (MI) 1339
SHIRES, Nancy P. . . . . . (NC) 1131
BROCKMAN, William S. . (NJ) 138
FLICK, Susan E. . . . . . . (NJ) 385
GREEN, Donald T. . . . . . (NJ) 461
SAWYCKY, Roman A. . . (NJ) 1086
GILES, Marta M. . . . . . . (NY) 434
LEW, Susan . . . . (NY) 722
MILLER, Philip L. . . . . . . (NY) 841
NICKERSON, Donna L. . (NY) 902
NUZZO, Nancy B. . . . . . (NY) 912
PERONE, Karen L. . . . . . (NY) 959
WOOD, Thor E. . . . . (NY) 1365
FIDLER, Linda M. . . . . . . (OH) 375
ROUTH, Sheila J. . . . . . . (OH) 1061
SHAMP, B K. . . . . (OH) 1120
SPERRY, Linda S. . . . . . (OH) 1174
RHYNE, Barbara B. . . . . (OR) 1026
GOODMAN, John E. . . . (PA) 449
GROSSMAN, Robert M. . (PA) 473
KENT, Frederick J. . . . . . (PA) 642
NIEWEG, Clinton F. . . . . (PA) 904
ROOT, Deane L. . . . . . . (PA) 1054
WOOD, Linda L. . . . . . . (PA) 1364
WADDINGTON, Susan R. (RI) 1290
WUJCIK, Dennis S. . . . . (TN) 1374
MCBRIDE, Jerry L. . . . . . (VT) 792
BRAGER, Beverly J. . . . . (WI) 127
BURR, Charlotte A. . . . . (WI) 163
FOERSTER, Trey . . . . . . (WI) 387

MUSIC (Cont'd)
Music

Music acquisitions for college libraries
Music administration & reference
Music & audiovisual cataloging
Music & audiovisual librarianship
Music & computer indexing
Music & dance librarianship
Music & dance reference
Music & fine arts reference
Music & folklore research
Music & performing arts librarianship
Music & sound recordings
Music & sound recordings cataloging
Music & theater
Music archives
Music arranging & orchestrating
Music articles
Music, arts & recreation
Music at the Library of Congress
Music, Audiovisual
Music autographs
Music bibliography

RATNER, Sabina T. . . . . (PQ) 1010
SMILEY, Marilynn J. . . . . (NY) 1151
HALL, Bonlyn G. . . . . . . (VA) 487
ALMQUIST, Sharon G. . . (TX)   17
SEAMAN, Sally G. . . . . . (IL) 1109
KELLER, Kate V. . . . . . . (PA) 635
HECK, Thomas F. . . . . . (OH) 519
HEUTTE, Frederic A. . . . (MD) 535
DAVIS, Joy V. . . . . (GA) 279
MCCULLOH, Judith M. . . (IL) 801
MAYER, George L. . . . . (NY) 789
WATTS, Richard S. . . . . (CA) 1310
SNODGRASS, Wilson D. (TX) 1163
WILSON, Fredric W. . . . (NY) 1351
BOWLING, Lance C. . . . (CA) 121
NIGHTINGALE, Daniel . . (PA) 904
GRAY, Michael H. . . . . . (DC) 460
WILKINS, Marilyn W. . . . (LA) 1340
ANDERSON, Gillian B. . . (DC)   23
AYRES, Edwin M. . . . . . (TX)   43
MACNUTT, Richard P. . . (ENG) 758
SMITH, Dorman H. . . . . (AZ) 1154
ADAMSON, Danette . . . (CA)   6
COLBY, Edward E. . . . . (CA) 230
DUGGAN, Mary K. . . . . (CA) 324
ELLIOTT, Patricia G. . . . (CA) 344
FRY, Stephen M. . . . . . (CA) 407
MOULTON, Suzanne L. . (CO) 873
KELLER, Michael A. . . . . (CT) 635
PRUETT, James W. . . . . (DC) 996
TEMPERLEY, Nicholas . . (IL) 1230
FLING, Robert M. . . . . . (IN) 385
MCKNIGHT, Mark C. . . . (LA) 812
EVENSEN, Robert L. . . . (MA) 358
OCHS, Michael . . . . . . (MA) 915
SHEETS, Robin R. . . . . (MD) 1125
BLACK-SHIER, Mary L. . (MI) 102
DRUESEDOW, John E. . (NC) 320
WURSTEN, Richard B. . . (NC) 1374
DIAMOND, Harold J. . . . (NY) 299
FOLTER, Siegrun H. . . . . (NY) 388
HILL, George R. . . . . . . (NY) 539
ELLIKER, Calvin . . . . . . (PA) 343
YOUNG, James B. . . . . (PA) 1382
BRENNAN, Patricia B. . . (RI) 133
PEAKE, Luise E. . . . . . . (SC) 952
REED, Marcia E. . . . . . . (WA) 1015
WENK, Arthur B. . . . . . (PQ) 1324
SCHUURSMA, Ann B. . . (NET) 1103

Music bibliography & cataloging
Music bibliography & discography
Music bibliography & history
Music bibliography & publishing
Music bibliography & reference
Music books
Music catalog
Music cataloging

HARTIG, Linda . . . . (WI) 508
MCCLELLAN, William M. . (IL) 796
VILES, Elza A. . . . . (TN) 1284
BRYCE, Maria C. . . . . . . (ON) 152
HAEFLIGER, Kathleen A. (NY) 482
BAHR, Edward R. . . . . . (MS)   45
MCINTOSH, Nadia . . . . (MA) 809
FAIR, Kathy L. . . . . (AL) 361
EARNEST, Jeffrey D. . . . (AR) 332
EAGLESON, Laurie E. . . (AZ) 331
ADAMSON, Danette . . . (CA)   6
BOCHIN, Janet S. . . . . . (CA) 108
ELLIOTT, Patricia G. . . . (CA) 344
CARTER, Nancy F. . . . . (CO) 180
SAVIG, Norman I. . . . . . (CO) 1086
DAVIS, Deta S. . . . . (DC) 278
PRICE, Harry H. . . . . . . (DC) 992
DAVIS, Joy V. . . . . (GA) 279
HUGHES, Neil R. . . . . . (GA) 572
BURBANK, Richard D. . . (IL) 158
GOUDY, Allie W. . . . . . . (IL) 454
GRISCOM, Richard W. . . (IL) 471
WARD, Shirlene A. . . . . (IL) 1304
NELSON, Brenda . . . . . (IN) 893
SCHOONOVER, Phyllis J. (IN) 1098
BRATCHER, Perry R. . . . (KY) 129
POWELL, Martha C. . . . . (KY) 988
PRITCHARD, Elsie T. . . . (KY) 994
RICHARDSON, Susan C. (KY) 1030

MUSIC (Cont'd)
Music cataloging

THOMPSON, Jeannette C. (LA) 1240
FELDT, Candice K. . . . . (MA) 369
SHEETS, Robin R. . . . . (MD) 1125
PERRY-BOWDER, Libbie
E. . . . . (ME) 961
BLACK-SHIER, Mary L. . (MI) 102
BOWEN, Jennifer B. . . . (MI) 120
HILDEBRAND, Linda L. . (MI) 538
CHRISTENSEN, Beth E. . (MN) 211
YOUNGHOLM, Philip . . . (MN) 1383
WURSTEN, Richard B. . . (NC) 1374
BRKIC, Beverly T. . . . . (ND) 138
DOW, Carolyn E. . . . . . (NE) 315
TIBBITS, Edith J. . . . . . (NE) 1243
NEWHOUSE, Brian G. . . (NJ) 899
SKROBELA, Katherine C. (NJ) 1147
FLOERSHEIMER, Lee M. (NY) 385
FOLTER, Siegrun H. . . . (NY) 388
HARDISH, Patrick M. . . (NY) 500
RANSOM, Sarah B. . . . (NY) 1007
RORICK, William C. . . . (NY) 1054
VAN BIEMA, Mary E. . . (NY) 1272
WISE, Matthew W. . . . . (NY) 1357
BALCAS, Georgianne . . . (OH) 50
HAMBLEY, Susan L. . . . (OH) 490
KNAPP, David . . . . (OH) 663
ROBSON, Timothy D. . . . (OH) 1045
WEITZ, Jay N. . . . . (OH) 1320
ZASLOW, Barry J. . . . . (OH) 1386
RENFRO, Robert S. . . . (OR) 1023
EISENBERG, Peter L. . . (PA) 340
ELLIKER, Calvin . . . . . . (PA) 343
GERHART, Catherine A. . (PA) 428
STEPHENS, Norris L. . . (PA) 1188
YOUNG, James B. . . . . (PA) 1382
FAWVER, Darlene E. . . . (SC) 367
GARRETT, Stuart . . . . . (TN) 420
CAINE, William C. . . . . (TX) 171
CRAIG, Marilyn J. . . . . (TX) 254
GEARY, Gregg S. . . . . (TX) 424
POPE, Betty F. . . . . . . (TX) 983
BECKER, Charlotte B. . . (VA) 72
REED, Marcia E. . . . . . (WA) 1015
LAVERTY, Corinne Y. . . (ON) 703
MOHAMMED, Selima . . . (PQ) 852
Music cataloging & bibliography   DURIS, Richard M. . . . . (PA) 328
Music cataloging or Hebrew
cataloging   FRIEDLAND, Frances K. . (ON) 403
Music collection development   BOGNAR, Dorothy M. . . (CT) 111
FLING, Robert M. . . . . . (IN) 385
RORICK, William C. . . . (NY) 1054
WATANABE, Ruth T. . . . (NY) 1308
PATTERSON, Myron B. . (UT) 948
BRYCE, Maria C. . . . . . (ON) 152
Music collections   JAROSLOW, Sylvia W. . (NJ) 594
DENNIS, Christopher J. . (NF) 292
Music collections & archives   GREEN, Walter H. . . . . (MO) 463
Music consulting & discography   PATRYCH, Joseph . . . . (NY) 947
Music, dance, theatre arts   LUBRANO, Judith A. . . . (MA) 745
Music databases   CNATTINGIUS, Claes M. (SWE) 224
Music departments   GERSTENBERGER,
Martha F. . . . . (IA) 429
Music editing   BLOTNER, Linda S. . . . (MA) 106
BROUDE, Ronald . . . . . (NY) 141
Music editing & proofreading   NIGHTINGALE, Daniel . . (PA) 904
Music education   THOMPSON, Anna M. . . (IN) 1238
Music history   MARTIN, Vernon E. . . . (CT) 778
JELLINEK, George . . . . (NY) 596
LINDAHL, Charles E. . . (NY) 728
NOVITSKY, Edward G. . (NY) 911
PEAKE, Luise E. . . . . . (SC) 952
Music history & literature   DONALDSON, Anna L. . . (TX) 311
Music, history & women's studies   LOMBARDI, Mary L. . . . (CA) 738
Music history collections   SIMMONS, Hal . . . . . . (GA) 1140
Music in public libraries   WAZNIS, Betty . . . . . . (CA) 1311
Music indexing   RUSHING, Darla H. . . . (LA) 1068
BLOTNER, Linda S. . . . (MA) 106

MUSIC (Cont'd)
Music indexing & database
  preparation   HILL, George R. . . . . . . (NY) 539
Music industry databases   BLUME, August G. . . . . (CA) 107
Music librarianship   SMITH, Dorman H. . . . . (AZ) 1154
BERMAN, Marsha . . . . . (CA) 88
BOWLES, Garrett H. . . . (CA) 121
COLBY, Michael D. . . . . (CA) 230
FRY, Stephen M. . . . . . (CA) 407
HERSH, Daniel . . . . (CA) 533
HUNTER, David C. . . . . (CA) 576
KRAMLICH, Raymonde S. (CA) 676
ROBERTS, John H. . . . . (CA) 1040
TANNO, John W. . . . . . (CA) 1223
WILLIAMS, Valencia . . . (CA) 1347
MOULTON, Suzanne L. . (CO) 873
JOHNSON, Carolyn A. . . (CT) 602
GUNN, Thomas H. . . . . (FL) 477
SCHERUBEL, Melody . . . (IA) 1092
WORK, Dawn E. . . . . . . (IA) 1369
ADKINS, Marjorie R. . . . (IL) 6
GOUDY, Allie W. . . . . . (IL) 454
ROBERTS, Donald L. . . . (IL) 1039
WILLIAMS, Nyal Z. . . . . (IN) 1345
KORDA, Marion . . . . . . (KY) 671
CURTIS, Robert L. . . . . (LA) 267
DANKNER, Laura R. . . . (LA) 273
KEENAN, Elizabeth L. . . (MA) 634
OCHS, Michael . . . . . . (MA) 915
SLAPSYS, Richard M. . . (MA) 1148
HALE, Dawn L. . . . . . . (MD) 485
QUIST, Edwin A. . . . . . (MD) 1001
RAND, Pamela S. . . . . . (MD) 1006
BOWEN, Jennifer B. . . . (MI) 120
WURSTEN, Richard B. . . (NC) 1374
MORGAN, Paula M. . . . (NJ) 864
BRISTAH, Pamela J. . . . (NY) 137
CASSARO, James P. . . . (NY) 193
CORAL, Lenore . . . . . . (NY) 245
ERICSON, Margaret D. . . (NY) 353
GOTTLIEB, Jane E. . . . . (NY) 453
HAEFLIGER, Kathleen A. (NY) 482
KAUFMAN, Judith L. . . . (NY) 631
KINNEY, Daniel W. . . . . (NY) 653
RANSOM, Sarah B. . . . . (NY) 1007
SHUMAN, Kristen K. . . . (NY) 1134
SMIRAGLIA, Richard P. . (NY) 1152
SOMMER, Susan T. . . . . (NY) 1167
DRONE, Jeanette M. . . . (OH) 320
MCMAHON, Melody L. . . (OH) 814
PALKOVIC, Mark A. . . . (OH) 935
ROBSON, Timothy D. . . . (OH) 1045
VAN DER SCHALIE, Eric
J. . . . . (OH) 1274
ZAGER, Daniel A. . . . . (OH) 1385
DILWORTH, Kirby D. . . . (PA) 303
MERZ, Lawrie H. . . . . . (PA) 827
THOMPSON, Annie F. . . (PR) 1239
HERFURTH, Sharon M. . (TX) 530
MARLEY, Judith L. . . . . (TX) 772
SIMS, Phillip W. . . . . . . (TX) 1142
HALL, Bonlyn G. . . . . . (VA) 487
SONNEMANN, Gail J. . . (VA) 1167
WALKER, Diane P. . . . . (VA) 1295
REHBACH, Jeffrey R. . . (VT) 1017
KREPS, Lise E. . . . . . . (WA) 678
JONES, Richard E. . . . . (WI) 614
VINE, Rita F. . . . . (AB) 1285
COLQUHOUN, Joan E. . . (ON) 234
Music librarianship & teaching   BLACK, Dorothy M. . . . (PA) 101
Music librarianship & theology   PARKER, Charles G. . . . (PQ) 941
Music librarianship, reference   KOLCZYNSKI, Charlotte
A. . . . . (MA) 669
Music libraries   ANDERSON, Carol L. . . (CA) 22
FREEMAN, Kevin A. . . . (CA) 401
KRUMMEL, Donald W. . . (IL) 680
BLOTNER, Linda S. . . . (MA) 106
EVANS, Sally . . . . (MA) 358
DAUB, Peggy E. . . . . . (MI) 275
CORWIN, Dean W. . . . . (NJ) 248

MUSIC (Cont'd)

Music libraries

	WEISS, Sabrina L.	(NY)	1320
	ZASLAW, Neal	(NY)	1386
	LEWIS, Karen E.	(PA)	723
	SKINNER, Robert G.	(TX)	1146
	ARNESON, Arne J.	(WI)	33
Music libraries reference	FOLLET, Robert E.	(TX)	388
Music library	JOHNSON, Ellen S.	(KS)	604
	GOLDMAN, Brenda C.	(MA)	445
	PETERSON, Cynthia L.	(NC)	963
	BALCAS, Georgianne	(OH)	50
Music library administration	FISKEN, Patricia B.	(NH)	382
	VELLUCCI, Sherry L.	(NJ)	1282
Music library administration & mgmt	BOGNAR, Dorothy M.	(CT)	111
Music library & collection development	SUYEMATSU, Kiyo	(MN)	1212
Music library collection development	FISKEN, Patricia B.	(NH)	382
Music library public services	FISKEN, Patricia B.	(NH)	382
Music library supervision	SHARP, Avery T.	(TX)	1122
Music library surveys & standards	MCCLELLAN, William M.	(IL)	796
Music library work	CHRISTENSEN, Beth E.	(MN)	211
Music, literary criticism	FRANK, Mortimer H.	(NY)	397
Music literature abstracting	HOLMES, John H.	(PA)	553
Music magazines	BAHR, Edward R.	(MS)	45
Music material cataloging	GOODWIN, Charles B.	(TX)	450
Music materials	MARTIN, John B.	(AL)	776
	HOFFMAN, Christine A.	(NY)	547
Music materials acquisitions	FALCONER, Joan O.	(IA)	362
Music materials & recordings	GOODWIN, Charles B.	(TX)	450
Music materials cataloging	ROSS, Mary E.	(MI)	1058
Music materials, cataloging & processing	MEERVELD, Bert	(ON)	821
Music media	HAMMARGREN, Betty L.	(MN)	493
Music museums & archives	HASSE, John E.	(DC)	511
Music of the Shakers	CHRISTENSON, Donald E.	(OH)	211
Music performance materials	WELIVER, E D.	(MI)	1321
Music performing arts reference	HARDISH, Patrick M.	(NY)	500
Music preparation parts extraction	NIGHTINGALE, Daniel	(PA)	904
Music printing history	BOORMAN, Stanley H.	(NY)	115
Music processing	BENTON, Mary A.	(NJ)	84
Music publications	NOVITSKY, Edward G.	(NY)	911
Music publications, editorial	MAYER, George L.	(NY)	789
Music publications, reviewer	MAYER, George L.	(NY)	789
Music recordings	EGGERS, Lolly P.	(IA)	339
Music recordings sound restoration	PETRIE, Mildred M.	(FL)	965
Music reference	DIAL, Clarence M.	(AZ)	299
	COLBY, Edward E.	(CA)	230
	ELLIOTT, Patricia G.	(CA)	344
	SILVER, Martin A.	(CA)	1138
	SAVIG, Norman I.	(CO)	1086
	BURKAT, Leonard	(CT)	160
	DOPP, Bonnie J.	(DC)	312
	FALCONER, Joan O.	(IA)	362
	STRAIT, Constance J.	(IL)	1199
	WARD, Shirlene A.	(IL)	1304
	DOLAN-HEITLINGER, Eileen	(IN)	309
	FLING, Robert M.	(IN)	385
	TALALAY, Kathryn M.	(IN)	1220
	RUSTMAN, Mark M.	(KS)	1070
	POWELL, Martha C.	(KY)	988
	IRION, Millard F.	(MA)	584
	MOCKOVAK, Holly E.	(MA)	851
	BJORKE, Wallace S.	(MI)	100
	BLACK-SIIIER, Mary L.	(MI)	102
	DRUESEDOW, John E.	(NC)	320
	DOW, Carolyn E.	(NE)	315
	TIBBITS, Edith J.	(NE)	1243
	MARCO, Guy A.	(NJ)	769
	REDLICH, Barry	(NJ)	1014
	RORICK, William C.	(NY)	1054
	WILLNER, Channan P.	(NY)	1348
	OBERLE, Holly E.	(OH)	914
	HUBER, George K.	(PA)	569
	MEYER, Kenton T.	(PA)	830
	SAUNDERS, Sharon K.	(PA)	1084
	FAWVER, Darlene E.	(SC)	367
	GEARY, Gregg S.	(TX)	424
	MCTYRE, Ruthann B.	(TX)	818

MUSIC (Cont'd)

Music reference

	MCCART, Vernon A.	(VA)	794
Music reference & bibliographic instrc	BEAUMIER, Renald	(PQ)	70
Music reference & cataloging	BOGNAR, Dorothy M.	(CT)	111
Music reference & research	MOORE, Emily C.	(NC)	859
	PERRY-BOWDER, Libbie E.	(ME)	961
	BOZIWICK, George E.	(NY)	124
Music reference service	BRYCE, Maria C.	(ON)	152
Music reference works	PAVLAKIS, Christopher	(NY)	950
Music research	COLLINS, Richard H.	(CA)	233
	SUMMERS, Robert A.	(NJ)	1209
	CLAYPOOL, Richard D.	(NY)	220
Music research, writing, editing	GLASFORD, G R.	(NY)	440
Music reviewer	POLITIS, John V.	(PA)	981
Music sales databases	VERNON, James R.	(TX)	1283
Music scores collection development	BERMAN, Marsha	(CA)	88
Music specialist	AYARI, Kaye W.	(SC)	42
Music subject specialist	SILCOX, Tinsley E.	(TN)	1137
	JONES, June D.	(MB)	613
Music technical services	MCKNIGHT, Mark C.	(LA)	812
Music theatre research	LYNCH, Richard C.	(NY)	752
Music thematic indexing	LINCOLN, Harry B.	(NY)	728
Music theory	TEUTSCH, Walter	(CA)	1233
Music theory in translation	THYM, Jurgen	(NY)	1243
Music typesetting	WESTERN, Eric D.	(WI)	1327
Music uniform headings	MC HALE, Mary M.	(MD)	808
Musical Canadiana	KALLMANN, Helmut M.	(ON)	623
Musical databases	WESTERN, Eric D.	(WI)	1327
Musical historiography	GRAMENZ, Francis L.	(MA)	457
Musical iconography	BOWLES, Edmund A.	(NY)	121
Musical instruments	ELSTE, R O.	(WGR)	346
Musical performance practice	ZASLAW, Neal	(NY)	1386
Musical performance practices	BOWLES, Edmund A.	(NY)	121
Musical sound recordings	PALKOVIC, Mark A.	(OH)	935
Musical theater history & production	LONEY, Glenn M.	(NY)	739
Musical theatre research	WALL, Richard L.	(NY)	1297
Musician, songwriter	MARTUCCI, Louis U.	(CA)	779
Music-related buying & cataloging	RUSTMAN, Mark M.	(KS)	1070
Native American music	ROBERTS, Donald L.	(IL)	1039
19th century American religious music	CHRISTENSON, Donald E.	(OH)	211
19th century & 20th century music	HATCHER, Nolan C.	(GA)	511
Online music cataloging	MASTRANGELO, Marjorie J.	(DC)	782
	OLMSTED, Elizabeth H.	(KY)	921
Opera & vocal music	JELLINEK, George	(NY)	596
Orchestra & music preparation	GUNTHER, Paul B.	(MN)	478
Organ & church music	KENT, Frederick J.	(PA)	642
Philosophy, classics, music	CULLARS, John M.	(IL)	263
Piano music & consulting	PATRYCH, Joseph	(NY)	947
Polish music history	WILK, Wanda	(CA)	1339
Popular music	MILLER, Charles W.	(NJ)	836
Popular music bibliography	COOPER, B L.	(MI)	242
Popular music discography	COOPER, B L.	(MI)	242
Popular music theme structures	COOPER, B L.	(MI)	242
Print music	VOLLONO, Millicent D.	(NY)	1288
Public & private music education	MILLER, Charles W.	(NJ)	836
Public, music librarianship	MATYI, Stephen G.	(OH)	786
Public services, music libraries	BERMAN, Marsha	(CA)	88
Publishing music reference books	BALK, Leo F.	(NY)	52
Publishing music reprints, facsimiles	BALK, Leo F.	(NY)	52
Publishing new music editions	BALK, Leo F.	(NY)	52
Rare books, literature, music	AUSTIN, Kristi N.	(WA)	40
Rare books, music	STRINGFELLOW, William T.	(NY)	1202
Rare music	MACNUTT, Richard P.	(ENG)	758
Recorded music	BROGDEN, Stephen R.	(IA)	139
Reference, music	HORTON, Anna J.	(OH)	561
Reference, music & art	BLUM, Fred	(MI)	107
Reference service, music	MILL, Rodney H.	(DC)	835
Research in hlth, socty, music, foods	STARKEY, Bonnie F.	(WV)	1182
Research, music	LOWENS, Margery M.	(MD)	744
Scholarly music publishing	PAVLAKIS, Christopher	(NY)	950
Scores & solo music	WALKER, Elizabeth	(PA)	1295
Select music, records, cassettes	CAPPAERT, Lael R.	(MI)	180
Sheet music	HASSE, John E.	(DC)	511
Sheet music cataloging	HOUSE, Katherine L.	(KY)	563
Sheet music collector	SETON, Charles B.	(NY)	1117
Sheet music consultant	SETON, Charles B.	(NY)	1117

MUSIC (Cont'd)

Sound music publishing	BOBB, Barry L.	(MO)	108
Special music bibliographies	LYON, Bruce C.	(FL)	752
Teaching music history	SMILEY, Marilynn J.	(NY)	1151
20th century American popular music	SPECHT, Joe W.	(TX)	1172
20th century concert music	PIZER, Charles R.	(NY)	977
	PIZER, Elizabeth F.	(NY)	977
Women & music	DOPP, Bonnie J.	(DC)	312
	ERICSON, Margaret D.	(NY)	353
Writing on music	LAWRENCE, Arthur P.	(NY)	704

MUSICOLOGY (See also Music)

Musicological research & writing	GUSHEE, Marion S.	(IL)	478
Musicology	MOULTON, Suzanne L.	(CO)	873
	KELLER, Michael A.	(CT)	635
	BARON, John H.	(LA)	58
	MCKNIGHT, Mark C.	(LA)	812
	GRAMENZ, Francis L.	(MA)	457
	NESS, Arthur J.	(MA)	896
	CRAWFORD, David E.	(MI)	256
	ZASLAW, Neal	(NY)	1386
	ROEPKE, David E.	(OH)	1048
	ELLIKER, Calvin	(PA)	343
	WENK, Arthur B.	(PQ)	1324
Musicology, ethnomusicology, romanticism	HAEFLIGER, Kathleen A.	(NY)	482
Renaissance era musicology	PRUETT, James W.	(DC)	996

MYCOLOGY

Mycology	SCHMIDT, Jean M.	(MN)	1095

MYSTERY (See also Crime, Detective)

Fiction & mysteries	COFFEY, Dorothy A.	(MI)	227
Mystery collection	HOOKER, Joan M.	(NJ)	556
Mystery fiction	MAIO, Kathleen L.	(MA)	762
Mystery fiction books	O'BRIEN, Marlys H.	(MN)	915

MYTHOLOGY (See also Folk)

Folklore & mythology	SLATTERY, Carole C.	(MA)	1148
Folklore, mythology & customs	MCCANN, Judith B.	(ON)	794
Mythology bibliography & research	GARDNER, Sue A.	(NJ)	418

M300XT

Library systems, M300XT	VERMA, Prem V.	(WV)	1282

NACO

NACO liaison	COLLINS, Donna S.	(MD)	232
NACO name authority work	JONES, Edgar A.	(MA)	612

NAME

Cataloging & name authorities	SCHUITEMA, Joan E.	(OH)	1101
Corp author name formation & database	KANE, Astor V.	(VA)	624
Creating automated name authorities	DAWE, Heather L.	(ON)	282
NACO name authority work	JONES, Edgar A.	(MA)	612
Name authorities	BILEYDI, Lois G.	(MN)	96
Name authority records	SCHMIDT, Holly H.	(OR)	1095
Place name literature	POWELL, Margaret S.	(OH)	988
Subject & name authority control	BADING, Kathryn E.	(TX)	44

NARRATION

Script writing & narration	SANKER, Paul N.	(NY)	1081

NASA

NASA & Defense technical reports	BOYD, Effie W.	(TN)	122
NASA & DTIC online databases	GENTRY, Susan K.	(CA)	427
NASA, Dept of Defense, & DIALOG database	BOYD, Effie W.	(TN)	122

NASHVILLE

Nashville writers	HEARNE, Mary G.	(TN)	518

NATION

Nationwide real estate title reporting	FELDER, Bruce B.	(OH)	369

NATIONAL

Militia & National Guard history	WEAVER, Thomas M.	(DC)	1312
National advisory bodies	STEELE, Colin R.	(AUS)	1184
National affairs	TYLER, David M.	(NY)	1266
National & historical bibliography	KEMP, Thomas J.	(CT)	639
National & international cooperation	LINTON, William D.	(NIR)	731
National & international document supply	LINE, Maurice B.	(ENG)	730
National & international standards	ORNE, Jerrold	(NC)	926
National & trade bibliography	ROPER, Fred W.	(SC)	1054
National information networks	BLOCH, Uri	(ISR)	105
National information planning	CAMPBELL, Harry	(ON)	176
National information policies	MENOU, Michel J.	(ITL)	824
National language computing	SEDELOW, Walter A.	(AR)	1110
National libraries	LINE, Maurice B.	(ENG)	730
National library networks design	MAGALONI, Ana M.	(MEX)	759
National library newsletter	MILLENSON, Roy H.	(MD)	835
National program development	STORDAHL, Beth A.	(WA)	1198
National security information	RUSSELL, Marvin F.	(DC)	1069
Planning national information systems	MENOU, Michel J.	(ITL)	824
Public libraries national network	MAGALONI, Ana M.	(MEX)	759
Restoration of national landmarks	MCDONALD, Lois E.	(CT)	803

NATIONAL LIBRARY OF MEDICINE

National Library of Medicine cataloging	WARD, Penny T.	(CA)	1304
	GILBERT, Carole M.	(MI)	433
	ELY, Betty L.	(PA)	347
National Library of Medicine databases	HELBERS, Catherine A.	(NY)	523
	ELY, Betty L.	(PA)	347
	TREVANION, Margaret U.	(PA)	1255
	ASPRI, Jo A.	(RI)	37
National Library of Medicine MEDLARS	KAKOSCHKE, Mona S.	(ON)	622
Online searching, NLM, DIALOG, BRS	NELSON, Iris N.	(CA)	894

NATIVE (See also American (Indian), Cherokee)

Native American	BLACK, Lea J.	(ND)	101
	SUMNER, Delores T.	(OK)	1209
Native American collection	CULL, Roberta	(AZ)	263
Native American genealogy	AUTRY, Brick	(TX)	41
Native American libraries	MCCRACKEN, John R.	(CA)	799
Native American music	ROBERTS, Donald L.	(IL)	1039
Native Americans collections	MITTEN, Lisa A.	(PA)	850
Native Americans research	YOUNKIN, C G.	(TX)	1383
Native people's education	FINN, Julia P.	(PQ)	378
Native studies	FRITZ, Linda	(SK)	405
	TURNBULL, Keith	(SK)	1264
Northern & native people's research	FINN, Julia P.	(PQ)	378

NATURAL (See also Wildlife)

Energy reference & natural gas	MARSHALL, Alexandra P.	(ON)	773
Natural gas industry	DORNER, Steven J.	(VA)	313
Natural gas, petroleum & electricity	LOOS, Carolyn F.	(TX)	740
Natural history	SHIH, Diana	(NY)	1130
	SPAWN, Carol M.	(PA)	1172
Natural history & natural sciences	MORITZ, Thomas D.	(CA)	865
Natural history media	ALASTI, Aryt	(MA)	9
Natural history, rare books	DONAHUE, Katharine E.	(CA)	310
Natural history reference	JERYAN, Christine B.	(MI)	600
Natural language computing	SEDELOW, Sally Y.	(AR)	1110
Natural language information processing	HAYDEN, Richard F.	(CA)	515
Natural language processing	TRIVISON, Donna	(OH)	1257
	VLEDUTS-STOKOLOV, Natalia	(PA)	1286
Natural language search strategy	HAYDEN, Richard F.	(CA)	515

NATURAL (Cont'd)

Natural languages processing	METZLER, Douglas P. . .	(PA)	829
Natural resource archives	COOK, Terry G.	(ON)	240
Natural resources	RADEMACHER, Kurt A. .	(CA)	1002
	AYER, Carol A.	(MD)	42
	LOUET, Sandra	(ON)	742
Natural resources & environment ref	LARSEN, Lynda L.	(DC)	698
Natural resources literature searching	WAGNER, Barbara L. . . .	(CO)	1291
Natural resources reference	RODES, Barbara K.	(DC)	1047
Natural resources research	CLOSE, Elizabeth G. . . .	(UT)	223
Soil plant relations & natural resources	SCHNEIDER, Karl R. . . .	(MD)	1097

NATURE

Nature photographers & photography	ALASTI, Aryt	(MA)	9
Science, nature, & conservation science	PFOHL, Theodore E. . . .	(NY)	966

NAVAL (See also Armed Forces, Military, Navy)

Maritime & naval history	KNAPP, Peter J.	(CT)	663
Military & naval history	SHERIDAN, Robert N. . .	(NY)	1128
Military & naval literature	AIMONE, Alan C.	(NY)	8
Military & naval service	NICULA, J G.	(VA)	903
Naval directives	BURDEN, John	(NY)	158
Technical trades, naval ship repair	ANDERSON, Marcia M. .	(VA)	24

NAVY

Navy documentation	MCCLAIN, Deborah C. . .	(VA)	795
Navy, technical librarianship	DAVIDOFF, Marcia	(FL)	276

NCIP

Cataloging & NCIP	CLOUSTON, John S. . . .	(ON)	223
Collections management & NCIP	CLOUSTON, John S. . . .	(ON)	223

NEAR EAST

Near East bibliography	WERYHO, Jan W.	(PQ)	1325
Near East languages cataloging	HIRSCH, David G.	(NJ)	543
Near East selection	WERYHO, Jan W.	(PQ)	1325
Near East studies	MYERS-HAYER, Patricia A.	(DC)	885
Near Eastern manuscripts	ORMSBY, Eric	(PQ)	926

NEBRASKA

Nebraska state publications	FROBOM, Jerome B. . . .	(NE)	405

NECK

Otolaryngology, head & neck surgery	JOHNSTON, Bruce A. . .	(PA)	610

NEEDLE

Surgical needle development	MCGREGOR, Walter . . .	(NJ)	808

NEEDS

Analysis of information needs	HOSONO, Kimio	(JAP)	562
Archival needs evaluation	EDGERLY, Linda	(MA)	336
Children's services & space needs	WARGO, Peggy M.	(CT)	1305
Community needs assessment	HEIL, Kathleen A.	(MD)	521
Consulting & needs assessment	WEISFIELD, Cynthia F. .	(PA)	1319
End-user needs analysis	SHELBURNE, Elizabeth C.	(DC)	1125
Information needs & uses	CASE, Donald O.	(CA)	191
	WALDHART, Thomas J. .	(KY)	1294
	KIM, Soon C.	(SKO)	649
Information needs evaluations & analysis	HOLDEN, Douglas H. . . .	(ND)	550
Information needs of politicians	TILLOTSON, Greig S. . .	(AUS)	1245
Information needs, user studies	DURRANCE, Joan C. . . .	(MI)	328
Information systems needs assessment	ROBERTS, Lesley A. . . .	(DC)	1040
Library & archival need assessments	FOURIE, Denise K.	(CA)	393
Needs assessment	HOLT, Raymond M.	(CA)	554
	SIGLER, Ronald F.	(CA)	1137
	TABACHNICK, Sharon . .	(TN)	1219

NEEDS (Cont'd)

Needs assessment & evaluation	RUBIN, Rhea J.	(CA)	1064
Needs evaluation	ASSUNCAO, Isabel	(PQ)	37
Physical building needs	ROGERS, William F.	(OH)	1050
Public library needs assessment	EVANS, Patricia D.	(AB)	357
Small library needs	MCMILLAN, Mary M. . . .	(IN)	815
User needs assessment	ROCQUE, Bernice L. . . .	(NY)	1046
User needs determination	SAYER, John S.	(MD)	1086
User needs studies	SMITH-GREENWOLD, Kathryn R.	(NY)	1162

NEGOTIATIONS (See also Bargaining)

Contract negotiation	GROSSMAN, Allen N. . .	(NJ)	473
Labor negotiations	MORRIS, Irving	(NY)	866
Negotiations & drafting	PACE, Thomas	(NJ)	933
Reference negotiation & supervision	USTACH, Joanne B. . . .	(NY)	1270
Third party negotiations	CORVESE, Lisa A.	(NY)	248
Vendor & supplier negotiations	YODER, Susan M.	(CA)	1380

NEIGHBORHOOD (See also Branch, Community)

Branch & neighborhood services	SCHNEIDER, Francisca M.	(CA)	1097
Neighborhood libraries	KINNEY, Michael F.	(WI)	653
Neighborhood libraries public relations	LOCKETT, Sandra B. . . .	(WI)	736

NETHERLANDS (See Dutch)

NETWORKS (See also Consortia)

Administrative networking	PELLEY, Shirley N.	(OK)	955
Automated integrated library network	EMAHISER, Joan A.	(MI)	347
Automated library networks	HOUGH, Allen D.	(NY)	562
Automated networks	SMITH, Randolph R.	(CO)	1159
	WREGE, Ann S.	(CT)	1370
Automated system networking	MAINIERO, Elizabeth T. .	(CT)	761
Automation & networking	SIMPSON, Donald B. . . .	(IL)	1141
	PATRICK, Ruth J.	(MT)	947
	BETCHER, Melissa A. . .	(OH)	92
Automation networks	BROWN, Louise R.	(MA)	145
Automation plng, multitype networking	DIENER, Margaret M. . . .	(CA)	302
Bibliographic & resource sharing network	REDDY, Sigrid R.	(MA)	1014
Bibliographic networking	BILLINGS, Harold W. . . .	(TX)	96
Collection access & networks	JOHNSON, Carolynn K. .	(WA)	603
Communications & networking software	THOMAS, Hilary B.	(NY)	1236
Communications networks	THORSTEINSON, William A.	(NS)	1243
Community networking	BREDESON, Peggy Z. . .	(WI)	131
Computer networking	RANKIN, Jocelyn A.	(GA)	1007
	DONOVAN, Paul	(MA)	312
	O'NEILL, Sue	(MD)	924
Connectivity & networking	GROSVENOR, Philip G. .	(OH)	473
Consortia or networks	VICK, Kathleen	(PA)	1283
Cooperative networking	REYNOLDS, Dennis J. . .	(DC)	1025
Cooperative networks	HAHN, Ellen	(DC)	483
Corporate library network management	LAMB, Cheryl M.	(WI)	689
County network library services	MARSHALL, Ruth T. . . .	(GA)	775
Data & voice networking	VEDDER, Harvey B.	(PA)	1280
Data communication network management	GETZ, Malcolm	(TN)	430
Database networking & communications	PASCHAL, John M.	(OK)	945
Electronic network directories	MACLELLAND, Margaret A.	(ON)	757
Gas Net industry database management	DORNER, Steven J.	(VA)	313
Health library networks	PANTON, Linda A.	(ON)	938
Health science library networks	WILLIS, Dorothy B.	(NE)	1348
IBM-PC/XT network coordination	LYDEN, Edward W.	(TX)	750
Information databases & networks	WOODS, Richard F.	(FIJ)	1367
Information network, resource sharing	AGRAWAL, Surendra P.	(IND)	7
Information networks	TUROCK, Betty J.	(NJ)	1265
Integrated services digital network	GILHEANY, Stephen J. .	(CA)	435
Interlibrary cooperation & networking	WILKINS, Barratt	(FL)	1340
Interlibrary loan networking	GIBBS, Margareth	(IL)	431
	ICKES, Barbara J.	(PA)	581

NETWORKS (Cont'd)

Interlibrary loan networks	KNUTSON, Linda J.	(IL)	666
	BOAZ, Ruth L.	(TN)	108
	SEIDENBERG, Edward	(TX)	1112
International networking	BAKER, Dale B.	(OH)	48
	BROWN, Rowland C.	(OH)	147
Library & community relations networking	POSEL, Nancy R.	(PA)	985
Library & information networks	ENGLER, June L.	(GA)	350
	STUART-STUBBS, Basil F.	(BC)	1204
	MINAIKIT, Nonglak	(THA)	845
Library automation & networking	SLEETER, Ellen L.	(CA)	1148
	LAUGHLIN, Cheryl H.	(MS)	703
	VARIEUR, Normand L.	(NJ)	1278
Library cooperation & networking	NYQUIST, Corinne E.	(NY)	913
	MONTAG, John	(OH)	855
	BUNGE, Charles A.	(WI)	157
Library cooperatives, networking	CHAPMAN, Mary A.	(MI)	202
	MASSEY, Eleanor N.	(NJ)	782
Library information networks	RAWLINS, Gordon W.	(PA)	1010
Library local area network	MILLER, Richard A.	(VA)	841
Library network administration	BYRN, James H.	(VA)	169
Library network development	MCGINN, Howard F.	(NC)	806
Library network services	BEACHELL, Doria M.	(DC)	68
Library network systems development	BAADE, Harley D.	(TX)	43
Library networking	MALONEY, James J.	(CA)	764
	CAMPBELL, John D.	(CO)	176
	VOLZ, Edward J.	(CO)	1288
	GALVIN, Thomas J.	(IL)	415
	SEGAL, Joan S.	(IL)	1111
	HOLICKY, Bernard H.	(IN)	550
	CANOSE, Joseph A.	(NJ)	179
	DIENER, Ronald E.	(OH)	302
	SINK, Thomas R.	(OH)	1143
	WALTERS, Clarence R.	(OH)	1301
	BROADBENT, H E.	(PA)	138
	GREESON, Judy G.	(TN)	465
	COTTER, Gladys A.	(VA)	250
Library networking & automation	JACOB, Mary E.	(OH)	589
Library networks	PIKE, Lee E.	(AL)	973
	SHAW, Ward	(CO)	1124
	KROMMINGA, Patricia G.	(IA)	679
	MCKANN, Michael R.	(LA)	809
	LYON-HARTMANN, Becky J.	(MD)	752
	MARTIN, Susan K.	(MD)	778
	JOSE, Phyllis A.	(MI)	617
	WILLIAMS, James F.	(MI)	1343
	SPAULDING, Frank H.	(NJ)	1172
	KLEMPNER, Irving M.	(NY)	660
	REGAN, Muriel	(NY)	1017
	BLANCHARD, Mark A.	(OH)	103
	LIBERTINI, Arleen J.	(OR)	725
	TOWNLEY, Charles T.	(PA)	1253
	CAMERON, Constance B.	(RI)	174
	COOPER, Ellen R.	(TN)	242
	HUBBARD, William J.	(VA)	568
	MILLS, Fiolina B.	(VI)	844
	MACLELLAND, Margaret A.	(ON)	757
	DU BREUIL, Laval	(PQ)	322
Library networks & networking	TAYLOR, Arthur R.	(MO)	1226
Library networks & systems	ALBRIGHT, Elaine M.	(ME)	10
Library systems & networking	TREZZA, Alphonse F.	(FL)	1256
	CUNNINGHAM, Barbara M.	(MD)	265
Library systems & networks	WEECH, Terry L.	(IL)	1315
	BAKER, Elizabeth A.	(MA)	48
	HEISE, George F.	(NJ)	522
	HUMPHRY, John A.	(NY)	574
	ROSS, Kathleen A.	(NY)	1058
	DURANCE, Cynthia J.	(ON)	328
	COCHRANE, Thomas G.	(AUS)	226
Library systems networking	RUTHERFORD, Virginia L.	(GA)	1070
Local area computer networks	KEMPER, Marlyn J.	(FL)	639
Local area network research	PFUDERER, Helen A.	(TN)	966
Local area networking	ELAZAR, David H.	(ISR)	341

NETWORKS (Cont'd)

Local area networks	CARD, Sandra E.	(CA)	180
	MOORE, Richard K.	(CA)	861
	CHU, Ellen M.	(MD)	212
Local government information network	AHLIN, Nancy	(FL)	8
Local networks & systems	STEFFEY, Ramona J.	(TN)	1185
Medical library networking	MIDDLETON, Dale R.	(WA)	833
Medical library networks	MAY, Ruby S.	(IL)	789
Microcomputer network	KEASCHUK, Michael J.	(SK)	633
Microcomputer systems & networks	TALLY, Roy D.	(MN)	1221
Multi-library automation networks	KERSHNER, Lois M.	(CA)	644
	JONES-LITTEER, Corene A.	(ID)	616
Multi-library network	HAYES, Richard E.	(MA)	516
Multi-library networking	SENNER, Rachel	(SD)	1115
Multipoint delivery networks	MAYNARD, John C.	(ON)	790
Multitype library network development	JOHNSON, Duane F.	(KS)	603
Multitype library network facilitation	SNOWDEN, Deanna	(IN)	1164
Multitype library networking	STEINER, Janet E.	(NY)	1186
Multitype networks	MARTHEY, Rebecca J.	(IN)	775
	IMMROTH, Barbara F.	(TX)	582
National information networks	BLOCH, Uri	(ISR)	105
National library networks design	MAGALONI, Ana M.	(MEX)	759
Network administration	MEDINA, Sue O.	(AL)	820
	GRISHAM, Frank P.	(GA)	471
	BANFIELD, Eilzabeth S.	(NS)	54
Network & consortium administration	NEUFELD, Judith B.	(NY)	897
Network & consortium governance	MITCHELL, Joan M.	(PA)	849
Network coordination	FELLA, Sarah C.	(OR)	370
	DANIEL, Eileen	(ON)	272
	JANIK, Sophie	(PQ)	593
Network development	ASHTON, Rick J.	(CO)	36
	RENNINGER, Karen	(DC)	1023
	SPYERS-DURAN, Peter	(MI)	1177
	DANIELS, Bruce E.	(RI)	273
Network Library automation	VIERGEVER, Dan W.	(KS)	1284
Network management	KUKLINSKI, Joan L.	(MA)	683
	SPYKERMAN, Bryan R.	(UT)	1177
Network organization	PINGS, Vern M.	(FL)	974
Network planning & development	URICCHIO, William J.	(CT)	1269
Networking	LESH, Nancy L.	(AK)	718
	GUTHRIE, Virginia G.	(AL)	479
	WRIGHT, Kathryn D.	(AL)	1372
	BECKER, Joseph	(CA)	72
	BUSCH, Barbara	(CA)	165
	GRAHAM, Elaine	(CA)	456
	SARGENT, Dency C.	(CT)	1083
	CRAIG, James P.	(FL)	254
	HASSLER, William B.	(HI)	511
	CULBERTSON, Lillian D.	(IL)	263
	LUNDQUIST, Marie A.	(IL)	748
	DURKIN, Virginia M.	(IN)	328
	MORRILL, Walter D.	(IN)	866
	LAUFFER, Donna J.	(KS)	702
	SEVIER, Susan G.	(KS)	1117
	CUNNINGHAM, Robert L.	(MA)	265
	SACK, Jean C.	(MD)	1073
	ASHLEY, Roger S.	(MI)	36
	FLAHERTY, Kevin C.	(MI)	383
	ST. AMAND, Norma P.	(MI)	1075
	EBRO, Diane C.	(MN)	334
	VALANCE, Marsha J.	(MN)	1271
	HELMS, Mary E.	(MO)	525
	MCKEE, Eugenia V.	(MO)	810
	SCHELL, Nancy S.	(NC)	1091
	BELSTERLING, Jean I.	(NJ)	78
	MILLER, Virginia L.	(NJ)	843
	O'CONNOR, Elizabeth W.	(NJ)	916
	PENNIMAN, W D.	(NJ)	957
	RANDALL, Lynn E.	(NJ)	1006
	WOLFORD, Larry E.	(NJ)	1361
	CORSON, Cornelia M.	(NY)	248
	LEVINSON, Barbara	(NY)	721
	NEUMANN, Joan	(NY)	897
	MC CORMICK, Lisa L.	(OH)	798
	WALBRIDGE, Sharon L.	(OH)	1293
	JOHNSON, Edward R.	(OK)	604
	TEICH, Steven	(OR)	1230
	BECK, William L.	(PA)	72
	SAWYER, Warren A.	(SC)	1086

NETWORKS (Cont'd)

Networking

	TARLTON, Shirley M.	(SC)	1224
	HAND, M D.	(TX)	494
	SNELL, Marykay H.	(TX)	1163
	WETHERBEE, Louella V.	(TX)	1327
	COCHRANE, Lynn S.	(VA)	225
	MARSHALL, Nancy H.	(VA)	775
	PROSSER, Judith M.	(WV)	995
	MACK, Bonnie R.	(WY)	756
	PEPPER, David A.	(BC)	958
	SCHRYER, Michel J.	(ON)	1100
	DUPUIS, Onil	(PQ)	327
	ARORA, Ved P.	(SK)	34
Networking & automation	JOHNSON, Herbert F.	(GA)	605
Networking & consortia	BAUGHMAN, Steven A.	(GA)	66
Networking & consulting	WAGNER, Rod G.	(NE)	1292
Networking & cooperation	KATZ, Ruth M.	(NC)	630
	WILLEMSE, John	(SAF)	1341
Networking & statewide planning	STRONG, Gary E.	(CA)	1203
Networking, interlibrary loan	SCHUBACK COHN, Judith	(NJ)	1101
	WOLFE, Gary D.	(PA)	1360
Networking libraries	SLONE, Eugenia F.	(CT)	1150
Networking, NILRC	BAYER, Susan P.	(IL)	67
Networking, regional	SCHWARTZ, Lawrence C.	(NJ)	1104
Networking, resource sharing, systems	LOVE, Erika	(NM)	743
Networking systems	VONDRAN, Raymond F.	(TX)	1288
Networks	PRESLAN, Bruce H.	(CA)	991
	DAY, Mary M.	(KY)	283
	ROGERS, Joann V.	(KY)	1049
	GOVAN, James F.	(NC)	454
	JOHNSON, Joann	(OH)	606
	ZIPKOWITZ, Fay	(RI)	1389
	BURGESS, Edwin B.	(VA)	159
	ZUSSY, Nancy L.	(WA)	1391
	FORGET, Louis J.	(ON)	390
	BERNHARD, Paulette	(PQ)	89
	NOERR, Kathleen T.	(ENG)	907
Networks & consortia	VANVUREN, Darcy D.	(CA)	1277
	RAITHEL, Frederick J.	(MO)	1004
Networks & resource sharing	SEIDMAN, Ruth K.	(MA)	1112
	MARTIN, Noelene P.	(PA)	777
Networks & systems	CHESHIER, Robert G.	(OH)	206
Networks in libraries	SHANK, Russell	(CA)	1120
Networks, networking	DEJOHN, William T.	(MN)	288
Online networks	FREDERICK, Sidney C.	(IL)	399
	OLSEN, Wallace C.	(NY)	922
	BOWERS, Paul A.	(PA)	120
Private information exchange networks	BUSSMANN, Steve	(VA)	166
	EDWARDS, Wilmoth O.	(VA)	338
	FILIPPONE, Anne	(VA)	377
	KELLER, Jay	(VA)	635
	LITTLE, William	(VA)	734
	LOVETT, Bruce	(VA)	743
	MAJOR, Skip	(VA)	762
	NEWLAND, Barbara	(VA)	899
	RINALDI, Roberta	(VA)	1035
	RYAN, Maureen	(VA)	1071
	STRATT, Randy	(VA)	1200
Professional networks, electronic mail	LEHMAN, Tom	(MN)	713
Public libraries national network	MAGALONI, Ana M.	(MEX)	759
Reference networking	MYERS, R D.	(DC)	885
Reference services & networking	ARRINGTON, Susan J	(MD)	34
Regional library networks	LINTON, William D.	(NIR)	731
Regional networks	LOW, Jocelyn L.	(CT)	743
Resource sharing & networking	TYER, Travis E.	(IL)	1266
Resource sharing networks	KENT, Allen	(PA)	642
School libraries networking	MATTIE, Joseph J.	(NY)	786
School library systems, networking	WEBSTER, Patricia B.	(NY)	1315
Schools in library networks	KESTER, Diane D.	(NC)	645
Shared cataloging networking online	BROWN, Pauline	(AUS)	146
Shared services regional network	WILCOX, Linda M.	(ON)	1338
Small networks	AUBIN, Robert	(PQ)	38
State library service & networks	JOSEY, E J.	(PA)	618
Statewide & regional networks	WOODWARD, Robert C.	(ME)	1368
Statewide interlibrary loan networks	ROBERTSON, Linda L.	(IA)	1042
Statewide networking	DRUM, Eunice P.	(NC)	321
Systems & networking	FAIBISOFF, Sylvia G.	(OK)	361

NETWORKS (Cont'd)

Telecommunication networking	MAZUR, Ronald M.	(MA)	791
Telecommunications & networks	REMKIEWICZ, Frank L.	(CA)	1022
Telecommunications networking	WARREN, G G.	(KS)	1306
	DEFALCO, Joseph	(NY)	287
Transactions network markets	WRIGHT, Bernell	(NY)	1370
UNIX local area network	ROSE, Phillip E.	(CO)	1055
Using local area network for catalogs	HUGHES, Carol A.	(OK)	571

NEUROFIBROMATOSIS

Neurofibromatosis	RICCARDI, Vincent M.	(TX)	1026

NEUROLOGY

Neurology	NORDENG, Diane	(ND)	908
	SHAH, Neeta N.	(SC)	1119
	TREMBLAY, Gerald F.	(SC)	1255

NEUROPSYCHIATRIC

Neuropsychiatric collection	BURTON, Mary L.	(PA)	164

NEUROSCIENCES

Neurosciences databases & collections	WIGGINS, Theresa S.	(PA)	1337

NEUROSURGERY

Neurosurgery	NORDENG, Diane	(ND)	908

NEW

Administration of a new library	DERMODY, Rita R.	(TX)	294
Adult new reader materials	MCGRIFF, Mary E.	(NC)	808
Adult new readers publishing	RYAN, Jenny L.	(NY)	1071
Automation & new technologies	ROSSMAN, Muriel J.	(MN)	1059
Automation & new technology	ACCARDI, Joseph J.	(WI)	3
Beginning new library programs	POWELL, Mary E.	(TX)	988
CD-ROM & new technology	CEBULA, Theodore R.	(WI)	196
Design & construction of new facilities	PAPENFUSE, Edward C.	(MD)	939
Developing new business opportunities	MCLANE, John F.	(CT)	813
Developing new media facilities	SCHREIBMAN, Fay C.	(NY)	1099
Developing new music libraries	FLOERSHEIMER, Lee M.	(NY)	385
Development of new facilities	ROYCE, Carolyn S.	(NJ)	1063
Establishing new libraries	SMITH, Kathleen S.	(DC)	1156
Establishing new school libraries	GOODMAN, Helen C.	(TX)	449
Forecasting new media diffusion	KLOPFENSTEIN, Bruce C.	(OH)	662
Innovative services, new users	STRAWDER, Maxine S.	(TN)	1201
Microcomputer software, new technologies	VEANER, Allen B.	(ON)	1280
Microcomputers & new technology	ORR, Cynthia	(OH)	926
New American religions	SMITH, Robert E.	(IN)	1160
New & remodel buildings	COURTRIGHT, Harry R.	(PA)	252
New & used book trade	SORGENFREI, Robert K.	(CA)	1168
New building planning	GARDNER, W J.	(CO)	418
New buildings & renovations planning	VANN, John D.	(PA)	1276
New facilities construction	STEELE, Leah J.	(IL)	1184
New information product development	CARTER, Daniel H.	(TX)	189
New information technology	CHEN, Ching C.	(MA)	205
New librarian training & development	BUSH, Joyce	(NY)	165
New libraries	HAND, M D.	(TX)	494
New library collections	DENOBLE, Augustine D.	(OR)	293
New library creation	YURO, David A.	(NY)	1384
New library development	KELVER, Ann E.	(CO)	639
New library implementation	O'BRIEN, Kathleen	(DC)	914
New library planning	KOPAN, Ellen K.	(CA)	671
New library setup	HARMON, Jacqueline B.	(TX)	502
New library structures	BURGIS, Grover C.	(ON)	159
New library technology	ALIX, Cleta M.	(CA)	13
New media market analysis	KLOPFENSTEIN, Bruce C.	(OH)	662
New media usage studies	KLOPFENSTEIN, Bruce C.	(OH)	662
New product development	ELLSWORTH, Dianne J.	(CA)	345
	BROCK, Laurie N.	(CO)	138
	WHITE, Suellen S.	(CO)	1332
	FATTIBENE, James F.	(DC)	366
	KINLEY, Jo H.	(DC)	652
	TAYLOR, George A.	(DC)	1226

NEW (Cont'd)

New product development
GROSSMAN, David G. . . . (IL) 473
LESLIE, Donald S. . . . . . (MN) 718
KIESER, Scott P. . . . . . (NY) 647
MACFARLAND, Scott D. (NY) 755
LA MARCHE, David L. . . (ON) 689
New product potential consulting   HOPE, Thomas W. . . . . (NY) 557
New product testing   MARANGONI, Eugene G. (CA) 768
New publication development   NASSO, Christine . . . . . (MI) 889
SCHMITTROTH, John . . (MI) 1096
New service planning   BARNETT, Becky L. . . . . (GA) 57
New technologies   WILTSE, Helen C. . . . . . (GA) 1353
GORDON, Helen A. . . . (IN) 451
New technologies in libraries   VOROS, David S. . . . . . (PA) 1289
New technologies research   SHAW, Renata V. . . . . (DC) 1123
New technology   RISHER, Carol A. . . . . . (DC) 1036
New technology & libraries   MARSHALL, Mary E. . . . (OH) 774
New Testament   WHIPPLE, Caroline B. . . (IL) 1329
Organization of new facilities   SCHUSTER, Adeline (IL) 1103
Planning new library outlets   STREIN, Barbara M. . . . . (MD) 1201
Planning of new information services   SIECK, Steven K. . . . . . (NY) 1135
Preparing for automation & new lib bldg   INGIBERGSSON, Asgeir (AB) 582
Publishing new music editions   BALK, Leo F. . . . . (NY) 52
Research & development, new products   WINGATE, Dawn A. . . . . (CA) 1354
Software & new technology   DECKER, Leola M. . . . . (MD) 286
Starting new libraries   SIESS, Judith A. . . . . . . (OH) 1136
Start-up of new libraries   WOFSE, Joy G. . . . . . . (NY) 1359
Training & supervising new staff   RICHARDSON, Emma G. (NY) 1029
Training new staff   WANG, Margaret K. . . . . (DE) 1303
PHILLIPS, Richard F. . . . (NJ) 969

NEW ENGLAND

New England local history   SKILLIN, Glenn B. . . . . . (PA) 1146
17th century New England books   BISHOP, John . . . . (MA) 99

NEW HAMPSHIRE

New Hampshire legal materials   RINDEN, Constance T. . . (NH) 1035

NEW JERSEY

Cataloging New Jersey documents   HARDGROVE, David J. . . (NJ) 499
New Jersey bibliography   SINCLAIR, Donald A. . . . (NJ) 1142
New Jersey history   IRWIN, Barbara S. . . . . . (NJ) 584
New Jersey school law   VAN BUSKIRK, Elisabeth L. . . . . (NJ) 1272

NEW ORLEANS

New Orleans bibliography   JUMONVILLE, Florence M. (LA) 619
New Orleans historical sources   HARDY, D C. . . . . (LA) 500
New Orleans history   HARDY, D C. . . . . (LA) 500

NEW YORK

Local history of upstate New York   KABELAC, Karl S. . . . . . (NY) 620
New York law   WESTHUIS, Judith A. . . . (NY) 1327
New York legal research   MOLINARI, Joseph G. . . . (NY) 853
New York state & local documents   PANDIT, Jyoti P. . . . . . . (NY) 937
New York state documents   ESPOSITO, Michael A. . . (NY) 354
NY state library systems committee   PHILLIPS, Ruth M. . . . . . (NY) 969

NEWBERY

Newbery book club   DRZEWIECKI, Iris M. . . . (NY) 321

NEWFOUNDLAND

Newfoundland studies   DENNIS, Christopher J. . (NF) 292

NEWS (See also Events, Newsletters, Newspapers, Newsroom, Reporting)

Cataloging of television news tapes   KEATING, Michael F. . . . (OH) 633
Current news & information databases   JOBE, Shirley A. . . . . . (MA) 601
Daily news abstracting   LEVINTON, Juliette . . . . (NY) 721

NEWS (Cont'd)

Editing company news brief   WHITE, Jane F. . . . . (MI) 1331
Editing information news stories   LYONS, Ivan . . . . (NY) 753
Electronic mail news services   STILLMAN, Stanley W. . (NY) 1194
Equity research news service   MILLS, Andrew G. . . . . (MA) 843
Financial news & publishing   CASEY, Robert W. . . . . (NY) 192
General news   ROLLINS, Marilyn H. . . . (NC) 1051
Indexing news stories   SINCLAIR, John M. . . . . (AB) 1142
Library news   NYREN, Karl . . . . (NY) 913
Local news   VANCE, Carolyn J. . . . . (IL) 1272
News & business databases   WALLAS, Philip R. . . . . (MA) 1298
KARCICH, Grant J. . . . (ON) 627
News & events cataloging   MCGANN, Margot . . . . (DC) 805
News & events reference   MCGANN, Margot . . . . (DC) 805
News & information cataloging   TRIVEDI, Harish S. . . . . (OH) 1257
News & information storage & retrieval   TRIVEDI, Harish S. . . . . (OH) 1257
News & media databases   MCCOY-LARSON, Sandra (DC) 799
News clip editing   CANT, Elaine N. . . . . . . (CA) 179
News databases   BEVERIDGE, David C. . . (DC) 93
DONOVAN, Elizabeth L. . (FL) 312
VAZQUEZ, Edward . . . . (NY) 1280
GRANT, Roberta L. . . . (ON) 458
LUSSIER, Richard . . . . (PQ) 749
News information services   DORSETT, Anita W. . . . . (TX) 313
News librarianship   HENDERSON, Linda L. . (RI) 526
News library organization   ROCKALL, Diane M. . . . (MI) 1046
News library systems   CANT, Elaine N. . . . . . . (CA) 179
News media   SUMMERS, Janice K. . . (MO) 1209
STEIN, Pamela H. . . . . . (NY) 1185
News media databases   WALSH, Barclay . . . . . (DC) 1299
News media librarianship   FURR, Susan H. . . . . . . (VA) 410
News media libraries   NEWCOMBE, Barbara T. (CA) 898
News media research   LEVINSON, Debra J. . . . (NY) 721
News medias   CHALIFOUX, Jean P. . . . (PQ) 197
News reference   ROBINSON, Robert C. . . (DC) 1044
News research   KIBBEE, Sally . . . . (CA) 646
FRIEDMAN, Judy B. . . . (NY) 404
Online news database   MCFARLANE, Agnes . . . (PQ) 805
Television news   PILKINGTON, James P. . (TN) 973
Television news film archives   WHITSON, Helene . . . . (CA) 1334
Topical news   CAMPO, Charles A. . . . . (ME) 177
Writing & editing news & features   CHEATHAM, Bertha M. . (NY) 204
Writing news releases   GIGLIO, Linda M. . . . . . (MI) 433

NEWSLETTERS (See also News)

Abstracting newsletter publications   KOVITZ, Nancy R. . . . . . (IL) 674
Advertising, newsletter production   WASERSTEIN, Gina S. . (PA) 1307
Books & newsletters, non-profit groups   TAFT, James R. . . . . . . (DC) 1219
Designing & editing newsletters   ENSEL, Ellen H. . . . . . . (CT) 350
Editing library newsletter   KULIBERT, Marie M. . . . (MI) 683
Editing newsletter   ROTH, Alison C. . . . . . . (CT) 1059
National library newsletter   MILLENSON, Roy H. . . . (MD) 835
Newsletter development   KASE-MCLAREN, Karen A. . . . . (NY) 628
Newsletter editing   BASART, Ann P. . . . . . . (CA) 62
CROCKETT, Darla J. . . . (CA) 259
WELLSMAN, Jennifer A. (NJ) 1323
Newsletter publishing   SEIDENBERG, Edward . . (TX) 1112
Newsletter publishing & editing   TAYLOR, David C. . . . . (NC) 1226
Newsletters   LONGO, Margaret K. . . . (CA) 740
Newsletters, directory   GAZZOLA, Kenneth E. . . (DC) 424
Newsletters, elections   THORSEN, Jeanne M. . . (WA) 1242
Preparation of departmental newsletters   CHAMBERS, E G. . . . . . (MI) 198
Publication services, books, newsletters   MOLLO, Terry . . . . (NY) 853
Publishing information newsletters   LYONS, Ivan . . . . (NY) 753
Publishing newsletters   SHALLEY, Doris P. . . . . . (PA) 1119
Telecommunications newsletter editing   IMPERIALE, Karen P. . . . (NJ) 582
Young adult book club newsletter   JACKSON, Nancy D. . . . (NY) 588

NEWSPAPERS (See also Editorial, News, Reporting)

Automation of newspaper archives	ENNS, Carol F.	(NB)	350
Bibliographic control of newspapers	FIELD, Kenneth C.	(BC)	375
Cataloging newspapers	GAIECK, Frederick W.	(OH)	412
	POLLARD, Margaret E.	(WI)	981
Catholic newspapers	AMES, Charlotte A.	(IN)	19
Community newspaper publication	COMPRI, Jeannine L.	(AB)	235
Computer newspaper indexing	SEMONCHE, Barbara P.	(NC)	1115
Computer-generated newspaper indexing	BOLDRICK, Samuel J.	(FL)	112
Computerized local newspaper indexing	KAGANN, Laurie K.	(IL)	621
Full-text newspaper library systems	DONCEVIC, Lois A.	(PA)	311
Indexing local newspapers	BROOKES, Barbara	(NY)	140
	VAN DE CASTLE, Raymond M.	(PA)	1273
Indexing newspaper articles	KHAN, Asma S.	(ON)	646
Indexing newspaper clips & photos	RICE, Margaret R.	(TX)	1027
Indexing newspaper photographs	BASNIGHT, Clara P.	(VA)	63
Local newspaper indexing	ALLING, M P.	(IA)	16
Microtext & newspapers	SCANNELL, Henry F.	(MA)	1087
Newspaper acquisition & cataloging	DANKY, James P.	(WI)	274
Newspaper & photo collections	SWARTZ, Patrice B.	(PA)	1214
Newspaper & publisher database systems	PASCHAL, John M.	(OK)	945
Newspaper archive systems	ROACH, Eddie D.	(OK)	1037
Newspaper archives	JONES, Martin J.	(NY)	614
Newspaper bibliography	HOVISH, Joseph J.	(IN)	563
Newspaper clip files	CROCKETT, Mary S.	(SC)	259
Newspaper clipping & indexing	WALSH, Barclay	(DC)	1299
Newspaper clipping files	VANCE, Carolyn J.	(IL)	1272
Newspaper clipping systems	KANE, Angelika R.	(PA)	624
Newspaper clippings	HEARN, Geraldine B.	(IL)	518
	KATZUNG, Judith	(MN)	630
	PARISOT, Beverly J.	(NE)	940
	SPINA, Nan H.	(NV)	1175
Newspaper clippings & photos	CHANCE, Peggy J.	(PA)	199
Newspaper clippings services	STILES, William G.	(ON)	1194
Newspaper clips	MOFFETT, Martha L.	(FL)	852
	PUSTAY, Marilyn J.	(MS)	998
Newspaper collections	BURROWS, Sandra	(ON)	163
Newspaper database	VANCE, Sandra L.	(IL)	1273
	PARISOT, Beverly J.	(NE)	940
Newspaper databases	KIBBEE, Sally	(CA)	646
	PAUL, Nora M.	(FL)	949
	PAPPALARDO, Marcia J.	(IL)	939
	TANNER, Allan B.	(KS)	1222
	SMITH, Linda L.	(KY)	1157
	GREENGRASS, Alan R.	(NY)	464
	PASCHAL, Linda P.	(OK)	945
	WILLMANN, Donna S.	(PA)	1348
	LOVELL, Bonnie A.	(TX)	743
	METCALF, Judith A.	(TX)	828
	WORCHEL, Harris M.	(TX)	1368
Newspaper indexes	BURROWS, Sandra	(ON)	163
Newspaper indexing	HINTZMAN, Bonnie	(AZ)	543
	HOCKEL, Kathleen N.	(CA)	545
	WELLS, Merle W.	(ID)	1322
	STEPHENS, Janet A.	(IL)	1188
	HAENICKE, Carol A.	(MI)	482
	LARZELERE, David W.	(MI)	700
	PEPPER, Alice A.	(MI)	958
	STEVENS, Robert R.	(MO)	1191
	KARES, Artemis C.	(NC)	627
	GARDNER, Jack I.	(NV)	418
	SCHLAERTH, Sally G.	(NY)	1093
	FRIEDMAN, Amy G.	(SC)	403
	MORRISON, Annette T.	(TN)	867
	NEU, Margaret J.	(TX)	896
	VAUGHN, Robert V.	(VI)	1280
	BRITTON, Pilaivan H.	(WA)	137
Newspaper indexing & cataloging	MCCARGAR, Susan E.	(TX)	794
Newspaper librarian	PARE, Gilles G.	(PQ)	940
Newspaper librarianship	BEVERIDGE, David C.	(DC)	93
	SHERR, Merrill F.	(NY)	1129
Newspaper libraries	GEIGER, Richard G.	(CA)	425
	OSTMANN, Sharon G.	(CA)	929
	ISAACS, Bob	(FL)	584
	JANUS, Bridget M.	(IA)	594
	BARNARD, Catherine A.	(NY)	57

NEWSPAPERS (Cont'd)

Newspaper libraries	PARCH, Grace D.	(OH)	939
	DISANTE, Linda B.	(PA)	305
	MOONEY, Shirley E.	(BC)	858
	HANDY, Mary J.	(ON)	495
	KIRSH, Julie	(ON)	655
Newspaper libraries development	DONCEVIC, Lois A.	(PA)	311
Newspaper library	MCCANLESS, Christel L.	(AL)	793
	FARLEY, Austin G.	(OK)	364
Newspaper library automation	ELLENBOGEN, Barbara R.	(MI)	343
	HUNTER, James J.	(OH)	576
	RHYDWEN, David A.	(ON)	1026
Newspaper library clipping	CLARK, Audrey M.	(UT)	216
Newspaper library consulting	IPPOLITO, Andrew V.	(NY)	583
Newspaper library databases	ROCKALL, Diane M.	(MI)	1046
Newspaper library management	HARDNETT, Carolyn J.	(MD)	500
	BULLOCK, Jessie M.	(PA)	156
Newspaper library systems	CASTER, Suzanne	(CA)	194
	SCOFIELD, James S.	(FL)	1106
	IRONS, Lynda R.	(ID)	584
	VANCE, Sandra L.	(IL)	1273
	FRANKLIN, Alyce B.	(KY)	397
Newspaper photo archives	PARISOT, Beverly J.	(NE)	940
Newspaper photo systems	KANE, Angelika R.	(PA)	624
Newspaper preservation	HARRISON, Karen A.	(ON)	507
Newspaper publishing	TRIGAUX, Robert	(DC)	1256
	ALLAN, John	(NY)	14
	BURKE, Edward	(NY)	160
	FINCH, Brian	(NY)	377
	FREY, Ned	(NY)	402
	HENDERSON, Brad	(NY)	526
	KRAUS, James	(NY)	676
	MALKIN, Peter	(NY)	763
	NOVEMBER, Robert S.	(NY)	911
	RUSLING, Con A.	(NY)	1068
	TYSON, David	(NY)	1267
	VELLA, Carl	(NY)	1281
	ZIMMERMAN, William	(NY)	1389
Newspaper reference	LOVELL, Bonnie A.	(TX)	743
	BURROWS, Sandra	(ON)	163
Newspaper research	ALLCORN, Mary E.	(MO)	14
	HARRIS, Belinda J.	(VA)	504
Newspapers	GRIMSLEY, Judy L.	(FL)	470
	WORK, Dawn E.	(IA)	1369
	OTTO, Kathryn D.	(KS)	930
	LEIBOWITZ, Faye R.	(PA)	713
	OVERTON, Margaret C.	(TN)	931
	REITMAN, Jo	(WI)	1022
Newspapers & periodicals	BURTON, Donna M.	(ON)	164
Newspapers, indexes	DAZE, Colleen J.	(NY)	283
Online newspaper	LANDRY, Denise C.	(LA)	693
Reference & research newspaper publshg	EGERTSON, Yvonne L.	(VA)	339
Researching newspapers	MORRISON, Annette T.	(TN)	867
Serials, newspapers	EVEY, Patricia G.	(PA)	359
Special newspaper libraries	BANKS, Marie M.	(OH)	54
Texas newspaper archives	MATHIS, Rama F.	(TX)	784
United States newspaper project	GULLEY, J L.	(GA)	477

NEWSROOM

Newsroom libraries	FARRAR, Lu A.	(KY)	365

NEXIS

LEXIS & NEXIS	KANJI, Zainab J.	(CA)	625
Online searches for NEXIS	BURROWS, Shirley	(NY)	163
Socioeconomic, LEXIS & NEXIS databases	MILUTINOVIC, Eunhee C.	(IL)	845

NICHE

Niche targeting & message development	GREEN, Randall N.	(DC)	462

NILRC

Networking, NILRC	BAYER, Susan P.	(IL)	67

NINETEENTH CENTURY

First editions, 19th century music	BRODY, Elaine	(NY)	139
Middle East 19th century photography	THOMAS, Ritchie D.	(OH)	1238
19th & 20th century art	SCHNEIDER, Karen	(DC)	1097
19th century American religious music	CHRISTENSON, Donald E.	(OH)	211
19th century & 20th century art	HATCHER, Nolan C.	(GA)	511
19th century & 20th century Engl lit	HATCHER, Nolan C.	(GA)	511
19th century & 20th century music	HATCHER, Nolan C.	(GA)	511
19th century British & American lit	COLEY, Betty A.	(TX)	231
19th century British theatre	DONOHUE, Joseph	(MA)	312
19th century literature	FECKO, Marybeth	(SC)	367
19th century manuscripts	RATNER, Sabina T.	(PQ)	1010
19th century Oregon history	EMMENS, Thomas A.	(OR)	348
19th century Pacific Northwest history	EMMENS, Thomas A.	(OR)	348
19th century photographs	RHINELANDER, Mary F.	(MA)	1025
	MORROW, Delores J.	(MT)	869
19th century technology	PRESGRAVES, Jim	(VA)	991
19th century US rare books	GARDNER, Ralph D.	(NY)	418

NOMENCLATURE (See also Terminological, Thesaurus, Vocabulary)

Chemical nomenclature	JUTERBOCK, Deborah K.	(NJ)	620
	NOCKA, Jean A.	(NJ)	906
Standard nomenclature & code for medcn	CASIRAGHI, Edoardo	(ITL)	192
Systematized nomenclature of medicine	NITZ, Andrew M.	(DC)	905

NON-BOOK (See also Audiovisual, Materials, Media)

Audiovisual & non-book media	HARRINGTON, Thomas R.	(DC)	504
Books & non-book cataloging	WU, Harriet	(CA)	1373
Cataloging, book & non-book	COTTINGHAM, Elsie E.	(IN)	250
Cataloging non-book materials	BUSER, Robin A.	(KY)	165
	MEYER, Kenton T.	(PA)	830
Cataloging, Slavic language, non-book	JENKS, Zoya E.	(PA)	597
Foreign language non-book materials	MCELWAIN, William	(IL)	804
Non-book cataloging	PEARMAN, Sara J.	(OH)	952
Non-book databases	PEARMAN, Sara J.	(OH)	952
Non-book library materials	BIVINS, Hulen E.	(AL)	100
Non-book material management	WEIHS, Jean	(ON)	1317
Non-book materials	CHESTER, Claudia J.	(CA)	207
	RODICH, Nancy A.	(MS)	1048
	ANGEL, Kenneth E.	(NY)	27
	KLEMPNER, Irving M.	(NY)	660
	READ, Jean B.	(NY)	1012
	HERRING, Billie G.	(TX)	533
	LIGHTHALL, Lynne I.	(BC)	727
	ELLIOTT, Lirlyn J.	(TRN)	344
Non-book mtrls & microcomputer software	INTNER, Sheila S.	(MA)	583
Non-book materials classification	HAMDY, Mohamed N.	(KWT)	491
Non-book materials online cataloging	KARON, Bernard L.	(MN)	627
Non-book media	SNOW, Maryly A.	(CA)	1164
Ordering & catlgng books & non-book mtrl	SPIEGEL, Bertha	(NY)	1174
Preservation of non-book material	ELLISON, John W.	(NY)	345

NONFICTION (See also Literature)

Adult trade nonfiction selection	WISOTZKI, Lila B.	(MD)	1358
Fiction & nonfiction	RARESHEID, Cynthia L.	(OH)	1008
Middle grade fiction & nonfiction acqs	BUCKLEY, Virginia L.	(NY)	154
Nonfiction & fiction writing	BRADWAY, Becky J.	(IL)	126
Nonfiction collection development	CANTWELL, Mary L.	(OH)	179
Non-fiction services	HALL, Clark J.	(IL)	487
Nonfiction trade books	RIBAROFF, Margaret F.	(CT)	1026
Popular fiction & nonfiction	GANYARD, Margaret E.	(MO)	416
Purchase of nonfiction material	LAMBERT, Sandra L.	(IL)	690
Writing children's non-fiction books	MARSTON, Hope I.	(NY)	775
Young adult fiction & nonfiction acqs	BUCKLEY, Virginia L.	(NY)	154
Young adult nonfiction & fiction	CROSS, Claudette S.	(CA)	260

NON-PRINT (See also Audiovisual, Literature, Materials, Media, Nonfiction)

Acquisition non-print media	SPEIRS, Gilmary	(PA)	1172
Acqs, processing print, non-print	FRENCH, Janet D.	(PA)	402
Bibliographic control, non-print media	TOTTEN, Herman L.	(TX)	1252

NON-PRINT (Cont'd)

Cataloging non-print materials	ADCOCK, Donald C.	(IL)	6
	GIBBS, Mary E.	(IL)	431
	WHYDE, John S.	(OH)	1335
Cataloging non-print media	MATTHEWS, Priscilla J.	(IL)	785
Cataloging print & non-print	HSIEH, Cynthia C.	(IL)	567
Cataloging visual non-print materials	VISKOCHIL, Larry A.	(IL)	1285
Computerizing print & non-print mtrls	BIANCHINO, Cecelia	(IN)	94
Copyright, non-print media	THOMAS, Fred	(MD)	1236
Non-print	MADDEN, Terence J.	(MI)	759
	PETERMAN, Kevin	(NY)	962
Non-print acquisition & access	KRANZ, Ralph	(UT)	676
Non-print catalog development	REHMS, Jane C.	(WA)	1017
Non-print cataloging	FAIR, Kathy L.	(AL)	361
	WOOLDRIDGE, Steven M.	(CA)	1368
	KELLEY, Colleen L.	(IN)	636
	BRATCHER, Perry R.	(KY)	129
	BADEN, Diane G.	(MA)	44
	BELL, Rebecca L.	(TN)	77
Non-print collection development	NUTTY, David J.	(IL)	912
	CHAPLOCK, Sharon K.	(WI)	201
Non-print curriculum materials	FISHER, Carolyn H.	(NY)	380
Non-print formats	ROLLIN, Marian B.	(CT)	1051
Non-print library development	BARRIE, John L.	(NY)	59
Non-print materials	POIRRIER, Sherry	(MA)	980
	JONES, David E.	(NJ)	612
	SPANGLER, William N.	(NJ)	1171
	WILDER, Nancy S.	(TX)	1339
	NORRGARD, Don K.	(ON)	909
Non-print materials collections	JOHNSON, Carolynn K.	(WA)	603
Non-print media	BESSER, Howard A.	(CA)	91
	DUBOIS, Henry J.	(CA)	322
	ERVITI, Debra L.	(CA)	353
	HANDMAN, Gary P.	(CA)	495
	WOOLDRIDGE, Steven M.	(CA)	1368
	HAMRELL, Larry G.	(FL)	494
	HOUGH, Leslie S.	(GA)	562
	COOPER, Susan C.	(IL)	243
	SOMMER, Ursula M.	(NJ)	1167
	KENSELAAR, Robert	(NY)	642
	RIVERA, Gregorio	(NY)	1037
	SCHABERT, Daniel R.	(NY)	1088
	BARNETT, Donald E.	(OR)	57
	VIGNOVICH, Ray L.	(WI)	1284
	GOODMAN, Henry J.	(AB)	449
Non-print media & audiovisuals	CURTIS, James A.	(NY)	267
Non-print media director	DINNESEN, Peter H.	(OH)	305
Non-print media librarianship	WHYTE, Sean	(VA)	1335
Non-print media services	VARNES, Richard S.	(CO)	1279
Non-print media utilization	THOMPSON, Elizabeth M.	(DC)	1239
	TOTTEN, Herman L.	(TX)	1252
Non-print production	THOMAS, James L.	(TX)	1237
Non-print research	LYNESS, Ann L.	(PA)	752
Non-print resources	COCHENOUR, Donnice K.	(OK)	225
Non-print services	CALLISON, Daniel J.	(IN)	174
	HOOPER, James E.	(TN)	557
	NORDEN, David J.	(VA)	908
Print & non-print cataloging	ROBERTS, Sallie H.	(OH)	1041
Print & non-print material cataloging	TIWANA, Shah J.	(IL)	1247
Print & non-print materials cataloging	BROWN, Biraj L.	(SDA)	142
Print & non-print teacher consulting	CARLISLE, Carol A.	(CT)	182
Printed & non-printed material catlgng	SZETO, Dorcas C.	(CA)	1218
Reviewing materials, print & non-print	SELWYN, Laurie	(TX)	1114
Selection & evaluation of non-print mtrl	AHN, Hyonah K.	(IL)	8
Selection of print & non-print material	GREENFIELD, Judith C.	(NY)	464
Yng adult & children's print & non-print	WOODS, Selina J.	(MA)	1367

NONPROFIT (See also Profit, Public)

Administration of non-profit corporation	TREBBY, Janis G.	(WI)	1255
Books & newsletters, non-profit groups	TAFT, James R.	(DC)	1219
Educational & non-profit archives	SCHUMACHER, Carolyn S.	(PA)	1102
Marketing non-profit agencies	RASSAM, Cynthia K.	(NM)	1009
Marketing non-profit services	LEISNER, Anthony B.	(IL)	714
Non-profit administration	BALL, Alice D.	(DC)	52

NONPROFIT (Cont'd)
Non-profit organizations | BOHLEN, Jeanne L. . . . . (DC) 111

NON-PUBLIC
Liaison with non-public schools | MACLEAN, Ellen G. . . . . (VI) 757

NON-USER
Non-user non-reader outreach
  services | FRANKLIN, Hardy R. . . . (DC) 397

NORTH
North American geology | WEST, Barbara F. . . . . . (TX) 1326
North American periodicals | NOBLE, Jean E. . . . . . . (CA) 906

NORTH CAROLINA
Cataloging North Carolina books | MCGLOHON, Leah L. . . (NC) 807
Civil War, North Carolina sources,
  units | WOODARD, John R. . . . (NC) 1365
North Carolina Baptists | WOODARD, John R. . . . (NC) 1365
North Carolina maritime activities | BUMGARNER, John L. . . (NC) 157
North Carolina rare books | TOMLINSON, Charles E. (NC) 1250

NORTHERN
Northern & native people's research | FINN, Julia P. . . . . (PQ) 378
Northern bibliography | KOBELKA, Carolynn L. . . (NT) 666
Northern Kentucky history | AVERDICK, Michael R. . . (KY) 41
Northern or polar materials | ALBRIGHT, Donald A. . . (NT) 10

NORTHWEST
Americana, Old Northwest Territory | MULLIGAN, William H. . . (MI) 877
19th century Pacific Northwest history | EMMENS, Thomas A. . . . (OR) 348
Pacific Northwest Americana | REESE, Gary F. . . . . . . (WA) 1016
Pacific Northwest history | CALDWELL, Richard C. . (WA) 172
Pacific Northwest regional local
  history | EMMENS, Thomas A. . . . (OR) 348

NOSTALGIA
Books on collectibles & nostalgia | JOHNSON, Nancy E. . . . (IA) 608

NOTICES
Listing notices, label copy | WOOD, Sallie B. . . . . . . (NY) 1365

NOTIS
NOTIS | CLOUD, Patricia D. . . . . . (IL) 223
 | WILLIAMS, Charles M. . . (IL) 1342
 | CURTIS, Ronald A. . . . . (OK) 267
 | REEB, Richard C. . . . . (WI) 1014
NOTIS acquisitions system | GALE, Sarah E. . . . . . . (IN) 413
NOTIS system | MARCINKO, Dorothy K. . (AL) 769
NOTIS training & procedures | ENGLE, Constance B. . . (MI) 349
OCLC & NOTIS systems | LASATER, Mary C. . . . (TN) 700

NOUVEAU
Research, art nouveau, Victorian art | STACY, Betty A. . . . . . . (VA) 1178

NOVELS
Novels in the classroom | PROCTOR, Deborah K. . (WY) 994

NUC
NUC database | JACKSON, Nancy G. . . . (VA) 588

NUCLEAR
Management of nuclear records | WOODLEY, Victoria B. . . (MI) 1366
Nuclear energy | KEIZUR, Berta L. . . . . . (CA) 635
Nuclear engineering | SHERMAN, Dottie . . . . (CT) 1128
 | DOENGES, John C. . . . . (DC) 308
 | NISH, Susan J. . . . . . . (PQ) 905

NUCLEAR (Cont'd)
Nuclear engineering sciences | MAYER, Erich J. . . . . . . (NY) 789
Nuclear fiction database | LENZ, Millicent A. . . . . . . (NY) 716
Nuclear high level waste | KING, Betty J. . . . . (WA) 650
Nuclear magnetic resonance
  bibliography | PARR, John R. . . . . (ON) 943
Nuclear power | WOODLEY, Victoria B. . . (MI) 1366
Nuclear power industry | SPARER, Saretta . . . . . . (NY) 1171
Nuclear quality assurance | KNIGHTLY, John J. . . . . (TN) 664
Nuclear regulations & quality admin | KING, Betty J. . . . . (WA) 650
Nuclear safety & nuclear engineering | TODOSOW, Helen K. . . . (NY) 1248
Nuclear science | GOLDMAN, Patricia J. . . (MD) 445
Nuclear science & engineering | WEBSTER, Lois S. . . . . (IL) 1314
Nuclear technology | ROBINSON, Doris T. . . . (CA) 1044
Nuclear training | BOBAN, Carol A. . . . . . . (IL) 108
Nuclear waste information | LANE, Sandra G. . . . . . . (NY) 694
Nuclear waste management | NISH, Susan J. . . . . . . (PQ) 905
Reviewing nuclear issues films | DOWLING, John . . . . . . (PA) 316

NUMERIC
Hybrid numeric bibliographic systems | SCULLY, Patrick F. . . . . (CA) 1109
Numeric & statistical databases | MOON, Jeffrey D. . . . . . (ON) 857
Numeric data files | TSANG, Daniel C. . . . . . (CA) 1260
Numeric databases | GERKEN, Ann E. . . . . . (CA) 429
Numerical online databases | PIGGOTT, Sylvia E. . . . . (PQ) 972
Report number formation | KANE, Astor V. . . . . . . (VA) 624

NUMISMATICS
Early Arab numismatics | MOLINE, Judi A. . . . . . . (MD) 853
Numismatic bibliography | CAMPBELL, Francis D. . (NY) 176
Numismatics | GREEN, Nancy W. . . . . . (CO) 462
 | HESSELBEIN, Krista M. . (OH) 534
 | FOERSTER, Trey . . . . . . (WI) 387
Rare numismatic books | CAMPBELL, Francis D. . (NY) 176

NURSING
Administering nursing book collection | DAUGHERTY, Carolyn M. (MD) 275
Clinical medicine & nursing | SMITH, Brian D. . . . . . . (NY) 1153
 | TREVANION, Margaret U. (PA) 1255
Computer-assisted nursing instruction | GUENTHER, Jody . . . . . (TX) 475
Media in nursing & medicine selection | REIT, Janet W. . . . . (VT) 1022
Medical & nursing | VANNORTWICK, Barbara
   | L. . . . . (NY) 1276
Medical & nursing books | CASSAR, Ann . . . . (PA) 193
Medical & nursing databases | JENNINGS, Patricia S. . (FL) 598
 | LIPPMAN, Anne F. . . . . . (MA) 732
Medical & nursing information
  services | JENNINGS, Patricia S. . . (FL) 598
Medical & nursing literature | KAISLER, Dolores H. . . . (MD) 622
Medical & nursing reference | SCHULTZ, Therese A. . . (IL) 1102
Medical & nursing resources | BRETSCHER, Susan M. . (NY) 134
Medical, nursing database | HINKEL, Jeannine M. . . . (MD) 542
Medical nursing databases | SEXTON, Sally V. . . . . . (OH) 1118
Medicine & nursing | REID, Carol L. . . . . (NY) 1018
Medicine, nursing | KAKOSCHKE, Mona S. . . (ON) 622
Medicine, nursing, allied health | KARCH, Linda S. . . . . . (NY) 627
 | COHEN, Nancy E. . . . . . (OH) 228
Medicine, nursing & allied health | BOROCK, Freddie . . . . . (NY) 116
Nursing | REINHARDT, Alice L. . . . (CA) 1021
 | KATSH, Sara . . . . (CO) 630
 | TOWERS, Lynn C. . . . . . (FL) 1252
 | MATTOX, Rosemary S. . . (KS) 786
 | MCCORMICK, Dorcas M. (LA) 798
 | SAHYOUN, Naim K. . . . . (MI) 1075
 | BERRY, Mary W. . . . . . . (NC) 90
 | NOFTLE, Dorothy B. . . . . (NH) 907
 | VARGO, Katherine J. . . . (NJ) 1278
 | GALLAGHER, Patricia E. (NY) 414
 | HAWKES, Warren G. . . . (NY) 513
 | LARKIN, Virgil C. . . . . . . (NY) 698
 | LEINHEISER, Diane R. . . (PA) 714
 | BOITE, Mary E. . . . . (ON) 111
Nursing, allied health book discounter | PUALWAN, Emily . . . . . (PA) 996
Nursing, allied health databases | PRIME, Eugenie E. . . . . (CA) 993
Nursing, allied health services | DORNER, Marian T. . . . . (OH) 313
Nursing & allied health | BALCERZAK, Judy A. . . (ID) 50

NURSING (Cont'd)

Nursing & allied health resources	MCCULLOCH, Elizabeth A.	(PA)	801
	PRINGLE, Robert M.	(WA)	993
Nursing & health sciences	AIRTH, Elizabeth J.	(TX)	9
Nursing bibliography	ANDREWS, Theodora A.	(IN)	27
Nursing book publishing	FORD, Andrew E.	(NY)	389
Nursing databases	DAUGHERTY, Carolyn M.	(MD)	275
	KATZER, Sylvia U.	(ON)	630
Nursing education	ECHOLS, Susan P.	(NE)	334
Nursing education & research	SOME, Barbara K.	(NJ)	1166
Nursing expert systems	HENDRICKSON, Maria F.	(NY)	527
Nursing history	LINEBACH, Laura M.	(MO)	730
Nursing home library	RING, Anne M.	(IL)	1035
Nursing information	WATKINS, Elizabeth A.	(NJ)	1309
	GUENTHER, Jody	(TX)	475
Nursing information & reference	BERG, Rebecca M.	(CO)	84
Nursing information resources	ALLEN, Margaret A.	(WI)	15
Nursing journals & books	KODER, Alma	(PA)	667
Nursing libraries	ROMANACE, Gisele R.	(IL)	1052
	COOK, Nedra J.	(TN)	240
Nursing library management	SHIFF, Linda S.	(ON)	1130
Nursing literature	SMITH, Julie L.	(CA)	1156
	GIBSON, Patricia M.	(IL)	432
	STEVENS, Sheryl R.	(MI)	1191
	GEARY, Linda L.	(OH)	424
	COOK, Peggy M.	(OK)	240
Nursing literature research	AUFIERO, Joan I.	(BC)	39
Nursing materials	KAMENOFF, Lovisa	(MA)	623
Nursing, medical selection, reference	TAPPANA, Kathy A.	(OK)	1223
Nursing, nutrition, community health	FOX, Lynne M.	(CO)	395
Nursing reference	CORCORAN, Virginia H.	(CT)	246
	JONES, Dixie A.	(LA)	612
Nursing research	SHIEH, Monica W.	(MO)	1129
	BRUCE, Marianne E.	(AB)	149
Nursing research & education	KELLEY, John F.	(PA)	636
Nursing school librarianship	BENISHEK, Kristine K.	(OH)	81
Nursing science databases, cataloging	DIMATTEO, Lucy A.	(NY)	304
Nursing subjects	TRIP, Barbara M.	(BC)	1257
School of nursing libraries	CARTER, Selina J.	(AL)	190
Science, biology & nursing bibliography	COOPER, Rosemarie A.	(IL)	243
Subject bibliography for nursing	CHAN, Lillian L.	(CA)	199
Women's history & nursing	PALMISANO-DRUCKER, Elsalyn	(NJ)	937

NUTRITION (See also Food)

Collection development, foods, nutrition	NIPP, Deanna	(NJ)	904
Food, agriculture, nutrition information	JOHNSON, Sheila A.	(NY)	609
Food & nutrition	HUNT, Jennie P.	(MD)	575
Food & nutrition collection development	SZILARD, Paula	(HI)	1218
Food & nutrition literature	CULBERTSON, Diana L.	(IL)	263
Food & nutrition reference	SZILARD, Paula	(HI)	1218
Foods & nutrition selection	LAMONTAGNE, Therese	(CA)	691
Nursing, nutrition, community health	FOX, Lynne M.	(CO)	395
Nutrition	HANSON, Donna M.	(ID)	498
Nutrition education & training	KREBS-SMITH, James J.	(MD)	677
Nutrition software	KREBS-SMITH, James J.	(MD)	677

OBJECTIVES

Goals & objectives	MACDONALD, Christine S.	(ON)	754
Personnel hiring, evaluating, objectives	NOLAN, Deborah A.	(MD)	907
Planning system goals & objectives	COURSON, M S.	(MD)	251
Setting goals & objectives	MARTIN, Ron G.	(IN)	778

OBSTETRICAL

Obstetrical databases	ANDERSEN, H F.	(MI)	21

OCCULT

Social science, occult reference	KLEIN, Victor C.	(LA)	659

OCCUPATIONAL (See also Career, Employment, Job, Vocational)

Databases, occupational health & safety	MCLAUGHLIN, W K.	(AB)	813
Occupational & post secondary texts	LESURE, Alan B.	(NY)	718
Occupational health	CHANDLER, Constance P.	(CO)	199
Occupational health & safety	LE BLANC, Judith E.	(OH)	708
	MORRISON, Brian H.	(ON)	867
	GREGOIRE, Fleurette	(PQ)	466
Occupational health & safety information	TUCKER, Mary E.	(NC)	1262
	ZUBA, Elizabeth J.	(AB)	1390
Occupational safety	KLEMARCZYK, Laurice D.	(CT)	660
	BOUTWELL, Barbara J.	(PA)	119
Occupational training	LESURE, Alan B.	(NY)	718

OCEANOGRAPHY (See also Marine)

Marine studies, oceanography	HALL, Alice W.	(DE)	486
Oceanography	BIELLE, Christian P.	(PQ)	95

OCLC

Cataloging, OCLC	SALGAT, Anne M.	(PA)	1076
Cataloging, RLIN, OCLC experience	YU, Hsiao M.	(IA)	1384
Enhance status OCLC	LABODDA, Marsha J.	(TX)	686
Interlibrary loan on OCLC	RISHWORTH, Susan K.	(DC)	1036
OCLC	PAUL, Jacqueline R.	(DE)	949
	NEWMAN, Lorna R.	(IL)	899
	KIBREAH, Golam	(IN)	646
	GROSS, Mary D.	(LA)	472
	NYSTROM, Kathleen A.	(MO)	913
	ABRAMS, Roger E.	(OH)	3
	PIECHNICK, Katarzyna M.	(PA)	971
	VALENTIN-MARTY, Jeannette	(PR)	1271
	ADDISON, Jane G.	(TX)	6
	HOADLEY, Irene B.	(TX)	545
	ALLSOP, Mary B.	(WI)	17
OCLC & literature searching	REILLY, Dayle A.	(MA)	1020
OCLC & NOTIS systems	LASATER, Mary C.	(TN)	700
OCLC audiovisual format	TEMPLE, Harold L.	(IL)	1230
OCLC, bibliofile	BISSETT, Claudia K.	(NH)	100
OCLC cataloging	MITCHAM, Janet C.	(AR)	848
	O'BRIEN, Mary C.	(OR)	915
	GOING, Susan C.	(SC)	444
	CASEY, Wayne T.	(VA)	192
OCLC cataloging systems	MYERS, Victor C.	(MO)	885
OCLC database	ARMSTRONG, Ruth C.	(NY)	32
OCLC database searching	ROBERTS, Lisa G.	(GA)	1041
OCLC interlibrary loan	RONDESTVEDT, Helen F.	(TN)	1053
OCLC map cataloging	STORM, Jill	(DC)	1198
OCLC, MARC tagging	LEONG, Carol L.	(IL)	717
OCLC operations	KNOCH, Daniel L.	(MI)	665
OCLC searching	BRUNER, Linda J.	(VA)	150
OCLC systems	ANDERSON, Elizabeth M.	(PA)	22
OCLC training & development	WILD, Judith W.	(NY)	1338
OCLC use	NOONAN, Patricia K.	(TN)	908
Online cataloging, OCLC, RLIN	TURITZ, Mitch L.	(CA)	1263

OFF-CAMPUS

Off-campus library services	HEARTH, Fred E.	(CA)	519
	BURICH, Nancy J.	(KS)	160
	SLADE, Alexander L.	(BC)	1147
Off-campus service	NOLAND, Jon	(CA)	908

OFFICE (See also Business)

Government Printing Office publications	MAST, Joanne	(PA)	782
Law office automation	GRIFFITH, Cary J.	(MN)	469
Law office, library automation	LEITER, Richard A.	(NE)	714
Library & office automation	MOORE, Penelope F.	(VA)	861
Library office automation	ROSE, Phillip E.	(CO)	1055
Management & office automation	LEONARD, Lucinda E.	(VA)	716
Mending office management	DURNIAK, Barbara A.	(NY)	328
Microcomputers in library offices	INGRAHAM, Alice L.	(PA)	582
Office administration	BOSTON, Mary T.	(CO)	118
Office & information technology	VASILAKIS, Mary	(PA)	1279

OFFICE (Cont'd)

Office automation	CIRCIELLO, Jean M. . . .	(CA)	215
	COVEY, William C.	(FL)	252
	CHUNG, Alison L.	(IL)	213
	DESROCHES, Richard A.	(MA)	295
	PRICE, Douglas S.	(MD)	992
	STIGLEMAN, Sue E. . . .	(NC)	1194
	D'ALLEYRAND, Marc R.	(NY)	270
	MARTIN, Thomas H. . . .	(NY)	778
	MASYR, Caryl L.	(NY)	783
	PERSKY, Gail M.	(NY)	961
	GILLILAND, Anne J. . . .	(OH)	436
	JOSEPH, Patricia A. . . .	(PA)	617
	RAMBO, Neil H.	(TX)	1005
	BERGERON, Pierrette . .	(PQ)	86
Office design	CALDWELL, John M. . . .	(PA)	172
Office maintenance	DUNN, Susan M.	(IA)	327
Office management	INGERSOL, Robert S. . .	(MO)	582
	VOIT, Irene E.	(NV)	1287
Office systems	LOWENSTEIN, Richard A.	(CT)	744
Office systems automation	SYPERT, Clyde F.	(CA)	1217
OMB Circular A-76	STALLINGS, Elizabeth A.	(DC)	1179
One-person offices	MAKIN, Mollie D.	(OH)	762
Secretarial & office skills	EDWARDS, Barnett A. . .	(NY)	337

OFFICIAL

Foreign official publications	MARLEAU, Gilles	(ON)	772
International official publications	MARLEAU, Gilles	(ON)	772
Official documents	MURRAY-LACHAPELLE, Rosemary F.	(ON)	882
Official publications	BERNIER, Gaston	(PQ)	89

OHIO

Ohio documents	RYAN, Richard A.	(OH)	1071

OIL (See also Petroleum)

Oil & gas	CAMBRIA, Roberto	(NY)	174
	POWELL, Alan D.	(TX)	987
Oil & gas company	WRIGHT, Craig W.	(TX)	1371
Oil & gas databases	PARKINSON, Susan L. . .	(AB)	943
Oil & gas exploration	DURIE, Debbie L.	(AB)	328
Oil & gas reference	DILLARD, Lois A.	(TX)	303

OKLAHOMA

Oklahoma collection	THORNE, Larry R.	(OK)	1242
Oklahoma history	SUMNER, Delores T. . . .	(OK)	1209
Oklahoma State University collection	BLEDSOE, Kathleen E. . .	(OK)	105

OLD (See also Antiquarian, Early, Out-of-Print, Rare)

Americana, Old Northwest Territory	MULLIGAN, William H. . . .	(MI)	877
Cataloging old documents	BOECKMAN, Frances B. .	(MS)	109
Old & rare books	O'BRIEN, Francis M.	(ME)	914
Old & rare sound recordings	CHANDLER, Thomas V. . .	(CA)	200
Old Testament	MERRILL, Arthur L.	(MN)	826

OLDER (See also Aging, Elderly, Senior)

Disabled, older adults	DUPERREAULT, Marilyn J.	(SK)	327
Impaired older adult services	LEONARD, Gloria J.	(WA)	716
Older adult services	KANNER, Elliott E.	(Il)	625
	MILLER, Junelle	(IN)	839
	BOLIN, Nancy C.	(MD)	112
Services to older population	CLARKE, Charlotte C. . .	(MN)	218

OLYMPIC

Olympic games collection development	GHENT, Gretchen K. . . .	(AB)	430

ONCOLOGY

Clinical oncology	BLOOMSTONE, Ajaye . .	(LA)	106
Medical records & oncology	BRENNER, Lawrence . . .	(MA)	133
Oncology information	LEBRUN, Anne	(ON)	708
Orthopedic & oncology pediatrics	KELLER, Nancy H.	(LA)	635

O'NEILL

Research, Eugene O'Neill life works	MCDONALD, Lois E. . . .	(CT)	803

ONE-PERSON

Consulting & managing one-person libs	DALY, Eudice	(CA)	271
Law enforcement, one-person library	ZIMMERMAN, Donna K. . .	(IN)	1388
Managing a one-person library	SPONDER, Dorothy R. . .	(DC)	1175
	KATES, Jacqueline R. . .	(MA)	629
	MCVICAR, Ann L.	(TX)	818
One & two-person libraries	STEVENS-RAYBURN, Sarah L.	(MD)	1191
One-person hospital medical libraries	SHELDON, Marie A.	(NY)	1126
One-person librarian	DUX-IDEUS, Sherrie L. . .	(NE)	330
One-person librarianship	BELLIS, Gloria K.	(TX)	78
	THOM, Pat A.	(WI)	1235
	SLINEY, Marjory T.	(IRE)	1149
One-person libraries	ASMUTH, Gretchen W. .	(DC)	36
	BLAKE, Martha A.	(IL)	103
	LONGMAN, Judith J. . . .	(IL)	740
	VAN HOORN, Audra G. . .	(IL)	1275
	WEBSTER, Lois S.	(IL)	1314
	HILL, Elizabeth C.	(KY)	539
	BARRINGER, Nancy F. .	(MA)	59
	MACE, Mary B.	(MA)	754
	PILE, Deborah R.	(MA)	973
	JENNINGS, Martha F. . .	(MI)	598
	NESBURG, Janet A.	(MI)	896
	SHAFFER, Nancy R. . . .	(NC)	1119
	FRIHART, Anne F.	(NJ)	404
	SIEGEL, Robin D.	(NJ)	1136
	BARNARD, Catherine A.	(NY)	57
	BOROCK, Freddie	(NY)	116
	LEYDEN, Annette	(NY)	724
	ST. CLAIR, Guy	(NY)	1075
	HAMILTON, Dennis O. . .	(OH)	492
	YOUNG, Thomas E.	(OK)	1383
	O'BRIEN, Alberta T.	(PA)	914
	PETRAK, Janet C.	(PA)	965
	VIGORITO, Patricia M. . .	(RI)	1284
	PATERSON, Elizabeth N. .	(VT)	947
	MUNDSTOCK, Aileen M. .	(WI)	879
	SEEBAUM, Carol J.	(WY)	1111
	BRESING, Sheindel H. . .	(PQ)	133
One-person libraries or biblgph instrc	KLEIN, Penny	(NY)	659
One-person library	ELLIOTT, Valerie E.	(CA)	344
	FALTZ, Judy A.	(CA)	363
	NEMETH, Martha C.	(CA)	895
	STUMBERG, Mary S. . . .	(CA)	1205
	MILLER, Charles G.	(CO)	836
	SASSO, Patricia A.	(CT)	1083
	BOHLEN, Jeanne L.	(DC)	111
	BARAGER, Wendy A. . . .	(FL)	55
	RIEKEN, Marietta K. . . .	(IA)	1033
	WINWARD, Coleen C. . .	(ID)	1356
	TERWILLIGER, Doris H. .	(MI)	1232
	BERGERON, Cheri Y. . .	(MT)	86
	FURR, Margaret H.	(NC)	410
	LAMBE, Catherine V. . . .	(NC)	690
	BARRICK, Judy H.	(NE)	59
	REDDING, Kathleen A. . .	(NE)	1013
	COLLISHAW, Jackie J. . .	(NJ)	233
	HODNETT, Diane M. . . .	(NJ)	546
	WATKINS, Elizabeth A. . .	(NJ)	1309
	WHITE, Joyce G.	(NJ)	1331
	CORNETT, John L.	(NM)	247
	JACKSON, Ella J.	(NV)	587
	GROSS, Elinor L.	(NY)	472
	ROTMAN, Elaine C.	(NY)	1060
	SANCHEZ, Eliana P. . . .	(NY)	1079
	TUBOLINO, Karen M. . . .	(NY)	1261
	MULDER, Marjorie M. . . .	(OH)	876
	DENGEL, Bette S.	(PA)	292
	PASKOWSKY, Carol	(PA)	946
	SHAPIRO, Ruth T.	(PA)	1121
	SOULTOUKIS, Donna Z. .	(PA)	1169
	WHITMAN, Joan T.	(PA)	1333
	WILLIAMS, Ruth J.	(PA)	1346
	TRIVETT, Martha S.	(TN)	1257

ONE-PERSON (Cont'd)

One-person library

GRAY, Gloria M.	(TX)	460
WRIGHT, Craig W.	(TX)	1371
HEYER, Terry L.	(UT)	535
MCMURRIN, Jean A.	(UT)	815
HAUCK, Janice B.	(VA)	512
SASSER, Ann B.	(VA)	1083
GUNSON, Murray J.	(AB)	478
WALKER, Elizabeth A.	(PQ)	1295

One-person library administration   ALFONSI-GIN, Mary A.   (IL)   13
One-person library management

KENNEDY, Joanne	(CA)	641
MILLIGAN, Jane M.	(MA)	843
COTE-THIBODEAU, Donna E.	(ME)	249
RUDA, Donna R.	(NY)	1065
LUPPINO, Julie B.	(SC)	749
PETERS, Mary N.	(TX)	962
WEST, Deborah C.	(TX)	1326

One-person library operation   MARTIN, Jody S.   (IN)   776
One-person library systems   REINALDO DA SILVA, Joann T.   (MB)   1021
One-person offices   MAKIN, Mollie D.   (OH)   762
One-person professional libraries   BENEDETTI, Joan M.   (CA)   80
One-person special libraries   WHELAN, Julia S.   (MA)   1329
One-person special library

HOLTON, Janet E.	(CO)	555
MIKSICEK, Barbara L.	(MO)	834
MARSHAK, Bonnie L.	(NY)	773

One-professional libraries   BELL, Karen L.   (GA)   77
One-professional library management   TURK, Sally   (CA)   1263
Operation of one-person library   HARRINGTON, Anne W.   (PA)   503
Running a one-person library   PUPIUS, Nijole K.   (IL)   998

ONLINE (See also OPAC)

Alcohol information online	MITCHELL, Andrea L.	(CA)	848
Automation, online retrieval services	BEACHELL, Doria M.	(DC)	68
Automation online systems	STEPHENS, Jerry W.	(AL)	1188
Bibliographic instruction & online	BURR, Charlotte A.	(WI)	163
Bibliographic instruction of online	WARD, Sandra N.	(CA)	1304
Biomedical research online & manual	LETT, Rosalind K.	(GA)	719
Biomedical searching online	DOBBS, David L.	(OH)	307
Business databases online searching	MCDAVID, Michael W.	(GA)	801
	CANNING, Joan M.	(NY)	178
Business online databases	PHILLIPS, Sylvia E.	(TX)	969
Business online research	BURYLO, Michelle A.	(PA)	164
CAS online end-user training	ROSS, Johanna C.	(CA)	1058
Cataloging online	CAREY, Jane G.	(FL)	181
Computer srchng, online info retrieval	SOUTH, Ruth E.	(OR)	1169
Computer systems & online research	REED, Carol R.	(HI)	1014
Demonstrating online systems	SOPELAK, Mary J.	(NY)	1168
Designing online systems	BELTON, Jennifer H.	(DC)	78
Developing online services	TIBBETTS, David W.	(NY)	1243
Development of online database	SWANBERG, Lisa A.	(DC)	1213
Documentation of online systems	SOPELAK, Mary J.	(NY)	1168
Educational online & CD-ROM searches	LIVELY, Nancy J.	(MD)	734
End-user online product design	LIPPERT, Margret G.	(OH)	732
End-user online training	HARBERT, Cathy E.	(MD)	499
	MACKSEY, Julie A.	(MI)	757
ERIC database online	MISSAR, Charles D.	(MD)	847
Humanities online databases	MACEWAN, Bonnie J.	(MO)	755
	LEWIS, Linda K.	(NM)	723
Implementing online cataloging system	FISHER, Carl D.	(VA)	380
Improvement of online retrieval	LIBBEY, Miles A.	(NJ)	725
Integrated online library systems	WEISS, William B.	(CA)	1320
	MARQUARDT, Steve R.	(WI)	772
Interactive online databases	PODWOL, Sharon L.	(NY)	979
Interlibrary loans online	TURLEY, Georgia P.	(WA)	1263
Legal research reference online manual	VON PFEIL, Helena P.	(DC)	1288
Library & online reference	MCDOWELL, Judith H.	(OH)	804
Library online integrated systems	KING, Maryde F.	(NY)	651
Library online systems	MADISON, Olivia M.	(IA)	759
	SONNEMANN, Gail J.	(VA)	1167
Life sciences databases online	DAVIDSON, Lloyd A.	(IL)	276
Manage online databases	CONNORS, Martin G.	(MI)	238
Management of online services	GOODWIN, Jane G.	(VA)	450
Manual & online bibliography	KREITZBURG, Marilyn J.	(PA)	677

ONLINE (Cont'd)

Manual online reference services	GINSLER, Mindy F.	(ON)	438
Manuscript cataloging online	CRONENWETT, Philip N.	(NH)	260
Market research, online & manual	MAXWELL, Christine Y.	(CA)	788
Marketing CD-ROM & online products	HUDES, Nan	(NY)	569
Marketing online database systems	POOL, Madlyn K.	(VA)	982
Marketing online services	JONES, Michael W.	(VA)	614
Medical database online searching	HEETER, Judith A.	(MN)	520
	VUGRIN, Margaret Y.	(TX)	1289
Medical databases online	SCHWARTZ, Dorothy D.	(NY)	1104
Medical online bibliographic searching	HARMAN, Susan E.	(MD)	502
Medical online databases	NELSON, Norma	(NY)	894
Medical reference & online databases	HARBERT, Cathy E.	(MD)	499
NASA & DTIC online databases	GENTRY, Susan K.	(CA)	427
Non-book materials online cataloging	KARON, Bernard L.	(MN)	627
Numerical online databases	PIGGOTT, Sylvia E.	(PQ)	972
Online	WELLSMAN, Jennifer A.	(NJ)	1323
	ROBINSON, Chantal	(PQ)	1043
Online abstracting	HORNE, Ernest L.	(MI)	560
Online acquisitions	GIBBS, Nancy J.	(AL)	431
Online aerospace & defense searching	RICH, Denise A.	(PA)	1027
Online analysis	MATTOX, Rosemary S.	(KS)	786
Online analysis of labor	ANDERSEN, H F.	(MI)	21
Online & CD-ROM searching	KACHALA, Bohdanna I.	(NY)	621
Online & CD-ROM systems	MAXWELL, Christine Y.	(CA)	788
Online & current awareness reference	LOGAN, Nancy L.	(ON)	737
Online & database	REINKE, Carol R.	(MI)	1021
Online & indexing services	STILES, William G.	(ON)	1194
Online & in-print reference	KING, Laurie L.	(MA)	651
Online & manual information services	GALBRAITH, Barry E.	(NY)	413
Online & manual searching	BOGART, Betty B.	(MA)	110
Online authority control	BERRINGER, Virginia M.	(OH)	90
	FRIEDLAND, Frances K.	(ON)	403
Online bibliographic control	HORNE, Ernest L.	(MI)	560
Online bibliographic database searching	SUBRAMANIAN, Jane M.	(NY)	1206
Online bibliographic databases	CALCAGNO, Philip M.	(IL)	172
Online bibliographic instruction	SPAANS, David N.	(DC)	1170
Online bibliographic retrieval	ROSS, Nina M.	(PA)	1058
Online bibliographic search	TU, Shu C.	(MA)	1261
Online bibliographic searching	WYBORNEY, Charles E.	(CA)	1374
	WESTON, E P.	(IL)	1327
	COLLINS, Mary E.	(IN)	233
	BEZERA, Elizabeth A.	(MA)	93
	LEE, Susan M.	(MT)	711
	NASE, Lois M.	(NJ)	888
	CURRY, Lenora Y.	(NY)	266
	HARDY, Gayle J.	(NY)	500
	PERRY, Claudia A.	(NY)	960
	TUCKER, Debbie B.	(OH)	1261
	JOHNSON, Jane W.	(VA)	605
Online bibliographic services	CANICK, Maureen L.	(DC)	178
	HARTZ, Mary K.	(DC)	509
	HILDITCH, Bonny M.	(MD)	539
	DESCHENE, Dorice	(OH)	294
Online bibliographic systems	MONTGOMERY, Michael S.	(NJ)	856
Online bibliographic training	PERRY, Claudia A.	(NY)	960
Online biochemistry searching	SIESS, Judith A.	(OH)	1136
Online biology searching	CHEN, Flora F.	(SK)	205
Online business databases	SAMUELS, Lois A.	(CT)	1079
	KANE, Nancy J.	(MA)	625
	MAKAREWICZ, Grace E.	(BC)	762
Online business information	ROMERO, Georg L.	(CA)	1052
	CRIM, Elias F.	(IL)	258
Online business searching	STREHL, Susan J.	(DC)	1201
	BURKE, Vivienne C.	(WA)	160
Online catalog	KIRKLAND, Janice J.	(CA)	655
	MERCADO, Marilyn J.	(FL)	825
	WILEY, Theresa K.	(KY)	1339
	CHU, Wendy N.	(NJ)	213
Online catalog database	BOWLES, Carol A.	(CA)	121
Online catalog development	BERGER, Michael G.	(CA)	85
	CLAYTON, William R.	(GA)	220
	GLEIM, David E.	(NC)	441
Online catalog development & use	BAKER, Paula J.	(OH)	49
Online catalog development evaluation	CLARK, Sharon E.	(IL)	218

ONLINE (Cont'd)

Online catalog instruction	KIRESEN, Evelyn M.	(CA)	654
	KNOWLES, Em C.	(CA)	665
	ABBOTT, Randy L.	(FL)	1
	BECK, Susan E.	(MO)	71
	NOWAKOWSKI, Frances C.	(NS)	911
Online catalog issues	RITCH, Alan W.	(CA)	1036
Online catalog maintenance	KIRKBRIDE, Amey L.	(OH)	654
	BABER, Elizabeth A.	(TX)	43
Online catalog management	STUBBS, Linda T.	(DC)	1204
	SELLBERG, Roxanne J.	(IN)	1113
Online catalog systems	PERONE, Karen L.	(NY)	959
Online catalog training	NOLAN, Christopher W.	(TX)	907
Online cataloging	GILLESPIE, Veronica M.	(DC)	435
	OSGOOD, James B.	(IL)	928
	WARTZOK, Susan G.	(IN)	1307
	CLOUGH, Linda F.	(MA)	223
	HORNE, Ernest L.	(MI)	560
	ROZENE, Janette B.	(NY)	1064
	ZIPPER, Masha	(NY)	1390
	FELL, Sally B.	(OH)	370
	WALBRIDGE, Sharon L.	(OH)	1293
	JAMES, Denise T.	(SC)	592
	VAN ORDEN, Richard D.	(UT)	1276
	HUANG, Paul T.	(NS)	568
	BOWEN, Tom G.	(ON)	120
	BURCHELL, Patricia M.	(ON)	158
	THOMSON, Donna K.	(ON)	1241
	WISE, Eileen M.	(ON)	1356
	CHAUMONT, Elise	(PQ)	204
	DANIS, Rolland J.	(PQ)	273
	RIOPEL, Jean M.	(PQ)	1035
Online cataloging databases	LINSKY, Leonore K.	(MA)	731
Online cataloging, OCLC, RLIN	TURITZ, Mitch L.	(CA)	1263
Online cataloging system	RICHARD, Sheila A.	(VA)	1028
Online cataloging systems	FRIEDLAND, Frances K.	(ON)	403
Online catalogs	BARANOWSKI, George V.	(CA)	55
	BROWNRIGG, Edwin B.	(CA)	149
	DWYER, James R.	(CA)	330
	MONTGOMERY, Teresa L.	(CA)	856
	SASSE, Margo	(CA)	1083
	WILLIAMS, Joan F.	(CA)	1344
	PRITCHARD, Sarah M.	(DC)	994
	RATESH, Ioana	(DC)	1009
	CAMPBELL, John L.	(GA)	176
	GORDON, Elaine H.	(IL)	451
	VARNER, Carroll H.	(IL)	1278
	READY, Sandra K.	(MN)	1012
	FOX, Judith A.	(MO)	395
	DAVIS, Jinnie Y.	(NC)	279
	BRKIC, Beverly T.	(ND)	138
	JUNION, Gail J.	(NY)	620
	MORRIS, Jennifer D.	(NY)	866
	SHERBY, Louise S.	(NY)	1127
	LOGAN, Susan J.	(OH)	737
	SLOVASKY, Stephen	(OH)	1150
	SOUCIE, Yan Y.	(OR)	1169
	KALIN, Sarah G.	(PA)	623
	SUTHERLAND, Carl T.	(SC)	1211
	COOPER, Jean L.	(VA)	243
	SALT, David P.	(SK)	1077
Online catalogs & systems	FORKES, David	(ON)	390
Online CD-ROM database searching	GRABINSKY, Warren B.	(BC)	455
Online CD-ROM databases	SEARS, Jonathan R.	(MD)	1110
Online chemical searching	PETRY, Robyn E.	(IL)	965
Online chemistry searching	CHEN, Flora F.	(SK)	205
Online circulation system	BONNET, Janice M.	(CA)	114
Online circulation systems	EDWARDS, Dana S.	(IL)	337
	FOLEY, Mary D.	(KY)	387
Online computer	BAZE, Mary P.	(WA)	68
Online computer applications	ROSENFELD, Joseph S.	(OH)	1056
Online computerized binding preparation	HECKMAN, Stephen P.	(IN)	520
Online coordination	BREMER, Thomas A.	(MT)	132
Online coordination & searching	TAYLOR, Douglas M.	(AL)	1226
Online database	RAQUET, Jacqueline R.	(GA)	1008
	RUSSELL, Barbara J.	(TX)	1068
Online database access	LOGAN, Elisabeth L.	(FL)	737
Online database & medical databases	FRANK, Agnes T.	(NY)	396

ONLINE (Cont'd)

Online database construction & searching	CHAMIS, Alice Y.	(OH)	198
Online database consultation	LAMB, Connie	(UT)	689
Online database design	LEMASTERS, Joann T.	(OH)	715
Online database development	KISSMAN, Henry M.	(MD)	656
	POQUETTE, Mary L.	(MN)	984
	DIETLE, Craig I.	(NY)	302
	CLASPER, James W.	(OH)	219
	SYEN, Sarah	(PA)	1217
Online database, electronic publishing	HERRICK, Carol L.	(OH)	532
Online database industry	CUADRA, Carlos A.	(CA)	262
	KNOPPERS, Jake V.	(ON)	665
Online database instruction	PARKER, Joan M.	(CA)	942
Online database maintenance	ISGANITIS, Jamie C.	(NY)	585
Online database management	CSENGE, Maragaret L.	(NY)	262
	TOWNLEY, Richard L.	(NY)	1253
Online database product development	JENKINS, George A.	(FL)	597
Online database reference	BEAVERS, Janet W.	(ISR)	71
Online database research	NIXON, Judith A.	(MD)	906
On-line database searching	PALMA, Nancy C.	(PA)	935
Online database services	KANTER, Elliot J.	(CA)	625
	SMITH, Robert B.	(PA)	1160
	HOSONO, Kimio	(JAP)	562
Online database training	KAVANAGH, Janette R.	(CO)	631
Online databases	PEARSON, Peter E.	(AL)	953
	BARANOWSKI, George V.	(CA)	55
	BIEK, David E.	(CA)	95
	LOW, Kathleen	(CA)	743
	NEWTON, Deborah A.	(CA)	900
	NING, Mary J.	(CA)	904
	QUINT, Barbara E.	(CA)	1000
	REYNOLDS, Diane C.	(CA)	1025
	TSAI, Sheh G.	(CA)	1260
	WILLIAMS, Donna S.	(CA)	1342
	GAGNE, Susan P.	(CT)	412
	DRAGOVICH, Pamela M.	(DC)	318
	JEMIOLA, Nancy E.	(DC)	596
	MITCHELL, Elaine M.	(DC)	848
	BRESLAUER, Lester M.	(FL)	133
	EVERETT, David D.	(FL)	358
	BECKER, Jacquelyn B.	(IL)	72
	REED, Janet S.	(IL)	1015
	BOLAND, Mary J.	(MA)	111
	FOX, Susan	(MA)	395
	LEWONTIN, Amy	(MA)	724
	WEINSCHENK, Andrea	(MA)	1318
	ERLICK, Louise S.	(MD)	353
	JACK, Robert F.	(MD)	586
	MARCACCIO, Kathleen Y.	(MI)	768
	HUYGEN, Michaele L.	(MT)	580
	WOOD, Judith B.	(NC)	1364
	ALLEN, Robert R.	(NY)	16
	CASE, Ann M.	(NY)	191
	COHEN, Hannah V.	(NY)	228
	FORCE, Stephen	(NY)	389
	LEVINSON, Debra J.	(NY)	721
	NERBOSO, Donna L.	(NY)	895
	TUCKERMAN, Susan	(NY)	1262
	O'GORMAN, Jack	(OH)	918
	GLOECKNER, Paul B.	(PA)	441
	HODGSON, Cynthia A.	(PA)	546
	LAURITO, Gerard P.	(PA)	703
	METZ, Betty A.	(PA)	828
	FELSTED, Carla M.	(TX)	370
	SHAPLEY, Ellen M.	(TX)	1122
	BERWICK, Philip C.	(VA)	91
	HAMMOND, Theresa M.	(VA)	494
	THOMAS, Mary E.	(VA)	1237
	CIMPL, Kathleen A.	(WI)	214
	GRAY, Sandra A.	(ON)	460
	PROULX, Steven D.	(ON)	996
	FLORIAN, Trudel	(PQ)	385
	ALI, Syed N.	(BRN)	13
Online databases & CD-ROM	GERSH, Barbara S.	(CA)	429
Online databases, business & financial	GARMAN, Nancy J.	(KY)	419
Online databases marketing	DAWSON, Debra A.	(CA)	282
Online development & marketing	ANDREWS, Chris C.	(CT)	26
Online documentation	RADUAZO, Dorothy M.	(DC)	1002

ONLINE (Cont'd)

Online editing	GOLDBERG, Judy W.	(NY)	444
Online electronic catalog instruction	HITT, Charles J.	(MN)	544
Online electronic information services	HARRISON, Burgess A.	(CT)	506
Online full-text retrieval	WHITMAN, Mary L.	(PA)	1333
Online help aids	JARVIS, William E.	(PA)	595
Online high school instruction	GARDNER, Laura L.	(MO)	418
Online indexing of business reports	SEASE, Sandra A.	(NY)	1110
Online industry	GORDON, Helen A.	(IN)	451
Online information delivery	HERNANDEZ, Tamsen M.	(NY)	532
Online information marketing	ROACH, Eddie D.	(OK)	1037
Online information research	ROYAL, Linda G.	(VA)	1063
Online information retrieval	ANDERSON, Clifford D.	(CA)	22
	GRENIER, Myra T.	(CA)	467
	FINE, Sandra R.	(DC)	377
	KOVITZ, Nancy R.	(IL)	674
	JACK, Robert F.	(MD)	586
	HAM, Beverly V.	(MN)	490
	MULTER, Ell P.	(MO)	878
	CALLANAN, Ellen M.	(NJ)	173
	HSIAO, Shu Y.	(NY)	567
	LOWE, Ida B.	(NY)	743
	MARTINEZ-NAZARIO, Ronaldo	(PR)	779
	MILLS, Catherine H.	(RI)	843
	DOBSON, Christine B.	(TX)	307
	ACCARDI, Joseph J.	(WI)	3
	SWEETLAND, James H.	(WI)	1215
	MACKENZIE, Shirley A.	(ON)	756
Online information retrieval & storage	WILLIAMS, Martha E.	(IL)	1345
Online information retrieval, business	OSTROW, Rona	(NY)	929
Online information retrieval, databases	RAITT, David I.	(NET)	1004
Online information services	EL-HADIDY, Bahaa	(FL)	342
	PEAKE, Sharon K.	(OH)	952
	GRAY, Paul W.	(TX)	460
Online information systems	SULLIVAN, Edward A.	(CA)	1207
	SWEENEY, Urban J.	(CA)	1215
	HEARTY, John A.	(DC)	519
	WILSON, Lizabeth A.	(IL)	1351
	SMITH, Jo T.	(NJ)	1156
	HILL, Linda L.	(OK)	540
	BILLINSKY, Christyn G.	(SC)	96
	GENNARO, John L.	(VA)	427
	YAMANAKA, Tai	(JAP)	1377
Online information, US & foreign	PINSON, Mark	(MA)	975
Online instruction	FEINGLOS, Susan J.	(NC)	369
	SNOW, Bonnie	(PA)	1164
Online interaction	SARACEVIC, Tefko	(NJ)	1082
Online legal database	KERN, Sharon P.	(IA)	643
Online legal databases	HASKO, John J.	(NY)	510
Online legal indexing compilation	WONG, Patricia M.	(CA)	1363
Online legal research	SKRUKRUD, Nora L.	(CA)	1147
	CALVERT, Lois M.	(CO)	174
	ROSS, Margery M.	(DC)	1058
Online legal research services	WEBSTER, Deborah K.	(NC)	1314
Online library applications	ALMQUIST, Deborah T.	(MA)	17
Online library catalogs	HILDRETH, Charles R.	(IL)	539
Online library systems	HOFFMAN, Herbert H.	(CA)	548
	CARRISON, Dale K.	(MN)	187
	KANAFANI, Kyung C.	(MO)	624
	TAYLOR, Arlene G.	(NY)	1226
	SEUSS, Herbert J.	(WI)	1117
Online literature, sci & tech searching	WALLACE, Wendy L.	(NJ)	1298
Online literature search	CHUNG, Helen S.	(NC)	213
Online literature searching	CRUM, Norman J.	(CA)	262
	GLYNN, Jeannette E.	(CA)	442
	HUNT, Richard K.	(CA)	575
	BODI, Sonia E.	(IL)	109
	BRINKMAN, Carol S.	(KY)	136
	KRESSE, Kerry L.	(KY)	678
	SHEPARD, Margaret E.	(MI)	1127
	OBERC, Susanne F.	(OH)	913
	ROHMILLER, Ellen L.	(OH)	1051
	BERGER, Lewis W.	(PA)	85
	FU, Clare S.	(PA)	407
	KELLAND, John L.	(RI)	635
	WORLEY, Merry P.	(TX)	1369
	PARHAM, Sandra H.	(VA)	940
	LAMB, Cheryl M.	(WI)	689
Online mainframe databases	RICHARDS, Stella	(PQ)	1028

ONLINE (Cont'd)

Online management & training	KIBBEE, Josephine Z.	(IL)	646
Online, manual search strategy	BATES, Marcia J.	(CA)	64
Online medical & legal systems	MORRIS, Timothy J.	(DC)	867
Online medical & scientific databases	REITANO, Maimie V.	(NY)	1022
Online medical database searching	TIBBS, Jo A.	(FL)	1244
Online medical databases	CUTTS, William B.	(CO)	268
	REAM, Diane F.	(FL)	1013
	GOLDMAN, Richard	(PA)	446
Online medical literature search	ABRAMSON, Lawrence J.	(MI)	3
Online medical searches	ROWBERG, Alan H.	(WA)	1062
Online medical searching	POSTLEWAIT, Cheryl A.	(KS)	986
Online microcomputer application	VIDMANIS, Visvaldis E.	(MA)	1283
Online microcomputer cataloging	BERNSTEIN, Elaine S.	(ON)	89
Online music cataloging	MASTRANGELO, Marjorie J.	(DC)	782
	OLMSTED, Elizabeth H.	(KY)	921
Online networks	FREDERICK, Sidney C.	(IL)	399
	OLSEN, Wallace C.	(NY)	922
	BOWERS, Paul A.	(PA)	120
Online news database	MCFARLANE, Agnes	(PQ)	805
Online newspaper	LANDRY, Denise C.	(LA)	693
Online operations	TURIEL, David	(NY)	1263
Online patent searching	TERANIS, Mara	(WI)	1231
Online processing	STRIEDIECK, Suzanne S.	(PA)	1202
	HOLLOWAY, Geraldine B.	(TX)	552
Online product design development	ODHO, Marc	(ON)	917
Online public access catalogs	BISOM, Diane B.	(CA)	99
	DRIVER, Linda A.	(CA)	320
	GLASSMAN, Penny L.	(MA)	440
	STERLING, Judith K.	(MD)	1189
	FABIAN, William M.	(MO)	360
	HOWE, Ernest A.	(AB)	565
Online records linking	HARRIS, Virginia B.	(VA)	506
Online reference	DERSHEM, Larry D.	(CA)	294
	LEE, Don A.	(CA)	709
	ZELINKA, Mary A.	(DC)	1387
	PRENDERGAST, Kathleen M.	(IL)	990
	ELFSTRAND, Stephen F.	(MN)	342
	HUNTER, James J.	(OH)	576
	HORWITZ, Seth	(PA)	561
	ENNS, Carol F.	(NB)	350
	BANFIELD, Eilzabeth S.	(NS)	54
	WARD, William D.	(ON)	1304
	COLLISTER, Edward A.	(PQ)	233
Online reference retrieval	ELLIOT, Hugh	(DC)	343
Online reference searches	MANNING, Mary J.	(IL)	766
Online reference service	PHIFER, Kenneth O.	(MD)	967
Online reference services	STEVENS, Paula F.	(AZ)	1190
	BRUMAN, Janet L.	(CA)	150
	CHADWICK, Sharon S.	(CA)	197
	SPURGEON, Kathy R.	(CT)	1176
	HARPER, Laura G.	(MS)	503
	CLASPER, James W.	(OH)	219
	WALKER, Richard D.	(WI)	1296
	SERMAT-HARDING, Kaili I.	(ON)	1116
Online reference systems	LAZARUS, Josephine G.	(CO)	706
Online research	CASTER, Suzanne	(CA)	194
	GIFFORD, Becky J.	(CA)	433
	WILLIAMS, Lisa B.	(CA)	1344
	KAHN, Victoria	(DC)	622
	PAVEK, C C.	(DC)	950
	JACOBSON, William R.	(IL)	590
	MARTIN, Jody S.	(IN)	776
	MACLEOD, Valerie R.	(KY)	757
	MAGUIRE, Linda H.	(MA)	760
	PERECMAN, Carol J.	(MI)	958
	AUSTIN, Fay A.	(NJ)	40
	FARAONE, Maria B.	(NY)	363
	SHAPIRO, Barbara G.	(NY)	1121
	SOROBAY, Roman T.	(NY)	1169
	MEHR, Joseph O.	(RI)	821
	PARTRIDGE, Cathleen F.	(UT)	945
	MCINTOSH, Julia E.	(PQ)	809
Online research & reference	YOUNG, Sandra C.	(KY)	1383
Online research training	WEEKS, Olivia L.	(NC)	1315

ONLINE (Cont'd)

Online retrieval

GALLERY, M C.	(CA)	414
PAIK, Nan H.	(CA)	935
BOWERS, Sandra L. . . .	(CO)	121
BELLARDO, Trudi	(DC)	78
PEPETONE, Diane S. . . .	(IA)	957
BAILEY, Joanne P.	(IN)	46
WALLACE, Danny P. . . .	(IN)	1297
GERKE, Ray	(MA)	428
SEELEY, Catherine R. . .	(ME)	1111
STEPHENS, Karen L. . . .	(MI)	1188
MILLER, Betty	(NY)	836
ST. JACQUES, Suzanne L.	(ON)	1075

Online retrieval services

DEBROWER, Amy M. . .	(MD)	285
MARSHALL, Patricia K. .	(NY)	775

Online retrieval systems

DRUMMOND, Louis E. . .	(DC)	321
TAHIR, Mary M.	(MD)	1220
STEFFEY, Ramona J. . . .	(TN)	1185
GALBRAITH, Paula L. . .	(TX)	413

Online scientific databases — SAMUELS, Lois A. . . . . . (CT) 1079

Online searching

BROWN, Lorene B.	(GA)	145
LAWRENCE, Robert E. .	(OR)	705

Online services

BENNION, Bruce C.	(CA)	82
DAVIS, Rebecca A.	(CA)	280
WILLHITE, Sherry	(CA)	1341
WILSON, Wayne V.	(CA)	1353
WATERS, W R.	(CO)	1309
KRAMER, William J.	(DC)	675
STOUT, Robert J.	(IA)	1199
RAYMAN, Ronald A. . . .	(IL)	1011
WRIGHT, Joyce C.	(IL)	1372
LANDRY, Abbie V.	(LA)	693
BANDER, Edward J.	(MA)	54
BRITTEN, William A. . . .	(MD)	137
KOTZIN, Sheldon	(MD)	673
LACROIX, Eve M.	(MD)	686
GAMACHE, Kathleen A. .	(MI)	416
KARP, Nancy S.	(MI)	628
KLEIN, Regina D.	(MO)	659
LEBEAU, Chris	(NE)	707
STEPHENS, Ann E.	(NE)	1187
CASSEL, Jeris F.	(NJ)	193
APPEL, Marsha C.	(NY)	29
BARTENBACH, Wilhelm K.	(NY)	60
O'CONOR, William C. . .	(NY)	916
SANDERS, Robin S. . . .	(NY)	1080
VITART, Jane A.	(NY)	1286
WATERS, Betsy M.	(NY)	1308
DALRYMPLE, Tamsen . .	(OH)	271
GREEN, Lynda C.	(OH)	462
SIMONS, Linda K.	(OH)	1141
BEDDOES, Thomas P. . .	(PA)	73
RAC-FEDORIJCZUK, Karola C.	(PA)	1001
TUCCI, Valerie K.	(PA)	1261
RHOLES, Julia M.	(TX)	1026
HARRISTON, Victoria R.	(VA)	507
WINIARSKI, Marilee E. . .	(VA)	1355
THOMPSON, Jean T. . . .	(WI)	1240
DEBRUIJN, Deborah I. . .	(AB)	285
BICE, Lee A.	(ON)	94

Online srvs & bibliographic utilities — MORGAN, Ferrell . . . . . . (CA) 864

Online services & end-user services — SATTERTHWAITE, Rebecca K. . . . . (MD) 1084

Online services & public libraries — MALONEY, James J. . . . (CA) 764

Online services librarian — MAGEE, Patricia A. . . . . (NY) 759

Online services management — FARAH, Barbara D. . . . . (MA) 363

Online services, searching — WARDEN, Carolyn L. . . . (NY) 1304

Online shopping & travel — WALSH, Mark L. . . . . . . (CT) 1300

Online software documentation — GIRILL, T R. . . . . (CA) 438

Online specialization — LEI, Polin P. . . . . (AZ) 713

Online statistical database — CHANG, Joseph I. . . . . . (NJ) 200

Online subject access interfaces — BATES, Marcia J. . . . . . (CA) 64

Online system management — REINBOLD, Janice K. . . . (OK) 1021

Online systems

INGEBRETSEN, Dorothy L.	(CA)	582
SIMPSON, Evelyn L. . . .	(CA)	1141
STREHL, Daniel J.	(CA)	1201
TYSON, Betty B.	(CA)	1267
LOWENSTEIN, Richard A.	(CT)	744

ONLINE (Cont'd)

Online systems

ORLOSKE, Margaret Q. .	(CT)	926
PEMBERTON, Jeffery K. .	(CT)	956
QUAKE, Ron	(CT)	999
FOWLIE, Linda K.	(DC)	394
PAVEK, C C.	(DC)	950
BIBBY, Elizabeth A.	(GA)	94
CUNNINGHAM, Robert L.	(MA)	265
FERNALD, Anne C.	(MA)	373
IRWIN, Ruth A.	(MD)	584
VONDERHAAR, Mark N. .	(MD)	1288
VELLIKY, Mary M.	(MI)	1281
ABBOTT, George L.	(NY)	1
BERTUCA, David J.	(NY)	91
CAREN, Loretta	(NY)	181
KOSTENBAUDER, Scott	(NY)	673
SAHLEM, James R.	(NY)	1075
MOUNTS, Earl L.	(PA)	873
SYEN, Sarah	(PA)	1217
PHILLIPS, Patricia A. . . .	(TN)	968
ROTHBART, Linda S. . . .	(VA)	1060
STEIN, Karen E.	(VA)	1185
ASHTON, Margaret A. . .	(ON)	36

Online systems & database — MATTHEWS, Elizabeth W. (IL) 785

Online systems & indexing — MALCOLM, J P. . . . . (MI) 762

Online systems & policy — ARRINGTON, Susan J. . . (MD) 34

Online systems & services — GREEN-MALONEY, Nancy (CA) 465

Online systems design

MCLAREN, M B.	(NM)	813
NORMORE, Lorraine F. . .	(OH)	909

Online systems development — WOODSMALL, Rose M. . . (MD) 1367

Online systems evaluation — WOODSMALL, Rose M. . . (MD) 1367

Online systems marketing — GABOR, John M. . . . . . . (NY) 411

Online systems programming — SKROBELA, Katherine C. (NJ) 1147

Online systems research — PITCHON, Cindy A. . . . . (PA) 976

Online systems testing — TRUBKIN, Loene . . . . . . (BC) 1259

Online systems training — HUGGENS, Gary D. . . . . (DC) 571

Online technical services — WILSON, Virginia G. . . . . (MA) 1353

Online technology & searching — KREMER, Jill L. . . . . (PA) 677

Online thesauri, dictionary research — LIBBEY, Miles A. . . . . . (NJ) 725

Online training

DAWSON, Debra A.	(CA)	282
BOLSTER, Kathryn	(CT)	113
RADUAZO, Dorothy M. .	(DC)	1002
MEREDITH, Meri	(IN)	825
ORENSTEIN, Ruth M. . .	(MA)	925
KENTON, Charlotte	(MD)	642
CUTLER, Judith	(PA)	268
DINGLE, Susan	(PA)	304
CAPUTO, Richard P. . . .	(VA)	180
MCKENNEY, Linda S. . .	(VA)	811
FRITZ, Richard J.	(ON)	405

Online training & development

MULL, Richard G.	(CA)	876
DRUMMOND, Louis E. . .	(DC)	321
CARUSO, Nicholas C. . .	(PA)	190
WONG, Lusi	(ON)	1363

Online training & management — SINGLETON, Cynthia B. . (ON) 1143

Online training & marketing — HOCK, Randolph E. . . . . (MA) 545

Online union serial listing — PARRAVANO, Ellen A. . . (NY) 944

Online verifications — TURNER, Freya A. . . . . . (OH) 1264

Overseas online distributors — YAMAKAWA, Takashi . . (JAP) 1376

Performing online & computer searches — DUCHARME, Judith C. . . (NM) 322

Pharmaceutical searching online — SNOW, Bonnie . . . . (PA) 1164

Public access online catalogs — PHENIX, Katharine J. . . . (LA) 967

Public online catalogs — KELLEY, Betty H. . . . . . . (TX) 636

Real estate online database marketing — JENKINS, George A. . . . (FL) 597

Reference & online — STEVELMAN, Sharon R. . . (AB) 1190

Reference & online info retrieval — YOUNGEN, Gregory K. . (IN) 1383

Reference & online services

FRANK, Donald G.	(AZ)	396
SCOTT, Ralph L.	(NC)	1108

Reference online literature searching — DUNKEL, Lisa M. . . . . . . (CA) 326

Reference service online databases — DUNN, Lucia S. . . . . (IL) 327

Remote access online catalogs — KALIN, Sarah G. . . . . . . (PA) 623

Research, online & print — RABAI, Terezia . . . . (IL) 1001

Sales & marketing online services — CLARK, Rick . . . . (NJ) 218

Science, general & online reference — GRAZIANO, Eugene . . . . (CA) 460

Search online — PAPADEMETRIOU, Athanasia . . . . (MA) 938

Searching & indexing online databases — KREPS, Lise E. . . . . . . (WA) 678

ONLINE (Cont'd)

Searching online databases BICK, Barbara K. . . . . . . (MO) 94
Serials control & online databases CHAPMAN, Elwynda K. . (DC) 202
Shared cataloging networking online BROWN, Pauline . . . . . . (AUS) 146
Staff online training CAGAN, Penny M. . . . . . (NY) 170
State online catalog department NAUGLE, Gretchen R. . . (NE) 889
Super searcher online systems CONGER, Lucinda D. . . (DC) 236
Technical searching online VAN BRUNT, Amy S. . . . (NY) 1272
Traditional or online research HUMPHRIES, Joy D. . . . (WV) 574
Training users of ILS, online catalog PRESLAR, M G. . . . . . . (TN) 991
Working online on DOBIS DAWE, Heather L. . . . . . (ON) 282
Writing programs, online card catalog JORDAN, Sharon L. . . . . (WA) 617

ONLINE SEARCHING (See also Database Searching, Online)

Agriculture & biology online searching GRAINGER, Bruce . . . . . (PQ) 457
Agriculture & medicine online
searching STUBBAN, Vanessa L. . . . (KS) 1204
Art online searching KORENIC, Lynette M. . . . (CA) 671
Biomedical online database searching COAN, La V. . . . . (MI) 224
Business & legal online database
srchng NICOL, Margaret W. . . . . (NY) 903
Business online searching TERTELL, Susan M. . . . . (MN) 1232
POLLARD, Bobbie T. . . . (NY) 981
TRICKEY, Katherine M. . . (TX) 1256
CAS online database searching ROSS, Johanna C. . . . . . (CA) 1058
CAS online searching DESS, Howard M. . . . . . (NJ) 295
Cataloging & online searching GABBIANELLI, Patrice A. (NJ) 411
Cataloging, online searching,
reference PHILLIPS, Rosemary . . . (ON) 969
Chemical & technical online searching SPECTOR, Janice B. . . . (MI) 1172
Chemicals & patents online searching NEWMAN, Robert M. . . . (TX) 899
Chemistry reference & online
searching STANLEY, Eileen H. . . . . (LA) 1180
Computer online searching WAI, Lily C. . . . . (ID) 1292
TRICKEY, Katherine M. . . (TX) 1256
Database online searching SINGER, Susan A. . . . . . (NJ) 1143
Database retrieval & online searching ROTHSCHILD, M C. . . . (VA) 1060
Early training for online searching MINEMIER, Betty M. . . . (NY) 845
End-user online searching WHITLEY, Katherine M. . (AZ) 1333
Engineering & business online
searching ARROWOOD, Nina R. . . (NJ) 35
Engineering databases online
searching SCHNEIDER, Tatiana . . . (ON) 1097
Financial services online searching JORDAN, Charles R. . . . (IL) 616
STENGER, Brenda E. . . . (IL) 1187
Food technology online searching LAMANNA, Joan M. . . . . (CA) 689
General online searches GRAY, Dorothy A. . . . . . (KY) 459
General online searching LAMBROU, Angella . . . . (PQ) 691
Health care & hospitals online
searching CLINTON, Janet C. . . . . . (PA) 222
Health sciences medical online
searching STANKE, Judith U. . . . . . (MN) 1180
Health sciences online searching MATER, Dee A. . . . . (NC) 783
Instruction of online database
searching LOVELAND, Catherine R. (OH) 743
Library administration, online
searching SIARNY, William D. . . . . (IL) 1134
Life science online searching WILLIAMS, Mitsuko . . . . (IL) 1345
Management of online searching KOGA, James S. . . . . . . (CA) 668
Manual & online searching HOLDEN, Douglas H. . . . (ND) 550
Math databases online searching CARTER, Jackson H. . . . (NM) 189
Medical & business online searching BLACKBURN-FOSTER,
Brenda . . . . (KY) 102
Medical & law online searching BERK, Nancy G. . . . . . . (AZ) 87
Medical & science online searching RANSOM, Christina R. . . (NY) 1007
Medical databases, online searching FEINGLOS, Susan J. . . . (NC) 369
CLINTON, Janet C. . . . . . (PA) 222
Medical online searching JONES, Dixie A. . . . . . . (LA) 612
WARNER, Elizabeth R. . . (PA) 1305
TRICKEY, Katherine M. . . (TX) 1256
Microcomputer systems online
searching ROTHSTEIN, Pauline M. . (NY) 1060
Microcomputers, online searching GUSTAFSON, Ruth . . . . (NJ) 478
Online database search analyst JOHNSON, Stephen C. . (OH) 609
Online database search services ACKER, Robert L. . . . . . (IL) 3
Online database searching STRAITON, T H. . . . . . . (AL) 1199
BALDWIN, Claudia A. . . (CA) 51
DEENEY, Kay E. . . . . . (CA) 286
FORBES, Fred R. . . . . . . (CA) 389

ONLINE SEARCHING (Cont'd)

Online database searching

KUCZMA, Michelle . . . . . (CA) 682
LO, Grace C. . . . . (CA) 735
PAGE, Kathryn . . . . (CA) 934
PETTEY, Brent . . . . (CA) 965
SHAWL, Janice H. . . . . . (CA) 1124
SINCLAIR, Lorelei P. . . . . (CA) 1142
WHITE, Phillip M. . . . . . . (CA) 1332
ZYROFF, Ellen S. . . . . . . (CA) 1392
BANKHEAD, Jean M. . . . (CO) 54
FOX, Lynne M. . . . . (CO) 395
KAVANAGH, Janette R. . (CO) 631
CLARIE, Thomas C. . . . . (CT) 216
DELUCIA, Christina . . . . (CT) 290
SMITH, Lydia K. . . . . (CT) 1157
HOLLENBACH, Karen L. (DC) 551
ROARK, Robin D. . . . . . (DC) 1038
SKARR, Robert J. . . . . . (DC) 1145
CAMPBELL, John L. . . . (GA) 176
CARPENTER, David E. . (GA) 184
DENNISON, Jacquelyn H. (GA) 292
GUBISTA, Kathryn R. . . . (GA) 475
WEEG, Barbara E. . . . . . (IA) 1315
GARDNER, Trudy A. . . . . (IL) 418
POINTON, Louis R. . . . . (IL) 980
SCHAPIRO, Benjamin H. (IL) 1090
STEWART, Jamie K. . . . (IL) 1192
TIWANA, Shah J. . . . . . . (IL) 1247
NIXON, Judith M. . . . . . . (IN) 906
WATTS, Tim J. . . . . (IN) 1310
YOUNG, Carolyn K. . . . . (KS) 1381
NEELY, Glenda S. . . . . . (KY) 892
TURNER, Rebecca M. . . (KY) 1265
JONES, Philip L. . . . . . . (LA) 614
EDWARDS, Betty . . . . . . (MA) 337
JACQUES, Donna M. . . . (MA) 591
LEIGHTON, Helene L. . . (MA) 714
CHEEKS, Cellestine . . . . (MD) 204
DADSON, Theresa E. . . . (MD) 269
WILSEY, Charlotte A. . . . (MD) 1349
CROOKS, James E. . . . . (MI) 260
DYKHUIS, Randy . . . . . . (MI) 331
EMAHISER, Joan A. . . . . (MI) 347
SCOTT, Jane . . . . (MI) 1107
SMITH, Catherine A. . . . (MI) 1153
HLAVSA, Larry B. . . . . . . (MN) 544
ANDREWS, Mark J. . . . . (MO) 27
DROSS, Polly C. . . . . . . (MO) 320
REIMAN, David A. . . . . . (MO) 1020
KING, Donald R. . . . . . . (NJ) 650
LANGSCHIELD, Linda S. (NJ) 696
MCDERMOTT, Ellen . . . . (NJ) 801
PAULLIN, William D. . . . (NJ) 950
TILLMAN, Hope N. . . . . . (NJ) 1245
SCHOTT, Mark E. . . . . . (NM) 1099
BERGER, Pam P. . . . . . . (NY) 86
CARPENTER, Dale . . . . (NY) 184
COHEN, Ann E. . . . . (NY) 227
CONEY, Kim C. . . . . (NY) 236
FRANKE, Gail E. . . . . . . (NY) 397
KAZANJIAN, Donna S. . . (NY) 632
LANDOLFI, Lisa M. . . . . (NY) 693
LILLY, Elise M. . . . . (NY) 727
RALBOVSKY, Edward A. (NY) 1004
SHALLENBERGER, Anna
F. . . . . (NY) 1119
SHAPIRO, Fred R. . . . . . (NY) 1121
STIEVATER, Susan M. . . (NY) 1194
WOFSE, Joy G. . . . . (NY) 1359
BOWIE, Angela B. . . . . . (OH) 121
NEYMAN, Sandra B. . . . (OH) 900
WALDEN, Graham R. . . . (OH) 1294
WILKS, Cheri L. . . . . (OH) 1341
MCQUITTY, Jeanette N. . (OK) 817
CABLE, Leslie G. . . . . . . (OR) 170
CHU, John S. . . . . (PA) 212
COOPER, Linda . . . . (PA) 243
CRAWFORD, Gregory A. (PA) 256
HELLER, Patricia A. . . . . (PA) 524

ONLINE SEARCHING (Cont'd)

Online database searching

RICHVALSKY, Neil F.	(PA)	1031
SEABORN, Frances L.	(PA)	1109
TINSLEY, Geraldine L.	(PA)	1246
BRENNAN, Patricia B.	(RI)	133
KING, Evlyn J.	(SC)	651
MCCULLEY, P M.	(SC)	800
SMITH, Stephen C.	(SC)	1161
NORRIS, Carol B.	(TN)	909
PONNAPPA, Biddanda P.	(TN)	982
RAWNSLEY, Virgilia I.	(TN)	1011
CRAIG, Thomas B.	(TX)	254
HENDERSON, Lennijo P.	(TX)	526
LOOS, Carolyn F.	(TX)	740
LOWRY, Andretta G.	(TX)	745
MARLEY, Judith L.	(TX)	772
MITCHE, Cynthia R.	(TX)	848
POWELL, Alan D.	(TX)	987
SPEARS, Norman L.	(TX)	1172
SPECHT, Alice W.	(TX)	1172
GREFE, Richard F.	(VA)	465
REEVES, Lois H.	(VA)	1017
SINWELL, Carol A.	(VA)	1144
JOHNSON, Dana E.	(WA)	603
LOPEZ, Loretta K.	(WA)	741
NELSON, Christine	(WA)	893
TRUPIANO, Rose M.	(WI)	1259
PARIS, Terrence L.	(NS)	940

Online database searching & abstracting

HOYT, Henry M.	(NY)	566

Online database searching & reference

SALM, Kay E.	(CA)	1077

Online database searching & training

WELLS, David B.	(NV)	1322

Online search

BAIN, Janice W.	(FL)	47
LIGHTNER, Karen J.	(PA)	727
LIU, Kitty P.	(UT)	734

Online search analysis

WILLIAMS, Elizabeth L.	(TN)	1343

Online search coordination

PATTON, Linda L.	(FL)	949

Online search, data manipulation

FOURNIER, Susan K.	(MD)	393

Online search reference

DUSABLON-BOTTEGA, Nicole	(PQ)	329

Online search service

PALLARDY, Judy S.	(MO)	935
DORR, Lorna B.	(NC)	313
PENCHANSKY, Mimi B.	(NY)	956

Online search service consulting

KLINGLER, Thomas E.	(OH)	662

Online search services

CLIFFORD, Susan G.	(CA)	222
COMPTON, Lawrence E.	(GA)	235
DICARLO, Michael A.	(LA)	300
HINEGARDNER, Patricia G.	(MD)	542
LARSON, Signe E.	(OR)	700

Online search services development

COCHRANE, Maryjane S.	(VA)	226

Online search systems

SHUMAN, Bruce A.	(MI)	1134

Online search theory

ROBERT, Berring C.	(CA)	1039

Online search training

COCHRANE, Maryjane S.	(VA)	226

Online search training & development

ROBERTS, Sally M.	(IL)	1041

Online searcher

EWING, Alison L.	(AZ)	359
CRAMPON, Jean E.	(CA)	255
ARSENAULT, Patricia A.	(MA)	35
FITZPATRICK, Nancy C.	(MI)	383
DARNOWSKI, Christina M.	(NY)	275
NEUBERG, Karen S.	(NY)	897
RONDESTVEDT, Helen F.	(TN)	1053
PHILLIPS, Toni M.	(TX)	969
FISHER, Rita C.	(WA)	381
MCNALLY, Brian D.	(NB)	815

Online searcher training

KLINGLER, Thomas E.	(OH)	662

Online searchers

WILLOUGHBY, Nona C.	(NY)	1349

Online searches

EMMICK, Nancy J.	(CA)	348
GREEN, Carol A.	(ID)	461
PEPLOW, Richard C.	(IL)	958
SONDALLE, Barbara J.	(IL)	1167
GOEL, Krishan S.	(MD)	443

Online searches for NEXIS

BURROWS, Shirley	(NY)	163

Online searching

PINNELL-STEPHENS, June A.	(AK)	975
DABBS, Mary L.	(AL)	269
FIELD, Kathy M.	(AL)	375
FOREMAN, Anne P.	(AL)	390

ONLINE SEARCHING (Cont'd)

Online searching

LAUGHLIN, Steven G.	(AL)	703
AWE, Susan C.	(AZ)	42
BIGLIN, Karen E.	(AZ)	96
COLE, Mitzi M.	(AZ)	231
FEAZEL, Edythe J.	(AZ)	367
FORE, Janet S.	(AZ)	390
GILREATH, Charles L.	(AZ)	437
JOSEPHINE, Helen B.	(AZ)	617
MACHOVEC, George S.	(AZ)	755
MAUTNER, Robert W.	(AZ)	787
MEAD, Thomas L.	(AZ)	819
MOUNT, Jack D.	(AZ)	873
MULVIHILL, Joann	(AZ)	878
STEEL, Virginia	(AZ)	1183
STEWART, Douglas J.	(AZ)	1192
WELLIK, Kay E.	(AZ)	1321
ADAMS, Linda L.	(CA)	5
BAGBY, Felicia R.	(CA)	45
BERGMAN, Emily A.	(CA)	86
BERRING, Robert C.	(CA)	90
BIDWELL, Lynne H.	(CA)	95
BRUNDAGE, Christina A.	(CA)	150
CHAMPLIN, Peggy	(CA)	198
CHICK, Cynthia L.	(CA)	208
CLARENCE, Judy	(CA)	216
CONNELL, William S.	(CA)	237
CRANFORD, Theodore N.	(CA)	255
DEBOER, Kee K.	(CA)	284
DUBOIS, Henry J.	(CA)	322
DUZAK, Sandra J.	(CA)	330
GEBHARD, Patricia	(CA)	424
GERSTLE, Steven M.	(CA)	429
HAMOR, Monica E.	(CA)	494
HARMON, Robert B.	(CA)	502
JUNG, Soon J.	(CA)	620
KANJI, Zainab J.	(CA)	625
KENNEDY, Charlene F.	(CA)	640
KIEFER, Karen N.	(CA)	647
KINNELL, Susan K.	(CA)	653
KLEINER, Donna H.	(CA)	660
LEWARK, Kathryn W.	(CA)	722
LEWIS, Cookie A.	(CA)	722
LINDEN, Margaret J.	(CA)	729
LONDON, Glenn S.	(CA)	738
MACEK, Rosanne M.	(CA)	755
MARKS, Larry	(CA)	771
MASON, Elsbeth S.	(CA)	781
MAYES, Elizabeth A.	(CA)	789
MIELKE, Marsha K.	(CA)	833
MULLEN, Cecilia P.	(CA)	877
NEWCOMBE, Barbara T.	(CA)	898
OLMSTEAD, Nancy L.	(CA)	921
OPPENHEIM, Michael R.	(CA)	925
PARISE, Marina P.	(CA)	940
POST, Linda C.	(CA)	986
RAZE, Nasus B.	(CA)	1012
ROBINSON, Doris T.	(CA)	1044
ROCKMAN, Ilene F.	(CA)	1046
ROSS, Mary A.	(CA)	1058
SAWYER, Anne R.	(CA)	1086
SHANMAN, Roberta	(CA)	1120
SHARP, Linda F.	(CA)	1122
STANEK, Suzanne	(CA)	1179
STEINMANN, Lois S.	(CA)	1186
THELIN, Sonya R.	(CA)	1234
VARAT, Nancy L.	(CA)	1278
WALTERS, Roberta J.	(CA)	1301
WATSON, Benjamin	(CA)	1309
WEEDMAN, Judith	(CA)	1315
WIBLE, Joseph G.	(CA)	1335
WILLARD, Ann M.	(CA)	1341
YANEZ, Elva K.	(CA)	1377
ZEBROWSKI, Cheryl K.	(CA)	1387
ERNEST, Douglas J.	(CO)	353
KRISMANN, Carol H.	(CO)	678
MALYSHEV, Nina A.	(CO)	764
MATTINGLY, Debra B.	(CO)	786
NELSON, Marie L.	(CO)	894

ONLINE SEARCHING (Cont'd)
Online searching

REITER, Ellie W. . . . . . . (CO) 1022
SMITH, Sallye W. . . . . . . (CO) 1160
SZABO, Kathleen S. . . . . (CO) 1218
WATTERSON, Jane L. . . (CO) 1310
HAAG, Nancy R. . . . . . . (CT) 480
HERMAN, Felicia G. . . . . (CT) 531
JUKNIS, Ann M. . . . . (CT) 619
KRITEMEYER, Ann C. . . (CT) 679
MCKINNEY, Linda R. . . . (CT) 812
MCPHERSON, Mary A. . (CT) 817
NATALE, Barbara G. . . . . (CT) 889
PIERCE, Anne L. . . . . . . (CT) 971
ROGERS, Mary E. . . . . . (CT) 1050
WENDELL, Florence P. . (CT) 1323
WIEHN, John F. . . . . (CT) 1336
BANKS, Jane L. . . . . (DC) 54
BATES, Mary E. . . . . (DC) 64
BERNSTEIN, Lee S. . . . . (DC) 89
CARLSON, Julia F. . . . . (DC) 182
CHASE, Linda S. . . . . . . (DC) 203
CHURCHVILLE, Lida H. . (DC) 213
CILIBERTI, Nancy A. . . . (DC) 214
CLEMMER, Dan O. . . . . (DC) 221
COLETTI, Jeannette D. . . (DC) 231
DOUMATO, Lamia . . . . . (DC) 314
FELDMAN, Ellen S. . . . . (DC) 369
FLAM, Floris . . . . (DC) 383
JOHNSON, Elaine B. . . . (DC) 604
LANE, Elizabeth S. . . . . . (DC) 694
MODLIN, Marilyn J. . . . . (DC) 851
PICCIANO, Laura . . . . . . (DC) 970
RADUAZO, Dorothy M. . (DC) 1002
SARANGAPANI, Chetluru (DC) 1082
SCHNEIDER, Hennie R. . (DC) 1097
SWEETLAND, Loraine F. (DC) 1215
SYLVESTER, Carol . . . . (DC) 1217
TABER, Sally A. . . . . (DC) 1219
TAYLOR, Joan R. . . . . . . (DC) 1227
VAN SYCKLE, Georgiana (DC) 1277
JOHNSON, Hilary C. . . . (DE) 605
PIFALO, Victoria . . . . . . (DE) 972
THORNTON, Alice J. . . . (DE) 1242
WOLFF, Stephen G. . . . . (DE) 1361
ATKINS, Donna A. . . . . . (FL) 37
BARTHE, Margaret R. . . (FL) 61
BATTISTE, Anita L. . . . . (FL) 65
BECKNER, Barbara J. . . (FL) 73
BILAL, Dania M. . . . . (FL) 96
CATES, Jo A. . . . . (FL) 194
COHEN, Kathleen F. . . . . (FL) 228
GEBET, Russell W. . . . . (FL) 424
HAYES, L S. . . . . (FL) 516
HOLLMANN, Pauline V. . (FL) 552
HUDSON, Phyllis J. . . . . (FL) 569
LITTON, Sally C. . . . . . . (FL) 734
MAHAN, Cheryl A. . . . . . (FL) 760
PELLEN, Rita M. . . . . . . (FL) 955
PFARRER, Theodore R. . (FL) 966
PINTOZZI, Chestalene . . (FL) 975
TEW, Robin L. . . . . (FL) 1233
TIPPLE, Roberta L. . . . . (FL) 1246
TOOLE, Gregor K. . . . . . (FL) 1250
TORNABENE, Charles . . (FL) 1251
WOODS, Susan E. . . . . . (FL) 1367
BANJA, Judith A. . . . . . . (GA) 54
BAUSCH, Donna K. . . . . (GA) 67
CANN, Sharon F. . . . . . . (GA) 178
CASSELL, Judy A. . . . . . (GA) 193
COFFMAN, Joseph W. . . (GA) 227
CRAWFORD, Sherrida J. (GA) 257
FARMER, Nancy R. . . . . (GA) 364
GRELL, Holly J. . . . . (GA) 467
GUERIN, Roberta T. . . . . (GA) 476
MENEELY, William E. . . (GA) 824
MORELAND, Virginia F. . (GA) 863
NITSCHKE, Eric R. . . . . (GA) 905
PAULK, Betty D. . . . . . . (GA) 950
PAULK, Sara L. . . . . (GA) 950

ONLINE SEARCHING (Cont'd)
Online searching

STAHL, D G. . . . . (GA) 1178
STATOM, Susan T. . . . . (GA) 1183
THAXTON, Lyn . . . . (GA) 1234
TOMAJKO, Kathy L. . . . . (GA) 1249
WHEELER, Carol L. . . . . (GA) 1328
WRIGHT, Dianne H. . . . . (GA) 1371
BEVERIDGE, Mary I. . . . (IA) 93
CLARK, Maeve K. . . . . . (IA) 217
ENGEL, Kevin R. . . . . . . (IA) 348
HOEVEN, Helen D. . . . . . (IA) 547
SHAW, James T. . . . . . . (IA) 1123
TYCKOSON, David A. . . . (IA) 1266
ANDERSON, Charles R. . (IL) 22
BEAN, Janet R. . . . . (IL) 69
BLAKE, Martha A. . . . . . (IL) 103
BROWN, Patricia L. . . . . (IL) 146
CAREY, Kevin J. . . . . . . (IL) 181
CARNELLI, Sandra R. . . (IL) 183
CIBULSKIS, Elizabeth R. (IL) 214
COLLINS, Janet . . . . (IL) 232
CZARNECKI, Cary J. . . . (IL) 268
FIELD, Connie N. . . . . . . (IL) 375
GIANGRANDE, Mark G. . (IL) 430
HANRATH, Linda C. . . . . (IL) 497
HUANG, Samuel T. . . . . (IL) 568
HURD, Julie M. . . . . (IL) 577
JOHNSON, Charlotte L. . (IL) 603
JUSTICE, Sylvia H. . . . . (IL) 620
KELLER, Steven W. . . . . (IL) 636
LEVIN, Joan E. . . . . (IL) 720
MARECEK, Robert J. . . . (IL) 770
MICHAEL, Ann B. . . . . . (IL) 831
MOULTON, James C. . . . (IL) 873
MUELLER, Julie M. . . . . (IL) 875
NIELSEN, Brian . . . . (IL) 903
ONGLEY, David C. . . . . . (IL) 924
OSGOOD, James B. . . . . (IL) 928
PENKA, Carol B. . . . . . . (IL) 956
PICKETT, Mary J. . . . . . (IL) 970
ROOSE, Tina . . . . (IL) 1053
ROTT, Richard A. . . . . . . (IL) 1060
SENN, Mary S. . . . . (IL) 1115
SHAW, Debora . . . . (IL) 1123
SLAWNIAK, Patricia M. . (IL) 1148
SPARKS, Joanne L. . . . . (IL) 1171
STUNKARD, Gilbert L. . . (IL) 1205
SVENSSON, C G. . . . . . (IL) 1212
SWANSON, Don R. . . . . (IL) 1213
TAN, Elizabeth L. . . . . . . (IL) 1222
TEGLER, Patricia . . . . . . (IL) 1230
WALLACE, Richard E. . . (IL) 1298
WELCH, Eric C. . . . . (IL) 1321
WHITNEY, Ruth . . . . (IL) 1334
BAUMGARTNER, Kurt O. (IN) 66
BERTRAM, Lee A. . . . . . (IN) 91
BONNER, Robert J. . . . . (IN) 114
BROWN, Sandra S. . . . . (IN) 147
CORBETT, Ann L. . . . . . (IN) 245
ELLSWORTH, Marlene A. (IN) 345
ENSOR, Pat L. . . . . (IN) 350
GALOW, Donald G. . . . . (IN) 415
GRIFFITTS, Joan K. . . . . (IN) 469
MEEK, Janet E. . . . . (IN) 821
MEYER, Ellen R. . . . . . . (IN) 830
MILLER, Constance R. . . (IN) 836
MILLER, Jeanne L. . . . . . (IN) 839
MITCHELL, Cynthia E. . . (IN) 848
MUSTO, Frederick W. . . (IN) 883
OGLES, Lynn C. . . . . . . (IN) 918
RIES, Steven T. . . . . (IN) 1033
SUTHERLAND, Timothy L. (IN) 1211
VAN CAMP, Ann J. . . . . (IN) 1272
WIGGINS, Gary D. . . . . . (IN) 1337
ZIMMERMAN, Brenda M. (IN) 1388
CARVER, Jane W. . . . . . (KS) 191
COFFEE, E G. . . . . (KS) 226
DRESSLER, Alta L. . . . . (KS) 319
LAUFFER, Donna J. . . . . (KS) 702

ONLINE SEARCHING (Cont'd)
Online searching

ROTH, Sally . . . . (KS) 1059
VUKAS, Rachel R. . . . . . (KS) 1290
WAY, Harold E. . . . . (KS) 1311
WILDE, Lucy E. . . . . (KS) 1338
WILLIAMS, Brian W. . . . . (KS) 1342
BARRISH, Alan S. . . . . . (KY) 60
PRIOR, Barbara Q. . . . . . (KY) 993
PRITCHARD, Elsie T. . . . (KY) 994
WALL, Celia J. . . . . (KY) 1297
WILEY, Theresa K. . . . . . (KY) 1339
WILLIAMS, Helen E. . . . (KY) 1343
FLEURY, Mary E. . . . . . . (LA) 385
HANKEL, Marilyn L. . . . . (LA) 496
MARIX, Mary L. . . . . (LA) 770
MAXSTADT, John M. . . . (LA) 788
WOJKOWSKI, Suhad K. (LA) 1359
CAIN, Susan H. . . . . (MA) 171
CARNAHAN, Paul A. . . . (MA) 183
COLLINS, John W. . . . . (MA) 232
COOPER WYMAN,
    Rosalind . . . . (MA) 244
COPPOLA, H P. . . . . (MA) 245
COPPOLA, Peter A. . . . . (MA) 245
DAVIS, Barbara M. . . . . . (MA) 277
DENTON, Francesca L. . . (MA) 293
GELB, Linda . . . . (MA) 425
HARZBECKER, Joseph J. (MA) 510
ISAACS, Cynthia W. . . . (MA) 584
MAST, Susan B. . . . . . . (MA) 782
METCALF, Marjorie . . . . (MA) 828
MURRAY, Lynn T. . . . . . (MA) 882
NELSON, Margaret R. . . (MA) 894
PICCININO, Rocco . . . . . (MA) 970
PLUNKET, Linda . . . . . . (MA) 979
PREVE, Roberta J. . . . . . (MA) 992
RIVARD, Timothy D. . . . . (MA) 1037
ROSENBERG, Barbra E. (MA) 1055
ROTMAN, Laurie D. . . . . (MA) 1060
RUTTER, Nancy R. . . . . (MA) 1070
SCHUELER, Dolores . . . (MA) 1101
SCHWARTZ, Candy S. . . (MA) 1104
WASOWICZ, Laura E. . . (MA) 1308
ALEXANDER, Estelle R. . (MD) 12
ANDREWS, Loretta K. . . (MD) 26
BOGAGE, Alan R. . . . . . (MD) 110
BOURKOFF, Vivienne R. (MD) 119
FELDMAN, Eleanor C. . . (MD) 369
HOOFNAGLE, Bettea J. . (MD) 556
KLEIN, Ilene R. . . . . (MD) 659
KOSMIN, Linda J. . . . . . (MD) 672
KRUSE, Kathryn W. . . . . (MD) 681
MOLTER, Maureen M. . . (MD) 853
PEARSE, Nancy J. . . . . . (MD) 952
PERKINS, Earle R. . . . . . (MD) 959
RAFATS, Jerome M. . . . (MD) 1003
SCHWARTZ, Betsy J. . . . (MD) 1104
WILLIAMS, Mary A. . . . . (MD) 1345
BAKER, Alison . . . . (ME) 47
WHITE, Lucinda M. . . . . (ME) 1331
ACKERMAN, Katherine K. (MI) 4
BENNETT, Christine H. . . (MI) 81
BRYANT, Barton B. . . . . (MI) 152
CONWAY, Michael J. . . . (MI) 239
HERBST, Linda R. . . . . . (MI) 530
JAZBINSCHEK, Jerri . . . (MI) 596
SCHAAFSMA, Roberta A. (MI) 1088
SIEVING, Pamela C. . . . . (MI) 1136
VANDERLAAN, Sharon J. (MI) 1274
WOJCIKIEWICZ, Carol A. (MI) 1359
YARBROUGH, Joseph W. (MI) 1378
BARRETT, Darryl D. . . . . (MN) 59
HAASE, Gretchen E. . . . (MN) 480
HOLT, Constance W. . . . (MN) 554
OLSEN, Stephen . . . . . . (MN) 922
OUSE, David J. . . . . (MN) 930
SINHA, Dorothy P. . . . . . (MN) 1143
BARNES, Everett W. . . . (MO) 57
BHULLAR, Pushpajit D. . (MO) 93

ONLINE SEARCHING (Cont'd)
Online searching

ELS, Nancy T. . . . . (MO) 346
FREEMAN, C L. . . . . (MO) 400
GAFFEY, Mary V. . . . . . (MO) 411
GINGRICH, Linda K. . . . . (MO) 437
HIBBELER, Sara J. . . . . (MO) 536
HUBBLE, Gerald B. . . . . (MO) 568
JOSEPH, Miriam E. . . . . (MO) 617
MOORE, Barbara S. . . . . (MO) 858
RILEY, Ruth A. . . . . (MO) 1034
SMITH, Valerie K. . . . . . (MO) 1161
STEVENS, Robert R. . . . (MO) 1191
STEWART, J A. . . . . (MO) 1192
TIMBERLAKE, Patricia P. (MO) 1245
VERBECK, Alison F. . . . . (MO) 1282
VOSS, Kathryn J. . . . . . . (MO) 1289
WITTIG, Glenn R. . . . . . (MS) 1358
ADAMS, Elizabeth L. . . . (NC) 4
ANTONE, Allen L. . . . . . (NC) 29
COLLINS, Donald E. . . . . (NC) 232
FRANK, Linda V. . . . . . . (NC) 397
HEBERT, Robert A. . . . . (NC) 519
MCKAY, Alberta S. . . . . (NC) 809
MIDDLETON, Beverly D. (NC) 833
MILLER, Barry K. . . . . . . (NC) 836
MINEIRO, Barbara E. . . . (NC) 845
NYE, Julie B. . . . . (NC) 912
SEGAL, Jane D. . . . . (NC) 1111
SKLADANOWSKI,
    Lawrence M. . . . . . . (NC) 1146
SUMMERFORD, Steven L. (NC) 1209
WHITE, Sherry J. . . . . . . (NC) 1332
EGBERS, Gail L. . . . . . . (NE) 339
GENDLER, Carol J. . . . . (NE) 426
LU, Janet C. . . . . (NE) 745
BERTHIAUME, Dennis A. (NH) 90
BECK, Susan J. . . . . (NJ) 72
DEDERT, Patricia L. . . . . (NJ) 286
DE WITT, Benjamin L. . . (NJ) 298
DOUGLASS, Leslie A. . . (NJ) 314
FRIEDMAN, Ruth . . . . . . (NJ) 404
GENTNER, Claudia A. . . (NJ) 427
GEORGE, Muriel S. . . . . (NJ) 428
HAWKINS, Donald T. . . . (NJ) 514
HUTCHINSON, Barbara J. (NJ) 579
JONES, Anita M. . . . . . . (NJ) 610
KORNFELD, Carol E. . . . (NJ) 672
MALAKOFF, Diane L. . . . (NJ) 762
MARTINEZ, Jane A. . . . . (NJ) 779
PAWSON, Robert D. . . . (NJ) 951
RANDALL, Lynn E. . . . . (NJ) 1006
REESE, Carol H. . . . . . . (NJ) 1016
RIHACEK, Karen S. . . . . (NJ) 1034
ROSENSTEIN, Susan J. . (NJ) 1057
SCOTT, Miranda D. . . . . (NJ) 1107
STEPIEN, Karen K. . . . . (NJ) 1189
TALAR, Anita . . . . (NJ) 1220
TIEDRICH, Ellen K. . . . . (NJ) 1244
VLOYANETES, Jeanne M. (NJ) 1286
ZIMMERMAN, Elisabeth K. (NJ) 1388
RICHARD, Harris M. . . . . (NM) 1027
ABBITT, Viola I. . . . . (NY) 1
BARTH, John E. . . . . (NY) 61
BENSON, James A. . . . . (NY) 83
BERGER, Paula E. . . . . . (NY) 86
BURNS, Violanda O. . . . (NY) 163
BUSTAMANTE, Corazon
    R. . . . . (NY) 166
COMEAU, Amy R. . . . . . (NY) 234
DAVIS, Robert J. . . . . . . (NY) 280
DEGOLYER, Christine C. (NY) 288
DENOTO, Dorothy E. . . . (NY) 293
ESWORTHY, Lori L. . . . . (NY) 355
FORD, George H. . . . . . . (NY) 389
GIGLIOTTI, Mary J. . . . . (NY) 433
GOODHARTZ, Gerald . . (NY) 448
GROSS, Gretchen . . . . . (NY) 472
HAND, Sally C. . . . . (NY) 494
HANE, Paula J. . . . . (NY) 495

ONLINE SEARCHING (Cont'd)
Online searching

HRYVNIAK, Joseph T. . . (NY) 567
JOHNSON, Steven P. . . (NY) 609
KNAPP, Sara D. . . . . (NY) 663
LAUER, Jonathan D. . . . . (NY) 702
LOCASCIO, Aline M. . . . (NY) 735
MACKSEY, Susan A. . . . (NY) 757
MANNING, Jo A. . . . . . . (NY) 766
MCGRATH, Antoinette M. (NY) 807
MUSKUS, Elizabeth A. . . . (NY) 883
NARCISO, Susan D. . . . (NY) 888
PILACHOWSKI, David M. . (NY) 973
PISTILLI, Susan A. . . . . . (NY) 976
RIECHEL, Rosemarie . . . (NY) 1033
RIGNEY, Shirley A. . . . . (NY) 1034
ROOT, Christine . . . . (NY) 1053
ROSEN, Nathan A. . . . . . (NY) 1055
RUBINO, Cynthia C. . . . . (NY) 1065
SEER, Gitelle . . . . (NY) 1111
SEULOWITZ, Lois . . . . . . (NY) 1117
SLOAN, Carol L. . . . . . . (NY) 1149
SMITH, Marian J. . . . . . . (NY) 1157
STEWART, Linda G. . . . (NY) 1192
STRAM, Lynn R. . . . . . . (NY) 1200
STRIFE, Mary L. . . . . . . (NY) 1202
SUTHERLAND-NEHRING,
    Laurie A. . . . . (NY) 1211
SVENNINGSEN, Karen L. (NY) 1212
THOM, Janice E. . . . . . . (NY) 1235
TUOHEY, Jeanne D. . . . . (NY) 1263
WAGNER, A B. . . . . (NY) 1291
WAHLERT, George A. . . (NY) 1292
WALKER, M G. . . . . (NY) 1296
WALSH, Daniel P. . . . . . (NY) 1299
WELLS, Margaret R. . . . . (NY) 1322
WESTERLING, Mary L. . . (NY) 1327
WILLER, Kenneth H. . . . (NY) 1341
WILLIAMS, David W. . . . (NY) 1342
WINDSOR, Donald A. . . (NY) 1354
BLANCHARD, Mark A. . . (OH) 103
BORUCKI, Jennifer A. . . . (OH) 117
BOX, Krista J. . . . . (OH) 122
BRANCHICK, Susan E. . . (OH) 127
BRANDT, Michael H. . . . (OH) 128
BROWN, Stephen P. . . . (OH) 147
CLARK, Kay S. . . . . (OH) 217
DUDLEY, Durand S. . . . . (OH) 323
GREEN, Denise D. . . . . . (OH) 461
HECHT, Judith N. . . . . . . (OH) 519
HELLING, James T. . . . . (OH) 524
HODGES, Pauline R. . . . (OH) 546
JARABEK, Leona T. . . . . (OH) 594
KLINGLER, Thomas E. . . (OH) 662
KOBULNICKY, Michael . (OH) 666
MERCADO, Heidi . . . . . . (OH) 825
MILLER, Clayton M. . . . . (OH) 836
MONTAG, John . . . . (OH) 855
NASRALLAH, Wahib T. . (OH) 888
OLSZEWSKI, Lawrence J. (OH) 923
PIETY, John S. . . . . (OH) 972
PRYSZLAK, Lydia M. . . . (OH) 996
ROHMILLER, Thomas D. (OH) 1051
SANDULEAK, Barbara . . (OH) 1081
SCHLOMAN, Barbara F. (OH) 1094
SKUTNIK, John S. . . . . . (OH) 1147
STROZIER, Sandra L. . . (OH) 1203
VARMA, Valsamani . . . . (OH) 1278
WARNER, Susan B. . . . . (OH) 1305
BATT, Fred . . . . (OK) 64
GUTIERREZ, Carolyn A. . (OK) 479
ROBERTS, Linda L. . . . . (OK) 1041
FRANTZ, Paul A. . . . . . . (OR) 398
HENDERSON, Carol G. . (OR) 526
HORAN, Patricia F. . . . . (OR) 559
RASH, David W. . . . . . . (OR) 1009
SHAVER, Donna B. . . . . (OR) 1123
SLOAN, Maureen G. . . . (OR) 1149
ALDRIDGE, Carol J. . . . . (PA) 11
AL SADAT, Amira A. . . . (PA) 17

ONLINE SEARCHING (Cont'd)
Online searching

ANDRILLI, Ene M. . . . . . (PA) 27
BECKER, Linda C. . . . . . (PA) 72
BELANGER, David L. . . . (PA) 75
BENGALI, Zarin P. . . . . . (PA) 80
BURSTEIN, Karen . . . . . (PA) 164
BURTON, Cynthia R. . . . (PA) 164
CARTULARO, Teresa C. . (PA) 190
DEEGAN, Rosemary L. . . (PA) 286
ENDRES, Maureen D. . . . (PA) 348
EPSTEIN, Barbara A. . . . (PA) 351
ERDREICH, Gina B. . . . . (PA) 352
FARREN, Ann L. . . . . . . (PA) 365
FEDRICK, Mary A. . . . . . (PA) 368
FENICHEL, Carol H. . . . . (PA) 371
FILLER, Mary A. . . . . . . (PA) 377
FUCHS, Karola M. . . . . . (PA) 408
GREEN, Patricia L. . . . . . (PA) 462
HESP, Judith A. . . . . (PA) 534
JUDGE, Joseph M. . . . . . (PA) 619
KASPERKO, Jean M. . . . (PA) 629
KIRCHER, Linda M. . . . . (PA) 654
KLEIN, Joanne S. . . . . . . (PA) 659
LINDBERG, Richard L. . . (PA) 728
LYONS, Evelyn L. . . . . . (PA) 753
MARLOW, Kathryn E. . . . (PA) 772
MERRIAM, Doris E. . . . . (PA) 826
MINES, Denise C. . . . . . (PA) 846
MORGANTI, Deena J. . . (PA) 864
POLITIS, John V. . . . . . . (PA) 981
QUINTILIANO, Barbara . (PA) 1000
RIDGEWAY, Patricia M. . (PA) 1032
RITTENHOUSE, Robert J. (PA) 1036
SAXMAN, Susan E. . . . . (PA) 1086
SCHREIBER-COIA,
    Barbara J. . . . . (PA) 1099
SENECAL, Kristin S. . . . (PA) 1115
STESIS, Karen R. . . . . . (PA) 1189
STRAWBRIDGE, Donna L. (PA) 1201
SWARTZ, Patrice B. . . . (PA) 1214
WAGNER, Darla L. . . . . . (PA) 1291
WEINER, Betty . . . . (PA) 1318
WEINGRAM, Ida . . . . . . (PA) 1318
WILLIAMSON, Susan G. (PA) 1348
WOOD, M S. . . . . (PA) 1364
WOODRUFF, William M. (PA) 1366
MAURA-SARDO, Mariano
    A. . . . . (PR) 787
CAMERON, Constance B. (RI) 174
KRAUSSE, Sylvia C. . . . (RI) 676
SHERIDAN, Jean . . . . . . (RI) 1127
SIEBURTH, Janice F. . . . (RI) 1135
CROSS, Joseph R. . . . . . (SC) 260
HOLLEY, E J. . . . . (SC) 551
SCHMITT, John P. . . . . . (SC) 1096
SILVERMAN, Susan M. . (SC) 1139
WEATHERS, Virginia W. (SC) 1312
WILLIAMS, Betty H. . . . . (SC) 1342
CASPERS, Mary E. . . . . (SD) 193
HALLMAN, Clark N. . . . . (SD) 489
ARMONTROUT, Brian A. (TN) 32
BURN, Harry T. . . . . (TN) 161
EKKEBUS, Allen E. . . . . (TN) 341
MABBOTT, Deborah D. . (TN) 753
MADER, Sharon B. . . . . (TN) 759
PARK, Elizabeth H. . . . . (TN) 941
PRESLAR, M G. . . . . . . (TN) 991
SCHER, Rita S. . . . . (TN) 1092
WALKER, Mary E. . . . . . (TN) 1296
ANDERSON, Margaret . . (TX) 24
BEAN, Norma P. . . . . . . (TX) 69
BELL, Joy A. . . . . (TX) 77
CASTO, Lisa A. . . . . (TX) 194
COTTER, Stacy L. . . . . . (TX) 250
DUFFY, Suzanne . . . . . . (TX) 324
FLESHMAN, Nancy A. . . (TX) 384
GARCIA, Beatriz H. . . . . (TX) 417
HOLAB-ABELMAN, Robin
    S. . . . . (TX) 550

ONLINE SEARCHING (Cont'd)
Online searching

KONDRASKE, Linda N.	(TX)	670
OGDEN, William S.	(TX)	918
PEDERSEN, Wayne A.	(TX)	954
PELOQUIN, Margaret I.	(TX)	955
SCHRAEDER, Diana C.	(TX)	1099
SHARP, Charlotte J.	(TX)	1122
SHEA, Kathleen	(TX)	1124
SUDENGA, Sara A.	(TX)	1206
TEVEBAUGH, Joyce E.	(TX)	1233
WESTBROOK, Brenda S.	(TX)	1326
WHITTLESEY, Jane M.	(TX)	1334
WILBUR, Sharon F.	(TX)	1338
HINDMARSH, Douglas P.	(UT)	542
LAMB, Connie	(UT)	689
MORRISON, David L.	(UT)	868
NOEL, Eileen V.	(UT)	907
REED, Vernon M.	(UT)	1015
YANG, Basil P.	(UT)	1377
CAHILL, Linda J.	(VA)	171
CARR, Timothy B.	(VA)	186
CASH, Susan R.	(VA)	192
CHRISTOLON, Blair B.	(VA)	212
GILL, Gerald L.	(VA)	435
HAUSMAN, Patricia R.	(VA)	513
HINKLE, Mary R.	(VA)	542
HURD, Douglas P.	(VA)	577
KNIGHT, Nancy H.	(VA)	664
POLLOCK, Ethel L.	(VA)	981
PRETLOW, Delores Z.	(VA)	992
SELLIN, Jon B.	(VA)	1114
STARR, Marian U.	(VA)	1182
STEIN, Karen E.	(VA)	1185
LEE, Donna K.	(VT)	709
JEWELL, Timothy D.	(WA)	600
PRITCHARD, Jackie L.	(WA)	994
RICIGLIANO, Lorraine M.	(WA)	1031
SLIVKA, Enid M.	(WA)	1149
VYHNANEK, Louis	(WA)	1290
ALLSOP, Mary B.	(WI)	17
COSTELLO, Janice M.	(WI)	249
DIETZ, Kathryn A.	(WI)	302
KELLY, Barbara J.	(WI)	637
LIVNY, Efrat	(WI)	735
SCHMIDT, Mary A.	(WI)	1095
POWELL, Ruth A.	(WV)	988
NELSON, Michael L.	(WY)	894
DEGINNUS, Roxie	(AB)	287
DROESSLER, Judith B.	(AB)	320
GASHUS, Karin C.	(AB)	421
GEE, Sharon	(AB)	425
KUJANSUU, Sylvia S.	(AB)	683
LANE, Barbara K.	(AB)	694
REICHARDT, Randall P.	(AB)	1018
WAUGH, Alan L.	(AB)	1310
MAROTZ, Karen V.	(BC)	772
PEPPER, David A.	(BC)	958
PITERNICK, Anne B.	(BC)	976
SAINT, Barbara J.	(BC)	1075
BLANCHARD, Jim	(MB)	103
MARSHALL, Kenneth E.	(MB)	774
ROUTLEDGE, Patricia A.	(MB)	1062
MORASH, Claire E.	(NS)	862
BAYNE, Jennifer M.	(ON)	67
BELL, Hope A.	(ON)	77
BERNSTEIN, Elaine S.	(ON)	89
BOWEN, Tom G.	(ON)	120
CASEY, Victoria L.	(ON)	192
DANCE, Barbara L.	(ON)	272
GALSWORTHY, Peter R.	(ON)	415
GOLD, Sandra	(ON)	444
GRANATSTEIN, M E.	(ON)	457
JOHNSON, John E.	(ON)	606
JUOZAPAVICIUS, Danguole T.	(ON)	620
KORNUTA, Helen	(ON)	672
LARSON, Anna M.	(ON)	699
LEONARDO, Joan M.	(ON)	717
MACDONALD, Patricia A.	(ON)	754

ONLINE SEARCHING (Cont'd)
Online searching

MITCHELL, Faye F.	(ON)	848
MORRISON, Carol A.	(ON)	868
NEILL, Sharon E.	(ON)	892
O'NEILL, Louise N.	(ON)	924
PAL, Gabriel	(ON)	935
RODGER, Jane	(ON)	1047
RUSSELL, Moira	(ON)	1069
SHIP, Martin I.	(ON)	1131
URQUHART, Dawn M.	(ON)	1270
WALLACE, Kathryn M.	(ON)	1297
WELLS, Nancy E.	(ON)	1322
APPLEBY, Judith A.	(PQ)	30
BIELLE, Christian P.	(PQ)	95
CANTIN, Gemma	(PQ)	179
CHAGNON, Danielle G.	(PQ)	197
DESCHATELETS, Gilles H.	(PQ)	294
DUMONT, Monique	(PQ)	325
GAMEIRO, Maria H.	(PQ)	416
GARDNER, Lucie	(PQ)	418
GARNETT, Joyce C.	(PQ)	419
GREGOIRE, Fleurette	(PQ)	466
LEMYRE, Nicole	(PQ)	715
MACFARLANE, Judy A.	(PQ)	755
MAHARAJ, Diana J.	(PQ)	760
RICHARD, Marc	(PQ)	1028
SMYTH, John	(PQ)	1162
TREVICK, Selma D.	(PQ)	1255
TRUDEL, Florian	(PQ)	1259
VONKA, Stephanie	(PQ)	1288
WADE, C A.	(PQ)	1290
VANDER LAAN, Lubbert	(SK)	1274
MIRABELLI, Gerardo	(CSR)	847
SANDFELDER, Paula M.	(HKG)	1080
ELAZAR, David H.	(ISR)	341
TWEEDALE, Dellene M.	(NZD)	1266
MARTIN, Nannette	(SDA)	777

Online searching & automation	STERN, David	(IL)	1189
	SIEGERT, Lindy E.	(NS)	1136
Online searching & biblgph retrieval	KING, Hannah M.	(DC)	651
Online searching & business databases	MICKEY, Melissa B.	(IL)	833
Online searching & computer applications	RANKIN, Carol A.	(NY)	1007
Online searching & consulting	CUEVAS, John R.	(CA)	263
Online searching & databases	COCHRANE, Maryjane S.	(VA)	226
Online searching & education	SCHROEDER, Eileen E.	(NY)	1100
Online searching & end-users	SCHATZ, Cindy A.	(MA)	1090
Online searching & library automation	FU, Ting W.	(HKG)	407
Online searching & management	STANLEY, Jean B.	(OH)	1180
Online searching & management thereof	FISHER, H L.	(CA)	381
Online searching & medical databases	MARTIN, Patricia W.	(MI)	777
Online searching & psychology databases	GOSLING, Carolyn	(VA)	453
Online searching & reference	DAVENPORT, Constance B.	(CA)	275
	HAMMOND, Elizabeth D.	(GA)	493
	COFFEY, James R.	(NJ)	227
	CHUANG, Felicia S.	(TX)	213
	MILLER, Veronica E.	(VI)	843
Online searching & retrieval	COOK, Kathleen M.	(CA)	240
Online searching & search coordination	ROBERTS, Sally M.	(IL)	1041
Online searching & search services	JONES, B E.	(ON)	611
Online searching & services	SCHNEIDER, Stewart P.	(RI)	1097
Online searching & technical database	LEREW, Ann A.	(CO)	717
Online searching & training	SCHWARTZ, Diane G.	(MI)	1104
Online searching behavior	FIDEL, Raya	(WA)	374
Online searching, biomedical literature	INGUI, Bettejean	(CO)	583
Online searching, brokerage, insurance	ENGLISH, Christopher C.	(NJ)	350
Online searching business databases	BRADLEY, Anne	(IL)	125
	ROSTAMI, Janet	(ON)	1059
Online searching, computers	STRAKA, Kathy M.	(CT)	1199
Online searching coordinator	WILKINSON, David W.	(CA)	1340
Online searching, database searching	HURYCH, Jitka M.	(IL)	578

ONLINE SEARCHING (Cont'd)

Online searching databases	KIRBY, Diana G.	(MD)	654
Online searching, DIALOG	GROVES, Helen G.	(TX)	474
Online searching, DIALOG, STN	O'NEILL, Patricia E.	(GA)	924
Online searching education	GOWDY, Laura E.	(IL)	455
	CONWAY, Michael J.	(MI)	239
Online searching, end-user training	KASALKO, Sally G.	(AR)	628
Online searching, engineering	SHLIONSKY, Anatoly	(PQ)	1132
Online searching, engineering databases	LYLE, Martha E.	(SC)	751
Online searching, especially full-text	REIFSNYDER, Betsy S.	(DC)	1020
Online searching for business	LEIGHTON, Victoria C.	(GA)	714
Online searching for general business	ENGLISH, Christopher C.	(NJ)	350
Online searching for medical databases	HILL, Barbarie F.	(OH)	539
Online searching gateways	HORWITZ, Seth	(PA)	561
Online searching, geology	METIVIER, Donna M.	(TX)	828
Online searching in community colleges	BERNHARDT, Frances	(VA)	89
Online searching in medical databases	SHEDLOCK, James	(IL)	1124
Online searching in medicine	TAYLOR, Margaret P.	(ON)	1227
Online searching in schools	CAIN, Carolyn L.	(WI)	171
Online searching legal	WELSH, Eric L.	(VA)	1323
Online searching, medical databases	CRUMP, Joyce A.	(CA)	262
	CESANEK, Sylvia B.	(FL)	196
	QUAIN, Julie R.	(NY)	999
	KRIVDA, Marita J.	(PA)	679
	ROSEN, Gloria K.	(PA)	1055
	FORD, Mary R.	(TX)	389
	KIELLY, Marion J.	(PE)	647
Online searching, MEDLARS databases	SZILARD, Paula	(HI)	1218
Online searching, MEDLINE	SNIDER, Jacqueline I.	(IA)	1163
Online searching, multiple systems	LINCOLN, Carol S.	(KY)	728
Online searching, NLM, DIALOG, BRS	NELSON, Iris N.	(CA)	894
Online searching of business databases	MCDEVITT-PARKS, Kathryn B.	(CA)	802
Online searching of databases	CHAPMAN, Ruby M.	(IL)	202
	MCDERMOTT, Margaret H.	(MO)	802
Online searching of scientific databases	WERT, Lucille M.	(IL)	1325
Online searching of various subjects	LAMPRECHT, Sandra J.	(CA)	691
Online searching reference	MITCHELL, Annmarie D.	(CA)	848
Online searching, school libraries	LATHROP, Ann	(CA)	701
Online searching, science & engineering	WILLS, Luella G.	(VA)	1349
Online searching science databases	WHITE, Larry R.	(CA)	1331
	COONS, William W.	(NY)	242
Online searching science, tech databases	RAEDER, Aggi W.	(CA)	1003
Online searching, scientific databases	MORRIS, Sharon D.	(MD)	867
Online searching services	FALK, Joyce D.	(CA)	362
Online searching, social sciences	GORAL, Miki	(CA)	451
Online searching, systems	LAMBERT, Nancy	(CA)	690
	BROWN, Cynthia D.	(NY)	142
Online searching, teaching, services	STWODAH, M I.	(VA)	1206
Online searching, technical databases	PRESTON, Deirdre R.	(WA)	991
Online searching techniques	SANDERS, Kathryn A.	(AR)	1080
Online searching training	MILLER, Susan E.	(LA)	842
	MOORE, Barbara S.	(MO)	858
	LINCOVE, David A.	(OH)	728
Online searching with students	DANIELS, Ann A.	(IN)	273
Physical scis databases online searching	CARTER, Jackson H.	(NM)	189
Public services, online searching	GILLETTE, Meredith	(WI)	435
Records management & online searching	IRONS, Carol A.	(IL)	584
Reference & online searcher	OSORIO, Nestor L.	(IL)	928
Reference & online searching	PETERMAN, Claudia A.	(CA)	962
	HAMDY, Amira	(CO)	491
	CASSEDY, Barbara S.	(DC)	193
	DOENGES, John C.	(DC)	308
	LOOMIS, Barbara	(IL)	740
	ELLIOTT, Barbara J.	(IN)	343
	DYKMAN, Elaine K.	(NJ)	331
	COHEN, Rosemary C.	(NY)	229

ONLINE SEARCHING (Cont'd)

Reference & online searching	RUTHERFORD, Frederick S.	(ON)	1070
	SCHMIDT, Diana M.	(ON)	1095
Reference, online database searching	MORGAN, Linda M.	(CA)	864
Reference, online searches	SYMES, Dal S.	(WA)	1217
Reference online searching	BENNETT, Michael W.	(CA)	82
	YU, Hsiao M.	(IA)	1384
	MIKOLYZK, Thomas A.	(IL)	834
	WEE, Lily K.	(IL)	1315
	MOSER, Emily F.	(VA)	870
Reference service & online searching	ESTES, Pamela J.	(AR)	355
Reference services & online searching	REID, Valerie L.	(MI)	1019
Science & engineering online searching	BRUNNER, A M.	(TX)	151
Science & medical online searching	LAMANN, Amber N.	(NY)	689
Science & technology online searching	POLLIS, Angela R.	(PA)	981
Scientific & technical online searches	TOMMEY, Richard J.	(CA)	1250
Scientific, technical online searching	ENGLISH, Bernard L.	(NJ)	350
Social sciences online searching	MYERS, Robert C.	(KS)	885
	MOORE, Kathryn L.	(NC)	860
	OSTROWSKY, Edith	(NY)	929
	BULL, Jerry J.	(PQ)	156
Technical & business online searching	DIETRICH, Peter J.	(NY)	302
Technical online searching	HARMON, Patricia A.	(CT)	502
	BOYLE, Stephen	(IL)	124
Tech online searching	PEDERSEN, Dennis C.	(MN)	954
Training for online searchers	HAWK, Susan A.	(MD)	513
Training for online searching	BROWN, Helen A.	(NE)	144
	HORWITZ, Seth	(PA)	561
Training of online search techniques	KAMINECKI, Ronald M.	(IL)	624
User support for online searching	BROWN, Helen A.	(NE)	144

OPAC

OPAC	NEWMAN, Linda D.	(OH)	899

OPERA

Opera	TEUTSCH, Walter	(CA)	1233
Opera & classical discography	COLLINS, William J.	(CA)	233
Opera & vocal music	JELLINEK, George	(NY)	596
Opera history	MOSES, Julian M.	(NY)	871
Opera singers & operatic history	FARKAS, Andrew	(FL)	364
Operas on videocassettes	HEDLUND, Dennis M.	(NJ)	520

OPERATIONS (See also Administration, Management, Organization)

Administrative operations	BRANN, Andrew R.	(OH)	128
All small library operations	ORFIRER, Lenore F.	(CA)	925
Archives administration & operations	ROTHMAN, John	(NY)	1060
Association organization & operation	PARSONS, Augustine C.	(OH)	944
Automation, systems operations	SIMPSON, W S.	(WI)	1142
Bookmobile operation	WIRICK, Terry L.	(PA)	1356
Branch library operations	TREJO-MEEHAN, Tamiye	(IL)	1255
Branch operations	STORCK, Bernadette R.	(FL)	1198
	PINDER, Jo A.	(MD)	974
Business library organization, operation	RABER, Nevin W.	(IN)	1001
Business operations	CLEMENS, Bonnie J.	(GA)	220
	HEATH, Henry H.	(MD)	519
	KEANE, John J.	(PA)	633
CLSI operations	LIGHT, Karen M.	(RI)	726
Computer operating	GAMBLE, Marian L.	(MI)	416
Computer operation	PROSSER, Judith M.	(WV)	995
Computerized library operation	SHIAU, Ian L.	(FL)	1129
Editorial & microform operations	DEL CERVO, Diane M.	(CT)	289
General operations	CLARK, William E.	(MI)	218
General special library operations	NEILSON, Ann	(ON)	892
High school library operations	CHANDRA, Jane H.	(NC)	200
Independent telephone operations	KAPLAN, Rosalyn L.	(IL)	626
Institutional library operation	ELLIOTT, Kay M.	(IA)	344
Library management & operation	CROCKER, Judith A.	(NM)	259
Library operation	GRAY, Tomysena F.	(CA)	460
Library operation & administration	EGAN, Terence W.	(AZ)	338

OPERATIONS (Cont'd)

Library operations	JONES, Robert P.	(FL)	614
	VOSS, Kathryn J.	(MO)	1289
	LIEBERFELD, Lawrence	(NY)	726
	WEINER, Betty	(PA)	1318
	NADEAU, Johan	(PQ)	885
Library operations & purchasing	HEATH, Henry H.	(MD)	519
Library operations & services	MCCONNELL, Pamela J.	(OH)	798
Library operations, management	MANN, Thomas	(CA)	766
	BARNUM, Deborah C.	(CT)	58
Library operations research	WYLLYS, Ronald E.	(TX)	1375
Library system operations	CARDEN, Marguerite	(FL)	180
Library systems operation	BYRN, James H.	(VA)	169
Management of publishing operations	BOYD, Joseph W.	(IL)	122
Media center management & operation	BRAUER, Regina	(NY)	129
Media center operation & administration	EGAN, Terence W.	(AZ)	338
Microcomputer operation	YAU, Linda S.	(CA)	1378
OCLC operations	KNOCH, Daniel L.	(MI)	665
One-person library operation	MARTIN, Jody S.	(IN)	776
Online operations	TURIEL, David	(NY)	1263
Operating & capital budgets	RAPHAEL, Mary E.	(DC)	1008
Operation & management	JEFFCOAT, Phyllis C.	(AR)	596
Operation of one-person library	HARRINGTON, Anne W.	(PA)	503
Operational development	HABER, Walter H.	(PA)	481
Operations	MILLER, G D.	(WA)	837
	SCHUTTE, Raymond R.	(WA)	1103
Operations management	WALKER, Patricia A.	(CA)	1296
	FULLER, Ruth V.	(GA)	409
	BACON, Lois C.	(MA)	44
	ATRI, Pushkala V.	(TX)	38
Operations research	KRAFT, Donald H.	(LA)	674
Organization & operation	TREISTER, Cyril C.	(CA)	1255
Overseas operations	SULLIVAN, Robert C.	(DC)	1208
Personnel & operations planning	LEATHER, Deborah J.	(VA)	707
Postal operations	WEERASINGHE, Jean Y.	(ON)	1316
Professional library operating	CHAPMAN, Peggy H.	(NC)	202
Record center operations	EDWARDS, Steven M.	(WA)	338
School & university library operations	KELLY, Myla S.	(CA)	638
School library operations	EGAN, Janet M.	(CA)	338
Systems operations	THORSTEINSON, William A.	(NS)	1243
Technical operations	MENEGAUX, Edmond A.	(MD)	824
	BRANN, Andrew R.	(OH)	128
	TIPLER, Stephen B.	(ON)	1246
Technical services operation	STEWART, William L.	(WY)	1193
Technical services operations	FRANZEK, Karyn	(MA)	398
Total library operations	HEINRICH, Mark A.	(MI)	522

OPHTHALMIC

Ophthalmic sciences	DRAPER, Linda J.	(MO)	318
Ophthalmology	WINNIKE, Mary E.	(IL)	1355
	JOHNSTON, Bruce A.	(PA)	610
	CASTAGNO, Lucio A.	(BRA)	194
Ophthalmology research	MOUNT, Albertina F.	(NY)	873

OPINION

Public opinion polls	BOVA, Patrick	(IL)	120

OPTICAL

CD-ROM, optical information systems	DESMARAIS, Norman P.	(RI)	295
Expert & optical information systems	SCHNEIDER, Karl R.	(MD)	1097
Key trainer for the optical disk	BEAN, Charles W.	(DC)	69
Laser optic publishing services	ALCOCK, Anthony J.	(CA)	11
Laser optical technology	KERR, Robert C.	(CO)	644
Library optical disk applications	SWORA, Tamara	(DC)	1217
Optical applications	CHEN, Ching C.	(MA)	205
Optical card applications	GALE, John C.	(VA)	413
Optical character recognition	MAYDET, Steven I.	(NJ)	789
	ERDT, Terrence	(PA)	352
	HARTT, Richard W.	(VA)	509
Optical data products, CD-ROM	STEFFEY, Ramona J.	(TN)	1185
Optical disc products	SPALA, Jeanne L.	(CA)	1170
Optical disk	VONDERHAAR, Mark N.	(MD)	1288
	BETCHER, Melissa A.	(OH)	92
Optical disk & CD-ROM	ROSE, Steven C.	(CA)	1055

OPTICAL (Cont'd)

Optical disk applications	WEBB, Duncan C.	(CA)	1313
	ROBERTSON, Michael A.	(NY)	1042
Optical disk collection development	QUIGLEY, Suzanne L.	(OH)	999
Optical disk conversion	BARRETT, Darryl D.	(MN)	59
Optical disk database system	BENGE, Bruce	(OK)	80
Optical disk information archiving	PASCHAL, John M.	(OK)	945
Optical disk publishing	ZOELLICK, Bill	(CO)	1390
Optical disk storage & retrieval	ELMAN, Stanley A.	(CA)	345
Optical disk systems	ABBOTT, George L.	(NY)	1
	HODGSON, Cynthia A.	(PA)	546
Optical disk technology	BOSS, Richard W.	(DC)	117
	PRICE, Joseph W.	(DC)	992
	REGAZZI, John J.	(NY)	1017
	ARJONA, Sandra K.	(PA)	31
	ALI, Syed N.	(BRN)	13
Optical disks & CD-ROM	TALLY, Roy D.	(MN)	1221
Optical disks, gateways	MARSHALL, Mary E.	(OH)	774
Optical disks in libraries	RASMUSSEN, Mary L.	(MN)	1009
Optical information system	HEIDENREICH, Fred L.	(AZ)	521
Optical information systems	ANDRE, Pamela Q.	(MD)	26
	MARMION, Daniel K.	(TX)	772
	DEBUSE, Raymond	(WA)	285
	REMINGTON, David G.	(WA)	1022
Optical laser disk products	HANIFORD, K L.	(MO)	496
Optical media	CARSON, Susan A.	(CA)	188
Optical media in libraries	DUCHESNE, Roderick M.	(ON)	322
Optical scanning & storage	SPANGLER, Bruce	(CO)	1171
Optical storage	CAMPBELL, Brian G.	(BC)	176
Optical storage & publishing	HERTHER, Nancy K.	(MN)	533
Optical storage media technology	GALL, Bert A.	(TN)	413
Optical storage technologies	HELGERSON, Linda W.	(VA)	524
Optical storage technology	LIGHTBOWN, Parke P.	(CA)	726
Optical technologies	MCCONNELL, Karen S.	(TX)	797
Optical video disk	GALL, Bert A.	(TN)	413

OPTICS

Optics	LATHAM, Mary R.	(MA)	701

ORAL

Local history & oral history	MUELLER, Jane L.	(CA)	875
Oral & written communication	EBERHARD, Neysa C.	(KS)	334
Oral communication	HAYES, L S.	(FL)	516
Oral histories	CHERPAK, Evelyn M.	(RI)	206
Oral history	BENNETT, Celestine C.	(CA)	81
	BURNS, John F.	(CA)	162
	GOODSTEIN, Judith R.	(CA)	450
	DEANE, Roxanna	(DC)	284
	MOSS, William W.	(DC)	872
	ROSS, Rodney A.	(DC)	1058
	LESLIE, Elizabeth J.	(GA)	718
	ERICKSEN, Paul A.	(IL)	352
	KRASEAN, Thomas K.	(IN)	676
	MCSHANE, Stephen G.	(IN)	818
	BIRDWHISTELL, Terry L.	(KY)	98
	NOWICKE, Carole E.	(MI)	911
	WAGNER, Cherryl A.	(MI)	1291
	BAKER, Tracey I.	(MN)	50
	BRILEY, Carol A.	(MO)	136
	WARNER, Wayne E.	(MO)	1305
	MCCULLOUGH, Jack W.	(NJ)	801
	SOMMER, Ursula M.	(NJ)	1167
	COLMAN, Gould P.	(NY)	233
	DISHON, Robert M.	(NY)	305
	GUREWITSCH, Bonnie	(NY)	478
	LACHATANERE, Diana	(NY)	686
	GOERLER, Raimund E.	(OH)	443
	BLUTH, John F.	(PA)	108
	WRAY, Wendell L.	(PA)	1370
	CONRAD, James H.	(TX)	238
	DRUMMOND, Donald R.	(TX)	321
	COLLINS, Sara D.	(VA)	233
	PENGELLY, Joe	(ENG)	956
Oral history catalog publication	KENDRICK, Alice M.	(NY)	640
Oral history collections	GRELE, Ronald J.	(NY)	467
Oral history consulting	GRELE, Ronald J.	(NY)	467
	MORRISSEY, Charles T.	(VT)	869
Oral history interview training	KENDRICK, Alice M.	(NY)	640

ORAL (Cont'd)

Oral history interviewing	CAMERON, Sam A.	(TN)	175
Oral history interviewing techniques	STEPHENSON, Shirley E.	(CA)	1189
Oral history program design	KENDRICK, Alice M. . . .	(NY)	640
Oral history projects	JONES, Martin J.	(NY)	614
Oral history teaching	GRELE, Ronald J.	(NY)	467
Oral interpretation	ZALESKI, Mary A.	(WA)	1385
Oral reviews	FOX, Estella E.	(KY)	394
Slavic literatures & oral poetry	POPOVIC, Tanya V. . . .	(NY)	983
Video & oral history archives	JAGOE, Katherine P. . . .	(TX)	591

ORANGE COUNTY

Community history, Orange County	FRANK, Anne E.	(CA)	396

ORCHESTRA

Music arranging & orchestrating	NIGHTINGALE, Daniel . .	(PA)	904
Orchestra & music preparation	GUNTHER, Paul B.	(MN)	478
Orchestra librarianship	GROSSMAN, Robert M. .	(PA)	473

ORDERS (See also Acquisitions, Approval, Buying, Purchasing)

Audiovisual ordering	SPERRY, Linda S.	(OH)	1174
Book ordering	BECKNER, Barbara J. . . .	(FL)	73
	MCLENNA, D S.	(TX)	814
Cataloging & book ordering	VIERGEVER, Dan W. . . .	(KS)	1284
Cataloging & ordering	CAMPBELL, Mary K. . . .	(TX)	177
Cataloging, ordering, processing	GERMINDER, Robin L. . .	(NJ)	429
Continuations & standing orders	BACON, Lois C.	(MA)	44
Library management & serials orders	VON PFEIL, Helena P. . .	(DC)	1288
Mail order	PAGE, Dennis N.	(ND)	934
Order & catalog materials	JOHNSON, Elizabeth L. . .	(NE)	604
Order plans, order procedures	KAVANAGH, Susan E. . . .	(ON)	631
Order records	VANCE, Mary L.	(MS)	1273
Order supervision	KNEIL, Gertrude M.	(PA)	664
Ordering	TRIMINGHAM, Robert . .	(CA)	1256
Ordering & catlgng books & non-book mtrl	SPIEGEL, Bertha	(NY)	1174
Ordering architectural, engrng books	SPAHR, Cheryl L.	(OH)	1170
Ordering books	GLASS, Gerald	(PQ)	440
Periodical collection & ordering	PELZER, Adolf	(MI)	955
Publishing & mail order	HAAS, Carolyn B.	(IL)	480
Religious women's orders	DEUTSCH, N E.	(MO)	297
Selection & ordering	LONNING, Roger D.	(MN)	740
Serials, standing orders	MCCANN, Jett C.	(GA)	794
Standing order selection & management	ROMANASKY, Marcia C.	(NJ)	1052
Standing orders	HUDSON, Gary A.	(SD)	569
Standing orders & serials	MCCANN, Judith B.	(ON)	794
Standing orders, continuations	BEN-SIMON, Julie E. . . .	(WA)	83
Supervising all book orders	DOYLE, Patricia A.	(TX)	317
Verifying citations & ordering	WILLIS, Joan K.	(CA)	1348

ORDINANCES (See also Law, Legal)

Codes of ordinances	HENDERSON, Laurel E. .	(GA)	526

ORDNANCE (See also Arms, Defense)

Ordnance	KOCH, Kathy R.	(CA)	667

OREGON

19th century Oregon history	EMMENS, Thomas A. . . .	(OR)	348
Oregon library law	GINNANE, Mary J.	(OR)	437
Oregoniana	MOBERG, F A.	(OR)	851

ORGAN

Organ & church music	KENT, Frederick J.	(PA)	642
Organ performance	ROEPKE, David E.	(OH)	1048
Researching reed organ history	RICHARDS, James H. . .	(TX)	1028

ORGANIC

Organic chemistry searching	COGHLAN, Jill M.	(MA)	227

ORGANIZATION (See also Administration, Arrangement, Branch, Department, Intra-Organization, Management, Reorganization, Taxation, Workflow)

Academic library organization	RICHARDS, James H. . .	(NM)	1028
Acquisition & organization	FILIATRAULT, Andre Y. . .	(PQ)	376
Administration & organization	WOODBURY, Marda . . .	(CA)	1366
	MEDEIROS, Joseph . . .	(NY)	820
	FEDRICK, Mary A.	(PA)	368
	BOYLAN, Merle N.	(WA)	123
	CAMERON, Bruce	(SK)	174
Administration organization, personnel	HEISE, George F.	(NJ)	522
Administrative planning & organization	SIMON, Bradley A.	(OK)	1140
Archival organization	HOFFBERG, Judith A. . .	(CA)	547
	BAUMSTEIN, Paschal M. .	(NC)	66
	HOOKS, Michael Q.	(TX)	556
Archive organization	MAASS, Eleanor A.	(PA)	753
Archives organization & training	KEATS, Susan E.	(MA)	633
Art history slide organizing	GRAY, Shirley M.	(NY)	460
Association organization & operation	PARSONS, Augustine C. .	(OH)	944
Audiovisual materials organization	SHEFFO, Belinda M. . . .	(PA)	1125
Automation & organizing libraries	HARRIS, Marie	(DC)	505
Bibliographic organization	CARPENTER, Michael A. .	(LA)	185
	BOLL, John J.	(WI)	112
Bibliographic organization control	HENDERSON, Kathryn L.	(IL)	526
Business library organization, operation	RABER, Nevin W.	(IN)	1001
Bylaws of organizations	DUJSIK, Gerald	(IL)	324
Collection organization	JANKOWSKI, Susan H. . .	(WI)	593
Collection organizing	SUGGS, John K.	(WA)	1206
Conference organizing	HOGAN, Thomas H.	(NJ)	549
Consulting in information organizations	PRUSAK, Laurence	(MA)	996
Corporate library organz & development	NIELSEN, Sonja M.	(MA)	903
Creating & organizing architectural libs	ROTHMAN, Marilyn R. . .	(CO)	1060
Creating & organizing private libraries	ROTHMAN, Marilyn R. . .	(CO)	1060
Database organization	DENIGER, Constant	(PQ)	292
Description, organization of information	BIERBAUM, Esther G. . .	(IA)	95
District library organz & supervision	DICK, Norma P.	(CA)	300
Electrochemical information organization	LANGKAU, Claire M. . . .	(OH)	696
Federal government organization	DOWNS, Charles F.	(DC)	317
Friends & citizen organizing	FADDEN, Donald M.	(PA)	360
Friends of libraries organization	MARSHALL, John D. . . .	(TN)	774
Friends of libs organizing & developing	DOLNICK, Sandy F.	(IL)	310
Friends organizations	STRAUTMAN, Randolph B.	(GA)	1201
Industrial & organizational psychology	FULMER, Dina J.	(PA)	409
Information center mgmt & organization	ALBERTUS, Donna M. . .	(NY)	10
Information flow in organizations	DANIEL, Evelyn H.	(NC)	272
Information for managers & organization	KATZER, Jeffrey	(NY)	630
Information management & organization	KADEC, Sarah T.	(MD)	621
Information organization	NYBERG, Lelia J.	(CA)	912
Intergovernmental organization documents	WESTFALL, Gloria D. . .	(IN)	1327
Internal data organization	MORROW, Ellen B.	(PA)	869
International congress organization	WALCKIERS, Marc A. . .	(BEL)	1293
Intl govt organizations' documentation	WILLIAMSON, Linda E. .	(IL)	1347
Intl Governmental Organizations Pubns	RUHLIN, Michele T.	(UT)	1066
International organization documents	SHAABAN, Marian F. . . .	(IN)	1118
International organization publications	RYAN, Richard A.	(OH)	1071
International organizations	CLARIE, Thomas C.	(CT)	216
	GUILBERT, Manon M. . .	(ON)	476
	HAJNAL, Peter I.	(ON)	484
Law & business library organization	HELBURN, Judith D. . . .	(TX)	523
Law library organization	SMITH, Susan A.	(CA)	1161
Law library upkeep & organization	RIGGS, Judith M.	(CA)	1034
Library development & organization	NIEMI, Peter G.	(WI)	903
Library government & organization	SABSAY, David	(CA)	1073
Library management & organization	CREAGHE, Norma S. . . .	(CA)	257
	SHERMAN, Mary A.	(OK)	1128

ORGANIZATION (Cont'd)

Library organization — HERSBERGER, Rodney M. (CA) 533
PERKINS, Steven C. (CA) 959
RIGGS, Judith M. (CA) 1034
JENKINS, Althea H. (FL) 597
SINTZ, Edward F. (FL) 1144
BARNHART, Arlene C. (MA) 58
KROST, Mary G. (MD) 680
WOLLAM, Martha A. (MD) 1361
COGSWELL, James A. (MN) 227
NAUEN, Lindsay B. (MN) 889
ABERNATHY, William F. (MO) 2
SEVERANCE, Robert W. (NC) 1117
MAYESKI, John K. (NE) 790
HAAS, Elaine H. (NY) 480
TAPIERO, Judith (NY) 1223
GEISEY, Barbara T. (OH) 425
RUSSELL, Elizabeth (RI) 1068
HALE, Relda D. (TN) 485
HANSON, Roger K. (UT) 498
CAHILL, Linda J. (VA) 171
GRINSTEAD, Beth K. (WA) 471
MUTSCHLER, Herbert F. (WA) 883
SMITH, Anne C. (ON) 1152
JOBA, Judith C. (PQ) 601
Library organization & administration — JONES, William G. (IL) 615
COLLINS, Evron S. (OH) 232
ROUSE, Charlie L. (OK) 1061
Library organization & maintenance — HAM, Beverly V. (MN) 490
Library organization & management — BEASLEY, Clarence W. (FL) 69
MURPHY, Marcy (IN) 881
LORENZ, John G. (MD) 741
ASP, William G. (MN) 37
SANDERS, John B. (MO) 1080
TUROCK, Betty J. (NJ) 1265
SHERIDAN, Robert N. (NY) 1128
HAMILTON, Elizabeth J. (VA) 492
Library organization & planning — CUMMING, Linda L. (CO) 264
Library organization development — YAVARKOVSKY, Jerome (NY) 1378
Library planning & organization — PARKS, Mary L. (CA) 943
VOHRA, Pran (SK) 1287
Library systems organization — HURD, Sandra H. (MA) 577
Lib systems organization & management — CHITWOOD, Julius R. (IL) 209
DIMATTIA, Ernest A. (CT) 304
MARKUSON, Carolyn A. (MA) 772
MEAHL, D D. (MI) 819
WRIGHT, Linda G. (WV) 1372
Management & organizational behavior — DENIS, Laurent G. (ON) 292
Mgmt & organizational effectiveness — RIZZO, John R. (MI) 1037
Management of serials organization — DONAHUE, Janice E. (FL) 310
Manuscript organization & description — ONN, Shirley A. (AB) 924
Media center organization — FOERTIN, Yves P. (PQ) 387
Medical library materials organization — DOLL, Harriet A. (PA) 309
Multitype library organizations — MORRISON, Carol J. (IL) 868
Museum & archival cataloging, organz — DEE, Camille C. (NY) 286
Network organization — PINGS, Vern M. (FL) 974
News library organization — ROCKALL, Diane M. (MI) 1046
Non-profit organizations — BOHLEN, Jeanne L. (DC) 111
Organization — HAZEKAMP, Phyllis W. (CA) 517
FURST, Joyce P. (NC) 410
RYAN, Donald L. (NY) 1070
POPECKI, Jeanne M. (VT) 983
TEANEY, Carol R. (MO) 1229
COAN, Mary L. (NY) 224
FOLCARELLI, Ralph J. (NY) 387
Organization & association leadership — BEDARD, Bernard J. (PQ) 73
Organization & facilities — STROUGAL, Patricia G. (GA) 1203
Organz & indexing of manufacturer catlgs — SCHUSTER, Adeline (IL) 1103
Organization & management — FRADKIN, Bernard (IL) 395
POWNALL, David E. (AUS) 989
Organization & microfilm pubn with index — FALK, Candace S. (CA) 362
Organization & operation — TREISTER, Cyril C. (CA) 1255
Organization & personnel — HERNANDEZ, Ramon R. (MI) 532
Organization & planning — ETTER, Patricia A. (AZ) 355
Organization & subject classification — HAYNES, Kathleen J. (OH) 516
Organization & workflow — MORRIS, Dilys E. (IA) 866

ORGANIZATION (Cont'd)

Organization change — ROBINSON, Barbara M. (MD) 1043
Organization delivery — SMITH, William K. (MI) 1161
Organization development — BLALOCK, Louise (CT) 103
SULLIVAN, Maureen (CT) 1208
STEPHEN, Ross G. (NJ) 1187
TOWNLEY, Charles T. (PA) 1253
Organz devlpmnt & communication systems — HUNT, Suellyn (NY) 575
Organization effectiveness — SEARS, Carlton A. (NY) 1110
Organization in development — COLE, Jack W. (MN) 230
Organization of author conferences — HIRABAYASHI, Joanne (CA) 543
Organization of congregational libraries — HANNAFORD, Claudia L. (OH) 496
Organization of information — BERRING, Robert C. (CA) 90
BRITE, Agnes (MA) 137
WATERSTREET, Darlene E. (WI) 1309
Organization of library collections — HORTON, Kathy L. (IL) 561
Organization of library materials — DESSER, Darrilyn (NY) 296
Organization of materials — YOUNG, Dorothy E. (PA) 1381
Organization of meetings & courses — ROBERTS, Kenneth H. (FRN) 1040
Organization of new facilities — SCHUSTER, Adeline (IL) 1103
Organization of recorded knowledge — HALSEY, Richard S. (NY) 490
Organization of rural school libraries — GOODMAN, Roslyn L. (AK) 449
Organization of special libraries — WOOLF, Amy K. (KS) 1368
MCCONNIE, Mary (TRN) 798
Organization planning — RILEY, Robert H. (NJ) 1034
FRAMEL, Phyllis M. (TX) 395
Organization, planning & administration — HOELLE, Dolores M. (NJ) 547
Organization theory — CEPPOS, Karen F. (CA) 196
Organization, training & development — FEINER, Arlene M. (IL) 369
ENGELBERT, Peter J. (IN) 348
KING, Willard B. (NC) 652
Organizational & personnel development — MAHMOODI, Suzanne H. (MN) 760
Organizational archives — KRAFT, Katherine G. (MA) 675
Organizational behavior — JOHNSON, Margaret A. (MN) 607
RUNYON, Robert S. (NE) 1067
Organizational behavior management — COFFMAN, M H. (MA) 227
Organizational change — EHRHORN, Jean H. (HI) 339
SMALL, Sally S. (PA) 1151
BUSCH, B J. (AB) 165
Organizational communication training — RUBEN, Brent D. (NJ) 1064
Organizational consulting — GARDNER, Jeffrey J. (DC) 418
Organizational development — TOMPKINS, Philip (CA) 1250
CHAMBERS, Joan L. (CO) 198
GRAY, Carolyn M. (MA) 459
TREFRY, Mary G. (NY) 1255
WEBB, Gisela M. (TX) 1313
ISOBE, Darron T. (UT) 585
NORDEN, David J. (VA) 908
WALLS, Francine E. (WA) 1299
Organizational dynamics & communication — CRETH, Sheila D. (IA) 258
Organizational management — BAKER, Gordon N. (GA) 48
Organizational papers — HERIOT, Ruthanne (WV) 531
Organizational planning — KINCHEN, Robert P. (NY) 650
Organizational planning & communications — LOWRY, Charles B. (TX) 745
Organizational psychology — BUSH, Nancy W. (AL) 165
Organizational structure — MORAN, Robert F. (IN) 862
Organizational studies — TAYLOR, William R. (TN) 1229
Organizational theory — GEORGE, Shirley H. (IA) 428
MCBURNEY, Margot B. (ON) 792
Organizing & problem solving — GREENBERG, Roberta D. (NY) 463
Organizing art exhibitions — FORMAN, Camille L. (CT) 390
Organizing, cataloging church libraries — HAMMER, Louise K. (IL) 493
Organizing, clippings pamphlets reports — HORN, Zoia (CA) 559
Organizing collections — JACOBS, Mildred H. (MO) 589
Organizing existing library collections — KOPAN, Ellen K. (CA) 671
Organizing libraries — KAST, Gloria E. (CA) 629
Organizing libraries from scratch — SANCHEZ, Eliana P. (NY) 1079
Organizing library for handicapped — BULLOCK, Frances E. (NY) 156
Organizing materials since 1870 — DOUET, Madeleine J. (NY) 313
Organizing miscellaneous materials — JONES, Dora A. (SD) 612
Organizing problem areas — BERG, David C. (MN) 84
Organizing reference collections — HAZEL, Debora E. (NC) 517

ORGANIZATION (Cont'd)

Organizing, reorganizing libraries — OFFERMAN, Mary C. . . . . (IA) 917
Organizing small libraries — FIRTH, Margaret A. . . . . (MA) 379
Organizing small special libraries — MCMANAMON, Mary J. . (MA) 814
Organizing special collections — ROSENSHIELD, Jill K. . . (WI) 1057
Patent organization & searching — MASTERS, Fred N. . . . . (CT) 782
Photo & slide organizational systems — ROBERTSON, Retha M. . (OK) 1042
Photo organizing — CANT, Elaine N. . . . . . . (CA) 179
Photographic collection organization — VOGT-O'CONNOR, Diane L. . . . . (DC) 1287
Planning & organization — ROSENFELD, Joel C. . . . (IL) 1056
Planning & organizing — BUHR, Rosemary E. . . . . (MO) 156
Processing & organization of collections — AUTRY, Carolyn . . . . (IN) 41
Professional organizations — O'HALLORAN, James V. (NY) 918
Proprietary documents organization — LAVIN, Margaret A. . . . . (NJ) 703
Public library management & organization — TREZZA, Alphonse F. . . . (FL) 1256
Public library organization — DEFASSIO, Sharon L. . . (PA) 287
Public library organizing & managing — AUSTIN, Neal F. . . . . . . (NC) 40
Resource for entire organization — FINNUCAN, Louise A. . . (CT) 379
Resources organization & development — HURD, Sandra H. . . . . . (MA) 577
School library organization — WEEKS, Patsy L. . . . . . (TX) 1315
SORENSEN, Richard J. . (WI) 1168
School library organization & evaluation — BAGAN, Beverly S. . . . . (VA) 45
Slide collection organization & devlpmnt — PRINS, Johanna W. . . . . (NY) 993
Small library administration & organz — REINGOLD, Judith S. . . . (NH) 1021
Small library organization — LOW, Frederick E. . . . . (NY) 743
Small special library organization — BEAL, Gretchen F. . . . . (TN) 68
Special library organization — OWEN, Karen V. . . . . . (VA) 931
ROSS, Evelyn M. . . . . (AB) 1058
SNYDER, Elizabeth A. . . (ENG)1164
Special library organization & design — BURNS, Marie T. . . . . . (IL) 162
Special library organization, management — COOKE, Geraldine A. . . . (AB) 241
Standards organization & distribution — RICE, Gerald W. . . . . . . (NH) 1027
Systems organization — COVILL, Bruce . . . . (NJ) 252
Technical services organization — WAITE, Ellen J. . . . . . . (IL) 1293
HERVEY, Norma J. . . . . (MN) 533
Technical services organization & admin — JOB, Rose A. . . . . (MO) 601
Vertical files organization, maintenance — GODFREY, Florence L. . . (NJ) 442
Workshop organization — BURKS, C J. . . . . (UT) 161
Youth service organization liaisonship — WRONKA, Gretchen M. . (MN) 1373

ORIENTAL (See also Asia)

Oriental language terminal — WANG, Gary Y. . . . . . . (MA) 1302

ORIENTATION

History selection & orientation — APPLEBY, Judith A. . . . . (PQ) 30
Library instruction & orientation — MACKENZIE, Shirley A. . (ON) 756
Library orientation — BURKE, Donna J. . . . . . (FL) 160
HONTZ, M E. . . . . (NJ) 556
GEISEY, Barbara T. . . . (OH) 425
ROBERTS, Sallie H. . . . (OH) 1041
MACLOWICK, Frederick B. (MB) 757
PAWLEY, Carolyn P. . . . (ON) 951
Library orientation & instruction — CLARK, Wendolyn H. . . . (AL) 218
MORRIS, Karen T. . . . . (OK) 867
Library orientation & outreach — BOELKE, Joanne H. . . . (IL) 110
Library orientation lessons — KEENE, Roberta E. . . . . (NV) 634
Library trustee orientation — GROSS, Richard F. . . . . (ME) 472
Orientation — PARIS, Terrence L. . . . . (NS) 940
ARMSTRONG, Jennifer E. (ON) 32
ROURKE, Lorna E. . . . . (ON) 1061
MOSER, Beryl R. . . . . . (PQ) 870
Orientation & bibliographic instruction — ARMSTRONG, Mary L. . (AB) 32
LAKHANPAL, Sarv K. . . (SK) 689
Orientation & instruction — KAYE, Karen . . . . (CA) 632
Orientation & research strategy — BIANCHINO, Cecelia . . . (IN) 94
Orientations — SMITH, Marilynn C. . . . . (SDA)1157
Orientations & interlib loan reference — BAYER, Susan P. . . . . . (IL) 67
Patron orientation — WELSCH, Melissa W. . . . (LA) 1323
Public services & orientations — LEVESQUE, Nancy B. . . (BC) 719

ORIENTATION (Cont'd)

Service orientation — HEISTER, Carla G. . . . . (IL) 523
Student orientation & training — RICE, Anna C. . . . . (NJ) 1026
Training & orientation — WINIARZ, Elizabeth . . . (PQ) 1355
Training & orienting — WAGNER, Judith O. . . . (OH) 1292
User education & orientation — PATTERSON, Charlean P. (PA) 948
User education, library orientation — SEARCY HOWARD, Linda M. . . . . (BC) 1109

ORIGINAL

Cataloging, original & retrospective — SCHEITLE, Janet M. . . . (VA) 1091
Cataloging original materials — SCHUMANN, Iris T. . . . . (TX) 1103
Original cataloging — WILSON, Betty R. . . . . . (IL) 1350
MAGUIRE, Shirley E. . . . (MI) 760
SCOTT, Randall W. . . . . (MI) 1108
MANY, Florence L. . . . . (NJ) 767
PRITCHARD, Barbara . . . (PA) 994
HAWLEY, Laurie J. . . . . (TX) 514
LACY, Yvonne M. . . . . (TX) 687
Original cataloging romance languages — SALINERO, Amelia . . . . (NY) 1076
Original cataloging, science — KARON, Bernard L. . . . . (MN) 627
Original cataloging Slavic materials — KORT, Richard L. . . . . . (MA) 672
Original cataloging using computers — HANNAFORD, Claudia L. (OH) 496
Original media slide programs — OWENS, Martha A. . . . . (VA) 932
Original monograph cataloging — LINSKY, Leonore K. . . . (MA) 731

ORTHODONTIC

Orthodontic research — GILTINAN, Celia E. . . . . (MO) 437

ORTHOPEDICS

Orthopedic & oncology pediatrics — KELLER, Nancy H. . . . . . (LA) 635
Orthopedics — RAY, Laura E. . . . . (OH) 1011
Orthopedics & sports medicine — CLEMENTS, Betty H. . . . (GA) 221

OSI

Bibliographic OSI protocol — ARBEZ, Gilbert J. . . . . . . (ON) 30
OSI communication protocols — MACLELLAND, Margaret A. . . . . (ON) 757

OTOLARYNGOLOGY

Otolaryngology — WINNIKE, Mary E. . . . . . (IL) 1355
CASTAGNO, Lucio A. . . (BRA) 194
Otolaryngology, head & neck surgery — JOHNSTON, Bruce A. . . (PA) 610

OUTLETS (See also Branch)

Planning new library outlets — STREIN, Barbara M. . . . . (MD) 1201

OUT-OF-PRINT (See also Antiquarian, Early, Old, Rare)

Out-of-print — THOMAS, David H. . . . . (MI) 1236
Out-of-print books — MONIE, Willis J. . . . . (NY) 855
BRAUTIGAM, David K. . . (PA) 130
FOUTS, Judith F. . . . . . (TX) 393
Out-of-print material — GAGE, Laurie E. . . . . . . (ENG) 412
Out-of-print recordings — DONAHUE, Louise . . . . . (NJ) 310
Out-of-print scholarly books — SOMERS, Wayne F. . . . (NY) 1167
Out-of-print searching — ZULA, Floyd M. . . . . (LA) 1391
KRAEHE, Mary A. . . . . . (VA) 674
Rare & out-of-print art books — DAVIS, L C. . . . . (CA) 280
Rare & out-of-print books — SMITH, Nolan E. . . . . . (CT) 1159
Rare, out-of-print records — SMITH, Walter H. . . . . . (VA) 1161

OUTPLACEMENT

Outplacement — GENTNER, Claudia A. . . (NJ) 427

OUTPUT

Output measures — SHELKROT, Elliot L. . . . . (PA) 1126

OUTREACH (See also Community, Extension, Marketing, Promotion, Underserved, Unserved)

Art gallery outreach learning centers	PATTERSON, Grace L. . .	(NY)	948
Bookmobile & outreach services	LEONARD, Gloria J.	(WA)	716
Branch, bookmobile, outreach services	BEECH, Vivian W.	(NC)	74
Children's outreach	HESS, M S.	(CA)	534
Children's outreach services	LYTLE, Marian M.	(NC)	753
Community outreach	COOPER, Ginnie	(CA)	242
	SCLAR, Marta L.	(CA)	1106
	MEISSNER, Edie A.	(MN)	822
	BRETING, Elizabeth C. . .	(MO)	133
	OCHS, Phyllis E.	(NY)	915
	GUMPPER, Mary F.	(OH)	477
	BURNETT, Wayne C. . . .	(ON)	162
	DE RONDE, Paula D. . . .	(ON)	294
Community outreach & marketing	WALTER, Virginia A. . . .	(CA)	1300
Community outreach services	PALMORE, Sandra N. . .	(IL)	937
	HARVELL, Valeria G. . . .	(NJ)	509
Correctional institution outreach	PETIT, J M.	(OH)	965
Extension & outreach	ENGELBERT, Alan M. . . .	(WI)	348
Extension & outreach services	MEIZNER, Kathie L.	(MD)	822
Hispanic outreach	SIMAS, Therese C.	(CA)	1139
Hospital outreach	SCHNEIDER, Marcia G. . .	(CA)	1097
Hospital outreach services to children	WALSH, Mary A.	(PQ)	1300
Library orientation & outreach	BOELKE, Joanne H.	(IL)	110
Library outreach	CONRAD, Celia B.	(CT)	238
	HIGGINBOTHAM, Richard C.	(IL)	537
	SADLER, Graham H. . . .	(VA)	1073
Library outreach & public relations	LAWTON, Bethany L. . . .	(DC)	705
Library outreach & publicity	BURKE, Lauri K.	(RI)	160
Library outreach programs	KARASICK, Alice W. . . .	(CA)	627
Library outreach services	HEISER, Jane C.	(MD)	523
Non-user non-reader outreach services	FRANKLIN, Hardy R. . . .	(DC)	397
Outreach	GORAL, Barbara J.	(CO)	451
	DRUSCHEL, Pauline H. . .	(MI)	321
	DAVIS, Emmett A.	(MN)	279
	WRIGHT, Linda D.	(NC)	1372
	ALEY, Judy M.	(NJ)	12
	RAZZANO, Barbara W. . .	(NJ)	1012
	GAWLER, Ann C.	(NY)	423
	TABEN, Eva M.	(NY)	1219
	LEATHERMAN, Donald G.	(TX)	707
	ACKERMAN, Frances W.	(PQ)	3
Outreach activities	BISHOP, Beverly D.	(GA)	99
	LARSON, Jean A.	(MD)	699
Outreach administration	KLAUBER, Julie B.	(NY)	658
Outreach & bookmobile services, literacy	JONES, Charlotte W. . . .	(WA)	611
Outreach & extension services	ALLEN, Debra C.	(SC)	14
Outreach & membership	LEVINE, Lillian S.	(OH)	720
Outreach & programming	BENNETT, Samuel J. . . .	(KS)	82
	DEMARCO, Elizabeth A. .	(NY)	291
Outreach & public relations	MANNING, Helen M. . . .	(TX)	766
Outreach, bookmobile	KELLEY, H N.	(IL)	636
Outreach for handicapped & homebound	BRYANT, Judith W.	(NJ)	152
Outreach libraries	HEMENWAY, Patti J. . . .	(IL)	525
Outreach library services	NORMAN, Nita V.	(AZ)	909
	BATSON, Darrell L.	(NV)	64
Outreach programming	GUTHRIE, Chab C.	(OH)	479
Outreach programs, services	BRAUN, Robin E.	(MA)	130
Outreach projects	MURDOCK, Everlyne K. .	(SC)	879
Outreach service & programming	JULIEN, Dorothy C.	(FL)	619
Outreach services	KENNEDY, Rose M.	(CA)	641
	JAMES, Stephen E.	(GA)	592
	MYRON, Victoria L.	(IA)	885
	DEMETRAKAKES, Jennifer B.	(IL)	291
	COLOKATHIS, Jane . . .	(MN)	234
	VALANCE, Marsha J. . . .	(MN)	1271
	ALICEA, Ismael	(NY)	13
	DOTSON, Mildred E. . . .	(NY)	313
	FOGLESONG, Marilee . .	(NY)	387
	BERRY, Diana M.	(OH)	90
	LOVEJOY, Eunice G. . . .	(OH)	743
	SPEAR, Linda A.	(OH)	1172
	BROWN, William A.	(VA)	148

OUTREACH (Cont'd)

Outreach services	MYERS, Antoinette B. . . .	(WA)	884
	BRANDEL, Pamela A. . . .	(WI)	128
	CROOKS, Sylvia A.	(BC)	260
Outreach services, community services	LONG, Judith N.	(IL)	739
Outreach services to special groups	HAABNIIT, Ene	(BC)	480
Outreach services to the community	MARTIN, Brian G.	(NY)	775
Outreach to ethnic minorities	BETANCOURT, Ingrid T. .	(NJ)	92
Outreach to special populations	REILLY, Carol H.	(NC)	1020
Outreach workshops	BUTLER, Randall R.	(CA)	167
Professional outreach to faculty	RIDINGER, Robert B. . . .	(IL)	1032
Programming & outreach	KAPLAN, Paul M.	(IL)	626
	SODERSTRUM, Ann L. . .	(IL)	1165
Public library outreach	BAER, Robert L.	(WA)	45
Public library outreach & bookmobiles	HOLE, Carol C.	(FL)	550
Public library outreach services	MEYERS, Arthur S.	(IN)	830
Public programming & outreach	WURL, Joel F.	(MN)	1374
Public relations & outreach	DAVIS, Denyvetta	(OK)	278
Senior citizen's outreach	OSTROUMOV, Tatiana . .	(CA)	929
Special & outreach library services	PARTRIDGE, James C. . .	(MD)	945

OVERSEAS (See also Foreign, Global, International, World)

General library consulting overseas	BERGQUIST, Christine F.	(DC)	87
Overseas consulting	CANDELMO, Emily	(NY)	178
Overseas online distributors	YAMAKAWA, Takashi . .	(JAP)	1376
Overseas operations	SULLIVAN, Robert C. . . .	(DC)	1208
Overseas STM subscription agents	YAMAKAWA, Takashi . .	(JAP)	1376

PAC

PAC in school	GRABINSKY, Warren B.	(BC)	455

PACIFIC

Art of the Pacific	TIMBERLAKE, Cynthia A.	(HI)	1245
Asia & South Pacific	WARPHEA, Rita C.	(VA)	1306
Asia Pacific business collection	CHAN, Diana L.	(BC)	199
Hawaii & the Pacific reference	ASHFORD, Marguerite K.	(HI)	36
Hawaii, Pacific	HORIE, Ruth H.	(HI)	559
Hawaiian & Pacific business periodicals	SCHULTZ, Elaine V.	(HI)	1102
Hawaiian & Pacific history	TIMBERLAKE, Cynthia A.	(HI)	1245
19th century Pacific Northwest history	EMMENS, Thomas A. . . .	(OR)	348
Pacific islands history	SHELDEN, Patricia R. . . .	(HI)	1125
Pacific Northwest Americana	REESE, Gary F.	(WA)	1016
Pacific Northwest history	CALDWELL, Richard C. .	(WA)	172
Pacific Northwest regional local history	EMMENS, Thomas A. . . .	(OR)	348
South Pacific studies	CREELY, Kathryn L.	(CA)	257

PACKAGING

Flexable packaging information analysis	MILLS, Catherine H.	(RI)	843
Packaged goods	FEUERSTEIN, Robin . . .	(NY)	374
Packaging industry	TRUE, Jacqueline J.	(IL)	1259
Packaging of information services	TIBBETTS, David W. . . .	(NY)	1243
Plastics & packaging	MCCULLEY, P M.	(SC)	800
Special interest packages	COURTOT, Marilyn E. . . .	(MD)	251
Statistical packages	ITNYRE, Jacqueline H. . .	(CA)	585

PAGEFORM

Automated pageform catalogs	GRUTCHFIELD, Walter .	(NY)	475

PAINTING

Contemporary Mexican painting	KIRKING, Clayton C. . . .	(AZ)	655
Painting & drafting	GLABICKI, Paul	(PA)	439
Paintings, drawings, water colors	MELTON, Howard E. . . .	(OK)	823
Paintings of J J Lankes	LANKES, J B.	(VA)	696

PALEOGRAPHY

Greek paleography	MATHIESEN, Thomas J.	(UT)	784
Paleography	BENOIT, Gerald	(CA)	82
	JORDAN, Louis E.	(IN)	616

PAMPHLETS (See also Vertical)
Building, weeding pamphlet collection ADAMS, Velma L. . . . . . (MS) 6
Indexing & collecting pamphlets RHYNAS, Don M. . . . . . (ON) 1026
Organizing, clippings pamphlets
  reports HORN, Zoia . . . . (CA) 559
Pamphlet file TURNER, Sue E. . . . . . . (PA) 1265
Pamphlet file coordination ROBINSON, David A. . . . (OH) 1043
Pamphlet file development LINDSTROM, Elaine C. . (OH) 730
Pamphlet file maintenance LAROSA, Thomas J. . . . (NY) 698

PAPER (See also Conservation, Preservation)
Art of paper conservation MOORE, Harold H. . . . . . (GA) 859
Book & paper conservation SUNDSTRAND, Jacquelyn
  K. . . . . (CA) 1210
  HANTHORN, Ivan E. . . . (IA) 499
Conservation of paper GRAUE, Luz B. . . . . (CA) 458
Library consulting, paper conservation MUELLER, Jane L. . . . . . (CA) 875
Paper & photographic conservation BUMGARNER, John L. . . (NC) 157
Paper book preservation MOLTKE-HANSEN, David (SC) 853
Paper conservation GARLICK, Karen . . . . . . (DC) 419
  METZLER, Valerie . . . . . (IL) 829
  LOMBARDO, Daniel J. . . (MA) 738
Paper document conservation MOORE, Harold H. . . . . . (GA) 859
Paper preservation SWIFT, David L. . . . . (TN) 1216
Preservation of books & paper HUTTNER, Sidney F. . . . (OK) 579
Pulp & paper databases STAHL, Hella . . . . (PQ) 1178
Pulp & paper literature GAGNON, Vernon N. . . . (OR) 412
Pulp & paper science, technology HALL, Deanna M. . . . . . (GA) 487
Pulp, paper & forestry information MARTINEZ, Linda W. . . . (WA) 779
Term paper assistance MORRIS, Karen T. . . . . . (OK) 867

PAPERMAKING
History of papermaking BIDWELL, John . . . . . . (CA) 95

PAPERS (See also Manuscripts)
Ernest Hemingway personal papers DESNOYERS, Megan F. . (MA) 295
Historical papers ROTH, Stacy F. . . . . (NJ) 1059
Organizational papers HERIOT, Ruthanne . . . . . (WV) 531
Papers processing DESNOYERS, Megan F. . (MA) 295
Personal papers KRAFT, Katherine G. . . . (MA) 675
  HERIOT, Ruthanne . . . . . (WV) 531
  STEELE, Apollonia L. . . . (AB) 1184
Personal papers, manuscripts MASLYN, David C. . . . . (RI) 780
Presidential & executive papers NESBITT, John R. . . . . . (MO) 896
Presidential papers HUMPHREY, David C. . . (TX) 573
Processing papers & records
  collections ERICKSEN, Paul A. . . . . (IL) 352

PARALEGAL
Paralegal instruction ALCORN, Marianne S. . . (AZ) 11
Utilization of paralegal personnel GILMER, Wesley . . . . . . (KY) 437

PARAPROFESSIONALS
Paraprofessional training WILSON, Susan W. . . . . (MD) 1353
Paraprofessionals WOODARD, Beth S. . . . (IL) 1365
Paraprofessionals in libraries HILL, Suzanne P. . . . . . (MD) 541
Supervision of paraprofessional staff ANDERES, Susan M. . . . (CA) 21
Training paraprofessionals JAGODZINSKI, Cecile M. (IL) 591

PARAPSYCHOLOGY (See also Extrasensory)
Parapsychology NORMAN, Wayne R. . . . (NY) 909

PARASITOLOGY
Parasitology HANFMAN, Deborah A. . (MD) 495

PARENT (See also Family)
Children's literature for parents WINKLER, Carol A. . . . . (MO) 1355
Early childhood & parenting SCHWARZLOSE, Sally F. (IL) 1105
Parent education PETERSON, Carolyn S. . (FL) 963
  NEVETT, Micki S. . . . . . (NY) 897
Parent groups, development of
  reading WALDEN, Katherine G. . (CT) 1294

PARISH
Church & parish libraries WHITE, Joyce L. . . . . . . (CO) 1331
Parish histories AMES, Charlotte A. . . . . (IN) 19
Parish libraries SULLIVAN, Mary A. . . . . (GA) 1208
  GARBIN, Angelo U. . . . . (IL) 417
Parish records WIEDERAENDE, Robert C. (IA) 1336

PARLIAMENTARY (See also Government, Legislative)
Government & parliamentary libraries PARE, Richard . . . . (ON) 940
Parliamentary history DIONNE, Guy . . . . (PQ) 305
Parliamentary librarianship SPICER, Erik J. . . . . . . (ON) 1174
  TILLOTSON, Greig S. . . (AUS)1245
Parliamentary procedure VELTEMA, John H. . . . . (MI) 1282

PARTNERSHIPS (See also Cooperation)
School & library partnerships ARRIVEE, Sally D. . . . . . (MI) 34

PART-TIME
Training & development of part-timers DINDAYAL, Joyce S. . . . (NY) 304

PASTORAL (See also Ministry, Pastoral)
Lutheran pastoral ministry SMITH, Robert E. . . . . . . (IN) 1160
Pastoral SHAH, Neeta N. . . . . . . (SC) 1119
Pastoral ministry O'LEARY, Teresa M. . . . (NJ) 920
Theology, pastoral studies, philosophy STALZER, Rita M. . . . . . (IL) 1179

PATENTS
Automotive patent & trademark
  research WREN, James A. . . . . . . (MI) 1370
Business & patent sources GALBRAITH, Barry E. . . (NY) 413
Chemical, patent databases STAVETSKI, Norma K. . . (NJ) 1183
Chemical patent searching WEHNER, Karen B. . . . . (TN) 1316
Chemical patents, literature databases UMFLEET, Ruth A. . . . . . (TX) 1268
Chemicals & patents online searching NEWMAN, Robert M. . . . (TX) 899
Government documents & patents GREALY, Deborah J. . . . (CO) 461
Online patent searching TERANIS, Mara . . . . (WI) 1231
Patent abstracting CIERZNIEWSKI, Robert J. (MI) 214
Patent & trademark databases HU, Robert T. . . . . (IL) 568
  HAYWARD, Diane J. . . . (NY) 517
Patent & trademark information DI MUCCIO, Mary J. . . . (CA) 304
  CROCKETT, Martha L. . . (DC) 259
Patent & trademark reference MOORE, John R. . . . . . . (IL) 860
Patent & trademark research JACOBSON, William R. . (IL) 590
Patent & trademark searching SCHUELER, Dolores . . . (MA) 1101
Patent, chemical & business
  databases TAYLOR, Donna I. . . . . . (NJ) 1226
Patent database & information
  retrieval ROSENTHAL, Francine C. (OH) 1057
Patent databases NOVACK, Dona A. . . . . . (CA) 910
  MOUNTFORD, Eve . . . . (CT) 873
  SAARI, David S. . . . . . . (IN) 1072
  ALLISON, Kenneth J. . . . (NJ) 17
  GARNER, Linda J. . . . . . (NJ) 419
  SKIDANOW, Helene . . . . (NJ) 1146
  WARDEN, Carolyn L. . . . (NY) 1304
  HANF, Elizabeth P. . . . . . (PA) 495
  ERWIN, Mary J. . . . . (TN) 353
  WEI, Carl K. . . . . (ON) 1316
  CORNELIUS, Peter K. . . (LUX) 246
Patent databases & searching LINEPENSEL, Kenneth C. (IN) 730
Patent documentation JONES, Michael W. . . . . (VA) 614
Patent drafting & prosecution SIMMONS, Edlyn S. . . . (OH) 1139
Patent information JACOBS, Leslie R. . . . . . (MA) 589
  WAGNER, Louis F. . . . . (OH) 1292
  DONOVAN, Kathryn M. . (PA) 312
  DIXON, Michael D. . . . . (VA) 306
  MEREK, Charles J. . . . . . (VA) 825
Patent information databases PLATAU, Gerard O. . . . . (OH) 977
Patent information retrieval SIMMONS, Edlyn S. . . . (OH) 1139
Patent literature COX, Bruce B. . . . . (MO) 253
  ADAMS, Dena R. . . . . . . (NM) 4
  RIFFLE, Linda . . . . (OH) 1034
Patent novelty searches AUGHEY, Kathleen M. . . (NJ) 39
Patent organization & searching MASTERS, Fred N. . . . . (CT) 782

PATENTS (Cont'd)

Patent research	SULZER, John H.	(PA)	1209
	MEREK, Charles J.	(VA)	825
Patent research & database	ENNIS, Mary J.	(OH)	350
Patent search	CHU, Insoo L.	(CA)	212
Patent searches	FULLER, Kathleen B.	(OH)	408
Patent searching	LAMBERT, Nancy	(CA)	690
	KOLBIN, Ronda I.	(CT)	669
	GEVIRTZMAN, Joyce L.	(MA)	430
	JUTERBOCK, Deborah K.	(NJ)	620
	BUTCHER, Sharon L.	(OH)	166
	RATLIFF, Priscilla	(OH)	1009
Patent training	MEREK, Charles J.	(VA)	825
Patents	HALL, Deborah N.	(AR)	487
	HONEYCUTT, Mary L.	(AR)	556
	ZEIDLER, Patricia L.	(CA)	1387
	SMISEK, Thomas P.	(MN)	1152
	THOMAS, Katharine S.	(NC)	1237
	DE WITT, Benjamin L.	(NJ)	298
	BROWN, Eulalie W.	(NM)	143
	MIMNAUGH, Ellen N.	(OH)	845
	SCHWEITZER, Margaret C.	(PA)	1105
	POYER, Robert K.	(SC)	989
	FAIRLEY, Craig R.	(ON)	361
Patents & chemistry	POOL, Madlyn K.	(VA)	982
Patents & trademarks	ANDERSEN, Thomas K.	(CA)	21
	GROOT, Elizabeth N.	(CA)	472
	JOHNSON, Johanna H.	(TX)	606
Patents reference	WALKER, Barbara J.	(GA)	1295
Patents, science & business databases	TUNG, Sandra J.	(CA)	1263
Patents, technical	WILLIAMS, Robert C.	(AK)	1346
Scientific & technical patents	STANGL-WALKER, Teresa L.	(ON)	1180
Scientific patent databases	POKLAR, Mary J.	(CA)	980
Searching patent & chemical databases	MILES, Donald D.	(PA)	834
United States patents	DAHMANN, Rosemary G.	(OH)	270
	JOHNS, John E.	(OH)	601
	KECK, Kerry A.	(TX)	633

PATHFINDERS

Pathfinders & bibliographies	MORGAN, Pamela S.	(NF)	864

PATHOLOGY

Pathology	PATEL, Patricia C.	(DC)	947
Speech pathology	SNOW, Marina	(CA)	1164

PATIENTS (See also Clients, Consumer, Customer, Patrons, User)

Consumer & patient health information	LINDNER, Katherine L.	(NJ)	729
Hospital patient librarianship	MC LAIN, Swan M.	(GA)	813
Patient & consumer subjects	CESARD, Mary A.	(NJ)	196
Patient & health information	POMERANTZ, Karyn L.	(MD)	982
Patient care information requirements	JACOBSEN, Teresa T.	(IL)	590
Patient education	PROTTSMAN, Mary F.	(AL)	995
	ELSESSER, Lionelle H.	(MO)	346
	SERLING, Kitty	(MO)	1116
	WISEMAN, Karin M.	(NY)	1357
	JONES, Ruth A.	(WA)	615
Patient health information	DEWEY, Marjorie C.	(MA)	298
Patient index file maintenance	PARR, John R.	(ON)	943
Patient interview systems	COOK, Galen B.	(SC)	240
Patients library	RALSTON, Anne C.	(MD)	1004
Psychiatric patient library services	MERRILL, Susan S.	(MD)	827
Psychiatric patients	MASON, Martha A.	(NY)	781
Services to patients	SANDE, Alice E.	(MN)	1079
Staff & patients development	RALSTON, Anne C.	(MD)	1004
Therapeutic patient program planning	ABDULLAH, Bilquis	(NY)	2

PATRONS (See also Clients, Consumer, Customer, Patients, User)

Assisting patrons of library	VANDERBECK, Maria	(CA)	1273
Handicapped patrons	BURKE, Saretta K.	(OH)	160
Innovative patron involvement techniques	SWANTON, Susan I.	(NY)	1214

PATRONS (Cont'd)

Patron & inventory control	RAHN, Erwin P.	(NY)	1003
Patron assistance	BISSO, Arthur J.	(GA)	100
	KALER, Dorothy C.	(NM)	623
Patron computer services	WEBER, Julie A.	(IL)	1314
Patron data entry	WALKER, Laura L.	(IL)	1295
Patron education	ANDERSON, Marcia	(SC)	24
Patron orientation	WELSCH, Melissa W.	(LA)	1323
Patron training	FRITZ, Donald D.	(MI)	405
Patron-initiated reference requests	LAROSA, Thomas J.	(NY)	698
Patron-staff library communications	BROWN, Carol J.	(TX)	142
Patron-staff systems training	GATTEN, Jeffrey N.	(OH)	422
Problem patrons	SPARKMAN, Mickey M.	(TX)	1171
Services to disabled patrons	LEVERING, Mary B.	(DC)	719
Working with patrons	BERG, David C.	(MN)	84

PAVEMENTS

Civil engineering, pavements, structures	MOBLEY, Arthur B.	(DC)	851

PAY (See also Compensation, Salary)

Pay & benefit administration	LEBRUN, Marlene M.	(MD)	708
Pay equity	GALLOWAY, Sue	(CA)	415
	DOWELL, David R.	(IL)	315
	RAY, Jean M.	(IL)	1011
	FEYE-STUKAS, Janice	(MN)	374
Payroll processing	MOY, Clarence T.	(NY)	874
Personnel & payroll	VOIT, Irene E.	(NV)	1287
Personnel pay & equity	JOHANSON, Cynthia J.	(DC)	601

PAYABLE

Budget & accounts payable	VOIT, Irene E.	(NV)	1287
Paying subscriptions	GAYNOR, Joann T.	(NY)	424
Receivable & payable accounts	CHAPP, Debra R.	(IL)	202

PEACE

Information for world peace & humanity	KIANG, C K.	(IN)	646
Peace & social justice	KLINE, Victoria E.	(CA)	661
Peace materials & reference	MEYER, Jimmy E.	(OH)	830
Peace research & education	KOCSIS, Jeanne	(MA)	667
Peace studies	HOHL, Robert J.	(IN)	550
War & peace studies	YAMAMOTO, Conrad S.	(CA)	1376
Women's studies & peace research	HAMILTON-PENNELL, Christine	(CO)	492

PEDIATRICS

Orthopedic & oncology pediatrics	KELLER, Nancy H.	(LA)	635
Pediatric medicine	GREEN, Deidre E.	(ON)	461
Pediatric reference	TURNER, Tamara A.	(WA)	1265
Pediatrics	SHAPIRO, Leonard P.	(CA)	1121
Pediatrics collection development	ALLOCCO, Claudia	(NJ)	17

PENNSYLVANIA

Pennsylvania county records	STAYER, Jonathan R.	(PA)	1183
Pennsylvania genealogy	STAYER, Jonathan R.	(PA)	1183
Pennsylvania law	SMITH, Eugene J.	(PA)	1155
Pennsylvania state documents	SWAN, Christine H.	(PA)	1213

PENSION (See also Benefits, Retirement)

Pension plans	BIRSCHEL, Dee B.	(WI)	99

PERCEPTION

Extrasensory perception	NORMAN, Wayne R.	(NY)	909

PERFORMANCE

Computer performance	DIENER, Ronald E.	(OH)	302
Evaluation of vendor performance	ANDERSON, E A.	(MN)	22
Library performance measures	KANIA, Antoinette M.	(NY)	625
Music performance materials	WELIVER, E D.	(MI)	1321
Musical performance practice	ZASLAW, Neal	(NY)	1386

PERFORMANCE (Cont'd)

Musical performance practices	BOWLES, Edmund A.	(NY)	121
Organ performance	ROEPKE, David E.	(OH)	1048
Performance & collection evaluation	JENSEN, L B.	(ON)	599
Performance & program evaluation	MARRIOTT, Lois I.	(CA)	773
Performance historian	LOMONACO, Martha S. .	(NY)	738
Performance measurement	BORCHUCK, Fred P.	(TN)	116
Personnel admin, performance appraisal	VEANER, Allen B.	(ON)	1280
Planning & performance measurement	SKIDMORE, Stephen C. .	(OK)	1146

PERFORMING

Collection development, performing arts	DIMMICK, Mary L.	(PA)	304
Fine & performing arts	HOFFMAN, Irene M.	(CA)	548
Fine & performing arts bibliography	GROVES, Percilla E.	(BC)	474
Freelance performing arts research	BRAYTON, Roy S.	(NY)	130
Music & performing arts librarianship	MAYER, George L.	(NY)	789
Music performing arts reference	HARDISH, Patrick M. . . .	(NY)	500
Performing arts	LEMMON, Alfred E.	(LA)	715
	VAN HOVEN, William D. .	(NC)	1276
	CHACH, Maryann	(NY)	196
	HIGGINS, Steven	(NY)	538
	SOMMER, Susan T.	(NY)	1167
	WOOD, Thor E.	(NY)	1365
	MCGLINN, Frank C.	(PA)	806
Performing arts administration	BUCK, Richard M.	(NY)	154
Performing arts archives	WOODS, Alan L.	(OH)	1366
	PRITCHARD, Jane E. . . .	(ENG)	994
Performing arts librarianship	KUNSELMAN, Joan D. . .	(CA)	684
	DIDHAM, Reginald A. . . .	(MA)	301
	DUCLOW, Geradline . . .	(PA)	322
Performing arts libraries, museums	GOLDING, Alfred S.	(OH)	445
Performing arts publishing	PINE, Ralph	(NY)	974
Performing arts reference	WISE, Matthew W.	(NY)	1357
Performing arts reference, research	DEE, Camille C.	(NY)	286
Performing arts reference work	VELEZ, Sara B.	(NY)	1281
Performing arts research	MILLER, Hester M.	(NM)	838
Performing arts selection & bibliography	VAN NIEL, Eloise S.	(HI)	1276
Performing arts, speech communication	KELLY, Richard J.	(MN)	638
Performing online & computer searches	DUCHARME, Judith C. . .	(NM)	322
Reference, fine & performing arts	DOCTOROW, Erica	(NY)	307

PERIODICALS (See also Journals, Magazines, Newsletters, Newspapers, Serials)

Academic periodical department	KEIST, Sandra H.	(NM)	635
Administration of periodicals collection	SMITH, Cynthia A.	(OH)	1153
Antiquarian periodicals	OKERSON, Ann L.	(NY)	920
Arkansas periodical index	MCKEE, Elizabeth C. . . .	(AR)	810
Art historical periodicals	ALLENTUCK, Marcia E. .	(NY)	16
Back-issue of periodicals	MCGILVERY, Laurence .	(CA)	806
Book & periodical indexing	KOEHNLEIN, Bill	(NY)	667
Book & periodical publishing	MECKLER, Alan M.	(CT)	820
	WOOD, Richard T.	(MI)	1365
Business periodical databases	MARKERT, Patricia B. . .	(NY)	771
Business periodicals	REGNER, Erlinda J.	(IL)	1017
	MARCACCIO, Kathleen Y.	(MI)	768
Current periodicals management	JOHNS, Jean B.	(OH)	601
Engineering periodicals	PIENITZ, Eleanor	(NY)	971
Foreign & domestic periodicals	LONG, Roger J.	(IL)	739
General reference & periodicals	SANCHEZ, Sara M.	(FL)	1079
Hawaiian & Pacific business periodicals	SCHULTZ, Elaine V.	(HI)	1102
History of periodicals	NOURIE, Alan R.	(IL)	910
Indexing books & periodicals	O'LEARY, Mary E.	(MN)	920
Indexing of business periodicals	PEDALINO, M C.	(NY)	954
Indexing periodical articles	BRISTOW, Barbara A. . .	(NY)	137
Indexing periodical literature	VARKENTINE, Aganita . .	(CA)	1278
Legal periodicals	CRAWFORD, Nola N. . . .	(NJ)	257
Marketing technical periodicals	FERRERE, Cathy M.	(NY)	373
Medical periodicals	MCGILL, Thomas J.	(NJ)	806
Mexican periodicals	OROZCO-TENORIO, Jose M.	(MEX)	926
Newspapers & periodicals	BURTON, Donna M.	(ON)	164

PERIODICALS (Cont'd)

North American periodicals	NOBLE, Jean E.	(CA)	906
Periodical agents	MARKS, Cicely P.	(MD)	771
Periodical & book indexing	KEMP, Thomas J.	(CT)	639
	AGEE, Victoria V.	(MD)	7
	THICKITT, Lisa	(NC)	1235
Periodical collection & ordering	PELZER, Adolf	(MI)	955
Periodical control	KRAMER, Helen A.	(CA)	675
Periodical database	HAGOOD, Patricia C. . . .	(NY)	483
Periodical directories	HAGOOD, Patricia C. . . .	(NY)	483
Periodical indexing	CRAVENS, Vickie L. . . .	(MO)	256
	TERHUNE, R S.	(OH)	1231
	HALLMAN, Clark N.	(SD)	489
Periodical literature indexing	FOX, Elyse H.	(MA)	394
Periodical room supervision	LAROSA, Thomas J.	(NY)	698
Periodical system automation	REED, Virginia R.	(IL)	1015
Periodicals	FREDERIKSEN, Patience A.	(AK)	400
	JAIN, Celeste C.	(CA)	591
	JESSUP, Carrie	(CA)	600
	MORRISEY, Locke J. . . .	(CA)	867
	PETERSON, Anita R. . . .	(CA)	962
	COE, Gloria M.	(DE)	226
	HENDERSON, Patricia A.	(FL)	526
	LICHTENFELS, David D.	(FL)	725
	REDDY, Michael B.	(IL)	1013
	FINK, Madonna	(KS)	378
	KING, Charles D.	(KY)	650
	MCFARLING, Patricia G.	(KY)	805
	FARNER, Susan G.	(MN)	365
	MOXNESS, Mary J.	(MN)	874
	SMITH, Rachel H.	(MS)	1159
	COOPER, Ruth K.	(NC)	243
	HEUBERGER, Karen W. .	(NC)	535
	ROWLAND, Janet M. . . .	(NC)	1062
	GAVRISH, Diane L.	(NH)	423
	KIETZMAN, William D. . .	(NH)	647
	HEGG, Judith L.	(NJ)	521
	KAHN, Leslie A.	(NJ)	622
	KRUSE, Theodore H. . . .	(NJ)	681
	SNELSON, Pamela	(NJ)	1163
	VAN FLEET, James A. . .	(NJ)	1275
	BRICKER, Naomi S.	(NY)	135
	FEICK, Christina L.	(NY)	368
	JANOWSKY, Cara A. . .	(NY)	593
	O'HALLORAN, James V.	(NY)	918
	OSTROWSKY, Edith . . .	(NY)	929
	PODELL, Diane K.	(NY)	979
	MCCALL, Patricia	(OK)	793
	APOSTOLOS, Margaret M.	(PA)	29
	CATHEY, Gail L.	(PA)	195
	PARTIN, Gail A.	(PA)	945
	DERRICK, Mitzi J.	(SC)	294
	GILL, Linda S.	(TN)	435
	SNODDERLY, Louise D. .	(TN)	1163
	BAILEY, Anne M.	(TX)	46
	CORLEY, Carol W.	(TX)	246
	WILLIAMS, Greta A.	(VA)	1343
	BEN-SIMON, Julie E. . . .	(WA)	83
	NELSON, Christine	(WA)	893
	HUPP, Mary A.	(WV)	577
	LEBLANC, Amedee	(NB)	708
	CHAUMONT, Elise	(PQ)	204
	PAGEAU, Denise	(PQ)	934
	SAUCIER, Danielle	(PQ)	1084
	BARBERENA, Elsa	(MEX)	55
	LUSK, Betty M.	(SAF)	749
Periodicals, abstracting & indexing	RICHARD, Marie F.	(PQ)	1028
Periodicals acquisition	RINE, Joseph L.	(MN)	1035
Periodicals acquisition & check-in	KESSINGER, Pamela C. .	(IL)	644
Periodicals, acquisitions	ROBICHAUD, Marcel J. .	(NY)	1042
Periodicals & journals	LAFAYE, Cary D.	(SC)	687
Periodicals & serials	GOWAN, Christa I.	(CA)	455
	SUBRAMANIAN, Jane M.	(NY)	1206
	ROBERTS, Marica L. . . .	(TN)	1041
	DANKY, James P.	(WI)	274
Periodicals cataloging	FLUK, Louise R.	(PQ)	386
Periodicals coordinating	ZIRBES, Colette M.	(WI)	1390
Periodicals management	BEAVERS, Janet W.	(ISR)	71
Periodicals processing	GATES, Jane P.	(CA)	421

PERIODICALS (Cont'd)

Periodicals reference	WILLIAMS, Pauline C. . .	(AL)	1346
	CHEVRIER, Francine . . .	(PQ)	207
Religious periodicals	HILL, Lawrence H.	(PA)	540
Scientific & technical early periodicals	KRONICK, David A.	(TX)	679
Serials & periodicals	SCHWARTZKOPF,		
	Rebecca B.	(MN)	1105
	TRIBIT, Donald K.	(PA)	1256
Serials periodicals, public relations	PATTERSON, Grace L. . .	(NY)	948
Theological & religious periodicals	HAYES, Bonaventure F. .	(NY)	515
Victorian periodicals	ROBERTS, Helene E. . . .	(MA)	1040

PERMISSIONS (See also Clearance, Copyright, Rights)

Copyright permissions	IFFLAND, Carol D.	(IL)	581
Permissions	TAPHORN, Joseph B. . . .	(NY)	1223
Permissions & licensing rights	MARKERT, Patricia B. . .	(NY)	771
Rights & permissions	PRONIN, Monica	(NY)	995

PERSIAN

Translating Persian	BAGHAL-KAR, Vali E. . .	(TX)	45

PERSONAL

Administration & personal manuscript col	CUMMINGS, Hilary A. . .	(OR)	264
Consumer products, personal care	SILVERMAN, Susanne . .	(CT)	1139
Ernest Hemingway personal papers	DESNOYERS, Megan F. .	(MA)	295
Personal & microcomputers	GARCIA, Joseph E.	(MI)	417
Personal documentation	YAMAZAKI, Hisamichi . .	(JAP)	1377
Personal film, theatre library	TUDIVER, Lillian	(NY)	1262
Personal information systems	BURTON, Hilary D.	(CA)	164
Personal injury law	KOEING, Sherman	(FL)	667
Personal management	AUGER, Bernard	(PQ)	39
Personal papers	KRAFT, Katherine G. . . .	(MA)	675
	HERIOT, Ruthanne	(WV)	531
	STEELE, Apollonia L. . .	(AB)	1184
Personal papers, manuscripts	MASLYN, David C.	(RI)	780
Personal univ-quality art collections	BLAIR, Madeline S.	(DC)	102

PERSONAL COMPUTERS

Mainframe & personal computer software	POLLARD, Louise	(UT)	981
Microcomputer support IBM PC	DEEMER, Selden S.	(GA)	286
Microcomputers & personal computers	YOUNT, Natalie W.	(WA)	1384
PC applications	MADDOCK, Jerome T. . .	(CO)	759
	MCGINNIS, Joan M. . . .	(NH)	806
PC bulletin boards	ROSE, Phillip E.	(CO)	1055
PC communications	DENNETT, Stephen C. . .	(CA)	292
PC software	ADDISON, Paul H.	(IN)	6
PC-based retrieval systems	CIUFFETTI, Peter D. . . .	(MA)	215
Personal computer applications	MITCHELL, Elaine M. . . .	(DC)	848
	BENNETT, Lee L.	(IL)	82
	MUNTEAN, Deborah E. . .	(MN)	879
	HANEY, Kevin M.	(NJ)	495
	HOLLEY, James L.	(NY)	551
	MASH, S D.	(NY)	780
	ROACH, Linda	(PA)	1038
Personal computer applications in libs	PESCHEL, Susan M. . . .	(WI)	961
Personal computer database, sales	NASON, Stanley J.	(NY)	888
Personal computer database training	MULLINS, James R.	(TX)	878
Personal computer databases	ROBSON, Amy K.	(IL)	1045
	SULLIVAN, Michael M. . .	(VA)	1208
Personal computer desktop publishing	BALCOM, Karen S.	(TX)	51
Personal computer development & training	JONES, Jennifer R.	(NY)	613
Personal computer hardware & software	MILLER, Ann M.	(ON)	835
Personal computer lab	BRENNAN, Edward P. . .	(MD)	132
Personal computer library systems	KLEIN, Joanne S.	(PA)	659
Personal computer software	TABKE, Robert	(CA)	1219
	BEFELER, Mike	(CO)	74
	NG, Pauline	(IL)	900
Personal computer software applications	SABATINI, Joseph D. . . .	(NM)	1072
Personal computer software development	MAYDET, Steven I.	(NJ)	789

PERSONAL COMPUTERS (Cont'd)

Personal computer software, legal forms	KUEHNLE, Emery C. . . .	(OH)	682
Personal computer system management	ROSENFELD, Jane D. . .	(NY)	1056
Personal computer systems & software	TOWNLEY, Richard L. . .	(NY)	1253
Personal computer training	KRONISH, Priscilla T. . . .	(NY)	680
Personal computer use	WOOLARD, Wilma L. . . .	(IL)	1368
Personal computer user guide composition	MILLER, Ann M.	(ON)	835
Personal computers	DEWOLF, Timothy B. . . .	(CA)	298
	TASHIMA, Marie	(CA)	1224
	LATOUR, Catherine M. . .	(DC)	701
	WILLIAMS, Pamela D. . .	(FL)	1345
	MOZGA, John P.	(IL)	874
	YORKS, Melissa L.	(MD)	1381
	CARON, Theodore F. . . .	(MN)	184
	AU, Ka N.	(NJ)	38
	MCGOEY, Richard P. . . .	(NM)	807
	COOK, Pamela D.	(NY)	240
	EISENBERG, Michael B. .	(NY)	340
	SOLOMON, Samuel H. . .	(NY)	1166
	BACON, Agnes K.	(OH)	44
	LINDSAY, Lorin H.	(TX)	729
	VAN SCHAIK, Jo A.	(TX)	1277
	COSGRIFF, John C.	(VA)	248
Personal computers & applications	DOOLING, Marie	(NY)	312
Personal computers & library systems	FEDORS, Maurica R. . . .	(NJ)	368
Personal computers for library admin	CALHOUN, Ellen	(NJ)	172
Personal computers in libraries	SALM, Kay E.	(CA)	1077
	VLCEK, Randall	(IL)	1286
	KERSTETTER, Virginia M.	(VA)	644
Personal computers in special libraries	DUNCAN, Rebecca	(CA)	325
Personal computing	LUKOS, Geraldine F. . . .	(MA)	748
Personal computing in libraries	BANKHEAD, Elizabeth M.	(CO)	54
Using PC software in library	DIETRICH, Peter J.	(NY)	302

PERSONNEL (See also Appraisal, Assistants, Benefits, Employee, Employment, Job, Paraprofessional, Part-Time, Placement, Professional, Reduction, Recruitment, Temporary, Workers)

Administration & personnel	FORTIER, Jan M.	(MA)	391
	ROCK, Sue W.	(NJ)	1046
Administration & personnel management	HAGLE, Claudette S. . . .	(TX)	483
Administration organization, personnel	HEISE, George F.	(NJ)	522
Administration, personnel, budget	DAVID, Indra M.	(MI)	276
Administration, personnel, budget, space	ROSENFELD, Mary A. . .	(DC)	1056
Administration, personnel management	MCCARTHY, Germaine A.	(MA)	794
Budget & personnel administration	HEMPHILL, Jean F.	(CO)	525
Budget & personnel management	MORITZ, William D.	(WI)	865
Budget, personnel actions administration	CURTIS, George H.	(MO)	267
Budget, personnel, systems development	HARRIS, Linda S.	(DC)	505
Budget, reference, personnel	FARKAS, Charles R. . . .	(NY)	364
Engineering library personnel	LOOMIS, Barbara	(IL)	740
File room personnel supervision	DICKERSON, Mary J. . .	(TX)	300
Finance & personnel	PERRY, Rodney B.	(NY)	961
Library administration & personnel	ALITO, Martha A.	(DC)	13
	SNYDER, Carolyn A. . . .	(IN)	1104
Library, information personnel services	GOSSAGE, Wayne	(NY)	453
Library personnel	WIGLEY, Marylou	(CA)	1337
	ANDERSON, Lemoyne W.	(CO)	24
	BEASLEY, Clarence W. .	(FL)	69
	LIBBEY, George H.	(GA)	725
	DEWEY, Barbara I.	(IA)	298
	DELZELL, Robert F.	(MO)	290
	KAUFMAN, Judith L. . . .	(NY)	631
	REGAN, Muriel	(NY)	1017
	TURNER, Gurley	(NY)	1264
	LEHMAN, Lois J.	(VA)	713
	BAGG, Deborah L.	(WA)	45
Library personnel administration	NICHOLS, Elizabeth D. . .	(CA)	901
	BOWDEN, Philip L.	(IL)	120

PERSONNEL (Cont'd)

Library personnel classification	HEARTH, Fred E.	(CA)	519
Library personnel issues	GAUGHAN, Thomas M.	(NC)	422
Library personnel management	GUY, Jeniece N.	(IL)	479
	TROVER, Larry E.	(OH)	1258
	PERSON, Ruth J.	(PA)	961
Library personnel placement	BERGER, Carol A.	(IL)	85
Library personnel recruiting	WALSH, Deborah T.	(IL)	1299
Library services & personnel	FLEMING, Anne	(ON)	384
Management & personnel	KUPERMAN, Agota M.	(DC)	684
Management & personnel administration	JONES, Anne	(NY)	611
Management personnel	SCHABEL, Donald J.	(KY)	1088
	WASIELEWSKI, Eleanor B.	(MD)	1308
Managing & administering personnel	ROUDEBUSH, Lawanda C.	(IA)	1061
Motivation personnel management	STEPHENS, Jerry W.	(AL)	1188
Organization & personnel	HERNANDEZ, Ramon R.	(MI)	532
Organizational & personnel development	MAHMOODI, Suzanne H.	(MN)	760
Personnel	COOPER, Richard S.	(CA)	243
	COSTELLO, Robert C.	(CA)	249
	ELGIN, Susan R.	(CA)	342
	HAYDEN, Ronald L.	(CA)	515
	KISLITZIN, Elizabeth H.	(CA)	656
	MCQUOWN, Eloise	(CA)	817
	PORTER-ROTH, Anne	(CA)	985
	SHARROW, Marilyn J.	(CA)	1122
	WELLS, H L.	(CA)	1322
	BOSWELL, Peggy B.	(CO)	118
	SCHWARZ, Shirlee	(CT)	1105
	DELANCEY, James F.	(DC)	288
	CASON, Maidel K.	(DE)	193
	BURDICK, Lois B.	(FL)	158
	WILLIAMS, Ann W.	(FL)	1342
	CLARK, Tommy A.	(GA)	218
	CLEMENS, Bonnie J.	(GA)	220
	ROBISON, Carolyn L.	(GA)	1045
	TOPE, Diana R.	(GA)	1251
	TYLER, Audrey Q.	(GA)	1266
	BLACK, William K.	(IA)	102
	STICK, Dorothy J.	(IA)	1193
	BECK, Richard J.	(ID)	71
	BOWEN, Christopher F.	(IL)	120
	CHENOWETH, Rose M.	(IL)	206
	GREENFIELD, Jane W.	(IL)	464
	HESSLER, Nancy R.	(IL)	534
	MYERS, Margaret R.	(IL)	884
	QUERY, Lance D.	(IL)	999
	WILSON, W R.	(IL)	1353
	BRISTOW, Ann	(IN)	137
	WARREN, Hugh P.	(IN)	1306
	WILLIAMS, Nyal Z.	(IN)	1345
	DANKNER, Laura R.	(LA)	273
	LEINBACH, Philip E.	(LA)	714
	SALTER, Jeffrey L.	(LA)	1077
	BOZONE, Billie R.	(MA)	124
	GILROY, Rupert E.	(MA)	437
	GROSE, B D.	(MA)	472
	HILL, Barbara M.	(MA)	539
	LEVITT, Irene S.	(MA)	721
	MCFARLAN, Karen N.	(MA)	804
	SMITH, Barbara J.	(ME)	1153
	O'CONNELL, Catherine A.	(MI)	915
	SANDSTEDT, Carl R.	(MO)	1081
	HANSEL, Patsy J.	(NC)	497
	JONES, John W.	(NC)	613
	LITTLETON, Isaac T.	(NC)	734
	SEVERANCE, Robert W.	(NC)	1117
	SUTTON, Judith K.	(NC)	1211
	COUGHLIN, Caroline M.	(NJ)	250
	COUMBE, Robert E.	(NJ)	251
	SEISER, Virginia	(NM)	1113
	DONOVAN, Ruth H.	(NV)	312
	KRANICH, Nancy C.	(NY)	676
	LEARMONT, Carol L.	(NY)	707
	LERNER, Arthur	(NY)	717
	WELLS, Gladysann	(NY)	1322
	BUCK, Jeremy R.	(OH)	153
	DRAPP, Laureen	(OH)	318

PERSONNEL (Cont'd)

Personnel	ENGLISH, Raymond A.	(OH)	350
	JACOBER, Sheryl A.	(OH)	589
	MACKENZIE, Alberta E.	(OH)	756
	ROGERS, William F.	(OH)	1050
	TRUCKSIS, Theresa A.	(OH)	1259
	WALLACH, John S.	(OH)	1298
	KEENE, Janis C.	(OK)	634
	MEYERS, Duane H.	(OK)	830
	SMITH, Donald R.	(OK)	1154
	REEVES, Marjorie A.	(OR)	1017
	GILBERT, Nancy L.	(PA)	434
	HOCKER, Justine L.	(PA)	545
	MILLER, Mary C.	(PA)	840
	WHITTAKER, Edward L.	(PA)	1334
	JAMES, Denise T.	(SC)	592
	BRACEY, Ann E.	(TX)	124
	CAMERON, Dee B.	(TX)	174
	HORNAK, Anna F.	(TX)	559
	PROGAR, Dorothy R.	(TX)	995
	RILEY, Richard K.	(TX)	1034
	ALBRECHT, Sterling J.	(UT)	10
	OGDEN, Howard A.	(VA)	918
	NEILL, Priscilla	(WI)	892
	WRIGHT, Linda G.	(WV)	1372
	OSBORN, Lucie P.	(WY)	927
	DENIS, Laurent G.	(ON)	292
	EVANS, Calvin D.	(PQ)	356
Personnel administration	COOLMAN, Jacqueline	(CA)	241
	TERRY, Josephine R.	(CA)	1232
	YEH, Irene K.	(CA)	1379
	DIMATTIA, Ernest A.	(CT)	304
	SHOLTZ, Katherine J.	(CT)	1132
	PANZERA, Donald P.	(DC)	938
	CANELAS, Dale B.	(FL)	178
	EHRHORN, Jean H.	(HI)	339
	CRETH, Sheila D.	(IA)	258
	JENKINS, Darrell L.	(IL)	597
	LI, Dorothy W.	(IL)	724
	MCCABE, Ronald B.	(IL)	793
	PETERSON, Fred M.	(IL)	963
	VOLKMANN, Carl W.	(IL)	1287
	RAWLES-HEISER, Carolyn	(IN)	1010
	CLOHERTY, Lauretta M.	(MA)	223
	KEOUGH, Francis P.	(MA)	643
	LEBRETON, Jonathan A.	(MD)	708
	WILKINSON, Billy R.	(MD)	1340
	SCHWARTZ, Diane G.	(MI)	1104
	SCHRAMM, Betty V.	(MO)	1099
	COGGINS, Timothy L.	(NC)	227
	LANEY, Elizabeth J.	(NC)	695
	RODNEY, Mae L.	(NC)	1048
	KARMAZIN, Sharon M.	(NJ)	627
	KUUSKMAE, Mati	(NY)	685
	ROGERS, Irene	(NY)	1049
	ROSSOFF, Judith H.	(NY)	1059
	WENDT, Mary E.	(NY)	1324
	CUPP, Christian M.	(OH)	265
	GARTEN, Edward D.	(OH)	420
	HELSER, Fred L.	(OH)	525
	BONAMICI, Andrew R.	(OR)	113
	HELICHER, Karl W.	(PA)	524
	NEAL, James G.	(PA)	890
	GALLOWAY, Margaret E.	(TX)	415
	GOLDBERG, Rhoda L.	(TX)	444
	TODD, Fred W.	(TX)	1248
	OLSEN, Randy J.	(UT)	921
	GHERMAN, Paul M.	(VA)	430
	HASKELL, John D.	(VA)	510
	WEAVER, Carolyn G.	(WA)	1312
	ROOS, Tedine J.	(WY)	1053
	KHOUZAM, Monique	(PQ)	646
Personnel administration & development	SHELDON, L S.	(CO)	1126
Personnel admin, performance appraisal	VEANER, Allen B.	(ON)	1280
Personnel & administration	MILLER, Marcia M.	(IN)	840
Personnel & budget management	WONG, Clark C.	(CA)	1362
Personnel & budgeting	MCCOOL, Donna L.	(WA)	798

PERSONNEL (Cont'd)

Personnel & budgeting administrative	LETTIERI, Robin M.	(NY)	719
Personnel & friends of the library	ALMONY, Robert A.	(MO)	17
Personnel & labor relations	APPEL, Anne M.	(CA)	29
Personnel & operations planning	LEATHER, Deborah J.	(VA)	707
Personnel & payroll	VOIT, Irene E.	(NV)	1287
Personnel & professional systems	PEISCHL, Thomas P.	(MN)	955
Personnel & staff development	SCHERREI, Rita A.	(CA)	1092
	OCHSNER, Renata E.	(IL)	915
	ST. CLAIR, Gloriana S.	(OR)	1075
Personnel communications	ELDREDGE, Jonathan D.	(NM)	342
Personnel computing	ENGER, Kathy B.	(IA)	349
Personnel development	BIRCH, Grace M.	(CT)	97
	FUJINO, Amy H.	(HI)	408
	ISACCO, Jeanne M.	(NC)	584
Personnel development & management	CLEMONS, John E.	(GA)	221
Personnel evaluation & development	YUEH, Norma N.	(NJ)	1384
	ROBERTSON, Billy O.	(TN)	1041
Personnel evaluation system	VIELE, George B.	(NC)	1283
Personnel evaluations	GREESON, Judy G.	(TN)	465
Personnel hiring, evaluating, objectives	NOLAN, Deborah A.	(MD)	907
Personnel issues	BIGGS, Debra R.	(MI)	95
Personnel management	LANE, Robert B.	(AL)	694
	HILLMAN, Stephanie	(CA)	541
	MOFFEIT, Tony A.	(CO)	852
	SULLIVAN, Maureen	(CT)	1208
	HEISS, Harry G.	(DC)	523
	BADGER, Lynn C.	(FL)	44
	MARSHALL, Maggie L.	(IL)	774
	RUBIN, Richard E.	(IL)	1065
	VARNET, Harvey	(IL)	1279
	GALBRAITH, Leslie R.	(IN)	413
	TUCKER, John M.	(IN)	1261
	KONESKI-WHITE, Bonnie L.	(MA)	670
	SUDDUTH, William E.	(MA)	1206
	AUER, Margaret E.	(MI)	39
	HAENICKE, Carol A.	(MI)	482
	KIRBY, Frederick J.	(MI)	654
	MOSS, Josievet	(MI)	872
	WOODFORD, Arthur M.	(MI)	1366
	KING, Jack B.	(MN)	651
	ANDERSON, James F.	(MS)	23
	BARTON, Phillip K.	(NC)	62
	KAUP, Jermain A.	(ND)	631
	DAVIS, Hiram L.	(NM)	279
	WU, Painan R.	(NY)	1373
	CALL, J R.	(OH)	173
	COLEMAN, Judith	(OH)	231
	HILDEBRAND, Carol I.	(OR)	538
	SHAW, Elizabeth L.	(OR)	1123
	HESS, Marjorie A.	(PA)	534
	WEBRECK, Susan J.	(PA)	1314
	KELLEY, Gloria	(SC)	636
	WARREN, Charles D.	(SC)	1306
	ALLMAND, Linda F.	(TX)	17
	CARGILL, Jennifer S.	(TX)	181
	GAMEZ, Juanita L.	(TX)	416
	ICE, Priscilla T.	(WA)	581
	SHAFFER, Maryann	(WA)	1119
	COGSWELL, Howard L.	(NB)	227
	LEVIS, Joel	(ON)	721
	SKEITH, Mary E.	(ON)	1145
	GLASS, Gerald	(PQ)	440
Personnel management & administration	SCOTT, Thomas L.	(MN)	1108
	GIORDANO, Frederick S.	(NY)	438
Personnel management & labor relations	FRANCIS, Derek R.	(BC)	396
Personnel management & staff development	PARENT, Roger H.	(IL)	940
Personnel management & training	DEMPSEY, Pamela M.	(NM)	291
Personnel management consulting	SMITH, Catherine	(NC)	1153
Personnel management, public libraries	HAGLOCH, Susan B.	(OH)	483
Personnel matters	VARIEUR, Normand L.	(NJ)	1278
Personnel pay & equity	JOHANSON, Cynthia J.	(DC)	601
Personnel, planning	LARSON, Mildred N.	(WI)	699

PERSONNEL (Cont'd)

Personnel, planning & budgeting	BROOM, Susan E.	(FL)	141
Personnel policies & administration	RITTER, Philip W.	(NC)	1036
Personnel policy	LEBRUN, Marlene M.	(MD)	708
Personnel problem solving	HARDIN, Willie	(AR)	500
Personnel problems	MUELLER, Elizabeth	(IL)	875
Personnel records	MOY, Clarence T.	(NY)	874
Personnel recruitment	MCINDOO, Larry R.	(CA)	809
Personnel recruitment & selection	MARTZ, David J.	(DC)	779
	MCMEEN, Frances E.	(NY)	815
Personnel relations	DUFORE, Thomas H.	(AZ)	324
Personnel resource	LEVESQUE, Janet A.	(RI)	719
Personnel services	CONDREY, Barbara K.	(CA)	236
Personnel structure	DOWELL, David R.	(IL)	315
Personnel supervision	COFFEY, James R.	(NJ)	227
Personnel systems	CLIFT, Scott B.	(MA)	222
	CANNON, Robert E.	(NC)	179
Personnel training	O'BRIEN, Marlys H.	(MN)	915
	GOLDSTEIN, Cynthia N.	(WA)	446
	BREDESON, Peggy Z.	(WI)	131
Personnel training & development	SCHWARZMANN, Diane D.	(CA)	1105
	GRAY, Karen S.	(IL)	460
	SEIDMAN, Ruth K.	(MA)	1112
	VON WAHLDE, Barbara	(NY)	1288
Personnel training & evaluation	EYLES, Heberle H.	(FL)	359
Personnel work	MC LAUGHLIN, Terry L.	(IL)	813
Planning & personnel administration	PHILLIPS, Carol B.	(TX)	967
Recruitment of personnel	STOFFEL, Lester L.	(IL)	1196
Research for media personnel	BROWN, Phyllis J.	(TN)	147
Special education personnel development	RUDDOCK, Velda I.	(CA)	1065
Staff development, media personnel	BURKE, Grace W.	(GA)	160
Staffing personnel	GROSS, Dorothy E.	(IL)	472
Student personnel	BUTLER, James C.	(MS)	166
Training & development of personnel	WILLIAMS, Nancy F.	(GA)	1345
Training information desk personnel	DUCHARME, Judith C.	(NM)	322
Training personnel	HACKMAN, Mary H.	(MD)	481
Training student-related personnel	WALLER, Elaine J.	(MI)	1298
Training technical services personnel	GOODWIN, Vania M.	(IN)	450
Utilization of paralegal personnel	GILMER, Wesley	(KY)	437

PESTICIDES

Pesticides	BLALOCK, Charlotte R.	(DC)	103
Pesticides information	SPURLING, Norman K.	(MD)	1177

PETROCHEMICALS

Petrochemicals	JENKINS-PENDER, Maureen	(AB)	597
Petroleum refining & petrochemicals	HOFFMAN, Allen	(NY)	547

PETROLEUM (See also Oil)

Earth science, geology & petroleum	DEPETRO, Thomas G.	(TX)	293
Indexing of petroleum-related material	TERLIZZI, Joseph M.	(NY)	1232
Natural gas, petroleum & electricity	LOOS, Carolyn F.	(TX)	740
Petroleum	BIGGS, Barbara R.	(LA)	95
Petroleum & energy database indexing	SHERRILL, Jooolyn T.	(NY)	1129
Petroleum & energy law	DUDLEY, Durand S.	(OH)	323
Petroleum bibliographic info systs	HILL, Linda L.	(OK)	540
Petroleum databases	STARK, Philip H.	(CO)	1182
Petroleum exploration & production	ANDERSON, Margaret	(TX)	24
Petroleum geology	SHANKS, Katherine N.	(OK)	1120
Petroleum industry information	ROBERTSON, Betty M.	(NY)	1041
Petroleum information	BREWER, Stanley E.	(TX)	134
Petroleum reference	MURRAY, James T.	(OK)	882
Petroleum refining & petrochemicals	HOFFMAN, Allen	(NY)	547
Petroleum related collections	GASHUS, Karin C.	(AB)	421
Software chemical, petroleum engineering	WILSON, John W.	(TX)	1351
Technical petroleum information	STURDIVANT, Clarence A.	(CO)	1205

PHARMACEUTICAL (See also Drugs, Pharmacology)

Managing pharmaceutical information	DRUKKER, Alexander E. .	(DE)	320
Medical & pharmaceutical literature	TANEN, Lee J.	(NJ)	1222
Medical, pharmaceutical & bus databases	DUDLEY, Debbra C.	(NJ)	323
Medical pharmaceutical chemical database	MOYNIHAN, Mary B. . . .	(CT)	874
Medical, pharmaceutical writing	CARVER, Mary	(NY)	191
Pharmaceutical	BOISVERT, Diane	(PQ)	111
Pharmaceutical & biotechnology info	DIXON, Michael D.	(VA)	306
Pharmaceutical & medical databases	ROSENTHAL, Francine C.	(OH)	1057
Pharmaceutical & medical information	LAUTENSCHLAG, Elisabeth C.	(PA)	703
Pharmaceutical chemistry	BONDAROVICH, Mary F.	(NJ)	113
Pharmaceutical databases	DUTKA, Jeanne L.	(NJ)	329
	MILLINGTON, Kathleen A.	(NJ)	843
Pharmaceutical industry	KOZAK, Marlene G.	(IL)	674
Pharmaceutical information	HULL, Peggy F.	(NC)	573
	CLEMANS, Margaret H. . .	(VA)	220
	WACASEY, Mary M.	(PQ)	1290
Pharmaceutical information scientist	THOMPSON, Reubin C. . .	(NC)	1241
Pharmaceutical, medical, bus databases	MCMASTER, Deborah L.	(CT)	815
Pharmaceutical, medical, business ref	MCMASTER, Deborah L.	(CT)	815
Pharmaceutical reference	WALTON, Carol G.	(NC)	1301
Pharmaceutical research info systems	PEETERS, Marc D.	(BEL)	954
Pharmaceutical sciences bibliography	ANDREWS, Theodora A.	(IN)	27
Pharmaceutical sciences reference	PIERMATTI, Patricia A. .	(NJ)	972
Pharmaceutical searching online	SNOW, Bonnie	(PA)	1164
Pharmaceuticals	KELLY, Claire B.	(PQ)	637
Pharmacy	ELDER, Nancy I.	(TX)	342
Pharmacy bibliography	ARTH, Janet M.	(MN)	35
Pharmacy computer systems	FASSETT, William E. . . .	(WA)	366
Pharmacy reference & bibliography	MANNARINO, Elizabeth R.	(OR)	766
Scientific & pharmaceutical databases	BARNETT, Philip	(NY)	58

PHARMACOLOGY (See also Drugs, Pharmaceutical)

Editing medical & pharmacological texts	HAMILTON, Gloria R. . . .	(PA)	492
Indexing medical & pharmacological texts	HAMILTON, Gloria R. . . .	(PA)	492
Pharmacological databases	WEIS, Ann M.	(NY)	1319
Pharmacology	SNELL, Charles E.	(CA)	1163
Pharmacology & toxicology	COSMIDES, George J. . .	(MD)	249
Rewriting medical & pharmacological text	HAMILTON, Gloria R. . . .	(PA)	492

PHILADELPHIA (See also Pennsylvania)

Library system of Philadelphia	GREEN, Rose B.	(PA)	462
Philadelphia architects	LAVERTY, Bruce	(PA)	703
Philadelphia, general history	LAVERTY, Bruce	(PA)	703
Philadelphia history	WOLF, Edwin	(PA)	1360
Public materials of Philadelphia	BRENNAN, Ellen	(PA)	132

PHILANTHROPY (See also Gifts)

Philanthropic databases	TAFT, James R.	(DC)	1219
	KLETZIEN, S D.	(PA)	661
Philanthropy	HARDING, Mary H.	(NY)	500
Philanthropy research	GONZALEZ, Suzanna S.	(CT)	448

PHILATELY

Philately	HESSELBEIN, Krista M. .	(OH)	534

PHILOLOGICAL (See also Literature)

Philological research & writing	HUMEZ, Nicholas D.	(ME)	573

PHILOSOPHY

Cataloging history, philosophy, religion	YU, Priscilla C.	(IL)	1384
Cataloging theology & philosophy	ROONEY, Eugene M. . . .	(DC)	1053
Col development, philosophy & religion	STEWART, Douglas J. . .	(AZ)	1192
History & philosophy of librarianship	STIELOW, Frederick J. . .	(MD)	1194
Humanities & philosophy bibliography	HANNAFORD, William E.	(PA)	496
Philosophical bibliography	BYNAGLE, Hans E.	(WA)	168

PHILOSOPHY (Cont'd)

Philosophy	OAKLANDER, Linda G. . .	(MI)	913
Philosophy, classics, music	CULLARS, John M.	(IL)	263
Philosophy of librarianship	BERGEN, Daniel P.	(NY)	85
	SORGEN, Herbert J. . . .	(NY)	1168
	ENGLE, Michael O.	(OR)	349
	NEILL, Sam D.	(ON)	892
Religion & philosophy	BUTKIS, John F.	(CA)	166
	FOLLICK, Edwin D.	(CA)	388
	NOLAN, Christopher W. .	(TX)	907
Religion & philosophy bibliography	HIGGINBOTHAM, Richard C.	(IL)	537
	ALTMANN, Thomas F. . .	(WI)	18
Religion, theology & philosophy	TROUTMAN, Joseph E. .	(GA)	1258
Subject specialist in philosophy	LAMB, Robert S.	(IN)	690
Theology, pastoral studies, philosophy	STALZER, Rita M.	(IL)	1179

PHONE

Touch-tone phone entry	ELASIK, Ronald G.	(MD)	341

PHONODISC

Phonodisc historical research	GRENDYSA, Peter A. . . .	(WI)	467

PHONOGRAPH (See also Discography, Disk, Recordings)

Antique phonograph records archives	JACOBSEN, Arnold	(MI)	590
Appraising record & phonograph cols	FABRIZIO, Timothy C. . .	(NY)	360
Early phonograph recordings, 1890-1930	RIGGS, Quentin T.	(CA)	1034
Historical phonograph records	BRYAN, Martin F.	(VT)	151
Historical records, phonographs	STRONG, Darrell G.	(PA)	1203
Phonograph	BOWLING, Lance C.	(CA)	121
Phonograph record collections	EVANS, David H.	(TN)	356
Phonograph recordings & rare books	BROWNE, J P.	(CA)	148
Phonographs & recordings	WITT, Kenneth W.	(MN)	1358
Recording dates phonograph records	STRONG, Darrell G.	(PA)	1203

PHONORECORDS

Phonorecordings	WOOD, Linda L.	(PA)	1364
Phonorecords or sound recordings	HASSE, John E.	(DC)	511

PHOTOCOPYING (See also Reprographics)

Document, reprint, photocopy supply	KOSTENBAUDER, Scott	(NY)	673
Microforms, equipment, photocopy	GREEN, Walter H.	(MO)	463
Photocopy reprints publishing	BROWN, G R.	(FL)	144
Photocopying	BENNETT, Richard F. . . .	(FL)	82
Reprography & photocopy	TRIBIT, Donald K.	(PA)	1256

PHOTOGRAPHS (See also Pictures, Slides)

Archival & photographic administration	DENSKY, Lois R.	(NJ)	293
Archival photographs	BAUS, J W.	(IN)	67
Cataloging & classifying photographs	KOSHER, Helene J.	(CA)	672
Cataloging & indexing photographs	GRAUE, Luz B.	(CA)	458
Cataloging photographs	CLARK, David L.	(CA)	216
	ZARCONE, Beth B.	(NY)	1386
	STONE, Gerald K.	(ON)	1197
Cataloging photographs & documents	FROST, Debra R.	(CO)	406
Cataloging photographs, collections mgmt	ROARK, Carol E.	(TX)	1038
Film & photograph research	GOTTFRIED, Erika D. . . .	(NY)	453
Historic photographs	LANDIS, Lawrence A. . . .	(TX)	693
	JACOB, Diane B.	(VA)	589
Historical photographs	BRENNER, M D.	(AK)	133
	D'ANTONIO, Lynn M. . . .	(AZ)	274
	ABRAHAM, Terry	(ID)	3
	CALDWELL, Richard C. .	(WA)	172
	ENGEMAN, Richard H. . .	(WA)	349
	HILL, Edwin L.	(WI)	539
Historical photos	ARONER, Miriam D.	(CA)	34
Indexing newspaper clips & photos	RICE, Margaret R.	(TX)	1027
Indexing newspaper photographs	BASNIGHT, Clara P. . . .	(VA)	63
Indexing photographs	SINCLAIR, John M.	(AB)	1142
John F Kennedy film & photographs	GOODRICH, Allan B. . . .	(MA)	449
Kennedy family photographs	GOODRICH, Allan B. . . .	(MA)	449

PHOTOGRAPHS (Cont'd)

Local history & photograph collections	BABBITT, Dennis L.	(IN)	43
Map & air photo collections	SUTHERLAND, Johnnie D.	(GA)	1211
Maps, aerial photos, atlases	EASTON, William W. . . .	(IL)	333
Marketing photos to public institutions	HENDERSON, Ellen B. . .	(CA)	526
Newspaper & photo collections	SWARTZ, Patrice B.	(PA)	1214
Newspaper clippings & photos	CHANCE, Peggy J.	(PA)	199
Newspaper photo archives	PARISOT, Beverly J. . . .	(NE)	940
Newspaper photo systems	KANE, Angelika R.	(PA)	624
19th century photographs	RHINELANDER, Mary F.	(MA)	1025
	MORROW, Delores J. . .	(MT)	869
Paper & photographic conservation	BUMGARNER, John L. . . .	(NC)	157
Photo & slide organizational systems	ROBERTSON, Retha M. . .	(OK)	1042
Photo archives	FURR, Susan H.	(VA)	410
Photo collection development	FRANKLIN, Alyce B. . . .	(KY)	397
Photo collections	LARZELERE, David W. . .	(MI)	700
	NEU, Margaret J.	(TX)	896
Photo duplication services	VISKOCHIL, Larry A. . . .	(IL)	1285
Photo filing systems	SCARANO, Lisa C.	(NY)	1087
Photo indexing	LYONS, Valerie S.	(GA)	753
Photo ISAR	TIFFT, Jeanne D.	(DC)	1244
Photo morgue design & implementation	DAMOTH, Douglas L. . . .	(NY)	272
Photo organizing	CANT, Elaine N.	(CA)	179
Photo research & indexing	FRANKLIN, Alyce B. . . .	(KY)	397
Photo storage & retrieval	HAMMOND, Theresa M. .	(VA)	494
Photograph collection	THOMPSON, Mary A. . .	(KS)	1240
	SUMNERS, Bill F.	(TN)	1209
Photograph collection administration	OKEEFE, Julia C.	(CA)	919
Photograph collection management	PINSON, Patricia A. . . .	(WY)	975
Photograph collections	REIFMAN, Deborah S. . .	(CA)	1019
	O'DONOGHUE, Patrice .	(TX)	917
	WILSON, Michael E.	(TX)	1352
	MOHOLT, Megan L.	(WA)	852
Photograph curator	BECK, Alison M.	(TX)	71
Photograph reference & cataloging	STERN, Teena B.	(CA)	1189
Photograph storage & retrieval	STEVENS, Paula F.	(AZ)	1190
Photographic archives	BERGEN, Philip S.	(MA)	85
	COTTEN, Jerry W.	(NC)	250
	HALLER, Douglas M. . . .	(PA)	489
	SCHULZ, Constance B. .	(SC)	1102
	STONE, Gerald K.	(ON)	1197
	HANDE, D A.	(SK)	494
Photographic archives & research	SPINA, Marie C.	(NY)	1175
Photographic collection	LINN, Mott R.	(PA)	731
Photographic collection management	OETTING, Edward C. . . .	(AZ)	917
Photographic collection organization	VOGT-O'CONNOR, Diane L.	(DC)	1287
Photographic collections	MUNOFF, Gerald J.	(IL)	879
	POIRRIER, Sherry	(MA)	980
	KIRWAN, Kathleen	(NY)	656
Photographic conservation	MATTENSON, Murray M. .	(IL)	785
	SARETZKY, Gary D. . . .	(NJ)	1082
Photographic copy work	DESJARDINS, Andrea C. .	(MA)	295
Photographic history	VISKOCHIL, Larry A. . . .	(IL)	1285
Photographic libraries	ZARCONE, Beth B.	(NY)	1386
Photographic preservation	COIR, Mark A.	(MI)	229
Photographic productions & publications	SPINA, Marie C.	(NY)	1175
Photographs	ESCHER, Nancy	(CA)	354
	SIMPSON, Mildred	(CA)	1142
	VANSLYKE, Lisa M.	(CA)	1277
	SMITH, Rebecca A.	(FL)	1159
	HEARN, Geraldine B. . . .	(IL)	518
	ELLIOTT, Joan M.	(IN)	344
	CRAWFORD, Anthony R. .	(KS)	256
	CREIGHTON, Alice S. . .	(MD)	258
	SILVER, Marcy R.	(MD)	1138
	STOCKDALE, Kay L. . . .	(NC)	1195
	O'KEEFE, Laura K.	(NY)	919
	DUCKETT, Kenneth W. .	(OR)	322
	WINROTH, Elizabeth C. .	(OR)	1355
	ANDRICK, Annita A. . . .	(PA)	27
	SILVERMAN, Marc B. . .	(PA)	1138
	SPAWN, Carol M.	(PA)	1172
	LETSON, Dawn E.	(TX)	719
	WHITE, Elizabeth B. . . .	(TX)	1331
Photographs as historical documents	CHRISTOPHER, Paul . . .	(CA)	212
Photographs collections management	STONE, Gerald K.	(ON)	1197
Photographs of Pittsburgh	KURTIK, Frank J.	(PA)	685

PHOTOGRAPHS (Cont'd)

Photography & things photographic	STOCKFLETH, Craig G. . .	(CA)	1195
Photos	CROCKETT, Mary S. . . .	(SC)	259
Prints & photographs	FELACO, Maja K.	(DC)	369
	IBACH, Marilyn	(DC)	581
	BAKER, Tracey I.	(MN)	50
Rare book photographic services	MCKENNEY, Kathryn K. .	(DE)	811
Rare books, photographs, ephemerae	HARDY, D C.	(LA)	500
Rare jazz records, films & photographs	BRADLEY, Jack	(MA)	126
Research photographs	ROARK, Carol E.	(TX)	1038
Researching historic photos & film	LUSKEY, Judith	(DC)	749
Slides & photographs	SNOW, Maryly A.	(CA)	1164
	BRAUNSTEIN, Mark M. . .	(RI)	130
Visual resources, slides & photographs	GREWENOW, Peter W. . .	(NY)	467

PHOTOGRAPHY (See also Photographs, Slides)

Aerial photography	STARK, Peter L.	(OR)	1181
Art & historical photography	FALK, Peter H.	(CT)	362
Bibliography of photography	RULE, Amy E.	(AZ)	1067
Cinematography & photography	ISOBE, Darron T.	(UT)	585
History of photography	RULE, Amy E.	(AZ)	1067
	MENTHE, Melissa	(NJ)	825
History of photography bibliography	HUGHSTON, Milan R. . . .	(TX)	572
Middle East 19th century photography	THOMAS, Ritchie D.	(OH)	1238
Nature photographers & photography	ALASTI, Aryt	(MA)	9
Photography	STONE, Joyce L.	(CO)	1197
	REYNOLDS, Jon K.	(DC)	1025
	SEITZ, Phillip R.	(DC)	1113
	BEETHAM, Donald W. . .	(NJ)	74
	HAYNIE, Altie V.	(TX)	517
	OTTO, Susan J.	(WI)	930
	MENARD, Michael J. . . .	(WY)	823
Photography & things photographic	STOCKFLETH, Craig G. . .	(CA)	1195
Photography & urban history	GRAY, Priscilla M.	(PA)	460
Photography archives	HENDERSON, Ellen B. . .	(CA)	526
Photography library	HOFFKNECHT, Carmen L.	(CA)	547
Photography referral	HOFFKNECHT, Carmen L.	(CA)	547
Photography resources information	HOFFKNECHT, Carmen L.	(CA)	547
Selection, photography	WACHEL, Kathleen B. . .	(IA)	1290
Still photography consultant, appraiser	MACAULEY, C C.	(CA)	754
Travel photography & lectures	PETERSON, Mildred O. . .	(IL)	964
Writing & photography	FREY, Roxanne C.	(IL)	403

PHOTOJOURNALISM

| Photojournalism | EUKEY, Jim O. . . . . | (WI) | 356 |

PHYSICAL

Acquisitions, physical sciences	MERRYMAN, Margaret M.	(VA)	827
Blind & physically handicapped	COLEMAN, James M. . .	(AL)	231
Chemical & physical scis database srchng	REDALJE, Susanne J. . .	(WA)	1013
Chemistry & physical sciences databases	BECK, Diane J.	(CA)	71
Life sciences & physical sciences	WILLIAMS, Robert C. . . .	(AK)	1346
Physical building needs	ROGERS, William F.	(OH)	1050
Physical education & dance	MAYRAND, Lise M.	(PQ)	791
Physical facilities	GILROY, Rupert E.	(MA)	437
Physical facilities management	WEBB, Gisela M.	(TX)	1313
Physical handicapped services	BIVINS, Hulen E.	(AL)	100
Physical handicaps	HAYNES, Douglas E. . . .	(NM)	516
Physical, life scis & engrng reference	MURPHY, Joan F.	(CA)	880
Physical medicine & rehabilitation	SHANEFIELD, Irene D. . .	(PQ)	1120
Physical planning	LEITH, Anna R.	(BC)	714
Physical preparation	SULLIVAN, Stephen W. . .	(NY)	1208
Physical processing	GAUDET, Dodie E.	(MA)	422
	CHILDRESS, Eric R. . . .	(NC)	208
	UHLMAN, Carol K.	(WA)	1268
	THOMSON, Donna K. . .	(ON)	1241
Physical science indexing	SERDZIAK, Edward J. . .	(CA)	1116
Physical science reference	BARATTA, Maria	(NJ)	55
Physical sciences & collection devlpmnt	MACEWEN, Virginia B. .	(DC)	755
Physical sciences & engineering	HADDEN, Robert L. . . .	(MD)	481
Physical sciences & mathematics	CRONEIS, Karen S.	(TX)	260
Physical sciences bibliography	SEILER, Susan L.	(FL)	1112

PHYSICAL (Cont'd)
Physical sciences collection
development — DESS, Howard M. . . . . . (NJ) 295
Physical sciences databases — HILDITCH, Bonny M. . . . (MD) 539
THAYER, Martha B. . . . . (WA) 1234
Physical scis databases online
searching — CARTER, Jackson H. . . . (NM) 189
Physical sciences, earth sciences — VIERICH, Richard W. . . . (CA) 1284
Physical sciences reference — LARUSSA, Carol J. . . . . (CA) 700
SOUTHERN, Mary A. . . . (NC) 1170
GALKOWSKI, Patricia E. (RI) 413
THAYER, Martha B. . . . . (WA) 1234
Physically handicapped reading
services — MCCASLIN, Cheryl A. . . . (TX) 795
Planning physical quarters — JAFFARIAN, Sara . . . . . (MA) 591
Reference, physical sci & engineering — SIEBURTH, Janice F. . . (RI) 1135
Special physical education — GRIFFITH, Joan C. . . . . . (NH) 469

PHYSICIANS
Teaching physicians GRATEFUL
MED — SCHELL, Catherine L. . . (WY) 1091
Women physicians — CHAFF, Sandra L. . . . . . (PA) 197

PHYSICS (See also Astrophysics, Metaphysics, Solar (Physics))
Chemistry & physics — ORCUTT, Roberta K. . . . (NV) 925
HELWIG, Karen A. . . . . . (WI) 525
Chemistry engineering & physics — SCHALIT, Michael . . . . . (CA) 1089
Chemistry, physics, soil science — VIERICH, Richard W. . . . (CA) 1284
Electronics & physics databases — WOLF, Noel C. . . . . (AZ) 1360
Engineering physics & chemical
databases — GENTRY, Susan K. . . . . (CA) 427
Health physics — SHERMAN, Dottie . . . . . (CT) 1128
Mathematics, physics, statistics — CZIFFRA, Peter . . . . (NJ) 269
Physics — STERN, David . . . . (IL) 1189
THORP, Raymond G. . . (ENG)1242
Physics & astronomy reference — SCHNOOR, Harriet E. . . (IL) 1098
Physics & chemistry — KAN, Halina S. . . . . (NJ) 624
Physics & life sciences — COHEN, Rosemary C. . . (NY) 229
Physics & math reference — DAVIDOFF, Gary N. . . . . (IL) 276
Physics collection development — WOELL, Yvette N. . . . . . (IL) 1359
Physics databases — DAVIDOFF, Gary N. . . . . (IL) 276
BRACKETT, Norman S. . (MI) 124
LERNER, Rita G. . . . . . . (NY) 717
Physics databases & reference — WOELL, Yvette N. . . . . . (IL) 1359
Physics literature — WANAT, Camille A. . . . . (CA) 1302
PRIMACK, Alice L. . . . . (FL) 993
Reviewing physics films — DOWLING, John . . . . . . (PA) 316
Science & physics reference — STEINBERG, Marilyn H. . (MA) 1185
Science, physics, mathematics — HOOKER, Ruth H. . . . . . (CA) 556
Semiconductor physics — COOK, Sherry M. . . . . . . (CA) 240
Solar physics — STRAND, Kathryn . . . . . (CO) 1200

PHYSIOLOGY
Anatomy, physiology, & microbiology — MANDERSCHEID, Dorothy
H. . . . . (MI) 765

PIANO
Piano discographies — YRIGOYEN, Robert P. . . (NJ) 1384
Piano music & consulting — PATRYCH, Joseph . . . . . (NY) 947
Piano research & cataloging — YRIGOYEN, Robert P. . . (NJ) 1384
Researching piano history &
technology — RICHARDS, James H. . . (TX) 1028

PICOCOMPUTERS
Microcomputers & picocomputers — TIERNAN, Linda M. . . . . (NH) 1244

PICTURES (See also Photographs, Portraits, Print)
Acquisition of eductnl motion pictures — CHAVES, Francisco M. . . (FL) 204
Acquisition of motion pictures &
videos — TALIT, Lynn . . . . (CT) 1221
Cataloging of eductnl motion pictures — CHAVES, Francisco M. . . (FL) 204
Director of pictorial resrch collection — GORDON, Thelma S. . . . (CT) 452
Motion picture & television archiving — FIELDING, Raymond E. . (TX) 376
Motion picture & television research — BRADY, Eileen E. . . . . . . (WA) 126

PICTURES (Cont'd)
Motion picture production research — PLUMB, Carolyn G. . . . . (CA) 978
Motion picture research — NAZARIAN, Anahid . . . . (CA) 890
Motion pictures — DEUTSCH, James I. . . . . (DC) 296
Motion pictures & television — SCHLOSSER, Anne G. . . (CA) 1094
Pictorial collections — OSTROW, Stephen E. . . . (DC) 929
Picture books — BUCKLEY, Virginia L. . . . (NY) 154
Picture books, early childhood — GREENE, Ellin P. . . . . . (NJ) 464
Picture collection cataloging — NATHEWS, Ann . . . . . . (AL) 889
Picture collection control — REDDINGTON, Mary E. . . (OH) 1013
Picture collection management — ANDERSON, James C. . . (KY) 23
Picture collections — EARLS, M L. . . . . (ON) 332
Picture file — MACIUSZKO, Kathleen L. (OH) 755
Picture research — DEANE, Roxanna . . . . . . (DC) 284
ELTZROTH, Elsbeth L. . . (GA) 519
Picture researcher — TODD, Rose A. . . . . (PQ) 1248
Picture searching — BAERWALD, Susan M. . (MO) 45
Research for motion picture, television — NELSON-HARB, Sally R. . (CA) 895
Slides & picture files design — KEAVENEY, Sydney S. . (NY) 633
Writing & editing pictorial histories — LUSKEY, Judith . . . . (DC) 749

PILOT
Pilot training — HARPER, Marie F. . . . . . (AL) 503

PIRACY
Piracy — RISHER, Carol A. . . . . . . (DC) 1036

PITTSBURGH (See also Pennsylvania)
General history of Pittsburgh — KURTIK, Frank J. . . . . . . (PA) 685
Photographs of Pittsburgh — KURTIK, Frank J. . . . . . . (PA) 685

PLACE
Place name literature — POWELL, Margaret S. . . (OH) 988

PLACEMENT
Career development & placement — ANSELMO, Edith H. . . . . (NJ) 28
Career planning & placement — SCOTT, Melissa C. . . . . (MI) 1107
Graduate placement — MATARAZZO, James M. . (MA) 783
Library & info science placement — WELSH, Barbara W. . . . (PA) 1323
Library development & placement — MUELLER, Elizabeth . . . . (IL) 875
Library personnel placement — BERGER, Carol A. . . . . . (IL) 85
Library placement — DEWEY, Barbara I. . . . . . (IA) 298
Placement — LEARMONT, Carol L. . . . (NY) 707
Staff interviewing, placement &
devlpmnt — MOODY, Marilyn D. . . . . (PA) 857
Student placement — MELVILLE, Karen E. . . . . (ON) 823

PLANNING (See also Goals, Objectives, Plans)
Academic libraries planning — QUERY, Lance D. . . . . . (IL) 999
Academic library budgeting &
planning — SMITH, Gordon W. . . . . . (CA) 1155
Academic library building planning — ELLSWORTH, Ralph E. . (CO) 345
MCDONALD, John P. . . . (CT) 802
GALVIN, Hoyt R. . . . . . (NC) 415
PARK, Leland M. . . . . . . (NC) 941
ROUSE, Roscoe . . . . (OK) 1061
SIEGMANN, Starla C. . . (WI) 1136
Administration & planning — WATSON, Ellen I. . . . . . (AR) 1309
DUNKLY, James W. . . . . (MA) 326
TRICARICO, Mary A. . . . (MA) 1256
GUY, Wendell A. . . . . . . (NY) 479
NICHOLS, James T. . . . . (OH) 901
SEKERAK, Robert J. . . . (VT) 1113
DAHLGREN, Anders C. . (WI) 269
Administration planning &
development — ZIPKOWITZ, Fay . . . . . . (RI) 1389
Administration, systems, planning — LARKIN, Patrick J. . . . . (NY) 698
Administrative planning & evaluation — TERNAK, Armand T. . . . (FL) 1232
Administrative planning & organization — SIMON, Bradley A. . . . . (OK) 1140
Archival planning — JIMERSON, Randall C. . . (CT) 600
Automated systems plng &
implementation — PATTERSON, Robert H. . . (OK) 948
Automation implementation &
planning — WALSH, Joanna M. . . . . (MA) 1299

PLANNING (Cont'd)

Automation planning	STANGL, Peter	(CA)	1180
	SNELSON, Pamela	(NJ)	1163
	SILVERMAN, Scott H.	(PA)	1138
	LANG, Elizabeth A.	(SD)	695
	WOOSTER, Linda I.	(WA)	1368
Automation planning, coordinating	DEMYANOVICH, Peter	(NJ)	291
Automation plng, multitype networking	DIENER, Margaret M.	(CA)	302
Branch planning & development	SMITH, Robert F.	(TN)	1160
Branches & long-range planning	HOLT, Raymond M.	(CA)	554
Budget & planning	DYER, Charles R.	(CA)	330
	CHESLEY, Thea B.	(IL)	207
	POLACH, Frank	(NJ)	980
Budget planning	SCHATZ, Natalie M.	(MA)	1090
Budget planning & control	CHRISTIANSON, Ellory J.	(MN)	212
Budgeting & planning	RILEY, Richard K.	(TX)	1034
Budgeting & program planning	HEINTZELMAN, Susan K.	(NY)	522
Building & planning	MEANS, Raymond B.	(NE)	820
Building & space planning	CLARK, Alice S.	(CA)	216
	ROHLF, Robert H.	(MN)	1050
	WATERS, Richard L.	(TX)	1308
Building construction plng & development	MARTIN, Mason G.	(MO)	777
Building planning	DAVIDSON, Donald C.	(CA)	276
	GAY, Elizabeth K.	(CA)	423
	SPINKS, Paul	(CA)	1175
	TERRY, Josephine R.	(CA)	1232
	BARRETT, Donald J.	(CO)	59
	MAGRATH, Lynn L.	(CO)	760
	D'ALESSANDRO, Edward A.	(DC)	270
	BUSTETTER, Stanley R.	(FL)	166
	KETCHERSID, Arthur L.	(FL)	645
	SCHULTHEISS, Louis A.	(IL)	1101
	JOHNSON, Duane F.	(KS)	603
	DE BEAR, Richard S.	(MI)	284
	CARMACK, Mona	(MN)	183
	METZ, T J.	(MN)	828
	ORNE, Jerrold	(NC)	926
	BERNSTEIN, Judith R.	(NM)	89
	DE KLERK, Ann M.	(PA)	288
	TANIS, James R.	(PA)	1222
	BALDWIN, Joe M.	(TX)	51
	HENINGTON, David M.	(TX)	528
Building planning, academic libraries	DORR, Ralze W.	(KY)	313
Building planning & construction	STEWART, George R.	(AL)	1192
Building planning & renovation	BARRY, James W.	(PA)	60
Building planning & space allocation	RAWLEY, Wayne	(IA)	1010
Building program, planning	HUNSBERGER, Charles W.	(NV)	574
Building programs & planning	PETERSON, Stephen L.	(CT)	964
Building, space planning	MCKEE, Christopher	(IA)	810
	TELATNIK, George M.	(NY)	1230
Buildings & facilities planning	HAKA, Clifford H.	(MI)	484
Buildings & space planning	SIGLER, Ronald F.	(CA)	1137
Business planning	JACOBUS, Nancy M.	(CA)	590
	HALL, Alix M.	(NY)	486
Business planning & development	BARTLETT, Jay P.	(NY)	61
Career path planning	SIMON, Ralph C.	(IN)	1141
Career planning & development	ARNOLD, Barbara J.	(WI)	33
Career planning & placement	SCOTT, Melissa C.	(MI)	1107
Certified financial planner	ROSS, Ric	(CA)	1058
City & urban planning	SLOCUM, Charlotte A.	(NC)	1150
City planning librarianship	BYRNE, Elizabeth D.	(CA)	169
Collection planning	GAREY, Anita I.	(CA)	418
Conference & workshop planning	MOON, Ilse	(FL)	857
Conference planning	MCCARTNEY, Jean A.	(MO)	794
Construction planning	SHAPIRO, June R.	(NY)	1121
Consulting & move planning	MILLER, Scott W.	(NY)	842
Consulting & planning	SIZEMORE, William C.	(WV)	1145
Consulting, library space planning	SCHWARZ, Shirlee	(CT)	1105
Cooperative planning	MICHAELIS, Kathryn S.	(WI)	831
Cooperative planning & teaching	SCOTT, William H.	(BC)	1108
Cooperative planning teaching	MACRAE, Lorne G.	(AB)	758
Corporate archives planning	EDGERLY, Linda	(MA)	336
Corporate planning	MACDONALD, Christine S.	(ON)	754
Corporate planning & strategy	MARKS, Larry	(CA)	771
Curriculum planning	HAMEL, Eleanor C.	(PR)	491
Data communications planning	BARNETT, Becky L.	(GA)	57

PLANNING (Cont'd)

Database lib srvs, plng & implementing	MADDEN, Doreitha R.	(NJ)	758
Defense planning & budgeting	BROWN, George F.	(MA)	144
Design & planning of library buildings	TRELEASE, Robert J.	(IL)	1255
Disaster planning	PEPPER, Jerold L.	(NY)	958
	FU, Paul S.	(OH)	407
	BALON, Brett J.	(SK)	53
Disaster planning & preservation	TOOLEY, Katherine J.	(OK)	1250
Disaster planning for recovery	MOON, Myra J.	(CO)	857
Disaster recovery planning	EULENBERG, Julia N.	(WA)	356
Equipment maintenance, replacement plng	CHRISTIANSON, Ellory J.	(MN)	212
Estate planning	MESMER, Frank B.	(NH)	827
Evaluation & planning	RODERER, Nancy K.	(NY)	1047
	MOMBILLE, Pedro	(PR)	854
Facilitation of group planning	TONEY, Stephen R.	(MD)	1250
Facilities design & planning	HOWLAND, Margaret E.	(MA)	566
Facilities planning	SIMON, William H.	(CT)	1141
	BOSS, Richard W.	(DC)	117
	GRANT, George C.	(FL)	458
	CURLEY, Arthur	(MA)	265
	DALY, Kathleen E.	(MI)	271
	STONE, Jason R.	(NJ)	1197
	SCHLOMAN, Barbara F.	(OH)	1094
	HABER, Walter H.	(PA)	481
	PIERCE, William S.	(PA)	972
	PHILLIPS, Louida V.	(TX)	968
	SENG, Mary A.	(TX)	1115
Facilities planning & design	BANNERMAN-WILLIAMS, Cheryl F.	(TN)	54
Facilities planning & remodeling	BUCKINGHAM, Betty J.	(IA)	154
Facilities programming & planning	MERRIFIELD, Thomas C.	(CA)	826
Facility layout & planning	MURDOCH, Arthur W.	(ON)	879
Facility planning	HAMILTON, Rita	(AZ)	492
	BECKER, Joseph	(CA)	72
	WARREN, Charles D.	(SC)	1306
Facility planning school media	COMEAU, Reginald A.	(NH)	234
Family planning	WINTERS, Wilma E.	(MA)	1356
	ZIMMERMAN, Hugh N.	(NY)	1389
Family planning, population, soc mktg	WILLSON, Katherine H.	(CT)	1349
Finances & financial planning	TABORN, Kym M.	(CA)	1219
Financial planning	MARTIN, Murray S.	(MA)	777
	SUDALL, Arthur D.	(NJ)	1206
Financial planning & reporting	SELLGREN, James A.	(MI)	1114
Financing & construction building plng	KELLUM-ROSE, Nancy P.	(CA)	637
Furniture, shelving, space planning	WATSON, Joyce N.	(ON)	1309
Future planning	JONES, C L.	(PA)	611
Health information resources planning	BYRD, Gary D.	(NC)	168
Health planning research	FLETCHER, Nancy S.	(WI)	384
Higher education planning	JORDAN, Robert T.	(DC)	617
Information for strategic planning	HANSEN, Kathelen L.	(MN)	497
Information management & planning	JENKINS, Ann A.	(CA)	597
Information management, plng, & systs	KOZAK, Marlene G.	(IL)	674
Information policy & planning	JACKSON, Miles M.	(HI)	588
Information services planning	PRENTICE, Ann E.	(TN)	990
Information strategic planning	JACOBSEN, Teresa T.	(IL)	590
Information system & services planning	KITTUR, Krishna N.	(IND)	657
	PARMING, Marju R.	(DC)	943
Information systems planning	ABLES, Timothy D.	(MS)	2
	FABRE DE MORLHON, Christiane	(ITL)	360
Information systems planning, consulting	GROTE, Janet H.	(NY)	473
Information systems strategic planning	PEETERS, Marc D.	(BEL)	954
Information technology planning	BURNS, Christopher	(MA)	162
	TAUBER, Stephen J.	(MA)	1225
Institutional planning	KARL, Roger M.	(TN)	627
Interior planning & design	DE BEAR, Richard S.	(MI)	284
	MICHAELS, David L.	(VA)	832
International information planning	CAMPBELL, Harry	(ON)	176
Knowledge of family planning	ROBERTS, Gloria A.	(NY)	1040
Land use planning	HANDROW, Margaret M.	(TX)	495
Law library facilities planning	MERRIFIELD, Thomas C.	(CA)	826
Law library management & planning	ARANDA-COODOU, Patricio	(DC)	30
Law library planning & design	KREMER, Jill L.	(PA)	677

PLANNING (Cont'd)

Law library space planning — CHICK, Cynthia L. (CA) 208
RAE, E A. (ON) 1002
Layout & planning — BAYLIS, Ted (MA) 67
Library administration & planning — AKEROYD, Richard G. (CT) 9
BONE, Larry E. (NY) 113
CLARK, Robert L. (OK) 218
BAKER, Douglas (WI) 48
Library & archive planning — SWINBURNE, Ralph E. (NY) 1216
Library architectural planning — ZAFREN, Herbert C. (OH) 1385
Library building & planning — LOOMIS, Barbara L. (CA) 740
MARSHALL, Ruth T. (GA) 775
Library building design & planning — MCCABE, James P. (PA) 793
Library building planning — ANDERSON, Herschel V. (AZ) 23
DAVIS, Douglas A. (CA) 278
JONES, Wyman (CA) 615
NOVAK, Gloria J. (CA) 910
JONES, William G. (IL) 615
LEE, Sang C. (NY) 711
BRAWNER, Lee B. (OK) 130
BEAUMIER, Renald (PQ) 70
Library building planning & design — SICKLES, Linda C. (MI) 1135
Library building, planning, construction — BROWN, Louise R. (MA) 145
Library conference planning — SUTHERLAND, Thomas A. (KY) 1211
Library construction, planning — SIMON, Bradley A. (OK) 1140
Library design & space planning — DAVIS, Glenn G. (IL) 279
Library design & systems planning — KAPNICK, Laura B. (NY) 626
Library facilities planning — MERRIFIELD, Thomas C. (CA) 826
SPURLOCK, Sandra E. (NM) 1177
MCADAMS, Nancy R. (TX) 792
Library facility planning — MOSLEY, Shelley E. (AZ) 872
COHEN, Aaron (NY) 227
Library furniture & space planning — GRANT, Robert S. (MI) 458
Library furniture, space planning — TUCKER, Richard B. (NH) 1262
Library interior planning & design — MICHAELS, Andrea A. (VA) 831
Library interior space planning — STEWART, John D. (VA) 1192
Library management & planning — LUSTER, Arlene L. (HI) 750
HORTON, Kathy L. (IL) 561
BAKER, Sylva S. (PA) 49
COCHRANE, Thomas G. (AUS) 226
Library media center facilities planning — FROST, Rebecca H. (PA) 406
Library organization & planning — CUMMING, Linda L. (CO) 264
Library planning — ANDERSON, Herschel V. (AZ) 23
CREAGHE, Norma S. (CA) 257
WHITE, Lelia C. (CA) 1331
LANCE, Keith C. (CO) 692
ZICH, Robert G. (DC) 1388
RICHMOND, Diane A. (IL) 1030
BENDER, Nancy W. (MA) 79
DUGAN, Robert E. (MA) 324
MOSS, Karen M. (MA) 872
GRIFFITHS, Jose M. (MD) 469
WELLISCH, Hans H. (MD) 1322
HENDRICKSON, Kent H. (NE) 527
ODELL, Glendon T. (NJ) 916
BIDDLE, Stanton F. (NY) 94
KUHNER, Robert A. (NY) 683
MOUNT, Ellis (NY) 873
WU, Painan R. (NY) 1373
WYATT, James F. (NY) 1374
DICKERSON, Lon R. (WA) 300
ZWEIZIG, Douglas L. (WI) 1392
MORTON, Robert E. (ON) 870
THODY, Susan I. (ON) 1235
Library planning & administration — STUDER, William J. (OH) 1204
KACENA, Carolyn (TX) 621
Library planning & budgeting — RAMSEY, Inez L. (VA) 1006
Library planning & construction — ROBINSON, Joel M. (OK) 1044
Library planning & design — OGLETREE, Elizabeth H. (PA) 918
Library planning & development — MCDAVID, Sara J. (GA) 801
JOSLIN, Ann (ID) 618
OAKS, Claire (IL) 913
LUCAS, Jean M. (OH) 746
NADEAU, Johan (PQ) 885
Library planning & evaluation — JENKINS, Darrell L. (IL) 597
ROBINSON, Charles W. (MD) 1043
BRAWNER, Lee B. (OK) 130
Library planning & layout consulting — WEINZIMMER, William A. (NY) 1318
Library planning & management — KAWAMOTO, Chizuko (CA) 632
Library planning & moving — LINDEN, Margaret J. (CA) 729

PLANNING (Cont'd)

Library planning & organization — PARKS, Mary L. (CA) 943
VOHRA, Pran (SK) 1287
Library planning & systems — DUANE, Carol A. (OH) 321
Library planning services — MAY, Robert E. (SC) 789
Library research & planning — ALBRITTON, Rosie L. (MO) 10
Library services planning, development — NIEMI, Peter G. (WI) 903
Library space planning — SCHAFER, Jay G. (CO) 1089
BATTEN, Henry R. (GA) 64
O'BRIEN, Marjorie S. (MA) 914
BOWLES, Nancy J. (NY) 121
VINCENT-DAVISS, Diana (NY) 1284
METZENBACHER, Gary W. (OR) 828
GARRISON, Guy G. (PA) 420
MITTAG, Erika (TX) 850
Library space planning, construction — NEIKIRK, Harold D. (MD) 892
Library strategic, long-range planning — MANN, Thomas (CA) 766
Library strategic planning — KANE, Bartholomew A. (HI) 624
COHEN, Aaron (NY) 227
Library strategies planning — VANDERELST, Wil (ON) 1274
Library system planning — PLACE, Philip A. (FL) 977
Library systems planning — PEMPE, Ruta (DC) 956
SCHALAU, Robert D. (MS) 1089
Local systems planning — HILLMANN, Diane I. (NY) 541
Long-range & strategic planning — BETTENCOURT, Nancy J. (CO) 92
VELLUCCI, Matthew J. (MD) 1282
BAUER, Margaret D. (PA) 65
Long-range library planning — SAGER, Donald J. (WI) 1074
Long-range planning — MARRIOTT, Lois I. (CA) 773
MANCINI, Donna D. (GA) 764
ANTHONY, Carolyn A. (IL) 28
HAWLEY, Marsha S. (IL) 514
WILFORD, Valerie J. (IL) 1339
WOODARD, Marcia S. (IN) 1366
RADEMACHER, Richard J. (KS) 1002
STEPHAN, Sandra S. (MD) 1187
NOBLE, Valerie (MI) 906
SWEEN, Roger (MN) 1214
WEISS, Kay M. (MN) 1320
ANDERSEN, Robert J. (NY) 21
MULLER, Claudya B. (NY) 877
JOHNSON, Corinne E. (OH) 603
KOZLOWSKI, Ronald S. (OH) 674
SALMON, Kay H. (OR) 1077
ALBRECHT, Lois K. (PA) 10
BROWN, David E. (PA) 143
HEDRICK, David T. (PA) 520
MANNING, Helen M. (TX) 766
Long-range planning & implementation — DIEHL, Carol L. (WI) 301
Long-range planning programs — CHAMBERLAIN, Ruth B. (MA) 197
Long-range strategic planning — NEEDHAM, George M. (OH) 891
LSCA criteria & planning — CLARK, Robert L. (OK) 218
Management & planning — NING, Mary J. (CA) 904
WISMER, Donald (ME) 1357
LANDAU, Herbert B. (NY) 692
Management & planning facilities — NEUBAUER, Richard A. (MA) 896
Management & planning studies — KING, Donald W. (MD) 650
Management & strategic planning — MALCOLM, J P. (MI) 762
Mgmt, planning, budgeting, supervising — ZAENGER, Kathleen L. (MI) 1385
Management, planning, systems — FLOERSHEIMER, Lee M. (NY) 385
Manpower planning — HUNT, Suellyn (NY) 575
Market planning, segmentation, research — HERRICK, Carol L. (OH) 532
Market research & planning — PERRON, Michelle M. (NH) 960
Market research, planning & development — LINDAHL, Ann L. (CA) 728
WEINGAND, Darlene E. (WI) 1318
Marketing & planning — VANCE, Julia M. (MD) 1273
Marketing & strategic planning
Marketing communications, strategic plng — WASERSTEIN, Gina S. (PA) 1307
Meeting planning — CORNOG, Martha (PA) 247
Meeting planning, management — ZOOK, Ruth A. (CO) 1390
Moving & space planning — BALKIN, Ruth G. (NY) 52
GOLDMAN, Martha A. (NY) 445
National information planning — CAMPBELL, Harry (ON) 176
Network planning & development — URICCHIO, William J. (CT) 1269

PLANNING (Cont'd)

Networking & statewide planning	STRONG, Gary E.	(CA)	1203
New building planning	GARDNER, W J.	(CO)	418
New buildings & renovations planning	VANN, John D.	(PA)	1276
New library planning	KOPAN, Ellen K.	(CA)	671
New service planning	BARNETT, Becky L.	(GA)	57
Organization & planning	ETTER, Patricia A.	(AZ)	355
Organization planning	RILEY, Robert H.	(NJ)	1034
	FRAMEL, Phyllis M.	(TX)	395
Organization, planning & administration	HOELLE, Dolores M.	(NJ)	547
Organizational planning	KINCHEN, Robert P.	(NY)	650
Organizational planning & communications	LOWRY, Charles B.	(TX)	745
Personnel & operations planning	LEATHER, Deborah J.	(VA)	707
Personnel, planning	LARSON, Mildred N.	(WI)	699
Personnel, planning & budgeting	BROOM, Susan E.	(FL)	141
Physical planning	LEITH, Anna R.	(BC)	714
Planning	HIEB, Louis A.	(AZ)	537
	CALDWELL, Kenneth R.	(CA)	172
	LAWRENCE, Gary S.	(CA)	704
	LUKE, Keye L.	(CA)	747
	OYLER, David K.	(CA)	932
	RICHMOND, Elizabeth B.	(CO)	1030
	RICHMOND, Rick	(CO)	1030
	BENN, James R.	(CT)	81
	KOEL, Ake I.	(CT)	667
	MIELKE, Linda	(FL)	833
	WILLIAMS, Ann W.	(FL)	1342
	JOHNSON, Anne C.	(IA)	602
	LINDVALL, Robert J.	(IL)	730
	MUNOFF, Gerald J.	(IL)	879
	SEGAL, Joan S.	(IL)	1111
	LAUGHLIN, Sara G.	(IN)	703
	WITTORF, Robert H.	(IN)	1359
	SCHAD, Jasper G.	(KS)	1088
	NOLAN, Deborah A.	(MD)	907
	SANDS, George A.	(MD)	1081
	TONEY, Stephen R.	(MD)	1250
	BRENNER, Saundra H.	(MO)	133
	DAVIS, Jinnie Y.	(NC)	279
	GRANT, George E.	(NJ)	458
	EVELAND, Ruth A.	(NY)	358
	MANBECK, Virginia B.	(NY)	764
	MATZEK, Richard A.	(NY)	786
	NEWMAN, George C.	(NY)	899
	SEARS, Carlton A.	(NY)	1110
	O'CONNOR, Deborah F.	(OH)	916
	JONES, Beverly A.	(OK)	611
	KEENE, Janis C.	(OK)	634
	LITTLE, Paul L.	(OK)	733
	BONAMICI, Andrew R.	(OR)	113
	WEBB, John	(OR)	1313
	AXAM, John A.	(PA)	42
	REIFF, Harry B.	(PA)	1019
	DANIELS, Bruce E.	(RI)	273
	LINDENFELD, Joseph F.	(TN)	729
	RICHARDS, Timothy F.	(TN)	1028
	OWEN, Amy	(UT)	931
	BECKER, Roger V.	(WA)	72
	KRUEGER, Karen J.	(WI)	680
	KERR, Audrey M.	(MB)	644
Planning & administration	JANES, Nina	(CO)	593
	PETERSON, Stephen L.	(CT)	964
Planning & application of technology	DIDIER, Elaine K.	(MI)	301
Planning & budget, university libraries	DORR, Ralze W.	(KY)	313
Planning & budgeting	CLIFTON, Joe A.	(CA)	222
	NICKERSON, Susan L.	(CA)	902
	FORTIER, Jan M.	(MA)	391
	HOLMGREN, Edwin S.	(NY)	553
Planning & budgeting for library service	WINSON, Gail I.	(CA)	1355
Planning & budgeting systems	NERODA, Edward W.	(MT)	895
Planning & construction of lib buildings	HEAD, Anita K.	(DC)	518
Planning & coordinating training	TOWNSEND, Carolyn J.	(PA)	1253
Planning & coordination	KERSCHNER, Joan G.	(NV)	644
Planning & design of library buildings	BEWLEY, Lois M.	(BC)	93
Planning & developing	REID, Peg L.	(IL)	1019

PLANNING (Cont'd)

Planning & development	BOTHMER, A J.	(CO)	118
	ORRICO, James T.	(CT)	926
	STRAKA, Kathy M.	(CT)	1199
	HENEHAN, Alva D.	(FL)	528
	CLAPP, David F.	(IL)	215
	KINZER, Kathryn	(MD)	653
	SPELLER, Benjamin F.	(NC)	1172
	TRUCKSIS, Theresa A.	(OH)	1259
	EVANS, Nancy H.	(PA)	357
	GALLOWAY, Margaret E.	(TX)	415
	MCCARGAR, Susan E.	(TX)	794
	TERWILLIGER, Gloria P.	(VA)	1232
	CONABLE, Gordon M.	(WA)	235
	FIELDEN, Stanley	(SK)	376
Planning & development, administration	WALSH, Lynn R.	(FL)	1299
Planning & establishing library systems	STANKIEWICZ, Carol A.	(CT)	1180
Planning & evaluation	DESSY, Blane K.	(AL)	296
	VAN HOUSE, Nancy A.	(CA)	1275
	BOLT, Nancy M.	(CO)	113
	WYCHE, Louise E.	(DE)	1374
	BALCOM, Kathleen M.	(IL)	51
	SLATER, Susan B.	(MD)	1148
	SMITH, Catherine	(NC)	1153
	ROBERTSON, Retha M.	(OK)	1042
	FELIX, Sally T.	(PA)	370
Planning & evaluation of info srvs	MCCLURE, Charles R.	(NY)	797
Planning & grant review	SCHUTT, Cheryl M.	(CT)	1103
Planning & implementation, library	PETERSON, Dennis R.	(IA)	963
Planning & management	MILLER, Edward P.	(AZ)	837
	SIGLER, Ronald F.	(CA)	1137
Planning & moving libraries	CARDENAS, Martha L.	(TX)	180
Planning & moving of law libraries	PLUNKET, Joy H.	(MA)	978
Planning & organization	ROSENFELD, Joel C.	(IL)	1056
Planning & organizing	BUHR, Rosemary E.	(MO)	156
Planning & performance measurement	SKIDMORE, Stephen C.	(OK)	1146
Planning & personnel administration	PHILLIPS, Carol B.	(TX)	967
Planning & policy development	MILLER, Richard T.	(MO)	841
Planning & policy making	BROWN, Lucinda A.	(KY)	145
Planning & program development	BLACK, Frances P.	(OH)	101
Planning & proposal writing	VAUGHN, Frances A.	(TX)	1280
Planning & redesigning libraries	PROCOPIO, Concetta E.	(MA)	994
Planning & renovating libraries	JOHNSON, Ruth E.	(OH)	608
Planning & reorganizing library space	WORTHINGTON, A P.	(CA)	1369
Planning & research	JONES, Charlotte W.	(WA)	611
Planning & strategic management	BRADBURY, Daniel J.	(MO)	125
Planning area library services	BLASINGAME, Ralph	(NJ)	104
Planning, budgeting, & supervision	THAKER, Virbala M.	(CA)	1234
Planning buildings	EVANS, Frank B.	(DC)	357
Planning consultation	MCCRACKEN, Ronald W.	(ON)	799
Planning, evaluation & management	SHELDON, Brooke E.	(TX)	1125
Planning for automation & videodiscs	VOGT-O'CONNOR, Diane L.	(DC)	1287
Planning for services	ROYCE, Carolyn S.	(NJ)	1063
Planning for small libraries	SHANNON, Marcia A.	(MA)	1120
Planning librarian	MATTY, Paul D.	(AZ)	786
Planning library assignments	GULICK, Eleanor L.	(NJ)	477
Planning library buildings	PALMER, David W.	(MI)	936
	BREEN, M F.	(NY)	131
	SNAPP, Elizabeth M.	(TX)	1162
	OROZCO-TENORIO, Jose M.	(MEX)	926
Planning library development activities	ROBERTS, Kenneth H.	(FRN)	1040
Planning library media centers	APPEL MOSESOF, Rhoda S.	(NJ)	29
Planning library services	DURBIN, Roger	(OH)	328
	RIVERA-ALVAREZ, Miguel A.	(PR)	1037
Planning national information systems	MENOU, Michel J.	(ITL)	824
Planning new library outlets	STREIN, Barbara M.	(MD)	1201
Planning of new information services	SIECK, Steven K.	(NY)	1135
Planning physical quarters	JAFFARIAN, Sara	(MA)	591
Planning process	BENDER, Betty W.	(WA)	79
Planning pub lib services & facilities	CURTIS, Jean E.	(MI)	267
Planning resources	GOODY, Cheryl S.	(HI)	450
Planning small corporate libraries	MONTAG, Diane	(CO)	855
Planning studies	WATERS, Richard L.	(TX)	1308

PLANNING (Cont'd)

Planning system goals & objectives	COURSON, M S.	(MD)	251
Planning systems & services	EVANS, Frank B.	(DC)	357
Planning two-year learning resource ctr	BOOK, Imogene I.	(SC)	115
Policy & planning	DURANCE, Cynthia J.	(ON)	328
Policy development & planning	MARTIN, Mason G.	(MO)	777
Population & family planning	BARROWS, William D.	(NC)	60
Preservation, planning, & programming	BROWN, Charlotte B.	(PA)	142
Product planning	HERRICK, Carol L.	(OH)	532
Program & space planning	EHRHORN, Jean H.	(HI)	339
Program planner	SIMPSON, Leslie T.	(MO)	1142
Program planning	SMITH, Jane B.	(AL)	1155
	PIKE, Nancy M.	(FL)	973
	MCCORMICK, Sheila P.	(MA)	799
	YUEH, Norma N.	(NJ)	1384
	DEUTSCH, Karen A.	(NY)	296
Program planning & foundation evaluation	JONES, C L.	(PA)	611
Program planning & implementation	HESS, Marjorie A.	(PA)	534
Programming, planning & evaluating	PEISCHL, Thomas P.	(MN)	955
Project planning & development	STONE, Clarence W.	(IDN)	1197
Project planning & implementation	NEAL, Jan	(CA)	890
Public library administration & planning	STEINFELD, Michael	(MA)	1186
Public library building planning	KEOUGH, Francis P.	(MA)	643
	GALVIN, Hoyt R.	(NC)	415
Public library facility planning	HARRIS, Patricia L.	(ND)	505
Public library planning	TURNER, Anne M.	(CA)	1264
	RODGER, Eleanor J.	(IL)	1047
	KEOUGH, Francis P.	(MA)	643
Public library planning & building	MCGRIFF, Ronald I.	(MN)	808
Public library planning & construction	BROWNLEE, Jerry W.	(FL)	148
Public library planning & evaluation	SMITH, David R.	(MN)	1154
Public relations planning	SHUMAN, Marilyn J.	(IL)	1134
Public services policies, planning	ICKES, Barbara J.	(PA)	581
Public transportation & urban planning	PRESBY, Richard A.	(CA)	990
Referendum campaign planning	FLEMING, Lois D.	(FL)	384
Regional planning	DONG, Tina	(MA)	311
Renovation & expansion planning	KELSH, Virginia J.	(CA)	639
Research & development project planning	KOZAK, Marlene G.	(IL)	674
Resource planning	WEISS, Egon A.	(NY)	1320
School curriculum planning	HUSTED, Ruth E.	(OK)	578
School library planning	KARPISEK, Marian E.	(UT)	628
	YAEGER, Luke R.	(VA)	1376
School project planning	ANDRIST, Shirley A.	(SK)	27
Service planning & development	CRIST, Margaret L.	(MA)	259
Small libraries building planning	MILLIKEN, Ruth L.	(FL)	843
Space planning	COOPER, Richard S.	(CA)	243
	WALLACE, Marie G.	(CA)	1297
	COCO, Al	(CO)	226
	MARIANI, Carolyn A.	(CT)	770
	WARD, Victoria M.	(DC)	1304
	ALFRED, Judith C.	(IN)	13
	POSTLEWAIT, Cheryl A.	(KS)	986
	LEARY, Margaret R.	(MI)	707
	AXEL-LUTE, Paul	(NJ)	42
	ANDERSON, Carol L.	(NY)	22
	FREIFELD, Roberta I.	(NY)	401
	MASYR, Caryl L.	(NY)	783
	HARVAN, Christine C.	(PA)	509
	PIERCE, William S.	(PA)	972
	ROACH, Linda	(PA)	1038
	CEBRUN, Mary J.	(TX)	196
	DAHLGREN, Jean E.	(TX)	269
	HELBURN, Judith D.	(TX)	523
	HOOTON, Virginia A.	(TX)	557
	CADA, Elizabeth J.	(ON)	170
Space planning & design	TEICH, Steven	(OR)	1230
Space planning & development	JOHNSON, Timothy J.	(IL)	609
Space planning & moving libraries	FOX, Marylou P.	(CA)	395
Space planning & utilization	NELSON, Norman L.	(OK)	895
	MCADAMS, Nancy R.	(TX)	792
Space planning facilities	FRALEY, Ruth A.	(NY)	395
Space planning, legal	MOYER, Holley M.	(NJ)	874
Space planning, management	KENDRICK, Curtis L.	(NY)	640
Space planning of law libraries	WELKER, Kathy J.	(OH)	1321

PLANNING (Cont'd)

Special libraries planning & development	ASTON, Jennefer	(IRE)	37
Special library land use & planning	MARTINEZ, Barbara A.	(CA)	779
Special library planning	THOMAS, Margaret J.	(MI)	1237
	DEVERA, Rosalinda M.	(NY)	297
Special library planning, developing	SELZER, Nancy S.	(DE)	1114
Statewide library planning	NIX, Larry T.	(WI)	905
Statewide library planning & services	ASP, William G.	(MN)	37
Statewide planning library services	DREW, Sally J.	(WI)	319
Strategic information planning	HORTON, Forest W.	(DC)	561
Strategic market planning	TELFER, Margaret E.	(NC)	1230
Strategic planning	ANDERSON, Dorothy J.	(CA)	22
	DOWLIN, Kenneth E.	(CO)	316
	MANNING, Leslie A.	(CO)	766
	LUTHER, M J.	(GA)	750
	HARRIS, Jeanne G.	(IL)	504
	LYNCH, Hugh J.	(IL)	751
	MAYFIELD, Maurice K.	(IL)	790
	PARENT, Roger H.	(IL)	940
	SHERRY, Diane H.	(IL)	1129
	VIRGO, Julie A.	(IL)	1285
	ARNOLD, Stephen E.	(KY)	34
	DOVE, Samuel	(MD)	315
	GROCKI, Daniel J.	(MD)	471
	ROBINSON, Barbara M.	(MD)	1043
	PORTER, Jean F.	(MI)	984
	WAITE, William F.	(NJ)	1293
	COVINGTON, Robert D.	(NV)	252
	BORBELY, Jack	(NY)	116
	BRAUDE, Robert M.	(NY)	129
	HUNTER, Karen A.	(NY)	576
	JACOB, Mary E.	(OH)	589
	TRUBKIN, Loene	(BC)	1259
	FAGERLUND, M L.	(SWZ)	361
Strategic planning & marketing	OLSON, Christine A.	(MD)	922
	BERGFELD, C D.	(NY)	86
	PARKER, Arthur D.	(ON)	941
Strategic planning & teambuilding	TYSON, John C.	(VA)	1267
Strategic planning for libraries	ARDEN, Caroline	(VA)	31
Strategic planning for library systems	MATHESON, Nina W.	(MD)	783
Strategic systems planning	BURNS, Barrie A.	(ON)	162
Supervision & planning	BLASE, Nancy G.	(WA)	104
System automation planning	RHEIN, Jean F.	(FL)	1025
Systems planning	TITUS, Elizabeth M.	(IL)	1247
	HIGH, Walter M.	(NC)	538
	ROHDY, Margaret A.	(PA)	1050
	WALL, H D.	(PA)	1297
	CORBIN, John	(TX)	245
Systems planning & design	STANLEY, Dale R.	(CA)	1180
Systems planning & implementation	SHOCKLEY, Cynthia W.	(MD)	1132
Technical services planning	WALBRIDGE, Sharon L.	(OH)	1293
Technical services workflow planning	LINSE, Mary M.	(MO)	731
Technology planning	CAMPBELL, Bonnie	(ON)	176
Therapeutic patient program planning	ABDULLAH, Bilquis	(NY)	2
Top-down information systems planning	TELFER, Margaret E.	(NC)	1230
Unit level planning	MOODY, Marilyn D.	(PA)	857
University library planning	SMITH, Eldred R.	(MN)	1154
Urban affairs planning	BEAL, Gretchen F.	(TN)	68
Urban planning	RAVENHALL, Mary	(IL)	1010
	DONG, Tina	(MA)	311
Urban planning & development	CROWE, Gloria J.	(AZ)	261
Urban planning bibliography	CHIBNIK, Katharine R.	(NY)	207
Workshop planner & producer	LYNCH, Minnie L.	(LA)	752

PLANS

Acquisitions & lesson plans	JORDAN, Sharon L.	(WA)	617
Approval plan development	HAMILTON, Marsha J.	(OH)	492
Approval plan management	WARZALA, Martin L.	(CT)	1307
	GRANTIER, John R.	(NY)	458
Approval plans	MARSHALL, David L.	(DC)	774
	HARDY, Eileen D.	(MA)	500
	DUCHIN, Douglas	(NH)	322
	KAPOOR, Jagdish C.	(NH)	626
	NARDINI, Robert F.	(NH)	888
Approval plans & continuations	JAGER, Conradus	(MA)	591
Building plans	BRANDON, Alfred N.	(FL)	128
Buildings, financing plans	SANDSTEDT, Carl R.	(MO)	1081

PLANS (Cont'd)

Business plan consulting	MOSLEY, Thomas E. . . .	(OK)	872
Business plan development	MILLER, Ronald F.	(CA)	842
Employee assistance plans	BELLEFONTAINE, Arnold G.	(DC)	78
Long-range plans	FINAN, Patrick E.	(OH)	377
Monitoring approval plans for Hispanics	SALINERO, Amelia	(NY)	1076
Order plans, order procedures	KAVANAGH, Susan E. . .	(ON)	631
Pension plans	BIRSCHEL, Dee B.	(WI)	99
Plan programs & services	GREENFIELD, Judith C. .	(NY)	464
Programming buildings & plan review	HOLT, Raymond M. . . .	(CA)	554

PLANTS (See also Botany, Horticulture)

Agricultural, plant science information	MITCHELL, Steve	(CA)	849
Plant safety & reliability	HASTINGS, Constance M.	(TN)	511
Plant science	STRANSKY, Maria	(MD)	1200
Soil plant relations & natural resources	SCHNEIDER, Karl R. . . .	(MD)	1097
Taxonomy of plants	STIEBER, Michael T. . . .	(PA)	1193

PLASTICS

Plastic resins	VOSS, Ingrid M.	(IL)	1289
Plastics & packaging	MCCULLEY, P M.	(SC)	800
Plastics industry information sources	KANE, Nancy J.	(MA)	625
Plastics libraries	BERGIN, Karen S.	(MI)	86
Rubber, plastics & polymer science	HOLLIS, William F.	(OH)	552

PLAY

Language of play direction	TRAPIDO, Joel	(HI)	1254
Plays collection development	CENTING, Richard R. . . .	(OH)	196

PLAYWRITING

Prose & playwriting	HECK-RABI, Louise E. . .	(MI)	520

POETRY (See also Literature)

California historical research, poetry	MOORE, Richard K.	(CA)	861
Contemporary literature, poetry, fiction	HUDZIK, Robert T.	(OH)	570
Contemporary poetry	MOREY, Frederick L. . . .	(MD)	863
Creative writing of poetry	GREEN, Rose B.	(PA)	462
Emily Dickinson, poet, info	MOREY, Frederick L. . . .	(MD)	863
French poetry	CARRINGTON, Samuel M.	(TX)	186
Literature, poetry	KARATNYTSKY, Christine A.	(NY)	627
Modern English poetry	KAISER, John R.	(PA)	622
Modern poetry	PARCHUCK, Jill A.	(CA)	940
Poetry	KNIFFEL, Leonard J. . . .	(MI)	664
	CAMMACK, Bruce P. . . .	(NY)	175
	NICHOLSON, Myreen M.	(VA)	902
Poetry & librarianship	MOFFEIT, Tony A.	(CO)	852
Poetry collection development	CENTING, Richard R. . . .	(OH)	196
Poetry video production & distribution	LESNIAK, Rose	(NY)	718
Prose & poetry translation	TABORY, Maxim	(NC)	1219
Slavic literatures & oral poetry	POPOVIC, Tanya V.	(NY)	983
Small press poetry	FOX, Willard	(LA)	395
Storytelling, poetry, holiday themes	BAUER, Caroline F.	(CA)	65
Victorian literature, fiction, poetry	FISHER, Benjamin F. . . .	(MS)	380
Women's poetry	GUY, Patricia A.	(CA)	479

POLAR (See also Arctic)

Alaska & polar regions reference service	LAKE, Gretchen L.	(AK)	688
Northern or polar materials	ALBRIGHT, Donald A. . .	(NT)	10
Polar databases	GOMEZ, Michael J.	(WGR)	447

POLICE (See also Law)

Police & law enforcement	RAMM, Dorothy V.	(IL)	1005
Police science	ZIMMERMAN, Donna K. .	(IN)	1388
Police training & law enforcement	MERRYWEATHER, J M.	(ON)	827

POLICY (See also Procedures)

Access policies	POSTAR, Adeen J.	(DC)	986
Administration & policy development	DILUCIA, Samuel J.	(HI)	303
Administrative policy for command	ROY, Alice R.	(VA)	1063
Canadian government information policy	ROSE, Frances E.	(BC)	1054
Circulation policies & procedures	COOK, Anita I.	(NE)	239
Circulation policy	BULERIN-LUGO, Josefina	(PR)	156
Collection development policies	CASSERLY, Mary F. . . .	(ME)	193
	DESJARLAIS-LUETH, Christine	(RI)	295
Collection policy & development	WARTLUFT, David J. . . .	(PA)	1307
Conservation policy	FOX, Peter K.	(IRE)	395
Cost recovery policies	BYRD, Harvey C.	(MD)	169
Domestic reference fiscal policy	ANDERSON, John M. . . .	(DC)	23
Environmental information & data policy	SNODGRASS, Rex J. . .	(NC)	1163
Federal information policy	HARPER, Lucy B.	(OH)	503
	MASON, Marilyn G.	(OH)	781
Federal library policy	HEANUE, Anne A.	(DC)	518
	KLASSEN, Robert L. . . .	(DC)	657
Fiscal & monetary policy	BRINNER, Roger E.	(MA)	136
Government information policies	ARDEN, Caroline	(VA)	31
Government information policy	SERBAN, William M. . . .	(LA)	1116
Health policy research	JENSEN, Joseph E.	(MD)	599
History & public policy	PREER, Jean L.	(DC)	990
Information geopolitics & policy	AINES, Andrew A.	(MD)	8
Information policies	BERGER, Patricia W. . . .	(MD)	86
	JACOB, Mary E.	(OH)	589
	MACDONALD, Alan H. . .	(AB)	754
Information policy	SCHILLER, Anita R.	(CA)	1093
	BARRETT, G J.	(DC)	59
	MILEVSKI, Sandra N. . . .	(DC)	835
	PEYTON, David	(DC)	966
	RATH, Charla M.	(DC)	1009
	ENGLER, June L.	(GA)	350
	MCDERMOTT, Patrice . .	(IL)	802
	HEIM, Kathleen M.	(LA)	521
	DANIEL, Evelyn H.	(NC)	272
	KLEMPNER, Irving M. . .	(NY)	660
	BEARMAN, Toni C.	(PA)	69
	SY, Karen J.	(WA)	1217
	HOWARD, Helen A.	(PQ)	564
Information policy administration	DE TONNANCOUR, P R.	(TX)	296
Information policy & planning	JACKSON, Miles M.	(HI)	588
Information policy & security	KNOPPERS, Jake V. . . .	(ON)	665
Information policy development	SPATH, Charles E.	(TN)	1171
Information policy issues	CHARTRAND, Robert L.	(DC)	203
Library administration & policy	BILLY, George J.	(NY)	97
Library & information policy	MOORE, Bessie B.	(DC)	858
Library collections policies	TAGGART, William R. . .	(BC)	1220
Library policy analysis	DOWDING, Martin R. . . .	(ON)	315
Library policy development	LIPTON, Connie F.	(MI)	732
Management & policy creation	WILLIAMSON, Michael W.	(ON)	1347
Medical public policy	SCUKA, Aletta N.	(DC)	1108
National information policies	MENOU, Michel J.	(ITL)	824
Online systems & policy	ARRINGTON, Susan J. .	(MD)	34
Personnel policies & administration	RITTER, Philip W.	(NC)	1036
Personnel policy	LEBRUN, Marlene M. . . .	(MD)	708
Planning & policy development	MILLER, Richard T.	(MO)	841
Planning & policy making	BROWN, Lucinda A.	(KY)	145
Policy analysis	PEYTON, David	(DC)	966
	SLATER, Susan B.	(MD)	1148
	WILLETT, Holly G.	(WI)	1341
Policy & control of library systems	MORALES, Milton F. . . .	(MO)	862
Policy & planning	DURANCE, Cynthia J. . .	(ON)	328
Policy development	LIEBERFELD, Lawrence .	(NY)	726
Policy development & planning	MARTIN, Mason G.	(MO)	777
Policy formation	ROBINSON, Barbara M. .	(MD)	1043
Policy formulation	TURNBULL, Keith	(SK)	1264
Policy formulation & development	HOWLAND, Margaret E. .	(MA)	566
Policy manuals	NAVRATIL, Jean	(NY)	890
Privacy & access policies	NASH, Cherie A.	(UT)	888
Public administration & policy	LEISTER, Jack	(CA)	714
Public policy	BROCKMAN, Norbert C.	(KEN)	138
Public policy & libraries	MOLZ, Redmond K.	(NY)	854
Public policy databases	PILGRIM, Auriel J.	(DC)	973
Public policy development	FORD, Gary E.	(MO)	389
Public policy studies	SHULER, John A.	(OR)	1133
Public services policies, planning	ICKES, Barbara J.	(PA)	581

POLICY (Cont'd)

Publishing policy development info	KLEIMAN, Gerald S.	(DC)	659
Reference services policy statements	INGRAHAM, Alice L.	(PA)	582
Reorganization of internal policies	LOMEN, Nancy L.	(NY)	738
School library policy development	ANDERSON, Pauline H.	(NY)	25
School media policy development	ADAMS, Helen R.	(WI)	5
Science & information policy	ROSENBERG, Kenyon C.	(VA)	1056
Small library policy development	EVANS, Patricia D.	(AB)	357
Social policy	REPPY, Charlotte D.	(MD)	1024
State policy development	ATKINS, Gregg T.	(CA)	38
Teacher evaluation policys	KRATZ, Hans G.	(AB)	676
Telecommunications & information policy	RIPLEY, Joseph M.	(KY)	1035
US information policy	JUERGENSMEYER, John E.	(IL)	619
Writing & editing policy manuals	COURSON, M S.	(MD)	251
Writing policies & procedures	KNIGHT, Rita C.	(AZ)	664

POLISH

Polish collection development	MITCHELL, Annmarie D.	(CA)	848
Polish folklore storytelling	MAZUREK, Adam P.	(MD)	791
Polish music history	WILK, Wanda	(CA)	1339

POLITICS (See also Geopolitics)

Cuban political prisoners	PEREZ, Maria L.	(FL)	958
Educational politics	FLOWERS, Helen F.	(NY)	386
Foreign trade, political science	LERNER, Arthur	(NY)	717
History & political science	AULD, Hampton M.	(NC)	39
History & politics	TAYLOR, Marion E.	(CA)	1227
History, political science bibliography	THOMPSON, Ann M.	(OH)	1238
Information needs of politicians	TILLOTSON, Greig S.	(AUS)	1245
Legal & political studies	NGUYEN, Vy K.	(PQ)	901
Libraries & politics	SPICER, Erik J.	(ON)	1174
Lobbying & political action	WARD, Robert C.	(VT)	1304
Political	WILSON, C D.	(LA)	1350
Political action	HOLMGREN, Edwin S.	(NY)	553
Political & business research	KAPNICK, Laura B.	(NY)	626
Political & sociological databases	BOILARD, Gilberte	(PQ)	111
Political barriers to information	BIRNEY, Ann E.	(KS)	98
Political history	PAPAZIAN, Pierre	(NJ)	939
Political liaison	MULLER, William A.	(WV)	877
Political lobbying	HALL, Edward B.	(MD)	487
Political lobbying for libraries	KIEFFER, Marian L.	(IA)	647
Political process	WILSON, David C.	(GA)	1350
	WILSON, Evie	(WA)	1350
	MITTERMEYER, Diane	(PQ)	850
Political research & reference	TAYLOR, Loretta C.	(ON)	1227
Political risk reports	NAPOLITANO, Wanda M.	(NY)	887
	SULLIVAN, Daniel M.	(NY)	1207
Political science	MARTIN, Fenton S.	(IN)	776
	BRUMM, Gordon L.	(MA)	150
	SINCLAIR, Regina A.	(MO)	1143
	OSTROWSKY, Edith	(NY)	929
	SHIROMA, Susan G.	(NY)	1131
	SMITH, Diane H.	(PA)	1154
	CHANCE, Truett L.	(TX)	199
	DIONNE, Guy	(PQ)	305
	GUILMETTE, Pierre	(PQ)	476
Political sci & psychology col devlpmnt	SOUTH, Ruth E.	(OR)	1169
Political science & theory	FENTON, Heike	(NY)	371
Political science bibliography	WERTHEIMER, Marilyn L.	(CO)	1325
Political science book selection	YORK, Grace A.	(MI)	1381
Political science collection development	TURNER, Patricia	(MN)	1265
Political science reference	LITTLE, Rosemary A.	(NJ)	734
	KINGSLEY, Marcia S.	(VA)	652
Politics & government	LOWENTHAL, Jane E.	(DC)	744
Politics, legislation & libraries	VERNON, Christie D.	(VA)	1283
Politics of library automation	PHELAN, Mary C.	(MA)	967
Politics of public librarianship	SHAVIT, David	(IL)	1123
Politics of subject headings	MICHEL, Dee A.	(CA)	832
Public relations & political support	RAY, Gordon L.	(BC)	1011
Research & reference for politicians	O'KEEFE, Kevin T.	(NT)	919
Selection in history & political science	WRIGHT, Joanna S.	(IL)	1371
20th century political collections	VOGT, Sheryl B.	(GA)	1287
World politics	BEESON, Lone C.	(CA)	74

POLLS

Public opinion polls	BOVA, Patrick	(IL)	120

POLLUTION (See also Environment)

Air pollution	SMITH, Shirley M.	(NV)	1161

POLYMERS

Biomedical polymers	STAVETSKI, Norma K.	(NJ)	1183
Polymer information	KLEMM, Carol B.	(NJ)	660
Polymer science	JUDGE, Joseph M.	(PA)	619
Polymer science & technology	HILL, Elizabeth C.	(KY)	539
Polymers	JAZBINSCHEK, Jerri	(MI)	596
Rubber, plastics & polymer science	HOLLIS, William F.	(OH)	552

POPULAR

American popular entertainments	LOMONACO, Martha S.	(NY)	738
American popular music	WELLS, Paul F.	(TN)	1323
Early popular songs	RIGGS, Quentin T.	(CA)	1034
Popular culture	DEUTSCH, James I.	(DC)	296
	EZELL, Johanna V.	(PA)	360
Popular culture bibliography	SCOTT, Randall W.	(MI)	1108
Popular fiction & nonfiction	GANYARD, Margaret E.	(MO)	416
Popular literature	SCHLIPF, Frederick A.	(IL)	1094
Popular materials in libraries	MCMULLEN, Charles H.	(VA)	815
Popular music	MILLER, Charles W.	(NJ)	836
Popular music bibliography	COOPER, B L.	(MI)	242
Popular music discography	COOPER, B L.	(MI)	242
Popular music theme structures	COOPER, B L.	(MI)	242
Popular reading	KIES, Cosette N.	(IL)	647
Popular reading interests	ROSENBERG, Betty	(CA)	1056
Publishing & popular literature	TAYLOR, Margaret T.	(MI)	1227
Selecting popular materials	CROW, Rebecca N.	(TX)	261
20th century American popular music	SPECHT, Joe W.	(TX)	1172

POPULATION (See also Census)

Family planning, population, soc mktg	WILLSON, Katherine H.	(CT)	1349
Library service for special populations	DALTON, Phyllis I.	(NV)	271
Library service to special populations	KIRSCHENBAUM, Arthur S.	(DC)	655
Outreach to special populations	REILLY, Carol H.	(NC)	1020
Population & family planning	BARROWS, William D.	(NC)	60
Population law	HEACOCK, Pamela P.	(MA)	518
Populations	WINTERS, Wilma C.	(MA)	1356
Service to special populations	CUNNINGHAM, William D.	(MD)	265
	JOHNSON, Nancy B.	(NY)	608
Service to special populations & seniors	RICKERT, Carol A.	(IL)	1032
Services for special populations	MARKARIAN, Rita J.	(NY)	771
Services to an aging population	MOORE, Bessie B.	(DC)	858
Services to older population	CLARKE, Charlotte C.	(MN)	218
Services to special populations	SPAZIANI, Carol	(IA)	1172
	MCCONNELL, Lorelei C.	(NJ)	797
Special populations	RAZZANO, Barbara W.	(NJ)	1012
	KLAUBER, Julie B.	(NY)	658

PORTABLE

Energy efficient portable library	POWELL, Anice C.	(MS)	988

PORTRAITS (See also Pictures)

Catalog of portraits of botanists	STIEBER, Michael T.	(PA)	1193

PORTUGUESE

Spanish & Portuguese languages	NEUGEBAUER, Rhonda L.	(KS)	897

POSTAL (See also Mail)

Postal operations	WEERASINGHE, Jean Y.	(ON)	1316

POTTER

Beatrice Potter	DOWNUM, Evelyn R.	(AZ)	317

POWER (See also Energy)

Electric power databases	JUDY, Joseph R.	(CA)	619
Nuclear power	WOODLEY, Victoria B.	(MI)	1366
Nuclear power industry	SPARER, Saretta	(NY)	1171
Power engineering	SEABERG, Eileen J.	(IL)	1109

PRECIS

PRECIS	LALIBERTE, Madeleine A.	(PQ)	689

PRECOLUMBIAN

Precolumbian art	GRIFFISS, M K.	(TN)	469

PREDICTIONS

Trend predictions & monitoring	BUNCE, George D.	(ENG)	157

PREPRESS

Electronic prepress publishing systems	BRAWLEY, Paul H.	(IL)	130
Prepress scanning technology	HILL, Kristin E.	(CA)	540

PRESCHOOL (See also Early, Toddlers)

Children's literature, preschool	WINFREE, Barbara S.	(LA)	1354
Children's programming for preschoolers	BELCHEE, Nancy O.	(NC)	76
Preschool & early childhood programs	REZNICK, Evi P.	(GA)	1025
Preschool programming	LANGSAM, Christine E.	(AR)	696
	WILLIAMS, Deborah H.	(NY)	1342
Preschool programs	KING, Cynthia	(CA)	650
Preschool storyhours	ZINMAN, Sandra	(NY)	1389
Preschool storytelling	SELANDER, Lucy M.	(MN)	1113
Preschool to grade nine	CHAPIN, Joan R.	(NJ)	201
Storytime for preschoolers	WALKER, Tamara E.	(TX)	1296

PRESENTATIONS

Effective presentations & slide shows	SANKER, Paul N.	(NY)	1081
Exhibits, audiovisual presentations	SHIDELER, John C.	(WA)	1129
Marketing of services, presentations	CURRAN, William M.	(PQ)	266
Product presentations	BAKES, Floy L.	(NJ)	50
Technical presentation	VILLERE, Dawn N.	(CA)	1284
Training & public presentations	MADDEN, Susan B.	(WA)	758

PRESERVATION (See also Conservation, Paper)

Analogue disc preservation	WAYLAND, Terry T.	(TX)	1311
Archival conservation & preservation	MARRELLI, Nancy M.	(PQ)	773
Archival preservation	CHRISTOPHER, Paul	(CA)	212
	MULDREY, Mary H.	(LA)	876
	GRIFFIN, Marie E.	(NJ)	468
Archival preservation techniques	TAMMARO, James M.	(NY)	1221
Archives & preservation	COURSEY, W T.	(GA)	251
Archives, historic building preservation	RABINS, Joan W.	(TX)	1001
Binding & book preservation	SNELL, Patricia P.	(CA)	1163
Building design for preservation	OGDEN, Barclay W.	(CA)	918
Cataloging & preserving archival mtrls	FALCONE, Elena C.	(NY)	362
Collection preservation	SAGE-GAGNE, Waneta	(FL)	1074
Conservation & preservation	BUTLER, Randall R.	(CA)	167
	CARROON, Robert G.	(CT)	187
	DE PEW, John N.	(FL)	293
	NAKANO, Kimberly L.	(HI)	887
	KLEEBERGER, Patricia L.	(MD)	658
	LATOUR, Terry S.	(MS)	701
	ALTERMAN, Deborah H.	(NJ)	18
	GRAUER, Sally M.	(NY)	458
	O'CONNELL, Brian E.	(NY)	915
	PEPPER, Jerold L.	(NY)	958
	BAUER, Barbara B.	(PA)	65
	REPP, Robert M.	(PA)	1024
	RUGGERE, Christine A.	(PA)	1066
Conservation & preservation services	HECKMAN, Stephen P.	(IN)	520
Conservation & preservation techniques	HOLT, David A.	(KY)	554
Disaster planning & preservation	TOOLEY, Katherine J.	(OK)	1250
Document preservation	PICKENS, Nancy C.	(KY)	970

PRESERVATION (Cont'd)

Film & television preservation	SALZ, Kay	(NY)	1078
Historic preservation	SIMS, Sally R.	(MD)	1142
	MORGAN, Anne E.	(BC)	863
Historic recordings preservation	PETRIE, Mildred M.	(FL)	965
Historic theaters & preservation	LONEY, Glenn M.	(NY)	739
Library & archive preservation	GARLICK, Karen	(DC)	419
Lib material, acquisition, preservation	KALRA, Bhupinder S.	(IL)	623
Library materials preservation	HAVENS, Shirley E.	(NY)	513
Library preservation	SCHROCK, Nancy C.	(MA)	1100
	YEAGER, Gerry	(MD)	1378
	STAM, David H.	(NY)	1179
Library preservation administration	JONES, Maralyn	(CA)	614
Local history, genealogy, preservation	BROWN, Donald R.	(PA)	143
Manuscripts general preservation	MICHAELIS, Patricia A.	(KS)	831
Microfiche preservation	COOPER, Carol D.	(NY)	242
Microfilming preservation	MARKHAM, Robert P.	(IL)	771
Newspaper preservation	HARRISON, Karen A.	(ON)	507
Paper book preservation	MOLTKE-HANSEN, David	(SC)	853
Paper preservation	SWIFT, David L.	(TN)	1216
Photographic preservation	COIR, Mark A.	(MI)	229
Preservation	ALLISON, Terry L.	(CA)	17
	BEVERAGE, Stephanie L.	(CA)	93
	WAKEFORD, Paul J.	(CA)	1293
	BOLLIER, John A.	(CT)	112
	SIGGINS, Jack A.	(CT)	1137
	STUEHRENBERG, Paul F.	(CT)	1205
	WALKER, Robin G.	(CT)	1296
	JEFFERSON, Karen L.	(DC)	596
	NAINIS, Linda	(DC)	886
	SUNG, Carolyn H.	(DC)	1210
	ZIMMERMANN, Carole R.	(DC)	1389
	DEBOLT, W D.	(FL)	284
	EIMAS, Richard	(IA)	340
	FENSTERMANN, Duane W.	(IA)	371
	STOPPEL, William A.	(IA)	1198
	ALEXANDER, Liz C.	(IL)	12
	BROWN, Norman B.	(IL)	146
	FRIEDER, Richard D.	(IL)	403
	MATTENSON, Murray M.	(IL)	785
	PENCE, Cheryl S.	(IL)	956
	WILLIAMS, Sara R.	(KS)	1346
	CAIN, Charlene C.	(LA)	171
	BOLSHAW, Cynthia L.	(MA)	112
	CARPENTER, Kenneth E.	(MA)	185
	BYRNES, Margaret M.	(MD)	169
	DURBIN, Ramona J.	(MD)	328
	HUMPHREYS, Betsy L.	(MD)	573
	MCCALLISTER, Myrna J.	(ME)	793
	OVERMIER, Judith A.	(MN)	931
	RACINE, John D.	(MO)	1001
	HIGGINS, Matthew J.	(NH)	538
	WALLIN, Cornelia B.	(NH)	1298
	DENSKY, Lois R.	(NJ)	293
	SWARTZBURG, Susan G.	(NJ)	1214
	WILINSKI, Grant W.	(NJ)	1339
	ANTHONY, Donald C.	(NY)	28
	BERGMANN, Allison M.	(NY)	86
	DAVIS, Mary B.	(NY)	280
	DECANDIDO, Graceanne A.	(NY)	285
	DEMAS, Samuel G.	(NY)	291
	FRUSCIANO, Thomas J.	(NY)	406
	HARRIS, Carolyn L.	(NY)	504
	NELSON, Robert J.	(NY)	895
	TAYLOR, Robert N.	(NY)	1228
	WARD, Christine W.	(NY)	1303
	COHEN, Susan J.	(OH)	229
	DENHAM, Patricia K.	(OH)	292
	SCHOONMAKER, Dina B.	(OH)	1098
	SEELY, Edward	(OH)	1111
	LOWELL, Howard P.	(OK)	744
	DUCKETT, Kenneth W.	(OR)	322
	TERRY, Carol S.	(RI)	1232
	KELLEY, Gloria	(SC)	636
	JONES, Roger G.	(TN)	615
	BRENNAN, Mary H.	(TX)	132
	BUCKNALL, Carolyn F.	(TX)	154
	HIMMEL, Richard L.	(TX)	542

PRESERVATION (Cont'd)

Preservation
	HOLLAND, Michael E.	(TX)	551
	WELLVANG, James K.	(TX)	1323
	CHAMBERLAIN, William R.	(VA)	197
	CREW, Roger T.	(VA)	258
	DUKE, John K.	(VA)	324
	MENGES, Gary L.	(WA)	824
	GARLOCK, Gayle N.	(ON)	419
	TURKO, Karen A.	(ON)	1263
	MOLLER, Hans	(PQ)	853
	INGLES, Ernie B.	(SK)	582

Preservation administration
	FORTSON, Judith	(CA)	392
	OGDEN, Barclay W.	(CA)	918
	MOON, Myra J.	(CO)	857
	BENNETT, Scott B.	(IL)	82
	BAKER, John P.	(NY)	48
	DARLING, Pamela W.	(NY)	275
	ROZENE, Janette B.	(NY)	1064
	SWARTZELL, Ann G.	(NY)	1214
	BOOMGAARDEN, Wesley L.	(OH)	115
	HEIDTMANN, Toby	(OH)	521
	PATTERSON, Robert H.	(OK)	948

Preservation & arrangement of records
	YOUNKIN, C G.	(TX)	1383

Preservation & conservation
	HAYES, Melinda K.	(CA)	516
	MAINELLI, Helen K.	(CA)	761
	MILLBROOKE, Anne	(CT)	835
	PIZER, Irwin H.	(IL)	977
	WITHEE, Jane S.	(IL)	1358
	GIETSCHIER, Steven P.	(MO)	433
	BELL, Mary F.	(NY)	77
	SEEMANN, Ann M.	(NY)	1111
	STERN, Marc J.	(NY)	1189
	SUNDT, Christine L.	(OR)	1210
	GYESZLY, Suzanne D.	(TX)	479
	MASON, Timothy D.	(TX)	781
	KARRER, Jonathan K.	(VA)	628
	MOLLER, Hans	(PQ)	853
	DE MACEDO, Maria L.	(PTG)	290

Preservation & conservation literature	HUEMER, Christina G.	(ITL)	570
Preservation & lib disaster prevention	DITXLER, Carol J.	(MD)	306
Preservation, binding, restoration	ALLEN, Doris L.	(CA)	14
Preservation consulting	MILEVSKI, Robert J.	(DC)	834
Preservation database development	ZIMMERMANN, Carole R.	(DC)	1389
Preservation education	JONES, Maralyn	(CA)	614
	HANTHORN, Ivan E.	(IA)	499
Preservation education & training	OGDEN, Barclay W.	(CA)	918
Preservation management	MAHER, William J.	(IL)	760
	SEWELL, Robert G.	(NY)	1117
Preservation microfilm cataloging	JONES, Edgar A.	(MA)	612
Preservation microfilming	CHACE, Myron B.	(DC)	196
	FERRARESE, Mary A.	(DC)	373
	SWORA, Tamara	(DC)	1217
	UNGER, Carol P.	(MD)	1269
	BAKER, John P.	(NY)	48
	SWARTZELL, Ann G.	(NY)	1214
	BOOMGAARDEN, Wesley L.	(OH)	115
Preservation of archival records	CALMES, Alan R.	(DC)	174
Preservation of books & paper	HUTTNER, Sidney F.	(OK)	579
Preservation of documentary materials	YOUNG, Julia M.	(MS)	1382
Preservation of legislative records	EFIRD, Frank K.	(IL)	338
Preservation of library materials	MERRILL-OLDHAM, Jan	(CT)	827
	CLOONAN, Michele V.	(IL)	223
	HENDERSON, William T.	(IL)	527
	MCNEILL, Janice M.	(IL)	816
	DARLING, Pamela W.	(NY)	275
	PYATT, Timothy D.	(OR)	999
	SAMET, Janet S.	(PA)	1078
	LANDRUM, John H.	(SC)	693
	DAVIS, Susan W.	(TN)	281
	POLLARD, Margaret E.	(WI)	981
	WHITCOMB, Dorothy V.	(WI)	1330
Preservation of maps in books	KLIMLEY, Susan	(NY)	661
Preservation of materials	SMITH, Ledell B.	(LA)	1157
Preservation of non-book material	ELLISON, John W.	(NY)	345

PRESERVATION (Cont'd)

Preservation of rare books	HALEY, Marguerite R.	(WA)	486
Preservation of records	LONG, Brideen	(WI)	739
Preservation of research materials	ROGERS, Rutherford D.	(CT)	1050
Preservation of sound recordings	KINNEY, Daniel W.	(NY)	653
Preservation, planning, & programming	BROWN, Charlotte B.	(PA)	142
Preservation program development	CHILD, Margaret S.	(DC)	208
Preservation techniques	HEIZER, Carolyn H.	(TX)	523
Preservation technology	WELSH, William J.	(DC)	1323
Preserving memorabilia	KESSLER, Selma P.	(NJ)	645
Rare book preservation	BEDARD, Laura A.	(DC)	73
Record preservation	KING, Eleanor M.	(PA)	650
Risk management & preservation	SEAL, Robert A.	(TX)	1109
Serials acquisitions & preservation	IRVIN, Judy C.	(LA)	584

PRESIDENCY

American presidency history	ELZY, Martin I.	(GA)	347
Presidential & executive papers	NESBITT, John R.	(MO)	896
Presidential archives	SMITH, Nancy K.	(TX)	1158
Presidential papers	HUMPHREY, David C.	(TX)	573

PRESS (See also Printing, Publishing)

Alternative press	TSANG, Daniel C.	(CA)	1260
	EMBARDO, Ellen E.	(CT)	347
Alternative press publication	FROST, Michelle	(CA)	406
Fine press	PASCAL, Barbara R.	(CA)	945
Fine press publisher	ALTERMAN, Deborah H.	(NJ)	18
Fine printing, private presses	MATHEWS, Richard B.	(FL)	784
Small press distribution	LEISNER, Anthony B.	(IL)	714
Small press poetry	FOX, Willard	(LA)	395
Small press publications	ROM, Cristine C.	(OH)	1052
Small press publishing	KNIFFEL, Leonard J.	(MI)	664
	SILVER, Gary L.	(MI)	1138
	THEWS, Dorothy D.	(MN)	1234
	CARTER, Charles R.	(BC)	189
Small presses	CARPENTER, Eric J.	(OH)	184

PREVENTION (See also Protection)

Accident prevention research	BISSON, Jacques	(PQ)	100
Preservation & lib disaster prevention	DITXLER, Carol J.	(MD)	306

PRICING (See also Cost)

International serials pricing	HAMAKER, Charles A.	(LA)	490
Library materials prices	LYNDEN, Frederick C.	(RI)	752
Securities pricing	FORD, George H.	(NY)	389
Stock & bond pricing	SOSTACK, Maura	(NY)	1169

PRIMARY

Library systems, primary	MILLER, Ellen L.	(VA)	837
Primary & secondary research	STARESINA, Lois J.	(MI)	1181
	MILGRIM, Martin S.	(NJ)	835
Primary education	CROTTS, Carolyn D.	(KS)	261
Primary school children's libraries	CARPENTER, Janella A.	(NC)	184
Primary through third grade libraries	BURKE, Mary E.	(TN)	160

PRINT (See also Books, Pictures)

Acquisitions, circulation, print media	GOODWYN, Betty R.	(AL)	450
Acqs, processing print, non-print	FRENCH, Janet D.	(PA)	402
Audiovisual print specialist	PHEGAN, Dolores M.	(TX)	967
Cataloging print & non-print	HSIEH, Cynthia C.	(IL)	567
Cataloging print media	KEARNEY, Jeanne E.	(NJ)	633
Computerizing print & non-print mtrls	BIANCHINO, Cecelia	(IN)	94
Conservation of print materials	COUPER, Richard W.	(NJ)	251
Early printed books	NORTON, Margaret W.	(IL)	910
Early printed books of 1450-1600	WITTEN, Laurence	(CT)	1358
Fine print cataloging	REDLICH, Barry	(NJ)	1014
Fine prints	OSTROW, Stephen E.	(DC)	929
	DANE, William J.	(NJ)	272
Historical prints	CRESSWELL, Donald H.	(PA)	258
Large print	MASSIS, Bruce E.	(NY)	782
	BORCHERT, Catherine G.	(OH)	116
Libraries for print handicapped	MINOR, Dorothy C.	(FL)	846
Literacy & large print	LEGO, Jane B.	(VA)	712

PRINT (Cont'd)

Lute prints & manuscripts	NESS, Arthur J.	(MA)	896
Maps, printed ephemera	SILVER, Marcy L.	(MD)	1138
Print	BOARDMAN, Edna M.	(ND)	108
Print & audiovisual communications	NORTON, Alice	(CT)	910
Print & computerized reference	MCDONALD, Michael L.	(DC)	803
Print & non-print cataloging	ROBERTS, Sallie H.	(OH)	1041
Print & non-print material cataloging	TIWANA, Shah J.	(IL)	1247
Print & non-print materials cataloging	BROWN, Biraj L.	(SDA)	142
Print & non-print teacher consulting	CARLISLE, Carol A.	(CT)	182
Print cataloging	GREESON-SCHARDL, Tamra J.	(GA)	465
Print music	VOLLONO, Millicent D.	(NY)	1288
Print selection	GILBERT, Donna J.	(OH)	433
Printed & non-printed material catlgng	SZETO, Dorcas C.	(CA)	1218
Printed circuit boards	ZANG, Patricia J.	(VA)	1386
Prints	SILVER, Marcy L.	(MD)	1138
Prints & photographs	FELACO, Maja K.	(DC)	369
	IBACH, Marilyn	(DC)	581
	BAKER, Tracey I.	(MN)	50
Research, online & print	RABAI, Terezia	(IL)	1001
Reviewing materials, print & non-print	SELWYN, Laurie	(TX)	1114
Selection of print & non-print material	GREENFIELD, Judith C.	(NY)	464
Yng adult & children's print & non-print	WOODS, Selina J.	(MA)	1367

PRINTING (See also Press, Publishing, Reprints, Type)

Archival printing	WAYLAND, Terry T.	(TX)	1311
Books & printing history	LOWE, Mildred	(NY)	744
Corporate printing & publishing	ARNSDORF, Dennis A.	(DC)	34
Early printing & publishing	GONIWIECHA, Mark C.	(AK)	447
Electronic printing & publishing	GRIMES, Judith E.	(MD)	470
Financial printing & publishing	ARNSDORF, Dennis A.	(DC)	34
Fine printing & incunabula	MENTHE, Melissa	(NJ)	825
Fine printing, limited editions	KIRSHENBAUM, Sandra D.	(CA)	655
Fine printing, private presses	MATHEWS, Richard B.	(FL)	784
Government Printing Office publications	MAST, Joanne	(PA)	782
History books & printing	COLBY, Robert A.	(NY)	230
History of American printing	MCCORISON, Marcus A.	(MA)	798
History of books & printing	KIRSHENBAUM, Sandra D.	(CA)	655
	THOMPSON, Susan O.	(NY)	1241
	JOHNSON, Bryan R.	(VA)	602
	BREGMAN, Alvan M.	(ON)	131
History of fine printing	DANE, William J.	(NJ)	272
History of printing	WELLS, James M.	(IL)	1322
	WINGER, Howard W.	(IL)	1355
	HALPORN, Barbara	(IN)	490
	BRODY, Catherine T.	(NY)	139
	TICHENOR, Irene	(NY)	1244
	FLAKE, Chad J.	(UT)	383
	ETTLINGER, John R.	(NS)	356
History of printing & publishing	DUGGAN, Mary K.	(CA)	324
Laser printing	DICK, John H.	(IL)	300
Laser printing distribution	CONTESSA, William B.	(NY)	239
Legal, medical, corporate printer	SCULLIN, Frank E.	(PA)	1109
Legal printing & publishing	ARNSDORF, Dennis A.	(DC)	34
Letterpress printing	JOHNSON, Bryan R.	(VA)	602
Modern fine printing	COLE, Maud D.	(NY)	231
Music printing history	BOORMAN, Stanley H.	(NY)	115
Non-impact printing technology	HILL, Kristin E.	(CA)	540
Printing & graphics art	WEISER, Douglas E.	(MI)	1319
Printing & publishing	LASH, David B.	(NY)	700
	CHALIFOUX, Jean P.	(PQ)	197
Printing & publishing history	BIDWELL, John	(CA)	95
Printing & publishing in Asia	DIEHL, Katharine S.	(TX)	302
Printing databases	LAMMERT, Diana P.	(PA)	691
Printing, design & production	NAGLE, Ann	(NY)	886
Printing history	SILVER, Joel B.	(IN)	1138
Publishing & printing	MEHNERT, Robert B.	(MD)	821
Publishing & printing histories	BUSHMAN, James L.	(OR)	165
Rare books, printing history	ALLEN, Susan M.	(CA)	16
Spanish printing & publishing	RAMER, James D.	(AL)	1005

PRINTMAKING

Electrographic printmaking	NEADERLAND, Louise O.	(NY)	890

PRISON (See also Correctional, Inmate, Institutions)

Cuban political prisoners	PEREZ, Maria L.	(FL)	958
Library service in prisons	GROSSHANS, Merilyn P.	(NV)	473
Library services to prisoners	CHESLEY, Thea B.	(IL)	207
Prison education	GALLER, Anne M.	(PQ)	414
Prison law libraries	BOTTA, Jean C.	(NY)	118
Prison librarianship	HARTZ, Frederic R.	(GA)	509
	LONG, Gary	(LA)	739
	PEARSON, Barbara F.	(WA)	952
Prison libraries	SASSE, Margo	(CA)	1083
	EATON, Barbara F.	(CO)	333
	GILLESPIE, David M.	(MD)	435
	BOTTA, Jean C.	(NY)	118
	ROMALIS, Carl	(NY)	1052
	SUVAK, Daniel S.	(OH)	1212
Prison library management	ROMALIS, Carl	(NY)	1052
Prison library service	MOSIER, Eric M.	(CA)	871
Prisoner's access law	WARNER, Marnie M.	(MA)	1305
Reference service to prisoners	COLOKATHIS, Jane	(MN)	234
Service to prison inmates	REHNBERG, Marilyn J.	(MN)	1017

PRIVACY

Privacy & access policies	NASH, Cherie A.	(UT)	888

PRIVATE (See also Non-Public)

Creating & organizing private libraries	ROTHMAN, Marilyn R.	(CO)	1060
Fine printing, private presses	MATHEWS, Richard B.	(FL)	784
Marketing in private practice	CLARKE, Elba C.	(GA)	218
Private information exchange networks	BUSSMANN, Steve	(VA)	166
	EDWARDS, Wilmoth O.	(VA)	338
	FILIPPONE, Anne	(VA)	377
	KELLER, Jay	(VA)	635
	LITTLE, William	(VA)	734
	LOVETT, Bruce	(VA)	743
	MAJOR, Skip	(VA)	762
	NEWLAND, Barbara	(VA)	899
	RINALDI, Roberta	(VA)	1035
	RYAN, Maureen	(VA)	1071
	STRATT, Randy	(VA)	1200
Private jazz archivist	ROBINSON, David F.	(VA)	1043
Private law firm administration	SCHIPPER, Joan A.	(CA)	1093
	KLEBBA, Lisa A.	(MO)	658
Private law firm consulting	PLUNKET, Joy H.	(MA)	978
Private law firms	GOLDMAN, Teri B.	(MO)	446
Private law libraries	WALLACE, Marie G.	(CA)	1297
Private law library	ROLLINS, James H.	(CA)	1051
	KOSLOSKE, Verleah B.	(DC)	672
Private law library management	KISSANE, Mary K.	(MO)	656
Private legal database indexing	LEVINTON, Juliette	(NY)	721
Private library research	MAZEFSKY, Gertrude T.	(PA)	791
Private manuscripts & records	GRAHAM, Robert W.	(IL)	456
Private records	BREEDLOVE, Michael A.	(AL)	131
Private records cataloging	BREEDLOVE, Michael A.	(AL)	131
Private schools libraries	JOHNSON, Guy M.	(NY)	605
Processing private manuscript cols	GILSON, Barbara J.	(NY)	437
Public & private academic libraries	EASTERLY, Ambrose	(TN)	333
Public & private music education	MILLER, Charles W.	(NJ)	836
Public or private law	STAYNER, Delsie A.	(CA)	1183
Researcher for private funding sources	ROBERTSON, Ina N.	(IL)	1042

PROBLEM

Bibliographic problem solving	JOHNSON, Everett J.	(DC)	604
Bibliographic problems	BROWN, Sharon D.	(MD)	147
Creative problem solving	WRIGHT-HESS, Anne H.	(NY)	1373
Organizing & problem solving	GREENBERG, Roberta D.	(NY)	463
Organizing problem areas	BERG, David C.	(MN)	84
Personnel problem solving	HARDIN, Willie	(AR)	500
Personnel problems	MUELLER, Elizabeth	(IL)	875
Problem patrons	SPARKMAN, Mickey M.	(TX)	1171
Problem solving	RICHARDS, Timothy F.	(TN)	1028
Resource person & problem solver	ALGAZE, Selma B.	(FL)	13

PROCEDURES (See also Policy)

Appellate procedure	WRIGHT, Jacqueline S. .	(AR)	1371
Automation procedure writing	PALMER, Marguerite C. .	(WV)	936
Circulation policies & procedures	COOK, Anita I.	(NE)	239
Circulation procedures	PORTER, Eva L.	(NJ)	984
Collection development procedures	AUER, Margaret E.	(MI)	39
Facilitate legal procedures to court	SIENDA, Madeline M. . .	(WA)	1136
Forms & procedures management	GENESEN, Judith L.	(IL)	427
Governmental procurement procedures	HAAS, Eva L.	(NY)	480
Information management procedures	HENDERSON, Madeline M.	(MD)	526
Library procedures	PELLINI, Nancy M.	(MA)	955
NOTIS training & procedures	ENGLE, Constance B. . .	(MI)	349
Order plans, order procedures	KAVANAGH, Susan E. . . .	(ON)	631
Parliamentary procedure	VELTEMA, John H.	(MI)	1282
Procedural systems analysis	NYBERG, Lelia J.	(CA)	912
Procedure & guideline writing	STRONG, Sunny A.	(WA)	1203
Procedure manual development	KOSTIS, Leigh W.	(PA)	673
Procedure manuals	PLOTSKY, Andrea G. . . .	(CA)	978
Reference training & procedures	HELSLEY, Alexia J.	(SC)	525
Rehabilitation procedures	MATTHEWS, Geraldine M.	(WI)	785
Science library procedures	STEEVES, Henry A.	(MA)	1184
Special library systems & procedures	CAMOZZI-EKBERG, Patricia L.	(WA)	175
Updating library procedures	CHOMENKO, Tamara L. . .	(MB)	210
Writing policies & procedures	KNIGHT, Rita C.	(AZ)	664
Writing procedures manuals	ZYNJUK, Nila L.	(MD)	1392

PROCEEDINGS

Acquisitions, serials & proceedings	LEFEBVRE, Veronica A. .	(MD)	712
Cataloging conference proceedings	CARTER, Judith A.	(AZ)	189
Publishing, professional proceedings	JACOBS, Horace	(CA)	589

PROCESS

Alumina production, bayer process	PHEGAN, Dolores M. . . .	(TX)	967
Budget process	JOHNSON, Wayne H. . .	(WY)	609
Budgeting & tax levying process	PLAISTED, Glen L.	(KS)	977
Budgeting process	GOEHNER, Donna M. . .	(IL)	443
Interpersonal comm & group processes	FLOOD, Barbara J.	(PA)	385
Manufacturing processes & applications	GROEN, Paulette E.	(MI)	471
Planning process	BENDER, Betty W.	(WA)	79
Political process	WILSON, David C.	(GA)	1350
	WILSON, Evie	(WA)	1350
	MITTERMEYER, Diane . .	(PQ)	850
Process engineering	GOLBITZ, Peter	(ME)	444
	KINGMA, Sharyn L.	(ME)	652
Teaching research process	PARR, Michael P.	(MI)	944
Technical process	SABINE, Davida M.	(SC)	1072
Technical processes	SONIN, Hille	(CA)	1167
	BLAKE-O'HOGAN, Kathleen E.	(NY)	103
	EARLE, Mary E.	(OH)	332

PROCESSING

Acquisitions & materials processing	LESNIK, Pauline	(NY)	718
Acqs, processing print, non-print	FRENCH, Janet D.	(PA)	402
Administer circulation, processing	STAINBROOK, Lynn M. . .	(WI)	1178
Archival processing	ODOM, Jane H.	(DC)	917
	ELTZROTH, Elsbeth L. . .	(GA)	346
	FRENCH, Melodee J. . . .	(GA)	402
	BOECKMAN, Frances B. .	(MS)	109
	DISHON, Robert M.	(NY)	305
	OAKHILL, Harold W. . . .	(NY)	913
	OVERTON, Julie M.	(OH)	931
	LEVITT, Martin L.	(PA)	721
	SNYDER, Theresa	(PA)	1165
Archival processing & description	SICILIANO, Peg P.	(MI)	1135
Archive & manuscript processing	THWEATT, John H.	(TN)	1243
Archives & manuscripts processing	BECK, Alison M.	(TX)	71
Archives processing	WOOD, Steven R.	(UT)	1365
Archives processing & reference	BLACK, J A.	(TX)	101
Automated language processing	BORKO, Harold	(CA)	116
Automated technical processing	TAYYEB, Rashid	(NS)	1229
Automatic text processing	SALTON, Gerard	(NY)	1077

PROCESSING (Cont'd)

Bibliographic tape processing	MCQUEEN, Judith D. . . .	(MD)	817
Book processing	WEISER, Douglas E. . . .	(MI)	1319
Book processing services	NAGEL, Lawrence D. . . .	(CA)	886
Cataloging & manuscript processing	WESTERBERG, Kermit B. .	(IL)	1326
Cataloging & processing	KOEL, Maria O.	(CT)	667
	ISHIMOTO, Carol F.	(MA)	585
	HESS, Marjorie A.	(PA)	534
Cataloging & processing manuscripts	WHITTINGTON, Erma P. .	(NC)	1334
Cataloging & processing of materials	BIANCHI, Karen F.	(WA)	93
Cataloging, ordering, processing	GERMINDER, Robin L. . .	(NJ)	429
Cataloging, processing & annotating	BARNARD, Sandra K. . . .	(CA)	57
Centralized processing	DICK, Norma P.	(CA)	300
	DAWSON, Lawrence	(WI)	282
Centralized processing union catalog	BENSON, Laurel D.	(MN)	83
Collection processing	MATTHEOU, Antonia . . .	(NY)	785
	VANDOREN, Sandra S. . .	(PA)	1275
Collections processing	HEISS, Harry G.	(DC)	523
	MEVERS, Frank C.	(NH)	829
Computer word processing	COUP, William A.	(FL)	251
Computerized processing	TABAR, Margaret E.	(MN)	1219
Data processing	PEMPE, Ruta	(DC)	956
	BREEN, Joanell C.	(IL)	131
	CHUNG, Alison L.	(IL)	213
	MYLES, Bobbie	(MA)	885
	CLARK, William E.	(MI)	218
	VETH, Terry R.	(MN)	1283
	SHAFFER, Richard P. . . .	(NY)	1119
	WILSON, Fredric W.	(NY)	1351
	HYNUM, Jill A.	(WI)	580
Data processing & computers	MCBRIDE, Jessica W. . .	(NY)	792
Data processing & production	BORKENSTEIN, Donald M.	(NY)	116
Data processing hardware & software	KOOLISH, Ruth K.	(CA)	671
Data processing management	CANGANELLI, Patrick W. .	(IN)	178
Data processing research	REIST, Paul A.	(CA)	1022
	SMITH, Lydia K.	(CT)	1157
Data processing systems	CLASQUIN, Frank F. . . .	(MA)	219
Database processing	ALLEN, Norene F.	(KS)	15
Editorial processing	ARJONA, Sandra K.	(PA)	31
Electronic data processing systems	MOUNIR, Khalil O.	(NY)	873
Engineering, data processing	FLEMING, Jack C.	(ON)	384
Food processing technology databases	MCNAUGHT, Hugh W. . .	(ON)	816
Freedom of information processing	DOLAN, Maura E.	(DC)	309
Geoscience information, processing mgmt	BICHTELER, Julie H. . . .	(TX)	94
Government document processing	HARTMAN, Anne M. . . .	(NY)	508
Image processing	CALMES, Alan R.	(DC)	174
	THOMA, George R.	(MD)	1235
Image processing software	DAVISSON, Darell D. . . .	(CA)	281
Information processing	CRIM, Dewey H.	(GA)	258
	ROTHMAN, John	(NY)	1060
	SCHUTT, Dedre A.	(NY)	1103
	CARNEY, Marillyn L. . . .	(VA)	183
Information processing & control	SPATH, Charles E.	(TN)	1171
Information processing consulting	ETZI, Richard	(NY)	356
Information processing technology	SAFFADY, William	(NY)	1074
Invoice processing	BURKHARD, Polly S. . . .	(PA)	161
Law information processing	ARAJ, Houda	(PQ)	30
Library technical processing	RUNKLE, Martin D.	(IL)	1067
Machine file processing	MARTIN, Robert A.	(FL)	778
Manuscript processing	MILLER, Leon C.	(AR)	839
	SHARP, Alice L.	(CO)	1122
	NEWHALL, Ann C.	(CT)	898
	HODGSON, Janet B. . . .	(KY)	546
	GIFFORD, Paul M.	(MI)	433
	JESSEE, W S.	(MN)	600
	TRASK, Benjamin H. . . .	(VA)	1254
	WEBER, Anita M.	(VA)	1313
Manuscript processing & collecting	HULL, Mary M.	(TX)	572
Manuscript processing & description	KAPLAN, Diane E.	(CT)	626
Manuscripts & archival processing	WHITE, William T.	(MN)	1332
Manuscripts, archives processing	BOOTHE, Nancy L.	(TX)	116
Manuscripts processing	PAUL, Andrea I.	(NE)	949
Manuscripts processing & cataloging	BOUCHE, Nicole L.	(CA)	118
Manuscripts processing & reference	WELLS, Anne S.	(MS)	1322
Manuscripts solicitation & processing	GRABOWSKI, John J. . .	(OH)	455
MARC data processing	SEGEL, Bernard J.	(DC)	1112
MARC tape processing	HAMILTON, Fae K.	(MA)	492
Material tracking & processing	KILLHEFFER, Robert E. .	(CT)	648

PROCESSING (Cont'd)

Multilingual text processing	DEERWESTER, Scott C.	(IL)	287
Music materials, cataloging & processing	MEERVELD, Bert	(ON)	821
Music processing	BENTON, Mary A.	(NJ)	84
Natural language information processing	HAYDEN, Richard F.	(CA)	515
Natural language processing	TRIVISON, Donna	(OH)	1257
	VLEDUTS-STOKOLOV, Natalia	(PA)	1286
Natural languages processing	METZLER, Douglas P.	(PA)	829
Non-Roman alphabet data processing	AGENBROAD, James E.	(DC)	7
Online processing	STRIEDIECK, Suzanne S.	(PA)	1202
	HOLLOWAY, Geraldine B.	(TX)	552
Papers processing	DESNOYERS, Megan F.	(MA)	295
Payroll processing	MOY, Clarence T.	(NY)	874
Periodicals processing	GATES, Jane P.	(CA)	421
Physical processing	GAUDET, Dodie E.	(MA)	422
	CHILDRESS, Eric R.	(NC)	208
	UHLMAN, Carol K.	(WA)	1268
	THOMSON, Donna K.	(ON)	1241
Post-processing	JACK, Robert F.	(MD)	586
Processing	MULLER, Charles W.	(FL)	877
	JONES, Thomas Q.	(IN)	615
	RAINWATER, Mark T.	(MS)	1004
	SAMPLES, Judith L.	(OH)	1078
	COKINOS, Elizabeth G.	(TX)	229
	NOLAN, Edward W.	(WA)	907
Processing accessioned material	RHEAUME, Irene M.	(MD)	1025
Processing & cataloging manuscripts	ETTER, Patricia A.	(AZ)	355
Processing & organization of collections	AUTRY, Carolyn	(IN)	41
Processing archival collections	HAWES, Grace M.	(CA)	513
	VIOL, Robert W.	(OH)	1285
Processing archival materials	SANDERS, Robert L.	(CA)	1080
	WADE, D J.	(MO)	1290
Processing archives & manuscripts	SIEBERS, Bruce L.	(MI)	1135
Processing books for shelving	HEYDUCK, Marilyn J.	(IL)	535
Processing center supervision	WINTER, Bernadette G.	(IL)	1356
Processing gifts	TAYLOR, Carolyn L.	(MO)	1226
Processing management	STEVENS, Michael L.	(MA)	1190
Processing manuscript collections	BOYD, Sandra E.	(MS)	123
	TEICHMAN, Raymond J.	(NY)	1230
Processing manuscripts & archives	CHESTNUT, Paul I.	(DC)	207
Processing materials	LONNING, Roger D.	(MN)	740
Processing media	BRANDT, Garnet J.	(IA)	128
Processing of archival materials	RABCHUK, Gordon K.	(PQ)	1001
Processing of records	HOOKS, Michael Q.	(TX)	556
Processing papers & records collections	ERICKSEN, Paul A.	(IL)	352
Processing private manuscript cols	GILSON, Barbara J.	(NY)	437
Records accessioning & processing	SCOTT, Paul R.	(TX)	1108
Serial processing	HSU, Karen M.	(NY)	567
Serials processing	BAILEY, Dorothy C.	(GA)	46
	CIANFARINI, Margaret	(MD)	214
	MCCUTCHEON, Dianne E.	(MD)	801
	KOVACIC, Mark E.	(OH)	673
Serials processing, holdings conversion	RONEN, Naomi	(MA)	1053
Technical processing	RICHMOND, John W.	(AZ)	1030
	COLALILLO, Robert M.	(CA)	230
	REDFIELD, Dale E.	(CA)	1014
	TARCZY, Stephen I.	(CA)	1224
	AVRAM, Henriette D.	(DC)	42
	TERRY, Susan N.	(DC)	1232
	BINAU, Myra I.	(MD)	97
	TAYLOR, Donna I.	(NJ)	1226
	MANES, Estelle L.	(OK)	765
	JACKSON, Joseph A.	(TN)	587
	TAYLOR, Karen E.	(ON)	1227
Technical processing & acquisitions	BOGGESS, John J.	(MD)	110
Technical processing & cataloging	WHITE, Ardeen L.	(VA)	1330
Technical processing center admin	ENGELBERT, Alan M.	(WI)	348
Technical processing, govt documents	ADAMS, Leonard R.	(MA)	5
Technical processing services	KOPPER, John A.	(MN)	671
Text processing	BUCKLAND, Lawrence F.	(MA)	154
Word processing	EMMONS, Mary E.	(AK)	348
	MORGAN, Bradford A.	(SD)	863
	GOERDT, Arthur L.	(TX)	443
Word processing, biblgph preparation	MANDEL, Douglas J.	(IL)	765

PROCESSING (Cont'd)

Word processing, record management systs	KEE, Walter A.	(NC)	634
Word processing software development	SCHWARTZ, James M.	(SD)	1104

PROCUREMENT (See also Acquisitions, Buying, Purchasing)

CD-ROM buyer procurement support	MILLER, Davic C.	(CA)	836
Federal computer & telecom procurement	DODSON, Whit	(VA)	308
Federal procurement support	SLOAN, Cheryl A.	(MD)	1149
Government procurement	AVERY, Galen V.	(OH)	41
Governmental procurement procedures	HAAS, Eva L.	(NY)	480
Library systems procurement	FRIEDMAN, Terri L.	(MA)	404
Literature procurement	GALLAGHER, Eileen W.	(PA)	414
Media appraisal & procurement	HOLSINGER, Katherine	(AZ)	554
Procurement	CIMBALA, Diane J.	(NJ)	214
	ROBINSON, Mitchell L.	(NY)	1044
Procurement & acquisitions	ROY, Alice R.	(VA)	1063
Procurement & cataloging	JONES, Stephanie R.	(LA)	615
Publications procurement	CROWTHER, Carol	(CA)	262

PRODUCT

Acquisitions & product development	YANNOTTA, Peter J.	(NJ)	1377
Bibliographic database products & srvs	PAUL, Rameshwar N.	(MD)	949
Bibliographic product analysis	FARINA, Robert A.	(DC)	363
Bibliographic products	LAWALL, Marie	(VA)	704
Bibliographic products & services	SEGEL, Bernard J.	(DC)	1112
	SETTLER, Leo H.	(DC)	1117
	PARENT, Ingrid T.	(ON)	940
CD-ROM product design	MCCLELLAND, Bruce A.	(NY)	796
CD-ROM product development	SPENCER, John T.	(CA)	1173
CD-ROM product marketing	CORCHADO, Veronica A.	(CA)	245
Company, product, & industry data	DLOTT, Nancy B.	(MA)	306
Consumer products, health care	SILVERMAN, Susanne	(CT)	1139
Consumer products markets	COMPTON, Erlinda R.	(TX)	235
Consumer products, personal care	SILVERMAN, Susanne	(CT)	1139
Custom data products	LA MARCHE, David L.	(ON)	689
Database product development	ROSEN, Theresa H.	(PA)	1055
	TRUBKIN, Loene	(BC)	1259
Electronic product development	BING, Robert H.	(NY)	97
Electronic products	MCGILL, Thomas J.	(NJ)	806
End-user online product design	LIPPERT, Margret G.	(OH)	732
Financial information products	TIERNEY, Richard H.	(NY)	1244
Industrial products	YANCHAR, Joyce M.	(MA)	1377
Information product design & development	DAY, Melvin S.	(VA)	283
Information product design & maintenance	PISCITELLI, Rosalie A.	(NY)	976
Information product development	HART, Patricia H.	(MI)	507
	BARTLETT, Jay P.	(NY)	61
Information product development mgmt	BRAM, Leon L.	(NJ)	127
Information product management	LEHMANN, Edward J.	(VA)	713
Information product market development	SAYER, John S.	(MD)	1086
Information products	MUZZO, Steven E.	(IL)	883
Information products development	ABLES, Timothy D.	(MS)	2
Leasing technical products	MONOSSON, Adolf S.	(MA)	855
Literature search product liability	KENNEDY, Joanna C.	(GA)	641
Market research & product	CUTLER, Judith	(PA)	268
Market research, product development	LEVITAN, Karen B.	(MD)	721
Marketing bibliographic products	STEVENS, Roberta A.	(DC)	1191
Marketing CD-ROM & online products	HUDES, Nan	(NY)	569
Marketing information products	GERSH, Barbara S.	(CA)	429
Marketing library products & services	ELLSWORTH, Dianne J.	(CA)	345
New information product development	CARTER, Daniel H.	(TX)	189
New product development	ELLSWORTH, Dianne J.	(CA)	345
	BROCK, Laurie N.	(CO)	138
	WHITE, Suellen S.	(CO)	1332
	FATTIBENE, James F.	(DC)	366
	KINLEY, Jo H.	(DC)	652
	TAYLOR, George A.	(DC)	1226
	GROSSMAN, David G.	(IL)	473
	LESLIE, Donald S.	(MN)	718

PRODUCT (Cont'd)

New product development

	KIESER, Scott P.	(NY)	647
	MACFARLAND, Scott D.	(NY)	755
	LA MARCHE, David L.	(ON)	689
New product potential consulting	HOPE, Thomas W.	(NY)	557
New product testing	MARANGONI, Eugene G.	(CA)	768
Online database product development	JENKINS, George A.	(FL)	597
Online product design development	ODHO, Marc	(ON)	917
Optical data products, CD-ROM	STEFFEY, Ramona J.	(TN)	1185
Optical disc products	SPALA, Jeanne L.	(CA)	1170
Optical laser disk products	HANIFORD, K L.	(MO)	496
Product databases	WINDSOR, Donald A.	(NY)	1354
Product development	DONINI, Elizabeth A.	(CA)	311
	BOGENSCHNEIDER, Duane R.	(CT)	110
	HUXSAW, Charles F.	(IL)	580
	JONES, Gerry U.	(MD)	613
	BARTENBACH, Wilhelm K.	(NY)	60
	MOLINE, Gloria	(NY)	853
	O'CONOR, William C.	(NY)	916
	REDEL, Judy A.	(NY)	1014
	REED, Buzz	(OH)	1014
	SYEN, Sarah	(PA)	1217
Product development & management	FOUSER, Jane G.	(IL)	393
Product development & marketing	JOHNSON, Emily P.	(MD)	604
Product development & valuation	MOFFITT, Michael D.	(MA)	852
Product literature	SATTLER, Pauline	(MI)	1084
	KOELLE, Joyce G.	(NJ)	667
Product management	BARNETT, Becky L.	(GA)	57
	KIESER, Scott P.	(NY)	647
Product management & development	RYAN, R P.	(VA)	1071
Product marketing	JAIN, Nem C.	(MA)	592
Product planning	HERRICK, Carol L.	(OH)	532
Product presentations	BAKES, Floy L.	(NJ)	50
Product, publication acquisition	QUINLIN, Margaret M.	(MD)	1000
Product rollouts & marketing	CORVESE, Lisa A.	(NY)	248
Product safety & liability research	MOUZON, Margaret W.	(MI)	874
Products liability	PATTELA, Rao R.	(PA)	947
Real estate CD-ROM product development	JENKINS, George A.	(FL)	597
Reference product & publishing mgmt	BRAM, Leon L.	(NJ)	127
Research & development, new products	WINGATE, Dawn A.	(CA)	1354
Sales, marketing, product development	ALESSI, Dana L.	(TX)	11
Software products	KAHN, Martin F.	(NY)	622
Soyfoods product development	GOLBITZ, Peter	(ME)	444
	KINGMA, Sharyn L.	(ME)	652
Special products production	ROTHSCHILD, M C.	(VA)	1060
System & product development	MILLER, Ronald F.	(CA)	842
Systems & product development	ABELES, Tom	(MN)	2
Tobacco products	LINCOLN, Carol S.	(KY)	728
Wood products research	SCHARMER, Roger C.	(WI)	1090

PRODUCTION

Advertising, newsletter production	WASERSTEIN, Gina S.	(PA)	1307
Alumina production, bayer process	PHEGAN, Dolores M.	(TX)	967
Audio book production	CYLKE, Frank K.	(DC)	268
Audio library production	MASSIS, Bruce E.	(NY)	782
Audiovisual equipment & productions	BURMAN, Marilyn P.	(WY)	161
Audiovisual instruction & production	FALLON, Marianna L.	(IN)	362
Audiovisual materials production	CARLISLE, Carol A.	(CT)	182
Audiovisual production	BEEBE, Richard J.	(CA)	74
	WESTBROOK, Patricia C.	(CT)	1326
	DEANS, Janice P.	(FL)	284
	BADGER, Barbara	(IL)	44
	TUGGLE, Ann M.	(IL)	1262
	NEWTON, Evah B.	(IN)	900
	O'LOUGHLIN, Marilyn L.	(MD)	921
	EDWARDS, Rosa C.	(NC)	338
	HAY, Mary K.	(WI)	515
Audiovisual production training	RUNYON, Steven C.	(CA)	1067
Automated bibliography production	CHERVENAK, Joseph F.	(CO)	206
Automated magazine production	HAVENS, Shirley E.	(NY)	513
Book production	FITZGERALD, Ardra F.	(CA)	382
	HUCHTING, Mary	(IL)	569
	KRAMER-GREENE, Judith	(NY)	675

PRODUCTION (Cont'd)

Braille production	CYLKE, Frank K.	(DC)	268
Catalog, index & directory production	BUCKLAND, Lawrence F.	(MA)	154
CD-ROM & CD-I prog design & production	DAVISSON, Darell D.	(CA)	281
CD-ROM catalog production	CUMMINGS, Christopher H.	(UT)	264
CD-ROM production	BATOR, Eileen F.	(MD)	64
Children's film production	DAVENPORT, Thomas R.	(VA)	276
Consultant, film & video production	HEMPEL, Gordon J.	(IL)	525
Data processing & production	BORKENSTEIN, Donald M.	(NY)	116
Database design & production	BATES, Ruthann I.	(MD)	64
	BRUNELLE, Bette S.	(NY)	150
	LAM, Vinh T.	(ON)	689
Database producer services	ZIRPOLO, Frank	(NY)	1390
Database production	LUEVANE, Marsha A.	(CO)	747
	GOERS, Willona G.	(IA)	443
	DEPKE, Robert W.	(IL)	293
	REMEIKIS, Lois A.	(IL)	1022
	ROTT, Richard A.	(IL)	1060
	JAMES, Bonnie B.	(KY)	592
	WEINBERG, Gail B.	(MN)	1317
	ROLETT, Virginia V.	(NH)	1051
	BARTENBACH, Wilhelm K.	(NY)	60
	GORDON, Marjorie	(NY)	451
	LAWRENCE, Barbara	(NY)	704
	LEWICKY, George I.	(NY)	722
	MOLINE, Gloria	(NY)	853
	MOONEY, Martha T.	(NY)	858
	SHAPIRO, Barbara G.	(NY)	1121
	KELLY, Maureen C.	(PA)	638
	CARROLL, Bonnie C.	(TN)	187
	OLIVETTI, L J.	(VA)	921
	FAST, Louise	(ON)	366
	OLMSTEAD, Marcia E.	(ON)	921
	KLOK, Buddhi	(PQ)	662
	AITCHISON, Thomas M.	(ENG)	9
Database production & design	CORNICK, Ron	(IL)	247
Database production & development	BROWNRIDGE, James R.	(ON)	149
Database production & indexing	SPENCER, John T.	(CA)	1173
Database production & maintenance	STEVENS, Paula F.	(AZ)	1190
Database systems production	BRENNER, Everett H.	(NY)	133
Databases, user producing	WELLS, Christine	(VA)	1322
Document production	DENNETT, Stephen C.	(CA)	292
Documentary production training	WILLIAMS, Carroll W.	(NM)	1342
Documentation production	FITZGERALD, Ardra F.	(CA)	382
Film & television production	COHEN, Frederick	(NY)	228
	KLUGHERZ, Dan	(NY)	662
Film & video production	WHITE, Matthew H.	(IL)	1331
	CABEZAS, Sue A.	(MA)	170
Film & video writing & production	TALIT, Lynn	(CT)	1221
Film production	BORUZKOWSKI, Lilly A.	(IL)	117
	CEDERHOLM, Theresa D.	(MA)	196
	MONDELL, Cynthia B.	(TX)	854
Film research, television production	LIMBACHER, James L.	(MI)	727
Food industry database production	INGISH, Karen S.	(IL)	582
Graphics production	HART, Thomas L.	(FL)	507
Grimm tales production & direction	DAVENPORT, Thomas R.	(VA)	276
Information-products produced harmlessly	THURSTON, Ethel H.	(NY)	1243
Instructional media production	POWELL, Patricia K.	(TX)	988
	REHMS, Jane C.	(WA)	1017
Language of dramatic production	TRAPIDO, Joel	(HI)	1254
Media & theatrical production	GOODMAN, John E.	(PA)	449
Media design, production & utilization	LIGGAN, Mary K.	(VA)	726
Media production	SMITH, Margie G.	(CA)	1157
	TAWYEA, Edward W.	(IL)	1225
	GERRING, Cheryl B.	(MD)	429
	HRYVNIAK, Joseph T.	(NY)	567
	YANOFF, Marcy S.	(NY)	1377
	LOCKETT, Iva	(TX)	736
Media production & evaluation	BELT, Jane	(WA)	78
Medical database production	TINGLEY, Dianne E.	(MD)	1246
Motion picture production research	PLUMB, Carolyn G.	(CA)	978
Multi-image production	ISOBE, Darron T.	(UT)	585
Musical theater history & production	LONEY, Glenn M.	(NY)	739
Non-print production	THOMAS, James L.	(TX)	1237
Petroleum exploration & production	ANDERSON, Margaret	(TX)	24

PRODUCTION (Cont'd)

Photographic productions & publications	SPINA, Marie C.	(NY)	1175
Poetry video production & distribution	LESNIAK, Rose	(NY)	718
Printing, design & production	NAGLE, Ann	(NY)	886
Producing & directing	GURIEVITCH, Grania B.	(NY)	478
Producing informational films	HOFFER, Thomas W.	(FL)	547
Producing training user aids	TOWNSEND, Carolyn J.	(PA)	1253
Producing translations database	NOWAK, Ildiko D.	(IL)	911
Production	LEE, Judith C.	(CA)	710
	LANGE, Clare M.	(MA)	695
Production & validation	SOUTHWICK, Margaret A.	(VA)	1170
Production audiovisuals	SOLIN, Myron	(NY)	1166
Production, film & video	BEATTY, R M.	(IN)	70
Production of find-aids	RABCHUK, Gordon K.	(PQ)	1001
Production system design	HODGE, Gail M.	(PA)	546
Public information video production	RANCER, Susan P.	(NC)	1006
Record producing	ROBINSON, Margaret L.	(DC)	1044
Slide & tape production	SHAMBARGER, Peter E.	(MD)	1120
Software production	FITZGERALD, Ardra F.	(CA)	382
Soybean production, mktg, & utilization	GIBSON, Marianne	(MO)	432
Special products production	ROTHSCHILD, M C.	(VA)	1060
Spine labels & automated production	CHILDRESS, Eric R.	(NC)	208
Student audiovisual productions	PROCTOR, Deborah K.	(WY)	994
Student media production	JONES, Wanda F.	(AR)	615
	MCKINNEY, Barbara J.	(AR)	812
Student video production	FREEMAN, Evangeline M.	(NC)	400
Teaching, audiovisual production	POWELL, Patricia K.	(TX)	988
Television production	SHAMBARGER, Peter E.	(MD)	1120
	MARTIN, Richard T.	(NC)	778
	MCLAREN, M B.	(NM)	813
Television production & distribution	WILSON, George N.	(TX)	1351
Television, radio production	BAYLES, Carmen L.	(CT)	67
Union catalog production	TSUI, Josephine	(ON)	1260
Video production	LARSON, Teresa B.	(IA)	700
	GREEN, Donald T.	(NJ)	461
	WHITLOW, Cherrill M.	(NM)	1333
	PETERMAN, Kevin	(NY)	962
	QUINN, David J.	(NY)	1000
	CLANCY, Ron	(BC)	215
Video program production	SPANGLER, William N.	(NJ)	1171
Videodisc design & productions	HAUSMAN, Julie	(IA)	513
Videotape production	PHILLIPS, Donald J.	(FL)	968
Videotape productions	PARKER, Eleanor V.	(OK)	941
Visual resources production	FREEMAN, Carla C.	(NY)	400
Workshop planner & producer	LYNCH, Minnie L.	(LA)	752

PRODUCTION/DISTRIBUTION

Production/distribution	SPALA, Jeanne L.	(CA)	1170

PRODUCTIVITY (See also Measurement)

Information & productivity research	KOENIG, Michael E.	(NY)	668
Productivity management	NEWBERG, Ellen J.	(MT)	898

PROFESSIONAL (See also Paraprofessionals)

Academic staff professional development	WHEELER, Helen R.	(CA)	1329
Continuing educ & professional devlpmnt	BRIDGE, Frank R.	(TX)	135
Continuing professional education	VARLEJS, Jana	(NJ)	1278
Criticism of professional literature	SHAPIRO, Lillian L.	(NY)	1121
Editing professional books	FRANKLIN, Robert M.	(NC)	398
Editing professional publications	SCHEETZ, Mary D.	(PA)	1091
Education & professional development	MCCRANK, Lawrence J.	(AL)	800
Education of information professionals	HALSEY, Richard S.	(NY)	490
Educ, training & professional devlpmnt	AMAN, Mohammed M.	(WI)	19
Ethics for information professionals	HORN, David E.	(MA)	559
Health professionals & training	BISCHOFF, Frances A.	(VA)	99
Information publishing, professionals	RICCOBONO, Joseph V.	(CT)	1026
International profsnl & academic publshg	SMITH, Richard A.	(CA)	1159
Library & information profession educ	GALVIN, Thomas J.	(IL)	415
Library professional literature	WYNAR, Bohdan S.	(CO)	1375
Marketing professional services	FROST, Roxanna	(WA)	406
One-person professional libraries	BENEDETTI, Joan M.	(CA)	80
Personnel & professional systems	PEISCHL, Thomas P.	(MN)	955

PROFESSIONAL (Cont'd)

Profession certification	KWAN, Julie K.	(CA)	685
Professional acting	MYERS, Maria P.	(NY)	884
Professional & reference books	BUCENEC, Nancy L.	(NY)	153
	TOPEL, Iris N.	(NY)	1251
Professional & reference publishing	QUINLIN, Margaret M.	(MD)	1000
Professional & special library direction	ROTHMAN, Marilyn R.	(CO)	1060
Professional association	DEARSTYNE, Bruce W.	(NY)	284
Professional association involvement	BEARD, Charles E.	(GA)	69
Professional book publishing	KING, Timothy B.	(NY)	652
Professional collection education	CORCORAN, Frances E.	(IL)	245
Professional conditions of academic libs	VINE, Rita F.	(AB)	1285
Professional continuing education	WILFORD, Valerie J.	(IL)	1339
Professional development	COPLER, Judith A.	(IN)	244
	DANIELS, Pam	(NY)	273
	KONKEL, Mary S.	(OH)	670
	TOMAN, Jocelyn B.	(PA)	1249
	OAKE, Rhena E.	(AB)	913
	MCQUEEN, Lorraine	(ON)	817
Professional development of archivists	THOMAS, Evangeline M.	(KS)	1236
Professional development of librarians	EDWARDS, Ralph M.	(AZ)	337
Professional education	MILLER, Sylvia G.	(NC)	843
Professional education & training progs	ROBERTS, Kenneth H.	(FRN)	1040
Professional education at Master's level	MATARAZZO, James M.	(MA)	783
Professional education collection	HABER, Elinor L.	(NY)	480
Professional ethics	ARDEN, Caroline	(VA)	31
Professional information	NISENOFF, Sylvia	(VA)	905
Professional involvement	GRAF, David L.	(WI)	455
Professional libraries	RUDDICK, Patsy R.	(KS)	1065
Professional library education	SIBAI, Mohamed M.	(SDA)	1134
Professional library operating	CHAPMAN, Peggy H.	(NC)	202
Professional library services	DEAN, Martha L.	(CA)	283
Professional materials	LAMBERTH, Linda E.	(TX)	690
Professional networks, electronic mail	LEHMAN, Tom	(MN)	713
Professional organizations	O'HALLORAN, James V.	(NY)	918
Professional outreach to faculty	RIDINGER, Robert B.	(IL)	1032
Professional publications & reviewing	CHEATHAM, Bertha M.	(NY)	204
Professional publishing	DANNE, William H.	(IL)	274
	OLDERR, Steven	(IL)	920
Professional puppeteering	HILDEBRANT, Darrel D.	(ND)	539
Professional reference accounting pubns	HALPIN, Gerard B.	(ON)	490
Professional reference law publications	HALPIN, Gerard B.	(ON)	490
Professional research	MARSHALL, Deborah M.	(IL)	774
Professional seminars	HALPIN, Gerard B.	(ON)	490
Professional society publishing	FERRERE, Cathy M.	(NY)	373
Professional staff supervision	WINTER, Bernadette G.	(IL)	1356
Professional standards	SASS, Samuel	(MA)	1083
Professional storytelling	GRAY, Raymond L.	(PA)	460
Professional, technical books	BOWMAN, James K.	(NY)	121
Professional technical trade texts	ABRAMOFF, Lawrence J.	(MA)	3
Professional training & development	PINGS, Vern M.	(FL)	974
Professional trends & issues	PHELPS, Thomas C.	(DC)	967
Professional workshops	DAVIS, Virginia K.	(ON)	281
Professional writing	PROCES, Stephen L.	(WI)	994
Publishing professional books & journals	GRAYSON, Martin	(NY)	460
Publishing, professional proceedings	JACOBS, Horace	(CA)	589
Sociology of professional education	PAGE, Jacqueline M.	(MO)	934
Supervision of professional staff	KRISTIAN, Alice	(NY)	679
Teacher/librarian professional devlpmnt	GUILBERT, N P.	(MB)	476
Values & professional ethics	HALL, Homer J.	(NJ)	488
Visual resources professional	HEHMAN, Jennifer L.	(IN)	521
Women in the profession	KADANOFF, Diane G.	(MA)	621
Writing & editing professional books	WEISBURG, Hilda K.	(NJ)	1319
Writing for professional journals	EAGLEN, Audrey B.	(OH)	331

PROFESSORSHIP

Professorship	WHITE, William	(VA)	1332

PROFIT

Libraries as profit centers	LUPPINO, Julie B.	(SC)	749
Not for profit libraries	BARNUM, Sally J.	(IL)	58

PROGRAMMING (See also Programs)

Adult & children's programming	CHRISTNER, Terry A. . .	(KS)	212
	HILDEBRANT, Darrel D. . .	(ND)	539
Adult library programming	KUSZMAUL, Marcia J. . .	(IL)	685
	BURKE, Lauri K.	(RI)	160
Adult programming	POIRIER, Maria K.	(CT)	980
	ROEHLING, Steven R. . .	(GA)	1048
	WEISS, Cynthia A.	(IA)	1320
	JACOB, Merle L.	(IL)	589
	ROBY, B D.	(KY)	1045
	MCCORMICK, Emily S. . .	(NC)	798
	BRODERICK, Therese L. .	(NY)	139
	GILLESPIE, Gerald V. . . .	(NY)	435
	SPYROS, Marsha L.	(NY)	1177
	YEE, J E.	(WA)	1379
Adult programming & instruction	UTSUNOMIYA, Leslie D.	(BC)	1270
Adult programming & services	DEMETRAKAKES, Jennifer B.	(IL)	291
Adult services & programming	BINGHAM, Elizabeth E.	(LA)	97
Adult services, programming	OLSON, Joann M.	(SC)	922
APL programming	ETZI, Richard	(NY)	356
Applications programming	CANGANELLI, Patrick W.	(IN)	178
Art films reference & programming	WARREN, Ann R.	(NH)	1306
Arts & humanities adult programming	SMOTHERS, Joyce W. . .	(NJ)	1162
Arts & humanities programming	GANN, Daniel H.	(IN)	416
Building programming	MCADAMS, Nancy R. . .	(TX)	792
Children's & young adult programming	WALSH, Lynn R.	(FL)	1299
Children's book selection & programming	GENDRON, Michele M. .	(PA)	426
Children's books & programming	BADERTSCHER, Kimberlin H.	(IN)	44
Children's literature & programming	NG, Carol S.	(CA)	900
	HEITMAN, Lynn	(IL)	523
	NOAH, Carolyn B.	(MA)	906
	REID, Margaret B.	(OH)	1018
Children's materials & programming	MACRURY, Mary E.	(NS)	758
Children's media programming	GAFFNEY, Maureen	(NY)	412
Children's programming	STOWE, Jean E.	(AR)	1199
	BECKER, Teresa J.	(AZ)	72
	BAILEY, Darlene L.	(CA)	46
	WINKLER, Jean J.	(CO)	1355
	KELLY, Anne V.	(FL)	637
	SOVANSKI, Vincent G. . .	(IL)	1170
	BICKEL, Bernice M.	(IN)	94
	TIMKO, Patricia A.	(IN)	1246
	RASKIN, Susan R.	(MA)	1009
	ROBERTS, Susan P. . . .	(MD)	1041
	RAFAL, Marian D.	(MI)	1003
	VOIGHT, Nancy R.	(MI)	1287
	DORNBERGER, Julie L. .	(NC)	313
	FARIAS, Elizabeth H. . . .	(NC)	363
	FREEDMAN, Barbara G. .	(NC)	400
	LYTLE, Marian M.	(NC)	753
	HODGES, Lois F.	(NY)	546
	LOUISDHON-WALTER, Marie L.	(NY)	742
	OLDERSHAW, Anne . . .	(NY)	920
	SIVULICH, Sandra S. . . .	(NY)	1145
	USTACH, Joanne B.	(NY)	1270
	PAPA, Deborah M.	(OH)	938
	RUHL, Jodi S.	(OH)	1066
	STICHA, Denise S.	(PA)	1193
	DAVIS, Mary F.	(TX)	280
	MACFARLANE, Francis X.	(TX)	755
	MCCONNELL, Ruth M. . .	(TX)	798
	PARNES, Daria M.	(VA)	943
	POWERS, Linda J.	(VA)	989
	SIPOLA, Debra L.	(WI)	1144
	LUTHY, Jean M.	(AB)	750
	MARSH, Mary L.	(NS)	773
	ADDY, Kathryn J.	(ON)	6
	GAGNON, Andre	(SK)	412
Children's programming & services	WOOLF, Amy K.	(KS)	1368
	MCLEAN, Paulette A. . .	(ON)	814
Children's programming for preschoolers	BELCHEE, Nancy O. . . .	(NC)	76
Children's programming or services	KILLEEN, Erlene B.	(VA)	648
Children's programming, puppets	NORMAN, Nita V.	(AZ)	909
Children's room programming	KIBREAH, Golam	(IN)	646

PROGRAMMING (Cont'd)

Children's services & programming	WARREN, Catherine S. . .	(MS)	1306
	HARTUNG, Nancy F. . . .	(TN)	509
Children's services programming	HUNTER, Julie A.	(NC)	576
Community programming	GRAYBIEL, Luisa	(SK)	460
Computer programming	ZHANG, Foster J.	(CA)	1387
	SMITH, Randolph R. . . .	(CO)	1159
	HEINRITZ, Fred J.	(CT)	522
	DREWETT, William O. . .	(IL)	319
	SLACH, June E.	(MI)	1147
	KANAFANI, Kyung C. . . .	(MO)	624
	MCGLOHON, Charlotte L.	(NC)	807
	YERKEY, A N.	(NY)	1380
	SCHEEREN, Judith A. . .	(PA)	1090
	MINAIKIT, Nonglak	(THA)	845
Computer programming for libraries	ANDERSEN, Eileen	(WA)	21
Computer programming in BASIC	BRETT, Lorraine F.	(IN)	134
Computer training & programming	NEUWILLER, Charlene . .	(WGR)	897
Computer use & programming	CLAPP, David F.	(IL)	215
Continuing education programming	TREBBY, Janis G.	(WI)	1255
Continuing medical education programming	BEDARD, Martha A.	(MA)	73
Craft programming	EDGREN, Gale R.	(IL)	336
Creative programming	WOODARD, Marcia S. . .	(IN)	1366
	PRUITT, Brenda F.	(NY)	996
Custom computer programming	GILLETTE, Robert S. . . .	(TX)	435
Custom microcomputer programming	MARSH, Elizabeth C. . . .	(OH)	773
Database applications programming	ROSENFELD, Jane D. . . .	(NY)	1056
Database programming	MICHELS, Fredrick A. . .	(MI)	832
	RUBIN, Myra P.	(NY)	1064
	SULLIVAN, Robert G. . . .	(NY)	1208
dBASE III programming	MCCAFFERY, Laurabelle	(IN)	793
Display & programming	CLARK, Janet L.	(NV)	217
Early childhood programming	PHELPS, Thomas C. . . .	(DC)	967
Educational programming	ZACHARY, Patricia A. . . .	(OK)	1385
Elementary library programming			
Exhibition & programming of AV materials	SCHREIBMAN, Fay C. . .	(NY)	1099
Exhibits & public programming	MESSINEO, Leonard L. . .	(KS)	828
Facilities programming & planning	MERRIFIELD, Thomas C.	(CA)	826
Film & video programming	THOMPSON, Elizabeth M.	(DC)	1239
	CANTWELL, Mary L. . . .	(OH)	179
Film & video reviewing & programming	BRAUN, Robert L.	(NY)	130
Film programming & research	VOURVOULIAS, Sabrina M.	(NY)	1289
Film programming for adults	JEFFERY, Phyllis D.	(AL)	596
Film, video selection & programming	BUCHANAN, Gerald . . .	(MS)	153
Humanities programming	PALMER, Virginia E.	(OH)	937
	BENDER, Evelyn	(PA)	79
International television programming	PAEN, Alexander L.	(CA)	934
Juvenile & young adult programming	HOUSEWARD, Bernice A.	(MI)	563
Library buildings & programming	YATES, Ella G.	(VA)	1378
Library financing & building programming	HELLUM-BERMAN, Bertha D.	(CA)	524
Library programming	HOLLOWAY, Patricia W.	(CT)	552
	HUPP, Sharon W.	(CT)	577
	PIANE, Mimi	(IN)	969
	WALTERS, Carol G.	(NC)	1301
	OBLOY, Elaine C.	(OH)	914
	PONTIUS, Louise	(TX)	982
	DE RONDE, Paula D. . . .	(ON)	294
Library programming for children	GRAHAM, Marilyn L. . . .	(PA)	456
Library promotion & spcl programming	WARREN, Catherine S. . .	(MS)	1306
Library systems & programming	MOORE, Phyllis C.	(CA)	861
	PITT, William B.	(MD)	976
Management & programming	CUMMINS, Julie A.	(NY)	264
Managing cultural programming	BRODERICK, John C. . .	(DC)	138
Material selection & programming	BRUNTON, Marilyn H. . .	(MN)	151
Mentally ill library programming	VAN DER VOORN, Neal P.	(WA)	1274
Micro & mainframe programming	BRITTON, Jeffrey W. . . .	(NJ)	137
Microcomputer programming & instruction	CARROLL, James K. . . .	(KS)	187
Microcomputer programming & training	ANDREWS, Mark J.	(MO)	27
Minicomputer programming	JACKSON, Charles G. . .	(NY)	587
Multimedia programming	GAREN, Robert J.	(MI)	418
Municipal cable television programming	VARNES, Richard S. . . .	(CO)	1279

PROGRAMMING (Cont'd)

Online systems programming	SKROBELA, Katherine C.	(NJ)	1147
Outreach & programming	BENNETT, Samuel J.	(KS)	82
	DEMARCO, Elizabeth A.	(NY)	291
Outreach programming	GUTHRIE, Chab C.	(OH)	479
Outreach service & programming	JULIEN, Dorothy C.	(FL)	619
Preschool programming	LANGSAM, Christine E.	(AR)	696
	WILLIAMS, Deborah H.	(NY)	1342
Preservation, planning, & programming	BROWN, Charlotte B.	(PA)	142
Programming	HOUGHTON, Sally L.	(AR)	563
	ELLIS, Ruth M.	(CA)	345
	MELLICAN, Nancy J.	(FL)	822
	RITZ, Paul S.	(FL)	1037
	SKUBISH, Barbara E.	(FL)	1147
	STAMPFL, Barbara A.	(FL)	1179
	WALKER, Terri L.	(GA)	1296
	PENROD, Saundra K.	(IN)	957
	MCKENZIE, Joe M.	(KS)	811
	MCLEOD, Debra A.	(KS)	814
	DIEMER, Irvin T.	(KY)	302
	GIBBS, Beatrice E.	(MD)	431
	JOHNSON, Jerry D.	(MD)	606
	MOORE, Craig P.	(MD)	859
	BOSE, Deborah L.	(MI)	117
	JAEGER, Sally J.	(MI)	591
	BERGER, Morey R.	(NJ)	86
	CHAMBERLIN, Cynthia C.	(NJ)	198
	RANIERI, Bernice A.	(NJ)	1007
	BREGMAN, Joan R.	(NY)	131
	SIMON, Patricia B.	(NY)	1140
	SYWAK, Myron	(NY)	1217
	TYNES, Jacqueline K.	(NY)	1267
	ROYSTER, Peggy K.	(OK)	1063
	PECK, Marian B.	(PA)	953
	WEISFIELD, Cynthia F.	(PA)	1319
	WHEELER, Martha M.	(PA)	1329
	MARMION, Daniel K.	(TX)	772
	KITE, Yvonne D.	(UT)	657
	SANDERS, William D.	(UT)	1080
	ANDERSON, Valerie J.	(VA)	25
	FRENCH, Randy A.	(VA)	402
	MAYER-HENNELLY, Mary B.	(VA)	789
	FAWCETT, Patrick J.	(MB)	367
	REID, Marion I.	(MB)	1019
	CORDUKES, Laura L.	(ON)	246
	WILBURN, Gene	(ON)	1338
	HIRON, Barbara A.	(PQ)	543
	BRILL, Kathryn R.	(ENG)	136
Programming & community relations	TANG, Grace L.	(NY)	1222
Programming & exhibits	ROTH, Claire J.	(NY)	1059
Programming & outreach	KAPLAN, Paul M.	(IL)	626
	SODERSTRUM, Ann L.	(IL)	1165
Programming & public relations	CHELTON, Mary K.	(MD)	204
	POLLOK, Karen E.	(VA)	981
Programming & publicity	OLIANSKY, Joseph D.	(MA)	920
Programming & reader advisor	MARCKS, Carol J.	(LA)	769
Programming applications	UCHIDA, Deborah K.	(HI)	1267
Programming buildings & plan review	HOLT, Raymond M.	(CA)	554
Programming COBOL	ZYNJUK, Nila L.	(MD)	1392
Programming development & implementation	TRASATTI, Margaret S.	(NV)	1254
Programming for children	SCHLANSER, Deborah B.	(CA)	1093
	FORD, Gale I.	(MI)	389
Programming for children & youth	MANCALL, Jacqueline C.	(PA)	764
Programming for children in libraries	POLISHUK, Bernard	(WA)	980
Programming for elderly	RING, Anne M.	(IL)	1035
Programming for young children	FADER, Ellen G.	(CT)	360
Programming for young people	JANSON, Sherryl A.	(AZ)	594
Programming languages	SKOVIRA, Robert J.	(PA)	1147
	EASTMAN, Caroline M.	(SC)	333
Programming, planning & evaluating	PEISCHL, Thomas P.	(MN)	955
Programming, public relations	LARSON, Mildred N.	(WI)	699
Public & cultural programming	BLANDY, Susan G.	(NY)	104
Public library adult programming	MEYERS, Arthur S.	(IN)	830
Public library programming	GRALAPP, Marcelee G.	(CO)	457
	ROBERTS, Susan P.	(MD)	1041
Public library programming & publicity	MORRISON, Meris E.	(VT)	868

PROGRAMMING (Cont'd)

Public programming	FRIDLEY, Russell W.	(ME)	403
	SCHWARTZ, Virginia C.	(WI)	1105
Public programming & outreach	WURL, Joel F.	(MN)	1374
Public programming & publications	MOLTKE-HANSEN, David	(SC)	853
Public programming coordination	ATCHISON, Fres D.	(KS)	37
Public programming for adults	MACKNIGHT, Judith M.	(NY)	757
Public relations & programming	CADDELL, Claude W.	(IN)	170
Public relations programming	NORTON, Tedgina	(TN)	910
Public service programming	CALLAHAN, Helen H.	(CT)	173
Radio programming via satellite	WILLIAMS, Fred	(GA)	1343
SAS programming application	ROSTAMI, Janet	(ON)	1059
School library programming	SCALES, Pat R.	(SC)	1087
Special activities programming	MACINICK, James W.	(NY)	755
Storyhour programming & storytelling	ANTHONY, Rose M.	(WI)	29
Storytelling & programming techniques	PELLOWSKI, Anne	(NY)	955
System design & programming	LARSON, Ray R.	(CA)	699
Systems design & programming	RAO, Paladugu V.	(IL)	1008
Teaching & programming	LANGA, Patricia A.	(TX)	695
Very basic computer programming	EIS, Myrna M.	(KS)	340
Video programming	REIDER, William L.	(MD)	1019
Youth programming	DURSTON, Corinne L.	(BC)	329

PROGRAMS

Accreditation & program evaluation	MITCHELL, Joan M.	(PA)	849
Administering school library programs	JACKSON, Gloria D.	(CA)	587
Administration of school lib media progs	KLASING, Jane P.	(FL)	657
Administrative special programs	FELLA, Sarah C.	(OR)	370
Adult library programs	SARLES, Christie V.	(NH)	1083
Adult programs	BALCOM, William T.	(IL)	51
	O'BRYANT, Alice A.	(MT)	915
	NYERGES, Michael S.	(NY)	912
Approval programs	NAGEL, Lawrence D.	(CA)	886
Approval programs, continuations	SCHRIFT, Leonard B.	(NY)	1100
Archive program	KERR, Kevin G.	(IL)	644
Audio & video programs	LOCKE, William G.	(NY)	736
Audiovisual programs	SLONE, Eugenia F.	(CT)	1150
	LAY, Shirley	(MD)	705
Automation records programs	BUTLER, Tyrone G.	(NY)	167
Beginning new library programs	POWELL, Mary E.	(TX)	988
Bibliographic instruction programs	DEWAR, Jo E.	(FL)	298
Book examination programs	NICHTER, Alan	(FL)	902
Branch library services & programs	ALSTON-REEDER, Lizzie A.	(NC)	18
Budgeting & program planning	HEINTZELMAN, Susan K.	(NY)	522
Building program	MAINIERO, Elizabeth T.	(CT)	761
Building program devlpmnt & construction	MOODY, Marilyn D.	(PA)	857
Building program, planning	HUNSBERGER, Charles W.	(NV)	574
Building programs	COBURN, Morton	(IL)	225
	STOFFEL, Lester L.	(IL)	1196
	BOWLING, Carol L.	(SC)	121
Building programs & feasibility study	WRIGHT, Paul L.	(KY)	1372
Building programs & furnishings	POWELL, Mary E.	(TX)	988
Building programs & planning	PETERSON, Stephen L.	(CT)	964
Building programs & space utilization	PALMATIER, Susan M.	(NH)	936
Capital building program	HALL, Edward B.	(MD)	487
CD-ROM & CD-I prog design & production	DAVISSON, Darell D.	(CA)	281
Children's & young adult programs	SOMERVILLE, Mary R.	(KY)	1167
	O'BRYANT, Alice A.	(MT)	915
Children's literature & programs	TOM, Chow L.	(HI)	1249
Children's literature programs	FOERTIN, Yves P.	(PQ)	387
Children's program	MORRIS, Kim	(NY)	867
Children's programs	WILLIS, Jan L.	(MS)	1348
	ZINMAN, Sandra	(NY)	1389
	SAULSBURY, Margie M.	(TX)	1084
Children's public library programs	BOTHAM, Jane	(WI)	118
Circuit librarian programs	ANTES, E J.	(PA)	28
Circuit library program	LEVINE, Lillian S.	(OH)	720
Clinical librarianship program	TRAVERS, Jane E.	(NY)	1254
Competitive assessment program	MOYNIHAN, Mary B.	(CT)	874
Computer library-oriented programs	O'BRIEN, Doris J.	(CT)	914
Computer programs for children	VOORS, Mary R.	(IN)	1289
Computer-managed programs	BROWN, Anita P.	(NJ)	142
Consulting libs, children's programs	WALDEN, Katherine G.	(CT)	1294

PROGRAMS (Cont'd)

Subject	Name	State	Page
Cooperative community programs	MAINIERO, Elizabeth T.	(CT)	761
Cooperative programs for libraries	JURIST, Susan	(CA)	620
Coordinating K-12 library programs	CHAPMAN, Peggy H.	(NC)	202
Coordination of literary programs	CALLAHAN, Helen H.	(CT)	173
Coordinator, library technology program	DAANE, Jeanette K.	(AZ)	269
Cultural programs on videocassettes	HEDLUND, Dennis M.	(NJ)	520
Database programs	EARLEY, Dorothy A.	(NE)	332
Designing media programs	COOK, Sybilla A.	(OR)	240
Developing community support programs	NATHAN, Frances E.	(NY)	889
Developing programs for adults	FISCHER, Anna M.	(PA)	379
Development of school library programs	MEIER, Patricia L.	(IA)	821
	PETERSON, Miriam E.	(IL)	964
Early childhood program services	SCHWABACHER, Sara A.	(NY)	1104
Educational program development	MACKAMAN, Frank H.	(IL)	756
Educational programs	CLARY, Rochelle L.	(CA)	219
Evaluating federal library programs	KIRSCHENBAUM, Arthur S.	(DC)	655
Evaluation of school library programs	HUNT, Linda A.	(VA)	575
Exemplary school library program	ROADS, Clarice D.	(OK)	1038
Exhibit program	HIEBER, Douglas M.	(IA)	537
Exhibitions & friends programs	STODDARD, Roger E.	(MA)	1196
Facilities for school programs	HOLTER, Charlotte S.	(MD)	554
Federal library programs	WELCH, John T.	(NC)	1321
Federal program administration	CROCKETT, Martha L.	(DC)	259
Friends of the library program	HERRING, Mark Y.	(TN)	533
Galleries & arts programs	WILKINSON, Billy R.	(MD)	1340
Graduate media programs	TEMPLE, Leroy E.	(CT)	1230
Graduate program services	NETZ, David H.	(MI)	896
Grant program administration	LEWIS, Alan D.	(MN)	722
Grant program evaluations	EATENSON, Ervin T.	(TX)	333
Grants administration & program devlpmnt	WRIGHT, Paul L.	(KY)	1372
High school media programs	KIRK, Mary L.	(IA)	654
Information program development	FRIERSON, Eleanor G.	(DC)	404
Initiating programs	TERZIAN, Shohig S.	(CA)	1232
Interactive videodisc programs	STEELE, Tom M.	(NC)	1184
International library & information prog	GRAY, Dorothy L.	(DC)	459
Internship programs	EISENBACH, Elizabeth R.	(CA)	340
Learning resource programs	CLARKE, Tobin D.	(CA)	219
Learning resources programs	HUNSUCKER, David L.	(NC)	575
Library adult education programs	REILLY, Jane A.	(IL)	1020
Library & media skills programs	MC NAIR, Marian B.	(OH)	815
Library automation programs	SIMON, Anne E.	(NY)	1140
Library building program writing	STEWART, John D.	(VA)	1192
Library building programs	MCPHERSON, Kenneth F.	(NJ)	817
Library literacy programs	LAW, Aileen E.	(SC)	704
Library media program development	HOBBS, Henry C.	(MB)	545
Library media programs & services	WURBS, Sue A.	(WY)	1374
Library outreach programs	KARASICK, Alice W.	(CA)	627
Library program evaluations	EATENSON, Ervin T.	(TX)	333
Library programs	BIRCH, Grace M.	(CT)	97
	JENKINS, Lydia E.	(DC)	597
	THOMAS, Jacquelyn H.	(NH)	1236
Library programs for aging	KRAMER, Mollie W.	(NY)	675
Library programs supervision	ROOZEN, Nancy L.	(WI)	1054
Library service programs	MCPHERSON, Kenneth F.	(NJ)	817
Library skills program	MCBURNEY, Lynnea R.	(TX)	792
Library technician program coordination	MCDONALD, Marilyn M.	(CA)	803
Literacy program	POWELL, Anice C.	(MS)	988
	MCCONNELL, Lorelei C.	(NJ)	797
Literacy program coordination	STEWART, Jeanne E.	(MS)	1192
Literacy prog development & evaluation	MADDEN, Doreitha R.	(NJ)	758
Literacy programs	BRONSON, Diane A.	(GA)	140
	LINTNER, Barbara J.	(IL)	731
	WESTNEAT, Helen C.	(OH)	1327
	RADOFF, Leonard I.	(TX)	1002
Literacy programs in libraries	PARK, Janice R.	(MI)	941
Literacy programs in public libraries	CARD, Judy	(TN)	180
Literature & programs children's srvs	HUDDLESTON, Marsha E.	(IL)	569
Local history, books, programs	JAMISON, Susan C.	(DE)	593
Long-range planning programs	CHAMBERLAIN, Ruth B.	(MA)	197
Management, administration, programs	LEHMAN, Tom	(MN)	713

PROGRAMS (Cont'd)

Subject	Name	State	Page
Management & supervision of lib programs	PETERSON, Miriam E.	(IL)	964
Managing school library programs	HACKMAN, Mary H.	(MD)	481
Marketing programs	LUTHER, M J.	(GA)	750
Master degree program	WILLIAMS, Carroll W.	(NM)	1342
Media center programs	PAULEY, Charles W.	(MN)	950
Media services program	PHILLIPS, Luouida V.	(TX)	968
Minority service programs	GOMEZ, Martin J.	(IL)	447
National program development	STORDAHL, Beth A.	(WA)	1198
Oral history program design	KENDRICK, Alice M.	(NY)	640
Original media slide programs	OWENS, Martha A.	(VA)	932
Outreach programs, services	BRAUN, Robin E.	(MA)	130
Overseeing Talking Book program	STEWART, Jeanne E.	(MS)	1192
Performance & program evaluation	MARRIOTT, Lois I.	(CA)	773
Plan programs & services	GREENFIELD, Judith C.	(NY)	464
Planning & program development	BLACK, Frances P.	(OH)	101
Preschool & early childhood programs	REZNICK, Evi P.	(GA)	1025
Preschool programs	KING, Cynthia	(CA)	650
Preservation program development	CHILD, Margaret S.	(DC)	208
Professional education & training progs	ROBERTS, Kenneth H.	(FRN)	1040
Program administration	GRAY, Dorothy L.	(DC)	459
Program & collection development	JAFFARIAN, Sara	(MA)	591
Program & space planning	EHRHORN, Jean H.	(HI)	339
Program consultant	BROWN, Gerald R.	(MB)	144
Program consulting	CLAVER, M P.	(AL)	219
Program coordination	MANBECK, Virginia B.	(NY)	764
	LOCKETT, Iva	(TX)	736
Program design	WILLIAMSON, Phyllis B.	(MT)	1348
Program development	GOLDBERG, Susan S.	(AZ)	445
	MARKEY, Penny S.	(CA)	771
	ATKIN, Michael I.	(DC)	37
	WYCHE, Louise E.	(DE)	1374
	WARNER, Wayne G.	(GA)	1305
	CRISPEN, Joanne	(IL)	259
	JOHNSON, Carol A.	(MD)	602
	KUNZ, Margarett N.	(MD)	684
	KELLOGG, Joanne T.	(ME)	637
	MYHRE, Char	(MN)	885
	HYMAN, Karen D.	(NJ)	580
	GUY, Wendell A.	(NY)	479
	WILSTED, Thomas P.	(NY)	1353
	PIPER, Paula	(PA)	975
	NORTON, Tedgina	(TN)	910
	GOW, Susan P.	(BC)	454
	LA CHAPELLE, Jennifer R.	(ON)	686
Program development & evaluation	WALLACE, Michael T.	(DC)	1298
Program development & management	WASSERMAN, Ricki F.	(NY)	1308
	PETERSON, Denise D.	(OK)	963
Program development, fundraising	PIKE, Kermit J.	(OH)	972
Program evaluation	MEDINA, Sue O.	(AL)	820
	PENNINGTON, Walter W.	(AL)	957
	WILLIAMS, Delmus E.	(AL)	1342
	CHELTON, Mary K.	(MD)	204
	HARER, John B.	(MD)	501
	WAYLAND, Marilyn T.	(MI)	1311
	MULLER, Claudya B.	(NY)	877
Program management	CRANOR, Alice T.	(DC)	255
	TESMER, Nancy	(OH)	1233
Program management for libraries	HARRIS, Linda S.	(DC)	505
Program planner	SIMPSON, Leslie T.	(MO)	1142
Program planning	SMITH, Jane B.	(AL)	1155
	PIKE, Nancy M.	(FL)	973
	MCCORMICK, Sheila P.	(MA)	799
	YUEH, Norma N.	(NJ)	1384
	DEUTSCH, Karen A.	(NY)	296
Program planning & foundation evaluation	JONES, C L.	(PA)	611
Program planning & implementation	HESS, Marjorie A.	(PA)	534
Programs	LAMBERT, Sandra L.	(IL)	690
	BURKE, Joseph A.	(NY)	160
	READ, Jean B.	(NY)	1012
Programs & services	SALVADORE, Maria B.	(DC)	1078
Programs for inner-city libraries	O'BRIEN, Anne M.	(MA)	914
Promotions, publicity & programs	HANNAFORD, Claudia L.	(OH)	496
Public information programs	PAISLEY, William J.	(CA)	935
Public libraries, adult programs	WRIGHT, Kathryn D.	(AL)	1372
Public library building programs	SMITH, Elizabeth M.	(CA)	1154
	WELCH, John T.	(NC)	1321

PROGRAMS (Cont'd)

Public programs	TRZECIAK, William J. . .	(CA)	1260
	BRENNAN, Deborah B. .	(RI)	132
	EVANS, Gwynneth	(ON)	357
Public relations & program coordination	MOORE, Virginia B.	(DC)	861
Public relations & programs	GRAVES, Sid F.	(MS)	459
Public service programs	STOLT, Wilbur A.	(OK)	1196
Publishing program management info	KLEIMAN, Gerald S.	(DC)	659
Reading programs	WALKER, Tamara E.	(TX)	1296
Records management programs	SAYED, Joyce P.	(CA)	1086
Reference & programs for children	HACHMEISTER, Helen M.	(WI)	481
Reference & resource programs	HOBBS, Henry C.	(MB)	545
Remedial action programs	PFUDERER, Helen A. . . .	(TN)	966
School curriculum programs	WEISLAK, Susan L.	(TX)	1319
School library media program	PATRICK, Retta B.	(AK)	947
School library media programs	DEWEESE, Don B.	(AR)	298
	WHITNEY, Karen A.	(AZ)	1334
	GREENBERG, Marilyn W.	(CA)	463
	WEIGEL, James S.	(CT)	1316
	HART, Thomas L.	(FL)	507
	BROCK, Kathy T.	(GA)	138
	HOLTER, Charlotte S. . . .	(MD)	554
	SMINK, Anna R.	(MD)	1152
	MATECUN, Marilyn L. . . .	(MI)	783
	MILLER, Robert H.	(MN)	842
	APPEL MOSESOF, Rhoda S.	(NJ)	29
	BARRON, Robert E.	(NY)	60
	RICHARDSON, Constance H.	(NY)	1029
	ROSCELLO, Frances R. .	(NY)	1054
	EHRHARDT, Margaret W.	(SC)	339
	EISENSTEIN, Jill M.	(TN)	341
	LANKFORD, Mary D. . . .	(TX)	696
	WIEMAN, Jean M.	(WA)	1336
	FOLKE, Carolyn W.	(WI)	387
	HOPKINS, Dianne M. . . .	(WI)	557
School library program development	BELL, Jo A.	(TX)	77
School library programs	LOWRIE, Jean E.	(MI)	744
	VANCE, Kenneth E.	(MI)	1273
	PAULEY, Charles W. . . .	(MN)	950
	FRENCH, Janet D.	(PA)	402
School library skills program	JOHNSON, Guy M.	(NY)	605
School media programs	TUGWELL, Helen M. . . .	(NC)	1262
Special programs	NICHOLS, Dolores D. . . .	(TN)	901
Special programs of services for deaf	STEELE, Leah J.	(IL)	1184
Special programs, public relations	LARSON, Josephine	(NC)	699
Staff development programs	FIELD, Judith J.	(MI)	375
Stage scripts & programs	WOODS, Alan L.	(OH)	1366
Standards for school programs	HOLTER, Charlotte S. . . .	(MD)	554
State records center program management	BITTLE, Christine M. . . .	(OK)	100
Statewide library program consulting	LEWIS, Alan D.	(MN)	722
Story & author programs	LOPEZ, Silvia P.	(FL)	741
Storytelling programs & workshops	GREENE, Ellin P.	(NJ)	464
Supervising school library media progs	KLASING, Jane P.	(FL)	657
Symphony computer programs	BURNS, Robert W.	(CO)	163
Systs analysis, microcomputer program	NEWCOMER, Susan N. . .	(CA)	898
Therapeutic patient program planning	ABDULLAH, Bilquis	(NY)	2
Toddler story programs	BROUSE, Ann G.	(NY)	141
Training & development programs	BUTLER, David W.	(CA)	166
Training & program development	MELTON, Vivian B.	(OH)	823
Video program coordination	SIEBL, Linda M.	(NY)	1135
Video program production	SPANGLER, William N. . .	(NJ)	1171
Volunteer literacy programs	TATE, Elizabeth L.	(MD)	1225
Volunteer program coordinator	SALVATORE, Gayle E. . .	(LA)	1078
Writing building programs	DAHLGREN, Jean E. . . .	(TX)	269
Writing programs, online card catalog	JORDAN, Sharon L.	(WA)	617
Young adult programs	TYSON, Edith S.	(OH)	1267
	TOMLIN, Celia K.	(UT)	1250
Youth programs	HUISKAMP, Julie G. . . .	(IA)	572
Youth services & programs	BRANZBURG, Marian G.	(MI)	129

PROJECTS

Alaska collection development project	INNES-TAYLOR, Catherine E.	(AK)	583
Archival acquisition projects	MORRISSEY, Charles T.	(VT)	869
Automation project management	MILLSAP, Gina J.	(MO)	844
Automation projects	FIELD, Judith J.	(MI)	375
Basalt waste isolation project	TRAUB, Teresa L.	(WA)	1254
Building projects	KINCHEN, Robert P. . . .	(NY)	650
Congressional projects in archives	HARWOOD, James L. . .	(DC)	510
Construction project administration	WALTERS, Daniel L. . . .	(WA)	1301
Cooperative library projects	SPECHT, Joe W.	(TX)	1172
Cooperative serials projects	UPHAM, Lois N.	(SC)	1269
Database conversion projects	DIXON, Edith M.	(WI)	306
Database development project management	TELFER, Margaret E. . . .	(NC)	1230
Drug abuse training projects	CNATTINGIUS, Claes M.	(SWE)	224
Fiscal projects & reference in archives	HARWOOD, James L. . .	(DC)	510
Fundraising for research projects	THOMAS, Evangeline M.	(KS)	1236
Gateway project management	MALONEY, James J. . . .	(CA)	764
Information marketing projects	VAN HALM, Johan	(NET)	1275
Inquiry in research project	SENATOR, Rochelle B. .	(CT)	1115
Learning disabled library projects	WILLIAMS, Eve A.	(NB)	1343
Library building projects	BEDSOLE, Dan T.	(VA)	73
Library design & moving projects	SCHUBACK COHN, Judith	(NJ)	1101
Library project administration	MCCAUGHTRY, Dorothy H.	(CT)	795
Library projects	LEON, Carmencita H. . . .	(PR)	716
Linked systems project	GLAZIER, Ed	(CA)	440
	SCHUITEMA, Joan E. . .	(OH)	1101
Local history research projects	WOLFE, Barbara M.	(NY)	1360
Multitype cooperative projects	DORST, Thomas J.	(IL)	313
Oral history projects	JONES, Martin J.	(NY)	614
Outreach projects	MURDOCK, Everlyne K. .	(SC)	879
Project administration	HORACEK, Paula B. . . .	(CA)	558
Project evaluation	SPYKERMAN, Bryan R. .	(UT)	1177
Project management	MOYER, Barbara A.	(CA)	874
	ENGERRAND, Steven W.	(GA)	349
	JANSSON, John F.	(IL)	594
	MILLER, Thomas R.	(IL)	843
	RUSSELL, Janet	(IL)	1069
	BATOR, Eileen F.	(MD)	64
	FIELD, Judith J.	(MI)	375
	DINERMAN, Gloria	(NJ)	304
	FISHER, Douglas A.	(PA)	380
	HOFFMAN, David R.	(PA)	547
	MENDINA, Guy T.	(TN)	824
	MOORE, Mary Y.	(WA)	860
	BROOME, Diana M.	(BC)	141
	HALE, Linda L.	(BC)	485
	CAMPBELL, Bonnie	(ON)	176
	FOX, Rosalie	(ON)	395
	LEUNG, Frank F.	(ON)	719
Project management & administration	MANBECK, Virginia B. . .	(NY)	764
Project management & coordination	BAADE, Harley D.	(TX)	43
Project management & development	DEL CERVO, Diane M. . .	(CT)	289
Project planning & development	STONE, Clarence W. . . .	(IDN)	1197
Project planning & implementation	NEAL, Jan	(CA)	890
Projects management	ST. AMANT, Robert	(ON)	1075
Promoting literacy projects	KRETTEK, Josephine G. .	(IA)	678
Promotions & special projects	THORSEN, Jeanne M. . .	(WA)	1242
Public library building projects	SMITH, David R.	(MN)	1154
Reconversion projects	BISSETT, Claudia K. . . .	(NH)	100
Research & development project planning	KOZAK, Marlene G.	(IL)	674
Research projects, fee-based	HARRIS, Virginia B.	(VA)	500
Retrospective conversion projects	PAYNE, Leila M.	(TX)	951
School project planning	ANDRIST, Shirley A. . . .	(SK)	27
School-wide projects	MEESE, Jane E.	(OH)	821
Special projects	MCWHORTER, Jimmie M.	(AL)	818
	PARK, Dona F.	(IA)	941
	ENGLISH, Cynthia J. . . .	(MA)	350
	KONESKI-WHITE, Bonnie L.	(MA)	670
	JONES, Kendra A.	(TN)	613
	ALTHEN, Elsa D.	(VA)	18
	ROUSSEAU, Denis	(PQ)	1061
Special projects management	FARLEY, Alfred E.	(KS)	364
Special projects research, automation	RHYNAS, Don M.	(ON)	1026
Specialized research projects	BEHNKE, Charles	(WI)	75

PROJECTS (Cont'd)

Supervision of SDI projects	SHALLENBERGER, Anna F.	(NY)	1119
Training & project implementation	BEDOR, Kathleen M.	(MN)	73
	HSU, Elizabeth L.	(NY)	567
United States newspaper project	GULLEY, J L.	(GA)	477

PROMOTION (See also Advertising, Community, Marketing, Merchandising, Outreach, Public Relations, Publicity)

Advertising & promotional literature	LONGO, Margaret K.	(CA)	740
Book promotion & publicity	BIANCO, David P.	(MI)	94
Database documentation & promotion ideas	MILLER, Carmen L.	(WA)	836
Database promotion & support	CRAUMER, Patricia A.	(PA)	255
Direct mail promotion management	OGREN, Mark S.	(IL)	918
Health promotion	RICHETELLE, Alberta L.	(CT)	1030
In-house promotion	KLEINMUNTZ, Dalia S.	(IL)	660
Library marketing & promotion	SIMPSON, F T.	(IA)	1141
Library promotion	SMOKEY, Sheila C.	(CA)	1162
	PETERSON, Denise D.	(OK)	963
	HOWARD, Elizabeth A.	(TX)	564
	SWITZER, Catherine M.	(WI)	1216
Library promotion & marketing	EASTMAN, Ann H.	(VA)	333
Library promotion & spcl programming	WARREN, Catherine S.	(MS)	1306
Library promotions	SHELKROT, Elliot L.	(PA)	1126
Library reading promotion	COLE, John Y.	(DC)	231
Library systems, management & promotion	CHAN, Margy	(ON)	199
Literacy & reading promotion	ALLEN, Richard H.	(NE)	16
Marketing promotion	GAREN, Robert J.	(MI)	418
Promote reading	MAYER, Mary C.	(OH)	789
Promoting conservation	REINSTEIN, Julia B.	(NY)	1021
Promoting Dewey decimal classification	KRAMER-GREENE, Judith	(NY)	675
Promoting literacy projects	KRETTEK, Josephine G.	(IA)	678
Promoting reference books	ROMIG, Thomas L.	(MI)	1053
Promoting regional American history	REINSTEIN, Julia B.	(NY)	1021
Promotion	VITART, Jane A.	(NY)	1286
Promotion & public relations	MULLER, Mary M.	(TX)	877
	SELLERS, Wayne C.	(TX)	1114
	HARRISON, Karen A.	(ON)	507
Promotion of library services	SPIEGELMAN, Barbara M.	(PA)	1174
Promotional communications	LAMBERT, Shirley A.	(CO)	690
Promotional publications	FRISCH, Corrine A.	(IL)	405
Promotions	WOLFE, Lisa A.	(WA)	1361
Promotions & special projects	THORSEN, Jeanne M.	(WA)	1242
Promotions, publicity & programs	HANNAFORD, Claudia L.	(OH)	496
Public relations & promotion	MCLAUGHLIN, Pamela W.	(NY)	813
Public relations & promotions	LEAMON, David L.	(MI)	707
Publicity & promotion	DRAGOTTA, Linda L.	(PA)	318
Reading promotion, advisory	SHANNON, Kathleen L.	(IL)	1120
Reading promotion & library skills	GOLDBERG, Linda B.	(KY)	444
Special events promotion	GOODRICH, Nita K.	(AZ)	449
Young adult books promotion & publicity	JACKSON, Nancy D.	(NY)	588

PROOFREADING (See also Editing)

Editing & proofreading	KNICKERBOCKER, Wendy	(MD)	664
	BAKISH, David J.	(NY)	50
Editing, proofreading, bibliographies	BRADWAY, Becky J.	(IL)	126
Music editing & proofreading	NIGHTINGALE, Daniel	(PA)	904
Proofreading	KAPLAN, Tiby	(FL)	626
	BUFFINGTON, Karyl L.	(KS)	155
Proofreading & translation	SMYTH, John	(PQ)	1162
Proofreading, writing, editing, indexing	GAGNON, Donna M.	(CA)	412
Technical & general proofreading	JOSLYN, Camille	(VA)	618

PROPERTY (See also Copyright)

Copyright & intellectual property	JENSEN, Mary B.	(SD)	599
Intellectual property	CONNOR, Billie M.	(CA)	237

PROPOSALS (See also Grants)

Development & funding proposals	BAKER, Sylva S.	(PA)	49
Development of grant proposals	WALCH, Victoria I.	(VA)	1293
Grant proposal writing	MORAN, Irene E.	(CA)	862

PROPOSALS (Cont'd)

Grant proposals	TARAN, Nadia P.	(MD)	1223
Grant proposals & administration	CABEZAS, Sue A.	(MA)	170
Grants, research & proposal writing	SECKELSON, Linda E.	(NY)	1110
Planning & proposal writing	VAUGHN, Frances A.	(TX)	1280
Proposal writing & database searching	KUHL, Danuta	(VA)	682
Proposal writing & fundraising	GOLDBERG, Susan S.	(AZ)	445

PROPRIETARY

Proprietary data retrieval	ROBERTSON, Betty M.	(NY)	1041
Proprietary database design	WAITE, William F.	(NJ)	1293
Proprietary documents organization	LAVIN, Margaret A.	(NJ)	703
Proprietary research	GAZZOLA, Kenneth E.	(DC)	424
Proprietary technical report systems	ECKROADE, Carlene B.	(DE)	335

PROPULSION

Propulsion systems	KITCHENS, Philips H.	(AL)	657

PROSE (See also Literature)

Editing, discography, prose	SHAPIRO, Burton J.	(MD)	1121
Prose & playwriting	HECK-RABI, Louise E.	(MI)	520
Prose & poetry translation	TABORY, Maxim	(NC)	1219

PROSECUTION

Patent drafting & prosecution	SIMMONS, Edlyn S.	(OH)	1139
Prosecution	VINCENT-DAVISS, Diana	(NY)	1284

PROTECTION (See also Prevention)

Consumer protection law	ENGLISH, Susan B.	(VA)	350
Environmental protection	WOLFE, Theresa L.	(NY)	1361
	BELLEFONTAINE, Gillian	(ON)	78
Fire protection in libraries & museums	MORRIS, John	(CA)	866
Protection of animal environment	THURSTON, Ethel H.	(NY)	1243

PROTESTANT

Protestant & Episcopal Church clergy	HYDE, E C.	(MO)	580

PROTOCOLS

Bibliographic OSI protocol	ARBEZ, Gilbert J.	(ON)	30
OSI communication protocols	MACLELLAND, Margaret A.	(ON)	757

PROVINCIAL

Maintaining province archives	STRECK, Helen T.	(KS)	1201
Province history, articles & lectures	STRECK, Helen T.	(KS)	1201
Provincial & municipal government	WEATHERHEAD, Barbara A.	(ON)	1312
Provincial government publications	ROSE, Frances E.	(BC)	1054
Writing province history	STRECK, Helen T.	(KS)	1201

PSYCHIATRY

Child psychiatry	WALLER, Carolyn A.	(RI)	1298
Computers & psychiatry	LESAGE, Jacques	(PQ)	717
Forensic psychiatry	STARESINA, Lois J.	(MI)	1181
Psychiatric & psychological databases	KINZIE, Lenora A.	(KS)	653
	WIGGINS, Theresa S.	(PA)	1337
Psychiatric database	LESAGE, Jacques	(PQ)	717
Psychiatric literature	COHAN, Lois	(NY)	227
	TOMASULO, Patricia A.	(NY)	1249
Psychiatric patient library services	MERRILL, Susan S.	(MD)	827
Psychiatric patients	MASON, Martha A.	(NY)	781
Psychiatric staff	MASON, Martha A.	(NY)	781
Psychiatry	LABREE, Rosanne	(MA)	686
	OWSLEY, Lucile C.	(NC)	932
	NORDENG, Diane	(ND)	908
	PIERCE, Shirley M.	(OK)	972
	EPSTEIN, Barbara A.	(PA)	351
	SOULTOUKIS, Donna Z.	(PA)	1169
	SHAH, Neeta N.	(SC)	1119
	HEUER, Jane T.	(WY)	535

PSYCHIATRY (Cont'd)
Psychiatry & mental health	FREDENBURG, Anne M.	(MD)	399
Psychiatry & psychology	WALTON, Linda J.	(RI)	1301
Psychiatry collection development	ASBELL, Mildred S.	(CT)	35
Psychiatry library management	STRICKLAND, F J.	(PA)	1202
Psychiatry, psychology, mental health	WARD, Nancy E.	(MI)	1304
Psychiatry reference services	ASBELL, Mildred S.	(CT)	35
Psychology & psychiatry reference	DEWEY, Marjorie C.	(MA)	298

PSYCHOANALYTIC (See also Psychology)
Cumulating psychoanalytic indexes	KLUMPNER, George H.	(IL)	663
Developing psychoanalytic indexes	KLUMPNER, George H.	(IL)	663
Psychoanalysis	REGNER-HYATT, Anne L.	(CA)	1017
Psychoanalytic library management	STRICKLAND, F J.	(PA)	1202
Psychoanalytic research	ROSS, David J.	(NY)	1058

PSYCHOKINESIS
Psychokinesis	NORMAN, Wayne R.	(NY)	909

PSYCHOLOGY (See also Parapsychology, Psychoanalytic)
Adlerian psychology references	KAHN, Paul J.	(CA)	622
Biology, psychology, geology	RONNERMANN, Gail	(NY)	1053
Computerized psychological databases	WALES, Patricia L.	(CT)	1294
Counseling psychology	GERITY, Louise P.	(OR)	428
Economics & psychological acquisitions	RICHARDSON, Linda B.	(VA)	1029
Education & psychology bibliography	BAUNER, Ruth E.	(IL)	67
Education & psychology databases	LEUNG, Terry S.	(CA)	719
	GERKE, Ray	(MA)	428
Education & psychology reference	MULVIHILL, Joann	(AZ)	878
Education & psychology research	LEUNG, Terry S.	(CA)	719
Education, psychology, human development	HENEBRY, Carolyn L.	(TX)	528
Educational & psychological databases	TU, Shu C.	(MA)	1261
General reference, psychology reference	COYLE, Leslie P.	(CA)	253
History of psychology	POPPLESTONE, John A.	(OH)	984
Humanistic psychology archivist	GRAZIANO, Eugene	(CA)	460
Industrial & organizational psychology	FULMER, Dina J.	(PA)	409
Medical & psychological databases	KNOBLOCH, Shirley S.	(DC)	665
	DAVIS, Anne C.	(MI)	277
	PLASO, Kathy A.	(PA)	977
	STILMAN, Ruth	(PQ)	1194
Med, psychological, educational database	KLINE, Eve P.	(PA)	661
Medical psychology databases	BLADEN, Marguerite	(CA)	102
Medical psychology information research	BLADEN, Marguerite	(CA)	102
Online searching & psychology databases	GOSLING, Carolyn	(VA)	453
Organizational psychology	BUSH, Nancy W.	(AL)	165
Political sci & psychology col devlpmnt	SOUTH, Ruth E.	(OR)	1169
Psychiatric & psychological databases	KINZIE, Lenora A.	(KS)	653
	WIGGINS, Theresa S.	(PA)	1337
Psychiatry & psychology	WALTON, Linda J.	(RI)	1301
Psychiatry, psychology, mental health	WARD, Nancy E.	(MI)	1304
Psychological collection development	LUNDGREN, Janan L.	(IL)	748
Psychological database searching	LINTON, Helen W.	(MA)	731
Psychological databases	LUNDGREN, Janan L.	(IL)	748
	VAN CAMP, Ann J.	(IN)	1272
Psychological literature	PORTER, Suzanne	(DC)	985
Psychology	BIRCH, Tobeylynn	(CA)	98
	MILLER, James G.	(CA)	838
	BINGHAM, Karen H.	(IL)	97
	BROWN, Patricia B.	(IL)	146
	COOK, Margaret K.	(IL)	240
	COUPE, Jill M.	(MD)	251
	BURHANS, Barbara C.	(MI)	159
	OWSLEY, Lucile C.	(NC)	932
	NAISMITH, Rachael	(PA)	887
	MCKENNEY, Linda S.	(VA)	811
Psychology & behavioral sciences	BAXTER, Pam M.	(IN)	67
Psychology & education bibliography	JOHNSON, Linda B.	(CA)	607
Psychology & mental health	LARMOUR, Rosamond E.	(VA)	698

PSYCHOLOGY (Cont'd)
Psychology & psychiatry reference	DEWEY, Marjorie C.	(MA)	298
Psychology, behavioral science databases	KAUFFMAN, Inge S.	(CA)	631
Psychology bibliography	WHELAN, Julia S.	(MA)	1329
Psychology databases	BANKS-ISZARD, Kimberly K.	(NY)	54
Psychology of information use	BODART-TALBOT, Joni	(KS)	109
Psychology of library use	EATON, Elizabeth G.	(NC)	333
Psychology reference & bibliography	KAUFFMAN, Inge S.	(CA)	631
Psychology reference & cataloging	HUFFINE, Lucinda J.	(OR)	571
Reference in psychology	GIRARD, Luc	(PQ)	438
Reference, psychology bibliography	CROSBY-MUILENBURG, Corryn	(CA)	260
Social psychology	MILLER, Everett G.	(MD)	837
Social work & school psychology	LUNT, Ruth B.	(NY)	749

PSYCHOMETRICS
Bibliography of psychometrics	JORDAN, Robert P.	(IA)	616

PUBLIC (See also Nonprofit)
Automated circulation, public catalog	NIEMEYER, Karen K.	(IN)	903
Business & public affairs research	COCHRAN, Catherine	(MI)	225
Cable television public access	PEARSON, Roger L.	(IL)	953
Canadian public company information	BONIN, Denise R.	(BC)	114
Computers & public access	HERMAN, Felicia G.	(CT)	531
Consultant, public, special libraries	WILLIAMS, Edwin E.	(CT)	1343
Distribution of public domain software	SHAW, Ben B.	(TX)	1123
Exhibits & public programming	MESSINEO, Leonard L.	(KS)	828
Florida public health history	HALL, M C.	(FL)	488
Generalist - public schools	YOUNG, Barbara A.	(FL)	1381
History & public policy	PREER, Jean L.	(DC)	990
Information services to public	KLAUSMEIER, Arno M.	(WI)	658
Librarians & public speaking	MCPEAK, James J.	(OH)	817
Library & public administration	KERSCHNER, Joan G.	(NV)	644
Library exhibitions & public education	WOODWARD, Daniel	(CA)	1368
Library management, public	WILSON, William J.	(WI)	1353
Library public & reference services	KLEINER, Janellyn P.	(LA)	660
Library public awareness	BOYARSKI, Jennie S.	(KY)	122
Marketing photos to public institutions	HENDERSON, Ellen B.	(CA)	526
Medical public policy	SCUKA, Aletta N.	(DC)	1108
Microcomputer public access centers	LARSON, Teresa B.	(IA)	700
Microcomputers & public access	RAPPAPORT, Susan E.	(NY)	1008
Online public access catalogs	BISOM, Diane B.	(CA)	99
	DRIVER, Linda A.	(CA)	320
	GLASSMAN, Penny L.	(MA)	440
	STERLING, Judith K.	(MD)	1189
	FABIAN, William M.	(MO)	360
	HOWE, Ernest A.	(AB)	565
Politics of public librarianship	SHAVIT, David	(IL)	1123
Public access & local cable	BARNETT, Donald E.	(OR)	57
Public access catalogs	SHAPTON, Gregory B.	(CA)	1122
Public access computers	MCCOY, Judy I.	(TX)	799
	BLUME, Scott	(WA)	107
Public access law	WARNER, Marnie M.	(MA)	1305
Public access microcomputer services	BROWN, Janis F.	(CA)	144
Public access microcomputers	MUDD, Isabelle G.	(AK)	875
	LEWIS, Jean R.	(AZ)	723
	HARRIS, Roger L.	(CA)	506
	FORREST, Charles G.	(IL)	390
	MILLS, Elaine L.	(KS)	844
	UPPGARD, Jeannine	(MA)	1269
	MCCANN, Susan F.	(NH)	794
	POLLY, Jean A.	(NY)	981
	RIVERA, Gregorio	(NY)	1037
	HOFFACKER, Antoinette C.	(PA)	547
	PIELE, Linda J.	(WI)	971
Public access online catalogs	PHENIX, Katharine J.	(LA)	967
Public access to information	HALLINAN, Patricia R.	(NY)	489
Public access to law	DUNN, Mary B.	(NY)	327
Public administration	COLSON, Harold G.	(AL)	234
	GOODYEAR, Mary L.	(CO)	450
	BLALOCK, Louise	(CT)	103
	ACKERMAN, F C.	(DC)	3
	JAQUES, Thomas F.	(LA)	594
	GARDNER, Jack I.	(NV)	418
	SHIROMA, Susan G.	(NY)	1131

PUBLIC (Cont'd)

Public administration

SILVER, Linda R. ...... (OH) 1138
FOREHAND, Margaret P. (VA) 390
ADAMS, Karen G. ..... (SK) 5
Public administration & policy   LEISTER, Jack .... (CA) 714
Public administration research   ETTER, Constance L. .. (IL) 355
Public affairs   STEWART, Ruth A. .... (DC) 1193
MEHNERT, Robert B. ... (MD) 821
DYER, Esther R. .... (NY) 330
EMERICK, Kenneth F. .. (PA) 347
Public affairs & administration   FU, Tina C. .... (WI) 407
Public affairs & diplomacy   STEERE, Paul J. ...... (DC) 1184
Public affairs & public administration   FERRALL, J E. .... (AZ) 373
Public affairs & public relations   MILLER, Deborah ...... (IL) 837
Public affairs information   CATHCART, Marilyn S. . (MN) 195
Public affairs research   GJELTEN, Daniel R. ... (MN) 439
Public & community relations   DRESP, Donald F. ..... (NM) 319
O'NEIL, Margaret M. ... (NY) 924
Public & court records management   COATES, Paul F. ...... (KY) 224
Public & cultural programming   BLANDY, Susan G. .... (NY) 104
Public & current affairs   MCFARLANE, Agnes ... (PQ) 805
Public & institutions libs consulting   MADDEN, Doreitha R. .. (NJ) 758
Public & private academic libraries   EASTERLY, Ambrose .. (TN) 333
Public & private music education   MILLER, Charles W. ... (NJ) 836
Public & school library cooperation   LEITLE, Barbara K. ..... (MO) 714
Public & staff library microcomputing   ROBERTSON, Michael A. (NY) 1042
Public & staff relations   FRANKLIN, Robert D. ... (VA) 398
Public & state libraries   LYMAN, Helen H. ..... (NY) 751
Public & state library development   LASETER, Ernest P. ... (AL) 700
SHELDON, Brooke E. ... (TX) 1125
Public & technical services   RIGGS, Donald E. ..... (AZ) 1034
Public circulation & access services   DREW, Wilfred E. ...... (NY) 319
Public documents   PARROTT, Margaret S. .. (NC) 944
Public education   TOWNSEND, Catherine M. (SC) 1253
Public events management   EZELL, Charlaine L. .... (MI) 360
Public finance   SHIH, Philip C. .... (IN) 1130
Public finance research   MARSHALL, Marion B. ... (DC) 774
Public, fine arts librarianship   MATYI, Stephen G. .... (OH) 786
Public health   PRUHS, Sharon .... (CA) 996
ALECCIA, Janet A. .... (IL) 11
FRANKLIN, Annette E. .. (IL) 397
GALLAGHER, Philip J. ... (NJ) 414
KRONENFELD, Michael R. (SC) 679
Public health administration   HORAK, Ellen B. ...... (CT) 558
Public health areas   SONG, Seungja Y. ..... (WA) 1167
Public health databases   MOORE, Catherine I. ... (MA) 859
Public health literature   MUNSEY, Joyce E. .... (MD) 879
Public historical research   CHRISTENSEN, Erin S. . (CO) 211
Public history   SCHEIPS, Paul J. ...... (MD) 1091
Public history administration   PRICE, William S. ...... (NC) 993
Public information   PEDAK-KARI, Maria ... (MD) 954
ROBINSON, Jolene A. .. (NY) 1044
HORNAK, Anna F. ..... (TX) 559
HENDERSON, Harriet ... (VA) 526
Public information & relations   WELLS, Gladysann .... (NY) 1322
Public information programs   PAISLEY, William J. ... (CA) 935
Public information strategies   CROWTHER, Warren W. (CSR) 262
Public information systems   SMITH, Peggy C. ..... (OK) 1159
Public information video production   RANCER, Susan P. .... (NC) 1006
Public involvement   DUNN, Susan M. ...... (IA) 327
Public lands   BAIRD, Dennis W. ..... (ID) 47
Public legal education   HEBDITCH, Suzan A. ... (AB) 519
Public legal information & education   TOMCHYSHYN, Theresa
M. .... (SK) 1249
Public library staff training   WYNN, Vivian R. ...... (OH) 1375
Public management information
systems   CROWTHER, Warren W. (CSR) 262
Public materials of Philadelphia   BRENNAN, Ellen ...... (PA) 132
Public microcomputer access   SMITH, Valerie M. ..... (OH) 1161
Public, music librarianship   MATYI, Stephen G. .... (OH) 786
Public online catalogs   KELLEY, Betty H. ...... (TX) 636
Public opinion polls   BOVA, Patrick .... (IL) 120
Public or private law   STAYNER, Delsie A. ... (CA) 1183
Public policy   BROCKMAN, Norbert C. (KEN) 138
Public policy & libraries   MOLZ, Redmond K. .... (NY) 854
Public policy databases   PILGRIM, Auriel J. ..... (DC) 973
Public policy development   FORD, Gary E. .... (MO) 389
Public policy studies   SHULER, John A. ...... (OR) 1133

PUBLIC (Cont'd)

Public programming   FRIDLEY, Russell W. .... (ME) 403
SCHWARTZ, Virginia C. . (WI) 1105
Public programming & outreach   WURL, Joel F. .... (MN) 1374
Public programming & publications   MOLTKE-HANSEN, David (SC) 853
Public programming coordination   ATCHISON, Fres D. .... (KS) 37
Public programming for adults   MACKNIGHT, Judith M. . (NY) 757
Public programs   TRZECIAK, William J. .. (CA) 1260
BRENNAN, Deborah B. .. (RI) 132
EVANS, Gwynneth ..... (ON) 357
Public reader services   BOWER, Beverly L. .... (FL) 120
OTTAVIANO, Doris B. ... (RI) 930
Public records   HURLBERT, Roger W. ... (CA) 577
Public reference   SIMONS, Maurice M. ... (CA) 1141
Public reference services   HUTCHINS, Kathleen D. . (MA) 579
BANDEMER, June E. .... (PA) 54
Public regional library administration   KENT, Charles D. ...... (ON) 642
Public relations   BURDASH, David H. .... (DE) 158
BLANDY, Susan G. .... (NY) 104
Public relations & public affairs   JONES, Elin D. .... (DC) 612
Public relations & public information   KUSZMAUL, Marcia J. ... (IL) 685
Public relations & training   CARDEN, Marguerite ... (FL) 180
Public school   DIERCKS, Eileen K. .... (IL) 302
Public school librarian, K-12   KOHRT, Ruth D. .... (IA) 669
Public school librarianship   STURGEON, Mary C. .... (AR) 1205
WILLIAMSON, Lanelle S. (TX) 1347
Public school libraries   WRIGHT, Pauline W. .... (AR) 1372
BUFFALOE, Catherine S. (GA) 155
HULLUM, Cheri J. ..... (GA) 573
BRUMBACK, Elsie ..... (NC) 150
BLESH, Tamara E. ..... (NH) 105
MCCULLEY, Lois P. ..... (TX) 800
STAAS, Gretchen L. .... (TX) 1177
Public school library administration   PORMEN, Paul E. ...... (OH) 984
Public school library collections   SPAULDING, Nancy J. .. (TX) 1172
Public school library expansion   SPAULDING, Nancy J. .. (TX) 1172
Public school library instruction   SPAULDING, Nancy J. .. (TX) 1172
Public school library media   HAMILTON, Betty D. .... (TX) 491
Public, school library mergers   BROWN, Freddiemae E. . (TX) 144
Public school multimedia   METTLING, Cora E. .... (KS) 828
Public schools   MURRAY, Bruce C. ..... (MD) 881
Public science & technology
reference   COHEN, Jackson B. ..... (NY) 228
Public secondary school   STEWART, Joanne R. ... (IL) 1192
Public services   HOGAN, Sharon A. ..... (LA) 549
Public speaking & workshops   GRAUER, Sally M. ..... (NY) 458
Public speaking training   BARKER, Lillian H. ...... (MD) 56
Public technical speaking   KAMINECKI, Ronald M. .. (IL) 624
Public transportation & urban planning   PRESBY, Richard A. .... (CA) 990
Public use microcomputers   FERGUSON, Chris D. .... (CA) 372
Public utilities   MALUMPHY, Sharon M. . (OH) 764
Public utility   SCULLY, Patrick F. ..... (CA) 1109
Public utility information   BOBAN, Carol A. .... (IL) 108
Public utility management   ERTZ, Ginger E. .... (PA) 353
Publicity, public & community
relations   PIANE, Mimi .... (IN) 969
Reference & public service   PELLEY, Shirley N. ..... (OK) 955
Reference, public & technical services   OPATOW, Judith ...... (NY) 925
Reference, public services   REED, Marcia C. .... (CA) 1015
School & public youth services   WUNDERLICH, Nina M. .. (IL) 1374
Small & medium, public   HOFFMANN, Maurine L. .. (IL) 548
Small public library administration   YOUNG, Lynne M. ..... (MN) 1382
Staff & public computer training   MCMURRAY, Sallylou .. (OH) 815
State, special & public lib consulting   PHILLIPS, Ray S. .... (TX) 969
Subject bibliography for public health   CHAN, Lillian L. .... (CA) 199
Training & public information   GILLIGAN, Julie .... (NY) 436
Training & public presentations   MADDEN, Susan B. .... (WA) 758
University-level public reference   MCCANN, Judith B. .... (ON) 794
Videotaping for public access   ASHFORD, Richard K. ... (MD) 36
Youth public school services   ROSEN, Elizabeth M. ... (CA) 1055

PUBLIC LIBRARY (See also Branch, Community, Public)

Administration & public library   BROWN, Lucinda A. ..... (KY) 145
Adult services in public libraries   HAHN, Maureen .... (PA) 484
Automated public library systems   MEAGHER, Janet H. ... (MA) 819
Branch management public libraries   REILLY, Jane A. .... (IL) 1020
Children's librarian, public library   POBANZ, Becky L. ..... (MI) 979
Children's public library programs   BOTHAM, Jane .... (WI) 118
Children's public library services   WILLETT, Holly G. ..... (WI) 1341

PUBLIC LIBRARY (Cont'd)

Collection development, public library
Computers & public libraries — BASSNETT, Peter J. (ON) 63
Consultant to public libraries — HINDMARSH, Douglas P. (UT) 542
Consulting in public libraries — CLARK, Jay B. (TX) 217
Consulting, public libraries — CRANE, Karen R. (AK) 255
Consulting to public libraries — VANDERLYKE, Barbara A. (CT) 1274
Directing a public library — VALENTINE, Patrick M. (NC) 1271
Directing public libraries — CANAVAN, Roberta N. (NJ) 178
KING, Dennis W. (NY) 650
Early public library development — MCNAMARA, Shelley G. (ME) 816
Friends of public libraries — PHELAN, Mary C. (MA) 967
General administration, public libraries — KRALISZ, Victor F. (TX) 675
General public library consulting — WUNDERLICH, Nina M. (IL) 1374
LAW, Aileen E. (SC) 704
General public lib service development — RUBY, Carmela M. (CA) 1065
Handicapped center, public library — ROATCH, Mary A. (AZ) 1038
Literacy programs in public libraries — CARD, Judy (TN) 180
Management of public libraries — MOORE, Thomas L. (NC) 861
Management of public library — JONKE, Grace M. (MD) 616
Marketing for public libraries — LUEDER, Dianne B. (IL) 747
EISNER, Joseph (NY) 341
CORBUS, Lawrence J. (OH) 245
Marketing public libraries — MOORE, Thomas L. (NC) 861
Marketing the public library — CAMERON, Bruce (SK) 174
Materials selection, public libraries — LEE, Lauren K. (GA) 710
Music in public libraries — WAZNIS, Betty (CA) 1311
Online services & public libraries — MALONEY, James J. (CA) 764
Personnel management, public libraries — HAGLOCH, Susan B. (OH) 483
Planning pub lib services & facilities — CURTIS, Jean E. (MI) 267
Public librarianship — FOOS, Donald D. (FL) 388
ADKINS, Marjorie R. (IL) 6
SHEARER, Kenneth D. (NC) 1124
CAMPAGNA, Roxane R. (NY) 175
LOWE, Mary E. (PA) 744
WINGLE, Rita M. (PA) 1355
Public libraries — STEPHENS, Annabel K. (AL) 1187
ALTMAN, Ellen (AZ) 18
CONNOR, Anne C. (CA) 237
GOLD, Anne M. (CA) 444
GOODRICH, Jeanne D. (CA) 449
HOLM, Blair I. (CA) 552
KILLIAN, Richard M. (CA) 648
LEVY, Mary J. (CA) 722
MINUDRI, Regina U. (CA) 847
STARR, Carol L. (CA) 1182
TERRY, Josephine R. (CA) 1232
WINGATE, Eliza C. (CA) 1354
WOOD, Linda M. (CA) 1364
CARRINGTON, Virginia F. (CT) 186
HOLSTINE, Lesa G. (FL) 554
MCCROSSAN, John A. (FL) 800
NOAH, Julia T. (FL) 906
COFFMAN, Joseph W. (GA) 227
BAKER, Sharon L. (IA) 49
NELSON, Mary L. (IA) 894
PLUEMER, Bonnie J. (IA) 978
SCHEETZ, George H. (IA) 1090
BYRNE, Janice M. (IL) 169
CAMPBELL, Ray (IL) 177
GORDON, Diane M. (IL) 451
JACKSON, Susan M. (IL) 588
KIES, Cosette N. (IL) 647
KOSCIELSKI, Roberta L. (IL) 672
LYNCH, Mary J. (IL) 752
MAGNUSSEN, Ruth A. (IL) 760
REDINGTON, Deirdre E. (IL) 1014
WHITNEY, Ruth (IL) 1334
KASER, John A. (IN) 628
KRULL, Jeffrey R. (IN) 680
PUNGITORE, Verna L. (IN) 997
AVANT, Julia K. (LA) 41
CRAWLEY, Carolyn S. (LA) 257
CASEY, Genevieve M. (MI) 192
WILSON, Patricia L. (MI) 1352
ENGBERG, Linda L. (MN) 348
EATON, Elizabeth G. (NC) 333
FEEHAN, Patricia E. (NC) 368

PUBLIC LIBRARY (Cont'd)

Public libraries — SUTTON, Judith K. (NC) 1211
FREAUF, Louis E. (NE) 399
LOTZ, Marilyn R. (NJ) 742
TUROCK, Betty J. (NJ) 1265
BURNHAM, Helen A. (NY) 162
DESCH, Carol A. (NY) 294
FIRTH, Jennifer L. (NY) 379
HOPKINS, Barbara A. (NY) 557
LEWIS, Frances R. (NY) 723
MOLZ, Redmond K. (NY) 854
MOUNIR, Khalil A. (NY) 873
PARKER, Margaret S. (NY) 942
RANSOM, Stanley A. (NY) 1007
KLINCK, Cynthia A. (OH) 661
PARCH, Grace D. (OH) 939
STORCK, John N. (OH) 1198
RYAN, Kathleen M. (OK) 1071
WOODRUM, Patricia A. (OK) 1366
CHILDERS, Thomas A. (PA) 208
DOW, Sally C. (PA) 315
LEONARD, Peter C. (PA) 716
LOCKE, Jill L. (PA) 736
ORSBURN, Elizabeth C. (PA) 927
TROWELL, Amy U. (SC) 1258
DRESCHER, Judith A. (TN) 319
HOFFMAN, Frank W. (TX) 548
MASON, Florence M. (TX) 781
ROY, Loriene (TX) 1063
BENNE, Mae M. (WA) 81
HARFST, Linda L. (WI) 501
KINNEY, Michael F. (WI) 653
WILLIAMSON, Judy D. (WV) 1347
REDFORD, Marcia E. (AB) 1014
LEHNERT, Sharon A. (ON) 713
ALLARD, Diane (PQ) 14
BOUCHARD, Martin (PQ) 118
LONDON, Eleanor (PQ) 738
MITTERMEYER, Diane (PQ) 850
Public libraries administration — OAKS, Claire (IL) 913
VOJTECH, Kathryn (IL) 1287
CRABB, Elizabeth A. (TX) 254
GOLDEN, Helene (PQ) 445
Public libraries, adult programs — WRIGHT, Kathryn D. (AL) 1372
Public libraries & adult services — FARACE, Virginia K. (FL) 363
Public libraries & public relations — WINCKLER, Paul A. (NY) 1354
Public libraries automated systems — NEAL, Jan (CA) 890
Public libraries consulting — CASSELL, Kay A. (NY) 193
Public libraries, medium-sized — WILLIAMS, Ann W. (FL) 1342
Public libraries national network — MAGALONI, Ana M. (MEX) 759
Public libraries public relations — VOJTECH, Kathryn (IL) 1287
Public libraries reference — VOJTECH, Kathryn (IL) 1287
Public library — VANDERBURG, Mary A. (FL) 1274
PARKER, Dorothy J. (GA) 941
HOLMES, Norman W. (IL) 553
YAMAMOTO, M C. (IN) 1377
CUNNINGHAM, William D. (MD) 265
ARNETT, Stanley K. (MI) 33
THIELE, Barbara J. (NJ) 1235
CANUTI, Teresa D. (NY) 179
RAYWARD, W B. (AUS) 1011
Public library administration — KELLEY, Sally J. (AR) 637
PACK, Nancy C. (AR) 933
TROMATER, Raymond B. (AR) 1257
BROWN, Donna M. (CA) 143
BUCKLEY, James W. (CA) 154
CONOVER, Robert W. (CA) 238
FARRIER, George F. (CA) 365
KELLUM-ROSE, Nancy P. (CA) 637
KLINE, Victoria E. (CA) 661
LANGE, Clifford E. (CA) 695
NELSON, Helen M. (CA) 893
SHAPTON, Gregory B. (CA) 1122
STORSTEEN, Linda L. (CA) 1198
TEMA, William J. (CA) 1230
BETTENCOURT, Nancy J. (CO) 92
MAGRATH, Lynn L. (CO) 760
HOLLOWAY, Patricia W. (CT) 552
JOHMANN, Nancy (CT) 601

PUBLIC LIBRARY (Cont'd)
Public library administration

FRANKLIN, Hardy R.	(DC)	397
RAPHAEL, Mary E.	(DC)	1008
BREEDEN, Wendy R.	(FL)	131
MOUNCE, Marvin W.	(FL)	873
HUNTER, Julie V.	(GA)	576
JAMES, Stephen E.	(GA)	592
STEWART, Carol J.	(GA)	1192
TOPE, Diana R.	(GA)	1251
HORNE, Norman P.	(HI)	560
GEIB, Jerry H.	(IA)	425
LIND, Beverly F.	(IA)	728
MINTER, Elizabeth D.	(IA)	846
BROWN, Diana M.	(IL)	143
DEMPSEY, Frank J.	(IL)	291
GOLDHOR, Herbert	(IL)	445
HARRIS, Robert A.	(IL)	506
HOFFMANN, Maurine L.	(IL)	548
LARSON, Carol	(IL)	699
LOCASCIO, John F.	(IL)	735
MCCULLY, William C.	(IL)	801
MECHTENBERG, Paul	(IL)	820
MEISELS, Henry R.	(IL)	822
NOVAK, Lorrine M.	(IL)	911
OLDERR, Steven	(IL)	920
OSERMAN, Stuart	(IL)	928
PODESCHI, Gwen	(IL)	979
ROSENFELD, Joel C.	(IL)	1056
SCHLIPF, Frederick A.	(IL)	1094
SHAVIT, David	(IL)	1123
WEST, Barbara G.	(IL)	1326
ZENKE, Mary H.	(IL)	1387
BOLTE, William F.	(IN)	113
GNAT, Raymond E.	(IN)	442
HOLMAN, Mary J.	(IN)	553
LAUBE, Lois R.	(IN)	702
OZINGA, Connie J.	(IN)	933
ROBLEE, Martha A.	(IN)	1045
BEATTIE, Brian	(KS)	70
MUTH, Thomas J.	(KS)	883
BAKER, Janet R.	(MA)	48
BUSH, Margaret A.	(MA)	165
DYGERT, Michael H.	(MA)	331
HILTON, Robert C.	(MA)	541
JAMES, Flaherty C.	(MA)	592
LATHAM, Ronald B.	(MA)	701
RAMSAY, John E.	(MA)	1005
COLLINS, Elizabeth H.	(MD)	232
CURRY, Anna A.	(MD)	266
GALE, Roswita W.	(MD)	413
GRIFFEN, Agnes M.	(MD)	468
ROBINSON, Charles W.	(MD)	1043
WOODWARD, Robert C.	(ME)	1368
HORN, Anna E.	(MI)	559
O'CONNELL, Catherine A.	(MI)	915
SHERIDAN, Clare A.	(MI)	1127
TATE, David L.	(MI)	1225
WOODFORD, Arthur M.	(MI)	1366
FUGAZZI, Elizabeth B.	(MN)	408
HOSLETT, Andrea E.	(MN)	561
YOUNG, Jerry H.	(MN)	1382
ALEXANDER, Susanna	(MO)	12
FRANKLIN, Jill S.	(MO)	397
GAERTNER, Donell J.	(MO)	411
GRAVES, Sid F.	(MS)	459
MACNEILL, Daniel S.	(MS)	758
SCHALAU, Robert D.	(MS)	1089
SCHLESINGER, Deborah L.	(MT)	1094
GADDIS, Dale W.	(NC)	411
RITTER, Philip W.	(NC)	1036
STEPHENS, Doris G.	(NC)	1188
TAYLOR, Michael Y.	(NC)	1228
WELCH, John T.	(NC)	1321
HARRIS, Patricia L.	(ND)	505
REA, Linda M.	(NE)	1012
BECKERMAN, Edwin P.	(NJ)	72
BENNETT, Rowland F.	(NJ)	82
BOGIS, Nana E.	(NJ)	110

PUBLIC LIBRARY (Cont'd)
Public library administration

FADLALLA, Gerald J.	(NJ)	361
HECHT, James M.	(NJ)	519
MCCOY, W K.	(NJ)	799
SUDALL, Arthur D.	(NJ)	1206
HUNSBERGER, Charles W.	(NV)	574
CUMMINS, A B.	(NY)	264
EISNER, Joseph	(NY)	341
FLUCKIGER, Adrienne N.	(NY)	386
GOLDEN, Fay A.	(NY)	445
MITTELGLUCK, Eugene L.	(NY)	850
O'CONNOR, William J.	(NY)	916
ROUNDS, Joseph B.	(NY)	1061
STREIT, Ann M.	(NY)	1202
TRUDELL, Robert J.	(NY)	1259
VERBESEY, J R.	(NY)	1282
COOK, Charles T.	(OH)	239
CROMER, Kenneth L.	(OH)	260
FURL, Michael	(OH)	410
O'CONNOR, Deborah F.	(OH)	916
REBENACK, John H.	(OH)	1013
BRAWNER, Lee B.	(OK)	130
MEEKS, James D.	(OR)	821
CRONEBERGER, Robert B.	(PA)	260
HORVATH, Robert T.	(PA)	561
KAMPER, Albert F.	(PA)	624
KEISER, Barbara J.	(PA)	635
MULLEN, Francis X.	(PA)	877
THOMAS, Scott E.	(PA)	1238
TYNAN, Laurie F.	(PA)	1267
BUNDY, Annalee M.	(RI)	157
COOPER, William C.	(SC)	244
HEIMBURGER, Bruce R.	(SC)	521
LINE, Faith A.	(SC)	730
NORTON, Tedgina	(TN)	910
DOUGLAS, Virginia G.	(TX)	314
RASKA, Ginny	(TX)	1009
GIACOMA, Pete J.	(UT)	430
HENDERSON, Harriet	(VA)	526
JOHNSON, Kenneth P.	(VA)	606
BRENNAN, Cindy L.	(WA)	132
WIRT, Michael J.	(WA)	1356
DAWSON, Terry P.	(WI)	282
LAMB, Donald K.	(WI)	689
PENNINGTON, Jerome G.	(WI)	957
SAGER, Donald J.	(WI)	1074
BEWLEY, Lois M.	(BC)	93
FREVE, Reay H.	(NS)	402
SKRZESZEWSKI, Stan E.	(ON)	1147
BOYER, Denis P.	(PQ)	123
MATTE, Pierre V.	(PQ)	785
SHAW, Shiow J.	(TAI)	1124

Public library administration & planning	STEINFELD, Michael	(MA)	1186
Public library administration, budget	NIEMI, Peter G.	(WI)	903
Public library administrative activities	WALSH, Florence C.	(NJ)	1299
Public library, adult education	BROWN, Freddiemae E.	(TX)	144
Public library adult programming	MEYERS, Arthur S.	(IN)	830
Public library adult reference	DAVIS, Joy V.	(GA)	279
Public library adult services	ROLSTAD, Gary O.	(IL)	1052
Public library advocacy	POSEL, Nancy R.	(PA)	985
Public library architecture	DEL SORDO, Jean S.	(MD)	290
Public library automated consortia	O'BRIEN, Anne M.	(MA)	914
Public library automation	SCHLESINGER, Deborah L.	(MT)	1094
Public library book selection	OTT, Bill	(IL)	930
Public library branch administration	MOLZ, Jean B.	(MD)	854
	PITTMAN, Dorothy E.	(MD)	976
Public library branch management	BERGMANN, Sue A.	(GA)	87
	BROWN, Merrikay E.	(NC)	146
Public library branch supervision	DOWDLE, Glen L.	(TX)	315
Public library branch work	RUDER, Clarice M.	(FL)	1065
Public library branches	MAGNUSSEN, Ruth A.	(IL)	760
Public library building design	BARTON, Phillip K.	(NC)	62
	MURPHY, Richard W.	(VA)	881
Public library building planning	KEOUGH, Francis P.	(MA)	643
	GALVIN, Hoyt R.	(NC)	415

PUBLIC LIBRARY (Cont'd)

Public library building programs	SMITH, Elizabeth M.	(CA)	1154
	WELCH, John T.	(NC)	1321
Public library building projects	SMITH, David R.	(MN)	1154
Public library buildings	DEAKYNE, William J. . . .	(CT)	283
	LUSHINGTON, Nolan . . .	(CT)	749
	BECKER, Josephine M. .	(FL)	72
	CHITWOOD, Julius R. . .	(IL)	209
	SCHABEL, Donald J. . . .	(KY)	1088
	FINNEY, Lance C.	(MD)	379
	YOUNG, Jerry F.	(MN)	1382
	COUMBE, Robert E. . . .	(NJ)	251
	HALL, Alan C.	(OH)	486
Public library children's services	KASPER, Barbara	(CT)	629
	STEMME, Virginia L. . .	(ND)	1186
	BANTA, Gratia J.	(OH)	55
Public library collection development	THOMPSON, Betsy J. . .	(IA)	1239
	MOLZ, Jean B.	(MD)	854
	FOGAL, Annabel E.	(PA)	387
Public library construction	MULKEY, Jack C.	(AR)	876
	FORK, Donald J.	(DC)	390
	FORSEE, Joe B.	(GA)	391
	COLLIER, Virginia S. . .	(TN)	232
Public library consultant	PHILLIPS, Clifford R. . .	(CA)	968
	JOHNSON, Jean G. . . .	(NH)	605
Public library consultation	BECKERMAN, Edwin P. .	(NJ)	72
	WAGGONER, Susan M. .	(PA)	1291
Public library consulting	GOLDBERG, Susan S. . .	(AZ)	445
	MERRILL, Mary G.	(CT)	827
	LOCKE, John W.	(IL)	736
	MOORMAN, John A. . . .	(IL)	862
	HELLARD, Ellen G. . . .	(KY)	524
	KLEE, Edward L.	(KY)	658
	PERRY, Emma B.	(MA)	960
	SCHLESINGER, Deborah L.	(MT)	1094
	FREEMAN, Larry S. . . .	(SC)	401
	NOLTE, Alice I.	(SC)	908
	GUBBIN, Barbara A. . . .	(TX)	475
	DOWNEY REIDA, Linda K.	(UT)	316
	MORRISON, Meris E. . . .	(VT)	868
	SAGER, Lynn S.	(WI)	1074
Public library cooperation	SONDALLE, Barbara J. .	(IL)	1167
Public library database	ABRAM, Persis R.	(ON)	3
Public library development	MULKEY, Jack C.	(AR)	876
	ROBERTSON, Linda L. .	(IA)	1042
	KIRK, Sherwood	(IL)	654
	KLEE, Edward L.	(KY)	658
	ALBRECHT, Lois K. . . .	(PA)	10
	FELIX, Sally T.	(PA)	370
	KEOGH, Judith L.	(PA)	643
	CALLAHAM, Betty E. . .	(SC)	173
	CHAIT, William	(SC)	197
	CASSELL, Marianne K. .	(VT)	193
	NIX, Larry T.	(WI)	905
	FRANCIS, Derek R. . . .	(BC)	396
Public library development & admin	POSEL, Nancy R.	(PA)	985
Public library development consulting	FUNK, Elizabeth A. . . .	(PA)	410
Public library direction	NICHOLS, Joyce N.	(NY)	901
Public library facilities	THRASHER, Jerry A. . . .	(NC)	1243
Public library facility planning	HARRIS, Patricia L. . . .	(ND)	505
Public library friends group	KOCHOFF, Stephen T. . .	(NY)	667
Public library functions	BARKE, Judith P.	(ON)	56
Public library funding	HUNSBERGER, Charles W.	(NV)	574
	LAMB, Donald K.	(WI)	689
Public library fundraising	THRASHER, Jerry A. . . .	(NC)	1243
Public library, generalist	HANSEN, Paula J.	(PA)	498
Public library governance	SHANNON, Marcia A. . .	(MA)	1120
Public library information & referral	GUMPPER, Mary F. . . .	(OH)	477
Public library information services	MOLZ, Jean B.	(MD)	854
Public library labor relations	BRANDWEIN, Larry	(NY)	128
Public library management	MARTIN, Rosemary S. . .	(AR)	778
	PACK, Nancy C.	(AR)	933
	COOPER, Ginnie	(CA)	242
	JOHNSON, Carolyn E. . .	(CA)	602
	TURNER, Anne M.	(CA)	1264
	DOWLIN, Kenneth E. . . .	(CO)	316
	ARNOLD, Arleen B.	(CT)	33
	BALCOM, Kathleen M. . .	(IL)	51

PUBLIC LIBRARY (Cont'd)

Public library management			
	STEELE, Leah J.	(IL)	1184
	WARREN, Janet B.	(KS)	1306
	SCHABEL, Donald J. . . .	(KY)	1088
	STEENSLAND, Ronald P.	(KY)	1184
	COADY, Reginald P. . . .	(LA)	224
	CHAMBERLAIN, Ruth B.	(MA)	197
	FLANNERY, Susan M. . .	(MA)	383
	KELLSTEDT, Jenny	(MA)	637
	PURCELL, Kathleen V. .	(MD)	998
	TRELEVEN, Richard L. . .	(MD)	1255
	RAZ, Robert E.	(MI)	1012
	BYRNE, Roseanne	(MN)	169
	VINNES, Norman M. . . .	(MN)	1285
	SANDERS, Jan W.	(MO)	1080
	MOXLEY, Melody A. . . .	(NC)	874
	SAYRE, Edward C.	(NM)	1087
	FRANZ, David A.	(NY)	398
	HOLLEY, James L.	(NY)	551
	LIU, Carol F.	(NY)	734
	PHILLIPS, Ruth M.	(NY)	969
	RANSOM, Stanley A. . . .	(NY)	1007
	COLEMAN, Judith	(OH)	231
	HALL, Alan C.	(OH)	486
	HARRIS, Margaret J. . . .	(OH)	505
	WALDER, Antoinette L. .	(OH)	1294
	LONG, Sarah A.	(OR)	740
	BAUER, Margaret D. . . .	(PA)	65
	GARRISON, Guy G.	(PA)	420
	CHAIT, William	(SC)	197
	NESSE, Mark A.	(WA)	896
	GATES, Mary D.	(WI)	422
Public library management & organization	TREZZA, Alphonse F. . . .	(FL)	1256
Public library management service	MITCHELL, Joyce L. . . .	(NC)	849
Public library media collections	FLYNN, Barbara L.	(IL)	386
Public library multilingual services	BELL, Irena L.	(ON)	77
Public library, multitype systems	WELCH, Steven J.	(IL)	1321
Public library needs assessment	EVANS, Patricia D.	(AB)	357
Public library organization	DEFASSIO, Sharon L. . .	(PA)	287
Public library organizing & managing	AUSTIN, Neal F.	(NC)	40
Public library outreach	BAER, Robert L.	(WA)	45
Public library outreach & bookmobiles	HOLE, Carol C.	(FL)	550
Public library outreach services	MEYERS, Arthur S.	(IN)	830
Public library planning	TURNER, Anne M.	(CA)	1264
	RODGER, Eleanor J. . . .	(IL)	1047
	KEOUGH, Francis P. . . .	(MA)	643
Public library planning & building	MCGRIFF, Ronald I.	(MN)	808
Public library planning & construction	BROWNLEE, Jerry W. . .	(FL)	148
Public library planning & evaluation	SMITH, David R.	(MN)	1154
Public library programming	GRALAPP, Marcelee G. .	(CO)	457
	ROBERTS, Susan P. . . .	(MD)	1041
Public library programming & publicity	MORRISON, Meris E. . . .	(VT)	868
Public library public relations	HAGLOCH, Susan B. . . .	(OH)	483
Public library public services	GREGGS, Elizabeth M. .	(WA)	465
Public library reference	MILLER, Margaret R. . . .	(FL)	840
	WALKER, Constance T. .	(NC)	1295
	GRAVITZ, Ina A.	(NY)	459
Public library reference service	VANYOUNG, Sayre	(CA)	1278
Public library reference services	GANN, Daniel H.	(IN)	416
Public library reference work	LINDBERG, Richard L. .	(PA)	728
Public library references	POTELICKI, Athalene O. .	(OH)	986
Public library, school cooperation	LONG, Judith N.	(IL)	739
Public library service	RAMIREZ, William L. . . .	(CA)	1005
	WEIGEL, James S.	(CT)	1316
	ROBINSON, Lois C.	(FL)	1044
	LANE, Linda A.	(GA)	694
	TAYLOR, Mary L.	(HI)	1227
	BOGNANNI, Kathleen J. .	(IA)	111
	VANDERGRIFT, Kay E. .	(NJ)	1274
	PERILLO, Marie J.	(NY)	958
	TISDALE, Barbara	(NY)	1247
	MCFERREN, Priscilla G. .	(PA)	805
	WHITEHILL, Margaret . .	(WGR)	1332
Public library service delivery	O'BRIEN, Patrick M.	(TX)	915
Public library services	FREITAS-OBREGON, Brenda J.	(HI)	401
	RITTER, Philip W.	(NC)	1036
	HILL, Malcolm K.	(NY)	540

PUBLIC LIBRARY (Cont'd)

Public library services
SHEEHAN, Robert C. . . .	(NY)	1125
GALLIVAN, Marion F. . . .	(PA)	414
NESSE, Mark A.	(WA)	896

Public library standards
HUISKAMP, Julie G. . . .	(IA)	572
TODD, Alexander W. . . .	(IL)	1248
EICHELBERGER, Marianne	(KS)	339
NEEDHAM, George M. . .	(OH)	891

Public library system — ELDREDGE, Jeffrey R. . . . (HI) 342

Public library system administration — JONES, Wyman . . . . (CA) 615

Public library systems
LAND, Edward P.	(AL)	692
SIEBENMORGEN, Ruth .	(CA)	1135
LUND, Ethel B.	(IA)	748
GOMEZ, Martin J.	(IL)	447
MORRISON, Samuel F. .	(IL)	868
PEARSON, Roger L. . . .	(IL)	953
KING, Kenneth	(MI)	651
LEAMON, David L.	(MI)	707
WEBER, Ruth A.	(NJ)	1314
GENCO, Barbara A. . . .	(NY)	426
LINDAUER, Dinah	(NY)	728
PANZ, Richard	(NY)	938
RANSOM, Stanley A. . . .	(NY)	1007
COOK, Charles T.	(OH)	239
SELLE, Donna M.	(OR)	1113
KEISER, Barbara J.	(PA)	635
PROMOS, Marianne	(PA)	995
WAGGONER, Susan M. .	(PA)	1291
PEARCE, Douglas A. . . .	(RI)	952
MESSINEO, Anthony . . .	(SC)	828
COLLIER, Virginia S. . . .	(TN)	232
CRABB, Elizabeth A. . . .	(TX)	254
GUBBIN, Barbara A.	(TX)	475
MATHIS, Rama F.	(TX)	784
LAYTON, A J.	(UT)	705
SCHUURMAN, Guy	(UT)	1103
MATTE, Pierre V.	(PQ)	785

Public library systems analysis — SHELTON, John L. . . . . . (GA) 1126

Public library systems development — BOAZ, Ruth L. . . . . (TN) 108

Public library systems management — DILLARD, Thomas W. . . (NC) 303

Public library technology — GRALAPP, Marcelee G. . . (CO) 457

Public library trustee
FAHERTY, Robert L. . . .	(DC)	361
KIRSCHENBAUM, Arthur S.	(DC)	655
HARRER, Gustave A. . . .	(FL)	503
KOHRT, Ruth D.	(IA)	669
COLE, Jack W.	(MN)	230
MANTHEY, Carolyn M. . .	(NJ)	767

Public library trustee board — GRUHL, Andrea M. . . . . (DC) 474

Public library trustee relations — JANK, David A. . . . . (MA) 593

Public library trustees
LANGE, Clifford E.	(CA)	695
GRALAPP, Marcelee G. . .	(CO)	457
LARSON, Phyllis S.	(PA)	699

Public library trusteeship — GORDON, Lewis A. . . . . (IL) 451

Public library user education — HANSON, Jan E. . . . . . . (NY) 498

Public library user services — SMITHEE, Jeannette P. . . (NY) 1161

Public service, public library — MILES, Ruby A. . . . . (TX) 834

Reference, public library — RITZ, Mary E. . . . . (CA) 1037

Reference services in public libraries — ANDERSON, Charles R. . . (IL) 22

Regional public libraries — BOESE, Robert A. . . . . . (MN) 110

Regional public library system — SCOTT, Thomas L. . . . . (MN) 1108

Regional school, public library holding — BENSON, Laurel D. . . . . (MN) 83

Rural public libraries
TROMATER, Raymond B.	(AR)	1257
ALLENSWORTH, James H.	(CA)	16
HARRIET, Conklin W. . . .	(IL)	503
CASSELL, Marianne K. .	(VT)	193

Rural public library systems — O'BRIEN, Marlys H. . . . . (MN) 915

School & public libraries - youth — SHAEVEL, Evelyn F. . . . (IL) 1118

School & public library administration — VEITCH, Carol J. . . . . . (NC) 1281

School & public library cooperation — BRAINARD, Elsie K. . . . (MA) 127

School & public library coordination — MORROW, Blaine V. . . . . (MI) 869

School & public library management — MILLER, Marilyn L. . . . . . (NC) 840

School & public library relations — DRACH, Marian C. . . . . . (MD) 317

Sharing with public library — VELTEMA, John H. . . . . (MI) 1282

Small & medium public library buildings — FARACE, Virginia K. . . . (FL) 363

PUBLIC LIBRARY (Cont'd)

Small public libraries
KADANOFF, Diane G. . . .	(MA)	621
FLOWER, Eileen D.	(OH)	386
FRENCH, Michael	(OH)	402
CASSELL, Marianne K. .	(VT)	193
BRENNAN, Cindy L.	(WA)	132
OTTOSEN, Charles F. . .	(AB)	930

Small public library administration
MUDD, Isabelle G.	(AK)	875
OVERSTREET, Allen J. .	(FL)	931
LINTNER, Barbara J. . . .	(IL)	731
MOTT, Schuyler L.	(ME)	872
WAGGONER, Susan M. .	(PA)	1291
KNODLE, Shirley M.	(WI)	665
EVANS, Patricia D.	(AB)	357
KIRKPATRICK, Jane E. .	(ON)	655

Small public library buildings — RASKA, Ginny . . . . (TX) 1009

Small public library collections — RASKA, Ginny . . . . (TX) 1009

Small public library development
PARRY, David R.	(CO)	944
HAWKINS, Paul J.	(KS)	514
SCHERBA, Sandra A. . .	(MI)	1092

Small public library issues — HAYES, Richard E. . . . . (MA) 516

Small public library management — LAPIERRE, France . . . . (PQ) 697

Small public library services — LEVIN, Elizabeth A. . . . . (MI) 720

Small public library systems — ELDRIDGE, Jane A. . . . . (MA) 342

Small rural public libraries — PANZ, Richard . . . . (NY) 938

State & public library management — WALTERS, Clarence R. . . (OH) 1301

Teaching graduate public libs course — VALENTINE, Patrick M. . . (NC) 1271

Trustees of public libraries — MOORE, Bessie B. . . . . . (DC) 858

US public library history — HECK-RABI, Louise E. . . . (MI) 520

Urban public libraries
SONDHEIM, John W. . . .	(MD)	1167
ROBERTS, Jean A.	(MO)	1040

Urban public library management — ICKES, Barbara J. . . . . . (PA) 581

Urban public library service — HEID, Gregory G. . . . . . . (GA) 521

PUBLIC RELATIONS (See also Advertising, Community, Marketing, Outreach, Promotion, Publicity)

Administration & public relations — GARDINER, Judith R. . . . (NJ) 417

Advertising & public relations — PEARSON, Jo A. . . . . . . (IA) 952

Advertising, public relations consulting — FRISBIE, Richard . . . . . . (IL) 405

Child advocate, public relations — BANTA, Gratia J. . . . . . . (OH) 55

Collection development, public relations — KNIGHT, Shirley D. . . . . (NJ) 664

Conferencing & public relations — WILLIAMS, Susan S. . . . (MI) 1346

Consultation, public relations — HARRIS, Linda S. . . . . . . (DC) 505

Development & public relations — REEVES, Joan R. . . . . . . (RI) 1016

Displays & public relations — COONEY, Mata M. . . . . . (NV) 242

Editing, writing, public relations — WEISENBURGER, Patricia J. . . . . (KS) 1319

Fundraising & public relations — TERNAK, Armand T. . . . (FL) 1232

Fundraising, public relations — FISCHLER, Barbara B. . . (IN) 380

Innovation & public relations — SCHALAU, Robert D. . . . (MS) 1089

Institutional public relations
FRISBIE, Margery	(IL)	405
CLARK, Charlene K.	(TX)	216

Library outreach & public relations — LAWTON, Bethany L. . . . (DC) 705

Library public relations
NORTON, Alice	(CT)	910
HOWINGTON, Lee R. . . .	(GA)	566
DEMPSEY, Frank J.	(IL)	291
HELLER, Dawn H.	(IL)	524
KEATS, Susan E.	(MA)	633
MCKAY, Ann	(ME)	809
TATE, David L.	(MI)	1225
CARLSON, Stan W.	(MN)	182
BRYANT, David S.	(NJ)	152
MCNEAL, Betty	(NV)	816
GODWIN, Mary J.	(NY)	443
SHUMAN, Susan E.	(NY)	1134
MAZEFSKY, Gertrude T.	(PA)	791
LAMBERTH, Linda E. . . .	(TX)	690
BAGAN, Beverly S.	(VA)	45
REAM, Daniel L.	(VA)	1012
THORSEN, Jeanne M. . .	(WA)	1242
DIEHL, Carol L.	(WI)	301
BRYAN, Carol L.	(WV)	151
BERCOVITCH, Sari	(ON)	84

Library public relations writing — BRYAN, Carol L. . . . . . . (WV) 151

Management & public relations — HUFFER, Mary A. . . . . . (MD) 570

Management, public relations, grants — KISER, Mary D. . . . . (FL) 656

Marketing, advertising, public relations — BETTENCOURT, Nancy J. (CO) 92

PUBLIC RELATIONS (Cont'd)

Marketing & public relations	FEINBERG, Beryl L.	(DC)	368
	KIES, Cosette N.	(IL)	647
	LEWIS, Thomas F.	(MA)	724
	PECK, Shirley S.	(MD)	953
	MUETH, Elizabeth C. . . .	(MO)	875
	WALTERS, Carol G.	(NC)	1301
	SWEENEY, Richard T. . .	(NY)	1215
	CRAUMER, Patricia A. . .	(PA)	255
	BROWN, Carol J.	(TX)	142
	MAIOLI, Jerry R.	(WA)	762
	LACROIX, Yvon A.	(PQ)	687
Marketing, public relations	SPIEGELMAN, Barbara M.	(PA)	1174
Neighborhood libraries public relations	LOCKETT, Sandra B.	(WI)	736
Outreach & public relations	MANNING, Helen M. . . .	(TX)	766
Programming & public relations	CHELTON, Mary K.	(MD)	204
	POLLOK, Karen E.	(VA)	981
Programming, public relations	LARSON, Mildred N. . . .	(WI)	699
Promotion & public relations	MULLER, Mary M.	(TX)	877
	SELLERS, Wayne C. . . .	(TX)	1114
	HARRISON, Karen A. . . .	(ON)	507
Public affairs & public relations	MILLER, Deborah	(IL)	837
Public libraries & public relations	WINCKLER, Paul A.	(NY)	1354
Public libraries public relations	VOJTECH, Kathryn	(IL)	1287
Public library public relations	HAGLOCH, Susan B. . . .	(OH)	483
Public relations	GALBRAITH, William B. . .	(AK)	413
	BUCKNER, Rebecca S. .	(AL)	154
	COOPER, Regina G. . . .	(AL)	243
	STEWART, Sharon L. . . .	(AL)	1193
	ARN, Nancy L.	(AR)	33
	GOODRICH, Nita K.	(AZ)	449
	MOSLEY, Shelley E.	(AZ)	872
	BALLOU, Eleanor F.	(CA)	53
	CLIFTON, Joe A.	(CA)	222
	HILLMAN, Stephanie . . .	(CA)	541
	JACOBS, Nina F.	(CA)	589
	KAYE, Karen	(CA)	632
	LANGE, Clifford E.	(CA)	695
	MCQUOWN, Eloise	(CA)	817
	MORAN, Irene E.	(CA)	862
	REAGAN, Bob	(CA)	1012
	ROSS, Ruth K.	(CA)	1058
	TARTER, Blodwen	(CA)	1224
	THAKER, Virbala M.	(CA)	1234
	WIGLEY, Marylou	(CA)	1337
	WALTERS, Suzanne . . .	(CO)	1301
	CALLAHAN, Helen H. . .	(CT)	173
	POIRIER, Maria K.	(CT)	980
	SERGEL, Carol K.	(CT)	1116
	BELLEFONTAINE, Arnold G.	(DC)	78
	KITZMILLER, Virginia G. .	(DC)	657
	LITTLEJOHN, Grace M. . .	(DC)	734
	ROBERTS, Lesley A. . . .	(DC)	1040
	BECKER, Josephine M. .	(FL)	72
	GRUBMAN, Donna Y. . .	(FL)	474
	HALES, John D.	(FL)	486
	HOLSTINE, Lesa G.	(FL)	554
	WULF, Karlinne V.	(FL)	1374
	BAKER, Gordon N.	(GA)	48
	FENNELL, Janice C.	(GA)	371
	HALE, Ruth C.	(GA)	485
	TRAINOR, Donna J.	(GA)	1253
	VAUGHAN, Elinor F. . . .	(GA)	1279
	WILLIS, Roni M.	(GA)	1348
	LUSTER, Arlene L.	(HI)	750
	PLADERA, Lucretia	(HI)	977
	SPAZIANI, Carol	(IA)	1172
	BRICKMAN, Sally F. . . .	(IL)	135
	CLAYTON, Nina A.	(IL)	220
	DEMETRAKAKES, Jennifer B.	(IL)	291
	FRISCH, Corrine A.	(IL)	405
	JOHNSON, Joanne D. . .	(IL)	606
	KEELER, Janice S.	(IL)	634
	KRAUSE, Roberta A. . . .	(IL)	676
	MCCABE, Ronald B. . . .	(IL)	793
	MCELROY, Beth A.	(IL)	804
	NELSON, Maggie E. . . .	(IL)	894
	OAKS, Claire	(IL)	913

PUBLIC RELATIONS (Cont'd)

Public relations	ROBERTSON, Deborah G.	(IL)	1041
	SORENSEN, Mark W. . .	(IL)	1168
	STARRATT, Joseph A. .	(IL)	1182
	TUGGLE, Ann M.	(IL)	1262
	WALLACE, Linda K.	(IL)	1297
	DEYOUNG, Charles D. . .	(IN)	298
	MILLER, Marcia M.	(IN)	840
	RAWLES-HEISER, Carolyn	(IN)	1010
	SABA, Bettye M.	(IN)	1072
	CHRISTNER, Terry A. . .	(KS)	212
	DRUSE, Judith A.	(KS)	321
	QUIRING, Virginia M. . .	(KS)	1000
	AVERDICK, Michael R. . .	(KY)	41
	WALL, Celia J.	(KY)	1297
	MCKANN, Michael R. . . .	(LA)	809
	COPLAN, Kate M.	(MD)	244
	KNOBBE, Mary L.	(MD)	665
	MEHNERT, Robert B. . . .	(MD)	821
	SNYDER, Denny L.	(MD)	1164
	WILLIAMS, J L.	(MD)	1343
	GOTTLIEB, Robert A. . . .	(ME)	453
	DELLER, A M.	(MI)	289
	DIDIER, Elaine K.	(MI)	301
	EZELL, Charlaine L.	(MI)	360
	GAREN, Robert J.	(MI)	418
	KERSHNER, Stephen A. .	(MI)	644
	LIPTON, Howard	(MI)	732
	ROBLING, John S.	(MI)	1045
	ST. AMAND, Norma P. . .	(MI)	1075
	SCHERBA, Sandra A. . .	(MI)	1092
	TATE, Carole A.	(MI)	1225
	HAEUSER, Michael J. . .	(MN)	482
	OLSON, Chris D.	(MN)	922
	READY, Sandra K.	(MN)	1012
	FORD, Gary E.	(MO)	389
	MCCARTNEY, Jean A. . .	(MO)	794
	WARREN, Catherine S. .	(MS)	1306
	NEWBERG, Ellen J.	(MT)	898
	COUSINS, Gloria D.	(NC)	252
	DAVIDSON, Laura B. . . .	(NC)	276
	ESTES, Elizabeth W. . . .	(NC)	355
	HAUPERT, Thomas J. . .	(NC)	512
	JONES, John W.	(NC)	613
	SOUTHERLAND, Carol A.	(NC)	1169
	JOHNSON, Jean G.	(NH)	605
	BURDEN, Geraldine R. . .	(NJ)	158
	CASEY, Mary A.	(NJ)	192
	COHEN, Adrea G.	(NJ)	227
	KARMAZIN, Sharon M. .	(NJ)	627
	KERN, Stella V.	(NJ)	643
	PAPAZIAN, Pierre	(NJ)	939
	SMOTHERS, Joyce W. .	(NJ)	1162
	WEST, Shirley L.	(NJ)	1326
	CAROLLO, Michael T. . .	(NV)	184
	RICE, Dorothy F.	(NV)	1027
	BERNER, Andrew J.	(NY)	88
	BOBINSKI, Mary F.	(NY)	108
	CARTER, Darline L.	(NY)	189
	CLAYBORNE, Jon L. . . .	(NY)	219
	CROCKER, Susan O. . . .	(NY)	259
	FARKAS, Charles R. . . .	(NY)	364
	GINSBURG, Joanne R. .	(NY)	438
	GLASER, Gloria T.	(NY)	439
	KLIMEK, Chester R.	(NY)	661
	LEWIS, Frances R.	(NY)	723
	MORRISON, J M.	(NY)	868
	NAGLE, Ann	(NY)	886
	NOTTINGHAM, Sharon E.	(NY)	910
	NOVIK, Sandra P.	(NY)	911
	O'GRADY, Jean P.	(NY)	918
	PHILLIPS, Ruth M.	(NY)	969
	SAUNDERS, Dorette . . .	(NY)	1084
	WITT, Susan T.	(NY)	1358
	DONAHUGH, Robert H. .	(OH)	310
	FENDER, Kimber L.	(OH)	371
	GERWIN, Barbara L. . . .	(OH)	430
	KAUER, Patricia M.	(OH)	630
	KOZLOWSKI, Ronald S. .	(OH)	674

PUBLIC RELATIONS (Cont'd)

Public relations

LATSHAW, Patricia H. . . (OH) 701
PASQUAL, Patricia E. . . (OH) 946
PEAKE, Sharon K. . . . . . (OH) 952
RUHL, Jodi S. . . . . (OH) 1066
SCHWELK, Jennifer C. . . (OH) 1105
SHIVERDECKER, Darlene
  J. . . . . (OH) 1132
MEYERS, Duane H. . . . . (OK) 830
NELSON, Norman L. . . . . (OK) 895
SKVARLA, Donna J. . . . (OK) 1147
VESELY, Marilyn L. . . . . (OK) 1283
LONG, Sarah A. . . . . (OR) 740
BLEIER, Carol S. . . . . . . (PA) 105
FADDEN, Donald M. . . . . (PA) 360
NEMEYER, Carol A. . . . . (PA) 895
POWERS, Beverly A. . . . (PA) 989
SMITH, Barbara J. . . . . . (PA) 1153
TANNER, Anne B. . . . . . (PA) 1222
TERRY, Terese M. . . . . . (PA) 1232
WHEELER, Martha M. . . . (PA) 1329
WINGLE, Rita M. . . . . . . (PA) 1355
CAIRNS, Roberta A. . . . . (RI) 171
JOHNSON, Minnie M. . . . (SC) 607
BAER, Ellen H. . . . . (TN) 45
BANNERMAN-WILLIAMS,
  Cheryl F. . . . . (TN) 54
DRESCHER, Judith A. . . . (TN) 319
LEE, Geoffrey J. . . . . (TN) 710
GROSS, Iva H. . . . . (TX) 472
LARSON, Jeanette C. . . . (TX) 699
PROGAR, Dorothy R. . . . (TX) 995
THOMAS, Greg . . . . (TX) 1236
BURKS, C J. . . . . (UT) 161
KARPISEK, Marian E. . . . (UT) 628
BURGESS, Dean . . . . . . (VA) 159
MAYER-HENNELLY, Mary
  B. . . . . (VA) 789
OWENS, Martha A. . . . . (VA) 932
SMITH, Ruth S. . . . . (VA) 1160
WEBB, Barbara A. . . . . . (VA) 1313
WOODALL, Nancy C. . . . (VA) 1365
FOLEY, Katherine E. . . . . (WA) 387
WOLFE, Lisa A. . . . . (WA) 1361
OHLEMACHER, Janet H. (WI) 919
PITEL, Vonna J. . . . . (WI) 976
TASNADI, Deborah L. . . (WI) 1224
WASICK, Mary A. . . . . . (WI) 1308
SIMPSON, Susan M. . . . (WY) 1142
STAFFORD, Leva L. . . . . (WY) 1178
BAILEY, Madeleine J. . . . (AB) 46
NADEAU, Sylvie . . . . (NB) 886
ARMBRUST, Susan P. . . (ON) 31
DE RONDE, Paula D. . . . (ON) 294
HORNE, Alan J. . . . . (ON) 560
MCLEAN-LOWE, Dallas . (ON) 814
MELVILLE, Karen E. . . . . (ON) 823
PICARD, Albert . . . . (ON) 970
POWELL, Wyley L. . . . . (ON) 989
CHEVRIER, Francine . . . (PQ) 207
RABCHUK, Gordon K. . . (PQ) 1001
LABUIK, Karen L. . . . . . (SK) 686
BRILL, Kathryn R. . . . . . (ENG) 136
IMOISI, Ann U. . . . . (NGR) 582

Public relations & advertising   GAMBRELL, Drucilla S. . . (AL) 416
Public relations & art   NICHOLSON, Myreen M. . (VA) 902
Public relations & communication   GOTHBERG, Helen M. . . (AZ) 453
Public relations & communications   TOMLIN, Marsha A. . . . . (OH) 1250
Public relations & development   LEBRETON, Jonathan A. (MD) 708
Public relations & education   ROBERTS, Anne F. . . . . (NY) 1039
Public relations & fundraising   ROCHELEAU, Kathleen D. (MA) 1046
  STICHA, Denise S. . . . . (PA) 1193
Public relations & marketing   CARTLEDGE, Ellen G. . . (CT) 190
  JOHNSON, Veronica A. . . (MI) 609
  ELDREDGE, Jonathan D. (NM) 342
Public relations & merchandising   FLUM, Judith G. . . . . . . (CA) 386
Public relations & outreach   DAVIS, Denyvetta . . . . . . (OK) 278
Public relations & political support   RAY, Gordon L. . . . . (BC) 1011

PUBLIC RELATIONS (Cont'd)

Public relations & program
  coordination   MOORE, Virginia B. . . . . (DC) 861
Public relations & programming   CADDELL, Claude W. . . (IN) 170
Public relations & programs   GRAVES, Sid F. . . . . . . (MS) 459
Public relations & promotion   MCLAUGHLIN, Pamela W. (NY) 813
Public relations & promotions   LEAMON, David L. . . . . (MI) 707
Public relations & public affairs   JONES, Elin D. . . . . (DC) 612
Public relations & public information   KUSZMAUL, Marcia J. . . (IL) 685
Public relations & publications   KUHN, Warren B. . . . . . (IA) 682
Public relations & publicity   ULBRICH, David E. . . . . (VA) 1268
Public relations & training   WAGGENER, Jean B. . . (TN) 1291
Public relations between firm & clients   BARNUM, Deborah C. . . (CT) 58
Public relations, community
  involvement   BEATTIE, Brian . . . . (KS) 70
Public relations, desktop publishing   WEIDEMANN, Margaret A. (NY) 1316
Public relations, exhibits, displays   DAANE, Jeanette K. . . . . (AZ) 269
Public relations for archives   WALSH, G M. . . . . (ON) 1299
Public relations for libraries   PERRY, Edward C. . . . . (CA) 960
  OLSON, Christine A. . . . (MD) 922
Public relations for school libraries   WHITE, Ann T. . . . . (SC) 1330
Public relations, including publishing   EVANS, Gwynneth . . . . . (ON) 357
Public relations information   EBERHARD, Neysa C. . . (KS) 334
Public relations, lobbying, training   SANKER, Paul N. . . . . . (NY) 1081
Public relations management   FONTAINE, Sue . . . . . . (NY) 388
Public relations, marketing   SAULMON, Sharon A. . . (OK) 1084
Public relations planning   SHUMAN, Marilyn J. . . . (IL) 1134
Public relations programming   NORTON, Tedgina . . . . . (TN) 910
Public relations, publications   MONTANA, Edward J. . . (MA) 855
Public relations, publicity   GODBEY, Esther R. . . . . (AR) 442
  MARGOLIS, Bernard A. . (MI) 770
  MOSES, Lynn M. . . . . . (PA) 871
Public relations, publishing, budgeting   ARROWOOD, Donna J. . (CA) 34
Public relations responsibilities   LETTIERI, Robin M. . . . . (NY) 719
Public relations, rural-small libraries   KNIEVEL, Helen A. . . . . (OR) 664
Public relations, school district   NIEMEYER, Karen K. . . . (IN) 903
Public relations staff training   NORTON, Alice . . . . (CT) 910
Public relations writing   POMERLEAU, Suzanne M. (FL) 982
Public relations, writing & publishing   ROUSE, Roscoe . . . . (OK) 1061
Public services & public relations   PETERSON, Paul A. . . . (MO) 964
Publicity & public relations   CARLSON, Alan C. . . . . (CA) 182
  ERLICH, Martin . . . . (CA) 353
  BEAN, Rick J. . . . . (IL) 69
  WEIKUM, James M. . . . . (MN) 1317
  DINERMAN, Gloria . . . . . (NJ) 304
School library media public relations   BALL, Diane A. . . . . (OH) 52
Serials periodicals, public relations   PATTERSON, Grace L. . . (NY) 948
Small library public relations   KIRKPATRICK, Jane E. . (ON) 655
Special programs, public relations   LARSON, Josephine . . . . (NC) 699

PUBLIC SERVICES (See also Library Services, Public)

Academic library public services   HOSEL, Harold V. . . . . . (CA) 561
  DAVID, Indra M. . . . . . . (MI) 276
  CRANE, John G. . . . . . . (NH) 255
Academic public service   ADELMAN, Jean S. . . . . (PA) 6
Administration & public services   HORRELL, Jeffrey L. . . . (NY) 560
Administration of public services   ROBINSON, Margaret G. (CA) 1044
Administration, public services   MORAN, William S. . . . . (NH) 862
  UVA, Peter A. . . . . (NY) 1270
Adult public services   GREEN, Vera A. . . . . . . (PA) 462
Automation of public services   ANDERSON, Kari D. . . . (VA) 24
Circulation, public services   FLIEGEL, Deborah A. . . . (WI) 385
College public services   LANDMAN, Lillian L. . . . (NY) 693
Community college, public service   MILES, Ruby A. . . . . . . (TX) 834
Coordinating public services   TITUS, Barbara E. . . . . . (DE) 1247
General public service, circulation   HOLMES, Nancy M. . . . . (GA) 553
General reference, public services   WHITTINGTON, Christine
  A. . . . . (PA) 1334
Information & public services   CAREN, Loretta . . . . (NY) 181
Information desk & public service   PAWLEY, Carolyn P. . . . (ON) 951
Library administration, public services   HAWKINS, Mary J. . . . . (KS) 514
Library management, public services   HENDRIX, Wilma P. . . . . (TN) 528
Library public services   TRAINER, Karin A. . . . . (CT) 1253
  WATSON, Peter G. . . . . (ID) 1310
  MCNEAL, Betty . . . . (NV) 816
Management & adult public services   SZETO, Dorcas C. . . . . (CA) 1218
Management & public services   COOK, Anita I. . . . . (NE) 239

PUBLIC SERVICES (Cont'd)

Management of public services — MARTIN, Ron G. . . . . . . (IN) 778
HANNA, Hildur W. . . . . . (MI) 496
DALRYMPLE, Tamsen . . (OH) 271
Microcomputers in public services — MARTIN, Ron G. . . . . . . (IN) 778
Music library public services — FISKEN, Patricia B. . . . . (NH) 382
Public library public services — GREGGS, Elizabeth M. . . (WA) 465
Public service — REICHEL, Mary . . . . (AZ) 1018
CASTAGNOZZI, Carol A. . (CA) 194
KUBIC, Joseph C. . . . . . (CA) 682
MARTIN, Rebecca R. . . . (CA) 778
MILLER, Elissa R. . . . . . (CA) 837
REYNOLDS, Diane C. . . (CA) 1025
WASHINGTON, Sigrid M. . (DC) 1308
SMITH-EPPS, E P. . . . . . (GA) 1161
DUCHOW, Sally . . . . . . (IL) 322
KIM, Chung S. . . . . (IL) 648
SHERMAN, Sarah . . . . . (IL) 1128
WESTON, Ann B. . . . . . (IL) 1327
REEVES, Cathy L. . . . . . (KS) 1016
MILLER, Norma B. . . . . . (KY) 841
RIVES, Lydia L. . . . . . . (KY) 1037
TATELMAN, Susan D. . . (MA) 1225
JAEGER, Sally J. . . . . . (MI) 591
HELTSLEY, Mary K. . . . . (MN) 525
WILROY, Joann . . . . . . (MS) 1349
GLEIM, Sharon S. . . . . . (NC) 441
SLOCUM, Charlotte A. . . (NC) 1150
SOUTHERN, Mary A. . . . (NC) 1170
YOUNG, Betty I. . . . . . . (NC) 1381
CHADWICK, Janina A. . . (OH) 197
HETTINGER, Susan F. . . (OH) 534
RYAN, Sharon K. . . . . . (OH) 1071
SNIDER, Sondra L. . . . . (OH) 1163
ALDRIDGE, Betsy B. . . . (OK) 11
SMITH, Donald R. . . . . . (OK) 1154
PEFFER, Margery E. . . . (PA) 954
THOMPSON, Sandra K. . (PA) 1241
VAN DE CASTLE,
Raymond M. . . . . . . (PA) 1273
BLAIR, Lynne M. . . . . . (TN) 102
MENDINA, Guy T. . . . . (TN) 824
BROWN, Muriel W. . . . . (TX) 146
MOLTZAN, Janet R. . . . (TX) 854
JONES, Ruth J. . . . . . . (UT) 615
WEBB, Barbara A. . . . . (VA) 1313
KAPLAN, Lesly A. . . . . . (WA) 626
MILLER, G D. . . . . (WA) 837
SEARING, Susan E. . . . . (WI) 1109
HUDSON, Susan P. . . . . (BC) 570
VIIERANS, Mary E. . . . . (BC) 1284
BELLAMY, Patricia C. . . (ON) 78
GILLHAM, Virginia A. . . . (ON) 436
GRATTAN, Robert . . . . . (FRN) 458
Public service administration — JOHNSTON, Judy F. . . . . (FL) 610
BALACHANDRAN,
Sarojini . . . . (MO) 50
OELZ, Erling R. . . . . . . (MT) 917
Public service & instruction — JAFFE, Lee D. . . . . (CA) 591
Public service & reference — DONOVAN, William A. . . . (IL) 312
THOMPSON, Anna M. . . (IN) 1238
SUYEMATSU, Kiyo . . . . (MN) 1212
CHODACKI, Roberta A. . . (NY) 210
PFOHL, Theodore E. . . . (NY) 966
CLAYTON, J G. . . . . . . (SC) 220
WING, Marjorie . . . . (AB) 1354
Public service & tours — HORTON, Anna J. . . . . . (OH) 561
Public service assistance — CEBULA, Theodore R. . . (WI) 196
Public service information desk — SPENSLEY, Malcolm C. . . (NY) 1173
Public service librarianship — GREEN, Carol C. . . . . . . (WA) 461
Public service management — GILREATH, Charles L. . . (AZ) 437
FOREMAN, Gertrude E. . (MN) 390
Public service programming — CALLAHAN, Helen H. . . (CT) 173
Public service programs — STOLT, Wilbur A. . . . . . . (OK) 1196
Public service, public library — MILES, Ruby A. . . . . . . (TX) 834
Public service reference — NOYES, Nicholas . . . . . . (ME) 911
WOESTHOFF, Catherine
F. . . . . (NY) 1359
Public service, science reference — HUDSON, Donna T. . . . . (NC) 569
Public service supervision — THOMAS, Greg . . . . (TX) 1236

PUBLIC SERVICES (Cont'd)

Public service to children
Public service training
Public services

SENN, Sharon L. . . . . . . (WA) 1115
BARKER, Lillian H. . . . . (MD) 56
HONEYCUTT, Mary L. . . (AR) 556
SANDERS, Kathryn A. . . (AR) 1080
KESSLER, Katheryn M. . (AZ) 645
RENEKER, Maxine H. . . . (AZ) 1023
BENNETT, Celestine C. . (CA) 81
BLANK, Karen L. . . . . . (CA) 104
BOORKMAN, Jo A. . . . . (CA) 115
CHAN, Carl C. . . . . (CA) 199
CONNOR, Anne C. . . . . (CA) 237
DUFFY, Karen R. . . . . . (CA) 324
HOWLAND, Joan S. . . . . (CA) 566
JAMES, Olive C. . . . . . (CA) 592
LAGIER, Jennifer B. . . . (CA) 688
MAWDSLEY, Katherine F. (CA) 787
SCHMIDT, C J. . . . . . . (CA) 1095
SEHR, Dena P. . . . . . . (CA) 1112
KANE, Katherine . . . . . (CO) 625
VARNES, Richard S. . . . (CO) 1279
HUGHES, John M. . . . . (CT) 571
LA FOGG, Mary C. . . . (CT) 688
CHANG, Helen S. . . . . . (DC) 200
GRANT, George C. . . . . (FL) 458
MARTIN, James R. . . . . (FL) 776
WILLIAMS, Thomas L. . . (FL) 1347
WILLOCKS, Robert M. . . (FL) 1349
ANDERSON, Thomas G. . (GA) 25
BOYD, Ruth V. . . . . (GA) 123
CHENEY, Philip M. . . . . (GA) 206
O'NEILL, Patricia E. . . . (GA) 924
RUSSELL, Ralph E. . . . . (GA) 1069
WILLIS, Roni M. . . . . . . (GA) 1348
BECK, Marianne J. . . . . (IA) 71
PIKE, George H. . . . . . . (ID) 972
BRACHMANN, Kathleen
A. . . . . (IL) 124
BROWN, Mary J. . . . . . (IL) 146
COATSWORTH, Patricia
A. . . . . (IL) 224
DUTTON, Lee S. . . . . . (IL) 329
MEEKER, Robert B. . . . (IL) 821
SACHS, Iris P. . . . . (IL) 1073
SCHREIBER, Robert E. . (IL) 1099
SWANSON, Patricia K. . (IL) 1213
LOGSDON, Robert L. . . (IN) 737
MOORE, Thomas J. . . . (IN) 861
SNYDER, Carolyn A. . . . (IN) 1164
STARKEY, Edward D. . . (IN) 1182
YOUNG, Philip H. . . . . . (IN) 1383
STEWART, Henry R. . . . (KS) 1192
AVERDICK, Michael R. . . (KY) 41
MARTIN, June H. . . . . . (KY) 777
STURM, Rebecca R. . . . (KY) 1205
CANTILLAS, Caroline M. . (LA) 179
KHOURY, Nancy L. . . . . (LA) 646
SALTER, Jeffrey L. . . . . (LA) 1077
FELDMAN, Laurence M. . (MA) 369
IRION, Millard F. . . . . . . (MA) 584
LEAHY, Lynda C. . . . . . (MA) 706
MOCKOVAK, Holly E. . . (MA) 851
PEARCE, Jean K. . . . . . (MA) 952
WALSH, Jim . . . . (MA) 1299
WESTLING, Ellen R. . . . (MA) 1327
CLARK, David S. . . . . . (MD) 216
CUMMINGS, John P. . . . (MD) 264
HALL, Mary A. . . . . (MD) 488
HOFSTETTER, Eleanore
O. . . . . (MD) 549
LYON-HARTMANN, Becky
J. . . . . (MD) 752
PISA, Maria G. . . . . . . (MD) 975
REILLY, Deborah D. . . . (MD) 1020
SZCZCPANIAK, Adam S. . (MD) 1218
WILT, Larry J. . . . . (MD) 1353
BUCKLEY, Francis J. . . . (MI) 154
CONWAY, Paul L. . . . . . (MI) 239
HAKA, Clifford H. . . . . . (MI) 484
KERSHNER, Stephen A. . (MI) 644

PUBLIC SERVICES (Cont'd)
Public services

O'CONNELL, Catherine A.	(MI)	915
PEREZ-STABLE, Maria A.	(MI)	958
SHAPIRO, Beth J.	(MI)	1121
STOFFLE, Carla J.	(MI)	1196
OBERMAN, Cerise G.	(MN)	914
MEADOR, John M.	(MO)	819
ONSAGER, Lawrence W.	(MO)	924
PARMENTER, Julie	(MO)	943
ALLEN, Regina L.	(NC)	15
GAUGHAN, Thomas M.	(NC)	422
LUBANS, John	(NC)	745
SEIBERT, Karen S.	(NC)	1112
BIRDSALL, Douglas G.	(ND)	98
ETTL, Lorraine R.	(ND)	356
LU, Janet C.	(NE)	745
WISE, Sally H.	(NE)	1357
BOYLE, Jeanne E.	(NJ)	124
BUTCHER, Patricia S.	(NJ)	166
GREENBERG, Evelyn	(NJ)	463
HODGE, Patricia A.	(NJ)	546
HUTCHINSON, Barbara J.	(NJ)	579
IRVINE, James S.	(NJ)	584
KENNEDY, Kathleen A.	(NJ)	641
KRANIS, Janet C.	(NJ)	676
SMITH, Reginald W.	(NJ)	1159
GRAY, Robert G.	(NV)	460
CHRISMAN, Diane J.	(NY)	211
JAY, Donald F.	(NY)	595
KRANICH, Nancy C.	(NY)	676
MONACO, Ralph A.	(NY)	854
MOORE, Ann L.	(NY)	858
PILACHOWSKI, David M.	(NY)	973
SHERBY, Louise S.	(NY)	1127
BENTLEY, Stella	(OH)	83
BETCHER, William M.	(OH)	92
BLOMQUIST, Laura G.	(OH)	106
CAIN, Linda B.	(OH)	171
CARY, Mary K.	(OH)	191
FENDER, Kimber L.	(OH)	371
MCNEER, Elizabeth J.	(OH)	816
PURSEL, Janet E.	(OH)	998
WELLINGTON, Jean S.	(OH)	1322
COCHENOUR, John J.	(OK)	225
HILKER, Emerson W.	(OK)	539
SAULMON, Sharon A.	(OK)	1084
JENSEN, Gary D.	(OR)	598
WAND, Patricia A.	(OR)	1302
DALE, Charles F.	(PA)	270
ENGLERT, Mary A.	(PA)	350
GINSBURG, Mary L.	(PA)	438
MUDRICK, Kristine E.	(PA)	875
PATTERSON, Charlean P.	(PA)	948
STRAUSS, Richard F.	(PA)	1201
GUILLEMARD DE COLON, Teresita	(PR)	476
CAIRNS, Roberta A.	(RI)	171
PERRY, Beth I.	(RI)	960
TAYLOR, Merrily E.	(RI)	1227
DENNIS, Everett J.	(SC)	292
REIMER, Mary S.	(SC)	1021
VASSALLO, John A.	(SC)	1279
BEST, Edwin J.	(TN)	92
GILL, Linda S.	(TN)	435
HELGUERA, Byrd S.	(TN)	524
HOOPER, James E.	(TN)	557
MITCHELL, Aubrey H.	(TN)	848
SCHER, Rita S.	(TN)	1092
VEACH, Lynn H.	(TN)	1280
WILLIAMS, Elizabeth L.	(TN)	1343
BIGLEY, John E.	(TX)	96
BRACEY, Ann E.	(TX)	124
FORD, Barbara J.	(TX)	389
GARAZA, Noemi	(TX)	417
GROSS, Sally L.	(TX)	472
HARTNESS, Ann	(TX)	508
KERLEY, Izoro D.	(TX)	643
RODE, Shelley J.	(TX)	1047
WELCH, C B.	(TX)	1321

PUBLIC SERVICES (Cont'd)
Public services

WERKING, Richard H.	(TX)	1324
BERWICK, Philip C.	(VA)	91
BROWN, Barbara J.	(VA)	142
COCHRANE, Lynn S.	(VA)	225
GREGORY, Carla L.	(VA)	466
HAYS, Peggy W.	(VA)	517
MAYER-HENNELLY, Mary B.	(VA)	789
NICULA, J G.	(VA)	903
WHITE, Lynda S.	(VA)	1331
SOUFFRONT, Blanche L.	(VI)	1169
ALEXANDER, Malcolm D.	(WA)	12
ARCHBOLD, Barbara C.	(WA)	30
BIRD, Viola A.	(WA)	98
BUCKINGHAM, Rebecca M.	(WA)	154
GILDENHAR, Janet	(WA)	434
HENINGER, Irene C.	(WA)	528
MENGES, Gary L.	(WA)	824
RICKELTON, Esther G.	(WA)	1031
SHAFFER, Maryann	(WA)	1119
CENTER, Sue L.	(WI)	196
PIELE, Linda J.	(WI)	971
SAGER, Lynn S.	(WI)	1074
SHARMA, Ravindra N.	(WI)	1122
ESKRIDGE, Virginia C.	(WV)	354
BALDWIN, David A.	(WY)	51
BURMAN, Marilyn P.	(WY)	161
WIEBE, Frieda	(BC)	1336
MACLOWICK, Frederick B.	(MB)	757
ISRAEL, Kathleen	(ON)	585
LAITMAN, Sheila	(ON)	688
ACKERMAN, Frances W.	(PQ)	3
FERAHIAN, Salwa	(PQ)	371
MCKENZIE, Donald R.	(PQ)	811
POON, Paul W.	(HKG)	983

Public services administration	SHELTON, Kathryn H.	(AK)	1126
	ADAMS, Judith A.	(AL)	5
	CLARK, Alice S.	(CA)	216
	LEWIS, Alfred J.	(CA)	722
	MCELROY, Neil J.	(CA)	804
	CLEMENS, Bonnie J.	(GA)	220
	BINGHAM, Karen H.	(IL)	97
	VANCIL, David E.	(IN)	1273
	LIPPINCOTT, Joan K.	(NY)	732
	THOMAS, Deborah A.	(PA)	1236
	JOSEPH, Margaret A.	(TX)	617
Public services & access	STROUP, Elizabeth F.	(DC)	1203
Public services & orientations	LEVESQUE, Nancy B.	(BC)	719
Public services & public relations	PETERSON, Paul A.	(MO)	964
Public services & reference	BASART, Ann P.	(CA)	62
	THELIN, Sonya R.	(CA)	1234
	SCHEIN, Lorraine S.	(NY)	1091
	APPLETON, Brenda F.	(BC)	30
Public services & references	GRANITZ, Adrienne D.	(VA)	457
Public services development	NEWMAN, Marianne L.	(OH)	899
Public services, general reference	DRAGOTTA, Linda L.	(PA)	318
Public services high quality	TURNER, Kathleen G.	(WA)	1264
Public services in health sciences	BLACK, Lawrence	(NY)	101
Public services in libraries	MURPHY, Marcy	(IN)	881
Public services information	MURRAY, Bruce C.	(MD)	881
Public services, law	BLAKE, Timothy J.	(LA)	103
Public services learning for disabled	KEYS, Marshall	(MA)	645
Public services management	NITECKI, Danuta A.	(MD)	905
	DEYOUNG, Gail O.	(MI)	298
	MALOY, Frances	(NY)	764
	CONIGLIO, Jamie W.	(VA)	236
	LEGERE, Monique E.	(ON)	712
Public services, music libraries	BERMAN, Marsha	(CA)	88
Public services, online searching	GILLETTE, Meredith	(WI)	435
Public services policies, planning	ICKES, Barbara J.	(PA)	581
Public services reference	STEPHENS, Diana C.	(HI)	1188
	COAN, La V.	(MI)	224
Public services reference & information	GRAY, Patricia B.	(VA)	460
Public services, reference services	LANE, David M.	(NH)	694
Public services, research & reference	FRENCH, Thomas R.	(OH)	402
Public services systems	BAKER, Shirley K.	(MA)	49

PUBLIC SERVICES (Cont'd)

Reference & public service	SCHAPIRO, Benjamin H.	(IL)	1090
	WOLF, Joy G.	(MN)	1360
	MARKSON, Eileen	(PA)	771
	FOWLER, Margaret A.	(MB)	394
Reference & public services	GELFAND, Julia M.	(CA)	426
	BOLLIER, John A.	(CT)	112
	WRIGHT, Joyce C.	(IL)	1372
	HEWISON, Nancy S.	(IN)	535
	KRESSE, Kerry L.	(KY)	678
	HILDITCH, Bonny M.	(MD)	539
	LEV, Yvonne T.	(MD)	719
	HALL, Lawrence E.	(MI)	488
	WALDERA, Katherine A.	(ND)	1294
	CRESCENZI, Jean D.	(NJ)	258
	SCHUT, Grace W.	(NJ)	1103
	ZULEWSKI, Gerald J.	(NJ)	1391
	TEVEBAUGH, Joyce E.	(TX)	1233
	MERCHANT, Thomas L.	(WI)	825
	DANCIK, Deborah B.	(AB)	272
	DEBRUIJN, Deborah I.	(AB)	285
Reference, public services	SUMMERS, Sheryl H.	(MI)	1209
	SAUNDERS, William B.	(PA)	1085
Special library public service	GOLDMAN, Nancy L.	(CA)	445
Supervision of public services	COUSINS, Gloria D.	(NC)	252
Technical & public services	RAMBLER, Linda K.	(PA)	1005
Training & public service	DERRICKSON, Margaret	(NY)	294

PUBLICATIONS (See also Imprints)

Abstracting newsletter publications	KOVITZ, Nancy R.	(IL)	674
Advising a student publication	MASON, John A.	(IL)	781
Alternative press publication	FROST, Michelle	(CA)	406
Archival publications consltng & editing	MARRELLI, Nancy M.	(PQ)	773
Artists' books & publications	HOFFBERG, Judith A.	(CA)	547
British & Commonwealth govt publications	BEAN, Charles W.	(DC)	69
Business & government publications	IVES, Peter B.	(NM)	586
Business reference publications	DITMARS, Robert D.	(NJ)	305
	SIMON, David H.	(NJ)	1140
Canadian federal government publications	ROSE, Frances E.	(BC)	1054
Canadian government publications	WIHBEY, Francis R.	(ME)	1337
	NIELSON, Paul F.	(MB)	903
Catalog editing & publication	HENDRICKSON, Norma K.	(DC)	527
Cataloging in publication	PARENT, Ingrid T.	(ON)	940
	SIMARD, Luc	(ON)	1139
CD-ROM publications	MCSPADDEN, Robert M.	(OH)	818
Community newspaper publication	COMPRI, Jeannine L.	(AB)	235
Congressional publications	SEELE, Ronald E.	(DC)	1111
Criminal justice publications	KUEHNLE, Emery C.	(OH)	682
Current awareness publications	CURTIS, Richard A.	(CA)	267
Economic outlook publications	HARTMAN, David G.	(MA)	508
Editing & designing publications	SHUMAN, Marilyn J.	(IL)	1134
Editing in-house publications	MINOR, Barbara B.	(NY)	846
Editing professional publications	SCHEETZ, Mary D.	(PA)	1091
Editing publications	WOLFSON, Catherine L.	(AZ)	1361
Federal & depository publications	FOSTER, Leslie A.	(WI)	392
Federal & state government publications	BROWN, Philip L.	(SD)	146
Federal government publications	STRAITON, T H.	(AL)	1199
	CALDWELL, George H.	(DC)	172
	EWING, Jerry L.	(MO)	359
	PANDIT, Jyoti P.	(NY)	937
Federal publications	SCULLY, Mark F.	(DC)	1109
	PARSONS, Kathy A.	(IA)	945
	KECK, Kerry A.	(TX)	633
Federal Register publications	BYRNE, John E.	(DC)	169
Federal, state, local govt publications	NAKATA, Yuri	(OR)	887
Films, publications & teaching aids	FORREST, Phyllis E.	(DC)	391
Foreign government publications	MAACK, David J.	(WA)	753
Foreign official publications	MARLEAU, Gilles	(ON)	772
French language publication	BERNARD, Marie L.	(AB)	88
Government document publications	DOUGLAS-BONNELL, Eileen	(PQ)	314
Government documents & publications	SINGH, Swarn L.	(KS)	1143
	HENSON, Stephen	(LA)	530
	WALSH, Jim	(MA)	1299

PUBLICATIONS (Cont'd)

Government documents, publications, info			
Government information, publications	WILLIAMSON, Linda E.	(IL)	1347
	HINZ, Julianne P.	(UT)	543
Government Printing Office publications			
Government publication	MAST, Joanne	(PA)	782
Government publications	WHITBECK, George W.	(IN)	1329
	HOGAN, Catherine R.	(AL)	549
	REAGAN, Agnes L.	(AR)	1012
	ANDERSEN, Thomas K.	(CA)	21
	DINTRONE, Charles V.	(CA)	305
	HAGEN, Dennis D.	(CA)	483
	HORN, Judy K.	(CA)	559
	LINVILLE, Herbert	(CA)	731
	MITTAN, Rhonda L.	(CA)	850
	MOONEY, Margaret T.	(CA)	858
	BYRNE, Timothy L.	(CO)	169
	SCHULZE, Suzanne S.	(CO)	1102
	KONERDING, Erhard F.	(CT)	670
	DANIELSON, Wilfred D.	(DC)	273
	PUCCIO, Joseph A.	(DC)	997
	MECRAY, Freida S.	(DE)	820
	ROEHLING, Steven R.	(GA)	1048
	STEVENS, Robert D.	(HI)	1190
	KOHLER, Carolyn W.	(IA)	668
	MOODY, Marilyn K.	(IA)	857
	VAN DE VOORDE, Philip E.	(IA)	1274
	WILKINSON, Patrick J.	(IA)	1340
	MANCUYAS, Natividad D.	(IL)	764
	NOLLEN, Sheila H.	(IL)	908
	STEWART, James A.	(IL)	1192
	STRANGE, Michele M.	(IL)	1200
	WEECH, Terry L.	(IL)	1315
	DAVISON, Ruth M.	(IN)	281
	FRY, Bernard M.	(IN)	406
	HAYES, Stephen M.	(IN)	516
	SCHMIDT, Kathy W.	(IN)	1095
	VIOLETTE, Judith L.	(IN)	1285
	KLOSTERMANN, Helen M.	(KS)	662
	CAMMARATA, Paul J.	(KY)	175
	MCANINCH, Sandra L.	(KY)	792
	BURG, Barbara A.	(MA)	159
	PARKER, Susan E.	(MA)	942
	BEHLES, Patricia A.	(MD)	74
	SCHWARZKOPF, Leroy C.	(MD)	1105
	GUNN, Arthur C.	(MI)	477
	ELLIOTT, Gwendolyn W.	(MN)	344
	LA BISSONIERE, William R.	(MN)	686
	KESSLER, Ridley R.	(NC)	645
	FETZER, Mary K.	(NJ)	374
	PROFETA, Patricia C.	(NJ)	995
	BROWN, Eulalie W.	(NM)	143
	MCGUIRE, Laura H.	(NM)	808
	HERMAN, Edward	(NY)	531
	LARSEN, Joan A.	(NY)	698
	WELSH, Harry E.	(NY)	1323
	YUKAWA, Masako	(NY)	1384
	HARPER, Lucy B.	(OH)	503
	SALT, Elizabeth A.	(OH)	1077
	BAHR, Alice H.	(PA)	45
	BARON, Herman	(PA)	58
	FERYOK, Joseph A.	(PA)	374
	MORPHET, Norman D.	(PA)	865
	SCHNEIDER, Stewart P.	(RI)	1097
	VOCINO, Michael C.	(RI)	1286
	ROBINSON, William C.	(TN)	1045
	WEDIG, Eric M.	(TN)	1315
	JOHNSON, Johanna H.	(TX)	606
	LEE, Frank	(TX)	709
	MORRIS, Pamela A.	(TX)	867
	MORRISON, David L.	(UT)	868
	SMITH, Ruth S.	(VA)	1160
	FUGATE, Cynthia S.	(WA)	408
	MAACK, David J.	(WA)	753
	SY, Karen J.	(WA)	1217
	GERLACH, Donald E.	(WI)	429

PUBLICATIONS (Cont'd)
Government publications

	HEBDITCH, Suzan A.	(AB)	519
	DODSON, Suzanne C.	(BC)	308
	FOOTE, Martha L.	(ON)	388
	HAJNAL, Peter I.	(ON)	484
	LAND, Reginald B.	(ON)	692
	MONTY, Vivienne	(ON)	857
	RHYNAS, Don M.	(ON)	1026

Government publications, access to info	WHITAKER, Constance C.	(OH)	1329
Government publications & databases	FELDMAN, Eleanor C.	(MD)	369
Government publications collections	MILLER, Mary E.	(PA)	840
Government publications reference srv	CALHOUN, Ellen	(NJ)	172
Hard-copy publication	OLMSTEAD, Marcia E.	(ON)	921
Index publications	LEINBACH, Anne E.	(PA)	714
Indexing journals, serial publications	POST, Joyce A.	(PA)	986
Institutional publications	GOODMAN, L D.	(CA)	449
International government publications	ALEXANDER, Liz C.	(IL)	12
	MAACK, David J.	(WA)	753
Intl Governmental Organizations Pubns	RUHLIN, Michele T.	(UT)	1066
International official publications	MARLEAU, Gilles	(ON)	772
International organization publications	RYAN, Richard A.	(OH)	1071
Jazz publications	COHEN, Frederick S.	(NY)	228
Journals, technical publications	FINDLING, Carol A.	(NE)	377
Legal & tax publications	FLEMING, Jack C.	(ON)	384
Library publications	ARIEL, Joan	(CA)	31
	BERNER, Andrew J.	(NY)	88
	WOO, Janice	(NY)	1363
	NAISMITH, Rachael	(PA)	887
Library publications & publicity	BUSER, Robin A.	(KY)	165
Library publications, user aids	OSTROW, Rona	(NY)	929
Library systems, research & publications	MWALIMU, Charles	(DC)	884
Local government publications & records	HEWLETT, Carol C.	(TN)	535
Manuscripts & publications acquisitions	VIOL, Robert W.	(OH)	1285
Minority publications	DANKY, James P.	(WI)	274
Music publications	NOVITSKY, Edward G.	(NY)	911
Music publications, editorial	MAYER, George L.	(NY)	789
Music publications, reviewer	MAYER, George L.	(NY)	789
Nebraska state publications	FROBOM, Jerome B.	(NE)	405
New publication development	NASSO, Christine	(MI)	889
	SCHMITTROTH, John	(MI)	1096
Official publications	BERNIER, Gaston	(PQ)	89
Oral history catalog publication	KENDRICK, Alice M.	(NY)	640
Photographic productions & publications	SPINA, Marie C.	(NY)	1175
Preparing current awareness publications	MILTON, Ardyce A.	(WI)	845
Product, publication acquisition	QUINLIN, Margaret M.	(MD)	1000
Professional publications & reviewing	CHEATHAM, Bertha M.	(NY)	204
Professional reference accounting pubns	HALPIN, Gerard B.	(ON)	490
Professional reference law publications	HALPIN, Gerard B.	(ON)	490
Promotional publications	FRISCH, Corrine A.	(IL)	405
Provincial government publications	ROSE, Frances E.	(BC)	1054
Public programming & publications	MOLTKE-HANSEN, David	(SC)	853
Public relations & publications	KUHN, Warren B.	(IA)	682
Public relations, publications	MONTANA, Edward J.	(MA)	855
Publication	PEATTIE, Noel	(CA)	953
	WELLINGTON, Carol S.	(MA)	1321
	SCHLESSINGER, Bernard S.	(TX)	1094
	BOWES, Laurie A.	(ON)	121
Publication clearance	SEAGER, Janice R.	(NJ)	1109
Publication development	QUINLIN, Margaret M.	(MD)	1000
Publication, quarterly & annual indexes	SIVE, Mary R.	(CT)	1144
Publication sales	MIDDLETON, Carl H.	(DC)	833
Publication services, books, newsletters	MOLLO, Terry	(NY)	853
Publications	AUSTIN, Stephen	(CA)	40
	FLANAGAN, Leo N.	(CT)	383
	WOODS, Susan E.	(FL)	1367
	YATES, Donald N.	(IN)	1378

PUBLICATIONS (Cont'd)
Publications

	CARPENTER, Kenneth E.	(MA)	185
	KONESKI-WHITE, Bonnie L.	(MA)	670
	MENDELL, Stefanie	(NC)	823
	POUND, Mary E.	(TX)	987
	BRIERE, Jean M.	(ON)	135

Publications about handicapped persons	HOLT, June C.	(MA)	554
Publications & communications	MOORE, Grace G.	(LA)	859
Publications design & development	STEPHENSON, Judy A.	(KY)	1188
Publications development	KITZMILLER, Virginia G.	(DC)	657
	COLBORN, Robert J.	(MD)	230
Publications distribution management	LEONARD, Lawrence E.	(DC)	716
Publications editing & writing	SHIRES, Nancy P.	(NC)	1131
Publications management	MORSE, June E.	(VA)	869
Publications procurement	CROWTHER, Carol	(CA)	262
Reference & publications	KAHLER, Mary E.	(DC)	622
Reference book publications	KNAPPMAN, Edward W.	(NY)	663
Reference publication design	STONE, Nancy Y.	(MI)	1197
Research & publication	LANDIS, Dennis C.	(RI)	693
Reviewing for publication	FOX, Estella E.	(KY)	394
Scholarly publication in video	O'CONNOR, Brian C.	(CA)	915
Scientific & technical publications	ELSBREE, John J.	(VA)	346
Serials, government publications	ZIMMERMAN, Martha B.	(MD)	1389
Small press publications	ROM, Cristine C.	(OH)	1052
State & local government publications	SULZER, John H.	(PA)	1209
State publication	PARSONS, Kathy A.	(IA)	945
State publications	WEDIG, Eric M.	(TN)	1315
	KECK, Kerry A.	(TX)	633
Statute publication	MCKEE, James E.	(MN)	810
Tax publishings	DANNE, William H.	(IL)	274
Technical publications	VARA, Margaret E.	(OH)	1278
	FREEDMAN, Bernadette	(PA)	400
Travel directory publications	BUZAN, Norma J.	(MI)	168
United Nations publications	RUHLIN, Michele T.	(UT)	1066
United States federal publications	SLOAN, Tom W.	(AL)	1150
	MCCLEARY, William E.	(LA)	796
United States government publications	DOWNS, Charles F.	(DC)	317
	TRAUTMAN, Maryellen	(DC)	1254
	WOODWARD, Lawrence W.	(DC)	1368
	WIHBEY, Francis R.	(ME)	1337
	FROBOM, Jerome B.	(NE)	405
	POWELL, Margaret S.	(OH)	988
	BELEU, Steve	(OK)	76
	BERWIND, Anne M.	(TN)	91
	BRADLEY, C D.	(TX)	125
World economic outlook publications	HARTMAN, David G.	(MA)	508
Writing for publication	WEAVER, Carolyn G.	(WA)	1312

PUBLICITY (See also Advertising, Promotion, Public Relations)

Book promotion & publicity	BIANCO, David P.	(MI)	94
Collection development & publicity	HAMMER, Louise K.	(IL)	493
Exhibits & publicity	COPLAN, Kate M.	(MD)	244
Library outreach & publicity	BURKE, Lauri K.	(RI)	160
Library publications & publicity	BUSER, Robin A.	(KY)	165
Marketing & publicity	ASU, Glynis V.	(WI)	37
Programming & publicity	OLIANSKY, Joseph D.	(MA)	920
Promotions, publicity & programs	HANNAFORD, Claudia L.	(OH)	496
Public library programming & publicity	MORRISON, Meris E.	(VT)	868
Public relations & publicity	ULBRICH, David E.	(VA)	1268
Public relations, publicity	GODBEY, Esther R.	(AR)	442
	MARGOLIS, Bernard A.	(MI)	770
	MOSES, Lynn M.	(PA)	871
Publicity	POIRIER, Maria K.	(CT)	980
	ELDER, Jane D.	(FL)	342
	GRUBMAN, Donna Y.	(FL)	474
	JACKSON, Audrey N.	(LA)	586
	POMERANTZ, Bruce F.	(OH)	982
	FRENCH, Randy A.	(VA)	402
Publicity & displays	PIKE, Nancy M.	(FL)	973
Publicity & promotion	DRAGOTTA, Linda L.	(PA)	318
Publicity & public relations	CARLSON, Alan C.	(CA)	182
	ERLICH, Martin	(CA)	353
	BEAN, Rick J.	(IL)	69
	WEIKUM, James M.	(MN)	1317

PUBLICITY (Cont'd)

Publicity & public relations
  DINERMAN, Gloria . . . . . (NJ) 304
Publicity, public & community
  relations PIANE, Mimi . . . . (IN) 969
Publicity, reference LARSON, Josephine . . . . (NC) 699
Writing & display publicity BOYD, Ruth E. . . . . (CO) 122
Young adult books promotion &
  publicity JACKSON, Nancy D. . . . (NY) 588

PUBLISHING (See also Incunabula, Micropublishing, Prepress, Press, Printing)

Adult new readers publishing RYAN, Jenny L. . . . . (NY) 1071
Advertising databases & publishing LITTLE, Dean K. . . . . (OH) 733
Art & reference publishing MCGILVERY, Laurence . (CA) 806
Automated publishing support GRIMES, Judith E. . . . . . (MD) 470
Bibliographic data publishing TARR, Susan M. . . . . . . (DC) 1224
Bibliography & publishing WOLTER, John A. . . . . . (DC) 1362
Book & directory publishing CSENGE, Maragaret L. . . (NY) 262
Book & journal publishing FAHERTY, Robert L. . . . (DC) 361
Book & periodical publishing MECKLER, Alan M. . . . . (CT) 820
  WOOD, Richard T. . . . . . (MI) 1365
Book publishing WALCH, Timothy G. . . . . (DC) 1293
  ALLEN, Walter C. . . . . . . (IL) 16
  KING, Kenneth . . . . (MI) 651
  SHIDELER, John C. . . . . (WA) 1129
  DITTMER, Luther A. . . . . (WGR) 306
Book publishing, writing & editing EASTMAN, Ann H. . . . . . (VA) 333
Bookselling & publishing DOLE, Wanda V. . . . . . . (PA) 309
Business & industrial publishing SAFRAN, Scott A. . . . . . (NY) 1074
Business & information publishing HOLLY, James H. . . . . . . (CA) 552
Business development, electronic
  publshg GROSSMAN, Allen N. . . (NJ) 473
Business publishing KLAUS, Roger D. . . . . . . (IL) 658
CD-ROM database publishing POOLEY, Christopher G. . (MA) 983
CD-ROM publisher CHRISTIANSEN, Eric G. (OH) 211
CD-ROM publishing MILLER, Davic C. . . . . . (CA) 836
  DICK, John H. . . . . (IL) 300
  STEPHENSON, Jon R. . . (PA) 1188
  LEDOUX, Marc A. . . . . . (PQ) 708
CD-ROM publishing applications KNOERDEL, Joan E. . . . (MD) 665
Children's book publishing SUTHERLAND, Zena B. . (IL) 1211
  EPSTEIN, Connie C. . . . . (NY) 351
Children's books, publishing &
  libraries BOTHAM, Jane . . . . . . (WI) 118
Classification schedules publishing DERSHEM, Larry D. . . . . (CA) 294
College software publishing NEEDHAM, Michael V. . . (CA) 891
College textbook publisher THORNTON, Jack N. . . . (CA) 1242
College textbook publishing NEEDHAM, Michael V. . . (CA) 891
Computer desktop publishing MOLLO, Terry . . . . (NY) 853
Consulting information, publishing CHICOREL, Marietta S. . (AZ) 208
Consulting to educational publishers MOSELEY, Cameron S. . (NY) 870
Contemporary publishing GATES, Jean K. . . . . . . (FL) 422
Corporate electronic publishing
  systems PETERSON, George B. . (MD) 963
Corporate printing & publishing ARNSDORF, Dennis A. . (DC) 34
Data preparation electronic publishing KERR, Robert C. . . . . . (CO) 644
Database information publishing RICCOBONO, Joseph V. (CT) 1026
Database publishing HOLLY, James H. . . . . . (CA) 552
  SCLAR, Herbert . . . . (CA) 1106
  ATKIN, Michael I. . . . . . . (DC) 37
  TRIGAUX, Robert . . . . . . (DC) 1256
  URBACH, Peter F. . . . . . (MA) 1269
  MCRAE, Alexander D. . . (MD) 818
  HART, Patricia H. . . . . . . (MI) 507
  WERLING, Anita L. . . . . (MI) 1324
  ALLAN, John . . . . (NY) 14
  BURKE, Edward . . . . . . (NY) 160
  FINCH, Brian . . . . (NY) 377
  FREY, Ned . . . . (NY) 402
  HENDERSON, Brad . . . . (NY) 526
  KRAUS, James . . . . (NY) 676
  MACFARLAND, Scott D. (NY) 755
  MALKIN, Peter . . . . (NY) 763
  NOVEMBER, Robert S. . (NY) 911
  REDEL, Judy A. . . . . . . (NY) 1014
  RUSLING, Con A. . . . . . (NY) 1068
  SIMON, Peter E. . . . . . . (NY) 1140
  TYSON, David . . . . (NY) 1267

PUBLISHING (Cont'd)

Database publishing
  VELLA, Carl . . . . (NY) 1281
  ZIMMERMAN, William . . (NY) 1389
Database publishing & development PRICKETT, Dan S. . . . . . (OH) 993
Database publishing applications KNOERDEL, Joan E. . . . (MD) 665
Desktop publishing CISLER, Stephen A. . . . . (CA) 215
  COYLE, Leslie P. . . . . . . (CA) 253
  ELLIOT, Hugh . . . . (DC) 343
  DICK, John H. . . . . (IL) 300
  MCKENZIE, Duncan J. . . (IL) 811
  VACCARO, William J. . . . (IL) 1270
  BOZOIAN, Paula . . . . . . (MA) 124
  PAPALAMBROS, Rita G. (MA) 939
  BRUTON, Robert T. . . . . (MN) 151
  KEIM, Robert . . . . (MN) 635
  BROWN, Stanley W. . . . (NH) 147
  ANDERSON, Eric S. . . . (OH) 22
  PITCHON, Cindy A. . . . . (PA) 976
  KRUSE, Luanne M. . . . . (TX) 681
  LIVNY, Efrat . . . . (WI) 735
  WESTERN, Eric D. . . . . . (WI) 1327
Dictionary publishing NAULT, William H. . . . . . (IL) 889
Directory compilation & publishing SCARBOROUGH,
  Katharine T. . . . . (CA) 1087
Directory publishing D'ADOLF, Steven P. . . . . (CA) 269
  KIMMEL, Mark R. . . . . . (MD) 649
  MARLOW, Cecilia A. . . . (MI) 772
  SCHMITTROTH, John . . (MI) 1096
  GREENFIELD, Stanley R. (NY) 464
  DARLINGTON, Susan . . (PQ) 275
Early printing & publishing GONIWIECHA, Mark C. . (AK) 447
Editing & publishing ALLEY, Brian . . . . (IL) 16
  EBERHART, George M. . (IL) 334
  RICHMOND, Robert W. . (KS) 1031
  GATTIS, R G. . . . . (MI) 422
  READE, Judith G. . . . . . (NS) 1012
Editorial publishing PLOTNIK, Arthur . . . . . . (IL) 978
  PEDOLSKY, Andrea D. . (NY) 954
Editorials & publishing STEVENS, Stanley D. . . . (CA) 1191
Electronic prepress publishing
  systems BRAWLEY, Paul H. . . . . (IL) 130
Electronic printing & publishing GRIMES, Judith E. . . . . . (MD) 470
Electronic publishing BUTLER, Matilda L. . . . . (CA) 167
  CARSON, Susan A. . . . . (CA) 188
  LIGHTBOWN, Parke P. . (CA) 726
  PAISLEY, William J. . . . . (CA) 935
  SPIGAI, Fran . . . . (CA) 1174
  ZOELLICK, Bill . . . . (CO) 1390
  SABOSIK, Patricia E. . . . (CT) 1073
  LEE, Joel M. . . . . (IL) 710
  MANDEL, Douglas J. . . . (IL) 765
  REEDY, Martha J. . . . . . (MA) 1015
  BEATTY, Samuel B. . . . . (MD) 70
  MCRAE, Alexander D. . . (MD) 818
  MEYER, Alan H. . . . . . . (MD) 829
  PATRICIU, Florin S. . . . . (MD) 947
  STEIGER, Bettie A. . . . . (MD) 1185
  ADLER, Robert J. . . . . . . (MI) 7
  SMILLIE, Pauline A. . . . . (MI) 1151
  KEIM, Robert . . . . (MN) 635
  DEMAS, Samuel G. . . . . (NY) 291
  PAUL, Sandra K. . . . . . . (NY) 949
  REGAZZI, John J. . . . . . (NY) 1017
  SIMON, Peter F . . . . (NY) 1140
  MAYNARD, John C. . . . . (ON) 790
  OLSHEN, Toni . . . . (ON) 922
  CUSWORTH, George R. . (ENG) 267
Electronic publishing & merchandising MOFFITT, Michael D. . . . (MA) 852
Electronic publishing consulting BERUL, Lawrence H. . . . (MD) 91
Electronic publishing contracting BROWN-SPRUILL, Debra
  K. . . . . (NY) 149
Electronic publishing service CONTESSA, William B. . (NY) 239
Encyclopedia publishing GOSDEN, George . . . . . (NY) 452
Financial news & publishing CASEY, Robert W. . . . . . (NY) 192
Financial printing & publishing ARNSDORF, Dennis A. . (DC) 34
Financial publishing TIERNEY, Richard H. . . . (NY) 1244
Fine press publisher ALTERMAN, Deborah H. . (NJ) 18
Fundraising, book publishing & writing GRAVES, Sid F. . . . . (MS) 459
General publishing business JACHINO, Robert J. . . . . (NY) 586

PUBLISHING (Cont'd)

General reference publishing	NAULT, William H.	(IL)	889
History of printing & publishing	DUGGAN, Mary K.	(CA)	324
Information publishing	GREENWAY, Helen B.	(CT)	465
	SEVERTSON, Susan M.	(VA)	1117
Information publishing, professionals	RICCOBONO, Joseph V.	(CT)	1026
Information science, publishing research	DINGLE, Susan	(PA)	304
International profsnl & academic publshg	SMITH, Richard A.	(CA)	1159
Intl publishing, student editions	HARMON, James R.	(NY)	502
Journal & magazine publishing	BRAWLEY, Paul H.	(IL)	130
Journals publishing	COHEN, Bill	(NY)	228
	HUNTER, Karen A.	(NY)	576
	KING, Timothy B.	(NY)	652
Laser optic publishing services	ALCOCK, Anthony J.	(CA)	11
Law book publishing	DANNE, William H.	(IL)	274
	MORSE, Alan L.	(NY)	869
	KUEHNLE, Emery C.	(OH)	682
	WALSH, Sharon T.	(PA)	1300
Law publishing	HALE, William B.	(NY)	486
	GATES, Robert G.	(OH)	422
Legal database publishing	STERN, Michael P.	(MD)	1189
Legal information publishing	HALL, Brian H.	(CO)	487
Legal printing & publishing	ARNSDORF, Dennis A.	(DC)	34
Legal publishing	DEGLER, Stanley E.	(DC)	287
	KLAUS, Roger D.	(IL)	658
	DESMOND, Andrew R.	(NY)	295
	CUSWORTH, George R.	(ENG)	267
Legal publishing & databases	COLBORN, Robert J.	(MD)	230
Legal publishing & indexing	SHERRILL, Jocelyn T.	(NY)	1129
Library & information publishing	GOLD, Renee L.	(NY)	444
Library publishing	STEWART, Donald E.	(IL)	1192
Library research & publishing	WOOD, Richard J.	(SC)	1365
Library science editing & publishing	CASINI, Barbara P.	(PA)	192
Library science publishing	COHEN, Bill	(NY)	228
Magazine publishing	MACIUSZKO, Kathleen L.	(OH)	755
	BROWN, Kent L.	(PA)	145
Magazine publishing & editing	LEHURAY, Stephen D.	(MD)	713
Management of publishing operations	BOYD, Joseph W.	(IL)	122
Market entry foreign publishers	PICKETT, Doyle C.	(NJ)	970
Medical book publishing	FORD, Andrew E.	(NY)	389
Medical publishing	TAKACS, Sharon N.	(IL)	1220
	PATTERSON, Anne S.	(MD)	948
Mergers & acquisitions in publishing	BODDORF, James E.	(NY)	109
	DRONZEK, Ronald	(NY)	320
	HADLEY, J M.	(NY)	482
	HALE, Paul E.	(NY)	485
	HUNNEWELL, Walter	(NY)	574
	LAMB, David C.	(NY)	689
	SCHULTE, Anthony M.	(NY)	1101
	SHAPIRO, Marvin L.	(NY)	1121
	STEVENSON, Jeffery T.	(NY)	1191
	SUHLER, John S.	(NY)	1207
	VERONIS, John J.	(NY)	1283
Microcomputer appls/electronic publshg	HULSEY, Richard A.	(MI)	573
Microform publishing	DUPONT, A J.	(HI)	327
	SEVERTSON, Susan M.	(VA)	1117
Music bibliography & publishing	BRYCE, Maria C.	(ON)	152
Newsletter publishing	SEIDENBERG, Edward	(TX)	1112
Newsletter publishing & editing	TAYLOR, David C.	(NC)	1226
Newspaper & publisher database systems	PASCHAL, John M.	(OK)	945
Newspaper publishing	TRIGAUX, Robert	(DC)	1256
	ALLAN, John	(NY)	14
	BURKE, Edward	(NY)	160
	FINCH, Brian	(NY)	377
	FREY, Ned	(NY)	402
	HENDERSON, Brad	(NY)	526
	KRAUS, James	(NY)	676
	MALKIN, Peter	(NY)	763
	NOVEMBER, Robert S.	(NY)	911
	RUSLING, Con A.	(NY)	1068
	TYSON, David	(NY)	1267
	VELLA, Carl	(NY)	1281
	ZIMMERMAN, William	(NY)	1389
Nursing book publishing	FORD, Andrew E.	(NY)	389
On demand publishing	SCLAR, Herbert	(CA)	1106
On-demand publishing	FITZSIMMONS, Joseph J.	(MI)	383

PUBLISHING (Cont'd)

Online database, electronic publishing	HERRICK, Carol L.	(OH)	532
Optical disk publishing	ZOELLICK, Bill	(CO)	1390
Optical storage & publishing	HERTHER, Nancy K.	(MN)	533
Performing arts publishing	PINE, Ralph	(NY)	974
Personal computer desktop publishing	BALCOM, Karen S.	(TX)	51
Photocopy reprints publishing	BROWN, G R.	(FL)	144
Prerevolutionary Russian publishing	BEAVEN, Miranda J.	(MN)	71
Printing & publishing	LASH, David B.	(NY)	700
	CHALIFOUX, Jean P.	(PQ)	197
Printing & publishing history	BIDWELL, John	(CA)	95
Printing & publishing in Asia	DIEHL, Katharine S.	(TX)	302
Professional & reference publishing	QUINLIN, Margaret M.	(MD)	1000
Professional book publishing	KING, Timothy B.	(NY)	652
Professional publishing	DANNE, William H.	(IL)	274
	OLDERR, Steven	(IL)	920
Professional society publishing	FERRERE, Cathy M.	(NY)	373
Public relations, desktop publishing	WEIDEMANN, Margaret A.	(NY)	1316
Public relations, including publishing	EVANS, Gwynneth	(ON)	357
Public relations, publishing, budgeting	ARROWOOD, Donna J.	(CA)	34
Public relations, writing & publishing	ROUSE, Roscoe	(OK)	1061
Publish high tech reference books	CONNORS, Martin G.	(MI)	238
Publisher	FOX, Elyse H.	(MA)	394
Publisher & library relations	HUNTER, Karen A.	(NY)	576
Publisher of electronic services	HYLAND, Barbara	(ON)	580
Publisher of legal translations	SCHLACKS, Charles	(CA)	1093
Publishers & publishing	CONNORS, Linda E.	(NJ)	238
Publishing	NEAVILL, Gordon B.	(AL)	891
	CHICOREL, Marietta S.	(AZ)	208
	PARRY, Pamela J.	(AZ)	944
	HAMILTON, David M.	(CA)	491
	KENEFICK, Mary L.	(CA)	640
	PERKINS, David L.	(CA)	959
	PLATE, Kenneth H.	(CA)	977
	ASH, Lee M.	(CT)	•35
	BALAY, Robert E.	(CT)	50
	GONZALEZ, Suzanna S.	(CT)	448
	KRAMER, Sheldon I.	(CT)	675
	SILVERSTEIN, Jeffrey S.	(CT)	1139
	BERNARD, Patrick S.	(DC)	88
	FARINA, Robert A.	(DC)	363
	PRATT, Dana J.	(DC)	990
	STEWART, Ruth A.	(DC)	1193
	CRIM, Dewey H.	(GA)	258
	BUCKLEY, Ja A.	(IL)	154
	DAVIS, Maryellen K.	(IL)	280
	DI MAURO, Paul	(IL)	304
	FLAGG, Gordon E.	(IL)	383
	HELLER, Dawn H.	(IL)	524
	MALINOWSKY, H R.	(IL)	763
	WRIGHT, Helen K.	(IL)	1371
	ISCA, Joseph J.	(IN)	585
	MIELE, Madeline F.	(MA)	833
	PRINDLE, Paul E.	(MA)	993
	SILVEY, Anita L.	(MA)	1139
	BREWER, Annie M.	(MI)	134
	DOUGHERTY, Ann P.	(MI)	313
	LIMBACHER, James L.	(MI)	727
	MAXWELL, Bonnie J.	(MI)	788
	RUFFNER, Frederick G.	(MI)	1066
	RUNCHOCK, Rita M.	(MI)	1067
	AMRON, Irving	(NJ)	20
	EDELMAN, Hendrik	(NJ)	335
	HOGAN, Thomas H.	(NJ)	549
	HORROCKS, Norman	(NJ)	561
	KOONTZ, John	(NJ)	671
	COHEN, Bill	(NY)	228
	HAUSRATH, Donald C.	(NY)	513
	IPPOLITO, Andrew V.	(NY)	583
	LERNER, Rita G.	(NY)	717
	SADER, Marion	(NY)	1073
	SCHUMAN, Patricia G.	(NY)	1103
	WITSENHAUSEN, Helen A.	(NY)	1358
	CORRIGAN, John T.	(PA)	247
	FISHER, Douglas A.	(PA)	380
	NEMEYER, Carol A.	(PA)	895
	HAMILTON, Wellington M.	(VA)	492
	KUNEY, Joseph H.	(VA)	684
	GERARD, James W.	(VT)	428

PUBLISHING (Cont'd)

Publishing

	MCCORMICK, Jack M. .	(WA)	798
	CHOUINARD, Germain . .	(PQ)	211
	LUSSIER, Richard	(PQ)	749
	GREEN, Jeffrey P.	(ENG)	462
Publishing administration	WEIDA, William A.	(OH)	1316
Publishing advice	ROBLING, John S.	(MI)	1045
Publishing & book distribution	GSTALDER, Herbert W. .	(NY)	475
Publishing & book trade	STUART-STUBBS, Basil F.	(BC)	1204
Publishing & consulting	DUMONT, Monique	(PQ)	325
Publishing & mail order	HAAS, Carolyn B.	(IL)	480
Publishing & marketing children's books	MASON, H J.	(NY)	781
Publishing & popular literature	TAYLOR, Margaret T. . . .	(MI)	1227
Publishing & printing	MEHNERT, Robert B. . . .	(MD)	821
Publishing & printing histories	BUSHMAN, James L. . . .	(OR)	165
Publishing book development	THOMPSON, Anne E. . . .	(AZ)	1238
Publishing consulting	FRISBIE, Richard	(IL)	405
Publishing database editing & design	THOMPSON, Anne E. . . .	(AZ)	1238
Publishing development	BOEHM, Ronald J.	(CA)	109
Publishing editing	THOMPSON, Anne E. . . .	(AZ)	1238
Publishing field	MCMANAMON, Mary J. . .	(MA)	814
Publishing for librarians	ESHELMAN, William R. .	(OH)	354
Publishing history	CLARK, Harry	(OK)	217
	GREEN, James N.	(PA)	462
	METZGER, Philip A.	(PA)	829
Publishing indexes	FAST, Louise	(ON)	366
Publishing information newsletters	LYONS, Ivan	(NY)	753
Publishing management	LEE, Judith C.	(CA)	710
Publishing monthly sales lists	SMITH, Walter H.	(VA)	1161
Publishing music reference books	BALK, Leo F.	(NY)	52
Publishing music reprints, facsimiles	BALK, Leo F.	(NY)	52
Publishing new music editions	BALK, Leo F.	(NY)	52
Publishing newsletters	SHALLEY, Doris P.	(PA)	1119
Publishing on CD-ROM	NICKEL, R S.	(PA)	902
Publishing policy development info	KLEIMAN, Gerald S.	(DC)	659
Publishing practices	TAYLOR, Raymond M. . . .	(NC)	1228
Publishing professional books & journals	GRAYSON, Martin	(NY)	460
Publishing, professional proceedings	JACOBS, Horace	(CA)	589
Publishing program management info	KLEIMAN, Gerald S.	(DC)	659
Publishing, reference	DAUB, Albert W.	(NJ)	275
Publishing reference books	BRYFONSKI, Dedria A. .	(MI)	152
Publishing research	LAGIES, Meinhart J.	(CA)	688
Publishing systems	KOPPELMAN, William H. .	(NY)	671
	PAUL, Sandra K.	(NY)	949
Publishing technology applications info	KLEIMAN, Gerald S.	(DC)	659
Reference & publishing	ROBERTS, Anne F.	(NY)	1039
Reference & research newspaper publshg	EGERTSON, Yvonne L. .	(VA)	339
Reference book publishing	MARLOW, Cecilia A. . . .	(MI)	772
	YOUNG, Margaret L. . . .	(MN)	1382
Reference book publishing & marketing	WHITELEY, Sandra M. . .	(IL)	1333
Reference product & publishing mgmt	BRAM, Leon L.	(NJ)	127
Reference publishing	LEACH, Sandra S.	(TN)	706
Reprint publishing	BOYD, Kenneth W.	(GA)	122
Sales, marketing & publishing	BECK, Arthur R.	(CT)	71
Scholarly & reference book publishing	BERKNER, Dimity S. . . .	(NY)	87
Scholarly music publishing	PAVLAKIS, Christopher .	(NY)	950
Scholarly publishing	MCCULLOH, Judith M. . .	(IL)	801
Secondary school publishing	IRELAND, Laverne H. . . .	(CA)	583
Small press publishing	KNIFFEL, Leonard J. . . .	(MI)	664
	SILVER, Gary L.	(MI)	1138
	THEWS, Dorothy D.	(MN)	1234
	CARTER, Charles R. . . .	(BC)	189
Sound music publishing	BOBB, Barry L.	(MO)	108
Spanish printing & publishing	RAMER, James D.	(AL)	1005
Tax publishing	KLAUS, Roger D.	(IL)	658
Teaching collection devlpmnt, publishing	HUMPHRY, James	(NY)	574
Technical publishing	DUNN, Richard L.	(PA)	327
Teletext electronic publishing	WILLIAMS, Fred	(GA)	1343
Textbook publishing	BROWN, Kent L.	(PA)	145
Writing, editing & publishing	JOHNSON, Richard D. . . .	(NY)	608

PULP

Pulp & paper databases	STAHL, Hella	(PQ)	1178
Pulp & paper literature	GAGNON, Vernon N. . . .	(OR)	412
Pulp & paper science, technology	HALL, Deanna M.	(GA)	487
Pulp, paper & forestry information	MARTINEZ, Linda W. . . .	(WA)	779

PUPPETRY

Children's programming, puppets	NORMAN, Nita V.	(AZ)	909
Experience in puppetry	BECKER, Barbara S. . . .	(NE)	72
Professional puppeteering	HILDEBRANT, Darrel D. .	(ND)	539
Puppet center	DUFF, Margaret K.	(CO)	323
Puppetry	JAMES, Karen G.	(KY)	592
	STEELE, Anitra T.	(MO)	1184
	KEEFE, Betty	(NE)	634
	WILLIAMS, Deborah H. .	(NY)	1342
	SCHWALB, Ann W.	(PA)	1104
	MEYER, Laura M.	(WA)	830
Puppets	PAULIN, Mary A.	(MI)	950
Storytelling & puppetry	LOWE, Joy L.	(LA)	744
	DELLER, A M.	(MI)	289
Storytelling with props & puppets	BROUSE, Ann G.	(NY)	141
Storytelling with puppets	CHAMPLIN, Constance J.	(IN)	198
Storytime & puppets	MITCHELL, Jan E.	(FL)	848

PURCHASING (See also Approval, Buying, Orders, Procurement, Requisition, Shopping)

Administration, purchasing, cataloging	HEDGES, Bonnie L.	(VA)	520
All media budget & purchase	DU CARMONT, M C. . . .	(LA)	322
Audiovisual equipment purchasing	SHARP, Betty L.	(TX)	1122
Book selection & purchase	GENSHAFT, Carole M. . .	(OH)	427
Budgeting & purchasing	ESPER, Elizabeth	(FL)	354
Cooperative purchase	LAUGHLIN, Beverly E. . .	(LA)	702
Curriculum-related material purchasing	SKELLY, Laurie J.	(MN)	1146
Government purchasing & marketing	KEATING, Michael F. . . .	(OH)	633
Library operations & purchasing	HEATH, Henry H.	(MD)	519
Library purchasing	EVERINGHAM, Neil G. . .	(VA)	358
Preview, evaluate & purchase films	NEBEL, Jean C.	(CA)	891
Purchase & acquisition	COMRAS, Rema	(FL)	235
Purchase & classification of books	LACAILLADE, Jacqueline	(PQ)	686
Purchase evaluation	MINNICH, Conrad H. . . .	(OH)	846
Purchase of nonfiction material	LAMBERT, Sandra L. . . .	(IL)	690
Purchasing	DANIEL, Alfred I.	(DE)	272
	STICK, Dorothy J.	(IA)	1193
	NIXON, Judith A.	(MD)	906
	MILLER, Marjorie M.	(PA)	840
	LAMOUREUX, Michele . .	(PQ)	691
Purchasing & acquisitions	RICHARD, Marie F.	(PQ)	1028
Purchasing & cataloging	MUNSEY, Joyce L.	(MD)	879
Purchasing & management	BERGER, Brenda L.	(NJ)	85
Purchasing medical books	POLLARD, Joan B.	(VA)	981
Purchasing research materials	KELLER, Dorothy B.	(CA)	635
Rare books purchase & sales	MCKITTRICK, Bruce W. .	(PA)	812
Selecting & purchasing books	JACKSON, Mildred E. . .	(MN)	588
Video & film purchasing	RICHIE, Mark L.	(NJ)	1030
Videotape purchasing & circulation	BARGAR, Arthur W.	(CT)	56

QL

QL database	KHAN, Asma S.	(ON)	646

QUACKERY

Health fraud & quackery	SERLING, Kitty	(MO)	1116

QUAKER

Quaker bibliography	DENSMORE, Christopher	(NY)	293

QUALITATIVE

Qualitative research methods	MELLON, Constance A. .	(NC)	822

QUALITY
Data quality   PIKE, Christine M. . . . . . (NJ) 972
Database design & quality control   VEGTER, Amy H. . . . . . . (NY) 1281
Database management & quality
  control   HOMAN, J M. . . . . (MI) 555
Database quality control   KOLMAN, Roberta F. . . . (HI) 669
General reference high quality   TURNER, Kathleen G. . . (WA) 1264
Library quality assurance   HOLST, Ruth M. . . . . (WI) 554
Micrographics & image quality   BAGG, Thomas C. . . . . . (MD) 45
Nuclear quality assurance   KNIGHTLY, John J. . . . . (TN) 664
Nuclear regulations & quality admin   KING, Betty J. . . . . . . (WA) 650
Public services high quality   TURNER, Kathleen G. . . (WA) 1264
Quality assurance   FREDENBURG, Anne M. . (MD) 399
Quality circles   WORDEN, Diane D. . . . . (MI) 1369
  CROCKER, Jane L. . . . . (NJ) 259
Quality control   AMELUNG, Richard C. . . (MO) 19
  DAVIS, Carol C. . . . . (OH) 277
Quality control & training   NADZIEJKA, David E. . . (WI) 886
Software system quality control   KOLMAN, Roberta F. . . . (HI) 669
  VEGTER, Amy H. . . . . . . (NY) 1281

QUANTITATIVE
Economic, statistical & quantitative std   KING, Donald W. . . . . . . (MD) 650
Quantitative analysis   FRETWELL, Gordon E. . . (MA) 402
Quantitative methods   TAGUE, Jean M. . . . . . . (ON) 1220

QUEBEC
Quebec legal bibliography   TANGUAY, Guy . . . . (PQ) 1222

QUESTIONING
Questioning techniques, lit discussions   SENATOR, Rochelle B. . (CT) 1115

QUILT
Quilt research & documentation,
  indexing   PARKER, Mary A. . . . . . (SC) 942

QUOTATIONS
Literary quotations   SHIPPS, Anthony W. . . . (IN) 1131
Stock & bond quotations   PAYNE, Linda C. . . . . . . (NY) 951

RACISM
Racism, sexism in media   ADAMS, Elaine P. . . . . . (TX) 4

RADIO (See also Broadcasting)
Film, television & radio   YEE, Martha M. . . . . (CA) 1379
  DAVIDSON, Steven I. . . . (NY) 276
Journalism, radio & television   CAROTHERS, Diane F. . . (IL) 184
Movies & radio formats consultation   SMITH, Walter H. . . . . . (VA) 1161
Radio & telecommunications   MERRYWEATHER, J M. . . (ON) 827
Radio archives   JOHNSON, Jane D. . . . . (CA) 605
Radio programming via satellite   WILLIAMS, Fred . . . . . . (GA) 1343
Television, radio production   BAYLES, Carmen L. . . . . (CT) 67

RADIOACTIVE
Radioactive waste   SHERMAN, Dottie . . . . . (CT) 1128
Radioactive waste management   CURRY, Lenora Y. . . . . . (NY) 266
  TRAUB, Teresa L. . . . . . (WA) 1254

RADIOECOLOGY
Radioecology   PFUDERER, Helen A. . . . (TN) 966

RADIOLOGY
Radiology information   EKSTRAND, Nancy L. . . (NC) 341

RAILROADS
Railroad archives   MUSICH, Gerald D. . . . . (WI) 883
Railroad history   MUTSCHLER, Charles V. . (WA) 883
Railroads   KOENEMAN, Joyce W. . . (DC) 668

RAIN
Acid rain   STOSS, Frederick W. . . . (NY) 1198

RARE (See also Antiquarian, Early, Editions, Manuscripts, Old, Out-of-Print, Unique)
Acquisition & evaluation of rare
  records   WAXMAN, Jack . . . . (FL) 1311
Acquisition of rare books   BUFF, Iva H. . . . . (NY) 155
Aeronautical history rare books   BARRETT, Donald J. . . . (CO) 59
Archival & rare books   YUILLE, Willie K. . . . . . (MD) 1384
  ROSS, David J. . . . . (NY) 1058
Archives & music rarities   WALKER, Elizabeth . . . . (PA) 1295
Archives & rare books   LARSGAARD, Mary L. . . (CO) 698
  STEVENS, Marjorie . . . . (MI) 1190
  TAYLOR, Carolyn L. . . . (MO) 1226
  HILL, Susan E. . . . . (TX) 540
  EDMONDS, Susan M. . . (WA) 336
  DESOMOGYI, Aileen A. . (ON) 295
Archives, rare books   RAY, Joyce M. . . . . (TX) 1011
Art & language rare books   COE, Miriam M. . . . . (LA) 226
Buying & selling of rare books   MARTIN, John W. . . . . . (IL) 776
Cataloging & collecting rare
  recordings   BROWNE, J P. . . . . (CA) 148
Cataloging rare books   LAND, Barbara J. . . . . . (CA) 692
  SMIRENSKY, Helen K. . . (NY) 1152
Cataloging, rare books, reference   STUFF, Marjorie . . . . . . (NE) 1205
Children's rare books   SEDNEY, Frances V. . . . (MD) 1111
Chinese rare books   KECSKES, Lily C. . . . . . (DC) 633
Education for rare books   BELANGER, Terry . . . . (NY) 76
Fundraising for rare books   IVES, Sidney E. . . . . . . (FL) 586
Hebrew manuscripts & rare books   KOHN, Roger S. . . . . . (NY) 668
Historical libraries & rare books   MERRIAM, Louise A. . . (WI) 826
History of books & rare books   WINCKLER, Paul A. . . . (NY) 1354
History of medical literature, rare bks   MIMS, Dorothy H. . . . . . (GA) 845
Japanese rare books   SEWELL, Robert G. . . . (NY) 1117
Legal bibliography, rare books   TRIFFIN, Nicholas . . . . (NY) 1256
Library school teaching of rare books   HEANEY, Howell J. . . . (PA) 518
Managing & appraising rare books   MICHAELS, Carolyn L. . (SC) 831
Manuscripts & rare books   YOUNG, Noraleen A. . . (IN) 1382
  ROUNDTREE, Lynn P. . . (LA) 1061
Manuscripts & rare books literary
  resrch   REIMAN, Donald H. . . . . (NY) 1020
Medical rare books   POND, Frederick C. . . . . (NY) 982
Natural history, rare books   DONAHUE, Katharine E. . (CA) 310
19th century US rare books   GARDNER, Ralph D. . . . (NY) 418
North Carolina rare books   TOMLINSON, Charles E. . (NC) 1250
Old & rare books   O'BRIEN, Francis M. . . . (ME) 914
Old & rare sound recordings   CHANDLER, Thomas V. . (CA) 200
Phonograph recordings & rare books   BROWNE, J P. . . . . (CA) 148
Preservation of rare books   HALEY, Marguerite R. . . (WA) 486
Rare & out-of-print art books   DAVIS, L C. . . . . (CA) 280
Rare & out-of-print books   SMITH, Nolan E. . . . . . . (CT) 1159
Rare & scholarly books   KIEFFER, Jay . . . . (CA) 647
Rare & special collection   PERSHE, Frank F. . . . . . (MO) 961
Rare art books   POCKROSE, Sheryl R. . . (OH) 979
Rare book acquisition & cataloging   COX, Shelley M. . . . . . . (IL) 253
Rare book appraisal   MARSHALL, Mary G. . . . (IL) 774
  HEANEY, Howell J. . . . . (PA) 518
Rare book cataloging   ZALL, Elisabeth W. . . . . (CA) 1386
  ROONEY, Eugene M. . . . (DC) 1053
  MARSHALL, Mary G. . . . (IL) 774
  MUELLER, Robert W. . . . (IL) 875
  RENSHAW, Marita . . . . . (IL) 1023
  SALAZAR, Pamela R. . . (NY) 1076
  FRITZ, William R. . . . . . (SC) 405
  GISSENDANNER,
   Cassandra S. . . . . (SC) 438
  HUMMEL, Ray O. . . . . . (VA) 573
  STAFFORD, Leva L. . . . (WY) 1178
Rare book collection   CAUSLEY, Monroe S. . . (NJ) 195
Rare book collections   SMITH, Ledell B. . . . . . (LA) 1157
  MULVIHILL, Maureen E. . (NY) 878
Rare book curator   PINKHAM, Eleanor H. . . (MI) 974
Rare book dealer   TWENEY, George H. . . . (WA) 1266
Rare book dealership   CADY, Richard H. . . . . . (IL) 170
Rare book librarianship   DUNLAP, Barbara J. . . . (NY) 326
Rare book library administration   KNACHEL, Philip A. . . . (DC) 663
Rare book library history   BELANGER, Terry . . . . (NY) 76
Rare book photographic services   MCKENNEY, Kathryn K. . (DE) 811

RARE (Cont'd)

Rare book preservation
Rare book research
Rare book sales
Rare books

BEDARD, Laura A.	(DC)	73
MONDLIN, Marvin	(NY)	854
MUELLER, Robert W.	(IL)	875
BRITT, Mary C.	(AL)	137
NELSON, Michael B.	(AL)	894
PFAU, Julia G.	(AL)	966
RAMER, James D.	(AL)	1005
ALSMEYER, Henry L.	(AR)	18
HARRISON, John A.	(AR)	506
MCNEIL, William K.	(AR)	816
MCLACHLAN, Ross W.	(AZ)	812
O'NEIL, Mary A.	(AZ)	924
STUART, Gerard W.	(AZ)	1204
AHLSTROM, Romaine	(CA)	8
AHOUSE, John B.	(CA)	8
BARROW, Jerry	(CA)	60
BENOIT, Gerald	(CA)	82
BEVERAGE, Stephanie L.	(CA)	93
BIDWELL, John	(CA)	95
CARNES, Suzanne M.	(CA)	183
DAVIS, James	(CA)	279
DIMUNATION, Mark G.	(CA)	304
DRAKE, Dorothy M.	(CA)	318
EDELSTEIN, J M.	(CA)	335
ELLIOTT, C D.	(CA)	343
EWEN, Eric P.	(CA)	359
FAY, Evelyn V.	(CA)	367
GOODSTEIN, Judith R.	(CA)	450
GRIFFIN, Thomas E.	(CA)	469
HAMILTON, David M.	(CA)	491
HARLAN, Robert D.	(CA)	502
HAYES, Melinda K.	(CA)	516
HOLLEMAN, Marian P.	(CA)	551
HUNTER, David C.	(CA)	576
JORDAN, Joan A.	(CA)	616
KRAKAUER, Elizabeth	(CA)	675
KUHNER, David A.	(CA)	683
LEVY, Jane	(CA)	721
LOWMAN, Matt P.	(CA)	744
LUTTRELL, Jordan D.	(CA)	750
MONTGOMERY, John W.	(CA)	856
PARCHUCK, Jill A.	(CA)	940
PERRY, Edward C.	(CA)	960
REED, Marcia C.	(CA)	1015
SHAFFER, Ellen	(CA)	1119
SNYDER, Henry L.	(CA)	1164
STALKER, Laura A.	(CA)	1178
THOMAS, Vivian	(CA)	1238
TREGGIARI, Arnaldo	(CA)	1255
VOSPER, Robert	(CA)	1289
WHITSON, Helene	(CA)	1334
WREDEN, William P.	(CA)	1370
WRIGLEY, Elizabeth S.	(CA)	1373
YEUNG, Esther Y.	(CA)	1380
ZEIDBERG, David S.	(CA)	1387
BOYD, Ruth E.	(CO)	122
MASON, Ellsworth G.	(CO)	781
NEILON, Barbara L.	(CO)	892
QUINLAN, Nora J.	(CO)	1000
ASH, Lee M.	(CT)	35
BENEDICT, Williston R.	(CT)	80
CROOKER, Cynthia L.	(CT)	260
EMBARDO, Ellen E.	(CT)	347
FRANKLIN, Ralph W.	(CT)	398
HOLMER, Paul L.	(CT)	553
KAIMOWITZ, Jeffery H.	(CT)	622
LEAB, Katharine K.	(CT)	706
PELTIER, Karen V.	(CT)	955
RESTOUT, Denise T.	(CT)	1024
SAMUEL, Harold E.	(CT)	1079
SCHIMMELPFENG, Richard H.	(CT)	1093
SILVERSTEIN, Louis H.	(CT)	1139
WAIT, Gary E.	(CT)	1293
WEIMERSKIRCH, Philip J.	(CT)	1317
BARRINGER, George M.	(DC)	59
BARRY, Paul J.	(DC)	60
BURNEY, Thomas D.	(DC)	162
BYERS, Laura T.	(DC)	168

RARE (Cont'd)

Rare books

CRAWFORD, Elva B.	(DC)	256
DOGGETT, Rachel H.	(DC)	308
KALKUS, Stanley	(DC)	623
KRIVATSY, Nati H.	(DC)	679
LASNER, Mark S.	(DC)	700
MWALIMU, Charles	(DC)	884
PORTER, Suzanne	(DC)	985
SERVERINO, Roberto	(DC)	1116
TURTELL, Neal T.	(DC)	1265
VASLEF, Irene	(DC)	1279
PUFFER, Nathaniel H.	(DE)	997
SCHREYER, Alice D.	(DE)	1100
BOLDRICK, Samuel J.	(FL)	112
CLOPINE, John J.	(FL)	223
DEBOLT, W D.	(FL)	284
DE VARONA, Esperanza B.	(FL)	297
HOLLOWAY, David R.	(FL)	552
HURTES, Reva	(FL)	578
JACOBSON, June B.	(FL)	590
MATHEWS, Richard B.	(FL)	784
HOUGH, Leslie S.	(GA)	562
JORDAN, Casper L.	(GA)	616
OVERBECK, James A.	(GA)	931
EIMAS, Richard	(IA)	340
BELAN, Judith A.	(IL)	75
BERGER, Sidney E.	(IL)	86
BOLEF, Doris	(IL)	112
BURROWS, Thomas W.	(IL)	163
CLOONAN, Michele V.	(IL)	223
COBB, David A.	(IL)	224
CROTZ, D K.	(IL)	261
GILLFILLAN, Nancy M.	(IL)	435
GODLEWSKI, Susan G.	(IL)	442
HALIBEY, Areta V.	(IL)	486
HEYMAN, Jerome S.	(IL)	536
HOLZENBERG, Eric J.	(IL)	555
HORST, Stanley E.	(IL)	561
KINGERY, Victor P.	(IL)	652
KLESTINSKI, Martha A.	(IL)	661
KOCH, David V.	(IL)	667
LANIER, Donald L.	(IL)	696
LOWMAN, Judith T.	(IL)	744
MATTHEWS, Elizabeth W.	(IL)	785
MAYLONE, R R.	(IL)	790
MOORE, Milton C.	(IL)	860
NASH, N F.	(IL)	888
OWNES, Dorothy J.	(IL)	932
PETERSON, Scott W.	(IL)	964
PODESCHI, John B.	(IL)	979
POSNER, Frances A.	(IL)	985
RENSHAW, Marita	(IL)	1023
RYAN, Diane M.	(IL)	1070
WELLS, James M.	(IL)	1322
DARBEE, Leigh	(IN)	274
RUDOLPH, L C.	(IN)	1066
SILVER, Joel B.	(IN)	1138
SPRINGER, Joe A.	(IN)	1176
TURNER, Nancy K.	(IN)	1265
VANCIL, David E.	(IN)	1273
DEGRUSON, Eugene H.	(KS)	288
HAURY, David A.	(KS)	512
JOHNSON, Georgina	(KS)	604
MEDER, Marylouise D.	(KS)	820
VANDER VELDE, John J.	(KS)	1274
BUNDY, David D.	(KY)	157
HUFF, James E.	(KY)	570
MARTIN, June H.	(KY)	777
MILLS, Constance A.	(KY)	844
ROBERTS, Gerald F.	(KY)	1040
WARTH, L T.	(KY)	1307
COMBE, David A.	(LA)	234
DRAUGHON, Ralph B.	(LA)	318
FOX, Willard	(LA)	395
HAMSA, Charles F.	(LA)	494
JUMONVILLE, Florence M.	(LA)	619
MARTIN, Robert S.	(LA)	778
PERRAULT, Anna H.	(LA)	959

RARE (Cont'd)
Rare books

SHIFLETT, Orvin L. . . . . (LA) 1130
TURNER, I B. . . . . (LA) 1264
ASCHMANN, Althea . . . (MA) 35
CAYLOR, Lawrence M. . . (MA) 195
FISCHER, Marge . . . . . . (MA) 380
HAMMOND, Wayne G. . . (MA) 494
HANKAMER, Roberta A. . (MA) 496
HAPIJ, Maria S. . . . . (MA) 499
HOPKINS, Benjamin . . . . (MA) 557
KENDALL, John D. . . . . . (MA) 640
LEWONTIN, Amy . . . . . . (MA) 724
LUBRANO, Judith A. . . . (MA) 745
MCGARRY, Marie L. . . . (MA) 805
MORTIMER, Ruth . . . . . (MA) 870
OLDHAM, Ellen M. . . . . . (MA) 920
RHINELANDER, Mary F. . (MA) 1025
SCOTT, Alison M. . . . . . (MA) 1106
SEEGRABER, Frank J. . . (MA) 1111
SLAPSYS, Richard M. . . (MA) 1148
STICKNEY, Zephorene L. . (MA) 1193
STRAND, Bethany . . . . . (MA) 1200
WALSH, James E. . . . . . (MA) 1299
WARRINGTON, David R. . (MA) 1307
WASOWICZ, Laura E. . . (MA) 1308
CREIGHTON, Alice S. . . (MD) 258
FARREN, Donald . . . . . . (MD) 365
FILBY, P W. . . . . (MD) 376
FORSHAW, William S. . . (MD) 391
GIORDANO, Peter . . . . . (MD) 438
HIRTLE, Peter B. . . . . . . (MD) 544
JACKSON, Doris G. . . . . (MD) 587
KIM, Sunnie I. . . . . (MD) 649
SHAY, Donald E. . . . . . . (MD) 1124
TATE, Vernon D. . . . . . . (MD) 1225
TEIGEN, Philip M. . . . . . (MD) 1230
SAEGER, Edwin J. . . . . . (ME) 1074
BUTZ, Helen S. . . . . (MI) 168
CRAWFORD, David E. . . (MI) 256
DRAPER, James P. . . . . (MI) 318
FRANCIS, Gloria A. . . . . (MI) 396
GAYLOR, Robert G. . . . . (MI) 423
KOCH, Henry C. . . . . . . (MI) 667
KEY, Jack D. . . . . (MN) 645
KUKLA, Edward R. . . . . (MN) 683
OVERMIER, Judith A. . . (MN) 931
RULON-MILLER, Robert . (MN) 1067
WENTE, Norman G. . . . . (MN) 1324
DEL CASTILLO, Mireya . (MO) 289
GLENN, Ardis L. . . . . . . (MO) 441
GULSTAD, Wilma B. . . . (MO) 477
HALL, Holly . . . . (MO) 487
HOWELL, Margaret A. . . (MO) 565
JENKINS, Harold R. . . . . (MO) 597
O'DELL, Charles A. . . . . (MO) 916
OFSTAD, Odessa L. . . . . (MO) 917
SHIRKY, Martha H. . . . . (MO) 1131
JONES, Dolores B. . . . . (MS) 612
KELLY, John M. . . . . (MS) 638
VERICH, Thomas M. . . . (MS) 1282
MILLS, Douglas E. . . . . . (MT) 844
BRABHAM, Robert F. . . . (NC) 124
CHENAULT, Elizabeth A. . (NC) 205
MCNAMARA, Charles B. . (NC) 816
SCOTT, Ralph L. . . . . . . (NC) 1108
SEVERANCE, Robert W. . (NC) 1117
WILKINSON, Fleeta M. . . (NC) 1340
MURDOCK, Douglas W. . (NE) 879
BROWN, Stanley W. . . . (NH) 147
BRODOWSKI, Joyce H. . (NJ) 139
CARLISLE, Scott G. . . . . (NJ) 182
COLLINS, Sarah F. . . . . (NJ) 233
FARRELL, Mark R. . . . . . (NJ) 365
FERGUSON, Stephen . . . (NJ) 372
GENNETT, Robert G. . . . (NJ) 427
HUDSON, Julie . . . . (NJ) 569
JONES, Arthur E. . . . . . . (NJ) 611
JOYCE, William L. . . . . . (NJ) 618
KOONTZ, John . . . . (NJ) 671

RARE (Cont'd)
Rare books

SINCLAIR, Donald A. . . . (NJ) 1142
WILINSKI, Grant W. . . . . (NJ) 1339
ZULEWSKI, Gerald J. . . . (NJ) 1391
CHEN, Laura F. . . . . (NM) 205
BLESSE, Robert E. . . . . . (NV) 105
KADANS, Joseph M. . . . (NV) 621
BAGNALL, Whitney S. . . (NY) 45
BARR, Jeffrey A. . . . . . . (NY) 58
BERGMANN, Allison M. . (NY) 86
CAPRIELIAN, Arevig . . . (NY) 180
CHANEY, Bev . . . . (NY) 200
CIOLLI, Antoinette . . . . . (NY) 214
CLARK, Diane A. . . . . . . (NY) 216
COLE, Maud D. . . . . (NY) 231
CRYSTAL, Bernard R. . . (NY) 262
DOCTOROW, Erica . . . . (NY) 307
DOWD, Philip M. . . . . . . (NY) 315
EDDY, Donald D. . . . . . . (NY) 335
ELLENBOGEN, Rudolph S. (NY) 343
FOLTER, Roland . . . . . . (NY) 388
GADBOIS, Frank W. . . . . (NY) 411
GAFFNEY, Ellen E. . . . . . (NY) 412
GELLER, Lawrence D. . . (NY) 426
GLASER, June E. . . . . . . (NY) 439
GRECH, Anthony P. . . . . (NY) 461
GRIFFITH, Sheryl . . . . . . (NY) 469
HEFNER, Xavier M. . . . . (NY) 520
JUNG, Norman O. . . . . . (NY) 620
JURIST, Janet . . . . (NY) 620
KASTEN, Seth E. . . . . . . (NY) 629
LESTER, Lillian . . . . (NY) 718
LOHF, Kenneth A. . . . . . (NY) 737
MACKECHNIE, Nancy S. (NY) 756
MAYO, Hope . . . . (NY) 790
MENT, David M. . . . . . . (NY) 824
MERKIN, David . . . . (NY) 826
MONIE, Willis J. . . . . (NY) 855
MOONEY, James E. . . . . (NY) 858
NEEDHAM, Paul . . . . . . (NY) 891
OSTWALD, Mark F. . . . . (NY) 929
PAULSON, Barbara A. . . (NY) 950
PEPPER, Jerold L. . . . . . (NY) 958
RAMER, Bruce J. . . . . . . (NY) 1005
SENTZ, Lilli . . . . (NY) 1115
SOMERS, Wayne F. . . . . (NY) 1167
STALKER, Dianne S. . . . (NY) 1178
THOMPSON, Susan O. . . (NY) 1241
VESLEY, Roberta A. . . . . (NY) 1283
WALSH, Daniel P. . . . . . (NY) 1299
ADOMEIT, Ruth E. . . . . . (OH) 7
BAIN, George W. . . . . . . (OH) 47
BIRK, Nancy . . . . (OH) 98
EAST, Dennis . . . . (OH) 332
GILDZEN, Alex J. . . . . . . (OH) 434
IRWIN, James W. . . . . . . (OH) 584
JENKINS, Fred W. . . . . . (OH) 597
LORANTH, Alice N. . . . . (OH) 741
MACIUSZKO, Jerzy J. . . (OH) 755
PIKE, Kermit J. . . . . (OH) 972
SMITH, Thomas A. . . . . . (OH) 1161
VANBRIMMER, Barbara A. (OH) 1272
BENDER, Nathan E. . . . . (OK) 79
BLEDSOE, Kathleen E. . . (OK) 105
GOODMAN, Marcia M. . . (OK) 449
LARSEN, Nancy E. . . . . (OK) 698
BAUER, Marilyn A. . . . . . (OR) 65
INGRAHAM-SWETS,
  Leonoor . . . . (OR) 582
OTNES, Harold M. . . . . . (OR) 930
PYATT, Timothy D. . . . . (OR) 999
DAVIS, Samuel A. . . . . . (PA) 281
DEIBLER, Barbara E. . . . (PA) 288
GREEN, James N. . . . . . (PA) 462
HEANEY, Howell J. . . . . (PA) 518
HEDRICK, David T. . . . . (PA) 520
HORROCKS, Thomas A. . (PA) 561
JOHNSEN, Mary C. . . . . (PA) 602
LEAHY, Mary S. . . . . . . (PA) 707

RARE (Cont'd)
Rare books

LIEBERMAN, Ronald ...	(PA)	726
LUNDY, M W.	(PA)	748
MAASS, Eleanor A.	(PA)	753
MANN, Charles W.	(PA)	766
MCGLINN, Frank C.	(PA)	806
MERZ, Lawrie H.	(PA)	827
METZGER, Philip A.	(PA)	829
MORRIS, Leslie A.	(PA)	867
MORSE, Alfred W.	(PA)	869
NEGHERBON, Vincent R.	(PA)	892
NEITZ, Cordelia M.	(PA)	892
NELSON, Vernon H.	(PA)	895
PAKALA, Denise M.	(PA)	935
ROOT, Deane L.	(PA)	1054
RUGGERE, Christine A. .	(PA)	1066
SWIGART, William E. ...	(PA)	1216
TRAISTER, Daniel H. ...	(PA)	1253
WOOLMER, J H.	(PA)	1368
YOLTON, Jean S.	(PA)	1380
ZORICH, Phillip J.	(PA)	1390
CASAS DE FAUNCE, Maria	(PR)	191
LANDIS, Dennis C.	(RI)	693
MASLYN, David C.	(RI)	780
PEARCE, Douglas A. ...	(RI)	952
CHOPESIUK, Ronald J. .	(SC)	210
HAMILTON, Ben	(SC)	491
RIDGE, Davy J.	(SC)	1032
THOMPSON, Harry F. ..	(SD)	1239
BRANTIGAN-STOWELL, Martha J.	(TN)	129
HARWELL, Sara J.	(TN)	509
LLOYD, James B.	(TN)	735
BOOTHE, Nancy L.	(TX)	116
CABLE, Carole L.	(TX)	170
CONRAD, James H.	(TX)	238
CULP, Paul M.	(TX)	264
FARMER, David	(TX)	364
GARNER, Jane	(TX)	419
GOODWIN, Willard	(TX)	450
GOULD, Karen K.	(TX)	454
HOOD, Sandra D.	(TX)	556
KENDALL, Lyle H.	(TX)	640
LAVENDER, Kenneth ...	(TX)	703
LOYD, Roger L.	(TX)	745
MACDONALD, Hugh ...	(TX)	754
MERSKY, Roy M.	(TX)	827
PAYNE, John R.	(TX)	951
RASCHE, Richard R.	(TX)	1008
RICE, Ralph A.	(TX)	1027
SALL, Larry D.	(TX)	1076
STONE, Marvin H.	(TX)	1197
THOMAS, Page A.	(TX)	1238
WHITE, Elizabeth B.	(TX)	1331
FLAKE, Chad J.	(UT)	383
LARSEN, A D.	(UT)	698
BERWICK, Philip C.	(VA)	91
CHAMBERLAIN, William R.	(VA)	197
GORDON, Vesta L.	(VA)	452
JAFFE, John G.	(VA)	591
KARRER, Jonathan K. ..	(VA)	628
KELLY, Ardie L.	(VA)	637
PINEL, Stephen L.	(VA)	974
SARTAIN, Sara M.	(VA)	1083
THOMPSON, Anthony B.	(VA)	1239
TYSINGER, Barbara R. .	(VA)	1267
SINGER, George C.	(VT)	1143
SWIFT, Esther M.	(VT)	1216
LANE, Steven P.	(WA)	694
LIPTON, Laura E.	(WA)	732
CORBLY, James E.	(WI)	245
EDMONDS, Michael	(WI)	336
HILL, Edwin L.	(WI)	539
SADLON, Ramona J. ...	(WI)	1074
BARNES, Jean S.	(WV)	57
CRESSWELL, Stephen ..	(WV)	258
NATHANSON, David ...	(WV)	889

RARE (Cont'd)
Rare books

STROUD, John N.	(WV)	1203
STOPKA, Christina K.	(WY)	1198
KUJANSUU, Asko J.	(AB)	683
LOVENBURG, Susan L. .	(AB)	743
STEELE, Apollonia L. ...	(AB)	1184
ROBERTSON, Guy M. .	(BC)	1041
ROSEVEAR, E C.	(NB)	1057
ETTLINGER, John R.	(NS)	356
ALSTON, Sandra	(ON)	18
HOFFMAN, Susan J. ...	(ON)	548
KOTIN, David B.	(ON)	673
LANDON, Richard G. ...	(ON)	693
MORLEY, William F.	(ON)	865
PULLEYBLANK, Mildred C.	(ON)	997
SEBANC, Mark F.	(ON)	1110
THOMSON, Dorothy F. ..	(ON)	1241
VAN DER BELLEN, Liana	(ON)	1273
WISEMAN, John A.	(ON)	1357
RATNER, Sabina T.	(PQ)	1010
GAGE, Laurie E.	(ENG)	412
MACNUTT, Richard P. ..	(ENG)	758
GARRETA, J C.	(FRN)	420
DE MACEDO, Maria L. ..	(PTG)	290
BARBEN, Tanya A.	(SAF)	55

Rare books administration
KENAMORE, Jane A. .... (TX) 640

Rare books, Americana
REESE, William S. ..... (CT) 1016

Rare books & archives
BEDARD, Laura A. .... (DC) 73
INGLES, Ernie B. .... (SK) 582

Rare books & artifacts
SPOTTED EAGLE, Joy . (MT) 1175

Rare books & bibliography
CRESSWELL, Donald H. (PA) 258

Rare books & genealogy
SABA, Bettye M. ...... (IN) 1072

Rare books & hand bookbinding
SMITH, Margit J. ...... (ENG) 1157

Rare books & literary manuscripts
EBELING-KONING, Blanche T. .... (MD) 334

Rare books & manuscripts

ROBROCK, David P.	(AZ)	1045
ESCHER, Nancy	(CA)	354
HORWITZ, Steven F. ...	(CA)	561
LEERHOFF, Ruth E. ...	(CA)	712
SORGENFREI, Robert K.	(CA)	1168
WHITING, F B.	(CA)	1333
WOODWARD, Daniel ...	(CA)	1368
BOGENSCHNEIDER, Duane R.	(CT)	110
PARKS, Stephen	(CT)	943
SCHMIDT, Alesandra M.	(CT)	1095
WILKIE, Everett C.	(CT)	1340
BEDARD, Laura A.	(DC)	73
ADAMS, Barbara M.	(DE)	4
IVES, Sidney E.	(FL)	586
TIMBERLAKE, Cynthia A.	(HI)	1245
ADAMS, Larry D.	(IA)	5
CULLEN, Charles T.	(IL)	263
GERDES, Neil W.	(IL)	428
GUSHEE, Marion S.	(IL)	478
MCCOY, Ralph E.	(IL)	799
MASON, Alexandra	(KS)	780
MILLER, Robert H.	(KY)	842
ENGLISH, Cynthia J. ...	(MA)	350
LANCASTER, John	(MA)	692
LOMBARDO, Daniel J. ..	(MA)	738
MELNICK, Ralph	(MA)	823
STODDARD, Roger E. .,	(MA)	1196
GWYN, Ann S.	(MD)	479
ALLENTUCK, Marcia E. .	(NY)	16
DUPONT, Inge	(NY)	327
RACHOW, Louis A.	(NY)	1001
WILSON, Fredric W.	(NY)	1351
HANSON, Norma S.	(OH)	498
MCCALLUM, Brenda W.	(OH)	793
BAKER, Sylva S.	(PA)	49
BAKY, John S.	(PA)	50
KOREY, Marie E.	(PA)	671
WOLF, Edwin	(PA)	1360
COLEY, Betty A.	(TX)	231
HENDERSON, Cathy ...	(TX)	526
KLEPPER, Bobbie J. ...	(TX)	660
LEACH, Sally S.	(TX)	706

RARE (Cont'd)

Rare books & manuscripts

NOLAN, Edward W. . . . . (WA) 907

Rare books & modern manuscripts HUTTNER, Sidney F. . . . (OK) 579
Rare books & reference work HARADA, Ryukichi . . . . . (JAP) 499
Rare books & special collections WALCOTT, M A. . . . . . . (FL) 1294
BROWN, Norman B. . . . . (IL) 146
TUCHMAN, Maurice S. . (MA) 1261
GOLDSBERG, Elizabeth D. (MD) 446
RAME, Mary E. . . . . (NY) 1005
SZMUK, Szilvia E. . . . . . (NY) 1218
ZAFREN, Herbert C. . . . . (OH) 1385
POST, Jeremiah B. . . . . . (PA) 986
RAINWATER, Jean M. . . (RI) 1004
BJORKLUND, Edi . . . . . (WI) 100
MILLER, Beth M. . . . . . . (ON) 836
Rare books appraisal GLENN, Ardis L. . . . . . . (MO) 441
DU BOIS, Paul Z. . . . . . (NJ) 322
Rare books, archives, & reference KAPLAN, Sylvia Y. . . . . . (IL) 626
Rare books cataloging REITH, Louis J. . . . . . . (DC) 1022
HOUSE, Katherine L. . . . (KY) 563
LANE, Mary J. . . . . (LA) 694
KISTLER, Ellen D. . . . . . (MO) 656
MYERS, Victor C. . . . . . (MO) 885
CALLINAN, Mary H. . . . (NY) 174
GOERNER, Tatiana . . . . (NY) 443
Rare books, college archives GALLAGHER, Mary E. . . (MA) 414
Rare books, exhibits NICKERSON, Donna L. . (NY) 902
Rare books for children MCNAMARA, Shelley G. (ME) 816
Rare books, history of medicine FREY, Emil F. . . . . (TX) 402
Rare books in theology VANDEGRIFT, J R. . . . . (DC) 1273
Rare books, literature, music AUSTIN, Kristi N. . . . . . (WA) 40
Rare books, manuscripts ZINN, Nancy W. . . . . . . (CA) 1389
HASWELL, Hollee . . . . . (NY) 511
Rare books, manuscripts, & archives FIELD, William N. . . . . . (NJ) 376
Rare books, medical JENKINS, Glen P. . . . . . (OH) 597
Rare books, music STRINGFELLOW, William
T. . . . . (NY) 1202
Rare books of bibliography DOAK, Wesley A. . . . . . (OR) 306
Rare books, photographs, ephemerae HARDY, D C. . . . . (LA) 500
Rare books, printing history ALLEN, Susan M. . . . . . (CA) 16
Rare books purchase & sales MCKITTRICK, Bruce W. . (PA) 812
Rare books, special collections SPONDER, Dorothy R. . . (DC) 1175
JONES, Christine S. . . . . (TN) 611
Rare books subject collections WOLFE, Marice . . . . . . (TN) 1361
Rare books, West Americana DOBBERTEEN, Sara J. . (OK) 307
Rare books, West Virginia MARTIN, June R. . . . . . (WV) 777
Rare children's books COUGHLAN, Margaret N. (DC) 250
SPIRT, Diana L. . . . . . . (NY) 1175
BROWN, Muriel W. . . . . (TX) 146
Rare children's books in English JOHNSON, Carolyn E. . . (CA) 602
Rare classical recordings CAMPBELL, R A. . . . . . (HI) 177
Rare jazz records, films &
photographs BRADLEY, Jack . . . . . . (MA) 126
Rare juvenile books MATHER, Becky R. . . . . (IA) 783
Rare law books BOYER, Larry M. . . . . . (DC) 123
REES, Warren D. . . . . . (MN) 1016
Rare maps WALSTROM, Jon L. . . . (MN) 1300
HUDSON, Alice C. . . . . . (NY) 569
Rare medical books JENSEN, Joseph E. . . . . (MD) 599
KEYS, Thomas E. . . . . . (MN) 645
WHITCOMB, Dorothy V. . (WI) 1330
Rare military affairs items AIMONE, Alan C. . . . . . (NY) 8
Rare music MACNUTT, Richard P. . . (ENG) 758
Rare numismatic books CAMPBELL, Francis D. . (NY) 176
Rare or historical recordings FABRIZIO, Timothy C. . . (NY) 360
Rare, out-of-print records SMITH, Walter H. . . . . . (VA) 1161
Rare record appraisal ALLEN, Douglas R. . . . . (FL) 14
Rare record cataloging ALLEN, Douglas R. . . . . (FL) 14
Rare recordings LAZZARONI, Philip S. . . (MD) 706
MOSES, Julian M. . . . . . (NY) 871
Rare Sisters of Mercy books MULDREY, Mary H. . . . . (LA) 876
Rare sound recordings GERBER, Warren C. . . . (NJ) 428
Rare sound recordings archives MAWHINNEY, Paul C. . . (PA) 787
Special collections, rare books SAHAK, Judy H. . . . . . . (CA) 1075
MENGES, Gary L. . . . . . (WA) 824
Special collections, rare books,
archive NAINIS, Linda . . . . (DC) 886
Theological rare books KANSFIELD, Norman J. . (NY) 625

READER

Adult & young adult readers advisory TREMBLAY, Carolyn B. . . (NH) 1255
Adult new reader materials MCGRIFF, Mary E. . . . . . (NC) 808
Adult new readers publishing RYAN, Jenny L. . . . . . . (NY) 1071
Adult reference, reader's advisory GELINAS, Jeanne L. . . . (MN) 426
Adult reference, reader's services PORTER, Eva L. . . . . . . (NJ) 984
Advising readers EISENSTADT, Rosa M. . . (SC) 341
CD-ROM reader distribution LESLIE, Nathan . . . . . . (ON) 718
LOWRY, Douglas B. . . . . (ON) 745
LOWRY, John D. . . . . . . (ON) 745
Children's reader services THOMAS, Victoria K. . . . (IN) 1238
Children's reference & reader
assistance BECKER, Teresa J. . . . . (AZ) 72
Circulation, reader services ADAMS, Velma L. . . . . . (MS) 6
General reader's advisory work BURKE, Lauri K. . . . . . . (RI) 160
Library administration, reader services STWODAH, M I. . . . . . . (VA) 1206
Library instruction & reader's advisory LINDGREN, Beverly P. . . (IL) 729
Materials selection & reader services TANG, Grace L. . . . . . . (NY) 1222
Programming & reader advisor MARCKS, Carol J. . . . . . (LA) 769
Public reader services BOWER, Beverly L. . . . . (FL) 120
OTTAVIANO, Doris B. . . (RI) 930
Reader advising CLEMINSHAW, Barbara B. (NY) 221
WIRICK, Terry L. . . . . . (PA) 1356
Reader advisor COLEMAN, James M. . . . (AL) 231
Reader advisories JONES, Mary L. . . . . . . (IL) 614
Reader advisory CHAMBERS, Donald A. . (HI) 198
GILBERT, Donna J. . . . . (OH) 433
Reader & technical services SHERWIG, Mary J. . . . . (NY) 1129
Reader guidance SCALES, Pat R. . . . . . . (SC) 1087
Reader service WILLIAMS, Nancy F. . . . (GA) 1345
Reader services OLIVE, J F. . . . . (AL) 921
MYERS, Sara J. . . . . . . (CO) 885
STODDARD, Charles E. . (CT) 1196
MCCAY, Lynne K. . . . . . (DC) 795
CARILLO, Sherry J. . . . . (FL) 181
KANNER, Elliott E. . . . . (IL) 625
PARSON, Lethiel C. . . . . (MA) 944
BELL, Bernice . . . . (MS) 76
FREEMAN, Lucile . . . . . (MT) 401
DENSON, Janeen J. . . . . (NC) 293
MCBETH, Deborah E. . . . (NM) 792
MEANS, Spencer . . . . . (NY) 820
BERG, Susan . . . . (VA) 85
MURPHY, Joyce . . . . . . (BC) 880
KATZ, Bernard M. . . . . . (ON) 630
MORAN, Teresita C. . . . (PHP) 862
Reader services, reference MUELLER, Jane L. . . . . (CA) 875
CARRIGAN, Marietta R. . (WA) 186
Reader's adviser's services SHEEHAN, Robert C. . . . (NY) 1125
Reader's advisories KELLOGG, Joanne T. . . . (ME) 637
Reader's advisory GALLAHAR, Christine M. . (FL) 414
COLLINS, Eugenia A. . . . (GA) 232
BROWN, Nancy E. . . . . . (IL) 146
CALTVEDT, Sarah C. . . . (IL) 174
JACOB, Merle L. . . . . . . (IL) 589
GILLIES, Irene B. . . . . . (MA) 436
MCCORMICK, Sheila P. . (MA) 799
HIRSCH, Dorothy K. . . . (MD) 543
HERTZ, Sylvia . . . . (MI) 533
ORMOND, Sarah C. . . . . (MI) 926
YOUNG, Lynne M. . . . . . (MN) 1382
AYLWARD, Judith A. . . . (MO) 43
MASSEY, Nancy O. . . . . (NC) 782
GREENBERG, Ruth S. . . (NJ) 463
VAN WIEMOKLY, Jane G. (NJ) 1277
ALVAREZ, Ronald . . . . . (NY) 19
DEMARCO, Elizabeth A. . (NY) 291
KUCINSKI, B J. . . . . . . (OH) 682
JORDAN, Linda K. . . . . . (OK) 616
KITE, Yvonne D. . . . . . . (UT) 657
RODGER, Elizabeth A. . . (ON) 1047
Readers advisory book information IRGON, Deborah A. . . . . (NJ) 583
Reader's advisory, reference work CORDUKES, Laura L. . . . (ON) 246
Readers' advisory service NITZBERG, Dale B. . . . . (MD) 905
Reader's advisory service &
reference HUNTER, Julie A. . . . . . (NC) 576
Readers advisory services LAWRENCE, Scott W. . . (CT) 705
Readers guidance BAKER, Sharon L. . . . . (IA) 49
Reader's guidance & reference SHEARIN, Cynthia E. . . . (NJ) 1124
Readers service ALDRICH, Willie L. . . . . (NC) 11

READER (Cont'd)

Readers services	HUFFMAN, Carol P.	(IL)	571
	GALLAGHER, Mary E.	(MA)	414
	HOVORKA, Marjorie J.	(MA)	563
	MAUL, Shirley A.	(NY)	787
	ELLSON, Linda R.	(OR)	345
	SPRANKLE, Anita T.	(PA)	1176
	IMOISI, Ann U.	(NGR)	582
Reader's theater reading aloud	BAUER, Caroline F.	(CA)	65
Reference & reader adviser service	ROUSE, Charlie L.	(OK)	1061
Reference & reader advisory	LIGGAN, Mary K.	(VA)	726
Reference & reader services	GOODWYN, Betty R.	(AL)	450
	SELF, Sharon W.	(GA)	1113
	GONNEVILLE, Priscilla R.	(MA)	447
	CLUNE, John R.	(NY)	223
	HILL, Ruth J.	(TN)	540
	BARBEN, Tanya A.	(SAF)	55
Reference & reader's advisory	HOLMES, Nancy M.	(GA)	553
	KELLSTEDT, Jenny	(MA)	637
	BAILEY, Carol A.	(MD)	46
	O'NEIL, Margaret M.	(NY)	924
Reference & readers advisory services	OLENDER, Karen L.	(NC)	920
Reference & readers services	KNAUFF, Elisabeth S.	(DC)	663
	DREW, Wilfred E.	(NY)	319
	FREW, Martha G.	(OH)	402
Reference, reader advising	ASLESEN, Rosalie V.	(SD)	36
Reference, reader guidance	WEICK, Robert J.	(IN)	1316
Reference service to readers	CHO, Sung Y.	(DC)	209
Trade books for beginning readers	BAUER, Carolyn J.	(OK)	65
Young adult readers advisory	BENOIT, Ursula L.	(ON)	83

READING

Adult reading interests & materials	FERSTL, Kenneth L.	(TX)	374
Adult reading services	MULAWKA, Chet	(CT)	876
Blind reading services	MCCASLIN, Cheryl A.	(TX)	795
Books & reading	RABBAN, Elana	(NY)	1001
Children's literature, reading	MCGOWN, Sue W.	(TX)	807
Children's reading environment	TAKEUCHI, Satoru	(JAP)	1220
Joy of reading	POOL, Jeraldine B.	(TX)	982
Junior high reading encouragement	LEWIS, Marjorie	(NY)	723
Library reading promotion	COLE, John Y.	(DC)	231
Literacy & reading comprehension	SIEGEL, Martin A.	(IL)	1136
Literacy & reading promotion	ALLEN, Richard H.	(NE)	16
Parent groups, development of reading	WALDEN, Katherine G.	(CT)	1294
Physically handicapped reading services	MCCASLIN, Cheryl A.	(TX)	795
Popular reading	KIES, Cosette N.	(IL)	647
Popular reading interests	ROSENBERG, Betty	(CA)	1056
Promote reading	MAYER, Mary C.	(OH)	789
Reader's theater reading aloud	BAUER, Caroline F.	(CA)	65
Reading	ROCHMAN, Hazel P.	(IL)	1046
	BLATT, Gloria T.	(MI)	104
	LIGGETT, Julie A.	(PA)	726
Reading development	LYONS, Dean E.	(ME)	753
Reading disabilities literature	SPARKS, Martha E.	(NC)	1171
Reading encouragement	OLSEN, Katherine M.	(UT)	921
Reading for enjoyment	CULLIS, Lois I.	(ON)	263
Reading guidance	MCCARTHY, Carrol B.	(DE)	794
	CRAVER, Susan J.	(IA)	256
	PARK, Dona F.	(IA)	941
	MOSKOWITZ, May K.	(MI)	871
	WIENER, Sylvia B.	(NY)	1330
	KENT, Rose M.	(OH)	642
	NORRIS, Gale K.	(SC)	909
	FORTIN, Clifford C.	(WI)	391
Reading guidance & children's literature	KONNEKER, Rachel C.	(NC)	670
Reading habits research	LANGERMAN, Shoshana P.	(ISR)	695
Reading, listening & viewing guidance	RING, Constance B.	(NY)	1035
Reading motivation	PAULIN, Mary A.	(MI)	950
Reading motivation, children	TRAINER, Leslie F.	(PAK)	1253
Reading programs	WALKER, Tamara E.	(TX)	1296
Reading promotion, advisory	SHANNON, Kathleen L.	(IL)	1120
Reading promotion & library skills	GOLDBERG, Linda B.	(KY)	444
Reading specialization	FISHER, Joan W.	(MD)	381
Reading teaching	BARTON, Barbara I.	(BAH)	61

READING (Cont'd)

Reading, writing, literacy consulting	MCDONOUGH, Timothy M.	(CA)	803
Reference & reading services	CUNNINGHAM, Barbara M.	(MD)	265
Sociology of reading	COLBY, Robert A.	(NY)	230
Teacher education, reading specialist	AUSTIN, Mary C.	(HI)	40
User acclamation to reading	FRANCOS, Alexis	(PA)	396
Young adult reading guidance	MALTBY, Florence H.	(MO)	764

REAL ESTATE

Nationwide real estate title reporting	FELDER, Bruce B.	(OH)	369
Real estate	WONG, Mabel K.	(IL)	1363
	HODNETT, Diane M.	(N.J)	546
Real estate analysis	LEVINE, Linda A.	(NY)	720
Real estate & legislative databases	KITZMILLER, Virginia G.	(DC)	657
Real estate CD-ROM product development	JENKINS, George A.	(FL)	597
Real estate databases	BRUTON, Robert T.	(MN)	151
Real estate online database marketing	JENKINS, George A.	(FL)	597
Real estate rentals management	COMPRI, Jeannine L.	(AB)	235
Real estate research	ROSENBERGER, Constance G.	(PA)	1056
Valuation & taxation of real property	BEVERLEY, Barbara S.	(NY)	93

REAL-TIME

Real-time financial information	REEDY, Martha J.	(MA)	1015
Real-time fixed income research	MILLS, Andrew G.	(MA)	843

RECEPTORS

Biochemistry, steroid hormone receptors	MCFARLAND, Robert T.	(MO)	805

RECLASSIFICATION (See also Classification, Conversion)

Cataloging & reclassification	HOOSE, Beverly D.	(CT)	557
	YEH, Thomas Y.	(WA)	1379
Reclassification	MANSFIELD, Fred	(IL)	767
	RAJEC, Elizabeth M.	(NY)	1004
	POST, Phyllis C.	(OH)	986
	SANDERS, Melodie	(OK)	1080
	RUSSELL, Barbara J.	(TX)	1068
Reclassification of libraries	JOHNSON, Ruth E.	(OH)	608

RECONNAISSANCE

Reconnaissance systems	VAN VELZER, Verna J.	(CA)	1277
	DONOHUE, Christine N.	(CT)	311

RECONSTITUTION

Book repair & reconstitution	GLEESON, Joyce M.	(IL)	441

RECONVERSION

Reconversion projects	BISSETT, Claudia K.	(NH)	100

RECORDINGS (See also Analogue, CD, CD-I, CD-ROM, Cassette, Compact, Discography, Disk, Phonodisc, Phonograph, Records, Sound, Tape)

Appraisals of sound recordings	SMOLIAN, Steven J.	(MD)	1162
Audio recording & archives	RUNYON, Steven C.	(CA)	1067
Audio recording & engineering	SUMMERHILL, Craig A.	(MI)	1209
Audio recordings	WARD, Shirlene A.	(IL)	1304
Band music recordings research	MITZIGA, Walter J.	(IL)	850
Cataloging & collecting rare recordings	BROWNE, J P.	(CA)	148
Cataloging band recordings	MITZIGA, Walter J.	(IL)	850
Cataloging music & sound recordings	DORFMAN, Ethel L.	(NY)	312
	POWELL, Virginia L.	(PA)	989
Cataloging of sound recordings	SCHUURSMA, Ann B.	(NET)	1103
Cataloging scores & sound recordings	MURRAY, Diane E.	(MI)	881
	WALLER, Elaine J.	(MI)	1298
Cataloging sound recordings	BJORKE, Wallace S.	(MI)	100
CD, LP, 45, 78 & Edison recordings	BAHR, Edward R.	(MS)	45
Classical music sound recordings	HALSEY, Richard S.	(NY)	490

RECORDINGS (Cont'd)

Designing recordings catalogs	GLASFORD, G R.	(NY)	440
Discographer, recording archivist	NOVITSKY, Edward G.	(NY)	911
Early phonograph recordings, 1890-1930	RIGGS, Quentin T.	(CA)	1034
Early recording artists, 1890-1930	RIGGS, Quentin T.	(CA)	1034
Film & video recordings	OLIVER, Scot	(KY)	921
Historic recordings preservation	PETRIE, Mildred M.	(FL)	965
Historical archive recordings	BUCHSBAUM, Robert E.	(OH)	153
Historical recording ledgers	WOOD, Sallie B.	(NY)	1365
History of recorded sound	FABRIZIO, Timothy C.	(NY)	360
Jazz recordings & musicians	COHEN, Frederick S.	(NY)	228
Music & sound recordings	WATTS, Richard S.	(CA)	1310
Music & sound recordings cataloging	SNODGRASS, Wilson D.	(TX)	1163
Music materials & recordings	GOODWIN, Charles B.	(TX)	450
Music recordings	EGGERS, Lolly P.	(IA)	339
Music recordings sound restoration	PETRIE, Mildred M.	(FL)	965
Musical sound recordings	PALKOVIC, Mark A.	(OH)	935
Old & rare sound recordings	CHANDLER, Thomas V.	(CA)	200
Organization of recorded knowledge	HALSEY, Richard S.	(NY)	490
Out-of-print recordings	DONAHUE, Louise	(NJ)	310
Phonograph recordings & rare books	BROWNE, J P.	(CA)	148
Phonographs & recordings	WITT, Kenneth W.	(MN)	1358
Phonorecords or sound recordings	HASSE, John E.	(DC)	511
Preservation of sound recordings	KINNEY, Daniel W.	(NY)	653
Rare classical recordings	CAMPBELL, R A.	(HI)	177
Rare or historical recordings	FABRIZIO, Timothy C.	(NY)	360
Rare recordings	LAZZARONI, Philip S.	(MD)	706
	MOSES, Julian M.	(NY)	871
Rare sound recordings	GERBER, Warren C.	(NJ)	428
Rare sound recordings archives	MAWHINNEY, Paul C.	(PA)	787
Recorded & braille materials & sources	WILSON, Barbara L.	(RI)	1350
Recorded media consultation, appraisal	MACAULEY, C C.	(CA)	754
Recorded music	BROGDEN, Stephen R.	(IA)	139
Recorded sound	MUNSICK, Lee R.	(NJ)	879
	COLQUHOUN, Joan E.	(ON)	234
Recorded sound archives	GAUNT, Sandra L.	(OH)	423
Recorded sound cataloging	GAUNT, Sandra L.	(OH)	423
Recorded sound collections	STEEL, Suzanne F.	(MS)	1183
Recorded sound research & training	GAUNT, Sandra L.	(OH)	423
Recording catalogs	CAMPBELL, R A.	(HI)	177
Recording dates phonograph records	STRONG, Darrell G.	(PA)	1203
Recordings selection	MENDRO, Donna C.	(TX)	824
Researching history of recording	PENGELLY, Joe	(ENG)	956
Scores & recordings	FARRINGTON, James	(CT)	365
Sound recording	GRAY, Michael H.	(DC)	460
Sound recording cataloging & databases	KLINGER, William E.	(OH)	661
Sound recording collection development	SAUNDERS, Sharon K.	(PA)	1084
Sound recording history & technology	KLINGER, William E.	(OH)	661
Sound recording indexing	CALDWELL, John M.	(PA)	172
Sound recordings	COLBY, Edward E.	(CA)	230
	FARRINGTON, James	(CT)	365
	WARREN, Richard	(CT)	1306
	MILLER, Anthony G.	(GA)	835
	EPSTEIN, Dena J.	(IL)	351
	NELSON, Brenda	(IN)	893
	JOHNSON, Ellen S.	(KS)	604
	GAGNON, Ronald A.	(MA)	412
	PRISTASH, Kenneth	(MA)	993
	WELIVER, E D.	(MI)	1321
	BOWERS, Sherri	(NY)	121
	KENSELAAR, Robert	(NY)	642
	LEW, Susan	(NY)	722
	PIZER, Charles R.	(NY)	977
	PIZER, Elizabeth F.	(NY)	977
	VOLLONO, Millicent D.	(NY)	1288
	WELLS, Phyllis L.	(NY)	1323
	WELLS, Paul F.	(TN)	1323
	MILLER, Karl F.	(TX)	839
	ELSTE, R O.	(WGR)	346
Sound recordings books	MAWHINNEY, Paul C.	(PA)	787
Sound recordings cataloging	NUZZO, Nancy B.	(NY)	912
	FOLLET, Robert E.	(TX)	388
Sound recordings collection	ROSENBURG, Betsy R.	(CT)	1056

RECORDINGS (Cont'd)

Sound recordings collection development	EARNEST, Jeffrey D.	(AR)	332
	FOLLET, Robert E.	(TX)	388
Sound recordings collections	ERICSON, Margaret D.	(NY)	353
Sound recordings databases	MAWHINNEY, Paul C.	(PA)	787
Tape recording graduate textbooks	BULLOCK, Frances E.	(NY)	156
Transcribing archive recordings	PENGELLY, Joe	(ENG)	956

RECORDS (See also Archives, Government)

Acquisition & evaluation of rare records	WAXMAN, Jack	(FL)	1311
Acquisition, cataloging of record col	MECHTENBERG, Paul	(IL)	820
Acquisitions, bks, records, music scores	SILVER, Martin A.	(CA)	1138
Administration of government records	WALCH, Victoria I.	(VA)	1293
American 20th century records	ASHKENAS, Bruce F.	(VA)	36
Antique phonograph records archives	JACOBSEN, Arnold	(MI)	590
Appraisal & records disposition	BRADSHER, James G.	(DC)	126
Appraising government records	BENGE, Joy L.	(TX)	80
Appraising record & phonograph cols	FABRIZIO, Timothy C.	(NY)	360
Architectural records	LATHROP, Alan K.	(MN)	701
Architectural records & drawings	BRUNK, Thomas W.	(MI)	150
Archival architectural records	BAUS, J W.	(IN)	67
Archival methods & records management	CAIN, Charlene C.	(LA)	171
Archives administration, land records	TEMPLE, Wayne C.	(IL)	1230
Archives & record management	OSTERFIELD, George T.	(OH)	928
Archives & records	HOLDEN, Harley P.	(MA)	550
Archives & records center management	CAMPBELL, Margaret E.	(NS)	177
Archives & records management	NEWCOMER, Susan N.	(CA)	898
	CANTELON, Philip L.	(MD)	179
	STIELOW, Frederick J.	(MD)	1194
	BLOUIN, Francis X.	(MI)	107
	REHKOPF, Charles F.	(MO)	1017
	PRICE, William S.	(NC)	993
	ERLANDSSON, Alf M.	(NY)	353
	LAIST, Sharon B.	(NY)	688
	CLARK, Robert L.	(OK)	218
	MURRAY, Lucia M.	(OR)	882
	CEBRUN, Mary J.	(TX)	196
	GRACY, David B.	(TX)	455
	EULENBERG, Julia N.	(WA)	356
	ROBERTSON, Guy M.	(BC)	1041
	ARDERN, Christine M.	(ON)	31
	MURDOCH, Arthur W.	(ON)	879
Archives & records management teaching	WHALEN, Lucille	(NY)	1328
Archives, labor records	RABINS, Joan W.	(TX)	1001
Archives, records management education	RHOADS, James B.	(WA)	1026
Archiving corporate records	LEMON, Nancy A.	(OH)	715
Audiovisual records	STERN, Marc J.	(NY)	1189
Authority record conversion	STUBBS, Linda T.	(DC)	1204
Automated medical records	LONG, John M.	(MN)	739
Automation of records centers	SMITH, David F.	(NY)	1154
Automation records programs	BUTLER, Tyrone G.	(NY)	167
Business records disaster recovery	EULENBERG, Julia N.	(WA)	356
Business records storage	EIGEMAN, Laurence E.	(IN)	340
Buying & selling 78 & LP records	SMOLIAN, Steven J.	(MD)	1162
California county records	WEBBER, Steven L.	(CA)	1313
Cataloging administrative records	WHEELER, Elaine	(NY)	1328
Cataloging LP records	SCHWANN, William J.	(MA)	1104
Church & denominational records	WOODARD, John R.	(NC)	1365
Church record & manuscripts	HILAND, Gerard P.	(OH)	538
Client record maintenance	EMMONS, Mary E.	(AK)	348
Collectible records 1950s, 1960s	MENNIE, Don	(NJ)	824
Collecting college records	VARGA, Nicholas	(MD)	1278
Colonial records	STEPHENS, Alonzo T.	(TN)	1187
Colorado territorial records	KETELSEN, Terry	(CO)	645
Computer-aided indexing for records	FROST, Debra R.	(CO)	406
Computerized medical records	STEAD, William W.	(NC)	1183
Congressional records	ODOM, Jane H.	(DC)	917
Corporate archives & records center	PEGLER, Ross J.	(FL)	954
Corporate archives & records centers	CLAYTON, John M.	(DE)	220
Corporate records & archives	RUNYON, Judith A.	(CA)	1067
Corporate records management	SALMON, Robin R.	(SC)	1077

RECORDS (Cont'd)

County records administration & archives	WEAVER, Clifton W.	(AL)	1312
Database record guide cataloging	MCKNIGHT, Jesse H.	(FL)	812
Describing & cataloging records	SIEBERS, Bruce L.	(MI)	1135
Description of legislative records	EFIRD, Frank K.	(IL)	338
Designing records management systems	BOWKER, Scott W.	(NY)	121
Develop medical record systems	KISH, Veronica R.	(PA)	656
Editing bibliographical records	WANG, Ann C.	(DC)	1302
Education archives & records	DEARSTYNE, Bruce W.	(NY)	284
Evaluation of records	MOSES, Julian M.	(NY)	871
Exploration records management	MOORE, Guusje Z.	(TX)	859
Financial records	VANCE, Mary L.	(MS)	1273
French archival records & manuscripts	KOHN, Roger S.	(NY)	668
Geological & geophysical records	MATLOCK, Teresa A.	(TX)	784
Government archives & records	HACKMAN, Larry J.	(NY)	481
Government records	SAYED, Joyce P.	(CA)	1086
	RUSSELL, Marvin F.	(DC)	1069
	CHAPDELAINE, Susan A.	(MA)	201
	NEWBORG, Gerald G.	(ND)	898
	NEAL, James H.	(TN)	890
Government records administration	OLSON, David J.	(NC)	922
Government records management	BOCKMAN, Eugene J.	(NY)	109
Historical phonograph records	BRYAN, Martin F.	(VT)	151
Historical records	MILLBROOKE, Anne	(CT)	835
	GIAQUINTA, C J.	(IA)	431
	EAST, Dennis	(OH)	332
	BROCHU, Frederick	(PQ)	138
	ORTIZ MONASTERIO, Leonor	(MEX)	927
Historical records of California	HANEL, Mary A.	(CA)	495
Historical records, phonographs	STRONG, Darrell G.	(PA)	1203
Inactive records management	RYAN, Betsey A.	(KS)	1070
Inactive records storage	KERR, Kevin G.	(IL)	644
Indian records	SCHMIDT HACKER, Margaret H.	(TX)	1096
Information & records management	KATTLOVE, Rose W.	(CA)	630
	OPEM, John D.	(IL)	925
	VAN BRUNT, Virginia	(MD)	1272
Information & records retrieval	LEE, William D.	(CA)	711
Institutional records	TENER, Jean F.	(AB)	1231
Jazz record computer cataloging	WEAVER, James B.	(FL)	1312
Legal records	MCREYNOLDS, R M.	(DC)	818
Legal records systems	KANE, Dorothea S.	(VA)	624
Legislative record technique	MERINGOLO, Joseph A.	(MD)	826
Library & data records administration	HURT, Nancy S.	(TX)	578
Library & records management	BLUM, Linda C.	(CA)	107
	CONNER, Norma	(NY)	237
Library & records management consulting	GAGNON, Donna M.	(CA)	412
Library records management	EVERINGHAM, Neil G.	(VA)	358
Local government publications & records	HEWLETT, Carol C.	(TN)	535
Local government records	WEBBER, Steven L.	(CA)	1313
	MOORE, Karl R.	(IL)	860
	HOLLAND, Michael E.	(TX)	551
	SCHAADT, Robert L.	(TX)	1088
Local Records	LEVSTIK, Frank R.	(KY)	721
Louis D Brandeis records	HODGSON, Janet B.	(KY)	546
Machine-readable catalog records	GUILES, Kay D.	(DC)	476
Maintenance of records	LONG, Brideen	(WI)	739
Management of information, records	WELCH, Donald A.	(TX)	1321
Management of nuclear records	WOODLEY, Victoria B.	(MI)	1366
Management records administration	AUSTIN, Ralph A.	(NY)	40
Manuscripts & records bibl control	KELLER, William B.	(DC)	636
MARC record formats	ESPLEY, John L.	(VA)	354
MARC record upgrade	CHIU, Ida K.	(TX)	209
Medical record systems	KISH, Veronica R.	(PA)	656
Medical records	SPOTTED EAGLE, Joy	(MT)	1175
	MENDELSON, Martin	(WA)	823
Medical records & oncology	BRENNER, Lawrence	(MA)	133
Microfilming & records management	KNARZER, Arlene	(IL)	663
Municipal records	LA CHAPELLE, Jennifer R.	(ON)	686
Name authority records	SCHMIDT, Holly H.	(OR)	1095
Online records linking	HARRIS, Virginia B.	(VA)	506
Order records	VANCE, Mary L.	(MS)	1273
Parish records	WIEDERAENDE, Robert C.	(IA)	1336
Pennsylvania county records	STAYER, Jonathan R.	(PA)	1183

RECORDS (Cont'd)

Personnel records	MOY, Clarence T.	(NY)	874
Phonograph record collections	EVANS, David H.	(TN)	356
Preservation & arrangement of records	YOUNKIN, C G.	(TX)	1383
Preservation of archival records	CALMES, Alan R.	(DC)	174
Preservation of legislative records	EFIRD, Frank K.	(IL)	338
Preservation of records	LONG, Brideen	(WI)	739
Private manuscripts & records	GRAHAM, Robert W.	(IL)	456
Private records	BREEDLOVE, Michael A.	(AL)	131
Private records cataloging	BREEDLOVE, Michael A.	(AL)	131
Processing of records	HOOKS, Michael Q.	(TX)	556
Processing papers & records collections	ERICKSEN, Paul A.	(IL)	352
Public & court records management	COATES, Paul F.	(KY)	224
Public records	HURLBERT, Roger W.	(CA)	577
Rare jazz records, films & photographs	BRADLEY, Jack	(MA)	126
Rare, out-of-print records	SMITH, Walter H.	(VA)	1161
Rare record appraisal	ALLEN, Douglas R.	(FL)	14
Rare record cataloging	ALLEN, Douglas R.	(FL)	14
Record acquisition & cataloging	BARGAR, Arthur W.	(CT)	56
Record & cassette selection	ANDERSON, Gail	(AB)	23
Record & tape collection	GORDON, Thelma S.	(CT)	452
Record, cassette & score cataloging	DONIO, Dorothy	(FL)	311
Record center operations	EDWARDS, Steven M.	(WA)	338
Record centers	MCCREARY, Gail A.	(MS)	800
Record collection	MARTUCCI, Louis U.	(CA)	779
Record collection development	MILLER, Charles W.	(NJ)	836
Record management	STEVENSON, Katherine	(IL)	1191
Record preservation	KING, Eleanor M.	(PA)	650
Record producing	ROBINSON, Margaret L.	(DC)	1044
Record reviewing	SEIBERT, Donald C.	(NY)	1112
Record reviews	LAMBERT, John W.	(NC)	690
Recording dates phonograph records	STRONG, Darrell G.	(PA)	1203
Records accessioning & processing	SCOTT, Paul R.	(TX)	1108
Records administration	ROSS, Rodney A.	(DC)	1058
Records & archival management	SANTORO, Corrado A.	(MB)	1082
Records & archives management	CAN, Hung V.	(PQ)	177
Records & collection management	WALKER, Heather C.	(DC)	1295
Records & documentation management	GRITZKA, Gerda M.	(PQ)	471
Records & info development & documtn	GRAHAM, Su D.	(CO)	456
Records & information filing & retrieval	GRAHAM, Su D.	(CO)	456
Records & information management	PHILLIPS, Donna M.	(IA)	968
	MUNTEAN, Deborah E.	(MN)	879
	ROFES, William L.	(NY)	1049
	MANARIN, Louis H.	(VA)	764
	STIRLING, Dale A.	(WA)	1195
Records & library management	SHANNON, Norma M.	(OR)	1120
Records & micrographics management	GENESEN, Judith L.	(IL)	427
Records appraisal	HONHART, Frederick L.	(MI)	556
	HAVENER, Ralph S.	(MO)	513
Records appraisal & scheduling	NASH, Cherie A.	(UT)	888
Records center	BROWNE, Jeri A.	(CA)	148
	WAGNER, Albin	(RI)	1291
Records declassification	HUMPHREY, David C.	(TX)	573
Records description	DOWD, Mary J.	(DC)	315
Records disposition	GORDON, Martin K.	(VA)	451
Records documentation systems	HAMILTON, Meredith L.	(IL)	492
Records inventory	DELOACH, Lynda J.	(MN)	290
Records management	NEWTON, Virginia A.	(AK)	900
	BRIDGES, Edwin C.	(AL)	135
	JONES, Allen W.	(AL)	610
	OETTING, Edward C.	(AZ)	917
	BROWNE, Jeri A.	(CA)	148
	BURSON, Sherrie L.	(CA)	164
	GABBERT, Gretchen W.	(CA)	411
	GOUDELOCK, Carol V.	(CA)	454
	HUNT, Judy L.	(CA)	575
	JENSEN, Marilyn A.	(CA)	599
	LARSON, Donald A.	(CA)	699
	MASTERS, Robin J.	(CA)	782
	MUSICK, Nancy W.	(CA)	883
	NEMCHEK, Lee R.	(CA)	895
	NYBERG, Lelia J.	(CA)	912
	PLATE, Kenneth H.	(CA)	977

RECORDS (Cont'd)
Records management

WITTMANN, Cecelia V. . .	(CA)	1358
FELDMAN, Rosalie M. . .	(CO)	369
GAUSS, Nancy V.	(CO)	423
MACARTHUR, Marit S. .	(CO)	754
NEWMAN, John	(CO)	899
WOLFE, F M.	(CO)	1360
MCGREGOR, M C.	(CT)	808
PALMQUIST, David W. .	(CT)	937
SIMON, William H.	(CT)	1141
CARTLEDGE, Connie L. .	(DC)	190
CASSEDY, James G. . . .	(DC)	193
NEWTON, Robert C. . . .	(DC)	900
O'BRIEN, Kathleen	(DC)	914
PACIFICO, Michele F. . .	(DC)	933
PAUL, Karen D.	(DC)	949
PROVINE, Dorothy S. . . .	(DC)	996
SHOREBIRD, Thomas S.	(DC)	1132
YOST, F D.	(DC)	1381
FRANCIS, Diane S.	(DE)	396
THOMAN, Nancy L.	(DE)	1236
TRYON, Roy H.	(DE)	1260
LANNING, E K.	(GA)	696
LONG, Linda E.	(GA)	739
ALDERSON, Karen A. . .	(IA)	11
WELLS, Merle W.	(ID)	1322
BURNS, Marie T.	(IL)	162
CULBERTSON, Diana L. .	(IL)	263
FARRELL, Patricia H. . . .	(IL)	365
GAYNON, David B.	(IL)	424
HANRATH, Linda C.	(IL)	497
KERR, Kevin G.	(IL)	644
MACKEY, Denise R.	(IL)	756
SORENSEN, Mark W. . .	(IL)	1168
STEGH, Leslie J.	(IL)	1185
SYVERSON, Kathleen A.	(IL)	1217
BISHOP, Barbara N.	(IN)	99
SOWINSKI, Carolyn M. .	(IN)	1170
YATES, Donald N.	(IN)	1378
BELL, Mary M.	(KY)	77
FOGLE, Dianna L.	(KY)	387
HAY, Charles C.	(KY)	515
CHAPDELAINE, Susan A.	(MA)	201
CYPHERS, James E. . . .	(MA)	268
EMOND, Kathleen A. . . .	(MA)	348
HORN, David E.	(MA)	559
HUENNEKE, Judith A. . .	(MA)	570
HUGGINS, Dean A.	(MA)	571
MCLAIN, Guy A.	(MA)	813
SCHWARTZ, Candy S. . .	(MA)	1104
STICKNEY, Zephorene L.	(MA)	1193
HOLLOWAK, Thomas L.	(MD)	552
KADEC, Sarah T.	(MD)	621
MERZ, Nancy M.	(MD)	827
PFLUG, Warner W.	(MI)	966
DEWAELSCHE, Thomas M.	(MO)	297
MCCREARY, Gail A. . . .	(MS)	800
OLSON, David J.	(NC)	922
SAYE, Jerry D.	(NC)	1086
GRAY, David P.	(ND)	459
BROWN, Jeanne I.	(NJ)	145
KAUFFMAN, Betty G. . . .	(NJ)	631
MAZZEI, Peter J.	(NJ)	791
MOSS, Susan K.	(NJ)	872
PARAS, Lucille P.	(NJ)	939
SIMMONS, Ruth J.	(NJ)	1140
VOGT, Herwart C.	(NJ)	1287
BEJNAR, Thaddeus P. . .	(NM)	75
MILLER, Bryan M.	(NM)	836
ROCHA, Guy L.	(NV)	1045
AUBRY, John C.	(NY)	38
BERNTSEN, Robert M. . .	(NY)	90
BONACORDA, James J.	(NY)	113
BOROSON, Sarah	(NY)	116
BUTLER, Tyrone G.	(NY)	167
CROCKETT, Denise J. . .	(NY)	259
D'ALLEYRAND, Marc R.	(NY)	270
FREIFELD, Roberta I. . . .	(NY)	401

RECORDS (Cont'd)
Records management

GRANKA, Bernard D. . . .	(NY)	457
HERBERT, Annette F. . .	(NY)	530
HOMMEL, Claudia	(NY)	555
HUDAK, Barbara M.	(NY)	569
HUNTER, Gregory S. . . .	(NY)	576
JONES, Sarah C.	(NY)	615
KLINE, Harriet	(NY)	661
LAFEVER, C R.	(NY)	687
MASYR, Caryl L.	(NY)	783
PARRIS, Angela P.	(NY)	944
POMRENZE, Seymour J.	(NY)	982
ROBERTSON, Betty M. .	(NY)	1041
SAFFADY, William	(NY)	1074
SEEBER, Frances M. . . .	(NY)	1111
SETTANNI, Joseph A. . .	(NY)	1117
TAMMARO, James M. . .	(NY)	1221
TAYLOR, Patricia A.	(NY)	1228
UZZO, Beatrice C.	(NY)	1270
WILSTED, Thomas P. . . .	(NY)	1353
GARTEN, Edward D. . . .	(OH)	420
GILLILAND, Anne J.	(OH)	436
GOERLER, Raimund E. . .	(OH)	443
SULLIVAN, Frances L. . .	(OH)	1207
LOWELL, Howard P. . . .	(OK)	744
FILSON, Laurie	(OR)	377
THELEN, Richard L.	(OR)	1234
ANDEL, June	(PA)	21
KIRCHER, Linda M.	(PA)	654
VANDOREN, Sandra S. .	(PA)	1275
WAGNER, Albin	(RI)	1291
EZELL, Margaret M.	(SC)	360
KINTNER, Susan B.	(SC)	653
KOHL, Michael F.	(SC)	668
MCCOY, Gail	(SC)	799
SUTHERLAND, Carl T. . .	(SC)	1211
WILLIAMS, Robert V. . . .	(SC)	1346
NORTON, Nancy P.	(TN)	910
PEMBERTON, J M.	(TN)	956
THWEATT, John H.	(TN)	1243
ANDERSON, Margaret . .	(TX)	24
AULBACH, Louis F.	(TX)	39
BENGE, Joy L.	(TX)	80
DAVIS, Connie J.	(TX)	278
DILLARD, Lois A.	(TX)	303
DUMONT, Paul E.	(TX)	325
HIMMEL, Richard L.	(TX)	542
HOLLAND, Michael E. . .	(TX)	551
HOOTON, Virginia A. . . .	(TX)	557
KESHISHIAN, Maria L. . .	(TX)	644
KLEIN, Mindy F.	(TX)	659
MATLOCK, Teresa A. . .	(TX)	784
MCCANN, Debra W. . . .	(TX)	794
PHILLIPS, Toni M.	(TX)	969
SCHAADT, Robert L. . . .	(TX)	1088
SCOTT, Paul R.	(TX)	1108
BAILEY, Clint R.	(UT)	46
HEFNER, Loretta L.	(UT)	520
SCOTT, Patricia L.	(UT)	1107
FIENCKE, Elaine L.	(VA)	376
GOLDBERG, Lisbeth S. .	(VA)	444
HUFF, Patricia M.	(VA)	570
KANE, Dorothea S.	(VA)	624
TATALIAS, Jean A.	(VA)	1225
HERNDON, Stan J.	(VT)	532
EDWARDS, Steven M. . .	(WA)	338
RHOADS, James B.	(WA)	1026
SCHUTTE, Raymond R. .	(WA)	1103
BLUE, Richard I.	(WI)	107
CONDON, John J.	(WI)	236
HYNUM, Jill A.	(WI)	580
KOVAN, Allan S.	(WI)	673
RYAN, Carol E.	(WI)	1070
SHUTKIN, Sara A.	(WI)	1134
GISHLER, John R.	(AB)	438
BEYEA, Marion L.	(NB)	93
CHAN, Margy	(ON)	199
HARDY, John L.	(ON)	500
LAFRANCHISE, David . .	(ON)	688

RECORDS (Cont'd)

Records management

SERMAT-HARDING, Kaili I. . . . . (ON) 1116
WILLIAMSON, Nancy J. . (ON) 1347
BROCHU, Frederick . . . . (PQ) 138
CAYA, Marcel . . . . . . (PQ) 195
PAPILLON, Yves . . . . . . (PQ) 939
TESSIER, Mario C. . . . . . (PQ) 1233
VAILLANCOURT, Alain . (PQ) 1270
ORTIZ MONASTERIO, Leonor . . . . (MEX) 927
FAGERLUND, M L. . . . . (SWZ) 361

Records management & archives PEARLSTEIN, Toby . . . . (MA) 952
OGAWA, Chiyoko . . . . . (JAP) 918
Records management & control REID, Angea S. . . . . (MA) 1018
Records management & librarianship ORTIZ, Diane . . . . (NV) 927
Records management & micrographics WALSH, G M. . . . . (ON) 1299
Records management & micrographics systs BRIMSEK, Tobi A. . . . . . (DC) 136
Records management & online searching IRONS, Carol A. . . . . . . (IL) 584
Records management & services HOWINGTON, Tad C. . . (TX) 566
Records management, archives PRESTON, Deirdre R. . . (WA) 991
Records management consulting FREEMAN, Carla . . . . . . (DC) 400
Records management in academia SCHULTZ, Charles R. . . (TX) 1101
Records management programs SAYED, Joyce P. . . . . . . (CA) 1086
Records management, retention scheduling NEWHALL, Ann C. . . . . (CT) 898
Records management systems HENDERSON, Deborah A. (ON) 526
Records management systems analysis BALON, Brett J. . . . . . . (SK) 53
Records management training MOORE, Gwen A. . . . . . (UT) 859
NASH, Cherie A. . . . . . (UT) 888
Records managing RITTER, Helen . . . . (NY) 1036
Records reference service SCOTT, Paul R. . . . . . . (TX) 1108
Records research, college history NELSON, Robert J. . . . . (NY) 895
Records retention UHLMAN, Carol K. . . . . (WA) 1268
Records retention, municipal BROWNE, Jeri A. . . . . . . (CA) 148
Records retention research BOWKER, Scott W. . . . . (NY) 121
Records retention scheduling SANDERS, Robert L. . . . (CA) 1080
SAYED, Joyce P. . . . . . . (CA) 1086
Records retention-disposition scheduling GRAHAM, Su D. . . . . . . (CO) 456
Records services HOLLINGS, Marie F. . . . (SC) 552
Records surveys & inventories FOURIE, Denise K. . . . . (CA) 393
Reference on university records HODGSON, Janet B. . . . (KY) 546
Religious record keeping SWEENEY, Shelley T. . . (SK) 1215
Score & record cataloging SEIBERT, Donald C. . . . (NY) 1112
Select music, records, cassettes CAPPAERT, Lael R. . . . . (MI) 180
Serial records CHATTERTON, Leigh A. (MA) 204
Serials records ASHLEY, Elizabeth . . . . (CA) 36
Serials records control CLASQUIN, Frank F. . . . (MA) 219
State agency records KETELSEN, Terry . . . . (CO) 645
WILLIAMS, Gene J. . . . (NC) 1343
State & local government records DEARSTYNE, Bruce W. . (NY) 284
State & local records WAGGENER, Jean B. . . (TN) 1291
State records center program management BITTLE, Christine M. . . . (OK) 100
Storage & retrieval of records & docums RAC-FEDORIJCZUK, Karola C. . . . . (PA) 1001
Student records databases THOMPSON, Jane K. . . . (VT) 1240
Subject authority records SCHMIDT, Holly H. . . . . (OR) 1095
Systems analysis & records management SIEGERT, Lindy E. . . . . (NS) 1136
Training & development records mgmt CORNELIUS, Charlene E. (WI) 246
Training & records development BUTLER, Tyrone G. . . . (NY) 167
Training in records management ARDERN, Christine M. . . (ON) 31
Treasury Department fiscal records SHERMAN, William F. . . (DC) 1128
20th century diplomatic records PFEIFFER, David A. . . . (DC) 966
20th century military records PFEIFFER, David A. . . . (DC) 966
University records LYSY, Peter J. . . . . (IN) 753
Use of historical records DENSMORE, Christopher (NY) 293
Vital records management MONTGOMERY, Suzanne L. . . . . (VA) 856
Word processing, record management systs KEE, Walter A. . . . . (NC) 634
78 rpm records SAVADA, Morton J. . . . . (NY) 1085

RECREATION

Music, arts & recreation WILKINS, Marilyn W. . . . (LA) 1340
Sports, recreation & leisure GRODSKI, Renata . . . . . (ON) 471

RECRUITMENT

Admissions & recruiting ARNOLD, Barbara J. . . . (WI) 33
Executive recruiting GAMBER, Deborah D. . . (CT) 416
FELDMAN, Linda A. . . . . (IL) 369
Executive search & recruitment BRYANT, Nancy J. . . . . (GA) 152
Library, information exec recruitment GOSSAGE, Wayne . . . . (NY) 453
Library personnel recruiting WALSH, Deborah T. . . . (IL) 1299
Library recruitment RODRIGUEZ, Ronald . . . (CA) 1048
Personnel recruitment MCINDOO, Larry R. . . . (CA) 809
Personnel recruitment & selection MARTZ, David J. . . . . . (DC) 779
MCMEEN, Frances E. . . . (NY) 815
Recruiting responsibilities supervisory LETTIERI, Robin M. . . . . (NY) 719
Recruiting temporary & permanent workers JOHNSON, Linnea R. . . . (IL) 607
Recruitment NYHAN, Constance W. . . (CA) 912
TANNER, Anne B. . . . . . (PA) 1222
Recruitment of librarians DEWEY, Barbara I. . . . . (IA) 298
Recruitment of personnel STOFFEL, Lester L. . . . (IL) 1196
Staff training, development, recruitment PURCELL, Marcia L. . . . (NY) 998
Volunteer recruitment SCHNEIDER, Marcia G. . (CA) 1097

REDESIGN

Creating or redesigning libraries BELTON, Jennifer H. . . . (DC) 78
Planning & redesigning libraries PROCOPIO, Concetta E. (MA) 994

REDUCTION

Reduction in force SHAFFER, Maryann . . . . (WA) 1119

REFEREEING

Refereeing system YAMAZAKI, Shigeaki . . . (JAP) 1377

REFERENCE (See also Atlases, Databases, Dictionaries, Directories, Encyclopedias, Information, Referral, Searching, Services)

Academic librarianship & reference SINGH, Swarn L. . . . . . . (KS) 1143
Academic library reference NELSON, Michael L. . . . . (WY) 894
Academic library reference service WEIMER, Sally W. . . . . (CA) 1317
Academic library reference services GREENE, Cathy C. . . . . (MA) 463
Academic reference ROBAR, Terri J. . . . . (FL) 1038
LAUDERDALE, Diane S. (IL) 702
VOGEL, Jane G. . . . . . . (NC) 1286
BUDGE, William D. . . . . (NY) 155
EISENBERG, Phyllis B. . . (VA) 340
OLIVETTI, L J. . . . . (VA) 921
Academic reference services LEHMAN, Douglas K. . . . (FL) 712
Academic reference work BOPP, Richard E. . . . . . (IL) 116
Academic science & technology reference COHEN, Jackson B. . . . . (NY) 228
Accounting & audit reference MCDEVITT-PARKS, Kathryn B. . . . . (CA) 802
Accounting, auditing & taxation ref HETZLER, Jill K. . . . . . . (WA) 534
Accounting auditing reference SWANTEK, Kathleen M. . (IL) 1214
Accounting reference HENEKS, Julia A. . . . . . (DC) 528
FLEISHMAN, Lauren Z. . (NY) 384
DUPUIS, Marcel . . . . (PQ) 327
Acquisition reference technical service WIENER, Sylvia B. . . . . (NY) 1336
Adlerian psychology references KAHN, Paul J. . . . . (CA) 622
Administration & reference PENNER, Elaine C. . . . . (TX) 957
GLENN, Lucy D. . . . . . . (VA) 441
Administration reference O'CONNELL, Susan . . . . (NY) 915
Administration, reference, research KNIGHT, Shirley D. . . . . (NJ) 664
Administration, reference services BURGESS, Rita N. . . . . (PA) 159
Administrative reference PADUA, Flores N. . . . . (PR) 934
Adult & children reference POTTER, Robert E. . . . . (FL) 987
Adult & children's reference service KAPUR, Geraldine P. . . . (MI) 626
Adult & reference specialist MACK, Phyllis G. . . . . . (NY) 756
Adult reference MURPHY, Patricia A. . . . (CA) 881
SIMAS, Therese C. . . . . (CA) 1139
SMITH, Heather . . . . . . (CA) 1155
WALSH, Donamarie F. . . (CA) 1299

REFERENCE (Cont'd)

Adult reference
- INGERSOLL, Lyn L. . . . . (DC) 582
- BRYAN, Michael G. . . . . (FL) 151
- AUSTIN, Sandra G. . . . . (IL) 40
- MILLER, Glenda G. . . . . (IL) 838
- NOTOWITZ, Joshua D. . . (MD) 910
- YERMAN, Roslyn F. . . . . (MI) 1380
- ZARYCZNY, Wlodzimierz A. . . . . (MI) 1386
- FARIAS, Elizabeth H. . . . (NC) 363
- WHITE, Sherry J. . . . . . . (NC) 1332
- THONER, Jane T. . . . . . (NJ) 1242
- ENG, Mamie . . . . (NY) 348
- KRAMPITZ, Barbara E. . (NY) 676
- KRISTIAN, Alice . . . . (NY) 679
- GRANTS, Yvette M. . . . . (OH) 458
- BRADY, Josiah B. . . . . . (TN) 126
- EDWARDS, Susan E. . . . (WA) 338
- WAGNER, Sabina H. . . . (WA) 1292
- WASICK, Mary A. . . . . . (WI) 1308
- BROSSEAU, Lise . . . . . . (PQ) 141

Adult reference & services — LOCKETT, Sandra B. . . . . (WI) 736
Adult reference, reader's advisory — GELINAS, Jeanne L. . . . (MN) 426
Adult reference, reader's services — PORTER, Eva L. . . . . . . (NJ) 984
Adult reference service
- HICKS, Cynthia S. . . . . . (CA) 536
- MALLER, Mark P. . . . . . (IL) 763

Adult reference services
- GROOMS, Richard O. . . . (AL) 472
- FARNHAM, Shera M. . . . (AZ) 365
- HERSH, Daniel . . . . (CA) 533
- ROBINSON, Lois C. . . . . (FL) 1044
- MEYER, Barbara G. . . . . (IL) 829
- MAY, Cecilia J. . . . . (KS) 788
- KUBICK, Dan P. . . . . (NE) 682
- BJORKLUND, Katharine B. (NM) 100
- MULLEN, Francis X. . . . . (PA) 877

Adult services & reference
- DENNIE, David L. . . . . . (DC) 292
- HENSON, Ruby P. . . . . . (MI) 530
- GILLESPIE, Gerald V. . . . (NY) 435

Advertising marketing reference service — OWENS, Tina M. . . . . . . (IL) 932
Aeronautics & aerospace reference — LEONARDO, Joan M. . . . (ON) 717
Agricultural economics reference
- PERMAN, Karen A. . . . . (IL) 959
- REEDMAN, M R. . . . . . . (MB) 1015

Agricultural reference
- MATHEWS, Eleanor R. . . (IA) 784
- DECKER, Leola M. . . . . (MD) 286
- KINCH, Michael P. . . . . . (OR) 649

Agricultural science reference — GAGE, Marilyn K. . . . . . (OK) 412
Agricultural sciences reference & bibl — MANNARINO, Elizabeth R. (OR) 766
Agriculture reference
- HARPER, Judy A. . . . . . (MB) 503
- SIMUNDSSON, Elva D. . . (MB) 1142

Alaska & arctic information reference — SOKOLOV, Barbara J. . . (AK) 1165
Alaska & polar regions reference service — LAKE, Gretchen L. . . . . (AK) 688
Alcoholism & substance abuse reference — WEINBERG, Gail B. . . . . (MN) 1317
American art reference
- FALK, Peter H. . . . . (CT) 362
- LYNAGH, Patricia M. . . . (DC) 751

American music reference — JACKSON, Richard H. . . (NY) 588
Anthropology reference — DAVIES, Mary K. . . . . . (DC) 277
Architectural reference — GRANADOS, Rose A. . . . (CA) 457
Architecture reference — AVERILL, Laurie J. . . . . (RI) 41
Architecture research & reference — WRIGHT, Sylvia H. . . . . (NY) 1373
Archival reference
- BAKER, Russell P. . . . . . (AR) 49
- MILLER, Leon C. . . . . . . (AR) 839
- CASSEDY, James G. . . . (DC) 193
- OAKHILL, Harold W. . . . (NY) 913

Archives processing & reference — BLACK, J A. . . . . (TX) 101
Archives reference
- BRILEY, Carol A. . . . . . . (MO) 136
- KUCHERENKO, Eugenia (OH) 682

Armenology reference — AVDOYAN, Levon . . . . . (DC) 41
Arms race materials & reference — MEYER, Jimmy E. . . . . . (OH) 830
Art & architecture reference — KEMPE, Deborah A. . . . . (NY) 639
Art & architecture specialized ref — BEGLO, Jo N. . . . . (ON) 74
Art & literature reference — REID, Kendall M. . . . . . (VA) 1018
Art & music reference — BARNETT, Jean D. . . . . (OR) 57
Art & reference publishing — MCGILVERY, Laurence . (CA) 806
Art & women's studies reference — ALLEN, Susan M. . . . . . (CA) 16
Art films reference & programming — WARREN, Ann R. . . . . . (NH) 1306
Art history reference — SMITH, Beryl K. . . . . . . (NJ) 1153

REFERENCE (Cont'd)

Art reference
- CARSCH, Ruth E. . . . . . (CA) 187
- ROSS, Alexander D. . . . . (CA) 1057
- DOUMATO, Lamia . . . . . (DC) 314
- LYNAGH, Patricia M. . . . (DC) 751
- BIRNEY, Ann E. . . . . (KS) 98
- MANNING, Mary L. . . . . (MN) 766
- SIMPSON, Leslie T. . . . . (MO) 1142
- CLARK, Diane E. . . . . . . (MS) 216
- MCARTHUR, Anne . . . . (NJ) 792
- REDLICH, Barry . . . . (NJ) 1014
- BRAUCH, Patricia O. . . . (NY) 129
- DEMARCO, Elizabeth A. . (NY) 291
- FREEMAN, Carla C. . . . (NY) 400
- WIERZBA, Christine . . . . (NY) 1337
- TOTH, Georgina G. . . . . (OH) 1252
- BISSELL, Joann S. . . . . . (PA) 100
- TACK, A C. . . . . (PA) 1219
- AVERILL, Laurie J. . . . . . (RI) 41

Art reference literature — WALKER, William B. . . . (NY) 1296
Art reference services — KORENIC, Lynette M. . . . (CA) 671
Arts & humanities reference — GRILIKHES, Sandra B. . . (PA) 470
Arts reference — DOLAN-HEITLINGER, Eileen . . . . (IN) 309
- LIKNESS, Craig S. . . . . . (TX) 727
Auction catalog reference services — TIEMAN, Robert S. . . . . (CA) 1244
Audiovisual & general reference — PIKUL, Diane M. . . . . . . (CT) 973
Audiovisual & library science reference — RUSIEWSKI, Charles B. . (IL) 1068
Audiovisual reference
- GARRETT, Melinda R. . . (OH) 420
- KASOW, Harriet . . . . . . (ISR) 629

Automated reference service — JOHNSON, Carolynn K. . (WA) 603
Automated reference services — JOHNSON, Charlotte L. . (IL) 603
- MASSEY-BURZIO, Virginia (MA) 782
Automated reference systems — BECK, Susan E. . . . . . . (MO) 71
Automated reference work — GORDON, Martin K. . . . . (VA) 451
Award reference books — SIEGMAN, Gita . . . . (MD) 1136
Banking & agriculture reference — PHILLIPS, Lena M. . . . . . (MD) 968
Banking, finance & business reference — MIRANDA, Esmeralda C. (MN) 847
Banking reference — MERBACH, Peggy O. . . . (CA) 825
Bibliographic instruction & reference — PATTERSON, Grace L. . . (NY) 948
- TORNQUIST, Kristi M. . . (WI) 1251
Bibliographic reference service — YU, Priscilla C. . . . . (IL) 1384
Bibliography & reference — SEEGRABER, Frank J. . . (MA) 1111
Bibliography & reference services — WANG, Chi . . . . (DC) 1302
Biography reference — DOPP, Bonnie J. . . . . . . (DC) 312
Biological science medicine reference — CHASTAIN-WARHEIT, Christine C. . . . . (DE) 203
Biological science reference
- MACLEAN, Jayne T. . . . (MD) 757
- GAGE, Marilyn K. . . . . . (OK) 412

Biological sciences reference & bibl — MANNARINO, Elizabeth R. (OR) 766
Biology reference — WILLIAMS, Doris C. . . . . (NY) 1343
Biology reference & selection — WINIARZ, Elizabeth . . . . (PQ) 1355
Biomedical & health reference — MYER, Nancy E. . . . . . . (NM) 884
Biomedical reference
- WEGLARZ, Catherine R. . (NJ) 1316
- KANESHIRO, Kellie N. . . (TX) 625
- VAN REENEN, Johannes A. . . . . (BC) 1277

Biomedical reference service — FURUMOTO, Viola G. . . (HI) 410
Biomedical reference services — COSKEY, Rosemary B. . . (MD) 248
Biomedical references — CONNOR, Elizabeth . . . . (MD) 237
Bio-medical science reference — MOORE, John R. . . . . . (IL) 860
Botanical reference & bibliography — SCHALLERT, Ruth F. . . . (DC) 1089
Botany reference
- MARKHAM, James W. . . (CA) 771
- TEETER, Enola J. . . . . . (PA) 1229

Budget, reference, personnel — FARKAS, Charles R. . . . (NY) 364
Building reference collection — COFFEY, Dorothy A. . . . (MI) 227
Business & advertising reference — BUSSEY, Holly J. . . . . . (NY) 165
Business & economics reference
- KRISTIE, William J. . . . . (CA) 679
- LARSEN, Lynda L. . . . . . (DC) 698
- WIZA, Judith M. . . . . . . (KY) 1359
- DODGE, Michael R. . . . . (NC) 308

Business & finance reference — NARCISO, Susan D. . . . (NY) 888
Business & general reference
- BOLL, Charles K. . . . . . (NJ) 112
- CARR, Timothy B. . . . . . (VA) 186

Business & humanities reference — GROVES, Helen G. . . . . (TX) 474
Business & industrial reference — PFOHL, Theodore E. . . . (NY) 966
Business & industry reference & resrch — LUXNER, Dick . . . . (NJ) 750

REFERENCE (Cont'd)

Business & law reference — PERELLA, Susanne B. . . (DC) 958

Business & marketing reference — WHITT, Diane M. . . . . . . (IL) 1334
CLIFT, Crystal A. . . . . . . (MN) 222

Business & religious reference sources — FEW, John E. . . . . (CA) 374

Business & science reference — MEYERS, Kathleen H. . . (AZ) 831

Business & technical reference — WILLIAMS, Constance H. (CO) 1342
REILLY, Dayle A. . . . . . . (MA) 1020

Business databases & reference — SCOTT, Miranda D. . . . . (NJ) 1107

Business, economic & mining reference — KIEFER, Karen N. . . . . . . (CA) 647

Business materials reference — CANNING, Joan M. . . . . . (NY) 178

Business reference — ENGEBRETSON, Mary E. (AL) 348
KENDRICK, Aubrey W. . (AL) 640
AWE, Susan C. . . . . (AZ) 42
HAWBAKER, A C. . . . . . (AZ) 513
BENSON-TALLEY, Lois I. (CA) 83
BRONARS, Lori A. . . . . . (CA) 140
CARSCH, Ruth E. . . . . . . (CA) 187
CLAEYS, Luisa T. . . . . . (CA) 215
COSTELLO, M R. . . . . . (CA) 249
DUFFY, Karen R. . . . . . . (CA) 324
EICHELBERGER, Susan . (CA) 339
FROST, Michelle . . . . . . (CA) 406
GERSTLE, Steven M. . . . (CA) 429
GORDON, Wendy R. . . . (CA) 452
HOFFMAN, Irene M. . . . . (CA) 548
JACOBSEN, Lavonne . . . (CA) 590
KENNEDY, Charlene F. . (CA) 640
MOORE-EVANS, Angela (CA) 862
STEELMAN, Lucille A. . . (CA) 1184
STERNHEIM, Karen . . . . (CA) 1189
WENDROFF, Catriona . . . (CA) 1323
WILKINSON, David W. . . (CA) 1340
SANI, Martha J. . . . . (CO) 1081
SHORE, Julia M. . . . . . . (CT) 1132
UBYSZ, Priscilla M. . . . . (CT) 1267
ZYGMONT, Carolyn A. . . (CT) 1392
BLANDAMER, Ann W. . . (DC) 103
CARDWELL, Diane O. . . (DC) 181
POSNIAK, John R. . . . . . (DC) 985
STREHL, Susan J. . . . . . (DC) 1201
UPDEGROVE, Robert A. (DC) 1269
WENGEL, Linda . . . . (DC) 1324
LADNER, Sharyn J. . . . . (FL) 687
MCKAY, Peter Z. . . . . . . (FL) 810
MORRIS, Steve R. . . . . . (FL) 867
PFARRER, Theodore R. . (FL) 966
COONIN, Bryna R. . . . . . (GA) 242
MACK, Debora S. . . . . . . (GA) 756
BRADLEY, Anne . . . . . . (IL) 125
BURGH, Scott G. . . . . . . (IL) 159
GARDNER, Margaret L. . (IL) 418
GIAMBRONE, Richard J. (IL) 430
GROSCH, Mary F. . . . . . (IL) 472
HAMILTON, Dawn J. . . . . (IL) 492
HILBURGER, Mary J. . . . (IL) 538
HUSFELDT, Jerry J. . . . . (IL) 578
MADDEN, Michael J. . . . (IL) 758
MASON, Margaret E. . . . (IL) 781
MOULTON, James C. . . . (IL) 873
SWANTEK, Kathleen M. . (IL) 1214
WAGNER, Ralph D. . . . . (IL) 1292
NEELY, Glenda S. . . . . . (KY) 892
BROWN, Sue S. . . . . (LA) 147
HANKEL, Marilyn L. . . . . (LA) 496
BENDER, Helen F. . . . . . (MA) 79
COLEMAN, James R. . . . (MA) 231
DANIELLS, Lorna M. . . . (MA) 273
EWING, Lydia M. . . . . . . (MA) 359
FEIDLER, Anita J. . . . . . (MA) 368
MAGUIRE, Patricia V. . . (MA) 760
JACKSON, Carleton . . . . (MD) 587
HEGEDUS, Mary E. . . . . (MI) 521
LEB, Joan P. . . . . (MI) 707
RING, Donna M. . . . . (MI) 1035
WHITE, Jane F. . . . . (MI) 1331
ANDERSON, Rebekah E. (MN) 25
CLARKE, Norman F. . . . (MN) 219

REFERENCE (Cont'd)

Business reference — GADE, Rachel P. . . . . . . (MN) 411
REYNEN, Richard G. . . . (MN) 1025
TERTELL, Susan M. . . . . (MN) 1232
VAN WHY, Carol B. . . . . (MN) 1277
HUND, Flower L. . . . . . . (MO) 574
REINHOLD, Edna J. . . . . (MO) 1021
HEBERT, Robert A. . . . . (NC) 519
MILLER, Barry K. . . . . . . (NC) 836
AU, Ka N. . . . . (NJ) 38
BARZELATTO, Elba G. . . (NJ) 62
CHANG, Bernadine A. . . (NJ) 200
GREENBLATT, Ruth . . . . (NJ) 463
LATINI, Samuel A. . . . . . (NJ) 701
OTT, Linda G. . . . . (NJ) 930
SKYZINSKI, Susan E. . . (NJ) 1147
TIPTON, Roberta L. . . . . (NJ) 1247
ABBITT, Viola I. . . . . (NY) 1
APPEL, Marsha C. . . . . . (NY) 29
BEALER, Jane A. . . . . . . (NY) 68
BULSON, Christine . . . . . (NY) 156
CARLSON, Robert E. . . . (NY) 182
COONEY, Martha D. . . . . (NY) 242
DIMARTINO, Diane J. . . . (NY) 303
DREIFUSS, Richard A. . . (NY) 319
HECKMAN, Lucy T. . . . . (NY) 519
HRYVNIAK, Joseph T. . . (NY) 567
JOHNSON, David J. . . . . (NY) 603
MACLEAN, Paul . . . . (NY) 757
NERBOSO, Donna L. . . . (NY) 895
REID, Richard C. . . . . . . (NY) 1019
ROSENFELD, Jane D. . . (NY) 1056
ROWAN, Diane M. . . . . . (NY) 1062
RUBINO, Cynthia C. . . . . (NY) 1065
RYAN, James J. . . . . (NY) 1071
SCIATTARA, Diane M. . . (NY) 1106
SOUDERS, Marilyn N. . . (NY) 1169
STERLING, Sheila . . . . . (NY) 1189
TIFFEAULT, Alice A. . . . (NY) 1244
VENER, Lucille . . . . (NY) 1282
CARY, Mary K. . . . . (OH) 191
HELSER, Fred L. . . . . . . (OH) 525
IRELAND, Clara R. . . . . . (OH) 583
KEATING, Michael F. . . . (OH) 633
LINDSTROM, Elaine C. . . (OH) 730
MAURER, Lewis R. . . . . (OH) 787
POPOVICH, Charles J. . . (OH) 984
CATTIE, Mary M. . . . . . . (PA) 195
DEWANE, Kathleen M. . . (PA) 298
GRIFFITH, Dorothy A. . . (PA) 469
KALIN, Sarah G. . . . . . . (PA) 623
KIRCHER, Linda M. . . . . (PA) 654
THOMPSON, Dorothea M. (PA) 1239
WRIGHT, Barbara C. . . . (PA) 1370
CRAVEN, Trudy W. . . . . (SC) 256
MCREE, John W. . . . . . . (SC) 818
SILER, Freddie B. . . . . . (SC) 1137
SMITH, Stephen C. . . . . (SC) 1161
DEAN, Leann F. . . . . (SD) 283
MADER, Sharon B. . . . . . (TN) 759
DAVIS, Carolyn . . . . (TX) 278
GAMEZ, Juanita L. . . . . . (TX) 416
GRIMES, Carolyn E. . . . . (TX) 470
HOLMAN, Linda E. . . . . . (TX) 553
MORRIS, Pamela A. . . . . (TX) 867
SPECHT, Alice W. . . . . . (TX) 1172
WEATHERS, Jerry D. . . . (TX) 1312
WISE, Olga B. . . . . (TX) 1357
CASH, Susan R. . . . . . . (VA) 192
MERRIFIELD, Mark D. . . (VA) 826
REID, Kendall M. . . . . . . (VA) 1018
TOSIANO, Barbara A. . . (VA) 1252
BURKE, Vivienne C. . . . . (WA) 160
PASSARELLI, Anne B. . . (WA) 946
BELL, Hope A. . . . . (ON) 77
SEDGWICK, Dorothy L. . (ON) 1111
DUPUIS, Marcel . . . . (PQ) 327

Business reference & instruction — BATISTA, Emily J. . . . . . (PA) 64
Business reference & legal research — SEAMAN, Sally G. . . . . . (IL) 1109

REFERENCE (Cont'd)

Business reference & research — MATTHEWSON, David S. (CT) 786
TEW, Robin L. (FL) 1233
WASYLENKO, Lydia W. (NY) 1308
ETCHINGHAM, John B. (RI) 355
Business reference bibliography — BROWN, Charlotte D. (VA) 142
Business reference databases — LEE, Soon H. (IL) 711
DITMARS, Robert D. (NJ) 305
Business reference information — PINSON, Mark (MA) 975
Business reference insurance — ALDRICH, Linda W. (CA) 11
Business reference materials — GORDON, Donna M. (AB) 451
Business reference publications — DITMARS, Robert D. (NJ) 305
SIMON, David H. (NJ) 1140
Business reference resources — SINWELL, Carol A. (VA) 1144
Business reference service — MOORE, Sheryl R. (TX) 861
TIRRELL, Brenda P. (TX) 1247
Business reference services — SLOCUM, Hannah R. (CA) 1150
STRAUSS, Diane (NC) 1201
SMITH, Sweetman R. (NY) 1161
MILLER, Clayton M. (OH) 836
STANLEY, Jean B. (OH) 1180
SEARS, Robert W. (OK) 1110
COORSH, Katalin (ON) 244
Business reference sources — EDWARDS, Betty (MA) 337
CARMACK, Norma J. (TX) 183
Business reference specialist — DICKSON, Laura K. (NE) 301
Business reference tools — LANDOLFI, Lisa M. (NY) 693
Business, science, & technology ref — REGNER, Erlinda J. (IL) 1017
RICHMOND, Diane A. (IL) 1030
Business, science reference & research — LEDBETTER, Sherry H. (MD) 708
Byzantine & medieval studies reference — AVDOYAN, Levon (DC) 41
Cartographic materials reference service — COOMBS, James A. (MO) 241
Cataloging & reference — DENNIS, Mary R. (IA) 292
RAMBO, Helen M. (ID) 1005
CHUNG, Hai C. (NJ) 213
CALDWELL, John M. (PA) 172
Cataloging & reference services — ANTHONY, Paul L. (IL) 29
Cataloging, online searching, reference — PHILLIPS, Rosemary (ON) 969
Cataloging, rare books, reference — STUFF, Marjorie A. (NE) 1205
Cataloging reference — EARLY, Stephen T. (WA) 332
SIEMENS, Bessie M. (MEX)1136
Cataloging, reference, & circulation — MANDAL, Mina R. (NY) 764
Cataloging reference, serials — VAN STRATEN, Daniel G. (WI) 1277
CD-ROM library reference information — HATVANY, Bela R. (MA) 512
Ceramic technology reference — CULLEY, Paul T. (NY) 263
Chemical & business reference — WILLARD, Ann M. (CA) 1341
Chemical engineering references — MONTGOMERY, Kimberly K. (AL) 856
Chemical literature & reference — YAGELLO, Virginia E. (OH) 1376
Chemical reference — AVERY, May S. (IL) 42
Chemistry & engineering reference — BECK, Diane J. (CA) 71
Chemistry & geology reference — HOBBS, Kathleen M. (ON) 545
Chemistry databases & reference — MILLER, Dennis P. (OH) 837
Chemistry reference — HUBER, Charles F. (CA) 568
EVANS, Sylvia D. (MD) 358
DESS, Howard M. (NJ) 295
Chemistry reference & online searching — STANLEY, Eileen H. (LA) 1180
Children & adult reference & referral — DAYO, Ayo (TX) 283
Children & young adult reference — TUPPER, Bobbie (HI) 1263
Children's literature reference — HURLEY, Doreen S. (PA) 577
Children's reference — SMITH, Heather (CA) 1155
LAPOLT, Margaret B. (CT) 697
REGNER, Erlinda J. (IL) 1017
ANDERSON, Valerie J. (VA) 25
BROSSEAU, Lise (PQ) 141
Children's reference & reader assistance — BECKER, Teresa J. (AZ) 72
Children's reference materials — DRACH, Priscilla L. (OH) 318
Circulation & reference — RINE, Joseph L. (MN) 1035
Circulation & reference services — WATTERSON, Jane L. (CO) 1310
Classical antiquity, reference — AVDOYAN, Levon (DC) 41
Classical Greek & Latin reference — CRITTENDEN, Robert R. (CA) 259
Clinical medical reference bibliography — KINNAIRD, Cheryl D. (IL) 653
Clinical medicine reference — ECKERT, Daniel L. (WI) 335

REFERENCE (Cont'd)

Clinical support & reference — MOORE, Sara L. (DC) 861
Compiling film reference books — TUDIVER, Lillian (NY) 1262
Computer hardware & software reference — ROBSON, Amy K. (IL) 1045
Computer reference service coordination — KONG, Leslie M. (CA) 670
Computer reference service, scientific — WANAT, Camille A. (CA) 1302
Computer reference services — HOGAN, Eddy (CA) 549
TAYLOR, Anne E. (TX) 1226
Computer-assisted reference — SCHOLAND, Julia E. (CA) 1098
TALALAY, Kathryn M. (IN) 1220
RICCI, Patricia L. (MN) 1026
Computer-assisted reference service — BALDWIN, Charlene M. (AZ) 51
Computer-assisted reference services — WILKINSON, David W. (CA) 1340
Computer-based legal reference — HARBISON, John H. (DC) 499
Computer-based reference — LIDSKY, Ella (NY) 725
FOWLER, Margaret A. (MB) 394
Computer-based reference service — COSTELLO, M R. (CA) 249
SPURLOCK, Pauline (CA) 1177
BOROSON, Sarah (NY) 116
REINALDO DA SILVA, Joann T. (MB) 1021
JUOZAPAVICIUS, Danguole T. (ON) 620
PAPOUTSIS, Fotoula (ON) 939
KELLY, Claire B. (PQ) 637
Computer-based reference services — BEARD, Craig W. (AR) 69
NEELY, Jesse G. (CA) 892
STEELE, Noreen O. (CT) 1184
MCNAMARA, Emma J. (DC) 816
PACIFICI, Sabrina I. (DC) 933
DEWBERRY, Claire D. (GA) 298
LOTZ, Marsha A. (IL) 742
ROMANO, Katherine V. (IL) 1052
WONG, Mabel K. (IL) 1363
MAYEAUX, Thurlow M. (LA) 789
WOJCIKIEWICZ, Carol A. (MI) 1359
WOODARD, Beth E. (MI) 1365
BEST-NICHOLS, Barbara J. (NC) 92
BUSH, Renee B. (NY) 165
DREZEN, Richard (NY) 319
HEWITT, Mary L. (NY) 535
PIENITZ, Eleanor (NY) 971
RICE, Cecelia E. (NY) 1027
SHADE, Ronald H. (NY) 1118
GATTEN, Jeffrey N. (OH) 422
LUST, Jeanette M. (OH) 749
BAKER, Judith M. (PA) 48
KATUCKI, June P. (PA) 630
PIERCE, Miriam D. (PA) 971
SCHWARZ, Betty P. (PA) 1105
JOHNSON, Johanna H. (TX) 606
MCCONNELL, Karen S. (TX) 797
NOREM, Monica R. (TX) 908
SHIH, Chia C. (TX) 1130
LARMOUR, Rosamond E. (VA) 698
CRANDALL, Michael D. (WA) 255
MOFJELD, Pamela A. (WA) 852
PASSARELLI, Anne B. (WA) 946
EKLAND, Patricia A. (BC) 341
JESKE, Margo (ON) 600
BONNELLY, Claude (PQ) 114
FIORE, Francine (PQ) 379
KITTUR, Krishna N. (IND) 657
LEE, Lucy T. (TAI) 710
Computerization, technical services, ref — HEISE, George F. (NJ) 522
Computerized reference service — MIDDLETON, Robert K. (TX) 833
Computerized reference services — LA BORDE, Charlotte A. (CA) 686
BILLY, George J. (NY) 97
BROMLEY, Alice V. (NY) 140
GOLDSTEIN, Cynthia N. (WA) 446
Congress reference — JONES, Catherine A. (DC) 611
Consumer health selection, reference — TAPPANA, Kathy A. (OK) 1223
Cooperative reference — ROOSE, Tina (IL) 1053
Cooperative reference services — GIBBS, Margareth (IL) 431
Corporate documents & reference — NOVICK, Ruth (NY) 911

REFERENCE (Cont'd)

Corporate reference	ADAMO, Marilyn H.	(NY)	4
	JOHNSON, John E.	(ON)	606
Current events reference	VANDEGRIFT, Barbara P.	(DC)	1273
Database reference services	LUNG, Chan S.	(NY)	748
Database searching, research, reference	BEDOR, Kathleen M.	(MN)	73
Dental literature reference	WILLIAMS, Ann T.	(TX)	1342
Dental reference	STROTHER, Elizabeth A.	(LA)	1203
Desk reference	KUGLER, Sharon	(NY)	682
Developing countries reference	BOYLE, James E.	(DC)	123
Documents reference	SHAABAN, Marian F.	(IN)	1118
	PARHAM, Kay B.	(OK)	940
Domestic reference fiscal policy	ANDERSON, John M.	(DC)	23
Earth science reference	MURRAY, James T.	(OK)	882
Earth sciences reference & research	SORROUGH, Gail L.	(CA)	1169
Earthquake engineering reference service	SVIHRA, S J.	(CA)	1212
Economic statistics reference	RANDOLPH, Susan E.	(DC)	1007
Economics & finance reference	MAYNARD, Elizabeth	(OH)	790
Economics reference	GROSCH, Mary F.	(IL)	472
Editing of reference works	HARNER, James L.	(OH)	503
Editing reference books	BRAUNSTEIN, Mark M.	(RI)	130
Education & psychology reference	MULVIHILL, Joann	(AZ)	878
Education for reference	DINGLE, Susan	(PA)	304
Education reference	TISE, Barbara L.	(CA)	1247
	ALTHAGE, Celia J.	(IL)	18
	BROWN, Sue S.	(LA)	147
	TYLER, Carolyn S.	(SC)	1266
Education reference & instruction	HINKLE, Mary R.	(VA)	542
Education ref collection development	DAVIS, Maryellen K.	(IL)	280
Education reference service	MCKEE, Elizabeth C.	(AR)	810
Education, social science reference	ROBERTSON, Ina N.	(IL)	1042
Education specialized reference services	BROWN, M S.	(FL)	145
Educational reference, research	FARRIS, Loretta	(PA)	365
Educational reference services	MISSAR, Charles D.	(MD)	847
Educational resources management & ref	ILACQUA, Anne K.	(MA)	581
Electronic media reference	HATVANY, Bela R.	(MA)	512
Electronic reference services	FLEMMING, Tom	(ON)	384
Energy & business reference	WEBER, Robert F.	(OR)	1314
Energy reference & library management	BLANDAMER, Ann W.	(DC)	103
Energy reference & natural gas	MARSHALL, Alexandra P.	(ON)	773
Engineering & business reference	KAUFENBERG, Jane M.	(MN)	630
Engineering & manufacturing reference	NESBITT, Olive K.	(PA)	896
Engineering & materials reference	WOODLOCK, Stephanie	(PA)	1366
Engineering & science reference	MULLEN, Cecilia P.	(CA)	877
	TINSLEY, Geraldine L.	(PA)	1246
Engineering information & reference	SCHEIN, Lorraine S.	(NY)	1091
Engineering reference	ANDREWS, Karen L.	(CA)	26
	GRANADOS, Rose A.	(CA)	457
	LARUSSA, Carol J.	(CA)	700
	RANCATORE, Celeste L.	(CA)	1006
	BLAKE, Martha A.	(IL)	103
	SCHRAMM, Mary T.	(IL)	1099
	BARRY, Richard A.	(NY)	60
	MURRAY, James T.	(OK)	882
	WARD, Suzanne M.	(TN)	1304
	LINDSEY, Thomas K.	(TX)	730
Engineering reference information	ST. AUBIN, Kendra J.	(MA)	1075
Engineering standards reference	MOORE, John R.	(IL)	860
Environmental reference	RODES, Barbara K.	(DC)	1047
	BARATTA, Maria	(NJ)	55
Environmental reference & research	JOHNSON, Mary E.	(CA)	607
Evaluation of reference services	BUNGE, Charles A.	(WI)	157
Expert system in reference	MICCO, Helen M.	(PA)	831
Expert systems for reference service	RICHARDSON, John V.	(CA)	1029
Expert systems in reference	EKLAND, Patricia A.	(BC)	341
Extensive reference	REDDINGTON, Mary E.	(OH)	1013
Federal & California law reference	CH'NG, Saw K.	(CA)	209
Federal government documents reference	LINDSEY, Thomas K.	(TX)	730
Federal legislative reference	COCHRAN, Catherine	(MI)	225
Film reference	GOLDMAN, Nancy L.	(CA)	445
Financial reference	VAZQUEZ, Edward	(NY)	1280
Financial reference sources	STONER, Ronald P.	(IL)	1198
Financial reporting reference	JOHNSON, John E.	(ON)	606

REFERENCE (Cont'd)

Fine arts reference	DONIO, Dorothy	(FL)	311
	MORR, Lynell A.	(FL)	866
	SCHERER, Herbert G.	(MN)	1092
	DOGU, Hikmet S.	(UT)	309
Fine arts reference services	MENDRO, Donna C.	(TX)	824
Fiscal projects & reference in archives	HARWOOD, James L.	(DC)	510
Food & nutrition reference	SZILARD, Paula	(HI)	1218
Food industry reference	DEPKE, Robert W.	(IL)	293
Food science reference	PERMAN, Karen A.	(IL)	959
Foreign & international law reference	TARNAWSKY, Marta	(PA)	1224
	WEISBAUM, Earl	(TX)	1319
Foreign language reference & cataloging	MCCLAREY, Catherine A.	(IL)	796
Forestry reference	KINCH, Michael P.	(OR)	649
Fundraising reference	ABBITT, Viola I.	(NY)	1
Genealogical reference	DECKER, John W.	(MN)	286
	OVERTON, Julie M.	(OH)	931
	SPERRY, Kip	(UT)	1174
Genealogical reference service	PARKER, John C.	(CA)	942
Genealogical research & reference	CARTER, Janet K.	(TX)	189
Genealogy reference	CRITTENDEN, Robert R.	(CA)	259
	CLARK, Diane E.	(MS)	216
	BAKER, Zachary M.	(NY)	50
	TURNER, Robert L.	(VA)	1265
General academic reference	OPPENHEIM, Michael R.	(CA)	925
General adult reference	AMESTOY, Helen M.	(CA)	20
General & business reference	HAULE, Laura M.	(IL)	512
	KONOVALOFF, Maria S.	(NY)	670
	WEEKS, Gerald M.	(BC)	1315
General & government documents reference	BALSARA, Aspi	(NF)	53
General & humanities reference	SANDERS, Lou M.	(MS)	1080
	DEDONATO, Ree	(NY)	286
General & medical reference	SMITH, Thomas E.	(DC)	1161
	CRABTREE, Anna B.	(MO)	254
	MICHAELS, Debbie D.	(NJ)	832
	THOMAS, Mary E.	(VA)	1237
General & reference service	LAKE, Gretchen L.	(AK)	688
General & science reference	FRIEDMAN, Ruth	(NJ)	404
General & subject reference	TZE-CHUNG, Li	(IL)	1267
General business reference	MCGARVEY, Eileen B.	(NY)	805
General law reference	WOOD, Elizabeth B.	(OH)	1364
General legal, corporate & tax reference	RAUCH, Anne	(NY)	1010
General legal reference	REID, Pauline	(NY)	1019
General librarian reference cataloging	GOSDECK, David M.	(WI)	452
General library reference	KAGANN, Laurie K.	(IL)	621
	ELLIS, Janet L.	(SC)	344
General reference	MITCHELL, Micheal L.	(AK)	849
	TAYLOR, Douglas M.	(AL)	1226
	HINTZMAN, Bonnie	(AZ)	543
	BUTKIS, John F.	(CA)	166
	CHOUDHURY, Lori B.	(CA)	211
	COOVER, Robert W.	(CA)	244
	EMERY, Frances D.	(CA)	348
	GORDON, Wendy R.	(CA)	452
	HANFT, Margie E.	(CA)	495
	HEPP, Thomas A.	(CA)	530
	LAMBREV, Garrett I.	(CA)	691
	MORRISON, Deborah L.	(CA)	868
	RAMIREZ, Anthony L.	(CA)	1005
	TISE, Barbara L.	(CA)	1247
	HURLEY, Faith P.	(DC)	577
	KLEIN, Kristine J.	(DC)	659
	TABB, Winston	(DC)	1219
	WOLFF, Stephen G.	(DE)	1361
	BYRD, Beverly P.	(FL)	168
	FAHNERT, Elizabeth K.	(FL)	361
	SAMUELS, David H.	(FL)	1079
	SMITH, Robyn H.	(FL)	1160
	STRADER, Helen B.	(FL)	1199
	SUGDEN, Martin D.	(FL)	1206
	FLICK, Frances J.	(IA)	385
	PARROTT, Lynn K.	(IA)	944
	SCHERUBEL, Melody J.	(IA)	1092
	ALLAN, Nancy P.	(IL)	14
	ANDERSON, Byron P.	(IL)	21
	FAIRCHILD, Constance A.	(IL)	361
	FORBES, Lydia B.	(IL)	389

REFERENCE (Cont'd)
General reference

KAYAIAN, Mary S. . . . . . (IL) 632
KING, David E. . . . . (IL) 650
KINNERSLEY, Ruth T. . . (IL) 653
PERSON, Roland C. . . . . (IL) 961
SENN, Mary S. . . . . (IL) 1115
SMYERS, Richard P. . . . (IN) 1162
WHITE, Lois A. . . . . . . (IN) 1331
MESNER, Lillian R. . . . . . (KY) 827
TEN HOOR, Joan M. . . . . (KY) 1231
BALL, Dannie J. . . . . (LA) 52
BYERS, Cora M. . . . . . . (LA) 168
LANDRY, Abbie V. . . . . . (LA) 693
CRANE, Hugh M. . . . . . . (MA) 255
JOHNSON, Dorothy A. . . (MA) 603
PANGALLO, Karen L. . . (MA) 938
CREST, Sarah E. . . . . . . (MD) 258
DAVISH, William . . . . . . (MD) 281
CORRADINI, Diane M. . . (MI) 247
SATTERTHWAITE, Diane
A. . . . . (MI) 1084
TSAI, Fu M. . . . . (MI) 1260
BARNES, Everett W. . . . (MO) 57
GREGORY, Kirk . . . . (MO) 466
REINHOLD, Edna J. . . . . (MO) 1021
HAUSE, Aaron H. . . . . . (MT) 512
ADAMS, Elizabeth L. . . . (NC) 4
DODGE, Michael R. . . . . (NC) 308
SPOON, James M. . . . . . (NC) 1175
LEBEAU, Chris . . . . (NE) 707
GRANT, Nancy A. . . . . . (NH) 458
BARZELATTO, Elba G. . (NJ) 62
BEEDE, Benjamin R. . . . (NJ) 74
GAYNOR, William A. . . . (NJ) 424
HOOKER, Joan M. . . . . . (NJ) 556
SKYZINSKI, Susan E. . . (NJ) 1147
BUTLER, Barbara E. . . . . (NV) 166
BROWN, Ronald L. . . . . (NY) 147
BUELOW, Mary E. . . . . . (NY) 155
CHRISTENSON, Janet S. (NY) 211
CORBIN, Evelyn D. . . . . (NY) 245
FINCH, Frances . . . . (NY) 377
GILES, Marta M. . . . . . . (NY) 434
HULTZ, Karen W. . . . . . (NY) 573
KLAVANO, Ann M. . . . . (NY) 658
PRICE, Susan W. . . . . . . (NY) 992
REMUSAT, Suzanne L. . (NY) 1023
ROSEN, Nathan A. . . . . (NY) 1055
SALTUS, Winifred T. . . . (NY) 1077
SWORDS, Susan . . . . . . (NY) 1217
FERGUSON, George E. . (OH) 372
ROBINSON, David A. . . . (OH) 1043
TYSON, Edith S. . . . . . . (OH) 1267
WOLFF, Cynthia J. . . . . . (OK) 1361
BISSELL, Joann S. . . . . (PA) 100
BOLGER, Dorita F. . . . . . (PA) 112
BRICKER, Will S. . . . . . . (PA) 135
CATTIE, Mary M. . . . . . . (PA) 195
FELLER, Judith M. . . . . . (PA) 370
JEAN, Lorraine A. . . . . . (PA) 596
KNEIL, Gertrude M. . . . . (PA) 664
LICHTENBERG, Elsa R. . (PA) 725
SCHANER, Marian E. . . . (PA) 1090
VERHAAREN, John E. . . (PA) 1282
WALLACE, Wilma E. . . . (TN) 1298
AIRTH, Elizabeth J. . . . . (TX) 9
BUCHWALD, Donald M. . (TX) 153
DEILY, Carole C. . . . . . . (TX) 288
EASON, Lisa H. . . . . (TX) 332
PALMER, Judith L. . . . . . (TX) 936
TINSMAN, William A. . . (TX) 1246
WILLIAMS, Ann T. . . . . . (TX) 1342
WEISS, Stephen C. . . . . (UT) 1320
DAVIS, Wylma P. . . . . . . (VA) 281
JORDAN, Caroline D. . . . (VA) 616
LIEBERMAN, Sharon A. . (VA) 726
MERRIFIELD, Mark D. . . (VA) 826
TURNER, Robert L. . . . . (VA) 1265
GROVER, Iva S. . . . . . . (WA) 474

REFERENCE (Cont'd)
General reference

LEASURE, Lois A. . . . . . (WV) 707
WOOD, Alberta A. . . . . . (NF) 1363
RODGER, Elizabeth A. . . (ON) 1047
BUTLER, Patricia . . . . . . (PQ) 167
GREGOIRE, Fleurette . . . (PQ) 466

General reference & adult services   FOSTER, Joan . . . . (MA) 392
General reference & business   DOLMON, Barbara N. . . . (IL) 310
General reference & information   BUSH, Rhoda H. . . . . . . (MD) 165
    LINDSAY, Jean S. . . . . . (NY) 729
General reference & periodicals   SANCHEZ, Sara M. . . . . (FL) 1079
General reference & research   WEISS, Paula K. . . . . . . (IL) 1320
General reference high quality   TURNER, Kathleen G. . . (WA) 1264
General reference, psychology
    reference   COYLE, Leslie P. . . . . . . (CA) 253
General reference, public services   WHITTINGTON, Christine
    A. . . . . (PA) 1334
General reference publishing   NAULT, William H. . . . . (IL) 889
General reference service   BRIDGMAN, Amy R. . . . (CA) 135
    LEVIN, Joan E. . . . . (IL) 720
    OWENS, Tina M. . . . . . . (IL) 932
    SMITH, Richard G. . . . . (IL) 1160
    DALLAS, Larayne J. . . . (TX) 270
General reference services   GUARINO, John P. . . . . (CA) 475
    CANICK, Maureen L. . . . (DC) 178
    TSCHERNY, Alexander . (DC) 1260
    LYON, Bruce C. . . . . . . (FL) 752
    PRIOR, Barbara Q. . . . . (KY) 993
    LAPAS, Martha E. . . . . . (NC) 697
    KLEHN, Victoria L. . . . . (TX) 658
General reference work   SWEEDLER, Ulla S. . . . . (CA) 1214
    FICKES, Raymond C. . . . (NC) 374
General references   GREENBERG, Eva M. . . (OH) 463
General science reference   FERGUSON, Elizabeth E. (CT) 372
    LANDRY, Francis R. . . . . (MA) 693
General university reference service   ROBERTS, Sally M. . . . . (IL) 1041
Geographical reference   PESCHEL, Susan M. . . . (WI) 961
Geological references   DAVIS, Connie J. . . . . . . (TX) 278
Geoscience reference   MESSICK, Carol H. . . . . (VA) 828
Gerontological reference services   HARTZ, Mary K. . . . . . . (DC) 509
Government documents & maps
    reference   WALKER, Barbara J. . . . (GA) 1295
Government documents reference   WEATHERLY, Cynthia D. (AL) 1312
    COONIN, Bryna R. . . . . (GA) 242
    CAIN, Charlene C. . . . . . (LA) 171
    SUDDUTH, William E. . . (MA) 1206
Government publications reference
    srv   CALHOUN, Ellen . . . . . . (NJ) 172
Government reference   BELL, Hope A. . . . . (ON) 77
Graduate reference   STRAUSS, Diane . . . . . . (NC) 1201
Hawaii & the Pacific reference   ASHFORD, Marguerite K. (HI) 36
Health & humanities sciences
    reference   CHASE, Judith H. . . . . . . (OR) 203
Health care administration reference
    srv   HAMILTON, Elizabeth J. . (VA) 492
Health care reference   NANSTIEL, Barbara L. . . (PA) 887
Health care reference & databases   LEE, Soon H. . . . . (IL) 711
Health reference services   TURNER, Ray . . . . (KY) 1265
Health science reference   LIPPMAN, Anne F. . . . . . (MA) 732
    ARTH, Janet M. . . . . (MN) 35
    PATTERSON, Charlean P. (PA) 948
Health sciences reference   BELL, R E. . . . . (CA) 77
    KAMENOFF, Lovisa . . . . (MA) 623
    SULLIVAN, Joanne L. . . (MD) 1207
    WENGER, Milton B. . . . (NY) 1324
    GIOVENALE, Sharon . . . (RI) 438
High school reference   HOLBROCK, Mary A. . . . (IL) 550
    KAPLAN, Lois J. . . . . . . (OH) 626
High technology reference   CARSCH, Ruth E. . . . . . (CA) 187
Hispanic studies reference library   HOOPES, Maria S. . . . . (AZ) 557
Historical reference   BENTLEY, Elna J. . . . . . (AL) 83
    BERGEN, Philip S. . . . . (MA) 85
History & art reference   PINSON, Patricia A. . . . (WY) 975
History & general reference   HOUSE, Katherine L. . . . (KY) 563
History, art reference   STOPKA, Christina K. . . . (WY) 1198
History of medicine, reference   JENKINS, Glen P. . . . . . (OH) 597
History reference   MONROE, William S. . . . (NY) 855
History reference & bibliography   CUDD, John M. . . . . (KY) 263
History, reference librarian   EMMICK, Nancy J. . . . . . (CA) 348

REFERENCE (Cont'd)

Home economics reference	GAGE, Marilyn K.	(OK)	412
Horticultural reference	TEETER, Enola J.	(PA)	1229
Hospital administration reference	SCHULTZ, Therese A.	(IL)	1102
Hospital reference	NESBITT, Olive K.	(PA)	896
Humanities & fine arts reference	COHN, Alan M.	(IL)	229
Humanities & general reference	COSSEY, M E.	(KY)	249
Humanities & social science reference	LO, Henrietta W.	(CA)	735
	TAKAHASHI, Annabelle T.	(HI)	1220
	HOLLEY, E J.	(SC)	551
	MACLENNAN, Oriel C.	(NS)	757
Humanities & social sciences reference	JOHNSON, Diane D.	(CA)	603
	ECKWRIGHT, Gail Z.	(ID)	335
Humanities reference	BLEILER, Richard J.	(AL)	105
	CURRY, Janette M.	(AL)	266
	OLSRUD, Lois C.	(AZ)	923
	HERZIG, Stella J.	(CA)	534
	COLLIER, Bonnie	(CT)	232
	MILLER, Margaret R.	(FL)	840
	PALMER, Carole L.	(IL)	936
	TUCKER, John M.	(IN)	1261
	LANDRY, Francis R.	(MA)	693
	KAHN, Leslie A.	(NJ)	622
	MONTGOMERY, Michael S.	(NJ)	856
	DUNLAP, Barbara J.	(NY)	326
	WALL, Richard L.	(NY)	1297
	BRYANT, James M.	(TX)	152
	LIKNESS, Craig S.	(TX)	727
	SMITH, Charles R.	(TX)	1153
	ONN, Shirley A.	(AB)	924
Humanities reference & bibliography	BYRE, Calvin S.	(IL)	169
	CUDD, John M.	(KY)	263
	FISHER, Kim N.	(PA)	381
Humanities ref, collection development	NOURIE, Alan R.	(IL)	910
Humanities reference librarian	POLIT, Carlos E.	(IN)	980
Humanities, social science reference	REIK, Constance	(NH)	1020
Information access & reference	LARY, Marilyn S.	(GA)	700
Information & reference	WERNE, Kenneth L.	(CO)	1324
	MOTIHAR, Kamla	(NY)	872
Information & reference services	MURTEN, Holly T.	(CA)	882
	GRAHAM, Sylvia R.	(TN)	456
Information, reference & referral	GUSS, Emily R.	(IL)	478
Information reference computers	MAJOR, Marla J.	(MI)	762
Information, reference services	MARTIN, Elaine R.	(DC)	776
Information retrieval & reference	DONNELLY, Kathleen	(OH)	311
Information services & reference	TOWNSEND, Silas H.	(PA)	1253
	CAMPBELL, Laurie G.	(ON)	177
Information services reference	MOORE, Jean B.	(NJ)	860
Innovative reference services	NIPPERT, Carolyn C.	(PA)	904
Insurance & business reference	GEE, Ka C.	(NY)	424
Insurance reference	COOK, Pamela D.	(NY)	240
	IVES, Jean E.	(OH)	586
	NUERNBURG, Donna S.	(WI)	912
Interlibrary loans, reference	KOLBIN, Ronda I.	(CT)	669
Japanese studies & reference	MAKINO, Yasuko	(IL)	762
Japanese subjects reference services	GONNAMI, Tsuneharu	(BC)	447
Jazz history reference	JERDE, Curtis D.	(LA)	599
Journalism reference & research	CATES, Jo A.	(IL)	194
Judaica reference	SALTZMAN, Robbin R.	(IL)	1077
Junior high reference	SHEPARD, Jon R.	(OH)	1127
Latin American & general reference	GROTHEY, Mina J.	(NM)	473
Law & legislation reference	ROCHE, Richard G.	(IL)	1046
Law & legislative reference	RINDEN, Constance T.	(NH)	1035
Law/legal reference	LATEGOLO, Meldie A.	(DC)	701
Law library reference services	MATZ, Ruth G.	(MA)	786
Law materials reference	TENOR, Randell B.	(PA)	1231
Law reference	HEATHER, Joleen	(CA)	519
	SCHIPPER, Joan A.	(CA)	1093
	GAULT, Robin R.	(FL)	423
	HEMPHILL, Lia S.	(FL)	525
	ENGELBERT, Peter J.	(IN)	348
	JOHNSON, David J.	(NY)	603
	KUMAR, C S.	(NY)	684
	SMITH, Diane H.	(PA)	1154
	BRAUTIGAM, Patsy R.	(TX)	130
	MORRIS, Pamela A.	(TX)	867
	ORLANDO, Karen T.	(WV)	926

REFERENCE (Cont'd)

Law reference, government documents	KAUL, Kanhya L.	(MI)	631
Law reference services	BLAKE, Timothy J.	(LA)	103
Legal & accounting reference	ROESCH, Gay E.	(CO)	1049
Legal & business reference	GERIG, Reginald R.	(DC)	428
	ANES, Joy R.	(IL)	27
	HIBBELER, Sara J.	(MO)	536
Legal & general reference	BRANN, Andrew R.	(OH)	128
Legal & non-legal research & reference	BENNIN, Cheryl S.	(NY)	82
Legal bibliography reference	NELSON, Mary A.	(MO)	894
Legal, business & general reference	WAY, Kathy A.	(CA)	1311
Legal information & reference work	OREJANA, Rebecca D.	(PHP)	925
Legal reference	LEWIS, Timothy A.	(AL)	724
	MAYS, Allison P.	(AR)	791
	FRIEDMAN, Zena K.	(AZ)	404
	OLEARY, Jennie L.	(AZ)	920
	SCHNEIDER, Elizabeth K.	(AZ)	1097
	CHICK, Cynthia L.	(CA)	208
	FRIEDRICH, Barbara J.	(CA)	404
	JEROME, Michael S.	(CA)	599
	KARR, Linda	(CA)	628
	KAWAMOTO, Chizuko	(CA)	632
	KUCZMA, Michelle	(CA)	682
	LAMARTINE, Elisabeth A.	(CA)	689
	OPPENHEIM, Michael R.	(CA)	925
	PALMER, Catherine C.	(CA)	936
	PAPERMASTER, Cynthia L.	(CA)	939
	PERITORE, Laura D.	(CA)	958
	SHOSTROM, Marian L.	(CA)	1133
	STAHL, Ramona J.	(CA)	1178
	STREIKER, Susan L.	(CA)	1201
	WHISMAN, Linda A.	(CA)	1329
	BINTLIFF, Barbara A.	(CO)	97
	FAAS, Caroline	(CT)	360
	JERNIGAN, Denise D.	(CT)	599
	SATTERLUND, Lisa L.	(CT)	1084
	BAXTER, Janet L.	(DC)	67
	CAREY, Marsha C.	(DC)	181
	CILIBERTI, Nancy A.	(DC)	214
	DOWLING, Shelley L.	(DC)	316
	ERICSON, Richard J.	(DC)	353
	KAHN, Victoria	(DC)	622
	LARSEN, Lynda L.	(DC)	698
	LOCKWOOD, David J.	(DC)	736
	MAXON, William N.	(DC)	787
	RUGE, Audrey L.	(DC)	1066
	SMITH, Clara M.	(DC)	1153
	DANIELS, Westwell R.	(FL)	273
	GEBET, Russell W.	(FL)	424
	MELNICOVE, Annette R.	(FL)	823
	MORRIS, Steve R.	(FL)	867
	SMITH, Mary D.	(FL)	1158
	WATERS, Sally G.	(FL)	1308
	CAMBELL, Miriam A.	(GA)	174
	TUTTLE, Jane S.	(GA)	1265
	WONG, Irene K.	(HI)	1362
	BAUMANN, Walter R.	(IL)	66
	COLLINS, Janet	(IL)	232
	EMRE, Serpil A.	(IL)	348
	HOUDEK, Frank G.	(IL)	562
	LEWIS, Sherman L.	(IL)	724
	WLEKLINSKI, William A.	(IL)	1359
	MATTS, Constance	(IN)	786
	WATTS, Tim J.	(IN)	1310
	BREDEMEYER, Carol	(KY)	131
	DUGGAN, James E.	(LA)	324
	TOWLES, Anne S.	(LA)	1252
	CLOUGH, Linda F.	(MA)	223
	RANDALL, Kristie C.	(MA)	1006
	RONEN, Naomi	(MA)	1053
	AMATRUDA, William T.	(MD)	19
	DULL, Karen A.	(MD)	324
	HOLDEN, Nancy K.	(MD)	550
	SPIVEY, Lynne G.	(MD)	1175
	BRAITHWAITE, Heather J.	(MI)	127
	REES, Warren D.	(MN)	1016
	ELAM, Kristy L.	(MO)	341

REFERENCE (Cont'd)
Legal reference

GREGORY, Kirk	(MO)	466
MILLES, James G.	(MO)	843
COHEN, Edward S.	(NC)	228
DUVAL, Barbara C.	(NC)	329
WILLIAMS, Lisa W.	(NC)	1344
FORSMAN, Avis B.	(NE)	391
GENDLER, Carol J.	(NE)	426
CRAWFORD, Nola N.	(NJ)	257
LITTLE, Rosemary A.	(NJ)	734
SCHRIEK, Robert W.	(NJ)	1100
SEADER, Jane M.	(NJ)	1109
MORLEY, Sarah K.	(NM)	865
SOUTHWICK, Susan A.	(NV)	1170
ADAMO, Marilyn H.	(NY)	4
ALIFANO, Alison F.	(NY)	13
ARMSTRONG, Joanne D.	(NY)	32
BARRETT, Lizabeth A.	(NY)	59
BERGER, Paula E.	(NY)	86
BRILL, Krista C.	(NY)	136
COOPER, Jo E.	(NY)	243
DONG, Alvin L.	(NY)	311
JAROSEK, Joan E.	(NY)	594
KASPAR, Eileen	(NY)	629
KJOLSTAD-ERLANDSSON, Britt S.	(NY)	657
SAHLEM, James R.	(NY)	1075
WIERZBA, Christine	(NY)	1337
WILLIAMS, David W.	(NY)	1342
FISHER, Jo A.	(OH)	381
GREEN, Lynda C.	(OH)	462
VOELKER, James R.	(OH)	1286
KANE, Kathy	(OK)	625
PIPER, Larry W.	(OR)	975
ARMSTRONG, Nancy A.	(PA)	32
BERGER, Joellen	(PA)	85
MAST, Joanne	(PA)	782
SCHAEFER, John A.	(PA)	1089
SPIVACK, Amy D.	(PA)	1175
STEWART, Barbara R.	(PA)	1192
SWARTHOUT, Judy L.	(PA)	1214
VARGAS, Gwen S.	(PA)	1278
WEINGRAM, Ida	(PA)	1318
TORRES-TAPI, Manual A.	(PR)	1251
ALEXANDER, Jacqueline P.	(RI)	12
GATES, Diane E.	(TX)	421
GRUBEN, Karl T.	(TX)	474
LANGSTON, Sally J.	(TX)	696
TEMPLETON, Virginia E.	(TX)	1231
TRAFFORD, Susan M.	(TX)	1253
BISSETT, John P.	(VA)	100
LIEBERMAN, Sharon A.	(VA)	726
SAUR, Cindy S.	(VA)	1085
HARBOLD, Mary J.	(WA)	499
KOSLOV, Marcia J.	(WI)	672

Legal reference & management	HARBISON, John H.	(DC)	499
Legal reference & research	LEVINE, Patricia M.	(AL)	720
	NORBIE, Dorothy E.	(CO)	908
	BARNUM, Deborah C.	(CT)	58
	BROQUE, Suzanne	(CT)	141
	LUBIN, Joan S.	(CT)	745
	MATTHEWSON, David S.	(CT)	786
	HOTCHKISS, Mary A.	(DC)	562
	AUSTIN, John R.	(IL)	40
	NYBERG, Cheryl R.	(IL)	912
	MAZZEI, Peter J.	(NJ)	791
	JACKSON, George R.	(OH)	587
Legal reference service	COLOKATHIS, Jane	(MN)	234
	VIGLIATURO, Kristy	(MO)	1284
Legal reference services	KING, Kamla J.	(DC)	651
	SHEINWALD, Franette	(NY)	1125
	WEILANT, Edward	(OH)	1317
	COTE, Carolee T.	(TX)	249
	WARREN, Gail	(VA)	1306
Legal references & databases	FOSKO, Maureen E.	(NJ)	392

REFERENCE (Cont'd)

Legal research & reference	MAYERS, Karen A.	(CA)	789
	VEGA, Carolyn L.	(CA)	1281
	HUGHES, John M.	(CT)	571
	NEWTON, Stephanne K.	(DC)	900
	EICHER, Thomas E.	(IA)	339
	SHAPIRO, Fred R.	(NY)	1121
	TRIFFIN, Nicholas	(NY)	1256
	SUHRE, Carol A.	(OH)	1207
	PARTIN, Gail A.	(PA)	945
	BULERIN-LUGO, Josefina	(PR)	156
Legal research reference	REYNOLDS, Diane C.	(CA)	1025
Legal research, reference & writing	KISSANE, Mary K.	(MO)	656
Legal research reference online manual	VON PFEIL, Helena P.	(DC)	1288
Legislative & legal reference	BROWNE, Lynda S.	(DC)	148
	QUINN, Karen H.	(RI)	1000
Legislative reference	JERNIGAN, Denise D.	(CT)	599
	BEALL, Barbara A.	(DC)	68
	KENNEDY, Lynne	(DC)	641
	DULL, Karen A.	(MD)	324
	BALLENTINE, Rebecca S.	(NC)	53
	HALPEREN, Vivian P.	(NC)	489
	MCVEY, Susan C.	(OK)	818
	BAXA, Jay W.	(VA)	67
Legislative reference & research	GRAY, Kevin P.	(NY)	460
Library & online reference	MCDOWELL, Judith H.	(OH)	804
Library & reference center management	MISSAR, Charles D.	(MD)	847
Library education reference instruction	JOHNSON, Denise J.	(WI)	603
Library information & reference services	STUART, Gerard W.	(AZ)	1204
Library instruction & reference	BECK, Erla P.	(IN)	71
	HADDERMAN, Margaret	(OR)	482
Library public & reference services	KLEINER, Janellyn P.	(LA)	660
Library reference	FRICK, Elizabeth A.	(NS)	403
Library reference service	COOPER, William C.	(SC)	244
Library reference services	WEHNER, Karen B.	(TN)	1316
Library reference skills	HALLBERG, Sharon P.	(CA)	489
Library science reference	TYLER, Carolyn S.	(SC)	1266
Library system, reference & research	ROTHENBERG, Mark H.	(NY)	1060
Library systems, reference	BLOKH, Basheva	(NY)	106
Library systems, reference referral	GUY, Patricia A.	(CA)	479
Life science reference	CURTIS, Susan C.	(GA)	267
Life sciences reference	TALBERT, David M.	(NC)	1220
	PASTER, Amy L.	(PA)	946
	KELLAND, John L.	(RI)	635
Linguistics, bibliography, reference	KELLY, Richard J.	(MN)	638
Literature & history reference	BARNETT, Jean D.	(OR)	57
Literature & language reference	THEWS, Dorothy D.	(MN)	1234
Literature searching & reference	HOMAN, J M.	(MI)	555
Local government reference	FREEDMAN, Phyllis D.	(PA)	400
Local historical reference	DECKER, John W.	(MN)	286
Local history & genealogy reference	WIENER, Alissa L.	(MN)	1336
Local history, audiovisual, reference	WOOD, Lois R.	(IL)	1364
Louisiana reference	MARSHALL, Susan O.	(LA)	775
Lutheran history & reference	WOHLRABE, John C.	(MO)	1359
Management consulting reference	FLEISHMAN, Lauren Z.	(NY)	384
Management, reference	BAILEY, George M.	(CA)	46
Managing reference & research studies	BRODERICK, John C.	(DC)	138
Manual & automated reference	MCGOWAN, Anna T.	(DC)	807
Manual medical reference	VAIL, Evelyn J.	(IL)	1270
Manual online reference services	GINSLER, Mindy F.	(ON)	438
Manuscripts & archival reference	KAPLAN, Diane E.	(CT)	626
Manuscripts processing & reference	WELLS, Anne S.	(MS)	1322
Manuscripts reference	BOWEN, Laurel G.	(IL)	120
Map & geography reference	PERRY, Joanne M.	(OR)	960
Map reference	WYMAN, Kathleen M.	(ON)	1375
Marine affairs, research & reference	ETCHINGHAM, John B.	(RI)	355
Marine biology reference	MARKHAM, James W.	(CA)	771
Marine science reference	HALE, Kay K.	(FL)	485
Mathematics reference	SCHNOOR, Harriet E.	(IL)	1098
	FUNKHOUSER, Richard L.	(IN)	410
Medical & health sciences reference	STANKE, Judith U.	(MN)	1180
Medical & nursing reference	SCHULTZ, Therese A.	(IL)	1102
Medical & reference databases	BINAU, Myra I.	(MD)	97
Medical care information & reference	CAHALAN, Thomas H.	(MA)	171
Medical care reference	SKIDMORE, Kerry F.	(UT)	1146

REFERENCE (Cont'd)

Medical databases & reference

Medical databases, reference,
  cataloging
Medical history reference
Medical, hospital reference
Medical reference

HUTCHINSON, Beck ... (FL) 579
REES, Pamela C. ...... (IA) 1016
DUNCAN, Bettye M. .... (MS) 325

MARK, Ronnie J. .... (NY) 770
RUGGERE, Christine A. . (PA) 1066
STRAUSS, Carol D. .... (IL) 1201
CLEMMONS, Nancy W. . (AL) 221
HARRIS, Jay .... (AL) 504
SHEARER, Barbara S. ... (AL) 1124
WILLIAMS, Nelle T. .... (AL) 1345
CLOUGHERTY, Leo P. ... (AR) 223
CONNOR, Paul L. ...... (CA) 238
CONTINI, Janice L. ..... (CA) 239
CRUMP, Joyce A. ..... (CA) 262
POTTER, Laurene ..... (CA) 987
TISE, Barbara L. .... (CA) 1247
SIMON, Nancy L. ...... (CO) 1140
EBINGER, Meada G. .... (CT) 334
LEVINE, Marion H. ..... (CT) 720
PENN, Elinor K. .... (CT) 957
SCURA, Georgia A. .... (CT) 1109
APOSTLE, Lynne M. .... (DC) 29
ANDERSON, Gail C. ... (GA) 23
BELL, Mamie J. .... (GA) 77
DENNISON, Jacquelyn H. (GA) 292
SCHNICK, Robert M. .... (GA) 1097
KRAUS, Marilyn J. ...... (IA) 676
BALCERZAK, Judy A. ... (ID) 50
AMBROSE, Karen S. .... (IL) 19
BEAN, Janet R. .... (IL) 69
EGGERS, Thomas D. ... (IL) 339
IWAMI, Russell A. ..... (IL) 586
SCHNOOR, Harriet E. ... (IL) 1098
WHITE, Anne E. .... (IL) 1330
BRAHMI, Frances A. ... (IN) 127
CORBETT, Ann L. ..... (IN) 245
ELLSWORTH, Marlene A. (IN) 345
RICHWINE, Margaret W. (IN) 1031
CARVER, Jane W. ..... (KS) 191
YOUNG, Stephanie O. ... (KY) 1383
JONES, Dixie A. .... (LA) 612
NOLAN-MITCHELL,
  Patricia .... (LA) 908
BEDARD, Martha A. .... (MA) 73
GELLER, Miriam R. .... (MA) 426
HARRIS, John C. ...... (MA) 504
BACKUS, Joyce E. ..... (MD) 44
BRANCH, Katherine E. ... (MD) 127
GOLDSTEIN, Helene B. . (MD) 446
HARRIMAN, Jenny F. .. (MD) 503
HUNT, Jennie P. ...... (MD) 575
KRUSE, Kathryn W. ..... (MD) 681
SATTERTHWAITE,
  Rebecca K. .... (MD) 1084
BRISTOR, Patricia R. .... (MI) 137
BURHANS, Barbara C. ... (MI) 159
ROBBINS, Lora A. ..... (MI) 1039
WILLIAMS, Gayle A. .... (MI) 1343
GLASGOW, Vicki L. .... (MN) 440
MUELLER, Mary G. .... (MN) 875
SINHA, Dorothy P. .... (MN) 1143
IGLAUER, Carol .... (MO) 581
JOHNSON, E D. ...... (MO) 604
SMITH, Valerie K. ...... (MO) 1161
BARROWS, William D. ... (NC) 60
FEINGLOS, Susan J. .... (NC) 369
TALBERT, David M. .... (NC) 1220
REINGOLD, Judith S. .... (NH) 1021
CONNICK, Kathleen D. ... (NJ) 237
NAGELE, Nancy C. ..... (NJ) 886
REGENBERG, Patricia B. (NJ) 1017
SPRUNG, George ..... (NJ) 1176
CURTIS, James A. ..... (NY) 267
HESSLEIN, Shirley B. .... (NY) 534
NELSON, Norma ...... (NY) 894
POONITHARA, Pradee P. (NY) 983
ROWELL, Regina A. .... (NY) 1062
SOLLENBERGER, Julia F. (NY) 1166

REFERENCE (Cont'd)

Medical reference

Medical reference administration

Medical reference & information
  services
Medical reference & literature
Medical reference & online databases
Medical reference & research

Medical reference databases

Medical reference service
Medical reference services

Medical reference sources
Medical references

Medical, scientific, technical reference
Medically-related reference
Medicine & allied health reference
Medicine, engineering reference
Mental health field reference
Mental health reference

Merger & acquisition reference
Michigan reference
Microcomputer reference

UVA, Peter A. .... (NY) 1270
WESTERMANN, Mary L. (NY) 1327
CONNERS, Margaret S. . (OH) 237
GALLANT, Jennifer J. .. (OH) 414
MULARSKI, Carol A. ... (OH) 876
ROSENTHAL, Barbara G. (OH) 1057
JORDAN, Cathryn M. ... (OR) 616
ANTES, E J. .... (PA) 28
FARNY, Diane M. ...... (PA) 365
GILLILAND, Lee P. ..... (PA) 436
GRIFFITH, Dorothy A. ... (PA) 469
LEINHEISER, Diane R. ... (PA) 714
MCNABB, Corrine R. ... (PA) 815
MOWERY, Susan G. ... (PA) 874
NANSTIEL, Barbara L. .. (PA) 887
NEUMANN, Pamela A. ... (PA) 897
RAINEY, Nancy B. ..... (PA) 1004
SCHANER, Marian E. ... (PA) 1090
STESIS, Karen R. ...... (PA) 1189
GABLE, Sarah H. ...... (SC) 411
HIPPS, Gary M. ...... (SC) 543
WARREN, Karen T. ..... (SC) 1306
SELIG, Susan A. ...... (TN) 1113
FRIDLEY, Bonnie J. .... (TX) 403
KNOTT, Teresa L. ... (TX) 665
PEDERSEN, Judy K. ... (TX) 954
WARD, Deborah H. .... (TX) 1303
WILSON, Barbara A. ... (TX) 1349
WISE, Olga B. .... (TX) 1357
WORLEY, Merry P. ..... (TX) 1369
TURMAN, Lynne U. ..... (VA) 1264
SEKERAK, Robert J. .... (VT) 1113
WEINSTOCK, Joanna S. (VT) 1318
HARBOLD, Mary J. ..... (WA) 499
MILES, Pamela W. ..... (WA) 834
STOCK, Carole G. .... (WA) 1195
HOLST, Ruth M. .... (WI) 554
MADSEN, Joyce ...... (WI) 759
NUERNBURG, Donna S. (WI) 912
WHITCOMB, Dorothy V. . (WI) 1330
AUBIN, Robert .... (PQ) 38
WALUZYNIEC, Hanna .. (PQ) 1302
SMITH, Marilynn C. ... (SDA)1157
HEIDENREICH, Fred L. . (AZ) 521

MAHONY, Doris D. ..... (MI) 761
NOYES, Suzanne N. .... (MA) 911
HARBERT, Cathy E. .... (MD) 499
KIEFER, Rosemary M. .. (FL) 647
SNYDER, Lisa A. ...... (MAL)1165
FRYER, Regina K. ..... (CT) 407
MARSHAK, Bonnie L. ... (NY) 773
MACK, Bonnie R. ...... (WY) 756
ANTONIEWICZ, Carol M. (WI) 29
MOON, Peter S. .... (CT) 858
STEPHENS, Gretchen .. (IN) 1188
WELSCH, Melissa W. .... (LA) 1323
LAMBREMONT, Jane A. (NC) 691
BREGMAN, Joan R. .... (NY) 131
DORNER, Marian T. ..... (OH) 313
KERSTETTER, Virginia M. (VA) 644
SINGER, Eleanore M. ... (ON) 1143
HANKS, Ellen T. .... (TX) 496
OBLOY, Elaine C. ...... (OH) 914
HESZ, Bianka M. ...... (PA) 534
MAYO, Helen G. ...... (TX) 790
LIN, Louise .... (ON) 727
TIFFEAULT, Alice A. .... (NY) 1244
SHRIER, Helene F. ..... (NY) 1133
NEELAND, Ellen L. .... (TX) 891
COSGRIFF, John C. .... (VA) 248
KIMBLE, Valerie F. ..... (OK) 649
VAN DER VOORN, Neal
  P. .... (WA) 1274
ROUP, Carol E. ...... (ON) 1061
ANTONETZ, Dolores ... (NY) 29
CALLARD, Carole ..... (MI) 173
SMITH, Karen F. ...... (NY) 1156

REFERENCE (Cont'd)

Microcomputers applications reference	MILLER, Susan E.	(LA)	842
Military & aeronautics reference	KYSELY, Elizabeth C.	(CO)	685
Military history, business reference	ROTHENBERG, Mark H.	(NY)	1060
Minnesota reference	CLARKE, Norman F.	(MN)	219
Municipal government reference	BRADDOCK, Virginia O.	(CO)	125
Municipal government reference services	TAYLOR, Patricia A.	(NY)	1228
Municipal reference	NORDBY, Leslie L.	(CA)	908
	MARTINES, Karen E.	(OH)	779
	HERFURTH, Sharon M.	(TX)	530
Municipal reference & services	FOREHAND, Margaret P.	(VA)	390
Music administration & reference	HALL, Bonlyn G.	(VA)	487
Music & dance reference	HEUTTE, Frederic A.	(MD)	535
Music & fine arts reference	DAVIS, Joy V.	(GA)	279
Music bibliography & reference	HAEFLIGER, Kathleen A.	(NY)	482
Music librarianship, reference	KOLCZYNSKI, Charlotte A.	(MA)	669
Music libraries reference	FOLLET, Robert E.	(TX)	388
Music performing arts reference	HARDISH, Patrick M.	(NY)	500
Music reference	DIAL, Clarence M.	(AZ)	299
	COLBY, Edward E.	(CA)	230
	ELLIOTT, Patricia G.	(CA)	344
	SILVER, Martin A.	(CA)	1138
	SAVIG, Norman I.	(CO)	1086
	BURKAT, Leonard	(CT)	160
	DOPP, Bonnie J.	(DC)	312
	FALCONER, Joan O.	(IA)	362
	STRAIT, Constance J.	(IL)	1199
	WARD, Shirlene A.	(IL)	1304
	DOLAN-HEITLINGER, Eileen	(IN)	309
	FLING, Robert M.	(IN)	385
	TALALAY, Kathryn M.	(IN)	1220
	RUSTMAN, Mark M.	(KS)	1070
	POWELL, Martha C.	(KY)	988
	IRION, Millard F.	(MA)	584
	MOCKOVAK, Holly E.	(MA)	851
	BJORKE, Wallace S.	(MI)	100
	BLACK-SHIER, Mary L.	(MI)	102
	DRUESEDOW, John E.	(NC)	320
	DOW, Carolyn E.	(NE)	315
	TIBBITS, Edith J.	(NE)	1243
	MARCO, Guy A.	(NJ)	769
	REDLICH, Barry	(NJ)	1014
	RORICK, William C.	(NY)	1054
	WILLNER, Channan P.	(NY)	1348
	OBERLE, Holly E.	(OH)	914
	HUBER, George K.	(PA)	569
	MEYER, Kenton T.	(PA)	830
	SAUNDERS, Sharon K.	(PA)	1084
	FAWVER, Darlene E.	(SC)	367
	GEARY, Gregg S.	(TX)	424
	MCTYRE, Ruthann B.	(TX)	818
	MCCART, Vernon A.	(VA)	794
	BEAUMIER, Renald	(PQ)	70
Music reference & bibliographic instrc	BOGNAR, Dorothy M.	(CT)	111
Music reference & cataloging	MOORE, Emily C.	(NC)	859
Music reference & research	PERRY-BOWDER, Libbie E.	(ME)	961
	BOZIWICK, George E.	(NY)	124
Music reference service	BRYCE, Maria C.	(ON)	152
Music reference works	PAVLAKIS, Christopher	(NY)	950
Natural history reference	JERYAN, Christine B.	(MI)	600
Natural resources & environment ref	LARSEN, Lynda L.	(DC)	698
Natural resources reference	RODES, Barbara K.	(DC)	1047
News & events reference	MCGANN, Margot	(DC)	805
News reference	ROBINSON, Robert C.	(DC)	1044
Newspaper reference	LOVELL, Bonnie A.	(TX)	743
	BURROWS, Sandra	(ON)	163
Nursing information & reference	BERG, Rebecca M.	(CO)	84
Nursing, medical selection, reference	TAPPANA, Kathy A.	(OK)	1223
Nursing reference	CORCORAN, Virginia H.	(CT)	246
	JONES, Dixie A.	(LA)	612
Oil & gas reference	DILLARD, Lois A.	(TX)	303
Online & current awareness reference	LOGAN, Nancy L.	(ON)	737
Online & in-print reference	KING, Laurie L.	(MA)	651
Online database reference	BEAVERS, Janet W.	(ISR)	71

REFERENCE (Cont'd)

Online database searching & reference	SALM, Kay E.	(CA)	1077
Online reference	DERSHEM, Larry D.	(CA)	294
	LEE, Don A.	(CA)	709
	ZELINKA, Mary A.	(DC)	1387
	PRENDERGAST, Kathleen M.	(IL)	990
	ELFSTRAND, Stephen F.	(MN)	342
	HUNTER, James J.	(OH)	576
	HORWITZ, Seth	(PA)	561
	ENNS, Carol F.	(NB)	350
	BANFIELD, Eilzabeth S.	(NS)	54
	WARD, William D.	(ON)	1304
	COLLISTER, Edward A.	(PQ)	233
Online reference retrieval	ELLIOT, Hugh	(DC)	343
Online reference searches	MANNING, Mary J.	(IL)	766
Online reference service	PHIFER, Kenneth O.	(MD)	967
Online reference services	STEVENS, Paula F.	(AZ)	1190
	BRUMAN, Janet L.	(CA)	150
	CHADWICK, Sharon S.	(CA)	197
	SPURGEON, Kathy R.	(CT)	1176
	HARPER, Laura G.	(MS)	503
	CLASPER, James W.	(OH)	219
	WALKER, Richard D.	(WI)	1296
	SERMAT-HARDING, Kaili I.	(ON)	1116
Online reference systems	LAZARUS, Josephine G.	(CO)	706
Online research & reference	YOUNG, Sandra C.	(KY)	1383
Online search reference	DUSABLON-BOTTEGA, Nicole	(PQ)	329
Online searching & reference	DAVENPORT, Constance B.	(CA)	275
	HAMMOND, Elizabeth D.	(GA)	493
	COFFEY, James R.	(NJ)	227
	CHUANG, Felicia S.	(TX)	213
	MILLER, Veronica E.	(VI)	843
Online searching reference	MITCHELL, Annmarie D.	(CA)	848
Organizing reference collections	HAZEL, Debora E.	(NC)	517
Orientations & interlib loan reference	BAYER, Susan P.	(IL)	67
Patent & trademark reference	MOORE, John R.	(IL)	860
Patents reference	WALKER, Barbara J.	(GA)	1295
Patron-initiated reference requests	LAROSA, Thomas J.	(NY)	698
Peace materials & reference	MEYER, Jimmy E.	(OH)	830
Pediatric reference	TURNER, Tamara A.	(WA)	1265
Performing arts reference	WISE, Matthew W.	(NY)	1357
Performing arts reference, research	DEE, Camille C.	(NY)	286
Performing arts reference work	VELEZ, Sara B.	(NY)	1281
Periodicals reference	WILLIAMS, Pauline C.	(AL)	1346
	CHEVRIER, Francine	(PQ)	207
Person-to-person reference	MANNING, Mary J.	(IL)	766
Petroleum reference	MURRAY, James T.	(OK)	882
Pharmaceutical, medical, business ref	MCMASTER, Deborah L.	(CT)	815
Pharmaceutical reference	WALTON, Carol G.	(NC)	1301
Pharmaceutical sciences reference	PIERMATTI, Patricia A.	(NJ)	972
Pharmacy reference & bibliography	MANNARINO, Elizabeth R.	(OR)	766
Photograph reference & cataloging	STERN, Teena B.	(CA)	1189
Physical, life scis & engrng reference	MURPHY, Joan F.	(CA)	880
Physical science reference	BARATTA, Maria	(NJ)	55
Physical sciences reference	LARUSSA, Carol J.	(CA)	700
	SOUTHERN, Mary A.	(NC)	1170
	GALKOWSKI, Patricia E.	(RI)	413
	THAYER, Martha B.	(WA)	1234
Physics & astronomy reference	SCHNOOR, Harriet E.	(IL)	1098
Physics & math reference	DAVIDOFF, Gary N.	(IL)	276
Physics databases & reference	WOELL, Yvette N.	(IL)	1359
Political research & reference	TAYLOR, Loretta C.	(ON)	1227
Political science reference	LITTLE, Rosemary A.	(NJ)	734
	KINGSLEY, Marcia S.	(VA)	652
Preparing indexes & legal reference	HOYT, Henry M.	(NY)	566
Print & computerized reference	MCDONALD, Michael L.	(DC)	803
Professional & reference books	BUCENEC, Nancy L.	(NY)	153
	TOPEL, Iris N.	(NY)	1251
Professional & reference publishing	QUINLIN, Margaret M.	(MD)	1000
Professional reference accounting pubns	HALPIN, Gerard B.	(ON)	490
Professional reference law publications	HALPIN, Gerard B.	(ON)	490
Promoting reference books	ROMIG, Thomas L.	(MI)	1053
Providing information from references	JOHNSON, Elaine B.	(DC)	604

REFERENCE (Cont'd)

Psychiatry reference services	ASBELL, Mildred S.	(CT)	35
Psychology & psychiatry reference	DEWEY, Marjorie C.	(MA)	298
Psychology reference & bibliography	KAUFFMAN, Inge S. . . .	(CA)	631
Psychology reference & cataloging	HUFFINE, Lucinda J. . . .	(OR)	571
Public libraries reference	VOJTECH, Kathryn	(IL)	1287
Public library adult reference	DAVIS, Joy V.	(GA)	279
Public library reference	MILLER, Margaret R. . . .	(FL)	840
	WALKER, Constance T. . .	(NC)	1295
	GRAVITZ, Ina A.	(NY)	459
Public library reference service	VANYOUNG, Sayre	(CA)	1278
Public library reference services	GANN, Daniel H.	(IN)	416
Public library reference work	LINDBERG, Richard L. . .	(PA)	728
Public library references	POTELICKI, Athalene O. .	(OH)	986
Public reference	SIMONS, Maurice M. . . .	(CA)	1141
Public reference services	HUTCHINS, Kathleen D. .	(MA)	579
	BANDEMER, June E. . . .	(PA)	54
Public science & technology reference	COHEN, Jackson B.	(NY)	228
Public service & reference	DONOVAN, William A. . . .	(IL)	312
	THOMPSON, Anna M. . . .	(IN)	1238
	SUYEMATSU, Kiyo	(MN)	1212
	CHODACKI, Roberta A. . .	(NY)	210
	PFOHL, Theodore E. . . .	(NY)	966
	CLAYTON, J G.	(SC)	220
	WING, Marjorie	(AB)	1354
Public service reference	NOYES, Nicholas	(ME)	911
	WOESTHOFF, Catherine F.	(NY)	1359
Public service, science reference	HUDSON, Donna T.	(NC)	569
Public services & reference	BASART, Ann P.	(CA)	62
	THELIN, Sonya R.	(CA)	1234
	SCHEIN, Lorraine S.	(NY)	1091
	APPLETON, Brenda F. . .	(BC)	30
Public services & references	GRANITZ, Adrienne D. . .	(VA)	457
Public services, general reference	DRAGOTTA, Linda L. . . .	(PA)	318
Public services reference	STEPHENS, Diana C. . . .	(HI)	1188
	COAN, La V.	(MI)	224
Public services reference & information	GRAY, Patricia B.	(VA)	460
Public services, reference services	LANE, David M.	(NH)	694
Public services, research & reference	FRENCH, Thomas R. . . .	(OH)	402
Publicity, reference	LARSON, Josephine	(NC)	699
Publish high tech reference books	CONNORS, Martin G. . . .	(MI)	238
Publishing music reference books	BALK, Leo F.	(NY)	52
Publishing, reference	DAUB, Albert W.	(NJ)	275
Publishing reference books	BRYFONSKI, Dedria A. . .	(MI)	152
Quick reference	LEITCH, Karen E.	(DC)	714
	HUGHES, Joan L.	(MO)	571
	HARADA, Ryukichi	(JAP)	499
Rare books & reference work	KAPLAN, Sylvia Y.	(IL)	626
Rare books, archives, & reference	MUELLER, Jane L.	(CA)	875
Reader services, reference	CARRIGAN, Marietta R. .	(WA)	186
Reader's advisory, reference work	CORDUKES, Laura L. . . .	(ON)	246
Reader's advisory service & reference	HUNTER, Julie A.	(NC)	576
Reader's guidance & reference	SHEARIN, Cynthia E. . . .	(NJ)	1124
Ready reference	POLK, Diana B.	(IL)	981
Ready reference service	SMITH, Maureen M.	(OH)	1158
Records reference service	SCOTT, Paul R.	(TX)	1108
Reference	BOEHMER, Elaine	(AK)	109
	BRAUND-ALLEN, Julianna E.	(AK)	130
	COLSON, Marcia B.	(AK)	234
	FREDERIKSEN, Patience A.	(AK)	400
	GALBRAITH, William B. .	(AK)	413
	HALES, David A.	(AK)	486
	PIERCE, Linda I.	(AK)	971
	THOMAS, Margie J.	(AK)	1237
	ATKINSON, Joan L.	(AL)	38
	DANCE, Betty A.	(AL)	272
	HALL, Patricia N.	(AL)	488
	HAMILTON, Ann H.	(AL)	491
	HARRIS, Linda S.	(AL)	505
	LIAW, Barbara C.	(AL)	725
	MCNAMARA, Jay	(AL)	816
	MERRILL, Martha	(AL)	826
	NICHOLS, Amy S.	(AL)	901
	NICHOLS, Shirley G. . . .	(AL)	901

REFERENCE (Cont'd)

Reference

ROBERTS, Eddie F.	(AL)	1039
SCALES, Diann R.	(AL)	1087
SPILLERS, Doris H.	(AL)	1174
STIEG, Margaret F.	(AL)	1193
VENABLE, Douglas R. . .	(AL)	1282
WISE, Kenda C.	(AL)	1357
FOSTER, Lynn	(AR)	392
GODBEY, Esther R.	(AR)	442
HALL, Deborah N.	(AR)	487
KASTANOTIS, William C. .	(AR)	629
KELLEY, Sally J.	(AR)	637
RICK, Jean A.	(AR)	1031
STOWE, Jean E.	(AR)	1199
BIGLIN, Karen E.	(AZ)	96
BRZOZOWSKI, Margery E.	(AZ)	152
CAMPBELL, Dierdre A. . .	(AZ)	176
DANIELS, Delores E. . . .	(AZ)	273
EDGINGTON, Linda A. . . .	(AZ)	336
FEAZEL, Edythe J.	(AZ)	367
HASSELL, Robert H. . . .	(AZ)	511
HOWARD, Pamela F. . . .	(AZ)	564
KESSLER, Katheryn M. . .	(AZ)	645
KIRKING, Clayton C. . . .	(AZ)	655
KLATT, Dixie K.	(AZ)	657
KOLBER, Denise	(AZ)	669
LEWIS, Jean R.	(AZ)	723
LONG, Carla J.	(AZ)	739
MCBRIDE, Patricia A. . . .	(AZ)	792
MILLER, Larry A.	(AZ)	839
MOHR, Mary C.	(AZ)	852
MULVIHILL, Joann	(AZ)	878
POSSNER, Roger D. . . .	(AZ)	986
ROTHLISBERG, Allen P. .	(AZ)	1060
SORENSEN, Lee R.	(AZ)	1168
TEVIS, Raymond H.	(AZ)	1233
WATT, Mary J.	(AZ)	1310
WHITE, Edward H.	(AZ)	1330
WILLIAMS, Karen B.	(AZ)	1344
ALLABACK, Patricia G. . .	(CA)	13
AMARA, Margaret F. . . .	(CA)	19
ANDERSEN, Leslie N. . .	(CA)	21
ARIARATNAM, Lakshmi V.	(CA)	31
ARNDAL, Robert E.	(CA)	33
BAILEY, Rolene M.	(CA)	46
BATTAGLIA, Bonnie J. . .	(CA)	64
BELANGER, Sandra E. . .	(CA)	75
BENNETT, Carson W. . . .	(CA)	81
BERNHART, Barbara M. .	(CA)	89
BEVERAGE, Stephanie L.	(CA)	93
BIBEL, Barbara M.	(CA)	94
BIDWELL, Lynne H.	(CA)	95
BONNET, Janice M.	(CA)	114
BOOKHEIM, Louis W. . . .	(CA)	115
BOYER, Laura M.	(CA)	123
BREWSAUGH, Susan J.	(CA)	134
BROOKS, Mary A.	(CA)	140
BROWN, Carol G.	(CA)	142
BRUEGGEMAN, Peter L.	(CA)	149
CACCESE, Vincent	(CA)	170
CAIN, Anne H.	(CA)	171
CANNON, Eleanor	(CA)	179
CARR, Richard D.	(CA)	186
CARROLL, Lois E.	(CA)	187
CELLE, Deborah A.	(CA)	196
CHAVEZ, Linda	(CA)	204
CLARENCE, Judy	(CA)	216
CLARK, Patricia A.	(CA)	217
CLINE, Cheryl L.	(CA)	222
CROSS, Mabel L.	(CA)	260
DAVIS, Charles E.	(CA)	278
DEBOER, Kee K.	(CA)	284
DEVEREAUX, Amy E. . .	(CA)	297
DIFFERDING, Jane B. . .	(CA)	302
DOLLEN, Charles J.	(CA)	310
DONALDSON, Maryanne T.	(CA)	311
DOUGLAS, Carolyn T. . .	(CA)	314

REFERENCE (Cont'd)
Reference

DUZAK, Sandra J. . . . . . (CA) 330
ELLIOTT, Valerie E. . . . . (CA) 344
ELNOR, Nancy G. . . . . . (CA) 346
FINLEY, Mary M. . . . . . . (CA) 378
FISHER, Alice J. . . . . . . (CA) 380
FORBES, Fred R. . . . . . . (CA) 389
FRANK, Anne E. . . . . . . (CA) 396
FREUDENBERGER, Elsie
    L. . . . . (CA) 402
GAREY, Anita I. . . . . (CA) 418
GARNER, Carolyn L. . . . (CA) 419
GEBHARD, Patricia . . . . (CA) 424
GIBBONS, Carolbeth . . . (CA) 431
GLENDENNING, Barbara
    J. . . . . (CA) 441
GLYNN, Jeannette E. . . . (CA) 442
GOLDMACHER, Sheila L. (CA) 445
GOLDSMITH, Jan E. . . . (CA) 446
GOODWATER, Leanna K. (CA) 450
GORAL, Miki . . . . (CA) 451
GRASSIAN, Esther S. . . (CA) 458
GUEDON, Mary S. . . . . . (CA) 475
HADLEY, Alice E. . . . . . . (CA) 482
HAMOR, Monica E. . . . . (CA) 494
HARMON, Robert B. . . . (CA) 502
HAUSSMANN, Virginia D. (CA) 513
HECKART, Ronald J. . . . (CA) 519
HESSEL, William H. . . . . (CA) 534
HICKS, Mary F. . . . . (CA) 537
HIMMEL, Ned A. . . . . . . (CA) 542
HIXON, Donald L. . . . . . . (CA) 544
HOFLAND, Freda B. . . . . (CA) 548
HOLLAND, Rebecca J. . . (CA) 551
HOLTZMAN, Douglas A. (CA) 555
HOUSEL, Mary B. . . . . . (CA) 563
HUNG, Joanne Y. . . . . . . (CA) 574
HUNT, Deborah S. . . . . . (CA) 575
HUSTON, Esther L. . . . . (CA) 578
JESSUP, Carrie . . . . (CA) 600
JESTES, Edward C. . . . . (CA) 600
JOHNSON, Clifford R. . . (CA) 603
JOHNSON, Peter A. . . . . (CA) 608
JORGENSEN, Venita . . . (CA) 617
KANTER, Elliot J. . . . . . . (CA) 625
KATZ, Janet R. . . . . (CA) 630
KING, Kitty G. . . . . (CA) 651
KISLITZIN, Elizabeth H. . (CA) 656
KLUGMAN, Simone . . . . (CA) 662
KOBZINA, Norma G. . . . (CA) 666
KUBIC, Joseph C. . . . . . (CA) 682
KYROPOULOS, Mary S. (CA) 685
LAND, Barbara J. . . . . . . (CA) 692
LEE, Don A. . . . . (CA) 709
LEE, Myung J. . . . . (CA) 711
LEVINE, Beryl . . . . (CA) 720
LITTLEJOHN, Alice C. . . (CA) 734
LO, Grace C. . . . . (CA) 735
LOMAX, Ronald C. . . . . . (CA) 738
LONDON, Glenn S. . . . . (CA) 738
LUEBKE, Margaret F. . . . (CA) 747
LUKE, Keye L. . . . . (CA) 747
MARTIN, Roger M. . . . . . (CA) 778
MASON, Elsbeth S. . . . . (CA) 781
MASWAN, Yurita . . . . . . (CA) 783
MCCORMICK, Mona . . . (CA) 798
MCGREEVY, Kathleen T. (CA) 808
MCNAMEE, Gilbert W. . . (CA) 816
MELTZER, Ellen J. . . . . . (CA) 823
MILFORD, Charles C. . . . (CA) 835
MILLER, Elissa R. . . . . . (CA) 837
MILLER, Jean R. . . . . . . (CA) 839
MILO, Albert J. . . . . (CA) 845
MOORE, Evia B. . . . . . . (CA) 859
MORRISEY, Locke J. . . . (CA) 867
MURTHA, Edward J. . . . (CA) 883
MYERS, Nancy J. . . . . . . (CA) 884
NICKERSON, Louann M. (CA) 902
NOE, Christopher J. . . . . (CA) 906

REFERENCE (Cont'd)
Reference

OKA, Susan Y. . . . . (CA) 919
OLSON, Sharon L. . . . . . (CA) 923
OWENS, Robert L. . . . . . (CA) 932
PAGE, Kathryn . . . . (CA) 934
PANTAGES, Sandra K. . . (CA) 938
PARKS, Mary L. . . . . (CA) 943
PEATTIE, Noel . . . . (CA) 953
PETERSON, Anita R. . . . (CA) 962
PILLING, George P. . . . . (CA) 973
PIONTEK, Frank P. . . . . (CA) 975
POOLE, Jay M. . . . . (CA) 983
PORTILLA, Teresa M. . . (CA) 985
POSTER, Susan E. . . . . (CA) 986
PRITCHARD, Eileen E. . . (CA) 994
REEDER, Ray A. . . . . . . (CA) 1015
REIST, Paul A. . . . . (CA) 1022
REYNOLDS, Judith L. . . (CA) 1025
RICHARDSON, Helen R. (CA) 1029
ROOSHAN, Gertrude I. . . (CA) 1053
RYAN, Ann . . . . (CA) 1070
SANDFORD, Betsy R. . . (CA) 1080
SCHILLER, Anita R. . . . (CA) 1093
SCHLACHTER, Gail A. (CA) 1093
SCHMIDT, Ford C. . . . . (CA) 1095
SEGAL, Naomi R. . . . . . (CA) 1112
SHERLOCK, John A. . . . (CA) 1128
SHERMAN, Judith E. . . . (CA) 1128
SIMS, Sidney B. . . . . . . (CA) 1142
SMALLEY, Topsy N. . . . (CA) 1151
SMITH, Catherine M. . . . (CA) 1153
STANEK, Suzanne . . . . . (CA) 1179
STEUBEN, Raymond L. . (CA) 1190
SUBLER, Joyce A. . . . . . (CA) 1206
SULLIVAN, Alice F. . . . . (CA) 1207
TASH, Steven J. . . . . . . (CA) 1224
TEBO, Jay D. . . . . (CA) 1229
TESTA, Barbara E. . . . . . (CA) 1233
THOMPSON, Don K. . . . (CA) 1239
THOMPSON, James A. . (CA) 1240
THORNE, Marco G. . . . . (CA) 1242
TORKELSON, Jon A. . . . (CA) 1251
TRZECIAK, William J. . . (CA) 1260
VADEBONCOEUR,
    Elizabeth J. . . . . (CA) 1270
VRATNY-WATTS, Janet
    M. . . . . (CA) 1289
WADE, Sherry A. . . . . . . (CA) 1290
WALSH, Donamarie F. . . (CA) 1299
WARD, Sandra N. . . . . . (CA) 1304
WAZNIS, Betty . . . . (CA) 1311
WETTS, Hazel H. . . . . . . (CA) 1328
WHITSON, William L. . . . (CA) 1334
WILLIAMS, Donna S. . . . (CA) 1342
WOLLTER, Patricia M. . . (CA) 1361
WONG, Maida L. . . . . . . (CA) 1363
WOO, Winnie H. . . . . . . (CA) 1363
WYKLE, Helen H. . . . . . . (CA) 1375
ZIEGLER, Janet M. . . . . (CA) 1388
ASPER, Mary K. . . . . . . (CO) 37
BRAGDON, Lynn . . . . . . (CO) 127
DOBBS, Ann R. . . . . (CO) 307
ERNEST, Douglas J. . . . (CO) 353
FINK, Deborah . . . . (CO) 378
GOODRICH, Margaret . . (CO) 449
GRATE, Jon F. . . . . (CO) 458
HENDRICKSON, Charles
    R. . . . . (CO) 527
JARAMILLO, George R. . (CO) 594
JOHNSON, K S. . . . . . . (CO) 606
LEREW, Ann A. . . . . (CO) 717
MOOMEY, Margaret M. . (CO) 857
OTTOSON, Robin D. . . . (CO) 930
RITTEN, Karla J. . . . . . . (CO) 1036
SHIELDS, Caryl L. . . . . . (CO) 1129
STEWART, Anna C. . . . . (CO) 1192
STRAND, Kathryn . . . . . (CO) 1200
SWEET, Sally K. . . . . . . (CO) 1215
SZABO, Kathleen S. . . . . (CO) 1218

REFERENCE (Cont'd)
Reference

VERCIO, Roseanne . . . . (CO) 1282
WATERS, W R. . . . . (CO) 1309
WERTHEIMER, Marilyn L. (CO) 1325
WILDER, Mary K. . . . . . . (CO) 1339
ANDRONIK, Catherine M. (CT) 27
BALAY, Robert E. . . . . . (CT) 50
BALDINI, Lois D. . . . . . . (CT) 51
BENAMATI, Dennis C. . . (CT) 79
BOHRER, Karen M. . . . . (CT) 111
BROOKS, Robert E. . . . . (CT) 140
BUNKER, Patricia J. . . . . (CT) 157
CARNEGLIA, Anna L. . . (CT) 183
CHEESEMAN, Bruce S. . (CT) 204
COLUCCI, Mildred A. . . . (CT) 234
DELUCIA, Christina . . . . (CT) 290
FERNANDEZ, Nenita . . . (CT) 373
HAAG, Nancy R. . . . . . . (CT) 480
HURLEY, Trudy M. . . . . . (CT) 577
ICHINOSE, Mitsuko . . . . (CT) 581
KNAPP, Peter J. . . . . . . (CT) 663
KUHR, Patricia S. . . . . . (CT) 683
MARTIN, Walter F. . . . . . (CT) 779
MCELHANEY, William E. (CT) 804
MCKINNEY, Linda R. . . . (CT) 812
MCPHERSON, Mary A. . (CT) 817
MOYNIHAN, Mary B. . . . (CT) 874
NATALE, Barbara G. . . . (CT) 889
PACKER, Joan G. . . . . . (CT) 934
REITER, Elizabeth A. . . . (CT) 1022
SPURGEON, Kathy R. . . (CT) 1176
STONE, Ellen C. . . . . . . (CT) 1197
SWIFT, Janet B. . . . . (CT) 1216
WETMORE, Judith M. . . (CT) 1328
WILLARD, Anne H. . . . . (CT) 1341
WILLIAMS, Judy R. . . . . (CT) 1344
ASMUTH, Gretchen W. . (DC) 36
ATKINSON, Rose M. . . . (DC) 38
AUERBACH, Bob S. . . . . (DC) 39
BARBEE, Norman N. . . . (DC) 55
BEATON, Barbara E. . . . (DC) 70
BERGAN, Helen J. . . . . . (DC) 85
BONYNGE, Jeanne R. . . (DC) 115
BROWNE, Lynda S. . . . . (DC) 148
CAMPBELL, Doris . . . . . (DC) 176
CHANG, Helen S. . . . . . (DC) 200
CHASE, Linda S. . . . . . . (DC) 203
CHEVERIE, Joan F. . . . . (DC) 207
CLARK, Margery M. . . . . (DC) 217
CLARY, Ann R. . . . . (DC) 219
CLEMMER, Dan O. . . . . (DC) 221
COLETTI, Jeannette D. . . (DC) 231
COLWELL, Carolyn J. . . (DC) 234
DAVIDSON, Dero H. . . . (DC) 276
DRAGOVICH, Pamela M. (DC) 318
FARKAS, Susan A. . . . . (DC) 364
FELACO, Maja K. . . . . . . (DC) 369
FELDMAN, Ellen S. . . . . (DC) 369
FIGUERAS, Myriam . . . . (DC) 376
FLAM, Floris . . . . (DC) 383
FLYNN, Richard M. . . . . (DC) 387
GAMSON, Arthur L. . . . . (DC) 416
GOREN, Morton S. . . . . (DC) 452
GRUHL, Andrea M. . . . . (DC) 474
HARRINGTON, Thomas R. (DC) 504
HOPPER, Mildry S. . . . . (DC) 558
HUDGINS, Peggy . . . . . . (DC) 569
JEMIOLA, Nancy E. . . . . (DC) 596
JENSEN, Doris J. . . . . . . (DC) 598
KOVER, Steven J. . . . . . (DC) 674
KUBAL, Gene J. . . . . (DC) 681
KUPERMAN, Agota M. . . (DC) 684
LATOUR, Catherine M. . . (DC) 701
LOMAX, Denise W. . . . . (DC) 738
LONG, Caroline C. . . . . . (DC) 739
MACEWEN, Virginia B. . . (DC) 755
MARTIN, Kathleen S. . . . (DC) 777
MCGILL, Theodora . . . . . (DC) 806
NEVIN, Barbara B. . . . . . (DC) 898

NEWTON, Robert C. . . . (DC) 900
NIBLEY, Elizabeth B. . . . (DC) 901
PICCIANO, Laura . . . . . . (DC) 970
POSTAR, Adeen J. . . . . (DC) 986
QUINN, Susan . . . . (DC) 1000
REIFSNYDER, Betsy S. . (DC) 1020
RUSH, Candace M. . . . . (DC) 1068
SCHNEIDER, Hennie R. . (DC) 1097
SCHUERMANN, Lois J. . (DC) 1101
SKARR, Robert J. . . . . . (DC) 1145
SMITH, Martin A. . . . . . . (DC) 1158
STACKPOLE, Laurie E. . (DC) 1178
STORM, Jill . . . . (DC) 1198
SWANBERG, Lisa A. . . . (DC) 1213
TOWELL, Jane M. . . . . . (DC) 1252
TRIMBLE, Kathleen L. . . (DC) 1256
VAN NIMMEN, Jane . . . (DC) 1276
VAROUTSOS, Mary A. . . (DC) 1279
VINCENT, Susan R. . . . . (DC) 1284
WASSERMAN, Krystyna (DC) 1308
YASUMATSU, Janet R. . (DC) 1378
ADAMS, Barbara M. . . . (DE) 4
BROWN, Sarah C. . . . . . (DE) 147
JAMISON, Susan C. . . . (DE) 593
PIFALO, Victoria . . . . . . (DE) 972
TRUMBORE, Jean F. . . . (DE) 1259
ABBOTT, Randy L. . . . . (FL) 1
ADAMS, Gustav C. . . . . (FL) 4
ALBAIR, Catherine M. . . (FL) 9
ALZOFON, Sammy R. . . (FL) 19
ATKINS, Donna A. . . . . . (FL) 37
BATTISTE, Anita L. . . . . (FL) 65
BENNETT, Renae M. . . . (FL) 82
BROMBERG, Johanna . . (FL) 139
BROOMALL, Susan G. . . (FL) 141
BURKE, Donna J. . . . . . . (FL) 160
BYRD, Susan G. . . . . . . (FL) 169
CAREY, Jane G. . . . . . . (FL) 181
CARILLO, Sherry J. . . . . (FL) 181
CESANEK, Sylvia B. . . . (FL) 196
COHEN, Kathleen F. . . . . (FL) 228
CONKLIN, Candace V. . . (FL) 236
CURRY, John W. . . . . . . (FL) 266
DE MEO, Mary A. . . . . . . (FL) 291
DRAKE, Grady . . . . (FL) 318
ELDER, Jane D. . . . . (FL) 342
FRANCIS, Barbara W. . . (FL) 396
GALLAHAR, Christine M. (FL) 414
HARRIS, Frank D. . . . . . (FL) 504
HARRIS, Martha J. . . . . . (FL) 505
HENDERSON, Patricia A. (FL) 526
HOLLMANN, Pauline V. . (FL) 552
HUDSON, Phyllis J. . . . . (FL) 569
HUSKEY, Janet S. . . . . . (FL) 578
JOHNSON, Susan J. . . . (FL) 609
JOHNSON, Theresa P. . . (FL) 609
JONES, Douglas M. . . . . (FL) 612
JULIEN, Dorothy C. . . . . (FL) 619
KANE, Joseph P. . . . . . . (FL) 624
KASKEY, Sid . . . . (FL) 629
LIANZI, Theresa L. . . . . (FL) 725
LICHTENFELS, David D. . (FL) 725
LITTLER, June D. . . . . . . (FL) 734
LITTON, Sally C. . . . . . . (FL) 734
MAHAN, Cheryl A. . . . . . (FL) 760
MARION, Gail E. . . . . . . (FL) 770
MOFFETT, Martha L. . . . (FL) 852
NOAH, Julia T. . . . . (FL) 906
PELLEN, Rita M. . . . . . . (FL) 955
RICHARDSON, Margaret
    B. . . . . (FL) 1029
RITZ, Paul S. . . . . (FL) 1037
ROBARTS, Phyllis G. . . . (FL) 1038
ROVIROSA, Dolores F. . . (FL) 1062
SEILER, Susan L. . . . . . (FL) 1112
SNYDER, Jean . . . . (FL) 1165
SOULE, Maria J. . . . . . . (FL) 1169
STEINBERG, Celia L. . . . (FL) 1185

REFERENCE (Cont'd)
Reference

TAYLOR, Rose M.	(FL)	1228
TIBBS, Jo A.	(FL)	1244
TIPPLE, Roberta L.	(FL)	1246
TOIFEL, Peggy W.	(FL)	1248
TOOLE, Gregor K.	(FL)	1250
VANDERBURG, Mary A.	(FL)	1274
WEISS, Susan	(FL)	1320
WILLIAMS, Pamela D.	(FL)	1345
WINE, H E.	(FL)	1354
WOODS, Susan E.	(FL)	1367
ALLEN, William R.	(GA)	16
AMMERMAN, Jackie W.	(GA)	20
BALL, Ardella P.	(GA)	52
BANJA, Judith A.	(GA)	54
BISHOP, Beverly D.	(GA)	99
BISSELL, Susan J.	(GA)	100
BOYD, Ruth V.	(GA)	123
BRACKNEY, Kathryn S.	(GA)	125
BRADLEY, Gail P.	(GA)	125
BROCKMAN, B D.	(GA)	138
BUSTOS, Roxann R.	(GA)	166
CARPENTER, David E.	(GA)	184
CHAMBERS, Shirley M.	(GA)	198
COLLINS, Eugenia A.	(GA)	232
COLLINS, Patrick	(GA)	233
COMPTON, Lawrence E.	(GA)	235
CORRELL, Emily N.	(GA)	247
DEENEY, Marian A.	(GA)	286
ELLIS, Marie C.	(GA)	345
GARFINKLE, Gail J.	(GA)	419
GLISSON, Patricia A.	(GA)	441
HAAR, John M.	(GA)	480
HALE, Ruth C.	(GA)	485
HARDIN, Barbara A.	(GA)	500
HICKMAN, Michael L.	(GA)	536
HOWARD, Rachel L.	(GA)	564
KRONE, Judith P.	(GA)	679
LARSEN, Mary T.	(GA)	698
LINKER, Rita S.	(GA)	731
LOWERY, Phyllis C.	(GA)	744
LYONS, Valerie S.	(GA)	753
MALCOLM, Carol L.	(GA)	762
MILLER, Jack E.	(GA)	838
MONTGOMERY, Denise L.	(GA)	856
MOSLEY, Mary M.	(GA)	871
NITSCHKE, Eric R.	(GA)	905
NITSCHKE, Marie M.	(GA)	905
PATON, John C.	(GA)	947
PAULK, Sara L.	(GA)	950
ROEHLING, Steven R.	(GA)	1048
SEARCY, David L.	(GA)	1109
SHERMAN, John R.	(GA)	1128
SOUTHWICK, Mary L.	(GA)	1170
STATOM, Susan T.	(GA)	1183
SUMNER, Ellen L.	(GA)	1209
TEMPLETON, Mary E.	(GA)	1231
TORRENTE, Kathryn J.	(GA)	1251
WILLIAMS, Anita	(GA)	1342
WILLIAMS, Howell M.	(GA)	1343
WILLIAMS, Sara E.	(GA)	1346
WILLIS, Roni M.	(GA)	1348
WRIGHT, Dianne H.	(GA)	1371
FUKUDA, Jodel L.	(HI)	408
MORGAN, Sally W.	(HI)	864
URAGO, Gail M.	(HI)	1269
BERNING, Robert W.	(IA)	89
BROWN, Jeanine B.	(IA)	144
CAMP, Emily E.	(IA)	175
CHAUDOIN, Sheila M.	(IA)	204
CLARK, Maeve K.	(IA)	217
CLAYBURN, Marginell P.	(IA)	220
DAVENPORT, Ronald D.	(IA)	276
ENGER, Kathy B.	(IA)	349
HESS, Sandra K.	(IA)	534
HILAND, Leah F.	(IA)	538
HILL, Fay G.	(IA)	539
HUNTING, Susan K.	(IA)	576
KNEFEL, Mary A.	(IA)	664

REFERENCE (Cont'd)
Reference

OHRLUND, Ava L.	(IA)	919
RIESBERG, Eunice L.	(IA)	1033
SCHACHT, John N.	(IA)	1088
SHAW, James T.	(IA)	1123
SHISLER, Shirley M.	(IA)	1131
SORENSON, Debra J.	(IA)	1168
STOUT, Robert J.	(IA)	1199
THEOBALD, Joanice	(IA)	1234
TYCKOSON, David A.	(IA)	1266
WEEG, Barbara E.	(IA)	1315
WEISS, Cynthia A.	(IA)	1320
ZORDELL, Pamela K.	(IA)	1390
PIKE, George H.	(ID)	972
STOLZ, Marty R.	(ID)	1196
TAYLOR, Adrien P.	(ID)	1225
WILLIAMS, Brenda M.	(ID)	1342
ABBOTT, John C.	(IL)	1
ADAMSHICK, Robert D.	(IL)	6
ALBSMEYER, Betty J.	(IL)	11
ALEXANDER, Lynetta L.	(IL)	12
ALLEN, Walter C.	(IL)	16
ANDERSON, Nancy E.	(IL)	24
AUFDENKAMP, Joann	(IL)	39
BAIR, Alice E.	(IL)	47
BAUNER, Ruth E.	(IL)	67
BEAN, Rick J.	(IL)	69
BECKER, John C.	(IL)	72
BENGTSON, Marjorie C.	(IL)	80
BEN-SHIR, Rya H.	(IL)	83
BJORNCRANTZ, Leslie B.	(IL)	100
BLACK, Kenneth L.	(IL)	101
BODI, Sonia E.	(IL)	109
BOUGHTON, Ruth E.	(IL)	119
BOURKE, Jacqueline K.	(IL)	119
BROSK, Carol A.	(IL)	141
BRYAN, Mila	(IL)	152
BRYANT, Eugenia D.	(IL)	152
BURNSIDE, Diane B.	(IL)	163
BURRUSS, Marsha A.	(IL)	163
CALHOUN, Michele	(IL)	172
CALTVEDT, Sarah C.	(IL)	174
CAMPANA, Deborah A.	(IL)	175
CARNELLI, Sandra R.	(IL)	183
CARY, Jan E.	(IL)	191
CHEN, Robert P.	(IL)	205
CICHON, Marilyn T.	(IL)	214
CLARKE, Susan M.	(IL)	219
CLAYTON, Nina A.	(IL)	220
COOPER, Rosemarie A.	(IL)	243
DARLING, Elizabeth A.	(IL)	274
DAVIS, Sandra B.	(IL)	281
DAWOOD, Rosemary	(IL)	282
DI MAURO, Paul	(IL)	304
EFIRD, Frank K.	(IL)	338
FARRELL, Patricia H.	(IL)	365
FAUST, Julia B.	(IL)	366
FAYNZILBERG, Irina	(IL)	367
FISHER, Marshall	(IL)	381
FITZGERALD, Adena H.	(IL)	382
FRY, Roy H.	(IL)	406
GRODINSKY, Deborah	(IL)	471
HALL, Clark J.	(IL)	487
HAMILTON, D A.	(IL)	491
HAMMOND, Louise H.	(IL)	494
HARRIS, Jane F.	(IL)	504
HEISTER, Carla G.	(IL)	523
HENRY, Nancy J.	(IL)	529
HILBURGER, Mary J.	(IL)	538
HILGERT, Elvire R.	(IL)	539
HINTZ, Jeanne E.	(IL)	543
HOGAN, Mary R.	(IL)	549
HUFFMAN, Carol P.	(IL)	571
JOHNSON, Keran C.	(IL)	606
JONES, Dorothy E.	(IL)	612
JUSTICE, Sylvia H.	(IL)	620
KEENAN, Mary T.	(IL)	634
KELLER, Steven W.	(IL)	636
KISSINGER, Patricia A.	(IL)	656

REFERENCE (Cont'd)
Reference

KLESTINSKI, Martha A. . . (IL) 661
KLINGBERG, Susan . . . . . (IL) 661
KLOCKENGA, Gary R. . . . (IL) 662
KOWITZ, Aletha A. . . . . (IL) 674
LAMBERT, Sandra L. . . . (IL) 690
LANDIS, Martha . . . . (IL) 693
LARSEN, John C. . . . . . (IL) 698
MARTIN, Bennie E. . . . . (IL) 775
MCCARTHY, Mary C. . . (IL) 794
MCFARLAND, Mary A. . (IL) 805
MCGILL, Sara L. . . . . . (IL) 806
MCHENRY, Renee E. . . . (IL) 808
MCHUGH, William A. . . . (IL) 809
MILLER, Marian I. . . . . . (IL) 840
MORRISON, Carol J. . . . (IL) 868
MORROW, Mary D. . . . . (IL) 869
MULHERIN, William S. . . (IL) 876
NEAL, Karen F. . . . . . . (IL) 890
NELSON, Barbara L. . . . (IL) 893
NEWMAN, Gerald L. . . . (IL) 899
NEWMAN, Lorna R. . . . . (IL) 899
NORWOOD, Pamela Z. . (IL) 910
OCHSNER, Renata E. . . (IL) 915
O'SHEA, Cornelius M. . . (IL) 928
OSWALT, Karen K. . . . . (IL) 929
PEARSON, Karen L. . . . (IL) 952
PENDERGRASS, Margaret
    E. . . . . (IL) 956
PEPLOW, Richard C. . . . (IL) 958
PHILLIPS, Dorothy E. . . . (IL) 968
PICCOLI, Roberta A. . . . (IL) 970
PORTER, Carol . . . . (IL) 984
POULTNEY, Judy R. . . . . (IL) 987
PRIOR, Janice L. . . . . . . (IL) 993
RECKS, Dorcas E. . . . . . (IL) 1013
REDDY, Michael B. . . . . (IL) 1013
ROBERTSON, S D. . . . . (IL) 1042
SANDERS, Charlene R. . (IL) 1079
SCOTT, Sharon E. . . . . . (IL) 1108
SHAFER, Anne E. . . . . . (IL) 1119
SODOWSKY, Kay M. . . . (IL) 1165
SORENSON, Liene S. . . (IL) 1168
SPEARMAN, Donna G. . (IL) 1172
SPRINGBORN, Janice T. (IL) 1176
STELLING, Dwight D. . . . (IL) 1186
STENGER, Brenda E. . . . (IL) 1187
STEPHENS, Janet A. . . . (IL) 1188
STEWART, Jamie K. . . . (IL) 1192
STROUSE, Roger L. . . . . (IL) 1203
STUART, Mary P. . . . . . (IL) 1204
SYED, Mariam A. . . . . . (IL) 1217
THOMAS, Marcia L. . . . . (IL) 1237
TIWANA, Nazar H. . . . . . (IL) 1247
TODD, Margaret . . . . (IL) 1248
UDDIN, Shantha C. . . . . (IL) 1267
VANCURA, Joyce B. . . . (IL) 1273
VILARO, Annette B. . . . . (IL) 1284
WALSH, Deborah T. . . . . (IL) 1299
WALSH, Susan E. . . . . . (IL) 1300
WATSON, Robert E. . . . . (IL) 1310
WESTON, Ann B. . . . . . (IL) 1327
WHEELER, Claudia J. . . (IL) 1328
WIMMER, Laura M. . . . . (IL) 1354
BERTRAM, Lee A. . . . . . (IN) 91
COHEN, Karen S. . . . . . (IN) 228
COLLINS, Mary E. . . . . . (IN) 233
DARBEE, Leigh . . . . (IN) 274
DEANE, Paul D. . . . . . . (IN) 284
GREMMELS, Gillian S. . . (IN) 467
HARLAN, John B. . . . . . (IN) 502
HAYES, Stephen M. . . . . (IN) 516
HICKLING, Jeanne . . . . . (IN) 536
HOHL, Robert J. . . . . . . (IN) 550
JONES, Deborah A. . . . . (IN) 612
JONES, Thomas Q. . . . . (IN) 615
KIDDIE, Jeanette A. . . . . (IN) 646
KONDELIK, Marlene R. . (IN) 670
KRAMER, Arlene H. . . . . (IN) 675

REFERENCE (Cont'd)
Reference

LOGSDON, Robert L. . . . (IN) 737
MAXWELL, Donald W. . . (IN) 788
MCCAFFERY, Laurabelle (IN) 793
MEEK, Janet E. . . . . (IN) 821
MILLER, Marsha A. . . . . (IN) 840
MURDOCK, J L. . . . . . . (IN) 879
MUSTO, Frederick W. . . (IN) 883
NORMAN, Orval G. . . . . (IN) 909
OGLES, Lynn C. . . . . . . (IN) 918
SABA, Bettye M. . . . . . . (IN) 1072
SCHMIDT, Kathy W. . . . (IN) 1095
SMITH, Lary . . . . (IN) 1156
SOWARDS, Steven W. . . (IN) 1170
TIMMER, Julia B. . . . . . . (IN) 1246
TRIBBLE, Judith E. . . . . (IN) 1256
WOLCOTT, Laurie J. . . . (IN) 1359
WOODARD, Marcia S. . . (IN) 1366
BENNETT, Samuel J. . . . (KS) 82
DOMBOURIAN MOORE,
    Ann . . . . (KS) 310
DRESSLER, Alta L. . . . . (KS) 319
FINK, Madonna . . . . (KS) 378
GALLOWAY, Mary A. . . . (KS) 415
GAYNOR, Kathy A. . . . . (KS) 424
GERMANN, Malcolm P. . (KS) 429
HAURY, David A. . . . . . . (KS) 512
HORTIN, Judith K. . . . . . (KS) 561
MARSH, Martha M. . . . . (KS) 773
MELICK, Cal G. . . . . (KS) 822
REIMER, Sylvia D. . . . . . (KS) 1021
RHODES, Saralinda A. . . (KS) 1026
SNYDER, Fritz . . . . (KS) 1164
STUHR-ROMMEREIM,
    Rebecca A. . . . . . . (KS) 1205
WIEBE, Margaret A. . . . . (KS) 1336
BENNETT, Donna S. . . . (KY) 81
CRABB, George W. . . . . (KY) 254
DARE, Philip N. . . . . (KY) 274
DEBUSMAN, Paul M. . . . (KY) 285
DIEMER, Irvin T. . . . . . . (KY) 302
HAWLEY, Mary B. . . . . . (KY) 514
MOORE, Elaine E. . . . . . (KY) 859
RINEY, Judith N. . . . . . . (KY) 1035
SCHLENE, Vickie J. . . . . (KY) 1094
STURM, Rebecca R. . . . (KY) 1205
THOMPSON, Ann B. . . . (KY) 1238
TURNER, Rebecca M. . . (KY) 1265
ZIMMER, Connie W. . . . (KY) 1388
ABRAHAM, Sandra H. . . (LA) 3
CHEW, Susan M. . . . . . . (LA) 207
COPELAND, Patricia S. . (LA) 244
DESSINO, Jacquelyn A. . (LA) 296
DICARLO, Michael A. . . . (LA) 300
FLEURY, Mary E. . . . . . . (LA) 385
HEBERT, Madeline . . . . . (LA) 519
HUSSEY, Sandra R. . . . . (LA) 578
JONES, Philip L. . . . . . . (LA) 614
JOSEPH, Eleanor C. . . . (LA) 617
MATTMILLER, C F. . . . . (LA) 786
MIDDLETON, Francine K. (LA) 833
MOONEY, Sandra T. . . . (LA) 858
NACHOD, Katherine B. . . (LA) 885
PERRAULT, Anna H. . . . (LA) 959
SARKODIE-MENSAH,
    Kwasi . . . . (LA) 1083
SHAUGHNESSY, Megan (LA) 1123
SNOW, Maxine L. . . . . . (LA) 1164
STAFFORD, Cecilia D. . . (LA) 1178
STANDEFER, Steven R. . (LA) 1179
WITTKOPF, Barbara J. . . (LA) 1358
WOJKOWSKI, Suhad K. . (LA) 1359
WOOD, Julienne L. . . . . (LA) 1364
YOUNG, Amanda M. . . . (LA) 1381
ANDERSON, A J. . . . . . (MA) 21
BAILEY, Leeta L. . . . . . . (MA) 46
BEARDEN, Eithne C. . . . (MA) 69
BENDER, Helen F. . . . . . (MA) 79
BEZERA, Elizabeth A. . . . (MA) 93

REFERENCE (Cont'd)
Reference

BIRD, Nora J.	(MA)	98
BLAKE, Michael R.	(MA)	103
BURG, Barbara A.	(MA)	159
CARNAHAN, Paul A.	(MA)	183
CARVER, Jane C.	(MA)	191
CHRISTOPHER, Irene	(MA)	212
CODAIR, Frederick R.	(MA)	226
COHEN, Christina M.	(MA)	228
COLBY, Beverly	(MA)	230
CONDON, Mary M.	(MA)	236
COOLIDGE, Christina L.	(MA)	241
COOPER WYMAN, Rosalind	(MA)	244
DAVIS, Barbara M.	(MA)	277
DODSON, Nancy C.	(MA)	308
DUCKETT, Joan	(MA)	322
DUNKLY, James W.	(MA)	326
DUTCHER, Henry D.	(MA)	329
FENG, Yen T.	(MA)	371
FRAZIER, Nancy E.	(MA)	399
FRIEDMAN, Fred T.	(MA)	403
GARBER, Suzanne	(MA)	417
GIBBS, Paige	(MA)	431
GILLIAM, Ellen M.	(MA)	436
GROVE, Shari T.	(MA)	474
HUDSON, Robert E.	(MA)	570
KELEHER, Carolyn P.	(MA)	635
KNAPP, Leslie C.	(MA)	663
KOVED, Ruth B.	(MA)	674
LEE, Marilyn M.	(MA)	710
MERRIAM, Joyce	(MA)	826
METCALF, Marjorie	(MA)	828
MINTON, Alix M.	(MA)	846
MOLTZ, Sandra S.	(MA)	854
MORNER, Claudia J.	(MA)	865
MURRAY, Lynn T.	(MA)	882
NASON, Jennifer L.	(MA)	888
NELSON, Margaret R.	(MA)	894
NESS, Pamela M.	(MA)	896
NORMAN-CAMP, Melody	(MA)	909
PANAGOPOULOS, Beata D.	(MA)	937
PAPADEMETRIOU, Athanasia	(MA)	938
PAPADEMETRIOU, George C.	(MA)	938
PEARCE, Jean K.	(MA)	952
PLUNKET, Linda	(MA)	979
PORTSCH-SNOW, Joanne	(MA)	985
ROTMAN, Laurie D.	(MA)	1060
SAUER, David A.	(MA)	1084
SAUNDERS, Leslie E.	(MA)	1084
SCHUELER, Dolores	(MA)	1101
SHERER, Elaine R.	(MA)	1127
SHIH, Jenny	(MA)	1130
SIEGEL, Bette L.	(MA)	1136
SMITH, Barbara A.	(MA)	1152
STANLEY, Ellen	(MA)	1180
STOCKARD, Joan	(MA)	1195
SWANN, Thomas E.	(MA)	1213
WALKER, Mary M.	(MA)	1296
WEBBER, Cynthia J.	(MA)	1313
WELLINGTON, Carol S.	(MA)	1321
WILLIAMS, Carole C.	(MA)	1342
WOOD, Ann L.	(MA)	1363
WOODARD, Paul E.	(MA)	1366
ZIEPER, Linda R.	(MA)	1388
ALEXANDER, Estelle R.	(MD)	12
AYER, Carol A.	(MD)	42
BOURKOFF, Vivienne R.	(MD)	119
BRADLEY, Wanda L.	(MD)	126
BROGDON, Jennie L.	(MD)	139
BYERLY, Imogene J.	(MD)	168
CHAPUT, Linda J.	(MD)	202
CHIESA, Adele M.	(MD)	208
COLE, Anna B.	(MD)	230
COOK, Daraka S.	(MD)	239
COUPE, Jill M.	(MD)	251

REFERENCE (Cont'd)
Reference

DYSART, Marcia J.	(MD)	331
FORBES, John B.	(MD)	389
GALLAGHER, Charles F.	(MD)	413
GIBBONS, Katherine Y.	(MD)	431
GOLDSBERG, Elizabeth D.	(MD)	446
GROSSHANS, Maxine Z.	(MD)	473
HAMMETT, Marcia G.	(MD)	493
HINEGARDNER, Patricia G.	(MD)	542
HOFMANN, Patricia P.	(MD)	548
HOMAN, Frances M.	(MD)	555
KELLS, Laura J.	(MD)	637
KLEIN, Ilene R.	(MD)	659
LABASH, Stephen P.	(MD)	685
LARSEN, Lida L.	(MD)	698
MEYER, William P.	(MD)	830
PANDA, Rosamond E.	(MD)	937
PEARSE, Nancy J.	(MD)	952
PECK, Ann D.	(MD)	953
PRATT, Laura C.	(MD)	990
PRIMER, Ben	(MD)	993
QUINN, Carol J.	(MD)	1000
RAFATS, Jerome M.	(MD)	1003
REILLY, Deborah D.	(MD)	1020
ROBERTS, Cynthia H.	(MD)	1039
SOLOMON, Fern R.	(MD)	1166
THAPAR, Shashi P.	(MD)	1234
THIES, Gail M.	(MD)	1235
TRELEVEN, Richard L.	(MD)	1255
VAN CAMPEN, Rebecca J.	(MD)	1272
WILLIAMS, Pamela S.	(MD)	1346
WOLF, Dorothy L.	(MD)	1360
ALLEY, Katherine S.	(ME)	16
BAKER, Alison	(ME)	47
BILODEAU, Judith M.	(ME)	97
SAEGER, Edwin J.	(ME)	1074
SHANKLAND, Anne H.	(ME)	1120
SMITH, Barbara J.	(ME)	1153
THOR, Angela M.	(ME)	1242
ARNETT, Stanley K.	(MI)	33
ARVIN, Charles S.	(MI)	35
ASHLEY, Roger S.	(MI)	36
BAKER, Jean S.	(MI)	48
BEAL, Sarell W.	(MI)	68
BECK, Mary C.	(MI)	71
BINONIEMI, Amanda M.	(MI)	97
BROW, Judith A.	(MI)	141
BURINSKI, Walter W.	(MI)	160
CAMMENGA, Cheryl G.	(MI)	175
CAPPAERT, Lael R.	(MI)	180
CARLSON, Susan L.	(MI)	182
CHAMBERS, E G.	(MI)	198
CHAPMAN, Mary A.	(MI)	202
CONWAY, Lauren K.	(MI)	239
COREY, Glenn M.	(MI)	246
DAVIDSEN, Susanna L.	(MI)	276
D'ELIA, Joseph G.	(MI)	289
DOYLE, James M.	(MI)	317
DURIVAGE, Mary J.	(MI)	328
GAMBLE, Marian L.	(MI)	416
GAYLOR, Robert G.	(MI)	423
GIFFORD, Paul M.	(MI)	433
GLIKIN, Ronda	(MI)	441
GOLDSTEIN, Doris R.	(MI)	446
HAENICKE, Carol A.	(MI)	482
HAGE, Christine C.	(MI)	482
HERTZ, Sylvia	(MI)	533
HEYMOSS, Jennifer M.	(MI)	536
HILDEBRAND, Linda L.	(MI)	538
HOMANT, Sue J.	(MI)	555
HORN, Anna E.	(MI)	559
IRWIN, Lawrence L.	(MI)	584
ISAACSON, David K.	(MI)	584
JOSE, Phyllis A.	(MI)	617
KARP, Nancy S.	(MI)	628
KING, Kathryn L.	(MI)	651
KIRKLAND, Ruth M.	(MI)	655

REFERENCE (Cont'd)
Reference

KONDAK, Ann . . . . (MI)   670
LEE, Lucy W. . . . . (MI)   710
LIGHT, Lin . . . . (MI)   726
LILLEY, Barbara A. . . . . (MI)   727
LINDSTROM, Susan C. . (MI)   730
LUKASIEWICZ, Barbara . (MI)   747
MASLOW, Linda S. . . . . (MI)   780
MATZO, Deborah J. . . . . (MI)   786
MEADOWS, Brenda L. . . (MI)   819
MICHAUD, John C. . . . . (MI)   832
MORELAND, Patricia L. . (MI)   863
NICHOLS, Darlene P. . . (MI)   901
NIETHAMMER, Leslee . . (MI)   904
NUFFER, Roy A. . . . . . . (MI)   912
PORTER, Jean F. . . . . . . (MI)   984
SANFORD, John D. . . . . (MI) 1081
SCHNEIDER, Janet M. . . (MI) 1097
SCOTT, Jane . . . . (MI) 1107
SHEPARD, Margaret E. . (MI) 1127
SIEVING, Pamela C. . . . . (MI) 1136
SMITH, Peter A. . . . . (MI) 1159
SPENCE, Theresa S. . . . (MI) 1173
STREETER, Linda D. . . . (MI) 1201
STUCK, Judy K. . . . . (MI) 1204
THUNELL, Allen E. . . . . . (MI) 1243
VAN ALLEN, Neil K. . . . . (MI) 1271
VANDERLAAN, Robert J. . (MI) 1274
VANDERLAAN, Sharon J. . (MI) 1274
VANDER MEER, Patricia
   F. . . . . (MI) 1274
VIGES, R J. . . . . (MI) 1284
WALKER, Joe L. . . . . . . (MI) 1295
WESTBROOK, Jo L. . . . (MI) 1326
WILSON, Amy S. . . . . . . (MI) 1349
WISCHMEYER, Carol A. . (MI) 1356
WISE, Virginia J. . . . . . . (MI) 1357
YETMAN, Nancy J. . . . . (MI) 1380
ZAENGER, Kathleen L. . . (MI) 1385
BAKER, Tracey I. . . . . . . (MN)   50
BAUM, Marsha L. . . . . . . (MN)   66
CARON, Theodore F. . . . (MN)   184
COVER, Teresa A. . . . . . (MN)   252
ELLIOTT, Gwendolyn W. . (MN)   344
FENTON, Patricia F. . . . . (MN)   371
GANGL, Susan D. . . . . . (MN)   416
GAVIN, Donna J. . . . . . . (MN)   423
HALES-MABRY, Celia E. . (MN)   486
HOLT, Constance W. . . . (MN)   554
JANZEN, Deborah K. . . . (MN)   594
JOHNSON, Deborah S. . . (MN)   603
MOXNESS, Mary J. . . . . (MN)   874
OUSE, David J. . . . . (MN)   930
REHNBERG, Marilyn J. . (MN) 1017
REIERSON, Pamela M. . (MN) 1019
ROLONTZ, Linda . . . . . . (MN) 1051
SHOPTAUGH, Terry L. . . (MN) 1132
TURNER, Patricia . . . . . . (MN) 1265
WALDEN, Barbara L. . . . (MN) 1294
WESTBY, Jerry L. . . . . . (MN) 1326
YOUNG, Lynne M. . . . . . (MN) 1382
ALLCORN, Mary E. . . . . (MO)   14
ALLEN, Ronald . . . . (MO)   16
BHULLAR, Puohpajit D. . (MO)   93
BOETTCHER, Joel W. . . (MO)   110
BREWER, O J. . . . . (MO)   134
DELIVUK, John A. . . . . . (MO)   289
DEWEESE, June L. . . . . (MO)   298
DILLARD, Bonita D. . . . . (MO)   303
ELLEBRACHT, Eleanor V. (MO)   343
GEARIN, Louvan A. . . . . (MO)   424
HALLIER, Sara J. . . . . . . (MO)   489
HANSEN, Charles A. . . . (MO)   497
HOCHSTETLER, Donald
   D. . . . . (MO)   545
HUFFMAN, Robert F. . . . (MO)   571
KIEL, Becky . . . . (MO)   647
KNORR, Martin R. . . . . . (MO)   665
LAWS, Janet E. . . . . (MO)   705

REFERENCE (Cont'd)
Reference

LOCKHART, Carol A. . . . (MO)   736
LUH, Ming . . . . (MO)   747
MASON, Laura L. . . . . . . (MO)   781
PARKES, Darla J. . . . . . (MO)   942
RILEY, Ruth A. . . . . (MO) 1034
SHIPLEY, Anne C. . . . . . (MO) 1131
STEWART, J A. . . . . (MO) 1192
BECK, Allisa L. . . . . (MS)   71
BLACK, Bernice B. . . . . . (MS)   101
BRELAND, June M. . . . . (MS)   132
DUNAWAY, Charjean L. . (MS)   325
HART, Julie C. . . . . (MS)   507
HAUTH, Allan C. . . . . . . (MS)   513
KIRBY, Donald J. . . . . . . (MS)   654
RAINWATER, Mark T. . . (MS) 1004
ROGERS, Margaret N. . . (MS) 1049
SMITH, Judy S. . . . . (MS) 1156
TUCKER, Ellis E. . . . . . . (MS) 1261
WILLIAMS, Eddie A. . . . (MS) 1343
WILLIS, Jan L. . . . . (MS) 1348
LEE, Susan M. . . . . (MT)   711
AHLERS, Glen P. . . . . . . (NC)   8
ALLEN, Lynne B. . . . . . . (NC)   15
ALLEN, Regina L. . . . . . . (NC)   15
ANTONE, Allen L. . . . . . (NC)   29
BACKMAN, Carroll H. . . (NC)   44
BEATTIE, Barbara C. . . . (NC)   70
BERGER, Kenneth W. . . (NC)   85
BUSH, Mary E. . . . . (NC)   165
CARMICHAEL, James V. (NC)   183
CARRINGTON, Bessie M. (NC)   186
CAWLEY, Marianne . . . . (NC)   195
COHEN, Edward S. . . . . (NC)   228
COLLINS, Donald E. . . . (NC)   232
COTTER, Michael G. . . . (NC)   250
DAVIDSON, Laura B. . . . (NC)   276
DEBRECZENY, Gillian M. (NC)   285
DEVITO, Robert M. . . . . (NC)   297
ELKINS, Anne M. . . . . . . (NC)   343
ELMORE, Lisa E. . . . . . . (NC)   346
FARKAS, Doina C. . . . . . (NC)   364
FRANK, Linda V. . . . . . . (NC)   397
GARTRELL, Ellen G. . . . (NC)   420
GERMAIN, Claire M. . . . (NC)   429
HEUBERGER, Karen W. . (NC)   535
HICKS, Michael . . . . (NC)   537
HORTON, James T. . . . . (NC)   561
HULL, Laurence O. . . . . (NC)   572
KARES, Artemis C. . . . . (NC)   627
LEONARD, Teresa G. . . . (NC)   717
MATOCHIK, Michael J. . (NC)   784
MAXWELL, Daisy D. . . . (NC)   788
MCCALLUM, Dorothy T. . (NC)   793
MCGLOHON, Leah L. . . (NC)   807
MILLER, Lewis R. . . . . . . (NC)   840
OSER, Anita K. . . . . (NC)   928
PARRISH, Nancy B. . . . . (NC)   944
PETERSON, Cynthia L. . (NC)   963
POZO, Frank J. . . . . (NC)   989
REES, Joe C. . . . . (NC) 1016
RICE, Patricia A. . . . . . . (NC) 1027
SEGAL, Jane D. . . . . (NC) 1111
SHEARY, Edward J. . . . . (NC) 1124
SHEPHERD, Gay W. . . . (NC) 1127
SPENCER, Linda A. . . . . (NC) 1173
STEPHENSON, Marilyn R. (NC) 1188
SUTTON, Ellen D. . . . . . (NC) 1211
TABORY, Maxim . . . . . . (NC) 1219
TUCKER, Mae S. . . . . . . (NC) 1262
WASILICK, Michael J. . . (NC) 1308
WATT, Richard S. . . . . . (NC) 1310
WEBSTER, Deborah K. . (NC) 1314
WEEKS, Olivia L. . . . . . . (NC) 1315
WHITMORE, Sharon S. . (NC) 1334
WILGUS, Anne B. . . . . . (NC) 1339
WILKINSON, Fleeta M. . (NC) 1340
WILLIAMS, Wiley J. . . . . (NC) 1347
WINDHAM, Shirley L. . . (NC) 1354

REFERENCE (Cont'd)
Reference

WOOD, Kelly S.	(NC)	1364
WORRELL, Diane F.	(NC)	1369
BIRDSALL, Douglas G.	(ND)	98
BRATTON, Phyllis A.	(ND)	129
NIENOW, Beth M.	(ND)	904
PEDERSON, Randy L.	(ND)	954
ROBERTSON, Pamela S.	(ND)	1042
EGBERS, Gail L.	(NE)	339
FELTON, John D.	(NE)	370
KENDRA, William E.	(NE)	640
LEITER, Richard A.	(NE)	714
MUNDELL, Jacqueline L.	(NE)	878
PAUL, Andrea I.	(NE)	949
SARTORI, Eva M.	(NE)	1083
SLOAN, Patricia K.	(NE)	1149
TOLLMAN, Thomas A.	(NE)	1249
GAVRISH, Diane L.	(NH)	423
KIETZMAN, William D.	(NH)	647
KOZIKOWSKI, Derek M.	(NH)	674
LANDAU, Cynthia R.	(NH)	692
MADDEN, Robert J.	(NH)	758
PERLUNGHER, Richard A.	(NH)	959
REED, Barbara E.	(NH)	1014
VORBEAU, Barbara E.	(NH)	1289
ANDERMAN, Lynea	(NJ)	21
ASSENHEIMER, Judy	(NJ)	37
AVENICK, Karen	(NJ)	41
BARTZ, Stephanie	(NJ)	62
BECK, Susan J.	(NJ)	72
BELCHER, Emily M.	(NJ)	76
BELSTERLING, Jean I.	(NJ)	78
BITTER, Jane L.	(NJ)	100
BOYLE, Jeanne E.	(NJ)	124
BROWN, Linda M.	(NJ)	145
BULYA, Larissa	(NJ)	157
BURDEN, Geraldine R.	(NJ)	158
BYOUK, Nancy K.	(NJ)	168
CALLANAN, Ellen M.	(NJ)	173
CAPARROS, Ilona S.	(NJ)	179
CARMER, Ann R.	(NJ)	183
CARNAHAN, Joan A.	(NJ)	183
CASSEL, Jeris F.	(NJ)	193
CHAIKIN, Mary C.	(NJ)	197
CHAMBERLIN, Cynthia C.	(NJ)	198
CHELARIU, Ana R.	(NJ)	204
COHEN, Adrea G.	(NJ)	227
COHEN, Susan K.	(NJ)	229
DONOHUE, Nancy W.	(NJ)	312
ELIASON, Elisabetha S.	(NJ)	342
FIELD, Jack	(NJ)	375
GEORGE, Mary W.	(NJ)	427
GOLDSMITH, Maxine K.	(NJ)	446
GREENBERG, Evelyn	(NJ)	463
HIGGINS, Flora T.	(NJ)	537
KALDENBERG, Katherine A.	(NJ)	622
KAPLAN, Susan J.	(NJ)	626
KRANIS, Janet C.	(NJ)	676
LEE, J S.	(NJ)	710
LEVINE, Riesa E.	(NJ)	721
LIND, Judith Y.	(NJ)	728
LIOU, Pearl S.	(NJ)	732
LUXNER, Ann F.	(NJ)	750
MAMAN, Marie	(NJ)	764
MCADOO, Jannifer C.	(NJ)	792
MCLAUGHLIN, Dorothy M.	(NJ)	813
MEYERS, Elsa M.	(NJ)	831
MILLER, Mary A.	(NJ)	840
MILLER, Virginia L.	(NJ)	843
NEDSWICK, Robert	(NJ)	891
NEWMAN, Lisa A.	(NJ)	899
OGONEK, Donna L.	(NJ)	918
OTT, Linda G.	(NJ)	930
PAULLIN, William D.	(NJ)	950
PISKORIK, Elizabeth	(NJ)	976
PORTUGAL, Rhoda	(NJ)	985
POVILAITIS, Leanna J.	(NJ)	987
REINHARDT, Eileen	(NJ)	1021

REFERENCE (Cont'd)
Reference

ROTHENBERG, Patricia	(NJ)	1060
SANDERS, Mary C.	(NJ)	1080
SCARPELLINO, Rebecca A.	(NJ)	1088
SCHUELER, Frances S.	(NJ)	1101
SLOAN, Ruth C.	(NJ)	1149
STONE, Jason R.	(NJ)	1197
STRATTON, Elizabeth G.	(NJ)	1200
TOMAR, Jeanne	(NJ)	1249
TUTWILER, Dorothea F.	(NJ)	1266
VAN FLEET, James A.	(NJ)	1275
WALLACE, Wendy L.	(NJ)	1298
WANGGAARD, Janice H.	(NJ)	1303
WELLSMAN, Jennifer A.	(NJ)	1323
WHITING, Elaine M.	(NJ)	1333
WILEN, Rosamond L.	(NJ)	1339
WILSON, Myoung C.	(NJ)	1352
WOODLEY, Robert H.	(NJ)	1366
WROBLEWSKI, Christine	(NJ)	1373
ZIMMERMAN, Elisabeth K.	(NJ)	1388
BARBER, Helen M.	(NM)	55
BROWN, Eulalie W.	(NM)	143
HUMPHREY, Thomas W.	(NM)	573
KLOPFER, Jerome J.	(NM)	662
LEWIS, Linda K.	(NM)	723
MCBETH, Deborah E.	(NM)	792
WALKER, Mary J.	(NM)	1296
ZAMORA, Gloria J.	(NM)	1386
DION, Kathleen L.	(NV)	305
GREFRATH, Richard W.	(NV)	465
MANLEY, Charles W.	(NV)	765
AKEY, Stephen	(NY)	9
ALLERTON, Ellen M.	(NY)	16
ALVAREZ, Ronald	(NY)	19
ANDERSON, Birgitta M.	(NY)	21
BALDWIN, Betty J.	(NY)	51
BARNELLO, Inga H.	(NY)	57
BAUM, Nathan	(NY)	66
BEHAR, Evelyn W.	(NY)	74
BELL, Mary F.	(NY)	77
BENDES, Adele N.	(NY)	79
BENSEN, Mary L.	(NY)	83
BERGER, Paula E.	(NY)	86
BERKEBILE, Sue A.	(NY)	87
BERRY, Gayle C.	(NY)	90
BIRO, Juliane	(NY)	99
BOURKE, Thomas A.	(NY)	119
BRAUN, Robert L.	(NY)	130
BRICKER, Naomi S.	(NY)	135
BRODERICK, Therese L.	(NY)	139
BROWNE, Scott M.	(NY)	148
BURKEY, Lynne	(NY)	161
BURNETTE, Michaelyn	(NY)	162
BUSH, Joyce	(NY)	165
BUZZANGA, Heidi S.	(NY)	168
CAGAN, Penny M.	(NY)	170
CAHN, Mary Z.	(NY)	171
CARUSO, Janet A.	(NY)	190
CHAMBERLAIN, Erna B.	(NY)	197
CINQUE, Douglas V.	(NY)	214
CLANCY, Kathy	(NY)	215
CLINE, Herman H.	(NY)	222
CONEY, Kim C.	(NY)	236
COONEY, Joan D.	(NY)	242
COOPER, Catherine M.	(NY)	242
DAY, Ross	(NY)	283
DERRICKSON, Margaret	(NY)	294
DIETRICH, Peter J.	(NY)	302
DOEZEMA, Linda P.	(NY)	308
DORN, Robert J.	(NY)	313
DOYLE, James J.	(NY)	317
DUTIKOW, Irene V.	(NY)	329
DWORKIN, Victoria G.	(NY)	330
EDWARDS, Rita F.	(NY)	337
EISENBERG, Debra	(NY)	340
EYMAN, David H.	(NY)	359
FEIGER, Cherie S.	(NY)	368
FENTON, Joan T.	(NY)	371

REFERENCE (Cont'd)
Reference

FRANCIS, Barbara B. . . . . (NY) 396
FRANKE, Gail E. . . . . . . (NY) 397
FRASER, Charlotte R. . . (NY) 399
FREIDES, Thelma . . . . . . (NY) 401
GAWLER, Ann C. . . . . . (NY) 423
GERACI, Diane . . . . (NY) 428
GOLD, Hilary G. . . . . . . (NY) 444
GRAVLEE, Diane D. . . . . (NY) 459
GREENE, Margaret A. . . (NY) 464
HAAS, Marilyn L. . . . . . . (NY) 480
HABER, Mark N. . . . . . . (NY) 481
HAIMOVSKY, Kira A. . . . (NY) 484
HALPIN, James R. . . . . . (NY) 490
HAND, Sally C. . . . . (NY) 494
HASKO, John J. . . . . (NY) 510
HIGGINS, Steven . . . . . . (NY) 538
HORNICK-LOCKARD,
    Barbara A. . . . . (NY) 560
HUFFORD, Jon R. . . . . . (NY) 571
IRWIN, Iris . . . . (NY) 584
JAFFE, Steven . . . . (NY) 591
JANOWSKY, Cara A. . . . (NY) 593
JOYCE, Therese . . . . . . (NY) 618
JUDD, Blanche E. . . . . . (NY) 618
JUHL, M E. . . . . (NY) 619
JUNG, Norman O. . . . . . (NY) 620
KAHN, Laura . . . . (NY) 622
KAIN, Joan P. . . . . (NY) 622
KARKHANIS, Sharad . . . (NY) 627
KASSIN, Abby L. . . . . . . (NY) 629
KENEFICK, Colleen M. . . (NY) 640
KING, Charles L. . . . . . (NY) 650
KING, Christine E. . . . . (NY) 650
KINYATTI, Njoki W. . . . . (NY) 653
KLINGLE, Philip A. . . . . (NY) 662
KOCH, Judith L. . . . . . . (NY) 667
KOLATA, Judith . . . . (NY) 669
KONDZELA, Jeanette M. (NY) 670
KRAUSS, Susan E. . . . . (NY) 676
KUPERMAN, Aaron W. . (NY) 684
KUPFERBERG, Natalie . . (NY) 684
LANG, Jovian P. . . . . . . (NY) 695
LAUER, Jonathan D. . . . . (NY) 702
LEWANDOWSKI, Virginia
    M. . . . . (NY) 722
LEWIS, David W. . . . . . . (NY) 723
LINDAHL, Charles E. . . . (NY) 728
LISZCZYNSKYJ, Halyna
    A. . . . . (NY) 733
LOCHER, Cornelia E. . . . (NY) 736
LOCKETT, Barbara A. . . . (NY) 736
LUBETSKI, Edith E. . . . . (NY) 745
MACINICK, James W. . . (NY) 755
MACK, Theodore D. . . . (NY) 756
MACKECHNIE, Nancy S. (NY) 756
MACKNIGHT, Judith M. . (NY) 757
MARTIN, Helen . . . . (NY) 776
MASH, S D. . . . . (NY) 780
MCGOWAN, Kathleen M. (NY) 807
MCGRATH, Antoinette M. (NY) 807
MCLAUGHLIN, Denis F. . (NY) 813
MELITO, Joyce A. . . . . . (NY) 822
MIHRAM, Danielle . . . . . (NY) 834
MILLER, Barbara K. . . . . (NY) 835
MOUSTAFA, Theresa A. . (NY) 874
MUELLER, Leta A. . . . . . (NY) 875
NAPOLITANO, Joan A. . (NY) 887
NAYLOR, David L. . . . . . (NY) 890
NELSON, Winifred S. . . . (NY) 895
NESBIT, Kathryn W. . . . . (NY) 896
NICOL, Margaret W. . . . . (NY) 903
NORDSTROM, Virginia . . (NY) 908
NUZZO, Nancy B. . . . . . (NY) 912
OCHS, Phyllis E. . . . . . . (NY) 915
OHMAN, Elisabeth T. . . . (NY) 919
OVERGAARD, Lynn H. . (NY) 931
PARKHURST, Kathleen A. (NY) 942
PATTISON, Frederick W. (NY) 948

REFERENCE (Cont'd)
Reference

PENNELL, Peggy P. . . . . (NY) 957
PERRY, Claudia A. . . . . . (NY) 960
PILACHOWSKI, David M. (NY) 973
PLATT, Mary L. . . . . (NY) 977
POTTER, Janet L. . . . . . (NY) 987
POWELL, Jill H. . . . . (NY) 988
PRAGER, George A. . . . (NY) 989
RAME, Mary E. . . . . (NY) 1005
RANHAND, Jori L. . . . . . (NY) 1007
REEPMEYER, Marie C. . (NY) 1016
RICKER, Shirley E. . . . . . (NY) 1031
RIDER, William J. . . . . . (NY) 1032
RITCHIE, David G. . . . . . (NY) 1036
ROBERTS, Gloria A. . . . (NY) 1040
ROOT, Christine . . . . (NY) 1053
ROSS, Ellen T. . . . . (NY) 1058
ROSSWURM, K M. . . . . . (NY) 1059
ROTHSTEIN, Pauline M. . (NY) 1060
RUBEY, Daniel R. . . . . . (NY) 1064
SALBER, Cecilia T. . . . . (NY) 1076
SALBER, Peter J. . . . . . . (NY) 1076
SANDERS, Robin S. . . . (NY) 1080
SCHENK, Kathryn L. . . . (NY) 1091
SCHLUCKEBIER, Leslie F. (NY) 1094
SCHMIDTMANN, Nancy
    K. . . . . (NY) 1096
SCHNEIDER, Adele . . . . (NY) 1096
SCHOENBAUM, Rhoda A. (NY) 1098
SCHROEDER, Eileen E. . (NY) 1100
SEER, Gitelle . . . . (NY) 1111
SEGAL, Judith . . . . (NY) 1112
SERBACKI, Mary . . . . . . (NY) 1116
SHAFFER, Kay L. . . . . . . (NY) 1119
SHALLENBERGER, Anna
    F. . . . . (NY) 1119
SHAPIRO, Barbara S. . . (NY) 1121
SHAPIRO, Martin P. . . . . (NY) 1121
SHELANDER, Frances R. (NY) 1125
SHUMAN, Jay A. . . . . . . (NY) 1134
SIMMONS, Rebecca A. . (NY) 1140
SINGER, Phyllis Z. . . . . . (NY) 1143
SLUSS, Sara B. . . . . (NY) 1150
SMITH, Mark J. . . . . (NY) 1158
SMITH, Melanie W. . . . . (NY) 1158
SPRAGG, Edwin B. . . . . (NY) 1175
STANTON, Lee W. . . . . . (NY) 1181
STEIN, Arlene B. . . . . . . (NY) 1185
STEIN, Marsha . . . . (NY) 1185
STIEVATER, Susan M. . . (NY) 1194
SUBRAMANIAN, Jane M. (NY) 1206
SVENNINGSEN, Karen L. (NY) 1212
SWERDLOVE, Dorothy L. (NY) 1215
SZMUK, Szilvia E. . . . . . (NY) 1218
TANNENBAUM, Robin L. (NY) 1222
TANZER, Barbara . . . . . . (NY) 1223
THOMSON, Diane G. . . . (NY) 1241
TOTH, Gregory M. . . . . . (NY) 1252
TUOHEY, Jeanne D. . . . . (NY) 1263
VANDELINDER, Bonnie L. (NY) 1273
VAUGHN, Susan J. . . . . (NY) 1280
VERDIBELLO, Muriel F. . (NY) 1282
VON BROCKDORFF, Eric (NY) 1288
WAGNER, Janet S . . . . (NY) 1291
WALSH, Daniel P. . . . . . (NY) 1299
WISHART, H L. . . . . (NY) 1357
WOLF, Carolyn M. . . . . . (NY) 1359
WOLFE, N J. . . . . (NY) 1361
WOLOZIN, Sara . . . . (NY) 1362
YOCHYM, Cynthia M. . . . (NY) 1380
YOUNG, Dorothy B. . . . . (NY) 1381
ZIESELMAN, Paula M. . . (NY) 1388
ZUBROW, Marcia L. . . . . (NY) 1391
ADAMS, Liese A. . . . . . . (OH) 5
ANDERSON, Janice L. . . (OH) 23
BAGBY, Ross F. . . . . . . (OH) 45
BAKER, Narcissa L. . . . . (OH) 49
BALCON, William J. . . . (OH) 51
BELL, Gladys S. . . . . (OH) 77

REFERENCE (Cont'd)
Reference

BEY, Leon S.	(OH)	93
BEYNEN, Gijsbertus K.	(OH)	93
BOX, Krista J.	(OH)	122
BRANCH, Susan	(OH)	127
BRINK, David R.	(OH)	136
BURKE, Saretta K.	(OH)	160
CLARK, Kay S.	(OH)	217
CURRIE, William W.	(OH)	266
DAHMANN, Rosemary G.	(OH)	270
DEAN, Winifred F.	(OH)	284
DOMBEY, Kathryn W.	(OH)	310
EHRHARDT, Allyn	(OH)	339
EMRICK, Nancy J.	(OH)	348
ENGEL, Carl T.	(OH)	348
ENGLISH, Raymond A.	(OH)	350
ESBIN, Martha P.	(OH)	354
FARAGO, Kathleen M.	(OH)	363
FINET, Scott	(OH)	378
FOSTER, Julia A.	(OH)	392
FRENCH, Michael	(OH)	402
GALLICCHIO, Virginia G.	(OH)	414
GEARY, James W.	(OH)	424
GEARY, Linda L.	(OH)	424
GILBERT, Donna J.	(OH)	433
GREEN, Denise D.	(OH)	461
GROHL, Arlene P.	(OH)	471
GUSS, Margaret B.	(OH)	478
HARPER, Lucy B.	(OH)	503
HENDERSON, Shirley A.	(OH)	527
HETTINGER, Susan F.	(OH)	534
HODGES, Pauline R.	(OH)	546
HUGE, Sharon A.	(OH)	571
HURLEY, Geraldine C.	(OH)	577
JAMISON, Martin P.	(OH)	593
JARABEK, Leona T.	(OH)	594
JOHNS, John E.	(OH)	601
JONES, Alice W.	(OH)	610
KAUER, Patricia M.	(OH)	630
KERBOW, Sandra C.	(OH)	643
KIRBAWY, Barbara L.	(OH)	653
KOBULNICKY, Michael	(OH)	666
KUCHERENKO, Eugenia	(OH)	682
KUCINSKI, B J.	(OH)	682
LANTZ, Elizabeth A.	(OH)	697
LERNER, Esther T.	(OH)	717
MALUCHNIK, Kathryn K.	(OH)	764
MCCOY, Betty J.	(OH)	799
MICHNAY, Susan E.	(OH)	832
MOHLER, Dorothy C.	(OH)	852
MOORE, Susan J.	(OH)	861
NEYMAN, Sandra B.	(OH)	900
NOLAN, Marianne	(OH)	907
OLSZEWSKI, Lawrence J.	(OH)	923
ORLANDO, Jacqueline M.	(OH)	926
PHILLIPS, Judith Z.	(OH)	968
POCKROSE, Sheryl R.	(OH)	979
POMERANTZ, Bruce F.	(OH)	982
PRESNELL, Jenny L.	(OH)	991
PROPAS, Sharon W.	(OH)	995
PURSCH, Lenore D.	(OH)	998
RHOADES, Nancy L.	(OH)	1025
RHODES, Glenda T.	(OH)	1026
ROHMILLER, Thomas D.	(OH)	1051
ROMARY, Michael P.	(OH)	1052
RYAN, Mary E.	(OH)	1071
SANKOT, Janice M.	(OH)	1081
SCHAEFGEN, Susan M.	(OH)	1089
SCHLOMAN, Barbara F.	(OH)	1094
SCOTT, Melvia A.	(OH)	1107
SIESS, Judith A.	(OH)	1136
SIMPSON, Alice H.	(OH)	1141
SLANE, Barbara A.	(OH)	1147
SMITH, Timothy D.	(OH)	1161
SWAIN, Richard H.	(OH)	1212
SWEENY, Mary K.	(OH)	1215
TOLZMANN, Don H.	(OH)	1249
TUCKER, Debbie B.	(OH)	1261
VANBRIMMER, Barbara A.	(OH)	1272

REFERENCE (Cont'd)
Reference

VARMA, Valsamani	(OH)	1278
VOIGT, Kathleen J.	(OH)	1287
WANSER, Jeffery C.	(OH)	1303
WEAVER, Alice O.	(OH)	1312
WEHMEYER, Jeffrey M.	(OH)	1316
WEIDMAN, Jeffrey	(OH)	1316
WELLS, Catherine A.	(OH)	1322
WILKS, Cheri L.	(OH)	1341
WILLIAMS, Karen J.	(OH)	1344
WILSON, Leigh K.	(OH)	1351
WORTMAN, William A.	(OH)	1369
ZAPOROZHETZ, Laurene E.	(OH)	1386
COOPER, Sylvia J.	(OK)	243
FLINNER, Beatrice E.	(OK)	385
FULK, Mary C.	(OK)	408
GOLDSBERRY, Maureen E.	(OK)	446
GUTIERREZ, Carolyn A.	(OK)	479
HACKER, Connie J.	(OK)	481
JORDAN, Linda K.	(OK)	616
MCCALL, Patricia	(OK)	793
MCVEY, Susan C.	(OK)	818
MELIK, Ella M.	(OK)	822
NASH, Helen B.	(OK)	888
THORNE, Larry R.	(OK)	1242
VARNER, Joyce	(OK)	1279
WEISS, Catharine H.	(OK)	1320
AMSBERRY, Dan F.	(OR)	20
BILLETER, Anne M.	(OR)	96
BROWNE, Joseph P.	(OR)	148
CABLE, Leslie G.	(OR)	170
CONNORS, Kathleen M.	(OR)	238
CRUMB, Lawrence N.	(OR)	262
DENOBLE, Augustine D.	(OR)	293
ELLSON, Linda R.	(OR)	345
GREEY, Kathleen M.	(OR)	465
HENDERSON, Carol G.	(OR)	526
JUDKINS, Dolores Z.	(OR)	619
MCDANIELS, Patricia R.	(OR)	801
MORRISON, Perry D.	(OR)	868
O'DONOVAN, Patricia A.	(OR)	917
RASH, David W.	(OR)	1009
SAYRE, Samuel R.	(OR)	1087
SOUTH, Ruth E.	(OR)	1169
WRIGHT, Janet K.	(OR)	1371
ALSTADT, Nancy A.	(PA)	18
ANDRILLI, Ene M.	(PA)	27
AZZOLINA, David S.	(PA)	43
BONTA, Bruce D.	(PA)	114
BROWN, Donald R.	(PA)	143
BRYANT, Lillian D.	(PA)	152
BUCK, Patricia K.	(PA)	154
CARRIER, Esther J.	(PA)	186
CATHEY, Gail L.	(PA)	195
CHAMBERLIN, Richard R.	(PA)	198
CLEVELAND, Susan E.	(PA)	221
COHEN, Laurie J.	(PA)	228
CULBERTSON, Judith D.	(PA)	263
CUTLER, Judith	(PA)	268
DEEGAN, Rosemary L.	(PA)	286
DONOVAN, Judith G.	(PA)	312
ERDICK, Joseph W.	(PA)	352
EVES, Judith A.	(PA)	359
FROMM, Roger W.	(PA)	405
FULLER, Edward H.	(PA)	408
GEORGE, Rachel	(PA)	428
GIBLIN, Carol C.	(PA)	431
GRZESIAK, Margaret M.	(PA)	475
HALL, Martha H.	(PA)	488
HARKE, Toby H.	(PA)	501
HESP, Judith A.	(PA)	534
HOLSTON, Kim R.	(PA)	554
HOLUB, Joseph C.	(PA)	555
HORN, Roger G.	(PA)	559
JABLONOWSKI, Mary D.	(PA)	586
JACOBS, Mark D.	(PA)	589
JOHNSON, Joan E.	(PA)	606

REFERENCE (Cont'd)
Reference

JONES, Annabel B.	(PA)	611
KING, Mimi	(PA)	652
KIRBY, Martha Z.	(PA)	654
KREDEL, Stephen F.	(PA)	677
KRZYS, Richard A.	(PA)	681
LEHMANN, Stephen R.	(PA)	713
LEVY, Anne W.	(PA)	721
LIEM, Frieda	(PA)	726
LYTLE, Marguerite S.	(PA)	753
MALCOM, Dorothy L.	(PA)	763
MARCHETTI, Honey B.	(PA)	768
MARTIN, Shelby A.	(PA)	778
MAXWELL, Barbara A.	(PA)	788
MCCOY, James F.	(PA)	799
MCGINNESS, Mary B.	(PA)	806
MCKOWN, Cornelius J.	(PA)	812
MEREDITH, Phyllis C.	(PA)	825
MORGANTI, Deena J.	(PA)	864
MORROW, Ellen B.	(PA)	869
MUDRICK, Kristine E.	(PA)	875
NAISMITH, Rachael	(PA)	887
O'NEILL, Philip M.	(PA)	924
PENROSE, Anna M.	(PA)	957
POE, Terrence C.	(PA)	979
PRITCHARD, Barbara	(PA)	994
PROCTOR, David J.	(PA)	994
QUINTILIANO, Barbara	(PA)	1000
REED, Gertrude	(PA)	1015
REILLY, Rebecca S.	(PA)	1020
RICHARDSON, Joy A.	(PA)	1029
RIDGEWAY, Patricia M.	(PA)	1032
RITTENHOUSE, Robert J.	(PA)	1036
RITTER, Ralph E.	(PA)	1037
ROBERTSON, Robert B.	(PA)	1042
ROSE, Dianne E.	(PA)	1054
ROSENBERGER, Merry G.	(PA)	1056
SAXMAN, Susan E.	(PA)	1086
SCHWALB, Ann W.	(PA)	1104
SEABORN, Frances L.	(PA)	1109
SENECAL, Kristin S.	(PA)	1115
SHULENBERGER, Catherine T.	(PA)	1133
SIMONE-HOHE, M J.	(PA)	1141
SOWICZ, Eugenia V.	(PA)	1170
SPINNEY, Molly P.	(PA)	1175
STAYER, Jonathan R.	(PA)	1183
SULLIVAN, Jennifer B.	(PA)	1207
TAMKEVICZ, Julia H.	(PA)	1221
TERRY, Terese M.	(PA)	1232
TRIPP, Audrey J.	(PA)	1257
USES, Ann K.	(PA)	1270
VAN DE CASTLE, Raymond M.	(PA)	1273
WAGNER, Darla L.	(PA)	1291
WEBER ROOCHVARG, Lynn E.	(PA)	1314
WEIHERER, Patricia D.	(PA)	1317
WEIS, Aimee L.	(PA)	1319
WELLE, Jacob P.	(PA)	1321
WESTERMAN, Melvin E.	(PA)	1327
WILLIAMSON, Susan G.	(PA)	1348
WOZNIAK, Grace I.	(PA)	1369
WYATT, Patricia A.	(PA)	1374
YOUNG, Dorothy E.	(PA)	1381
ZABEL, Diane M.	(PA)	1385
ALSTON, Jane C.	(PR)	18
DELGADO-NUNEZ, Milton	(PR)	289
GARCIA-RUIZ, Maritza L.	(PR)	417
HIDALGO, Nilda R.	(PR)	537
JARAMILLO, Juana S.	(PR)	594
NEGRON-GAZTAMBIDE, Olguita	(PR)	892
PEREZ, Sarai	(PR)	958
RODRIGUEZ, Vidalina	(PR)	1048
CAMERON, Lucille W.	(RI)	175
COOPER, Jacquelyn B.	(RI)	243
FARK, Ronald K.	(RI)	364
FUTAS, Elizabeth	(RI)	411

REFERENCE (Cont'd)
Reference

KEEFE, Margaret J.	(RI)	634
LIGHT, Karen M.	(RI)	726
OTTAVIANO, Doris B.	(RI)	930
SIBULKIN, Lucille	(RI)	1135
WALTON, Linda J.	(RI)	1301
ANDERSON, Marcia	(SC)	24
ARMISTEAD, Myra A.	(SC)	32
BAND, Richard A.	(SC)	53
BELL, David B.	(SC)	76
BOONE, Shirley W.	(SC)	115
CHANDLER, Dorothy S.	(SC)	199
DERRICK, Mitzi J.	(SC)	294
FRIEDMAN, Amy G.	(SC)	403
GOING, Susan C.	(SC)	444
HUX, Roger K.	(SC)	579
JOHNSON, Minnie M.	(SC)	607
LAWSON, James F.	(SC)	705
LYLE, Martha E.	(SC)	751
MARTIN, Neal A.	(SC)	777
OLINGER, Elizabeth B.	(SC)	920
OLSON, Joann M.	(SC)	922
POYER, Robert K.	(SC)	989
RAINES, Thomas A.	(SC)	1004
SEAMAN, Sheila L.	(SC)	1109
SILVERMAN, Susan M.	(SC)	1139
SINDEL, Amy C.	(SC)	1143
SLIFE, Joye D.	(SC)	1149
TAPLEY, Bridgette M.	(SC)	1223
TAYLOR, Dennis S.	(SC)	1226
WEATHERS, Virginia W.	(SC)	1312
WILLIAMS, Betty H.	(SC)	1342
WILLIAMS, Guynell	(SC)	1343
BROWN, Philip L.	(SD)	146
LISTER, Lisa F.	(SD)	732
LUGER, Mary J.	(SD)	747
OSTHUS, Mary J.	(SD)	928
THOELKE, Elisabeth A.	(SD)	1235
ALDERFER, Jane B.	(TN)	11
BERWIND, Anne M.	(TN)	91
CHEN, Helen M.	(TN)	205
CHENEY, Frances N.	(TN)	206
CLELAND, Nancy D.	(TN)	220
COOK, Nedra J.	(TN)	240
FORBES, Evelyn H.	(TN)	388
FULTON, Dixie W.	(TN)	409
HENDRIX, Wilma P.	(TN)	528
KOHUT, David R.	(TN)	669
LEWIS, Rosalyn	(TN)	724
LOCKWOOD, Bonnie J.	(TN)	736
MURGAI, Sarla R.	(TN)	880
MYERS, Marcia J.	(TN)	884
MYERS, William F.	(TN)	885
PARK, Elizabeth H.	(TN)	941
PENNINGTON, Melanie L.	(TN)	957
RAWNSLEY, Virgilia I.	(TN)	1011
RIDENOUR, Lisa R.	(TN)	1032
SCHER, Rita S.	(TN)	1092
SHABB, Cynthia H.	(TN)	1118
SMITH, Lori D.	(TN)	1157
SOLBERG, Judy L.	(TN)	1166
VIERA, Ann R.	(TN)	1284
WALLACE, Alan H.	(TN)	1297
WILLIAMS, Elizabeth L.	(TN)	1343
WORLEY, Joan H.	(TN)	1369
WRIGHT, David A.	(TN)	1371
YALCINTAS, Rana	(TN)	1376
ALLEN, Peggy G.	(TX)	15
ANDERSON, Mark	(TX)	24
ATKINS, Winston	(TX)	38
BAILEY, Anne M.	(TX)	46
BEAN, Norma P.	(TX)	69
BENSON, Joyce	(TX)	83
BLACK, Katherine S.	(TX)	101
BRUNNER, A M.	(TX)	151
BUTKOVICH, Nancy J.	(TX)	166
BUTLER, Marguerite L.	(TX)	166
CAMERON, Dee B.	(TX)	174
CAMPBELL, Mary K.	(TX)	177

REFERENCE (Cont'd)
Reference

REFERENCE (Cont'd)
Reference

COOKSEY, Martha L. . . . (TX) 241
CORREDOR, Javier . . . . (TX) 247
COTTER, Stacy L. . . . . . (TX) 250
CRAIG, Thomas B. . . . . . (TX) 254
CRISSINGER, John D. . . (TX) 259
DAVIS, Cynthia V. . . . . . (TX) 278
DAVIS, Mary F. . . . . (TX) 280
DAVIS, Philip M. . . . . (TX) 280
DIXON, Donna S. . . . . . . (TX) 306
DONALDSON, Anna L. . (TX) 311
EWALT, Rosalind H. . . . . (TX) 359
FRANKSON, Marie S. . . (TX) 398
FRANZELLO, Joseph J. . (TX) 398
GARAZA, Noemi . . . . . . (TX) 417
GRAY, Wayne D. . . . . . . (TX) 460
GROSS, Sally L. . . . . . . (TX) 472
GUTIERREZ, Margo . . . . (TX) 479
GYESZLY, Suzanne D. . . (TX) 479
HAMBRIC, Jacqueline B. (TX) 491
HARLOW, Sally S. . . . . . (TX) 502
HEIZER, Carolyn H. . . . . (TX) 523
HENDERSON, Lennijo P. (TX) 526
HENEBRY, Carolyn L. . . (TX) 528
HENRICKS, Duane E. . . . (TX) 529
HOOD, Sandra D. . . . . . . (TX) 556
HOWELL, Gladys M. . . . . (TX) 565
HYMAN, Ferne B. . . . . . (TX) 580
JESER-SKAGGS, Sharlee
    A. . . . . (TX) 600
KENNEDY, Johnnye . . . . (TX) 641
KHADER, Majed J. . . . . . (TX) 645
LEVINE, Harriet L. . . . . . (TX) 720
LOPICCOLO, Cathy J. . . (TX) 741
LOWRY, Andretta G. . . . . (TX) 745
LYDERS, Josette A. . . . . (TX) 750
MALLORY, Elizabeth J. . (TX) 763
MAULDIN, Lou A. . . . . . . (TX) 787
MAULSBY, Tommie L. . . (TX) 787
MCCURDY, Sandra A. . . (TX) 801
MCKAY, Mary F. . . . . . . (TX) 810
METZGER, Oscar F. . . . (TX) 829
MILLER, Susan A. . . . . . (TX) 842
MUCK, Bruce E. . . . . (TX) 874
MYCUE, David J. . . . . . . (TX) 884
NEALE, Marilee . . . . (TX) 891
OSWALT, Paul K. . . . . . (TX) 929
PARTON, William A. . . . (TX) 945
PEDEN, Rita Y. . . . . (TX) 954
PEYTON, Janice L. . . . . . (TX) 966
SCAMMAN, Carol J. . . . (TX) 1087
SCHWERBEL, Jeannette
    E. . . . . (TX) 1105
SMITH, Dayna F. . . . . . . (TX) 1154
SMITH, Nancy K. . . . . . . (TX) 1158
SPARKMAN, Glenda K. . (TX) 1171
SPENCER, Catherine K. . (TX) 1173
SPOEDE, Mary H. . . . . . (TX) 1175
SUDENGA, Sara A. . . . . (TX) 1206
TEOH, George M. . . . . . (TX) 1231
THEISS, Diane M. . . . . . (TX) 1234
TODD, Leslie N. . . . . (TX) 1248
TOLMAN, Kimberly S. . . (TX) 1249
TOURAINE, Linda S. . . . (TX) 1252
TROST, Theresa K. . . . . (TX) 1258
VUGRIN, Margaret Y. . . . (TX) 1289
WASSENICH, Red . . . . . (TX) 1308
WAYLAND, Sharon L. . . (TX) 1311
WEATHERS, Barbara H. . (TX) 1312
WILLIAMS, Suzanne C. . (TX) 1346
WYGANT, Alice C. . . . . . (TX) 1375
CASADY, Richard L. . . . (UT) 191
CHENG, Nancy H. . . . . . (UT) 206
ELLEFSEN, David . . . . . (UT) 343
FUJIMOTO, Jan D. . . . . . (UT) 408
HAGGERTY, Maxine R. . (UT) 483
KITE, Yvonne D. . . . . . . (UT) 657
LAYTON, A J. . . . . (UT) 705
LYMAN, Lovisa . . . . (UT) 751

MARCHANT, Cathy . . . . (UT) 768
MCMURRIN, Jean A. . . . (UT) 815
MOGREN, Paul A. . . . . . (UT) 852
REDDICK, Mary J. . . . . . (UT) 1013
SMITH, Nathan M. . . . . . (UT) 1159
TALBERT, Dorothy R. . . (UT) 1220
ZEDNEY, Francis L. . . . (UT) 1387
BADER, Susan G. . . . . . (VA) 44
BENKE, Robin P. . . . . . . (VA) 81
BRAINARD, Blair . . . . . . (VA) 127
CIPRIANI, Debra A. . . . . (VA) 215
CLAYMAN, Ida H. . . . . . (VA) 220
COOPER, Nancy C. . . . . (VA) 243
DANIEL, Mary H. . . . . . . (VA) 272
DEWEY, Helen W. . . . . . (VA) 298
DRYE, Jerry L. . . . . (VA) 321
DUNLEAVY, Theresa G. . (VA) 326
GILL, Gerald L. . . . . (VA) 435
GREGORY, Carla L. . . . . (VA) 466
GRIFFLER, Carl W. . . . . (VA) 469
HARRISTON, Victoria R. . (VA) 507
HAUSMAN, Patricia R. . . (VA) 513
HAYS, Peggy W. . . . . . . (VA) 517
HIGBEE, Florence . . . . . (VA) 537
HOLLOWAY, Johnna H. . (VA) 552
HUETER, Eike . . . . (VA) 570
JACKSON, F C. . . . . (VA) 587
KARRER, Jonathan K. . . (VA) 628
KENNEY, Donald J. . . . . (VA) 641
KIEWITT, Eva L. . . . . . . (VA) 647
LEHMAN, James O. . . . . (VA) 712
LESTER, Linda L. . . . . . . (VA) 718
LONG, Elizabeth T. . . . . (VA) 739
MCKELVEY, Mary J. . . . (VA) 810
MCLAUGHLIN, Elaine C. (VA) 813
METZ, Paul D. . . . . (VA) 828
OBRIST, Cynthia W. . . . (VA) 915
POWERS, Linda J. . . . . . (VA) 989
RASMUSSEN, Lane D. . (VA) 1009
REEVES, Lois H. . . . . . . (VA) 1017
RICHARD, Sheila A. . . . (VA) 1028
RITTER, Allison C. . . . . . (VA) 1036
RUDOLF, Christine T. . . . (VA) 1066
SARTAIN, Sara M. . . . . . (VA) 1083
SELF, James R. . . . . (VA) 1113
SHEPARD, E L. . . . . (VA) 1126
SONNEMANN, Gail J. . . (VA) 1167
SPENCE, Addie F. . . . . . (VA) 1173
STARR, Marian U. . . . . . (VA) 1182
SWAINE, Cynthia W. . . . (VA) 1212
TAI, Elizabeth L. . . . . . . (VA) 1220
TIPPER, Maryellen . . . . . (VA) 1246
WARD, Carol T. . . . . (VA) 1303
WEEKS, Linda F. . . . . . . (VA) 1315
WELSH, Eric L. . . . . (VA) 1323
YELICH, Hope H. . . . . . . (VA) 1379
DURFEE, Tamara . . . . . . (VT) 328
EVANS, Nancy I. . . . . . . (VT) 357
HERNDON, Stan J. . . . . (VT) 532
LAMSON, Maria W. . . . . (VT) 691
LAPIDOW, Amy R. . . . . . (VT) 697
LUZER, Nancy H. . . . . . . (VT) 750
MCCULLOUGH, Doreen J. (VT) 801
MOORE, Russell S. . . . . (VT) 861
RAUM, Hans L. . . . . (VT) 1010
THOMPSON, Judith H. . . (VT) 1240
ALEXANDER, Malcolm D. (WA) 12
ALKIRE, Leland G. . . . . . (WA) 13
ANDERSON, Christine M. (WA) 22
BOLLING, Thomas E. . . . (WA) 112
BRADY, Eileen E. . . . . . . (WA) 126
BREKKE, Elaine C. . . . . (WA) 132
BURSON, Scott F. . . . . . (WA) 163
EARLY, Stephen T. . . . . (WA) 332
FENKER, John A. . . . . . . (WA) 371
FOLEY, Katherine E. . . . (WA) 387
FRALEY, David B. . . . . . (WA) 395
GILCHRIST, Debra L. . . . (WA) 434

REFERENCE (Cont'd)
Reference

GREENWOOD, Alma I. . . (WA) 465
HENSLEY, Randall B. . . . (WA) 529
HILL, Ann M. . . . . (WA) 539
ICE, Priscilla T. . . . . (WA) 581
JONES, Faye E. . . . . (WA) 613
KNOLL, Betty A. . . . . . . (WA) 665
LIPTON, Laura E. . . . . . (WA) 732
LOPEZ, Loretta K. . . . . . (WA) 741
NELSON, Christine . . . . . (WA) 893
NEWELL, Rick K. . . . . . . (WA) 898
PETTIT, Donna K. . . . . . (WA) 965
REDALJE, Susanne J. . . (WA) 1013
RICIGLIANO, Lorraine M. (WA) 1031
SCOTT-MILLER, Gwen . (WA) 1108
SHELDEN, Lucinda D. . . (WA) 1125
WADDEN, Emily E. . . . . (WA) 1290
WOOSTER, Linda I. . . . . (WA) 1368
WYNN, Debra D. . . . . . . (WA) 1375
YONGMAN, Zhang . . . . (WA) 1380
ZIEGLER, Ronald M. . . . (WA) 1388
ZIKE, Ruth D. . . . . (WA) 1388
AHL, Ruth E. . . . . (WI) 8
ALTMANN, Thomas F. . . (WI) 18
BURR, Charlotte A. . . . . (WI) 163
CARROLL, Barbara T. . . (WI) 187
CIMPL, Kathleen A. . . . . (WI) 214
CONRAD, Kay A. . . . . . . (WI) 238
DELAUCHE, Jean E. . . . (WI) 289
EBERT, John J. . . . . (WI) 334
ENGELDINGER, Eugene
    A. . . . . (WI) 349
FLIEGEL, Deborah A. . . . (WI) 385
FORTIN, Clifford C. . . . . (WI) 391
FOSTER, Leslie A. . . . . . (WI) 392
GREEN, Thomas A. . . . . (WI) 462
HANAMAN, Nancy J. . . . (WI) 494
HARTIG, Linda . . . . (WI) 508
HOOTKIN, Neil M. . . . . . (WI) 557
HOPWOOD, Susan H. . . (WI) 558
HORNUNG, Susan D. . . . (WI) 560
JESUDASON, Melba . . . (WI) 600
JOHNSON, Denise J. . . . (WI) 603
KALVONJIAN, Araxie . . . (WI) 623
KELLY, Barbara J. . . . . . (WI) 637
KILANDER, Ann H. . . . . (WI) 647
KRAJNAK, Patricia A. . . (WI) 675
MARKOWETZ, Marianna
    C. . . . . (WI) 771
MCCLEMENTS, Nancy A. (WI) 796
PAUL, Nancy A. . . . . (WI) 949
PIETERS, Donald L. . . . . (WI) 972
PUHEK, Esther L. . . . . . (WI) 997
RINGER, Susan G. . . . . . (WI) 1035
SCHINK, Sandra C. . . . . (WI) 1093
SCHULTZ, Ellen A. . . . . (WI) 1102
SCOFIELD, Constance V. (WI) 1106
SECHREST, Sandra L. . . (WI) 1110
SIMPSON, Carolyn A. . . (WI) 1141
SINGH, Rosemary A. . . . (WI) 1143
STRUBE, Kathleen . . . . . (WI) 1203
THOMPSON, Glenn J. . . (WI) 1239
TOBIN, R J. . . . . (WI) 1247
TRUPIANO, Rose M. . . . (WI) 1259
VAN ESS, James E. . . . . (WI) 1275
WEISMAN, Suzy . . . . . . (WI) 1319
WESTON, Karen A. . . . . (WI) 1327
BARNES, Jean S. . . . . . (WV) 57
CRESSWELL, Stephen . . (WV) 258
GAUMOND, George R. . . (WV) 423
HOWARD, Elizabeth F. . . (WV) 564
POWELL, Ruth A. . . . . . (WV) 988
REENSTJERNA, Frederick
    R. . . . . (WV) 1016
RUSSELL, Richard A. . . . (WV) 1069
WATSON, Carolyn R. . . . (WV) 1309
HOFF, Vickie J. . . . . (WY) 547
JACKSON, Sue H. . . . . . (WY) 588
OSTRYE, Anne T. . . . . . (WY) 929

REFERENCE (Cont'd)
Reference

RAO, Dittakavi N. . . . . . . (WY) 1008
SIMPSON, Susan M. . . . (WY) 1142
BOUCHER, Michel . . . . . (AB) 118
DELONG, Kathleen M. . . (AB) 290
HEBDITCH, Suzan A. . . . (AB) 519
KISSAU, Arlene M. . . . . (AB) 656
KUJANSUU, Sylvia S. . . (AB) 683
LANE, Barbara K. . . . . . (AB) 694
REICHARDT, Randall P. . (AB) 1018
ASHCROFT, Susan M. . . (BC) 35
BARTON, Joan A. . . . . . (BC) 62
BELL, Barbara . . . . (BC) 76
DEVAKOS, Elizabeth R. . (BC) 297
DYKSTRA, Stephanie . . . (BC) 331
GROVES, Percilla E. . . . . (BC) 474
HAMILTON, Donald E. . . (BC) 492
INSELBERG, Diana E. . . (BC) 583
MANSBRIDGE, John . . . (BC) 767
MILLER, Gordon . . . . (BC) 838
TROWSDALE, Robert G. (BC) 1258
WHITE, Donald J. . . . . . . (BC) 1330
BLANCHARD, Jim . . . . . (MB) 103
CHOMENKO, Tamara L. . (MB) 210
DELONG, Linwood R. . . . (MB) 290
MARTEN, Mary L. . . . . . (MB) 775
WRIGHT, Patrick D. . . . . (MB) 1372
EADIE, Tom . . . . (NB) 331
CAMERON, H C. . . . . . . (NF) 174
HEINO, Dan R. . . . . (NF) 522
TILLOTSON, Joy G. . . . . (NF) 1245
COLBORNE, Michael B. . (NS) 230
PARIS, Terrence L. . . . . (NS) 940
BANFILL, Christine . . . . . (ON) 54
BLACK, Sandra M. . . . . . (ON) 101
BOJIN, Minda A. . . . . . . (ON) 111
BREZINA, Jennifer R. . . . (ON) 134
COLVIN, Alison J. . . . . . (ON) 234
COURNOYER, Joanne . . (ON) 251
D'AMBOISE, Marion J. . . (ON) 271
DAVIS, Wendy A. . . . . . (ON) 281
DESOMOGYI, Aileen A. . (ON) 295
GALSWORTHY, Peter R. (ON) 415
GIBSON, Elizabeth A. . . . (ON) 432
GOLTZ, Eileen A. . . . . . . (ON) 447
GRANT, Roberta L. . . . . (ON) 458
GREENWOOD, Jan . . . . (ON) 465
HAUCK, Danuta . . . . (ON) 512
KEYS, Sandra A. . . . . . . (ON) 645
LAMBERT, Deborah B. . . (ON) 690
LOVE, Barbara . . . . (ON) 743
MACKENZIE, Shirley A. . (ON) 756
MCLEAN, Paulette A. . . . (ON) 814
MITCHELL, Faye F. . . . . (ON) 848
NORRGARD, Don K. . . . (ON) 909
OUIMET, Jacinthe . . . . . (ON) 930
QUIXLEY, James V. . . . . (ON) 1001
RAY, Cathy J. . . . . (ON) 1011
SCHRYER, Michel J. . . . (ON) 1100
SMITH, Ruth P. . . . . (ON) 1160
STEWART, Elizabeth A. . (ON) 1192
URQUHART, Dawn M. . . (ON) 1270
VUKOV, Vesna . . . . (ON) 1290
WALDRON, Nerine R. . . (ON) 1294
WARD, William D. . . . . . (ON) 1304
WHITE, Janette H. . . . . . (ON) 1331
ASTBURY, Effie C. . . . . (PQ) 37
AUGER, Bernard . . . . . . (PQ) 39
BAILLARGEON, Daniele . (PQ) 47
BAZINET, Jeanne . . . . . (PQ) 68
BERGERON, Gilles I. . . . (PQ) 86
BIELLE, Christian P. . . . . (PQ) 95
BOILARD, Gilberte . . . . . (PQ) 111
BOUCHARD, Martin . . . . (PQ) 118
BOUCHER, Lorna M. . . . (PQ) 118
BRETON, Lise . . . . (PQ) 133
CYR, Solange . . . . (PQ) 268
DANIS, Rolland J. . . . . . (PQ) 273
DAUNAIS, Marie J. . . . . (PQ) 275

REFERENCE (Cont'd)
Reference

DIMITRESCU, Ioana	(PQ)	304
DUMOULIN, Nicole L. ...	(PQ)	325
FILIATRAULT, Sylvie	(PQ)	376
FINNEMORE, Mary A. ...	(PQ)	378
FONTAINE, Nicole	(PQ)	388
FORTIN, Jean L.	(PQ)	391
FORTIN, Johanne	(PQ)	392
GARDNER, Lucie	(PQ)	418
GAUDREAU, Louis	(PQ)	422
GELINAS, Gratien	(PQ)	426
GELINAS, Michel R.	(PQ)	426
GELINAS, Sylvain	(PQ)	426
GRAINGER, Bruce	(PQ)	457
GRITZKA, Gerda M.	(PQ)	471
HERLINGER, Peggy	(PQ)	531
HEROUX, Genevieve ...	(PQ)	532
HIRON, Barbara A.	(PQ)	543
HOFFMAN, Sandra D. ...	(PQ)	548
JUNEAU, Jocelyne B. ...	(PQ)	620
LAFRENIERE, Myriam ..	(PQ)	688
LATOUR, Pierre	(PQ)	701
LEMIEUX, Louise	(PQ)	715
LEMYRE, Nicole	(PQ)	715
LESSARD, Josee	(PQ)	718
MAILLOUX, Jean Y.	(PQ)	761
MANSEAU, Edith	(PQ)	767
MARION, Guylaine	(PQ)	770
MARION, Luce	(PQ)	770
MAYRAND, Lise M.	(PQ)	791
MENARD, Francoise	(PQ)	823
MONDOU, Cecile	(PQ)	854
MOSER, Beryl R.	(PQ)	870
PAGEAU, Denise	(PQ)	934
PARKER, Charles G.	(PQ)	941
RIOPEL, Jean M.	(PQ)	1035
ROBIN, Madeleine	(PQ)	1043
ROBINSON, Chantal ...	(PQ)	1043
ROUSSEAU, Denis	(PQ)	1061
ROY, Christine	(PQ)	1063
SHEERAN, Ruth J.	(PQ)	1125
TAILLON, Yolande A. ...	(PQ)	1220
TESSIER, Mario C.	(PQ)	1233
MACK, A Y.	(SK)	756
RUSSELL, Vija	(SK)	1069
BEATTIE, Kathleen M. ...	(AUS)	70
DEROODE, Clifford H. ..	(FRN)	294
BALDWIN, Robert D.	(JAM)	52
KAWASHIMA, Hiroko ...	(JAP)	632
ABDEL-MOTEY, Yaser Y.	(KWT)	2
LUSK, Betty M.	(SAF)	749
ALI, Farooq M.	(SDA)	13

Reference, acquisitions librarianship	ENGLAND, Ellen M.	(VA)	349
Reference activities	EVERITT, Janet M.	(MI)	359
Reference administration	KASALKO, Sally G.	(AR)	628
	CAIN, Anne H.	(CA)	171
	HAHN, Ellen	(DC)	483
	WILER, Linda L.	(FL)	1339
	BRAUCH, Patricia O.	(NY)	129
	PHILLIPS, Linda L.	(TN)	968
	DUPUIS, Marcel	(PQ)	327
Reference, American ethnic studies	RENKIEWICZ, Frank A. ..	(MI)	1023
Reference & access	PROSSER, Judy A.	(CO)	995
	JACOBS, Richard A.	(DC)	590
	RUSH, James S.	(DC)	1068
	WALLER, M C.	(KY)	1298
	CREW, Roger T.	(VA)	258
Reference & acquisitions	FENLON, Mary P.	(KS)	371
Reference & adult materials	FELTON, Barbara M.	(IN)	370
Reference & adult services	BEEBE, Richard J.	(CA)	74
	VANDERLYKE, Barbara A.	(CT)	1274
	WAGNER, George L.	(CT)	1291
	ATWOOD, Virginia W. ...	(ID)	38
	KALRA, Bhupinder S. ...	(IL)	623
	WILSEY, Charlotte A. ...	(MD)	1349
	DESIREY, Janice M.	(MN)	295
	AULD, Hampton M.	(NC)	39
	TAYLOR, Anne C.	(NJ)	1226
	BARRETT, John C.	(NY)	59

REFERENCE (Cont'd)
Reference & adult services

	DESCH, Carol A.	(NY)	294
	LA SORTE, Antonia J. ...	(NY)	700
	ROECKEL, Alan G.	(NY)	1048
	SELVAR, Jane C.	(NY)	1114
	VELA-CREIXELL, Mary I.	(TX)	1281
	WEBER, Joan L.	(WA)	1314
	TALIS, Ross M.	(WI)	1221
Reference & aging issues	TABER, Sally A.	(DC)	1219
Reference & archives	MACKENZIE, Alberta E. .	(OH)	756
Reference & audiovisual service	PINE, Nancy M.	(FL)	974
Reference & automated services	O'HANLON, Nancyanne .	(OH)	919
Reference & bibliographic instruction	PETERS, Marion C.	(CA)	962
	NORONHA, Marilyn S. ...	(CT)	909
	COHN, William L.	(FL)	229
	MALANCHUK, Peter P. .	(FL)	762
	CANN, Sharon F.	(GA)	178
	GIAQUINTA, C J.	(IA)	431
	HUFFORD, Gordon L.	(IN)	571
	MCDONALD, Stanley M.	(MA)	803
	SIGALA, Stephanie C. ..	(MO)	1137
	FARRELL, Michele A.	(NY)	365
	HARDY, Gayle J.	(NY)	500
	LYONS, Evelyn L.	(PA)	753
	LEGET, Max	(SD)	712
	CONIGLIO, Jamie W.	(VA)	236
	HOWE, Patricia A.	(VA)	565
	EDMONDS, Michael	(WI)	336
	NECHKA, Ada M.	(AB)	891
	LEVESQUE, Nancy B. ..	(BC)	719
Reference & bibliographic works	NGUYEN, Vy K.	(PQ)	901
Reference & bibliography	JOHNSON, Elizabeth G. .	(AL)	604
	RAMER, James D.	(AL)	1005
	WOLD, Shelley T.	(AR)	1359
	MAACK, Mary N.	(CA)	753
	RAFAEL, Ruth K.	(CA)	1003
	BARTHELL, Daniel W. ..	(DC)	61
	CAHALANE, Edmond P. .	(DC)	171
	TRUETT, Carol A.	(HI)	1259
	CUNNINGHAM, William D.	(MD)	265
	SLAVENS, Thomas P. ...	(MI)	1148
	CARROLL, C E.	(MO)	187
	COLBY, Robert A.	(NY)	230
	STERN, Liselotte B.	(NY)	1189
	SANTAVICCA, Edmund F.	(OH)	1082
	BURNS, Richard K.	(PA)	162
	CLARKSON, Mary C.	(TX)	219
	THORNE, Bonnie B.	(TX)	1242
	CORBEIL, Lizette	(PQ)	245
Reference & bibliography services	MUNDELL, Eric L.	(IN)	878
Reference & bibliography work	LAMPRECHT, Sandra J. .	(CA)	691
Reference & cataloging	NELSON, Mary L.	(IA)	894
	BROWN-MAY, Patricia A.	(MI)	148
	FACINELLI, Jaclyn R.	(OH)	360
	FILIATRAULT, Andre Y. .	(PQ)	376
Reference & circulation	OVERTON, Margaret C. .	(TN)	931
	HARPER, Marsha W.	(TX)	503
	CASEY, Wayne T.	(VA)	192
Reference & collection development	NING, Mary J.	(CA)	904
	SIBLEY, Elizabeth A. ...	(CA)	1135
	POINTON, Louis R.	(IL)	980
	STALZER, Rita M.	(IL)	1179
	TRINKAUS-RANDALL, Gregor	(MA)	1257
	NDENGA, Viola W.	(MI)	890
	CASTO, Lisa A.	(TX)	194
	BERNIER, Gaston	(PQ)	89
Reference & collection maintenance	WILES-HAFFNER, Meredith L.	(PA)	1339
Reference & collection management	BRUCE, Robert K.	(MN)	149
Reference & computer information search	MOORHEAD, Kenneth E.	(CT)	862
Reference & computer services	POSES, June A.	(PA)	985
Reference & consultation	DUBOIS, Henry J.	(CA)	322
Reference & consultation services	SINCLAIR, Lorelei P. ...	(CA)	1142
Reference & database searching	SHELTON, Kathryn H. ...	(AK)	1126
	ALITO, Martha A.	(DC)	13
	THOMPSON, Susan J. ..	(IN)	1241
	MATHAI, Aleyamma	(NJ)	783

REFERENCE (Cont'd)

Reference & database searching
- BATES, Ellen .... (NY) 63
- FRASENE, Joanne R. .... (NY) 399
- KATZ, Jacqueline E. .... (NY) 630
- MURRAY, Elizabeth F. .. (NY) 881
- JENSEN, Mary B. ...... (SD) 599
- HELWIG, Karen A. ..... (WI) 525

Reference & documents — CRETINI, Blanche M. .... (LA) 258
Reference & education — LESSARD, Elizabeth B. ... (NH) 718
Reference & education bibliography — ROBERTS, Francis X. .... (CO) 1040
Reference & fiction training — BARKER, Lillian H. ..... (MD) 56
Reference & humanities — PEDERSOLI, Heleni M. ... (AL) 954
Reference & indexing
- MEVERS, Frank D. ...... (NH) 829
- MORRIS, Trisha A. ..... (OH) 867

Reference & information
- GOEBEL, Heather L. ..... (AZ) 443
- JOHMANN, Nancy ..... (CT) 601
- RAILSBACK, Patsy S. .... (IA) 1003
- CORNETT, John L. .... (NM) 247
- KUJOORY, Parvin ..... (TX) 683
- WILSON, Brenda J. .... (UT) 1350
- TOMCHYSHYN, Theresa M. .... (SK) 1249
- BARBERENA, Elsa ..... (MEX) 55

Reference & information management — LAWSON, Venable A. .... (GA) 705
Reference & information research — THOMPSON, Myra D. ... (OH) 1240
Reference & information retrieval
- HEINZ, Catharine F. .... (DC) 522
- MOORE, Patricia R. .... (NC) 860
- RICE, Anna C. .... (NJ) 1026
- BEAUDRIE, Ronald A. ... (NY) 70
- STOAN, Stephen K. .... (TX) 1195

Reference & info retrieval systems — MASON, Michael L. .... (NJ) 781
Reference & information science
- EASTMAN, Franklin R. .. (CA) 333
- BRANDEL, Pamela A. ... (WI) 128
- NEILL, Sam D. .... (ON) 892

Reference & information service
- PINTOZZI, Chestalene .. (FL) 975
- KIM, Chung S. .... (IL) 648
- TAYLOR, Rebecca A. ... (LA) 1228
- ANDREWS, Mark J. ..... (MO) 27
- SMITH, Nancy M. ...... (MO) 1159
- ROBINSON, W D. ..... (ON) 1045

Reference & information services
- HERON, David W. ..... (CA) 532
- SHORT, Virginia .... (CA) 1132
- JAY, Hilda L. .... (CT) 596
- DANNECKER, Joyce H. . (FL) 274
- BARD, Therese B. ..... (HI) 56
- RICE, James G. .... (IA) 1027
- KLEKOWSKI, Lynn M. ... (IL) 660
- JACKSON, Arlyne A. ... (MA) 586
- MOORE, Craig P. ...... (MD) 859
- PITTMAN, Dorothy E. ... (MD) 976
- FISCHER, Catherine S. .. (MN) 379
- OBERMAN, Cerise G. ... (MN) 914
- ROSSMAN, Muriel J. ... (MN) 1059
- SPICER, Orlin C. ...... (MO) 1174
- BRUCE, Nancy G. ..... (NC) 149
- PARROTT, Margaret S. . (NC) 944
- STEPHENS, Ann E. .... (NE) 1187
- MCDERMOTT, Ellen .... (NJ) 801
- GRAY, Robert G. ...... (NV) 460
- DOYAL, Patricia A. ..... (NY) 317
- ORR, Coleridge W. ..... (NY) 926
- WELLS, Margaret R. ... (NY) 1322
- NEAL, James G. ...... (PA) 890
- SCHNEIDER, Stewart P. . (RI) 1097
- KRATZ, Abby R. ...... (TX) 676
- BROADWAY, Marsha D. (UT) 138
- VANDERBERG, E S. ... (VA) 1273
- SHERMAN, Jacob R. ... (VT) 1128
- KEMP, Barbara E. ..... (WA) 639
- DAWSON, Terry P. .... (WI) 282
- PARSONS, Patricia S. .. (WI) 945
- SEARCY HOWARD, Linda M. .... (BC) 1109
- BUDNICK, Carol ...... (MB) 155
- KEARNS, Linda J. ..... (ON) 633
- SCOTT, Judith W. ..... (ON) 1107
- PROVOST, Paul E. .... (PQ) 996

Reference & information specialist — MISTARAS, Evangeline . (IL) 848

REFERENCE (Cont'd)

Reference & instruction
- ROCKMAN, Ilene F. .... (CA) 1046
- WILDE, Lucy E. .... (KS) 1338
- BAILEY, Madeleine J. .... (AB) 46

Reference & instruction academic support — VERNON, Christie D. .... (VA) 1283
Reference & instructional services
- HINCKLEY, Ann T. ..... (CA) 542
- NESBIT, Angus B. ..... (IL) 896

Reference & interlibrary loan
- ROUDEBUSH, Lawanda C. (IA) 1061
- LACROIX, Eve M. ..... (MD) 686
- NAIRN, Charles E. ..... (MI) 886
- CARR, Charles E. ...... (NJ) 185

Reference & interlibrary loans
- HUTCHINS, Mary J. .... (IL) 579
- GENTRY, Etherlene H. ... (MS) 427
- LIN, Susan T. .... (NY) 728

Reference & internal database creation — IRONS, Carol A. .... (IL) 584
Reference & legal databases — BONADIA, Roseann .... (NY) 113
Reference & legal research
- TATELMAN, Susan D. .. (MA) 1225
- HAASE, Gretchen E. ... (MN) 480

Reference & library administration — AYALA, John L. .... (CA) 42
Reference & library instruction — STARKEY, Edward D. .. (IN) 1182
Reference & literature education — NORRIS, Carol B. ..... (TN) 909
Reference & media — WILLER, Kenneth H. ... (NY) 1341
Reference & online — STEVELMAN, Sharon R. . (AB) 1190
Reference & online info retrieval — YOUNGEN, Gregory K. . (IN) 1383
Reference & online searcher — OSORIO, Nestor L. ..... (IL) 928
Reference & online searching
- PETERMAN, Claudia A. . (CA) 962
- HAMDY, Amira .... (CO) 491
- CASSEDY, Barbara S. .. (DC) 193
- DOENGES, John C. .... (DC) 308
- LOOMIS, Barbara ..... (IL) 740
- ELLIOTT, Barbara J. ... (IN) 343
- DYKMAN, Elaine K. .... (NJ) 331
- COHEN, Rosemary C. .. (NY) 229
- RUTHERFORD, Frederick S. .... (ON) 1070
- SCHMIDT, Diana M. ..... (ON) 1095

Reference & online services
- FRANK, Donald G. ..... (AZ) 396
- SCOTT, Ralph L. ...... (NC) 1108

Reference & programs for children — HACHMEISTER, Helen M. (WI) 481
Reference & public service
- SCHAPIRO, Benjamin H. (IL) 1090
- WOLF, Joy G. .... (MN) 1360
- PELLEY, Shirley N. ..... (OK) 955
- MARKSON, Eileen ..... (PA) 771
- FOWLER, Margaret A. .. (MB) 394

Reference & public services
- GELFAND, Julia M. .... (CA) 426
- BOLLIER, John A. ..... (CT) 112
- WRIGHT, Joyce C. ..... (IL) 1372
- HEWISON, Nancy S. ... (IN) 535
- KRESSE, Kerry L. ..... (KY) 678
- HILDITCH, Bonny M. ... (MD) 539
- LEV, Yvonne T. .... (MD) 719
- HALL, Lawrence E. ..... (MI) 488
- WALDERA, Katherine A. (ND) 1294
- CRESCENZI, Jean D. .... (NJ) 258
- SCHUT, Grace W. .... (NJ) 1103
- ZULEWSKI, Gerald J. .... (NJ) 1391
- TEVEBAUGH, Joyce E. . (TX) 1233
- MERCHANT, Thomas L. . (WI) 825
- DANCIK, Deborah B. ... (AB) 272
- DEBRUIJN, Deborah I. .. (AB) 285

Reference & publications — KAHLER, Mary E. ...... (DC) 622
Reference & publishing — ROBERTS, Anne F. ..... (NY) 1039
Reference & reader adviser service — ROUSE, Charlie L. ..... (OK) 1061
Reference & reader advisory — LIGGAN, Mary K. ...... (VA) 726
Reference & reader services
- GOODWYN, Betty R. .... (AL) 450
- SELF, Sharon W. ...... (GA) 1113
- GONNEVILLE, Priscilla R. (MA) 447
- CLUNE, John R. .... (NY) 223
- HILL, Ruth J. .... (TN) 540
- BARBEN, Tanya A. .... (SAF) 55

Reference & reader's advisory
- HOLMES, Nancy M. .... (GA) 553
- KELLSTEDT, Jenny ..... (MA) 637
- BAILEY, Carol A. ...... (MD) 46
- O'NEIL, Margaret M. .... (NY) 924

Reference & readers advisory services — OLENDER, Karen L. .... (NC) 920

REFERENCE (Cont'd)

Reference & readers services	KNAUFF, Elisabeth S. . . .	(DC)	663
	DREW, Wilfred E.	(NY)	319
	FREW, Martha G.	(OH)	402
Reference & reading services	CUNNINGHAM, Barbara		
	M.	(MD)	265
Reference & reference scheduling	WALDEN, Graham R. . .	(OH)	1294
Reference & referral	LEVY, Judith B.	(CA)	721
	WESTERBERG, Kermit B.	(IL)	1326
	GREENBERG, Ruth S. . .	(NJ)	463
	SWINEHART, Katharine J.	(OH)	1216
	DENGROVE, Richard A. .	(VA)	292
Reference & referral service	WAGNER, Barbara L. . .	(CO)	1291
Reference & referrals	FREY, Roxanne C.	(IL)	403
Reference & research	LASETER, Ernest P. . . .	(AL)	700
	AARON, Kathleen F. . . .	(CA)	1
	COLLINS, Judith A.	(CA)	232
	GRANGER, Dorothy J. . .	(CA)	457
	HOTZ, Sharon M.	(CA)	562
	LENSCHAU, Jane A. . . .	(CA)	715
	MAH, Jeffery	(CA)	760
	MASTERS, Robin J.	(CA)	782
	MULLER, Malinda S. . . .	(CA)	877
	SCHMIDT, Alesandra M.	(CT)	1095
	GREENE, Danielle L. . .	(DC)	463
	MCCOY-LARSON, Sandra	(DC)	799
	SMITH, Mary P.	(DC)	1158
	WRIGHT, Arthuree M. . .	(DC)	1370
	AHLIN, Nancy	(FL)	8
	BOGGUS, Tamara K. . . .	(FL)	110
	DALLET, Jane L.	(FL)	270
	HARTON, Pamela J. . . .	(FL)	508
	SCHWABEL, Lexie W. . .	(FL)	1104
	UCHIDA, Deborah K. . . .	(HI)	1267
	ANTON, Tess	(IL)	29
	LASHER, Esther L.	(IN)	700
	TEITELBAUM, Gene W. .	(KY)	1230
	LANDRY, Denise C.	(LA)	693
	COPPOLA, H P.	(MA)	245
	FOX, Susan	(MA)	395
	FRYDRYK, Teresa E. . . .	(MA)	407
	GRIGORIS, Lygia	(MA)	470
	MEAGHER, Janet H. . . .	(MA)	819
	ZUGBY, Lillian C.	(MD)	1391
	PARTHUM, John W. . . .	(MI)	945
	DOLAN, Mary M.	(MN)	309
	RAFTER, Susan	(MN)	1003
	FERRIGNO, Helen F. . . .	(NH)	373
	DUDLEY, Debbra C. . . .	(NJ)	323
	MACKINTOSH, Pamela J.	(NJ)	757
	MANY, Florence L.	(NJ)	767
	CAROLLO, Michael T. . .	(NV)	184
	CAMPBELL, Francis D. .	(NY)	176
	CLOWE, Isabel B.	(NY)	223
	EDWARDS, Harriet M. . .	(NY)	337
	GREENBERG, Linda	(NY)	463
	KASTEN, Seth E.	(NY)	629
	PETERS, Jean R.	(NY)	962
	PINEDA, Conchita J. . . .	(NY)	974
	RODGERS, Judith P. . . .	(OH)	1047
	SULLIVAN, Frances L. . .	(OH)	1207
	FELDMAN, Marianne L. .	(OR)	369
	BENGALI, Zarin P.	(PA)	80
	KREITZBURG, Marilyn J.	(PA)	677
	MCCOY, Gail	(SC)	799
	RASCHE, Richard R. . . .	(TX)	1008
	KIESSLING, Mary S. . . .	(UT)	647
	LIN, John T.	(VA)	727
	COHEN, Jane L.	(WA)	228
	HUGHES, Dorothy S. . . .	(WA)	571
	STEWART, Jane	(WA)	1192
	MARCUS, Terry C.	(WI)	769
	FRASER, Gail L.	(AB)	399
	HARDY, Kenneth J.	(AB)	501
	BOWEN, Tom G.	(ON)	120
	CHIU, Lily F.	(ON)	209
	OZAKI, Hiroko	(ON)	932
	THIVIERGE, Lynda M. . .	(PQ)	1235
Reference & research assistance	GURAYA, Harinder	(NS)	478
Reference & research databases	JONES, Stephanie R. . . .	(LA)	615

REFERENCE (Cont'd)

Reference & research in management	CHOUDHURY, Lori B. . . .	(CA)	211
Reference & research information	MCCARTNEY, Margaret		
	M.	(NY)	794
Reference & research materials	TUDOR, Dean F.	(ON)	1262
Reference & research newspaper publshg	EGERTSON, Yvonne L. .	(VA)	339
Reference & research services	HURLBERT, Irene W. . . .	(CA)	577
	PRITCHARD, Sarah M. .	(DC)	994
	ADAMOWICZ, Joanne C.	(MA)	4
	KING, Trina E.	(NY)	652
	FREEMAN, Michael S. . .	(PA)	401
	BARRUS, Phyl	(TX)	60
Reference & reserves	COONEY, Mata M.	(NV)	242
Reference & resource programs	HOBBS, Henry C.	(MB)	545
Reference & scholarly books	SCHORR, Alan E.	(AK)	1099
Reference & searching	FORD, Mary R.	(TX)	389
Reference & teaching	PATTERSON, Myron B. .	(UT)	948
Reference & technical services	RAO, Rama K.	(PA)	1008
Reference & technical services teaching	ROVELSTAD, Mathilde V.	(DC)	1062
Reference & training staff	WHITE, Joyce L.	(CO)	1331
Reference & user education	KIBBEE, Josephine Z. . . .	(IL)	646
Reference & user services	EAST, Catherine R.	(DC)	332
	TERRY, Susan N.	(DC)	1232
	EUSTACE, Susan J.	(MD)	356
Reference & Virginiana collection	EHLKE, Nancy K.	(VA)	339
Reference archivist	LEMMON, Alfred E.	(LA)	715
Reference, art & architecture	OLSON, Joann D.	(OH)	922
Reference, arts & humanities	DIAL, Clarence M.	(AZ)	299
Reference assistance	DOWNS, Sandra P.	(CA)	317
	MOORE, Patsy H.	(DC)	861
	COALTER, Milton J.	(KY)	224
	PLUNKET, Joy H.	(MA)	978
	FISH, Paula H.	(NC)	380
	KELLER, Katarina S. . . .	(NY)	635
	LINCOVE, David A.	(OH)	728
	LAFAYE, Cary D.	(SC)	687
	LEVY, Sharon J.	(VA)	722
	ZIRBES, Colette M.	(WI)	1390
	TULLY, Sharon I.	(MB)	1262
Reference, biblical/religious studies	GILNER, David J.	(OH)	437
Reference, bibliographic	RUBY, Irple P.	(NE)	1065
Reference, bibliographic instruction	THOMAS, Mary C.	(CA)	1237
Reference bibliography	ECKLUND, Kristin A. . . .	(CA)	335
Ref, bibliography, humanities, soc scis	DAVIS, Donald G.	(TX)	278
Reference book design	FRANKLIN, Robert M. . .	(NC)	398
Reference book design & research	KLINE, Victoria E.	(CA)	661
Reference book publications	KNAPPMAN, Edward W.	(NY)	663
Reference book publishing	MARLOW, Cecilia A. . . .	(MI)	772
	YOUNG, Margaret L. . . .	(MN)	1382
Reference book publishing & marketing	WHITELEY, Sandra M. . .	(IL)	1333
Reference book reviewing	JENSEN, Joan W.	(CT)	598
	MEYERS, Arthur S.	(IN)	830
Reference book reviews	HOGAN, Patricia M.	(IL)	549
Reference books	WOOD, Raymund F.	(CA)	1364
	WYNAR, Bohdan S.	(CO)	1375
	HAYES, James L.	(CT)	515
	STEWART, Donald E. . .	(IL)	1192
	WRIGHT, Helen K.	(IL)	1371
	BREWER, Annie M.	(MI)	134
	CROWLEY, Ellen T.	(MI)	261
	MACFARLAND, Scott D.	(NY)	755
	SPIER, Margaret M.	(NY)	1174
	HEINZKILL, J R.	(OR)	522
	VELA, Leonor G.	(SPN)	1281
Reference books evaluation	MCSWEENEY, Josephine	(NY)	818
Reference building & service	ADAMS, Velma L.	(MS)	6
Reference, business & technical	POST, Linda C.	(CA)	986
Reference, business sources	MACKEY, Wendy W. . . .	(MA)	757
Reference, Canadian studies	WILLIAMSON, Michael W.	(ON)	1347
Reference career centers	HAWKE, Susan J.	(PQ)	513
Reference, cataloging & acquisitions	KOPAN, Ellen K.	(CA)	671
Reference, chemical & medical databases	WINGATE, Dawn A.	(CA)	1354
Reference collection development	MARIE, Jacquelyn	(CA)	770
	PORTILLA, Teresa M. . .	(CA)	985
	WATERS, Marie B.	(CA)	1308
	BROWN, Pia T.	(FL)	147

REFERENCE (Cont'd)

Reference collection development			
	MIDDLETON, Beverly D.	(NC)	833
	MOORE, Kathryn L.	(NC)	860
	REIK, Constance	(NH)	1020
	COMER, Cynthia H.	(OH)	234
	SCHMITT, John P.	(SC)	1096
	DANIEL, Mary H.	(VA)	272
	SKELTON, W M.	(ON)	1146
	BARLOW, Elizabeth A.	(SK)	57
Reference collections	SMITH, Phillip A.	(CA)	1159
	SAMMATARO, John A.	(MA)	1078
	MCCRACKEN, Ronald W.	(ON)	799
Reference, company information	BOODIS, Maxine S.	(PA)	115
Reference, cooperative	GOULDING, Mary A.	(IL)	454
Reference database searching	HALL, Alice W.	(DE)	486
	MASON, Marjorie L.	(IL)	781
	FLEURY, Bruce E.	(LA)	385
	OSBORNE, Nancy S.	(NY)	927
	BANNEN, Carol A.	(WI)	54
Reference databases	HAYDEN, Ronald L.	(CA)	515
	BRISTOW, Ann	(IN)	137
Reference department	ANDREWS, Margaret	(MA)	27
	BOWEN, Ethel B.	(MS)	120
	MARYNOWYCH, Roman V.	(NJ)	780
Reference department management	DUCKETT, Joan	(MA)	322
Reference desk	CLOHESSY, Antoinette M.	(CO)	223
	WRIGHT, Joanna S.	(IL)	1371
	KULIBERT, Marie M.	(MI)	683
	SALPETER, Janice L.	(NY)	1077
	CARTULARO, Teresa C.	(PA)	190
	FERYOK, Joseph A.	(PA)	374
	MORGAN, Nancy T.	(SC)	864
Reference desk assistance	BROWN, Carolyn M.	(GA)	142
Reference desk coverage	HARRISON, James O.	(GA)	506
Reference desk service	SCHWARTZ, Philip J.	(TX)	1105
Reference editing	REGAN, Lesley E.	(MI)	1017
Reference end-user service	EDWARDS, Willie M.	(MI)	338
Reference engineering subjects	PERTELL, Grace M.	(IL)	961
Reference, especially Canadian studies	EVANS, Gwynneth	(ON)	357
Reference evaluation	BENHAM, Frances	(AL)	80
Reference file development, cataloging	TYLER, Kim E.	(OR)	1266
Reference film & television	TODD, Rose A.	(PQ)	1248
Reference, fine & performing arts	DOCTOROW, Erica	(NY)	307
Reference for art	MCKEE, George D.	(NY)	810
Reference for education	WILKE, Janet S.	(KS)	1339
Reference, general humanities	OLSON, Joann D.	(OH)	922
Reference, humanities	BLUM, Fred	(MI)	107
Reference, humanities & social sciences	ROUTH, Spencer	(AUS)	1061
Reference, humanities bibliography	KRAUSSE, Sylvia C.	(RI)	676
Reference in business college	SULLIVAN, Cecil G.	(NY)	1207
Reference in cinema	BEAUCLAIR, Rene	(PQ)	70
Reference in education	DICKSTEIN, Ruth H.	(AZ)	301
	BEUTHEL, Ellengail	(CO)	93
	GIRARD, Luc	(PQ)	438
Reference in fermentation technology	BOND, Mary J.	(CO)	113
Reference in French studies	GIRARD, Luc	(PQ)	438
Reference in mathematics & statistics	MERCADO, Heidi	(OH)	825
Reference in psychology	GIRARD, Luc	(PQ)	438
Reference in the social sciences	LAUBE, Lois R.	(IN)	702
Reference in women's & ethnic studies	MARIE, Jacquelyn	(CA)	770
Reference in women's studies	DICKSTEIN, Ruth H.	(AZ)	301
Reference including databases	LARISON, Brenda	(IL)	697
Reference information	EVANS, June C.	(NC)	357
	MINNICH, Conrad H.	(OH)	846
	KING, Olive E.	(ON)	652
Reference, information & referral	HOPPER, Lorraine E.	(TX)	558
Reference, information management	MULCAHY, Bryan L.	(GA)	876
Reference information retrieval	STEPANICK, John R.	(FL)	1187
Reference information service	CHRISTOLON, Blair B.	(VA)	212
Reference information services	ALLENSWORTH, James H.	(CA)	16
	WHITE, Lucinda M.	(ME)	1331
	SHIP, Martin I.	(ON)	1131
Reference instruction	ROBINS, Nora D.	(AB)	1043

REFERENCE (Cont'd)

Reference languages & literature	WARREN, Peggy A.	(ON)	1306
Reference, law	KRIKORIAN, Rosanne	(CA)	678
	HEITZ, Kathleen R.	(GA)	523
Reference law librarian	BURGALASSI, Anthony J.	(NY)	159
Reference, legal databases	BLOUGH, Keith A.	(OH)	106
Reference librarian	ANNETT, Susan E.	(CA)	28
	SARAVIS, Judith A.	(MA)	1082
Reference librarianship	WATERS, Marie B.	(CA)	1308
	PERDUE, Robert W.	(FL)	958
	SCOTT, Rupert N.	(GA)	1108
	ADKINS, Marjorie R.	(IL)	6
	HEMENWAY, Patti J.	(IL)	525
	HUCHTING, Mary	(IL)	569
	KRAMER, Ruth M.	(IL)	675
	MARKHAM, Robert P.	(IL)	771
	ENSOR, Pat L.	(IN)	350
	ARNOLD, Peggy	(MI)	34
	COREY, Marjorie	(MI)	246
	HUPP, Stephen L.	(MI)	577
	KEYSER, Sue C.	(VA)	645
	GERLACH, Donald E.	(WI)	429
	GRANATSTEIN, M E.	(ON)	457
	RIDER, Lillian M.	(PQ)	1032
	TILLOTSON, Greig S.	(AUS)	1245
Reference library	EVANS, Rina A.	(CA)	358
Reference library marketing	LEINBACH, Anne E.	(PA)	714
Reference library service	ARMONTROUT, Brian A.	(TN)	32
Reference literature	ULINCY, Loretta D.	(PA)	1268
Reference local history	GOLDENKOFF, Isabel M.	(NY)	445
Reference management	MYERS, R D.	(DC)	885
	QUINLAN, Judy B.	(GA)	1000
	DUCKWORTH, Paul M.	(MO)	322
	WOOD, M S.	(PA)	1364
	MACDONALD, Hugh	(TX)	754
	SHEETS, Janet E.	(TX)	1125
	THOMPSON, Jean T.	(WI)	1240
Reference materials	MECRAY, Freida S.	(DE)	820
	SKRAMOUSKY, Mary C.	(NJ)	1147
	SCHMALBERG, Aaron	(OH)	1094
	SKELLEY, Grant T.	(WA)	1145
Reference materials, teaching, services	STWODAH, M I.	(VA)	1206
Reference, medical databases	WRIGHT, Barbara A.	(NC)	1370
Reference, music	HORTON, Anna J.	(OH)	561
Reference, music & art	BLUM, Fred	(MI)	107
Reference negotiation & supervision	USTACH, Joanne B.	(NY)	1270
Reference networking	MYERS, R D.	(DC)	885
Reference on university records	HODGSON, Janet B.	(KY)	546
Reference, online database searching	MORGAN, Linda M.	(CA)	864
Reference online literature searching	DUNKEL, Lisa M.	(CA)	326
Reference, online searches	SYMES, Dal S.	(WA)	1217
Reference online searching	BENNETT, Michael W.	(CA)	82
	YU, Hsiao M.	(IA)	1384
	MIKOLYZK, Thomas A.	(IL)	834
	WEE, Lily K.	(IL)	1315
	MOSER, Emily F.	(VA)	870
Reference or information service	HOFFMAN, Frank W.	(TX)	548
Reference, physical sci & engineering	SIEBURTH, Janice F.	(RI)	1135
Reference product & publishing mgmt	BRAM, Leon L.	(NJ)	127
Reference, psychology bibliography	CROSBY-MUILENBURG, Corryn	(CA)	260
Reference, public & technical services	OPATOW, Judith	(NY)	925
Reference, public library	RITZ, Mary E.	(CA)	1037
Reference, public services	REED, Marcia C.	(CA)	1015
	SUMMERS, Sheryl H.	(MI)	1209
	SAUNDERS, William B.	(PA)	1085
Reference publication design	STONE, Nancy Y.	(MI)	1197
Reference publishing	LEACH, Sandra S.	(TN)	706
Reference, reader advising	ASLESEN, Rosalie V.	(SD)	36
Reference, reader guidance	WEICK, Robert J.	(IN)	1316
Reference referral	HAHN, Ellen	(DC)	483
Reference related to film	DIAMANT, Betsy	(ISR)	299
Reference related training	AARON, Kathleen F.	(CA)	1
Reference, research	WYBORNEY, Charles E.	(CA)	1374
	RAINWATER, Barbara C.	(CO)	1004
	RAQUET, Jacqueline R.	(GA)	1008
	THOMPSON, Barbara F.	(NC)	1239
	LEE, Judy A.	(NY)	710
	MCKILLIP, Rita J.	(WI)	811

REFERENCE (Cont'd)

Reference, research & bibliography	DICKSON, Katherine M. .	(MD)	301
Reference research assistance	INGLE, Bernita W.	(GA)	582
Reference research services	COHEN, Ann E.	(NY)	227
Reference resources	JONES, Mary L.	(IL)	614
	VOSS, Joyce M.	(IL)	1289
	SINWELL, Carol A.	(VA)	1144
Reference science	LEE, P M.	(ON)	711
Reference, science & technology	HUYGEN, Michaele L. . .	(MT)	580
Reference search	KINGSBERY, Evelyn B. . .	(TX)	652
Reference searches	GORDON, Shirlee J.	(OH)	452
Reference searching	COOPER, William E. . . .	(CA)	244
Reference service	BOROVANSKY, Vladimir		
	T.	(AZ)	117
	DICKINSON, Donald C. .	(AZ)	300
	GILREATH, Charles L. . .	(AZ)	437
	RICE, Virginia E.	(AZ)	1027
	CASTONGUAY, Russell .	(CA)	194
	DEAN, Terry J.	(CA)	284
	DRUMMOND, Herbert . .	(CA)	321
	GLITZ, Beryl	(CA)	441
	MINICK, Donna J.	(CA)	846
	O'CONNOR, Thomas F. .	(CA)	916
	RITCH, Alan W.	(CA)	1036
	ROSS, Ruth K.	(CA)	1058
	SMITH, Phillip A.	(CA)	1159
	SWAFFORD, William M. .	(CA)	1212
	WUERTZ, Eva L.	(CA)	1373
	CLENDINNING, David . .	(CT)	221
	JENSEN, Joan W.	(CT)	598
	LI, Hong C.	(CT)	724
	LEONARD, Angela M. . .	(DC)	716
	MARTIN, John H.	(FL)	776
	POMERLEAU, Suzanne M.	(FL)	982
	CLARK, Jane F.	(GA)	217
	JONES, Helen C.	(GA)	613
	TAYLOR, Mary L.	(HI)	1227
	MAYER, Dale C.	(IA)	789
	BEAN, Bobby G.	(IL)	69
	CHOLDIN, Marianna T. . .	(IL)	210
	GRIEGER, Sharon L. . . .	(IL)	468
	HUANG, Samuel T.	(IL)	568
	KESSINGER, Pamela C. .	(IL)	644
	LIM, Peck B.	(IL)	727
	PARK, Chung I.	(IL)	940
	RUDNIK, Mary C.	(IL)	1065
	TROFIMUK, Janette A. . .	(IL)	1257
	WHITAKER, Geraldine M.	(IL)	1329
	GUTSCHENRITTER,		
	Victoria M.	(IN)	479
	JARBOE, Betty M.	(IN)	594
	SHIPPS, Anthony W. . . .	(IN)	1131
	SPULBER, Pauline	(IN)	1176
	FLAHERTY, Margaret P. .	(KY)	383
	KEENAN, Elizabeth L. . .	(MA)	634
	BENDER, Cynthia F.	(MD)	79
	BOGAGE, Alan R.	(MD)	110
	COURTOIS, Martin P. . .	(MI)	251
	LUFT, William	(MI)	747
	SMITH, Paul M.	(MI)	1159
	STANGER, Keith J.	(MI)	1180
	ERWIN, Patricia J.	(MN)	353
	FISHEL, Teresa A.	(MN)	380
	SIBLEY, Marjorie H.	(MN)	1135
	DORR, Lorna B.	(NC)	313
	HARDIE, Karen R.	(NC)	499
	WRIGHT, Larry L.	(NC)	1372
	GILL, Bernard I.	(ND)	435
	FAWCETT-BRANDON,		
	Pamela S.	(NJ)	367
	LIN, Fumei C.	(NJ)	727
	REESE, Carol H.	(NJ)	1016
	DODSON, Carolyn	(NM)	308
	SCHOTT, Mark E.	(NM)	1099
	CLARK, Camille S.	(NV)	216
	BAXTER, Paula A.	(NY)	67
	BENEDICT, Marjorie A. .	(NY)	80
	GILLIGAN, Mary A.	(NY)	436
	LUTZ, Alexandra	(NY)	750
	PARK, T P.	(NY)	941

REFERENCE (Cont'd)

Reference service			
	COMER, Cynthia H.	(OH)	234
	KARRE, David J.	(OH)	628
	KAWAKAMI, Toyo S. . . .	(OH)	632
	LEIBOLD, Cynthia K. . . .	(OH)	713
	MONTAG, John	(OH)	855
	MEADOR, Joan S.	(OK)	819
	HEINZKILL, J R.	(OR)	522
	BEDDOES, Thomas P. . .	(PA)	73
	FERNANDEZ, Josefina L.	(PR)	373
	BRENNAN, Patricia B. . .	(RI)	133
	DAVIDSON, Nancy M. . .	(SC)	276
	ALEXANDER, Mary B. . .	(TN)	12
	JACKSON, Harriett D. . .	(TN)	587
	MARSHALL, John D. . . .	(TN)	774
	RONDESTVEDT, Helen F.	(TN)	1053
	RUDOLPH, N J.	(TN)	1066
	BOWMAN, Laura M. . . .	(TX)	122
	HAGLE, Claudette S. . . .	(TX)	483
	ROY, Loriene	(TX)	1063
	SCHWARTZ, Charles A. .	(TX)	1104
	HURT, Charlene S.	(VA)	577
	BARZELAY, Mary S. . . .	(VI)	62
	BETZ-ZALL, Jonathan R. .	(WA)	92
	BLASE, Nancy G.	(WA)	104
	NOFSINGER, Mary M. . .	(WA)	907
	HAU, Edward T.	(AB)	512
	MOFFAT, N L.	(AB)	852
	BRODIE, Nancy E.	(ON)	139
	DUNN, Mary J.	(ON)	327
	PARROTT, James R. . . .	(ON)	944
	THAUBERGER, Marianne		
	T.	(SK)	1234
	NGUYEN, Michael V. . . .	(AUS)	900
Reference service administration	TROMBLEY, Patricia A. .	(TX)	1258
Reference service & collection			
devlpmnt	WILCOX, Patricia F.	(WI)	1338
Reference service & online searching	ESTES, Pamela J.	(AR)	355
Reference service, collection			
management	WILLIAMS, Calvin	(MI)	1342
Reference service development	EDWARDS, Rela G.	(TN)	337
Reference service in the sciences	ELLSBURY, Susan H. . . .	(MS)	345
Reference service management	SCHWARTZ, Virginia C. .	(WI)	1105
Reference service, music	MILL, Rodney H.	(DC)	835
Reference service online databases	DUNN, Lucia S.	(IL)	327
Reference service provision	CANN, Cheryle J.	(MO)	178
Reference service to prisoners	COLOKATHIS, Jane . . .	(MN)	234
Reference service to readers	CHO, Sung Y.	(DC)	209
Reference services	CALHOUN, Margie B. . . .	(AL)	172
	DABBS, Mary L.	(AL)	269
	FIELD, Kathy M.	(AL)	375
	GATLING, James L.	(AL)	422
	SLOAN, Tom W.	(AL)	1150
	BEARD, Craig W.	(AR)	69
	MISENHEIMER, Paula S. .	(AR)	847
	MORRISON, Margaret L. .	(AR)	868
	REAGAN, Agnes L.	(AR)	1012
	COLE, Mitzi M.	(AZ)	231
	NAMSICK, Lynn J.	(AZ)	887
	BELL, Christina D.	(CA)	76
	BENNION, Bruce C.	(CA)	82
	BRITTON, Helen H.	(CA)	137
	CHWEH, Steven S.	(CA)	214
	CLARY, Rochelle L.	(CA)	219
	COBB, Jean L.	(CA)	224
	CRUM, Norman J.	(CA)	262
	DOWNEY, Christine D. . .	(CA)	316
	DUNN, Kathleen K.	(CA)	327
	ESQUEVIN, Christian R. .	(CA)	354
	FORMAN, Jack	(CA)	390
	FREEMAN, Kevin A.	(CA)	401
	HOCKEL, Kathleen N. . .	(CA)	545
	HUDSON, Jane	(CA)	569
	JAMES, Olive C.	(CA)	592
	KHATTAB, Hosneya M. . .	(CA)	646
	KLECKER, Anita N.	(CA)	658
	LAWRENCE, John R. . . .	(CA)	704
	LEVIN, Marc A.	(CA)	720
	LEWALLEN, David D. . . .	(CA)	722

REFERENCE (Cont'd)
Reference services

LEWIS, Phyllis N. . . . . . . (CA) 724
PARISE, Marina P. . . . . . (CA) 940
PETTEY, Brent . . . . (CA) 965
PUGH, Mary J. . . . . (CA) 997
REYES, Helen M. . . . . . . (CA) 1024
ROLLING, George M. . . (CA) 1051
SCHWARZMANN, Diane
    D. . . . . (CA) 1105
STOCKWELL, Judith R. . (CA) 1196
SULLIVAN, Kathleen A. . (CA) 1207
TIENHAARA, Kaarina I. . (CA) 1244
URBANIC, Allan J. . . . . . (CA) 1269
WATSON, Benjamin . . . . (CA) 1309
WILLIS, Glee M. . . . . (CA) 1348
BANKHEAD, Jean M. . . . (CO) 54
LAMPREY, Patricia M. . . (CO) 691
MALYSHEV, Nina A. . . . (CO) 764
BRADBERRY, Richard P. (CT) 125
CLARIE, Thomas C. . . . . (CT) 216
GAGNE, Susan P. . . . . . (CT) 412
IANNUZZI, Patricia A. . . (CT) 581
MILLBROOKE, Anne . . . (CT) 835
ROGERS, Mary E. . . . . . (CT) 1050
TRAVER, Julia M. . . . . . (CT) 1254
WENDELL, Florence P. . (CT) 1323
ANGLE, Joanne G. . . . . . (DC) 28
CHESTNUT, Paul I. . . . . (DC) 207
CHILD, Margaret S. . . . . (DC) 208
HILL, Victoria C. . . . . (DC) 541
LEONE, Rosemarie G. . . (DC) 717
PILGRIM, Auriel J. . . . . . (DC) 973
ROSENBERG, Jane A. . . (DC) 1056
STROUP, Elizabeth F. . . (DC) 1203
TOOHEY, Anne K. . . . . . (DC) 1250
MANUEL, Larry L. . . . . . (DE) 767
AHMAD, Carol F. . . . . . . (FL) 8
BARTHE, Margaret R. . . (FL) 61
EVERETT, David D. . . . . (FL) 358
SCHWENN, Janet M. . . . (FL) 1105
TERWILLEGAR, Jane C. (FL) 1232
CAMPBELL, John L. . . . (GA) 176
CHENEY, Philip M. . . . . (GA) 206
LAWSON, A V. . . . . (GA) 705
MORELAND, Virginia F. . (GA) 863
PARKER, Dorothy J. . . . . (GA) 941
STILLWATER, Rebecca S. (GA) 1194
WHEELER, Carol L. . . . . (GA) 1328
UYEHARA, Harry Y. . . . . (GU) 1270
ALLING, M P. . . . . (IA) 16
ENGEL, Kevin R. . . . . . . (IA) 348
HAYSLETT, Dawn C. . . . (IA) 517
HOEVEN, Helen D. . . . . (IA) 547
MATHEWS, Eleanor R. . . (IA) 784
PARSONS, Kathy A. . . . (IA) 945
HANSON, Donna M. . . . (ID) 498
BINGHAM, Karen H. . . . (IL) 97
CZARNECKI, Cary J. . . . (IL) 268
DONAHOE, Patricia A. . . (IL) 310
ENGRAM, Sandra K. . . . (IL) 350
FULTON, Tara L. . . . . . . (IL) 409
GEYER, Robert I. . . . . . . (IL) 430
GLANZ, Lenore M. . . . . . (IL) 439
GOWDY, Laura E. . . . . . (IL) 455
GRISSO, Karl M. . . . . . . (IL) 471
HANSEN, Andrew M. . . . (IL) 497
HANSEN, Roland C. . . . (IL) 498
KAUTZ-WARTH, Linda S. (IL) 631
KELLEY, Rhona S. . . . . . (IL) 636
KRUPKA, Karen K. . . . . (IL) 680
MARANO, Nancy H. . . . . (IL) 768
MARSHALL, Jerilyn A. . . (IL) 774
MCNEILL, Janice M. . . . (IL) 816
MILLER, Doris A. . . . . . . (IL) 837
PALMORE, Sandra N. . . (IL) 937
RETTIG, James R. . . . . . (IL) 1024
SHAW, Joyce M. . . . . . . (IL) 1123
SMITH, Lester K. . . . . . . (IL) 1157
SVENSSON, C G. . . . . . (IL) 1212

REFERENCE (Cont'd)
Reference services

TROY, Shannon M. . . . . (IL) 1258
WHITELEY, Sandra M. . . (IL) 1333
WHITNEY, Ruth . . . . (IL) 1334
WOOLSEY, Mary E. . . . . (IL) 1368
BAILEY, Joanne P. . . . . . (IN) 46
BONNER, Robert J. . . . . (IN) 114
BRISTOW, Ann . . . . (IN) 137
DAY, Thomas L. . . . . (IN) 283
GUYDON, Janet H. . . . . (IN) 479
JACKSON, Susan M. . . . (IN) 588
LISTON, Karen A. . . . . . (IN) 733
MCNAIR, James . . . . . . (IN) 815
MEYER, Ellen R. . . . . . . (IN) 830
MITCHELL, Cynthia E. . . (IN) 848
PASK, Judith M. . . . . (IN) 946
POPP, Mary F. . . . . (IN) 984
SUTHERLAND, Timothy L. (IN) 1211
ATCHISON, Fres D. . . . . (KS) 37
MYERS, Robert C. . . . . . (KS) 885
NEELEY, James D. . . . . (KS) 891
SNOKE, Elizabeth R. . . . (KS) 1163
VUKAS, Rachel R. . . . . . (KS) 1290
FOWLER, James W. . . . . (KY) 393
GRAY, Dorothy A. . . . . . (KY) 459
SHEPHERD-SHLECHTER,
    Rae . . . . (KY) 1127
COLON, Carlos W. . . . . . (LA) 234
CUROL, Helen B. . . . . . . (LA) 266
DANTIN, Doris B. . . . . . . (LA) 274
FERGUSON, Gary L. . . . (LA) 372
GIAMALVA, Lolah C. . . . (LA) 430
HASCHAK, Paul G. . . . . (LA) 510
HIMEL, Sandra M. . . . . . (LA) 542
KING, Anne M. . . . . (LA) 650
KONTROVITZ, Eileen R. (LA) 671
MAXSTADT, John M. . . . (LA) 788
ANDERSON, Wanda E. . (MA) 25
CAHALAN, Thomas H. . . (MA) 171
COHEN, Martha J. . . . . . (MA) 228
DELZELL, William R. . . . (MA) 290
GERKE, Ray . . . . (MA) 428
GREEN, Kathleen A. . . . (MA) 462
HERNON, Peter . . . . (MA) 532
JONES, Frederick S. . . . (MA) 613
KANG, Wen . . . . (MA) 625
WHEALAN, Ronald E. . . (MA) 1328
WURTZEL, Barbara S. . . (MA) 1374
BRITTEN, William A. . . . (MD) 137
CONNER, P Z. . . . . (MD) 237
ERLICK, Louise S. . . . . . (MD) 353
HANFMAN, Deborah A. . (MD) 495
HARER, John B. . . . . . . (MD) 501
HARMAN, Susan E. . . . . (MD) 502
HINSON, Karen C. . . . . . (MD) 543
KIRBY, Diana G. . . . . . . (MD) 654
LIZER, Bonnie S. . . . . . . (MD) 735
MERIKANGAS, Robert J. (MD) 826
REPENNING, Julie A. . . . (MD) 1023
TURNER, David E. . . . . . (MD) 1264
WILSON, William G. . . . (MD) 1353
GOODWIN, Bryan D. . . . (ME) 450
CONWAY, Paul L. . . . . . (MI) 239
HALL, Jo A . . . . (MI) 488
MATTESON, James S. . . (MI) 785
PELZER, Adolf . . . . (MI) 955
RADEMACHER, Matthew
    J. . . . . (MI) 1002
SCHAAFSMA, Roberta A. (MI) 1088
SICKLES, Linda C. . . . . . (MI) 1135
SIEBERS, Bruce L. . . . . (MI) 1135
CATHCART, Marilyn S. . (MN) 195
ESSLINGER, Guenter W. (MN) 355
GROSSMAN, Michael P. (MN) 473
HLAVSA, Larry B. . . . . . (MN) 544
HUBER, Kristina R. . . . . (MN) 569
ISMAIL, Noha S. . . . . . . (MN) 585
PIEHL, Kathleen K. . . . . (MN) 971
SPETLAND, Charles G. . (MN) 1174

REFERENCE (Cont'd)
Reference services

WEIKUM, James M.	(MN)	1317
BLANKENSHIP, Phyllis E.	(MO)	104
HENRY, Peggy L.	(MO)	529
HICKS, James M.	(MO)	537
MACKEY, Neosha A.	(MO)	756
MCDERMOTT, Margaret H.	(MO)	802
POWELL, Ronald R.	(MO)	988
REIMAN, David A.	(MO)	1020
TIMBERLAKE, Patricia P.	(MO)	1245
WADE, D J.	(MO)	1290
GRAVES, Gail T.	(MS)	459
BERGUP, Bernice	(NC)	87
CARPENTER, Jennifer K.	(NC)	184
IRVING, Ophelia M.	(NC)	584
MCGRIFF, Mary E.	(NC)	808
PHILBECK, Jo S.	(NC)	967
SEXTON, Spencer K.	(NC)	1118
WEANT, Rebecca E.	(NC)	1311
GARD, Betty A.	(ND)	417
BERNARDI, John V.	(NE)	88
BERTHIAUME, Dennis A.	(NH)	90
REIK, Constance	(NH)	1020
HAWLEY, George S.	(NJ)	514
LANGSCHIELD, Linda S.	(NJ)	696
MCCONNELL, Lorelei C.	(NJ)	797
MCCOY, W K.	(NJ)	799
MEYER, Mary L.	(NJ)	830
NASE, Lois M.	(NJ)	888
PROFETA, Patricia C.	(NJ)	995
RAFFERTY, Stephen P.	(NJ)	1003
WANG, Hsi H.	(NJ)	1303
KRAEMER, Mary P.	(NM)	674
CONWAY, Susan L.	(NV)	239
CURLEY, Elmer F.	(NV)	265
MASTALIR, Janet K.	(NV)	782
WELLS, David B.	(NV)	1322
ZINK, Steven D.	(NV)	1389
BULSON, Christine	(NY)	156
COOPER, Carol D.	(NY)	242
EAMES, Robert W.	(NY)	332
FIRTH, Jennifer L.	(NY)	379
FRANZ, David A.	(NY)	398
GAFFNEY, Denis C.	(NY)	412
GARGAN, William M.	(NY)	419
GRUNDT, Leonard	(NY)	475
HESLER, June P.	(NY)	534
HEWITT, Vivian D.	(NY)	535
HOLT, Lisa A.	(NY)	554
KATZ, William A.	(NY)	630
KLEIN, Stephen C.	(NY)	659
LACKS, Bernice K.	(NY)	686
LARSEN, Joan A.	(NY)	698
LAURENCE, Katherine S.	(NY)	703
MARSH, John S.	(NY)	773
MCSWEENEY, Josephine	(NY)	818
MULLEN, Marion L.	(NY)	877
OCKENE, David L.	(NY)	915
ROGERS, Elizabeth S.	(NY)	1049
SALITA, Christine T.	(NY)	1076
SULOUFF, Patricia T.	(NY)	1208
SWANSON, Dorothy T.	(NY)	1213
VIA, Barbara J.	(NY)	1283
WAHLERT, George A.	(NY)	1292
YUKAWA, Masako	(NY)	1384
BLOCK, Bernard A.	(OH)	106
DALRYMPLE, Tamsen	(OH)	271
HUGHES, Marcelle E.	(OH)	572
KOLLAR, Mary E.	(OH)	669
MAYER, Mary C.	(OH)	789
MILLER, William	(OH)	843
NASRALLAH, Wahib T.	(OH)	888
PARR, Virginia H.	(OH)	944
SIMONS, Linda K.	(OH)	1141
TIPKA, Donald A.	(OH)	1246
VIOL, Robert W.	(OH)	1285
BATT, Fred	(OK)	64
BRICK, Sarah E.	(OK)	134

REFERENCE (Cont'd)
Reference services

BUTHOD, J C.	(OK)	166
HUESMANN, James L.	(OK)	570
MCQUITTY, Jeanette N.	(OK)	817
MURPHY, Peggy A.	(OK)	881
FRANTZ, Paul A.	(OR)	398
HORAN, Patricia F.	(OR)	559
SCHIWEK, Joseph A.	(OR)	1093
ALDRIDGE, Carol J.	(PA)	11
CHANG, Shirley L.	(PA)	201
CRAWFORD, Gregory A.	(PA)	256
CROWE, Virginia M.	(PA)	261
DIMMICK, Mary L.	(PA)	304
EVITTS, Beth A.	(PA)	359
FORD, Sylverna V.	(PA)	390
GINSBURG, Mary L.	(PA)	438
GUENTHER, Nancy A.	(PA)	476
KNAPP, Mabel J.	(PA)	663
LINGLE, Virginia A.	(PA)	730
MILLER, Mary E.	(PA)	840
OGLETREE, Elizabeth H.	(PA)	918
PAWLIK, Deborah A.	(PA)	951
SEPP, Frederick C.	(PA)	1115
SHELLENBERGER, Dawn M.	(PA)	1126
THOMAS, Deborah A.	(PA)	1236
BERNAL-ROSA, Emilia	(PR)	88
RAINWATER, Jean M.	(RI)	1004
YOUNG, Arthur P.	(RI)	1381
BAKER, Steven L.	(SC)	49
FREEMAN, Larry S.	(SC)	401
LANDRUM, John H.	(SC)	693
MCREE, John W.	(SC)	818
MURDOCK, Everlyne K.	(SC)	879
NORRIS, Gale K.	(SC)	909
RIDGE, Davy J.	(SC)	1032
CASPERS, Mary E.	(SD)	193
HALLMAN, Clark N.	(SD)	489
SMITH, Rise L.	(SD)	1160
CARTER, Barbara W.	(TN)	189
GIVENS, Mary K.	(TN)	439
GOLDSMITH, Arthur	(TN)	446
HARRISON, Richard H.	(TN)	507
HAYMES, Don	(TN)	516
LEWIS, Carol E.	(TN)	722
MANNING, Dale	(TN)	766
BARRINGER, Sallie H.	(TX)	60
BELL, Joy A.	(TX)	77
GARCIA, Beatriz H.	(TX)	417
HARTNESS, Ann	(TX)	508
HAWLEY, Laurie J.	(TX)	514
JARMUSZ, Ruth M.	(TX)	594
KRALISZ, Victor F.	(TX)	675
METCALF, Judith A.	(TX)	828
MOSS, Charmagne L.	(TX)	872
MUELLER, Peggy	(TX)	875
NEU, Margaret J.	(TX)	896
SAFLEY, Ellen D.	(TX)	1074
TIME, Ming M.	(TX)	1245
TONGATE, John T.	(TX)	1250
TYLER-WHITE, Patricia G.	(TX)	1266
WILLIAMS, Suzi	(TX)	1346
HALL, Blaine H.	(UT)	487
HINDMARSH, Douglas P.	(UT)	542
JOHNSON, Jeffery O.	(UT)	606
CAHILL, Linda J.	(VA)	171
CHAPPELL, Barbara A.	(VA)	202
COSGROVE-DAVIES, Lisa A.	(VA)	248
FANNON, Elizabeth L.	(VA)	363
GIBSON, Robert S.	(VA)	432
GOODWIN, Jane G.	(VA)	450
GREFE, Richard F.	(VA)	465
JENNERICH, Elaine Z.	(VA)	598
MCCULLEY, Lucretia	(VA)	800
PARKER, John A.	(VA)	942
PARNES, Daria M.	(VA)	943
REAM, Daniel L.	(VA)	1012
SELLIN, Jon B.	(VA)	1114

REFERENCE (Cont'd)

Reference services

THOMPSON, Evan L.	(VT)	1239
ANDERSEN, Eileen	(WA)	21
CHRISTIANSEN, Claire B.	(WA)	211
SCHREINER, Suzanne M.	(WA)	1100
BOULANGER, Mary E.	(WI)	119
CHRISTMAN, Inese R.	(WI)	212
GRUEL, Janice L.	(WI)	474
MANDERNACK, Scott B.	(WI)	765
MCGILL, Nancy A.	(WI)	806
RISTIC, Jovanka	(WI)	1036
SHUTKIN, Sara A.	(WI)	1134
STANTON, Vida C.	(WI)	1181
MARTIN, June R.	(WV)	777
SCOBELL, Elizabeth H.	(WV)	1106
HARRINGTON, Carolyn B.	(WY)	504
ANDREWS, Christina A.	(AB)	26
ENGLESAKIS, Marina F.	(AB)	350
SEYEDMAHMOUD, Donna A.	(AB)	1118
SHORES, Sandra J.	(AB)	1132
CROOKS, Sylvia A.	(BC)	260
GARRAWAY, Babs L.	(BC)	420
HOPKINS, Richard L.	(BC)	558
KELNER, Gregory H.	(BC)	638
ROTHSTEIN, Samuel	(BC)	1060
WILLISON, Maureen I.	(BC)	1348
MARSHALL, Kenneth E.	(MB)	774
LOGAN, Penelope A.	(NS)	737
READE, Judith G.	(NS)	1012
SUTHERLAND, J E.	(NS)	1211
BENDIG, Regina	(ON)	79
BILLINGSLEY, Andrew G.	(ON)	96
DUFF, Ann M.	(ON)	323
FRAUMENI, Michael A.	(ON)	399
KANNEL, Ene	(ON)	625
KRALIK, Jane M.	(ON)	675
MULLERBECK, Aino	(ON)	877
PAL, Gabriel	(ON)	935
PAPOUTSIS, Fotoula	(ON)	939
PARK, Nancy R.	(ON)	941
COLLISTER, Edward A.	(PQ)	233
DESCHATELETS, Gilles H.	(PQ)	294
DOUGLAS-BONNELL, Eileen	(PQ)	314
DUCHESNEAU, Pierre	(PQ)	322
GAMEIRO, Maria H.	(PQ)	416
LAMONTAGNE, Jacqueline	(PQ)	691
WATIER-LALONDE, Chantal	(PQ)	1309
MAHOUD ALY, Usama E.	(EGY)	761
COBOLET, Guy P.	(FRN)	225
OGBAA, Clara K.	(NGR)	918
VELA, Leonor G.	(SPN)	1281
ESTERMANN-WISKOTT, Yolande	(SWZ)	355
HU, James S.	(TAI)	567
LIN, Chih F.	(TAI)	727
SENG, Harris B.	(TAI)	1115
YANG, Mei H.	(TAI)	1377
ELLIOTT, Lirlyn L.	(TRN)	344

Reference services administration	VIOLETTE, Judith L.	(IN)	1285
Reference services & collections	NEUBAUER, Richard A.	(MA)	896
	SAMMATARO, Linda J.	(TN)	1078
Reference services & consultation	WONG, Anita	(ON)	1362
Reference services & instruction	KENT, Rose M.	(OH)	642
Reference services & management skills	THOMAS, Fannette H.	(MD)	1236
Reference services & materials	BUNGE, Charles A.	(WI)	157
Reference services & micrographics	EISEN, David J.	(IN)	340
Reference services & networking	ARRINGTON, Susan J.	(MD)	34
Reference services & online searching	REID, Valerie L.	(MI)	1019
Reference services & special collections	CORSARO, James	(NY)	248
Reference services coordinating	QUEEN, Margaret E.	(CA)	999
Reference services delivery	EILERS, Marsha J.	(IN)	340
Reference services, engineering	OMAR, Elizabeth A.	(MD)	923

REFERENCE (Cont'd)

Reference services, ethnic & general	FISHER, Edith M.	(CA)	380
Reference services in engineering	MORRIS, Louis M.	(MD)	867
Reference services in life sciences	SOWELL, Steven L.	(IN)	1170
Reference services in public libraries	ANDERSON, Charles R.	(IL)	22
Reference services management	CROOKS, Joyce M.	(CA)	260
	POEHLMAN, Dorothy J.	(DC)	979
	WATSON, Paula D.	(IL)	1310
Reference services, medical databases	BROWN, Biraj L.	(SDA)	142
Reference services policy statements	INGRAHAM, Alice L.	(PA)	582
Reference services, social sciences	ANDREWS, Loretta K.	(MD)	26
Reference services, theology	KENDALL, Charles T.	(IN)	640
Reference services to federal agencies	CHO, Sung Y.	(DC)	209
Reference skill teaching	GRIFFIN, Charlene F.	(KY)	468
Reference skills	LOPATIN, Edith K.	(NY)	740
Reference, social science & humanities	WIZA, Judith M.	(KY)	1359
Reference, social sciences	BLUM, Fred	(MI)	107
Reference, social sciences & humanities	MCCLEARY, William E.	(LA)	796
Reference sources	HASELWOOD, Eldon L.	(NE)	510
Reference sources & services	HARLAN, Robert D.	(CA)	502
	ROPER, Fred W.	(SC)	1054
	MEHRAD, Jafar	(IRN)	821
Reference, special collections	MCQUAIL, Edward J.	(WV)	817
Reference specialist	SCHAAF, Robert W.	(DC)	1088
Ref, staff development	KEMPF, Andrea C.	(KS)	639
Reference standards	GOULDING, Mary A.	(IL)	454
Reference statistics	JOSEPH, Margaret A.	(TX)	617
Reference, student assistance	DAUGHERTY, Carolyn M.	(MD)	275
Reference teaching	EISENBACH, Elizabeth R.	(CA)	340
	CLARKE, Norman F.	(MN)	219
Reference, teaching & evaluation	CROWLEY, Terence	(CA)	262
Reference, technical & marketing	GARVEY, Nancy G.	(NJ)	421
Reference, technology	MARCOTTE, Marcel	(PQ)	769
Reference theory	BURNS, Nancy R.	(CA)	162
Reference tools, writing	BOAST, Carol	(IL)	108
Reference training	CROOKS, Joyce M.	(CA)	260
	MICHEL, William D.	(MN)	832
	THOMPSON, Ronelle K.	(SD)	1241
	THAUBERGER, Marianne T.	(SK)	1234
Reference training & procedures	HELSLEY, Alexia J.	(SC)	525
Reference unit administration	APPLEBY, Judith A.	(PQ)	30
Reference user services	LUND, Patricia A.	(WI)	748
Reference, veterinary & human medicine	VEENSTRA, Robert J.	(AL)	1281
Reference work	ZLATOS, Christy L.	(AL)	1390
	DICKINSON, Dan C.	(CA)	300
	FLOWERS, Pat	(CA)	386
	KRAMER, Helen A.	(CA)	675
	PANSKI, Saul J.	(CA)	938
	VARKENTINE, Aganita	(CA)	1278
	REITER, Ellie W.	(CO)	1022
	ROGERS, Brian D.	(CT)	1049
	HANFORD, Sally	(DC)	495
	ZICH, Robert G.	(DC)	1388
	GREEN, Carol A.	(ID)	461
	BURNS, Mary F.	(IL)	162
	SHERMAN, William F.	(IL)	1128
	STEVENS, Rolland E.	(IL)	1191
	SWITZER, Joann H.	(IN)	1216
	WILKINS, Marilyn W.	(LA)	1340
	MCGARRY, Marie L.	(MA)	805
	ROSENBAUM, David	(MI)	1055
	KEYS, Thomas E.	(MN)	645
	KALER, Dorothy C.	(NM)	623
	PIERSON, Robert M.	(NM)	972
	STAM, Deirdre C.	(NY)	1179
	WOOTEN, Jean A.	(NY)	1368
	LUCAS, Linda S.	(SC)	746
	WOHLSCHLAG, Sarah A.	(TX)	1359
	HEDGES, Bonnie L.	(VA)	520
	STEIN, Karen E.	(VA)	1185
	RICKERSON, Carla	(WA)	1031
	FRASER, Elizabeth L.	(WV)	399
	DEGINNUS, Roxie	(AB)	287
	DUFFUS, Sylvia J.	(AB)	323

REFERENCE (Cont'd)
Reference work

	EAGLETON, Kathleen M.	(MB)	331
	WALLACE, Kathryn M.	(ON)	1297
	KIELLY, Marion J.	(PE)	647
	HETU, Sylvie	(PQ)	534
Reference work, administration	HERBST, Linda R.	(MI)	530
Reference work & bibliographies	EARL, Susan R.	(NC)	332
Reference work & database searching	DIBARTOLO, Amy L.	(NY)	299
Reference work & medical databases	FRATIES, Marie L.	(MI)	399
Reference work in education	BEIMAN, Frances M.	(NJ)	75
Reference work, interlibrary loans	LEHWALDT, Marliese	(ON)	713
Reference works compilation	SABLE, Martin H.	(WI)	1072
References	RAYMAN, Ronald A.	(IL)	1011
References & bibliographic instruction	KOK, Victoria T.	(VA)	669
References in medicine	HIGGINBOTHAM, Cecelia B.	(LA)	537
Religion & education reference	GRIMES, Timothy P.	(MI)	470
Religion reference	BOISCLAIR, Regina A.	(PA)	111
Research & reference	MAJOR, Caryl M.	(AZ)	762
	DICKSON, Constance P.	(DC)	301
	HIGBEE, Joan F.	(DC)	537
	FULLER, Ruth V.	(GA)	409
	PEURYE, Lloyd M.	(IL)	966
	FERGUSON, Roberta J.	(MA)	372
	SUTTON, Joyce A.	(MA)	1211
	ARNEJA, Harbhajan S.	(NY)	33
	HARDING, Mary H.	(NY)	500
	PALMER, Paul R.	(NY)	936
	RANKIN, Carol A.	(NY)	1007
	SEEBER, Frances M.	(NY)	1111
	NISENOFF, Sylvia	(VA)	905
Research & reference for politicians	O'KEEFE, Kevin T.	(NT)	919
Research & reference services	SLINGER, Michael J.	(IN)	1149
Research & reference training	ROSS, Theodosia B.	(GA)	1059
Research reference	FALVEY, Genemary H.	(NY)	363
Scandinavian reference services	TIBLIN, Mariann E.	(MN)	1244
Scholarly & reference book publishing	BERKNER, Dimity S.	(NY)	87
School reference work	BANICK, Albert N.	(NY)	54
Science & business reference	EYLES, Heberle H.	(FL)	359
Science & engineering reference	HODGSON, Elizabeth A.	(NY)	546
	PANCAKE, Edwina	(VA)	937
	FISHER, Rita C.	(WA)	381
Science & engineering reference service	BALDWIN, Charlene M.	(AZ)	51
Science & engineering reference services	TABACHNICK, Sharon	(TN)	1219
Science & medical reference	LACY, Yvonne M.	(TX)	687
Science & physics reference	STEINBERG, Marilyn H.	(MA)	1185
Science & technical reference	ENRICI, Pamela L.	(MN)	350
Science & technical reference services	DEBROWER, Amy M.	(MD)	285
Science & technology reference	SABIN, Robert G.	(AL)	1072
	BRONARS, Lori A.	(CA)	140
	LEE, Lydia H.	(CA)	710
	ZEIDLER, Patricia L.	(CA)	1387
	MARCUS, Stephanie M.	(DC)	769
	CHADWICK, Alena F.	(MA)	196
	HANSEN, Joanne J.	(MI)	497
	ADAMS, Dena R.	(NM)	4
	SHIPPEY, Susan S.	(NY)	1131
	DUVALLY, Charlotte F.	(PA)	330
	CRAVEN, Trudy W.	(SC)	256
	BICHTELER, Julie H.	(TX)	94
	WHEELER, Marjorie W.	(TX)	1329
	HASELBAUER, Kathleen J.	(WA)	510
Science & technology reference & resrch	LUXNER, Dick	(NJ)	750
Science & technology reference service	TIRRELL, Brenda P.	(TX)	1247
Science & technology reference work	NITZBERG, Dale B.	(MD)	905
Science bibliography & reference	DEGOLYER, Christine C.	(NY)	288
Science, general & online reference	GRAZIANO, Eugene	(CA)	460
Science reference	FORE, Janet S.	(AZ)	390
	MAUTNER, Robert W.	(AZ)	787
	MOUNT, Jack D.	(AZ)	873
	CULOTTA, Wendy A.	(CA)	264
	DODSON, Snowdy D.	(CA)	308
	O'HEARN, Sarah A.	(CA)	919

REFERENCE (Cont'd)
Science reference

	PRITCHARD, Eileen E.	(CA)	994
	ROTH, Dana L.	(CA)	1059
	OSTROFF, Cynthia R.	(CT)	929
	NELSON, Marilyn L.	(DC)	894
	PRIMACK, Alice L.	(FL)	993
	GUBISTA, Kathryn R.	(GA)	475
	WALD, Marlena M.	(GA)	1294
	DAVIS, Richard A.	(IL)	280
	MICHAELSON, Robert C.	(IL)	832
	SHOTWELL, Richard T.	(IL)	1133
	SMITH, Linda C.	(IL)	1157
	THORNHILL, Robert E.	(IL)	1242
	FRANKLIN, Janice C.	(KS)	397
	STUBBAN, Vanessa L.	(KS)	1204
	HAGEDORN, Dorothy L.	(LA)	482
	MARSHALL, Susan O.	(LA)	775
	GELB, Linda	(MA)	425
	KENT, Caroline M.	(MA)	642
	KHAN, Syed M.	(MA)	646
	RUBENS, Donna J.	(MN)	1064
	KEMPF, Jody L.	(NM)	639
	HEATON, Shelley J.	(NV)	519
	LIFSHIN, Arthur	(NY)	726
	POWIS, Katherine E.	(NY)	989
	STEWART, Linda G.	(NY)	1192
	WILLIAMS, Esther L.	(NY)	1343
	BOLEK, Ann D.	(OH)	112
	FELTES, Carol A.	(OH)	370
	HOUDEK, G R.	(OH)	562
	KINCH, Michael P.	(OR)	649
	LAWRENCE, Robert E.	(OR)	705
	EARL, Martha F.	(TN)	332
	DUFFY, Suzanne	(TX)	324
	HUNTER, John H.	(TX)	576
	JACKSON, Ruth L.	(TX)	588
	CARTER-LOVEJOY, Steven H.	(VA)	190
	MOFJELD, Pamela A.	(WA)	852
	PRITCHARD, Jackie L.	(WA)	994
	ROOS, Tedine J.	(WY)	1053
	DROESSLER, Judith B.	(AB)	320
	KREIDER, Janice A.	(BC)	677
	IVANOCHKO, Robert W.	(SK)	585
	RESCH, Peter T.	(SK)	1024
Science reference service	WHITLEY, Katherine M.	(AZ)	1333
Science reference services	YUCHT, Donald J.	(NY)	1384
Science reference sources	LOCKHART, Carol A.	(MO)	736
Sciences reference	RICKER, Alison S.	(OH)	1031
Scientific & medical reference	LANEY-SHEEHAN, Susan	(AR)	695
Scientific & technical reference	CUMMINGS, Helen H.	(DC)	264
	KING, Hannah M.	(DC)	651
	BLASCHAK, Mary M.	(MI)	104
Scientific & technical ref & research	MILLER, Dennis P.	(OH)	837
Scientific reference	STRIFE, Mary L.	(NY)	1202
Scientific reference & research	STOKES, Claire Z.	(MN)	1196
Scientific reference services	KOSMIN, Linda J.	(MD)	672
Scientific, technical & reference books	PECK, Brian T.	(FL)	953
Sci-tech reference	SAYLOR, Linda	(CA)	1086
	STOCKER, Randi L.	(IN)	1195
	COLLINS, Mitzi L.	(VA)	233
Selection, admin, reference, cataloging	MALTBY, Florence H.	(MO)	764
Serials & reference	CLARK, Peter W.	(WI)	217
Serials reference	PUCCIO, Joseph A.	(DC)	997
16mm film selection & reference	LOCKE-GAGNON, Rebecca A.	(OH)	736
Slavic bibliography & reference	TURCHYN, Andrew	(IN)	1263
Slavic reference, Russian language	PRICE, Susan W.	(NY)	992
Social science & humanities reference	BILAL, Dania M.	(FL)	96
	PATTON, Linda L.	(FL)	949
	WESTON, E P.	(IL)	1327
Social science, general reference	TUDIVER, Lillian	(NY)	1262
Social science, occult reference	KLEIN, Victor C.	(LA)	659
Social science reference	HALL, Susan W.	(CT)	488
	WAI, Lily C.	(ID)	1292
	ELS, Nancy T.	(MO)	346
	REINHOLD, Edna J.	(MO)	1021
	TOMPKINS, Louise	(NJ)	1250

REFERENCE (Cont'd)

Social science reference

MACOMBER, Nancy ...	(NY)	758
NOLAN, John A.	(NY)	907
SHEEHAN, Robert C. ...	(NY)	1125
HOLMES, Jill M.	(OK)	553
HOVDE, David M.	(OK)	563
RICHARDSON, Linda B. .	(VA)	1029
JEWELL, Timothy D. ...	(WA)	600

Social science reference services MILLER, Clayton M. ..... (OH) 836
WEILANT, Edward ..... (OH) 1317
Social sciences & business reference HATTENDORF, Lynn C. . (IL) 512
Social sciences & humanities
reference COCHRANE, Kerry L. .. (IL) 225
TURLEY, Harriet M. .... (NY) 1264
TOLBERT, Jean F. ..... (TX) 1248
ST. JACQUES, Suzanne L. (ON) 1075
Social sciences & religion reference PHILLIPS, Robert L. .... (TX) 969
Social sciences reference TUCKER, John M. ..... (IN) 1261
DRISCOLL, Jacqueline .. (MI) 320
SCIATTARA, Diane M. ... (NY) 1106
WYLLIE, Stanley C. .... (OH) 1375
CARR, Caryn J. .... (PA) 185
LUIKART, Nancy B. .... (TX) 747
DAVIS, Wylma P. ...... (VA) 281
BULL, Jerry J. .... (PQ) 156
Social sciences reference & research HOWREY, Mary M. ..... (IL) 566
Social sciences reference courses LI, Richard T. .... (IL) 725
Social sciences, reference services DIMATTEO, Lucy A. .... (NY) 304
Social studies reference WHITE, Carol A. ...... (GA) 1330
Social work reference REGUEIRO, Judith E. ... (PA) 1017
Solving difficult reference questions DUCHARME, Judith C. .. (NM) 322
Southeast Asian reference services ASHMUN, Lawrence F. .. (NY) 36
Southwest history reference services D'ANTONIO, Lynn M. ... (AZ) 274
Special library reference UMANA, Christine J. ... (MA) 1268
Special reference POSEY, Sussann F. ..... (MD) 985
Specialized business reference LEVINSON, Catherine K. . (NC) 721
Standard reference DIEHL, Katharine S. .... (TX) 302
State government reference REES, Pamela C. ...... (IA) 1016
Student supervision, reference OLSEN, Sarah G. ...... (IL) 922
Subject reference WYNNE, Allen .... (CO) 1375
Supervision of reference librarians MUTCH, Donald G. .... (ON) 883
System reference EGAN, Elizabeth M. .... (IL) 338
Tax & accounting reference BLUM, Linda C. .... (CA) 107
Tax law reference REID, Pauline .... (NY) 1019
Tax reference MOORE-EVANS, Angela . (CA) 862
HENEKS, Julia A. ...... (DC) 528
JOHNSON, David J. .... (NY) 603
DANIELSON, Connie S. . (IA) 273
Teacher & reference skills TRIM, Kathryn .... (MI) 1256
Teaching, reference librarian SABLE, Martin H. ...... (WI) 1072
Teaching reference service SLOAN, Mary J. .... (GA) 1149
Teaching reference skills BERNAT, Mary A. ..... (VEN) 88
Teaching research & reference skills GABRIEL, Linda .... (NJ) 411
Technical & business reference THOM, Pat A. .... (WI) 1235
Technical & scientific reference SIMPSON, Alice H. ..... (OH) 1141
Technical cataloging & reference LEE, Dora T. .... (CA) 709
Technical reference WORSTER, Carol L. ..... (IL) 1369
FEIDLER, Anita J. ..... (MA) 368
EIPERT, Susan L. ...... (WA) 340
Technical reference & searching DESOIER, Jacqueline J. .. (CA) 295
Technical service & reference KRIEGER, Tillie .... (NY) 678
Telecommunications & film reference GRILIKHES, Sandra B. ... (PA) 470
Telecommunications reference MCGARVEY, Eileen B. .. (NY) 805
Telecommunications, research,
reference ROGGENKAMP, Alice M. (NY) 1050
Telephone & ready reference RIECHEL, Rosemarie ... (NY) 1033
Telephone & written reference PLUMER, F I. .... (NY) 978
Telephone reference BEECHER, Sally .... (MA) 74
Telephone reference service BENDER, Cynthia F. .... (MD) 79
PHIFER, Kenneth O. .... (MD) 967
Test & measurements reference KAUFFMAN, Inge S. .... (CA) 631
Texana reference HULL, Mary M. .... (TX) 572
Textile reference SILER, Freddie B. ...... (SC) 1137
Theatre reference WILMETH, Don B. ..... (RI) 1349
Theological reference HAYES, Bonaventure F. . (NY) 515
HUNN, Marvin T. ...... (TX) 574
GILCHRIST-DOBSON,
Norma J. ...... (NS) 434
GUNN, Shirley A. ...... (NGR) 477

REFERENCE (Cont'd)

Theological reference service OLSON, Ray A. .... (MN) 923
Theological reference services OLSEN, Robert A. ...... (TX) 921
Theological reference works WELLS, Keith P. ...... (IL) 1322
Theology & religion reference CAMP, Thomas E. ..... (TN) 175
Theology or banking reference JORDAN, Charles R. ... (IL) 616
Theology reference SIVIGNY, Robert J. .... (VA) 1144
Traditional & computer reference AUSTIN, Martha L. ..... (WA) 40
Training for reference services MILLSAP, Gina J. ..... (MO) 844
Transportation reference & databases CORNELL, Pamela J. ... (MN) 246
Undergraduate reference JASPER, Richard P. .... (MI) 595
TOLBERT, Jean F. ..... (TX) 1248
United States documents reference SPAHR, Janet E. ...... (VA) 1170
University-level public reference MCCANN, Judith B. .... (ON) 794
Urban affairs reference DANIEL, Eileen .... (ON) 272
Urban affairs reference service LOGAN, Mary A. ...... (MD) 737
Video selection & reference LOCKE-GAGNON,
Rebecca A. ...... (OH) 736
Visual & sound material reference DRIESSEN, Karen C. ... (MT) 320
Visual arts reference SHERIDAN, Helen A. ... (MI) 1127
Water management, reference
service PLOCKELMAN, Cynthia H. (FL) 978
Young adult reference ZANARINI, Linda S. .... (NE) 1386
Young adult reference services GROOMS, Richard O. ... (AL) 472
Youth reference work DURSTON, Corinne L. .. (BC) 329
Zoo related subjects reference KENYON, Kay A. ...... (DC) 643

REFERENDUMS (See also Bond, Elections)

Bond issue & tax referendums BECKER, Josephine M. . (FL) 72
Library tax elections & referendums AVANT, Julia K. .... (LA) 41
Referendum campaign planning FLEMING, Lois D. ..... (FL) 384

REFERRAL (See also Reference)

Arctic information referral SOKOLOV, Barbara J. ... (AK) 1165
Children & adult reference & referral DAYO, Ayo .... (TX) 283
Community information & referral FERDUN, Georgenne M. . (CA) 372
MATZKE, Ellen S. ..... (MI) 786
SEKELY, Maryann ...... (NY) 1113
Community information & referral
service LIGHT, Jane E. .... (CA) 726
Information & referral CROWLEY, Terence ... (CA) 262
FISHER, Alice J. ...... (CA) 380
NICKERSON, Louann M. (CA) 902
TSCHERNY, Elena .... (DC) 1260
JOSEPH, Eleanor C. ..... (LA) 617
HEIL, Kathleen A. ...... (MD) 521
ZARYCZNY, Wlodzimierz
A. ...... (MI) 1386
VALANCE, Marsha J. ... (MN) 1271
BEAGLE, Donald R. .... (NC) 68
PARRISH, Nancy B. .... (NC) 944
REILLY, Carol H. ...... (NC) 1020
WALDERA, Katherine A. (ND) 1294
ELENAUSKY, Edward V. (NJ) 342
CRONEBERGER, Robert
B. ...... (PA) 260
GIBLIN, Carol C. ...... (PA) 431
NEWPORT, Dorothea D. . (PA) 900
BREDESON, Peggy Z. .. (WI) 131
MATTHEWS, Geraldine M. (WI) 785
WIERUCKI, Karen A. ... (ON) 1337
Information & referral service CARRINGTON, Ruth ... (NY) 186
ELLIS, Kathy M. .... (BC) 344
Information & referral services PAQUETTE, John F. .... (CA) 939
COLON, Carlos W. ..... (LA) 234
HSU, Elizabeth L. ...... (NY) 567
Information, reference & referral GUSS, Emily R. .... (IL) 478
Library systems, reference referral GUY, Patricia A. .... (CA) 479
Photography referral HOFFKNECHT, Carmen L. (CA) 547
Public library information & referral GUMPPER, Mary F. .... (OH) 477
Reference & referral LEVY, Judith A. .... (CA) 721
WESTERBERG, Kermit B. (IL) 1326
GREENBERG, Ruth S. .. (NJ) 463
SWINEHART, Katharine J. (OH) 1216
DENGROVE, Richard A. . (VA) 292
Reference & referral service WAGNER, Barbara L. ... (CO) 1291
Reference & referrals FREY, Roxanne C. ..... (IL) 403
Reference, information & referral HOPPER, Lorraine E. ... (TX) 558

REFERRAL (Cont'd)
Reference referral — HAHN, Ellen . . . . (DC) 483
Referral — BOIVIN-OSTIGUY, Jocelyne . . . . (PQ) 111

REFORMATION
Renaissance & Reformation history — REITH, Louis J. . . . . (DC) 1022

REFORMS
Social reforms, minorities — MOREY, Frederick L. . . . (MD) 863

REGIONAL
Administration on regional level — PURCELL, Marcia L. . . . (NY) 998
Branch & regional library layouts — COBURN, Morton . . . . . . (IL) 225
Development of regional cooperation — CANAVAN, Roberta N. . . (NJ) 178
Library management, regional young adult — CHARVAT, Catherine T. . (OH) 203
Library regional systems — CHRISTENSON, John D. (MN) 211
Local & regional history interpretation — LEAHY, M J. . . . . (AK) 706
Networking, regional — SCHWARTZ, Lawrence C. (NJ) 1104
Pacific Northwest regional local history — EMMENS, Thomas A. . . . (OR) 348
Promoting regional American history — REINSTEIN, Julia B. . . . . (NY) 1021
Public regional library administration — KENT, Charles D. . . . . . . (ON) 642
Regional archives — MOORE, Karl R. . . . . (IL) 860
Regional computer applications — NELSON, James B. . . . . (NY) 894
Regional cooperative library systems — HURREY, Katharine C. . . (MD) 577
Regional coordination — WEITKEMPER, Larry D. . (MO) 1320
Regional databases — FELMY, John C. . . . . (DC) 370
MARBAN, Ricio . . . . (GUA) 768
Regional development — PHILIP, John J. . . . . (OH) 967
Regional educational media centers — FITZGERALD, Ruth F. . . (MI) 382
Regional film library — HOFSTAD, Alice M. . . . . (MN) 548
Regional history — GRAHAM, Robert W. . . . (IL) 456
MUTSCHLER, Charles V. (WA) 883
Regional history, genealogy — PROPER, David R. . . . . . (MA) 995
Regional information library — OAKES, Patricia A. . . . . . (AK) 913
Regional libraries — HALES, John D. . . . . (FL) 486
WASH, Melba W. . . . . . . (TN) 1307
OSTRANDER, Richard E. (WA) 929
RIDLER, Elizabeth A. . . . (SK) 1032
Regional library cooperation — JENNINGS, Martha F. . . (MI) 598
Regional library development — LANDRUM, Margaret C. . (CO) 693
LOPEZ, Deborah A. . . . . (FL) 741
NELSON, James B. . . . . (NY) 894
RAY, Gordon L. . . . . (BC) 1011
Regional library networks — LINTON, William D. . . . . (NIR) 731
Regional library service system — OWEN, Mary J. . . . . (CO) 932
Regional library systems — FALK, Louise G. . . . . (IA) 362
SPRAUER, Linda J. . . . . (OR) 1176
SLOAN, Lynette S. . . . . . (TN) 1149
DAVIS, Joyce . . . . (TX) 279
JORDAN, Peter A. . . . . . (AB) 616
CAMPBELL, Joylene E. . (SK) 177
HARADA, Ryukichi . . . . . (JAP) 499
Regional medical biography — REDMON, Sherrill . . . . . . (KY) 1014
Regional multitype library systems — BERNER, Karen J. . . . . . (NE) 88
Regional networks — LOW, Jocelyn L. . . . . (CT) 743
Regional planning — DONG, Tina . . . . (MA) 311
Regional public libraries — BOESE, Robert A. . . . . . (MN) 110
Regional public library system — SCOTT, Thomas L. . . . . (MN) 1108
Regional school, public library holding — BENSON, Laurel D. . . . . (MN) 83
Regional services — SCHALK-GREENE, Katherine . . . . (NJ) 1089
Regional system administration — LE BUTT, Katherine L. . . (NB) 708
Regional systems — KISSNER, Arthur J. . . . . (MA) 656
Regional trade — WILSON, John W. . . . . . (TX) 1351
Regional union catalog automation — PARRAVANO, Ellen A. . . (NY) 944
School region lib, media coordination — RIVERA, Antonio . . . . . . (NY) 1037
School, regional services consulting — BUCKINGHAM, Betty J. . (IA) 154
Shared services regional network — WILCOX, Linda M. . . . . . (ON) 1338
State & regnl literature & history bibl — RAZER, Robert L. . . . . . . (AR) 1012
Statewide & regional networks — WOODWARD, Robert C. (ME) 1368
Televised regional services — POWER, Colleen J. . . . . (CA) 989

REGISTRATION
Registration — PROSSER, Judy A. . . . . (CO) 995

REGULATIONS
Business & regulatory research — MERINGOLO, Joseph A. (MD) 826
Collect specific regulatory documents — HARDY, Kenneth J. . . . . (AB) 501
Copyright laws & regulations — KATZ, Bernard M. . . . . . (ON) 630
Energy regulatory matters — PARK, Nancy R. . . . . . . (ON) 941
Environmental & health regulations — LE BLANC, Judith E. . . . (OH) 708
Environmental laws & regulations — KAYES, Mary J. . . . . . . · (WI) 632
Federal acquisition regulations — SMITH, David A. . . . · (VA) 1153
Federal regulations — NOWAK, Geraldine D. . . (DC) 911
Federal regulations on CD-ROM — CHRISTIANSEN, Eric G. (OH) 211
Florida building regulations — FOSTER, Helen M. . . . . . (FL) 392
Gas industry regulation — DORNER, Steven J. . . . . (VA) 313
Government regulations — DUFFY, Brenda F. . . . . (DC) 324
Government regulations on environment — GROOT, Elizabeth N. . . . (CA) 472
Legal, legislative & regulatory database — JOHNSON, Jacqueline B. (DC) 605
Legislative & regulatory information — JOHNSON, Jacqueline B. (DC) 605
Litigation & regulatory support — SCULLY, Patrick F. . . . . (CA) 1109
Nuclear regulations & quality admin — KING, Betty J. . . . . (WA) 650
Regulatory information — RATHGEBER, Jo F. . . . (NC) 1009
Regulatory information access — MCRAE, Alexander D. . . (MD) 818
Regulatory issues — GOLDSMITH, Carol C. . . (NJ) 446
Regulatory research — MALEK, Stanislaw A. . . . (PQ) 763
Securities & commodities regulatory — JOHNSON, G V. . . . . . . (IL) 604
Securities regulation — DATTALO, Elmo F. . . . . (DC) 275
Securities regulations — GREEN, Randall N. . . . . (DC) 462
Telecom regulatory information — MASON-WARD, Lesley . (ON) 781
Telecommunications regulation — GOLDSMITH, Carol C. . . (NJ) 446
Trade regulation — TAYLOR, Raymond M. . . (NC) 1228

REHABILITATION
Cognitive rehabilitation & computers — SHANEFIELD, Irene D. . . (PQ) 1120
Disability & rehabilitation evaluation — SMITH, Kathleen A. . . . . (MD) 1156
Physical medicine & rehabilitation — SHANEFIELD, Irene D. . . (PQ) 1120
Rehabilitation — TISHLER, Amnon . . . . . (NY) 1247
CASINI, Barbara P. . . . . (PA) 192
Rehabilitation collection development — COUCH, Susan H. . . . . . (PA) 250
Rehabilitation information — COUCH, Susan H. . . . . . (PA) 250
Rehabilitation medicine — KALUZSA, Karen L. . . . (IL) 623
Rehabilitation procedures — MATTHEWS, Geraldine M. (WI) 785
Special education & rehabilitation — VELLEMAN, Ruth A. . . . (NY) 1281
Vocational rehabilitation library — CHAPERO, Alicia . . . . . . (NY) 201

RELATIONAL
Creating relational database — PEGLER, Ross J. . . . . . . (FL) 954
Relational database design — CAMOZZI-EKBERG, Patricia L. . . . . (WA) 175
WARD, Maryanne . . . . . (WA) 1304
Relational databases design & use — ROBINSON, David F. . . . (VA) 1043

RELATIONS
Academic library relations — KOYAMA, Janice T. . . . . (CA) 674
Administration board relationships — MEADOWS, Donald F. . . (BC) 819
Authority & bibliographic relationships — CARNEY, Marilyn L. . . . (VA) 183
City government relations — WEST, Shirley L. . . . . . (NJ) 1326
Commercial client relations — VALANDRA, Kent T. . . . (NY) 1271
Communication, info, lib relationships — VOIGT, Melvin J. . . . . . . (CA) 1287
Community group relations — SMOTHERS, Joyce W. . (NJ) 1162
Community relations — ARMITAGE, Constance . (CO) 32
O'SHEA, Cornelius M. . . (IL) 928
WOODY, Jacqueline B. . (MD) 1368
MAXWELL, Martha A. . . (MO) 788
ROBERTS, Jean A. . . . . (MO) 1040
FONTAINE, Sue . . . . . . (NY) 388
BRUCE, Dennis L. . . . . (SC) 149
Community relations & services — WHITNEY, Howard F. . . . (MA) 1334
Customer relations — HUGHES, Marilyn A. . . . (PA) 572
Employee relations — LIBBEY, George H. . . . . . (GA) 725
WEATHERFORD, John W. (MI) 1311
GOODINGS, Sally A. . . . (ON) 449
Federal relations — HEANUE, Anne A. . . . . . (DC) 518
Foreign relations research — QUARTELL, Robert J. . . (NY) 999

RELATIONS (Cont'd)

Government relations	WOOD, Linda M.	(CA)	1364
	MCDONOUGH, Roger H.	(NJ)	803
	THENELL, Janice C.	(OR)	1234
	SHELKROT, Elliot L.	(PA)	1126
Governmental relations	KINCHEN, Robert P.	(NY)	650
	BRUCE, Dennis L.	(SC)	149
Governmental relations & lobbying	GODWIN, Mary J.	(NY)	443
Human relations	MISSAVAGE, Leonard	(FL)	848
	SUMMERFORD, Steven L.	(NC)	1209
Human relations skill development	LENOX, Mary F.	(MO)	715
Human resources & labor relations	HARE, Judith E.	(ON)	501
Industrial labor relations	FRASER, Charlotte R.	(NY)	399
Industrial relations	CHAPLAN, Margaret A.	(IL)	201
	WATSON, Marjorie O.	(NJ)	1310
	LA MARCHE, David L.	(ON)	689
Information of international relations	RIGNEY, Janet M.	(NY)	1034
International library relations	HUTCHINSON, Beck	(FL)	579
	MASSIS, Bruce E.	(NY)	782
International library relationships	TSUNEISHI, Warren M.	(DC)	1260
International relations	BEESON, Lone C.	(CA)	74
	DIMATTIA, Ernest A.	(CT)	304
	LOWENTHAL, Jane E.	(DC)	744
	PANOFSKY, Hans E.	(IL)	938
International relations & exchange	MCCOOL, Donna L.	(WA)	798
Interpersonal relations	SMITH, Nathan M.	(UT)	1159
Labor relations	BOISSE, Joseph A.	(CA)	111
	MCINDOO, Larry R.	(CA)	809
	TAUSKY, Janice	(MA)	1225
	STUDDIFORD, Abigail M.	(NJ)	1204
	BUCK, Jeremy R.	(OH)	153
	SMITH, Ellen A.	(OH)	1154
	FARK, Ronald K.	(RI)	364
	LEATHER, Deborah J.	(VA)	707
Legislative relations	FONTAINE, Sue	(NY)	388
Library & archives relation	KOEL, Maria O.	(CT)	667
Library & community relations	HEFFINGTON, Carl O.	(GA)	520
Library & community relations networking	POSEL, Nancy R.	(PA)	985
Library boards, community relations	GIBSON, Barbara H.	(CT)	431
Library, faculty relationship	FARBER, Evan I.	(IN)	363
Media relations	REAGAN, Bob	(CA)	1012
Personnel & labor relations	APPEL, Anne M.	(CA)	29
Personnel management & labor relations	FRANCIS, Derek R.	(BC)	396
Personnel relations	DUFORE, Thomas H.	(AZ)	324
Programming & community relations	TANG, Grace L.	(NY)	1222
Public & community relations	DRESP, Donald F.	(NM)	319
	O'NEIL, Margaret M.	(NY)	924
Public & staff relations	FRANKLIN, Robert D.	(VA)	398
Public information & relations	WELLS, Gladysann	(NY)	1322
Public library labor relations	BRANDWEIN, Larry	(NY)	128
Public library trustee relations	JANK, David A.	(MA)	593
Public relations	BURDASH, David H.	(DE)	158
	BLANDY, Susan G.	(NY)	104
	CARDEN, Marguerite	(FL)	180
Publicity, public & community relations	PIANE, Mimi	(IN)	969
Publisher & library relations	HUNTER, Karen A.	(NY)	576
School & public library relations	DRACH, Marian C.	(MD)	317
School library community relations	HASBROUCK, Clara H.	(TN)	510
Soil plant relations & natural resources	SCHNEIDER, Karl R.	(MD)	1097
Staff development & human relations	MIAH, Abdul J.	(VA)	831
Staff development, human relationships	SMITH, Robert F.	(TN)	1160
Structure-activity relationships	LASSLO, Andrew	(TN)	700
Trustee/librarian relations	BALCOM, Kathleen M.	(IL)	51
Vendor & library relations	GOEHNER, Donna M.	(IL)	443
Vendor relations	FERRELL, Mary S.	(CA)	373
	AXTMANN, Margaret M.	(NY)	42

RELIGION (See also Church, Evangelicalism, Evangelism, Inter-Faith, Scriptures, Spiritual and names of specific denominations)

American religion	SHUSTER, Robert D.	(IL)	1134
Archives, religious	HAURY, David A.	(KS)	512
Biblical & religious studies	WUNDERLICH, Clifford S.	(MA)	1374
Bibliography, European hist & religion	ROBERTS, Susanne F.	(CT)	1041
Bibliography of religious studies	STARKEY, Edward D.	(IN)	1182

RELIGION (Cont'd)

Business & religious reference sources	FEW, John E.	(CA)	374
Cataloging history, philosophy, religion	YU, Priscilla C.	(IL)	1384
Cataloging theology & religion	WUNDERLICH, Clifford S.	(MA)	1374
Children's religious literature	PEARL, Patricia D.	(VA)	952
Church history & religion cataloging	MITCHELL, Annmarie D.	(CA)	848
Collecting state religious history	ROLLER, Twila J.	(NM)	1051
Collection development in religion	PETERSON, Stephen L.	(CT)	964
Col development, philosophy & religion	STEWART, Douglas J.	(AZ)	1192
Comparative religion research	SMITH, Robert E.	(IN)	1160
Computers in religion	ANDERSON, Norman E.	(MA)	24
Ethnic & religious archives	GRACE, William M.	(PA)	455
Liberal arts, religion, music cataloging	LUSK, Betty M.	(SAF)	749
New American religions	SMITH, Robert E.	(IN)	1160
19th century American religious music	CHRISTENSON, Donald E.	(OH)	211
Religion	BRANDT, Steven R.	(CA)	128
	MILLER, Everett G.	(MD)	837
	GAYNOR, William A.	(NJ)	424
	BORCHERT, Catherine G.	(OH)	116
	PAKALA, James C.	(PA)	935
	GILLUM, Gary P.	(UT)	436
Religion & ancient history databases	FRAZER, Ruth F.	(FL)	399
Religion & education reference	GRIMES, Timothy P.	(MI)	470
Religion & humanities databases	HILGERT, Elvire R.	(IL)	539
Religion & philosophy	BUTKIS, John F.	(CA)	166
	FOLLICK, Edwin D.	(CA)	388
	NOLAN, Christopher W.	(TX)	907
Religion & philosophy bibliography	HIGGINBOTHAM, Richard C.	(IL)	537
	ALTMANN, Thomas F.	(WI)	18
Religion & theology bibliography	MCGARTY, Jean R.	(MI)	805
Religion databases	OLSON, Ray A.	(MN)	923
Religion reference	BOISCLAIR, Regina A.	(PA)	111
Religion research tools/methodology	BOISCLAIR, Regina A.	(PA)	111
Religion, theology & philosophy	TROUTMAN, Joseph E.	(GA)	1258
Religious acquisitions	REYNOLDS, Dorsey	(PA)	1025
Religious archives	BAKER, Russell P.	(AR)	49
	WHITE, Joyce L.	(CO)	1331
	JANSSEN, Gene R.	(MN)	594
	BODLING, Kurt A.	(MO)	109
	DEUTSCH, N E.	(MO)	297
	SULLIVAN, Majella M.	(NY)	1208
	YAKEL, Elizabeth	(NY)	1376
	CLAYTON, J G.	(SC)	220
	WILLIAMSON, Jane K.	(TN)	1347
	LOCH, Edward J.	(TX)	735
	BROCKMAN, Norbert C.	(KEN)	138
Religious archives administration	JOHNSON, Timothy J.	(IL)	609
Religious book selection	SMITH, Newland F.	(IL)	1159
	HILL, Lawrence H.	(PA)	540
Religious books	DOLLEN, Charles J.	(CA)	310
	MEDER, Stephen A.	(MI)	820
	HEISER, W C.	(MO)	523
	HEFNER, Xavier M.	(NY)	520
Religious books, evangelism	FERM, Lois R.	(MN)	373
Religious collections	LAMBREV, Garrett I.	(CA)	691
Religious community archives	PATTERSON, Mary E.	(WA)	948
Religious databases	OTTOSON, Robin D.	(CO)	930
Religious denomination archives	WARNER, Wayne E.	(MO)	1305
Religious education	PARSLEY, Brantley H.	(AL)	944
	HIBLER, James P.	(MI)	536
	OFFERMANN, Glenn W.	(MN)	917
Religious library	FREESE, Melanie L.	(NY)	401
Religious periodicals	HILL, Lawrence H.	(PA)	540
Religious record keeping	SWEENEY, Shelley T.	(SK)	1215
Religious resources	GLEASON, Ruth I.	(IN)	440
Religious studies	WOOD, James F.	(FL)	1364
	KAPOOR, Jagdish C.	(NH)	626
Religious studies bibliography	CRIDLAND, Nancy C.	(IN)	258
Religious women	MISNER, Barbara	(WI)	847
Religious women's orders	DEUTSCH, N E.	(MO)	297
Sexuality & religion issues	MAZUR, Ronald M.	(MA)	791
Social sciences & religion reference	PHILLIPS, Robert L.	(TX)	969
Teaching religion courses	BOISCLAIR, Regina A.	(PA)	111
Theological & religious periodicals	HAYES, Bonaventure F.	(NY)	515
Theology & religion collection devlpmnt	CAMP, Thomas E.	(TN)	175
Theology & religion reference	CAMP, Thomas E.	(TN)	175

RELIGION (Cont'd)

Theology, religion	FIEG, Eugene C.	(IL)	375
Women & religion	HURT, Charlene S.	(VA)	577
Young adult religious literature	PEARL, Patricia D.	(VA)	952

REMEDIAL

Remedial action programs	PFUDERER, Helen A.	(TN)	966

REMODELING (See also Building, Facilities, Renovation)

Facilities planning & remodeling	BUCKINGHAM, Betty J.	(IA)	154
Facility remodeling	KRABBE, Natalie	(OR)	674
Library renovation & remodeling	MCCRACKEN, Ronald W.	(ON)	799
Maintenance & remodeling facilities	EVANS, Constance L.	(KS)	356
New & remodel buildings	COURTRIGHT, Harry R.	(PA)	252
Remodeling, renovation, furniture layout	WALSH, Robert R.	(NY)	1300

RENAISSANCE

Ancient & Renaissance manuscripts	WITTEN, Laurence	(CT)	1358
English renaissance manuscripts	YEANDLE, Laetitia	(DC)	1378
Medieval & Renaissance literature	WHITE, D J.	(MO)	1330
Medieval & Renaissance studies	DILLON, John B.	(WI)	303
Renaissance & Baroque art	OSTROW, Stephen E.	(DC)	929
Renaissance & Reformation history	REITH, Louis J.	(DC)	1022
Renaissance art	FURTAK, Rosemary	(MN)	410
Renaissance era musicology	PRUETT, James W.	(DC)	996

RENOVATION (See also Building, Facilities, Remodeling)

Building & capital renovation	NYERGES, Michael S.	(NY)	912
Building & renovation	TOMPKINS, Philip	(CA)	1250
Building design & renovation	WU, Harry P.	(MI)	1373
	CADA, Elizabeth J.	(ON)	170
Building planning & renovation	BARRY, James W.	(PA)	60
Building renovation	STAHL, Wilson M.	(NC)	1178
	SZILASSY, Sandor	(NJ)	1218
Building renovation & additions	JOHNSTON, James R.	(IL)	610
Building renovation supervision	BURNS, Mary F.	(IL)	162
Building renovations	TITUS, H M.	(DE)	1247
Library design & renovation	BIHLER, Charles H.	(CT)	96
Library renovation & remodeling	MCCRACKEN, Ronald W.	(ON)	799
Library renovation, construction	WILLIAMS, Edwin E.	(CT)	1343
Library renovations	FRANCK, Jane P.	(NY)	396
New buildings & renovations planning	VANN, John D.	(PA)	1276
Planning & renovating libraries	JOHNSON, Ruth E.	(OH)	608
Remodeling, renovation, furniture layout	WALSH, Robert R.	(NY)	1300
Renovation	MILLS, Helen L.	(TX)	844
Renovation & expansion planning	KELSH, Virginia J.	(CA)	639

REORGANIZATION (See also Management, Organization)

Academic library reorganization	SZILASSY, Sandor	(NJ)	1218
Lrng resrch ctr mgmt & reorganization	MIAH, Abdul J.	(VA)	831
Library reorganization	MCGRAW, Scott C.	(IL)	807
	ELLENBOGEN, Barbara R.	(MI)	343
Organizing, reorganizing libraries	OFFERMAN, Mary C.	(IA)	917
Planning & reorganizing library space	WORTHINGTON, A P.	(CA)	1369
Reorganization	GAPEN, D K.	(WI)	416
Reorganization, clean-up, weeding	HANLON, Patricia S.	(IL)	496
Reorganization of collections	GORMAN, Audrey J.	(NJ)	452
Reorganization of internal policies	LOMEN, Nancy L.	(NY)	738
Reorganization of technical services	HENN, Barbara J.	(IN)	528
Reorganizing law firm libraries	BYRNE, Jeanne M.	(TX)	169

REPAIR (See also Bindings, Bookbinding, Conservation, Restoration)

Binding & repair	WOODS, Janet R.	(WY)	1367
Book repair	KALLENBERG, Mary E.	(AK)	623
Book repair & reconstitution	GLEESON, Joyce M.	(IL)	441
Bookbinding repair	LANE, David R.	(CA)	694
Book-binding, repair, conservation	AUSTIN, Kristi N.	(WA)	40
Computers & computer repair	RADER, H J.	(WV)	1002
Repair & conservation of documents	JORDAN, Ervin L.	(VA)	616
Technical trades, naval ship repair	ANDERSON, Marcia M.	(VA)	24

REPORTING (See also News, Newspapers)

Appraisal reporting	FELDER, Bruce B.	(OH)	369
Financial planning & reporting	SELLGREN, James A.	(MI)	1114
Financial reporting reference	JOHNSON, John E.	(ON)	606
Merger & acquisition reporting	GREEN, Randall N.	(DC)	462
Nationwide real estate title reporting	FELDER, Bruce B.	(OH)	369
Reporter	ELWELL, Christopher S.	(CT)	347
Reporting	GRANT, George E.	(NJ)	458
Research & reporting	PARK, Chung I.	(IL)	940
Research information for reporters	RICE, Margaret R.	(TX)	1027
Theft reporting	LEAB, Katharine K.	(CT)	706

REPORTS

Article, report, & review writing	EDELSON, Ken	(NJ)	335
Cataloging of technical reports	KLEIBER, Michael C.	(CA)	658
Collection of marketing research reports	COVIENSKY, Lana	(ON)	252
Department of Defense & AFR reports	BURDEN, John	(NY)	158
Historical research, report preparation	STINE, Roy S.	(NC)	1194
Index & abstract technical reports	CIBULSKIS, Elizabeth R.	(IL)	214
Industry reports	HENDERSON, Joanne L.	(DE)	526
Market analysis business reports	KASE-MCLAREN, Karen A.	(NY)	628
Market research reports	NAPOLITANO, Wanda M.	(NY)	887
	SULLIVAN, Daniel M.	(NY)	1207
	MASON-WARD, Lesley	(ON)	781
NASA & Defense technical reports	BOYD, Effie W.	(TN)	122
Online indexing of business reports	SEASE, Sandra A.	(NY)	1110
Organizing, clippings pamphlets reports	HORN, Zoia	(CA)	559
Political risk reports	NAPOLITANO, Wanda M.	(NY)	887
	SULLIVAN, Daniel M.	(NY)	1207
Proprietary technical report systems	ECKROADE, Carlene B.	(DE)	335
Report collections	LATYSZEWSKYJ, Maria A.	(ON)	702
Report editing, management systems	KEE, Walter A.	(NC)	634
Report literature	HECHT, Judith N.	(OH)	519
Report number formation	KANE, Astor V.	(VA)	624
Research & analytical report writing	MEYER, Andrea P.	(CO)	829
Research reports	CLINE, Margery C.	(CA)	222
	DOYLE, Patricia A.	(TX)	317
Resource reports	COURTOT, Marilyn E.	(MD)	251
Software development, library reports	HENDERSON, John E.	(PA)	526
Technical report document retrieval	WHITE, Chandlee	(MA)	1330
Technical report management	CONKLING, Thomas W.	(PA)	236
Technical reports	THOMPSON, Bryan	(CA)	1239
	TYSON, Betty B.	(CA)	1267
	BYRNE, Timothy L.	(CO)	169
	SAUNDERS, Laurel B.	(NM)	1084
	BURDEN, John	(NY)	158
	CURRY, Lenora Y.	(NY)	266
	GRUBER, Linda R.	(PA)	474
	HARRIS, Maureen	(SC)	505
	PINELLI, Thomas E.	(VA)	974
Writing & editing scientific reports	LAUTENSCHLAG, Elisabeth C.	(PA)	703

REPOSITORY

Script repository	FREEMAN, John P.	(TX)	401

REPRESENTATION

Buyer & seller representation	PICKETT, Doyle C.	(NJ)	970
Indexing representations	WOOD, Judith B.	(NC)	1364
Knowledge representation	DIENER, Richard A.	(MD)	302
	WEI, Yin M.	(OH)	1316

REPRINTS

Database management, reprint files	MENZUL, Faina	(NJ)	825
Document, reprint, photocopy supply	KOSTENBAUDER, Scott	(NY)	673
Photocopy reprints publishing	BROWN, G R.	(FL)	144
Publishing music reprints, facsimiles	BALK, Leo F.	(NY)	52
Reprint publishing	BOYD, Kenneth W.	(GA)	122
Reprints	GAUNT, James R.	(FL)	423
	ASTIFIDIS, Maria	(NY)	37

REPROGRAPHICS (See also Photocopying, Reprints, Telefacsimile)
Reprographics   FERRARESE, Mary A. . . . (DC)   373
Reprographics, microformatting   WARD, Christine W. . . . . (NY) 1303
Reprography & photocopy   TRIBIT, Donald K. . . . . . (PA) 1256

RESEARCH (See also Searching, Surveys)
Abstracting & research   HADDERMAN, Margaret . (OR)   482
Academic & research libraries   DAIN, Phyllis . . . . (NJ)   270
Academic & research libraries book
  sales   SCHRIFT, Leonard B. . . . (NY) 1100
Academic, research, & special
  libraries   YASSA, Lucie M. . . . . . (CA) 1378
Academic research libraries   STEINKE, Cynthia A. . . . (MN) 1186
Academy Awards research   STOCKSTILL, Patrick E. . (CA) 1195
Accident prevention research   BISSON, Jacques . . . . . (PQ)   100
Accounting & auditing research   VEASLEY, Mignon M. . . . (CA) 1280
                                        EMERSON, Beth A. . . . . (TX)   347
Accounting & tax research   KLOPPER, Susan M. . . . . (GA)   662
                                        HAYWARD, Sheila S. . . . (MA)   517
                                        SNAY, Sylvia A. . . . . . . (MI) 1162
Accounting & taxation research   FROST, Roxanna . . . . . . (WA)   406
Accounting research   GROFT, Mary L. . . . . . . (IL)   471
                                        DINGLEY, Doris A. . . . . (MN)   305
                                        ROSENBERGER,
                                          Constance G. . . . . . (PA) 1056
                                        HOPKINS, Terry F. . . . . (TX)   558
                                        SMITH, Kraleen S. . . . . (TX) 1156
Accounting, tax research   STEPHENS, Stefanie N. . (AZ) 1188
Actuarial science research   CHAPA, Joan I. . . . . . . (IL)   201
Ad hoc research   RUBINSTEIN, Ed . . . . . (NY) 1065
Administration & research   CARROLL, Dewey E. . . . (TX)   187
Administration of research libraries   FORTH, Stuart . . . . (PA)   391
Administration, reference, research   KNIGHT, Shirley D. . . . . (NJ)   664
Advanced legal research   NISSENBAUM, Robert J. (OH)   905
Advertising & marketing research   STEINMANN, Lois S. . . . (CA) 1186
                                        MACIVER, Linda B. . . . . (MA)   756
                                        ROCHLEN, Rita E. . . . . (MI) 1046
                                        GESKE, Aina S. . . . . . . (NY)   430
Advertising research   PETRUGA, Patricia L. . . . (ON)   965
Aerospace industry research   BELL, Karen L. . . . . (GA)   77
Aerospace related research   JOHNSON, Marlys J. . . . (MN)   607
African & Middle Eastern research   WITHERELL, Julian W. . (DC) 1358
Afro-American, American lit resrch   BAKISH, David J. . . . . . (NY)   50
Agribusiness research   BLUMENFELD, Judith K. (MN)   107
Agricultural research   NOGA, Dolores A. . . . . . (AB)   907
Applied arts research   FRANKLIN, Linda C. . . . (NY)   398
Architectural research   BAERWALD, Susan M. . . (MO)   45
Architecture research   GRETES, Frances C. . . . (NY)   467
                                        FLESHMAN, Nancy A. . . (TX)   384
Architecture research & reference   WRIGHT, Sylvia H. . . . . (NY) 1373
Archival research   KREPS, Lise E. . . . . . . (WA)   678
Archives & research   BRUNK, Thomas W. . . . . (MI)   150
Art historical research   WYKLE, Helen H. . . . . . (CA) 1375
                                        KNOWLES, Susan W. . . . (TN)   665
Art history research   YARNALL, James L. . . . . (DC) 1378
                                        TRINKOFF, Elaine . . . . . (NY) 1257
                                        CICCONE, Amy N. . . . . . (VA)   214
Art research   KLEIN, Kristine J. . . . . . (DC)   659
                                        COREY, Glenn M. . . . . . (MI)   246
Art research methodology   JONES, Lois S. . . . . . . (TX)   613
Arts & humanities research &
  development   PIERCE, Mildred L. . . . . (NV)   971
Automated legal research   GOTT, Gary D. . . . . . . (ND)   453
                                        GREENBERG, Charles J. (NY)   463
Automotive industry research   GIGLIO, Linda M. . . . . . (MI)   433
Automotive patent & trademark
  research   WREN, James A. . . . . . (MI) 1370
Band music recordings research   MITZIGA, Walter J. . . . . (IL)   850
Banking research   LASKOWITZ, Roberta G. (NY)   700
Behavioral sciences & education
  research   SWARTZ, Jon D. . . . . . (TX) 1214
Biblical research   KIRKESY, Oliver M. . . . . (MI)   655
Bibliographic research   KRUKONIS, Perkunas P. (MA)   680
                                        FORSYTH, Karen R. . . . (MI)   391
                                        SCHMIDT, Diana M. . . . (ON) 1095
                                        SAUCIER, Danielle . . . . (PQ) 1084
Bibliographical instruction & research FREITAG, Wolfgang M. . (MA)   401

RESEARCH (Cont'd)
Bibliographical research   DEUTSCH, James I. . . . (DC)   296
                                        FIGUEREDO, Danilo H. . . (NY)   376
                                        NYQUIST, Corinne E. . . (NY)   913
                                        BRETON, Lise . . . . (PQ)   133
Bibliography & research   ETTER, Patricia A. . . . . (AZ)   355
Bibliography & research guides   LITT, Dorothy E. . . . . . (NY)   733
Biographical research   BERGAN, Helen J. . . . . (DC)   85
                                        ARMEIT, Marilyn . . . . . (NY)   32
Biographical research for artists   BAILEY, Tuuli T. . . . . . . (AZ)   47
Biomedical literature research,
  indexing   COMPTON, Joan C. . . . . (CA)   235
Biomedical research online & manual   LETT, Rosalind K. . . . . (GA)   719
Black music research   DE LERMA, Dominique R. (MD)   289
                                        GRENDYSA, Peter A. . . (WI)   467
Book research   FRANK, Peter R. . . . . . (CA)   397
                                        FELDMAN, Linda A. . . . (IL)   369
Broadcasting & communications
  research   SLOCUM, Leslie E. . . . . (NY) 1150
Broadcasting research   KATZ, Doris B. . . . . . . (NY)   630
Broker analysis research   HEFFRON, Betsy A. . . . (NY)   520
Business, advertising & legal research FISHER, Daphne V. . . . (PA)   380
Business & corporate research   DENOTO, Dorothy E. . . (NY)   293
Business & economic research   DUFFY, Brenda F. . . . . (DC)   324
Business & finance database
  research   STOOPS, Louise . . . . . (NY) 1198
Business & finance research   ARMEIT, Marilyn . . . . . (NY)   32
                                        CLOWE, Isabel B. . . . . (NY)   223
                                        MAYOPOULOS, Karen L. (NY)   791
Business & financial research   SOROBAY, Roman T. . . (NY) 1169
Business & industry reference &
  resrch   LUXNER, Dick . . . . (NJ)   750
Business & industry research   RATZABI, Arlene . . . . . (NY) 1010
Business & legal research   WHITTLESEY, Jane M. . (TX) 1334
Business & marketing research   TUCKERMAN, Susan . . . (NY) 1262
Business & public affairs research   COCHRAN, Catherine . . (MI)   225
Business & regulatory research   MERINGOLO, Joseph A. (MD)   826
Business & tax research   WATERS, Susan S. . . . . (DC) 1309
Business & technology research   SOVNER-RIBBLER, Judith (MA) 1170
                                        MENNELLA, Dona M. . . (MD)   824
Business information & research   RUTKOWSKI, Hollace A. (PA) 1070
Business information sources &
  research   CVELJO, Katherine . . . . (TX)   268
Business management & research   KIRSHBAUM, Priscilla J. (CO)   655
Business market research   DEHN, Lydia A. . . . . . . (CA)   288
Business, marketing & advertising
  resrch   PIDALA, Veronica C. . . . (NY)   971
Business, marketing research   LEWARK, Kathryn W. . . (CA)   722
Business online research   BURYLO, Michelle A. . . . (PA)   164
Business reference & legal research   SEAMAN, Sally G. . . . . (IL) 1109
Business reference & research   MATTHEWSON, David S. (CT)   786
                                        TEW, Robin L. . . . . (FL) 1233
                                        WASYLENKO, Lydia W. . (NY) 1308
                                        ETCHINGHAM, John B. . (RI)   355
Business research   ADAMS, Linda L. . . . . . (CA)   5
                                        GERSH, Barbara S. . . . . (CA)   429
                                        GHAZARIAN, Salpi H. . . (CA)   430
                                        MILLER, Ralph D. . . . . . (CA)   841
                                        BRUNER, Robert B. . . . . (CO)   150
                                        KRISMANN, Carol H. . . (CO)   678
                                        SMART, Marriott W. . . . (CO) 1151
                                        SOLOMON, Arnold D. . . (DC) 1166
                                        BRYANT, Nancy J. . . . . (GA)   152
                                        COOPER, Glenn . . . . . . (GA)   243
                                        BARNUM, Sally J. . . . . . (IL)   58
                                        GROFT, Mary L. . . . . . . (IL)   471
                                        REED, Janet S. . . . . . . (IL) 1015
                                        HAYWARD, Sheila S. . . . (MA)   517
                                        KELLEY, Barbara C. . . . (MI)   636
                                        POQUETTE, Mary L. . . . (MN)   984
                                        BAERWALD, Susan M. . . (MO)   45
                                        THOMPSON, Barbara F. (NC) 1239
                                        JONES, Deborah A. . . . . (NJ)   612
                                        LAUB, Barbara J. . . . . . (NJ)   702
                                        COOPER, Catherine M. . (NY)   242
                                        GROSS, Gretchen . . . . . (NY)   472
                                        HUBBARD, Susan E. . . . (NY)   568
                                        KATZ, Doris B. . . . . . . (NY)   630
                                        MANN, Amy S. . . . . . . (NY)   765
                                        MINTZ, Anne P. . . . . . . (NY)   847

RESEARCH (Cont'd)

Business research

	ROSENFELD, Lillian E. . .	(NY)	1056
	TYLER, David M.	(NY)	1266
	BORUCKI, Jennifer A. . .	(OH)	117
	BOWIE, Angela B.	(OH)	121
	POPOVICH, Charles J. . .	(OH)	984
	SKUTNIK, John S.	(OH)	1147
	MOSLEY, Thomas E. . . .	(OK)	872
	KASPERKO, Jean M. . . .	(PA)	629
	WHITAKER, Cynthia D. .	(PA)	1329
	QUINN, Joan M.	(TN)	1000
	FELSTED, Carla M.	(TX)	370
	MCCLURE, Margaret R. .	(TX)	797
	HARMALA, Amy A.	(WA)	502
	WATERSTREET, Darlene E.	(WI)	1309
	CARVALHO, Sarah V. . .	(ON)	191
	CASEY, Victoria L.	(ON)	192
	ELLERT, Barbara M. . . .	(ON)	343
	SEDGWICK, Dorothy L. .	(ON)	1111
	DARLINGTON, Susan . .	(PQ)	275
Business resrch, acquisitions, & instrc	CAMERON, Constance B.	(RI)	174
Business research analysis	JACKSON, Craig A.	(ON)	587
Business research & databases	MORRIS, Ann	(IL)	866
Business research in databases	HOPKINS, Terry F.	(TX)	558
Business research services	ADAMO, Clare	(CT)	4
Business, science reference & research	LEDBETTER, Sherry H. .	(MD)	708
Business/technical information research	MICHAEL, Ann B.	(IL)	831
CAD/CAM & AI research	POLK, Diana B.	(IL)	981
California historical research, poetry	MOORE, Richard K. . . .	(CA)	861
Canadian studies research	FOX, Rosalie	(ON)	395
Canadiana bio-bibliographical research	DOWDING, Martin R. . .	(ON)	315
Cataloging research	YEE, Martha M.	(CA)	1379
	VAJDA, Elizabeth A. . . .	(NY)	1271
Chemical & agronomy research	GAMBRELL, Drucilla S. .	(AL)	416
Chemical research	AUER, E E.	(NJ)	39
Classification research	RICHMOND, Phyllis A. . .	(OH)	1030
Clinical medicine research	BRUCE, Marianne E. . . .	(AB)	149
Clinical research	OWENS, Clayton S.	(AZ)	932
Collection development research	ST. CLAIR, Gloriana S. .	(OR)	1075
Collection of marketing research reports	COVIENSKY, Lana	(ON)	252
College & research libraries	TURNER, Frank L.	(TX)	1264
College library service research	MICIKAS, Lynda L.	(PA)	832
Communication & research	DALRYMPLE, Prudence W.	(IL)	271
Communication research	CASE, Donald O.	(CA)	191
	PULVER, Thomas B. . . .	(DC)	997
Communications industry market research	LEIGHTON, Victoria C. . .	(GA)	714
Company & industry research	THAU, Richard	(NJ)	1234
Company research	BELL, Steven J.	(PA)	77
Comparative religion research	SMITH, Robert E.	(IN)	1160
Competitive research, analyses	SOUDER, Edith I.	(PA)	1169
Computer industry research	KRUSE, Luanne M.	(TX)	681
Computer research & retrieval	WOLFE, Bardie C.	(FL)	1360
Computer stock market research	HEFFRON, Betsy A.	(NY)	520
Computer system research & development	DIEHL, Mark	(IL)	302
Computer systems & online research	REED, Carol R.	(HI)	1014
Computer-assisted legal research	DOHERTY, Walter E. . . .	(AZ)	309
	WIEBELHAUS, Richard J.	(AZ)	1336
	CASTETTER, Karla M. . .	(CA)	194
	GRIGST, Denise J.	(CA)	470
	JONES, Michael D.	(CA)	614
	MOORE, Gregory B. . . .	(CA)	859
	WERNER, O J.	(CA)	1325
	WATERS, Sally G.	(FL)	1308
	GRIFFITH, Cary J.	(MN)	469
	ELAM, Kristy L.	(MO)	341
	COCHRAN, J W.	(MS)	225
	O'CONNOR, Sandra L. . .	(NC)	916
	DESMOND, Andrew R. . .	(NY)	295
	D'AMORE, Denice M. . . .	(OH)	272
	HARVAN, Christine C. . .	(PA)	509
	SHAW, Ben B.	(TX)	1123

RESEARCH (Cont'd)

Computer-assisted research	JOHNSRUD, Thomas E. .	(CA)	609
	SHELAR, James W.	(DC)	1125
	HINSON, Karen C.	(MD)	543
	MCKENZIE, Elizabeth M.	(MO)	811
	CARRINGTON, Bessie M.	(NC)	186
	BEJNAR, Thaddeus P. . .	(NM)	75
	MCGOEY, Richard P. . . .	(NM)	807
	GLOECKNER, Donna S. .	(NY)	441
Computer-associated legal research	MOYER, Holley M.	(NJ)	874
Computer-based research	SKRUKRUD, Nora L. . . .	(CA)	1147
Computerized legal research	ANDREWS, Sylvia L. . . .	(IN)	27
	HANLEY, Thomas L. . . .	(OH)	496
	SIMON, Dale	(OR)	1140
Computerized legal research instruction	STOPPEL, Ellen K.	(IA)	1198
Computerized research	REDDY, Michael B.	(IL)	1013
Conference testing, resrch & development	ARBEZ, Gilbert J.	(ON)	30
Congressional & legislative research	CARR, Timothy B.	(VA)	186
Congressional research	SEELE, Ronald E.	(DC)	1111
Consulting & research	DANTON, J P.	(CA)	274
Copyright research	MISSAR, Margaret M. . .	(DC)	847
Corporate giving research	KLETZIEN, S D.	(PA)	661
Corporate intelligence research	DETWILER, Susan M. . .	(IN)	296
Corporate legal research databases	MORRIS, Ann	(IL)	866
Corporate research	CALLAHAN, Joan	(MA)	173
	GOETZ, Helen L.	(NY)	443
	KRAMER, Allan F.	(NY)	675
	THOM, Janice E.	(NY)	1235
Corporate research & devlpmnt info systs	BURCSU, James E.	(NC)	158
Current affairs & journalism research	BEAUDET, Normand . . .	(PQ)	70
Current affairs, general research	ROBINSON, Betty J. . . .	(CA)	1043
Curriculum & research skills	PITLUK, Paula K.	(CA)	976
Custom research	MOORHEAD, John D. . .	(IL)	862
Custom research, library & archives	TURNER, Ellis S.	(MD)	1264
Dance research	JEROME, Michael S. . . .	(CA)	599
Data processing research	REIST, Paul A.	(CA)	1022
	SMITH, Lydia K.	(CT)	1157
Database market research	MAYERS, Henry L.	(MI)	789
Database research	LARSON, Donald A.	(CA)	699
	VILLERE, Dawn N.	(CA)	1284
	ALBAIR, Catherine M. . .	(FL)	9
	GIANNINI, Evelyn L. . . .	(IL)	431
	EDER, Sonya	(PQ)	336
	FORRESTER, John H. . .	(ITL)	391
Database research, high schools	WARAKSA, Raymond P.	(CT)	1303
Database researching	AARON, Rina S.	(NY)	1
Database searching, research, reference	BEDOR, Kathleen M. . . .	(MN)	73
Demographic research	MARSCHNER, Robyn J. .	(CO)	773
Dental research	LYNN, Kenneth C.	(MD)	752
Development research	WILLIAMS, Lisa B.	(CA)	1344
Director of pictorial resrch collection	GORDON, Thelma S. . . .	(CT)	452
Directories research	REDEL, Judy A.	(NY)	1014
Discreet research	EGGLESTON, Phyllis A. .	(AK)	339
Documentation & research	LEFFALL, Dolores C. . . .	(DC)	712
Doing connected research	RHEAUME, Irene M. . . .	(MD)	1025
Donor prospect research	ANDERSON, Clifford D. .	(CA)	22
Drug research	SUPEAU, Cynthia	(CT)	1210
Earth sciences reference & research	SORROUGH, Gail L. . . .	(CA)	1169
Ecological research	PRESBY, Richard A. . . .	(CA)	990
Economic & labor research	KIBILDIS, Melba	(MI)	646
Economic research	BRUNER, Robert B.	(CO)	150
Economic research & analysis	COOPER, J P.	(MA)	243
Economics research	MALEK, Stanislaw A. . . .	(PQ)	763
Editing short research topics	MCCRAY, Evelina W. . . .	(LA)	800
Editing, writing, researching	MANNING, Jo A.	(NY)	766
Editorial research & development	SOKOLOFF, Michele . . .	(PA)	1165
Education & psychology research	LEUNG, Terry S.	(CA)	719
Education research	COLLINS, John W.	(MA)	232
	PERKUS, Paul C.	(NY)	959
Educational & historical research	KLEIN, Victor C.	(LA)	659
Educational reference, research	FARRIS, Loretta	(PA)	365
Educational research	JACKSON, Gloria D. . . .	(CA)	587
	STOCKTON, Ken R. . . .	(DC)	1196
	KAYAIAN, Mary S.	(IL)	632
	VAN BUSKIRK, Elisabeth L.	(NJ)	1272

RESEARCH (Cont'd)

Educational research
HITT, Gail D.	(NY)	544

Electric utility research — HORAH, Richard H. (GA) 558
Electronic tax research — SPEYER, Thomas W. (NY) 1174
Electronics & computing research — CRABTREE, Sandra A. (CA) 254
Employee benefits research — GRANDE, Paula G. (NY) 457
Energy & environment research — STANLEY, Eileen H. (LA) 1180
Engineering & medical research — SARAIDARIDIS, Susan B. (MA) 1082
Engineering & science research — SOKOV, Asta M. (PQ) 1166
Engineering research — SHAFER, Leona M. (NJ) 1119
BLAUERT, Mary A. (PA) 105
SMART, Doris M. (WA) 1151
Engineering research, databases — EVANS, M R. (CA) 357
Entertainment research — PLUMB, Carolyn G. (CA) 978
PRUETT, Barbara J. (DC) 996
Environment research — WEISENBURGER, Patricia J. (KS) 1319
Environmental reference & research — JOHNSON, Mary E. (CA) 607
Environmental research — LARASON, Larry (LA) 697
LANK, Dannette H. (WI) 696
Environmental research & info service — FELICETTI, Barbara W. (MA) 370
Environmental research areas — PRESBY, Richard A. (CA) 990
Epidemiologic research databases — HOLMES, John H. (PA) 553
Equity research archival database — MILLS, Andrew G. (MA) 843
Equity research news service — MILLS, Andrew G. (MA) 843
Ethics research — MOLINARI, Joseph G. (NY) 853
Evaluation research — LUND, Patricia A. (WI) 748
Evaluation research, curriculum software — HERB, Elizabeth D. (OH) 530
Evaluation research, information systems — SIEGEL, Elliot R. (MD) 1136
Evaluative & developmental research — LIPETZ, Ben A. (NY) 732
Faculty research support — BRENNAN, Edward P. (MD) 132
Family & local history research — WILLIAMS, Janet L. (OR) 1344
Family research — HORNUNG, Susan D. (WI) 560
Federal & state law research — VARGA, William R. (DC) 1278
Federal, state, & government research — KIRSHBAUM, Priscilla J. (CO) 655
Film & photograph research — GOTTFRIED, Erika D. (NY) 453
Film & television research — MICHAELS, Joan M. (CA) 832
GLADSTONE, Mark A. (NJ) 439
Film programming & research — VOURVOULIAS, Sabrina M. (NY) 1289
Film research — SUMMERS, Robert A. (NJ) 1209
MONTGOMERY, Patrick (NY) 856
DUCLOW, Geradline (PA) 322
Film research, television production — LIMBACHER, James L. (MI) 727
Finance & business information research — SINGER, Susan A. (NJ) 1143
Financial analysis research — HEFFRON, Betsy A. (NY) 520
Financial & business research — THAU, Richard (NJ) 1234
Financial research — SAYRS, Judith A. (WI) 1087
Financial research & modeling — COOPER, J P. (MA) 243
Fine arts research — MILLER, Hester M. (NM) 838
Fine arts researcher — HEHMAN, Jennifer L. (IN) 521
Fire research — JASON, Nora H. (MD) 595
Fire science research — SALY, Alan J. (NY) 1078
Food industry research & development — WILTON, Greg J. (MB) 1353
Food marketing & research — SWANSON, Mary A. (NY) 1213
Food service research — DEPKE, Robert W. (IL) 293
Foreign & international law research — GOLDBERG, Jolande E. (DC) 444
Foreign & international legal research — ARANDA-COODOU, Patricio (DC) 30
Foreign law research — KAVASS, Igor I. (TN) 631
Foreign relations research — QUARTELL, Robert J. (NY) 999
Foundation research — DICK, Ellen A. (IL) 300
KLETZIEN, S D. (PA) 661
Freelance performing arts research — BRAYTON, Roy S. (NY) 130
Freelance research — HEISER, Nancy E. (ME) 523
GRIFFITH, Dorothy A. (PA) 469
Funding research — HERFURTH, Sharon M. (TX) 530
Fundraising & development research — EVERETT, Amy E. (DE) 358
Fundraising for research projects — THOMAS, Evangeline M. (KS) 1236
Genealogical computing & research — O'BRIEN, Doris J. (CT) 914
Genealogical research — LEVIS, Gail A. (IL) 721
WILLSON, Richard E. (IL) 1349
ESALA, Lillian H. (MN) 354
SUELFLOW, August R. (MO) 1206

RESEARCH (Cont'd)

Genealogical research
RUGG, John D.	(OH)	1066

LAMAR, Christine L. (RI) 689
GOODFELLOW, Marjorie E. (PQ) 448
Genealogical research & documentation — PARKER, Mary A. (SC) 942
Genealogical research & reference — CARTER, Janet K. (TX) 189
Genealogy research — MAPP, Erwin E. (FL) 768
FREEMAN, Patricia E. (NM) 401
GRAVLEE, Diane D. (NY) 459
General & legal research — GIANNINI, Evelyn L. (IL) 431
General business & corporate research — POJE, Mary E. (NY) 980
General business research — KAZANJIAN, Donna S. (NY) 632
BELL, Steven J. (PA) 77
General reference & research — WEISS, Paula K. (IL) 1320
General research — GOTTFRIED, Erika D. (NY) 453
HOFFMAN, David M. (NY) 547
Geotechnical & geological research — JEROME, Susanne M. (AZ) 599
Geriatric information & research — BENSING, Karen M. (OH) 83
Glass & ceramics research — DREIFUSS, Richard A. (NY) 319
Government research — MISSAR, Margaret M. (DC) 847
RABER, Steven (NY) 1001
Grants, research & proposal writing — SECKELSON, Linda E. (NY) 1110
Health & safety research — GAMBRELL, Drucilla S. (AL) 416
Health care management research — BELL, Steven J. (PA) 77
Health effects research writing — MUNRO, Nancy B. (TN) 879
Health planning research — FLETCHER, Nancy S. (WI) 384
Health policy research — JENSEN, Joseph E. (MD) 599
Health risk analysis research — MUNRO, Nancy B. (TN) 879
Health science library educ, research — LOVE, Erika (NM) 743
Health services administration research — PLOTSKY, Andrea G. (CA) 978
Health services research — ANDERSON, Marilyn M. (IN) 24
KERN, Donald C. (MA) 643
Helping researchers, Methodist history — ROLLER, Twila J. (NM) 1051
High technology custom research services — JAGIELLOWICZ, Jadzia (ON) 591
High tech research & devlpmnt consulting — HERTHER, Nancy K. (MN) 533
Highway research transportation info — MOBLEY, Arthur B. (DC) 851
Historical & archival research — MCGAUGHRAN, Roberta W. (DC) 805
Historical & evaluation research — DU MONT, Rosemary R. (OH) 325
Historical & genealogical research — HELSLEY, Alexia J. (SC) 525
Historical children's books, research — GILBERT, Ophelia R. (MO) 434
Historical research — CLARK, David L. (CA) 216
JOHNSON, Paul A. (CA) 608
MASON, Ellsworth G. (CO) 781
WOLFE, F M. (CO) 1360
ALDRICH, Michele L. (DC) 11
PINKETT, Harold T. (DC) 974
BOPP, Richard E. (IL) 116
LEVIS, Gail A. (IL) 721
METZLER, Valerie (IL) 829
SNOKE, Elizabeth R. (KS) 1163
KELLS, Laura J. (MD) 637
MCNAMARA, Shelley G. (ME) 816
FRYE, Dorothy T. (MI) 407
SMITH, Michael O. (MI) 1158
SULTANOF, Jeff B. (NJ) 1208
ROCHA, Guy L. (NV) 1045
ROBINSON, Mitchell L. (NY) 1044
BAGBY, Ross F. (OH) 45
RUGG, John D. (OH) 1066
GIMPL, Caroline A. (OR) 437
LAMAR, Christine L. (RI) 689
SILVA, Phyllis C. (RI) 1138
CRIST, Lynda L. (TX) 259
GOLTZ, Eileen A. (ON) 447
CHANDLER, George (ENG) 200
Historical research & archives — HECKMAN, Marlin L. (CA) 520
Historical research & development — JONSON, Laurence F. (IA) 616
Historical research & writing — BROOKS, Jerrold L. (NC) 140
HESS, James W. (NY) 534
MORRISSEY, Charles T. (VT) 869
DIBIASE, Linda P. (WA) 299
Historical research consultation — ESALA, Lillian H. (MN) 354

RESEARCH (Cont'd)

Historical research for archaeologist	STINE, Roy S.	(NC)	1194
Historical research, indexing & writing	DENNIS, Mary R.	(IA)	292
Historical research, report preparation	STINE, Roy S.	(NC)	1194
Historical researching	SNYDER, Theresa	(PA)	1165
Historico-theological research	CAMILLI, E M.	(PA)	175
History of research libraries	BELANGER, Terry	(NY)	76
History research & writing	SHIDELER, John C.	(WA)	1129
Hospitality industry culinary research	JOHNSON, Sheila A.	(NY)	609
Human resources research	BRUNER, Robert B.	(CO)	150
Humanities research	JOY, Patricia L.	(CT)	618
	STIELOW, Frederick J.	(MD)	1194
Humanities research & bibliography	DWOSKIN, Beth M.	(MI)	330
Humanities research, literature	TIBBO, Helen R.	(MD)	1244
Indexer, researcher, bibliographer	BELCHER, Emily M.	(NJ)	76
Indexing research & teaching	WEINBERG, Bella H.	(NY)	1317
Industry research	O'BRIEN, Barbara E.	(IL)	914
	NOBLE, James K.	(NY)	906
Information & productivity research	KOENIG, Michael E.	(NY)	668
Info & research, business & technical	SPINA, Marie C.	(NY)	1175
Information linguistics research	WEINBERG, Bella H.	(NY)	1317
Information media research	SETTANNI, Joseph A.	(NY)	1117
Information research	PECK, Brian T.	(FL)	953
Information retrieval research	COOPER, William S.	(CA)	244
	HUESTIS, Jeffrey C.	(MO)	570
	FOX, Edward A.	(VA)	394
Information science, publishing research	DINGLE, Susan	(PA)	304
Information science research	MARCUS, Richard S.	(MA)	769
	MARSHALL, Joanne G.	(ON)	774
Information support for researchers	JONES, Kendra A.	(TN)	613
Information systems research	SNYDER, Cathrine E.	(TN)	1164
Information systems research & devlpmnt	TONKERY, Thomas D.	(NY)	1250
Inquiry in research project	SENATOR, Rochelle B.	(CT)	1115
Institutional research	STILLMAN, Mary E.	(PA)	1194
Instruction in research methods	TROTTI, John B.	(VA)	1258
Insurance research	FIELD, Connie N.	(IL)	375
Interdisciplinary research	BAUGHMAN, James C.	(MA)	66
Interdisciplinary research & instruction	STONE, Nancy Y.	(MI)	1197
International law research	TRIFFIN, Nicholas	(NY)	1256
	FOX, James R.	(PA)	394
International market research	HANSEN, Kathelen L.	(MN)	497
	SHELTON, Anita L.	(NY)	1126
International marketing research	TAYLOR, Alice J.	(CA)	1226
International trade research	MATTERA, Joseph J.	(NY)	785
Investment research	AVITABILE, Susan L.	(MA)	42
	RUBIN, Ellen R.	(NY)	1064
Iron Range Minnesota research	ESALA, Lillian H.	(MN)	354
Japanese & Korean law research	CHO, Sung Y.	(DC)	209
Journalism reference & research	CATES, Jo A.	(FL)	194
Labor research	MOLINARI, Joseph G.	(NY)	853
Latin America research	FIGUEREDO, Danilo H.	(NY)	376
Latvian bibliography & research	OZOLINS, Karl L.	(MN)	933
Leadership research	WALLS, Francine E.	(WA)	1299
Lrng resrch ctr mgmt & reorganization	MIAH, Abdul J.	(VA)	831
Legal & business research	CAIN, Susan H.	(MA)	171
Legal & general research	DUMAINE, Paul R.	(RI)	325
Legal & non-legal research & reference	BENNIN, Cheryl S.	(NY)	82
Legal database research	CINQUE, Douglas V.	(NY)	214
	ROCKWOOD, Susan M.	(PA)	1046
Legal database researcher	WOODRUFF, Brenda B.	(OH)	1366
Legal legislative research	BRESLIN, Ellen R.	(NY)	133
Legal reference & research	LEVINE, Patricia M.	(AL)	720
	NORBIE, Dorothy E.	(CO)	908
	BARNUM, Deborah C.	(CT)	58
	BROQUE, Suzanne	(CT)	141
	LUBIN, Joan S.	(CT)	745
	MATTHEWSON, David S.	(CT)	786
	HOTCHKISS, Mary A.	(DC)	562
	AUSTIN, John R.	(IL)	40
	NYBERG, Cheryl R.	(IL)	912
	MAZZEI, Peter J.	(NJ)	791
	JACKSON, George R.	(OH)	587
Legal research	ALCORN, Marianne S.	(AZ)	11
	WHITE, Edward H.	(AZ)	1330
	BERRING, Robert C.	(CA)	90
	BIRNIE, Elizabeth B.	(CA)	98
	BRAZIL, Lynne E.	(CA)	130

RESEARCH (Cont'd)

Legal research

	GINSBURG, Helen W.	(CA)	438
	GRIGST, Denise J.	(CA)	470
	HENKE, Dan	(CA)	528
	HOLLINGSWORTH, Dena M.	(CA)	552
	HUSTON, Esther L.	(CA)	578
	LEWIS, Alfred J.	(CA)	722
	LEWIS, Cookie A.	(CA)	722
	MACLEOD, June F.	(CA)	757
	OPPEDAL, Teresa A.	(CA)	925
	ROBERT, Berring C.	(CA)	1039
	RODICH, Lorraine E.	(CA)	1047
	ROLLINS, James H.	(CA)	1051
	RUNYON, Judith A.	(CA)	1067
	SMITH, Catherine M.	(CA)	1153
	SMITH, Susan A.	(CA)	1161
	STROMME, Gary L.	(CA)	1203
	TAYLOR, Susan E.	(CA)	1228
	TRIVISON, Margaret A.	(CA)	1257
	WEBB, Gayle E.	(CA)	1313
	WINSON, Gail I.	(CA)	1355
	CALVERT, Lois M.	(CO)	174
	COCO, Al	(CO)	226
	BURKE, Jane D.	(CT)	160
	COHEN, Morris L.	(CT)	228
	MARIANI, Carolyn A.	(CT)	770
	DURAKO, Frances G.	(DC)	328
	GEHRINGER, Susanne E.	(DC)	425
	MCDERMOTT, Patricia M.	(DC)	802
	NEVIN, Barbara B.	(DC)	898
	NORRIS, Loretta W.	(DC)	909
	PACIFICI, Sabrina I.	(DC)	933
	STOCKTON, Sue T.	(DC)	1196
	THOMPSON, Johanna W.	(DC)	1240
	WOLFE, Susan J.	(DC)	1361
	EFRON, Muriel C.	(FL)	338
	OVERSTREET, Allen J.	(FL)	931
	TAYLOR, Betty W.	(FL)	1226
	WOLFE, Bardie C.	(FL)	1360
	BAUSCH, Donna K.	(GA)	67
	COOPER, Glenn	(GA)	243
	GROOVER, Marion D.	(GA)	472
	GUERIN, Roberta T.	(GA)	476
	WEINGARTH, Darlene	(GU)	1318
	REED, Carol R.	(HI)	1014
	DONAHUE, Karin V.	(IL)	310
	DOYLE, Francis R.	(IL)	317
	FREY, Roxanne C.	(IL)	403
	HUTCHINS, Richard G.	(IL)	579
	MARTIN, Bennie E.	(IL)	775
	PERSYN, Mary G.	(IN)	961
	CONNOR, Lynn S.	(KY)	238
	GILMER, Wesley	(KY)	437
	DULEY, Kay E.	(LA)	324
	FISHER, Collette J.	(LA)	380
	DUCKETT, Joan	(MA)	322
	HAYES, Alison M.	(MA)	515
	LAMBERT, Lyn D.	(MA)	690
	MCLELLAN, Mary T.	(MA)	814
	CAMILLO, Janet H.	(MD)	175
	BONGE, Barbara M.	(MI)	114
	KONDAK, Ann	(MI)	670
	TURNER, Ann S.	(MN)	1264
	GIBSON, Helen R.	(MO)	432
	HUNT, Lori A.	(MO)	575
	KLEBBA, Lisa A.	(MO)	658
	MCKENZIE, Elizabeth M.	(MO)	811
	SCHELL, Rosalie F.	(MO)	1091
	STRAUSE, Robert C.	(MO)	1200
	TEANEY, Carol R.	(MO)	1229
	WHITE, Cheryl L.	(MO)	1330
	WEST, Carol C.	(MS)	1326
	GASAWAY, Laura N.	(NC)	421
	HANNUM-MCPHERSON, Melissa A.	(NC)	497
	MURPHY, Malinda M.	(NC)	881
	WEZELMAN, Joy L.	(ND)	1328
	LOMAX, Anne M.	(NE)	738

RESEARCH (Cont'd)

Legal research

ERBE, Evalina S. ...... (NJ) 352
GORDON, Kaye B. ..... (NJ) 451
BEJNAR, Thaddeus P. . . (NM) 75
MCGOEY, Richard P. . . . (NM) 807
MORGAN, James E. . . . (NV) 864
BERNSTEIN, Mark P. . . . (NY) 89
CARTAFALSA, Joan C. . (NY) 188
CHICCO, Giuliano ..... (NY) 208
COLE, Charles D. ...... (NY) 230
CURCI, Lucy .... (NY) 265
DAVENPORT, Margaret J. (NY) 275
DIGIOVANNA, Josephine
A. .... (NY) 303
GRECH, Anthony P. ..... (NY) 461
HAYWARD, Diane J. . . . (NY) 517
KUPERMAN, Aaron W. . (NY) 684
LASKOWITZ, Roberta G. (NY) 700
LILLY, Elise M. .... (NY) 727
LOCKE, William G. ..... (NY) 736
MANN, Amy S. .... (NY) 765
NEWMAN, Marie S. ..... (NY) 899
O'GRADY, Jean P. ..... (NY) 918
PAGEL, Scott B. .... (NY) 934
PINSLEY, Lauren J. ..... (NY) 975
RAUM, Tamar .... (NY) 1010
VAJDA, Carolyn M. ..... (NY) 1271
CHRISTY, Patricia A. .... (OH) 212
GILL, Judith L. .... (OH) 435
HOLOCH, S A. .... (OH) 553
LEONARD, James ..... (OH) 716
MCFARLAND, Anne S. .. (OH) 804
ORLANDO, Jacqueline M. (OH) 926
SPOHR, Cynthia L. ..... (OH) 1175
WERNERSBACH,
Geraldine S. .... (OH) 1325
CORNEIL, Charlotte E. . . (OK) 246
DUCEY, Richard E. ..... (OK) 322
BAUER, Marilyn A. ..... (OR) 65
DAVID, Kay O. .... (OR) 276
ARMSTRONG, Nancy A. (PA) 32
BEYER, Robyn L. ...... (PA) 93
HORVATH, Patricia M. . . (PA) 561
REGUEIRO, Judith E. . . (PA) 1017
SILVERMAN, Marc B. . . (PA) 1138
SULZER, John H. ...... (PA) 1209
SABATER-SOLA, Rigel . (PR) 1072
LABEDZ, Elizabeth K. .... (RI) 686
BARKAN, Steven M. .... (TX) 56
BLACK, Elizabeth A. .... (TX) 101
CHAMPION, Walter T. . . (TX) 198
CORBIN, John .... (TX) 245
GARDNER, Linda ...... (TX) 418
GILBERT, Barry .... (TX) 433
HAMBLETON, James E. . . (TX) 490
HOUSTON, Barbara B. . . (TX) 563
MAGNER, Mary F. ..... (TX) 759
OLM, Jane G. .... (TX) 921
PARKER, David F. ..... (TX) 941
TRANFAGLIA, Twyla L. . . (TX) 1254
CALHOUN, Clayne M. .. (VA) 172
SCHAEFER, Mary E. ... (VA) 1089
TOSIANO, Barbara A. .. (VA) 1252
ABAZARNIA, Diane B. . . (VT) 1
LAWSON, Annetta ..... (WA) 705
PERLSON, Beverly J. ... (WI) 959
ESKRIDGE, Virginia C. .. (WV) 354
DEYOUNG, Marie ..... (NS) 298
HEARDER-MOAN, Wendy
P. .... (ON) 518
ARAJ, Houda .... (PQ) 30
TANGUAY, Guy .... (PQ) 1222
SAKAMOTO, Hiroshi ... (JAP) 1076
RUNGSANG, Rebecca J. (THA) 1067

Legal research & bibliography
SCHANCK, Peter C. ... (KS) 1090
Legal research & compliance
KNARZER, Arlene ..... (IL) 663
Legal research & database searching
ELAM, Joice B. .... (GA) 341
Legal research & databases
HEINEN, Margaret A. ... (MI) 522
EDMONDS, Edmund P. . (VA) 336

Legal research & material
Legal research & reference
FOWLES, Alison C. .... (PQ) 394
MAYERS, Karen A. .... (CA) 789
VEGA, Carolyn L. ...... (CA) 1281
HUGHES, John M. ..... (CT) 571
NEWTON, Stephanne K. (DC) 900
EICHER, Thomas E. .... (IA) 339
SHAPIRO, Fred R. ..... (NY) 1121
TRIFFIN, Nicholas ..... (NY) 1256
SUHRE, Carol A. ...... (OH) 1207
PARTIN, Gail A. .... (PA) 945
BULERIN-LUGO, Josefina (PR) 156

Legal research & resources management
DEMPSEY, Pamela M. . . (NM) 291
Legal research & teaching
PIERCE, Ann E. .... (ME) 971
Legal research & writing
BRIDGMAN, David L. . . . (CA) 135
KRIKORIAN, Rosanne . . (CA) 678
EDWARDS, John D. .... (IA) 337
POINTON, Louis R. ..... (IL) 980
COCHRAN, J W. ...... (MS) 225
COGGINS, Timothy L. . . (NC) 227
GIANNATTASI, Gerard E. (NY) 430
HANLEY, Thomas L. ... (OH) 496
Legal research & writing teaching
MURRAY, James M. .... (WA) 882
Legal research assistance
GERLOTT, Eleanor L. .... (PA) 429
Legal research, bibliography
DUNCAN, Rebecca .... (CA) 325
Legal research curriculum
COYLE, Christopher B. . . (OH) 253
Legal research in international law
KLECKNER, Simone M. . (NY) 658
Legal research instruction
CASTETTER, Karla M. . . (CA) 194
STREIKER, Susan L. .... (CA) 1201
BRENNAN, Edward P. . . (MD) 132
BAUM, Marsha L. ...... (MN) 66
LEITER, Richard A. ..... (NE) 714
KENNEDY, Bruce M. ... (NY) 640
KOSTER, Gregory E. ... (NY) 673
ZUBROW, Marcia L. ... (NY) 1391
Legal research, LEXIS
PATTELA, Rao R. ..... (PA) 947
Legal research reference
REYNOLDS, Diane C. . . (CA) 1025
Legal research, reference & writing
KISSANE, Mary K. ..... (MO) 656
Legal research reference online manual
VON PFEIL, Helena P. . . (DC) 1288
Legal research retrieval systems
EVERLOVE, Nora J. ..... (FL) 359
Legal research teaching
PREBLE, Leverett L. ..... (DC) 990
Legal research training
SHEAR, Joan A. ...... (MA) 1124
Legal research training & development
COYLE, Christopher B. . . (OH) 253
GORDON, Kaye B. ...... (NJ) 451
Legislative history research
GRAY, Kevin P. .... (NY) 460
Legislative reference & research
LATEGOLO, Meldie A. . . (DC) 701
Legislative research
MILLER, William S. . . . (DC) 843
OAKS, Robert K. ...... (DC) 913
KELLERSTRASS, Amy L. (IL) 636
LARISON, Brenda ..... (IL) 697
MCLELLAN, Mary T. . . . (MA) 814
GORDON, Kaye B. ...... (NJ) 451
CAHN, Mary Z. .... (NY) 171
CHENICK, Michael J. . . . (RI) 206
GEISAR, Barbara J. ..... (WI) 425
DEYOUNG, Marie ..... (NS) 298

Library & information science research
PRABHA, Chandra G. . . (OH) 989
BOWERS, Paul A. ..... (PA) 120
ELLIOTT, Pirkko E. ..... (ENG) 344
Library development, research, grants
COLLARD, R M. ...... (CO) 232
Library evaluation & research
MULLINER, Kent ...... (OH) 878
Library operations research
WYLLYS, Ronald E. ... (I X) 1375
Library research
GRENIER, Myra T. ..... (CA) 467
PIERCE, Patricia J. ..... (CA) 971
LANCE, Keith C. ...... (CO) 692
ZICH, Robert G. ...... (DC) 1388
SCOFIELD, James S. . . . (FL) 1106
ATKINS, Stephen E. .... (IL) 38
KELLY, Raymond T. ..... (IL) 638
ALBRIGHT, John B. .... (MD) 10
RICE, Rosamond H. .... (MD) 1027
BROWN, Ina A. .... (NJ) 144
STEVENS, Sharon G. ... (NJ) 1191
BUTTLAR, Lois J. ...... (OH) 167
MCDONALD, Joseph A. . (PA) 802
WOLF, Richard E. ...... (VA) 1360

RESEARCH (Cont'd)

Library research

	ZWEIZIG, Douglas L. . . .	(WI)	1392
	HOPKINS, Richard L. . . .	(BC)	558
	MOLLER, Hans	(PQ)	853
	ONONOGBO, Raphael U.	(NGR)	924
Library research & demonstration	STEVENS, Frank A.	(DC)	1190
Library research & fundraising	MOLLER, Hans	(PQ)	853
Library research & planning	ALBRITTON, Rosie L. . . .	(MO)	10
Library research & publishing	WOOD, Richard J.	(SC)	1365
Library research in ancient history	SEAVER, James E.	(KS)	1110
Library research in Jewish history	SEAVER, James E.	(KS)	1110
Library research in medieval history	SEAVER, James E.	(KS)	1110
Library research instruction	LODER, Michael W.	(PA)	736
Library research methods	SMITH, Nathan M.	(UT)	1159
	CHANG, Henry C.	(VI)	200
Library research service	SCHALIT, Michael	(CA)	1089
Library research skills instruction	ROSENBERG, Harlene Z.	(NJ)	1056
Library research, statistical method	HITT, Charles J.	(MN)	544
Library research strategies instruction	KUNSELMAN, Joan D. . .	(CA)	684
Library science researcher	NITECKI, Joseph Z.	(NY)	905
Library skills & research education	YOUNG, Marjie D.	(TX)	1382
Library system, reference & research	ROTHENBERG, Mark H.	(NY)	1060
Library systems research	POWELL, James R.	(MI)	988
Library systems, research & publications	MWALIMU, Charles	(DC)	884
Library trend research	LAGIES, Meinhart J.	(CA)	688
Life & health insurance research	HILL, Judith L.	(PA)	540
Limited basic research	DUNN, Susan M.	(IA)	327
Literary research	HO, Paul J.	(FL)	545
Literary research consultation	MASON, Michael L.	(NJ)	781
Literature research	CONRAD, Celia B.	(CT)	238
Literature searching & research	SPARK, Catherine L. . . .	(ON)	1171
Local area network research	PFUDERER, Helen A. . . .	(TN)	966
Local history research	MATTIS, George E.	(VA)	786
Local history research projects	WOLFE, Barbara M.	(NY)	1360
Long-term corporate research	SOSTACK, Maura	(NY)	1169
Management chemical information research	STOBAUGH, Robert E. . .	(OH)	1195
Management, consulting & research	RUDD, Janet K.	(CA)	1065
Mgmt of independent research libraries	MCCORISON, Marcus A.	(MA)	798
Management of medical & research data	COLLINS, Kenneth A. . .	(MD)	233
Management of research activity	RUSSELL, John T.	(DC)	1069
Managing reference & research studies	BRODERICK, John C. . .	(DC)	138
Managing research libraries	MILES, Donald D.	(PA)	834
Manual library research	SPEARMAN, Marie A. . .	(WA)	1172
Manuscripts & rare books literary resrch	REIMAN, Donald H. . . .	(NY)	1020
Manuscripts, archives resrchr guidance	BOOTHE, Nancy L.	(TX)	116
Marine affairs, research & reference	ETCHINGHAM, John B. . .	(RI)	355
Market & industry research	LANDRY, Ronald	(IL)	694
Market & marketing research	OLSEN, Stephen	(MN)	922
Market planning, segmentation, research	HERRICK, Carol L.	(OH)	532
Market research	EVANS, Deborah L.	(CA)	356
	WARNOCK, Patric F. . . .	(CA)	1305
	BROCK, Laurie N.	(CO)	138
	HALL, Brian H.	(CO)	487
	WHITE, Suellen S.	(CO)	1332
	STAHL, D G.	(GA)	1178
	KOVITZ, Nancy R.	(IL)	674
	DELTANO, Pauline T. . . .	(MA)	290
	GEER, Elizabeth F.	(MA)	425
	ISAACS, Cynthia W. . . .	(MA)	584
	SAUNDERS, Leslie E. . .	(MA)	1084
	FRYSER, Benjamin S. . .	(MD)	407
	KORBER, Nancy	(NH)	671
	FRIHART, Anne R.	(NJ)	404
	PAVELY, Richard W. . . .	(NJ)	950
	RILEY, Robert H.	(NJ)	1034
	GOETZ, Helen L.	(NY)	443
	GRETES, Frances C. . . .	(NY)	467
	HALL, Alix M.	(NY)	486
	KRAMER, Allan F.	(NY)	675
	GROSVENOR, Philip G. .	(OH)	473
	SHAPLEY, Ellen M.	(TX)	1122

RESEARCH (Cont'd)

Market research

	PETRUGA, Patricia L. . . .	(ON)	965
Market research & analysis	ROE, Georgeanne T. . . .	(MA)	1048
Market research & planning	PERRON, Michelle M. . .	(NH)	960
Market research & product	CUTLER, Judith	(PA)	268
Market research, business intelligence	MIMNAUGH, Ellen N. . . .	(OH)	845
Market research consulting	STILLMAN, Stanley W. .	(NY)	1194
Market research databases	UMFLEET, Ruth A.	(TX)	1268
Market research for the info industry	SOVNER-RIBBLER, Judith	(MA)	1170
Market research, online & manual	MAXWELL, Christine Y. .	(CA)	788
Market research, planning & development	LINDAHL, Ann L.	(CA)	728
Market research, product development	LEVITAN, Karen B.	(MD)	721
Market research reports	NAPOLITANO, Wanda M.	(NY)	887
	SULLIVAN, Daniel M. . . .	(NY)	1207
	MASON-WARD, Lesley .	(ON)	781
Marketing & marketing research	FRIEND, Gary I.	(DC)	404
	AHERN, Camille P.	(NH)	8
Marketing research	MARKS, Larry	(CA)	771
	GASKINS, Stephen D. . .	(GA)	421
	CHAPMAN, Ruby M. . . .	(IL)	202
	KILBERG, Jacqueline L. .	(NY)	648
	WASERSTEIN, Gina S. .	(PA)	1307
	BALDWIN, Mark F.	(RI)	52
	FLESHMAN, Nancy A. . .	(TX)	384
Marketing research & analysis	EVANS, Shirley A.	(OH)	358
Marketing research resources management	SEULOWITZ, Lois	(NY)	1117
Media, audiovisual market research	HOPE, Thomas W.	(NY)	557
Media research of current events	BROWN, Phyllis J.	(TN)	147
Medical & legal research	BEDARD, Evelyn M. . . .	(TX)	73
Medical information & research	SMITH, Sharon	(CSR)	1160
Medical information research	WHITESIDE, Lee A.	(FL)	1333
Medical psychology information research	BLADEN, Marguerite . . .	(CA)	102
Medical reference & research	KIEFER, Rosemary M. . .	(FL)	647
	SNYDER, Lisa A.	(MAL)	1165
Medical research	HEMINGWAY, Beverly L.	(CA)	525
	SNELL, Charles E.	(CA)	1163
	ROYSTER, Jane G.	(KY)	1063
	HUMPHRIES, Anne W. .	(MD)	574
	TORDOFF, Brian G.	(MO)	1251
	KIRSCH, Anne S.	(NY)	655
	MIYAUCHI, Phyllis J. . . .	(NY)	850
	HARMALA, Amy A.	(WA)	502
	LIBRO, Teresa M.	(WI)	725
	HEUER, Jane T.	(WY)	535
Medico-legal research	BENNETT, Laura B.	(IL)	82
Mental health research	EVANS, Josephine K. . . .	(FL)	357
Meteorological research	MEACHAM, Mary	(OK)	819
Methods of literary research	ABBOTT, Craig S.	(IL)	1
Microcomputer applications research	STRAHAN, Michael F. . .	(ND)	1199
Microfilming data for resrch purposes	FROST, Debra R.	(CO)	406
Mining & geology research	STRACHAN, Pamela H. .	(ON)	1199
Minority services researching	ALLEN, Christina Y.	(WI)	14
Motion picture & television research	BRADY, Eileen E.	(WA)	126
Motion picture production research	PLUMB, Carolyn G.	(CA)	978
Motion picture research	NAZARIAN, Anahid	(CA)	890
Music & folklore research	MCCULLOH, Judith M. . .	(IL)	801
Music reference & research	PERRY-BOWDER, Libbie E.	(ME)	961
	BOZIWICK, George E. . .	(NY)	124
Music research	COLLINS, Richard H. . . .	(CA)	233
	SUMMERS, Robert A. . .	(NJ)	1209
	CLAYPOOL, Richard D. .	(NY)	220
	GLASFORD, G R.	(NY)	440
	LYNCH, Richard C.	(NY)	752
	WALL, Richard L.	(NY)	1297
Music research, writing, editing	GUSHEE, Marion S.	(IL)	478
Music theatre research	GARDNER, Sue A.	(NJ)	418
Musical theatre research	YOUNKIN, C G.	(TX)	1383
Musicological research & writing	CLOSE, Elizabeth G. . . .	(UT)	223
Mythology bibliography & research	SHAW, Renata V.	(DC)	1123
Native Americans research	MOLINARI, Joseph G. . .	(NY)	853
Natural resources research	LEVINSON, Debra J. . . .	(NY)	721
New technologies research	KIBBEE, Sally	(CA)	646
New York legal research	FRIEDMAN, Judy B.	(NY)	404
News media research			
News research			

RESEARCH (Cont'd)

Newspaper research	ALLCORN, Mary E.	(MO)	14
	HARRIS, Belinda J.	(VA)	504
Non-legal research	DONAHUE, Karin V.	(IL)	310
Non-print research	LYNESS, Ann L.	(PA)	752
Northern & native people's research	FINN, Julia P.	(PQ)	378
Nursing education & research	SOME, Barbara K.	(NJ)	1166
Nursing literature research	AUFIERO, Joan I.	(BC)	39
Nursing research	SHIEH, Monica W.	(MO)	1129
	BRUCE, Marianne E.	(AB)	149
Nursing research & education	KELLEY, John F.	(PA)	636
Online database research	NIXON, Judith A.	(MD)	906
Online information research	ROYAL, Linda G.	(VA)	1063
Online legal research	SKRUKRUD, Nora L.	(CA)	1147
	CALVERT, Lois M.	(CO)	174
	ROSS, Margery M.	(DC)	1058
Online legal research services	WEBSTER, Deborah K.	(NC)	1314
Online research	CASTER, Suzanne	(CA)	194
	GIFFORD, Becky J.	(CA)	433
	WILLIAMS, Lisa B.	(CA)	1344
	KAHN, Victoria	(DC)	622
	PAVEK, C C.	(DC)	950
	JACOBSON, William R.	(IL)	590
	MARTIN, Jody S.	(IN)	776
	MACLEOD, Valerie R.	(KY)	757
	MAGUIRE, Linda H.	(MA)	760
	PERECMAN, Carol J.	(MI)	958
	AUSTIN, Fay A.	(NJ)	40
	FARAONE, Maria B.	(NY)	363
	SHAPIRO, Barbara G.	(NY)	1121
	SOROBAY, Roman T.	(NY)	1169
	MEHR, Joseph O.	(RI)	821
	PARTRIDGE, Cathleen F.	(UT)	945
	MCINTOSH, Julia E.	(PQ)	809
Online research & reference	YOUNG, Sandra C.	(KY)	1383
Online research training	WEEKS, Olivia L.	(NC)	1315
Online systems research	PITCHON, Cindy A.	(PA)	976
Online thesauri, dictionary research	LIBBEY, Miles A.	(NJ)	725
Operations research	KRAFT, Donald H.	(LA)	674
Ophthalmology research	MOUNT, Albertina F.	(NY)	873
Orientation & research strategy	BIANCHINO, Cecelia	(IN)	94
Orthodontic research	GILTINAN, Celia E.	(MO)	437
Patent & trademark research	JACOBSON, William R.	(IL)	590
Patent research	SULZER, John H.	(PA)	1209
	MEREK, Charles J.	(VA)	825
Patent research & database	ENNIS, Mary J.	(OH)	350
Peace research & education	KOCSIS, Jeanne	(MA)	667
Performing arts reference, research	DEE, Camille C.	(NY)	286
Performing arts research	MILLER, Hester M.	(NM)	838
Pharmaceutical research info systems	PEETERS, Marc D.	(BEL)	954
Philanthropy research	GONZALEZ, Suzanna S.	(CT)	448
Philological research & writing	HUMEZ, Nicholas D.	(ME)	573
Phonodisc historical research	GRENDYSA, Peter A.	(WI)	467
Photo research & indexing	FRANKLIN, Alyce B.	(KY)	397
Photographic archives & research	SPINA, Marie C.	(NY)	1175
Piano research & cataloging	YRIGOYEN, Robert P.	(NJ)	1384
Picture research	DEANE, Roxanna	(DC)	284
	ELTZROTH, Elsbeth L.	(GA)	346
Picture researcher	TODD, Rose A.	(PQ)	1248
Planning & research	JONES, Charlotte W.	(WA)	611
Political & business research	KAPNICK, Laura B.	(NY)	626
Political research & reference	TAYLOR, Loretta C.	(ON)	1227
Practice development research	EMERSON, Beth A.	(TX)	347
Preservation of research materials	ROGERS, Rutherford D.	(CT)	1050
Primary & secondary research	STARESINA, Lois J.	(MI)	1181
	MILGRIM, Martin S.	(NJ)	835
Private library research	MAZEFSKY, Gertrude T.	(PA)	791
Product safety & liability research	MOUZON, Margaret W.	(MI)	874
Professional research	MARSHALL, Deborah M.	(IL)	774
Proprietary research	GAZZOLA, Kenneth E.	(DC)	424
Providing research & government info	CASO, Gasper	(MA)	193
Psychoanalytic research	ROSS, David J.	(NY)	1058
Public administration research	ETTER, Constance L.	(IL)	355
Public affairs research	GJELTEN, Daniel R.	(MN)	439
Public finance research	MARSHALL, Marion B.	(DC)	774
Public historical research	CHRISTENSEN, Erin S.	(CO)	211
Public services, research & reference	FRENCH, Thomas R.	(OH)	402
Publishing research	LAGIES, Meinhart J.	(CA)	688
Purchasing research materials	KELLER, Dorothy B.	(CA)	635
Qualitative research methods	MELLON, Constance A.	(NC)	822

RESEARCH (Cont'd)

Quilt research & documentation, indexing	PARKER, Mary A.	(SC)	942
Rare book research	MONDLIN, Marvin	(NY)	854
Reading habits research	LANGERMAN, Shoshana P.	(ISR)	695
Real estate research	ROSENBERGER, Constance G.	(PA)	1056
Real-time fixed income research	MILLS, Andrew G.	(MA)	843
Recorded sound research & training	GAUNT, Sandra L.	(OH)	423
Records research, college history	NELSON, Robert J.	(NY)	895
Records retention research	BOWKER, Scott W.	(NY)	121
Reference & information research	THOMPSON, Myra D.	(OH)	1240
Reference & legal research	TATELMAN, Susan D.	(MA)	1225
	HAASE, Gretchen E.	(MN)	480
Reference & research	LASETER, Ernest P.	(AL)	700
	AARON, Kathleen F.	(CA)	1
	COLLINS, Judith A.	(CA)	232
	GRANGER, Dorothy J.	(CA)	457
	HOTZ, Sharon M.	(CA)	562
	LENSCHAU, Jane A.	(CA)	715
	MAH, Jeffery	(CA)	760
	MASTERS, Robin J.	(CA)	782
	MULLER, Malinda S.	(CA)	877
	SCHMIDT, Alesandra M.	(CT)	1095
	GREENE, Danielle L.	(DC)	463
	MCCOY-LARSON, Sandra	(DC)	799
	SMITH, Mary P.	(DC)	1158
	WRIGHT, Arthuree M.	(DC)	1370
	AHLIN, Nancy	(FL)	8
	BOGGUS, Tamara K.	(FL)	110
	DALLET, Jane L.	(FL)	270
	HARTON, Pamela J.	(FL)	508
	SCHWABEL, Lexie W.	(FL)	1104
	UCHIDA, Deborah K.	(HI)	1267
	ANTON, Tess	(IL)	29
	LASHER, Esther L.	(IN)	700
	TEITELBAUM, Gene W.	(KY)	1230
	LANDRY, Denise C.	(LA)	693
	COPPOLA, H P.	(MA)	245
	FOX, Susan	(MA)	395
	FRYDRYK, Teresa E.	(MA)	407
	GRIGORIS, Lygia	(MA)	470
	MEAGHER, Janet H.	(MA)	819
	ZUGBY, Lillian C.	(MD)	1391
	PARTHUM, John W.	(MI)	945
	DOLAN, Mary M.	(MN)	309
	RAFTER, Susan	(MN)	1003
	FERRIGNO, Helen F.	(NH)	373
	DUDLEY, Debbra C.	(NJ)	323
	MACKINTOSH, Pamela J.	(NJ)	757
	MANY, Florence L.	(NJ)	767
	CAROLLO, Michael T.	(NV)	184
	CAMPBELL, Francis D.	(NY)	176
	CLOWE, Isabel B.	(NY)	223
	EDWARDS, Harriet M.	(NY)	337
	GREENBERG, Linda	(NY)	463
	KASTEN, Seth E.	(NY)	629
	PETERS, Jean R.	(NY)	962
	PINEDA, Conchita J.	(NY)	974
	RODGERS, Judith P.	(OH)	1047
	SULLIVAN, Frances L.	(OH)	1207
	FELDMAN, Marianne L.	(OR)	369
	BENGALI, Zarin P.	(PA)	80
	KREITZBURG, Marilyn J.	(PA)	677
	MCCOY, Gail	(SC)	799
	RASCHE, Richard R.	(TX)	1008
	KIESSLING, Mary S.	(UT)	647
	LIN, John T.	(VA)	727
	COHEN, Jane L.	(WA)	228
	HUGHES, Dorothy S.	(WA)	571
	STEWART, Jane	(WA)	1192
	MARCUS, Terry C.	(WI)	769
	FRASER, Gail L.	(AB)	399
	HARDY, Kenneth J.	(AB)	501
	BOWEN, Tom G.	(ON)	120
	CHIU, Lily F.	(ON)	209
	OZAKI, Hiroko	(ON)	932
	THIVIERGE, Lynda M.	(PQ)	1235
Reference & research assistance	GURAYA, Harinder	(NS)	478

RESEARCH (Cont'd)

Reference & research databases   JONES, Stephanie R. . . . (LA) 615
Reference & research in management   CHOUDHURY, Lori B. . . (CA) 211
Reference & research information   MCCARTNEY, Margaret
M. . . . . (NY) 794
Reference & research materials   TUDOR, Dean F. . . . . . (ON) 1262
Reference & research newspaper
   publshg   EGERTSON, Yvonne L. . (VA) 339
Reference & research services   HURLBERT, Irene W. . . . (CA) 577
PRITCHARD, Sarah M. . (DC) 994
ADAMOWICZ, Joanne C. (MA) 4
KING, Trina E. . . . . (NY) 652
FREEMAN, Michael S. . (PA) 401
BARRUS, Phyl . . . . (TX) 60
Reference book design & research   KLINE, Victoria E. . . . . . (CA) 661
Reference, research   WYBORNEY, Charles E. (CA) 1374
RAINWATER, Barbara C. (CO) 1004
RAQUET, Jacqueline R. . (GA) 1008
THOMPSON, Barbara F. (NC) 1239
LEE, Judy A. . . . . (NY) 710
MCKILLIP, Rita J. . . . . . (WI) 811
Reference, research & bibliography   DICKSON, Katherine M. . (MD) 301
Reference research assistance   INGLE, Bernita W. . . . . . (GA) 582
Reference research services   COHEN, Ann E. . . . . . . (NY) 227
Regulatory research   MALEK, Stanislaw A. . . (PQ) 763
Religion research tools/methodology   BOISCLAIR, Regina A. . . (PA) 111
Research   SCALES, Diann R. . . . . . (AL) 1087
ANDREW, Karen L. . . . (CA) 26
BENNETT, Celestine C. . (CA) 81
BOWMAN, Frances A. . . (CA) 121
CANTER, Judy A. . . . . . (CA) 179
DEMENT, Alice R. . . . . (CA) 291
GARDISER, Kathleen E. . (CA) 417
KIRESEN, Evelyn M. . . (CA) 654
LAWRENCE, Gary S. . . (CA) 704
LOVE, Sandra R. . . . . . (CA) 743
MUSICK, Nancy W. . . . (CA) 883
PRELINGER, Polly . . . . (CA) 990
RINGWALT, Arthur . . . . (CA) 1035
ROOSHAN, Gertrude I. . (CA) 1053
SCHLACHTER, Gail A. . (CA) 1093
SHEA, Ann W. . . . . (CA) 1124
SHOUSE, Richard . . . . (CA) 1133
STOCKS, Lee P. . . . . . . (CA) 1195
AMAN, Ann L. . . . . (CO) 19
BASA, Eniko M. . . . . . . (DC) 62
FALK, Diane M. . . . . . . (DC) 362
JENSEN, Doris J. . . . . . (DC) 598
JONES, Elin D. . . . . (DC) 612
MANNING, Martin J. . . . (DC) 766
MEADOWS, Beth W. . . . (DC) 819
ROBERTS, Lesley A. . . . (DC) 1040
WEAVER, Thomas M. . . (DC) 1312
YOUNG, Christina C. . . . (DC) 1381
COPELAND, Mildred A. . (FL) 244
DONOVAN, Elizabeth L. . (FL) 312
WEISS, Susan . . . . (FL) 1320
HUGHES, Glenda J. . . . (GA) 571
LAWLESS, Dorothy A. . . (GA) 704
MARTIN, Clarece . . . . . (GA) 775
MATHER, Mildred E. . . . (IA) 783
VERHOFF, Patricia A. . . (ID) 1282
ALPERIN, Goldie G. . . . (IL) 17
BURBANK, Richard D. . . (IL) 158
DICK, Ellen A. . . . . (IL) 300
ESTABROOK, Leigh S. . (IL) 355
GLANZ, Lenore M. . . . . (IL) 439
GOLDHOR, Herbert . . . . (IL) 445
GUINEE, Andrea M. . . . (IL) 476
LINDVALL, Robert J. . . . (IL) 730
NIELSEN, Brian . . . . (IL) 903
OSBORN, Walter . . . . . . (IL) 927
BARRISH, Alan S. . . . . . (KY) 60
BUSAM, Emma C. . . . . . (KY) 164
FRENCH, Robert B. . . . . (KY) 402
GERICKE, Paul W. . . . . . (LA) 428
JACKSON, Audrey N. . . (LA) 586
BARNHART, Arlene C. . . (MA) 58
COPPOLA, Peter A. . . . (MA) 245
KOVED, Ruth B. . . . . . . (MA) 674

RESEARCH (Cont'd)

Research
PELLINI, Nancy M. . . . . . (MA) 955
PERRY, Guest . . . . (MA) 960
PREVE, Roberta J. . . . . . (MA) 992
SARAVIS, Judith A. . . . . (MA) 1082
SHERER, Elaine R. . . . . (MA) 1127
WOODARD, Paul E. . . . (MA) 1366
CANTELON, Philip L. . . . (MD) 179
DAHLEN, Roger W. . . . . (MD) 269
SHAPIRO, Burton J. . . . . (MD) 1121
BALOK, Becki . . . . (MI) 53
BENSON, Peggy . . . . . . (MI) 83
CARLEN, Claudia . . . . . (MI) 181
CONWAY, Paul L. . . . . . (MI) 239
COREY, Marjorie . . . . . . (MI) 246
GAMACHE, Kathleen A. . (MI) 416
THOMAS, Laverne J. . . . (MI) 1237
MCDIARMID, Errett W. . . (MN) 802
MIRANDA, Esmeralda C. (MN) 847
CRAWFORD, Susan Y. . (MO) 257
HOWERTON, Betty J. . . (MO) 565
SHIPLEY, Anne C. . . . . (MO) 1131
FURST, Joyce P. . . . . . . (NC) 410
HAUPERT, Thomas J. . . (NC) 512
HEROLD, Virginia L. . . . (NC) 532
MORAN, Barbara B. . . . . (NC) 862
WEEKS, Olivia L. . . . . . . (NC) 1315
CUNNIFFE, Charlene M. . (NH) 265
THOMPSON, Debra J. . . (NH) 1239
KARETZKY, Stephen . . . (NJ) 627
KOONTZ, John . . . . (NJ) 671
SCHRIMPE, Janice E. . . (NJ) 1100
CLARK, Camille S. . . . . (NV) 216
ARMSTRONG, Joanne D. (NY) 32
BERKMAN, Robert I. . . . (NY) 87
BOWEN, Christopher E. . (NY) 120
CANDE, Lorraine N. . . . (NY) 178
DAMON, Shirley J. . . . . (NY) 272
DEVERS, Charlotte M. . . (NY) 297
GUBERT, Betty K. . . . . . (NY) 475
HAYES, Jude T. . . . . . . (NY) 516
HAYNES, Patricia . . . . . (NY) 516
KLATT, Wilma F. . . . . . . (NY) 658
LINDAHL, Charles E. . . . (NY) 728
MARGALITH, Helen M. . . (NY) 770
MEDEIROS, Joseph . . . . (NY) 820
NARCISO, Susan D. . . . (NY) 888
NEUBERG, Karen S. . . . (NY) 897
PIZER, Charles R. . . . . . (NY) 977
RANHAND, Jori L. . . . . . (NY) 1007
RHODES, Deborah L. . . . (NY) 1026
RITTER, Sally K. . . . . . . (NY) 1037
ROGINSKI, James W. . . (NY) 1050
ROY, Diptimoy . . . . (NY) 1063
SPERR BRISFJORD, Inez
L. . . . . (NY) 1173
TISDALE, Barbara . . . . . (NY) 1247
TORRONE, Joan M. . . . . (NY) 1251
VESLEY, Roberta A. . . . . (NY) 1283
WOLFE, Allis . . . . (NY) 1360
ZILAVY, Julie A. . . . . . . (NY) 1388
ARK, Connie E. . . . . (OH) 31
O'BRIEN, Betty A. . . . . . (OH) 914
VICTORY, Karen M. . . . . (OH) 1283
BAUER, Barbara B. . . . . (PA) 65
BLEIER, Carol S. . . . . . . (PA) 105
COOPER, Joanne S. . . . (PA) 243
COURTNEY, June M. . . . (PA) 251
DONCEVIC, Lois A. . . . . (PA) 311
GRAY, Priscilla M. . . . . . (PA) 460
HOLUB, Joseph C. . . . . . (PA) 555
HOWLEY, Deborah H. . . (PA) 566
KOHL, Arlene F. . . . . . . (PA) 668
LINN, Mott R. . . . . (PA) 731
LOCKETT, Cheryl L. . . . . (PA) 736
PARKER, Peter J. . . . . . (PA) 942
PARSONS, Muriel W. . . . (PA) 945
YAPLE, Deborah A. . . . . (PA) 1377
HIDALGO, Nilda R. . . . . . (PR) 537

RESEARCH (Cont'd)

Research

	RIVERA-ALVAREZ, Miguel A.	(PR)	1037
	HENDERSON, Linda L.	(RI)	526
	HUYGEN, Eva	(SC)	580
	MARTIN, Laquita V.	(TN)	777
	HURT, Nancy S.	(TX)	578
	MALCOLM, Jane B.	(TX)	762
	MEADOR, Cornie M.	(TX)	819
	MITCHE, Cynthia R.	(TX)	848
	MITCHELL, Cynthia R.	(TX)	848
	SHABOWICH, Stanley A.	(TX)	1118
	WEATHERS, Barbara H.	(TX)	1312
	WESTBROOK, Brenda S.	(TX)	1326
	VAN ORDEN, Richard D.	(UT)	1276
	COX, Tina S.	(VA)	253
	HARRISTON, Victoria R.	(VA)	507
	HAUCK, Janice B.	(VA)	512
	MCGINN, Ellen T.	(VA)	806
	WINFREE, Waverly K.	(VA)	1354
	BRZUSTOWICZ, Richard J.	(WA)	152
	KING, Betty J.	(WA)	650
	ASU, Glynis V.	(WI)	37
	ASHCROFT, Susan M.	(BC)	35
	HART, Elizabeth	(BC)	507
	ASHTON, Margaret A.	(ON)	36
	BUNCE, Catherine J.	(ON)	157
	CHOUDHURI, Kabita	(ON)	211
	FLOWER, M A.	(ON)	386
	KORNUTA, Helen	(ON)	672
	SPEISMAN, Stephen A.	(ON)	1172
	DUVAL, Marc	(PQ)	329
	FONTAINE, Nicole	(PQ)	388
	LACROIX, Yvon A.	(PQ)	687
	SANDFELDER, Paula M.	(HKG)	1080
	MEHRAD, Jafar	(IRN)	821
Research administration	RIKLI, Arthur E.	(MO)	1034
	POTEAT, James B.	(NY)	986
Research, American Indian studies	BLUMER, Thomas J.	(DC)	107
Research & analytical report writing	MEYER, Andrea P.	(CO)	829
Research & bibliography	STEFANCIC, Jean A.	(CA)	1185
Research & consultation sales	MIDDLETON, Carl H.	(DC)	833
Research & curriculum coordination	BANKHEAD, Elizabeth M.	(CO)	54
Research & development	CHANDLER, James	(CA)	200
	TSENG, Louisa	(MA)	1260
	KIRBY, Diana G.	(MD)	654
	LUCIER, Richard E.	(MD)	746
	MASYS, Daniel R.	(MD)	783
	DRAPER, James P.	(MI)	318
	ABELES, Tom	(MN)	2
	MCCLELLAND, Bruce A.	(NY)	796
	RAWLINS, Gordon W.	(PA)	1010
	BECKER, Roger V.	(WA)	72
	DE LIAMCHIN, Lana	(PQ)	289
	KLOK, Buddhi	(PQ)	662
Research & development in lib science	MEUNIER, Pierre	(PQ)	829
Research & development, new products	WINGATE, Dawn A.	(CA)	1354
Research & development project planning	KOZAK, Marlene G.	(IL)	674
Research & development research support	MUSKUS, Elizabeth A.	(NY)	883
Research & development, software	CHAPMAN, Ruby M.	(IL)	202
Research & editing	ROBINSON, Michaele M.	(CA)	1044
	CUTHBERT, John A.	(WV)	267
Research & education	CULLEN, Charles T.	(IL)	263
	WEST, Richard T.	(MD)	1326
	BRISFJORD, Inez S.	(NY)	136
Research & engineering databases	DE TONNANCOUR, P R.	(TX)	296
Research & evaluation	LOERTSCHER, David V.	(CO)	737
	HERNON, Peter	(MA)	532
	ROBBINS, Jane B.	(WI)	1038
Research & indexing	LE DORR, Lillian E.	(CA)	708
Research & information	DALY, Eudice	(CA)	271
Research & information retrieval	ROE, Georgeanne T.	(MA)	1048
	HACKNEY, Judith G.	(TX)	481
Research & information services	ROTHMAN, John	(NY)	1060

RESEARCH (Cont'd)

Research & library skills	LOPEZ, Silvia P.	(FL)	741
Research & management issues	FORD, Gary E.	(MO)	389
Research & publication	LANDIS, Dennis C.	(RI)	693
Research & reference	MAJOR, Caryl M.	(AZ)	762
	DICKSON, Constance P.	(DC)	301
	HIGBEE, Joan F.	(DC)	537
	FULLER, Ruth V.	(GA)	409
	PEURYE, Lloyd M.	(IL)	966
	FERGUSON, Roberta J.	(MA)	372
	SUTTON, Joyce A.	(MA)	1211
	ARNEJA, Harbhajan S.	(NY)	33
	HARDING, Mary H.	(NY)	500
	PALMER, Paul R.	(NY)	936
	RANKIN, Carol A.	(NY)	1007
	SEEBER, Frances M.	(NY)	1111
	NISENOFF, Sylvia	(VA)	905
Research & reference for politicians	O'KEEFE, Kevin T.	(NT)	919
Research & reference services	SLINGER, Michael J.	(IN)	1149
Research & reference training	ROSS, Theodosia B.	(GA)	1059
Research & reporting	PARK, Chung I.	(IL)	940
Research & statistics	ANDERSON, Beryl L.	(ON)	21
Research & teaching	CASTRO, Rafaela G.	(CA)	194
Research & writing	MOON, Ilse	(FL)	857
	LANDAU, Cynthia R.	(NH)	692
	GLATT, Carol R.	(NJ)	440
	FALARDEAU, Ernest R.	(NM)	361
	MILLER, Bryan M.	(NM)	836
	WAGNER, Stephen K.	(NY)	1292
Research & writing American history	SCHEIPS, Paul J.	(MD)	1091
Research architectural history	ROARK, Carol E.	(TX)	1038
Research, art nouveau, Victorian art	STACY, Betty A.	(VA)	1178
Research assistance	BRONARS, Lori A.	(CA)	140
	ZIRBES, Colette M.	(WI)	1390
Research, chemistry & metallurgy	SCHLOTT, Florenceann	(PA)	1094
Research collection development	KRUMMEL, Donald W.	(IL)	680
Research consulting	MIDDLETON, Carl H.	(DC)	833
	SANCHEZ, Jose L.	(DC)	1079
	ROWLAND, Lucy M.	(GA)	1062
Research databases	ALSOP, Robyn J.	(CO)	18
Research design	TAGUE, Jean M.	(ON)	1220
Research design & analysis	CHOBOT, Mary C.	(VA)	210
	LUECHT, Richard M.	(WI)	747
Research director	SMITH, Cynthia M.	(ON)	1153
Research, Eugene O'Neill life works	MCDONALD, Lois E.	(CT)	803
Research facilities management	LANOUETTE, Marie	(ON)	696
Research for exhibition development	SHERIDAN, Helen A.	(MI)	1127
Research for media personnel	BROWN, Phyllis J.	(TN)	147
Research for motion picture, television	NELSON-HARB, Sally R.	(CA)	895
Research for slide information	BAILEY, Tuuli T.	(AZ)	47
Research help	LE DORR, Lillian E.	(CA)	708
Research in American literature	BRODERICK, John C.	(DC)	138
Research in architecture	HUNT, Judy L.	(CA)	575
Research in children's literature	BISSETT, Donald J.	(MI)	100
	MONSON, Dianne L.	(MN)	855
Research in federal Indian law	HARRAGARRA WATERS, Deana J.	(CO)	503
Research in hlth, socty, music, foods	STARKEY, Bonnie F.	(WV)	1182
Research in law	LAEUCHLI, Ann J.	(CT)	687
Research in librarianship	BENNION, Bruce C.	(CA)	82
	MCCROSSAN, John A.	(FL)	800
	VALLEJO, Rosa M.	(PHP)	1271
Research in local history	CREAMER, Mary M.	(KY)	257
Research in medical informatics	FULLER, Sherrilynne S.	(MN)	409
Research in the study of literature	MILLER, Robert H.	(KY)	842
Research in theatre history	DONOHUE, Joseph	(MA)	312
Research information	LOCH, Edward J.	(TX)	735
	CHISUM, Emmett D.	(WY)	209
Research information for reporters	RICE, Margaret R.	(TX)	1027
Research legal databases	WOOD, Elizabeth B.	(OH)	1364
Research librarianship	AMAN, Ann L.	(CO)	19
	CRESCENT, Victoria L.	(PA)	258
Research libraries	BRYNTESON, Susan	(DE)	152
	SLOAN, Elaine F.	(IN)	1149
	SCOTT, Marianne F.	(ON)	1107
Research libraries management	DOWLER, Lawrence E.	(MA)	315
Research library administration	GRAZIANO, Eugene	(CA)	460
	SCHMIDT, C J.	(CA)	1095
	ROGERS, Rutherford D.	(CT)	1050
	PETERSON, Paul A.	(MO)	964

RESEARCH (Cont'd)

Research library administration
NITECKI, Joseph Z. . . . . (NY) 905
Research library collection
  development
KELLER, Michael A. . . . . (CT) 635
Research library management
LUCKER, Jay K. . . . . . . (MA) 746
EDELMAN, Hendrik . . . . (NJ) 335
Research library supervision
STRYCK, B C. . . . . . . (IL) 1203
Research management
JOHNSON, Minnie L. . . . (NJ) 607
FIDOTEN, Robert E. . . . . (PA) 375
Research managing, international
  team
CLARK, Joan . . . . (NJ) 217
Research material
CLARK, Audrey M. . . . . . (UT) 216
Research methodology
MAYES, Elizabeth A. . . . (CA) 789
GROTZINGER, Laurel A. (MI) 473
Research methodology & statistics
KATZER, Jeffrey . . . . . (NY) 630
Research methods
CHRISMAN, Larry G. . . . (FL) 211
AULD, Lawrence W. . . . . (IL) 40
BOOKSTEIN, Abraham . (IL) 115
PATEL, Jashu . . . . (IL) 947
WERT, Lucille M. . . . . . . (IL) 1325
HARTER, Stephen P. . . . (IN) 508
POWELL, Ronald R. . . . . (MO) 988
DAIN, Phyllis . . . . (NJ) 270
WYNAR, Lubomyr R. . . . (OH) 1375
HEAD, John W. . . . . . . (PA) 518
ROBINSON, William C. . (TN) 1045
MARCHANT, Maurice P. (UT) 768
STEPHENSON, Mary S. . (BC) 1188
HU, James S. . . . . (TAI) 567
Research methods & bibliographic
  instrc
TROUTMAN, Joseph E. . (GA) 1258
Research methods & cost analysis
WEBRECK, Susan J. . . . (PA) 1314
Research methods & systems
  analysis
FENSKE, Ruth E. . . . . . (IL) 371
Research methods in humanities
COHN, Alan M. . . . . . . (IL) 229
Research, music
LOWENS, Margery M. . . (MD) 744
Research of artists & exhibitions
GENSHAFT, Carole M. . . (OH) 427
Research on artists
SHERIDAN, Helen A. . . . (MI) 1127
Research on cartographic
  librarianship
STEVENS, Stanley D. . . . (CA) 1191
Research on cognitive learning
KOCHEN, Manfred . . . . . (MI) 667
Research on college faculty
HARDESTY, Larry L. . . . (FL) 499
Research on current awareness
  services
MONDSCHEIN, Lawrence
  G. . . . . (NJ) 854
Research on databases
BELANGER, Sylvie . . . . (PQ) 76
Research on East Germany
HUETING, Gail P. . . . . . (IL) 570
Research on information brokers
WALLS, Francine E. . . . . (WA) 1299
Research on management intelligence
  syst
KOCHEN, Manfred . . . . . (MI) 667
Research on risks & hazards
KASPERSON, Jeanne X. (MA) 629
Research on science of science
KOCHEN, Manfred . . . . . (MI) 667
Research on women artists
WASSERMAN, Krystyna (DC) 1308
Research on Women writers,
  1660-1800
MULVIHILL, Maureen E. (NY) 878
Research on world hunger
KASPERSON, Jeanne X. (MA) 629
Research on-demand
MACCALLUM, Barbara B. (NY) 754
Research, online & print
RABAI, Terezia . . . . . (IL) 1001
Research photographs
ROARK, Carol E. . . . . . (TX) 1038
Research projects, fee-based
HARRIS, Virginia B. . . . . (VA) 506
Research reference
FALVEY, Genemary H. . . (NY) 363
Research related to libraries
LYNCH, Mary J. . . . . . . (IL) 752
Research reports
CLINE, Margery C. . . . . (CA) 222
DOYLE, Patricia A. . . . . (TX) 317
Research retail & wholesale industries
LAMBE, Michael . . . . . . (NY) 690
Research services
ENGRAM, Sandra K. . . . (IL) 350
HAUGH, Amy J. . . . . . . (PA) 512
HELLER, Patricia A. . . . . (PA) 524
Research skill instruction
BROWN, Judith B. . . . . (MD) 145
Research skill teaching
PRIESING, Patricia L. . . (NJ) 993
Research skills
PLOWDEN, Martha W. . . (GA) 978
MENINGALL, Evelyn L. . (NJ) 824
AFROMSKY, Ellen S. . . . (NY) 7
Research skills education
BERGEN, Dessa C. . . . . (NY) 85
Research skills instruction
MAIN, Isabelle G. . . . . . (AZ) 761
Research skills teaching
MARTINAZZI, Toni . . . . (IL) 779
Research specialist
ARSENAULT, Patricia A. (MA) 35
SCOTT, Miranda D. . . . . (NJ) 1107
Research specialization
DUPLESSIS, Daniel . . . . (PQ) 327

RESEARCH (Cont'd)

Research support
STEVENSON, Michael I. . (MA) 1191
Research support for art
MCKEE, George D. . . . . (NY) 810
Research support services
KLIMIADES, Mario N. . . (AZ) 661
BROWN-WEBB, Deborah
  D. . . . . (TX) 149
PARE, Richard . . . . (ON) 940
Research techniques
FOLCARELLI, Ralph J. . . (NY) 387
Research training
CALLINAN, Ellen M. . . . (DC) 173
Research, women's studies
SMALLWOOD, Carol A. . (MI) 1151
Research, writing
BERNARD, Bobbi . . . . . (MA) 88
GREENBERG, Hinda F. . (NJ) 463
Research, writing & editing
CHRISTIANSON, Elin B. (IN) 212
Researcher
ELWELL, Christopher S. . (CT) 347
QUINTEN, Rebecca G. . . (OH) 1000
MICHAELS, Carolyn L. . . (SC) 831
EWUNES, Ernest L. . . . . (TX) 359
Researcher & bibliographer
LEONARD, Angela M. . . (DC) 716
Researcher, consultant, & analyst
KNIGHTLY, John J. . . . . (TN) 664
Researcher for private funding
  sources
ROBERTSON, Ina N. . . . (IL) 1042
Researcher of legal translations
SCHLACKS, Charles . . . (CA) 1093
Researching
SINOFSKY, Esther R. . . (CA) 1144
KURT, Edgar . . . . (IA) 684
MUISE, Anita M. . . . . . . (MA) 876
VINT, Patricia A. . . . . . . (MI) 1285
CLEMONS, Kenneth L. . (NC) 221
SCHEPP, Brad J. . . . . . (NJ) 1091
MATTHEOU, Antonia . . . (NY) 785
ULRICH, Pamela L. . . . . (WA) 1268
KRAFT, Gwen L. . . . . . (AK) 675
SHABERLY, Leanna J. . . (AZ) 1118
Researching & writing
Researching film distributors
Researching foreign archive
  institutions
OGAWA, Chiyoko . . . . . (JAP) 918
Researching foundations
DUCKWORTH, Paul M. . (MO) 322
Researching historic photos & film
LUSKEY, Judith . . . . . . (DC) 749
Researching historical material
HAZEL, Debora E. . . . . (NC) 517
Researching history of recording
PENGELLY, Joe . . . . . . (ENG) 956
Researching keyboard instruments
RICHARDS, James H. . . (TX) 1028
Researching, library systems
GIGANTE, Vickilyn M. . . (MD) 433
Researching material for the elderly
MCCRAY, Evelina W. . . . (LA) 800
Researching newspapers
MORRISON, Annette T. . (TN) 867
Researching piano history &
  technology
RICHARDS, James H. . . (TX) 1028
Researching reed organ history
RICHARDS, James H. . . (TX) 1028
Researching unavailable information
TERZIAN, Shohig S. . . . (CA) 1232
Resources of research libraries
JACKSON, William V. . . (TX) 588
Safety engineering research
HANSEN, Cheryl A. . . . . (IL) 497
Scholarly library research
HARMALA, Amy A. . . . . (WA) 502
School library research skills
SHERMAN, Madeline R. . (VT) 1128
Science & technology reference &
  resrch
LUXNER, Dick . . . . (NJ) 750
Science & technology research
MUSKUS, Elizabeth A. . . (NY) 883
Science & tech resrch & devlpmnt
  support
LOGAN, Nancy L. . . . . . (ON) 737
Science fiction & fantasy research
PELZ, Bruce E. . . . . . . (CA) 955
Science fiction, fantasy research
KAN, Katharine L. . . . . . (HI) 624
Science research
RUBEN, Jacquelen S. . . (CA) 1064
SINGLETON, Cynthia B. . (ON) 1143
Scientific & technical ref & research
MILLER, Dennis P. . . . . (OH) 837
Scientific & technical research
CRANDALL, Michael D. . (WA) 255
Scientific literature research
HAMILTON, Beth A. . . . . (IL) 491
Scientific reference & research
STOKES, Claire Z. . . . . . (MN) 1196
SDI in corporate research &
  development
MONDSCHEIN, Lawrence
  G. . . . . (NJ) 854
SDI use by basic research scientists
MONDSCHEIN, Lawrence
  G. . . . . (NJ) 854
SEC research & retrieval
GRISDELA, Margaret . . . (DC) 471
Secondary faculty research
MERRELL, Sheila J. . . . . (MO) 826
Secondary research
OSWALD, Edward E. . . . (FL) 929
Secondary research facilities
CROTTS, Carolyn D. . . . (KS) 261
Securities research
CROFT, Elizabeth G. . . . (NY) 260
Semiconductor research
CRABTREE, Sandra A. . (CA) 254
Social science research
GERKEN, Ann E. . . . . . (CA) 429
MISSAR, Margaret M. . . (DC) 847
EVERHART, Paul R. . . . (IL) 358
Social sciences reference & research
HOWREY, Mary M. . . . . (IL) 566
Social services research
ROBINSON, Jolene A. . . (NY) 1044
South Asian bibliography & research
SEN, Joyce H. . . . . (NY) 1115

RESEARCH (Cont'd)

Soyfoods market research	GOLBITZ, Peter	(ME)	444
	KINGMA, Sharyn L.	(ME)	652
Special projects research, automation	RHYNAS, Don M.	(ON)	1026
Specialized research projects	BEHNKE, Charles	(WI)	75
Sports research	QUARTELL, Robert J.	(NY)	999
Staff devlpmnt, research & development	BURKS, Alvin L.	(MS)	161
State & local historical research	CHRISTENSEN, Erin S.	(CO)	211
State & local history research	OAKES, Patricia A.	(AK)	913
Statistical research	RAILSBACK, Beverly D.	(NJ)	1003
Statistics & research methods	D'ELIA, George P.	(MN)	289
Story & visual research for films	FINE, Deborah J.	(CA)	377
Subject research	PEARSON, Judith G.	(CA)	952
Survey research	PIGGFORD, Roland	(MA)	972
	MCDONALD, Dennis D.	(MD)	802
Survey research for libraries	OLSON, Christine A.	(MD)	922
Systems research & development	COVILL, Bruce	(NJ)	252
Tax & accounting research	WHITTLESEY, Jane M.	(TX)	1334
Tax law research	MAXON, William N.	(DC)	787
Tax research	ROLLINS, James H.	(CA)	1051
	MCDERMOTT, Patricia M.	(DC)	802
	ELLIS, Gloria B.	(MI)	344
	DINGLEY, Doris A.	(MN)	305
	SLAMKOWSKI, Donna L.	(MN)	1147
	FRANKENSTEIN, Steven S.	(NY)	397
	EMERSON, Beth A.	(TX)	347
	SMITH, Kraleen S.	(TX)	1156
Taxation research	HOPKINS, Terry F.	(TX)	558
Taxation research, management consulting	VEASLEY, Mignon M.	(CA)	1280
Teaching & research	MCELHANEY, William E.	(CT)	804
	KEEFER, Ethel A.	(NY)	634
Teaching legal research	FOSTER, Lynn	(AR)	392
Teaching legal research skills	WHISMAN, Linda A.	(CA)	1329
	WELKER, Kathy J.	(OH)	1321
Teaching library & research skills	WIENER, Sylvia B.	(NY)	1336
Teaching library research	BROWN, Patricia L.	(OR)	146
Teaching library research skills	REILLY, Maureen E.	(CT)	1020
Teaching library skills & research	CARVER, Jane C.	(MA)	191
Teaching research & reference skills	BERNAT, Mary A.	(VEN)	88
Teaching research process	PARR, Michael P.	(MI)	944
Teaching research skill	HAYASHI, Chigusa	(NJ)	515
Teaching research skills	MISENHEIMER, Paula S.	(AR)	847
	THORNTON, Alice J.	(DE)	1242
	SMITH, Lena D.	(KY)	1157
	CRAMER, Eugene C.	(AB)	255
Teaching school library research skills	CARLISLE, Carol A.	(CT)	182
Technical & research libraries mgmt	CRENSHAW, Tena L.	(FL)	258
Technical & tech commercial research	CRABTREE, Sandra A.	(CA)	254
Technical information research	LAHR, Thomas F.	(VA)	688
Technical library research	SAUTER, Lyn F.	(WA)	1085
Technical research	ADLER, Naomi L.	(IL)	7
	HALASZ, Marilynn J.	(IL)	484
	WINQUIST, Elaine W.	(MA)	1355
	SEMKO, Melanie J.	(MD)	1115
	PIERCE, Mildred L.	(NV)	971
	OGDEN, Suzanne M.	(TX)	918
	ROBERTS, Ernest J.	(TX)	1040
Technical research libraries	DOUGLASS, Leslie A.	(NJ)	314
Telecommunication research	FOSKO, Maureen E.	(NJ)	392
Telecommunications research	KIRSHBAUM, Priscilla J.	(CO)	655
	GLADSTONE, Mark A.	(NJ)	439
	IMPERIALE, Karen P.	(NJ)	582
	JONES, Deborah A.	(NJ)	612
Telecommunications research & devlpmnt	DENMAN, Monica K.	(CT)	292
Telecommunications, research, reference	ROGGENKAMP, Alice M.	(NY)	1050
Theatre bibliographic researching	ULRICH, Paul S.	(WGR)	268
Theatre research	DUCLOW, Geraldine	(PA)	322
Theological bibliography & research	OZOLINS, Karl L.	(MN)	933
Theological research	PARKER, Mary A.	(SC)	942
Theological research & writing	WROTENBERY, Carl R.	(TX)	1373
Theological research methodology	TROUTMAN, Joseph E.	(GA)	1258
Theological research methods	ERDEL, Timothy P.	(JAM)	352
Trade magazine research	DAMOTH, Douglas L.	(NY)	272
Traditional or online research	HUMPHRIES, Joy D.	(WV)	574

RESEARCH (Cont'd)

Traditional research	CESARD, Mary A.	(NJ)	196
Training & development, legal research	MCGUIRL, Marlene C.	(DC)	808
Training research analysts	BERWICK, Mary C.	(PA)	91
Training technology research	SNYDER, Cathrine E.	(TN)	1164
Transportation information & research	ARMEIT, Marilyn	(NY)	32
Transportation safety research support	GATTIS, R G.	(MI)	422
US Customs law research	MATTERA, Joseph J.	(NY)	785
United States legal research	ARANDA-COODOU, Patricio	(DC)	30
University research lib administration	RUNKLE, Martin D.	(IL)	1067
Utilities research	FERME, Paul H.	(IL)	373
Venture capital research	SOROBAY, Roman T.	(NY)	1169
Visual resources & research	NIELSEN, Sonja M.	(MA)	903
Voluntary research	MARTIN, Teresa B.	(KS)	778
Welding library research	BAKER, Martha A.	(OH)	49
Westlaw computer-based research	SMITH, Susan A.	(CA)	1161
Westlaw research	SPRINGER, Michelle M.	(TX)	1176
Women's studies & peace research	HAMILTON-PENNELL, Christine	(CO)	492
Wood products research	SCHARMER, Roger C.	(WI)	1090

RESERVES (See also Circulation)

Circulation & faculty reserves	HARER, John B.	(MD)	501
Circulation & reserve	RASMUSSEN, Gordon E.	(IL)	1009
	DEBRECZENY, Gillian M.	(NC)	285
	THOMAS, Barbara C.	(TX)	1236
Circulation & reserve services	LACKS, Bernice K.	(NY)	686
	NECHKA, Ada M.	(AB)	891
Circulation & reserve systems & services	HENSHAW, Rod	(PA)	529
Circulation & reserves	HILL, Ann M.	(WA)	539
Circulation, reserve, interlibrary loan	MEAD-DONALDSON, Susan L.	(FL)	819
Legal & reserve book circulation	DINDAYAL, Joyce S.	(NY)	304
Reference & reserves	COONEY, Mata M.	(NV)	242
Reserve & Afro-American librarianship	GENTRY, Etherlene H.	(MS)	427
Reserve books	NAMSICK, Lynn J.	(AZ)	887
Reserves	NEWMYER, Joann C.	(CT)	900
	SWINTON, Cordelia W.	(PA)	1216
	SAUR, Cindy S.	(VA)	1085
Reserves & interlibrary loan	PARK, T P.	(NY)	941
Reserves, interlibrary loan	MILLSAP, Gina J.	(MO)	844

RESINS

Plastic resins	VOSS, Ingrid M.	(IL)	1289

RESOLUTION

Conflict resolution	PEISCHL, Thomas P.	(MN)	955

RESOLUTIONS

Indexing legislative resolutions	GEISAR, Barbara J.	(WI)	425

RESONANCE

Nuclear magnetic resonance bibliography	PARR, John R.	(ON)	943

RESOURCES (See also Collections, Materials, Sources)

Ad hoc resource service	STANAT, Ruth E.	(NY)	1179
Administration of learning resource ctr	BOOK, Imogene I.	(SC)	115
Adult services & resources	LYMAN, Helen H.	(NY)	751
Aerospace information resources	KITCHENS, Philips H.	(AL)	657
Agricultural resources	PEARSON, Jo A.	(IA)	952
Architecture & design resources	GRIGORIS, Lygia	(MA)	470
Area health education learning resources	JOHN, Stephanie C.	(MI)	601
Artists' resources	BYRNE, Nadene M.	(IL)	169
Audiovisual resources	FORREST, Charles G.	(IL)	390
	ZOGOTT, Joyce	(PA)	1390
Automated visual resources	LUSKEY, Judith	(DC)	749

RESOURCES (Cont'd)

Bibliographic & resource sharing network	REDDY, Sigrid R.	(MA)	1014
Biomedical information resources	BROERING, Naomi C.	(DC)	139
Board-operated resource centers	BERTRAND, Doreen M.	(ON)	91
Business & marketing info resources	BARTL, Richard P.	(NY)	61
Business, economic resources	ERWIN, Nancy S.	(OH)	353
Business information resources	MICKEY, Melissa B.	(IL)	833
Business reference resources	SINWELL, Carol A.	(VA)	1144
Business resources	EMBAR, Indrani M.	(IL)	347
	BURYLO, Michelle A.	(PA)	164
	PAGELL, Ruth A.	(PA)	934
	PIETZAK, Stephen D.	(PA)	972
	MIDGETT, Ann S.	(TX)	833
Career & education resources	WHITNEY, Howard F.	(MA)	1334
Career resources	SCOTT, Melissa C.	(MI)	1107
Children's media resources	WARNER, Wayne G.	(GA)	1305
Chiropractic resources & bibliography	PETERSON, Dennis R.	(IA)	963
Church history, theology resources	SUELFLOW, August R.	(MO)	1206
Collection building resource	WATSON, Joyce N.	(ON)	1309
Collection care & handling resources	MOON, Myra J.	(CO)	857
Collection development, resource sharing	FISCHLER, Barbara B.	(IN)	380
	HEANEY, Henry J.	(SCT)	518
Community college learning resources	KELLER, Jan K.	(CA)	635
	PERSON, Ruth J.	(PA)	961
Community college resources	PARADISE, Don M.	(PA)	939
Community information resources	DAVIS, Natalia G.	(NY)	280
Community resource development	MARKEY, Penny S.	(CA)	771
Computer industry resources	LAPENSKY, Barbara A.	(MN)	697
Computer resources	MONTGOMERY, Kimberly K.	(AL)	856
Computer resources for teachers	COLEMAN, Barbara K.	(OH)	231
Computer science resources	CARNES, Mary J.	(NE)	183
Computerized learning resources	STANKE, Judith U.	(MN)	1180
Computers resource specialist	CAMPANELLA, Alice D.	(MA)	175
Conservation of library resources	DEVENISH-CASSEL, Ann W.	(NY)	297
Continuing education, resource sharing	SHELDON, Brooke E.	(TX)	1125
Cooperation for resource sharing	BESEMER, Susan P.	(NY)	91
Current awareness resource materials	SEXTON, Spencer K.	(NC)	1118
Data resource management	VALENTINE, Scott	(ON)	1271
Defense & aerospace info resources	BARTL, Richard P.	(NY)	61
Early childhood resources	HERSCOVITCH, Pearl	(AB)	533
Education, instructional resources	STAVROLAKIS, Rachel G.	(GA)	1183
Education resource center	BADGER, Barbara	(IL)	44
Education resources	SCHROEDER, Eileen E.	(NY)	1100
Educational resources, curriculum	SACK, Jean C.	(MD)	1073
Educational resources management & ref	ILACQUA, Anne K.	(MA)	581
Employee benefits, home resource mgmt	JACQUES, Donna M.	(MA)	591
Energy & mineral resources information	HARDY, Kenneth J.	(AB)	501
Energy information resources	RIX, Dolores M.	(IL)	1037
Engineering library resources management	PFANN, Mary L.	(NJ)	966
Entrepreneur resources	SKONIECZNY, Jill	(MI)	1147
Environmental information resources	STOSS, Frederick W.	(NY)	1198
Establishing resource centers	KUHL, Danuta	(VA)	682
Film & video resources	ALLAN, David W.	(MN)	14
Geriatric information resources	STEPHENSON, Judy A.	(KY)	1188
Gifted resources dissemination	WARNER, Wayne G.	(GA)	1305
Graduate library training resource	HOLSINGER, Katherine	(AZ)	554
Health information resources planning	BYRD, Gary D.	(NC)	168
Health sciences information resources	ALMQUIST, Deborah T.	(MA)	17
Historical resources	KOBELKA, Carolynn L.	(NT)	666
Hospital administration resources	BRETSCHER, Susan M.	(NY)	134
Human resource development	CARROLL VIRGO, Julie	(IL)	187
	BLASINGAME, Ralph	(NJ)	104
Human resource management	SWEENEY, June D.	(DC)	1215
	RIDDLE, Raymond E.	(KS)	1032
	PINDER, Jo A.	(MD)	974
	WEBB, Gisela M.	(TX)	1313
	WILKINSON, John P.	(ON)	1340
Human resources	BOSTON, Mary T.	(CO)	118
	BRYANT, Nancy J.	(GA)	152
	CRANE, John G.	(NH)	255
	FULMER, Dina J.	(PA)	409

RESOURCES (Cont'd)

Human resources & labor relations	HARE, Judith E.	(ON)	501
Human resources development	SHERMAN, Mary A.	(OK)	1128
Human resources in library services	SAVARD, Rejean	(PQ)	1085
Human resources management	COFFMAN, M H.	(MA)	227
	MEADOWS, Donald F.	(BC)	819
Human resources research	BRUNER, Robert B.	(CO)	150
Humanities resources	MARCHAND, Janet H.	(CT)	768
Information management resources	STEIGER, Bettie A.	(MD)	1185
Information network, resource sharing	AGRAWAL, Surendra P.	(IND)	7
Information resource management	DENNISON, Lynn C.	(CA)	292
	MCCARTHY, John L.	(CA)	794
	STAN, Gail A.	(CA)	1179
	BEICHMAN, John C.	(MI)	75
	DANIEL, Evelyn H.	(NC)	272
	KOENIG, Michael E.	(NY)	668
	HODGSON, Cynthia A.	(PA)	546
	LYTLE, Richard H.	(PA)	753
	BURNS, Barrie A.	(ON)	162
Information resource systems	THOMAS, Margaret J.	(MI)	1237
Information resources	ROBBINS, Gordon D.	(TN)	1038
Information resources management	POEHLMAN, Dorothy J.	(DC)	979
	EVERETT, Amy E.	(DE)	358
	BROWN, Patricia L.	(IL)	146
	REITER, Richard R.	(IL)	1022
	MOBLEY, Kathleen S.	(KS)	851
	LEVITAN, Karen B.	(MD)	721
	NEWMAN, Wilda B.	(MD)	900
	PRICE, Douglas S.	(MD)	992
	HAMLIN, Eileen M.	(NY)	493
	MARCHAND, Donald A.	(NY)	768
	MARTIN, Thomas H.	(NY)	778
	RODERER, Nancy K.	(NY)	1047
	MOORE, Penelope F.	(VA)	861
Instructional media resources	ALLAN, David W.	(MN)	14
Instructional resources	DAVILA, Daniel	(NY)	277
	NOVIK, Sandra P.	(NY)	911
Integrated info resources management	KNOPPERS, Jake V.	(ON)	665
Integrated service for info resources	BERGERON, Pierrette	(PQ)	86
Interlibrary loan of genealogical resrcs	MEYERS, Martha L.	(MO)	831
Interlibrary loan, resource sharing	THOMPSON, Dorothea M.	(PA)	1239
Jewish library resources	SHEPARD, Jon R.	(OH)	1127
Learning resource center administration	BOROWSKI, Joseph F.	(IL)	117
Learning resource center col standards	BOOK, Imogene I.	(SC)	115
Learning resource centers	CARR, Charles E.	(AL)	185
Learning resource programs	CLARKE, Tobin D.	(CA)	219
Learning resource services	HISLE, W L.	(TX)	544
Learning resources	CODER, Ann	(CA)	226
	RONEY, Raymond G.	(CA)	1053
	SCHLATTER, M W.	(GA)	1093
	SORELL, Janice G.	(MN)	1168
	HAMMITT, Margaret R.	(NE)	493
	PONTIUS, Louise	(TX)	982
	SULLIVAN, Janice L.	(TX)	1207
	POLLOCK, Ethel L.	(VA)	981
Learning resources administration	BOONE, Morell D.	(MI)	115
	JASSAL, Raghbir S.	(NM)	595
Learning resources center	JOHNSON, Scott R.	(MS)	609
Learning resources center management	CAROL, Barbara B.	(OK)	184
Learning resources centers	FRIEDMAN, Arthur L.	(NY)	403
	ADAMS, Elaine P.	(TX)	4
Learning resources management	BERLING, John G.	(MN)	88
Learning resources programs	HUNSUCKER, David L.	(NC)	575
Legal research & resources management	DEMPSEY, Pamela M.	(NM)	291
Legal resources for non-lawyers	EWING, Florence E.	(CA)	359
Library & information resource systems	NELSON, James A.	(KY)	894
Library media resources	HUNT, Mary A.	(FL)	575
Library resource center management	SMITH, Noralee W.	(OH)	1159
Library resources teacher	ELLEBRACHT, Eleanor V.	(MO)	343
Manufacturing information resources	KELLER, Karen A.	(MI)	635
Marketing research resources management	SEULOWITZ, Lois	(NY)	1117
Medical & nursing resources	BRETSCHER, Susan M.	(NY)	134
Minority librarianship & resources	HARVELL, Valeria G.	(NJ)	509

RESOURCES (Cont'd)

Multitype resource sharing	MICHAELIS, Kathryn S. .	(WI)	831
Natural resource archives	COOK, Terry G.	(ON)	240
Natural resources	RADEMACHER, Kurt A. .	(CA)	1002
	AYER, Carol A.	(MD)	42
	LOUET, Sandra	(ON)	742
Natural resources & environment ref	LARSEN, Lynda L.	(DC)	698
Natural resources literature searching	WAGNER, Barbara L.	(CO)	1291
Natural resources reference	RODES, Barbara K.	(DC)	1047
Natural resources research	CLOSE, Elizabeth G.	(UT)	223
Networking, resource sharing, systems	LOVE, Erika	(NM)	743
Networks & resource sharing	SEIDMAN, Ruth K.	(MA)	1112
	MARTIN, Noelene P.	(PA)	777
Non-print resources	COCHENOUR, Donnice K.	(OK)	225
Nursing & allied health resources	MCCULLOCH, Elizabeth A.	(PA)	801
	PRINGLE, Robert M.	(WA)	993
Nursing information resources	ALLEN, Margaret A.	(WI)	15
Personnel resource	LEVESQUE, Janet A.	(RI)	719
Photography resources information	HOFFKNECHT, Carmen L.	(CA)	547
Planning resources	GOODY, Cheryl S.	(HI)	450
Planning two-year learning resource ctr	BOOK, Imogene I.	(SC)	115
Reference & resource programs	HOBBS, Henry C.	(MB)	545
Reference resources	JONES, Mary L.	(IL)	614
	VOSS, Joyce M.	(IL)	1289
	SINWELL, Carol A.	(VA)	1144
Religious resources	GLEASON, Ruth I.	(IN)	440
Resource allocation	LITTLE, Paul L.	(OK)	733
Resource allocations	MILLER, Richard T.	(MO)	841
Resource center development	EVANS, Stephen P.	(OH)	358
Resource center management	BECHOR, Malvina B.	(GA)	71
Resource centers	GREENBERG, Roberta D.	(NY)	463
Resource conservation	PLOCKELMAN, Cynthia H.	(FL)	978
Resource coordination	BRICK, Sarah E.	(OK)	134
Resource database development	SCHUELLER, Janette H.	(WA)	1101
Resource development	KING, Kenneth	(MI)	651
	FEDUNOK, Suzanne	(NY)	368
Resource for entire organization	FINNUCAN, Louise A.	(CT)	379
Resource management	KRIZ, Harry M.	(VA)	679
Resource materials on women	SNAPP, Elizabeth M.	(TX)	1162
Resource person & problem solver	ALGAZE, Selma B.	(FL)	13
Resource person to lib administration	WATSON, Joyce N.	(ON)	1309
Resource planning	WEISS, Egon A.	(NY)	1320
Resource recovery information	COLLISHAW, Jackie J. .	(NJ)	233
Resource reports	COURTOT, Marilyn E.	(MD)	251
Resource sharing	GRAHAM, Elaine	(CA)	456
	IVERSON, Diann S.	(CA)	585
	SCHWEERS, Lucy	(CO)	1105
	VOLZ, Edward J.	(CO)	1288
	BURGER, Leslie B.	(CT)	159
	DEJOHN, William T.	(MN)	288
	BUCHANAN, Gerald	(MS)	153
	NEAL, Michelle H.	(NC)	890
	NOLAN, John A.	(NY)	907
	WASHBURN, Keith E.	(NY)	1307
	WOLFE, N J.	(NY)	1361
	WAREHAM, Nancy L.	(OH)	1304
	HALGREN, Joanne V.	(OR)	486
	BRICE, Heather W.	(PA)	134
	JACKSON, Mary E.	(PA)	588
	KOLBE, Jane	(SD)	669
	COTTER, Gladys A.	(VA)	250
	WARD, Robert C.	(VT)	1304
	CLEMENT, Hope E.	(ON)	221
Resource sharing among libraries	CHEN, Catherine W.	(MI)	205
Resource sharing & networking	TYER, Travis E.	(IL)	1266
Resource sharing networks	KENT, Allen	(PA)	642
Resources	YOUNG, Eleanor C.	(CA)	1381
	PATTERSON, Charles D.	(LA)	948
Resources & technical services	WILKINS, Alice L.	(NC)	1340
Resources of research libraries	JACKSON, William V.	(TX)	588
Resources organization & development	HURD, Sandra H.	(MA)	577
	TRIBOLETTI, Kathleen	(DE)	1256
Resourcing	GOTHIA, Blanche	(TX)	453
School learning resource ctr consulting	BERTRAND, Doreen M.	(ON)	91
School library resource centers	RUDIE, Helen M.	(MN)	1065
School media center resources	PASKOFF, Beth M.	(LA)	946
Science resources			

RESOURCES (Cont'd)

Senior citizen resources	CARABATEAS, Clarissa D.	(NY)	180
Sexuality education resources	FORREST, Phyllis E.	(DC)	391
Shared resources management	MILLER, Charles E.	(FL)	836
Social science information resources	SHIELDS, Gerald R.	(NY)	1130
Soil plant relations & natural resources	SCHNEIDER, Karl R.	(MD)	1097
State information resource management	EVANS, Max J.	(UT)	357
Statistical resources	TAYLOR, Marcia E.	(MD)	1227
Storytime resources	CROTTS, Carolyn D.	(KS)	261
Teacher resource	ONUFFER, Joachim	(PA)	924
	BACON, Carey H.	(WA)	44
Teacher resource consultant	REESE, Virginia D.	(KY)	1016
Technical information resources	BARTL, Richard P.	(NY)	61
Theological resources	VANDELINDER, Bonnie L.	(NY)	1273
Visual arts resources	MCRAE, Linda	(FL)	818
Visual resource collection	AUCHSTETTER, Rosann M.	(IN)	38
Visual resource management	HOGAN, Kristine K.	(NY)	549
	FOWLER, Michele R.	(OH)	394
Visual resources	COATES, Ann S.	(KY)	224
	BOLSHAW, Cynthia L.	(MA)	112
	ROBERTS, Helene E.	(MA)	1040
	KUSNERZ, Peggy A.	(MI)	685
	BEETHAM, Donald W.	(NJ)	74
	CINLAR, Anne	(NJ)	214
	SCHAFFER, D J.	(NY)	1089
	PEARMAN, Sara J.	(OH)	952
	KLOS, Sheila M.	(OR)	662
	SUNDT, Christine L.	(OR)	1210
	LAZARUS, Karin	(PA)	706
	CASHMAN, Norine D.	(RI)	192
	JACOBY, Mary M.	(VA)	590
	UPDIKE, Christina B.	(VA)	1269
Visual resources & research	NIELSEN, Sonja M.	(MA)	903
Visual resources authority control	MOST, Gregory P.	(TX)	872
Visual resources classification	FREEMAN, Carla C.	(NY)	400
Visual resources curator	WYKLE, Helen H.	(CA)	1375
Visual resources database design	ELTZROTH, Elsbeth L.	(GA)	346
Visual resources databases	SCHAFFER, D J.	(NY)	1089
Visual resources, especially slides	CALLAHAN, Linda J.	(MA)	173
Visual resources library	MOST, Gregory P.	(TX)	872
Visual resources management, development	PRINS, Johanna W.	(NY)	993
Visual resources production	FREEMAN, Carla C.	(NY)	400
Visual resources professional	HEHMAN, Jennifer L.	(IN)	521
Visual resources, slides & photographs	GREWENOW, Peter W.	(NY)	467
Water resources	ORCUTT, Roberta K.	(NV)	925
Water resources & hydrology	HANSON, Donna M.	(ID)	498
Water resources cataloging	TORNABENE, Charles	(FL)	1251
Water resources databases	JENSEN, Raymond A.	(VA)	599
West African soils & water resources	CANDELMO, Emily	(NY)	178

RESPONSE

Response management system	POWELL, Timothy W.	(NY)	989

RESTORATION (See also Repair)

Music recordings sound restoration	PETRIE, Mildred M.	(FL)	965
Preservation, binding, restoration	ALLEN, Doris L.	(CA)	14
Restoration	DE MACEDO, Maria L.	(PTG)	290
Restoration of national landmarks	MCDONALD, Lois E.	(CT)	803
Sound archives, restoration	FRANK, Mortimer H.	(NY)	397
Sound restoration	SMOLIAN, Steven J.	(MD)	1162

RESUME

Resume assistance for librarians	KLEMENT, Susan P.	(ON)	660

RETAILING (See also Sales, Selling)

Home video retailing	WHITE, Matthew H.	(IL)	1331
Research retail & wholesale industries	LAMBE, Michael	(NY)	690
Retail financial technologies	RATH, Charla M.	(DC)	1009
Retailer of Black literature	MILLENDER, Dharathola	(IN)	835
Retailing	SPEECE, Yvonne M.	(OH)	1172

RETAILING (Cont'd)
Retailing statistical data   PALMER, Shirley ...... (CT)   937

RETARDATION (See also Disabled, Handicapped)
Mental retardation   HAYNES, Douglas E. ... (NM)   516
  GILSON, Robert .... (NY)   437
  HOWIE, Maryann ...... (NY)   566
  LEONARD, Peter C. .... (PA)   716
Services to mentally retarded   HOMAN, Frances M. ... (MD)   555

RETIREMENT (See also Benefits, Pension)
Retirement   LOVAS, Paula M. ...... (DC)   743

RETRIEVAL
Acquisitions & information retrieval	MOORE, Virginia B.	(DC)	861
Artificial intelligence based retrieval	VLADUTZ, George E.	(PA)	1286
Automated indexing & retrieval	MATLOCK, Teresa A.	(TX)	784
Automated information retrieval	SANDERS, Robert L.	(CA)	1080
Automated information retrieval systems	MACIAS-CHAPULA, Cesar A.	(MEX)	755
Automated storage & retrieval	LEVINE, Emil H.	(DC)	720
Automation, online retrieval services	BEACHELL, Doria M.	(DC)	68
Basic retrieval	HANDY, Mary J.	(ON)	495
Bibliographic retrieval	HALASZ, Marilynn J.	(IL)	484
Biotechnology information retrieval	SCHEPPER, Josee H.	(PQ)	1091
Cataloging & information retrieval	CARROLL, Dewey E.	(TX)	187
CD-ROM retrieval software	DITMARS, David W.	(OH)	305
Chemical databases & info retrieval	ROSENTHAL, Francine C.	(OH)	1057
Chemical information retrieval	SIMMONS, Edlyn S.	(OH)	1139
Chemical substance information retrieval	STOBAUGH, Robert E.	(OH)	1195
Clinical literature retrieval, databases	KINNAIRD, Cheryl D.	(IL)	653
Communication & information retrieval	NADEAU, Johan	(PQ)	885
Comparative automated retrieval systems	O'CONNOR, Sandra L.	(NC)	916
Computer research & retrieval	WOLFE, Bardie C.	(FL)	1360
Computer srchng, online info retrieval	SOUTH, Ruth E.	(OR)	1169
Computer storage & retrieval	MERRYWEATHER, J M.	(ON)	827
Computer-assisted text retrieval	PRICKETT, Dan S.	(OH)	993
Computerized database retrieval	WHITE, Chandlee	(MA)	1330
Computerized information retrieval	CARRIGAN, John L.	(CA)	186
	LEE, William D.	(CA)	711
	WILDE, Daniel U.	(CT)	1338
	MARCUS, Richard S.	(MA)	769
Computerized retrieval system	OSTROW, Dianne G.	(MD)	929
Congressional document retrieval	MILLER, William S.	(DC)	843
Data analysis & retrieval	YACOUBY, Ray S.	(MA)	1376
Database development & retrieval	SAUNDERS, Leslie E.	(MA)	1084
Database information retrieval	MAGNER, Mary F.	(TX)	759
Database retrieval	MEYER, Garry S.	(NY)	830
	BONIN, Denise R.	(BC)	114
	WARREN, Lois M.	(BC)	1306
Database retrieval & online searching	ROTHSCHILD, M C.	(VA)	1060
Database retrieval systems	ODHO, Marc	(ON)	917
Database storage & retrieval	KANTOR, Paul B.	(OH)	626
Document retrieval	CHAMPANY, Barry W.	(CA)	198
	BOGART, Betty B.	(MA)	110
	CAIN, Susan H.	(MA)	171
	DLOTT, Nancy B.	(MA)	306
	RAUM, Tamar	(NY)	1010
	FELL, Sally B.	(OH)	370
	GOURLAY, Una M.	(TX)	454
	SCHRAEDER, Diana C.	(TX)	1099
Document retrieval & cataloging	ELAM, Kim A.	(AK)	341
Document retrieval & federal agencies	TURNER, Ellis S.	(MD)	1264
Document retrieval & interlibrary loan	FELDMAN, Eleanor C.	(MD)	369
Document retrieval systems	WRIGHT, John H.	(FL)	1371
Document storage & retrieval systems	BAGG, Thomas C.	(MD)	45
Electrochemical information retrieval	LANGKAU, Claire M.	(OH)	696
Engineering information retrieval	CHANG, Frances M.	(DC)	200
Expert retrieval assistance systems	MARCUS, Richard S.	(MA)	769
Film & television database retrieval	SALZ, Kay	(NY)	1078
Full-text retrieval	LEVINE, Emil H.	(DC)	720
Full-text retrieval software	BENGE, Bruce	(OK)	80
Geoscience information retrieval	WICK, Constance S.	(MA)	1335
Government info index & retrieval	MASSA, Paul P.	(MD)	781

RETRIEVAL (Cont'd)
Improvement of online retrieval	LIBBEY, Miles A.	(NJ)	725
Indexing, abstracting & retrieval	JOHNSON, David K.	(NJ)	603
Indexing & retrieval	HARRIS, Michael A.	(CO)	505
Information & records retrieval	LEE, William D.	(CA)	711
Information & retrieval systems	ANDRADE, Rebecca	(CA)	26
Information retrieval	NEMCHEK, Lee R.	(CA)	895
	NEWMAN, Mark J.	(CA)	899
	SHANMAN, Roberta	(CA)	1120
	SHARP, Geoffrey H.	(CA)	1122
	CHANAUD, Jo P.	(CO)	199
	CONRAD, Celia B.	(CT)	238
	SUPEAU, Cynthia	(CT)	1210
	BELLARDO, Trudi	(DC)	78
	EDWARDS, Andrea Y.	(DC)	337
	LUNDEEN, Gerald W.	(HI)	748
	ANTON, Tess	(IL)	29
	BIRKHOLD, Martha S.	(IL)	98
	CAREY, Kevin J.	(IL)	181
	DEERWESTER, Scott C.	(IL)	287
	HILDRETH, Charles R.	(IL)	539
	JOHNSON, Anita D.	(IL)	602
	LANCASTER, Frederick W.	(IL)	691
	SMITH, Linda C.	(IL)	1157
	SWANSON, Don R.	(IL)	1213
	HARTER, Stephen P.	(IN)	508
	HICKLING, Jeanne	(IN)	536
	MARKEE, Katherine M.	(IN)	771
	BOYCE, Bert R.	(LA)	122
	KRAFT, Donald H.	(LA)	674
	RAGHAVAN, Vijay V.	(LA)	1003
	BOGART, Betty B.	(MA)	110
	DENTON, Francesca L.	(MA)	293
	DRESLEY, Susan C.	(MA)	319
	BRANDHORST, Wesley T.	(MD)	128
	BUCHAN, Ronald L.	(MD)	153
	CARR, Margaret M.	(MD)	186
	BALOK, Becki	(MI)	53
	EVERITT, Janet M.	(MI)	359
	ASPNES, Grieg G.	(MN)	37
	BURGIN, Robert E.	(NC)	159
	KISER, Anita H.	(NC)	656
	LOSEE, Robert M.	(NC)	742
	DATUS, Marie B.	(NE)	275
	AMIRZAFARI, Jamileh A.	(NJ)	20
	SARACEVIC, Tefko	(NJ)	1082
	BERRY, Gayle C.	(NY)	90
	CARICONE, Paul	(NY)	181
	CULLEN, Martin J.	(NY)	263
	CYPSER, Rudy J.	(NY)	268
	ETTLINGER, Sandra E.	(NY)	356
	KATZER, Jeffrey	(NY)	630
	KRONISH, Priscilla T.	(NY)	680
	PEARCE, Karla J.	(NY)	952
	SALTON, Gerard	(NY)	1077
	SCHAFFER, Rita K.	(NY)	1089
	BROWN, Rowland C.	(OH)	147
	HARTNER, Elizabeth P.	(PA)	508
	MICCO, Helen M.	(PA)	831
	PAUL, Thompson	(PA)	949
	CARLIN, Don	(TN)	182
	MCDONALD, Ethel Q.	(TN)	802
	ECHT, Sandy A.	(TX)	334
	HELFER, Robert S.	(TX)	523
	MOORE, Guusje Z.	(TX)	859
	WALKER, Constance M.	(TX)	1295
	LIU, Kitty P.	(UT)	734
	PITERNICK, Anne B.	(BC)	976
	NELSON, Michael J.	(ON)	894
	RIDLEY, A M.	(ON)	1033
	TAGUE, Jean M.	(ON)	1220
	THACH, Phat V.	(PQ)	1233
	WALKER, Elizabeth A.	(PQ)	1295
	BEATTIE, Kathleen M.	(AUS)	70
	CLEVERDON, Cyril W.	(ENG)	221
	BLOCH, Uri	(ISR)	105
	ELAZAR, David H.	(ISR)	341
	NASU, Yukio	(JAP)	889
	YAMAZAKI, Hisamichi	(JAP)	1377

RETRIEVAL (Cont'd)

Information retrieval & analysis — OWEN, Beth C. . . . . (MA) 931
Information retrieval & indexing — HUMPHREY, Susanne M. (MD) 573
Information retrieval & reference — DONNELLY, Kathleen . . . (OH) 311
Information retrieval & services — COFFEE, E G. . . . . (KS) 226
Information retrieval design system — KORNFELD, Carol E. . . . (NJ) 672
Information retrieval in Latin America — GREEN-MALONEY, Nancy (CA) 465
Information retrieval research — COOPER, William S. . . . (CA) 244
HUESTIS, Jeffrey C. . . . . (MO) 570
FOX, Edward A. . . . . (VA) 394
Information retrieval service — BOURNE, Charles P. . . . (CA) 119
Information retrieval services — WILLMANN, Donna S. . . (PA) 1348
Information retrieval software — RALBOVSKY, Edward A. (NY) 1004
NICHOL, Kathleen M. . . . (BC) 901
Information retrieval software design — BRUNELLE, Bette S. . . . (NY) 150
Information retrieval softwares — LEDOUX, Marc A. . . . . . (PQ) 708
Information retrieval system — SANO, Hikomaro . . . . . . (JAP) 1081
Information retrieval system design — MEYER, Alan H. . . . . . . (MD) 829
MCCLELLAND, Bruce A. (NY) 796
Information retrieval systems — CUADRA, Carlos A. . . . . . (CA) 262
GABBERT, Gretchen W. . (CA) 411
SHELBURNE, Elizabeth C. (DC) 1125
SCHIPMA, Peter B. . . . . (IL) 1093
EISENMANN, Laura M. . . (MA) 341
BONDAROVICH, Mary F. (NJ) 113
CHAPMAN, Janet L. . . . (NJ) 202
FRANTS, Valery . . . . (NJ) 398
GLAMM, Amy E. . . . . . . (VA) 439
SAUVE, Deborah A. . . . . (VA) 1085
REILLY, Brian O. . . . . . . (ON) 1020
ZHU, Xiaofeng . . . . (CHI) 1387
ROBERTSON, Stephen E. (ENG)1042
CHAUMIER, Jacques . . . (FRN) 204
Information retrieval systems design — ANDERSON, James D. . . (NJ) 23
Information retrieval technologies — HOLMES, Lyndon S. . . . (MA) 553
Information retrieval theories — HOSONO, Kimio . . . . . . (JAP) 562
Information retrieval thesaurus — ASIS, Moises . . . . (CUB) 36
Information storage & retrieval — KENDRICK, Brent L. . . . (DC) 640
CARR, Sallyann . . . . (FL) 186
CHERN, Jenn C. . . . . . . (GA) 206
GOODY, Cheryl S. . . . . . (HI) 450
BOOKSTEIN, Abraham . . (IL) 115
SHAW, Debora . . . . (IL) 1123
WALDHART, Thomas J. . (KY) 1294
BRIAND, Margaret M. . . . (MA) 134
GEORGE, Muriel S. . . . . (NJ) 428
AUSTIN, Ralph A. . . . . . (NY) 40
GREENBERG, Linda . . . . (NY) 463
WYLLYS, Ronald E. . . . . (TX) 1375
MORRISON, David L. . . . (UT) 868
BONNETT, Mary B. . . . . (VA) 114
SCHABAS, Ann H. . . . . . (ON) 1088
WILSON, Concepcion S. (AUS)1350
Information storage & retrieval theory — WILSON, Patrick . . . . . . (CA) 1352
Legal information retrieval education — BARBEN, Tanya A. . . . . (SAF) 55
Legal research retrieval systems — EVERLOVE, Nora J. . . . . (FL) 359
Material retrieval — CUNNINGHAM, Mary A. (NY) 265
Mechanized information retrieval — KENT, Allen . . . . (PA) 642
Medical information retrieval — WAKEFIELD, Jacqueline
M. . . . . (CA) 1293
MicroBASIS retrieval software — DITMARS, David W. . . . (OH) 305
Microcomputer information retrieval — WOODWARD, Anthony M. (ENG)1367
Microform storage & retrieval systems — SKARR, Robert J. . . . . . (DC) 1145
News & information storage & retrieval — TRIVEDI, Harish S. . . . . . (OH) 1257
Online bibliographic retrieval — ROSS, Nina M. . . . . (PA) 1058
Online full-text retrieval — WHITMAN, Mary L. . . . . (PA) 1333
Online information retrieval — ANDERSON, Clifford D. . (CA) 22
GRENIER, Myra T. . . . . . (CA) 467
FINE, Sandra R. . . . . . . (DC) 377
KOVITZ, Nancy R. . . . . . (IL) 674
JACK, Robert F. . . . . . . (MD) 586
HAM, Beverly V. . . . . . . (MN) 490
MULTER, Ell P. . . . . (MO) 878
CALLANAN, Ellen M. . . . (NJ) 173
HSIAO, Shu Y. . . . . (NY) 567
LOWE, Ida B. . . . . (NY) 743
MARTINEZ-NAZARIO,
Ronaldo . . . . (PR) 779
MILLS, Catherine H. . . . . (RI) 843

RETRIEVAL (Cont'd)

Online information retrieval — DOBSON, Christine B. . . (TX) 307
ACCARDI, Joseph J. . . . . (WI) 3
SWEETLAND, James H. . (WI) 1215
MACKENZIE, Shirley A. . (ON) 756
Online information retrieval & storage — WILLIAMS, Martha E. . . . (iL) 1345
Online information retrieval, business — OSTROW, Rona . . . . . . (NY) 929
Online information retrieval, databases — RAITT, David I. . . . . . . (NET)1004
Online reference retrieval — ELLIOT, Hugh . . . . (DC) 343
Online retrieval — GALLERY, M C. . . . . (CA) 414
PAIK, Nan H. . . . . (CA) 935
BOWERS, Sandra L. . . . (CO) 121
BELLARDO, Trudi . . . . . (DC) 78
PEPETONE, Diane S. . . . (IA) 957
BAILEY, Joanne P. . . . . . (IN) 46
WALLACE, Danny P. . . . (IN) 1297
GERKE, Ray . . . . (MA) 428
SEELEY, Catherine R. . . (ME) 1111
STEPHENS, Karen L. . . . (MI) 1188
MILLER, Betty . . . . (NY) 836
ST. JACQUES, Suzanne L. (ON) 1075
Online retrieval services — DEBROWER, Amy M. . . . (MD) 285
MARSHALL, Patricia K. . . (NY) 775
Online retrieval systems — DRUMMOND, Louis E. . . . (DC) 321
TAHIR, Mary M. . . . . . . (MD) 1220
STEFFEY, Ramona J. . . . (TN) 1185
GALBRAITH, Paula L. . . . (TX) 413
Online searching & biblgph retrieval — KING, Hannah M. . . . . . (DC) 651
Online searching & retrieval — COOK, Kathleen M. . . . . (CA) 240
Optical disk storage & retrieval — ELMAN, Stanley A. . . . . (CA) 345
Patent database & information
retrieval — ROSENTHAL, Francine C. (OH) 1057
Patent information retrieval — SIMMONS, Edlyn S. . . . . (OH) 1139
PC-based retrieval systems — CIUFFETTI, Peter D. . . . (MA) 215
Photo storage & retrieval — HAMMOND, Theresa M. . (VA) 494
Photograph storage & retrieval — STEVENS, Paula F. . . . . (AZ) 1190
Proprietary data retrieval — ROBERTSON, Betty M. . . (NY) 1041
Records & information filing &
retrieval — GRAHAM, Su D. . . . . . . (CO) 456
Reference & information retrieval — HEINZ, Catharine F. . . . (DC) 522
MOORE, Patricia R. . . . . (NC) 860
RICE, Anna C. . . . . (NJ) 1026
BEAUDRIE, Ronald A. . . (NY) 70
STOAN, Stephen K. . . . . (TX) 1195
Reference & info retrieval systems — MASON, Michael L. . . . . (NJ) 781
Reference & online info retrieval — YOUNGEN, Gregory K. . (IN) 1383
Reference information retrieval — STEPANICK, John R. . . . (FL) 1187
Research & information retrieval — ROE, Georgeanne T. . . . (MA) 1048
HACKNEY, Judith G. . . . (TX) 481
Retrieval systems — VON KEITZ, Wolfgang . . (WGR)288
Retrieval systems design — HOWARD, Susanna J. . . (NC) 564
Retrieval systems, text — BYRN, William H. . . . . . (MA) 169
Retrieving information for students — LONNING, Roger D. . . . . (MN) 740
Retrieving technical information — HALLSTROM, Curtis H. . . (MN) 489
Science information retrieval — BROWN, Cynthia D. . . . . (NY) 142
Scientific & technical info retrieval — HOWARD, Theresa M. . . (ENG) 564
Searching & retrieving archival
sources — FALK, Candace S. . . . . . (CA) 362
SEC research & retrieval — GRISDELA, Margaret . . . (DC) 471
Special collections catlgng & retrieval — KELLY, John P. . . . . (NJ) 638
Storage & retrieval of records &
docums — RAC-FEDORIJCZUK,
Karola C. . . . . (PA) 1001
Storage & retrieval system design — TRAVIS, Irene L. . . . . . . (VA) 1254
Teach information retrieval skills — SMITH, Margie G. . . . . . (CA) 1157
Technical information retrieval — NELSON, Alice R. . . . . . (CA) 893
SCHALIT, Michael . . . . . (CA) 1089
LAZARUS, Josephine G. (CO) 706
Technical report document retrieval — WHITE, Chandlee . . . . . (MA) 1330
Text management & retrieval systems — LOWENSTEIN, Richard A. (CT) 744
Text retrieval — HOWARD, Theresa M. . . (ENG) 564
Text retrieval systems — WEAVER, Maggie . . . . . (ON) 1312
Textile information storage & retrieval — LAWRENCE, Philip D. . . (VA) 704
Theory of information retrieval — MOOERS, Calvin N. . . . (MA) 857
ROBERTSON, Stephen E. (ENG)1042

RETROCONVERSION (See also Retrospective)

Retroconversion — HORGAN, Laura A. . . . . (MA) 559

RETROSPECTIVE (See also Conversion, Reconversion, Retroconversion)

Automated retrospective conversion	JOHNSON, Pat M.	(TX)	608
Catalog & retrospective conversion	CHAN, Margy	(ON)	199
Cataloging & retrospective conversion	ZIESELMAN, Paula M.	(NY)	1388
Cataloging, original & retrospective	SCHEITLE, Janet M.	(VA)	1091
Cataloging retrospective conversion	ROBERTSON, Pamela S.	(ND)	1042
Database retrospective conversion	MORGAN, Ferrell	(CA)	864
Inventory retrospective conversion	SCHMIDT, Mary A.	(TX)	1095
Retrospective cataloging	OSGOOD, James B.	(IL)	928
Retrospective cataloging & editing	HUGGENS, Gary D.	(DC)	571
Retrospective conversion	MOORE, Anne C.	(AZ)	858
	DRIVER, Linda A.	(CA)	320
	MAINELLI, Helen K.	(CA)	761
	NEAL, Jan	(CA)	890
	SASSE, Margo	(CA)	1083
	SCHOTTLAENDER, Brian E.	(CA)	1099
	SWEENEY, Suzanne	(CA)	1215
	THELIN, Sonya R.	(CA)	1234
	WILLIAMS, Mary S.	(CA)	1345
	HILL, John R.	(CT)	540
	LISOWSKI, Andrew H.	(DC)	732
	REED-SCOTT, Jutta R.	(DC)	1015
	SANDIQUE-OWENS, Amelia A.	(DC)	1080
	PINGS, Joan G.	(FL)	974
	WILLIAMS, Nancy L.	(FL)	1345
	WILSON, Lesley P.	(GA)	1351
	CURL, Margo W.	(ID)	265
	OSTRANDER, Gloria J.	(ID)	929
	IDDINGS, Daniel H.	(IL)	581
	JAGODZINSKI, Cecile M.	(IL)	591
	OWNES, Dorothy J.	(IL)	932
	WILLIAMS, Charles M.	(IL)	1342
	EBERSHOFF-COLES, Susan V.	(IN)	334
	PEC, Jean A.	(IN)	953
	WARTZOK, Susan G.	(IN)	1307
	DEARUJO, Georgia R.	(KY)	284
	KUKLINSKI, Joan L.	(MA)	683
	SMITH, Barbara G.	(MD)	1152
	SMITH, Mary P.	(MD)	1158
	BRUNHUMER, Sondra K.	(MI)	150
	DOMBROWSKI, Mark A.	(MI)	310
	ENGLE, Constance B.	(MI)	349
	GERLACH, William P.	(MI)	429
	MA, Helen Y.	(MI)	753
	CHAN, Jeanny T.	(MO)	199
	MYRICK, Judy C.	(MS)	885
	MAYES, Susan E.	(NC)	789
	GARZILLO, Robert R.	(NJ)	421
	LI, Marjorie H.	(NJ)	724
	WILEN, Rosamond L.	(NJ)	1339
	BANICKI, Cynthia A.	(NM)	54
	SAUNDERS, Laverna M.	(NV)	1084
	ANDERSON, Birgitta M.	(NY)	21
	BERTUCA, David J.	(NY)	91
	CHAPMAN, Renee D.	(NY)	202
	ERLAND, Virginia K.	(NY)	353
	GALGAN, Mary N.	(NY)	413
	KIM, Chung N.	(NY)	648
	LOW, Frederick E.	(NY)	743
	LUCKER, Amy E.	(NY)	746
	NICHOLS-RANDALL, Barbara L.	(NY)	902
	SALVAGE, Barbara A.	(NY)	1078
	STALKER, Dianne S.	(NY)	1178
	WERNER, Edward K.	(NY)	1324
	CALL, J R.	(OH)	173
	DAVIS, Linda M.	(OH)	280
	SAMPLES, Judith L.	(OH)	1078
	LOWRIMORE, R T.	(SC)	745
	THOMAS, Julie A.	(SC)	1237
	WALTON, Robert A.	(TX)	1301
	YEH, Helen S.	(TX)	1379
	NOEL, Eileen V.	(UT)	907
	SMITH, John R.	(MB)	1156
Retrospective conversion coordination	WALSH, Joanna M.	(MA)	1299

RETROSPECTIVE (Cont'd)

Retrospective conversion of serials	TUTTLE, Joseph C.	(NC)	1266
	POST, Phyllis C.	(OH)	986
Retrospective conversion projects	PAYNE, Leila M.	(TX)	951
Retrospective conversion services	HANIFORD, K L.	(MO)	496
Serials retrospective conversion	KING, Kenneth E.	(MI)	651

REVENUE

Revenue enhancement	HAMMER, Sharon A.	(CA)	493

REVIEWING (See also Appraisal, Assessment, Criticism, Evaluation)

Access review & coordination	GRAF, Thomas H.	(DC)	456
Access review databases	GRAF, Thomas H.	(DC)	456
Article, report, & review writing	EDELSON, Ken	(NJ)	335
Audiovisual & film reviewing	LOCKE, John W.	(IL)	736
Author interviews & reviews	HOLTZE, Sally H.	(NY)	555
Book & audiovisual software reviewer	LEIBOLD, Cynthia K.	(OH)	713
Book review	WALKER, Elinor	(MN)	1295
Book reviewer	HOFFMANN, Maurine L.	(IL)	548
	TASHJIAN, Virginia A.	(MA)	1224
Book reviewer & speaker	GLATT, Carol R.	(NJ)	440
Book reviewing	JANUS, Bridget M.	(IA)	594
	CALLAGHAN, Linda W.	(IL)	173
	DONOVAN, William A.	(IL)	312
	EPP, Ronald H.	(IL)	351
	MALLER, Mark P.	(IL)	763
	OTT, Bill	(IL)	930
	RETTIG, James R.	(IL)	1024
	WRIGHT, Helen K.	(IL)	1371
	BLANK, Annette C.	(MD)	104
	CIERZNIEWSKI, Robert J.	(MI)	214
	GREFRATH, Richard W.	(NV)	465
	BARTH, Joseph M.	(NY)	61
	JENNINGS, Vincent	(NY)	598
	SOUDERS, Marilyn N.	(NY)	1169
	HAGLOCH, Susan B.	(OH)	483
	MCKEE, Barbara J.	(OH)	810
	WIEHE, Janet C.	(OH)	1336
	JENKINS, Georgann K.	(PA)	597
	MACK, Sara R.	(PA)	756
	DEILY, Carole C.	(TX)	288
	TWENEY, George H.	(WA)	1266
Book reviewing & editing	GUSHEE, Marion S.	(IL)	478
Book reviewing, children's	PAGOTTO, Sarah L.	(PA)	934
Book reviews	DONOVAN, Diane C.	(CA)	312
	WENDROFF, Catriona	(CA)	1323
	JOHNSON, Eric W.	(CT)	604
	CZARNECKI, Cary J.	(IL)	268
	ROBERTSON, Deborah G.	(IL)	1041
	LEVEL, M J.	(KS)	719
	POLACHECK, Demarest L.	(OH)	980
	WEEKS, Patsy L.	(TX)	1315
Book selection & reviewing	CARROLL, Barbara T.	(WI)	187
Children's book reviewer	WAGNER, Sharon L.	(CA)	1292
Children's book reviewing	NICHOLS, Margaret M.	(AZ)	901
	WILSON, Phillis M.	(IL)	1352
	GILLIS, Ruth J.	(MN)	436
	WILLIAMS, Deborah H.	(NY)	1342
Children's social sciences reviewing	WOLL, Christina B.	(TX)	1361
Concert reviews	LAMBERT, John W.	(NC)	690
Critical reviews of literature	HENDERSON, Madeline M.	(MD)	526
Database development, indexing, reviews	WOODARD, Beth E.	(MI)	1365
Database searching & reviews	NITECKI, Danuta A.	(MD)	905
Editing & reviewing	RAZER, Robert L.	(AR)	1012
	BALLARD, Robert M.	(NC)	53
Editing book reviews	ESTES, Sally C.	(IL)	355
Editing law review articles	STEFANCIC, Jean A.	(CA)	1185
Editing, reviewing, young adult lib srvs	CAMPBELL, Patricia J.	(CA)	177
Fiction reviewing	SMITH, Maureen M.	(OH)	1158
Film & video reviewing & programming	BRAUN, Robert L.	(NY)	130
Film reviewer	SECKELSON, Linda E.	(NY)	1110
General exposition essays & reviews	HUMEZ, Nicholas D.	(ME)	573
Grantsmanship writing & reviewing	KELLEY, John F.	(PA)	636
IRM reviews & audits	HORTON, Forest W.	(DC)	561
Management reviews	STEELE, Colin R.	(AUS)	1184

REVIEWING (Cont'd)

Mandatory review declassification	BRILEY, Carol A.	(MO)	136
Media reviewer	CHAKLOSH, Cynthia L.	(MI)	197
Microcomputer software reviews	MANN, Carol A.	(TX)	765
Music publications, reviewer	MAYER, George L.	(NY)	789
Music reviewer	POLITIS, John V.	(PA)	981
Oral reviews	FOX, Estella E.	(KY)	394
Planning & grant review	SCHUTT, Cheryl M.	(CT)	1103
Professional publications & reviewing	CHEATHAM, Bertha M.	(NY)	204
Programming buildings & plan review	HOLT, Raymond M.	(CA)	554
Record reviewing	SEIBERT, Donald C.	(NY)	1112
Record reviews	LAMBERT, John W.	(NC)	690
Reference book reviewing	JENSEN, Joan W.	(CT)	598
	MEYERS, Arthur S.	(IN)	830
Reference book reviews	HOGAN, Patricia M.	(IL)	549
Review writing & editing	SILVER, Gary L.	(MI)	1138
Reviewer	ALABASTER, Carol	(AZ)	9
Reviewer of children's books	GOODRICH PETERSON, Marilyn	(KS)	450
Reviewing	DOBREZ, Cynthia K.	(IL)	307
	ROCHMAN, Hazel P.	(IL)	1046
	NOAH, Carolyn B.	(MA)	906
	SILVEY, Anita L.	(MA)	1139
	BURGESS, Eileen E.	(MD)	159
	GREGORY, Helen B.	(MI)	466
	WRIGHT, Larry L.	(NC)	1372
	LAWRENCE, Arthur P.	(NY)	704
	POLACHECK, Janet G.	(OH)	980
	CHENEY, Frances N.	(TN)	206
	SHUEY, Andrea L.	(TX)	1133
Reviewing AV & computer software	MILLER, John E.	(OH)	839
Reviewing audiovisual materials	RYBARCZYK, Barclay S.	(NY)	1071
Reviewing children's books	NIX, Kemie	(GA)	905
	CRAIGHEAD, Alice A.	(TX)	254
	POLISHUK, Bernard	(WA)	980
	KRUSE, Ginny M.	(WI)	681
Reviewing children's books & audiovisual	SHERMAN, Louise L.	(NJ)	1128
Reviewing, editing, writing	ARK, Connie E.	(OH)	31
Reviewing film, video & media	TROJAN, Judith L.	(NY)	1257
Reviewing for publication	FOX, Estella E.	(KY)	394
Reviewing genealogical materials	CRAWFORD, Carolyn	(CA)	256
Reviewing materials, print & non-print	SELWYN, Laurie	(TX)	1114
Reviewing nuclear issues films	DOWLING, John	(PA)	316
Reviewing physics films	DOWLING, John	(PA)	316
Reviewing strategies	OWENS, Irene E.	(PA)	932
Reviews & abstracts articles	GABBIANELLI, Patrice A.	(NJ)	411
Reviews of editing & writing	GORDON, Ruth I.	(CA)	452
Reviews, writing, editing	VAN NIEL, Eloise S.	(HI)	1276
Serials bibliographic control & review	STEINHAGEN, Elizabeth N.	(ID)	1186
Technical book reviewing	KRUPP, Robert G.	(NJ)	681
Writing book reviews	ESTES, Sally C.	(IL)	355
Writing reviews & editing	MATHES, Miriam S.	(WA)	783
Young adult literature reviewing	TUZINSKI, Jean H.	(NY)	1266
Young adult reviewing	SCHLANSER, Deborah B.	(CA)	1093
	BALL, Diane A.	(OH)	52
Young adult reviews	WADE, Sherry A.	(CA)	1290

REWRITING (See also Writing)

Rewriting medical & pharmacological text	HAMILTON, Gloria R.	(PA)	492

RHEUMATOLOGY

Rheumatology	RAY, Laura E.	(OH)	1011

RIGHTS

Constitution rights	JUERGENSMEYER, John E.	(IL)	619
Human rights implementation	KLOK, Buddhi	(PQ)	662
International human rights law	PERKINS, Steven C.	(CA)	959
Permissions & licensing rights	MARKERT, Patricia B.	(NY)	771
Rights & permissions	PRONIN, Monica	(NY)	995

RISK

Health risk analysis research	MUNRO, Nancy B.	(TN)	879
Health risk appraisal systems	ABRAMSON, Lawrence J.	(MI)	3
Library risk management	SCHMIDT, Theodore A.	(MT)	1096
Medical risk management consulting	THOMASSON, George O.	(CO)	1238
Political risk reports	NAPOLITANO, Wanda M.	(NY)	887
	SULLIVAN, Daniel M.	(NY)	1207
Research on risks & hazards	KASPERSON, Jeanne X.	(MA)	629
Risk management	REYNOLDS, Carol C.	(GA)	1025
Risk management & preservation	SEAL, Robert A.	(TX)	1109

RLIN

Cataloging, RLIN, OCLC experience	YU, Hsiao M.	(IA)	1384
Library systems & RLIN database	LEE, Doreen H.	(CA)	709
Online cataloging, OCLC, RLIN	TURITZ, Mitch L.	(CA)	1263
RLIN	SNYDER, Theresa	(PA)	1165
RLIN/AMC Database	BROWN, William E.	(CT)	148
RLIN automation	SOLOMON, Geri E.	(NY)	1166
RLIN database	KAPLAN, Diane E.	(CT)	626

ROBOTICS

Robotics	KOUNTZ, John C.	(CA)	673

ROMANCE

Cataloging romance languages	KELLEY, Ann C.	(IA)	636
Original cataloging romance languages	SALINERO, Amelia	(NY)	1076
Romance language cataloging	CRISTAN, Anita L.	(DC)	259
	JAVONOVICH, Kenneth L.	(IL)	595
Romance languages	CANTRELL, Clyde H.	(AL)	179
	SMITH, Mary P.	(MD)	1158
	SHIRKY, Martha H.	(MO)	1131
Romance languages & literature	POLIT, Carlos E.	(IN)	980

ROMANTICISM

American literature, romanticism	FISHER, Benjamin F.	(MS)	380
English literature, romantic	STAM, David H.	(NY)	1179
Musicology, ethnomusicology, romanticism	HAEFLIGER, Kathleen A.	(NY)	482

RUBBER

Rubber, plastics & polymer science	HOLLIS, William F.	(OH)	552

RURAL

Electronic rural libraries	HOLT, Suzy	(MT)	554
Organization of rural school libraries	GOODMAN, Roslyn L.	(AK)	449
Public relations, rural-small libraries	KNIEVEL, Helen A.	(OR)	664
Rural & small libraries	HULL, Catherine C.	(RI)	572
Rural branch libraries	MCCORMICK, Tamsie	(IN)	799
Rural health	TOVREA, Roxanna L.	(IA)	1252
	KATZER, Sylvia U.	(ON)	630
Rural health information transfer	BOISSY, Robert W.	(NY)	111
Rural librarianship	KRUGLET, Jo A.	(CO)	680
	HANKS, Gardner C.	(MN)	496
	HENDRICKS, Thom	(ND)	527
Rural libraries	HALES, John D.	(FL)	486
	CADDELL, Claude W.	(IN)	170
	CHRISTENSON, John D.	(MN)	211
	JANZEN, Deborah K.	(MN)	594
	SHAFFER, Nancy R.	(NC)	1119
	MINERVA, Jane R.	(NY)	846
	MING, Marilyn	(AB)	846
	GOODGER-HILL, Carol	(ON)	448
Rural library administration	BURNETT, James H.	(CO)	161
Rural library construction	MCCORMICK, Tamsie	(IN)	799
Rural library consulting	HAYNES, Jean	(NY)	516
Rural library development	PACEY, Brenda M.	(IL)	933
	LANGEVIN, Ann T.	(NV)	695
	GINNANE, Mary J.	(OR)	437
	KNIEVEL, Helen A.	(OR)	664
Rural library development & training	WILLIAMS, Susan S.	(MI)	1346
Rural library management	BREIT, Anitra D.	(WA)	132

RURAL (Cont'd)
Rural library service

	LAWSON, Martha G. . . .	(AR)	705
	UBEL, James A.	(IL)	1267
	SPILLERS, Roger E. . . .	(MN)	1174
	JOHNSON, Corinne E. . .	(OH)	603
	REID, Margaret B.	(OH)	1018
	WASH, Melba W.	(TN)	1307
	LABUIK, Karen L.	(SK)	686
Rural library services	MCCORMICK, Tamsie . .	(IN)	799
	BOESE, Robert A.	(MN)	110
	DEGRUYTER, M L.	(TX)	288
Rural library systems	CAMPBELL, Ray	(IL)	177
	HOWARD, Ada M.	(TX)	563
Rural public libraries	TROMATER, Raymond B.	(AR)	1257
	ALLENSWORTH, James H.	(CA)	16
	HARRIET, Conklin W. . . .	(IL)	503
	CASSELL, Marianne K. .	(VT)	193
Rural public library systems	O'BRIEN, Marlys H.	(MN)	915
Rural services	PHILIP, John J.	(OH)	967
Service to rural disadvantaged	POWELL, Anice C.	(MS)	988
Small & rural libraries	JENNINGS, Martha F. . .	(MI)	598
Small, rural library service	MILLER, Pearl F.	(IA)	841
Small rural public libraries	PANZ, Richard	(NY)	938

RUSSIAN (See also Soviet Union)

History of Russian, Soviet bibliography	WHITBY, Thomas J.	(CO)	1330
Prerevolutionary Russian publishing	BEAVEN, Miranda J. . .	(MN)	71
Russian & East European bibliography	BEAVEN, Miranda J. . . .	(MN)	71
Russian & East European studies	ROBERTSON, Howard W.	(OR)	1042
Russian & Soviet studies	WERTHEIMER, Marilyn L.	(CO)	1325
Russian bibliography	POLANSKY, Patricia A. .	(HI)	980
Russian collection development	BAER, Eberhard A.	(VA)	44
Russian criticism	ROYTMAN, Serafima . .	(NY)	1063
Russian history	YERBURGH, Mark R. . .	(VT)	1379
Russian history, revolutionary period	ST. AUBIN, Arleen K. . .	(MA)	1075
Russian library history	STUART, Mary P.	(IL)	1204
Slavic reference, Russian language	PRICE, Susan W.	(NY)	992

S/38

S/38 computer software	TODD, Hal W.	(FL)	1248

SAFETY (See also Accidents)

Automotive safety	VAN ALLEN, Neil K.	(MI)	1271
Databases, occupational health & safety	MCLAUGHLIN, W K. . . .	(AB)	813
Food safety information systems	CHATFIELD, Michele R. .	(DC)	203
Health & safety	BELLEFONTAINE, Gillian	(ON)	78
Health & safety at work	MERCIER, Diane	(PQ)	825
Health & safety research	GAMBRELL, Drucilla S. .	(AL)	416
Motor vehicle safety	DOERNBERG, David G. .	(DC)	308
Motorcycle safety	DAWSON, Lawrence . . .	(WI)	282
Nuclear safety & nuclear engineering	TODOSOW, Helen K. . . .	(NY)	1248
Occupational health & safety	LE BLANC, Judith E. . . .	(OH)	708
	MORRISON, Brian H. . . .	(ON)	867
	GREGOIRE, Fleurette . . .	(PQ)	466
Occupational health & safety information	TUCKER, Mary E.	(NC)	1262
	ZUBA, Elizabeth J.	(AB)	1390
Occupational safety	KLEMARCZYK, Laurice D.	(CT)	660
	BOUTWELL, Barbara J. .	(PA)	119
Plant safety & reliability	HASTINGS, Constance M.	(TN)	511
Product safety & liability research	MOUZON, Margaret W. .	(MI)	874
Safety & toxicology	WEISS, Barbara M.	(CT)	1319
Safety engineering research	HANSEN, Cheryl A.	(IL)	497
Safety, toxicology databases	WEISS, Barbara M.	(CT)	1319
Traffic safety	BARTH, Nancy L.	(CA)	61
Transportation safety research support	GATTIS, R G.	(MI)	422

SALARY (See also Compensation, Pay)

Salary & compensation analysis	FRETWELL, Gordon E. . .	(MA)	402
Strategies for salary issues	SHANNON, Marcia A. . .	(MA)	1120

SALES (See also Retailing, Selling, Vendor, Wholesale)

Academic & research libraries book sales	SCHRIFT, Leonard B. . .	(NY)	1100
Advertising sales management	KOBASA, Paul A.	(IL)	666
Antiquarian theatre books sales	KAHAN, Gerald	(GA)	621
Database marketing & sales	PAPPALARDO, Marcia J.	(IL)	939
Database sales	SINE, George H.	(IL)	1143
	GABOR, John M.	(NY)	411
Direct marketing & sales management	JOHNSON, Richard K. . .	(MD)	608
Equipment sales	MAY, Robert E.	(SC)	789
Gateway sales & marketing	GROSSMAN, Allen N. . .	(NJ)	473
Information sales & marketing	BARTLETT, Jay P.	(NY)	61
Marketing, advertising & sales	CORNICK, Ron	(IL)	247
Marketing & sales	MALCOLM, J P.	(MI)	762
	JAMIESON, Peter V. . . .	(NY)	593
	KOCHOFF, Stephen T. . .	(NY)	667
	MILLER, Frank W.	(NY)	837
	REED, Buzz	(OH)	1014
Marketing sales & customer service	KINLEY, Jo H.	(DC)	652
Music sales databases	VERNON, James R. . . .	(TX)	1283
Personal computer database, sales	NASON, Stanley J.	(NY)	888
Publication sales	MIDDLETON, Carl H. . . .	(DC)	833
Publishing monthly sales lists	SMITH, Walter H.	(VA)	1161
Rare book sales	MUELLER, Robert W. . .	(IL)	875
Rare books purchase & sales	MCKITTRICK, Bruce W. .	(PA)	812
Research & consultation sales	MIDDLETON, Carl H. . . .	(DC)	833
Sales	HARDT, James R.	(FL)	500
	GILL, John H.	(IN)	435
	LESLIE, Donald S.	(MN)	718
Sales & marketing	BARKALOW, Pat A.	(CA)	56
	POOLEY, Christopher G. .	(MA)	983
	ARTHUR, Christine	(NY)	35
	BAILEY, Joe A.	(NY)	46
	MELKIN, Audrey D.	(NY)	822
	SOLOMON, Samuel H. . .	(NY)	1166
Sales & marketing online services	CLARK, Rick	(NJ)	218
Sales & speaker	WILBUR, Helen L.	(NY)	1338
Sales consulting	IVAK, Patricia A.	(PA)	585
Sales, marketing & publishing	BECK, Arthur R.	(CT)	71
Sales, marketing, product development	ALESSI, Dana L.	(TX)	11
Subscription services, sales	NASON, Stanley J.	(NY)	888
Subscriptions sales management	KOBASA, Paul A.	(IL)	666
Telephone sales	DYER, Carolyn A.	(CT)	330
Used law book sales	BROWN, G R.	(FL)	144
	KILLIAN, Mary C.	(MI)	648

SANSKRIT

Sanskrit	NYE, James H.	(IL)	912

SAS

SAS programming application	ROSTAMI, Janet	(ON)	1059

SAT

SAT preparation	CARPENTER, Carole H. .	(DE)	184

SATELLITES

Communication satellites	LIU, Rosa	(DC)	734
Radio programming via satellite	WILLIAMS, Fred	(GA)	1343
Satellite communications	SCHABERT, Daniel R. . .	(NY)	1088
Satellite information ctrs establishment	LAVIN, Margaret A.	(NJ)	703
Satellite teleconferences	CONNOR, Elizabeth	(MD)	237
Satellite teleconferencing	LANSDALE, Metta T. . . .	(MI)	696
Secondary curriculum, satellite use	WILSON, M L.	(CO)	1352
Video, TV, satellite systems	HISS, Sheila M.	(FL)	544

SCANDINAVIAN (See also Swedish)

Scandinavian area studies	SPETLAND, Charles G. .	(MN)	1174
Scandinavian bibliography	THORSTENSSON, Edith J.	(MN)	1243
Scandinavian literature	MOLLER, Hans	(PQ)	853
Scandinavian reference services	TIBLIN, Mariann E.	(MN)	1244
Scandinavian studies	SWEEDLER, Ulla S. . . .	(CA)	1214

SCANNING

Optical scanning & storage	SPANGLER, Bruce	(CO)	1171
Prepress scanning technology	HILL, Kristin E.	(CA)	540

SCHOENBERG

Schoenberg	THYM, Jurgen	(NY)	1243

SCHOLARSHIP

Computer scholarship matching service	SHAW, Ben B.	(TX)	1123
Literary scholarship	LEWIS, John S.	(TX)	723
Out-of-print scholarly books	SOMERS, Wayne F.	(NY)	1167
Rare & scholarly books	KIEFFER, Jay	(CA)	647
Reference & scholarly books	SCHORR, Alan E.	(AK)	1099
Scholarly & reference book publishing	BERKNER, Dimity S.	(NY)	87
Scholarly & scientific communication	EDELMAN, Hendrik	(NJ)	335
Scholarly books	ASH, Lee M.	(CT)	35
	EDWARDS, David M.	(PA)	337
Scholarly communication	OSBURN, Charles B.	(AL)	927
	STIEG, Margaret F.	(AL)	1193
	GEORGE, Mary W.	(NJ)	427
	RICHARDS, Pamela S.	(NJ)	1028
	PURDY, Victor W.	(UT)	998
Scholarly communication for info tech	DOUGHERTY, Richard M.	(MI)	314
Scholarly communications	BRANIN, Joseph J.	(MN)	128
Scholarly databases	BEARMAN, David A.	(PA)	69
Scholarly journal coverage	WALSH, James A.	(PA)	1299
Scholarly law books	LUTTRELL, Jordan D.	(CA)	750
Scholarly library research	HARMALA, Amy A.	(WA)	502
Scholarly micropublishing	JOHNSON, Richard K.	(MD)	608
Scholarly music publishing	PAVLAKIS, Christopher	(NY)	950
Scholarly publication in video	O'CONNOR, Brian C.	(CA)	915
Scholarly publishing	MCCULLOH, Judith M.	(IL)	801

SCHOOL (See also Elementary, Grade, High, Junior, K-12, Kindergarten, Middle, Primary, Senior)

Administering school library programs	JACKSON, Gloria D.	(CA)	587
Administration, middle school library	GERLACH, Gretchen J.	(IL)	429
Administration of school libraries	LENOX, Mary F.	(MO)	715
	EGAN, Mary J.	(NY)	338
	SHAPIRO, Lillian L.	(NY)	1121
	ADRIAN, Donna J.	(PQ)	7
Administration of school lib media progs	KLASING, Jane P.	(FL)	657
Administrator, school library system	MORRISON, George J.	(NY)	868
Archdiocesan school system libraries	DALY, Sally A.	(PA)	271
Art museums & schools	LEIBOLD, Cheryl A.	(PA)	713
Audiovisual materials for schools	ELLIS, Caryl A.	(AZ)	344
Automating school libraries	KRENTZ, Roger F.	(WI)	677
Automation in school libraries	HAND, M D.	(TX)	494
Books for schools & libraries	RARESHEID, Cynthia L.	(OH)	1008
Cataloging school library media	SANDERS, Minda M.	(PA)	1080
Censorship in school libraries	SCHMUHL, Gayle B.	(OH)	1096
Centralized media services, schools	BERTRAND, Doreen M.	(ON)	91
Children's librarian, elementary school	POBANZ, Becky L.	(MI)	979
Collection development in schools	MARTINEZ, Helen	(NF)	779
Collection development, school	KENNEY, Ann J.	(OR)	641
Collection development, school libraries	CORNWELL, Linda L.	(IN)	247
College & school accreditation	FITZPATRICK, Kelly	(MD)	383
College & school library administration	BROWN, Thomas M.	(WV)	148
Computer applications in schools	WEST, Marian S.	(MI)	1326
Computer technology for high sch libs	TOLMAN, Bonnie B.	(MI)	1249
Computer use in school libraries	WHITNEY, Karen A.	(AZ)	1334
Computers in school libraries	PORMEN, Paul E.	(OH)	984
Computers in schools	MCDANIEL, Deanna J.	(OH)	801
Consultant to schools & libraries	HAAS, Carolyn B.	(IL)	480
Consulting services to schools	LEVEL, M J.	(KS)	719
Copyright, school library issues	WEBSTER, Patricia B.	(NY)	1315
Curriculum & school libraries	EGAN, Mary J.	(NY)	338
Database research, high schools	WARAKSA, Raymond P.	(CT)	1303
Declining enrollment & school closings	FLOWERS, Helen F.	(NY)	386
Developing school libraries	GRAY, Tomysena F.	(CA)	460
Development of school library programs	MEIER, Patricia L.	(IA)	821
	PETERSON, Miriam E.	(IL)	964

SCHOOL (Cont'd)

District school library administration	CURRIE, Bertha B.	(NS)	266
District, school library evaluation	LEVEILLEE, Louis R.	(RI)	719
Education for school librarianship	HAYCOCK, Kenneth R.	(BC)	515
	WHALEN, George F.	(ON)	1328
Elementary & high school libraries	SULLIVAN, Mary A.	(GA)	1208
Elementary & middle school	ROONEY, Merilyn H.	(IN)	1053
Elementary, junior & senior high schools	ABBOTT, Ruth J.	(TX)	1
	FITZGERALD, M A.	(MD)	382
	SCHULTE, Teresa M.	(WI)	1101
Elementary school librarian	TRIDLE, Jeanne A.	(AK)	1256
Elementary school librarianship	SULLIVAN, Geraldine M.	(IL)	1207
	TEEGARDEN, Maude B.	(KY)	1229
	FORD, Delores C.	(TX)	389
Elementary school libraries	ELLIS, Caryl A.	(AZ)	344
	SKEHAN, Patricia A.	(CA)	1145
	MORIARTY, Ann	(DC)	865
	GRANTHAM, Ann V.	(GA)	458
	BAKER, Ethelyn J.	(IL)	48
	HUNT, Margaret M.	(IN)	575
	LONG, Marilyn B.	(LA)	739
	NOLAN, Peggy H.	(LA)	907
	NOLES, Judy H.	(LA)	908
	MASSEY, Eleanor N.	(NJ)	782
	TUNISON, Janice A.	(NY)	1263
	CHERESNOWSKI, Linda M.	(PA)	206
	PASHEL, Susan M.	(PA)	945
	SACHS, Kathie B.	(PA)	1073
	MCGOWN, Sue W.	(TX)	807
Elementary school libraries admin	ZUCKER, Blanche W.	(NV)	1391
Elementary school library	SCHAEFER, Elizabeth K.	(IL)	1088
	BRUNO, Frances J.	(NY)	151
Elementary school library automation	MULLER, Madeline A.	(OH)	877
Elementary school library coordination	HERRON, Bettie J.	(AZ)	533
Elementary school library instruction	SHABERLY, Leanna J.	(AZ)	1118
Elementary school library skills	CANDE, Lorraine N.	(NY)	178
Elementary school library systems	BERRIE, Ellen T.	(ME)	90
Elementary school media	GREENWOOD, Anna S.	(DC)	465
	KILPATRICK, Marguerite C.	(GA)	648
	NEWTON, Evah B.	(IN)	900
	SCHEU, Jean W.	(MN)	1092
Elementary school media centers	BURGOON, Roger S.	(GA)	159
Elementary school media services	HARTMAN, Linda C.	(MO)	508
Elementary schools	DEES DAUGHERTY, Kristin	(WI)	287
Elementary, secondary school materials	PIEHL, Kathleen K.	(MN)	971
Establishing new school libraries	GOODMAN, Helen C.	(TX)	449
Establishing school libraries	KRENTZ, Roger F.	(WI)	677
Evaluation of school librarians	OLSEN, Katherine M.	(UT)	921
Evaluation of school library programs	HUNT, Linda A.	(VA)	575
Evaluation of school library services	BOMAR, Cora P.	(NC)	113
Evaluation school libraries	CRAIGHEAD, Alice A.	(TX)	254
Exemplary school library program	ROADS, Clarice D.	(OK)	1038
Facilities for school programs	HOLTER, Charlotte S.	(MD)	554
Facility planning school media	COMEAU, Reginald A.	(NH)	234
Film & video for schools	MAY, Frank C.	(CA)	788
General school media	WESTFALL, Martha L.	(IN)	1327
Generalist - public schools	YOUNG, Barbara A.	(FL)	1381
Grade school collection development	DRECHSEL, Marcella J.	(NJ)	319
Graduate school collections	SIMMONS, Hal	(GA)	1140
Graduate school teaching	MANES, Estelle L.	(OK)	765
Grammar school libraries	LANE, Mary K.	(NY)	694
High school administration	BOULA, Lillian Y.	(FL)	119
High school & elementary libraries	STUBBLEFIELD, J G.	(TX)	1204
High school curriculum development	MAIN, Isabelle G.	(AZ)	761
	KAPLAN, Lois J.	(OH)	626
High school curriculum implementation	MEANS, E P.	(KS)	820
High school curriculum support	DAVIS, Inez W.	(TN)	279
High school, junior high	JENSEN, Kathryn E.	(MA)	599
High school librarianship	LATIMER, Mary A.	(CA)	701
	SLANGA, Joanne	(MD)	1147
	CLUM, Audna T.	(NY)	223
	GODWIN, Frances L.	(TX)	443
	WILLIAMSON, Judy D.	(WV)	1347

SCHOOL (Cont'd)

High school libraries HEINTZ, Mary L. . . . . . . (AZ) 522
WOLFF, Mary K. . . . . . (CA) 1361
BEUTHEL, Ellengail . . . . (CO) 93
FALK, Louise G. . . . . . . (IA) 362
RODDY, Ruth . . . . (MD) 1047
ZANARINI, Linda S. . . . (NE) 1386
BROWN, Anita P. . . . . (NJ) 142
WEISBURG, Hilda K. . . (NJ) 1319
CARSTATER, Mary E. . . (NY) 188
LANE, Mary K. . . . . (NY) 694
MCCANN, Kathleen . . . . (NY) 794
SUSSMAN, Valerie J. . . . (NY) 1210
SZEMRAJ, Edward R. . . (NY) 1218
CHERESNOWSKI, Linda
M. . . . . (PA) 206
MILLS, Wanda R. . . . . . (TN) 844
GOTHIA, Blanche . . . . . . (TX) 453
HAY, Mary K. . . . . (WI) 515
MIDDLETON, Dorothy J. . (WY) 833
High school libraries & media centers PORTA, Mary D. . . . . . . (PA) 984
High school library HAZLETT, Florence E. . . (AZ) 517
WALTER, Maria . . . . (NY) 1300
MILLER, Marian A. . . . . (OH) 840
High school library administration GOZEMBA, Frances E. . . (MA) 455
High school library management OSTHUS, Mary J. . . . . (SD) 928
High school library operations CHANDRA, Jane H. . . . (NC) 200
High school library service TOLMAN, Bonnie B. . . . (MI) 1249
High school library system KING, Willard B. . . . . . (NC) 652
High school library teaching JEFFORDS, Margaret C. . (NY) 596
High school media GRADY, Alida J. . . . . . (FL) 455
High school media center KLOZA, Paula P. . . . . . (NJ) 662
High school media programs KIRK, Mary L. . . . . . . (IA) 654
High school media specialist THOMPSON, Myra D. . . (OH) 1240
High school reference HOLBROCK, Mary A. . . . (IL) 550
KAPLAN, Lois J. . . . . . (OH) 626
High school student services WONSEVER, Eithne C. . . (NY) 1363
High school students PESTUN, Aloysius J. . . . (CA) 961
High schools BAIRD, Patricia M. . . . . (MI) 47
PARTHUM, John W. . . . (MI) 945
Hospital & medical school LANDWIRTH, Trudy K. . . (IL) 694
Independent school librarianship SANDERS, Jacqueline C. (MD) 1080
Independent school libraries SANTINGA, Reda A. . . . (MI) 1082
MATTHEWS, Stephen L. (VA) 786
Independent secondary school
librarian REARDON, Elizabeth M. . (TN) 1013
Information services, school KENNEY, Ann J. . . . . . (OR) 641
International schools GAMAL, Sandra H. . . . . (NY) 416
International schools librarianship SERVENTE, Marcia M. . (ENG)1116
Judaica, Hebrew day schools HERTZ, Cynthia L. . . . . (NY) 533
Junior & senior high schools DANIEL, Donna M. . . . . (OH) 272
Junior high, middle school HAUG, Pauline C. . . . . . (WI) 512
Junior High school librarianship COOK, Anne S. . . . . . (TX) 239
K-12 school administration REMKIEWICZ, Frank L. . (CA) 1022
K-12 school libraries GAMAL, Sandra H. . . . . (NY) 416
K-12 school media LUKASIK, Marion F. . . . (IL) 747
Large high school library
administration SPICER, Orlin C. . . . . . (MO) 1174
Latin American school library
consulting CARDENAS, Mary E. . . . (SAF) 180
Law school libraries LUCAS, Ann . . . . (MI) 745
Law school library GHIDOTTI, Pauline A. . . (AR) 430
Law school professor DYER, Charles R. . . . . (CA) 330
Law schools LONG, Clare S. . . . . . . (OH) 739
Law schools, legal education COYLE, Christopher B. . . (OH) 253
Lecturer, school library service MARSH, Martha M. . . . . (KS) 773
Liaison with non-public schools MACLEAN, Ellen G. . . . (VI) 757
Library education & school librarians LYDERS, Josette A. . . . . (TX) 750
Library management, college, school CORRIGAN, John T. . . . (PA) 247
Library school accreditation FRANKIE, Suzanne O. . . (MI) 397
GREENE, Richard L. . . . (PQ) 464
Library school administration LOWE, Mildred . . . . (NY) 744
WHALEN, Lucille . . . . . (NY) 1328
Library school education ALLEN, Nancy S. . . . . . (MA) 15
MORGAN, Lynn K. . . . . (NY) 864
Library school education, music COOVER, James B. . . . . (NY) 244
Library school instruction HARRIS, Margaret J. . . . (OH) 505
Library school student groups COLEMAN, J G. . . . . . . (AL) 231
Library school teaching SIMMONS, Ruth J. . . . . (NJ) 1140
Library school teaching of rare books HEANEY, Howell J. . . . . (PA) 518

SCHOOL (Cont'd)

Library skills, high schools WARAKSA, Raymond P. . (CT) 1303
Library systems for schools MAUTINO, Patricia H. . . . (NY) 787
Management elementary school
libraries CRAIGHEAD, Alice A. . . (TX) 254
Managing elementary school libraries HOWELL, Wanda H. . . . (FL) 565
Managing school libraries WHITE, Ann T. . . . . (SC) 1330
Managing school library & media JANTZ, Helen N. . . . . . (KS) 594
Managing school library programs HACKMAN, Mary H. . . . (MD) 481
Media use in schools JOSEPH, Elizabeth T. . . . (PA) 617
Medical school administration WILSON, Marjorie P. . . . (MD) 1352
Medical school education MORGAN, Lynn K. . . . . . (NY) 864
Medical school libraries RANKIN, Jocelyn A. . . . . (GA) 1007
Microcomputer use in school libraries SCHMUHL, Gayle B. . . . (OH) 1096
Microcomputers in school libraries GREESON, Janet S. . . . . (AR) 465
LOWE, Joy L. . . . . (LA) 744
GROSE, Rosemary F. . . . (MA) 472
Middle school & young adult literature MILLER, Ellen L. . . . . . . (VA) 837
Middle school library media center
admin GOZEMBA, Frances E. . . (MA) 455
Middle school media centers EDWARDS, Barbara T. . . (TN) 337
Middle schools PITLUK, Paula K. . . . . . (CA) 976
New Jersey school law VAN BUSKIRK, Elisabeth
L. . . . . (NJ) 1272
Nursing school librarianship BENISHEK, Kristine K. . . (OH) 81
Online high school instruction GARDNER, Laura L. . . . . (MO) 418
Online searching in schools CAIN, Carolyn L. . . . . . (WI) 171
Online searching, school libraries LATHROP, Ann . . . . (CA) 701
Organization of rural school libraries GOODMAN, Roslyn L. . . (AK) 449
PAC in school GRABINSKY, Warren B. . (BC) 455
Primary school children's libraries CARPENTER, Janella A. . (NC) 184
Private schools libraries JOHNSON, Guy M. . . . . (NY) 605
Public & school library cooperation LEITLE, Barbara K. . . . . (MO) 714
Public library, school cooperation LONG, Judith N. . . . . . . (IL) 739
Public relations for school libraries WHITE, Ann T. . . . . (SC) 1330
Public relations, school district NIEMEYER, Karen H. . . . (IN) 903
Public school DIERCKS, Eileen K. . . . . (IL) 302
Public school librarian, K-12 KOHRT, Ruth D. . . . . . . (IA) 669
Public school librarianship STURGEON, Mary C. . . . (AR) 1205
WILLIAMSON, Lanelle S. (TX) 1347
Public school libraries WRIGHT, Pauline W. . . . (AR) 1372
BUFFALOE, Catherine S. (GA) 155
HULLUM, Cheri J. . . . . . (GA) 573
BRUMBACK, Elsie . . . . . (NC) 150
BLESH, Tamara E. . . . . . (NH) 105
MCCULLEY, Lois P. . . . . (TX) 800
STAAS, Gretchen L. . . . . (TX) 1177
Public school library administration PORMEN, Paul E. . . . . . (OH) 984
Public school library collections SPAULDING, Nancy J. . . (TX) 1172
Public school library expansion SPAULDING, Nancy J. . . (TX) 1172
Public school library instruction SPAULDING, Nancy J. . . (TX) 1172
Public school library media HAMILTON, Betty D. . . . (TX) 491
Public, school library mergers BROWN, Freddiemae E. . (TX) 144
Public school multimedia METTLING, Cora E. . . . . (KS) 828
Public schools MURRAY, Bruce C. . . . . (MD) 881
Public secondary school STEWART, Joanne R. . . (IL) 1192
Regional school, public library holding BENSON, Laurel D. . . . . (MN) 83
School LOTZ, Marilyn R. . . . . . (NJ) 742
School administration GEIB, Jerry H. . . . . (IA) 425
School & academic administration SPENCER, Albert F. . . . . (GA) 1173
School & children's librarian LANE, Margaret . . . . . . (MA) 694
School & children's libraries LANE, Margaret . . . . . . (MA) 694
School & children's library BLACKSHEAR, Martha J. (AL) 102
School & library media UTTS, Janet R. . . . . (NY) 1270
School & library partnerships ARRIVEE, Sally D. . . . . (MI) 34
School & library services HATFIELD, Frances S. . . (FL) 511
School & public libraries - youth SHAEVEL, Evelyn F. . . . (IL) 1118
School & public library administration VEITCH, Carol J. . . . . . (NC) 1281
School & public library cooperation BRAINARD, Elsie A. . . . . (MA) 127
School & public library coordination MORROW, Blaine V. . . . (MI) 869
School & public library management MILLER, Marilyn L. . . . . (NC) 840
School & public library relations DRACH, Marian C. . . . . (MD) 317
School & public youth services WUNDERLICH, Nina M. . (IL) 1374
School & university library operations KELLY, Myla S. . . . . . . (CA) 638
School collection development HULLUM, Cheri J. . . . . . (GA) 573
School curriculum planning HUSTED, Ruth E. . . . . . (OK) 578
School curriculum programs WEISLAK, Susan L. . . . . (TX) 1319
School district consulting HIRABAYASHI, Joanne . (CA) 543
School district coordinator GILBERT, Betty H. . . . . (AZ) 433
School district information systems SLYGH, Gyneth . . . . . . (WI) 1151

SCHOOL (Cont'd)

School district libraries — SZEMRAJ, Edward R. . . (NY) 1218
School district library administration — APPEL MOSESOF, Rhoda S. . . . . (NJ) 29
School district library services — BAGAN, Beverly S. . . . . (VA) 45
School district library supervision — BURGESON, Clair D. . . . (NY) 159
School district media centers — MOHN, Kari . . . . (AK) 852
School district media services — STAAS, Gretchen L. . . . . (TX) 1177
School learning resource ctr consulting — GOTHIA, Blanche . . . . . . (TX) 453
School librarian — PRESSNALL, Patricia E. . (CA) 991
RECHNITZ, Harriet L. . . . (DE) 1013
VITELLO, Susan . . . . (FL) 1286
STEBEN, Florence E. . . . (LA) 1183
FRIEND, Ann S. . . . . (MA) 404
School librarian education — ALSWORTH, Frances W. (OK) 18
HAMMEL, Philip J. . . . . . (SK) 493
School librarian media specialist — COACHMAN, Dorothea L. (NY) 224
School librarian's instructional role — MINEMIER, Betty M. . . . (NY) 845
School librarianship — MCCLAIN, Harriet V. . . . (AK) 795
ROYAL, Selvin W. . . . . . (AR) 1063
EASUN, M S. . . . . (CA) 333
GRAVES, Frances M. . . . (CA) 459
DUBEAU, Marsha . . . . . . (CT) 321
POLOMSKI, Linda . . . . . (CT) 982
MYERS, Victoria B. . . . . (DE) 885
VAN ORDEN, Phyllis J. . . (FL) 1276
TOM, Chow L. . . . . (HI) 1249
HANNON, Bobbie A. . . . (IL) 497
SCHORMANN, Marguerite T. . . . . (IL) 1099
STINCHCOMB, Maxine K. (IL) 1194
REEVES, Cathy L. . . . . . (KS) 1016
WILLIAMS, Helen E. . . . (MD) 1343
BERTRAND, Beverly P. . (MI) 91
HOERGER, Helen L. . . . . (MI) 547
BROOKS, S B. . . . . (MN) 141
BREIMEIER, Lois . . . . . . (MO) 132
FABIAN, William M. . . . . (MO) 360
SMITH, Sharon M. . . . . . (MO) 1160
BOYCE, Emily S. . . . . . . (NC) 122
BUSBIN, O M. . . . . (NC) 164
DICKINSON, Gail K. . . . . (NC) 301
FISH, Barbara M. . . . . . . (NC) 380
WILKINSON, Fleeta M. . (NC) 1340
HASELWOOD, Eldon L. . (NE) 510
GILLESPIE, John T. . . . . (NY) 435
HENDRICKS, Elaine M. . (NY) 527
KLEINBURD, Freda . . . . (NY) 659
MERRILL, Barbara P. . . . (NY) 826
MEYER, Albert . . . . (NY) 829
SCHEU, Susan P. . . . . . (NY) 1092
TALLMAN, Julie I. . . . . . (NY) 1221
DRIESSEN, Diane . . . . . (OH) 320
GILLMORE, Salley G. . . . (OH) 436
POJMAN, Paul E. . . . . . . (OH) 980
COCHENOUR, Donnice K. (OK) 225
GEARHART, Carol A. . . . (PA) 424
RUPERT, Elizabeth A. . . (PA) 1068
SHAW, Doris G. . . . . (PA) 1123
SCALES, Pat R. . . . . (SC) 1087
WATSON, Gail H. . . . . . (TN) 1309
BASS, Martha L. . . . . . . (TX) 63
GONZALEZ, Sharon M. . (TX) 448
SMITH, Lorraine K. . . . . . (TX) 1157
SHIELDS, Dorthy M. . . . . (UT) 1130
GREENAWALT, Ruth A. . (VA) 463
PYKE, Carol J. . . . . (VA) 999
WAMPLER, Dorris M. . . . (VA) 1302
SHELDEN, Lucinda D. . . (WA) 1125
TERESINSKI, Sally S. . . (WI) 1231
HOWARD, Elizabeth F. . . (WV) 564
OBERG, Dianne . . . . (AB) 913
WRIGHT, John G. . . . . . . (AB) 1371
HAMILTON, Donald E. . . (BC) 492
HAYCOCK, Carol A. . . . (BC) 515
WRIGHT, Jonathan C. . . (ON) 1371
GALLER, Anne M. . . . . . (PQ) 414
PHILLIPS, Yvonne A. . . . (PQ) 969
SLINEY, Marjory T. . . . . (IRE) 1149

SCHOOL (Cont'd)

School librarianship — PICACHE, Ursula D. . . . . (PHP) 970
School librarianship & education — BERNHARD, Paulette . . . (PQ) 89
School librarianship education — BUTLER, Christina . . . . . (OH) 166
MERRIAM, Doris E. . . . . (PA) 826
BLANKENBURG, Judith B. (VA) 104
School librarianship, media centers — RYUS, Phyllis K. . . . . (CA) 1072
School libraries — THOMAS, Margie J. . . . . (AK) 1237
COLEMAN, J G. . . . . (AL) 231
MCGARITY, Marysue . . . (AL) 805
HENSON, Aleene E. . . . . (AR) 529
SCHON, Isabel . . . . (AZ) 1098
EBY, James F. . . . . (CA) 334
LEE, Mildred C. . . . . (CA) 711
RICHARDSON, Helen R. (CA) 1029
SIGLER, Lorraine . . . . . . (CA) 1137
COSTA, Betty L. . . . . . . (CO) 249
MACY, Edwin L. . . . . (CO) 758
COGLISER, Luann L. . . . (CT) 227
KNOPP, Marie L. . . . . . . (CT) 665
MEUCCI, Victoria F. . . . . (CT) 829
NAVE, Greer G. . . . . (DC) 890
MINNICH, Nancy P. . . . . (DE) 846
BLOCK, Sandra S. . . . . . (FL) 106
BRACKWINKLE, Hilda L. (FL) 125
MCCAMMON, Carol G. . (FL) 793
MORGAN, Ina K. . . . . . . (FL) 864
PAULSON, Mary E. . . . . (FL) 950
BENNETT, Priscilla B. . . (GA) 82
BECK, Marianne J. . . . . . (IA) 71
DAVIS, Deanna S. . . . . . (IA) 278
KOLLASCH, Matthew A. . (IA) 669
MCGREW, Mary L. . . . . (IA) 808
GORDON, Diane M. . . . . (IL) 451
RICHARDSON, Selma K. (IL) 1030
SIVAK, Marie R. . . . . (IL) 1144
WIRIG, Joan S. . . . . (IL) 1356
ROBERTS, Linda A. . . . . (KS) 1041
ROGERS, Joann V. . . . . (KY) 1049
HEROY, Phyllis B. . . . . . (LA) 532
ROBINSON, Joyce W. . . (LA) 1044
BOSTLEY, Jean R. . . . . . (MA) 117
MELNICK, Ralph . . . . . . (MA) 823
PHELAN, Mary C. . . . . . (MA) 967
BOWERS, Rhoda E. . . . . (MD) 120
FISHER, Eleanor W. . . . . (MD) 381
BROOKS, Burton H. . . . . (MI) 140
SCHEU, Jean W. . . . . . . (MN) 1092
URBANSKI, Lawrence E. (MN) 1269
FUCHS, Curt R. . . . . (MO) 408
VAN MELER, Vandelia L. (MS) 1276
BRADBURN, Frances B. (NC) 125
MANN, Sallie E. . . . . (NC) 766
SANDERS, Elizabeth S. . (NC) 1080
YLINIEMI, Hazel A. . . . . . (ND) 1380
GRAZIER, Dorothy W. . . (NH) 460
BUMP, Ruth E. . . . . (NJ) 157
ODENHEIM, Claire E. . . (NM) 916
KEENE, Richard R. . . . . (NV) 634
KEENE, Roberta E. . . . . (NV) 634
MOY, Clarence T. . . . . . (NY) 874
OGBIN, Frances . . . . (NY) 918
ORGREN, Sally C. . . . . . (NY) 925
SCHOENBAUM, Rhoda A. (NY) 1008
SUSSMAN, Valerie J. . . . (NY) 1210
VOSE, Deborah R. . . . . . (NY) 1289
BLACK, Jeannie M. . . . . (OH) 101
ROGERS, Cassandra J. . (OH) 1049
SCHMALBERG, Aaron . . (OH) 1094
SHIVERDECKER, Darlene J. . . . . (OH) 1132
BAUER, Carolyn J. . . . . . (OK) 65
ANDERSON, C L. . . . . . (OR) 21
MCCONNELL, Robert D. (PA) 798
MORIARTY, Kathleen T. . (PA) 865
NOLAN, Joan . . . . (PA) 907
PARADISE, Don M. . . . . (PA) 939
RICHVALSKY, Neil F. . . (PA) 1031
SCHEEREN, William O. . (PA) 1090

SCHOOL (Cont'd)
School libraries

WOOLLS, Esther B. . . . . (PA) 1368
SMITH, Sara B. . . . . (SC) 1160
GILLILAND, Donna E. . . . (SD) 436
RATKIN, Annette L. . . . . (TN) 1009
TUDOR, Betty A. . . . . . . (TN) 1262
HOLDREN, Ann E. . . . . . (TX) 550
KERBY, Ramona A. . . . . (TX) 643
MANN, Carol A. . . . . (TX) 765
NORTH, Yvonne M. . . . . (TX) 910
STAAS, Gretchen L. . . . . (TX) 1177
THOMAS, James L. . . . . (TX) 1237
WHISENNAND, Cynthia S. (TX) 1329
WORTHY, Annie B. . . . . (TX) 1369
YOUNG, Nancy M. . . . . . (TX) 1382
BARBER, Gloria K. . . . . . (VA) 55
GEORGE, Melba R. . . . . (VA) 427
YOUNGER, Melinda M. . . (VA) 1383
ULRICH, Pamela L. . . . . (WA) 1268
HUMPHRIES, Lajean . . . (WI) 574
KEMPF, Arlys L. . . . . (WI) 639
MORROW, Kathryn M. . . (WI) 869
BRADLEY, Harold K. . . . (AB) 126
SCHMIDT, Raymond J. . . (AB) 1095
LIGHTHALL, Lynne I. . . . (BC) 727
SCOTT, William H. . . . . . (BC) 1108
BOUDREAU, Berthe . . . . (NB) 118
RUSSELL, Sharon A. . . . (NB) 1069
MARTINEZ, Helen . . . . . (NF) 779
CHURCHMAN, Alice M. . . (ON) 213
DEKKER, Barbara A. . . . (ON) 288
DEVOE, Dan L. . . . . (ON) 297
GREAVES, H P. . . . . (ON) 461
MOORE, Lawrence A. . . . (ON) 860
HAMBLETON, Alixe E. . . (SK) 490
MCLEOD, Karen E. . . . . (SK) 814
EUSEBIUS, Nima V. . . . . (IND) 356

School libraries & intellectual freedom   BLANKENBURG, Judith B. . (VA) 104
School libraries & media centers   CARR, Charles E. . . . . . (AL) 185
PELOVSKY, Suzy A. . . . . (CA) 955
WEICK, Robert J. . . . . . . (IN) 1316
HAWKINS, Marilyn J. . . . (MO) 514
MULLER, Madeline A. . . . (OH) 877
HERRING, Billie G. . . . . . (TX) 533

School libraries, children's literature   TERRY, Virginia W. . . . . (MO) 1232
School libraries K-12   BARTZ, Alice P. . . . . (PA) 62
School libraries networking   MATTIE, Joseph J. . . . . . (NY) 786
School library   RUSSELL, Sandra W. . . . (CA) 1069
YOUNG, Eleanor C. . . . . (CA) 1381
SLONE, Eugenia F. . . . . (CT) 1150
HADA, Jerrianne . . . . . . (KS) 481
WHITSON, Joyce G. . . . (KS) 1334
WINFREE, Barbara S. . . . (LA) 1354
MCCOLL, Rita M. . . . . . . (NC) 797
WISE, Martha K. . . . . (OH) 1357
WILSON, Donna R. . . . . (TN) 1350
MILES, Ruby A. . . . . (TX) 834
BARTON, Barbara I. . . . . (BAH) 61

School library administration   HAWKINS, Nina L. . . . . . (CA) 514
MILLER, Margaret S. . . . (CA) 840
HUGHES, Sondra K. . . . . (CO) 572
DAYTON, Diane . . . . (GA) 283
WHITE, Carol A. . . . . (GA) 1330
TRUETT, Carol A. . . . . . (HI) 1259
DONHAM, Jean O. . . . . . (IA) 311
HILAND, Leah F. . . . . . . (IA) 538
ADCOCK, Donald C. . . . (IL) 6
FISHER, Lois F. . . . . (IL) 381
KARON, Joyce E. . . . . . . (IL) 627
KRAMER, Pamela K. . . . (IL) 675
SHAFER, Anne E. . . . . . (IL) 1119
BIANCHINO, Cecelia . . . (IN) 94
LITTLE, Robert D. . . . . . (IN) 733
MOSLEY, Mattie J. . . . . . (LA) 871
BARTH, Edward W. . . . . (MD) 61
DEAN, Frances C. . . . . . (MD) 283
MOLLENKOPF, Carolyn M. (MD) 853
RANDAZZO, Corinne O. . (MS) 1006
SUMRALL, Ada M. . . . . . (MS) 1210

SCHOOL (Cont'd)
School library administration

HATHAWAY, Milton G. . . (NC) 512
GREENSPAN, Vivi S. . . . (NJ) 465
FREEMAN, Patricia E. . . (NM) 401
CORRY, Emmett . . . . . . (NY) 247
ELLIS, Kathleen V. . . . . . (NY) 344
JAFFE, Lawrence J. . . . . (PA) 591
MIZIK, Judy G. . . . . (PA) 850
WALKER, Sue A. . . . . . . (PA) 1296
FERNANDEZ, Josefina L. (PR) 373
MCANALLY, Charlotte L. . (TN) 792
SCOTT, Willodene A. . . . (TN) 1108
BURT, Lesta N. . . . . (TX) 164
CARDENAS, Martha L. . . (TX) 180
NISBY, Dora R. . . . . (TX) 904
PARIS, Janelle A. . . . . . . (TX) 940
WOLL, Christina B. . . . . (TX) 1361
KARPISEK, Marian E. . . (UT) 628
YOUNGER, Melinda M. . . (VA) 1383
BUELER, Roy D. . . . . . . (WA) 155
CZARNEZKI, Mary E. . . . (WI) 268

School library & media   STRICKLAND, Mary L. . . (NC) 1202
BRADLEY, Patricia L. . . . (SC) 126
School library & media administration   JOSEPH, Elizabeth T. . . (PA) 617
SKELLEY, Cornelia A. . . (WA) 1145
School library & media center   JENKS, Arlene I. . . . . . . (AK) 597
LEFF, Barbara Y. . . . . . . (CA) 712
FENWICK, Sara I. . . . . . (FL) 371
HIRSCH, Elizabeth . . . . (MA) 543
COURTNEY, Marjorie S. . (MO) 251
GARDNER, Janet K. . . . (NC) 418
RILEY, Marie R. . . . . (NJ) 1034
RUSSELL, Paula V. . . . . (TX) 1069
WU, Jean . . . . (TX) 1373
AXT, Randolph W. . . . . . (WI) 42

School library & media center management   SNYDER, Denny L. . . . . (MD) 1164
STEVENS, Elizabeth B. . . (NY) 1190
School library & media centers   DIERCKS, Eileen K. . . . . (IL) 302
KIRZINGER, Denise C. . . (KY) 656
DALBOTTEN, Mary S. . . (MN) 270
WEISENFELS, Marjorie A. (MO) 1319
HUNTER, Cecilia A. . . . . (TX) 576
MOELLENDICK, M J. . . . (WV) 851
KRATZ, Hans C. . . . . . . (AB) 676

School library & media collections   TERWILLEGAR, Jane C. (FL) 1232
School library & media services   RUSK, Alice C. . . . . (MD) 1068
School library & media specialists educ   PATTERSON, Lotsee . . . (OK) 948
School library automation   HALL, Howard L. . . . . . . (CA) 488
HECKLINGER, Ellen L. . . (CA) 519
KARON, Joyce E. . . . . . . (IL) 627
LYNN, Barbara A. . . . . . (KS) 752
HOLLEY, Rebecca M. . . . (LA) 551
PRESTEBAK, Jane R. . . (MN) 991
TUZINSKI, Jean H. . . . . (PA) 1266
HUNT, Linda A. . . . . (VA) 575
SORENSEN, Richard J. . (WI) 1168
GELINAS, Rene . . . . (PQ) 426

School library collection & development   BERK, Nancy G. . . . . . . (AZ) 87
School library community relations   HASBROUCK, Clara H. . . (TN) 510
School library computer systems   SLYGH, Gyneth . . . . (WI) 1151
School library computers   MCANALLY, Charlotte L. . (TN) 792
School library consulting   HARADA, Violet H. . . . . . (HI) 499
VAUGHN, Robert V. . . . . (VI) 1280
School library curricula   PALMER, Julia R. . . . . . (NY) 936
School library curriculum   KARON, Joyce E. . . . . . . (IL) 627
MIZIK, Judy G. . . . . (PA) 850
School library curriculum integration   ZEIGER, Hanna B. . . . . (MA) 1387
School library curriculum involvement   FREEMAN, Evangeline M. (NC) 400
School library development   TARANKO, Walter J. . . . (ME) 1223
GUILBERT, N P. . . . . . . (MB) 476
FINN, Julia P. . . . . (PQ) 378

School library development & management   BERKLUND, Nancy J. . . (MI) 87
School library direction   APEL, Catherine D. . . . . (WV) 29
School library education   SIGRIST, Staci E. . . . . . (OH) 1137
FUNK, Grace E. . . . . (BC) 410

SCHOOL (Cont'd)

School library evaluation	RANDAZZO, Corinne O.	(MS)	1006
	ANDERSON, Pauline H. .	(NY)	25
School library facilities	MARKUSON, Carolyn A.	(MA)	772
	ANDERSON, Pauline H. .	(NY)	25
	KAHLER, June	(TX)	621
School library instruction	MIZIK, Judy G.	(PA)	850
School library journalism	WILLIAMS, Eve A.	(NB)	1343
School library, K-5	GOODRICH, Carolyn B. .	(NY)	449
School library management	HILLIS, Patricia K.	(CA)	541
	DANIELSON, Connie S. .	(IA)	273
	MASON, John A.	(IL)	781
	ROBIEN, Eleanor K.	(IL)	1043
	SHAW, Louis P.	(IL)	1123
	CALLISON, Daniel J.	(IN)	174
	O'BRIEN, John F.	(MA)	914
	LATHAM, Candace	(NJ)	701
	SCOTT, Mellouise J.	(NJ)	1107
	MCCAULEY, Elfrieda B. .	(NM)	795
	BURGESON, Clair D.	(NY)	159
	ALTAN, Susan B.	(OH)	18
	WOLFORD, Betty K.	(OH)	1361
	BARRON, Daniel D.	(SC)	60
	HASBROUCK, Clara H. .	(TN)	510
	VAN ORSDEL, Darrell E.	(WI)	1276
	ALTURKAIT, Adela A.	(KWT)	19
School library media	MCKISSICK, Mabel F.	(CT)	812
	SRYGLEY, Sara K.	(FL)	1177
	PASCHAL, Eloise R.	(GA)	945
	SPENCE, Rethia C.	(GA)	1173
	TOLMAN, Lorraine E.	(MA)	1249
	DAVIS, Mavis W.	(MD)	280
	HELMICK, Aileen B.	(MO)	525
	STEMME, Virginia L.	(ND)	1186
	CONDIT, Martha O.	(NJ)	235
	BANICK, Albert N.	(NY)	54
	HARRIS, Martha	(NY)	505
	HERTZ, Cynthia L.	(NY)	533
	BACK, Andrew W.	(PA)	43
	COX, Carol A.	(PA)	253
	DALY, Sally A.	(PA)	271
	CALDWELL, Rossie B.	(SC)	172
	CASEY, Jean M.	(WI)	192
School library media administration	CARTER, Yvonne B.	(DC)	190
	YOUNG, Christina C.	(DC)	1381
	NOONAN, Eileen F.	(IL)	908
	MEANS, E P.	(KS)	820
	KULLESEID, Eleanor R.	(NY)	683
	CHISHOLM, Margaret	(WA)	209
School library media center	DOOLEY, Sally J.	(AZ)	312
	DAY, Bettie B.	(CA)	282
	WHALEY, Janie B.	(IN)	1328
	HOLLEY, Rebecca M.	(LA)	551
	COLYER, Judith A.	(MI)	234
	WALL, Marilyn M.	(MI)	1297
	MCDONALD, Frances B.	(MN)	802
	FIRSCHEIN, Sylvia H.	(NJ)	379
	DILLINGER, Mary A.	(TX)	303
	VEENSTRA, Geraldine B.	(TX)	1281
	HAUG, Pauline C.	(WI)	512
	MCKILLIP, Rita J.	(WI)	811
	KOGA, Setsuko	(JAP)	668
School library media center automation	JOYCE, Robert A.	(NC)	618
School library media center management	MILLER, John E.	(OH)	839
	STANTON, Vida C.	(WI)	1181
School library, media centers	SACHSE, Gladys M.	(AR)	1073
	BOWMAN, Kathleen A.	(CA)	122
	NIEMEYER, Kay M.	(CA)	903
	HEMPSTEAD, John	(CO)	525
	LOERTSCHER, David V.	(CO)	737
	HALE, Robert G.	(CT)	485
	LAPOLT, Margaret B.	(CT)	697
	WHITE, Charles H.	(CT)	1330
	FOSTER, Candice L.	(FL)	392
	HOLMES, Gloria P.	(FL)	553
	JONES, Winona N.	(FL)	615
	RAMEY, Linda K.	(FL)	1005
	ELIZABETH, Martin A.	(IA)	343

SCHOOL (Cont'd)

School library, media centers			
	MARTIN, Elizabeth A.	(IA)	776
	BIBLO, Mary	(IL)	94
	BEILKE, Patricia F.	(IN)	75
	HUNT, Margaret M.	(IN)	575
	SOLDNER, Nancy C.	(KS)	1166
	LIVINGSTON, Sarah M.	(KY)	735
	CARSTENS, Jane E.	(LA)	188
	STANTON, Martha	(MA)	1181
	FITZGERALD, Ruth F.	(MI)	382
	NICKEL, Mildred L.	(MI)	902
	OLSON, Lowell E.	(MN)	923
	SCHULZETENBERG, Anthony C.	(MN)	1102
	LITTLE, Nina M.	(NE)	733
	KUHLTHAU, Carol C.	(NJ)	682
	SEVERINGHAUS, Ethel L.	(NY)	1117
	SPIRT, Diana L.	(NY)	1175
	STAINO, Rocco A.	(NY)	1178
	VELLEMAN, Ruth A.	(NY)	1281
	ARK, Connie E.	(OH)	31
	AVERY, Jacqueline R.	(OH)	41
	MELTON, Vivian B.	(OH)	823
	COWEN, Linda L.	(OK)	253
	MURPHY, Diana G.	(PA)	880
	CARPENTER, Dorothy B.	(TN)	184
	SCOTT, Willodene A.	(TN)	1108
	IMMROTH, Barbara F.	(TX)	582
	KAHLER, June	(TX)	621
	REIFEL, Louie E.	(TX)	1019
	MILLS, Fiolina B.	(VI)	844
School lib media ctrs staff development	SMITH, Jane B.	(AL)	1155
School library media certification	SORENSEN, Richard J.	(WI)	1168
School library media computerization	LITTLE, Nina M.	(NE)	733
School library media consultation	DOWNES, Valerie	(IL)	316
School library media curriculum	LITTLE, Nina M.	(NE)	733
	ROSCELLO, Frances R.	(NY)	1054
School library media development	LUDWIG, Deborah M.	(CO)	746
	DOWNES, Valerie	(IL)	316
	VOSS, Anne E.	(NJ)	1289
School library media education	GRAZIER, Margaret H.	(MI)	461
School library media facilities	PATRICK, Retta B.	(AR)	947
	SHUMAN, Susan E.	(NY)	1134
	EHRHARDT, Margaret W.	(SC)	339
School library media improvement	MORRIS, Irving	(NY)	866
School library media instruction	RING, Constance B.	(NY)	1035
School library media management	GREGORY, Mary L.	(WA)	466
School library media program	PATRICK, Retta B.	(AR)	947
School library media programs	DEWEESE, Don B.	(AR)	298
	WHITNEY, Karen A.	(AZ)	1334
	GREENBERG, Marilyn W.	(CA)	463
	WEIGEL, James S.	(CT)	1316
	HART, Thomas L.	(FL)	507
	BROCK, Kathy T.	(GA)	138
	HOLTER, Charlotte S.	(MD)	554
	SMINK, Anna R.	(MD)	1152
	MATECUN, Marilyn L.	(MI)	783
	MILLER, Robert H.	(MN)	842
	APPEL MOSESOF, Rhoda S.	(NJ)	29
	BARRON, Robert E.	(NY)	60
	RICHARDSON, Constance II.	(NY)	1029
	ROSCELLO, Frances R.	(NY)	1054
	EHRHARDT, Margaret W.	(SC)	339
	EISENSTEIN, Jill M.	(TN)	341
	LANKFORD, Mary D.	(TX)	696
	WIEMAN, Jean K.	(WA)	1336
	FOLKE, Carolyn W.	(WI)	387
	HOPKINS, Dianne M.	(WI)	557
School library media public relations	BALL, Diane A.	(OH)	52
School library media services	GILBERT, Betty H.	(AZ)	433
	ROSE, David L.	(CA)	1054
	SKINNER, L M.	(FL)	1146
	DURAND, Joyce J.	(GA)	328
	UYEHARA, Harry Y.	(GU)	1270
	DEQUIN, Henry C.	(IL)	293
	TUGGLE, Ann M.	(IL)	1262

SCHOOL (Cont'd)

School library media services
MCNALLY, Crystal E. . . . (KS) 815
COOPER, Judy L. . . . . . (KY) 243
SMITH, Zelda G. . . . . . (MA) 1161
MONTGOMERY, Paula K. (MD) 856
KERESEY, Gayle . . . . . (NC) 643
VANDERGRIFT, Kay E. . (NJ) 1274
EISENBERG, Michael B. . (NY) 340
SHONTZ, Marilyn L. . . . (PA) 1132
BROADWAY, Marsha D. (UT) 138
BROWN, Dale W. . . . . (VA) 143
JONES, Sally L. . . . . . . (WA) 615
School library media skills
BUGHER, Kathryn M. . . (WI) 155
School library, media specialist
CAZZULINO, Clara P. . . (NY) 195
GRIFFIN, Cheryl J. . . . . (NY) 468
DURHAM, Wanda J. . . . (TN) 328
REARDON, Elizabeth M. . (TN) 1013
School library media specialization
ARKHURST, Joyce C. . . (NY) 31
School library media supervision
JAFFARIAN, Sara . . . . . (MA) 591
School library operations
EGAN, Janet M. . . . . . . (CA) 338
School library organization
WEEKS, Patsy L. . . . . . (TX) 1315
SORENSEN, Richard J. . (WI) 1168
School library organization & evaluation
BAGAN, Beverly S. . . . . (VA) 45
School library planning
KARPISEK, Marian E. . . (UT) 628
YAEGER, Luke R. . . . . (VA) 1376
School library policy development
ANDERSON, Pauline H. . (NY) 25
School library program development
BELL, Jo A. . . . . (TX) 77
School library programming
SCALES, Pat R. . . . . . (SC) 1087
School library programs
LOWRIE, Jean E. . . . . . (MI) 744
VANCE, Kenneth E. . . . (MI) 1273
PAULEY, Charles W. . . . (MN) 950
FRENCH, Janet D. . . . . (PA) 402
School library research skills
SHERMAN, Madeline R. . (VT) 1128
School library resource centers
BERTRAND, Doreen M. . (ON) 91
School library roles
SAVAGE, Daniel A. . . . (ON) 1085
School library service
SHELTON, Elease B. . . (GA) 1126
BOMAR, Cora P. . . . . . (NC) 113
POND, Patricia B. . . . . (OR) 982
SINCLAIR, Rose P. . . . . (TX) 1143
School library services
DEAN, Martha L. . . . . . (CA) 283
SERIS, Eileen J. . . . . . . (CO) 1116
SCARBROUGH, S J. . . . (MI) 1087
GERHARDT, Lillian N. . . (NY) 428
KENNEDY BRIGHT, Sandra . . . . (NY) 641
FRENCH, Janet D. . . . . (PA) 402
LINDSEY, Nancy L. . . . . (TN) 730
School library services & collections
DAIGNEAULT, Audrey I. (CT) 270
School library services for K-6
ROTSAERT, Stefanie C. . (NJ) 1060
School library skills
VALLAR, Cynthia L. . . . . (MD) 1271
School library skills program
JOHNSON, Guy M. . . . . (NY) 605
School library specialist
LOHRER, Alice . . . . (IL) 737
School library supervision
WIGET, Laurence A. . . . (AK) 1337
LOWERY, Phyllis C. . . . (GA) 744
MEYERS, Judith K. . . . . (KS) 831
RANDAZZO, Corinne O. (MS) 1006
ABBOTT, Ruth J. . . . . . (TX) 1
BUELER, Roy D. . . . . . (WA) 155
School library supervisor
WIDENER, Sarah A. . . . (TX) 1335
School library system
WOOD, Marilyn R. . . . . (IA) 1364
School library systems
BUBOLTZ, Dale D. . . . . (CA) 152
LUNARDI, Albert A. . . . . (CA) 748
MCMICHAEL, Sandra C. (FL) 815
UMANA, Christine J. . . . (MA) 1268
BAILIE, Donna L. . . . . . (NY) 47
LINDSLEY, Barbara N. . . (NY) 730
MATTIE, Joseph J. . . . . (NY) 786
ROSCELLO, Frances R. . (NY) 1054
SALUSTRI, Madeline . . . (NY) 1077
SIMON, Anne E. . . . . . . (NY) 1140
LEON, Carmencita H. . . (PR) 716
FILSON, Anne H. . . . . . (VA) 377
School library systems, networking
WEBSTER, Patricia B. . . (NY) 1315
School library training & development
BRUWELHEIDE, Janis H. (MT) 151
CURRIE, Bertha B. . . . . (NS) 266

SCHOOL (Cont'd)

School media
PENDLETON, Kim B. . . . (AK) 956
JAIN, Celeste C. . . . . . . (CA) 591
HILL, Marian W. . . . . . . (FL) 540
MOORE, Vivian L. . . . . . (FL) 861
DENNY, Mary C. . . . . . . (ID) 293
NEAL, Nancy J. . . . . (IL) 890
MATHEWS, Mary P. . . . (MD) 784
SCHULTZ, Christine K. . . (MI) 1102
WEST, Marian S. . . . . . (MI) 1326
GORDON, Muriel C. . . . (NJ) 451
School media administration
BURKE, Grace W. . . . . . (GA) 160
WILSON, Mary S. . . . . . (MS) 1352
School media center
JENSEN, Kathryn E. . . . (MA) 599
School media center administration
ROTH, Alvin R. . . . . (MN) 1059
JOYCE, Robert A. . . . . . (NC) 618
LATROBE, Kathy H. . . . . (OK) 701
LAUGHLIN, Mildred A. . . (OK) 703
School media center design
LEVEILLEE, Louis R. . . . (RI) 719
School media center evaluation
SLYGH, Gyneth . . . . . . (WI) 1151
School media center instruction
JOYCE, Robert A. . . . . . (NC) 618
School media center management
GARLAND, Kathleen . . . (NY) 419
School media center resources
RUDIE, Helen M. . . . . . (MN) 1065
School media centers
JOHNSEN, Ellen I. . . . . (IL) 601
KRAUSE, Roberta A. . . . (IL) 676
ROBINSON, Phyllis A. . . (MA) 1044
BUIST, Elaine R. . . . . . . (SC) 156
ANDIS, Norma B. . . . . . (TX) 26
LABODDA, Marsha J. . . (TX) 686
PRETLOW, Delores Z. . . (VA) 992
REINAGLE, Carol M. . . . (WI) 1021
School media children's services
AMISON, Mary V. . . . . . (NY) 20
School media libraries
MACLEAN, Ellen G. . . . (VI) 757
School media policy development
ADAMS, Helen R. . . . . . (WI) 5
School media programs
TUGWELL, Helen M. . . . (NC) 1262
School media services
BERG, Charlene J. . . . . (CA) 84
SYFERT, Samuel R. . . . (IL) 1217
ZAPPONE, William F. . . . (NY) 1386
KARRENBROCK, Marilyn H. . . . . (TN) 628
ZIMMERMAN, Nancy P. . (VA) 1389
School media specialist
RACZYNSKI, Mary K. . . (IL) 1002
BRUMIT, Nancy T. . . . . (OH) 150
HARDIN, Sue H. . . . . . . (SC) 500
School media specialization
SMITH, Noralee W. . . . . (OH) 1159
DAY, Pamela A. . . . . . . (WI) 283
School medical
KILPATRICK, Barbara A. (TN) 648
School of nursing libraries
CARTER, Selina J. . . . . . (AL) 190
School project planning
ANDRIST, Shirley A. . . . (SK) 27
School reference work
BANICK, Albert N. . . . . . (NY) 54
School region lib, media coordination
RIVERA, Antonio . . . . . . (NY) 1037
School, regional services consulting
BUCKINGHAM, Betty J. . (IA) 154
School services
MINNICH, Conrad H. . . . (OH) 846
School system library media management
KAUFMAN, Polly W. . . . (MA) 631
School visiting
SCHLAFF, Donna G. . . . (MA) 1093
Schools, collection development
DEVEREAUX, Amy E. . . (CA) 297
Schools, community colleges
SLICK, Myrna H. . . . . . . (PA) 1149
Schools in library networks
KESTER, Diane D. . . . . (NC) 645
School-wide computer coordination
LINDSEY, Nancy L. . . . . (TN) 730
School-wide projects
MEESE, Jane E. . . . . . . (OH) 821
Secondary school collections
RIFFEY, Robin S. . . . . . (OH) 1033
Secondary school librarianship
KLEINMAN, Elsa C. . . . (CA) 660
AUFSES, Harriet W. . . . (NY) 39
KENT, Candace D. . . . . (TN) 642
SHANNON, Theresa M. . (VA) 1121
KITTS, T J. . . . . (ON) 657
Secondary school libraries
CURTIN, Mimi V. . . . . . . (CA) 266
SKEHAN, Patricia A. . . . (CA) 1145
NOLES, Judy H. . . . . . . (LA) 908
MURTAGH, Mary B. . . . (NY) 882
HARDIN, Sue H. . . . . . . (SC) 500
WILLIAMS, Shelagh C. . . (ON) 1346
Secondary school library
SCHAFFER, Eamon . . . (CA) 1089
NICKELS, Anita B. . . . . (CO) 902
CARPENTER, Carole H. . (DE) 184
Secondary school library media centers
MILLER, George M. . . . . (MA) 837
Secondary school media centers
RAKE, Anthony I. . . . . . (IL) 1004
Secondary school publishing
IRELAND, Laverne H. . . (CA) 583

SCHOOL (Cont'd)

Secondary schools	JAY, Hilda L.	(CT)	596
	O'HEARON, Doris M.	(IL)	919
	WRIGHT, Deborah L.	(IL)	1371
Selection of materials for schools	POOLE, Rebecca S.	(CO)	983
Selection school library materials	HAMMEL, Philip J.	(SK)	493
Setting up school libraries	WRIGHT, Carolyn R.	(OK)	1370
Sexism in school materials	NILSEN, Alleen P.	(AZ)	904
Small high school collections	SHEPHERD, Rex L.	(IA)	1127
Small high school facilities	SHEPHERD, Rex L.	(IA)	1127
Social work & school psychology	LUNT, Ruth B.	(NY)	749
Staff development for school librarians	WHITE, Ann T.	(SC)	1330
Standards for school media centers	CAIN, Carolyn L.	(WI)	171
Standards for school programs	HOLTER, Charlotte S.	(MD)	554
Supervising school library management	BROWN, Atlanta T.	(DE)	142
Supervising school library media progs	KLASING, Jane P.	(FL)	657
Supervision of school librarians	VANDERGRIFF, Kathleen E.	(TN)	1274
Teaching in library school	WOOD, Raymund F.	(CA)	1364
Teaching school library research skills	CARLISLE, Carol A.	(CT)	182
Training school librarians	GAUDET, Jean A.	(VA)	422
University, school & library cooperation	BERLING, John G.	(MN)	88
Youth & school services	PACEY, Brenda M.	(IL)	933
Youth public school services	ROSEN, Elizabeth M.	(CA)	1055

SCIENCE (See also Bioscience, Geoscience, Neuroscience, Technology)

Academic science & technology reference	COHEN, Jackson B.	(NY)	228
Academic science librarianship	WANAT, Camille A.	(CA)	1302
Academic science libraries	YOCUM, Patricia B.	(MI)	1380
Academic science library design	STANKUS, Tony	(MA)	1180
Acquisitions, physical sciences	MERRYMAN, Margaret M.	(VA)	827
Actuarial science research	CHAPA, Joan I.	(IL)	201
Agricultural & scientific databases	PORTA, Maria A.	(IL)	984
Agricultural, plant science information	MITCHELL, Steve	(CA)	849
Agricultural science reference	GAGE, Marilyn K.	(OK)	412
Agricultural sciences	SIBIA, Tejinder S.	(CA)	1134
Agricultural sciences reference & bibl	MANNARINO, Elizabeth R.	(OR)	766
Airway science	COONS, Daniel E.	(DE)	242
Allied health, audiology, hearing sci	MCFARLAND, Robert T.	(MO)	805
American science	ELLIOTT, Clark A.	(MA)	343
Analysis of science library functions	ALEXANDER, Carol G.	(VA)	12
Aquatic sciences	MORITZ, Thomas D.	(CA)	865
Aquatic sciences & fisheries information	SEARS, Jonathan R.	(MD)	1110
Archival science	DOWNS, Charles F.	(DC)	317
Arts & sciences	KELLOGG, Rebecca B.	(AZ)	637
Arts, humanities & social sciences	LOMBARDI, Mary L.	(CA)	738
Atmospheric sciences	SMITH, Shirley M.	(NV)	1161
Audiovisual & library science reference	RUSIEWSKI, Charles B.	(IL)	1068
Baking science & technology	HORTIN, Judith K.	(KS)	561
Basic library science courses	SANDERS, John B.	(MO)	1080
Behavioral science	AJIBERO, Matthew I.	(NGR)	9
Behavioral sciences	SEGAL, Judith	(NY)	1112
Behavioral sciences & education research	SWARTZ, Jon D.	(TX)	1214
Behavioral sciences databases	BAXTER, Pam M.	(IN)	67
Bibliographic science instruction	DERKSEN, Charlotte R.	(CA)	294
Bibliography, social scis & humanities	PARROTT, Margaret S.	(NC)	944
Biochemistry & general sciences	ROMANIUK, Elena	(BC)	1052
Biological science bibliography	LUCHSINGER, Arlene E.	(GA)	746
Biological science medicine reference	CHASTAIN-WARHEIT, Christine C.	(DE)	203
Biological science reference	MACLEAN, Jayne T.	(MD)	757
	GAGE, Marilyn K.	(OK)	412
Biological sciences	BULLARD, Rita J.	(MI)	156
	HAMMARSKJOLD, Carolyn A.	(MI)	493
	SCHMIDT, Jean M.	(MN)	1095
	BUSH, Renee B.	(NY)	165
	ZIPF, Elizabeth M.	(PA)	1389
	LOPICCOLO, Cathy J.	(TX)	741
	BOISVENUE, Marie J.	(ON)	111
Biological sciences cataloging	HAWVER, Nancy	(CA)	515

SCIENCE (Cont'd)

Biological sciences reference & bibl	MANNARINO, Elizabeth R.	(OR)	766
Biomedical & applied science databases	LETT, Rosalind K.	(GA)	719
Biomedical & scientific databases	CARRIGAN, John L.	(CA)	186
Biomedical science information	POWELL, James R.	(MI)	988
Bio-medical science reference	MOORE, John R.	(IL)	860
Biomedical sciences	DURSO, Angeline M.	(CA)	329
	HADDEN, Robert L.	(MD)	481
Biomedical sciences cataloging	WURANGIAN, Nelia C.	(CA)	1374
Business & science databases	CALDWELL, Marlene	(TX)	172
Business & science reference	MEYERS, Kathleen H.	(AZ)	831
Business & scientific databases	MITCHELL, Cynthia R.	(TX)	848
Business & scientific information	BUNCE, George D.	(ENG)	157
Business & social sciences databases	KENYON, Sharmon H.	(CA)	643
	SLOCUM, Hannah R.	(CA)	1150
Business, science & industry	SUGDEN, Martin D.	(FL)	1206
Business science & technology database	DIMITRESCU, Ioana	(PQ)	304
Business, science, & technology ref	REGNER, Erlinda J.	(IL)	1017
	RICHMOND, Diane A.	(IL)	1030
Business, science reference & research	LEDBETTER, Sherry H.	(MD)	708
Business, social sciences	TAYLOR, Douglas M.	(AL)	1226
Chemical & physical scis database srchng	REDALJE, Susanne J.	(WA)	1013
Chemical databases, science databases	COSGRIFF, John C.	(VA)	248
Chemistry & physical sciences databases	BECK, Diane J.	(CA)	71
Chemistry, physics, soil science	VIERICH, Richard W.	(CA)	1284
Clinical science bibliography	LIMAYE, Asha A.	(IL)	727
Collection development health sciences	WARD, Penny T.	(CA)	1304
Collection development in life sciences	SOWELL, Steven L.	(IN)	1170
Collection development in science	WARD, Sandra N.	(CA)	1304
	WINN, Carolyn P.	(MA)	1355
	SUDENGA, Sara A.	(TX)	1206
Collection development, library science	VIA, Barbara J.	(NY)	1283
Collection development, science & tech	GREENE, Cathy C.	(MA)	463
Combustion science	KITCHENS, Philips H.	(AL)	657
Communication among scientists	WALKER, Richard D.	(WI)	1296
Compiling computer science bibliography	WEINER, Carolynn N.	(NY)	1318
Computer reference service, scientific	WANAT, Camille A.	(CA)	1302
Computer science	GUST, Kathleen D.	(CA)	478
	VARNER, James H.	(CO)	1279
	COPPOLA, H P.	(MA)	245
	MATTHEWS, Charles E.	(MA)	785
	BEDDES, Marianne T.	(NJ)	73
	HOUGHTON, Joan I.	(NY)	562
	HAHN, Susan H.	(PA)	484
	MYERS, Charles J.	(PA)	884
	BELL, Charise F.	(TX)	76
	GOODWIN, C R.	(AB)	450
	FUENTES, Ismael	(SPN)	408
Computer science & math	TIMBERS, Jill G.	(MI)	1245
Computer science collection development	ENSOR, Pat L.	(IN)	350
	TINSLEY, Geraldine L.	(PA)	1246
Computer science education	FOX, Edward A.	(VA)	394
Computer science, high tech industry	SLOAN, Maureen G.	(OR)	1149
Computer science library	SUBLETTE, Doris L.	(CA)	1206
Computer science literature	MCDANIEL, Sara H.	(GA)	801
Computer science resources	CARNES, Mary J.	(NE)	183
Computer science, start-up libraries	FUCHS, Karola M.	(PA)	408
Computer searching, biological sciences	CULOTTA, Wendy A.	(CA)	264
Computing science	BUCHANAN, Zoe A.	(ON)	153
Criminological & behavioral sciences	BEAUDET, Normand	(PQ)	70
Database searching, food sciences, chem	REED, Catherine A.	(NY)	1015
Decision, management science	KANTOR, Paul B.	(OH)	626
Earth & environmental sciences	RUDD, Janet K.	(CA)	1065
Earth science	NEWMAN, Linda P.	(NV)	899
Earth science databases	WEST, Barbara F.	(TX)	1326
Earth science, geology & petroleum	DEPETRO, Thomas G.	(TX)	293

SCIENCE (Cont'd)

Earth science information	ALBRIGHT, Donald A.	(NT)	10
Earth science reference	MURRAY, James T.	(OK)	882
Earth sciences	KRICK, Mary	(IL)	678
	HEISER, Lois	(IN)	523
	MERRYMAN, Margaret M.	(VA)	827
	HAU, Edward T.	(AB)	512
Earth sciences bibliography	DERKSEN, Charlotte R.	(CA)	294
Earth sciences reference & research	SORROUGH, Gail L.	(CA)	1169
Editing computer science magazines	WEINER, Carolynn N.	(NY)	1318
Education & behavioral sciences	WOMACK, Sharon K.	(NE)	1362
Education, behavioral sciences	O'BRIEN, Nancy P.	(IL)	915
Education of science librarians	ALEXANDER, Carol G.	(VA)	12
Education, social science reference	ROBERTSON, Ina N.	(IL)	1042
Energy & environmental science	CLARK, Peter W.	(WI)	217
Engineering & science information	LUCKER, Jay K.	(MA)	746
Engineering & science reference	MULLEN, Cecilia P.	(CA)	877
	TINSLEY, Geraldine L.	(PA)	1246
Engineering & science research	SOKOV, Asta M.	(PQ)	1166
Engineering, scintfc, chemical databases	PELLINI, Nancy M.	(MA)	955
Environmental sci & engineering database	DONG, Tina	(MA)	311
Environmental sciences	CARRICABURU, Robert	(CA)	186
	BROOKES, Barbara	(NY)	140
Exercise science	WINIARZ, Elizabeth	(PQ)	1355
Fantasy & science fiction	BRIDGE, Stephen W.	(IN)	135
Fire science research	SALY, Alan J.	(NY)	1078
Fire sciences & technology	GOLD, Sandra	(ON)	444
Food science	ARNOLD, Patricia K.	(TX)	34
	MUNDSTOCK, Aileen M.	(WI)	879
Food science & medical databases	FALCONE, Elena C.	(NY)	362
Food science & technology	WHITEMARSH, Thomas R.	(WI)	1333
Food science & textiles	MANDERSCHEID, Dorothy H.	(MI)	765
Food science, chemistry & technology	RILEY, Sarah A.	(MD)	1035
Food science reference	PERMAN, Karen A.	(IL)	959
Food science, technology	MARTIN, Irmgarde D.	(TX)	776
Foreign language scientific literature	SAMSON, Mary	(ON)	1079
Foreign scientific technical literature	BROPHY, Charles A.	(OH)	141
General & science reference	FRIEDMAN, Ruth	(NJ)	404
General science	MORRISSETT, Elizabeth	(AK)	868
	MANDERSCHEID, Dorothy H.	(MI)	765
General science reference	FERGUSON, Elizabeth E.	(CT)	372
	LANDRY, Francis R.	(MA)	693
General sciences	HALL, Forest A.	(DC)	487
Health & humanities sciences reference	CHASE, Judith H.	(OR)	203
Health, science & business collections	ARMSTRONG, Mary L.	(AB)	32
Health science cataloging	CAFFAREL, Agnes	(LA)	170
Health science databases	LEVY, Judith B.	(CA)	721
	HORAK, Ellen B.	(CT)	558
Health science information	NEVEU, Wilma B.	(LA)	897
	LONG, Susan S.	(MT)	740
Health science information services	SWATOS, Priscilla L.	(IL)	1214
Health science library administration	FULLER, Sherrilynne S.	(MN)	409
Health science library educ, research	LOVE, Erika	(NM)	743
Health science library networks	WILLIS, Dorothy B.	(NE)	1348
Health science literature	GREEN, Deidre E.	(ON)	461
Health science reference	LIPPMAN, Anne F.	(MA)	732
	ARTH, Janet M.	(MN)	35
	PATTERSON, Charlean P.	(PA)	948
Health sciences	FOLLICK, Edwin D.	(CA)	388
	HALL, Forest A.	(DC)	487
	HURYCH, Jitka M.	(IL)	578
	LANDWIRTH, Trudy K.	(IL)	694
	HILL, Elizabeth C.	(KY)	539
	LEWIS, Ruth E.	(MO)	724
	HARE, William J.	(NH)	501
	BAIN, Christine A.	(NY)	47
	BOROCK, Freddie	(NY)	116
	ROSEN, Wendy L.	(NY)	1055
	STERN, Marilyn	(NY)	1189
	JUDKINS, Dolores Z.	(OR)	619
	BRANDRETH, Elizabeth A.	(PA)	128
	KELLERMAN, Frank R.	(RI)	636
	LLOYD, Lynn A.	(RI)	735
	PUHEK, Esther L.	(WI)	997

SCIENCE (Cont'd)

Health sciences	SCHLUGE, Vicki L.	(WI)	1094
	ARMSTRONG, Jennifer E.	(ON)	32
Health sciences acquisitions	GRIMES, Maxyne M.	(FL)	470
Health sciences audiovisuals	MCLEAN, Martha L.	(TN)	814
Health sciences cataloging	NEUFELD, Sue E.	(IA)	897
	COLSON, Elizabeth A.	(TX)	234
Health sciences collection development	BRANDON, Alfred N.	(FL)	128
	NEUFELD, Sue E.	(IA)	897
Health sciences computer software	MCLEAN, Martha L.	(TN)	814
Health sciences database searching	NEUFELD, Sue E.	(IA)	897
Health sciences databases	BELL, R E.	(CA)	77
	KLEINMUNTZ, Dalia S.	(IL)	660
	KANNEL, Selma	(WA)	625
Health sciences including alternative	WOODBURY, Marda	(CA)	1366
Health sciences information resources	ALMQUIST, Deborah T.	(MA)	17
Health sciences information services	MATER, Dee A.	(NC)	783
Health sciences liaison	GIOVENALE, Sharon	(RI)	438
Health sciences librarianship	BERK, Robert A.	(IL)	87
	FENSKE, Ruth E.	(IL)	371
	WEST, Richard T.	(MD)	1326
	MCKININ, Emma J.	(MO)	811
	BRADIGAN, Pamela S.	(OH)	125
	EMPEY, Verla	(ON)	348
	SMITHIES, Roger	(ON)	1162
	CRAWFORD, David S.	(PQ)	256
	WILSON, Concepcion S.	(AUS)	1350
Health sciences libraries	GRAHAM, Elaine	(CA)	456
	BINGHAM, James L.	(KS)	97
	DRAYSON, Pamela K.	(MO)	318
Health sciences library administration	EATON, Elizabeth K.	(MA)	333
	ANDERSON, Rachael K.	(NY)	25
	RICHARDS, Daniel T.	(NY)	1028
Health sciences library management	KAFES, Frederick W.	(NJ)	621
Health sciences library services	FLOWER, M A.	(ON)	386
Health sciences literature	ROPER, Fred W.	(SC)	1054
Health sciences literature access	FLEMMING, Tom	(ON)	384
Health sciences medical online searching	STANKE, Judith U.	(MN)	1180
Health sciences online searching	MATER, Dee A.	(NC)	783
Health sciences reference	BELL, R E.	(CA)	77
	KAMENOFF, Lovisa	(MA)	623
	SULLIVAN, Joanne L.	(MD)	1207
	WENGER, Milton B.	(NY)	1324
	GIOVENALE, Sharon	(RI)	438
Health sciences selection	GIOVENALE, Sharon	(RI)	438
Health sciences specialization	KAYA, Kathryn A.	(MT)	632
Hearing sciences	CHARBONNEAU, Ronald P.	(CA)	202
History of health sciences	ZINN, Nancy W.	(CA)	1389
History of science	CHAMPLIN, Peggy	(CA)	198
	ELLIOTT, Clark A.	(MA)	343
	RAMER, Bruce J.	(NY)	1005
	WARNOW-BLEWETT, Joan N.	(NY)	1305
	GOODMAN, Marcia M.	(OK)	449
History of science & technology	ANDERSON, Marjorie E.	(ME)	24
	STAPLETON, Darwin H.	(NY)	1181
History of the health sciences	BRITT, Mary C.	(AL)	137
	EDDY, Leonard M.	(KY)	335
Hospital & health science libraries	CAMACHO, Nancy S.	(TX)	174
Indexing science journals	DOWNEN, Kathleen Z.	(NY)	316
Indexing scientific materials	GHOSH, Subhra	(NY)	430
International scientific bookselling	OVEREYNDER, Rombout E.	(NET)	931
Japanese life sciences information	WILLIAMS, Mitsuko	(IL)	1345
Japanese science & tech information	SHERMAN, Roger S.	(CA)	1128
	QUINN, Ralph M.	(NJ)	1000
Japanese science technology information	TALBOT, Dawn E.	(CA)	1220
Library & info science placement	WELSH, Barbara W.	(PA)	1323
Library information science history	MIKSA, Francis L.	(TX)	834
Library science	BLANCHARD, Mark A.	(OH)	103
	GARSON, Kenneth W.	(PA)	420
	RISHEL, Joseph F.	(PA)	1035
	WOZNIAK, Grace I.	(PA)	1369
	FOUDRAY, Rita C.	(TX)	393
	JULIAN, Charles A.	(WV)	619

SCIENCE (Cont'd)

Library science — HUANG, Shih H. . . . . . . (TAI) 568
Library science collection
development — DAVIS, Sally A. . . . . (WI) 281
Library science curriculum — SWIGGER, Keith . . . . . . (TX) 1216
Library science curriculum
development — SPILLERS, Roger E. . . . . (MN) 1174
Library science editing & publishing — CASINI, Barbara P. . . . . (PA) 192
Library science education — RICKS, Bonnie B. . . . . (AK) 1032
WOLD, Shelley T. . . . . (AR) 1359
BURICH, Nancy J. . . . . . (KS) 160
YATES, Dudley V. . . . . . (KY) 1378
PALMER, Forrest C. . . . . (VA) 936
Library science education
administration — FOOS, Donald D. . . . . . . (FL) 388
Library science in China — WEI, Karen T. . . . . (IL) 1316
Library science instruction — MCNALLY, Ruth C. . . . . (CA) 816
GLEESON, Joyce M. . . . (IL) 441
BAER, Eleanora A. . . . . . (MO) 45
LAINE, Rebecca R. . . . . . (VA) 688
Library science instructor — JOHNSON, Jean G. . . . . (NH) 605
Library science librarian — WEINSTEIN, Ellen B. . . . (NY) 1318
Library science literature — STEELE, Patricia A. . . . . (IN) 1184
Library science publishing — COHEN, Bill . . . . (NY) 228
Library science reference — TYLER, Carolyn S. . . . . . (SC) 1266
Library science researcher — NITECKI, Joseph Z. . . . (NY) 905
Library sciences instruction — KUTTEROFF, Ethel C. . . (NJ) 685
WYLLIE, Stanley C. . . . . (OH) 1375
Life science databases — MITCHELL, Steve . . . . . (CA) 849
WALSH, James A. . . . . . (PA) 1299
YERGER, George A. . . . . (PA) 1379
Life science online searching — WILLIAMS, Mitsuko . . . (IL) 1345
Life science reference — CURTIS, Susan C. . . . . . (GA) 267
Life sciences — LUDWIG, J D. . . . . (AK) 746
FINEMAN, Michael . . . . . (CA) 377
PARKER, Joan M. . . . . . (CA) 942
WALKER, Luise E. . . . . . (OR) 1295
ELDER, Nancy I. . . . . . . (TX) 342
Life sciences & physical sciences — WILLIAMS, Robert C. . . . (AK) 1346
Life sciences cataloging — PASTER, Amy L. . . . . . . (PA) 946
Life sciences collection development — KELLAND, John L. . . . . (RI) 635
Life sciences databases — POWER, Colleen J. . . . . (CA) 989
HEWISON, Nancy S. . . . (IN) 535
SAFFER-MARCHAND,
Melinda . . . . (MA) 1074
Life sciences databases online — DAVIDSON, Lloyd A. . . . (IL) 276
Life sciences information — SEARS, Jonathan R. . . . (MD) 1110
Life sciences literature — FLEURY, Bruce E. . . . . . (LA) 385
DODSON, Carolyn . . . . . (NM) 308
Life sciences, medical databases — BAUGH, L S. . . . . (IL) 65
Life sciences reference — TALBERT, David M. . . . . (NC) 1220
PASTER, Amy L. . . . . . . (PA) 946
KELLAND, John L. . . . . . (RI) 635
Linguistics & library science — WEISS, Paul J. . . . . (NY) 1320
Literature of science — MAYLES, William F. . . . . (IN) 790
Literature of science & technology — PINELLI, Thomas E. . . . . (VA) 974
Management of science libraries — ALEXANDER, Carol G. . . (VA) 12
Management science — HSIEH, Richard K. . . . . . (MD) 567
HOUGHTON, Joan I. . . . (NY) 562
GIBSON, Gladys N. . . . . (MB) 432
Maritime science information — SHIPMAN, Natalie W. . . (TX) 1131
Materials science — COOK, Sherry M. . . . . . . (CA) 240
BONHOMME, Mary S. . . (IN) 114
LANE, Sandra G. . . . . . . (NY) 694
Materials sciences databases — VAUGHAN, Ruth M. . . . (IL) 1280
Math & computer science databases — DAVIDOFF, Gary N. . . . (IL) 276
Mathematics & science instruction — STRAWN, Aimee S. . . . . (IL) 1201
Mathematics, statistics, computer sci — PIERCE, Miriam D. . . . . (PA) 971
Meat science & technology — WHITEMARSH, Thomas
R. . . . . (WI) 1333
Medical & health science databases — AIRTH, Elizabeth J. . . . . (TX) 9
Medical & health sciences reference — STANKE, Judith U. . . . . . (MN) 1180
Medical & science databases — ROBINSON, Betty J. . . . . (CA) 1043
HUNTER, John H. . . . . . (TX) 576
BOULANGER, Mary E. . . (WI) 119
Medical & science librarianship — EBRO, Diane C. . . . . (MN) 334
Medical & science online searching — RANSOM, Christina R. . . (NY) 1007
Medical & scientific books — FUGLE, Mary E. . . . . . . (NY) 408

SCIENCE (Cont'd)

Medical & scientific databases — VEENSTRA, Robert J. . . . (AL) 1281
GOUVEIA, Sara C. . . . . . (CA) 454
MALMGREN, Terri L. . . . (CA) 763
BERNSTEIN, Lee S. . . . . (DC) 89
TAN, Elizabeth L. . . . . . . (IL) 1222
HAWTHORNE, Dorothy M. (MN) 514
AUSTON, Ione . . . . (VA) 40
Medical & scientific journals — FUGLE, Mary E. . . . . . . (NY) 408
Medical & scientific librarianship — ANDERSON, Christine . . (CA) 22
Medical laboratory sciences — STANDING, Doris A. . . . . (ON) 1179
Medical science collection
development — DIMATTEO, Lucy A. . . . . (NY) 304
Medical sciences — CONNOLLY, Betty F. . . . (CA) 237
GREEN, Ellen W. . . . . . . (CA) 461
BULLARD, Rita J. . . . . . . (MI) 156
Medical, scientific, technical reference — TIFFEAULT, Alice A. . . . (NY) 1244
Medicine & life sciences — GUIDA, Pat . . . . (NJ) 476
Metals, metallurgical sci, engineering — HYSLOP, Marjorie R. . . . (OH) 580
Military science & military history — DOYLE, Frances M. . . . . (VA) 317
Minorities & women in science — JOHNSON, Sheila A. . . . (NY) 609
Natural history & natural sciences — MORITZ, Thomas D. . . . . (CA) 865
Nuclear engineering sciences — MAYER, Erich J. . . . . . . (NY) 789
Nuclear science — GOLDMAN, Patricia J. . . . (MD) 445
Nuclear science & engineering — WEBSTER, Lois S. . . . . . (IL) 1314
Nursing & health sciences — AIRTH, Elizabeth J. . . . . (TX) 9
Nursing science databases,
cataloging — DIMATTEO, Lucy A. . . . . (NY) 304
Online literature, sci & tech searching — WALLACE, Wendy L. . . . (NJ) 1298
Online medical & scientific databases — REITANO, Maimie V. . . . (NY) 1022
Online scientific databases — SAMUELS, Lois A. . . . . . (CT) 1079
Online searching of scientific
databases — WERT, Lucille M. . . . . . . (IL) 1325
Online searching, science &
engineering — WILLS, Luella G. . . . . . . (VA) 1349
Online searching science databases — WHITE, Larry R. . . . . . . (CA) 1331
COONS, William W. . . . . (NY) 242
Online searching science, tech
databases — RAEDER, Aggi W. . . . . . (CA) 1003
Online searching, scientific databases — MORRIS, Sharon D. . . . . (MD) 867
Ophthalmic sciences — DRAPER, Linda J. . . . . . (MO) 318
Original cataloging, science — KARON, Bernard L. . . . . (MN) 627
Patents, science & business
databases — TUNG, Sandra J. . . . . . . (CA) 1263
Pharmaceutical information scientist — THOMPSON, Reubin C. . . (NC) 1241
Pharmaceutical sciences bibliography — ANDREWS, Theodora A. (IN) 27
Pharmaceutical sciences reference — PIERMATTI, Patricia A. . (NJ) 972
Physical, life scis & engrng reference — MURPHY, Joan F. . . . . . (CA) 880
Physical science indexing — SERDZIAK, Edward J. . . (CA) 1116
Physical science reference — BARATTA, Maria . . . . . . (NJ) 55
Physical sciences & collection
devlpmnt — MACEWEN, Virginia B. . . (DC) 755
Physical sciences & engineering — HADDEN, Robert L. . . . . (MD) 481
Physical sciences & mathematics — CRONEIS, Karen S. . . . . (TX) 260
Physical sciences bibliography — SEILER, Susan L. . . . . . (FL) 1112
Physical sciences collection
development — DESS, Howard M. . . . . . (NJ) 295
Physical sciences databases — HILDITCH, Bonny M. . . . (MD) 539
THAYER, Martha B. . . . . (WA) 1234
Physical scis databases online
searching — CARTER, Jackson H. . . . (NM) 189
Physical sciences, earth sciences — VIERICH, Richard W. . . . (CA) 1284
Physical sciences reference — LARUSSA, Carol J. . . . . (CA) 700
SOUTHERN, Mary A. . . . (NC) 1170
GALKOWSKI, Patricia E. . (RI) 413
THAYER, Martha B. . . . . (WA) 1234
Physics & life sciences — COHEN, Rosemary C. . . (NY) 229
Plant science — STRANSKY, Maria . . . . . (MD) 1200
Police science — ZIMMERMAN, Donna K. . (IN) 1388
Polymer science — JUDGE, Joseph M. . . . . . (PA) 619
Polymer science & technology — HILL, Elizabeth C. . . . . . (KY) 539
Psychology & behavioral sciences — BAXTER, Pam M. . . . . . (IN) 67
Psychology, behavioral science
databases — KAUFFMAN, Inge S. . . . (CA) 631
Public science & technology
reference — COHEN, Jackson B. . . . . (NY) 228
Public service, science reference — HUDSON, Donna T. . . . . (NC) 569
Public services in health sciences — BLACK, Lawrence . . . . . (NY) 101
Pulp & paper science, technology — HALL, Deanna M. . . . . . (GA) 487
Reference, physical sci & engineering — SIEBURTH, Janice F. . . . (RI) 1135

SCIENCE (Cont'd)

Reference science	LEE, P M.	(ON)	711
Reference, science & technology	HUYGEN, Michaele L.	(MT)	580
Reference service in the sciences	ELLSBURY, Susan H.	(MS)	345
Reference services in life sciences	SOWELL, Steven L.	(IN)	1170
Research & development in lib science	MEUNIER, Pierre	(PQ)	829
Research on science of science	KOCHEN, Manfred	(MI)	667
Rubber, plastics & polymer science	HOLLIS, William F.	(OH)	552
Scholarly & scientific communication	EDELMAN, Hendrik	(NJ)	335
Science	DMOHOWSKI, Joseph F.	(CA)	306
	FINEMAN, Michael	(CA)	377.
	THUNELL, Allen E.	(MI)	1243
	BAIN, Christine A.	(NY)	47
	DAHMANN, Rosemary G.	(OH)	270
	VEITH, Charles R.	(OK)	1281
	SAURIOL, Guy L.	(ON)	1085
Science acquisitions	FLICK, Frances J.	(IA)	385
Science administration & buildings	SOMERVILLE, Arleen N.	(NY)	1167
Science agency government documents	CURTIS, Susan C.	(GA)	267
Science & business databases	SHAW, Debra S.	(OH)	1123
Science & business reference	EYLES, Heberle H.	(FL)	359
Science & computer science	MATTHEWS, Priscilla J.	(IL)	785
Science & engineering	SMITH, Martin A.	(DC)	1158
	FARAH, Barbara D.	(MA)	363
	BALACHANDRAN, Sarojini	(MO)	50
	FREEDMAN, Jack A.	(MS)	400
	HECHT, Judith N.	(OH)	519
	ZEIDNER, Christine M.	(UT)	1387
Science & engineering bibliography	MALINOWSKY, H R.	(IL)	763
Science & engineering cataloging	BRUNNER, A M.	(TX)	151
Science & engineering databases	BAUM, Ester B.	(AZ)	66
	WYLIE, Nethery A.	(CO)	1375
	SAUER, David A.	(MA)	1084
	POWELL, Jill H.	(NY)	988
	HOLLIS, William F.	(OH)	552
	LANG, Anita E.	(TX)	695
Science & engineering literature	MCGORRAY, John J.	(AZ)	807
	BUNTZEN, Joan L.	(CA)	157
	SASS, Samuel	(MA)	1083
Science & engineering online searching	BRUNNER, A M.	(TX)	151
Science & engineering reference	HODGSON, Elizabeth A.	(NY)	546
	PANCAKE, Edwina	(VA)	937
	FISHER, Rita C.	(WA)	381
Science & engineering reference service	BALDWIN, Charlene M.	(AZ)	51
Science & engineering reference services	TABACHNICK, Sharon	(TN)	1219
Science & history bibliography	LEE, J S.	(NJ)	710
Science & information policy	ROSENBERG, Kenyon C.	(VA)	1056
Science & medical collection development	HUNTER, John H.	(TX)	576
Science & medical databases	OSTROFF, Cynthia R.	(CT)	929
	MAYER, Erich J.	(NY)	789
Science & medical literature	MOSER, Emily F.	(VA)	870
Science & medical online searching	LAMANN, Amber N.	(NY)	689
Science & medical reference	LACY, Yvonne M.	(TX)	687
Science & medicine collection devlpmnt	MICHAELS, Debbie D.	(NJ)	832
Science & physics reference	STEINBERG, Marilyn H.	(MA)	1185
Science & serials cataloging	DODSON, Snowdy D.	(CA)	308
Science & social studies	ALBUM, Bernie	(CA)	11
Science & technical collection devlpmnt	PASTERCZYK, Catherine E.	(NM)	946
Science & technical databases	PASTERCZYK, Catherine E.	(NM)	946
Science & technical reference	ENRICI, Pamela L.	(MN)	350
Science & technical reference services	DEBROWER, Amy M.	(MD)	285
Science & technical serials	LEWANDOWSKI, Joseph J.	(CA)	722
Science & technological databases	TALBOT, Dawn E.	(CA)	1220
	BARRETT, Carol A.	(TX)	59

SCIENCE (Cont'd)

Science & technology	DAVIS, Frances F.	(AL)	279
	CONNOR, Billie M.	(CA)	237
	DIBLE, Joan B.	(CA)	299
	FELDMAN, Irwin	(CA)	369
	MCGARRY, Dorothy	(CA)	805
	REILLY, James H.	(CA)	1020
	SCLAR, Marta L.	(CA)	1106
	SIMS, Sidney B.	(CA)	1142
	CARTER, Ida	(IL)	189
	DAVIS, Jeannette	(MA)	279
	GIFFIN, Wendy L.	(MA)	433
	ARMSTRONG, Carole S.	(MI)	32
	HERBERT, Helen E.	(MI)	530
	MENDELSOHN, Loren D.	(MI)	823
	MONTGOMERY, Mary E.	(MI)	856
	CAREN, Loretta	(NY)	181
	COTY, Patricia A.	(NY)	250
	KAPLAN, Isabel C.	(NY)	626
	MASCIA, Regina B.	(NY)	780
	HSU, Helena S.	(OH)	567
	BROSKY, Catherine M.	(PA)	141
	CRONEIS, Karen S.	(TX)	260
	DEPETRO, Thomas G.	(TX)	293
	OGDEN, William S.	(TX)	918
	WILSON, John W.	(TX)	1351
	KRIZ, Harry M.	(VA)	679
	GREEN, Carol C.	(WA)	461
	JONES, David L.	(AB)	612
	WAUGH, Alan L.	(AB)	1310
	KENDALL, Sandra A.	(ON)	640
Science & technology bibliography	BAILEY, Martha J.	(IN)	46
	GLUCK, Myke H.	(NC)	442
	COHEN, Jackson B.	(NY)	228
Science & technology biogph instruction	SABIN, Robert G.	(AL)	1072
Science & technology cataloging	WALLACE, Wendy L.	(NJ)	1298
	LANDIS, Kay A.	(OH)	693
Science & technology collection devlpmnt	SABIN, Robert G.	(AL)	1072
	ANDREWS, Karen L.	(CA)	26
	ROHMANN, Gloria P.	(NY)	1050
Science & technology computer searching	CHADWICK, Alena F.	(MA)	196
Science & technology database searching	SENKUS, Linda J.	(CT)	1115
	SMISEK, Thomas P.	(MN)	1152
	HASELBAUER, Kathleen J.	(WA)	510
	SCHARMER, Roger C.	(WI)	1090
Science & technology databases	BROWN, Diane M.	(CA)	143
	ECKLUND, Lynn M.	(CA)	335
	GRENIER, Myra T.	(CA)	467
	LOVE, Sandra R.	(CA)	743
	MAH, Jeffery	(CA)	760
	SMITH, Sallye W.	(CO)	1160
	LONG, Caroline C.	(DC)	739
	KENNEDY, Joanna C.	(GA)	641
	MARECEK, Robert J.	(IL)	770
	VAUGHAN, Ruth M.	(!L)	1280
	ERDMANN, Charlotte A.	(IN)	352
	COLBY, Beverly	(MA)	230
	SEELEY, Catherine R.	(ME)	1111
	HEILEMAN, Gene C.	(MI)	521
	DUELTGEN, Ronald R.	(MN)	323
	KAN, Halina S.	(NJ)	624
	MCLAUGHLIN, Dorothy M.	(NJ)	813
	MAUTER, George A.	(NY)	787
	MONTALBANO, James J.	(NY)	855
	QUINN, Caroline E.	(OH)	1000
	HILKER, Emerson W.	(OK)	539
	DALLAS, Larayne J.	(TX)	270
	WONG, Lusi	(ON)	1363
Science & technology defense	JOHNSON, Mary E.	(CA)	607
Science & technology development	CHESLOCK, Rosalind P.	(MD)	207
Science & technology information	CULLEY, Paul T.	(NY)	263
	SALT, David P.	(SK)	1077
	ALI, Syed N.	(BRN)	13
Science & technology librarianship	SMITH, Eric J.	(NC)	1155

SCIENCE (Cont'd)

Science & technology libraries	MARKWORTH, Lawrence L.	(CA)	772
	NEUFELD, Irving H.	(CT)	897
	VANCURA, Joyce B.	(IL)	1273
	STEINKE, Cynthia A.	(MN)	1186
	PETERSON, Paul A.	(MO)	964
	MOUNT, Ellis	(NY)	873
Science & technology library consulting	PHINNEY, Hartley K.	(CO)	969
Science & technology literature	HEINRITZ, Fred J.	(CT)	522
	HOWARD, Helen A.	(PQ)	564
Science & technology online searching	POLLIS, Angela R.	(PA)	981
Science & technology reference	SABIN, Robert G.	(AL)	1072
	BRONARS, Lori A.	(CA)	140
	LEE, Lydia H.	(CA)	710
	ZEIDLER, Patricia L.	(CA)	1387
	MARCUS, Stephanie M.	(DC)	769
	CHADWICK, Alena F.	(MA)	196
	HANSEN, Joanne J.	(MI)	497
	ADAMS, Dena R.	(NM)	4
	SHIPPEY, Susan R.	(NY)	1131
	DUVALLY, Charlotte F.	(PA)	330
	CRAVEN, Trudy W.	(SC)	256
	BICHTELER, Julie H.	(TX)	94
	WHEELER, Marjorie W.	(TX)	1329
	HASELBAUER, Kathleen J.	(WA)	510
Science & technology reference & resrch	LUXNER, Dick	(NJ)	750
Science & technology reference service	TIRRELL, Brenda P.	(TX)	1247
Science & technology reference work	NITZBERG, Dale B.	(MD)	905
Science & technology research	MUSKUS, Elizabeth A.	(NY)	883
Science & tech resrch & devlpmnt support	LOGAN, Nancy L.	(ON)	737
Science & technology services	PHILLIPS, Linda L.	(TN)	968
Science & technology specialist	HOLLMANN, Pauline V.	(FL)	552
Science archives	GOODSTEIN, Judith R.	(CA)	450
Science bibliographic instruction	CULOTTA, Wendy A.	(CA)	264
	STANKUS, Tony	(MA)	1180
Science bibliography	LUDWIG, J D.	(AK)	746
	CHAMPLIN, Peggy	(CA)	198
	FLICK, Frances J.	(IA)	385
	MARSHALL, Jessica A.	(IA)	774
	PETERSON, Sally R.	(IA)	964
	MARION, Donald J.	(MN)	770
	CLARK, Camille S.	(NV)	216
	KREIDER, Janice A.	(BC)	677
Science bibliography & reference	DEGOLYER, Christine C.	(NY)	288
Science, biology & nursing bibliography	COOPER, Rosemarie A.	(IL)	243
Science books for children	JENSEN, Ann M.	(CA)	598
Science, branch librarianship	CAMPBELL, Susan M.	(PA)	177
Science cataloging	EDWARDS, Jennifer L.	(CA)	337
	MARKHAM, James W.	(CA)	771
Science classification	CANTIN, Gemma	(PQ)	179
Science collection development	WALTERS, Roberta J.	(CA)	1301
	KHAN, Syed M.	(MA)	646
	WILT, Charles F.	(OH)	1353
	STIRLING, Isabel A.	(OR)	1195
	SMITH, Charles R.	(TX)	1153
Science database searcher	PERDUE, Robert W.	(FL)	958
Science database searching	HART, David J.	(MI)	507
	DANFORD, Robert E.	(VA)	272
Science database searching, instruction	STIRLING, Isabel A.	(OR)	1195
Science databases	BRUEGGEMAN, Peter L.	(CA)	149
	KENNY-SLOAN, Linda	(CA)	642
	STANLEY, Eileen H.	(LA)	1180
	ELLSBURY, Susan H.	(MS)	345
	DICKERSON, Jimmy	(NC)	300
	OSEGUEDA, Laura M.	(NC)	927
	KEMPF, Jody L.	(NM)	639
	WILLIAMS, Esther L.	(NY)	1343
	HOUDEK, G R.	(OH)	562
	DANIEL, Mary H.	(VA)	272
	BLASE, Nancy G.	(WA)	104
	CHISMAN, Janet K.	(WA)	209

SCIENCE (Cont'd)

Sci databases, training & development	HOELLE, Dolores M.	(NJ)	547
Science education	BUBOLTZ, Dale D.	(CA)	152
Science, engineering	VARNER, James H.	(CO)	1279
Science, engineering & medical databases	ARIARATNAM, Lakshmi V.	(CA)	31
Science, engineering, & technology	GNAT, Jean M.	(IN)	442
Science fiction	HALL, Halbert W.	(TX)	487
	MACFARLANE, Francis X.	(TX)	755
	ESPLEY, John L.	(VA)	354
Science fiction alternative histories	COLLINS, William J.	(CA)	233
Science fiction & fantasy research	PELZ, Bruce E.	(CA)	955
Science fiction bibliography	KRIEGER, Lee A.	(NC)	678
	DAWSON, Terry P.	(WI)	282
Science fiction, fantasy research	KAN, Katharine L.	(HI)	624
Science fiction history	COLLINS, William J.	(CA)	233
Science, general & online reference	GRAZIANO, Eugene	(CA)	460
Science indexing	CANTIN, Gemma	(PQ)	179
Science information	HURD, Julie M.	(IL)	577
	CLANCY, Ron	(BC)	215
Science, info applications, of computers	MITCHELL, Steve	(CA)	849
Science information communication	FRY, Bernard M.	(IN)	406
Science information retrieval	BROWN, Cynthia D.	(NY)	142
Science information services	SOMERVILLE, Arleen N.	(NY)	1167
Science information sources	WOOD, Judith B.	(NC)	1364
Science librarianship	PARKER, Joan M.	(CA)	942
	BROWN, Steven A.	(GA)	147
	BLACK, George W.	(IL)	101
	OLSON, James	(IL)	922
	SWANSON, Patricia K.	(IL)	1213
	GARRABRANT, William A.	(NJ)	420
	WALCOTT, Rosalind	(NY)	1294
	TIMMERS, Debra A.	(WI)	1246
	MILNE, Dorothy J.	(NF)	845
	WALLACE, Kathryn M.	(ON)	1297
Science librarianship & management	STIRLING, Isabel A.	(OR)	1195
Science, libraries	HARRISON, John A.	(AR)	506
	KUHNER, David A.	(CA)	683
	NEELEY, Kathleen L.	(KS)	892
	RUSSELL, Keith W.	(MD)	1069
	SPURLOCK, Sandra E.	(NM)	1177
	HILLER, Steven Z.	(WA)	541
	ROBERTS, Elizabeth P.	(WA)	1039
Science library administration	HALE, Kay K.	(FL)	485
Science library management	RICKER, Alison S.	(OH)	1031
Science library procedures	STEEVES, Henry A.	(MA)	1184
Science literature	ALURI, Rao	(AZ)	19
	HOWARD, Joyce M.	(NY)	564
	WILSON, Concepcion S.	(AUS)	1350
Science, nature, & conservation science	PFOHL, Theodore E.	(NY)	966
Science, physics, mathematics	HOOKER, Ruth H.	(CA)	556
Science reference	FORE, Janet S.	(AZ)	390
	MAUTNER, Robert W.	(AZ)	787
	MOUNT, Jack D.	(AZ)	873
	CULOTTA, Wendy A.	(CA)	264
	DODSON, Snowdy D.	(CA)	308
	O'HEARN, Sarah A.	(CA)	919
	PRITCHARD, Eileen E.	(CA)	994
	ROTH, Dana L.	(CA)	1059
	OSTROFF, Cynthia R.	(CT)	929
	NELSON, Marilyn L.	(DC)	894
	PRIMACK, Alice L.	(FL)	993
	GUBISTA, Kathryn R.	(GA)	475
	WALD, Marlena M.	(GA)	1294
	DAVIS, Richard A.	(IL)	280
	MICHAELSON, Robert C.	(IL)	832
	SHOTWELL, Richard T.	(IL)	1133
	SMITH, Linda C.	(IL)	1157
	THORNHILL, Robert E.	(IL)	1242
	FRANKLIN, Janice C.	(KS)	397
	STUBBAN, Vanessa L.	(KS)	1204
	HAGEDORN, Dorothy L.	(LA)	482
	MARSHALL, Susan O.	(LA)	775
	GELB, Linda	(MA)	425
	KENT, Caroline M.	(MA)	642
	KHAN, Syed M.	(MA)	646
	RUBENS, Donna J.	(MN)	1064

SCIENCE (Cont'd)

Science reference
KEMPF, Jody L. . . . . (NM) 639
HEATON, Shelley J. . . . . (NV) 519
LIFSHIN, Arthur . . . . (NY) 726
POWIS, Katherine E. . . . (NY) 989
STEWART, Linda G. . . . (NY) 1192
WILLIAMS, Esther L. . . . (NY) 1343
BOLEK, Ann D. . . . . (OH) 112
FELTES, Carol A. . . . . . . (OH) 370
HOUDEK, G R. . . . . (OH) 562
KINCH, Michael P. . . . . . (OR) 649
LAWRENCE, Robert E. . . (OR) 705
EARL, Martha F. . . . . . . (TN) 332
DUFFY, Suzanne . . . . . . (TX) 324
HUNTER, John H. . . . . . (TX) 576
JACKSON, Ruth L. . . . . (TX) 588
CARTER-LOVEJOY,
Steven H. . . . . (VA) 190
MOFJELD, Pamela A. . . . (WA) 852
PRITCHARD, Jackie L. . . (WA) 994
ROOS, Tedine J. . . . . . . (WY) 1053
DROESSLER, Judith B. . (AB) 320
KREIDER, Janice A. . . . . (BC) 677
IVANOCHKO, Robert W. . (SK) 585
RESCH, Peter T. . . . . . . (SK) 1024
Science reference service
WHITLEY, Katherine M. . (AZ) 1333
Science reference services
YUCHT, Donald J. . . . . . (NY) 1384
Science reference sources
LOCKHART, Carol A. . . . (MO) 736
Science research
RUBEN, Jacquelen S. . . (CA) 1064
SINGLETON, Cynthia B. . (ON) 1143
Science resources
PASKOFF, Beth M. . . . . (LA) 946
Science services, library systems
WILLOCKS, Robert M. . . (FL) 1349
Science special libraries
HILL, Susan E. . . . . (TX) 540
Science technical literature &
databases
ROE, Eunice M. . . . . . . (PA) 1048
Science, technology & business
databases
TOSTEVIN, Patricia A. . . (WA) 1252
Science, technology engineering
database
TODOSOW, Helen K. . . . (NY) 1248
Science, technology, medicine
WOLF, Richard E. . . . . . (VA) 1360
Science writing
MAISEL, Merry W. . . . . . (CA) 762
Sciences
FERDUN, Georgenne M. . (CA) 372
Sciences & health sciences
WILSON, Jacqueline B. . . (CA) 1351
Sciences collection development
RICKER, Alison S. . . . . . (OH) 1031
Sciences reference
RICKER, Alison S. . . . . . (OH) 1031
Scientific & biomedical database mktg
ZAJDEL, George J. . . . . (PA) 1385
Scientific & business databases
AUGHEY, Kathleen M. . . (NJ) 39
Scientific & chemical indexing
BARNETT, Philip . . . . . . (NY) 58
Scientific & engineering databases
LANDAU, Herbert B. . . . (NY) 692
Scientific & medical databases
LANEY-SHEEHAN, Susan (AR) 695
Scientific & medical indexing
TRIMBLE, Kathy W. . . . . (CA) 1256
Scientific & med literature searching
TRIMBLE, Kathy W. . . . . (CA) 1256
Scientific & medical reference
LANEY-SHEEHAN, Susan (AR) 695
Scientific & pharmaceutical databases
BARNETT, Philip . . . . . . (NY) 58
Scientific & statistical databases
MCCARTHY, John L. . . . (CA) 794
Scientific & technical cataloging
ELSBREE, John J. . . . . . (VA) 346
Scientific & technical databases
LEVIN, Amy E. . . . . (DC) 720
ENRICI, Pamela L. . . . . . (MN) 350
CIARAMELLA, Mary A. . . (NJ) 214
ORTIZ, Cynthia . . . . (NV) 927
LETTIS, Lucy B. . . . . (NY) 719
LEMON, Nancy A. . . . . . (OH) 715
ELSBREE, John J. . . . . . (VA) 346
HOLLY, Janet S. . . . . . . (VA) 552
JOACHIM, Robert J. . . . . (VA) 600
Scientific & technical early periodicals
KRONICK, David A. . . . . (TX) 679
Scientific & technical information
DOUVILLE, Judith A. . . . (CT) 314
WALDHART, Thomas J. . . (KY) 1294
AINES, Andrew A. . . . . . (MD) 8
SMITH, Robert B. . . . . . (PA) 1160
WALKER, Richard D. . . . (WI) 1296
Scientific & technical info copyright
WOOD, Julienne L. . . . . (LA) 1364
Scientific & technical info
management
CARROLL, Bonnie C. . . . (TN) 187
SPATH, Charles E. . . . . (TN) 1171
Scientific & technical info retrieval
HOWARD, Theresa M. . . (ENG) 564
Scientific & technical information srvs
MOSER, Jane W. . . . . . (CA) 870
Scientific & technical intelligence
CRANOR, Alice T. . . . . . (DC) 255

SCIENCE (Cont'd)

Scientific & technical libraries
FEENEY, Karen E. . . . . . (CA) 368
PRUETT, Nancy J. . . . . . (NM) 996
Scientific & technical literature
FOREMAN, Anne P. . . . . (AL) 390
SNYDER, Richard L. . . . (PA) 1165
GARNETT, Joyce C. . . . (PQ) 419
JOBA, Judith A. . . . . . . (PQ) 601
Scientific & technical lit databases
MOBLEY, Emily R. . . . . (IN) 851
Scientific & technical online searches
TOMMEY, Richard J. . . . (CA) 1250
Scientific & technical patents
STANGL-WALKER,
Teresa L. . . . . (ON) 1180
Scientific & technical publications
ELSBREE, John J. . . . . . (VA) 346
Scientific & technical reference
CUMMINGS, Helen H. . . (DC) 264
KING, Hannah M. . . . . . (DC) 651
BLASCHAK, Mary M. . . . (MI) 104
Scientific & technical ref & research
MILLER, Dennis P. . . . . (OH) 837
Scientific & technical research
CRANDALL, Michael D. . (WA) 255
Scientific & technical searching
POLAND, Jean A. . . . . . (OK) 980
Scientific & technical translations
SAMSON, Mary . . . . . . (ON) 1079
Scientific bibliographic databases
PERRONE, Jeanne M. . . (DC) 960
Scientific bibliography
LAVKULICH, Joanne . . . (AB) 704
Scientific books editing
SKALLERUP, Amy G. . . (FL) 1145
Scientific, chemical, medical
databases
ANTOS, Brian F. . . . . . . (PA) 29
Scientific communication
SIEGEL, Elliot R. . . . . . . (MD) 1136
GRIFFITH, Belver C. . . . (PA) 469
KRONICK, David A. . . . . (TX) 679
Scientific database search
BAIR, Alice E. . . . . (IL) 47
Scientific database searching
BANKS, Mary E. . . . . . . (CT) 54
VELLIKY, Mary M. . . . . (MI) 1281
FREY, Luanne C. . . . . . (WI) 402
Scientific databases
FELLER, Amy I. . . . . (CA) 370
ROTH, Dana L. . . . . (CA) 1059
SEHR, Dena P. . . . . (CA) 1112
MOON, Mary G. . . . . . . (CT) 857
SARANGAPANI, Chetluru (DC) 1082
KINNA, Dorothy H. . . . . (MD) 652
CORRADO, Margaret M. . (NJ) 247
KNEE, Michael . . . . (NY) 663
KRAMER, Sally J. . . . . . (OH) 675
EDWARDS, David M. . . . (PA) 337
ATHA, Shirley A. . . . . . . (ON) 37
THORP, Raymond G. . . . (ENG)1242
Scientific documents
GIBSON, Joanne . . . . . . (CA) 432
Scientific indexing
ZOLNERZAK, Robert . . . (NY) 1390
Scientific information
HOPP, Ralph H. . . . . . . (MN) 558
O'GORMAN, Jack . . . . . (OH) 918
OWENS, Frederick H. . . . (PA) 932
Scientific information, automation
MCGREGOR, M C. . . . . (CT) 808
Scientific information databases
ZIAIAN, Monir . . . . (CA) 1387
Scientific information systems design
DIESING, Arthur C. . . . . (KY) 302
Scientific journals
YAMAZAKI, Shigeaki . . . (JAP)1377
Scientific libraries
BLANCHARD, J R. . . . . . (CA) 103
MENEGAUX, Edmond A. (MD) 824
Scientific library administration
BARKER, Victoria S. . . . (CO) 56
Scientific literature
ECKROADE, Carlene B. . (DE) 335
Scientific literature research
HAMILTON, Beth A. . . . (IL) 491
Scientific medical databases
DAVEY, Dorothy M. . . . (ON) 276
Scientific medical literature searches
DAVEY, Dorothy M. . . . (ON) 276
Scientific patent databases
POKLAR, Mary J. . . . . . . (CA) 980
Scientific reference
STRIFE, Mary L. . . . . . . (NY) 1202
Scientific reference & research
STOKES, Claire Z. . . . . (MN) 1196
Scientific reference services
KOSMIN, Linda J. . . . . . (MD) 672
Scientific serials
STANKUS, Tony . . . . . . (MA) 1180
FALVEY, Genemary H. . . (NY) 363
PARKKARI, John . . . . . . (ON) 943
Scientific tape film archives
SALY, Alan J. . . . . (NY) 1078
Scientific, technical & reference books
PECK, Brian T. . . . . (FL) 953
Scientific, technical business
databases
ALEXANDER, Mary B. . . (TN) 12
Scientific technical medical
KRIEGER, Robert E. . . . (FL) 678
Scientific, technical online searching
ENGLISH, Bernard L. . . . (NJ) 350
Scientific, technology databases
MACKSEY, Susan A. . . . (NY) 757
Scientific translation
SCHUTZ, Robert S. . . . . (OH) 1103
SDI use by basic research scientists
MONDSCHEIN, Lawrence
G. . . . . (NJ) 854
Selecting materials in sciences
KRONISH, Priscilla T. . . . (NY) 680
Selection of science materials
REED, Virginia R. . . . . . (IL) 1015
Social & behavioral sciences
KNAPP, Sara D. . . . . . . (NY) 663
Social sciences
WATSON, Marjorie O. . . (NJ) 1310

SCIENCE (Cont'd)

Soil science & computers	HANDROW, Margaret M.	(TX)	495
Sources & services in sci & technology	COOPER, Marianne	(NY)	243
Soviet science & technology	MARCUS, Stephanie M.	(DC)	769
Supercomputing, computational science	MAISEL, Merry W.	(CA)	762
Systems science	MILLER, James G.	(CA)	838
Teacher, computer science	EFFERTZ, Rose	(IL)	338
Teaching information science	FLOOD, Barbara J.	(PA)	385
Teaching library science	JEFFCOAT, Phyllis C.	(AR)	596
	HAZLETT, Florence E.	(AZ)	517
	KAST, Gloria E.	(CA)	629
	CULPEPPER, Jetta C.	(KY)	264
	KNORR, Martin R.	(MO)	665
Teaching library science courses	MATHES, Miriam S.	(WA)	783
	RUSSELL, Richard A.	(WV)	1069
Teaching undergraduate library science	MALTBY, Florence H.	(MO)	764
Technical & scientific reference	THOM, Pat A.	(WI)	1235
Technical, scientific information	ISGANITIS, Jamie C.	(NY)	585
Undergraduate science instruction	MICIKAS, Lynda L.	(PA)	832
Wildlife science	WEISS, Stephen C.	(UT)	1320
Worldwide scientific acquisitions	SNIDER, Elizabeth M.	(OH)	1163
Writing & editing scientific reports	LAUTENSCHLAG, Elisabeth C.	(PA)	703

SCIENTOLOGY

Church of Scientology	LITTLER, June D.	(FL)	734

SCIENTOMETRICS

Bibliometrics & scientometrics	HURT, Charlie D.	(AZ)	578

SCI-TECH

Business & sci-tech databases	GALTON, Gwen	(ON)	415
Sci-tech databases	EGGLESTON, Phyllis A.	(AK)	339
	WONG, Carol Y.	(CA)	1362
	REILLY, Francis S.	(DC)	1020
	SZE, Melanie C.	(NJ)	1218
	OBERLANDER, Deborah K.	(OH)	914
	GROSS, Margaret B.	(PQ)	472
	HETU, Sylvie	(PQ)	534
Sci-tech information	LAUB, Barbara J.	(NJ)	702
	MAASS, Eleanor A.	(PA)	753
Sci-tech libraries	WELLER, Leann C.	(KS)	1321
	TALCOTT, Ann W.	(NJ)	1221
Sci-tech library management	WONG, Carol Y.	(CA)	1362
Sci-tech reference	SAYLOR, Linda	(CA)	1086
	STOCKER, Randi L.	(IN)	1195
	COLLINS, Mitzi L.	(VA)	233

SCORES

Acquisitions, bks, records, music scores	SILVER, Martin A.	(CA)	1138
Cataloging scores & sound recordings	MURRAY, Diane E.	(MI)	881
	WALLER, Elaine J.	(MI)	1298
Monographs & scores cataloging	SUDDUTH, William E.	(MA)	1206
Music scores collection development	BERMAN, Marsha	(CA)	88
Record, cassette & score cataloging	DONIO, Dorothy	(FL)	311
Score & record cataloging	SEIBERT, Donald C.	(NY)	1112
Scores & recordings	FARRINGTON, James	(CT)	365
Scores & solo music	WALKER, Elizabeth	(PA)	1295

SCRIPT

Arabic script cataloging	WERYHO, Jan W.	(PQ)	1325
Non-Roman scripts	ALIPRAND, Joan M.	(CA)	13
Script clearances	PLUMB, Carolyn G.	(CA)	978
Script repository	FREEMAN, John P.	(TX)	401
Script writing & narration	SANKER, Paul N.	(NY)	1081
Scripts, manuscripts	KARATNYTSKY, Christine A.	(NY)	627
Stage scripts & programs	WOODS, Alan L.	(OH)	1366

SCRIPTURES

Col devlpmnt, theology, scriptures	MAINELLI, Helen K.	(CA)	761

SCULPTURE

American figurative sculpture	SALMON, Robin R.	(SC)	1077

SC350

SC350 & LS2000	STRICKLER, Candice S.	(TN)	1202

SDI (See also Information)

SDI	SHARP, Charlotte J.	(TX)	1122
SDI, current awareness	BUNTROCK, Robert E.	(IL)	157
SDI European information	BERLIET, Nathalie B.	(CT)	87
SDI in corporate research & development	MONDSCHEIN, Lawrence G.	(NJ)	854
SDI service	SCHAEFFER, Judith E.	(PA)	1089
SDI services	KOSTENBAUDER, Scott	(NY)	673
	DUFF, Ann M.	(ON)	323
SDI use by basic research scientists	MONDSCHEIN, Lawrence G.	(NJ)	854
Supervision of SDI projects	SHALLENBERGER, Anna F.	(NY)	1119

SEARCHING (See also Reference, Research)

Archival searching	RITTER, Helen	(NY)	1036
Automated searches	NORRIS, Loretta W.	(DC)	909
Bibliographic computer searching	KNAPP, Sara D.	(NY)	663
	NESBIT, Kathryn W.	(NY)	896
Bibliographic search	OLSON, Carol A.	(MN)	922
Bibliographic searching	LASETER, Shirley B.	(AL)	700
	DI MUCCIO, Mary J.	(CA)	304
	LAMBRECHT, Jay H.	(IL)	691
	LAMB, Robert S.	(IN)	690
	MANGIN, Julianne	(MD)	765
	FLOWERS, Janet L.	(NC)	386
	MEEHAN-BLACK, Elizabeth C.	(NC)	821
	SWANSON, Dorothy T.	(NY)	1213
	FUSELER-MCDOWELL, Elizabeth A.	(PA)	410
	COLE, Lorna P.	(ON)	231
Bibliographic searching & access	MARTIN, Noelene P.	(PA)	777
Bibliographical searching	MCTYRE, Ruthann B.	(TX)	818
Biomedical computerized lit searching	DORNER, Marian T.	(OH)	313
Biomedical literature searching	SMITH, Yvonne B.	(NJ)	1161
Biomedical searching	KENTON, Charlotte	(MD)	642
	CYGAN, Rose M.	(MI)	268
	MACKSEY, Julie A.	(MI)	757
Biomedical searching online	DOBBS, David L.	(OH)	307
Biotechnology search analyst	FRANZELLO, Joseph J.	(TX)	398
Business & marketing searching	BRANCHICK, Susan E.	(OH)	127
Business database searching	STERNHEIM, Karen	(CA)	1189
	ST. GEORGE, Susan M.	(CT)	1075
	MARANO, Nancy H.	(IL)	768
	OJALA, Marydee P.	(KS)	919
	ORENSTEIN, Ruth M.	(MA)	925
	SOSTACK, Maura	(NY)	1169
	FREY, Luanne C.	(WI)	402
Business databases online searching	MCDAVID, Michael W.	(GA)	801
	CANNING, Joan M.	(NY)	178
Business databases searching	FENTON, Patricia F.	(MN)	371
Business information search	MIWA, Makiko	(JAP)	850
Business searching	WEHNER, Karen B.	(TN)	1316
Chemical abstracts searching	BOLEK, Ann D.	(OH)	112
Chemical databases & searching	LINEPENSEL, Kenneth C.	(IN)	730
Chemical information, lit searching	JOHNSON, David K.	(NJ)	603
Chemical information searching	BUNTROCK, Robert E.	(IL)	157
Chemical literature search	CHU, Insoo L.	(CA)	212
Chemical literature searching	LAMBERT, Nancy	(CA)	690
	LERITZ, M K.	(CT)	717
	KASPERKO, Jean M.	(PA)	629
Chemical lit, substructure searching	SAARI, David S.	(IN)	1072
Chemical patent searching	WEHNER, Karen B.	(TN)	1316
Chemical searches	FULLER, Kathleen B.	(OH)	408

SEARCHING (Cont'd)

Category	Name	State	Page
Chemical searching	PACETTI, Karen C.	(IL)	933
	SKLADANOWSKI, Lawrence M.	(NC)	1146
	JUTERBOCK, Deborah K.	(NJ)	620
Chemical structure searching	LERITZ, M K.	(CT)	717
Chemical substructure searching	LEWIS, Dale E.	(NJ)	722
	DOBBS, David L.	(OH)	307
Chemistry searching	COHEN, Hannah V.	(NY)	228
	BRANCHICK, Susan E.	(OH)	127
Chem structures & substructure searching	MACKSEY, Julie A.	(MI)	757
Computer literature searching	BELANGER, Sandra E.	(CA)	75
	GLENDENNING, Barbara J.	(CA)	441
	MONTAG, Diane	(CO)	855
	MACKEY, Wendy W.	(MA)	757
	LAUTENSCHLAG, Elisabeth C.	(PA)	703
	KERSTETTER, Virginia M.	(VA)	644
	NOFSINGER, Mary M.	(WA)	907
Computer searches	KALRA, Bhupinder S.	(IL)	623
	KOLLIN, Richard P.	(PA)	669
	HOFFMAN, Sandra D.	(PQ)	548
Computer searching	COOPER, William E.	(CA)	244
	GIBBONS, Carolbeth	(CA)	431
	SCHWENN, Janet M.	(FL)	1105
	SCHACHT, John N.	(IA)	1088
	SNYDER, Fritz	(KS)	1164
	ADAMS, Deborah L.	(MI)	4
	SARTORI, Eva M.	(NE)	1083
	MAMAN, Marie	(NJ)	764
	BUTLER, Barbara E.	(NV)	166
	BATTOE, Melanie K.	(NY)	65
	BENEDICT, Marjorie A.	(NY)	80
	BUSH, Joyce	(NY)	165
	PURSCH, Lenore D.	(OH)	998
	STARRETT, Patricia L.	(OH)	1182
	VOIGT, Kathleen J.	(OH)	1287
	CONNORS, Kathleen M.	(OR)	238
	SAYRE, Samuel R.	(OR)	1087
	TENOR, Randell B.	(PA)	1231
	BAILEY, William G.	(TX)	47
	CHISHOLM, Clarence E.	(VA)	209
	DELONG, Kathleen M.	(AB)	290
	TULLY, Sharon I.	(MB)	1262
Computer searching, biological sciences	CULOTTA, Wendy A.	(CA)	264
Computer searching medical databases	TAPPANA, Kathy A.	(OK)	1223
	CAMPBELL, Shirley A.	(TX)	177
	ARMSTRONG, Jennifer E.	(ON)	32
Computer srchng, online info retrieval	SOUTH, Ruth E.	(OR)	1169
Computer-based search services	COOPER, Jean L.	(VA)	243
Computerized literature searching	HENTZ, Margaret B.	(CT)	530
	NESBIT, Angus B.	(IL)	896
	JONES, Deborah A.	(IN)	612
	DLOTT, Nancy B.	(MA)	306
	HALL, Robert G.	(MA)	488
Computerized searching	DAVIS, Anne C.	(MI)	277
Database cataloging & searching	VELEZ, Sara B.	(NY)	1281
Database computer searching	KING, Anne M.	(LA)	650
Database design & search	SCHWALLER, Marian C.	(MA)	1104
Database evaluation & searching	HEWISON, Nancy S.	(IN)	535
Database search strategy assistance	MARANGONI, Eugene G.	(CA)	768
Database searching	TRIMBLE, Kathleen L.	(DC)	1256
	WILLIAMS, Eddie A.	(MS)	1343
	JACQUES, Eunice L.	(NC)	591
Developing search profiles	RYERSON, George D.	(OH)	1071
DIALOG searches	MARCHANT, Cathy	(UT)	768
DIALOG searching	ASTIFIDIS, Maria	(NY)	37
	TOMLIN, Celia K.	(UT)	1250
	CARR, Carol L.	(WA)	185
Document searching	GRAF, Thomas H.	(DC)	456
Educational online & CD-ROM searches	LIVELY, Nancy J.	(MD)	734
Electronics searching	COGHLAN, Jill M.	(MA)	227
End-user search instruction	LIEBER, Ellen C.	(NY)	726
	CAMPBELL, Sandra M.	(AB)	177
End-user search systems	CHAPMAN, Janet L.	(NJ)	202

SEARCHING (Cont'd)

Category	Name	State	Page
End-user searching	HOGAN, Eddy	(CA)	549
	LITTLEJOHN, Alice C.	(CA)	734
	DAVIDSON, Lloyd A.	(IL)	276
	HURYCH, Jitka M.	(IL)	578
	GREENE, Cathy C.	(MA)	463
	TEITELBAUM, Sandra D.	(MD)	1230
	NASH, Stanley D.	(NJ)	888
	LIPPINCOTT, Joan K.	(NY)	732
	HALPERIN, Michael	(PA)	489
	BADER, Susan G.	(VA)	44
	STARR, Lea K.	(AB)	1182
	MARSHALL, Joanne G.	(ON)	774
	ST. JACQUES, Suzanne L.	(ON)	1075
End-user searching & education	GLASGOW, Vicki L.	(MN)	440
End-user searching & training	BATISTA, Emily J.	(PA)	64
End-user searching training	NESBIT, Kathryn W.	(NY)	896
	KONDRASKE, Linda N.	(TX)	670
ERIC searching	SCHWARTZ, Philip J.	(TX)	1105
	MCCART, Vernon A.	(VA)	794
Executive search	JONG, Jennifer L.	(NY)	616
Executive search & recruitment	BRYANT, Nancy J.	(GA)	152
Executive search firms	MARSHALL, Deborah M.	(IL)	774
Foundation collection searches	FRASER, Elizabeth L.	(WV)	399
General medical searching	LATTA, Barbara K.	(MN)	702
Health sciences database searching	NEUFELD, Sue E.	(IA)	897
Information management & data search	ZIAIAN, Monir	(CA)	1387
Information searches	SPAHR, Cheryl L.	(OH)	1170
Information searches, manual & computer	SHALLEY, Doris P.	(PA)	1119
Information searching	VAUGHN, Robert V.	(VI)	1280
Interlibrary loans, computer searching	SARGENT, Phyllis M.	(OR)	1083
International & domestic library search	FALK, Candace S.	(CA)	362
Legal database instruction & searching	ESKRIDGE, Virginia C.	(WV)	354
Legal database searches	TUTTLE, Jane S.	(GA)	1265
Legal database searching	RODICH, Lorraine E.	(CA)	1047
	RUGE, Audrey L.	(DC)	1066
	DULEY, Kay E.	(LA)	324
	CHERRY, Anna M.	(MN)	206
	KENNEDY, Bruce M.	(NY)	640
	WYNNE, Joseph J.	(VA)	1375
Legal database searching & training	KAUL, Kanhya L.	(MI)	631
LEXIS & Westlaw searching	BUTLER, Marguerite L.	(TX)	166
Library search	FOX, Frances J.	(AZ)	394
Literature search	EVES, Judith A.	(PA)	359
Literature search product liability	KENNEDY, Joanna C.	(GA)	641
Literature search supervision	CYGAN, Rose M.	(MI)	268
Literature searches	HAYES, Linda J.	(CA)	516
	HURTES, Reva	(FL)	578
	SUMMERS, Kathy B.	(VA)	1209
	MENDOZA, Anthanett C.	(WY)	824
Literature searching	BREWSAUGH, Susan J.	(CA)	134
	KATTLOVE, Rose W.	(CA)	630
	MURPHY, Joan F.	(CA)	880
	PETERSON, Gretchen N.	(CA)	963
	KELLY, Karon M.	(CO)	638
	LUEVANE, Marsha A.	(CO)	747
	WILLIAMS, Alexander	(FL)	1341
	MANGION, Barbara E.	(MA)	765
	REDFEARN, Linda E.	(MA)	1014
	OLIVER, James W.	(MI)	921
	METZGER, Eva C.	(NC)	829
	HOLDEN, Douglas H.	(ND)	550
	CHU, Wendy N.	(NJ)	213
	HAAS, Elaine H.	(NY)	480
	HOOD, Katherine T.	(NY)	556
	MUELLER, Leta A.	(NY)	875
	MOORE, Susan J.	(OH)	861
	ZAPOROZHETZ, Laurene E.	(OH)	1386
	HOWARD, Dianne D.	(PA)	564
	SCHWARZ, Betty P.	(PA)	1105
	MANNING, Helen M.	(TX)	766
Literature searching & astronomy	KNUDSEN, Helen Z.	(CA)	666
Literature searching & reference	HOMAN, J M.	(MI)	555
Literature searching & research	SPARK, Catherine L.	(ON)	1171
Manual literature searching	WELCH, Carol J.	(PA)	1321
Manual searching	SCHRAEDER, Diana C.	(TX)	1099

SEARCHING (Cont'd)

Marketing databases & searching	LINEPENSEL, Kenneth C.	(IN)	730
Marketing searching	RATHGEBER, Jo F.	(NC)	1009
Medical & chemical searching	RATHGEBER, Jo F.	(NC)	1009
Medical database online searching	HEETER, Judith A.	(MN)	520
	VUGRIN, Margaret Y.	(TX)	1289
Medical database searching	CLEMMONS, Nancy W.	(AL)	221
	SHEARER, Barbara S.	(AL)	1124
	COLALILLO, Robert M.	(CA)	230
	WAKEFIELD, Jacqueline M.	(CA)	1293
	HELENIUS, Majlen	(CT)	523
	MOON, Peter S.	(CT)	858
	WETMORE, Judith M.	(CT)	1328
	APOSTLE, Lynne M.	(DC)	29
	ANDERSON, Gail C.	(GA)	23
	BROWN, Carolyn M.	(GA)	142
	BALCERZAK, Judy A.	(ID)	50
	KELLEY, Rhona S.	(IL)	636
	SWANSON, Ruth M.	(IL)	1213
	RICHWINE, Margaret W.	(IN)	1031
	WEHLACZ, Joseph T.	(IN)	1316
	KRUSE, Kathryn W.	(MD)	681
	MORISSEAU, Anne L.	(MD)	865
	BRISTOR, Patricia R.	(MI)	137
	VAN TOLL, Faith	(MI)	1277
	ARTH, Janet M.	(MN)	35
	TORDOFF, Brian G.	(MO)	1251
	BELL, Cecelia L.	(MS)	76
	GRANDAGE, Karen K.	(NC)	457
	REISLER, Reina	(NJ)	1021
	ABLOVE, Gayle J.	(NY)	2
	EDSALL, Shirley A.	(NY)	336
	KELLER, Sharon A.	(NY)	635
	LIEBER, Ellen C.	(NY)	726
	UVA, Peter A.	(NY)	1270
	WESTERMANN, Mary L.	(NY)	1327
	BENSING, Karen M.	(OH)	83
	GIROUARD, J L.	(TX)	438
	HASELBAUER, Kathleen J.	(WA)	510
	WOOD-LIM, Eileen K.	(WA)	1366
	SCHELL, Catherine L.	(WY)	1091
	BRUCE, Marianne E.	(AB)	149
	SMITH, Marilynn C.	(SDA)	1157
Medical databases & searching	GLASGOW, Vicki L.	(MN)	440
Medical databases searching	KLECKER, Anita N.	(CA)	658
	WHITE, Anne E.	(IL)	1330
	GILBERT, Carole M.	(MI)	433
	HESLIN, Catherine M.	(PA)	534
Medical literature & searching	KATES, Jacqueline R.	(MA)	629
Medical literature searches	SIKORSKI, Charlene S.	(NY)	1137
Medical literature searching	RAINEY, Kathleen O.	(NJ)	1004
Medical online bibliographic searching	HARMAN, Susan E.	(MD)	502
Medical searches	NICKELS, Anita B.	(CO)	902
MEDLINE search training	KYKER, Penelope R.	(IN)	685
MEDLINE searches	NGUYEN, Michael V.	(AUS)	900
MEDLINE searching	HANSON, Elana L.	(CO)	498
	LINDNER, Katherine L.	(NJ)	729
	JUDKINS, Timothy C.	(OK)	619
Natural language search strategy	HAYDEN, Richard F.	(CA)	515
Natural resources literature searching	WAGNER, Barbara L.	(CO)	1291
OCLC & literature searching	REILLY, Dayle A.	(MA)	1020
OCLC searching	BRUNER, Linda J.	(VA)	150
Online aerospace & defense searching	RICH, Denise A.	(PA)	1027
Online & CD-ROM searching	KACHALA, Bohdanna I.	(NY)	621
Online & manual searching	BOGART, Betty B.	(MA)	110
Online bibliographic search	TU, Shu C.	(MA)	1261
Online bibliographic searching	WYBORNEY, Charles E.	(CA)	1374
	WESTON, E P.	(IL)	1327
	COLLINS, Mary E.	(IN)	233
	BEZERA, Elizabeth A.	(MA)	93
	LEE, Susan M.	(MT)	711
	NASE, Lois M.	(NJ)	888
	CURRY, Lenora Y.	(NY)	266
	HARDY, Gayle J.	(NY)	500
	PERRY, Claudia M.	(NY)	960
	TUCKER, Debbie B.	(OH)	1261
	JOHNSON, Jane W.	(VA)	605

SEARCHING (Cont'd)

Online biochemistry searching	SIESS, Judith A.	(OH)	1136
Online biology searching	CHEN, Flora F.	(SK)	205
Online business searching	STREHL, Susan J.	(DC)	1201
	BURKE, Vivienne C.	(WA)	160
Online chemical searching	PETRY, Robyn E.	(IL)	965
Online chemistry searching	CHEN, Flora F.	(SK)	205
Online coordination & searching	TAYLOR, Douglas M.	(AL)	1226
Online database construction & searching	CHAMIS, Alice Y.	(OH)	198
Online literature, sci & tech searching	WALLACE, Wendy L.	(NJ)	1298
Online literature search	CHUNG, Helen S.	(NC)	213
Online literature searching	CRUM, Norman J.	(CA)	262
	GLYNN, Jeannette E.	(CA)	442
	HUNT, Richard K.	(CA)	575
	BODI, Sonia E.	(IL)	109
	BRINKMAN, Carol S.	(KY)	136
	KRESSE, Kerry L.	(KY)	678
	SHEPARD, Margaret E.	(MI)	1127
	OBERC, Susanne F.	(OH)	913
	ROHMILLER, Ellen L.	(OH)	1051
	BERGER, Lewis W.	(PA)	85
	FU, Clare S.	(PA)	407
	KELLAND, John L.	(RI)	635
	WORLEY, Merry P.	(TX)	1369
	PARHAM, Sandra H.	(VA)	940
	LAMB, Cheryl M.	(WI)	689
Online, manual search strategy	BATES, Marcia J.	(CA)	64
Online medical database searching	TIBBS, Jo A.	(FL)	1244
Online medical literature search	ABRAMSON, Lawrence J.	(MI)	3
Online medical searches	ROWBERG, Alan H.	(WA)	1062
Online medical searching	POSTLEWAIT, Cheryl A.	(KS)	986
Online patent searching	TERANIS, Mara	(WI)	1231
Online reference searches	MANNING, Mary J.	(IL)	766
Online searching	BROWN, Lorene B.	(GA)	145
	LAWRENCE, Robert E.	(OR)	705
Online searching & search coordination	ROBERTS, Sally M.	(IL)	1041
Online searching & search services	JONES, B E.	(ON)	611
Online services, searching	WARDEN, Carolyn L.	(NY)	1304
Online technology & searching	KREMER, Jill L.	(PA)	677
Organic chemistry searching	COGHLAN, Jill M.	(MA)	227
Out-of-print searching	ZULA, Floyd M.	(LA)	1391
	KRAEHE, Mary A.	(VA)	674
Patent & trademark searching	SCHUELER, Dolores	(MA)	1101
Patent databases & searching	LINEPENSEL, Kenneth C.	(IN)	730
Patent novelty searches	AUGHEY, Kathleen M.	(NJ)	39
Patent organization & searching	MASTERS, Fred N.	(CT)	782
Patent search	CHU, Insoo L.	(CA)	212
Patent searches	FULLER, Kathleen B.	(OH)	408
Patent searching	LAMBERT, Nancy	(CA)	690
	KOLBIN, Ronda I.	(CT)	669
	GEVIRTZMAN, Joyce L.	(MA)	430
	JUTERBOCK, Deborah K.	(NJ)	620
	BUTCHER, Sharon L.	(OH)	166
	RATLIFF, Priscilla	(OH)	1009
Performing online & computer searches	DUCHARME, Judith C.	(NM)	322
Pharmaceutical searching online	SNOW, Bonnie	(PA)	1164
Picture searching	BAERWALD, Susan M.	(MO)	45
Prior art searches	ANTOS, Brian F.	(PA)	29
Reference & computer information search	MOORHEAD, Kenneth E.	(CT)	862
Reference & searching	FORD, Mary R.	(TX)	389
Reference online literature searching	DUNKEL, Lisa M.	(CA)	326
Reference search	KINGSBERY, Evelyn B.	(TX)	652
Reference searches	GORDON, Shirlee J.	(OH)	452
Reference searching	COOPER, William E.	(CA)	244
Science & technology computer searching	CHADWICK, Alena F.	(MA)	196
Science database searching, instruction	STIRLING, Isabel A.	(OR)	1195
Scientific & med literature searching	TRIMBLE, Kathy W.	(CA)	1256
Scientific & technical searching	POLAND, Jean A.	(OK)	980
Scientific medical literature searches	DAVEY, Dorothy M.	(ON)	276
Search assistance	GAROOGIAN, Rhoda	(NY)	420
Search online	PAPADEMETRIOU, Athanasia	(MA)	938

SEARCHING (Cont'd)

Search software	LESLIE, Nathan	(ON)	718
	LOWRY, Douglas B.	(ON)	745
	LOWRY, John D.	(ON)	745
Search strategies	DOYLE, James M.	(MI)	317
Search system software: front-end	WOODSMALL, Rose M.	(MD)	1367
Search training	LEACH, Sandra S.	(TN)	706
Searches	PROKESH, Jane	(TX)	995
Searching	YASUMATSU, Janet R.	(DC)	1378
	RANDTKE, Angela W.	(FL)	1007
	MCSWAIN, Christy A.	(PA)	818
Searching & indexing online databases	KREPS, Lise E.	(WA)	678
Searching & retrieving archival sources	FALK, Candace S.	(CA)	362
Searching databases	BROWN, Helen A.	(NE)	144
	WELCH, Donald A.	(TX)	1321
Searching medical databases	SCARFIA, Angela M.	(NY)	1087
	TANNENBAUM, Robin L.	(NY)	1222
	MILES, Donald D.	(PA)	834
Searching, MEDLINE	THOMAS, Yvonne	(CA)	1238
Searching online databases	BICK, Barbara K.	(MO)	94
Searching patent & chemical databases	MILES, Donald D.	(PA)	834
Searching, social science databases	WEIMER, Sally W.	(CA)	1317
Simultaneous remote search	GRAHAM, Deborah L.	(OR)	456
Special search services	JOHNSON, Everett J.	(DC)	604
Super searcher online systems	CONGER, Lucinda D.	(DC)	236
Technical information searching	FISLER, Charlotte D.	(PA)	382
Technical literature search	MIWA, Makiko	(JAP)	850
Technical literature searches	BARTLETT, Vernell W.	(MN)	61
Technical literature searching	WHITT, Diane M.	(IL)	1334
	YANCEY, Marianne	(OH)	1377
Technical reference & searching	DESOIER, Jacqueline J.	(CA)	295
Technical searching online	VAN BRUNT, Amy S.	(NY)	1272
Training end-users searching	BROWN, Carolyn M.	(GA)	142
Training of computer searchers	SOPELAK, Mary J.	(NY)	1168
Translations availability searches	NOWAK, Ildiko D.	(IL)	911

SEARS

Cataloging Lib of Congress, Dewey, Sears	RUSSELL, Richard A.	(WV)	1069

SEC

SEC databases	RUBIN, Ellen R.	(NY)	1064
SEC research & retrieval	GRISDELA, Margaret	(DC)	471

SECONDARY

Elementary & secondary education	MCDOWELL, Judith H.	(OH)	804
Elementary, secondary col devlpmnt	KUTTEROFF, Ethel C.	(NJ)	685
Elementary, secondary library education	CARTER, Yvonne B.	(DC)	190
Elementary, secondary school materials	PIEHL, Kathleen K.	(MN)	971
Independent secondary school librarian	REARDON, Elizabeth M.	(TN)	1013
Primary & secondary research	STARESINA, Lois J.	(MI)	1181
	MILGRIM, Martin S.	(NJ)	835
Public secondary school	STEWART, Joanne R.	(IL)	1192
Secondary curriculum, database searching	WILSON, M L.	(CO)	1352
Secondary curriculum, satellite use	WILSON, M L.	(CO)	1352
Secondary education	SHAPIRO, Lillian L.	(NY)	1121
Secondary education curriculum materials	LAURITO, Gerard P.	(PA)	703
Secondary faculty research	MERRELL, Sheila J.	(MO)	826
Secondary information	ARTHUR, Christine	(NY)	35
Secondary libraries	NYLUND, Carol L.	(TX)	912
Secondary library	ASTORGA, Alicia M.	(DE)	37
Secondary library curriculum	MERRELL, Sheila J.	(MO)	826
Secondary library materials selection	MERRELL, Sheila J.	(MO)	826
Secondary library media	CAMPA, Josephine	(MD)	175
Secondary research	OSWALD, Edward E.	(FL)	929
Secondary research facilities	CROTTS, Carolyn D.	(KS)	261
Secondary school collections	RIFFEY, Robin S.	(OH)	1033

SECONDARY (Cont'd)

Secondary school librarianship	KLEINMAN, Elsa C.	(CA)	660
	AUFSES, Harriet W.	(NY)	39
	KENT, Candace D.	(TN)	642
	SHANNON, Theresa M.	(VA)	1121
	KITTS, T J.	(ON)	657
Secondary school libraries	CURTIN, Mimi V.	(CA)	266
	SKEHAN, Patricia A.	(CA)	1145
	NOLES, Judy H.	(LA)	908
	MURTAGH, Mary B.	(NY)	882
	HARDIN, Sue H.	(SC)	500
	WILLIAMS, Shelagh C.	(ON)	1346
Secondary school library	SCHAFFER, Eamon	(CA)	1089
	NICKELS, Anita B.	(CO)	902
	CARPENTER, Carole H.	(DE)	184
Secondary school library media centers	MILLER, George M.	(MA)	837
Secondary school media centers	RAKE, Anthony I.	(IL)	1004
Secondary school publishing	IRELAND, Laverne H.	(CA)	583
Secondary schools	JAY, Hilda L.	(CT)	596
	O'HEARON, Doris M.	(IL)	919
	WRIGHT, Deborah L.	(IL)	1371
Secondary services	JENSEN, Raymond A.	(VA)	599

SECRETARIAL

Secretarial & office skills	EDWARDS, Barnett A.	(NY)	337
Secretarial arts	EDWARDS, Barnett A.	(NY)	337

SECURITIES (See also Bond, Investment, Stock)

Business, securities	FOWLIE, Linda K.	(DC)	394
Corporate & securities	PATTERSON, Patricia A.	(IL)	948
Securities	LASTRES, Steven A.	(NY)	701
Securities & commodities audits	JOHNSON, G V.	(IL)	604
Securities & commodities regulatory	JOHNSON, G V.	(IL)	604
Securities & commodities taxes	JOHNSON, G V.	(IL)	604
Securities & Exchange Commission	BARRETT, Michael D.	(NY)	59
Securities & Exchange Commission filings	GELINNE, Michael S.	(MO)	426
Securities industry	GROSSMAN, Adrian J.	(NY)	473
Securities pricing	FORD, George H.	(NY)	389
Securities regulation	DATTALO, Elmo F.	(DC)	275
Securities regulations	GREEN, Randall N.	(DC)	462
Securities research	CROFT, Elizabeth G.	(NY)	260
Tax & securities law	DOWLING, Shelley L.	(DC)	316

SECURITY

Copy services, security	ALMONY, Robert A.	(MO)	17
Defense & security	BARON, Herman	(PA)	58
Information policy & security	KNOPPERS, Jake V.	(ON)	665
Information security	ROFES, William L.	(NY)	1049
Library security	BYERS, Cora M.	(LA)	168
	LEBRETON, Jonathan A.	(MD)	708
	WALSH, Robert R.	(NY)	1300
	SALL, Larry D.	(TX)	1076
Material security & book theft	BAHR, Alice H.	(PA)	45
National security information	RUSSELL, Marvin F.	(DC)	1069
Security	CORDONI, Earl C.	(IL)	246
	JUDD, J V.	(NY)	619
	MOFFETT, William A.	(OH)	852
Security for libraries & archives	WALCH, Timothy G.	(DC)	1293
Security systems	BUTLER, James C.	(MS)	166

SELECTION (See also Acquisitions, Collection, Deselection, Weeding)

Administration & book selection	SNYDER, Esther M.	(ISR)	1164
Adult & children's book selection	GENCO, Barbara A.	(NY)	426
Adult book selection	COFFEY, Dorothy A.	(MI)	227
Adult materials selection	NICHTER, Alan	(FL)	902
Adult trade nonfiction selection	WISOTZKI, Lila B.	(MD)	1358
Audiovisual material selection	WOOD, Irene P.	(IL)	1364
Audiovisual materials selection	SHEFFO, Belinda M.	(PA)	1125
Audiovisual selection	TRIVISON, Margaret A.	(CA)	1257
	DOWD, Frank B.	(MD)	315
Audiovisual selection & advisory	ORMOND, Sarah C.	(MI)	926
Automation selection & implementation	DONALDSON, Timothy P.	(OH)	311
Biology reference & selection	WINIARZ, Elizabeth	(PQ)	1355

SELECTION (Cont'd)

Book & audiovisual media selection	YOUNG, Patricia S.	(TN)	1383
Book & journal selection	MAYRAND, Lise M.	(PQ)	791
Book & media selection	HUBER, Donald L.	(OH)	569
	MC NAIR, Marian B.	(OH)	815
Book & serial selection	VELEZ, Sara B.	(NY)	1281
Book selection	VOSS, Ruth A.	(AR)	1289
	CROWTHER, Carol	(CA)	262
	FRANK, Peter R.	(CA)	397
	STERLIN, Annette S.	(CA)	1189
	WINKLER, Jean J.	(CO)	1355
	ADAMS, Gustav C.	(FL)	4
	HENDERSON, Patricia A.	(FL)	526
	SKUBISH, Barbara E.	(FL)	1147
	GLISSON, Patricia A.	(GA)	441
	SUMNER, Ellen L.	(GA)	1209
	BRANDT, Garnet J.	(IA)	128
	CURRY, Jean K.	(IL)	266
	LEVIN, Joan E.	(IL)	720
	NELSON, Barbara L.	(IL)	893
	TIWANA, Nazar H.	(IL)	1247
	MILLER, Marsha A.	(IN)	840
	SHIPPS, Anthony W.	(IN)	1131
	SMYERS, Richard P.	(IN)	1162
	SCHEUERMAN, Luanne J.	(KS)	1092
	SMITH, Barbara J.	(ME)	1153
	CHAMBERS, E G.	(MI)	198
	GLIKIN, Ronda	(MI)	441
	KINGSTON, Jo A.	(MI)	652
	ORMOND, Sarah C.	(MI)	926
	VANDERLAAN, Robert J.	(MI)	1274
	WISCHMEYER, Carol A.	(MI)	1356
	BLANKENSHIP, Phyllis E.	(MO)	104
	LARSON, Josephine	(NC)	699
	ANDERSON, Janelle E.	(NJ)	23
	BERGER, Morey R.	(NJ)	86
	DOBRZYNSKI, Terenita	(NY)	307
	SALINERO, Amelia	(NY)	1076
	SZMUK, Szilvia E.	(NY)	1218
	BURKE, Ambrose L.	(OH)	160
	FREW, Martha G.	(OH)	402
	GORDON, Shirlee J.	(OH)	452
	LEWIS, Betty J.	(OH)	722
	PLUMMER, Karen A.	(OH)	978
	POLACHECK, Demarest L.	(OH)	980
	MADER, Marion C.	(PA)	759
	JACKSON, Harriett D.	(TN)	587
	YAPLE, Marilyn V.	(TX)	1378
	PETERSON, Francine	(UT)	963
	CHAMBERLAIN, M J.	(VA)	197
	POWERS, Linda J.	(VA)	989
	ZWICK, Susan G.	(VA)	1392
	POPECKI, Jeanne M.	(VT)	983
	SCOTT, John E.	(WV)	1107
	STAFFORD, Leva L.	(WY)	1178
	GOW, Susan P.	(BC)	454
	INSELBERG, Diana E.	(BC)	583
	MARTEN, Mary L.	(MB)	775
	WRIGHT, Patrick D.	(MB)	1372
	LAMBERT, Deborah B.	(ON)	690
	COUGHLIN, Violet L.	(PQ)	250
	FINNEMORE, Mary A.	(PQ)	378
	OUIMET, Yves	(PQ)	930
	ROY, Helene	(PQ)	1063
	STILMAN, Ruth	(PQ)	1194
Book selection & acquisition	LANGEVIN, Ann T.	(NV)	695
	GRAY, Patricia B.	(VA)	460
	MEHRAD, Jafar	(IRN)	821
Book selection & acquisitions	HARRINGTON, Charles W.	(LA)	504
Book selection & bibliography	WEISBAUM, Earl	(TX)	1319
Book selection & cataloging	MILLER, Jean J.	(CT)	838
Book selection & collection development	HOLSTINE, Lesa G.	(FL)	554
Book selection & evaluation	PATRON, Susan H.	(CA)	947
Book selection & purchase	GENSHAFT, Carole M.	(OH)	427
Book selection & reviewing	WAGNER, Sharon L.	(CA)	1292
Book selection, audiovisual services	DE CASTRO, Elinore H.	(PHP)	285
Book selection, bookmobiles	MONTANA, Edward J.	(MA)	855
Book selection catalog department	KING, Willard B.	(NC)	652

SELECTION (Cont'd)

Book selection, children's	LYTLE, Marian M.	(NC)	753
Books & audiovisual equipment selection	ANDIS, Norma B.	(TX)	26
Books & audiovisual materials selection	SCHILL, Julie G.	(PA)	1092
Branch adult book selection	RODGER, Elizabeth A.	(ON)	1047
Cataloging, selecting	ASLESEN, Rosalie V.	(SD)	36
Children & young adult selection	MATECUN, Marilyn L.	(MI)	783
Children's & young adult mtrls selection	ROBERTS, Sallie H.	(OH)	1041
Children's book selection	WISOTZKI, Lila B.	(MD)	1358
	RAFAL, Marian D.	(MI)	1003
	STEELE, Anitra T.	(MO)	1184
Children's book selection & programming	GENDRON, Michele M.	(PA)	426
Children's selection & development	SIPOLA, Debra L.	(WI)	1144
Collection selection & development	LANKFORD, Mary D.	(TX)	696
Construction site, architect selections	WRIGHT, Paul L.	(KY)	1372
Consumer health selection, reference	TAPPANA, Kathy A.	(OK)	1223
Coordinating materials selection	ZIEGLER, Fred	(AB)	1388
Current information selection	CYPSER, Rudy J.	(NY)	268
Document selection	LAHR, Thomas F.	(VA)	688
Educational film & video selection	MODICA, Mary L.	(SD)	851
English & French book selection	TAGGART, William R.	(BC)	1220
English & French books selection	DAVIS, Virginia K.	(ON)	281
English literature selector	THORSON, Connie C.	(NM)	1242
Evaluation & selection of library media	PETERSON, Miriam E.	(IL)	964
Evaluation selection	MACRAE, Lorne G.	(AB)	758
Fiction, books selection	SANDY, Marjorie M.	(MI)	1081
Fiction selection	SIMONS, Maurice M.	(CA)	1141
Film, video selection & programming	BUCHANAN, Gerald	(MS)	153
Film, video selection development	SHAPIRO, Leila C.	(MD)	1121
Fine arts book selection	SCHERER, Herbert G.	(MN)	1092
Foods & nutrition selection	LAMONTAGNE, Therese	(CA)	691
Foreign language literature selection	DOLAN-HEITLINGER, Eileen	(IN)	309
German selection	COULOMBE, Dominique C.	(RI)	250
Guiding children's book selection	SUTHERLAND, Helen G.	(CA)	1211
Health sciences selection	GIOVENALE, Sharon	(RI)	438
History selection & orientation	APPLEBY, Judith A.	(PQ)	30
Humanities selection	VOLAT-SHAPIRO, Helene M.	(NY)	1287
Instructional materials selection	WOBBE, Jean	(CA)	1359
Journal selection	RADA, Roy F.	(MD)	1002
Latin American selection	CLINE, Herman H.	(NY)	222
Latin American studies selection	KELLEY, Ann C.	(IA)	636
Legal materials selection	TENOR, Randell B.	(PA)	1231
Library boards selection & training	LIPTON, Connie F.	(MI)	732
Material selection	BONE, Larry E.	(NY)	113
	BEDDOES, Thomas P.	(PA)	73
	LINDENFELD, Joseph F.	(TN)	729
Material selection & programming	BRUNTON, Marilyn H.	(MN)	151
Materials evaluation & selection	HOWLAND, Margaret E.	(MA)	566
Materials selection	GOEBEL, Heather L.	(AZ)	443
	CROOKS, Joyce M.	(CA)	260
	HUND, Flower L.	(MO)	574
	BERLIN, Susan T.	(OH)	87
	HERSTAND, Joellen	(OK)	533
	LATROBE, Kathy H.	(OK)	701
	HOFFMAN, Elizabeth P.	(PA)	547
	TRIPP, Audrey J.	(PA)	1257
	COOPER, Jacquelyn B.	(RI)	243
	FOUTS, Judith F.	(TX)	393
	PENNER, Elaine C.	(TX)	957
	LAM, Letitia E.	(VA)	689
	WOODALL, Nancy C.	(VA)	1365
	FUNK, Grace E.	(BC)	410
Materials selection, all media	CLARK, Elizabeth K.	(MA)	216
Materials selection & cataloging	KENT, Rose M.	(OH)	642
Materials selection & reader services	TANG, Grace L.	(NY)	1222
Materials selection, collection devlpmnt	THOMPSON, Elizabeth M.	(DC)	1239
Materials selection, public libraries	LEE, Lauren K.	(GA)	710
Media in nursing & medicine selection	REIT, Janet W.	(VT)	1022
Media selection & evaluation	CHEEKS, Cellestine	(MD)	204
Media selection for curriculum	HILLER, Catherine C.	(CT)	541
Medieval era book selection	HILL, Lawrence H.	(PA)	540
Near East selection	WERYHO, Jan W.	(PQ)	1325
Nursing, medical selection, reference	TAPPANA, Kathy A.	(OK)	1223

SELECTION (Cont'd)

Performing arts selection & bibliography	VAN NIEL, Eloise S.	(HI)	1276
Personnel recruitment & selection	MARTZ, David J.	(DC)	779
	MCMEEN, Frances E.	(NY)	815
Political science book selection	YORK, Grace A.	(MI)	1381
Print selection	GILBERT, Donna J.	(OH)	433
Public library book selection	OTT, Bill	(IL)	930
Record & cassette selection	ANDERSON, Gail	(AB)	23
Recordings selection	MENDRO, Donna C.	(TX)	824
Religious book selection	SMITH, Newland F.	(IL)	1159
	HILL, Lawrence H.	(PA)	540
Secondary library materials selection	MERRELL, Sheila J.	(MO)	826
Select music, records, cassettes	CAPPAERT, Lael R.	(MI)	180
Select weed central adult circulation	DOYLE, Patricia A.	(TX)	317
Selected annotated bibliographics	PARKER, John C.	(CA)	942
Selecting & abstracting articles	HASSAN, Abe H.	(CA)	511
Selecting & purchasing books	JACKSON, Mildred E.	(MN)	588
Selecting materials in sciences	KRONISH, Priscilla T.	(NY)	680
Selecting popular materials	CROW, Rebecca N.	(TX)	261
Selection	ALABASTER, Carol	(AZ)	9
	RAFFERTY, Eve	(DC)	1003
	HUNT, Susan O.	(FL)	576
	BUFFALOE, Catherine S.	(GA)	155
	ELIZABETH, Martin A.	(IA)	343
	MARTIN, Elizabeth A.	(IA)	776
	LARSEN, John C.	(IL)	698
	LATZKE, Henry R.	(IL)	702
	SHERMAN, Janice E.	(IL)	1128
	LONGENECKER, William H.	(MD)	740
	MASON, Pamela R.	(MD)	781
	WESTBY, Jerry L.	(MN)	1326
	JUCHIMEK, Dianne M.	(NY)	618
	KAUER, Patricia A.	(OH)	630
	BRUCE, Robert D.	(AB)	149
	CHAN, Bruce A.	(ON)	199
	HOFFMAN, Sandra D.	(PQ)	548
	JETTE, Monika E.	(PQ)	600
Selection, admin, reference, cataloging	MALTBY, Florence H.	(MO)	764
Selection & acquisition	MISENHEIMER, Paula S.	(AR)	847
	MASTERS, Robin J.	(CA)	782
	NICHOLS, Dolores D.	(TN)	901
Selection & acquisition of library mtrls	SMITH, Cynthia A.	(OH)	1153
Selection & acquisitions	STAYNER, Delsie A.	(CA)	1183
	WILSON, Memory A.	(OH)	1352
	GILMORE, Carolyn	(PQ)	437
Selection & acquisitions of materials	MORRIS, Trisha A.	(OH)	867
Selection & collection development	WHEELER, Helen R.	(CA)	1329
	CUMLET, Harolyn S.	(LA)	264
	STURCKEN, Rodney A.	(LA)	1205
Selection & evaluation of non-print mtrl	AHN, Hyonah K.	(IL)	8
Selection & implementation	MILLER, Ann M.	(ON)	835
Selection & ordering	LONNING, Roger D.	(MN)	740
Selection for young people	IMONDI, Lenore R.	(RI)	582
Selection in history & political science	WRIGHT, Joanna S.	(IL)	1371
Selection, Italian literature	WACHEL, Kathleen B.	(IA)	1290
Selection of acquisition materials	BIANCHI, Karen F.	(WA)	93
Selection of books	ADRIAN, Donna J.	(PQ)	7
Selection of books & journals	THOMAS, Yvonne	(CA)	1238
Selection of children's materials	FORD, Marcia K.	(IN)	389
Selection of English books	DJEVALIKIAN, Sonia	(PQ)	306
Selection of library materials	PANKAKE, Marcia J.	(MN)	938
Selection of materials	PLOWDEN, Martha W.	(GA)	978
	GEORGE, Linda H.	(OH)	427
Selection of materials for schools	POOLE, Rebecca S.	(CO)	983
Selection of print & non-print material	GREENFIELD, Judith C.	(NY)	464
Selection of science materials	REED, Virginia H.	(IL)	1015
Selection, photography	WACHEL, Kathleen B.	(IA)	1290
Selection school library materials	HAMMEL, Philip J.	(SK)	493
Serials selection	GELENTER, Winifred H.	(MD)	426
Serials selection & control	KRIER, Mary M.	(MA)	678
Site selection	FRANKLIN, Robert D.	(VA)	398
16mm film selection	ANDERSON, Gail	(AB)	23
16mm film selection & reference	LOCKE-GAGNON, Rebecca A.	(OH)	736
Software selection	PUGH, W J.	(MD)	997

SELECTION (Cont'd)

Standing order selection & management	ROMANASKY, Marcia C.	(NJ)	1052
Technical material selection	WILLIAMS, Alexander	(FL)	1341
Video selection & projection	ROLLIN, Marian B.	(CT)	1051
Video selection & reference	LOCKE-GAGNON, Rebecca A.	(OH)	736
Young adult book selection	MOORE, Richard K.	(CA)	861
	WINSLOW, Carol M.	(IN)	1355
	WISOTZKI, Lila B.	(MD)	1358
	WRIGHT, Patricia Y.	(OK)	1372
Young adult fiction selection	TYSON, Edith S.	(OH)	1267
Young people's book selection	DAVIS, Inez W.	(TN)	279
Young teens book selection	RAPPELT, John F.	(NY)	1008

SELF-DEVELOPMENT

Individual & self-development	NOBLE, Valerie	(MI)	906

SELF-STUDY

Library self-study & evaluation	KANIA, Antoinette M.	(NY)	625
Standards & self-study	JOHNSON, Elizabeth G.	(AL)	604

SELLING (See also Retailing, Sales, Vendor, Wholesale)

Book selling	MARKS, Cicely P.	(MD)	771
Buyer & seller representation	PICKETT, Doyle C.	(NJ)	970
Buying & selling of American literature	MARTIN, John W.	(IL)	776
Buying & selling of English literature	MARTIN, John W.	(IL)	776
Buying & selling of rare books	MARTIN, John W.	(IL)	776
Buying & selling 78 & LP records	SMOLIAN, Steven J.	(MD)	1162

SEMICONDUCTOR

Semiconductor equipment & materials	SHERMAN, Roger S.	(CA)	1128
Semiconductor physics	COOK, Sherry M.	(CA)	240
Semiconductor research	CRABTREE, Sandra A.	(CA)	254

SEMINARS (See also Workshops)

Conducting training seminars	TOWNSEND, Carolyn J.	(PA)	1253
Consulting & seminars	ACKERMAN, Katherine K.	(MI)	4
Continuing education seminars	RUSH, James E.	(OH)	1068
Information gathering seminars	BERKMAN, Robert I.	(NY)	87
Library usage seminars	DECAMPS, Alice L.	(VA)	285
Management development seminars	SULLIVAN, Daniel M.	(NY)	1207
Professional seminars	HALPIN, Gerard B.	(ON)	490
Seminar development	SCHNEIDER, Hennie R.	(DC)	1097
Seminars	WILLIAMS, Joan F.	(CA)	1344
	GRIMES, John F.	(TX)	470
Training & seminars	TUNG, Sandra J.	(CA)	1263

SEMINARY

Theological seminary libraries	HAMMERLY, Hernan D.	(ARG)	493

SENIOR (See also Aging, Elderly, Older, Senior)

Academic, junior & senior highs	COLLINS, Judith A.	(CA)	232
Elementary, junior & senior high schools	ABBOTT, Ruth J.	(TX)	1
Junior & senior high schools	DANIEL, Donna M.	(OH)	272
Senior citizen resources	CARABATEAS, Clarissa D.	(NY)	180
Senior citizen's outreach	OSTROUMOV, Tatiana	(CA)	929
Seniors' deposits	GRAHAM, Heather F.	(MB)	456
Service to senior citizens	BORCHERT, Catherine G.	(OH)	116
Service to special populations & seniors	RICKERT, Carol A.	(IL)	1032
Services for seniors	CHAN, Arlene S.	(ON)	199
Young adult & senior citizen services	MYRON, Victoria L.	(IA)	885

SERIALS (See also Continuations, Journals, Magazines, Newsletters, Newspapers, Periodicals, Subscriptions)

Acquisition & cataloging serials	CHANG, Min M.	(CA)	200
Acquisitions & serials	TAYLOR, Patricia A.	(AZ)	1228
	PETRY, Robyn E.	(IL)	965

SERIALS (Cont'd)

Acquisitions & serials automation	MCCALLISTER, Myrna J.	(ME)	793
Acquisitions & serials technical srvs	KARASICK, Alice W.	(CA)	627
Acquisitions, books & serials	MIRANDA, Cecilia	(TX)	847
Acquisitions, monographic & serials	BENNETT, Lee L.	(IL)	82
Acquisitions, monographs & serials	WACHEL, Kathleen B.	(IA)	1290
Acquisitions, monographs, serials	BARKER, Joseph W.	(CA)	56
Acquisitions of books & serials	WARD, Dorothy S.	(AL)	1303
Acquisitions, serials	TAYLOR, Trish A.	(AZ)	1229
	MERRITT, Betty A.	(CA)	827
Acquisitions, serials & proceedings	LEFEBVRE, Veronica A.	(MD)	712
Acquisitions, serials maintenance	PICQUET, D C.	(TN)	971
Automated serial control systems	FONG, Wilfred W.	(WI)	388
Automated serials & acquisitions	ROYLE, Maryanne	(IL)	1063
Automated serials control	TALLMAN, Karen D.	(AZ)	1221
	KIRK, Darcy	(MA)	654
Automated serials management	REID, Janine A.	(VA)	1018
Automated serials management systems	CLAPPER, Mary E.	(MA)	216
Automation of serials & acquisitions	WAN, William W.	(TX)	1302
Bibliographic control of serials	KOMOROUS, Hana J.	(BC)	670
Book & serial collection	ELSTEIN, Rochelle S.	(IL)	346
Book & serial selection	VELEZ, Sara B.	(NY)	1281
Books & serials acquisitions	OSIER, Donald V.	(SDA)	928
Cataloging & classifying serials	WALKER, Elizabeth A.	(PQ)	1295
Cataloging & serials control	DRAPER, Linda J.	(MO)	318
Cataloging fine arts, serials	MILLS, Rolland W.	(PR)	844
Cataloging monographs & serials	NEVIN, Susanne	(MN)	898
Cataloging of serials, journals, etc	WARD, Dorothy S.	(AL)	1303
Cataloging reference, serials	VAN STRATEN, Daniel G.	(WI)	1277
Cataloging serials	WILLIAMS, Nancy L.	(FL)	1345
	ESMAN, Michael D.	(MD)	354
Cataloging serials, law, monographs	SPRANKLE, Vicki S.	(PA)	1176
Collection development & serials	ROGERS, Nancy H.	(AL)	1050
Collection development & serials control	BECHOR, Malvina B.	(GA)	71
CONSER serials cataloging	JONES, Edgar A.	(MA)	612
Cooperative serials agreements	ROBERTS, Elizabeth P.	(WA)	1039
Cooperative serials projects	UPHAM, Lois N.	(SC)	1269
Databases for serials, journals, etc	WARD, Dorothy S.	(AL)	1303
Datatrek computer catalog, serials	GENTRY, Susan K.	(CA)	427
Documents & serials	AIDE, Kathryn S.	(AL)	8
Exchange serials	BALL, Alice D.	(DC)	52
General & technical services serials	SZETO, Dorcas C.	(CA)	1218
Indexing journals, serial publications	POST, Joyce A.	(PA)	986
Interlibrary loan & serial management	WILLIAMS, Calvin	(MI)	1342
International serials pricing	HAMAKER, Charles A.	(LA)	490
Law serials	ROYLE, Maryanne	(IL)	1063
Legal serials cataloging	WOODS, Frances B.	(CT)	1367
Legal serials management	GOLIAN, Linda M.	(FL)	447
Library management & serials orders	VON PFEIL, Helena P.	(DC)	1288
Library systems, serials control	WANG, Anna M.	(OH)	1302
Management of serials organization	DONAHUE, Janice E.	(FL)	310
Medical serials	EGGERS, Thomas D.	(IL)	339
	BROWN, Sharon D.	(MD)	147
	WARREN, Karen T.	(SC)	1306
Medical serials acquisitions & control	WOODBURN, Judy I.	(NC)	1366
Monographic & serials acquisitions	PERRYMAN, Wayne R.	(TX)	961
	WAN, William W.	(TX)	1302
Monographic & serials cataloging	MORROW, Deborah	(MI)	869
Online union serial listing	PARRAVANO, Ellen A.	(NY)	944
Periodicals & serials	GOWAN, Christa I.	(CA)	455
	SUBRAMANIAN, Jano M.	(NY)	1206
	ROBERTS, Marica L.	(TN)	1041
	DANKY, James P.	(WI)	274
Retrospective conversion of serials	TUTTLE, Joseph C.	(NC)	1266
	POST, Phyllis C.	(OH)	986
Science & serials cataloging	DODSON, Snowdy D.	(CA)	308
Science & technical serials	LEWANDOWSKI, Joseph J.	(CA)	722
Scientific serials	STANKUS, Tony	(MA)	1180
	FALVEY, Genemary H.	(NY)	363
	PARKKARI, John	(ON)	943
Serial acquisitions	WILLMERING, William J.	(MD)	1348
	SCHUSTER, Bonnie H.	(MT)	1103
Serial & microform cataloging	NADESKI, Karen L.	(PA)	886
Serial & monograph acquisitions	WETZBARGER, Cecilia G.	(MD)	1328

SERIALS (Cont'd)

Serial cataloging	SCOTT, Sharon K.	(AZ)	1108
	HERRICK, Judith M.	(DC)	532
	HUGGENS, Gary D.	(DC)	571
	BLEIL, Leslie A.	(MI)	105
	SWETMAN, Barbara E.	(NY)	1216
Serial collection devlpmnt & management	CONWAY, Susan L.	(NV)	239
Serial control & collection development	MANDAL, Mina R.	(NY)	764
Serial department	MOORE, Mildred M.	(LA)	860
Serial development	BARRIE, John L.	(NY)	59
Serial holdings standards & formats	CLAPPER, Mary E.	(MA)	216
Serial holdings updating	DEES, Leslie M.	(GA)	287
Serial management	NOGA, Susan D.	(NY)	907
Serial processing	HSU, Karen M.	(NY)	567
Serial records	CHATTERTON, Leigh A.	(MA)	204
Serial services	CARSON, Howard C.	(VA)	188
Serial subscription service	WEED, Joe K.	(AL)	1315
Serials	MARTIN, John B.	(AL)	776
	O'NEAL, Kenneth W.	(AL)	924
	RODGERS, Patricia M.	(AL)	1047
	STEPHENS, James T.	(AL)	1188
	BLAND, Janet A.	(AR)	103
	HAYES, Franklin D.	(AR)	515
	HEITSHU, Sara C.	(AZ)	523
	KNEPP, Kenneth B.	(AZ)	664
	STOUT, Mary A.	(AZ)	1199
	TALLMAN, Karen D.	(AZ)	1221
	ANDERSON, David C.	(CA)	22
	CARD, Sandra E.	(CA)	180
	CARR, Richard D.	(CA)	186
	DONLEY, Leigh M.	(CA)	311
	EWEN, Eric P.	(CA)	359
	FAY, Evelyn V.	(CA)	367
	HAAS, Florence A.	(CA)	480
	LINVILLE, Herbert	(CA)	731
	MILFORD, Charles C.	(CA)	835
	MOORE, Evia B.	(CA)	859
	RANDALL, Michael H.	(CA)	1006
	RICHTER, Bertina	(CA)	1031
	STEFANCIC, Jean A.	(CA)	1185
	STOCKFLETH, Craig G.	(CA)	1195
	TSENG, Sally C.	(CA)	1260
	VANDEGRIFT, Glennda E.	(CA)	1273
	WANG, Connie	(CA)	1302
	ZEIDLER, Patricia L.	(CA)	1387
	BOYER, Carol C.	(CO)	123
	HENSLEY, Charlotta C.	(CO)	529
	MUELLER, Carolyn J.	(CO)	875
	PATERSON, Judy L.	(CO)	947
	COOMBS, Elisabeth G.	(CT)	241
	FU, Theresa L.	(CT)	407
	LAWRENCE, Carol A.	(CT)	704
	SORENSEN, Pamela	(CT)	1168
	BAILEY, Marian C.	(DC)	46
	BARTLEY, Linda K.	(DC)	61
	BLIXRUD, Julia C.	(DC)	105
	MCCRAY, Maceo E.	(DC)	800
	STACEY, Kathleen M.	(DC)	1177
	WOLFE, Susan J.	(DC)	1361
	ARMSTRONG, Ruth C.	(FL)	32
	GRIMES, Maxyne M.	(FL)	470
	MCCAMMON, Leslie V.	(FL)	793
	ORSER, Frank W.	(FL)	927
	TAYSOM, Daniel B.	(FL)	1229
	JOHNSON, Jane G.	(GA)	605
	RIEMER, John J.	(GA)	1033
	FALK, Mark F.	(IA)	362
	OSMUS, Lori L.	(IA)	928
	SKEERS, Timothy M.	(IA)	1145
	ADAMSHICK, Robert D.	(IL)	6
	BECKER, John C.	(IL)	72
	BLACKBURN, Joy M.	(IL)	102
	BLOSS, Alexander B.	(IL)	106
	BLOSS, Marjorie E.	(IL)	106
	BROWN, Norman B.	(IL)	146
	CHANG, Sookang H.	(IL)	201
	HASSERT, Rita M.	(IL)	511
	KIRKLAND, Kenneth L.	(IL)	655

SERIALS (Cont'd)
Serials

LEWIS, Martha S.	(IL)	724
MCBRIDE, Ruth B.	(IL)	792
SCHORMANN, Victor	(IL)	1099
SKIDMORE, Gail	(IL)	1146
SYED, Mariam A.	(IL)	1217
WENZEL, Duane E.	(IL)	1324
GOLOVIN, Naomi E.	(IN)	447
KUO, Ming M.	(IN)	684
PEC, Jean A.	(IN)	953
SANDSTROM, Pamela E.	(IN)	1081
WATTS, Tim J.	(IN)	1310
HATCHER, Marihelen	(KS)	511
TANNER, Jane E.	(KS)	1223
WILLIAMS, Sara R.	(KS)	1346
MAZUK, Melody	(KY)	791
STAPLETON, Diana L.	(KY)	1181
BRADLEY, Jared W.	(LA)	126
MATTMILLER, C F.	(LA)	786
MCREYNOLDS, Rosalee	(LA)	818
ROCHE, Alvin A.	(LA)	1045
DEARBORN, Susan C.	(MA)	284
DUFFEK, Elizabeth A.	(MA)	323
HOSTAGE, John B.	(MA)	562
JUDD, Eleanor M.	(MA)	618
KNAPP, Leslie C.	(MA)	663
KOLCZYNSKI, Charlotte A.	(MA)	669
LANDESMAN, Betty J.	(MA)	692
PROUTY, Sharman E.	(MA)	996
HANES, Alice H.	(MD)	495
STEINHOFF, Cynthia K.	(MD)	1186
TURKOS, Joseph A.	(MD)	1263
THOR, Angela M.	(ME)	1242
BREITENWISCHER, Rosalyn E.	(MI)	132
CARLSON, Susan L.	(MI)	182
FEDER, Carol S.	(MI)	367
HART, David J.	(MI)	507
LUCAS, Ann	(MI)	745
PUBLISKI, Patricia J.	(MI)	996
SALZER, Melodie A.	(MI)	1078
KOPPER, John A.	(MN)	671
CRAIG, Marian D.	(MO)	254
WINJUM, Roberta J.	(MO)	1355
DRAKE, Betty S.	(MS)	318
HAUSE, Aaron H.	(MT)	512
BRILEY, Anne S.	(NC)	136
BUSH, Mary E.	(NC)	165
CLARK, Marie L.	(NC)	217
COBB, Mary L.	(NC)	225
FARKAS, Doina C.	(NC)	364
FLOYD, Rebecca M.	(NC)	386
FOLTZ, Faye D.	(NC)	388
GLEIM, Sharon S.	(NC)	441
IRVING, Ophelia M.	(NC)	584
MCGEACHY, John A.	(NC)	805
STOCKDALE, Kay L.	(NC)	1195
FAWCETT, Georgene E.	(NE)	367
JOHNSON, Judy L.	(NE)	606
VORBEAU, Barbara E.	(NH)	1289
CHEN, Chiou S.	(NJ)	205
FAWCETT-BRANDON, Pamela S.	(NJ)	367
GAYNOR, William A.	(NJ)	424
HAJDAS, Susan A.	(NJ)	484
HEGG, Judith L.	(NJ)	521
GREFRATH, Richard W.	(NV)	465
ANGEL, Kenneth E.	(NY)	27
ARNOLD, Linda A.	(NY)	34
BARNELLO, Inga H.	(NY)	57
BATES, Ellen	(NY)	63
BEAUDRIE, Ronald A.	(NY)	70
DAVIS, Susan A.	(NY)	281
DAY, Ross	(NY)	283
DOEZEMA, Linda P.	(NY)	308
D'ONOFRIO, Erminio	(NY)	311
DOUGLAS, Jacqueline A.	(NY)	314
DUNCAN, Elizabeth C.	(NY)	325

SERIALS (Cont'd)
Serials

EARLY, Caroline L.	(NY)	332
FEICK, Christina L.	(NY)	368
FINN, Margaret M.	(NY)	378
GADBOIS, Frank W.	(NY)	411
HSU, Karen M.	(NY)	567
HULBERT, Linda A.	(NY)	572
LEE, Judy A.	(NY)	710
LEWIS, Gillian H.	(NY)	723
MASTRANGELO, Paul J.	(NY)	783
MEISELES, Linda	(NY)	822
MILLER, Heather S.	(NY)	838
NELSON, Winifred S.	(NY)	895
PAGELS, Helen H.	(NY)	934
RAUCH, Theodore G.	(NY)	1010
ROGERS, Jonathan B.	(NY)	1049
SHEVIAK, Jean K.	(NY)	1129
SOUDERS, Marilyn N.	(NY)	1169
YOCHYM, Cynthia M.	(NY)	1380
ARTZ, Theodora S.	(OH)	35
BELKIN, Betsey B.	(OH)	76
CHEEK, Fern M.	(OH)	204
FELTES, Carol A.	(OH)	370
HORTON, Anna J.	(OH)	561
LUPONE, George	(OH)	749
COBB, Sylvia R.	(OK)	225
HUESMANN, James L.	(OK)	570
O'DONOVAN, Patricia A.	(OR)	917
SOOHOO, Terry A.	(OR)	1167
ARMISTEAD, Henry T.	(PA)	32
CARTER, Ruth C.	(PA)	190
GREENE, Nancy S.	(PA)	464
GRZESIAK, Margaret M.	(PA)	475
HORN, Janice H.	(PA)	559
LEIBOWITZ, Faye R.	(PA)	713
MCCAWLEY, Christina W.	(PA)	795
MONTOYA, Leopoldo	(PA)	856
PHALAN, Mary A.	(PA)	967
RICE, Patricia O.	(PA)	1027
ROBINSON, Agnes F.	(PA)	1043
ROGERS, Linda S.	(PA)	1049
SAMET, Janet S.	(PA)	1078
SONDEN, Mary L.	(PA)	1167
TUCKER, Cornelia A.	(PA)	1261
WELLE, Jacob P.	(PA)	1321
DEVIN, Robin B.	(RI)	297
HELLER, Betty D.	(RI)	524
MARSH, Corrie V.	(RI)	773
TERRY, Carol S.	(RI)	1232
STRAUCH, Katina P.	(SC)	1200
RITTER, Linda B.	(SD)	1036
ABOUSHAMA, Mary F.	(TN)	2
GRACE, Loranne J.	(TN)	455
HOM, Sharon L.	(TN)	555
MCDONELL, W E.	(TN)	803
MCHOLLIN, Mattie L.	(TN)	809
PHILLIPS, Patricia A.	(TN)	968
STRICKLER, Candice S.	(TN)	1202
ALLEN, Joan W.	(TX)	15
ANDREWS, Virginia L.	(TX)	27
COFFEY, Sue E.	(TX)	227
CORLEY, Carol W.	(TX)	246
GUTHRIE, Melinda L.	(TX)	479
HENEBRY, Carolyn L.	(TX)	528
HOOD, Elizabeth	(TX)	556
JACKSON, Marian D.	(TX)	588
KELLEY, Carol M.	(TX)	636
MUCKLEROY, Sue A.	(TX)	875
PETERS, Mary N.	(TX)	962
SHAPIRO, Lenore M.	(TX)	1121
THOMAS, Donald L.	(TX)	1236
WILKERSON, Judith C.	(TX)	1339
NORSTEDT, Marilyn L.	(VA)	909
THOMPSON, Connie B.	(VA)	1239
CHADWICK, Leroy D.	(WA)	197
TRACY, Joan I.	(WA)	1253
PARSON, Karen L.	(WI)	944
SCHMIDT, Mary A.	(WI)	1095
KUJANSUU, Sylvia S.	(AB)	683

SERIALS (Cont'd)

Serials

OLSON, Hope A.	(AB)	922
DYKSTRA, Stephanie	(BC)	331
BENSON, Theodore L.	(MB)	83
TIFFANY, William C.	(NF)	1244
MCNAIR, Alison T.	(NS)	815
CLARKE, Bozena	(ON)	218
LAWLESS, Ruthmary G.	(ON)	704
RIPLEY, Victoria E.	(ON)	1035
STEPHENSON, Cheryl E.	(ON)	1188
WALDRON, Nerine R.	(ON)	1294
LAPOINTE, Louise	(PQ)	697
RUSSELL, Vija	(SK)	1069
HARKINS, Diane G.	(ENG)	501

Serials acquisition

GASKINS, Betty	(KY)	421
GELENTER, Winifred H.	(MD)	426
LEWIS, Diane M.	(VA)	723
DOI, Makiko	(WA)	309

Serials acquisition & cataloging

GRIFFITH, Joan C.	(NH)	469

Serials acquisition & control

KHOURY, Nancy L.	(LA)	646

Serials acquisitions

PALM, Miriam W.	(CA)	935
LONBERGER, Jana L.	(GA)	738
ERTL, Mary R.	(IA)	353
BAIRD, Lynn N.	(ID)	47
DELONG, Douglas A.	(IL)	290
SIEVERS, Arlene M.	(IN)	1136
WINJUM, Roberta J.	(MO)	1355
TAYLOR, David C.	(NC)	1226
TUTTLE, Marcia L.	(NC)	1266
SHROUT, Sally J.	(OK)	1133
D'ANDRAIA, Dana D.	(OR)	272
SWEARINGEN, Wilba S.	(TX)	1214

Serials acquisitions & control

SCHWARTZ, Marla J.	(VA)	1105

Serials acquisitions & preservation

IRVIN, Judy C.	(LA)	584

Serials administration

KASCUS, Marie A.	(CT)	628
STOPPEL, Ellen K.	(IA)	1198
HEPFER, Cynthia K.	(NY)	530
HEPFER, William E.	(NY)	530

Serials & acquisitions

LI, Dorothy W.	(IL)	724

Serials & cataloging

SELMER, Sylvia A.	(KY)	1114

Serials & government documents

PANDA, Rosamond E.	(MD)	937

Serials & integrated systems

CLINE, Sharon D.	(CA)	222

Serials & microforms

IRBY, Geraldine A.	(AL)	583

Serials & Middle East studies

NIELSON, Paula I.	(UT)	903

Serials & monographs cataloging

TAVARES, Cecelia M.	(MA)	1225
CHALMERS, Lois M.	(MD)	197
ROSENSHIELD, Jill K.	(WI)	1057

Serials & periodicals

SCHWARTZKOPF, Rebecca B.	(MN)	1105
TRIBIT, Donald K.	(PA)	1256

Serials & reference

CLARK, Peter W.	(WI)	217

Serials & union listing

HICKEY, John T.	(NY)	536

Serials, AV materials, automation

SOPER, Mary E.	(WA)	1168

Serials automation

STAYNER, Delsie A.	(CA)	1183
LOWELL, Gerald R.	(CT)	744
PRESLEY, Roger L.	(GA)	991
CHATTERTON, Leigh A.	(MA)	204
KING, Kenneth E.	(MI)	651
HELMS, Mary E.	(MO)	525
FINLAY, J A.	(NH)	378
HEPFER, Cynthia K.	(NY)	530
SHEVIAK, Jean K.	(NY)	1129
MOORE, Brian P.	(OH)	858
WOODS, Janet R.	(WY)	1367

Serials bibliographic control & review

STEINHAGEN, Elizabeth N.	(ID)	1186
GOLIAN, Linda M.	(FL)	447

Serials binding & acquisitions

Serials cataloging

CALLAHAN, Patrick F.	(AR)	173
RUSSELL, Carne	(AZ)	1068
ANDERES, Susan M.	(CA)	21
BULLARD, Sharon W.	(CA)	156
CHURUKIAN, Araxie P.	(CA)	213
FULSAAS, Esther M.	(CA)	409
HSIA, Ting M.	(CA)	567
TURITZ, Mitch L.	(CA)	1263
WU, Harriet	(CA)	1373
BARELA, Lori A.	(CO)	56
GLASBY, Dorothy J.	(DC)	439
HIRONS, Jean L.	(DC)	543

SERIALS (Cont'd)

Serials cataloging

WANG, Margaret K.	(DE)	1303
DONAHUE, Janice E.	(FL)	310
GOLIAN, Linda M.	(FL)	447
HARDIN, Barbara A.	(GA)	500
VIDOR, Ann B.	(GA)	1283
VISK, Linda S.	(GA)	1285
COLE, Jim E.	(IA)	230
MELROY, Virginia A.	(IA)	823
JONES, Ann L.	(IL)	611
LEONG, Carol L.	(IL)	717
TRIMMER, Keith R.	(IL)	1256
MCKOWEN, Dorothy K.	(IN)	812
MERING, Margaret V.	(LA)	826
TIMBERLAKE, Phoebe W.	(LA)	1245
PAYNE, Douglass B.	(MA)	951
WILSON, Virginia A.	(MA)	1353
KINGSTON, Mary L.	(MD)	652
WINZER, Kathleen M.	(MD)	1356
KING, Kenneth E.	(MI)	651
VAN CLEVE, Nancy J.	(MN)	1273
NIEMEYER, Mollie M.	(MO)	903
NYSTROM, Kathleen A.	(MO)	913
TUTTLE, Joseph C.	(NC)	1266
LANE, Alice L.	(NE)	694
STRIMAN, Brian D.	(NE)	1202
WOOL, Gregory J.	(NE)	1368
BARRETT, Beth R.	(NH)	59
FINLAY, J A.	(NH)	378
BORRIES, Michael S.	(NY)	117
CHAPMAN, Renee D.	(NY)	202
DECKER, Jean S.	(NY)	285
ROSENBERG-NUGENT, Nanci B.	(NY)	1056
SCHNEIDER, Judith A.	(NY)	1097
THOMAS, Catherine M.	(NY)	1236
ADREAN, Louis V.	(OH)	7
O'NEIL, Rosanna M.	(OH)	924
KANCHANAKPAN, Pongsak	(OK)	624
TOOLEY, Katherine J.	(OK)	1250
OSHEROFF, Shiela K.	(OR)	928
WIWEL, Pamela S.	(PA)	1359
YOLTON, Jean S.	(PA)	1380
KELLEY, Gloria	(SC)	636
THOMAS, Julie A.	(SC)	1237
RICHARDS, Susan L.	(SD)	1028
BROSS, Valerie	(TN)	141
PERRY, Glenda L.	(TN)	960
DOMA, Tshering	(TX)	310
LATTIMORE, Clare I.	(TX)	702
WAN, William W.	(TX)	1302
LEWIS, Diane M.	(VA)	723
SADOWSKI, Frank E.	(VA)	1074
SCHWARTZ, Marla J.	(VA)	1105
ROMANIUK, Elena	(BC)	1052
ANNETT, Adele M.	(ON)	28
GOODMAN, Julia M.	(ON)	449
FINLAY, Barbara J.	(PQ)	378
KRISHAN, Kewal	(SK)	678
HARKINS, Diane G.	(ENG)	501

Serials cataloging & holdings

WANG, Anna M.	(OH)	1302

Serials cataloging & management

COLLINS, Susan H.	(NB)	233

Serials cataloging & union listing

MURRAY, Diane E.	(MI)	881

Serials check-in & control

GERLOTT, Eleanor L.	(PA)	429

Serials collection development

CENTING, Richard R.	(OH)	196
BOCHTE, Terrence C.	(WI)	109

Serials control

WHITE, Larry R.	(CA)	1331
WILLARD, Ann M.	(CA)	1341
CARNEGLIA, Anna L.	(CT)	183
HOLLYFIELD, Diane S.	(DC)	552
PUGH, Thurman A.	(DC)	997
VISK, Linda S.	(GA)	1285
DARLING, Elizabeth A.	(IL)	274
EILERS, Marsha J.	(IN)	340
VIGEANT, Robert J.	(IN)	1284
FORFIA, Linda S.	(KS)	390
GASKINS, Betty	(KY)	421
SCULLIN, Janice J.	(MA)	1109

SERIALS (Cont'd)
Serials control

	MOLTER, Maureen M.	(MD)	853
	LARONGE, Philip V.	(MI)	698
	MOSHER, Robin A.	(MI)	871
	WHEATON, Julie A.	(MI)	1328
	MOONEY, Jennifer M.	(NJ)	858
	CARLSON, Robert E.	(NY)	182
	DECKER, Jean S.	(NY)	285
	FINCH, Frances	(NY)	377
	FOSTER, Selma V.	(NY)	392
	PERCELLI, Irene M.	(NY)	958
	RESCIGNO, Dolores S.	(NY)	1024
	RUIZ-VALERA, Phoebe L.	(NY)	1067
	GRABENSTATTER, Christine N.	(OH)	455
	LEE, Sooncha A.	(OH)	711
	MOORE, Maxwell J.	(OH)	860
	TANNEHILL, Robert S.	(OH)	1222
	WELLS, Catherine A.	(OH)	1322
	FACKLER, Naomi P.	(TX)	360
	KIMZEY, Ann C.	(TX)	649
	SWEARINGEN, Wilba S.	(TX)	1214
	ANDERSON, Janet A.	(UT)	23
	MERRYMAN, Margaret M.	(VA)	827
	MURDEN, Steven H.	(VA)	879
	CHRISTMAN, Inese R.	(WI)	212
	CRAWFORD, Josephine	(WI)	256
	MILLER, Julia E.	(WI)	839
	FU, Ting W.	(HKG)	407
Serials control & online databases	CHAPMAN, Elwynda K.	(DC)	202
Serials control systems	LONG, Roger J.	(IL)	739
Serials coordinating	MOORE, Sheryl R.	(TX)	861
Serials database	YUSTER, Leigh C.	(NY)	1385
Serials databases	HELMS, Mary E.	(MO)	525
Serials department	BOWEN, Ethel B.	(MS)	120
Serials education	ROGERS, Nancy H.	(AL)	1050
Serials, geology	BOYER, Ann T.	(WI)	123
Serials, government publications	ZIMMERMAN, Martha B.	(MD)	1389
Serials holdings, MARC format	VISK, Linda S.	(GA)	1285
Serials indexing	SHUPAK, Harris J.	(PA)	1134
Serials librarianship	BAUMGARDNER, Sandra A.	(DC)	66
	POSTLETHWAITE, Bonnie S.	(MA)	986
	CIPOLLA, Wilma R.	(NY)	215
	OKERSON, Ann L.	(NY)	920
	NICOL, Jessie T.	(TN)	902
	BROWN, Pauline	(AUS)	146
	ODSEN, Elizabeth R.	(AK)	917
Serials management	BATTISTELLA, Maureen S.	(AL)	65
	ANDERES, Susan M.	(CA)	21
	LIU, Susanna J.	(CA)	734
	PALM, Miriam W.	(CA)	935
	WONG, Cecilia	(CA)	1362
	BARELA, Lori A.	(CO)	56
	GLASBY, Dorothy J.	(DC)	439
	PRICE, Mary S.	(DC)	992
	SMITH, Thomas E.	(DC)	1161
	CARR, Mary L.	(FL)	186
	PEARSON, Karen L.	(IL)	952
	JOHNTING, Wendell E.	(IN)	610
	SIEVERS, Arlene M.	(IN)	1136
	HAMAKER, Charles A.	(LA)	490
	TIMBERLAKE, Phoebe W.	(LA)	1245
	WOJKOWSKI, Suhad K.	(LA)	1359
	BACON, Lois C.	(MA)	44
	DI BONA, Leslie F.	(MA)	299
	BROWN-MAY, Patricia A.	(MI)	148
	MORELAND, Patricia L.	(MI)	863
	SMOLER, Shelly	(MI)	1162
	WILDMAN, Linda	(MI)	1339
	TUTTLE, Marcia L.	(NC)	1266
	SCHOTT, Mark E.	(NM)	1099
	HARTMAN, Anne M.	(NY)	508
	NICHOLS-RANDALL, Barbara L.	(NY)	902
	PRAGER, George A.	(NY)	989
	SCHNEIDER, Helen S.	(NY)	1097

SERIALS (Cont'd)
Serials management

	SCHUTT, Dedre A.	(NY)	1103
	TUOHEY, Jeanne D.	(NY)	1263
	HARRINGTON, Sue A.	(OK)	504
	SHROUT, Sally J.	(OK)	1133
	CHAMBERLAIN, Carol E.	(PA)	197
	RICHARDS, Susan L.	(SD)	1028
	ANDERSON, Madeleine J.	(TX)	24
	MURPHY, Pency G.	(TX)	881
	DEBUSE, Judith S.	(WA)	285
	GELLATLY, Peter	(WA)	426
	KOMOROUS, Hana J.	(BC)	670
	MILANICH, Melanie M.	(ON)	834
	DARIS, Claude	(BEL)	274
Serials, newspapers	EVEY, Patricia G.	(PA)	359
Serials periodicals, public relations	PATTERSON, Grace L.	(NY)	948
Serials processing	BAILEY, Dorothy C.	(GA)	46
	CIANFARINI, Margaret	(MA)	214
	MCCUTCHEON, Dianne E.	(MD)	801
	KOVACIC, Mark E.	(OH)	673
Serials processing, holdings conversion	RONEN, Naomi	(MA)	1053
Serials records	ASHLEY, Elizabeth	(CA)	36
Serials records control	CLASQUIN, Frank F.	(MA)	219
Serials reference	PUCCIO, Joseph A.	(DC)	997
Serials retrospective conversion	KING, Kenneth E.	(MI)	651
Serials selection	GELENTER, Winifred H.	(MD)	426
Serials selection & control	KRIER, Mary M.	(MA)	678
Serials service	SWEARINGEN, Wilba S.	(TX)	1214
Serials services	GREEN, Walter H.	(MO)	463
Serials, standing orders	MCCANN, Jett C.	(GA)	794
Serials systems & management	VANDERPOORTEN, Mary B.	(AL)	1274
Serials union listing	MANEY, Lana E.	(TX)	765
Serials union listings	CRAWFORD-OPPENHIE-MER, Christine	(NY)	257
Serials union lists	BOUCHARD-HALL, Robert W.	(MA)	118
Serials vending	KETCHAM, Lee C.	(AL)	645
Standing orders & serials	MCCANN, Judith B.	(ON)	794
Union list of serials	PIKE, Lee E.	(AL)	973
	HAGGARD, Lynn	(TX)	483
	CHENG, Sheung O.	(TAI)	206
	WANG, Sin C.	(TAI)	1303
Union list serials	HIGGINS, Flora T.	(NJ)	537
Union listing, serials	MONTGOMERY, Teresa L.	(CA)	856
Union lists of serials	NEUFELD, Judith B.	(NY)	897
	ADREAN, Louis V.	(OH)	7

SERIES

Monographic series, authority control	DECKER, Jean S.	(NY)	285
Stratemeyer series books	THORNDILL, Christine M.	(WA)	1242

SET

Fuzzy set theory	KRAFT, Donald H.	(LA)	674

SEVENTEENTH CENTURY

17th century English books	SILVER, Joel B.	(IN)	1138
17th century French bibliography	CHAMBERS, Bettye T.	(DC)	198
17th century New England books	BISHOP, John	(MA)	99

SEWAGE (See also Waste)

Sewage & solid waste libraries	ANJOU-DURAZZO, Martel T.	(CA)	28
Sewage & toxic waste libraries	ANJOU-DURAZZO, Martel T.	(CA)	28
Sewage, water, & wastewater libraries	ANJOU-DURAZZO, Martel T.	(CA)	28

SEXISM

Racism, sexism in media	ADAMS, Elaine P.	(TX)	4
Sexism in school materials	NILSEN, Alleen P.	(AZ)	904

SEXUALITY
Human sexuality   WHITBY, Thomas J. . . . . (CO) 1330
Sex, drugs, & teenagers   LONG, Gary . . . . (LA) 739
Sex education databases   CAMPBELL, Patricia J. . . (CA) 177
Sexuality & religion issues   MAZUR, Ronald M. . . . . (MA) 791
Sexuality education resources FORREST, Phyllis E. . . . (DC) 391

SHAKERS
Music of the Shakers   CHRISTENSON, Donald E. (OH) 211
Shaker collection   ADAMS, Barbara M. . . . . (DE)   4
Shaker history   CHRISTENSON, Donald E. (OH) 211

SHAKESPEARE
Shakespeare   TARANOW, Gerda . . . . . (CT) 1223
                               WHITE, D J. . . . . (MO) 1330

SHARING (See also Cooperation)
Bibliographic & resource sharing
  network   REDDY, Sigrid R. . . . . . (MA) 1014
Collection development, resource
  sharing   FISCHLER, Barbara B. . . . (IN) 380
                               HEANEY, Henry J. . . . . . (SCT) 518
Continuing education, resource
  sharing   SHELDON, Brooke E. . . . . (TX) 1125
Cooperation for resource sharing BESEMER, Susan P. . . . (NY)   91
Information network, resource sharing AGRAWAL, Surendra P. (IND)   7
Interlibrary loan, resource sharing THOMPSON, Dorothea M. (PA) 1239
Literature sharing   CROCKER, Judith A. . . . (NM) 259
Multitype resource sharing   MICHAELIS, Kathryn S. . (WI) 831
Networking, resource sharing,
  systems   LOVE, Erika . . . . (NM) 743
                               SEIDMAN, Ruth K. . . . . . (MA) 1112
                               MARTIN, Noelene P. . . . (PA) 777
Resource sharing   GRAHAM, Elaine . . . . . . (CA) 456
                               IVERSON, Diann S. . . . . (CA) 585
                               SCHWEERS, Lucy . . . . . (CO) 1105
                               VOLZ, Edward J. . . . . . . (CO) 1288
                               BURGER, Leslie B. . . . . . (CT) 159
                               DEJOHN, William T. . . . . (MN) 288
                               BUCHANAN, Gerald . . . . (MS) 153
                               NEAL, Michelle H. . . . . . (NC) 890
                               NOLAN, John A. . . . . . . (NY) 907
                               WASHBURN, Keith E. . . . (NY) 1307
                               WOLFE, N J. . . . . (NY) 1361
                               WAREHAM, Nancy L. . . . (OH) 1304
                               HALGREN, Joanne V. . . . (OR) 486
                               BRICE, Heather W. . . . . (PA) 134
                               JACKSON, Mary E. . . . . (PA) 588
                               KOLBE, Jane . . . . (SD) 669
                               COTTER, Gladys A. . . . . (VA) 250
                               WARD, Robert C. . . . . . . (VT) 1304
                               CLEMENT, Hope E. . . . . (ON) 221
Resource sharing among libraries CHEN, Catherine W. . . . . (MI) 205
Resource sharing & networking TYER, Travis E. . . . . . . (IL) 1266
Resource sharing networks   KENT, Allen . . . . (PA) 642
Shared automated systems   MARTIN, Robert A. . . . . (FL) 778
Shared cataloging networking online BROWN, Pauline . . . . . (AUS) 146
Shared resources management   MILLER, Charles E. . . . . (FL) 836
Shared services regional network WILCOX, Linda M. . . . . . (ON) 1338
Sharing with public library   VELTEMA, John H. . . . . (MI) 1282

SHEET
Sheet music   HASSE, John E. . . . . . . (DC) 511
Sheet music cataloging   HOUSE, Katherine L. . . . (KY) 563
Sheet music collector   SETON, Charles B. . . . . (NY) 1117
Sheet music consultant   SETON, Charles B. . . . . (NY) 1117

SHELFLIST
Machine-readable shelflist conversion NOBLE, Barbara N. . . . . (MO) 906
Shelf & shelflist inventory   BADING, Kathryn E. . . . . (TX)   44

SHELVING
Design of shelving systems   BAYLIS, Ted . . . . (MA)   67
Furniture, shelving, space planning WATSON, Joyce N. . . . . (ON) 1309
Library shelving & equipment   DAVIS, Glenn G. . . . . . . (IL) 279
Library shelving & furniture   WEINZIMMER, William A. (NY) 1318
Manufacture of shelving systems BAYLIS, Ted . . . . (MA)   67
Processing books for shelving HEYDUCK, Marilyn J. . . . (IL) 535
Provide & install library shelving MCDONALD, Barbara J. . . (CA) 802
Shelving technical equipment   DE BEAR, Richard S. . . . (MI) 284

SHIP (See also Maritime)
Technical trades, naval ship repair ANDERSON, Marcia M. . (VA)   24

SHOPPING
Online shopping & travel   WALSH, Mark L. . . . . . . (CT) 1300

SHOWS (See also Presentations)
Effective presentations & slide shows SANKER, Paul N. . . . . . (NY) 1081
Library art shows   NANCE, Betty L. . . . . . . (TX) 887

SHUT-INS (See also Home (Bound))
Shut-ins   GRAHAM, Heather F. . . . (MB) 456

SIERRA LEONE
Libraries in Sierra Leone West Africa WATERS, Bill F. . . . . . . (MO) 1308

SIGNAGE
Library sign systems   MALLERY, Mary S. . . . . (MD) 763
Library signage   JOSEPH, Miriam E. . . . . (MO) 617

SIGNALS
Traffic signals   HATHAWAY, Kay E. . . . (VA) 512

SILENT
History of silent film   ALTOMARA, Rita E. . . . . (NJ)   18

SIMPLIFICATION
Work simplification   RYUS, Joseph E. . . . . . . (CA) 1072

SIMULATION
Computer-aided simulation   ALSANARRAI, Hafidh S. (SDA)   17
Management simulation training WRIGHT, Keith C. . . . . . (NC) 1372
Simulation   NELSON, Michael J. . . . . (ON) 894

SINATRA
Frank Sinatra archivist   ROSS, Ric . . . . (CA) 1058

SITE
Construction site, architect selections WRIGHT, Paul L. . . . . . (KY) 1372
Hanford site   TRAUB, Teresa L. . . . . . (WA) 1254
Site preparation for automation GREGORY, Roderick F. . . (NC) 466
Site selection   FRANKLIN, Robert D. . . . (VA) 398

SIXTEENTH CENTURY
16th century French bibliography CHAMBERS, Bettye T. . . . (DC) 198

SKILLS
Audiovisual skills   HSU, Peter T. . . . . (ON) 567
Branch adminstrv & supervisory skills SMITH-EPPS, E P. . . . . . (GA) 1161
Classes in library skills   BLALOCK, Virginia D. . . (TX) 103
Communication skills   OHLEMACHER, Janet H. (WI) 919
Computer literacy skills   VALLAR, Cynthia L. . . . . (MD) 1271
Computer skills instruction   JACOBS, Lois S. . . . . . . (MA) 589
Critical viewing skills   NEWMAN, Eileen M. . . . (NY) 899
Curriculum & research skills   PITLUK, Paula K. . . . . . (CA) 976

SKILLS (Cont'd)

Curriculum-based library skills   GOODRICH PETERSON,
   Marilyn . . . . (KS) 450
Directing library skills instruction   HACKMAN, Mary H. . . . (MD) 481
Elementary school library skills   CANDE, Lorraine N. . . . . (NY) 178
Human relations skill development   LENOX, Mary F. . . . . (MO) 715
Info skills & curriculum correlation   JONES, Wanda F. . . . . . (AR) 615
   MCKINNEY, Barbara J. . (AR) 812
Information skills curriculum   COWEN, Linda L. . . . . . (OK) 253
Information skills in curriculum   HAYCOCK, Kenneth R. . (BC) 515
Informational skills instruction   LOPEZ, Kathryn P. . . . . . (NM) 741
Information-seeking skills instruction   MICIKAS, Lynda L. . . . . (PA) 832
Instruction in information skills   COOK, Sybilla A. . . . . . . (OR) 240
Instruction in library skills   HILLER, Catherine C. . . . (CT) 541
Instruction of media skills   KOEPP, Sara H. . . . . . . (IA) 668
Instructional design & library skills   EFFERTZ, Rose . . . . (IL) 338
Integrated library media skills   WALKER, Sue A. . . . . . . (PA) 1296
Integrated library skills instruction   HUSTED, Ruth E. . . . . . (OK) 578
Integrating library skills   RICHARDSON, Constance
   H. . . . . (NY) 1029
Integration, library skills, curriculum   HOROWITZ, Marjorie B. . (NJ) 560
Interpersonal skills training &
   devlpmnt   KNIGHT, Shirley D. . . . . (NJ) 664
Junior high library skills   LEWIS, Marjorie . . . . (NY) 723
K-12 library skills   VELTEMA, John H. . . . . (MI) 1282
Library aides, library skills   ASLESEN, Rosalie V. . . . (SD) 36
Library & information skills   TALLMAN, Julie I. . . . . . (NY) 1221
Library & information skills instruction   RATZER, Mary B. . . . . . (NY) 1010
Library & media skill instruction   GOODMAN, Roslyn L. . . (AK) 449
Library & media skills programs   MC NAIR, Marian B. . . . . (OH) 815
Library instructional skills   LAMBERTH, Linda E. . . . (TX) 690
Library media skill instruction   RAMSEY, Inez L. . . . . . (VA) 1006
Library media skills   MEIER, Patricia L. . . . . . (IA) 821
   SULLIVAN, Jennifer B. . . (PA) 1207
Library media skills curriculum   MURTO, Kathleen A. . . . (WI) 883
Library media skills instruction   EHRICH, Joan C. . . . . . . (MA) 339
   TASSIA, Margaret R. . . . (PA) 1224
Library reference skills   HALLBERG, Sharon P. . . (CA) 489
Library research skills instruction   ROSENBERG, Harlene Z. (NJ) 1056
Library skill education for K-12   LAU, Ray D. . . . . (OK) 702
Library skills   GILSON, Myral A. . . . . . (AZ) 437
   MARTINAZZI, Toni . . . . . (IL) 779
   KEEFE, Betty . . . . (NE) 634
   GOLDBERG, Barbara W. (NJ) 444
   MASSEY, Eleanor N. . . . (NJ) 782
   KING, Evlyn J. . . . . (SC) 651
Library skills & research education   YOUNG, Marjie D. . . . . . (TX) 1382
Library skills classes   HOOVER, Gloria E. . . . . (TX) 557
Library skills curriculum   KAHLER, June . . . . (TX) 621
Library skills development   HOOVER, Clara G. . . . . (NE) 557
   NORRIS, Gale K. . . . . . . (SC) 909
Library skills education   WOLFE, Barbara M. . . . . (NY) 1360
Library skills for children   MCDANIEL, Deanna J. . . (OH) 801
Library skills, high schools   WARAKSA, Raymond P. . (CT) 1303
Library skills instruction   PENDLETON, Kim B. . . . (AK) 956
   CHESSMAN, Rebecca L. (CA) 207
   AKE, Mary W. . . . . (CO) 9
   DEANS, Janice P. . . . . . (FL) 284
   JACKSON, Nancy I. . . . . (FL) 588
   KRAMER, Pamela K. . . . (IL) 675
   SHANNON, Kathleen L. . (IL) 1120
   KELLY, Sarah A. . . . . . . (KY) 638
   PECK, Ruth M. . . . . (MA) 953
   FITZGERALD, M A. . . . . (MD) 382
   MONTGOMERY, Paula K. (MD) 856
   RUFF, Martha R. . . . . . . (MD) 1066
   WILLIAMS, J L. . . . . (MD) 1343
   SKELLY, Laurie J. . . . . . (MN) 1146
   FABIAN, William M. . . . . (MO) 360
   DRUKE-STICKLER, Janet
   A. . . . . (NH) 320
   DOMINESKE, Alice M. . . (NJ) 310
   AVERY, Linda S. . . . . . . (NM) 42
   BRAMLETT, Suzanne M. . (NM) 127
   DI BIANCO, Phyllis R. . . (NY) 299
   MCCOY, Joanne . . . . . . (OR) 799
   EMERICK, Michael J. . . . (PA) 347
   KOSTIS, Leigh W. . . . . . (PA) 673
   SMITH, Sara B. . . . . (SC) 1160

SKILLS (Cont'd)

Library skills instruction   BANNERMAN-WILLIAMS,
   Cheryl F. . . . . (TN) 54
   PONTIUS, Louise . . . . . . (TX) 982
   SMITH, Dorothy B. . . . . (TX) 1154
   OWENS, Martha A. . . . . (VA) 932
   YOUNGER, Melinda M. . (VA) 1383
   BACON, Carey H. . . . . . (WA) 44
   PITEL, Vonna J. . . . . . . (WI) 976
Library skills program   MCBURNEY, Lynnea R. . (TX) 792
Library skills teaching   HUGHES, Sondra K. . . . (CO) 572
   BECKING, Mara S. . . . . (IN) 73
   HIRSCH, Elizabeth . . . . (MA) 543
   BROWN, Anita P. . . . . . (NJ) 142
   WHITLOW, Cherrill M. . . (NM) 1333
Library study skills   KENNEY, Ann J. . . . . . . (OR) 641
Library use skills   BRUNER, Katharine E. . . (TN) 150
Management skills   DRAKE, Betty S. . . . . . . (MS) 318
Media skills   ROMAN, Susan . . . . (IL) 1052
Media skills instruction   BOWEN, Louise E. . . . . (GA) 120
   CHAPMAN-SIMPSON,
   Alisa M. . . . . (IA) 202
   KONNEKER, Rachel C. . (NC) 670
   SOUTHERLAND, Carol A. (NC) 1169
Medial skill instruction   SMITH, Judy B. . . . . . . (GA) 1156
Reading promotion & library skills   GOLDBERG, Linda B. . . (KY) 444
Reference services & management
   skills   THOMAS, Fannette H. . . (MD) 1236
Reference skill teaching   GRIFFIN, Charlene F. . . . (KY) 468
Reference skills   LOPATIN, Edith K. . . . . (NY) 740
Research & library skills   LOPEZ, Silvia P. . . . . . . (FL) 741
Research skill instruction   BROWN, Judith B. . . . . (MD) 145
Research skill teaching   PRIESING, Patricia L. . . . (NJ) 993
Research skills   PLOWDEN, Martha W. . . (GA) 978
   MENINGALL, Evelyn L. . (NJ) 824
   AFROMSKY, Ellen S. . . . (NY) 7
   BERGEN, Dessa C. . . . . (NY) 85
Research skills education   MAIN, Isabelle G. . . . . . (AZ) 761
Research skills instruction   MARTINAZZI, Toni . . . . . (IL) 779
Research skills teaching   BUGHER, Kathryn M. . . . (WI) 155
School library media skills   SHERMAN, Madeline R. . (VT) 1128
School library research skills   VALLAR, Cynthia L. . . . . (MD) 1271
School library skills   JOHNSON, Guy M. . . . . (NY) 605
School library skills program   EDWARDS, Barnett A. . . (NY) 337
Secretarial & office skills   EDWARDS, Andrea Y. . . (DC) 337
Skill development   GERRING, Cheryl B. . . . (MD) 429
Skill instruction   PHILLIPS, Louoida V. . . . (TX) 968
Standards & skills development   DATUS, Marie B. . . . . . . (NE) 275
Student library skills   BRAUER, Regina . . . . . . (NY) 129
Study & information skills   CARPENTER, Carole H. . (DE) 184
Study skills instruction   SMITH, Margie G. . . . . . (CA) 1157
Teach information retrieval skills   DANIELSON, Connie S. . (IA) 273
Teacher & reference skills   ROUSE, Charlie L. . . . . (OK) 1061
Teacher of library skills   MARTIN, Sandra D. . . . . (KY) 778
Teaching & implementation of lib skills   HEINRICH, Lois M. . . . . (MD) 522
Teaching elementary library skills   TOWNSEND, Rita M. . . . (PA) 1253
   SULLI, Gerard C. . . . . . . (CT) 1207
Teaching elementary media skills   WHISMAN, Linda A. . . . (CA) 1329
Teaching legal research skills   WELKER, Kathy J. . . . . (OH) 1321
   WIENER, Sylvia B. . . . . . (NY) 1336
Teaching library & research skills   CONOVER, Kathryn H. . . (FL) 238
Teaching library, audiovisual skills   REILLY, Maureen E. . . . (CT) 1020
Teaching library research skills   KLUESNER, Marvin P. . . (AL) 662
Teaching library skills   STARRETT, Mildred J. . . (AZ) 1182
   ALLABACK, Patricia G. . . (CA) 13
   KOSKY, Janet J. . . . . . . (CA) 672
   MILLS, Denise Y. . . . . . . (CA) 844
   SUTHERLAND, Helen G. (CA) 1211
   SELVERSTONE, Harriet S. (CT) 1114
   SOUTHARD, Sarah T. . . (CT) 1169
   MCCARTHY, Carrol B. . . (DE) 794
   COPELAND, Mildred A. . (FL) 244
   LOPEZ, Deborah A. . . . . (FL) 741
   ADCOCK, Betty L. . . . . (IL) 6
   JOHNSON, Keran C. . . . (IL) 606
   CRACE, Sallye C. . . . . . (KY) 254
   REESE, Virginia D. . . . . (KY) 1016
   BERNSTEIN, D S. . . . . . (MA) 89
   JACOBS, Lois S. . . . . . . (MA) 589

SKILLS (Cont'd)

Teaching library skills

THOMAS, Laverne J.	. . .	(MI)	1237
AYLWARD, Judith A.	. . .	(MO)	43
GULICK, Eleanor L.	. . . .	(NJ)	477
MATTER, Kathy L.	. . . . .	(NM)	785
SCHUBERT, Donald F.	. .	(NM)	1101
LEPINNET, Nancy M.	. .	(NY)	717
SOUTHCOMBE, Patricia A.	. . . .	(NY)	1169
SPIEGEL, Bertha	. . . . . .	(NY)	1174
WOLF, Catharine D.	. . . .	(NY)	1360
DISTEFANO, Marianne	. .	(OH)	305
BALDWIN, Janet M.	. . . .	(PA)	51
MORIARTY, Kathleen T.	. .	(PA)	865
WOLFE, Mary S.	. . . . . .	(PA)	1361
ALDRICH, Linda S.	. . . .	(RI)	11
IMONDI, Lenore R.	. . . .	(RI)	582
VANDERGRIFF, Kathleen E.	. . . .	(TN)	1274
DAVIS, Joan C.	. . . .	(TX)	279
FRIEDMAN, Tevia L.	. . .	(TX)	404
GREMONT, Joan C.	. . . .	(TX)	467
WEISLAK, Susan L.	. . . .	(TX)	1319
PETERSON, Francine	. .	(UT)	963
CHAMBERLAIN, M J.	. . .	(VA)	197
HOSKINS, Sylvia H.	. . . .	(VA)	561
DOLBEY, Mary B.	. . . . . .	(WA)	309
KNOLL, Betty A.	. . . . . .	(WA)	665

Teaching library skills & computers	YOUNG, Patricia S.	(TN)	1383
Teaching library skills & research	CARVER, Jane C.	(MA)	191
Teaching media skills	HUNT, Susan O.	(FL)	576
	WINSLOW, Carol M.	(IN)	1355
	CUNNINGHAM, Mary A.	(NY)	265
Teaching of library skill to students	GERMINDER, Robin L.	(NJ)	429
Teaching of library skills	BIANCHI, Karen F.	(WA)	93
Teaching reference skills	SLOAN, Mary J.	(GA)	1149
Teaching research & reference skills	BERNAT, Mary A.	(VEN)	88
Teaching research skill	HAYASHI, Chigusa	(NJ)	515
Teaching research skills	MISENHEIMER, Paula S.	(AR)	847
	THORNTON, Alice J.	(DE)	1242
	SMITH, Lena D.	(KY)	1157
	CRAMER, Eugene C.	(AB)	255
Teaching school library research skills	CARLISLE, Carol A.	(CT)	182
Teaching skills	ROBINSON, Gayle N.	(AL)	1044
	MERRILL, Barbara P.	(NY)	826
Writing library curriculum skills	SWITZER, Catherine M.	(WI)	1216

SLAVIC

Cataloging of Slavic materials	VERYHA, Wasyl	(ON)	1283
Cataloging, Slavic language, non-book	JENKS, Zoya E.	(PA)	597
Cataloging Slavic monographs	SMIRENSKY, Helen K. . . .	(NY)	1152
Descriptive cataloging, Slavic materials	MORGAN, Robert C. . . .	(VA)	864
Original cataloging Slavic materials	KORT, Richard L.	(MA)	672
Slavic & East European	CHOLDIN, Marianna T. . . .	(IL)	210
Slavic & East European librarianship	LEICH, Harold M.	(DC)	713
Slavic area specialist	MOLLOY, Molly F.	(AZ)	853
Slavic bibliography	ZALEWSKI, Wojciech . . .	(CA)	1385
	DOBCZANSKY, Jurij W. . .	(DC)	307
	LORKOVIC, Tatjana B. . . .	(IA)	741
	STUART, Mary P.	(IL)	1204
	GALIK, Barbara A.	(MI)	413
	CORRSIN, Stephen D. . . .	(NY)	247
	GOERNER, Tatiana	(NY)	443
	RAINWATER, Jean M. . . .	(RI)	1004
Slavic bibliography & reference	TURCHYN, Andrew	(IN)	1263
Slavic cataloging	MOLLOY, Molly F.	(AZ)	853
	KELLY, Mark M.	(DC)	638
	HOWE, Priscilla P.	(KS)	565
	URBANIC, Allan J.	(CA)	1269
	CANEVARI DE PAREDES, Donna A.	(SK)	178
Slavic collections	ALTENBERGER, Alicja . .	(MA)	18
Slavic exchange	HOWE, Priscilla P.	(KS)	565
Slavic languages	SABOVIK, Pavel	(AZ)	1073
	ESMAN, Michael D.	(MD)	354
	FORBES, John B.	(MD)	389

SLAVIC (Cont'd)

Slavic languages cataloging	CAPRIELIAN, Arevig . . .	(NY)	180
Slavic librarianship	ZALEWSKI, Wojciech . . .	(CA)	1385
	BEYNEN, Gijsbertus K. . .	(OH)	93
	SWENSEN, Dale S.	(UT)	1215
	MORGAN, Robert C. . . .	(VA)	864
Slavic literature	BRISKA, Boniface	(NY)	137
Slavic literatures & oral poetry	POPOVIC, Tanya V.	(NY)	983
Slavic materials	PRONEVITZ, Gregory . . .	(OH)	995
Slavic reference, Russian language	PRICE, Susan W.	(NY)	992
Slavic studies	RYAN, Frederick W.	(CA)	1071
	IRWIN, Lawrence L.	(MI)	584
	IVANOCHKO, Robert W.	(SK)	585
Slavic studies collection development	WAWRO, Wanda T.	(NY)	1311

SLIDES

American architecture slides	ROMEO, Sheryl R.	(DC)	1052
Architecture slide libraries	CINLAR, Anne	(NJ)	214
Architecture slides	STEWARD, Martha J. . .	(CA)	1192
Archiving art slides on video disks	SHARER, E J.	(CO)	1122
Art history slide organizing	GRAY, Shirley M.	(NY)	460
Art history slides	KRUPANSKI, Pamela M.	(MA)	680
Art slide collections	BLAIR, Madeline S.	(DC)	102
Art slide library systems	DULAN, Peter A.	(CO)	324
Automation of slide collections	HENDERSON, Joyce C.	(AZ)	526
Cataloging & classification of slides	HENDERSON, Joyce C.	(AZ)	526
Cataloging & classifying slides	KOSHER, Helene J.	(CA)	672
Cataloging art & architecture slides	FOWLER, Michele R. . . .	(OH)	394
Cataloging of art slides	BAILEY, Tuuli T.	(AZ)	47
Effective presentations & slide shows	SANKER, Paul N.	(NY)	1081
Management of slide collections	HENDERSON, Joyce C.	(AZ)	526
Original media slide programs	OWENS, Martha A.	(VA)	932
Photo & slide organizational systems	ROBERTSON, Retha M. . .	(OK)	1042
Research for slide information	BAILEY, Tuuli T.	(AZ)	47
16mm films, slides, & videocassettes	CRITCHLOW, Therese E.	(NJ)	259
Slide & tape production	SHAMBARGER, Peter E.	(MD)	1120
Slide classification	HAWKOS, Lise J.	(AZ)	514
Slide classification & cataloging	MCRAE, Linda	(FL)	818
Slide collection	KLEEBERGER, Patricia L.	(MD)	658
Slide collection development	GANGL, Susan D.	(MN)	416
Slide collection evaluation	PRINS, Johanna W.	(NY)	993
Slide collection organization & devlpmnt	PRINS, Johanna W.	(NY)	993
Slide collections	ABRAMS, Leslie E.	(SC)	3
	WHITE, Lynda S.	(VA)	1331
Slide curatorship	GUNN, Diane M.	(MI)	477
Slide indexing & cataloging	WALD, Ingeborg	(NY)	1294
Slide librarianship	KING, Carmen M.	(MI)	650
Slide libraries	CINLAR, Anne	(NJ)	214
Slide library	WAXMAN, Joanne	(ME)	1311
Slide library consulting	DULAN, Peter A.	(CO)	324
Slide library management	MCKENNEY, Kathryn K. .	(DE)	811
Slides & photographs	SNOW, Maryly A.	(CA)	1164
	BRAUNSTEIN, Mark M. . .	(RI)	130
Slides & picture files design	KEAVENEY, Sydney S. . .	(NY)	633
Supervising art slide library	LANTZ, Louise K.	(MD)	697
Visual resources, especially slides	CALLAHAN, Linda J. . . .	(MA)	173
Visual resources, slides & photographs	GREWENOW, Peter W. .	(NY)	467

SLSS

IBM Documentation of SLSS	KEALEY, Catherine M. . .	(ON)	632

SMALL

Administration of small academic libs	LANCASTER, Edith E. . .	(ID)	691
Administration of small libraries	VIGEANT, Robert J.	(IN)	1284
	HAY, Linda A.	(VT)	515
All small library operations	ORFIRER, Lenore F.	(CA)	925
Archives for small businesses	HOMMEL, Claudia	(NY)	555
Automation of medium & small libraries	BARRUS, Phyl	(TX)	60
Automation of small libraries	DICENSO, Jacquelyn C. .	(VT)	300
Cataloging small collections	KNOBBE, Mary L.	(MD)	665
Cataloging utilizing small computers	HOBBS, Henry C.	(MB)	545
Computers in small libraries	HENDRICKS, Thom	(ND)	527
Consulting for small & medium libraries	LEAMON, David L.	(MI)	707

SMALL (Cont'd)

Consulting large & small libraries	WEST, L P.	(IL)	1326
Development of small libraries	RUBY, Carolyn M.	(MO)	1065
General management, small special lib	GALLUP, Jane H.	(DC)	415
Improving small libraries	FORD, Marjorie F.	(CA)	389
Large computers & small libraries	STEVENS-RAYBURN, Sarah L.	(MD)	1191
Management of small libraries	BERK, Robert A.	(IL)	87
	STEINBERG, David L. ..	(VA)	1185
Managing small hospital libraries	KRATZ, Gale G.	(CA)	676
Managing small libraries	INGERSOLL, Lyn L.	(DC)	582
	LAURENSTEIN, Ann G. ..	(MO)	703
Managing small special libraries	KAMICHAITIS, Penelope H.	(PQ)	624
Managing small to medium law libraries	SCAMMAHORN, Lynne .	(PA)	1087
Marketing the small library	GARRISON, Michael G. .	(OH)	420
Organizing small libraries	FIRTH, Margaret A.	(MA)	379
Organizing small special libraries	MCMANAMON, Mary J. .	(MA)	814
Planning for small libraries	SHANNON, Marcia A. ...	(MA)	1120
Planning small corporate libraries	MONTAG, Diane	(CO)	855
Rural & small libraries	HULL, Catherine C.	(RI)	572
Setting up small libraries	LEESMENT, Helgi	(AB)	712
Small academic building design	LUCAS, Linda L.	(CA)	746
Small academic library management	DALY, Simeon	(IN)	271
Small & medium, public	HOFFMANN, Maurine L. .	(IL)	548
Small & medium public library buildings	FARACE, Virginia K.	(FL)	363
Small & rural libraries	JENNINGS, Martha F. ...	(MI)	598
Small archives	WEBBER, Steven L.	(CA)	1313
Small business automation	SEN, Joyce H.	(NY)	1115
Small business counseling	MESMER, Frank B.	(NH)	827
Small business information	ROWE, David G.	(PQ)	1062
	THIVIERGE, Lynda M. ..	(PQ)	1235
Small business start-up	MCWILLIAM, Deborah A.	(OH)	818
Small businesses	COORSH, Katalin	(ON)	244
	MCINTOSH, Julia E.	(PQ)	809
Small college library administration	OLSEN, Rowena J.	(KS)	921
	SPICER, Orlin C.	(MO)	1174
	GARRETSON, Henry C. .	(NY)	420
Small college library cooperation	OLSEN, Rowena J.	(KS)	921
Small college library management	OFFERMANN, Glenn W. .	(MN)	917
	PAWLIK, Deborah A.	(PA)	951
	CORMAN, Linda W.	(ON)	246
Small computer applications	ELWELL, Pamela M.	(OH)	347
Small computers	BOND, George	(NH)	113
Small database design	FOWELLS, Fumi T.	(MI)	393
Small database development	ENGLISH, Bernard L.	(NJ)	350
Small group training	FORD, Marjorie F.	(CA)	389
Small high school collections	SHEPHERD, Rex L.	(IA)	1127
Small high school facilities	SHEPHERD, Rex L.	(IA)	1127
Small law firms	WEZELMAN, Joy L.	(ND)	1328
Small libraries	BREIDT, Cheryll K.	(ID)	132
	MCFERRAN, Warren A. .	(MI)	805
	SHAFFER, Nancy R. ...	(NC)	1119
	MINERVA, Jane R.	(NY)	846
	HIRSCH, Barbara S.	(VT)	543
	ROBBERS, Sandra M. ..	(WI)	1038
	STANDING, Doris A. ...	(ON)	1179
	BASLER, Ellen L.	(SK)	63
Small libraries & library systems	FEYE-STUKAS, Janice ..	(MN)	374
Small libraries building planning	MILLIKEN, Ruth L.	(FL)	843
Small library administration	LEIDER, Karen S.	(DC)	713
	MORGAN, Sally W.	(HI)	864
	MCCLAREY, Catherine A.	(IL)	796
	PROCTOR, Judy C.	(IN)	995
	JOB, Rose A.	(MO)	601
	BALOG, Rita J.	(OH)	53
	PAKALA, James C.	(PA)	935
	MERCHANT, Thomas L. .	(WI)	825
Small library administration & organz	REINGOLD, Judith S. ...	(NH)	1021
Small library automation	LANGHORNE, Mary J. ..	(IA)	696
	MARKUSON, Carolyn A.	(MA)	772
	COOK, Nancy E.	(SD)	240
	PROVOST, Paul E.	(PQ)	996
Small library circulation automation	STOUT, Chester B.	(OH)	1198
Small library computer applications	MORRIS, R P.	(NC)	867
Small library computing	STARK, Ted	(IA)	1182

SMALL (Cont'd)

Small library consulting	DAVIDOFF, Marcia	(FL)	276
	BACKMAN, Carroll H. ..	(NC)	44
	BULLEY, Joan S.	(VA)	156
Small library development	NOTARSTEFANO, Vincent C.	(NY)	910
	GINNANE, Mary J.	(OR)	437
	KNIEVEL, Helen A.	(OR)	664
Small lib development & administration	HILL, Susan E.	(TX)	540
Small library establishment	STEFANACCI, Michal A.	(PA)	1185
Small library management	DAVIS, Becky C.	(CA)	277
	MORRISON, M C.	(DC)	868
	OGDEN, Nina M.	(ID)	918
	SIEVING, Pamela C. ...	(MI)	1136
	BARROWS, William D. ..	(NC)	60
	SHAPIRO, Ruth T.	(PA)	1121
	MCGOWAN, Anne W. ...	(WY)	807
Small library needs	MCMILLAN, Mary M. ...	(IN)	815
Small library organization	LOW, Frederick E.	(NY)	743
Small library policy development	EVANS, Patricia D.	(AB)	357
Small library positions	BRANSWELL, Sr M.	(NH)	129
Small library public relations	KIRKPATRICK, Jane E. .	(ON)	655
Small library services	DEGRUYTER, M L.	(TX)	288
Small library supervision	MOORE, Craig P.	(MD)	859
Small library systems	DAVEY, Dorothy M.	(ON)	276
Small museum libraries	BENEDETTI, Joan M. ...	(CA)	80
Small networks	AUBIN, Robert	(PQ)	38
Small press distribution	LEISNER, Anthony B. ...	(IL)	714
Small press poetry	FOX, Willard	(LA)	395
Small press publications	ROM, Cristine C.	(OH)	1052
Small press publishing	KNIFFEL, Leonard J. ...	(MI)	664
	SILVER, Gary L.	(MI)	1138
	THEWS, Dorothy D.	(MN)	1234
	CARTER, Charles R. ...	(BC)	189
Small presses	CARPENTER, Eric J. ...	(OH)	184
Small public libraries	KADANOFF, Diane G. ..	(MA)	621
	FLOWER, Eileen D.	(OH)	386
	FRENCH, Michael	(OH)	402
	CASSELL, Marianne K. .	(VT)	193
	BRENNAN, Cindy L.	(WA)	132
	OTTOSEN, Charles F. ..	(AB)	930
Small public library administration	MUDD, Isabelle G.	(AK)	875
	OVERSTREET, Allen J. .	(FL)	931
	LINTNER, Barbara J. ..	(IL)	731
	MOTT, Schuyler L.	(ME)	872
	YOUNG, Lynne M.	(MN)	1382
	WAGGONER, Susan M. .	(PA)	1291
	KNODLE, Shirley M.	(WI)	665
	EVANS, Patricia D.	(AB)	357
	KIRKPATRICK, Jane E. .	(ON)	655
Small public library buildings	RASKA, Ginny	(TX)	1009
Small public library collections	RASKA, Ginny	(TX)	1009
Small public library development	PARRY, David R.	(CO)	944
	HAWKINS, Paul J.	(KS)	514
	SCHERBA, Sandra A. ..	(MI)	1092
Small public library issues	HAYES, Richard E.	(MA)	516
Small public library management	LAPIERRE, France	(PQ)	697
Small public library services	LEVIN, Elizabeth A.	(MI)	720
Small public library systems	ELDRIDGE, Jane A.	(MA)	342
Small, rural library service	MILLER, Pearl F.	(IA)	841
Small rural public libraries	PANZ, Richard	(NY)	938
Small special libraries	CIBOCH, Lorraine A. ...	(WI)	214
Small special libraries consulting	HAMILTON, Patricia J. .	(SD)	492
Small special library administration	CLARK, Jane F.	(GA)	217
Small special library organization	BEAL, Gretchen F.	(TN)	68
Small special library supervision	DAYHOFF, Judith A. ...	(CO)	283
Special small library administration	BODNAR, Marta	(ON)	109

SOCIAL (See also Society)

American social history	ANDERSON, R J.	(PA)	25
Arts, humanities & social sciences	LOMBARDI, Mary L.	(CA)	738
Bibliography, social scis & humanities	PARROTT, Margaret S. .	(NC)	944
Business & social science	RUPPRECHT, Leslie P. .	(NJ)	1068
Business & social sciences databases	KENYON, Sharmon H. ..	(CA)	643
	SLOCUM, Hannah R. ...	(CA)	1150
Business, social sciences	TAYLOR, Douglas M. ...	(AL)	1226
Cataloging in social science	HAN, Kenneth P.	(CA)	494

SOCIAL (Cont'd)

Cataloging social sciences monographs	HARDGROVE, David J. .	(NJ)	499
Catholic social action archives	RUNKEL, Phillip M.	(WI)	1067
Children's social sciences reviewing	WOLL, Christina B.	(TX)	1361
Database searching & social sciences	FISHEL, Teresa A.	(MN)	380
Databases in social science & humanities	PRICE, Susan W.	(NY)	992
Economics & social sciences	TOTH, George S.	(DC)	1252
Education & social sciences databases	BROWN, M S.	(FL)	145
Education & the social sciences	WEST, Loretta G.	(OH)	1326
Education, social science reference	ROBERTSON, Ina N.	(IL)	1042
English social sciences	STURGIS, Marylee C.	(VA)	1205
ERIC & social sciences	MEEKER, Robert B.	(IL)	821
Family planning, population, soc mktg	WILLSON, Katherine H.	(CT)	1349
Government & social science databases	BASEFSKY, Stuart M.	(NC)	62
Humanities & social science bibliography	ROTHACKER, John M. .	(TN)	1059
Humanities & social science databases	TAKAHASHI, Annabelle T.	(HI)	1220
Humanities & social science reference	LO, Henrietta W.	(CA)	735
	TAKAHASHI, Annabelle T.	(HI)	1220
	HOLLEY, E J.	(SC)	551
	MACLENNAN, Oriel C.	(NS)	757
Humanities & social scis bibliography	MCELROY, Neil J.	(CA)	804
	MENZEL, John P.	(NJ)	825
Humanities & social sciences cols	EDWARDS, Willie M.	(MI)	338
Humanities & social sciences databases	STORM, Jill	(DC)	1198
Humanities & social sciences reference	JOHNSON, Diane D.	(CA)	603
	ECKWRIGHT, Gail Z.	(ID)	335
Humanities, social science reference	REIK, Constance	(NH)	1020
Law & social sciences	ESPOSITO, Michael A.	(NY)	354
Library instruction, social sciences	WEIMER, Sally W.	(CA)	1317
Literature & social sciences	NEVIN, Susanne	(MN)	898
Literature of social sciences	SHAW, Shiow J.	(TAI)	1124
Online searching, social sciences	GORAL, Miki	(CA)	451
Peace & social justice	KLINE, Victoria E.	(CA)	661
Ref, bibliography, humanities, soc scis	DAVIS, Donald G.	(TX)	278
Reference, humanities & social sciences	ROUTH, Spencer	(AUS)	1061
Reference in the social sciences	LAUBE, Lois R.	(IN)	702
Reference services, social sciences	ANDREWS, Loretta K.	(MD)	26
Reference, social science & humanities	WIZA, Judith M.	(KY)	1359
Reference, social sciences	BLUM, Fred	(MI)	107
Reference, social sciences & humanities	MCCLEARY, William E.	(LA)	796
Science & social studies	ALBUM, Bernie	(CA)	11
Searching, social science databases	WEIMER, Sally W.	(CA)	1317
Social & behavioral sciences	KNAPP, Sara D.	(NY)	663
Social economics documentation	VAN GARSSE, Yvan	(BEL)	1275
Social epistemology	FROEHLICH, Thomas J.	(NY)	405
Social, folk, & ceremonial dances	KELLER, Kate V.	(PA)	635
Social history archives	COOK, Terry G.	(ON)	240
Social impacts of telecommunications	RICE, Ronald E.	(CA)	1027
Social policy	REPPY, Charlotte D.	(MD)	1024
Social psychology	MILLER, Everett G.	(MD)	837
Social reforms, minorities	MOREY, Frederick L.	(MD)	863
Social responsibilities	SHERIDAN, John B.	(CO)	1127
Social science	WOLLTER, Patricia M.	(CA)	1361
	MISSAVAGE, Leonard	(FL)	848
	KOCSIS, Jeanne	(MA)	667
	VERBA, Sidney	(MA)	1282
	SCHELL, Rosalie F.	(MO)	1091
	BENSON, Harold W.	(NY)	83
Social science & computer indexing	LINDHEIMER, Elinor	(CA)	729
Social sci & humanities col development	DUPRE, Monique	(ON)	327
Social science & humanities librarians	HUPP, Stephen L.	(MI)	577
Social science & humanities reference	BILAL, Dania M.	(FL)	96
	PATTON, Linda L.	(FL)	949
	WESTON, E P.	(IL)	1327
Social science bibliographic instruction	NESBITT, Renee D.	(CA)	896
Social science bibliographies	DESSAINT, Alain Y.	(VA)	295

SOCIAL (Cont'd)

Social science bibliography	MCNAMARA, Jay	(AL)	816
	SCHILLER, Anita R.	(CA)	1093
	HALIBEY, Areta V.	(IL)	486
	GERACI, Diane	(NY)	428
	LUNT, Ruth B.	(NY)	749
	HOVDE, David M.	(OK)	563
Social science collection development	NESBITT, Renee D.	(CA)	896
	GROVE, Shari T.	(MA)	474
	MAJOR, Marla J.	(MI)	762
Social science database	DICKSTEIN, Ruth H.	(AZ)	301
	THIES, Gail M.	(MD)	1235
Social science database marketing	ZAJDEL, George J.	(PA)	1385
Social science database searching	GETCHELL, Charles M.	(NC)	430
Social science databases	ECKMAN, Charles D.	(CA)	335
	NESBITT, Renee D.	(CA)	896
	NEWMARK, Laura C.	(CA)	900
	SHOUSE, Richard	(CA)	1133
	FRANCIS, Barbara W.	(FL)	396
	BURNS, Marie T.	(IL)	162
	WISE, Mintron S.	(NC)	1357
	GERACI, Diane	(NY)	428
	REINSTEIN, Diana J.	(NY)	1021
	PARR, Virginia H.	(OH)	944
	ELSHAMI, Ahmed M.	(PA)	346
	ROSS, Nina M.	(PA)	1058
	DESSAINT, Alain Y.	(VA)	295
	MCCLEMENTS, Nancy A.	(WI)	796
	LANGERMAN, Shoshana P.	(ISR)	695
	KATAOKA, Yoko	(JAP)	629
Social science, general reference	TUDIVER, Lillian	(NY)	1262
Social science, history, education	NELSON, Michael L.	(WY)	894
Social science indexing	FLANZRAICH, Gerri	(NY)	384
	LANGERMAN, Shoshana P.	(ISR)	695
Social science information	SERBAN, William M.	(LA)	1116
	TAMURA, Shunsaku	(JAP)	1221
Social science information resources	SHIELDS, Gerald R.	(NY)	1130
Social science librarianship	BERGEN, Daniel P.	(NY)	85
Social science literature	WHITBECK, George W.	(IN)	1329
Social science, occult reference	KLEIN, Victor C.	(LA)	659
Social science reference	HALL, Susan W.	(CT)	488
	WAI, Lily C.	(ID)	1292
	ELS, Nancy T.	(MO)	346
	REINHOLD, Edna J.	(MO)	1021
	TOMPKINS, Louise	(NJ)	1250
	MACOMBER, Nancy	(NY)	758
	NOLAN, John A.	(NY)	907
	SHEEHAN, Robert C.	(NY)	1125
	HOLMES, Jill M.	(OK)	553
	HOVDE, David M.	(OK)	563
	RICHARDSON, Linda B.	(VA)	1029
	JEWELL, Timothy D.	(WA)	600
Social science reference services	MILLER, Clayton M.	(OH)	836
	WEILANT, Edward	(OH)	1317
Social science research	GERKEN, Ann E.	(CA)	429
	MISSAR, Margaret M.	(DC)	847
	EVERHART, Paul R.	(IL)	358
Social science subject cataloging	DEVERA, Rosalinda M.	(NY)	297
Social sciences	O'NEILL, Diane J.	(CA)	924
	PELLE, Catherine A.	(CA)	955
	SPENCER, Patricia O.	(CA)	1173
	MANDOUR, Cecile A.	(CT)	765
	HALL, Forest A.	(DC)	487
	HORCHLER, Gabriel F.	(DC)	559
	JONES, Milbrey L.	(DC)	614
	PENKIUNAS, Ruta M.	(DC)	956
	WILLETT, Charles	(FL)	1341
	WIBERLEY, Stephen E.	(IL)	1335
	MOON, Elizabeth A.	(IN)	857
	LASER, Debra L.	(MD)	700
	PERLUNGHER, Richard A.	(NH)	959
	WATSON, Marjorie O.	(NJ)	1310
	ANGEL, Kenneth E.	(NY)	27
	OCKENE, David L.	(NY)	915
	BONTA, Bruce D.	(PA)	114
	OTTAVIANO, Doris B.	(RI)	930
	KOHUT, David R.	(TN)	669
	SAMMATARO, Linda J.	(TN)	1078

SOCIAL (Cont'd)
Social sciences

	BOGIE, Thomas M.	(TX)	110
	WILSON, Thomas C. . . .	(TX)	1353
	MAXWELL, Littleton M. .	(VA)	788
	GAUMOND, George R. . .	(WV)	423
	BEAUMIER, Renald	(PQ)	70
Social sciences & art	BRADLEY, Jared W. . . .	(LA)	126
Social sciences & business	SAFLEY, Ellen D.	(TX)	1074
Social sciences & business databases	ALLERTON, Ellen M. . . .	(NY)	16
Social sciences & business reference	HATTENDORF, Lynn C. .	(IL)	512
Social sciences & education	ATCHISON, Fres D.	(KS)	37
Social sciences & history bibliography	BROWN, Philip L.	(SD)	146
Social sciences & humanities	WINTER, Michael F. . . .	(CA)	1356
	OTA, Leslie H.	(NJ)	930
	PENCHANSKY, Mimi B. .	(NY)	956
	ANDERSON, Madeleine J.	(TX)	24
Social sciences & humanities databases	COCHRANE, Kerry L. . .	(IL)	225
Social sciences & humanities reference	COCHRANE, Kerry L. . .	(IL)	225
	TURLEY, Harriet M.	(NY)	1264
	TOLBERT, Jean F.	(TX)	1248
	ST. JACQUES, Suzanne L.	(ON)	1075
Social sciences & management	GREEN, Kathleen A. . . .	(MA)	462
Social sciences & religion reference	PHILLIPS, Robert L. . . .	(TX)	969
Social sciences bibliographer	MISTARAS, Evangeline .	(IL)	848
	COHEN, Steven J.	(OH)	229
Social sciences bibliography	TSANG, Daniel C.	(CA)	1260
	MEDER, Marylouise D. . .	(KS)	820
	COUTTS, Brian E.	(KY)	252
	BEAL, Sarell W.	(MI)	68
	JOHNSON, Deborah S. .	(MN)	603
	SWINDLER, Luke	(NC)	1216
	HAGERMAN, George F. .	(NY)	483
Social sciences cataloging	NOTARSTEFANO, Vincent C.	(NY)	910
Social sciences collection development	MYERS, Robert C.	(KS)	885
	ROMANS, Lawrence M. .	(TN)	1052
Social sciences database searching	GOODWIN, Bryan D. . . .	(ME)	450
	MILLER, Mary E.	(PA)	840
	RICHARDSON, Linda B. .	(VA)	1029
Social sciences databases	ILACQUA, Anne K.	(MA)	581
	BIGGS, Debra R.	(MI)	95
	VANDER MEER, Patricia F.	(MI)	1274
	HARDING, Mary H.	(NY)	500
	GUSS, Margaret B.	(OH)	478
	HAAG, Enid E.	(WA)	480
	COURNOYER, Joanne . .	(ON)	251
Social sciences education	AMAN, Mary J.	(WI)	19
Social sciences, humanities & computers	WOGGON, Michele	(CA)	1359
Social sciences information sources	CONGER, Lucinda D. . . .	(DC)	236
Social sciences literature	WYNAR, Lubomyr R. . . .	(OH)	1375
Social sciences, mental health	HORNUNG, Susan D. . . .	(WI)	560
Social sciences online searching	MYERS, Robert C.	(KS)	885
	MOORE, Kathryn L.	(NC)	860
	OSTROWSKY, Edith . . .	(NY)	929
	BULL, Jerry J.	(PQ)	156
Social sciences reference	TUCKER, John M.	(IN)	1261
	DRISCOLL, Jacqueline . .	(MI)	320
	SCIATTARA, Diane M. . .	(NY)	1106
	WYLLIE, Stanley C.	(OH)	1375
	CARR, Caryn J.	(PA)	185
	LUIKART, Nancy B.	(TX)	747
	DAVIS, Wylma P.	(VA)	281
	BULL, Jerry J.	(PQ)	156
Social sciences reference & research	HOWREY, Mary M.	(IL)	566
Social sciences reference courses	LI, Richard T.	(IL)	725
Social sciences, reference services	DIMATTEO, Lucy A. . . .	(NY)	304
Social sciences, South Asia	WOOD, Ann L.	(MA)	1363
Social service	BENSON, Harold W. . . .	(NY)	83
Social services	OLEARY, Jennie L.	(AZ)	920
Social services research	ROBINSON, Jolene A. . .	(NY)	1044
Social studies	ZUK, Donna R.	(AB)	1391
Social studies curriculum	HIGGINS, Judith H.	(NY)	538
Social studies in information	WILSON, Patrick	(CA)	1352
Social studies of information	CEPPOS, Karen F.	(CA)	196

SOCIAL (Cont'd)

Social studies reference	WHITE, Carol A.	(GA)	1330
Social surveys	BOVA, Patrick	(IL)	120
Social theory	WINTER, Michael F. . . .	(CA)	1356
Social welfare legislation	AUSTIN, Monique C. . . .	(DC)	40
Social work	LI, Hong C.	(CT)	724
	WILLIAMS, James W. . .	(IL)	1344
	OWSLEY, Lucile C. . . .	(NC)	932
	BENSON, Harold W. . . .	(NY)	83
	EDWARDS, Rita F.	(NY)	337
Social work & history	CAGLE, Robert B.	(LA)	171
Social work & school psychology	LUNT, Ruth B.	(NY)	749
Social work & social sciences	WORTZEL, Murray N. . .	(NY)	1369
Social work library consulting	BUTLER, Evelyn	(PA)	166
Social work practice	REPPY, Charlotte D. . . .	(MD)	1024
Social work reference	REGUEIRO, Judith E. . . .	(PA)	1017
Subject analysis & social sciences	WRIGHT, Sylvia H.	(NY)	1373
Youth, childhood, social sciences	WOODBURY, Marda . . .	(CA)	1366

SOCIALISM

Socialism	DEGRUSON, Eugene H. .	(KS)	288

SOCIETY (See also Social, Sociology)

Historical society	COLLINS, Sarah F.	(NJ)	233
Historical society libraries	BOWERS, Rhoda E.	(MD)	120
Historical society, library admin	MILLER, Irene K.	(CT)	838
Impact of info technologies on society	FISHER, H L.	(CA)	381
Impacts of technology on society	MARCHAND, Donald A. .	(NY)	768
Libraries & American society	VANCE, Kenneth E. . . .	(MI)	1273
Library history, libraries in society	KUSNERZ, Peggy A. . . .	(MI)	685
Library in society	O'HARA, Frederic J. . . .	(NY)	919
	MCCHESNEY, Kathryn M.	(OH)	795
Professional society publishing	FERRERE, Cathy M. . . .	(NY)	373
Research in hlth, socty, music, foods	STARKEY, Bonnie F. . . .	(WV)	1182
Sociology, unification of society	COE, Miriam M.	(LA)	226
Systems technology for society	CHARTRAND, Robert L.	(DC)	203

SOCIOECONOMIC (See also Economics)

Biomedical & medical socioeconomic info	BANKS, Jane L.	(DC)	54
Socioeconomic databases	REILLY, Francis S.	(DC)	1020
Socioeconomic, LEXIS & NEXIS databases	MILUTINOVIC, Eunhee C.	(IL)	845

SOCIOLOGY

Economics & sociology	FIELD, Louise P.	(NY)	375
Heritage sociology & genealogy	SCHLOTT, Florenceann .	(PA)	1094
Political & sociological databases	BOILARD, Gilberte	(PQ)	111
Sociology	MANCUYAS, Natividad D.	(IL)	764
	WILLIAMS, James W. . .	(IL)	1344
Sociology of knowledge	PIERCE, Sydney J.	(GA)	972
Sociology of professional education	PAGE, Jacqueline M. . . .	(MO)	934
Sociology of reading	COLBY, Robert A.	(NY)	230
Sociology, unification of society	COE, Miriam M.	(LA)	226

SOFTWARE (See also Computers, Front-End, Gateways, Microsoftware and names of specific software packages, e.g. Symphony and types of software, e.g. Spreadsheets)

Acquisitions software development	LAREW, Christian K. . . .	(NJ)	697
Analytical software	ZURBRIGG, Lyn E.	(ON)	1391
Apple & Macintosh computer software	TRAVILLIAN, Mary W. . .	(IA)	1254
Audiovisual & microcomputer software	DAVIS, Shelley E.	(GA)	281
Audiovisual software	REIMAN, Anthony C. . . .	(NY)	1020
Audiovisual software & hardware	WARREN, Ann R.	(NH)	1306
Audiovisual software & services	DIAMOND, Shela W. . . .	(KY)	299
Audiovisual software cataloging	DUHAMELL, Lynnette H.	(IN)	324
	HORAN, Meredith L. . . .	(MD)	559
Automation software	ERLAND, Virginia K. . . .	(NY)	353
Avionics software	FRIEDMAN, Sandra M. . .	(CA)	404
Book & audiovisual software reviewer	LEIBOLD, Cynthia K. . . .	(OH)	713
Cataloging microcomputer software	CARTER, Judith A.	(AZ)	189
CD-ROM retrieval software	DITMARS, David W. . . .	(OH)	305
Chemical structure software evaluation	SOUTHWICK, Margaret A.	(VA)	1170

SOFTWARE (Cont'd)

Children's literature computer software — FEUERHELM, Jill A. (OR) 374
Children's literature, software — HOFMANN, Susan M. (PA) 548
Circulating software collections — POLLY, Jean A. (NY) 981
College software publishing — NEEDHAM, Michael V. (CA) 891
Communications & networking software — THOMAS, Hilary B. (NY) 1236
Communications software marketing — CORCHADO, Veronica A. (CA) 245
Computer & software technology — AMMERMAN, Jackie W. (GA) 20
Computer books & software — BLAKE, Harry W. (CA) 103
Computer hardware & software — GRIFFIN, Hillis L. (CA) 468
Computer hardware & software — FALK, Howard (NJ) 362
Computer hardware & software — FERRIN, Eric G. (PA) 373
Computer hardware & software — BELL, David B. (SC) 76
Computer hardware & software manuals — CASSAR, Ann (PA) 193
Computer hardware & software reference — ROBSON, Amy K. (IL) 1045
Computer literacy software — ROSEN, Elizabeth M. (CA) 1055
Computer software — CROSS, Claudette S. (CA) 260
Computer software — DAVENPORT, Constance B. (CA) 275
Computer software — SANDELL, Judy L. (CA) 1079
Computer software — JONES, David E. (NJ) 612
Computer software — STROZIER, Sandra L. (OH) 1203
Computer software database — CHICHESTER, Gerald C. (CT) 208
Computer software databases — KOOLISH, Ruth K. (CA) 671
Computer software evaluation — KELLY, Patricia M. (MA) 638
Computer software hardware — SHENASSA, Daryoosh (IL) 1126
Computer systems & software — BURTON, Mary L. (PA) 164
Computers & software — MAIN, Isabelle G. (AZ) 761
Data processing hardware & software — KOOLISH, Ruth K. (CA) 671
Database management software — YAU, Linda S. (CA) 1378
Database software — EDDISON, Elizabeth B. (MA) 335
Database software — LUCAS, Jean M. (OH) 746
Database software creation — GARMAN, Nancy J. (KY) 419
Databases & software consulting — GIGANTE, Vickilyn M. (MD) 433
DBMS software — HASKINS, Dawn A. (OH) 510
Digitize image manipulation software — BENGE, Bruce (OK) 80
Distribution of public domain software — SHAW, Ben B. (TX) 1123
Educational software — LATHROP, Ann (CA) 701
Educational software — BOLSTER, Kathryn (CT) 113
Evaluation of library software — SAVAGE, Gretchen S. (CA) 1085
Evaluation research, curriculum software — HERB, Elizabeth D. (OH) 530
Forms generation software — CONTESSA, William B. (NY) 239
French educational software — GELINAS, Rene (PQ) 426
Front-end software — KING, Joseph T. (CA) 651
Full-text retrieval software — BENGE, Bruce (OK) 80
Health sciences computer software — MCLEAN, Martha L. (TN) 814
IBM-PC microcomputers & software — COLE, David H. (MN) 230
Image processing software — DAVISSON, Darell D. (CA) 281
Information management software — HASKINS, Dawn A. (OH) 510
Information retrieval software — RALBOVSKY, Edward A. (NY) 1004
Information retrieval software — NICHOL, Kathleen M. (BC) 901
Information retrieval software design — BRUNELLE, Bette S. (NY) 150
Information retrieval softwares — LEDOUX, Marc A. (PQ) 708
InMagic software file management system — HOUSTON, Louise B. (ON) 563
Instructional software — FOLKE, Carolyn W. (WI) 387
Instructional software collection — OSTROM, Kriss T. (MI) 929
Integrated library software — MOSER, Maxine M. (CA) 871
Interactive software & films — FORD, Andrew E. (NY) 389
Knowledge software design — GRENIER, Serge (PQ) 467
Legal software — GRIFFITH, Cary J. (MN) 469
Library software — LUNDQUIST, Marie A. (IL) 748
Library software — BRIAND, Margaret M. (MA) 134
Library software development — THOMAS, James M. (OH) 1237
Library software development — FERRIN, Eric G. (PA) 373
Library software development — RUTHERFORD, Frederick S. (ON) 1070
Library software development — GROSS, Margaret B. (PQ) 472
Library software development & support — FEDECZKO, Joyce L. (IL) 367
Library statistics, spreadsheet software — KATES, Jacqueline R. (MA) 629
Library systems & software — DYKMAN, Elaine K. (NJ) 331
Library systems & software — KARCICH, Grant J. (ON) 627
Library systems & software — TOUCHETTE, Francois G. (PQ) 1252

SOFTWARE (Cont'd)

Library systems software — DITMARS, David W. (OH) 305
Mainframe & personal computer software — POLLARD, Louise (UT) 981
Medical software — RUMSEY, Eric T. (IA) 1067
Micro & mainframe library software — SPENCER, John T. (CA) 1173
MicroBASIS retrieval software — DITMARS, David W. (OH) 305
Microcomputer software — BENIDIR, Samia (CA) 80
Microcomputer software — CLANCY, Stephen L. (CA) 215
Microcomputer software — SILVERSTEIN, Jeffrey S. (CT) 1139
Microcomputer software — DOLAK, Frank J. (IN) 309
Microcomputer software — HANE, Paula J. (NY) 495
Microcomputer software — HERB, Elizabeth D. (OH) 530
Microcomputer software — MITCHELL, George D. (TX) 848
Microcomputer software — YOUNT, Natalie W. (WA) 1384
Microcomputer software — JONES, B E. (ON) 611
Microcomputer software cataloging — WEISS, Paul J. (NY) 1320
Microcomputer software collection mgmt — BEHNKE, Charles (WI) 75
Microcomputer software development — EVERSBERG, Bernhard (WGR) 359
Microcomputer software evaluation — MAY, Frank C. (CA) 788
Microcomputer software evaluation — MICHELS, Fredrick A. (MI) 832
Microcomputer software for libraries — YEH, Helen S. (TX) 1379
Microcomputer software industry — SLAVIN, Vicky J. (MA) 1148
Microcomputer software, new technologies — VEANER, Allen B. (ON) 1280
Microcomputer software reviews — MANN, Carol A. (TX) 765
Microcomputers & software — STANLEY, Nancy M. (PA) 1180
Microcomputers & software design — KARR, Ronald D. (MA) 628
Microcomputers, hardware & software — ZABEL, Patricia L. (TX) 1385
Mini & microcomputer software — COLEMAN, James R. (MA) 231
Non-book mtrls & microcomputer software — INTNER, Sheila S. (MA) 583
Nutrition software — KREBS-SMITH, James J. (MD) 677
Online software documentation — GIRILL, T R. (CA) 438
PC software — ADDISON, Paul H. (IN) 6
Personal computer hardware & software — MILLER, Ann M. (ON) 835
Personal computer software — TABKE, Robert (CA) 1219
Personal computer software — BEFELER, Mike (CO) 74
Personal computer software — NG, Pauline (IL) 900
Personal computer software applications — SABATINI, Joseph D. (NM) 1072
Personal computer software development — MAYDET, Steven I. (NJ) 789
Personal computer software, legal forms — KUEHNLE, Emery C. (OH) 682
Personal computer systems & software — TOWNLEY, Richard L. (NY) 1253
Research & development, software — CHAPMAN, Ruby M. (IL) 202
Reviewing AV & computer software — MILLER, John E. (OH) 839
S/38 computer software — TODD, Hal W. (FL) 1248
Search software — LESLIE, Nathan (ON) 718
Search software — LOWRY, Douglas B. (ON) 745
Search software — LOWRY, John D. (ON) 745
Search system software: front-end — WOODSMALL, Rose M. (MD) 1367
Software — QUAKE, Ron (CT) 999
Software — MOULTON, Lynda W. (MA) 873
Software — BROOKS, Martin (NY) 140
Software — HAUGH, Amy J. (PA) 512
Software & new technology — DECKER, Leola M. (MD) 286
Software applications — FUKAI, Eiko (IL) 408
Software applications in libraries — STEWART, Douglas J. (AZ) 1192
Software cataloging — DUMLAO, Mercedes G. (CA) 325
Software cataloging — FLUK, Louise R. (PQ) 386
Software, CD-ROM — EDWARDS, David M. (PA) 337
Software chemical, petroleum engineering — WILSON, John W. (TX) 1351
Software collection development — CHIANG, Katherine S. (NY) 207
Software configuration management — DURHAM, Mary J. (MA) 328
Software consultation — FARAONE, Maria B. (NY) 363
Software customization — SOUDER, Edith I. (PA) 1169
Software design — MULVANY, Nancy (CA) 878
Software design & development — RICKERSON, George T. (MO) 1031
Software development — MARLOR, Hugh T. (CA) 772
Software development — TARTER, Blodwen (CA) 1224
Software development — BEN-SHIR, Rya H. (IL) 83
Software development — O'REILLY, Daniel F. (MA) 925
Software development — YACOUBY, Ray S. (MA) 1376
Software development — NELSON, David W. (NH) 893

SOFTWARE (Cont'd)

Software development

	QUAIN, Julie R.	(NY)	999
	RALBOVSKY, Edward A.	(NY)	1004
	SULLIVAN, Michael M.	(VA)	1208
	SCHELL, Catherine L.	(WY)	1091
	FORRESTER, John H.	(ITL)	391
Software development, library reports	HENDERSON, John E.	(PA)	526
Software documentation	CONNELL, Christopher J.	(OH)	237
Software engineering	BAILEY, Charles W.	(NC)	46
	THOMAS, James M.	(OH)	1237
Software engineering collection	SOUCIE, Yan Y.	(OR)	1169
Software evaluation	LATHROP, Ann	(CA)	701
	GROSCH, Audrey N.	(MN)	472
	WILTSHIRE, Denise A.	(VA)	1354
	ATTINGER, Monique L.	(ON)	38
Software evaluation for libraries	ASSUNCAO, Isabel	(PQ)	37
Software for cataloging	LOWELL, Brian V.	(IL)	744
Software industry	PUGH, Ann E.	(MA)	997
Software lending	SHIRINIAN, George N.	(ON)	1131
Software manual distribution	BYERS, Cathy L.	(ON)	168
Software production	FITZGERALD, Ardra F.	(CA)	382
Software products	KAHN, Martin F.	(NY)	622
Software selection	PUGH, W J.	(MD)	997
Software support	BIRD, H C.	(TX)	98
	ATTINGER, Monique L.	(ON)	38
Software system quality control	KOLMAN, Roberta F.	(HI)	669
	VEGTER, Amy H.	(NY)	1281
Software systems training	DULAN, Peter A.	(CO)	324
Software testing	NELSON, David W.	(NH)	893
Software training	ROGERS, Jonathan B.	(NY)	1049
	NAULTY, Deborah M.	(PA)	889
	ATTINGER, Monique L.	(ON)	38
Software training & development	LIGHTERMAN, Mark	(FL)	726
Special library software	HASKINS, Dawn A.	(OH)	510
Strategic & decision software	BUNCE, George D.	(ENG)	157
Technical writing, software documtn	GREENE, Nancy S.	(PA)	464
Training library automation software	DOEHLERT, Irene C.	(CA)	308
Training on micros & software	KANNEL, Ene	(ON)	625
Using PC software in library	DIETRICH, Peter J.	(NY)	302
Utilization of computer software	CLEMENTS, Cynthia L.	(TX)	221
Word processing software development	SCHWARTZ, James M.	(SD)	1104

SOIL

Chemistry, physics, soil science	VIERICH, Richard W.	(CA)	1284
Soil plant relations & natural resources	SCHNEIDER, Karl R.	(MD)	1097
Soil science & computers	HANDROW, Margaret M.	(TX)	495
West African soils & water resources	CANDELMO, Emily	(NY)	178

SOLAR

Passive solar cooling techniques	LAKE, Mary S.	(AZ)	689
Solar physics	STRAND, Kathryn	(CO)	1200
Solar system astronomy	CHAPMAN, Jennalyn W.	(AZ)	202

SOLICITATION

Collection solicitation	INGERSOL, Robert S.	(MO)	582
Manuscripts solicitation & processing	GRABOWSKI, John J.	(OH)	455

SOLINET

SOLINET database searching	ROBERTS, Lisa G.	(GA)	1041

SONGS

American art song	SHERIDAN, Margaret G.	(PA)	1127
Early popular songs	RIGGS, Quentin T.	(CA)	1034

SONGWRITER

Musician, songwriter	MARTUCCI, Louis U.	(CA)	779

SOUND (See also Audio, Audiovisual, Media, Recordings)

Appraisals of sound recordings	SMOLIAN, Steven J.	(MD)	1162
Cataloging music & sound recordings	DORFMAN, Ethel L.	(NY)	312
	POWELL, Virginia L.	(PA)	989
Cataloging of sound recordings	SCHUURSMA, Ann B.	(NET)	1103
Cataloging scores & sound recordings	MURRAY, Diane E.	(MI)	881
	WALLER, Elaine A.	(MI)	1298
Cataloging sound recordings	BJORKE, Wallace S.	(MI)	100
Cataloging visual & sound materials	DRIESSEN, Karen C.	(MT)	320
Classical music sound archives	MAROTH, Frederick J.	(CA)	772
Classical music sound recordings	HALSEY, Richard S.	(NY)	490
History of recorded sound	FABRIZIO, Timothy C.	(NY)	360
Music & sound recordings	WATTS, Richard S.	(CA)	1310
Music & sound recordings cataloging	SNODGRASS, Wilson D.	(TX)	1163
Music recordings sound restoration	PETRIE, Mildred M.	(FL)	965
Musical sound recordings	PALKOVIC, Mark A.	(OH)	935
Old & rare sound recordings	CHANDLER, Thomas V.	(CA)	200
Phonorecords or sound recordings	HASSE, John E.	(DC)	511
Preservation of sound recordings	KINNEY, Daniel W.	(NY)	653
Rare sound recordings	GERBER, Warren C.	(NJ)	428
Rare sound recordings archives	MAWHINNEY, Paul C.	(PA)	787
Recorded sound	MUNSICK, Lee R.	(NJ)	879
	COLQUHOUN, Joan E.	(ON)	234
Recorded sound archives	GAUNT, Sandra L.	(OH)	423
Recorded sound cataloging	GAUNT, Sandra L.	(OH)	423
Recorded sound collections	STEEL, Suzanne F.	(MS)	1183
Recorded sound research & training	GAUNT, Sandra L.	(OH)	423
Sound archives	ROTH, Stacy F.	(NJ)	1059
	BLUTH, John F.	(PA)	108
Sound archives, restoration	FRANK, Mortimer H.	(NY)	397
Sound archiving	SERCOMBE, Laurel	(WA)	1116
Sound music publishing	BOBB, Barry L.	(MO)	108
Sound recording	GRAY, Michael H.	(DC)	460
Sound recording cataloging & databases	KLINGER, William E.	(OH)	661
Sound recording collection development	SAUNDERS, Sharon K.	(PA)	1084
Sound recording history & technology	KLINGER, William E.	(OH)	661
Sound recording indexing	CALDWELL, John M.	(PA)	172
Sound recordings	COLBY, Edward E.	(CA)	230
	FARRINGTON, James	(CT)	365
	WARREN, Richard	(CT)	1306
	MILLER, Anthony G.	(GA)	835
	EPSTEIN, Dena J.	(IL)	351
	NELSON, Brenda	(IN)	893
	JOHNSON, Ellen S.	(KS)	604
	GAGNON, Ronald A.	(MA)	412
	PRISTASH, Kenneth	(MA)	993
	WELIVER, E D.	(MI)	1321
	BOWERS, Sherri	(NY)	121
	KENSELAAR, Robert	(NY)	642
	LEW, Susan	(NY)	722
	PIZER, Charles R.	(NY)	977
	PIZER, Elizabeth F.	(NY)	977
	VOLLONO, Millicent D.	(NY)	1288
	WELLS, Phyllis L.	(NY)	1323
	WELLS, Paul R.	(TN)	1323
	MILLER, Karl F.	(TX)	839
	ELSTE, R O.	(WGR)	346
Sound recordings books	MAWHINNEY, Paul C.	(PA)	787
Sound recordings cataloging	NUZZO, Nancy B.	(NY)	912
	FOLLET, Robert E.	(TX)	388
Sound recordings collection	ROSENBURG, Betsy R.	(CT)	1056
Sound recordings collection development	EARNEST, Jeffrey D.	(AR)	332
	FOLLET, Robert E.	(TX)	388
Sound recordings collections	ERICSON, Margaret D.	(NY)	353
Sound recordings databases	MAWHINNEY, Paul C.	(PA)	787
Sound restoration	SMOLIAN, Steven J.	(MD)	1162
Visual & sound material acquisition	DRIESSEN, Karen C.	(MT)	320
Visual & sound material reference	DRIESSEN, Karen C.	(MT)	320

SOURCES (See also Resources)

Art & architectural documtn sources	ROBERTSON, Jack	(MD)	1042
Business & computer information sources	AHERN, Camille P.	(NH)	8
Business & marketing information sources	STEPIEN, Karen K.	(NJ)	1189
Business & patent sources	GALBRAITH, Barry E.	(NY)	413

SOURCES (Cont'd)

Business & religious reference sources	FEW, John E.	(CA)	374
Business information sources	STANYON, Kelly	(CT)	1181
	JACOBS, Leslie R.	(MA)	589
Business information sources & research	CVELJO, Katherine	(TX)	268
Business reference sources	EDWARDS, Betty	(MA)	337
	CARMACK, Norma J.	(TX)	183
Business sources	LOOMIS, Mary K.	(CT)	740
	MUTCH, Donald G.	(ON)	883
Canadian business information sources	KING, Alan S.	(ME)	650
Chemical databases & sources	GALBRAITH, Barry E.	(NY)	413
Civil War, North Carolina sources, units	WOODARD, John R.	(NC)	1365
Communications sources	ARNESON, Rosemary H.	(VA)	33
Computer info sources, end-user systems	GODT, Carol	(MO)	443
Corporate information sources	JACKSON, Craig A.	(ON)	587
Corporate sources	GRAY, Sandra A.	(ON)	460
Drug information sources	SEWELL, Winifred	(MD)	1118
Educational sources	STURM, Rebecca R.	(KY)	1205
Engineering information sources	PATIENCE, Alice	(OH)	947
Environmental sources	VAN BRUNT, Amy S.	(NY)	1272
Environmental sources & databases	HOTZ, Sharon M.	(CA)	562
Filing source code documentation	BOZE, Lucy G.	(GA)	124
Filing source code listings	BOZE, Lucy G.	(GA)	124
Financial reference sources	STONER, Ronald P.	(IL)	1198
Fine arts & architecture sources	SPENCER, Deirdre D.	(FL)	1173
Foundation sources	JOHNSEN-HARRIS, Amy	(RI)	602
German legal sources	MENZEL, William H.	(NY)	825
Government information sources	CROWLEY, Terence	(CA)	262
Health care information sources	MESSERLE, Judith R.	(MO)	828
Humanities sources & services	WINCKLER, Paul A.	(NY)	1354
Information sources & services	PIERCE, Sydney J.	(GA)	972
	TAYLOR, Margaret T.	(MI)	1227
	ESTES, Glenn E.	(TN)	355
Information sources & utilization	VOIGT, Melvin J.	(CA)	1287
Insurance sources	KUCSMA, Susan P.	(NY)	682
International information sources	WILLIAMS, Robert V.	(SC)	1346
Local history sources	GRABOWSKI, John J.	(OH)	455
Materials cataloging & sourcing	LOWELL, Brian V.	(IL)	744
Medical information sources	TEITELBAUM, Sandra D.	(MD)	1230
Medical reference sources	HANKS, Ellen T.	(TX)	496
Microcomputer information sources	MAYER, Erich J.	(NY)	789
New Orleans historical sources	HARDY, D C.	(LA)	500
Plastics industry information sources	KANE, Nancy J.	(MA)	625
Recorded & braille materials & sources	WILSON, Barbara L.	(RI)	1350
Reference, business sources	MACKEY, Wendy W.	(MA)	757
Reference sources	HASELWOOD, Eldon L.	(NE)	510
Reference sources & services	HARLAN, Robert D.	(CA)	502
	ROPER, Fred W.	(SC)	1054
	MEHRAD, Jafar	(IRN)	821
Researcher for private funding sources	ROBERTSON, Ina N.	(IL)	1042
Science information sources	WOOD, Judith B.	(NC)	1364
Science reference sources	LOCKHART, Carol A.	(MO)	736
Searching & retrieving archival sources	FALK, Candace S.	(CA)	362
Social sciences information sources	CONGER, Lucinda D.	(DC)	236
Sources & services in sci & technology	COOPER, Marianne	(NY)	243
Sources in women's studies	SMITH, Ellen A.	(OH)	1154
Sources of business information	OSWALD, Edward E.	(FL)	929
Sources of cartographic materials	MINTON, James O.	(AZ)	846
Sources of visual aids	WILSON, Barbara L.	(RI)	1350
Sourcing	FELDMAN, Linda A.	(IL)	369
Statistical sources	BILLINGSLEY, Andrew G.	(ON)	96
Utility information sources	KING, Alan S.	(ME)	650

SOUTH

Asia & South Pacific	WARPHEA, Rita C.	(VA)	1306
Collection development in South Asia	SEN, Joyce H.	(NY)	1115
Social sciences, South Asia	WOOD, Ann L.	(MA)	1363
South Africa	CASON, Maidel K.	(DE)	193
South American literature	WELCH, Thomas L.	(DC)	1321
South & Southeast Asia	HARPER, Marie F.	(AL)	503

SOUTH (Cont'd)

South Asian area studies	NELSON, David N.	(ND)	893
South Asian bibliography	NYE, James H.	(IL)	912
South Asian bibliography & research	SEN, Joyce H.	(NY)	1115
South Pacific studies	CREELY, Kathryn L.	(CA)	257
South Texas history	MITTELSTAEDT, Gerard E.	(TX)	850
Southern library history	CARMICHAEL, James V.	(NC)	183
Southern Lutheran history	FRITZ, William R.	(SC)	405
USSR, Asia, South American, Europe art	BLAIR, Madeline S.	(DC)	102

SOUTH CAROLINA

South Carolina history	SALMON, Robin R.	(SC)	1077
South Carolina Supreme Court	BARDIN, Angela D.	(SC)	56

SOUTHEAST

South & Southeast Asia	HARPER, Marie F.	(AL)	503
Southeast Asia	DUTTON, Lee S.	(IL)	329
	MILLER, David A.	(OH)	836
Southeast Asian languages	HICKEY, John T.	(NY)	536
Southeast Asian reference services	ASHMUN, Lawrence F.	(NY)	36
Southeast Asian studies	KOH, Siew B.	(IL)	668
	ASHMUN, Lawrence F.	(NY)	36
	BARNWELL, Jane L.	(OR)	58
Southeast Asian studies bibliography	GAMER, May L.	(MO)	416
Southeast Asian technical services	ASHMUN, Lawrence F.	(NY)	36

SOUTHWEST

American Southwest	KLIMIADES, Mario N.	(AZ)	661
Literature of American Southwest	BROGDEN, Stephen R.	(IA)	139
Southwest Afro-American	STEPHENS, Alonzo T.	(TN)	1187
Southwest collections	MILLER, Bryan M.	(NM)	836
Southwest history, reference services	D'ANTONIO, Lynn M.	(AZ)	274
Southwestern literature	POWELL, Lawrence C.	(AZ)	988

SOVIET UNION (See also Russian, Ukrainian)

Eastern Europe & Soviet Union	TOTH, George S.	(DC)	1252
History of Russian, Soviet bibliography	WHITBY, Thomas J.	(CO)	1330
Russian & Soviet studies	WERTHEIMER, Marilyn L.	(CO)	1325
Soviet film history	DAY, Martha T.	(VT)	282
Soviet science & technology	MARCUS, Stephanie M.	(DC)	769
Soviet Union	WYNAR, Bohdan S.	(CO)	1375
USSR, Asia, South American, Europe art	BLAIR, Madeline S.	(DC)	102

SOYBEAN

Soybean production, mktg, & utilization	GIBSON, Marianne	(MO)	432

SOYFOODS

Soyfoods market research	GOLBITZ, Peter	(ME)	444
	KINGMA, Sharyn L.	(ME)	652
Soyfoods product development	GOLBITZ, Peter	(ME)	444
	KINGMA, Sharyn L.	(ME)	652

SPACE (See also Aerospace, Architecture, Building, Construction, Design, Facilities, Interiors, Layout)

Administration, personnel, budget, space	ROSENFELD, Mary A.	(DC)	1056
Air & space law	FOX, James R.	(PA)	394
Building & space planning	CLARK, Alice S.	(CA)	216
	ROHLF, Robert H.	(MN)	1050
	WATERS, Richard L.	(TX)	1308
Building planning & space allocation	RAWLEY, Wayne	(IA)	1010
Building programs & space utilization	PALMATIER, Susan M.	(NH)	936
Building, space planning	MCKEE, Christopher	(IA)	810
	TELATNIK, George M.	(NY)	1230
Buildings & space planning	SIGLER, Ronald F.	(CA)	1137
Children's services & space needs	WARGO, Peggy M.	(CT)	1305
Civil, military, space databases	GAZZOLA, Kenneth E.	(DC)	424
Collection & space management	DUNN, Jamie N.	(MN)	326

SPACE (Cont'd)

Consulting, library space planning	SCHWARZ, Shirlee	(CT)	1105
Furniture, shelving, space planning	WATSON, Joyce N.	(ON)	1309
Law library space planning	CHICK, Cynthia L.	(CA)	208
	RAE, E A.	(ON)	1002
Library design & space planning	DAVIS, Glenn G.	(IL)	279
Library furniture & space planning	GRANT, Robert S.	(MI)	458
Library furniture, space planning	TUCKER, Richard B.	(NH)	1262
Library interior space planning	STEWART, John D.	(VA)	1192
Library space design	D'ANGELO, Paul P.	(NY)	272
Library space planning	SCHAFER, Jay G.	(CO)	1089
	BATTEN, Henry R.	(GA)	64
	O'BRIEN, Marjorie S.	(MA)	914
	BOWLES, Nancy J.	(NY)	121
	VINCENT-DAVISS, Diana	(NY)	1284
	METZENBACHER, Gary W.	(OR)	828
	GARRISON, Guy G.	(PA)	420
	MITTAG, Erika	(TX)	850
Library space planning, construction	NEIKIRK, Harold D.	(MD)	892
Moving & space planning	BALKIN, Ruth G.	(NY)	52
	GOLDMAN, Martha A.	(NY)	445
Planning & reorganizing library space	WORTHINGTON, A P.	(CA)	1369
Program & space planning	EHRHORN, Jean H.	(HI)	339
Space management	D'ALESSANDRO, Edward A.	(DC)	270
Space planning	COOPER, Richard S.	(CA)	243
	WALLACE, Marie G.	(CA)	1297
	COCO, Al	(CO)	226
	MARIANI, Carolyn A.	(CT)	770
	WARD, Victoria M.	(DC)	1304
	ALFRED, Judith C.	(IN)	13
	POSTLEWAIT, Cheryl A.	(KS)	986
	LEARY, Margaret R.	(MI)	707
	AXEL-LUTE, Paul	(NJ)	42
	ANDERSON, Carol L.	(NY)	22
	FREIFELD, Roberta I.	(NY)	401
	MASYR, Caryl L.	(NY)	783
	HARVAN, Christine C.	(PA)	509
	PIERCE, William S.	(PA)	972
	ROACH, Linda	(PA)	1038
	CEBRUN, Mary J.	(TX)	196
	DAHLGREN, Jean E.	(TX)	269
	HELBURN, Judith D.	(TX)	523
	HOOTON, Virginia A.	(TX)	557
	CADA, Elizabeth J.	(ON)	170
Space planning & design	TEICH, Steven	(OR)	1230
Space planning & development	JOHNSON, Timothy J.	(IL)	609
Space planning & moving libraries	FOX, Marylou P.	(CA)	395
Space planning & utilization	NELSON, Norman L.	(OK)	895
	MCADAMS, Nancy R.	(TX)	792
Space planning facilities	FRALEY, Ruth A.	(NY)	395
Space planning, legal	MOYER, Holley M.	(NJ)	874
Space planning, management	KENDRICK, Curtis L.	(NY)	640
Space planning of law libraries	WELKER, Kathy J.	(OH)	1321
Space reutilization	BELLIN, Bernard E.	(WI)	78
Space utilization	JACKSON, Susan M.	(IL)	588
	SAWYER, Miriam	(NJ)	1086
	KRABBE, Natalie	(OR)	674

SPANISH (See also Catalan, Chicano, Hispanic, Iberia, Mexican (American))

Bilingual services in Spanish	DIAZ, Magna M.	(PA)	299
Cataloging Italian & Spanish books	CHANG, Roselyne M.	(DC)	201
Cataloging Spanish materials	LABODDA, Marsha J.	(TX)	686
Juvenile books in Spanish	SCHON, Isabel	(AZ)	1098
Library services to the Spanish speaking	TSCHERNY, Elena	(DC)	1260
Service to Spanish speaking	MILLER, Elissa R.	(CA)	837
Services to Spanish speaking	RIVERA, Gregorio	(NY)	1037
	CROMER, Kenneth L.	(OH)	260
Spanish & Latin American bibliography	MORENO, Rafael	(PA)	863
Spanish & Latin American collections	BARZELATTO, Elba G.	(NJ)	62
Spanish & Portuguese languages	NEUGEBAUER, Rhonda L.	(KS)	897
Spanish archivist	LEMMON, Alfred E.	(LA)	715
Spanish bibliographies	CORREDOR, Javier	(TX)	247

SPANISH (Cont'd)

Spanish collection development	PAREDES-RUIZ, Eudoxio B.	(SK)	940
	CARDENAS, Mary E.	(SAF)	180
Spanish documents	DRIVER, Marjorie G.	(GU)	320
Spanish language acquisitions	PETERSON, Anita R.	(CA)	962
Spanish language & literature	COLLAZO, Maria L.	(PR)	232
Spanish language cataloging	JAVONOVICH, Kenneth L.	(IL)	595
Spanish language children's books	ZWICK, Louise Y.	(TX)	1392
Spanish language collection	CHAVEZ, Linda	(CA)	204
Spanish language collection development	SIMAS, Therese C.	(CA)	1139
	BETANCOURT, Ingrid T.	(NJ)	92
Spanish language collections	CADY, Steven R.	(CA)	170
Spanish language materials	NAVARRO, Frank A.	(CA)	889
	ANDERSON, Mark	(TX)	24
Spanish language services	PISANO, Vivian M.	(CA)	975
Spanish law	GONZALEZ, Armando E.	(DC)	448
Spanish literature	CHU, Felix T.	(IL)	212
Spanish materials	CALIMANO, Ivan E.	(TX)	173
Spanish printing & publishing	RAMER, James D.	(AL)	1005
Translation Spanish to English	DRIVER, Marjorie G.	(GU)	320

SPEAKING (See also Lecturing)

Book reviewer & speaker	GLATT, Carol R.	(NJ)	440
Choral speaking direction	ANTHONY, Rose M.	(WI)	29
Librarians & public speaking	MCPEAK, James J.	(OH)	817
Library services to the Spanish speaking	TSCHERNY, Elena	(DC)	1260
Motivational & informational speaker	LYNCH, Minnie L.	(LA)	752
Public speaking & workshops	GRAUER, Sally M.	(NY)	458
Public speaking training	BARKER, Lillian H.	(MD)	56
Public technical speaking	KAMINECKI, Ronald M.	(IL)	624
Sales & speaker	WILBUR, Helen L.	(NY)	1338
Service to Spanish speaking	MILLER, Elissa R.	(CA)	837
Services to Spanish speaking	CROMER, Kenneth L.	(OH)	260
Speaker on censorships	HORN, Zoia	(CA)	559
Speaking	X, Laura	(CA)	1376
	SCHRAG, Dale R.	(KS)	1099
	BERKLUND, Nancy J.	(MI)	87
Speaking & consulting	REID, Judith P.	(DC)	1018
Speaking on library services	NELSON, Maggie E.	(IL)	894
Speaking on local history	NELSON, Maggie E.	(IL)	894
Speaking, writing, automation	JOHNSON, Pat M.	(TX)	608

SPECIAL (See also Disabled, Exceptional, Handicapped)

Administrative special programs	FELLA, Sarah C.	(OR)	370
Adult special services	KRAMPITZ, Barbara E.	(NY)	676
Library promotion & spcl programming	WARREN, Catherine S.	(MS)	1306
Library service for special populations	DALTON, Phyllis I.	(NV)	271
Library service to special populations	KIRSCHENBAUM, Arthur S.	(DC)	655
Outreach services to special groups	HAABNIIT, Ene	(BC)	480
Outreach to special populations	REILLY, Carol H.	(NC)	1020
Promotions & special projects	THORSEN, Jeanne M.	(WA)	1242
Rare & special collection	PERSHE, Frank F.	(MO)	961
Service to special groups	VIGNOVICH, Ray L.	(WI)	1284
Service to special populations	CUNNINGHAM, William D.	(MD)	265
	JOHNSON, Nancy B.	(NY)	608
Service to special populations & seniors	RICKERT, Carol A.	(IL)	1032
Service to special users	LANG, Jovian P.	(NY)	695
Services for special populations	MARKARIAN, Rita J.	(NY)	771
Services to special groups teaching	WHALEN, Lucille	(NY)	1328
Services to special populations	SPAZIANI, Carol	(IA)	1172
	MCCONNELL, Lorelei C.	(NJ)	797
Special activities programming	MACINICK, James W.	(NY)	755
Special & institutional libraries	GRAY, Karen S.	(IL)	460
Special & outreach library services	PARTRIDGE, James C.	(MD)	945
Special art & architecture librarianship	BEGLO, Jo N.	(ON)	74
Special art collections	NESBURG, Janet A.	(MI)	896
Special col management & appraisal	WEISS, Egon A.	(NY)	1320
Special collections & special libraries	MATHEWS, Richard B.	(FL)	784
Spcl cols exploitation internationally	HEANEY, Henry J.	(SCT)	518
Special Dutch heritage center	SLIEKERS, Hendrik	(IL)	1149
Special education	HAYNES, Douglas E.	(NM)	516
Special education & rehabilitation	VELLEMAN, Ruth A.	(NY)	1281
Special education classes	TEEGARDEN, Maude B.	(KY)	1229

SPECIAL (Cont'd)

Special education libraries	DINNESEN, Peter H.	(OH)	305
Special education personnel development	RUDDOCK, Velda I.	(CA)	1065
Special events	BRENNAN, Deborah B.	(RI)	132
Special events, fairs, & festivals	CHASE, William D.	(MI)	203
Special events promotion	GOODRICH, Nita K.	(AZ)	449
Special focus database trainers	CARUSO, Nicholas C.	(PA)	190
Special government collection	KOCH, Patricia J.	(MT)	667
Special index databases	TSUI, Josephine	(ON)	1260
Special interest packages	COURTOT, Marilyn E.	(MD)	251
Special languages cataloging	MCCLOY, William B.	(IN)	797
Special libraries	MCCALLUM, David L.	(ON)	793
Special material cataloging	KROSCH, Penelope S.	(MN)	680
Special music bibliographies	LYON, Bruce C.	(FL)	752
Special newspaper libraries	BANKS, Marie M.	(OH)	54
Special physical education	GRIFFITH, Joan C.	(NH)	469
Special populations	RAZZANO, Barbara W.	(NJ)	1012
	KLAUBER, Julie B.	(NY)	658
Special products production	ROTHSCHILD, M C.	(VA)	1060
Special programs	NICHOLS, Dolores D.	(TN)	901
Special programs of services for deaf	STEELE, Leah J.	(IL)	1184
Special programs, public relations	LARSON, Josephine	(NC)	699
Special projects	MCWHORTER, Jimmie M.	(AL)	818
	PARK, Dona F.	(IA)	941
	ENGLISH, Cynthia J.	(MA)	350
	KONESKI-WHITE, Bonnie L.	(MA)	670
	JONES, Kendra A.	(TN)	613
	ALTHEN, Elsa E.	(VA)	18
	ROUSSEAU, Denis	(PQ)	1061
Special projects management	FARLEY, Alfred E.	(KS)	364
Special projects research, automation	RHYNAS, Don M.	(ON)	1026
Special reference	POSEY, Sussann F.	(MD)	985
Special search services	JOHNSON, Everett J.	(DC)	604
Special services	MOHR, Mary C.	(AZ)	852
	PLACE, Philip A.	(FL)	977
	TABEN, Eva M.	(NY)	1219
	HERZ, Michael J.	(VI)	534
	DUPERREAULT, Marilyn J.	(SK)	327
Special small library administration	BODNAR, Marta	(ON)	109
Special subject education cataloging	VERMA, Prem V.	(WV)	1282
State, special & public lib consulting	PHILLIPS, Ray S.	(TX)	969

SPECIAL COLLECTIONS

Alternative library, special collection	ANDREWS, Margaret	(MA)	27
American Indian special collections	THIEL, Mark G.	(WI)	1235
Archives & special collections	MCCRANK, Lawrence J.	(AL)	800
	CRAFT, Guy C.	(GA)	254
	MEADOR, Patricia L.	(LA)	819
	STEEL, Suzanne F.	(MS)	1183
	OSBORNE, Nancy S.	(NY)	927
	MCCALLUM, Brenda W.	(OH)	793
Art special collections	CASHMAN, Norine D.	(RI)	192
Automating special collections	WEAVER, Thomas M.	(DC)	1312
Automation of special collections	SMITH, David F.	(NY)	1154
	LLOYD, James B.	(TN)	735
Children's material special collections	DURSTON, Corinne L.	(BC)	329
Commercial use of special collections	KANE, Katherine	(CO)	625
Little magazines, special collections	FOX, Willard	(LA)	395
Manuscripts & special collections	SNIFFIN-MARINO, Megan G.	(MA)	1163
	CORSARO, James	(NY)	248
Organizing special collections	ROSENSHIELD, Jill K.	(WI)	1057
Rare books & special collections	WALCOTT, M A.	(FL)	1294
	BROWN, Norman B.	(IL)	146
	TUCHMAN, Maurice S.	(MA)	1261
	GOLDSBERG, Elizabeth D.	(MD)	446
	RAME, Mary E.	(NY)	1005
	SZMUK, Szilvia E.	(NY)	1218
	ZAFREN, Herbert C.	(OH)	1385
	POST, Jeremiah B.	(PA)	986
	RAINWATER, Jean M.	(RI)	1004
	BJORKLUND, Edi	(WI)	100
	MILLER, Beth M.	(ON)	836
Rare books, special collections	SPONDER, Dorothy R.	(DC)	1175
	JONES, Christine S.	(TN)	611
Reference services & special collections	CORSARO, James	(NY)	248

SPECIAL COLLECTIONS (Cont'd)

Reference, special collections	MCQUAIL, Edward J.	(WV)	817
Special collection administration	LEACH, Sally S.	(TX)	706
Special collection cataloging	LANE, Mary J.	(LA)	694
Special collection development	SMITH, Marvin E.	(CA)	1158
	TOCH, Terryann	(DC)	1248
	GROVER, Wilma S.	(FL)	474
	PETERSON, Denise D.	(OK)	963
Special collection for church groups	VANDEGRIFT, J R.	(DC)	1273
Special collection library systems	COLEMAN, David E.	(HI)	231
Special collections	PRUITT, Paul M.	(AL)	996
	DABRISHUS, Michael J.	(AR)	269
	ALLEN, Doris L.	(CA)	14
	BRISCOE, Peter M.	(CA)	136
	CHURUKIAN, Araxie P.	(CA)	213
	DAVIS, Charles E.	(CA)	278
	DMOHOWSKI, Joseph F.	(CA)	306
	HANFF, Peter E.	(CA)	495
	MCPHERON, William	(CA)	817
	STREETER, David	(CA)	1201
	SUNDSTRAND, Jacquelyn K.	(CA)	1210
	BOYD, Ruth E.	(CO)	122
	NEWMAN, John	(CO)	899
	BROWN, William E.	(CT)	148
	MARTZ, David J.	(DC)	779
	RUSSELL, John T.	(DC)	1069
	SCHREYER, Alice D.	(DE)	1100
	SAGE-GAGNE, Waneta	(FL)	1074
	SKALLERUP, Harry R.	(FL)	1145
	LESLIE, Elizabeth J.	(GA)	718
	MONTGOMERY, David E.	(IA)	856
	SHIPE, Timothy R.	(IA)	1131
	WIESE, Glenda C.	(IA)	1337
	BAMBERGER, Mary A.	(IL)	53
	LANIER, Donald L.	(IL)	696
	MEYER, Daniel	(IL)	830
	ROBISON, Carley R.	(IL)	1045
	BOGAN, Mary E.	(KS)	110
	THOMPSON, Mary A.	(KS)	1240
	ROBERTS, Gerald F.	(KY)	1040
	MARTIN, Robert S.	(LA)	778
	BATES, Susie M.	(MA)	64
	FRIEDMAN, Fred T.	(MA)	403
	LYDON, Mary E.	(MA)	751
	STRAND, Bethany	(MA)	1200
	WARRINGTON, David R.	(MA)	1307
	CURTIS, Peter H.	(MD)	267
	FARREN, Donald	(MD)	365
	FITZPATRICK, Kelly	(MD)	383
	GILLESPIE, David M.	(MD)	435
	PARASCANDOLA, John L.	(MD)	939
	HALL, Lawrence E.	(MI)	488
	NAIRN, Charles E.	(MI)	886
	GREENE, Mark A.	(MN)	464
	KUKLA, Edward R.	(MN)	683
	JONES, Dolores B.	(MS)	612
	LATOUR, Terry S.	(MS)	701
	VERICH, Thomas M.	(MS)	1282
	CADLE, Dean	(NC)	170
	CARMICHAEL, James V.	(NC)	183
	GRENDLER, Marcella	(NC)	467
	JONES, H G.	(NC)	613
	MILLER, Lewis R.	(NC)	840
	PHILBECK, Jo S.	(NC)	967
	TOOMER, Clarence	(NC)	1251
	YORK, Maurice C.	(NC)	1381
	BROWN, Stanley W.	(NH)	147
	MADDEN, Robert J.	(NH)	758
	FERGUSON, Stephen	(NJ)	372
	GRAHAM, Peter S.	(NJ)	456
	JOYCE, William L.	(NJ)	618
	LATINI, Samuel A.	(NJ)	701
	WALKER, Mary J.	(NM)	1296
	CLARK, Diane A.	(NY)	216
	DEVENISH-CASSEL, Ann W.	(NY)	297
	DOYAL, Patricia A.	(NY)	317
	EVANS, Ruth A.	(NY)	358

SPECIAL COLLECTIONS (Cont'd)
Special collections

FINCH, C H.	....	(NY)	377
HARRIS, Carolyn L.	.....	(NY)	504
HIGGINS, Virginia A.	...	(NY)	538
SEEMANN, Ann M.	....	(NY)	1111
WASYLENKO, Lydia W.	.	(NY)	1308
BRANDT, Michael H.	...	(OH)	128
ORAM, Richard W.	.....	(OH)	925
SCHOONMAKER, Dina B.		(OH)	1098
BENDER, Nathan E.	....	(OK)	79
BLEDSOE, Kathleen E.	..	(OK)	105
HUTTNER, Sidney F.	...	(OK)	579
JONES, Charles E.	....	(OK)	611
BROWN, Charlotte B.	...	(PA)	142
FULLER, Edward H.	.....	(PA)	408
LEVITT, Martin L.	......	(PA)	721
MANN, Charles W.	.....	(PA)	766
REPP, Robert M.	.....	(PA)	1024
STALLARD, Kathryn E.	..	(PA)	1179
TANIS, James R.	......	(PA)	1222
ZABROSKY, Frank A.	..	(PA)	1385
COLLAZO, Maria L.	....	(PR)	232
GONZALEZ-VELEZ, Isaura	(PR)		448
DUPLAIX, Sally T.	......	(RI)	327
CLAYTON, J G.	....	(SC)	220
KOHL, Michael F.	......	(SC)	668
GOLDSMITH, Arthur	...	(TN)	446
GRENGA, Kathy A.	....	(TN)	467
ATKINS, Winston	....	(TX)	38
FRANKUM, Katherine H.		(TX)	398
PAYNE, John R.	....	(TX)	951
WACHTER-NELSON, Ruth M.	....	(TX)	1290
BACHMAN, Katherine H.		(VA)	43
BOONE, Edward J.	......	(VA)	115
JACOB, John N.	......	(VA)	589
KOPP, James J.	....	(WA)	671
REESE, Gary F.	....	(WA)	1016
KOVAN, Allan S.	......	(WI)	673
KRUEGER, Gerald J.	....	(WI)	680
ARMSTRONG, Fredrick H.		(WV)	32
NATHANSON, David	...	(WV)	889
KOTIN, David B.	....	(ON)	673

Special collections administration
MULLANE, William H.	..	(AZ)	877
ZEIDBERG, David S.	....	(CA)	1387
GORDON, Vesta L.	.....	(VA)	452
KIMBALL, Gregg D.	....	(VA)	649
CUTHBERT, John A.	...	(WV)	267

Special collections & archives
ABRAHAM, Terry	....	(ID)	3
SPRANKLE, Anita T.	...	(PA)	1176
TATUM, George M.	....	(VA)	1225

Special collections & development
KASPERSON, Jeanne X.		(MA)	629

Special collections & special libraries
MATHEWS, Richard B.	..	(FL)	784

Special collections, archives
ROBBINS, Louise S.	...	(OK)	1039

Special collections, automotive
HELVERSON, Louis G.	...	(PA)	525

Special collections cataloging
HERMAN, Elizabeth	....	(CA)	531
PODESCHI, John B.	....	(IL)	979
CHAPERO, Alicia	......	(NY)	201

Special collections catlgng & retrieval
KELLY, John P.	....	(NJ)	638

Special collections development
MULLANE, William H.	..	(AZ)	877
KELLER, William B.	....	(DC)	636
CHAPERO, Alicia	......	(NY)	201

Special collections including archives
HOLLAND, Mary M.	....	(TX)	551

Special collections, rare books
SAHAK, Judy H.	......	(CA)	1075
MENGES, Gary L.	.....	(WA)	824

Special collections, rare books, archive
NAINIS, Linda	....	(DC)	886

Theatre special collection
COUCH, Nena L.	......	(OH)	250

SPECIAL LIBRARIES

Academic & special lib administration	BOWDEN, Philip L.	......	(IL)	120
Academic & special library management	PHINNEY, Hartley K.	....	(CO)	969
Academic, research, & special libraries	YASSA, Lucie M.	......	(CA)	1378
Architectural special library materials	STEWARD, Martha J.	..	(CA)	1192
Consultant, public, special libraries	WILLIAMS, Edwin E.	....	(CT)	1343
Designing special library systems	HAUSRATH, Donald C.	.	(NY)	513

SPECIAL LIBRARIES (Cont'd)

Establishing special libraries	WITMER, Tonya C.	....	(KS)	1358
General management, small special lib	GALLUP, Jane H.	....	(DC)	415
General special library operations	NEILSON, Ann	....	(ON)	892
Info center & special lib management	COOPER, Marianne	....	(NY)	243
Institution or special libraries	HOFFMAN, Frank W.	...	(TX)	548
Library systems for special libraries	SMITH, Adelaide M.	....	(NY)	1152
Management of special libraries	WINQUIST, Elaine W.	..	(MA)	1355
Management of special library	PALMISANO-DRUCKER, Elsalyn	....	(NJ)	937
Managing small special libraries	KAMICHAITIS, Penelope H.	....	(PQ)	624
	LUPPINO, Julie B.	......	(SC)	749
Marketing special libraries	CVELJO, Katherine	.....	(TX)	268
Medical & special libraries	SMITH-GREENWOLD, Kathryn R.	....	(NY)	1162
Medical & special library collections	SPARKS, Marie C.	......	(IN)	1171
Medical special librarianship	HALL, Elizabeth L.	.....	(WI)	487
Microcomputers in special libraries	WHELAN, Julia S.	....	(MA)	1329
One-person special libraries	HOLTON, Janet E.	....	(CO)	555
One-person special library	MIKSICEK, Barbara L.	..	(MO)	834
	MARSHAK, Bonnie L.	..	(NY)	773
Organization of special libraries	WOOLF, Amy K.	......	(KS)	1368
	MCCONNIE, Mary	....	(TRN)	798
Organizing small special libraries	MCMANAMON, Mary J.	.	(MA)	814
Personal computers in special libraries	DUNCAN, Rebecca	....	(CA)	325
Professional & special library direction	ROTHMAN, Marilyn R.	..	(CO)	1060
Science special libraries	HILL, Susan E.	....	(TX)	540
Small special libraries	CIBOCH, Lorraine A.	....	(WI)	214
Small special libraries consulting	HAMILTON, Patricia J.	..	(SD)	492
Small special library administration	CLARK, Jane F.	....	(GA)	217
Small special library organization	BEAL, Gretchen F.	.....	(TN)	68
Small special library supervision	DAYHOFF, Judith A.	...	(CO)	283
Special librarianship	NEWCOMER, Susan N.	.	(CA)	898
	POSNIAK, John R.	....	(DC)	985
	BIERBAUM, Esther G.	...	(IA)	95
	MELTON, Emily I.	......	(IL)	823
	LOGAN, Mary A.	......	(MD)	737
	HESS, Stanley W.	.....	(MO)	534
	PARTRIDGE, Cathleen F.		(UT)	945
	ARNOLD, Barbara J.	...	(WI)	33
	PARSONS, Patricia S.	..	(WI)	945
	TEES, Miriam H.	....	(PQ)	1229
	SLINEY, Marjory T.	.....	(IRE)	1149
Special librarianship & bibliography	BRITT, Mary C.	.....	(AL)	137
Special libraries	HURTT, Betty D.	....	(AL)	578
	SCHLOSSER, Anne G.	.	(CA)	1094
	MYERS, Victoria B.	....	(DE)	885
	BRESLAUER, Lester M.	.	(FL)	133
	ADAMSHICK, Robert D.	.	(IL)	6
	CHAPLAN, Margaret A.	.	(IL)	201
	FORD, Jennifer D.	.....	(IL)	389
	FRANKLIN, Annette E.	..	(IL)	397
	KING, David E.	....	(IL)	650
	SHOTWELL, Richard T.	.	(IL)	1133
	CHRISTIANSON, Elin B.		(IN)	212
	WHITE, Herbert S.	.....	(IN)	1331
	RICHMOND, Robert W.	.	(KS)	1031
	PASKOFF, Beth M.	....	(LA)	946
	PRESTON, Margaret P.	.	(MA)	992
	JOHNSON, Susan W.	..	(MD)	609
	ASPNES, Grieg G.	.....	(MN)	37
	MCINERNEY, Claire R.	.	(MN)	809
	GOLDMAN, Teri B.	....	(MO)	446
	BALLARD, Robert M.	...	(NC)	53
	HOWARD, Susanna J.	..	(NC)	564
	OLSON, Eric J.	....	(NC)	922
	ANDREWS, Margaret D.	.	(NY)	27
	COPLEN, Ron	....	(NY)	244
	GESKE, Aina S.	....	(NY)	430
	MOUNT, Ellis	....	(NY)	873
	REGAN, Muriel	....	(NY)	1017
	VAILLANCOURT, Pauline M.	....	(NY)	1271
	ROBIN, Annabeth	......	(OK)	1043
	DETLEFSEN, Ellen G.	..	(PA)	296
	KLINE, Eve P.	....	(PA)	661
	PLASO, Kathy A.	....	(PA)	977

SPECIAL LIBRARIES (Cont'd)

Subject	Name	State	Page
Special libraries	ROOT, Deane L.	(PA)	1054
	BILLINSKY, Christyn G.	(SC)	96
	JETT, Don W.	(TN)	600
	CEBRUN, Mary J.	(TX)	196
	JACKSON, Eugene B.	(TX)	587
	JACKSON, Ruth L.	(TX)	588
	MARTIN, Jean K.	(TX)	776
	MCCANN, Debra W.	(TX)	794
	REIFEL, Louie E.	(TX)	1019
	WISE, Olga B.	(TX)	1357
	HUMMEL, Ray O.	(VA)	573
	BLUE, Richard I.	(WI)	107
	MORGAN, Anne E.	(BC)	863
	PITERNICK, Anne B.	(BC)	976
	ANDERSON, Beryl L.	(ON)	21
	BASSETT, Betty A.	(ON)	63
	COONEY, Jane	(ON)	241
	FREEMAN, Elayne B.	(ON)	400
	WHITE, Janette H.	(ON)	1331
	PILLET, Sylvaine M.	(KEN)	973
	JONES, Roger A.	(SWZ)	615
Special libraries administration	FIRTH, Margaret A.	(MA)	379
	LEONARD, Ruth S.	(MA)	717
	COSKEY, Rosemary B.	(MD)	248
	SIGALA, Stephanie C.	(MO)	1137
	NORTON, Nancy P.	(TN)	910
Special libraries & collections	WATSON, Linda S.	(AL)	1309
Special libraries & information centers	STRABLE, Edward G.	(IL)	1199
Special libraries & services	SLAMKOWSKI, Donna L.	(MN)	1147
Special libraries automation	KALVINSKAS, Louanne A.	(CA)	623
Special libraries cataloging	ELROD, J M.	(BC)	346
Special libraries consultant	HUSBAND, Susan M.	(AZ)	578
Special libraries consulting	MCDONOUGH, Kathleen C.	(NH)	803
Special libraries management	SPURLOCK, Pauline	(CA)	1177
	ST. AUBIN, Kendra J.	(MA)	1075
	WILKINSON, William A.	(MO)	1340
	KING, Maryde F.	(NY)	651
	WILT, Charles F.	(OH)	1353
	VASILAKIS, Mary	(PA)	1279
	WILLIAMS, Robert V.	(SC)	1346
	OLIVETTI, L J.	(VA)	921
	STARR, Marian U.	(VA)	1182
Special libraries planning & development	ASTON, Jennefer	(IRE)	37
Special library	KLOSKY, Patricia W.	(DC)	662
	ASTORGA, Alicia M.	(DE)	37
	MAYER, Barbara D.	(NC)	789
Special library administration	MINTON, James O.	(AZ)	846
	ELMAN, Stanley A.	(CA)	345
	GOLDMAN, Nancy L.	(CA)	445
	SELZER, Nancy S.	(DE)	1114
	CULBERTSON, Diana L.	(IL)	263
	DAVIS, Elisabeth B.	(IL)	278
	KAYAIAN, Mary S.	(IL)	632
	MCNEILL, Janice M.	(IL)	816
	MOBLEY, Emily R.	(IN)	851
	TUTTLE, Walter A.	(NC)	1266
	VIXIE, Anne C.	(OR)	1286
	BOWLBY, Raynna M.	(RI)	121
	DUMAINE, Paul R.	(RI)	325
	BARLOGA, Carolyn J.	(WI)	57
	SUNDER-RAJ, P E.	(ON)	1210
Special library & archives management	CLASPER, James W.	(OH)	219
Special library automation	HARTT, Richard W.	(VA)	509
Special library cataloging	PYKE, Carol J.	(VA)	999
Special library collection development	POST, Linda C.	(CA)	986
Special library consulting	GOLDMAN, Ava R.	(FL)	445
	BARRISH, Alan S.	(KY)	60
	THOMAS, Margaret J.	(MI)	1237
	QUINTEN, Rebecca G.	(OH)	1000
	CARVER, Sue A.	(WA)	191
Special library department management	RYAN, Jenny L.	(NY)	1071
Special library design consulting	MAIN, Annette Z.	(PA)	761

SPECIAL LIBRARIES (Cont'd)

Subject	Name	State	Page
Special library development	ROSS, Mary A.	(CA)	1058
	STARESINA, Lois J.	(MI)	1181
	MORROW, Paula J.	(MO)	869
	DINNIMAN, Margo P.	(PA)	305
Special lib establishment & development	LOKETS BEISCHROT, Dina	(CT)	738
Special library general administration	AHRENSFELD, Jan	(IL)	8
Special library hospital settings	GROSS, Elinor L.	(NY)	472
Special library issues & management	MORRISON, Patricia	(CA)	868
Special library land use & planning	MARTINEZ, Barbara A.	(CA)	779
Special library management	ATKINSON, Calberta O.	(AL)	38
	CAMPBELL, Bill W.	(CA)	176
	COPPIN, Ann S.	(CA)	245
	HALEY, Roger K.	(DC)	486
	KNAUFF, Elisabeth S.	(DC)	663
	GOLDMAN, Ava R.	(FL)	445
	WHITESIDE, Lee A.	(FL)	1333
	MCDAVID, Sara J.	(GA)	801
	BERGER, Carol A.	(IL)	85
	FUKAI, Eiko	(IL)	408
	MICHAEL, Ann B.	(IL)	831
	SCHRAMM, Mary T.	(IL)	1099
	VELLIKY, Mary M.	(MI)	1281
	PRESTON, Jenny	(MO)	991
	CONNOLLY, Bruce E.	(NY)	237
	ERICKSON, Sandra E.	(NY)	352
	RATLIFF, Priscilla	(OH)	1009
	SPOHR, Cynthia L.	(OH)	1175
	HILL, Linda L.	(OK)	540
	PYKE, Carol J.	(VA)	999
	CAMPBELL, Corinne A.	(WA)	176
	CAMPBELL, Harry	(ON)	176
Special library, microelectronics	HARMON, Jacqueline B.	(TX)	502
Special library organization	OWEN, Karen V.	(VA)	931
	ROSS, Evelyn M.	(AB)	1058
	SNYDER, Elizabeth A.	(ENG)	1164
Special library organization & design	BURNS, Marie T.	(IL)	162
Special library organization, management	COOKE, Geraldine A.	(AB)	241
Special library planning	THOMAS, Margaret J.	(MI)	1237
	DEVERA, Rosalinda M.	(NY)	297
Special library planning, developing	SELZER, Nancy S.	(DE)	1114
Special library public service	GOLDMAN, Nancy L.	(CA)	445
Special library reference	UMANA, Christine J.	(MA)	1268
Special library services consulting	FUNK, Elizabeth A.	(PA)	410
Special library services evaluation	BERLIN, Arthur E.	(NH)	87
Special library software	HASKINS, Dawn A.	(OH)	510
Special library systems	SCHUTZBERG, Frances	(MA)	1103
	TROVER, Larry E.	(OH)	1258
	MURRAY, Lucia M.	(OR)	882
	FISHER, Daphne V.	(PA)	380
	LUMANDE, Edward	(ZAM)	748
Special library systems & procedures	CAMOZZI-EKBERG, Patricia L.	(WA)	175
Start-up of special libraries	GREENE, Danielle L.	(DC)	463
Supervising a special library	MCLAUGHLIN, Dorothy M.	(NJ)	813
Teaching administration, special libs	HUMPHRY, James	(NY)	574

SPECIALIZATION

Subject	Name	State	Page
Acquisitions specialization	MACDONALD, Wayne D.	(MA)	754
Architecture specialization	VAN DYKE, Stehpen H.	(NY)	1275
Art & architecture specialization	TEAGUE, Edward H	(FL)	1229
Audiovisual specialization	ROGINSKI, Donna J.	(IL)	1050
Business information specialization	SCOTT, Rupert N.	(GA)	1108
Chemical information specialization	ROUSE, Kendall G.	(WI)	1061
Chemistry subject specialization	DRUM, Carol A.	(FL)	320
Elementary medial specialization	SMITH, Judy B.	(GA)	1156
Fine art & handicraft specialization	MANNING, Mary J.	(IL)	766
Genealogy subject specialization	HAMILTON, Darlene E.	(WA)	491
Health sciences specialization	KAYA, Kathryn A.	(MT)	632
Home economics subject specialization	SANDERS, Nancy P.	(OH)	1080
Information specialization	ROOSHAN, Gertrude I.	(CA)	1053
	LEREW, Ann A.	(CO)	717
	RAND, Pamela S.	(MD)	1006
Library media specialization	MILLER, Sylvia G.	(NC)	843
Media specialization	MILLER, Marian A.	(OH)	840

SPECIALIZATION (Cont'd)
Online specialization   LEI, Polin P. . . . . (AZ)   713
Reading specialization   FISHER, Joan W. . . . . . . (MD)   381
Research specialization   DUPLESSIS, Daniel . . . . (PQ)   327
School library media specialization   ARKHURST, Joyce C. . . (NY)   31
School media specialization   SMITH, Noralee W. . . . . (OH)   1159
  DAY, Pamela A. . . . . (WI)   283

SPECIALIZED
Art & architecture specialized ref   BEGLO, Jo N. . . . . (ON)   74
Education specialized reference services   BROWN, M S. . . . . (FL)   145
Specialized business reference   LEVINSON, Catherine K. (NC)   721
Specialized cataloging & indexing   DE WITT, Benjamin L. . . (NJ)   298
Specialized database administration   BILES, Mark J. . . . . (NJ)   96
Specialized database construction   LIVNY, Efrat . . . . (WI)   735
Specialized research projects   BEHNKE, Charles . . . . . (WI)   75
Specialized services   ENSLEY, Robert F. . . . . . (IL)   350

SPECIFICATIONS
Budgets & specifications   MAY, Robert E. . . . . . . (SC)   789
Educational specifications   SMINK, Anna R. . . . . . . (MD)   1152
Government specifications & standards   AUSTIN, Stephen . . . . . (CA)   40
Internal specification maintenance   GRUEL, Janice L. . . . . . (WI)   474
Military specifications & standards   BARNES, Denise M. . . . (CT)   57
Specifications & standards   KING, Elizabeth . . . . . . (FL)   650
Standards & specifications   ROSS, Mary A. . . . . . . (CA)   1058
  WIEHN, John F. . . . . . . (CT)   1336
  MALUMPHY, Sharon M. . (OH)   764
  FENKER, John A. . . . . . (WA)   371
  FOX, Howard A. . . . . . . (WA)   394
  PHILLIPS, Rosemary . . . (ON)   969
System specification   TAUBER, Stephen J. . . (MA)   1225
Systems specifications development   HAWK, Susan A. . . . . . (MD)   513
Writing furniture specifications   DAHLGREN, Jean E. . . . (TX)   269

SPEECH
Performing arts, speech communication   KELLY, Richard J. . . . . (MN)   638
Speech pathology   SNOW, Marina . . . . (CA)   1164

SPIRITUAL
Spiritual book buying   HLUHANY, Patricia . . . . (PA)   544

SPORTS (See also Baseball)
Art, music & sports collection devlpmnt   BAKER, Paula J. . . . . . (OH)   49
Orthopedics & sports medicine   CLEMENTS, Betty H. . . (GA)   221
Sports   TYLER, David M. . . . . . (NY)   1266
Sports & entertainment law   EDMONDS, Edmund P. . (VA)   336
Sports ethics   CARGAS, Harry J. . . . . (MO)   181
Sports history   GIETSCHIER, Steven P. . (MO)   433
Sports information & databases   GHENT, Gretchen K. . . (AB)   430
Sports law   CHAMPION, Walter T. . . (TX)   198
Sports, recreation & leisure   GRODSKI, Renata . . . . (ON)   471
Sports research   QUARTELL, Robert J. . . (NY)   999

SPREADSHEETS
Library statistics, spreadsheet software   KATES, Jacqueline R. . . (MA)   629
Spreadsheets in libraries   BURNS, Robert W. . . . . (CO)   163

ST PAUL
St Paul history   HLAVSA, Larry B. . . . . . (MN)   544

STACK
Circulation & stack management   PARKER, Susan E. . . . . (MA)   942
Stack maintenance   WILSON, Karen A. . . . . (CA)   1351
  SWINTON, Cordelia W. . (PA)   1216
Stack management & remote storage   HENSHAW, Rod . . . . . . (PA)   529

STAFF (See also Continuing)
Academic staff professional development   WHEELER, Helen R. . . . (CA)   1329
Administration & staff development   HOGAN, Patricia M. . . . (IL)   549
  ALLDREDGE, Noreen S. (MT)   14
  LIN, John T. . . . . (VA)   727
Administration & staff supervision   IRONS, Carol A. . . . . . . (IL)   584
Administration training & staff mgmt   NANTON-COMISSIONG, Barbara L. . . . . (TRN)   887
Building & staff administration   BALCOM, William T. . . . (IL)   51
Cataloging staff supervision   TAVARES, Cecelia M. . . (MA)   1225
Computer training staff & students   DUHAMELL, Lynnette H. (IN)   324
Continuing education & staff development   TYER, Travis E. . . . . . . (IL)   1266
Developing appropriate staff   TERZIAN, Shohig S. . . . (CA)   1232
Educating staff   INGERSOLL, Lyn L. . . . . (DC)   582
End-user training, staff training   MEREDITH, Meri . . . . . . (IN)   825
Library administration & staff   FOWLER, Margaret A. . . (MB)   394
Library management, staff development   DE KLERK, Ann M. . . . . (PA)   288
  MCLEAN-LOWE, Dallas . (ON)   814
Library staff development   LIBBEY, George H. . . . . (GA)   725
Library staff training   MING, Marilyn . . . . (AB)   846
Library staff training & development   JOHNSON, Martha A. . . (VA)   607
Personnel & staff development   SCHERREI, Rita A. . . . . (CA)   1092
  OCHSNER, Renata E. . . (IL)   915
  ST. CLAIR, Gloriana S. . . (OR)   1075
Personnel management & staff development   PARENT, Roger H. . . . . (IL)   940
Professional staff supervision   WINTER, Bernadette G. . (IL)   1356
Psychiatric staff   MASON, Martha A. . . . . (NY)   781
Public & staff library microcomputing   ROBERTSON, Michael A. (NY)   1042
Public & staff relations   FRANKLIN, Robert D. . . . (VA)   398
Public library staff training   WYNN, Vivian R. . . . . . . (OH)   1375
Public relations staff training   NORTON, Alice . . . . (CT)   910
Reference & training staff   WHITE, Joyce L. . . . . . . (CO)   1331
Ref, staff development   KEMPF, Andrea C. . . . . (KS)   639
Scheduling substitute staff   QUEEN, Margaret E. . . . (CA)   999
School lib media ctrs staff development   SMITH, Jane B. . . . . . . (AL)   1155
Service development & staff training   RIECHEL, Rosemarie . . . (NY)   1033
Staff & patients development   RALSTON, Anne C. . . . . (MD)   1004
Staff & public computer training   MCMURRAY, Sallylou . . (OH)   815
Staff & services administration   ESPER, Elizabeth . . . . . . (FL)   354
Staff & student library assistance   TROY, Barbara J. . . . . . . (MI)   1258
Staff, board training & development   GIBSON, Barbara H. . . . (CT)   431
Staff development   BENHAM, Frances . . . . . (AL)   80
  OLIVE, J F. . . . . (AL)   921
  LAWSON, Martha G. . . . (AR)   705
  FRANK, Donald G. . . . . . (AZ)   396
  WILLIAMS, Karen B. . . . (AZ)   1344
  HAMMER, Sharon A. . . . (CA)   493
  KAVANAGH, Margaret M. (CA)   631
  LEE, Mildred C. . . . . (CA)   711
  LIU, Susanna J. . . . . (CA)   734
  MILLER, Margaret S. . . . (CA)   840
  NIEMEYER, Kay M. . . . . (CA)   903
  REYNOLDS, Judith L. . . . (CA)   1025
  THORNE, Marco G. . . . . (CA)   1242
  WHITLATCH, Jo B. . . . . (CA)   1333
  FOLEY, Georgiana . . . . . (CO)   387
  BLALOCK, Louise . . . . . (CT)   103
  STANN, Patsy H. . . . . . . (DC)   1180
  STROUP, Elizabeth F. . . . (DC)   1203
  WALKER, Heather C. . . . (DC)   1295
  TITUS, H M. . . . . (DE)   1247
  ALGAZE, Selma B. . . . . (FL)   13
  HENSON, Llewellyn L. . . (FL)   529
  JENKINS, Althea H. . . . . (FL)   597
  JOHNSON, Herbert F. . . (GA)   605
  RUSSELL, Ralph E. . . . . (GA)   1069
  STROUGAL, Patricia G. . (GA)   1203
  BELGUM, Kathie G. . . . . (IA)   76
  ELLIOTT, Kay M. . . . . . . (IA)   344
  CHITWOOD, Julius R. . . (IL)   209
  DEUEL, Marlene R. . . . . (IL)   296
  KNUTSON, Linda J. . . . . (IL)   666
  LUQUIRE, Wilson . . . . . . (IL)   749
  PETERSON, Fred M. . . . (IL)   963
  PETERSON, Kenneth G. . (IL)   964

STAFF (Cont'd)

Staff development
WICKS, Jerry R.	(IL)	1335
WILFORD, Valerie J.	(IL)	1339
CHAMPLIN, Constance J.	(IN)	198
LAUGHLIN, Sara G.	(IN)	703
LEACH, Ronald G.	(IN)	706
BOYARSKI, Jennie S.	(KY)	122
CAHALAN, Thomas H.	(MA)	171
LEVITT, Irene S.	(MA)	721
ANDERSON, Della L.	(MD)	22
BARTH, Edward W.	(MD)	61
CUNNINGHAM, Barbara M.	(MD)	265
DRACH, Marian C.	(MD)	317
TARAN, Nadia P.	(MD)	1223
GROSS, Richard F.	(ME)	472
D'ELIA, Joseph G.	(MI)	289
DUCKWORTH, Paul M.	(MO)	322
FISHER, Georgeann	(MO)	381
GARDNER, Laura L.	(MO)	418
ROBERTS, Jean A.	(MO)	1040
NEWBERG, Ellen J.	(MT)	898
BRILEY, Anne S.	(NC)	136
SIMPSON, Barbara T.	(NJ)	1141
BESEMER, Susan P.	(NY)	91
BINGHAM, Kathleen S.	(NY)	97
CONNOLLY, Bruce E.	(NY)	237
KENNEDY BRIGHT, Sandra	(NY)	641
SHERBY, Louise S.	(NY)	1127
THOMAS, Lucille C.	(NY)	1237
CHESKI, Richard M.	(OH)	207
DRAPP, Laureen	(OH)	318
MILLER, Ruth G.	(OH)	842
DICKSON, Theresa J.	(OK)	301
JOHNSON, Edward R.	(OK)	604
COULOMBE, Dominique C.	(RI)	250
RAINES, Thomas A.	(SC)	1004
WILLIAMS-JENKINS, Barbara J.	(SC)	1347
LANG, Elizabeth A.	(SD)	695
WATSON, Tom G.	(TN)	1310
BAKER, Nettie L.	(TX)	49
RILEY, Richard K.	(TX)	1034
YOUNG, J A.	(TX)	1382
CARVALHO, Sarah V.	(ON)	191
COCHRANE, Thomas G.	(AUS)	226

Staff development & continuing education	HIATT, Peter	(WA)	536
Staff development & human relations	MIAH, Abdul J.	(VA)	831
Staff development & motivation	AUSTIN, Neal F.	(NC)	40
Staff development & supervision	SCHWABACHER, Sara A.	(NY)	1104
Staff development & training	SULLIVAN, Maureen	(CT)	1208
	FIORE, Carole D.	(FL)	379
	APPS, Michelle L.	(MI)	30
	ALBRITTON, Rosie L.	(MO)	10
	MATER, Dee A.	(NC)	783
	NEWMAN, Marianne L.	(OH)	899
	RHODES, Glenda T.	(OH)	1026
	GOODMAN, Helen C.	(TX)	449
	HAYCOCK, Carol A.	(BC)	515
	NEAME, Roderick L.	(AUS)	891
Staff development for school librarians	WHITE, Ann T.	(SC)	1330
Staff development for teachers	FISH, Barbara M.	(NC)	380
Staff development, human relationships	SMITH, Robert F.	(TN)	1160
Staff development, media personnel	BURKE, Grace W.	(GA)	160
Staff development programs	FIELD, Judith J.	(MI)	375
Staff devlpmnt, research & development	BURKS, Alvin L.	(MS)	161
Staff duty coordination	BULLOCK, Jessie M.	(PA)	156
Staff evaluation	BLACKABY, Sandra L.	(WA)	102
Staff evaluation & development	SCHNEIDER, Frank A.	(WA)	1097
Staff inservice	SORELL, Janice G.	(MN)	1168
Staff interviewing, placement & devlpmnt	MOODY, Marilyn D.	(PA)	857
Staff management	COOPER, Jacquelyn B.	(RI)	243
	KRATZ, Abby R.	(TX)	676
	WAUGH, Alan L.	(AB)	1310

STAFF (Cont'd)

Staff management & development	FLEMMING, Tom	(ON)	384
Staff online training	CAGAN, Penny M.	(NY)	170
Staff scheduling	TAORMINA, Anthony P.	(NJ)	1223
Staff supervision	RESSMEYER, Ellen H.	(MA)	1024
	MLODZIANOWSKI, Mary L.	(MI)	850
Staff supervisor	MCTYRE, Ruthann B.	(TX)	818
Staff training	CARLSON, Alan C.	(CA)	182
	GLOGOFF, Stuart J.	(DE)	441
	FULTON, Tara L.	(IL)	409
	DEANE, Paul D.	(IN)	284
	SEXTON, Ebba J.	(KY)	1118
	HAVENER, Ralph S.	(MO)	513
	LANEY, Elizabeth J.	(NC)	695
	MASSEY, Nancy O.	(NC)	782
	ELLIS, Peter K.	(NY)	345
	GUMPPER, Mary F.	(OH)	477
	PURCELL, V N.	(OR)	998
	PEFFER, Margery E.	(PA)	954
	CHESHER, Joyce A.	(TX)	206
	HENSLEY, Randall B.	(WA)	529
	CLANCY, Ron	(BC)	215
	SPRY, Patricia	(ON)	1176
Staff training & development	STEWART, George R.	(AL)	1192
	MULLINS, Carolyn J.	(CA)	878
	FRANKLIN, Hardy R.	(DC)	397
	PHELPS, Thomas C.	(DC)	967
	SALVADORE, Maria B.	(DC)	1078
	STARCK, William L.	(DC)	1181
	TRAINOR, Donna J.	(GA)	1253
	REES, Pamela C.	(IA)	1016
	PICCOLI, Roberta A.	(IL)	970
	ROBY, B D.	(KY)	1045
	NEAU, Philip F.	(LA)	891
	COURSON, M S.	(MD)	251
	HEISER, Jane C.	(MD)	523
	WILLIAMS, J L.	(MD)	1343
	WILLIAMSON, Phyllis B.	(MT)	1348
	BEECH, Vivian W.	(NC)	74
	SCHULTZ, Gary J.	(ND)	1102
	HESS, Jayne L.	(NJ)	534
	TANG, Grace L.	(NY)	1222
	AXAM, John A.	(PA)	42
	CARD, Judy	(TN)	180
	ARD, Harold J.	(TX)	31
	WELCH, C B.	(TX)	1321
	WOHLSCHLAG, Sarah A.	(TX)	1359
	MACRURY, Mary E.	(NS)	758
	DINEEN, Diane M.	(ON)	304
	SMITH, Cynthia M.	(ON)	1153
	EL-DUWEINI, Aadel K.	(EGY)	342
Staff training & evaluation	LEE, Janis M.	(PA)	710
	TONGATE, John T.	(TX)	1250
Staff training, development, recruitment	PURCELL, Marcia L.	(NY)	998
Staff, volunteer supervision	CARTER, Susan M.	(IN)	190
Staffing	HOLDREN, Ann E.	(TX)	550
Staffing & development	CUTLER, C M.	(AB)	268
Staffing personnel	GROSS, Dorothy E.	(IL)	472
Student staffing & training	DIAL, Ron	(NY)	299
Supervise library faculty & staff	REID, Richard H.	(LA)	1019
Supervision & staff development	BRUCE, Robert K.	(MN)	149
Supervision & staff training	JACKSON, Harriett D.	(TN)	587
Supervision of editorial staff	STRATELAK, Nadia A.	(MI)	1200
Supervision of library staff	MOSER, Jane W.	(CA)	870
Supervision of paraprofessional staff	ANDERES, Susan M.	(CA)	21
Supervision of professional staff	KRISTIAN, Alice	(NY)	679
Supervision of student staff	GROSS, Dorothy E.	(IL)	472
Train, supervise & evaluate staff	DAYO, Ayo	(TX)	283
Training & development of library staff	JEANNENEY, Mary L.	(NY)	596
Training & development of staff	BRICKER, Will S.	(PA)	135
Training & staff development	RUDDOCK, Velda I.	(CA)	1065
	JUROW, Susan R.	(DC)	620
	TYLER, Audrey Q.	(GA)	1266
	CRIST, Margaret L.	(MA)	259
	HANSSEN, Nancy E.	(MA)	499
	GIORDANO, Frederick S.	(NY)	438
	HUNT, Suellyn	(NY)	575
Training & supervising circulation staff	MANOVILLE, Susanne	(PE)	767

STAFF (Cont'd)
Training & supervising new staff RICHARDSON, Emma G. (NY) 1029
Training new staff WANG, Margaret K. . . . . . (DE) 1303
  PHILLIPS, Richard F. . . . (NJ) 969
Training staff & users NDENGA, Viola W. . . . . . (MI) 890
Training, staff development, teaching FALANGA, Rosemarie E. (CA) 361
Training staff in technology SCHREFFLER, Lynne W. (PA) 1099

STAGE (See also Theater)
History & aesthetics stage design STOWELL, Donald C. . . . . (GA) 1199
Stage scripts & programs WOODS, Alan L. . . . . . . (OH) 1366

STANDARDS (See also Measurement)
Academic library standards KANIA, Antoinette M. . . . . (NY) 625
  BORCHUCK, Fred P. . . . . (TN) 116
Archival descriptive standards MACDERMAID, Anne . . . (ON) 754
Bibliographic standards GLAZIER, Ed . . . . (CA) 440
  ATTIG, John C. . . . . (PA) 38
Bibliographic standards & systems CARRINGTON, David K. (DC) 186
Cataloging standards WEISS, Paul J. . . . . (NY) 1320
Codes & standards SANDVIKEN, Gordon L. . (CA) 1081
  BONGARD, Nancy D. . . . (ON) 114
Data element standardization BREWER, Christina A. . . . (MD) 134
Data standards LEVINE, Emil H. . . . . (DC) 720
Drug information interchange
  standards FASSETT, William E. . . . . (WA) 366
Engineering codes & standards BERNSTEIN, Anna L. . . . . (DC) 89
Engineering standards RICCI, Patricia L. . . . . . . (MN) 1026
Engineering standards reference MOORE, John R. . . . . . . (IL) 860
Foreign & international standards OVERMAN, Joanne R. . . . (MD) 931
Government specifications &
  standards AUSTIN, Stephen . . . . . . (CA) 40
Industry standards AUSTIN, Stephen . . . . . . (CA) 40
  RANSOM-BERGSTROM,
    Janette F. . . . . (MI) 1008
  HAMPTON, Sylvia S. . . . . (RI) 494
  HOLAB-ABELMAN, Robin
    S. . . . . (TX) 550
Information standards KELLY, Maureen C. . . . . (PA) 638
International information standards KOLTAY, Emery I. . . . . . (NY) 670
Learning resource center col
  standards BOOK, Imogene I. . . . . . (SC) 115
Library & info technology standards MANNING, Ralph W. . . . . (ON) 767
Library standards SASS, Samuel . . . . (MA) 1083
  MCCONE, Gary K. . . . . . (MD) 797
Micrographic standards SHAFFER, Norman J. . . . . (DC) 1119
Microimagery & digitizing standards BAGG, Thomas C. . . . . . (MD) 45
Military specifications & standards BARNES, Denise M. . . . . (CT) 57
Music library surveys & standards MCCLELLAN, William M. (IL) 796
National & international standards ORNE, Jerrold . . . . (NC) 926
Professional standards SASS, Samuel . . . . (MA) 1083
Public library standards HUISKAMP, Julie G. . . . . (IA) 572
  TODD, Alexander W. . . . . (IL) 1248
  EICHELBERGER,
    Marianne . . . . (KS) 339
  NEEDHAM, George M. . . . (OH) 891
Reference standards GOULDING, Mary A. . . . (IL) 454
Serial holdings standards & formats CLAPPER, Mary E. . . . . (MA) 216
Specifications & standards KING, Elizabeth . . . . (FL) 650
Standard nomenclature & code for
  medcn CASIRAGHI, Edoardo . . . (ITL) 192
Standard reference DIEHL, Katharine S. . . . . (TX) 302
Standardization SCHLAG, Gretchen A. . . . (VA) 1093
Standards PERKINS, David L. . . . . . (CA) 959
  VAUGHAN, Ruth M. . . . . . (IL) 1280
  BRANDHORST, Wesley T. (MD) 128
  GREEN, Judith G. . . . . . . (NY) 462
  TANNEHILL, Robert S. . . . (OH) 1222
  CARSON, M S. . . . . (PA) 188
  GRUBER, Linda R. . . . . . (PA) 474
  KRUEGER, Karen J. . . . . (WI) 680
  DELSEY, Thomas J. . . . . (ON) 290
  MASON-WARD, Lesley . (ON) 781
Standards & certification information OVERMAN, Joanne R. . . . (MD) 931
Standards & evaluation WALL, H D. . . . . (PA) 1297
Standards & self-study JOHNSON, Elizabeth G. . (AL) 604
Standards & service measures WARGO, Peggy M. . . . . (CT) 1305
Standards & skills development PHILLIPS, Luouida V. . . . . (TX) 968

STANDARDS (Cont'd)
Standards & specifications ROSS, Mary A. . . . . (CA) 1058
  WIEHN, John F. . . . . (CT) 1336
  MALUMPHY, Sharon M. . . (OH) 764
  FENKER, John A. . . . . . . (WA) 371
  FOX, Howard A. . . . . (WA) 394
  PHILLIPS, Rosemary . . . (ON) 969
Standards definition LEMASTERS, Joann T. . . . (OH) 715
Standards development &
  implementation WHITMAN, Jean A. . . . . (MD) 1333
Standards for school media centers CAIN, Carolyn L. . . . . . . (WI) 171
Standards for school programs HOLTER, Charlotte S. . . . (MD) 554
Standards in information systems HENDERSON, Madeline
    M. . . . . (MD) 526
Standards indexing SHUPAK, Harris J. . . . . . (PA) 1134
Standards organization & distribution RICE, Gerald W. . . . . . . (NH) 1027
Technical standards PIETY, Jean Z. . . . . (OH) 972
  MARSHALL, Alexandra P. (ON) 773
Two-year college standards WALLACE, James O. . . . . (TX) 1297
United States voluntary standards
  index OVERMAN, Joanne R. . . . (MD) 931

STANDING
Continuations & standing orders BACON, Lois C. . . . . (MA) 44
Serials, standing orders MCCANN, Jett C. . . . . . (GA) 794
Standing order selection &
  management ROMANASKY, Marcia C. (NJ) 1052
Standing orders HUDSON, Gary A. . . . . . (SD) 569
Standing orders & serials MCCANN, Judith B. . . . . (ON) 794
Standing orders, continuations BEN-SIMON, Julie E. . . . (WA) 83

STANISLAVSKI
Stanislavski system MOORE, Sonia . . . . (NY) 861
Stanislavski's answer to spontaneity MOORE, Sonia . . . . (NY) 861
Stanislavski's ultimate technique MOORE, Sonia . . . . (NY) 861

START-UP
Computer science, start-up libraries FUCHS, Karola M. . . . . . (PA) 408
Library start-ups AIREY, Martha R. . . . . . . (ME) 9
Small business start-up MCWILLIAM, Deborah A. (OH) 818
Starting new libraries SIESS, Judith A. . . . . (OH) 1136
Start-up libraries BENDER, Elizabeth H. . . (MA) 79
Start-up of new libraries WOFSE, Joy G. . . . . (NY) 1359
Start-up of special libraries GREENE, Danielle L. . . . (DC) 463
Teaching archival start-up CASLIN, Adele . . . . (PA) 193

STATE (See also County, Government)
Advising, federal & state government CASEY, Daniel W. . . . . . (DC) 192
Collecting state religious history ROLLER, Twila J. . . . . . . (NM) 1051
Connecticut state documents ENSEL, Ellen H. . . . . (CT) 350
Federal & international state
  documents BASEFSKY, Stuart M. . . (NC) 62
Federal & state government
  publications BROWN, Philip L. . . . . . . (SD) 146
Federal & state law SCHUTT, Cheryl M. . . . . (CT) 1103
Federal & state law research VARGA, William R. . . . . (DC) 1278
Federal & state legislative materials CAMMARATA, Paul J. . . . (KY) 175
Federal & state library legislation HICKS, Frederick M. . . . . (IL) 537
Federal, state, & government
  research KIRSHBAUM, Priscilla J. (CO) 655
Federal, state, local govt publications NAKATA, Yuri . . . . (OR) 887
Liaison with state library MOSES, Lynn M. . . . . . . (PA) 871
Library management & statewide
  devlpmnt KLINCK, Patricia E. . . . . . (VT) 661
Louisiana state documents MARSHALL, Susan O. . . . (LA) 775
Nebraska state publications FROBOM, Jerome B. . . . (NE) 405
Networking & statewide planning STRONG, Gary E. . . . . . (CA) 1203
New York state & local documents PANDIT, Jyoti P. . . . . . . (NY) 937
New York state documents ESPOSITO, Michael A. . . . (NY) 354
NY state library systems committee PHILLIPS, Ruth M. . . . . . (NY) 969
Oklahoma State University collection BLEDSOE, Kathleen E. . . (OK) 105
Pennsylvania state documents SWAN, Christine H. . . . . (PA) 1213
Public & state libraries LYMAN, Helen H. . . . . . . (NY) 751
Public & state library development LASETER, Ernest P. . . . . (AL) 700
  SHELDON, Brooke E. . . . (TX) 1125
State agencies BARRON, Robert E. . . . . (NY) 60

STATE (Cont'd)

State agency law libraries	BOTTA, Jean C.	(NY)	118
State agency libraries	MOSIER, Eric M.	(CA)	871
	ELLIOTT, Kay M.	(IA)	344
State agency records	KETELSEN, Terry	(CO)	645
	WILLIAMS, Gene J.	(NC)	1343
State & federal documents	HOM, Sharon L.	(TN)	555
State & institution libraries	CASEY, Genevieve M.	(MI)	192
State & local documents	LUNDQUIST, David A.	(CA)	748
	SWAFFORD, William M.	(CA)	1212
	ESKOZ, Patricia A.	(CO)	354
	LEVY, Suzanne S.	(VA)	722
State & local government documents	HAMMOND, Louise H.	(IL)	494
State & local government publications	SULZER, John H.	(PA)	1209
State & local government records	DEARSTYNE, Bruce W.	(NY)	284
State & local historical research	CHRISTENSEN, Erin S.	(CO)	211
State & local history	SCHMIDT, Jean M.	(LA)	1095
	CURTIS, Peter H.	(MD)	267
State & local history research	OAKES, Patricia A.	(AK)	913
State & local records	WAGGENER, Jean B.	(TN)	1291
State & public library management	WALTERS, Clarence R.	(OH)	1301
State & regnl literature & history bibl	RAZER, Robert L.	(AR)	1012
State archives	BAKER, Russell P.	(AR)	49
	LOWELL, Howard P.	(OK)	744
	HELSLEY, Alexia J.	(SC)	525
State associations	GESSNER, Marianne	(MI)	430
	DANNUNZIO, Rebecca T.	(WV)	274
State collections	JONES, H G.	(NC)	613
State development & training	BIHLER, Charles H.	(CT)	96
State document cataloging	MITCHELL, Micheal L.	(AK)	849
	MITCHAM, Janet C.	(AR)	848
State document distribution	MITCHELL, Micheal L.	(AK)	849
State documents	RIESBERG, Eunice L.	(IA)	1033
	SWANSON, Byron E.	(IN)	1213
	YOUNG, Noraleen A.	(IN)	1382
	MOORE, Grace G.	(LA)	859
	NASON, Jennifer L.	(MA)	888
	SANDERS, Lou H.	(MS)	1080
	QUINN, Karen H.	(RI)	1000
	WILLIAMS, Saundra W.	(TN)	1346
	KELLOUGH, Jean L.	(TX)	637
	FOSTER, Leslie A.	(WI)	392
State government documents	ADAMS, Leonard R.	(MA)	5
State government reference	REES, Pamela C.	(IA)	1016
State information resource management	EVANS, Max J.	(UT)	357
	O'BRIEN, Anne M.	(MA)	914
State legislation	HALEY, Anne E.	(WA)	486
State legislature & library development	NIXON, Arless B.	(AZ)	906
State level services	FALSONE, Anne M.	(CO)	363
State librarianship	OWEN, Amy	(UT)	931
State libraries	BOLT, Nancy M.	(CO)	113
State library administration	TOPE, Diana R.	(GA)	1251
	ROBERTSON, Linda L.	(IA)	1042
	NIX, Larry T.	(WI)	905
State library agencies	DESSY, Blane K.	(AL)	296
	SUMMERS, Lorraine S.	(FL)	1209
	TREZZA, Alphonse F.	(FL)	1256
	ENGLER, June L.	(GA)	350
	KANE, Bartholomew A.	(HI)	624
	CADE, Roberta G.	(NY)	170
State library agency administration	WILKINS, Barratt	(FL)	1340
State library association	SUTTON, Sandra K.	(AL)	1211
State library legislation	HUBBS, Ronald B.	(CT)	568
State library legislation & funding	PECK, Ruth M.	(MA)	953
State library service & networks	JOSEY, E J.	(PA)	618
State library statistics	KAPOSTA, Joseph D.	(IN)	626
State of Florida documents	KONOP, Bonnie M.	(FL)	670
State of Maine	CAMPO, Charles A.	(ME)	177
State online catalog department	NAUGLE, Gretchen R.	(NE)	889
State policy development	ATKINS, Gregg T.	(CA)	38
State publication	PARSONS, Kathy A.	(IA)	945
State publications	WEDIG, Eric M.	(TN)	1315
	KECK, Kerry A.	(TX)	633
State records center program management	BITTLE, Christine M.	(OK)	100
State, special & public lib consulting	PHILLIPS, Ray S.	(TX)	969
Statewide & regional networks	WOODWARD, Robert C.	(ME)	1368
Statewide archival development	HACKMAN, Larry J.	(NY)	481

STATE (Cont'd)

Statewide audiovisual distribution	NAUGLE, Gretchen R.	(NE)	889
Statewide automation	HOPKINS, Benjamin	(MA)	557
Statewide interlibrary loan networks	ROBERTSON, Linda L.	(IA)	1042
Statewide library funding services	YATES, Ella G.	(VA)	1378
Statewide library planning	NIX, Larry T.	(WI)	905
Statewide library planning & services	ASP, William G.	(MN)	37
Statewide library program consulting	LEWIS, Alan D.	(MN)	722
Statewide library services	STEVENSON, Marilyn E.	(CA)	1191
	ROBLEE, Martha A.	(IN)	1045
Statewide networking	DRUM, Eunice P.	(NC)	321
Statewide planning library services	DREW, Sally J.	(WI)	319

STATISTICAL

Computer-readable statistical databases	HENSON, Jane E.	(IN)	529
Economic, statistical & quantitative std	KING, Donald W.	(MD)	650
Library research, statistical method	HITT, Charles J.	(MN)	544
Numeric & statistical databases	MOON, Jeffrey D.	(ON)	857
Online statistical database	CHANG, Joseph I.	(NJ)	200
Retailing statistical data	PALMER, Shirley	(CT)	937
Scientific & statistical databases	MCCARTHY, John L.	(CA)	794
Statistical analysis	COMPTON, Joan C.	(CA)	235
	RINGWALT, Arthur	(CA)	1035
	PIGGFORD, Roland	(MA)	972
	BUNCE, Catherine J.	(ON)	157
Statistical computing	JAMES, Brent C.	(UT)	592
Statistical consulting	JAIN, Nem C.	(MA)	592
Statistical financial databases	PRAVER, Robin I.	(NY)	990
Statistical modelling	KOUNTZ, John C.	(CA)	673
Statistical packages	ITNYRE, Jacqueline H.	(CA)	585
Statistical research	RAILSBACK, Beverly D.	(NJ)	1003
Statistical resources	TAYLOR, Marcia E.	(MD)	1227
Statistical sources	BILLINGSLEY, Andrew G.	(ON)	96

STATISTICS

Accounting & statistics	RZECZKOWSKI, Eugene M.	(DC)	1072
Budget & statistics	JENSEN, Charla J.	(UT)	598
Business & finance statistics	MEREDITH, Meri	(IN)	825
Census statistics	DICKMEYER, John N.	(IN)	301
Databases & statistics	HSU, Elizabeth L.	(NY)	567
Demographic statistics	COMPTON, Erlinda R.	(TX)	235
Economic statistics reference	RANDOLPH, Susan E.	(DC)	1007
Energy statistics	BAILEY, Linda S.	(TX)	46
Federal statistics	WILKINSON, Patrick J.	(IA)	1340
Foreign trade statistics	MORTON, Dorothy J.	(DE)	870
Gathering & disseminating statistics	CANTWELL, Mickey A.	(NY)	179
Hospital statistics	RICHARDSON, Alice W.	(PA)	1029
Library statistics	WONG, Cecilia	(CA)	1362
	KOHL, David F.	(CO)	668
	LANCE, Keith C.	(CO)	692
	GOLDHOR, Herbert	(IL)	445
	SONDHEIM, John W.	(MD)	1167
	FEYE-STUKAS, Janice	(MN)	374
	LEE, Chui C.	(NY)	709
	LYDERS, Richard A.	(TX)	751
	STUBBS, Kendon L.	(VA)	1204
	DINEEN, Diane M.	(ON)	304
	MANNING, Ralph W.	(ON)	767
	CHASSE, Jules	(PQ)	203
Library statistics, spreadsheet software	KATES, Jacqueline R.	(MA)	629
Management statistics	TANNEHILL, Robert S.	(OH)	1222
Manufacturing statistics	LANEY, Helen B.	(DC)	695
Mathematical statistics	SEILER, Susan L.	(FL)	1112
	PAUSCH, Lois M.	(IL)	950
Mathematics, physics, statistics	CZIFFRA, Peter	(NJ)	269
Mathematics, statistics, computer sci	PIERCE, Miriam D.	(PA)	971
Metal & general statistics	GOODINGS, Sally A.	(ON)	449
Mortality & morbidity statistics	MURPHY, Virginia A.	(WI)	881
Reference in mathematics & statistics	MERCADO, Heidi	(OH)	825
Reference statistics	JOSEPH, Margaret A.	(TX)	617
Research & statistics	ANDERSON, Beryl L.	(ON)	21
Research methodology & statistics	KATZER, Jeffrey	(NY)	630
State library statistics	KAPOSTA, Joseph D.	(IN)	626

STATISTICS (Cont'd)

Statistics	HURT, Charlie D.	(AZ)	578
	MORRIS, George H.	(CA)	866
	SCHLACHTER, Gail A. .	(CA)	1093
	BOOKSTEIN, Abraham . .	(IL)	115
	CLAPP, David F.	(IL)	215
	ROBERTSON, Pamela S.	(ND)	1042
	NELSON, Veneese C. . .	(UT)	895
	STUBBS, Kendon L. . . .	(VA)	1204
	MURDOCH, Martha T. . .	(WA)	879
	MACRURY, Mary E.	(NS)	758
Statistics & research methods	D'ELIA, George P.	(MN)	289
Statistics, definition, compilation	ARROWOOD, Donna J. .	(CA)	34
Statistics on libraries	LYNCH, Mary J.	(IL)	752

STATUS

Academic librarian status	KELLOGG, Rebecca B. .	(AZ)	637
	HOSEL, Harold V.	(CA)	561
Academic status	HOBBINS, Alan J.	(PQ)	545
Enhance status OCLC	LABODDA, Marsha J. . .	(TX)	686
Faculty governance & status	THORSON, Connie C. . .	(NM)	1242
Faculty status for librarians	GALLOWAY, R D.	(CA)	415
	SCEPANSKI, Jordan M. .	(CA)	1088
	MITCHELL, W B.	(NC)	849
Upgrading status of librarians	NANCE, Betty L.	(TX)	887

STATUTE

Statute publication	MCKEE, James E.	(MN)	810

STEAM

Steam history & technology	ARNOLD, Nancy K.	(PA)	34

STEROID

Biochemistry, steroid hormone receptors	MCFARLAND, Robert T.	(MO)	805

STM

Overseas STM subscription agents	YAMAKAWA, Takashi . .	(JAP)	1376
STM conference management	YAMAKAWA, Takashi . .	(JAP)	1376

STN

Online searching, DIALOG, STN	O'NEILL, Patricia E. . . .	(GA)	924

STOCK (See also Bond, Investment, Securities)

Computer stock market research	HEFFRON, Betsy A.	(NY)	520
Domestic stock & bonds	LAWSON, George F. . . .	(NY)	705
Film & video stock footage	SUMMERS, Robert A. . .	(NJ)	1209
Stock & bond pricing	SOSTACK, Maura	(NY)	1169
Stock & bond quotations	PAYNE, Linda C.	(NY)	951
Stock data	PAYNE, Linda C.	(NY)	951
Stock footage libraries	MONTGOMERY, Patrick .	(NY)	856
Stock/options trading data	ELASIK, Ronald G.	(MD)	341

STORAGE

Archives & storage	PROCTOR, Dixie L.	(FL)	994
Automated storage & retrieval	LEVINE, Emil H.	(DC)	720
Book storage & conservation	HERON, David W.	(CA)	532
Business records storage	EIGEMAN, Laurence E. .	(IN)	340
Computer storage & retrieval	MERRYWEATHER, J M.	(ON)	827
Database storage & retrieval	KANTOR, Paul B.	(OH)	626
Document storage & retrieval systems	BAGG, Thomas C.	(MD)	45
Inactive records storage	KERR, Kevin G.	(IL)	644
Information storage & retrieval	KENDRICK, Brent L. . . .	(DC)	640
	CARR, Sallyann	(FL)	186
	CHERN, Jenn C.	(GA)	206
	GOODY, Cheryl S.	(HI)	450
	BOOKSTEIN, Abraham . .	(IL)	115
	SHAW, Debora	(IL)	1123
	WALDHART, Thomas J. .	(KY)	1294
	BRIAND, Margaret M. . . .	(MA)	134
	GEORGE, Muriel S.	(NJ)	428
	AUSTIN, Ralph A.	(NY)	40

STORAGE (Cont'd)

Information storage & retrieval	GREENBERG, Linda	(NY)	463
	WYLLYS, Ronald E.	(TX)	1375
	MORRISON, David L. . . .	(UT)	868
	BONNETT, Mary B.	(VA)	114
	SCHABAS, Ann H.	(ON)	1088
	WILSON, Concepcion S.	(AUS)	1350
Information storage & retrieval theory	WILSON, Patrick	(CA)	1352
Library storage	STOCKTON, Gloria J. . .	(CA)	1196
Microform storage & retrieval systems	SKARR, Robert J.	(DC)	1145
News & information storage & retrieval	TRIVEDI, Harish S.	(OH)	1257
Online information retrieval & storage	WILLIAMS, Martha E. . . .	(IL)	1345
Optical disk storage & retrieval	ELMAN, Stanley A.	(CA)	345
Optical scanning & storage	SPANGLER, Bruce	(CO)	1171
Optical storage	CAMPBELL, Brian G. . . .	(BC)	176
Optical storage & publishing	HERTHER, Nancy K. . . .	(MN)	533
Optical storage media technology	GALL, Bert A.	(TN)	413
Optical storage technologies	HELGERSON, Linda W. .	(VA)	524
Optical storage technology	LIGHTBOWN, Parke P. .	(CA)	726
Photo storage & retrieval	HAMMOND, Theresa M. .	(VA)	494
Photograph storage & retrieval	STEVENS, Paula F.	(AZ)	1190
Stack management & remote storage	HENSHAW, Rod	(PA)	529
Storage & retrieval of records & docums	RAC-FEDORIJCZUK, Karola C.	(PA)	1001
Storage & retrieval system design	TRAVIS, Irene L.	(VA)	1254
Textile information storage & retrieval	LAWRENCE, Philip D. . .	(VA)	704
Weeding & storage	HAYTON, E E.	(ON)	517

STORYTELLING

Adult & juvenile storytelling	MACFARLANE, Francis X.	(TX)	755
Adult storytelling	VOSS, Joyce M.	(IL)	1289
Adult-level storytelling	POMERANTZ, Bruce F. .	(OH)	982
Children & storytelling	MOLLENKOPF, Carolyn M.	(MD)	853
Children's services, storytelling	STRATTON, Martha G. .	(IN)	1200
Editing information news stories	LYONS, Ivan	(NY)	753
Folklore & storytelling	HARDESTY, Vicki H. . . .	(OH)	499
Indexing news stories	SINCLAIR, John M.	(AB)	1142
Polish folklore storytelling	MAZUREK, Adam P. . . .	(MD)	791
Preschool storyhours	ZINMAN, Sandra	(NY)	1389
Preschool storytelling	SELANDER, Lucy M. . . .	(MN)	1113
Professional storytelling	GRAY, Raymond L.	(PA)	460
School-age storytelling	SELANDER, Lucy M.	(MN)	1113
Story & author programs	LOPEZ, Silvia P.	(FL)	741
Story & visual research for films	FINE, Deborah J.	(CA)	377
Storyhour	ANDERSEN-PUSEY, Vavene J.	(NM)	21
Storyhour programming & storytelling	ANTHONY, Rose M.	(WI)	29
Storyhours	RANIERI, Bernice A. . . .	(NJ)	1007
Storyhours for ages 2 to 9	COHN, Jeanette	(NJ)	229
Storyhours for toddlers through grade 2	SALUZZO, Mary S.	(NY)	1078
Storyhours, storytelling	BUTLER, Rebekah O. . . .	(NY)	167
Storyteller	SHERMAN, Louise L. . . .	(NJ)	1128
Storytelling	COLCLASURE, Marian S.	(AR)	230
	LANGSAM, Christine E. .	(AR)	696
	JANSON, Sherryl A.	(AZ)	594
	CHAMBERLIN, Leslie A.	(CA)	198
	KING, Cynthia	(CA)	650
	LAGIER, Jennifer B.	(CA)	688
	MULLINS, Carolyn J. . . .	(CA)	878
	DUFF, Margaret K.	(CO)	323
	BUSCH, Kathleen M. . . .	(CT)	165
	DAIGNEAULT, Audrey I. .	(CT)	270
	ROCKMAN, Connie C. . .	(CT)	1046
	HUNT, Susan O.	(FL)	576
	KINNEY, Molly S.	(FL)	653
	STINES, Joe R.	(FL)	1194
	COFFIE, Patricia R.	(IA)	227
	DOBREZ, Cynthia K. . . .	(IL)	307
	DOWNS, Jane B.	(IL)	317
	EFFERTZ, Rose	(IL)	338
	FEDERICI, Yolanda D. . .	(IL)	368
	GLEESON, Joyce M. . . .	(IL)	441
	MARTINAZZI, Toni	(IL)	779
	SULLIVAN, Peggy A. . . .	(IL)	1208
	PENROD, Saundra K. . . .	(IN)	957

STORYTELLING (Cont'd)
Storytelling

TEUBERT, Lola H. . . . . . (IN) 1233
VOORS, Mary R. . . . . . . (IN) 1289
BARTLETT, Gwenell J. . . (KS) 61
HEINTZMAN, Justina . . . (KY) 522
HERRON, Darl H. . . . . . . (KY) 533
JAMES, Karen G. . . . . . (KY) 592
MILLER, Barbara S. . . . . (KY) 835
HOLLEY, Rebecca M. . . . (LA) 551
MEINEL, Nancy T. . . . . . (LA) 822
KELLMAN, Lillian S. . . . . (MA) 637
RASKIN, Susan R. . . . . . (MA) 1009
SLATTERY, Carole C. . . . (MA) 1148
WEISCHEDEL, Elaine F. . (MA) 1319
ASHFORD, Richard K. . . (MD) 36
BLANK, Annette C. . . . . (MD) 104
GIBBS, Beatrice E. . . . . (MD) 431
MEIZNER, Kathie L. . . . (MD) 822
ARRIVEE, Sally D. . . . . . (MI) 34
BEDUNAH, Virginia M. . . (MI) 74
GREGORY, Helen B. . . . (MI) 466
MOSKOWITZ, May K. . . (MI) 871
RAWLINSON, Pamela . . (MI) 1011
TATE, Carole A. . . . . . . (MI) 1225
SIMMONS, Antoinette S. (MN) 1139
HUGHES, Donna J. . . . . (NC) 571
HUNTER, Julie A. . . . . . (NC) 576
MELLON, Constance A. . (NC) 822
KEEFE, Betty . . . . (NE) 634
CUTLER, Marsha L. . . . . (NV) 268
AMISON, Mary V. . . . . . (NY) 20
FUNK, Nancy J. . . . . . . (NY) 410
HODGES, Lois F. . . . . . (NY) 546
LOUISDHON-WALTER,
   Marie L. . . . . (NY) 742
MORRIS, Kim . . . . (NY) 867
OLDERSHAW, Anne . . . (NY) 920
ROSS, Kathleen A. . . . . (NY) 1058
SPIEGEL, Bertha . . . . . (NY) 1174
VOSE, Deborah R. . . . . (NY) 1289
WEIDEMANN, Margaret A. (NY) 1316
ALEXA, Cynthia M. . . . . (OH) 12
CLARK, Marilyn L. . . . . . (OH) 217
FLOWER, Eileen D. . . . . (OH) 386
FREW, Martha G. . . . . . (OH) 402
GUTHRIE, Chab C. . . . . (OH) 479
JANKY, Donna L. . . . . . (OH) 593
NOWAK, Leslie A. . . . . . (OH) 911
REID, Margaret B. . . . . . (OH) 1018
TAYLOR, Orphus R. . . . . (OH) 1228
KIMBLE, Valerie F. . . . . (OK) 649
ZACHARY, Patricia A. . . (OK) 1385
BAUMGARTNER, Barbara
   W. . . . . (PA) 66
FIELD, Carolyn W. . . . . (PA) 375
MARON-WOOD, Kathy M. (PA) 772
SACHS, Kathie B. . . . . . (PA) 1073
SCOTT, Lydia E. . . . . . . (PA) 1107
SMITH, Mary M. . . . . . . (PA) 1158
BIERDEN, Margaret W. . (RI) 95
CARPENTER, Charlotte L. (TX) 184
COKINOS, Elizabeth G. . (TX) 229
NISBY, Dora R. . . . . . . (TX) 904
SHANNON, Jerry B. . . . (TX) 1120
TANNER, Clarabel . . . . (TX) 1222
EDMUNDSON, Margaret
   B. . . . . (UT) 336
PETERSON, Francine . . . (UT) 963
GUILFORD, Diane E. . . . (VA) 476
WISECARVER, Betty A. . (VA) 1357
BETZ-ZALL, Jonathan R. . (WA) 92
BLUME, Scott . . . . (WA) 107
DOLBEY, Mary B. . . . . . (WA) 309
MEYER, Laura M. . . . . . (WA) 830
WISEMAN, Mary J. . . . . (WI) 1357
CHATTON, Barbara A. . . (WY) 204
NEILL, Sam D. . . . . (ON) 892
TRAINER, Leslie F. . . . . (PAK) 1253

Storytelling & drama
ROSS, Theodosia B. . . . . (GA) 1059

STORYTELLING (Cont'd)
Storytelling & folklore
BOLT, Janice A. . . . . (IL) 113
HERMAN, Gertrude B. . . (WI) 531
Storytelling & programming
   techniques
PELLOWSKI, Anne . . . . (NY) 955
Storytelling & puppetry
LOWE, Joy L. . . . . (LA) 744
DELLER, A M. . . . . (MI) 289
Storytelling, collection development
HOUSEWARD, Bernice A. (MI) 563
Storytelling for all ages
SALUZZO, Mary S. . . . . (NY) 1078
Storytelling instruction
NELSON, Olga G. . . . . . (OH) 895
Storytelling, poetry, holiday themes
BAUER, Caroline F. . . . . (CA) 65
Storytelling programs & workshops
GREENE, Ellin P. . . . . . (NJ) 464
Storytelling to children
KNOTT, Joan Y. . . . . . . (MI) 665
Storytelling with props & puppets
BROUSE, Ann G. . . . . . (NY) 141
Storytelling with puppets
CHAMPLIN, Constance J. (IN) 198
Storytime & puppets
MITCHELL, Jan E. . . . . . (FL) 848
Storytime for preschoolers
WALKER, Tamara E. . . . (TX) 1296
Storytime resources
CROTTS, Carolyn D. . . . (KS) 261
Storytimes
EDGREN, Gale R. . . . . . (IL) 336
Teaching storytelling
MACDONALD, Margaret
   R. . . . . (WA) 754
Toddler story programs
BROUSE, Ann G. . . . . . (NY) 141
Traditional storytelling
CORSARO, Julie A. . . . . (IL) 248

STRATEGIC
Information for strategic planning
HANSEN, Kathelen L. . . . (MN) 497
Information strategic planning
JACOBSEN, Teresa T. . . (IL) 590
Information systems strategic planning
PEETERS, Marc D. . . . . (BEL) 954
Library strategic, long-range planning
MANN, Thomas . . . . . . (CA) 766
Library strategic planning
KANE, Bartholomew A. . (HI) 624
COHEN, Aaron . . . . (NY) 227
Long-range & strategic planning
BETTENCOURT, Nancy J. (CO) 92
VELLUCCI, Matthew J. . . (MD) 1282
BAUER, Margaret D. . . . (PA) 65
Long-range strategic planning
NEEDHAM, George M. . . (OH) 891
Management & strategic planning
MALCOLM, J P. . . . . . . (MI) 762
Marketing & strategic planning
VANCE, Julia M. . . . . . . (MD) 1273
Marketing communications, strategic
   plng
WASERSTEIN, Gina S. . (PA) 1307
Planning & strategic management
BRADBURY, Daniel J. . . (MO) 125
Strategic & decision software
BUNCE, George D. . . . . (ENG) 157
Strategic business management
   services
CARTER, Daniel H. . . . . (TX) 189
Strategic corporate information
   analysis
BEICHMAN, John C. . . . (MI) 75
Strategic direction
CHANDLER, James . . . . (CA) 200
Strategic information planning
HORTON, Forest W. . . . (DC) 561
Strategic market planning
TELFER, Margaret E. . . . (NC) 1230
Strategic planning
ANDERSON, Dorothy J. . (CA) 22
DOWLIN, Kenneth E. . . . (CO) 316
MANNING, Leslie A. . . . (CO) 766
LUTHER, M J. . . . . (GA) 750
HARRIS, Jeanne G. . . . . (IL) 504
LYNCH, Hugh J. . . . . . . (IL) 751
MAYFIELD, Maurice K. . . (IL) 790
PARENT, Roger H. . . . . (IL) 940
SHERRY, Diane H. . . . . (IL) 1129
VIRGO, Julie A. . . . . . . (IL) 1285
ARNOLD, Stephen E. . . . (KY) 34
DOVE, Samuel . . . . (MD) 315
GROCKI, Daniel J. . . . . . (MD) 471
ROBINSON, Barbara M. . (MD) 1043
PORTER, Jean F. . . . . . (MI) 984
WAITE, William F. . . . . . (NJ) 1293
COVINGTON, Robert D. . (NV) 252
BORBELY, Jack . . . . . . (NY) 116
BRAUDE, Robert M. . . . (NY) 129
HUNTER, Karen A. . . . . (NY) 576
JACOB, Mary E. . . . . . . (OH) 589
TRUBKIN, Loene . . . . . (BC) 1259
FAGERLUND, M L. . . . . (SWZ) 361
Strategic planning & marketing
OLSON, Christine M. . . . (MD) 922
BERGFELD, C D. . . . . . (NY) 86
PARKER, Arthur D. . . . . (ON) 941
Strategic planning & teambuilding
TYSON, John C. . . . . . . (VA) 1267
Strategic planning for libraries
ARDEN, Caroline . . . . . (VA) 31
Strategic planning for library systems
MATHESON, Nina W. . . . (MD) 783
Strategic systems planning
BURNS, Barrie A. . . . . . (ON) 162

STRATEGIC (Cont'd)

Strategic use of information technology — MARCHAND, Donald A. . (NY) 768

STRATEGIES

Assessing corporate strategies — MCLANE, John F. . . . . (CT) 813
Business strategy — ERES, Beth K. . . . . (ISR) 352
Cooperative strategies, consortia — OFFERMANN, Glenn W. (MN) 917
Corporate planning & strategy — MARKS, Larry . . . . . . (CA) 771
Database search strategy assistance — MARANGONI, Eugene G. (CA) 768
Information seeking strategies — MARCHIONINI, Gary J. . (MD) 769
Library research strategies instruction — KUNSELMAN, Joan D. . (CA) 684
Library strategies planning — VANDERELST, Wil . . . . (ON) 1274
Natural language search strategy — HAYDEN, Richard F. . . (CA) 515
Online, manual search strategy — BATES, Marcia J. . . . . . (CA) 64
Orientation & research strategy — BIANCHINO, Cecelia . . . (IN) 94
Public information strategies — CROWTHER, Warren W. (CSR) 262
Reviewing strategies — OWENS, Irene E. . . . . . . (PA) 932
Search strategies — DOYLE, James M. . . . . . (MI) 317
Strategies for salary issues — SHANNON, Marcia A. . . (MA) 1120

STRATEMEYER

Stratemeyer series books — THORNDILL, Christine M. (WA) 1242

STRUCTURE (See also Substructure)

Chemical structure searching — LERITZ, M K. . . . . (CT) 717
Chemical structure software evaluation — SOUTHWICK, Margaret A. (VA) 1170
Chem structures & substructure searching — MACKSEY, Julie A. . . . . (MI) 757
Civil & structural engineering — SPIGELMAN, Cynthia A. (IL) 1174
Civil engineering, pavements, structures — MOBLEY, Arthur B. . . . . (DC) 851
Computer database structure — MARTINEZ, Jane A. . . . . (NJ) 779
New library structures — BURGIS, Grover C. . . . . (ON) 159
Organizational structure — MORAN, Robert F. . . . . . (IN) 862
Personnel structure — DOWELL, David R. . . . . . (IL) 315
Popular music theme structures — COOPER, B L. . . . . (MI) 242
Related structural materials — HYSLOP, Marjorie R. . . (OH) 580
Structure-activity relationships — LASSLO, Andrew . . . . . . (TN) 700

STUDENT (See also Internship, Study, Workstudy)

Adult students — NOLAND, Jon . . . . (CA) 908
Advising a student publication — MASON, John A. . . . . . . (IL) 781
Assisting students — FANSLOW, Malinda C. . . (TN) 363
Computer assistance to students — BLAIR, Sharon K. . . . . . . (SC) 103
Computer literacy for students — HUNTER, Cecilia A. . . . (TX) 576
Computer training staff & students — DUHAMELL, Lynnette H. . (IN) 324
Dyslexic adult students — THOMPSON, Jane K. . . . (VT) 1240
Foreign students & libraries — SARKODIE-MENSAH, Kwasi . . . . (LA) 1083
High school student services — WONSEVER, Eithne C. . (NY) 1363
High school students — PESTUN, Aloysius J. . . . (CA) 961
Intl publishing, student editions — HARMON, James R. . . . (NY) 502
Library school student groups — COLEMAN, J G. . . . . . . (AL) 231
Managing student workers — KEMP, Henrietta J. . . . . . (IA) 639
Media for gifted students — FITZPATRICK, Janis M. . (OH) 383
Online searching with students — DANIELS, Ann A. . . . . . (IN) 273
Reference, student assistance — DAUGHERTY, Carolyn M. (MD) 275
Retrieving information for students — LONNING, Roger D. . . . (MN) 740
Staff & student library assistance — TROY, Barbara J. . . . . . (MI) 1258
Student — O'NEIL, Mary A. . . . . . . (AZ) 924
Student & faculty services — MORRISSETT, Elizabeth (AK) 868
Student assistant management — FREEMAN, Evangeline M. (NC) 400
Student assistant training — MORRIS, Betty J. . . . . . (AL) 866
Student assisting — TUOHY, Eileen M. . . . . (CA) 1263
Student audiovisual productions — PROCTOR, Deborah K. . (WY) 994
Student development & libraries — LAWTON, Bethany L. . . . (DC) 705
Student library skills — DATUS, Marie B. . . . . . (NE) 275
Student media production — JONES, Wanda F. . . . . (AR) 615
— MCKINNEY, Barbara J. . (AR) 812
Student motivation — SKELLY, Laurie J. . . . . (MN) 1146
Student orientation & training — RICE, Anna C. . . . . (NJ) 1026
Student personnel — BUTLER, James C. . . . . (MS) 166
Student placement — MELVILLE, Karen E. . . . (ON) 823
Student records databases — THOMPSON, Jane K. . . . (VT) 1240

STUDENT (Cont'd)

Student services — HAMEL, Eleanor C. . . . . (PR) 491
Student staffing & training — DIAL, Ron . . . . (NY) 299
Student supervision & training — MCHUGH, William A. . . (IL) 809
Student supervision, reference — OLSEN, Sarah G. . . . . . (IL) 922
Student training & development — BARTZ, Alice P. . . . . . . (PA) 62
Student use of libraries — PARR, Michael P. . . . . . (MI) 944
— HAMILTON, Betty D. . . (TX) 491
Student video production — FREEMAN, Evangeline M. (NC) 400
Student work supervisor — SPURRIER, Suzanne F. . (AR) 1177
Supervising students — THOMPSON, Myra D. . . (OH) 1240
Supervision of student staff — GROSS, Dorothy E. . . . . (IL) 472
Teaching of library skill to students — GERMINDER, Robin L. . . (NJ) 429
Teaching students — SCHREFFLER, Lynne W. (PA) 1099
Training of medical students — LANDAU, Lucille . . . . . . (OH) 692
Training of student assistants — GLADIEUX, Mary B. . . . . (MO) 439
Training student aides — GORMAN, Mary B. . . . . (NY) 452
Training student library aids — AVERY, Linda S. . . . . . . (NM) 42
Training student-related personnel — WALLER, Elaine J. . . . . . (MI) 1298
Working with students & faculty — SOUTHARD, Sarah T. . . (CT) 1169

STUDY (See also Student)

Building programs & feasibility study — WRIGHT, Paul L. . . . . . . (KY) 1372
Communication study — ASHEIM, Lester E. . . . . (NC) 35
Graduate film study — FREEMAN, John P. . . . . (TX) 401
Library study skills — BRUNER, Katharine E. . . . (TN) 150
Research in the study of literature — MILLER, Robert H. . . . . . (KY) 842
Study & information skills — BRAUER, Regina . . . . . . (NY) 129
Study of children's literature — POVSIC, Frances F. . . . . (OH) 987
Study skills instruction — CARPENTER, Carole H. . . (DE) 184
User study — TAMURA, Shunsaku . . . . (JAP) 1221

SUBJECT (See also Headings)

Anthropology subjects — BARNWELL, Jane L. . . . . (OR) 58
Art subject — SMITH, Elizabeth J. . . . . (PA) 1154
Banking & finance subject field — GALLUP, Jane H. . . . . . . (DC) 415
Biomedical subjects — CRAIG, James L. . . . . . . (MA) 254
Business subjects — ENDRES, Maureen D. . . (PA) 348
— BELL, Barbara . . . . (BC) 76
Cataloging & subject analysis — TAYLOR, Arlene G. . . . . (NY) 1226
Cataloging, subject analysis — SOPER, Mary E. . . . . . (WA) 1168
Chemistry subject specialization — DRUM, Carol A. . . . . . . (FL) 320
Classification & subject analysis — DYKSTRA, Mary E. . . . . (NS) 331
Engineering subjects — SPARER, Saretta . . . . . (NY) 1171
Freemasonry & related subjects — HANKAMER, Roberta A. (MA) 496
Genealogy subject specialization — HAMILTON, Darlene E. . (WA) 491
General & subject reference — TZE-CHUNG, Li . . . . (IL) 1267
General subject indexing — LINDHEIMER, Elinor . . . . (CA) 729
Geography subjects — MILLER, Rosanna . . . . . . (AZ) 842
Home economics subject specialization — SANDERS, Nancy P. . . (OH) 1080
Hospital & clinical management subjects — BELT, Jane . . . . (WA) 78
Interlibrary loan, subject requests — LLOYD, H R. . . . . (PA) 735
Japanese subjects reference services — GONNAMI, Tsuneharu . . (BC) 447
Latin American subjects — CARRENO, Angela M. . . (NY) 186
Lib of Congress music subject headings — PRICE, Harry H. . . . . (DC) 992
Mathematics subject specialist — ANDERSON, Nancy D. . . (IL) 24
Medical subject specialist — WORTHINGTON, A P. . . (CA) 1369
Music subject specialist — SILCOX, Tinsley E. . . . (TN) 1137
— JONES, June D. . . . . . . (MB) 613
Nursing subjects — TRIP, Barbara M. . . . . (BC) 1257
Online searching of various subjects — LAMPRECHT, Sandra J. . (CA) 691
Online subject access interfaces — BATES, Marcia J. . . . . . (CA) 64
Organization & subject classification — HAYNES, Kathleen J. . . (OH) 516
Patient & consumer subjects — CESARD, Mary A. . . . . . (NJ) 196
Politics of subject headings — MICHEL, Dee A. . . . . . (CA) 832
Rare books subject collections — WOLFE, Marice . . . . . . (TN) 1361
Reference engineering subjects — PERTELL, Grace M. . . . (IL) 961
Social science subject cataloging — DEVERA, Rosalinda M. . (NY) 297
Special subject education cataloging — VERMA, Prem V. . . . . (WV) 1282
Subject access — COLLANTES, Lourdes Y. (NY) 232
— MANDEL, Carol A. . . . . (NY) 764
— WALKER, M G. . . . . . . (NY) 1296
— LYTLE, Richard H. . . . . (PA) 753
— MICCO, Helen M. . . . . (PA) 831
Subject access to ethnomusicology — SCHUURSMA, Ann B. . . (NET) 1103

SUBJECT (Cont'd)

Subject access to information — COLLINS, William P. . . . . (ISR) 233
Subject analysis — MICHEL, Dee A. . . . . (CA) 832
WEINTRAUB, D K. . . . . (CA) 1318
HARGRAVE, Charles W. . (DC) 501
CLACK, Doris H. . . . . . . (FL) 215
WILSON, Betty R. . . . . . (IL) 1350
LEWICKY, George I. . . . . (NY) 722
VIZINE-GOETZ, Diane . . (OH) 1286
DAILY, Jay E. . . . . (PA) 270
FUJIMOTO, Jan D. . . . . . (UT) 408
PORTEUS, Andrew C. . . (ON) 985
RENAUD, Monique M. . . (ON) 1023
ROLLAND-THOMAS,
Paule . . . . (PQ) 1051
TESSIER, Richard . . . . . (PQ) 1233
Subject analysis & classification — CROWTHER, Carol . . . . (CA) 262
Subject analysis & social sciences — WRIGHT, Sylvia H. . . . . . (NY) 1373
Subject & name authority control — BADING, Kathryn E. . . . . (TX) 44
Subject approach to information — WILLIAMSON, Nancy J. . . (ON) 1347
FOSKETT, Antony C. . . . (AUS) 392
Subject authority — PAGELS, Helen H. . . . . . (NY) 934
Subject authority control — HURLBERT, Irene W. . . . . (CA) 577
Subject authority records — SCHMIDT, Holly H. . . . . (OR) 1095
Subject bibliographer — MARKSON, Eileen . . . . . (PA) 771
Subject bibliographies — MARSCHNER, Robyn J. . . (CO) 773
SPARKS, Martha E. . . . . (NC) 1171
Subject bibliography — OLSON, Lowell E. . . . . . (MN) 923
MEYERS, Charles . . . . . (NY) 830
Subject bibliography for nursing — CHAN, Lillian L. . . . . (CA) 199
Subject bibliography for public health — CHAN, Lillian L. . . . . (CA) 199
Subject cataloging — MORRISSETT, Elizabeth . (AK) 868
ENYINGI, Peter . . . . (CA) 351
MILSTEAD, Jessica L. . . (CT) 845
DOBCZANSKY, Jurij W. . (DC) 307
HORCHLER, Gabriel F. . . (DC) 559
PENKIUNAS, Ruta M. . . (DC) 956
YASUMATSU, Janet R. . . (DC) 1378
CHAN, Lois M. . . . . (KY) 199
MAILLET, Lucienne G. . . (NY) 761
BALATTI, David R. . . . . . (ON) 50
WANG, Sing W. . . . . . . (AUS) 1303
Subject cataloging & classification — KIRKWOOD, Francis T. . . (ON) 655
Subject cataloging anthropology — CARNAHAN, Stephanie B. (DC) 183
Subject cataloging of law books — KREH, Fritz . . . . (WGR) 677
Subject classification — NEW, Gregory R. . . . . . . (DC) 898
LOVELL, Bonnie A. . . . . (TX) 743
Subject, English literature — SILVER, Diane L. . . . . . . (PA) 1138
Subject files — BENDES, Adele N. . . . . . (NY) 79
Subject headings — GOUDREAU, Ronald A. . (DC) 454
WRIGHT, Joseph F. . . . . (FL) 1372
POLSON, Billie M. . . . . . (NV) 982
Subject index database — KENEFICK, Mary L. . . . . (CA) 640
Subject indexing — MOOERS, Calvin N. . . . . (MA) 857
WELLISCH, Hans H. . . . (MD) 1322
CIARAMELLA, Mary A. . (NJ) 214
Subject reference — WYNNE, Allen . . . . (CO) 1375
Subject research — PEARSON, Judith G. . . . (CA) 952
Subject responsibilities — RICE, Virginia E. . . . . . . (AZ) 1027
Subject specialist in fine arts — PIRON, Alice M. . . . . . . (IL) 975
Subject specialist in philosophy — LAMB, Robert S. . . . . . . (IN) 690
Zoo related subjects reference — KENYON, Kay A. . . . . . (DC) 643

SUBMARINE

Submarine medicine databases — OMARA, Marie T. . . . . . (MD) 923

SUBSCRIPTIONS (See also Periodicals)

Administration of subscriptions — SMITH, Cynthia A. . . . . . (OH) 1153
Overseas STM subscription agents — YAMAKAWA, Takashi . . (JAP) 1376
Paying subscriptions — GAYNOR, Joann T. . . . . (NY) 424
Serial subscription service — WEED, Joe K. . . . . (AL) 1315
Subscription agencies — FEICK, Christina L. . . . . . (NY) 368
Subscription agency — GAUNT, James R. . . . . . (FL) 423
Subscription agency business
management — CLASQUIN, Frank F. . . . (MA) 219
Subscription agents — GROSSMANN, Pierre . . (BRA) 473
Subscription fulfillment — LYNCH, Hugh J. . . . . . . (IL) 751

SUBSCRIPTIONS (Cont'd)

Subscription services — CLINE, Sharon D. . . . . . (CA) 222
LONG, Roger J. . . . . (IL) 739
Subscription services, sales — NASON, Stanley J. . . . . (NY) 888
Subscriptions sales management — KOBASA, Paul A. . . . . . (IL) 666
West European subscription agencies — JAGER, Conradus . . . . (MA) 591

SUBSTANCES (See also Alcohol, Drugs)

Alcoholism & substance abuse
reference — WEINBERG, Gail B. . . . . (MN) 1317
Chemical substance information
retrieval — STOBAUGH, Robert E. . . (OH) 1195
Hazardous substances databanks — COSMIDES, George J. . . (MD) 249
Substance abuse literature — GANGLOFF, Tory W. . . . (OH) 416
Substance & alcohol abuse — ROLETT, Virginia V. . . . . (NH) 1051
Toxic substances information — MULTER, Ell P. . . . . (MO) 878

SUBSTRUCTURE (See also Structure)

Chemical lit, substructure searching — SAARI, David S. . . . . . . (IN) 1072
Chemical substructure searching — LEWIS, Dale E. . . . . . . (NJ) 722
DOBBS, David L. . . . . . (OH) 307
Chem structures & substructure
searching — MACKSEY, Julie A. . . . . (MI) 757

SUBSYSTEM

Interlibrary loan subsystem — THOMPSON, Karolyn S. . (MS) 1240

SUPERCOMPUTING

Supercomputing, computational
science — MAISEL, Merry W. . . . . . (CA) 762

SUPERVISION (See also Administration, Directing, Management)

Administration & staff supervision — IRONS, Carol A. . . . . . . (IL) 584
Administration & supervision — MILLER, Suzanne M. . . . (CA) 842
MOORE, Phyllis C. . . . . (CA) 861
LOSEY, Doris C. . . . . . . (FL) 742
BOLEF, Doris . . . . (IL) 112
BRAZILE, Orella R. . . . . (LA) 130
BROOKS, Jerrold L. . . . . (NC) 140
JACKSON, Nancy G. . . . (VA) 588
JORDAN, Ervin L. . . . . . (VA) 616
Administrative, supervising — MARK, Ronnie J. . . . . . . (NY) 770
Administrative supervision — BUTTERWORTH, Donald
Q. . . . . (KY) 167
HIRSCH, Dorothy K. . . . . (MD) 543
Archives supervision — CURTIS, George H. . . . . (MO) 267
Branch adminstrv & supervisory skills — SMITH-EPPS, E P. . . . . (GA) 1161
Branch supervising — PICHA, Charlotte G. . . . . (IN) 970
Branch supervision — JOHNSON, Beth . . . . . . (GA) 602
Building renovation supervision — BURNS, Mary F. . . . . . . (IL) 162
Cataloging & supervision — UMBERGER, Sheila S. . . (VA) 1268
Cataloging staff supervision — TAVARES, Cecelia M. . . (MA) 1225
Cataloging supervision — SIMS, Phillip W. . . . . . . (TX) 1142
Circulation supervision — STAHL, Ramona J. . . . . (CA) 1178
ESTES, Elizabeth W. . . . (NC) 355
Circulation supervisor — REINBOLD, Janice K. . . . (OK) 1021
Clerical supervision — WHITE, Larry R. . . . . . . (CA) 1331
Collection supervision & maintenance — CAMPBELL, Mary K. . . . (TX) 177
Department supervision — WOLF, Dorothy L. . . . . . (MD) 1360
Department supervision & decisions — EARL, Susan R. . . . . . . (NC) 332
Department supervisor — PAPA, Deborah M. . . . . (OH) 938
District library organz & supervision — DICK, Norma P. . . . . . . (CA) 300
District-wide coordination, supervision — VAUGHAN, Janet E. . . . (MN) 1279
Extension agency management,
supervision — GRAY, Patricia B. . . . . . (VA) 460
File room personnel supervision — DICKERSON, Mary J. . . (TX) 300
Filing supervision & training — ABRAMS, Roger E. . . . . (OH) 3
General supervision systems — DILLENSCHNEIDER,
Patricia A. . . . . (NJ) 303
Grant supervision — MOSES, Lynn M. . . . . . (PA) 871
Law library supervision — COX, Irvin E. . . . . (MD) 253
BEQUETTE, V L. . . . . . (MO) 84
Librarian & technician supervision — DEYOUNG, Gail O. . . . . (MI) 298
Library administration & supervision — GUYDON, Janet H. . . . . (IN) 479
Library building supervision — MALOY, Frances . . . . . (NY) 764

SUPERVISION (Cont'd)

Library coordinator supervision
Library management & supervision   FRIEDMAN, Tevia L. . . . (TX) 404
   HARRAGARRA WATERS,
     Deana J. . . . . (CO) 503
   CASTRO, Maritza . . . . . . (PR) 194
   EISENBERG, Phyllis B. . . (VA) 340
Library programs supervision   ROOZEN, Nancy L. . . . . (WI) 1054
Library supervision & management   GERLOTT, Eleanor L. . . . (PA) 429
Literature search supervision   CYGAN, Rose M. . . . . . . (MI) 268
Management, administration,
   supervisory   MARSHALL, Kathryn E. . . (IL) 774
Management & supervision   CROCKETT, Darla J. . . . (CA) 259
   MACEK, Rosanne M. . . . (CA) 755
   VETTER, Jean A. . . . . . . (IL) 1283
   PICCININO, Rocco . . . . . (MA) 970
   DAVIS, Denise . . . . (MD) 278
   KELLOGG, Joanne T. . . . (ME) 637
   FARHAT, Elizabeth M. . . (MI) 363
   TSAI, Fu M. . . . . (MI) 1260
   WILROY, Joann . . . . (MS) 1349
   AULD, Hampton M. . . . . (NC) 39
   MATHAI, Aleyamma . . . . (NJ) 783
   ROYSTER, Peggy K. . . . (OK) 1063
   MAYNARD, James E. . . . (SC) 790
   LEONARD, Gloria J. . . . . (WA) 716
   WEBER, Joan L. . . . . . . (WA) 1314
   BELLOWS, Leslie A. . . . (WI) 78
Management & supervision of lib
   programs   PETERSON, Miriam E. . . (IL) 964
Management & supervisory training   PARSONS, Jerry L. . . . . (CA) 945
Mgmt, planning, budgeting,
   supervising   ZAENGER, Kathleen L. . . (MI) 1385
Management, supervising   ·   MCDONOUGH, Douglas
     M. . . . . (RI) 803
Management, supervision & training   BOWLES, Carol A. . . . . (CA) 121
Middle management & supervision   BAILEY, Martha J. . . . . . (IN) 46
   HENRY, Peggy L. . . . . . . (MO) 529
Music library supervision   SHARP, Avery T. . . . . . . (TX) 1122
Order supervision   KNEIL, Gertrude M. . . . . (PA) 664
Periodical room supervision   LAROSA, Thomas J. . . . (NY) 698
Personnel supervision   COFFEY, James R. . . . . (NJ) 227
Planning, budgeting, & supervision   THAKER, Virbala M. . . . (CA) 1234
Processing center supervision   WINTER, Bernadette G. . (IL) 1356
Professional staff supervision   WINTER, Bernadette G. . (IL) 1356
Public library branch supervision   DOWDLE, Glen L. . . . . . (TX) 315
Public service supervision   THOMAS, Greg . . . . (TX) 1236
Recruiting responsibilities supervisory   LETTIERI, Robin M. . . . (NY) 719
Reference negotiation & supervision   USTACH, Joanne B. . . . (NY) 1270
Research library supervision   STRYCK, B C. . . . . (IL) 1203
School district library supervision   BURGESON, Clair D. . . . (NY) 159
School library media supervision   JAFFARIAN, Sara . . . . . (MA) 591
School library supervision   WIGET, Laurence A. . . . (AK) 1337
   LOWERY, Phyllis C. . . . . (GA) 744
   MEYERS, Judith K. . . . . (KS) 831
   RANDAZZO, Corinne O. . (MS) 1006
   ABBOTT, Ruth J. . . . . . . (TX) 1
   BUELER, Roy D. . . . . . . (WA) 155
School library supervisor   WIDENER, Sarah A. . . . (TX) 1335
Small library supervision   MOORE, Craig P. . . . . . (MD) 859
Small special library supervision   DAYHOFF, Judith A. . . . (CO) 283
Staff development & supervision   SCHWABACHER, Sara A. (NY) 1104
Staff supervision   RESSMEYER, Ellen H. . . (MA) 1024
   MLODZIANOWSKI, Mary
     L. . . . . (MI) 850
Staff supervisor   MCTYRE, Ruthann B. . . . (TX) 818
Staff, volunteer supervision   CARTER, Susan M. . . . . (IN) 190
Student supervision & training   MCHUGH, William A. . . . (IL) 809
Student supervision, reference   OLSEN, Sarah G. . . . . . (IL) 922
Student work supervisor   SPURRIER, Suzanne F. . (AR) 1177
Supervise all audiovisual   MARVEL, Frances J. . . . (CA) 780
Supervise all media   MARVEL, Frances J. . . . (CA) 780
Supervise & training librarians   EMERICK, John L. . . . . (PA) 347
Supervise corporate technical library   CARPENTER, Dale . . . . (NY) 184
Supervise library faculty & staff   REID, Richard H. . . . . . (LA) 1019
Supervising   RIVES, Lydia L. . . . . (KY) 1037
Supervising a special library   MCLAUGHLIN, Dorothy M. (NJ) 813
Supervising all book orders   DOYLE, Patricia A. . . . . (TX) 317
Supervising art slide library   LANTZ, Louise K. . . . . . (MD) 697
Supervising assistants   VANDERBECK, Maria . . (CA) 1273
Supervising branch library system   RADOFF, Leonard I. . . . (TX) 1002

SUPERVISION (Cont'd)

Supervising copy cataloging   KNIGHT, Rita C. . . . . . . (AZ) 664
Supervising day-to-day activities   DAYHOFF, Judith A. . . . (CO) 283
Supervising school library
   management   BROWN, Atlanta T. . . . . (DE) 142
Supervising school library media
   progs   KLASING, Jane P. . . . . . (FL) 657
Supervising students   THOMPSON, Myra D. . . (OH) 1240
Supervision   FIEGEN, Ann M. . . . . . . (AZ) 375
   REDFIELD, Elizabeth . . . (CA) 1014
   SULLIVAN, Alice F. . . . . (CA) 1207
   VOTAW, Floyd M. . . . . . (CA) 1289
   WALKER, Patricia A. . . . (CA) 1296
   FOLEY, Georgiana . . . . . (CO) 387
   MARTIN, Walter F. . . . . (CT) 779
   SWEENEY, June D. . . . . (DC) 1215
   WILLIAMS, Anita . . . . . . (GA) 1342
   BURBANK, Richard D. . . (IL) 158
   FAUST, Mary H. . . . . . . (IN) 366
   DYER, Victor E. . . . . . . (MA) 330
   DENNEY, Christine A. . . (MD) 292
   MILLER, Gloria . . . . (NC) 838
   AVENICK, Karen . . . . . . (NJ) 41
   ATKINS, Gene D. . . . . . (NM) 37
   SALTUS, Winifred T. . . . (NY) 1077
   FINET, Scott . . . . (OH) 378
   DICKSON, Theresa J. . . (OK) 301
   YAEGER, Luke R. . . . . . (VA) 1376
   DENIS, Laurent G. . . . . . (ON) 292
   WOOD, Ronald P. . . . . . (ON) 1365
   DE LUISE, Alexandra . . . (PQ) 290
Supervision & administration   THOMAS, Lucille C. . . . (NY) 1237
Supervision & management   BENZ, Lieselotte . . . . . . (NY) 84
   LAMBERT, Sarah E. . . . (TN) 690
Supervision & planning   BLASE, Nancy G. . . . . . (WA) 104
Supervision & staff development   BRUCE, Robert K. . . . . . (MN) 149
Supervision & staff training   JACKSON, Harriett D. . . (TN) 587
Supervision & training   YOST, F D. . . . . (DC) 1381
   BRADY, Mary M. . . . . . . (IL) 127
   RUIZ-VALERA, Phoebe L. (NY) 1067
   BYRNE, Helen E. . . . . . (OR) 169
   THOMPSON, Sandra K. . (PA) 1241
Supervision & training of employees   MCIVER, Stephanie P. . . (GA) 809
Supervision department library   YAGELLO, Virginia E. . . (OH) 1376
Supervision of editorial staff   STRATELAK, Nadia A. . . (MI) 1200
Supervision of interlibrary loan   WRIGHT, Joanna S. . . . (IL) 1371
Supervision of library staff   MOSER, Jane W. . . . . . (CA) 870
Supervision of paraprofessional staff   ANDERES, Susan M. . . (CA) 21
Supervision of professional staff   KRISTIAN, Alice . . . . . . (NY) 679
Supervision of public services   COUSINS, Gloria D. . . . (NC) 252
Supervision of reference librarians   MUTCH, Donald G. . . . . (ON) 883
Supervision of school librarians   VANDERGRIFF, Kathleen
     E. . . . . (TN) 1274
Supervision of SDI projects   SHALLENBERGER, Anna
     F. . . . . (NY) 1119
Supervision of student staff   GROSS, Dorothy E. . . . . (IL) 472
Supervision, training & development   BANKHEAD, Jean M. . . . (CO) 54
Supervision, training, cataloging   VAN STRATEN, Daniel G. (WI) 1277
Supervisor   TAYLOR, Melissa P. . . . (CT) 1227
   RIEKE, Judith L. . . . . . . (TN) 1033
Supervisory administration   HARVEY, Carl G. . . . . . (AB) 509
Supervisory & management training   GARDNER, Jeffrey J. . . . (DC) 418
Technical services supervision   PARRY, David R. . . . . . . (CO) 944
   WERT, Alice L. . . . . (IN) 1325
   BRENNAN, Christopher P. (NY) 132
Train, supervise & evaluate staff   DAYO, Ayo . . . . (TX) 283
Training & supervising circulation staff   MANOVILLE, Susanne . . (PE) 767
Training & supervising new staff   RICHARDSON, Emma G. (NY) 1029
Training & supervision   BRIERTY, Carol A. . . . . (FL) 135
   MCCUNE, Lois M. . . . . . (IN) 801
Training & supervision of volunteers   WILLIAMS, Suzanne C. . (TX) 1346
Training, supervising & development   FUN, Winnie W. . . . . . . (VA) 409
Workstudy employee supervision   FOX, Lynne M. . . . . (CO) 395

SUPPLY

Book supply   SCHMIEDL, Keith S. . . . (NY) 1096
Document, reprint, photocopy supply   KOSTENBAUDER, Scott (NY) 673
Information broker & supplier   POND, Frederick C. . . . . (NY) 982

SUPPLY (Cont'd)

Information supply	MAHAFFEY, Susan M. . .	(CA)	760
	GRANT, Mary M.	(NY)	458
Library books & supplies	AMIS, Terence K.	(NB)	20
National & international document supply	LINE, Maurice B.	(ENG)	730
Supply video & audio tapes	GRAY, Lee H.	(NJ)	460
Vendor & supplier negotiations	YODER, Susan M.	(CA)	1380

SUPPORT

Account support	FOUSER, Jane G.	(IL)	393
Administrative support	CASSEDY, Barbara S. . .	(DC)	193
	SKLODOSKI, Terrance E.	(KY)	1147
	OKUDA, Sachiko E. . . .	(ON)	920
Archival support	EDGERLY, Linda	(MA)	336
Automated publishing support	GRIMES, Judith E.	(MD)	470
Cataloging support	FINNI, John J.	(MA)	379
CD-ROM buyer procurement support	MILLER, David C.	(CA)	836
Clinical support & reference	MOORE, Sara L.	(DC)	861
Corporate administration support	HOOTKIN, Neil M.	(WI)	557
Curriculum support	YELVERTON, Mildred G.	(AL)	1379
	GUNDERSEN, Shirley S.	(IL)	477
	SCHAACK, Wilma J. . . .	(IL)	1088
Curriculum support for faculty	DAVIS, Deanna S.	(IA)	278
Customer service support	ROMERO, Georg L.	(CA)	1052
Customer support	LOCASCIO, Aline M. . . .	(NY)	735
	FOSTER, Anne	(ON)	392
Customer technical support	PIKE, Christine M.	(NJ)	972
Database promotion & support	CRAUMER, Patricia A. . .	(PA)	255
Database support & service	SOUDER, Edith I.	(PA)	1169
Decision support systems	RANDOLPH, Kevin H. . .	(CA)	1007
	SMITH, Peggy C.	(OK)	1159
	LATHROP, Irene M.	(RI)	701
Developing community support programs	NATHAN, Frances E. . . .	(NY)	889
Faculty research support	BRENNAN, Edward P. . .	(MD)	132
Federal procurement support	SLOAN, Cheryl A.	(MD)	1149
Fundraising information support	EVERETT, Amy E.	(DE)	358
High school curriculum support	DAVIS, Inez W.	(TN)	279
Information support for researchers	JONES, Kendra A.	(TN)	613
Information systems & decision support	BERGFELD, C D.	(NY)	86
Legal administrative support systems	CROCKETT, Denise J. . .	(NY)	259
Library software development & support	FEDECZKO, Joyce L. . . .	(IL)	367
Library support	REHKOP, Barbara L. . . .	(MO)	1017
Litigation & regulatory support	SCULLY, Patrick F.	(CA)	1109
Litigation support	EVANS, Deborah L.	(CA)	356
	SMITH, Catherine C. . . .	(CO)	1153
	KRONE, Judith P.	(GA)	679
	BERUL, Lawrence H. . . .	(MD)	91
Litigation support databases	LANK, Dannette H.	(WI)	696
Market support	LAUER, Marjorie A.	(ON)	702
Marketing support databases	POWELL, Timothy W. . .	(NY)	989
Media & instruction support	YEE, Sandra G.	(MI)	1379
Media support services	MICHAEL, Richard T. . . .	(RI)	831
Microcomputer applications & support	WILLIAMS, David W. . . .	(NY)	1342
Microcomputer support Apple Macintosh	DEEMER, Selden S.	(GA)	286
Microcomputer support IBM PC	DEEMER, Selden S.	(GA)	286
Microcomputer training support	STIGLEMAN, Sue E. . . .	(NC)	1194
Microcomputer user support	OWEN, Willy	(NC)	932
Public relations & political support	RAY, Gordon L.	(BC)	1011
Reference & instruction academic support	VERNON, Christie D. . . .	(VA)	1283
Research & development research support	MUSKUS, Elizabeth A. . .	(NY)	883
Research support	STEVENSON, Michael I. .	(MA)	1191
Research support for art	MCKEE, George D.	(NY)	810
Research support services	KLIMIADES, Mario N. . . .	(AZ)	661
	BROWN-WEBB, Deborah D.	(TX)	149
	PARE, Richard	(ON)	940
Science & tech resrch & devlpmnt support	LOGAN, Nancy L.	(ON)	737
Software support	BIRD, H C.	(TX)	98
	ATTINGER, Monique L. .	(ON)	38
Support & technical services	BROOM, Susan E.	(FL)	141
Support group liaison	SCHWARTZ, Virginia C. .	(WI)	1105

SUPPORT (Cont'd)

Supporting curriculum Grades K-4	MEINEL, Nancy T.	(LA)	822
Systems support	ALLEN, Stephanie O. . . .	(AZ)	16
Technical support	HENKEL, Grace E.	(NJ)	528
Technical support for archives	MURDOCH, Arthur W. . .	(ON)	879
Training & support	IVERSON, Diann S.	(CA)	585
Training & user support	VEATCH, Laurie L.	(DC)	1280
Transportation safety research support	GATTIS, R G.	(MI)	422
User support	LEUNG, Frank F.	(ON)	719
User support for online searching	BROWN, Helen A.	(NE)	144

SUPREME COURT

South Carolina Supreme Court	BARDIN, Angela D.	(SC)	56

SURGERY (See also Neurosurgery)

Otolaryngology, head & neck surgery	JOHNSTON, Bruce A. . .	(PA)	610
Surgical cataloging	RUBINSTEIN, Edith	(NY)	1065
Surgical instrument development	MCGREGOR, Walter . . .	(NJ)	808
Surgical needle development	MCGREGOR, Walter . . .	(NJ)	808

SURVEYS

Conducting & analyzing surveys	CANTWELL, Mickey A. .	(NY)	179
Financial information surveying	JONES, Frank	(VA)	613
In-house use surveys	MITCHELL, W B.	(NC)	849
Library surveys	AYLWARD, James F. . . .	(RI)	42
	BOWLBY, Raynna M. . . .	(RI)	121
	TSAI, Shaopan	(ON)	1260
Management studies & surveys	D'ALESSANDRO, Edward A.	(DC)	270
Music library surveys & standards	MCCLELLAN, William M. .	(IL)	796
Records surveys & inventories	FOURIE, Denise K.	(CA)	393
Social surveys	BOVA, Patrick	(IL)	120
Survey research	PIGGFORD, Roland	(MA)	972
	MCDONALD, Dennis D. .	(MD)	802
Survey research for libraries	OLSON, Christine A. . . .	(MD)	922
Surveys	COMPTON, Joan C.	(CA)	235
Surveys & evaluations	VELLUCCI, Matthew J. . .	(MD)	1282
User surveys	MACDONALD, Christine S.	(ON)	754

SUSPENDED

Cryonics & suspended animation	BRIDGE, Stephen W. . . .	(IN)	135

SWEDISH (See also Scandinavian)

Swedish translating	CARLSON, Kathleen A. .	(NM)	182

SWEDISH-AMERICAN

Swedish-American history	JOHNSON, Timothy J. . .	(IL)	609
Swedish-Americana collection development	WESTERBERG, Kermit B.	(IL)	1326

SYMBOLISM

Art & world symbolism	RONNBERG, Annmari . .	(NY)	1053

SYMPHONY

Symphony computer programs	BURNS, Robert W.	(CO)	163

SYNAGOGUE

Church & synagogue library consulting	KARON, Bernard L.	(MN)	627
Synagogue & center library	FIRSCHEIN, Sylvia H. . .	(NJ)	379
Synagogue libraries	HONOR, Naomi G.	(NY)	556

SYSTEMATICS

Botanical systematics & taxonomy	CHANDLER, Jody A. . . .	(UT)	200
Systematized nomenclature of medicine	NITZ, Andrew M.	(DC)	905
Zoological systematics & taxonomy	CHANDLER, Jody A. . . .	(UT)	200

SYSTEMS (See also Intersystems, MIS, Online and names of specific computerized library systems, e.g. CLSI, GEAC, NOTIS)

Academic information systems	JENKIN, Michael A.	(FL)	596
	WILSON, Marjorie P.	(MD)	1352
Academic library system	MOSBORG, Stella F.	(IL)	870
Academic library system administration	SMITH, Gordon W.	(CA)	1155
Acquisition systems	FAUST, Mary H.	(IN)	366
Acquisitions systems	SALGAT, Anne M.	(PA)	1076
Administration of system	HERSTAND, Joellen	(OK)	533
Administration systems analysis	CHRISTNER, Deborah S.	(CA)	212
Administration, systems, planning	LARKIN, Patrick J.	(NY)	698
Administrative & communications systems	MEADOWS, Donald F.	(BC)	819
Administrative & technical systems	KNIGHTLY, John J.	(TN)	664
Administrative system design	CLARKE, Elba C.	(GA)	218
Administrator, school library system	MORRISON, George J.	(NY)	868
Agricultural information systems	BURTON, Hilary D.	(CA)	164
	OLSEN, Wallace C.	(NY)	922
	LUMANDE, Edward	(ZAM)	748
AI expert systems	SIEGEL, Elliot R.	(MD)	1136
ALIS systems	BURCHELL, Patricia M.	(ON)	158
Analysis design information systems	DEBONS, Anthony	(PA)	285
Analysis of library systems	GOODFELLOW, Marjorie E.	(PQ)	448
Anthropological information systems	CLARK, Barton M.	(IL)	216
Archdiocesan school system libraries	DALY, Sally A.	(PA)	271
Archival control systems	MOTTRAM, Geoffrey	(IL)	873
Archival indexing systems	GORDON, Martin K.	(VA)	451
Archival information systems	EASTWOOD, Terence M.	(BC)	333
Archival systems	BURNS, John F.	(CA)	162
Art information systems	PETERSEN, Toni	(MA)	962
Art slide library systems	DULAN, Peter A.	(CO)	324
Artificial experience systems	KARR, Ronald D.	(MA)	628
Artificial intelligence, expert systems	VEENKER, Linda J.	(CA)	1281
	DIEHL, Mark	(IL)	302
Attorney information systems consulting	STERN, Michael P.	(MD)	1189
Automated acquisitions systems	BARKER, Joseph W.	(CA)	56
	TRIMINGHAM, Robert	(CA)	1256
	KAPOOR, Jagdish C.	(NH)	626
	HUDSON, Gary A.	(SD)	569
Automated administrative systems	ARROWOOD, Donna J.	(CA)	34
Automated & integrated library systems	GABRIEL, Linda	(NJ)	411
Automated archival systems	SZARY, Richard V.	(DC)	1218
Automated bibliographic systems	SZARY, Richard V.	(DC)	1218
Automated circulation system	LANE, Linda A.	(GA)	694
	ELDREDGE, Jeffrey R.	(HI)	342
Automated circulation systems	CASTONGUAY, Russell	(CA)	194
	EICHELBERGER, Susan	(CA)	339
	PARKS, Amy N.	(CT)	943
	SHURMAN, Richard L.	(IL)	1134
	PHENIX, Katharine J.	(LA)	967
	PURCELL, Kathleen V.	(MD)	998
	FARHAT, Elizabeth M.	(MI)	363
	HENRY, Peggy L.	(MO)	529
	ROSENBERG, Harlene Z.	(NJ)	1056
	MORRIS, Jennifer D.	(NY)	866
	RIEBEL, Ellis F.	(PA)	1033
	IVES, Gary W.	(VA)	585
	ICE, Priscilla T.	(WA)	581
	HAYES, Janice E.	(ON)	516
Automated information retrieval systems	MACIAS-CHAPULA, Cesar A.	(MEX)	755
Automated information systems	HUNE, Mary G.	(OH)	574
	NORTON, Nancy P.	(TN)	910
Automated information systems management	WEINSTEIN, Lois	(NY)	1318
Automated integrated library system	OBERC, Susanne F.	(OH)	913
Automated library circulation systems	ULRICH, Paul S.	(WGR)	268
Automated library control systems	YOUNG, Peter R.	(DC)	1383
Automated library, information systems	KANNEL, Ene	(ON)	625
Automated library system	MATTHEWS, Joseph R.	(CA)	785
	HUMMEL, Janice A.	(MD)	573

SYSTEMS (Cont'd)

Automated library systems	ODSEN, Elizabeth R.	(AK)	917
	MUIR, Scott P.	(AL)	876
	BLANK, Karen L.	(CA)	104
	BULLARD, Sharon W.	(CA)	156
	LEE, Hee J.	(CA)	710
	SOY, Susan K.	(CA)	1170
	BATES, Charles E.	(CO)	63
	HAYNAM, Kenneth W.	(CT)	516
	SKOP, Vera	(CT)	1147
	MITCHELL, Phyllis R.	(GA)	849
	OHRLUND, Bruce L.	(IA)	919
	HAMMER, Donald P.	(IL)	493
	HILDRETH, Charles R.	(IL)	539
	YATES, Dudley V.	(KY)	1378
	KNAACK, Linda M.	(MA)	663
	TAHIR, Mary M.	(MD)	1220
	MARTIN, John E.	(MI)	776
	MOSEY, Jeanette	(MI)	871
	BECK, Susan E.	(MO)	71
	RICKERSON, George T.	(MO)	1031
	DAVIDSON, Laura B.	(NC)	276
	MOREHOUSE, Valerie J.	(ND)	863
	ROCK, Sue W.	(NJ)	1046
	O'DONNELL, Maryann T.	(NY)	917
	SALAZAR, Pamela R.	(NY)	1076
	MCMURRAY, Sallylou	(OH)	815
	SHAW, Debra S.	(OH)	1123
	SHREWSBURY, Lynn D.	(OH)	1133
	FULLER, Elizabeth E.	(PA)	408
	LANDRUM, John H.	(SC)	693
	BEHRENS, Elizabeth A.	(TN)	75
	MILLS, Debra D.	(TN)	844
	UBALDINI, Michael W.	(TN)	1267
	ALLEN, Virginia M.	(TX)	16
	CLARK, Jay B.	(TX)	217
	MULLINS, James R.	(TX)	878
	PEDEN, Robert M.	(TX)	954
	KANE, Dorothea S.	(VA)	624
	SCOTT, Mona L.	(VA)	1107
	WEIST, Melody S.	(VA)	1320
	WILLIAMSON, Judy D.	(WV)	1347
	TAYYEB, Rashid	(NS)	1229
	PIGGOTT, Sylvia E.	(PQ)	972
Automated library systems implementation	DUMONT, Paul E.	(TX)	325
Automated microcomputer systems	ROSE, Pamela M.	(NY)	1055
Automated public library systems	MEAGHER, Janet H.	(MA)	819
Automated reference systems	BECK, Susan E.	(MO)	71
Automated serial control systems	FONG, Wilfred W.	(WI)	388
Automated serials management systems	CLAPPER, Mary E.	(MA)	216
Automated system implementation	STAHL, Wilson M.	(NC)	1178
Automated system networking	MAINIERO, Elizabeth T.	(CT)	761
Automated systems	BRUMAN, Janet L.	(CA)	150
	PISANO, Vivian M.	(CA)	975
	SZYNAKA, Edward M.	(CA)	1219
	BOWERS, Sandra L.	(CO)	121
	AUSTIN, Monique C.	(DC)	40
	APPELQUIST, Donald L.	(FL)	30
	MOUW, James R.	(IL)	874
	CIUCKI, Marcella A.	(IN)	215
	FUTA, Debra D.	(IN)	411
	MOORE, Thomas J.	(IN)	861
	BADEN, Diane G.	(MA)	44
	BAILEY, Carol A.	(MD)	46
	BLEGEN, John C.	(MD)	105
	GALLAGHER, Charles F.	(MD)	413
	O'BRIEN, Lee A.	(MD)	914
	GOSLING, William A.	(MI)	453
	ELFSTRAND, Stephen F.	(MN)	342
	CONNORS, Theresa	(MO)	238
	HAMMOND, John J.	(MO)	493
	MYERS, Carol B.	(NC)	884
	BLUMENTHAL, Sidney L.	(NJ)	107
	STAVETSKI, Norma K.	(NJ)	1183
	KLOPFER, Jerome J.	(NM)	662
	BORRESS, Lewis R.	(NY)	117
	DAVIS, Robert J.	(NY)	280
	HITT, Gail D.	(NY)	544

SYSTEMS (Cont'd)

Automated systems
LOLLIS, Martha J. ..... (NY) 738
SIVULICH, Kenneth G. ... (NY) 1145
UCHTORFF, Barbara J. .. (NY) 1267
RASKIN, Rosa S. ...... (OH) 1009
DAYO, Ayo .... (TX) 283
SARGENT, Charles W. ... (TX) 1082
WILSON, D K. .... (UT) 1350
CALLAHAN, John J. ... (VA) 173
UMBERGER, Sheila S. ... (VA) 1268
WINTERS, Sharon A. ... (VA) 1356
CONABLE, Irene H. ..... (WA) 235
BARUTH, Barbara P. .... (WI) 62
JEFFCOTT, Janet B. .... (WI) 596
TOOTH, John E. .... (MB) 1251
Automated systems & indexing TAYLOR, James B. .... (WA) 1227
Automated systems for archives HONHART, Frederick L. .. (MI) 556
Automated systems for circulation JOHNSON, Martha A. ... (VA) 607
Automated systems plng & implementation PATTERSON, Robert H. . (OK) 948
Automated systems training & development
BOWRIN-MARSH, Donna M. .... (CA) 122
LOCASCIO, Aline M. .... (NY) 735
Automatic identification systems PAVELY, Richard W. .... (NJ) 950
Automatic indexing system VLEDUTS-STOKOLOV, Natalia .... (PA) 1286
Automatic indexing, system design VLADUTZ, George E. .... (PA) 1286
Automating library systems YALCINTAS, Rana ..... (TN) 1376
Automation & information systems SAHLI, Nancy A. ...... (DC) 1075
Automation & library systems EZQUERRA, Isabel .... (FL) 360
FUN, Winnie W. .... (VA) 409
Automation & systems for libraries WELCH, Donald A. ...... (TX) 1321
Automation of library systems LAMANN, Amber N. .... (NY) 689
Automation online systems STEPHENS, Jerry W. .... (AL) 1188
Automation, system implementation NICHOLSON, Dianne L. .. (BC) 902
Automation systems CHU, Felix T. .... (IL) 212
EVANS, James M. ..... (LA) 357
Automation, systems analysis STAMBOULIEH, Nora .... (PQ) 1179
Automation systems & services RUBENS, Charlotte C. ... (CA) 1064
Automation, systems operations SIMPSON, W S. .... (WI) 1142
Bar code system design VOGT, Herwart C. ..... (NJ) 1287
Bibliographic automated systems BROWN, Rowland C. .... (OH) 147
Bibliographic citation systems BRANDT, Daryl S. ..... (IN) 128
Bibliographic control systems GUILES, Kay D. .... (DC) 476
Bibliographic information systems LARSON, Ray R. ...... (CA) 699
ODOM, Jane H. .... (DC) 917
WALL, Eugene .... (MD) 1297
LI, Marjorie H. .... (NJ) 724
Bibliographic instruction automated syst PALLARDY, Judy S. ... (MO) 935
Bibliographic standards & systems CARRINGTON, David K. (DC) 186
Bibliographic systems HENKE, Dan .... (CA) 528
TANTOCO, Dolores W. . (IN) 1223
KILGOUR, Frederick G. . (OH) 648
Book distribution systems KOLTAY, Emery I. ..... (NY) 670
Branch library systems LANDGRAF, Mary N. .... (CA) 692
Budget, personnel, systems development HARRIS, Linda S. ...... (DC) 505
Budgeting systems CANNON, Robert E. ..... (NC) 179
Business information system development LITTLE, Dean K. .... (OH) 733
Business information systems SHAFFER, Richard P. .... (NY) 1119
Calendar systems CHASE, William D. ..... (MI) 203
Canadian health care system BOITE, Mary E. .... (ON) 111
Cancer information systems DICKINSON, Patricia C. . (MD) 301
Cataloging & automated systems SEXTON, Ebba J. ...... (KY) 1118
Cataloging & cataloging systems PAGE, Jacqueline M. ... (MO) 934
Cataloging, library systems PERCELLI, Irene M. ..... (NY) 958
Cataloging on automated systems WONG, Ming K. .... (DC) 1363
Cataloging systems MANEY, Lana E. ...... (TX) 765
ZIMMERMAN, Suzan E. . (ON) 1389
CD-ROM, optical information systems DESMARAIS, Norman P. . (RI) 295
CD-ROM systems BEFELER, Mike .... (CO) 74
PRATT, Allan D. .... (CT) 989
MOES, Robert T. ...... (NY) 852
CD-ROM systems development GOOGINS, Jennifer J. ... (NY) 450
CD-ROM systems integration DAVISSON, Darell D. .... (CA) 281

SYSTEMS (Cont'd)

Chemical information systems BURCSU, James E. .... (NC) 158
LEWIS, Dale E. .... (NJ) 722
WAGNER, A B. .... (NY) 1291
DUANE, Carol A. ...... (OH) 321
VLADUTZ, George E. ... (PA) 1286
ROSENBERG, Murray D. (VA) 1056
Circulation & reserve systems & services HENSHAW, Rod ...... (PA) 529
Circulation control systems DODGE, Christopher N. . (MN) 308
Circulation system automation NOBLE, Barbara N. .... (MO) 906
Circulation systems FROHMBERG, Katherine A. .... (CA) 405
HESSLER, Nancy R. ... (IL) 534
DOELLMAN, Michael A. . (IN) 308
DOVE, Samuel .... (MD) 315
FARK, Ronald K. ...... (RI) 364
MILLER, G D. .... (WA) 837
CAPES, Judy L. .... (BC) 179
HAYTON, E E. .... (ON) 517
MAHARAJ, Diana J. .... (PQ) 760
Classification scheme & systems devlpmnt ELLIS, Kathy M. .... (BC) 344
Classification system development NEW, Gregory R. ...... (DC) 898
Classification systems PAULSON, Peter J. .... (NY) 950
Classification systems & catalogs GOLDBERG, Jolande E. . (DC) 444
Clinical systems BOLLINGER, Robert O. . (MI) 112
CLSI automated circulation system CALLANAN, Ellen M. ... (NJ) 173
Communication systems TILSON, Koleta B. ..... (TN) 1245
Communications systems ZOROWITZ, Richard D. . (IL) 1390
Communications systems design BLISS, David H. .... (IA) 105
Community college library systems HISLE, W L. .... (TX) 544
Community information systems REMINGTON, David G. . (WA) 1022
Comparative automated retrieval systems O'CONNOR, Sandra L. ... (NC) 916
Comparative library information systems CARPENTER, Raymond L. (NC) 185
Competitive intelligence systems MOBLEY, Kathleen S. .. (KS) 851
Competitor intelligence systems SEASE, Sandra A. ..... (NY) 1110
Computer applications & systems KIRKWOOD, Francis T. . (ON) 655
Computer circulation systems WAGNER, Robin O. .... (IL) 1292
Computer indexing systems SEMONCHE, Barbara P. (NC) 1115
Computer info sources, end-user systems GODT, Carol .... (MO) 443
Computer management systems GILLETTE, Robert S. ... (TX) 435
Computer system administration PETERSON, Barbara E. . (PA) 962
Computer system integration WANG, Gary Y. .... (MA) 1302
Computer system management GIANGRANDE, Mark G. . (IL) 430
HANAFEE, Valerie ..... (MI) 494
Computer system research & development DIEHL, Mark .... (IL) 302
Computer systems HALPIN, Peter .... (DC) 490
AAGAARD, James S. ... (IL) 1
GRIES, James P. ...... (IL) 468
BERNARD, Bobbi ..... (MA) 88
BENNETT, Harry D. .... (MD) 81
KOSCHIK, Douglas R. ... (MI) 672
WALKER, M G. .... (NY) 1296
KOOPMAN, Frances A. . (TX) 671
MCCORD, Stanley J. ... (TX) 798
SY, Karen J. .... (WA) 1217
VAILLANCOURT, Alain . (PQ) 1270
GOMEZ, Michael J. .... (WGR)447
Computer systems analysis CHRISTY, Ann K. ...... (DC) 212
Computer systems & databases SPARKS, Marie C. ..... (IN) 1171
Computer systems & online research REED, Carol R. .... (HI) 1014
Computer systems & software BURTON, Mary L. ..... (PA) 164
Computer systems design WHITEHEAD, James M. . (GA) 1332
Computer systems development POLLARD, Louise ..... (UT) 981
Computer systems for libraries ELLIOTT, Riette B. ..... (AL) 344
Computer systems in health BENNETT, David M. .... (AUS) 81
Computer systems integration SPYKERMAN, Bryan R. . (UT) 1177
Computer systems management MITCHELL, Betty J. .... (CA) 848
Computer systems training ROBAR, Terri J. .... (FL) 1038
Computer-assisted instruction lib syst DICARLO, Michael A. .... (LA) 300
Computer-based bibliographic info systs COCHRANE, Pauline A. . (NY) 226
Computer-based information systems SAWYER, Edmond J. ... (DC) 1086
PARK, Margaret K. .... (GA) 941
RUSH, James E. ...... (OH) 1068

SYSTEMS (Cont'd)

Computerization in library systems	LEE, Sulan I.	(AL)	711
Computerized circulation systems	HANRATH, Richard A.	(IL)	497
	UNDERHILL, Jan	(OK)	1268
	EMERICK, Michael J.	(PA)	347
Computerized information systems	DAY, Melvin S.	(VA)	283
Computerized instructional systems	FROST, Rebecca H.	(PA)	406
Computerized library information system	OMARA, Marie T.	(MD)	923
Computerized library systems	GRIFFIN, Hillis L.	(CA)	468
	MITCHELL, Joyce P.	(IL)	849
	DRUKE-STICKLER, Janet A.	(NH)	320
	CARTER, Jackson H.	(NM)	189
	SKIDMORE, Kerry F.	(UT)	1146
Computerized management systems	FROST, Rebecca H.	(PA)	406
Computerized retrieval system	OSTROW, Dianne G.	(MD)	929
Computerized system design	JOHNSON, Jane S.	(IL)	605
Computerized system in libraries	TILLETT, Barbara B.	(CA)	1245
Computerized systems	OLIVARES, Jose A.	(CA)	920
Computers & information systems	HORGAN, Laura A.	(MA)	559
Computers, management systems	CULL, Roberta	(AZ)	263
Consultation on setup, systems	RICHARDS, Stella	(PQ)	1028
Cooperative library systems	PIKE, Lee E.	(AL)	973
	KNUTSON, Linda J.	(IL)	666
	MCCULLY, William C.	(IL)	801
	BUFFINGTON, Karyl L.	(KS)	155
	PATRICK, Patricia M.	(NY)	947
	VERDIBELLO, Muriel F.	(NY)	1282
	WELLS, Mary K.	(TX)	1322
Cooperative medical library systems	JOHN, Stephanie C.	(MI)	601
Cooperative multitype library systems	JAGOE, Katherine P.	(TX)	591
Cooperative systems	MAXWELL, James G.	(OR)	788
	GOLDEN, Helene	(PQ)	445
Coordination of automated systems	THOMPSON, John W.	(IL)	1240
Copier vend systems	SCHULTZ, Michael W.	(AZ)	1102
Copier vending systems	MERKERT, Robert J.	(NJ)	826
Copyright compliance systems	WEIL, Ben H.	(NJ)	1317
Corporate electronic publishing systems	PETERSON, George B.	(MD)	963
Corporate research & devlpmnt info systs	BURCSU, James E.	(NC)	158
Corp information system implementation	GRENIER, Serge	(PQ)	467
County library systems	SMITH, David R.	(MN)	1154
	HARPER, Marjory B.	(TN)	503
County systems	SHIRTS, Russell B.	(UT)	1131
Critical care systems	PORTER, William R.	(TN)	985
Data processing systems	CLASQUIN, Frank F.	(MA)	219
Database & information system design	BATTY, Charles D.	(MD)	65
Database & system design	VANCE, Julia M.	(MD)	1273
Database & systems administration	KINLEY, Jo H.	(DC)	652
Database & systems analysis	ROCHELEAU, Kathleen D.	(MA)	1046
Database & systems consultant	CHAPMAN, Kathleen A.	(WA)	202
Database & systems design	CUTRONA, Cheryl	(PA)	268
Database full-text systems	PHILLIPS, J R.	(OK)	968
Database management system	ROBB, Thomas W.	(DC)	1038
	NASU, Yukio	(JAP)	889
Database management systems	ANDERSON, Clifford D.	(CA)	22
	CUADRA, Carlos A.	(CA)	262
	SHARP, Geoffrey H.	(CA)	1122
	WEISS, William B.	(CA)	1320
	CARR, Sallyann	(DC)	186
	CARR, Sallyann	(FL)	186
	WRIGHT, John H.	(FL)	1371
	VAN BRUNT, Virginia	(MD)	1272
	COX, Bruce B.	(MO)	253
	STEAD, William W.	(NC)	1183
	MOTT, Thomas H.	(NJ)	872
	FROEHLICH, Thomas J.	(NY)	405
	GUBIOTTI, Ross A.	(OH)	475
	EASTMAN, Caroline M.	(SC)	333
	SNYDER, Cathrine E.	(TN)	1164
	FASSETT, William E.	(WA)	366
	SCHUELLER, Janette H.	(WA)	1101
	COLE, Lorna P.	(ON)	231
Database management systems development	ROSENTHAL, Marylu C.	(MA)	1057

SYSTEMS (Cont'd)

Database management systems on computers	RAEDER, Aggi W.	(CA)	1003
Database retrieval systems	ODHO, Marc	(ON)	917
Database search systems	MEADOW, Charles T.	(ON)	819
Database searching & systems	WILLIAMS, Calvin	(MI)	1342
Database system development	ROWBERG, Alan H.	(WA)	1062
Database systems	HALPIN, Peter	(DC)	490
	EMBAR, Indrani M.	(IL)	347
	FITZPATRICK, Nancy C.	(MI)	383
	MITCHELL, Joyce A.	(MO)	849
	LEONARD, Teresa G.	(NC)	717
	KOPPELMAN, William H.	(NY)	671
	LEINBACH, Anne E.	(PA)	714
	WESSEL, Charles B.	(PA)	1325
	SACKETT-WILK, Susan A.	(TX)	1073
	NIGAM, Alok C.	(VA)	904
	ERICKSON, Randall D.	(WA)	352
Database systems & management	SIEGERT, Lindy E.	(NS)	1136
Database systems design	SHAPTON, Gregory B.	(CA)	1122
	KOSTINKO, Gail A.	(DC)	673
Database systems design & analysis	KAVANAGH, Janette R.	(CO)	631
Database systems design & development	SCHWARTZ, Betsy J.	(MD)	1104
Database systems development	ALBERTUS, Donna M.	(NY)	10
	AULBACH, Louis F.	(TX)	39
	JOHNSON, Pat M.	(TX)	608
Database systems, library indexing	FUNK, Carla J.	(IL)	409
Database systems production	BRENNER, Everett H.	(NY)	133
Databases & expert systems	MOLINE, Judi A.	(MD)	853
Databases & systems	OLSON, Rue E.	(IL)	923
Databases, library systems	QUEYROUZE, Mary E.	(TX)	999
Decision support systems	RANDOLPH, Kevin H.	(CA)	1007
	SMITH, Peggy C.	(OK)	1159
	LATHROP, Irene M.	(RI)	701
Defense marketing information systems	MAUTER, George A.	(NY)	787
Demonstrating online systems	SOPELAK, Mary J.	(NY)	1168
Dental information systems	DIEHL, Mark	(IL)	302
Descriptive systems	BURKE, Frank G.	(DC)	160
Design & eval of info systs & lib srvs	COCHRANE, Pauline A.	(NY)	226
Design of shelving systems	BAYLIS, Ted	(MA)	67
Designing medical information systems	LAZAROW-STETTEN, Jane K.	(MD)	706
Designing online systems	BELTON, Jennifer H.	(DC)	78
Designing records management systems	BOWKER, Scott W.	(NY)	121
Designing special library systems	HAUSRATH, Donald C.	(NY)	513
Desktop information management systems	HARTT, Richard W.	(VA)	509
Develop & design accounting systems	CHRISTIANSON, Ellory J.	(MN)	212
Develop medical record systems	KISH, Veronica R.	(PA)	656
Developing nations, information systems	JETT, Don W.	(TN)	600
Device control systems	ZOROWITZ, Richard D.	(IL)	1390
Dissemination systems	SIMS, Edward N.	(KY)	1142
Distributed information systems	DEERWESTER, Scott C.	(IL)	287
Document retrieval systems	WRIGHT, John H.	(FL)	1371
Document storage & retrieval systems	BAGG, Thomas C.	(MD)	45
Documentation of online systems	SOPELAK, Mary J.	(NY)	1168
Electronic communication systems	VAN VELZER, Verna J.	(CA)	1277
Electronic data processing systems	MOUNIR, Khalil A.	(NY)	873
Electronic document handling systems	SPANGLER, Bruce	(CO)	1171
Electronic information delivery systems	PENNIMAN, W D.	(NJ)	957
Electronic information systems	WOOD, Richard T.	(MI)	1365
Electronic mail system management	WAGNER, Judith O.	(OH)	1292
Electronic prepress publishing systems	BRAWLEY, Paul H.	(IL)	130
Elementary school library systems	BERRIE, Ellen T.	(ME)	90
End-user search systems	CHAPMAN, Janet L.	(NJ)	202
End-user systems	NICHOLS, Amy S.	(AL)	901
	MENEELY, William E.	(GA)	824
	SPARKS, Joanne L.	(IL)	1171
Ergonomics in system design	FONG, Wilfred W.	(WI)	388
Establishing lib & information systems	LEFFALL, Dolores C.	(DC)	712
Evaluation research, information systems	SIEGEL, Elliot R.	(MD)	1136
Executive information systems	HARRIS, Jeanne G.	(IL)	504

SYSTEMS (Cont'd)

Expert & optical information systems	SCHNEIDER, Karl R. . . .	(MD)	1097
Expert medical systems	RAMAKRISHNAN, T . . .	(LA)	1004
Expert retrieval assistance systems	MARCUS, Richard S.	(MA)	769
Expert system development	LINDER, Elliott	(NY)	729
Expert system in reference	MICCO, Helen M.	(PA)	831
Expert systems	FOX, Ann M.	(DC)	394
	PARK, Margaret K.	(GA)	941
	SAVAGE, Allan G.	(MD)	1085
	WATERS, Samuel T.	(MD)	1309
	METZLER, Douglas P. . . .	(PA)	829
	MEYER, Daniel E.	(PA)	830
	WILBURN, Clouse R. . . .	(TN)	1338
	PARROTT, James R. . . .	(ON)	944
Expert systems & AI	PITT, William B.	(MD)	976
Expert systems & artificial intelligence	CHANG, Roy T.	(IL)	201
	MOTT, Thomas H.	(NJ)	872
Expert systems & databases	SOERGEL, Dagobert . . .	(MD)	1165
Expert systems & human cognition	HARMON, Glynn	(TX)	502
Expert systems for reference service	RICHARDSON, John V. . .	(CA)	1029
Expert systems in medical databases	LONG, John M.	(MN)	739
Expert systems in reference	EKLAND, Patricia A.	(BC)	341
File systems design	HUFF, Patricia M.	(VA)	570
Filing system design	QUINN, Sidney	(MD)	1000
Filing systems	MCCREARY, Gail A.	(MS)	800
Financial industry trading systems	HALL, Robert C.	(NY)	488
Financial information systems	DEFALCO, Joseph	(NY)	287
Food safety information systems	CHATFIELD, Michele R. .	(DC)	203
Form file systems	GRIGST, Denise J.	(CA)	470
Full-text newspaper library systems	DONCEVIC, Lois A.	(PA)	311
Fund accounting systems	FRIEDMAN, Barbara S. .	(NY)	403
General supervision systems	DILLENSCHNEIDER, Patricia A.	(NJ)	303
Geographic information systems	CHAMMOU, Eliezer	(CA)	198
	SUTHERLAND, Johnnie D.	(GA)	1211
	BOURGEOIS, Ann M. . . .	(MI)	119
	REINHARD, Christine M.	(WI)	1021
Geological, geophysical data systems	AULBACH, Louis F.	(TX)	39
Grant accounting systems	FRIEDMAN, Barbara S. .	(NY)	403
Health care information systems	JACOBSEN, Teresa T. . . .	(IL)	590
Health information systems	JENKIN, Michael A.	(FL)	596
	POST, Joyce A.	(PA)	986
Health risk appraisal systems	ABRAMSON, Lawrence J.	(MI)	3
High school library system	KING, Willard B.	(NC)	652
Hospital information system	HOYT, Lester H.	(IN)	566
Hospital information systems	ANDERSON, Marilyn M. .	(IN)	24
	BUCHANAN, Holly S. . . .	(KY)	153
	LATHROP, Irene M.	(RI)	701
Human factors in computer systems	CHERRY, Joan M.	(ON)	206
Human system language interface	WEI, Yin M.	(OH)	1316
Hybrid numeric bibliographic systems	SCULLY, Patrick F.	(CA)	1109
IBM automation system	ROBERSON, Janis L. . . .	(TX)	1039
Imaging systems, electronic	GOUDELOCK, Carol V. . .	(CA)	454
Implementation of automated systems	HAAK, John R.	(HI)	480
	SMITH, Robert S.	(OH)	1160
Implementing online cataloging system	FISHER, Carl D.	(VA)	380
Index systems	CLIFT, Scott B.	(MA)	222
Indexing & information systems	MCCRANK, Lawrence J.	(AL)	800
Indexing system development	KLEMENT, Susan P. . . .	(ON)	660
Indexing systems	SAUNDERS, Vinette A. .	(DC)	1085
	FLOOD, Barbara J.	(PA)	385
	COTE, Jean P.	(PQ)	249
Indexing systems design	ANDERSON, James D. . .	(NJ)	23
Information & communication systems	RUBEN, Brent D.	(NJ)	1064
Information & library systems	OREJANA, Rebecca D. . .	(PHP)	925
Information & retrieval systems	ANDRADE, Rebecca . . .	(CA)	26
Information center management systems	WEIL, Ben H.	(NJ)	1317
Information database systems	RILEY, Sarah A.	(MD)	1035
Information delivery systems & analysis	GRIMES, A R.	(DC)	470
Information management, plng, & systs	KOZAK, Marlene G.	(IL)	674
Information management systems	WITTMANN, Cecelia V. .	(CA)	1358
	WEST, Richard T.	(MD)	1326
	BAADE, Harley D.	(TX)	43
	KLEIN, Mindy F.	(TX)	659
Information resource systems	THOMAS, Margaret J. . .	(MI)	1237
Information retrieval design system	KORNFELD, Carol E. . . .	(NJ)	672

SYSTEMS (Cont'd)

Information retrieval system	SANO, Hikomaro	(JAP)	1081
Information retrieval system design	MEYER, Alan H.	(MD)	829
	MCCLELLAND, Bruce A.	(NY)	796
Information retrieval systems	CUADRA, Carlos A.	(CA)	262
	GABBERT, Gretchen W. .	(CA)	411
	SHELBURNE, Elizabeth C.	(DC)	1125
	SCHIPMA, Peter B.	(IL)	1093
	EISENMANN, Laura M. .	(MA)	341
	BONDAROVICH, Mary F.	(NJ)	113
	CHAPMAN, Janet L. . . .	(NJ)	202
	FRANTS, Valery	(NJ)	398
	GLAMM, Amy E.	(VA)	439
	SAUVE, Deborah A.	(VA)	1085
	REILLY, Brian O.	(ON)	1020
	ZHU, Xiaofeng	(CHI)	1387
	ROBERTSON, Stephen E.	(ENG)	1042
	CHAUMIER, Jacques . . .	(FRN)	204
Information retrieval systems design	ANDERSON, James D. . .	(NJ)	23
Information science systems	HAMMER, Donald P. . . .	(IL)	493
	CANNATA, Arleen	(NY)	178
Information science, technology systems	JOHNSON, David K. . . .	(NJ)	603
Information system & services planning	KITTUR, Krishna N.	(IND)	657
Information system design	KOPP, Kurt W.	(MO)	671
	RUSHING, Jessie W. . . .	(TN)	1068
	MEADOW, Charles T. . .	(ON)	819
	VAN SLYPE, Georges . . .	(BEL)	1277
Information system design & management	FREEDMAN, Bernadette .	(PA)	400
	LAZAR, Peter	(HUN)	706
Information system development	JONES, Gerry U.	(MD)	613
	KOPP, Kurt W.	(MO)	671
	GUBIOTTI, Ross A.	(OH)	475
Information system evaluation	GRIFFITH, Belver C. . . .	(PA)	469
	VAN SLYPE, Georges . . .	(BEL)	1277
Information systems	SEDELOW, Sally Y.	(AR)	1110
	SEDELOW, Walter A. . . .	(AR)	1110
	HOTZ, Sharon M.	(CA)	562
	LEWIS, Gretchen S.	(CA)	723
	PALLONE, Kitty J.	(CA)	935
	PETERMAN, Claudia A. .	(CA)	962
	VARAT, Nancy L.	(CA)	1278
	SHAW, Ward	(CO)	1124
	ORRICO, James T.	(CT)	926
	FOX, Ann M.	(DC)	394
	FRANCIS, Diane S.	(DE)	396
	GRIES, James P.	(IL)	468
	COPLER, Judith A.	(IN)	244
	FRY, Bernard M.	(IN)	406
	ROMALEWSKI, Robert S.	(LA)	1052
	DOWLER, Lawrence E. . .	(MA)	315
	FERGUSON, Roberta J. .	(MA)	372
	KANG, Wen	(MA)	625
	O'REILLY, Daniel F.	(MA)	925
	YACOUBY, Ray S.	(MA)	1376
	ANDERSON, John E. . . .	(MD)	23
	JOHNSON, Susan W. . .	(MD)	609
	PAUL, Thomas A.	(MI)	949
	ABLES, Timothy D.	(MS)	2
	SNODGRASS, Rex J. . . .	(NC)	1163
	KELSEY, Ann L.	(NJ)	639
	PENNIMAN, W D.	(NJ)	957
	HARRISON, Susan F . . .	(NV)	507
	EISENBERG, Debra	(NY)	340
	SCHARF, Davida	(NY)	1090
	SIMONIS, James J.	(NY)	1141
	KILGOUR, Frederick G. .	(OH)	648
	KISER, Betsy N.	(OH)	656
	MCCONNELL, Pamela J.	(OH)	798
	ROMANOS, Vasso A. . .	(OH)	1052
	TRIVISON, Donna	(OH)	1257
	PETERSON, Barbara E. .	(PA)	962
	TOMASOVIC, Evelyn . . .	(PA)	1249
	TILSON, Koleta B.	(TN)	1245
	ANDERSON, Madeleine J.	(TX)	24
	VONDRAN, Raymond F. .	(TX)	1288
	LAHR, Thomas F.	(VA)	688
	MORSE, June E.	(VA)	869

SYSTEMS (Cont'd)

Information systems
	TATALIAS, Jean A.	(VA)	1225
	MCCORMICK, Jack M.	(WA)	798
	DYKSTRA, Mary E.	(NS)	331
	BIRKS, Grant F.	(ON)	98
	SIMARD, Denis	(PQ)	1139
	NEAME, Roderick L.	(AUS)	891
	IRURIA, Daniel M.	(KEN)	584
	LIM, Hucktee E.	(MLY)	727

Information systems analysis & design	BORKO, Harold	(CA)	116
	WILLIAMS, James G.	(PA)	1344
Information systems & decision support	BERGFELD, C D.	(NY)	86
Information systems & technologies	FRIERSON, Eleanor G.	(DC)	404
Information systems consultant	SHAMS, Kamruddin	(CA)	1120
Information systems, database design	FOURNIER, Susan K.	(MD)	393
Information systems design	MICHEL, Dee A.	(CA)	832
	TUNG, Sandra J.	(CA)	1263
	KENNEY, Brigitte L.	(CO)	641
	RADER, Ronald A.	(DC)	1002
	SOERGEL, Dagobert	(MD)	1165
	KELLER, Karen A.	(MI)	635
	WAGNER, A B.	(NY)	1291
	WARD, Edith	(NY)	1303
	HOLMES, John H.	(PA)	553
	LEONARD, Lucinda E.	(VA)	716
	BOOHER, Craig S.	(WI)	115
Information systems design, analysis	SYPERT, Clyde F.	(CA)	1217
Information systems design & development	WHITE, Suellen S.	(CO)	1332
	CLARK, Rick	(NJ)	218
Information systems design & evaluation	LEVITAN, Karen B.	(MD)	721
Information systems design & integration	CHU, John S.	(PA)	212
Information systems development	PARSONS, John W.	(DC)	945
	KOSMAN, Joyce E.	(IL)	672
	HOLMES, Lyndon S.	(MA)	553
	ETZI, Richard	(NY)	356
	BERGMAN, Rita F.	(VA)	86
	COTTER, Gladys A.	(VA)	250
	HOWARD, Theresa M.	(ENG)	564
Information systems engineering	LISTON, David M.	(MD)	732
Information systems management	TETTEH, Joseph A.	(LA)	1233
	MENOU, Michel J.	(ITL)	824
Information systems, microcomputers	ANDERSON, Axel R.	(WI)	21
Information systems needs assessment	ROBERTS, Lesley A.	(DC)	1040
Information systems planning	PARMING, Marju R.	(DC)	943
	ABLES, Timothy D.	(MS)	2
	FABRE DE MORLHON, Christiane	(ITL)	360
Information systems planning, consulting	GROTE, Janet H.	(NY)	473
Information systems research	SNYDER, Cathrine E.	(TN)	1164
Information systems research & devlpmnt	TONKERY, Thomas D.	(NY)	1250
Information systems strategic planning	PEETERS, Marc D.	(BEL)	954
In-house systems	DAVIDSON, Dero H.	(DC)	276
In-house systems automation	MOUNTFORD, Eve	(CT)	873
InMagic software file management system	HOUSTON, Louise B.	(ON)	563
Innovacq & Innopac systems	TEMPLE, Harold L.	(IL)	1230
Instructional systems technology	BERMAN, Arthur	(AR)	88
Integrated & automated library systems	WORMINGTON, Peggie	(CA)	1369
Integrated automated library systems	LASETER, Shirley B.	(AL)	700
	SIDMAN, George C.	(CA)	1135
	MOORE, Barbara N.	(MN)	858
Integrated circulation systems	CRISCO, Mary E.	(MD)	259
Integrated information systems	RAGHAVAN, Vijay V.	(LA)	1003
	CHIANG, Katherine S.	(NY)	207
Integrated library automation systems	SHURMAN, Richard L.	(IL)	1134
Integrated library system automation	BREEDLOVE, Elizabeth A.	(NJ)	131
Integrated library systems	ELMAN, Stanley A.	(CA)	345
	NASATIR, Marilyn	(CA)	888
	SWEENEY, Urban J.	(CA)	1215
	WOLF, Nola M.	(CA)	1360
	TODD, Hal W.	(FL)	1248

SYSTEMS (Cont'd)

Integrated library systems
	BALL, Mary A.	(IL)	52
	DREWETT, William O.	(IL)	319
	BOND, Marvin A.	(MD)	113
	HENDERSON, Susanne	(MD)	527
	MENEGAUX, Edmond A.	(MD)	824
	STERLING, Judith K.	(MD)	1189
	EPSTEIN, Rheda	(MN)	351
	KAN, Halina S.	(NJ)	624
	CHAPMAN, Renee D.	(NY)	202
	HOPKINS, Judith	(NY)	558
	FERRIN, Eric G.	(PA)	373
	RITTENHOUSE, Robert J.	(PA)	1036
	AIROLDI, Melissa	(TX)	9
	GALTON, Gwen	(ON)	415

Integrated online library systems	WEISS, William B.	(CA)	1320
	MARQUARDT, Steve R.	(WI)	772
Integrated systems	SHERIDAN, John B.	(CO)	1127
	LAKSHMAN, Malathi K.	(MD)	689
	HEMPEL, Ruth M.	(TX)	525
Integrated systems automation	BRIDGE, Frank R.	(TX)	135
Intl library & information systems	GOODMAN, Henry J.	(AB)	449
Investment information systems	CAHILL, Jack F.	(MA)	171
IOLS library systems	BENTE, June E.	(NJ)	83
Journal & interlibrary loan systems	ROBERTS, Linda L.	(OK)	1041
Knowledge acquisition for expert systems	MUSEN, Mark A.	(CA)	883
Knowledge systems	GOLDSCHMIDT, Peter G.	(MD)	446
Knowledge-based information system	WEI, Yin M.	(OH)	1316
Knowledge-based systems	HUMPHREY, Susanne M.	(MD)	573
K-12 library systems	JOHNSON, Elizabeth L.	(NE)	604
Large-scale information systems	SAYER, John S.	(MD)	1086
Law firm, information systems	EWING, Alison L.	(AZ)	359
Law library systems	BUTTS, Willie D.	(MD)	168
	BROWN, Vicki L.	(OH)	148
Law library systems design	RAUM, Tamar	(NY)	1010
Legal administrative support systems	CROCKETT, Denise J.	(NY)	259
Legal information systems	STERN, Michael P.	(MD)	1189
Legal records systems	KANE, Dorothea S.	(VA)	624
Legal research retrieval systems	EVERLOVE, Nora J.	(FL)	359
Library & archival systems	BARRY, Paul J.	(DC)	60
Library & archives systems	TONEY, Stephen R.	(MD)	1250
Library & information resource systems	NELSON, James A.	(KY)	894
Library & information systems	DEBUSE, Raymond	(WA)	285
	WARD, Maryanne	(WA)	1304
	CHANDLER, George	(ENG)	200
Library & information systems & tech	GRIFFITHS, Jose M.	(MD)	469
Library & information systems consulting	MADDOCK, Jerome T.	(CO)	759
Library & management systems	BLACKBURN, Joy M.	(IL)	102
Library automated systems	ALLEN, Linda G.	(FL)	15
	REDFEARN, Linda E.	(MA)	1014
	MURRAY, Diane E.	(MI)	881
	SHEVIAK, Jean K.	(NY)	1129
	NEAL, James G.	(PA)	890
	RAMBLER, Linda K.	(PA)	1005
	LINDBERG, Sandra	(VT)	728
Library automation & systems	MORROW, Deborah	(MI)	869
	LUCKER, Amy E.	(NY)	746
	RAWLINS, Gordon W.	(PA)	1010
Library automation & systems analysis	MAURA-SARDO, Mariano A.	(PR)	787
Library automation system	WANG, Gary Y.	(MA)	1302
Library automation system, Book Trak	JACKSON, Nancy I.	(FL)	588
Library automation systems	BARKALOW, Pat A.	(CA)	56
	JOHNSON, Mary L.	(CA)	607
	HENTZ, Margaret E.	(CT)	530
	CANICK, Maureen L.	(DC)	178
	TURNER, Susan A.	(DC)	1265
	BROWN, Pamela P.	(IL)	146
	HOWREY, Mary M.	(IL)	566
	BUCKLAND, Lawrence F.	(MA)	154
	STACK, Laurie A.	(MT)	1177
	STICKEL, William R.	(NJ)	1193
	KERSCHNER, Joan G.	(NV)	644
	RAHN, Erwin P.	(NY)	1003
	DAVIS, Linda M.	(OH)	280

SYSTEMS (Cont'd)

Library automation systems

CADY, Susan A.	(PA)	170
GOULD, Douglas A.	(UT)	454
ESPLEY, John L.	(VA)	354
DIXON, Edith M.	(WI)	306
DZIERZAK, Edward M.	(WV)	331

Library automation systems
management — HOWE, Patricia A. (VA) 565
Library communications systems — PLOTKIN, Nathan (CA) 978
Library computer systems — SEGEL, Bernard J. (DC) 1112

STELZLE, James J.	(NY)	1186
YAVARKOVSKY, Jerome	(NY)	1378
PIPER, Larry W.	(OR)	975
WOODS, Richard F.	(FIJ)	1367

Library computerization, systems — MILLER, Suzanne M. (CA) 842
Library computers & systems — SINK, Thomas R. (OH) 1143
Library delivery systems & services — STOCKTON, Gloria J. (CA) 1196
Library design & systems planning — KAPNICK, Laura B. (NY) 626
Library display systems design — RIBNICKY, Karen F. (CT) 1026
Library indexing systems — MAJURE, William D. (MS) 762
Library information management
systems — SMITH, Jessie C. (MD) 1156
Library information system — ZHANG, Foster J. (CA) 1387
Library information systems

KERR, Robert C.	(CO)	644
HERNANDEZ, Hector R.	(IL)	531
LUDWIG, Logan T.	(IL)	747
VAN HOUTEN, Stephen	(IL)	1275
ASSOUAD, Carol S.	(MD)	37
PAUL, Rameshwar N.	(MD)	949
JENSEN, Charla J.	(UT)	598

Library microcomputer systems — BAZILLION, Richard J. (ON) 68
Library network systems development — BAADE, Harley D. (TX) 43
Library networks & systems — ALBRIGHT, Elaine M. (ME) 10
Library of Congress classification syst — SAVAGE, Helen (MI) 1085
Library online integrated systems — KING, Maryde F. (NY) 651
Library online systems — MADISON, Olivia M. (IA) 759

SONNEMANN, Gail J.	(VA)	1167

Library planning & systems — DUANE, Carol A. (OH) 321
Library regional systems — CHRISTENSON, John D. (MN) 211
Library sign systems — MALLERY, Mary S. (MD) 763
Library system — CROWE, Linda D. (CA) 261

WINKLER, Jean J.	(CO)	1355
HAGEMEYER, Alice L.	(DC)	483
LANDESMAN, Betty J.	(MA)	692
JENG, Helene W.	(MD)	596
COUMBE, Robert E.	(NJ)	251
ANDREWS, Lois W.	(NM)	26
CHEN, Ching F.	(NY)	205
SCHNEIDER, J K.	(OH)	1097

Library system administration — SWAN, James A. (KS) 1213

WU, Harry P.	(MI)	1373
NETTLES, Jess	(MS)	896
LANGER, Frank A.	(WV)	695

Library system analysis — ROHLF, Robert H. (MN) 1050
Library system analysis & design — MORGAN, Ferrell (CA) 864
Library system budget funding — NETTLES, Jess (MS) 896
Library system consulting — LEWIS, Alan D. (MN) 722
Library system coordination — EBERSHOFF-COLES,
Susan V. (IN) 334
Library system development — MILLER, Dick R. (CA) 837

MAKAREWICZ, Grace E.	(BC)	762

Library system management — COBLE, Gerald M. (FL) 225
Library system of Philadelphia — GREEN, Rose B. (PA) 462
Library system operations — CARDEN, Marguerite (FL) 180
Library system planning — PLACE, Philip A. (FL) 977
Library system, reference & research — ROTHENBERG, Mark H. (NY) 1060
Library system-public service — CARDEN, Marguerite (FL) 180
Library systems — CHANEY, A V. (AK) 200

ELAM, Kim A.	(AK)	341
WEILAND, Karen B.	(AK)	1317
BUSH, Nancy W.	(AL)	165
HARRIS, Edwin R.	(AL)	504
LANCASTER III, Thomas A.	(AL)	692
LOWE, David	(AL)	743
MAYTON, Regina A.	(AL)	791
MCWHORTER, Jimmie M.	(AL)	818
MORRIS, Betty J.	(AL)	866
STEWART, George R.	(AL)	1192

SYSTEMS (Cont'd)

Library systems

VANDERPOORTEN, Mary B.	(AL)	1274
MULKEY, Jack C.	(AR)	876
TROMATER, Raymond B.	(AR)	1257
WATSON, Ellen I.	(AR)	1309
ALURI, Rao	(AZ)	19
BIERMAN, Kenneth J.	(AZ)	95
BUXTON, David T.	(AZ)	168
KNEPP, Kenneth B.	(AZ)	664
MACHOVEC, George S.	(AZ)	755
MCCRAY, Jeanette C.	(AZ)	800
MCGORRAY, John J.	(AZ)	807
ALIPRAND, Joan M.	(CA)	13
ALLENSWORTH, James H.	(CA)	16
AVENEY, Brian H.	(CA)	41
BALES, F K.	(CA)	52
BARANOWSKI, George V.	(CA)	55
BATES, Henry E.	(CA)	64
BECKER, Joseph	(CA)	72
BENGSTON, Carl E.	(CA)	80
BLUE, Margaret L.	(CA)	107
BRITTAIN, Cynthia E.	(CA)	137
BUNTZEN, Joan L.	(CA)	157
CHANG, Min M.	(CA)	200
COYLE, Karen E.	(CA)	253
DAILEY, Kazuko M.	(CA)	270
DEMENT, Alice R.	(CA)	291
DONINI, Elizabeth A.	(CA)	311
DWYER, James R.	(CA)	330
FARMAR, Donna M.	(CA)	364
FROHMBERG, Katherine A.	(CA)	405
GULLION, Susan L.	(CA)	477
HAMBRIDGE, Sally L.	(CA)	491
HAY, Wayne M.	(CA)	515
HEINES, Rodney M.	(CA)	522
HERDMAN, Elena	(CA)	530
HUANG, George W.	(CA)	568
JACOBUS, Nancy M.	(CA)	590
JADWIN, Rochelle J.	(CA)	591
JUDY, Joseph R.	(CA)	619
KARCHER, Tracey L.	(CA)	627
KATZ, Jeffrey P.	(CA)	630
KILLIAN, Richard M.	(CA)	648
KING, Kitty G.	(CA)	651
LEIGH, Carma R.	(CA)	714
LEWIS, Ralph W.	(CA)	724
LINDBERG, Susan J.	(CA)	729
MARLOR, Hugh T.	(CA)	772
MAYES, Elizabeth A.	(CA)	789
MCCRACKEN, John R.	(CA)	799
MCDONALD, Marilyn M.	(CA)	803
MCDONOUGH, Timothy M.	(CA)	803
MERKLEY, John P.	(CA)	826
MILLS, Denise Y.	(CA)	844
MOLLETT, Mike M.	(CA)	853
MONTGOMERY, Teresa L.	(CA)	856
MORSE, David H.	(CA)	869
MOSER, Elizabeth C.	(CA)	870
MULLER, Malinda S.	(CA)	877
NEWMAN, Mark J.	(CA)	899
PAI, Herman H.	(CA)	934
PARSONS, Jerry L.	(CA)	945
PENDLETON, Lynne G.	(CA)	956
PIERCE, Patricia J.	(CA)	971
PINCOCK, Rulon D.	(CA)	974
PLATE, Kenneth H.	(CA)	977
PLOTKIN, Nathan	(CA)	978
POST, William E.	(CA)	986
PRELINGER, Polly	(CA)	990
PRESLAN, Bruce H.	(CA)	991
REEDER, Norman L.	(CA)	1015
REIFMAN, Deborah S.	(CA)	1019
REILLY, James H.	(CA)	1020
RHEE, Susan F.	(CA)	1025
ROBERTS, Justine T.	(CA)	1040

SYSTEMS (Cont'd)
Library systems

ROSENBERG, Stuart L.	(CA)	1056
ROSENBERGER, Diane C.	(CA)	1056
SABSAY, David	(CA)	1073
SAUSEDO, Ann E.	(CA)	1085
SCHAFFER, Eamon	(CA)	1089
SCHMIDT, C J.	(CA)	1095
SCHRIEFER, Kent	(CA)	1100
SCRIBNER, Ruth B.	(CA)	1108
SEGUNDO, Fe P.	(CA)	1112
SERTIC, Kenneth J.	(CA)	1116
SEVIER, Jeffrey A.	(CA)	1117
SILBERSTEIN, Stephen M.	(CA)	1137
STOVEL, Madeleine D.	(CA)	1199
TAOKA, Wesley M.	(CA)	1223
TEMA, William J.	(CA)	1230
TOMMEY, Richard J.	(CA)	1250
TOMPKINS, Philip	(CA)	1250
TRAVER, Dorothy A.	(CA)	1254
WAWRZONEK, Mary S.	(CA)	1311
WEBB, Duncan C.	(CA)	1313
WINGATE, Eliza C.	(CA)	1354
WOO, Winnie H.	(CA)	1363
WOODS, Lawrence A.	(CA)	1367
ZEIND, Samir M.	(CA)	1387
ZIAIAN, Monir	(CA)	1387
ZYROFF, Ellen S.	(CA)	1392
BOND, Mary J.	(CO)	113
ESTES, Mark E.	(CO)	355
JONES, Donna R.	(CO)	612
QUINN, Candy L.	(CO)	1000
SHAW, Ward	(CO)	1124
WILLIAMS, Alma	(CO)	1341
BAYLES, Carmen L.	(CT)	67
CROWLEY, John D.	(CT)	261
CRUTCHER, Hope H.	(CT)	262
FLANAGAN, Leo N.	(CT)	383
LOWELL, Gerald R.	(CT)	744
MASTERS, Fred N.	(CT)	782
MASTERS, Kathy B.	(CT)	782
NEUFELD, Irving H.	(CT)	897
PARIKH, Kaumudi H.	(CT)	940
PARKS, Amy N.	(CT)	943
PORTER, Kathryn W.	(CT)	985
PRATT, Allan D.	(CT)	989
URICCHIO, William J.	(CT)	1269
ATKINSON, Rose M.	(DC)	38
AVRAM, Henriette D.	(DC)	42
BROERING, Naomi C.	(DC)	139
DELANCEY, James F.	(DC)	288
FLANNERY, Patrick D.	(DC)	383
FREEMAN, Carla	(DC)	400
GERIG, Reginald R.	(DC)	428
HALEY, Roger K.	(DC)	486
HO, James K.	(DC)	545
KALKUS, Stanley	(DC)	623
KEHOE, Patrick E.	(DC)	634
KOENEMAN, Joyce W.	(DC)	668
LISOWSKI, Andrew H.	(DC)	732
MCCRAY, Maceo E.	(DC)	800
MOTEN, Derryn E.	(DC)	872
PAGE, John S.	(DC)	934
PFUND, Leona I.	(DC)	966
PRICE, Joseph W.	(DC)	992
PULVER, Thomas B.	(DC)	997
SHEERAN, Carole A.	(DC)	1125
SHEN, I Y.	(DC)	1126
SHERWIN, Rosalie L.	(DC)	1129
STACKPOLE, Laurie E.	(DC)	1178
SYLVESTER, Carol	(DC)	1217
THOMPSON, Laurie L.	(DC)	1240
TRIMBLE, Kathleen L.	(DC)	1256
WILLSON, Elizabeth	(DC)	1349
BURDASH, David H.	(DE)	158
GLOGOFF, Stuart J.	(DE)	441
MANUEL, Larry L.	(DE)	767
THOMAN, Nancy L.	(DE)	1236
BROWNLEE, Jerry W.	(FL)	148
BUFKIN, Anne G.	(FL)	155

SYSTEMS (Cont'd)
Library systems

BURROWS, Suzetta C.	(FL)	163
CLOPINE, John J.	(FL)	223
CORNELL, Sylvia C.	(FL)	247
DALEHITE, Michele I.	(FL)	270
DONOVAN, Elizabeth L.	(FL)	312
GOSS, Theresa C.	(FL)	453
HENNINGS, Leroy	(FL)	528
HOPKINS, Joan A.	(FL)	558
ISAACS, Bob	(FL)	584
JONES, Robert P.	(FL)	614
MOJO, Anne Z.	(FL)	852
MULLER, Charles W.	(FL)	877
PETIT, Michael J.	(FL)	965
PROCTOR, Dixie L.	(FL)	994
RHEIN, Jean F.	(FL)	1025
STORCK, Bernadette R.	(FL)	1198
TAYLOR, Betty W.	(FL)	1226
TAYSOM, Daniel B.	(FL)	1229
TORNABENE, Charles	(FL)	1251
WHEELER, James M.	(FL)	1329
WILLIAMS, Nancy L.	(FL)	1345
BATTEN, Henry R.	(GA)	64
BECHOR, Malvina B.	(GA)	71
BRADLEY, Gail P.	(GA)	125
CRAFT, Guy C.	(GA)	254
DEES, Anthony R.	(GA)	287
DRAPER, James D.	(GA)	318
FISTE, David A.	(GA)	382
FLAVIN, Linda M.	(GA)	384
HENDRIX, Linda S.	(GA)	527
HENNER, Terry A.	(GA)	528
JORDAN, Casper L.	(GA)	616
LANDRAM, Christina L.	(GA)	693
LEWIS, Frank R.	(GA)	723
MCDANIEL, Sara H.	(GA)	801
OVERBECK, James A.	(GA)	931
STAHL, D G.	(GA)	1178
SURRENCY, Erwin C.	(GA)	1210
WARREN, Ruth M.	(GA)	1307
WIGHT, Nancy E.	(GA)	1337
WILTSE, Helen C.	(GA)	1353
JACKSON, Miles M.	(HI)	588
KANE, Bartholomew A.	(HI)	624
LUSTER, Arlene L.	(HI)	750
MATSUMORI, Donald M.	(HI)	784
NAJ, Linda M.	(HI)	887
URAGO, Gail M.	(HI)	1269
WILSON, Deetta C.	(HI)	1350
BROWN, Darmae J.	(IA)	143
HIRST, Donna L.	(IA)	543
MIDDLESWART, Patricia A.	(IA)	833
MORRIS, Dilys E.	(IA)	866
NAVARRE, Emily L.	(IA)	889
SHAW, Craig S.	(IA)	1123
SWANSON, P A.	(IA)	1213
COVINGTON, Eddis E.	(ID)	252
VERHOFF, Patricia A.	(ID)	1282
ALLEY, Brian	(IL)	16
BERRY, John W.	(IL)	90
BURNSIDE, Diane B.	(IL)	163
CHAMBERLIN, Edgar W.	(IL)	198
CLARK, Gerald L.	(IL)	217
ENSLEY, Robert F.	(IL)	350
FROST, Bruce Q.	(IL)	406
GARDNER, Trudy A.	(IL)	418
GIERING, Richard H.	(IL)	433
HAFNER, Arthur W.	(IL)	482
HAMILTON, Beth A.	(IL)	491
HARRIS, Thomas J.	(IL)	506
HAYES, Hazel I.	(IL)	515
HICKS, Frederick M.	(IL)	537
HUSLIG, Dennis M.	(IL)	578
HUTCHINS, Mary J.	(IL)	579
IDDINGS, Daniel H.	(IL)	581
JOHN, Nancy R.	(IL)	601
KANNER, Elliott E.	(IL)	625
KAPLAN, Sylvia Y.	(IL)	626

SYSTEMS (Cont'd)
Library systems

KELLERSTRASS, Amy L.	(IL)	636
KREINBRING, Mary	(IL)	677
LAMONT, Bridget L.	(IL)	691
LOCKRIDGE, Eunice A.	(IL)	736
LUNDQUIST, Marie A.	(IL)	748
LUQUIRE, Wilson	(IL)	749
MACKEY, Denise R.	(IL)	756
MANN, Vijai S.	(IL)	766
MCCLARREN, Robert R.	(IL)	796
MCKAY, Robert W.	(IL)	810
MCKEARN, Anne B.	(IL)	810
MEISELS, Henry R.	(IL)	822
MICKELBERRY, Mark B.	(IL)	833
MILLER, Bruce A.	(IL)	836
MOCH, Mary I.	(IL)	851
MOTTRAM, Geoffrey	(IL)	873
NIEHAUS, Barbara J.	(IL)	903
PERLMAN, Michael S.	(IL)	959
POULTNEY, Judy R.	(IL)	987
PROBST, Virginia M.	(IL)	994
RANDALL, Sara L.	(IL)	1006
SCHAACK, Wilma J.	(IL)	1088
SCHOLTZ, James C.	(IL)	1098
SCOTT, Alice H.	(IL)	1106
SOBKOWIAK, Emily J.	(IL)	1165
SPENCER, Joan M.	(IL)	1173
STALZER, Rita M.	(IL)	1179
STARRATT, Joseph A.	(IL)	1182
STOFFEL, Lester L.	(IL)	1196
SYVERSON, Kathleen A.	(IL)	1217
TEGLER, Patricia	(IL)	1230
UBEL, James A.	(IL)	1267
UDDIN, Shantha C.	(IL)	1267
WARRO, Edward A.	(IL)	1307
WERNETTE, Janice J.	(IL)	1325
WINNER, Ronald	(IL)	1355
WRIGHT, Donald E.	(IL)	1371
BOYCE, Harold W.	(IN)	122
CLEGG, Michael B.	(IN)	220
CORYA, William L.	(IN)	248
DOLAN, Robert T.	(IN)	309
LAUGHLIN, Sara G.	(IN)	703
POOR, William E.	(IN)	983
RANSIL, M M.	(IN)	1007
SELLBERG, Roxanne J.	(IN)	1113
SHEETS, Michael T.	(IN)	1125
VIGEANT, Robert J.	(IN)	1284
WITTORF, Robert H.	(IN)	1359
WOLCOTT, Laurie J.	(IN)	1359
ALLEN, Norene F.	(KS)	15
BUMBALOUGH, Bruce L.	(KS)	157
BURBACH, Jude	(KS)	158
BURCHILL, Mary D.	(KS)	158
EVANS, Constance L.	(KS)	356
GATTIN, Leroy M.	(KS)	422
HOWARD, Clinton N.	(KS)	564
MOBLEY, Kathleen S.	(KS)	851
MORELAND, Rachel S.	(KS)	863
POSTLEWAIT, Cheryl A.	(KS)	986
RIDDLE, Raymond E.	(KS)	1032
ROTH, Sally	(KS)	1059
VAN BENTEN, Virginia M.	(KS)	1272
WITMER, Tonya C.	(KS)	1358
BUTTERWORTH, Donald Q.	(KY)	167
DIESING, Arthur C.	(KY)	302
HERRON, Darl H.	(KY)	533
ROBINSON, Christie M.	(KY)	1043
SMITH, Lena D.	(KY)	1157
STROHECKER, Edwin C.	(KY)	1202
CARTEE, Lewis D.	(LA)	188
DAVIS, Margo	(LA)	280
DOMBOURIAN, Sona J.	(LA)	310
GOLDSTEIN, Cynthia H.	(LA)	446
LAUGHLIN, Beverly E.	(LA)	702
NUCKLES, Nancy E.	(LA)	912
POUNCY, Mitchell L.	(LA)	987
WICKER, W W.	(LA)	1335

SYSTEMS (Cont'd)
Library systems

YOUNG, Amanda M.	(LA)	1381
ANDERSON, Norman E.	(MA)	24
BENDER, Elizabeth H.	(MA)	79
BLAKE, Michael R.	(MA)	103
BOEHME, Richard W.	(MA)	109
BRITE, Agnes	(MA)	137
CAREY, Charlene E.	(MA)	181
CARNAHAN, Paul A.	(MA)	183
CHANDRASEKHAR, Ratna	(MA)	200
CLIFT, Scott B.	(MA)	222
COHEN, Martha J.	(MA)	228
DEARBORN, Susan C.	(MA)	284
DESROCHES, Richard A.	(MA)	295
FINNI, John J.	(MA)	379
FRIEDMAN, Terri L.	(MA)	404
GAGNON, Ronald A.	(MA)	412
GILLIAM, Ellen M.	(MA)	436
GIULIANO, Lillian C.	(MA)	439
GOLDBERG, Steven R.	(MA)	444
GRAY, Carolyn M.	(MA)	459
GREENBERG, Carolyn R.	(MA)	463
GRIFFITH, William R.	(MA)	469
HAYES, Maureen L.	(MA)	516
HENEGHAN, Mary A.	(MA)	528
HONESS, Mary E.	(MA)	555
INGERSOLL, Diane S.	(MA)	582
JACOBSON, Nancy C.	(MA)	590
KUKLINSKI, Joan L.	(MA)	683
LYDON, Mary E.	(MA)	751
MAGUIRE, Linda H.	(MA)	760
MASON, Hayden	(MA)	781
MAZURANIC, Joseph R.	(MA)	791
MCKIRDY, Colin	(MA)	812
MIELE, Madeline F.	(MA)	833
MOULTON, Lynda W.	(MA)	873
MYLES, Bobbie	(MA)	885
NIMS, Judith C.	(MA)	904
PELLEGRINI, Deborah A.	(MA)	955
PROCOPIO, Concetta E.	(MA)	994
RAMSAY, John E.	(MA)	1005
ROBINSON, Deanna C.	(MA)	1043
SARAIDARIDIS, Susan B.	(MA)	1082
SHARE, Donald S.	(MA)	1122
SNYDER, David A.	(MA)	1164
SUTTON, Joyce A.	(MA)	1211
TSENG, Louisa	(MA)	1260
WHEALAN, Ronald E.	(MA)	1328
ALBRIGHT, John B.	(MD)	10
ANDERSON, John E.	(MD)	23
BATOR, Eileen F.	(MD)	64
BLEGEN, John C.	(MD)	105
BROWN, Florence S.	(MD)	144
CARMAN, Carol A.	(MD)	183
CHEN, John H.	(MD)	205
CHIESA, Adele M.	(MD)	208
COOK, Daraka S.	(MD)	239
COSTABILE, Salvatore L.	(MD)	249
DAVIS, Bonnie D.	(MD)	277
DUDLEY, Robyn A.	(MD)	323
DUTCHER, Gale A.	(MD)	329
GALLAGHER, Elizabeth M.	(MD)	414
GOETZ, Arthur H.	(MD)	443
HALE, Dawn L.	(MD)	485
HILL, Norma L.	(MD)	540
HOWARD, Paul	(MD)	564
HURREY, Katharine C.	(MD)	577
JACKSON, Doris G.	(MD)	587
JOHNSON, Carol A.	(MD)	602
KADEC, Sarah T.	(MD)	621
KIM, Chung S.	(MD)	648
LYON-HARTMANN, Becky J.	(MD)	752
MARTINEZ-GOLDMAN, Aline	(MD)	779
MCCONE, Gary K.	(MD)	797
NEAL, Robert L.	(MD)	890
PECK, Shirley S.	(MD)	953

SYSTEMS (Cont'd)
Library systems

RICHTER, Mary L.	(MD)	1031
SCHULMAN, Jacque L.	(MD)	1101
TUCKER, Clark F.	(MD)	1261
WAGNER, Susan C.	(MD)	1292
WILLMERING, William J.	(MD)	1348
WOODS, Catharine C.	(MD)	1366
SHANKLAND, Anne H.	(ME)	1120
BEST, Donald A.	(MI)	92
DOUGHERTY, Richard M.	(MI)	314
GARCIA, Joseph E.	(MI)	417
GARNSEY, Alice M.	(MI)	419
GAURI, Kul B.	(MI)	423
MARGOLIS, Bernard A.	(MI)	770
MCDONALD, David R.	(MI)	802
MEAHL, D D.	(MI)	819
NUCKOLLS, Karen A.	(MI)	912
SAGAR, Mary B.	(MI)	1074
SLACH, June E.	(MI)	1147
SPECTOR, Janice B.	(MI)	1172
STAJNIAK, Elizabeth T.	(MI)	1178
VERGE, Colleen R.	(MI)	1282
VETTESE, Richard	(MI)	1283
WILLIAMS, James F.	(MI)	1343
ANDERSON, Margaret J.	(MN)	24
COGSWELL, James A.	(MN)	227
FARNER, Susan G.	(MN)	365
FEMAL, Mary B.	(MN)	370
FERM, Lois R.	(MN)	373
GROSCH, Audrey N.	(MN)	472
KISHEL, Deane A.	(MN)	656
RASMUSSEN, Mary L.	(MN)	1009
VETH, Terry R.	(MN)	1283
BROWN, Gerald D.	(MO)	144
CHUNG, Carolyn	(MO)	213
DOSS, Mamie	(MO)	313
FEDDERS, Cynthia S.	(MO)	367
GAMER, May L.	(MO)	416
HALBROOK, Barbara	(MO)	485
HOOVER, Jonnette L.	(MO)	557
KAISER, Patricia L.	(MO)	622
KOPP, Kurt W.	(MO)	671
MEIZNER, Karen L.	(MO)	822
MURPHY, Kathryn L.	(MO)	880
TOLSON, Stephanie D.	(MO)	1249
BATTAGLIA, Mary H.	(MS)	64
BELL, Bernice	(MS)	76
DUNAWAY, Charjean L.	(MS)	325
MYRICK, Judy C.	(MS)	885
WILLIAMS, Eddie A.	(MS)	1343
ALLDREDGE, Noreen S.	(MT)	14
CATES, Sheila A.	(MT)	195
ASPINALL, David L.	(NC)	37
BEAGLE, Donald R.	(NC)	68
BENNETT, David B.	(NC)	81
BIRD, Warren P.	(NC)	98
CAMPBELL, Jerry D.	(NC)	176
COLLINS, Melanie H.	(NC)	233
FISH, Paula H.	(NC)	380
FRAZELLE, Betty	(NC)	399
JACQUES, Eunice L.	(NC)	591
MACPHAIL, Jessica	(NC)	758
MCGLOHON, Charlotte L.	(NC)	807
MOORE, Thomas L.	(NC)	861
MURPHY, Malinda M.	(NC)	881
RHINE, Cynthia	(NC)	1025
ROBERTSON, W D.	(NC)	1042
SCHELL, Nancy S.	(NC)	1091
STEPHENS, Arial A.	(NC)	1187
STINE, Roy S.	(NC)	1194
THOMAS, Katharine S.	(NC)	1237
ULMSCHNEIDER, John E.	(NC)	1268
VON OESEN, Elaine	(NC)	1288
SORNSIN, Kathleen R.	(ND)	1168
NEWCOMER, Audrey P.	(NE)	898
RUBY, Irple P.	(NE)	1065
RUNYON, Robert S.	(NE)	1067
BERLIN, Arthur E.	(NH)	87
CRANE, John G.	(NH)	255

SYSTEMS (Cont'd)
Library systems

HAMILL, Martha L.	(NH)	491
HIGGINS, Matthew J.	(NH)	538
KENT, Jeffrey A.	(NH)	642
LIZOTTE, Jeanette S.	(NH)	735
ADAMS, June B.	(NJ)	5
BERGER, Morey R.	(NJ)	86
BIELAWSKI, Marvin F.	(NJ)	95
BRODOWSKI, Joyce H.	(NJ)	139
BROWN, Jeanne I.	(NJ)	145
CAPOOR, Asha	(NJ)	180
CHAO, Gloria F.	(NJ)	201
DENNIS, Deborah E.	(NJ)	292
GRAHAM, Peter S.	(NJ)	456
GREENBERG, Hinda F.	(NJ)	463
HIEBING, Dottie	(NJ)	537
KLATH, Nancy S.	(NJ)	657
KLEMM, Carol B.	(NJ)	660
LINNAMAA, Mari M.	(NJ)	731
MARYNOWYCH, Roman V.	(NJ)	780
MURO, Ernest A.	(NJ)	880
PANDELAKIS, Helene S.	(NJ)	937
RAFFERTY, Stephen P.	(NJ)	1003
ROSS, Robert D.	(NJ)	1058
SAWYER, Miriam	(NJ)	1086
SILVA, Nelly H.	(NJ)	1138
SIMPSON, Barbara T.	(NJ)	1141
SOBIN, Maryann D.	(NJ)	1165
SPAULDING, Frank H.	(NJ)	1172
SUDEKUM, Katharine	(NJ)	1206
TAYLOR, Donna I.	(NJ)	1226
WEISBROD, David L.	(NJ)	1319
WOLPERT, Scott L.	(NJ)	1362
HSU, Grace S.	(NM)	567
KALE, Shirley W.	(NM)	623
ROLLINS, Stephen J.	(NM)	1051
SUGNET, Christopher L.	(NM)	1206
DEACON, Mary D.	(NV)	283
PARKHURST, Carol A.	(NV)	942
ANTHONY, Donald C.	(NY)	28
ARNEJA, Harbhajan S.	(NY)	33
BADERTSCHER, David G.	(NY)	44
BALKEMA, John B.	(NY)	52
BARR, Janet L.	(NY)	58
BARRON, Robert E.	(NY)	60
BARTLE, Susan M.	(NY)	61
BELLI, Frank G.	(NY)	78
BERGER, Pam P.	(NY)	86
BERTCHUME, Gary	(NY)	90
BURTON, Robert E.	(NY)	164
CADE, Roberta G.	(NY)	170
CHITTAMPALLI, Padma S.	(NY)	209
CHIU, Liwa J.	(NY)	209
CHO-PARK, Jaung J.	(NY)	210
CHURCH, Virginia K.	(NY)	213
CLANCY, Kathy	(NY)	215
CLARE, Richard W.	(NY)	216
CLOUDSLEY, Donald H.	(NY)	223
COHEN, Rochelle F.	(NY)	229
CRAWFORD, Carter	(NY)	256
DAVIES, Carol A.	(NY)	277
ELLIS, Peter K.	(NY)	345
FASANA, Paul J.	(NY)	366
FIORILLO, Barbara A.	(NY)	379
FRANCK, Jane P.	(NY)	396
GEIBEN, Rodney F.	(NY)	425
GOODHARTZ, Gerald	(NY)	448
GRANKA, Bernard D.	(NY)	457
GRAVES, Howard E.	(NY)	459
GREEN, Joseph H.	(NY)	462
GREEN, Judith G.	(NY)	462
GROSS, Gretchen	(NY)	472
HARSHE, Florence E.	(NY)	507
HENDERSON, Janice E.	(NY)	526
HILL, Malcolm K.	(NY)	540
HODGES, Phyllis	(NY)	546
HOLMGREN, Edwin S.	(NY)	553
HOOVER, James L.	(NY)	557

SYSTEMS (Cont'd)
Library systems

HUTCHINSON, Ann P. . . . (NY) 579
JASSIN, Raymond M. . . . . (NY) 595
JONES, Jennifer R. . . . . (NY) 613
KENDRIC, Marisa A. . . . . (NY) 640
KOROLIK, Margarita N. . . . (NY) 672
KOSTER, Gregory E. . . . (NY) 673
KRAMER, Mollie W. . . . . (NY) 675
KRATZ, Charles E. . . . . . (NY) 676
LEE, Lolly P. . . . . (NY) 710
LEVINSON, Barbara . . . . (NY) 721
LEVINSON, Debra J. . . . (NY) 721
LEWIS, Frances R. . . . . . (NY) 723
MAGEE, Patricia A. . . . . (NY) 759
MANDAL, Mina R. . . . . . (NY) 764
MARTIN, Margaret B. . . . (NY) 777
MARTINEZ-RIVERA, Ivette (NY) 779
MATTIE, Joseph J. . . . . . (NY) 786
MATTURRO, Richard C. . (NY) 786
MCMORRAN, Charles E. (NY) 815
MEHL, Cathy A. . . . . . . (NY) 821
METZ, Ray E. . . . . (NY) 828
MILLER-KUMMERFELD,
    Elizabeth . . . . (NY) 843
MOONEY, James E. . . . . (NY) 858
MURDOCK, William J. . . (NY) 880
NESTA, Frederick N. . . . (NY) 896
NEUMANN, Joan . . . . . . (NY) 897
PAUL, Sandra K. . . . . . . (NY) 949
PENICH, Sonia S. . . . . . (NY) 956
PENNELL, Peggy P. . . . . (NY) 957
PERSKY, Gail M. . . . . . . (NY) 961
PICCIANO, Jacqueline L. (NY) 970
PIDALA, Veronica C. . . . (NY) 971
PRAVER, Robin I. . . . . . (NY) 990
PROVOST, Beverly A. . . . (NY) 996
RA, Marsha H. . . . . (NY) 1001
RANDALL, Lawrence E. . (NY) 1006
RICE, Cecelia E. . . . . . . (NY) 1027
RICHARDSON, John A. . (NY) 1029
ROBERTSON, Michael A. (NY) 1042
ROCQUE, Bernice L. . . . (NY) 1046
RODERER, Nancy K. . . . (NY) 1047
ROECKEL, Alan G. . . . . (NY) 1048
ROGERS, Elizabeth S. . . (NY) 1049
ROSS, David J. . . . . (NY) 1058
ROUNDS, Joseph B. . . . (NY) 1061
SCHMIEDL, Keith S. . . . (NY) 1096
SCHNEIDER, Judith A. . . (NY) 1097
SERCHUK, Barnett . . . . (NY) 1116
SHERIDAN, Robert N. . . (NY) 1128
SIAHPOOSH, Farideh T. (NY) 1134
SJOGREN, Mack D. . . . . (NY) 1145
SLATE, Ted . . . . (NY) 1148
SMITH, Dorothy C. . . . . (NY) 1154
STAINO, Rocco A. . . . . . (NY) 1178
STEIN, Marsha . . . . (NY) 1185
STRAM, Lynn R. . . . . . . (NY) 1200
THOMAS, Catherine M. . (NY) 1236
TORRONE, Joan M. . . . . (NY) 1251
UTTS, Janet R. . . . . (NY) 1270
VAN ZANTEN, Frank V. . (NY) 1278
WAGSCHAL, Sara G. . . . (NY) 1292
WASHBURN, Keith E. . . (NY) 1307
WEAS, Andrea T. . . . . . . (NY) 1311
WILLNER, Richard A. . . . (NY) 1349
WULFING, Joyce . . . . . . (NY) 1374
WYATT, James F. . . . . . (NY) 1374
ARNOLD, Gary J. . . . . . (OH) 33
BLACK, Larry D. . . . . . . (OH) 101
BOYD, Alan D. . . . . (OH) 122
BRANSCOMB, Lewis C. . (OH) 129
BRIELL, Robert D. . . . . . (OH) 135
BROWN, Stephen P. . . . (OH) 147
DAVIS, Yvonne M. . . . . . (OH) 281
DOWDELL, Marlene S. . . (OH) 315
GARDNER, Frank D. . . . (OH) 417
GEISEY, Barbara T. . . . . (OH) 425
GENAWAY, David C. . . . (OH) 426

SYSTEMS (Cont'd)
Library systems

GILNER, David J. . . . . . . (OH) 437
GIOFFRE, B J. . . . . (OH) 438
GOULD, Allison L. . . . . . (OH) 454
GRABENSTATTER,
    Christine N. . . . . (OH) 455
HUNT, James R. . . . . . . (OH) 575
JANKOWSKI, Dorothy A. (OH) 593
JANKY, Donna L. . . . . . . (OH) 593
JONES, Judykay . . . . . . (OH) 613
KNOBLAUCH, Carol J. . . (OH) 665
LESLIE, Camille J. . . . . . (OH) 718
LIPPERT, Margret G. . . . (OH) 732
LOWELL, Virginia L. . . . . (OH) 744
MOORE, Brian P. . . . . . . (OH) 858
NAM, Wonki K. . . . . (OH) 887
NEWMAN, Linda D. . . . . (OH) 899
PAK, Moo J. . . . . (OH) 935
REESE, Kathleen A. . . . . (OH) 1016
REPP, Joan M. . . . . (OH) 1024
RIFFLE, Linda . . . . (OH) 1034
RYAN, Mary E. . . . . (OH) 1071
SAHLING, Margaret E. . . (OH) 1075
SNIDER, Sondra L. . . . . (OH) 1163
STUDER, William J. . . . . (OH) 1204
TAVISS, Patricia A. . . . . (OH) 1225
TRIVEDI, Harish S. . . . . (OH) 1257
TRUCKSIS, Theresa A. . (OH) 1259
VARA, Margaret E. . . . . (OH) 1278
WALKER, Mary A. . . . . . (OH) 1296
YANCURA, Ann J. . . . . . (OH) 1377
BOOTENHOFF, Rebecca
    J. . . . . (OK) 116
CALLARD, Joanne C. . . (OK) 173
MOORE, Maxwell L. . . . . (OK) 860
PETERS, Lloyd A. . . . . . (OK) 962
RELPH, Martha H. . . . . . (OK) 1022
SKIDMORE, Stephen C. . (OK) 1146
STAIR, Fred . . . . (OK) 1178
BURNS, Carol J. . . . . . . (OR) 162
GAULKE, Mary F. . . . . . (OR) 423
JENSEN, Gary D. . . . . . (OR) 598
JOHNSON, Millard F. . . . (OR) 607
MILLER, Daniel J. . . . . . (OR) 836
MORGAN, James E. . . . (OR) 864
OLSEN, Clintena D. . . . . (OR) 921
ACKLER, Susan . . . . . . (PA) 4
BAHR, Alice H. . . . . (PA) 45
BARREAU, Deborah K. . . (PA) 58
BECK, William L. . . . . . . (PA) 72
BECKER, Linda C. . . . . . (PA) 72
BURKHARD, Polly S. . . . (PA) 161
CLINE, Nancy M. . . . . . . (PA) 222
COURTRIGHT, Harry R. . (PA) 252
DALE, Charles F. . . . . . . (PA) 270
DE KLERK, Ann M. . . . . (PA) 288
DIXON, Rebecca D. . . . . (PA) 306
EVANS, Nancy H. . . . . . (PA) 357
FANUCCI, Mary M. . . . . (PA) 363
FARNY, Diane M. . . . . . . (PA) 365
FISHMAN, Lee H. . . . . . (PA) 381
FREIVALDS, Dace I. . . . (PA) 402
FUCHS, Karola M. . . . . . (PA) 408
GLOECKNER, Paul D. . . (PA) 441
GREEN, Joyce M. . . . . . (PA) 462
GRIFFIN, Mary A. . . . . . (PA) 468
HARRISON, Susan B. . . (PA) 507
IOBST, Barbara J. . . . . . (PA) 583
KEOGH, Judith L. . . . . . (PA) 643
KING, Mimi . . . . (PA) 652
KOKOLUS, Cait C. . . . . (PA) 669
LARSON, Phyllis S. . . . . (PA) 699
MAXIN, Jacqueline A. . . (PA) 787
MCCAWLEY, Christina W. (PA) 795
MCSWAIN, Christy A. . . (PA) 818
MICHALAK, Jo A. . . . . . (PA) 832
MILLIGAN, Edna H. . . . . (PA) 843
MOORE, Curtis P. . . . . . (PA) 859
MYERS, James N. . . . . . (PA) 884

SYSTEMS (Cont'd)
Library systems

ORSAG, Ann . . . . (PA)   927
PAUSTIAN, P R. . . . . . (PA)   950
REES, G M. . . . . (PA)   1016
RYAN, Patricia M. . . . . (PA)   1071
SNOWTEN, Renee Y. . . (PA)   1164
SUMMERS, George V. . . (PA)   1209
WHITEHURST, Dori A. . . (PA)   1333
CASTRO, Maritza . . . . . (PR)   194
CONCEPCION, Luis . . . . (PR)   235
MARTINEZ-NAZARIO,
    Ronaldo . . . . (PR)   779
SANTIAGO, Maria . . . . . (PR)   1082
DESMARAIS, Norman P.   (RI)   295
GIEBLER, Albert C. . . . . (RI)   432
MEHR, Joseph O. . . . . . (RI)   821
ZIPKOWITZ, Fay . . . . . . (RI)   1389
BOWLING, Carol L. . . . . (SC)   121
DAVIS, Patsy M. . . . . . . (SC)   280
EISENSTADT, Rosa M. . . (SC)   341
GORDON, Clara B. . . . . (SC)   451
MARTIN, Neal A. . . . . . . (SC)   777
MITLIN, Laurance R. . . . (SC)   850
NEVILLE, Robert F. . . . . (SC)   898
RUST, Roxy J. . . . . (SC)   1070
SMITH, Nancy . . . . (SC)   1158
WARR, Virginia M. . . . . . (SC)   1306
BENNETT, Peg E. . . . . . (TN)   82
BUNTING, Anne C. . . . . (TN)   157
BURN, Harry T. . . . . (TN)   161
CUNNINGHAM, Helen . . (TN)   265
HOLDREDGE, Faith A. . . (TN)   550
LEISERSON, Annabelle . (TN)   714
SMITH, Philip M. . . . . . . (TN)   1159
TERRY, Carol D. . . . . . . (TN)   1232
VILES, Elza A. . . . . (TN)   1284
WILLIAMS, Marsha D. . . (TN)   1345
WILSON, Florence J. . . . (TN)   1351
ALMQUIST, Sharon G. . . (TX)   17
ANDIS, Norma B. . . . . . (TX)   26
ANDREWS, Virginia L. . . (TX)   27
ARMES, Patti . . . . (TX)   32
BAKER, Nettie L. . . . . . . (TX)   49
BALCOM, Karen S. . . . . (TX)   51
BIERI, Sandra J. . . . . (TX)   95
COOK, C C. . . . . (TX)   239
DIVELY, Reddy . . . . (TX)   306
DOWNINS, Jeffery G. . . (TX)   317
FREY, Emil F. . . . . (TX)   402
GARCIA, Lana C. . . . . . . (TX)   417
HARRISON, Karen M. . . (TX)   507
HOGAN, Sarah T. . . . . . (TX)   549
KACENA, Carolyn . . . . . (TX)   621
KELLEY, Carol M. . . . . . (TX)   636
KIM, David U. . . . . (TX)   648
KORKMAS, Carolyn C. . . (TX)   671
LEATHERBURY, Maurice
    C. . . . . (TX)   707
LINDSAY, Lorin H. . . . . . (TX)   729
LOCH, Edward J. . . . . . . (TX)   735
MARSHALL, Suzanne K.   (TX)   775
MARTIN, Jean K. . . . . . . (TX)   776
MASON, Florence M. . . . (TX)   781
MCCONNELL, Karen S. . (TX)   797
MERSKY, Roy M. . . . . . . (TX)   827
MURRAY, Margaret A. . . (TX)   882
POWELL, Alan D. . . . . . (TX)   987
RIEPMA, Helen J. . . . . . (TX)   1033
RUDDY, Mary K. . . . . . . (TX)   1065
ST. JOHN, Louise . . . . . (TX)   1075
SCHMIDT, Sherrie . . . . . (TX)   1096
SEAL, Robert A. . . . . . . (TX)   1109
SHEPHERD, Antoinette . . (TX)   1127
SINCLAIR, Rose P. . . . . (TX)   1143
TAYLOR, Nancy L. . . . . . (TX)   1228
THOMAS, Barbara C. . . . (TX)   1236
WALTON, Robert A. . . . . (TX)   1301
WATERS, Richard L. . . . (TX)   1308
WEBB, Sue E. . . . . (TX)   1313

SYSTEMS (Cont'd)
Library systems

WHISMAN, Loyse B. . . . (TX)   1329
WILKERSON, Judith C. . (TX)   1339
WOOD, Richard C. . . . . (TX)   1365
WOODALL, Cynthia P. . . (TX)   1365
YEH, Helen S. . . . . (TX)   1379
YOUNG, J A. . . . . (TX)   1382
ALBRECHT, Sterling J. . . (UT)   10
NIELSEN, Steven P. . . . . (UT)   903
REED, Vernon M. . . . . . (UT)   1015
ALTHEN, Elsa E. . . . . . . (VA)   18
BEDSOLE, Dan T. . . . . . (VA)   73
CARR, Jeanette A. . . . . . (VA)   185
CARTER-LOVEJOY,
    Steven H. . . . . (VA)   190
CIPRIANI, Debra A. . . . . (VA)   215
COSTA, Robert N. . . . . . (VA)   249
DAY, Melvin S. . . . . (VA)   283
GARRETSON, George D.   (VA)   420
GATTONE, Dean R. . . . . (VA)   422
GLENNON, Irene F. . . . . (VA)   441
HAMMOND, Theresa M. . (VA)   494
HANNA, Jill C. . . . . (VA)   496
HUGHES, J M. . . . . (VA)   571
KAISER, Donald W. . . . . (VA)   622
LEE, Carl R. . . . . (VA)   709
LESSER, Barbara . . . . . (VA)   718
MAGPANTAY, J A. . . . . (VA)   760
MELVIN, Kay H. . . . . (VA)   823
NORSTEDT, Marilyn L. . . (VA)   909
OSIA, Ruby R. . . . . (VA)   928
ROY, Alice R. . . . . (VA)   1063
SEVERTSON, Susan M. . (VA)   1117
SIMS, Martha J. . . . . (VA)   1142
STROHL, Leroy S. . . . . . (VA)   1202
WELLS, Christine . . . . . . (VA)   1322
WOODY, Janet C. . . . . . (VA)   1368
WYNNE, Joseph J. . . . . (VA)   1375
CASWELL, Jerry V. . . . . (VT)   194
REHBACH, Jeffrey R. . . . (VT)   1017
SEKERAK, Robert J. . . . (VT)   1113
ANDERSON, Christine M.   (WA)   22
BOYLAN, Merle N. . . . . . (WA)   123
DICKERSON, Lon R. . . . (WA)   300
ERICKSON, Randall D. . . (WA)   352
HARVEY, Suzanne . . . . . (WA)   509
JOHNSON, Dana E. . . . . (WA)   603
MCBRIDE, Anne . . . . . . (WA)   792
NEWELL, Rick K. . . . . . . (WA)   898
SMART, Doris M. . . . . . . (WA)   1151
VAN DYKE, Ruth L. . . . . (WA)   1275
BAKER, Douglas . . . . . . (WI)   48
BLUE, Richard I. . . . . . . (WI)   107
CIMPL, Kathleen A. . . . . (WI)   214
CRAWFORD, Josephine . (WI)   256
DAVIS, Phyllis B. . . . . . . (WI)   280
DAWSON, Lawrence . . . (WI)   282
GAPEN, D K. . . . . (WI)   416
MCCONNELL, Shirley M.   (WI)   798
MCKINNEY, Venora . . . . (WI)   812
MERRIAM, Louise A. . . . (WI)   826
ORCUTT, Linda S. . . . . . (WI)   925
REANDEAU, Walter E. . . (WI)   1013
ROBBERS, Sandra M. . . (WI)   1038
SCHWARZ, Joy L. . . . . . (WI)   1105
SWIFT, Leonard W. . . . . (WI)   1216
WHITE, James W. . . . . . (WI)   1331
FAULKNER, Ronnie W. . . (WV)   366
KALLAY, Ernest R. . . . . . (WV)   623
PROSSER, Judith M. . . . (WV)   995
RADER, H J. . . . . (WV)   1002
RULE, Judy K. . . . . (WV)   1067
FRALICK, Deborah L. . . . (AB)   395
FRASER, Gail L. . . . . . . (AB)   399
GASHUS, Karin C. . . . . . (AB)   421
HAYWARD, Edith C. . . . (AB)   517
JANJUA, Zaytoon . . . . . (AB)   593
JONES, Winstan M. . . . . (AB)   615
KENNEDY, Marcia G. . . . (AB)   641

SYSTEMS (Cont'd)
Library systems

LUNN, Rowena F.	(AB)	749
MANSON, Bill B.	(AB)	767
OAKE, Rhena E.	(AB)	913
PARKINSON, Susan L.	(AB)	943
SLOAN, Stephen M.	(AB)	1150
STARR, Jane E.	(AB)	1182
DOBBIN, Geraldine F.	(BC)	307
MAYFIELD, Betty L.	(BC)	790
CONVERSE, Wm R.	(MB)	239
FAWCETT, Patrick J.	(MB)	367
MARTEN, Mary L.	(MB)	775
POPE, Andrew T.	(NB)	983
ELLIS, Richard H.	(NF)	345
BIANCHINI, Lucian	(NS)	94
CAMPBELL, Margaret E.	(NS)	177
MACINTOSH, Ian R.	(NS)	755
ATHA, Shirley A.	(ON)	37
BARCLAY, Susan L.	(ON)	55
BERCOVITCH, Sari	(ON)	84
BISHOP, Heather F.	(ON)	99
BRIGGS, Geoffrey H.	(ON)	135
BRODIE, Nancy E.	(ON)	139
BROWN, Phyllis E.	(ON)	147
BURNS, Barrie A.	(ON)	162
CALBICK, Ian M.	(ON)	172
CAMPBELL, Bonnie	(ON)	176
DALRYMPLE, Odette	(ON)	271
DAVIS, Wendy A.	(ON)	281
DUNN, Mary J.	(ON)	327
FITZGERALD, Dorothy A.	(ON)	382
FORKES, David	(ON)	390
GOSS, Alison M.	(ON)	453
GRIMES, Deirdre E.	(ON)	470
JENSEN, L B.	(ON)	599
KAYE, Barbara J.	(ON)	632
KELLY, Glen J.	(ON)	637
KRALIK, Jane M.	(ON)	675
LEHWALDT, Marliese	(ON)	713
LEVIS, Joel	(ON)	721
LUNAU, Carrol D.	(ON)	748
MACDONALD, Marcia H.	(ON)	754
MCBURNEY, Margot B.	(ON)	792
MCCLYMONT, Karen A.	(ON)	797
MERILEES, Bobbie	(ON)	826
MORTON, Robert E.	(ON)	870
NORTH, John A.	(ON)	909
PARE, Richard	(ON)	940
PARENT, Ingrid T.	(ON)	940
PERRY, William B.	(ON)	961
POWELL, Wyley L.	(ON)	989
PROULX, Steven D.	(ON)	996
QUEINNEC, Young H.	(ON)	999
RIDLEY, A M.	(ON)	1033
ROBERTS, Nancy	(ON)	1041
ROSSMAN, Linda	(ON)	1059
ROUP, Carol E.	(ON)	1061
RYANS, Kathryn J.	(ON)	1071
SERMAT-HARDING, Kaili I.	(ON)	1116
SOULES, Aline E.	(ON)	1169
STEVENS, Mary	(ON)	1190
SUNDER-RAJ, P E.	(ON)	1210
TAYLOR, Karen E.	(ON)	1227
THODY, Susan I.	(ON)	1235
TIPLER, Stephen B.	(ON)	1246
TSUI, Josephine	(ON)	1260
VALENTINE, Scott	(ON)	1271
VANDOROS, Z	(ON)	1275
VAN ORDER, Mary J.	(ON)	1276
WALSH, Sandra A.	(ON)	1300
WEI, Carl K.	(ON)	1316
WEIR, Leslie	(ON)	1319
WELCH, Grace D.	(ON)	1321
YANCHINSKI, Roma N.	(ON)	1377
AUGER, Bernard	(PQ)	39
CAN, Hung V.	(PQ)	177
CHAREST, Ronald	(PQ)	203
COTE, Jean P.	(PQ)	249

SYSTEMS (Cont'd)
Library systems

	DE LIAMCHIN, Lana	(PQ)	289
	DU BREUIL, Laval	(PQ)	322
	DUSABLON-BOTTEGA, Nicole	(PQ)	329
	FINK, Norman	(PQ)	378
	HARVEY, Serge	(PQ)	509
	HOULE, Louis P.	(PQ)	563
	LUSSIER, Claudine	(PQ)	749
	MACFARLANE, Judy A.	(PQ)	755
	TESSIER, Mario C.	(PQ)	1233
	TRUDEL, Florian	(PQ)	1259
	VADNAIS, Martine	(PQ)	1270
	YOUNG, Patricia M.	(PQ)	1383
	FIELDEN, Stanley	(SK)	376
	JENSEN, Ken	(SK)	599
	WALCKIERS, Marc A.	(BEL)	1293
	NOERR, Kathleen T.	(ENG)	907
	CHAUMIER, Jacques	(FRN)	204
	YEN, David S.	(HKG)	1379
	AGRAWAL, Surendra P.	(IND)	7
	SATYANARAYANA, Vadhri V.	(IND)	1084
	BORCK, Liba	(ISR)	116
	DE WALERSTEIN, Linda S.	(MEX)	297
	VAN HALM, Johan	(NET)	1275
	TWEEDALE, Dellene M.	(NZD)	1266
	BASCOM, James F.	(SDA)	62
	CHOU, Nancy O.	(TAI)	210
	LIN, Chih F.	(TAI)	727
	YANG, Mei H.	(TAI)	1377
	MUKUNGU, Frederick N.	(UGN)	876
	GOMEZ, Michael J.	(WGR)	447
Library systems administration	WILLIAMS, Susan S.	(MI)	1346
	LIN, Susan T.	(NY)	728
	MILLS, Fiolina B.	(VI)	844
Library systems analysis	HEINRITZ, Fred J.	(CT)	522
	PARKS, Amy N.	(CT)	943
	SILVESTER, June P.	(MD)	1139
	MULLINER, Kent	(OH)	878
	LEUNG, Frank F.	(ON)	719
Library systems analysis & automation			
Library systems & acquisitions	ALBERTUS, Donna M.	(NY)	10
Library systems & analysis	BREWER, Joseph	(NY)	134
	ANDERSON, Thomas G.	(GA)	25
	TODD, Fred W.	(TX)	1248
Library systems & automation	BOSSEAU, Don L.	(CA)	117
	SUGRANES, Maria R.	(CA)	1207
	PITKIN, Gary M.	(CO)	976
	DONOHUE, Christine N.	(CT)	311
	CRIST, Margaret L.	(MA)	259
	MCDONALD, Stanley M.	(MA)	803
	STEVENS, Michael L.	(MA)	1190
	CHIANG, Ahushun	(MD)	207
	FREIBURGER, Gary A.	(MD)	401
	BUGG, Louise M.	(MI)	155
	COHEN, Rosemary C.	(NY)	229
	LISTOVITCH, Denise A.	(RI)	733
	HUBBARD, William J.	(VA)	568
	POPE, Nolan F.	(WI)	983
	BEAUMONT, Jane	(ON)	70
	PARKER, Arthur D.	(ON)	941
	GONZALEZ, Paloma	(PQ)	448
	RAITT, David I.	(NET)	1004
Library systems & children's services	POARCH, Margaret E.	(CA)	979
Library systems & cooperation	WILDER, David T.	(NY)	1338
Library systems & database consulting	DILORETO, Ann M.	(CA)	303
Library systems & database management	HUFFER, Mary A.	(MD)	570
Library systems & databases	HARTLEY, Gloria R.	(PA)	508
Library systems & design	HENDERSON, Deborah A.	(ON)	526
Library systems & management	SCHRIFT, Leonard B.	(NY)	1100
Library systems & networking	TREZZA, Alphonse F.	(FL)	1256
	CUNNINGHAM, Barbara M.	(MD)	265

SYSTEMS (Cont'd)

Library systems & networks	WEECH, Terry L.	(IL)	1315
	BAKER, Elizabeth A.	(MA)	48
	HEISE, George F.	(NJ)	522
	HUMPHRY, John A.	(NY)	574
	ROSS, Kathleen A.	(NY)	1058
	DURANCE, Cynthia J.	(ON)	328
	COCHRANE, Thomas G.	(AUS)	226
Library systems & programming	MOORE, Phyllis C.	(CA)	861
	PITT, William B.	(MD)	976
Library systems & RLIN database	LEE, Doreen H.	(CA)	709
Library systems & services	PRITCHARD, John A.	(NC)	994
Library systems & software	DYKMAN, Elaine K.	(NJ)	331
	KARCICH, Grant J.	(ON)	627
	TOUCHETTE, Francois G.	(PQ)	1252
Library systems, automation	ARNOLD, Donna W.	(CA)	33
	LEHMAN, Douglas K.	(FL)	712
	MCGINN, Thomas P.	(IL)	806
	MORRIS, Louis M.	(MD)	867
	PAWSON, Robert D.	(NJ)	951
Library systems consultation	GISHLER, John R.	(AB)	438
Library systems consulting	FEINER, Arlene M.	(IL)	369
	BECKMAN, Margaret L.	(ON)	73
Library systems design	GABBERT, Gretchen W.	(CA)	411
	WHITEHEAD, James M.	(GA)	1332
	O'NEIL, Rosanna M.	(OH)	924
	MCDONALD, Joseph A.	(PA)	802
	MAGALONI, Ana M.	(MEX)	759
Library systems design & layout	AKS, Gloria	(NY)	9
Library systems development	BAUMGARDNER, Sandra A.	(DC)	66
	HUESTIS, Jeffrey C.	(MO)	570
	DANIELS, Pam	(NY)	273
	TONKERY, Thomas D.	(NY)	1250
	BALDWIN, Mark F.	(RI)	52
Library systems development & training	CHAPMAN, Elwynda K.	(DC)	202
Library systems direction	SAYRE, Edward C.	(NM)	1087
Library systems DOBIS	DEEMER, Selden S.	(GA)	286
Library systems evaluation	GOODELL, John S.	(AUS)	448
Library systems for schools	MAUTINO, Patricia H.	(NY)	787
Library systems for special libraries	SMITH, Adelaide M.	(NY)	1152
Library systems installation	BRUNELL, David H.	(CO)	150
Library systems interfaces	CLAPPER, Mary E.	(MA)	216
	LAREW, Christian K.	(NJ)	697
Library systems, interlibrary loans	CLAYTOR, Jane B.	(MI)	220
Library systems, library microcomputers	JAFFE, John G.	(VA)	591
Library systems management	PRINTZ, Naomi J.	(CA)	993
	AVERSA, Elizabeth S.	(DC)	41
	RUSH, Candace M.	(DC)	1068
	BRESLAUER, Lester M.	(FL)	133
	STONE, Nancy Y.	(MI)	1197
	CAVINESS, Ann N.	(NY)	195
	DURBIN, Roger	(OH)	328
	DYE, Luella I.	(WV)	330
Library systems, management & promotion	CHAN, Margy	(ON)	199
Lib systems, microcomputer applications	ONSI, Patricia W.	(NY)	924
Library systems, M300XT	VERMA, Prem V.	(WV)	1282
Library systems networking	RUTHERFORD, Virginia L.	(GA)	1070
Library systems of Morocco	OUELLET, Louise M.	(PQ)	930
Library systems on microcomputers	TESSIER, Yves	(PQ)	1233
Library systems operation	BYRN, James H.	(VA)	169
Library systems organization	HURD, Sandra H.	(MA)	577
Lib systems organization & management	CHITWOOD, Julius R.	(IL)	209
Library systems planning	PEMPE, Ruta	(DC)	956
	SCHALAU, Robert D.	(MS)	1089
Library systems, primary	MILLER, Ellen L.	(VA)	837
Library systems procurement	FRIEDMAN, Terri L.	(MA)	404
Library systems, reference	BLOKH, Basheva	(NY)	106
Library systems, reference referral	GUY, Patricia A.	(CA)	479
Library systems research	POWELL, James R.	(MI)	988
Library systems, research & publications	MWALIMU, Charles	(DC)	884
Library systems, serials control	WANG, Anna M.	(OH)	1302
Library systems services	DEVENISH-CASSEL, Ann W.	(NY)	297

SYSTEMS (Cont'd)

Library systems software	DITMARS, David W.	(OH)	305
Library systems training	PHILLIPS, Rosemary	(ON)	969
Library systems, user services	O'DELL, M P.	(MD)	916
Library systems with branches	DAVIES, Jo	(WA)	277
Library technology & systems	BLACK, John B.	(ON)	101
Library technology, systems	MANN, Thomas	(CA)	766
Linked systems	BESSER, Howard A.	(CA)	91
	VEDDER, Harvey B.	(PA)	1280
Linked systems project	GLAZIER, Ed	(CA)	440
	SCHUITEMA, Joan E.	(OH)	1101
Local distribution of database systems	NASATIR, Marilyn	(CA)	888
Local library systems	SEVIER, Susan G.	(KS)	1117
	SMITH, Barbara G.	(MD)	1152
	THOMAS, James M.	(OH)	1237
Local networks & systems	STEFFEY, Ramona J.	(TN)	1185
Local system automation	KOUTNIK, Charles J.	(VA)	673
Local systems	CURTIS, Alison J.	(ON)	267
Local systems planning	HILLMANN, Diane I.	(NY)	541
Local systems training	BERRINGER, Virginia M.	(OH)	90
Mainframe-based chemical info systems	MEYER, Daniel E.	(PA)	830
Management & systems	CRAWFORD, Geraldine H.	(MI)	256
Management information systems	SCHERREI, Rita A.	(CA)	1092
	TRIOLO, Victor A.	(CT)	1257
	SHENASSA, Daryoosh	(IL)	1126
	RADEMACHER, Richard J.	(KS)	1002
	ANDERSON, John E.	(MD)	23
	MOTT, Thomas H.	(NJ)	872
	LITTLE, Paul L.	(OK)	733
	SKOVIRA, Robert J.	(PA)	1147
	BONNELLY, Claude	(PQ)	114
Management information systems for libs	SCHUELLER, Janette H.	(WA)	1101
Management of circulation systems	TREMBLAY, Carolyn B.	(NH)	1255
Management of information systems	MOSER, Jane W.	(CA)	870
Management of in-house database systems	LEMMON, Anne B.	(LA)	715
Management of library systems	FORGET, Louis J.	(ON)	390
Management, planning, systems	FLOERSHEIMER, Lee M.	(NY)	385
Management systems	PRICE, Douglas S.	(MD)	992
Managing information in systems	ARDERN, Christine M.	(ON)	31
Managing information services & systems	HALLSTROM, Curtis H.	(MN)	489
Managing systems development	PEMPE, Ruta	(DC)	956
Manual systems design	PISCITELLI, Rosalie A.	(NY)	976
Manufacture of shelving systems	BAYLIS, Ted	(MA)	67
Manufacturing database systems	SINE, George H.	(IL)	1143
Manufacturing information systems	BEICHMAN, John C.	(MI)	75
MARC-based systems	EVANS, Linda J.	(IL)	357
MARC-compatible systems	MOTTRAM, Geoffrey	(IL)	873
Marketing data systems	SEULOWITZ, Lois	(NY)	1117
Marketing information services & systems	LAROSA, Sharon M.	(MA)	698
Marketing information services, systems	EL-DUWEINI, Aadel K.	(EGY)	342
Marketing online database systems	POOL, Madlyn K.	(VA)	982
Marketing systems	BAUMGARTNER, Robert M.	(OH)	66
Medical databases & systems	SATTERTHWAITE, Rebecca K.	(MD)	1084
Medical end-user systems	TURMAN, Lynne U.	(VA)	1264
Medical info system analysis & design	HENDRICKSON, Maria F.	(NY)	527
Medical information systems	JENKIN, Michael A.	(FL)	596
	BAKER, Benjamin R.	(MD)	48
	HUMPHREYS, Betsy L.	(MD)	573
	JACOBS, Patt	(OR)	590
	PORTER, William R.	(TN)	985
	URATA, Kazuo	(JAP)	1269
Medical record systems	KISH, Veronica R.	(PA)	656
Microcomputer index systems	FISLER, Charlotte D.	(PA)	382
Microcomputer library systems	CURTIS, Alison J.	(ON)	267
Microcomputer library systems, Apple IIe	BOCHTE, Terrence C.	(WI)	109
Microcomputer system configuration	COVEY, William C.	(FL)	252
Microcomputer system implementation	OYER, Kenneth E.	(NE)	932
Microcomputer systems	MILLER, Leon C.	(AR)	839
	RUMSEY, Eric T.	(IA)	1067
	CANGANELLI, Patrick W.	(IN)	178
	FOGLE, Dianna L.	(KY)	387

SYSTEMS (Cont'd)

Microcomputer systems

	ANGLIN, Richard V.	(NY)	28
	DOBSON, Christine B. . . .	(TX)	307
	PUZIAK, Kathleen M. . . .	(WA)	998
Microcomputer systems & networks	TALLY, Roy D.	(MN)	1221
Microcomputer systems in libraries	PRATT, Allan D.	(CT)	989
Microcomputer systems online searching	ROTHSTEIN, Pauline M. .	(NY)	1060
Microcomputer-based chemical info system	MEYER, Daniel E.	(PA)	830
Microcomputer-based information systems	JOHNSON, Jane S.	(IL)	605
Microcomputer-based integrated systems	MEIKAMP, Kathie D. . . .	(DC)	822
Microcomputer-based library systems	MILLER, Randy S.	(IL)	841
Microform storage & retrieval systems	SKARR, Robert J.	(DC)	1145
Micrographic systems	PAVLAKIS, Christopher .	(NY)	950
	KESHISHIAN, Maria L. . .	(TX)	644
Micrographics systems	TAMMARO, James M. . .	(NY)	1221
Multilink systems	BRANDEAU, John H. . .	(NY)	128
Multitype library system	PACEY, Brenda M.	(IL)	933
Multitype library systems	WRIGHT, Kathryn D. . . .	(AL)	1372
	HARRIET, Conklin W. . . .	(IL)	503
	ROOSE, Tina	(IL)	1053
	TYER, Travis E.	(IL)	1266
	ELDRED, Heather A. . . .	(WI)	342
Multitype library systems, cooperation	KNEPEL, Nancy	(CO)	664
Municipal information systems	BOCKMAN, Eugene J. . .	(NY)	109
Museum database systems	YARNALL, James L. . . .	(DC)	1378
Museum information systems	BEARMAN, David A. . . .	(PA)	69
Networking, resource sharing, systems	LOVE, Erika	(NM)	743
Networking systems	VONDRAN, Raymond F. . .	(TX)	1288
Networks & systems	CHESHIER, Robert G. . .	(OH)	206
News library systems	CANT, Elaine N.	(CA)	179
Newspaper & publisher database systems	PASCHAL, John M.	(OK)	945
Newspaper archive systems	ROACH, Eddie D.	(OK)	1037
Newspaper clipping systems	KANE, Angelika R.	(PA)	624
Newspaper library systems	CASTER, Suzanne	(CA)	194
	SCOFIELD, James S. . . .	(FL)	1106
	IRONS, Lynda V.	(ID)	584
	VANCE, Sandra L.	(IL)	1273
	FRANKLIN, Alyce B. . . .	(KY)	397
Newspaper photo systems	KANE, Angelika R.	(PA)	624
NOTIS acquisitions system	GALE, Sarah E.	(IN)	413
NOTIS system	MARCINKO, Dorothy K. .	(AL)	769
Nursing expert systems	HENDRICKSON, Maria F.	(NY)	527
NY state library systems committee	PHILLIPS, Ruth M.	(NY)	969
OCLC & NOTIS systems	LASATER, Mary C.	(TN)	700
OCLC cataloging systems	MYERS, Victor C.	(MO)	885
OCLC systems	ANDERSON, Elizabeth M.	(PA)	22
Office systems	LOWENSTEIN, Richard A.	(CT)	744
Office systems automation	SYPERT, Clyde F.	(CA)	1217
One-person library systems	REINALDO DA SILVA, Joann T.	(MB)	1021
Online & CD-ROM systems	MAXWELL, Christine Y. .	(CA)	788
Online bibliographic systems	MONTGOMERY, Michael S.	(NJ)	856
Online catalog systems	PERONE, Karen L.	(NY)	959
Online cataloging system	RICHARD, Sheila A. . . .	(VA)	1028
Online cataloging systems	FRIEDLAND, Frances K. .	(ON)	403
Online catalogs & systems	FORKES, David	(ON)	390
Online circulation system	BONNET, Janice M. . . .	(CA)	114
Online circulation systems	EDWARDS, Dana S. . . .	(IL)	337
	FOLEY, Mary D.	(KY)	387
Online information systems	SULLIVAN, Edward A. . .	(CA)	1207
	SWEENEY, Urban J. . . .	(CA)	1215
	HEARTY, John A.	(DC)	519
	WILSON, Lizabeth A. . . .	(IL)	1351
	SMITH, Jo T.	(NJ)	1156
	HILL, Linda L.	(OK)	540
	BILLINSKY, Christyn G. .	(SC)	96
	GENNARO, John L.	(VA)	427
	YAMANAKA, Tai	(JAP)	1377
Online library systems	HOFFMAN, Herbert H. . .	(CA)	548
	CARRISON, Dale K. . . .	(MN)	187
	KANAFANI, Kyung C. . .	(MO)	624
	TAYLOR, Arlene G.	(NY)	1226

SYSTEMS (Cont'd)

Online library systems	SEUSS, Herbert J.	(WI)	1117
Online medical & legal systems	MORRIS, Timothy J.	(DC)	867
Online reference systems	LAZARUS, Josephine G.	(CO)	706
Online retrieval systems	DRUMMOND, Louis E. . .	(DC)	321
	TAHIR, Mary M.	(MD)	1220
	STEFFEY, Ramona J. . . .	(TN)	1185
	GALBRAITH, Paula L. . .	(TX)	413
Online search systems	SHUMAN, Bruce A.	(MI)	1134
Online searching, multiple systems	LINCOLN, Carol S.	(KY)	728
Online searching, systems	LAMBERT, Nancy	(CA)	690
	BROWN, Cynthia D.	(NY)	142
Online system management	REINBOLD, Janice K. . . .	(OK)	1021
Online systems	INGEBRETSEN, Dorothy L.	(CA)	582
	SIMPSON, Evelyn L. . . .	(CA)	1141
	STREHL, Daniel J.	(CA)	1201
	TYSON, Betty B.	(CA)	1267
	LOWENSTEIN, Richard A.	(CT)	744
	ORLOSKE, Margaret Q. .	(CT)	926
	PEMBERTON, Jeffery K.	(CT)	956
	QUAKE, Ron	(CT)	999
	FOWLIE, Linda K.	(DC)	394
	PAVEK, C C.	(DC)	950
	BIBBY, Elizabeth A.	(GA)	94
	CUNNINGHAM, Robert L.	(MA)	265
	FERNALD, Anne C.	(MA)	373
	IRWIN, Ruth A.	(MD)	584
	VONDERHAAR, Mark N.	(MD)	1288
	VELLIKY, Mary M.	(MI)	1281
	ABBOTT, George L.	(NY)	1
	BERTUCA, David J.	(NY)	91
	CAREN, Loretta	(NY)	181
	KOSTENBAUDER, Scott	(NY)	673
	SAHLEM, James R.	(NY)	1075
	MOUNTS, Earl L.	(PA)	873
	SYEN, Sarah	(PA)	1217
	PHILLIPS, Patricia A. . . .	(TN)	968
	ROTHBART, Linda S. . . .	(VA)	1060
	STEIN, Karen E.	(VA)	1185
	ASHTON, Margaret A. . .	(ON)	36
Online systems & database	MATTHEWS, Elizabeth W.	(IL)	785
Online systems & indexing	MALCOLM, J P.	(MI)	762
Online systems & policy	ARRINGTON, Susan J. . .	(MD)	34
Online systems & services	GREEN-MALONEY, Nancy	(CA)	465
Online systems design	MCLAREN, M B.	(NM)	813
	NORMORE, Lorraine F. .	(OH)	909
Online systems development	WOODSMALL, Rose M. .	(MD)	1367
Online systems evaluation	WOODSMALL, Rose M. .	(MD)	1367
Online systems marketing	GABOR, John M.	(NY)	411
Online systems programming	SKROBELA, Katherine C.	(NJ)	1147
Online systems research	PITCHON, Cindy A.	(PA)	976
Online systems testing	TRUBKIN, Loene	(BC)	1259
Online systems training	HUGGENS, Gary D.	(DC)	571
Optical disk database system	BENGE, Bruce	(OK)	80
Optical disk systems	ABBOTT, George L.	(NY)	1
	HODGSON, Cynthia A. . .	(PA)	546
Optical information system	HEIDENREICH, Fred L. .	(AZ)	521
Optical information systems	ANDRE, Pamela Q.	(MD)	26
	MARMION, Daniel K. . . .	(TX)	772
	DEBUSE, Raymond	(WA)	285
	REMINGTON, David G. .	(WA)	1022
Organz devlpmnt & communication systems	HUNT, Suellyn	(NY)	575
Patient interview systems	COOK, Galen B.	(SC)	240
Patron staff systems training	GATTEN, Jeffrey N.	(OH)	422
PC-based retrieval systems	CIUFFETTI, Peter D. . . .	(MA)	215
Periodical system automation	REED, Virginia R.	(IL)	1015
Personal computer library systems	KLEIN, Joanne S.	(PA)	659
Personal computer system management	ROSENFELD, Jane D. . .	(NY)	1056
Personal computer systems & software	TOWNLEY, Richard L. . .	(NY)	1253
Personal computers & library systems	FEDORS, Maurica R. . . .	(NJ)	368
Personal information systems	BURTON, Hilary D.	(CA)	164
Personnel & professional systems	PEISCHL, Thomas P. . . .	(MN)	955
Personnel evaluation system	VIELE, George B.	(NC)	1283
Personnel systems	CLIFT, Scott B.	(MA)	222
	CANNON, Robert E.	(NC)	179
Petroleum bibliographic info systs	HILL, Linda L.	(OK)	540

SYSTEMS (Cont'd)

Specialty	Name		Page
Pharmaceutical research info systems	PEETERS, Marc D.	(BEL)	954
Pharmacy computer systems	FASSETT, William E.	(WA)	366
Photo & slide organizational systems	ROBERTSON, Retha M.	(OK)	1042
Photo filing systems	SCARANO, Lisa C.	(NY)	1087
Planning & budgeting systems	NERODA, Edward W.	(MT)	895
Planning & establishing library systems	STANKIEWICZ, Carol A.	(CT)	1180
Planning national information systems	MENOU, Michel J.	(ITL)	824
Planning system goals & objectives	COURSON, M S.	(MD)	251
Planning systems & services	EVANS, Frank B.	(DC)	357
Policy & control of library systems	MORALES, Milton F.	(MO)	862
Procedural systems analysis	NYBERG, Lelia J.	(CA)	912
Production system design	HODGE, Gail M.	(PA)	546
Proprietary technical report systems	ECKROADE, Carlene B.	(DE)	335
Propulsion systems	KITCHENS, Philips H.	(AL)	657
Public information systems	SMITH, Peggy C.	(OK)	1159
Public libraries automated systems	NEAL, Jan	(CA)	890
Public library, multitype systems	WELCH, Steven J.	(IL)	1321
Public library system	ELDREDGE, Jeffrey R.	(HI)	342
Public library system administration	JONES, Wyman	(CA)	615
Public library systems	LAND, Edward P.	(AL)	692
	SIEBENMORGEN, Ruth	(CA)	1135
	LUND, Ethel B.	(IA)	748
	GOMEZ, Martin J.	(IL)	447
	MORRISON, Samuel F.	(IL)	868
	PEARSON, Roger L.	(IL)	953
	KING, Kenneth	(MI)	651
	LEAMON, David L.	(MI)	707
	WEBER, Ruth A.	(NJ)	1314
	GENCO, Barbara A.	(NY)	426
	LINDAUER, Dinah	(NY)	728
	PANZ, Richard	(NY)	938
	RANSOM, Stanley A.	(NY)	1007
	COOK, Charles T.	(OH)	239
	SELLE, Donna M.	(OR)	1113
	KEISER, Barbara J.	(PA)	635
	PROMOS, Marianne	(PA)	995
	WAGGONER, Susan M.	(PA)	1291
	PEARCE, Douglas A.	(RI)	952
	MESSINEO, Anthony	(SC)	828
	COLLIER, Virginia S.	(TN)	232
	CRABB, Elizabeth L.	(TX)	254
	GUBBIN, Barbara A.	(TX)	475
	MATHIS, Rama F.	(TX)	784
	LAYTON, A J.	(UT)	705
	SCHUURMAN, Guy	(UT)	1103
	MATTE, Pierre V.	(PQ)	785
Public library systems analysis	SHELTON, John L.	(GA)	1126
Public library systems development	BOAZ, Ruth L.	(TN)	108
Public library systems management	DILLARD, Thomas W.	(NC)	303
Public management information systems	CROWTHER, Warren W.	(CSR)	262
Public services systems	BAKER, Shirley K.	(MA)	49
Publishing systems	KOPPELMAN, William H.	(NY)	671
	PAUL, Sandra K.	(NY)	949
Reconnaissance systems	VAN VELZER, Verna J.	(CA)	1277
	DONOHUE, Christine N.	(CT)	311
Records documentation systems	HAMILTON, Meredith L.	(IL)	492
Records management & micrographics systs	BRIMSEK, Tobi A.	(DC)	136
Records management systems	HENDERSON, Deborah A.	(ON)	526
Records management systems analysis	BALON, Brett J.	(SK)	53
Refereeing system	YAMAZAKI, Shigeaki	(JAP)	1377
Reference & info retrieval systems	MASON, Michael L.	(NJ)	781
Regional cooperative library systems	HURREY, Katharine C.	(MD)	577
Regional library service system	OWEN, Mary J.	(CO)	932
Regional library systems	FALK, Louise G.	(IA)	362
	SPRAUER, Linda J.	(OR)	1176
	SLOAN, Lynette S.	(TN)	1149
	DAVIS, Joyce	(TX)	279
	JORDAN, Peter A.	(AB)	616
	CAMPBELL, Joylene E.	(SK)	177
	HARADA, Ryukichi	(JAP)	499
Regional multitype library systems	BERNER, Karen J.	(NE)	88
Regional public library system	SCOTT, Thomas L.	(MN)	1108
Regional system administration	LE BUTT, Katherine L.	(NB)	708
Regional systems	KISSNER, Arthur J.	(MA)	656
Report editing, management systems	KEE, Walter A.	(NC)	634

SYSTEMS (Cont'd)

Specialty	Name		Page
Research methods & systems analysis	FENSKE, Ruth E.	(IL)	371
Research on management intelligence syst	KOCHEN, Manfred	(MI)	667
Researching, library systems	GIGANTE, Vickilyn M.	(MD)	433
Response management system	POWELL, Timothy W.	(NY)	989
Retrieval systems	VON KEITZ, Wolfgang	(WGR)	288
Retrieval systems design	HOWARD, Susanna J.	(NC)	564
Retrieval systems, text	BYRN, William H.	(MA)	169
Rural library systems	CAMPBELL, Ray	(IL)	177
	HOWARD, Ada M.	(TX)	563
Rural public library systems	O'BRIEN, Marlys H.	(MN)	915
School district information systems	SLYGH, Gyneth	(WI)	1151
School library computer systems	SLYGH, Gyneth	(WI)	1151
School library system	WOOD, Marilyn R.	(IA)	1364
School library systems	BUBOLTZ, Dale D.	(CA)	152
	LUNARDI, Albert A.	(CA)	748
	MCMICHAEL, Sandra C.	(FL)	815
	UMANA, Christine J.	(MA)	1268
	BAILIE, Donna L.	(NY)	47
	LINDSLEY, Barbara N.	(NY)	730
	MATTIE, Joseph J.	(NY)	786
	ROSCELLO, Frances R.	(NY)	1054
	SALUSTRI, Madeline	(NY)	1077
	SIMON, Anne E.	(NY)	1140
	LEON, Carmencita H.	(PR)	716
	FILSON, Anne H.	(VA)	377
School library systems, networking	WEBSTER, Patricia B.	(NY)	1315
School system library media management	KAUFMAN, Polly W.	(MA)	631
Science services, library systems	WILLOCKS, Robert M.	(FL)	1349
Scientific information systems design	DIESING, Arthur C.	(KY)	302
Search system software: front-end	WOODSMALL, Rose M.	(MD)	1367
Security systems	BUTLER, James C.	(MS)	166
Serials & integrated systems	CLINE, Sharon D.	(CA)	222
Serials control systems	LONG, Roger J.	(IL)	739
Serials systems & management	VANDERPOORTEN, Mary B.	(AL)	1274
Setting up library systems in law firms	BYRNE, Jeanne M.	(TX)	169
Shared automated systems	MARTIN, Robert A.	(FL)	778
Small libraries & library systems	FEYE-STUKAS, Janice	(MN)	374
Small library systems	DAVEY, Dorothy M.	(ON)	276
Small public library systems	ELDRIDGE, Jane A.	(MA)	342
Software system quality control	KOLMAN, Roberta F.	(HI)	669
	VEGTER, Amy H.	(NY)	1281
Software systems training	DULAN, Peter A.	(CO)	324
Solar system astronomy	CHAPMAN, Jennalyn W.	(AZ)	202
Special collection library systems	COLEMAN, David E.	(HI)	231
Special library systems	SCHUTZBERG, Frances	(MA)	1103
	TROVER, Larry E.	(OH)	1258
	MURRAY, Lucia M.	(OR)	882
	FISHER, Daphne V.	(PA)	380
	LUMANDE, Edward	(ZAM)	748
Special library systems & procedures	CAMOZZI-EKBERG, Patricia L.	(WA)	175
Standards in information systems	HENDERSON, Madeline M.	(MD)	526
Stanislavski system	MOORE, Sonia	(NY)	861
Storage & retrieval system design	TRAVIS, Irene L.	(VA)	1254
Strategic planning for library systems	MATHESON, Nina W.	(MD)	783
Strategic systems planning	BURNS, Barrie A.	(ON)	162
Super searcher online systems	CONGER, Lucinda D.	(DC)	236
Supervising branch library system	RADOFF, Leonard I.	(TX)	1002
System analysis	STRIBLING, Lorraine R.	(CA)	1202
	CORTEZ, Edwin M.	(DC)	248
	DODSON, Whit	(VA)	308
System analysis & design	DIENER, Carol W.	(MD)	302
System & product development	MILLER, Ronald F.	(CA)	842
System automation planning	RHEIN, Jean F.	(FL)	1025
System design	SARGENT, Charles W.	(TX)	1082
	CARNEY, Marillyn L.	(VA)	183
	LUNIN, Lois F.	(VA)	749
	BLOCH, Uri	(ISR)	105
System design & development	HALPIN, Peter	(DC)	490
System design & programming	LARSON, Ray R.	(CA)	699
System development	CIRCIELLO, Jean M.	(CA)	215
	PATTON, Glenn E.	(OH)	949
System documentation	PETTOLINA, Anthony M.	(NY)	965
System library management	DOCKINS, Glenn	(IL)	307

SYSTEMS (Cont'd)

Specialty	Name		Page
System management	HOMEYARD, Marjorie A.	(FL)	555
System reference	EGAN, Elizabeth M.	(IL)	338
System specification	TAUBER, Stephen J.	(MA)	1225
Systems	BARKEY, Patrick T.	(CA)	56
	MILLER, R B.	(CA)	841
	GIBBONS, Katherine Y.	(MD)	431
	KRUG, Ruth A.	(NM)	680
	JONES, Sarah C.	(NY)	615
	JUDD, J V.	(NY)	619
	SPORE, Stuart	(NY)	1175
	DENTON, A W.	(TN)	293
	HENINGTON, David M.	(TX)	528
	HARRIS, Richard J.	(VA)	506
	BLACK, Sandra M.	(ON)	101
	FORGET, Louis J.	(ON)	390
	SHEPHERD, Murray C.	(ON)	1127
	LEIDE, John E.	(PQ)	713
Systems analysis	BALES, F K.	(CA)	52
	EPSTEIN, Susan B.	(CA)	351
	HADLEY, Peter H.	(CA)	482
	HALL, Anthony	(CA)	487
	KAZLAUSKAS, Edward J.	(CA)	632
	GUERRIERO, Donald A.	(DC)	476
	LEWIS, Robert J.	(DC)	724
	PARMING, Marju R.	(DC)	943
	COVEY, William C.	(FL)	252
	LOGAN, Elisabeth L.	(FL)	737
	SHEPARD, Clayton A.	(IN)	1126
	MCKIRDY, Pamela R.	(MA)	812
	ASSOUAD, Carol S.	(MD)	37
	LABEAU, Dennis	(MI)	685
	KANAFANI, Kyung C.	(MO)	624
	STACK, Laurie A.	(MT)	1177
	FRANTS, Valery	(NJ)	398
	HEINEMAN, Stephanie R.	(NY)	522
	HSIAO, Shu Y.	(NY)	567
	LANDAU, Herbert B.	(NY)	692
	JOSEPH, Patricia A.	(PA)	617
	HUNN, Marvin T.	(TX)	574
	SWIGGER, Keith	(TX)	1216
	DEBARDELEBEN, Marian Z.	(VA)	284
	STEPHENSON, Mary S.	(BC)	1188
	FAWCETT, Patrick J.	(MB)	367
	DYSART, Jane I.	(ON)	331
	LA CHAPELLE, Jennifer R.	(ON)	686
Systems analysis & design	STOVEL, Madeleine D.	(CA)	1199
	LISTON, David M.	(MD)	732
	CONNORS, William E.	(NY)	238
	WAGNER, Stephen K.	(NY)	1292
	REDMER, Paul C.	(VA)	1014
	BALON, Brett J.	(SK)	53
	ARTEAGA, Georgina	(MEX)	35
Systems analysis & development	HILL, Helen K.	(OK)	540
Systems analysis & records management	SIEGERT, Lindy E.	(NS)	1136
Systems analysis, micro	COX, Bruce B.	(MO)	253
Systs analysis, microcomputer program	NEWCOMER, Susan N.	(CA)	898
Systems analyst	ENGERRAND, Steven W.	(GA)	349
Systems & automation	LOWELL, Felice K.	(FL)	744
Systems & database development	HOWELL, M G.	(NY)	565
Systems & networking	FAIBISOFF, Sylvia G.	(OK)	361
Systems & product development	ABELES, Tom	(MN)	2
Systems & technology	NEWMAN, George C.	(NY)	899
Systems automation	FORSMAN, Rick B.	(CO)	391
Systems automation consultant	GRAMINSKI, Denise M.	(NY)	457
Systems design	ELLIS, Ruth M.	(CA)	345
	WHITE, Cecil R.	(CA)	1330
	WEST, L P.	(IL)	1326
	MORGAN, James J.	(IN)	864
	GOLDSCHMIDT, Peter G.	(MD)	446
	WEISFIELD, Cynthia F.	(PA)	1319
	YODER, William M.	(VA)	1380
	MCCUBBIN, George M.	(ON)	800
Systems design & programming	RAO, Paladugu V.	(IL)	1008
Systems designing	BORBELY, Jack	(NY)	116

SYSTEMS (Cont'd)

Specialty	Name		Page
Systems development	LANE, Robert B.	(AL)	694
	LANDGRAF, Mary N.	(CA)	692
	SMILLIE, Pauline A.	(MI)	1151
	BINGHAM, Kathleen S.	(NY)	97
	RUBIN, Myra P.	(NY)	1064
	SIMON, Peter E.	(NY)	1140
	WEINER, Betty	(PA)	1318
	MAYFIELD, David M.	(UT)	790
	CAMPBELL, Brian G.	(BC)	176
Systems development & implementation	JENKINS, Ann A.	(CA)	597
	ANDERSON, Eliane G.	(TX)	22
Systems engineering	LISTON, David M.	(MD)	732
Systems implementation	NIEMEYER, Mollie M.	(MO)	903
Systems management	COVILL, Bruce	(NJ)	252
	WILBURN, Gene	(ON)	1338
Systems operations	THORSTEINSON, William A.	(NS)	1243
Systems optimization	THORSTEINSON, William A.	(NS)	1243
Systems organization	COVILL, Bruce	(NJ)	252
Systems planning	TITUS, Elizabeth M.	(IL)	1247
	HIGH, Walter M.	(NC)	538
	ROHDY, Margaret A.	(PA)	1050
	WALL, H D.	(PA)	1297
	CORBIN, John	(TX)	245
Systems planning & design	STANLEY, Dale R.	(CA)	1180
Systems planning & implementation	SHOCKLEY, Cynthia W.	(MD)	1132
Systems research & development	COVILL, Bruce	(NJ)	252
Systems science	MILLER, James G.	(CA)	838
Systems specifications development	HAWK, Susan A.	(MD)	513
Systems support	ALLEN, Stephanie O.	(AZ)	16
Systems technology for society	CHARTRAND, Robert L.	(DC)	203
Systems theory	BURNS, Nancy R.	(CA)	162
Systems training	GIBSON, Timothy T.	(TX)	432
Systems, training & development	ARSENAULT, Patricia A.	(MA)	35
Technical services & systems	BONK, Sharon C.	(NY)	114
	LINCOLN, Robert S.	(MB)	728
Technical services automated systems	BAIRD, Lynn N.	(ID)	47
Technology & systems	RIGGS, Donald E.	(AZ)	1034
Technology systems	BECKER, Roger V.	(WA)	72
Telecommunication monitor & test systems	NELSON, David W.	(NH)	893
Text management & retrieval systems	LOWENSTEIN, Richard A.	(CT)	744
Text retrieval systems	WEAVER, Maggie	(ON)	1312
Text systems	CLARK, Gerald L.	(IL)	217
Top-down information systems planning	TELFER, Margaret E.	(NC)	1230
Training & development micrographic syst	CORNELIUS, Charlene E.	(WI)	246
Training & system implementation	JOHNSON, Jane S.	(IL)	605
Training for systems	VANDERPOORTEN, Mary B.	(AL)	1274
Training for systems use	UPHAM, Lois N.	(SC)	1269
Training on automated systems	WELCH, Grace D.	(ON)	1321
Training systems design, analysis	SYPERT, Clyde F.	(CA)	1217
Travel & tourism information systems	MOLL, Joy K.	(NJ)	853
Trends in computer systems	BILES, Mark J.	(NJ)	96
Turnkey automated information systems	SIDMAN, George C.	(CA)	1135
University filing systems	SWEENEY, Shelley T.	(SK)	1215
UNIX System	HAWKINS, Donald T.	(NJ)	514
UNIX systems administration	SULLIVAN, Edward A.	(CA)	1207
Usability of computer systems	CHERRY, Joan M.	(ON)	206
User interface, automated systems	SACKETT-WILK, Susan A.	(TX)	1073
User-friendly systems	KING, Joseph T.	(CA)	651
Video, TV, satellite systems	HISS, Sheila M.	(FL)	544
Videotex systems	PAL, Gabriel	(ON)	935
Word processing, record management systs	KEE, Walter A.	(NC)	634
Working with county library system	WINGLE, Rita M.	(PA)	1355

TAGGING

Specialty	Name		Page
OCLC, MARC tagging	LEONG, Carol L.	(IL)	717

TAKEOVER
Takeover defense .... SLUSSER, W P. ...... (NY) 1150

TALENTED (See also Gifted)
Gifted & talented bibliography .... GRAVITZ, Ina A. ...... (NY) 459
Gifted & talented education ...... ABILOCK, Debbie ..... (CA)   2
Gifted & talented services .... TALLEY, Loretta K. .... (IA) 1221

TALES (See also Folk)
Grimm tales production & direction .. DAVENPORT, Thomas R. (VA) 276

TALKING (See also Booktalking)
Overseeing Talking Book program .. STEWART, Jeanne E. .. (MS) 1192
Talking books .... JENNINGS, Mary ...... (AK) 598
                                 COLEMAN, James M. .. (AL) 231
                                 WAZNIS, Betty .... (CA) 1311
                                 KELLEY, H N. .... (IL) 636
                                 PARK, T P. .... (NY) 941
Talking books service .... LADUE, Annette S. ..... (NY) 687
Young adult book talks .... OSSOLINSKI, Lynn .... (NV) 928

TANDY
Library uses, Tandy databases .... TUGGLE, Pamela C. ... (VA) 1262

TAPE (See also Recordings)
Audio tapes, audio books .... SANDY, Marjorie M. .... (MI) 1081
Bibliographic tape processing .... MCQUEEN, Judith D. ... (MD) 817
Cataloging of television news tapes . KEATING, Michael F. ... (OH) 633
MARC tape processing .... HAMILTON, Fae K. ..... (MA) 492
Record & tape collection .... GORDON, Thelma S. .... (CT) 452
Scientific tape film archives ..... SALY, Alan J. .... (NY) 1078
Slide & tape production .... SHAMBARGER, Peter E. . (MD) 1120
Supply video & audio tapes ...... GRAY, Lee H. .... (NJ) 460
Tape recording graduate textbooks . BULLOCK, Frances E. .. (NY) 156
Video tape .... KELLY, Sarah A. ...... (KY) 638

TARIFF (See also Export)
Tariff & trade .... PARSONAGE, Dianne L. (ON) 944

TAXATION
Accounting & tax .... BLAIR, William W. ..... (PA) 103
Accounting & tax research .... KLOPPER, Susan M. .... (GA) 662
                                 HAYWARD, Sheila S. .... (MA) 517
                                 SNAY, Sylvia A. .... (MI) 1162
Accounting & taxation .... TICE, Kathleen A. ...... (CA) 1244
Accounting & taxation research ... FROST, Roxanna .... (WA) 406
Accounting, auditing & taxation ref . HETZLER, Jill K. ...... (WA) 534
Accounting, tax research .... STEPHENS, Stefanie N. .. (AZ) 1188
Bond issue & tax referendums .... BECKER, Josephine M. .. (FL)   72
Budgeting & tax levying process .. PLAISTED, Glen L. ..... (KS) 977
Business & tax research .... WATERS, Susan S. .... (DC) 1309
Electronic tax research .... SPEYER, Thomas W. .... (NY) 1174
General legal, corporate & tax
  reference .... RAUCH, Anne .... (NY) 1010
Law & tax libraries .... TAYLOR, Kathryn E. ... (CA) 1227
                                 BALKIN, Ruth G. ...... (NY)   52
Law & tax library consulting .... EVERLOVE, Nora J. .... (FL) 359
Legal & tax publications .... FLEMING, Jack C. ..... (ON) 384
Library tax elections & referendums . AVANT, Julia K. .... (LA)   41
Securities & commodities taxes ... JOHNSON, G V. .... (IL) 604
Tax & accounting reference ...... BLUM, Linda C. .... (CA) 107
Tax & accounting research .... WHITTLESEY, Jane M. .. (TX) 1334
Tax & securities law .... DOWLING, Shelley L. ... (DC) 316
Tax collection .... SCHIELACK, Tricia J. ... (TX) 1092
Tax databases .... GIBSON, Timothy T. .... (TX) 432
Tax elections .... BENOIT, Anthony H. .... (LA)   82
Tax law .... FISHER, Jean K. ...... (MA) 381
                                 HOWE, Paula E. .... (TX) 565
Tax law reference .... REID, Pauline .... (NY) 1019
Tax law research .... MAXON, William N. .... (DC) 787
Tax libraries .... KOENDERINCK, Myrla J. . (AB) 668
Tax publishing .... KLAUS, Roger D. ...... (IL) 658
Tax publishings .... DANNE, William H. ..... (IL) 274

TAXATION (Cont'd)
Tax reference .... MOORE-EVANS, Angela .. (CA) 862
                                 HENEKS, Julia A. ...... (DC) 528
                                 JOHNSON, David J. .... (NY) 603
Tax research .... ROLLINS, James H. .... (CA) 1051
                                 MCDERMOTT, Patricia M. (DC) 802
                                 ELLIS, Gloria B. .... (MI) 344
                                 DINGLEY, Doris A. ..... (MN) 305
                                 SLAMKOWSKI, Donna L. . (MN) 1147
                                 FRANKENSTEIN, Steven
                                   S. .... (NY) 397
                                 EMERSON, Beth A. ..... (TX) 347
                                 SMITH, Kraleen S. ..... (TX) 1156
Tax-accounting databases .... BARRETT, Carol A. ..... (TX)   59
Taxation .... BONYNGE, Jeanne R. .. (DC) 115
                                 SHEERAN, Carole A. ... (DC) 1125
                                 HEIDKA, Patricia L. .... (IL) 521
                                 CRAIG, Wendy E. ...... (ON) 254
Taxation research .... HOPKINS, Terry F. ..... (TX) 558
Taxation research, management
  consulting .... VEASLEY, Mignon M. ... (CA) 1280
Taxes .... CARTELLI, Alessandra J. (PA) 188
                                 PLEFKA, Cathleen S. ... (PA) 978
Tax-related information .... ENSEL, Ellen H. .... (CT) 350
Valuation & taxation of real property . BEVERLEY, Barbara S. . (NY)   93

TAXONOMY
Botanical systematics & taxonomy . CHANDLER, Jody A. ... (UT) 200
Taxonomy of librarianship .... JORDAN, Robert T. .... (DC) 617
Taxonomy of plants .... STIEBER, Michael T. ... (PA) 1193
Zoological systematics & taxonomy . CHANDLER, Jody A. ... (UT) 200

TEACHING (See also Courses, Instruction, Instructional, Lecturing, Lessons, Professorship, Skills, Tutoring)
Archives & records management
  teaching .... WHALEN, Lucille ...... (NY) 1328
Assisting teachers .... FANSLOW, Malinda C. .. (TN) 363
Bibliography teaching .... SCHMITZ, Eugenia E. .. (WI) 1096
Cataloging administration & teaching . AYRAULT, Margaret W. . (HI)   43
Cataloging teaching .... SCHMITZ, Eugenia E. .. (WI) 1096
Children's literature teaching .... SCHMITZ, Eugenia E. .. (WI) 1096
Children's srvs, teaching, acquisitions . BACHAND, Alice J. ..... (KS)   43
Classroom teaching .... MCCARTHY, Carmen H. . (PR) 794
Clinical teaching .... RAMAKRISHNAN, T ... (LA) 1004
College & university teaching ..... GUENTHER, Charles J. . (MO) 475
Computer resources for teachers .. COLEMAN, Barbara K. .. (OH) 231
Computers & teaching .... BRODMAN, Estelle ..... (NJ) 139
Cooperative planning & teaching .. SCOTT, William H. .... (BC) 1108
Cooperative planning teaching .... MACRAE, Lorne G. ..... (AB) 758
Cooperative teaching .... WILLIAMS, Eve A. ..... (NB) 1343
Curriculum & teacher assistance .. MILLER, Marian A. ..... (OH) 840
Curriculum teaching materials .... FISHER, Joan W. ...... (MD) 381
Econometrics teaching .... JAIN, Nem C. .... (MA) 592
Education of teacher librarians ... BROWN, Jean I. .... (NF) 144
Educational materials for teachers .. MAY, Frank C. .... (CA) 788
Elementary teaching .... SKEHAN, Patricia A. ... (CA) 1145
Films, publications & teaching aids . FORREST, Phyllis E. ... (DC) 391
Foreign language teaching .... HSU, Patrick K. .... (TX) 567
Graduate school teaching .... MANES, Estelle L. ..... (OK) 765
High school library teaching ..... JEFFORDS, Margaret C. . (NY) 596
Indexing research & teaching .... WEINBERG, Bella H. ... (NY) 1317
Instruction, teaching .... CARUSO, Genevieve O. . (MI) 190
Instructional materials, teacher educ . PRILLAMAN, Susan M. .. (NC) 993
Intellectual freedom teaching .... EISENBACH, Elizabeth R. (CA) 340
Lecturing & teaching .... ROMAN, Susan .... (IL) 1052
Legal research & teaching .... PIERCE, Ann E. .... (ME) 971
Legal research & writing teaching .. MURRAY, James M. ... (WA) 882
Legal research teaching .... PREBLE, Leverett L. ... (DC) 990
Librarian & teacher teams ...... LESH, Jane G. .... (CA) 718
Libraries in teacher education .... SAVAGE, Daniel A. .... (ON) 1085
Lib education teaching &
  administration .... SULLIVAN, Peggy A. ... (IL) 1208
Library resources teacher .... ELLEBRACHT, Eleanor V. (MO) 343
Library school teaching .... SIMMONS, Ruth J. ..... (NJ) 1140
Library school teaching of rare books . HEANEY, Howell J. .... (PA) 518

TEACHING (Cont'd)

Library skills teaching	HUGHES, Sondra K.	(CO)	572
	BECKING, Mara S.	(IN)	73
	HIRSCH, Elizabeth	(MA)	543
	BROWN, Anita P.	(NJ)	142
	WHITLOW, Cherrill M.	(NM)	1333
	KENNEY, Ann J.	(OR)	641
Library teaching assistance courses	STRANC, Mary C.	(NY)	1200
Library use in teaching	JOHNSON, B L.	(CA)	602
Library use teaching	RAPPELT, John F.	(NY)	1008
Media center management & teaching	CLEAVER, Betty P.	(OH)	220
Medical librarian teaching	SUGA, Toshinobu	(JAP)	1206
Microcomputer teaching	MANN, Sallie E.	(NC)	766
Music librarianship & teaching	BLACK, Dorothy M.	(PA)	101
Online searching, teaching, services	STWODAH, M I.	(VA)	1206
Oral history teaching	GRELE, Ronald J.	(NY)	467
Print & non-print teacher consulting	CARLISLE, Carol A.	(CT)	182
Reading teaching	BARTON, Barbara I.	(BAH)	61
Reference & teaching	PATTERSON, Myron B.	(UT)	948
Reference & technical services teaching	ROVELSTAD, Mathilde V.	(DC)	1062
Reference materials, teaching, services	STWODAH, M I.	(VA)	1206
Reference skill teaching	GRIFFIN, Charlene F.	(KY)	468
Reference teaching	EISENBACH, Elizabeth R.	(CA)	340
	CLARKE, Norman F.	(MN)	219
Reference, teaching & evaluation	CROWLEY, Terence	(CA)	262
Research & teaching	CASTRO, Rafaela G.	(CA)	194
Research skill teaching	PRIESING, Patricia L.	(NJ)	993
Research skills teaching	MARTINAZZI, Toni	(IL)	779
Service to teachers	AVERY, Linda S.	(NM)	42
Services to special groups teaching	WHALEN, Lucille	(NY)	1328
Staff development for teachers	FISH, Barbara M.	(NC)	380
Teach information retrieval skills	SMITH, Margie G.	(CA)	1157
Teacher	VITELLO, Susan	(FL)	1286
	SWARENS, Darrell F.	(IN)	1214
Teacher & administrator	COLYER, Judith A.	(MI)	234
Teacher & reference skills	DANIELSON, Connie S.	(IA)	273
Teacher, computer science	EFFERTZ, Rose	(IL)	338
Teacher consultation	GERRING, Cheryl B.	(MD)	429
Teacher education	GILLAN, Dennis P.	(NJ)	435
	BROWN, Jean I.	(NF)	144
Teacher education, reading specialist	AUSTIN, Mary C.	(HI)	40
Teacher evaluation policys	KRATZ, Hans G.	(AB)	676
Teacher, inservice in technology	HOFSTAD, Alice M.	(MN)	548
Teacher librarian	CADY, Ruth A.	(CA)	170
	CHONCOFF, Joyce L.	(IN)	210
Teacher/librarian cooperatives	ANDRIST, Shirley A.	(SK)	27
Teacher/librarian in service	DICK, Norma P.	(CA)	300
Teacher/librarian professional devlpmnt	GUILBERT, N P.	(MB)	476
Teacher librarianship	LINDSAY, Jane A.	(WI)	729
Teacher of library skills	ROUSE, Charlie L.	(OK)	1061
Teacher resource	ONUFFER, Joachim	(PA)	924
	BACON, Carey H.	(WA)	44
Teacher resource consultant	REESE, Virginia D.	(KY)	1016
Teacher training	NEWMAN, Eileen M.	(NY)	899
Teacher use of libraries	JOHNSON, Harlan R.	(AZ)	605
Teaching	JOHNSON, Robert K.	(AZ)	608
	DOUGLAS, Carolyn T.	(CA)	314
	EVANS, G E.	(CA)	357
	HOLLEMAN, Marian P.	(CA)	551
	CLOPINE, John J.	(FL)	223
	PINGS, Joan G.	(FL)	974
	BORUZKOWSKI, Lilly A.	(IL)	117
	WEICK, Robert J.	(IN)	1316
	MATHEWS, Mary P.	(MD)	784
	TIMBERS, Jill G.	(MI)	1245
	WISE, Virginia J.	(MI)	1357
	MCDIARMID, Errett W.	(MN)	802
	DOBRUNZ, Sally J.	(MO)	307
	LATHAM, Candace	(NJ)	701
	THIRD, Bettie J.	(NJ)	1235
	GILLESPIE, John T.	(NY)	435
	HERTZ, Cynthia L.	(NY)	533
	SIKORSKI, Charlene S.	(NY)	1137
	STEWART, Vicki	(OK)	1193
	OLSEN, Clintena D.	(OR)	921
	BROWN, David E.	(PA)	143
	FENICHEL, Carol H.	(PA)	371

TEACHING (Cont'd)

Teaching	MILLER, Marjorie M.	(PA)	840
	MILLER, Sheila K.	(PA)	842
	PAGOTTO, Sarah L.	(PA)	934
	SCHEEREN, Judith A.	(PA)	1090
	STALLARD, Kathryn E.	(PA)	1179
	BUTLER, Marguerite L.	(TX)	166
	KUNEY, Joseph H.	(VA)	684
	TERESINSKI, Sally S.	(WI)	1231
	MARCHAND, Jacques	(PQ)	768
	KISHIMOTO, Hiroko	(JAP)	656
Teaching academic library services	TRYON, Jonathan S.	(RI)	1259
Teaching administration, special libs	HUMPHRY, James	(NY)	574
Teaching adventures in attitudes	SCHLAFF, Donna G.	(MA)	1093
Teaching Afro-American literature	PERRY, Margaret	(IN)	960
Teaching & development	MALLALIEU, Robert K.	(NJ)	763
	WOLPERT, Scott L.	(NJ)	1362
Teaching & implementation of lib skills	MARTIN, Sandra D.	(KY)	778
Teaching & lecturing library admin	GRIFFEN, Agnes M.	(MD)	468
Teaching & programming	LANGA, Patricia A.	(TX)	695
Teaching & research	MCELHANEY, William E.	(CT)	804
	KEEFER, Ethel A.	(NY)	634
Teaching & training	BLACK, Dorothy M.	(PA)	101
	BEAUMONT, Jane	(ON)	70
Teaching archival management	YOUNKIN, C G.	(TX)	1383
Teaching archival start-up	CASLIN, Adele	(PA)	193
Teaching at university level	SWARTZ, Jon D.	(TX)	1214
Teaching audiovisual education	WIRTANEN, James	(ND)	1356
Teaching, audiovisual production	POWELL, Patricia K.	(TX)	988
Teaching beginning cataloging	ALSWORTH, Frances W.	(OK)	18
Teaching cataloging	KATO, Hisae	(JAP)	629
Teaching cataloging & classification	MILLER, Sarah J.	(NJ)	842
Teaching children & adolescent lit	SANDERS, John B.	(MO)	1080
Teaching children's literature	WALDEN, Katherine G.	(CT)	1294
	NIX, Kemie	(GA)	905
	ADCOCK, Betty L.	(IL)	6
Teaching collection development	TRYON, Jonathan S.	(RI)	1259
Teaching collection devlpmnt, publishing	HUMPHRY, James	(NY)	574
Teaching elementary library skills	HEINRICH, Lois M.	(MD)	522
	TOWNSEND, Rita M.	(PA)	1253
Teaching elementary media skills	SULLI, Gerard C.	(CT)	1207
Teaching folklore course	MICHNAY, Susan E.	(OH)	832
Teaching graduate public libs course	VALENTINE, Patrick M.	(NC)	1271
Teaching in library school	WOOD, Raymund F.	(CA)	1364
Teaching information science	FLOOD, Barbara J.	(PA)	385
Teaching intellectual freedom	TRYON, Jonathan S.	(RI)	1259
Teaching legal research	FOSTER, Lynn	(AR)	392
Teaching legal research skills	WHISMAN, Linda A.	(CA)	1329
	WELKER, Kathy J.	(OH)	1321
Teaching library administration	MCNEAL, Archie L.	(FL)	816
Teaching library & research skills	WIENER, Sylvia B.	(NY)	1336
Teaching library, audiovisual skills	CONOVER, Kathryn H.	(FL)	238
Teaching library concepts	ONELLI, Patricia M.	(NJ)	924
Teaching library research	BROWN, Patricia L.	(OR)	146
Teaching library research skills	REILLY, Maureen E.	(CT)	1020
Teaching library science	JEFFCOAT, Phyllis C.	(AR)	596
	HAZLETT, Florence E.	(AZ)	517
	KAST, Gloria E.	(CA)	629
	CULPEPPER, Jetta C.	(KY)	264
	KNORR, Martin R.	(MO)	665
Teaching library science courses	MATHES, Miriam S.	(WA)	783
	RUSSELL, Richard A.	(WV)	1069
Teaching library skills	KLUESNER, Marvin P.	(AL)	662
	STARRETT, Mildred J.	(AZ)	1182
	ALLABACK, Patricia G.	(CA)	13
	KOSKY, Janet J.	(CA)	672
	MILLS, Denise Y.	(CA)	844
	SUTHERLAND, Helen G.	(CA)	1211
	SELVERSTONE, Harriet S.	(CT)	1114
	SOUTHARD, Sarah T.	(CT)	1169
	MCCARTHY, Carrol B.	(DE)	794
	COPELAND, Mildred A.	(FL)	244
	LOPEZ, Deborah A.	(FL)	741
	ADCOCK, Betty L.	(IL)	6
	JOHNSON, Keran C.	(IL)	606
	CRACE, Sallye C.	(KY)	254
	REESE, Virginia D.	(KY)	1016
	BERNSTEIN, D S.	(MA)	89

TEACHING (Cont'd)

Teaching library skills

	JACOBS, Lois S.	(MA)	589
	THOMAS, Laverne J.	(MI)	1237
	AYLWARD, Judith A.	(MO)	43
	GULICK, Eleanor L.	(NJ)	477
	MATTER, Kathy L.	(NM)	785
	SCHUBERT, Donald F.	(NM)	1101
	LEPINNET, Nancy M.	(NY)	717
	SOUTHCOMBE, Patricia A.	(NY)	1169
	SPIEGEL, Bertha	(NY)	1174
	WOLF, Catharine D.	(NY)	1360
	DISTEFANO, Marianne	(OH)	305
	BALDWIN, Janet M.	(PA)	51
	MORIARTY, Kathleen T.	(PA)	865
	WOLFE, Mary S.	(PA)	1361
	ALDRICH, Linda S.	(RI)	11
	IMONDI, Lenore R.	(RI)	582
	VANDERGRIFF, Kathleen E.	(TN)	1274
	DAVIS, Joan C.	(TX)	279
	FRIEDMAN, Tevia L.	(TX)	404
	GREMONT, Joan C.	(TX)	467
	WEISLAK, Susan L.	(TX)	1319
	PETERSON, Francine	(UT)	963
	CHAMBERLAIN, M J.	(VA)	197
	HOSKINS, Sylvia H.	(VA)	561
	DOLBEY, Mary B.	(WA)	309
	KNOLL, Betty A.	(WA)	665
Teaching library skills & computers	YOUNG, Patricia S.	(TN)	1383
Teaching library skills & research	CARVER, Jane C.	(MA)	191
Teaching library technicians	TILLOTSON, Joy G.	(NF)	1245
Teaching library usage	BOSTLEY, Jean R.	(MA)	117
Teaching linguistics	WILLIAMSON, Susan G.	(PA)	1348
Teaching literature appreciation	MERRILL, Barbara P.	(NY)	826
Teaching materials	ANDERSON, Virginia L.	(IN)	25
Teaching media skills	HUNT, Susan O.	(FL)	576
	WINSLOW, Carol M.	(IN)	1355
	CUNNINGHAM, Mary A.	(NY)	265
Teaching music history	SMILEY, Marilynn J.	(NY)	1151
Teaching non-automated library work	LINNENBRUEGGE, Gertrude R.	(WA)	731
Teaching of library skill to students	GERMINDER, Robin L.	(NJ)	429
Teaching of library skills	BIANCHI, Karen F.	(WA)	93
Teaching physicians GRATEFUL MED	SCHELL, Catherine L.	(WY)	1091
Teaching, reference librarian	TRIM, Kathryn	(MI)	1256
Teaching reference service	SABLE, Martin H.	(WI)	1072
Teaching reference skills	SLOAN, Mary J.	(GA)	1149
Teaching religion courses	BOISCLAIR, Regina A.	(PA)	111
Teaching research & reference skills	BERNAT, Mary A.	(VEN)	88
Teaching research process	PARR, Michael P.	(MI)	944
Teaching research skill	HAYASHI, Chigusa	(NJ)	515
Teaching research skills	MISENHEIMER, Paula S.	(AR)	847
	THORNTON, Alice J.	(DE)	1242
	SMITH, Lena D.	(KY)	1157
	CRAMER, Eugene C.	(AB)	255
Teaching school library research skills	CARLISLE, Carol A.	(CT)	182
Teaching skills	ROBINSON, Gayle N.	(AL)	1044
	MERRILL, Barbara P.	(NY)	826
Teaching storytelling	MACDONALD, Margaret R.	(WA)	754
Teaching students	SCHREFFLER, Lynne W.	(PA)	1099
Teaching, technical & business info	CHAMIS, Alice Y.	(OH)	198
Teaching technical services	SOPER, Mary E.	(WA)	1168
Teaching, training & development	ROTHENBERG, Mark H.	(NY)	1060
Teaching undergraduate courses	FREEMAN, C L.	(MO)	400
Teaching undergraduate library science	MALTBY, Florence H.	(MO)	764
Teaching use of library	KATZ, Claire G.	(CT)	630
	RICHARDSON, Margaret B.	(FL)	1029
	MEINEL, Nancy T.	(LA)	822
	PELZER, Adolf	(MI)	955
Teaching use of media center	DAVIES, Gordon D.	(MD)	277
Teaching writing	BATES, Barbara S.	(PA)	63
Teaching writing & editing	BLUMER, Thomas J.	(DC)	107
Television teaching	RECTOR, Wendell H.	(CT)	1013
Training & development, teaching	CURRAN, William M.	(PQ)	266

TEACHING (Cont'd)

Training & teaching	PIERRE, Zenata W.	(OR)	972
Training & teaching library courses	KUJOORY, Parvin	(TX)	683
Training, staff development, teaching	FALANGA, Rosemarie E.	(CA)	361
Video as teaching tool	LESH, Jane G.	(CA)	718

TEAM

Librarian & teacher teams	LESH, Jane G.	(CA)	718
Research managing, international team	CLARK, Joan	(NJ)	217
Strategic planning & teambuilding	TYSON, John C.	(VA)	1267
Team building	MUNGER, Freda R.	(OR)	879
Team management	LUTHER, M J.	(GA)	750

TECHNICAL (See also Cataloging, Classification, Geotechnical, Processing, Technology)

Abstracting & indexing technical data	HOWARD, Susanna J.	(NC)	564
Abstracting & technical writing	FISHER, Daphne V.	(PA)	380
Acquisition reference technical service	WIENER, Sylvia B.	(NY)	1336
Acquisitions & serials technical srvs	KARASICK, Alice W.	(CA)	627
Acquisitions, technical services	BATTAGLIA, Bonnie J.	(CA)	64
	MORGAN, Linda M.	(CA)	864
	COFFEY, James R.	(NJ)	227
Administration of technical services	ANDERSON, David C.	(CA)	22
	GLEIM, David E.	(NC)	441
	LANGE, Elizabeth A.	(SC)	695
Administrative & technical systems	KNIGHTLY, John J.	(TN)	664
Aerospace technical literature	BOYD, Effie W.	(TN)	122
All aspects of technical services	HAMBURGER, Roberta L.	(OK)	491
Automated technical processing	TAYYEB, Rashid	(NS)	1229
Automation & technical services	CLEVENGER, Judy B.	(AR)	221
Automation of technical services	MCDONALD, Michael L.	(DC)	803
	KLINK, Carol A.	(IL)	662
Automotive technical innovations	WREN, James A.	(MI)	1370
Business & technical databases	DONAHUE, Karin V.	(IL)	310
	WEBER, Robert F.	(OR)	1314
	WHITEHURST, Dori A.	(PA)	1333
	ARMSTRONG, Denise M.	(SAF)	32
Business & technical engineering	GRIFFITTS, Joan K.	(IN)	469
Business & technical information	RUTHERFORD, Frederick S.	(ON)	1070
Business & technical reference	WILLIAMS, Constance H.	(CO)	1342
	REILLY, Dayle A.	(MA)	1020
Cataloging & technical services	SHAPIRO, Leonard P.	(CA)	1121
	LOPEZ, Deborah A.	(FL)	741
	LUNG, Mon Y.	(KS)	748
	LEONARD, Ruth S.	(MA)	717
	ANDERMAN, Lynea	(NJ)	21
	ENG, Mamie	(NY)	348
	MALINCONICO, S M.	(NY)	763
	ANDERSON, Elizabeth M.	(PA)	22
	ROCKWOOD, Susan M.	(PA)	1046
	MARTIN, Nannette	(SDA)	777
Cataloging of technical reports	KLEIBER, Michael C.	(CA)	658
Cataloging technical documents	PATTEN, Frederick W.	(CA)	947
Cataloging, technical services	MESNER, Lillian R.	(KY)	827
	BALDWIN, Betty J.	(NY)	51
	ROBICHAUD, Marcel J.	(NY)	1042
	TRINKAUS, Tanya	(RI)	1256
Chemical & technical online searching	SPECTOR, Janice B.	(MI)	1172
Circulation & technical services	BENGSTON, Carl E.	(CA)	80
Commercial technical services	JACOBS, Peter J.	(CA)	590
Computer & technical liaison	EVANS, Mark S.	(FL)	357
Computerization of technical services	PICCOLI, Roberta A.	(IL)	970
Computerization, technical services, ref	HEISE, George F.	(NJ)	522
Customer & technical services	LEE, Doreen H.	(CA)	709
Customer technical support	PIKE, Christine M.	(NJ)	972
Defense technical information	HALL, Robert G.	(MA)	488
Editing of technical materials	WOODLOCK, Stephanie	(PA)	1366
Energy & technical databases	LOOP, Jacqueline N.	(ID)	740
Engineering & technical databases	POZO, Frank J.	(NC)	989
	VIXIE, Anne C.	(OR)	1286
	MIDGETT, Ann S.	(TX)	833
Engineering & technical library	MCDANIELS, Patricia R.	(OR)	801
Evaluation of technical information	HALL, Homer J.	(NJ)	488
Foreign scientific technical literature	BROPHY, Charles A.	(OH)	141

TECHNICAL (Cont'd)

General & technical services serials	SZETO, Dorcas C.	(CA)	1218
Geological technical info management	DICKERSON, Mary J.	(TX)	300
Head of technical services	ROCK, Sue W.	(NJ)	1046
Head, technical services	SOUZA, Margaret A.	(CA)	1170
Index & abstract technical reports	CIBULSKIS, Elizabeth R.	(IL)	214
Info & research, business & technical	SPINA, Marie C.	(NY)	1175
Japanese technical & business databases	QUINN, Ralph M.	(NJ)	1000
Japanese technl literature abstracting	FOWELLS, Fumi T.	(MI)	393
Japanese technical translations	QUINN, Ralph M.	(NJ)	1000
Journals, technical publications	FINDLING, Carol A.	(NE)	377
Law library technical services	ADAN, Adrienne	(CA)	6
	PIPER, Patricia L.	(CA)	975
	NASSERDEN, Marilyn D.	(AB)	889
Leasing technical products	MONOSSON, Adolf S.	(MA)	855
Library technical areas	COHEN, Rochelle F.	(NY)	229
Library technical assistants	HARWOOD, Judith A.	(IL)	510
Library technical processing	RUNKLE, Martin D.	(IL)	1067
Library technical services	STUART, Gerard W.	(AZ)	1204
	DOERRER, David H.	(FL)	308
	JOHNSON, Richard D.	(NY)	608
	MOORE, Jane R.	(NY)	859
	LYNDEN, Frederick C.	(RI)	752
	DUMONT, Paul E.	(TX)	325
	REMINGTON, David G.	(WA)	1022
Library technical services admin	NICHOLS, Elizabeth D.	(CA)	901
Management of technical services	SLOCA, Sue E.	(DC)	1150
	STEVENS, Roberta A.	(DC)	1191
	BETH, Dana L.	(MO)	92
	KAWAGUCHI, Miyako	(VA)	632
Managing a scientific, technical library	GIBSON, Gladys N.	(MB)	432
Managing technical services	DJEVALIKIAN, Sonia	(PQ)	306
Manual & automated technl applications	MERRITT, Betty A.	(CA)	827
Manual technical cataloging	WHITT, Diane M.	(IL)	1334
Manufacturing lib technical furniture	VAN PELT, Peter J.	(NY)	1277
Mapping, technical libraries	RUDD, Janet K.	(CA)	1065
Marketing, technical liaison	ZIRPOLO, Frank	(NY)	1390
Marketing technical periodicals	FERRERE, Cathy M.	(NY)	373
Medical library technical services	WOODBURN, Judy I.	(NC)	1366
Medical, scientific, technical reference	TIFFEAULT, Alice A.	(NY)	1244
Medical technical services	LAWRENCE, Carol A.	(CT)	704
Microcomputers & technical services	JOHNSON, Gary M.	(MD)	604
Microcomputers in technical services	RODICH, Nancy A.	(MS)	1048
Music technical services	MCKNIGHT, Mark C.	(LA)	812
NASA & Defense technical reports	BOYD, Effie W.	(TN)	122
Navy, technical librarianship	DAVIDOFF, Marcia	(FL)	276
Online searching & technical database	LEREW, Ann A.	(CO)	717
Online searching, technical databases	PRESTON, Deirdre R.	(WA)	991
Online technical services	WILSON, Virginia G.	(MA)	1353
Patents, technical	WILLIAMS, Robert C.	(AK)	1346
Professional, technical books	BOWMAN, James K.	(NY)	121
Professional technical trade texts	ABRAMOFF, Lawrence J.	(MA)	3
Proprietary technical report systems	ECKROADE, Carlene B.	(DE)	335
Public & technical services	RIGGS, Donald E.	(AZ)	1034
Public technical speaking	KAMINECKI, Ronald M.	(IL)	624
Reader & technical services	SHERWIG, Mary J.	(NY)	1129
Reference & technical services	RAO, Rama K.	(PA)	1008
Reference & technical services teaching	ROVELSTAD, Mathilde V.	(DC)	1062
Reference, business & technical	POST, Linda C.	(CA)	986
Reference, public & technical services	OPATOW, Judith	(NY)	925
Reference, technical & marketing	GARVEY, Nancy G.	(NJ)	421
Reorganization of technical services	HENN, Barbara J.	(IN)	528
Resources & technical services	WILKINS, Alice L.	(NC)	1340
Retrieving technical information	HALLSTROM, Curtis H.	(MN)	489
Science & technical collection devlpmnt	PASTERCZYK, Catherine E.	(NM)	946
Science & technical databases	PASTERCZYK, Catherine E.	(NM)	946
Science & technical reference	ENRICI, Pamela L.	(MN)	350
Science & technical reference services	DEBROWER, Amy M.	(MD)	285
Science & technical serials	LEWANDOWSKI, Joseph J.	(CA)	722
Science technical literature & databases	ROE, Eunice M.	(PA)	1048

TECHNICAL (Cont'd)

Scientific & technical cataloging	ELSBREE, John J.	(VA)	346
Scientific & technical databases	LEVIN, Amy E.	(DC)	720
	ENRICI, Pamela L.	(MN)	350
	CIARAMELLA, Mary A.	(NJ)	214
	ORTIZ, Cynthia	(NV)	927
	LETTIS, Lucy B.	(NY)	719
	LEMON, Nancy A.	(OH)	715
	ELSBREE, John J.	(VA)	346
	HOLLY, Janet S.	(VA)	552
	JOACHIM, Robert J.	(VA)	600
Scientific & technical early periodicals	KRONICK, David A.	(TX)	679
Scientific & technical information	DOUVILLE, Judith A.	(CT)	314
	WALDHART, Thomas J.	(KY)	1294
	AINES, Andrew A.	(MD)	8
	SMITH, Robert B.	(PA)	1160
	WALKER, Richard D.	(WI)	1296
Scientific & technical info copyright	WOOD, Julienne L.	(LA)	1364
Scientific & technical info management	CARROLL, Bonnie C.	(TN)	187
	SPATH, Charles E.	(TN)	1171
Scientific & technical info retrieval	HOWARD, Theresa M.	(ENG)	564
Scientific & technical information srvs	MOSER, Jane W.	(CA)	870
Scientific & technical intelligence	CRANOR, Alice T.	(DC)	255
Scientific & technical libraries	FEENEY, Karen E.	(CA)	368
	PRUETT, Nancy J.	(NM)	996
Scientific & technical literature	FOREMAN, Anne P.	(AL)	390
	SNYDER, Richard L.	(PA)	1165
	GARNETT, Joyce C.	(PQ)	419
	JOBA, Judith C.	(PQ)	601
Scientific & technical lit databases	MOBLEY, Emily R.	(IN)	851
Scientific & technical online searches	TOMMEY, Richard J.	(CA)	1250
Scientific & technical patents	STANGL-WALKER, Teresa A.	(ON)	1180
Scientific & technical publications	ELSBREE, John J.	(VA)	346
Scientific & technical reference	CUMMINGS, Helen H.	(DC)	264
	KING, Hannah M.	(DC)	651
	BLASCHAK, Mary M.	(MI)	104
Scientific & technical ref & research	MILLER, Dennis P.	(OH)	837
Scientific & technical research	CRANDALL, Michael D.	(WA)	255
Scientific & technical searching	POLAND, Jean A.	(OK)	980
Scientific & technical translations	SAMSON, Mary	(ON)	1079
Scientific, technical & reference books	PECK, Brian T.	(FL)	953
Scientific, technical business databases	ALEXANDER, Mary B.	(TN)	12
Scientific technical medical	KRIEGER, Robert E.	(FL)	678
Scientific, technical online searching	ENGLISH, Bernard L.	(NJ)	350
Service & technical databases	DUFF, Ann M.	(ON)	323
Shelving technical equipment	DE BEAR, Richard S.	(MI)	284
Southeast Asian technical services	ASHMUN, Lawrence F.	(NY)	36
Supervise corporate technical library	CARPENTER, Dale	(NY)	184
Support & technical services	BROOM, Susan E.	(FL)	141
Teaching, technical & business info	CHAMIS, Alice Y.	(OH)	198
Teaching technical services	SOPER, Mary E.	(WA)	1168
Technical & business online searching	DIETRICH, Peter J.	(NY)	302
Technical & business reference	GABRIEL, Linda	(NJ)	411
Technical & engineering databases	ALBRIGHT, Sue R.	(CA)	10
Technical & engineering documents	SCHULTZ, Arnold J.	(MN)	1101
Technical & engineering information	HARTLEY, Gloria R.	(PA)	508
Technical & general editing	JOSLYN, Camille	(VA)	618
Technical & general proofreading	JOSLYN, Camille	(VA)	618
Technical & public services	RAMBLER, Linda K.	(PA)	1005
Technical & research libraries mgmt	CRENSHAW, Tena L.	(FL)	258
Technical & scientific reference	THOM, Pat A.	(WI)	1235
Technical & tech commercial research	CRABTREE, Sandra A.	(CA)	254
Technical assistance	MOELLENDICK, M J.	(WV)	851
Technical book reviewing	KRUPP, Robert G.	(NJ)	681
Technical cataloging	JADWIN, Rochelle J.	(CA)	591
Technical cataloging & reference	SIMPSON, Alice H.	(OH)	1141
Technical collection development	SAKAI, Diane H.	(HI)	1076
Technical communications	NADZIEJKA, David E.	(WI)	886
Technical corporate libraries	BERGIN, Karen S.	(MI)	86
Technical database development	D'ADOLF, Steven P.	(CA)	269
Technical databases	LEE, Dora T.	(CA)	709
	WRIGHT, Betty A.	(CA)	1370
	HARRIS, Michael A.	(CO)	505
	PRESTON, Lawrence N.	(CO)	991
	LADNER, Sharyn J.	(FL)	687
	CARTER, Ida	(IL)	189

TECHNICAL (Cont'd)

Technical databases

Technical databases	MASON, Dorothy L.	(IN)	781
	WILSON, Sharon L.	(OH)	1353
	DINNIMAN, Margo P.	(PA)	305
	KLEIN, Joanne S.	(PA)	659
	ERWIN, Mary J.	(TN)	353
	HULSE, Phyllis	(TX)	573
	BEHR, Alice S.	(WV)	75
	KAMICHAITIS, Penelope H.	(PQ)	624
	POGUE, Basil G.	(SK)	979
Technical databases, engineering	FINGERMAN, Susan M.	(MA)	378
Technical documentation	SPINKS, Paul	(CA)	1175
	QUINN, Candy L.	(CO)	1000
	SCOTT, Mona L.	(VA)	1107
	REILLY, Brian O.	(ON)	1020
Technical editing	DAVIS, Marianne W.	(CA)	280
	RIDER, Philip R.	(IL)	1032
	BARRETT, Joyce C.	(NJ)	59
	CASSELL, Gerald S.	(TN)	193
	HACKNEY, Judith G.	(TX)	481
Technical editing, consumer electronics	MENNIE, Don	(NJ)	824
Technical editor	HINTON, N E.	(KS)	543
Technical education	RICE, Joyce I.	(MS)	1027
Technical indexing	BAIR, Alice E.	(IL)	47
Technical indexing & abstracting	WILLS, Luella G.	(VA)	1349
Technical information	JENKINS, Ann A.	(CA)	597
	OKEY, Susan T.	(IN)	920
	MATTHEWS, Charles E.	(MA)	785
	YUILLE, Willie K.	(MD)	1384
	KEOGH, Jeanne M.	(OH)	643
	LANGKAU, Claire M.	(OH)	696
	BERGER, Lewis W.	(PA)	85
	DRAKE, James B.	(ON)	318
	FAIRLEY, Craig R.	(ON)	361
Technical information acquisition	RICE, Gerald W.	(NH)	1027
Technical information acquisitions	MONTGOMERY, Suzanne L.	(VA)	856
Technical information center management	EYLES, Heberle H.	(FL)	359
	HALL, Deanna M.	(GA)	487
Technical information centers	PERELLA, Susanne B.	(DC)	958
Technical information indexing	BRETON, Ernest J.	(DE)	133
Technical information management	SAYLOR, Linda	(CA)	1086
	MAYER, June C.	(NJ)	789
	DE TONNANCOUR, P R.	(TX)	296
Technical information research	LAHR, Thomas F.	(VA)	688
Technical information resources	BARTL, Richard P.	(NY)	61
Technical information retrieval	NELSON, Alice R.	(CA)	893
	SCHALIT, Michael	(CA)	1089
	LAZARUS, Josephine G.	(CO)	706
Technical information searching	FISLER, Charlotte D.	(PA)	382
Technical information services	LERNER, Frederick A.	(NH)	717
	HASSAN, Mohammad Z.	(NY)	511
	STAIR, Fred	(OK)	1178
Technical information specialist	COOK, Kathleen M.	(CA)	240
Technical liaison	ANDEL, June	(PA)	21
Technical libraries	FRIEDMAN, Sandra M.	(CA)	404
	WILKINSON, William A.	(MO)	1340
Technical library development	WHITMAN, Jean A.	(MD)	1333
Technical library management	REITER, Martha B.	(CT)	1022
	FILLER, Mary A.	(PA)	377
Technical library research	SAUTER, Lyn F.	(WA)	1085
Technical literature	KORNFELD, Carol E.	(NJ)	672
	SWINBURNE, Ralph E.	(NY)	1216
Technical literature search	MIWA, Makiko	(JAP)	850
Technical literature searches	BARTLETT, Vernell W.	(MN)	61
Technical literature searching	WHITT, Diane M.	(IL)	1334
	YANCEY, Marianne	(OH)	1377
Technical management	GAGNON, Donna M.	(CA)	412
	BLISS, David H.	(IA)	105
Technical material selection	WILLIAMS, Alexander	(FL)	1341
Technical online searching	HARMON, Patricia A.	(CT)	502
	BOYLE, Stephen	(IL)	124
Technical operations	MENEGAUX, Edmond A.	(MD)	824
	BRANN, Andrew R.	(OH)	128
	TIPLER, Stephen B.	(ON)	1246

TECHNICAL (Cont'd)

Technical petroleum information	STURDIVANT, Clarence A.	(CO)	1205
Technical presentation	VILLERE, Dawn N.	(CA)	1284
Technical process	SABINE, Davida M.	(SC)	1072
Technical processes	SONIN, Hille	(CA)	1167
	BLAKE-O'HOGAN, Kathleen E.	(NY)	103
	EARLE, Mary E.	(OH)	332
Technical processing	RICHMOND, John W.	(AZ)	1030
	COLALILLO, Robert M.	(CA)	230
	REDFIELD, Dale E.	(CA)	1014
	TARCZY, Stephen I.	(CA)	1224
	AVRAM, Henriette D.	(DC)	42
	TERRY, Susan N.	(DC)	1232
	BINAU, Myra I.	(MD)	97
	TAYLOR, Donna I.	(NJ)	1226
	MANES, Estelle L.	(OK)	765
	JACKSON, Joseph A.	(TN)	587
	TAYLOR, Karen E.	(ON)	1227
Technical processing & acquisitions	BOGGESS, John J.	(MD)	110
Technical processing & cataloging	WHITE, Ardeen L.	(VA)	1330
Technical processing center admin	ENGELBERT, Alan M.	(WI)	348
Technical processing, govt documents	ADAMS, Leonard R.	(MA)	5
Technical processing services	KOPPER, John A.	(MN)	671
Technical publications	VARA, Margaret E.	(OH)	1278
	FREEDMAN, Bernadette	(PA)	400
Technical publishing	DUNN, Richard L.	(PA)	327
Technical reference	LEE, Dora T.	(CA)	709
	WORSTER, Carol L.	(IL)	1369
	FEIDLER, Anita J.	(MA)	368
	EIPERT, Susan L.	(WA)	340
Technical reference & searching	DESOIER, Jacqueline J.	(CA)	295
Technical report document retrieval	WHITE, Chandlee	(MA)	1330
Technical report management	CONKLING, Thomas W.	(PA)	236
Technical reports	THOMPSON, Bryan	(CA)	1239
	TYSON, Betty B.	(CA)	1267
	BYRNE, Timothy L.	(CO)	169
	SAUNDERS, Laurel B.	(NM)	1084
	BURDEN, John	(NY)	158
	CURRY, Lenora Y.	(NY)	266
	GRUBER, Linda R.	(PA)	474
	HARRIS, Maureen	(SC)	505
	PINELLI, Thomas E.	(VA)	974
Technical research	ADLER, Naomi L.	(IL)	7
	HALASZ, Marilynn J.	(IL)	484
	WINQUIST, Elaine W.	(MA)	1355
	SEMKO, Melanie J.	(MD)	1115
	PIERCE, Mildred L.	(NV)	971
	OGDEN, Suzanne M.	(TX)	918
	ROBERTS, Ernest J.	(TX)	1040
Technical research libraries	DOUGLASS, Leslie A.	(NJ)	314
Technical, scientific information	ISGANITIS, Jamie C.	(NY)	585
Technical searching online	VAN BRUNT, Amy S.	(NY)	1272
Technical service	SNODGRASSE, Elaine	(FL)	1163
	GHALI, Raouf S.	(NY)	430
	HUANG, Paul T.	(NS)	568
Technical service administration	PERCELLI, Irene M.	(NY)	958
Technical service & reference	KRIEGER, Tillie	(NY)	678
Technical services	ROSS, Rosemary E.	(AK)	1058
	GREGORY, Vicki L.	(AL)	466
	MAYTON, Regina A.	(AL)	791
	MAYS, Allison P.	(AR)	791
	HEITSHU, Sara C.	(AZ)	523
	JOHNSON, Robert K.	(AZ)	608
	POTTER, William G.	(AZ)	987
	ATKINS, Gregg T.	(CA)	38
	BIEK, David E.	(CA)	95
	CHWEH, Steven S.	(CA)	214
	COLLINS, Judith A.	(CA)	232
	CUNNINGHAM, Jay L.	(CA)	265
	DAILEY, Kazuko M.	(CA)	270
	ECKMAN, Charles D.	(CA)	335
	ENYINGI, Peter	(CA)	351
	FEENEY, Karen E.	(CA)	368
	GREGOR, Dorothy D.	(CA)	466
	HADLEY, Alice E.	(CA)	482
	HANFF, Peter E.	(CA)	495
	HOWLAND, Joan S.	(CA)	566
	LEONHARDT, Thomas W.	(CA)	717

TECHNICAL (Cont'd)
Technical services

LEUNG, Shirley W. . . . . . (CA) 719
LINVILLE, Herbert . . . . . (CA) 731
MILLER, R B. . . . . (CA) 841
MILLER, Suzanne M. . . . (CA) 842
MORSE, David H. . . . . . (CA) 869
ORTOPAN, Leroy D. . . . (CA) 927
PAI, Herman H. . . . . . . (CA) 934
RHEE, Susan F. . . . . . . (CA) 1025
ROLEN, Helen T. . . . . . (CA) 1051
RUBENS, Charlotte C. . . (CA) 1064
SIMON, Vaughn L. . . . . (CA) 1141
TILLETT, Barbara B. . . . (CA) 1245
WALTERS, Mary D. . . . . (CA) 1301
WERNER, Gloria . . . . . . (CA) 1324
WHITE, Kathleen M. . . . (CA) 1331
WILLIAMS, Leonette M. . (CA) 1344
BURKE, Marianne D. . . . (CO) 160
FORSMAN, Rick B. . . . . (CO) 391
FULMER, Russell F. . . . (CO) 409
GARZA, Rosario . . . . . . (CO) 421
MITCHELL, Marilyn J. . . (CO) 849
PITKIN, Gary M. . . . . . . (CO) 976
BALMER, Mary . . . . (CT) 53
BENAMATI, Dennis C. . . (CT) 79
COOMBS, Elisabeth G. . . (CT) 241
FAAS, Caroline . . . . . . (CT) 360
HENTZ, Margaret B. . . . (CT) 530
KELSEY, Mary J. . . . . . (CT) 639
KOEL, Ake I. . . . . (CT) 667
SCOTT, Joseph W. . . . . (CT) 1107
STEVENS, Hannah M. . . (CT) 1190
BEDARD, Laura A. . . . . (DC) 73
CIMERMANIS, Ilze V. . . (DC) 214
DENHAM, Maryanne H. . (DC) 292
LEIDER, Karen S. . . . . . (DC) 713
PAGE, John S. . . . . (DC) 934
RATESH, Ioana . . . . . . (DC) 1009
SETTLER, Leo H. . . . . . (DC) 1117
SHERWIN, Rosalie L. . . (DC) 1129
SPONDER, Dorothy R. . . (DC) 1175
TANSEY, Francis J. . . . . (DC) 1223
THOMPSON, Laurie L. . . (DC) 1240
ULRICH, Sue . . . . (DE) 1268
ALLEN, Linda G. . . . . . . (FL) 15
ALLISON, Anne M. . . . . (FL) 17
BROMBERG, Johanna . . (FL) 139
CHRISMAN, Larry G. . . (FL) 211
CLACK, Doris H. . . . . . . (FL) 215
CUBBERLEY, Carol W. . (FL) 263
FOSTER, Candice L. . . . (FL) 392
GRIMES, Maxyne M. . . . (FL) 470
KETCHERSID, Arthur L. . (FL) 645
TREYZ, Joseph H. . . . . (FL) 1256
WILLOCKS, Robert M. . . (FL) 1349
BAIN, Michael L. . . . . . . (GA) 47
BAKER, Barry B. . . . . . . (GA) 47
BATTEN, Henry R. . . . . (GA) 64
COHRS, Joyce S. . . . . . (GA) 229
DEENEY, Marian A. . . . (GA) 286
HANSON, Kathy H. . . . . (GA) 498
LUKAS, Vicki A. . . . . . . (GA) 747
MASSEY, Katha D. . . . . (GA) 782
PAULK, Betty D. . . . . . . (GA) 950
AYRAULT, Margaret W. . (HI) 43
KOTO, Ann S. . . . . (HI) 673
MAZZOLA, Patricia R. . . (HI) 791
BENTZ, Dale M. . . . . . . (IA) 84
BROWN, Darmae J. . . . (IA) 143
DICKES, Janis H. . . . . . (IA) 300
HIRST, Donna L. . . . . . . (IA) 543
ROBINSON, Caitlin M. . . (IA) 1043
FUNABIKI, Ruth P. . . . . (ID) 409
BLOSS, Marjorie E. . . . . (IL) 106
CLELAND, Camille S. . . (IL) 220
CULBERTSON, Lillian D. (IL) 263
DALE, Doris C. . . . . (IL) 270
D'AVERSA, Concettina M. (IL) 276
DILLEY, Richard A. . . . . (IL) 303

ETTER, Constance L. . . . (IL) 355
FUNK, Carla J. . . . . (IL) 409
HANSEN, Eleanore E. . . (IL) 497
HENDERSON, Kathryn L. (IL) 526
HOLZBERLEIN, Deanne B. (IL) 555
HORNY, Karen L. . . . . . (IL) 560
KNOBLAUCH, Mark G. . (IL) 665
LAMB, Sara G. . . . . (IL) 690
MCGREGOR, James W. (IL) 808
MCKEARN, Anne B. . . . (IL) 810
POOLE, Connie . . . . . . (IL) 983
PORTER, Carol . . . . (IL) 984
PRIOR, Janice L. . . . . . . (IL) 993
REIMER, Elizabeth A. . . (IL) 1020
SCHMIDT, Karen A. . . . (IL) 1095
STRAWN, Gary L. . . . . . (IL) 1201
TEGLER, Patricia . . . . . (IL) 1230
VARNER, Carroll H. . . . (IL) 1278
VONDRUSKA, Eloise M. (IL) 1288
WARRO, Edward A. . . . (IL) 1307
ARNOLD, Joann M. . . . . (IN) 33
ASHER, Richard E. . . . . (IN) 36
CIUCKI, Marcella A. . . . (IN) 215
COTTINGHAM, Elsie E. . (IN) 250
EBERSHOFF-COLES,
    Susan V. . . . . (IN) 334
GUNNELLS, Danny C. . . (IN) 477
JOHNTING, Wendell E. . (IN) 610
LE GUERN, Charles A. . (IN) 712
MCCLOY, William B. . . . (IN) 797
SACZAWA, Rosemary . . (IN) 1073
STANLEY, Luana K. . . . (IN) 1180
WARREN, Lois B. . . . . . (IN) 1306
GRASS, Charlene G. . . . (KS) 458
HOWARD, Clinton N. . . (KS) 564
MELICK, Cal G. . . . . (KS) 822
VAN SICKLE, Mary L. . . (KS) 1277
NILES, Judith F. . . . . . . (KY) 904
RICHARDSON, Susan C. (KY) 1030
FLORENT, Marguerite R. (LA) 385
MOORE, Mildred M. . . . (LA) 860
REID, Marion T. . . . . . . (LA) 1019
SHORT, Peggy S. . . . . . (LA) 1132
BETTENCOURT, Ronald J. (MA) 92
BOYCE, Barbara S. . . . . (MA) 122
DESJARDINS, Andrea C. (MA) 295
GAGNON, Ronald A. . . . (MA) 412
GATES, James L. . . . . . (MA) 421
GRAY, Carolyn M. . . . . (MA) 459
HALE, Janice L. . . . . . . (MA) 485
HARVEY, Paul W. . . . . . (MA) 509
LANDESMAN, Betty J. . (MA) 692
TRINKAUS-RANDALL,
    Gregor . . . . (MA) 1257
WILLIAMS, Carole C. . . (MA) 1342
BOND, Marvin A. . . . . . (MD) 113
BROADY, Jessie . . . . . . (MD) 138
CRISCO, Mary E. . . . . . (MD) 259
HENDERSON, Susanne . (MD) 527
KALTENBORN, Helen P. (MD) 623
STERLING, Judith K. . . . (MD) 1189
TATE, Elizabeth L. . . . . (MD) 1225
WAGNER, Susan C. . . . (MD) 1292
ARVIN, Charles S . . . . . (MI) 35
BRENNAN, Jean M. . . . (MI) 132
BUCKLEY, Francis J. . . . (MI) 154
BUGG, Louise M. . . . . . (MI) 155
GAURI, Kul B. . . . . (MI) 423
GOSLING, William A. . . (MI) 453
KOBEL, Rose A. . . . . . . (MI) 666
KOSCHIK, Douglas R. . . (MI) 672
LARONGE, Philip V. . . . (MI) 698
SERPENTO, Mary M. . . (MI) 1116
SMITHSON, Paul G. . . . (MI) 1162
THOMAS, David H. . . . . (MI) 1236
TUCKER, Florence R. . . (MI) 1261
YETMAN, Nancy J. . . . . (MI) 1380
COLLINS, Mary F. . . . . . (MN) 233

TECHNICAL (Cont'd)
Technical services

TECHNICAL (Cont'd)
Technical services

EPSTEIN, Rheda	(MN)	351
HARWOOD, Karen L.	(MN)	510
KING, Jack B.	(MN)	651
AMELUNG, Richard C.	(MO)	19
CHAN, Jeanny T.	(MO)	199
HOHENSTEIN, Margaret L.	(MO)	549
JUNG, Mary K.	(MO)	620
SPALDING, Helen H.	(MO)	1171
TIPSWORD, Thomas N.	(MO)	1246
MOMAN, Orthella P.	(MS)	854
BREEZE, Hope	(NC)	131
CHENG, Chao S.	(NC)	206
COBB, Mary L.	(NC)	225
DRUM, Eunice P.	(NC)	321
HEROLD, Virginia L.	(NC)	532
HUNT, Margaret R.	(NC)	575
LUBANS, John	(NC)	745
MATOCHIK, Michael J.	(NC)	784
NUTTER, Susan K.	(NC)	912
TAYLOR, Christine M.	(NC)	1226
TUTTLE, Marcia L.	(NC)	1266
WALTNER, Nellie L.	(NC)	1301
BIALAC, Verda H.	(NE)	93
GRABE, Lauralee F.	(NE)	455
BENTE, June E.	(NJ)	83
BIELAWSKI, Marvin F.	(NJ)	95
BITTER, Jane L.	(NJ)	100
CAPOOR, Asha	(NJ)	180
CRESCENZI, Jean D.	(NJ)	258
DILLENSCHNEIDER, Patricia A.	(NJ)	303
EBELING, Elinor H.	(NJ)	334
GRAHAM, Peter S.	(NJ)	456
GRIFFIN, Marie E.	(NJ)	468
HALASZ, Etelka B.	(NJ)	484
LEE, Minja P.	(NJ)	711
ROMANKO, Karen A.	(NJ)	1052
STICKEL, William R.	(NJ)	1193
TUTTLE, Helen W.	(NJ)	1265
WHITE, Robert W.	(NJ)	1332
ATKIN, Shifra	(NY)	37
BERRYMAN, Karen L.	(NY)	90
BOREK, Mary A.	(NY)	116
CHICARELLA, Joseph T.	(NY)	207
CINQUE, Deborah G.	(NY)	214
CONNOLLY, Bruce E.	(NY)	237
CORRSIN, Stephen D.	(NY)	247
DOOLING, Marie	(NY)	312
EDENS, John A.	(NY)	336
FASANA, Paul J.	(NY)	366
FRANZ, David A.	(NY)	398
GALASSO, Nancy	(NY)	412
GUZMAN, Diane J.	(NY)	479
HOPKINS, Judith	(NY)	558
HUMPHRY, John A.	(NY)	574
KEATING, Faith	(NY)	633
LOW, Frederick E.	(NY)	743
MARSHAK, Bonnie L.	(NY)	773
MEYERS, Charles	(NY)	830
MOLINE, Gloria	(NY)	853
MORRIS, Leslie R.	(NY)	867
ONSI, Patricia W.	(NY)	924
PARR, Mary Y.	(NY)	944
PINSLEY, Lauren J.	(NY)	975
RANDALL, Lawrence E.	(NY)	1006
RICHARDSON, John A.	(NY)	1029
ROBBINS, Sara E.	(NY)	1039
ROGERS, Irene	(NY)	1049
ROSSOFF, Judith H.	(NY)	1059
RYAN, Constance V.	(NY)	1070
SCHNEIDER, Adele	(NY)	1096
SIMPSON, Charles W.	(NY)	1141
STRAM, Lynn R.	(NY)	1200
TAYLOR, Arlene G.	(NY)	1226
TOYAMA, Ryoko	(NY)	1253
VON WAHLDE, Barbara	(NY)	1288
WAGSCHAL, Sara G.	(NY)	1292
YUKAWA, Masako	(NY)	1384

TECHNICAL (Cont'd)
Technical services

ANDERSON, Carl A.	(OH)	21
BETCHER, William M.	(OH)	92
CROWE, William J.	(OH)	261
DURBIN, Roger	(OH)	328
FROMMEYER, L R.	(OH)	405
GREEN, Gary A.	(OH)	461
HEARD, Jeffrey L.	(OH)	518
HUNT, James R.	(OH)	575
KELTON, Jon D.	(OH)	639
KENT, Joel S.	(OH)	642
KOVACIC, Mark E.	(OH)	673
LUPONE, George	(OH)	749
RYAN, Sharon K.	(OH)	1071
SEELY, Edward	(OH)	1111
TOEDTMAN, Janet J.	(OH)	1248
TUROCI, Esther M.	(OH)	1265
VANBRIMMER, Barbara A.	(OH)	1272
WINANS, Diane D.	(OH)	1354
DAVIS, Joyce N.	(OK)	279
GUTIERREZ, Carolyn A.	(OK)	479
HILL, Helen K.	(OK)	540
MOORE, Maxwell L.	(OK)	860
TOOLEY, Katherine J.	(OK)	1250
BRUSEAU, Laurence L.	(OR)	151
BURKHOLDER, Sue A.	(OR)	161
FISCHER, Karen	(OR)	379
REEVES, Marjorie A.	(OR)	1017
ST. CLAIR, Gloriana S.	(OR)	1075
BILLS, Linda G.	(PA)	96
CADY, Susan A.	(PA)	170
CARTER, Ruth C.	(PA)	190
DALE, Charles F.	(PA)	270
ELSHAMI, Ahmed M.	(PA)	346
HANSON, Eugene R.	(PA)	498
HARRISON, Susan B.	(PA)	507
HINTON, Frances	(PA)	543
KAMPER, Albert F.	(PA)	624
MESSICK, Karen J.	(PA)	828
MUDRICK, Kristine E.	(PA)	875
MYERS, James N.	(PA)	884
RICHARDSON, Joy A.	(PA)	1029
SCHWIND, Penelope	(PA)	1106
SHAPERA, Gladys S.	(PA)	1121
SILVERMAN, Karen S.	(PA)	1138
STRIEDIECK, Suzanne S.	(PA)	1202
WEBSTER, Connie L.	(PA)	1314
MUNOZ-SOLA, Haydee	(PR)	879
CAMP, Mary A.	(SC)	175
ROSS, Gary M.	(SC)	1058
TARLTON, Shirley M.	(SC)	1224
UPHAM, Lois N.	(SC)	1269
COOK, Nancy E.	(SD)	240
CRANMER, Donna C.	(SD)	255
RANEY, Leon	(SD)	1007
BUNTING, Anne C.	(TN)	157
DENTON, Ann L.	(TN)	293
MCHOLLIN, Mattie L.	(TN)	809
AYRES, Edwin M.	(TX)	43
BAXTER, Barbara A.	(TX)	67
ELAM, Craig S.	(TX)	341
HSU, Patrick K.	(TX)	567
HURT, Nancy S.	(TX)	578
INKS, Cordelia R.	(TX)	583
LANDINGHAM, Alpha M.	(TX)	692
MATHIS, Rama F.	(TX)	784
MCKAY, Mary F.	(TX)	810
SNODGRASS, Wilson D.	(TX)	1163
SPARKMAN, Glenda K.	(TX)	1171
HOLLEY, Robert P.	(UT)	551
BLAKE, Mary K.	(VA)	103
BRAUN, Mina H.	(VA)	129
BROOKS, Terri A.	(VA)	141
GWIN, James E.	(VA)	479
HARRIS, Richard J.	(VA)	506
HEYMAN, Berna L.	(VA)	536
LEHMAN, Lois J.	(VA)	713
LINN, Cynthia S.	(VA)	731
MELVIN, Kay H.	(VA)	823

TECHNICAL (Cont'd)

Technical services

	REID, Janine A.	(VA)	1018
	SUMMERS, Kathy B. . . .	(VA)	1209
	WOODY, Janet C.	(VA)	1368
	LINDBERG, Sandra	(VT)	728
	HAGAN, Dalia L.	(WA)	482
	LOKEN, Sarah F.	(WA)	738
	MORGAN, Erma J.	(WA)	864
	STEVENS, Peter H.	(WA)	1190
	CHRISTMAN, Inese R. . .	(WI)	212
	HARFST, Linda L.	(WI)	501
	HOUKOM, Susan L.	(WI)	563
	JAMBREK, William L. . . .	(WI)	592
	MEERDINK, Richard E. . .	(WI)	821
	MERRIAM, Louise A. . . .	(WI)	826
	PATANE, John R.	(WI)	946
	PAUL, Nancy A.	(WI)	949
	PENNINGTON, Jerome G.	(WI)	957
	REEB, Richard C.	(WI)	1014
	YOUNGER, Jennifer A. . .	(WI)	1383
	BEHR, Alice S.	(WV)	75
	DANNUNZIO, Rebecca T.	(WV)	274
	MCKEE, Jean A.	(WV)	810
	HARRINGTON, Carolyn B.	(WY)	504
	BOULTBEE, Paul G. . . .	(AB)	119
	KAVANAGH, Elizabeth G.	(AB)	631
	MACRAE, Lorne G.	(AB)	758
	ROONEY, Sieglinde E. . .	(AB)	1053
	ZIEGLER, Fred	(AB)	1388
	NICHOLLS, Pat	(MB)	901
	GRIMES, Deirdre E. . . .	(ON)	470
	HOOGKAMER, Dawne . .	(ON)	556
	KRYGSMAN, Nancy T. .	(ON)	681
	LATYSZEWSKYJ, Maria A.	(ON)	702
	LUNAU, Carrol D.	(ON)	748
	MURRAY-LACHAPELLE, Rosemary F.	(ON)	882
	RIDLEY, A M.	(ON)	1033
	SAVIC, Edward I.	(ON)	1086
	SCOLLIE, F B.	(ON)	1106
	YKELENSTAM, Priscilla I.	(PE)	1380
	CHASSE, Jules	(PQ)	203
	DARBON, Ginette	(PQ)	274
	BALDWIN, Robert D. . . .	(JAM)	52
	MORAN, Teresita C. . . .	(PHP)	862
Technical services, acquisitions	SMITH, Kathleen S. . . .	(DC)	1156
	DOLAN, Robert T.	(IN)	309
	SANTIAGO, Maria	(PR)	1082
Technical services, acqs & cataloging	MAZZEI, Peter J.	(NJ)	791
Technical services administration	BIERMAN, Kenneth J. . .	(AZ)	95
	HENSLEY, Charlotta C. .	(CO)	529
	MANNING, Leslie A. . . .	(CO)	766
	DAVIS, Betty B.	(IN)	277
	MUELLER, Jeanne G. . . .	(IN)	875
	WAGAR, Joanna M.	(MI)	1291
	MARION, Phyllis C.	(MN)	770
	RACINE, John D.	(MO)	1001
	BREEDLOVE, Elizabeth A.	(NJ)	131
	HARRINGTON, Sue A. . .	(OK)	504
	BOYLAN, Lorena A.	(PA)	123
	RICHARDS, Barbara G. .	(PA)	1028
	ROHDY, Margaret A. . . .	(PA)	1050
	BENGTSON, Betty G. . .	(TN)	80
	LYNCH, Frances H.	(TN)	751
	BATEMAN, Robert A. . . .	(AB)	63
Technical services & automation	SEBRIGHT, Terence F. . .	(FL)	1110
Technical services & cataloging	SPURRIER, Suzanne F. .	(AR)	1177
	MENDENHALL, Bethany R.	(CA)	824
	ELLIOTT, Barbara J.	(IN)	343
	THOMAS, Victoria K. . . .	(IN)	1238
	ECKERSON, Gale E. . . .	(MA)	334
	JACKSON, Nancy G. . . .	(VA)	588
Technical services & collection devlpmnt	FEINER, Arlene M.	(IL)	369
Technical services & management	FENSTERMANN, Duane W.	(IA)	371
Technical services & microcomputers	NIEMEYER, Karen K. . . .	(IN)	903

TECHNICAL (Cont'd)

Technical services & systems	BONK, Sharon C.	(NY)	114
	LINCOLN, Robert S. . . .	(MB)	728
Technical services automated systems	BAIRD, Lynn N.	(ID)	47
Technical services automation	KELSEY, Mary J.	(CT)	639
	STARCK, William L. . . .	(DC)	1181
	FROSCHER, Jean L. . . .	(FL)	406
	STRYCK, B C.	(IL)	1203
	INTNER, Sheila S.	(MA)	583
	DRUM, Eunice P.	(NC)	321
	JUDKINS, Timothy C. . . .	(OK)	619
	GRADY, Agnes M.	(TN)	455
	AIROLDI, Melissa	(TX)	9
	FESSLER, Vera F.	(VA)	374
	DJEVALIKIAN, Sonia . . .	(PQ)	306
Technical services cataloging	HUSKEY, Janet S.	(FL)	578
	LORNE, Lorraine K.	(MI)	741
	SUMMERS, Sheryl H. . . .	(MI)	1209
	HAMDY, Mohamed N. . .	(KWT)	491
Technical services, circulation	CLAER, Joycelyn H. . . .	(TX)	215
Technical services computer applications	FRANCQ, Carole	(IN)	396
Technical services coordination	ALLEN, Joan W.	(TX)	15
	MATHIS, Margaret H. . . .	(TX)	784
Technical services, indexing	HALES, David A.	(AK)	486
Technical services, law	LINNANE, Mary L.	(IL)	731
Technical services, library automation	BIGLIN, Karen E.	(AZ)	96
Technical services management	LESH, Nancy L.	(AK)	718
	BISHOFF, Lizbeth J.	(CA)	99
	JOHNSON, Thomas L. . .	(CA)	609
	MILLER, Dick R.	(CA)	837
	LEONARD, Lawrence E. .	(DC)	716
	HELGE, Brian L.	(IL)	524
	PETERSEN, Karla D. . . .	(IL)	962
	FRANZEK, Karyn	(MA)	398
	HEWITT, Joe A.	(NC)	535
	MYERS, Carol B.	(NC)	884
	SAUNDERS, Laverna M.	(NV)	1084
	DUNCAN, Elizabeth C. . .	(NY)	325
	JUNION, Gail J.	(NY)	620
	TRAMDACK, Philip J. . . .	(OH)	1254
	CORBIN, John	(TX)	245
	PAYNE, Leila M.	(TX)	951
	NICHOLSON, Dianne L. .	(BC)	902
Technical services operation	STEWART, William L. . .	(WY)	1193
Technical services operations	FRANZEK, Karyn	(MA)	398
Technical services organization	WAITE, Ellen J.	(IL)	1293
	HERVEY, Norma J.	(MN)	533
Technical services organization & admin	JOB, Rose A.	(MO)	601
Technical services planning	WALBRIDGE, Sharon L. .	(OH)	1293
Technical services supervision	PARRY, David R.	(CO)	944
	WERT, Alice L.	(IN)	1325
	BRENNAN, Christopher P.	(NY)	132
Technical services training development	WANG, Anna M.	(OH)	1302
Technical services workflow planning	LINSE, Mary M.	(MO)	731
Technical standards	PIETY, Jean Z.	(OH)	972
	MARSHALL, Alexandra P.	(ON)	773
Technical support	HENKEL, Grace E.	(NJ)	528
Technical support for archives	MURDOCH, Arthur W. . .	(ON)	879
Technical trades, naval ship repair	ANDERSON, Marcia M. .	(VA)	24
Technical writer	HINTON, N E.	(KS)	543
Technical writing	BLITZ, Ruth R.	(CA)	105
	MARCHIANO, Marilyn C.	(CA)	768
	WRIGHT, Betty A.	(CA)	1370
	RIDER, Philip R.	(IL)	1032
	SILVESTER, June P. . . .	(MD)	1139
	SLOAN, Cheryl A.	(MD)	1149
	GASTON, Judith A.	(MN)	421
	SPYROS, Marsha L. . . .	(NY)	1177
	SWEENEY, Del	(PA)	1215
	HARDIN, Nancy E.	(TN)	500
	SACKETT-WILK, Susan A.	(TX)	1073
	SANDERS, William D. . .	(UT)	1080
	SCHAEFER, Mary E. . . .	(VA)	1089
	FOSKETT, Antony C. . . .	(AUS)	392

TECHNICAL (Cont'd)

Technical writing & editing	GIRILL, T R.	(CA)	438
	JACOBS, Horace	(CA)	589
	WEIL, Ben H.	(NJ)	1317
Technical writing, editing	URKEN, Madeline	(NJ)	1270
Technical writing, software documtn	GREENE, Nancy S.	(PA)	464
Textbook & technical book databases	JACKRELL, Thomas L.	(NJ)	586
Thesaurus construction, technical	GENUARDI, Michael T.	(MD)	427
Training technical services personnel	GOODWIN, Vania M.	(IN)	450
Vocational & technical libraries	SLICK, Myrna H.	(PA)	1149

TECHNICIAN

Education & training library technicians	ANASTASIOU, Joan D.	(BC)	21
Librarian & technician supervision	DEYOUNG, Gail O.	(MI)	298
Library technician education	WILSON, Lucy	(OH)	1351
Library technician program coordination	MCDONALD, Marilyn M.	(CA)	803
Library technician training	SELING, Kathy A.	(WA)	1113
	DAVIDSON-ARNOTT, Frances E.	(ON)	277
Teaching library technicians	TILLOTSON, Joy G.	(NF)	1245
Technician training	GAMSON, Arthur L.	(DC)	416

TECHNIQUES

Administration management techniques	BENOIT, Anthony H.	(LA)	82
Archival preservation techniques	TAMMARO, James M.	(NY)	1221
Archival techniques	SPEISMAN, Stephen A.	(ON)	1172
Automated collection devlpmnt techniques	LAREW, Christian K.	(NJ)	697
Automated techniques	FISHBEIN, Meyer H.	(MD)	380
Book illustration techniques	DONAHUE, Katharine E.	(CA)	310
Budgeting & cost recovery techniques	FOX, Marylou P.	(CA)	395
Conservation & preservation techniques	HOLT, David A.	(KY)	554
Innovative patron involvement techniques	SWANTON, Susan I.	(NY)	1214
Legislative record technique	MERINGOLO, Joseph A.	(MD)	826
Management techniques	SCHUBERT, Donald F.	(NM)	1101
Online searching techniques	SANDERS, Kathryn A.	(AR)	1080
Oral history interviewing techniques	STEPHENSON, Shirley E.	(CA)	1189
Passive solar cooling techniques	LAKE, Mary S.	(AZ)	689
Preservation techniques	HEIZER, Carolyn H.	(TX)	523
Questioning techniques, lit discussions	SENATOR, Rochelle B.	(CT)	1115
Research techniques	FOLCARELLI, Ralph J.	(NY)	387
Stanislavski's ultimate technique	MOORE, Sonia	(NY)	861
Storytelling & programming techniques	PELLOWSKI, Anne	(NY)	955
Training of online search techniques	KAMINECKI, Ronald M.	(IL)	624

TECHNOECONOMICS

Business, marketing & technoeconomics	GUIDA, Pat	(NJ)	476

TECHNOLOGY (See also Biotechnology, Science, Technical, Technoeconomics)

Academic science & technology reference	COHEN, Jackson B.	(NY)	228
Advanced info telecommunication tech	GOODMAN, Henry J.	(AB)	449
Application of info technology in libs	AMAN, Mohammed M.	(WI)	19
Application of videotext technology	BROWNRIDGE, James R.	(ON)	149
Applications of information technology	CHARTRAND, Robert L.	(DC)	203
Appropriate technology	FREEDMAN, Phyllis D.	(PA)	400
Audiovisual technology, computer appls	NOLAN, Joan	(PA)	907
Automation & new technologies	ROSSMAN, Muriel J.	(MN)	1059
Automation & new technology	ACCARDI, Joseph J.	(WI)	3
Baking science & technology	HORTIN, Judith K.	(KS)	561
Business & technology	BOSMA, Elske M.	(ON)	117
Business & technology research	SOVNER-RIBBLER, Judith	(MA)	1170
	MENNELLA, Dona M.	(MD)	824
Business science & technology database	DIMITRESCU, Ioana	(PQ)	304

TECHNOLOGY (Cont'd)

Business, science, & technology ref	REGNER, Erlinda J.	(IL)	1017
	RICHMOND, Diane A.	(IL)	1030
CD-ROM & new technology	CEBULA, Theodore R.	(WI)	196
CD-ROM technology	WILSON, Wayne V.	(CA)	1353
	WATSON, Paula D.	(IL)	1310
	CROSS, Jennie B.	(MI)	260
	HURLEY, Geraldine C.	(OH)	577
CD-ROM technology management	PHILLIPS, J R.	(OK)	968
Ceramic technology reference	CULLEY, Paul T.	(NY)	263
Chemistry & technology	GUIDA, Pat	(NJ)	476
Collection development, science & tech	GREENE, Cathy C.	(MA)	463
Communication technology in libraries	SHANK, Russell	(CA)	1120
Communications technology	THOMA, George R.	(MD)	1235
Computer & software technology	AMMERMAN, Jackie W.	(GA)	20
Computer & telecommunications technology	BAILEY, Charles W.	(NC)	46
Computer high tech databases	CHICHESTER, Gerald C.	(CT)	208
Computer science, high tech industry	SLOAN, Maureen G.	(OR)	1149
Computer technology	JARAMILLO, George R.	(CO)	594
	SHAPIRO, Barbara G.	(NY)	1121
	TEPE, Ann S.	(OH)	1231
	DRIEHAUS, Rosemary H.	(PA)	320
Computer technology directory	LEE, Douglas E.	(NY)	709
Computer technology for high sch libs	TOLMAN, Bonnie B.	(MI)	1249
Coordinator, library technology program	DAANE, Jeanette K.	(AZ)	269
Database technology	DEBUSE, Raymond	(WA)	285
Education technology	HINDS, Vira C.	(NY)	542
Educational media & technology	GASTON, Judith A.	(MN)	421
	BENDER, Evelyn	(PA)	79
Educational technology	BERG, Charlene J.	(CA)	84
	LUDWIG, Deborah M.	(CO)	746
	PORTER, Kathryn W.	(CT)	985
	WHITE, Charles R.	(CT)	1330
	BADER, Shelley	(DC)	44
	KLASING, Jane P.	(FL)	657
	STABLER, William H.	(FL)	1177
	WILLARD, Gayle K.	(KS)	1341
	ALLAN, David W.	(MN)	14
	WALKER, Judith A.	(NC)	1295
	SJURSON, Gail M.	(NE)	1145
	ELY, Donald P.	(NY)	347
	WAGNER, A C.	(NY)	1291
	DEMARS, Patricia	(VA)	291
	BOLDUC, Yves	(PQ)	112
Educational technology & media	KRANCH, Douglas A.	(IA)	676
Educational technology application	STARKEY, Richard E.	(MA)	1182
Educational technology, audiovisual	SPENCER, Albert F.	(GA)	1173
Electronic technology	ZUCK, Gregory J.	(KS)	1391
Emerging communication media technology	HOPE, Thomas W.	(NY)	557
Energy technology	MARCIL, Louise	(PQ)	769
Engineering technologies	HARE, William J.	(NH)	501
Fire sciences & technology	GOLD, Sandra	(ON)	444
Food processing technology databases	MCNAUGHT, Hugh W.	(ON)	816
Food science & technology	WHITEMARSH, Thomas R.	(WI)	1333
Food science, chemistry & technology	RILEY, Sarah A.	(MD)	1035
Food science, technology	MARTIN, Irmgarde D.	(TX)	776
Food technology	WRIGHT, Nancy M.	(PA)	1372
Food technology online searching	LAMANNA, Joan M.	(CA)	689
High technology	VUGRINECZ, Anna E.	(CA)	1289
	PEERS, Charles T.	(MA)	954
	CAMBRIA, Roberto	(NY)	174
High technology consulting	JAGIELLOWICZ, Jadzia	(ON)	591
High technology custom research services	JAGIELLOWICZ, Jadzia	(ON)	591
High tech databases	PRONIN, Monica	(NY)	995
	JAGIELLOWICZ, Jadzia	(ON)	591
High technology industries	LEWIS, Gretchen S.	(CA)	723
High technology information	ROARK, Robin D.	(DC)	1038
High technology reference	CARSCH, Ruth E.	(CA)	187
High tech research & devlpmnt consulting	HERTHER, Nancy K.	(MN)	533
History of science & technology	ANDERSON, Marjorie E.	(ME)	24
	STAPLETON, Darwin H.	(NY)	1181
History of technology	HARDING, Robert S.	(DC)	500

TECHNOLOGY (Cont'd)

Specialty	Name	State	No.
Imaging technology	HILL, Kristin E.	(CA)	540
Impact of information technologies	DIENER, Richard A.	(MD)	302
Impact of info technologies on society	FISHER, H L.	(CA)	381
Impacts of technology	SURPRENANT, Thomas T.	(NY)	1210
Impacts of technology on society	MARCHAND, Donald A.	(NY)	768
Info industry & technology tracking	SIECK, Steven K.	(NY)	1135
Information processing technology	SAFFADY, William	(NY)	1074
Information retrieval technologies	HOLMES, Lyndon S.	(MA)	553
Information science & computer tech	NEWMAN, Wilda B.	(MD)	900
Information science & technology	HARMON, Glynn	(TX)	502
Information science, technology systems	JOHNSON, David K.	(NJ)	603
Information systems & technologies	FRIERSON, Eleanor G.	(DC)	404
Information technologies	MASON, Marilyn G.	(OH)	781
	WERSIG, Gernot	(WGR)	325
Information technologies & services	CARTER, Daniel H.	(TX)	189
Information technologies education	BOONE, Morell D.	(MI)	115
Information technology	BUTLER, Matilda L.	(CA)	167
	CASE, Donald O.	(CA)	191
	HELFER, Doris S.	(CA)	523
	PAISLEY, William J.	(CA)	935
	WALTER, Virginia A.	(CA)	1300
	DREWES, Arlene T.	(DC)	319
	PRICE, Joseph W.	(DC)	992
	DRAKE, Miriam A.	(GA)	318
	DOWELL, David R.	(IL)	315
	PARK, Chung I.	(IL)	940
	WATERS, Samuel T.	(MD)	1309
	D'ALLEYRAND, Marc R.	(NY)	270
	SWEENEY, Richard T.	(NY)	1215
	PRICKETT, Dan S.	(OH)	993
	ERES, Beth K.	(ISR)	352
	MINAIKIT, Nonglak	(THA)	845
Information technology & management	FIDOTEN, Robert E.	(PA)	375
Information technology applications	BISHOP, Sarah G.	(DC)	99
	MILEVSKI, Sandra N.	(DC)	835
Information technology assessment	DUCHESNE, Roderick M.	(ON)	322
Information technology economics	MCSPADDEN, Robert M.	(OH)	818
Information technology management	MCKIRDY, Pamela R.	(MA)	812
	BECKMAN, Margaret L.	(ON)	73
Information technology planning	BURNS, Christopher	(MA)	162
	TAUBER, Stephen J.	(MA)	1225
Instruction using media & technology	TREGLOAN, Donald C.	(MI)	1255
Instructional media & technology	GOFF, Linda J.	(CA)	443
	LEAHY, Michael D.	(CT)	707
	VAN MELER, Vandelia L.	(MS)	1276
Instructional systems technology	BERMAN, Arthur	(AR)	88
Instructional technology	ROYAL, Selvin W.	(AR)	1063
	ALBUM, Bernie	(CA)	11
	KELLY, Myla S.	(CA)	638
	HALE, Robert G.	(CT)	485
	RECTOR, Wendell H.	(CT)	1013
	TEMPLE, Leroy E.	(CT)	1230
	FORK, Donald J.	(DC)	390
	CAMPA, Josephine	(MD)	175
	CHANDLER, Devon	(MT)	199
	MARTIN, Richard T.	(NC)	778
	SURPRENANT, Thomas T.	(NY)	1210
	BROWN, Dale W.	(VA)	143
Instructional technology specialist	MCGHEE, Patricia L.	(WI)	806
Integration of media & technology	TREGLOAN, Donald C.	(MI)	1255
Interdisciplinary technology	ADAMS, Judith A.	(AL)	5
Japanese science & tech information	SHERMAN, Roger S.	(CA)	1128
	QUINN, Ralph M.	(NJ)	1000
Japanese science technology information	TALBOT, Dawn E.	(CA)	1220
Keywording cement & concrete technology	SPIGELMAN, Cynthia A.	(IL)	1174
Laser optical technology	KERR, Robert C.	(CO)	644
Leveraging information technologies	MCLANE, John F.	(CT)	813
Library & information systems & tech	GRIFFITHS, Jose M.	(MD)	469
Library & info technology standards	MANNING, Ralph W.	(ON)	767
Library automation & technology	MCQUEEN, Judith D.	(MD)	817
	WAGNER, Rod G.	(NE)	1292
Library technology	HEATH, Henry H.	(MD)	519
	PRIESING, Patricia L.	(NJ)	993
	DE GENNARO, Richard	(NY)	287
	MILLER, Ellen L.	(NY)	837

TECHNOLOGY (Cont'd)

Specialty	Name	State	No.
Library technology	PAGELL, Ruth A.	(PA)	934
	DIONNE, Charlotte A.	(NB)	305
Library technology & systems	BLACK, John B.	(ON)	101
Library technology, systems	MANN, Thomas	(CA)	766
Literature of science & technology	PINELLI, Thomas E.	(VA)	974
Management & budgeting info technologies	LOWRY, Charles B.	(TX)	745
Managing library automation & technology	LEACH, Ronald G.	(IN)	706
Manufacturing technology acquisition	STEVENS, Michael	(IL)	1190
Maritime law & technology	COMEAU, Amy R.	(NY)	234
Meat science & technology	WHITEMARSH, Thomas R.	(WI)	1333
Media & technology in libraries	CHISHOLM, Margaret	(WA)	209
Media & technology services	BRUMBACK, Elsie	(NC)	150
Media technologies	AJIBERO, Matthew I.	(NGR)	9
Medical technology	COLEMAN, David E.	(HI)	231
Microcomputer software, new technologies	VEANER, Allen B.	(ON)	1280
Microcomputer technology	RUBIN, Myra P.	(NY)	1064
	PICHETTE, William H.	(TX)	970
Microcomputers & new technology	ORR, Cynthia	(OH)	926
Microcomputing technologies	TOOEY, Mary J.	(MD)	1250
Microelectronics technologies databases	WOLF, Noel C.	(AZ)	1360
Microfilm technologies	HOWINGTON, Tad C.	(TX)	566
Microforms technology	WIHBEY, Francis R.	(ME)	1337
New information technology	CHEN, Ching C.	(MA)	205
New library technology	ALIX, Cleta M.	(CA)	13
New technologies	WILTSE, Helen C.	(GA)	1353
	GORDON, Helen A.	(IN)	451
New technologies in libraries	VOROS, David S.	(PA)	1289
New technologies research	SHAW, Renata V.	(DC)	1123
New technology	RISHER, Carol A.	(DC)	1036
New technology & libraries	MARSHALL, Mary E.	(OH)	774
19th century technology	PRESGRAVES, Jim	(VA)	991
Non-impact printing technology	HILL, Kristin E.	(CA)	540
Nuclear technology	ROBINSON, Doris T.	(CA)	1044
Office & information technology	VASILAKIS, Mary	(PA)	1279
Online literature, sci & tech searching	WALLACE, Wendy L.	(NJ)	1298
Online searching science, tech databases	RAEDER, Aggi W.	(CA)	1003
Online technology & searching	KREMER, Jill L.	(PA)	677
Optical disk technology	BOSS, Richard W.	(DC)	117
	PRICE, Joseph W.	(DC)	992
	REGAZZI, John J.	(NY)	1017
	ARJONA, Sandra K.	(PA)	31
	ALI, Syed N.	(BRN)	13
Optical storage media technology	GALL, Bert A.	(TN)	413
Optical storage technologies	HELGERSON, Linda W.	(VA)	524
Optical storage technology	LIGHTBOWN, Parke P.	(CA)	726
Optical technologies	MCCONNELL, Karen S.	(TX)	797
Planning & application of technology	DIDIER, Elaine K.	(MI)	301
Polymer science & technology	HILL, Elizabeth C.	(KY)	539
Prepress scanning technology	HILL, Kristin E.	(CA)	540
Preservation technology	WELSH, William J.	(DC)	1323
Public library technology	GRALAPP, Marcelee G.	(CO)	457
Public science & technology reference	COHEN, Jackson B.	(NY)	228
Publish high tech reference books	CONNORS, Martin G.	(MI)	238
Publishing technology applications info	KLEIMAN, Gerald S.	(DC)	659
Pulp & paper science, technology	HALL, Deanna M.	(GA)	487
Reference in fermentation technology	BOND, Mary J.	(CO)	113
Reference, science & technology	HUYGEN, Michaele L.	(MT)	580
Reference, technology	MARCOTTE, Marcel	(PQ)	769
Researching piano history & technology	RICHARDS, James H.	(TX)	1028
Retail financial technologies	RATH, Charla M.	(DC)	1009
Scholarly communication for info tech	DOUGHERTY, Richard M.	(MI)	314
Science & technological databases	TALBOT, Dawn E.	(CA)	1220
Science & technology	BARRETT, Carol A.	(TX)	59
	DAVIS, Frances F.	(AL)	279
	CONNOR, Billie M.	(CA)	237
	DIBLE, Joan B.	(CA)	299
	FELDMAN, Irwin	(CA)	369
	MCGARRY, Dorothy	(CA)	805
	REILLY, James H.	(CA)	1020

TECHNOLOGY (Cont'd)

Science & technology

SCLAR, Marta L. . . . . . . (CA) 1106
SIMS, Sidney B. . . . . (CA) 1142
CARTER, Ida . . . . (IL) 189
DAVIS, Jeannette . . . . . . (MA) 279
GIFFIN, Wendy L. . . . . . (MA) 433
ARMSTRONG, Carole S. . (MI) 32
HERBERT, Helen E. . . . . (MI) 530
MENDELSOHN, Loren D. . (MI) 823
MONTGOMERY, Mary E. . (MI) 856
CAREN, Loretta . . . . (NY) 181
COTY, Patricia A. . . . . . (NY) 250
KAPLAN, Isabel C. . . . . . (NY) 626
MASCIA, Regina B. . . . . (NY) 780
HSU, Helena S. . . . . (OH) 567
BROSKY, Catherine M. . (PA) 141
CRONEIS, Karen S. . . . . (TX) 260
DEPETRO, Thomas G. . . . (TX) 293
OGDEN, William S. . . . . (TX) 918
WILSON, John W. . . . . . (TX) 1351
KRIZ, Harry M. . . . . (VA) 679
GREEN, Carol C. . . . . . . (WA) 461
JONES, David L. . . . . . . (AB) 612
WAUGH, Alan L. . . . . . . (AB) 1310
KENDALL, Sandra A. . . . (ON) 640

Science & technology bibliography   BAILEY, Martha J. . . . . . (IN) 46
GLUCK, Myke H. . . . . . . (NC) 442
COHEN, Jackson B. . . . . (NY) 228

Science & technology biogph
instruction   SABIN, Robert G. . . . . . . (AL) 1072

Science & technology cataloging   WALLACE, Wendy L. . . . (NJ) 1298
LANDIS, Kay A. . . . . (OH) 693

Science & technology collection
devlpmnt   SABIN, Robert G. . . . . . . (AL) 1072
ANDREWS, Karen L. . . . (CA) 26
ROHMANN, Gloria P. . . . (NY) 1050

Science & technology computer
searching   CHADWICK, Alena F. . . (MA) 196

Science & technology database
searching   SENKUS, Linda J. . . . . . (CT) 1115
SMISEK, Thomas P. . . . . (MN) 1152
HASELBAUER, Kathleen
J. . . . . (WA) 510
SCHARMER, Roger C. . . (WI) 1090

Science & technology databases   BROWN, Diane M. . . . . . (CA) 143
ECKLUND, Lynn M. . . . . (CA) 335
GRENIER, Myra T. . . . . . (CA) 467
LOVE, Sandra R. . . . . . . (CA) 743
MAH, Jeffery . . . . (CA) 760
SMITH, Sallye W. . . . . . (CO) 1160
LONG, Caroline C. . . . . . (DC) 739
KENNEDY, Joanna C. . . (GA) 641
MARECEK, Robert J. . . . (IL) 770
VAUGHAN, Ruth M. . . . . (IL) 1280
ERDMANN, Charlotte A. . (IN) 352
COLBY, Beverly . . . . (MA) 230
SEELEY, Catherine R. . . (ME) 1111
HEILEMAN, Gene C. . . . (MI) 521
DUELTGEN, Ronald R. . . (MN) 323
KAN, Halina S. . . . . (NJ) 624
MCLAUGHLIN, Dorothy M. (NJ) 813
MAUTER, George A. . . . (NY) 787
MONTALBANO, James J. (NY) 855
QUINN, Caroline E. . . . . (OH) 1000
HILKER, Emerson W. . . . (OK) 539
DALLAS, Larayne J. . . . . (TX) 270
WONG, Lusi . . . . (ON) 1363

Science & technology defense   JOHNSON, Mary E. . . . . (CA) 607
Science & technology development   CHESLOCK, Rosalind P. (MD) 207
Science & technology information   CULLEY, Paul T. . . . . . . (NY) 263
SALT, David P. . . . . (SK) 1077
ALI, Syed N. . . . . (BRN) 13
Science & technology librarianship   SMITH, Eric J. . . . . (NC) 1155
Science & technology libraries   MARKWORTH, Lawrence
L. . . . . (CA) 772
NEUFELD, Irving H. . . . . (CT) 897
VANCURA, Joyce B. . . . (IL) 1273
STEINKE, Cynthia A. . . . (MN) 1186
PETERSON, Paul A. . . . . (MO) 964

TECHNOLOGY (Cont'd)

Science & technology libraries   MOUNT, Ellis . . . . (NY) 873
Science & technology library
consulting   PHINNEY, Hartley K. . . . (CO) 969
Science & technology literature   HEINRITZ, Fred J. . . . . . (CT) 522
HOWARD, Helen A. . . . . (PQ) 564
Science & technology online
searching   POLLIS, Angela R. . . . . . (PA) 981
Science & technology reference   SABIN, Robert G. . . . . . . (AL) 1072
BRONARS, Lori A. . . . . . (CA) 140
LEE, Lydia H. . . . . (CA) 710
ZEIDLER, Patricia L. . . . (CA) 1387
MARCUS, Stephanie M. . (DC) 769
CHADWICK, Alena F. . . (MA) 196
HANSEN, Joanne J. . . . . (MI) 497
ADAMS, Dena R. . . . . . . (NM) 4
SHIPPEY, Susan S. . . . . (NY) 1131
DUVALLY, Charlotte F. . . (PA) 330
CRAVEN, Trudy W. . . . . (SC) 256
BICHTELER, Julie H. . . . (TX) 94
WHEELER, Marjorie W. . (TX) 1329
HASELBAUER, Kathleen
J. . . . . (WA) 510
Science & technology reference &
resrch   LUXNER, Dick . . . . (NJ) 750
Science & technology reference
service   TIRRELL, Brenda P. . . . . (TX) 1247
Science & technology reference work   NITZBERG, Dale B. . . . . (MD) 905
Science & technology research   MUSKUS, Elizabeth A. . . (NY) 883
Science & tech resrch & devlpmnt
support   LOGAN, Nancy L. . . . . . (ON) 737
Science & technology services   PHILLIPS, Linda L. . . . . . (TN) 968
Science & technology specialist   HOLLMANN, Pauline V. . (FL) 552
Science, engineering, & technology   GNAT, Jean M. . . . . (IN) 442
Science, technology & business
databases   TOSTEVIN, Patricia A. . . (WA) 1252
Science, technology engineering
database   TODOSOW, Helen K. . . . (NY) 1248
Science, technology, medicine   WOLF, Richard E. . . . . . (VA) 1360
Scientific, technology databases   MACKSEY, Susan A. . . . (NY) 757
Software & new technology   DECKER, Leola M. . . . . . (MD) 286
Sound recording history & technology   KLINGER, William E. . . . (OH) 661
Sources & services in sci &
technology   COOPER, Marianne . . . . (NY) 243
Soviet science & technology   MARCUS, Stephanie M. . (DC) 769
Steam history & technology   ARNOLD, Nancy K. . . . . (PA) 34
Strategic use of information
technology   MARCHAND, Donald A. . (NY) 768
Systems & technology   NEWMAN, George C. . . . (NY) 899
Systems technology for society   CHARTRAND, Robert L. (DC) 203
Teacher, inservice in technology   HOFSTAD, Alice M. . . . . (MN) 548
Technical & tech commercial
research   CRABTREE, Sandra A. . (CA) 254
Technological literature   TANEN, Lee J. . . . . (NJ) 1222
Technological university library admin   SNYDER, Richard L. . . . (PA) 1165
Technology   HALPIN, Jerome H. . . . . (CA) 490
MCGOWAN, John P. . . . (IL) 807
SILVERBERG, Mary E. . . (MA) 1138
STANTON, Martha . . . . . (MA) 1181
KOTZIN, Sheldon . . . . . . (MD) 673
MCKEE, Eugenia V. . . . . (MO) 810
BAIN, Christine A. . . . . . (NY) 47
VEITH, Charles R. . . . . . (OK) 1281
EVERHART, Nancy L. . . (PA) 358
SAURIOL, Guy L. . . . . . . (ON) 1085
Technology & end-users   RUSSELL, Keith W. . . . . (MD) 1069
Technology & information transfer   HATTERY, Lowell H. . . . (MD) 512
Technology & systems   RIGGS, Donald E. . . . . . (AZ) 1034
Technology assessment   LAWRENCE, Gary S. . . . (CA) 704
MOYER, Barbara A. . . . . (CA) 874
RATH, Charla M. . . . . . . (DC) 1009
HODGE, Gail M. . . . . . . (PA) 546
Technology collection development   SMITH, Charles R. . . . . . (TX) 1153
Technology databases   CURRY, John A. . . . . . . (IL) 266
HECHT, Joseph A. . . . . . (OH) 519
Technology for libraries   DOWLIN, Kenneth E. . . . (CO) 316
Technology gatekeeper   BLISS, David H. . . . . (IA) 105
Technology implementation   BJORNER, Susan N. . . . (MA) 100
Technology information   WALKER, Patricia A. . . . (MO) 1296

TECHNOLOGY (Cont'd)

Technology integration with curriculum	TROUTNER, Joanne J.	(IN)	1258
Technology library development	HARMON, Jacqueline B.	(TX)	502
Tech online searching	PEDERSEN, Dennis C.	(MN)	954
Technology planning	CAMPBELL, Bonnie	(ON)	176
Technology systems	BECKER, Roger V.	(WA)	72
Technology transfer	WILDE, Daniel U.	(CT)	1338
	SWEENEY, Del	(PA)	1215
	LEHMANN, Edward J.	(VA)	713
Technology-computers & video	HOFSTAD, Alice M.	(MN)	548
Telecommunications technology	MARGOLIS, Suzanne M.	(MI)	770
Television, computers, & other tech	EGAN, Mary J.	(NY)	338
Training staff in technology	SCHREFFLER, Lynne W.	(PA)	1099
Training technology research	SNYDER, Cathrine E.	(TN)	1164
Video technology	REIDER, William L.	(MD)	1019
Writer, designer, technology	SEITZ, Robert J.	(NY)	1113

TEENAGERS (See also Adolescent, Young Adult, Youth)

Evaluating teenage books	ESTES, Sally C.	(IL)	355
Sex, drugs, & teenagers	LONG, Gary	(LA)	739
Teenage literature	STEINBERG, Eileen	(PA)	1185
Teenagers	WALKER, Elinor	(MN)	1295
Young teens book selection	RAPPELT, John F.	(NY)	1008

TELECOMMUNICATION (See also Communication)

Advanced info telecommunication tech	GOODMAN, Henry J.	(AB)	449
Computer & telecommunications technology	BAILEY, Charles W.	(NC)	46
Federal computer & telecom procurement	DODSON, Whit	(VA)	308
International telecommunication	LIU, Rosa	(DC)	734
International telecommunications	CANNATA, Arleen	(NY)	178
Library automation & telecommunications	BALCOM, Karen S.	(TX)	51
Library telecommunications	BRUMAN, Janet L.	(CA)	150
	CISLER, Stephen A.	(CA)	215
Library telecommunications consulting	BOWDEN, Philip L.	(IL)	120
Microcomputers & telecommunications	LEWONTIN, Amy	(MA)	724
Radio & telecommunications	MERRYWEATHER, J M.	(ON)	827
Social impacts of telecommunications	RICE, Ronald E.	(CA)	1027
Telecom database	HAMPTON, Sylvia S.	(RI)	494
Telecom regulatory information	MASON-WARD, Lesley	(ON)	781
Telecommunication monitor & test systems	NELSON, David W.	(NH)	893
Telecommunication networking	MAZUR, Ronald M.	(MA)	791
Telecommunication research	FOSKO, Maureen E.	(NJ)	392
Telecommunication services	GAUJARD, Pierre G.	(MD)	422
Telecommunication training & development	IFFLAND, Carol D.	(IL)	581
Telecommunications	MILLS, Peggy	(AR)	844
	BROWNRIGG, Edwin B.	(CA)	149
	CLARKE, Tobin D.	(CA)	219
	DEENEY, Kay E.	(CA)	286
	FALSONE, Anne M.	(CO)	363
	KENNEY, Brigitte L.	(CO)	641
	NICKEL, Edgar B.	(CO)	902
	BUCK, Dayna E.	(DC)	153
	KEMPER, Marlyn J.	(FL)	639
	AAGAARD, James S.	(IL)	1
	CARLSON, Robert P.	(IL)	182
	KAPLAN, Rosalyn L.	(IL)	626
	ROMANO, Katherine V.	(IL)	1052
	COLE, David H.	(MN)	230
	SANDNESS, John G.	(MN)	1081
	WILSON, Mary S.	(MS)	1352
	OWEN, Willy	(NC)	932
	CARNES, Mary J.	(NE)	183
	MARSH, Paul W.	(NE)	773
	BOND, George	(NH)	113
	BEDDES, Marianne T.	(NJ)	73
	PRAQ, Lora B.	(NJ)	989
	SUNDAY, Donald E.	(NJ)	1210
	THOM, Janice E.	(NY)	1235
	HERB, Elizabeth D.	(OH)	530
	TAYLOR, Rosemarie K.	(PA)	1228

TELECOMMUNICATION (Cont'd)

Telecommunications	ARMES, Patti	(TX)	32
	RYDESKY, Mary M.	(TX)	1071
	SAMSON, Robert C.	(TX)	1079
	KAISER, Donald W.	(VA)	622
	DU BREUIL, Laval	(PQ)	322
Telecommunications access	WRIGHT, Bernell	(NY)	1370
Telecommunications & data communications	CASTO, Lisa A.	(TX)	194
Telecommunications & film reference	GRILIKHES, Sandra B.	(PA)	470
Telecommunications & information policy	RIPLEY, Joseph M.	(KY)	1035
Telecommunications & info transfer	RESNIK, Linda I.	(DC)	1024
Telecommunications & media	WEINGAND, Darlene E.	(WI)	1318
Telecommunications & networks	REMKIEWICZ, Frank L.	(CA)	1022
Telecommunications, computers	KISHEL, Deane A.	(MN)	656
Telecommunications database	TERRELL, Jane A.	(VA)	1232
Telecommunications databases	MASTERS, Kathy B.	(CT)	782
	BATES, Mary E.	(DC)	64
Telecommunications, distance learning	SCHABERT, Daniel R.	(NY)	1088
Telecommunications information	COOPER, Linda	(PA)	243
Telecommunications, microcomputers	OHLMAN, Herbert	(SWZ)	919
Telecommunications networking	WARREN, G G.	(KS)	1306
	DEFALCO, Joseph	(NY)	287
Telecommunications newsletter editing	IMPERIALE, Karen P.	(NJ)	582
Telecommunications reference	MCGARVEY, Eileen B.	(NY)	805
Telecommunications regulation	GOLDSMITH, Carol C.	(NJ)	446
Telecommunications research	KIRSHBAUM, Priscilla J.	(CO)	655
	GLADSTONE, Mark A.	(NJ)	439
	IMPERIALE, Karen P.	(NJ)	582
	JONES, Deborah A.	(NJ)	612
Telecommunications research & devlpmnt	DENMAN, Monica K.	(CT)	292
Telecommunications, research, reference	ROGGENKAMP, Alice M.	(NY)	1050
Telecommunications services	VEDDER, Harvey B.	(PA)	1280
Telecommunications technology	MARGOLIS, Suzanne M.	(MI)	770
Three-party telecommunications	GRAHAM, Deborah L.	(OR)	456

TELECONFERENCES (See also Conferences)

Satellite teleconferences	CONNOR, Elizabeth	(MD)	237
Satellite teleconferencing	LANSDALE, Metta T.	(MI)	696
Teleconferencing	MACKINTOSH, Mary L.	(CA)	757

TELEFACSIMILE (See also Facsimiles)

Telefacsimile	JOHN, Stephanie C.	(MI)	601
Telefacsimile applications	BROWN, Steven A.	(GA)	147

TELEMARKETING (See also Marketing)

Telemarketing	PRAQ, Lora B.	(NJ)	989
	CLAYBORNE, Jon L.	(NY)	219
	WORTON, Geoffrey P.	(NY)	1369
Telemarketing management	OGREN, Mark S.	(IL)	918

TELEMATICS

Computers, telematics	KRATZ, Hans G.	(AB)	676

TELEPHONE

History of telephony	SWINBURNE, Ralph E.	(NY)	1216
Independent telephone operations	KAPLAN, Rosalyn L.	(IL)	626
Telephone & ready reference	RIECHEL, Rosemarie	(NY)	1033
Telephone & written reference	PLUMER, F I.	(NY)	978
Telephone information	BRADY, Mary T.	(NY)	127
Telephone reference	BEECHER, Sally	(MA)	74
Telephone reference service	BENDER, Cynthia F.	(MD)	79
	PHIFER, Kenneth O.	(MD)	967
Telephone sales	DYER, Carolyn A.	(CT)	330

TELETEXT (See also Videotex)

Teletext electronic publishing	WILLIAMS, Fred	(GA)	1343
Videotex & teletext	SHAFFER, Richard P.	(NY)	1119

TELEVISION (See also Broadcasting, Cable, ITV)

Audiovisual & television	KUBIC, Joseph C.	(CA)	682
Cable television	CHAMBERLIN, Leslie A.	(CA)	198
	RITZ, Mary E.	(CA)	1037
	MILLER, Robert	(IL)	841
	SIVULICH, Sandra S.	(NY)	1145
Cable television & broadcast television	WALSH, Mark L.	(CT)	1300
Cable television public access	PEARSON, Roger L.	(IL)	953
Cataloging of television news tapes	KEATING, Michael F.	(OH)	633
Cinema & television	THOMPSON, Don K.	(CA)	1239
Community cable television	PORMEN, Paul E.	(OH)	984
Educational television	VOLPATTI, Rechilde	(ON)	1288
Film & television archives	JOHNSON, Jane D.	(CA)	605
Film & television database retrieval	SALZ, Kay	(NY)	1078
Film & television distribution	KLUGHERZ, Dan	(NY)	662
Film & television media	MONACO, James	(NY)	854
Film & television preservation	SALZ, Kay	(NY)	1078
Film & television production	COHEN, Frederick	(NY)	228
	KLUGHERZ, Dan	(NY)	662
Film & television research	MICHAELS, Joan M.	(CA)	832
	GLADSTONE, Mark A.	(NJ)	439
Film & TV information	ALLEN, Nancy H.	(MI)	15
Film research, television production	LIMBACHER, James L.	(MI)	727
Film, television & radio	YEE, Martha M.	(CA)	1379
	DAVIDSON, Steven I.	(NY)	276
Film, theatre, television	KARATNYTSKY, Christine A.	(NY)	627
Instructional television	BURGESS, Barbara J.	(IA)	159
International television programming	PAEN, Alexander L.	(CA)	934
Journalism, radio & television	CAROTHERS, Diane F.	(IL)	184
Motion picture & television archiving	FIELDING, Raymond E.	(TX)	376
Motion picture & television research	BRADY, Eileen E.	(WA)	126
Motion pictures & television	SCHLOSSER, Anne G.	(CA)	1094
Municipal cable television programming	VARNES, Richard S.	(CO)	1279
Reference film & television	TODD, Rose A.	(PQ)	1248
Research for motion picture, television	NELSON-HARB, Sally R.	(CA)	895
Televised regional services	POWER, Colleen J.	(CA)	989
Television	CHACH, Maryann	(NY)	196
Television archives	SCHREIBMAN, Fay C.	(NY)	1099
Television broadcasting	KLEM, Marjorie R.	(NC)	660
Television commercial databases	LOFTHOUSE, Patricia A.	(IL)	737
Television, computers, & other tech	EGAN, Mary J.	(NY)	338
Television industry & communication	POTEAT, James B.	(NY)	986
Television, library applications	RITZ, Mary E.	(CA)	1037
Television news	PILKINGTON, James P.	(TN)	973
Television news film archives	WHITSON, Helene	(CA)	1334
Television production	SHAMBARGER, Peter E.	(MD)	1120
	MARTIN, Richard T.	(NC)	778
	MCLAREN, M B.	(NM)	813
Television production & distribution	WILSON, George N.	(TX)	1351
Television, radio production	BAYLES, Carmen L.	(CT)	67
Television teaching	RECTOR, Wendell H.	(CT)	1013
Video, TV, satellite systems	HISS, Sheila M.	(FL)	544

TEMPORARY

Placing temporary library workers	JOHNSON, Linnea R.	(IL)	607
	KLINGBERG, Jane E.	(IL)	661
Recruiting temporary & permanent workers	JOHNSON, Linnea R.	(IL)	607

TENNESSEE (See also Nashville)

Tennessee Afro-American	STEPHENS, Alonzo T.	(TN)	1187
Tennessee history	COTHAM, James S.	(TN)	249

TERMINOLOGICAL (See also Nomenclature, Thesaurus, Vocabulary)

Terminological documentation	RICHER, Suzanne	(ON)	1030
Thesaurus & terminological databases	MOUREAU, Magdeleine	(FRN)	873
Thesaurus preparation, textile terms	LAWRENCE, Philip D.	(VA)	704

TERRITORY

Americana, Old Northwest Territory	MULLIGAN, William H.	(MI)	877
Colorado territorial records	KETELSEN, Terry	(CO)	645

TESTAMENT (See also Bible)

New Testament	WHIPPLE, Caroline B.	(IL)	1329
Old Testament	MERRILL, Arthur L.	(MN)	826

TESTING (See also Measurement)

Alternatives to test animals	THURSTON, Ethel H.	(NY)	1243
Civil service testbooks	LUNSTEDT, Ralph A.	(CA)	749
Conference testing, resrch & development	ARBEZ, Gilbert J.	(ON)	30
New product testing	MARANGONI, Eugene G.	(CA)	768
Online systems testing	TRUBKIN, Loene	(BC)	1259
Software testing	NELSON, David W.	(NH)	893
Telecommunication monitor & test systems	NELSON, David W.	(NH)	893
Test & measurements reference	KAUFFMAN, Inge S.	(CA)	631
Test cataloging	JORDAN, Robert P.	(IA)	616
Test collection development	JORDAN, Robert P.	(IA)	616
Test collections	WHEELER, Claudia J.	(IL)	1328
	MANDEL, Debra H.	(MA)	764

TEXAS

South Texas history	MITTELSTAEDT, Gerard E.	(TX)	850
Texana	HARPER, Sarah H.	(TX)	503
Texana reference	HULL, Mary M.	(TX)	572
Texas & Northeastern Mexico history	GAUSE, George R.	(TX)	423
Texas history & genealogy	SMITH, Michael K.	(TX)	1158
Texas newspaper archives	MATHIS, Rama F.	(TX)	784

TEXT

Author, children's textbooks	BISSETT, Donald J.	(MI)	100
Automated text analyses	VON KEITZ, Wolfgang	(WGR)	288
Automatic text processing	SALTON, Gerard	(NY)	1077
Bibliography & textual	ROYTMAN, Serafima	(NY)	1063
Bibliography & textual studies	BERGER, Sidney E.	(IL)	86
College textbook publisher	THORNTON, Jack N.	(CA)	1242
College textbook publishing	NEEDHAM, Michael V.	(CA)	891
College textbooks	BARCOMB, Wayne A.	(MA)	55
Computer-assisted text retrieval	PRICKETT, Dan S.	(OH)	993
Computer-based text editing	LUDGIN, Donald H.	(ME)	746
Curriculum textbook cataloging	ONUFFER, Joachim	(PA)	924
Curriculum textbooks	MEWS, Alison J.	(NF)	829
Data, text input	FISHER, Douglas A.	(PA)	380
Editing chemical & medical text	GRIFFITHS, Mary C.	(MD)	469
Editing medical & pharmacological texts	HAMILTON, Gloria R.	(PA)	492
Editorial & textual criticism	REIMAN, Donald H.	(NY)	1020
English language text data	SCHULTZ, Arnold J.	(MN)	1101
Enumerative & textual bibliographies	ABOYADE, Beatrice O.	(NGR)	2
Indexing medical & pharmacological texts	HAMILTON, Gloria R.	(PA)	492
Medical texts	MCGILL, Thomas J.	(NJ)	806
Multilingual text processing	DEERWESTER, Scott C.	(IL)	287
Occupational & post secondary texts	LESURE, Alan B.	(NY)	718
Professional technical trade texts	ABRAMOFF, Lawrence J.	(MA)	3
Retrieval systems, text	BYRN, William H.	(MA)	169
Rewriting medical & pharmacological text	HAMILTON, Gloria R.	(PA)	492
Tape recording graduate textbooks	BULLOCK, Frances E.	(NY)	156
Text book indexing	WEIR, Alexandra L.	(PA)	1319
Text conversion	BEATTY, Samuel B.	(MD)	70
Text database design & development	CHU, John S.	(PA)	212
Text database development	BRIMSEK, Tobi A.	(DC)	136
	BOYLE, Stephen	(IL)	124
	LAFRANCHISE, David	(ON)	688
Text databases	HENDERSON, Ronald L.	(MD)	527
Text management & retrieval systems	LOWENSTEIN, Richard A.	(CT)	744
Text manipulation	HENDERSON, Ronald L.	(MD)	527
Text processing	BUCKLAND, Lawrence F.	(MA)	154
Text retrieval	HOWARD, Theresa M.	(ENG)	564
Text retrieval systems	WEAVER, Maggie	(ON)	1312
Text systems	CLARK, Gerald L.	(IL)	217
Textbases & databases	KRUSS, Daniel M.	(IL)	681
Textbook & circulation cataloging	WILSON, Carole F.	(CA)	1350
Textbook & technical book databases	JACKRELL, Thomas L.	(NJ)	586
Textbook publishing	BROWN, Kent L.	(PA)	145
Textual & enumerative bibliography	WHITE, D J.	(MO)	1330

TEXT (Cont'd)

Textual database management	SCHWARTZ, James M.	(SD)	1104
Textual editing	YEANDLE, Laetitia	(DC)	1378
	BIRK, Nancy	(OH)	98

TEXTILES (See also Clothing)

Clothing & textiles literature	FETTERMAN, Nelma I.	(AB)	374
Food science & textiles	MANDERSCHEID, Dorothy H.	(MI)	765
Textile databases	BEST-NICHOLS, Barbara J.	(NC)	92
Textile information storage & retrieval	LAWRENCE, Philip D.	(VA)	704
Textile reference	SILER, Freddie B.	(SC)	1137
Textiles	PINKNEY, Helen L.	(OH)	975
Textiles databases & books	DAVIS, Jeannette	(MA)	279
Thesaurus preparation, textile terms	LAWRENCE, Philip D.	(VA)	704

THAI

Indexing Thai law	RUNGSANG, Rebecca J.	(THA)	1067

THEATER (See also Acting, Drama, Costumes, Play, Playwriting, Stage)

American musical theatre archives	ROSENBURG, Betsy R.	(CT)	1056
American theatre history	ARCHER, Stephen M.	(MO)	31
Antiquarian theatre books sales	KAHAN, Gerald	(GA)	621
Appraisal of theatre collections	KAHAN, Gerald	(GA)	621
Author of books on theatre	WILMETH, Don B.	(RI)	1349
Chronology, British-American theater	LONEY, Glenn M.	(NY)	739
Current & historical theatre	BUCK, Richard M.	(NY)	154
Experimental theatre	DACE, Tish	(MA)	269
Film & theater memorabilia	WESOLOWSKI, Paul G.	(PA)	1325
Film, theatre, television	KARATNYTSKY, Christine A.	(NY)	627
French & theater	NELSON, Ian C.	(SK)	893
Historic theaters & preservation	LONEY, Glenn M.	(NY)	739
History of the theatre	TARANOW, Gerda	(CT)	1223
International theatre	BURDICK, Elizabeth B.	(NY)	158
Media & theatrical production	GOODMAN, John E.	(PA)	449
Music & theater	WILSON, Fredric W.	(NY)	1351
Music, dance, theatre arts	LUBRANO, Judith A.	(MA)	745
Music theatre research	LYNCH, Richard C.	(NY)	752
Musical theater history & production	LONEY, Glenn M.	(NY)	739
Musical theatre research	WALL, Richard L.	(NY)	1297
19th century British theatre	DONOHUE, Joseph	(MA)	312
Personal film, theatre library	TUDIVER, Lillian	(NY)	1262
Reader's theater reading aloud	BAUER, Caroline F.	(CA)	65
Research in theatre history	DONOHUE, Joseph	(MA)	312
Theater	BRACKEN, James K.	(IN)	124
	FUSCO, Marilyn A.	(PA)	410
Theatre & drama	SHAPIRO, Barbara S.	(NY)	1121
Theater archives	FRITZ, Donald D.	(MI)	405
	COLEMAN, Faith	(NY)	231
Theatre arts	SNOW, Marina	(CA)	1164
Theatre bibliographic researching	ULRICH, Paul S.	(WGR)	268
Theatre bibliography	RAKSHI, Sri R.	(NY)	1004
	BALL, John L.	(ON)	52
Theatre biographical indexing	ULRICH, Paul S.	(WGR)	268
Theatre books & memorabilia	BOWLEY, Craig	(NY)	121
Theatre collection	MCCABE, James P.	(PA)	793
Theatre collections development	KAHAN, Gerald	(GA)	621
Theatre database	MCCULLOUGH, Jack W.	(NJ)	801
Theatre ephemera	WOODS, Alan L.	(OH)	1366
Theatre history	OGDEN, Dunbar H.	(CA)	918
	LENTHALL, Franklyn	(ME)	715
	WALLIN, Cornelia B.	(NH)	1298
	MYERS, Maria P.	(NY)	884
	TAYLOR, Robert N.	(NY)	1228
	WILMETH, Don B.	(RI)	1349
Theater history & bibliography	HECK, Thomas F.	(OH)	519
Theatre language	TRAPIDO, Joel	(HI)	1254
Theatre librarianship	WALL, Richard L.	(NY)	1297
Theatre library association contributor	EPPES, William D.	(NY)	351
Theatre materials	O'CONNELL, Brian E.	(NY)	915
Theatre reference	WILMETH, Don B.	(RI)	1349
Theatre research	DUCLOW, Geradline	(PA)	322
Theatre special collection	COUCH, Nena L.	(OH)	250
Theatrical collection development	CURTIN-STEVENSON, Mary C.	(MA)	266

THEATER (Cont'd)

20th century American theater	LOMONACO, Martha S.	(NY)	738

THEFT (See also Crime, Security)

Material security & book theft	BAHR, Alice H.	(PA)	45
Theft reporting	LEAB, Katharine K.	(CT)	706

THEME

Music thematic indexing	LINCOLN, Harry B.	(NY)	728
Popular music theme structures	COOPER, B L.	(MI)	242
Storytelling, poetry, holiday themes	BAUER, Caroline F.	(CA)	65

THEOLOGY (See also Bible)

Anglican theology	KEARNEY, Robert D.	(NY)	633
Bible & theology collection development	ZINK, Esther L.	(ND)	1389
Cataloging & theology	LLOVIO, Kay M.	(CA)	735
	ROBINSON, Nancy D.	(KY)	1044
Cataloging theology & philosophy	ROONEY, Eugene M.	(DC)	1053
Cataloging theology & religion	WUNDERLICH, Clifford S.	(MA)	1374
Church history, theology resources	SUELFLOW, August R.	(MO)	1206
Circulation, theology	BULLOCK, Frances E.	(NY)	156
Collection building in theology	ZIMPFER, William E.	(MA)	1389
Collection development, theology	KENDALL, Charles T.	(IN)	640
Col devlpmnt, theology, scriptures	MAINELLI, Helen K.	(CA)	761
Cooperative theological lib development	WARTLUFT, David J.	(PA)	1307
Indexing, theology	LALIBERTE, Madeleine A.	(PQ)	689
Management, theological library	HICKS, Barbara A.	(ON)	536
Music librarianship & theology	PARKER, Charles G.	(PQ)	941
Rare books in theology	VANDEGRIFT, J R.	(DC)	1273
Reference services, theology	KENDALL, Charles T.	(IN)	640
Religion & theology bibliography	MCGARTY, Jean R.	(MI)	805
Religion, theology & philosophy	TROUTMAN, Joseph E.	(GA)	1258
Theological & religious periodicals	HAYES, Bonaventure F.	(NY)	515
Theological bibliography	MILLER, William C.	(MO)	843
	FERRIBY, Peter G.	(NJ)	373
	TAYLOR, Sharon A.	(NJ)	1228
	WARTLUFT, David J.	(PA)	1307
	FRITZ, William R.	(SC)	405
	HAYMES, Don	(TN)	516
	IBACH, Robert D.	(TX)	581
Theological bibliography & research	OZOLINS, Karl L.	(MN)	933
Theological, bibl, collection devlpmnt	ERDEL, Timothy P.	(JAM)	352
Theological books	GAGE, Laurie E.	(ENG)	412
Theological collection development	BURDICK, Oscar C.	(CA)	158
	MINDEMAN, George A.	(CA)	845
	HADIDIAN, Dikran Y.	(PA)	482
	SALGAT, Anne M.	(PA)	1076
	OLSEN, Robert A.	(TX)	921
Theological collections	HAIR, William B.	(TN)	484
	STROUD, John N.	(WV)	1203
Theological databases	DARR, William E.	(IN)	275
Theological librarianship	WENDEROTH, Christine	(GA)	1323
	GRUMBLING, Dennis K.	(IL)	474
	THOMPSON, John W.	(IL)	1240
	DEERING, Ronald F.	(KY)	287
	MCLEOD, Herbert E.	(NC)	814
	KASTEN, Seth E.	(NY)	629
	MAURER, Eric	(NY)	787
	SAYRE, John L.	(OK)	1087
	KRUPP, Robert A.	(OR)	681
	CAMILLI, E M.	(PA)	175
	DERRICK, Mitzi J.	(SC)	294
	BAKER, Bonnie U.	(TN)	48
	LOYD, Roger L.	(TX)	745
	MANEY, James W.	(TX)	765
	PAYSON, Evelyn H.	(WI)	951
	CORMAN, Linda W.	(ON)	246
Theological libraries	MARKHAM, Robert P.	(IL)	771
	DELIVUK, John A.	(MO)	289
	BAKER, Steven L.	(SC)	49
Theological library administration	ALDRICH, Willie L.	(NC)	11
Theological library services	CHEATHAM, Gary L.	(OK)	204
Theological literature	HART, Elizabeth	(BC)	507
Theological materials cataloging	RZECZKOWSKI, Eugene M.	(DC)	1072

THEOLOGY (Cont'd)

Theological rare books	KANSFIELD, Norman J. .	(NY)	625
Theological reference	HAYES, Bonaventure F. .	(NY)	515
	HUNN, Marvin T.	(TX)	574
	GILCHRIST-DOBSON, Norma J.	(NS)	434
	GUNN, Shirley A.	(NGR)	477
Theological reference service	OLSON, Ray A.	(MN)	923
Theological reference services	OLSEN, Robert A.	(TX)	921
Theological reference works	WELLS, Keith P.	(IL)	1322
Theological research	PARKER, Mary A.	(SC)	942
Theological research & writing	WROTENBERY, Carl R. . .	(TX)	1373
Theological research methodology	TROUTMAN, Joseph E. .	(GA)	1258
Theological research methods	ERDEL, Timothy P.	(JAM)	352
Theological resources	VANDELINDER, Bonnie L.	(NY)	1273
Theological seminary libraries	HAMMERLY, Hernan D. .	(ARG)	493
Theology	LYONS, Sarah P.	(CO)	753
	HESS, Sandra K.	(IA)	534
	HELGE, Brian L.	(IL)	524
	WHIPPLE, Caroline B. . .	(IL)	1329
	CAREY, John T.	(MD)	181
	OSTERFIELD, George T. .	(OH)	928
	GEORGE, Rachel	(PA)	428
	GILBERT, Thomas F. . . .	(PA)	434
	RANDALL, Laura H.	(TX)	1006
Theology & biblical backgrounds	ANDERSON, Norman E. .	(MA)	24
Theology & ethics	DAVISH, William	(MD)	281
Theology & religion collection devlpmnt	CAMP, Thomas E.	(TN)	175
Theology & religion reference	CAMP, Thomas E.	(TN)	175
Theology, biblical studies	MUNDAY, Robert S.	(PA)	878
Theology cataloging	BURKE, Ambrose L.	(OH)	160
Theology collection development	ROONEY, Eugene M. . . .	(DC)	1053
	BUNDY, David D.	(KY)	157
	SIVIGNY, Robert J.	(VA)	1144
Theology, inclusive	HILGERT, Elvire R.	(IL)	539
Theology journals	MONGOLD, Alice D. . . .	(TX)	854
Theology or banking reference	JORDAN, Charles R. . . .	(IL)	616
Theology, pastoral studies, philosophy	STALZER, Rita M.	(IL)	1179
Theology reference	SIVIGNY, Robert J.	(VA)	1144
Theology, religion	FIEG, Eugene C.	(IL)	375

THEORY

Archival history & theory	BRICHFORD, Maynard J. .	(IL)	134
Archival theory	KIMBALL, Gregg D.	(VA)	649
Bibliographical theory	HOWARD-HILL, Trevor .	(SC)	564
Canadian archival theory	COOK, Terry G.	(ON)	240
Feminist theory	MCDERMOTT, Patrice . .	(IL)	802
Fuzzy set theory	KRAFT, Donald H.	(LA)	674
History of architectural theory	ARNTZEN, Etta M.	(IL)	34
Information retrieval theories	HOSONO, Kimio	(JAP)	562
Information storage & retrieval theory	WILSON, Patrick	(CA)	1352
Music theory	TEUTSCH, Walter	(CA)	1233
Music theory in translation	THYM, Jurgen	(NY)	1243
Online search theory	ROBERT, Berring C.	(CA)	1039
Organization theory	CEPPOS, Karen F.	(CA)	196
Organizational theory	GEORGE, Shirley H. . . .	(IA)	428
	MCBURNEY, Margot B. .	(ON)	792
Political science & theory	FENTON, Heike	(NY)	371
Reference theory	BURNS, Nancy R.	(CA)	162
Social theory	WINTER, Michael F.	(CA)	1356
Systems theory	BURNS, Nancy R.	(CA)	162
Theory development	SCHRADER, Alvin M. . . .	(AB)	1099
Theory of information retrieval	MOOERS, Calvin N.	(MA)	857
	ROBERTSON, Stephen E.	(ENG)	1042

THERAPY (See also Bibliotherapy, Rehabilitation)

Biblio/poetry therapy	HYNES, Arleen M.	(MN)	580
Therapeutic patient program planning	ABDULLAH, Bilquis	(NY)	2

THESAURUS (See also Dictionaries, Nomenclature, Terminological, Vocabulary)

Database thesaurus preparation	KENTON, Charlotte	(MD)	642
Indexing, abstracting & thesaurus bldg	SUIDAN, Randa H.	(IL)	1207
Indexing & thesaurus development	LAFRANCHISE, David . .	(ON)	688
Indexing languages & thesauri	PAUL, Rameshwar N. . . .	(MD)	949
Information retrieval thesaurus	ASIS, Moises	(CUB)	36

THESAURUS (Cont'd)

Online thesauri, dictionary research	LIBBEY, Miles A.	(NJ)	725
Set up & management of a thesaurus	AMNOTTE, Celine	(PQ)	20
Thesauri	FRIERSON, Eleanor G. . .	(DC)	404
	MASON, Hayden	(MA)	781
	WORDEN, Diane D.	(MI)	1369
	MORIN-LABATUT, Gisele	(ON)	865
Thesauri construction	HEWINS, Elizabeth H. . .	(TX)	535
Thesauri development	HARGRAVE, Charles W. .	(DC)	501
Thesauri updating	MARION, Guylaine	(PQ)	770
Thesaurus	BERTRAND-GASTALDY, Suzanne	(PQ)	91
Thesaurus & classification construction	BATTY, Charles D.	(MD)	65
Thesaurus & terminological databases	MOUREAU, Magdeleine .	(FRN)	873
Thesaurus building	FRIED, Suzanne C.	(NY)	403
Thesaurus buildup	PILLET, Sylvaine M.	(KEN)	973
Thesaurus construction	SPRUNG, Lori L.	(CA)	1176
	SVENONIUS, Elaine	(CA)	1212
	LYNCH, Jacqueline	(MA)	751
	PETERSEN, Toni	(MA)	962
	AMATRUDA, William T. .	(MD)	19
	LASER, Debra L.	(MD)	700
	SOERGEL, Dagobert . . .	(MD)	1165
	BRENNER, Everett H. . . .	(NY)	133
	MOLHOLT, Pat	(NY)	852
	PHILLIPS, Sylvia E.	(TX)	969
	LECOMPTE, Louis L. . . .	(PQ)	708
	VAN SLYPE, Georges . .	(BEL)	1277
Thesaurus construction & maintenance	KLEIMAN, Helen M.	(DC)	659
Thesaurus construction & management	VAN HALM, Johan	(NET)	1275
Thesaurus construction, technical	GENUARDI, Michael T. .	(MD)	427
Thesaurus design & maintenance	LINDER, Elliott	(NY)	729
Thesaurus design & preparation	FEINBERG, Hilda W. . . .	(GA)	368
Thesaurus development	BOOTH, Barbara A.	(CA)	116
	MILSTEAD, Jessica L. . .	(CT)	845
	IBACH, Marilyn	(DC)	581
	CURTIN-STEVENSON, Mary C.	(MA)	266
	HOOD, Martha W.	(MD)	556
	RADA, Roy F.	(MD)	1002
	PASQUARIELLA, Susan K.	(NY)	946
	SEKELY, Maryann	(NY)	1113
	SHELLENBERGER, Dawn M.	(PA)	1126
Thesaurus elaboration & indexing	BRETON, Lise	(PQ)	133
Thesaurus maintenance	MUTTER, Letitia N.	(NY)	883
Thesaurus preparation, textile terms	LAWRENCE, Philip D. . .	(VA)	704
Vocabulary & thesaurus construction	SAVAGE, Gretchen S. . .	(CA)	1085

THINKING (See also Thought)

Critical thinking	SENATOR, Rochelle B. .	(CT)	1115
Critical viewing & thinking	BRAUN, Robert L.	(NY)	130

THIRD WORLD (See also Developing Countries)

Acquisitions, including Third World	HENN, Barbara J.	(IN)	528
Third World development	FAESY, Nancy N.	(CT)	361
Third World information	HOWELL, John B.	(IA)	565

THOUGHT (See also Thinking)

Jewish life & thought	BEN-ZVI, Hava	(CA)	84

THRIFT (See also Banking)

Financial & thrift industry	CALLINAN, Mary H.	(NY)	174

THURBER

James Thurber collection	BRANSCOMB, Lewis C. .	(OH)	129

TIBETAN

Tibetan language materials	SCHOENING, Jeffrey D. .	(MA)	1098

TIME
Time management .... MCGOVERN, Gail J. ... (CA) 807
                                         SMITH-EPPS, E P. ...... (GA) 1161

TITLE
Foreign title acquisitions .... SIEVERS, Arlene M. .... (IN) 1136
Nationwide real estate title reporting .. FELDER, Bruce B. ...... (OH) 369

TOBACCO
Tobacco .... PURYEAR, Pamela E. .. (NC) 998
Tobacco information .... DEBARDELEBEN, Marian
                                         Z. .... (VA) 284
Tobacco products .... LINCOLN, Carol S. ..... (KY) 728

TODDLERS (See also Preschool)
Storyhours for toddlers through grade
2 .... SALUZZO, Mary S. .... (NY) 1078
Toddler story programs .... BROUSE, Ann G. ...... (NY) 141

TOPICAL (See also Current)
Topical indexing .... OVERTON, Julie M. .... (OH) 931
Topical news .... CAMPO, Charles A. .... (ME) 177

TOPONYMY
Toponymy .... PETERSON, Charles B. . (DC) 963

TOURISM (See also Travel)
Travel & tourism .... JANSEN, Guenter A. ... (NY) 593
Travel & tourism information systems ... MOLL, Joy K. .... (NJ) 853

TOURS
Public service & tours .... HORTON, Anna J. ..... (OH) 561
Walking tours on cassette .... ECKRICH, Herman J. ... (CT) 335

TOWN
Town, township, county history .... CARTER, Susan M. .... (IN) 190

TOXICOLOGY (See also Hazards)
Chemical & toxicological databases ..... COSMIDES, George J. ... (MD) 249
Chemical & toxicology database
searching .... TAYLOR, Melissa P. .... (CT) 1227
Chemical toxicology .... NOWAK, Geraldine D. .. (DC) 911
                                         MORRISON, Brian H. ... (ON) 867
Database searching, toxicology &
medical .... LEMMON, Anne B. ..... (LA) 715
Medical & toxicology databases .... MORRISON, Brian H. ... (ON) 867
Medical, toxicological databases .... CONNER, Shirley D. .... (CT) 237
Medicine, toxicology .... SCHATZ, Cindy A. ..... (MA) 1090
Medicine, toxicology, & biochemistry ... JOHNSON, Susan W. .. (MD) 609
Pharmacology & toxicology .... COSMIDES, George J. ... (MD) 249
Safety & toxicology .... WEISS, Barbara M. .... (CT) 1319
Safety, toxicology databases .... WEISS, Barbara M. .... (CT) 1319
Sewage & toxic waste libraries .... ANJOU-DURAZZO, Martel
                                         T. .... (CA) 28
Toxic substances information .... MULTER, Ell P. .... (MO) 878
Toxicological database searching .... MCDONELL, W E. ..... (TN) 803
Toxicological evaluation .... MUNRO, Nancy B. ..... (TN) 879
Toxicological information .... EVERITT, Janet M. .... (MI) 359
Toxicology .... CHANDLER, Constance P. (CO) 199
                                         CHASTAIN-WARHEIT,
                                         Christine C. .... (DE) 203
                                         STOSS, Frederick W. ... (NY) 1198
                                         BOUTWELL, Barbara J. . (PA) 119
                                         KRONENFELD, Michael R. (SC) 679
                                         LEE, Diana W. .... (AB) 709
Toxicology archive administration ...... YOUNG, Carolyn K. .... (KS) 1381
Toxicology bibliographies .... HAUTH, Carol A. ...... (CA) 513
Toxicology databases .... BURSON, Sherrie L. .... (CA) 164
                                         KLEMARCZYK, Laurice D. (CT) 660
                                         SMITH, Yvonne B. ..... (NJ) 1161
                                         LIBERTINI, Arleen J. ... (OR) 725

TOXICOLOGY (Cont'd)
Toxicology databases
                                         WICKS, Pamela J. ..... (PA) 1335
Toxicology, industrial medicine .... SELZER, Nancy S. ..... (DE) 1114
Toxicology information .... KERNS, John T. .... (CA) 644
                                         WEHLACZ, Joseph T. ... (IN) 1316
Toxicology information & literature .... EICKENHORST, Joanna
                                         W. .... (CT) 339
Toxicology information, databases ...... DEXTER, Patrick J. .... (MD) 298
Toxicology information services .... KISSMAN, Henry M. ... (MD) 656
Toxicology libraries .... ELY, Betty L. .... (PA) 347

TOY
Toy libraries .... GOVERNS, Molly K. .... (HI) 454
                                         SEDNEY, Frances V. ... (MD) 1111

TRACKING
Competitive tracking, benchmarking ..... LEWARK, Kathryn W. .. (CA) 722
Competitor tracking .... CURTIS, Richard A. .... (CA) 267
Data tracking .... BISHOP, John .... (MA) 99
Info industry & technology tracking .... SIECK, Steven K. ...... (NY) 1135
Material tracking & processing .... KILLHEFFER, Robert E. . (CT) 648

TRADE (See also Business, Commerce, Industry)
Adult trade nonfiction selection .... WISOTZKI, Lila B. ..... (MD) 1358
Book trade .... KAVANAGH, Susan E. ... (ON) 631
Books sold through trade .... GAUNT, James R. ..... (FL) 423
Children's trade books .... RIBAROFF, Margaret F. . (CT) 1026
Foreign trade, political science .... LERNER, Arthur .... (NY) 717
Foreign trade statistics .... MORTON, Dorothy J. ... (DE) 870
Grain trade .... EMOND, Lucille I. ...... (MB) 348
                                         REEDMAN, M R. ...... (MB) 1015
Indexing film & broadcast trade
journals .... HOFFER, Thomas W. .... (FL) 547
International trade .... PRUETT, Barbara J. .... (DC) 996
International trade database .... PFLEIDERER, Stephen D. (DC) 966
International trade databases .... BECK, Douglas J. ...... (DC) 71
International trade research .... MATTERA, Joseph J. ... (NY) 785
Library, book trade market .... BUCENEC, Nancy L. .... (NY) 153
National & trade bibliography .... ROPER, Fred W. ...... (SC) 1054
New & used book trade .... SORGENFREI, Robert K. (CA) 1168
Nonfiction trade books .... RIBAROFF, Margaret F. . (CT) 1026
Professional technical trade texts ..... ABRAMOFF, Lawrence J. (MA) 3
Publishing & book trade .... STUART-STUBBS, Basil
                                         F. .... (BC) 1204
Regional trade .... WILSON, John W. ...... (TX) 1351
Tariff & trade .... PARSONAGE, Dianne L. . (ON) 944
Technical trades, naval ship repair .... ANDERSON, Marcia M. . (VA) 24
Trade association information
management .... HILL, Susan M. .... (DC) 540
Trade books for beginning readers ...... BAUER, Carolyn J. .... (OK) 65
Trade information .... MAROTZ, Karen V. ..... (BC) 772
                                         JONES, Roger A. ...... (SWZ) 615
Trade magazine research .... DAMOTH, Douglas L. ... (NY) 272
Trade magazines & directories .... DALY, Charles P. ...... (NJ) 271
Trade regulation .... TAYLOR, Raymond M. .. (NC) 1228

TRADEMARKS
Automotive patent & trademark
research .... WREN, James A. ...... (MI) 1370
Copyright, trademark .... MESMER, Frank D. ..... (NH) 827
Mastersearch of trademarks on CD ...... NICKEL, R S. .... (PA) 902
Patent & trademark databases .... HU, Robert T. .... (IL) 568
                                         HAYWARD, Diane J. ... (NY) 517
Patent & trademark information .... DI MUCCIO, Mary J. .... (CA) 304
                                         CROCKETT, Martha L. .. (DC) 259
Patent & trademark reference .... MOORE, John R. ...... (IL) 860
Patent & trademark research .... JACOBSON, William R. . (IL) 590
Patent & trademark searching .... SCHUELER, Dolores ... (MA) 1101
Patents & trademarks .... ANDERSEN, Thomas K. . (CA) 21
                                         GROOT, Elizabeth N. ... (CA) 472
                                         JOHNSON, Johanna H. . (TX) 606
Trademarks, banking, accounting
services .... FLEMING, Jack C. ..... (ON) 384
Trademarks database .... SIEGEL, Marilyn .... (MI) 1136

TRADING
Financial industry trading systems   HALL, Robert C. . . . . . .   (NY)   488
Stock/options trading data   ELASIK, Ronald G. . . . . .   (MD)   341

TRAFFIC (See also Highway)
Traffic engineering   HATHAWAY, Kay E. . . .   (VA)   512
Traffic safety   BARTH, Nancy L. . . . . . .   (CA)   61
Traffic signals   HATHAWAY, Kay E. . . .   (VA)   512

TRAINING (See also Education, Inservice, Instruction, Skills, Staff, Teaching)
Administration, training &
  development   BOAZ, Martha T. . . . . . .   (CA)   108
Administration training & staff mgmt   NANTON-COMISSIONG,
    Barbara L.   (TRN)   887
Adult literacy tutor trainer   KORNITSKY, Judith M.   (FL)   672
Archival training   JONES, Allen W. . . . . . .   (AL)   610
      BARTKOWSKI, Patricia .   (MI)   61
Archives organization & training   KEATS, Susan E. . . . . . .   (MA)   633
Archives training   TOUCHETTE, Francois G.   (PQ)   1252
Archives, training & development   RABINS, Joan W. . . . . .   (TX)   1001
Archivists training & development   SANTORO, Corrado A. . .   (MB)   1082
Audiovisual production training   RUNYON, Steven C. . . .   (CA)   1067
Audiovisual training   HARLOW, Aileen W. . . . .   (CT)   502
Audiovisual training & development   STUCKWICH, Chris E. . .   (LA)   1204
      CLEMONS, Kenneth L. . .   (NC)   221
Automated systems training &
  development   BOWRIN-MARSH, Donna
    M. . . . .   (CA)   122
      LOCASCIO, Aline M. . . .   (NY)   735
Bibliotherapy training   HYNES, Arleen M. . . . . .   (MN)   580
CAS online end-user training   ROSS, Johanna C. . . . .   (CA)   1058
Cataloging, training   STUHLMAN, Daniel D. . .   (IL)   1205
      WARTZOK, Susan G. . .   (IN)   1307
      COPELAND, Alice T. . . .   (NJ)   244
Cataloging, training & development   KEATTS, Rowena W. . . .   (TX)   633
Catlgng training, devlpmnt &
  instruction   JIZBA, Laurel . . . .   (MI)   600
CD-ROM development & training   HORNIG-ROHAN, James
    E. . . . .   (PA)   560
Children's librarian training   BREEN, Karen B. . . . . . .   (NY)   131
Children's libn training & development   BOTHAM, Jane . . . .   (WI)   118
Church libraries training &
  development   RODDA, Dorothy J. . . . .   (PA)   1047
Computer input & training   THACKER, Timothy M. . . .   (WV)   1233
Computer literacy training   NEWHARD, Eleanor M. .   (CA)   899
      ARNY, Philip H. . . . .   (LA)   34
Computer systems training   ROBAR, Terri J. . . . . . .   (FL)   1038
Computer training   FERDUN, Georgenne M. .   (CA)   372
      FISHER, Georgeann . . . .   (MO)   381
      RAPPAPORT, Susan E. .   (NY)   1008
      STOCK, Carole G. . . . . .   (WA)   1195
Computer training & development   TABORN, Kym M. . . . . .   (CA)   1219
Computer training & programming   NEUWILLER, Charlene . .   (WGR)   897
Computer training staff & students   DUHAMELL, Lynnette H.   (IN)   324
Computer usage training   BERG, David C. . . . . . .   (MN)   84
Computerized literature training   WONG, Ming S. . . . . . .   (DC)   1363
Conducting training seminars   TOWNSEND, Carolyn J. . .   (PA)   1253
Conservation training specialist   MILEVSKI, Robert J. . . .   (DC)   834
Consultation & training   BRZUSTOWICZ, Richard
    J. . . . .   (WA)   152
Continuing education & training   HOWARD, Mary R. . . . . .   (GA)   564
      CHOBOT, Mary C. . . . . .   (VA)   210
Continuing educ, training &
  development   WELLS, Mary K. . . . . . .   (TX)   1322
Customer services, training   HECHT, Joseph A. . . . . .   (OH)   519
Database demonstrations & training   FRYER, Regina K. . . . . .   (CT)   407
Database demos & training   WRIGHT, Larry L. . . . . .   (NC)   1372
      MOON, Fletcher F. . . . . .   (TN)   857
Database instruction & training   WILCOX, Patricia F. . . .   (WI)   1338
Database search service, trainer   CARR, Caryn J. . . . . . .   (PA)   185
Database training   JUDY, Joseph R. . . . . . .   (CA)   619
      ROSS, Margery M. . . . . .   (DC)   1058
      ALZOFON, Sammy R. . . .   (FL)   19
      PAPPALARDO, Marcia J.   (IL)   939
      EARLEY, Dorothy A. . . . .   (NE)   332
      ARTHUR, Christine . . . . .   (NY)   35
      HOWARD, Joyce M. . . .   (NY)   564

TRAINING (Cont'd)
Database training
      RAUCH, Anne . . . .   (NY)   1010
      GOSLING, Carolyn . . . . .   (VA)   453
Database training & demonstration   SANDULEAK, Barbara . .   (OH)   1081
Database training & development   PASCHAL, Linda P. . . . .   (OK)   945
      NEAL, James H. . . . . . .   (TN)   890
Database training & documentation   ACKERMAN, Katherine K.   (MI)   4
Development & training   BEGG, Karin E. . . . . . .   (MA)   74
      DAMON, Shirley J. . . . . .   (NY)   272
      NEGHERBON, Vincent R.   (PA)   892
Documentary production training   WILLIAMS, Carroll W. . . .   (NM)   1342
Drug abuse training projects   CNATTINGIUS, Claes M.   (SWE)   224
Early training for online searching   MINEMIER, Betty M. . . .   (NY)   845
Education & training   BELLARDO, Trudi . . . . .   (DC)   78
      BLOUIN, Francis X. . . . .   (MI)   107
      COVVEY, H D. . . . .   (MB)   252
      ELLIOTT, Pirkko E. . . . . .   (ENG)   344
      POON, Paul W. . . . .   (HKG)   983
      LAZAR, Peter . . . .   (HUN)   706
      KIM, Soon C. . . . .   (SKO)   649
      CHOU, Nancy O. . . . . . .   (TAI)   210
Education & training library
  technicians   ANASTASIOU, Joan D. .   (BC)   21
Education training & development   WILSON, Jacqueline B. .   (CA)   1351
Educ, training & professional devlpmnt   AMAN, Mohammed M. . .   (WI)   19
Electronics training   GRIEVE, Shelley . . . . . .   (OH)   468
End-user online training   HARBERT, Cathy E. . . . .   (MD)   499
      MACKSEY, Julie A. . . . .   (MI)   757
End-user searching & training   BATISTA, Emily J. . . . . .   (PA)   64
End-user searching training   NESBIT, Kathryn W. . . . .   (NY)   896
      KONDRASKE, Linda N. . .   (TX)   670
End-user services & training   BRUNDAGE, Christina A.   (CA)   150
End-user training   DAVIS, Rebecca A. . . . .   (CA)   280
      DEENEY, Kay E. . . . . . .   (CA)   286
      MANTHEY, Teresa M. . .   (CA)   767
      MIELKE, Marsha K. . . . .   (CA)   833
      PETERS, Marion C. . . . .   (CA)   962
      SHERMAN, Judith E. . . .   (CA)   1128
      SIMON, Nancy L. . . . . . .   (CO)   1140
      BANKS, Jane L. . . . .   (DC)   54
      JOHNSON, Hilary C. . . .   (DE)   605
      HSU, Pi Y. . . . .   (FL)   567
      BEVERIDGE, Mary I. . . . .   (IA)   93
      BUNTROCK, Robert E. . . .   (IL)   157
      BUTTON, Katherine H. . . .   (MA)   167
      LOSCALZO, Anita B. . . . .   (MA)   741
      OPPENHEIM, Roberta A. .   (MA)   925
      HERIN, Nancy J. . . . .   (MD)   531
      OSEGUEDA, Laura M. . . .   (NC)   927
      AUGHEY, Kathleen M. . . .   (NJ)   39
      GREENBERG, Charles J.   (NY)   463
      SAFRAN, Scott A. . . . . .   (NY)   1074
      SOLLENBERGER, Julia F.   (NY)   1166
      SEXTON, Sally V. . . . . . .   (OH)   1118
      MADER, Sharon B. . . . . .   (TN)   759
      LEE, Donna K. . . . .   (VT)   709
End-user training & consultation   INGUI, Bettejean . . . . . .   (CO)   583
End-user training & development   STRAHAN, Michael F. . . .   (ND)   1199
End-user training for MEDLINE
  computer   POND, Frederick C. . . . .   (NY)   982
End-user training, staff training   MEREDITH, Meri . . . . . .   (IN)   825
Filing supervision & training   ABRAMS, Roger E. . . . .   (OH)   3
GEAC training & development   WERT, Alice L. . . . .   (IN)   1325
General library, training   PFEIFFER, Mary A. . . . .   (NY)   966
Graduate library training resource   HOLSINGER, Katherine .   (AZ)   554
Group training & development   BURGER, Leslie B. . . . .   (CT)   159
Health professionals & training   BISCHOFF, Frances A. .   (VA)   99
Information management training   STARK, Philip H. . . . . . .   (CO)   1182
Information training   CHICOREL, Marietta S. .   (AZ)   208
      ADDISON, Paul H. . . . . .   (IN)   6
In-house training   ROACH, Linda . . . .   (PA)   1038
Inservice training   PATRICK, Patricia M. . . .   (NY)   947
      VANDERGRIFF, Kathleen
    E. . . . .   (TN)   1274
      BURKS, C J. . . . .   (UT)   161
Interpersonal communication training   RUBEN, Brent D. . . . . .   (NJ)   1064
Interpersonal communications training   KOSHER, Helene J. . . . .   (CA)   672
Interpersonal skills training &
  devlpmnt   KNIGHT, Shirley D. . . . .   (NJ)   664

TRAINING (Cont'd)

Key trainer for the optical disk	BEAN, Charles W.	(DC)	69
Laubach tutor training	TEUBERT, Lola H.	(IN)	1233
Leadership training	SKELLEY, Cornelia A.	(WA)	1145
Legal database searching & training	KAUL, Kanhya L.	(MI)	631
Legal databases training	STREIKER, Susan L.	(CA)	1201
Legal research training	SHEAR, Joan A.	(MA)	1124
Legal research training & development	COYLE, Christopher B.	(OH)	253
Legal training & development	STEELE, Tom M.	(NC)	1184
LEXIS & Westlaw training	WINSON, Gail I.	(CA)	1355
Librarian training	WALTER, Raimund E.	(WGR)	1300
Librarians training & development	BARTZ, Alice P.	(PA)	62
Library automation training	MILLER, Randy S.	(IL)	841
Library boards selection & training	LIPTON, Connie F.	(MI)	732
Library education, training & devlpmnt	EGAN, Terence W.	(AZ)	338
Library management, training, devlpmnt	WILLIAMS, Edwin E.	(CT)	1343
Library staff training	MING, Marilyn	(AB)	846
Library staff training & development	JOHNSON, Martha A.	(VA)	607
Library systems development & training	CHAPMAN, Elwynda K.	(DC)	202
Library systems training	PHILLIPS, Rosemary	(ON)	969
Library technician training	SELING, Kathy A.	(WA)	1113
	DAVIDSON-ARNOTT, Frances E.	(ON)	277
Library training & development	TOMMEY, Richard J.	(CA)	1250
Library training & education	MILLER, Beth M.	(ON)	836
Local systems training	BERRINGER, Virginia M.	(OH)	90
Management & supervisory training	PARSONS, Jerry L.	(CA)	945
Management & training	MILLS, Victoria A.	(AZ)	844
	WRIGHT, Joseph F.	(FL)	1372
Management simulation training	WRIGHT, Keith C.	(NC)	1372
Management, supervision & training	BOWLES, Carol A.	(CA)	121
Management training	BOBAN, Carol A.	(IL)	108
	FORRESTER, John H.	(ITL)	391
Management training & consulting	SCEPANSKI, Jordan M.	(CA)	1088
Management, training & development	SLOCUM, Hannah R.	(CA)	1150
	PERRY, Emma B.	(MA)	960
	RIZZO, John R.	(MI)	1037
Management training, instruction	KLEIN, Victor C.	(LA)	659
MARC training & development	HENSEN, Steven L.	(NC)	529
Media education training & development	FORTIN, Clifford C.	(WI)	391
Media specialists training & development	RIVERA, Antonio	(NY)	1037
Medical computer training & development	HORNIG-ROHAN, James E.	(PA)	560
Medical databases training	REID, Carolyn A.	(NY)	1018
MEDLARS training	VEEKEN, Mary L.	(ON)	1280
MEDLINE search training	KYKER, Penelope R.	(IN)	685
MEDLINE training	HARRIMAN, Jenny F.	(MD)	503
	KINNA, Dorothy H.	(MD)	652
Microcomputer applications & training	MARSH, Elizabeth C.	(OH)	773
	MARMION, Daniel K.	(TX)	772
Microcomputer programming & training	ANDREWS, Mark J.	(MO)	27
Microcomputer training	ALURI, Rao	(AZ)	19
	JAJKO, Pamela J.	(CA)	592
	KARCHER, Tracey L.	(CA)	627
	CARLSON, Robert P.	(IL)	182
	FOURNIER, Susan K.	(MD)	393
	CONWAY, Michael J.	(MI)	239
	STOUT, Chester D.	(OH)	1198
	BRADLEY, John	(PA)	126
	FISLER, Charlotte D.	(PA)	382
	ZOGOTT, Joyce	(PA)	1390
	QUEYROUZE, Mary E.	(TX)	999
Microcomputer training & development	ELAM, Kristy L.	(MO)	341
	CHAPMAN, Kathleen A.	(WA)	202
	GRAF, David L.	(WI)	455
Microcomputer training database searches	KENNEDY, James W.	(OK)	641
Microcomputer training support	STIGLEMAN, Sue E.	(NC)	1194
Microcomputer use & training	NELSON, Margaret R.	(MA)	894
Microcomputing & database training	KATZ, Jacqueline E.	(NY)	630
MIS training	JACOBS, Patt	(OR)	590
Monographic cataloging unit training	DONAHUE, Janice E.	(FL)	310

TRAINING (Cont'd)

New librarian training & development	BUSH, Joyce	(NY)	165
NOTIS training & procedures	ENGLE, Constance B.	(MI)	349
Nuclear training	BOBAN, Carol A.	(IL)	108
Nutrition education & training	KREBS-SMITH, James J.	(MD)	677
Occupational training	LESURE, Alan B.	(NY)	718
OCLC training & development	WILD, Judith W.	(NY)	1338
Online bibliographic training	PERRY, Claudia A.	(NY)	960
Online catalog training	NOLAN, Christopher W.	(TX)	907
Online database searching & training	WELLS, David B.	(NV)	1322
Online database training	KAVANAGH, Janette R.	(CO)	631
Online management & training	KIBBEE, Josephine Z.	(IL)	646
Online research training	WEEKS, Olivia L.	(NC)	1315
Online search training	COCHRANE, Maryjane S.	(VA)	226
Online search training & development	ROBERTS, Sally M.	(IL)	1041
Online searcher training	KLINGLER, Thomas E.	(OH)	662
Online searching & training	SCHWARTZ, Diane G.	(MI)	1104
Online searching, end-user training	KASALKO, Sally G.	(AR)	628
Online searching training	MILLER, Susan E.	(LA)	842
	MOORE, Barbara S.	(MO)	858
	LINCOVE, David A.	(OH)	728
Online systems training	HUGGENS, Gary D.	(DC)	571
Online training	DAWSON, Debra A.	(CA)	282
	BOLSTER, Kathryn	(CT)	113
	RADUAZO, Dorothy M.	(DC)	1002
	MEREDITH, Meri	(IN)	825
	ORENSTEIN, Ruth M.	(MA)	925
	KENTON, Charlotte	(MD)	642
	CUTLER, Judith	(PA)	268
	DINGLE, Susan	(PA)	304
	CAPUTO, Richard P.	(VA)	180
	MCKENNEY, Linda S.	(VA)	811
	FRITZ, Richard J.	(ON)	405
Online training & development	MULL, Richard G.	(CA)	876
	DRUMMOND, Louis E.	(DC)	321
	CARUSO, Nicholas C.	(PA)	190
	WONG, Lusi	(ON)	1363
Online training & management	SINGLETON, Cynthia B.	(ON)	1143
Online training & marketing	HOCK, Randolph E.	(MA)	545
Oral history interview training	KENDRICK, Alice M.	(NY)	640
Organization, training & development	FEINER, Arlene M.	(IL)	369
	ENGELBERT, Peter J.	(IN)	348
	KING, Willard B.	(NC)	652
Organizational communication training	RUBEN, Brent D.	(NJ)	1064
Paraprofessional training	WILSON, Susan W.	(MD)	1353
Patent training	MEREK, Charles J.	(VA)	825
Patron training	FRITZ, Donald D.	(MI)	405
Patron-staff systems training	GATTEN, Jeffrey N.	(OH)	422
Personal computer database training	MULLINS, James R.	(TX)	878
Personal computer development & training	JONES, Jennifer R.	(NY)	613
Personal computer training	KRONISH, Priscilla T.	(NY)	680
Personnel management & training	DEMPSEY, Pamela M.	(NM)	291
Personnel training	O'BRIEN, Marlys H.	(MN)	915
	GOLDSTEIN, Cynthia N.	(WA)	446
	BREDESON, Peggy Z.	(WI)	131
Personnel training & development	SCHWARZMANN, Diane D.	(CA)	1105
	GRAY, Karen S.	(IL)	460
	SEIDMAN, Ruth K.	(MA)	1112
	VON WAHLDE, Barbara	(NY)	1288
Personnel training & evaluation	EYLES, Heberle H.	(FL)	359
Pilot training	HARPER, Marie F.	(AL)	503
Planning & coordinating training	TOWNSEND, Carolyn J.	(PA)	1253
Police training & law enforcement	MERRYWEATHER, J M.	(ON)	827
Preservation education & training	OGDEN, Barclay W.	(CA)	918
Producing training user aids	TOWNSEND, Carolyn J.	(PA)	1253
Professional education & training progs	ROBERTS, Kenneth H.	(FRN)	1040
Professional training & development	PINGS, Vern M.	(FL)	974
Public library staff training	WYNN, Vivian R.	(OH)	1375
Public relations & training	CARDEN, Marguerite	(FL)	180
	WAGGENER, Jean B.	(TN)	1291
Public relations, lobbying, training	SANKER, Paul N.	(NY)	1081
Public relations staff training	NORTON, Alice	(CT)	910
Public service training	BARKER, Lillian H.	(MD)	56
Public speaking training	BARKER, Lillian H.	(MD)	56
Quality control & training	NADZIEJKA, David E.	(WI)	886
Recorded sound research & training	GAUNT, Sandra L.	(OH)	423

TRAINING (Cont'd)

Records management training	MOORE, Gwen A.	(UT)	859
	NASH, Cherie A.	(UT)	888
Reference & fiction training	BARKER, Lillian H.	(MD)	56
Reference & training staff	WHITE, Joyce L.	(CO)	1331
Reference related training	AARON, Kathleen F.	(CA)	1
Reference training	CROOKS, Joyce M.	(CA)	260
	MICHEL, William D.	(MN)	832
	THOMPSON, Ronelle K.	(SD)	1241
	THAUBERGER, Marianne T.	(SK)	1234
Reference training & procedures	HELSLEY, Alexia J.	(SC)	525
Research & reference training	ROSS, Theodosia B.	(GA)	1059
Research training	CALLINAN, Ellen M.	(DC)	173
Rural library development & training	WILLIAMS, Susan S.	(MI)	1346
School library training & development	BRUWELHEIDE, Janis H.	(MT)	151
	CURRIE, Bertha B.	(NS)	266
Sci databases, training & development	HOELLE, Dolores M.	(NJ)	547
Search training	LEACH, Sandra S.	(TN)	706
Service development & staff training	RIECHEL, Rosemarie	(NY)	1033
Small group training	FORD, Marjorie F.	(CA)	389
Software systems training	DULAN, Peter A.	(CO)	324
Software training	ROGERS, Jonathan B.	(NY)	1049
	NAULTY, Deborah M.	(PA)	889
	ATTINGER, Monique L.	(ON)	38
Software training & development	LIGHTERMAN, Mark	(FL)	726
Staff & public computer training	MCMURRAY, Sallylou	(OH)	815
Staff, board training & development	GIBSON, Barbara H.	(CT)	431
Staff development & training	SULLIVAN, Maureen	(CT)	1208
	FIORE, Carole D.	(FL)	379
	APPS, Michelle L.	(MI)	30
	ALBRITTON, Rosie L.	(MO)	10
	MATER, Dee A.	(NC)	783
	NEWMAN, Marianne L.	(OH)	899
	RHODES, Glenda T.	(OH)	1026
	GOODMAN, Helen C.	(TX)	449
	HAYCOCK, Carol A.	(BC)	515
	NEAME, Roderick L.	(AUS)	891
Staff online training	CAGAN, Penny M.	(NY)	170
Staff training	CARLSON, Alan C.	(CA)	182
	GLOGOFF, Stuart J.	(DE)	441
	FULTON, Tara L.	(IL)	409
	DEANE, Paul D.	(IN)	284
	SEXTON, Ebba J.	(KY)	1118
	HAVENER, Ralph S.	(MO)	513
	LANEY, Elizabeth J.	(NC)	695
	MASSEY, Nancy O.	(NC)	782
	ELLIS, Peter K.	(NY)	345
	GUMPPER, Mary F.	(OH)	477
	PURCELL, V N.	(OR)	998
	PEFFER, Margery E.	(PA)	954
	CHESHER, Joyce A.	(TX)	206
	HENSLEY, Randall B.	(WA)	529
	CLANCY, Ron	(BC)	215
	SPRY, Patricia	(ON)	1176
Staff training & development	STEWART, George R.	(AL)	1192
	MULLINS, Carolyn J.	(CA)	878
	FRANKLIN, Hardy R.	(DC)	397
	PHELPS, Thomas C.	(DC)	967
	SALVADORE, Maria B.	(DC)	1078
	STARCK, William L.	(DC)	1181
	TRAINOR, Donna J.	(GA)	1253
	REES, Pamela C.	(IA)	1016
	PICCOLI, Roberta A.	(IL)	970
	ROBY, B D.	(KY)	1045
	NEAU, Philip F.	(LA)	891
	COURSON, M S.	(MD)	251
	HEISER, Jane C.	(MD)	523
	WILLIAMS, J L.	(MD)	1343
	WILLIAMSON, Phyllis B.	(MT)	1348
	BEECH, Vivian W.	(NC)	74
	SCHULTZ, Gary J.	(ND)	1102
	HESS, Jayne L.	(NJ)	534
	TANG, Grace L.	(NY)	1222
	AXAM, John A.	(PA)	42
	CARD, Judy	(TN)	180
	ARD, Harold J.	(TX)	31
	WELCH, C B.	(TX)	1321
	WOHLSCHLAG, Sarah A.	(TX)	1359

TRAINING (Cont'd)

Staff training & development	MACRURY, Mary E.	(NS)	758
	DINEEN, Diane M.	(ON)	304
	SMITH, Cynthia M.	(ON)	1153
	EL-DUWEINI, Aadel K.	(EGY)	342
Staff training & evaluation	LEE, Janis M.	(PA)	710
	TONGATE, John T.	(TX)	1250
Staff training, development, recruitment	PURCELL, Marcia L.	(NY)	998
State development & training	BIHLER, Charles H.	(CT)	96
Student assistant training	MORRIS, Betty J.	(AL)	866
Student orientation & training	RICE, Anna C.	(NJ)	1026
Student staffing & training	DIAL, Ron	(NY)	299
Student supervision & training	MCHUGH, William A.	(IL)	809
Student training & development	BARTZ, Alice P.	(PA)	62
Supervise & training librarians	EMERICK, John L.	(PA)	347
Supervision & staff training	JACKSON, Harriett D.	(TN)	587
Supervision & training	YOST, F D.	(DC)	1381
	BRADY, Mary M.	(IL)	127
	RUIZ-VALERA, Phoebe L.	(NY)	1067
	BYRNE, Helen E.	(OR)	169
	THOMPSON, Sandra K.	(PA)	1241
Supervision & training of employees	MCIVER, Stephanie P.	(GA)	809
Supervision, training & development	BANKHEAD, Jean M.	(CO)	54
Supervision, training, cataloging	VAN STRATEN, Daniel G.	(WI)	1277
Supervisory & management training	GARDNER, Jeffrey J.	(DC)	418
Systems training	GIBSON, Timothy T.	(TX)	432
Systems, training & development	ARSENAULT, Patricia A.	(MA)	35
Teacher training	NEWMAN, Eileen M.	(NY)	899
Teaching & training	BLACK, Dorothy M.	(PA)	101
	BEAUMONT, Jane	(ON)	70
Teaching, training & development	ROTHENBERG, Mark H.	(NY)	1060
Technical services training development	WANG, Anna M.	(OH)	1302
Technician training	GAMSON, Arthur L.	(DC)	416
Telecommunication training & development	IFFLAND, Carol D.	(IL)	581
Train, supervise & evaluate staff	DAYO, Ayo	(TX)	283
Trainer, administration	MORRIS, Effie C.	(CA)	866
Training	ALLEN, Stephanie O.	(AZ)	16
	HAMILTON, Rita	(AZ)	492
	FRANKEL, Kate M.	(CA)	397
	HEDDEN, Judy A.	(CA)	520
	INGEBRETSEN, Dorothy L.	(CA)	582
	KATZ, Jeffrey P.	(CA)	630
	KAZLAUSKAS, Edward J.	(CA)	632
	KERSHNER, Lois M.	(CA)	644
	MULVANY, Nancy	(CA)	878
	ROSE, Steven C.	(CA)	1055
	SHIRASAWA, Sharon V.	(CA)	1131
	SUGRANES, Maria R.	(CA)	1207
	HENSINGER, James S.	(CO)	529
	LEFFALL, Dolores C.	(DC)	712
	WILLSON, Elizabeth	(DC)	1349
	SMITH, Linda L.	(FL)	1157
	BAUGHMAN, Steven A.	(GA)	66
	DEES, Leslie M.	(GA)	287
	RHEAY, Mary L.	(GA)	1025
	PEPETONE, Diane S.	(IA)	957
	BALL, Mary A.	(IL)	52
	FOUSER, Jane G.	(IL)	393
	RABAI, Terezia	(IL)	1001
	RANDALL, Sara L.	(IL)	1006
	WAJENBERG, Arnold S.	(IL)	1293
	MORELAND, Rachel S.	(KS)	863
	BLACKBURN-FOSTER, Brenda	(KY)	102
	WASHINGTON, Idella A.	(LA)	1307
	DYER, Victor E.	(MA)	330
	INGERSOLL, Diane S.	(MA)	582
	STAACK, Katherine A.	(MA)	1177
	WEISS, Bernice O.	(MA)	1320
	BOGAGE, Alan R.	(MD)	110
	DAHLEN, Roger W.	(MD)	269
	KIGER, Anne F.	(MD)	647
	LAZAROW-STETTEN, Jane K.	(MD)	706
	LOSINSKI, Julia M.	(MD)	742
	PURCELL, Kathleen V.	(MD)	998

TRAINING (Cont'd)
Training

GILBERT, Carole M.	(MI)	433
PONOMARENKO, Ella . .	(MI)	982
BYRNE, Roseanne	(MN)	169
MARCHANT, Thomas O.	(MO)	768
WILLIS, Dorothy B.	(NE)	1348
BAKES, Floy L.	(NJ)	50
DUDLEY, Debbra C.	(NJ)	323
PIERCE, Mildred L.	(NV)	971
CHEN, Barbara A.	(NY)	205
DENNIS, Anne R.	(NY)	292
O'DONNELL, Maureen D.	(NY)	917
REDDINGTON, Mary E. .	(OH)	1013
RICHARDSON, Ulrike L. .	(OH)	1030
SKVARLA, Donna J. . . .	(OK)	1147
ANDERSON, Elizabeth M.	(PA)	22
DUCK, Patricia M.	(PA)	322
GILBERT, Nancy L.	(PA)	434
MARLOW, Kathryn E. . . .	(PA)	772
SILVERMAN, Karen S. . .	(PA)	1138
SWOPE, Paula J.	(PA)	1217
BIRD, H C.	(TX)	98
CAMP, Joyce H.	(TX)	175
LINDSAY, Lorin H.	(TX)	729
MULLER, Mary M.	(TX)	877
PENNER, Elaine C.	(TX)	957
THOMPSON, Christine E.	(TX)	1239
WILSON, Barbara A. . . .	(TX)	1349
LUH, Lydia Y.	(VA)	747
MCLANE, Kathleen	(VA)	813
WINIARSKI, Marilee E. . .	(VA)	1355
KETCHELL, Debra S. . . .	(WA)	645
DAVIS, Phyllis B.	(WI)	280
SIEBERSMA, Dan	(WY)	1135
NICHOL, Kathleen M. . .	(BC)	901
MIRABELLI, Gerardo . . .	(CSR)	847
EL-MASRY, Mohammed .	(EGY)	345
CHAUMIER, Jacques . . .	(FRN)	204
FABRE DE MORLHON,		
Christiane	(ITL)	360
CHUO, Josephine Y.	(TAI)	213

Training, abstracting & indexing	AUSTON, Ione	(VA)	40
Training aids & manuals	CORNICK, Ron	(IL)	247
Training & advising	BREWER, Helen L.	(VA)	134
Training & coaching	AUER, Margaret E.	(MI)	39
Training & collection development	DAVIS, Denise	(MD)	278
	SALEY, Stacey	(NY)	1076
Training & conference management	HUFFER, Mary A.	(MD)	570
Training & consulting	STRONG, Sunny A.	(WA)	1203
	MIWA, Makiko	(JAP)	850
Training & continuing education	DREWETT, William O. . .	(IL)	319
	HYMAN, Karen D.	(NJ)	580
Training & curriculum development	HARADA, Violet H.	(HI)	499
Training & customer services	CHAMPANY, Barry W. . . .	(CA)	198
Training & development	CHANEY, A V.	(AK)	200
	ELAM, Kim A.	(AK)	341
	JENKS, Arlene I.	(AK)	597
	KOLB, Audrey P.	(AK)	669
	PARHAM, Robert B.	(AK)	940
	WEILAND, Karen B.	(AK)	1317
	COLEMAN, L Z.	(AL)	231
	HARRIS, Edwin R.	(AL)	504
	MOORE, Patricia S.	(AL)	861
	BRADLEY, Florene J. . . .	(AR)	125
	PIERSON, Betty	(AR)	972
	JOHNSON, Harlan R. . . .	(AZ)	605
	LEI, Polin P.	(AZ)	713
	LONG, Carla J.	(AZ)	739
	PHIPPS, Shelley E.	(AZ)	969
	WELLIK, Kay E.	(AZ)	1321
	ALFORD, Thomas E. . . .	(CA)	13
	BLITZ, Ruth R.	(CA)	105
	BUSCH, Barbara	(CA)	165
	CASTER, Suzanne	(CA)	194
	CASTRO, Rafaela G.	(CA)	194
	CHURCH, Sonia J.	(CA)	213
	CONTINI, Janice L.	(CA)	239
	CROSBY-MUILENBURG,		
	Corryn	(CA)	260

TRAINING (Cont'd)
Training & development

DRAKE, Dorothy M.	(CA)	318
ECKLUND, Lynn M.	(CA)	335
ELGIN, Susan R.	(CA)	342
ELNOR, Nancy G.	(CA)	346
FARMER, Lesley S.	(CA)	364
FAY, Evelyn V.	(CA)	367
FOX, Marylou P.	(CA)	395
FROST, Shirley E.	(CA)	406
GELMAN-KMEC, Marsha	(CA)	426
GILMAN, Lelde B.	(CA)	436
GORDON, Ruth I.	(CA)	452
GRIFFIN, Hillis L.	(CA)	468
HALE, Kaycee	(CA)	485
HIMMEL, Ned A.	(CA)	542
HUANG, George W.	(CA)	568
HUTCHESON, Don S. . . .	(CA)	578
KATZ, Janet R.	(CA)	630
KIRBY, Barbara L.	(CA)	653
LOOMIS, Barbara L.	(CA)	740
MAIN, Linda Y.	(CA)	761
MCGOVERN, Gail J.	(CA)	807
MCINDOO, Larry R.	(CA)	809
MCKENZIE, Harry	(CA)	811
MCNAMEE, Gilbert W. . .	(CA)	816
MEGLIO, Delores D.	(CA)	821
MONTGOMERY, John W.	(CA)	856
MORRISON, Patricia . . .	(CA)	868
NEELY, Jesse G.	(CA)	892
NELSON, Alice R.	(CA)	893
NICKELSON-DEARIE,		
Tammy A.	(CA)	902
O'NEILL, Diane J.	(CA)	924
PATRON, Susan H.	(CA)	947
PRINTZ, Naomi J.	(CA)	993
QUEEN, Margaret E.	(CA)	999
REVEAL, Arlene H.	(CA)	1024
REYES, Helen M.	(CA)	1024
RINGWALT, Arthur	(CA)	1035
RITCH, Alan W.	(CA)	1036
RODRIGUEZ, Ronald . . .	(CA)	1048
RONEY, Raymond G. . . .	(CA)	1053
RUBIN, Rhea J.	(CA)	1064
SAHAK, Judy H.	(CA)	1075
SAUSEDO, Ann E.	(CA)	1085
SIGMAN, Paula M.	(CA)	1137
SZABO, Carolyn J.	(CA)	1218
TAOKA, Wesley M.	(CA)	1223
TARCZY, Stephen I.	(CA)	1224
THOMPSON, James A. .	(CA)	1240
TREGGIARI, Arnaldo . . .	(CA)	1255
TREISTER, Cyril C.	(CA)	1255
UEBELE, Dorothy B.	(CA)	1268
VEGA, Carolyn L.	(CA)	1281
VOTAW, Floyd M.	(CA)	1289
WEINTRAUB, D K.	(CA)	1318
WELLS, H L.	(CA)	1322
WILLIAMS, Mary S.	(CA)	1345
WORMINGTON, Peggie .	(CA)	1369
ZEIND, Samir M.	(CA)	1387
BRUNELL, David H.	(CO)	150
GOODYEAR, Mary L. . . .	(CO)	450
MURRAY, William A. . . .	(CO)	882
QUINN, Candy L.	(CO)	1000
RICHMOND, Elizabeth B.	(CO)	1030
CORCORAN, Virginia H.	(CT)	246
DIMATTIA, Susan S. . . .	(CT)	304
FINNUCAN, Louise A. . .	(CT)	379
HELENIUS, Majlen	(CT)	523
JAY, Hilda L.	(CT)	596
ROTH, Alison C.	(CT)	1059
STANKIEWICZ, Carol A.	(CT)	1180
STANYON, Kelly	(CT)	1181
YOUNG, Marianne F. . . .	(CT)	1382
ATKINSON, Rose M. . . .	(DC)	38
BENDER, David R.	(DC)	79
BORYS, Cynthia A.	(DC)	117
BROWN, Dale S.	(DC)	143
CANNAN, Judith P.	(DC)	178

TRAINING (Cont'd)
Training & development

CARTER, Yvonne B. . . .	(DC)	190
EVANS, Frank B.	(DC)	357
HALEY, Roger K.	(DC)	486
HARRIS, Marie	(DC)	505
HOA, Quynh N.	(DC)	545
KENDRICK, Brent L. . . .	(DC)	640
KUPERMAN, Agota M. . .	(DC)	684
LAWTON, Bethany L.	(DC)	705
LEE, Amy C.	(DC)	709
LITTLEJOHN, Grace M. . .	(DC)	734
MARCUM, Deanna B. . .	(DC)	769
MWALIMU, Charles	(DC)	884
SMITH, Kathleen S.	(DC)	1156
SWEENEY, June D.	(DC)	1215
SWEETLAND, Loraine F.	(DC)	1215
UNVER, Amira V.	(DC)	1269
VASLEF, Irene	(DC)	1279
WRIGHT, Arthuree M. . . .	(DC)	1370
YARNALL, James L. . . .	(DC)	1378
HITCHENS, Howard B. . .	(DE)	544
BADGER, Lynn C.	(FL)	44
BONFILI, Barbara J.	(FL)	114
BROWN, Jeanette L.	(FL)	144
CARNAHAN, Mabel A. . .	(FL)	183
DALEHITE, Michele I. . . .	(FL)	270
EL-HADIDY, Bahaa	(FL)	342
FENWICK, Sara I.	(FL)	371
FLEMING, Lois D.	(FL)	384
GOGGIN, Margaret K. . .	(FL)	444
GOSS, Theresa C.	(FL)	453
GULLETTE, Irene	(FL)	477
JOHNSTON, Judy F. . . .	(FL)	610
KASKEY, Sid	(FL)	629
LOWELL, Felice K.	(FL)	744
MISSAVAGE, Leonard . .	(FL)	848
O'CONNOR-LEVY, Linda L.	(FL)	916
PHILLIPS, Donald J.	(FL)	968
PROCTOR, Dixie L.	(FL)	994
SMITH, Alice G.	(FL)	1152
WILER, Linda L.	(FL)	1339
BALL, Ardella P.	(GA)	52
BAUER, Leslie L.	(GA)	65
CLARK, Tommy A.	(GA)	218
CRAFT, Guy C.	(GA)	254
GIBSON, Ricky S.	(GA)	432
KLOPPER, Susan M. . . .	(GA)	662
LAZENBY, Gail R.	(GA)	706
LEWIS, Frank R.	(GA)	723
MARKWELL, Linda G. . .	(GA)	772
MCLAUGHLIN, Laverne L.	(GA)	813
PLOWDEN, Martha W. . . .	(GA)	978
PRESLEY, Roger L.	(GA)	991
RAQUET, Jacqueline R. .	(GA)	1008
ROAN, Tattie W.	(GA)	1038
TOOKES, Amos J.	(GA)	1250
WALKER, Terri L.	(GA)	1296
EPIL, Charlene M.	(HI)	351
FUKUDA, Jodel L.	(HI)	408
JACKSON, Miles M.	(HI)	588
SPENCER, Caroline P. . .	(HI)	1173
CRETH, Sheila D.	(IA)	258
DUTCHER, Terry R.	(IA)	329
GEORGE, Shirley H.	(IA)	428
RUNGE, Kay K.	(IA)	1067
SHEPHERD, Rex L.	(IA)	1127
SWANSON, P A.	(IA)	1213
JONES-LITTEER, Corene A.	(ID)	616
TATE, Karen E.	(ID)	1225
BOWEN, Christopher F. . .	(IL)	120
CHUNG, Alison L.	(IL)	213
CORDONI, Earl C.	(IL)	246
DESSOUKY, Ibtesam . . .	(IL)	296
EVERHART, Paul R.	(IL)	358
FORD, Jennifer D.	(IL)	389
GORDON, Elaine H.	(IL)	451
GOULDING, Mary A. . . .	(IL)	454

TRAINING (Cont'd)
Training & development

GRUNDKE, Patricia J. . .	(IL)	475
GUY, Jeniece N.	(IL)	479
HAFNER, Arthur W.	(IL)	482
HANRATH, Richard A. . .	(IL)	497
HAYES, Hazel I.	(IL)	515
HUSLIG, Dennis M.	(IL)	578
KAPLAN, Sylvia Y.	(IL)	626
KARSTEN, Eileen S. . . .	(IL)	628
KIENE, Andrea L.	(IL)	647
KINNEY, M R.	(IL)	653
LOFTHOUSE, Patricia A.	(IL)	737
LUDWIG, Logan T.	(IL)	747
MAGNUSSEN, Ruth A. . .	(IL)	760
MANN, Vijai S.	(IL)	766
MARSHALL, Kathryn E. .	(IL)	774
MAYFIELD, Maurice K. . .	(IL)	790
MCGINN, Thomas P. . . .	(IL)	806
MENZIES, Pamela C. . . .	(IL)	825
MIFFLIN, Michael J.	(IL)	833
MOZGA, John P.	(IL)	874
PATEL, Jashu	(IL)	947
PIRON, Alice M.	(IL)	975
REITER, Richard R.	(IL)	1022
SCHAACK, Wilma J. . . .	(IL)	1088
SHAEVEL, Evelyn F. . . .	(IL)	1118
SHERMAN, Janice E. . . .	(IL)	1128
VOLKMANN, Carl W. . . .	(IL)	1287
VONDRUSKA, Eloise M. .	(IL)	1288
WALSH, Deborah T.	(IL)	1299
WERNETTE, Janice J. . .	(IL)	1325
WEST, L P.	(IL)	1326
WOODARD, Beth S. . . .	(IL)	1365
ALLEN, Joyce S.	(IN)	15
ALLEN, Patricia J.	(IN)	15
BEILKE, Patricia F.	(IN)	75
BERRY, Marjorie L.	(IN)	90
BONHOMME, Mary S. . .	(IN)	114
BROTON, Cecilianne S. .	(IN)	141
BUDD, Anne D.	(IN)	155
DUHAMELL, Lynnette H.	(IN)	324
GUERRA, Angela M. . . .	(IN)	476
GUYDON, Janet H.	(IN)	479
KRAMER, Arlene H.	(IN)	675
LASHER, Esther L.	(IN)	700
MILLER, Jeanne L.	(IN)	839
MORGAN, James J.	(IN)	864
TIMMER, Julia B.	(IN)	1246
BRADEN, Jan	(KS)	125
COOKE, Bette L.	(KS)	241
EVANS, Constance L. . .	(KS)	356
QUIRING, Virginia M. . . .	(KS)	1000
VOSS, Ernestine D.	(KS)	1289
BUSAM, Emma C.	(KY)	164
HALL, Juanita J.	(KY)	488
JAMES, William	(KY)	592
KOLLOFF, Fred C.	(KY)	669
LINCOLN, Carol S.	(KY)	728
MARTIN, Sandra D.	(KY)	778
NELSON, James A.	(KY)	894
SOMERVILLE, Mary R. . .	(KY)	1167
BRAZILE, Orella R.	(LA)	130
CRETINI, Blanche M. . . .	(LA)	258
CUROL, Helen B.	(LA)	266
DANKNER, Laura R. . . .	(LA)	273
GROSS, Mary D.	(LA)	472
JACKSON, Audrey N. . .	(LA)	586
MARCKS, Carol J.	(LA)	769
SMITH, Ledell B.	(LA)	1157
STEWART, Mary E.	(LA)	1193
ANDERSON, Cheryl M. .	(MA)	22
BOEHME, Richard W. . . .	(MA)	109
BOLAND, Mary J.	(MA)	111
BRAUN, Robin E.	(MA)	130
BRITE, Agnes	(MA)	137
CHANDRASEKHAR, Ratna	(MA)	200
COHEN, Martha J.	(MA)	228
COLLINS, John W.	(MA)	232

TRAINING (Cont'd)
Training & development

EMOND, Kathleen A. . . . (MA) 348
FERGUSON, Roberta J. . (MA) 372
HIMMELSBACH, Carl J. . (MA) 542
LADD, Dorothy P. . . . . . (MA) 687
LEIGHTON, Helene L. . . (MA) 714
MARCY, Henry O. . . . . . (MA) 769
MCCARTHY, Germaine A. (MA) 794
MCDOWELL, Sylvia A. . . (MA) 804
MCLAUGHLIN, Lee R. . . (MA) 813
MEAGHER, Janet H. . . . (MA) 819
NEUBAUER, Richard A. . (MA) 896
NOAH, Carolyn B. . . . . (MA) 906
POLLARD, Russell O. . . . (MA) 981
SCHWARTZ, Frederick E. (MA) 1104
SOVNER-RIBBLER, Judith (MA) 1170
TUCHMAN, Helene L. . . (MA) 1261
UMANA, Christine J. . . . (MA) 1268
VOIGT, John F. . . . . . . (MA) 1287
BOLIN, Nancy C. . . . . . (MD) 112
BRADLEY, Wanda L. . . . (MD) 126
BUCHAN, Patricia C. . . . (MD) 153
BYERLY, Imogene J. . . . (MD) 168
COLLINS, Donna S. . . . . (MD) 232
COOPER, Judith C. . . . . (MD) 243
DAVIS, Bonnie D. . . . . . (MD) 277
DOVE, Samuel . . . . (MD) 315
GLOCK, Martha H. . . . . (MD) 441
GOLDSBERG, Elizabeth D. (MD) 446
GRAVES, Louise H. . . . . (MD) 459
HALL, Mary A. . . . . (MD) 488
HILL, Norma L. . . . . (MD) 540
HOOFNAGLE, Bettea J. . (MD) 556
JACKSON, Carleton . . . . (MD) 587
JACKSON, Doris G. . . . . (MD) 587
JENG, Helene W. . . . . . (MD) 596
KAESSINGER, Carla S. . (MD) 621
LANDRY, Mary E. . . . . . (MD) 693
LAY, Shirley . . . . (MD) 705
LIZER, Bonnie S. . . . . . . (MD) 735
MALLERY, Mary S. . . . . (MD) 763
MARCHIONINI, Gary J. . (MD) 769
MORISSEAU, Anne L. . . (MD) 865
PEARSE, Nancy J. . . . . . (MD) 952
PEDAK-KARI, Maria . . . . (MD) 954
RICHTER, Mary L. . . . . . (MD) 1031
SCHNEIDER, Karl R. . . . (MD) 1097
SCHULMAN, Jacque L. . (MD) 1101
SCHULTZ, Barbara A. . . (MD) 1101
STEPHAN, Sandra S. . . . (MD) 1187
STREIN, Barbara M. . . . . (MD) 1201
SUMLER, Claudia B. . . . (MD) 1209
SUTTON, Sharan D. . . . . (MD) 1212
TOOEY, Mary J. . . . . (MD) 1250
VANCE, Julia M. . . . . . . (MD) 1273
WALLER, Madalyn M. . . (MD) 1298
WASIELEWSKI, Eleanor
   B. . . . . (MD) 1308
ZIMMERMAN, Martha B. (MD) 1389
BINDSCHADLER, Valerie
   V. . . . . (MI) 97
BISSETT, Donald J. . . . . (MI) 100
CARUSO, Genevieve O. . (MI) 190
CRAWFORD, Geraldine H. (MI) 256
CROOKS, James E. . . . . (MI) 260
CURTIS, Jean E. . . . . . . (MI) 267
EL MOUCHI, Joan S. . . . (MI) 346
FORSYTH, Karen R. . . . . (MI) 391
KRENITSKY, Michael V. . (MI) 677
MA, Helen Y. . . . . (MI) 753
MATTESON, James S. . . (MI) 785
MCKINNEY, Ceola S. . . . (MI) 812
PAUL, Thomas A. . . . . . (MI) 949
POWELL, James R. . . . . (MI) 988
ROCKALL, Diane M. . . . (MI) 1046
SICILIANO, Peg P. . . . . . (MI) 1135
SMITH, Nancy J. . . . . . . (MI) 1158
STREETER, Linda D. . . . (MI) 1201
TRENNER, Claudine F. . . (MI) 1255

TRAINING (Cont'd)
Training & development

WOODARD, Beth E. . . . . (MI) 1365
CLARKE, Charlotte C. . . (MN) 218
DALBOTTEN, Mary S. . . (MN) 270
HANKS, Gardner C. . . . . (MN) 496
JENSEN, Wilma M. . . . . (MN) 599
MAHMOODI, Suzanne H. (MN) 760
MCINERNEY, Claire R. . (MN) 809
SANDE, Alice E. . . . . (MN) 1079
WRONKA, Gretchen M. . (MN) 1373
ALEXANDER, Susanna . (MO) 12
BECK, Sara R. . . . . (MO) 71
BROWN, Gerald D. . . . . (MO) 144
ELSESSER, Lionelle H. . . (MO) 346
JENKINS, Harold R. . . . . (MO) 597
KISSANE, Mary K. . . . . . (MO) 656
LENOX, Mary F. . . . . (MO) 715
LINSE, Mary M. . . . . (MO) 731
MACKEY, Neosha A. . . . (MO) 756
NESBITT, John R. . . . . . (MO) 896
RIKLI, Arthur E. . . . . (MO) 1034
SHAUGHNESSY, Thomas
   W. . . . . (MO) 1123
SPALDING, Helen H. . . . (MO) 1171
SULLIVAN, Marilyn G. . . (MO) 1208
YOUNG, Virginia G. . . . . (MO) 1383
BELL, Bernice . . . . (MS) 76
HAUTH, Allan C. . . . . . . (MS) 513
TOWERY, Margaret G. . . (MS) 1252
WALL, Norma F. . . . . . . (MS) 1297
WILROY, Joann . . . . (MS) 1349
BRANDON, Janice R. . . . (MT) 128
CHAPMAN, Peggy H. . . . (NC) 202
CHUNG, Helen S. . . . . . (NC) 213
FERGUSSON, David G. . (NC) 372
HANSEL, Patsy J. . . . . . (NC) 497
HUTTON, Jean R. . . . . . (NC) 579
LAMBREMONT, Jane A. (NC) 691
MURCHISON, Margaret B. (NC) 879
RICHARDSON, Beverly S. (NC) 1029
ROLLINS, Marilyn H. . . . (NC) 1051
SCHELL, Nancy S. . . . . . (NC) 1091
SMITH, Catherine . . . . . (NC) 1153
THOMPSON, Reubin C. . (NC) 1241
TUCKER, Mae S. . . . . . . (NC) 1262
YOUNG, Tommie M. . . . (NC) 1383
KENT, Jeffrey A. . . . . . . (NH) 642
PALMATIER, Susan M. . (NH) 936
ANSELMO, Edith H. . . . . (NJ) 28
BARATTA, Maria . . . . . . (NJ) 55
BERGER, Brenda L. . . . . (NJ) 85
BUCK, Anne M. . . . . (NJ) 153
CHAIKIN, Mary C. . . . . . (NJ) 197
COHEN, Adrea G. . . . . . (NJ) 227
DRECHSEL, Marcella J. . (NJ) 319
FAVORS, Thelma L. . . . . (NJ) 366
GILHEANY, Rosary S. . . (NJ) 434
GRAY, Lee H. . . . . (NJ) 460
HALASZ, Etelka B. . . . . . (NJ) 484
HSU, Hsiu H. . . . . (NJ) 567
KALDENBERG, Katherine
   A. . . . . (NJ) 622
KAZIMIR, Edward O. . . . (NJ) 632
LEE, Minja P. . . . . (NJ) 711
LYNN-NELSON, Gayle . . (NJ) 752
MCGREGOR, Walter . . . (NJ) 808
ODERWALD, Sara M. . . (NJ) 916
REINHARDT, Eileen . . . . (NJ) 1021
SUDALL, Arthur D. . . . . . (NJ) 1206
THRESHER, Jacquelyn E. (NJ) 1243
ANDREWS, Lois W. . . . . (NM) 26
SAMPSON, Ellanie S. . . . (NM) 1078
DONOVAN, Ruth H. . . . . (NV) 312
MORGAN, James E. . . . (NV) 864
ABDULLAH, Bilquis . . . . (NY) 2
ALICEA, Ismael . . . . (NY) 13
ALLERTON, Ellen M. . . . (NY) 16
ARAYA, Rose M. . . . . . . (NY) 30
ARLINGTON, Bill . . . . . . (NY) 31

TRAINING (Cont'd)
Training & development

BAILEY, Joe A. . . . . (NY) 46
BARTENBACH, Martha A. (NY) 60
BAUM, Christina D. . . . . (NY) 66
BENZ, Lieselotte . . . . (NY) 84
BLAKE-O'HOGAN,
  Kathleen E. . . . . (NY) 103
BORRESS, Lewis R. . . . (NY) 117
BRISFJORD, Inez S. . . . (NY) 136
BROWN, Cynthia D. . . . . (NY) 142
BURKE, Joseph A. . . . . . (NY) 160
CALVANO, Margaret . . . (NY) 174
CARTER, Darline L. . . . . (NY) 189
CHANG, Daphne Y. . . . . (NY) 200
CHIANG, Nancy . . . . (NY) 207
CIOPPA, Lawrence . . . . . (NY) 214
COHEN, Rochelle F. . . . . (NY) 229
COOK, Jeannine S. . . . . (NY) 240
DAVIES, Carol A. . . . . . (NY) 277
DICKERSON, D J. . . . . . (NY) 300
FEIGER, Cherie S. . . . . . (NY) 368
GALVIN, Jeanne D. . . . . (NY) 415
GATNER, Elliott S. . . . . . (NY) 422
GESKE, Aina S. . . . . . . (NY) 430
GILLIGAN, Mary A. . . . . (NY) 436
GUBERT, Betty K. . . . . . (NY) 475
HEINTZELMAN, Susan K. (NY) 522
HENDERSON, Janice E. . . (NY) 526
HOPKINS, Lee B. . . . . . (NY) 558
IRONS, Florence E. . . . . (NY) 584
JOHNSON, Nancy B. . . . (NY) 608
KACHALA, Bohdanna I. . (NY) 621
KENDRIC, Marisa A. . . . (NY) 640
KRATZ, Charles E. . . . . . (NY) 676
KRISTIAN, Alice . . . . (NY) 679
LANE, Elizabeth L. . . . . . (NY) 694
LEARMONT, Carol L. . . . (NY) 707
LEE, Sylvia . . . . (NY) 711
LEHNOFF-ONGIRSKI,
  Hannelore . . . . (NY) 713
LEVINE, Margaret A. . . . (NY) 720
LOCHER, Cornelia E. . . . (NY) 736
LOWE, Ida B. . . . . (NY) 743
MARK, Ronnie J. . . . . . . (NY) 770
MARTIN, Margaret B. . . . (NY) 777
MAUTINO, Patricia H. . . . (NY) 787
MCCARTNEY, Margaret
  M. . . . . (NY) 794
MCLAUGHLIN, Pamela W. (NY) 813
MEDEIROS, Joseph . . . . (NY) 820
MEHL, Cathy A. . . . . (NY) 821
MILLER-KUMMERFELD,
  Elizabeth . . . . (NY) 843
MURDOCK, William J. . . . (NY) 880
NARBY, Ann E. . . . . (NY) 888
PALMER, Robert B. . . . . (NY) 936
PALMIERI, Lucien E. . . . (NY) 937
PENICH, Sonia S. . . . . . (NY) 956
QUAIN, Julie R. . . . . (NY) 999
REEPMEYER, Marie C. . . (NY) 1016
ROCQUE, Bernice L. . . . (NY) 1046
ROHMANN, Gloria P. . . . (NY) 1050
ROSAR, Virginia W. . . . . (NY) 1054
SALTUS, Winifred T. . . . (NY) 1077
SCARANO, Lisa C. . . . . (NY) 1087
SHELTON, Anita L. . . . . (NY) 1126
SHERWIG, Mary J. . . . . (NY) 1129
SIMCOE, Darryl D. . . . . (NY) 1139
SMITH, Annie J. . . . . . . (NY) 1152
SPAIN, Frances L. . . . . . (NY) 1170
SPERR BRISFJORD, Inez
  L. . . . . (NY) 1173
STOOPS, Louise . . . . . . (NY) 1198
TICE, Margaret E. . . . . . (NY) 1244
TRAGER, Phyllis H. . . . . (NY) 1253
TREFRY, Mary G. . . . . . (NY) 1255
VAILLANCOURT, Pauline
  M. . . . . (NY) 1271
WENDT, Mary E. . . . . . . (NY) 1324

TRAINING (Cont'd)
Training & development

WESTERLING, Mary L. . . (NY) 1327
WIGG, Ristiina M. . . . . . (NY) 1337
WILBUR, Helen L. . . . . . (NY) 1338
WILEY, Deborah E. . . . . (NY) 1339
WOODS, Regina C. . . . . (NY) 1367
ARNOLD, Gary J. . . . . . (OH) 33
BAILEY, Lois E. . . . . . . (OH) 46
BAKER, Carole A. . . . . . (OH) 48
BALL, Diane A. . . . . (OH) 52
BAYER, Bernard I. . . . . . (OH) 67
BLACK, Frances P. . . . . (OH) 101
BOWIE, Angela B. . . . . . (OH) 121
CHRISTOU, Corilee S. . . (OH) 212
CLARK, Marilyn L. . . . . . (OH) 217
CONLIFFE, Bobbi L. . . . . (OH) 236
CRAM, Mary E. . . . . (OH) 255
DZIEDZINA, Christine A. (OH) 331
ERWIN, Nancy S. . . . . . (OH) 353
GILROY, Dorothy A. . . . . (OH) 437
GROHL, Arlene P. . . . . . (OH) 471
HAMBLEY, Susan L. . . . (OH) 490
JACOBER, Sheryl A. . . . (OH) 589
JOHNSON, Debbie L. . . . (OH) 603
KELLER, Marlo L. . . . . . (OH) 635
NOLAN, Patrick B. . . . . . (OH) 907
PAK, Moo J. . . . . (OH) 935
PALMER, Virginia E. . . . (OH) 937
REESE, Gregory L. . . . . (OH) 1016
REPP, Joan M. . . . . (OH) 1024
RODDA, Donna S. . . . . . (OH) 1047
SCHUITEMA, Joan E. . . (OH) 1101
SHARP, Linda C. . . . . . (OH) 1122
TEPE, Ann S. . . . . (OH) 1231
TILLMAN, Linda M. . . . . (OH) 1245
WAGAR, Elsa A. . . . . . . (OH) 1290
BOOTENHOFF, Rebecca
  J. . . . . (OK) 116
COCHENOUR, John J. . . (OK) 225
MADAUS, J R. . . . . (OK) 758
MATHIS, Barbara B. . . . (OK) 784
STURDIVANT, Nan J. . . (OK) 1205
WEAVER, Pamela J. . . . (OK) 1312
WRIGHT, Patricia Y. . . . . (OK) 1372
BILLETER, Anne M. . . . . (OR) 96
BOES, Rachel M. . . . . . (OR) 110
FELDMAN, Marianne L. . (OR) 369
GAULKE, Mary F. . . . . . (OR) 423
SALMON, Kay H. . . . . . (OR) 1077
SHAVER, Donna B. . . . . (OR) 1123
TASHJIAN, Sharon A. . . (OR) 1224
ALBRECHT, Lois K. . . . . (PA) 10
AMICONE, Janice L. . . . (PA) 20
BACK, Andrew W. . . . . . (PA) 43
BROADBENT, H E. . . . . (PA) 138
BROWN, David E. . . . . . (PA) 143
BRYANT, Lillian D. . . . . . (PA) 152
CRAUMER, Patricia A. . . (PA) 255
DOW, Elizabeth H. . . . . (PA) 315
FARREN, Ann L. . . . . . . (PA) 365
FREIVALDS, Dace I. . . . (PA) 402
FU, Clare S. . . . . (PA) 407
GARRISON, Guy G. . . . . (PA) 420
GRIFFIN, Mary A. . . . . . (PA) 468
HUGHES, Marilyn A. . . . (PA) 572
IVAK, Patricia A. . . . . . . (PA) 585
JOSEPH, Elizabeth T. . . . (PA) 617
KEOGH, Judith L. . . . . . (PA) 643
KIMMEL, Margaret M. . . . (PA) 649
MESSICK, Karen J. . . . . (PA) 828
MILLIGAN, Edna H. . . . . (PA) 843
NAISMITH, Patricia A. . . (PA) 887
ORSAG, Ann . . . . (PA) 927
POLLIS, Angela R. . . . . . (PA) 981
PROMOS, Marianne . . . . (PA) 995
ROSS, Nina M. . . . . (PA) 1058
RUPERT, Elizabeth A. . . . (PA) 1068
SCHEEREN, Judith A. . . (PA) 1090
SCHNEIDER, Louise H. . (PA) 1097

TRAINING (Cont'd)
Training & development

SIMONE-HOHE, M J. . . . . (PA) 1141
SNOWTEN, Renee Y. . . . (PA) 1164
STANLEY, Nancy M. . . . . (PA) 1180
SWEENEY, Del . . . . (PA) 1215
SWIGART, William E. . . . (PA) 1216
WHITMAN, Mary L. . . . . (PA) 1333
WOODRUFF, William M. . (PA) 1366
WRIGHT, Irene R. . . . . . (PA) 1371
YAPLE, Deborah A. . . . . (PA) 1377
YERGER, George A. . . . (PA) 1379
GUILLEMARD DE
    COLON, Teresita . . . . (PR) 476
LEON, Carmencita H. . . . (PR) 716
PADUA, Flores N. . . . . . (PR) 934
DAVIS, Patsy M. . . . . . . (SC) 280
HIPPS, Gary M. . . . . (SC) 543
SMITH, Nancy . . . . (SC) 1158
DERTIEN, James L. . . . . (SD) 294
COOKE, Anna L. . . . . . . (TN) 240
EDWARDS, Rela G. . . . . (TN) 337
SELIG, Susan A. . . . . . . (TN) 1113
SLOAN, Lynette S. . . . . . (TN) 1149
WILBURN, Clouse R. . . . (TN) 1338
WILLIAMS, Marsha D. . . (TN) 1345
ALMQUIST, Sharon G. . . (TX) 17
ANDERSON, Eliane G. . . (TX) 22
ARNOLD, Gaye C. . . . . . (TX) 33
BELL, Jo A. . . . . (TX) 77
BIERI, Sandra J. . . . . (TX) 95
CAMPBELL, Shirley A. . . (TX) 177
CARDENAS, Martha L. . (TX) 180
DOWNINS, Jeffery G. . . (TX) 317
FISCHER, Beverly J. . . . (TX) 379
GOERDT, Arthur L. . . . . (TX) 443
GOTHIA, Blanche . . . . . . (TX) 453
GUTHRIE, Melinda L. . . . (TX) 479
HOOTON, Virginia A. . . . (TX) 557
HORNAK, Anna F. . . . . . (TX) 559
KELLOUGH, Jean L. . . . . (TX) 637
KLAPPERSACK, Dennis . (TX) 657
LEE, Regina H. . . . . (TX) 711
MACBETH, Helen L. . . . . (TX) 754
MARKS, Mary L. . . . . . . (TX) 771
MAULSBY, Tommie L. . . (TX) 787
MAYO, Helen G. . . . . . . (TX) 790
MERCHANT, Cheryl N. . (TX) 825
MONTGOMERY, Wanda
    W. . . . . (TX) 856
MUELLER, Peggy . . . . . . (TX) 875
PHILLIPS, Carol B. . . . . . (TX) 967
ROBERTS, Ernest J. . . . (TX) 1040
RODE, Shelley J. . . . . . . (TX) 1047
SCHUMANN, Iris T. . . . . (TX) 1103
SELWYN, Laurie . . . . . . (TX) 1114
SHIH, Chia C. . . . . (TX) 1130
SNELL, Marykay H. . . . . (TX) 1163
VAUGHN, Frances A. . . . (TX) 1280
WILSON, Thomas C. . . . (TX) 1353
DAY, J D. . . . . (UT) 282
HEFNER, Loretta L. . . . . (UT) 520
JENSEN, Charla J. . . . . . (UT) 598
OLSEN, Randy J. . . . . . . (UT) 921
SCOTT, Patricia L. . . . . . (UT) 1107
ANDERSON, Marcia M. . (VA) 24
BISCHOFF, Frances A. . (VA) 99
CAPUTO, Anne S. . . . . . (VA) 180
DARDEN, Sue E. . . . . . . (VA) 274
DODSON, Whit . . . . (VA) 308
DUNNIGAN, Mary C. . . . (VA) 327
HABAN, Mary F. . . . . . . (VA) 480
HUMMEL, Ray O. . . . . . . (VA) 573
KNIGHT, Nancy H. . . . . . (VA) 664
LEATHER, Deborah J. . . (VA) 707
LEE, Carl R. . . . . (VA) 709
LOY, Dennis C. . . . . (VA) 745
ROBISON, Dennis E. . . . (VA) 1045
SCHEITLE, Janet M. . . . . (VA) 1091
SPRENGER, Suzanne F. (VA) 1176

TRAINING (Cont'd)
Training & development

STURGIS, Sibyl A. . . . . . (VA) 1205
TYSON, John C. . . . . . . (VA) 1267
ULBRICH, David E. . . . . (VA) 1268
VAN SICKLEN, Lindsay L. (VA) 1277
WOODALL, Nancy C. . . (VA) 1365
BATTEY, Jean D. . . . . . . (VT) 64
REED, Sally G. . . . . (VT) 1015
BAGG, Deborah L. . . . . . (WA) 45
CARRIGAN, Marietta R. . (WA) 186
DEDAS, Madelyn W. . . . (WA) 286
GILDENHAR, Janet . . . . (WA) 434
JENNERICH, Edward J. . (WA) 598
JONES, Faye E. . . . . (WA) 613
PRESS, Nancy O. . . . . . (WA) 991
SAUTER, Sylvia E. . . . . . (WA) 1085
SKELLEY, Cornelia A. . . (WA) 1145
STORDAHL, Beth A. . . . (WA) 1198
TOLLIVER, Barbara J. . . (WA) 1248
ULRICH, Pamela L. . . . . (WA) 1268
WEBER, Joan L. . . . . . . (WA) 1314
WIEMAN, Jean M. . . . . . (WA) 1336
BELLOWS, Leslie A. . . . (WI) 78
BLACKWELDER, Mary B. (WI) 102
EBERT, John J. . . . . (WI) 334
GORSEGNER, Betty D. . (WI) 452
HEITKEMPER, Elsie M. . (WI) 523
KRCHMAR, Sandra L. . . (WI) 677
LUECHT, Richard M. . . . (WI) 747
PITEL, Vonna J. . . . . (WI) 976
WEINGAND, Darlene E. . (WI) 1318
FIDLER, Leah J. . . . . (WV) 375
COTTAM, Keith M. . . . . . (WY) 250
OSBORN, Lucie P. . . . . . (WY) 927
BOUEY, Elaine F. . . . . . . (AB) 119
HARVEY, Carl G. . . . . . . (AB) 509
AUFIERO, Joan I. . . . . . . (BC) 39
HAABNIIT, Ene . . . . (BC) 480
HAYCOCK, Kenneth R. . (BC) 515
LEITH, Anna R. . . . . (BC) 714
SIFTON, Patricia A. . . . . (BC) 1137
WEESE, Dwain W. . . . . . (BC) 1316
PENNEY, Pearce J. . . . . (NF) 957
LYNCH, Darrell B. . . . . . (NS) 751
TAYLOR, Hugh A. . . . . . (NS) 1227
ARMBRUST, Susan P. . . (ON) 31
BAYNE, Jennifer M. . . . . (ON) 67
BLACK, Jane L. . . . . (ON) 101
FITZGERALD, Dorothy A. (ON) 382
GREENWOOD, Jan . . . . (ON) 465
GUHERIDGE, Allison A. . (ON) 476
HSU, Peter T. . . . . (ON) 567
KENDALL, Sandra A. . . . (ON) 640
KING, Olive E. . . . . (ON) 652
LAM, Vinh T. . . . . (ON) 689
MACDONALD, Marcia H. (ON) 754
MORIN-LABATUT, Gisele (ON) 865
OLSHEN, Toni . . . . (ON) 922
RODGER, Stephen J. . . . (ON) 1047
SELLERS, Alexander G. . (ON) 1114
SMITH, Anne C. . . . . (ON) 1152
TEMPLIN, Dorothy . . . . . (ON) 1231
TUDOR, Dean F. . . . . . . (ON) 1262
VALENTINE, Scott . . . . . (ON) 1271
WALSH, Sandra A. . . . . (ON) 1300
WEBB, Mary J. . . . . (ON) 1313
WEIHS, Jean . . . . (ON) 1317
WEIR, Leslie . . . . (ON) 1319
WILBURN, Marion T. . . . (ON) 1338
BOLDUC, Yves . . . . (PQ) 112
DESROCHERS, Monique (PQ) 295
FERAHIAN, Salwa . . . . . (PQ) 371
FOERTIN, Yves P. . . . . . (PQ) 387
GAUDREAU, Louis . . . . (PQ) 422
GODIN, Maud . . . . (PQ) 442
JANIK, Sophie . . . . (PQ) 593
KOBER, Gary L. . . . . . . (PQ) 666
MANSEAU, Edith . . . . . . (PQ) 767
MENARD, Francoise . . . (PQ) 823

TRAINING (Cont'd)

Training & development

Specialty	Name	State	Page
	PIGGOTT, Sylvia E.	(PQ)	972
	RICHARDS, Stella	(PQ)	1028
	SIMON, Marie L.	(PQ)	1140
	FIELDEN, Janet	(SK)	376
	MCLEOD, Karen E.	(SK)	814
	MOSS, Loretta E.	(CSR)	872
	GRATTAN, Robert	(FRN)	458
	WACHTER, Margery C.	(FRN)	1290
	YEN, David S.	(HKG)	1379
	STONE, Clarence W.	(IDN)	1197
	DUFFIN, Elizabeth A.	(IRE)	323
	HADDAD, Aida N.	(ISR)	481
	WASERMAN, Barbara	(ISR)	1307
	MANSINGH, Laxmi	(JAM)	767
	BROCKMAN, Norbert C.	(KEN)	138
	IRURIA, Daniel M.	(KEN)	584
	SNYDER, Lisa A.	(MAL)	1165
	BARBERENA, Elsa	(MEX)	55
	BOOM, Ramon A.	(MEX)	115
	ABOYADE, Beatrice O.	(NGR)	2
	AFOLAYAN, Matthew A.	(NGR)	7
	ONONOGBO, Raphael U.	(NGR)	924
	DE CASTRO, Elinore H.	(PHP)	285
	VALLEJO, Rosa M.	(PHP)	1271
	ROSSOUW, Steve F.	(SAF)	1059
	LIN, Chih F.	(TAI)	727
	YANG, Mei H.	(TAI)	1377
Training & development, legal research	MCGUIRL, Marlene C.	(DC)	808
Training & development management	HOCKER, Justine L.	(PA)	545
Training & development micrographic syst	CORNELIUS, Charlene E.	(WI)	246
Training & development of library staff	JEANNENEY, Mary L.	(NY)	596
Training & development of part-timers	DINDAYAL, Joyce S.	(NY)	304
Training & development of personnel	WILLIAMS, Nancy F.	(GA)	1345
Training & development of staff	BRICKER, Will S.	(PA)	135
Training & development programs	BUTLER, David W.	(CA)	166
Training & development records mgmt	CORNELIUS, Charlene E.	(WI)	246
Training & development, retreats	CLUFF, E D.	(TX)	223
Training & development, teaching	CURRAN, William M.	(PQ)	266
Training & development workshops	TAYLOR, Arthur R.	(MO)	1226
Training & documentation	ANDREWS, Chris C.	(CT)	26
	ANDERSON, Thomas G.	(GA)	25
	ECKERSON, Gale E.	(MA)	334
	SARAIDARIDIS, Susan B.	(MA)	1082
	WUNDERLICH, Clifford S.	(MA)	1374
	BOBKA, Marlene S.	(MD)	108
	CHAPMAN, Janet L.	(NJ)	202
	MLYNAR, Mary	(OH)	850
Training & education	KAGER, Jeffrey F.	(PA)	621
	CORBEIL, Lizette	(PQ)	245
	KOGA, Setsuko	(JAP)	668
	BASCOM, James F.	(SDA)	62
Training & instruction	CARTER-LOVEJOY, Steven H.	(VA)	190
Training & instructional development	JASSAL, Raghbir S.	(NM)	595
Training & orientation	WINIARZ, Elizabeth	(PQ)	1355
Training & orienting	WAGNER, Judith O.	(OH)	1292
Training & program development	MELTON, Vivian B.	(OH)	823
Training & project implementation	BEDOR, Kathleen M.	(MN)	73
	HSU, Elizabeth L.	(NY)	567
Training & public information	GILLIGAN, Julie	(NY)	436
Training & public presentations	MADDEN, Susan B.	(WA)	758
Training & public service	DERRICKSON, Margaret	(NY)	294
Training & records development	BUTLER, Tyrone G.	(NY)	167
Training & seminars	TUNG, Sandra J.	(CA)	1263
Training & staff development	RUDDOCK, Velda I.	(CA)	1065
	JUROW, Susan R.	(DC)	620
	TYLER, Audrey Q.	(GA)	1266
	CRIST, Margaret L.	(MA)	259
	HANSSEN, Nancy E.	(MA)	499
	GIORDANO, Frederick S.	(NY)	438
	HUNT, Suellyn	(NY)	575
Training & supervising circulation staff	MANOVILLE, Susanne	(PE)	767
Training & supervising new staff	RICHARDSON, Emma G.	(NY)	1029
Training & supervision	BRIERTY, Carol A.	(FL)	135
	MCCUNE, Lois M.	(IN)	801
Training & supervision of volunteers	WILLIAMS, Suzanne C.	(TX)	1346
Training & support	IVERSON, Diann S.	(CA)	585
Training & system implementation	JOHNSON, Jane S.	(IL)	605
Training & teaching	PIERRE, Zenata W.	(OR)	972
Training & teaching library courses	KUJOORY, Parvin	(TX)	683
Training & training materials	MARBAN, Ricio	(GUA)	768
Training & translating	DRUKKER, Alexander E.	(DE)	320
Training & use of volunteers	KILLEEN, Erlene B.	(VA)	648
Training & user documentation	DIXON, Edith M.	(WI)	306
Training & user education	SEELEY, Catherine R.	(ME)	1111
Training & user support	VEATCH, Laurie L.	(DC)	1280
Training & workshops	ROSSMAN, Muriel J.	(MN)	1059
Training art educators & docents	GENSHAFT, Carole M.	(OH)	427
Training attorneys on databases	DONNELLY, Kathleen	(OH)	311
Training, bibliographic instruction	WIBLE, Joseph G.	(CA)	1335
Training catalogers	WANG, Ann C.	(DC)	1302
Training children's services volunteers	OVERMYER, Elizabeth C.	(CA)	931
Training development	CASTRO, Maritza	(PR)	194
Training development & administration	WALTERS, Carol G.	(NC)	1301
Training, development, & documentation	KAPLAN, Robin	(CA)	626
Training documentation	HIRONS, Jean L.	(DC)	543
	GAROOGIAN, Rhoda	(NY)	420
Training elementary library volunteers	HLUHANY, Patricia	(PA)	544
Training end-users	REID, Valerie L.	(MI)	1019
	ETTL, Lorraine R.	(ND)	356
Training end-users searching	BROWN, Carolyn M.	(GA)	142
Training for adult services	SPYROS, Marsha L.	(NY)	1177
Training for automation use	JUERGENS, Bonnie	(TX)	619
Training for catalogers	TRUMPLER, Elisabeth	(PA)	1259
Training for church librarians	JENSEN, Wilma M.	(MN)	599
Training for online searchers	HAWK, Susan A.	(MD)	513
Training for online searching	BROWN, Helen A.	(NE)	144
	HORWITZ, Seth	(PA)	561
Training for reference services	MILLSAP, Gina J.	(MO)	844
Training for systems	VANDERPOORTEN, Mary B.	(AL)	1274
Training for systems use	UPHAM, Lois N.	(SC)	1269
Training in cataloging	STEWART, Richard A.	(IL)	1193
Training in microcomputer use	ANGLIN, Richard V.	(NY)	28
	DYER, Barbara M.	(TN)	330
Training in microcomputers	PLAZA, Joyce S.	(NJ)	978
Training in records management	ARDERN, Christine M.	(ON)	31
Training indexers	BERNAL, Rose M.	(NY)	88
Training indexing & classification	LOMBARDI, Mary L.	(CA)	738
Training information analysts	HALL, Homer J.	(NJ)	488
Training information desk personnel	DUCHARME, Judith C.	(NM)	322
Training information specialists & users	COURRIER, Yves G.	(FRN)	251
Training library assistants	SHEARIN, Cynthia E.	(NJ)	1124
Training library automation software	DOEHLERT, Irene C.	(CA)	308
Training library volunteers	OFFERMAN, Mary C.	(IA)	917
Training new staff	WANG, Margaret K.	(DE)	1303
	PHILLIPS, Richard F.	(NJ)	969
Training non-professionals	HAMMER, Louise K.	(IL)	493
Training of boards of trustees	STIEGEMEYER, Nancy H.	(MO)	1193
Training of catalogers	GRIFFIN, Karen D.	(OR)	468
Training of computer searchers	SOPELAK, Mary J.	(NY)	1168
Training of medical students	LANDAU, Lucille	(OH)	692
Training of online search techniques	KAMINECKI, Ronald M.	(IL)	624
Training of student assistants	GLADIEUX, Mary B.	(MO)	439
Training of volunteers	FOX, Estella E.	(KY)	394
	AROKSAAR, Richard D.	(WA)	34
Training on automated systems	WELCH, Grace D.	(ON)	1321
Training on micros & software	KANNEL, Ene	(ON)	625
Training paraprofessionals	JAGODZINSKI, Cecile M.	(IL)	591
Training personnel	HACKMAN, Mary H.	(MD)	481
Training research analysts	BERWICK, Mary C.	(PA)	91
Training school librarians	GAUDET, Jean A.	(VA)	422
Training staff & users	NDENGA, Viola W.	(MI)	890
Training, staff development, teaching	FALANGA, Rosemarie E.	(CA)	361
Training staff in technology	SCHREFFLER, Lynne W.	(PA)	1099
Training student aides	GORMAN, Mary B.	(NY)	452
Training student library aids	AVERY, Linda S.	(NM)	42
Training student-related personnel	WALLER, Elaine J.	(MI)	1298
Training, supervising & development	FUN, Winnie W.	(VA)	409
Training systems design, analysis	SYPERT, Clyde F.	(CA)	1217
Training technical services personnel	GOODWIN, Vania M.	(IN)	450
Training technology research	SNYDER, Cathrine E.	(TN)	1164
Training the blind	BEIMAN, Frances M.	(NJ)	75

TRAINING (Cont'd)

Training users of ILS, online catalog	PRESLAR, M G.	(TN)	991
Training workshops	HIRONS, Jean L.	(DC)	543
Trustee training & education	STEVENSON, Marilyn E.	(CA)	1191
User & specialist training	CROWTHER, Warren W.	(CSR)	262
User documentation & training	DIENER, Carol W.	(MD)	302
User library training	SCHAPIRO, Benjamin H.	(IL)	1090
User services & training	BAZAN, Lorraine R.	(CA)	68
User training	CHU, Felix T.	(IL)	212
	SLAWNIAK, Patricia M. .	(IL)	1148
	CUTLER, C M.	(AB)	268
User training & documentation	GREEN-MALONEY, Nancy	(CA)	465
Volunteer training	YEE, J E.	(WA)	1379
Westlaw & LEXIS training	DOWLING, Shelley L. ...	(DC)	316
Writing, editing, & training	SYMES, Dal S.	(WA)	1217

TRANSACTIONS

Financial information & transaction	RANDOLPH, Kevin H. ...	(CA)	1007
Transactions network markets	WRIGHT, Bernell	(NY)	1370

TRANSCRIPTIONS

Disc transcriptions	GERBER, Warren C. ...	(NJ)	428
Transcribing archive recordings	PENGELLY, Joe	(ENG)	956

TRANSFER

Community information transfer	SHIRK, John C.	(MN)	1131
Information transfer	JASON, Nora H.	(MD)	595
International information transfer	GREENFIELD, Stanley R.	(NY)	464
Medical information transfer	SEWELL, Winifred	(MD)	1118
Rural health information transfer	BOISSY, Robert W.	(NY)	111
Technology & information transfer	HATTERY, Lowell H. ...	(MD)	512
Technology transfer	WILDE, Daniel U.	(CT)	1338
	SWEENEY, Del	(PA)	1215
	LEHMANN, Edward J. ..	(VA)	713
Telecommunications & info transfer	RESNIK, Linda I.	(DC)	1024
User education & information transfer	BOROVANSKY, Vladimir T.	(AZ)	117

TRANSIT

Mass transit information	KANE, Deborah A.	(TX)	624

TRANSLATION

Abstracting & translating	SPRY, Patricia	(ON)	1176
Abstracting, editing, translation	REITH, Louis J.	(DC)	1022
Bibliography, translating, editing	KRAMER-GREENE, Judith	(NY)	675
Bilingual translation	CHANG, Joseph I.	(NJ)	200
Foreign language translating	HOMNACK, Mark	(CA)	555
Foreign language translation	SICILIANO, Peg P.	(MI)	1135
French, Arabic, English translation	YASSA, Lucie M.	(CA)	1378
Music theory in translation	THYM, Jurgen	(NY)	1243
Proofreading & translation	SMYTH, John	(PQ)	1162
Prose & poetry translation	TABORY, Maxim	(NC)	1219
Scientific translation	SCHUTZ, Robert S.	(OH)	1103
Swedish translating	CARLSON, Kathleen A. .	(NM)	182
Training & translating	DRUKKER, Alexander E. .	(DE)	320
Translating	SABOVIK, Pavel	(AZ)	1073
	WARREN, Lois B.	(IN)	1306
	WALD, Ingeborg	(NY)	1294
Translating Persian	BAGHAL-KAR, Vali E. ..	(TX)	45
Translation	GUENTHER, Charles J. .	(MO)	475
	MONTEIRO, George	(RI)	856
	HUYGEN, Eva	(SC)	580
	FRANZELLO, Joseph J. .	(TX)	398
	GRENIER, Serge	(PQ)	467
Translation Spanish to English	DRIVER, Marjorie G. ...	(GU)	320
Writing & translating	LIU, David T.	(TX)	734

TRANSLATIONS

Cataloging translations	NOWAK, Ildiko D.	(IL)	911
Editor of legal translations	SCHLACKS, Charles ...	(CA)	1093
Japanese technical translations	QUINN, Ralph M.	(NJ)	1000
Producing translations database	NOWAK, Ildiko D.	(IL)	911
Publisher of legal translations	SCHLACKS, Charles ...	(CA)	1093
Researcher of legal translations	SCHLACKS, Charles ...	(CA)	1093

TRANSLATIONS (Cont'd)

Scientific & technical translations	SAMSON, Mary	(ON)	1079
Translations	WRIGHT, Kathleen J. ...	(CA)	1372
	GREENE, Danielle L. ...	(DC)	463
	HOPPER, Mildry S.	(DC)	558
	PRITCHARD, Robert W. .	(MA)	994
	THOMPSON, Michael E. .	(MD)	1240
	ROSENSTEIN, Susan J. .	(NJ)	1057
Translations availability searches	NOWAK, Ildiko D.	(IL)	911
Translations databases	SAMSON, Mary	(ON)	1079
Translations identification	HIMMELSBACH, Carl J. .	(MA)	542
Turkish literature, English translations	BILEYDI, Lois G.	(MN)	96

TRANSPORTATION (See also Highway, Maritime, Railroads, Transit)

Highway research transportation info	MOBLEY, Arthur B.	(DC)	851
Public transportation & urban planning	PRESBY, Richard A. ...	(CA)	990
Transportation	HOFSTADTER, Marc E. .	(CA)	549
	MAYERS, Karen A.	(CA)	789
	KOENEMAN, Joyce W. .	(DC)	668
	GROSSMAN, David G. ...	(IL)	473
	RAMM, Dorothy V.	(IL)	1005
	PEARLSTEIN, Toby	(MA)	952
	OYER, Kenneth E.	(NE)	932
	BLOECHLE, Marie K. ...	(TX)	106
	HATHAWAY, Kay E.	(VA)	512
	BROOKING, Ruth P. ...	(ON)	140
	BUISMAN, Maria J.	(ON)	156
	CROXFORD, Agnes M. .	(ON)	262
Transportation accidents	BARTH, Nancy L.	(CA)	61
Transportation databases	BROWN-WEBB, Deborah D.	(TX)	149
	WARREN, Lois M.	(BC)	1306
Transportation history of California	HANEL, Mary A.	(CA)	495
Transportation information	REILLY, Francis S.	(DC)	1020
	KANE, Deborah A.	(TX)	624
Transportation information & research	ARMEIT, Marilyn	(NY)	32
Transportation reference & databases	CORNELL, Pamela J. ...	(MN)	246
Transportation safety research support	GATTIS, R G.	(MI)	422
Urban transportation	KAWABATA, Julie	(OR)	632

TRAVEL (See also Tourism)

Corporate travel	HERNDON, Stan J.	(VT)	532
Online shopping & travel	WALSH, Mark L.	(CT)	1300
Travel & tourism	JANSEN, Guenter A. ...	(NY)	593
Travel & tourism information systems	MOLL, Joy K.	(NJ)	853
Travel directory publications	BUZAN, Norma J.	(MI)	168
Travel for the handicapped	SHANEFIELD, Irene D. ...	(PQ)	1120
Travel industry databases	OGREN, Mark S.	(IL)	918
Travel photography & lectures	PETERSON, Mildred O. .	(IL)	964

TREASURY

Treasury Department fiscal records	SHERMAN, William F. ..	(DC)	1128

TREATIES

International law & treaties	MCDONALD, Ellen J. ...	(MA)	802
International treaty indexing	KAVASS, Igor I.	(TN)	631

TRENDS

Future trends in libraries	SMALLS, Mary L.	(SC)	1151
Library trend research	LAGIES, Meinhart J.	(CA)	688
Market trends	BRAIMON, Margie S. ...	(NJ)	127
Professional trends & issues	PHELPS, Thomas C. ...	(DC)	967
Trend predictions & monitoring	BUNCE, George D.	(ENG)	157
Trends in computer systems	BILES, Mark J.	(NJ)	96

TRIBAL

Development of tribal & Indian libraries	PATTERSON, Lotsee ...	(OK)	948
Tribal history & culture	HENDRICKS, Thom	(ND)	527

TROUBLESHOOTING

General troubleshooting | SULLIVAN, Stephen W. . . | (NY) | 1208
Troubleshooting information
  bottlenecks | SAUTER, Sylvia E. . . . . . | (WA) | 1085

TRUSTEESHIP (See also Boards)

Friends & trustees groups | WINSLOW, Carol M. . . . | (IN) | 1355
Library trustee | MILLENDER, Dharathola . | (IN) | 835
| EARNSHAW, Donald C. . | (MO) | 332
| CONDIT, Martha O. . . . | (NJ) | 235
Library trustee education | PANZ, Richard . . . . | (NY) | 938
Library trustee matters | KREAMER, Jean T. . . . | (LA) | 677
Library trustee orientation | GROSS, Richard F. . . . | (ME) | 472
Library trustees | CARRINGTON, Virginia F. | (CT) | 186
Library trusteeship | MILLER, Deborah . . . . . . | (IL) | 837
| KIRKESY, Oliver M. . . . . | (MI) | 655
Library trusteeship, educ &
  development | WILLIAMS, Lorraine O. . | (ON) | 1344
Public library trustee | FAHERTY, Robert L. . . . | (DC) | 361
| KIRSCHENBAUM, Arthur
  S. . . . . | (DC) | 655
| HARRER, Gustave A. . . . | (FL) | 503
| KOHRT, Ruth D. . . . . . | (IA) | 669
| COLE, Jack W. . . . . . . | (MN) | 230
| MANTHEY, Carolyn M. . . | (NJ) | 767
Public library trustee board | GRUHL, Andrea M. . . . . | (DC) | 474
Public library trustee relations | JANK, David A. . . . . . . | (MA) | 593
Public library trustees | LANGE, Clifford E. . . . . | (CA) | 695
| GRALAPP, Marcelee G. . | (CO) | 457
| LARSON, Phyllis S. . . . . | (PA) | 699
Public library trusteeship | GORDON, Lewis A. . . . . | (IL) | 451
Training of boards of trustees | STIEGEMEYER, Nancy H. | (MO) | 1193
Trustee | KONZEN, Brian E. . . . . . | (IL) | 671
Trustee consulting | SWAN, James A. . . . . . . | (KS) | 1213
Trustee development | MOORE, Mary Y. . . . . . | (WA) | 860
Trustee education | SWAN, James A. . . . . . . | (KS) | 1213
Trustee education consulting | LYNCH, Minnie L. . . . . | (LA) | 752
Trustee educator | YOUNG, Virginia G. . . . | (MO) | 1383
Trustee/librarian relations | BALCOM, Kathleen M. . . | (IL) | 51
Trustee training & education | STEVENSON, Marilyn E. | (CA) | 1191
Trustees | BERRY, Louise P. . . . . . | (CT) | 90
Trustees & friends | CRABB, Elizabeth A. . . . | (TX) | 254
Trustees of public libraries | MOORE, Bessie B. . . . . | (DC) | 858
Trusteeship | WUNDERLICH, Nina M. . | (IL) | 1374
| MOLONEY, Kevin F. . . . | (MA) | 853
| JACKSON, Elmer M. . . . | (MD) | 587
| REEVES, Joan R. . . . . . | (RI) | 1016
Trusteeship in governance | BAUGHMAN, James C. . | (MA) | 66
Trusteeships | ALLAIN, Alexander P. . . . | (LA) | 13

TUNE

Hymn tune indexing | TEMPERLEY, Nicholas . . | (IL) | 1230

TURKISH

Turkish literature, English translations | BILEYDI, Lois G. . . . . . | (MN) | 96

TURNKEY (See also Computers)

Turnkey automated information
  systems | SIDMAN, George C. . . . . | (CA) | 1135
Turnkey vendor | MATTHEWS, Joseph R. . | (CA) | 785

TUTORING (See also Instruction, Teaching)

Adult literacy tutor trainer | KORNITSKY, Judith M. . | (FL) | 672
Computer tutorials database
  searching | CARUSO, Nicholas C. . . | (PA) | 190
Laubach tutor training | TEUBERT, Lola H. . . . . | (IN) | 1233
Tutoring English as a foreign
  language | NORRIS, Loretta W. . . . | (DC) | 909

TWENTIETH CENTURY

American 20th century records | ASHKENAS, Bruce F. . . | (VA) | 36
19th & 20th century art | SCHNEIDER, Karen . . . | (DC) | 1097
19th century & 20th century art | HATCHER, Nolan C. . . | (GA) | 511
19th century & 20th century Engl lit | HATCHER, Nolan C. . . | (GA) | 511

TWENTIETH CENTURY (Cont'd)

19th century & 20th century music | HATCHER, Nolan C. . . | (GA) | 511
20th century American history | BARTHELL, Daniel W. . . | (DC) | 61
20th century American popular music | SPECHT, Joe W. . . . . | (TX) | 1172
20th century American theater | LOMONACO, Martha S. . | (NY) | 738
20th century concert music | PIZER, Charles R. . . . . | (NY) | 977
| PIZER, Elizabeth F. . . . . | (NY) | 977
20th century diplomatic records | PFEIFFER, David A. . . . | (DC) | 966
20th century literature | CAMMACK, Bruce P. . . | (NY) | 175
| ROYTMAN, Serafima . . | (NY) | 1063
| FECKO, Marybeth . . . . . | (SC) | 367
20th century military records | PFEIFFER, David A. . . . | (DC) | 966
20th century political collections | VOGT, Sheryl B. . . . . . . | (GA) | 1287

TWO-PERSON

One & two-person libraries | STEVENS-RAYBURN,
  Sarah L. . . . . | (MD) | 1191
Two-person community hospital
  library | WILLOUGHBY, Nona C. . | (NY) | 1349
Two-person libraries | MITCHELL, Mary H. . . . . | (ON) | 849

TWO-YEAR (See also College, Community, Junior)

Planning two-year learning resource
  ctr | BOOK, Imogene I. . . . . . | (SC) | 115
Two-year college standards | WALLACE, James O. . . . | (TX) | 1297

TYPE

Computer typesetting & interfacing | MEDINA, Ildefonso M. . | (NY) | 820
Computerized typesetting | GRIES, James P. . . . . . . | (IL) | 468
Foreign language typesetting | HOMNACK, Mark . . . . . . | (CA) | 555
Music typesetting | WESTERN, Eric D. . . . . . | (WI) | 1327
Type design & typography | KIRSHENBAUM, Sandra
  D. . . . . | (CA) | 655
Typecoding of indexes | GARCIA, Kathleen J. . . . | (NY) | 417
Typesetting | HENDERSON, Ronald L. | (MD) | 527
Typesetting & graphic design | MILLER, Thomas R. . . . . | (IL) | 843
Typesetting from databases | LABEAU, Dennis . . . . . . | (MI) | 685

UKRAINIAN (See also Soviet Union)

Ukrainian Canadians | VERYHA, Wasyl . . . . | (ON) | 1283
Ukrainian studies | DOBCZANSKY, Jurij W. . | (DC) | 307
| YANCHINSKI, Roma N. . | (ON) | 1377

UNDERGRADUATE (See also College, University)

Teaching undergraduate courses | FREEMAN, C L. . . . . | (MO) | 400
Teaching undergraduate library
  science | MALTBY, Florence H. . . . | (MO) | 764
Undergraduate librarianship | FERGUSON, Chris D. . . . | (CA) | 372
| FLOWERS, Pat . . . . | (CA) | 386
Undergraduate libraries | HARWOOD, Judith A. . . | (IL) | 510
| TAYLOR, David C. . . . . . | (NC) | 1226
| PUNIELLO, Francoise S. . | (NJ) | 997
| CIPOLLA, Wilma R. . . . . | (NY) | 215
Undergraduate library education | BUTLER, Christina . . . . . | (OH) | 166
Undergraduate reference | JASPER, Richard P. . . . . | (MI) | 595
| TOLBERT, Jean F. . . . . . | (TX) | 1248
Undergraduate science instruction | MICIKAS, Lynda L. . . . . | (PA) | 832
Undergraduate services | WALKER, Paula B. . . . . . | (WA) | 1296

UNDERGROUND

Underground literature | PEREZ, Maria L. . . . . . . | (FL) | 958
Underground writing & ephemera | BJORKLUND, Edi . . . . . | (WI) | 100

UNDERSERVED

Services to the underserved, literacy | RUBY, Carmela M. . . . . | (CA) | 1065

UNION

Automated union catalogs & indexes | JAGOE, Katherine P. . . . | (TX) | 591
CD-ROM union catalogs | BEISER, Karl A. . . . . | (ME) | 75
Centralized processing union catalog | BENSON, Laurel D. . . . . | (MN) | 83
Online union serial listing | PARRAVANO, Ellen A. . . | (NY) | 944
Regional union catalog automation | PARRAVANO, Ellen A. . . | (NY) | 944

UNION (Cont'd)
Serials & union listing — HICKEY, John T. . . . . . . (NY) 536
Serials cataloging & union listing — MURRAY, Diane E. . . . . (MI) 881
Serials union listing — MANEY, Lana E. . . . . . (TX) 765
Serials union listings — CRAWFORD-OPPENHIE-MER, Christine . . . . . (NY) 257
Serials union lists — BOUCHARD-HALL, Robert W. . . . . (MA) 118
Union — LINVILLE, Marcia L. . . . . (HI) 731
Union catalog production — TSUI, Josephine . . . . (ON) 1260
Union catalogues — MCQUEEN, Lorraine . . . . (ON) 817
— ARORA, Ved P. . . . . (SK) 34
Union list — TRACY, Joan I. . . . . (WA) 1253
Union list coordination — ARNN, Judith A. . . . . (TX) 33
Union list of serials — PIKE, Lee E. . . . . (AL) 973
— HAGGARD, Lynn . . . . . . (TX) 483
— CHENG, Sheung O. . . . . (TAI) 206
— WANG, Sin C. . . . . (TAI) 1303
Union list serials — HIGGINS, Flora T. . . . . . (NJ) 537
Union listing — CHANG, Sookang H. . . . . (IL) 201
— CHATTERTON, Leigh A. (MA) 204
— KINGSTON, Mary L. . . . (MD) 652
— HARTMAN, Anne M. . . . (NY) 508
— MOORE, Brian P. . . . . . (OH) 858
— WARREN, Karen T. . . . . (SC) 1306
— WALKER, Bonnie M. . . . (TX) 1295
— POLLARD, Margaret E. . . (WI) 981
Union listing, serials — MONTGOMERY, Teresa L. (CA) 856
Union listings — O'DONOVAN, Patricia A. . (OR) 917
— CHIU, Ida K. . . . . (TX) 209
Union lists — HAAS, Florence A. . . . . . (CA) 480
— MCCUTCHEON, Dianne E. (MD) 801
— MCQUEEN, Lorraine . . . . (ON) 817
Union lists of serials — NEUFELD, Judith B. . . . . (NY) 897
— ADREAN, Louis V. . . . . . (OH) 7

UNIONS (See also Labor)
Administration, especially labor unions — LANDRY, Mary E. . . . . . (MD) 693
Administration plus unions — DONAHUGH, Robert H. . . (OH) 310
Credit unions — ZYSKOWSKI, Dianne D. . (MI) 1392
Librarians & labor unions — POTTER, Janet L. . . . . . (NY) 987

UNIQUE (See also Rare)
Unique books — PASCAL, Barbara R. . . . (CA) 945

UNITED NATIONS
United Nations documents — SHELDEN, Patricia R. . . . (HI) 1125
— BOYCE, Barbara S. . . . . (MA) 122
— MCDONALD, Ellen J. . . . (MA) 802
— PANDIT, Jyoti P. . . . . . . (NY) 937
United Nations publications — RUHLIN, Michele T. . . . . (UT) 1066

UNITED STATES (See also Federal, Government)
Canadian & US companies & industries — ORLANDO, Richard P. . . (PQ) 926
Canadian & United States history — OTTOSEN, Charles F. . . . (AB) 930
Government, US & European history — HERTZ, Sylvia . . . . (MI) 533
Hispanics in the United States — PEREZ-LOPEZ, Rene . . . (VA) 958
Library buildings consultant, Japan, USA — GITLER, Robert L. . . . . . (CA) 438
19th century US rare books — GARDNER, Ralph D. . . . (NY) 418
Online information, US & foreign — PINSON, Mark . . . . (MA) 975
United States & international documents — ELAM, Joice B. . . . . (GA) 341
US & international marketing — MIELE, Madeline F. . . . . (MA) 833
United States & women's history — GALLOWAY, Sue . . . . . (CA) 415
US Bureau of Census materials — MACKEY, Wendy W. . . . (MA) 757
United States census maps — SCHULZE, Suzanne S. . . (CO) 1102
United States Civil War history — CAHILL, Colleen R. . . . . (PA) 171
United States Coast Guard — SHERMAN, William F. . . (DC) 1128
US Customs law research — MATTERA, Joseph J. . . . (NY) 785
United States Customs Service — SHERMAN, William F. . . (DC) 1128
US documents — SACHSE, Gladys M. . . . . (AR) 1073
— FINLEY, Mary M. . . . . . . (CA) 378
— WESTFALL, Gloria D. . . . (IN) 1327
— HANSSEN, Nancy E. . . . (MA) 499

UNITED STATES (Cont'd)
US documents — COBB, Sylvia R. . . . . (OK) 225
United States documents reference — SPAHR, Janet E. . . . . . . (VA) 1170
United States federal documents — HAUSE, Aaron H. . . . . . . (MT) 512
United States federal publications — SLOAN, Tom W. . . . . . . (AL) 1150
— MCCLEARY, William E. . (LA) 796
United States government & documents — MORENO, Rafael . . . . . . (PA) 863
US government documents — IRBY, Geraldine A. . . . . . (AL) 583
— COSTELLO, M R . . . . . (CA) 249
— SANSOBRINO, Jean C. . (CA) 1081
— HURLEY, Trudy M. . . . . (CT) 577
— MELNICOVE, Annette R. . (FL) 823
— COLLINS, Patrick . . . . . (GA) 233
— WAI, Lily C. . . . . (ID) 1292
— BECK, Mary C. . . . . . . (MI) 71
— ESSLINGER, Guenter W. (MN) 355
— LAUGHLIN, Cheryl H. . . (MS) 703
— KENDRA, William E. . . . (NE) 640
— BEAUDRIE, Ronald A. . . (NY) 70
— FELLER, Judith M. . . . . (PA) 370
— WRIGHT, Barbara C. . . . (PA) 1370
— TINSMAN, William A. . . (TX) 1246
— DAVIS, Wylma P. . . . . . (VA) 281
— HAYS, Peggy W. . . . . . (VA) 517
US government documents, business — TAYLOR, William R. . . . (TN) 1229
United States government publications — DOWNS, Charles F. . . . . (DC) 317
— TRAUTMAN, Maryellen . (DC) 1254
— WOODWARD, Lawrence W. . . . . (DC) 1368
— WIHBEY, Francis R. . . . (ME) 1337
— FROBOM, Jerome B. . . . (NE) 405
— POWELL, Margaret S. . . (OH) 988
— BELEU, Steve . . . . (OK) 76
— BERWIND, Anne M. . . . (TN) 91
— BRADLEY, C D. . . . . . . (TX) 125
United States historical census — SCHULZE, Suzanne S. . . (CO) 1102
US history — DALY, John E. . . . . (IL) 271
— KENDALL, John D. . . . . (MA) 640
— POHL, Gunther E. . . . . . (NY) 979
— SMITH, Michael K. . . . . (TX) 1158
— SHERMAN, Madeline R. . (VT) 1128
US history bibliography — RHODES, Saralinda A. . . (KS) 1026
US information policy — JUERGENSMEYER, John E. . . . . (IL) 619
United States law — WESTHUIS, Judith A. . . . (NY) 1327
United States legal research — ARANDA-COODOU, Patricio . . . . (DC) 30
US MARC formats — JANK, David A. . . . . . . (MA) 593
— CARSON, M S. . . . . . . (PA) 188
US model development — YANCHAR, Joyce M. . . . (MA) 1377
United States newspaper project — GULLEY, J L. . . . . (GA) 477
United States patents — DAHMANN, Rosemary G. (OH) 270
— JOHNS, John E. . . . . . (OH) 601
— KECK, Kerry A. . . . . . . (TX) 633
US public library history — HECK-RABI, Louise E. . . (MI) 520
United States voluntary standards index — OVERMAN, Joanne R. . . (MD) 931
United States Western mining history — MC CAULEY, Philip F. . . (SD) 795
United States women's history — MOSELEY, Eva S. . . . . . (MA) 870
Western United States history — MC CAULEY, Philip F. . . (SD) 795

UNIVERSITY (See also Academic, Campus, College, Graduate, Higher, Off-Campus, Undergraduate)
Administering university archives — MATTHEW, Jeannette M. . (IN) 785
Administration of university libraries — JENNERICH, Edward J. . . (WA) 598
College & university archives — REYNOLDS, Jon K. . . . . (DC) 1025
— MAHER, William J. . . . . (IL) 760
— BARTKOWSKI, Patricia . (MI) 61
— DUNLAP, Barbara J. . . . (NY) 326
— STOUT, Leon J. . . . . . . (PA) 1198
College & university libraries — BERRY, John W. . . . . . . (IL) 90
— WILLIAMSON, William L. (WI) 1348
College & university library admin — GITLER, Robert L. . . . . . (CA) 438
— KONDELIK, John P. . . . . (IN) 670
— YOUNG, Tommie M. . . . (NC) 1383
— ALEXANDER, Shirley B. . (TX) 12

UNIVERSITY (Cont'd)

College & university teaching — GUENTHER, Charles J. . . (MO) 475
College, university archives — BERKELEY, Edmund . . . (VA) 87
Creating university archives — MATTHEW, Jeannette M. (IN) 785
Future of university libraries — CLUFF, E D. . . . . (TX) 223
General administration, univ libraries — DORR, Ralze W. . . . . . . (KY) 313
General university reference service — ROBERTS, Sally M. . . . (IL) 1041
Librarians in university governance — COLLINS, Evron S. . . . (OH) 232
Local history & university archives — WALKER, Mary J. . . . . . (NM) 1296
Loss control in libraries & universities — MORRIS, John . . . . (CA) 866
Oklahoma State University collection — BLEDSOE, Kathleen E. . . (OK) 105
Personal univ-quality art collections — BLAIR, Madeline S. . . . . (DC) 102
Planning & budget, university libraries — DORR, Ralze W. . . . . . . (KY) 313
Reference on university records — HODGSON, Janet B. . . . (KY) 546
Role of library in the university — SMITH, Eldred R. . . . . . . (MN) 1154
School & university library operations — KELLY, Myla S. . . . . (CA) 638
Teaching at university level — SWARTZ, Jon D. . . . . (TX) 1214
Technological university library admin — SNYDER, Richard L. . . . (PA) 1165
Universities — MCDONELL, W E. . . . . (TN) 803
University administration — TIRRO, Frank P. . . . . (CT) 1247
— SWARTZ, Jon D. . . . . . . (TX) 1214
University archives — D'ANTONIO, Lynn M. . . . (AZ) 274
— WHITSON, Helene . . . . . (CA) 1334
— WITTHUS, Rutherford W. (CO) 1358
— JIMERSON, Randall C. . . (CT) 600
— BAMBERGER, Mary A. . . (IL) 53
— GRAHAM, Robert W. . . . (IL) 456
— LEONARD, Kevin B. . . . . (IL) 716
— MEYER, Daniel . . . . (IL) 830
— TURNER, Nancy K. . . . . (IN) 1265
— CRAWFORD, Anthony R. . (KS) 256
— BIRDWHISTELL, Terry L. (KY) 98
— SCHMIDT, Jean M. . . . . (LA) 1095
— BOLES, Frank . . . . (MI) 112
— GRESSITT, Alexandra S. . (MS) 467
— SIMMONS, Ruth J. . . . . . (NJ) 1140
— SOLOMON, Geri E. . . . . (NY) 1166
— STERN, Marc J. . . . . (NY) 1189
— GALLAGHER, Dennis J. . (PA) 414
— LANDIS, Lawrence A. . . . (TX) 693
— DANIELS, Jerome P. . . . (WI) 273
— HARADA, Ryukichi . . . . . (JAP) 499
University filing systems — SWEENEY, Shelley T. . . (SK) 1215
University libraries — SALMON, Stephen R. . . (CA) 1077
— CANELAS, Dale B. . . . . . (FL) 178
— TREYZ, Joseph H. . . . . . (FL) 1256
University libraries consulting — SHAPIRO, S R. . . . . (NY) 1121
University library — GHALI, Raouf S. . . . . . . (NY) 430
University library administration — BLANCHARD, J R. . . . . . (CA) 103
— HOLLAND, Harold E. . . . (CA) 550
— VOSPER, Robert . . . . . . (CA) 1289
— FUSTUKJIAN, Samuel Y. (FL) 410
— BISHOP, David F. . . . . . . (GA) 99
— SMITH, Eldred R. . . . . . (MN) 1154
— ORNE, Jerrold . . . . (NC) 926
— DALTON, Jack . . . . (NY) 271
— SMITH, John B. . . . . . . (NY) 1156
— BOBICK, James E. . . . . . (OH) 108
— BRANSCOMB, Lewis C. . (OH) 129
— PATTERSON, Robert H. . (OK) 948
— ROUSE, Roscoe . . . . . . (OK) 1061
— LYNDEN, Frederick C. . . (RI) 752
— RANEY, Leon . . . . (SD) 1007
— JAX, John J. . . . . (WI) 595
University library automation — HAMMOND, Jane L. . . . (NY) 493
University library cataloging — BARKER, Victoria S. . . . (CO) 56
University library cooperation — DUPUIS, Onil . . . . (PQ) 327
University library management — BERGER, Michael G. . . . (CA) 85
University library planning — SMITH, Eldred R. . . . . . (MN) 1154
University of Florida documents — KONOP, Bonnie M. . . . (FL) 670
University records — LYSY, Peter J. . . . . (IN) 753
University research lib administration — RUNKLE, Martin D. . . . . (IL) 1067
University, school & library
cooperation — BERLING, John G. . . . . . (MN) 88
University-level public reference — MCCANN, Judith B. . . . (ON) 794

UNIX

UNIX local area network — ROSE, Phillip E. . . . . (CO) 1055
UNIX System — HAWKINS, Donald T. . . . (NJ) 514
UNIX systems administration — SULLIVAN, Edward A. . . (CA) 1207

UNSERVED

Serving unserved — KIRK, Sherwood . . . . (IL) 654

URBAN (See also City)

City & urban planning — SLOCUM, Charlotte A. . . (NC) 1150
Photography & urban history — GRAY, Priscilla M. . . . . . (PA) 460
Public transportation & urban planning — PRESBY, Richard A. . . . (CA) 990
Urban affairs — NORDBY, Leslie L. . . . . (CA) 908
— CASEY, Victoria L. . . . . (ON) 192
Urban affairs planning — BEAL, Gretchen F. . . . . (TN) 68
Urban affairs reference — DANIEL, Eileen . . . . (ON) 272
Urban affairs reference service — LOGAN, Mary A. . . . . . (MD) 737
Urban & intergovernmental affairs — ORTIZ, Diane . . . . (NV) 927
Urban history — DALY, John E. . . . . (IL) 271
Urban history, Boston — BERGEN, Philip S. . . . . . (MA) 85
Urban history documentation — KELLER, William B. . . . . (DC) 636
Urban main library — PRESSING, Kirk L. . . . . . (IL) 991
Urban planning — RAVENHALL, Mary . . . . (IL) 1010
— DONG, Tina . . . . (MA) 311
Urban planning & development — CROWE, Gloria J. . . . . . (AZ) 261
Urban planning bibliography — CHIBNIK, Katharine R. . . (NY) 207
Urban public libraries — SONDHEIM, John W. . . . (MD) 1167
— ROBERTS, Jean A. . . . . (MO) 1040
Urban public library management — ICKES, Barbara J. . . . . . (PA) 581
Urban public library service — HEID, Gregory G. . . . . . (GA) 521
Urban transportation — KAWABATA, Julie . . . . . (OR) 632

USER (See also Clients, Consumer, Customer, End-User, Patients, Patrons)

Administration of user services — WILSON, Lizabeth A. . . . (IL) 1351
Assistance to users — STILLMAN, June S. . . . . (FL) 1194
Behavior information users — BOISSY, Robert W. . . . . (NY) 111
Databases, user producing — WELLS, Christine . . . . . (VA) 1322
Educating information users — KUHLTHAU, Carol C. . . . (NJ) 682
Human factors user interface — MCALLISTER, Caryl K. . . (WI) 792
Information needs, user studies — DURRANCE, Joan C. . . . (MI) 328
Information use & users — WILKINSON, John P. . . . (ON) 1340
Information, user interface — HUTTON, Emily A. . . . . . (WA) 579
Innovative services, new users — STRAWDER, Maxine S. . . (TN) 1201
Library & information user education — EL-DUWEINI, Aadel K. . . (EGY) 342
Library instruction & user education — LIPPINCOTT, Joan K. . . . (NY) 732
Library publications, user aids — OSTROW, Rona . . . . . . (NY) 929
Library systems, user services — O'DELL, M P. . . . . (MD) 916
Library user education — HENNER, Terry A. . . . . . (GA) 528
— PALMER, Virginia E. . . . (OH) 937
— CHISMAN, Janet K. . . . (WA) 209
— FRICK, Elizabeth A. . . . . (NS) 403
Library user studies — WHITLATCH, Jo B. . . . . (CA) 1333
Library users committee — BARBEE, Norman N. . . . (DC) 55
Library users groups — BRANDT, Daryl S. . . . . . (IN) 128
Microcomputer user support — OWEN, Willy . . . . (NC) 932
Personal computer user guide
composition — MILLER, Ann M. . . . . . . (ON) 835
Producing training user aids — TOWNSEND, Carolyn J. . (PA) 1253
Public library user education — HANSON, Jan E. . . . . . . (NY) 498
Public library user services — SMITHEE, Jeannette P. . (NY) 1161
Reference & user education — KIBBEE, Josephine Z. . . (IL) 646
Reference & user services — EAST, Catherine R. . . . . (DC) 332
— TERRY, Susan N. . . . . . (DC) 1232
— EUSTACE, Susan J. . . . (MD) 356
Reference user services — LUND, Patricia A. . . . . (WI) 748
Service to special users — LANG, Jovian P. . . . . . (NY) 695
Training & user documentation — DIXON, Edith M. . . . . . (WI) 306
Training & user education — SEELEY, Catherine R. . . (ME) 1111
Training & user support — VEATCH, Laurie L. . . . . (DC) 1280
Training information specialists &
users — COURRIER, Yves G. . . . (FRN) 251
Training staff & users — NDENGA, Viola W. . . . . (MI) 890
Training users of ILS, online catalog — PRESLAR, M G. . . . . . . (TN) 991
Use & user studies — DEGRUYTER, M L. . . . . (TX) 288
User acclamation to reading — FRANCOS, Alexis . . . . . (PA) 396

USER (Cont'd)

User & information management education	BERNARD, Molly S.	(WA)	88
User & specialist training	CROWTHER, Warren W.	(CSR)	262
User assistance	GRIFFIN, Martha R.	(GA)	468
User documentation & training	DIENER, Carol W.	(MD)	302
User education	MORRISON, Margaret L.	(AR)	868
	CARAVELLO, Patti S.	(CA)	180
	CASTAGNOZZI, Carol A.	(CA)	194
	FRY, Thomas K.	(CA)	407
	MCMASTER, Deborah L.	(CT)	815
	APOSTLE, Lynne M.	(DC)	29
	WILLIAMS, Mitsuko	(IL)	1345
	HARZBECKER, Joseph J.	(MA)	510
	BRANCH, Katherine A.	(MD)	127
	HUMPHRIES, Anne W.	(MD)	574
	SIMS, Sally R.	(MD)	1142
	SCHWARTZ, Diane G.	(MI)	1104
	STOFFLE, Carla J.	(MI)	1196
	VAN TOLL, Faith	(MI)	1277
	POLLARD, Bobbie T.	(NY)	981
	MULARSKI, Carol A.	(OH)	876
	MILLER, Naomi	(PA)	841
	SEEDS, Robert S.	(PA)	1111
	WARNER, Elizabeth R.	(PA)	1305
	THOMPSON, Annie F.	(PR)	1239
	WELCH, C B.	(TX)	1321
	BADER, Susan G.	(VA)	44
	MCCULLEY, Lucretia	(VA)	800
	NOFSINGER, Mary M.	(WA)	907
	STRUBE, Kathleen	(WI)	1203
	WU, Edith Y.	(HKG)	1373
User education & information transfer	BOROVANSKY, Vladimir T.	(AZ)	117
User education & orientation	PATTERSON, Charlean P.	(PA)	948
User education coordination	FREY, Barbara J.	(CT)	402
User education, library orientation	SEARCY HOWARD, Linda M.	(BC)	1109
User information	FRANCOS, Alexis	(PA)	396
User interface	VAUGHAN, John	(NY)	1279
User interface, automated systems	SACKETT-WILK, Susan A.	(TX)	1073
User interface design	HURLEY, Geraldine C.	(OH)	577
User interface development	VEATCH, Laurie L.	(DC)	1280
User interfaces	EASTMAN, Caroline M.	(SC)	333
User interfaces & database frontends	CURRAN, George L.	(NY)	266
User library training	SCHAPIRO, Benjamin H.	(IL)	1090
User needs assessment	ROCQUE, Bernice L.	(NY)	1046
User needs determination	SAYER, John S.	(MD)	1086
User needs studies	SMITH-GREENWOLD, Kathryn R.	(NY)	1162
User requirements analysis	DIENER, Carol W.	(MD)	302
User services	PENNINGTON, Walter W.	(AL)	957
	HUSBAND, Susan M.	(AZ)	578
	JOHNSON, Charlotte L.	(IL)	603
	FRETWELL, Gordon E.	(MA)	402
	VARGHA, Rebecca B.	(NC)	1278
	EVANS, Nancy R.	(PA)	357
	CARTER, Barbara W.	(TN)	189
	ELDRIDGE, Virginia L.	(TN)	342
	ARNESON, Rosemary H.	(VA)	33
	RYAN, R P.	(VA)	1071
	WEESE, Dwain W.	(BC)	1316
	FRANK, Elizabeth W.	(TKY)	397
User services & training	BAZAN, Lorraine R.	(CA)	68
User studies	NAHL-JAKOBOVITS, Diane	(HI)	886
	BESANT, Larry X.	(KY)	91
	D'ELIA, George P.	(MN)	289
User study	TAMURA, Shunsaku	(JAP)	1221
User support	LEUNG, Frank F.	(ON)	719
User support for online searching	BROWN, Helen A.	(NE)	144
User surveys	MACDONALD, Christine S.	(ON)	754
User training	CHU, Felix T.	(IL)	212
	SLAWNIAK, Patricia M.	(IL)	1148
	CUTLER, C M.	(AB)	268
User training & documentation	GREEN-MALONEY, Nancy	(CA)	465
User-friendly systems	KING, Joseph T.	(CA)	651
Writing of user documentation	WHITMAN, Mary L.	(PA)	1333

UTILITIES

Bibliographic utilities	SHIRASAWA, Sharon V.	(CA)	1131
	DUDLEY, Robyn A.	(MD)	323
	MORRIS, Jennifer D.	(NY)	866
	SLATER, Ronald J.	(ON)	1148
Bibliographic utility	PRESLAN, Bruce H.	(CA)	991
Cataloging utilities	BULLARD, Sharon W.	(CA)	156
Computer utilities for education	COLCLASURE, Marian S.	(AR)	230
Electric utilities	JOHNSON, Doris E.	(CT)	603
	STANLEY, Nelda J.	(LA)	1180
	BALL, Susan C.	(WA)	52
Electric utilities & energy	FARKAS, Susan A.	(DC)	364
Electric utility	FELDMAN, Rosalie M.	(CO)	369
Electric utility engineering	WEBER, Robert F.	(OR)	1314
Electric utility research	HORAH, Richard H.	(GA)	558
Energy, electric utility industry	MUIR, Scott P.	(AL)	876
Information utilities	MORGAN, Bradford A.	(SD)	863
Library utilities	MADISON, Olivia M.	(IA)	759
	BOES, Rachel M.	(OR)	110
Online srvs & bibliographic utilities	MORGAN, Ferrell	(CA)	864
Public utilities	MALUMPHY, Sharon M.	(OH)	764
Public utility	SCULLY, Patrick F.	(CA)	1109
Public utility information	BOBAN, Carol A.	(IL)	108
Public utility management	ERTZ, Ginger E.	(PA)	353
Utilities research	FERME, Paul H.	(IL)	373
Utility information sources	KING, Alan S.	(ME)	650
Water utility management	ERTZ, Ginger E.	(PA)	353

UTOPIAN

Utopian literature	YAMAMOTO, Conrad S.	(CA)	1376

VALIDATION

Authority validation	BATTOE, Melanie K.	(NY)	65
Production & validation	SOUTHWICK, Margaret A.	(VA)	1170

VALUATION (See also Appraisal)

Appraising current market value	MONDLIN, Marvin	(NY)	854
Product development & valuation	MOFFITT, Michael D.	(MA)	852
Valuation & taxation of real property	BEVERLEY, Barbara S.	(NY)	93

VALUES

Values & professional ethics	HALL, Homer J.	(NJ)	488

VBI

Data broadcasting on VBI	WILLIAMS, Fred	(GA)	1343

VEHICLES (See also Motorcycle)

Armored vehicles	HOLT, David A.	(KY)	554
Motor vehicle safety	DOERNBERG, David G.	(DC)	308

VENDOR (See also Sales, Selling, Retailing, Wholesale)

Copier vend systems	SCHULTZ, Michael W.	(AZ)	1102
Copier vending systems	MERKERT, Robert J.	(NJ)	826
Database vendor	EWING, Alison L.	(AZ)	359
	HYLAND, Barbara	(ON)	580
Evaluation of vendor performance	ANDERSON, E A.	(MN)	22
Inventory control, vendor management	MCGRAW, Scott C.	(IL)	807
Library automation vending	NASATIR, Marilyn	(CA)	888
Library vendor services	HULL, Debbie M.	(NY)	572
Serials vending	KETCHAM, Lee C.	(AL)	645
Turnkey vendor	MATTHEWS, Joseph R.	(CA)	785
Vendor & library relations	GOEHNER, Donna M.	(IL)	443
Vendor & supplier negotiations	YODER, Susan M.	(CA)	1380
Vendor consulting for libraries	MURO, Ernest A.	(NJ)	880
Vendor relations	FERRELL, Mary S.	(CA)	373
	AXTMANN, Margaret M.	(NY)	42

VENTURE

Co-joint ventures	NICKEL, R S.	(PA)	902
Venture capital research	SOROBAY, Roman T.	(NY)	1169

VERIFICATION
Bibliographic verification	NIELSON, Paula I.	(UT)	903
	ALLISON, Scott	(AB)	17
	HOBBS, Brian	(AB)	545
Online verifications	TURNER, Freya A.	(OH)	1264
Verifying citations & ordering	WILLIS, Joan K.	(CA)	1348

VERTICAL (See also Pamphlets)
Vertical file	GOLDMACHER, Sheila L.	(CA)	445
	STEWART, Anna C.	(CO)	1192
	TODD, Suzanne L.	(MI)	1248
	MALLORY, Elizabeth J.	(TX)	763
Vertical file on artists	MCNULTY, Karen	(CT)	817
Vertical files	CHESTER, Claudia J.	(CA)	207
	WATT, Richard S.	(NC)	1310
Vertical files organization, maintenance	GODFREY, Florence L.	(NJ)	442

VETERINARY
Agricultural veterinary databases	NEELEY, Dana M.	(TX)	891
Reference, veterinary & human medicine	VEENSTRA, Robert J.	(AL)	1281
Veterinary medical librarianship	STEPHENS, Gretchen	(IN)	1188
Veterinary medical libraries consulting	KERKER, Ann E.	(IN)	643
Veterinary medicine	WILLARD, Gayle K.	(KS)	1341
	LOUBIERE, Sue	(LA)	742
	SAFFER-MARCHAND, Melinda	(MA)	1074
	CARLSON, Livija I.	(MN)	182
	WILSON, Marijo S.	(NY)	1352
	SESSIONS, Robert	(WI)	1117
Veterinary medicine bibliography	KERKER, Ann E.	(IN)	643
Veterinary medicine databases	DE WALERSTEIN, Linda S.	(MEX)	297
Veterinary medicine information	COOK, Elaine	(ENG)	239

VHS
VHS innovation	REIDER, William L.	(MD)	1019

VICTIMS
Victims of violent crime	ARBELBIDE, Cindy L.	(TX)	30

VICTORIAN
Research, art nouveau, Victorian art	STACY, Betty A.	(VA)	1178
Victorian art	ROBERTS, Helene E.	(MA)	1040
Victorian literature & bibliography	LASNER, Mark S.	(DC)	700
Victorian literature, fiction, poetry	FISHER, Benjamin F.	(MS)	380
Victorian periodicals	ROBERTS, Helene E.	(MA)	1040

VIDEO (See also Audiovisual, Film, Media, VHS, Videotex)
Acquisition of motion pictures & videos	TALIT, Lynn	(CT)	1221
Administrator, film & video library	MORRISON, George J.	(NY)	868
Archiving art slides on video disks	SHARER, E J.	(CO)	1122
Audio & video collection	BERGER, Brenda L.	(NJ)	85
Audio & video programs	LOCKE, William G.	(NY)	736
Audiovisual & 16mm film & video	FISH, Marie	(CA)	380
Audiovisual, film, video	ENGLE, Joyce C.	(NJ)	349
Audiovisuals & video media	DIAL, Ron	(NY)	299
Audiovisuals, film & video	MINOR, Barbara G.	(MN)	846
Ballets on videocassettes	HEDLUND, Dennis M.	(NJ)	520
Bibliography in film & video field	CYR, Helen W.	(MD)	268
Children's films & videotapes	GAFFNEY, Maureen	(NY)	412
Computer & video based instruction	BUTLER, David W.	(CA)	166
Computer & video education	KRAUSE, Roberta A.	(IL)	676
Computer-based interactive video	HAUSMAN, Julie	(IA)	513
Consultant, film & video production	HEMPEL, Gordon J.	(IL)	525
Contemporary art & video	HORIGAN, Evelyn A.	(CA)	559
Creating video disks for art	SHARER, E J.	(CO)	1122
Cultural programs on videocassettes	HEDLUND, Dennis M.	(NJ)	520
Developing video collections	PURCELL, Marcia L.	(NY)	998
Documentary films & videotapes	RICHTER, Robert	(NY)	1031
Educational film & video evaluation	MODICA, Mary L.	(SD)	851
Educational film & video selection	MODICA, Mary L.	(SD)	851

VIDEO (Cont'd)
Educational films & videotapes	FISHER, Carolyn H.	(NY)	380
Educational video	MACINTYRE, Ronald R.	(NY)	755
Fashion & costume video	HALE, Kaycee	(CA)	485
Film & video	POOLE, Rebecca S.	(CO)	983
	GASTON, Judith A.	(MN)	421
	HADDOCK, Mable	(OH)	482
Film & video acquisition	HUGHES, Rolanda L.	(IN)	572
	HAYNES, Jean	(NY)	516
Film & video archiving	WEATHERFORD, Elizabeth	(NY)	1311
Film & video collection	HANFT, Margie E.	(CA)	495
Film & video collection coordination	NEBEL, Jean C.	(CA)	891
Film & video collection development	MOORE, Emily C.	(NC)	859
Film & video collections	FLYNN, Barbara L.	(IL)	386
	TUGGLE, Pamela C.	(VA)	1262
Film & video consultant, appraiser	MACAULEY, C C.	(CA)	754
Film & video distribution	BLANK, Les	(CA)	104
	WHITE, Matthew H.	(IL)	1331
	CABEZAS, Sue A.	(MA)	170
Film & video for schools	MAY, Frank C.	(CA)	788
Film & video librarianship	AYARI, Kaye W.	(SC)	42
Film & video libraries	BARNES, Robert W.	(NY)	57
Film & video library	WEISER, Douglas E.	(MI)	1319
	LINK, Margaret A.	(NC)	730
	SOUTHARD, Ruth K.	(TX)	1169
Film & video library administration	THOMAS, Fred	(MD)	1236
Film & video library management	HOLSINGER, Katherine	(AZ)	554
Film & video media	JENNINGS, Mary	(AK)	598
Film & video production	WHITE, Matthew H.	(IL)	1331
	CABEZAS, Sue A.	(MA)	170
Film & video programming	THOMPSON, Elizabeth M.	(DC)	1239
	CANTWELL, Mary L.	(OH)	179
Film & video recordings	OLIVER, Scot	(KY)	921
Film & video resources	ALLAN, David W.	(MN)	14
Film & video reviewing & programming	BRAUN, Robert L.	(NY)	130
Film & video services	DEAN, Martha L.	(CA)	283
Film & video stock footage	SUMMERS, Robert A.	(NJ)	1209
Film & video writing & production	TALIT, Lynn	(CT)	1221
Film library & video library	GORDON, Thelma S.	(CT)	452
Film, video selection & programming	BUCHANAN, Gerald	(MS)	153
Film, video selection development	SHAPIRO, Leila C.	(MD)	1121
Home video retailing	WHITE, Matthew H.	(IL)	1331
Instructional video/ITV	BOYNTON, John W.	(ME)	124
Interactive art video disks	SHARER, E J.	(CO)	1122
Interactive video	TROUTNER, Joanne J.	(IN)	1258
Interactive video disk development	HORNIG-ROHAN, James E.	(PA)	560
Interactive videodisc	CHAPLOCK, Sharon K.	(WI)	201
Interactive videodisc programs	STEELE, Tom M.	(NC)	1184
Literary videos	LESNIAK, Rose	(NY)	718
Managing film & video libraries	HAYNES, Jean	(NY)	516
Media, audiovisual equipment, video	RUBIN, Ellen B.	(NY)	1064
Media services, audio & video	SLYHOFF, Merle J.	(PA)	1151
On-site interactive video	PODWOL, Sharon L.	(NY)	979
Operas on videocassettes	HEDLUND, Dennis M.	(NJ)	520
Optical video disk	GALL, Bert A.	(TN)	413
Planning for automation & videodiscs	VOGT-O'CONNOR, Diane L.	(DC)	1287
Poetry video production & distribution	LESNIAK, Rose	(NY)	718
Production, film & video	BEATTY, R M.	(IN)	70
Public information video production	RANCER, Susan P.	(NC)	1006
Reviewing film, video & media	TROJAN, Judith L.	(NY)	1257
Scholarly publication in video	O'CONNOR, Brian C.	(CA)	915
16mm film & video	GOTTLIEB, Delia	(NY)	453
16mm films, slides, & videocassettes	CRITCHLOW, Therese E.	(NJ)	259
Student video production	FREEMAN, Evangeline M.	(NC)	400
Supply video & audio tapes	GRAY, Lee H.	(NJ)	460
Technology-computers & video	HOFSTAD, Alice M.	(MN)	548
Video	EBY, James F.	(CA)	334
	SEITZ, Phillip R.	(DC)	1113
	MOGLE, Dawn E.	(IN)	852
	VOLLNOGLE, Leslie A.	(IN)	1288
	WILLIAMS, Danby O.	(KY)	1342
	KREAMER, Jean T.	(LA)	677
	MADDEN, Terence J.	(MI)	759
	MILLER, Lynn F.	(NJ)	840
	GURN, Robert M.	(NY)	478
	SLOAN, William J.	(NY)	1150

VIDEO (Cont'd)
Video

Video | WEBB, Barbara A. . . . . . (VA) 1313
Video & audio services manager | EVANS, Mark S. . . . . . . (FL) 357
Video & cable services | DRESANG, Eliza T. . . . . (WI) 319
Video & film collection development | GORSEGNER, Betty D. . . (WI) 452
Video & film purchasing | RICHIE, Mark L. . . . . (NJ) 1030
Video & oral history archives | JAGOE, Katherine P. . . (TX) 591
Video applications | BIRMINGHAM, Frank R. . . (MN) 98
Video as teaching tool | LESH, Jane G. . . . . (CA) 718
Video/audiovisual | LARSON, Catherine A. . . (IA) 699
Video cassettes | SKUBISH, Barbara E. . . . (FL) 1147
Video cataloging, indexing & abstracting | LOFTHOUSE, Patricia A. (IL) 737
Video collection | NEWMARK-KRUGER, Barbara . . . . (NJ) 900
| WITT, Susan T. . . . . (NY) 1358
Video collection consultant | REID, Margaret L. . . . . . . (IL) 1019
Video collection development | WISE, Ronnie W. . . . . . . (MS) 1357
| CANTWELL, Mary L. . . . (OH) 179
Video collections | MILLER, Michael D. . . . . (NY) 841
Video courses | HARLOW, Aileen W. . . . (CT) 502
Video disk instructional design | CONNELL, William S. . . . (CA) 237
Video journalism | PLOTNIK, Arthur . . . . . . (IL) 978
Video media & equipment | MITCHELL, George D. . . (TX) 848
Video production | LARSON, Teresa B. . . . . (IA) 700
| GREEN, Donald T. . . . . . (NJ) 461
| WHITLOW, Cherrill M. . . (NM) 1333
| PETERMAN, Kevin . . . . . (NY) 962
| QUINN, David J. . . . . . . (NY) 1000
| CLANCY, Ron . . . . (BC) 215
Video program coordination | SIEBL, Linda M. . . . . . . (NY) 1135
Video program production | SPANGLER, William N. . (NJ) 1171
Video programming | REIDER, William L. . . . . . (MD) 1019
Video selection & projection | ROLLIN, Marian B. . . . . (CT) 1051
Video selection & reference | LOCKE-GAGNON, Rebecca A. . . . . . . (OH) 736
Video tape | KELLY, Sarah A. . . . . . . (KY) 638
Video technology | REIDER, William L. . . . . . (MD) 1019
Video, TV, satellite systems | HISS, Sheila M. . . . . (FL) 544
Videocassette collection building | AROS, Andrew A. . . . . . (CA) 34
Videocassette consulting | REID, Peg L. . . . . (IL) 1019
Videocassettes & AV materials | SCHOLTZ, James C. . . . (IL) 1098
Video-database interfaces | KRUSS, Daniel M. . . . . . (IL) 681
Videodisc design & productions | HAUSMAN, Julie . . . . . . (IA) 513
Videos | RUSSELL, Marilyn L. . . . (KS) 1069
| HABINSKI, Carol A. . . . . (OH) 481
Videotape | TABAR, Margaret E. . . . . (MN) 1219
Videotape librarianship | BOGIS, Nana E. . . . . . (NJ) 110
Videotape production | PHILLIPS, Donald J. . . . . (FL) 968
Videotape productions | PARKER, Eleanor V. . . . (OK) 941
Videotape purchasing & circulation | BARGAR, Arthur W. . . . . (CT) 56
Videotaping | BIGGS-WILLIAMS, Evelyn A. . . . . (AL) 95
Videotaping for public access | ASHFORD, Richard K. . . (MD) 36
Wholesaling of audio & video materials | JACOBS, Peter J. . . . . . (CA) 590
Writer for film & video | BEATTY, R M. . . . . (IN) 70

VIDEOTEX
Application of videotext technology | BROWNRIDGE, James R. (ON) 149
Videotex | KEIM, Robert . . . . (MN) 635
Videotex & teletext | SHAFFER, Richard P. . . . (NY) 1119
Videotex services | HOLLY, James H. . . . . . (CA) 552
| WRIGHT, Bernell . . . . . . (NY) 1370
Videotex systems | PAL, Gabriel . . . . (ON) 935

VIEWING
Critical viewing & thinking | BRAUN, Robert L. . . . . . (NY) 130
Critical viewing skills | NEWMAN, Eileen M. . . . (NY) 899
Reading, listening & viewing guidance | RING, Constance B. . . . . (NY) 1035

VIRGINIANA
Reference & Virginiana collection | EHLKE, Nancy K. . . . . . (VA) 339

VIROLOGY
Information virology, molecular biology | PERLMAN, Stephen E. . . . (NY) 959

VISUAL (See also Audiovisual, Media)
Administration of visual collections | SHAW, Renata V. . . . . . (DC) 1123
Automated visual resources | LUSKEY, Judith . . . . (DC) 749
Cataloging visual & sound materials | DRIESSEN, Karen C. . . . (MT) 320
Cataloging visual non-print materials | VISKOCHIL, Larry A. . . . (IL) 1285
Contemporary visual arts information | HOFFBERG, Judith A. . . (CA) 547
K-12 visual education | LACY, Lyn E. . . . . (MN) 687
Sources of visual aids | WILSON, Barbara L. . . . . (RI) 1350
Story & visual research for films | FINE, Deborah J. . . . . . . (CA) 377
Visual & sound material acquisition | DRIESSEN, Karen C. . . . (MT) 320
Visual & sound material reference | DRIESSEN, Karen C. . . . (MT) 320
Visual anthropology | WILLIAMS, Carroll W. . . (NM) 1342
Visual arts | DEW, T R. . . . . (CO) 297
| THISTLE, Dawn R. . . . . . (MA) 1235
Visual arts reference | SHERIDAN, Helen A. . . . (MI) 1127
Visual arts resources | MCRAE, Linda . . . . (FL) 818
Visual communication | WERSIG, Gernot . . . . . . (WGR) 325
Visual materials | RYAN, Diane M. . . . . (IL) 1070
Visual resource collection | AUCHSTETTER, Rosann M. . . . . (IN) 38
Visual resource management | HOGAN, Kristine K. . . . . (NY) 549
| FOWLER, Michele R. . . . (OH) 394
Visual resources | COATES, Ann S. . . . . . . (KY) 224
| BOLSHAW, Cynthia L. . . (MA) 112
| ROBERTS, Helene E. . . . (MA) 1040
| KUSNERZ, Peggy A. . . . (MI) 685
| BEETHAM, Donald W. . . (NJ) 74
| CINLAR, Anne . . . . (NJ) 214
| SCHAFFER, D J. . . . . . . (NY) 1089
| PEARMAN, Sara J. . . . . (OH) 952
| KLOS, Sheila M. . . . . . . (OR) 662
| SUNDT, Christine L. . . . . (OR) 1210
| LAZARUS, Karin . . . . . . (PA) 706
| CASHMAN, Norine D. . . (RI) 192
| JACOBY, Mary M. . . . . . (VA) 590
| UPDIKE, Christina B. . . . (VA) 1269
Visual resources & research | NIELSEN, Sonja M. . . . . (MA) 903
Visual resources authority control | MOST, Gregory P. . . . . . (TX) 872
Visual resources classification | FREEMAN, Carla C. . . . . (NY) 400
Visual resources curator | WYKLE, Helen H. . . . . . (CA) 1375
Visual resources database design | ELTZROTH, Elsbeth L. . . (GA) 346
Visual resources databases | SCHAFFER, D J. . . . . . . (NY) 1089
Visual resources, especially slides | CALLAHAN, Linda J. . . . (MA) 173
Visual resources library | MOST, Gregory P. . . . . . (TX) 872
Visual resources management, development | PRINS, Johanna W. . . . . (NY) 993
Visual resources production | FREEMAN, Carla C. . . . . (NY) 400
Visual resources professional | HEHMAN, Jennifer L. . . . (IN) 521
Visual resources, slides & photographs | GREWENOW, Peter W. . . (NY) 467

VISUALLY (See also Blind, Braille, Large, Talking)
Service to visually impaired | POPP, Mary F. . . . . (IN) 984

VOCABULARY (See also Dictionaries, Nomenclature, Terminological, Thesaurus)
Controlled vocabularies | NADZIEJKA, David E. . . (WI) 886
Controlled vocabulary development | WALL, Eugene . . . . (MD) 1297
Controlled vocabulary indexing | LINDER, Elliott . . . . (NY) 729
Vocabulary & thesaurus construction | SAVAGE, Gretchen S. . . (CA) 1085
Vocabulary development | LOO, Shirley . . . . (DC) 740

VOCAL
French solo vocal music | VOLLEN, Gene E. . . . . . (KS) 1287
Opera & vocal music | JELLINEK, George . . . . . (NY) 596

VOCATIONAL (See also Career, Employment, Job, Occupational)
Business law vocational education | DIAL, Ron . . . . (NY) 299
Vocational & technical libraries | SLICK, Myrna H. . . . . . . (PA) 1149
Vocational collection development | SAKAI, Diane H. . . . . . . (HI) 1076
Vocational education | DAY, Virginia M. . . . . . . (MA) 283
Vocational materials | AYALA, John L. . . . . (CA) 42

VOCATIONAL (Cont'd)
Vocational materials development   WHITE, Charles R. . . . . . (CT) 1330
Vocational rehabilitation library   CHAPERO, Alicia . . . . . . (NY) 201

VOLCANOLOGY
Volcanology   NIELSEN, Elizabeth A. . . (DC) 903

VOLUNTEERS
County museums volunteer
   librarianship   HOWE, Mary T. . . . . (IL) 565
Friends & volunteers   PALMATIER, Susan M. . . (NH) 936
Literacy volunteerism   DIRKSEN, Jean . . . . (SK) 305
Staff, volunteer supervision   CARTER, Susan M. . . . . (IN) 190
Training & supervision of volunteers   WILLIAMS, Suzanne C. . (TX) 1346
Training & use of volunteers   KILLEEN, Erlene B. . . . . (VA) 648
Training children's services volunteers   OVERMYER, Elizabeth C. (CA) 931
Training elementary library volunteers   HLUHANY, Patricia . . . . (PA) 544
Training library volunteers   OFFERMAN, Mary C. . . . (IA) 917
Training of volunteers   FOX, Estella E. . . . . (KY) 394
   AROKSAAR, Richard D. . (WA) 34
Use of volunteers   SLIVKA, Regina . . . . . . (MI) 1149
Volunteer coordination   ALLEN, Stephanie O. . . (AZ) 16
   SPAZIANI, Carol . . . . . (IA) 1172
Volunteer literacy programs   TATE, Elizabeth L. . . . . (MD) 1225
Volunteer management   HAUSSMANN, Virginia D. (CA) 513
Volunteer program coordinator   SALVATORE, Gayle E. . (LA) 1078
Volunteer recruitment   SCHNEIDER, Marcia G. . (CA) 1097
Volunteer services   KENNEDY, Rose M. . . . (CA) 641
   STANLEY, Sydney J. . . . (CA) 1180
   PARTRIDGE, James C. . (MD) 945
   SMITH, Dorothy B. . . . . (TX) 1154
Volunteer training   YEE, J E. . . . . (WA) 1379
Volunteers   DOLNICK, Sandy F. . . . (IL) 310
   HEITKEMPER, Elsie M. . (WI) 523
Volunteers management   KLAUS, Susan B. . . . . . (OH) 658
Work with volunteers   TITUS, Barbara K. . . . . (DE) 1247

WAR
Civil War   TEMPLE, Wayne C. . . . (IL) 1230
Civil War historical collections   JORDAN, Ervin L. . . . . (VA) 616
Civil War history   BERENT, Irwin M. . . . . (VA) 84
Civil War, North Carolina sources,
   units   WOODARD, John R. . . . (NC) 1365
Electronic warfare   VAN VELZER, Verna J. . (CA) 1277
United States Civil War history   CAHILL, Colleen R. . . . (PA) 171
War & peace studies   YAMAMOTO, Conrad S. . (CA) 1376
World War II bibliography   ZIEGLER, Janet M. . . . (CA) 1388

WASHINGTON (See also Government, United States)
Washington affairs & legislation   MILLENSON, Roy H. . . . (MD) 835

WASTE (See also Sewage)
Basalt waste isolation project   TRAUB, Teresa L. . . . . (WA) 1254
Hazardous waste   LAWSON, James R. . . . (ME) 705
   WOLFE, Theresa L. . . . (NY) 1361
Hazardous waste, energy &
   environment   HASTINGS, Constance M. (TN) 511
Hazardous wastes   BUISMAN, Maria J. . . . (ON) 156
   CROXFORD, Agnes M. . (ON) 262
Nuclear high level waste   KING, Betty J. . . . . (WA) 650
Nuclear waste information   LANE, Sandra G. . . . . . (NY) 694
Nuclear waste management   NISH, Susan J. . . . . . . (PQ) 905
Radioactive waste   SHERMAN, Dottie . . . . (CT) 1128
Radioactive waste management   CURRY, Lenora Y. . . . . (NY) 266
   TRAUB, Teresa L. . . . . (WA) 1254
Sewage & solid waste libraries   ANJOU-DURAZZO, Martel
   T. . . . . (CA) 28
Sewage & toxic waste libraries   ANJOU-DURAZZO, Martel
   T. . . . . (CA) 28
Sewage, water, & wastewater libraries   ANJOU-DURAZZO, Martel
   T. . . . . (CA) 28
Solid, hazardous waste management   KAYES, Mary J. . . . . . (WI) 632
Water & wastewater engineering   SANSOBRINO, Jean C. . (CA) 1081
Water & wastewater treatment   LEE, Diana W. . . . . (AB) 709

WATER (See also Hydrogeology, Hydrology)
Paintings, drawings, water colors   MELTON, Howard E. . . . (OK) 823
Sewage, water, & wastewater libraries   ANJOU-DURAZZO, Martel
   T. . . . . (CA) 28
Water & air analysis   LEE, Diana W. . . . . (AB) 709
Water & wastewater engineering   SANSOBRINO, Jean C. . (CA) 1081
Water & wastewater treatment   LEE, Diana W. . . . . (AB) 709
Water management, reference
   service   PLOCKELMAN, Cynthia H. (FL) 978
Water resources   ORCUTT, Roberta K. . . . (NV) 925
Water resources & hydrology   HANSON, Donna M. . . . (ID) 498
Water resources cataloging   TORNABENE, Charles . . (FL) 1251
Water resources databases   JENSEN, Raymond A. . . (VA) 599
Water utility management   ERTZ, Ginger E. . . . . . . (PA) 353
West African soils & water resources   CANDELMO, Emily . . . . (NY) 178

WATERMARKS
Incunabula, watermarks   KRAKAUER, Elizabeth . . (CA) 675

WEEDING (See also Collections, Deselection, Selection)
Building, weeding pamphlet collection   ADAMS, Velma L. . . . . . (MS) 6
Inventory & weeding   TURLEY, Georgia P. . . . (WA) 1263
Reorganization, clean-up, weeding   HANLON, Patricia S. . . . (IL) 496
Select weed central adult circulation   DOYLE, Patricia A. . . . . (TX) 317
Weeding   NELSON, Veneese C. . . (UT) 895
Weeding & storage   HAYTON, E E. . . . . (ON) 517
Weeding collections   MARTIN, Jess A. . . . . . (TN) 776

WELDING
Welding library research   BAKER, Martha A. . . . . (OH) 49

WELFARE
Animal welfare information   LARSON, Jean A. . . . . . (MD) 699
Social welfare legislation   AUSTIN, Monique C. . . . (DC) 40

WEST VIRGINIA
Rare books, West Virginia   MARTIN, June R. . . . . . (WV) 777

WESTERN
Cataloging Western European
   monographs   SORURY, Kathryn L. . . . (IN) 1169
Collection devlpmnt, Western
   Americana   CLARK, Robert M. . . . . (MT) 218
History, American West   EMERSON, Tamsen L. . . (WY) 347
Libraries in Sierra Leone West Africa   WATERS, Bill F. . . . . . . (MO) 1308
Rare books, West Americana   DOBBERTEEN, Sara J. . (OK) 307
United States Western mining history   MC CAULEY, Philip F. . . (SD) 795
West African soils & water resources   CANDELMO, Emily . . . . (NY) 178
West European academic
   monographs   JAGER, Conradus . . . . (MA) 591
West European studies   FINEMAN, Charles S. . . (IL) 377
West European subscription agencies   JAGER, Conradus . . . . (MA) 591
Western American Jewish history   ARONER, Miriam D. . . . (CA) 34
Western European area studies   BROGAN, Martha L. . . . (MN) 139
Western European collection
   development   HUETING, Gail P. . . . . . (IL) 570
Western European humanities   DILLON, John B. . . . . . (WI) 303
Western European language materials   NEVIN, Susanne . . . . . (MN) 898
Western European languages &
   literature   BYRE, Calvin S. . . . . . . (IL) 169
Western Jewish history   ABRAMS, Jeanne E. . . . (CO) 3
Western United States history   MC CAULEY, Philip F. . . (SD) 795

WESTLAW
Legal databases, LEXIS & Westlaw   MURPHY, Malinda M. . . . (NC) 881
Legal databases, Westlaw, LEXIS   SWAN, Christine H. . . . (PA) 1213
LEXIS & Westlaw   GOTT, Gary D. . . . . . . (ND) 453
LEXIS & Westlaw searching   BUTLER, Marguerite L. . . (TX) 166
LEXIS & Westlaw training   WINSON, Gail I. . . . . . . (CA) 1355
Westlaw   OWENS, Robert L. . . . . (CA) 932
   ROCHE, Alvin A. . . . . . (LA) 1045
   O'CONNOR, Sandra L. . (NC) 916
   PATTELA, Rao R. . . . . (PA) 947

WESTLAW (Cont'd)
Westlaw & LEXIS training — DOWLING, Shelley L. .... (DC) 316
Westlaw computer-based research — SMITH, Susan A. ...... (CA) 1161
Westlaw database searching — SHEINWALD, Franette .. (NY) 1125
Westlaw research — SPRINGER, Michelle M. . (TX) 1176
Westlaw specialist — SUHRE, Carol A. ...... (OH) 1207

WHITE HOUSE
White House conferences — MILEVSKI, Sandra N. .... (DC) 835

WHOLESALE
Book wholesaling — STEVENS, Sharon G. .... (NJ) 1191
Research retail & wholesale industries — LAMBE, Michael .... (NY) 690
Wholesaling of audio & video materials — JACOBS, Peter J. ..... (CA) 590

WIESEL
Work of Elie Wiesel — CARGAS, Harry J. ..... (MO) 181

WILDER
Laura Ingalls Wilder — DOWNUM, Evelyn R. .... (AZ) 317

WILDLIFE (See also Natural)
Wildlife science — WEISS, Stephen C. .... (UT) 1320

WILLIAMSBURG (See also Virginiana)
18th century Williamsburg imprints — BERG, Susan .... (VA) 85

WISCONSIN (See also Milwaukee)
Wisconsin law — BEMIS, Michael F. ..... (WI) 79
— PAUL, Sara J. .... (WI) 949
Wisconsin library law — BAKER, Douglas ...... (WI) 48

WITNESSES
Library & expert witnesses databases — MAULSBY, Tommie L. ... (TX) 787

WOMEN (See also Feminism, Sexism)
American women's studies — DICKSON, Katherine M. . (MD) 301
Art & women studies — PUNIELLO, Francoise S. . (NJ) 997
Art & women's studies bibliography — ALLEN, Susan M. ...... (CA) 16
Art & women's studies reference — ALLEN, Susan M. ...... (CA) 16
Bibliography, women's studies — BJORKLUND, Edi ...... (WI) 100
Black, women & management studies — JONES-TRENT, Bernice R. (VA) 616
History, humanities, women's studies — FALK, Joyce D. .... (CA) 362
Library history, women — GROTZINGER, Laurel A. (MI) 473
Library instruction, women's studies — OSBORNE, Nancy S. ... (NY) 927
Military families & women — HARPER, Marie F. ...... (AL) 503
Minorities & women in science — JOHNSON, Sheila A. .... (NY) 609
Music, history & women's studies — LOMBARDI, Mary L. .... (CA) 738
Reference in women's & ethnic studies — MARIE, Jacquelyn ..... (CA) 770
Reference in women's studies — DICKSTEIN, Ruth H. .... (AZ) 301
Religious women — MISNER, Barbara ...... (WI) 847
Religious women's orders — DEUTSCH, N E. ...... (MO) 297
Research on women artists — WASSERMAN, Krystyna (DC) 1308
Research on Women writers, 1660-1800 — MULVIHILL, Maureen E. . (NY) 878
Research, women's studies — SMALLWOOD, Carol A. . (MI) 1151
Resource materials on women — SNAPP, Elizabeth M. .. (TX) 1162
Sources in women's studies — SMITH, Ellen A. .... (OH) 1154
United States & women's history — GALLOWAY, Sue ..... (CA) 415
United States women's history — MOSELEY, Eva S. ..... (MA) 870
Women — GERITY, Louise P. ..... (OR) 428
Women & libraries — STARR, Carol L. ...... (CA) 1182
Women & music — DOPP, Bonnie J. ..... (DC) 312
— ERICSON, Margaret D. ... (NY) 353
Women & religion — HURT, Charlene S. ...... (VA) 577
Women artists — FALK, Peter H. .... (CT) 362
— RITCHIE, Verna F. ..... (IA) 1036
Women in Africa — CASON, Maidel K. ..... (DE) 193
Women in librarianship — MOSLANDER, Charlotte D. (NY) 871

WOMEN (Cont'd)
Women in libraries — IRVINE, Betty J. .... (IN) 584
— PHENIX, Katharine J. .... (LA) 967
Women in the profession — KADANOFF, Diane G. .... (MA) 621
Women physicians — CHAFF, Sandra L. ..... (PA) 197
Women studies — BURSTEIN, Rose A. ..... (NY) 164
— FEINBERG, Renee ...... (NY) 369
— OWENS, Irene E. ...... (PA) 932
— FUGATE, Cynthia S. ..... (WA) 408
Women's art history — FURTAK, Rosemary .... (MN) 410
Women's center — ROBBINS, Diane D. ..... (NY) 1038
Women's collection — LOWMAN, Judith T. ..... (IL) 744
Women's collections — CHAFF, Sandra L. ..... (PA) 197
Women's health — VANHINE, Pamela M. .... (DC) 1275
Women's history — MILLER, Janet .... (IL) 838
— KRAFT, Katherine G. .... (MA) 675
Women's history & nursing — PALMISANO-DRUCKER, Elsalyn .... (NJ) 937
Women's information services — NERBOSO, Donna L. .... (NY) 895
Women's issues — KONDELIK, Marlene R. . (IN) 670
Women's poetry — GUY, Patricia A. .... (CA) 479
Women's studies — MILLS, Victoria A. ...... (AZ) 844
— ARIEL, Joan .... (CA) 31
— ELDREDGE, Mary ..... (CA) 342
— FROST, Michelle ...... (CA) 406
— HUMPHREYS, Nancy K. (CA) 574
— SIBLEY, Elizabeth A. ... (CA) 1135
— MCGAUGHRAN, Roberta W. .... (DC) 805
— PRITCHARD, Sarah M. . (DC) 994
— MANCUYAS, Natividad D. (IL) 764
— BIRNEY, Ann E. .... (KS) 98
— ENGELHART, Anne D. .. (MA) 349
— FELDT, Candice K. ..... (MA) 369
— GRIGG, Susan .... (MA) 470
— MAIO, Kathleen L. ..... (MA) 762
— BIGGS, Debra R. ...... (MI) 95
— DRISCOLL, Jacqueline .. (MI) 320
— KAHN, Leslie A. .... (NJ) 622
— MILLER, Lynn F. .... (NJ) 840
— REED, Elizabeth M. ..... (OH) 1015
— EZELL, Johanna V. ..... (PA) 360
— DRYDEN, Sherre H. ..... (SC) 321
— RAY, Joyce M. .... (TX) 1011
— WEBSTER, Linda ...... (TX) 1314
— MCGOWAN, Sarah M. ... (WI) 807
— SEARING, Susan E. .... (WI) 1109
Women's studies & peace research — HAMILTON-PENNELL, Christine .... (CO) 492
Women's studies collection — BRANT, Susan L. ..... (WI) 129
Women's studies collection development — REDFERN, Bernice I. .... (CA) 1014
— CANEVARI DE PAREDES, Donna A. .... (SK) 178
Women's studies information — HICKS, Barbara A. .... (ON) 536
Women's studies librarianship — RUDISELL, Carol A. .... (DE) 1065
— COMER, Cynthia H. .... (OH) 234
Women's studies, Middle East — BEZIRGAN, Basima .... (IL) 93

WOOD
Manufacturing wood library furniture — VAN PELT, Peter J. ..... (NY) 1277
Wood products research — SCHARMER, Roger C. ... (WI) 1090

WOODCUTS
Woodcuts of J J Lankes — LANKES, J B. .... (VA) 696

WORD (See also Software)
Computer word processing — COUP, William A. .... (FL) 251
Word processing — EMMONS, Mary E. ..... (AK) 348
— MORGAN, Bradford A. .. (SD) 863
— GOERDT, Arthur L. .... (TX) 443
Word processing, biblgph preparation — MANDEL, Douglas J. .... (IL) 765
Word processing, record management systs — KEE, Walter A. .... (NC) 634
Word processing software development — SCHWARTZ, James M. . (SD) 1104

WORKERS (See also Personnel)

Managing student workers	KEMP, Henrietta J.	(IA)	639
Placing permanent library workers	JOHNSON, Linnea R.	(IL)	607
	KLINGBERG, Jane E.	(IL)	661
Placing temporary library workers	JOHNSON, Linnea R.	(IL)	607
	KLINGBERG, Jane E.	(IL)	661
Recruiting temporary & permanent workers	JOHNSON, Linnea R.	(IL)	607

WORKFLOW (See also Organization)

Cataloging management & workflow	CLARK, Sharon E.	(IL)	218
Organization & workflow	MORRIS, Dilys E.	(IA)	866
Revision of workflow	PHILLIPS, Richard F.	(NJ)	969
Technical services workflow planning	LINSE, Mary M.	(MO)	731
Workflow analysis	LOWELL, Virginia L.	(OH)	744
Workflow & cataloging	HERVEY, Norma J.	(MN)	533

WORKSHOPS (See also Instruction, Seminars, Training)

Conference & workshop planning	MOON, Ilse	(FL)	857
Interlibrary loan workshops	SCHWEERS, Lucy	(CO)	1105
Outreach workshops	BUTLER, Randall R.	(CA)	167
Professional workshops	DAVIS, Virginia K.	(ON)	281
Public speaking & workshops	GRAUER, Sally M.	(NY)	458
Storytelling programs & workshops	GREENE, Ellin P.	(NJ)	464
Training & development workshops	TAYLOR, Arthur R.	(MO)	1226
Training & workshops	ROSSMAN, Muriel J.	(MN)	1059
Training workshops	HIRONS, Jean L.	(DC)	543
Workshop design & coordination	WEBSTER, Linda	(TX)	1314
Workshop logistics	SPARKMAN, Mickey M.	(TX)	1171
Workshop organization	BURKS, C J.	(UT)	161
Workshop planner & producer	LYNCH, Minnie L.	(LA)	752
Workshops	SMITH, Harold F.	(MO)	1155
	MENDELL, Stefanie	(NC)	823
Workshops & institutes	LYNCH, Mary D.	(PA)	752
Workshops on computers	YARBROUGH, Joseph W.	(MI)	1378

WORKSTUDY

Workstudy employee supervision	FOX, Lynne M.	(CO)	395

WORLD (See also Global, International)

Art & world symbolism	RONNBERG, Annmari	(NY)	1053
Information for world peace & humanity	KIANG, C K.	(IN)	646
Research on world hunger	KASPERSON, Jeanne X.	(MA)	629
World economic outlook publications	HARTMAN, David G.	(MA)	508
World history	OSWALT, Paul K.	(TX)	929
World librarianship	KRZYS, Richard A.	(PA)	681
World politics	BEESON, Lone C.	(CA)	74
World War II bibliography	ZIEGLER, Janet M.	(CA)	1388
Worldwide exchange agreements	SNIDER, Elizabeth M.	(OH)	1163
Worldwide scientific acquisitions	SNIDER, Elizabeth M.	(OH)	1163

WORM

WORM applications	GALE, John C.	(VA)	413

WRITING (See also Authors, Copywriting, Essays, Exposition, Paleography, Reports, Reviewing, Rewriting)

Abstracting & technical writing	FISHER, Daphne V.	(PA)	380
Administration including grant writing	LYNCH, Mary D.	(PA)	752
Applied arts, writing & editing	FRANKLIN, Linda C.	(NY)	398
Article, report, & review writing	EDELSON, Ken	(NJ)	335
Article writing	STUDWELL, William E.	(IL)	1204
Automation procedure writing	PALMER, Marguerite C.	(WV)	936
Book publishing, writing & editing	EASTMAN, Ann H.	(VA)	333
Book writing	STUDWELL, William E.	(IL)	1204
Communications, writing, editing	EATENSON, Ervin T.	(TX)	333
Computer applications to writing	SCHWARTZ, James M.	(SD)	1104
Creative writing of poetry	GREEN, Rose B.	(PA)	462
Curriculum writing	JENKINS, Lydia E.	(DC)	597
Database documentation chapter writing	MARANGONI, Eugene G.	(CA)	768
Discography, writing	MORAN, William R.	(CA)	862
Documentation writer	EPPES, William D.	(NY)	351

WRITING (Cont'd)

Editing & writing	FILES, Patricia T.	(CA)	376
	WISMER, Donald	(ME)	1357
	BLUMBERG-MCKEE, Hazel	(MN)	107
	TANNER, Anne B.	(PA)	1222
	TAYLOR, Nancy L.	(TX)	1228
	CHAGNON, Danielle G.	(PQ)	197
Editing, writing	GOTTLIEB, Robert A.	(ME)	453
Editing, writing & design	MOLLO, Terry	(NY)	853
Editing, writing, public relations	WEISENBURGER, Patricia J.	(KS)	1319
Editing, writing, researching	MANNING, Jo A.	(NY)	766
Editor & writer	NIEHAUS, Barbara J.	(IL)	903
Editor, writer	GROTE, Janet H.	(NY)	473
Film & video writing & production	TALIT, Lynn	(CT)	1221
Freelance writing	RUGG, John D.	(OH)	1066
Fundraising, book publishing & writing	GRAVES, Sid F.	(MS)	459
Grant & other writing & editing	WRIGHT-HESS, Anne H.	(NY)	1373
Grant proposal writing	MORAN, Irene E.	(CA)	862
Grant writing	MCWHORTER, Jimmie M.	(AL)	818
	MARTZ, David J.	(DC)	779
	KIEFFER, Marian L.	(IA)	647
	ROBISON, Diana E.	(IL)	1045
	SOMERVILLE, Mary R.	(KY)	1167
	HELO, Martin	(MA)	525
	TRICARICO, Mary A.	(MA)	1256
	DEL SORDO, Jean S.	(MD)	290
	MORROW, Paula J.	(MO)	869
	CLARK, Robert M.	(MT)	218
	LINDSLEY, Barbara N.	(NY)	730
	FINAN, Patrick E.	(OH)	377
	LONG, Sarah A.	(OR)	740
	BRICE, Heather W.	(PA)	134
	EVERHART, Nancy L.	(PA)	358
	MITCHELL, Joan M.	(PA)	849
	YATES, Diane G.	(PA)	1378
Grant writing, administration	SARLES, Christie V.	(NH)	1083
Grant writing & external funding	FELLA, Sarah C.	(OR)	370
Grant writing & fundraising	DUPLAIX, Sally J.	(RI)	327
Grant writing & implementation	BRENNAN, Deborah B.	(RI)	132
Grants, research & proposal writing	SECKELSON, Linda E.	(NY)	1110
Grantsmanship writing & reviewing	KELLEY, John F.	(PA)	636
Health effects research writing	MUNRO, Nancy B.	(TN)	879
Historical research & writing	BROOKS, Jerrold L.	(NC)	140
	HESS, James W.	(NY)	534
	MORRISSEY, Charles T.	(VT)	869
	DIBIASE, Linda P.	(WA)	299
Historical research, indexing & writing	DENNIS, Mary R.	(IA)	292
Historical writing	CHRISTENSEN, Erin S.	(CO)	211
	PINKETT, Harold T.	(DC)	974
	FRIDLEY, Russell W.	(ME)	403
History research & writing	SHIDELER, John C.	(WA)	1129
Law & business writing & editing	HOYT, Henry M.	(NY)	566
Legal research & writing	BRIDGMAN, David L.	(CA)	135
	KRIKORIAN, Rosanne	(CA)	678
	EDWARDS, John D.	(IA)	337
	POINTON, Louis R.	(IL)	980
	COCHRAN, J W.	(MS)	225
	COGGINS, Timothy L.	(NC)	227
	GIANNATTASI, Gerard E.	(NY)	430
	HANLEY, Thomas L.	(OH)	496
Legal research & writing teaching	MURRAY, James M.	(WA)	882
Legal research, reference & writing	KISSANE, Mary K.	(MO)	656
Legal writing	WEST, Carol C.	(MS)	1326
	LEONARD, James	(OH)	716
	MCFARLAND, Anne S.	(OH)	804
Library building program writing	STEWART, John D.	(VA)	1192
Library history writing	MCCRIMMON, Barbara S.	(FL)	800
Library public relations writing	BRYAN, Carol L.	(WV)	151
Manual writing	NEW, Gregory R.	(DC)	898
Medical, pharmaceutical writing	CARVER, Mary	(NY)	191
Medical writing	BEATTY, William K.	(IL)	70
Medical writing & editing	CLEMENTS, Betty H.	(GA)	221
	SPARKS, Martha E.	(NC)	1171
Music research, writing, editing	GLASFORD, G R.	(NY)	440
Musicological research & writing	GUSHEE, Marion S.	(IL)	478
Nashville writers	HEARNE, Mary G.	(TN)	518
Nonfiction & fiction writing	BRADWAY, Becky J.	(IL)	126
Oral & written communication	EBERHARD, Neysa C.	(KS)	334

WRITING (Cont'd)

Peer book writing instructor	KORNITSKY, Judith M. .	(FL)	672
Philological research & writing	HUMEZ, Nicholas D.	(ME)	573
Planning & proposal writing	VAUGHN, Frances A. . . .	(TX)	1280
Procedure & guideline writing	STRONG, Sunny A.	(WA)	1203
Professional writing	PROCES, Stephen L. . . .	(WI)	994
Proofreading, writing, editing, indexing	GAGNON, Donna M. . . .	(CA)	412
Proposal writing & database searching	KUHL, Danuta	(VA)	682
Proposal writing & fundraising	GOLDBERG, Susan S. . . .	(AZ)	445
Public relations writing	POMERLEAU, Suzanne M.	(FL)	982
Public relations, writing & publishing	ROUSE, Roscoe	(OK)	1061
Publications editing & writing	SHIRES, Nancy P.	(NC)	1131
Reading, writing, literacy consulting	MCDONOUGH, Timothy M.	(CA)	803
Reference tools, writing	BOAST, Carol	(IL)	108
Research & analytical report writing	MEYER, Andrea P.	(CO)	829
Research & writing	MOON, Ilse	(FL)	857
	LANDAU, Cynthia R. . . .	(NH)	692
	GLATT, Carol R.	(NJ)	440
	FALARDEAU, Ernest R. . .	(NM)	361
	MILLER, Bryan M.	(NM)	836
	WAGNER, Stephen K. . . .	(NY)	1292
Research & writing American history	SCHEIPS, Paul J.	(MD)	1091
Research on Women writers, 1660-1800	MULVIHILL, Maureen E. . .	(NY)	878
Research, writing	BERNARD, Bobbi	(MA)	88
	GREENBERG, Hinda F. .	(NJ)	463
Research, writing & editing	CHRISTIANSON, Elin B. .	(IN)	212
Researching & writing	KRAFT, Gwen L.	(AK)	675
Review writing & editing	SILVER, Gary L. . . . . . .*	(MI)	1138
Reviewing, editing, writing	ARK, Connie E.	(OH)	31
Reviews of editing & writing	GORDON, Ruth I.	(CA)	452
Reviews, writing, editing	VAN NIEL, Eloise S.	(HI)	1276
Science writing	MAISEL, Merry W.	(CA)	762
Script writing & narration	SANKER, Paul N.	(NY)	1081
Speaking, writing, automation	JOHNSON, Pat M.	(TX)	608
Teaching writing	BATES, Barbara S.	(PA)	63
Teaching writing & editing	BLUMER, Thomas J. . . .	(DC)	107
Technical writer	HINTON, N E.	(KS)	543
Technical writing	BLITZ, Ruth R.	(CA)	105
	MARCHIANO, Marilyn C.	(CA)	768
	WRIGHT, Betty A.	(CA)	1370
	RIDER, Philip R.	(IL)	1032
	SILVESTER, June P. . . .	(MD)	1139
	SLOAN, Cheryl A.	(MD)	1149
	GASTON, Judith A.	(MN)	421
	SPYROS, Marsha L.	(NY)	1177
	SWEENEY, Del	(PA)	1215
	HARDIN, Nancy E.	(TN)	500
	SACKETT-WILK, Susan A.	(TX)	1073
	SANDERS, William D. . .	(UT)	1080
	SCHAEFER, Mary E. . . .	(VA)	1089
	FOSKETT, Antony C. . . .	(AUS)	392
Technical writing & editing	GIRILL, T R.	(CA)	438
	JACOBS, Horace	(CA)	589
	WEIL, Ben H.	(NJ)	1317
Technical writing, editing	URKEN, Madeline	(NJ)	1270
Technical writing, software documtn	GREENE, Nancy S.	(PA)	464
Telephone & written reference	PLUMER, F I.	(NY)	978
Theological research & writing	WROTENBERY, Carl R. . .	(TX)	1373
Underground writing & ephemera	BJORKLUND, Edi	(WI)	100
Writer	DALY, Jay	(MA)	271
	SHARMA, Ravindra N. . .	(WI)	1122
Writer & history archives	NEWTON, Virginia A. . . .	(AK)	900
Writer, designer, technology	SEITZ, Robert J.	(NY)	1113
Writer for film & video	BEATTY, R M.	(IN)	70
Writing	MCKENZIE, Harry	(CA)	811
	ROSS, Rodney A.	(DC)	1058
	DANIEL, Alfred I.	(DE)	272
	MARTIN, Clarece	(GA)	775
	CRAWFORD, Daniel R. . .	(IA)	256
	BORUZKOWSKI, Lilly A.	(IL)	117
	BOSTIAN, Irma R.	(IL)	117
	CAMP, John F.	(IL)	175
	DOWNS, Jane B.	(IL)	317
	SHUMAN, Marilyn J. . . .	(IL)	1134
	WIREN, Eleanor C.	(IN)	1356
	HUGGINS, Dean A.	(MA)	571
	MCDOWELL, Sylvia A. . .	(MA)	804

WRITING (Cont'd)

Writing	PALMER, David W.	(MI)	936
	RENKIEWICZ, Frank A. .	(MI)	1023
	HYNES, Arleen M.	(MN)	580
	STIEGEMEYER, Nancy H.	(MO)	1193
	SCHEPP, Brad J.	(NJ)	1091
	GUBITS, Helen S.	(NY)	475
	KARNEZIS, Kristine C. . .	(NY)	627
	REINSTEIN, Julia B.	(NY)	1021
	WULKER, Clare	(OH)	1374
	BOYTINCK, Paul	(PA)	124
	CORNOG, Martha	(PA)	247
	HOSKINS, Sylvia H.	(VA)	561
	HALE, Linda L.	(BC)	485
	KISHIMOTO, Hiroko	(JAP)	656
Writing about Afro-American literature	PERRY, Margaret	(IN)	960
Writing & directing educational films	HARTLEY, Elda E.	(CT)	508
Writing & display publicity	BOYD, Ruth E.	(CO)	122
Writing & editing	COYLE, Leslie P.	(CA)	253
	DOWNEY, Lynn A.	(CA)	316
	MACKINTOSH, Mary L. .	(CA)	757
	MILLER, Ralph D.	(CA)	841
	SCARBOROUGH, Katharine T.	(CA)	1087
	MEYER, Andrea P.	(CO)	829
	GRAY, Dorothy L.	(DC)	459
	KENDRICK, Brent L. . . .	(DC)	640
	KIEFER, Rosemary M. . .	(FL)	647
	KNOBLAUCH, Mark G. . .	(IL)	665
	PEARSON, Lois R.	(IL)	952
	HOOK-SHELTON, Sara A.	(IN)	556
	ROTH, Sally	(KS)	1059
	STEVENSON, Michael I. .	(MA)	1191
	HEISER, Nancy E.	(ME)	523
	MAGNUSON, Norris A. . .	(MN)	759
	DECANDIDO, Graceanne A.	(NY)	285
	WRIGHT, Sylvia H.	(NY)	1373
	FRY, Mildred C.	(OH)	406
	MILLER, William	(OH)	843
	RATLIFF, Priscilla	(OH)	1009
	SULLIVAN, Frances L. . .	(OH)	1207
	LARSON, Signe E.	(OR)	700
	BLEIER, Carol S.	(PA)	105
	CUTRONA, Cheryl	(PA)	268
	ZIPF, Elizabeth M.	(PA)	1389
	BAKER, Bonnie U.	(TN)	48
	GEARY, Kathleen A.	(TX)	424
	BELLAMY, Patricia C. . .	(ON)	78
Writing & editing news & features	CHEATHAM, Bertha M. . .	(NY)	204
Writing & editing pictorial histories	LUSKEY, Judith	(DC)	749
Writing & editing policy manuals	COURSON, M S.	(MD)	251
Writing & editing professional books	WEISBURG, Hilda K. . . .	(NJ)	1319
Writing & editing scientific reports	LAUTENSCHLAG, Elisabeth C.	(PA)	703
Writing & indexing	VAILLANCOURT, Pauline M.	(NY)	1271
Writing & monitoring grants	TRIVISON, Margaret A. . .	(CA)	1257
Writing & photography	FREY, Roxanne C.	(IL)	403
Writing & translating	LIU, David T.	(TX)	734
Writing & writing	RANHAND, Jori L.	(NY)	1007
Writing book reviews	ESTES, Sally C.	(IL)	355
Writing building programs	DAHLGREN, Jean E. . . .	(TX)	269
Writing children's non-fiction books	MARSTON, Hope I.	(NY)	775
Writing documentation	ROTH, Alison C.	(CT)	1059
Writing/editing	ERLICK, Louise V.	(MD)	353
	HUNTER, Joy W.	(TN)	576
Writing, editing & indexing	PALMER, Marguerite C. . .	(WV)	936
Writing, editing & publishing	JOHNSON, Richard D. . .	(NY)	608
Writing, editing, & training	SYMES, Dal S.	(WA)	1217
Writing for children	WHITEHEAD, Jane	(TN)	1332
Writing for professional journals	EAGLEN, Audrey B.	(OH)	331
Writing for publication	WEAVER, Carolyn G. . . .	(WA)	1312
Writing furniture specifications	DAHLGREN, Jean E. . . .	(TX)	269
Writing history, federal communication	AINES, Andrew A.	(MD)	8
Writing, Hollywood costumes	NELSON-HARB, Sally R. .	(CA)	895
Writing institutional histories	CANTELON, Philip L. . . .	(MD)	179
Writing library & literature curriculum	JACKSON, Gloria D. . . .	(CA)	587
Writing library curriculum skills	SWITZER, Catherine M. . .	(WI)	1216

WRITING (Cont'd)

Writing manuscript guide entries	HULL, Mary M.	(TX)	572
Writing news releases	GIGLIO, Linda M.	(MI)	433
Writing of manuals	SCOTT, Patricia L.	(UT)	1107
Writing of user documentation	WHITMAN, Mary L.	(PA)	1333
Writing on music	LAWRENCE, Arthur P.	(NY)	704
Writing policies & procedures	KNIGHT, Rita C.	(AZ)	664
Writing procedures manuals	ZYNJUK, Nila L.	(MD)	1392
Writing programs, online card catalog	JORDAN, Sharon L.	(WA)	617
Writing province history	STRECK, Helen T.	(KS)	1201
Writing reviews & editing	MATHES, Miriam S.	(WA)	783
Writing United Methodist history	ROLLER, Twila J.	(NM)	1051
Written & audiovisual documentation	MARCHAND, Jacques	(PQ)	768
Written business communication	SILVA, Mary E.	(WA)	1138
Written communication	ROBINSON, Jolene A.	(NY)	1044

WYOMING

Wyoming history	CHISUM, Emmett D.	(WY)	209

XYLOPHONE

Marimba, xylophone collection	GERHARDT, Edwin L.	(MD)	428

YOUNG

Children & young people services	BARRON, Daniel D.	(SC)	60
Children's & young people's literature	BRUNER, Katharine E.	(TN)	150
Children's literature for young children	BALDWIN, Ruth M.	(FL)	52
Programming for young children	FADER, Ellen G.	(CT)	360
Programming for young people	JANSON, Sherryl A.	(AZ)	594
Selection for young people	IMONDI, Lenore R.	(RI)	582
Young people's book selection	DAVIS, Inez W.	(TN)	279
Young people's library services	FAHERTY, Gladys W.	(MD)	361
Young people's literature	MILLER, Barbara S.	(KY)	835
	MCGARRY, Marie L.	(MA)	805
	SCHOLTEN, Frances	(MD)	1098
Young people's services	SCHEUERMAN, Luanne J.	(KS)	1092
Young teens book selection	RAPPELT, John F.	(NY)	1008

YOUNG ADULT (See also Adolescent, Teenagers, Young, Youth)

Acquisitions, young adult materials	CORLEE, Lisa	(OK)	246
Adult & young adult collection devlpmnt	STEVENSON, Sheila M.	(IL)	1191
Adult & young adult readers advisory	TREMBLAY, Carolyn B.	(NH)	1255
Adult & young adult services	CHALLENER, Marcee M.	(FL)	197
	SADLER, Shirley L.	(IL)	1073
	STEVENSON, Sheila M.	(IL)	1191
	REILLY, Deborah D.	(MD)	1020
Audiovisual for young adults	CHARVAT, Catherine T.	(OH)	203
Children & young adult books	GILBERT, Ophelia R.	(MO)	434
	MCELDERRY, Margaret K.	(NY)	804
Children & young adult library services	PARIS, Janelle A.	(TX)	940
Children & young adult literature	MARR, Charles A.	(CA)	773
	HATHAWAY, Milton G.	(NC)	512
	BURT, Lesta N.	(TX)	164
Children & young adult reference	TUPPER, Bobbie	(HI)	1263
Children & young adult selection	MATECUN, Marilyn L.	(MI)	783
Children & young adult services	SRYGLEY, Sara K.	(FL)	1177
	BARRETT, John C.	(NY)	59
	PANCOE, Deborra S.	(PA)	937
	STATTON, Alison H.	(TX)	1183
	FLETCHER, Robert A.	(WA)	385
	SHELDEN, Lucinda D.	(WA)	1125
Children & young adults	PROVOST, Beverly A.	(NY)	996
Children & young adults booktalking	ROCHMAN, Hazel P.	(IL)	1046
Children's & young adult books	JONES, Trevelyn E.	(NY)	615
Children's & young adult librarianship	TALBERT, Dorothy R.	(UT)	1220
Children's & young adult literature	ROSEN, Elizabeth M.	(CA)	1055
	DAIGNEAULT, Audrey I.	(CT)	270
	FISHER, Margery M.	(CT)	381
	SPENCER, Albert F.	(GA)	1173
	LOWE, Joy L.	(LA)	744
	EHRICH, Joan C.	(MA)	339
	WERNER, Laura L.	(MO)	1325
	O'BRYANT, Alice A.	(MT)	915
	BUSBIN, O. M.	(NC)	164
	HERBERT, Barbara R.	(NJ)	530

YOUNG ADULT (Cont'd)

Children's & young adult literature	VANDERGRIFT, Kay E.	(NJ)	1274
	MASCIA, Regina B.	(NY)	780
	LATROBE, Kathy H.	(OK)	701
	LAUGHLIN, Mildred A.	(OK)	703
	ANTHONY, Rose M.	(WI)	29
	DRESANG, Eliza T.	(WI)	319
	HOWARD, Elizabeth F.	(WV)	564
	SALTMAN, Judith M.	(BC)	1077
	HAMBLETON, Alixe E.	(SK)	490
Children's & young adult mtrls selection	ROBERTS, Sallie H.	(OH)	1041
Children's & young adult programming	WALSH, Lynn R.	(FL)	1299
Children's & young adult programs	SOMERVILLE, Mary R.	(KY)	1167
	O'BRYANT, Alice A.	(MT)	915
Children's & young adult services	CANTILLAS, Caroline M.	(LA)	179
	HOMAN, Frances M.	(MD)	555
	GORMAN, Audrey J.	(NJ)	452
	RAZZANO, Barbara W.	(NJ)	1012
	CHEATHAM, Bertha M.	(NY)	204
	LAUGHLIN, Mildred A.	(OK)	703
	BROADWAY, Marsha D.	(UT)	138
	CHAUVETTE, Catherine A.	(VA)	204
	JONES, Norma L.	(WI)	614
Children's & young adult work	BARNARD, Sandra K.	(CA)	57
Editing, reviewing, young adult lib srvs	CAMPBELL, Patricia J.	(CA)	177
Education, young adults	SCHULTZ, Cathern J.	(WI)	1101
Juvenile & young adult col development	GOLEY, Elaine P.	(TX)	447
Juvenile & young adult literature	HOUSEWARD, Bernice A.	(MI)	563
Juvenile & young adult programming	HOUSEWARD, Bernice A.	(MI)	563
Library management, regional young adult	CHARVAT, Catherine T.	(OH)	203
Library materials for young adults	NOONAN, Eileen F.	(IL)	908
Library service to young adults	BEDNAR, Sheila	(NY)	73
Literature for children & young adults	FISHER, Joan W.	(MD)	381
Materials & services for young adults	BARD, Therese B.	(HI)	56
	MILLER, Marilyn L.	(NC)	840
	MILLER, Ellen L.	(VA)	837
Middle school & young adult literature	KIMMEL, Margaret M.	(PA)	649
Services for children & young adults	ROBERTS, Scott J.	(MI)	1041
Services to young adults	MCLAUGHLIN, Hilda S.	(TX)	813
Young adult	MOORE, Mary L.	(CA)	860
	CONKLIN, Candace V.	(FL)	236
	CARNELLI, Sandra R.	(IL)	183
	COHEN, Susan K.	(NJ)	229
	NEDSWICK, Robert	(NJ)	891
	HOFFMAN, Barbara E.	(NY)	547
	BELVIN, Robert J.	(OH)	78
	PETIT, J M.	(OH)	965
	MORRIS, Karen L.	(VA)	867
Young adult & audiovisual services	HULTZ, Karen W.	(NY)	573
Young adult & children's materials	STURGEON, Mary C.	(AR)	1205
Yng adult & children's print & non-print	WOODS, Selina J.	(MA)	1367
Young adult & children's services	POMERLEAU, Suzanne M.	(FL)	982
	SVEINSSON, Joan L.	(TX)	1212
	CURRIE, Bertha B.	(NS)	266
Young adult & senior citizen services	MYRON, Victoria L.	(IA)	885
Young adult bibliographic instruction	REIF, Lenore S.	(IL)	1019
Young adult book club newsletter	JACKSON, Nancy D.	(NY)	588
Young adult book selection	MOORE, Richard K.	(CA)	861
	WINSLOW, Carol M.	(IN)	1355
	WISOTZKI, Lila B.	(MD)	1358
	WRIGHT, Patricia Y.	(OK)	1372
Young adult book talks	OSSOLINSKI, Lynn	(NV)	928
Young adult books	BURGESS, Eileen E.	(MD)	159
	HOLTZE, Sally H.	(NY)	555
	WARD, Peter K.	(NY)	1304
Young adult books, acquisition & editing	JACKSON, Nancy D.	(NY)	588
Young adult books & materials	WILLIAMS, Helen E.	(MD)	1343
Young adult books promotion & publicity	JACKSON, Nancy D.	(NY)	588
Young adult collection development	MEYERS, Kathleen H.	(AZ)	831
	RUBINSTEIN, Roslyn	(NY)	1065
Young adult education	MCKEE, Barbara J.	(OH)	810
Young adult fiction	BRADBURN, Frances B.	(NC)	125

YOUNG ADULT (Cont'd)

Young adult fiction & nonfiction acqs	BUCKLEY, Virginia L. . . .	(NY)	154
Young adult fiction selection	TYSON, Edith S.	(OH)	1267
Young adult librarianship	CLARK, Patricia A.	(CA)	217
	GERARD, Sandra C. . . .	(CA)	428
	MANOR, Lawanda	(DC)	767
	HEMENWAY, Patti J. . . .	(IL)	525
	MUNDY, Suzanne W. . . .	(MA)	879
	HABINSKI, Carol A. . . .	(OH)	481
Young adult literature	NILSEN, Alleen P.	(AZ)	904
	CAMPBELL, Patricia J. . . .	(CA)	177
	JAIN, Celeste C.	(CA)	591
	WILKINSON, Evalyn S. . .	(GA)	1340
	KOLLASCH, Matthew A. .	(IA)	669
	HOLBROCK, Mary A. . . .	(IL)	550
	JACKSON, Susan M. . . .	(IN)	588
	DRUSE, Judith A.	(KS)	321
	LYNN, Barbara A.	(KS)	752
	JACOBSON-BEYER, Harry E.	(KY)	590
	MOSLEY, Mattie J.	(LA)	871
	GALLAGHER, Mary E. . .	(MA)	414
	LEVINE, Susan H.	(MD)	721
	BIELICH, Paul S.	(MI)	95
	ROBERTS, Scott J.	(MI)	1041
	SIBLEY, Carol H.	(MN)	1134
	BELCHER, Nancy S. . . .	(MO)	76
	RANCER, Susan P. . . .	(NC)	1006
	RENICK, Paul R.	(ND)	1023
	GRAZIER, Dorothy W. . .	(NH)	460
	FICHTELBERG, Susan . .	(NJ)	374
	GROSSHANS, Merilyn P. .	(NV)	473
	CUSEO, Allan A.	(NY)	267
	FLOWERS, Helen F. . . .	(NY)	386
	HIGGINS, Judith H.	(NY)	538
	HOPKINS, Lee B.	(NY)	558
	LENZ, Millicent A.	(NY)	716
	LONG, Joanna R.	(NY)	739
	RYBARCZYK, Barclay S. .	(NY)	1071
	RIFFEY, Robin S.	(OH)	1033
	SCHWELK, Jennifer C. . .	(OH)	1105
	WYNN, Vivian R.	(OH)	1375
	ALSWORTH, Frances W. .	(OK)	18
	COWEN, Linda L.	(OK)	253
	HALE, Carolyn R.	(PA)	485
	MILLER, Mary E.	(PA)	840
	YOUREE, Beverly B. . . .	(TN)	1384
	CARTER, Betty B.	(TX)	189
	HOLLAND, Deborah K. . .	(TX)	550
	WIDENER, Sarah A. . . .	(TX)	1335
	BIGELOW, Therese G. . .	(VA)	95
	KNAPP, Marilyn S.	(VA)	663
	ANDERSEN, Eileen	(WA)	21
	CHATTON, Barbara A. . .	(WY)	204
	OBERG, Dianne	(AB)	913
	KOSTIAK, Adele E. . . .	(ON)	673
Young adult literature & services	BUSH, Margaret A. . . .	(MA)	165
	VEITCH, Carol J.	(NC)	1281
Young adult literature reviewing	TUZINSKI, Jean H.	(PA)	1266
Young adult materials	ROSENBERG, Melvin H. .	(CA)	1056
	DEQUIN, Henry C.	(IL)	293
	ZVIRIN, Stephanie H. . .	(IL)	1392
	WHITLOW, Cherrill M. . .	(NM)	1333
	PASHEL, Susan M.	(PA)	945
	TYSON, Christy	(WA)	1267
Young adult materials & services	MITCHELL, Carolyn	(CO)	848
	ROGERS, Joann V.	(KY)	1049
	WRIGHT, John G.	(AB)	1371
Young adult media	HUNT, Mary A.	(FL)	575
Young adult nonfiction & fiction	CROSS, Claudette S. . . .	(CA)	260
Young adult programs	TYSON, Edith S.	(OH)	1267
	TOMLIN, Celia K.	(UT)	1250
Young adult readers advisory	BENOIT, Ursula L.	(ON)	83
Young adult reading guidance	MALTBY, Florence H. . .	(MO)	764
Young adult reference	ZANARINI, Linda S. . . .	(NE)	1386
Young adult reference services	GROOMS, Richard O. . .	(AL)	472
Young adult religious literature	PEARL, Patricia D.	(VA)	952
Young adult reviewing	SCHLANSER, Deborah B. .	(CA)	1093
	BALL, Diane A.	(OH)	52
Young adult reviews	WADE, Sherry A.	(CA)	1290

YOUNG ADULT (Cont'd)

Young adult service	BEAN, Bobby G.	(IL)	69
	MILLER, Marcia M.	(IN)	840
Young adult services	ATKINSON, Joan L.	(AL)	38
	GUTHRIE, Virginia G. . . .	(AL)	479
	LEWIS, Jean R.	(AZ)	723
	BANGE, Stephanie D. . . .	(CA)	54
	CONDIT, Larry D.	(CA)	235
	FARMER, Lesley S.	(CA)	364
	FLUM, Judith G.	(CA)	386
	LAPERRIERE, Renee J. .	(CA)	697
	MINUDRI, Regina U.	(CA)	847
	SCRIBNER, Ruth B.	(CA)	1108
	STARR, Carol L.	(CA)	1182
	SAVAGE, Judith G.	(CT)	1085
	WALLACE, Michael T. . .	(DC)	1298
	ROBERTS, Judith M. . . .	(DE)	1040
	SIMMONS, Elizabeth M. .	(DE)	1139
	HARBER, Patty S.	(GA)	499
	SEARCY, David L.	(GA)	1109
	FREITAS-OBREGON, Brenda J.	(HI)	401
	SPENCER, Caroline P. . .	(HI)	1173
	BOGNANNI, Kathleen J. .	(IA)	111
	DUTCHER, Terry R.	(IA)	329
	KOLLASCH, Matthew A. .	(IA)	669
	TALLEY, Loretta K.	(IA)	1221
	BABANOURY, Betty G. . .	(IL)	43
	BOUGHTON, Ruth E. . . .	(IL)	119
	CALLAGHAN, Linda W. . .	(IL)	173
	DAVIS, Carol L.	(IL)	278
	LAWSON, Mary L.	(IL)	705
	NEAL, Nancy J.	(IL)	890
	SCHOLTZ, James C. . . .	(IL)	1098
	HEROY, Phyllis B.	(LA)	532
	SANTA, Elizabeth C. . . .	(LA)	1082
	SOTO, Donna G.	(LA)	1169
	FLANNERY, Susan M. . .	(MA)	383
	SMITH, Zelda G.	(MA)	1161
	CHELTON, Mary K.	(MD)	204
	EDWARDS, Margaret A. .	(MD)	337
	JONES, Cynthia A.	(MD)	612
	LAPIDES, Linda F.	(MD)	697
	LOSINSKI, Julia M.	(MD)	742
	O'LOUGHLIN, Marilyn L. .	(MD)	921
	SANDERS, Jacqueline C. .	(MD)	1080
	TITCOMB, Anne S.	(MD)	1247
	WOODY, Jacqueline B. . .	(MD)	1368
	DELLER, A M.	(MI)	289
	MAYES, Jane M.	(MI)	789
	PARTHUM, John W.	(MI)	945
	REASONER, Mary B. . . .	(MI)	1013
	GROSSMAN, Michael P. .	(MN)	473
	VAUGHAN, Janet E. . . .	(MN)	1279
	EAGLE, Opal C.	(MO)	331
	WYNNE, Tia J.	(MT)	1375
	ELMORE, Lisa E.	(NC)	346
	HUGHES, Donna J.	(NC)	571
	BRYANT, Judith W.	(NJ)	152
	CARR, Charles E.	(NJ)	185
	HONTZ, M E.	(NJ)	556
	MAYNES, Kathleen R. . .	(NJ)	790
	NEWMARK-KRUGER, Barbara	(NJ)	900
	PELLETIER, Karen E. . . .	(NJ)	955
	SCARPELLINO, Rebecca A.	(NJ)	1088
	SHEARIN, Cynthia E. . . .	(NJ)	1124
	STARRETT, Mary J.	(NJ)	1182
	THONER, Jane T.	(NJ)	1242
	VARLEJS, Jana	(NJ)	1278
	BENNETT, Deborah L. . .	(NM)	81
	CASSEL, Susan D.	(NY)	193
	EBER, Beryl E.	(NY)	334
	FIRTH, Jennifer L.	(NY)	379
	FOGLESONG, Marilee . .	(NY)	387
	GERHARDT, Lillian N. . .	(NY)	428
	HANSON, Jan E.	(NY)	498
	MEIGS, Carolyn R.	(NY)	821
	PASSOFF, Barbara F. . .	(NY)	946

YOUNG ADULT (Cont'd)

Young adult services

	RABIN, Alan H.	(NY)	1001
	ROSENBERG-NUGENT, Nanci B.	(NY)	1056
	RUBINSTEIN, Roslyn	(NY)	1065
	STARK, Li S.	(NY)	1181
	WEMETT, Lisa C.	(NY)	1323
	CHARVAT, Catherine T.	(OH)	203
	DOMBEY, Kathryn W.	(OH)	310
	HUEBSCHER, Mary	(OH)	570
	POLACHECK, Janet G.	(OH)	980
	SLEEMAN, Linda E.	(OH)	1148
	WESTNEAT, Helen C.	(OH)	1327
	WYNN, Vivian R.	(OH)	1375
	GREBEY, Betty H.	(PA)	461
	JENGAJI-EL, Taifa	(PA)	596
	LYTLE, Marguerite S.	(PA)	753
	SHONTZ, Marilyn L.	(PA)	1132
	SHEA, Margaret	(RI)	1124
	CONLEY, Janis E.	(TN)	236
	KARRENBROCK, Marilyn H.	(TN)	628
	MCIVER, Lynne A.	(TX)	809
	ROBINS, Barbara D.	(TX)	1043
	SPRADLING, Nancy L.	(TX)	1175
	FARR, Patricia A.	(VA)	365
	GEORGE, Melba R.	(VA)	427
	MADDEN, Susan B.	(WA)	758
	NELSON, Judy T.	(WA)	894
	WAITY, Gloria J.	(WI)	1293
	RHYNES, H B.	(AB)	1026
	WHITE, Valerie L.	(AB)	1332
	SALTMAN, Judith M.	(BC)	1077
	AMEY, Lorne J.	(NS)	20
	RABY, Eva F.	(PQ)	1001
Young adult services & literature	EDMONDS, M L.	(IL)	336
Young adult services & materials	SHAEVEL, Evelyn F.	(IL)	1118
Young adult services delivery	TYSON, Christy	(WA)	1267
Young adult services, literature	RUBIN, Ellen B.	(NY)	1064
Young adult specialist	BRUGNOLOTTI, Phyllis T.	(NY)	150
	JOHNSON, Patrelle E.	(NY)	608
Young adult work	GRAVITZ, Ina A.	(NY)	459
Young adults	FOWLER, Brian R.	(CA)	393
	CLANCY, Catherine M.	(MA)	215
	BOSE, Deborah L.	(MI)	117
	SHAPIRO, Barbara S.	(NY)	1121
	SUSSMAN, Valerie J.	(NY)	1210
	GOLDSBERRY, Maureen E.	(OK)	446
Young adults & children's services	WASHINGTON, Idella A.	(LA)	1307
Young adults services	PILLING, George P.	(CA)	973

YOUTH (See also Adolescent, Children, Teenagers, Young, Young Adult)

Children & youth literature	OAKLEY, Adeline D.	(MA)	913
Children & youth services	CHURCH, Sonia J.	(CA)	213
	KAN, Katharine L.	(HI)	624
Children & youth services, bibliotherapy	SMITH, Alice G.	(FL)	1152
Children's & youth services	BOGGUS, Tamara K.	(FL)	110
	KERESEY, Gayle	(NC)	643
Foreign libraries for youth	JACKSON, Clara O.	(OH)	587
Library service for youth	LONG, Joanna R.	(NY)	739
Library services to youth	JACKSON, Clara O.	(OH)	587
Literature for youth	JACKSON, Clara O.	(OH)	587
Programming for children & youth	MANCALL, Jacqueline C.	(PA)	764
School & public libraries - youth	SHAEVEL, Evelyn F.	(IL)	1118
School & public youth services	WUNDERLICH, Nina M.	(IL)	1374
Service to disabled youth	HARRIS, Karen H.	(LA)	505
Service to gifted youth	HARRIS, Karen H.	(LA)	505
Working with youth	GORDON, Ruth I.	(CA)	452
Youth & school services	PACEY, Brenda M.	(IL)	933
Youth, childhood, social sciences	WOODBURY, Marda	(CA)	1366
Youth librarianship	LOCKE, Jill L.	(PA)	736
Youth library services	DENNEHY, Margaret	(NY)	292
Youth library use education	USHIRODA, Christine H.	(HI)	1270
Youth literature & services	BODART-TALBOT, Joni	(KS)	109
Youth literature appreciation	USHIRODA, Christine H.	(HI)	1270

YOUTH (Cont'd)

Youth participation in libraries	TYSON, Christy	(WA)	1267
Youth programming	DURSTON, Corinne L.	(BC)	329
Youth programs	HUISKAMP, Julie G.	(IA)	572
Youth public school services	ROSEN, Elizabeth M.	(CA)	1055
Youth reference work	DURSTON, Corinne L.	(BC)	329
Youth service organization liaisonship	WRONKA, Gretchen M.	(MN)	1373
Youth services	GILDEN, Susanna C.	(CA)	434
	STOCKWELL, Judith R.	(CA)	1196
	WONG, Patricia M.	(CA)	1363
	ROBINSON, Cathy A.	(DC)	1043
	CHALLENER, Marcee M.	(FL)	197
	CHIMERAKIS, Mary A.	(FL)	208
	FIORE, Carole D.	(FL)	379
	LOSEY, Doris C.	(FL)	742
	NICKELSBURG, Marilyn M.	(IA)	902
	DAVIS, Carol L.	(IL)	278
	DECKER, Judy J.	(IL)	286
	MCMAHON, Judith L.	(IL)	814
	MORGAN, Miriam M.	(IL)	864
	SOVANSKI, Vincent G.	(IL)	1170
	STINCHCOMB, Maxine K.	(IL)	1194
	ASHFORD, Richard K.	(MD)	36
	CURTIS, Kathleen W.	(MI)	267
	BEHLER, Patricia A.	(MO)	74
	EATON, Elizabeth G.	(NC)	333
	FEEHAN, Patricia E.	(NC)	368
	STRICKLAND, Patricia J.	(NJ)	1202
	BARTLE, Susan M.	(NY)	61
	BIRO, Juliane	(NY)	99
	SIMON, Anne E.	(NY)	1140
	BARRICK, Susan K.	(OH)	59
	PETERSON, Douglas L.	(UT)	963
	CAYWOOD, Carolyn A.	(VA)	195
	FOREHAND, Margaret P.	(VA)	390
	WILSON, Evie	(WA)	1350
	WISEMAN, Mary J.	(WI)	1357
Youth services & programs	BRANZBURG, Marian G.	(MI)	129

ZIONISM

Israel, Zionism	BEN-ZVI, Hava	(CA)	84

ZOO

Zoo related subjects reference	KENYON, Kay A.	(DC)	643

ZOOLOGY

Collection development zoology	CACCESE, Vincent	(CA)	170
Zoological systematics & taxonomy	CHANDLER, Jody A.	(UT)	200
Zoology	GUBISTA, Kathryn R.	(GA)	475

ZYINDEX

ZyIndex use with Bernoulli	LINEWEAVER, Joe R.	(MN)	730

Employer Index

Professionals, with their current positions, are indexed by employers. Employers are listed alphabetically and further sorted by state (Canadian province or country).

A

A A L (WI)
KLAVER, Timothy J. (Info Sci Spclst) 658

A C Nielsen Co (IL)
STELK, W E. (VP, Group Mgmt Staff) 1186

A C Nielsen Co (NY)
BEHANNA, William R. (Client Srv Exec) 74

A Chance to Grow (MN)
DAVIS, Emmett A. (Lib Dir) 279

A E Staley Manufacturing Co (IL)
WALLACE, Richard E. (Technl Info Ctr Mgr) 1298

A H Robins Co (VA)
CLEMANS, Margaret H. (Documtn Spclst) 220
VAN SICKLEN, Lindsay L. (Ref Libn) 1277

A J G Associates (NY)
GROSSMAN, Adrian J. (Consult) 473

A Lib Service (CA)
DAVIS, Becky C. (Dir) 277

A R E Clinic (AZ)
DIAL, Zona P. (Lib Dir) 299

A T and E Laboratories Inc (OR)
VIXIE, Anne C. (Mgr of Info Srvs) 1286

A T Kearney Inc (FL)
CARR, Sallyann (Resrch Mgr) . . . 186

A T Kearney Inc (IL)
LARSEN, Linda E. (Mgr) 698

Aaron Cohen Associates (NY)
COHEN, Aaron (Principal) 227
COHEN, Elaine 228

ABBE Regional Lib System (SC)
BOWLING, Carol L. (Dir) 121

Abbeville-Greenwood Regional Lib (SC)
HEIMBURGER, Bruce R. (Dir) . . . 521

Abbott Laboratories (IL)
HOFF, Carole 547
LEWIS, Martha S. (Serials Libn) . . 724
MANDEL, Douglas J. (Info Scitst II) 765
OPEM, John D. (Info Srvs Mgr) . . 925
SWANSON, Ruth M. (Info Scitst) 1213

Abbott Laboratories (PQ)
HEROUX, Genevieve (Libn) 532

ABC-CLIO (CA)
BOEHM, Ronald J. (Pres) 109
BYRNE, Pam 169
KINNELL, Susan K. (Online Coordntr Asst Edit) 653

ABC-CLIO (CO)
BROCK, Laurie N. (Resrch Editor) 138

ABC Schwann Publications Inc (MA)
SCHWANN, William J. (Founder & Publshr) 1104

ABC Unified Sch District (CA)
PITLUK, Paula K. (Libn & Mentor Tchr) 976

Abilene Christian Univ (TX)
ALEXANDER, Shirley B. (Catlg Libn) 12
ANDERSON, Madeleine J. (Perdcls & Religious Std Asst Libn) 24
HARPER, Marsha W. (Asst Libn for Pub Srvs) 503
WALKER, Bonnie M. (Technl Prcsng Head) 1295

Abilene State Sch (TX)
ALLEN, Peggy G. (Libn I) 15

Abington Free Lib (PA)
GINSBURG, Mary L. (Ref Libn) . . 438
POSEL, Nancy R. (Dir of Libs) . . 985

Abington Memorial Hospital (PA)
PASKOWSKY, Carol (Libn) 946

Abraham Baldwin Agricultural Coll (GA)
SELLERS, Brenda A. (Readers Srvs & Ref Libn) 1114

Abstract/Info Retrieval (PA)
AUGUST, Sidney (Info Spclst) 39

Academia Perpetuo Socorro (PR)
DE DEL VALLE, Heida C. (Libn) . 286

Academic & General Book Shop (PQ)
GLASS, Gerald (Bk Store Dir & Owner) 440

Academic Press Inc (FL)
VANCE, Blake F. (Dir of Sales & Mktg) 1272

Academy for Educational Development (DC)
BETTS, Ardith M. (Sr Libn) 92
MARA, Ruth M. (Deputy Proj Dir) 768
TIFFT, Jeanne D. (Prog Analyst) 1244

The Academy of American Poets (NY)
CAMMACK, Bruce P. (Archvst) . 175

Academy of Motion Picture Arts & Scis (CA)
OKA, Susan Y. (Asst Libn) 919
STOCKSTILL, Patrick E. (Academy Histn) 1195

Academy of Natural Scis of Philadelphia (PA)
BAKER, Sylva S. (Lib Srvs Vice Pres) 49
SPAWN, Carol M. (Manuscript & Archs Libn) 1172

Academy of Saint Joseph (NY)
WALTER, Maria (Lib Media Spclst) 1300

The Academy of the New Church (PA)
SULLIVAN, Jennifer B. (Dir of Lib Media Ctr) 1207

Academy School (VT)
HAY, Linda A. (Lib Media Specialist) 515

Acadia Univ (NS)
BATES, Iain J. (Univ Libn) 64

Access Information Associates (TX)
HOLAB-ABELMAN, Robin S. (Libn) 550
SMITH, Dayna F. (Libn) 1154

Access Information Services (AB)
LEESMENT, Helgi (Freelance Lib Consult) 712

Access Innovations Inc (NM)
HLAVA, Marjorie M. (Pres) 544

Access Publishing Co (NY)
STILLMAN, Stanley W. (Edit & Publshr) 1194

Acres International Ltd (AB)
ROSS, Evelyn M. (Libn) 1058

Acres International Ltd (ON)
D'AMBOISE, Marion J. (Libn) . . . 271

Acron Pub Lib District (IL)
NOVELLI, Jean L. (Dir) 911

Acton Information Resources Mgmt Ltd (BC)
ACTON, Patricia 4

Actraining Services (MD)
KAESSINGER, Carla S. (Vice Pres for Devlpmnt) 621

Acurex Corp (CA)
STOCKS, Lee P. (Lib Srvs Mgr) 1195

Adams County Pub Lib (CO)
DOBBS, Ann R. (Branch Libn II) . 307

Adams County Pub Lib (WI)
STEINKRAUS, Ann M. (Dir) . . . 1186

Adams McCullough & Beard (NC)
WILLIAMS, Lisa W. (Libn) 1344

Adath Yeshurun Synagogue (FL)
FRIEDMAN, Sylvia (Judaica Libn) 404

Addiction Research Foundation (ON)
CHAN, Margy (Lib Srvs Mgr) . . . 199

Addison Gilbert Hospital (MA)
CHEVES, Vera L. (Libn) 207

Addison Trail High Sch (IL)
JOHNSEN, Ellen I. (Libn) 601

Addison-Wesley Publishing Co (CA)
HALL, Elede T. (Info Srvs Spclst) 487

Adelphi Univ (NY)
DOCTOROW, Erica (Head, Fine Arts Lib) 307
EDWARDS, Rita F. (Ref Libn & Soc Work Spclst) 337
KELLY, Donald V. (Asst to the Dean for Col Devlpmnt) 637
LIFSHIN, Arthur 726
SCHNEIDER, Judith A. (Serials Catlgr) 1097
SMITH, Adelaide M. (Libn) 1152

Adirondack Museum (NY)
PEPPER, Jerold L. (Libn) 958

Adirondack Research Ctr (NY)

Adlai E Stevenson High Sch (IL)

Adler Pollock & Sheehan (RI)
Administrative Office of the US Courts (DC)

Administrative Office of the US Courts (KY)

Adolph Coors Co (CO)
Adorers of the Blood of Christ (KS)

Adrian Coll (MI)

Adriance Memorial Lib (NY)

Advanced Info Consult (MI)
Advanced Information Management (CA)

Advanced Library Systems Inc (MA)
Advanced Systems Design Inc (CO)
Advanced Technology Laboratories (WA)

Advocate Computerization Services Inc (PA)

Aerodyne Research Inc (MA)
Aerojet Strategic Systems Co (CA)

Aerospace Corp (CA)

Aerospace Industries Assn of America Inc (DC)

Aetna Life & Casualty (CT)

Affiliated Pathologists (TX)
Africa News Service (NC)

After Image Inc (CA)
Agee Indexing Services (MD)
Agency of Administration (VT)
Agenda Technology (MA)
Agribusiness Associates Inc (MA)

Agriculture Canada (AB)

Agriculture Canada (MB)
Agriculture Canada (ON)

Agridata Network (WI)
Agua Fria Union High Sch (AZ)
AI&U (CA)
Air Academy High Sch (CO)
Air Products & Chemicals Inc (PA)

KING, Maryde F. (Biblgphr) 651
KRUEGER, Sharon B. (Ref Libn) 680
DUMAINE, Paul R. (Libn) 325

ERICSON, Richard J. (Lawbook Sect Chief) 353
HARRIS, Linda S. (Adminstrv Libn) 505
THOMAS, Patricia A. (Lib Dir) .. 1238

COATES, Paul F. (Micrographics & Arch Supvsr) 224
BOND, Mary J. (Info Spclst) ... 113
STRECK, Helen T. (Archvst & Histn) 1201
ARNDT, Arleen (Tech Srvs Libn) 33
WALSH, Robin S. (Branch Head) 1300
BRYANT, Barton B. 152

CONDREY, Barbara K. (Persnl Spclst) 236
PORTER-ROTH, Anne (VP) ... 985
SAMMATARO, John A. (Pres) . 1078
HULL, Stephen P. 573

GRINSTEAD, Beth K. (Corprt Records Adminstr & Libn) 471
WEISFIELD, Cynthia F. (Pres & Sr Systs Analyst) 1319
MAST, Susan B. (Info Spclst) ... 782
MIRONENKO, Rimma (Head Resrch Libn) 847
HOCKING, Theresa R. (Libn, Indxr) 546

RUTEMILLER, Annette M. (Lib Asst) 1070
DOMINIANNI, Beth S. (Corpte Info Ctr Adminstr) 310
PORTER, Kathryn W. (Mgr) 985
TAYLOR, Melissa P. (Technl Libn) 1227
WEINSTEIN, Daniel L. (Resrch Libn) 1318
FORD, Mary R. (Med Libn) 389
WHITMORE, Sharon S. (Libn & Bk Rvw Edit) 1334
HENDERSON, Ellen B. (Pres) .. 526
AGEE, Victoria V. (Dir) 7
YACAVONI, A J. (Asst Dir) ... 1376
BYRN, William H. (Principal) 169
KENNEDY, Amy J. (Info Systs Coordntr) 640
CUTLER, C M. (Lib Area Coordntr) 268
SIMUNDSSON, Elva D. (Libn) . 1142
BOISVENUE, Marie J. (Entomology Libn) 111
FRAUMENI, Michael A. (Libn) ... 399
GAZELEY, Joan E. (Technl Srvs Actg Chief) 424
MORTON, Margaret L. (Lib Div Dir) 870
WEENING, Richard W. 1315
WHITNEY, Karen A. (Lib Dir) .. 1334
ROSE, Steven C. (Pres) 1055
WILSON, M L. (Lib Media Dir) . 1352
BURYLO, Michelle A. (Corp Bus Info Ctr Supvsr) 164
DRAGOTTA, Linda L. (Lib Srvs Supvsr) 318
SMITH, Robert B. (Sr Info Spclst) 1160
TUCCI, Valerie K. (Info Srvs Mgr) 1261

Aircraft Technical Publishers (CA)

Airdrie Municipal Lib (AB)
Akerman Senterfitt & Eidson (FL)

Akron Beacon Journal (OH)

Akron City Hospital (OH)

Akron Pub Schs (OH)

Akron-Summit County Pub Lib (OH)

Aktion Das Frohliche Krankenzimmer (WGR)
Akzo Chemic America (IL)

Akzo Chemie America (IL)
Alabama Christian Sch of Religion (AL)

Alabama Department of Archives & History (AL)

Alabama Department of Education (AL)

Alabama Lib Association (AL)

Alabama Lib Exchange Inc (AL)
Alabama Power Co (AL)
Alabama Pub Lib Service (AL)

Alabama Regional Lib (AL)
Alabama State Univ (AL)

Alabama Supreme Court & State Law Lib (AL)

Alachua County Lib District (FL)

Alameda County Law Lib (CA)

Alameda County Lib (CA)

DONINI, Elizabeth A. (Resrc Ctr Mgr) 311
OTTOSEN, Charles F. (Dir) 930
SMITH, Mary D. (Dir of Lib Srvs) 1158
TIERNEY, Catherine M. (Chief Libn) 1244
CREELAN, Marilee M. (Hospital Libs Dir) 257
GEARY, Linda L. (Ref Libn) 424
PHILLIPS, Judith Z. (Ref Libn) .. 968
MAYER, Mary C. (Sch Media Spclst) 789
BERRY, Diana M. (Head, Mobile Srvs Dept) 90
HAWK, Steven (Dir) 513
LATSHAW, Patricia H. (Comunty Relations Dir) 701
NOWAK, Leslie A. (Chlds Libn) .. 911
REED, Elizabeth M. (Chld's Libn) 1015
WAGNER, Evelyn M. (Coordntr of Srvs to Chld, Yng Teens) . 1291

ADENEY, Carol D. (Resrchr) 6
PETRY, Robyn E. (Co Technl Lib Head Libn) 965
PACETTI, Karen C. (Asst Libn) .. 933

LANCASTER III, Thomas A. (Lrng Resrcs Ctr Dir) 692

BREEDLOVE, Michael A. (Archvst I) 131
BRIDGES, Edwin C. (Dir) 135
PENDLETON, Debbie D. (Quality Control Archvst) 956

SMITH, Jane B. (Educ Spclst in Lib Media) 1155
SUTTON, Sandra K. (Exec Secy) 1211
WEBSTER, Sherry (Exec Secy) 1315
PIKE, Lee E. (Dir) 973
KING, Karen H. (Libn) 651
COLEMAN, James M. (Reader Adv) 231
DESSY, Blane K. (Dir) 296
STEPHENS, Alice G. (Lib Operations Div Head) 1187
BIVINS, Hulen E. (Regnl Libn) ... 100
PEDERSOLI, Heleni M. (Col Devlpmnt Libn) 954

LEWIS, Timothy A. (Asst State Law Libn) 724
BECKER, Josephine M. (Circ Supvsr) 72
HOLE, Carol C. (Outreach Supvsr) 550
WILLIAMS, Ann W. (Lib Dir) ... 1342
KENSINGER, Colleen O. (Technl Srvs Libn) 642
LOMAX, Ronald C. (Ref Libn) ... 738
OWENS, Robert L. (Ref Libn) ... 932
APPEL, Anne M. (Deputy Cnty Libn) 29
COOPER, Ginnie (Cnty Libn) ... 242
CROOKS, Joyce M. (Info Coordntr) 260
FLUM, Judith G. (Yng Adult, Pub Relations Coordntr) 386
OVERMYER, Elizabeth C. (Chlds Libn) 931
PANTAGES, Sandra K. (Branch Mgr) 938
PISANO, Vivian M. (Catlgng Supvsr) 975

Alamo Community Coll District (TX)
HOLLOWAY, Geraldine B. (Tech Srvs Head) 552
METZGER, Oscar F. (Chairman, Lrng Resrcs) 829

Alamosa Southern Peaks Lib (CO)
SHELDON, L S. (Dir) 1126

Alan Patricof Associates (NY)
RUBIN, Myra P. (Info Mgr) 1064

Alaska Court Libs (AK)
ODSEN, Elizabeth R. (Technl Srvs Libn) 917

Alaska Department of Administration (AK)
KINNEY, John M. (State Archvst) 653

Alaska Department of Education (AK)
CRANE, Karen R. (Alaska State Libn) 255
KOLB, Audrey P. (Libn & Coordntr) 669
MITCHELL, Micheal L. (State Docums Libn) 849

Alaska Health Sciences Lib (AK)
ANDRESS, Loretta M. (Libn) 26

Alaska Pacific Univ (AK)
MORRISSETT, Elizabeth (Lib Dir) 868

Alaska State Archives & Records Service (AK)
NEWTON, Virginia A. (Deputy State Archvst) 900

Alaska State Lib (AK)
JENNINGS, Mary (Libn) 598
SHELTON, Kathryn H. (Pub Srvs Libn) 1126
SMITH, George V. (Deputy Dir) . 1155
SIMPSON, Susan M. (Pub Srvs Head) 1142

Albany County Pub Lib (WY)

The Albany Herald (GA)
MEREY-KADAR, Ervin R. (Libn, Ed Correspondent) 825

Albany International Research Co (MA)
DAVIS, Jeannette (Resrch Libn) . 279

Albany Law Sch (NY)
PINSLEY, Lauren J. (Catlgr) 975

Albany Medical Center Archives (NY)
MOORE, Rue I. (Exec Assoc Dean) 861

Albany Medical Coll of Union Univ (NY)
MARTIN, Lyn M. (Catlg Libn) . . . 777
POLAND, Ursula H. (Prof Emeritus) 980

Albany Pub Lib (NY)
BRODERICK, Therese L. (Adult Learner Libn) 139
DRATCH-KOVLER, Carol A. (AV Libn) 318
GILLESPIE, Gerald V. (Head, Adult Srvs) 435
LEWIS, Frances R. (Pub Relations Dir) 723
MIDDLETON, Marcia S. (Ref & Microcomputer Libn) 833
O'CONNOR, William J. (Dir) 916
PATRICK, Patricia M. (Chld's Srvs Head) 947
SACCO, Gail A. (Branch Libn) . 1073

Albemarle County (VA)
KEYSER, Sue C. (Libn) 645

Albert Einstein Coll of Medicine (NY)
LAMPORT, Bernard (Analysis of Scintfc Info Spclst) 691
LINDNER, Charlotte K. (Lib Dir) . 729
NELSON, Norma (Ref Libn) 894

Albert Einstein Medical Center (PA)
SCHANER, Marian E. (Lib Dir) . 1090

Albert Westmorland Kent Regional Lib (NB)
POTVIN, Claude (Regnl Libn) . . . 987

Albert Whitman & Co (IL)
BOYD, Joseph W. (Pres) 122

Alberta Agriculture (AB)
BATEMAN, Robert A. (Head Libn) 60
NOGA, Dolores A. (Ref Libn) . . . 907
STARR, Jane E. (Technl Srvs Head) 1182

Alberta Alcohol & Drug Abuse Commission (AB)
REIMER, Bette J. (Libn) 1020

Alberta Community & Occupational Health (AB)
MCLAUGHLIN, W K. (Lib Srvs Branch Dir) 813
CLUBB, Barbara H. (Asst Dir) . . . 223

Alberta Culture Lib Services (AB)

Alberta Economic Development & Trade (AB)
GORDON, Donna M. (Departmental Libn) 451

Alberta Education (AB)
ANDREWS, Christina A. (Info Spclst) 26
KRATZ, Hans G. (Dir) 676

Alberta Environment Lib (AB)

Alberta Environmental Centre (AB)
Alberta Municipal Affairs (AB)

Alberta Research Council (AB)

Alberta Vocational Center (AB)

Albertus Magnus Coll (CT)

Albion Central Sch District (NY)

Albion Coll (MI)

Albion Pub Lib (MI)
Albright & Wilson American Inc (ON)
Albright Coll (PA)

Albright-Knox Art Gallery (NY)
Albuquerque Pub Lib (NM)

Albuquerque Pub Schs (NM)

ALCOA Laboratories (PA)

Alcohol Research Group (CA)
ALCOLAC Inc (MD)
Alderson-Broaddus Coll (WV)
Aldine Independent Sch District (TX)

Alex Brown & Sons Inc (MD)

The Alexander Consulting Group Inc (MA)

Alexander County Lib (NC)

Alexander Mitchell Pub Lib (SD)
Alexandria City Pub Schools (VA)

Alexandria Hospital (VA)

The Alexandria Institute (CO)
Alexandria Pub Lib (MN)
Alexandria Pub Lib (VA)

Alfred I Du Pont Institute (DE)
Alfred Wegener Institute (WGR)

Algoma Univ Coll (ON)

Algonquin Area Pub Lib (IL)

Algonquin Coll of Applied Arts & Tech (ON)

Alhambra Elementary Schs (AZ)

Alice & Hamilton Fish Lib (NY)

Alice Norton Pub Relations (CT)

All Saints Catholic Church (TX)

FRALICK, Deborah L. (Head of Lib Srv) 395
LEE, Diana W. (Info Srvs Head) . 709
BAYRAK, Bettie (Departmental Libn) 68
GEE, Sharon (Dir of Info Srvs) . . . 425
BRUCE, Robert D. (Libn) 149
ENGLESAKIS, Marina F. (Libn) . . 350
KELLY, Thomas A. (Asst Libn & Archvst) 638
LYNCH, M W. (Dir) 751
MERRILL, Barbara P. (Sch Lib Media Spclst) 826
CARSON, Claudia A. (Head of Technl Srvs) 188
OBERG, Larry R. (Dir of Libs) . . . 914
KNOTT, Joan Y. (Chlds Libn) . . . 665
LOGAN, Nancy L. (Corprt Libn) . 737
DEEGAN, Rosemary L. (Instrcnl & Biblgph Srvs Libn) 286
HANNAFORD, William E. (Lib Dir) 496
STILLMAN, Mary E. (Spcl Asst to the Pres) 1194
SCHENK, Kathryn L. (Asst Libn) 1091
SABATINI, Joseph D. (Head of Main Lib) 1072
AVERY, Linda S. (Libn) 42
CARLSON, Kathleen A. (Libn) . . 182
WHITLOW, Cherrill M. (Libn) . . 1333
MOUNTS, Earl L. (Ref Info Scientist) 873
MITCHELL, Andrea L. (Libn) 848
BLUTE, Mary R. (Resrch Libn) . . 107
SIZEMORE, William C. (Pres) . . 1145
WALKER, Tamara E. (Lrng Resrc Coordntr) 1296
QUINDLEN, Ruthann (Resrch Analyst) 999
JACQUES, Donna M. (Info Spclst) 591
LAWRENCE, Virginia W. (Chlds Libn) 705
STEPHENS, Doris G. (Dir) 1188
RAVE, David A. (Dir) 1010
BROWN, Dale W. (Dir of Libs & Instrnl Resrcs) 143
HAMILTON, Elizabeth J. (Med Lib Dir) 492
KERR, Robert C. (Pres) 644
HELGESON, Victoria L. (Dir) . . . 524
EFFRON, Barbara L. (Chlds Libn) 338
HINDMAN, Pamela J. (Chlds Libn) 542
MERRIFIELD, Mark D. (Bus Ref Libn) 826
PLITT, Jeanne G. (Dir of Libs) . . . 978
RUDOLF, Christine T. (Ref Libn) 1066
NOLTING, Carl E. (Med Libn) . . . 908
GOMEZ, Michael J. (Libn & Head of Automation) 447
BAZILLION, Richard J. (Chief Libn & Assoc Prof) 68
VLCEK, Randall (Admnstrv Libn) 1286
BREGAINT, Bernard J. (Head of Ref Sect) 131
HAUCK, Danuta (Pub & Technl Srvs Dept Head) 512
GILBERT, Betty H. (Sch Lib Media Spclst) 433
STARRETT, Mildred J. (Libn) . . 1182
BALDWIN, Geraldine S. (Lib Dir) 51
NORTON, Alice (Owner/Operator) 910
BELLAVANCE, Maria I. (Libn) 78

Allain-Le Breton Co (LA)

ALLAIN, Alexander P. (Gen Mgr, Gen Counsel) 13

Allard K Lowenstem Pub Lib (NY)

FIRTH, Jennifer L. (Yng Adult Libn) 379

Allegan Pub Lib (MI)

ROOP, Donna K. (Lib Dir) 1053

Allegany County Board of Education (MD)

FAHERTY, Gladys W. (Media Spclst) 361

Allegany County Lib System (MD)

NEAL, Robert L. (Dir) 890

Allegheny Coll (PA)

BURTON, Cynthia R. (Data Srvs Libn) 164
STALLARD, Kathryn E. (Instr) .. 1179

Allegheny County Law Lib (PA)

MAST, Joanne (Catlg, Ref Libn) . 782

Allegheny Ludlum Steel (PA)

GALLAGHER, Eileen W. (Libn) .. 414

Allelix Inc (ON)

ATHA, Shirley A. (Head, Info Srvs) 37

Allen B Veaner Associates (ON)

VEANER, Allen B. (Principal) .. 1280

Allen-Bradley Co (WI)

MILTON, Ardyce A. (Asst Libn) .. 845

Allen County Pub Lib (IN)

BUDD, Anne D. (Perdcl Source Index, Proj Supvsr) 155
CLEGG, Michael B. (Branch Operations Mgr) 220
DEANE, Paul D. (Mgr) 284
DICKMEYER, John N. (Mgr of Bus & Tech) 301
KRULL, Jeffrey R. (Dir) 680
MCCAFFERY, Laurabelle (Readers Srvs Libn) 793
REARDON, Ann L. (Catlgr) ... 1013
ROGERS, Martha J. (Libn) 1050
SANDSTROM, Pamela E. (Acqs Srvs Mgr) 1081
STANLEY, Luana K. (Systs Mgr) 1180
VOORS, Mary R. (Chlds Srvs Libn) 1289
WITCHER, Curt B. (Asst Mgr) .. 1358

Allendale-Hampton-Jasper Regional Lib (SC)

DRYDEN, Donald W. (Lib Dir) ... 321

Allentown Coll (PA)

MCCABE, James P. (Lib Dir) ... 793
WELLE, Jacob P. (Asst Libn) .. 1321

The Allentown Hospital (PA)

IOBST, Barbara J. (Dir of Lib Srvs) 583

Allentown Osteopathic Medical Center (PA)

SCHWARTZ, Linda M. (Med Libn) 1104

Allentown Pub Lib (PA)

STEPHANOFF, Kathryn (Lib Dir) 1187

Allergan Inc (CA)

CURTIS, Richard A. (Info Spclst) 267
NOVACK, Dona A. (Lit Analysis Supvsr) 910
WIERZBA, Heidemarie B. (Corprt Info Ctr Mgr) 1337

Allerton Pub Lib (IL)

LINTNER, Barbara J. (Dir) ... 731

Allied Aerospace Co (MD)

DOVE, Samuel (Sr Technl Libn) . 315

Allied Automotive (MI)

BLASCHAK, Mary M. (Resrch Libn) 104

Allied Irish Banks Plc (IRE)

LAMBKIN, Anthony (Archvst) ... 690

Allied Signal (IL)

GAUMOND, Suzanne M. (Mgr of Technl Info Ctr) 423

Allied Signal (NJ)

MASILAMANI, Mary P. (Bus Info Spclst) 780

Allstate Insurance Co (IL)

BRUEMMER, Alice 149
JUSTIE, Julie H. (Lib Srvs Supvsr) 620

Ally Gargano M C A Advertising Ltd (NY)

COHEN, Marsha C. (Vice Pres & Resrch Info Srvs Mgr) 228

Alma Coll (MI)

DOLLARD, Peter A. (Lib Dir) ... 309
GERLACH, William P. (Retro Con, Ref Libn) 429
HALL, Lawrence E. (Ref Libn & Coll Archvst) 488
PALMER, Catherine S. (Lib Automation Coordntr) 936
RATHGEBER, Jo F. (Technl & Regulatory Info Spclst) 1009

Almay Inc (NC)

WEAVER, Nancy B. (Indxr) 1312

Alpha Byte & Co (MO)

Alpha Park Pub Lib District (IL)

JACKSON, Susan M. (Dir) 588
KAUTZ-WARTH, Linda S. (Pub Srvs Libn) 631

Alpha Regional Lib (WV)

RADER, H J. (Dir) 1002

Alschuler Grossman & Pines (CA)

GRIGST, Denise J. (Libn) 470

Alsip-Merrionette Park Lib (IL)

BLIETZ, Cynthia S. (Ref Libn) ... 105

Alston & Bird (GA)

STROUGAL, Patricia G. (Head Libn) 1203

Altadena Lib District (CA)

TEMA, William J. (Dist Libn) ... 1230

Altana Films (NY)

KLUGHERZ, Dan (Producer & Distributor) 662

Altheimer & Gray (IL)

ANES, Joy R. (Libn) 27

Altruruan Pub Lib (NM)

ANDERSEN-PUSEY, Vavene J. (Libn) 21

Alumax Inc (CA)

LINDAHL, Ann L. (Info Spclst, Planning & Devlpmnt) 728

Aluminum Co of America (PA)

PETERSON, Barbara E. (Hlth Info Adminstr) 962
SAPP, V J. 1082
WHITAKER, Cynthia D. (Resrch Spclst) 1329

Alvernia Coll (PA)

JONES, M C. (Dir of Lib Srvs) .. 614

Alverno Coll (WI)

DELAUCHE, Jean E. (Lib Dir) ... 289
SAGER, Lynn S. (Pub Srvs Dir) 1074
SHUTKIN, Sara A. (Records Mgr & Libn) 1134

Alvin C York Veterans Admin Medical Ctr (TN)

HUNTER, Joy W. (Chief Lib Srv) 576

AM Systems Inc (MD)

MEYER, Alan H. (Pres) 829

Amagansett Elementary Sch (NY)

BRUNO, Frances J. (Lib Media Spclst) 151

Amarillo Pub Lib (TX)

GROSS, Iva H. (Head of AV Dept) 472
RUDDY, Mary K. (Technl & Circ Srvs Coordntr) 1065

AMAX Inc (CT)

DVORIN, Nancy T. (Asst Libn) . 330
GRAYSON, Virginia S. (Libn) ... 460

Ambassador Coll (CA)

WALTHER, Richard E. (Lib Dir) . 1301

Ambassador Coll (TX)

CRISSINGER, John D. (Lib Dir) . 259

Amber Univ (TX)

HENDERSON, Lennijo P. (Asst Dir of Lib Resrc Ctr) 526
LOWRY, Andretta G. (Lib Resrc Ctr Dir) 745

Amerada Hess Petroleum (TX)

MOORE, Guusje Z. (Supvsr, Exploration Files) 859

American Academy of Dermatology (IL)

STLUKA, Thomas H. (Dir of Mem Srvs) 1195

American Academy of Orthopedic Surgeons (TN)

HARALSON, Robert H. (Chairman) 499

The American Alpine Club (NY)

FLETCHER, Patricia A. (Libn) ... 385

American Antiquarian Society (MA)

BARNHILL, Georgia B. (Graphic Arts Cur) 58
BURKETT, Nancy H. (Asst Libn) . 161
MCCORISON, Marcus A. (Dir & Libn) 798
WASOWICZ, Laura E. (Sr Catlgr, Am Chlds Lit) 1308

American Assn for Counseling & Devlpmnt (VA)

NISENOFF, Sylvia (Profsnl Info Spclst) 905

Am Assn for the Advancement of Science (DC)

ALDRICH, Michele L. (Archvst & Comp Srvs Mgr) 11

American Assn of Advertising Agencies (NY)

APPEL, Marsha C. (Mem Info Srvs Mgr) 29
FENTON, Joan T. (Info Spclst) .. 371
HUBBARD, Susan E. (Info Spclst) 568
MORRIS, Margaret J. (Staff Exec) 867
ZILAVY, Julie A. (Info Spclst) .. 1388

Am Assn of Gynecologic Laparoscopists (CA)

PHILLIPS, Jordan M. (Board Chairman) 968

American Association of Law Libs (IL)

JEPSON, William H. (Exec Dir) .. 599

American Association of Orthodontists (MO)
GILTINAN, Celia E. (Libn) 437

American Assn of Petroleum Geologists (OK)
SHANKS, Katherine N. (Libn) . . 1120

American Association of Retired Persons (DC)
HARTZ, Mary K. (Resrc Spclst) . 509
LATOUR, Catherine M. (Sr Resrc Spclst) 701
LOVAS, Paula M. (Natl Gerontology Resrc Ctr Dir) . . 743
RAFFERTY, Eve (Technl Srvs Mgr) 1003
TABER, Sally A. (Resrc Spclst) . 1219

American Assn of State Colls & Univs (DC)
STOCKTON, Ken R. (Assn Resrch Info Asst) 1196

American Association of Univ Women (DC)
MCGAUGHRAN, Roberta W. (Libn) 805

American Banker - Bond Buyer (DC)
TRIGAUX, Robert (Washington Bureau Chief) 1256

American Banker - Bond Buyer (NY)
ALLAN, John (Edit, The Bond Buyer) 14
BURKE, Edward (Exec VP) 160
CASEY, Robert W. (Managing Edit) 192
FINCH, Brian (Sr VP) 377
FREY, Ned (VP) 402
HENDERSON, Brad (Product Devlpmnt Dir) 526
KRAUS, James (Edit, Audiotex) . . 676
LEVINE, Margaret A. (Database Srvs Mgr) 720
MALKIN, Peter (Sr VP) 763
NOVEMBER, Robert S. (Exec VP) 911
RUSLING, Con A. (Exec VP) . . 1068
TIERNEY, Richard H. (Pres & Chief Exec Ofcr) 1244
TYSON, David (Assoc Edit, Am Banker) 1267
VELLA, Carl (Sr VP) 1281
ZIMMERMAN, William (Edit, Am Banker) 1389

American Bankers Association (DC)
GERVINO, Joan (Dir of Lib & Info Srvs) 429
WENGEL, Linda (Info Srvs Mgr) 1324

American Bible Society (NY)
WOSH, Peter J. (Archvst & Records Mgr) 1369
YAKEL, Elizabeth (Proj Archvst) 1376

The American Botanist (IL)
CROTZ, D K. (Self-employed) . . . 261

Am Ctr for Stanislavski Theatre Art Inc (NY)
MOORE, Sonia (Pres) 861

American Chemical Society (DC)
HEARTY, John A. (Mgr of Electronic Publshg) 519

American Chemical Society (OH)
BAKER, Dale B. (Dir Emeritus) . . . 48

The American Coll (PA)
HILL, Judith L. (Libn) 540

American Coll in Paris (FRN)
STONE, Toby G. (Coll Libn) . . . 1197

American Coll of Cardiology (MD)
GOLDSTEIN, Helene B. (Lib Dir) 446
LAFFREY, Laurel W. (Asst Dir) . . 687

Am Coll of Obstetricians & Gynecologists (DC)
MEIKAMP, Kathie D. (Technl Srvs Libn) 822
VANHINE, Pamela M. (Head Libn) 1275

American Coll of Radiology (VA)
RICHARD, Sheila A. (Libn) 1028

American Coll Testing Program (IA)
RENTER, Lois I. (Head Libn) . . . 1023

American Companies Inc (KS)
LYNN, Barbara A. (Lib Mktg Coordntr) 752

American Connection (CT)
BERLIET, Nathalie B. (Pres) 87

American Council for the Arts (NY)
EISENBERG, Alan J. (Info Mgr) . 340

American Council on Education (DC)
FONT, Mary M. (Dir, Lib & Info Srvs) 388

American Craft Council (NY)
SECKELSON, Linda E. (Lib Dir) 1110

American Cyanamid Co (CT)
MOUNTFORD, Eve (Info Scitst) . 873
REITER, Martha B. (Technl Info Srvs Mgr) 1022

American Cyanamid Co (NJ)
AUGHEY, Kathleen M. (Lit Scitst) 39
JONES, Anita M. (Info Scientist) . 610
MOSENKIS, Sharon L. 870

American Cyanamid Co (NY)
HOWELL, M G. (Technl Info Srvs Head) 565

American Defense Preparedness Assoc (VA)
CLARKE, Robert F. 219

American Dental Association (IL)
KOWITZ, Aletha A. (Dir, Bureau of Lib Srvs) 674
PILARSKI, James P. (Head of Indexing) 973

American Educational Complex (TX)
MOSS, Charmagne L. (Ref Libn) . 872

American Electronic Labs Inc (PA)
BLAUERT, Mary A. (Libn) 105

American Express Co (UT)
POLLARD, Louise (Systs Libn) . . 981

American Family Mutual Insurance Group (WI)
BELLOWS, Leslie A. (Profsnl Devlpmnt Libn) 78

American Family Records Association (MO)
KARNS, Kermit B. (Consult) 627

American Farm Bureau Federation (IL)
SCHULTZ, Susan (Resrch Libn) 1102

American Field Services International (NY)
GELLER, Lawrence D. (Archvst) . 426

American Film & Video Association (NY)
TROJAN, Judith L. (Editor-in-Chief) 1257

American Film Institute (CA)
SCHLOSSER, Anne G. (Lib Dir) 1094

American Fork City (UT)
TOMLIN, Celia K. (Dir) 1250

American Foundation for the Blind (NY)
ELLIS, Peter K. (Technl Srvs Libn) 345

American Gas Association (VA)
DORNER, Steven J. (Industry Info Srvs Dir) 313

American Guild of Organists (NY)
LAWRENCE, Arthur P. (Assoc Edit of The Am Organist) 704

American Hospital Association (IL)
FOSTER, Eloise C. (Dir) 392
PINKOWSKI, Patricia E. (Staff Spclst) 975
POOLE, Connie (Asst Dir & Mgr) 983
WENZEL, Duane E. (Col Devlpmnt Staff Spclst) 1324

American Hospital Association (MD)
KIGER, Anne F. (Staff Spclst, Indexing) 647

American Humane Association (CO)
ALSOP, Robyn J. (Resrc Ctr Libn) 18

American Inst for Property Liability (PA)
HOLSTON, Kim R. (Libn) 554

Am Inst of Aeronautics & Astronautics (NY)
BUSTAMANTE, Corazon R. (Asst Circ Libn) 166
LAWRENCE, Barbara (Adminstr) 704
WORTON, Geoffrey P. (Mktg Dir) 1369

American Institute of Architects (DC)
KIMBERLIN, Robert L. (Ref Srvs Libn) 649
ROMEO, Sheryl R. (Libn, Technl Srvs) 1052

American Institute of Baking (KS)
HORTIN, Judith K. (Libn) 561

American Institute of Business (IA)
GRIFFIN, Kathryn A. (Lib Dir) . . . 468

Am Inst of Certified Pub Accountants (NY)
BEHAR, Evelyn W. (Asst Libn) . . . 74
NELOMS, Karen H. (Lib Srvs Dir) 893
ROSENFELD, Lillian E. (Libn) . . 1056

American Institute of Physics (NY)
HOWITT, Jeff (Mktg Srvs Mgr) . . 566
LERNER, Rita G. (Mgr of Books Div) 717
MARKS, Robert H. 771
PARISI, Paul A. 940
WARNOW-BLEWETT, Joan N. (Ctr for Hist of Physics Assoc Mgr) 1305

American International Coll (MA)
DELZELL, William R. (Technl Srv Catlgr) 290

American International Group (NY)
GOLLOP, Sandra G. (Sr Info Spclst) 447
STRAZDON, Maureen E. (Asst Dir) 1201

American Jewish Committee (NY)
HOROWITZ, Cyma M. (Lib Dir) . 560
RITTER, Helen (Records Mgr & Archvst) 1036

American Journal of Nursing Co (NY)
PATTISON, Frederick W. (Libn) . 948

American Kennel Club (NY)
VESLEY, Roberta A. (Lib Dir) . . 1283

American Latvian Association (MI)
BUNDZA, Maira (Libn) 157

American Law Institute (PA)
HOLUB, Joseph C. (Assoc Libn) . 555
WALSH, Sharon T. (Dir, Ofc of Bks) 1300

American Legion (IN)
HOVISH, Joseph J. (Asst Libn & Musm Cur) 563

American Lib Association (CT)
BECK, Arthur R. (Advertising Mgr) 71
SABOSIK, Patricia E. (Edit & Publshr) 1073

American Lib Association (DC)
COOKE, Eileen D. (Assoc Exec Dir & Dir) 241
HEANUE, Anne A. (Assoc Dir) . . 518

American Lib Association (IL)
BERRY, John W. (Executive Dir) . . 90
BRAWLEY, Paul H. (Editor-in-Chief) 130
CARLSON, Robert P. (Deputy ALANET Syst Mgr) 182
CLINE, Helen R. (Managing Edit) 222
DAVIS, Maryellen K. (Prog Ofcr) . 280
EBERHART, George M. (Editor of Coll & Resrch Libs News) . . 334
ELLEMAN, Barbara J. (Chlds Books Edit) 343
EPP, Ronald H. (Managing Edit of CHOICE Mag) 351
ESTES, Sally C. (Editor of Books for Yng Adults) 355
FLAGG, Gordon E. (Am Libs Mag Assoc Edit) 383
GALVIN, Thomas J. (Exec Dir) . 415
GUY, Jeniece N. (Asst Dir) 479
HANSEN, Andrew M. (RASD Exec Dir) 497
HUCHTING, Mary (Prodctn Editor) 569
KAYE, Marilyn J. (Edit) 632
KNUTSON, Linda J. (Lib & Info Tech Assn Exec Dir) 666
KOBASA, Paul A. (Asst Dir for Mktg/Publshg Srvs) 666
KRUG, Judith F. (Dir of Ofc for Intellectual Freedom) 680
KUSZMAUL, Marcia J. (Pub Info Ofc Mktg Mgr) 685
LEE, Joel M. (Sr Mgr of Info Tech Publshg) 710
LYNCH, Mary J. (Ofc for Resrch Dir) 752
MCDERMOTT, Patrice (Asst Dir) 802
MELTON, Emily I. (Headquarters Libn) 823
MULLER, Karen (Exec Dir) 877
MYERS, Margaret R. (Dir of Ofc for Lib Persnl Resrcs) 884
OTT, Bill (Editor of Books for Adults) 930
PARENT, Roger H. (Deputy Exec Dir) 940
PEARSON, Lois R. (Am Libs Assoc Edit) 952
PLOTNIK, Arthur (Am Libs Mag Edit) 978
ROBERTSON, Deborah G. (Pub Info Ofcr) 1041
ROCHMAN, Hazel P. (Asst Edit of Bks for Yng Adults) 1046
ROMAN, Susan (Exec Dir, Assn for Lib Srv to Chld) 1052

American Lib Association (IL)
SCARRY, Patricia A. (Membership Srv Dir) 1088
SEGAL, Joan S. (Exec Dir) 1111
SHAEVEL, Evelyn F. (Exec Dir) . 1118
WALLACE, Linda K. (Pub Info Ofc Dir) 1297
WHITE, Howard S. (Lib Tech Reports Editor) 1331
WHITELEY, Sandra M. (Edit Ref Bks Bltn) 1333
WILSON, Phillis M. (Asst Libn) . 1352
WOOD, Irene P. (Nonprint Mtrls Rvsw Editor) 1364
WRIGHT, Helen K. (Asst Dir of Publshg Srvs) 1371
ZVIRIN, Stephanie H. (Asst Editor of Books for Yng Adults) 1392

The American Lib in Paris (FRN)
GRATTAN, Robert (Dir) 458

American Lib Trustee Association (AZ)
WISENER, Joanne C. (Immediate Past-President) . . 1357

American Lib Trustee Association (MD)
DAVIS, Herbert A. (Pres) 279

American Lutheran Church (IA)
WIEDERAENDE, Robert C. (Archvst) 1336

American Lutheran Church (MN)
DANIELS, Paul A. (Asst Archvst) 273

American Management Association (NY)
JONES, Anne (Libn & Database Adminstr) 611
LAMBKIN, Claire A. (Chief Libn) . 691

American Management Systems Inc (VA)
GLAMM, Amy E. (Systs Analyst) 439
YODER, William M. (Principal) . 1380

American Mathematical Society (MI)
PONOMARENKO, Ella (Head Libn) 982

American Mathematical Society (RI)
KUSMA, Taissa T. 685

American Medical Association (DC)
BANKS, Jane L. (Lib Mgr) 54

American Medical Association (IL)
FUNK, Carla J. (Automation & Technl Srvs Dir) 409
GRAVES, Karen J. (Info Srvs Dir) 459
HAFNER, Arthur W. (Lib & Info Mgmt Dir) 482
JAGODZINSKI, Cecile M. (Technl Srvs Mgr) 591
MUELLER, Julie M. (Resrch Assoc) 875

American Medical International (CO)
GUTH, Karen K. (Hospital Libn) . . 478

American Museum of Natural History (NY)
KITT, Sandra E. (Libn) 657
SHIH, Diana (Sr Catlgng Libn) . . 1130

American Newspaper Publishers Assn (VA)
EGERTSON, Yvonne L. (Libn) . . 339

American Nuclear Insurers (CT)
SHERMAN, Dottie (Lib Dir) 1128

American Nuclear Society (IL)
WEBSTER, Lois S. (Info Resrcs Mgr) 1314

American Numismatic Association (CO)
GREEN, Nancy W. (Libn) 462

American Numismatic Society (NY)
CAMPBELL, Francis D. (Libn) . . . 176

American Optometric Association (MO)
DRAPER, Linda J. (Head of Technl Srvs) 318

American Overseas Book Co (MD)
MARKS, Cicely P. (Regnl Dir) . . . 771

American Petroleum Institute (DC)
SCHUERMANN, Lois J. (Acting Libn) 1101

American Petroleum Institute (NY)
BRENNER, Everett H. (Centl Abstctng & Indexing Srv Mgr) . 133
HOFFMAN, Allen (Editor) 547
LINDER, Elliott (Sr Edit) 729
SHERRILL, Jocelyn T. (Bus Indxr) 1129
TERLIZZI, Joseph M. (Technl Indexing Edit) 1232

American Pharmaceutical Association (DC)
KUTTY, Lalitha M. (Libn) 685

American Philosophical Society (PA)
CARROLL-HORROCKS, Elizabeth (Manuscripts Libn) . . 187
LEVITT, Martin L. (Asst Manuscript Libn) 721
American Plywood Assn (WA) PRESTON, Deirdre R. (Supvsr) . . 991
American Psychological Association (VA)
DESSAINT, Alain Y. (Assoc Edit, Psychological Abstrcs) . . 295
GOSLING, Carolyn (Mgr User Srvs PsycINFO) 453
GRANICH, Lois 457
KNIGHT, Nancy H. (Database Educ Spclst) 664
LARMOUR, Rosamond E. (Indxr & Srch Analyst) 698
MCKENNEY, Linda S. (Database Educ Spclst) 811
American Pub Works Association (CO)
CHRISTENSEN, Erin S. (Histn) . . 211
American Reading Council (NY)
PALMER, Julia R. (Exec Dir) 936
SCHWABACHER, Sara A. (Assoc Dir) 1104
American Record Collector's Exchange (NY)
MOSES, Julian M. (Dir) 871
American Sch in London (ENG)
BRILL, Kathryn R. (Libn & Activites Coordntr) 136
SERVENTE, Marcia M. (Head Libn) 1116
American Society for Information Science (DC)
MORRISON, Steve (Dir of Comms) 868
RATH, Charla M. (Mem Srvs Dir) 1009
RESNIK, Linda I. (Exec Dir) 1024
American Society for Metals Intl (OH)
WEIDA, William A. (Mtrls Info Mgr) 1316
American Society for Microbiology (MD)
SHAY, Donald E. (Archvst) 1124
American Society for Testing Materials (PA)
SHUPAK, Harris J. (Sr Indxr) . . 1134
American Society for Training & Devlpmnt (MD)
CHAPUT, Linda J. (Info Ctr Spclst) 202
American Society for Training & Devlpmnt (VA)
OLIVETTI, L J. (Info Ctr Mgr) . . . 921
American Society of Artists Inc (LA) COE, Miriam M. (LA State Rep) . 226
American Society of Civil Engineers (NY)
EDWARDS, Melanie G. (Info Products Mgr) 337
American Society of Hospital Pharmacists (MD)
HANES, Alice H. (Libn) 495
MORISSEAU, Anne L. (Database & User Srvs Coordntr) 865
American Sound & Video (NJ)
GRAY, Lee H. (VP, Gen Systs Mgr) 460
American Soybean Association (MO) GIBSON, Marianne (Libn) 432
American Speech, Language & Hearing Assn (MD)
ZAHARKO, Nancy W. (Libn) . . . 1385
American Systems Engineering Corp (VA)
WISECARVER, Betty A. (Technl Libn) 1357
American Technological Univ (TX)
GUTHRIE, Melinda L. (Univ Libn) 479
American Theological Lib Association (IL)
FIEG, Eugene C. (Catlgr) 375
HURD, Albert E. (Exec Dir, Religion Indexes) 577
MARKHAM, Robert P. (Dir of Progs) 771
ATLA Religion Indexes (IL) TREESH, Erica (Edit) 1255
American Translators International (CA)
HOMNACK, Mark (Intl Dir) 555
American Trucking Associations (VA) ROTHBART, Linda S. (Dir of Info Srvs) 1060
American Univ (DC)
CHASE, Linda S. (Ref Libn) 203
KEHOE, Patrick E. (Prof of Law & Dir of the Law Lib) 634
SANDIQUE-OWENS, Amelia A. (Assoc Law Libn for Catlgng) 1080

American Univ (DC)
ZICH, Joanne A. (Govt Docums & Non-Print Media Libn) 1388
American Univ of Beirut (LEB) HANHAN, Leila M. (Acting Med Libn) 495
American Water Works Association (CO)
LUEVANE, Marsha A. (Technl Info Spclst) 747
American Worlds Books (CT) SMITH, Nolan E. (Proprietor) . . . 1159
Americus City Board of Education (GA)
PASCHAL, Eloise R. (Career Media Spclst) 945
Amerika-Gedenkbibliothek (WGR) ULRICH, Paul S. (Head of Computerized Circ Syst) 1268
Ameritech Services Inc (IL) METCALFE, Douglas N. (Mgr) . . 828
Ames Pub Lib (IA) KENAGY, Charles R. (Asst Dir) . . 640
LARSON, Teresa B. (Media Srvs Coordntr) 700
LAWSON, George T. (Dir) 705
RAILSBACK, Patsy S. (Ref Libn) 1003
STUART, Kimberly A. (Technl Srvs Coordntr) 1204
Amherst Coll (MA)
BAILEY, Leeta L. (Asst Ref Libn) 46
BRIDEGAM, Willis E. (Coll Libn) . 135
EVANS, Sally (Music Libn) 358
LANCASTER, John (Cur of Spcl Cols) 692
Amherst Pub Lib (NY)
ALLENBACH, Norma A. (Libn) . . . 16
BOBINSKI, Mary F. (Dir) 108
AMIGOS Bibliographic Council Inc (TX)
CHIU, Ida K. (Pgmr & Analyst) . . 209
DOWNINS, Jeffery G. (Pub Srvs Mgr) 317
MARMION, Daniel K. (Lib Liaison Ofcr) 772
WETHERBEE, Louella V. (Exec Dir) 1327
WHITE, Douglas A. (Programming Mgr) 1330
Amityville Pub Lib (NY) PAVLAK, Anne C. (Dir) 950
Amoco Corp (IL)
AVERY, May S. (Info Spclst) 42
BUNTROCK, Robert E. (Resrch Assoc) 157
STRYCK, B C. (Resrch Supvsr) 1203
Amoco Production Co (OK) EGGERT, Paula A. 339
Amoco Production Co (TX) JOHANSEN, Priscilla P. (Info Spclst) 601
Amon Carter Museum (TX)
HUGHSTON, Milan R. (Assoc Libn) 572
ROARK, Carol E. (Asst Cur of Photographs) 1038
Amos Memorial Pub Lib (OH)
BELVIN, Robert J. (Exec Dir) . . . 78
WILSON, Memory A. (Branch Coordntr) 1352
Amos Press (OH) HESSELBEIN, Krista M. (Libn) . . 534
Amron Information Services (NJ) AMRON, Irving (Pres) 20
Amtec Information Services Inc (CA) KILKER, Paul V. (Executive VP) . 648
An Idea Place (WI) WAITY, Gloria J. (Freelance Libn & Consult) 1293
Anaheim Pub Lib (CA) EARNEST, Patricia 332
Anaheim Union High Sch District (CA)
HALL, Howard L. (Libn & Media Spclst) 488
Analysis & Computer Systems Inc (MA)
ROSENTHAL, Marylu C. (Technl Libn) 1057
Analytics Inc (NJ) HENKEL, Grace E. (Chief Libn) . . 528
Anchorage Municipal Libs (AK) BRAUND-ALLEN, Julianna E. (Chlds Libn) 130
LUDWIG, J D. (Sci Libn) 746
MACLEAN, Barbara A. (Col Devlpmnt Coordntr) 757
PIERCE, Linda I. (Bus & Docums Libn) 971
PUTZ, Paul D. (Catlgng Head) . . 998
WILLIAMS, Robert C. (Head, Ref & Reader Srvs) 1346

Anchorage Museum of History and Art (AK)
BRENNER, M D. (Musm Archvst) 133

Anchorage Sch District (AK)
TRIDLE, Jeanne A. (Elem Media Spclst) 1256
WIGET, Laurence A. (Lib & Media Supvsr) 1337

Ancilla Coll (IN)
BOCKMAN, Glenda C. (Libn) . . 109

Anderson Clayton Foods (TX)
MARTIN, Irmgarde D. (Supvsr Technl Info Srvs) 776

Anderson Coll (IN)
COTTINGHAM, Elsie E. (Technl Srvs Libn) 250

Anderson County District 4 Schs (SC)
DIXON, Linda A. (Sch Media Spclst) 306

Anderson Publishing Co (OH)
GATES, Robert G. (Exec Vice Pres) 422
KUEHNLE, Emery C. (Secy) 682

Anderson Russell Killsolick (NY)
KAIN, Joan P. (Libn) 622

Anderson Univ (IN)
KENDALL, Charles T. (Lib Dir) . . 640

Andover Newton Theological Sch (MA)
HARRISON, Sylvia E. (Head, Technl Srvs) 507
O'NEAL, Ellis E. (Libn Emeritus) . 923
YOUNT, Diana (Spcl Cols Libn) 1384

Andover Pub Schools (MA)
FREEDMAN, Annetta R. (Media Srvs Dir) 400

Andrew W Mellon Foundation (NY)
MOTIHAR, Kamla (Lib Dir) 872

Andrew Wilson Co (MA)
LEWIS, Thomas F. (Dist Sales Mgr) 724

Andrews Univ (MI)
SOPER, Marley H. (Dir) 1168
WALLER, Elaine J. (Music Mtrls Libn) 1298
WILDMAN, Linda (Asst Prof of Lib Sci & Perdcls Libn) 1339

Anglican Bibliopole (NY)
KEARNEY, Robert D. (Self-employed) 633

Anglo American Corp of South Africa (SAF)
ARMSTRONG, Denise M. (Head of Info Srvs) 32

Anglo-American Sch of Moscow (NY)
VOSE, Deborah R. (Libn) 1289

Anheuser Busch Co Inc (MO)
LAURENSTEIN, Ann G. (Corp Libn) 703
VOLLMAR, William J. (Archs & Records Admin Mgr) 1288

Ann Arbor Pub Lib (MI)
CAPPAERT, Lael R. (Ref Libn) . . 180
COFFEY, Dorothy A. (Head Libn) 227
DALY, Kathleen E. (Head Libn) . . 271

Ann Arbor Pub Schs (MI)
HERNANDEZ, Ramon R. (Dir of Pub Libs) 532

Annapolis & Anne Arundel County Lib (MD)
HALL, Edward B. (Lib Adminstr) . 487

Anne Arundel Community Coll (MD)
STEINHOFF, Cynthia K. (Acqs Libn) 1186

Anne Arundel County Board of Education (MD)
JACKSON, Doris G. (Media Spclst) 587
SHAMBARGER, Peter E. (Media Spclst) 1120
SMITH, Jan E. (Media Spclst) . . 1155

Anne Arundel County Circuit Court (MD)
SIMISON, Joan B. (Law Libn) . . 1139

Anne Arundel County Pub Lib (MD)
AUGER, Brian K. (Branch Mgr) . . . 39
COURSON, M S. (Branch Mgr) . 251
KELLER, Susan J. (Branch Mgr) . 636
MAZUREK, Adam P. (Branch Mgr) 791
PINDER, Jo A. (Assoc Adminstr) 974
PURCELL, Kathleen V. (Spcl Projs Libn) 998
SUMLER, Claudia B. (Branch Mgr) 1209

Anne Arundel County Pub Sch System (MD)
LIVELY, Nancy J. (Libn) 734
STIGALL, Judith N. (Media Spclst) 1194

Anoka County Lib (MN)
WEEKS, Diane M. (Head of Catlgng) 1315
YOUNG, Jerry F. (Dir) 1382

Anoka Pub Lib (MN)
Anotherplace Research Service (MI)
Ansbach American High Sch (NY)

Antigo Unified Sch District (WI)
Antillian Coll (PR)
Antioch Univ (PA)

Antiquarian Bookselling Firm (PA)

Aoyama Gakuin Univ (JAP)

Apache I-6 Sch District (OK)

Apache Junction Unified Sch District 43 (AZ)

Appalachian Hall (NC)
Appalachian State Univ (NC)

Appalshop Inc (KY)

Apple Computer Inc (CA)

Appleton Pub Lib (WI)

Appollo Computer Inc (MA)

Appomattox County Lib (VA)
Aqudas Achim Synagogue (IA)
Aquinas Coll (MI)
Arabian Horse Trust (CO)
ARAMCO (SDA)

Arapahoe Lib District (CO)

Archdiocese of Boston (MA)

Archdiocese of Boston (SC)
Archdiocese of Cincinnati (OH)

Archdiocese of Dubuque Archives (IA)
Archdiocese of Hartford (CT)
Archdiocese of Los Angeles (CA)

Archdiocese of New York (NY)

Archdiocese of Newark (NJ)

Archdiocese of St Louis (MO)
Archdiocese of San Antonio (TX)
Archdiocese of Santa Fe (NM)

Archdiocese of Washington (DC)
Archer Daniels Midland Co (IL)
Architect of the Capitol (DC)

SHANLEY, Dennis M. (Lib Dir) . 1120
STARESINA, Lois J. 1181
MEIGS, Carolyn R. (Media Splcst) 821
RETZER, Cathy E. (Elem Libn) . 1024
PEREZ, Sarai (Lib Dir) 958
SAUNDERS, William B. (Dir, Resrc Ctr) 1085
MCKITTRICK, Bruce W. (Pres) . . 812
KOGA, Setsuko (Prof) 668
HUSTED, Ruth E. (K-12 Lib Media Spclst) 578

GILSON, Myral A. (Elem Libn) . . 437
WHORTON, Pamela J. (Sch Libn) 1334
MAYER, Barbara D. (Med Libn) . 789
ANTONE, Allen L. (Head of Ref Srvs) 29
BARKER, Richard T. (Libn) 56
BUSBIN, O M. (Prof of Lib Sci) . . 164
GOLDEN, Susan L. (Instr & Libn) 445
HATHAWAY, Milton G. (Asst Prof) 512
NAYLOR, Alice P. (Prof) 890
OLSON, Eric J. (Col Libn) 922
WISE, Mintron S. (Ref Libn) . . . 1357
OLIVER, Scot (Dir of Film Distribution) 921
BIDWELL, Lynne H. (Info Spclst) 95
DEWEY, Barney L. (VP) 298
ERTEL, Monica (Info Srvs Mgr) . . 353
MACEK, Rosanne M. (Info Srvs Supvsr) 755
VRATNY-WATTS, Janet M. (Sr Info Spclst) 1289
DAWSON, Terry P. (Asst Dir for Access) 282
KELLY, Barbara J. (Ref Libn & Online Coordntr) 637
PENNINGTON, Jerome G. (Dir) . 957
MATTHEWS, Charles E. (Mgr, Technl Info Srvs) 785
KEMPTER, Albert H. (Lib Dir) . . . 640
GINSBERG, Marjorie E. (Libn) . . 438
MARTIN, Rose M. (Head) 778
BOYD, Ruth E. (Libn & Archvst) . 122
BASCOM, James F. (Sr Surgeon) 62
BRUNTON, David W. (Mgr) 151
WILDER, Mary K. (Ref Coordntr) 1339
CLARK, Mary E. (Vice-Principal & Libn) 217
EPPARD, Philip B. (Archvst) 351
PARKER, Mary A. (Libn) 942
HILAND, Gerard P. (Dir of Archs) 538
KURT, Edgar (Dir) 684
JASKEL, Mary A. (Archvst) 595
WOLFF, Mary K. (High Sch Libn) 1361
FERNANDEZ, M L. (Head Libn & Chairman) 373
REINHARDT, Eileen (Libn/Media Spclst, Adminstr) 1021
BEDAN, Lucille D. (Libn) 73
LOCH, Edward J. (Archvst) 735
FALARDEAU, Ernest R. (Archdiocesan Ecumenical Ofcr) 361
BARRY, Paul J. (Archvst) 60
PERMAN, Karen A. (Libn) 959
CARTLEDGE, Connie L. (Records Mgmt Div Head) . . . 190

The Architects Collaborative (MA)
GRIGORIS, Lygia (Interiors Resrc Spclst) 470
HARTMERE, Anne 508
TENNEY, Kimberly M. (Corp Libn) 1231

Archive Film Productions Inc (NY)
MONTGOMERY, Patrick (Pres) . . 856

Arch for Resrch in Archetypal Symbolism (NY)
RONNBERG, Annmari (Curator) 1053

Archive of Contemporary Music (NY)
GEORGE, B 427
WHEELER, David 1328

Archives & Museum Informatics (PA)
BEARMAN, David A. (Info Tech Consult) 69

Archives for the Performing Arts (CA)
VANSLYKE, Lisa M. (Archvst) . 1277

Archives Museums & Historical Department (WY)
YELVINGTON, Julia A. (Dir) . . . 1379

Archives of Industrial Society (PA)
KURTIK, Frank J. (Asst Curator) . 685

Archives Traces de Montreal (PQ)
CHAGNON, Danielle G. (Libn) . . 197

ARCO (CA)
BOWMAN, Frances A. (Mgr) . . 121
HAUTH, Carol A. (Mgr, Info Systs, Safety, Hlth, Env) 513
WRIGHT, Betty A. (Technl Info Spclst) 1370

ARCO Chemical Co (PA)
WHITEHURST, Dori A. (Bus & Tech Info Spclst) 1333

ARCO Oil & Gas Co (TX)
PROKESH, Jane (Head Libn) . . 995

ARCO Pipe Line Co (KS)
RYAN, Betsey A. (Info Srvs Supvsr) 1070

Area Corp (CA)
YU, Simone 1384

Argo-Summit Bedford Park Pub Schs (IL)
WIRIG, Joan S. (Lib AV Coordntr) 1356

Argonne National Laboratory (IL)
DAVIDOFF, Gary N. (Technl Libn) 276
GREGORY, Melissa R. (Acqs and Serials Sects Head) 466
WILSON, Majorie A. 1352
WOELL, Yvette N. (Technl Libn) 1359

Aries Systems Corp (MA)
HOLMES, Lyndon S. (Pres) 553

Arizona Department of Economic Security (AZ)
OLEARY, Jennie L. (Libn I) 920

Arizona Department of Education (AZ)
EDGINGTON, Linda A. (Libn II) . . 336
RIDGEWAY, Merrilyn S. (Sch Lib Media Consult) 1032

Arizona Dept of Lib, Archs & Pub Records (AZ)
FRIEDMAN, Zena K. (Resrch Lib Dir) 404
MCCOLGIN, Michael A. (Conservator) 797

Arizona State Capitol (AZ)
TURGEON, Sharon (Dir of Archvs & Pub Records) 1263

Arizona State Univ (AZ)
ALCORN, Marianne S. (Ref Libn) 11
BOROVANSKY, Vladimir T. (Head of Noble Sci & Engrng Lib) 117
FERRALL, J E. (Ref Libn) 373
GEMPELER, Constance M. (Music Catlg Libn) 426
HAWKOS, Lise J. (Art Slide Col Cur) 514
HOWARD, Pamela F. (Latin-American Area Spclst) . 564
JOSEPHINE, Helen B. (Info Mgr) 617
KNEPP, Kenneth B. (Assoc Libn & Catlg Libn) 664
MACHOVEC, George S. (Lib Tech & Systs Head) 755
MILLER, Rosanna (Map Col Head) 842
MOLLOY, Molly F. (Slavic Catlgr & Area Spclst) 853
MULVIHILL, Joann (Ref Libn & Educ & Psy Subj Spclst) 878
NILSEN, Alleen P. (Asst Dean) . . 904
OETTING, Edward C. (Head, Archvs & Manuscripts) 917
POTTER, William G. (Assoc Univ Libn) 987

Arizona State Univ (AZ)
RENEKER, Maxine H. (Pub Srvs Assoc Univ Libn) 1023
RIGGS, Donald E. (Univ Libn) . . 1034
SCHON, Isabel (Prof) 1098
STEEL, Virginia (Access Srvs Actg Head) 1183
STEWART, Douglas J. (Ref Libn & Subj Spclst) 1192
VATHIS, Alma C. (Visiting Asst Libn) 1279
WU, Ai H. (Chinese Catlg Libn & Area Spclst) 1373

Arizona State Univ West (AZ)
KOLBER, Denise (Visiting Libn) . . 669

Arizona Theatre Co (AZ)
GOLDBERG, Susan S. (Managing Dir) 445

Arizona Western Coll (AZ)
SHACKELFORD, Eileen R. (Dir) 1118

Arkansas Arts Center (AR)
MCCOY, Evelyn G. (Sr Dir) 799

Arkansas Coll (AR)
WATSON, Ellen I. (Dir, Mabee Lrng Resrc Ctr) 1309

Arkansas History Commission (AR)
BAKER, Russell P. (Deputy Dir) . . 49
FERGUSON, John L. (State Histn) 372

Arkansas Lib Association (AR)
IVEY, Frank (Exec Dir) 586

Arkansas Parks & Tourism Commission (AR)
MCNEIL, William K. (Folklorist, Ozark Folk Ctr) 816

Arkansas State Lib (AR)
HALL, Deborah N. (Ref Libn) . . . 487
HALL, John J. (Lib Prog Advisor II) 488
HONEYCUTT, Mary L. (State Lib Srvs Coordntr) 556
MITCHAM, Janet C. (Catlgng Srvs Coordntr) 848
MULKEY, Jack C. (Asst State Libn) 876
MURPHEY, John A. (State Libn) . 880
PITTS, Cynthia F. (Col Devlpmnt Srvs Coordntr) 976

Arkansas State Univ (AR)
BLAND, Janet A. (Head Orders & Perdcls Libn) 103
BRENNER, Willis F. (Docums Libn) 133
GREEN, Douglas A. (Libn) 461

Arkansas Supreme Court (AR)
WRIGHT, Jacqueline S. (Libn & Dir) 1371

Arkansas Tech Univ (AR)
VAUGHN, William A. (Lib Dir) . . 1280

Arkansas Valley Regional Lib Srv System (CO)
JONES, Donna R. (Dir) 612

Arlington County Department of Libs (VA)
BRITTO, Mary M. (Chlds Libn) . . 137
BROWN, Charles M. (Dir of Libs) 142
COLLINS, Sara D. (Virginiana Libn) 233
COOPER, Nancy C. (Ref Libn) . . 243
FISHER, Carl D. (Head of Catlgng) 380
HABERLAND, Jody (Pub Srvs Supvsr, Fiction, Fine Arts) . . . 481
WEILERSTEIN, Deborah E. (Chlds Srvs Coordntr) 1317

Arlington County Pub Schs (VA)
LAM, Letitia E. (High Sch Libn) . . 689

Arlington Heights Memorial Lib (IL)
BROWN, Pamela P. (Head, Technl Srvs) 146
DEMPSEY, Frank J. (Exec Libn) . 291
HANRATH, Richard A. (Circ Srvs Head) 497
SHUMAN, Marilyn J. (Pub Info Ofcr) 1134

Arlington Independent Sch District (TX)
KERBY, Ramona A. (Elem Sch Libn) 643

Arlington Pub Lib (VA)
SWICEGOOD, Mary R. (Media Prcsng Ctr Supvsr) 1216

Arlington Pub Schs (VA)
YAEGER, Luke R. (Sch Libs Supvsr) 1376

Arma Unified Sch District 246 (KS)
ROBERTS, Linda A. (Lib Media Spclst) 1041

Armed Forces Institute of
  Pathology (DC)   PATEL, Patricia C. (Libn) 947
Armstrong State Coll (GA)   BALL, Ardella P. (Asst Prof of
                                     Lib Sci) 52
Armstrong World Industries Inc (PA) FILLER, Mary A. (Technl Lib
                                     Mgr) 377
                                   JUDGE, Joseph M. (Tech Srch
                                     & Transfer Assoc) 619
ArmTeis (CT)   CRUTCHER, Hope H. (Libn) 262
Army & Navy Club (DC)   SPONDER, Dorothy R. (Libn) .. 1175
Arnall Golden & Gregory (GA)   CAMBELL, Miriam A. (Asst Law
                                     Libn) 174
Arnold & Porter (DC)   SEELE, Ronald E. (Legislativ
                                     Resrch Dir) 1111
                                   SHELAR, James W. (Chief
                                     Libn) 1125
Arnold's Archives (MI)   JACOBSEN, Arnold (Owner &
                                     Archvst) 590
Arnprior Pub Lib (ON)   BARKE, Judith P. (Chief Libn) 56
Arnstein Gluck Lehr & Milligan (IL) DRAKE, Francis L. (Lib Srvs
                                     Dir) 318
Aromat Corp (NJ)   CHANG, Joseph I. (Adminstrv
                                     Asst to Pres) 200
Art Gallery of Ontario (ON)   ARDERN, Christine M. (Mgr of
                                     Adminstrv Srvs & Archs) 31
Art Institute of Boston (MA)   DESJARDINS, Andrea C. (Libn) . 295
Art Institute of Chicago (IL)   BYRNE, Nadene M. (Sch Lib
                                     Dir) 169
                                   GODLEWSKI, Susan G. (Assoc
                                     Dir) 442
                                   HANSEN, Roland C. (Reader
                                     Srvs Libn) 498
                                   WALSH, Susan E. (Sr Ref Libn) 1300
Art Libs Society of North
  America (AZ)   PARRY, Pamela J. (Exec Dir) ... 944
Art Museum Lib Consortium (NY)   LUCKER, Amy E. (Proj
                                     Coordntr) 746
Art Preservation Information
  Service (IA)   JONSON, Laurence F.
                                     (Independent Conservator &
                                     Consult) 616
Arthur Andersen & Co (AZ)   STEPHENS, Stefanie N. (Libn) . 1188
Arthur Andersen & Co (CA)   FOX, Marylou P. (Head Libn) ... 395
                                   MCDEVITT-PARKS, Kathryn B.
                                     (Ref Libn) 802
Arthur Andersen & Co (GA)   KLOPPER, Susan M. (Libn) 662
Arthur Andersen & Co (IL)   GUINEE, Andrea M. (Resrch
                                     Assoc) 476
                                   HARRIS, Jeanne G. (Sr Mgr) ... 504
                                   JAMESON, Martha E. (Resrch
                                     Assoc) 592
                                   MURRAY, Marilyn R. (Dir, Lib
                                     Srvs) 882
                                   O'BRIEN, Barbara E. (Mktg
                                     Libn) 914
                                   SWANTEK, Kathleen M. (Asst
                                     Libn) 1214
Arthur Andersen & Co (MA)   FISHER, Jean K. (Libn) 381
Arthur Andersen & Co (MI)   SNAY, Sylvia A. (Lib Supvsr) .. 1162
                                   STREETER, Linda D. (Libn) ... 1201
Arthur Andersen & Co (MN)   DINGLEY, Doris A. (Lib
                                     Adminstr) 305
Arthur Andersen & Co (MO)   KETTERING, Marguerite L.
                                     (Libn) 645
Arthur Andersen & Co (NC)   MOORE, Patricia R. (Libn) 860
Arthur Andersen & Co (PA)   CARTELLI, Alessandra J. (Libn) . 188
                                   PLEFKA, Cathleen S. (Lib
                                     Supvsr) 978
Arthur D Little Inc (MA)   ADAMOWICZ, Joanne C. (Libn) ... 4
                                   COLBY, Beverly (Info Spclst) ... 230
                                   HIBBERD, Cynthia M. (Mgr) 536
                                   MACKEY, Wendy W. (Sr Ref
                                     Asst) 757
                                   MOFFITT, Michael D. (Info Srvs
                                     Practice Mgr) 852
                                   REEDY, Martha J. (Consult) ... 1015
                                   SACERDOTE, George S. (Info
                                     Srvs Dir) 1073
                                   WOLPERT, Ann J. (Dir of Libs) . 1362
Arthur Kill Correctional Facility (NY) ROMALIS, Carl (Sr Libn) 1052

Arthur Young & Co (NY)   CARLSON, Robert E. (Asst
                                     Libn) 182
                                   MCBRIDE, Jessica W. (Resrch
                                     Srvs Adminstr) 792
Arthur Young & Co (TX)   BARRETT, Carol A. (Lib
                                     Adminstr) 59
                                   HOPKINS, Terry F. (Lib Dir) 558
Arthur Young & Co (WI)   HOOTKIN, Neil M. (Libn) 557
Artworks (CA)   PASCAL, Barbara R.
                                     (Co-owner) 945
Arvey Hodes Costello & Burman (IL) HARRINGTON, Margaret V.
                                     (Libn) 504
Asbury Theological Seminary (KY)   BUNDY, David D. (Col Devlpmnt
                                     Libn) 157
                                   BUTTERWORTH, Donald Q.
                                     (Asst Dir) 167
                                   FAUPEL, David W. (Lib Srvs
                                     Dir) 366
Ascension Parish (LA)   HILL, Sue A. (Head Libn) 540
ASFETM (PQ)   MERCIER, Diane (Archvst) 825
Asheville-Buncombe Lib System (NC) HEROLD, Virginia L. (Head of
                                     Technl Srvs) 532
                                   PERRY, Douglas F. (Dir of Libs) . 960
Asheville City Schs (NC)   BROWN, Nancy E. (Media
                                     Coordntr) 146
Ashford & Wriston (HI)   REED, Carol R. (Law Libn) 1014
Ashland Chemical Co (OH)   LANDIS, Kay A. (Info Resrch
                                     Chemist) 693
                                   MILLER, Dennis P. (Sr Resrch
                                     Chemist) 837
                                   RATLIFF, Priscilla (Technl Info
                                     Ctr Supvsr) 1009
Ashland County Law Lib
  Association (OH)   RHOADES, Nancy L. (Libn) ... 1025
Ashland Exploration Inc (TX)   MATLOCK, Teresa A. (Info
                                     Coordntr) 784
Ashland Oil (KY)   YOUNG, Sandra C. (Technl Info
                                     Resrch Analyst) 1383
Ashley Book Company (VT)   SINGER, George C. (Proprietor) 1143
Ashtabula County District Lib (OH) WARREN, Dorothea C.
                                     (Trustee) 1306
Ashtabula County Law Lib
  Association (OH)   BROWN, Vicki L. (Cnty Law
                                     Libn) 148
Asia Pacific Foundation of
  Canada (BC)   BROOME, Diana M. (Info Srvs
                                     Dir) 141
                                   CESARD, Mary A. (Pres) 196
ASKMAC (NJ)   BALDWIN, Eleanor M. (Lib
ASM International (OH)   Supvsr) 51
                                   SANDULEAK, Barbara (Info
                                     Srvs Mgr) 1081
Aspen Publishers Inc (MD)   PATTERSON, Anne S. (Editrl
                                     Dir of Clinical Medcn) 948
                                   QUINLIN, Margaret M. (Editrl
                                     Dir, Allied Hlth & Educ) 1000
Aspen Systems Corp (DC)   LOMAX, Denise W. (Libn) 738
Aspen Systems Corp (MD)   BATES, Ruthann I. (Prog Dir) 64
                                   BYRD, Harvey C. (Vice Pres) ... 169
                                   CHIANG, Ahushun (Prog Plng
                                     Dir) 207
                                   GAVIN, Andrew 423
                                   GROCKI, Daniel J. (Sr Info
                                     Designer & Consult) 471
                                   JOHNSON, Carol A. (Prog Dir) .. 602
                                   JOHNSON, Emily P. (Proj Mgr) .. 604
                                   KNOERDEL, Joan E. (Systs
                                     Consult) 665
                                   MCDONALD, Dennis D. (Mktg
                                     Dir) 802
                                   PEARSE, Nancy J. (Supvsr of
                                     Lib Srvs) 952
                                   USDIN, B T. (Info Syst
                                     Designer) 1270
                                   VANCE, Julia M. (Sr Systs
                                     Analyst) 1273
Aspen Systems Corp (NY)   BRINBERG, Herbert R. (Bd of
                                     Dirs Mem) 136
Associated Lib Service Inc (NY)   WUNDERLICH, Penina (Assoc
                                     Lib Srv Libn) 1374

Associated Mennonite Biblical Seminaries (IN)
Associated Press (NY)

SANER, Eileen K. (Lib Dir) 1081
PEDERSON, Christopher 954
PISTILLI, Susan A. (Chief News Libn) 976
SHAPIRO, Barbara G. (Libn) ... 1121

Association for Computing Machinery (NY)

WEINER, Carolynn N. (Assignment Edit) 1318

Association for Higher Educ (TX)

JAGOE, Katherine P. (Dir of Lib Progs & Srvs) 591

Assn for Information & Image Management (MD)

COURTOT, Marilyn E. (Dir, Standards & Tech) 251
STEIGER, Bettie A. (Exec Dir) .. 1185

Assn for Lib & Info Science Education (PA)
Association for Recorded Sound Cols (VA)
Assn for Volntry Surgical Contraception (NY)
Association of American Publishers Inc (DC)

PHILLIPS, Janet C. (Exec Secy) . 968

ROCHLIN, Phillip (Exec Dir) ... 1046

RECORD, William J. (Libn) 1013

RISHER, Carol A. (Copyright & New Tech Dir) 1036

Association of American Railroads (DC)

KOENEMAN, Joyce W. (Lib Srvs Supvsr) 668

Assn of Americans & Canadians in Israel (ISR)

WASERMAN, Barbara (Volunteer Chlds Libn) 1307

Association of Christian Librarians (OH)
Association of Coll & Research Libs (IL)

BROCK, Lynn A. (Exec Dir) 138

BOURDON, Cathleen J. (Deputy Exec Dir) 119

Association of Operating Room Nurses (CO)

BERG, Rebecca M. (Asst Libn) ... 84
KATSH, Sara (Libn) 630

Association of Research Libs (DC)

BARRETT, G J. (Federal Relations Ofcr) 59
JUROW, Susan R. (Prog Ofcr for Trng) 620
REED-SCOTT, Jutta R. (Col Devlpmnt Spclst) 1015

Assn of Teachers of Preventive Medicine (DC)

ANGLE, Joanne G. (Dir of Prevention Educ Resrc Ctr) ... 28

Assn of the Bar of the City of New York (NY)

BURGALASSI, Anthony J. (Reader Srvs Libn) 159
GRECH, Anthony P. (Libn and Cur) 461
RUIZ-VALERA, Phoebe L. (Head of Technl Srvs) 1067
WILLIAMS, David W. (Reader Srvs Libn) 1342

Assumption Coll (MA)

GONNEVILLE, Priscilla R. (Catlgr & Ref Libn) 447

Astoria Sch District (OR)

KORPELA, Betty L. (Lib, Media Spclst) 672

At Your Service, The Informative Network (CA)
AT&T Bell Laboratories (CO)

CUEVAS, John R. (Co-Dir) 263
ROSE, Phillip E. (Ref Libn) 1055
VARNER, James H. (Persnl & Info Srvs Dist Mgr) 1279

AT&T Bell Laboratories (IL)

CHAPMAN, Ruby M. (Ref Info Spclst) 202
FURLONG, Robert E. (Lib Mgr) .. 410
ROMANO, Katherine V. (Mkt Info Resrch Spclst) 1052

AT&T Bell Laboratories (NJ)

BALLARD, Bruce W. 53
BROWN, Ina A. (Libs & Info Systs Spcl Projs Mgr) 144
CANOSE, Joseph A. (Integrated Info Srvs Mgr) 179
CLARK, Joan (Mgr) 217
ENGLISH, Bernard L. (Technl Lib Mgr) 350
ENGLISH, Christopher C. (Info Spclst) 350

AT&T Bell Laboratories (NJ)

GOLDSMITH, Carol C. (Mktg Dept Staff Supvsr) 446
GRANT, George E. (Plng & Reporting Systs Mgr) 458
HAWKINS, Donald T. (Sr Info Tech Scitst) 514
IMPERIALE, Karen P. (Resrch Mgr) 582
JONES, Deborah A. (Resrch Mgr) 612
KAUFFMAN, Betty G. (Resrc & Technl Srvs Mgr) 631
LEVY, Louise R. (Mktg Spclst) .. 721
LEWIS, Dale E. (Info Scitst) 722
LUNAS, Leslie K. (Intl Technl Info Spclst) 748
MCDERMOTT, Ellen (Resrchr & Info Spclst) 801
ODERWALD, Sara M. (Ref Libn) 916
PEABODY, Kenneth W. 951
PENNIMAN, W D. (Libs & Info Systs Dir) 957
PRAQ, Lora B. (Resrch Spclst) .. 989
QUINN, Ralph M. (Japanese Info Spclst) 1000
RIHACEK, Karen S. (Technl Ref Libn) 1034
SINGER, Susan A. (Info Spclst) 1143
SPAULDING, Frank H. (Lib Netwk Mgr) 1172
STANTON, Robert O. (Libs & Info Srvs Mgr) 1181
STEPIEN, Karen K. (Mktg Info Spclst) 1189
ZIMMERMAN, Elisabeth K. (Ref Libn) 1388

AT&T Bell Laboratories (NY)

O'TOOLE, James F. (Div Mgr) .. 930
ROGGENKAMP, Alice M. (Mgr) 1050
SWINBURNE, Ralph E. (Corp Archvst) 1216

AT&T Bell Laboratories (PA)

WAGNER, Darla L. (Technl Ref Libn) 1291

AT&T Communications (NJ)

SCHRIMPE, Janice E. (Resrch Mgr) 1100

AT&T Consumer Products (IN)

MASON, Dorothy L. (Technl Info Libn) 781

AT&T Conversant Systems (OH)

EVANS, Shirley A. (Mktg Planner) 358

AT&T Technical Training Services (OH)

GRIEVE, Shelley (Technl Writer & Course Devlpr) 468

AT&T Technologies Inc (NJ)

SCOTT, Miranda D. (Info Spclst Libn) 1107

AT&T Technology Systems (VA)
ATE Management & Service Co Inc (OH)

ZANG, Patricia J. (Libn) 1386

FENDER, Kimber L. (Mgr, Info Srvs) 371

Ateneo de Manila Univ (PHP)
Athabasca Univ (AB)

MORAN, Teresita C. (Libn) 862
DWORACZEK, Marian (Asst Univ Libn & Head of Tech Srvs) 330

Athenaeum of Philadelphia (PA)

LAVERTY, Bruce (Archvst) 703
MOSS, Roger W. (Exec Dir) 872

Athens Regional Lib (GA)

TAYLOR, Prudence A. (Chlds Libn) 1228

Athol Pub Lib (MA)
Atlanta Arts Alliance (GA)
Atlanta Board of Education (GA)

ROSE, Christine P. (Dir) 1054
MILLER, Jack E. (Musm Libn) ... 838
LOWERY, Phyllis C. (Lib Media Spclst) 744
ROSS, Theodosia B. (Lib Media Spclst) 1059

Atlanta Christian Coll (GA)
Atlanta-Fulton Pub Lib (GA)

BAIN, Michael L. (Libn) 47
BRADLEY, Gail P. (Col Devlpmnt Libn) 125
BRIGHTHARP, Wilma S. (Chlds Libn) 136
BUDLONG, Thomas F. (Branch Mgr) 155

Atlanta-Fulton Pub Lib (GA)

CHUPP, Linda D. (Devlpmnt Ofcr) 213
DAVIS, Joy V. (Branch Mgr) 279
HEID, Gregory G. (Centrl Libn) . . 521
HICKMAN, Michael L. (Libn I) . . . 536
JOHNSON, Beth (Branch Mgr, Chlds Libn) 602
JORDAN, Casper L. (Deputy Dir) 616
LANE, Linda A. (Lib Sr Assoc) . . 694
LEE, Lauren K. (Col Mgmt Ofcr) . 710
MACK, Debora S. (Govt Docums Head & Asst Dept Head) 756
MCIVER, Stephanie P. (Asst Branch Srvs Adminstr) 809
MILLER, Anthony G. (Music Subject Spclst) 835
PICKENS, Lynne R. (Head, Chlds Dept) 970
ROBERTS, Vann R. (Finance & Plng Admin Asst) 1041
SEARCY, David L. (Branch Mgr) 1109
SMITH-EPPS, E P. (Branch Srvs Adminstr) 1161
TYLER, Audrey Q. (Persnl & Staff Devlpmnt Ofcr) 1266
WILLIAMS, Howell M. (Libn I) . . 1343

Atlanta Historical Society (GA)
DICKENS, Rosa L. (Manuscripts Archvst) 300
WIGHT, Nancy E. (Resrch Asst) 1337

Atlanta Information Services (GA)
ROAN, Tattie W. (Pres) 1038

Atlanta Journal Constitution (GA)
LYONS, Valerie S. (Photo Libn) . 753

Atlanta Pub Schs (GA)
LINCOLN, Joanne (Libn) 728
PLOWDEN, Martha W. (Media Spclst) 978

Atlanta Univ (GA)
BROWN, Lorene B. (Dean of Lib Sch) 145
COFFMAN, Joseph W. (Asst Prof) 227
CRAFT, Guy C. (Lib Dir) 254
JAMES, Stephen E. (Assoc Prof) 592
MISRA, Jayasri T. (Prcsng & Archvst Libn) 847
SPENCER, Albert F. (Asst Prof of Lib & Info Std) 1173
TROUTMAN, Joseph E. (Dir, Div of Theol Srvs) 1258

Atlantic City Free Pub Lib (NJ)
CROSS, Roberta A. (Local Info Mgr) 261

Atlantic Community Schs (IA)
CRAVER, Susan J. (Libn) 256

Atlantic County Lib (NJ)
CAPELLA, Jeanne M. (Jr Libn) . . 179
PAULLIN, William D. (Asst Dir & Coordntr of Ref Srvs) 950

Atlantic Electric (NJ)
LEVINE, Riesa E. (Corprt Libn) . . 721

Atlantic Health Service Corp (FL)
CREERON, Carolyn E. (Circuit Libn) 257

Atlantic Lottery Corp (NB)
ENNS, Carol F. (Libn) 350

Atlantic Research Corp (VA)
WALDE, Norma J. (Corprt Libn) 1294

Atlantic Sch of Theology (NS)
GILCHRIST-DOBSON, Norma J. (Ref Libn) 434

Atlantic Union Coll (MA)
PARSON, Lethiel C. (Lib Dir) . . . 944
SBACCHI, Margareta E. (Head of Technl Srvs) 1087

AtlantiCare Medical Center (MA)
ALMQUIST, Deborah T. (Lib Srvs Dir) 17

Atomic Energy of Canada Limited (MB)
GIBSON, Gladys N. (Libn) 432

Atomic Energy of Canada Limited (ON)
ALBURGER, Thomas P. (Libn) . . . 11
GALTON, Gwen (Sect Head, Lib & Procedures) 415
LEWIS, Leslie (Technl Info Ofcr) . 723

Atomic Energy of Canada Limited (PQ)
NISH, Susan J. (Libn) 905

Atomic Industrial Forum (MD)
GOLDMAN, Patricia J. (Lib Mgr) . 445

Attleboro Pub Lib (MA)
STITT, Walter B. (Dir) 1195

Auburn Memorial Hospital (NY)

Auburn-Placer County Lib (CA)

Auburn Pub Lib (MA)

Auburn Pub Lib (ME)

Auburn Pub Lib (WA)

Auburn Sch District 408 (WA)

Auburn Univ (AL)

Auckland City Council (NZD)

Audio Response Services Inc (MD)

Augie Blume & Associates Inc (CA)

Auglaize County Pub Lib (OH)

Augsburg Coll (MN)

Augsburg Publishing Co (MN)

Augusta Coll (GA)
Augusta Genealogical Society (GA)
Augusta Regional Lib (GA)
Augusta-Richmond County Pub Lib (GA)

Augusta Technical Institute (GA)

Augustana Coll (IL)

TOMLIN, Anne C. (Med Libn) . . 1250
SANBORN, Dorothy C. (County Libn) 1079
RAMSAY, John E. (Dir) 1005
HILYARD, Nann B. (Dir) 542
GOLDSTEIN, Cynthia N. (Ref & Catlgng Libn) 446
WALBURN, Joyce M. (High Sch Libn) 1293
ADAMS, Judith A. (Humanities Dept Head) 5
BEST, Rickey D. (Archvst, Spcl Cols Libn) 92
CANTRELL, Clyde H. (Prof & Dir of Libs Emeritus) 179
COLSON, Harold G. (Soc Sci Ref Libn) 234
FAIR, Kathy L. (Non-print, Music, Docums Catlgr) . . . 361
FRIEDMAN, Richard E. (Art & Architecture Lib Head) 404
GIBBS, Nancy J. (Approval Plan Libn) 431
GIBBS, Robert C. (Asst Univ Libn for Ref & Info Srvs) . . . 431
GREGORY, Vicki L. (Head of Systs & Operations Dept) 466
HARRIS, Edwin R. (Automated Srvs Libn) 504
JONES, Allen W. (Hist & Archvl Admin Prof) 610
MARCINKO, Dorothy K. (Acqs Dept Head) 769
MARTIN, John B. (Biblgph Ctl Coordntr) 776
MCCRANK, Lawrence J. (Dean AUM Lib and Resrc Ctr) 800
NELSON, Barbara K. (Order Libn) 893
NELSON, Michael B. (Soc Scis Catlgr) 894
SABIN, Robert G. (Sci & Tech Biblgphr) 1072
STRAITON, T H. (Head, Microforms and Docums Dept) 1199
VEENSTRA, Robert J. (Head of Lib) 1281
WRIGHT, Kathryn D. (Southeast AL Multitype Syst Dir) 1372
ZLATOS, Christy L. (Ref Libn) . 1390
TWEEDALE, Dellene M. (Commerce Sci & Tech Dept Head) 1266
ELASIK, Ronald G. (Mktg Dir) . . . 341
BLUME, August G. (Pres) 107
FREW, Martha G. (Chlds Libn) . . 402
FURL, Michael (Lib Dir) 410
ANDERSON, Margaret J. (Head Libn) 24
SIBLEY, Marjorie H. (Prof Emeritus) 1135
JANSSEN, Gene R. (Libn, Archvst) 594
BUSTOS, Roxann R. (Asst Libn) . 166
RANDALL, Gordon E. (Catlgr) . . 1006
CALHOUN, Wanda J. (Dir) 172

LAYMON, Diane L. (Branch Mgr) 705
WALKER, Alice O. (Local Hist Libn) 1295
DUTTWEILER, Robert W. (Lib Dir) 329
BELAN, Judith A. (Spcl Cols Libn) 75
CALDWELL, John (Dir) 172
CONWAY, Colleen M. (Catlgr) . . 239
MASON, Marjorie L. (Head of Pub Srvs) 781

Augustana Coll (IL)
MILLER, Marian I. (Ref Libn) 840
WESTERBERG, Kermit B.
(Archvst & Libn) 1326

Augustana Coll (SD)
HAGEMEIER, Deborah A.
(Biblgph Access Libn) 483
THOELKE, Elisabeth A. (Pub
Srvs Libn) 1235
THOMPSON, Harry F. (Archvst
& Manuscript Curator) 1239
THOMPSON, Ronelle K. (Dir) .. 1241

Auraria Lib (CO)
MACARTHUR, Marit S. (State
Pubns Catlgr) 754

Aurora Pub Lib (CO)
SMITH, Randolph R. (Technl
Srvs Coor) 1159

Aurora Pub Lib (IL)
ISELY, Megan M. (Ref Libn) 585
STEPHENS, Janet A. (Libn I) .. 1188

Aurora Pub Schools (CO)
MURRAY, William A. (Media
Srvs Dir) 882

Aurora Univ (IL)
MCKEARN, Anne B. (Head,
Access Srvs) 810

Austen Riggs Center (MA)
LINTON, Helen W. (Libn) 731

Austin Community Coll (TX)
AIROLDI, Melissa (Technl Srvs
Libn) 9
HISLE, W L. (Dir of Lrng Resrc
Srvs) 544
PELOQUIN, Margaret I. (Head
Libn, Riverside Campus) ... 955
SOWELL, Cary L. (Head Libn) . 1170
WASSENICH, Red (Ref Libn) .. 1308

Austin Co (OH)
MAKELA, Helen M. (Info Resrcs
Coordntr) 762

Austin Independent Sch District (TX)
SMITH, Dorothy B. (Libn) 1154

Austin Peay State Univ (TN)
BERWIND, Anne M. (Head, Info
Srvs Lib) 91
CARLIN, Don (Info Srvs Libn) ... 182
JOYCE, Donald F. (Dir) 618
MCMAHAN, Elnor W. (Catlgng
Dept Head) 814

Austin Preparatory Sch (MA)
MILLER, George M. (Lib Media
Ctr Dir) 837

Austin Pub Lib (MN)
HAYS, Robert M. (Dir) 517

Austin Pub Lib (TX)
DAYO, Ayo (Libn) 283
DEGRUYTER, M L. (Branch
Head) 288
GAMEZ, Juanita L. (Branch
Libn) 416
MIDDLETON, Robert K. (Info
Srvs Supvsr) 833
SKINNER, Vicki F. (Mgmt Srvs
Assoc Dir) 1146

Austintown Pub Schs (OH)
PORMEN, Paul E. (Media
Coordntr) 984

Australian Lib Journal (AUS)
ADAMS, Jenny (Exec Dir) 5
LEVETT, John (Edit) 720

Australian National Univ (AUS)
STEELE, Colin R. (Univ Libn) .. 1184

Austrian Lance & Stewart (NY)
ROJAS, Alexandra A. (Legal
Libn) 1051

Autex Systems Inc (MA)
LANDGREBE, George W.
(Pres) 692

Automated Sciences Group Inc (MD)
SPURLING, Norman K. (PDMS
Data Coordntr) 1177

Automatic Switch Co (NJ)
GABBIANELLI, Patrice A. (Libn) . 411

**Automobile Aerospace &
Agricultural** (MI)
KIBILDIS, Melba (Libn) 646

Avalanche Development Co (CO)
ZOELLICK, Bill (Vice Pres) 1390

Avalon Pub Lib (PA)
OSTRUM, Roxane M. (Lib Dir) .. 929

AVCO Systems Textron (MA)
HALL, Robert G. (Info Spclst &
Ref Libn) 488

Averett Coll (VA)
GRANT, Juanita G. (Lib Dir) 458

Avery Fisher (CA)
STANLEY, Dale R. (Resrch Info
Scitst) 1180

Avery International (CA)
KALVINSKAS, Louanne A.
(Database Design Adminstr) .. 623

Avon Products Inc (NY)
BOROSON, Sarah (Prog
Leader) 116

Aye-Aye Press (VI)
VAUGHN, Robert V. (Owner) .. 1280

Ayerst Laboratories (NY)
BARNETT, Philip (Info Scitst) 58
CURRAN, George L. (Sr Libn &
Info Scitst) 266
SCHNEIDER, Helen S. (Sr Info
Scitst) 1097

Ayerst Laboratories Research (NJ)
ALLISON, Kenneth J. (Chemical
Info Scitst) 17
WALLMARK, John S. (Sr Info
Scitst) 1298

Azusa Pacific Univ (CA)
SZETO, Dorcas C. (Perdcl Libn) 1218

B

B M C Durfee High Sch (MA)
BETTENCOURT, Ronald J.
(Catlgr) 92

**Babcock & Wilcox Research &
Development** (OH)
CARTER, James W. (Mgr,
Corpte Info Ctr) 189

Babson Coll (MA)
MAGUIRE, Patricia V. (Asst Dir
for User Srvs) 760
MALLER, Alma L. (Spcl Projs
Ref Libn) 763

Bad Axe High Sch (MI)
MAYES, Jane M. (High Sch
Libn) 789

Badger Infosearch (WI)
WATERSTREET, Darlene E.
(Proprietor) 1309

Baha'i World Centre (ISR)
BEAVERS, Janet W. (Head of
Periodicals Sect) 71
COLLINS, William P. (Head
Libn) 233
MOULD, Edith L. (Catlgng Libn) . 873

**Bahamas Ministry of
Education** (BAH)
BARTON, Barbara I. (Teacher &
Libn) 61

Bailey Hill Sch (OR)
FEUERHELM, Jill A. (Lib Media
Spclst) 374

Bain & Co Inc (MA)
BLAKE, Michael R. (Resrch Ref
Libn) 103
EISENMANN, Laura M. (Mgr) ... 341

**Baird Holm McEachen Pedersen et
al** (NE)
LOMAX, Anne M. (Law Libn) ... 738

Baker & Botts (TX)
DAVIS, Cynthia V. (Ref Libn) ... 278
HOPKINS, Joyce A. (Catlg Libn) . 558
JOITY, Donna M. (Acqs Libn) ... 610

Baker & Daniels (IN)
SCHMIDT, Paula O. (Libn) ... 1095

Baker & Hostetler (OH)
RODGERS, Judith P. (Libn) ... 1047

Baker & Taylor (IL)
COOPER, Susan C. (Acad Srvs
Rep) 243

Baker & Taylor (NJ)
CAPOOR, Asha (Lib Srvs &
Database Admin Dir) 180
LAREW, Christian K. (Mktg Dir) . 697
ROMANASKY, Marcia C. (Dir of
Pub Lib Mktg) 1052
SANDLER, Gary D. (Catlgr) ... 1081
STEVENS, Sharon G. (Market
Resrch Mgr) 1191
SUDEKUM, Katharine (Lib Systs
Rep) 1206

Baker Coll (MI)
ARNOLD, Peggy (Ref Libn) 34
VOELZ, Laura D. (Acqs Libn) .. 1286

Baker Spielvogal Bates (NY)
SCHACHTER, Bert (Vice Pres
& Mgr) 1088

Bakersfield City Sch District (CA)
WICKEY, Marjorie J. (Tchr &
Libn) 1335

**Balch Institute for Ethnic
Studies** (PA)
ANDERSON, R J. (Lib Dir) 25
SUTTON, David H. (Archvst) .. 1211
VANDOREN, Sandra S.
(Archvst II) 1275

Baldwin Borough Pub Lib (PA)
HARKINS, Anna W. (Libn) 501

Baldwin Pub Lib (MI)
KERSHNER, Stephen A. (Lib
Dir) 644
MARTIN, John E. (Head of
Technl Srvs) 776
ORMOND, Sarah C. (Adult
Reading Head) 926
SWEENEY, Thomas F. (Bd of
Dirs Mem) 1215

Baldwin Pub Lib (NY)
HOPKINS, Barbara A. (Dir) 557

Baldwin-Wallace Coll (OH)

Baldwin-Whitehall Sch District (PA)

Baldwinsville Pub Lib (NY)

Balkin Lib Management Services (NY)

Ball Aerospace Systems Division (CO)

Ball State Univ (IN)

HAMBLEY, Susan L. (Head Music Libn & Lib Dir) 490
MACIUSZKO, Jerzy J. (Retired) . 755
JENKINS, Georgann K. (Sch Libn & AV Coordntr) 597
LAUBACHER, Marilyn R. (Lib Dir) 702

BALKIN, Ruth G. (Owner) 52

DAYHOFF, Judith A. (Supvsr, Lib Operations) 283
PRESTON, Lawrence N. (Info Spclst) 991
BEILKE, Patricia F. (Prof of Lib & Info Sci) 75
DOLAK, Frank J. (Eductnl Resrcs Catlgr) 309
FAUST, Mary H. (Acqs Fiscal Ctl Libn) 366
HARLAND, Phyllis A. (Architecture Libn) 502
HODGE, Stanley P. (Dir of Cols Develpmnt) 546
KELLEY, Colleen L. (Instr, Eductnl Resrcs Catlgr) 636
KUO, Ming M. (Cols Devlpmnt Libn) 684
MCGINNIS, Mildred M. (Acqs Search & Order Libn) 806
MOORE, Thomas J. (Dir of Lib Pub Srvs) 861
RANSIL, M M. (Lib Automation Proj Coordntr) 1007
SACZAWA, Rosemary (Head, Catlgng Srvs) 1073
TURNER, Nancy K. (Univ Archvst) 1265
WILLIAMS, Nyal Z. (Music Libn) 1345
WOOD, Michael B. (Dean of Univ Libs) 1364

Ballen Booksellers International Inc (NY)

Ballet Rambert (ENG)

Ballston Spa Pub Lib (NY)

Baltimore City (MD)

Baltimore City Law Lib (MD)

Baltimore County Board of Education (MD)

Baltimore County Board of Lib Trustees (MD)

Baltimore County Pub Lib (MD)

SCHRIFT, Leonard B. (Pres & Chief Exec Ofcr) 1100
PRITCHARD, Jane E. (Archvst) . 994
HUMPHREY, Virginia S. (Lib Dir) 573
HOLLOWAK, Thomas L. (City Archvst & Records Mgmt Ofcr) 552
COX, Irvin E. (Law Libn) 253

HEINRICH, Lois M. (Lib Media Spclst) 522
MOLLENKOPF, Carolyn M. (Dept Chairman, Lib/Media Generalist) 853

TURNER, David E. (Libn) 1264
BAILEY, Carol A. (Ref Libn) 46
EICKHOFF, Jane S. (Branch Mgr) 339
HAIRE, Jennifer C. (Lib Mgr) 484
HEMPHILL, Franklin B. (Asst Dir & Lib Building Consult) 525
JONKE, Grace M. (Branch Mgr) . 616
LISS, Nancy J. (Pub Srvs Libn II) 732
MOLZ, Jean B. (Assoc Dir) 854
MORRONE, Kay O. (Branch Mgr) 869
ROBINSON, Charles W. (Dir) . . 1043
VALLAR, Cynthia L. (Ref Libn) . 1271
WISOTZKI, Lila B. (Mtrls Selection Asst Head) 1358
ZAIDEL, Jack N. (Branch Mgr) . 1385

Baltimore County Pub Schs (MD)

ANDERSON, Della L. (Instrcl Spclst) 22
DRACH, Marian C. (Lib & Media Srvs Supvsr) 317

Baltimore County Pub Schs (MD)

Baltimore Gas & Electric Co (MD)

Baltimore Sun (MD)

Bamado Central Sch District (NY)

Bananas Records & Tapes (FL)

Bancroft-Parkman Inc (CT)

Bangor Pub Lib (ME)

Bangor Publishing Co (ME)

Bangs Independent Sch District (TX)

Bank Marketing Association (IL)

Bank of America (CA)

Bank of America (NY)

Bank of Boston-in-House Counsel (MA)

Bank of Hawaii (HI)

Bank of Montreal (ON)

Bank of Montreal (PQ)

Bank of Nova Scotia (ON)

Bank Street Coll of Education (NY)

Bankers Trust Co of New York (NY)

Baptist Book Stores (TX)

Baptist Hospital of Miami (FL)

Baptist Hospitals-Louisville (KY)

Baptist Memorial Health Care System (TN)

Baptist Memorial Hospital (AL)

Baptist Missionary Assn Theological Sem (TX)

Bar Ilan Univ (ISR)

Barat Coll (IL)

Barberton Pub Lib (OH)

Barksdale Air Force Base (LA)

Barnard College (NY)

Barnes & Thornburg (IN)

Barnesville Exempted Village Schs (OH)

HACKMAN, Mary H. (Coordntr) . 481
REIDER, William L. (Spclst in Instrcl Srvs) 1019
HUMMEL, Janice A. (Trng Resrc Coordntr) 573
HARDNETT, Carolyn J. (Chief Libn) 500
BURGESON, Clair D. (Dir of Libs and AV) 159
ALLEN, Douglas R. (Owner) 14
LEAB, Katharine K. (Exec Edit & Data Base Mgr) 706
WOODWARD, Robert C. (Dir) . 1368
CAMPO, Charles A. (Chief Libn) . 177
WEEKS, Patsy L. (Lrng Resrcs Coordntr) 1315
CORNICK, Ron (Database Mgr) . 247
JORDAN, Charles R. (Info Spclst) 616
REMEIKIS, Lois A. (Dir of Info Srvs Dept) 1022
STENGER, Brenda E. (Info Spclst) 1187
ANDERSON, Connie J. (Lib & Info Srvs Mgr) 22
GLYNN, Jeannette E. (Tech Lib Mgr) 442
POLLACH, Karen F. (Catlgr) 981
REIST, Paul A. (Resrch Libn) . 1022
WAY, Kathy A. (Law Libn) 1311
BATES, Ellen (Libn) 63

VAN BEEK, Susan (Head Law Libn) 1272
CHAFE, Douglas A. (Info Spclst) . 197
SCHULTZ, Elaine V. (Info Spclst) 1102
BOSMA, Elske M. (Mgr, Bus Info Ctr) 117
ORLANDO, Richard P. (Resrch Coordntr) 926
PIGGOTT, Sylvia E. (Info Ctr Mgr) 972
NOKES, Jane E. (Corpte Archvst) 907
KULLESEID, Eleanor R. (Lib Srvs Dir) 683
GINSBURG, Carol L. (Vice Pres) 438
SHALLENBERGER, Anna F. (Intern Resrch Libn) 1119
VERNON, James R. (Clerk) . . . 1283
REAM, Diane F. (Dir of Hlth Scis Lib Srvs) 1013
JOHNSON, Garry B. (Dir of Lib Srvs) 604
OWEN, Richard L. (Resrc Libn) . . 932
BUCKNER, Rebecca S. (Med Libn) 154
BLAYLOCK, James C. (Libn) . . . 105
SNYDER, Esther M. (Law Lib Dir) 1164
JEFFORDS, Rebecca J. (Ref Libn) 596
KIRBAWY, Barbara L. (Dir) 653
PAPA, Deborah M. (Chlds Libn) . 938
SWINEHART, Katharine J. (Sr Ref Libn) 1216
WOOD, Julienne L. (Dir, Base Lib) 1364
TUCKER, Mary E. (Systems Libn) 1262
RIES, Steven T. (Ref Libn) 1033

THOMPSON, Myra D. (High Sch Libn) 1240

Barrett Smith Schapiro Simon &
  Armstrong (NY)   SULLIVAN, Stephen W.
        (Technician) 1208
Barrie Pub Lib (ON)   ADDY, Kathryn J. (Chlds Libn) 6
        MULLEN, Gail C. (Lib Dir) 877
Barrington Area Lib (IL)   ALLAN, Nancy P. (Ref Libn) 14
        BRYAN, Mila (Adult Srvs Head) . 152
        POLL, Diane R. (Technl Srvs
        Head) 981
        SUGDEN, Barbara L. (Head
        Libn) 1206
Barrington Pub Lib (RI)   BURKE, Lauri K. (Comunty Srvs
        Libn) 160
Barrington Pub Schs (IL)   KARON, Joyce E. (Media Srvs
        Coordntr) 627
Barrister Information Systems (NY) WAGNER, Stephen K. (Sales
        Info & Pubn Mgr) 1292
Barron & Stadfeld (MA)   MOLONEY, Kevin F. (Partner) . . 853
Barron Collier High Sch (FL) HAINES, Nancy H. (Lib Media
        Spclst) 484
Barry Univ (FL)   PINE, Nancy M. (Catlgr) 974
Barton Lib (AR)   ARN, Nancy L. (Union Cnty
        Libn) 33
Bartow County Pub Lib System (GA) HOWINGTON, Lee R. (Lib Exec
        Div) 566
        LINKER, Rita S. (Pub Srvs Libn) . 731
Baruch Coll of the City Univ of New
  York (NY)   BIDDLE, Stanton F. (Prof &
        Chief Libn) 94
        DIMARTINO, Diane J. (Ref Libn
        & Data Base Searcher) 303
        HEUMAN, Rabbi F. (Assoc Prof) . 535
        HILL, George R. (Assoc Prof &
        Music Biblgphr) 539
        LOWE, Ida B. (Actg Asst Dean) . 743
        MEANS, Spencer (Reader Srvs
        Coordntr) 820
        OSTROW, Rona (Assoc Prof) . . . 929
        POLLARD, Bobbie T. (Asst
        Prof) 981
        PRAGER, George A. (Serials
        Mgr) 989
        SLUSS, Sara B. (Ref Libn) 1150
Basalt Regional Lib District (CO) WINKLER, Jean J. (Dir) 1355
Bascom Palmer Eye Institute (FL) HURTES, Reva (Lib Dir) 578
Baseline Inc (NY)   MONACO, James (Pres) 854
BASF Corp (MI)   SPECTOR, Janice B. (Supvsr) . . 1172
        SWEET, Robert E. (Resrch llbn) . 1215
BASF Corp (NJ)   VOGT, Herwart C. (Info Resrcs
        Mgr) 1287
BASF Corp (TX)   TYLER-WHITE, Patricia G. (Info
        Spclst) 1266
Bassel Sullivan & Leake (ON) FOOTE, Martha L. (Libn) 388
Bassist Coll (OR)   SCHIWEK, Joseph A. (Libn) . . . 1093
        THURSTON, Nancy W. (Libn) . 1243
Bath Memorial Hospital (ME) MCKAY, Ann (Libn) 809
Bathgate Wegener Wouters &
  Newmann (NJ)   ERBE, Evalina S. (Libn) 352
Bathurst Sch District 42 (NB) RUSSELL, Sharon A. (Dist Tchr
        & Libn) 1069
Battelle Memorial Institute (OH) FELTES, Carol A. (Mgr, Lib and
        Technl Info Srvs) 370
        GUBIOTTI, Ross A. (Projects
        Mgr) 475
        TROVER, Larry E. (Technl Info
        Srvs Mgr) 1258
        WARNER, Susan B. (Biblgph
        Info Spclst) 1305
Battelle Northwest Laboratory (WA) DANIEL, Eunice L. (Technl Info
        Spclst) 272
        SAMPLE, Charles R. (Ref
        Spclst) 1078
Batten Barton Durstine Osborn (IL) DELANEY, Jerry (Info Srvs Dir) . . 289
Battery March Financial
  Management Co (MA) AVITABILE, Susan L. (Consult) . . . 42
Baxter Healthcare Corp (CA) JACOBUS, Nancy M. (Info Srvs
        Mgr) 590
Baxter Healthcare Corp (IL) ALLEN, Dorothy L. (Catlgng
        Spclst) 14

Baxter Travenol Laboratories Inc (IL) GARDNER, Margaret L. (Info
        Spclst) 418
        SHERRY, Diane H. (Info Resrc
        Ctrs Mgr) 1129
        TAN, Elizabeth L. (Supvsr & Info
        Spclst) 1222
Bay Area Air Quality Management
  District (CA)   LENSCHAU, Jane A. (Lib
        Technican) 715
Bay Area Lib & Information
  System (CA)   GUY, Patricia A. (Sr Ref Libn) . . . 479
Bay Area Reference Center (CA) SHOUSE, Richard (Resrch Libn) 1133
Bay City Independent Sch
  District (TX)   HOWARD, Elizabeth A. (Sch
        Libn) 564
Bay County Lib System (MI) PEARSONS, Sheila M. (Branch
        Libn) 953
Bay County Sch Board (FL) MILLER, Merna B. (Lib Media
        Spclst) 841
Bay Medical Center (MI) KORMELINK, Barbara A. (Dir of
        Libs) 671
Bay Shore Pub Schs (NY) FLOWERS, Helen F. (Lib Media
        Spclst) 386
Bay View Association (MI) DOERR, Jane P. (Dir) 308
Bay Village Schs (OH) SCHWELK, Jennifer C. (Lib
        Media Spclst) 1105
Bayero Univ (NGR)   AJIBERO, Matthew I. (Lectr I) 9
Bayfront Medical Center Inc (FL) CESANEK, Sylvia B. (Hlth Scis
        Libn) 196
Bayley Seton Hospital (NY) SHELDON, Marie A. (Med Libn) 1126
Baylor Hlth Scis Lib (TX) THOMAS, Donald L. (Info
        Access Libn) 1236
Baylor Sch (TN)   HOOPER, James E. (Interim
        Libn) 557
Baylor Univ (TX)   COLEY, Betty A. (Libn) 231
        GEARY, Gregg S. (Music Ref
        Asst) . . . . : 424
        GUENTHER, Jody (Lrng Resrcs
        Ctr Dir) 475
        HILLMAN, Kathy R. (Acqs Libn
        & Asst Prof) 541
        HUGHES, Sue M. (Lib Dir) 572
        KENDRICK, Susan (Asst Law
        Libn) 640
        SEAMAN, Helen D. (Asst Acqs
        Libn) 1109
        SHARP, Avery T. (Music Libn &
        Assoc Prof) 1122
        SHEETS, Janet E. (Ref Srvs
        Head) 1125
        SPARKMAN, Glenda K. (Catlg
        Dept Head) 1171
        TOLBERT, Jean F. (Ref Libn) . . 1248
Bayne-Jones Army Community
  Hospital (LA)   HIGGINBOTHAM, Cecelia B.
        (Med Libn) 537
Bayonne Pub Lib (NJ) CHUNG, Hai C. (Jr Libn) 213
Bayouland Lib System (LA) LAUGHLIN, Beverly E. (Dir) 702
Bayside Indexing Service (CA) MULVANY, Nancy (Owner) 878
Baystate Medical Center (MA) HUNTER, Isabel (Hlth Scis Lib
        Dir) 576
Bayville Free Lib (NY) BERTINO, Lorna L. (Dir) 91
BBDO (NY)   SANTORO, Tesse F. (Info
        Resrc Ctr Mgr) 1082
BBN Communications Corp (MA) DURHAM, Mary J. (Sect Mgr,
        Software Release Srvs) 328
BCCLS Computer Consortium (NJ) ROUX, Yvonne R. (Trng
        Coordntr) 1062
BDM Corp Inc (OH)   ROHMILLER, Thomas D.
        (Technl Libn) 1051
BDM Corp Inc (VA)   WHITE, Ardeen L. (Libn) 1330
BDM Management Services
  Corp (WA)   PARR, Loraine E. (Staff Mem) . . . 943
BEA Associates (NY) HEFFRON, Betsy A. (Resrch
        Libn) 520
Beachwood City Schs (OH) CHAMPLIN, Lydia F. (Libn &
        Media Spclst) 198
Beaconsfield Pub Lib (PQ) HIRON, Barbara A. (Yng
        People's Libn) 543

Beaumont Independent Sch District (TX) — NISBY, Dora R. (Lib Srvs Dir) . . . 904
Beauty Without Cruelty USA (NY) — THURSTON, Ethel H. (Chair) . 1243
Beaver Country Day Sch (MA) — SMITH, Zelda G. (Asst Libn) . . . 1161
Beaver County Federated Lib System (PA) — BRUBAKER, Dale L. (Technl Srvs Head) 149
Beaver County Law Lib (PA) — DENGEL, Bette S. (Law Libn) . . . 292
Beaver County Times (PA) — DISANTE, Linda B. (Head Libn) . 305
Bechtel Civil Inc (CA) — SORROUGH, Gail L. (Libn) 1169
Bechtel Information Services (VA) — JONES, Frank (Technl Mgr) 613
Bechtel Power Corp (CA) — DUMLAO, Mercedes G. (Data Prcsng Libn) 325
MAH, Jeffery (Asst Chief Libn) . . 760
Becker-Hayes Inc (CA) — BECKER, Joseph (Pres) 72
Becker Junior Coll (MA) — VIDMANIS, Visvaldis E. (Dir of Eductnl Resrcs) 1283
Becker Poliakoff & Streitfeld (FL) — KOEING, Sherman (Law Libn) . . . 667
Beckerman Associates Inc (DC) — BECKERMAN, George (Pres) 72
Beckman Instruments (CA) — MILLER, Jean R. (Lib & Info Srvs Mgr) 839
Becton Dickinson & Co (NJ) — CHANG, Bernadine A. (Mktg Info Spclst) 200
DYKMAN, Elaine K. (Corprt Libn) 331
MENZUL, Faina (Coprt Info Ctr Mgr) 825
Bedford Park Pub Lib District (IL) — HAFFNER, Barbara (Lib Dir) 482
Bedford Pub Lib (MA) — MAIER, Robert C. (Lib Dir) 761
Behringer Ingelheim Pharmaceuticals Inc (CT) — HENTZ, Margaret B. (Info Scitst) . 530
Beinecke Lib (CT) — WYNNE, Marjorie G. 1375
Belhaven Coll (MS) — ADAMS, Velma L. (Night Libn) 6
Bell Canada (ON) — COVIENSKY, Lana (Mgr of Mktg Info Ctr) 252
Bell Canada (PQ) — MALEK, Stanislaw A. (Econ Info Ctr Mgr) 763
SYKES, Stephanie L. (Dir) 1217
YOUNG, Patricia M. (Law Libn) . 1383
Bell Canada Enterprises (PQ) — FOWLES, Alison C. (Libn) 394
Bell Communications Research (IL) — IFFLAND, Carol D. (Assoc Mgr) . 581
Bell Communications Research (NJ) — BEDDES, Marianne T. (Technl Ref Libn) 73
BUCK, Anne M. (Lib & Info Srvs Dir) 153
GLADSTONE, Mark A. (Staff Mgr) 439
KAPLAN, Susan J. (Ref Libn) . . . 626
MILLER, Virginia L. (Technl Ref Libn) 843
MOONEY, Jennifer M. (Technl Catlgr) 858
SCHNEIDER, Lynette C. (Mgr, Lib Netwk Support Srvs) . . . 1097
SUNDAY, Donald E. (Staff Mgr) 1210
Bell Helicopter Textron Canada (PQ) — GRITZKA, Gerda M. (Documtn Techgst) 471
Bell Laboratories (MA) — CONDON, Mary M. (Ref Libn) . . 236
Bell-Northern Research (TX) — CASTO, Lisa A. (Info Spclst) . . . 194
Bell-Northern Research (ON) — BIRKS, Grant F. (Info Support Mgr) 98
MASON-WARD, Lesley (Mktg Analyst) 781
SELLERS, Alexander G. (Lrng Resrc Ctr Mgr) 1114
Bell-Northern Research (PQ) — DIMITRESCU, Ioana (Info Spclst) 304
Bell of Pennsylvania (PA) — VEDDER, Harvey B. (Syst Design Consult) 1280
Bellaire Pub Lib (OH) — KNIESNER, John T. (Dir) 664
Belle Valley Sch District 119 (IL) — DOMESCIK, Carol J. (Libn) 310
Belle Vernon Area Sch District (PA) — PARADISE, Don M. (Lib Supvsr) 939
Bellerose Sch District (NY) — CANDE, Lorraine N. (Sch Library-Media Spclst) 178
Belleville Pub Lib (IL) — KIRCHGRABER, Nancy B. (Head, Technl Processes Dept) 654
Belleville Pub Lib (NJ) — BRYANT, David S. (Lib Dir) 152
COHEN, Adrea G. (Asst Lib Dir) . 227

Bellevue Community Coll (WA) — DECOSTER, Barbara L. (Technl Processes Libn) 286
WALLS, Francine E. (Libn & Faculty Mem) 1299
Bellevue Hospital (OH) — WAGAR, Elsa A. (Catlgr) 1290
Bellevue Pub Lib (IA) — KIEFFER, Marian L. (Dir) 647
Bellevue Pub Schs (NE) — KEEFE, Betty (Media Spclst) 634
Bellevue Pub Schs (WA) — ERICKSON, Jane (Libn) 352
SHERMAN-PETERSON, Ronald A. (Head Catlgr) 1128
SKELLEY, Cornelia A. (Dir of Instrcl Mtrls) 1145
Bellingham Pub Lib (WA) — BLUME, Scott (Head of Chlds Srvs) 107
MCCAIN, Claudia J. (Dir) 793
Bellingham Sch District 501 (WA) — ANDERSEN, Eileen (Sch Lib Media Spclst) 21
Bellsouth Enterprises (GA) — CONLIN, Peter A. (Staff Mgr) . . . 236
Bellsouth Services (GA) — BARNETT, Becky L. (Product Mgr) 57
Bellwood Pub Lib (IL) — HARRIS, Robert A. (Lib Dir) 506
Belmont Abbey Coll (NC) — BAUMSTEIN, Paschal M. (Archvst & Histn) 66
MAYES, Susan E. (Catlg Libn) . . 789
Belmont Coll (TN) — GMEINER, Timothy J. (Music Libn) 442
GRENGA, Kathy A. (Ref & Serials Libn) 467
Belmont Pub Schs (MA) — PHELAN, Mary C. (Substitute Sch Libn) 967
WOODS, Selina J. (Lib Media Spclst) 1367
Belmont Sch District (CA) — CHESSMAN, Rebecca L. (Dist Libn) 207
Beloit Corp (WI) — THOM, Pat A. (Technl Libn) . . . 1235
Beloit Pub Lib (WI) — ALLEN, Christina Y. (Support Srvs Dir) 14
BREDESON, Peggy Z. (Asst Dir) 131
SIMPSON, W S. (Asst Dir of Support Srvs) 1142
STAINBROOK, Lynn M. (Support Srvs Dir) 1178
Belt Collins & Associates (HI) — GOODY, Cheryl S. (Libn) 450
Belton Independent Sch District (TX) — MARKS, Mary L. (Jr High Sch Libn) 771
Bemidji State Univ (MN) — ELLIOTT, Gwendolyn W. (Govt Pubns Libn) 344
KISHEL, Deane A. (Univ Libn) . . . 656
Benchmark Films (NY) — SOLIN, Myron (Pres) 1166
Bend Research Inc (OR) — WEBER, Nola S. (Resrch Libn) . 1314
Bendel State Lib Board (NGR) — IMOISI, Ann U. (Libn I) 582
Benedictine Coll (KS) — BURBACH, Jude (Head Libn) . . . 158
FENLON, Mary P. (Assoc Libn, Ref) 371
Benedictine Sisters of Chicago (IL) — REILLY, Jane A. (Writer & Resrchr) 1020
Benedictine Society of Virginia (VA) — LIGGAN, Mary K. (Dir of Libs) . . . 726
Benesch Friedlander Coplan & Aronoff (OH) — DONNELLY, Kathleen (Head Libn) 311
Benjamin Franklin Univ (DC) — LEWIS, Robert J. (Lib Dir) 724
Bennington Free Lib (VT) — PRICE, Michael L. (Dir) 992
Bentley Coll (MA) — BELASTOCK, Tjalda N. (Assoc Lib Dir, Info Srvs) 76
LEWONTIN, Amy (Ref Libn & Biographical Instr) 724
Benton Harbor Area Schs (MI) — PELZER, Adolf (Pub High Sch Libn) 955
Benton Harbor Lib Board (MI) — KIRBY, Frederick J. (Lib Dir) 654
Berea Coll (KY) — HAWLEY, Mary B. (Acqs Libn) . . . 514
KIRK, Thomas G. (Coll Libn) 654
ROBERTS, Gerald F. (Head of Archs & Spcl Cols) 1040
Bergen Brunswig Corp (CA) — LA BORDE, Charlotte A. (Corprt Lib Mgr) 686
Bergen County Coop Lib Syst Comp Cnsrtm (NJ) — WHITE, Robert W. (Exec Dir) . . 1332
Bergen Pines County Hospital (NJ) — GONZALES, Victoria E. (Med Libn) 448

Bering Strait Sch District (AK) GOODMAN, Roslyn L. (Media
                                   Spclst) 449
Berkeley Heights Pub Lib (NJ)   LIND, Judith Y. (Ref Dept Head) . 728
Berkeley Heights Pub Schs (NJ)   WICHELMAN, Ruthann (Media
                                   Spclst) 1335
Berkeley Preparatory Sch (FL)   MCCAMMON, Carol G. (Libn) . . 793
Berkeley Pub Lib (CA)   MINUDRI, Regina U. (Dir of Lib
                                   Srvs) 847
                                 SCHNEIDER, Francisca M.
                                   (Supvsng Libn) 1097
Berkeley Sch (NJ)   RANDALL, Lynn E. (Lrng Resrc
                                   Ctr Dir) 1006
Berkeley Unified Sch District (CA) FRANKEL, Kate M. (Elem Field
                                   Libn) 397
Berklee Coll (MA)   VOIGT, John F. (Lib Dir) 1287
Berkman Ruslander Pohl Lieber &
  Engel (PA)   ORSAG, Ann (Head Libn) 927
Berks County Pub Lib System (PA) WAGGONER, Susan M.
                                   (Adminstr) 1291
Berkshire Athenaeum (MA)   FUCHS, John M. (Dir) 408
Berkshire Museum (MA)   MACE, Mary B. (Libn) 754
Berkshire Sch (MA)   CARVER, Jane C. (Asst Dir) 191
Berlex Laboratories Inc (NJ)   LINGELBACH, Lorene N. (Lib
                                   Srvs Mgr) 730
                                 MILLINGTON, Kathleen A. (Info
                                   Srvs Libn) 843
                                 SKIDANOW, Helene (Sr Info
                                   Scitst) 1146
Berlin Board of Education (CT)   KATZ, Claire G. (Sch Lib Media
                                   Spclst) 630
Bernalillo County Pub Lib (NM)   TAFT, Patricia S. (Trustee) 1219
Bernard M Baruch Coll (NJ)   LEE, Minja P. (Coordntr) 711
Bernards Township Lib (NJ)   JIULIANO, Margaret C. (Dir) . . . 600
Bernardsville Pub Lib (NJ)   BURDEN, Geraldine R. (Dir) 158
Bernice P Bishop Museum (HI)   ASHFORD, Marguerite K. (Head
                                   Libn) 36
                                 HORIE, Ruth H. (Ref Libn) 559
Bernstein Shur Sawyer & Nelson (ME) STANTON, Linda J. (Law Libn) . 1181
Berrien County Intermediate Sch
  District (MI)   FITZGERALD, Ruth F. (Dir of
                                   Regnl Eductnl Media Ctr) 382
Berul Associates Ltd (MD)   BERUL, Lawrence H. (Pres) 91
Berwick Group (MA)   BIANCANELLO, Anthony R.
                                   (Pres) 93
Bessemer Trust Co N A (NY)   STOOPS, Louise (Info Srvs
                                   Mgr) 1198
Beta Comp Indexing (NY)   GARCIA, Kathleen J. (Freelance
                                   Indxr) 417
Beth Israel Hospital (MA)   DALY, Jay (Dir, Med Lib) 271
Beth Israel Medical Center (NY) GALLAGHER, Patricia E.
                                   (Technl Srvs Libn) 414
                                 SCHWARTZ, Dorothy D. (Sr
                                   Med Libn) 1104
                                 SYFERT, Samuel R. (Jr & Sr
                                   High Libn) 1217
Bethany Community Unit 301 (IL)
Bethel Coll (IN)   TUCKER, Dennis C. (Dir of Lib
                                   Srvs) 1261
Bethel Coll (KS)   SCHRAG, Dale R. (Dir of Libs) . 1099
Bethel Park Pub Lib (PA)   MCGINNESS, Mary B. (Ref &
                                   Docums Libn) 806
Bethel Sch District 403 (WA)   ULRICH, Pamela L. (Lib Media
                                   Spclst) 1268
Bethel Theological Seminary (MN) MAGNUSON, Norris A. (Resrc
                                   Ctr Dir & Prof of Hist) 759
Bethesda Naval Hospital (MD)   MEYER, Gerald E. (Adminstrv
                                   Libn) 830
Bethesda Oak Hospital (OH)   GITLIN, Rebecca A. (Med Libn) . 439
Bethlehem Central Schs (NY)   GRAVLEE, Diane D. (Retired) . . . 459
Bethlehem Pub Lib (NY)   CARLSON, Marie S. (Head of
                                   AV Srvs) 182
Bethlehem Pub Lib (PA)   BERK, Jack M. (Lib Dir) 87
                                 THOMAS, Lynda H. (Info Libn) . 1237
Bethlehem Steel Corp (PA)   HENDLEY, David D. (Law Libn) . 527
Betsy Ross Publications (MI)   BUZAN, Norma J. (Owner) 168
Bettendorf Community Sch
  District (IA)   MEIER, Patricia L. (Lib Media
                                   Spclst) 821
Bettendorf Pub Lib & Information
  Center (IA)   CLOW, Faye E. (Dir) 223

Better Business Bureau, NIA Publshg
  Co (OH)   LITTLE, Dean K. (Membership &
                                   Advertising Sales Mgr) 733
Betts Patterson & Mines PS (WA) WILLIAMS, Janet M. (Libn) 1344
Betz Libs Inc (TX)   WEST, Deborah C. (Libn) 1326
Bev Chaney Books (NY)   CHANEY, Bev (Owner) 200
Beverly Hills Pub Lib (CA)   ANNETT, Susan E. (Libn) 28
                                 GREGORY, Timothy P. (Lib &
                                   Comnty Srvs Asst Dir) 466
                                 PIONTEK, Frank P. (Ref
                                   Supvsr) 975
Beverly Hills Unified Sch District (CA) DOUGLAS, Carolyn T. (Head
                                   Libn) 314
                                 GIRARD, Valerie V. (Libn) 438
Beverly Pub Lib (MA)   SCULLY, Thomas F. (Lib Dir) . . 1109
Bexley Pub Lib (OH)   CHADWICK, Janina A. (Head of
                                   Circ Dept) 197
BF Goodrich Research & Developmnt
  Center (OH)   BUTCHER, Sharon L. (Info
                                   Spclst) 166
Bharat Heavy Electricals Ltd (IND) SATYANARAYANA, Vadhri V.
                                   (Sr Info Ofcr) 1084
BHP Utah Minerals International (CA) KIEFER, Karen N. (Mgr Info
                                   Srvs Lib) 647
Bi-County Community (MI)   WILLIAMS, Gayle A. (Libs Dir) . 1343
Biblical Theological Seminary (PA) PAKALA, Denise M. (Technl
                                   Srvs Libn) 935
                                 PAKALA, James C. (Libn) 935
                                 RITTER, Ralph E. (Profsnl Srvs
                                   Libn) 1037
Biblio-File Inc (NY)   LANDMAN, Lillian L. (Owner) . . 693
Bibliographical Center for
  Research (CO)   BRUNELL, David H. (Exec Dir) . . 150
                                 GARZA, Rosario (Mem Srvs
                                   Libn) 421
                                 HENSINGER, James S.
                                   (MicroSystems & Srvs Mgr) . . 529
                                 KAVANAGH, Janette R. (Ref
                                   Systs & Srvs Mgr) 631
Bibliographical Center for
  Research (IA)   SCHMIDT, Sandra L. (Mem
                                   Srvs Libn) 1096
Bibliographical Society of
  America (NY)   TICHENOR, Irene (Exec Secy) . 1244
Bibliomation Inc (CT)   ROTH, Alison C. (Trng Libn) . . . 1059
Bibliotheque Centrale de Pret (PQ) FINK, Norman (Mgr) 378
Bibliotheque Municipale de
  Dorval (PQ)   DAUNAIS, Marie J. (Head Libn) . 275
Bibliotheque Nationale (FRN)   GARRETA, J C. (Chief Cur) 420
Bibliotheque Regionale de
  Saint-Jean (NB)   NADEAU, Sylvie (Dir) 886
Big Spring State Hospital (TX)   BRADBERRY, Anna L. (Med
                                   Libn) 125
Big Valley Joint Unified Sch
  District (CA)   MAIN, Steven B. (Tchr & Libn) . . 761
Billerca Pub Lib (MA)   FLAHERTY, Barbara A. (Dir) . . . 383
Billy Graham Evangelistic
  Association (MN)   FERM, Lois R. (Resrch
                                   Coordntr) 373
Bingham Dana & Gould (MA)   ANZALONE, Filippa M. (Law Lib
                                   Dir) 29
Binghamton Psychiatric Center (NY) MASON, Martha A. (Sr Libn) . . 781
Biogen Research Corp (MA)   JONES, Rebekah A. (Libn) 614
Biokoor (ISR)   BORCK, Liba (Info Mgr) 116
Biomedical Information Services (NJ) KUSHINKA, Kerry L. 685
BioSciences Information Service (PA) ELIAS, Arthur W. (Mktg &
                                   Distribution Dir) 342
                                 HODGE, Gail M. (Resrch &
                                   Devlpmnt Head) 546
                                 KIESEL, Bruce H. 647
                                 ZIPF, Elizabeth M. (Technl
                                   Consult to the Pres) 1389
BIOSIS (PA)   FARREN, Ann L. (Sr Educ
                                   Spclst) 365
                                 FISHER, Douglas A. (Projs
                                   Adminstr) 380
                                 KELLY, Maureen C. (Dir) 638
                                 KENNEDY, H E. (Pres) 641
                                 SYEN, Sarah (Product Devlpmnt
                                   Sect Chief) 1217

BIOSIS (PA)
TOWNSEND, Carolyn J. (Educ & Trng Group Leader) 1253
VLEDUTS-STOKOLOV, Natalia (Coordntr, Resrch & Devlpmnt Dept) 1286
WALSH, James A. (Head, Biblgph Control Dept) 1299
WASERSTEIN, Gina S. (Sect Chief) 1307
WEINER, Betty (Libn) 1318
YERGER, George A. (Educ Spclst) 1379

Biospherics Inc (MD)
KNICKERBOCKER, Wendy (Catlgr) 664

Birmingham Museum of Art (AL)
GRIFFITH, Ethel T. (Libn) 469

Birmingham Pub Lib (AL)
DAY, Janeth N. (Assoc Dir) ... 282
GUTHRIE, Virginia G. (Regnl Branch Coordntr) 479
HOGAN, Catherine R. (Govt Docums Dept Libn) 549
MCCARTHY, Sherri L. (Libn) ... 794
STEWART, George R. (Dir) ... 1192
VENABLE, Douglas R. (Libn I) ... 1282

Birmingham-Southern Coll (AL)
PENNINGTON, Walter W. (Lib Dir) 957

Birzeit Univ (ISR)
HADDAD, Aida N. (Head Libn) .. 481

Bishop County High Sch (CA)
NAGY, Helen C. (Libn) 886

Bishop Denis J O'Connell High Sch (VA)
MCKELVEY, Mary J. (Libn) 810

Bishop Fenwick High Sch (MA)
CODAIR, Frederick R. (Sch Libn) 226

Bishop Foley High Sch (MI)
UZENSKI, Helen R. (Media Spclst) 1270

Bishop Gallagher High Sch (MI)
SLIVKA, Regina (Media Srvs Dir) 1149

Bishop Kearney High Sch (NY)
LANE, Mary K. (Libn) 694

Bishop McCort High Sch (PA)
PORTA, Mary D. (Libn) 984

Bishop Noll Institute (IN)
BERG, Rita J. (Media Ctr Dir) 85

Bishop O'Reilly High Sch (PA)
FANUCCI, Mary M. (Libn) 363

Bishop Rosecrans High Sch (OH)
SIGRIST, Staci E. (Head Libn) . 1137

Bishop Tucker Theological Coll (UGN)
MUKUNGU, Frederick N. (Coll Libn) 876

Bishop Walsh Middle/High School (MD)
PRICE, Consuelo (Media Ctr Dir) 992

Bishop's Univ (PQ)
SHEERAN, Ruth J. (Catlgr) 1125

Bismarck State Coll (ND)
NELSON, Colleen M. (Catlgr) ... 893

Bissell & Karn Inc (CA)
HUNT, Deborah S. (Corprt Libn) . 575

Black Gold Cooperative Lib System (CA)
SOY, Susan K. (Syst Dir) 1170

Black Hills Regional Eye Institute (SD)
EVANS, Jane (Libn) 357

Black Hills State Coll (SD)
JONES, Dora A. (Spcl Cols Libn) 612

Blackburn Coll (IL)
FORBES, Lydia B. (Ref Libn) ... 389

Blackwell North America (OR)
MILLER, Daniel J. (Mgr, Sales & Srv, Technl Srvs Div) 836
SCHMIDT, Holly H. (MARC Consult & Corprt Libn) 1095

Blackwell's (TX)
ALESSI, Dana L. (Dir, Monographic & Selection Srvs) 11

Blackwell's Periodicals Division (NY)
FEICK, Christina L. (Serials Spclst) 368

Bladen County Board of Education (NC)
KERESEY, Gayle (Media Coordntr) 643

Blaine Sch District 503 (WA)
BACON, Carey H. (Dist Libn) 44

Blair Academy (NJ)
JOHNSON, Holly P. (Dir of Lib Srvs) 605

Blair Memorial Lib (MI)
LEVIN, Elizabeth A. (Dir) 720

Blake Cassels & Graydon (ON)
MORRIS, Sandra M. (Asst Libn) . 867
URQUHART, Dawn M. (Asst Libn) 1270

Blessing Coll of Nursing (IL)
ROMANACE, Gisele R. (Lib Srvs Dir) 1052

Blind & Physically Handicapped Regnl Lib (VI)
HERZ, Michael J. (Regnl Libn) .. 534

Block Drug Co Inc (NJ)
LEICHTMAN, Anne B. (Technl Libn) 713

Bloomfield Board of Education (CT)
CARLISLE, Carol A. (Lib Media Spclst) 182

Bloomfield Coll (NJ)
GILLAN, Dennis P. (Head Libn) .. 435

Bloomfield Hills Schs (MI)
ASHLEY, Roger S. (Dir of Andover Media Ctr) 36

Bloomfield Township Pub Lib (MI)
HERBST, Linda R. (Head of Ref) 530
RAFAL, Marian D. (Head of Youth Srvs) 1003
SANDY, Marjorie M. (Adult Reading Dept Head) 1081

Bloomingdale Pub Schs (MI)
POST, Roger (Libn) 986

Bloomington High Sch (CA)
MILLS, Denise Y. (Sch Libn) ... 844

Bloomington Pub Lib (IL)
HUFFMAN, Carol P. (Head of Technl Srvs Dept) 571
KELLEY, H N. (Extension Srvs Libn) 636
KUBIAK, Matthew C. (Dir) ... 682
WOOD, Lois R. (Lib Assoc) ... 1364

Bloomsburg Univ of Pennsylvania (PA)
ENDRES, Maureen D. (Ref Libn & Online Srch Srv Coordntr) .. 348
FROMM, Roger W. (Ref Libn & Univ Archvst) 405
FROST, William J. (Ref Coll Libn) 406
VANN, John D. (Dir of Lib Srvs) 1276

Bloorview Children's Hospital (ON)
LAMBERT, Deborah B. (Libn) ... 690

Blount County Commission (AL)
WEAVER, Clifton W. (Records Adminstr & Archvst) 1312

Blue Cross & Blue Shield Association (IL)
AHRENSFELD, Jan (Head Libn) ... 8

Blue Cross Blue Shield of Florida (FL)
JENKIN, Michael A. (Vice Pres) . 596

Blue Grass Regional Lib Center (TN)
SLOAN, Lynette S. (Regnl Dir) . 1149
WAGGENER, Jean B. (Asst Dir) 1291
WOZNY, Jay (Dir) 1370

Blue Island Pub Lib (IL)
MOORE, Vivian L. (Elem Sch Media Spclst) 861

Blue Lake Elementary Sch (FL)
BUCCO, Louise F. (Libn) ... 153

Blue Ridge Community Coll (VA)
RITTER, Allison C. (Reader Srvs Libn) 1036

Blue Ridge Regional Lib (VA)
FISLER, Charlotte D. (Independent Consult Broker) . 382

Blue Valley Information (PA)
ELLIOTT, Barbara J. (Asst Dir) .. 343
WOOD, Sallie B. (Listing Editor) 1365

Bluffton-Wells County Pub Lib (IN)
JENKINS, John A. 597

BMG Music/RCA (NY)
TAYLOR, George A. (Mktg Mgr) 1226

BNA Inc (DC)
BARR, Janet L. (Sch Lib Syst Dir) 58
HABER, Elinor L. (Libn) 480
WHEELER, Allison S. (Sch Lib Media Spclst) 1328

Board of Cooperative Educational Srvs (NY)
CLARY, Ann R. (Chief Libn) 219
RATESH, Ioana (Technl Srvs Libn) 1009
VINCENT, Susan R. (Ref Libn) . 1284

Bd of Governors of the Federal Rsv Syst (DC)
BEATTIE, Brian (Lib Dir) 70

Board of Trustees (KS)
BALOG, Rita J. (Libn Dir) 53

Board of Trustees (OH)
SEITZ, Robert J. (Pres) 1113

Bob Seitz Communications (NY)
HEINRICH, Mark A. (Libn) 522

Bodman Longley & Dahling (MI)
MCMASTER, Deborah L. (Info Scitst) 815

Boehringer Ingelheim Pharmaceuticals Inc (CT)
MOYNIHAN, Mary B. (Info Scientist) 874
SUPEAU, Cynthia (Info Scitst III) 1210
WARD, Carol T. (Technl Lib Mgr) 1303

Boeing Co (VA)
BAGG, Deborah L. (Lib Technl Processes Supvsr) 45

Boeing Co (WA)
CAMPBELL, Corinne A. (Technl Libs Mgr) 176
CRANDALL, Michael D. (Resrch Libn) 255
LAUGHLIN, Catherine (Libn) 703

Boeing Co (WA)
SILVA, Mary E. (Libn) 1138
Bogart-Brociner Associates (MA)
BOGART, Betty B. (Exec Ofcr) . . 110
Boise Cascade Corp (OR)
GAGNON, Vernon N. (Libn) 412
Boise Pub Lib (ID)
ROBERTSON, Naida
(Volunteer, Circ Dept) 1042
Boise State Univ (ID)
CRANE, David E. (Catlg Libn
Head) 255
HANSEN, Ralph W. (Assoc
Libn) 498
OSTRANDER, Gloria J. (Acqs
Libn) 929
TAYLOR, Adrien P. (Head Ref
Libn) 1225
Bolivar County Lib (MS)
STEWART, Jeanne E.
(Extension Srvs Libn) 1192
WISE, Ronnie W. (Dir) 1357
Bon Secours Hospital (MI)
FRATIES, Marie L. (Asst Libn) . . 399
Bond System (NJ)
STAMP, Raymond T. (Executive
VP) 1179
Bondurant Mixson and Elmore (GA)
KRONE, Judith P. (Info Srvs Dir) . 679
Bonifay Elementary Sch (FL)
HOWELL, Wanda H. (Libn) 565
Bonneville Power Admin (OR)
CONNORS, Jean M. (Law Libn) . 238
Bonneville Telecommunications (UT)
MEIER, Joe (Mktg VP) 821
Bonnie Campbell & Associates (ON)
CAMPBELL, Bonnie (Pres) 176
Book Seminars Inc (FL)
GOGGIN, Margaret K.
(Co-owner, Secy & Treas) . . . 444
Books for Libraries (NY)
SHAPIRO, S R. (Pres) 1121
Books Unlimited Inc (NJ)
YANNOTTA, Peter J. (Pres) . . . 1377
Books Worth Buying (MD)
RUSS, Kennetta P. (Edit) 1068
The Bookwatch (CA)
DONOVAN, Diane C. (Editor &
West Coast Rep) 312
Bookworm & Silverfish-ABAA (VA)
PRESGRAVES, Jim (Proprietor) . 991
Boone County Pub Lib (KY)
BROWN, Lucinda A. (Dir) 145
Booneville Sch System (MS)
BARAGONA, Lynn C. (Libn &
Media Spclst) 55
Boonville Correctional Center (MO)
JOB, Rose A. (Libn) 601
**Boothbay Playhouse Foundation
Inc** (ME)
LENTHALL, Franklyn (Boothbay
Theatre Musm Cur &
Founder) 715
Boots Pharmaceuticals Inc (LA)
TETTEH, Joseph A. (Med Info
Syst Adminstr) 1233
Booz Allen & Hamilton Inc (MD)
GRIMES, Judith E. (Assoc) 470
WETZBARGER, Cecilia G.
(Consult) 1328
Booz Allen & Hamilton Inc (NY)
LANDES, J C. (Financial Srvs
Resrchr) 692
WILLNER, Richard A. (Resrch
Srvs Mgr) 1349
Booz Allen & Hamilton Inc (VA)
CIPRIANI, Debra A. (Consult) . . . 215
Borden & Elliot (ON)
DENTON, Vivienne K. (Libn) 293
**Borgelt Powell Peterson & Frauen
SC** (WI)
PERLSON, Beverly J. (Law
Libn) 959
Borgess Medical Center (MI)
HARVEY, Norma L. (Lib Mgr) . . . 509
Borough of Paramus (NJ)
MOORE, Jean B. (Ref Head) . . . 860
Borough of Park Ridge (NJ)
LINNAVUORI, Julie R. (Lib Dir) . . 731
Bose McKinney & Evans (IN)
BOOHER, William V. (Libn) 115
Boston Athenaeum (MA)
ENGLISH, Cynthia J. (Resrch
Spclst) 350
Boston Coll (MA)
BEGG, Karin E. (Asst Univ Lib) . . 74
BEST, Eleanor L. (Catlg Libn) . . . 92
CHANNING, Rhoda K. (Asst
Univ Libn) 201
CHATTERTON, Leigh A.
(Serials Libn) 204
CONSTANCE, Joseph W.
(Archvst) 238
GROVE, Shari T. (Ref Biblgphr) . 474
KHAN, Syed M. (Ref Libn,
Biblgphr & Coordtr) 646
KIRK, Darcy (Asst Libn for
Technl Srvs) 654
LIPPMAN, Anne F. (Nursing Ref
Biblgphr) 732
MORNER, Claudia J. (Asst Univ
Libn for Access Srvs) 865
SHEAR, Joan A. (Ref Libn) 1124

Boston Conservatory (MA)

Boston Consulting Group (IL)

**Boston Department of Health &
Hospitals** (MA)

Boston Edison Co (MA)

Boston Globe Newspaper Co (MA)
Boston Pub Lib (MA)

Boston Pub Schs (MA)

**Boston Redevelopment
Authority** (MA)
Boston Univ (MA)

DIDHAM, Reginald A. (Head
Libn) 301
EMBAR, Indrani M. (Info Srvs
Dir) 347
PEPLOW, Richard C. (Technl
Srvs Libn) 958

BRENNER, Lawrence (Sr Med
Libn) 133
HORN, David E. (Records Mgmt
Spclst &Corprt Archvst) 559
JOBE, Shirley A. (Lib Mgr) 601
BEECHER, Sally (Hum Cur) 74
BELANGER, Janet B. (Acsq
Libn III) 75
BENDER, Helen F. (Ref Libn) . . . 79
CEDERHOLM, Theresa D.
(Devlpmnt Ofcr) 196
CLANCY, Catherine M. (Yng
Adult Lit Spclst) 215
CORNWALL, Scot J. (Book
Stack Cols & Reader Srvs
Cur) 247
CRIST, Margaret L. (Plng &
Adminstrv Coordntn Asst Dir) . 259
CURLEY, Arthur (Dir & Libn) 265
DOHERTY, John J. (Asst Dir) . . . 309
GRIFFIN, Fredericia (Catlgr) 468
HENRY, Susan L. (Generalist) . . . 529
HORN, Joseph A. (Sr Catlgr &
Classifier) 559
KOLCZYNSKI, Charlotte A.
(Music Ref Libn I) 669
KORT, Richard L. (Slavic Catlgr) . 672
LANG, Rosalie A. (Asst to Dir
for Persnl) 695
MCCORMICK, Sheila P. (Adult
Srvs Libn) 799
MOORACHIAN, Rose (Branch
Libs Supvsr) 858
MYLES, Bobbie (Systs Libn) 885
PARKS, P D. (Catlgr &
Classifier) 943
ROGAN, Michael J. (Ref Libn I) . 1049
RUTKOVSKIS, Gunnars (Asst
Resrcs Dir & Resrcs Libn) . . . 1070
ST. AUBIN, Arleen K. (Sr Catlgr
& Classifier) 1075
SCANNELL, Henry F. (Ref Libn
II) 1087
SCHLAFF, Donna G. (Chlds
Libn) 1093
SCHUELER, Dolores (Sci Ref
Libn) 1101
ELAM, Barbara C. (Dir of Lib &
Media Srvs) 341
KAUFMAN, Polly W. (Lib Media
Srvs Prog Dir) 631

SUTTON, Joyce A. (Head Libn) . 1211
ANDERSON, Wanda E. (Bio
Biblgphr) 25
CHRISTOPHER, Irene (Chief
Libn) 212
CLIFT, Scott B. (Sr Systs
Analyst) 222
FREEHLING, Dan J. (Law Lib
Dir & Assoc Prof of Law) 400
GATES, James L. (Head of
Technl Srvs) 421
GRAMENZ, Francis L. (Music
Lib Head) 457
HARZBECKER, Joseph J. (Info
Srvs Libn) 510
HUDSON, Robert E. (Biblgph
Instrc Coordntr) 570
ILACQUA, Anne K. (Head) 581
LADD, Dorothy P. (Assoc Dir) . . . 687
LAUCUS, John (Dir of Lib) 702

Boston Univ (MA)
MOULTON, Catherine A. (Catlg Dept Head) 873
PAYNE, Douglass B. (Comp Systs Coordntr) 951
PERINO, Elaine S. (Online Searcher & Ref Libn) 958
PETROFF, Loumona J. (Catlgr) . . 965
PLUNKET, Linda (Ref Libn) . . . 979
SAUER, David A. (Biblgphr) . . . 1084
SESKIN, Ann H. (Catlg Libn) . . . 1116
SNYDER, David A. (Systs Libn) . 1164
TOLMAN, Lorraine E. (Prof Emeritus) 1249
WEINSCHENK, Andrea (Comp Srvs Coordntr) 1318
ZIEPER, Linda R. (Hist Biblgphr) 1388
ZIMPFER, William E. (Lib Dir) . 1389

Bostonian Society (MA)
BERGEN, Philip S. (Libn) 85

Botanica The Wichita Gardens (KS)
WOOLF, Amy K. (Libn) 1368

Botsford General Hospital (MI)
ADAMS, Deborah L. (Dir, Lib & Media Srvs) 4
ELLISON, J T. (Archvst) 345

Boulder Pub Lib (CO)

Boult Cummings Connors & Berry (TN)
BOURNER, Elizabeth A. (Law Libn) 119

Bowditch & Dewey (MA)
HILL, Byron C. (Libn) 539

Bowdoin Coll (ME)
SAEGER, Edwin J. (Rare Book Catlgr) 1074
SHANKLAND, Anne H. (Art Libn) 1120

Bowie State Coll (MD)
PENISTON, William A. (Archvst & Spcl Cols Libn) 956

Bowker Electronic Publishing (CA)
MALONEY, James J. (CD-ROM Sales Mgr) 764

Bowker Electronic Publishing (NY)
ALLEN, Robert R. (Dir of Sales) . 16
HUDES, Nan (Mktg Mgr) 569

Bowling Green State Univ (OH)
BURLINGAME, Dwight F. (Vice Pres) 161
COLLINS, Evron S. (Map Libn) . . 232
CURRIE, William W. (Asst Libn & Asst Prof of Humanities) . . . 266
FIDLER, Linda M. (Head of Music Lib) 375
HARNER, James L. (Prof of Eng) 503
KLOPFENSTEIN, Bruce C. (Asst Prof) 662
MCCALLUM, Brenda W. (Asst Prof & Lib Head) 793
MILLER, Ruth G. (Dean of Libs & Lrng Resrcs) 842
MILLER, William (Libs & Lrng Resrcs Assoc Dean) 843
POVSIC, Frances F. (Head of Curr Resrc Ctr) 987
PURSEL, Janet E. (Lib User Educ Coordntr) 998
REPP, Joan M. (Access Srvs Dir) 1024
SLOVASKY, Stephen (Head, Catlgng Dept) 1150
ZAPOROZHETZ, Laurene E. (Dir, Info Srvs) 1386

Bowman Gray Sch of Medicine (NC)
EKSTRAND, Nancy L. (Clinical Libn & Asst Prof) 341
JOHNSTON, Rebecca M. (Catlgng Head) 610
SIBLEY, Shawn C. (Lib Dir) . . . 1135

Bowne & Co Inc (NY)
VONZIEGESAR, Franz (Chairman) 1289

Boyce & Frausto APC (CA)
TABORN, Kym M. (Adminstrv Asst) 1219

Boyertown Area Sch District (PA)
EMERICK, John L. (Supvsr, Lib Media Srvs) 347

BP America (OH)
MCCONNELL, Pamela J. (Technl Info Spclst II) 798
WAGNER, Louis F. (Chemist & Attorny) 1292

Bracewell & Patterson (TX)
YANCY, Susan M. (Law Libn) . . 1377

Bracken County Board of Education (KY)
TEEGARDEN, Maude B. 1229

Braddock General Hospital (PA)
SHAPIRO, Ruth T. (Med Libn) . 1121

Bradley Univ (IL)
HANSEN, Eleanore E. (Biblgph Srvs Libn) 497

Braintree Pub Schs (MA)
ROBINSON, Phyllis A. (Libn & Media Spclst) 1044

Brampton Pub Lib & Art Gallery (ON)
BURGIS, Grover C. (Dir & Secy-Treas) 159
CHAN, Bruce A. (Col Devlpmnt Libn) 199

Brandeis Univ (MA)
CARNAHAN, Paul A. (Ref Libn) . 183
COOPER WYMAN, Rosalind (Reader Srvs Libn) 244
EVENSEN, Robert L. (Asst Dir, Col Mgmt & Creative Arts) . . . 358
GELB, Linda (Sr Reader Srvs Libn) 425
GILROY, Rupert E. (Assoc Univ Libn) 437
GRAY, Carolyn M. (Asso Dir for Technl & Reader Srvs) 459
MASSEY-BURZIO, Virginia (Ref Dept Head) 782
STRAND, Bethany (Rare Bks & Spcl Cols Catlgr) 1200

Brandon General Hospital (MB)
EAGLETON, Kathleen M. (Lib Srvs Dir) 331

Brandon Univ (MB)
JONES, June D. (Music Spclst & Catlgr) 613
SZIVOS, Maria (Extension Libn) 1218

Brandywine Hospital (PA)
KELLEY, John F. (Dir, Resrch Srvs) 636

Braswell Memorial Lib (NC)
ELKINS, Anne M. (Dir) 343

Braxton Associates (MA)
KING, Laurie L. (Info Srvs Dir) . . . 651
PREVE, Roberta J. (Info Srvs) . . . 992

Brazil Pub Lib (IN)
PROCTOR, Judy C. (Lib Dir) . . . 995

Brazoria County Lib System (TX)
BROWN, Steven L. (Dir) 147

Brazosports Facts (TX)
RICE, Margaret R. (Libn) 1027

Breck Sch (MN)
TABAR, Margaret E. (Media Spclst) 1219

Breckenridge Community Schs (MI)
HOERGER, Helen L. (Sch Libn) . 547

Breed Abbott & Morgan (NY)
BARRA, Carol H. (Libn) 58
GREENE, Margaret A. (Asst Libn) 464
NOVICK, Ruth (Law Libn) 911
VAUGHAN, Elinor F. (Lrng & Lib Resrcs Dir) 1279

Brehau Coll (GA)
LANDINGHAM, Alpha M. (Bookseller) 692

Brentanoj (TX)
RAPPELT, John F. (Jr High Sch Libn) 1008

Brentwood Pub Schs (NY)
RINEY, Judith N. (Lib Srvs Dir) . 1035

Brescia Coll (KY)
BRETON, Ernest J. (Consult) . . . 133

Breton & Associates Inc (DE)
HARRIS, Frank D. (Lib Dir) 504

Brevard County (FL)
MCFARLAND, George S. (Law Lib Dir) 804

Brevard County Law Lib (FL)
MELNICOVE, Annette R. (Law Libn) 823

Brewton-Parker Coll (GA)
PHILLIPS, Don (Dir of Lib) 968

Briar Cliff Coll (IA)
THEOBALD, Joanice (Assoc Libn) 1234

Briarcliff Manor Pub Lib (NY)
FARKAS, Charles R. (Lib Dir) . . . 364

Briarcliffe Coll (NY)
NOTARSTEFANO, Vincent C. (Lib Srvs Coordntr) 910

Briarwood Christian High Sch (AL)
OLIVE, J F. (Dir of Media Srvs) . . 921

Brick Row Book Shop (CA)
LOWMAN, Matt P. (Mgr) 744

Bridgeport Hospital (CT)
STEMMER, Katherine R. (Dir of Hlth Scis Lib & AV Srvs) . . . 1186

Bridgeport Pub Lib (CT)
JOHMANN, Nancy (Asst City Libn) 601
MINERVINO, Louise (City Libn) . . 846
MULAWKA, Chet (Head of the Popular Lib) 876
SLOMSKI, Monica J. (Libn) . . . 1150

Bridgeport Pub Schs (CT)
BERRYHILL, Ellen K. (Sch Lib Media Spclst) 90

Bridgewater Coll (VA)
GREENAWALT, Ruth A. (Lib Dir) 463

Bridgewater State Coll (MA)
BATES, Susie M. (Spcl Cols & Archs) 64
CHANDRASEKHAR, Ratna (Ref Libn) 200
NEUBAUER, Richard A. (Lib Sci Prof) 896
OAKLEY, Adeline D. (Assoc Prof Emeritus) 913
TU, Shu C. (Ref Libn) 1261
WEBBER, Cynthia J. (Ref Libn) 1313

Briggs and Morgan (MN)
MUNTEAN, Deborah E. (Info Srvs Mgr) 879

Briggs Lawrence County Pub Lib (OH)
REID, Margaret B. (Dir) 1018

Brigham & Women's Hospital (MA)
DUBNER, Nancy (Med Libn) 321

Brigham Young Univ (UT)
ALBRECHT, Sterling J. (Univ Libn) 10
BROADWAY, Marsha D. (Asst Prof) 138
CHANDLER, Jody A. (Musm Libn) 200
FLAKE, Chad J. (Cur of Spcl Cols) 383
GELDMACHER, Bonnie R. (Asst Acqs Libn) 425
GILLUM, Gary P. (Ancient Std Libn) 436
GOULD, Douglas A. (Circ Libn) . . 454
HALL, Blaine H. (Engl Lang & Lit Libn) 487
ISOBE, Darron T. (AV Srvs Mgr & Technician) 585
JONES, Ruth J. (Circ Libn) 615
LAMB, Connie (Comp-Assisted Resrch Srvs Supvsr) 689
LARSEN, A D. (Assoc Univ Libn) 698
LYMAN, Lovisa (Govt Docums Law Libn) 751
MARCHANT, Maurice P. (Prof of Lib and Info Sci) 768
MATHIESEN, Thomas J. (Prof of Music & Assoc Dean Honors) 784
NELSON, Veneese C. (Col Devlpmnt Libn) 895
NIELSON, Paula I. (Biblgphc Dept Head) 903
OLSEN, Randy J. (Asst Univ Libn for Col Devlpmnt) 921
PURDY, Victor W. (Asst Prof) . . . 998
ROWLEY, Edward D. (Univ Archvst & Cur) 1063
SHIELDS, Dorthy M. (Assoc Prof) 1130
SMITH, Nathan M. (Sch of Lib & Info Scis Dir) 1159
SWENSEN, Dale S. (Serials Catlgr) 1215
WIGGINS, Marvin E. (Bibl Instr Coordntr) 1337
YANG, Basil P. (Sr Microform & Genealogy Catlgr) 1377

Bristol Board of Education (CT)
LEAHY, Michael D. (Lib Media Tchr) 707

Bristol High Sch (RI)
ALDRICH, Linda S. (Head Libn) . . 11

Bristol-Myers Products (CT)
MCGREGOR, M C. (Resrch Scitst & Microbiologist) 808

Bristol-Myers Products (NJ)
BONDAROVICH, Mary F. (Mgr) . 113

Bristol Pub Lib (VA)
POWERS, Linda J. (Chld's Libn) . 989

British Columbia Institute of Technology (BC)
WEEKS, Gerald M. (Info Srvs Coordntr) 1315

British Lib (ENG)
LINE, Maurice B. (Dir Gen) 730

Broadcast Music Inc (NY)
STRINGFELLOW, William T. (Cur) 1202

Broadcast Pioneers Lib (DC)
HEINZ, Catharine F. (Dir) 522

Broadview Associates (NJ)
GOLDSTEIN, Bernard (Partner) . . 446
POPPEL, Harvey (Partner) 984

Brobeck Phleger & Harrison (CA)
BESTE, Ian R. (Law Libn) 92

Brock Univ (ON)
MCKENZIE, Alice M. (Head Libn) 811
RUSSELL, Moira (Docums Spclst) 1069

Brockton Hospital (MA)
KAMENOFF, Lovisa (Mgr of Lib Srvs) 623

Brockton Pub Lib (MA)
WHITE, Sheree L. (Adult Srvs, Ref Libn) 1332

Brockville Pub Lib Board (ON)
HOWELL, Raymond C. (Chief Libn) 565

Brodart Co (NC)
WINKEL, Lois (Edit, Elem Sch Lib Col) 1355

Brodart Co (PA)
FOGAL, Annabel E. (Catlgng Supvsr) 387
SHEAFFER, Marc L. (Technl Consultant) 1124

BroMenn Healthcare (IL)
STROYAN, Susan E. (Hlth Scis Lib Dir) 1203

Bronson Bronson & McKinnon (CA)
SAWYER, Sandra (Libn) 1086

Bronx High Sch of Science (NY)
SUSSMAN, Valerie J. (Libn) . . . 1210

Bronx Municipal Hospital Center (NY)
DAVIDSON, Silvia (Libn) 276

Brookdale Community Coll (NJ)
ANTCZAK, Janice (Prof) 28
EBELING, Elinor H. (Dir, Lrng Resrcs Ctr) 334
KEARNEY, Jeanne E. (Technl Srvs Catlgr) 633
REESE, Carol H. (Media Spclst) 1016
VLOYANETES, Jeanne M. (Media Spclst) 1286

Brookdale Hospital Medical Center (NY)
STRAUSMAN, Jeanne (Asst Med Libn) 1201

Brooke County Pub Lib (WV)
ANTIGO, Dolores A. (Dir) 29

Brookfield High Sch (CT)
SLONE, Eugenia F. (Lib Media Spclst) 1150

Brookfield Pub Lib (IL)
TODD, Margaret (Asst Libn) . . . 1248

Brookfield Publishing Co (VT)
GERARD, James W. (Pres) 428

Brookgreen Gardens (SC)
SALMON, Robin R. (Archvst) . . 1077

Brookhaven Memorial Hospital M C (NY)
BOROCK, Freddie (Med Libn) . . . 116

Brookhaven National Laboratory (NY)
ALBERTUS, Donna M. (Lib Mgr) 10
COHEN, Rosemary C. (Ref Libn) 229
GALLI, Marilyn C. 414
LANE, Sandra G. (Sr Libn) 694
SERCHUK, Barnett (Technl Srvs Head) 1116
TODOSOW, Helen K. (Sr Libn & Mgr) 1248

Brookings Institution (DC)
FAHERTY, Robert L. (Dir of Pubns) 361

Brookline Pub Schs (MA)
MARKUSON, Carolyn A. (Supvsr of Libs and Instrcl Mtrls) 772

Brooklyn Coll of the City Univ of NY (NY)
BRAUCH, Patricia O. (Head of Ref) 129
CORRSIN, Stephen D. (Deputy Assoc Libn, Technl Srvs) 247
FEINBERG, Renee (Ref Libn) . . . 369
GARGAN, William M. (Assoc Prof & Asst Head of Ref) 419
HIGGINBOTHAM, Barbra B. (Chief Libn) 537
HORNE, Dorice L. (Biogph Instr Coordntr) 560
KUPFERBERG, Natalie (Sci & Ref Libn) 684
LESTER, Lillian (Spcl Cols Libn & Archvst) 718
LONEY, Glenn M. (Prof of Theater) 739
MEISELES, Linda (Principal Serials Libn) 822
VAUGHN, Susan J. (Assoc Libn for Col Devlpmnt) 1280
WILD, Judith W. (Catlgr & Asst Prof) 1338

Brooklyn Law Sch (NY) — ROBBINS, Sara E. (Law Libn & Asst Prof of Law) 1039

Brooklyn Museum (NY) — GUZMAN, Diane J. (Wilbour Libn) 479
KERR, Virginia M. (Assoc Libn for Technl Srvs) 644

Brooklyn Pub Lib (NY) — AKEY, Stephen (Libn) 9
AVERY, Theodore M. (Retired) .. 42
BRANDWEIN, Larry (Dir) 128
CANNING, Joan M. (Bus Libn) .. 178
DAVIS, Natalia G. (Asst Branch Libn) 280
DUCHAC, Kenneth F. (Dir Emeritus) 322
GENCO, Barbara A. (Asst Coordntr) 426
HAMILTON, Reatha B. (Asst Branch Libn & Jr Libn) 492
HARKAVY, Ira B. (Trustee) 501
JOHNSON, Sheila A. (Ref Libn) . 609
KALKHOFF, Ann L. (Branch Libn & Chlds Libn) 623
KIMMONS, Anita L. (Chlds Libn) 649
KLEIMAN, Allan M. (Srv to the Aging Chief) 658
KUPERMAN, Aaron W. (Libn) ... 684
MILLER, Roy D. (Exec Asst to the Dir) 842
MILLS, David L. (Branch Libn) .. 844
NYREN, Dorothy E. (Chief of Centl Lib & Spcl Srvs) ... 913
ROYTMAN, Serafima (Libn) ... 1063
SALPETER, Janice L. (Youth Srvs Libn) 1077
TICE, Margaret E. (Sr Libn) 1244
TUDIVER, Lillian (Libn) 1262
VOGEL, Dorothy H. (Asst Bus Libn) 1286
YOUNG, Dorothy B. (Sr Libn) .. 1381

Brooklyn Sch Districts (NY) — MEYERS, Charles (Sch Libn) .. 830

Broome County Pub Lib (NY) — COHEN, Ann E. (Info Srvs Libn) . 227
SEARS, Carlton A. (Dir) 1110
WILLIAMS, Deborah H. (Chlds Srvs Coordntr) 1342

Brother Martin High Sch (LA) — SALVATORE, Gayle E. (Head Libn) 1078

Broude Brothers Limited (NY) — BROUDE, Ronald (Pres & Exec Edit) 141

Broughton Hospital (NC) — BUSH, Mary E. (Libn) 165

Brouse & McDowell (OH) — MCDOWELL, C B. (Attorney) ... 803

Broward Community Coll (FL) — DRAKE, Grady (Lib Srvs Dir) ... 318

Broward County Lib (FL) — ALGAZE, Selma B. (Coordntr of Branches) 13
BURKE, Donna J. (Branch Libn) . 160
GOLDMAN, Ava R. (Govt Docums Libn) 445
GRUBMAN, Donna Y. (Pub Info Ofcr) 474
HARTON, Pamela J. (Libn) 508
KORNITSKY, Judith M. (Literacy Spclst) 672
MILLER, Margaret R. (Lib Assoc) 840
MULLER, Charles W. (Asst Head of Technl Srvs) 877
SMITH, Robyn H. (Ref Libn) ... 1160
SOURS, Katherine M. (Libn IV Head Gen Cols) 1169

Broward County Schs (FL) — JACKSON, Nancy I. (Media Spclst) 588

Brown and Caldwell Consulting Engineers (CA) — SPURLOCK, Pauline (Lib Dir) .. 1177

Brown & Williamson Tobacco Corp (KY) — DIESING, Arthur C. (Sr Resrch Chemist) 302
LINCOLN, Carol S. (Resrch Libn) 728

Brown Healey Bock Architects (IA) — HEALY, Edward H. (Pres) 518

Brown Maroney Rose Barber & Dye (TX) — BIERI, Sandra J. (Libn) 95

Brown Rudnick Freed & Gesmer (MA) — MURRAY, Lynn T. (Law Libn) .. 882

Brown Univ (RI) — ADAMS, Thomas R. (John Hay Prof, Bibl & Univ Biblgphr) 6
BELL, Carole R. (Gifts & Col Maintenance Libn) 76
BOWLBY, Raynna M. (Med Lib Coordntr) 121
BUZZELL, Bonnie G. (Pembroke Libn) 168
CASHMAN, Norine D. (Slides & Photographs Cur) 192
COULOMBE, Dominique C. (Catlg Libn Asst Head) 250
DESJARLAIS-LUETH, Christine (Col Devlpmnt Coordntr) 295
FARK, Ronald K. (Head Circ Libn) 364
GALKOWSKI, Patricia E. (Sci Ref Libn) 413
HELLER, Betty D. (Scis Serials Libn) 524
KELLERMAN, Frank R. (Ref Libn) 636
LANDIS, Dennis C. (European Americana Edit) 693
LYNDEN, Frederick C. (Asst Univ Libn for Technl Srvs) ... 752
MARSH, Corrie V. (Acqs Dept Head) 773
MONTEIRO, George (Prof of Engl & Am Lit) 856
RAINWATER, Jean M. (Reader Srvs Libn) 1004
STONE, Howard P. (Catlg Libn) 1197
TAYLOR, Merrily E. (Univ Libn) . 1227
WILMETH, Don B. (Prof) 1349

Browne Bortz & Coddington Inc (CO) — MARSCHNER, Robyn J. (Info Spclst) 773

Brownfield Independent Sch District (TX) — HAMILTON, Betty D. (Dir) 491

Browning-Ferris Industries Inc (TX) — MAGNER, Mary F. (Corprt Libn) . 759

Brownsburg Pub Lib (IN) — PEARSON, Wanda H. (Dir) 953

Brownstein Zeidman & Schoner (DC) — COUSINS, Richard F. (Law Libn) 252

BRS Information Technologies (HI) — KOLMAN, Roberta F. (Product Devlpmnt Mgr) 669

BRS Information Technologies (IL) — MIFFLIN, Michael J. (Regnl Representative) 833

BRS Information Technologies (NY) — BROWN, Jane E. (Bus Div Dir) .. 144
BRUNELLE, Bette S. (Product Devlpmnt Dir) 150
GABOR, John M. (Sales Dir) ... 411
HULL, Debbie M. (VP) 572
KAHN, Martin F. (Pres) 622
KELLY, Jane A. 637
MCCLELLAND, Bruce A. (New Product Design Mgr) 796
PALMER, Lloyd G. (Vice Pres) .. 936
QUAIN, Julie R. (Lib Srvs Med Product Mgr) 999
RALBOVSKY, Edward A. (Online Srvs Dir) 1004
RUGOFF, Iris L. 1066
VEGTER, Amy H. (Dir) 1281
ZIRPOLO, Frank (Producer Srvs Mgr) 1390

BRS Information Technologies (PA) — NORRIS, Carole 909
SWOPE, Paula J. (Regnl Rep) . 1217

BRS Information Technologies (TX) — GALBRAITH, Paula L. (Sr Regnl Rep) 413

Bruce County Pub Lib (ON) — FLEMING, Anne (Asst Libn) 384

Bruce Guadalupe Community Sch (WI) — MCKILLIP, Rita J. (Resrc Ctr Dir) 811

Brunswick Junior Coll (GA) — BOYD, Ruth V. (Assoc Libn) 123

Bryan Cave McPheeters & McRoberts (ENG) — SNYDER, Elizabeth A. (Law Libn) 1164

Bryan Coll (TN)

WRIGHT, David A. (Dir of Lib
   Srvs) 1371

**Bryan County Board of
   Education** (GA)

GLISSON, Patricia A. (Media
   Spclst) 441

Bryan Memorial Hospital (NE)   ECHOLS, Susan P. (Libn) 334

Bryant Coll (RI)   CAMERON, Constance B. (Asst
   Libn, Ref Dept) 174

Bryant Pub Lib (NY)   WYDEN, Elaine S. (Dir) 1374

Bryn Mawr Coll (PA)   BILLS, Linda G. (Automation
   Coordntr) 96

LAZARUS, Karin (Visual Resrcs
   Actg Adminstrv Head) 706

LEAHY, Mary S. (Rare Bk Dept
   Head) 707

LUNDY, M W. (Rare Bk Catlgr) . . 748

MARKSON, Eileen (Head) 771

PRINGLE, Anne N. (Sci Libn) . . . 993

REED, Gertrude (Asst Dir, Pub
   Srvs) 1015

REGUEIRO, Judith E. (Ref Libn) 1017

SCHWIND, Penelope (Asst Dir
   for Technl Srvs) 1106

SILVERMAN, Scott H. (Catlgng
   Libn) 1138

TANIS, James R. (Dir of Libs) . . 1222

Bryn Mawr Sch (MD)   SANDERS, Jacqueline C. (Head
   Libn) 1080

Buchanan Ingersoll P C (PA)   HORVATH, Patricia M. (Head
   Libn) 561

Buchart-Horn Inc (PA)   HARTLEY, Gloria R. (Libn) 508

Buckman Laboratories (TN)   FITZER, Maureen D. (Resrcs
   Technician) 382

MCDONELL, W E. (Technl Info
   Ctr Mgr) 803

Bucknell Univ (PA)   BOYTINCK, Paul (Head of
   Catalog Dept) 124

DE KLERK, Ann M. (Lib Srvs
   Dir) 288

JENKS, George M. (Col
   Devlpmnt Libn) 597

JENKS, Zoya E. (Catlg Libn) 597

LEWIS, Karen E. (Music Dept
   Libn) 723

**Bucks County Community
   College** (PA)

BRADLEY, John (Dir of Lib
   Srvs) 126

Bucks County Free Lib (PA)   BURSK, Mary A. (Asst Branch
   & Chlds Libn) 163

GILMOUR, Marianne S. (Chlds
   Srvs Coordntr) 437

KALTWASSER, Patricia F.
   (Libn) 623

STRAUSS, Richard F. (Libn) . . . 1201

WHITTAKER, Edward L. (Asst
   Dir) 1334

Budd Larner Gross Picillo et al (NJ)   LEVEROCK, Lisa A. (Law Libn) . 719

Buena Park Lib District (CA)   RITZ, Mary E. (Libn & Cable TV
   Coordntr) 1037

**Buffalo & Erie County Historical
   Society** (NY)

BELL, Mary F. (Lib & Archs Dir) . . 77

Buffalo & Erie County Pub Lib (NY)   CHODACKI, Roberta A. (Music
   Libn) 210

CHRISMAN, Diane J. (Deputy
   Dir) 211

CLOUDSLEY, Donald H. (Dir) . . . 223

COLLINS, Ruth A. (Persnl Dir) . . 233

DORFMAN, Ethel L. (Catlgr) 312

GURN, Robert M. (AV Dept
   Head) 478

MAYER, Erich J. (Libn) 789

MOHN, Wallace D. (Deputy Dir) . 852

REINSTEIN, Julia B. (Lib
   Trustee) 1021

ROSENFELD, Jane D. (Libn) . . 1056

ROUNDS, Joseph B. (Dir
   Emeritus) 1061

STELZLE, James J. (Libn I) . . . 1186

WILLET, Ruth J. (Head, Hist &
   Govt Dept) 1341

Buffalo Bill Historical Center (WY)

Buffalo News (NY)

Buffalo Plains Sch Division 21 (SK)

**Bulloch County Board of
   Education** (GA)

Bur Oak Lib System (IL)

Bureau Marcel van Dijk (BEL)
Bureau Marcel van Dijk (FRN)
Bureau of Archives & History (PA)

Bureau of History (MI)

Bureau of Indian Affairs (NM)

Bureau of Jewish Education (OH)
Bureau of Land Management (MT)

Bureau of National Affairs Inc (DC)

Bureau of National Affairs Inc (IN)
Burgdorf Health Center (CT)
**Burkville Independent Sch
   District** (TX)
**Burlington County Audiovisual Aids
   Ctr** (NJ)
Burlington County Lib (NJ)

Burlington Pub Lib (IA)

Burlington Pub Lib (WI)
Burlington Pub Lib (ON)

Burndy Lib (CT)

Burnham Hospital (IL)

Burns & Levinson (MA)

Burns Clinic Medical Center (MI)

Burns Doane Swecker & Mathis (VA)

**Burnt Hills-Ballston Lake Central
   Schs** (NY)
Burr and Burton Seminary (VT)

Burr-Brown Corp (AZ)
Burroughs Wellcome Co (NC)

PINSON, Patricia A. (Asst Libn
   & Archvst) 975

STOPKA, Christina K. (Libn,
   Archvst) 1198

SCHLAERTH, Sally G. (Head
   Libn) 1093

MCLEOD, Karen E. (Lib
   Coordntr) 814

BURGOON, Roger S. (Lib
   Media Spclst) 159

SPEARMAN, Donna G. (Ref
   Libn) 1172

VAN SLYPE, Georges (Dir) 1277

CHAUMIER, Jacques (Dir) 204

WHIPKEY, Harry E. (State
   Archvst & Dir) 1329

BIGELOW, Martha M. (Dir) 95

MILLER, Bertha H. (Deputy Dir) . 836

MCCAULEY, Elfrieda B.
   (Toadlena Boarding Sch
   Libn) 795

KATZ, Lawrence M. (Asst Dir) . . 630

KOCH, Patricia J. (Lib
   Technician) 667

BALL, Thomas W. (Client Srvs
   Mgr) 52

DEGLER, Stanley E. (Vice Pres
   & Exec Edit) 287

KING, Kamla J. (Lib Mgr) 651

KLEIMAN, Helen M. (Assoc
   Edit, Indexing Srvs) 659

MODLIN, Marilyn J. (Online
   Srvs Libn) 851

PILK, Emily G. (Asst to Pres) . . . 973

HAWKINS, John W. (Pres) 514

CONRAD, Celia B. (Med Libn) . . 238

TEDDER, Dorothy L. (Libn) 1229

RICHIE, Mark L. (Exec Dir) 1030

ALEY, Judy M. (AV Insts Libn) . . . 12

CARR, Charles E. (Principal
   Libn Readers Adv) 185

CRAWFORD, Lynn D. (Technl
   Srvs Coordntr) 257

KALDENBERG, Katherine A.
   (Branch Libn) 622

RILEY, Marie R. (Sr Libn) 1034

FOWLER, Linda J. (Chlds Srvs
   Head) 394

JOHNSON, Anne C. (Asst Dir,
   Head Adult Srvs) 602

PROCES, Stephen L. (Dir) 994

JARVIS, A W. (Head, Technl
   Srvs) 595

WEIMERSKIRCH, Philip J.
   (Asst Dir) 1317

BENNINGTON, April A.
   (Medical Libn) 82

HEACOCK, Pamela P. (Law
   Libn) 518

KELLY, Kay (Lib Dir & Coordntr
   CME) 638

VODRA, Carol (Adminstr and
   Law Libn) 1286

EGAN, Mary J. (Dir of Libs) 338

ELLIS, Margaret D. (Head Libn
   & Media Spclst) 345

WOLF, Noel C. (Corprt Libn) . . . 1360

BURCSU, James E. (Head,
   Scitfc Documtn Dept) 158

CARPENTER, Vincent P. (Drug
   Info Scientst) 185

MCCONNELL, Judith J.
   (Catlgng Libn) 797

THOMPSON, Reubin C.
   (Chemical Info Scientst) 1241

Burroughs Wellcome Co (NC)

TROMBITAS, Ildiko D. (Technl Info Dept Head) 1258
WALTON, Carol G. (Info Spclst) 1301

Burson-Marsteller (NY)
MACCALLUM, Barbara B. (Info Spclst) 754

Burton Pub Lib (OH)
DONALDSON, Timothy P. (Catlgr & Automation Systs Mgr) 311
VARGA, Carol C. (Dir) 1278

Bush Hartt & Kingsbury Inc (VA)
HARTT, Richard W. (Pres) 509
Bushy Run Research Center (PA)
ELY, Betty L. (Lib Consult) . . . 347
Business & Technology Online (NY)
SHELTON, Anita L. (Dir) 1126
Business Information Services (MA)
DLOTT, Nancy B. (Pres) 306
Business International Corp (DC)
MIDDLETON, Carl H. (VP and Washington Rep) 833

Business International Electronic (NY)
CAPPS, Ian M. (Sr VP) 180
Business Research Corp (MA)
GALVIN, Carol K. 415
LEASON, Jane (Indxr) 707

Business Week (NY)
MUNDER, Barbara (Director) . . . 879
Businessfacts (CA)
ADAMS, Joyce A. (Info Consult) . . . 5
Butler & Binion (TX)
BULL, Margarita A. (Lib Dir) 156
Butler Area Pub Lib (PA)
POWERS, Beverly A. (Dir) 989
Butler County Law Lib (OH)
SHEW, Anita K. (Law Libn) 1129
Butler Hospital (RI)
WALTON, Linda J. (Med Libn) . 1301
Butler Pub Lib (NJ)
GARDNER, Sue A. (Dir) 418
Butler R-V Sch District (MO)
FISHER, Georgeann (Dir of Curr & Instrc) 381
Butler Univ (IN)
JONES, Deborah A. (Ref Dept Head) 612
KONDELIK, John P. (Dir) 670
SCHOONOVER, Phyllis J. (Music & Fine Arts Libn) 1098
Butte County Lib (CA)
BROWN, Carol G. (Branch Libn) . 142
TERRY, Josephine R. (Dir) 1232
Butterfield Press (CA)
LEACH, Elizabeth A. (Asst Publshr & Indxr) 706
Butterworth & Co Ltd (ENG)
CUSWORTH, George R. (Chief Executive) 267
Byers Casgrain (PQ)
EDER, Sonya (Documentalist) . . . 336
BYLS Press (IL)
STUHLMAN, Daniel D. (Pres) . . 1205
Byram Hills High Sch (NY)
BERGER, Pam P. (Lib Media Spclst) 86
BYTE Information Exchange (NH)
BOND, George (Exec Editor) 113

C

C Berger & Co (IL)
BERGER, Carol A. (Pres) 85
BROWN, Patricia B. (Info Specialist) 146
FAUST, Julia B. (Persnl Srvs Dir) 366
JOHNSON, Linnea R. (Staff Recruitment Consult) 607
KLINGBERG, Jane E. (Temporary Srvs Coordntr) . . . 661
RUSSELL, Janet (Spcl Projs Coordntr) 1069
STRABLE, Edward G. (Sr Consult) 1199
WALSH, Deborah T. (Staff Recruiter) 1299
C-E-L Regional Lib (GA)
ROEHLING, Steven R. (Asst Head of Ref) 1048
C-I-L Inc (ON)
DUNBAR, Janet M. (Lib Technician) 325
WEAVER, Maggie (Libn) 1312
C J Bellamy & Associates (AUS)
BENNETT, David M. (Sr Consultant) 81
C S R Louis Frechette (PQ)
GELINAS, Rene (Lrng Aids Consult) 426
C/W Mars Inc (MA)
ECKERSON, Gale E. (User Srvs Supvsr) 334
CAB International (ENG)
COOK, Elaine (Regional Sales Mgr) 239
Cabarrus County Schs (NC)
KISER, Anita H. (Media Coordntr) 656
Cabarrus Memorial Hospital (NC)
MILLER, Nancy H. (Med Libn) . . 841

Cabell County Board of Education (WV)
APEL, Catherine D. (Huntington High Sch Libn) 29
Cabell County Pub Lib (WV)
RULE, Judy K. (Dir) 1067
Cable News Network (GA)
ALLEN, William R. (Libn) 16
Cabot Corp (MA)
DAVIS, Barbara M. (Technl Info Mgr) 277
REID, Angea S. (Libn) 1018
Cabot Corp (PA)
FU, Clare S. (Libn) 407
Cabot Institute of Applied Arts & Tech (NF)
MORGAN, Pamela S. (Libn) 864
RAHAL, M P. (Mgr, Eductnl Resrcs) 1003
Cabrini Medical Center (NY)
KASSIN, Abby L. (Asst Libn) . . . 629
MAXWELL, Marjo V. (Info Engineer) 788
Caci Inc (OH)
HUCK, Dan (VP & Div Dir) 569
SULLIVAN, Michael M. (PC Systs Mktg Dir) 1208
Caci Inc (VA)
MOTTRAM, Geoffrey (Pres) 873
Cactus Software (IL)
KENNEDY, Frances C. (Libn) . . . 641
Caddo Parish Schs (LA)
BEST, Donald A. (Lib Dir) 92
Cadillac-Wexford County Pub Lib (MI)
CAHN, Mary Z. (Asst Libn) 171
Cahill Gordon & Reindel (NY)
DAVENPORT, Margaret J. (Libn) 275
LUNG, Chan S. (Asst Libn) 748
SHORE, Julia M. (Libn) 1132
Cahill Larkin & Co (CT)
GERHARDT, Lillian N. (Editor-in-Chief of Sch Lib Jnl) 428
Cahners Magazines (NY)
CAIN, Robert B. (Pres) 171
Cain Associates Architects (MI)
GAMAL, Sandra H. (Libn) 416
Cairo American Coll (NY)
CASE, Doris A. (Elem Sch Libn) . 191
Cairo Unit Sch District 1 (IL)
EL-MASRY, Mohammed (Asst Prof) 345
Cairo Univ (EGY)
MAHOUD ALY, Usama E. (Prof of Lib & Info Sci) 761
Calcasieu Parish Pub Lib (LA)
LEE, Lynda M. (Dir) 710
Caldwell Coll (NJ)
HODGE, Patricia A. (Dir of Lib) . . 546
STICKEL, William R. (Cataloger) 1193
Calgary Board of Education (AB)
MACRAE, Lorne G. (Dir) 758
Calgary Pub Lib (AB)
ANDERSON, Gail (Dept Head, Arts & Recreation) 23
HARDMAN, Joye A. (Chlds Coordntr) 500
MANSON, Bill B. (Asst Dir) 767
REID, Patricia M. (Branch Head) 1019
RHYNES, H B. (Part-time employee) 1026
WAUGH, Alan L. (Dept Head) . . 1310
WHITE, Valerie L. (Young Adult Srvs Coordntr) 1332
WING, Marjorie (Dept Head, Soc Scis) 1354
Calgene Inc (CA)
JOHNSON, Deanna L. (Libn) . . . 603
Calgon Corp (PA)
KASPERKO, Jean M. (Plng Analyst) 629
SCHWARZ, Betty P. (Info Ctr Mgr) 1105
California Academy of Sciences (CA)
MORITZ, Thomas D. (Academy Libn) 865
TSAI, Sheh G. (Lib Page) 1260
California Book Supply (CA)
LUNSTEDT, Ralph A. (Owner) . . 749
California Community Colls (CA)
MARRIOTT, Lois I. (Lib Srvs & Plng Systs Coordntr) 773
California Department of Corrections (CA)
LEFFERS, Mary J. (Sr Libn) 712
California Department of Education (CA)
KLEINMAN, Elsa C. (Libn) 660
California Dept of Food & Agriculture (CA)
KAWAMOTO, Chizuko (Supvsng Libn) 632
California Department of General Srvs (CA)
GRANADOS, Rose A. (Technl Libn) 457
California Department of Justice (CA)
RAFFALOW, Janet W. (Supvsng Libn) 1003
California Department of Transportation (CA)
HANEL, Mary A. (Sr Libn & Histl Records Ofcr) 495

California Division of Mines & Geology (CA)

BRUNTON, Angela (Sr Libn) 151

California Family Study Center (CA)

GREENWOLD, Amy (Lib Dir) ... 465

California Institute of Technology (CA)

ANDERSON, Virginia 25
BRUDVIG, Glenn L. (Info Resrcs Dir) 149
CARD, Sandra E. (Systs Devlpmnt Ofcr) 180
CHANG, Min M. (Head, Technl Srvs) 200
CHOUDHURY, Lori B. (Mgmt Lib Head) 211
GOODSTEIN, Judith R. (Inst Archvst) 450
KNUDSEN, Helen Z. (Astrophysics Libn) 666
ROTH, Dana L. (Sci & Engrng Libs Head) 1059

California Institute of the Arts (CA)

HANFT, Margie E. (Film, Video & Ref Libn) 495
HORIGAN, Evelyn A. (Art & Slide Libn) 559

California Lib Association (CA)

FERRELL, Mary S. (Exec Dir) ... 373

California Maritime Academy (CA)

LANE, David R. (Technl Srvs Libn) 694

California Medical Center at Los Angeles (CA)

FITZGERALD, Diana S. (Dir of Lib & Info Srvs) 382

California Polytechnic State Univ (CA)

DOBB, Linda S. (Head, Catlgng Dept) 307
HANSEN, Phyllis J. (Asst Catlgr) 498
PRITCHARD, Eileen E. (Ref Libn) 994
ROCKMAN, Ilene F. (Libn & Asst Dept Head) 1046
STEWARD, Martha J. (Dir, Intrcl Resrc Ctr) 1192
WALCH, David B. (Dean of Lib Srvs) 1293

CA Postsecondary Education Commission (CA)

TESTA, Elizabeth M. (Lib Srvs Dir) 1233

California Sch of Professional Psy (CA)

BERGMAN, Emily A. (Asst Libn) .. 86
BIRCH, Tobeylynn (Lib Dir) 98
KAUFFMAN, Inge S. (Dir) 631

California State Board of Equalization (CA)

AKEY, Sharon A. (Sr Libn) 9

California State Coll at Bakersfield (CA)

KIRKLAND, Janice J. (Head of Biblgph Ctl) 655
WINTER, Eugenia B. (Acqs Libn & Bibl) 1356

California State Court of Appeals (CA)

GOMEZ, Cheryl J. (Law Libn) ... 447
RODICH, Lorraine E. (Libn) 1047

California State Lib (CA)

ANDERSEN, Thomas K. (Govt Pubns Head) 21
CUNNINGHAM, Jay L. (Asst Chief, State Lib Srvs) 265
GILBERT, Carol L. (Conversion Proj Libn) 433
GLOVER, Frank J. (Ref Libn) ... 442
HAGEN, Dennis D. (Libn) 483
HUSTON, Esther L. (Sr Libn) ... 578
LOW, Kathleen (Online Ref Libn) 743
MCGOVERN, Gail J. (Lib Consult) 807
SILVER, Cy H. (Consult) 1138
STRONG, Gary E. (State Libn) . 1203

California State Polytechnic Univ (CA)

ADAMSON, Danette (Catlg Libn & Music Biblgphr) 6
DUNN, Kathleen K. (Ref Dept Head) 327

California State Polytechnic Univ (CA)

HSIA, Ting M. (Serials Catlg Libn) 567
KOGA, James S. (Online Ref Srv Coordntr) 668
LAMONTAGNE, Therese (Circ Srvs Libn) 691
LIM, Sue C. (Catlg Dept Head) .. 727

California State Univ at Bakersfield (CA)

HERSBERGER, Rodney M. (Dir of Libs) 533

California State Univ at Chico (CA)

ARIARATNAM, Lakshmi V. (Ref & Instrc Libn) 31
DWYER, James R. (Head, Biogph Srvs) 330
HUANG, George W. (Prof) 568
LO, Henrietta W. (Assoc Libn) ... 735
NISSLEY, Meta J. (Head, Acq & Col Mgmt) 905
POST, William E. (Asst Univ Libn) 986
POWER, Colleen J. (Regnl Srvs Coordntr) 989
RYAN, Frederick W. (Deputy Univ Libn) 1071
SESSIONS, Judith A. (Univ Libn) 1117

California State Univ at Dominguez Hills (CA)

BALDWIN, Claudia A. (Ref Libn) 51
DUNKLEE, Joanna E. (Catlg Dept Head) 326
OPPENHEIM, Michael R. (Asst Libn & Asst Prof) 925
SUNDSTRAND, Jacquelyn K. (Archvst) 1210

California State Univ at Fresno (CA)

BOCHIN, Janet S. (Music Catlgr) 108
HILLMAN, Stephanie (Asst Univ Libn) 541
RICHTER, Bertina (Assoc Libn) . 1031

California State Univ at Fullerton (CA)

ANDERSEN, Leslie N. (Music Libn) 21
BRIL, Patricia L. (Col Devlpmnt Ofcr) 136
STEPHENSON, Shirley E. (Assoc Dir of Oral Hist Prog) 1189

California State Univ at Hayward (CA)

CASTAGNOZZI, Carol A. (Head of Pub Srvs) 194
REEDER, Ray A. (Music Libn) .. 1015
ROSE, Melissa M. (Lib Dir) 1055

California State Univ at Long Beach (CA)

AHOUSE, John B. (Spcl Col Libn) 8
BENSON-TALLEY, Lois I. (Sr Asst Libn) 83
BRITTON, Helen H. (Assoc Dir) . 137
CULOTTA, Wendy A. (Assoc Libn) 264
DEBOER, Kee K. (Soc Scis Libn) 284
DUBOIS, Henry J. (Col Devlpmnt Coordntr) 322
KOUNTZ, John C. (Devlpmnt Assoc Dir) 673
LITTLEJOHN, Alice C. (Sr Asst Libn) 734
NESBITT, Renee D. (Sr Asst Libn) 896
PARKER, Joan M. (Sr Asst Libn) 942
SCEPANSKI, Jordan M. (Dir, Univ Lib & Lrng Resrcs) 1088
SIMS, Sidney B. 1142
SINCLAIR, Lorelei P. (Asst Libn) 1142
SMITH, Gordon W. (Assoc Dir of Lib Affairs) 1155
WILLIAMS, Valencia (Coordntr) 1347

California State Univ at Los Angeles (CA)

GREENBERG, Marilyn W. (Prof) . 463
HOFFMAN, Irene M. (Lib Instrc Coordntr) 548
ROLLING, George M. (Humanities & Soc Scis Libn) 1051
SULLIVAN, Suzanne E. (Asst Univ Libn) 1208
WALTERS, Mary D. (Asst Univ Libn for Col Devlpmnt) 1301
WILKINSON, David W. (Bus Libn & Online Srchg Coordntr) 1340

California State Univ at Northridge (CA)

CREAGHE, Norma S. (Assoc Dir of Libs) 257
DAVIS, Douglas A. (Coordntr of Physical Plng) 278
DODSON, Snowdy D. (Sci Libn) . 308
DURAN, Karin J. (Instrcl Mtrls Lab Dir) 328
ECKLUND, Kristin A. (Ref & Bibl Dept Assoc Libn) 335
EICHELBERGER, Susan (Circ Dept Chair) 339
FINLEY, Mary M. (Libn) 378
PERKINS, David L. (Head of Col Devlpmnt) 959
TANIS, Norman E. (Dir of Univ Libs) 1222
WONG, Clark C. (Asst Dir for Lib Admin) 1362

California State Univ at Sacramento (CA)

ANDREW, Karen L. (Intermittent Asst Ref Libn) 26
DRUMMOND, Herbert (Humanities Ref Libn) 321
GOFF, Linda J. (Lib Instrc Libn) . . 443
GRAVES, Frances M. (Coordntr, Lib Credential Prog) 459
HICKS, Mary F. (Asst Libn) 537
KONG, Leslie M. (Assoc Soc Sci & Bus Ref Libn) 670
KRISTIE, William J. (Sr Asst Libn) 679
PARSONS, Jerry L. (Asst Univ Libn for Systs) 945
SNOW, Marina (Humanities Ref Libn) 1164
TRIMINGHAM, Robert (Acqs Libn) 1256

California State Univ at San Bernardino (CA)

PARISE, Marina P. (Sr Asst Libn) 940

California State Univ at Stanislaus (CA)

AMRHEIN, John K. (Lib Dir) 20
BENNETT, Agnes H. (Catlg Libn) 81
PARKER, John C. (Head of Pub Srv & Asst Lib Dir) 942
SANTOS, Bob (Biblgphr) 1082

California Training and Resource Network (CA)

RUDDOCK, Velda I. (Info Dissemination Spclst) 1065

California Univ of Pennsylvania (PA)

BARREAU, Deborah K. (Systs Libn) 58
BECK, William L. (Dean of Lib Srvs) 72
NOLF, Marsha L. (Biogph Instrc Libn) 908

California Western Sch of Law (CA)

BOOKHEIM, Louis W. (Ref Libn, Dir of Pub Srvs) 115
GARCIA, Mary E. (Acqs Libn) . . . 417
ROSS, Robert D. 1058

Call-it Co Inc (IA)
Callaghan & Co (IL)

DANNE, William H. (Sr VP of Publshg & Operations) 274
GRIES, James P. (Mgmt Info Srvs Dir) 468
HACKNER, Barry M. (VP of Mktg) 481

Callaghan & Co (IL)

HUXSAW, Charles F. (Dir) 580
KLAUS, Roger D. (Edit-in-Chief) . 658
LYNCH, Hugh J. (VP of Finance) 751
SCUDELLARI, Anthony E. (Pres & Chief Exec Ofcr) 1108

Callaway Educational Association (GA)

GIBSON, Ricky S. (Libn) 432

Calligraphic Arts Guild of Toronto (ON)

FREEMAN, Elayne B. (Libn) 400

Calocerinos & Spina Consulting (NY)

AUSTIN, Ralph A. (Libn, Scientific & Technl Info) . . 40

Calspan Corp (NY)

MILLER, Betty (Mgr, Tech Info Ctr) 836

Caltex Petroleum Corp (TX)

HUMMEL, Muriel H. (Corprt Libn) 573

Calumet City Pub Lib (IL)

EDGREN, Gale R. (Youth Svrs Libn) 336

Calumet Coll (IN)

BROTON, Cecilianne S. (Libn & AV Asst Prof) 141

Calumet Pub Hospital (MI)

BINONIEMI, Amanda M. (Hospital Libn) 97

Calvary Baptist Theological Seminary (PA)

KROLL, Anna L. (Catlgr) 679

Calvert County Pub Lib (MD)

HAMMETT, Marcia G. (Asst Dir) . 493
HOFMANN, Patricia P. (Ref Libn) 548

Calvin Coll & Seminary (MI)

CARLSON, Susan L. (Ref Libn) . 182
DE KLERK, Peter (Theol Libn) . . 288
MONSMA, Marvin E. (Lib Dir) . . 855

Camas Pub Lib (WA)
Cambria Records & Publishing (CA)

BRENNAN, Cindy L. (Dir) 132
BOWLING, Lance C. (Publshr & Edit) 121

Cambridge Analytical Associates (MA)
Cambridge Pub Lib (MA)

DAMICO, Nancy B. (Libn) 272
CLOHERTY, Lauretta M. (Asst Dir of Persnl Admin & AV Srvs) 223
CRANE, Hugh M. (Asst Ref Dept Head) 255

Cambridge Pub Lib (ON)

SKELTON, W M. (Adminstrv Srvs Coordntr) 1146

Cambridge Research Institute (MA)
Cambridge Scientific Abstracts (MD)

SMART, William R. (Sr VP) . . . 1151
SEARS, Jonathan R. (Managing Editor) 1110

Camden Catholic High Sch (NJ)
Camden County Lib (NJ)

BROWN, Anita P. (Libn) 142
AVENICK, Karen (Supvsr of Ref Dept) 41
DENNIS, Deborah E. (Syst Libn) . 292
LADOF, Nina S. (Lib Dir) 687
ROMISHER, Sivya S. (Coordntr) 1053
ROTHENBERG, Patricia (Ref Libn) 1060

Camden County Vocational Technical Sch (NJ)
Camden Free Pub Lib (NJ)

GORDON, Muriel C. (Libn) 451
DILLENSCHNEIDER, Patricia A. (Supvsng Libn) 303
WEST, Shirley L. (Lib Dir) 1326

Cameron Univ (OK)

RABURN, Josephine R. (Div Head) 1001

Camp Dresser & McKee Inc (MA)
Camp Lejeune Naval Hospital (NC)

CARROLL, Virginia L. (Libn) 187
FRAZELLE, Betty (Lib Technician) 399

Campbell County Board of Education (TN)

HENSON, Susie K. (High Sch Libn) 530

Campbell County Pub Lib (KY)

LILLIE, Jean N. (Technl Srvs Libn) 727

Campbell County Pub Lib (WY)
Campbell County Sch District (WY)

SIEBERSMA, Dan (Dir) 1135
PROCTOR, Deborah K. (Elem Lib Media Spclst) 994
WURBS, Sue A. (Dir Media Srvs) 1374

Campbell-Ewald Co (MI)

ROSE, Sharon G. (Libn) 1055
STEPEK, Susan B. (Sr Vice Pres & Ref Ctr Mgr) 1187

Campbell Mithun Inc (IL)
Campbell Soup Co (NJ)

LELLENBERG, Nancy A. (Libn) . 714
KESSLER, Selma P. (Consult) . . 645

Campbell Univ (NC)
SORVARI, Kare C. (Libn) 1169
WEEKS, Olivia L. (Asst Law Libn) 1315

Camrose Lutheran Coll (AB)
INGIBERGSSON, Asgeir (Head Libn) 582

Canada Cement Lafarge (PQ)
SHLIONSKY, Anatoly (Engrng Libn) 1132

Canada Department of External Affairs (ON)
GUILBERT, Manon M. (Intl Docums & Microfilms Libn) . . . 476

Canada Department of Fisheries & Oceans (MB)
MARSHALL, Kenneth E. (Regnl Libn) 774

Canada Department of Fisheries & Oceans (NS)
SUTHERLAND, J E. (Lib Srvs Head) 1211

Canada Employment Immigration Commission (ON)
SUNDER-RAJ, P E. (Lib Srvs Dir) 1210
JORDAN, Peter A. (Regnl Libn) . 616

Canada Environment Canada (AB)
Canada Inst for Scientific & Technl Info (NF)
TILLOTSON, Joy G. (Branch Head) 1245

Canada Inst for Scientific & Technl Info (ON)
IRELAND, Michael A. (Catlgng Libn) 583
LATYSZEWSKYJ, Maria A. (Technl Srvs Libn) 702
REILLY, Brian O. (Documtn Spclst Libn) 1020
SAMSON, Mary (Head of Index Scintfc Translations) 1079
SMITH, Elmer V. (Dir) 1154

Canada Inst for Scientific & Technl Info (PQ)
SCHEPPER, Josee H. (Head of Biotechnology Branch) 1091
VENNE, Louise (Branch Head) . 1282

Canada Law Book Inc (ON)
CAMPBELL, Catherine J. 176
Canada Post Corp (ON)
WEERASINGHE, Jean Y. (Corprt Libn) 1316

Canada Systems Group (ON)
BYERS, Cathy L. (Libn) 168
Canadian Association of Research Libs (ON)
MCCALLUM, David L. (Exec Dir) 793
Canadian Bankers' Association (ON)
LEAMEN, Nancy J. (Head Libn) . 707
Canadian Broadcasting Corp (ON)
EARLS, M L. (Ref & Design Libs Head Libn) 332

Canadn Ctr for Occupational Hlth/Safety (ON)
LAM, Vinh T. (Data Base Devlpmnt Mgr) 689

Canadian Center for Occupational Safety (ON)
BROWNRIDGE, James R. (Mgr, Proj Devlpmnt Group) 149

Canadian Centre for Architecture (PQ)
DE LUISE, Alexandra (Acqs Libn) 290

Canadian Department of Agriculture (PQ)
LUSSIER, Claudine (Libn) 749
Canadian Federal Government (ON)
KAYE, Barbara J. (Women's Bureau Ref Ctr Catlgr) 632

Canadian Federation of Independent Bus (ON)
COORSH, Katalin (Libn & Mgr) . . 244
Canadian Gas Assn (ON)
KARCICH, Grant J. (Mgr of Lib & Info Systs) 627

Canadian Geriatrics Research Society (ON)
SABLJIC, John A. (Libn) 1072
YANCHINSKI, Roma N. (Head Libn) 1377

Canadian Grain Commission (MB)
BLANCHARD, Jim (Libn) 103
Canadian Health Libs Association (ON)
KENT, Diana 642

Canadian Imperial Bank of Commerce (ON)
MILLER, Ann M. (Ofc Automation Consult) 835

Canadian Jewish Congress (PQ)
NEFSKY, Judith L. (Dir, Archs) . . 892
Canadian Lib Association (ON)
BOWES, Laurie A. (Dir of Publshg) 121
COONEY, Jane (Exec Dir) 241
PORTER, David E. (Finance & Admin Dir) 984

Canadian Marconi Co (PQ)
Canadian Mental Health Association (ON)

Canadian Natl Institute for the Blind (ON)

Canadian National Railway Co (PQ)

Canadian Nurses Association (ON)
Canadn Organz for Devlpmnt Through Educ (ON)
Canadian Pacific Rail (PQ)

Canadian Press (ON)
Canadian Standards Association (ON)

Canadian Tobacco Manufactures' Council (PQ)

Canadian Wheat Board (MB)

GONZALEZ, Paloma (Asst Libn) . 448

ROUP, Carol E. (Lib Srvs & Resrch Coordntr) 1061

HAYES, Janice E. (Mgr of Lib Srvs) 516
HAGOPIAN, Shake (Info Appls Analyst) 483
SHIFF, Linda S. (Libn Mgr) 1130

ST. AMANT, Robert (Prog Ofcr) 1075
BERARDINUCCI, Heather R. (Technl Srvs Libn) 84
KHAN, Asma S. (Libn) 646

MARSHALL, Alexandra P. (Info Spclst) 773

CLARKE, Robert F. (Info Spclst) . 219
TREVICK, Selma D. (Assoc Libn) 1255
EMOND, Lucille I. (Lib Technician) 348
REEDMAN, M R. (Libn) 1015

Cancer Control Agy of British Columbia (BC)
NOBLE, David (Head Libn) 906
Caney Fork Regional Lib Center (TN)
HOLDREDGE, Faith A. (Dir) 550
Canisius Coll (NY)
NELSON, Robert J. (Archvst) . . . 895
PERONE, Karen L. (Catlg Libn) . . 959
TELATNIK, George M. (Lib Dir) . 1230
Canmore Pub Lib (AB)
LUTHY, Jean M. (Libn) 750
Cannon's Business Coll (HI)
DILUCIA, Samuel J. (Libn) 303
Canterbury Sch (CT)
BOLSTER, Kathryn (Dir) 113
CAPCON Lib Network (DC)
REYNOLDS, Dennis J. (Exec Dir) 1025
WILLSON, Elizabeth (Mem Srvs Mgr) 1349
Cape Breton Regional Lib (NS)
MACINTOSH, Ian R. (Chief Libn) 755
Cape Cod Hospital (MA)
FRAZIER, Nancy E. (Med Libn) . . 399
Cape Fear Valley Medical Center (NC)
BEATTIE, Barbara C. (Dir of Lib Srvs) 70
Cape Girardeau Pub Lib (MO)
MAXWELL, Martha A. (Dir) 788
Cape Henlopen Sch District (DE)
ROBERTS, Judith M. (Libn) . . . 1040
Capehart and Scatchard (NJ)
WILLIAMSON, Carol L. (Law Libn) 1347
Capital Area Health Foundation (PA)
CAPITANI, Cheryl A. (Dir of Lib & Media Srvs) 180
Capital Newspapers (NY)
MATTURRO, Richard C. (Lib Systs Dir) 786
Capital Sch District (DE)
FITZPATRICK, Barbara L. (Elem Sch Libn) 382
Capital Univ (OH)
ORLANDO, Jacqueline M. (Ref Libn) 926
Capitol City Press (LA)
MATTMILLER, C F. (Libn) 786
Capitol Region Lib Council (CT)
PARKS, Amy N. (Network Mgr) . 943
SARGENT, Dency C. (Exec Dir) 1083
URICCHIO, William J. (Assoc Dir for Automated Srvs) 1269
Carabateas Responsive Information Srv (NY)
CARABATEAS, Clarissa D. (Owner) 180
Caramics Process Systems Corp (MA)
SCHUTZBERG, Frances (Experience Ctr Dir) 1103
Carbon County Sch District 1 (WY)
HOFF, Vickie J. (Media Spclst) . . 547
Carbon Lehigh Intermediate Unit 21 (PA)
GOODMAN, John E. (Instrcl Mtrls Srv Dir) 449
Carbondale Pub Lib (IL)
CAMPBELL, Ray (Lib Dir) 177
Cardinal Glennon Coll (MO)
GLADIEUX, Mary B. (Chief Libn) 439
Cardinal Spellman Philatelic Museum (MA)
KOVED, Ruth B. (Libn) 674
Cardinal Stritch Coll (WI)
GILLETTE, Meredith (Head Libn) 435
CareerTrack Inc (CO)
MEYER, Andrea P. (Resrch Spclst) 829

Cargill Inc (MN)

ANDERSON, Marcia L. (Law
   Libn) 24
PETERSON, Julia C. (Info Ctr
   Mgr) 963

Caribbean Graduate Sch of
   Theology (JAM)

ERDEL, Timothy P. (Libn &
   Lectr in Theol Std) . . . 352

Cariboo Coll (BC)

LEVESQUE, Nancy B. (Head
   Libn) 719

Caritas High Sch (AB)

COMPRI, Jeannine L. (Libn) 235

Carl & Lily Pforzheimer Foundation
   Inc (NY)

REIMAN, Donald H. (Edit) 1020

Carleton Coll (MN)

GREENE, Mark A. (Coll
   Archvst) 464
METZ, T J. (Coll Libn) 828
NILES, Ann A. (Asst Coll Libn) . . 904
SANFORD, Carolyn C.
   (Biblgphr) 1081

Carleton Univ (ON)

BRIGGS, Geoffrey H. (Univ
   Libn) 135
CAMPBELL, Laurie G. (Info
   Srvs & Col Devlpmnt Libn) . . . 177
CLARKE, Bozena (Head of
   Serials) 218
ROGERS, Dorothy S. (Head of
   Catlgng) 1049
ROSSMAN, Linda (Syst
   Devlpmnt Asst Libn) 1059
SCHNEIDER, Tatiana (Ref Libn) . . 1097

Carlisle Pub Lib (IA)

BERNING, Robert W. (Lib Dir) . . . 89

Carlow Coll (PA)

MITCHELL, Joan M. (Dir of Lib
   Srvs) 849

Carlsbad City Lib (CA)

LANGE, Clifford E. (Dir) 695

Carlson Marketing Group (OH)

QUINTEN, Rebecca G. (Mgr,
   Mktg Resrch Info Ctr) 1000

Carlton Fields Ward Emmanuel
   Smith et al (FL)

GEBET, Russell W. (Law Libn) . . 424

Carlyle Systems Inc (CA)

BARANOWSKI, George V.
   (Systs Analyst) 55
NASATIR, Marilyn (Systs
   Analysis Dir) 888
SALMON, Stephen R. (Chair of
   the Bd) 1077

Carmel Clay Schs (IN)

DANIELS, Ann A. (Media Dept
   Chair) 273
NIEMEYER, Karen K. (Dir of
   Media Srvs) 903

Carmody & Torrance (CT)

HODGES, Ann C. (Libn) 546

Carnegie Corp of New York (NY)

HAYNES, Patricia (Files &
   Archs Supvsr) 516

Carnegie Endowment for Intl
   Peace (DC)

LOWENTHAL, Jane E. (Libn) . . . 744

Carnegie Foundation
   Advancement (NJ)

GREENBERG, Hinda F. 463

Carnegie Free Lib (PA)

HORVATH, Robert T. (Dir) 561

Carnegie Lib of Pittsburgh (PA)

BLANCHFIELD, Georgette (Pub
   Relations Dir) 103
BROSKY, Catherine M. (Sci &
   Tech Dept Head) 141
CRONEBERGER, Robert B.
   (Dir) 260
DILWORTH, Kirby D. (Asst
   Head) 303
FALGIONE, Joseph F. (Assoc
   Dir) 362
GREEN, Vera A. (Sr Staff Libn) . . 462
KAMPER, Albert F. (Dist Srvs
   Coordntr) 624
KONOPKA, Amelia S. (Chlds
   Libn) 670
LEONARD, Peter C. (Div Head,
   West End Branch) 716
MARON-WOOD, Kathy M.
   (Chlds Libn) 772
PEFFER, Margery E. (Asst
   Head, Sci & Tech Dept) 954
POTTER, Donald C. (Actg Dir) . . . 987
REPP, Robert M. (Spcl Cols &
   Preservation Ofcr) 1024
SAUNDERS, Sharon K. (Libn) . 1084

Carnegie Lib of Pittsburgh (PA)

SCOTT, Lydia E. (Div Head) . . . 1107
SHAPERA, Gladys S. (Asst Dir) 1121
STRAWBRIDGE, Donna L.
   (Staff Libn) 1201
TACK, A C. (Music & Art Dept
   Staff Libn) 1219
THOMPSON, Sandra K.
   (Branch Libn & Div Head) . . 1241

Carnegie Mellon Univ (PA)

EVANS, Nancy H. (Data & Info
   Srvs Mgr) 357
FITZGERALD, Patricia A. (Sci &
   Tech Libs Head) 382
FORD, Sylverna V. (Asst to the
   Dir of Libs) 390
JOHNSEN, Mary C. 602
LINKE, Erika C. (Acqs & Col
   Devlpmnt Libn) 731
MARCHETTI, Honey B. (Sci
   Info Spclst) 768
NAISMITH, Rachael (Ref Libn &
   Pubns Coordntr) 887
PISCIOTTA, Henry A. (Fine Arts
   Libn) 976
RICHARDS, Barbara G. (Technl
   Processes Dept Head) 1028
STIEBER, Michael T. (Archvst &
   Assoc Prof of Biology) 1193
THOMPSON, Dorothea M. (Ref
   Libn) 1239
TINSLEY, Geraldine L. (Comp
   Sci Libn) 1246
WILES-HAFFNER, Meredith L.
   (Sci Info Spclst) 1339

Carnegie-Stout Pub Lib (IA)

CLARK, Maeve K. (Asst Dir &
   Head of Adult Srvs) 217
METZGER, Eva C. (Pres) 829

Carolina Library Services Inc (NC)

FISH, Paula H. (Libn) 380

Carolina Power & Light Co (NC)

SANDS, George A. (Lib Admin) 1081

Caroline County Pub Lib (MD)

DUFORE, Thomas H. (Corp Dir
   of Compensation) 324

Carondelet Health Services Inc (AZ)

CARRINGTON, Virginia F.
   (Eductnl Consult) 186

Carrington Co (CT)

Carrizo Springs Independent Sch
   District (TX)

POWELL, Mary E. (Libn &
   Media Spclst) 988

Carroll Coll (WI)

EVANS, Russel C. (Catlg Libn) . . 358
VAN ESS, James E. (Assoc Dir) 1275

Carroll County Board of
   Education (GA)

MITCHELL, Phyllis R. (Media
   Spclst) 849

Carroll County Pub Lib (AR)

STOWE, Jean E. (Libn) 1199

Carroll County Pub Lib (MD)

DAVIS, Denise (Branch Libn) . . . 278
MCCARTY, Emily H. (Spcl Projs
   Coordntr) 795
ROBERTS, Susan P. (Prog
   Coordntr) 1041
WOLF, Dorothy L. (Adult Srvs
   Supvsr) 1360

Carroll County Schools (MS)

NEILL, Laquita B. (Media Dir) . . . 892

The Carroll Group Inc (IL)

CARROLL VIRGO, Julie (VP) . . . 187
VIRGO, Julie A. (Vice Pres &
   Treasurer) 1285

Carroll Independent Sch District (TX)

BROWN, Judith A. (Dist Libn) . . . 145

Carrollton-Farmers Branch (TX)

BLAIR, Elaine K. (Libn) 102

Carson-Newman Coll (TN)

SELF, George A. (Circ Libn) . . . 1113
SNODDERLY, Louise D. (Perdcl
   Libn) 1163
STURM, H P. (Med Libn) 1205
URENECK, Dolores (Lib Mgr) . . 1269

Carson-Tahoe Hospital (NV)

Carter-Wallace Inc (NJ)

Carthage Central Schs (NY)

MOSES, Camelia T. (Elem Sch
   Libn & Media Spclst) 871

Carthage Pub Lib (IL)

ROBISON, Diana E. (Dir & Libn) 1045

Caruso Associates Inc (PA)

CARUSO, Nicholas C. (VP &
   Treas) 190

Carver Associates (NY)

CARVER, Mary (Owner & Pres) . 191

Cary Medical Center (ME)

COTE-THIBODEAU, Donna E.
   (Med Libn) 249

Cary Memorial Lib (MA) HILTON, Robert C. (Lib Dir) 541
MCCARTHY, Germaine A. (Media Spclst, Coordntr) 794

Case Western Reserve Univ (OH) BALCAS, Georgianne (Music Lib Dir) 50
BELL, Gladys S. (Database Ref Srvs Coordntr) 77
BENTLEY, Stella (Asst Dir for Pub Srvs & Col Mgmt) 83
BOBICK, James E. (Assoc Dir of Libs) 108
CHESHIER, Robert G. (Lib Dir) .. 206
COTE, Susan J. (Dir of Univ Libs) 249
HANSON, Norma S. (Spcl Cols Head) 498
HARRISON, Dennis I. (Univ Archvst) 506
LEDOUX, Mary E. (AV & Ref Libn) 709
LEVINE, Lillian S. (Extramural Coordntr) 720
MAHOVLIC, Leanne M. (Circuit Libn) 761
PINCHES, Mary F. (Assoc Prof Emeritus and Libn) 974
RAY, Laura E. (Neomac Libn) .. 1011
RICHMOND, Phyllis A. (Prof Emeritus) 1030
ROBSON, Timothy D. (Bibgph Srvs Acting Head) 1045
STANLEY, Jean B. (Col Mgmt and Ref Libn) 1180
WELLS, Catherine A. (Pub Srvs Libn) 1322

Cass County Lib (MI) FEDEROWSKI, Marjorie S. (Dir) . 368
Cass County Pub Lib (MO) FRANKLIN, Jill S. (Dir) 397
Cassar Technical Services (PA) CASSAR, Ann (Freelance Indxr) . 193
WIDLUND, Harriet L. (Indxr) ... 1336
Casson Calligaro & Mutryn (DC) JOHNSON, Maria S. (Law Libn) . 607
Castle Junior Coll (NH) BRANSWELL, Sr M. (Jr Coll Libn) 129
Castleton State Coll (VT) LUZER, Nancy H. (Ref Libn) 750
Castro County (TX) AUTRY, Brick (Dir) 41
HOWELL, Gladys M. (Asst Dir) . 565
Catalina Foothills Sch District (AZ) DOOLEY, Sally J. (Sch Libn) ... 312
Catalyst (NY) CROCKER, Susan O. (Info Ctr Dir) 259
Catawba County Pub Lib System (NC) PRITCHARD, John A. (Dir of Lib Scis) 994
Cate Sch (CA) ALLABACK, Patricia G. (Libn) 13
Cathedral-Carmel Sch (LA) LONG, Marilyn B. (Sch Libn) 739
Cathedral High Sch (CA) GERARD, Sandra C. (Libn) 428
Catherine McAuley Health Center (MI) DEY, Anita C. (Asst Libn) 298
LANSDALE, Metta T. (Lib Srvs Mgr) 696
MARTIN, Patricia W. (Asst Libn) . 777
Catholic Archives of Texas (TX) BRYSON, Gary B. (Archvst) 152
Catholic Bishop of Chicago (IL) GARBIN, Angelo U. (Pastor) 417
Catholic Diocese of Jackson (MS) BOECKMAN, Frances B. (Archvst) 109
Catholic Diocese of Mobile (AL) ROBINSON, Gayle N. (Sch Media Spclst) 1044
Catholic Diocese of Rochester (NY) MCNAMARA, Robert F. (Archvst) 816
Catholic Diocese of Wilmington (DE) TRIBOLETTI, Kathleen (Resource Dir) 1256
Catholic Lib Association (PA) CORRIGAN, John T. (Exec Dir) . 247
CORRINGAN, John T. (Exec Dir) 247
MORGAN, Dorothy H. (Perdcl Indxr) 863
Catholic Med Center of Brooklyn & Queens (NY) WOODS, Regina C. (Med Libs Dir) 1367
Catholic Univ of America (DC) AVERSA, Elizabeth S. (Visiting Asst Prof) 41
BELLARDO, Trudi (Asst Prof) 78
CORTEZ, Edwin M. (Assoc Prof) 248

Catholic Univ of America (DC) HORNE, Esther E. 560
PREER, Jean L. (Asst Prof) 990
ROVELSTAD, Mathilde V. (Prof of Lib Sci) 1062
STANN, Patsy H. (Head) 1180
STONE, Elizabeth W. (Prof Emeritus) 1197
TOOHEY, Anne K. (Ref Libn) .. 1250
Catholic Univ of Puerto Rico (PR) DELGADO-NUNEZ, Milton (Libn I) 289
GUILLEMARD DE COLON, Teresita (Ref Libn) 476
MEJILL-VEGA, Gregorio (Catlgr) 822
PADUA, Flores N. (Law Lib Dir) . 934
RODRIGUEZ, Vidalina (Head of Puerto Rico Col) 1048
SANTIAGO, Maria (Acqs Law Libn) 1082
Catlin Gabel Sch (OR) KENNEY, Ann J. (Libn) 641
Catonsville Community Coll (MD) COOK, Daraka S. (Pub Srvs Libn) 239
HILL, Suzanne P. (Dir of Lib Srvs) 541
PECK, Shirley S. (Pub Relations Coordntr) 953
Cayuga Community Coll (NY) LOLLIS, Martha J. (Technl Srvs Libn) 738
MICHAEL, Douglas O. (Dir of Learning Resrcs Ctr) 831
CBH Publishing Inc (IL) HAAS, Carolyn B. (Author, Consult) 480
CBN Univ (VA) KIEWITT, Eva L. (Assoc Dean of Libs) 647
LEHMAN, Lois J. (Dean of Libs) . 713
SIVIGNY, Robert J. (Ref Libn) .. 1144
WELSH, Eric L. (Law Ref Libn) . 1323
CBS Inc (NY) D'ALLEYRAND, Marc R. (Dir, Records Mgmt) 270
KAPNICK, Laura B. (Dir) 626
SALZ, Kay (Deputy Archvst) ... 1078
WOLOZIN, Sara (Mgr) 1362
CCH Computax Inc (CA) PHILLIPS, Clifford R. (Lib Mgr) .. 968
CCM Associates (CA) MACAULEY, C C. (Pres) 754
CCX Direct Marketing Network (AR) WOMBLE, Jim (Executive VP) . 1362
CDB Enterprises Inc (MD) BATTY, Charles D. (Pres) 65
CDT Inc (AZ) SCHULTZ, Michael W. (Pres) .. 1102
CEAC Computers Inc (VA) KAISER, Donald W. (Mgr Customer Support Eastern US) 622
Cecil Community Coll (MD) DENNEY, Christine A. (Asst Libn) 292
Cecil County Pub Lib (MD) BRAMMER, Linda A. (Dir) 127
O'BRIEN, Lee A. (Asst Adminstr) 914
Cecil County Pub Schs (MD) THOMAS, Fred (Media Spclst & Dir) 1236
CECM (PQ) LAPOINTE, Georgette (Dir) 697
CECV (PQ) VAILLANCOURT, Alain (Archvst) 1270
Cedar Crest and Muhlenberg Colls (PA) BAHR, Alice H. (Proj & Online Syst Libn) 45
Cedar Falls High Sch (IA) KOLLASCH, Matthew A. (Lib Media Spclst) 669
Cedar Rapids Community Sch District (IA) MCGREW, Linda L. (Elem Sch Lib Media Spclst) 808
WRIGHT, Dian A. (Media Spclst) 1371
Cedar Rapids Gazette (IA) JANUS, Bridget M. (Libn & Bk Edit) 594
Cedar Rapids Medical Education Program (IA) NELSON, Donald A. (Asst Dir) .. 893
Cedar Rapids Pub Lib (IA) DAVENPORT, Ronald D. (Ref Libn) 276
HAYSLETT, Dawn C. (Adult Srvs Head) 517

Cedarburg Pub Schs (WI) — PITEL, Vonna J. (H S Lib Media Dir, Dist Coordntr) 976

Cedars-Sinai Medical Center (CA) — GREEN, Ellen W. (Dir of Libs) . . 461

Cedarville Coll (OH) — BROWN, Stephen P. (Assoc Dir of Lib Srvs) 147

Centenary Coll (NJ) — ACKROYD-KELLY, Elaine S. (Techni Srvs Libn) 4
STEEN, Carol N. (Lrng Resrcs Dir) 1184

Centennial Coll of Applied Arts & Tech (ON) — WOOD, Ronald P. (Dir) 1365

Centennial Sch District (PA) — FRENCH, Janet D. (Lib Coordntr) 402

Ctr de Recherche Industrielle du Quebec (PQ) — FLORIAN, Trudel (Chief of Documtn Group) 385
TRUDEL, Florian (Documtn Ctr Mgr) 1259

Ctr for Advanced Study in Behavioral Sci (CA) — AMARA, Margaret F. (Libn) 19

Center for Business Research (NY) — COOPER, Catherine M. (Libn) . . 242

Center for Creative Leadership (NC) — HARDIE, Karen R. (Ref Libn) . . . 499

Center for Creative Photography (AZ) — RULE, Amy E. (Photographic Archs Libn) 1067

Center for Environmental Information Inc (NY) — STOSS, Frederick W. (Mgr of Info Srvs) 1198

Center for Forensic Economic Studies (PA) — DEWANE, Kathleen M. (Info Mgr) 298

Ctr for Holocaust Std Documtn & Research (NY) — GUREWITSCH, Bonnie (Libn & Archvst) 478

Center for Naval Analyses (VA) — HANNA, Jill C. (Dir of Info Srvs) . 496

Center for Neurological Services (FL) — WHITESIDE, Lee A. (Libn) 1333

Center for Research Libs (IL) — HELGE, Brian L. (Catlgng Dept Head) 524
NARU, Linda A. 888
PETERSEN, Karla D. (Dir Technl Srvs Div) 962
SIMPSON, Donald B. (Pres) . . . 1141

Center for the Gifted (MI) — HALSTED, Judith W. (Eductnl Consult) 490

Ctr Hospitalier Notre-Dame-de-la-Merci (PQ) — TESSIER, Mario C. (Med Libn) . 1233

Ctr of Information & Land Documentation (CUB) — ASIS, Moises (Info Sci Spclst & Analyst) 36

Centers for Disease Control (GA) — STANSELL, Janet S. (Technl Info Spclst) 1181

Central America Resource Center (TX) — MCCANN, Charlotte P. (Refugee Legal Support Srv Coordntr) 793

Central Am Research Inst for Industry (GUA) — MARBAN, Ricio (Documtn & Info Div) 768

Central and South West Services (TX) — WHISMAN, Loyse B. (Libn) . . . 1329

Central Arkansas Lib System (AR) — KASTANOTIS, William C. (Ref Srvs Head) 629
MARTIN, Rosemary S. (Dir) 778
RAZER, Robert L. (Technl Srvs Head) 1012

Central Catholic High Sch (IL) — JOHNSON, Keran C. (Libn & Media Spclst) 606

Central Catholic High Sch (OH) — MOHLER, Dorothy C. (Lib Media Spclst) 852

Central Coll (IA) — CAMP, Emily E. (Ref Libn) 175

Central Coll (KS) — MCIRVIN, Jane P. (Lib Dir) 809

Central Columbia Sch District (PA) — FROST, Rebecca H. (Elem Lib Media Spclst) 406

Central Connecticut State Univ (CT) — KASCUS, Marie A. (Serials Dept Head) 628
PACKER, Joan G. (Head Ref Libn) 934
TEMPLE, Leroy E. (Dir of Media Srvs) 1230

Central DuPage Hospital (IL) — ROWE, Dorothy B. (Libn) 1062

Central High Sch (CT) — WARAKSA, Raymond P. (Lib Media Spclst) 1303

Central Iowa Regional Lib (IA) — HILL, Fay G. (Ref & Resrch Libn) 539

Central Kansas Lib System (KS) — SWAN, James A. (Adminstr) . . . 1213

Central Maine Medical Center (ME) — GREVEN, Maryanne L. (Lib Dir) . 467

Central Maine Power Co (ME) — KING, Alan S. (Supvsr of Lib Srvs) 650

Central Massachusetts Regional Lib Syst (MA) — CHAMBERLAIN, Ruth B. (Regnl Adminstr) 197

Central Methodist Coll (MO) — HOCHSTETLER, Donald D. (Pub Srvs Libn) 545

Central Michigan Univ (MI) — MULLIGAN, William H. (Dir) 877
SHIRLEY, David B. (Docums Libn) 1131
TIMBERS, Jill G. (Ref Libn & Biblgphr) 1245
WEATHERFORD, John W. (Libs Dir) 1311

Central Michigan Univ (VA) — KINGSLEY, Marcia S. (Regnl Libn) 652

Central Mississippi Regional Lib System (MS) — JOHNSON, Max C. (Technl Srvs Coordntr) 607

Central Missouri State Univ (MO) — GILBERT, Ophelia R. (Chlds & Yng Peoples Libn) 434
HELMICK, Aileen B. (Assoc Prof & Dept Chair) 525
HUND, Flower L. (Bus & Econ Libn) 574
NIEMEYER, Mollie M. (Catlg Libn) 903
SADLER, Philip A. (Assoc Prof, Chlds Lit) 1073
SCHELL, Rosalie F. (Assoc Dir) 1091
SLATTERY, Charles E. (Humanities Libn & Asst Prof) 1148
WALKER, Stephen R. (Catlgr) . 1296
WHITE, D J. (Assoc Prof of Engl) 1330

Central New York Lib Resources Council (NY) — SMITHEE, Jeannette P. (Asst Dir) 1161
WASHBURN, Keith E. (Exec Dir) 1307

Central Oregon Community Coll (OR) — FISCHER, Karen (Dir of Lib & Media Srvs) 379
HENDERSON, Carol G. (Faculty Libn) 526

Central Pennsylvania District Lib (PA) — WOLFE, Gary D. (Dist Ctr Adminstr) 1360

Central Piedmont Community Coll (NC) — OPLINGER, Mary P. (Lib Srvs Dir) 925

Central Rappahannock Regional Lib (VA) — FARR, Patricia A. (Yng Adult Coordntr) 365
VANDERBERG, E S. (Head of Ref Dept) 1273

Central Regional Education Center (NC) — BRADBURN, Frances B. (Sch Media Progs Coordntr) 125

Central Sch District (NY) — MINEMIER, Betty M. (Sch Lib Media Spclst) 845

Central State Griffin Memorial Hospital (OK) — PIERCE, Shirley M. (Med Libn) . . 972

Central State Univ (OK) — ALSWORTH, Frances W. (Lib Media Educ Assoc Prof) 18
CURTIS, Ronald A. (Technl Srvs Asst Dir) 267
RYLANDER, Carolyn S. (Head of Catlgng) 1072

Central Suffolk Hospital (NY) — KIRSCH, Anne S. (Med Libn) . . . 655

Central Texas Coll (NY) — SIEBL, Linda M. (Libn) 1135

Central Washington Hospital (WA) — BELT, Jane (Med Libn & Contng Educ Coordntr) 78

Central Washington Univ (WA) — ALEXANDER, Malcolm D. (Assoc Prof & Head of Ref) . . . 12
DOI, Makiko (Serials Libn, Assoc Prof) 309

Central Washington Univ (WA)
SCHNEIDER, Frank A. (Lib Srvs Dean) 1097
VILLAR, Susanne P. (Assoc Prof, Govt Docums Libn) . . . 1284
YEH, Thomas Y. (Dept Head) . . 1379

Central Wesleyan Coll (SC)
SABINE, Davida M. (Asst Libn) . 1072

Centrale des Bibliotheques (PQ)
PELLETIER, Rosaire (Docums Analyst & Evaluator) 955

Centre d'Animation, de Developpement (PQ)
BRETON, Lise (Libn) 133

Centre Doc (PQ)
PARE, Gilles G. (Le Devoir) 940

Centre for Christian Studies (ON)
TELFORD, Shelagh S. (Libn) . . 1230

Centre Hospitalier Cote-des-Neiges (PQ)
JUNEAU, Jocelyne B. (Chief Libn) 620

Centre Hospitalier Hotel-Dieu Sherbrooke (PQ)
FONTAINE, Nicole (Documtn Technician) 388

Centre Hospitalier Robert-Giffard (PQ)
PLAMONDON, Yolande M. (Lib Chief) 977

Centre Hospitalier St-Joseph (PQ)
DE-ROUYN, Solange (Head of Lib Srvs) 294

Centre Marie-Vincent (PQ)
BAZINET, Jeanne (Libn) 68

Centro Adventista de Estudios Superiores (CSR)
MOSS, Loretta E. (Lib Dir) 872

Century Companies of America (IA)
RIEKEN, Marietta K. (Libn) 1033

CER Corp (NV)
JACKSON, Ella J. (Libn) 587

Certaintaid Corp (PA)
RAC-FEDORIJCZUK, Karola C. (Libn & Records Mgr) 1001

Cetus Corp (CA)
KARCHER, Tracey L. (Database Adminstr) 627
POKLAR, Mary J. (Scintfc Info Spclst) 980

CFM Documentazione (ITL)
FABRE DE MORLHON, Christiane (Mgr) 360

CFS Continental Inc (IL)
DEPKE, Robert W. (Resrch Srvs Mgr) 293

CFSSCK (CA)
LEE, Myung J. (Asst Ref Lib) . . . 711

CGS (WA)
STOCK, Carole G. (Self-employed) 1195

Chabot Coll (CA)
BUTLER, David W. (Assoc Dean of Instrc) 166
LUCAS, Linda L. (Asst Dean of Instrc, Lrng Resrcs) 746
SASSE, Margo (Catlgr) 1083

Chadron Pub Schs (NE)
HAMMITT, Margaret R. (Elem Libn & Media Spclst) 493

Chadron State Coll (NE)
BRENNAN, Terrence F. (Dir, Lib Srvs) 133
SHRADER, Juanita J. (Lib Asst) 1133

Chadwyck-Healey Inc (VA)
HAMILTON, Wellington M. (Vice Pres & Exec Edit) 492
SEVERTSON, Susan M. (Pres) . 1117

Challenge House (NC)
FOREMAN, Kenneth J. (Exec Edit) 390

Chamberlain Hrdlicka White Johnson et al (TX)
TRAFFORD, Susan M. (Lib Dir) 1253

Chamberlain Manufacturing Corp (IL)
CARTER, Ida (Technl Libn) 189

Chamberlayne Junior Coll (MA)
FRIEND, Ann S. (Libn) 404

Chaminade-Julienne High Sch (OH)
DISTEFANO, Marianne (Libn) . . 305

Champaign Pub Lib & Information Center (IL)
MCCABE, Ronald B. (Lib Dir) . . 793

Champion International Corp (CT)
COLUCCI, Mildred A. (Info Spclst) 234

Champion International Corp (NY)
COHEN, Hannah V. (Libn) 228
RIGNEY, Shirley A. (Technl Info Spvsr) 1034

Champlain Coll (VT)
POPECKI, Jeanne M. (Lib Dir) . . 983

Champlain Regional Coll (PQ)
HERLINGER, Peggy (Resrc Ctr Coordntr) 531
PETRYK, Louise O. (Coordntr of Resrc Ctr) 965

Channelmark Corp (CA)
TARTER, Blodwen (Mktg Dir) . . 1224

Chanute Pub Sch (KS)
TUNNELL, Mary D. (Eductnl Media Dir) 1263

Chanute Unified Sch District 413 (KS)
DRUSE, Judith A. (Sch Lib Media Spclst) 321

Chapel Hill Pub Lib (NC)
CAMERON, Mary T. (Chlds Libn) 175

Chapman & Cutler (IL)
KOWALEWSKI, Denis S. (Libn) . 674
STEWART, Jamie K. (Ref Libn) 1192

Chapman Coll (CA)
SHAWL, Janice H. (Assoc Prof) 1124
WILSON, Wayne V. (Dir of the Lib) 1353

Chappaqua Central Sch District (NY)
DI BIANCO, Phyllis R. (Lib Media Spclst) 299

Chappaqua Lib (NY)
PLATT, Mary L. (Ref Libn) 977

Charles A Cannon Memorial Lib (NC)
DILLARD, Thomas W. (Lib Dir) . . 303
HULL, Laurence O. (Ref Libn) . . 572

Charles A Ransom District Lib (MI)
PARK, Janice R. (Dir) 941

Charles Babbage Institute (MN)
BRUEMMER, Bruce H. (Archvst) 149

Charles City Pub Lib (IA)
STARK, Ted (Dir) 1182

Charles County Pub Lib (MD)
TRELEVEN, Richard L. (Branch Chief) 1255

Charles E Merriam Center for Pub Admin (IL)
COATSWORTH, Patricia A. (Lib Dir) 224
GREEN, Randall N. (VP) 462

Charles E Simon & Co (DC)
GRISDELA, Margaret (Chief Exec Ofcr) 471

Charles P Young Management Services (IL)
SMITH, Denis J. (Operator I) . . . 1154

Charles Schlacks Jr Publisher (CA)
SCHLACKS, Charles 1093

Charles Stark Draper Laboratory Inc (MA)
COFFMAN, M H. (Technl Info Ctr Mgr) 227
ROTMAN, Laurie D. (Asst Libn) 1060

Charles Stewart Mott Foundation (MI)
BROWN, Eve C. (Records Mgmt Supvsr) 144

Charleston Carnegie Pub Lib (IL)
MCDOWELL, Myrnella J. (Catlgr) 804

Charleston County Lib (SC)
RAINES, Thomas A. (Deputy Dir) 1004
SINDEL, Amy C. (Ref Dept Libn I) 1143
TROWELL, Amy U. (Actg Libn) . 1258

Charleston County Records Center (SC)
HOLLINGS, Marie F. (Records Mgr) 552

Charleston County Sch District (SC)
BRADLEY, Patricia L. (Sch Lib Media Spclst) 126
MITCHUM, Grace M. (Media Spclst) 850

Charleston Lib Society (SC)
SADLER, Catherine E. (Head Libn) 1073

Charlestown-Clark County Pub Lib (IN)
MCCORMICK, Tamsie (Dir) 799

Charlotte Law Lib Associates (NC)
HANNUM-MCPHERSON, Melissa A. (Law Libn) 497

Charlotte-Mecklenburg Schs (NC)
CARPENTER, Janella A. (Media Spclst) 184
MILLER, Gloria (Lib Supvsr) 838
MASON, Hayden (Libn) 781

Chas T Main Inc (MA)
NEUBERG, Karen S. (Sr Libn) . . 897

Chase Manhattan Bank (NY)
CHASE, William D. (Editor) 203

Chase's Annual Events (MI)

Chatham-Effingham-Liberty Regional Lib (GA)
BROCKMAN, B D. (Branch Libn) 138

Chattanooga-Hamilton County (TN)
GRIFFISS, M K. (Dept of Fine Arts & AV Head) 469
HARTUNG, Nancy F. (Chlds Dept Supvsr) 509
MCFARLAND, Jane E. (Dir) 805

Chautauqua-Cattaraugus Lib System (NY)
HAYNES, Jean (Film & Video Libn) 516
LEE, Sylvia (Automation Coordntr) 711
JOHNSON, G V. (Partner) 604

Checkers Simon & Rosner (IL)
WITT, Susan T. (Libn) 1358

Cheektowaga Central Schs (NY)
USTACH, Joanne B. (Chld's Libn & Asst Branch Mgr) . . . 1270

Cheektowaga Pub Lib (NY)

Chelmsford Pub Lib (MA)
RAUCH, Ellen C. (Dir) 1010

Cheltenham Township Pub Sch District (PA)
LIGGETT, Julie A. (Engl as a Second Lang Tchr) 726

Chemcyclopedia (VA)

Chemical Abstracts Service (OH)

Chemical Bank (NY)

Chem-Nuclear Systems Inc (SC)

Chem Systems Inc (NY)
Chenango Memorial Hospital (NY)
Cherokee County Pub Lib (SC)
Cherokee County Sch System (GA)

Cherokee Regional Lib (GA)
Cherry Creek Pub Schs (CO)

Cherry Hill Free Pub Lib (NJ)
Cheseborough-Ponds Inc (CT)

Cheshire Pub Lib (CT)

Chestatee Regional Lib (GA)
Chester County Hospital (PA)

Chester County Lib & District`
   Center (PA)

Chester County Pub Lib (SC)

Chesterfield County Pub Lib (VA)

Chesterton High Sch (IN)

Chestnut Hill Hospital (PA)
Chestnut Lodge Hospital (MD)
Chevron Chemical Co (CA)
Chevron Corp (CA)

Chevron Environmental Health
   Center Inc (CA)

KUNEY, Joseph H. (Consult &
   Editor) 684
BENINTENDI, Cheri (CAS
   Workshop Coordntr) 81
COPENHAVER, Ida L. (Chem
   Mgr) 244
HODGES, Pauline R. (Asst Libn) . 546
LANGSTAFF, Elizabeth M. 696
LEMASTERS, Joann T. (Sr Syst
   Engineer) 715
MOORE, Maxwell J. (Assoc
   Libn) 860
NICHOL, Marian P. (Asst Mgr) . . 901
NORMORE, Lorraine F. (Resrch
   Scitst) 909
PLATAU, Gerard O. (Sr Asst for
   Editrl Operations) 977
RYERSON, George D. (Sr Edit) 1071
SNIDER, Elizabeth M. (Asst
   Acqs Libn) 1163
STEPP, Dena F. (Product
   Devlpmnt Spclst) 1189
STOBAUGH, Robert E. (Mgr of
   Resrch Dept) 1195
TANNEHILL, Robert S. (Lib
   Srvs Mgr) 1222
WATSON, Judith E. (Sr Editor) . 1309
O'DONNELL, Maureen D. (Libn) . 917
PENNELL, Peggy P. (Libn) 957
KINTNER, Susan B. (Docum Ctl
   Adminstr) 653
GRANDY, Maryann M. 457
SLOCUM, Ann L. (Libn) 1150
EDEN, David E. (Dir) 336
SALTER, Nellie C. (Media
   Spclst) 1077
WOODLEE, Rick G. (Asst Dir) . 1366
BANKHEAD, Elizabeth M. (Lib
   Coordntr) 54
KUAN, Jenny W. (Ref Libn) 681
SUPRYNOWICZ, Mary M.
   (Resrch Libn) 1210
POIRIER, Maria K. (Asst Dir) ... 980
WREGE, Ann S. (Lib Dir) 1370
BRONSON, Diane A. (Asst Dir) . 140
HARRINGTON, Anne W. (Med
   Staff Libn) 503

FISCHER, Anna M. (Head of
   Adult Srvs) 379
KEOGH, Judith L. (Asst Dir for
   Consult Srvs) 643
LINDBERG, Richard L. (Ref
   Libn) 728
SILVER, Diane L. (Col Devlpmnt
   Libn) 1138
MURDOCK, Everlyne K. (Head
   of Adult Srvs) 879
DUNAWAY, Carolyn D. (Technl
   Srvs Libn) 325
WAGENKNECHT, Robert E.
   (Lib Dir) 1291
BECKING, Mara S. (Sch Lib
   Media Spclst) 73
MOWERY, Susan G. (Med Libn) . 874
SMITH, Karen G. (Libn) 1156
LOPEZ, Frank D. (Resrch Libn) . . 741
BROWN, Barbara L. (Libn &
   Catlgr) 142
HERDMAN, Elena (Technl Srvs
   Supvsr) 530
LINDEN, Margaret J. (Mgr) 729
WOO, Winnie H. (Head Catlgr &
   Ref Libn) 1363

BURSON, Sherrie L. (Info
   Analyst) 164
KERNS, John T. (Info Srvs
   Supvsr) 644

Chevron Geoscience (LA)

Chevron Information Technology
   Co (CA)

Chevron Oil Field Research Co (CA)

Chevron Research Co (CA)

Chevron USA Inc (CA)

Chevron USA Inc (TX)

Chi Systems Inc (MI)

Chicago Board of Education (IL)

Chicago Board Options
   Exchange (IL)

The Chicago Defender (IL)

Chicago Historical Society (IL)

Chicago Mercantile Exchange (IL)
Chicago Pub Lib (IL)

ROMALEWSKI, Robert S.
   (Analyst) 1052
STAN, Gail A. (Database
   Coordntr) 1179
COPPIN, Ann S. (Technl Info
   Srvs Supvsr) 245
DESOIER, Jacqueline M. (Technl
   Lib Supvsr) 295
LAMBERT, Nancy (Technl Info
   Analyst) 690
RILEY, Constance L. 1034
WAWRZONEK, Mary S. (Mgr) . 1311
WHITE, Larry R. (Info Analyst) . 1331
O'HEARN, Sarah A. (Technl
   Info Srvs Supvsr) 919
BREWER, Stanley E. (Lib
   Supvsr) 134
RIEMANN, Frederick A. (Chief
   Law Libn) 1033
TERWILLIGER, Doris H.
   (Resrch Libn) 1232
BAKER, Ethelyn J. (Lib Tchr) 48
HANLON, Patricia S. (Tchr &
   Libn) 496
KELLY, Raymond T. (Head
   Libn) 638
MUELLNER, John P. (Head
   Libn) 875
LAGRUTTA, Charles J. (Systs
   Libn) 688
ADKINS, Marjorie R. (Libn
   Newspaper Morgue) 6
EVANS, Linda A. (Assoc Cur) ... 357
MCGILL, Sara L. (Asst Libn) ... 806
MCNEILL, Janice M. (Libn) 816
MOTLEY, Archie (Archvs &
   Manuscripts Cur) 872
RYAN, Diane M. (Photo
   Archvst) 1070
VISKOCHIL, Larry A. (Prints &
   Photographs Cur) 1285
FROST, Bruce Q. (Mgr) 406
AHN, Hyonah K. (AV Srvs
   Head) 8
AUSTIN, Sandra G. (Ref I Libn) .. 40
BROWN, Eva R. (Dir, Multitype
   Lib Syst Devlpmnt) 143
BYRNE, Janice M. (Branch
   Head) 169
CAPANO, Laura M. (Libn 1) ... 179
CARLSON, Claudette J.
   (Branch Head) 182
CLAPP, David F. (Head Libn) ... 215
COBURN, Morton (Lib Plng &
   Bldg Progs Dir) 225
DAVIS, Sandra B. (Ref Asst) ... 281
DAWOOD, Rosemary (Head of
   Lit & Lang Div) 282
DONOVAN, William A. (First
   Asst, Film & Video Ctr) 312
DUFF, John B. (Commissioner) .. 323
FLYNN, Barbara L. (Head,
   Film/Video Center) 386
GOMEZ, Martin J. (Northwest
   Dist Chief) 447
GUSS, Emily R. (Branch Mgr) ... 478
HERNANDEZ, Hector R.
   (Hispanic Srvs Coordntr) 531
HOGAN, Thomas J. (Libn) 549
HUDDLESTON, Marsha E. (Libn
   II, Chlds Srvs) 569
HUSFELDT, Jerry J. (Libn I) ... 578
JAVONOVICH, Kenneth L.
   (Romance Langs Catlgr) 595
JONES, Mary L. (Branch Libn) .. 614
KIM, Chung S. (Branch Head) ... 648
KNOBLAUCH, Mark G. (Technl
   Srvs Div Dir) 665

Chicago Pub Lib (IL)

LOCKRIDGE, Eunice A. (Chlds Libn) 736
MCELWAIN, William (Foreign Lang Sect Head) 804
MEYER, Barbara G. (Branch Head) 829
MILLER, Glenda G. (Libn I) 838
MILLER, Robert (Cur) 841
MOORE, John R. (Engrng Sect Head) 860
MORRISON, Samuel F. (Deputy Commissioner & Chief Libn) .. 868
OAKS, Claire (Resrch Analyst) .. 913
O'SHEA, Cornelius M. (Asst Dir) . 928
REGNER, Erlinda J. (Bus Ref Libn) 1017
REID, Margaret L. (Chief of Southwest Dist) 1019
REID, Peg L. (Southwest Dist Chief) 1019
RICHMOND, Diane A. (Sci & Tech Info Ctr Head) 1030
SADLER, Shirley L. (Libn I) 1073
SCHWEGEL, Richard C. (Head Music Info Ctr) 1105
SCOTT, Alice H. (Deputy Commissioner) 1106
STEELE, Leah J. (Regnl Lib Dir) 1184
STEWART, Richard A. (Head Catlgr) 1193
STRAIT, Constance J. (Recorded Sound Libn) 1199
STROUSE, Roger L. (Libn I) ... 1203
THORNHILL, Robert E. (Libn I) .. 1242
TIBBITS, George D. (Catlgr) ... 1244
TREJO-MEEHAN, Tamiye (Northeast Dist Chief) 1255
TRIMMER, Keith R. (Libn II) ... 1256
TUTEUR, Civia M. (Chld's Libn) 1265
VACCARO, William J. (Asst Head of AV Sect) 1270

Chicago Research & Trading Group Ltd (IL)
REITER, Richard R. (Infor Resrcs Mgr) 1022

Chicago Research Group Inc (IL)
MARSHALL, Deborah M. (Pres) . 774

Chicago Ridge Pub Lib (IL)
LOTZ, Marsha A. (Adult Srvs Libn) 742

Chicago State Univ (IL)
BOLT, Janice A. (Assoc Prof) ... 113
CHANG, Sookang H. (Head) 201
MANCUYAS, Natividad D. (Govt Pubns Libn) 764
MEEKER, Robert B. (Ref Dept Head) 821
MEYER, Beverly R. (Catlgr) 829
MOORE, Annie M. (Interlib Loan Libn) 858
ONGLEY, David C. (Ref Libn) ... 924
PATEL, Jashu (Prof) 947

Chicago Sun Times (IL)
PERLMAN, Michael S. (Syst Libn) 959

Chicago Transit Authority (IL)
CULBERTSON, Lillian D. (Supvsr, Lib Srvs) 263
GENESEN, Judith L. (Info Srvs Dir) 427
KERR, Kevin G. (Records Storage Coordntr) 644

Chicago Tribune (IL)
HUSCHEN, Mary (Resrch Srvs Mgr) 578
JANSSON, John F. (Edit, Info Systs) 594
PAPPALARDO, Marcia J. (Online Mktg Mgr) 939
ROTT, Richard A. (Mgr, Online Systs) 1060

Chickasaw Lib System (OK)
ROBINSON, Joel M. (Dir) 1044

Chief Judge Lake Superior Court (IN)
ENGELBERT, Peter J. (Head Law Libn) 348

Children's Hospital (CO)
KLENK, Anne S. (Med Libn) 660

Children's Hospital (LA)
KELLER, Nancy H. (Med libn) ... 635

Children's Hospital (MA)

Children's Hospital & Medical Center (WA)

Children's Hospital Medical Center (CA)

Children's Hospital Medical Center (OH)

Children's Hospital National Medical Ctr (DC)

Children's Hospital of Eastern Ontario (ON)

Children's Hospital of Michigan (MI)
Children's Hospital of Pittsburgh (PA)
Children's House Inc (NJ)
Children's Literature for Children (GA)
Children's Memorial Hospital (IL)
Children's Museum of Oak Ridge (TN)

Children's Specialized Hospital (NJ)
Chilton Co (PA)
China Evangelical Seminary (TAI)

Chinese Univ of Hong Kong (HKG)

Chinook Regional Lib (SK)
Chipola Junior Coll (FL)

Chippewa Valley Schs (MI)

Choate Hall & Stewart (MA)

Choice Magazine (CT)
Chris Olson & Associates (MD)
Christ Hospital (NJ)

Christ Hospital & Medical Center (IL)
Christ the King Sch (FL)

Christ the King Seminary (NY)

Christian Brothers Coll (TN)
Christian Center Elementary Sch (MA)
Christian Theological Seminary (IN)

Christina Sch District (DE)

Christopher Burns Inc (MA)
Christopher Newport Coll (VA)

Chrysler Corp (MI)

Chrysler Museum (VA)
Chubb & Son Inc (NJ)

Chulalongkorn Univ (THA)

Church & Synagogue Lib Association (OR)
Church Farm Sch (PA)
Church of Jesus Christ Latter-day Saints (UT)

GELLER, Miriam R. (Radiology Dept Libn) 426

TURNER, Tamara A. (Hospital Lib Dir) 1265

SHAPIRO, Leonard P. (Med Libn) 1121

HALIBEY-BILYK, Christine M. (Asst Dir) 486
HILL, Barbarie F. (Dir) 539
STROZIER, Sandra L. (Lib Dir) . 1203

INGERSOLL, Lyn L. (Family Libn) 582

TAYLOR, Margaret P. (Lib Srvs Dir) 1227
KLEIN, Michele S. (Lib Srvs Dir) . 659
SCHEETZ, Mary D. (Info Spclst) 1091
EDELSON, Ken (Editor) 335

NIX, Kemie (Exec Dir) 905
WARD, Meg 1304

ALDERFER, Jane B. (Resrc Coordntr & Libn) 11
GLASSER, Anne (Medical Libn) . 440
SWEELY, Christine A. (Mgr) ... 1214
CHENG, Sheung O. (Libn) 206
WANG, Sin C. (Lib Dir) 1303
WU, Edith Y. (Prob Asst Libn) .. 1373
YEN, David S. (Univ Libn) 1379
KEASCHUK, Michael J. (Dir) ... 633
STABLER, William H. (Lrng Resrcs Ctr Dir) 1177
MATECUN, Marilyn L. (Sch Lib Media Spclst) 783
MURPHY, Eva B. (Libn) 880
BALAY, Robert E. (Ref Edit) 50
OLSON, Christine A. (Principal) .. 922
PANDELAKIS, Helene S. (Libn) . 937
VARGO, Katherine J. (Libn) ... 1278
KELLY, Janice E. (Chief Libn) ... 637
LOPEZ, Deborah A. (Libn, Media Spclst) 741
HAYES, Bonaventure F. (Lib Dir) 515
DENTON, A W. (Dir) 293

BERNSTEIN, D S. (Head Libn) ... 89
GALBRAITH, Leslie R. (Libn, Assoc Prof of Bibl) 413
BROWN, Atlanta T. (Dist Chairperson, Lib Media) 142
MYERS, Victoria B. (Libn & Media Spclst) 885
THORNTON, Alice J. (Libn) ... 1242
BURNS, Christopher (Pres) 162
DANIEL, Mary H. (Ref Srvs Libn) 272
PERECMAN, Carol J. (Mktg Libn) 958
CICCONE, Amy N. (Chief Libn) . 214
LINNAMAA, Mari M. (Libn, Info Spclst) 731
MINAIKIT, Nonglak (Dept of Lib Sci Head) 845

BURSON, Lorraine E. (Exec Dir) . 163
SHAW, Doris G. (Libn) 1123

CASADY, Richard L. (Catlgr II) .. 191
CLEMENT, Charles R. (Catlgng Mgr) 221
CUMMINGS, Christopher H. (Lead Pgmr & Analyst) 264
KIESSLING, Mary S. (Supvsr of Gen Ref) 647

Church of Jesus Christ Latter-day Saints (UT)
MAYFIELD, David M. (Dir) 790
REED, Vernon M. (Lib Systs User Spclst) 1015

Church of the Nazarene Headquarters (MO)
INGERSOL, Robert S. (Archs Dir) 582

Church World Service (IN)
HUGHES, Rolanda L. (Media Ctr Dir) 572

Churches of Christ in Australia (AUS)
SMITH, Lindsay L. (Libn) 1157

CH2M Hill Inc (FL)
PROCTOR, Dixie L. (Sr Record Mgmt Spclst & Libn) 994

CH2M Hill Inc (OR)
O'BRIEN, Mary C. (Centl Lib Srvs Coord) 915
SHANNON, Norma M. (Mgr of Records & Libs) 1120

CH2M Hill Inc (VA)
MONTGOMERY, Suzanne L. (Records & Libs Mgr) 856

Ciba-Corning Diagnostics (OH)
MULDER, Marjorie M. (Libn) .. 876

CIBA-GEIGY Corp (NC)
JACQUES, Eunice L. (Libn) ... 591
THOMAS, Katharine S. (Info Scientist/Libn) 1237

CIBA-GEIGY Corp (NJ)
WAITE, William F. (Srch & Archvl Srvs Mgr) 1293

CIBA-GEIGY Pharmaceuticals Co (NJ)
JUTERBOCK, Deborah K. (Lit Scitst) 620

Cicero Pub Lib (IL)
MALLER, Mark P. (Head of Ref Srvs) 763
WEBER, Julie A. (Ref Libn) ... 1314

CIGNA Corp (CT)
BROQUE, Suzanne (Law Libn) .. 141
CHEESEMAN, Bruce S. (Assoc Archvst) 204
LIU, Jessie (Bus Resrc Ctr Unit Asst Mgr) 734

Cincinnati Ctr for Devlpmntl Disorders (OH)
GILROY, Dorothy A. (Chief Resrch Libn) 437

Cincinnati Law Lib Association (OH)
FRENCH, Thomas R. (Administrv Asst Libn) 402

Cincinnati Milacron Inc (OH)
CLASPER, James W. (Corporate Libn & Supvsr) ... 219
PATIENCE, Alice (Mgr, Info Resrc Ctr) 947

Cincinnati Pub Schs (OH)
MC NAIR, Marian B. (Sch Libs K-12 Supvsr) 815
SHIVERDECKER, Darlene J. (Libn) 1132

Cincinnati Technical Coll (OH)
TUCKER, Debbie B. (Coordntr, Info Srvs) 1261

Cineaste (NY)
CROWDUS, Gary A. (Editor) ... 261

Cinematheque Quebecoise (PQ)
BEAUCLAIR, Rene (Head Libn) .. 70

Circle District Historical Society (AK)
OAKES, Patricia A. (Histn & Archvst) 913

Circleville Bible Coll (OH)
BAILEY, Lois E. (Head Libn) 46

The Citadel (SC)
MAYNARD, James E. (Coordntr of User Srvs) 790
WOOD, Richard J. (Lib Srvs Dir) 1365

Citibank North America (NY)
SANCHEZ, Eliana P. (Libn & Asst Mgr) 1079
WILKINS, Peggy (VP) 1340

Citicorp (NY)
PINEDA, Conchita J. (Mgr) ... 974

Citicorp Development (NY)
GREENBERG, Walter E. (VP) ... 463

Citicorp Electronic Securities (NY)
CIRILLO, Kenneth 215

Citicorp Information Business (NY)
GREENHOUSE, Lee R. (Vice Pres) 464

Citizens General Hospital (PA)
TEOLIS, Marilyn G. (Libn) 1231

City & Borough of Juneau Sch District (AK)
BELFLOWER, Elizabeth D. (Libn) 76

City and County of Denver (CO)
GEHRES, Eleanor M. (Western Hist Dept Mgr) 425
GIGNAC, Solange G. (Horticultural Libn) 433

City and County of Grand Forks (ND)
STEMME, Virginia L. (Chlds Libn) 1186

City & County of Honolulu (HI)
AKAO, Pamela S. (Head Libn) 9

City & County of San Francisco (CA)
GUARINO, John P. (Libn I) 475
SCHMIDT, Robert R. (Sr Libn II) 1096

City Coll of San Francisco (CA)
FEW, John E. (Lib Info Tech Chair) 374
SCHOLAND, Julia E. (Libn, Lib Automation) 1098
SMYTH, Mary B. (Lib Mgr) 1162

City Coll of the City Univ of New York (NY)
ALLENTUCK, Marcia E. (Prof of Hist & Art) 16
CLINE, Herman H. (Asst Prof & Ref Libn) 222
DOUGLAS, Jacqueline A. (Serials Libn) 314
DUNLAP, Barbara J. (Archs & Spcl Cols Chief) 326
FRANKLIN, Laurel F. (Head of Catlg Div) 398
HINDS, Vira C. (Dir of Affirmative Action) 542
KUHNER, Robert A. (Lib Plng Officer) 683
MOORE, Jane R. (Prof & Chief Libn) 859
PERKUS, Paul C. (Libn & Archvst) 959
RAJEC, Elizabeth M. (Prof & Head of Acqs) 1004
WRIGHT, Sylvia H. (Assoc Prof, Chief, Architecture Lib) 1373

City Colleges of Chicago (IL)
LOCKE, John W. (Lib Dept Chairman) 736

City of Abilene (TX)
WOODALL, Cynthia P. (City Libn) 1365

City of Albany (OR)
SUGGS, Wayne L. (Lib Dir) .. 1206

City of Alma (PQ)
BOUCHARD, Martin (Lib Dir) ... 118

City of Alva (OK)
THORNE, Larry R. (Head Libn) . 1242

City of Amarillo (TX)
DOYLE, Patricia A. (Acqs Libn) .. 317
SNELL, Marykay H. (Dir of Lib Srvs) 1163
THOMAS, Greg (Asst City Libn) 1236

City of Appleton (WI)
VIGNOVICH, Ray L. (Asst Dir for Prog) 1284

City of Arlington (TX)
LEATHERMAN, Donald G. (Outreach Dept Head) 707

City of Auburn Hills (MI)
EL MOUCHI, Joan S. (Lib Dir) .. 346

City of Aylmer (PQ)
MACKEY, Laurette (Mgr) 756

City of Baltimore (MD)
DULL, Karen A. (Ref Libn) 324
LEDBETTER, Sherry H. (Bus, Sci & Tech Dept Head) 708
NOTOWITZ, Joshua D. (Extension Libn) 910

City of Baton Rouge (LA)
HASCHAK, Paul G. (Ref & Catlg Libn) 510

City of Bayonne (NJ)
HALASZ, Etelka B. (Principal Libn) 484

City of Baytown (TX)
KLEHN, Victoria L. (Libn) 658

City of Beaconsfield (PQ)
BADGER, Carole (Chlds Libn) 44

City of Bellaire (TX)
ALFORD, Mary A. (Asst Dir) 13

City of Bellevue (NE)
YAPLE, Marilyn V. (Lib Dir) ... 1378

City of Berkeley (CA)
JACKA, David C. (Dir) 586
VANYOUNG, Sayre (Ref Libn) . 1278

City of Berkley (MI)
KAPUR, Geraldine P. (Libn) 626

City of Boucherville (PQ)
MORSE, Celia B. (Lib Dir) 869

City of Boulder (CO)
DUBOIS, Florian (Lib Dir) 322
BRADDOCK, Virginia O. (Coordntr, Municipal Govt Ref Ctr) 125
GRALAPP, Marcelee G. (Lib Dir) 457
VARNES, Richard S. (Operations Dir) 1279
VOLC, Judith G. (Chlds Srvs Coordntr) 1287

City of Boynton Beach (FL)
COUP, William A. (Ref Libn) 251
FARACE, Virginia K. (Lib Dir) .. 363

City of Brentwood (TN)
NORTON, Tedgina (Lib Dir) 910

City of Bridgeport (CT)
PALMQUIST, David W. (City Records Mgt) 937

City of Bristol (CT)
CALLAHAN, Helen H. (Readers' Advisor) 173
WILSON, Eleanor L. (Head of Technl Processes) 1350

City of Bryan (TX)
MOUNCE, Clara B. (City Libn) . . 873

City of Burbank (CA)
BROWNE, Jeri A. (Records Mgmt Coordntr) 148
MICHAELS, Joan M. (Lib Asst) . . 832
RICHARDS, Marcia M. (Lib Dir) . 1028

City of Burlingame (CA)
BERGSING, Patricia M. (City Libn) 87

City of Calexico (CA)
MERKLEY, John P. (Dir) 826

City of Calgary (AB)
KLUMPENHOUWER, Richard (Archvst) 662

City of Cambridge (MA)
SAKEY, Joseph G. (Dir of Libs & Comms) 1076

City of Cannon Falls (MN)
WOLF, Joy G. (Lib Dir) 1360

City of Carlsbad (CA)
KENNEDY, Charlene F. (Head Ref Libn) 640

City of Charleston (SC)
MCCOY, Gail (Records Retention Supvsr) 799

City of Chesapeake (VA)
FOREHAND, Margaret P. (Dir of Libs & Resrch Srvs) 390
REID, Kendall M. (Ref Libn) . . . 1018

City of Chicago (IL)
BENIGNO, Linda J. (Chief of Ref Srvs) 80
STEWART, James A. (Govt Pubns Libn) 1192
TIWANA, Shah J. (Libn III) 1247

City of Chula Vista (CA)
BLUE, Margaret L. (Principal Libn & Head of Technl Srv) . . 107
BROWN, Paula D. (Head of Adult & Info Srvs) 146

City of Clearwater (FL)
MIELKE, Linda (Lib Dir) 833

City of Cleveland (TX)
SMITH, Barbara F. (Cnty Certftn Lib Dir) 1152

City of Commerce (CA)
CONOVER, Robert W. (Dir of Lib Srvs) 238

City of Coolidge (AZ)
FRANSEN, Gary K. (Lib Dir) 398

City of Coppel (TX)
BIGGERSTAFF, Judi L. (Lib Dir) . . 95

City of Corpus Christi (TX)
GEORGE, Aubrey W. (Ref Head & Info Srvs) 427

City of Corvallis (OR)
SALMON, Kay H. (Lib Dir) 1077

City of Council Bluffs (NE)
BERNARDI, John V. (Ref Libn) . . . 88

City of Crete (NE)
HARDING, Margaret A. (Dir) 500

City of Davenport (IA)
MONTGOMERY, David E. (City Archvst & Spcl Col Supvsr) . . 856

City of Dearborn (MI)
MARQUIS, Rollin P. (City Libn) . . 773

City of Denton (TX)
ORR, Joella A. (Lib Dir) 926

City of Detroit (MI)
MOSS, Josievet (Affirmative Action Coordntr) 872

City of Dorval (PQ)
BOUMAN, Judith C. (Head Libn) . 119

City of Dover (DE)
MILLER, Paula J. (Lib Dir) 841

City of Dover (NH)
TREMBLAY, Carolyn B. (Circ Libn) 1255

City of Dubuque (IA)
MINTER, Elizabeth D. (Lib Dir) . . 846

City of Duluth (MN)
SCHROEDER, Janet K. (Dir) . . . 1100

City of Dunedin (FL)
NOAH, Julia T. (Info Srvs Dir) . . . 906
SKUBISH, Barbara E. (Dir of Adult Srvs) 1147

City of East Detroit (MI)
TODD, Suzanne L. (Ref Libn) . . 1248

City of East Providence (RI)
CAIRNS, Roberta A. (Dir of Lib Srvs) 171

City of Edinburg (TX)
HOPPER, Lorraine E. (Bilingual Ref Libn) 558
NANCE, Betty L. (Lib Srvs Dir) . . 887
MARTIN, Ann F. (City Libn) 775

City of El Paso de Robles (CA)
City of El Segundo (CA)
KIRBY, Barbara L. (Lib Dir) 653

City of Elmhurst (IL)
STEWART, Virginia R. (Dir) 1193

City of Englewood (CO)
WINKLE, Sharon L. (Lib Dir) . . . 1355

City of Escondido (CA)
BRIDGMAN, Amy R. (Libn) 135

City of Eugene (OR)
HILDEBRAND, Carol I. (Asst City Libn) 538
MEEKS, James D. (City Libn) . . . 821

City of Evanston (IL)
WRIGHT, Donald E. (Dir) 1371

City of Fort Atkinson (WI)
GATES, Mary D. (Dir) 422

City of Fort Worth (TX)
BRACEY, Ann E. (Pub Srvs Coordntr) 124

City of Frankenmuth (MI)
MCEWEN, Mary A. (Libn) 804

City of Fullerton (CA)
JOHNSON, Carolyn E. (City Libn) 602

City of Garland (TX)
CRABB, Elizabeth A. (Coordntr) . 254

City of Glendale (AZ)
MOSLEY, Shelley E. (Lib Mgr) . . 872

City of Glendale (CA)
FISH, Marie (Lib Srvs Supvsr) . . . 380
RAMSEY, Jack (Dir of Libs) . . . 1006

City of Grand Haven (MI)
AMES, Mark J. (Lib Dir) 20

City of Grapevine (TX)
ROBERSON, Janis L. (Lib Dir) . . 1039

City of Greensboro (NC)
VIELE, George B. (Lib Dir) 1283

City of Guthrie (OK)
ROYSTER, Peggy K. (Dir) 1063

City of Hamilton Board of Education (ON)
PAPOUTSIS, Fotoula (Asst Libn) 939

City of Harlingen (TX)
MILLS, Helen L. (Lib Dir) 844

City of Harper Woods (MI)
ARRIVEE, Sally D. (Dir) 34

City of Hayward (CA)
EAGER, Nancy A. (Supvsng libn) 331

City of Hialeah (FL)
COMRAS, Rema (Lib Dir) 235

City of High Point (NC)
AUSTIN, Neal F. (Dir of Lib Srvs) 40
DORNBERGER, Julie L. (Chlds Srvs Head) 313
HAWN, Elizabeth L. (Adult Srvs Head) 514
MORRIS, R P. (Asst Dir of Libs) . 867
NDENGA, Viola W. (Dir) 890

City of Highland Park (MI)
City of Hope National Medical Center (CA)
CARRIGAN, John L. (Info Spclst) 186

City of Houston (TX)
DEPETRO, Thomas G. (Libn II) . . 293
RADOFF, Leonard I. (Chief, Branch Srvs) 1002

City of Hudson (WI)
TIETZ, Kathleen E. (Lib Dir) . . . 1244

City of Hull (PQ)
BOYER, Denis P. (Dir) 123
CHEVRIER, Francine (Asst Dir) . . 207

City of Irving (TX)
LEVINE, Harriet L. (Info Srvs Libn) 720
MARION, Gail E. (Ref Libn) 770

City of Jacksonville (FL)
EASON, Lisa H. (Dir) 332

City of Keller (TX)
NOZICK, Sandy B. (Lib Dir) 911

City of King (CA)
City of Kingsport (TN)
FANSLOW, Malinda C. (Libn) . . . 363

City of Kirbyville (TX)
SAULSBURY, Margie M. (Lib Dir) 1084

City of Kirkland (PQ)
CLEMENT, Clarie (Lib Dir) 221

City of La Baie (PQ)
LEBEL, Anne (Dir) 707

City of La Grande (OR)
ELAM, Barbara J. (Lib Dir) 341

City of La Marque (TX)
NEALE, Marilee (Dir) 891

City of Lamar (CO)
BURNETT, James H. (Dir) 161

City of Largo (FL)
MURPHEY, Barbara A. (Lib Dir) . 880

City of Las Cruces (NM)
DRESP, Donald F. (Lib Dir) 319

City of Las Vegas (NV)
ORTIZ, Diane (Mgmt Analyst) . . . 927

City of Le Gardeur (PQ)
MARTIN, Ginette (Lib Dir) 776

City of Levis (PQ)
LAMOUREUX, Michele (Lib Dir) . 691

City of Liberty (TX)
PICKETT, Ellen W. (Lib Dir) 970

City of Lincoln (OR)
HERINGER, Patricia G. (Lib Dir) . 531

City of Livonia (MI)
DELLER, A M. (City Libn Dir) . . . 289
TRENNER, Claudine F. (Branch Libn) 1255

City of Lodi (CA)
LACHENDRO, Leonard L. (City Libn) 686

City of Lompoc (CA)
STARR, Carol L. (Lib Dir) 1182

City of Long Beach (CA)
NEWHARD, Eleanor M. (Dept Libn I) 899

City of Longueuil (PQ)
OUIMET, Yves (Dir) 930

City of Los Angeles (CA)
MCINDOO, Larry R. (Mgmt Recruiting Ofcr) 809

City of Lowell (MA)
O'BRIEN, Anne M. (City Libn & Dir) 914

City of Lubbock (TX)
CHAPMAN, Katherine (Asst Dir) . 202

City of Mascouche (PQ)
ALLARD, Diane (Lib Dir) 14

City of Mattoon (IL)
GRAFTON, Mona R. (City Libn) . 456

City of McKinney (TX)
DOYLE, Patricia L. (Lib Dir) 317

City of Memphis (TN)
JACKSON, Harriett D. (Branch Head) 587

City of Mesa (AZ)
ANDERSON, Herschel V. (Lib Dir) 23

City of Miami (OK)
WALLEN, Joyce M. (Lib Dir) . . . 1298

City of Middlebury (VT)
REED, Sally G. (Dir) 1015

City of Milton-Freewater (OR)
SARGENT, Phyllis M. (Lib Dir) . 1083

City of Montello (WI)
TANNER, Linda L. (Dir) 1223

City of Monterey (CA)   LAGIER, Jennifer B.
(Bookmoblie Libn) 688
City of Montreal (PQ)   MEUNIER, Pierre (Resrch Libn) .. 829
THACH, Phat V. (Libn) 1233
City of Montreal-Est (PQ)   KO, Jean S. (Dir) 666
City of Montreal-Nord (PQ)   DENOMMEE, Celine (Dir) 293
City of Mt Pleasant (MI)   KRUUT, Evald (Dir of Lib Srvs) .. 681
City of Myrtle Beach (SC)   BOONE, Shirley W. (City Libn) .. 115
City of New Haven (CT)   HAYNAM, Kenneth W. (Libn III) . 516
City of New York (NY)   BOCKMAN, Eugene J.
(Commissioner) 109
DISHON, Robert M. (Grad Intern
Archvst) 305
City of Newport Beach (CA)   CHWEH, Steven S. (Technl
Srvs Head) 214
City of Newport News (VA)   HENDERSON, Harriet (Dir) 526
City of Newton (MA)   TASHJIAN, Virginia A. (Lib Dir) . 1224
City of Norfolk (VA)   BOONE, Edward J. (Adminstrv
Asst) 115
DARDEN, Sue E. (Lib Dir) 274
GRAY, Patricia B. (Sr Libn &
Branch Head) 460
MARSHALL, Jane C. (Libn) 774
City of Oak Creek (WI)   TASNADI, Deborah L. (City
Libn) 1224
City of Oakland (CA)   WONG, Patricia M. (Chlds Libn) 1363
City of Oceanside (CA)   NELSON, Helen M. (Lib Dir) 893
City of Oldsmar (FL)   MELLICAN, Nancy J. (Lib Dir) .. 822
City of Orange (CA)   LEO, Karen A. (Lib Dir) 716
City of Orlando (FL)   AHLIN, Nancy (Libn & Mgr) ... 8
City of Oxnard (CA)   SMITH, Heather (Libn II) 1155
City of Palmdale (CA)   STORSTEEN, Linda L. (Lib Dir) 1198
City of Pasadena (CA)   SZYNAKA, Edward M. (Dir) ... 1219
City of Petersburg (AK)   JENKINS, Joyce K. (City Libn) .. 597
City of Philadelphia (PA)   ERTZ, Ginger E. (Libn) 353
City of Phoenix (AZ)   DIAL, Clarence M. (Libn IV) 299
City of Plattsburgh (NY)   MCCAUSLAND, Sharon H. (Ref
Libn) 795
City of Pointe-Claire (PQ)   COTE, Claire (Dir of Lib &
Cultural Srvs) 249
LAPERRIERE, Celine (Technl
Srvs Dir) 697
City of Ponca City (OK)   SKIDMORE, Stephen C. (City
Libn) 1146
City of Poquoson (VA)   TAI, Elizabeth L. (Lib Dir) 1220
City of Portland (OR)   VAN HORN, Neal F. (Libn) 1275
City of Portsmouth (NH)   PRIDHAM, Sherman C. (Lib Dir) . 993
City of Red Wing (MN)   BRANDT, Janet E. (Technl Srvs
Libn) 128
City of Redwood City (CA)   DUFFY, Karen R. (Asst Lib Dir) .. 324
City of Regina (SK)   BALON, Brett J. (Record Systs
Coordntr) 53
City of Richmond (CA)   CONTRERAS, Marie (City Libn) . 239
City of Richmond (VA)   COSTA, Robert N. (City Libn) ... 249
City of Riverview (MI)   NAPOLITAN, Jacquetta (City
Libn) 887
City of Rochester (MN)   TAYLOR, Judith K. (Dir) 1227
City of Rockland (ON)   DALRYMPLE, Odette (Chief
Adminstr) 271
City of Rogers (AR)   KELLEY, Sally J. (Head Libn) ... 637
City of Rosemere (PQ)   LAPIERRE, France (Dir) 697
City of Roseville (CA)   NICKERSON, Susan L. (Dir) 902
City of Roswell (GA)   MARTIN, Clarece (Archvst) 775
City of Round Rock (TX)   RICKLEFS, Dale L. (Dir) 1032
City of Safety Harbor (FL)   DE MEO, Mary A. (Libn) 291
City of Saginaw (TX)   COPELAND, Sara O. (Lib Dir) .. 244
City of St-Bruno de Montarville (PQ)   BERNARDIN, Luce (Dir) 88
City of Saint-Eustache (PQ)   KHOUZAM, Monique (Dir of
Cultural Srvs) 646
City of St Hubert (PQ)   DUMOULIN, Nicole L. (Libn) 325
City of Saint-Laurent (PQ)   DJEVALIKIAN, Sonia (Technl
Srvs Head) 306
FORTIN, Johanne (Ref Libn) 392
SIMON, Marie L. (Head Libn) .. 1140
City of St Leonard Pub Lib (PQ)   CORBEIL, Lizette (Ref Libn) 245
City of St Paul (MN)   EPSTEIN, Rheda (Technl Srvs
Mgr) 351
City of Sainte-Foy (PQ)   AUGER, Claudette (Dir) 39

City of San Antonio (TX)   GRUENBECK, Laurie (Branch
Mgr) 474
MCCONNELL, Ruth M. (Chlds
Libn) 798
MYLER, Josephine P. (Libn) ... 885
SEXTON, Irwin (Dir) 1118
City of San Benito (TX)   GARAZA, Noemi (Lib Dir) 417
City of San Diego (CA)   DER PARSEGHIAN, Anahid A.
(Libn II) 294
City of San Francisco (CA)   GOODRICH, Jeanne D. (City
Libn) 449
City of San Jose (CA)   CARPIO, Virginia A. (Asst City
Libn) 185
FLETCHER, Homer L. (City
Libn) 384
City of San Rafael (CA)   STRATFORD, Vaughn M. (Dir) . 1200
City of Santa Ana (CA)   MORGAN, Ferrell (Centl Lib
Head & Asst Lib Dir) 864
City of Santa Fe (TX)   MCLENNA, D S. (Lib Dir) 814
City of Santa Monica (CA)   MITCHELL, Betty J. (Info
Systems Mgr) 848
City of Schertz (TX)   DOUGLAS, Virginia G. (Dir) 314
City of Scottsdale (AZ)   SAFERITE, Linda L. (Dir) 1074
City of Seattle (WA)   CLINE, Robert S. (City Archvst) . 222
City of Sept-Iles (PQ)   BOUDREAU, Jocelyne (Chief
Libn) 119
City of Sherman (TX)   WALLER, Hope C. (Lib Dir) ... 1298
City of Sierra Vista (AZ)   POSSNER, Roger D. (Pub Srvs
Libn) 986
City of Silsbee (TX)   JOHNSON, Cathy (Actg Libn) .. 603
City of Sioux Falls (SD)   DERTIEN, James L. (Libn) 294
City of Soda Springs (ID)   TATE, Karen E. (Dir) 1225
City of South Portland (ME)   ALEXANDER, William D. (Lib
Dir) 12
City of Spencer (IA)   MYRON, Victoria L. (Dir) 885
City of Spokane (WA)   SHELDEN, Lucinda D. (Chlds
Libn) 1125
City of Springfield (IL)   WHITAKER, Geraldine M. (Ref
& Info Head) 1329
City of Ste-Therese (PQ)   NADEAU, Leonard (Dir) 886
City of Sunnyvale (CA)   BRITTAIN, Cynthia E. (Catlgr) ... 137
COMSTOCK, Evelyn B.
(Adminstrv Libn) 235
DI MUCCIO, Mary J. (Adminstrv
Libn) 304
SIMMONS, Beverley J. (Dir of
Libs) 1139
City of Tarpon Springs (FL)   O'BRIEN, Elizabeth M. (Lib Dir) .. 914
City of Tempe (AZ)   JANSON, Sherryl A. (Chlds
Srvs Supvsr) 594
City of Temple (TX)   TIME, Ming M. (Head of Ref) .. 1245
City of Texas City (TX)   MONCLA, Carolyn S. (Lib Dir) .. 854
City of The Colony (TX)   SVEINSSON, Joan L. (Lib Dir) .. 1212
City of Thousand Oaks (CA)   SMITH, Marvin E. (Lib Dir) ... 1158
WALTERS, Roberta J. (Libn) ... 1301
WIGLEY, Marylou (Deputy Dir) . 1337
City of Toledo (OR)   JORGENSEN, Blythe M. (Lib
Dir) 617
City of Topeka (KS)   CARROLL, James K. (User
Srvs Supvsr) 187
City of Trois-Rivieres (PQ)   BESSETTE, Madeleine (Col
Devlpmnt & Evaluation Libn) ... 91
City of Tualatin (OR)   HARDIE, Susan H. (Lib Dir) ... 500
City of Tyler (TX)   ALBERTSON, Christopher A.
(City Libn) 10
HARPER, Sarah H. (Sr Libn) 503
City of Valdez (AK)   LEAHY, M J. (Musm & Arch
Dir) 706
WEILAND, Karen B. (Lib Dir) .. 1317
City of Verona (WI)   KNODLE, Shirley M. (Lib Dir) .. 665
City of Vineland (NJ)   GREENBLATT, Ruth (Sr Libn) .. 463
City of Virginia Beach (VA)   BARKLEY, Carolyn L. (Centl
Libn) 56
CARR, Jeanette A. (Catlgng &
Prcsng Libn) 185
CAYWOOD, Carolyn A. (Libn) .. 195
DUNLEAVY, Theresa G. (Ref
Libn II) 326
LOHMAN, Toni A. (Col Mgmt
Libn) 737

City of Virginia Beach (VA)
SIMS, Martha J. (Dir) 1142
ZWICK, Susan G. (Biblgphr) . . . 1392
City of Waco (TX)
PROGAR, Dorothy R. (Dir of
Libs) 995
City of Watauga (TX)
MCCURDY, Sandra A. (Dir) 801
City of Waterbury (CT)
YOUNG, Marianne F. (Technl
Srvs Dept Head) 1382
City of West Haven (CT)
ABBOTT, Kathleen A. (Lib
Media Spclst) 1
City of White Cloud (MI)
HARPER, Nancy L. (Dir & Libn) . 503
City of Windsor (ON)
WALSH, G M. (Mncpl Archvst) . 1299
City of Winnipeg (MB)
BENSON, Theodore L. (Acqs
Libn) 83
GRAHAM, Heather F.
(Extension & Bookmobile
Head) 456
MARTEN, Mary L. (Area Libn) . . 775
REINALDO DA SILVA, Joann
T. (Lib Srvs Asst III) 1021
SMITH, John R. (Head Catlgr) . 1156
City of Woodburn (OR)
SPRAUER, Linda J. (Lib Dir) . . . 1176
City of Woodland (CA)
KELLUM-ROSE, Nancy P. (Lib
Srvs Dir) 637
City of Yonkers (NY)
SCHAVRIEN, Judith L. (Branch
Adminstr) 1090
City Polytechnic of Hong Kong (HKG)
POON, Paul W. (Assoc Libn) . . . 983
City Univ of London (ENG)
ROBERTSON, Stephen E.
(Reader in Info Sci) 1042
City Univ of New York (NY)
ANGEL, Kenneth E. (Supvsr) 27
BRODY, Catherine T. (Dir of
Archs) 139
RA, Marsha H. (Dir, Univ Lib
Automated Srvs) 1001
KOLBIN, Ronda I. (Libn) 669
Clairol Inc (CT)
Clapp & Eisenberg (NJ)
BORCHERT, Janis L. (Law
Libn) 116
Claremont Coll (CA)
BAILEY, George M. (Assoc Dir
of Libs) 46
BARKEY, Patrick T. (Dir of Libs) . . 56
KUHNER, David A. (Lib Consult) . 683
MOSER, Judith E. (Original
Catlgng Head) 871
Claremont Unified Sch District (CA)
ROSE, David L. (Dir, Instrc
Support) 1054
Claremont Univ Center (CA)
SAHAK, Judy H. (Asst Dir of
Libs & Libn) 1075
Clarion Community Sch (IA)
FLETCHALL, Josephine V.
(Libn) 384
Clarion Univ of Pennsylvania (PA)
DECKER, Debra E. (Serials
Coordntr) 285
DINGLE, Susan (Asst Prof) 304
EMERICK, Kenneth F. (Asst
Prof & Catlgr) 347
HARTSOCK, Ralph M.
(Non-Book Formats Catlgr) . . . 508
HEAD, John W. (Assoc Prof) . . . 518
HORN, Janice H. (Technl Srvs
Coordntr) 559
HORN, Roger G. (Cols Libn) 559
MCCABE, Gerard B. (Dir of
Libs) 792
PERSON, Ruth J. (Coll of Lib
Sci Dean) 961
TOWNSEND, Silas H. (Ref
Libn) 1253
Claritas Limited Partnership (MD)
PATRICIU, Florin S. (Chief
Operating Ofcr) 947
Clark Art Institute (MA)
ERICKSON, Peter B. (Libn for
Catlgng and Serials) 352
Clark Boardman Co Ltd (NY)
MORSE, Alan L. (Pres & Chief
Exec Ofcr) 869
Clark County Community Coll (NV)
MASTALIR, Janet K. (Ref Libn) . . 782
Clark County Lib District (NV)
MOUJAES, Sylva S. (Ref Libn) . . 873
Clark County Pub Lib (KY)
WILLIAMS, Danby O. (Dir) 1342
Clark County Sch District (NV)
GROSSHANS, Merilyn P. (Libn) . 473
KEENE, Richard R. (Libn) 634
KEENE, Roberta E. (Libn) 634
Clark Equipment Co (IN)
EIGEMAN, Laurence E. (Corprt
Records Mgr & Archvst) 340

Clark Klein & Beaumont (MI)
GAMACHE, Kathleen A. (Libn) . . 416
Clark Ladner Fortenbaugh &
Young (PA)
HAAS, Carol C. (Law Libn) 480
Clark Memorial Lib (RI)
HULL, Catherine C. (Dir) 572
Clark Pub Lib (NJ)
CHAPIN, Joan R. (Chlds Libn) . . 201
JONES, Sandra K. (Dir) 615
Clark Thomas Winters & Newton (TX)
TRANFAGLIA, Twyla L. (Law
Libn) 1254
Clark Univ (MA)
KASPERSON, Jeanne X.
(Resrch Libn) 629
ROCHELEAU, Kathleen D. (Asst
Resrch Libn) 1046
Clarksburg-Harrison Pub Lib (WV)
THACKER, Timothy M. (Head,
Technl Srvs) 1233
Clarksdale & Coahoma County (MS)
GRAVES, Sid F. (Dir) 459
Clarkson Univ (NY)
BERRY, Gayle C. (Head of Ref) . . 90
NOLTE, James S. (Libn) 908
STAHL, J N. (Libn & Eductnl
Resrcs Ctr Assoc Dir) 1178
Class (CA)
ALIX, Cleta M. (Mgr, Resrch &
Devlpmnt & Mktg) 13
CHAMPANY, Barry W. (Product
Mgr) 198
SHIRASAWA, Sharon V. (Sr
Coordntr) 1131
Classic Software Inc (FL)
TODD, Hal W. (Sales Mgr) 1248
Clatsop Community Coll (OR)
DUNN, Carolyn A. (Dir of Lib
Srvs) 326
Clausen Miller Gorman Caffrey &
Witous (IL)
FINNER, Susan L. (Head Libn) . . 378
Clayton County Board of
Education (GA)
BAKER, Gordon N. (Lib/Media
Spclst/Coordntr Comp Educ) . . 48
GRANTHAM, Ann V. (Media
Spclst) 458
Clayton County Lib System (GA)
STEWART, Carol J. (Dir of Lib
Srvs) 1192
Clayton Environmental
Consultants (MI)
COREY, Marjorie (Libn & Info
Spclst) 246
Clayton State Coll (GA)
BROCKMEIER, Kristina C. (Lib
Srvs Dir) 138
Clear Creek Baptist Bible Coll (KY)
BROOKS, Carolyn B. (Dir of Lib
Srvs) 140
Clear Creek Independent Sch
District (TX)
POWELL, Patricia K. (AV Libn) . . 988
Clearwater Pub Lib (FL)
HAMRELL, Larry G. (Libn) 494
RITZ, Paul S. (Libn II) 1037
Cleburne High Sch (TX)
CARDENAS, Martha L. (Libn) . . . 180
Clemson Univ (SC)
ABRAMS, Leslie E. (Branch
Head) 3
ARMISTEAD, Myra A. (Ref
Libn) 32
HARRIS, Maureen (Pub Docum
Unit Head) 505
JOHNSON, Steven D. (Head of
Monograph Acqs Unit) 609
KOHL, Michael F. (Spcl Cols
Head) 668
LYLE, Martha E. (Engrng Ref
Libn) 751
MEYER, Richard W. (Assoc Dir
of Libs) 830
MORGAN, Nancy T. (Biblgph
Instrc Coordntr) 864
SILER, Freddie B. (Bus, Textile
Ref Libn) 1137
TAYLOR, Dennis S. (Univ
Archvst) 1226
THOMAS, Julie A. (Biblgph
Database Libn) 1237
Clermont Coll (OH)
MARCOTTE, Frederick A. (Coll
Libn) 769
Clermont County Law Lib (OH)
SUHRE, Carol A. (Dir) 1207
Clermont County Pub Lib (OH)
POMERANTZ, Bruce F. (Adult
Srvs Coordntr) 982
Clermont Mercy Hospital (OH)
STONE, Diane L. (Libn) 1197

Cleveland Area Metropolitan Lib System (OH)
FRY, Mildred C. (Proj Libn) 406
WAREHAM, Nancy L. (Exec Dir) 1304

Cleveland Board of Education (OH)
MELTON, Vivian B. (Dir) 823

Cleveland Chiropractic Coll (CA)
FOLLICK, Edwin D. (Dean of Student Affairs) 388

Cleveland City Schs (TN)
SMITH, Judy R. (Libn) 1156

Cleveland Clinic Foundation (OH)
DORNER, Marian T. (Med Libn) . 313
ENGLANDER, Marlene S. (Med Libn) 349
HALLERBERG, Gretchen A. (Mgr) 489

Cleveland Consulting Associates (OH)
GRAY, Elisabeth M. (Info & Resrc Spclst) 459

Cleveland Diocese (OH)
BRADEN, Carol A. (Head Libn) . . 125

Cleveland Health Sciences Lib (OH)
JENKINS, Glen P. (Rare Bk Libn, Archvst) 597

Cleveland Heights Univ Heights Pub Lib (OH)
HORVATH, Camilla K. (Chlds Srvs Supvsr) 561

Cleveland Institute of Art (OH)
FOWLER, Michele R. (Slide Libn) 394
ROM, Cristine C. (Lib Dir) 1052

Cleveland Institute of Music (OH)
MCMAHON, Melody L. (Dir) 814

Cleveland Marshall Coll of Law (OH)
FINET, Scott (Deputy Dir) 378

Cleveland Metropolitan General Hospital (OH)
BENSING, Karen M. (Libn) 83
DZIEDZINA, Christine A. (Chief Libn) 331

Cleveland Museum of Art (OH)
ABID, Ann B. (Head Libn) 2
ADREAN, Louis V. (Serials Libn) 7
LANTZ, Elizabeth A. (Catlg Libn) 697
PEARMAN, Sara J. (Slide Libn) . 952
TOTH, Georgina G. (Assoc Ref Libn) 1252

Cleveland Museum of Natural History (OH)
FLAHIVE, Mary E. (Musm Archvst) 383

Cleveland Orchestra (OH)
CALMER, Charles E. (Eductnl Activities Dir) 174

Cleveland Psychiatric Institute (OH)
PETIT, J M. (Libn) 965

Cleveland Pub Lib (OH)
BOWIE, Angela B. (Dir of Cleveland Resrch Ctr) 121
FARRELL, Maureen C. (Map Libn) 365
JUNEJA, Derry C. (Acqs Dept Head) 620
KOLLAR, Mary E. (Bus Econ & Labor Dept Asst Head) 669
LORANTH, Alice N. (Fine Arts & Spcl Cols Dept Head) 741
MARTINES, Karen E. (Head of Pub Admin Lib) 779
MASON, Marilyn G. (Dir) 781
PIETY, Jean Z. (Sci & Tech Dept Head) 972
PRYSZLAK, Lydia M. (Libn II) . . 996
SEELY, Edward (Head of Technl Srvs) 1111
SHAMP, B K. (Libn) 1120
TIPKA, Donald A. (Head of Gen Ref) 1246

Cleveland State Community Coll (TN)
BASKETT, D A. (Head Libn) 63

Cleveland State Univ (OH)
DEAN, Winifred F. (Ref Biblgphr Soc Scis) 284
LUPONE, George (Deputy Dir) . . 749
MONGAN, Janet (Asst Dir for Info Srvs) 854
NISSENBAUM, Robert J. (Law Lib Dir & Assoc Prof of Law) . 905
NOLAN, Marianne (Asst Head of Ref) 907
RADER, Hannelore B. (Dir of Libs) 1002
ROSENFELD, Joseph S. (Catlgng Libn) 1056

Cleveland State Univ (OH)
SANTAVICCA, Edmund F. (Head, Col Mgmt Srvs) 1082
SWAIN, Richard H. (Head, Ref Srvs) 1212
TRAMDACK, Philip J. (Catlgng Head) 1254

Clifton Pub Lib (NJ)
CHAMBERLIN, Cynthia C. (Libn & Branch Mgr) 198

Clinch-Powell Regional Lib (TN)
GREESON, Judy G. (Regnl Lib Dir) 465

Clinch Valley Coll (VA)
BENKE, Robin P. (Col Devlpmnt Libn & Lib Sci Prof) 81

Clinicom International (MB)
COVVEY, H D. (Pres) 252

Clinton Community Sch District 15 (IL)
ADCOCK, Betty L. (Elem Sch Libn) 6

Clinton-Essex-Franklin Lib System (NY)
RANSOM, Stanley A. (Dir) 1007
ROGERS, Elizabeth S. (Head) . . 1049

Clinton Memorial Hospital (OH)
TOMLIN, Marsha A. (Info Resrcs Dir) 1250

Clinton Pub Lib (IA)
SEGER, Robert M. (Dir) 1112

Clio Group Inc (PA)
GRAY, Priscilla M. (Resrch Histn) 460

Closter Pub Lib (NJ)
DLUGOS, Carolyn M. (Chlds Libn) 306
LUXNER, Ann F. (Dir) 750

Clover Park Vocational-Technical Inst (WA)
SELING, Kathy A. (Instr & Coordntr) 1113

Clovis Unified Sch District (CA)
DICK, Norma P. (Support Systs Dir) 300
HENDRIX, Linda S. (Sales Rep) . 527

CLSI Inc (GA)
CLSI Inc (MA)
BRIAND, Margaret M. (Software Engineer) 134
FRIEDMAN, Terri L. (Bid Dept Mgr) 404
GLASSMAN, Penny L. (Product Mgr) 440
GRIFFITH, William R. (Mktg Vice Pres) 469
INGERSOLL, Diane S. (Sales Rep) 582
JANK, David A. (Sr Staff Consult) 593
LANDESMAN, Betty J. (Product Mgr) 692
MIELE, Madeline F. (International Market Devlpmnt Mgr) 833
SANTOSUOSSO, Joseph P. (Product Mgr) 1082
SCHWARTZ, Frederick E. (Mgr Inst Support Group) 1104
PORTER, Jean F. (Pres) 984

CMP Associates Inc (MI)
CMQ Communications (ON)
BECHER, Henry (VP & Gen Mgr) 71

CNR Partners (CT)
STANKIEWICZ, Carol A. (Mgr of Resrc Ctr) 1180

CNR Partners (NY)
UNNOLD, Terry (Plng & Devlpmnt VP) 1269

Coalinga-Huron Lib District (CA)
GUIDINGER, Delmar J. (Dist Libn) 476

Coastal Carolina Community Coll (NC)
MARTIN, Richard T. (Media Coordntr & Libn) 778

Coatesville Area Pub Lib (PA)
NEWPORT, Dorothea D. (Dir & Head Libn) 900

Cobb County Board of Education (GA)
SLOAN, Mary J. (Lib Media Spclst) 1149

Cobb County Pub Lib (GA)
RHEAY, Mary L. (Pub Lib Dir) . . 1025

Cobb County Pub Lib System (GA)
COHRS, Joyce S. (Technl Operations Head) 229
LAZENBY, Gail R. (Asst Dir) 706

COBE Laboratories Inc (CO)
HOLTON, Janet E. (Resrch & Devlpmnt Libn) 555

Cobre Consolidated Sch District (NM)
KEIST, Sandra H. (Lib & Media Dir) 635

Coburn Croft and Putzell (MO)	KISSANE, Mary K. (Libn & Attorney) 656	
Coca-Cola Co (GA)	CASSELL, Judy A. (Libn & Mgr of Mktg Info Ctr) 193	
	COOPER, Glenn (Law Lib Mgr) . . 243	
Cocoa Beach Pub Lib (FL)	ARMSTRONG, Ruth C. (Head of Ref) 32	
Codex Corp (MA)	EDWARDS, Betty (Info Srvs Libn) 337	
	WRIGHT, Victoria L. (Corporate Lib Supvsr) 1373	
Coe Coll (IA)	YU, Hsiao M. (Ref & Catlg Libn) 1384	
Coffeyville Community Coll (KS)	HENDERSON, Rosemary (Dir of Lrng Resrcs Ctr) 527	
Coffeyville Pub Lib (KS)	BUFFINGTON, Karyl L. (Dir) 155	
Cohen Brown Management Group (CA)	VARAT, Nancy L. (Info Resrcs Spclst) 1278	
Cohen Shapiro Polisher Sheikman & Cohen (PA)	KREMER, Jill L. (Libn) 677	
	METZ, Betty A. (Libn) 828	
Colby-Sawyer Coll (NH)	TATE, Joanne D. (Ref Libn) . . . 1225	
Colchester-East Hants Regional Lib (NS)	FREVE, Reay H. (Chief Libn) . . . 402	
	MARSH, Mary L. (Chlds Srvs Libn) 773	
Cold Spring Harbor Laboratory (NY)	FALVEY, Genemary H. (Libn & Info Spclst) 363	
Cole & Corette (DC)	MCDONALD, Michael L. (Libn) . . 803	
Colegio Adventista del Plata (ARG)	HAMMERLY, Hernan D. (Dir of Libs) 493	
Colegio Internacional de Caracas (VEN)	BERNAT, Mary A. (Head Libn) . . . 88	
Colegio Nueva Granada (COL)	CARDENAS, Mary E. (Instrcl Media Coordntr) 180	
Colegio Puertorriqueno de Ninas (PR)	FERNANDEZ, Josefina L. (Head Libn) 373	
Colfax Pub Schs (WI)	WASSINK, Patricia L. (Media Spclst) 1308	
Colgate Rochester Divinity Sch (NY)	BRENNAN, Christopher P. (Asst Libn for Technl Srvs) 132	
	KANSFIELD, Norman J. (Dir of Lib Srvs) 625	
	VANDELINDER, Bonnie L. (Asst Libn for Pub Srvs) 1273	
Colgate Univ (NY)	GREEN, Judith G. (Univ Libn) . . . 462	
	PILACHOWSKI, David M. (Assoc Univ Libn) 973	
	SIMCOE, Darryl D. (Dir) 1139	
Colle & McVoy Advertising (MN)	HARNDEN, Donna J. (Info Spclst) 502	
Coll Andre-Grasset (PQ)	LUSSIER, Jean P. (Dir) 749	
Coll Board of New York (NY)	AUBRY, John C. (Archvst & Records Mgr) 38	
Coll de l'Abitibi-Temiscamingue (PQ)	TREMBLAY, Levis (Technl Srvs Head) 1255	
CEGEP at Chicoutimi (PQ)	HARVEY, Serge (Head Libn) 509	
CEGEP at Jonquiere (PQ)	LAPOINTE, Louise (Prof) 697	
CEGEP at Limoilou (PQ)	GODIN, Maud (Ref Mgr) 442	
CEGEP at St-Felicien (PQ)	LAMBERT, Yvan (Libn) 690	
CEGEP at Sorel-Tracy (PQ)	RIOPEL, Jean M. (Libn) 1035	
CEGEP at Trois-Rivieres (PQ)	BAILLARGEON, Daniele (Ref Libn) 47	
	SIMARD, Denis (AV Lib Dir) . . . 1139	
Coll des Eudistes de Rosemont (PQ)	AUGER, Bernard (Head Libn) . . . 39	
Coll du Sacre-Coeur (PQ)	DEMERS, Madeleine M. (Lib Dir) 291	
Coll Francois-Xavier Garneau (PQ)	PAGEAU, Denise (Lib Technician in Lib Srvs) 934	
Coll Jesus-Marie de Sillery (PQ)	LAMONTAGNE, Jacqueline (Libn) 691	
Coll Lionel-Groulx (PQ)	PARADIS, Jacques (Tchr in Lib Sci) 939	
Coll Marie-Victorin (PQ)	CHARETTE, Rejean (Coordntr) . . 203	
Coll Montmorency (PQ)	CHAUMONT, Elise (Documtn Technician) 204	
	DANIS, Rolland J. (Technl Srvs Libn) 273	
Coll Notre-Dame-de-L'Assomption (PQ)	ROY, Lucille Y. (Head Libn) . . . 1063	
Coll of Basic Education (KWT)	ABDEL-MOTEY, Yaser Y. (Tchr of Lib & Info Sci) 2	
Coll of Charleston (SC)	NEVILLE, Robert F. (Catlgng Dept Head) 898	
	ROSS, Gary M. (Asst Dir for Technl Srvs) 1058	
	SCHMITT, John P. (Ref Srvs Head) 1096	
	SEAMAN, Sheila L. (Asst Dir for Pub Srvs) 1109	
	STRAUCH, Katina P. (Head, Col Devlpmnt Dept) 1200	
Coll of Chicoutimi (PQ)	GAUDREAU, Louis (Ref Libn) . . . 422	
Coll of DuPage (IL)	BERGER, Marianne C. (Ref Libn) 85	
	FRADKIN, Bernard (Dean) 395	
	GEYER, Robert I. (Libn) 430	
	TEMPLE, Harold L. (Technl Srvs Libn) 1230	
Coll of Great Falls (MT)	LEE, Susan M. (Readers Srv Libn) 711	
Coll of Health Sciences (VA)	SEAMANS, Nancy H. (Dir) 1109	
Coll of Insurance (NY)	ROSIGNOLO, Beverly A. (Chief Libn) 1057	
Coll of Mt St Joseph (OH)	ALBRECHT, Cheryl C. (Lib Dir) . . 10	
Coll of New Caledonia (BC)	MAYFIELD, Betty L. (Head of Technl Srvs) 790	
	PLETT, Katherine (Lib Dir) 978	
Coll of New Rochelle (NY)	GRECO, Gloria T. (Lib Automation Plng Coordntr) . . . 461	
	MOSLANDER, Charlotte D. (Circ Libn) 871	
	RUSSO, Mary (Archvst) 1070	
Coll of Notre Dame (CA)	GUEDON, Mary S. (Ref Libn) . . . 475	
	PELLE, Catherine A. (Libn & Lib Dir) 955	
	RAMSEY, Robert D. (Art Prof & Christian Art Archs Dir) 1006	
Coll of Our Lady of the Elms (MA)	BRENNAN, Mary E. (Libn) 132	
	GALLAGHER, Mary E. (Asst Libn) 414	
Coll of Physicians of Philadelphia (PA)	FULTON, June H. 409	
	HORROCKS, Thomas A. (Histl Cols of the Lib Cur) 561	
	NEUMANN, Pamela A. (Ref Libn) 897	
	POSES, June A. (Asst Libn for Pub Srvs) 985	
Coll of St Catherine (MN)	HARWOOD, Karen L. (Head of Technl Srvs) 510	
	HOLT, Constance W. (Info Srvs Libn) 554	
	KINNEY, Janet S. (Libs & Media Srvs Dir) 653	
	MCINERNEY, Claire R. (Asst Prof) 809	
Coll of St Elizabeth (NJ)	MANTHEY, Carolyn M. (Circ Libn) 767	
	ROUSEK, Marie B. (Dir of Lib) . 1061	
Coll of St Joseph (VT)	MCCULLOUGH, Doreen J. (Asst Libn) 801	
Coll of St Rose (NY)	CORDING, A C. (Technl Srvs Libn) 246	
	NEAT, Charles M. (Archvst) 891	
Coll of St Thomas (MN)	OZOLINS, Karl L. (Lib Dir) 933	
Coll of San Mateo (CA)	ATKINS, Gregg T. (Lib Dir) 38	
Coll of Staten Island (NY)	O'DONNELL, Michael J. (Lib Instrc Coordntr) 917	
	SVENNINGSEN, Karen L. (Ref Libn & Instr) 1212	
Coll of the Albemarle (NC)	COOK-WOOD, Holly M. (Libn) . . 241	
	LEE, Charles D. (Lrng Resrcs Ctr Dir) 709	
Coll of the Canyons (CA)	KELLER, Jan K. (Lrng Resrcs Asst Dean) 635	

Coll of the Holy Cross (MA)
STANKUS, Tony (Sci Libn) 1180
THISTLE, Dawn R. (Music
Visual Arts Libn) 1235

Coll of the Southwest (NM)
TUBESING, Richard L. (Coll
Libn) 1261

Coll of William & Mary (VA)
BARRICK, Susan O. (Lib Dir) 59
BLUE, Kathryn J. (Sr Catlgr) 107
BROWN, Charlotte D. (Dir) 142
EDMONDS, Edmund P. (Law
Libn & Assoc Prof of Law) ... 336
HASKELL, John D. (Assoc Univ
Libn) 510
HAUSMAN, Patricia R. (Physics
& Geology Libn) 513
HEDGES, Bonnie L. (Music
Faculty) 520
HEYMAN, Berna L. (Asst Univ
Libn for Automation) 536
MAGPANTAY, J A. (Systs Mgr) . 760
MARSHALL, Nancy H. (Univ
Libn) 775
YELICH, Hope H. (Ref Libn) ... 1379

Coll of Wooster (OH)
GUSTAFSON, Julia C. (Ref
Libn) 478
POWELL, Margaret S. (Docums
& Ref Libn) 988

Collegiate Sch Inc (NY)
BRUGNOLOTTI, Phyllis T.
(Head Libn) 150

**Collin County Community Coll
District** (TX)
CORREDOR, Javier (Ref &
Periodicals Libn) 247

Collin County Law Lib (TX)
BALCOMBE, Judith A. (Law Lib
Dir) 51

Collins Correctional Facility (NY)
KING, Charles L. (Libn) 650
Colobiere Center (MI)
MEDER, Stephen A. (Libn) 820
**Colonial Penn Information
Service** (CO)
CAMERON, Richard D. (Pres &
Chief Executive Ofcr) 175

**Colonial Williamsburg
Foundation** (VA)
BERG, Susan (Reader Srvs
Libn) 85
GROVE, Pearce S. (Dir) 473
HASKELL, Mary B. (Technl
Srvs Libn) 510
DAVIS, Mary F. (Technl Libn) ... 280
YEN, Marilyn L. (Lib Asst) 1379

Colony Pub Lib (TX)
Colorado Academy (CO)
**Colorado Alliance of Research
Libs** (CO)
GARRALDA, John C. (Sr Libn) .. 420
SHAW, Ward (Exec Dir) 1124

Colorado Coll (CO)
JONES-EDDY, Julie (Govt
Docums Libn) 615
NEILON, Barbara L. (Spcl Cols
Cur) 892
SHERIDAN, John B. (Head
Libn) 1127

**Colorado Department of
Education** (CO)
BOLT, Nancy M. (State Libn) ... 113
GORAL, Barbara J. (Dir) 451
LANCE, Keith C. (Resrch &
Budget Ofcr) 692
ROBERTS, Katherine M.
(Consult & Correctional Libn) 1040

**Colorado Endowment for the
Humanities** (CO)
SHARER, E J. (Resrc Ctr Dir) .. 1122
Colorado Historical Society (CO)
KANE, Katherine (Dir of Pub Srv
and Access) 625
SHARP, Alice L. (Libn) 1122

**Colorado Independent Sch
District** (TX)
GODWIN, Frances L. (High Sch
Libn & AV Coordntr) 443
Colorado Lib Association (CO)
HAMILTON-PENNELL,
Christine (Exec Dir) 492

**Colorado National Bankshares
Inc** (CO)
FUJII, Cynthia M. (Consult) 408
Colorado Sch District 11 (CO)
DALBY, Richard F. (Libn, Media
Spclst) 270
Colorado Sch of Mines (CO)
FULMER, Russell F. (Asst Dir
for Technl Srvs) 409
LARSGAARD, Mary L. (Asst Dir
for Spcl Cols) 698

Colorado Sch of Mines (CO)
LEREW, Ann A. (Ref Libn) 717
PHINNEY, Hartley K. (Dir of the
Lib) 969

**Colorado Springs Fine Arts
Center** (CO)
DEW, T R. (Libn & Archvst) 297
Colorado State Lib (CO)
EATON, Barbara F. (Instnl Lib
Srv Supvsr) 333
HEMPSTEAD, John (Sch Lib
Media Consultant) 525
LINSLEY, Priscilla M. (Supvsr) . 731
WAGNER, Barbara L. (Prog
Mgr) 1291
Colorado State Univ (CO)
AMAN, Ann L. (Prospect Resrch
& Mgmt Coordntr) 19
ANDERSON, Lemoyne W. (Dir
of Libs Emeritus) 24
BURNS, Robert W. (Asst Dir) ... 163
CHAMBERS, Joan L. (Dir of
Libs) 198
ERNEST, Douglas J. (Soc Sci &
Humanities Libn) 353
JOHNSON, K S. (Sci & Tech
Dept Head) 606
LANGE, Holley R. (Catlg Libn) .. 695
LINDGREN, William F. (Catlg
Dept Head) 729
MOON, Myra J. (Preservation
Libn) 857
NEWMAN, John (Spcl Cols
Libn, Univ Archvst) 899
SCHMIDT, Fred C. (Docums
Dept Head) 1095

**Colquitt County Board of
Education** (GA)
BOWEN, Louise E. (Media
Spclst) 120
MOYE, Edna B. (Head of Sch
Lib & Media Ctr Dept) 874

Colton Pub Lib (CA)
HOLM, Blair I. (Chlds Srvs Libn) . 552
Columbia Christian Coll (OR)
ELLSON, Linda R. (Libn) 345
Columbia Coll (CA)
STEUBEN, Raymond L. (Dir of
Lib Srvs) 1190
Columbia Coll (IL)
HSIEH, Cynthia C. (Catlg Libn) .. 567
Columbia Coll (SC)
CROSS, Mary R. (Technl Srvs
Head) 260
VASSALLO, John A. (Ref Libn) 1279

Columbia Daily Tribune (MO)
SUMMERS, Janice K.
(Newsroom Libn) 1209
Columbia Heights Pub Schs (MN)
VAUGHAN, Janet E. (Libn) 1279
Columbia Hospital (WI)
HOLST, Ruth M. (Lib Srvs Dir) .. 554
**Columbia-Lafayette-Ouachita-Calho-
un Lib** (AR)
BRADLEY, Florene J. (Libn) 125
Columbia Museum of Art (OH)
GENSHAFT, Carole M. (Resrc
Ctr Coordntr) 427
Columbia Pub Schs (MO)
FUCHS, Curt R. (Media Srvs
Dir) 408
WERNER, Laura L. (Lib Media
Spclst) 1325
Columbia State Community Coll (TN)
HARRISON, Richard H. (Asst
Libn Ref Srvs) 507
LIGHT, Marvin J. (Lrng Resrcs
Ctr Dir) 726
Columbia Theological Seminary (GA)
MARONEY, Daryle M. (Technl
Srvs Libn) 772
OVERBECK, James A. (Dir of
the Lib) 931
WENDEROTH, Christine (Assoc
Libn) 1323
Columbia Univ (NJ)
DAIN, Phyllis (Prof of Lib Srv) ... 270
Columbia Univ (NY)
ANDERSON, Rachael K. (Hlth
Scis Libn Dir) 25
ARMSTRONG, Joanne D. (Ref
Head) 32
BAGNALL, Whitney S. (Spcl
Law Cols Libn) 45
BANKS-ISZARD, Kimberly K.
(Psy Libn) 54
BATTIN, Patricia (Vice Pres of
Info Srvs & Univ Libn) 64
BELANGER, Terry (Assoc Prof) .. 76

Columbia Univ (NY)

BERNSTEIN, Mark P. (Ref Libn) . . 89
BERTCHUME, Gary (Catlgr) 90
BORRIES, Michael S. (Serials
Catlgr) 117
CHIBNIK, Katharine R. (Ref Libn
& Catlgr) 207
CHO-PARK, Jaung J. (Lib Sci
Doctor Prog) 210
CRYSTAL, Bernard R. (Asst
Libn for Manuscripts) 262
CURTIS, James A. (Media Srvs
Libn) 267
DELLA-CAVA, Olha (Libn) 289
ELLENBOGEN, Rudolph S.
(Asst Libn for Rare Bks) 343
FEDUNOK, Suzanne (Asst Dir
for Resrc Devlpmnt) 368
FRANCK, Jane P. (Lib Dir) 396
GOODMAN, Edward C. (Gen
Edit) 449
GREENBERG, Charles J.
(Media & Instrcl Srvs Libn) . . . 463
GRELE, Ronald J. (Oral Hist
Resrch Ofc Dir) 467
GREWENOW, Peter W.
(Curator, Visual Resrcs Col) . . 467
HAEFLIGER, Kathleen A.
(Music Libn & Head, Music
Lib) 482
HAGSTROM, Jack W. (Prof of
Pathology & Dir) 483
HARRIS, Carolyn L.
(Preservation Dept Head) 504
HASWELL, Hollee (Cur) 511
HOLLIDAY, Geneva R. (Ref,
Interlib Loan Libn) 552
HOOVER, James L. (Law Libn
& Law Prof) 557
JACKSON, Charles G. (Univ
Med Ofcr & Psychiatrist) . . . 587
KEMPE, Deborah A. (Indxr &
Ref Libn) 639
KLIMLEY, Susan (Geological
Scis Libn) 661
LEARMONT, Carol L. (Sch of
Lib Srv Assoc Dean) 707
LESNIK, Pauline (Head of
Resrcs) 718
LEWIS, David W. (Lehman Libn) . 723
LOHF, Kenneth A. (Libn) 737
MANDEL, Carol A. (Technl Srvs
Dir) 764
MAY, Jonathan B. (Docums Srv
Ctr Head) 788
MENT, David M. (Head of Spcl
Cols) 824
MOLZ, Redmond K. (Melvil
Dewey Prof of Lib Srv) 854
MOUNT, Ellis (Sch of Lib Srv
Resrch Scholar) 873
PAGEL, Scott B. (Asst Law Libn
for Pub Srvs) 934
PALMER, Paul R. (Cur & Libn) . . 936
PASQUARIELLA, Susan K.
(Head Libn) 946
PAULSON, Barbara A. (Spcl
Cols Libn) 950
PEARCE, Karla J. (Asst Dir of
Sci & Engrng Div) 952
PETERS, Paul E. (Asst Univ
Libn for Systs) 962
RAUCH, Theodore G. (Serials
Biblgphr & Unit Head) 1010
RICHARDS, Daniel T. (Asst Hlth
Scis Libn) 1028
RODERER, Nancy K. (Hlth Scis
Systs Libn) 1047
SHERBY, Louise S. (Deputy
Head for Admin) 1127

Columbia Univ (NY)

SMIRAGLIA, Richard P. (Sr
Lectr) 1152
STALKER, Dianne S. (Rare Bk
Catlgr) 1178
STOLLER, Michael E. (Hist
Biblgphr) 1196
TAYLOR, Arlene G. (Assoc
Prof) 1226
THOMAS, Catherine M. (Serials
Catlgr & Recon Supvsr) 1236
THOMPSON, Susan O. (Assoc
Prof) 1241
TOYAMA, Ryoko (Head, Access
Srvs) 1253
WEDGEWORTH, Robert W.
(Dean) 1315
WOO, Janice (Indxr & Ref Libn) 1363
ZUMBERGE, Gloria A. (Base
Libn) 1391

Columbus Air Force Base (MS)

Columbus & Franklin County Pub
Lib (OH)

FELLOWS, Barbara G. (Asst
Dir) 370
MAURER, Lewis R. (Asst Mgr &
Adult Srvs Libn) 787

Columbus City Schs (NE)

TAYLOR, Joie L. (Dir of Prcsng
& Coordntr, Elem Lib) 1227

Columbus Diocesan Schs (OH)

FITZPATRICK, Janis M. (Lib &
Media Srvs Coordntr) 383

Columbus Dispatch (OH)   HUNTER, James J. (Libn) 576
Columbus Hospital (IL)   FINNERTY, James L. (Dir,
                             Corprt, Med Lib) 379
Columbus Law Lib Association (OH) BLOUGH, Keith A. (Lib Dir) 106
                             BRANN, Andrew R. (Assoc
                             Libn) 128
Columbus Pub Schs (OH)   HERB, Elizabeth D. (Supvsr) . . . 530
                             SMITH, Noralee W. (Resrc Libn) 1159
Columbus Pub Schs (WI)   CZARNEZKI, Mary E. (Elem &
                             Jr High Sch Libn) 268
Columbus Sch for Girls (OH) ALTAN, Susan B. (Sr Libn) 18
Combs Moorhead Associates Inc (IL) MOORHEAD, John D.
                             (Principal) 862
Combustion Engineering Inc (CT) CARTLEDGE, Ellen G. (Info
                             Resrc Ctr Mgr) 190
                             GAGNE, Susan P. (Info Spclst) . . 412
Comerica Inc (MI)   LILLEY, Barbara A. (Asst Libn) . . 727
                             STANTON, Beth L. (Resrch Lib
                             Mgr) 1181
Comission Scolaire Regnl de
Chambly (PQ)   GELINAS, Sylvain (Dir) 426
Commerce Clearing House Inc (IL) GIERING, Richard H. (Mgr) 433
Commercial Appeal (TN)   TERRY, Carol D. (Lib Dir) 1232
Commission on Pub Records (IN) NEWMAN, John J. (State
                             Archvst) 899
Commission Scolaire de
Drummondville (PQ)   HEON, Gerard (Tchg Spclst) 530
Commission Scolaire des
Laurentides (PQ)   FILIATRAULT, Andre Y. (Sch
                             Libn) 376
Commission Scolaire Regnl La
Verendrye (PQ)   MARCHAND, Jacques
                             (Documtn Ctr Mgr) 768
Commonwealth Edison Co (IL) BOBAN, Carol A. (Lrng Resrc
                             Ctr Coordntr) 108
                             PERTELL, Grace M. (Asst Libn) . 961
Commonwealth High Sch (PR)   HAMEL, Eleanor C. (Libn) 491
Commonwealth of Kentucky (KY) NELSON, James A. (State Libn
                             & Commissioner) 894
Commonwealth of
Massachusetts (MA)   CASO, Gasper (Dir) 193
                             CYPHERS, James E. (State
                             Records Analyst) 268
                             HOAGLAND, E L. (Law Libn) . . . 545
                             LAMBERT, Lyn D. (Law Libn) . . . 690
                             LEE, Marilyn M. (Libn I) 710
                             MCGOWAN, Owen T. (Libs Dir) . 807
                             MCLELLAN, Mary T. (Asst Dir) . . 814
                             PIGGFORD, Roland (Dir) 972
                             SASS, Samuel (Chairman) 1083
                             SCHWALLER, Marian C. (Libn) 1104

Commonwealth of Massachusetts (MA)
WARNER, Marnie M. (Law Lib Coordntr) 1305

Commonwealth of Pennsylvania (PA)
DEIBLER, Barbara E. (Rare Bk Libn/Asst Coordntr Col Mgmt) 288
FADDEN, Donald M. (Mem PA Governor's Advsy Council) . . . 360
FOUST, Judith M. (Lib Devlpmnt Div Dir) 393
SMITH, Eugene J. (Law Sect Head) 1155

Commonwealth of Virginia (VA)
BAXA, Jay W. (Legislative Ref Libn) 67
SNAIR, Dale S. (Instnl Consult) . 1162

Commtek Publishing Co (ID)
GREEN, Carol A. (Libn) 461

The Communication Studio Inc (NY)
VAUGHAN, John (Creative Dir) . 1279

Community & Occupational Hlth Lib (AB)
LAVKULICH, Joanne (Libn) 704

Community Center & Lib Association (PA)
SCHNEIDER, Louise H. (Lib Dir) 1097

Community Coll of Allegheny County (PA)
KING, Mimi (Ref Libn & Head of Serials) 652

Community Coll of Baltimore (MD)
BRADLEY, Wanda L. (Acq, Ref Libn) 126
SHAPIRO, Burton J. (Editor, Critic & Producer) 1121

Community Coll of Philadelphia (PA)
BRADLEY, James S. (Libn) 126
DALE, Charles F. (Ref Libn) . . . 270
JOHNSON, Joan E. (Acqs Libn) . 606
WEIS, Aimee L. (Libn & Assoc Prof) 1319

Community Consolidated Sch District 21 (IL)
NEAL, Nancy J. (Tchr Libn & Media Spclst) 890

Community Consolidated Sch District 62 (IL)
CORCORAN, Frances E. (Instrcl Mtrls Ctr Coordntr) 245

Community General Hospital (NY)
REINSTEIN, Diana J. (Med Libn) 1021

Community Hospitals of Central CA Inc (CA)
NELSON, Iris N. (Med Libn) 894
WARD, Penny T. (Lib Srvs Mgr) 1304

Community Lib of Castle Shannon (PA)
HENDERSON, John E. (Lib Dir) . 526

Community Medical Center (PA)
MCNABB, Corrine R. (Libn) . . . 815

Community Memorial Hospital (NJ)
REISLER, Reina (Med Libn) . . . 1021

Community Reformed Church of Colonie (NY)
SEVERINGHAUS, Ethel L. (Church Libn) 1117

Community Unit Sch District 118 (IL)
RAKE, Anthony I. (Libn & AV Dir) 1004

Community Unit Sch District 15 (IL)
LUKASIK, Marion F. (Comunty Unit Libn, AV Libn) 747

Community Unit Sch District 3 (IL)
BOGARDUS, Roberta S. (Dist Libn) 110

Compton Community Coll (CA)
PANSKI, Saul J. (Assoc Prof, Lib) 938

CompTron Research Inc (CA)
COMPTON, Joan C. (Pres) 235

Computer Ability (TX)
BIRD, H C. (Owner) 98

Computer Aided Planning (MI)
FITZPATRICK, Nancy C. (Database Libn) 383

Computer Business (CA)
HASSAN, Abe H. (Managing Edit & Proprietor) 511

The Computer Co (VA)
CARNEY, Marillyn L. (Mgr Lib Systs) 183

Computer Consultants (SDA)
ALSANARRAI, Hafidh S. (Consult) 17

Computer Corp of America (VA)
BERGMAN, Rita F. (Resrch & Systs Branch Mgr) 86

Computer Data Systems Inc (MD)
ZYNJUK, Nila L. (Pgmr & Analyst) 1392

Computer Industry Almanac Inc (TX)
KRUSE, Luanne M. (Managing Editor) 681

Computer Sciences Corp (CA)
LEVINE, Warren D. (Market Sector Devlpmnt Consult) 721

Computer Sciences Corp (NM)
HSU, Grace S. (Sr Technl Libn) . 567

Comp-U-Card International Inc (CT)
WALSH, Mark L. (Natl Sales Dir) 1300

Comquest Inc (PA)
DRIEHAUS, Rosemary H. (Pres) . 320

Comsat Technology Products Co (DC)
BOYER, Nate (Bus Network Sales Mgr) 123

Comstow Information Services (MA)
MOULTON, Lynda W. (Pres) . . 873

Con Diesel Mobile Equipment (CT)
BARNES, Denise M. (Technl Libn) 57

Conant Pub Lib (MA)
CORNELL, Barbara M. (Lib Dir) . 246

Concord Coll (WV)
BROWN, Thomas M. (Dir of Libs) 148

Concord Pike Lib (DE)
TITUS, H M. (Lib Dir) 1247

Concord Sch District (NH)
KENT, Jeffrey A. (Coordntr) 642

Concordia Coll (IL)
LATZKE, Henry R. (Lib Srvs Dir) 702

Concordia Coll (MI)
DAVIDSEN, Susanna L. (Pub Srvs Dir) 276

Concordia Coll (MN)
OFFERMANN, Glenn W. (Head Libn) 917
RUDIE, Helen M. (Asst Prof) . . 1065

Concordia Coll (NE)
MEIER, Marjorie A. (Asst Libn) . . 821

Concordia Coll (NY)
ANDERSON, Birgitta M. (Asst to the Dir of Lib Srvs) 21
HUEBNER, Mary A. (Dir of Lib Srvs) 570

Concordia Historical Institute (MO)
BODLING, Kurt A. (Asst Dir, Ref & Info Srvs) 109
WOHLRABE, John C. (Asst Dir, Archvst, Libn) 1359

Concordia Publishing House (MO)
BOBB, Barry L. (Dir, Music Pubn) 108

Concordia Theological Seminary (IN)
WARTZOK, Susan G. (Technl Srvs Libn) 1307

Concordia Unified Sch District 333 (KS)
BRADLEY, Susanne A. (Libn/Media Spclst) 126

Concordia Univ (PQ)
APPLEBY, Judith A. (Asst Libn) . . 30
BOUCHER, Lorna M. (Ref Libn) . 118
GALLER, Anne M. (Assoc Prof) . 414
GAMEIRO, Maria H. (Ref Libn) . . 416
HAWKE, Susan J. (Asst Libn) . . . 513
HOFFMAN, Sandra D. (Bus Ref Libn) 548
KATZ, Solomon B. (Catlgng Libn) 630
MAHARAJ, Diana J. (Computer-assisted Reader Srvs Libn) 760
MARRELLI, Nancy M. (Univ Archvst) 773
MATE, Albert V. (Dir of Libs) 783
WINIARZ, Elizabeth (Ref & Selection Libn) 1355

Conemaugh Valley Memorial Hospital (PA)
WILSON, Fred L. (Hlth Scis Libn) 1351

Coney Island Hospital (NY)
MARK, Ronnie J. (Med Lib Dir) . . 770

The Conference Board Inc (NY)
HERNANDEZ, Tamsen M. (Dir, Info Srvs) 532

Conference Board of Canada (ON)
BUCHANAN, Zoe A. (Info Spclst) 153
ROSTAMI, Janet (Online Spclst) 1059

Congressional Information Service Inc (MD)
JOHNSON, Richard K. (Dir of Comms) 608
MASSA, Paul P. (Pres & Chief Exec Ofcr) 781
MCRAE, Alexander D. (Dir of Resrch) 818
STERN, Michael P. (Resrch VP) 1189
TAYLOR, Marcia E. (Comms Coordntr) 1227
VONDERHAAR, Mark N. (Asst Resrch Dir) 1288

Congressional Quarterly Inc (DC)
ALITO, Martha A. (Lib Dir) 13
VEATCH, Laurie L. (Account Rep) 1280

Congressional Research Services (DC) — BAUMGARDNER, Sandra A. (Lib Resrcs Head) 66
FLAM, Floris (Arts & Scis Team Leader) 383

Congressman Bill Archer (DC) — CARLSON, Julia F. (Legislative Aide) 182

Connecticut Coll (CT) — JOHNSON, Carolyn A. (Music Libn) 602
ROGERS, Brian D. (Coll Libn) . . 1049
SORENSEN, Pamela (Serials Libn & Automation Coordntr) 1168
TARANOW, Gerda (Engl Prof) . 1223
WALDEN, Katherine G. (Instr) . . 1294

Connecticut Department of Education (CT) — HALE, Robert G. (Coordntr) 485
WHITE, Charles R. (Educ Consult) 1330

Connecticut Dept of Mental Health (CT) — KRUK, Pauline A. (Libn II) 680

Connecticut Department of Transportation (CT) — JUKNIS, Ann M. (Libn II) 619

Connecticut Historical Society (CT) — SCHMIDT, Alesandra M. (Ref Lib) 1095
WAIT, Gary E. (Catlg Libn) 1293
WILKIE, Everett C. (Head Libn) . 1340
WILLARD, Anne H. (Archvst & Libn) 1341

Connecticut Lib Association (CT) — SIMPSON, Jeanne (Exec Secy) 1142

Connecticut State Lib (CT) — AKEROYD, Richard G. (State Libn) 9
BURGER, Leslie B. (Dir of Netwk Srvs) 159
BURKE, Jane D. (Sr Libn) 160
FAAS, Caroline (Sr Libn) 360
HORRIGAN, John J. (Sr Libn) . . 560
JERNIGAN, Denise D. (Head of Law/Legislative Ref Unit) 599
JONES, Mark H. (State Archvst) . 614
MERRILL, Mary G. (Consult) 827
O'BRIEN, Doris J. (Lib Clerk) 914
PRESEMPERE, Dominic A. (Adminstr) 991
SCHUTT, Cheryl M. (Lib Srv & Construction Act Coordntr) . . 1103
SULLIVAN, Martha J. (Unit Head) 1208
VANDERLYKE, Barbara A. (Lib Dir) 1274

Connecticut Valley Hospital (CT) — ASBELL, Mildred S. (Med Lib Dir) 35

The Connetquot Central Sch Dist of Islip (NY) — JENSEN, Patricia K. (Substitute Libn) 599

Conoco Inc (TX) — WEST, Barbara F. (Libn) 1326

Conrad Pub Lib (IA) — GALLENTINE, Richard J. (Trustee) 414
MILLER, Pearl F. (Dir) 841

Conseillers en Information Inc (PQ) — DUBEAU, Pierre (Info Broker) . . . 321

Consoer Townsend & Associates (IL) — SCHRAMM, Mary T. (Technl Lib & Info Ctr Mgr) 1099

Consolidated Edison Co (NY) — JAFFE, Steven (Libn) 591

Consolidated Edison of New York Inc (NY) — DIETRICH, Peter J. (Assoc Libn) 302

Consolidated Sch District 1 (MO) — HARTMAN, Linda C. (Media Spclst) 508

Consolidated Sch District 62 (IL) — MARTINAZZI, Toni (Libn) 779

Consortium for Health Info & Lib Srvs (PA) — VICK, Kathleen (Exec Dir) 1283

Consortium of Univs (DC) — LEMKE, Darrell H. (Lib Progs Coordntr) 715

Constitution Island Association (NY) — MARTIN, Janet L. (Archvst & Libn) 776

Consumer & Corporate Affairs Canada (ON) — HEROUX, Rejean W. (Chief Libn) 532

Consumers' Gas Co Ltd (ON) — IVEY, Donna M. 586

Consumers Power Co (MI) — SMITH, Catherine A. (Libn) 1153

Consumers Union (NY) — INGRAM, Saralyn (Lib Div Head) 583

Contel Federal Systems (MD) — VAN BRUNT, Virginia (Technl Libn) 1272

Continental Illinois National Bank (IL) — ALTGILBERS, Cynthia J. (Sr Info Analyst) 18
MOULTON, James C. (Sr Info Analyst) 873
REED, Janet S. (Mgr & 2nd VP) 1015

Continental Information Systems (NY) — GRANKA, Bernard D. (Lib Coordntr) 457

Continental Insurance Co (NY) — GAINES, Irene A. (Info Spclst) . . 412

Contra Costa County Lib (CA) — ALEXANDER, Diane A. (Branch Libn) 12
CISLER, Stephen A. (Branch Libn) 215
KENNEDY, Rose M. (Lib Comunty Srvs Coordntr) 641
LARKIN, Sally S. (Libn) 698
SIEGEL, Ernest (Cnty Libn) 1136

Control Data Corp (MN) — AXDAL, Joan L. (Ref Libn) . . 42
CLIFT, Crystal A. (Mgr) 222
GRIFFITH, Cary J. (Law Libn) . . . 469
JESSEE, W S. (Archs Consult) . . 600
LEHMAN, Tom (LOGIN Info Srvs Mgr) 713

Controlled Therapeutics Corp (PA) — MCSWAIN, Christy A. (Dir of Info Srvs) 818

Converse Coll (SC) — FAWVER, Darlene E. (Music Libn) 367

Converse Consultants NW (WA) — CHAPMAN, Kathleen A. (Libn & Info Mgr) 202

Cook County Law Lib (IL) — HAMMOND, Louise H. (Law Libn) 494
LAM, Judy (Law Libn) 689
MANN, Vijai S. (Ref Libn) 766
MARTIN, Bennie E. (Exec Law Libn) 775
NARANJO-BOSCH, Antonio A. (Chief Libn) 888

Cook Memorial Pub Lib District (IL) — LAMBERT, Sandra L. (Asst Chlds Libn) 690
SULLIVAN, Eileen M. (Chlds Srvs Dir) 1207

Cooper Heller Research (PA) — COOPER, Linda (Pres) 243
HELLER, Patricia A. (Resrch Dir) 524

Cooper Laboratories (CA) — HEMINGWAY, Beverly L. (Info Spclst) 525

Cooper Union - Advancement of Sci & Art (NY) — VAJDA, Elizabeth A. (Head Libn) 1271

Cooperative Lib Agency for Systs & Srvs (CA) — ELLSWORTH, Dianne J. (Products & Srvs Dir) 345
HAAS, Florence A. (Data Base Srvs Sr Coordntr) 480
LEE, Doreen H. (Customer & Technl Srvs Coordntr) 709
MILLER, Ronald F. (Exec Dir) . . . 842
MORRIS, Susan M. (Coordntr) . . 867

Cooperative Services (IL) — CROSS, Mabel A. (Asst Libn) . . . 260
MEARNS, Mary A. (Libn) 820

Coopers & Lybrand (CA) — HENEKS, Julia A. (Libn) 528

Coopers & Lybrand (DC) —
Coopers & Lybrand (NY) — BATTINO, Bill 65
BERGFELD, C D. (Mktg Mgr) 86
GRANDE, Paula G. (Resrch Mgr) 457
HALL, Alix M. (Cosultng Mgr, Info & Comm Group) 486
KILBERG, Jacqueline L. (Ref Libn) 648
PORTA, Catherine M. (Lib Asst) . 984
POWELL, Timothy W. (Mktg Mgr) 989

Coopers & Lybrand (OH) — IRELAND, Clara R. (Corprt Libn) . 583

Coopers & Lybrand (PA) — BLAIR, William W. (Libn) 103
BOODIS, Maxine S. (Libn) 115

Coopers & Lybrand (ON)
ATTINGER, Monique L. (Assoc Consult) 38
MCCALLUM, Anita J. (Info Ctr Mgr) 793

Coordinating Board for Higher Education (MO)
BEHLER, Patricia A. (Assoc) 74
MOORE, Barbara S. (Resrch Assoc & Ref Libn) 858

Coordinating Council of Literary Mags (NY)
CASSELL, Kay A. (Executive Dir) 193

Coos Bay Pub Lib (OR)
RASH, David W. (Asst Dir) 1009

Copiague Pub Schs (NY)
ADAMS, Grover C. (Lib Srvs Coordntr) 4

Copley Los Angeles Newspapers (CA)
ANDRADE, Rebecca (Chief Libn) 26

Copley Newspapers (CA)
CARNES, Suzanne M. (Sr Libn) . 183

Copyright Information Services (WA)
MILLER, Jerome K. (Pres) 839

Coquitlam Pub Lib (BC)
DUNCAN, Deborah J. (Chlds Coordntr) 325
UTSUNOMIYA, Leslie D. (Adult, Community Srvs Coordntr) . . 1270

Corbett Coll (MN)
HILBER, Leocadia (Libn) 538

Corbit-Calloway Memorial Lib (DE)
JAMISON, Susan C. (Dir) 593

Corcoran Gallery of Art (DC)
KOVACS, Katherine M. (Consultng Archvst) 673

Corinth Sch System (NY)
KOCH, Fran C. (Media Spclst) . . 667

Corn Belt Lib System (IL)
MC LAUGHLIN, Terry L. (Instnl Srvs Coordntr) 813
MEISELS, Henry R. (Dir) 822
POULTNEY, Judy R. (Interlib Loan Libn) 987

Cornell Coll (IA)
FALK, Mark F. (AV/Serials Libn) . 362

Cornell Medical Center (NY)
TOMASULO, Patricia A. (Head Libn) 1249

Cornell Univ (NY)
ASHMUN, Lawrence F. (Southeast Asia Libn) 36
AXTMANN, Margaret M. (Acqs Libn) 42
BRAUDE, Robert M. (Libn & Asst Dean for Info Srvs) 129
CARSON, Anne R. (Interlib Srvs Libn) 188
CASSARO, James P. (Asst Music Libn) 193
CHIANG, Katherine S. (Comp Files Libn) 207
CLARKE, D S. (Assoc Catlg Libn) 218
COLMAN, Gould P. (Univ Archvst) 233
COONS, William W. (Information Litcy Spclst) 242
CORAL, Lenore (Music Libn) . . . 245
DEMAS, Samuel G. (Col Devlpmnt Head) 291
DIEFENBACH, Dale A. (Foreign & Intl Law Libn) 301
EDDY, Donald D. (Dept Head) . . . 335
FINCH, C H. (Asst Univ Libn) . . . 377
HAMMOND, Jane L. (Prof of Law & Law Libn) 493
HASKO, John J. (Assoc Law Libn) 510
HILLMANN, Diane I. (Technl Srvs Head) 541
HUNTER, Carolyn O. 576
KENNEDY, Bruce M. (Pub Srvs Libn) 640
KIM, Chung N. (Catlg Libn) 648
LAURENCE, Katherine S. (Actg Sch of Hotel Admin Libn) . . 703
LIPPINCOTT, Joan K. (Pub Srvs Head) 732
MILLER, J G. (Prof Emeritus) . . . 838
OLSEN, Wallace C. (Agricultural Info Scitst) 922
PICCIANO, Jacqueline L. (Access Srvs Head) 970

Cornell Univ (NY)
POWELL, Jill H. (Asst Ref Libn) . 988
REID, Carolyn A. (Assoc Dir) . . 1018
SALTON, Gerard (Prof of Comp Sci) 1077
SCHNEDEKER, Donald W. (Bus Info Srvs Libn) 1096
SERCAN, Cecilia S. (NEH Dante Catlgng Proj Dir) 1116
SLOCUM, Robert B. (Assoc Catlg Libn) 1150
SPRAGG, Edwin B. (Info Srv Coordntr) 1175
STEWART, Linda G. (Online Coordntr) 1192
THOMSON, Diane G. (Eductnl Srvs Head) 1241
WALD, Ingeborg (Slide Libn) . . . 1294
WAWRO, Wanda T. (Slavic Biblgphr) 1311
WEISS, Paul J. (Catlgr) 1320
WILSON, Marijo S. (Catlgr, Catlg Editor & Database Mgr) 1352
ZASLAW, Neal (Music Prof) . . . 1386

Cornerstone Technologies (CA)
RADWIN, Mark 1002

Corning Community Coll (NY)
HORNICK-LOCKARD, Barbara A. (Lib Dir) 560

Corning Glass Works (NY)
DREIFUSS, Richard A. (Technl Info Ctr Supvsr) 319

Cornwall Pub Lib (NY)
KONDZELA, Jeanette M. (Ref Libn) 670

Cornwall Pub Lib (ON)
HARSANYI, Nancy L. (Chief Libn) 507

Coronado Pub Lib (CA)
MURTEN, Holly T. (Sr Libn) 882

Coronet Recording Co (OH)
BUCHSBAUM, Robert E. (Chairman of the Bd) 153

Corporate Report (MN)
MINOR, Barbara G. (Resrch Dir) . 846

Corp Mgmt & Marketing Consultants Inc (NJ)
PAVELY, Richard W. (Pres) 950

Corp of the City of Hamilton (ON)
BROWN, Phyllis E. (Data Base Srvs Head) 147

Corp of the President (UT)
CLEMENT, Patsy (Catlgr) 221

Corp Technology Information Services Inc (MA)
PEERS, Charles T. (Managing Editor) 954
POMERANTZ, Michael H. 982

Corpus Christi Caller-Times (TX)
NEU, Margaret J. (Lib Dir) 896

Corpus Christi Catholic Church (GA)
SULLIVAN, Mary A. (Ref Educ Prog Coordntr) 1208

Corpus Christi Pub Libs (TX)
CANALES, Herbert G. (Libs Dir) . 178

Corpus Christi State Univ (TX)
BUCHWALD, Donald M. (Head of Circ) 153
TROMBLEY, Patricia A. (Coodntr of Ref Srvs) 1258

Cortland City Sch District (NY)
HATCH, Nancy W. (Lib Media Spclst) 511

Costabile Associates Inc (MD)
BOEHR, Diane L. (Lib Consult) . . 109
COSTABILE, Salvatore L. (Pres) 249

Cote Saint-Luc Pub Lib (PQ)
PHILLIPS, Lena M. (Libn) 968

Cottage Hospital (CA)
WINZER, Kathleen M. (Libn) . . . 1356

Cottey Coll (MO)
YU, Pei (Libn) 1384

Cottonwood-Oak Creek Elem Sch District 6 (AZ)
LONDON, Eleanor (Chief Libn) . . 738

FAY, Evelyn V. (Chief Libn) 367

KIEL, Becky (Ref Libn) 647

HERRON, Bettie J. (Sch Dist Libn) 533

Cotulla Independent Sch District (TX)
BARBOUR, James C. (Head Libn) 55

Coudert Brothers (NY)
RUBENS, Jane C. (Attorney-in-Charge of the Lib) 1064

Council for Exceptional Children (VA)
MCLANE, Kathleen (Prog Mgr, Info Srvs) 813

Council of Family & Chld Caring Agencies (NY)
ROBINSON, Jolene A. (Assoc for Pub Info) 1044

Council of State Governments (KY)
SIMS, Edward N. (Dir of State
Srvs) 1142

Council on Foreign Relations (NY)
ETHERIDGE, Virginia (Actg Lib
Dir) 355
MILLER, Barbara K. (Asst Libn) . 835

Council on Lib Resources Inc (DC)
DEAN, Barbara C. (Prog Assoc) . 283
HAAS, Warren J. (Pres) 480
KEMPNER, Maximilian
(Chairperson) 639
MARCUM, Deanna B. (VP) 769
THOMPSON, Mary A.
(Secretary-Treasurer) 1240

**Country Dance & Song Society of
America** (PA)
KELLER, Kate V. (Cur) 635

**Country Day Sch of the Sacred
Heart** (MD)
WILLIS, Susan C. (Lower Sch
Libn) 1348

Country Music Foundation Inc (TN)
BELL, Rebecca L. (Serials Libn
& Non-Print Catlgr) 77
SEEMANN, Charles H. (Deputy
Dir for Col and Resrch) 1111

County-City Lib (TX)
MCSWEENEY, Bonnie (Head
Libn) 818

County Coll of Morris (NJ)
COHN, John M. (Dir) 229
JONES, David E. (Catlg Libn) . . . 612
KELSEY, Ann L. (Assoc Dir) 639

County of Barrhead (AB)
SLEMKO, M Y. (Dir) 1148

County of Cape May (NJ)
HSU, Hsiu H. (Supvsng Libn) . . . 567

County of Chester (PA)
HOFFACKER, Antoinette C.
(Asst Dir) 547

**County of Dallas & City of
Rowlett** (TX)
CROUCH, Vivian E. (Dir) 261

County of Henrico (VA)
FINCH, Mildred E. (Technl Srvs
Dir) 377
SADLER, Graham H. (Lib Dir) . . 1073
TEMPLE, Patricia C. (Area Libn) 1230

County of Los Alamos (NM)
BJORKLUND, Katharine B.
(Adult Srvs Libn) 100
KRAEMER, Mary P. (Head of
Ref & Info Srvs) 674

County of Los Angeles (CA)
DEFATO, Joan (Plant Sci Libn) . . 287

County of Morris (NJ)
LYNN-NELSON, Gayle (Law
Libn) 752

County of Richmond (NY)
KLINGLE, Philip A. (Sr Law
Libn) 662

County of San Luis Obispo (CA)
SCHLANSER, Deborah B.
(Branch Lib Mgr) 1093

County of Shasta (CA)
MCCRACKEN, John R. (Lib
Srvs Dir) 799

County of Sonoma (CA)
SAYED, Joyce P. (Records
Mgmt Coordntr) 1086

County of Victoria (ON)
GIBSON, Mary B. (Chief Libn) . . 432

County of Volusia (FL)
WHEELER, James M. (Cnty Lib
Syst Dir) 1329

County of Wayne (MI)
MISNER, Joyce V. (Chlds Libn) . 847

County of Winnebago (IL)
LINDVALL, Robert J. (Law Libn) . 730

County of Yolo (CA)
STEPHENS, Mary L. (Cnty
Libn) 1188

Coutts Lib Service (NY)
GRANTIER, John R. (Technl
Srvs VP) 458
SCHMIEDL, Keith S. (Pres) . . . 1096
REIS, Howard (VP, Bus Plng) . . 1021

Covidea (NY)
MAHAR, Ellen P. (Libn) 760

Covington and Burling (DC)
DECKER, Charlotte J. (Libn) . . . 285

Covington Latin Sch (KY)
FILIATRAULT, Sylvie (Libn) 376

Cowansville Institution (PQ)
FANARAS, William F. (Pres) . . . 363

Cowles Information Services (MN)
NANES, Evelyn M. (Law Libn) . . 887

Cozen & O'Connor (PA)
CARUSO, Joy L. (Mgr of Info
Srvs) 190

CPC International Inc (IL)
AVERILL, M S. (Info Resrch
Analyst) 41

CPC International Inc (NJ)
BROWN, Jeanne I. (Info Spclst) . 145
MALAKOFF, Diane L. (Info
Spclst) 762

Craft & Folk Art Museum (CA)
BENEDETTI, Joan M. (Musm
Libn) 80

Cranbrook Academy of Art (MI)
DYKI, Judy (Lib Dir) 331
GUNN, Diane M. (Asst Libn,
Slide Cur) 477

**Cranbrook Educational
Community** (MI)

Cranbrook Institute of Science (MI)

Crandall Lib (NY)

Crane McDowell & Co Inc (MN)

Cranford Board of Education (NJ)

Cravath Swaine & Moore (NY)

Crawford Adventist Academy (ON)

Crawfordsville District Pub Lib (IN)

Cray Research Inc (MN)

CRC Press (FL)

Creamer Dickson Basford Inc (NY)

Creative Consulting & Design (GA)

**Creative Information Retrieval
Services** (TN)

Credit Union National Assn (WI)

Credit Valley Hospital (ON)

Cree Sch Board (PQ)

Creighton Univ (NE)

Cresco Pub Lib (IA)

**Creswell Munsell Fultz & Zirbel
Inc** (IA)

Cretin-Derham Hall (MN)

**Crew-Noble Information
Services** (CA)

**Crittenden County Board of
Education** (KY)

Crittenton Hospital (MI)

Crompton & Knowles Corp (PA)

Crosby Heafey Roach & May (CA)

**Crossroads Sch for Arts and
Sciences** (CA)

Croton Free Lib (NY)

Crouse Irving Memorial Hospital (NY)

Crow Segal Management Co Inc (FL)

Crowder Coll (MO)

Crowe & Dunlevy (OK)

Crowell & Moring (DC)

**Crowley Independent Sch
District** (TX)

**Crown Point Community Sch
Corp** (IN)

Crownsville Hospital Center (MD)

CRSS Inc (TX)

Crum & Forster Insurance Co (NJ)

Crystal Lake Pub Lib (IL)

CSI (NY)

COIR, Mark A. (Dir of Archs &
Histl Cols) 229
ST. AMAND, Norma P. (Libn) . . 1075

JERYAN, Christine B. (Head
Libn & Proj Coordntr) 600
KARGE, James R. (Head) 627
HAM, Beverly V. (Info Spclst) . . . 490
GERMINDER, Robin L. (Sch
Libn K-8) 429
ADAMO, Marilyn H. (Asst Dir of
Lib Srvs) 4
BONADIA, Roseann (Head, Ref
Srvs & Info Spclst) 113
GRAY, Kevin P. (Info Spclst) . . . 460
MCLEAN, Paulette A. (Media
Centre Dir) 814
DAY, Thomas L. (Ref Srvs
Head) 283
LAPENSKY, Barbara A. (Libn) . . 697
SKALLERUP, Amy G. (Sr Edit) . 1145
BOTKIN, Karen R. (Resrch &
Info Srvs Mgr) 118
STOWELL, Donald C. (Partner) . 1199

MOON, Fletcher F. (Info Broker,
Consult) 857
SAYRS, Judith A. (Ref Libn) . . . 1087
KORNUTA, Helen (Hlth Scis
Libn) 672
GOSSELIN, Claude (Sch Libn) . . 453
GRABE, Lauralee F. (Technl
Srvs Dept Head) 455
LEBEAU, Chris (Ref Libn for
Online Srvs) 707
MEANS, Raymond B. (Lib Dir) . . 820
MURDOCK, Douglas W. (Catlg
Libn) 879
HUISKAMP, Julie G. (Dir) 572

PEARSON, Jo A. (Info Srvs
Mgr) 952
BROOKS, S B. (Head Libn) 141

CREW-NOBLE, Sara M.
(Consultant, Info Srvs) 258

HERRON, Darl H. (Elem Libn) . . . 533
LEE, Lucy W. (Med Lib Dir) 710
HANF, Elizabeth P. (Sr Info
Chemist) 495
SKRUKRUD, Nora L. (Libn) . . . 1147

EVTUHOV, Tanya (Libn) 359
BURNHAM, Helen A. (Croton
Free Lib Trustee & Co-chair) . 162
SHELANDER, Frances R. (Dir
of Lib Resrcs) 1125
STEALEY, Marjorie J.
(Executive Secy) 1183
SCHADE, Barbara L. (LRC Dir) . 1088
CORNEIL, Charlotte E. (Law
Libn) 246
CALLINAN, Ellen M. (Lib Mgr) . . 173

CRAIGHEAD, Alice A. (Elem
Sch Libn) 254

SUTTINGER, Mary C. (Media
Spclst) 1211
MERRILL, Susan S. (Libn) 827
FLESHMAN, Nancy A. (Resrch
Libn) 384
MACKINTOSH, Pamela J. (Info
Srvs Spclst) 757
THOMPSON, Melia M. (Bus Info
Ctr Supvsr) 1240
SPRINGBORN, Janice T. (Ref
Libn) 1176
KRIEGER, Tillie (Perdcls Mgr) . . . 678

Cuadra Associates Inc (CA)
CUADRA, Carlos A. (Pres) 262
KURANZ, John 684
PELTO, Charles (Mktg Support
    Asst) 955
Cuadra Associates Inc (NY)
SMITH, David F. (Consult) 1154
Cubic Corp (CA)
COOK, Kathleen M. (Libn &
    Mgr) 240
MOSER, Maxine M. (Technl Lib
    Mgr) 871
Cubic Defense Systems (CA)
MOSER, Elizabeth C. (Libn) 870
CUH2A (NJ)
MOSS, Susan K. (Libn) 872
Cumberland Books (NJ)
KOONTZ, John (Bookseller &
    Publshr) 671
**Cumberland County Pub Lib & Info
    Center** (NC)
ASPINALL, David L. (Head of
    Technl Srvs) 37
DEVITO, Robert M. (Info Srvs
    Head) 297
FREEDMAN, Barbara G. (Chlds
    Libn & Branch Head) 400
HANSEL, Patsy J. (Asst Dir) 497
HUNTER, Julie A. (Chlds Libn &
    Interim Branch Head) 576
KRIEGER, Lee A. (Coordntr) 678
MCGRIFF, Mary E. (Info Srvs
    Libn) 808
THRASHER, Jerry A. (Dir) 1243
Cumberland County Sch System (NC)
GARDNER, Janet K. (Media
    Coordntr) 418
Cumberland Pub Lib (RI)
LEVESQUE, Janet A. (Dir) 719
Cumberland Trail Lib System (IL)
DOCKINS, Glenn (Exec Dir) 307
HARRIS, Thomas J.
    (Headquarters Coordntr) 506
Cumberland Univ (TN)
KARL, Roger M. (Dir) 627
ROBERTSON, Sally A. (Asst
    Lib & Dir of LRC) 1042
Cummins Engine Co Inc (IN)
MEREDITH, Meri (Bus Libn) 825
POOR, William E. (Lib Srvs
    Mgr) 983
Curative Rehabilitation Center (WI)
BOCHTE, Terrence C. (Libn) . . . 109
Currier Lib (VA)
MATTHEWS, Stephen L. (Libn
    & Media Coordntr) 786
Curry Coll (MA)
KEYS, Marshall (Acting Dean) . . . 645
Curtis Institute of Music (PA)
EISENBERG, Peter L. (Catlg
    Libn) 340
MEYER, Kenton T. (Asst Libn) . . 830
WALKER, Elizabeth (Head Libn) 1295
Cutchague Free Lib (NY)
MINERVA, Jane R. (Dir) 846
Cuyahoga Community Coll (OH)
GORDON, Shirlee J. (Ref Libns) . . 452
MEYER, Jimmy E. (Libn) 830
Cuyahoga County Pub Lib (OH)
ALEXA, Cynthia M. (Chlds Libn,
    Pub Srvs Libn II) 12
BERLIN, Susan T. (Adult/Yng
    Adult Mtrls Selection Mg) 87
BINA, Marcella A. (Chlds Libn) . . . 97
BLAHA, Linda N. (Regnl Chlds
    Srvs Mgr) 102
CHARVAT, Catherine T.
    (Regional Head, Young Adult
    Srvs) 203
DRACH, Priscilla L. (Mgr Chlds
    Srvs) 318
DZURENKO, Joann T. (Branch
    Mgr) 331
EAGLEN, Audrey B. (Order
    Dept Mgr) 331
EVERETT, Janet J. (Regnl
    Chlds Srvs Mgr) 358
GRANTS, Yvette M. (Libn) 458
GREENBERG, Eva M. (Adult
    Srvs Libn) 463
GREENLEE, Joanne E. (Ref
    Spclst) 465
HARRIS, Margaret J. (Regnl
    Mgr) 505
HUEBSCHER, Mary (Pub Srvs
    Libn) 570
KOZLOWSKI, Ronald S.
    (Executive Dir) 674

Cuyahoga County Pub Lib (OH)
LOWELL, Virginia L. (Technl
    Srvs Dir) 744
NANCE, Lena L. (Branch Lib
    Mgr) 887
OBLOY, Elaine C. (Consumer
    Hlth Educ Spclst) 914
POTELICKI, Athalene O.
    (Branch Mgr) 986
ROBINSON, Doris J. (Regnl
    Chlds Srvs Mgr) 1043
SILVER, Linda R. (Deputy Dir) . 1138
SLEEMAN, Linda E. (Pub Srvs
    & Chlds Libn) 1148
VAN DER SCHALIE, Eric J.
    (Subject Spclst Libn) 1274
VANKE, Judith P. (Libn II) 1276
WYNN, Vivian R. (Regnl Adult
    Srvs Mgr) 1375
Cuyahoga Falls City Schs (OH)
KLAUS, Susan B. (Elem Lib
    Coordntr) 658
**Cuyahoga Falls General
    Hospital** (OH)
MAKIN, Mollie D. (Med Libn) 762
CVPH Medical Center (NY)
RANSOM, Christina R. (Med
    Libn) 1007
Cyprus Minerals Co (CO)
SMART, Marriott W. (Dir) 1151

D

D B Weldon Lib (ON)
LEE, Robert (Dir of Libs) 711
D&B Computing Service Inc (CT)
LEE, Frank B. (Sr VP) 709
Dade County Pub Schs (FL)
ADAMS, Gustav C. (Libn) 4
CHAVES, Francisco M. (Film
    Spclst) 204
PHILLIPS, Donald J. (Media
    Spclst) 968
SEGOR, Phyllis L. (Media
    Spclst) 1112
Daily News of Los Angeles (CA)
REIFMAN, Deborah S. (Chief
    Libn) 1019
The Daily Press (VA)
HAMMOND, Theresa M. (Lib
    Srvs Dir) 494
Dakota County (MN)
MACDONALD, Roderick (Dir) . . . 754
Dakota State Coll (SD)
SMITH, Rise L. (Pub Srvs Libn) 1160
Dakota Wesleyan Univ (SD)
RITTER, Linda B. (Asst Libn) . . 1036
Dalhart Independent Sch District (TX)
YOUNG, Nancy M. (Lib Resrc
    Spclst Dir/Coordntr) 1382
Dalhousie Univ (NS)
AMEY, Lorne J. (Assoc Prof) 20
BIRDSALL, William F. (Univ
    Libn) 98
DYKSTRA, Mary E. (Prof & Dir) . 331
ETTLINGER, John R. (Prof) 356
FRICK, Elizabeth A. (Assoc
    Prof) 403
HAMILTON, Elizabeth 492
HSIUNG, Lai Y. (Head of
    Catlgng) 567
MACLENNAN, Oriel C. (Ref
    Libn) 757
MCNAIR, Alison T. (Profsnl
    Libn) 815
NOWAKOWSKI, Frances C.
    (Ref Libn III) 911
READE, Judith G. (Libn) 1012
SIEGERT, Lindy E. (Asst Prof) . 1136
Dallas Area Rapid Transit (TX)
BLOECHLE, Marie K. (Asst
    Libn) 106
KANE, Deborah A. (Libn) 624
Dallas County (TX)
BENGE, Joy L. (Records Mgr &
    Archvst) 80
**Dallas County Community Coll
    District** (TX)
BAKER, Linda L. (Circ Libn) 49
DUMONT, Paul E. (Technl Srvs
    Dir) 325
EWALT, Rosalind H. (Biogph
    Catlgng Spclst) 359
Dallas County Law Lib (TX)
CLEE, June E. (Libn) 220
HOOD, Lawrence E. (Dir) 556

Dallas Independent Sch District (TX)

DANIELS, Cynthia E. (Media Spclst) 273
MCCASLIN, Cheryl A. (Media Coordntr) 795
MCLAUGHLIN, Hilda S. (Libn) . . 813
SPENCER, Barbara L. (Media Coordntr) 1173
YOUNG, J A. (Libn) 1382

Dallas Morning News (TX)

LOVELL, Bonnie A. (Text Libn) . . 743
METCALF, Judith A. (Ref Editor) 828

Dallas Pub Lib (TX)

ALLEN, Sarabeth (Mgr) 16
BOCKSTRUCK, Lloyd D. (Genealogy Section Supvsr) . . 109
BOGIE, Thomas M. (Div Mgr) . . . 110
BROWN, Muriel W. (Chld's Lit Spclst) 146
CROW, Rebecca N. (Current Col Head) 261
DAVIS, Carolyn (Asst Mgr) 278
EWUNES, Ernest L. (Lib Mgr) . . . 359
FOUDRAY, Rita C. (Subj Spclst) . 393
FOUTS, Judith F. (Selection Srvs Libn) 393
GRAY, Wayne D. (Cntl Lib Adminstr) 460
HARRIS, Andrea L. (Asst Dir) . . . 504
HERFURTH, Sharon M. (Grants Info Srv Libn) 530
JOHNSON, Johanna H. (Patent Libn & Asst Mgr) 606
KRALISZ, Victor F. (Media Devlpmnt Mgr) 675
MENDRO, Donna C. (Recordings Libn) 824
MOLTZAN, Janet R. (Asst Dir, Pub Srvs) 854
O'BRIEN, Patrick M. (Dir) 915
OSWALT, Paul K. (Asst Mgr of Hist & Soc Scis Div) 929
SHUEY, Andrea L. (Branch Mgr) 1133
SLAUGHTER, William J. (Adminstrv Srvs Dir) 1148
SMITH, Michael K. (Ref Libn & Subject Spclst) 1158
STAMELOS, Ellen A. (Catlg Div Mgr) 1179
STONE, Marvin H. (Fine Bks Div Mgr) 1197

Dallas Theological Seminary (TX)

HUNN, Marvin T. (Ref Libn & Syst Analyst) 574
IBACH, Robert D. (Lib Dir) 581

Dallas Times Herald (TX)

WALDEN, Elaine B. (Libn) 1294

Dalles-Wasco County Pub Lib (OR)

DOOLEY, Sheila M. (Lib Dir) 312

Dalton Coll (GA)

LARY, Marilyn S. (Dir of Lrng Resrc Ctr) 700

Dalton Community Lib (PA)

THOMAS, Scott E. (Dir) 1238

Dana Coll (NE)

PETERSON, Vivian A. (Lib Dir) . . 964

Dana-Farber Cancer Institute (MA)

BERNIER, Esta S. (Libn) 89

Daniel Boone Regional Lib (MO)

ANDREWS, Mark J. (Pub Srvs Libn) 27
BELCHER, Nancy S. (Chld's Libn) 76
MARTIN, Mason G. (Dir) 777
MILLSAP, Gina J. (Circ & Comp Srvs Head) 844
WATERS, Bill F. (Chlds Libn) . . 1308

Daniel Carter Consulting (TX)

CARTER, Daniel H. (Pres) 189

Daniel Webster Coll (NH)

BARRETT, Beth R. (Catlg Libn) . . 59
JACKSON, Patience K. (Lib Dir) . 588

Dann Pecar Newman Talesnick & Kleiman (IN)

WHITEMAN, Merlin P. (Attorney) 1333

Dansville Pub Lib (NY)

CANUTI, Teresa D. (Dir) 179

Danville Area Community Coll (IL)

DUCHOW, Sally (Ref & Instrctnl Libn) 322
KESSINGER, Pamela C. (Reader Srvs Libn) 644

Danville-Boyle County Pub Lib (KY)

BENSON, Karl A. (Lib dir) 83
DEARUJO, Georgia R. (Libn) . . . 284

Danville Community Coll (VA)

Danville Pub Lib (IN)

Danyl Corp (NJ)

DAP Inc (OH)

D'Arcy Masius Benton & Bowles (MI)

D'Arcy Masius Benton & Bowles (NY)
Darien Lib (CT)

Darien Pub Lib (IL)

Darien Pub Sch System (CT)

Darlington County Lib (SC)

Dartmouth Coll (NH)

Dartmouth District Sch Board (NS)

Dartmouth-Hitchcock Medical Center (NH)

Dartmouth Pub Lib (MA)
Dartmouth Regional Lib (NS)
Dartmouth Regional Vocational Sch (NS)

Dastrup/Vondruska Associates Ltd (IL)

Data Architects Inc (MA)
The Data Brokers (MD)
Data Center (CA)
The Data Desk (MA)
Data General Corp (CO)

Data General Corp (MA)

Data General Services Inc (MA)
DATA Inc (CA)

DATA Inc (CT)

Data Matrix (WA)

Data Resources (DC)

Data Resources (IL)

Data Resources (MA)

JOHNSON, Martha A. (Lrng Resrcs Dir) 607
KIBREAH, Golam (Chlds Srvs Head, Adminstrv Asst) 646
MERKERT, Robert J. (VP, Mktg) 826
SULLIVAN, Frances L. (Technl Info Spclst) 1207
ROCHLEN, Rita E. (Lib Info Spclst) 1046
SIDEN, Harriet F. (Libn) 1135
BURKE, J L. (Chief Libn) 160
BERRY, Louise P. (Dir) 90
CARNAHAN, Anne D. (Chld's Srvs Head) 183
BOUGHTON, Ruth E. (Adult Srvs Libn) 119
GILBERT, Marion M. (Lib Media Spclst) 433
SOUTHARD, Sarah T. (Lib Media Spclst) 1169
JAMES, Denise T. (Technl Srvs Libn & Admin Asst) 592
LANGSTON, William E. (Dir) . . . 696
WARR, Virginia M. (Branch Libn) 1306
BROWN, Stanley W. (Cur of Rare Books) 147
CRANE, John G. (Circ Srvs Libn) 255
CRONENWETT, Philip N. (Chief) 260
FINNEGAN, Gregory A. (Humanities & Soc Sci Ref Biblgphr) 378
FISKEN, Patricia B. (Music Libn) . 382
MORAN, William S. (Humanities & Soc Scis Libn) 862
OTTO, Margaret A. (Libn) 930
REED, Barbara E. (Art Libn) . . . 1014
WALLIN, Cornelia B. (Theatre Col Cur) 1298
LYNCH, Darrell B. (Sch Lib Srvs Supvsr) 751
BUNDY, John F. (Asst Biomedical Libn) 157
STANLEY, Ellen (Ref Libn) 1180
LEWIS, Aileen M. (Chief Libn) . . . 722
HUANG, Paul T. (Libn) 568
VONDRUSKA, Eloise M. (Resrch Adminstr) 1288
PUGH, Ann E. (Corprt Libn) 997
O'LEARY, Mick 920
CHESTER, Claudia J. (Libn) 207
CAIN, Susan H. (Pres) 171
BETTENCOURT, Nancy J. (Mktg Progs Mgr) 92
FERGUSON, Roberta J. (Mktg Spclst) 372
COPPOLA, H P. (Sr Info Spclst) . 245
D'ADOLF, Steven P. (Vice Pres Product Devlpmnt) 269
GONZALEZ, Suzanna S. (Pubns Mgr & Libn) 448
ERICKSON, Randall D. (President) 352
FELMY, John C. (Dir, Sales & Mktg Devlpmnt) 370
MUZZO, Steven E. (Industrial Consulting Dir) 883
BRINNER, Roger E. (Chief Economist & Group VP) 136
BROWN, George F. (Exec VP) . . 144
FELDMAN, Stanley J. (Sr Vice Pres) 369
HATFIELD, Philip A. (Vice Pres & Controller) 511

Data Resources (NY)

Data Resources (ON)
Data Retrieval Corp (WI)
Data Search & Retrieval Inc (OK)
Data-Star (PA)
Data Trek Inc (CA)

Database Directory Service (NY)

Database Services Inc (CA)
Databooks (MA)
DataCenter (CA)

DataChase Inc (IL)

Datalogics Inc (IL)
Datapoint Canada Inc (ON)
Datapro Research Corp (NJ)

Dataquest Inc (CA)

Datatek Corp (OK)

DATATIMES Corp (OK)

Datex Inc (MA)
Daughters of Charity St Vincent DePaul (NY)

Daughters of the American Revolution (DC)
Daughters of the Republic of Texas (TX)
Dauphin County Lib System (PA)

Davenport Films (VA)

Davenport Pub Lib (IA)

The Davey Co (NJ)

David Lipscomb Coll (TN)

David Lloyd Swift Paper Preservation (TN)
David Rexford Smith Consulting Librarian (MN)

David Sarnoff Research Center (NJ)

Davidson Coll (NC)

Davidson Community Coll (NC)

Davie County Pub Lib (NC)
Davies Medical Center (CA)
Davis & Schorr Art Books (CA)
Davis Coll of Business (OH)
Davis County Lib (UT)

Davis Graham & Stubbs (CO)

CORVESE, Lisa A. (Dir, Mktg & New Bus Devlpmnt) 248
ESSMAN, Tallaine G. (VP of Financial Instns Group) 355
ZURBRIGG, Lyn E. (Gen Mgr) . 1391
ERICKSON, Thomas (VP) 353
MOSLEY, Thomas E. (Pres) 872
CRAUMER, Patricia A. (Dir) 255
PIERCE, Patricia J. (Product Devlpmnt Dir) 971
MILLER, Barbara (VP & Publshr) 835
SPIGAI, Fran (Pres) 1174
ABRAMOFF, Lawrence J. (Pres) 3
HORN, Zoia (Right to Know Proj Dir) 559
CURRY, John A. (Info Srvs Dir) . 266
LANDRY, Ronald (Pres) 694
BROWN, Steven A. (Pres) 147
KEYS, Sandra A. (Technl Libn) . . 645
LOMBARDO, William J. (Mktg VP) 738
SCHEPP, Brad J. (Assoc Editor) 1091
FINLEY, O R. (Exec VP & Gen Mgr) 378
PASCHAL, Linda P. (Newspaper Support Srvs Mgr) 945
ROACH, Eddie D. (Electronic Publshg Mgr) 1037
PASCHAL, John M. (Vice Pres of Operations) 945
CUCCHIARO, Stephen J. (Pres) . 263

WHEELER, Elaine (Provincial Archvst) 1328

CRAWFORD, Elva B. (Archvst) . 256

HOOD, Sandra D. (Libn) 556
GIBLIN, Carol C. (Ref Libn) 431
WEBSTER, Connie L. (Dir of Technl Srvs) 1314
DAVENPORT, Thomas R. (Pres) 276
MURRAY, Rochelle A. (Chlds Dept Head) 882
OHRLUND, Ava L. (Head of Extension Srvs) 919
ROUDEBUSH, Lawanda C. (Human Resrcs Dir, Bus Libn) 1061
RUNGE, Kay K. (Dir) 1067
BROOKS, Alfred C. (Sales & Customer Srv Vice Pres) . . . 140
PERRY, Myrna G. (Assoc Libn) . . 960
WARD, James E. (Lib Dir) 1304

SWIFT, David L. (Owner) 1216

SMITH, David R. (Consltng Libn) 1154
CHU, Wendy N. (Lib & Info Srvs Mgr) 213
PARK, Leland M. (Lib Dir) 941
WOOD, Kelly S. (Asst Catlgr) . 1364
THOMAS, John B. (Lrng Resrcs Dean) 1237
HOYLE, Ruth A. (Dir) 566
SHEW, Anne L. (Med Libn) 1129
DAVIS, L C. (Partner) 280
BASILE, Anne J. (Libn) 63
GIACOMA, Pete J. (Asst Dir) . . 430
LAYTON, A J. (Dir) 705
BURNS, Linda L. (Legislative Info Spclst) 162
WOLFE, F M. (Archvst, Records Mgr) 1360

Davis Hockenberg Wine Brown et al (IA)

Davis Hoxie Faithfull & Hapgood (NY)
Davis Markel & Edwards (NY)
Davis Polk & Wardwell (DC)

Davis Polk & Wardwell (NY)

Davis Senior High Sch (CA)
Davis Wright & Jones Lib (WA)

Dawson Coll (PQ)

Dawson Independent Sch District (TX)
Dayton & Montgomery County Pub Lib (OH)

Dayton Art Institute (OH)

Dayton Board of Education (OH)

Dayton City Schs (OH)

Dayton-Montgomery County Pub Lib (OH)

Dayton Newspapers Inc (OH)
dba Info-Access (WA)

DCM Associates (CA)

DDB Needham Worldwide Inc (CA)

DDB Needham Worldwide Inc (NY)

De Kalb Pub Lib (IL)
Deaconess Hospital (MO)
Dean Jr College (MA)
Dean Witter Reynolds (NY)
Dearborn & Ewing (TN)
Dearborn Board of Education (MI)

Dearborn Div of W R Grace & Co (IL)
Dearborn Pub Schs (MI)

Debevoise & Plimpton (NY)
DEC CD-ROM Publishing (MA)

DEC Videotex Marketing Group (MA)
Decatur High Sch Lib (AL)
Decatur Memorial Hospital (IL)
Decatur Pub Lib (IL)
Dechert Price & Rhoads (NY)
Decision Resources Corp (DC)
Dedham Board of Lib Trustees (MA)
Dedham Pub Lib (MA)

Deer Park Community Schools (OH)
Deer Park Pub Lib (TX)
Deer Valley Unified Sch District (AZ)
Deere & Co (IL)

KERN, Sharon P. (Info Resrcs Mgr) 643
HAYWARD, Diane J. (Law Libn) . 517
BENNIN, Cheryl S. (Law Libn) . . . 82
MARTIN, Kathleen S. (Washington Libn) 777
MAGEE, Patricia A. (Automated Legal Resrch Libn) 759
PERRY, Paula J. (Technl Srvs Libn) 960
HALLBERG, Sharon P. (Libn) . . . 489
ANDERSON, Christine M. (Assoc Libn) 22
GILMORE, Carolyn (Libn) 437
MOSER, Beryl R. (Mgr) 870

SPRADLING, Nancy L. (Libn) . . 1175

BEY, Leon S. (Ref Libn) 93
BUCK, Jeremy R. (Deputy Dir) . 153
NEWMAN, Marianne L. (Ref Libn) 899
WALLACH, John S. (Dir) 1298
WESTNEAT, Helen C. (Ref Libn) 1327
WILSON, Letitia A. (Chld & Yng Adult Srvs Coordntr) 1351
WYLLIE, Stanley C. (Soc Sci & Genealogy Ref Libn) 1375
DUNWOODIE, Jane A. (Libn) . . 327
PINKNEY, Helen L. (Libn Emeritus & Cur of Textiles) . . . 975
JOHNSON, Floy W. (Music Educator) 604
TAYLOR, Orphus R. (Sch Psychologist) 1228

LINDSTROM, Elaine C. (Ref Libn) 730
TRIVEDI, Harish S. (Ref Lib Dir) 1257
SPEARMAN, Marie A. (Owner, Mgr, Online Database Analyst) 1172
MILLER, Davic C. (Managing Partner) 836
STEINMANN, Lois S. (Info Srvs Mgr) 1186
BROMLEY, Alice V. (Vice Pres, Mgr of Info Ctr) 140
GOLDEN, Urla M. (Dir) 445
IGLAUER, Carol (Chief Libn) . . . 581
DACHS, Jerald K. (Dir of Lib) . . 269
DAVID, Julia A. (Resrch Libn) . . 276
JULIAN, Julie L. (Law Libn) . . . 619
MCCARTY, Linda A. (Media Spclst) 795
MITCHELL, Martha M. (Libn) . . 849
CRAWFORD, Geraldine H. (Medic Spclst, Head) 256
JAROSEK, Joan E. (Asst Libn) . 594
HAYES, Kathleen M. (Mktg Comms Mgr) 516
PAGE, Bill (Mktg Mgr) 934
MORRIS, Betty J. (Head Libn) . . 866
ROGINSKI, Donna J. (Libn) . . . 1050
SEIDL, James C. (City Libn) . . . 1112
WIERZBA, Christine (Libn) . . . 1337
CARR, Sallyann (Info Spclst) . . . 186
ALLEN, Paul B. (Chairman) 15
HARVEY, Paul W. (Technl Srvs Head) 509
HEFFRON, Sheila F. (Dist Libn) . 520
CATES, Susan W. (Lib Dir) 195
BROWN, I C. (Libn) 144
HAGBERG, Betty S. (Lib Srvs Mgr) 482
POLK, Diana B. (Sr Ref Libn) . . . 981
STEGH, Leslie J. (Archvst) 1185

Deerfield Academy (MA)
COHEN, Christina M. (Ref Libn & Archvst) 228
KELLY, Patricia M. (Asst Libn) . . 638
VON KRIES, Beverley A. (Dir) . 1288

Deerfield Pub Lib (IL)
BEAN, Rick J. (Adult Srvs Ref Libn) 69
CALLAGHAN, Linda W. (Youth Srvs Coordntr) 173
MCCABE, Peggy J. (Coordntr of Pub Srvs & Spcl Projs) 793

Defense Inst of Security Assistance Mgmt (OH)
KNASIAK, Theresa J. (Lib Dir) . . 663

Defense/Intelligence Agency (DC)
CRANOR, Alice T. (Prog Analyst) 255

Defense Language Institute (CA)
CHAN, Carl C. (Catlgng Libn) . . . 199

Defense Systems Management Coll (VA)
TIPPER, Maryellen (Ref Libn) . . 1246

Defense Technical Information Center (VA)
COTTER, Gladys A. (Chief of Info Systs Div) 250
LAHR, Thomas F. (Prog Analyst) 688
LESSER, Barbara (Admin Libn) . . 718
ROTHSCHILD, M C. (Info Scis Intern) 1060
RYAN, R P. (Ofc of User Srvs Dir) 1071
SCHLAG, Gretchen A. (Supervisory Adminstrv Libn) 1093
SEDLCOK, Barbara J. (Technl Srvs Asst Libn) 1111
TIBBETS, Celeste (Ref Libn) . . . 1243

Defiance Coll (OH)
DeKalb Coll (GA)
DeKalb County (GA)
BERGMANN, Sue A. (Branch Mgr) 87

DeKalb County Sch System (GA)
BUFFALOE, Catherine S. (Libn) . 155
HULLUM, Cheri J. (Libn) 573

DeKalb Pub Lib System (GA)
HUNTER, Julie V. (Adminstrv Libn) 576
LOAR, Barbara J. (Dir) 735
LUKAS, Vicki A. (Automation Coordntr) 747

DeKalb Sch System (GA)
DOUGLASS, Charlene K. (Media Spclst) 314

Del Valle High Sch (TX)
LABODDA, Marsha J. (Libn) 686

Delaware Academy of Medicine (DE)
ELLIOTT, Gwendolyn T. (Circuit Riding Med Libn) 344
PIFALO, Victoria (Libn) 972

Delaware County Daily Times (PA)
CHANCE, Peggy J. (Newspaper Libn) 199

Delaware County District Lib (OH)
SAMPLES, Judith L. (Technl Srvs Head, Automation Mgr) 1078

Delaware County Lib System (PA)
BELANGER, David L. (Head/Automated Srvs Div) . . 75
COURTRIGHT, Harry R. (Syst Adminstr) 252
DOW, Sally C. (Asst Syst Adminstr, Consult Libn) 315
LARSON, Phyllis S. (Pres, Bd of Lib Directors) 699

Delaware Law Sch Lib (DE)
PAUL, Jacqueline R. (Head Catlgr) 949

Delaware State Coll (DE)
COONS, Daniel E. (Coll Libs Dir) 242

Delaware Technical and Community Coll (DE)
ABED, Donna M. (Asst Lib Dir) 2
TRUMBORE, Jean F. (Ref Libn) 1259

Delaware Valley Sch District (PA)
HOFMANN, Susan M. (Libn) 548

Delgado Community Coll (LA)
CUMLET, Harolyn S. (Coordntr of Acqs & Col Dev) 264
REPMAN, Denise C. (Catlgng Coordntr) 1023

Deloitte Haskins & Sells (CA)
Deloitte Haskins & Sells (IL)
MOORE-EVANS, Angela (Libn) . 862
COTILLAS, Therese G. (Libn) . . 250
JACOBSEN, Teresa T. (Supvsr) . 590

Deloitte Haskins & Sells (MN)
REYNEN, Richard G. (Libn) . . . 1025

Deloitte Haskins & Sells (NY)
KRAUSS, Susan E. (Ref Libn) . . 676
LIN, Tung F. (Asst Libn) 728

Deloitte Haskins & Sells (AB)
KOENDERINCK, Myrla J. (Libn) . 668

Deloitte Haskins & Sells (ON)
MACDONALD, Yvonne M. (Info Srvs Supvsr) 754

Delta Coll (MI)
Delta State Univ (MS)

Dement Research Assocs (CA)
DEMENT, Alice R. (Owner & Consult) 291

Deming Pub Lib (NM)
GREEN, Bradley A. (Dir) 461

The Denali Press (AK)
SCHORR, Alan E. (Editrl Dir & Publshr) 1099

Denison Pub Lib (TX)
BAILEY, Alvin R. (Dir) 46

Denison Univ (OH)
MAURER, Charles B. (Libs Dir) . . 787

Denmark Technical Coll (SC)
BOOK, Imogene I. (Lrng Resrc Ctr Dir) 115

Denton Pub Lib (TX)
TOURAINE, Linda S. (Spcl Srvs Libn) 1252

Denver Art Museum (CO)
GOODRICH, Margaret (Libn) 449

Denver Conservation Baptist Seminary (CO)
LYONS, Sarah P. (Libn/Assoc Prof of Bibl) 753

Denver Pub Lib (CO)
ASHTON, Rick J. (City Libn) 36
BOSWELL, Peggy B. (Branch Lib Mgr) 118
BOYER, Carol C. (Catlgng Supvsr) 123
CLOHESSY, Antoinette M. (Sr Libn) 223
CUMMING, Linda L. (Centl Lib Dir) 264
FOLEY, Georgiana (Dept Mgr) . . 387
TREFZ, Robert O. (Catlgng Spclst) 1255
VOLZ, Edward J. (Interlib Loan Mgr) 1288
WALTERS, Suzanne (Dir of Mktg & Devlpmnt) 1301

Denver Pub Schs (CO)
BEUTHEL, Ellengail (Libn) 93

Denver Seminary (CO)
OTTOSON, Robin D. (Ref Libn) . 930

Department for Libs and Archives (KY)
HELLARD, Ellen G. (Field Srvs Dir) 524

Department of Archives & History (MS)
HILLIARD, Elbert R. (Dir) 541

Department of Archives & History (SC)
MCDOWELL, William L. (Deputy Dir) 804

Department of Commerce (WA)
MCCORMICK, Jack M. (Scintfc Pubns Ofc Chief) 798

Department of Cultural Resources (NC)
HOY, Suellen N. (Asst Dir) 566
PRICE, William S. (Dir) 993

Department of External Affairs (ON)
LAFRANCHISE, David (Database Administr) 688

Department of Fisheries and Oceans (BC)
KELLER, Susan E. (Libn) 636

Department of Pub Instruction (WI)
DREW, Sally J. (Dir) 319
FOLKE, Carolyn W. (Bureaur Dir) 387

Department of Pub Libraries (VA)
STEWART, John D. (Asst Lib Dir) 1192

Department of State (FL)
KELLEY, Randall (Dir) 636
MORRELL, Ross (Asst Dir) 866

Department of State (NJ)
IAZOVONE, Cesear (Dir) 581

Department of State (VA)
SUMMERS, Kathy B. (Lib Technician) 1209

Department Regional Industrial Expansion (PQ)
LAPLANTE, Carole (Chief) 697

DePaul Health Center (MO)
LANEMAN, Joan A. (Lib Dir) . . . 695

DePaul Univ (IL)
ACKER, Robert L. (Asst Ref Libn & Music Libn) 3
BADGER, Barbara (Media Libn & Head Audio Visual Srvs) . . . 44
BROWN, Doris R. (Dir of Libs) . . 143
CLARKE, Susan M. (Asst Ref Libn) 219
COOPER, Rosemarie A. (Ref Libn) 243
DORST, Thomas J. (Coordntr) . . 313
GASKELL, Judith A. (Dir) 421
GORDON, Elaine H. (Instrc Libn) 451

DePaul Univ (IL)
BROW, Judith A. (Ref Libn) 141
BAHR, Edward R. (Prof of Music) 45
MACON, Myra (Lib Srvs Dir) . . . 758

DePaul Univ (IL)

KIRKLAND, Kenneth L. (Serials
Libn) 655
LINNANE, Mary L. (Technl Srvs
Assoc Libn Head) 731
MULHERIN, William S. (Asst
Law Libn) 876
OLSON, James (Asst Ref Libn) . . 922
SINKUS, Raminta (Head Catlgr) 1144

DePauw Univ (IN)

BRADLEY, Johanna (Dir of Libs) . 126
GREMMELS, Gillian S. (Pub
Srvs Coordntr) 467

Derry Pub Lib (NH)

BISSETT, Claudia K. (Catlg
Libn) 100

Derwent Inc (VA)

HARDSOG, Ellen L. (Dir) 500
DIXON, Michael D. (Pres) 306
FORMAN, Jeffrey L. (E Regnl
Sales Mgr) 390

**Des Plaines Valley Pub Lib
District** (IL)

CHAPP, Debra R. (Asst Libn) . . . 202

Deschutes County Lib (OR)

BYRNE, Helen E. (Chlds Srvs
Dir) 169

Deseret News Publishing Co (UT)

CLARK, Audrey M. (Head Libn) . 216

Desert Research Institute (NV)

SMITH, Shirley M. (Lib Resrch
Spclst) 1161

Designs for Information Inc (NY)

MILLER, Ellen L. (Vice Pres,
Info Srvs) 837

DeSisto Schs (FL)

COHN, William L. (Libs Dir) 229

DeSoto Inc (IL)

KOZELKA, Catherine C. (Info
Ctr Mgr) 674
WHITT, Diane M. (Info Resrcs
Spclst) 1334

Detroit Board of Education (MI)

THOMAS, Laverne J. (Middle
Sch Libn) 1237

Detroit Coll of Law (MI)

HANNA, Hildur W. (Pub Srvs
Libn) 496
LORNE, Lorraine K. (Assoc
Libn) 741

Detroit Edison Co (MI)

WOODLEY, Victoria B. (Work
Leader, Info Syst) 1366

Detroit Free Press (MI)

PEPPER, Alice A. (Libn) 958

The Detroit News (MI)

HAVLENA, Betty W. (Chief
Libn) 513

Detroit Pub Lib (MI)

BOWEN, Jennifer B. (Music
Catlgr) 120
BUCKLEY, Francis J. (Assoc
Dir for Pub Srvs) 154
CURTIS, Jean E. (Deputy Dir) . . . 267
FRANCIS, Gloria A. (Rare Bk
Room Chief) 396
GAREN, Robert J. (Pub
Relations Coordntr) 418
GRIMES, Timothy P. (Libn II) . . . 470
HAUSMAN, Lisa M. (Libn II) 513
HENSON, Ruby P. (Adult Srvs
Libn) 530
KNIFFEL, Leonard J. (Libn III) . . . 664
LAROSE, Margaret (Assoc Dir
of Persnl) 698
MA, Helen Y. (Copy Catlg Dept
Chief) 753
MATZKE, Ellen S. (Libn II) 786
OLDENBURG, Joseph F. (Asst
Dir, Main Lib) 920
TSAI, Fu M. (Chief Libn) 1260
TUCKER, Florence R. (Assoc
Dir of Support Srvs) 1261
WISCHMEYER, Carol A. (Subj
Spclst) 1356
ZARYCZNY, Wlodzimierz A.
(Asst Dept Head) 1386

Detroit Pub Schs (MI)

BIELICH, Paul S. (Libn) 95
HUNTER, Dorothea A. (Lib
Media Spclst) 576
WALL, Marilyn M. (Media
Spclst) 1297

Detroit Receiving Hospital (MI)

MUDLOFF, Cherrie M. (Med
Libn) 875

Devers Independent Sch District (TX)

COKINOS, Elizabeth G. (Libn) . . . 229

Devon Aire Community Sch (FL)

BLOCK, Sandra S. (Media
Spclst) 106

DeVry Institute of Technology (GA)

CHAMBERS, Shirley M. (Dir of
Lrng Resrc Ctr) 198

DeVry Institute of Technology (IL)

BOWDEN, Philip L. (Lrng Resrc
Ctr Dir) 120

DeVry Institute of Technology (TX)

COCHRAN, Carolyn (Lrng
Resrc Ctr Dir) 225

DeVry Technical Institute (NJ)

BOYLE, Jean E. (Lrng Resrcs
Ctr Dir) 124
LIOU, Pearl S. (Lrng Resrc Ctr
Co-Dir) 732

**Dewey Ballantine Bushby Palmer &
Wood** (NY)

SEER, Gitelle (Head Libn) 1111

DeWitt Sch System (AR)

HUDSPETH, Holly C. (Libn) 570

The Dexter Corp (CT)

MASTERS, Fred N. (Mgr) 782

Diablo Valley Coll (CA)

DOLVEN, Mary (Dir of Lib Srvs) . 310

**DIALOG Information Services
Inc** (CA)

BOURNE, Charles P. (Dir,
General Info Div) 119
CORCHADO, Veronica A. (Sr
Mktg Rep) 245
DEHN, Lydia A. (Bus News
Product Mgr) 288
FROST, Michelle (Info Spclst) . . . 406
GREEN-MALONEY, Nancy
(Edit, Latin Am Coordntr) . . . 465
HOLLOWAY, Dona W. (Sr
Product Analyst) 552
HUDNUT, Sophie 569
MAR, Sandy (Assoc Mktg Rep) . . 768
MARANGONI, Eugene G. (Info
Spclst) 768
ROMERO, Georg L. (Customer
Support Supvsr) 1052
SHARP, Geoffrey H. (Bus Info
Srvs Dir) 1122
SIMONS, Robert A. (Co
Counsel) 1141
SUMMIT, Roger K. (Pres) 1209
TAOKA, Wesley M. (Sr Product
Analyst) 1223
WOGGON, Michele (Product
Analyst) 1359
YODER, Susan M. (Legal &
Govt Info Product Mgr) 1380

DIALOG Information Services Inc (IL)

KAMINECKI, Ronald M. (Mgr) . . . 624
LEE, Ann H. (Regnl Rep) 709

**DIALOG Information Services
Inc** (MA)

HOCK, Randolph E. (Regnl Mgr) . 545
JACOBS, Leslie R. (New
England Regnl Rep) 589

DIALOG Information Services Inc (NY)

ESPO, Hal (Sr Product Analyst) . 354
KACHALA, Bohdanna I. (Regnl
Rep) 621

**DIALOG Information Services
Inc** (PA)

SNOW, Bonnie (Staff Regnl
Rep) 1164

DIALOG Information Services Inc (TX)

CAMP, Joyce H. (Southwest
Region Mgr) 175

**DIALOG Information Services
Inc** (VA)

CAPUTO, Anne S. (Classroom
Instrc Prog Mgr) 180
CAPUTO, Richard P. (Southeast
Regnl Mgr) 180

Dialogue Across America (VA)

BERENT, Irwin M. (Dir) 84

DIANE Publishing Co (PA)

BARON, Herman (Pres &
Publshr) 58

Dickinson Coll (PA)

JACOB, Scott J. (Catlgr) 589
POE, Terrence C. (Libn) 979

Dickinson-Higginson Press (MD)

MOREY, Frederick L.
(Editor-Publisher) 863

Dickinson Sch of Law (PA)

FOX, James R. (Law Lib Dir &
Prof of Law) 394
JONES, Debra A. (Assoc Libn) . . 612
PARTIN, Gail A. (Asst Libn) 945
SWARTHOUT, Judy L. (Circ &
Ref Libn) 1214

Dickinson Wright Moon Van Dusen et al (MI)
DARGA, Carol M. (Technl Srvs Libn) 274
HANAFEE, Valerie (Mgr, Info Srvs) 494

Dickstein Shapiro & Morin (DC) DURAKO, Frances G. (Lib Dir) . . 328
Digital Equipment Corp (MA) ADAMS, Michael Q. 5
ANDREWS, Peter J. (Systs Analyst) 27
BAKER, Elizabeth A. (Hudson Info Ctr Mgr) 48
DONOVAN, Paul (Comp Networking Consult) 312
GARDNER, Catherine P. (Market Info Spclst) 417
GEER, Elizabeth F. (Info Consult Supvsr) 425
GILLIAM, Ellen M. (Technl Info Spclst) 436
MAGUIRE, Linda H. (Mgr) . . 760
OWEN, Beth C. (Principal Info Analyst) 931

Digital Equipment Corp (MI) BEICHMAN, John C. (Software Spclst) 75
Digital Equipment Corp (NH) AHERN, Camille P. (Corprt Market Resrch Systs Mgr) 8
FERRIGNO, Helen F. (Systs Analyst & Catalgr) 373
KORBER, Nancy (Mktg Info Spclst) 671
KOZIKOWSKI, Derek M. (Technl Libn) 674
VORBEAU, Barbara E. (Serials Libn) 1289

Digital Information Group (CT) ELWELL, Christopher S. (Sr Editor) 347
SILVERSTEIN, Jeffrey S. (Publshr) 1139

Dike Community Schs (IA) MIDDLESWART, Patricia A. (Elem Sch Lib Media Spclst) . . 833
Dillon Read & Co Inc (NY) BOWLES, Nancy J. (Lib Dir) 121
SCHAFFER, Rita K. (Assoc Libn) 1089

Dilworth Paxson Kalish & Kauffman (PA)
PARKER, Lettice M. (Asst Libn) . 942
WYATT, Patricia A. (Head Libn) 1374

Dinse Erdmann & Clapp (VT) ABAZARNIA, Diane B. (Libn, Paralegal) 1
Diocese of Allentown (PA) MORIARTY, Kathleen T. (Libn) . 865
Diocese of Brooklyn (NY) STAFFORD, Catherine H. (Libn) 1178
Diocese of Green Bay (WI) LONG, Brideen (Archvst for the Green Bay Diocese) 739
Diocese of Olympia (WA) HANSEN, Peggy A. (Archvst, Records Mgr) 498
Diocese of Rockville Centre (NY) GRAHAM, Loretta (Media Coordntr) 456
Diocese of Sioux City (IA) CUMMINGS, Kevin (Archvst) . . . 264
Diocese of Wichita (KS) SHARMA, Shirley K. (Sec Sch Libn) 1122

Dirksen Congressional Research Center (IL)
MACKAMAN, Frank H. (Executive Dir) 756

Disciples of Christ Historical Society (TN)
MCWHIRTER, David I. (Dir of Lib & Archs) 818

Disclosure Information Group (MD) HOFFMAN, Diane J. 547
HYTLA, Sheila G. (Spcl Projs Mgr) 581
INKELLIS, Barbara G. (Gen Counsel) 583

Disclosure Information Group (NY) ARTHUR, Christine (Sr Mktg Rep) 35
GRUENBERG, Michael L. (Natl Sales Mgr) 474

Discography Series (NY) WEBER, Jerome F. (Edit and Publshr) 1314
DC General Hospital (DC) MOORE, Sara L. (Chief Libn) . . . 861
DC Pickett Associates (NJ) PICKETT, Doyle C. (Pres & Chief Exec Ofcr) 970

District of Columbia Pub Lib (DC)

District of Columbia Pub Schs (DC)

District 15 Sch Board (NB)
Dittlinger Memorial Lib (TX)
Divine Word Seminary Lib (WI)

Division of State Archives & Pub Records (CO)

Division of State History (UT)

Dixie Regional Lib System (MS)

Dixon Homestead Lib (NJ)

Dixon Pub Lib (IL)
Dixon-Turner Research Associates (MD)
DMA Aerospace Center (MO)

Doctors Medical Center (CA)

Document Conservation Center (GA)
Documentary Educational Resources Inc (MA)

Dodd Mead Publisher (NY)

Dodge City Community Coll (KS)

Dofasco Inc (ON)
Doherty Rumble & Butler (MN)
Dolby Laboratories (CA)
Dolton Pub Lib (IL)

Dome Petroleum Limited (AB)

BERGAN, Helen J. (Deputy Coordntr) 85
CIMERMANIS, Ilze V. (Head, Technl Srvs Dept) 214
DEANE, Roxanna (Chief of the Washingtoniana Div) 284
DOPP, Bonnie J. (Chief) 312
FRANKLIN, Hardy R. (Lib Dir) . . 397
HAGEMEYER, Alice L. (Libn for the Deaf Comunty) 483
JOHNSON, Brenda V. (Asst Dir) . 602
JONES, Elin D. (Pub Info Ofcr) . . 612
MOLUMBY, Lawrence (Deputy Dir) 854
RAPHAEL, Mary E. (Exec Asst to the Dir) 1008
RAY, Kathryn C. (Asst Div Chief) 1011
ROBINSON, Cathy A. (Libn) . . . 1043
SALVADORE, Maria B. (Coordntr of Chlds Srvs) 1078
SWEENEY, June D. (Supvsr) . . 1215
THOMPSON-JOYNER, Rita S. (Catlg Div Chief) 1241
TSCHERNY, Elena (Coordntr of Comunty Info Srv) 1260
WALLACE, Michael T. (Chief of Yng Adult Srvs Div) 1298
WASHINGTON, Sigrid M. (Regnl Branch Libn) 1308
EDWARDS, Andrea Y. (Sch Lib Media Spclst) 337
HARRIS, Marie (Actg Supvsng Dir) 505
JENKINS, Lydia E. (Lib Media Spclst) 597
LITTLEJOHN, Grace M. (Dir of Med Srvs) 734
MANOR, Lawanda (Sch Libn) . . . 767
MOORE, Virginia B. (Libn) 861
ROBINSON, Sandra N. (Lib Media Spclst) 1044
WILLIAMS, Eve A. (Tchr & Libn) 1343
MCENTEE, Mary F. (AV Libn) . . . 804
KREINUS, Anthony A. (Head Libn) 677

KETELSEN, Terry (State Archvst) 645
HAYMOND, Jay M. (Coordntr, Cols & Resrch) 516
HART, Julie C. (Dir) 507
WILLIS, Jan L. (Extension Libn) 1348
SCHUELER, Frances S. (Head of Ref & Catlgng) 1101
GILLFILLAN, Nancy M. (Lib Dir) . 435

TURNER, Ellis S. (Pres) 1264
BICK, Barbara K. (Ref Libn) 94
MECHANIC, Margaret A. (Technl Lib Chief) 820
LUEBKE, Margaret F. (Med Libn) 747
MOORE, Harold H. (Owner) 859

CABEZAS, Sue A. (Exec Vice-Pres) 170
DEE, Camille C. (Contribr, Best Plays Series) 286
REEVES, Cathy L. (Lrng Resrcs Ctr Dir) 1016
DUFF, Ann M. (Resrch Libn) . . . 323
TURNER, Ann S. (Libn) 1264
EVANS, M R. (Info Spclst) 357
FITZGERALD, Adena H. (Technl Srvs Libn) 382
HARDY, Kenneth J. (Libn) 501
HARVEY, Carl G. (Libs & Records Mgmt Supvsr) 509

Dominican Central Province (IL) WRIGHT, David F. (Provincial Archvst) ... 1371
Dominican Coll (CA) DIENER, Margaret M. (Lib Dir) .. 302
Dominican Coll (NY) ARNEJA, Harbhajan S. (Asst Prof & Asst Libn) ... 33
Dominican House of Studies (DC) NITZ, Andrew M. (Catlgr) ... 905
RZECZKOWSKI, Eugene M. (Lib Bus Mgr) 1072
VANDEGRIFT, J R. (Libn) ... 1273
Dominican Sisters of Edmonds (WA) HALEY, Marguerite R. (Archvst) . 486
Domino's Farms Archives & Galleries Corp (MI) MATTHEWS, Darwin C. (Corprt Archvst) ... 785
Domino's Pizza (MI) ELLENBOGEN, Barbara R. (Info Spclst) ... 343
Don A Turner County Law Lib (CA) WEBB, Duncan C. (Dir) ... 1313
Donaldson Lufkin & Jenrette (NY) CLOWE, Isabel B. (Ref Libn) ... 223
Donmar Associates (NY) ANTHONY, Donald C. (Pres) ... 28
Donnelley Marketing Information (CT) HILL, Gary L. (VP & Gen Mgr) .. 539
Donnelly Coll (KS) VAN BENTEN, Virginia M. (Media Ctr Dir) ... 1272
Donnelly Corp (MI) YETMAN, Nancy J. (Libn) ... 1380
Donohue & Associates Inc (WI) CONDON, John J. (Lib Dir) ... 236
Donohue/McCaughtry Inc (CT) DONOHUE, Christine N. (Pres) .. 311
MCCAUGHTRY, Dorothy H. (Principal) ... 795
MOON, Peter S. (Info Prfsnl) .. 858
Doraville City Lib (GA) DRAPER, James D. (Dir) ... 318
Dorchester County Pub Lib (MD) DEL SORDO, Jean S. (Lib Adminstr) ... 290
Dorothy Thomas Co (NY) THOMAS, Dorothy (Owner) ... 1236
Dorr Genealogy Lib (CA) LE DORR, Lillian E. (Owner) ... 708
Double Joy Studios (WI) EUKEY, Jim O. (Mgr) ... 356
Douglas Aircraft Co (CA) BREWSAUGH, Susan J. (Libn) .. 134
Douglas County Board of Commissioners (GA) WARREN, Ruth M. (Head Libn) 1307
Douglas County Board of Education (GA) BISSELL, Susan J. (Libn) ... 100
BROCK, Kathy T. (Sch Lib Media Spclst) ... 138
Douglas County District Court (NE) GENDLER, Carol J. (Libn) ... 426
Douglas County Lib (NV) STURM, Danna G. (Chlds Libn) 1205
Douglas County Lib System (OR) CLELAND, Mary V. (Technl Srvs Head) ... 220
Douglas County Pub Lib (CO) CONNOR, Evelyn (Dir) ... 238
Dover General Hospital & Medical Center (NJ) RYAN, Mary E. (Head Libn) ... 1071
Dover Pub Lib (OH) COOLEY, Daniel R. (Dir) ... 241
Dow Chemical Canada Inc (ON) CHAPMAN, Phyllis C. (Libn) ... 202
RUTHERFORD, Frederick S. (Info Spclst) ... 1070
Dow Chemical Co (MI) JAZBINSCHEK, Jerri (Patent Info Spclst) ... 596
STEINER, Doris L. (Legal Lib Supvsr) ... 1186
Dow Chemical Co (OH) QUINN, Caroline E. (Technl Info Spclst) ... 1000
Dow Chemical USA (TX) WOLFE, Carl F. (Sr Resrch Libn) ... 1360
HORCHER, Ann M. (Info Retrieval Supvsr) ... 559
Dow Corning Corp (MI)
Dow Jones & Co Inc (NJ) BAKES, Floy L. (Account Devlpmnt Mgr) ... 50
GROSSMAN, Allen N. (Dir of Bus Devlpmnt & Info Srvs) .. 473
LOGAN, Harold J. (Bus Devlpmnt Deputy Dir) ... 737
PACE, Thomas (Comms Counsel) ... 933
RODEAWALD, Patricia M. (Proj Mgr) ... 1047
TURNER, Tim L. (Mktg Dir) ... 1265
VALENTI, Carl M. ... 1271
WARD, Catherine J. (Edit) ... 1303
Dowdell Lib (NJ) MCCOY, W K. (Dir) ... 799
Dowling Coll (NY) BEAUDRIE, Ronald A. (Head Ref Libn) ... 70
GUY, Wendell A. (Dir of Lrng Resrcs) ... 479

Downers Grove Pub Lib (IL) BALCOM, Kathleen M. (Lib Dir) .. 51
BOWEN, Christopher F. (Asst Libn) ... 120
BROWN, Nancy E. (Lit & AV Libn) ... 146
KLEKOWSKI, Lynn M. (Ref Libn) ... 660
NEAL, Karen F. (Ref Libn) ... 890
SCHULTZ, Lois B. (Chlds Libn) . 1102
Downingtown Area Sch District (PA) AMICONE, Janice L. (Libn) ... 20
GREBEY, Betty H. (Lib Dept Head) ... 461
JAFFE, Lawrence J. (Libn) ... 591
Downs Rachlin and Martin (VT) BROWNE, Wynne W. (Libn) ... 148
Dr Robert L Yeager Health Center (NY) GROSS, Elinor L. (Libn) ... 472
Dr Samuel L Bossard Memorial Lib (OH) GUTHRIE, Chab C. (Chlds Srvs Dir) ... 479
Dr William M Scholl Coll (IL) KLEIN, Richard S. (Dir of Lib Srvs) ... 659
Drackett Company (OH) ENNIS, Mary J. (Libn & Patent Consultant) ... 350
Drake Univ (IA) EDWARDS, John D. (Law Lib Dir & Prof of Law) ... 337
SKEERS, Timothy M. (Serials Libn) ... 1145
STOPPEL, Ellen K. (Assoc Law Libn & Assoc Prof) ... 1198
STOPPEL, William A. (Dir of Libs) ... 1198
Drama Book Publishers (NY) PINE, Ralph (Editor-in-Chief) ... 974
Draughons Junior Coll (TN) TURNER, Deborah M. (Libn) ... 1264
Dresser Industries Inc (NJ) SZE, Melanie C. (Info Spclst) .. 1218
Dresser Industries Inc (TX) GIBSON, Timothy T. (Sr Tax Libn) ... 432
Drew Univ (NJ) BROCKMAN, William S. (Ref Libn) ... 138
COPELAND, Alice T. (Head, Catlgng Dept) ... 244
COUGHLIN, Caroline M. (Lib Dir) ... 250
FERRIBY, Peter G. (Catlgr) ... 373
FRIEDMAN, Ruth (Ref Libn) ... 404
JONES, Arthur E. (Dir Emeritus & Spcl Cols Libn) ... 611
SNELSON, Pamela (Access Srvs Coordntr) ... 1163
WANGGAARD, Janice H. (Govt Docums Dept Staff Mem) ... 1303
Drew Univ Lib (NJ) CONNORS, Linda E. (Col Devlpmnt Coordntr) ... 238
Drexel Burnham Lambert (NY) RIPIN, Laura G. (Lib Dir) ... 1035
Drexel Univ (PA) CHILDERS, Thomas A. (Info Resch Ctr Dir) ... 208
DUVALLY, Charlotte F. (Engrng Libn) ... 330
GARRISON, Guy G. (Kroeger Prof of Lib Sci) ... 420
GARSON, Kenneth W. (Ref Libn) ... 420
GRIFFITH, Belver C. (Prof) ... 469
LABORIE, Tim ... 686
LYTLE, Richard H. (Dean of the Coll of Info Std) ... 753
MANCALL, Jacqueline C. (Assoc Prof, Lib & Info Sci) . 764
MARVIN, Stephen G. (Head, Govt Docums) ... 780
PAUL, Thompson (Asst Prof) ... 949
SNYDER, Richard L. (Libs Dir) . 1165
TANNER, Anne B. (Asst Dean) . 1222
TRUMPLER, Elisabeth (Catlgng Head) ... 1259
WELSH, Barbara W. (Placement Dir) ... 1323
Dreyfus Corp (NY) DIFEDE, Robert F. (Info Spclst) . 302
DRI/McGraw-Hill (MA) WYSS, David A. (Sr Vice Pres) 1376
Drury Coll (MO) SINCLAIR, Regina A. (Asst Prof) ... 1143

Duane Morris & Heckscher (PA)
Dublin Local Schs (OH)

Dublin Pub Libs (IRE)
Duchesne Academy (TX)

Duke Power Co (NC)
Duke Univ (NC)

BERGER, Joellen (Libn) 85
LOVELAND, Catherine R. (Lib
    Media Spclst) 743
SLINEY, Marjory T. (Libn) 1149
WEATHERS, Barbara H. (High
    Sch Libn) 1312
SKINNER, Linda W. (Libn) 1146
ADAMS, Elizabeth L. (Ref Libn) . . . 4
BASEFSKY, Stuart M. (Docums
    Ref and Maps Libn) 62
BERGER, Kenneth W. (Ref
    Libn) 85
BIRD, Warren P. (Assoc Prof &
    Lib Dir) 98
BREEZE, Hope (Div Head) 131
BYRD, Robert L. (Manuscripts
    Cur) 169
CAMPBELL, Jerry D. (Vice
    Provost & Univ Libn) 176
CARRINGTON, Bessie M. (Ref
    Libn) 186
CLARK, Marie L. (Head, Pub
    Docums, Maps Dept) 217
DENSON, Janeen J. (Circ Libn) . 293
DRUESEDOW, John E. (Music
    Lib Dir) 320
DUNN, Elizabeth B. (Asst Ref
    Libn) 326
EZZELL, Joline R. (Spcl Projs
    Libn) 360
FARRIS, Joyce L. (Original
    Catlgng Section Head) 365
FEINGLOS, Susan J. (Online
    Srvs Coordntr) 369
GARTRELL, Ellen G. (Asst Cur
    for Reader Srvs) 420
GERMAIN, Claire M. (Asst Libn
    & Sr Lectr) 429
HEBERT, Robert A. (Pub Srvs
    Libn) 519
HENSEN, Steven L. (Asst
    Curator for Technl Srvs) 529
HINSON, Doris M. (Catlgr) 543
KLINE, Lawrence O.
    (Monographic Catlgng Dept
    Head) 661
LAVINE, Marcia M. (Ref Libn,
    Coordntr, User Educators) . . . 703
LUBANS, John (Assoc Univ
    Libn) 745
MIDDLETON, Beverly D. (Ref
    Libn) 833
MOORE, Scott L. (Archvl Asst) . . 861
NELIUS, Albert A. (Circ Dept
    Head) 893
PORTER, Katherine R. (Chem
    Lib Head & Sci Coordntr) 985
REES, Joe C. (Ref Libn) 1016
SMITH, Eric J. (Engrng Libn) . . . 1155
SOUTHERN, Mary A. (Math &
    Physics Libn) 1170
STEAD, William W. (Assoc Prof
    of Medcn & Nephrology) . . . 1183
TRUMBULL, Jane (Catlgng
    Dept Head) 1259
TUTTLE, Joseph C. (Libn) 1266
VOGEL, Jane G. (Ref Libn) 1286
WOODBURN, Judy I. (Coordntr
    of Technl Srvs) 1366
YOUNG, Betty I. (Libn) 1381

Duluth Pub Lib (MN)
OUSE, David J. (Ref & Info Srvs
    Head) 930
Dumbarton Oaks Research Lib (DC)
BYERS, Laura T. (Libn) 168
VASLEF, Irene (Lib Dir) 1279
Dumont Board of Education (NJ)
MAYNES, Kathleen R. (Instrcl
    Media Spclst) 790
Dun & Bradstreet Canada Ltd (ON)
LA MARCHE, David L. (Natl
    Mktg Mgr) 689
SOMMERS, Patrick C. (VP of
    Corprt Mktg) 1167

Dun & Bradstreet Corp (CA)
Dun & Bradstreet Corp (DC)

Dun & Bradstreet Corp (IL)
Dun & Bradstreet Corp (NC)

Dun & Bradstreet Corp (NJ)

Dun & Bradstreet Corp (NY)

Dun & Bradstreet Credit Services (NJ)

**Dun & Bradstreet Information
    Resources** (PA)

Dun & Bradstreet International (NY)

Duncanville Pub Lib (TX)
Dundalk Community Coll (MD)

**Dundee Township Pub Lib
    District** (IL)

Dunedin Pub Lib (FL)

Dunham Pub Lib (NY)

HARMON, Gary (Regnl VP) 502
FRIEND, Gary I. (Govt Info Srvs
    Mgr) 404
MCGINTY, James P. (Govt
    Mktg Group VP) 806
MORROW, Murrey (Regnl VP) . . 869
MCZORN, Bonita A. (Bus
    Analyst & Data Spclst) 819
AMICO, Robert (Product Mgmt
    Dir) 20
BARTOS, Phil (Pres) 62
BLOOM, Robert (VP of Market
    Devlpmnt) 106
CLARK, Rick (Online Srvs Dir) . . 218
COLEMAN, Peggy (Trng &
    Documtn Mgr) 231
DITMARS, Robert D. (VP &
    Publshr) 305
DOLAN, Joseph (VP of Admin) . . 309
DONAHUE, Delaine R. (Sr VP) . . 310
EUSTIS, Peter (Sr VP of Bus
    Devlpmnt) 356
GREENBERG, Charles (Regnl
    Sales Mgr) 463
HACKETT, William F. (VP of
    Mktg & Plng) 481
HANEY, Kevin M. (Mgr, New
    Product Devlpmnt) 495
HORNE, Stephen (Dir of Direct
    Mktg Srvs) 560
ITZ, Richard A. (Online Product
    Mgr) 585
KAHOFER, Stephen O. (Dir of
    Sales & Mktg Srvs) 622
KONTOGOURIS, Venetia (VP
    of Product Devlpmnt) 671
KREINER, Joseph (VP of
    Specialized Market Mgmt) . . . 677
LEHMKUHL, Charles (VP of Info
    Systs & Srvs) 713
MCCARTHY, Thomas M. (Sr
    VP of Client Srvs) 794
PAIGE, Richard (VP of
    Database Mgmt & Devlpmnt) . 935
POLUSZNY, Joseph P. (VP of
    Finance) 982
REISBERG, Gerald (VP of
    Direct Mktg Srvs) 1021
SIMON, David H. (Product Mgr) 1140
WILKENING, Barry (VP of
    Operations) 1339
WOODS, William (Sr VP of
    Mktg & Plng) 1367
GOOGINS, Jennifer J. (Assoc
    Dir of Systs & Mktg Std) 450
ALDEN, Pamela V. (Asst VP,
    Product Plng & Resrch) 11
MILGRIM, Martin S. (Resch Proj
    Dir) 835
OLD, Forrest R. 920
ROTHMAN, Joan (Dir of Online
    Srvs) 1060

DONOHUE, Delaine R. (Sr Vice
    Pres) 312
JURKOWICH, George J.
    (Communications VP) 620
BRYAN, Carla W. (Lib Dir) 151
LANDRY, Mary E. (Dir of Lib
    Srvs) 693
MILLER, Everett G. (Prof,
    Minister & Adminstr) 837

MECHTENBERG, Paul (Head
    Libn) 820
POTTER, Robert E. (Technl
    Srvs Dir) 987
SHINN, Sydniciel (Lib Dir) 1131
SHEFFER, Karen M. (Chlds
    Libn) 1125

Dunkirk Pub Schs (NY) GEIBEN, Rodney F. (High Sch Libn) 425

Dun's Marketing Services (NJ) BROWNE, Pat (Advertising & Comms Dir) 148
PIKE, Christine M. (Technl Support Liaison) 972

Dunsnet (CT) MACHALE, Jesslyn C. (Product Consult) 755

DuPage County Health Department (IL) ALECCIA, Janet A. (Lib Srvs Coordntr) 11

DuPage County Law Lib (IL) EGGERT, Charlean D. (Law Libn) 339

DuPage High Sch District 88 (IL) WRIGHT, Deborah L. (Lib Dir) . 1371

DuPage Lib System (IL) FEINER, Arlene M. (Consultant/Coordinator) 369
LUEDER, Dianne B. (Asst Dir) . . . 747
MORRISON, Carol J. (Info Netwk Coordntr) 868
SHURMAN, Richard L. (Lib Automation Coordntr) 1134

Duplin County Lib (NC) HADDEN, Linda W. (Dir) 481

Dupont Critical Care Inc (IL) KOZAK, Marlene G. (Info & Resrch Plng Dir) 674

Duquesne Univ (PA) KERCHOF, Kathryn K. (Instr of Comp Sci) 643
PUGLIESE, Paul J. (Exec Dir) . . 997
RISHEL, Joseph F. (Asst Prof of Hist) 1035
ROBINSON, Agnes F. (Assit Law Libn & Technl Srv Head) 1043

Duracell Inc (MA) GEVIRTZMAN, Joyce L. (Mgr, Tech Info Ctr) 430

Durham Academy (NC) OSBORN, Dorothy H. (Dir of Libs) 927

Durham City Schs (NC) CLEMONS, Kenneth L. (AV Coordntr) 221

Durham Coll of Applied Arts (ON) BARCLAY, Susan L. (Lib & Media Srvs Dept Head) 55

Durham County Lib (NC) GADDIS, Dale W. (Dir) 411
SIPPEN, Kathi H. (AV Libn) . . . 1144

Durham County Schs (NC) FISH, Barbara M. (Ctr Coordntr) . 380

Durham Herald Co Inc (NC) BARBEE, Lisa M. (Lib Asst, Microfilm) 55
SEMONCHE, Barbara P. (Lib Dir) 1115

Dusty Strings Dulcimer Co (WA) KREPS, Lise E. (Music Store Ordering, Sales Clerk) 678

Dutchess County (NY) LAFEVER, C R. (Records Mgmt Ofcr) 687

Duval County Pub Schs (FL) BONFILI, Barbara J. (Libn & Media Spclst) 114
COTE, Sarah A. (Lib Media Spclst) 249
MCMICHAEL, Sandra C. (Media Srvs Coordntr) 815
YOUNG, Barbara A. (Lib Supvsr) 1381

Dwight Sch (NY) ELLIS, Kathleen V. (Libn & Tchr) 344

Dyess Grove Inc (TX) RICE, Ralph A. (Resrchr & Appraiser) 1027

Dyke Coll (OH) TRIVISON, Donna (Dir) 1257

Dymanic Bioreactors (CA) ANJOU-DURAZZO, Martel T. (Self-employed) 28

Dynamic Information (CA) MARSINKO, Randy 775
WLADAS, Edward 1359

Dynatrend Inc (MA) DRESLEY, Susan C. (Technl Ref Ctr Supvsr) 319
HUSSEY, Laurie L. (Sr Info Analyst) 578

DYNIX Inc (MD) DUDLEY, Robyn A. (Automation Spclst) 323

DYNIX Inc (UT) PETERSON, Douglas L. (Lib Support Rep) 963
WILSON, D K. (Vice Pres & Gen Mgr) 1350

E

E B Crawford Memorial Lib (NY) DORN, Robert J. (Lib Dir) 313
E C Jordan Co (ME) LAWSON, James R. (Libn) 705
E C Lively Elementary Sch (TX) WHISENNAND, Cynthia S. (Sch Libn) 1329
E F Houghton & Co (PA) SCHWEITZER, Margaret C. (Libn) 1105
E F Hutton Co Inc (NY) STERLING, Sheila (Asst VP) . 1189
E F Keon Co (NJ) KEON, Edward F. (Pres) 643
E I DuPont Co (SC) SUTHERLAND, Carl T. (Libn) . . 1211
E I DuPont de Nemours & Co Inc (DE) GRILLO, Anthony L. (Coordntr of Multiclient Std) 470
MORTON, Dorothy J. (Sr Analyst) 870
SELZER, Nancy S. (Libn) 1114
E I DuPont de Nemours & Co Inc (IL) SYVERSON, Kathleen A. (Sr Info Analyst) 1217
E I DuPont de Nemours & Co Inc (MA) LEEDS, Pauline R. (Lib Srvs Supvsr) 711
E I DuPont de Nemours & Co Inc (VA) WILLS, Luella G. (Technl Libn) . 1349
E M Warburg Pincus & Co Inc (NY) SOROBAY, Roman T. (Resrch Libn) 1169
E O Coffman Middle Sch (TN) EDWARDS, Barbara T. (Libn) . . . 337
E P Dutton (NY) BUCKLEY, Virginia L. (Lodestar Books Editrl Dir) 154
E R Squibb & Sons Inc (NJ) GEORGE, Muriel S. (Resrch Info Ctr Sect Head) 428
MCLAUGHLIN, Dorothy M. (Supvsr of Lib Operations) . . . 813
PHILLIPS, Carol H. (Sci Info Spclst) 967
WEISS, Susan (Technl Libn) . . . 1320
E-Systems Inc (FL) PARKS, Dennis H. (Lib, Archs Dir) 943
EAA Aviation Foundation Inc (WI) ARMITAGE, Constance (Dir) 32
Eagle County Pub Lib (CO) BOEHME, Vada M. (Sch Libn) . . 109
Eanes Independent Sch District (TX) HOOVER, Gloria E. (Sch Libn) . . 557
WIDENER, Sarah A. (Lib Srvs Dir) 1335
Earl K Long Memorial Hospital (LA) FINLEY, Jean B. (Dir of Lib Srvs) 378
Earle Palmer Brown Companies (MD) MASTROIANNI, Richard L. (Libn & Resrchr) 783
Earlham Coll (IN) FARBER, Evan I. (Lib Dir) 363
Easley Information Service (WA) EASLEY, Janet T. (Partner) 332
East Albemarle Regional Lib (NC) SANDERS, Anne D. (Dir) 1079
East Arkansas Community Coll (AR) BERMAN, Arthur (Dir, Lrng Resrc Ctr) 88
East Baton Rouge Parish Lib (LA) ABRAHAM, Sandra H. (Libn I) 3
BINGHAM, Elizabeth E. (Adult Srvs Head) 97
MARCKS, Carol J. (Libn I) 769
East Baton Rouge Parish Sch Board (LA) HEROY, Phyllis B. (Supvsr of Libs) 532
ROBINSON, Joyce W. (Libn) . . 1044
STEBEN, Florence E. (Libn) . . . 1183
East Brunswick Pub Lib (NJ) KARMAZIN, Sharon M. (Asst Dir) 627
KHEEL, Susan T. (Ref & Info Srvs Head) 646
STONE, Jason R. (Facilities Plng Coordntr) 1197
East Carolina Univ (NC) BOCCACCIO, Mary A. (Cur of Manuscripts) 108
BOYCE, Emily S. (Chair & Prof) . 122
CHENG, Chao S. (Acqs Libn) . . . 206
COLLINS, Donald E. (Assoc Prof) 232
COTTER, Michael G. (Docums Libn) 250
DALTON, Lisa K. (Libn) 271
DODGE, Michael R. (Asst Prof & Ref Libn) 308
GLUCK, Myke H. (Sci-Tech Biblgphr & Ref Libn) 442
KARES, Artemis C. (Coordntr of Ref Srvs & Col Devlpmnt) . . . 627

East Carolina Univ (NC)

KATZ, Ruth M. (Dir of Acad Lib
 Srvs & Prof) 630
KESTER, Diane D. (Lectr) 645
LANIER, Gene D. (Prof & Dir of
 Graduate Std) 696
LAPAS, Martha E. (Ref Libn) 697
LENNON, Donald R. (Spcl Cols
 Coordntr & Assoc Prof) 715
MCGLOHON, Leah L. (Ref
 Libn) 807
MELLON, Constance A. (Asst
 Prof) 822
SCOTT, Ralph L. (Assoc Prof,
 Govt Docums Head) 1108
SHIRES, Nancy P. (Ref, Catlgng
 Libn) 1131
SPEER, Susan C. (Systs Libn) . 1172
STEPHENSON, Marilyn R. (Ref
 Libn) 1188

East Central Coll (MO)
PARKS, Gary D. (Dir of Lrng
 Resrcs) 943

East Central Regional Lib (MN)
BOESE, Robert A. (Dir) 110

East Central Univ (OK)
COULTER, Cynthia M. (Acqs
 Libn) 251
HUESMANN, James L. (Asst
 Libn) 570
ROBBINS, Louise S. (Catlgng,
 Govt Docum, Spcl Cols Libn) 1039

East Chicago Pub Lib (IN)
BERRY, Marjorie L. (Supvsng
 Libn) 90
SMYERS, Richard P. (Ref Libn) 1162
TIMMER, Julia B. (Supvsng
 Libn) 1246

**East Cleveland Board of
 Education** (OH)
AVERY, Jacqueline R. (Head
 Libn & Lib Coordntr) 41

East Cleveland Municipal Court (OH)
KEENON, Una H. (Judge) 634

East Cleveland Pub Lib (OH)
REESE, Gregory L. (Asst Dir) . . 1016
VENABLE, Andrew A. (Lib Dir) . 1282

East Detroit Memorial Lib (MI)
REID, Bette C. (Ref Libn) 1018

East Irondequoit Pub Lib (NY)
HULTZ, Karen W. (Yng Adult &
 AV Libn) 573

East Islip Pub Lib (NY)
HEINTZELMAN, Susan K. (Dir) . . 522

East Kootenay Community Coll (BC)
WHITELEY, Catherine M. (Mgr
 of Learning Resrcs) 1333

East Lansing Pub Lib (MI)
POBANZ, Becky L. (Chlds Libn) . 979

East Lyme Pub Lib (CT)
DEAKYNE, William J. (Dir) 283

East Meadow Pub Lib (NY)
EDWARDS, Harriet M. (Asst
 Dir) 337
FRANZEN, John F. (Acting Dir) . 398
WALKER, Laura L. (Head of
 Adult Srvs) 1295

East Moline Pub Lib (IL)
SHEARES, Ora M. (Libn) 1124

East Orange Board of Education (NJ)
EISEN, Marc M. (Asst Lib Dir) . . 340

East Orange Pub Lib (NJ)
IRGON, Deborah A. (Sr Libn) . . . 583
JONES, Dorothy S. (Lib Dir) 612
MATHAI, Aleyamma (Principal
 Libn in charge of Circ) 783

East Providence School Dist (RI)
LUBER, Arlene R. (Elem Media
 Spclst) 745

East St Louis Sch District 189 (IL)
BEAN, Bobby G. (Jr High Libn) . . 69

**East Side Union High Sch
 District** (CA)
MCDONOUGH, Timothy M.
 (Soh Libn, Dist Lib Coordntr) . 803

East Stroudsburg Univ (PA)
FELLER, Judith M. (Assoc Prof,
 Govt Docums Libn) 370
RIEBEL, Ellis F. (Circ Libn) 1033
SUMMERS, George V. (Univ Lib
 Dir) 1209

East Tennessee State Univ (TN)
ABOUSHAMA, Mary F. (Technl
 Srvs Libn) 2
BORCHUCK, Fred P. (Lib Dir) . . 116
FISHER, Janet S. (Asst Dean
 for Lrng Resrcs) 381
NORRIS, Carol B. (Online
 Srchng Libn & Asst Prof) . . . 909
RIDENOUR, Lisa R. (Interlib
 Loan Libn & Instr) 1032

East Tennessee State Univ (TN)

SCHER, Rita S. (Asst Dir of Libs
 for Reader Srvs) 1092
WILLIAMS, Elizabeth L. (Asst
 Libn) 1343

East Texas Baptist Univ (TX)
MAGRILL, Rose M. (Lib Dir) . . . 760

East Texas State Univ (TX)
CONRAD, James H. (Univ
 Archvst) 238

**Eastern Baptist Theological
 Seminary** (PA)
GILBERT, Thomas F. (Dir of
 Lrng Resrcs) 434

Eastern Coll (PA)
SAUER, James L. (Lib Dir) 1084

**Eastern Connecticut Lib
 Association** (CT)
DAW, May B. (Consult) 282

Eastern Connecticut State Univ (CT)
HOOSE, Beverly D. (Univ Libn
 Asst) 557
MOORHEAD, Kenneth E. (Ref &
 Curr Ctr Libn) 862
NEWMYER, Joann C. (Instrcl
 Srvs Libn) 900

Eastern Counties Regional Lib (NS)
MACRURY, Mary E. (Branch
 Srvs Coordntr) 758

**Eastern Idaho Regional Medical
 Center** (ID)
WINWARD, Coleen C. (Med
 Libn) 1356

Eastern Illinois Univ (IL)
CHEN, Robert P. (Docums Srvs
 Coordntr, Prof) 205
GRISSO, Karl M. (Head of Col
 Mgmt Srvs) 471
ISOM, Bill V. (Circ Srvs Head) . . 585
KAPLAN, Sylvia Y. (Asst Prof) . . 626
LIBBEY, Maurice C. (Acq Srvs
 Head) 725
LUQUIRE, Wilson (Dean of Lib
 Srvs & Prof) 749
NESBIT, Angus B. (Ref Libn) . . . 896
POLLARD, Frances M. (Exec
 Asst for Lib Srvs) 981
RAO, Paladugu V. (Acting Dean
 of Lib Srvs) 1008

Eastern Kentucky Univ (KY)
BARKSDALE, Milton K. (Col
 Devlpmnt Coordntr) 57
CRABB, George W. (Ref Libn) . . 254
FLAHERTY, Margaret P. (Ref
 Libn) 383
HAY, Charles C. (Archvst) 515
KOLLOFF, Fred C. (Dir, Div TV
 & Radio) 669
MARTIN, June H. (Coordntr, Lib
 Pub Srvs/Asst to Dean) 777
STAPLETON, Diana L. (Asst
 Perdcls Libn) 1181
THOMAS, Carol J. (Catlg Sect
 Chief) 1236
TURNER, Rebecca M. (Ref
 Sect Chief) 1265

**Eastern Lancaster County Sch
 District** (PA)
SCHREFFLER, Lynne W. (Info
 and Tech Coordntr) 1099

Eastern Lib System (NE)
BERNER, Karen J. (Adminstr) . . . 88

Eastern Maine Medical Center (ME)
JAGELS, Suellen T. (Lib Dir) . . . 591

**Eastern Massachusetts Regnl Lib
 System** (MA)
HENEGHAN, Mary A. (Regnl
 Adminstr) 528
MONTANA, Edward J. (Asst
 Regnl Adminstr, Pub Srvs) . . 855

**Eastern Mennonite Coll
 Seminary** (VA)
LEHMAN, James O. (Libs Dir) . . 712

Eastern Michigan Univ (MI)
BEAL, Sarell W. (Assoc Prof &
 Soc Scis Libn) 68
BECK, Mary C. (US Docums
 Libn) 71
BLUM, Fred (Ref Libn & Prof) . . . 107
BOONE, Morell D. (Lrng Resrcs
 & Tech Dean) 115
BULLARD, Rita J. (Libn) 156
DRABENSTOTT, Jon D. (Assoc
 Dean for Lib Srvs) 317
GLIKIN, Ronda (Humanities
 Libn) 441

Eastern Michigan Univ (MI)

HANSEN, Joanne J. (Coordntr) . . 497
KING, Carmen M. (Asst Prof and Slide Libn) 650
KIRKENDALL, Carolyn A. (IMC Libn) 654
RACZ, Twyla M. (Col Devlpmnt Coordntr) 1001
STANGER, Keith J. (Coordntr, Access Srvs) 1180
YEE, Sandra G. (Asst Dean) . . . 1379

Eastern Montana Coll (MT)

HAUSE, Aaron H. (Docums Serials & Maps Libn) 512
NERODA, Edward W. (Lib Srvs Dir) 895

Eastern New Mexico Univ (NM)

DOWLIN, C E. (Dir) 316
HUMPHREY, Thomas W. (Lib & Lrng Resrcs Dir) 573
MCBETH, Deborah E. (Pub Srvs Libn) 792
MCGUIRE, Laura H. (Docums Libn) 808
SCHOTT, Mark E. (Serials & Ref Libn) 1099
WALKER, Mary J. (Spcl Cols Libn) 1296

Eastern Oklahoma District Lib System (OK)

VARNER, Joyce (Asst Ref Libn) 1279

Eastern State Sch & Hospital (PA)

SORG, Elizabeth A. (Libn) 1168

Eastern Virginia Medical Sch (VA)

POLLOCK, Ethel L. (Lrng Resrcs Coordntr) 981

Eastern Washington State Histl Society (WA)

NOLAN, Edward W. (Cur) 907

Eastern Washington Univ (WA)

ALKIRE, Leland G. (Libn) 13
BAUMANN, Charles H. (Univ Libn) 66
MUTSCHLER, Charles V. (Asst Archvst) 883
TRACY, Joan I. (Asst Libn) 1253

Eastham Pub Lib (MA)

ELDRIDGE, Jane A. (Dir) 342

Eastman Chemicals Div of Eastman Kodak (TN)

WEHNER, Karen B. (Resrch Info Scitst) 1316

Eastman Dental Center (NY)

GLASER, June E. (Libn) 439

Eastman Kodak Co (NY)

BAILEY, Joe A. (Info Resrcs Coordntr) 46
BARTL, Richard P. (Libn) 61
MOUREY, Deborah A. (Bus Analyst) 874
REITANO, Maimie V. (Group Leader) 1022
SEASE, Sandra A. (Private Consult) 1110

Eastman Kodak Co (TN)

CASSELL, Gerald S. (Technl Info Assoc) 193
PRESLAR, M G. (Resrch Libn) . . 991
UBALDINI, Michael W. (Sr Technl Info Scitst) 1267

Eastman Pharmaceuticals (PA)

MILES, Donald D. (Lib Srvs Mgr) 834

Easton Area Pub Lib (PA)

BAUER, Barbara B. (Spcl Cols Cur) 65
MOSES, Lynn M. (Supvsr of Coop Srvs & Dist Consult) . . . 871

Easylink Information Service (NJ)

MCCARTHY, Martin 794

Eaton Corp (CA)

LARSON, Donald A. (Records Mgr) 699

Eaton Corp (MI)

MONTGOMERY, Mary E. (Resrch Libn) 856

EATON/Cutler-Hamer (WI)

SEUSS, Herbert J. (Consult) . . . 1117

Eau Claire Sch District (WI)

BUGHER, Kathryn M. (Catalgr) . . 155

EBASCO Services Inc (NY)

AKS, Gloria (Supvsr of Libs) 9
NOGA, Susan D. (Technl Srvs Libn) 907
VAN BRUNT, Amy S. (Ref Libn) 1272

Eberstadt Fleming Inc (NY)

THOM, Janice E. (Dir of Lib Srvs) 1235

EBS Univ (NY)

FIEGAS, Barbara E. (Acqs Head) 375

EBSCO Industries Inc (AL)

STEPHENS, James T. (Pres) . . 1188

EBSCO Industries Inc (CA)

EBSCO Industries Inc (VA)

EBSCO Subscription Services (AL)

SPALA, Jeanne L. (Adminstrv Mgr) 1170
CARSON, Howard C. (Vice Pres, Gen Mgr) 188
KETCHAM, Lee C. 645
MCKAY, Dashiell P. (Trng Coordntr) 809
ROGERS, Nancy H. (Sales Mgr) 1050
VANDERPOORTEN, Mary B. (Dir of Lib Srvs) 1274
WEED, Joe K. (VP & Dir of Mktg) 1315

EBSCO Subscription Services (CA)

CLINE, Sharon D. (Sales Rep) . . 222
LOHNES, Richard B. (Sales Rep) 737

EBSCO Subscription Services (TX)

SWEARINGEN, Wilba S. (Rep) 1214

Eccles-Lesher Memorial Lib (PA)

SCHILL, Julie G. (Dir) 1092

Eckerd Coll (FL)

HARDESTY, Larry L. (Dir of Lib Srvs) 499
BURKHARD, Polly S. (Asst Libn) 161
PENROD, Saundra K. (Dir, Chlds Srvs) 957

Eckert Seamans Cherin, & Mellott (PA)

SMITH, Sirleine M. (Adminstr) . . 1161

Eckhart Pub Lib (IN)

ROY, Helene (Sch Libn) 1063

Ecole Demosthene (PQ)

LEMIEUX, Louise (Sch Libn) . . . 715

Ecole les Melezes (PQ)

COBOLET, Guy P. (Prof) 225

Ecole Natl Superieure des Bibliothecaire (FRN)

LEMYRE, Nicole (Ref Srvs Coordntr) 715

Ecole Polytechnique (PQ)

THIBAUDEAU, Louise (Head of Pub Srvs) 1235

Ecology & Environment Inc (NY)

WOLFE, Theresa L. (Libn) 1361

Ecology Center of Ann Arbor (MI)

STONE, Nancy Y. (Staff Coordntr & Libn) 1197

Economic Council of Canada (ON)

BONAVERO, Leonard C. (Lib Mgr) 113

Ecorse Public Schs (MI)

MCKINNEY, Ceola S. (Libn & Media Spclst) 812

Ector County Lib (TX)

COPELAND, David R. (Acqs Libn) 244

Ecumenical Music & Liturgy Resource Lib (NE)

BARRICK, Judy H. (Founding Dir) 59

Edgar Allan Poe Middle Sch (TX)

THEISS, Diane M. (Libn & Media Spclst) 1234

Edgartown Pub Lib (MA)

NORTON, Linda N. (Head Libn) . 910

Edgecombe County Memorial Lib (NC)

YORK, Maurice C. (Ref & Local Hist Libn) 1381

Edgerton Elem Sch (CT)

DAIGNEAULT, Audrey I. (Sch Lib Media Spclst) 270

Edgewater Hospital (IL)

JONES, Gwendolyn C. (Med Libn) 613

Edgewood Coll (WI)

BEYENKA, Barbara L. (Archvst) . . 93
CLARK, Peter W. (Serials Libn) . 217
COSTELLO, Janice M. (Dir of Lib) 249
HOWDEN, Regis (Libn) 565
LAESSIG, Joan M. (Asst Libn) . . 687

Edgewood High Sch (WI)

DIMENT, Elna N. (Sch Libn) 304

Edina Public Schs (MN)

LEAHY, Sheila A. (Catlg Dept Head) 707

Edinburg Pub Lib (TX)

SCOTT, Mellouise J. (Media Spclst & Libn) 1107

Edison Board of Education (NJ)

FROSCHER, Jean L. (Asst Dir, Lrng Resrcs Devlpmnt) 406
HUGHES, Joyce M. (Catlgr) . . . 572
SCHWENN, Janet M. (Ref Libn) 1105

Edison Community Coll (FL)

FARKAS, Susan A. (Gen Ref Libn) 364
JOHNSON, Jacqueline B. (Legislative Ref Libn) 605
MORSE, June E. (Mgr) 869
NELSON, Christine (Ref Libn) . . 893

Edison Electric Institute (DC)

Editorial Experts Inc (VA)

Edmonds Community Coll (WA)

Edmondson Junior Coll (TN)

TAMM-DANIELS, Ana L. (Libn) 1221

Edmonton Pub Lib (AB)
BERNARD, Marie L. (Asst Supvsr) 88
DUFFUS, Sylvia J. (Bus Libn) . . . 323
RICHARDS, Vincent P. (Lib Dir) 1029
SINCLAIR, John M. (Chief Libn) 1142

Edmonton Sun (AB)

Ednor Enterprises (WV)
MCQUAIL, Edward J. (Assoc & Partner) 817

EDS Corp (MD)
PETERSON, George B. (Gen Mgr, Electronic Publshr Srvs) . 963

Educational & Industrial Television (NY)
DAMOTH, Douglas L. (Resrch Editr) 272

Educational Broadcasting Corp (NY)
DAWSON, Victoria A. (Mgr, Resrch Lib) 282

Educational Film & Video Association (NY)
MACINTYRE, Ronald R. (Exec Dir) 755

Educational Testing Service (NJ)
AMIRZAFARI, Jamileh A. (Info Analyst) 20
HALPERN, Marilyn (Lib Mgr) . . . 489
SARETZKY, Gary D. (Archvst) . 1082
WILLIAMS, Janet L. (Lib & Ref Srvs Dir) 1344

Edward Hospital (IL)
AMBROSE, Karen S. (Libn) 19

Edward R Murrow High Sch (NY)
ZAPPONE, William F. (High Sch Libn) 1386

Edward T Rabbit & Co Books for Children (VA)
REMICK, Katherine G. (Bookseller/Owner) 1022

Edwards & Angell (RI)
ALEXANDER, Jacqueline P. (Head Libn) 12

Edwards-Knox Central Sch (NY)
BRIZENDINE, Margaret K. (Lib Media Spclst) 137

Edwin L Cox Sch of Business (TX)
MASON, Florence M. (Consult) . . 781

EI Intl (ID)
LOOP, Jacqueline N. (Libn) 740

EIC Intelligence Inc (NY)
JAMIESON, Peter V. (Sales Vice Pres) 593
KOLLEGGER, James G. (Pres) . . 669
PRONIN, Monica (Vice Pres) . . . 995
VITART, Jane A. (Mktg Srvs Mgr) 1286

Eighteen East Consulting (PA)
CUTRONA, Cheryl (Self-employed) 268

Eisenhower Foundation (KS)
STROWIG, Calvin (Pres) 1203

El Camino Coll (CA)
RONEY, Raymond G. (Dean, Instrcl Srvs) 1053

El Camino Hospital (CA)
JAJKO, Pamela J. (Dir) 592

El Dorado County Free Lib (CA)
AMOS, Jeanne L. (Chlds Libn) . . . 20
BATTAGLIA, Bonnie J. (Ref, Acqs & Catlgng Libn I) 64

El Dorado Sch District 15 (AR)
MISENHEIMER, Paula S. (Lib Media Spclst) 847

El Monte Union High Sch District (CA)
CONNELL, William S. (Libn) 237

El Paso Community Coll (TX)
MALLORY, Elizabeth J. (Ref Libn) 763
TAYLOR, Anne E. (Pub Srvs Libn) 1226

El Paso Herald-Post (TX)
MCCARGAR, Susan E. (Libn) . . . 794

El Paso Independent Sch District (TX)
CAMERON, Dee B. (Sch Libn) . . 174

El Paso Pub Lib (TX)
ANDERSON, Mark (Branch Supvsr) 24
DILLINGER, Mary A. (Chlds Srvs Libn) 303
DOWDLE, Glen L. (Veterans Park Branch Libn) 315
FISCHER, Beverly J. (Chlds Consult) 379
ROBERTS, Glenda S. (Head of Catlgng) 1040
RODERICK, Mary P. (Libn II) . . 1047

El Pueblo de los Angeles State Park (CA)
STERN, Teena B. (Archvst & Resrch Historian) 1189

Ela Area Pub Lib District (IL)
DEMETRAKAKES, Jennifer B. (Comunty Srvs Libn) 291
LARSON, Carol (Adminstrv Libn) 699

Elaine Day Latourelle & Associates (WA)
OMURA, Michael (VP) 923

Eldorado Memorial Lib (IL)

Eldredge Pub Lib (MA)

Electric Power Research Institute (CA)

Electronic Data Systems (MD)

Electronic Data Systems (MI)

Electronic Data Systems (TX)

Electronic Information (ON)

Electronic Information Systems (MD)

The Electronic Scribe (ME)

Elf Aquitaine Inc (NY)

Elf Aquitaine Petroleum (TX)

Elgin Sch District 46 (IL)

Eli Lilly & Co (IN)

Elinor Lindheimer Indexing Services (CA)

Elizabeth Board of Education (NJ)

Elizabeth General Medical Center (NJ)

Elizabeth Pub Lib (NJ)

Elizabeth Seton Coll (NY)

Elizabethtown Coll (PA)

Elk Grove Unified Sch District (CA)

Elkhart Pub Lib (IN)

Elko County Lib (NV)

Ellensburg Pub Lib (WA)

Elliot Hospital (NH)

Ellis Computer Services (CA)

Ellis Fischel State Cancer Center (MO)

Elmhurst Coll (IL)

Elmhurst Memorial Hospital (IL)

Elmhurst Pub Lib (IL)

Elmira & Chemung County (NY)

Elmira City Sch District (NY)

Elmont Pub Lib (NY)

Elms Coll (MA)

Elmwood Park Pub Lib (IL)

Elmwood Park Pub Lib (NJ)

Elon Coll (NC)

Elsevier Science Publishers (NY)

FUNKHOUSER, Brenda K. (Head Libn) 410
GILLIES, Irene B. (Head Libn) . . . 436

JUDY, Joseph R. (Technl Info Ctrs Mgr) 619
PARKER, Stephen B. (Libn) 942
SLOAN, Cheryl A. (Fed Proposal Writers Mgr) 1149
MARGOLIS, Suzanne M. (Head Libn) 770
WILDER, Nancy S. (Supvsr) . . . 1339
FOSTER, Anne (VP) 392
GAUJARD, Pierre G. (Pres) 422
LUDGIN, Donald H. (Proprietor) . . 746
CAMBRIA, Roberto (Mgr, Resrch & Documtn Ctr) 174
POWELL, Alan D. (Mgr) 987
LONG, Sara E. (Lib & Media Srvs Coordntr) 739
BERTRAM, Lee A. (Scintfc Ref Libn) 91
WEHLACZ, Joseph T. (Toxicologist, Info Spclst) . . . 1316

LINDHEIMER, Elinor (Indxr) 729
RICE, Anna C. (Eductnl Media Spclst, High Sch Libn) 1026

BOSS, Catherine M. (Dir, Hlth Sci Lib) 117
DEMYANOVICH, Peter (Supvsng Libn & Syst Mgr) . . 291
LATINI, Samuel A. (Sr Ref Libn) . 701
SKRAMOUSKY, Mary C. (Lib Intern) 1147
SULLIVAN, Marion M. (Lib Dir) . . 1208
BARD, Nelson P. (Head Libn) 56
SCRIBNER, Ruth B. (Libn) 1108
DOELLMAN, Michael A. (Assoc Dir of Adult Srvs) 308
EILERS, Marsha J. (Ref Srvs Assoc Dir) 340
MILLER, Junelle (Catlgr, Asst Dept Head, Technl Srvs) 839
MADSEN, Carol (Asst Dir & Asst Coordntr) 759
WILLBERG, Carolyn S. (Dir of Lib) 1341
REINGOLD, Judith S. (Hlth Scis Libn) 1021
ELLIS, Ruth M. (Comp Consult) . 345

O'DELL, Charles A. (Med Libn) . . 916
DARLING, Elizabeth A. (Technl Srvs Libn) 274
KLATT, Melvin J. (Lib Dir) 658
NG, Pauline (Dir) 900
CALTVEDT, Sarah C. (Head of Adult Srvs) 174
BROUSE, Ann G. (Head of Technl Srvs) 141
KEEFER, Ethel A. (Lib Media Spclst) 634
CORBIN, Evelyn D. (Adult Srvs Libn) 245
STARKEY, Richard E. (Asst Prof of Lib Sci and Media Libn) 1182
HOFFMANN, Maurine L. (Adminstrv Libn) 548
GROSSBERG, Aileen D. (Chlds Libn) 473
JONES, Plummer A. (Head Libn & Dir of Lrng Resrcs) 614
SHEPHERD, Gay W. (Ref & Biblgph Instrc Libn) 1127
HUNTER, Karen A. (Vice Pres & Chairman Asst) 576

Eltzroth-Gillette Research Services (GA)

Elyria Pub Lib (OH)

Emergency Care Research Institute (PA)

Emerson Coll (MA)

Emerson Pub Lib (NJ)

Emma Pendleton Bradley Hospital (RI)

Emma S Clark Memorial Lib (NY)

Emmanuel Coll (GA)

Emmet O'Neal Lib (AL)

Emory & Henry Coll (VA)

Emory Univ (GA)

ELTZROTH, Elsbeth L. (Self-Employed) 346
BURRIER, Donald H. (Dir) 163

KATUCKI, June P. (Head Libn) . . 630
ALCORN, Cynthia W. (Col Devlpmnt Dept Head) 11
BEZERA, Elizabeth A. (Asst Dir, Pub Srv) 93
CURTIN-STEVENSON, Mary C. (Systs Devlpmnt Libn) 266
MOSKOWITZ, Michael A. (Lib Dir) 871
TRIPP, Maureen A. (Media Libn) 1257
SPOHN, Veronica G. (Dir) 1175

WALLER, Carolyn A. (Med Libn) 1298
COOK, Jeannine S. (Dir) 240
HOWARD, Rachel L. (Libn) 564
MOORE, Patricia S. (Dir) 861
JENNERICH, Elaine Z. (Lib Dir) . 598
AMMERMAN, Jackie W. (Ref Libn Intern) 20
BENEVICH, Lauren A. (Ref Libn) 80
BISHOP, Beverly D. (Ref Archvst) 99
BROWN, Carolyn M. (Ref Libn) . 142
CLEMONS, John E. (Assoc Prof & Assoc Dir) 221
DEEMER, Selden S. (Lib Systms Mgr) 286
ELAM, Joice B. (Sr Ref Libn) . . 341
ENGLER, June L. (Assoc Prof) . . 350
JESCHKE, Channing 600
JOHNSON, Herbert F. (Dir of Libs) 605
LAWSON, A V. (Dir) 705
LAWSON, Venable A. (Dir, Div of Lib & Info Mgmt) 705
LESLIE, Elizabeth J. (Grad Asst & Bookkeeper) 718
MARKWELL, Linda G. (Grady Branch Libn) 772
MILLS, Robin K. (Law Libn & Law Prof) 844
MORTON, Ann W. (Div Libn) . . . 870
NITSCHKE, Eric R. (Ref Libn) . . . 905
NITSCHKE, Marie M. (Ref Libn) . 905
O'NEILL, Patricia E. (Chem Libn) 924
PIERCE, Sydney J. (Asst Prof) . . 972
TEMPLETON, Mary E. (Bus Ref Libn) 1231
TORRENTE, Kathryn J. (Educ Coordntr) 1251
TUTTLE, Jane S. (Ref Libn) . . . 1265
VISK, Linda S. (Serials Ctl Dept Head) 1285

Empire Blue Cross & Blue Shield (NY)

CHANG, Daphne Y. (Corprt Libn) 200
DYER, Esther R. (Pub Affairs Resrch & Info Srvs Dir) 330
ROSHON, Nina C. (Mgr, Prog Srvs) 1057
RUBIN, David S. (Resrchr & Analyst) 1064

Emporia State Univ (KS)

BEEZLEY, Jo A. (Lib Asst II) . . . 74
BIRNEY, Ann E. (Asst Dean) . . . 98
BODART-TALBOT, Joni (Sch of Lib & Info Mgmt Asst Prof) . . 109
BOGAN, Mary E. (Spcl Cols Libn, Univ Archvst) 110
GROVER, Robert J. (Dean, Sch of Lib & Info Sci) 474
HALE, Martha L. (Dean) 485
KLOSTERMANN, Helen M. (Technl Srvs Dept Head) 662

Emporia State Univ (KS)

Encino-Tarzana Friends of the Lib (CA)

Encyclopaedia Britannica Inc (IL)

Endicott Coll (MA)

Energy Mines & Resources of Canada (ON)

Energy Research Group Inc (MA)

Energy Resource Conservation Board (AB)

Enfield Board of Education (CT)

Engelhard Corp (NJ)

Engineering Information Inc (NY)

Englewood Hospital (NJ)

Englewood Pub Lib (NJ)

English-Speaking Union (NY)

Enoch Pratt Free Lib (MD)

Ensworth School (TN)

Enumclaw Pub Lib (WA)

Enviroment Health Associates Inc (CA)

Environment Canada (ON)

MEDER, Marylouise D. (Prof) . . . 820
STEWART, Henry R. (Dir) 1192

BROWN, Marie H. (Exhibit Cur) . 146
HOTIMLANSKA, Leah D. (Bibl Edit) 562
SCHROEDER, Anne M. (Bibl Edit) 1100
UDDIN, Shantha C. (Assoc Libn) 1267
DUSCHATKO, Rebecca F. (Lib Dir) 329

JESKE, Margo (Libn) 600
MAYRAND, Florian (Technl Srvs Asst Head) 791
SCOLLIE, F B. (Head of Lib Srvs) 1106
WILSON, Valerie E. (Chief Libn) 1353
WINQUIST, Elaine W. (Mgr of Info Resources) 1355

JOHNSON, Liz 607
DUBEAU, Marsha (Lib Media Spclst) 321
FEDORS, Maurica R. (Technl Info Spclst) 368
SOBIN, Maryann D. (Technl Info Ctr Libn) 1165
BERGER, Mary C. (Plng & Product Devlpmnt Div Mgr) 85
BERRYMAN, Karen L. (Acq & Catlgng Dept Head) 90
BROWN-SPRUILL, Debra K. (Database Mgmt Dept Head) . 149
CABEEN, Samuel K. (Dir) 170
LANDAU, Herbert B. (Pres) 692
MCCOY, Barbara S. 799
MOLINE, Gloria (Database Production Div Mgr) 853
LINDNER, Katherine L. (Med Lib Dir) 729
HECHT, James M. (Dir) 519
GRAY, Karen (Libn) 460
ANDREWS, Loretta K. (Educ Spclst) 26
ARRINGTON, Susan J. (Head, Govt Ref Srv) 34
BENDER, Cynthia F. (Gen Info Dept Asst Head) 79
BLANK, Annette C. (Lib Col Devlpmnt Spclst) 104
BLEGEN, John C. (Asst Dir) 105
BROWN, Florence S. (Extension Div Chief) 144
CURRY, Anna A. (Dir) 266
CYR, Helen W. (AV Dept Head) . 268
DYSART, Marcia J. (Ref Libn) . . 331
ELDER, Richard H. (Head, Technl Srvs) 342
FINNERTY, Michael B. 379
HEISER, Jane C. (Adminstr) 523
HIRSCH, Dorothy K. (Asst Head, Fiction Dept) 543
LAPIDES, Linda F. (Head, Ofc of Materials Mgmt) 697
LOGAN, Mary A. (Libn) 737
SLEEMAN, William E. (Ref Libn) 1148
SONDHEIM, John W. (Chief) . . 1167
WALLER, Madalyn M. (Branch Mgr) 1298
BURKE, Mary E. (Libn) 160
BAER, Robert L. (Lib Dir) 45

LONDON, Glenn S. (Info Srvs Mgr) 738
SAVIC, Edward I. (Catlgr) 1086

Environment Canada-Parks (AB) GUNSON, Murray J. (Regnl Libn) 478
LIGHTFOOT, Robert J. (Regnl Mgr Resident & Realy Srvs) . 726

Environmental Law Institute (DC) LARSEN, Lynda L. (Libn) 698

Environmental Research Institute (MI) PUBLISKI, Patricia J. (Info Resrc Spclst I) 996

Environmental Science & Engineering Inc (FL) CIVITARESE, Kathleen A. (Libn) . 215

Episcopal Church (LA) NOLAN, Peggy H. (Libn) 907

Episcopal Diocese of Connecticut (CT) CARROON, Robert G. (Archvst & Historiographer) 187

Episcopal Diocese of Missouri (MO) REHKOPF, Charles F. (Registrar) 1017

Episcopal Divinity Sch (MA) DUNKLY, James W. (Dir of Libs) 326

Episcopal High Sch (LA) CHEW, Susan M. (Libn) 207

Episcopal High Sch (TX) HAND, M D. (Head Libn) 494

Episcopal Theol Sem of the Southwest (TX) BOOHER, Harold H. (Libn and Prof of Theol Lit) 115

Epoch Research Corp (JAP) MIWA, Makiko (Pres) 850

The Epstein Collection (DC) VAN NIMMEN, Jane (Cur) . . . 1276

Epstein School (GA) REZNICK, Evi P. (Libn & Media Spclst) 1025

Equatorial Communication Service (CA) PARKER, Edwin B. (Pres) 941

Equifax Inc (GA) MCDAVID, Michael W. (Corprt Info Resrcs Mgr) 801

Equitable Archives (NY) MATTHEOU, Antonia (Asst Archvst) 785

Ergosyst Associates Inc (KS) BURCH, John L. (Pres) 158
HINTON, N E. (Managing Edit, Pubns Database) 543

ERIC Clearinghouse (IN) HENSON, Jane E. (Asst Dir) 529

ERIC Clearinghouse (NJ) OLSON, Lucie M. (Info Spclst) . . 923

ERIC Processing & Reference Facility (MD) EUSTACE, Susan J. (Acqs & Ref Libn) 356

Erie Community Coll North (NY) MORAN, Sylvia J. (Lib Coor) . . . 862

Erie County Historical Society (PA) ANDRICK, Annita A. (Libn Archvst) 27

Erie County Lib System (PA) GALLIVAN, Marion F. (Dist Consult) 414
WIRICK, Terry L. (Adult Srvs Libn) 1356

Ernst & Whinney (NY) REID, Richard C. (Info Spclst) . . 1019

Ernst & Whinney (WA) UHLMAN, Carol K. (Lib Asst) . . 1268

ERT Inc (MA) ROBINSON, Deanna C. (Mgr, Info Ctr) 1043

Esala Associates Information/Research (MN) ESALA, Lillian H. (Dir) 354

ESL Inc/Subsidiary of TRW (CA) VAN VELZER, Verna J. (Resrch Libn) 1277

Espial Productions Ltd (ON) CAMPBELL, Harry (Gen Mgr) . . . 176

Essex Community Coll (MD) BROADY, Jessie (Actng Dir) 138
HSIEH, Rebecca T. (AV Lib Coordntr) 567
THOMAS, Fannette H. (Ref Libn & Asst Dir) 1236

Essex Fells Board of Education (NJ) ROTSAERT, Stefanie C. (Libn) . 1060

Essex Institute (MA) FOUNTAIN, Eugenia F. (Ref Libn) 393

Esso Petroleum Canada (ON) GASPAR, Noel J. (Info Srvs Head) 421

Esso Resources Canada Ltd (AB) GASHUS, Karin C. (Staff Libn) . . 421

Estevan Comprehensive Sch Board (SK) ANDRIST, Shirley A. (Tchr & Libn) 27

Ethicon Inc (NJ) LITTLE, Karen M. (Asst Info Scientist) 733
MCGREGOR, Walter (Dir) 808
STAVETSKI, Norma K. (Sect Mgr, Technl Info Ctr) 1183

Ethyl Corp (LA) FOOS, Ferol A. (Bus Libn) 388
LEMMON, Anne B. (Info Spclst) . 715

Etobicoke Board of Education (ON) CHURCHMAN, Alice M. (Lrng Mtrls Coordntr) 213

Etobicoke Pub Lib Board (ON) BUNCE, Catherine J. (Resrch Libn) 157
DETERVILLE, Linda C. (Chlds Libn) 296
LAITMAN, Sheila (Pub Srvs Libn) 688

Euclid Pub Lib (OH) COLEMAN, Judith (Dir) 231

Eugene Shool District 4J (OR) THOMPSON, Paulette (Lib Media Spclst) 1241

Eunice Municipal Sch (NM) ANDREWS, Lois W. (High Sch Libn) 26

Eureka Public Lib (IL) THOMAS, Marcia L. (Dir) 1237

European Commission Host Organisation (LUX) CORNELIUS, Peter K. (Database Devlpmnt Spclst) . . 246

European Space Agency-ESTEC (NET) RAITT, David I. (Head, Lib & Info Srvs) 1004

European Stars & Stripes (WGR) NEUWILLER, Charlene (Comp Appls Instr) 897

Evaluative Technologies Inc (MD) POSEY, Sussann F. (Libn & Catlgr) 985

Evanston Hospital (IL) ANTON, Tess (Libn) 29
FEINBERG, Linda J. (Asst Libn) . 368

Evanston Pub Lib (IL) ANDERSON, Charles R. (Pub Srvs Asst Dir) 22
JOHNSON, Marjorie M. (Branch Head & Staff Libn) 607
KRIIGEL, Barbara J. (Technl Srvs Mgr) 678
SCHOR, Abby R. (Col Devlpmnt Libn) 1099
SCHWARZLOSE, Sally F. (Chlds Libn) 1105
SUNDELL, Elizabeth B. (Art, Music, AV Libn) 1210

Evanston Township High Sch (IL) GOLDBERGER, Virginia F. (AV Libn) 445
SHAFER, Anne E. (Michael Resrc Ctr Libn) 1119

Evansville-Vanderburgh County Pub Lib (IN) ALLEN, Patricia J. (Asst Dir) 15
BICKEL, Bernice M. (Head) 94
TEUBERT, Lola H. (Young Adult Libn, Literacy Consult) 1233

Evansville-Vanderburgh Sch Corp (IN) BAIN, Leslie E. (Libn) 47
WINSLOW, Carol M. (Media Spclst) 1355

Evening Post Publishing Co (SC) CROCKETT, Mary S. (Chief Libn) 259

Eveready Battery Co Inc (OH) LANGKAU, Claire M. (Technl Info Mgr) 696

Everett Pub Lib (WA) NESSE, Mark A. (Dir) 896

Evergreen Sch District (CA) SUTHERLAND, Helen G. (Lib Media Spclst) 1211

Evergreen Sch District (WA) CONABLE, Irene H. (Libn) 235

Excelsior Springs Sch District 40 (MO) HOOVER, Jonnette L. (Media Coordntr) 557

Executive Office of the US President (DC) HOTCHKISS, Mary A. (White House Law Libn) 562
MCCOY-LARSON, Sandra (Ref Libn) 799

Executive Telecom System Inc (IN) GILL, John H. (Natl Sales Mgr) . . 435
GUERRA, Angela M. (Srv Support Mgr) 476
HANKINS, John (Pres) 496
HASHEM, Judy A. (Database & Technl Srvs Mgr) 510

Exeter Hospital Inc (NH) REED, Alice (Med Libn) 1014

Experience Inc (MN) BLUMENFELD, Judith K. (Info Mgr) 107

Experimente Old and Rare Books (NY) RAMER, Bruce J. (Owner) 1005

Export-Import Bank of the US (DC) MCGILL, Theodora (Libn) 806
POSNIAK, John R. (Asst Libn) . . 985

Exxon Biomedical Sciences Inc (NJ) — DEDERT, Patricia L. (Head of Info Srvs) 286
SEAGER, Janice R. (Info Analyst) 1109
Exxon Chemical Co (TX) — NEWMAN, Robert M. (Info Analyst) 899
Exxon Co USA (LA) — BIGGS, Barbara R. (Libn) 95
Exxon Production Research Co (TX) — CEBRUN, Mary J. (Libn) ... 196
PARRIS, Lou B. (Supvsr, Info Ctr) 944
Exxon Research & Engineering Co (NJ) — BARRETT, Joyce C. (Info Spclst) 59
CHAPMAN, Janet L. (Proj Analyst) 202
JOHNSON, David K. (Staff Chemist) 603
LAVIN, Margaret A. (Info Analyst) 703
Eye & Ear Hospital of Pittsburgh (PA) — JOHNSTON, Bruce A. (Med Lib & Lrng Resrc Ctr Dir) 610

F

F C Adams Pub Lib (MA) — OLIANSKY, Joseph D. (Dir) 920
F W Faxon Co (MA) — KRUKONIS, Perkunas P. (Biblgph Resrchr) 680
F W Faxon Co (NJ) — CIMBALA, Diane J. (Northeast Regnl Rep) 214
F Y I Associates (TX) — SCHRAEDER, Diana C. (Info Spclst) 1099
Facts On File Inc (CA) — KLINE, Victoria E. (Ref Bk Writer) 661
Facts On File Inc (NY) — KNAPPMAN, Edward W. (Exec Vice Pres) 663
Faegre & Benson (MN) — DUNN, Jamie N. (Dir of Lib Srvs) 326
Fairbanks North Star Borough Pub Lib (AK) — GALBRAITH, William B. (Ref & Pub Relations Libn) 413
Fairbanks North Star Borough Sch Dist (AK) — THOMAS, Margie J. (Libn) 1237
Fairchild Research Center (CA) — COOK, Sherry M. (Systs Libn) .. 240
Fairchild Semiconductor (CA) — CRABTREE, Sandra A. (Mgr, Technl Info Ctr) 254
Fairchild Weston Systems Inc (PA) — KOHL, Arlene F. (Technl Libn) .. 668
Fairfax County Board of Education (VA) — GIEGERICH, M P. (Lib Media Spclst) 433
Fairfax County Pub Lib (VA) — CHAUVETTE, Catherine A. (Regnl Chld's Libn) 204
CLAY, Edwin S. (Dir of Libs) 219
COLEMAN, Karen S. (Assoc Dir of Support Srvs) 231
DEWEY, Helen W. (Libn I) 298
EHLKE, Nancy K. (Libn) 339
FESSLER, Vera F. (Assoc Dir of Technl Operations) 374
GOODWIN, Jane G. (Evaluation & Info Devlpmnt Coordntr) ... 450
JONES, Sue P. (Asst Branch Mgr) 615
LEVY, Suzanne S. (VA Room Libn) 722
MONK, Joanne (Acqs Lib Prog Coordntr) 855
PARNES, Daria M. (Libn I) 943
WEBB, Barbara A. (Assoc Dir) . 1313
WOODALL, Nancy C. (Trng Coordntr) 1365
Fairfax County Pub Schs (VA) — FILSON, Anne H. (Sch Lib Media Spclst) 377
GRIEVE, Karen R. (Sch Libn) ... 468
GUILFORD, Diane E. (Head Libn) 476
HUNT, Linda A. (Lib Srvs Coordntr) 575
KNAPP, Marilyn S. (Head Libn) .. 663

Fairfax County Pub Schs (VA) — TYSINGER, Barbara R. (Catlgng Head) 1267
Fairfield Community High Sch (IL) — MAYNARD, Marilyn K. (Lrng Ctr Dir) 790
Fairfield Community Sch District (IA) — DANIELSON, Connie S. (Media Spclst) 273
Fairfield County Lib (OH) — NEEDHAM, George M. (Lib Dir) . 891
Fairfield County Lib (SC) — MCMASTER, Sarah D. (Dir) 815
Fairfield Pub Lib (CT) — WARGO, Peggy M. (Asst Dir) .. 1305
Fairfield Pub Lib (NJ) — WROBLEWSKI, Christine (Dir) . 1373
Fairfield Republic Co (NY) — MAUTER, George A. (Technl Info Ctr Adminstr) 787
Fairfield Univ (CT) — BRYAN, Barbara D. (Univ Libn) . 151
COOMBS, Elisabeth G. (Asst Libn for Technl Srvs) 241
HAAG, Nancy R. (Head Ref Libn) 480
HEFZALLAH, Mona G. (Head Catlgr) 521
MAROUSEK, Kathy A. (Asst Dir for Dental Lib) 772
SOMMER, Ursula M. (Media Srvs Dir) 1167
Fairmont State Coll (WV) — HUPP, Mary A. (Coordntr/Assoc Prof/Perdcls Libn) 577
POWELL, Ruth A. (Ref Technl Srvs Libn) 988
WEMETT, Lisa C. (Asst Dir) ... 1323
Fairport Pub Lib (NY) — FEMAL, Mary B. (Med Libn) ... 370
Fairview Southdale Hospital (MN) — HELMAN, Sarah M. (Sch Lib Media Spclst) 524
Falcon Sch District 49 (CO) — OLSEN, Stephen (Info Srvs Mgr) 922
Fallon McElligott (MN) — FOSTER, Joan (Head, Ref & Adult Srvs) 392
Falmouth Pub Lib (MA) — FALSONE, Anne M. (Pres) 363
Falsone Management Consultants (CO) — LIEBERMAN, Ronald (Dir) 726
The Family Album ABAA (PA) —
Family Court of the State of Delaware (DE) — FRANCIS, Diane S. (Info Resrc Mgr) 396
Family Health Foundation of America (MO) — CRAIG, Marian D. (Technl Srvs Libn) 254
GIBSON, Patricia A. (VP, Info Srvs & Systs) 432
RUBY, Carolyn M. (Med Ref Libn) 1065
Family Health International (NC) — BARROWS, William D. (Info Coordntr) 60
Family History Lib (UT) — SPERRY, Kip (Col Devlpmnt Spclst) 1174
Family Service America (WI) — HORNUNG, Susan D. (Libn) 560
MCGILL, Nancy A. (Dir, Severson Natl Info Ctr) 806
Farella Braun & Martel (CA) — MACKLER, Mark E. (Asst Libn) .. 757
Fargo Pub Lib (ND) — SCHULTZ, Gary J. (Lib Dir) ... 1102
Fargo Pub Schs (ND) — QUAMME, Beverly J. (Sch Media Spclst) 999
YLINIEMI, Hazel A. (Instrcl Resrcs Dir) 1380
Faribault Regional Center (MN) — HELTSLEY, Mary K. (Libn) 525
Farm Credit Administration (VA) — REDMER, Paul C. (Records & Projs Div Chief) 1014
Farmers Branch Pub Lib (TX) — KELLEY, Betty H. (Dir) 636
Farmingdale Pub Lib (NY) — MASCIA, Regina B. (Chlds & Yng Adult Libn) 780
Farmingdale Sch District (NY) — MCNAMARA, Marie F. (Sch Lib Media Spclst) 816
Farmington Community Lib (MI) — PAPAI, Beverly D. (Dir) 938
SUMMERS, Sheryl H. (Libn 2 Head of Technl Srvs Law Libn) 1209
THEEKE, Tina M. (Branch Head) 1234
Farmington High Sch (NH) — GAGNON, Ruth (Lib Media Supvsr) 412
Farmington Pub Schs (CT) — LAWRENCE, Scott W. (Elem Lib Media Spclst) 705

Farmington Village Green & Lib Assn (CT)
GIBSON, Barbara H. (Dir of Lib Srvs) 431

Farmland Industries Inc (MO)
HUDSON, Rosetta A. (Info Spclst) 570

Farser Valley Regional Lib (BC)
GARRAWAY, Babs L. (Pub Srvs Libn) 420

Fashion Inst of Design & Merchandising (CA)
HALE, Kaycee (Exec Dir of Resrc & Resrch Ctr) 485
HARRIS, Kathryn S. (Resrc & Resrch Ctr Coordntr) 505

Fashion Institute of Technology (NY)
MARTIN, Richard (Exec Dir) 778
ROZENE, Janette B. (Spcl Cols & Non-print Catlgr & Libn) . . 1064
SMITH, Sweetman R. (Ref Libn) 1161

Father Lopez High Sch (FL)
DEANS, Janice P. (Media Spclst) 284

Faulkner County Lib (AR)
VOSS, Ruth A. (Dir) 1289

Faulkner Univ (AL)
NEWMAN, Sharon K. (Law Lib Dir) 900

Faxon Co (GA)
LUTHER, M J. (Southern Sales Rep) 750

Faxon Co (MA)
BACON, Lois C. (Continuation Srvs Mgr) 44
CLAPPER, Mary E. (Lib Vendor Interface Srvs Mgr) 216
DEARBORN, Susan C. (Sales Rep) 284
KNAPP, Leslie C. (Rsrch Asst) . . 663
POSTLETHWAITE, Bonnie S. (Mgr) 986

Faxon Co (VA)
REID, Janine A. (Operations Mgr) 1018

Faxon Inc (MA)
ROWE, Richard R. (Pres) 1062

Fayette County Board of Education (KY)
MARTIN, Sandra D. (Elem Sch Media Libn) 778

Fayetteville Area Health Educ Fndtn Inc (NC)
WRIGHT, Barbara A. (Dir of Lib & Info Srvs) 1370

Fayetteville City Schs (TN)
YOUNG, Patricia S. (Elem Sch Libn) 1383

Fayetteville Free Lib (NY)
MOORE, Ann L. (Lib Dir) 858

Fayetteville Publishing Co (NC)
MAXWELL, Daisy D. (Newspaper Libn) 788

Fayetteville Sch District 1 (AR)
DEWEESE, Don B. (Adminstrv Asst for Info Srvs) 298

Federal Business Development Bank (PQ)
MCINTOSH, Julia E. (External Database Coordntr) 809
ROWE, David G. (Head Libn) . . 1062
THIVIERGE, Lynda M. (Ref Libn) 1235

Federal Deposit Insurance Corp (DC)
LEWIS, Noreen B. (Technl Srvs Libn) 724
SMITH, Kathleen S. (Lead Libn & Regnl Srvs Libn) 1156

Federal Emergency Management Agency (MD)
CHIESA, Adele M. (Lrng Resrc Ctr Chief) 208

Federal German Ministry for Econ Cooprtn (WGR)
LOTZ, Rainer E. (Sr Govt Official) 742

Federal Government (MD)
MEZZAPELLE, Alice S. (Ret Libn) 831

Federal Home Loan Bank of Atlanta (GA)
LAWLESS, Dorothy A. (Lib Srvs Mgr) 704

Federal Home Loan Bank of Boston (MA)
HAYES, Maureen L. (Libn) 516

Federal Home Loan Bank of Dallas (TX)
TALLEY, Pat L. (Resrch Libn) . . 1221

Federal Home Loan Bank of New York (NY)
LEVINTON, Juliette (Mgr, Lib Srvs) 721

Federal Home Loan Bank of San Francisco (CA)
GOVAARS, Inga (Adminstr of Lib Srvs) 454

Federal Home Loan Bank of Seattle (WA)
FEATHERS, John E. (Lib Technician) 367

Federal Reserve Bank of Chicago (IL)
BECKER, John C. (Resrch Libn) . . 72
PHILLIPS, Dorothy E. (Lib Adminstr) 968

Federal Reserve Bank of Cleveland (OH)
MAYNARD, Elizabeth (Libn) 790

Federal Reserve Bank of Minneapolis (MN)
SWAN, Janet (Lib & Records Srvs Mgr) 1213

Federal Reserve Bank of New York (NY)
CONGDON, Rodney H. (Chief Law Libn) 236
LASKOWITZ, Roberta G. (Asst Chief Law Libn) 700
TRUEBLOOD, Emily H. (Chief Libn) 1259
WOOTEN, Jean A. (Asst Chief Libn) 1368

Federal Reserve Bank of Philadelphia (PA)
ALDRIDGE, Carol J. (Ref Libn & Info Spclst) 11
NAULTY, Deborah M. (Info Srvs Supvsr) 889

Federal Reserve Bank of Richmond (VA)
CANNON, Ruth M. (Libn) 179
CASH, Susan R. (Assoc Libn) . . . 192
THOMPSON, Connie B. (Assoc Libn) 1239

Federal Reserve Bank of San Francisco (CA)
ROSENBERGER, Diane C. (Systs Libn) 1056

Federal Trade Commission (DC)
PERELLA, Susanne B. (Lib Dir) . 958

Federal Univ of Technology (NGR)
ONONOGBO, Raphael U. (Principal Libn) 924

Federation, Am Socty, Experimental Bio (MD)
ERLICK, Louise S. (Libn) 353

FEDLINK (DC)
BEACHELL, Doria M. (Netwk Libn) 68

FEICO (NY)
NEWCOMB, Jonathan (Pres) . . . 898

Feit & Ahrens (NY)
HERBERT, Annette F. (Libn & File Supvsr) 530

Felician Coll (IL)
GALLAGHER, Eileen M. (Assoc Libn) 414
MOCH, Mary I. (Dir, Lib Srvs) . . . 851

Felician Coll (NJ)
KARETZKY, Stephen (Lib Dir) . . 627

Felician Sisters (IL)
RUDNIK, Mary C. (Asst to Provincial Admin) 1065

Fellers Snider Blankenship Bailey et al (OK)
BOOTENHOFF, Rebecca J. (Head Libn) 116

Fenco Engineers Inc (ON)
BUISMAN, Maria J. (Lib Technician) 156
CROXFORD, Agnes M. (Chief Libn) 262

Feng Chia Univ (TAI)
YANG, Mei H. (Lib Dir) 1377

Ferguson Lib (CT)
ARNOLD, Arleen B. (Dir of Adminstrv Srvs) 33
DIMATTIA, Ernest A. (Pres and Exec Dir) 304
FERRARI, Kathleen M. (Temporary Acqs Asst) 373
GOLOMB, Katherine A. (Dir of Pub Srvs) 447
ROCKMAN, Connie C. (Chlds Srvs Supvsr) 1046
WILLIAMS, Judy R. (Adult Ref) 1344

Fernbank Science Center (GA)
LARSEN, Mary T. (Libn) 698

Ferris Independent Sch District (TX)
REECE, Sue A. (High Sch Libn) 1014

Ferro Corp (OH)
FULLER, Kathleen B. (Lib Supvsr) 408

Fiberglas Canada Inc (ON)
BICE, Lee A. (Info Spclst) 94

Fidelity Management & Research Co (MA)
CAHILL, Jack F. (Resrch Coordntr) 171

Fiduciary Trust Co International (NY)
ARMEIT, Marilyn (Resrch Lib Mgr) 32

Field Lib (NY)
FALCONE, Edward M. (Dir) 362

Field Museum of National History (IL)　CALHOUN, Michele (Ref Libn) . . 172
MILLER, Janet
(Archvst/Registrar) 838
Film Audio Services Inc (NJ)　SUMMERS, Robert A. (Pres) . . 1209
Film Comm (IL)　HEMPEL, Gordon J. (Pres) 525
The Filson Club (KY)　HOUSE, Katherine L. (Libn,
Catlgr) 563
Finance/Treasury Board Lib (ON)　FIRTH, Leslie (Catlg Libn) 379
Financial Advice & Support Inc (CA)　ROSS, Ric (Pres) 1058
The Financial Post (ON)　GUHERIDGE, Allison A. (Info
Spclst & Trainer) 476
ODHO, Marc (Product Devlpmnt
Mgr) 917
FIND/SVP Inc (NY)　BINGHAM, Kathleen S. (Exec
Vice Pres) 97
DENNIS, Anne R. (Info Resorcs
Dept Dir) 292
GARVIN, Andrew P. (Chairman
& Chief Exec Ofcr) 421
Finder Information Tools Inc (GA)　SMITH, Judith A. (VP of New
Products) 1156
Findlay City Schools (OH)　HARDESTY, Vicki H. (Libn) 499
Findlay Coll (OH)　SCHIRMER, Robert W. (Dir) . . . 1093
STEVENS, Donna H. (Technl
Srvs Libn) 1190
**Findlay-Hancock County Pub
Lib** (OH)　DICKINSON, Luren E. (Dir) 301
DUDLEY, Durand S. (Technl
Srvs Dept Supvsr) 323
HABINSKI, Carol A. (AV & Yng
Adult Libn, Dept Head) 481
JANKY, Donna L. (Coordntr,
Chlds Srvs) 593
LUST, Jeanette M. (Ref,
Genealogy Libn) 749
Fine Arts Center at Cheekwood (TN)　KNOWLES, Susan W. (Cur of
Cols) 665
Fine Print Publishing (CA)　KIRSHENBAUM, Sandra D.
(Edit & Publshr) 655
Finger Lakes Lib System (NY)　MORRIS, Jennifer D. (Assoc Dir
& Technl Srvs Head) 866
PANZ, Richard (Lib Syst Dir) . . . 938
PARKHURST, Kathleen A. (Ref
& Interlib Loan Head) 942
Finger Lakes Times (NY)　BARNARD, Catherine A. (Libn) . . . 57
Finley Junior High (NY)　NEWMAN, Eileen M. (Lib &
Media Spclst) 899
**Finley Kumble Wagner Heine et
al** (CA)　JEROME, Michael S. (Asst Libn) . 599
PALMER, Catherine C. 936
**Finley Kumble Wagner Heine et
al** (NY)　SCIOLINO, Elaine T. (Libn) 1106
Finneytown Local Sch (OH)　KENT, Rose M. (Lib Media Srvs
Coordntr) 642
Firehouse Communications (NY)　SALY, Alan J. (Managing Edit) . 1078
Firelands Community Hospital (OH)　BARNUM, Denise I. (Med Libn) . . 58
Fireman's Fund Insurance Co (CA)　ALDRICH, Linda W. (Libn) 11
GHILOTTI, Linda L. (Lib Dir) 430
First Baptist Church (TX)　SCHMIDT, Mary A. (Dir) 1095
First Boston Corp (NY)　LANDOLFI, Lisa M. (Ref Libn) . . . 693
First Church of Christ Scientist (MA)　HUENNEKE, Judith A. (Records
Mgmt Analyst) 570
**First Church of God Christian
Sch** (CA)　GRAY, Tomysena F. (Libn) 460
First Covenant Church (WA)　STORDAHL, Beth A. (Archvst) . 1198
First Information Service (AZ)　BAUM, Ester B. (Proprietor) 66
**First Judicial District of
Pennsylvania** (PA)　DIAZ, Nelson A. (Judge) 299
First Manhattan Co (NY)　SUSMAN, Beatrice (Libn) 1210
**First Manhattan Consulting
Group** (NY)　TAPIERO, Judith (Resrch Dir &
Libn) 1223
First National Bank of Chicago (IL)　ADLER, Naomi L. (Technl
Resrch Libn) 7
PROBST, Virginia M. (Corprt
Info Ctr Asst Mgr) 994
First Presbyterian Church (OH)　ROEPKE, David E. (Organist &
Choirmaster) 1048
First Presbyterian Church (VA)　PEARL, Patricia D. (Libn) 952

First Regional Lib (MS)　ANDERSON, James F. (Dir) 23
ROGERS, Margaret N. (Acqs
Libn) 1049
WARREN, Catherine S.
(Headquarters Libn) 1306
WILROY, Joann (Asst Dir) 1349
Fisk Univ (TN)　SHOCKLEY, Ann A. (Assoc
Libn for Spcl Cols & Archvst) 1132
Fisons Corp (MA)　CAREY, Charlene E. (Libn) 181
Fitchburg Pub Lib (MA)　KISSNER, Arthur J. (Dir) 656
Fitzgerald-Ben Hill County Lib (GA)　HEFFINGTON, Carl O. (Dir) 520
PAULK, Sara L. (Asst Dir) 950
Flagler County Abstract Co (FL)　MCKNIGHT, Jesse H. (Pres) . . . 812
**Flagstaff City-Coconino County Pub
Lib** (AZ)　DOWNUM, Evelyn R. (Chlds
Libn) 317
GRANADE, Victoria A. (Assoc
Dir & Head of Technl Srvs) . . 457
MOHR, Mary C. (Libn) 852
Flaming Rainbow Univ (OK)　FULK, Mary C. (Libn) 408
**Flinders Univ of South
Australia** (AUS)　BROWN, Pauline (Libn) 146
Flinflon Sch Division 46 (MB)　HOBBS, Henry C. (Tchr Libn) . . . 545
The Flint Journal (MI)　LARZELERE, David W. (Chief
Libn) 700
Flint Pub Lib (MI)　CHAMBERS, E G. (First Asst) . . 198
JAEGER, Sally J. (Head Libn) . . . 591
KINGSTON, Jo A. (Branch
Head) 652
OAKLANDER, Linda G. (Libn) . . . 913
SCHAAFSMA, Roberta A. (Gen
Ref Head) 1088
STILLEY, Cynthia S. (Srvs for
Chld & Yng Teens Supvsr) . . 1194
Flint River Regional Lib (GA)　CHENEY, Philip M. (Pub Srvs
Coordntr) 206
HATCHER, Nolan C. (Libn) 511
STRAUTMAN, Randolph B.
(Branch Srvs Coordntr) 1201
**Flintridge Sacred Heart
Academy** (CA)　HA, Marie S. (Libn) 480
Florence County Lib (SC)　MCREE, John W. (Info Srvs
Libn) 818
Florham Park Pub Lib (NJ)　BYOUK, Nancy K. (Dir) 168
Florida Atlantic Univ (FL)　DONAHUE, Janice E. (Coll
Organz Head) 310
HOLLMANN, Pauline V. (Libn) . . 552
MOORE, Dahrl E. (Libn) 859
PELLEN, Rita M. (Asst Ref Dept
Head) 955
SKALLERUP, Harry R. (Libs
Dir) 1145
WILER, Linda L. (Ref Dept
Head) 1339
Florida Bankers Association (FL)　BARAGER, Wendy A. (Libn) 55
Florida Bar (FL)　DALLET, Jane L. (Pub Info &
Bar Srvs Libn) 270
**Florida Center for Lib
Automation** (FL)　DALEHITE, Michele I. (Asst Dir
for Prog Devlpmnt) 270
HOGUE, Margaret A. (User Srvs
Libn) 549
Florida Coll (FL)　TABOR, Curtis H. (Lib Dir) 1219
**Florida Department of
Agriculture** (FL)　JACOBSON, June B. (Libn II) . . . 590
**Florida Department of
Corrections** (FL)　OVERSTREET, Allen J. (Libn &
Law Lib Supvsr) 931
Florida Department of Education (FL)　SKINNER, L M. (Prog Spclst) . . 1146
**Florida Division of Blind
Services** (FL)　MINOR, Dorothy C. (Technl
Srvs & Ref Libn) 846
**Florida Federal State Loan
Association** (FL)　GELEADI, Ruth H. (Collector II
for Repayment Dept) 425
Florida Hospital (FL)　BECKNER, Barbara J. (Libn) 73
Florida Institute of Technology (FL)　HENSON, Llewellyn L. (Libs Dir) . 529
SHIAU, Ian L. (Catlgr) 1129

Florida International Univ (FL)
CARILLO, Sherry J. (Reader Srvs Asst Dir) 181
DOWNS, Antonie B. (Assoc Dir of Libs) 317
MCCAMMON, Leslie V. (Serials Libn) 793
MEAD-DONALDSON, Susan L. (Head of Biblgph Control Dept) 819
MILLER, Laurence A. (Libs Dir) . . 839
MIRANDA, Salvador (Asst Dir for Col Devlpmnt) 847
MORRIS, Steve R. (Bus Ref Libn) 867

Florida Keys Community Coll (FL)
SOULE, Maria J. (Libn) 1169

Florida Power Corp (FL)
CORNWELL, Douglas W. (Libn) . 247

Florida State Hospital (FL)
BEASLEY, Clarence W. (Dir, Lib Srvs) 69

Florida State Univ (FL)
BILAL, Dania M. (Ref Libn) 96
BURDICK, Lois B. (Asst Dir, Admin Srvs) 158
CLACK, Doris H. (Prof) 215
CLARKSON, Jane S. (Univ Libn) 219
CONAWAY, Charles W. (Assoc Prof) 235
DE PEW, John N. (Assoc Prof) . . 293
DONNELL, Marianne (Maps Libn) 311
EVANS, Mark S. (Spcl Media Libn) 357
GAULT, Robin R. (Head of Pub Srvs) 423
HART, Thomas L. (Prof of Lib & Info Std) 507
HOFFER, Thomas W. (Prof of Comm) 547
HUNT, Mary A. (Prof & Assoc Dean) 575
LOGAN, Elisabeth L. (Asst Prof) . 737
MARTIN, James R. (Asst Dir for Pub Srvs) 776
MILLER, Charles E. (Univ Libs Dir) 836
PATTON, Linda L. (Assoc Univ Libn) 949
SCHROEDER, Edwin M. (Dir) . . 1100
SHINN, Allen E. (Dept Head) . . 1130
SRYGLEY, Sara K. (Prof Emeritus) 1177
STONE, Alva T. (Catlg Libn) . . . 1196
SUMMERS, F W. (Dean) 1209
TOOLE, Gregor K. (Assoc Univ Libn) 1250
TREZZA, Alphonse F. (Prof, Sch of Lib & Info Std) 1256
VAN ORDEN, Phyllis J. (Prof) . . 1276

Flower Films & Video (CA)
BLANK, Les (Producer Dir & Owner) 104

FluiDyne Engineering Corp (MN)
JOHNSON, Marlys J. (Technl Libn) 607

Fluor Corp (CA)
LEE, William D. (Sr Info Spclst) . 711

Fluor Daniel (IL)
SEABERG, Eileen J. (Libn) 1109

FMC Corp (CA)
KOCH, Kathy R. (Info Spclst) . . . 667
LUKE, Keye L. (Info Srvs Supvsr) 747
RANCATORE, Celeste L. (Info Spclst II, Ref) 1006
SMOKEY, Sheila C. (Lib Srvs Mgr) 1162

FMC Corp (MN)
MOE, Sandra J. (Sr Info Spclst) . 851

FMC Corp (NJ)
MAYER, June C. (Mgr) 789

Focus Research Systems Inc (CT)
CHICHESTER, Gerald C. (Chairman & Chief Exec Ofcr) 208
TALSKY, Gene R. (VP, New Bus Devlpmnt) 1221

FOI Services Inc (MD)
BOBKA, Marlene S. (Mktg Dir) . . 108

Foley & Lardner (DC)
BARDE, Karla I. (Ofc Adminstr & Libn) 56

Foley & Lardner (WI)
Foley Hoag & Eliot (MA)
Folger Shakespeare Lib (DC)
LINK, Noreen M. (Head Libn) . . . 730
NORMAN-CAMP, Melody (Libn) . 909
DOGGETT, Rachel H. (Accessions Libn) 308
KNACHEL, Philip A. (Assoc Dir) . 663
KRIVATSY, Nati H. (Ref Libn) . . . 679
YEANDLE, Laetitia (Manuscripts Cur) 1378

Follett Library Book Co (IL)
RICHARDSON, Vickie W. (Lib Consult) 1030

Follett Software Co (IL)
MILLER, Randy S. (Software Support Technician) 841

Fond Du Lac Pub Lib (WI)
CONRAD, Kay A. (Ref Dept Head) 238
RINGER, Susan G. (Asst Ref Libn & Govt Docums Libn) . . 1035

Fondulac District Lib (IL)
PIRES, Priscilla J. (Adult Srvs Libn) 975

Fontana Regional Lib (NC)
MODLIN, John W. (Dir) 851
NEWSOM, Jeanette D. (Libn) . . . 900

Fontbonne Academy (MA)
UMANA, Christine J. (Lib & Media Spclst) 1268

Fontbonne Coll Lib (MO)
BAER, Eleanora A. (Staff Member) 45

Food & Agriculture Organization (ITL)
JOLING, Carole G. (Chief Libn) . . 610

Food & Drug Administration (DC)
MCGOWAN, Anna T. (BRC Libn) 807

Food & Drug Administration (MD)
ASSOUAD, Carol S. (Deputy Dir) 37

Food Marketing Institute (DC)
MCBRIDE, Barbara L. 792

Foote Cone & Belding Communication (IL)
NELSON, Dwayne L. (Libn) 893
WERNETTE, Janice J. (Mgr of Info Srvs) 1325

Foothill-De Anza Community Coll District (CA)
MCDONALD, Marilyn M. (Lrng Resrcs Dean) 803
MINTZ, Anne P. (Info Srvs Dir) . . 847
WIKANDER, Lawrence E. (Cur) 1338

Forbes Inc (NY)
Forbes Lib (MA)
Forbes Magazine (NY)
BENDES, Adele N. (Info Spclst) . . 79

Ford Foundation (NY)
HARDING, Mary H. (Libn) 500
LAIST, Sharon B. (Archvst) 688
SAYWARD, Nick H. (Investment Srvs Libn) 1087

Ford Microelectronics (CO)
LAZARUS, Josephine G. (Sr Libn) 706

Ford Motor Co (MI)
BALOK, Becki (Resrch Analyst) . . 53
ESTRY, Donna S. (Supvsr, Technl Info Sect) 355

Fordham Univ (NJ)
Fordham Univ (NY)
FRANTS, Valery (Asst Prof) 398
DINDAYAL, Joyce S. (Circ Libn) 304
ESSIEN, Victor K. (Intl & Foreign Law Libn) 354
HITT, Gail D. (Instnl Resrch Dir) . 544
KANE, Patrice M. (Ref Libn & Bibl Instrc) 625
MURPHY, Anne M. (Dir of Libs) . 880
TRACY, Janet R. (Law Libn) . . . 1253

Foreign Mission Board (VA)
CASEY, Wayne T. (Lib Srvs Catlgr) 192
MACLEOD, James M. (Lib Srvs Supvsr) 757

Foresight Inc (PA)
ALBRECHT, Lois K. (Consult) 10

Forest Grove City Lib (OR)
FALZON, Judith A. (Acqs) 363

Forest Hills Sch District (OH)
LEIBOLD, Cynthia K. (Media Spclst) 713

Forest Inst of Professional Psychology (IL)
LUNDGREN, Janan L. (Lib Srvs Dir) 748

Forest Press (NY)
KRAMER-GREENE, Judith (In-house Editor) 675
PAULSON, Peter J. (Exec Dir) . . 950

Forintek Canada Corp (BC)
JOHNSON, Marione 607

Forrest General Hospital (MS)
DUNCAN, Bettye M. (Med Libn) . 325

Forsyth County Pub Lib (NC)
BELCHEE, Nancy O. (Libn II & Chlds Libn) 76
BROWN, Merrikay E. (Libn III) . . 146
ELMORE, Lisa E. (Libn II) 346

Forsyth County Pub Lib (NC)
FERGUSSON, David G.
(Headquarters Libn) 372
ROBERTS, William H. (Dir) 1041
ROWLAND, Janet M. (Perdcls
& Pub Docums Head) 1062
WEEKS, Arthur L. (Head of
Extension Div) 1315
WHITE, Sherry J. (Bus, Sci,
Industry Dept Head) 1332

Forsyth Dental Center (MA)
OPPENHEIM, Roberta A. (Lib
and Info Dir) 925

Forsyth Memorial Hospital (NC)
COBB, Margaret L. (Dir, Med
Lib) 225

Fort Bend County (TX)
JARMUSZ, Ruth M. (Head) . . . 594

**Fort Bend Independent Sch
District** (TX)
DIXON, Donna S. (Lrng Resrcs
Spclst) 306
LOCKETT, Iva (Coordntr, Lib
Media Srvs) 736

Fort Caspar Museum (WY)
MENARD, Michael J. (Musm
Dir) 823

**Fort Frances Rainy River Board of
Educ** (ON)
KITTS, T J. (Arts Head & Libn) . . 657

Fort Hays State Univ (KS)
DIRKS, Martha W. (Assoc Prof
of Lib Sci) 305
WARREN, G G. (Dir) 1306

**Fort Lauderdale
News/Sun-Sentinel** (FL)
BROWN, Jeanette L. (Lib Srvs
Asst Mgr) 144

Ft Lauderdale Sun-Sentinel (FL)
ALBAIR, Catherine M. (Libn) 9

Fort Lee Pub Lib (NJ)
ALTOMARA, Rita E. (Lib Dir) 18

Fort Lewis Coll (CO)
PATERSON, Judy L. (Technl
Srvs Libn) 947

Fort Lupton Pub Schs (CO)
MATSUNAGA, Fay L. (Primary
& Elem Libn) 785

**Fort McMurray Regional
Hospital** (AB)
BRUCE, Marianne E. (Lrng
Resrcs Ctr Coordntr) 149

Fort Morgan Pub Lib (CO)
KRUGLET, Jo A. (Lib Dir) 680

**Fort Myers Lee County Pub Lib
System** (FL)
TIPPLE, Roberta L. (Sch Media
Spclst) 1246

Fort Sanders Regional Med Ctr (TN)
COOK, Nedra J. (Med &
Nursing Libn) 240

**Fort Saskatchewan Municipal Lib
Board** (AB)
REDFORD, Marcia E. (Lib Dir) . 1014

Fort Smith Pub Lib (AR)
LARSON, Larry (Dir & Libn) 699

Fort Thomas Board of Education (KY)
DOAN, Janice K. (Elem Sch
Libn) 307

Fort Vancouver Regional Lib (WA)
CONABLE, Gordon M. (Assoc
Dir) 235
EDWARDS, Susan E. (Dist Ref
Libn) 338
HUTTON, Emily A. (Yng
People's Libn) 579

**Fort Wayne Area III Lib Srvs
Authority** (IN)
LISTON, Karen A. (Ref Ctr Dir) . . 733

Fort Wayne Community Schs (IN)
WEICK, Robert J. (Media Tchr) . 1316

**Fort Worth Museum of Science &
History** (TX)
MAULDIN, Lou A. (Libn) 787

Fort Worth Pub Lib (TX)
ALLMAND, Linda F. (Lib Dir) 17
ARD, Harold J. (Bus, Sci &
Tech Mgr) 31
BALSAM, Frances G. (Libn II &
Catlgr) 53
DAVIS, Philip M. (Libn I) 280
DIXON, Catherine A. (Asst Dir) . . 306
MUELLER, Peggy (Ref Ctr Mgr) . 875

Fort Worth Star-Telegram (TX)
SANDEFUR, Kristin T. (Head
Libn) 1079

Fortin & Assoc (PQ)
FOERTIN, Yves P. (Lib Consult) . 387

Foster Associates Inc (DC)
BLANDAMER, Ann W. (Head
Libn) 103

Foth & Van Duke & Associates (WI)
JOBELIUS, Nancy L. (Libn) 601

**Foulston Siefkin Powers &
Eberhardt** (KS)
BERARD, Sue A. (Law Libn) 84

The Foundation Center (NY)
CAVINESS, Ann N. (Pub Srvs
Dir) 195
DERRICKSON, Margaret (Libn) . . 294

The Foundation Center (OH)
PASQUAL, Patricia E. (Dir of
Cleveland Field Ofc) 946

**Fndtn, Children With Lrng
Disabilities** (NY)
GILLIGAN, Julie (Dir of Comm
& Pub Affairs) 436

Foundation for Blood Research (ME)
SPIEGEL, Nancy C. (Libn) 1174

**Foundation of the Federal Bar
Assn** (DC)
FLYNN, Richard M. (Head Libn) . 387

Founders Society (MI)
WAGNER, Cherryl A. (Assoc
Archvst) 1291

**Fountain-Ft Carson Sch District
8** (CO)
POOLE, Rebecca S. (Dir of Lib
Srvs) 983

**Fountain Valley Regional
Hospital** (CA)
SCHULZ, Judith H. (Med Libn) . 1102

Fountaindale Pub Lib District (IL)
ANDERSON, Karen T.
(Adminstrv Srvs Dir) 23
HACKETT, Nancy J. (Head Libn
& Head of Chlds Srvs) 481
TODD, Alexander W. (Dir) 1248

Four County Lib System (NY)
HILL, Malcolm K. (Dir) 540

Four Winds Hospital (NY)
STERN, Deborah S. (Libn) 1189

Fox Chapel Area Sch District (PA)
MILLER, Marjorie M. (Libn, Dept
Head) 840

Fox Chase Cancer Center (PA)
NISTA, Ann S. (Libn) 905

Fox Valley Technical Institute (WI)
PARSON, Karen L. (Lib
Technician) 944

Framework for Information Inc (NY)
FREIFELD, Roberta I. (Exec
Vice Pres) 401
MASYR, Caryl L. (Pres) 783

Framingham Pub Lib (MA)
JAMES, Flaherty C. (Dir) 592

Framingham State Coll (MA)
BOEHME, Richard W. (Technl
Srvs Head) 109
KRIER, Mary M. (Acqs & Serials
Libn) 678
MCDONALD, Stanley M. (Lib
Dir) 803

Framingham Union Hospital (MA)
CLEVESY, Sandra R. (Lib Srvs
Dir) 222

Frances Morrison Lib (SK)
BUCKLE, Judith (Chlds Srvs
Coordntr) 154

Francis Bacon Foundation Inc (CA)
WRIGLEY, Elizabeth S. (Dir) . . . 1373

Francis Marion Coll (SC)
DOVE, Herbert P. (Dir) 314
HUX, Roger K. (Asst Ref Libn) . . 579
MARTIN, Neal A. (Ref Libn &
Dept Head) 777

Franford Hospital (PA)
ROSE, Dianne E. (Libn) 1054

**Frank & Effa Laubach Memorial
Lib** (PA)
HESS, Marjorie A. (Volunteer
Libn) 534

**Frank B Hall Consulting
Company** (NY)
CLARKE, Elizabeth S. (Assoc
Libn) 218

Frankel & Co (IL)
KOVITZ, Nancy R. (Mgr Info
Ctr) 674

Frankfort Community Pub Lib (IN)
CADDELL, Claude W. (Dir) 170

Frankfort Pub Lib Dist (IL)
NOVAK, Lorrine M. (Adminstrv
Libn) 911

Franklin & Johnson County Lib (IN)
EWICK, Joann (Libn) 359

Franklin & Marshall Coll (PA)
BROWN, Charlotte B. (Coll
Archvst) 142

Franklin Coll (IN)
FALLON, Marianna L. (Instrcl
Media Libn) 362

Franklin County Sch System (TN)
WATSON, Gail H. (Libn) 1309

**Franklin D Roosevelt Four Freedoms
Fndtn** (NY)
GOODMAN, Frederica (Exec
Dir) 449
VANDEN HEUVEL, William J.
(Pres) 1273

Franklin Fixtures Inc (MA)
BAYLIS, Ted (Pres) 67

Franklin Furnace Archive Inc (NY)
HOGAN, Matthew (Cur &
Archvst) 549

Franklin Institute (MA)
GIFFIN, Wendy L. (Libn & Dir) . . 433

**Franklin Lakes Board of
Education** (NJ)
GOLDBERG, Barbara W. (Sch
Libn/Media Spclst) 444

Franklin-McKinley Sch District (CA)
BERG, Charlene J. (Principal) . . . 84
MERSHON, J L. (Libn) 827

The Franklin Mint (PA)   CUTLER, Judith (Sr Resrchr) . . . 268
HOWLEY, Deborah H. (Resrch
Libn) 566
PITCHON, Cindy A. (Info
Spclst) 976

Franklin Park Pub Lib (IL)   BOYLE, Lawrence C. (Info Srvs
Head) 124
VOSS, Joyce M. (Readers' Srvs
Head) 1289
WATSON, Robert E. (Asst Dir) . 1310

Franklin Pierce Coll (NH)   GRISWOLD, Esther A. (Dir, Lib
Resrc Ctr) 471
STEARNS, Melissa M. (Head,
Technl Srvs) 1183

Franklin Pierce Law Center (NH)   LANDAU, Cynthia R. (Asst Law
Libn) 692

Franklin Pub Lib (WI)   BELLIN, Bernard E. (Lib
Coordntr) 78
SANCHEZ, Alexander J. (Chlds
Srvs Libn) 1079

**Franklin Regional Medical
Center** (PA)   GILLILAND, Lee P. (Chief Med
Libn) 436

Franklin Research Center (VA)   GOLDENBERG, Joan M. (Proj
Dir) 445

Franklin Univ (OH)   EHRHARDT, Allyn (Libn) 339
HELSER, Fred L. (Asst Libn) 525

Franklin Watts Inc (NY)   VESTAL, Jeanne G. (Vice Pres
& Editrl Dir) 1283

Fraser Hickson Institute (PQ)   ACKERMAN, Frances W. (Circ
Head) 3

Fraser Valley Coll (BC)   HARRIS, Winifred E. (Lrng
Resrcs Dir) 506
SIFTON, Patricia A. (Lib
Technician Prog Coordntr) . . 1137

Fraser Valley Regional Lib (BC)   CHAN, Mary L. (Area Chlds
Libn) 199
GOW, Susan P. (Area Chlds
Libn) 454
HUDSON, Susan P. (Chlds
Libn) 570
KIERANS, Mary E. (E Centl
Area Coordntr) 647
RAY, Gordon L. (Exec Dir) 1011
SEARCY HOWARD, Linda M.
(Area Ref Libn) 1109
VIIERANS, Mary E. (Area
Coordntr) 1284

Fred Alger Management Inc (NY)   HERMAN, Marsha (Libn) 531
Fred Meyer Charitable Trust (OR)   FERGUSON, Douglas K. (Prog
Dir) 372

**Fredercik County Board of
Education** (MD)   FISHER, Eleanor W. (Libn,
Media Spclst) 381
Frederic R Harris Inc (NY)   CANDELMO, Emily (Libn) 178
**Frederick Cancer Research
Facility** (MD)   KINNA, Dorothy H. (Online Srch
Coordntr) 652
Frederick Cohen Productions (NY)   COHEN, Frederick (Pres) 228
Frederick County Pub Libs (MD)   FISHER, Joan W. (Chlds Srvs
Dir) 381
JOHNSON, Jerry D. (Asst Dir,
Extension) 606

Free Lib of Philadelphia (PA)   AXAM, John A. (Area Adminstr) . . 42
BARR, Marilyn P. (Ritnor Chldc
Branch Libn) 58
BAUMGARTNER, Barbara W.
(Lib Coordntr I) 66
BLUM, Irma (Chlds Libn) 107
BOARDMAN, Richard C. (Head,
Map Col) 108
BOND, Mary W. (Trustee
Emerita) 113
BRICKER, Will S. (Branch Mgr) . 135
CARSON, Sheila M. (Asst Head
of Mtrls Selection) 188
CATTIE, Mary M. (Libn II) 195
DIAZ, Magna M. (Adult & Yng
Adult Bilingual Libn) 299
DUCLOW, Geradline (Cur) 322

Free Lib of Philadelphia (PA)   EVEY, Patricia G. (Ref & Info
Libn, Spcl Srvs) 359
FOY, Lorraine M. (Branch Head
Libn) 395
GENDRON, Michele M. (Branch
Libn) 426
GLOVER, Peggy D. (Deputy Dir) . 442
GREEN, Rose B. (Mem of Bd of
Directors) 462
HALE, Carolyn R. (Regional
Libn) 485
HANSEN, Paula J. (Chlds Libn) . 498
HARKE, Toby H. (Adult & Yng
Adult Libn) 501
HARRISON, Susan B. (Lib Info
Systs Mgr) 507
HELVERSON, Louis G. (Info &
Ref Libn) 525
HINTON, Frances (Chief,
Prcsng Div) 543
ICKES, Barbara J. (Asst Chief) . . 581
JENGAJI-EL, Taifa (Branch
Libn) 596
KENT, Frederick J. (Music Dept
Head) 642
KOREY, Marie E. (Dept Head) . . 671
LIGHTNER, Karen J. (Libn) 727
MAXWELL, Barbara A. (Chlds
Dept Head) 788
MAYOVER, Steven J. (Chief,
Cntl Pub Srvs Div) 791
MCCONKEY, Jill T. (Libn II) 797
MCGLINN, Frank C. (Trustee &
Dir) 806
MCLAUGHLIN, Patricia A.
(Young Adult Libnn) 813
MOODY, Marilyn D. (Extension
Srvs Div Chief) 857
MULLEN, Helen M. (Coordntr,
Ofc of Work with Chld) 877
NEWCOMBE, Jack A.
(Extension Div Asst Chief) . . . 898
NIGHTINGALE, Daniel (Music
Proj Spclst) 904
ORSBURN, Elizabeth C. (Films
& Video Dept Head) 927
POST, Jeremiah B. (Print &
Picture Cur) 986
PROMOS, Marianne (Head
Libn, Art Dept) 995
RAIVELY, Martha M. (Asst to
Head of Mtrls Section) 1004
REIFF, Harry B. (Northwest
Area Adminstr) 1019
ROSENSTEEL, J R. (Adminstrv
Asst to the Pres) 1057
SHELKROT, Elliot L. (Pres &
Dir) 1126
SNOWTEN, Renee Y. (Roving
Ref Libn) 1164
SULLIVAN, Kathryn A. (Branch
Head) 1208
TERRY, Joseph D. (Adult
Spclst, Book Selection) 1232
VERHAAREN, John E. (Branch
Libn) 1282
WOOD, Linda L. (Asst Head) . . 1364
WRIGHT, Irene R. (Chld's Dept
Head) 1371

Free Pub Lib of Bayonne (NJ)   DAYETTE, Patricia E. (Bus Sci
& Industry Dept Sr Libn) 283

**Free Pub Lib of Berkeley
Heights** (NJ)   COHEN, Susan K. (Ref Libn) . . . 229
Free Pub Lib of Council Bluffs (IA)   NELSON, Mary L. (Head Adult
Srvs) 894
PARROTT, Lynn K. (Catlgr &
Ref Libn) 944

Free Pub Lib of Elizabeth (NJ) BOLL, Charles K. (Supvsng Libn) 112
SAWYCKY, Roman A. (Asst Dir) 1086

Free Pub Lib of Livingston (NJ) ROBERTS, Leila J. (Lib Dir) . . . 1040

Free Pub Lib of Monroe Township (NJ) BOGIS, Nana E. (Lib Dir) 110

Free Pub Lib of Stratford (NJ) RODERICK, Ruth C. (Dir) 1047

Free Pub Lib of Union (NJ) GARDINER, Judith R. (Asst Lib Dir) 417
MARYNOWYCH, Roman V. (Libn) 780

Free Pub Lib of Woodbridge (NJ) BECKERMAN, Edwin P. (Dir) 72
SPANGLER, William N. (Branch & AV Coordntr) 1171

Free Univ of Berlin (WGR) WERSIG, Gernot (Prof) 1325

Freedom-Gaiswold Sch (OH) MICHNAY, Susan E. (Media Spclst K-12) 832

The Freedonia Gazette (PA) WESOLOWSKI, Paul G. (Editor-in-Chief, Archvst) . . . 1325

The Freedonia Group (OH) BAUMGARTNER, Robert M. (Vice Pres, Treasurer) 66

Freehold Area Hospital (NJ) SIEGEL, Robin D. (Med Libn) . . 1136

Freelance Library Services (OH) EVANS, Stephen P. (Freelance Libn) 358

Freeport Memorial Lib (NY) EDWARDS, Guy P. (Libn Trainee) 337
OPATOW, Dave (Dir) 924

Freeport Pub Lib (IL) LOCASCIO, John F. (City Libn) . 735

Fremont County Lib (WY) HEUER, William J. (Dir of Libs) . . 535

Fremont Pub Lib Dist (IL) ROSE, Marta A. (Adult Srvs Libn) 1055

Fremont Sch District (CO) HART, Karen L. (Lib Media Spclst) 507

French Institute-Alliance Francaise (NY) GITNER, Fred J. (Lib Dir) 439

Fresno County Pub Lib (CA) CARLSON, Alan C. (Reader's Srvs Supvsr) 182
COBB, Karen B. (Assoc Cnty Libn) 225

Fresno Pacific Coll (CA) BRANDT, Steven R. (Lib Srvs Dir) 128
PAULS, Adonijah (Technl Srvs Dir) 950

Friends Academy (NY) FOLCARELLI, Ralph J. (Sch Libn) 387

Friends Hospital (PA) SOULTOUKIS, Donna Z. (Libn, Search Analyst) 1169

Friends of the Libraries USA (IL) DOLNICK, Sandy F. (Exec Dir) . . 310

Friends of the St Paul Pub Lib (MN) MEISSNER, Edie A. (Prog Ofcr) . 822

Friends Select Sch (PA) PANCOE, Deborra S. (Libn) 937

Friends Seminary (NY) WARNER, Elaine (Lib Media Spclst) 1305

Friends Univ (KS) GAYNOR, Kathy A. (Ref Libn & Asst Prof) 424

Frisbie Communications (IL) FRISBIE, Richard (Owner) 405

Frisch Dudek & Slattery Ltd (WI) PETERSON, Christine E. (Libn) . . 963

Frito-Lay Inc (TX) ARNOLD, Patricia K. (Mgr of Technl Info) 34
HAWLEY, Laurie J. (Ref Libn) . . . 514
OGDEN, Suzanne M. (Lib Srvs Mgr) 918

Front Free Lib (WV) LANGER, Frank A. (Owner & Libn) 695

Frost & Jacobs (OH) DAVIS, Yvonne M. (Law Libn) . . . 281

Frost & Sullivan Inc (NY) BORKENSTEIN, Donald M. (Sr Vice Pres) 116
NAPOLITANO, Wanda M. (Mgr, Product Admin) 887
SULLIVAN, Daniel M. (Pres) . . . 1207
SULLIVAN, Diane M. (Pres) . . . 1207

Frostburg State Coll (MD) GILLESPIE, David M. (Lib Dir) . . 435
WILLIAMS, Pamela S. (Ref & Biblgph Instrc) 1346

Fruehauf Corp (MI) SCOTT, Jane (Libn) 1107

FSI Archives of Recorded Sound (NJ) GERBER, Warren C. (Dir) 428

Fulbright & Jaworski (TX) HOLLAND, Jane D. (Dir of Lib Srvs) 550
VELA-CREIXELL, Mary I. (Law Libn) 1281

Fulcrum Technologies Inc (ON)

Fuller & Henry (OH)

Fuller Theological Seminary (CA) EDDISON, E P. (Mktg Dir) 335
SCOTT, Melvia A. (Law Libn) . . 1107
YEUNG, Esther Y. (Technl Srvs Head) 1380

Fullerton Pub Lib (CA) MILO, Albert J. (Adult Srvs Coordntr) 845
MUELLER, Jane L. (Libn) 875

Fulton County Board of Education (GA) HANSON, Kathy H. (Media Spclst) 498
SMITH, Judy B. (Media Spclst) . 1156

Fulton County Government (GA) PARKER, Dorothy J. (Adult Srvs Libn/Head of Ref) 941

Fulton County Pub Lib (IN) LASHER, Esther L. (Dir) 700

Funk & Wagnalls Inc (NJ) BRAM, Leon L. (Vice Pres & Editrl Dir) 127
O'BRIEN, Kathleen (Resrch Libn) 914

Furash & Co (DC) CLAYTON, J G. (Pub Srvs Asst Lib Dir) 220

Furman Univ (SC) SHIDELER, John C. (Pres) 1129
UBYSZ, Priscilla M. (Info Spclst) 1267

Futurepast: The Hist Co (WA)
Futures Group (CT) WILLSON, Katherine H. (Info Srvs Mgr) 1349

G

G D Searle (IL) SLAWNIAK, Patricia M. (Sr Info Spclst) 1148

G E Plastics (MA) KANE, Nancy J. (Info Resrce Ctr Adminstr) 625

G F Stron Rehabilitation Centre (BC) TROWSDALE, Robert G. (Libn) . 1258

G P Putham Sons (NY) GAUCH, Patricia L. (Author) 422

Gabbert Information & Lib Services (CA) GABBERT, Gretchen W. (Pres & Owner) 411

Gabriel Dumont Institute (SK) TURNBULL, Keith (Dir, Progs & Srvs) 1264

Gadsden Independent Sch Dist (NM) ODENHEIM, Claire E. (Dist Lib Coord) 916

GAF Corp (NJ) GARCIA, Ceil K. (Chemical Info Spclst) 417

Gage Postal Books (ENG) GAGE, Laurie E. (Proprietor) 412

Gail Borden Pub Lib District (IL) SOVANSKI, Vincent G. (Asst Chlds Libn) 1170

Gale Research Co (DC) MISSAR, Margaret M. (Resrch Consult) 847

Gale Research Co (MI) BIANCO, David P. (Bk Publicity Mgr) 94
BREWER, Annie M. (Sr Edit & Dir of Lib) 134
BRYFONSKI, Dedria A. (Publshr, Editrl Dir & Exec VP) 152
CLARK, William E. (Sr VP of Operations) 218
CONNORS, Martin G. (Sr Editor) 238
CROWLEY, Ellen T. (VP & Assoc Editrl Dir) 261
DRAPER, James P. (Sr Asst Edit) 318
LABEAU, Dennis (Dir, Editrl Data Systs) 685
MARCACCIO, Kathleen Y. (Edit) 768
MARLOW, Cecilia A. (Edit & Supvsr) 772
NASSO, Christine (Bio Div Dir) . . 889
PAUL, Thomas A. (Pres) 949
ROMIG, Thomas L. (Promotion Dir) 1053
RUFFNER, Frederick G. (Chairman & Chief Exec Ofcr) 1066
RUNCHOCK, Rita M. (Assoc Edit) 1067
SAVAGE, Helen (Edit) 1085

Gale Research Co (MI)
  SCHMITTROTH, John (Dir, New Product Devlpmnt) 1096
  SELLGREN, James A. 1114
  TARBERT, Gary C. (Exhibits Coordntr) 1224
Gale Research Co (MN)
  DARNAY, Brigitte T. (Sr Edit) .. 275
  YOUNG, Margaret L. (Edit) .. 1382
Gale Research Co (NY)
  GEISER, Elizabeth A. (Sr VP for Bus Devlpmnt) 425
  HUBBARD, Roy (Vice Pres) 568
Galena Park Independent Sch District (TX)
  SINCLAIR, Rose P. (Sch Libn) . 1143
Gales Ferry Board of Education (CT)
  HILLER, Catherine C. (Sch Media Spclst) 541
Galesburg Pub Lib (IL)
  BABANOURY, Betty G. (Chlds Dept Head) 43
Gallaudet Univ (DC)
  CHANG, Helen S. (Pub Srvs Libn) 200
  DAY, John M. (Univ Libn) 282
  HARRINGTON, Thomas R. (Media Libn) 504
  HURLEY, Faith P. (Info Resrcs Libn) 577
  LAWTON, Bethany L. (Bibliographic Instrcl Libn) 705
Gallery Association of New York State (NY)
  VOURVOULIAS, Sabrina M. (Film Coordntr & Exhibits Asst) 1289
Gannett Co Inc (VA)
  WELLS, Christine (Dir Lib Srvs & USA Today Lib Dir) 1322
Gannett News Media Services (DC)
  WOODHULL, Nancy (VP, News) 1366
Gannon Univ (PA)
  DAVIES, Grace A. (Archvst & Gift Bks Libn) 277
  LAURITO, Gerard P. (Libn) 703
Garden City Community Coll (KS)
  RUDDICK, Patsy R. (Dir of Lib Srvs) 1065
Garden City Pub Lib (ID)
  SCHIFF, Margaret M. (Dir) 1092
Garden City Pub Lib (NY)
  PIRODSKY, Nancy E. (Chlds Srvs Head) 975
  ROECKEL, Alan G. (Dir) 1048
  SHERWOOD, Nancy (Technl Srvs Head) 1129
Gardere & Wynne (TX)
  GARDNER, Linda (Info Mgr) 418
  LUETHEMEYER, Kaethryn (Asst Libn) 747
Gardner Advertising Co (MO)
  FINGERS, Deborah L. (Info Ctr Mgr) 378
Gardner Carton & Douglas (IL)
  DONAHUE, Karin V. (Info Srvs) . 310
Gardner-S Wilmington Township High Sch (IL)
  MCCLAREY, Catherine A. (Actg Libn & Spanish Tchr) 796
Garfield County Pub Lib (CO)
  GARYPIE, Renwick (Dir) 421
Garland County Community Coll (AR)
  MILLS, Peggy (Lrng Resrc Ctr Dir) 844
Garland Independent Sch District (TX)
  STAAS, Gretchen L. (Consult for Lib & Media Srvs) 1177
Garland Publishing Inc (NY)
  BALK, Leo F. (Exec Editor) 52
Garner Pub Lib (IA)
  GROTH, Robert E. (Dir) 473
Garrett Canada (ON)
  THODY, Susan I. (Engrng Libn) . 1235
Garrett-Evangelical, Seabury-Western Sem (IL)
  HAGEN, Loren R. (Catlg Libn) ... 483
  THOMPSON, John W. (Head of Biogph Ctl) 1240
Garrett Seabury Seminaries (IL)
  SMITH, Newland F. (Col Mgmt Libn) 1159
Gartner Group Inc (CT)
  LAZINGER, Susan S. (Assoc Libn) 706
  MASTERS, Kathy B. (Lib Srvs Dir) 782
Garvey Associates (NJ)
  GARVEY, Nancy G. (Pres) 421
Garvin Information Services (NY)
  PROSKE, James (VP, Info Srvs) . 995
Gary Community Sch Cooperation (IN)
  MCNAIR, James (Libn) 815
Gary Public Lib (IN)
  GUYDON, Janet H. (Head Libn, Dir) 479

Gas Research Institute (IL)
  MICHAEL, Ann B. (Lib Srvs Mgr) 831
  SUVARNAMANI, Nuj 1212
Gaston Coll (NC)
  HUNSUCKER, David L. (Dir of Lib & Media Ctr) 575
Gaston County Schs (NC)
  YARBROUGH, Doris A. (Media Coordntr) 1378
Gaston-Lincoln Regional Lib (NC)
  RITTER, Philip W. (Dir of Lib) .. 1036
Gates Pub Lib (NY)
  SWANTON, Susan I. (Lib Dir) .. 1214
Gateway Productions Inc (LA)
  YOUNG, Ruth H. (Vice Pres) .. 1383
Gateway Technical Coll (WI)
  KALVONJIAN, Araxie (Technl Processes Libn) 623
Gaylord Hospital (CT)
  EBINGER, Meada G. (Med Libn) . 334
  PENN, Elinor K. (Med Libn) 957
The Gazette (PQ)
  MCFARLANE, Agnes (Chief Libn) 805
GE Fanuc Automation Inc (VA)
  COX, Tina S. (Lib Mgr) 253
GE/RCA Astro Space Division (PA)
  SOWICZ, Eugenia V. (Lib Supvsr) 1170
GEAC Computers Inc (VA)
  GATTONE, Dean R. (Mgr, Customer Support) 422
  WEIST, Melody S. (Mktg Pub Relations Mgr) 1320
Gear Computers International (ON)
  MORTON, Robert E. (Gen Mgr) . 870
Geary Consulting (TX)
  GEARY, Kathleen A. (Consult) . 424
Geauga County Pub Lib (OH)
  CORBUS, Lawrence J. (Dir) 245
  GUMPPER, Mary F. (Mgr, Middlefield Branch) 477
  O'CONNOR, Deborah F. (Libn) .. 916
  ORR, Cynthia (Chester Lib Mgr) . 926
  WINANS, Diane D. (Support Srvs Mgr) 1354
Gee & Jenson Engrng-Architects-Planners (FL)
  FOSTER, Helen M. (Lib & Centl Records Mgr) 392
Gellman Research Associates (PA)
  FINN, Dorothy K. (Libn) 378
Gelman Sciences Inc (MI)
  BENSON, Peggy (Libn) 83
Gemological Institute Of America (CA)
  DIRLAM, Dona M. (Sr Resrch Libn) 305
GenCorp (OH)
  HOLLIS, William F. (Head, Info Ctr) 552
General American Investors Co Inc (NY)
  JONES, Jennifer R. (Dir of Info Srvs) 613
General Archives of Puerto Rico (PR)
  NIEVES, Miguel A. (Dir) 904
General Assembly of North Carolina (NC)
  HALPEREN, Vivian P. (Libn) 489
General Cable Co (NJ)
  DE WITT, Benjamin L. (Technl Info Srvs Mgr) 298
Gen Conference of Seventh-day Adventists (DC)
  SWEETLAND, Loraine F. (Dir of Lib Srvs) 1215
General Conference/Seventh-Day Adventist (DC)
  YOST, F D. (Ofc of Archs Dir & Statistics Libn) 1381
General Conference/Seventh-Day Adventist (SAF)
  LUSK, Betty M. (Perdcls & Technl Srvs Libn) 749
General Council of the Assemblies of God (MO)
  WARNER, Wayne E. (Archs Dir) 1305
General Council of the Bar of Ireland (IRE)
  ASTON, Jennefer (Libn) 37
General Datacomm Industries (CT)
  WIEHN, John F. (Corprt Libn) .. 1336
General Dynamics Corp (CA)
  ARNDAL, Robert E. (Chief Libn) .. 33
General Dynamics Corp (MI)
  MAGUIRE, Shirley E. (Sr Adminstrv Analyst) 760
General Dynamics Corp (TX)
  DE TONNANCOUR, P R. (Resrch Lib & Info Srvs Dir) .. 296
General Electric Co (CA)
  ROBINSON, Doris T. (Ref Libn) 1044
General Electric Co (CT)
  ESCARILLA, Jose G. (Adminstr) . 354
  FROST, Mary K. (Corprt Info Tech Lib Mgr) 406
General Electric Co (MA)
  MOLTZ, Sandra S. (Supvsr) 854
General Electric Co (MD)
  HENDERSON, Susanne (Lib Srvs Mgr) 527
General Electric Co (NJ)
  PFANN, Mary L. (Libn) 966

General Electric Co (NY) HEWITT, Julia F. (Mgr) 535
OLIVER, Patricia A. 921
SMITH, Marian J. (Online Srvs Libn) 1157
WARDEN, Carolyn L. (Srch Libn) 1304

General Electric Co (PA) RICH, Denise A. (Technl Info Spclst) 1027

General Foods Corp (NJ) TAYLOR, Donna I. (Assoc Info Spclst) 1226

General Foods Corp (NY) HOUGHTON, Joan I. (Supervisory Info Spclst) 562
SEULOWITZ, Lois (Mgr) 1117
SWANSON, Mary A. (Mktg Sr Info Spclst) 1213
VAJDA, Carolyn M. (Law Libn) . 1271
WEINSTEIN, Lois (Technl Info Mgr) 1318

General Mills Inc (MN) ANGUS, Jacqueline A. (Supvsr, Lib Srvs) 28
GALT, Judith A. (Info Spclst) 415
HALLSTROM, Curtis H. (Technl Info Srvs Mgr) 489
HONEBRINK, Andrea C. (Mgr) . . 555

General Motors Corp (MI) BRISTOR, Patricia R. (Biomedical Libn) 137
COCHRAN, Catherine (Govt Resrch Unit Supvsr) 225
HORNE, Ernest L. (Sr Libn) 560
SHEPARD, Margaret E. (Sr Libn) 1127
STEPHENS, Karen L. (Info Spclst) 1188
VAN ALLEN, Neil K. (Staff Libn) 1271

General Railway Signal Co (NY) ERICKSON, Sandra E. (Sr Technl Libn) 352

General Research Corp (CA) BOWRIN-MARSH, Donna M. (Customer Rep) 122

General Telephone of California (CA) DENNISON, Lynn C. (Info Resrc Mgmt) 292

General Theological Seminary (NY) HOOGAKKER, David A. (Assoc Libn) 556

Genesee Community Coll (NY) LANE, Elizabeth J. (Assoc Dean, Learning Resrc Ctr) . . . 694

Genesee District Lib (MI) ARVIN, Charles S. (Head of Acqs & Prcsng) 35
GAMBLE, Marian L. (Dir) 416

Geneseo Pub Lib District (IL) REDINGTON, Deirdre E. (Lib Dir) 1014

Genetic Systems Corp/Oncogen (WA) WILDER, Patricia A. (Libn) 1339
Geneva Pub Lib Dist (IL) HINTZ, Jeanne E. (Actg Dir) 543
Genix Corp (PA) PUPO, Raul (Pres) 998
George & Elsie Wood Lib (CA) STOCKWELL, Judith R. (Pub Srvs & Ref Libn) 1196

George B Dedrick Pub Lib (IL) GILBORNE, Jean E. (Pub Libn) . . 434
George Brown Coll of Applied Arts & Tech (ON) HARDY, John L. (Archvst) 500
George C Marshall Foundation (VA) JACOB, John N. (Archvst Libn) . . 589
WEBER, Anita M. (Asst Archvst) 1313

George Mason Univ (VA) ALTHEN, Elsa E. (Spcl Projs Libn) 18
BERWICK, Philip C. (Dir of Law Lib) 91
CONIGLIO, Jamie W. (Assoc Libn for Pub Srvs) 236
HURT, Charlene S. (Lib Dir) 577
MCGINN, Ellen T. (Law Libn) . . . 806
SAUR, Cindy S. (Pub Srvs Libn) 1085
SCHWARTZ, Marla J. (Serials Libn) 1105
SONNEMANN, Gail J. (Humanities Ref Libn) 1167
TATUM, George M. (Resrc Devlpmnt Libn) 1225

George Peabody Coll for Teachers (TN) ROTHACKER, John M. (Assoc Prof of Lib Sci) 1059

George Washington Univ (DC) APOSTLE, Lynne M. (User Educ Libn) 29
BADER, Shelley (Dir) 44
BARTHELL, Daniel W. (Subject Spclst, Ref Libn) 61
DEUTSCH, James I. (Instr in Am Civilization) 296
HEAD, Anita K. (Prof of Law & Law Libn) 518
HOLLYFIELD, Diane S. (Acqs Head) 552
KELLER, William B. (Head, Spcl Cols) 636
LONG, Caroline C. (Engrng Subject Spclst) 739
MACEWEN, Virginia B. (Ref Libn) 755
MARTIN, Elaine R. (Asst Dir, Info & Instrcl Srvs) 776
NIBLEY, Elizabeth B. (Actg Head, Media Resrcs) 901
PORTER, Suzanne (Col Devlpmnt Libn) 985
ROGERS, Sharon J. (Univ Libn) 1050
SANCHEZ, Jose L. (Ref Libn/Pol Sci Subject Spclst) . 1079
STEBELMAN, Scott D. (Coordntr for Biogph Instn) . . 1183
THOMPSON, Laurie L. (Asst Dir, Lib Operations) 1240
UNVER, Amira V. (Serials Coordntr) 1269

George West Indpendent Sch District (TX) ROBINS, Barbara D. (High Sch Libn) 1043

Georgetown Univ (DC) BARRINGER, George M. (Spcl Cols Libn) 59
BEDARD, Laura A. (Spcl Cols Libn) 73
BEDARD, Laura A. (Spcl Cols Libn) 73
BRAVY, Gary J. (Media & Ref Libn) 130
BROERING, Naomi C. (Biomedical Info Resrc Ctr Dir) 139
CHAMBERS, Bettye T. (Visiting Asst Prof) 198
CHEVERIE, Joan F. (Asst Ref Libn) 207
COLWELL, Carolyn J. (Asst Ref Libn) 234
DELANCEY, James F. (Assoc Univ Libn) 288
DENHAM, Maryanne H. (Automation Libn) 292
DOWLING, Shelley L. (Actg Head of Pub Srvs) 316
HELMINSKI, James C. (Asst to Sci Libn) 525
JACKSON, Elisabeth S. (Assoc Law Libn, Dir of Admin) 587
JOINER, Mary J. (Ref Libn) 610
KELLY, Mark M. (Catlgr) 638
MARSHALL, David L. (Asst Head of Acqs) 774
MAXON, William N. (Sr Ref Libn) 787
NAINIS, Linda (Asst Law Libn for Col Mgmt) 886
NOLEN, Anita L. (Archvst) 908
OAKLEY, Robert L. (Lib Dir & Assoc Prof of Law) 913
POSTAR, Adeen J. (Coordntr of External Srvs) 986
REITH, Louis J. (Rare Bk Catlgr) 1022
REYNOLDS, Jon K. (Univ Archvst) 1025
SERVERINO, Roberto (Assoc Prof of Italian) 1116

Georgetown Univ (DC)

SHAIMES, Karen 1119
SMITH, Elizabeth W. (Asst Libn) 1154
STACEY, Kathleen M. (Acqs
Libn) 1177

Georgia Coll (GA)

FENNELL, Janice C. (Dir of
Libs) 371
SCOTT, Rupert N. (Info Srvs
Coordntr) 1108

Georgia Department of Archives & History (GA)

BECHOR, Malvina B.
(Advanced Archvst) 71
DEES, Anthony R. (Archs Asst
Dir) 287
ENGERRAND, Steven W.
(Operations Analyst) 349

Georgia Department of Education (GA)

FORSEE, Joe B. (Dir) 391
MARSHALL, Ruth T.
(Southwest Regnl Lib Dir) 775
TOPE, Diana R. (Deputy Dir) . . . 1251

Georgia Department of Human Resources (GA)

CLARK, Jane F. (Sr Libn) 217

Georgia Division of Pub Lib Services (GA)

CORRELL, Emily N. (Libn) 247

Georgia Institute of Technology (GA)

BAILEY, Dorothy C. (Ctl Dept
Head) 46
BRACKNEY, Kathryn S.
(Architecture Libn) 125
DEES, Leslie M. (Serials Catlgr) . 287
DRAKE, Miriam A. (Dir of Libs) . 318
DREW, Frances K. (Medals Cur) . 319
GARFINKLE, Gail J. (Ref Libn &
Asst to the Dir of Libs) 419
GRIFFIN, Martha R. (Ref Libn) . . 468
HALE, Ruth C. (Pub Relations
Asst Dir) 485
KENNEDY, Joanna C. (Ref
Libn) 641
KYLE, Robert J. 685
LONBERGER, Jana L. (Acqs
Libn) 738
SHERMAN, John R. (Ref Libn) . 1128
TOMAJKO, Kathy L. (Resrch
Info Srvs Head) 1249
VIDOR, Ann B. (Dept Head) . . . 1283
WALKER, Barbara J. (Libn &
Asst Prof) 1295
WHITE, Carol A. (Dept of
Resrch Info Srvs Libn) 1330
WILTSE, Helen C. (Assoc Dir) . 1353

Georgia-Pacific Corp (GA)

GROOVER, Marion D. (Law
Libn & Resrch Attorney) 472
HALL, Deanna M. (Mgr, Technl
Info Resrcs) 487
LONG, Linda E. (Corprt Records
Mgr) 739
RAQUET, Jacqueline R. (Technl
Info Spclst) 1008

Georgia Power Co (GA)

INGLE, Bernita W. (Corprt
Archvst) 582
MANNING, Katherine J. 766

Georgia Southern Coll (GA)

BROWN, Edna E. (Prof & Assoc
Dir of Libs) 143
HARRISON, James O. (Head
Ref Libn) 506
JOHNSON, Jane G. (Acqs Dept
Head) 605

Georgia Southwestern Coll (GA)

MCLAUGHLIN, Laverne L.
(Asst Prof Head Technl Srv) . . 813

Georgia State Univ (GA)

ANDERSON, David G. (Head,
Catlgng Dept) 22
BANJA, Judith A. (Ref Spclst) . . . 54
CANN, Sharon F. (Educ Libn) . . . 178
CHRISTIAN, Gayle R. (Ref &
Docums Libn) 211
HOUGH, Leslie S. (Dir, Spcl
Cols) 562
HUGHES, Glenda J. (Asst Prof,
Map Libn) 571

Georgia State Univ (GA)

JOHNSON, Nancy P. (Law
Libn) 608
JONES, Helen C. (Asst Prof &
Ref Libn) 613
MENEELY, William E. (Sci
Biblgphr) 824
MORELAND, Virginia F. (Ref
Dept Head) 863
MOSBY, Anne P. (Ref Libn &
Online Coordntr) 870
PRESLEY, Roger L. (Acqs Dept
Head) 991
ROBISON, Carolyn L. (Assoc
Univ Libn) 1045
RUSSELL, Ralph E. (Univ Libn) . 1069
STILLWATER, Rebecca S. (Ref
Libn) 1194
THAXTON, Lyn (Soc Sci
Biblgphr) 1234

Georgia Technical Research Institute (GA)

GRELL, Holly J. (Resrch Assoc) . 467

Georgian Court Coll (NJ)

HERBERT, Barbara R. (Dir,
Instrcl Media Ctr) 530
HUTCHINSON, Barbara J. (Dir
of Lib Srvs) 579

Gerald R Ford Foundation (MI)

GRIFFIN, Robert P. (Chairman) . . 469

Germantown Central Sch (NY)

LINDSLEY, Barbara N. (Sch Lib
Media Spclst) 730

Germantown Pub Lib (OH)

BANTA, Gratia J. (Asst Dir &
Chlds Libn) 55

Gershman Brickner & Bratton Inc (VA)

GOLDBERG, Lisbeth S. (Info
Ctr Dir) 444

Getty Center for the History of Art (CA)

HERMAN, Elizabeth (Spcl Cols
Catlg Libn) 531
REED, Marcia C. (Assoc Libn) . 1015
TIEMAN, Robert S. (Auction
Catlg Dept Supvsr) 1244
WHITE, Kathleen M. (Lib Asst
2) 1331

Gettysburg Coll (PA)

HEDRICK, David T. (Spcl Cols
Libn) 520

Gibson Dunn & Crutcher (CA)

HOLLINGSWORTH, Dena M.
(Online Info Spclst) 552

Gibson Dunn & Crutcher (DC)

DICKSON, Constance P. (Libn) . . 301

Gilbert Commonwealth Inc (MI)

HERBERT, Helen E. (Libn) 530

Gilbert Pub Schs (AZ)

TRZICKY, Richard F. (Lib Media
Spclst) 1260

The Gillette Co (MA)

FOX, Susan (Mgr, Info Srvs) 395

Gillette Medical Evaluation Laboratories (MD)

DEXTER, Patrick J. (Info Srvs
Supvsr) 298

Gilman Sch (MD)

RUFF, Martha R. (Chlds Libn) . . 1066

Girls Preparatory Sch (TN)

LAMBERT, Sarah E. (Head
Libn) 690

Gishler Group Lib & Info System Consults (AB)

GISHLER, John R. (Sr Consult) . . 438

GJM Associates (NY)

MOLLO, Terry (Self-employed) . . 853

Glassboro State Coll (NJ)

GARRABRANT, William A.
(Circ, Interlib Loan & Sci
Libn) 420
GAYNOR, William A. (Perdcls
Libn) 424
KENNEDY, Kathleen A. (Asst
Pub Srvs Dir) 641
SZILASSY, Sandor (Dir of Libs) 1218

Glassboro State Coll (PA)

MEREDITH, Phyllis C. (Branch
Libn) 825

Glaxo Inc (NC)

HULL, Peggy F. (Lib & Info Srvs
Mgr) 573
MCKAY, Alberta S. (Technl Info
Spclst) 809

Glen Ellyn Sch District 41 (IL)

ADCOCK, Donald C. (Lib Srvs
Dir) 6

Glen Loch Elementary Sch (TX)

MILLER, Carol A. (Media Ctr
Spclst & Elem Sch Libn) 836

Glen Ridge Pub Lib (NJ)

LOOS, Jean E. (Dir) 740

Glen Rock Pub Lib (NJ)

FADLALLA, Gerald J. (Lib Dir) . . 361

Glenbard North High Sch (IL)   SONDALLE, Barbara J. (Media
                                            Dept Chair) 1167
Glenbrook Hospital (IL)   PERLES, Paul (Med Libn) 959
Glenbrook North High Sch (IL)   WICKS, Jerry R. (Instrcl Mtrls
                                            Srvs Coordntr) 1335
**Glendale Adventist Medical
  Center** (CA)   GUPTA, Ann D. (Libn) 478
                                           PRIME, Eugenie E. (Dir) 993
Glendale Community Coll (CA)   THOMAS, Mary C. (Libn) 1237
**Glendale Heights Community
  Hospital Inc** (IL)   APOSTOLOPOULOS, Sophia
                                            S. (Med Libn) 29
Glendale Pub Lib (CA)   WONG, Maida L. (Subsitite
                                            Libn) 1363
Glendale Unified Sch District (CA)   BRACE, Joyce B. (Libn) 124
**Glendale Union High Sch
  District** (AZ)   MAJOR, Caryl M. (Media Dir) . . . 762
Glenelg Country Sch (MD)   PICKWORTH, Hannah S. (Sec
                                            Sch Libn) 971
Glenfield Middle Sch (NJ)   HOROWITZ, Marjorie B. (Sch
                                            Lib, Media Spclst) 560
Glenn Books Inc (MO)   GLENN, Ardis L. (Pres) 441
Glenside Pub Lib District (IL)   VOJTECH, Kathryn (Admintrv
                                            Libn) 1287
Glenview Pub Lib (IL)   MOSS, Barbara J. (Catlgr &
                                            Head of Technl Srvs) 872
Glenville State Coll (WV)   FAULKNER, Ronnie W. (Lib Dir) . 366
                                          RUSSELL, Richard A. (Pub Srvs
                                            Libn) 1069
                                          VERMA, Prem V. (Technl Srvs
                                            Head) 1282
The Glidden Co (OH)   BACON, Agnes K. (Data Admin
                                            & User Support Asst Mgr) . . . 44
                                          STARRETT, Patricia L. (Technl
                                            Libn) 1182
Glide Sch District 12 (OR)   COOK, Sybilla A. (Lib Media
                                            Spclst) 240
Global Engineering Documents (CA)   AUSTIN, Stephen (Gen Mgr) 40
The Globe and Mail (ON)   HYLAND, Barbara (Dir of
                                            Electronic Publshg) 580
                                          VALPY, Amanda M. (Head Libn) 1271
Globe Unified Sch District 1 (AZ)   DWAN, Sandra K. (Libn) 330
Glocester Manton Free Pub Lib (RI)   LOXLEY, Donna J. (Dir) 745
Gloucester County Coll (NJ)   BOLESTA, Linda (Ref Libn) 112
                                          CROCKER, Jane L. (Lib, Media
                                            Ctr Dir) 259
Gloucester County Lib (NJ)   COUMBE, Robert E. (Dir) 251
Gloucester Pub Lib (ON)   NEILL, Sharon E. (Head, Technl
                                            Srvs) 892
                                          PICARD, Albert (Branch Head,
                                            Chef de Succursale) 970
Glover Memorial Hospital (MA)   LOSCALZO, Anita B. (Med
                                            Libn) 741
Gloversville Free Lib (NY)   STREIT, Ann M. (Dir) 1202
**GMI Engineering & Management
  Institute** (MI)   MEADOWS, Brenda L. (Ref
                                            Libn) 819
Goethe Institute (CA)   BERNHART, Barbara M. (Libn) . . . 89
Goldberg & Simpson P S C (KY)   VOYLES, James R. (Tax
                                            Partner) 1289
**Golden Gate Baptist Theological
  Seminary** (CA)   ASHLEY, Elizabeth (Technl Srvs
                                            Dir) 36
                                          KUBIC, Joseph C. (Readers
                                            Srvs Libn) 682
                                          WHITE, Cecil R. (Dir of Libs) . . . 1330
Golden Gate Univ (CA)   CODER, Ann (Gen Lib Dir) 226
                                          WENDROFF, Catriona (Ref
                                            Srvs Head) 1323
Golden Rule Insurance Co (IN)   SOWINSKI, Carolyn M. (Corpte
                                            Archvst) 1170
Golden West High Sch (CA)   PELOVSKY, Suzy A. (Lib Media
                                            Spclst) 955
Golder Assocs (WA)   EIPERT, Susan L. (Libn) 340
Goldey Beacom Coll (DE)   BEACH, Rose M. (Dir) 68
                                          COE, Gloria M. (Lib Dir) 226
Goldman Sachs & Co (NY)   KOLATA, Judith (Dir, Info Ctr) . . . 669
                                          POJE, Mary E. (Sr Ref Libn) 980
Goldman Sachs & Co (JAP)   KATAOKA, Yoko (Libn) 629

Goldome Bank (NY)   CALLINAN, Mary H. (Mgr of
                                            Info Ctr) 174
Golembe Associates (DC)   GALLUP, Jane H. (Libn) 415
Gonzaga Univ (WA)   MURRAY, James M. (Dir & Asst
                                            Prof) 882
                                          WYNN, Debra D. (Catlg Libn) . . 1375
Good Samaritan Hospital (OR)   LIBERTINI, Arleen J. (Libn) 725
**Good Samaritan Hospital & Health
  Center** (OH)   ROBINSON, Elizabeth A. (Libn)   1044
**Good Samaritan Hospital & Medical
  Center** (OR)   BROWN, Patricia L. (Technl
                                            Srvs Libn) 146
Good Shepherd Lutheran Sch (IL)   STELLING, Dwight D. (Tchr) . . . 1186
Goodall Memorial Lib (ME)   SMITH, Barbara J. (Asst Libn) . 1153
Goodland Pub Lib (KS)   WARREN, Janet B. (Dir) 1306
Goodman & Goodman (ON)   RODGER, Jane (Libn) 1047
Goodspeed Opera House (CT)   ROSENBURG, Betsy R. (Libn &
                                            Archvst) 1056
Goodyear Tire & Rubber Co (OH)   SMITH, Cynthia A. (Staff Resrch
                                            Lit Chemist) 1153
**Gordon-Conwell Theological
  Seminary** (MA)   ANDERSON, Norman E. (Ref &
                                            Technl Srvs Assoc Libn) 24
                                          DVORAK, Robert (Dir of the Lib) . 330
**Gordon County Board of
  Education** (GA)   OWINGS, Priscilla A. (Media
                                            Spclst) 932
Gordon Feinblatt Rothman et al (MD) BAVAR, Betty J. (Law Libn) 67
Gorman Publishing Co (IL)   INGISH, Karen S. (Info Spclst) . . 582
Goshen Coll (IN)   AMSTUTZ, Mary (Assoc Libn) . . . 21
                                          MILNE, Sally J. (Assoc Libn,
                                            Ref & Instrc) 845
                                          SPRINGER, Joe A. (Cur) 1176
Goshen Pub Lib (IN)   MCCARTNEY, Shirley R. (Dir) . . 795
Gospel Missionary Union (MO)   JACOBS, Mildred H. (Libn &
                                            Tchr) 589
Gossage Regan Associates Inc (NY)   COPLEN, Ron (Operations Mgr) . 244
                                          GESKE, Aina S. (GRA People
                                            Counselor) 430
                                          GOSSAGE, Wayne (Prinicpal) . . 453
                                          REGAN, Muriel (Principal) 1017
                                          TURNER, Gurley (Mgr) 1264
Gottlieb Memorial Hospital (IL)   OSTERTAG, Ina (Med Libn) . . . 928
Goucher Coll (MD)   LANTZ, Louise K. (Art Asst) . . . 697
                                          LEV, Yvonne T. (Col Devlpmnt
                                            Libn) 719
                                          MAGNUSON, Nancy (Lib Dir) . . . 759
Gould Inc (FL)   HAYES, L S. (Mgr, Technl Info
                                            Ctr) 516
Goulston & Storrs (MA)   HAYES, Alison M. (Law Libn) . . . 515
                                          MARX, Peter (Partner) 780
Government of Alberta (AB)   HU, Shih S. (Chief Provincial
                                            Law Libn) 568
                                          KUJANSUU, Sylvia S. (Serials
                                            Lib) 683
Government of Canada (ON)   RICHER, Suzanne (Chief Libn) . 1030
                                          VANDOROS, Z (Head of Technl
                                            Srvs) 1275
Government of Canada (PQ)   BERGERON, Pierrette
                                            (Integrated Srv for Info
                                            Resrcs Mgr) 86
                                          MAILLOUX, Jean Y. (Classftn
                                            Libn) 761
Government of Manitoba (MB)   TOOTH, John E. (Instrcl Resrcs
                                            Dir) 1251
Government of New Brunswick (NB)   BEYEA, Marion L. (Provincial
                                            Archvst) 93
**Government of Northern Mariannas
  Islands** (CM)   TIGHE, Ruth L. (Libn) 1244
Government of Ontario (ON)   VANDERELST, Wil (Dir) 1274
                                          WHALEN, George F. (Educ
                                            Ofcr, Libn) 1328
**Government of Prince Edward
  Island** (PE)   YKELENSTAM, Priscilla I.
                                            (Head of Technl Srvs) 1380
Government of Saskatchewan (SK)   ADAMS, Karen G. (Provincial
                                            Libn) 5
                                          ARORA, Ved P. (Bibliographic
                                            Srvs Head) 34

Government of the District of Columbia (DC)
PROVINE, Dorothy S. (State Archvst) 996

Government of the Northwest Territories (NT)
BAER, Susan E. (Libn) 45
O'KEEFE, Kevin T. (Resrch Ofcr) 919

Government of the US Virgin Islands (VI)
CHANG, Henry C. (Dir) 200
SOUFFRONT, Blanche L. (Asst Dir) 1169

Govt Relations Consultants (MD)
MILLENSON, Roy H. (Edit, Urban Libs Exchange) 835

Governors State Univ (IL)
TROY, Shannon M. (Lib Faculty) 1258
VARNET, Harvey (Univ Lib Dir) . 1279

Grace A Dow Memorial Lib (MI)
DYKHUIS, Randy (Ref Libn) 331
KOBEL, Rose A. (User Srvs Supvsr) 666

Grace Coll & Theological Seminary (IN)
DARR, William E. (Dir of Lib Srvs) 275

Grace Episcopal Church (OH)
CONNERS, Margaret S. (Volunteer Libn) 237

Graceland Coll (IA)
SHELTON, Diane E. (Lib Dir) . . 1126

Graduate Cardiology Consultants Inc (PA)
KREULEN, Thomas (Cardiology Dir) 678

The Graduate Hospital (PA)
FARNY, Diane M. (Dir of Lib Srvs) 365

Graduate Theological Union (CA)
BERLOWITZ, Sara B. (Head of Catlgng) 88
BISCHOFF, Mary L. (Assoc Dir) . . 99
BURDICK, Oscar C. (Assoc Libn for Col Devlpmnt) 158
CHOQUETTE, Diane L. (Head of Pub Srvs Dept) 210
CLARENCE, Judy (Ref Head) . . . 216
WILLIAMS, Mary S. (Head, Technl Srvs) 1345

Grafton/Midview Pub Lib (OH)
DIAL, David E. (Dir) 299

Graham & Dunn (WA)
DOWD, Mary M. (Law Libn) 315

Graham Independent Sch District (TX)
HINSON, Susan K. (Libn) 543

Graham Information Management Services (CO)
GRAHAM, Su D. (Sr Assoc & Consult) 456

Grand Ave Christian Church (MT)
FREEMAN, Lucile (Church Libn) . 401

Grand Blanc High Sch (MI)
BERTRAND, Beverly P. (High Sch Libn) 91

Grand Canyon Coll (AZ)
BRZOZOWSKI, Margery E. (Pub Srvs Libn) 152
FEAZEL, Edythe J. (Co-Director of Lib Srvs) 367
GROSSNICKLE, Jane L. (Co-Director of Lib) 473

Grand Forks Pub Lib (ND)
PAGE, Dennis N. (Dir) 934

Grand Forks Pub Sch Dist (ND)
RENICK, Paul R. (Media Dir) . . 1023

Grand Haven Pub Schs (MI)
BROOKS, Burton H. (Instrcl Media Srvs Dir) 140

Grand Lodge of Masons (MA)
HANKAMER, Roberta A. (Libn) . . 496

Grand Rapids Pub Lib (MI)
BOSE, Deborah L. (Libn I) 117
MATTESON, James S. (Libn) . . . 785
RAZ, Robert E. (Lib Dir) 1012

Grand Rapids Pub Lib (MN)
VALANCE, Marsha J. (Lib Dir) . 1271

Grand Rapids Pub Schs (MI)
COLYER, Judith A. (Media Spclst) 234

Grand Valley State Coll (MI)
FORD, Stephen W. (Lib Dir) 390
KING, Kathryn L. (Ref Libn) 651
VANDERLAAN, Sharon J. (Ref Libn) 1274

Grand View Hospital (PA)
BEACH, Linda M. (Med Libn) 68

Grande Prairie Pub Lib (AB)
SMITH, Linda A. (Chlds Libn) . . 1157

Grandview Heights Pub Lib (OH)
CANTWELL, Mary L. (Col Devlpmnt & Adult Srv Libn) . . 179
ROBINSON, David A. (Ref Libn) 1043

Grant Hospital of Chicago (IL)
KLEINMUNTZ, Dalia S. (Dir) . . . 660

Grant/Jacoby Inc (IL)
GATES, Carol M. (Info Srvs Mgr) 421

Grant Macewan Community Coll (AB)
FELL, Anthony M. (Lib Technician Prog Head) 370

Grant Medical Center (OH)
COHEN, Nancy E. (Med Libn) . . . 228

Granville County Lib System (NC)
STEPHENS, Arial A. (Dir of Libs) 1187

Grapevine Pub Lib (TX)
MCCOY, Judy I. (Media Libn) . . . 799

Graphic Arts Techical Foundation (PA)
LAMMERT, Diana P. (Libn & Edit) 691

Gray Cary Ames & Frye (CA)
MACLEOD, June F. (Lib Srvs Dir) 757

Gray Panthers Project Fund (PA)
HOPPER, Jean G. (Info Spclst) . . 558

Grayslake Community High Sch (IL)
ROBIEN, Eleanor K. (Libn) 1043

Great Falls Pub Lib (MT)
O'BRYANT, Alice A. (Chlds Libn) 915

Great Falls Pub Schs District 1 (MT)
WILLIAMSON, Phyllis B. (Supvsr of Lib Media Srvs) . . 1348

Great Lakes Chemical Corp (IN)
ADDISON, Paul H. (Info Support Spclst) 6
CHANDIK, Barbara V. (Info Spclst) 199
LINEPENSEL, Kenneth C. (Sr Info Spclst) 730

Great Lakes Industries (IL)
GORDON, Lewis A. (Pres) 451

Great Neck Pub Lib (NY)
TRINKOFF, Elaine (Ref Libn) . . 1257

Great River Lib System (IL)
ALBSMEYER, Betty J. (Coordntr, Consltng Srvs) 11
GRAY, Karen S. (Asst Exec Dir) . 460
TYER, Travis E. (Exec Dir) 1266

Great River Regional Lib (MN)
BERNDTSON, Janet L. (Libn in Technl Srvs) 88
CARMACK, Mona (Dir) 183
COLE, David H. (Technl Srvs Coordntr) 230

Great Valley Sch District (PA)
BALDWIN, Janet M. (High Sch Libn) 51

Greater Albany Pub Schs (OR)
OLSEN, Clintena D. (Lib Media Spclst) 921

Greater Amsterdam School District (NY)
TUNISON, Janice A. (Media Spclst) 1263

Greater Baltimore Medical Center (MD)
CONNOR, Elizabeth (Med Libn) . 237

Greater Cincinnati Chamber (OH)
ROTTE, Marge E. (Resrch Data Ctr Mgr) 1060

Greater Cincinnati Lib Consortium (OH)
JOHNSON, Joann (Exec Dir) . . . 606

Greater Clark County Schs (IN)
WHALEY, Janie B. (Lib Media Spclst) 1328

Greater Vancouver Lib Federation (BC)
CLANCY, Ron (Coordntr) 215

Greater Victoria Hospital Society (BC)
VAN REENEN, Johannes A. (Chief Libn) 1277

Greece Central Sch District (NY)
CUSEO, Allan A. (Libn) 267

Greece Pub Lib (NY)
SHAPIRO, June R. (Lib Dir) . . . 1121

Greeley & Hansen Engineers (IL)
CICHON, Marilyn T. (Libn) 214

Greeley Medical Clinic (CO)
CUTTS, William B. (Physician, Internist, Gereactrics) 268

Green Bay Board of Education (WI)
MURTO, Kathleen A. (Lib Media Spclst) 883

Green County District Lib (OH)
MULHERN, Raymond A. (Dir) . . . 876

Green Hills Pub Lib District (IL)
CARY, Jan E. (Lib Dir) 191
SODOWSKY, Kay M. (Ref Libn) 1165

Green Mountain Power Corp (VT)
HERNDON, Stan J. (Info Resrcs Adminstr) 532

Greenbaum Rowe Smith Raven Davis et al (NJ)
SEADER, Jane M. (Law Libn) . . 1109

Greenberg Traurig Askew Hoffman et al (FL)
EFRON, Muriel C. (Law Libn) . . . 338

Greenburgh Pub Lib (NY)
GILES, Marta M. (Ref Libn) 434
LEW, Susan (Technl Srvs Head) . 722
TRUDELL, Robert J. (Dir) 1259
TYNES, Jacqueline K. (Adult Srvs Head) 1267
WENDOLSKI, Alice D. (Adult Srvs Libn) 1323

Greene County Department of Social Srvs (NY)
MAURER, Eric (Case Mgr) 787

Greene County District Lib (OH)
KELTON, Jon D. (Automation Project Mgr) 639
OVERTON, Julie M. (Coordntr of Local Hist) 931

Greene County District Lib (OH)

Greene County Lib System (PA)

Greenebaum Doll & McDonald (KY)

Greenfield Community Coll (MA)

Greenhills Sch (MI)
Greensboro Pub Lib (NC)

Greensboro Pub Schs (NC)

Greensfelder Hemker et al (MO)
Greenville Coll (IL)
Greenville County Lib (SC)

Greenville Higher Education Consortium (SC)
Greenville Hospital System (SC)
Greenville Pub Lib (OH)
Greenville Technical Coll (SC)
Greenwich High Sch (CT)

Greenwich Lib (CT)

Greenwood Press (CT)

Greenwood Pub Lib (IN)
Greenwood Sch District 50 (SC)

Gregg Corp (MA)
Gregory-Portland Independent Sch Dist (TX)
Greiner Inc (FL)
Grey Advertising (NY)
Grey Nuns of the Sacred Heart (PA)
Griffin Hospital (CT)

Griffin-Spalding Board of Education (GA)

Griffin-Spalding County Schs (GA)

Grimm-McPherson & Associates (NJ)

Grimsby Public Lib (ON)
Grinnell Coll (IA)

Grolier Educational Corp (CT)
Grolier Electronic Publishing Inc (NY)

Groom & Nordberg Chartered (DC)
Grosse Pointe Pub Lib (MI)

Grosse Pointe Pub Sch System (MI)

Grossmont Coll (CA)

Grossmont-Cuyamaca Community Coll Dist (CA)
Grossmont Union High Sch District (CA)

WALDER, Antoinette L. (Head) . 1294
TURNER, Sue E. (Spcl Cols & Srvs Libn) 1265
CONNOR, Lynn S. (Lib & Info Srvs Dir) 238
FOGLE, Dianna L. (Libn II) 387
HOWLAND, Margaret E. (Lib Dir) 566
SANTINGA, Reda A. (Libn) . . . 1082
WATT, Richard S. (Libn I) 1310
WINDHAM, Shirley L. (Head, Main Lib Pub Srvs) 1354
SANDERS, Elizabeth S. (Media Spclst) 1080
GIBSON, Helen R. (Law Libn) . . . 432
HOPKINS, Jane L. (Lib Dir) 558
AYARI, Kaye W. (AV Dir) 42
EISENSTADT, Rosa M. (Branch Mgr) 341
MESSINEO, Anthony (Lib Dir) . . . 828

HIPPS, Gary M. (Exec Dir) 543
TOWELL, Fay J. (Dir of Libs) . . 1252
RUHL, Jodi S. (Adminstrv Asst) . 1066
OLINGER, Elizabeth B. (Lib Dir) . 920
MARCHAND, Janet H. (Media Spclst & Sr Tchr) 768
LUSHINGTON, Nolan (Dir) 749
SKOP, Vera (Circ Head) 1147
YARMAL, Ann (Chld's Libn) . . . 1378
SIVE, Mary R. (Indexing & Abstctng Srvs Mgr) 1144
DAVIS, Bernice (Libn) 277
BUIST, Elaine R. (Lib Media Spclst) 156
HEACOCK, Gregg (Pres) 518

COOK, Anne S. (Sch Libn) 239
SCHWABEL, Lexie W. (Libn) . . . 1104
DAGATA, Marie (Libn) 269
FOGARTY, Catherine B. (Libn) . . 387
FINNUCAN, Louise A. (Hlth Scis Lib Dir) 379

ROGERS, Jan F. (Media Coordntr) 1049
WILKINSON, Evalyn S. (Sch Lib Media Spclst) 1340
MCPHERSON, Kenneth F. (Self-employed) 817
CHURCH, Barry S. (Chief Libn) . 213
BONATH, Gail J. (Asst Libn for Technl Srvs) 113
ENGEL, Kevin R. (Sci Libn) 348
MCKEE, Christopher (Coll Libn) . . 810
HAYES, James L. (Pres) 515

ARGANBRIGHT, David (Exec VP & Operations Chief) 31
TOWNLEY, Richard L. (Info Srvs Vice Pres) 1253
GREENE, Danielle L. (Libn) 463
HANSON, Charles D. (Dir of Libs) 498
MORROW, Blaine V. (Automated Srvs Coordntr) . . . 869
GREGORY, Helen B. (Chlds Srvs Chief) 466
ROBERTS, Scott J. (Libn) 1041
STEPHENS, John H. (Elem Sch Libn) 1188
LEVINE, Beryl (Instrcl, Pub Srvs Libn) 720

HEPP, Thomas A. (Libn) 530

CURTIN, Mimi V. (Sch Libn & Media Spclst) 266

Groton Board of Education (CT)

Groton Public Lib & Information Center (CT)
Group Health Association of America (DC)

Group L Corp (VA)

Grove City Pub Lib (OH)

Gruen Gruen & Associates (CA)

Grumman Aerospace Corp (NY)

Grumman/Butkus Associates (IL)
Grumman Corp (NY)

GS Associates (MD)

GSD & M Advertising (TX)

GTE Communication Systems (AZ)
GTE Government Systems Corp (MA)

GTE Laboratories (MA)

GTE Spacenet Corp (VA)
Guam Territorial Law Lib (GU)

Guelph Pub Lib (ON)

Guggenheim Memorial Foundation (NY)
Guilford Coll (NC)
Guilford County Schs (NC)

Guilford Township Historical Collection (IN)

Gulf Canada Resources Limited (AB)

Gulf Comprehensive High Sch (FL)
Gulf Publishing Co (TX)
Gulf States Utilities Co (TX)

Gundersen-Lutheran Medical Center (WI)

Gunn Memorial Lib Board of Directors (CT)

Gunster Yoakley Criser & Stewart (FL)

Gurdon Pub Schs (AR)

Gustavus Adolphus Coll (MN)

Guthrie Clinic Ltd (PA)
Gwynedd Mercy Coll (PA)

LACKORE, Lois P. (Media Spclst) 686
REITER, Elizabeth A. (Ref Libn) 1022
SWANBERG, Lisa A. (Resrch Libn) 1213
DYER, Daniel (Chairman of the Board) 330
BARRICK, Susan K. (Youth Srvs Div Head) 59
BLACK, Frances P. (Asst Dir for Pub Srvs) 101
SULLIVAN, Edward A. (Info Spclst) 1207
BURDEN, John (Technl Libn) . . . 158
WESTERLING, Mary L. (Asst Chief Libn) 1327
GRUMMAN, David L. (Pres) 475
LOVISOLO, Lois (Archvst & Histn) 743
SIEGMAN, Gita (Sole Proprietor & Edit) 1136
POWERS, Sally J. (Info Srvs Dir) 989
LENNON, Suzanne 715
TAUBER, Stephen J. (Sr Member, Technl Staff) 1225
GRAHAM, Katherine I. (Info Spclst) 456
REDFEARN, Linda E. (Ref Libn) . 1014
BROOKS, Terri A. (Libn) 141
WEINGARTH, Darlene (Territorial Law Libn) 1318
KEARNS, Linda J. (Ref & Info Srvs Libn) 633
TANSELLE, G T. 1223
POWELL, Lucy A. (Acqs Libn) . . 988
KLEM, Marjorie R. (Libn, Northwest Sr High Sch) 660
RANCER, Susan P. (Media Coordntr) 1006
MILLER, Ida M. (Catlgr & Field Agent) 838
PARKINSON, Susan L. (Sr Libn) 943
GRADY, Alida J. (Media Spclst) . 455
WILSON, John W. (Sales Mgr) . . 1351
MCCONNELL, Karen S. (Systs Analyst) 797
CIMPL, Kathleen A. (Lib Srvs Dir) 214
COSTA, Shirley W. (Head Libn) . 249
PRITCHARD, Teresa N. (Dir of Resrch Srvs) 994
WRIGHT, Pauline W. (Libn & Media Spclst) 1372
ESSLINGER, Guenter W. (Govt Docums & Ref Libn) 355
FISTER, Barbara R. (Bibliographic Instruction Libn) 382
HAEUSER, Michael J. (Lrng Resrcs Dir) 482
HERVEY, Norma J. (Assoc Prof & Head of Technl Srvs) 533
THORSTENSSON, Edith J. (Scandinavian Libn, Coll Archvst) 1243
ANTES, E J. (Editrl Consult) 28
CRESCENT, Victoria L. (Ref Libn) 258

H

H A Simons Ltd (BC)

H & G Associates (MD)

H J Heinz Co (PA)

H Leslie Perry Memrl Lib (NC)

H P Kraus Rare Books and
Manuscripts (NY)

H W Wilson Co (MA)

H W Wilson Co (NY)

PEPPER, David A. (Corprt Libn) . 958
GIGANTE, Vickilyn M. (Resrch
Consult) 433
WRIGHT, Nancy M. (Libn) 1372
SHAFFER, Nancy R. (Asst Dir) . 1119

FOLTER, Roland (Dir) 388
LUKOS, Geraldine F. (Asst Edit) . 748
BARTENBACH, Wilhelm K.
(Product Devlpmnt Dir) 60
BATTOE, Melanie K. (Indxr) . . . 65
BRISTOW, Barbara A. 137
CARRICK, Bruce R. (Vice Pres) . 186
CASE, Ann M. (Assoc Dir of
Indexing Srvs) 191
CHEN, Barbara A. (Asst to Dir
of Indexing Srvs) 205
CLAYBORNE, Jon L.
(Telemarketing Mgr) 219
CORNELL, Charles R. (Editor) . . 246
DEEBRAH, Grace J. (Catlgr &
Indxr) 286
DOWNEN, Kathleen Z. (Sci
Indxr) 316
ENTIN, Paula B. (Catlgr) 351
FISHER, Maureen C. (Catlgr &
Indxr) 381
FORCE, Stephen (Dir,
Production Srvs) 389
GAROOGIAN, Rhoda
(WilsonLine Info Syst Dir) 420
GHOSH, Subhra (Indxr) 430
GODWIN, Mary J. (Asst Edit) . . . 443
GOLDBERG, Judy W. (Catlgr) . . . 444
HEWITT, Mary L. (Editor, Educ
Index) 535
HILLEGAS, Ferne E. (Catlgr) . . . 541
HOWARD, Joyce M. (Editor) . . . 564
HSIAO, Shu Y. (Catlgr) 567
KING, Trina E. (Editor) 652
LEWICKY, George I. (Vice Pres
& Dir) 722
LOCASCIO, Aline M. (Systs
Spclst) 735
MARK, Linda R. (Assoc Edit) . . . 770
MILLER, Frank W. (VP & Dir of
Mktg) 837
MOONEY, Martha T. (Edit) 858
NELSON, Milo G. (Editor) 894
PEDALINO, M C. (Indexer) 954
PEHE, Jana (Asst Edit) 954
REGAZZI, John J. (Vice Pres &
Dir of Comp Srvs) 1017
RENTSCHLER, Cathy (Edit, Lib
Lit) 1023
ROY, Diptimoy (Indxr) 1063
SCOFIELD, Andrea (Indxr) 1106
SHAH, Syed M. (Edit) 1119
SOPELAK, Mary J. (Systs
Spclst) 1168
TRAGER, Phyllis H. (Syst
Spclst) 1253

Hacienda La Puente Unified Sch
District (CA)

Hackley Hospital (MI)

Hackley Pub Lib (MI)

Haddonfield Board of Education (NJ)

Hage Fundsearch (MN)

Hahnemann Univ (PA)

SIGLER, Lorraine (Libn) 1137
MARSHALL, Betty J. (Libn) 773
KIRKLAND, Ruth M. (Ref Libn) . 655
GULICK, Eleanor L. (High Sch
Lib Media Spclst) 477
HAGE, Elizabeth A. (Dir) 482
BAKER, Judith M. (Assoc Libn
for Pub Srvs) 48
DONOVAN, Judith G. (Ref Libn,
Srch Analyst) 312
FENICHEL, Carol H. (Dir of Lib) . 371
HODGE, Margaret T. (Technl
Srvs Libn) 546

Haight Gardner Poor & Havens (NY)

Haines City Pub Lib (FL)

COMEAU, Amy R. (Head Libn) . 234
BARTHE, Margaret R. (Dir) 61

Haines Lundberg Waehler (NY)

Halcyon Associates (NY)

Hales Corners Pub Lib (WI)

Half Hollow Hills Community Lib (NY)

SPINA, Marie C. (Photography
Coordntr, Archvst) 1175
FLECK, Donald R. (Pres) 384
SIPOLA, Debra L. (Chlds Libn) . 1144
MOY, Clarence T. (Adminstrv
Aide) 874
NICHOLS, Gerald D. (Dir) 901
WOODS, Janice T. (Branch
Libn) 1367

Haliburton County Pub Lib (ON)

Halifax Area Sch District (PA)

Halifax City Regional Lib (NS)

LEVIS, Joel (Cnty Libn) 721
BLACKWAY, Madeline E. (Libn) . 102
COLBORNE, Michael B. 230
MACKENZIE, Heather L. 756

Halifax County-South Boston
Regional Lib (VA)

Halifax District Sch Board (NS)

ULBRICH, David E. (Asst Dir &
Branch Libn) 1268
CURRIE, Bertha B. (Sch Lib
Srvs Supvsr) 266

Hall Hill O'Donnell Taylor Manning et
al (NC)

Hallmark Communications (MO)

TAYLOR, Raymond M.
(Attorney & Partner) 1228
KOE, Bruce G. (Corprt Devlpmnt
Dir) 667

Hamblen County Lib Board (TN)

Hamburg Pub Lib (PA)

Hamden Lib (CT)

EDWARDS, Rela G. (Dir) 337
WINGLE, Rita M. (Libn) 1355
MAINIERO, Elizabeth T. (Lib
Dir) 761
MALOY, Frances (Pub Srv Dir) . 764
SWETMAN, Barbara E. (Catlgr) 1216

Hamilton Coll (NY)

Hamilton County Department of
Education (TN)

BRUNER, Katharine E. (Libn) . . . 150
VANDERGRIFF, Kathleen E.
(Coordntr of Media Srvs) . . . 1274

Hamilton-Fulton-Montgomery
BOCES (NY)

BAILIE, Donna L. (Sch Lib Syst
Dir) 47

Hamilton General Hospital (ON)

MCKINLAY, Bessie J. (Med
Libn) 811

Hamilton Law Association (ON)

HEARDER-MOAN, Wendy P.
(Libn & Exec Secy) 518

Hamilton Pub Lib (ON)

LEHNERT, Sharon A. (Branch
Head) 713

Hamilton Township Free Pub Lib (NJ)

HOOKER, Joan M. (Ref Dept
Head) 556

Hamilton Township Pub Lib (NJ)

ENGLE, Joyce C. (Head, Circ
Dept) 349
PORTER, Eva L. (Technl Srvs
Principal Libn Head) 984

Hamlin Memorial Lib (ME)

MOTT, Schuyler L. (Board of
Trustees Pres) 872

Hamline Univ (MN)

KING, Jack B. (Univ Libn) 651

Hammer Mountain Book Halls (NY)

SOMERS, Wayne F. (Owner) . . 1167

Hammermill Paper Co (PA)

YAPLE, Deborah A. (Corprt Lib
Coordntr) 1377

Hammond Academy Lower Sch (SC)

JACOCKS, Marcia W. (Libn) . . . 590

Hammond Pub Lib (IN)

MEYERS, Arthur S. (Dir) 830
MILLER, Marcia M. (Asst Dir) . . 840

Hammond Sch City (IN)

ROONEY, Merilyn H. (Media
Spclst) 1053

Hamot Medical Center (PA)

TAUBER, Jean A. (Dir of Lib
Srvs) 1225

Hampden-Sydney Coll (VA)

MORRISON, Jane B. (Reclass
Libn) 868
NORDEN, David J. (Dir) 908

Hampton Books (SC)

Hampton Pub Lib (VA)

HAMILTON, Ben (Owner) 491
BIGELOW, Therese G. (Chlds &
Yng Adult Srvs Coordntr) 95
JORDAN, Caroline D. (Ref Libn) . 616
OGDEN, Howard A. (Lib Dir) . . . 918
WINTERS, Sharon A. (Systs
Libn) 1356

Hampton Univ (VA)

DENDY, Adele S. (Dir of Univ
Libs & Satellite Ctrs) 291

Hanau American High Sch (NY)

Handley Lib (VA)

Handy Associates Inc (NY)

Hanhasset Pub Schs (NY)

PRINZ, Jane A. (Media Spclst) . 993
MILLER, Richard A. (Lib Dir) . . . 841
KAZANJIAN, Donna S. (Libn) . . 632
CAZZULINO, Clara P. (Lib
Media Spclst) 195

Hanover Coll (IN)   MORRILL, Walter D. (Dir of Libs) 866
        SOWARDS, Steven W. (Asst Ref Lib) 1170

Hanover Pub Lib (PA)   MCFERREN, Priscilla G. (Dir) ... 805
Hanson Lind Meyer Inc (IA)   PEPETONE, Diane S. (Dir of Info Systs) 957
Harcourt Brace Jovanovich (CA)   LAGIES, Meinhart J. (Edit in Chief) 688
Harcourt Brace Jovanovich (DC)   CAROW, Marsha (VP) 184
Harcourt Brace Jovanovich (FL)   JOLINSKI, Jenny R. (Info Srvs Mgr) 610
Harcourt Brace Jovanovich (OH)   MACIUSZKO, Kathleen L. (Info Mgr) 755
Hardee County Pub Lib (FL)   MAPP, Erwin E. (Dir) 768
Hardin County Schs (KY)   DAY, Mary M. (Lib Coordntr) 283
Hardin-Simmons Univ (TX)   BRADLEY, C D. (Perdcls & Docums Libn) 125
        CAMPBELL, Mary K. (Educ Libn) 177
        DAHLSTROM, Joe F. (Dir of Univ Libs) 269
        DONALDSON, Anna L. (Music & Interlib Loan Libn) 311
        SPECHT, Alice W. (Assoc Dir of Univ Libs) 1172
Harding Lawson Associates (CA)   HOTZ, Sharon M. (Chief Corprt Libn) 562
Harding Univ (AR)   BEARD, Craig W. (Ref Libn) 69
        HAYES, Franklin D. (Perdcls Libn) 515
        SPURRIER, Suzanne F. (Circ & Technl Srvs) 1177
Harding Univ (TN)   BAKER, Bonnie U. (Asst Libn) ... 48
        MEREDITH, Don L. (Head Libn) . 825
Harford County Lib (MD)   CLARK, David S. (Branch Libn) .. 216
        CRISCO, Mary E. (Automation & Tech Srvs Coordntr) 259
        LEBRUN, Marlene M. (Adminstrv Asst, Personnel & Finance) 708
        MASSEY, James E. (AV Coordntr & Operations Mgr) .. 782
        PITTMAN, Dorothy E. (Branch Libn) 976
        SEDNEY, Frances V. (Coordntr of Chlds Srvs) 1111
        SHAUCK, Stephanie M. (Sr Chlds Libn, Branch Libn) ... 1123
        STREIN, Barbara M. (Adult Srvs Coordntr) 1201
        WASIELEWSKI, Eleanor B. (Asst Dir) 1308
Harlem Hospital (NY)   MANDAL, Mina R. (Dept Sr Libn) 764
Harlem Valley Psychiatric Center (NY)   LEWANDOWSKI, Virginia M. (Mental Hlth Libn) 722
Harlequin Enterprises (NY)   JACKSON, Nancy D. (Sr Edit) .. 588
Harnett County Lib (NC)   COLLINS, Melanie H. (Technl Srvs Comp Systs Coordntr) .. 233
Harrington Institute of Interior Design (IL)   SCHUSTER, Adeline (Head Libn) 1103
Harris Beach Wilcox Rubin & Levey (NY)   BARRETT, Lizabeth A. (Law Libn) 59
Harris Corp (NY)   PIENITZ, Eleanor (Chief Libn) ... 971
Harris Corp Government Systems Sector (FL)   CAREY, Jane G. (Admin Lib Srvs) 181
Harris County Law Lib (TX)   EICHSTADT, John R. (Dir) 339
Harris County Pub Lib (TX)   GOLDBERG, Rhoda L. (Asst Cnty Libn) 444
        NOREM, Monica R. (Ref Libn) .. 908
Harris-Hess Associates (VA)   HARRIS, Virginia B. (Partner) ... 506
Harris-Stowe State Coll (MO)   GUENTHER, Charles J. (Adjunct Prof of French & Engl) 475
        KNORR, Martin R. (Dir, Lib Srvs) 665

Harris-Stowe State Coll (MO)   SHAPIRO, Marian S. (Technl Srvs Coordntr) 1121
        WOOD, Arline L. 1363

Harrison Central Schs (NY)
Harrison County Board of Education (WV)   DANNUNZIO, Rebecca T. (Sch Libn) 274
Harrison Memorial Hospital (WA)   KANNEL, Selma (Lib Srv Dir) ... 625
Harrison Sch District (CO)   SITTER, Clara M. (Lib Media Spclst) 1144
Harrold Independent Sch District (TX)   MCIVER, Lynne A. (Sch Libn) ... 809
Harry S Truman Lib Institute (MO)   OLSON, James C. (Pres) 922
Hart County Pub Lib (GA)   BISSO, Arthur J. (Dir) 100
Hart County Pub Lib (KY)   GRIDER, Patty B. (Dir) 467
Hart Crowser Associates Inc (WA)   SMITH, Sophia A. 1161
Hartford Courant (CT)   MCKULA, Kathleen S. (News Libn) 812
Hartford Hospital (CT)   CORCORAN, Virginia H. (Sr Libn) 246
        LAMB, Gertrude (Dir) 690
Hartford Insurance Group (CT)   KLEMARCZYK, Laurice D. (Technl Resrch Srvs Dir) 660
        SMITH, Lydia K. (Lib Adminstr) . 1157
        WOODWORTH, Bonnie J. (Corprt Libn) 1368
Hartford Pub Lib (CT)   BERBERICH, Patricia L. (Assoc Libn) 84
        BURGAN, John S. (Chief Libn) .. 159
        KING, Judith D. (Ref Libn) 651
        MARTIN, Vernon E. (Art & Music Dept Head) 778
        SCHULTZE, Salvatrice G. (Coordntr of Chlds Srvs) 1102
        SCHERBA, Sandra A. (Dir) 1092
Hartland Consolidated Schs (MI)
Hartley Film Foundation (CT)   HARTLEY, Elda E. (Founder & Pres) 508
Hartnel Coll (CA)   DICKENS, Jan (Instrcl Srvs Dir) . 300
Hartwick Coll (NY)   CHIANG, Nancy (Technl Srv Head) 207
        VON BROCKDORFF, Eric (Libs Dir) 1288
        WOLF, Carolyn M. (Head of Pub Srvs) 1359
Harvard Business Sch (MA)   EWING, Lydia M. (Ref Libn) 359
        JUDD, Eleanor M. (Acqs Dept Head) 618
Harvard Coll (MA)   DAMES, Barbara B. (Interlib Loan Libn) 271
Harvard Divinity Sch (MA)   WILSON, Virginia G. (Serials Catlgr) 1353
Harvard Law Sch (MA)   DUCKETT, Joan (Head of Ref) .. 322
        HOSTAGE, John B. (Catlgr) .. 562
        LEIGHTON, Lee W. (Catlgng Asst Libn) 714
        RONEN, Naomi (Ref Libn) 1053
        THOMAS, Jonathan R. (Ref Libn) 1237
Harvard Sch of Pub Health (MA)   ALPERT, Hillel R. 17
        HAUSER, Betty W. 512
Harvard Univ (MA)   ALTENBERGER, Alicja (Catlgr & Ref Libn) 18
        ASCHMANN, Althea (Rare Bk and Monograph Catlgr) 35
        BROW, Ellen H. (Book Selector for Ibero-America) 141
        BURG, Barbara A. (Ref Libn) .. 159
        CARPENTER, Kenneth E. (Resrch Resrcs Asst Dir) 185
        CHILDERS, Martha P. (Romance Lang Catlgr) 208
        COLLINS, John W. (Libn) 232
        DESIMONE, Dorothy H. (Catlgr) . 295
        DI BONA, Leslie F. (Head of Technl Srvs) 299
        DOWLER, Lawrence E. (Libn) ... 315
        DRAKE, Robert E. (Libn & Archvst) 318
        DUDA, Heidi E. (Ref Libn) ... 323
        ELLIOTT, Clark A. (Assoc Cur) . 343
        ERICKSON, Alan E. (Sci Spclst) . 352

Harvard Univ (MA)

FENG, Yen T. (Roy E Larsen Libn) 371
FREITAG, Wolfgang M. (Libn) . . . 401
FUNG, Margaret C. (Assoc in Resrch) 409
HAIL, Christopher (Asst Libn) . . . 484
HAMILTON, Malcolm 492
HOLDEN, Harley P. (Curator of the Harvard Univ Archs) 550
IRION, Millard F. (Pub Srvs Asst) 584
ISHIMOTO, Carol F. (Assoc Libn for Catlgng & Prcsng) . . . 585
JONES, Edgar A. (Sr Catlgr for CONSER & Preservation) . . . 612
KENT, Caroline M. (Ref Dept Head) 642
MAHARD, Martha (Asst Cur) . . 760
MCFARLAN, Karen N. (Univ Persnl Libn) 804
MOCKOVAK, Holly E. (Pub Srvs Libn) 851
MOREN, Harold M. (Acqs Libn) . . 863
OCHS, Michael (Libn & Sr Lectr on Music) 915
PANAGOPOULOS, Beata D. (Serials Catlgr) 937
PANTZER, Katharine F. 938
PARKER, Susan E. (Circ Srvs Libn) 942
PEDERSON, Daniel E. (Ref Libn) 954
PERRY, Emma B. (Assoc Libn for Admin) 960
POLLARD, Russell O. (Technl Srvs Head) 981
ROBERTS, Helene E. (Cur of Visual Cols) 1040
SCHATZ, Cindy A. (Libn II, Online Srch Spclst) 1090
SKLAR, Hinda F. (Head of Technl Srvs) 1146
SOLBRIG, Dorothy J. (Libn) . . . 1166
STEVENSON, Michael I. (Bus Info Analyst) 1191
STODDARD, Roger E. (Cur of Rare Books) 1196
VERBA, Sidney (Dir) 1282
WALSH, James E. (Keeper of Printed Books) 1299
WARRINGTON, David R. (Spcl Cols Asst Libn) 1307
WEISS, Bernice O. (Catlg Libn) . 1320
WICK, Constance S. (Libn) 1335
WINTERS, Wilma E. (Libn) 1356
WUNDERLICH, Clifford S. (Catlgr) 1374
YACKLE, Jeanette F. (Ref Libn for Foreign & Intl Law) 1376

Harverford Coll (PA)
ROBERTSON, Robert B. (Catlgng Libn) 1042

Harvey Pub Lib (IL)
AUFDENKAMP, Joann (Ref Libn) 39
OCHSNER, Renata E. (Adminstrv Llbn) 915

Harvin Clarendon County Lib (SC)
GILBERT, Sybil M. (Dir) 434

Harza Engineering Co (IL)
IRONS, Carol A. (Lib Srvs Mgr) . 584

Hassard Bonnington Rogers & Huber (CA)
CONLEY, Linda A. (Libn) 236

Hastings Coll (NE)
GARDNER, Charles A. (Dir) 417

Hastings Pub Lib (MI)
SCHONDELMAYER, Barbara B. (Lib Dir) 1098

Hastings Pub Lib (NE)
REA, Linda M. (Lib Dir) 1012

Hastings Pub Schs (NY)
AFROMSKY, Ellen S. (Lib Media Spclst) 7

Hathaway Brown Sch (OH)
LARSON, Gretchen S. (Head Libn) 699

Hattiesburg Pub Lib System (MS)
SANFORD, Janice R. (Chlds Libn) 1081

Haut-Saint-Jean Regional Lib Board (NB)

Haverford Coll (PA)

Haverford Sch (PA)

Haverford Township Free Lib (PA)

Haverhill Pub Lib (MA)

Haverstraw Kings Daughters Pub Lib (NY)
Havre-Hill County Lib (MT)
Hawaii Institute of Geophysics (HI)
Hawaii Judiciary (HI)

Hawaii Medical Lib Inc (HI)

Hawaii Pub Radio (HI)

Hawaii State Department of Archives (HI)

Hawaii State Department of Education (HI)

Hawaii State Lib (HI)
Hawaii State Pub Lib System (HI)

Hawaii Supreme Court (HI)

Hawaiian Electric Co Inc (HI)

Haworth Press Inc (NY)

Haworth Press Inc (WA)

Hay Management Consultants (ON)
Hayes Seay Mattern & Mattern (VA)
Hays Pub Lib (KS)

Hayt Hayt & Landau (NY)

Haywood County Pub Lib (NC)
Haywood County Schs (NC)
Hazen Pub Sch (AR)

HBM/CREAMER Inc (MA)

HBW Associates Inc (TX)

HCA Wesley Medical Center (KS)
HCT Corp (OH)
Health & Welfare Canada (ON)

Health Data Institute (MA)
Health Insurance Plan of Greater NY (NY)

CHIASSON, Gilles (Regnl Dir) . . . 207
FREEMAN, Michael S. (Libn of the Coll) 401
BROWN, David E. (Dir, Instrcl Media Resrc Ctr) 143
ROGERS, Linda S. (Asst Libn for Online Srvs) 1049
HOCKER, Justine L. (Emeritus Dir) 545
HOFFMAN, Elizabeth P. (Dir) . . . 547
LEE, Janis M. (Assoc Dir) 710
HUTCHINS, Kathleen D. (Asst Ref Libn) 579

GUBITS, Helen S. (Lib Dir) 475
RITTER, Ann L. (Catlgng Libn) . 1036
PRICE, Patricia 992
KOTO, Ann S. (Law Libn) 673
TANAKA, Momoe (State Law Libn) 1222
BREINICH, John A. (Dir) 132
FETTES, Virginia M. (Ref Libn) . . 374
CAMPBELL, R A. (Music Dir & Libn) 177

ITAMURA, Ruth S. (State Archvst) 585

FUJINO, Amy H. (Dist Adminstr) . 408
HARADA, Violet H. (Sch Lib Srvs Spclst) 499
HERRICK, Johanna W. (Sch Libn) 532
KANE, Bartholomew A. (State Libn) 624
TSUTSUMI, Carole K. (Libn) . . . 1261
WARNER, Joyce E. (Elem Sch Libn) 1305
GOTANDA, Masae (Dir) 453
LINVILLE, Marcia L. (Chlds Spclst) 731
PLADERA, Lucretia (Adminstr) . . 977
SCHINDLER, Jo A. (Bus, Sci, & Tech Unit Head) 1093
SPENCER, Caroline P. (East Oahu Lib Dist Adminstr) 1173
TAYLOR, Mary L. (Branch Libn) 1227
TENCATE, Sri P. (Libn III) 1231
WONG, Irene K. (Pub Srvs Libn) 1362
UCHIDA, Deborah K. (Corprt Libn) 1267
COHEN, Bill (Publshr) 228
FRALEY, Ruth A. (Edit) 395
RIZZO, John D. (Edit) 1037
GELLATLY, Peter (Sr Edit, Libnshp) 426
ABRAM, Stephen K. 3
COLLINS, Mitzi L. (Corprt Libn) . . 233
MILLER, Melanie A. (Lib Dir) . . . 841
THOMPSON, Mary A. (KS Rm Libn) 1240
MULCAHY, Brian J. (Head Law Libn) 876
ARMITAGE, Katherine Y. (Dir) . . . 32
LESUEUR, Joan K. (Libn) 718
JEFFCOAT, Phyllis C. (High Sch Libn) 596
ROSENBERG, Barbra E. (Info Srvs Dept Mgr) 1055
WATERS, Richard L. (Principal Consult) 1308
BRADEN, Jan (Dir of Lib Srvs) . 125
BANKS, Marie M. (Head Libn) . . . 54
STABLEFORD, Bonita A. (Lib Srvs Chief) 1177
WAKS, Jane B. (Libn) 1293

MOUNIR, Khalil A. (MIS Libn) . . . 873

Health Sciences Communications Assn (MO)
ELSESSER, Lionelle H. (Exec Dir) 346

Heartland Health Systems (MO)
HUGHES, Joan L. (Hlth Sci Libn) 571

Heartland Hospital West (MO)
GARNER, Sherril (Med Libn) 419

Heath/Zenith Data Systems (MI)
WOJCIKIEWICZ, Carol A. (Technl Libn) 1359

Hebrew Academy of Atlanta (GA)
KARP, Hazel B. (Media Spclst) . . 628

Hebrew Arts Sch (NY)
FLOERSHEIMER, Lee M. (Lib Dir) 385

Hebrew Coll (MA)
TUCHMAN, Maurice S. (Lib Dir) 1261

Hebrew Union Coll (OH)
GILNER, David J. (Pub Srvs Libn) 437
ZAFREN, Herbert C. (Dir of Libs) 1385

Hebrew Univ of Jerusalem (ISR)
KASOW, Harriet (Video Libn) . . . 629

Heckman Bindery Inc (IN)
HECKMAN, Stephen P. (Pres) . . 520

Hecksville High Sch Lib (NY)
MCCARTNEY, Margaret M. (Dir of Ref) 794

Hedendaagse Dokumentatie (BEL)
VAN GARSSE, Yvan (Lib Dir) . . 1275

Heery Architects and Engineers (GA)
ALLEN, Laurie C. (Libn) 15

Heidrick & Struggles (CA)
LEWIS, Gretchen S. (Resrch Mgr) 723

Heidrick & Struggles (IL)
MASON, Margaret E. (Corp Libn) 781

Heidrick & Struggles Inc (NY)
JONG, Jennifer L. (Resrch Assoc) 616

Heidrick Partners Inc (IL)
FELDMAN, Linda A. (Exec Srch Assoc) 369

Helene Curtis Inc (IL)
BECKER, Jacquelyn B. (Mgr of Technl Info Srvs) 72
CLAGGETT, Laura K. (Corp Libn) 215

Helene Fuld Sch of Nursing (NJ)
SOME, Barbara K. (Libn) 1166

Hellenic Coll (MA)
PAPADEMETRIOU, Athanasia (Asst Libn & Catlgr) 938
PAPADEMETRIOU, George C. (Lib Dir) 938

Hellmuth Obata & Kassabaum (MO)
BAERWALD, Susan M. (Libn) 45

Hemenway & Barnes (MA)
MOYER, Diane E. (Firm Libn) . . . 874

Hemmings Motor News (VT)
GILCHER, Edwin (Prodctn Staff Mem) 434

Hempfield Area Sch District (PA)
SCHEEREN, William O. (Sch Libn) 1090

Hempstead Public Lib (NY)
STEFANI, Carolyn R. (Asst Dir) 1185

Henderson Community Methodist Hospital (KY)
ROYSTER, Jane G. (Med Libn) . 1063

Henderson County (NC)
MARSHALL, Elizabeth C. (Dir) . . 774

Henderson District Pub Lib (NV)
CLARK, Janet L. (Dir) 217

Henderson State Univ (AR)
WOODS, L B. (Dir of Lrng Resrcs) 1367

Hendrix Coll (AR)
ALSMEYER, Henry L. (Dir of Libs) 18

Hennepin County Law Lib (MN)
GRANDE, Anne W. (Dir) 457

Hennepin County Lib (MN)
BYRNE, Roseanne (Principal Libn) 169
DESIREY, Janice M. (AV Catlgr) 295
DODGE, Christopher N. (Lib Asst) 308
ENGBERG, Linda L. (Deputy Dir) 348
FISCHER, Catherine S. (Sr Govt Docums Libn) 379
FRYMIRE, Jane K. (Sr Mgmt Info Spclst) 407
GELINAS, Jeanne L. (Principal Libn) 426
GROSSMAN, Michael P. (Libn) . . 473
ISMAIL, Noha S. (Ref Libn) 585
ROHLF, Robert H. (Dir) 1050
ROLF, Robert H. (Dir & Lib Building Consult) 1051
WRONKA, Gretchen M. (Chlds Srvs Sr Libn) 1373

Hennepin County Lib Board (MN)
COLE, Jack W. (Pres) 230

Hennigan & Mercer (CA)
KARR, Linda (Libn) 628

Henrico County Pub Schs (VA)

Henrietta Egleston Children's Hospital (GA)

Henrietta Independent Sch District (TX)

Henrietta Szold Institute (ISR)

Henry Carter Hill Lib Inc (CT)

Henry E Huntington Lib (CA)

Henry Ford Hospital (MI)

Henry Ford Museum and Greenfield Village (MI)

Henry Waldinger Memorial Lib (NY)

Herald & Review (IL)

Herbert Green Middle Sch (CA)

Herbert H Lehman Coll (NY)

Herbert Hoover Presidential Lib Assn Inc (IA)

Hercules Inc (DE)

Hercules Inc (UT)

Heritage North (WA)

Herman Miller Inc (MI)

Herner and Co (VA)

Herrick Pub Lib (MI)

Herricks Pub Schs (NY)

Hershey Foods Corp (PA)

Hesston Coll (KS)
Hesston Pub Lib (KS)

Hewlett-Packard Co (CA)

Hewlett-Packard Co (MA)

Hewlett-Packard Co (WA)
Hewlett-Woodmere Pub Lib (NY)

Hicksville Pub Lib (NY)
Hicksville Pub Schs (NY)

Hidalgo Lib (PR)
High Density Systems Inc (NY)
High Plains Regional Lib Service System (CO)
High Point City (NC)

GEORGE, Melba R. (Libn) 427
KANE, Dorothea S. (Records Adminstr) 624

BELL, Mamie J. (Libn) 77

MCKAY, Mary F. (Dist Lib Media Dir) 810
LANGERMAN, Shoshana P. (Head of the Info Retrieval Ctr) 695

CUMMINGS, Gary J. (Dir) 264
SPIRO GREEN, Becky A. (Catlgng Libn) 1175
ZALL, Elisabeth W. (Rare Book Catlgr) 1386

REID, Valerie L. (Asst Libn) 1019
STEVENS, Sheryl R. (Asst Libn) 1191

HEYMOSS, Jennifer M. (Asst Libn) 536
ENG, Mamie (Adult Srvs Libn) . . . 348
HEARN, Geraldine B. (Lib Supvsr) 518
KOSKY, Janet J. (Sch Libn) 672
WORTZEL, Murray N. (Perdcls Div Chier) 1369

DENNIS, Mary R. (Resrchng Indexing & Writing) 292
FAWCETT, John T. (Exec Dir) . . 367
KAUTZ, Richard C. (Pres & Chairman) 631
HENDERSON, Joanne L. (Lib Supvsr) 526
PARTRIDGE, Cathleen F. (Lib & Info Srvs Supvsr) 945
STIRLING, Dale A. (Records Mgr & Archvst) 1195
WAGENVELD, Linda M. (Mgr, Resrc Ctr) 1291
DAY, Melvin S. (Sr VP) 283
LUNIN, Lois F. (VP) 749
STEIN, Rene S. 1185
CORRADINI, Diane M. (Ref Libn) 247
LIGHT, Lin (Head of Technl Srvs) 726
HARRIS, Martha (Sch Lib Media Spclst) 505
WOODRUFF, William M. (Comms Ctr Mgr) 1366
WIEBE, Margaret A. (Libn) 1336
EICHELBERGER, Marianne (Libn) 339
COFFIN, Theodore Q. (Perdcl Acqs) 227
DUNBAR, Miriam B. 325
GUST, Kathleen D. (Info Spclst) . 478
HUNG, Joanne Y. (Info Spclst) . . 574
RAZE, Nasus B. (Sr Info Analyst) 1012
VUGRINECZ, Anna E. (Sr Mktg Info Analyst) 1289
SARAIDARIDIS, Susan B. (Lib Mgr) 1082
VAN DYKE, Ruth L. (Lib Mgr) . . 1275
DESCIORA, Susan O. (Dir) 294
VOLLONO, Millicent D. (Music Spclst) 1288
SWORDS, Susan (Ref Libn) . . . 1217
WICHMANN, Jane M. (Sch Libn) 1335
HIDALGO, Nilda R. (Libn) 537
PAVLAKIS, Christopher (Pres) . . 950

KNEPEL, Nancy (Dir) 664
ALSTON-REEDER, Lizzie A. (Head of Branch Srv) 18

High Point Coll (NC)   GAUGHAN, Thomas M. (Lib
                                Srvs Dir) 422
High Point Pub Lib (NC)   ELLIS, Kem B. (Adult Srvs Div
                                Asst II) 345
                                EVANS, June C. (Divsnl Asst I) . . 357
                                HICKS, Michael (Technl Srvs
                                Div Asst) 537
                                MOORE, Emily C. (AV Srvs Div
                                Head) 859
                                SPOON, James M. (Div Asst,
                                Info Srvs) 1175
                                TOMLINSON, Charles E.
                                (Technl Srvs Head) 1250
Highland Community Coll (IL)   WELCH, Eric C. (Lrng Resrcs
                                Dir) 1321
Highland Hospital (CA)   MORGAN, Linda M. (Med Libn) . 864
Highland Hospital (NY)   ROBBINS, Diane D. (Hlth Scis
                                Lib Dir) 1038
Highland Park Hospital (IL)   PRIOR, Janice L. (Med Libn) . . . 993
Highland Park Pub Lib (IL)   BRACHMANN, Kathleen A. (Dir
                                of Chlds Srvs) 124
                                GREENFIELD, Jane W.
                                (Adminstr) 464
                                KAPLAN, Paul M. (Dir of Adult
                                Srvs) 626
Highland Park Pub Lib (NJ)   JONES, Dorothy C. (Libn) 612
Highland Pub Lib (NY)   RANKIN, Carol A. (Lib Dir) 1007
Highland Sch District (WA)   JORDAN, Sharon L. (Dist Libn
                                K-12) 617
Highlights for Children (PA)   BROWN, Kent L. (Editor) 145
Highline Community Coll (WA)   BOSLEY, Dana L. (Technl Srvs
                                Libn) 117
                                TURLEY, Georgia P. (Lib
                                Technician III) 1263
                                WILSON, Anthony M. (Prof) 1349
Highsmith Co Inc (WI)   VAN ORSDEL, Darrell E. (Sales
                                Mgr) 1276
Hildebrandt Inc (NJ)   MOYER, Holley M. (Info & Lib
                                Srvs) 874
Hill & Barlow (MA)   WELLINGTON, Carol S. (Law
                                Libn) 1321
Hill & Knowlton Inc (IL)   KEELER, Janice S. (Supvsr,
                                Resrch & Info Srvs) 634
Hill Beats & Nash (NY)   RABER, Steven (Libn) 1001
Hill Holliday Connors Cosmopulos
  Inc (MA)   LEVINSON, Gail (Info Resrcs
                                Senior Analyst) 721
Hill Lewis Adams Goodrich & Tait (MI) SERPENTO, Mary M. (Libn &
                                Legal Asst) 1116
Hill Van Santen Steadman &
  Simpson (IL)   PETERSON, Scott W.
                                (Attorney) 964
Hillcrest Hospital (OH)   LYNAM, Nancy J. (Med Libn) . . . 751
Hillcrest Medical Center (OK)   COOK, Peggy M. (Libn) 240
Hillsborough Community Coll (FL) GIUNTA, Victoria J. (Ref, Media
                                Libn) 439
                                WOOD, James F. (Ref Libn) . . . 1364
Hillsborough County (NH)   THOMPSON, Debra J. (Head
                                Libn) 1239
Hillsdale Coll (MI)   KNOCH, Daniel L. (Technl Srvs
                                Libn) 665
Hillside Associates (RI)   MILLS, Catherine H. (Info
                                Analyst) 843
Hillside Pub Lib (NY)   ITKIN, Stanley (Dir) 585
Hilo Hospital (HI)   HAMASU, Claire (Libn) 490
Hinckley Allen Tobin &
  Silverstein (RI)   CHENICK, Michael J. (Asst
                                Libn) 206
                                LABEDZ, Elizabeth K. (Head
                                Libn) 686
Hinds Junior Coll (MS)   MYRICK, Judy C. (Catlg Libn) . . 885
                                WALL, Norma F. (Dist Dir) 1297
Hinsdale High Sch District 86 (IL) PETERS, Janet E. (Libn) 962
Hinsdale Pub Lib (IL)   CZARNECKI, Cary J. (Head of
                                Ref Dept) 268
                                SODERSTRUM, Ann L. (Head
                                of Circulation) 1165
Hinsdale Township High Sch
  Central (IL)   GRIFFIN, Thelma J. (Head, Lib
                                Media Ctr) 469

Hiram Coll (OH)   DUFFETT, Gorman L. (Head
                                Libn) 323
                                WANSER, Jeffery C. (Ref &
                                Govt Docums Head) 1303
Hirschler Fleischer Weinberg Cox &
  Allen (VA)   MOSER, Emily F. (Libn) 870
Hispanic Baptist Theological
  Seminary (TX)   WALLACE, James O. (Libn) . . . 1297
Historic Deerfield Inc (MA)   PROPER, David R. (Libn) 995
                                PROUTY, Sharman E. (Asst
                                Libn) 996
Historic New Orleans Collection (LA) DRAUGHON, Ralph B.
                                (Manuscripts Cur) 318
                                JUMONVILLE, Florence M.
                                (Head Libn) 619
                                LEMMON, Alfred E. (Ref
                                Archvst & Head of Reader
                                Srvs) 715
Historical Concepts Inc (NY)   WOLFE, Allis (Pres) 1360
Histl Fndtn of the Cumberland
  Church (TN)   WILLIAMSON, Jane K.
                                (Archvst) 1347
Histl Fndtn Presbyterian & Reform
  Church (NC)   BROOKS, Jerrold L. (Exec Dir) . . 140
                                STOCKDALE, Kay L. (Libn) 1195
Historical Museum of Southern
  Florida (FL)   SMITH, Rebecca A. (Resrch
                                Mtrls Cur) 1159
Histl Socty of Oak Park & River
  Forest (IL)   KELM, Carol R. (Cur) 638
Historical Society of
  Pennsylvania (PA)   PARKER, Peter J. (Dir) 942
                                SNYDER, Theresa (Proj
                                Archvst) 1165
Historical Society of Seattle (WA) CALDWELL, Richard C. (Libn,
                                Div Head) 172
History Associates Inc (MD)   CANTELON, Philip L. (Pres) 179
                                KELLS, Laura J. (Histn) 637
                                MERZ, Nancy M. (Archs &
                                Records Srvs Dir) 827
Hkyconeechee Regnl Lib (NC)   MASSEY, Nancy O. (Dir) 782
Hmmm Corp (FL)   LIGHTERMAN, Mark (Vice
                                Pres) 726
Hoag Memorial Hospital
  Presbyterian (CA)   SCHULTZ, Ute M. (Med Libn) . . 1102
Hobart Brothers Company (OH)   BAKER, Martha A. (Libn) 49
Hobart Township Community Sch
  Corp (IN)   CHONCOFF, Joyce L. (Libn) . . . 210
                                HUNT, Margaret M. (Lib Media
                                Spclst) 575
Hoechst Celanese Corp (NJ)   PAPROCKI, Mary E. (Info
                                Spclst) 939
                                URKEN, Madeline (Sr Info
                                Spclst) 1270
Hoechst Celanese Corp (TX)   UMFLEET, Ruth A. (Info Spclst) 1268
Hoffmann-LaRoche Inc (NJ)   CORRADO, Margaret M.
                                (Technl Ref Libn) 247
Hoffmann-LaRoche Ltd (ON)   HOARE, Colin G. (Asst Mgr) . . . 545
Hofstra Univ (NY)   ANDREWS, Charles R. (Dean
                                of Lib Srvs) 26
                                ARMSTRONG, Ruth C. (Head
                                Catlgr) 32
                                CINQUE, Deborah G. (Acqs &
                                Serial Libn) 214
                                COONEY, Joan D. (Ref Libn) . . . 242
                                COONEY, Martha D. (Bus Libn,
                                Asst Prof) 242
                                FREESE, Melanie L. (Catlg Libn) . 401
                                GIANNATTASI, Gerard E. (Asst
                                Dir of the Law Lib) 430
                                GRAVES, Howard E. (Head,
                                Catlg Libn) 459
                                HIGGINS, Virginia A. (Catlg
                                Libn) 538
                                JENNINGS, Vincent (Docums,
                                Map Libn) 598
                                KRATZ, Charles E. (Asst Dean
                                of Pub Srvs) 676
                                STERN, Marc J. (Univ Archvst) . 1189

Hofstra Univ (NY)
WAGNER, Janet S. (Head of Ref Srvs) 1291

Hogan & Hartson (DC)
DUVALL, John E. (Catlgr) 329

Holbrook Public Lib (MA)
MEAGHER, Janet H. (Dir) 819

Holladay Park Medical Center (OR)
OLSON-URLIE, Carolyn T. (Libn) 923

Holland & Knight (FL)
DOWLER, John W. (Law Libn) .. 315

Hollins Coll (VA)
BECKER, Charlotte B. (Catlgr & Music Libn) 72
DIERCKS, Thelma C. (Asst Libn & Lectr in Music) 302
HILL, Nancy A. (Head Catlgr) ... 540
OBRIST, Cynthia W. (Catlgr) ... 915
SCHNEIDER, Holle E. (Circ Libn) 1097
THOMPSON, Anthony B. (Archvst) 1239

Hollis Social Lib (NH)
SHERWOOD, Janet R. (Libn & Dir) 1129

Hollister Incorporated (IL)
CUNNINGHAM, Elizabeth A. (Corprt Libn) 265

Hollywood Presbyterian Medical Center (CA)
KING, Joseph T. (Chief Med Libn) 651

Holmes & Narver Services Inc (NY)
RUDA, Donna R. (Libn) 1065

Holmes Coll of The Bible (SC)
SLIFE, Joye D. (Lib Dir) 1149

Holmes Junior Coll (MS)
RICE, Joyce I. (Libn) 1027

Holmes Public Lib (MA)
MCGRATH, Margaret A. (Lib Dir) 807

Holmes Roberts & Owen (CO)
ESTES, Mark E. (Head Libn) 355

Holton-Arms Sch (MD)
SMINK, Anna R. (Head Libn) .. 1152

Holy Cross High Sch (CT)
PARIKH, Kaumudi H. (Libn) 940
RECTOR, Wendell H. (AV Dir) . 1013

Holy Cross Hospital (FL)
MCCLAIN, Mary P. (Libn) 796

Holy Family Coll (PA)
MCDONALD, Joseph A. (Dir of Lib Srvs) 802
MICIKAS, Lynda L. (Asst Prof of Bio) 832

Holy Family Medical Center (WI)
ECKERT, Daniel L. (Mgr Lrng Resrcs) 335

Holy Family Sch (LA)
LAROSE, Louise K. (Libn) 698

Holy Ghost Sch (LA)
WINFREE, Barbara S. (Sch Libn) 1354

Holy Name Hospital (NJ)
HOVER, Leila M. (Lib Srvs Dir) .. 563

Holy Names Coll (CA)
HOWATT, Helen C. (Lib Dir) 565
MAINELLI, Helen K. 761

Holy Rosary Academy (TN)
CUNNINGHAM, Helen (Sch Lib Media Spclst) 265

Holy Spirit Association (TN)
CONVERY, Sukhont K. (Missionary) 239

Holy Trinity Sch (DC)
MORIARTY, Ann (Elem Sch Libn) 865

Holyoke Community Coll (MA)
DUTCHER, Henry D. (Asst Pub Srvs Libn) 329

Holzmacher Mclendon & Murrell PC (NY)
UZZO, Beatrice C. (Dir & Records Mgr) 1270

Home Mission Board SBC (GA)
COURSEY, W T. (Libn) 251

Home Oil Co Limited (AB)
FRASER, Gail L. (Supvsr, Lib & Info Srvs) 399
LANE, Barbara K. (Indxr) 694

Homewood Pub Lib (AL)
GROOMS, Richard O. (Ref Asst) 472

Honeywell Bull Inc (MA)
BENDER, Elizabeth H. (Corprt Info Ctr Mgr) 79
PAPALAMBROS, Rita G. (Supvsr) 939

Honeywell Inc (CA)
CARRICABURU, Robert (Libn) .. 186

Honeywell Inc (MN)
BARTLETT, Vernell W. (Info Scientist) 61
KAUFENBERG, Jane M. (Asst Libn) 630
MUSUMECI, Joann 883
SPURLOCK, Sandra E. (Libn) .. 1177

Honeywell Inc (NM)
CHU, Tat C. (Asst Libn II) 213

Hong Kong Baptist Coll (HKG)
FU, Ting W. (Asst Libn I) 407

Honigman Miller Schwartz & Cohn (MI)
HEINEN, Margaret A. (Libn) 522

Hood River County Lib (OR)
KNUDSON, June (Dir) 666

Hoover Institution (CA)
HAWES, Grace M. (Archvl Spclst) 513
JAJKO, Edward A. (Middle East Cur) 592

Hoover Presidential Lib (IA)
MAYER, Dale C. (Archvst & Manuscripts Cur) 789

Hoover Pub Lib (AL)
ANDREWS, Linda R. (Dir) 26

Hopatcong Board of Education (NJ)
FEAKINS, Lois S. (Media Ctr Libn) 367

Hope Coll (MI)
JENSEN, David P. (Libs Dir) 598
MURRAY, Diane E. (Technl & Automated Srvs Libn) 881

Hope Reports Inc (NY)
HOPE, Thomas W. (Pres) 557

Hope Sch District 32 (BC)
SCOTT, William H. (Tchr & Libn) 1108

Hopewell Valley Regional Sch District (NJ)
PRIESING, Patricia L. (Media Srvs Supvsr) 993

Hopital Christ-Roi (PQ)
GELINAS, Gratien (Med Libn) ... 426

Hopital Dr G L Dumont (NB)
BRIDEAU, Marthe (Libn) 135

Hopital du Sacre-Coeur (PQ)
LESSARD, Josee (Documtn Technician) 718

Hopital Notre-Dame (PQ)
ALLARD, Andre (Head Libn) 14

Hopital Riviere-des-Prairies (PQ)
AUBIN, Robert (Lib Head) 38

Hopital Saint-Luc (PQ)
DUCHESNEAU, Pierre (Lib Srvs Chief) 322

Hopital Sainte-Justine (PQ)
LECOMPTE, Louis L. (Head Libn) 708

Hopkinton Junior-Senior High Sch (MA)
FONTES, Patricia J. (Libn) 388

Hoquiam Sch Dist 28 (WA)
GREGORY, Mary L. (Lib Media Spclst) 466

Horace Mann Sch (NY)
PEELE, Marla H. (Elem Sch Libn) 954

Horizon Information Services (CA)
TONKERY, Dan (Pres) 1250

Horn Book Magazine (MA)
SILVEY, Anita L. (Edit in Chief) . 1139

Horry County Memorial Lib (SC)
LOWRIMORE, R T. (Technl Srvs Libn) 745
BELL, David B. (Head Libn) 76

Horry County Sch District (SC)
ROTMAN, Elaine C. (Lib Srvs Dir) 1060

Hospital Association of New York State (NY)
RICHARDSON, Alice W. (Resrch Fndtn Assoc & Libn) 1029

Hospital Association of Pennsylvania (PA)
PATTERSON, Jennifer J. (Data Resrcs Mgr) 948

Hospital Corp of America (TN)
GREEN, Deidre E. (Dir, Hospital Lib) 461

Hospital for Sick Children (ON)
DIN, Munir U. (Med Libn) 304

Hospital for Special Surgery (NY)
WALES, Patricia L. (Lib Srvs Dir) 1294

Hospital of Saint Raphael (CT)

Hospital of the Univ of Pennsylvania (PA)
CLEVELAND, Susan E. (Lib Dir) . 221

Hospital Sisters Health Plan Inc (IL)
KNARZER, Arlene (Spcl Projs Adminstr) 663

Hotel Dieu Hospital (LA)
CAFFAREL, Agnes (Hlth Sci Libn) 170

Houghton Coll (NY)
DOEZEMA, Linda P. (Ref Libn & Coll Archvst) 308
LAUER, Jonathan D. (Dir) 702

Houghton Mifflin Co (MA)
HOGAN, Margaret A. (Promotions Mgr) 549
MURPHY, Marilyn S. (Sr Info Spclst) 881
PERRY, Guest (Dir Corprt Lib) .. 960

Housatonic Community Coll (CT)
HARLOW, Aileen W. (Media Libn) 502

House Ear Institute (CA)
CHARBONNEAU, Ronald P. (Resrch Libn) 202
MULE, Gabriel (Acqs & Serials Libn & Lib Adminstr) 876

House of Assembly (NF)
RICHARDS, Norma J. (Legislative Libn) 1028

House of Commons (ON)
TAYLOR, Loretta C. (Libn & Resrchr) 1227

Houston Academy of Medicine (TX)
BAXTER, Barbara A. (Col Devlpmnt Dir) 67
COLSON, Elizabeth A. (Catlgng Dir) 234

Houston Academy of Medicine (TX)
GARCIA, Beatriz H. (Info Srvs Libn) 417
IGNATIEV, Laura (Circ Srvs Head) 581
KANESHIRO, Kellie N. (Info Srvs Libn) 625
LYDERS, Richard A. (Exec Dir) . . 751
MANN, Caroline E. (Dir of Serials) 765
RAMBO, Neil H. (Asst Dir) 1005
WHITE, Elizabeth B. (Dir, Histl Resrch Ctr) 1331
WILSON, Barbara A. (Ref Desk Coordntr & Educ Libn) 1349

Houston Baptist Univ (TX)
NOBLE, Ann A. (Tech Srvs Head) 906

Houston Community Coll (TX)
KLAPPERSACK, Dennis (Dir of Libs) 657
TEOH, George M. (Catlgr) 1231

Houston County Pub Libs (GA)
MERK, P E. (Branch Libn) 826

Houston Independent Sch District (TX)
BLALOCK, Virginia D. (Elem Sch Libn) 103
HOLDREN, Ann E. (Dir of Lib Srvs) 550
MILES, Ruby A. (Sch Libn & Comunty Coll Libn) 834
WU, Jean (Sch Libn) 1373

Houston Lighting & Power Co (TX)
ANDERSON, Eliane G. (Sr Records Analyst) 22
LOOS, Carolyn F. (Records Analyst) 740

Houston Museum of Fine Arts (TX)
ROBINSON, Kathleen M. (Archvst) 1044

Houston Post (TX)
WORCHEL, Harris M. (Asst Chief Libn) 1368

Houston Pub Lib (TX)
BROWN, Carol J. (Asst Chief) . . 142
BROWN, Freddiemae E. (Regnl Branch Libn) 144
BRYANT, James M. (Ref Libn, Humanities) 152
CLARK, Jay B. (Technl Srv Div Chief) 217
ENDELMAN, Sharon B. (Coordntr) 348
GOLEY, Elaine P. (Juvenile Spclst) 447
GUBBIN, Barbara A. (Coordntr) . 475
HANDROW, Margaret M. (Libn II) 495
HENINGTON, David M. (Dir) 528
HOLMAN, Linda E. (Ref Libn) . . . 553
HORNAK, Anna F. (Asst Dir) . . . 559
MOORE, Sheryl R. (Ref and Serials Libn) 861
POTIER, Gwendolyn J. (Branch Mgr) 986
SELLIN, Linda M. (Interlib Loan Mgr) 1114
TIRRELL, Brenda P. (Mgr of Bus Sci & Tech Dept) 1247
WILSON, Michael E. (Architectural Archvst) 1352
WOHLSCHLAG, Sarah A. (Manager) 1359
ZWICK, Louise Y. (Chlds Libn) . 1392

Howard County Lib (MD)
BOGAGE, Alan R. (Ref Spclst) . . 110
HILL, Norma L. (Asst Dir) 540
JONES, Cynthia A. (Yng Adult Spclst) 612

Howard County Pub Schs (MD)
O'LOUGHLIN, Marilyn L. (Lib Media Spclst) 921

Howard Payne Univ (TX)
PARTON, William A. (Univ Libn) . 945

Howard Univ (DC)
ACKERMAN, F C. (Assoc Libn) . . . 3
BATTLE, Thomas C. (Dir) 65
HAITH, Dorothy M. (Dir of Univ Libs) 484
HO, James K. (Asst Dir) 545
JEFFERSON, Karen L. (Cur) 596

Howard Univ (DC)
LEONARD, Angela M. (Asst Libn) 716
MCCRAY, Maceo E. (Assoc Libn) 800
RICHARDSON, Deborra A. (Music Libn) 1029
SMITH, Clara M. (Asst Libn for Pub Srvs) 1153
WRIGHT, Arthuree M. (Libn & Ref Supvsr) 1370

Howe Military Sch (IN)
VANZUILEN, Darlene A. (Libn) . 1278

Howell Carnegie Lib (MI)
ZAENGER, Kathleen L. (Dir) . . . 1385

Howrey & Simon (DC)
BEALL, Barbara A. (Legislative Libn) 68
FELDMAN, Ellen S. (Asst Lib Dir) 369

Hoyle Morris & Kerr (PA)
SMITH, Linda D. (Libn) 1157

Hoyt Galvin & Associates (NC)
GALVIN, Hoyt R. (Principal) 415

HTB Inc (OK)
ROBERTSON, Retha M. (Libn) . 1042

Hudson City Sch District (NY)
HENDRICKS, Elaine M. (Sch Lib Media Spclst) 527

Hudson Valley Community Coll (NY)
BLANDY, Susan G. (Assoc Prof & Asst Libn) 104
ROOT, Christine (Prof, Ref and Online Srchng) 1053
WALSH, Daniel P. (Asst Libn) . . 1299

Huffer Associates (MD)
HUFFER, Mary A. (Pres) 570

Huffman Independent Sch District (TX)
SHARP, Betty L. (Dir of AV & Libn) 1122

Hufstedler Miller Carlson & Beardsley (CA)
DONALDSON, Maryanne T. (Libn) 311

Hugh MacMillan Medical Center (ON)
BERNSTEIN, Elaine S. (Libn) 89

Hughes Aircraft Co (CA)
CAMPBELL, Bill W. (Mgr of Info Srvs Dept) 176
CLIFFORD, Susan G. (Technl Lib Mgr) 222
GOUDELOCK, Carol V. (Sr Libn) 454
MORRISEY, Locke J. (Perdcls Libn) 867
PATTEN, Frederick W. (Catlg Libn) 947
PAUL, Donald C. (Head Libn) . . 949
SEVIER, Jeffrey A. (Head, Technl Lib) 1117
STERLIN, Annette S. (Technl Processes Supvsr) 1189
TAYLOR, Alice J. (Sr Libn) 1226

Hughes & Luce (TX)
RODAWALT, Valarie J. (Law Libn) 1046

Hughes Communications Inc (CA)
SUTTON, Joanna M. (Resrch Info Ctr Supvsr) 1211

Hughes Hubbard & Reed (NY)
GREEN, Charlene (Asst Libn) . . . 461
RISH, Jennifer G. (Libn) 1035
ROSS, Ellen T. (Ref Libn) 1058

Hughes Thorsness Gantz Powell & Brundin (AK)
ELAM, Kim A. (Head Libn) 341

Hughston Sports Medicine Foundation (GA)
CLEMENTS, Betty H. (Libn) 221

Human Resources Center (NY)
TISHLER, Amnon (Resrch Libn) 1247

Human Resources Development Group (BC)
HAYCOCK, Carol A. (Pres) 515

Human Resources Sch (NY)
VELLEMAN, Ruth A. (Lib Dir) . . 1281

Humana Hospital (AZ)
BERK, Nancy G. (Med Staff Lib Dir) 87

Humber College (ON)
HOOGKAMER, Dawne (Lib Technician) 556

Humboldt State Univ (CA)
CHADWICK, Sharon S. (Sci Ref Libn) 197
CROSBY-MUILENBURG, Corryn (Head of Info Srvs) . . . 260
KENYON, Sharmon H. (Bus Libn) 643
MAGLADRY, George C. (Acqs Libn) 759
OYLER, David K. (Univ Libn & Dir of Media Srvs) 932

Humboldt State Univ (CA)

The Hun Sch of Princeton (NJ)
Hunter Coll of the City Univ of New York (NY)

WIMMER, Ted (Col Devlpmnt Coordntr) 1354
FOX, Mary A. (Lib Srvs Head) . . 395

AUFSES, Harriet W. (Libn in Charge) 39
BRAUER, Regina (Libn) 129
SALAZAR, Pamela R. (Catlgr) . 1076
SEGAL, Judith (Asst Libn) 1112
ROSENBERG, Harlene Z. (Eductnl Media Spclst) 1056

Hunterdon Central High Sch (NJ)

WHITE, Joyce G. (Med Libn) . 1331

Hunterdon Medical Center (NJ)
TYNAN, Laurie F. (Dir) 1267
Huntingdon County Lib (PA)
Huntington Beach Pub Lib (CA)
HAYDEN, Ronald L. (Lib Dir) . . 515
Huntington Lib (CA)
HODSON, Sara S. (Assoc Cur of Manuscripts) 546
MCLOONE, Harriet V. (Asst Curator) 814
WOODWARD, Daniel (Libn) . 1368

Huntington Memorial Hospital (CA)
ZEIND, Samir M. (Mgr) 1387
Huntington Pub Lib (NY)
MCGRATH, Antoinette M. (Ref Srvs Head) 807
ROSEN, Albert (Bd of Trustees Mem) 1055
WULFING, Joyce (Lib I, Head of Technl Srvs Dept) 1374

Hunton & Williams (DC)
FUTRELL, Iva M. (Law Libn) . . . 411
Hunton & Williams (NC)
MURPHY, Malinda M. (Law Libn) 881

Huntsville-Madison County Pub Lib (AL)
COOPER, Regina G. (Col Devlpmnt & Pub Info Head) . . 243
LIAW, Barbara C. (Head) 725
MCCANLESS, Christel L. (Lib Consult) 793

The Huntsville Times (AL)
COX, Sharon P. (Chld's Asst Libn) 253
Huron County Pub Lib (ON)
CHAPMAN, Mary A. (Ref & Interlib Loan Dept Head) 202
Huron Valley Lib System (MI)
MONTGOMERY, Wanda W. (Libn) 856
Hurst-Euless-Bedford ISD (TX)

Hurt Richardson Garner Todd & Cadenhead (GA)
GUERIN, Roberta T. (Law Libn) . 476
Hutchinson Pub Lib (KS)
CHRISTNER, Terry A. (Pub Info Ofcr) 212
RATZLAFF, Marcella J. (Asst Dir) 1010
Hutchinson Pub Schs (KS)
SOLDNER, Nancy C. (Lib Media Srvs Coordntr) 1166
GOLD, Susan L. (Asst VP) 444
Huttonline E F Hutton (NY)
BRENNAN, Jean M. (Libn) 132
Hutzel Hospital (MI)
Hyde County Board of Education (NC)
MANN, Sallie E. (Lib Media Supvsr) 766

I

I E Associates Inc (MN)
ABELES, Tom (Pres) 2
I M Pei & Partners (NY)
BURROUGHS, Christine M. (Libn) 163
I P Sharp Associates Limited (IL)
FOUSER, Jane G. (Account Mgr) 393
I P Sharp Associates Limited (NY)
GENEREAUX, Peter R. 427
I P Sharp Associates Limited (ON)
KEITH, David A. (Database Srvs Dir) 635
I S Grupe Inc (IL)
SCHIPMA, Peter B. (Pres) . . . 1093
ICCROM (ITL)
HUEMER, Christina G. (Asst Libn) 570
ICD/CCNAA (GA)
CHERN, Jenn C. (Info Assoc) . . . 206
Ice Miller Donadia & Ryan (IN)
OVERSHINER, Barbara A. (Law Libn) 931
ICI Americas Inc (DE)
MECRAY, Freida S. (Ref Libn) . . 820
THOMAN, Nancy L. (Syst Analyst) 1236
IDA Ireland (IRE)
KELLY, Jerry (Sr VP) 638
Idaho Falls Pub Lib (ID)
ATWOOD, Virginia W. (Ref Dept Head) 38
HOLLAND, Paul E. (Dir) 551

Idaho State Historical Society (ID)
Idaho State Lib (ID)

WELLS, Merle W. (Histn and Archvst) 1322
BOLLES, Charles A. (Libn) 112
FORD, Karin E. (Acting Assoc Dir for Info Srvs) 389
JOSLIN, Ann (Assoc Dir, Lib Dvlpmnt) 618

Idaho State Univ (ID)
WATSON, Peter G. (Univ Libn) . 1310
The Idaho Statesman (ID)
IRONS, Lynda R. (Libn) 584
Idox (CA)
O'CONNOR, Brian C. (Sr Consult) 915
O'NEILL, Sue (Libn) 924
IIT Research Institute (MD)
MYERS, Sara J. (Lib Dir & Asst Prof) 885
Iliff Sch of Theology (CO)
SWATOS, Priscilla L. (Hlth Info Srvs Coordntr) 1214
Illini Hospital (IL)
THOMPSON, Bert A. (Lib Srv Dir) 1239
Illinois Benedictine Coll (IL)
LINDGREN, William D. (Dir) . . . 729

Illinois Central Coll (IL)
IL Coalition Against Sexual Assault (IL)
BRADWAY, Becky J. (Spcl Projects Coordntr) 126
Illinois Coll (IL)
ZUIDERVELD, Sharon R. (Catlgr) 1391
Illinois Coll of Optometry (IL)
BAIR, Alice E. (Pub Srv Libn) 47
DUJSIK, Gerald (Lrng Resrcs Dir) 324
HEIDKA, Patricia L. (Info Centl Mgr) 521
Illinois CPA Society (IL)
CHESLEY, Thea B. (Lib Srvs Coordntr) 207

Illinois Department of Corrections (IL)
MILUTINOVIC, Eunhee C. (Libn) 845
Illinois Dept of Employment Security (IL)
FORD, Jennifer D. (Lib Dir) 389
OLSON, Rue E. (Lib Srvs Dir) . . . 923
Illinois Dept of Mental Health (IL)
Illinois Farm Bureau (IL)
BOWEN, Laurel G. (Cur of Manuscripts) 120
Illinois Historic Preservation Agency (IL)
BLOSS, Marjorie E. (Technl Srvs & Automation Asst Dir) . . 106
Illinois Institute of Technology (IL)
DOWELL, David R. (Dir of Libs) . 315
GLANZ, Lenore M. (Lib Asst) . . . 439
JONES, Ann L. (Serials Libn) . . . 611
PICKETT, Mary J. (Ref & Interlib Loan Libn) 970
STEVENS, Michael (Info Spclst) 1190
STRZYNSKI, John C. (Intl Law Libn) 1204
VANCURA, Joyce B. (Ref Dept Head) 1273
Illinois Library Association (IL)
MILLER, Deborah (Govtl Srvs Dir) 837
Illinois Natural History Survey (IL)
HEISTER, Carla G. (Technl Libn) 523
Illinois Prairie District Pub Lib (IL)
FREDERICKSEN, Grant A. (Dir) . 400
Illinois Sch District 144 (IL)
O'SHEA, Margaret A. (Media Spclst) 928
Illinois Secretary of State (IL)
SORENSEN, Mark W. (Records Mgmt & Info Srvs Supvsr) . . 1168
TEMPLE, Wayne C. (Chief Deputy Dir) 1230
Illinois State Archives (IL)
MOORE, Karl R. (Archvst & Supvsr) 860
Illinois State Board of Education (IL)
SIVAK, Marie R. (State Sch Lib & Media Supvsr) 1144
Illinois State Geological Survey (IL)
KRICK, Mary (Libn) 678
SUIDAN, Randa H. (Asst Libn) . 1207
WASSON, Patricia G. (Asst to the Libn) 1308
Illinois State Historical Lib (IL)
FERGUSON, Bonnie E. (Histl Docums Conservator) 372
Illinois State Lib (IL)
BOSTIAN, Irma R. (Edit, IL Libs) . 117
KELLERSTRASS, Amy L. (Mgmt Consult) 636
LAMONT, Bridget L. (Dir) 691
PENCE, Cheryl S. (Preservation Ofcr) 956

Illinois State Lib (IL)

PENDERGRASS, Margaret E. (Catlgr) 956
SHERWOOD, Arlyn K. (Map Libn) 1129

Illinois State Univ (IL)

ALEXANDER, Lynetta L. (Catlgr) 12
BROWN, Mary J. (Music Libn & Lib Sci Assoc Prof) 146
DELOACH, Marva L. (Head) 290
DELONG, Dianne S. (Catlgr) 290
DELONG, Douglas A. (Acqs Libn) 290
EASTON, William W. (Map Libn) 333
GOEHNER, Donna M. (Technl Srvs Assoc Univ Libn) 443
GOWDY, Laura E. (Spcl Cols Libn & Archvst) 455
MATTHEWS, Priscilla J. (Catlg Libn) 785
NOURIE, Alan R. (Assoc Univ Libn) 910
PETERSON, Fred M. (Univ Libn) 963
THAKORE, Manhar (Col Devlpmnt Coordntr) 1234

Illinois State Veterans Home (IL) EGGERS, Thomas D. (Libn) 339
Illinois State Water Survey (IL) DESSOUKY, Ibtesam (Head Libn) 296
JOHNSON, Anita D. (Info Resrc Spclst) 602
MEI, Angela L. (Asst Libn) 821
Illinois Valley Lib System (IL) NIEHAUS, Barbara J. (Lib Technician) 903
WILFORD, Valerie J. (Exec Dir) 1339
Image Management Corp (CO) DULAN, Peter A. (Self-employed) 324
Imaging Update (CA) HILL, Kristin E. (Pres) 540
IME Ltd (ENG) NOERR, Kathleen T. (Pres) 907
Imed Corp (CA) ALBRIGHT, Sue R. (Lib Supvsr) . . 10
Immaculate Conception High Sch (IL) MASON, John A. (Head Libn) . . . 781
Immaculate Heart Academy (NJ) DONOHOE, Monica M. (Lib Media Coordntr) 311
IMNET (NY) SHAPP, Lenore 1122
Imo State Univ at Okigwe (NGR) OGBAA, Clara K. (Lectr) 918
Imperial Corp of America (CA) MORRISON, Patricia (Corprt Libn) 868
Imperial Oil Limited (ON) CZARNOTA, Les (Info Spclst) . . 268
RYANS, Kathryn J. (Info Resrch Supvsr) 1071
Imperial Savings Bank (CA) GAGNON, Donna M. (Lib Records & Mgmt Consultant) . 412
Imperial Tobacco (PQ) MUKHERJEE, Yolande (Corp Libn) 876
Incarnate Word Academy (MO) EIKEN, Mary A. (Libn) 340
Incarnate Word Coll (TX) DUNCAN, Lucy E. (Head of Technl Srvs) 325

Incorporated Village of Lynbrook (NY) PARK, T P. (Ref Libn) 941
Independence Regional Health Center (MO) VOSS, Kathryn J. (Libn) 1289
Independence Township (MI) ROSE, Anne (Head of Chlds Srvs) 1054
Independent Sch District 16 (MN) BURESH, Reggie F. (Dist Media Coordntr) 158
Independent Sch District 241 (MN) LONNING, Roger D. (Media Spclst) 740
Independent Sch District 271 (MN) VAN SOMEREN, Betty A. (Resrc Ctr Dir) 1277
Independent Sch District 30 (OK) STEWART, Vicki (Elem Lib Coord) 1193
Independent Sch District 621 (MN) HAJICEK, Nancy K. (Libn) 484
Independent Sch District 625 (MN) ROTH, Alvin R. (Asst Supvsr) . . 1059
Independent Sch District 742 (MN) SORELL, Janice G. (Lrng Resrcs Facilitator) 1168
Independent Sch District 813 (MN) POST, Diana (Libn & Media Generalist) 986
Independent Sch District 94 (MN) URBANSKI, Lawrence E. (Libn) 1269

Independent Sch Lib Media Center (NM)

Independent Schs Multi-Media Center Inc (NY)
Independent Sector (DC)
Index & Information Srvs (CA)

Index Group Inc (MA)

The Indexer (ENG)
Indian & Northern Affairs Canada (NT)

Indian Council of Soc Science Research (IND)
Indian Oasis (AZ)
Indian Prairie Sch District 204 (IL)
Indian River County Board (FL)
Indian River County Lib (FL)
Indian Trails Pub Lib District (IL)

Indian Village Historical Collection Inc (MI)

Indiana Area Sch District (PA)
Indiana Commission on Pub Records (IN)

Indiana Department of Education (IN)

Indiana Historical Society (IN)

Indiana House of Representatives (IN)

Indiana Institute of Technology (IN)
Indiana Law Enforcement Academy (IN)
Indiana Lib Association (IN)

IN MOTION Film & Video Production Mag (MD)

Indiana Prov Congregation of Holy Cross (IN)
Indiana State Lib (IN)

FREEMAN, Patricia E. (Consult & Auth) 401

FISHER, Carolyn H. (Dir) 380
BOHLEN, Jeanne L. (Assoc Dir) . 111
SERDZIAK, Edward J. (Indexing Srvs Dir) 1116
HAYWARD, Sheila S. (Resrch Assoc) 517
BELL, Hazel (Edit) 77

ALBRIGHT, Donald A. (Regnl Libn) 10

AGRAWAL, Surendra P. (Dir) 7
CULL, Roberta (Dist Coordntr) . . . 263
YOUNG, Nancy J. (Dir) 1382
WALSH, Lynn R. (Lib Dir) 1299
KISER, Mary D. (Lib Dir) 656
LEVIN, Joan E. (Ref Libn) 720
WRIGHT, Joanna S. (Ref Libn) . 1371

BRUNK, Thomas W. (Pres & Archvst) 150
MILLER, Sheila K. (Libn) 842

JONES, Thomas Q. (Records Analyst and Archvst) 615
CORNWELL, Linda L. (Lrng Resrc Consult) 247
AUTRY, Carolyn (Lib Asst) 41
DARBEE, Leigh (Head, Ref & Biblgph Srvs) 274
KRASEAN, Thomas K. (Field Srvs Div Dir) 676
MUNDELL, Eric L. (Ref Libn) . . . 878

STAPLES, James A. (Caucus Asst) 1181
HICKLING, Jeanne (Libn) 536

ZIMMERMAN, Donna K. (Libn) . 1388
MARTELLO, Joyce M. (Exec Dir) 775

LEHURAY, Stephen D. (Publshr & Edit) 713

CONNELLY, James T. (Archvst) . 237
ASHER, Richard E. (Catlg Mgmt Libn) 36
CONRADS, Douglas L. (Head of Serials & Fed Docums Sect) . 238
EWICK, Charles R. (State Libn) . 359
KAPOSTA, Joseph D. (Lib Info Coordntr) 626
KONDELIK, Marlene R. (Ref Libn) 670
LOGSDON, Robert L. (Assoc Dir, Pub Srvs) 737
ROBLEE, Martha A. (Extension Div Head) 1045
SCHMIDT, Kathy W. (Asst Docums Libn) 1095
SIMON, Ralph C. (Head, Data Srvs Div) 1141
SWANSON, Byron E. (Head, IN Div) 1213
WOODARD, Marcia S. (Lib Plng Consult) 1366
YOUNG, Noraleen A. (Ref Libn) 1382

Indiana State Univ at Terre Haute (IN) ANDERSON, Virginia L. (Dept Head Asst) 25
DAVIS, Betty B. (Dir of Technl Srvs) 277
DAVIS, H S. (Dept Head) 279
ENSOR, Pat L. (Coordntr, Database Srchng) 350

Indiana State Univ at Terre Haute (IN)

GALE, Sarah E. (Acqs Dept Head) 413

LAMB, Robert S. (Circ Dept Head) 690

LEACH, Ronald G. (Dean of Lib Srvs) 706

LITTLE, Robert D. (Chairperson and Prof of Lib Sci) 733

LYLE, Jack W. (Docums Libn) ... 751

MARTIN, Ron G. (Dir of Pub Srvs) 778

MCGIVERIN, Rolland H. (Tchg Mtrls, Microforms & Media Head) 806

MILLER, Marsha A. (Instrc Libn) . 840

NORMAN, Orval G. (Head, Ref Dept) 909

SWARENS, Darrell F. (Asst Prof of Educ) 1214

THOMPSON, Susan J. (Head, Sci Lib) 1241

TRIBBLE, Judith E. (Ref Libn) .. 1256

VANCIL, David E. (Head, Rare Books, Spcl Cols) 1273

Indiana Univ at Bloomington (IN)

AUCHSTETTER, Rosann M. (Ref Libn) 38

BAILEY, Joanne P. (Ref Libn) 46

BAUS, J W. (Asst Archvst) 67

BECK, Erla P. (Col Devlpmnt Coordntr) 71

BRISTOW, Ann (Head, Ref Dept) 137

CALLISON, Daniel J. (Asst Prof) 174

COPLER, Judith A. (Mgr) 244

CRIDLAND, Nancy C. (Hist Subject Spclst) 258

DAVISON, Ruth M. (Libn, US Govt Pubns) 281

FARRELL, David (Assoc Dean, Col Mgmt) 365

FLING, Robert M. (Assoc Coll Devlpmnt Libn) 385

FRY, Bernard M. (Prof Emeritus) . 406

HALPORN, Barbara (Libn) 490

HARTER, Stephen P. (Assoc Prof) 508

HEISER, Lois (Head, Geology Lib) 523

HENN, Barbara J. (Asst Head) .. 528

IRVINE, Betty J. (Acting Persnl Ofcr) 584

JACKSON, Susan M. (Asst Prof) 588

JARBOE, Betty M. (Assoc Libn) . 594

KASER, David (Distinguished Prof) 628

KUDRYK, Oleg (Libn Emeritus & Consult) 682

LAIR, Nancy C. (Lectr) 688

LEE, Thomas H. (East Asian Libn) 711

MARTIN, Fenton S. 776

MCCLOY, William B. (Head of Techn Srvs) 797

MCCUNE, Lois M. (Asst Dept Head) 801

MILLER, Constance R. (Comp Assisted Info Srvs Coordntr) .. 836

MURPHY, Marcy (Assoc Prof) .. 881

MUSTO, Frederick W. (Ref Libn) 883

NELSON, Brenda (Visiting Affiliate Libn) 893

NIEKAMP, Dorothy R. (Assoc Libn Catlgr) 903

POPP, Mary F. (Assoc Libn, Ref & Instrc Libn) 984

Indiana Univ at Bloomington (IN)

PUNGITORE, Verna L. (Asst Prof) 997

RABER, Nevin W. (Libn Emeritus) 1001

READ, Glenn F. (Latin-Am Std Libn) 1012

RUDOLPH, Ellen T. (Gifts Libn) . 1066

RUDOLPH, L C. (Libn Emeritus) 1066

RUFSVOLD, Margaret I. (Prof Emeritus) 1066

SELDIN, Daniel T. (Head of the Geography and Map Lib) ... 1113

SELLBERG, Roxanne J. (Head of Catlg Mgmt Dept) 1113

SEREBNICK, Judith (Assoc Prof) 1116

SHAABAN, Marian F. (Intl Docums Libn) 1118

SHEPARD, Clayton A. 1126

SHIPPS, Anthony W. (Libn for Engl & Theatre) 1131

SILVER, Joel B. (Reader Srvs Head) 1138

SLOAN, Elaine F. (Dean of Univ Libs) 1149

SNYDER, Carolyn A. (Pub Srvs Assoc Dean) 1164

SORURY, Kathryn L. (Catlgr) .. 1169

SOWELL, Steven L. (Biology Lib Head) 1170

SPULBER, Pauline (Ref Libn) .. 1176

STEELE, Patricia A. (Head of Sch of Lib & Info Sci Lib) ... 1184

TALALAY, Kathryn M. (Ref Libn, Sch of Music) 1220

THOMAS, Joseph W. (Catlgr) .. 1237

TURCHYN, Andrew (Libn Emeritus & Prof Emeritus) ... 1263

WALLACE, Danny P. (Asst Prof) 1297

WENNER, Alexander W. (Catlgr) 1324

WESTFALL, Gloria D. (Foreign Docums Libn) 1327

WHITBECK, George W. (Assoc Dean & Assoc Prof) 1329

WHITE, Herbert S. (Dean & Prof) 1331

WIGGINS, Gary D. (Lib Head) . 1337

ZIMMERMAN, Brenda M. (Grad Asst) 1388

Indiana Univ at Indianapolis (IN)

BRAHMI, Frances A. (Info Srvs Dir) 127

BROWN, Sandra S. (Media Coordntr) 147

CORBETT, Ann L. (Ref Libn) ... 245

ELLSWORTH, Marlene A. (Ref Libn) 345

FRANCQ, Carole (Catlg Acqs Libn) 396

HEHMAN, Jennifer L. (Asst Head Libn, Slide Libn) 521

HOOK-SHELTON, Sara A. (Head Libn) 556

JOHNTING, Wendell E. (Asst Dir for Techn Srvs) 610

MATTS, Constance (Asst Dir for Reader Srvs) 786

MUELLER, Jeanne G. (Dir, Techn Srvs) 875

RICHWINE, Margaret W. (Ref Libn) 1031

SWITZER, Joann H. (Ref Libn & Srchr) 1216

Indiana Univ at South Bend (IN)

MARSHELEK, Sonja E. (Ref Libn) 775

MULLINS, James L. (Dir of Lib Srvs) 878

Indiana Univ East (IN)

Indiana Univ Northwest (IN)

Indiana Univ of Pennsylvania (PA)

Indiana Univ-Purdue Univ at Fort Wayne (IN)

Indiana Univ-Purdue Univ at Indianapolis (IN)

Indiana Univ Southeast (IN)
Indianapolis-Marion County Pub Lib (IN)

HUFFORD, Gordon L. (Dir, Lib/Lrng Resrcs Ctr) 571

ARNOLD, Joann M. (Technl Srvs Head) 33
BAVER, Cynthia M. (Asst Libn) . . . 67
MCSHANE, Stephen G. (Archvst & Cur Asst Libn) . . . 818
MORAN, Robert F. (Dir of Lib Srvs) 862
SUTHERLAND, Timothy L. (Asst Libn of Ref) 1211
WHITE, Lois A. (Head of Ref) . . 1331
CHAMBERLIN, Richard R. (Ref Coordntr) 198
ELLIKER, Calvin (Music Libn) . . . 343
KROAH, Larry A. (Libs and Media Resrcs Dir) 679
MICCO, Helen M. (Comp Sci Dept Assoc Prof) 831
RAHKONEN, Carl J. (Acting Music Libn) 1003
RAMBLER, Linda K. (Assoc Dir of Libs and Media Resrcs) . . 1005
SHIVELY, Daniel C. (Catlgng Coordntr) 1132
ZORICH, Phillip J. (Spcl Cols Libn) 1390

HUNSBERGER, Willard D. (Asst Dir/Admin Srvs) 574
SIEVERS, Arlene M. (Serials Libn) 1136
TRUESDELL, Cheryl B. (Interlib Loan Dept Head) 1259
VIOLETTE, Judith L. (Asst Dir for Info Srvs) 1285

BALDWIN, James A. (Head of Acqs) 51
BONNER, Robert J. (Assoc Libn) 114
FISCHLER, Barbara B. (Dir of Libs) 380
GNAT, Jean M. (Pub Srvs Head) 442
GOODWIN, Vania M. (Head, Catlgng Dept) 450
HUETTNER, Janet S. 570
MATTHEW, Jeannette M. (Archvst & Spcl Cols Libn) . . . 785
MAYLES, William F. (Sci, Engrng & Tech Libn) 790
SCHMIDT, Steven J. (Circ & Interlib Loan Libn) 1096
STARKEY, Edward D. (Pub Srvs Head) 1182
STOCKER, Randi L. (Ref Libn) . . 1195
WILLIAMS, Maudine (Head of Pub Srvs) 1345
BISHOP, Barbara N. (Archvst) . . . 99

ALLEN, Janice K. (Chld's Libn) . . . 15
BRIDGE, Stephen W. (Chlds Libn) 135
COHEN, Harriet A. (Newspaper & Perdcl Div Head) 228
COLLINS, Marian M. (Adult Ref Libn) 233
DOLAN-HEITLINGER, Eileen (Ref Libn) 309
DOWNEY, Lawrence J. (Assoc Dir of Centl Srvs) 316
DUNCAN, Maureen E. (Libn) . . . 325
EBERSHOFF-COLES, Susan V. (Technl Srvs Supvsr) 334
FELTON, Barbara M. (Warren Branch Adminstr) 370
GANN, Daniel H. (Arts Div Head) 416
GNAT, Raymond E. (Dir) 442

Indianapolis-Marion County Pub Lib (IN)

Indianapolis Museum of Art (IN)
Indianhead Federated Lib System (WI)

Industrial Accident Prevention Assn (ON)

Industrial Risk Insurers (CT)
Industrial Technology Institute (MI)

INET 2000 (ON)

Infax Corp (MD)
INFO FLO (SC)

Infocon Inc (CO)
Infolink (NY)
INFOMART (TX)

INFOMART (ON)

INFOMED (CSR)

InfoQuest (MO)

Inform II (PQ)
Informaco Inc (NY)

Information Access Co (CA)

Information Access Co (OH)
Information/Access On-Line (NC)
Information America Inc (GA)
Information Companies of America (VA)
Information Connection (PA)
Information Conservation Inc (NC)
Information Consultants Inc (DC)
Info Consulting (CA)
Information Consulting Inc (OH)
Information Coordinators Inc (MI)

Information Corner: Health Scis Lib Srvs (ON)

Information Counts (CA)

Information Dimensions Inc (OH)

Information for Business (CA)
Info Globe (ON)

The Information Group (CA)

The Information Guild (MA)

LAUBE, Lois R. (Soc Sci Div Head) 702
LILES, William E. (Branch Adminstr) 727
MCCANON, Marilyn (Assoc Dir of Extension Srvs) 794
THOMPSON, Anna M. (Music Libn) 1238
SU, Julie C. (Catlgng Libn) 1206

ROBBERS, Sandra M. (Lib Devlpmnt Coordntr) 1038

HARMS PENNER, Dolores T. (Resrc Libn) 502
SASSO, Patricia A. (Libn) 1083
KELLER, Karen A. (Database Design Spclst) 635
SOLOSKY, A. G. (Bus Devlpmnt Dir) 1166
JONES, Gerry U. (Pres) 613
MICHAELS, Carolyn L. (Consult) 831
KENNEY, Brigitte L. (Pres) 641
TUCKERMAN, Susan (Owner) . 1262
DOBSON, Christine B. (Lib Srvs Mgr) 307
PEDEN, Robert M. (Lib Systs Coordntr) 954
TRICKEY, Katherine M. (Ref Libn) 1256
ZABEL, Patricia L. (Ref Libn) . . 1385
BLOXAM, Gerald S. (Sr VP & Gen Mgr) 107
SMITH, Sharon (Med Doctor & Surgeon) 1160
REHKOP, Barbara L. (Info Spclst) 1017
LEDOUX, Marc A. (Pres) 708
BOWKER, Scott W. (Sr Consult) 121
GRIFFIN, Michael D. (Indxr, Edit) 468
MEGLIO, Delores D. (Vice Pres) . 821
PORTUGAL, Dolores 985
HOWARD, Susanna J. (Owner) . 564
MADDEN, Mary A. (Principal) . . . 758

SMITH, David A. (Consult) 1153
ANDEL, June (Owner) 21
FAIRFIELD, John R. (Pres) 361
REGAN, William J. (Mktg VP) . . 1017
POST, Linda C. (Consult) 986
MIMNAUGH, Ellen N. (Pres) 845
STRATELAK, Nadia A. (Managing Editor) 1200

FLOWER, M A. (Hlth Scis Lib Consult) 386
FALANGA, Rosemarie E. (Owner) 361
BRINKMAN, Barry J. (Consult Srvs Mgr) 136
DITMARS, David W. (Market Devlpmnt Mgr) 305
HASKINS, Dawn A. (Product Mktg Rep) 510
KNOBLAUCH, Carol J. (Lib Products Support) 665
MOORE, Brian P. (Techlib Group Mgr) 858
MARKS, Larry (Owner) 771
MILLER, Katherine J. (Database Coordntr) 839
KAPLAN, Robin (Info Consult, Dir) 626
WARNER, Alice S. (Owner) . . . 1305

Information Handling Services (CO) | SZABO, Kathleen S. (Sr Indxr) . 1218
WHITE, Suellen S. (Sr Mgr of Market Resrch) 1332
WEATHERSBY, Anne 1312

Information Inc (DC)
Information Industry Association (DC) | ALLEN, Kenneth B. (Sr Vice Pres for Govt Relations) 15
ANGERMAN, Judith (Membership Devlpmnt Dir) . . 27
ATKIN, Michael I. (Dir of Mktg) . . . 37
CAUGHMAN, Alison Y. (Finance & Admin Dir) 195
CUNNINGHAM, Linda (Dir of Meetings) 265
PEYTON, David (Govt Relations Dir) 966
ZURKOWSKI, Paul G. (Pres) . . 1391

Info Management (DC) | FREEMAN, Carla (Consult) 400
Information Management Associates (WI) | ACCARDI, Joseph J. (Consult & Info Broker) 3

Information Management Consultants Inc (OH) | CHAMIS, Alice Y. (Owner/Consult) 198

Information Management Services (ON) | KNOPPERS, Jake V. (Sr Vice Pres) 665

Info Mania (CA) | LEWIS, Cookie A. (Pres) 722
Information Masters (OR) | LARSON, Signe E. (Pres) 700
Information on Demand Inc (CA) | MAXWELL, Christine Y. (Pres) . . 788
PEARSON, Judith G. (Resrch Assoc) 952

Information Outlet (IN) | GRIFFITTS, Joan K. (Info Broker) 469

Information PLUS (TX) | WESTBROOK, Brenda S. (Owner) 1326

Information Professionals (CO) | ROESCH, Gay E. (Info Spclst) . 1049
Info-Recherche (PQ) | DARLINGTON, Susan (Dir) 275
Information Research Analysts (PA) | SOUDER, Edith I. (Info Counselor) 1169

Information Research Center Inc (NC) | O'CONNOR, Sandra L. (Dir & Partner) 916

Information Resources (ON) | KLEMENT, Susan P. (Principal) . 660
Information Resources Management Service (DC) | CARR, Frank J. (Commissioner) . 185
MCDONOUGH, Francis A. (Deputy Commissioner) 803
NEUSTADT, Margaret L. (Exec Dir) 897

Information Resources Unlimited (AK) | EGGLESTON, Phyllis A. (Independent Info Broker) 339
Info-Search (TX) | SHAW, Ben B. (Info Srch Broker) 1123

Info Srvs & Consulting (CO) | ZOOK, Ruth A. (Mgr) 1390
The Information Source (CA) | EVANS, Deborah L. (Owner) 356
Information Sources Inc (CA) | KOOLISH, Ruth K. (Pres) 671
Information Systems (CO) | RICHMOND, Elizabeth B. (Self-employed Consult) 1030
Information Systems (TX) | GRIMES, John F. (Info Systs Pres) 470

Information Systems Consultants Inc (DC) | BOSS, Richard W. (Sr Consult) . . 117
Information Systems International (HKG) | SANDFELDER, Paula M. (Info Broker) 1080

Information Transform (WI) | EPSTEIN, Hank 351
Information Ventures Inc (PA) | KLEINSTEIN, Bruce H. (Pres) . . 660
Info Webb (CA) | WEBB, Ty (Owner) 1313
Information Workstation Group (VA) | GALE, John C. (Pres) 413
Informative Design Group Inc (DC) | DAWSON, Barbara J. (Archvl Srvs Dir) 282

Informed Sources (CA) | DALY, Eudice (Self-employed Lib Consult) 271
Informed Sources Inc (WV) | GREATHOUSE, Brenda J. (Med Info Spclst) 461

Inforonics Inc (MA) | BUCKLAND, Lawrence F. (Pres) 154
FINNI, John J. (Lib Systs Analyst) 379
Infoserv Associates (NJ) | KORNFELD, Carol E. (Pres) . . . 672
Infotec Development Inc (CO) | MILLIGAN, Steven M. (Libn) 843
Infotech (VT) | SCHWERIN, Julie B. 1106
Infotelligence (CT) | NEUFELD, Irving H. (Self-employed) 897

INFOUR (CA) | BUTLER, Brett B. 166
CARSON, Susan A. (Resrch Assoc) 188
FOLEY, Donna H. (Med Libn) . . . 387

Ingalls Memorial Hospital (IL)
Ingalls Memorial Library Association (MA) | LANE, Margaret (Volunteer) 694
Ingalls Quinn & Johnson (MA) | MACIVER, Linda B. (Mgr of Info Srvs) 756
Ingersoll-Rand Co (NJ) | SHINER, Sharon L. (Corprt Libn) 1130
Ingham Medical Center (MI) | KEDDLE, David G. (Dir of Chi Med Lib) 634
Inglewood Pub Lib (CA) | PETERSON, Anita R. (Libn) 962
Ingram Distribution Group Inc (TN) | PRICE, Larry C. (Dir of Mktg) . . . 992
Ingram-Rude Information Researchers (MI) | INGRAM, Elizabeth T. (Info Broker) 583
Inland Lib System (CA) | AARON, Kathleen F. (Ref Coordntr) 1
SIMON, Vaughn L. (Dir) 1141
Inlex Inc (CA) | BRUMAN, Janet L. (Proposal Dept Mgr) 150
DOEHLERT, Irene C. (Trng Mgr) 308
HAY, Wayne M. (Customer Support Rep) 515
MATTHEWS, Joseph R. (VP, Operations) 785
SIDMAN, George C. (Pres) 1135
WEISS, William B. (Client Srvs Rep) 1320
WILLIAMS, Joan F. (Client Srvs Dir) 1344
Inmagic Inc (MA) | EDDISON, Elizabeth B. (Chairman & Vice Pres) 335
Inman Unified Sch District 448 (KS) | EIS, Myrna M. (Elem Libn) 340
Innovative Interfaces Inc (CA) | FROHMBERG, Katherine A. (Lib Systs Analyst) 405
SILBERSTEIN, Stephen M. (Exec VP) 1137
Inquiry Inc (PA) | WEBER, A C. (Owner) 1313
Institut Catholique de Montreal (PQ) | LALONDE, Diane (Libn) 689
Institut de Readaptation de Montreal (PQ) | BOYER, Maryse (Head of Lib) . . . 123
Institut de Recherche en Sante (PQ) | GREGOIRE, Fleurette (Libn) 466
Institut de Recherches Cliniques (PQ) | SMYTH, John (Asst Libn) 1162
Institut d'Etudes Sociales (SWZ) | ESTERMANN-WISKOTT, Yolande (Tchr & Adminstr) . . . 355
Institut Francais du Petrole (FRN) | MOUREAU, Magdeleine (Deputy Dir) 873
Institut Philippe-Pinel (PQ) | BEAUDET, Normand (Resrchr) . . . 70
LESAGE, Jacques (Psychiatrist) . 717
Institut Roland-Saucier (PQ) | SAUCIER, Danielle (Lib Dir) . . . 1084
Institute for Basic Research (NY) | BLACK, Lawrence (Libn) 101
Institute for Defense Analyses (VA) | SWEENEY, Joan L. (Resrch Libn) 1215
Institute for East-West Security Studies (NY) | DEVERA, Rosalinda M. (Libn) . . . 297
Institute for Scientific Information (PA) | EDWARDS, David M. (Vice Pres of Publshg) 337
FREEDMAN, Bernadette (Editrl Srvs Dir) 400
FUSELER-MCDOWELL, Elizabeth A. (Mgr, Biblgph Resrch) 410
GARFIELD, Eugene (Pres & Chief Exec Ofcr) 418
LEINBACH, Anne E. (Dir, Mktg & Product Mgmt) 714

Institute for Scientific
Information (PA)

MEYER, Daniel E. (Mgr, New
Product Devlpmnt) 830
ROSEN, Theresa H. (Asst Vice
Pres) 1055
SCHAEFFER, Judith E.
(Ascatopics Coordntr) 1089
SCHREIBER-COIA, Barbara J.
(Online Info Resrcs Mgr) . . . 1099
VLADUTZ, George E. (Basic
Resrch Mgr) 1286
WALKER, Kate 1295
ZAJDEL, George J. (Mktg
Adminstr) 1385

Inst of Advanced Law Study (NV) KADANS, Joseph M. (Libn &
Dean) 621

Institute of Canadian Bankers (PQ) VONKA, Stephanie (Resrch
Libn) 1288

Inst of Electrical & Electronic
Engnrs (NY) FERRERE, Cathy M. (Mktg Mgr) . 373

Institute of Gas Technology (IL) RIX, Dolores M. (Libn) 1037

Institute of Medieval Music
Limited (WGR) DITTMER, Luther A. (Pres) 306

Institute of Paper Chemistry (WI) BOOHER, Craig S. (Libn) 115
NADZIEJKA, David E. (Resrch
Fellow) 886
TIMMERS, Debra A. (Libn) 1246

Institute of Pennsylvania
Hospital (PA) STRICKLAND, F J. (Libn) 1202

Inst of Sedimentary & Petroleum
Geology (AB) HAU, Edward T. (Asst Libn) . . . 512

Institute of Textile Technology (VA) LAWRENCE, Philip D. (Edit) . . . 704
LOY, Dennis C. (Sr Edit) 745

Institution of Electrical
Engineers (ENG) AITCHISON, Thomas M. (Dir of
INSPEC) 9

Instituto Tecnologico Autonomo de
Mexico (MEX) OROZCO-TENORIO, Jose M.
(Lib Dir) 926

Institutu Tecnologico de
Durango (MEX) LAU, Jesus G. (Libn) 702

Instrumentation Laboratory (MA) KATES, Jacqueline R. (Lib Srvs
Mgr) 629

Insurance Corp of British
Columbia (BC) MAKAREWICZ, Grace E. (Mgr) . 762

Insurance Information Institute (NY) GORDON, Marjorie (Dir of Info
Srvs) 451

Integrated Research & Information
Srvs (CA) PLOTSKY, Andrea G. (Info
Spclst) 978

Intel Corp (AZ) MCGORRAY, John J. (Info
Spclst) 807

Intel Corp (CA) HAMBRIDGE, Sally L. (Syst
Adminstr) 491

Intel Corp (OR) STARNES, Jane K. (Technl
Libn) 1182

Intelsat (DC) LIU, Rosa (Libn) 734

Inter American Univ of Puerto
Rico (PR) SABATER-SOLA, Rigel (Law
Lib Dir) 1072

InterAmerica Research Associates
Inc (VA) SAUVE, Deborah A. (Sr Assoc
& Info Mgr) 1085

Interez Inc (KY) HILL, Elizabeth C. (Info Spclst) . . 539
Interior Planning Consultants (IL) DAVIS, Glenn G. (Sr Lib Facility
Consult) 279

Interlochen Center for the Arts (MI) WELIVER, E D. (Music Lib Dir) . 1321

Intermountain Community Lrng &
Info Srvs (UT) SPYKERMAN, Bryan R. (Proj
Mgr) 1177

Intermountain Health Care Inc (UT) JAMES, Brent C. (Dir of Med
Resrch) 592

Internal Medicine Associates (PA) GOLDMAN, Richard (VP &
Practicing Physician) 446

Intl Association for Financial
Planning (GA) MCDAVID, Sara J. (Mgr, Info
Ctr) 801

IBM Canada Ltd (ON) LAUER, Marjorie A. (Mktg Libn) . 702

IBM Corp (CO)

IBM Corp (CT)

IBM Corp (GA)
IBM Corp (MA)
IBM Corp (NY)

IBM Corp (WI)
International Crops Research
Institute (IND)

International Data Corp (MA)

International Data Corp (NY)

International Data Corp (VA)

International Development Research
Ctr (ON)

International Energy Agency (FRN)

Intl Food Policy Research
Institute (DC)

Intl Foundation of Employee Benefit
Plan (WI)

International Information Networks
Inc (MN)

International Minerals & Chemical
Corp (IN)
International Monetary Fund (DC)

International Museum of
Photography (NY)

Intl Pentecostal Holiness
Church (OK)

International Sch of Theology (CA)

International Signal & Control
Group (PA)
International Society of Copier
Artists (NY)

WILLIAMS, Constance H. (Sr
Libn) 1342
LOWENSTEIN, Richard A.
(Program Adminstr) 744
PRATT, Allan D. (Lib Consult) . . . 989
MCDANIEL, Sara H. (Sr Libn) . . . 801
WHITE, Chandlee (Intern Libn) . 1330
BEVERIDGE, Walter W. 93
BOWLES, Edmund A. (Sr Prog
Adminstr) 121
CYPSER, Rudy J. (Dir, Technl
Comm) 268
KOSTENBAUDER, Scott
(Technl Info Retrieval Ctr
Mgr) 673
RANKINE, L J. 1007
ROFES, William L. (Prog Mgr of
Records & Info Mgmt) 1049
SHADE, Ronald H. (Info
Analyst) 1118
SJOGREN, Mack D.
(Pgmr/Libn) 1145
TAPHORN, Joseph B. (Consltng
Attorney) 1223
MCALLISTER, Caryl K. 792

SINHA, Pramod K. (Sr Documtn
Ofcr) 1143
BAKST, Shelley D. (Sr Analyst) . . 50
CAFFREY, Timothy J. (Mktg &
Bus Devlpmnt Dir) 170
KANE, Jean B. (Mgr, Creative
Srvs) 624
MCGOVERN, Patrick J.
(Chairman) 807
GROTE, Janet H. (Mgr, Info
Srvs) 473
DODSON, Whit (Vice Pres &
Resrch Dir) 308

MORIN-LABATUT, Gisele (Prog
Ofcr) 865
WACHTER, Margery C. (Head
Libn) 1290

KLOSKY, Patricia W. (Head
Libn) 662

BIRSCHEL, Dee B. (Dir of Info
Srvs & Pubns) 99
CHRISTMAN, Inese R. (Asst
Libn) 212
KRAJNAK, Patricia A. (Libn) 675
MILLER, Julia E. (Libn) 839

HANSEN, Kathelen L. (Chief
Info Ofcr) 497

SHANE, T C. (Info Scientist) . . . 1120
ARANDA-COODOU, Patricio
(Law Libn) 30
CUMMING, Leighton H. (Sr
Projs Libn) 264
FRIERSON, Eleanor G. (Asst
Projs Libn) 404
TURNER, Susan A. (Automation
Systs Libn) 1265

SIMMONS, Rebecca A. (Serials
Libn) 1140

HARGIS-LYTLE, Betty L. (Asst
Archvst, Secy) 501
MINDEMAN, George A. (Lib
Dir) 845

STEFANACCI, Michal A. (Libn) 1185

NEADERLAND, Louise O. (Dir) . . 890

International Technology Group (CA)   WARNOCK, Patric F. (Dir of Resrch Operations) 1305

ITT Advanced Technology Center (CT)   DENMAN, Monica K. (Staff Supvsr & Libn) 292

ITT Corp (NY)   HUNTER, Gregory S. (Corprt Records & Micrographics Mgr) 576
NARCISO, Susan D. (Resrch & Lib Srvs Mgr) 888

ITT Defense Communications (NJ)   REISMAN, Rita C. (Technl Libn) 1021

ITT Gilfillan Inc (CA)   VILLERE, Dawn N. (Sr Technl Libn) 1284

ITT Rayonier Inc (WA)   TOSTEVIN, Patricia A. (Libn & Info Spclst) 1252

ITT Telecom (NC)   HAY, Gerald M. (Libn) 515

International Theatre Institute (NY)   BURDICK, Elizabeth B. (Dir & Organizer) 158

International Thomson (DC)   TAFT, James R. (The Taft Group Pres) 1219

International Thomson (ON)   BROWN, Michael (President) ... 146

International Thomson Book (CA)   SMITH, Richard A. (Pres) 1159

International Thomson Business Press Inc (NJ)   DALY, Charles P. (Pres & Chief Exec Ofcr) 271
SCHAEFER, Donald A. (Chairman/Chief Exec Ofcr) . 1088

International Thomson Lib Service (VA)   ASLESON, Robert F. 36

International Thomson Organization Ltd (NY)   HALL, Robert C. (Intl Financial Netwk Group Pres) 488
JACHINO, Robert J. (Exec VP) .. 586

International Thomson Profsnl Publshg (ON)   FLEMING, Jack C. (Chairman, Chief Exec Ofcr) 384

International Trade Centre (SWZ)   JONES, Roger A. (Trade Info Consult) 615

International Trade Commission (DC)   SCHNEIDER, Hennie R. (Supvsr Ref Libn) 1097

International Trade Education Associates (NY)   MATTERA, Joseph J. (Info Spclst) 785

Interpublic Group of Companies (NY)   FEUERSTEIN, Robin (Info Dir) .. 374

Invest/Net Group Inc (FL)   WRIGHT, John H. (Dir of Mktg) . 1371

Iolani Sch (HI)   MITCHELL, Jeanette E. (Libn) .. 848

Iona Coll (NY)   LARKIN, Patrick J. (Chief Libn) .. 698

Iowa City Community Sch District (IA)   DONHAM, Jean O. (Dist Lib Media Coordntr) 311
KOSHATKA, Beverly V. (Lib Media Spclst) 672
PARK, Dona F. (Media Spclst/Libn) 941
REHMKE, Denise M. (Lib Media Spclst) 1017

Iowa City High Sch (IA)   HARMON, Charles T. (Libn) 502

Iowa City Pub Lib (IA)   CARTER, Jeanette F. (Info Srvs Coordntr) 189
EGGERS, Lolly P. (Dir) 339
SPAZIANI, Carol (Comunty Srvs Coordntr) 1172

Iowa Department of Education (IA)   BUCKINGHAM, Betty J. (Eductnl Media Consult) 154

Iowa Department of Human Services (IA)   ELLIOTT, Kay M. (Lib Dir) 344

Iowa Hospital Association (IA)   TOVREA, Roxanna L. (Lib Dir) . 1252

Iowa Lib Association (IA)   STOVALL, Naomi (Exec Secy) . 1199

Iowa Lutheran Hospital (IA)   KROMMINGA, Patricia G. (Eductnl Media Dir) 679

Iowa Northwest Regional Lib (IA)   FALK, Louise G. (Northwest Regnl Lib Trustee) 362

Iowa State Archives (IA)   MCCONNELL, Edward (State Archvst) 797

Iowa State Lib (IA)   GEORGE, Shirley H. (State Libn) 428

Iowa State Univ (IA)   BLACK, William K. (Asst Dir for Adminstrv Srvs) 102
COLE, Jim E. (Serials Catlgr) ... 230
DOBSON, Cynthia (Soc Sci Biblgphr & Assoc Prof) 307

Iowa State Univ (IA)   GALEJS, John E. (Col Devlpmnt Asst Dir) 413
HANTHORN, Ivan E. (Conservation Spclst) 499
KLINE, Laura S. (Univ Archvst) .. 661
KUHN, Warren B. (Dean & Dir of Lib Srvs) 682
MADISON, Olivia M. (Monographs Dept Head) 759
MATHEWS, Eleanor R. (Info Srvs Libn) 784
MOODY, Marilyn K. (Head of Access Srvs) 857
MORRIS, Dilys E. (Asst Dir, Technl Srvs) 866
ORR, Margaret H. (Order Dept Head) 926
OSMUS, Lori L. (Head, Serials Catlgng Sect) 928
PARSONS, Kathy A. (Info Srvs Libn) 945
PETERSON, Lorna (Asst Prof) .. 964
PETERSON, Sally R. (Veterinary Med Libn) 964
TYCKOSON, David A. (Info Srvs Libn) 1266
VAN DE VOORDE, Philip E. (Info Srvs Dept Head) 1274

Iowa Wesleyan Coll (IA)   SCHERUBEL, Melody (Assoc Libn) 1092

IR Concepts Inc (TX)   FRAMEL, Phyllis M. (Conslting Assoc) 395

Irell & Manella (CA)   HAMOR, Monica E. (Ref Libn) .. 494

Irondequoit Pub Lib (NY)   OLDERSHAW, Anne (Chlds Libn) 920

Irving Independent Sch District (TX)   LANKFORD, Mary D. (Dir of Lib & Media Srvs) 696

Irving Pub Lib (TX)   AYRES, Edwin M. (Technl Srvs Libn) 43
PALMER, Judith L. (Pub Srvs Libn) 936

Irvington Pub Lib (NJ)   MCCONNELL, Lorelei C. (Ref Dept Head) 797

Irvington Unified Sch District (NY)   GINSBERG, Barbara (Sch Media Spclst) 438

Irwin Army Hospital (KS)   WHITESIDE, Phyllis J. 1333

Isham Lincoln Beale (IL)   RABAI, Terezia (Mgr, Info Srvs) 1001

ISI (NJ)   JUNKINS, Katherine V. (Info Spclst) 620

Island Trees Pub Lib (NY)   KING, Dennis W. (Dir) 650

Islip Pub Lib (NY)   KLATT, Wilma F. (Ref Libn) 658

Israel Aircraft Industries (ISR)   ELAZAR, David H. (Technl Info Ctr Mgr) 341

Israel Film Arch Jerusalem Cinematheque (ISR)   DIAMANT, Betsy (Lib Dir) 299

Israeli Ministry of Energy (ISR)   HOFFMANN, Eliahu W. (Israeli Database Devlopmnt Head) .. 548

Issaquah Sch Dist (WA)   FLETCHER, Robert A. (Sch Libn) 385

ISU Inc (NH)   ROLETT, Virginia V. (Pres) 1051

IT Corp (CO)   HAMDY, Amira (Resrch Libn) ... 491

Itasca Community Lib (IL)   HOGAN, Patricia M. (Adminstrv Libn) 549

Item Data Inc (IL)   LOWELL, Brian V. (Pres) 744
SINE, George H. (Mktg Vice Pres) 1143

Ithaca Coll (NY)   ERICSON, Margaret D. (Asst Music & Audio Libn) 353
HICKEY, John T. (Catlg Libn) ... 536
JACKSON, Sue H. (Med Libn) .. 588

Ivinson Memorial Hospital (WY)   LOGAN, Penelope A. (Hospital Libn) 737

Izaak Walton Killam Children's Hospital (NS)   FRANK, Elizabeth W. (Assoc Libn) 397

Izmir Amerikan Lisesi (TKY)

J

J & A Assoc Inc (CO)
MONTAG, Diane (Supvsr of Info Srvs) 855

J & J Lubrano (MA)
LUBRANO, Judith A. (Antiquarian Bookseller) 745

J C Penney Co Inc (NY)
MOLITERNO, Daniel A. (Mktg Info Ctr Mgr) 853

J P Morgan Securities (NY)
HUDAK, Barbara M. (Info Mgr) . . 569

J Paul Getty Center (CA)
EDELSTEIN, J M. (Sr Biblgphr & Resrc Coordntr) 335
MENDENHALL, Bethany R. (Assoc Libn) 824
NOBLE, Jean E. (Lib Asst III) . . 906
SLEETER, Ellen L. (Info Systs Libn) 1148
YASSA, Lucie M. (Serials Catlgr) 1378

J Paul Getty Trust (CA)
HALBROOK, Anne M. (Libn) 485

J Paul Getty Trust (MA)
PETERSEN, Toni (Art & Architecture Thesaurus Dir) . . 962

J Pierpont Morgan Lib (NY)
NEEDHAM, Paul (Cur of Printed Bks & Binding) 891

J Sargeant Reynolds Community Coll (VA)
BLAKE, Mary K. (Media Prcsng Coordntr) 103
MIAH, Abdul J. (Lrng Resrcs Ctr Dir) 831

J Sterling Morton High Schs (IL)
SHERMAN, William F. (Head Libn) 1128

J Walter Thompson Co (IL)
HALVORSON, Eric H. (Dir, Info Srvs) 490
KEARNEY, Sharon M. (Info Spclst) 633
LOFTHOUSE, Patricia A. (Indxr & Abstctr) 737
OWENS, Tina M. (Sr Info Spclst) 932
PICCOLI, Roberta A. (Info Srvs Mgr) 970

J Walter Thompson Co (NY)
GOODSELL, Joan W. (Asst Mgr) 450
KELLEY, Dennis L. (Mgr) 636

Jack Chitwood Consultant (IL)
CHITWOOD, Julius R. (Libs & Info Srvs Consult) 209

Jackson & Hinds Lib System (MS)
BALLARD, Thomas H. (Dir) 53
DUNAWAY, Charjean L. (Asst Dir) 325

Jackson Board of Education (NJ)
REGAN, Barbara M. (Libn & Media Spclst) 1017

Jackson County Dept of Mgmt Info Srvs (OR)
THELEN, Richard L. (Records Srvs Techn, County Archvst) 1234

Jackson County Lib System (OR)
BILLETER, Anne M. (Ref Srvs Head) 96
GORDON, Patricia H. (Libn) 451
PURCELL, V N. (Technl Srvs Libn) 998

Jackson District Lib (MI)
BUXBAUM, Sharolyn (Ref Libn) . 168
LEAMON, David L. (Dir) 707

Jackson-George Regional Lib (MS)
SMITH, Janet E. (Branch Libn) . 1155

Jackson-George Regional Lib System (MS)
MAJURE, William D. (Systs & Resrcs Mgr) 762

The Jackson Laboratory (ME)
BAKER, Alison (Libn) 47

Jackson-Madison County General Hospital (TN)
FARMER, Linda G. (Dir, Lrng Ctr) 364

Jackson-Madison County Lib (TN)
AUD, Thomas L. (Dir) 39

Jackson Memorial Hospital (FL)
TOWERS, Lynn C. (Libn) 1252

Jackson Printing Inc (MD)
JACKSON, Elmer M. (Proprietor) 587

Jackson Pub Libs (FL)
LITTON, Sally C. (Dept Libn, Bus, Sci & Industry Dept) 734

Jackson State Univ (MS)
GENTRY, Etherlene H. (Asst Prof of Lib Sci) 427
MOMAN, Orthella P. (Asst Dean of Libs) 854
SANDERS, Lou H. (Asst Prof of Lib Sci, Asst Libn) 1080

Jackson Walker Winstead Cantwell et al (TX)

Jacksonville Country Day School (FL)
STELBRINK, Mary H. (Libn) . . . 1186

Jacksonville Pub Libs (FL)
CARNAHAN, Mabel A. (Branch Mgr) 183
CORNELL, Sylvia C. (Asst Dir of Libs) 247
DISMORE, Joan M. (Part-time) . 305
GREEN, Madonna (Ref Lib) 462
SMITH, Margaret N. (Branch Lib Supvsr) 1157
SUGDEN, Martin D. (Ref Libn) . 1206
WILLIAMS, Judith L. (Dir) 1344

Jacksonville State Univ (AL)
MERRILL, Martha (Soc Scis Libn) 826
TAYLOR, Douglas M. (Ref Libn) 1226

Jacksonville Univ (FL)
GUNN, Thomas H. (Lib Dir) 477

Jacob Edwards Lib (MA)
LATHAM, Ronald B. (Dir) 701

Jacobs Engineering Group (TX)
DAVIS, Sara (Info Spclst) 281

Jacobus Pharmaceutical Co (NJ)
JACOBUS, David P. (Pres) 590

JAI Info (PQ)
WADE, C A. (Info Broker) 1290

Jal Pub Schs (NM)
BRAMLETT, Suzanne M. (Sch Libn) 127
GOODFELLOW, Jacklyn M. (Sch Libn) 448

Jamaica Hospital (NY)
MANSBACH, Carolyn (Dir) 767

Jamaica National Investment (NY)
EDWARDS, Diane H. (Sr Regnl Mgr) 337

Jamaica National Investment Promotion (NY)
PHILLIPS, Angela B. (Resrch Ofcr) 967
SAUNDERS, Dorette (Pub Relations Coordntr) 1084

James Agee Film Project (TN)
SPEARS, Ross (Dir & Filmmaker) 1172

James E Rush Assoc Inc (OH)
RUSH, James E. (Pres) 1068

James Jerome Hill Reference Lib (MN)
MARKHAM, Scott C. (Catlgr) . . . 771
WHITE, William T. (Curator) . . . 1332

James M Montgomery Consulting Engineers (CA)
HELGESON, Duane M. (Corprt Libn) 524

James Madison Univ (VA)
ARNESON, Rosemary H. (Loan Srvs Libn & Lib Coordntr) 33
BLANKENBURG, Judith B. (Lib Sci & Eductnl Media Asst Prof) 104
FOX, Barbara S. (Col Devlpmnt Libn) 394
GILL, Gerald L. (Bus Ref Libn) . 435
HABAN, Mary F. (Prof of Lib Sci) 480
PALMER, Forrest C. (Prof of Lib Sci & Docum Libn) 936
RAMSEY, Inez L. (Assoc Prof) . 1006
ROBISON, Dennis E. (Univ Libn) 1045
UPDIKE, Christina B. (Art Slide Cur) 1269

James N Gamble Institute of Med Research (OH)
MC CORMICK, Lisa L. (Info Srvs & Resrch Libn) 798

James Prendergast Lib Association (NY)
KOCH, Judith L. (Ref Libn) 667
MORRIS, Kim (Chlds Libn) 867

James River Corp (WI)
LAMB, Cheryl M. (Info Scitst) . . 689

James S Copley Lib (CA)
MCPHAIL, Martha E. (Libn) 817

Jameson Memorial Hospital (PA)
WHITMAN, Joan T. (Libn) 1333

Jamestown Area Sch District (PA)
MCCONNELL, Robert D. (Libn K-12) 798

Jamestown Coll (ND)
BRATTON, Phyllis A. (Dir) 129

Jamestown Philomenian Lib (RI)
BELL, Judith H. (Dir) 77

Janes Publishing Co Inc Ltd (NY)
MCHALE, Joseph T. (Vice Pres & Dir) 808

Janesville Pub Lib (WI)
ENGELBERT, Alan M. (Support Srvs Coordntr) 348
HARFST, Linda L. (Authority Ctl Libn) 501
HELWIG, Karen A. (Ref Libn) . . . 525

Janesville Pub Lib (WI)

Janssen Pharmaceutica Inc (NJ)

Janssen Research Foundation (BEL)
Jay County Pub Lib (IN)

Jayell Enterprises (MI)
Jazz Record Center (NY)
JDA Inc (TX)

Jean Walling Civic Center (NJ)

Jeanne Byrne Lib Service Inc (TX)

Jeannette Pub Lib (PA)
Jefferson Community Coll (KY)

Jefferson County Board of Education (KY)

Jefferson County Board of Education (TN)

Jefferson County Law Lib (AL)
Jefferson County Pub Lib (CO)

Jefferson County Pub Schs (KY)

Jefferson County Pub Schs (TN)
Jefferson Davis Parish (LA)

Jefferson Davis State Junior Coll (AL)
Jefferson-Madison Regional Lib (VA)

Jefferson Parish (LA)

Jefferson Parish Pub Sch System (LA)

Jefferson Township Pub Lib (IN)
The Jelem Co (CT)
Jenison Pub Schs (MI)

Jenks & Associates, Lib Consultants (AK)

Jenner & Block (IL)

Jennison Associates Capital Corp (NY)

Jerry Alper Inc (NY)

Jerry FitzGerald & Associates (CA)

Jersey City Pub Lib (NJ)

Jersey City State Coll (NJ)

KRUEGER, Karen J. (Dir) 680
MONDSCHEIN, Lawrence G. (Resrch Adminstr) 854
SILVA, Nelly H. (Resrch Info Srvs Mgr) 1138
PEETERS, Marc D. (VP) 954
CLAMME, Rosalie A. (Dir) . . . 215
FORD, Marcia K. (Chlds Libn) . . 389
LIMBACHER, James L. (Pres) . . 727
COHEN, Frederick S. (Owner) . . . 228
DAHLGREN, Jean E. (Lib Planner) 269
BERGER, Brenda L. (Media Srvs Dept Head) 85
BYRNE, Jeanne M. (Pres & Owner) 169
BALAS, Janet L. (Asst Libn) 50
SCHLENE, Vickie J. (Pub Srvs Head) 1094

BING, Dorothy A. (Lib Media Spclst) 97
CRACE, Sallye C. (Elem Sch Libn) 254
JACOBSON-BEYER, Harry E. (Libn) 590
SMITH, Lena D. (Libn) 1157

LINDSEY, Nancy L. (Pub Sch Libn) 730
HAND, Linda M. (Law Libn) 494
LAMPREY, Patricia M. (Head of Ref & Adult Srvs) 691
KELLY, Sarah A. (Media Spclst) . 638
LIVINGSTON, Sarah M. (Consult) 735
TACKETT, Janet S. (Media Ctr Spclst) 1219
JONES, Anne G. (Libn) 611
PATTERSON, Trudy J. (Adminstrv Parish Libn) 948
BIGGS-WILLIAMS, Evelyn A. (Libn) 95
ANDERSON, Valerie J. (Chlds Libn) 25
BERNE, Beth (Technl Srvs Head) 88
EVERINGHAM, Neil G. (Asst Dir of Finance) 358
MORRIS, Karen L. (Ref Libn) . . . 867
BENOIT, Anthony H. (Dir) 82
STUCKWICH, Chris E. (AV Dept Head) 1204
STURCKEN, Rodney A. (Acqs Libn) 1205

FAVORITE, Grealdine J. (Libn) . . 366
WASHINGTON, Idella A. (Libn) . 1307
BOLTE, William F. (Dir) 113
MILSTEAD, Jessica L. (Pres) . . . 845
VELTEMA, John H. (Media Srvs Dir) 1282

JENKS, Arlene I. (Principal Consult) 597
BAUMANN, Walter R. (Lib Asst) . . 66
CHUNG, Alison L. (Dir, Mgmt Info Syst) 213

RANSOM, Cynthia E. (Asst Vice Pres) 1007
OKERSON, Ann L. (Lib Srvs Mgr) 920
FITZGERALD, Ardra F. (Co-owner) 382
BRYANT, Judith W. (Principal Libn & Chld's Branch Head) . . 152
AUSTIN, Fay A. (Catlg Libn) 40

Jersey Shore Medical Center (NJ)
Jervis Pub Lib (NY)

Jesuit Coll Preparatory Sch (TX)

Jesuit-Krauss-McCormick Lib (IL)

Jet Propulsion Laboratory (CA)

Jewish Braille Institute of America Inc (NY)

Jewish Federation Council (CA)
Jewish Federation of Nashville (TN)

Jewish Guild for the Blind (NY)
Jewish Historical Museum (NET)
Jewish Pub Lib (PQ)
Jewish Rehabilitation Hospital (PQ)

JHK & Associates (CA)
JHK & Associates (VA)
Jikei Univ Sch of Medicine (JAP)

JNB Associates (NJ)
Joel Barlow High Sch (CT)

Joel R Pitlor Inc (MA)

Johan Van Halm & Associates (NET)
John A Logan Coll (IL)

John Abbott Coll (PQ)

John & Mable Ringling Museum of Art (FL)
John B Podeschi Bibliographer (IL)

John C Hart Memorial Lib (NY)

John Carroll Univ (OH)

John Coutts Lib Srvs (ON)

John Curtis Lib (MA)
John F Kennedy Lib Foundation Inc (MA)
John F Kennedy Medical Center (IL)

John F Kennedy Memorial Hospital (CA)
John F Kennedy Univ (CA)

John F Ross Collegiate & Vocational Inst (ON)

John Hancock Mutual Life Insurance (MA)
John J Pershing Veterans Administration (MO)

John Jay Coll of Criminal Justice, CUNY (NY)

John M Wing Foundation (IL)

PALMISANO-DRUCKER, Elsalyn (Lib Dir & Faculty) . . . 937
ESWORTHY, Lori L. (Ref Libn) . . 355
FOWLER, Carole F. (Dir) 393
SULLIVAN, Janice L. (Head Libn) 1207
HILGERT, Elvire R. (Pub Srv Libn) 539
PULVER, Emilie G. (Principal Catlgr) 997
WHIPPLE, Caroline B. (Dir) 1329
CASTAGNO, Judith M. (Info Srvs Supvsr) 193

JAHR, Joanne B. (Lib Srvs Administr) 591
BEN-ZVI, Hava (Head Libn) 84
RATKIN, Annette L. (Dir of Lib & Archs) 1009
MASSIS, Bruce E. (Lib Dir) 782
CAHEN, Joel J. (Asst Dir) 171
RABY, Eva F. (Head) 1001
SHANEFIELD, Irene D. (Med Libn) 1120
PAQUETTE, John F. (Libn) 939
HATHAWAY, Kay E. (Libn) 512
URATA, Kazuo (Assoc Prof and Assoc Dir) 1269
YAMAZAKI, Shigeaki (Lectr) . . . 1377
BRITTON, Jeffrey W. (Dir) 137
CROWLEY, John D. (Dir, Lib/Media Ctr) 261
ISAACS, Cynthia W. (Info Srvs Dir) 584
VAN HALM, Johan (Owner) . . . 1275
BARRETTE, Linda J. (Libn, Dir of Computing) 59
DE LIAMCHIN, Lana (Resrch & Devlpmnt Dean) 289
DOUGLAS-BONNELL, Eileen (Lib Info & Serials Coordntr) . . 314
MORR, Lynell A. (Art Libn) 866
PODESCHI, John B. (Descriptive Biblgphr & Bibl Consult) 979
HALLINAN, Patricia R. (Ref Head, Technl Srvs Libn) 489
BALCON, William J. (Asst Libn) . . 51
PIETY, John S. (Dir) 972
SWEENY, Mary K. (Ref Head) . 1215
PORTEUS, Andrew C. (Biblgphr Ofcr) 985
FRIEDMAN, Fred T. (Lib Dir) . . . 403

CULLINANE, John J. (Pres) 263
SCHULTZ, Therese A. (Med Libn) 1102

DICKINSON, Dan C. (Med Libn) . 300
SMITH, Susan A. (Law Libn, Asst Univ Libn & Prof) 1161

WRIGHT, Jonathan C. (Head, Lib Resrc Ctr) 1371

RENDALL, Margot L. (Law Libn) 1023

AKIYAMA, Wilfrid S. (Chief, Lib Srvs) 9

LUTZKER, Marilyn L. (Deputy Chief Libn & Assoc Prof) 750
MARGOLIES, Alan (Prof of Engl) 770
ROWLAND, Eileen (Chief Libn) . 1062
WELLS, James M. (Custodian Emeritus) 1322

John Marshall Law Sch (IL)

KEISER, Mary P. (Catlgr) 635
LI, Dorothy W. (Asst Law Libn) . . 724
PETERSON, Randall T. (Dir of
    Lib Srvs) 964
REDDY, Michael B. (Ref Libn) . . 1013
WLEKLINSKI, William A. (Head
    of Ref) 1359

John McIntire Pub Lib (OH)

SMITH, Jacqueline (Adult Srvs
    Head) 1155

John Muir Memorial Hospital (CA)

REYES, Helen M. (Med Libn) . . 1024

John Read Middle Sch (CT)

MITCHELL, Lucy A. (Libn,
    Media Spclst) 849

John Sayer Associates (MD)

SAYER, John S. (Principal) 1086

John Snow Inc (MA)

FRYDRYK, Teresa E. (Lib Mgr) . . 407

John Stevens Robling Ltd (MI)

ROBLING, John S. (Managing
    Dir) 1045

John Wiley & Sons Inc (NY)

ARLINGTON, Bill (Human
    Resrcs Plng & Devlpmnt
    Mgr) 31
FORD, Andrew E. (VP & Gen
    Mgr, Medical Div) 389
HARMON, James R. (Gen Mgr,
    Intl Div) 502
JOHNSON, Richard O. (Corprt
    Devlpmnt VP) 608
KING, Timothy B. (VP &
    Publshr) 652
LESURE, Alan B. (Vice Pres &
    Gen Mgr) 718
MELKIN, Audrey D. (Lib Sales
    Mgr) 822
WILEY, Deborah E. (Vice
    Chairman) 1339
WITSENHAUSEN, Helen A.
    (Corprt Libn) 1358

John XXIII Pastoral Center (WV)

HUMPHRIES, Joy D. (Libn,
    Comp Pgmr) 574

Johns Hopkins Univ (MD)

BEARSS, Daniel H. (Asst Head,
    Acqs Dept) 69
BOURKOFF, Vivienne R. (Head,
    Interlib Loan) 119
BRANCH, Katherine A. (Ref &
    Circ Srvs Head) 127
BUTTER, Karen A. (Assoc Dir
    of Info Syst Srvs) 167
COOPER, David J. (Humanities
    Biblgphr) 242
COUPE, Jill M. (Ref Head) 251
DEBROWER, Amy M. (Ref
    Libn) 285
FLORANCE, Valerie (Info
    Resrcs Mgmt Asst Dir) 385
FLOWER, Kenneth E.
    (Adminstrv Srvs Assoc Dir) . . 386
GILLISPIE, James E. 436
GWYN, Ann S. (Assoc Dir for
    Spcl Cols) 479
HALE, Dawn L. (Catlgng Dept
    Head) 485
HEATH, Henry H. (Bldg Mgr) . . . 519
HILDITCH, Bonny M. (Online
    Srvs Coordntr) 539
KIM, Chung S. (Catlgng Dept
    Head) 648
KOEHLER, Barbara M. (Catlgng
    Libn) 667
KOSMIN, Linda J. (Readers'
    Srvs Supvsr) 672
LOWENS, Margery M. (Prof) . . . 744
LUCIER, Richard E. (Asst
    Resrch & Devlpmnt Dir) 746
MARTIN, Susan K. (Lib Dir) 778
MATHESON, Nina W. (Dir
    Assoc Prof of Med Info) 783
NEWMAN, Wilda B. (Info
    Resrcs Mgr) 900
PERKINS, Earle R. (Info
    Retrieval Libn) 959
PETTERSON, Marjorie M.
    (Acqs Coordntr) 965

Johns Hopkins Univ (MD)

PUGH, W J. (Psychiatry &
    Neurosciences Libn) 997
QUIST, Edwin A. (Music Libn) . . 1001
ROBERTS, Cynthia H. (Sr Ref
    Libn) 1039
SATTERTHWAITE, Rebecca K.
    (Online Srvs Coordntr) 1084
SCHAAF, Elizabeth (Archvst) . . 1088
SMITH, Mary P. (Catlgng
    Coordntr) 1158
WOODS, Catharine C. (Systs
    Libn) 1366

Johnsburg Central Sch (NY)

SULLIVAN, Linda R. (Sch Lib
    Media Spclst) 1208

Johnson & Johnson (NJ)

PARAS, Lucille P. (Resrch Lib
    Info Ctr Mgr) 939

**Johnson & Johnson Baby Products
Co** (NJ)

RONDELLI, Marilyn H. (Mgr of
    Bus & Technl Info) 1053

Johnson & Swanson (TX)

DEWBERRY, Betty B. (Law
    Libn) 298
GATES, Diane E. (Asst Libn) . . . 421
SUMMERFORD, Steven L. (Ref
    Libn) 1209

Johnson C Smith Univ (NC)

TRIVETT, Martha S. (Dir) 1257

**Johnson City Medical Center
Hospital** (TN)

BROWN, Phyllis J. (Newsroom
    Libn) 147

Johnson City Press (TN)

Johnson Controls Inc (WI)

ALLSOP, Mary B. (Asst Libn) 17
RAUSCH, Marian 1010

**Johnson County Board of
Commissioners** (KS)

LANGWORTHY, Asher C. (Lib
    Bd Vice Chairman) 696

**Johnson County Community
Coll** (KS)

KEMPF, Andrea C. (Pub Srvs
    Libn) 639

Johnson County Lib (KS)

DRESSLER, Alta L. (Ref Libn) . . 319
EVANS, Constance L. (Branch
    Systs Dept Head) 356
LAUFFER, Donna J. (Deputy
    Cnty Libn) 702
MCLEOD, Debra A. (Chlds Col
    Coordntr) 814
WAY, Harold E. (Head of Centl
    Lib) 1311

Johnson Free Pub Lib (NJ)

OLSON, Marilyn A. (Chlds Libn) . 923

Johnson Publishing Co (IL)

MENZIES, Pamela C. (Libn) 825

Johnsonburgh Pub Lib (PA)

NELSON, Wilburta B. (Asst
    Libn) 895

**Johnston County & Smithfield Pub
Lib** (NC)

CLAYTON, Sue N. (Catlgr) 220

Johnston County Schools (NC)

KONNEKER, Rachel C. (Sch
    Media Coordntr) 670

Johnston Sch Department (RI)

SHANLEY, Elaine (Libn & Tchr) 1120

Joint Center for Political Studies (DC)

PILGRIM, Auriel J. (Info Resrcs
    Dir) 973
SYLVESTER, Carol (Technl
    Srvs Libn) 1217

**Joint Computer Programs for
Libs** (IL)

MITCHELL, Joyce P. (Systs
    Libn) 849

**Joint Free Pub Lib of
Morristown** (NJ)

DENSKY, Lois R. (Archvst) 293

Joint Sch District 2 of Meridian (ID)

DENNY, Mary C. (Libn & Media
    Generalist) 293

Joliet Pub Lib (IL)

HALL, Clark J. (Non-Fiction
    Srvs Libn) 487
JOHNSTON, James R. (Lib Dir) . 610
MOZGA, John P. (Asst Dir) 874

Jones Day Reavis & Pogue (CA)

SCHIPPER, Joan A. (Head
    Libn) 1093

Jones Day Reavis & Pogue (DC)

SHEELER, Harva L. (Head Libn) 1125

Jones Day Reavis & Pogue (NY)

GOLDMAN, Martha A. (Libn) . . . 445

Jones Day Reavis & Pogue (OH)

GREEN, Lynda C. (Online Srvs
    Libn) 462

Jones Day Reavis & Pogue (TX)

GRIMES, Carolyn E. (Asst Libn) . 470
HOOTON, Virginia A. (Records
    Mgr) 557
LEE, Frank (Head Libn) 709

Jones Library Inc (MA)

LOMBARDO, Daniel J. (Spcl Col Cur) 738

Joni L Cassidy Cataloguing Services (NJ)

CASSIDY, Joni L. (Owner) 193

Jordan Elbridge Sch District (NY)

BERGEN, Dessa C. (Lib Media Spclst) 85

Joseph Downs Manuscript & Micofilm Coll (DE)

ADAMS, Barbara M. (Asst Libn) . . . 4

Joseph E Seagram Co (NY)

GROSS, Alice 472

Josephite Fathers and Brothers (MD)

HOGAN, Peter E. (Archvst) 549

Journal/Sentinel Inc (WI)

KRCHMAR, Sandra L. (Ref & Resrch Person) 677

REITMAN, Jo (Mgr) 1022

Judah L Magnes Museum (CA)

ARONER, Miriam D. (Photo Archvst) 34

RAFAEL, Ruth K. (Archvst & Libn) 1003

Judson Coll (AL)

YELVERTON, Mildred G. (Lib Dir) 1379

Juergensmeyer and Assocs (IL)

JUERGENSMEYER, John E. (Attorney) 619

Julie Rohr Academy (FL)

MITCHELL, Jan E. (Media Spclst) 848

Julliard Sch (NY)

GOTTLIEB, Jane E. (Head Libn) . 453

Juniata Coll (PA)

WILSON, Martin P. (Asst Dean/Lrng Resrcs & Coll Libn) 1352

Justan Enterprises (TX)

JUERGENS, Bonnie (Partner) . . . 619

STANDIFER, Hugh A. (Partner)   1179

K

K G Saur Inc (NY)

COOPER, Carol D. (Exec VP) . . . 242

KADEC Info Management Co (MD)

KADEC, Sarah T. (Info Mgmt Consult & Pres) 621

Kaiser Aluminum & Chemical Corp (CA)

ROOSHAN, Gertrude I. (Mgr) . . 1053

Kaiser Engineers Inc (CA)

ZACHER, Elaine F. (Technl Libn) 1385

Kaiser Engineers Inc (TN)

MCDONALD, Ethel Q. (Sr Database Analyst) 802

Kaiser Foundation Hospital (CA)

SAWYER, Anne R. (Med Libn) . 1086

Kaiser Permanente Hospitals & Hlth Plan (CA)

CRAWFORD, Marilyn L. (Lib Dir) 257

Kaiser Permanente Medical Center (CA)

BALOGH, Leeni I. (Med Libn) 53

BENNETT, Michael W. (Hlth Scis Libn) 82

Kaiser Permanente Medical Center (HI)

FUKUDA, Jodel L. (Med Libn) . . . 408

Kalamazoo Coll (MI)

PINKHAM, Eleanor H. (Dir of Libs & Media Srvs) 974

SMITH, Carol P. (Ref Libn) 1153

SMITHSON, Paul G. (Assoc Dir) 1162

Kalamazoo Institute of Arts (MI)

NESBURG, Janet A. (Libn) 896

SHERIDAN, Helen A. (Asst to Dir for Cols Exhibitions) 1127

Kalamazoo Pub Lib (MI)

LARSON, Catherine A. (Local Hist Spclst) 699

RIFE, Mary C. (Chlds Srvs Div Dir) 1033

Kalamazoo Pub Schs (MI)

WILLIAMS, S J. (Sch Libn) 1346

Kalamazoo Regional Psychiatric Hospital (MI)

AEBLI, Carol L. (Lib Dir) 7

Kalamazoo Valley Community Coll (MI)

APPS, Michelle L. (Adminstrv Asst) 30

Kalida Board of Educ (OH)

MILLER, Marian A. (Libn) 840

Kalispell Regional Hospital (MT)

LONG, Susan S. (Libn) 740

KALSEC Inc (MI)

SAGAR, Mary B. (Lib Mgr) 1074

Kaman Tempo (CA)

GALLERY, M C. (Info spclst) 414

Kanawha County Pub Lib (WV)

FRASER, Elizabeth L. (Ref, Interlib Loan, Fndtn Libn) 399

LEASURE, Lois A. (Ref Libn) . . . 707

MARTIN, June R. (Chief Ref Libn) 777

PALMER, Marguerite C. (Technl Writer, Branch Consult) 936

Kanawha County Pub Lib (WV)

WRIGHT, Linda G. (Lib Dir) . . . 1372

Kane County 16th Circuit Court (IL)

POINTON, Louis R. (Legal Resrchr, Asst Law Libn) 980

Kaneohe Regional Lib (HI)

CHAMBERS, Donald A. (Adult Ref Libn) 198

Kaneville Pub Lib (IL)

HANKES, Janice R. (Lib Dir) 496

Kannapolis City Schs (NC)

DAVIS, Judy R. (Media Coordntr) 279

Kansas City Art Institute (MO)

GAMER, May L. (Lib Dir) 416

Kansas City Pub Lib (KS)

BENNETT, Samuel J. (Branch Coordntr) 82

GARRISON, Teresa J. (Asst Dir of Pub Srvs) 420

MILLS, Elaine L. (Comp Systs Coordntr) 844

RIDDLE, Raymond E. (Dir) 1032

RUSSELL, Marilyn L. (Fine Arts Coordntr) 1069

VAN SICKLE, Mary L. (Technl Srvs Coordntr) 1277

Kansas City Pub Lib (MO)

BRADBURY, Daniel J. (Lib Dir) . . 125

BRETING, Elizabeth C. (Chlds & Comunty Srvs Assoc Dir) 133

HAMMOND, John J. (Assoc Dir) . 493

HANSEN, Charles A. (Pub Srvs Coordntr, Ref) 497

PARMENTER, Julie (Libn) 943

TOMS, Merrill F. (Assoc Dir) . . . 1250

Kansas Newman Coll (KS)

FORTE, Joseph E. (Lib Dir) 391

Kansas State Department of Education (KS)

LEVEL, M J. (Prog Spclst) 719

Kansas State Historical Society (KS)

DECKER, Eugene (State Archvst) 285

MICHAELIS, Patricia A. (Cur of Manuscripts) 831

RICHMOND, Robert W. (Asst Exec Dir & Treas) 1031

Kansas State Lib (KS)

FLANDERS, Bruce L. 383

JOHNSON, Duane F. (State Libn) 603

VOSS, Ernestine D. (Dir of Lib Devlpmnt) 1289

Kansas State Univ (KS)

COFFEE, E G. (Libn) 226

CRAWFORD, Anthony R. (Univ Archst) 256

GRASS, Charlene G. (Col & Technl Srvs Acting Assoc Dean) 458

MADSEN, Debora L. (Acqs Libn) 759

MORELAND, Rachel S. (Automation Devlpmnt Dept Actg Chair) 863

PRENTICE, Margaret A. (Orginal Monograph Catlgr) . . 990

QUIRING, Virginia M. (Assoc Dean) 1000

STUBBAN, Vanessa L. (Sci Ref Libn & Biblgphr) 1204

TALAB, Rosemary S. (Asst Prof) 1220

VANDER VELDE, John J. (Spcl Cols Libn) 1274

WEISENBURGER, Patricia J. (Chair of Branch Srvs) 1319

WILDE, Lucy E. (Humanities, Ref & Bibl) 1338

WILLARD, Gayle K. (Head Libn) 1341

WILLIAMS, Sara R. (Preservation Libn) 1346

Kansas Supreme Court (KS)

VINCENT, Claire E. (Asst Law Libn) 1284

Karr Tuttle Koch Campbell Mawer et al (WA)

HOLT, Barbara C. (Law Libn) . . . 554

YONGMAN, Zhang (Lib Asst) . . 1380

Kaskaskia Lib System (IL)

CHAMBERLIN, Edgar W. (Exec Dir) 198

ENSLEY, Robert F. (Asst Exec Dir) 350

Katharine Gibbs Sch (MA)   BUTLER, Ann S. (Libn) 166
Katharine Gibbs Sch (NY)   EDWARDS, Barnett A. (Dir of
                                     Lib) 337
Katherine Ackerman and Assoc (MI) ACKERMAN, Katherine K.
                                     (Pres) 4
Kativik Sch Board (PQ)   FINN, Julia P. (Libn) 378
Katonah Village Lib (NY)   KELLOGG, Marya S. (Technl
                                     Srvs) 637
Kattlove & Associates (CA)   KATTLOVE, Rose W. (Pres) 630
                                   WITTMANN, Cecelia V. (Systs
                                     Designer) 1358
Kaukauna Area Schs (WI)   SWITZER, Catherine M.
                                     (Coordntr of Sch Lib Srvs) . . 1216
Kaye Scholer Fierman Hays &
  Handler (NY)   GOODHARTZ, Gerald (Head
                                     Libn) 448
                                   PARRIS, Angela P. (Technl
                                     Srvs Libn) 944
Kazmaier Associates Inc (MA)   SAUNDERS, Leslie E. (Corprt
                                     Resrch Libn) 1084
The KBL Group Inc (MD)   LEVITAN, Karen B. (Pres) 721
KCOP Television Inc-Los
  Angeles (CA)   WALDOW, Mitch (Assignment
                                     Mgr) 1294
Kean Coll of New Jersey (NJ)   KALIF, Alexander J. (Technl
                                     Srvs Libn) 623
                                   SIMPSON, Barbara T. (Lib Srvs
                                     Dir) 1141
Kearney Pub Lib & Information
  Center (NE)   NORMAN, Ronald V. (Dir) 909
Kearney State Coll (NE)   MAYESKI, John K. (Lib Dir) 790
Kearsley Community Schs (MI)   KIRN, Marjorie A. (Media Spclst) . 655
Keene High Sch (NH)   PERLUNGHER, Richard A.
                                     (Head Libn) 959
Keene Pub Lib (NH)   LESSER, Charlotte B. (Youth
                                     Srvs Head) 718
                                   PERLUNGHER, Jane R. (Lib
                                     Dir) 959
Keene State Coll (NH)   MADDEN, Robert J. (Ref & Spcl
                                     Cols Libn) 758
                                   VINCENT, Charles P. (Lib Dir) . 1284
Keim Enteprises (MN)   KEIM, Robert (Consult) 635
Keio Univ (JAP)   HOSONO, Kimio (Prof) 562
                                   TAMURA, Shunsaku (Assoc
                                     Prof) 1221
Kelbry Enterprises (TX)   HEWINS, Elizabeth H. (Owner) . . 535
Kelco Division of Merck & Co (CA) WILLARD, Ann M. (Info Spclst) 1341
Keller Independent Sch District (TX) BERRY, Mary A. (Libn) 90
Kellogg Community Coll (MI)   SCHUCKEL, Sally B. (Info
                                     Retrieval Coordntr) 1101
Kellogg Co (MI)   HULSEY, Richard A. (Technl
                                     Info Supvsr) 573
Kelly Communications (VA)   CAHILL, Linda J. (Libn) 171
Keltoi Cybernetics (MA)   BISHOP, John (Dir) 99
Kenai Peninsula Borough Sch
  District (AK)   MOHN, Kari (Dist Media
                                     Coordntr) 852
                                   PENDLETON, Kim B. (Sch
                                     Media Coordntr) 956
Kendall Coll of Art & Design (MI) HORNBACH, Ruth M. (Head
                                     Libn) 559
Kendall Whaling Museum (MA)   FRAZIER, James A. (Asst Cur
                                     for Manuscripts) 399
Kendall Young Lib (IA)   WEISS, Cynthia A. (Dir) 1320
Kenilworth Pub Lib (NJ)   FLICK, Susan E. (Dir) 385
Kenmore Mercy Hospital (NY)   TUBOLINO, Karen M. (Libn) . . . 1261
Kennedy Cooington Lobdell &
  Hickman (NC)   FURST, Joyce P. (Libn) 410
Kennedy Inst for Handicapped
  Children (MD)   HOOFNAGLE, Bettea J. (Info
                                     Srvs Head) 556
Kennedy Jenks Chilton Consltng
  Engineers (CA)   SANSOBRINO, Jean C. (Corprt
                                     Libn) 1081
Kennedy-King Coll (IL)   OSGOOD, James B. (Catlgr &
                                     Asst Libn) 928
Kennedy Space Center (FL)   ATKINS, Donna A. (Asst
                                     Docums Libn) 37
Kennesaw Coll (GA)   HARDIN, Barbara A. (Asst Libn) . 500
Kenneth King Associates (MI)   KING, Kenneth (Pres) 651

Kenneth Leventhal & Co (CA)   DOSER, Virginia A. (Libn) 313
Kenneth W Rendell Inc (MA)   RENDELL, Kenneth W. (Pres) . . 1023
Kennewick Sch District 17 (WA)   KNOLL, Betty A. (Lib Media
                                     Spclst) 665
Kenosha Memorial Hospital (WI)   PUHEK, Esther L. (Hlth Scis
                                     Libn) 997
Kenosha Pub Lib (WI)   BAKER, Douglas (Dir) 48
                                   JAMBREK, William L. (Technl
                                     Srvs Mgr) 592
                                   THOMSON, Kathleen R. (West
                                     Branch Lib Head) 1241
Kenrick Seminary (MO)   PAGE, Jacqueline M. (Head
                                     Libn) 934
Kent County Lib Board (MI)   THOMAS, Louise V. (Chair) . . . 1237
Kent County Lib System (MI)   CAMMENGA, Cheryl G.
                                     (Branch Mgr, Libn II) 175
                                   DEYOUNG, Gail O. (East Grand
                                     Rapids Lib Mgr) 298
                                   GARCIA, Joseph O. (Dir) 417
                                   STADELMAN, Kathleen M.
                                     (Libn I) 1178
Kent County Memorial Hospital (RI) ASPRI, Jo A. (Libn) 37
Kent County Pub Lib (MD)   BRIGGS, Anne F. (Dir) 135
                                   REILLY, Deborah D. (Asst Dir) . 1020
Kent County Pub Schs (MD)   HUNTINGTON, Joan L. (Media
                                     Spclst) 576
Kent Free Lib (OH)   CELIGOJ, Carmen Z. (Dir) 196
Kent Lib Association (CT)   CUSTER, Deborah P. (Head
                                     Libn) 267
Kent State Univ (OH)   BIRK, Nancy (Assoc Cur for
                                     Spcl Cols) 98
                                   BUTTLAR, Lois J. (Sch of Lib
                                     Sci Asst Prof) 167
                                   DU MONT, Rosemary R. (Sch
                                     of Lib Scis Dean) 325
                                   GATTEN, Jeffrey N. (Systs
                                     Libn) 422
                                   GEARY, James W. (Assoc Prof
                                     & Lib Adminstr) 424
                                   GILDZEN, Alex J. (Spcl Cols
                                     Cur) 434
                                   JACKSON, Clara O. (Prof
                                     Emerita) 587
                                   KERSTETTER, John (Dir) 644
                                   KIRKBRIDE, Amey L. (Libn) . . . 654
                                   KOBULNICKY, Michael (Lib Dir) . 666
                                   KREYCHE, Michael R.
                                     (Coordntr of Automation) 678
                                   MCCHESNEY, Kathryn M. (Asst
                                     Prof) 795
                                   NELSON, Olga G. (Tchg Fellow) . 895
                                   SCHLOMAN, Barbara F. (Asst
                                     Prof) 1094
                                   TOLLIVER, Don L. (Dir of Libs) . 1248
                                   WHYDE, John S. (Film/Video
                                     Ref & Acqs Supvsr) 1335
                                   WYNAR, Lubomyr R. (Prof &
                                     Dir of Lib Std Ctr) 1375
Kenton Assocs (MD)   KENTON, Charlotte (Consult &
                                     Biblgphr) 642
Kenton County Pub Lib (KY)   AVERDICK, Michael R. (Assoc
                                     Dir) 41
Kentucky Baptist Convention Inc (KY) YEISER, Doris B. (Archvst &
                                     Exec Ofc & Comms Consult) 1379
Kentucky Country Day Sch (KY)   GOLDBERG, Linda B. (Lower
                                     Sch Libn) 444
Kentucky Department for Libs &
  Archives (KY)   KLEE, Edward L. (Asst Dir of
                                     Field Srvs) 658
                                   LEVSTIK, Frank R. (Archs &
                                     Records Adminstr) 721
                                   PICKENS, Nancy C.
                                     (Conservator Sr) 970
                                   WRIGHT, Paul L. (Construction
                                     Adminstr) 1372
Kentucky Department of
  Education (KY)   COOPER, Judy L. (Consult) 243
Kentucky Department of Pub
  Advocacy (KY)   LYNES, Tezeta G. (Law Libn) . . . 752

Kentucky Historical Society (KY)   BELL, Mary M. (Archvst & Histn) 77

Kentucky Lib Association (KY)   UNDERWOOD, Mary S. (Exec Secy) 1269

Kentucky Wesleyan Coll (KY)   MCFARLING, Patricia G. (Head of Technl Srvs) 805
YATES, Dudley V. (Chairperson & Dir, Lib Lrng Ctr) 1378

Kenyon & Kenyon (NY)   CULLEN, Martin J. (Head Law Libn) 263

Kenyon Coll (OH)   GREENSLADE, Thomas B. (Coll Archvst) 465
QUIGLEY, Suzanne L. (AV Libn) 999
WILT, Charles F. (Sci Libn) 1353

Keramont Research & Advanced Ceramics (AZ)   HUSBAND, Susan M. (Corprt Libn) 578

Kern County (CA)   WADE, Sherry A. (Ref Libn) . . . 1290

Kern County Lib System (CA)   COOPER, William E. (Comp Search Libn) 244
GARDNER, Laura L. (Technl Srvs Supvsr) 418
NICKERSON, Louann M. (Centl Region Libn) 902
YOON, Sandra G. (Chlds Libn) . 1380

Kershaw County Lib (SC)   ALBRIGHT, Penny E. (Dir) 10
OLSON, Joann M. (Adult Srvs Coordntr, Ref) 922

Kessler, Merci & Associates (IL)   KESSLER, Howard E. (Principal Architect) 645

Kewanee Pub Lib (IL)   HARRIET, Conklin W. (Lib Dir) . . 503

Keyand Coll (AB)   JARVIS, Marylea (Lib Srvs Coordntr) 595

Keycom Electronic Publishing (IL)   AVERY, Cliff (VP & Edit) 41

Keystone Local Schools (OH)   SCHMUHL, Gayle B. (K-8 Libn) 1096

Kidder Peabody & Co Inc (NY)   ANTONETZ, Dolores (Sr Ref Libn) 29
DARNOWSKI, Christina M. (Ref Libn) 275
DOOLING, Marie (Technl Srvs Libn) 312

Kilgore Junior Coll (TX)   CLAER, Joycelyn H. (Catlg Libn) 215
JACKSON, Marian D. (Acqs Libn) 588

Kilgore Memorial Lib (NE)   SCHULZ, Stanley D. (Dir) 1102

Killingly Junior High Sch (CT)   WEIGEL, James S. (Lib Media Spclst) 1316

Kilpatrick & Cody (GA)   LISI, Susan C. (Adminstv Comp Srvs) 732

Kimball Grade Schs (NE)   DATUS, Marie B. (Libn Media Dir) 275

Kimbell Art Museum (TX)   DOWNING, Jeannette D. (Libn) . 316
SHIH, Chia C. (Catlgr, Assoc Libn) 1130

Kimberly-Clark Corp (WI)   DIETZ, Kathryn A. (Legal Libn) . . 302
RYAN, Carol E. (Records Mgr & Archvst) 1070

Kinderhook Regional Lib (MO)   CRAVENS, Vickie L. (Extension Libn) 256

King Abdulaziz Univ (SDA)   KHAN, Mohammed A. (Lctr & Libn) 646

King & Spalding (GA)   FRY, Mary A. (Info Mgr) 406

King Coll (TN)   HERRING, Mark Y. (Lib Dir) 533

King County Lib System (WA)   ARCHBOLD, Barbara C. (Regnl Coordntr) 30
BEN-SIMON, Julie E. (Head of Acqs) 83
DUBOIS, Delores M. (Head Libn) 322
FOWLER, Ellen T. (Chlds Libn) . 393
GREGGS, Elizabeth M. (Head Libn) 465
JOHNSON, Carolyn K. (Deputy Libn) 603
MACDONALD, Margaret R. (Chlds Libn) 754
MADDEN, Susan B. (Coordntr of Yng Adult Srvs) 758

King County Lib System (WA)   MORGAN, Erma J. (Deputy Libn for Technl Srvs) 864
MUTSCHLER, Herbert F. (Dir) . . 883
NELSON, Judy T. (Chlds, Yng Adult Libn) 894
PETTIT, Donna K. (Libn) 965
POLISHUK, Bernard (Coordntr, Chlds Srvs) 980
RICKELTON, Esther G. (Regnl Coordntr) 1031
THOMPSON, Rosalind R. (Chlds Libn) 1241
THORSEN, Jeanne M. (Pub Info Coordntr) 1242
TOLLIVER, Barbara J. (Deputy Libn for Pub Srvs & Asst Dir) 1248
WAGNER, Sabina H. (Asst Head Libn) 1292
WALTERS, Daniel L. (Deputy Libn) 1301

King Fahd Hospital (SDA)   KIRKWOOD, Brenda S. (Med Libn) 655

King Faisal Hospital & Research Center (SDA)   BROWN, Biraj L. (Clinical Libn, Acting Libn) 142

King Khalid Eye Specialist Hospital (SDA)   MARTIN, Nannette (Med Libn & Dept Head) 777

King Research Inc (MD)   GRIFFITHS, Jose M. (Vice Pres) 469
KING, Donald W. (Pres) 650

King Saud Univ (SDA)   ALI, Farooq M. (Acqs Libn) 13
BUTT, Abdul W. (Med Libn) 167
SIBAI, Mohamed M. (Asst Prof) 1134

Kingman Unified Sch District 331 (KS)   HADA, Jerrianne (High Sch Libn) 481

King's Coll (PA)   MECH, Terrence F. (Lib Dir) 820
TOMASOVIC, Evelyn (Resrch & Records Dir) 1249

Kingsborough Coll of the City Univ of NY (NY)   CLUNE, John R. (Chief Libn) . . . 223
KARKHANIS, Sharad (Prof) 627
ORR, Coleridge W. (Interlib Loan Libn) 926
SCHNEIDER, Adele (Assoc Prof) 1096

Kingsley Lib Equipment Co (CA)   KINGSLEY, Eleanor V. (Pres) . . . 652

Kingston Psychiatric Hospital (ON)   MORLEY, Mae L. (Libn) 865

Kingsville Independent Sch District (TX)   MERCHANT, Cheryl N. (Coordntr of Libs) 825

Kinkaid Sch (TX)   WILLIAMS, Suzanne C. (Libn) . 1346

Kinsmen Rehabilitation Foundation of BC (BC)   ELLIS, Kathy M. (Libn & Asst Mgr) 344

Kinston-Lenoir County Pub Lib (NC)   FICKES, Raymond C. (Ref Libn) . 374

Kirkland & Ellis Lib (IL)   TEGLER, Patricia (Syst Libn) . . 1230

Kirkpatrick & Lockhart (DC)   DATTALO, Elmo F. (Libn) 275

Kirkpatrick & Lockhart (PA)   VARGAS, Gwen S. (Libn) 1278

Kirksville Coll of Osteopathic Medicine (MO)   ONSAGER, Lawrence W. (Lib Dir) 924

Kirkus Reviews (NY)   LONG, Joanna R. (Chlds & Yng Adults Editor) 739

Kirkwood R-7 Sch District (MO)   LEWIS, Marilee V. (Libn) 723

Kitchener Pub Lib (ON)   CORSTON, Christine F. (Coordntr, Info Srvs) 248
HOFFMAN, Susan J. (Local Hist Libn & Archvst) 548
COATES, Penny A. (Libn) 224

Kitchener Waterloo Record (ON)   O'BRIEN, Marlys H. (Dir) 915

Kitchigami Regional Lib (MN)   WEISS, Kay M. (Adminstv Libn) 1320

Kitsap Regional Lib (WA)   CARLSON, Sandra L. (Centl Branch Srvs Head) 182
HENINGER, Irene C. (Dir) 528

Kittery Sch Department (ME)   MOY, Agnes U. (Libn & Media Spclst) 874

Kleberg Dyer Redford & Weil (TX) HOUSTON, Barbara B. (Libn) . . . 563

Kluwer (DC) EVERTS, Arjaan (Executive VP) . 359

Kluwer Law Book Publishers Inc (NY) BERNSTEIN, Sidney (Chief
'Executive Ofcr) 89

KMS Fusion Inc (MI) BENNETT, Christine H. (Technl
Libn) 81

**Knight-Ridder Business
Information** (KS) OWENS, Charles E. (Sr VP) . . . 932

Knoll Pharmaceuticals (NJ) LUSTIG, Joanne (Med & Scintfc
Info Mgr) 750

BUTLER, Matilda L. (Pres) 167

PAISLEY, William J. (Executive
Vice Pres) 935

Knowledge Access International (CA)

**Knowledge Industry Publications
Inc** (NY) CSENGE, Maragaret L. (Asst
VP & Exec Edit) 262

Knox Coll (IL) ROBISON, Carley R. (Archives
Curator) 1045

Knox County Pub Lib System (TN) CARTER, Barbara W.
(Subsitute) 189

COTHAM, James S. (Head of
McClung Histl Col) 249

DYER, Barbara M. (Asst Head
Technl Srvs) 330

Knox County Schs (TN) LOCKWOOD, Bonnie J. (Sch
Libn) 736

Knoxville Journal (TN) JACKSON, Phyllis J. (Libn) 588

Knoxville Pub Lib (IA) VINER, Mamie N. (Dir) 1285

Kokomo-Howard County Pub Lib (IN) KIDDIE, Jeanette A. (Ref & AV
Libn) 646

Kollsman (NH) RICE, Gerald W. (Info Spclst) . . 1027

Korn/Ferry International (CA) HADLEY, Peter H. (User Design
Analyst) 482

KPMG Peat Marwick (PQ) MACFARLANE, Judy A. (Mgr) . . 755

Kraft Inc (IL) BIRKHOLD, Martha S. (Info
Spclst) 98

**Kramer Levin Nessen Kamin &
Frankel** (NY) CHICCO, Giuliano (Libn) 208

CINQUE, Douglas V. (Asst Libn) . 214

Kratter Law Lib (CA) BRISCOE, Georgia K. (Technl
Srvs Head) 136

**Kraus-Thomson Organization
Limited** (NY) GSTALDER, Herbert W. (Pres) . . 475

Krieger Publishing Co Inc (FL) KRIEGER, Robert E. (Chair of
the Board) 678

LANGA, Patricia A. (Libn) 695

Krum Independent Sch District (TX)

Kultur Home Video (NJ) HEDLUND, Dennis M. (Pres and
Founder) 520

Kummerfeld Associates Inc (NY) MILLER-KUMMERFELD,
Elizabeth (Pres) 843

Kutak Rock & Campbell (DC) HARBISON, John H. (Law Libn) . 499

Kutak Rock & Campbell (NE) FORSMAN, Avis B. (Law Libn) . 391

Kutztown Area Sch District (PA) EMERICK, Michael J. (Media
Spclst) 347

Kutztown Univ (PA) APOSTOLOS, Margaret M.
(Microtext & Perdcls Libn) 29

GEARHART, Carol A. (Asst
Prof of Lib Sci) 424

GOLDSTAUB, Curt S. (Head
Catlgr) 446

SAFFORD, Herbert D. (Lib Srvs
Dir) 1074

SIMONE-HOHE, M J. (Prof) . . . 1141

SPRANKLE, Anita T. (Readers'
Srvs Libn) 1176

Kuwait Univ (KWT) HAMDY, Mohamed N. (Libs Dir) . 491

Kwantlen Coll (BC) FRANCIS, Derek R. (Dir of Srvs
to Students) 396

Kyodo News International Inc (NY) NAKAZATO, Kazuo (Corprt
Plng Mgr) 887

STEIN, Pamela H. (Online Srvs
Dir) 1185

KZF Inc (OH) HAMILTON, Dennis O.
(Adminstrv Srvs Mgr) 492

L

L E Phillips Memorial Pub Lib (WI) MERRIAM, Louise A. (Support
Srvs Libn) 826

L M Warren Inc (BC) WARREN, Lois M. (Pres) 1306

La Canada Memorial Lib (CA) MORAN, William R. (Trustee) . . . 862

La Crosse Pub Lib (WI) GROSKOPF, Amy L. (Archvst) . 472

WHITE, James W. (Lib Dir) 1331

La Follette High Sch (WI) CAIN, Carolyn L. (Dir) 171

La Grange Coll (GA) LEWIS, Frank R. (Lib Dir) 723

La Grange Memorial Hospital (IL) GRUNDKE, Patricia J. (Dir of
Lib Resrcs) 475

La Jolla Country Day Sch (CA) VANSONNENBERG, Catherine
(Head Libn) 1277

**La Jolla Museum of Contemporary
Art** (CA) RICHARDSON, Gail (Libn) 1029

La Porte County Pub Lib (IN) CLINE, James D. (Ref & Circ
Srvs Coordntr) 222

GUNNELLS, Danny C.
(Coordntr of Extension &
Technl Srvs) 477

La Presse Newspaper (PQ) CHALIFOUX, Jean P. (Consult) . 197

La Reine High Sch (MD) SLANGA, Joanne (Lib Media
Spclst) 1147

La Salle Univ (PA) BAKY, John S. (Biblgphr Rare
Bks & Manuscripts) 50

MCNAMARA, Emma J. (Head
Libn & Coordntr) 816

PUGH, Thurman A. (Col
Devlpmnt & Acqs Libn) 997

Labat-Anderson Inc (DC) BRUNER, Linda J. (Catlgng
Technician) 150

Labat-Anderson Inc (VA) LEHWALDT, Marliese (Head
Libn) 713

Labatt Brewing Co Limited (ON) FUENTES, Ismael (Computers
Div Mgr) 408

Laboratorios Grifols SA (SPN) DESTEFANO, Daniel A. (Dir of
Med Lib) 296

Laboure Coll (MA) PRUHS, Sharon (Med Dir, Med
Libn II) 996

**LAC Health Services
Administration** (CA) PAPARELLI, Marita E. 939

Lackawanna Bar Association (PA) REES, G M. (Adminstr) 1016

Lackawanna County Lib System (PA) CAMPION, Carol M. (Head
Libn) 177

Lackawanna Junior Coll (PA) BEDNAR, Sheila (Sch Lib Media
Spclst) 73

Lackawanna Sch District (NY) WARD, Nancy E. (Med Libn) . . 1304

Lafayette Clinic (MI) NARBETH, Thomas G. (Technl
Srvs Head) 888

Lafayette Coll (PA) DOMBOURIAN, Sona J. (Asst
Dir) 310

Lafayette Pub Lib (LA) NEWTON, Evah B. (Media Srvs
Supvsr) 900

Lafayette Sch Corp (IN) HUMPHRIES, Lajean (Libn) 574

LaFollette & Sinykin (WI) LOW, Frederick E. (Coordntr of
Technl Srvs) 743

**LaGuardia Coll of the City Univ of
NY** (NY) GILSON, Barbara J. (Asst
Archvst) 437

LaGuardia Community Coll (NY) TRAINER, Leslie F. (Libn) 1253

Lahore American Society (PAK) JANZEN, Deborah K. (Sunday
Supvsr) 594

Lake Agassiz Regional Lib (MN) OLSON, Chris D. (Pub Info
Spclst) 922

OSTAZEWSKI, Theodore (Head
of Technl Srvs) 928

Lake Bluff Pub Lib (IL) LAMB, Sara G. (Head Libn) 690

Lake Charles Memrl Hospital (LA) SCHREMP, Mary J. (Med Lib
Dir) 1100

Lake County (IL) FERME, Paul H. (Resrch Libn) . . 373

**Lake County Bd of County
Commissioners** (FL) BREEDEN, Wendy R. (Lib
Coordntr) 131

Lake County Historical Society (OH) ENGEL, Carl T. (Libn) 348

Lake County Lib (CO) PARRY, David R. (Cnty Lib Dir) . 944

Lake County Pub Lib (IN)

CIUCKI, Marcella A. (Chief of Technl Srvs) 215
KETCHUM, Irene F. (Trustee) . . . 645
MOGLE, Dawn E. (AV Srvs Head) 852
PICHA, Charlotte G. (Branch Supvsr) 970
YAMAMOTO, M C. (Chief of Extension Srv) 1377

Lake Forest Coll (IL)
BRIGGS, Martha T. (Asst Libn) . . 135
MIKOLYZK, Thomas A. (Asst Libn) 834
MILLER, Arthur H. (Coll Libn) . . 835

Lake Forest Country Day Sch (IL)
DANOFF, Fran (Libn) 274

Lake Hospital System Inc (OH)
SHELDON, Holly L. (Hlth Sci Libn) 1126

Lake Lanier Lib (GA)
SHELTON, John L. (Dir) 1126

Lake Region Community Coll (ND)
EVENSEN, Sharon L. (Libn) . . . 358

Lake Superior State Coll (MI)
MICHELS, Fredrick A. (Lib AV Dir) 832
NAIRN, Charles E. (Ref, Interlib Loan Libn) 886

Lake View Elementary Sch (WI)
DEES DAUGHERTY, Kristin (Sch Libn) 287

Lake Worth Independent Sch District (TX)
DUNCAN, Donna P. (Sch Libn) . . 325

Lakeland Christian Sch (FL)
VITELLO, Susan (Libn) 1286

Lakeland Community Coll (OH)
MAGNER, Mary J. (Dir of Lib Srvs) 759

Lakeland Library Region (SK)
RIDLER, Elizabeth A. (Regnl Libn) 1032

Lakeland Pub Lib (FL)
SAGE-GAGNE, Waneta (Spcl Col Libn) 1074
STAMPFL, Barbara A. (Adult Srvs Libn) 1179

Lakeland Sch District (NY)
SALUSTRI, Madeline (Dist Lib Srvs Chairperson) 1077

Lakeshore General Hospital (PQ)
FIORE, Francine (Libn) 379

Lakewood Board of Education (OH)
COLEMAN, Barbara K. (Lib Media Spclst) 231
FREDERICKA, Theresa (Lib Media Coordntr) 400
FORD, Delores C. (Sch Libn) . . . 389

Lakewood Elementary Sch (TX)

Lakewood Hospital (OH)
HUDSON, Jo A. (Dir, Med Lib) . . 569

Lakewood Pub Lib (NJ)
ANDERSON, Janelle E. (Dir) . . . 23

Lakewood Pub Lib (OH)
FARAGO, Kathleen M. (Ref Libn) 363
GIOFFRE, B J. (Deputy Dir) 438
HENDERSON, Shirley A. (Libn) . 527
RYAN, Mary E. (Ref Libn) 1071
SPERRY, Linda S. (Ref Libn) . . . 1174
TAYLOR, Patricia L. (Chlds Srvs Head) 1228

Lamar Univ (TX)
HOLLAND, Mary M. (Head of Govt Docums & Spcl Cols) . . . 551
MURRAY, Kathleen R. (Assoc Dir for Technl Srvs) 882
SPARKMAN, Mickey M. (Pub Srvs Assoc Dir) 1171
TURNER, Margaret A. (Eductnl Srvs Mgr) 1264

Lambton Coll (ON)

Lancaster Bible Coll (PA)
ROBBINS, Stephen L. (Head Libn) 1039

Lancaster Central Sch (NY)
DRZEWIECKI, Iris M. (Lib Media Spclst) 321
NEELAND, Margaret A. (Sch Media Spclst) 891

Lancaster County Law Lib (PA)
GERLOTT, Eleanor L. (Law Libn) 429

Lancaster County Lib (SC)
BAND, Richard A. (Dir) 53

Lancaster Mennonite Historical Society (PA)
ZEAGER, Lloyd (Libn) 1387

Lancaster Newspapers Inc (PA)
BULLOCK, Jessie M. (Lib Mgr) . . 156

Lancaster Theological Seminary (PA)
SALGAT, Anne M. (Dir of Lib Srvs) 1076

Lancaster Town Lib (MA)
FISCHER, Marge (Dir) 380

Lander Coll (SC)
FECKO, Marybeth (Ref Libn and Catlgr) 367
GOING, Susan C. (Catlgr) 444
HARE, Ann T. (Lib Catlgr) 501

Lander Coll (SC)
WILLIAMS, Betty H. (Ref & Interlib Loan) 1342

Lander Valley Regional Medical Center (WY)
HEUER, Jane T. (Med Libn) 535

Landmark Coll (VT)
THOMPSON, Jane K. (Registrat, Resrch Data Coordntr) 1240

Landon Sch (MD)
BROWN, Judith B. (Libn & Media Spclst) 145

Lane Coll (TN)
COOKE, Anna L. (Lib Dir) 240

Lane Education Service District (OR)
MAXWELL, James G. (Superintendent) 788

Lane Powell Moss & Miller (WA)
LAWSON, Annetta (Asst Libn) . . 705
MCFADDEN, Denyse I. (Libn) . . . 804

Lane Pub Lib (OH)
RHODES, Glenda T. (Branch Head) 1026
TAVISS, Patricia A. (Systems Mgr) 1225

Lange Simpson Robinson & Somerville (AL)
FEENKER, Cherie D. (Libn) 368

Langley Publications Inc (VA)
HELGERSON, Linda W. (Editor) . 524

Lankenau Hospital (PA)
KODER, Alma (Libn) 667

Lansdale Sch of Business (PA)
WEBER ROOCHVARG, Lynn E. (Libn) 1314

Lansing Catholic Central High Sch (MI)
BROWN, Joan (Media Dir) 145

Lansing Community Coll (MI)
MAJOR, Marla J. (Ref Libn) 762
RADEMACHER, Matthew J. (Ref & Col Devlpmnt Libn) . . 1002

Lansing General Hospital (MI)
HEINLEN, Bethany A. (Med Libn) 522

Lansing Pub Lib (MI)
CONWAY, Lauren K. (Ref Libn) . 239
STRAUSS, Laura C. (Asst Dir) . 1201
VIGES, R J. (Libn) 1284

Lapeer County Lib (MI)

Lapeer General Hospital (MI)

LaQuita Martin Lib Management Inc (TN)
MARTIN, Laquita V. (Pres) 777

Laramie County Lib System (WY)
BYERS, Edward W. (Cnty Libn) . 168
OSBORN, Lucie P. (Asst Dir) . . . 927

Larchmont Pub Lib (NY)
BARRETT, John C. (Libn) 59
HESLER, June P. (Ref) 534

Laredo State Univ (TX)
BRESIE, Mayellen (Dir) 133
BROMBERG, Johanna (Technl Srvs, AV) 139

Largo Lib (FL)
BOYD, Kenneth W. (Pres) 122

Larlin Corp (GA)

Las Vegas-Clark County Lib District (NV)
BATSON, Darrell L. (Adminstr) . . 64
CUTLER, Marsha L. (Young People's Libn) 268
DAVENPORT, Marilyn G. (Graphic Artist) 275
GARDNER, Jack I. (Adminstr) . . . 418
HUNSBERGER, Charles W. (Lib Dir) 574
LANGEVIN, Ann T. (Extension Adminstr) 695
LAUB, Mary M. (Lib Trustee) . . . 702
MORGAN, James E. (Lib Head) . 864
TRASATTI, Margaret S. (Dist Programming Coordntr) 1254
VOIT, Irene E. (Bus Ofc Mgr) . . 1287
WELLS, David B. (Ref Dept Head) 1322

Las Virgenes Unified Sch District (CA)
ROGALSKY, Virginia R. (Libn) . 1049

LaSalle Hig Sch (OH)
BLACK, Jeannie M. (Libn) 101

LaSalle Parish Police Jury (LA)
RAMBO, Gloria P. (Lib Dir) 1005

Laser Magnetic Storage International (NY)
MOES, Robert T. (Vice Pres of Sales & Mktg CD-ROM) 852

Laser Resources Inc (NY)
CONTESSA, William B. (Pres & Chief Exec Ofcr) 239
SHULSINGER, Don (Mktg VP) . . 1133

Laserdata Inc (MA)
TEANEY, Carol R. (Law Libn) . . 1229

Lashly Baer & Hamel PC (MO)
KACZOROWSKI, Monice M. (Assoc Libn Catlg, Ref) 621

Latham & Watkins (CA)
VEGA, Carolyn L. (Law Libn) . . 1281
WALLACE, Marie G. (Libs Dir) . 1297

Latham & Watkins (IL)
COLLINS, Janet (Libn) 232

Latham & Watkins (NY)
LEWIS, Anne (Dir of Lib) 722

Latin Sch of Chicago (IL)
RUMNEY, Leslie W. (Lower Sch
Libn) 1067
Laubach Literacy International (NY)
RYAN, Jenny L. (Libn) 1071
Lauentian Univ (ON)
GOLTZ, Eileen A. (Head, Pub
Docums) 447
Laupenval Sch Board (PQ)
ADRIAN, Donna J. (Lib Consult) . . . 7
Laurel Henderson & Associates (GA)
HENDERSON, Laurel E.
(Owner) 526
Laurel Pub Lib (DE)
STRANGE, Elizabeth B. (Dir) . . 1200
Lauren Rogers Museum of Art (MS)
CLARK, Diane E. (Musm Libn) . . 216
Laurence Witten Rare Books (CT)
WITTEN, Laurence (Owner) . . . 1358
Laurens County Lib (SC)
COOPER, William C. (Dir) 244
Laurentian Hospital (ON)
HAMILTON, Simone (Libn) . . 492
Laurentian Univ (ON)
KELLY, Glen J. (Lib Automation
Proj Coordntr) 637
SLATER, Ronald J. (Asst Libn &
Catlgr) 1148
Lauri Ann West Memorial Lib (PA)
RAO, Rama K. (Asst Libn) 1008
Laval Univ (PQ)
BONNELLY, Claude (Assoc
Chief Libn) 114
CANTIN, Gemma (Libn) 179
CARTIER, Celine (Lib Dir) 190
GUERETTE, Charlotte M. (Chlds
Lit Prof) 476
GUILMETTE, Pierre (Spcl Libn) . 476
JULIEN, Guy (Subject Heading
Indxr) 619
LALIBERTE, Madeleine A.
(Libn) 689
ROBIN, Madeleine (Art &
Architecture Libn) 1043
TAILLON, Yolande A. (Subject
Spclst Libn) 1220
TESSIER, Yves (Head of Map
Lib) 1233
LavaLin Inc (PQ)
MARCOTTE, Marcel (Chief
Libn) 769
Laventhol & Horwath (PA)
ABRAMS, Joan R. (Info Spclst) . . . 3
ROSENBERGER, Constance G.
(Info Spclst) 1056
SHELLENBERGER, Dawn M.
(Info Spclst) 1126
Laventhol & Horwath (ON)
ASHTON, Margaret A. (Head
Libn) 36
Law & Order (TX)
GARCIA, Lana C. (Owner) 417
Law Book Exchange (FL)
BROWN, G R. (Pres) 144
Law Lib Association of Geavga
County (OH)
MOSELEY, Audrey (Law Libn) . . 870
Law Lib Consultants Inc (MN)
BEDOR, Kathleen M. (Consult) . . . 73
Law Lib Management Inc (NY)
JASSIN, Raymond M. (Pres) 595
Law Library Microfrom
Consortium (HI)
DUPONT, A J. (Exec Dir) 327
Law Lib of Louisiana (LA)
KERN, Elizabeth (Acqs Libn) 643
SHULL, Janice K. (Catlg & Ref
Libn) 1133
Law Lib of Montgomery County (PA)
ZANAN, Arthur S. (Dir) 1386
Lawrance Memorial Hospital of
Medford (MA)
HARRIS, John C. (Hospital Libn) . 504
Lawrence Berkeley Laboratory (CA)
GRIFFIN, Hillis L. (Lab Libn) 468
MCCARTHY, John L. (Comp
Scitst) 794
Lawrence County High Sch (AL)
SPILLERS, Doris H. (Secondary
Sch Lib Media Spclst) 1174
Lawrence Hospital (NY)
LARKIN, Virgil C. (Lib Mgr) 698
Lawrence Institute of Tech (MI)
COCOZZOLI, Gary R. (Dir of
the Lib) 226
Lawrence Livermore National
Laboratory (CA)
BURTON, Hilary D. (Technl Info
Spclst) 164
FISHER, H L. (Resrch Info
Group Head) 381
HUNT, Richard K. (Branch Lib
Mgr) 575
KEIZUR, Berta L. (Technl Info
Spclst) 635
LAI, Dennis (Info Spclst) 688
LOVE, Sandra R. (Technl Info
Spclst) 743
Lawrence Pub Lib (KS)
MAY, Cecilia J. (Ref Dept Head) . 788
MAYO, Wayne (Lib Dir) 791

Lawrence Pub Lib (MA)
WHITNEY, Howard F. (Adult
Srvs Head) 1334
Lawry's Foods Inc (CA)
NEWCOMER, Susan N. (Corprt
Libn & Records Admin) 898
Lawyers Co-Operative Publishing
Co (NY)
HALE, William B. (VP & Secy) . . 486
KARNEZIS, Kristine C.
(Managing Edit) 627
LOCKE, William G. (Pub
Relations Rep) 736
The Lawyers Review (PHP)
OREJANA, Rebecca D. (Exec
Edit) 925
Lazard Freres & Co (NY)
BENJAMIN, R D. 81
SMITH, Sharon M. (Lib Srvs
Mgr) 1160
LDA Publishing (NY)
IPPOLITO, Andrew V. (Publshr) . 583
LDF Community Schs (IA)
WOOD, Marilyn R. (Media
Spclst) 1364
LDS Hospital (UT)
HEYER, Terry L. (Lib Dir) 535
Le Mars Pub Lib (IA)
SIMPSON, F T. (Lib Dir) 1141
Le Moyne Coll (NY)
BARNELLO, Inga H. (Soc Scis
& Ref Libn) 57
POPOVIC, Tanya V. (Catlgng
Libn) 983
SIMONIS, James J. (Lib Dir) . . . 1141
Le Phillips Memorial Pub Lib (WI)
LARSON, Mildred N. (Asst to
the Dir) 699
Leach & Garner Co (MA)
MANGION, Barbara E. (Info
Spclst) 765
Leading Edge Products (MA)
ORENSTEIN, Ruth M. (Mgr of
Online Srvs) 925
Leading National Advertisers (NY)
KOURY, Kyra (Dir of Mktg &
Sales) 673
League Insurance Companies (MI)
ZYSKOWSKI, Dianne D. (Libn) . 1392
Leamington Pub Lib (ON)
NICHOLSON, Jill A. (Chief Libn) . 902
Leander Independent Sch
District (TX)
SMITH, Lorraine K. (Libn) 1157
Lear Siegler Inc (CA)
BAGBY, Felicia R. (Spcl Libn) 45
Lear Siegler Inc (MI)
BRACKETT, Norman S. (Technl
Lib Mgr) 124
Lear Siegler Inc (NJ)
SHAFER, Leona M. (Technl
Libn) 1119
Learned Information Inc (NJ)
BAKER, Rita (Asst Editor of Info
Today) 49
BILBOUL, Roger R. (Chairman) . . . 96
HOGAN, Thomas H. (Pres) 549
SMITH, Bev (Editor of Info
Today) 1153
The Learning Tree Ltd (ON)
DAVIS, Virginia K. (VP for Lib
Srvs) 281
Lebanon Community Sch Corp (IN)
WESTFALL, Martha L. (Media
Spclst) 1327
Lebanon County Lib System (PA)
MOORE, Curtis P. (Adminstr) . . . 859
Lebhar-Friedman Inc (NY)
KRAMER, Allan F. (Sr Resrch
Mgr) 675
LAMBE, Michael (Resrch Dir) . . . 690
WESELTEER, Ruth (Libn) 1325
LeBoeuf Lamb Leiby & MacRae (CA)
WOODS, Marcia G. (Libn) 1367
LeBoeuf Lamb Leiby & MacRae (NY)
CHICCO, Meg (Head Libn) 208
FRANKENSTEIN, Steven S.
(Tax Libn) 397
Lee Coll (TX)
INKS, Cordelia R. (Asst Libn for
Technl Srvs) 583
Lee County Lib System (FL)
DIAL, Carolyn E. (Libn II) 299
HOLSTINE, Lesa G. (Pub Srvs
Head) 554
WALTON, Terence M.
(Coordntr, Col Devlpmnt &
Mgmt) 1302
Lee County Lib System (NC)
BEAGLE, Donald R. (Dir) 68
MATOCHIK, Michael J. (Asst
Dir) 784
Lee County Sch Board (FL)
ASFOUR, Karen R. (Media
Spclst) 35
Lee Lib Association (MA)
MASSUCCO, Georgia A. (Lib
Dir) 782
Leffall Enterprises Inc (DC)
LEFFALL, Dolores C. (Lib & Info
Sci Spclst) 712
Legacy Books (PA)
BURNS, Richard K. (Edit) 162
Legal Aid Bureau Inc (MD)
BUTTS, Willie D. (Libn) 168

Legal Aid Society (NY)
COHEN, Rochelle F. (Lib Srvs Dir) 229

Legal Assistance Foundation (IL)
RYDEN, John (Libn) 1071

Legal Infomation Management (CA)
DILORETO, Ann M. (Consult) ... 303

Legal Information Services (MA)
FOX, Elyse H. (Law Lib Consult) . 394

Legal Research Services (IL)
HUTCHINS, Richard G. (Dir & Owner) 579

Legal Services Corp of Alabama (AL)
FRANKS, Janice (Law Libn & Resrch Asst) 398

Legi-Slate Inc (DC)
GROVE, Curtis C. (Pres) 473

Legislative Assembly of Alberta (AB)
MCDOUGALL, Donald B. (Legislature Libn) 803

Legislative Assembly of British Columbia (BC)
BARTON, Joan A. (Legislative Libn) 62

Legislative Assembly of Ontario (ON)
LAND, Reginald B. (Exec Dir) ... 692

Legislative Assembly of Puerto Rico (PR)
TORRES-TAPI, Manual A. (Libn V) 1251

Legislative Intent Service (CA)
STALLARD, Thomas W. (Dir) .. 1179

Legislative Lib of Fredericton (NB)
SWANICK, Eric L. (Legislative Libn) 1213

Legislative Lib of Manitoba (MB)
NIELSON, Paul F. (Head of Technl Srvs) 903

Legislative Reference Lib (MN)
CATHCART, Marilyn S. (Dir) ... 195

Legislative Research Unit (IL)
LARISON, Brenda (Head Libn) .. 697

Lehigh County Historical Society (PA)
GRIFFITHS, June B. (Libn) 469

Lehigh Univ (PA)
CADY, Susan A. (Assoc Dir for Technl Srvs) 170
JARVIS, William E. (Col Devlpmnt & Acqs Libn) 595
METZGER, Philip A. (Spcl Cols Cur) 829
NIPPERT, Carolyn C. (Lib Dir) . 904

Lehigh Valley Hospital Center (PA)

Lehman Coll of the City Univ of New York (NY)
DEMANDY, Claire (Catlg Sect Chief) 291
DIAMOND, Harold J. (Music & Fine Arts Libn & Assoc Prof) . 299
FOLTER, Siegrun H. (Catlgr) ... 388
GEE, Ka C. (Instr & Libn) 424
RIDER, William J. (Ref Libn) ... 1032
RUBEY, Daniel R. (Humanities Libn) 1064
SHANNON, Michael O. (Prof & Assoc Libn) 1120
VOROS, David S. (Lib Dir) 1289

Leigh County Community Coll (PA)
Leila Hospital & Health Center (MI)
MOSHER, Robin A. (Libn) 871

Lenape Regional High Sch District (NJ)
DONOHUE, Nancy W. (Media Coordntr) 312
STARRETT, Mary J. (Media Coordntr) 1182

Lenape Valley Regional High Sch (NJ)
KUTTEROFF, Ethel C. (Media Dir) 685

Lenoir County Board of Education (NC)
SOUTHERLAND, Carol A. (Lib Media Coordntr) 1169

Lenox Hill Hospital (NY)
DANSKER, Shirley E. (Chief Libn) 274
MORROW, Mary D. (Info Ctr Dir) 869
MUNSON, Kathleen J. (Info Spclst) 879

Leo Burnett Co (IL)
THERIAULT, Susan L. (Dir) ... 1234

Leominster Pub Lib (MA)
BUSTETTER, Stanley R. (Lib Adminstr) 166

Leon County Pub Lib (FL)
HOLMES, Gloria P. (Eductnl Media Dir) 553

Leon County Pub Schs (FL)

Leonard Burkat/Program Note Service (CT)
BURKAT, Leonard (Head) 160

Leonard Street & Deinard (MN)
CUMMINGS, Patricia K. (Law Libn) 264
ROLONTZ, Linda (Asst Libn) ... 1051

Leonia Board of Education (NJ)
SHERMAN, Louise L. (Elem Sch Lib Media Spclst) 1128

Leonia Pub Lib (NJ)
PAWSON, Robert D. (Ref Libn) . 951

Lepper Lib Association (OH)
MCPEAK, James J. (Dir) 817

Les Franciscains (PQ)
PAPILLON, Yves (Archvst) 939

Les Pretres de Saint-Sulpice de Montreal (PQ)
AUMONT, Gerard (Provincial Secy) 40

Lesley Coll (MA)
DURANCEAU, Ellen F. (Catlgr) .. 328
STAVIS, Ruth L. (Tchg Resrcs Libn) 1183

Lethbridge Pub Lib (AB)
RAND, Duncan D. (Chief Libn) . 1006

LeTourneau Coll (TX)
GRAY, Paul W. (Dir of Lib & AV Srvs) 460

Levi Heywood Memorial Lib (MA)
HALES, Margaret L. (Chlds Srvs Supvsr & Actg Asst Dir) 486

Levine Huntley Schmidt & Beaver (NY)
LOVARI, John A. (Info Mgr) 743

Lewin & Associates Inc (DC)
ELLIOT, Hugh (Hlth Practice Libn) 343
FEINBERG, Beryl L. (Energy Info Spclst) 368

Lewis & Clark Coll (OR)
FLYNN, Lauri R. (Asst Law Libn) 387
GERITY, Louise P. (Coordntr of Ref Srvs) 428

Lewis and Clark Community Coll (IL)
HUMPHRIES, Beverly H. (Libn) .. 574

Lewis & Clark Lib (MT)
SCHLESINGER, Deborah L. (Lib Dir) 1094

Lewis & Rice Law Firm (MO)
WHITE, Cheryl L. (Libn) 1330

Lewis & Roca (AZ)
DOHERTY, Walter E. (Law Libn) . 309

Lewis Egerton Smoot Memorial Lib (VA)
SCHEPMOES, Rita D. (Lib Dir) . 1091

Lewis Mitchell & Moore (VA)
MOORE, Dianne T. (Lib Dir) 859

Lewiston City Lib (ID)
WILLIAMS, Brenda M. (Technl Srvs Coordntr) 1342

Lexecon Inc (IL)
SMITH, Judy E. (Resrch Mgr & Libn) 1156

LEXIK House Publishers (NY)
BARNHART, David K. (Editor & Publshr) 58

Lexington Community Coll (KY)
BIRCHFIELD, Martha J. (Head Libn) 98

Lexington Herald-Leader (KY)
FARRAR, Lu A. (Libn) 365

Lexington Pub Lib (KY)
SMITH, Linda L. (Libn) 1157
MILLER, Norma B. (Branch Mgr) 841
SCHABEL, Donald J. (Asst Dir for Lib Srvs) 1088
STEENSLAND, Ronald P. (Lib Dir) 1184

Lexington Pub Lib (MA)
STANTON, Martha (Coordntr, Instrcl Mtrls & Srvs) 1181

Lexington Pub Schs (MA)
BENDER, Nancy W. (Lib Media Spclst) 79

Lexington RV Sch District (MO)
ROSS, Shirley D. (Lib Media Spclst) 1059

Lexington Sch District 2 (SC)
BRANTON, Mildred M. (Media Spclst & Libn) 129
HARDIN, Sue H. (Media Spclst) . 500

Lexington Theological Seminary (KY)
DARE, Philip N. (Head Libn) 274

Libbey Owens Ford Co (OH)
KEOGH, Jeanne M. (Libn) 643

Liberty High Sch (MS)
BURKS, Alvin L. (Lib Media Dir) . 161

Liberty Mutual Insurance Co (MA)
CALLAHAN, Joan (Resrcs Supvsr) 173
PROCOPIO, Concetta E. (Dir of Law Libs) 994

Liberty Publishing Co (FL)
HO, Paul J. (Dir) 545

Liberty Univ (VA)
KAWAGUCHI, Miyako (Chairman, Technl Srvs Dept) 632
KRAMER, Pamela K. (Ref Libn) . 675

Libertyville High Sch (IL)

Libertyville United Methodist Church (IL)
HOOVER, Margaret R. (Volunteer Church Libn) 557

Libonia Pub Lib (MI)
VOIGHT, Nancy R. (Chlds Srvs Libn) 1287

Libra Associates Inc (MD)
BAKER, Benjamin R. (Treas & Dir) 48

Libraries Inc (IL)
DICK, Ellen A. (Pres) 300

Libs of the Claremont Colleges (CA)
ALLEN, Susan M. (Asst to the Dir) 16

Libraries Unlimited (CO)

LAMBERT, Shirley A. (Mktg Dir) . 690
LOERTSCHER, David V. (Sr
    Acqs Edit) 737
WYNAR, Bohdan S. (Pres,
    Editor-in-Chief) 1375

Library and Information
** Services** (CO)

COLLARD, R M. (Dir, Lib & Info
    Srvs) 232

Lib Association of Portland (OR)

LARSON, Betty (Dir of
    Extension) 699
MIKKELSEN, June L. (Dir of
    Central) 834

Library Association Publishing
** Limited** (ENG)

ELLIOTT, Pirkko E. (Editor) 344

Lib Automation Products (NY)

ERLAND, Virginia K. (Dir of
    Mktg & Customer Support) . . . 353

Library Binding Institute (NY)

GRAUER, Sally M. (Exec Dir) . . . 458

Library Bureau Inc (NY)

VAN PELT, Peter J. (Pres) 1277

The Library CO-OP Inc (NJ)

DINERMAN, Gloria (Pres) 304

Lib Co of Burlington (NJ)

ZULEWSKI, Gerald J. (Lib Dir) . 1391

Lib Co of Philadelphia (PA)

GREEN, James N. (Cur of
    Printed Bks) 462
VAN HORNE, John C. (Libn) . . 1275
WOLF, Edwin (Libn Emeritus) . . 1360

Lib Co of the Baltimore Bar (MD)

FISHMAN, David H. (Pres) 381

Library Concepts (CA)

FOURIE, Denise K. (Principal
    Consult) 393

Lib Consulting Services (CT)

SCHWARZ, Shirlee (Pres) 1105

Lib Cooperative of Macomb (MI)

CUNNINGHAM, Tina Y. (Libn) . . 265

Lib Council of Metropolitan
** Milwaukee** (WI)

TREBBY, Janis G. (Exec Dir) . . 1255

Library Design Associates Inc (MI)

DE BEAR, Richard S. (Pres &
    Lib Bldg Consult) 284
MCCLINTOCK, Janet (Dir of
    Design) 797

Library Equipment/Space Design
** Inc** (SC)

MAY, Robert E. (President) 789

Lib Hi Tech News (MI)

MCDERMOTT, Rebecca
    (Managing Editor) 802
WALL, C E. (Editor) 1297

Library Information Specialist
** Inc** (CO)

SUDOL, Barbara A. (Resrc
    Access, Lib Spclst) 1206

Lib Innovators (CA)

PLOTKIN, Nathan (Pres) 978

Lib Journal (NY)

BERRY, John N.
    (Editor-in-Chief) 90
FLETCHER, Janet (Book Rvw
    Editor) 384
FOX, Bette L. (Sr Editor) 394

Library Management & Services (TX)

HELBURN, Judith D.
    (Self-employed Dir) 523

Library Management Services (PA)

MACBETH, Eileen M. (Law
    Libn, Pres) 754

Lib Management Services Ltd (PA)

SCAMMAHORN, Lynne (Law
    Libn) 1087

Library Management Systems (CA)

BALABAN, Robin M. (Libn) 50

Library Management Systems
** Inc** (MI)

KILLIAN, Mary C. (Vice Pres) . . . 648

Lib of Administrative Sciences (PQ)

COURTEMANCHE, Pierre O.
    (Gen Mgr) 251

Lib of Congress (DC)

AGENBROAD, James E. (Sr
    Syst Analyst) 7
ALBIN, Michael W. (Chief,
    Order Div) 10
ALEXANDER, Virginia A. (Sr
    Descriptive Catlgr) 12
ANDERSON, Gillian B. (Music
    Spclst) 23
ANDERSON, John M. (Ref
    Spclst) 23
AUSTIN, Judith P. (Gen
    Reading Rooms Head) 40
AUSTIN, Monique C. (Technl
    Info Spclst) 40
AVDOYAN, Levon (Classics &
    Byzantine Std Ref Spclst) 41
AVRAM, Henriette D. (Asst Libn
    for Prcsng Srvs) 42
BARTLEY, Linda K. (CONSER
    Operations Coordntr) 61

Lib of Congress (DC)

BASA, Eniko M. (Serials Catlgr) . . 62
BEALL, Julianne (Dewey
    Decimal Classftn Asst Editor) . . 69
BEAN, Charles W. (Serial Ref
    Spclst) 69
BEATON, Barbara E. (Ref Libn) . . 70
BELLEFONTAINE, Arnold G.
    (Exec Ofcr) 78
BENJAMIN, Marilyn (Catlgng
    Edit) 81
BERNARD, Patrick S. (Principal
    Edit, Natl Union Catlg) 88
BLIXRUD, Julia C. (Sect Head) . . 105
BLUMER, Thomas J. (Sr Edit) . . . 107
BOORSTIN, Daniel J. (Libn of
    Congress) 115
BOWMAN, James R. (Sr
    Descriptive Catlgr) 122
BOYER, Larry M. (Asst Chief,
    Main Reading Room) 123
BRIDGE, Peter H. (Exchange &
    Gift Div Chief) 135
BRODERICK, John C. (Resrch
    Srvs Asst Libn) 138
BROWN, Maxine M. (Computer
    Systs Analyst) 146
BURNEY, Thomas D. (Rare Bk
    Spclst) 162
CAHALANE, Edmond P. (Sr
    Descriptive Catlgr) 171
CALDWELL, George H. (Sr
    Spclst in US Govt Docums) . . 172
CANNAN, Judith P. (Chief) 178
CARNAHAN, Stephanie B.
    (Subject Catlgr) 183
CARRINGTON, David K. (Head
    of Technl Srvs Sect) 186
CASTRO-KLAREN, Sara
    (Hispanic Div Chief) 194
CHACE, Myron B. (Head, Spcl
    Srvs Section) 196
CHANG, Roselyne M. (Libn &
    Catlgr) 201
CHARTRAND, Robert L. (Sr
    Spclst in Info Policy & Tech) . . 203
CHESTNUT, Paul I. (Ref &
    Reader Srv Sect Head) 207
CHO, Sung Y. (Far Eastern Law
    Div Asst Chief) 209
CHRISTY, Ann K. (Systems
    Analyst) 212
COLE, John Y. (Dir) 231
COUGHLAN, Margaret N.
    (Chlds Lit Ref Spclst) 250
CRISTAN, Anita L. (Descriptive
    Catlgr) 259
CURRAN, Donald C. (Assoc
    Libn of Congress) 266
CYLKE, Frank K. (Dir) 268
D'ALESSANDRO, Edward A.
    (Spcl Asst for Plng Mgmt) . . . 270
DAVIS, Deta S. (Sr Music
    Catlgr) 278
DOBCZANSKY, Jurij W. (Slavic
    Catlgr) 307
DRAGOVICH, Pamela M. (Ref
    Libn) 318
DRUMMOND, Louis E. (Spclst,
    Automated Info Resrcs) 321
ELSASSER, Katharine K.
    (Head, Hum I Sect) 346
EWALD, Robert B. (Sr
    Descriptive Catlgng Spclst) . . . 359
FARINA, Robert A. (Lib
    Customer Srv Analyst) 363
FAY, Peter J. (Head Libn) 367
FELACO, Maja K. (Ref Spclst) . . . 369
FERRARESE, Mary A. (Biblgph
    Srvs Asst Chief) 373

Lib of Congress (DC)

FILSTRUP, E C. (Overseas Operations Div Chief) 377
FLATNESS, James A. (Sr Ref Libn) 384
FOX, Ann M. (Sr Descriptive Catlgr) 394
GARLICK, Karen (Paper Conservator) 419
GILLESPIE, Veronica M. (Biblgph Conversion Spclst) . . 435
GLASBY, Dorothy J. (Asst Chief, Serial Record Div) 439
GOLDBERG, Jolande E. (Law Classftn Spclst) 444
GONZALEZ, Armando E. (Asst Chief) 448
GOUDREAU, Ronald A. (Edit of Subject Headings) 454
GUDE, Gilbert (Dir) 475
GUILES, Kay D. (Sr Descriptive Catlgng Spclst) 476
HAHN, Ellen (Chief) 483
HARRISON, Harriet W. (Head, Prcsng Sect) 506
HAWKINS, Sandra J. (Sr Descriptive Catlgr & Law Spclst) 514
HENDRICKSON, Norma K. (Spcl Catlgs Sect Asst Head) . 527
HERMAN, Steven J. (Chief of Cols Mgmt Div) 531
HERRICK, Judith M. (Asst Head) 532
HIATT, Robert M. (Asst to the Dir of Catlgng) 536
HICKERSON, Joseph C. (Head) . 536
HIGBEE, Joan F. (Libn) 537
HILL, Victoria C. (Head, Main Reading Room) 541
HIRONS, Jean L. (Head, CONSER Minimal Level Catlgng) 543
HORCHLER, Gabriel F. (Soc Scis I Sect Head) 559
HSIA, Tao T. (Far Eastern Law Chief) 567
HUGGENS, Gary D. (Quality Ctl Analyst) 571
HUTSON, James H. (Manuscript Div Chief) 579
IBACH, Marilyn (Video Disk Proj Catlgr) 581
JABBOUR, Alan (Dir) 586
JAGUSCH, Sybille A. (Chief of Chlds Lit) 591
JOHANSON, Cynthia J. (Asst Chief) 601
JOHNSON, Everett J. (Cols Improvement Section Head) . . 604
JONES, Catherine A. (Chief, Congressional Ref Div) 611
JWAIDEH, Zuhair E. (Near Eastern & African Law Chief) . 620
KAHLER, Mary E. (Sr Spclst, Hispanic Biblgph) 622
KENNEDY, Lynne (Resrc Devlpmnt Spclst) 641
KENYON, Carleton W. (Law Libn) 643
KESSINGER, Judith A. (Asst Principal Subject Catlgr) 644
KNOWLTON, John D. (Spclst in Lib of Congress Hist and) 665
KRAUS, David H. (Actg Chief) . . 676
LANE, Elizabeth S. (Intern) 694
LEICH, Harold M. (Russian & Soviet Area Spclst Lib) 713
LEVERING, Mary B. (Chief, Netwk Div) 719

Lib of Congress (DC)

LIGGETT, Suzanne L. (Coordntr, Natl Coop Catlgng Project) 726
LISOWSKI, Andrew H. (Sr Automation Plng Spclst) 732
LOO, Shirley (Info Ctl & Automated Systs Spclst) 740
MARCUS, Stephanie M. (Sci Ref Libn) 769
MARTON, Victor (Head of Info Sect) 779
MASTRANGELO, Marjorie J. (Copyright Spclst & Sr Catlgr) 782
MATHESON, William (Rare Bk & Spcl Cols Div Chief) 784
MCCAY, Lynne K. (Sr Team Leader) 795
MCGUIRE, Brian (Archvst) 808
MCGUIRL, Marlene C. (Div Chief) 808
MCKINLEY, Sylvia J. (Copyright Catlgr) 811
MCNELLIS, Claudia H. (Comp Systs Analyst) 817
MEDINA, Rubens (Hispanic Law Chief) 820
MICHENER, David H. (Pubn Quality Ctl Analyst) 832
MILEVSKI, Robert J. (Supervisory Conservator & Sect Head) 834
MILL, Rodney H. (Music Spclst & Ref Libn) 835
MORRIS, Timothy J. (Ref Libn) . . 867
MWALIMU, Charles (Sr Legal Spcslt) 884
MYERS, R D. (Telephone Ref & Bibl Sect Head) 885
MYERS-HAYER, Patricia A. (Sr. Arabic Catlgr) 885
NELSON, Marilyn L. (Ref Libn) . . 894
NEW, Gregory R. (Asst Edit) 898
NEWSOM, Jon (Actg Chief) 900
NYGREN, Deborah A. (Descriptive Catlgr) 912
OSTROFF, Harriet (Edit, Natl Union Catlg of Mss Cols) 929
OSTROVE, Geraldine E. (Head of Reader Srvs) 929
OSTROW, Stephen E. (Prints & Photographs Div Chief) 929
OVERTON, Kathryn R. (Asst Edit, Bill Digest) 931
PANITZ, Barbara R. (Descriptive Catlgr) 938
PANZERA, Donald P. (Exec Ofcr of Prcsng Srvs Dept) . . . 938
PEMPE, Ruta (Sr Automation Plng Spclst) 956
PENKIUNAS, Ruta M. (Subj Catlgr) 956
PETERSON, Charles B. (Sr Map Catlgr) 963
PLETZKE, Linda (Asst Chief) . . . 978
PRATT, Dana J. (Dir of Publshg) 990
PREBLE, Leverett L. (Law Lib Reading Room Head) 990
PRICE, Harry H. (Music Catlgr) . . 992
PRICE, Joseph W. (Chief, Sci & Tech Div) 992
PRICE, Mary S. (Biogph Products & Srvs Dir) 992
PRITCHARD, Sarah M. (Ref Spclst, Women's Std) 994
PRUETT, James W. (Music Div Chief) 996

Lib of Congress (DC)

PUCCIO, Joseph A. (Serials Ref
Spclst) 997
RATHER, Lucia J. (Dir for
Catlgng) 1009
REID, Judith P. (Ref Spclst
Local Hist & Genealogy) 1018
REIFSNYDER, Betsy S. (Ref
Spclst) 1020
RILEY, James P. 1034
RIMER, J T. (Asian Div Chief) . . 1035
SAUDEK, Robert (Chief of
Motion Picture Brdcstng) . . . 1084
SCHAAF, Robert W. (Sr Spclst,
UN & Intl Docums) 1088
SCHEEDER, Donna 1090
SCUKA, Aletta N. (Ref Spclst) . 1108
SEGEL, Bernard J. (Lib Info
Systs Spclst) 1112
SETTLER, Leo H. (Asst to Dir
for Biblgph Srvs) 1117
SHAFFER, Norman J.
(Photoduplication Srv Chief) . 1119
SHAW, Renata V. (Prints &
Photographs Div Asst Chief) . 1123
SIPKOV, Ivan (Chief, European
Law Div) 1144
SMITH, Thomas E. (Head, Circ
Sect, Loan Div) 1161
SOLOMON, Alan C. (Head) . . . 1166
SOLOMON, Arnold D. (Sr Ref
Libn) 1166
SPAANS, David N. (Sr Systs
Analyst) 1170
SPARKS, Peter G. (Natl
Preservation Prog Dir) 1171
STANHOPE, Charles V.
(Adminstrv Ofcr) 1180
STARCK, William L. (Sr
Descriptive Catlgr) 1181
STARNER, James A. (Libn) . . . 1182
STEPHENSON, Richard W.
(Spclst in Am Cartographic
Hist) 1188
STEVENS, Roberta A.
(Customer Srvs Ofcr) 1191
STEWART, Ruth A. (Asst Libn
for Natl Progs) 1193
STREHL, Susan J. (Ref Libn) . 1201
STROUP, Elizabeth F. (Gen Ref
Dir) 1203
STUBBS, Linda T. (Name
Authority Conversion Sect
Head) 1204
SULLIVAN, Robert C. (Acqs &
Overseas Operations Dir) . . . 1208
SUNG, Carolyn H. (Acting Dir
for Preservation) 1210
SWORA, Tamara (Asst
Preservation Microfilming
Ofcr) 1217
TABB, Winston (Chief of Info &
Ref Div) 1219
TAPPER, Bruce (Editor) 1223
TARR, Susan M. (Chief, Catlgng
Distribution Srv) 1224
THURONYI, Geza T. (Proj
Head) 1243
TOTH, George S. (Slavic Catlgr) 1252
TRACZEWSKI, Elizabeth P.
(Copyright Catlgr) 1253
TSCHERNY, Alexander (Catlgr) 1260
TSUNEISHI, Warren M. (Area
Std Dir) 1260
VAN SYCKLE, Georgiana
(Catlgr) 1277
VARGA, William R. (Legal Ref
Spclst) 1278
WANG, Ann C. (Sr Descriptive
Catlgr) 1302

Lib of Congress (DC)

WANG, Chi (Head, Chinese &
Korean Sect) 1302
WARREN, Robert P. 1306
WELSH, William J. (Deputy
Libn) 1323
WIENER, Theodore (Sr Catlgr) . 1336
WIGGINS, Beacher J. (Asst to
Asst Libn for Prcsng Srvs) . . 1337
WISDOM, Donald F. (Serial &
Govt Pubns Chief) 1356
WITHERELL, Julian W. (African
& Middle Eastern Div Chief) . 1358
WOLFE, Susan J. (Subscription
& Microform Sect Head) 1361
WOLTER, John A. (Chief of
Geography & Map Div) 1362
WOMELDORF, Jack H. (Sr
Descriptive Catlgr) 1362
WOOD, Karen A. (Spcl Asst) . . 1364
YASUMATSU, Janet R.
(Subject Catlgr) 1378
YOUNG, Peter R. (Copyright
Catlgng Div Chief) 1383
ZICH, Robert G. (Office of Plng
and Devlpmnt Dir) 1388
ZIMMERMAN, Glen A. (Assoc
Libn for Mgmt) 1389
ZIMMERMANN, Carole R.
(Preservation Ofc Libn) 1389

Lib of Congress (FL)

BALLANTYNE, Lygia M. (Field
Dir of Rio De Janeiro Ofc) . . . 53

Lib of Congress (MD)

JOHNSON, Bruce C. (Lib
Customer Srvs Analyst) 602
VIRTA, Alan K. (Sr Catlgr) . . . 1285

Lib of Congress (NY)
Lib of Congress (VA)

JAY, Donald F. (Field Dir) 595
JACKSON, Nancy G. (Head,
NUC Editrl Sect I) 588
MORGAN, Robert C. (Catlgr) . . 864

Lib of Michigan (MI)

DUKELOW, Ruth H. (Lib
Establishment Spclst) 324
EZELL, Charlaine L. (Pub
Relations Spclst) 360
JOHNSON, Veronica A. (Govt
Relations Spclst) 609
WOLFE, Charles B. (State Law
Libn) 1360

Lib of Parliament (ON)

BROWN, Barbara E. (Catlgr) . . . 142
LEGAULT, Michel (Catlgr) 712
LEGERE, Monique E. (Pub Srvs
Div Chief) 712
MARLEAU, Gilles (Head) 772
PARE, Richard (Assoc
Parliamentary Libn) 940
STILES, William G. (Chief, Info
Dissemination Div) 1194

Lib of Parliament (PQ)

TESSIER, Richard (Subject
Analysis Spclst) 1233

Lib of the National Assembly of
Quebec (PQ)

PREMONT, Jacques (Chief Libn
or Dir) 990

Lib of the United States Courts (IL)

YOUNG, Peter W. (Asst Libn) . . 1383

Lib Systems & Services (DC)

PERRONE, Jeanne M. (Branch
Supvsr) 960

Lib Systems & Services (MD)

MCQUEEN, Judith D. (Netwk
Srvs Vice Pres) 817

Lib Tech Reports (IL)

CAMP, John F. (Asst Ed) . . . 175

Licking Memorial Hospital (OH)

FREYTAG, Lindsay J. (Med Lib
Consult) 403

Life Chiropractic Coll West (CA)

CARR, Richard D. (Pub Srvs
Libn) 186
WOODBURY, Marda (Lib Dir) . . 1366

Lifecard International (MD)
Ligonier Valley Lib (PA)

SCHERER, Dieter (Mktg Mgr) . . 1092
WHEELER, Martha M. (Chlds
Libn) 1329

Lillick McHose & Charles (CA)

HARDIN, Betty N. (Asst Libn) . . . 500
SPATH, Linda C. (Law Libn) . . . 1171

Limestone Hills Book Shop (TX)

KENDALL, Lyle H. (Dir) 640

Lincoln City Libs (NE)
DOW, Carolyn E. (Music Libn) .. 315
FELTON, John D. (Coordntr of Adult Srvs) 370

Lincoln County Sch District (OR)
KRABBE, Natalie (Instrcl Media Srvs Dir) 674

Lincoln Electric Co (OH)
KLINGER, William E. (Electronic Reliability Engineer) 661

Lincoln High Sch (MN)
HOFSTAD, Alice M. (Media Spclst) 548

Lincoln Lawrence Franklin Regional Lib (MS)
LEDET, Henry J. (Dir) 708

Lincoln Lib (IL)
FRISCH, Corrine A. (Head of Pub Relations) 405
VETTER, Jean A. (North Branch & West Branch Head) 1283
VOLKMANN, Carl W. (Lib Dir) . 1287

Lincoln Parish Lib (LA)
AVANT, Julia K. (Lib Dir) 41

Lincoln Park Zoological Society (IL)
SHAW, Joyce M. (Zoo Libn) ... 1123

Lincoln Telephone Co (NE)
CARNES, Mary J. (Info Resrc Libn) 183

Lincoln Township Pub Lib (MI)
BEDUNAH, Virginia M. (Dir) 74

Lincoln Trail Libs System (IL)
FREDERICK, Sidney C. (Automation Consultant) 399
PACEY, Brenda M. (Lib Devlpmnt Consult) 933

Lincoln Univ (PA)
OWENS, Irene E. (Circ & Readers' Srvs) 932

Lincolnwood Pub Lib District (IL)
WHITNEY, Ruth (Lib Dir) 1334

Linda Hall Lib (MO)
COX, Bruce B. (Docums Libn) ... 253
MARTIN, Louis E. (Dir) 777
PETERSON, Paul A. (Adminstrv Asst) 964

Linden Free Pub Lib (NJ)
CANAVAN, Roberta N. (Dir) 178
PISKORIK, Elizabeth (Sr Libn) ... 976

Lindenhurst Memorial Lib (NY)
MILNES, Patricia C. (Dir) 845
SALITA, Christine T. (Asst Dir) . 1076
WARD, Peter K. (Adult Srvs Libn) 1304

Lindsey Wilson Coll (KY)
FOWLER, James W. (Ref Srvs Head) 393

Linfield Coll (OR)
BENSON, Mary M. (Technl Srvs Libn/Assoc Prof) 83
CHMELIR, Lynn K. (Coll Libn) ... 209
ENGLE, Michael O. (Reader Srvs Libn & Assoc Prof) 349

Linfield Sch (CA)
BOWMAN, Kathleen A. (Sch Lib & Media Spclst) 122

Linguistics International Inc (MA)
PRINDLE, Paul E. (Chief Exec Ofcr) 993

LINK Resources Corp (NY)
FISCHER, Margaret T. (Chief of Resrch) 379
GAFFNER, Haines B. (Pres) 412
SIECK, Steven K. (VP, Electronic Srvs Group) 1135
WRIGHT, Bernell (Vice Pres, Electronic Comm) 1370

Linn-Benton Community Coll (OR)
FELLA, Sarah C. (Coordntr, Consumer Hlth Info Proj) 370

Linne Unified Sch District 223 (KS)
BACHAND, Alice J. (Sch Media Spclst) 43

Linowes & Blocher (DC)
KOSLOSKE, Verleah B. (Asst Libn) 672

Linowes & Blocher (MD)
CAMILLO, Janet H. (Libn) 175

L'Institut Canadien de Quebec (PQ)
MARQUIS, Julien (Chief, Technl Srvs) 773
MCKENZIE, Donald R. (Branch Srvs Chief) 811

Linx Union Middlesex Regional Lib Coop (NJ)
ROSENBERG, Gail L. (Exec Dir) 1056

Liposome Co (NJ)
GARNER, Linda J. (Info Spclst) .. 419

Liposome Technology Inc (CA)
HARRIS, Nina M. (Asst Libn) ... 505
JENSEN, Marilyn A. (Mgmt Info Syst Libn) 599

Lipshutz Frankel Greenblatt & King (GA)
LIPSHUTZ, Robert J. (Sr Partner) 732

Lisbon National Lib (PTG)
DE MACEDO, Maria L. (Head of Preservation & Conservation) . 290

Litchfield County Center for Higher Educ (CT)
JOY, Patricia L. (Dir) 618

Litchfield Pub Schs (CT)
VAN LEER, Jerilyn M. (Lib Media Coordntr) 1276

Lithgow Pub Lib (ME)
CROSBY, Barbara A. (Chief Libn) 260

Littion Guidance & Control Systems (CA)
MASON, Elsbeth S. (Ref Libn Docum Libn) 781

Little Co of Mary Hospital (IL)
KARNER, Rita (Libn) 627

Little Elm Independent Sch District (TX)
FRITSCH, Janet E. (Libn & Tutor) 405

Little Falls Pub Lib (NJ)
SAWYER, Miriam (Lib Dir) 1086

Little Hoop Community Coll (ND)
BLACK, Lea J. (Lib Aide) 101

Little Silver Pub Lib (NJ)
EDWARDS, Susan M. (Dir) 338

Littleton Pub Schs (CO)
AKE, Mary W. (Libn & Media Spclst) 9
SALLE, Ellen M. (Media Spclst) . 1076

Littleton Pub Schs (MA)
JENSEN, Kathryn E. (Lib Media Spclst) 599

Litton-Amecom Div (MD)
O'DELL, M P. (Mgr of Lib, Info Srvs) 916

Litton Industries (CA)
RUNYON, Judith A. (Corprt & Law Libn) 1067

Litton Industries (MA)
LATHAM, Mary R. (Libn) 701

Litton Systems Inc (CA)
CLIFTON, Joe A. (Info Srvs Mgr) 222
GILBRIDE, Irene L. 434

The Live Oak Press (CA)
HAMILTON, David M. (Pres) 491

Livermore Pub Lib (CA)
PALLONE, Kitty J. (Technl Srvs Coordntr) 935

Liverpool Pub Lib (NY)
GOLDEN, Fay A. (Dir) 445
POLLY, Jean A. (Pub & Comp Srvs Asst Dir) 981
ROSSOFF, Judith H. (Asst Dir, Support Srvs) 1059

Livingston & Wyoming Co Lib Systems (NY)
BARTLE, Susan M. (Spcl Projs Libn) 61

Livingstone Coll & Hood Theol Sem (NC)
ALDRICH, Willie L. (Head Libn) .. 11
FARHAT, Elizabeth M. (Branch Libn) 363

Livonia Pub Lib (MI)
DEUTSCH, Karen A. (Lib Dir) ... 296

Livonia Pub Lib (NY)
PERRY, Rebecca A. (Head Libn) 960

Lloyd Lib & Museum (OH)
PFISTER, Lawrence T. (Pres & Chief Exec Ofcr) 966

Lloyd S Maritime Data Network (CT)
MCGRAW, Scott C. (Pres) 807

LLSC Inc (IL)
MCADAM, Paul E. (Col Devlpmnt Libn) 791

LMTC (MD)

Lock Haven Univ of Pennsylvania (PA)
BRAVARD, Robert S. (Lib Srvs Dir) 130
CARRIER, Esther J. (Ref & Interlib Loan Libn) 186
CHANG, Shirley L. (Libn, Asst Prof) 201
PALMA, Nancy C. (Asst Reader Srvs Libn) 935
ENGLE, Madge (Law Libn) 349

Locke Reynolds Boyd & Weisell (IN)
HOLLAND, Deborah K. (Libn) ... 550

Lockhart Independent Sch Dist (TX)
CRUM, Norman J. (Supvsr of Online Resrch & Lit Srch) 262
ELMAN, Stanley A. (Adminstrv Srvs Mgmt Staff Spclst) 345

Lockheed-California Co (CA)
SAWYER, Edmond J. (Info Spclst) 1086
GABRIEL, Linda (Supvsr) 411

Lockheed Corp (DC)

Lockheed Electronics Co (NJ)
LEWIS, Ralph W. (Technl Info Ctr Mgr) 724

Lockheed Missiles & Space Co Inc (CA)
STANEK, Suzanne (Sr Technl Libn) 1179
TYSON, Betty B. (Sr Technl Libn) 1267
WOLF, Nola M. (Syst Mgr) 1360

Loctite Corp (CT)
LERITZ, M K. (Sr Libn) 717

Lodi Memorial Lib (NJ)
TAORMINA, Anthony P. (Lib Dir) 1223

Lodi Pub Lib (CA)
MAAS, Dorothy W. (Chlds Libn) . 753
YAMAMOTO, Conrad S. (Asst
Adult Srvs Libn) 1376

Logan Coll of Chiropractic (MO)
BUHR, Rosemary E. (Dir, Lrgn
Resrcs Ctr) 156

Logansport Cass County Pub Lib (IN)
SHIH, Philip C. (Dir) 1130

Logicon Inc (CA)
DAVENPORT, Constance B.
(Info Srvs Mgr) 275
SPRUNG, Lori L. (Libn II) 1176

Logicon Inc (MA)
EMOND, Kathleen A. (Proj Libn) . 348

Login Brothers Book Co (IL)
TAKACS, Sharon N. (Med Libn) 1220

Logistics Management Institute (MD)
SHOCKLEY, Cynthia W.
(Resrch Fellow) 1132

Loma Linda Univ (CA)
BUTLER, Randall R. (Assoc
Univ Archvst) 167
DAVIS, Charles E. (Dept of Pub
Srvs Chair) 278
HESSEL, William H. (Assoc Lib
Dir) 534
WALKER, James J. (Catlgng
Libn) 1295
WURANGIAN, Nelia C. (Dept of
Technl Srvs Chairperson) . . . 1374

Lombard Sch District 87 (IL)
TUGGLE, Ann M. (Lib Media
Srvs Dept Chair) 1262

Lombardi Indexing & Information
Services (CA)
LOMBARDI, Mary L. (Indxr &
Pres) 738

Lomond Publications Inc (MD)
HATTERY, Lowell H. (Publshr) . . 512
JOHNSON, Susan W. (Editrl
Asst) 609

London & Middlesex County (ON)
BENOIT, Ursula L. (Libn) 83

London Pub Libs & Museums (ON)
MITCHELL, Margaret M.
(Coordntr) 849

London Pub Lib (ON)
CADA, Elizabeth J. (Branch
Srvs Coordntr) 170

London Pub Lib Board (ON)
OSBORNE, Reed E. (Dir) 927

Long & Levit (CA)
NEWMAN, Mark J. (Libn) 899

Long Beach City Coll (CA)
AYALA, John L. (Assoc Prof &
Libn) 42

Long Beach Pub Lib (CA)
DARTT, Florence R. (Libn) 275
SALLSTROM, Marilee A. (Adult
Libn, Libn I) 1077

Long Beach Pub Lib (NY)
PILLA, Marianne L. (Head of
Chlds Srvs) 973

Long Beach Unified Schs (CA)
HECKLINGER, Ellen L. (Sch
Libn/Tchr) 519

Long Island Coll Hospital (NY)
WAHLERT, George A. (Staff
Med Libn) 1292

Long Island Jewish Medical
Center (NY)
ATKIN, Shifra (Actg Dir Hlth
Srvs Lib) 37
KING, Esther (Med Libn for Col
Organz) 651

Long Island Lib Resources
Council (NY)
NEUFELD, Judith B. (Asst Dir) . . 897

Long Island Univ (NY)
BARRIE, John L. (Lib & Comp
Srvs Dir) 59
BRISFJORD, Inez S. (Assoc
Prof of Info Sci) 136
GATNER, Elliott S. (Dir of Lib &
Prof of Hist, Emeritus) 422
GRANT, Mary M. (Dir) 458
IRWIN, Iris (Docums Libn) 584
KETCHAM, Susan E. (Catlgr) . . . 645
MAILLET, Lucionne G. (Dean) . . 761
MANN, Amy S. (Faculty Libn) . . . 765
MOFFAT, Edward S. (Assoc
Prof, Lib Sch) 852
O'HARA, Frederic J. (Lib & Info
Sci Prof) 919
PODELL, Diane K. (Perdcls Libn
& Assoc Prof) 979
SPERR BRISFJORD, Inez L.
(Assoc Prof) 1173
SPIRT, Diana L. (Prof Emeritus) 1175
SYWAK, Myron (Assoc Prof) . . 1217
WEINSTEIN, Ellen B. (Head, Lib
& Info Sci Lib) 1318
WENGER, Milton B. (Ref Libn) . 1324

Long Island Univ (NY)
WINCKLER, Paul A. (Lib & Info
Sci Prof) 1354
YUKAWA, Masako (Ref Srvs
Coordntr) 1384
ZUBARIK, Therese (Ref Libn) . . 1390

Longview Independent Sch
District (TX)
NYLUND, Carol L. 912

Longview Sch District (WA)
DOLBEY, Mary B. (Lib Media
Spclst) 309

Longwood Central Sch District (NY)
NARBY, Ann E. (High Sch Lib
Media Spclst) 888

Longwood Coll (VA)
HOWE, Patricia A. (Libn & Asst
Prof) 565
LAINE, Rebecca R. (Technl
Srvs Libn) 688
STWODAH, M I. (Asst
Prof/Head of Reader Srvs) . . 1206
TEETER, Enola J. (Libn) 1229

Longwood Gardens (PA)
HOUGHTON, Sally L. (Dir) 563

Lonoke County Lib System (AR)
GANGLOFF, Tory W. (Med
Libn) 416

Lorain Community Hospital (OH)

Lorain Pub Lib (OH)
CROMER, Kenneth L. (Asst Dir,
Supvsr of Branches) 260
RUSSO, Stephen A. (Adult Srvs
Supvsr) 1070
SMITH, Valerie M. (Chlds Srvs
Supvsr) 1161

Loras Coll (IA)
GIBSON, Michael D. (Archvst) . . 432
ZORDELL, Pamela K. (Pub Srvs
Libn) 1390

Lord Corp (PA)
HOWARD, Dianne D. (Info
Retrieval Supvsr) 564

Lord Day & Lord (NY)
FRANK, Penny G. (Head Libn) . . 397

Lord Selkirk Sch Division (MB)
PETROWSKI, Stan M. (Tchr
Libn) 965

Lorillard Inc (NC)
SKLADANOWSKI, Lawrence
M. (Lib Supvsr) 1146

L'Orsa Maggiore SRL (ITL)
PUSATERI, Liborio (Owner) 998

Los Alamos County Lib (NM)
SAYRE, Edward C. (Dir) 1087

Los Alamos National Laboratory (NM)
BEYER, Ann H. (Ref Libn) 93
CARTER, Jackson H. (Report
Libn) 189
COMSTOCK, Daniel L.
(Adminstrv Spclst) 235
FREED, J A. (Head Libn) 400
GODFREY, Lois E. (Asst Head
Libn) 442

Los Alamos Pub Schs (NM)
CROCKER, Judith A. (Lib &
Media Spclst) 259

Los Angeles County Law Lib (CA)
BARROW, Jerry (Catlgr) 60
ENYINGI, Peter (Technl Srvs
Libn) 351
IAMELE, Richard T. (Lib Dir) 581
MITTAN, Rhonda L. (Sr Catlgr) . . 850
REYNOLDS, Diane C. (Pub Srv
Libn) 1025
SNELL, Patricia P. (Catlgr &
Law Libn) 1163

Los Angeles County Medical
Association (CA)
CRUMP, Joyce A. (Ref Srvs
Head) 262
POTTER, Laurene (Med Ref
Libn) 987
TREISTER, Cyril C. (Med Ref
Libn) 1255

Los Angeles County Pub Lib (CA)
AMESTOY, Helen M. (Sr
Librarian-in-Charge) 20
AROS, Andrew A. (AV Libn) 34
ASAWA, Edward E. (Perdcls &
Acqs Libn) 35
BUTKIS, John F. (Ref Libn) 166
BUTTERWORTH, Linda M.
(Chlds Libn) 167
CASTONGUAY, Russell (Ref
Libn) 194
CHAVEZ, Linda (Chicano Resrc
Ctr Libn) 204
CURZON, Susan C. (Regnl
Adminstr) 267

Los Angeles County Pub Lib (CA)

DEVEREAUX, Amy E. (Chlds and Ref Libn) 297
HAUSSMANN, Virginia D. (Head Libn) 513
MARKEY, Penny S. (Chlds Srvs Coordntr) 771
PETERMAN, Claudia A. (Ref Libn) 962
RODRIGUEZ, Ronald (Technl Srvs Libn) 1048
ROSENBERG, Stuart L. (Libn-In-Charge) 1056
WAGNER, Sharon L. (Chlds Book Evaluator) 1292

Los Angeles Herald Examiner (CA)
SAUSEDO, Ann E. (Lib Dir) . . . 1085

Los Angeles ORT Technical Institute (CA)
SATER, Analya (Libn) 1083

Los Angeles Pub Lib (CA)
AHLSTROM, Romaine (Col Devlpmnt Mgr) 8
ALFORD, Thomas E. (Asst City Libn) 13
BEVERAGE, Stephanie L. (Libn) . . 93
BUCK, Donald (Bus Mgr) 153
CLARK, David L. (Consult & Histn) 216
CLARK, Patricia A. (Yng Adult Libn) 217
COLLINS, Richard H. (Libn) 233
CONNOR, Anne C. (Sr Libn) . . . 237
CONNOR, Billie M. (Dept Mgr) . . 237
ELLISON, Bettye H. (CA Room Libn) 345
GAY, Elizabeth K. (Centl Lib Dir) . 423
GINSBURG, Helen W. (Law Libn) 438
HICKS, Cynthia S. (Ref Libn) . . . 536
JONES, Wyman (City Libn) 615
KHATTAB, Hosneya M. (Adult Ref Libn) 646
LEE, Hee J. (Libn & Catlgr) 710
LEWIS, Phyllis N. (Libn) 724
MAZUR, Victoria P. (Libn) 791
NAVARRO, Frank A. (Coordntr) . 889
NG, Carol S. (Chils Libn) 900
NORDBY, Leslie L. (Principal Libn) 908
PATRON, Susan H. (Asst Coordntr of Chlds Srvs) 947
REAGAN, Bob (Pub Info Dir) . . 1012
ROH, Jae M. (Branch Libn) 1050
ROSENBERG, Melvin H. (Principal Libn, Art & Music) . 1056
RUBEN, Jacquelen S. (Ref Libn) 1064
SPENCER, Patricia O. (Libn & Subject Spclst) 1173
STREHL, Daniel J. (Sr Libn) . . . 1201
TESTA, Barbara E. (Chlds Libn) 1233
WALKER, Patricia A. (Branch Mgr) 1296
WALTER, Virginia A. (Dept Mgr) 1300
WILLIAMS, Sonja D. (Regnl Mgr) 1346
WINSTON, Gillian R. (Chlds Libn) 1356
ZEIDLER, Patricia L. (Sr Libn) . . 1387

Los Angeles Times (CA)
BROWN, Patricia L. 146
SIMPSON, Mildred (Graphics Libn) 1142

Los Angeles Times (DC)
WALSH, Barclay (Head Libn) . . 1299

Los Angeles Unified Sch District (CA)
BUBOLTZ, Dale D. (Lib Media Ctr Dir) 152
CROSS, Claudette S. (Libn) 260
HILLIS, Patricia K. (Sch Libn) . . . 541
MULLINS, Carolyn J. (Jr High Sch Libn) 878
SINOFSKY, Esther R. (Libn) . . . 1144
SKEHAN, Patricia A. (Sec Sch Libn) 1145

Los Angeles Unified Sch District (CA)

Lotus Development Corp (MA)

Louis A Weiss Memorial Hospital (IL)
Louisiana Coll (LA)
Louisiana Lib Association (LA)

Louisiana Retired Teachers (LA)

Louisiana Southern Univ (LA)

Louisiana State Lib (LA)

Louisiana State Penitentiary (LA)
Louisiana State Senate (LA)

Louisiana State Univ at Baton Rouge (LA)

SMITH, Margie G. (Lib Media Spclst) 1157
MCLAGAN, Donald L. (VP & Gen Mgr) 813
SLAVIN, Vicky J. (Mgr, Lib and Info Srvs) 1148
SACHS, Iris P. (Med Libn) 1073
SALLEY, Landrum (Lib Dir) 1076
AUCOIN, Sharilynn A. (Exec Dir) 38
MCCRAY, Evelina W. (Resrc Person) 800
TRIPLETT, Billy L. (Asst Prof of Med Lib Sci) 1257
ANJIER, Jennifer S. (Films & Recordings Sect Head) 28
CRETINI, Blanche M. (User Srvs Coordntr) 258
MOORE, Grace G. (Recorder of Docums & Lib Mgr) 859
LONG, Gary (Libn) 739
MCENANY, Arthur E. (Law Libn) 804

ARNY, Philip H. (Grad Asst) 34
BALL, Dannie J. (Resrch Assoc) . . 52
BOYCE, Bert R. (Prof) 122
BROWNING, Sandra B. (Supvsr) 148
CARPENTER, Michael A. (Asst Prof) 185
DANTIN, Doris B. (Lib Orientation & Instrc Coordntr) . 274
DUGGAN, James E. (Grad Asst) 324
FULLING, Richard W. (Docums Libn) 409
GIAMALVA, Lolah C. (Ref Libn) . 430
HAMAKER, Charles A. (Asst Dir, Col Devlpmnt) 490
HEBERT, Madeline (Ref Libn) . . . 519
HEIM, Kathleen M. (Dean) 521
HOGAN, Sharon A. (Dir of Libs) . 549
JOHNS, Mary E. (Head of Catlgng) 601
KLEINER, Janellyn P. (Head, Ref Srvs) 660
KRAFT, Donald H. (Prof & Chairman of Comp Sci) 674
LANE, Mary J. (Catlgr) 694
LOUBIERE, Sue (Libn) 742
MARTIN, Norma H. (Head of Catlg Dept) 777
MARTIN, Robert S. (Asst Dir of Libs for Spcl Cols) 778
MAXSTADT, John M. (Asst Libn) 788
MCCLEARY, William E. (Assoc Libn, Docums Dept Head) . . . 796
MERING, Margaret V. (Serials Catlgr) 826
MILLER, Susan E. (Ref Libn) . . . 842
MOONEY, Sandra T. (Head, Design Resrc Ctr) 858
NOLAN-MITCHELL, Patricia (Ref Libn) 908
NUCKLES, Nancy E. (Asst Libn) . 912
PASKOFF, Beth M. (Instr) 946
PATTERSON, Charles D. (Prof) . 948
PERRAULT, Anna H. (Head, Ref Col Devlpmnt) 959
PHENIX, Katharine J. (Instr) . . . 967
PHILLIPS, Faye (Head, LA & Lower MS Valley Cols) 968
REID, Marion T. (Assoc Dir for Technl Srvs) 1019
ROUNDTREE, Lynn P. (Manuscripts Cur) 1061

Louisiana State Univ at Baton Rouge (LA)

SCULL, Roberta A. (Info Srvs Dir) 1108
SHIFLETT, Orvin L. (Assoc Prof) 1130
STANLEY, Eileen H. (Assoc) . . 1180
WANK, Paul G. (Instrcl Mtrls Ctr Head) 1303
WITTKOPF, Barbara J. (Ref Libn) 1358
WOJKOWSKI, Suhad K. (Libn) . 1359

Louisiana State Univ at Eunice (LA)
MARSHALL, Susan O. (Sci Ref Libn) 775

Louisiana State Univ at Lafayette (LA)
RAMAKRISHNAN, T (Assoc Prof of Med) 1004

Louisiana State Univ at New Orleans (LA)
MARIX, Mary L. (Pub Srvs Head & Ref Libn) 770
STROTHER, Elizabeth A. (Head, Dental Lib) 1203

Louisiana State Univ at Shreveport (LA)
BROWN, Sue S. (Soc Sci Ref Libn) 147
KING, Anne M. (Ref Libn) 650
MEADOR, Patricia L. (Archvst & Assoc Libn) 819
MOSLEY, Mattie J. (Lib Sci Assoc Prof) 871

Louisiana Technical Univ (LA)
BYERS, Cora M. (Head, Circ Dept) 168
DICARLO, Michael A. (Lib Automation Head) 300
EVANS, James M. (Catlgr) 357
HAMILTON, William F. (Interlib Loan Libn) 492
HENSON, Stephen (Govt Docums Libn) 530
IRVIN, Judy C. (Serials Dept Head) 584
LOWE, Joy L. (Lib Sci Assoc Prof) 744
MCFADDEN, Sue J. (Bus & Econ Libn) 804
SHORT, Peggy S. (Asst in Acqs & Catlgng) 1132
VIDRINE, Jacqueline M. (Libn I) 1283
WICKER, W W. (Dir of Libs) . . . 1335

Louisville Academy of Music (KY)
FRENCH, Robert B. (Pres) 402

Louisville Free Pub Lib (KY)
DIEMER, Irvin T. (Lib Asst) 302
GARNAR, William H. (Asst Dir) . . 419
JAMES, Karen G. (Chlds Srvs Coordntr) 592
KING, Charles D. (Mag & Newpaper Room Sr Libn) 650
PTACEK, William H. (Dir) 996
ROBY, B D. (Lib Srvs Coordntr) 1045
SHEPHERD-SHLECHTER, Rae (Interlib Loan Libn Govt Docums Head) 1127
SOMERVILLE, Mary R. (Mgr of Chlds Srvs) 1167

Louisville Presbyterian Theological Sem (KY)
COALTER, Milton J. (Libn & Bibl & Resrch Assoc Prof) . . . 224
RICHARDSON, Susan C. (Technl Srvs Libn) 1030
WHITE, Ernest M. (Sem Archvst) 1331

Lovel Information Services (ON)
SMITH, Anne C. 1152

Lovelace Biomedical & Environmental (NM)
NEFF, Judy C. (Technl Libn) 892

Lovelace Medical Foundation (NM)
STRUB, Jeane E. (Med Libn) . . 1203

Lovenburg Lib Consultation (AB)
LOVENBURG, Susan L. (Freelance Lib Consult) 743

Low Country Area Health Education Center (SC)
DAVIS, Patsy M. (Hlth Scis Lib Dir) 280

Lowell General Hospital (MA)
BEDARD, Martha A. (Hlth Scis Lib Dir) 73

Lower Columbia Coll (WA)
BAKER, Robert K. (Asst Dean) . . . 49
RYAN, Patricia M. (Dir of Libs) . 1071

Lower Merion Lib Assn (PA)

Lower Merion Township Lib Association (PA)
SORET, Judith E. (Libn) 1168

Lower Naugatuck Valley Comunty Hlth Ctr (CT)
MARTIN, Walter F. (Clerical Asst) 779

Loyola Academy (IL)
REIF, Lenore S. (Resrc Ctr Dir) . 1019

Loyola-Blakefield Lib (MD)
RUSSELL, Rose M. (Libn) 1069

Loyola Coll (MD)
VARGA, Nicholas (Coll Archvst) 1278

Loyola Law Sch (CA)
HUFF-DUFF, Barbara (Acqs Libn) 570
SZEGEDI, Laszlo (Head Catlg Libn) 1218
WONG, Cecilia (Serials Libn) . . 1362

Loyola Marymount Univ (CA)
EVANS, G E. (Univ Libn) 357
SCHMIDT, Ford C. (Asst Ref Libn) 1095

Loyola-Notre Dame Lib (MD)
DAVISH, William (Ref Libn) 281
FRYER, Philip (AV Libn) 407
RAY, John G. (Asst Dir) 1011
TURKOS, Joseph A. (Acqs Libn) 1263

Loyola Univ of Chicago (IL)
BENNETT, Lee L. (Acq Libn) 82
DELANA, Genevieve A. (Lewis Towers Lib Dir) 288
DOYLE, Francis R. (Law Lib Dir & Prof of Law) 317
FRY, Roy H. (Govt Docums Libn) 406
FULTON, Tara L. (Ref Instrc Libn) 409
GIANGRANDE, Mark G. (Comp & Ref Libn) 430
HOLZENBERG, Eric J. (Rare Bk Catlgr) 555
KLINK, Carol A. (Acqs Libn) 662
LEWIS, Sherman L. (Ref Libn) . . 724
LUDWIG, Logan T. (Med Ctr Lib Dir) 747
MCCOY, Patricia S. (Catlgr, Soc Sci Biblgphr) 799
NEWMAN, Gerald L. (Head of Ref Dept) 899
NEWMAN, Lorna R. (Interlib Loan Libn) 899
NUTTY, David J. (AV Srvs Libn) . 912
RANDALL, Sara L. (Systs Libn) 1006
STALZER, Rita M. (Ref Libn, Biblgphr) 1179
SVED, Alexander (Head Catlgr) . 1212
WAITE, Ellen J. (Dir of Univ Libs) 1293
WARRO, Edward A. (Asst Dir, Automation & Technl Srvs) . . 1307
WICKREMERATNE, Swarna (Catlgr) 1335

Loyola Univ of New Orleans (LA)
BLAKE, Timothy J. (Ref Libn & Asst Prof) 103
DANKNER, Laura R. (Assoc Prof & Music Libn) 273
KELLY, Judy M. (Govt Docums) . 638
MCKNIGHT, Mark C. (Music & AV Catlg Libn) 812
MCREYNOLDS, Rosalee (Serials Libn) 818
RUSHING, Darla H. (Head of Catlgng) 1068
SNOW, Maxine L. (Ref Srvs Head) 1164
SWEAT, Mary L. (Univ Libn) . . . 1214

LRP Publications and Axon Group Co (PA)
LOCKETT, Cheryl L. (Index Devlpmnt Managing Edit) 736

LSI (NY)
PISCITELLI, Rosalie A. (Info Srvs Chief) 976

LSI (TX)
JOHNSON, Pat M. (VP) 608

LTV Steel Co (OH)
WOOLARD, Kathryn A. (Technl Libn) 1368

Lubbock City County Lib (TX) HARP, Marlene M. (Pub Srvs Dir) 503
Lucasfild Ltd (CA) FINE, Deborah J. (Resrch Dir) . . . 377
Lucius Beebe Memorial Lib (MA) MUNDY, Suzanne W. (Yng Adult Libn) 879
Ludlow Board of Education (KY) REESE, Virginia D. (Media Libn) 1016
Lueders Robertson & Konzen (IL) KONZEN, Brian E. (Trustee) . . . 671
Lukins & Annis (WA) WADDEN, Emily E. (Law Libn) . 1290
Lumberton Independent Sch District (TX) POOL, Jeraldine B. (Middle Sch Libn) 982
Lummus Crest Inc (NJ) CIARAMELLA, Mary A. (Chief Libn) 214
Lurie Sklar & Simon Ltd (IL) MABANAG, Teresita R. (Law Libn) 753
Luther Coll (IA) FENSTERMANN, Duane W. (Assoc Libn & Head of Technl Srvs) 371
KEMP, Henrietta J. (Circ & Ref Libn) 639
Luther Northwestern Theological Seminary (MN) OLSON, Carol A. (Acquisitions Libn) 922
OLSON, Ray A. (Ref Libn) 923
WENTE, Norman G. (Chief Libn) 1324
Lutheran Church in America (IL) WITTMAN, Elisabeth C. (Assoc Archvst) 1358
Lutheran Church Lib Asssociation (MN) JENSEN, Wilma M. (Exec Dir) . . 599
The Lutheran Church Missouri Synod (MO) SUELFLOW, August R. (Dir) . . . 1206
Lutheran Council in the USA (NY) KENDRICK, Alice M. (Dir, Records & Info Ctr) 640
Lutheran Family & Childrens Services (MO) STIEGEMEYER, Nancy H. (Pub Relations & Devlpmnt Coordntr) 1193
Lutheran General Hospital (IL) BLACKBURN, Joy M. (Systs Libn) 102
CRISPEN, Joanne (Lib & Resrch Admin Dir) 259
Lutheran High Sch East (MI) FRITZ, Donald D. (Libn) 405
Lutheran High Sch of Kansas City (MO) BOETTCHER, Joel W. (Libn & Tchr) 110
Lutheran Hospital (IN) AVEN, Lauralee (Lib Mgr) 41
Lutheran Theological Seminary at Phila (PA) WARTLUFT, David J. (Lib Dir & Faculty Secy) 1307
Lutheran Theological Southern Seminary (SC) DERRICK, Mitzi J. (Asst Libn) . . . 294
Luzerne Intermediate Unit 18 (PA) FARRIS, Loretta (Dir of Lib Media Examination Ctr) 365
Lynchburg Coll (VA) SCUDDER, Mary C. (Lib Dir) . . 1108
Lynchburg General Hospital (VA) STURGIS, Sibyl A. (Hlth Scis Libn) 1205
Lynchburg Pub Schs (VA) YOUNGER, Melinda M. (Media Libn) 1383
Lyndhurst Hospital (ON) CHONG, Jean L. (Libn) 210
Lyndhurst Pub Lib (NJ) BAYLESS, Bernie J. (Asst Libn) . . 67
PORTUGAL, Rhoda (Lib Dir) . . . 985
Lyndon Baines Johnson Foundation (TX) REED, Lawrence D. (Exec Dir) . 1015
Lyndon Baines Johnson Lib (TX) FRANKUM, Katherine H. (Libn & Biblgphr) 398
Lyons Pub Lib (KS) CRANE, Gerri G. (Lib Dir) 255
Lyster Hospital (AL) PROTTSMAN, Mary F. (Med Libn) 995

M

M/A-Com Government Systems (CA) ROSS, Mary A. (Libn) 1058
M & T Chemicals Inc (NJ) ESKA, Dorothy I. (Technl Indexing Supvsr) 354
TORRE, Louis P. 1251
M D Anderson Hospital (TX) JACKSON, Sara J. (Lib Dir) 588
M R Airey & Associates (ME) AIREY, Martha R. (Pres & Owner) 9
Mac Farlane & Co Inc (GA) GASKINS, Stephen D. (Consult) . 421

Macalester Coll (MN) CLEMMER, Joel G. (Dir) 221
FISHEL, Teresa A. (Head of Ref) 380
MacFarlane Ferguson Allison & Kelly (FL) GIBBS, Rosalyn D. (Firm Libn) . . 431
Machinery & Allied Products Institute (DC) DUFFY, Brenda F. (Resrch Asst) 324
MacKenzie Memorial Pub Lib (OH) JOHNSON, Ruth E. (Dir) 608
Maclean Hunter Limited (ON) OLSHEN, Toni (Client Srvs Mgr) . 922
Maclean Hunter Media (CT) PALMER, Shirley (Resrch Libn) . . 937
Maclean's Magazine (ON) GRANT, Roberta L. (Chief Libn) . 458
Macmillan Publishing Co (NY) BERNAL, Rose M. (Index Dept Supvsr) 88
HOWELL, Josephine T. (Bus Info Resrcs Mgr) 565
MCELDERRY, Margaret K. (Vice Pres & Publshr) 804
WHIPPLE, Judith R. (VP & Publshr) 1329
MacNeal Hospital (IL) BEN-SHIR, Rya H. (Hlth Sci Resrcs Ctr Mgr) 83
FEDECZKO, Joyce L. (Asst Libn) 367
Macomb Community Coll (MI) DOYLE, James M. (Pub Srv Libn) 317
GAURI, Kul B. (Dir of Acad Srvs) 423
LUFT, William (Head of Col Devlpmnt Div) 747
Macomb County Lib (MI) PALMER, Richard J. (Head Libn) 936
Macomb Intermediate Sch District (MI) WILKINSON, Eoin H. (Univ Libn) 1340
Macquarie Univ (AUS) BRUMIT, Nancy T. (Libn & Media Spclst) 150
Mad River Township Local Schs (OH) MYERS, Martha O. (Libn) 884
Madeira Sch (VA) JEFFCOTT, Janet B. (Info Resrc Ctr Syst Dir) 596
Madison Area Technical Coll (WI) POVILAITIS, Leanna J. (Supervising Libn) 987
Madison Borough Pub Lib (NJ) WILLIAMS, Patricia F. (Lib Media Spclst) 1346
Madison County Board of Education (AL) YERMAN, Roslyn F. (Head Ref Libn) 1380
Madison Heights Pub Lib (MI) BABBITT, Dennis L. (Dir) 43
WILLIS, Ione P. (Head, Technl Srvs) 1348
Madison-Jefferson County Pub Lib (IN) NELSON, Kathy J. (Educ & Med Lib Dir) 894
Madison Memorial Hospital (ID) BACH, Nancy C. (IMC Dir) 43
Madison Metropolitan Sch District (WI) DRESANG, Eliza T. (Media, Info & Comm Mgr) 319
KEMPF, Arlys L. (Lib Media Spclst) 639
PARFREY, Hilda W. (Info Media Ctr Dir) 940
SCHULTZ, Cathern J. (Media Spclst) 1101
Madison Pub Lib (IL) KERN, Frances L. (Lib Dir) 643
Madison Pub Lib (WI) ABLEIDINGER, Rose A. (Chlds Libn) 2
BRAGER, Beverly J. (Supvsr) . . . 127
HAWLEY, Joann C. (Branch Coordntr, Spcl Proj Coordntr) . 514
NIEMI, Peter G. (Dir) 903
Madison Sch Dist 321 (ID) COVINGTON, Eddis E. (Media Dir) 252
Madonna Coll (MI) BERRY, Charlene (Catlg Libn) 90
MLODZIANOWSKI, Mary L. (Lib Dir) 850
VINT, Patricia A. (Instrc Ctr Dir) 1285
Magee Rehabilitation Hospital (PA) COUCH, Susan H. (Lib Srvs Dir) 250
Magna International Inc (ON) JACKSON, Agnes M. (Libn & Resrchr) 586

Magnes Museum (CA)   LEVY, Jane (Libn) 721
The Magus Bookstore (WA)   AUSTIN, Kristi N. (Mgr) 40
Maharishi International Univ (IA)   SHAW, Craig S. (Adminstr) 1123
Maimonides Hospital Geriatric
   Centre (PQ)   BRESING, Sheindel H. (Libn) . . . 133
Maimonides Medical Center (NY)   FRIEDMAN, Lydia (Chief Med
      Libn) 404
Maine Department of Educ &
   Cultural Srvs (ME)   TARANKO, Walter J. (Media
      Coordntr) 1223
Maine Sch Administrative District
   74 (ME)   LYONS, Dean E. (Head Libn) . . . 753
Maine Sch Administrative District
   75 (ME)   BERRIE, Ellen T. (Lib Media
      Spclst) 90
Maine State Archives (ME)   SILSBY, Samuel S. (State
      Archvst) 1138
Maine State Lib (ME)   BEISER, Karl A. (State Lib
      Automation Proj Dir) 75
   BOYNTON, John W. (Dir of Lib
      Devlpmnt) 124
   NICHOLS, J G. (State Libn) . . . 901
   WISMER, Donald (Dir of Ref
      and Info Srvs Div) 1357
Mainstream Data (UT)   BENNION, John F. (VP of Mktg
      & Sales) 82
Malaspina Coll (BC)   BRIDGES, Douglas W. (Dir,
      Lrng Resrcs Ctr) 135
Malcahy & Wherry S C (WI)   LINTNER, Mary K. 731
Malcolm X Coll (IL)   PARK, Chung I. (Ref Libn) 940
Malden Hospital (MA)   O'BRIEN, Elizabeth J. (Med
      Libn) 914
Malone Coll (OH)   ANDERSON, Janice L. (Ref
      Libn) 23
   TERHUNE, R S. (Lib Srvs Dir) . 1231
   WHITEHEAD, Beatrice A.
      (Catlgr) 1332
Mamie Doud Eisenhower Birthplace
   Fndtn (IA)   ADAMS, Larry D. (Cur) 5
Manatee Community Coll (FL)   CARR, Mary L. (Pub Srvs Libn) . 186
Manatee County Pub Lib System (FL)   O'CONNOR-LEVY, Linda L.
      (Asst Dir) 916
   PATTISON, Joanne (Supvsr of
      Chlds Srvs) 948
   PLACE, Philip A. (Dir) 977
   TAYLOR, Rose M. (Libn I) 1228
Manatee County Sch Board (FL)   HUNT, Susan O. (Sch Lib &
      Media Spclst) 576
   SHAMP, Mary J. (Media Spclst) 1120
Manatee Memorial Hospital (FL)   MOSHER, Jeanette M. (Med
      Libn) 871
Manchester Coll (IN)   STEPHENSON, Doris F.
      (Catlgng Libn) 1188
Manchester Community Coll (CT)   NATALE, Barbara G. (Pub Srvs
      Libn III) 889
Manchester Historic Association (NH)   LESSARD, Elizabeth B. (Libn) . . . 718
Manchester Memorial Hospital (CT)   GLUCK, Jeannine C. (Med Libn) . 442
Manhattan Coll (NY)   BARRY, Richard A. (Engrng
      Libn) 60
   DOWD, Philip M. (Rare Books
      Cur) 315
   O'DONNELL, Mary A. (Assoc
      Prof of Engl & World Lit) 917
   WELSH, Harry E. (Libs Dir) 1323
Manhattan Comunty Coll, City Univ
   of NY (NY)   LOWRY, Lina M. (Chief Libn) . . . 745
Manhattan Eye Ear & Throat
   Hospital (NY)   WOFSE, Joy G. (Lib Srvs Dir) . . 1359
Manhattan High Sch (KS)   WHITSON, Joyce G. (Lib Media
      Spclst) 1334
Manhattan Pub Lib (KS)   ATCHISON, Fres D. (Head of
      Pub Srvs) 37
Manhattan Punch Line Theatre (NY)   BOWLEY, Craig (Exec Dir) 121
Manhattan Sch of Music (NY)   BRISTAH, Pamela J. (Catlgr) . . . 137
   HOFFMAN, Christine A. (Libn) . . 547
Manhattanville Coll (NY)   NICKERSON, Donna L. (Assoc
      Prof and Lib Catlgr) 902
   RAY, Donald L. (Biogph Srvs
      Libn) 1011

Manitoba Attorney-General (MB)   HERNANDEZ, Marilyn J. (Mgr
      of Legal Lib Resrcs) 531
Manitoba Education (MB)   TRAILL, Susan (Sch Lib
      Consult) 1253
Manitoba Legislative Lib (MB)   IRVINE, Joyce (Legislative Libn) . 584
Manitoba Research Council (MB)   WILTON, Greg J. (Info Srvs
      Mgr) 1353
Manitowoc Pub Lib (WI)   BENDIX, Linda A. (Ref Libn) 79
   OHLEMACHER, Janet H. (Pub
      Relations Supvsr) 919
   SINGH, Rosemary A. (Ref &
      Adult Srvs) 1143
Mankato State Univ (MN)   ALLAN, David W. (Media
      Spclst) 14
   BIRMINGHAM, Frank R. (Chair
      of Lib Media Educ) 98
   CARRISON, Dale K. (Dir of Proj
      for Automated Lib Systs) 187
   FARNER, Susan G. (Circ Syst
      Quality Ctl Grad Asst) 365
   HITT, Charles J. (Instrc Libn) . . . 544
   MCDONALD, Frances B.
      (Assoc Prof) 802
   MOORE, Barbara N. (Systs
      Libn) 858
   PEISCHL, Thomas P. (Dean of
      the Lib) 955
   PIEHL, Kathleen K. (Educ & Ref
      Libn) 971
   READY, Sandra K. (Asst Dean
      of the Lib) 1012
   SCHWARTZKOPF, Rebecca B.
      (Perdcl & Map Libn) 1105
   SUYEMATSU, Kiyo (Music Libn
      and Tchr) 1212
Manlius Lib (NY)   FERGUSON, Jane M. (Adult
      Srvs, Ref, AV Libn) 372
Mannes Coll of Music (NY)   DAVIS, Deborah G. (Head Libn) . 278
   VAN BIEMA, Mary E. (Catlgr) . . 1272
Mansfield General Hospital (OH)   BENISHEK, Kristine K. (Lib Dir) . . . 81
Mansfield-Richland County Pub
   Lib (OH)   GARRETT, Melinda R. (Head,
      AV and Spcl Srvs) 420
   KIECZYKOWSKI, Edward M.
      (Dir) 647
Mansfield Univ (PA)   DOWLING, John (Prof of
      Physics) 316
   NESBIT, Larry L. (Dir of Lib Srv
      & Instrcl Resrcs) 896
   SEABORN, Frances L. (Educ
      Libn) 1109
   RAUM, Tamar (Law Libn) 1010
Manufacturers Hanover (NY)   CITROEN, Julie M. (Head Libn) . 215
Manufacturers Life Insurance
   Co (ON)   CHANDLER, Constance P.
Manville Corp (CO)   (Libn) 199
Maple Grove Junior-Senior High
   Sch (NY)   BJORKQUIST, Donna M. (High
      Sch Libn) 100
Maplewood Memorial Lib (NJ)   BENNETT, Rowland F. (Lib Dir) . . 82
Marakon Associates (CA)   GARDISER, Kathleen E.
      (Resrch Srvs Mgr) 417
Maranacook Community Schs (ME)   BAYLISS, Edna M. (Media
      Spclst) 67
Marathon County Pub Lib (WI)   PETERSON, Diane S. (Libn I) . . . 963
Marathon Oil Co (CO)   GREALY, Deborah J. (Assoc
      Technl Libn) 461
   STURDIVANT, Clarence A.
      (Technl Info Supvsr) 1205
Marathon Oil Co (OH)   WHIPPLE, Connie S. (Law Libn) 1329
Marathon Oil Co (TX)   DICKERSON, Mary J. (Assoc
      Technl Info Spclst) 300
   GILBERT, Barry (Law Libn) 433
Marathon Software & Services
   Inc (NJ)   SKROBELA, Katherine C. (Sr
      Consult) 1147
Marblehead Pub Schs (MA)   EHRICH, Joan C. (Lib Media
      Spclst) 339
MARC Inc (TX)   COMPTON, Erlinda R. (Mgr,
      Info Srvs) 235

Marcellus Community Schools (MI)	TATE, Carole A. (Libn) 1225	Mars Hill Coll (NC)	CADLE, Dean (Spcl Cols Libn) . . 170
Mare Island Naval Shipyard (CA)	WONG, Carol Y. (Physical Sci & Engrng Libn) 1362		PETERSON, Cynthia L. (Instrcl Srvs Libn) 963
Marian Coll (IN)	STUSSY, Susan A. (Head Libn) 1205	Marsh & McLennan Inc (NY)	AARON, Rina S. (Libn) 1
Marian Court Junior Coll (MA)	LINDSAY, Mary A. (Chief Libn) . . 729		COOK, Pamela D. (Asst Mgr, Asst Vice Pres) 240
Marian Health Center (IA)	PHILLIPS, Donna M. (Head Libn) 968		KUCSMA, Susan P. (Mgr) 682
Marian High Sch (IN)	BIANCHINO, Cecelia (Libn) 94	Marshall Cavendish Corp (NY)	GOSDEN, George (Vice Pres) . . 452
Maricopa County Community Coll System (AZ)		Marshall Law Lib (MD)	GROSSHANS, Maxine Z. (Asst Libn Info Srvs) 473
	ALLEN, Stephanie O. (Acqs & Catlgng Proj Team) 16	Marshall/Plumb Research Associates (CA)	
	DAANE, Jeanette K. (Eductnl Srvs Libn) 269		PLUMB, Carolyn G. (Legal Resrchr & Partner) 978
	MILLER, Larry A. (Head Libn) . . . 839	Marshall Univ (WV)	DZIERZAK, Edward M. (Hlth Scis Libs Dir) 331
	THEILMANN, James W. (Dir of Lib Srvs) 1234		FIDLER, Leah J. (Technl Srvs Libn, Libn IV) 375
Maricopa County Law Lib (AZ)	MEERIANS, Patti L. (Acqs Libn) . 821		REENSTJERNA, Frederick R. (Asst Housing Mgr) 1016
Maricopa County Superior Court (AZ)	SCHNEIDER, Elizabeth K. (Dir) . 1097		
Marietta City Schs (GA)	KILPATRICK, Marguerite C. (Media Spclst) 648	Marshalltown Area Education Agency 6 (IA)	TRAVILLIAN, Mary W. (Media Srvs Dir) 1254
	STAVROLAKIS, Rachel G. (Lib Media Spclst) 1183	Marshalltown Community Schs (IA)	BURGESS, Barbara J. (Elem Media Spclst) 159
Marietta Coll (OH)	NEYMAN, Sandra B. (Readers Srvs Head) 900	Marshfield Clinic (WI)	ZIMMERMANN, Albert J. (Med Libn & Edit) 1389
Marietta Memorial Hospital (OH)	KERBOW, Sandra C. (Med Libn) 643	Marshfield Pub Lib (WI)	BRANDEL, Pamela A. (Supvsr of Info of Adult Srvs) 128
Marigold Lib System (AB)	LUNN, Rowena F. (Coordntr of Lib Srvs) 749	Martin & Martin Info Consultants Inc (TX)	MARTIN, Jean K. (Vice Pres) . . 776
Marin County Free Lib (CA)	EMERY, Frances D. (Ref Libn) . . 348	Martin County Pub Lib (FL)	HENNINGS, Leroy (Dir) 528
	HAMMER, Sharon A. (Cnty Libn) 493	Martin Marietta (MD)	CARR, Margaret M. (Bus Info Ctr Mgr) 186
	LAPERRIERE, Renee J. (Libn I) . 697		CHESLOCK, Rosalind P. (Technl Info Srvs Mgr) 207
	ZALE, Phyllis J. (Ref Libn) 1385		FELDMAN, Eleanor C. (Info Spclst) 369
Marine Technology Society (VA)	MATON, Joanne T. (Consult) . . . 784		MORRIS, Sharon D. (Assoc Info Spclst) 867
Mariners' Museum (VA)	CREW, Roger T. (Archvst) 258		RICHTER, Mary L. (Lib Srvs Supvsr) 1031
	KELLY, Ardie L. (Libn) 637		SCHWARTZ, Betsy J. (Info Systs Spclst) 1104
Marion Coll (IN)	BOYCE, Harold W. (Lib Srvs Dir) 122	Martin Marietta Aerospace (CO)	REITER, Ellie W. (Ref Libn) 1022
Marion County Lib (SC)	MCAULAY, Louise S. (Lib Dir) . . 792	Martin Marietta Data Systems (CA)	FRIEDMAN, Sandra M. (Sr Pubns Spclst & Technl Libn) . . 404
Marion County Pub Lib System (IN)	BADERTSCHER, Kimberlin H. (Chlds Libn) 44	Martin Marietta Energy Systems (TN)	ALEXANDER, Mary B. (Ref Libn) 12
	COHEN, Karen S. (Ref Libn) . . . 228		DELKER, Kathy M. 289
	TIMKO, Patricia A. (Chlds Libn) . 1246		EKKEBUS, Allen E. (Centl Resrch Lib Head) 341
Marion Pub Lib (OH)	GERWIN, Barbara L. (Ref, Adult Srvs Libn) 430		GOVE, N B. (Comp Consult) 454
Maritime Resource Management Service Inc (NS)	CAMPBELL, Margaret E. (Libn) . . 177		NORTON, Nancy P. (Mgr of Info Srvs) 910
Maritime Telephone & Telegraph (NS)	BANFIELD, Eilzabeth S. (Libn) . . . 54		ROBBINS, Gordon D. (Mgr of Info Resrcs) 1038
Maritz Inc (MO)	DEKEN, Jean M. (Mgr of Lib Srvs) 288		SNYDER, Cathrine E. (Resrch Assoc) 1164
Mark Mitchell Associates (NH)	MITCHELL, Mark B. (Proprietor) . 849		STRICKLER, Candice S. (Technl Libn II) 1202
Mark Producing Inc (TX)	AULBACH, Louis F. (Supvsr Info & Records Mgmt) 39		VEACH, Lynn H. (Head, Bio Lib) 1280
Market New Service Inc (CA)	MURPHY, Robert (Pres) 881	Martin Memorial Lib (PA)	FUNK, Ann L. (Film Coordntr) . . . 409
Market Opinion Research (MI)	KELLEY, Barbara C. (Libn) 636	Martindale-Hubbell Inc (NJ)	PECON, Sally N. (Adminstrv Asst & Corprt Libn) 953
Marketing Intelligence Service (NY)	BROOK, Rick 140	Martineau & Walker (PQ)	AMNOTTE, Celine (Documentalist) 20
Markon Inc (VA)	KUHL, Danuta (Libn) 682	Martins Ferry Pub Lib (OH)	STORCK, John W. (Dir) 1198
Markscope Inc (NY)	ETZI, Richard (Pres) 356	Martinsburg Lib Commission (WV)	BEALL, C E. (Chairman) 68
Marlboro Central Sch District (NY)	BAKER, Marie A. (Lib Media Spclst) 49	Martinus Nijhoff International (MA)	JAGER, Conradus (N Amer Area Mgr) 591
Marlborough Pub Lib (MA)	GIULIANO, Lillian C. (Dir) 439	Maruzen Co Ltd (JAP)	YAMANAKA, Tai (Asst Mgr of Plng) 1377
MARLF (DE)	HUKILL, Jane E. (Pres) 572	Marvin Memorial Lib (OH)	BAVIN, Ann L. (Chlds Libn) 67
The Marquardt Company (CA)	LEE, Lydia H. (Supvsr, Lib) 710		WOOD, Ann F. (Dir) 1363
Marquette Univ (WI)	GARDNER, William M. (Libs Dir) 418	Mary Bird Perkins Cancer Center (LA)	BLOOMSTONE, Ajaye (Libn) . . . 106
	GILL, Norman N. (McBeath Sr Resrch Scholar) 435	Mary C Chobot and Associates (VA)	CHOBOT, Mary C. (Pres) 210
	HOPWOOD, Susan H. (Ref & Info Srvs Coordntr) 558	Mary Gaither Marshall Rare Book Consult (IL)	
	POLLARD, Margaret E. (Preservation Libn) 981		MARSHALL, Mary G. (Self-employed Consult) 774
	RUNKEL, Phillip M. (Asst Archvst) 1067		
	THIEL, Mark G. (Asst Archvst) . 1235		
Married Mettle Press (NJ)	ALTERMAN, Deborah H. (Proprietor) 18		
Mars & Co (CT)	ST. GEORGE, Susan M. (Resrch Libn) 1075		

Mary Immaculate Seminary (PA) KOKOLUS, Cait C. (Dir of the Lib) 669

Mary Lou Johnson-Hardin County Dist Lib (OH) PETTY, Sue W. (Dir) 965

Mary S Senn & Associates (IL) SENN, Mary S. 1115

Mary Washington Coll (VA) ANDERSON, Kari D. (Ref Libn) . . 24

MULVANEY, John P. (Col Devlpmnt Libn) 878

STROHL, Leroy S. (Lib Dir) . . . 1202

Mary Washington Hospital (VA) BULLEY, Joan S. (Lib Dir) 156

Maryknoll Sch of Theology (NY) O'HALLORAN, James V. (Assoc Libn) 918

Maryland Coll of Art & Design (MD) PRATT, Laura C. (Head Libn) . . . 990

Maryland Dept of Health & Mental Health (MD) MUNSEY, Joyce E. (Assoc Libn) 879

Maryland Dept of Legislative Reference (MD) CARMAN, Carol A. (Legislative Libn) 183

Maryland Dept of State Planning Lib (MD) JENG, Helene W. (Libn) 596

Maryland Historical Society (MD) SILVER, Marcy L. (Prints & Photographs Libn) 1138

STUART, Karen A. (Lib Dir) . . . 1204

Maryland Lib Association (MD) GREENFIELD, Robert E. (Exec Secy) 464

MD Software (WY) SCHELL, Catherine L. (Info Consult) 1091

Maryland State Archives (MD) PRIMER, Ben (Ref Srvs Assoc Dir) 993

THAPAR, Shashi P. (Libn) 1234

Maryland State Department of Education (MD) BOLIN, Nancy C. (Comunty Srvs Consultant) 112

HILDEBRANDT, Irene (Sch Lib Media Srvs) 539

MONTGOMERY, Paula K. (Chief of Sch Lib Media Srvs) 856

PARTRIDGE, James C. (Spclst, Comunty Srvs) 945

STEPHAN, Sandra S. (Staff Devlpmnt & Contng Educ Spclst) 1187

TAYLOR, Nettie B. (Asst State Supvsr for Libs) 1228

WILLIAMS, J L. (Sch Lib Media Srvs/Educ Tech Spclst) 1343

Maryland State Lib (MD) SZCZCPANIAK, Adam S. (Assoc Libn) 1218

Maryland State Lib for the Blind (MD) FINNEY, Lance C. (Dir) 379

Marymount Coll (KS) WHITE, George R. (Dir of Lib Srvs) 1331

Marymount High Sch (CA) TUOHY, Eileen M. (Head Libn) . 1263

Marymount Junior Sch (VA) PYKE, Carol J. (Libn) 999

Marymount Univ (VA) CARR, Timothy B. (Ref Libn) . . . 186

LEATHER, Deborah J. (Lib & Lrng Srvs Dean) 707

Maryvale Sch District (NY) SZEMRAJ, Edward R. (Lib & Media Coordntr) 1218

Maryville Coll (MO) MCKEE, Eugenia V. (Head of Technl Srvs) 810

Maryville Coll (TN) WORLEY, Joan H. (Dir) 1369

Marywood Coll (PA) FEDRICK, Mary A. (Dir of the Lib) 368

MILLER, Mary E. (Prof) 840

SPEIRS, Gilmary (Comms Libn) 1172

Mascoutah Sch District 19 (IL) SCHAACK, Wilma J. (High Sch Media Spclst) 1088

Mason City Community Schs (IA) CHAPMAN-SIMPSON, Alisa M. (Media Spclst) 202

Mason County Board of Education (WV) WILLIAMSON, Judy D. (Libn) . . 1347

Mason-McDuffie Real Estate Inc (CA) DOWNEY, Lynn A. (Archvst) . . . 316

Massachusetts Archives at Columbia Point (MA) WHITAKER, Albert H. (Archvst) 1329

Massachusetts Audubon Society (MA) COHEN, Martha J. (Environmental libn) 228

Massachusetts Bay Community Coll (MA)

Massachusetts Board of Lib Commissioners (MA)

Massachusetts Coll of Art (MA)

Massachusetts Coll of Pharmacy (MA)

Massachusetts Department of Pub Health (MA)

Massachusetts Dept of the Attorney Gen (MA)

Massachusetts Eye & Ear Infirmary (MA)

Massachusetts Financial Service Center (MA)

Massachusetts General Hospital (MA)

Massachusetts Horticultural Society (MA)

Massachusetts Institute of Technology (MA)

Massachusetts Lib Association (MA) BOZOIAN, Paula (Exec Secy) . . . 124

Massachusetts Maritime Academy (MA) RESSMEYER, Ellen H. (Asst Libn) 1024

MA Municipal Wholestate Electric Co (MA) MACDONALD, Wayne D. (Docum Control Technician) . . 754

Massachusetts Mutual Life Insurance Co (MA) CLOUGH, Linda F. (Law Libn) . . . 223

Massachusetts Rehabilitation Commission (MA) HOLT, June C. (Lib Dir) 554

Massachusetts Sch of Professional Psy (MA) WHELAN, Julia S. (Libn) 1329

Massachusetts State Lib (MA) DONG, Tina (Pub Srvs Libn) 311

Massachusetts State Transportation Lib (MA) PEARLSTEIN, Toby (Chief Libn & Archvst) 952

SHERER, Elaine R. (Resrch Libn) 1127

DUGAN, Robert E. (Lib Plng & Devlpmnt Head) 324

LEVITT, Irene S. (Head of Admin & Support Srvs) 721

SHANNON, Marcia A. (Spcl Projs Consult) 1120

HOPKINS, Benjamin (Lib Dir) . . . 557

HILL, Barbara M. (Libn) 539

MOORE, Catherine I. (Libn) 859

MATZ, Ruth G. (Chief Libn) 786

NIMS, Judith C. (Lib Dir) 904

MCGEE, Ruby T. (Info & Docums Spclst) 805

BUTTON, Katherine H. (Comp Srch Analyst) 167

LEIGHTON, Helene A. (Asst Dir, Head of Comp Srch Ctr) 714

SCHNEIDER, Elizabeth 1097

SCULLIN, Janice J. (Libn for Serials Control) 1109

WESTLING, Ellen R. (Info Srvs Asst Dir) 1327

NESS, Pamela M. (Technl Srvs Libn) 896

BAKER, Shirley K. (Assoc Pub Srvs Dir) 49

BELLO, Susan E. (Asst Acqs Libn) 78

BIRD, Nora J. (Asst Sci Libn for Chem) 98

BJORNER, Susan N. (Info Spclst) 100

CONNELLY, Ramona S. (Tech Pubns Catlgr) 237

DAVY, Edgar W. (Head Libn) . . . 281

GREEN, Kathleen A. (Asst Libn & Rev Srvs Coordntr) 462

GREENBERG, Carolyn R. (Systs Libn) 463

GREENE, Cathy C. (Physical Scis Libn) 463

JACKSON, Arlyne A. (Assoc Libn & Cols Mgr) 586

KNAACK, Linda M. (Libn) 663

LUCKER, Jay K. (Dir of Libs) . . . 746

MARCUS, Richard S. (Principal Resrch Scitst) 769

MCDOWELL, Sylvia A. (Adminstrv Libn) 804

WEBBER, Donna E. (Assoc Archvst & Records Mgt) 1313

Massachusetts Trial Court (MA)
FLYNN, Kathleen M. (Law Libn) . 386
KANE, Lois B. (Dept Libn) 625

MA Vocational Curriculum Research Center (MA)
DAY, Virginia M. (Libn) 283

Massachusetts Water Resource Authority (MA)
LYDON, Mary E. (Libn) 751

Massao County Medical Center (NY)
MERRIGAN, Paul G. (Lib Dir) . . . 826

Massapequa Pub Schs (NY)
SPIEGEL, Bertha (Sch Lib Media Spclst) 1174

Massillon Pub Lib (OH)
LESLIE, Camille J. (Adminstr) . . 718

Masters Coll & Seminary (CA)
VOTAW, Floyd M. (Dir of Lib Srvs) 1289

Mastics-Moriches-Shirley Community Lib (NY)
VERBESEY, J R. (Dir) 1282

Matanuska-Susitna Community Coll (AK)
COLSON, Marcia B. (Comunty Coll Libn) 234

Maude Shunk Lib (WI)
BAKULA, Patricia A. (Youth Libn) 50

Maupin Taylor Ellis & Adams PA (NC)
LAMBE, Catherine V. (Libn) 690

Maurice M Pine Free Pub Lib (NJ)
NEDSWICK, Robert (Yng Adult Libn) 891

Max Robinson Institute (OR)
EMMENS, Thomas A. (Dir) 348

Maxima Corp (DC)
DEARNBARGER, Dennis (Catlgr & Interlib Loan Coordntr) 284

Maxima Corp (TN)
CLELAND, Nancy D. (Resrch Spclst Info Prcsng) 220

Mayers & Associates (MI)
MAYERS, Henry L. (Owner) 789

Mayfield City Sch District (OH)
GILLMORE, Salley G. (Head Libn) 436

Mayo Clinic (MN)
CARON, Theodore F. (Chief Catlgr) 184
ERWIN, Patricia J. (Head, Ref Libn) 353
GINN, Marjorie J. (Acqs Lib) 437
HAWTHORNE, Dorothy M. (Ref Libn) 514
KEY, Jack D. (Libn) 645
KOPPER, John A. (Technl Prcsng Srvs Supvsr & Libn) . . 671
PALMER, Joy J. (Catlgng Libn) . . 936
SANDE, Alice E. (Spcl Projs Coordntr) 1079

Mays & Valentine (VA)
WARD, Brenda H. (Libn) 1303

Maytag Aircraft Corp (FL)
GOODIER, Darlene P. (Lib Mgr) . 448

Mayville District Pub Lib (MI)
GARNSEY, Alice M. (Lib Dir) . . . 419

Mayville State Univ (ND)
KARAIM, Betty J. (Lib Srvs Dir) . 627

McAdams Planning Consultants Inc (TX)
MCADAMS, Nancy R. (Pres) . . . 792

McAlester Pub Schs (OK)
WRIGHT, Carolyn R. (Lib Media Spclst) 1370

McAllen Memorial Lib (TX)
MITTELSTAEDT, Gerard E. (Lib Dir) 850

McCallie Sch (TN)
REARDON, Elizabeth M. (Head Libn) 1013

McCamish Ingram Martin & Brown PC (TX)
HURT, Nancy S. (Dir, Info Srvs) . 578

McClelland Engineers Inc (TX)
ALIMOHAMMAD, Habiba (Libn) . . 13

McCollister McCleary & Fazio (LA)
TOWLES, Anne S. (Law Libn) . 1252

McConnell Air Force Base (KS)
DOMBOURIAN MOORE, Ann (Base Libn) 310

McCook Community Coll (NE)
RUBY, Irple P. (Lib Dir) 1065

McCord Memorial Lib (PA)
TRIPP, Audrey J. (Dir) 1257

McCormick & Co Inc (MD)
RILEY, Sarah A. (Info Scitst & Systs Analyst) 1035

McCormick Middle Sch (SC)
TOWNSEND, Catherine M. (Media Spclst) 1253

McCutchen Black Verleger & Shea (CA)
ANNAND, Stewart S. (Libn) 28

McDermott Will & Emery (IL)
COVOTSOS, Louis J. (Head Libn) 252
TAYLOR, Terry S. (Online Srvs Libn) 1229

McDonnell Douglas Computer Systems (CA)
MARLOR, Hugh T. (Pgmr/Analyst) 772

McDonnell Douglas Corp (CA)
BARKALOW, Pat A. (Account Mgr) 56
LO, Grace C. (Ref & Catlgng Libn) 735
MACKINTOSH, Mary L. (Info Resrc Ctr Mgr) 757
WORMINGTON, Peggie (Mkt Support Analyst) 1369

McDonnell Douglas Corp (MO)
PRESTON, Jenny (Mgr, Lib Srvs) 991
TOLSON, Stephanie D. (Sr Libn) 1249

McDowell Pub Lib (WV)
MULLER, William A. (Dir) 877

McFarland & Co Inc (NC)
FRANKLIN, Robert M. (Pres) . . . 398

McGill Univ (PQ)
CAYA, Marcel (Dir Gen of Musm) 195
COUGHLIN, Violet L. (Mem, Lib Sch Advisory Council) 250
CRAWFORD, David S. (Asst Life Scis Area Libn) 256
CURRAN, William M. (Branch Libs & Pub Relations) 266
EVANS, Calvin D. (Area Libn) . . . 356
FERAHIAN, Salwa (Pub Srvs Supvsr) 371
FINLAY, Barbara J. (Asst Technl Srvs Libn) 378
GARNETT, Joyce C. (Area Libn) 419
GRAINGER, Bruce (Pub Srvs Head) 457
GROEN, Frances K. (Life Scis Libn) 471
HOBBINS, Alan J. (Acqs Head) . 545
HOWARD, Helen A. (Dir, Grad Sch of Lib & Info Std) 564
LAMBROU, Angella (Ref Libn Online Srvs) 691
LEIDE, John E. (Prof) 713
MACLEAN, Eleanor A. (Biological Scis Libn) 757
MITTERMEYER, Diane (Asst Prof) 850
MOHAMMED, Selima (Fine Arts & Music Catlgr) 852
MOLLER, Hans (Resrch & Devlpmnt Libn) 853
MOLLER, Hans (Resrch & Devlpmnt Libn) 853
MORRISON, H D. (Ref Libn) 868
ORMSBY, Eric (Dir of Libs) 926
RICHARD, Marc (Ref Libn) 1028
RIDER, Lillian M. (Head, Educ Lib) 1032
TEES, Miriam H. (Assoc Prof) . . 1229
WALUZYNIEC, Hanna (Head of Ref) 1302
WERYHO, Jan W. (Islamic Std Catlgr) 1325

McGinnis Lochridge & Kilgore (TX)
HILL, Susan E. (Law Libn) 540
O'MARA, Joan (Law Libn) 923

McGlinchey Stafford Mintz Cellini & Lang (LA)
DAVIS, Margo (Law Libn) 280

McGraw-Hill Book Co (NY)
ALMAN, Richard D. (Group VP) . . 17
BRAGG, Sanford B. (Vice Pres for Financial Mktg) 127
MARKERT, Patricia B. (Editrl Licensing Mgr) 771
SMITH, Richard L. (Staff Srvs Exec VP) 1160
SOLOMON, Samuel H. (VP) . . . 1166

McGraw-Hill Bookstores (NY)
BOWMAN, James K. (VP & Gen Mgr) 121

McGraw-Hill Inc (CA)
BLAKE, Harry W. (Gen Mgr) 103

McGraw-Hill Inc (CO)
HALL, Brian H. (Pres) 487

McGraw-Hill Inc (DC)
BECK, Douglas J. (Vice Pres of Intl Products) 71
GIGLIO, William 433
GRIMES, A R. (Sr Managing Consult) 470

McGraw-Hill Inc (DC)

MCKELVEY, Michael J. (VP, Federal Govt Consulting) 811

McGraw-Hill Inc (MA)

CARTER, Walter F. (Vice Pres & Steel Srv Dir) 190
CATON, Christopher N. (Vice Pres) 195
HARTMAN, David G. (Sr Vice Pres & Chief Intl Economist) . 508
JAIN, Nem C. (Tech Mktg Dir) . 592
O'REILLY, Daniel F. (Info Systs Devlpmnt VP) 925
PHILLIPS, Steven G. (VP) 969
YACOUBY, Ray S. (Info Systs & Tech Vice Pres) 1376
YANCHAR, Joyce M. (Resrch Dir) 1377

McGraw-Hill Inc (NH)

PERRON, Michelle M. (Plng & Resrch Dir) 960

McGraw-Hill Information Systems (NJ)

MAYDET, Steven I. (Electronic Products Mgr) 789

McGraw-Hill Information Systems (NY)

JENSEN, Fred O. (VP, Plng & Devlpmnt) 598

McGraw-Hill International Book Co (NY)

HARDEN, Jon B. (Plng & Devlpmnt Dir) 499

McGraw-Hill Publications Co (NY)

ROWLANDS, Marvin L. (Plng VP) 1063

McGregor Subscription Services Inc (IL)

LONG, Roger J. (Gen Sales Mgr) 739

McGuire Woods Battle & Boothe (VA)

ROBERTS, Ann B. (Lib Srvs Dir) 1039

MCI Communications Corp (DC) BATES, Mary E. (Corp Libn) 64
McKeesport Hospital (PA) ZUNDEL, Karen M. (Dir) 1391
McKenna Connor & Cuneo (CA) CHICK, Cynthia L. (Law Libn) .. 208
McKim Advertising Ltd (ON) PETRUGA, Patricia L. (Libn) 965
McKinley Memorial Lib (OH)

MCMURRAY, Sallylou (Lib Media Spclst) 815
STOUT, Chester B. (Dir) 1198

McKinsey & Co (CA)

KRAEMER, Linda L. (Mgr of Info Srvs) 674

McKinsey & Co (DC)

LEITCH, Karen E. (Info Spclst) .. 714
TOCH, Terryann (Energy Info Coordntr) 1248

McKinsey & Co (NY)

BERGMANN, Allison M. (Recruiting Info Analyst) 86
CARICONE, Paul (Info Spclst) . 181
KLINE, Harriet (Firm Info Spclst) . 661

McKinsey & Co (OH)

BORUCKI, Jennifer A. (Mgr of Info Srvs) 117
VICTORY, Karen M. (Info Spclst) 1283

McKinsey & Co (TX)

PORRAS, Susan M. (Info Srvs Mgr) 984

McKinzie Publishing Co (CA) MCKENZIE, Harry (Writer) 811
McLane Graf Raulerson & Middleton PA (NH) GUEDEA, Elizabeth J. (Libn) 475
McLaren General Hospital (MI)

MORELAND, Patricia L. (Asst Med Libn) 863

McLean Hospital (MA) LABREE, Rosanne (Dir) 686
McMaster Meighen (PQ) CHAREST, Ronald (Librarian-in-Chief) 203
McMaster Univ (ON)

BENDIG, Regina (Catlgng Libn) ... 79
FITZGERALD, Dorothy A. (Dir, Hlth Scis Lib) 382
FLEMMING, Tom (Pub Srvs Head) 384
HAYNES, Robert B. (Faculty of Hlth Scis Prof) 517
HAYTON, E E. (Circ Srvs Coordntr) 517
HILL, Graham R. (Univ Libn) 539
PANTON, Linda A. (Netwk Coordntr) 938
RIDLEY, A M. (Systs & Technl Srvs Head) 1033

McMaster Univ (ON)

THOMSON, Donna K. (Catlg Standards Libn) 1241

McMillan Binch (ON)

GULLIVER, Joanne V. (Mgr, Lib Srvs) 477

McMillan Memorial Lib (WI) WILSON, William J. (Dir) 1353
McMurry Coll (TX)

HAGGARD, Lynn (Ref, Circ & Interlib Loan Libn) 483
SPECHT, Joe W. (Lib Dir) 1172

McNees Wallace & Nurick (PA) ANDREWS, Evelyn F. (Libn) 26
McNeese State Univ (LA)

CAGLE, Robert B. (Prof and Docums Libn) 171
CUROL, Helen B. (Ref Libn) 266
KHOURY, Nancy L. (Head of Pub Srvs) 646
REID, Richard H. (Dir of Libs) .. 1019

McNeil Consumer Products Co (PA)

BECKER, Linda C. (Sr Technl Info Spclst) 72

McNeil Pharmaceutical (PA)

STANLEY, Kerry G. (Info Srvs Mgr) 1180
WICKS, Pamela J. (Info Spclst) . 1335

McNeil Specialty Products Co (NJ)

DOUGLASS, Leslie A. (Info Srvs Mgr) 314

McPherson Coll (KS)

JOHNSON, H J. (Asst Libn) 605
OLSEN, Rowena J. (Libn) 921

McPherson Pub Lib (KS) OBERLY, Beverly R. (Lib Dir) ... 914
McPherson's America Inc (CT)

RICCOBONO, Joseph V. (Pres, US Publshg Operations) 1026

Mead Data Central (AZ)

EWING, Alison L. (Account Exec) 359

Mead Data Central (CA)

KANJI, Zainab J. (Sr Accounts Rep) 625
TABKE, Robert (Gen Mgr) 1219

Mead Data Central (CO)

CALVERT, Lois M. (Account Exec, Law Sch Prog) 174

Mead Data Central (DC)

ROSS, Margery M. (Account Exec) 1058

Mead Data Central (MA)

WALLAS, Philip R. (Sr Account Exec) 1298

Mead Data Central (OH)

CHRISTOU, Corilee S. (Info Ctr Market Planner) 212
COYLE, Christopher B. (Law Sch Prog Dir) 253
HERRICK, Carol L. (Market Resrch Mgr) 532
JOHNSON, John R. (Small Law Firm Market Dir) 606
LONG, Clare S. (Law Sch Account Exec) 739
NERO, Robert A. (Vice Pres of Worldwide Sales) 895
PEAKE, Sharon K. (Mgr, Pub Comms) 952
PRICKETT, Dan S. (Strategic Plng Mgr) 993
REED, Buzz (Dir of Sales Prog Integration) 1014
SIMPSON, Jack W. 1142
SPOHR, Cynthia L. (Product Spclst) 1175

Mead Data Central (OR) SIMON, Dale (Account Exec) .. 1140
Mead Data Central (PA) IVAK, Patricia A. (Sr Account Rep) 585
Mead Data Central (TX) NEWMAN, Patricia O. (Law Schs Account Exec) 899
WEGMANN, Pamela A. (Branch Mgr) 1316

Mead Data Central (ON) RODGER, Stephen J. (Account Exec) 1047
Mead Imaging (OH) ROHMILLER, Ellen L. (Libn) .. 1051
Mead Pub Lib (WI) PETZOLD, Mary E. (Interlib Loan & Asst Info Srv Libn) ... 966
VAN STRATEN, Daniel G. (Supvsr of Technl Srvs) 1277

Meadville/Lombard Theological Sch (IL) GERDES, Neil W. (Head Libn) .. 428
Mease Health Care (FL) JENNINGS, Patricia S. (Med Libn) 598

Mechanic's Institute Lib (CA) — PABST, Kahleen T. (Dir) 933
SULLIVAN, Alice F. (Staff Supvsr) 1207

Meckler Corp (CT) — MECKLER, Alan M. (Publshr) . . . 820
Meckler Publishing (CA) — QUINT, Barbara E. (Edit, Database Scrchr) 1000

Medford Pub Lib (MA) — SHANK, Beverly C. (Comunty Srvs Libn) 1120

Medgar Evens Coll of the City Univ of NY (NY) — BAKISH, David J. (Prof of Enlg & Hum) 50

Media & Methods Magazine (PA) — SOKOLOFF, Michele (Edit) 1165
Media Applications (CA) — HOFFMAN, William J. (Owner and Consult) 548

Media Center for Children (NY) — BRAUN, Robert L. (Info Dir & Editor) 130
GAFFNEY, Maureen (Exec Dir) . . 412

Media General Inc (VA) — DILLON, James L. (VP) 303
OWEN, Karen V. (Libn) 931

Media Projects & New Day Films (TX) — MONDELL, Cynthia B. (Filmmaker & Distributor) 854

Media Resource Center (NE) — DUX-IDEUS, Sherrie L. (Libn) . . . 330
Medical & Chirurgical Faculty (MD) — HARMAN, Susan E. (Ref & Circ Libn) 502
JENSEN, Joseph E. (Dir of Resrch & Info Systs) 599

Med Associates Health Center (WI) — MADSEN, Joyce (Med Libn) 759
Medical Center Hospital (TX) — NEELAND, Ellen L. (Med Libn) . . 891
Medical Center Inc (PA) — COGHLAN, Patricia M. (Dir, Hlth Scis Lib) 227

Medical Center of Delaware (DE) — CHASTAIN-WARHEIT, Christine C. (Dir of Med Libs) . 203

Medical Coll of Georgia (GA) — ANDERSON, Gail C. (Educ Coordntr, Ref Srvs) 23
BASLER, Thomas G. (Prof and Dir of Libs) 63
DAVIS, Shelley E. (AV Libn) 281
DENNISON, Jacquelyn H. (Ref Srvs Head) 292
FLAVIN, Linda M. (Head of Catlgng) 384
HENNER, Terry A. (Online Srvs Coordntr) 528
MCCANN, Jett C. (Head of Serials Dept, Govt Docums) . . 794
MIMS, Dorothy H. (Spcl Cols Libn) 845
SCHLATTER, M W. (Head of AV Srvs) 1093
TRAINOR, Donna J. (Circ Srvs & Interlib Loan Head) 1253

Medical Coll of Hampton Roads (VA) — HARRIS, Richard J. (Systs & Technl Srvs Coordntr) 506

Medical Coll of Pennsylvania (PA) — CHAFF, Sandra L. (Dir & Archvst/Resrch Instr) 197
HORNIG-ROHAN, James E. (Comp Assisted Lrng Lab Dir) 560
KIRBY, Martha Z. (Ref Libn & Srch Analyst) 654
MILLER, Naomi (Clinical Libn) . . . 841
MONTOYA, Leopoldo (Technl Srvs Asst Libn) 856
WIGGINS, Theresa S. (Assoc Libn) 1337

Medical Coll of Wisconsin (WI) — ANTONIEWICZ, Carol M. (Ref Libn) 29
ASU, Glynis V. (Spcl Srvs Libn) . . 37
BLACKWELDER, Mary B. (Assoc Dir for User Srvs) 102
BRENNEN, Patrick W. (Dir of Libs) 133
HOUKOM, Susan L. (Asst Dir for Technl Srvs) 563
KIRKALI, Meral (Catlg & Ref Libn) 654
STRUBE, Kathleen (Clinical Ref Libn) 1203
WONG, Elizabeth M. (Pub Srvs Libn) 1362

Medical Economics Co Inc (NJ) — MCGILL, Thomas J. (Pres) 806
Med-Info Search (CO) — GILBERT, Ruth E. (Info Broker) . . 434
Medical Information Services (ON) — DAVEY, Dorothy M. (Owner & Operator) 276
Medical Information Specialists (CO) — SMITH, Catherine C. (Owner) . . 1153
Medical Liability Consultants Program (CO) — THOMASSON, George O. (Risk Mgr) 1238
Medical Lib Association (IL) — MAYFIELD, Maurice K. (Educ Dir) 790
PALMER, Raymond A. (Exec Dir) 936
Medical Logic International (SC) — COOK, Galen B. (Pres) 240
Medical Research Council (SAF) — ROSSOUW, Steve F. (Dir) 1059
Medical Univ of South Carolina (SC) — ANDERSON, Marcia (Ref Libn) . . . 24
POYER, Robert K. (Pub Srvs Coordntr) 989
SAWYER, Warren A. (Dir of Libs & Lrng Resrc Ctrs) 1086
TREMBLAY, Gerald F. (Med Informatics Resrch Fellow) . . 1255
Medina County District Lib (OH) — SMITH, Robert S. (Dir) 1160
Medtronic Inc (MN) — LO, Maryanne H. (Technl Info Spclst) 735
Meeker Regional Lib District (CO) — NICKEL, Robbie L. (Lib Dir) 902
Meharry Medical Coll (TN) — CAMERON, Sam A. (Archvst & Archs Dir) 175
EARL, Martha F. (Med Ref Libn) . 332
GOODALE, Adebonojo L. (Lib Dir) 448
HAMBERG, Cheryl J. (Head of Ref) 490
MCHOLLIN, Mattie L. (Asst Dir of Technl Srvs) 809
WATTS, Adalyn (Ref Libn) 1310
WILLIAMS, Marsha D. (Systs Libn) 1345

Melbourne Coll of Advanced Education (AUS) — POWNALL, David E. (Chief Libn) 989

Meldrum & Fewsmith Inc (OH) — SKUTNIK, John S. (Supvsr, Bus Info Srvs) 1147

Melin Nelson Associates (NY) — NELSON, Nancy M. (Principal) . . 894
Mellon Bank (PA) — GREEN, Joyce M. (Mktg Resrc Ctr Mgr) 462

Melton Co Inc (OK) — MELTON, Howard E. (Mgr) 823
Memorial Hall Lib (MA) — JACOBSON, Nancy C. (Lib Dir) . 590
Memrl Hospital Martinsville & Henry Cnty (VA) — SHERRARD, Mary A. (Med Libn) 1129

Memorial Hospital of Burlington County (NJ) — O'CONNOR, Elizabeth W. (Med Libn) 916

Memorial Hospital of Colorado Springs (CO) — HANSON, Elana L. (Lib Dir) 498
Memorial Hospital of Danville (VA) — SASSER, Ann B. (Med Libn) . . . 1083
Memorial Hospital of Easton Maryland (MD) — MOLTER, Maureen M. (Med Libn) 853
Memorial Hospital of Fremont (OH) — KELLER, Marlo L. (Dir, Eductnl Srvs) 635
Memorial Hospital of South Bend (IN) — MILLER, Jeanne L. (Lib Mgr) . . . 839
Memorial Hospital of York (PA) — HOMICK, Elaine (Med Libn) . . . 555
Memorial Hospitals Association (CA) — HAMMETT, Susan A. (Dir) 493
SHAMS, Kamruddin (Info Systs Vice Pres) 1120
Memorial Lib (IL) — RICKERT, Carol A. (Comunty Srvs Dept Head) 1032
Memorial Sloan-Kettering Cancer Center (NY) — ABBITT, Viola I. (Donor Resrch Mgr) 1
BECKER, Jeanne (Dir) 72
Memorial Univ of Newfoundland (NF) — BALSARA, Aspi (Asst Govt Docums Libn) 53
BROWN, Jean I. (Asst Prof) 144
DENNIS, Christopher J. (Libn I) . . 292
ELLIS, Richard H. (Univ Libn) . . . 345
HEINO, Dan R. (Ref & Spcl Projs Libn) 522
MEWS, Alison J. (Libn) 829

Memorial Univ of Newfoundland (NF)

MILNE, Dorothy J. (Sci Colls Libn & Biblgphr) 845

TIFFANY, William C. (Head of Acqs and Perdcls) 1244

WOOD, Alberta A. (Map Libn) . . 1363

Memory Lane & Record Finder (VA)

SMITH, Walter H. (Owner) 1161

Memphis & Shelby County Pub Lib (TN)

BAER, Ellen H. (Pub Relations Ofcr) 45

BRADY, Josiah B. (Libn II) 126

CARD, Judy (Staff Devlpmnt Ofcr) 180

DRESCHER, Judith A. (Dir of Libs) 319

LINDENFELD, Joseph F. (Head Libn) 729

RICHARDSON, Merle J. (Asst Dir for Technl Srvs) 1029

SMITH, Robert F. (Asst Dir for Branch Srvs) 1160

STRAWDER, Maxine S. (Branch Mgr) 1201

Memphis City Schs (TN)

BANNERMAN-WILLIAMS, Cheryl F. (Lib & Info Spclst) . . . 54

FARRIS, Mary E. (Lib Media Spclst) 365

Memphis State Univ (TN)

BEHRENS, Elizabeth A. (Technl Srvs Libn) 75

CO, Francisca (Sci & Tech Catlgr) 224

DENTON, Ann L. (Asst Head) . . . 293

EVANS, David H. (Music Prof) . . 356

HENDRIX, Wilma P. (Pub Srvs Assoc Dir) 528

HUGGINS, Annelle R. (Assoc Dir) 571

MADER, Sharon B. (Info Retrieval Libn, Asst Prof) 759

MENDINA, Guy T. (Systs & Circ Libn) 824

PARK, Elizabeth H. (Info Retrieval Libn) 941

POURCIAU, Lester J. (Libs Dir) . 987

RUDOLPH, N J. (Ref/Instrc Libn) 1066

SMITH, Philip M. (Catlg Dept Head) 1159

VILES, Elza A. (Assoc Prof & Head, Music Lib) 1284

WANG, Hueychyi V. (Catlgr) . . 1303

WARD, Suzanne M. (Engrng Libn) 1304

WEDIG, Eric M. (Asst Govern Docum Libn) 1315

WILLIAMS, Saundra W. (Head of Govt Docums) 1346

Menasha Pub Lib (WI)

LOCH-WOUTERS, Marge (Dir, Youth Srvs) 736

Mendocino Coll (CA)

MCGREEVY, Kathleen T. (Dir of Lib & AV Srvs) 808

Menlo Park Pub Lib (CA)

HOFLAND, Freda B. (Libn III) . . 548

Menninger Foundation (KS)

BRAND, Alice A. (Chief Libn) . . . 127

Mennonite Brethren Biblical Seminary (CA)

ENNS-REMPEL, Kevin M. (Archvst) 350

Mennonite Lib & Archives (KS)

HAURY, David A. (Dir & Archvst) 512

Mental Health Assn in Dutchess County (NY)

CARUSO, Janet A. (Libn) 190

Mental Health Center of Boulder County (CO)

ROTHMAN, Marilyn R. (Lib Dir) 1060

Mental Health Services of Southern OK (OK)

KIMBLE, Valerie F. (Libn) 649

Mequon-Thiensville Sch District (WI)

CASEY, Jean M. (Lib Media Spclst) 192

Mercantile Lib (NY)

ROTH, Claire J. (Lib Dir) 1059

Merced County Lib (CA)

KOBAYASHI, Deanna H. (Libn III, Pub Srvs Libn) 666

WILSON, Linda L. (Cnty Libn) . . 1351

Mercer County Lib (NJ)

GREENBERG, Ruth S. (Branch Head) 463

Mercer County Service Center (WV)

DYE, Luella I. (Pub Lib Dir) 330

Mercer Medical Center (NJ)

MARCHOK, Catherine W. (Hlth Scis Lib Dir) 769

Mercer Meidinger Hansen Inc (CA)

COSTELLO, Robert C. (Resrch & Info Coordntr) 249

Mercer Univ (GA)

BURKHART, Sue W. (Catologer) 161

CHANIN, Leah F. (Dir of Law Lib & Prof) 201

COLLINS, Patrick (Govt Docums & Ref Libn) 233

HARBER, Patty S. (Catlg Libn) . . 499

HOWARD, Mary R. (Lib Dir) 564

JACKSON, Elizabeth C. (Dir of Lib) 587

RANKIN, Jocelyn A. (Med Lib Dir) 1007

SIMMONS, Hal (Music Prof) . . . 1140

WILLIAMS, Nancy F. (Head, Reader Srvs & Col Devlpmnt) 1345

Merck & Co Inc (CA)

JENKINS, Ann A. (Info & Technl Systs Mgr) 597

Merck Frosst Canada Inc (PQ)

KELLY, Claire B. (Sr Resrch Libn) 637

WACASEY, Mary M. (Resrch Libn) 1290

Merck Sharp & Dohme (PA)

MAXIN, Jacqueline A. (Mgr, Lit Resrcs) 787

MESSICK, Karen J. (Lit Resrc Ctr Supvsr) 828

Mercy Academy (LA)

DU CARMONT, M C. (High Sch Libn) 322

Mercy Catholic Medical Center (PA)

CLINTON, Janet C. (Lib Srvs Chief) 222

Mercy Center for Health Care Services (IL)

Mercy Coll (NY)

BEAN, Janet R. (Lib Dir) 69

BONE, Larry E. (Libs Dir & Prof) . 113

KLAVANO, Ann M. (Ref and Bibliographic Instrc Lib) 658

MCLAUGHLIN, Denis F. (Libn) . . 813

REDDING, Kathleen A. (Libn) . . 1013

Mercy High School (NE)

Mercy Hospital (FL)

HOLLOWAY, David R. (Med Libn) 552

Mercy Hospital (IA)

SNIDER, Jacqueline I. (Med Libn) 1163

Mercy Hospital (IL)

WILLIAMSON, Harriet 1347

Mercy Hospital (MD)

KAISLER, Dolores H. (Libn) 622

Mercy Hospital (ME)

ANDERSON, Marjorie E. (Libn) . . 24

Mercy Hospital (NY)

GARVEY, Jeffrey M. (Libn) 421

KARCH, Linda S. (Med Libn) . . . 627

REID, Carol L. (Med Libn) 1018

Mercy Hospital (OH)

SINK, Thomas R. (Dir of Lib & AV Srvs) 1143

Mercy Hospital (PA)

BRANDRETH, Elizabeth A. (Libn) 128

NANSTIEL, Barbara L. (Info Srvs Dir) 887

Mercy Hospital & Medical Center (CA)

HABETLER, Anna M. (Lib Dir) . . 481

Mercy Medical Center (ID)

BALCERZAK, Judy A. (Libn) 50

Mercy Medical Center (WI)

GEBHARDT, Sharon E. (Lib Mgr) 424

Mercyhurst Coll (PA)

COOPER, Joanne S. (Lib Dir) . . . 243

Meredith Pub Lib (NH)

TORR, Lydia M. (Lib Dir) 1251

Meriden Pub Lib (CT)

BOGATZ, June H. (Asst Dir) 110

Meridian Community Unit Sch District 101 (IL)

SHAW, Louis P. (Dist Libn) 1123

Meridian Junior Coll (MS)

JOHNSON, Scott R. (Lib Dir) . . . 609

RAINWATER, Mark T. (Lib Aide) 1004

Meridian Pub Lib (MS)

MACNEILL, Daniel S. (Lib Dir) . . 758

Merilees Associates Inc (ON)

MERILEES, Bobbie (Lib & Info Systs Mgmt Consultant) 826

Merion Elem Sch (PA)

SILER, Marguerite S. (Libn) . . . 1138

Meritor Corporate Archives (PA)

KING, Eleanor M. (Archvst) 650

Meriweather County Board of Education (GA)
SHELTON, Elease B. (Media Spclst) 1126

Merrell Dow Pharmaceuticals Inc (OH)
CRETSOS, James M. 258
DOBBS, David L. (Sr Info Scientist) 307
ROSENTHAL, Francine C. (Patent Info Spclst) 1057
SCHUTZ, Robert S. (Scientific Translator) 1103
SIMMONS, Edlyn S. (Patent Info Supvsr) 1139

Merriam Center Lib (IL)
VALAUSKAS, Edward J. (Asst Dir) 1271

Merrill Lynch (NY)
BONACORDA, James J. (Info Mgr) 113
DREZEN, Richard (Ref Libn) 319
GREENBERG, Linda (Info Spclst) 463

Merrill Lynch Pierce Fenner & Smith (NY)
WALKER, Jeanette F. (Libn) .. 1295

Merrimack Pub Lib (NH)
MARSHALL, Margaret E. (Dir) .. 774

Mershon Sawyer Johnston Dunwody & Cole (FL)
SNYDER, Jean (Libn) 1165

Mesa Coll (CA)
FORMAN, Jack (Ref & Biogph Srvs Libn) 390

Mesa Coll (CO)
HENDRICKSON, Charles R. (Lib Dir & Head Libn) 527

Mesa Pub Lib (AZ)
BECKER, Teresa J. (Chlds Libn) .. 72
CZOPEK, Vanessa (Libn) 269
GREGORY, Joan A. (Head, Acqs/Cols Devlpmnt Coordntr) 466
MURPHY, Ellen A. (Supvsr Libn of Chlds Srvs) 880

Meserne Mumper & Hughes (CA)
ROLLINS, James H. (Law Libn) 1051

Mesiror Gelman Jaffe Cramer & Jamieson (PA)
PROCTOR, David J. (Libn) 994

Mesquite Independent Sch District (TX)
MANN, Carol A. (Libn) 765

Mesquite Pub Lib (TX)
BYROM, Jeanne (AV Libn) 170
LARSON, Jeanette C. (Pub Srvs Supvsr) 699

Messiah Coll (PA)
POWELL, Virginia L. (Assoc Prof for Catlgng & Ref) 989

Meta Micro Library Systems Inc (TX)
LEATHERBURY, Maurice C. (Pres) 707

Metallgesellschaft AG (WGR)
BECHTEL, Hans 71

Metamora Township High Sch (IL)
WOOLARD, Wilma L. (Lib Media Ctr Dir) 1368

Metcalf & Eddy Inc (MA)
CHAPDELAINE, Susan A. (Record Mgr) 201
MUISE, Anita M. (Libn) 876

Methodist Hospital (IN)
ANDERSON, Marilyn M. (Clinical Resrch Assoc) 24
HOYT, Lester H. (Med Data Prcsng Consultant) 566

Methodist Hospital (NY)
TANNER, Ellen B. (Hlth Scis Lib Dir) 1222

Methodist Hospital (TX)
GIROUARD, J L. (Hospital Libn) . 438

Methodist Hospital-North (TN)
PORTER, William R. (Dept Chief of Staff) 985

Methodist Hospital of Indiana Inc (IN)
ALLEN, Joyce S. (Lib Mgr) 15

Methodist Medical Center (IL)
WALTERS, Patsy M. (Asst Med Libn) 1301

Methodist Medical Center (TX)
JARVIS, Mary E. (Med Libn) 595

Methodist Theological Sch (OH)
FOSTER, Julia A. (Catlgng & Ref Libn) 392

Methuen Public School (MA)
JACOBS, Lois S. (Media Spclst) . 589

Metrics Research Corp (OH)
MCSPADDEN, Robert M. (Pres) . 818

Metro Health Center (PA)
WELCH, Carol J. (Med Libn) ... 1321

Metro Nashville Pub Schs (TN)
MCANALLY, Charlotte L. (Lib Consult) 792

METRO NY (NY)
BRANDEAU, John H. (Spcl Projs Coordntr) 128

METRO NY Metropolitan Reference & Resrch (NY)
BARTEN, Sharon S. (Med Libn) .. 60

Metro Toronto Reference Lib (ON)

Metroplitan Lib System (OK)

Metropolitan Business Systems Inc (NY)

Metropolitan Community Coll (MO)
Metropolitan Community Colls (MO)

Metropolitan Dade Pub Lib System (FL)

Metropolitan Data Services Group Inc (PA)
Metropolitan Hospital (MI)
Metropolitan Hospital (PA)

Metropolitan Lib Service Agency (MN)

Metropolitan Lib System (OK)

Metropolitan Museum of Art (NY)

Metropolitan-Nashville Bd of Education (TN)
Metropolitan Nashville General Hospital (TN)
Metropolitan Planning Commission (TN)

Metropolitan Sch District of Washington (IN)

Metropolitan Separate Sch Board (ON)

Metropolitan Technical Community Coll (NE)

Metropolitan Toronto Lib Board (ON)

Metropolitan Toronto Management (ON)

FRIEDLAND, Frances K. (Music Catlgr) 403
GUNDARA, Jaswinder (Langs & Lit Dept Mgr) 477
MEYERS, Duane H. (Assoc Dir for Mgmt Srvs) 830

D'ANGELO, Paul P. (Vice Pres of Mktg) 272
NELSON, Freda H. (Libn) 893
SCHWAAB, Beverly J. (Head Libn) 1103

LYON, Bruce C. (Asst Libn Class III) 752
STEPANICK, John R. (Ref Libn) 1187

BOWERS, Paul A. (List Mgr) ... 120
LOFTIS, Mary B. (Med Libn) 737
STESIS, Karen R. (Dir of Lib & Info Srvs) 1189

WELYGAN, Sylvia M. (Index Edit) 1323
BRAWNER, Lee B. (Exec Dir) .. 130
CORLEE, Lisa (Mtrls Selector) .. 246
DAVIS, Denyvetta (Lib Head) ... 278
FEHRENBACH, Laurie A. (Circ Clerk) 368
HERSTAND, Joellen (Chief of Mtrls Selection) 533
LITTLE, Paul L. (Chief of Plng Srvs) 733
MELIK, Ella M. (Pub Srvs Libn) .. 822
PETERSON, Denise D. (Head of Outreach Srvs) 963
COVERT, Nadine (Spcl Consult for Critical Inventory) 252
DAY, Ross (Libn) 283
PINES, Doralynn (Acqs Libn and Biblghpr) 974
WALKER, William B. (Arthur K Watson Chief Libn) 1296
WERNER, Edward K. (Asst Musm Catlgng & Ref Libn) .. 1324

DURHAM, Wanda J. (Libn) 328

PERRY, Glenda L. (Libn) 960

BEAL, Gretchen F. (Info Resrcs Coordntr) 68

CHAMPLIN, Constance J. (Media Srvs Coordntr) 198

BOWEN, Tom G. (Libn) 120
SEBANC, Mark F. (Archvst & Libn) 1110

MARSH, Paul W. (Instrcl Resrcs & Tech Dir) 773

BEETON, Elizabeth O. (Asst Dir of Tech Support Div) 74
KOTIN, David B. (Hist Dept Mgr) 673
LORENTOWICZ, Genia (Catlgng Dept Head) 741
MACDONALD, Christine S. (Plng Ofcr) 754
MCCUBBIN, George M. (Acqs & Cols Mgr) 800
MILANICH, Melanie M. (Ref Libn) 834
SCHWENGER, Frances S. (Dir) 1105
TSUI, Josephine (Mgr) 1260
WATSON, Joyce N. (Departmental Liaison Libn) . 1309

SMITH, Pamela 1159

Metropolitan Toronto Reference Lib (ON)
ALSTON, Sandra (Libn) 18
BAWA, Indira (Asst Mgr of Sci & Tech) 67
BURCHELL, Patricia M. (Catlgr) . 158
FAIRLEY, Craig R. (Libn) 361
JACKSON, Craig A. (Bus Ref Libn) 587
LAVERTY, Corinne Y. (Music Catlgng Supvsr) 703
MCCANN, Judith B. (Libn) 794
STANGL-WALKER, Teresa L. (Metroline Unit Libn) 1180

Metropolitan Toronto Separate Sch Board (ON)
PEPE, Berenice A. (Vocal Music Itinerant Tchr) 957

Metropolitan Water Dist of Southern CA (CA)
LEE, Dora T. (Libn) 709

Metuchen Board of Education (NJ)
MASSEY, Eleanor N. (Coordntr & Eductnl Media Spclst) 782

Metuchen High Sch (NJ)
HIGGINS, Marilyn E. (Eductnl Media Spclst) 538

Metuchen Pub Lib (NJ)
WANG, Hsi H. (Adult Srvs Libn) 1303

Meyer Boswell Books Inc (CA)
LUTTRELL, Jordan D. (Pres) . . . 750

MFI Associates Inc (NY)
RAHN, Erwin P. (Pres) 1003

MGIC Investment Corp (WI)
MCKEE, Margaret J. (Corprt Libn) 810

MHF Consulting Service (MD)
FISHBEIN, Meyer H. (Consult) . . 380

Miami Children's Hospital (FL)
COSCULLUELA, Marta (Chief Med Libn) 248

Miami-Dade Community Coll (FL)
BYRD, Susan G. (Ref & Coordntr of Biblgph Instr) 169
DEWAR, Jo E. (Lib Dir) 298
LEHMAN, Douglas K. (Dir, Lib Tech Srvs) 712
WINE, H E. (Readers' Srvs Libn) 1354

Miami-Dade Pub Lib System (FL)
BOLDRICK, Samuel J. (FL Col Head) 112
CARDEN, Marguerite (Asst Dir) . . 180
CHIMERAKIS, Mary A. (Chlds Libn) 208
DONIO, Dorothy (Fine Arts Libn) . 311
LIANZI, Theresa L. (Sci Libn) . . . 725
PEREZ, Maria L. (Ref Libn) 958
RYAN, Audrey H. (Prog Adminstr) 1070
SAMUELS, David H. (Ref Libn) . 1079
SINTZ, Edward F. (Dir) 1144
WULF, Karlinne V. (Branch Libn) 1374
YOUNG, Barbara N. (Head of Art Srvs) 1381

Miami Herald Publishing Co (FL)
DONOVAN, Elizabeth L. (Info Spclst) 312
PAUL, Nora M. (Lib Dir) 949

Miami Independent Sch District (TX)
LOTMAN, Marion O. (Sch Libn) . 742

The Miami News (FL)
WRIGHT, Joseph F. (Head Libn) 1372

Miami Shores Village (FL)
ESPER, Elizabeth (Libn & Dir) . . . 354
KELLY, Anne V. (Chlds Srvs Libn) 637

Miami Univ (OH)
MILLER, Clayton M. (Head, Soc Sci Dept) 836
OLSON, Joann D. (Hum Libn) . . . 922
QUAY, Richard H. (Actg Head, Soc Sci Dept) 999
SCHMALBERG, Aaron (Instr) . . 1094
WORTMAN, William A. (Humanities Libn) 1369
ZASLOW, Barry J. (Catlg Libn) . 1386

Miami Valley Hospital (OH)
SEXTON, Sally V. (Asst Libn of Ref Srvs) 1118

Michael Baker Jr Inc (PA)
WILLIAMS, Ruth J. (Libn) 1346

Michael Duren MD (TX)
DUREN, Norman (Med Ofc Comp Operator) 328

Michaels Associates Design Consultants (VA)
MICHAELS, Andrea A. (Pres) . . . 831
MICHAELS, David L. (Vice Pres) 832

Michigan Bell (MI)
SPRAGUE, Karol S. (Corp Libn) 1176

Michigan City Pub Lib (IN)
Michigan Consolidated Gas Co (MI)

Michigan Lib Association (MI)
Michigan Lib Consortium (MI)

Michigan Osteopathic Medical Center (MI)

Michigan State Univ (MI)

Michigan Technological Univ (MI)

Michigan Tech Univ (MI)

Microelectronics & Computer Tech Corp (TX)

Microelectronics Ctr of North Carolina (NC)

Microfor Inc (PQ)

Microform Inc (PA)
Micromedia Limited (ON)

DEYOUNG, Charles D. (Dir) 298
AMES, Kay L. (Corprt Lib Supvsr) 20
GESSNER, Marianne (Exec Dir) . 430
CONWAY, Michael J. (Automation Srvcs Coordntr) . 239
FLAHERTY, Kevin C. (Exec Dir) . 383

HOUGH, Carolyn A. (Lib Srvs Mgr) 562
ARMSTRONG, Carole S. (Head of Sci Libs) 32
BLACK-SHIER, Mary L. (Music Catlg Libn & Biblgphr) 102
BURINSKI, Walter W. (Ref Libn) . 160
CHAPIN, Richard E. (Dir of Libs) . 201
CLULEY, Leonard E. (Original Catlg Libn) 223
COOK, Kay A. (Monographic Acqs Head) 240
COURTOIS, Martin P. (Sci Ref Libn) 251
FRYE, Dorothy T. (Archvl Spclst) 407
HAKA, Clifford H. (Head of Access Srvs) 484
HAMMARSKJOLD, Carolyn A. (Branch Libn) 493
HONHART, Frederick L. (Univ Arch & Histl Cols Dir) 556
JIZBA, Laurel (Head of Original Catlgng) 600
KLOSWICK, John (Catlg Libn) . . 662
KOCH, Henry C. (Assoc Lib Dir Emeritus) 667
MANDERSCHEID, Dorothy H. (Sci Libn) 765
MEAHL, D D. (Docum Delivery Head & Systs Libn) 819
OLIVER, James W. (Chem Libn) . 921
OSTROM, Kriss T. (Circ & Assigned Reading Srvs Head) 929
REITER, Berle G. (Math Libn) . . 1022
RIVERA, Diana H. (Libn) 1037
SANFORD, John D. (Archvl Spclst) 1081
SCOTT, Randall W. (Catlg Libn) 1108
SHAPIRO, Beth J. (Deputy Dir) . 1121
THUNELL, Allen E. (Original Catlgr) 1243
WIEMERS, Eugene L. (Head of Soc Scis & Humanities Lib) . 1336
WOODARD, Beth E. (Soc Sci & Hum Ref Libn II) 1365
MORROW, Deborah (Automation Coordntr & Catlgr) 869
SPENCE, Theresa S. (Univ Archvst) 1173
THOMAS, David H. (Technl Srvs Div Head) 1236
KRENITSKY, Michael V. (Lib Dir Emeritus) 677

HARMON, Jacqueline B. (Corprt Info Ctr Dir) 502

MENDELL, Stefanie (Corprt Comms Mgr) 823
DENIGER, Constant (Gen Mgr) . . 292
LUSSIER, Richard (Projs Mgr) . . 749
RUOCCHIO, James P. (Pres) . . 1068
CASEY, Victoria L. (Resrch Coordntr) 192
DE STRICKER, Ulla (Bus Info Ctr Mgr) 296
FAST, Louise (VP & Gen Mgr) . . 366
GAGNE, Frank (Database Mktg & Devlpmnt Mgr) 412

Micromedia Limited (ON)	GIBSON, Robert (Pres) 432
	GRAY, Sandra A. (Info Spclst) . . 460
	OLMSTEAD, Marcia E. (Editrl
	Dept Mgr) 921
Microsoft Corp (WA)	YOUNT, Natalie W. (Info Resrcs
	Mgr) 1384
Mid-America Baptist Theological	
Seminary (TN)	HAIR, William B. (Dir of Lib
	Srvs) 484
	MABBOTT, Deborah D. (Technl
	Srvs Head) 753
Mid-America Nazarene Coll (KS)	GALLOWAY, Mary A. (Ref
	Libn) 415
Mid-Atlantic Preservation	
Service (PA)	JONES, C L. (Dir) 611
Mid Con Corp (IL)	ELL, Elizabeth L. (Chief Libn) . . . 343
Mid-Continent Pub Lib (MO)	AMOS, Billie E. (Libn) 20
	HENRY, Peggy L. (Branch Libn) . 529
	MEYERS, Martha L. (Ref Libn) . . 831
	MORALES, Milton F. (Bd of
	Trustees Pres) 862
	PLUMB, Warren G. (Pres,
	Trustee) 978
	STEELE, Anitra T. (Chlds
	Spclst) 1184
Mid-Hudson Lib System (NY)	MARKARIAN, Rita J. (Outreach
	Srvs Consult) 771
	SANKER, Paul N. (Pub
	Relations Consult) 1081
	VAN ZANTEN, Frank V. (Dir) . . 1278
	VERDIBELLO, Muriel F. (Dept
	Head of Interlib Loan & Ref) . 1282
	WIGG, Ristiina M. (Chlds Srvs
	Consult) 1337
Mid-Maine Medical Center (ME)	DAMON, Cora M. (Dir of Libs) . . 272
Mid-Mississippi Regional Lib	
System (MS)	RODICH, Nancy A. (Techn Srvs
	Libn) 1048
Mid-Missouri Lib Network (MO)	RAITHEL, Frederick J. (Network
	Dir) 1004
Mid-Peninsula Lib Cooperative (MI)	SILVER, Gary L. (Dir) 1138
Mid-South Bible Coll (TN)	ADAMS, Paul R. (Libn) 5
	PENNINGTON, Melanie L. (Asst
	Libn) 957
	GROSS, Richard F. (Libs Dir) . . . 472
Mid-State Coll (ME)	
Midcontinental Regnl Medical Lib	
Program (NE)	EARLEY, Dorothy A. (Online
	Srvs Instr) 332
Middle County Public Lib (NY)	HEINEMAN, Stephanie R. (Asst
	Dir) 522
Middle Tennessee State Univ (TN)	BURKHEART, Hilda S. (Catlg
	Libn) 161
	CRAIG, James D. (Libn) 254
	GILL, Linda S. (User Srvs
	Coordntr) 435
	MARSHALL, John D. (Prof,
	Univ Biblgphr) 774
	NEAL, James H. (Prof, Hist &
	Archvl Admin) 890
	SCOTT, Margaret W. (Col Mgmt
	Coordntr) 1107
	WELLS, Paul F. (Dir of Ctr for
	Popular Music) 1323
	YOUREE, Beverly B. (Assoc
	Prof) 1384
Middlebury Coll (VT)	ECKERT, Sharon S. (Asst Catlg
	Libn) 335
	MCBRIDE, Jerry L. (Music Libn) . 792
	POST, Jennifer C. (Cur of
	Flanders Ballad Col) 986
	RAUM, Hans L. (Assoc Libn) . . 1010
	REHBACH, Jeffrey R. (Systs
	Libn) 1017
	RUCKER, Ronald E. (Coll Libn) . 1065
Middlesex Community Coll (MA)	HALE, Janice L. (Sr Asst Libn) . 485
	HORGAN, Laura A. (Caltgr) 559
Middlesex County Coll (NJ)	MILLER, Mary A. (Client Srvs
	Libn) 840

Middlesex Memorial Hospital (CT)	BRECK, Evelyn M. (Dir, Hlth
	Scis Lib) 131
Middletown Board of Education (CT)	POLOMSKI, Linda (Tchr & Libn) . 982
Middletown Township Lib (NJ)	WOLFORD, Larry E. (Dir) 1361
Midland Coll (TX)	MIRANDA, Cecilia (Technl Srvs
	Libn) 847
Midland Lutheran Coll (NE)	BOYLE, Thomas E. (Lib Dir) 124
Midlands Technical Coll (SC)	LAFAYE, Cary D. (Ref &
	Perdcls Libn) 687
Midlothian Pub Lib (IL)	PETERSON, Carolyn R.
	(Adminstrv Libn) 963
	WINDHAM, Carol B. (Med Libn) 1354
Midway Hospital (MN)	ASPNES, Grieg G. (Mgr) 37
Midwest China Center (MN)	
Midwest Library Service (CA)	NAGEL, Lawrence D. (Western
	Regnl Mgr) 886
Midwest Research Institute (MO)	CARSON, Bonnie L. (Sr
	Chemical Info Scientist) 188
	DRAYSON, Pamela K. 318
Midwest Stock Exchange (IL)	BREEN, Joanell C. (Systs Libn) . 131
Midwestern State Univ (TX)	COFFEY, Sue E. (Serials Libn) . . 227
	HARVILL, Melba S. (Dir of Libs) . 509
Milbank Tweed Hadley & McCloy (DC)	CAREY, Marsha C. (Libn) 181
Milbank Tweed Hadley & McCloy (NY)	RESCIGNO, Dolores S. (Technl
	Srvs Libn) 1024
	SANDERS, Robin S. (Asst Libn) 1080
Miles & Stockbridge (MD)	COLE, Anna B. (Libn) 230
Miles City Unified Sch District (MT)	STERLING, Linda L. (Libn) 1189
Miles Laboratories (IN)	LE GUERN, Charles A. (Pubns
	Srvs Libn) 712
	SAARI, David S. (Info Scitst) . . . 1072
Miles Laboratories Inc (IN)	YATES, Donald N. (Supvsr
	Employee Communications) . 1378
Milford Hospital (CT)	WESTBROOK, Patricia C.
	(Libn) 1326
Milford Pub Lib (CT)	BARGAR, Arthur W. (Media
	Libn) 56
Milford Sch District (DE)	CARPENTER, Carole H. (Libn &
	Study Skills Tchr) 184
Millard Pub Schs (NE)	HOOVER, Clara G. (Libn) 557
Millcreek Township Sch District (PA)	KOSTIS, Leigh W. (Elem Libn) . . 673
Miller Canfield Paddock & Stone (MI)	GREEN, Katherine A. (Head
	Libn) 462
Miller Legislative Services (DC)	MILLER, William S. (Pres) 843
Millersville Univ (PA)	GLASS, Catherine C. (Head
	Catlgr) 440
	LOTLIKAR, Sarojini D. (Asst
	Prof & Catlg Libn) 742
	LYONS, Evelyn L. (Ref Libn &
	Online Scrchr) 753
	MERRIAM, Doris E. (Asst Prof
	of Lib Sci) 826
	PEASE, Elaine K. (Catlg Libn) . . 953
	SANDERS, Minda M. (Assoc
	Prof Emeritus) 1080
	TASSIA, Margaret R. (Lib Sci
	Dept Chair) 1224
	TRIBIT, Donald K. (Perdcl,
	Microforms Libn, Assoc Prof) 1256
	ZUBATSKY, David S. (Lib &
	Media Srvs Dean) 1390
Milliken & Co (GA)	KELLY, Patrick M. (Educ Market
	Mgr) 638
Milliken Research Corp (SC)	CRAVEN, Trudy W. (Lib Mgr) . . . 256
Millikin Univ (IL)	HALE, Charles E. (Lib Dir) 485
Milling Benson Woodward Hillyer et	
al (LA)	FISHER, Collette J. (Head Libn) . 380
Mills Coll (CA)	PANDOLFO, Steven P. (Coll
	Libn) 937
	STOCKFLETH, Craig G.
	(Technl Srvs Libn) 1195
Mills-Peninsula Hospitals (CA)	CHU, Sally C. (Hlth Scis Lib
	Med Libn) 212
Millsaps Coll (MS)	PARKS, James F. (Coll Libn) . . . 943
Milton Pub Lib (WI)	MERCHANT, Thomas L. (Dir) . . . 825
Milton Pub Schs (WI)	HAY, Mary K. (Lib/Media Spclst) . 515
Milwaukee Area Technical Coll (WI)	MEERDINK, Richard E. (Libn) . . . 821
Milwaukee Board of Sch	
Directors (WI)	PINGEL, Carol J. (Libn) 974
Milwaukee County (WI)	GEISAR, Barbara J. (Legislative
	Libn) 425

Milwaukee County Federated Lib System (WI)
SAGER, Donald J. (City Libn & Dir) 1074

Milwaukee County Historical Society (WI)
COONEY, Charles W. (Cur of Resrch Cols) 241

Milwaukee Institute of Art & Design (WI)
MARCUS, Terry C. (Head Libn) . 769

Milwaukee Metropolitan Sewerage District (WI)
LANK, Dannette H. (Technl Resrch Analyst) 696

Milwaukee Pub Lib (WI)
ALTMANN, Thomas F. (Asst Coordntr for Humanities) 18
BOTHAM, Jane (Chlds Srvs Coordntr) 118
CEBULA, Theodore R. (Sci Bus & Tech Coordntr) 196
KINNEY, Michael F. (Mgmt Libn IV) 653
LOCKETT, Sandra B. (Libn In-Charge) 736
MCKINNEY, Venora (Deputy City Libn) 812
RAAB, Kathleen M. (Asst City Libn) 1001
SCHULLER, Susan M. (Chlds Libn) 1101
SCHWARTZ, Virginia C. (Humanities Coordntr) 1105

Milwaukee Pub Museum (WI)
CHAPLOCK, Sharon K. (Dir, AV Ctr) 201
OTTO, Susan J. (Photograph Archvst) 930
TURNER, Judith C. (Musm Libn) 1264

Milwaukee Sch of Engineering (WI)
SCHMIDT, Mary A. (Lib Dir) . . 1095

Minatare Pub Schs (NE)
JOHNSON, Elizabeth L. (Lib Media Spclst) 604

Mind Science Foundation (TX)
MORTON, Diane E. (Info Coordntr) 870

Mine Safety Appliances Co (PA)
BOUTWELL, Barbara J. (Lib Srvs Supvsr) 119

Mineral Well Independent Sch System (TX)
CHESHER, Joyce A. (Elem Lib Coordntr) 206

Ministry of Agriculture (PQ)
BELANGER, Sylvie (Libn) 76

Ministry of Agriculture & Water Devlpmnt (ZAM)
LUMANDE, Edward (Libn) 748

Ministry of Communications (PQ)
COLLISTER, Edward A. (Head of Info & Ref) 233

Ministry of Consumer/Commercial Relation (ON)
NIXON, Audrey I. (Lib Technician) 906

Ministry of Education (PQ)
CYR, Solange (Head of Documtn Ctr) 268

Ministry of Energy and Resources (PQ)
MARCIL, Louise (Libn) 769

Ministry of Finance & National Economy (SDA)
MANSFIELD, Jerry W. (Info & Resrch Spclst) 767

Ministry of Foreign Affairs (SDA)
TAMEEM, Jamal A. (Libn) 1221

Ministry of Health & Welfare (MEX)
MACIAS-CHAPULA, Cesar A. (Dir) 755

Ministry of Labor & Consumer Services (BC)
MURPHY, Joyce (Libn) 880

Ministry of Law, Hunting & Fishing (PQ)
SAVARD, Madeleine (Head Libn) 1085

Ministry of the Solicitor General (ON)
MOORE, Heather J. (Chief of Ministry Lib & Ref Ctr) 859

Ministry of Tourism, Recreation, Culture (BC)
MORGAN, Anne E. (Branch Libn) 863

MINITEX (MN)
DEJOHN, William T. (Dir) 288
ROSSMAN, Muriel J. (OCLC & Ref Srvs Asst Dir) 1059
YOUNGHOLM, Philip (Sr Minitex/OCLC Coordntr) 1383

Minneapolis Coll of Art & Design (MN)
MANNING, Mary L. (Asst Libn) . . 766

Minneapolis Community Coll (MN)
RINE, Joseph L. (Head Lib) 1035

Minneapolis Pub Lib (MN)

Minneapolis Pub Schs (MN)
LACY, Lyn E. (Media Spclst) 687

Minnegasco Inc (MN)
FABIO, Janet L. (Supvsr, Lib & Records Srv) 360

Minnehaha County Lib (SD)
REDDY, Joan L. (Dir) 1013

Minnesota Attorney General (MN)
ANDERSON, Anita M. (Law Libn) 21

Minnesota Department of Education (MN)
ASP, William G. (Dir) 37
DALBOTTEN, Mary S. (Media & Tech Spclst) 270
FEYE-STUKAS, Janice (Lib Spclst) 374
LEWIS, Alan D. (Asst Dir & Supvsr of Lib Devlpmnt) 722
MILLER, Robert H. (Supvsr, Media and Tech) 842
SWEEN, Roger (Multitype Lib Cooprtn Spclst) 1214
TALLY, Roy D. (Mgmt Analyst) . 1221

Minnesota Dept of Energy & Econ Devlpmnt (MN)
FENTON, Patricia F. (Sr Libn) . . . 371

Minnesota Department of Human Services (MN)
LINEWEAVER, Joe R. 730

Minnesota Department of Revenue (MN)
SLAMKOWSKI, Donna L. (Sr Libn) 1147

Minnesota Department of Transportation (MN)
BALDWIN, Jerome C. (Info Srvs Section Dir) 51
CORNELL, Pamela J. (Info Srvs Mgr) 246

Minnesota Historical Society (MN)
BAKER, Tracey I. (Asst Libn) 50
HOLBERT, Sue E. (State Archvst) 550
WALSTROM, Jon L. (Map Cur) 1300
WIENER, Alissa L. (Ref Libn) . . 1336

Minnesota Lib Association (MN)
TOWNE, Pamela (Exec Dir) . . . 1252

Minnesota Office of Lib Devlpmnt & Srvs (MN)
MAHMOODI, Suzanne H. (Continuing Educ Spclst) 760

Minnesota Orchestral Association (MN)
GUNTHER, Paul B. (Libn) 478

Minnesota Pollution Control Agency (MN)
DOLAN, Mary M. (Libn) 309

Minnesota State Law Lib (MN)
COLOKATHIS, Jane (Outreach Libn) 234
GALLIGAN, Sara A. (Head of Techni Srvs) 414

Minnesota State Legislature (MN)
GJELTEN, Daniel R. (Ref Srvs Head) 439

Minnesota Valley Regional Lib (MN)
GAVIN, Donna J. (Adult Srvs Coordntr) 423
WEIKUM, James M. (Asst Dir) . 1317

BARRETT, Darryl D. (Libn II) 59
BRUCE, Robert K. (Hist & Travel Dept Head) 149
CORCORAN, Nancy L. (Libn) . . . 246
FUGAZZI, Elizabeth B. (Chief, Centl Lib) 408
GRIGGS, Cynthia B. (Catlgr) 470
HASENSTEIN, Virginia P. (Libn) . 510
HILL, Constance L. (Catlgr) 539
KANE, Dennis M. (Assoc Dir) . . . 624
KIMBROUGH, Joseph (Dir) 649
KUKLA, Edward R. (Dept Head, Spcl Col) 683
SELANDER, Lucy M. (Lib Asst) 1113
SHANNON, Zella J. (Assoc Dir) 1121
SIMMONS, Antoinette S. (Chld's Libn) 1139
SMISEK, Thomas P. (Asst Dept Head) 1152
TERTELL, Susan M. (Dept Head of Bus & Econ) 1232
THEWS, Dorothy D. (Lit & Languages Dept Head) 1234
VAN WHY, Carol B. (Bus & Econ Asst Head) 1277
VETH, Terry R. (Head of Electronic Data Prcsng Dept) 1283

Minot Pub Lib (ND)
Minot Pub Schs (ND)

Minot State Univ (ND)
Mintz Levin Cohr Ferris Glovsky & Popeo (DC)
Minuteman Lib Network (MA)

Miriam I & William H Crawford Books (PA)

Mishawaka Lib Services Authority (IN)
Mishawaka-Penn Pub Lib (IN)

Missile Systems Division (GA)

Mission Coll (CA)
Mission Consolidated Independent Schs (TX)

Mississauga Pub Lib System (ON)

Mississippi Baptist Medical Center (MS)
Mississippi Coll (MS)

Mississippi Dept of Archives and History (MS)

Mississippi Lib Association (MS)
Mississippi Lib Commission (MS)
Mississippi Power Co (MS)

Mississippi State Univ (MS)

Mississippi Univ for Women (MS)

Mississippi Valley State Univ (MS)
Missoula County (MT)

Missouri Baptist Hospital (MO)
Missouri Botanical Garden (MO)

Missouri Department of Health (MO)
Missouri Lib Association (MO)

Missouri Lib Network Cooperation (MO)
Missouri Southern State Coll (MO)

Missouri State Lib (MO)

KAUP, Jermain A. (Lib Dir) 631
BOARDMAN, Edna M. (Lib Media Spclst) 108
WIRTANEN, James (AV Libn) . 1356

PULVER, Thomas B. (Law Libn) . 997
BADEN, Diane G. (Head of Catlgng Ctr) 44
KUKLINSKI, Joan L. (Netwk Coordntr) 683
LINSKY, Leonore K. (Database Mgr) 731

CRAWFORD, Miriam I. (Bookseller) 257

STRATTON, Martha G. (Coordntr) 1200
EISEN, David J. (Lib Dir) 340
VOLLNOGLE, Leslie A. (Video Libn) 1288
DEWBERRY, Claire D. (Engrng Libn) 298
CARROLL, Lois E. (Media Libn) . 187

ANDIS, Norma B. (Dir of Lrng Resrcs) 26
PONTIUS, Louise (Lrng Resrcs Spclst) 982
DINEEN, Diane M. (Head of Centl Lib) 304
RYAN, Noel (Bldg Proj Mgr) . . . 1071

BELL, Cecelia L. (Hlth Sci Libn) . 76
HOWELL, John B. (Dir) 565
MCMILLAN, Carnette R. (Acqs Libn) 815
SMITH, Rachel H. (Catlgr) 1159
WEST, Carol C. (Law Lib Dir & Prof of Law) 1326
HENNEN, Earl M. (Manuscripts Cur (Archvst III)) 528
BELL, Bernice (Exec Secy) 76
WOODBURN, David M. (Dir) . . 1366
MCCREARY, Gail A. (Records Mgmt Supvsr) 800
BRELAND, June M. (Branch Libn) 132
CHRESSANTHIS, June D. (Serials Catlgr) 211
WELLS, Anne S. (Asst Prof Manuscripts Lib) 1322
PAYNE, David L. (Lib Srvs Dir & Prof) 951
BOWEN, Ethel B. (Serials Libn) . . 120
WYNNE, Tia J. (Chlds, Young Adult Libn) 1375
RENFER, Melissa (Med Libn) . 1023
NYSTROM, Kathleen A. (Head of Catlgng) 913
RILEY, Martha J. (Archvst) 1034
WOLF, Constance P. (Lib Dir) . . 1360
TORDOFF, Brian G. (Med Libn) 1251
MCCARTNEY, Jean A. (Exec Coordntr) 794

MERCANTE, Mary A. (Dir) 825
CONNORS, Theresa (Libn) 238
KEMP, Charles H. (Head Libn) . . 639
NODLER, Charles E. (Archvst, Libn) 906
REIMAN, David A. (Ref Libn) . . 1020
HIGHTOWER, Monteria (State Libn) 538
MILLER, Richard T. (Asst State Libn) 841
PARKES, Darla J. (Ref & Interlib Loan Libn) 942
WATSON, Janice D. (Libn) 1309

Missouri Training Center for Men (MO)
Mitchell Community Pub Lib (IN)
Mitchell Community Schs (IN)
Mitchell Information Services (TX)

Mitchell Memorial Lib (MS)

Mitel Corp (ON)

Mitel Corp (PQ)

Mitre Corp (MA)

Mitre Corp (VA)

Mitsubishi Research Institute Inc (JAP)

MJE Infoservices (TN)
MMI Preparatory Sch (PA)

Mobay Chemical Corp (KS)
Mobay Chemical Corp (PA)

Moberly Area Junior Coll (MO)
Mobil Chemical Co (NJ)

Mobil Exploration and Producing Srvs Inc (TX)
Mobil Oil Corp (NJ)

Mobil Oil Corp (NY)

Mobil Producing of Texas & New Mexico (TX)

Mobil Research & Development Corp (NJ)

Mobil Research & Development Corp (TX)

Mobil Solar Energy Corp (MA)
Mobile Coll (AL)

Mobile Infirmary Medical Center (AL)
Mobile Pub Lib (AL)

Modern Language Association (NY)

Modern Talking Picture Service (SD)

Modern Woodmen of America (IL)
Modrall Sperling Roehl Harris & Sisk (NM)
Mohawk Coll (ON)

BEQUETTE, V L. (Sch Libn) 84
HOLT, Vickie L. (Dir) 554
WOODRUFF, Gail R. (Sch Libn) 1366
MITCHE, Cynthia R. (Pres) 848
MITCHELL, Cynthia R. (Pres) . . . 848
ELLSBURY, Susan H. (Asst Prof & Ref Libn) 345
PHILLIPS, Rosemary (Corprt Lib Mgr) 969
RICHARD, Marie F. (Info & Documtn Mgr) 1028
JENNINGS, Margaret S. (Sr Writer & Editor) 598
JOACHIM, Robert J. (Ref Libn) . . 600
LIEBERMAN, Sharon A. (Ref Libn) 726
NIGAM, Alok C. (Technl Staff Mem) 904
TATALIAS, Jean A. (Info Srvs Mgr) 1225

NASU, Yukio (Sr Staff Researcher) 889
YAMAZAKI, Hisamichi (Mgr of Database Srvs Sect) 1377
ERWIN, Mary J. (Info Broker) . . . 353
EVERHART, Nancy L. (Lib Media Spclst) 358
YOUNG, Carolyn K. (Libn) 1381
ALSTADT, Nancy A. (Libn) 18
SCHLUETER, Betsy W. 1094
DARST, Valerie (Libn) 275
GURNEY, Eileen A. (Technl Info Spclst) 478

FREEMAN, Mary L. (Libn) 401
SMITH, Yvonne B. (Technl Info Spclst) 1161
DIGIOVANNA, Josephine A. (Head Libn) 303
MARSHALL, Patricia K. (Mgr, Analytical Resrch Srvs) 775
ROBERTSON, Betty M. (Records Mgmt Supvsr) 1041

BISHOP, Daran L. (Info Resrc Coordntr) 99

BITTER, Jane L. (Lib Supvsr) . . . 100
BULYA, Larissa (Technl Libn) . . . 157

SCHOOLFIELD, Dudley B. (Catlgr) 1098
BERGIN, Dorothy O. (Coordntr) . . . 86
PARSLEY, Brantley H. (Lib Dir) . . 944
ROBERTS, Eddie F. (Reader Srvs Libn) 1039
WESTOVER, Mary L. (Ref & Media Asst) 1327
HALL, Patricia N. (Med Lib Dir) . . 488
CALHOUN, Margie B. (Branch Libn) 172
CURRY, Janette M. (Hum Ref Libn) 266
JEFFERY, Phyllis D. (AV Libn) . . 596
LEFLORE, Walker B. (Pub Lib Bd Mem) 712
MCWHORTER, Jimmie M. (Spcl Projects Ofcr) 818
MACKESY, Eileen M. (Bibligphr Srvs Dir) 756
SPEARS, Dee E. 1172
MODICA, Mary L. (Resrcs Curr & Trng Coordntr) 851
LEVIS, Gail A. (Secy & Histn) . . . 721

GREENWOOD, Miriam J. (Libn) . 465
BLACK, Sandra M. (Chief Libn) . 101

Mohawk Valley Lib Association (NY)
PROVOST, Beverly A. (Chlds & Yng Adult Consult) 996
KASPER, Barbara (Chlds Libn) . . 629
CHENOWETH, Rose M. (Head, Extension Srvs) 206
SNYDER, Sherrie E. (Lib Dir) . . 1165
MAYER, Mary C. (Catlgr) 789

Mohegan Community Coll (CT)
Moline Pub Lib (IL)

Molloy Coll (NY)
Moncrief Army Community Hospital (SC)
WETHERBY, Ivor L. (Libn) 1328
Monenco Consultants Ltd (PQ)
KAMICHAITIS, Penelope H. (Libn) 624

Monessen Pub Lib (PA)
FERYOK, Joseph A. (Adult Srvs Libn) 374

Monmouth Coll (IL)
HAUGE, Harris R. (Head Libn) . . 512
Monmouth Coll (NJ)
SUTTON, Robert F. (Assoc Libn & Catlg Dept Head) 1211
VAN BENTHUYSEN, Robert F. (Cur of Spcl Cols) 1272

Monmouth County Lib (NJ)
BERGER, Morey R. (Asst Dir) 86
FIELD, Jack (Chief Libn, Headquarters) 375
FIELD, Margaret (Branch Coordntr) 375
HIGGINS, Flora T. (Branch Libn) . 537
KRANIS, Janet C. (Chief Libn) . . 676
PARR, Louise M. (Principal Libn) 943
SMOTHERS, Joyce W. (Supervising Libn) 1162

Monmouth Medical Center (NJ)
PACHMAN, Frederic C. (Dir) . . 933
Mono County Free Lib (CA)
REVEAL, Arlene H. (County Libn) 1024

Monosson Technology Enterprises (MA)
MONOSSON, Adolf S. (Publshr) . 855
Monroe Business Institute (NY)
KONOVALOFF, Maria S. (Libn) . 670
Monroe City Sch System (LA)
MEINEL, Nancy T. (Elem Libn) . . 822
Monroe County Historical Commission (MI)
KULL, Christine L. (Archvst) 683
Monroe County Lib System (MI)
MARGOLIS, Bernard A. (Dir) . . . 770
Monroe County Lib System (NY)
CUMMINS, Julie A. (Chlds Srvs Consult) 264
MORSE, Pat B. (Extension Libn) . 869
Monroe County Pub Lib (FL)
Monroe County Pub Lib (IN)
FARLEY, Janice S. (Asst Dir) . . . 364
KASER, Jane (Technl Srvs Asst Head) 628
Monroe County Pub Lib (PA)
KEISER, Barbara J. (Adult Srvs Libn) 635
Monroe Developmental Center (NY)
HOWIE, Maryann (Staff Libn) . . . 566
Monsanto Co (MO)
BACKES, Lynn B. 44
CHUNG, Carolyn (Libn) 213
GAFFEY, Mary V. (Sr Libn) 411
GELINNE, Michael S. (Bus Ref Libn) 426
KLEIN, Regina D. (Bus Lib Supvsr) 659
WILKINSON, William A. (Info Ctr Mgr) 1340
Monsanto Research Corp (OH)
MOORE, Susan J. (Libn) 861
Montague Area Pub Schs (MI)
SCARBROUGH, S J. (Media Spclst) 1087

Montana Coll of Mineral Sci and Tech (MT)
HUYGEN, Michaele L. (Ref Libn) 580

Montana Historical Society (MT)
CLARK, Robert M. (Head, Div of Archs and Lib) 218
HIBPSHMAN, Lawrence (State Archvst) 536
MORROW, Delores J. (Photograph Archvst) 869
Montana Lib Association (MT)
MAXWELL, Lawrence (Pres) . . . 788
Montana Office of Pub Instruction (MT)
BERGERON, Cheri Y. (Libn) 86
Montana State Lib (MT)
CATES, Sheila A. (Lib Devlpmnt Coordntr) 195
PARKER, Sara A. (State Libn) . . 942
Montana State Univ (MT)
ALLDREDGE, Noreen S. (Dean of Libs) 14
BRANDON, Janice R. (Head of Circ & Rsvs Dept) 128
BREMER, Thomas A. (Ref Libn) . 132

Montana State Univ (MT)
BRUWELHEIDE, Janis H. (Instrcl Media Assoc Prof) . . . 151
KAYA, Kathryn A. (Ref Libn) 632
MORTON, Bruce (Ref Dept Head) 870
STACK, Laurie A. (Systs Coordntr) 1177
STEPHENS, Marian G. (Docums Libn) 1188
Montclair Kimberly Academy (NJ)
GREENSPAN, Vivi S. (Libn) 465
Montclair Pub Lib (NJ)
GORMAN, Audrey J. (Youth Srvs Dept Mgr) 452
STRICKLAND, Patricia J. (Youth Srvs Spclst) 1202
Montclair State Coll (NJ)
HUGHES, Kathleen (Catlgr & Asst Prof) 572
MINTZ, Donald M. (Prof of Music) 847
RICHARDSON, Robert J. (Non-print Media Libn) 1030
STOCK, Norman (Col Devlpmnt & Acqs Libn) 1195
Monte Cristo Coll (CT)
MCDONALD, Lois E. (Assoc Cur) 803
Montefiore Hospital (PA)
ROSEN, Gloria K. (Med Lib Dir) 1055
Montefiore Medical Center (NY)
LIEBER, Ellen C. (Acting Dir) . . . 726
Montemorelos Univ (MEX)
SIEMENS, Bessie M. (Lib Dir) . . 1136
Monterey Bay Aquarium (CA)
MANKE, Merrill E. (Libn) 765
Monterey Bay Area Coop Lib Syst (CA)
SERTIC, Kenneth J. (Syst Coordntr) 1116
Monterey County (CA)
SHAFFER, Dallas Y. (Cnty Libn) 1119
Monterey County Lib (CA)
CHURCH, Sonia J. (Youth Srvs Coordntr) 213
Monterey Peninsula Coll (CA)
SMALLEY, Topsy N. (Pub Srvs Libn) 1151
Monterey Pub Lib (CA)
NEAL, Jan (Technl Srvs Head) . . 890
Montezuma Unified Sch District 371 (KS)
CROTTS, Carolyn D. (Sch Libn) . 261
Montgomery Coll (MD)
NOLAN, Deborah A. (Coll Dir) . . 907
Montgomery County Board of Education (AL)
FELDER, Jimmie R. (Head Libn) . 369
Montgomery County Community Coll (PA)
MARTIN, Shelby A. (Head Catlg Libn) 778
ROSENBERGER, Merry G. (Ref Libn) 1056
TERRY, Terese M. (Pub Srvs Libn) 1232
Montgomery County Department of Pub Libs (MD)
ALEXANDER, Estelle R. (Ref Libn) 12
BUSH, Rhoda H. (Ref Libn) 165
CHELTON, Mary K. (Lib Progs Coordntr) 204
DOWD, Frank B. (Acqs & Spcl Cols Mgr) 315
GALE, Roswita W. (Comunty Libn) 413
GRIFFEN, Agnes M. (Dir) 468
LINTON, Linda A. (Chlds Libn) . . 731
NITZBERG, Dale B. (Ref Libn) . . 905
PEDAK-KARI, Maria (Pub Info & Staff Devlpmnt Coordntr) 954
PHIFER, Kenneth O. (Ref Libn) . . 967
PILZER, Cecily R. (Chlds Libn 1) 973
SHAPIRO, Leila C. (Regnl Libn) 1121
SOLOMON, Fern R. (Sr Libn, Supvsr of Telephone Ref) . . . 1166
Montgomery County Department of Pub Libs (PA)
CATHEY, Gail L. (Ref Perdcl Libn) 195
GRIFFITH, Dorothy A. (Ref Libn) 469
PECK, Marian B. (Dir of Chlds Srvs) 953
Montgomery County Lib (MD)
GIBBS, Beatrice E. (Chlds Libn) . 431
Montgomery County Lib System (TX)
BALDWIN, Joe M. (Lib Dir) 51

Montgomery County Pub Lib (MD) MEIZNER, Kathie L. (Sr Libn) ... 822
Montgomery County Pub Schs (MD) BARALOTO, R A. (Evaluation & Selection Asst) 55
DAVIES, Gordon D. (Media Spclst) 277
DEAN, Frances C. (Dir) 283
KISSMAN, Elise C. (Media Spclst) 656
KNOX, Jo E. (Media Spclst) ... 666
MORGAN, Betty J. (Media Spclst) 863
Montgomery-Floyd Regional Lib (VA) COMPARIN, Ida (Asst Dir) 235
Montgomery Hospital (PA) O'BRIEN, Alberta T. (Libn) 914
Montgomery McCracken Walker & Rhoads (PA) BROWN, Georgeanne H. (Libn) . 144
Montini High Sch (IL) RACZYNSKI, Mary K. (Libn) ... 1002
Montreal Children's Lib (PQ) WALSH, Mary A. (Head Libn & Branch Coordntr) 1300
Montreal General Hospital (PQ) KOBER, Gary L. (Chief Libn) 666
STAMBOULIEH, Nora (Libn) ... 1179
Montrose County Sch District RE15 (CO) MACY, Edwin L. (Libn) 758
Moody Bible Institute Lib (IL) OSBORN, Walter (Ref Libn) 927
Moody's Investors Service (NY) BING, Robert H. (Asst VP & Municipal Products Mgr) .. 97
KOPPELMAN, William H. (Asst VP) 671
LAMBERT, Sheila S. (Sr VP & Publshr) 690
ZOTTOLI, Danny A. (VP and Dir, Info Srvs) 1390
Moore & Peterson (TX) TEMPLETON, Virginia E. (Libn) . 1231
Moore Business Forms Inc (NY) WATERS, Betsy M. (Info Ctr Supvsr) 1308
Moore Data Database Publishing (MN) RUBNIK, Louis J. (Pres) 1065
Moore Data Management Services (MN) BRUTON, Robert T. (Dir of Corprt Plng) 151
Moorhead Pub Lib (MN) BRUNTON, Marilyn H. (Youth Srvs Coordntr) 151
Moorhead State Univ (MN) SHOPTAUGH, Terry L. (Univ Archvst) 1132
SIBLEY, Carol H. (Curr Libn) .. 1134
Mor Institute for Medical Data (ISR) CAREL, Rafael S. (Med Dir) 181
Moraine Valley Community Coll (IL) D'AVERSA, Concettina M. (Technl Srvs Asst Libn) 276
HESSLER, Nancy R. (Lib Srvs Coordntr) 534
TEO, Elizabeth A. (Assoc Libn) . 1231
Moravian Archives (NC) HAUPERT, Thomas J. (Dir) 512
Moravian Archives (PA) NELSON, Vernon H. (Archvst) .. 895
Moravian Coll (PA) CRAWFORD, Gregory A. (Ref & Pub Srvs Libn) 256
Morehead State Univ (KY) BESANT, Larry X. (Dir of Libs) ... 91
HALL, Juanita J. (Head Catlgr) . 488
ISON, Betty S. (Coordntr) 585
PRITCHARD, Elsie T. (Acting Acqs Libn) 994
WILLIAMS, Helen E. (Lrng Resrc Ctr Head) 1343
Morehouse Sch of Medicine (GA) SWANSON, Joe (Catlg Libn) ... 1213
Morgan & Finnegan (NY) CURCI, Lucy (Libn) 265
Morgan Guaranty Trust Co (NY) SMITH, Melanie W. (Head Ref Libn) 1158
WARD, Victoria M. (Law Libn) . 1304
Morgan Lewis & Bockius (DC) LIPMAN, Renee E. (Libn) 732
Morgan Lewis & Bockius (FL)
Morgan Lewis & Bockius (MD) MERINGOLO, Joseph A. (Legislative Dir & Ref Libn) ... 826
Morgan Lewis & Bockius (PA) BEARDWOOD, Louise B. (Asst Libn) 69
ROACH, Linda 1038
Morgan Stanley & Co (NY) DESSER, Darrilyn (Lib Technl Srvs Asst Mgr) 296
ENGLER, Gretchen (Asst Resrch Mgr) 349
JONES, Sarah C. (VP) 615
LAWSON, George F. (Data Base Analyst) 705
Morgan Stanley & Co (NY) MAYOPOULOS, Karen L. (Resrch Libn) 791
VAZQUEZ, Edward (Database Asst) 1280
Morgan State Univ (MD) DE LERMA, Dominique R. (Prof of Music) 289
KUAN, David A. (Catlg Libn) ... 681
Morley Lib (OH) GARDNER, John R. (Dir) 418
The Morning Call (PA) SWARTZ, Patrice B. (Libn) 1214
Morningside Coll (IA) BOWEN, Kay (Technl Srvs Libn) 120
Morrill Memorial Lib (MA) HIMMELSBACH, Carl J. (Lib Dir) 542
Morris Architects (TX) WIEGMAN, John H. (Pres) 1336
Morris Coll (SC) GORDON, Clara B. (Lib Dir) 451
Morris County Board of Realtors (NJ) HODNETT, Diane M. (Libn) 546
Morris County Free Lib (NJ) MENZEL, John P. (Col Devlpmnt Coordntr) 825
OTT, Linda G. (Head of Ref) ... 930
VAN WIEMOKLY, Jane G. (Principal Libn) 1277
Morris County Lib (NJ) CAUSLEY, Monroe S. (Lib Dir) .. 195
Morris Larson King and Stamper (MO) GINGRICH, Linda K. (Law Libn) . 437
Morris Lib (IL) BLACK, George W. (Sci Libn) ... 101
Morrison & Foerster (CA) NEMCHEK, Lee R. (Law Libn & Records Ctr Supvsr) 895
OPPEDAL, Teresa A. (Law Libn) 925
Morristown Hamblen Pub Lib (TN) BROOKS, Judy B. (Asst Dir & Chlds Libn) 140
Morristown Memorial Hospital (NJ) SEARLE, Jo A. (Dir of Lib Srvs) 1110
The Morton Arboretum (IL) HASSERT, Rita M. (Technl Srvs Libn) 511
SHOTWELL, Richard T. (Lib Adminstr & Ref Libn) 1133
Morton F Plant Hospital (FL) SCHMID, Cynthia M. (Med Libn) 1094
Morton Grove Pub Lib (IL) GOLATA, John P. (Bd of Trustees Pres) 444
OSERMAN, Stuart (Trustee) 928
Morton High Sch District 201 (IL) DOWNES, Valerie (Lib Media Srvs Libn) 316
SHERMAN, Janice E. (Dir) 1128
Morton Pub Lib (IL) IRWIN, Ruth A. (Div Libn) 584
Morton Thiokol Inc (MD) WAID, Diana L. 1292
Morton Thiokol Inc (OH)
Moseley Associates Inc (NY) MOSELEY, Cameron S. (Pres & Chief Exec Ofcr) 870
Moses Brown Sch (RI) ODEAN, Kathleen F. (Libn) 916
Moses H Cone Hospital (NC) MACKLER, Leslie G. (Med Lib Dir) 757
Moses Taylor Hospital (PA) BABISH, Jo A. (Dir of Lib Srvs) .. 43
Moss Adams (WA) HETZLER, Jill K. (Info Spclst) ... 534
Moss Rehabilitation Hospital (PA) CASINI, Barbara P. (Educ Resrcs Dir) 192
KLUESNER, Marvin P. (Libn) ... 662
Mother Mary Mission Sch Lib (AL) O'HEARON, Doris M. (Dir, Resr Ctr) 919
Mother McAuley Liberal Arts High Sch (IL) RICH, Elisabeth (Libn) 1027
Motor Vehicle Manufacturers Association (MI) GIGLIO, Linda M. (Pub Relations Coordntr, Libn) 433
SIEGEL, Marilyn (Libn) 1136
VELLIKY, Mary M. (Technl Libn) 1281
WREN, James A. (Patent Dept Mgr) 1370
Motorola Inc (FL) LANGE, Joan K. (Technl Libn) .. 695
Motorola Inc (TX) MCVICAR, Ann L. (Mgr) 818
Mount Allison Univ (NB) EADIE, Tom (Univ Libn) 331
MCNALLY, Brian D. (Sci Govt Docums Libn) 815
Mount Auburn Hospital (MA) LANDRY, Francis R. (Asst Libn) . 693
Mount Carmel Health Center (OH) CHEEK, Fern M. (Ref Libn) 204
ELWELL, Pamela M. (Dir, Lib Srvs) 347
Mount Carmel Mercy Hospital (MI) SKONIECZNY, Jill (Dir, Med Lib) 1147
Mount Diablo Unified Sch District (CA) SKAPURA, Robert J. (Libn) ... 1145

Mount Holyoke Coll (MA)
CALLAHAN, Linda J. (Slide Cur) 173
EDMONDS, Anne C. (Coll Libn) . 336
VAN HOORN, Audra G. (Libn) . 1275

Mount Hope Township (IL)
Mt Kisco Pub Lib (NY)
BIRO, Juliane (Libn) 99
Mt Lebanon Pub Lib (PA)
HURLEY, Doreen S. (Chlds Libn & Catlgr) 577

Mount Mercy Coll (IA)
DICKES, Janis H. (Technl Srvs Libn) 300

Mt Olive Coll (NC)
BAREFOOT, Gary F. (Libn) 56
Mt Prospect Pub Lib (IL)
GRIEGER, Sharon L. (Col Devlpmnt Libn) 468
MARABOTTI, Denise M. (Chlds Srvs Asst Head) 768
TIWANA, Nazar H. (Ref Libn) .. 1247
Mt Prospect Pub Schs (IL)
GUNDERSEN, Shirley S. (Lib Srvs Dir) 477
Mount Royal Coll (AB)
BAILEY, Madeleine J. (Coll Libn) 46

Mount Saint Joseph Motherhouse (KY)
BUSAM, Emma C. (Archs & Musm Dir) 164
Mount St Mary's Coll (CA)
CONDON, Erika M. (Head Libn) . 236
POPOVITCH-KREKIC, Ruzica (Pub Srvs & Ref Libn) 984
Mount Saint Mary's Coll (MD)
FITZPATRICK, Kelly (Dir, Spcl Cols) 383
Mount St Vincent Univ (NS)
BIANCHINI, Lucian (Univ Libn) ... 94
GLENISTER, Peter (Catlg Libn) . 441
PARIS, Terrence L. (Pub Srvs Libn) 940
Mount Sinai Affiliation (NY)
SALEY, Stacey (Chief Med Libn) 1076

Mount Sinai Hospital Medical Center (IL)
SOBKOWIAK, Emily J. (Med & Nursing Libn) 1165
Mount Sinai Medical Center (FL)
EZQUERRA, Isabel (Med Lib Chief) 360
Mount Sinai Medical Center (NY)
MORGAN, Lynn K. (Lib Dir & Instr of Dept of Med Educ) .. 864
Mount Sinai Medical Center (OH)
LANDAU, Lucille (Project Coordntr and Clinical Libn) ... 692
RASKIN, Rosa S. (Med Libn) . 1009
Mount Vernon Coll (DC)
COCKE, Lucy S. (Lib Dir) 226
Mount Vernon Community Center Sch (VA)
OSIA, Ruby R. (Lib Media Spclst) 928
Mt Vernon Hospital (NY)
COAN, Mary L. (Dir of Lib & Info Srvs) 224
Mount Vernon Pub Lib (NY)
MITTELGLUCK, Eugene L. (Lib Dir) 850
O'DELL, Lorraine I. (Asst Dir) ... 916
ROSSWURM, K M. (Adults Srvs Head) 1059
Mt Vernon Sch District (WA)
JONES, Sally L. (Libn) 615
Mount Wachusett Community Coll (MA)
COOLIDGE, Christina L. (Asst Libn) 241

Mountain Area Health Education Center (NC)
BUTSON, Linda C. (Assoc Dir) .. 167
THIBODEAU, Patricia L. (Info & Media Srvs Dir) 1235
Mountain Bell (CO)
BOND, Bruce B. (Strategic Plng VP) 113
BRUNER, Robert B. (Human Resrcs Resrch) 150
Mountain Brook City Schs (AL)
GOODWYN, Betty R. (Libn) 450
Mountainside Hospital (NJ)
REGENBERG, Patricia B. (Hlth Scis Lib Dir) 1017
WATKINS, Elizabeth A. (Libn) .. 1309
Mountainside Publishing Co (MI)
DOUGHERTY, Ann P. (Assoc Edit) 313

Mountainwest Coll of Business & Tech (UT)
Mouzon Information Services (MI)
MCMURRIN, Jean A. (Libn) 815
MPR Associates Inc (DC)
MOUZON, Margaret W. (Owner) . 874
MSC Seminary Lib (PA)
BERNSTEIN, Anna L. (Libn) 89
CAMILLI, E. M. (Libn) 175
MSL International Inc (GA)
BRYANT, Nancy J. (Dir of Resrch) 152

MSL International Ltd (NY)
MSU System Services Inc (LA)

Mudge Rose Guthrie Alexander & Ferdon (NY)

Mueller Associates Inc (MD)

Mullen High Sch (CO)
Multipoint Communications Limited (ON)
Multnomah County Lib (OR)

Multnomah Law Lib (OR)
Mumps Medical Info Management Systems (IL)
Muncie Pub Lib (IN)

Mundelein Coll (IL)

Municipal Art Society (NY)
Municipal Information Lib (MN)

Municipality of Anchorage (AK)

Municipality of Metropolitan Seattle (WA)
Municipality of Metropolitan Toronto (ON)
Murdoch Magazines (DC)

Murdoch Magazines (NJ)
Murray City Pub Lib (UT)
Murray State Coll (OK)

Murray State Univ (KY)

Muscatine Community Schs (IA)

Muscogee County Sch District (GA)
Museum of Broadcasting (NY)

Museum of Contemporary Art (IL)

Museum of Fine Arts (MA)
Museum of Fine Arts (TX)

Museum of Jewish Heritage (NY)

Museum of Modern Art (NY)

RATZABI, Arlene (Resrch Assoc) 1010
STANLEY, Nelda J. (Sr Environ Analyst & Info Mgr) 1180

BRILL, Krista C. (Ref Libn) 136
MARTIN, Margaret B. (Info Srvs Dir) 777
MENEGAUX, Edmond A. (Libn, Technl Spclst) 824
TUCKER, Clark F. (Info Ctr Mgr) 1261
MILLER, Charles G. (Libn) 836

SMITH, Iain (VP) 1155
BARNETT, Jean D. (Hum Dept Mgr) 57
BURNS, Carol J. (Technl Srvs Dir) 162
JULAPHONGS, Martha M. (Finance Dir) 619
LONG, Sarah A. (Dir) 740
RENFRO, Robert S. (Catlg Libn) 1023
RHYNE, Barbara B. (Sr Music Libn) 1026
THENELL, Janice C. (Coordntr of Pub Relations) 1234
WRIGHT, Catherine A. (Black Resrc Ctr Coordntr) 1370
JURKINS, Jacquelyn J. (Dir) 620

KRUSS, Daniel M. (Pres) 681
KROEHLER, Beth A. (Spcl Projs Libn) 679
SCHAEFER, Patricia (Lib Dir) .. 1089
CURRY, Jean K. (Acqs & Perdcls Libn) 266
DONAHOE, Patricia A. (Dir) 310
SWIESZKOWSK, L S. (Dir) ... 1216
RAFTER, Susan (Head & Ref Libn) 1003
FREDERIKSEN, Patience A. (Ref Libn) 400

MCBRIDE, Anne (Libn) 792

DANIEL, Eileen (Sr Resrch Ofcr) . 272
GAZZOLA, Kenneth E. (Publshr) 424
KINLEY, Jo H. (Dir) 652
COVILL, Bruce (Systs Dir) 252
SLUSHER, Donna C. (Dir) 1150
KENNEDY, James W. (Lib, Lrng Resrc Ctr Dir) 641
BUSER, Robin A. (Catlgr & Instr) 165
CULPEPPER, Jetta C. (Head of Acqs) 264
HEIM, Keith M. (Head, Spcl Cols) 521
WALL, Celia J. (Circ Dept Head) 1297
MATHER, Becky R. (Media Spclst) 783
SELF, Sharon W. (Libn) 1113
DAVIDSON, Steven I. (Lib Srvs Dir) 276
PIRON, Alice M. (Libn & Outreach Coordntr for Schs) .. 975
ALLEN, Nancy S. (Lib Dir) 15
MOST, Gregory P. (Slide Libn) .. 872
SHEAROUSE, Linda N. (Libn) .. 1124
SCHREIBMAN, Fay C. (Proj Dir, Hall of Lrng) 1099
BAXTER, Paula A. (Assoc Ref Libn) 67
EKDAHL, Janis K. (Asst Lib Dir) . 341
PHILLPOT, Clive J. (Lib Dir) 969
SLOAN, William J. (Chief of Circulating Film Lib) 1150

Museum of Modern Art (NY)
STARR, Daniel A. (Assoc Libn, Catlgng) 1182

Museum of the American Indian (NY) DAVIS, Mary B. (Libn) 280
WEATHERFORD, Elizabeth (Assoc Cur) 1311

Museum of the City of New York (NY) COLEMAN, Faith (Asst Cur for the Archs, Theatre Col) 231
TAYLOR, Robert N. (Cur) 1228

Museum of Western Colorado (CO) PROSSER, Judy A. (Archvst & Registrar) 995

Museum Systems Enterprises (DC) YARNALL, James L. (Consult) . 1378

Music & Arts Programs of America Inc (CA) MAROTH, Frederick J. (Pres) ... 772

Music Lib Association (IL) GUSHEE, Marion S. (Book Rvw Edit) 478

Music Lib Association (MA) BLOTNER, Linda S. (Exec Secy) 106
HENDERSON, James P. (Bus Mgr) 526

Musical Arts Association (OH) ARNOLD, Judith M. (Archvst) 33

Muskegon Community Coll (MI) VANDERLAAN, Robert J. (Catlgr & Ref Libn) 1274

Muskegon County Lib (MI) MCFERRAN, Warren A. (Dir) ... 805
VETTESE, Richard (Asst Dir) .. 1283

Muskegon Schs (MI) HOUSEWARD, Bernice A. (Head, Chlds & Teens Dept) .. 563

Musser Pub Lib (IA) CHAUDOIN, Sheila M. (Asst Dir) 204
SORENSON, Debra J. (Technl Srvs Coordntr) 1168

Mutual Benificial Insurance Co (PA) SWIGART, William E. (Chairman of the Bd) 1216

Mutual Life of Canada (ON) ELLERT, Barbara M. (Libn & Resrchr) 343

Mutual of New York Financial Services (NY) GROSS, Gretchen (Mgr) 472

Mystic Seaport Museum (CT) STONE, Ellen C. (Ships Plans Col Mgr) 1197

N

N S Kline Inst for Psychiatric Research (NY) COHAN, Lois (Lib Dir) 227

N W Ayer Inc (NY) BUSSEY, Holly J. (Mgr) 165

Nabors Bid Tabulations Service (LA) JACKSON, Audrey N. (Pres & Owner) 586

Nagoya Univ of Commerce (JAP) TOGUCHI, Eiko (Asst Dir & Lecturer in Lib Sci) 1248

Nahant Pub Lib (MA) CISNEY, Douglas S. (Head Libn) 215

NAHB National Research Center (MD) HARBERT, Cathy E. (Libn) 499

Nairobi Evangelical Grad Sch of Theology (KEN) BOWEN, Dorothy N. (Dir of Lib Srvs) 120

Nalco Chemical Co (IL) BOYLE, Stephen (Info Srvs Supvsr) 124
STUNKARD, Gilbert L. (Info Scitst) 1205

NALINET (MD) CHEN, John H. (Dir) 205

Nancy Escher Inc (CA) ESCHER, Nancy (Pres) 354

Nantahala Regional Library (NC) ABBOTT, Dorothy D. (Acqs Libn) 1

Nantucket Historical Assn (MA) HARING, Jacqueline K. (Cur of Resrch Mtrls) 501

Napa City-County Lib (CA) CHAMBERLIN, Leslie A. (Head of Extension & Chlds Srvs) ... 198
HERSH, Daniel (Ref Libn) 533

Nardin Academy (NY) BREEN, M F. (Archvst) 131

Naremco Services Inc (NY) CROCKETT, Denise J. (Principal) 259

Nash Technical Coll (NC) FINCH, Lynette (Libn) 377

Nashua Pub Lib (NH) GRANT, Nancy A. (Ref Libn) ... 458
WARREN, Ann R. (Music Art Media Srvs Supvsr) 1306

Nashville Community High Sch District 99 (IL) RUSIEWSKI, Charles B. (Lib & Media Ctr Dir) 1068

Nassau Academy of Medicine (NY) WESTERMANN, Mary L. (Med Libn) 1327

Nassau Community Coll (NY) FRIEDMAN, Arthur L. (Lib Chairman) 403
GRUNDT, Leonard (Prof) 475

Nassau Lib System (NY) BARTENBACH, Martha A. (Microcomputer Spclst) 60
BOREK, Mary A. (Technl Srvs Chief) 116
GOTTLIEB, Delia (Media Spclst) . 453
GREEN, Joseph H. (Dir) 462

Natchez-Adams Pub Schs (MS) RANDAZZO, Corinne O. (Lib Media Srvs Dir) 1006

National Academy of Sciences (DC) MOBLEY, Arthur B. (Mgr) 851

National Aeronautics & Space Admin (DC) HARGRAVE, Charles W. (Acqs & Dissemination Branch Chief) 501

National Aeronautics & Space Admin (MD) BOGGESS, John J. (Acting Libn) 110

National Aeronautics & Space Admin (OH) FACINELLI, Jaclyn R. (Libn D-K Assocs) 360
JARABEK, Leona T. (Libn) 594

National Aeronautics & Space Admin (VA) PINELLI, Thomas E. (Visual & Printing Srvs Branch Head) .. 974

NASA/Ames Research Center Lib (CA) SANDFORD, Betsy R. (Catlgng & Ref Libn) 1080

NASA Lewis Research Center (OH) LONG, Melanie C. (Catlgng and Resrch Libn) 739
OBERC, Susanne F. (Libn, Sr Catlgr & Ref Libn) 913

NASA Scientific & Technl Info Facility (MD) BUCHAN, Ronald L. (Lexicographer) 153
JACK, Robert F. (Tech Utilization Database Systs Mgr) 586

National Agricultural Lib (MD) BROGDON, Jennie L. (Head, Ref Branch) 139
COLLINS, Donna S. (Slavic Languages Libn) 232
ESMAN, Michael D. 354
GELENTER, Winifred H. (Leader, Serials Unit) 426
GOLDSBERG, Elizabeth D. (Spcl Srvs Branch Head) 446
MCCONE, Gary K. (Head, Database Admin Branch) 797
RAFATS, Jerome M. (Ref Libn) 1003
RUSSELL, Keith W. (Pub Srvs Div Chief) 1069
THOMAS, Sarah E. (Technl Srvs Div Chief) 1238
WATERS, Samuel T. (Assoc Dir) 1309

National Air & Space Museum (DC) SMITH, Martin A. (Chief Branch Libn) 1158

National Archives & Records Admin (DC) BEAM, Christopher M. (Archvst) .. 69
BOHANAN, Robert D. (Comp Syst Analyst) 111
BRADSHER, James G. (Archvst) 126
BROWN, Linda (Asst Archvst for Pub Progs) 145
BURKE, Frank G. (Acting US Archvst) 160
BYRNE, John E. (Dir of the Fed Register) 169
CALMES, Alan R. (Preservation Ofcr) 174
CASSEDY, James G. (Archvst) .. 193
CHURCHVILLE, Lida H. (Spcl Projs Libn) 213
DE ARMAN, Charles L. (Supervisory Libn) 284

National Archives & Records Admin (DC)

DOWD, Mary J. (Editor) 315
DOWNS, Charles F. (Lib &
    Printed Archs Branch Chief) . . 317
EVANS, Frank B. (Deputy Asst
    Archvst) 357
GRAF, Thomas H. (Supervisory
    Archvst) 456
GUSTAFSON, Milton O. (Chief,
    Diplomatic Branch) 478
HARWOOD, James L. (Sr
    Archvst) 510
HEDLIN, Ethel W.
    (Machine-Readable Branch
    Chief) 520
JACOBS, Richard A. (Exec Dir) . 590
MCREYNOLDS, R M.
    (Legislative Archs Div Dir) . . 818
MEGRONIGLE, James C. (Actg
    Asst Archvst for Mgmt &
    Admin) 821
MOORE, James W. (Asst
    Archvst for Records Admin) . . 859
PACIFICO, Michele F. (Archvst) . 933
PETERSON, David F. (Asst
    Archvst for Fed Records Ctr) . 963
PFEIFFER, David A. (Archvst) . . . 966
PURDY, Virginia C. (Archvl
    Pubn Staff Dir) 998
RICHTER, Pat 1031
ROSS, Rodney A. (Supervisory
    Archvst) 1058
RUSH, James S. (Ref Archvst) . 1068
RUSSELL, Marvin F.
    (Surervisory Archvst) 1069
SHERMAN, William F. (Civil
    Archs Div Archvst) 1128
TRAUTMAN, Maryellen (US
    Govt Pubns Libn) 1254
WALCH, Timothy G. (Deputy Dir
    of Pubns Div) 1293
WEIHER, Claudine J. (Actg
    Deputy Archvst of the US) . . 1316

National Archives & Records Admin (GA)

ELZY, Martin I. (Supervisory
    Archvst) 347
FRENCH, Melodee J. (Archvl
    Spclst) 402
SCHEWE, Donald B. (Dir) 1092

National Archives & Records Admin (IA)

MATHER, Mildred E. (Archvst,
    Libn) 783

National Archives & Records Admin (MA)

DESNOYERS, Megan F.
    (Supervisory Archvst & Cur) . . 295
GOODRICH, Allan B.
    (Supervisory Archvst) 449
WHEALAN, Ronald E. (Head
    Libn) 1328

National Archives & Records Admin (MD)
National Archives & Records Admin (MI)

DIMKOFF, Diane L. (Archvst) . . . 304

CONWAY, Paul L. (Archvst) 239

National Archives & Records Admin (MO)

BRILEY, Carol A. (Archvst) 136
CURTIS, George H. (Asst Dir) . . . 267
DEWAELSCHE, Thomas M.
    (Supervisory Archvst) 297

National Archives & Records Admin (NJ)

BUCKWALD, Joel (New York
    Branch Dir) 155
KINAHAN-OCKAY, Mary (Arch
    Spclst) 649

National Archives & Records Admin (NY)

GRIFFITH, Sheryl (Libn) 469
SEEBER, Frances M. (Chief
    Archvst) 1111
TEICHMAN, Raymond J.
    (Supervisory Archvst) 1230

National Archives & Records Admin (TX)

HUMPHREY, David C. (Sr
    Archvst) 573
SCHMIDT HACKER, Margaret
    H. (Archvst) 1096
SMITH, Nancy K. (Archvst) 1158
TISSING, Robert W. (Archvst) . 1247

National Archives & Records Admin (VA)
National Archives & Records Admin (WA)
National Archives of Canada (ON)

ASHKENAS, Bruce F. (Archvst) . . 36

EDWARDS, Steven M. (Dir) 338
COOK, Terry G. (Chief) 240
GORDON, Robert S. (Dir) 451
KIDD, Betty H. (Div Dir) 646
ST. PIERRE, Normand (Dir) . . . 1075

National Archives of Japan (JAP)

OGAWA, Chiyoko (Clerical
    Asst) 918

National Archives of Mexico (MEX)

ORTIZ MONASTERIO, Leonor
    (Gen Dir) 927

National Assembly of Quebec (PQ)

BERNIER, Gaston (Asst Dir) 89
BOILARD, Gilberte (Ref Libn) . . . 111
DIONNE, Guy (Ref Libn) 305
FORTIN, Jean (Libn) 391
FORTIN, Jean L. (Head of Ref
    Div) 391
LEBEL, Clement (Technl Srvs
    Head) 707
NADEAU, Johan (Libn) 885
NGUYEN, Vy K. (Ref Libn) 901
WAIT, Elaine (Head of Pub
    User's Info Srv) 1292

Natl Assoc of Industrial & Office Parks (VA)
NAACP Legal Defense & Eductnl Fund Inc (NY)

HAUCK, Janice B. (Info Spclst) . . 512

GLOECKNER, Donna S. (Dir of
    Lib Srvs) 441

National Association of Accountants (NJ)

REDRICK, Miriam J. (Lib Srvs
    Mgr) 1014

National Association of Broadcasters (DC)

HILL, Susan M. (Dir of Lib &
    Info Ctr) 540

National Association of Home Builders (DC)

CAMPBELL, Doris (Assoc Libn) . 176
CLARK, Margery M. (Chief
    Libn) 217

National Assn of Insurance Commissioners (MO)

GINDRA, Janice J. (Resrch Lib
    Mgr) 437
SHIPLEY, Anne C. (Asst Resrch
    Libn) 1131

National Association of Letter Carriers (DC)
National Association of Manufacturers (DC)

RUSH, Candace M. (Info Spclst) 1068

LANEY, Helen B. (Libn) 695
WOOLSEY, Mary E. (Head,
    User Srvs) 1368

National Association of Realtors (IL)

WHITMAN, Jean A. (Quality
    Assurance Analyst) 1333

National Assn of Securities Dealers Inc (MD)

National Association of Universities (MEX)

BOOM, Ramon A. (Chairman) . . . 115

National Autonomous Univ of Mexico (TX)

MANEY, Lana E. (Lib Dir) 765

National Autonomous Univ of Mexico (MEX)

BARBERENA, Elsa (Head Libn) . . 55
DE WALERSTEIN, Linda S.
    (Head Libn) 297
RODRIGUEZ, Serafin L. (Lib
    Coordntr) 1048
SABOURIN, Agathe (Libn) 1073
WOODROW, Carolyn M. (Mgr
    Lib Srvs) 1366

National Bank of Canada (PQ)
National Bank of Detroit Bancorp (MI)

National Black Programming Consultants (OH)
National Broadcasting Co (NY)

HADDOCK, Mable (Exec Dir) . . . 482
FRIEDMAN, Judy B. (Mgr of Lib
    Info Srvs) 404
KATZ, Doris B. (Mgr of
    Broadcast & Bus Resrch) 630

National Broadcasting Co (NY)

LEVINSON, Debra J. (Lib Info Systs Mgr) 721

MAYER, Vera (New Info Srvs Vice Pres) 789

National Bureau of Standards (MD)

BAGG, Thomas C. (Systs Engineer) 45

BERGER, Patricia W. (Info Resrcs & Srvs Div Chief) 86

BOND, Marvin A. (Resrch Resrcs Devlpmnt Chief) 113

JASON, Nora H. (Project Libn) .. 595

KINGSTON, Mary L. (Serials Libn) 652

KLEIN, Sami W. 659

MOLINE, Judi A. (Comp Scitst) .. 853

OVERMAN, Joanne R. (Supervisory Technl Info Spclst) 931

National Cancer Center (JAP)

KAWASHIMA, Hiroko (Head Libn) 632

National Cancer Institute (MD)

DICKINSON, Patricia C. (Chief, Docum Ref Sect) 301

FRYSER, Benjamin S. (Technl Srvs Libn) 407

OSTROW, Dianne G. (Technl Sect Head) 929

TINGLEY, Dianne E. (Chief of Data Bank Resrch Branch) .. 1246

WILSON, Susan W. (Proj Mgr) . 1353

National Center for Atmospheric Research (CO)

GAUSS, Nancy V. (Archvst) 423

KELLY, Karon M. (Chief Libn) .. 638

STRAND, Kathryn (Libn) 1200

Natl Ctr for Earthquake Engrng Resrch (NY)

COTY, Patricia A. (Info Spclst) .. 250

Natl Ctr for Resrch in Vocational Educ (OH)

WAGNER, Judith O. (User Srvs Coordntr) 1292

Natl Center for Social Policy & Practice (MD)

REPPY, Charlotte D. (Dir of Info Srvs) 1024

National Central Lib (TAI)

CHOU, Nancy O. (Head of Acqs & Catlgng Dept) 210

OU-LAN, Nancy 930

National City Bank of Minneapolis (MN)

MIRANDA, Esmeralda C. (Libn) . 847

National City Pub Lib (CA)

MONROE, Shula H. (City Lib Dir) 855

National Clearinghouse for Alcohol Info (MD)

FREEDMAN, Lynn P. (Lib Mgr) .. 400

Natl Clearinghouse for Legal Srvs Inc (IL)

STEVENSON, Katherine (Libn) . 1191

National Coll of Chiropractic (IL)

IWAMI, Russell A. (Ref Libn) ... 586

WHITEHEAD, Joyce E. (Lrng Resrc Ctr Dir) 1332

National Coll of Naturopathic Medicine (OR)

KIRCHFELD, Friedhelm (Libn) ... 654

National Commission on Libs & Info Sci (DC)

CASEY, Daniel W. (Commissioner) 192

GRAY, Dorothy L. (Resrch Assoc) 459

MILEVSKI, Sandra N. (Resrch Assoc) 835

MOORE, Bessie B. (Vice Chair) . 858

YOUNG, Christina C. (Resrch Assoc) 1381

National Computer Network Corp (IL) MCDONALD, Tom (Dir of Mktg) . 803

National Council for Science & Tech (KEN)

IRURIA, Daniel M. (Info Sci Secy) 584

National Dairy Council (IL)

CULBERTSON, Diana L. (Lib Records Ctr Dir) 263

FARRELL, Patricia H. (Info Resrcs Asst Dir) 365

National Decision Systems (CA) GAY, Thomas R. (Executive VP) . 423

National Defense Univ (DC)

DAVIDSON, Dero H. (Libn) 276

JEMIOLA, Nancy E. (Ref Libn) .. 596

RUSSELL, John T. (Dir) 1069

VAROUTSOS, Mary A. (Ref Libn) 1279

National Defense Univ (VA)

NICULA, J G. (Reader Srvs Chief) 903

National Diet Lib (JAP)

SAKAMOTO, Hiroshi (Discriptive Catlgr) 1076

National Economic Research Associates (DC)

PAVEK, C C. (Libn & Info Spclst) 950

National Economic Research Associates (NY)

RYAN, James J. (Asst Libn) ... 1071

National Education Assn of New York (NY)

PINGITORE, Patricia E. (Resrch Spclst) 974

National Endowment for the Arts (DC)

MORRISON, M C. (Lib Dir) 868

National Endowment for the Humanities (DC)

COLETTI, Jeannette D. (Libn) ... 231

MARTZ, David J. (Prog Ofcr) ... 779

PHELPS, Thomas C. (Asst Dir/Div of Gen Progs) 967

ROSENBERG, Jane A. (Prog Ofcr) 1056

National Energy Board (ON)

KRALIK, Jane M. (Ref Libn) ... 675

PARK, Nancy R. (Lib Mgr) 941

National Enquirer (FL)

MOFFETT, Martha L. (Resrch Libn) 852

Natl Federation of Abstctng & Info Srvs (PA)

CORNOG, Martha (Spcl Projects Coordntr) 247

National Film Board of Canada (PQ)

BIDD, Donald W. (Chief Libn) ... 94

BUTLER, Patricia (Asst Libn) ... 167

TODD, Rose A. (Ref Lib Head) . 1248

National Fire Protection Association (MA)

BARNHART, Arlene C. (Libn) 58

Natl Fisheries Contaminant Research Ctr (MO)

HINDMAN, Axie A. (Libn) 542

National Food Processors Association (CA)

LAMANNA, Joan M. (Libn) 689

National Gallery of Art (DC)

DANIELS, Maygene (Archs Chief) 273

DOUMATO, Lamia (Head of Reader Srvs) 314

PHILBRICK, Ruth R. (Cur) 967

TURTELL, Neal T. (Exec Libn) . 1265

WEITZENKORN, Laurie (Asst Cur) 1320

WISNIEWSKI, Julia L. (Catlgr) . 1357

National Gallery of Canada (ON)

HUNTER, Jacqueline E. (Chief Libn) 576

National Geographic Society (DC)

BEVERIDGE, David C. (Supvsr) .. 93

BLOZIS, Jolene M. (Index Editor & Indexing Div Mgr) 107

DREWES, Arlene T. (Circ Libn) .. 319

FIFER-CANBY, Susan M. (Lib Dir) 376

FLANNERY, Patrick D. (Systs Libn) 383

SMITH, Mary P. (Assoc Dir) ... 1158

STORM, Jill (Map Libn) 1198

National Heart Lung & Blood Institute (MD)

YORKS, Melissa L. (Technl Info Spclst) 1381

Natl Histl Pubns & Records Commission (DC)

SAHLI, Nancy A. (Acting Dir of Records Prog) 1075

National Humanities Center (NC)

TUTTLE, Walter A. (Libn) 1266

VARGHA, Rebecca B. (Asst Libn) 1278

National Information & Documentation Ctr (EGY)

EL-DUWEINI, Aadel K. (Mktg, Comm & Scintfc Relations) ... 342

Natl Information Standards Organization (MD)

HARRIS, Patricia R. (Exec Dir) . 505

Natl Inst for Petroleum & Energy Resrch (OK)

STROMAN, Josh H. (Head Libn) 1202

National Inst of Environmental Hlth Scis (NC)

ROBERTSON, W D. (Lib Dir) . . 1042
WRIGHT, Larry L. (Biomedical Sci Libn) 1372

National Institutes of Health (MD)

CHU, Ellen M. (Libn) 212
COLLINS, Kenneth A. (Sect Chief) 233
GALLAGHER, Elizabeth M. (Technl Info Spclst) 414
GLOCK, Martha H. (Supvsr Libn/Deputy Head) 441
HARRIMAN, Jenny F. (Med Ref Libn) 503
KUNZ, Margarett N. (Acqs Head) 684
MASYS, Daniel R. (Dir) 783
TAHIR, Mary M. (Med Libn) . . . 1220
TEIGEN, Philip M. (Deputy Chief) 1230

National League of Cities (DC)

PICKETT, Olivia K. (Staff Assoc) 971

National Lib Bindery Co (GA)

TOLBERT, Jack W. 1248

National Lib of Canada (ON)

ALGAR, L E. (Catlgng Libn) 13
ARBEZ, Gilbert J. (OSI Protocols Ofcr) 30
AUBREY, Irene E. (Chief of Chlds Lit Srv) 38
BALATTI, David R. (Chief, Subject Analysis Div) 50
BELL, Irena L. (Asst Chief) 77
BISHOP, Heather F. (Systs Libn) 99
BRIERE, Jean M. (Sect Head) . . 135
BRODIE, Nancy E. (Asst Dir of Ref) 139
BRYCE, Maria C. (Head of Printed Col) 152
BURNS, Barrie A. (Info Analysis & Standards) 162
BURROWS, Sandra (Newspaper Spclst) 163
CAMLIOGLU, Ergun (Canadian Bk Exchange Chief) 175
CLEMENT, Hope E. (Assoc Natl Libn) 221
COLQUHOUN, Joan E. (Head, Recorded Sound Col) 234
DAWE, Heather L. (Catlgr) 282
DEAVY, Elizabeth A. (Actg Chief) 284
DELSEY, Thomas J. (Dir, Acqs & Bilgph Srvs Branch) 290
DUCHESNE, Roderick M. (Info Tech Assessment Mgr) 322
DUNN, Mary J. (Asst Ref Dir) . . . 327
DUPRE, Monique (Gifts & Exchange Sec Head) 327
DURANCE, Cynthia J. (Dir) 328
DUSSIAUME, Robert (Catlgr) . . . 329
EVANS, Gwynneth (Dir, External Relations) 357
FORGET, Louis J. (Dir, Lib Systs Ctr) 390
FOX, Rosalie (Sr Projs Ref Libn) . 395
GOODMAN, Julia M. (Head of Serials Sect) 449
KALLMANN, Helmut M. (Chief of Music Div) 623
KANNEL, Ene (Systs Lib Technician) 625
KAVANAGH, Susan E. (Monographs Unit Head) 631
KIRKWOOD, Francis T. (Annotator & Microcomputer Adminstr) 655
LANOUETTE, Marie (Asst Chief) 696
LAWLESS, Ruthmary G. (Asst Acqs Dir) 704
LEMOINE, Claude (Curator) 715

National Lib of Canada (ON)

LEUNG, Frank F. (Systs Libn) . . . 719
LUNAU, Carrol D. (Sr Adv for Systs & Analysis) 748
MACDONALD, Marcia H. (Sr Systs Libn) 754
MACDONALD, Patricia A. (Cols Libn) 754
MACLELLAND, Margaret A. (Netwk Ofcr) 757
MANNING, Ralph W. (Sr Coordntr for Standards) 767
MCKEEN, C E. (Spcl Asst to the Assoc Natl Libn) 810
MCQUEEN, Lorraine (Chief, Union Catlg Div) 817
OKUDA, Sachiko E. (Libn) 920
OZAKI, Hiroko (Ref Libn) 932
PARENT, Ingrid T. (Asst Dir Systs) 940
QUEINNEC, Young H. (Canadian MARC Ofc Chief) . 999
RENAUD, Monique M. (Head of French Sect) 1023
ROBERTS, Nancy (Sr Systs Libn) 1041
ROBINSON, W D. (Asst Chief of Lib Documtn Ctr) 1045
ROGERS, Helen F. 1049
SCHRYER, Michel J. (Fed Libs Liaison Ofcr) 1100
SCOTT, Judith W. (Sr Ref Libn) 1107
SCOTT, Marianne F. (Natl Libn) 1107
SIMARD, Luc (Catlgng in Publication Coordntr) 1139
SMALE, Carol (Asst Chief of Interlib Loan Div) 1151
TSAI, Shaopan (Project Ofcr) . . 1260
TURNER, Sharon (Govt Docums Catlgr) 1265
VALENTINE, Scott (Data Dictionary Adminstr) 1271
VAN DER BELLEN, Liana (Chief of Rare Bk Div) 1273
WEBBER, Reginald N. (Maintenance & Operations Mgr) 1313
WEIR, Leslie (Head, User Liaison Sect) 1319
WELCH, Grace D. (Sr Systs Libn) 1321
WILLIAMSON, Michael W. (Chief of Ref & Info Srvs) . . . 1347
ZIELINSKA, Marie F. (Chief, Multilingual Biblioservice) . . . 1388

National Lib of Medicine (MD)

AINES, Andrew A. (Scholar in Residence) 8
ALLEN, Cassandra (Col Access Sect Head) 14
ANDERSON, John E. (Info Systs Dir) 23
ARENALES, Duane W. (Technl Srvs Div Chief) 31
ARONSON, Jules (Comp Sci Branch Acting Chief) 34
BACKUS, Joyce E. (Ref Libn) 44
BARNES, Alvin (Staff Lib Head) . . 57
BECKELHIMER, Melvin (Develpmnt Branch Chief) 72
BECKWITH, Frances (Pubns & NLM Photo & Slide Cols) 73
BENNETT, Harry D. (Deputy Dir for Operations) 81
BLACK, Dennis E. (Ofc of Acqs Mgmt Chief) 101
BRAND, Jeanne L. (Intl Progs Branch Chief) 128
BROWN, Sharon D. (Libn) 147
BUCHAN, Patricia C. (Online Trng Coordntr) 153

National Lib of Medicine (MD)

BUCKNER, Donald (Spcl Asst
   for Htl Professions Educ) 154
BYRNES, Margaret M. (Head of
   Preservation Sect) 169
CAIN, James (Pub Srvs Div
   Deputy Chief) 171
CAMPBELL, Brian (Adminstrv
   Ofcr) 176
CARNEY, Kenneth G.
   (Executive Ofcr) 183
CHARUHAS, Joseph (Exhibits &
   Pubns) 203
CLEPPER, Peter A. (Prog Ofcr) . 221
COLAIANNI, Lois A. (Assoc Dir
   for Lib Operations) 229
COLTON, Karin (Com Mgmt
   Ass) 234
CONNER, P Z. (Lib Assoc) 237
COSMIDES, George J. (Deputy
   Dir) 249
COSTANZO, Sandra (Adminstrv
   Ofcr) 249
COX, John (Deputy Dir) 253
CURRY, Robert (Comp Srvs
   Branch Acting Chief) 266
DAHLEN, Roger W. (Chief) 269
DOSZKOCS, Tamas (Specl
   Asst for Resrch & Devlpmnt) . 313
DUFF, Judith A. (Adminstrv
   Ofcr) 323
DUTCHER, Gale A. (Systs Libn) . 329
FERGUSON, Tyrone (Acting
   Head) 372
GILKESON, Roger (NLM News
   Edit) 435
GOLDSMITH, James (Comp
   Operations Sect Head) 446
GOLDSTEIN, Charles M. (Info
   Tech Branch Chief) 446
GOODWIN, Linda (Conf
   Facilities Coordntr) 450
GOSHORN, Jeanne C.
   (Biomedical Info Srvs Sect
   Chief) 452
HAWK, Susan A. (Technl Info
   Spclst) 513
HAZARD, George F. (Chem Info
   Srvs Sect Chief) 517
HENDERSON, B E. (Deputy Dir) . 525
HERBERT, Charles E. (Asst Dir
   for Prog Plng & Coordtn) 530
HIRTLE, Peter B. (Modern
   Manuscripts Cur) 544
HOFFMAN, Christa F. (Catlgng
   Sect Head) 547
HORAN, Meredith L. (Libn) 559
HOWARD, Frances (Spcl Asst
   to the Assoc Dir) 564
HSIEH, Richard K. (Asst Dir for
   Intl Progs) 567
HUMPHREY, Susanne M. (Info
   Scientist) 573
HUMPHREYS, Betsy L. (Deputy
   Assoc Dir, Lib Operations) ... 573
HUNT, Jennie P. (Ref Libn) 575
JOHNSON, Frances E. (Prog
   Ofcr) 604
JOHNSON, Gary M. (Libn) 604
KEISTER, Lucinda (Head) 635
KENTON, David (Staff Asst) 643
KIM, Sunnie I. (Libn) 649
KIRBY, Diana G. (Lib Assoc) ... 654
KISSMAN, Henry M. (Assoc Dir
   of Specialized Info Srvs) 656
KOTZIN, Sheldon (Chief) 673
LACROIX, Eve M. (Chief of Pub
   Srvs Div) 686
LAKSHMAN, Malathi K. (Libn) .. 689
LINDBERG, Donald A. (Dir) 728

National Lib of Medicine (MD)

LYON-HARTMANN, Becky J.
   (Reg Med Lib Prog Coordntr) . 752
MAIKAIL, Jackie (Educ
   Coordntr) 761
MAIN, James S. (AV Prog
   Devlpmnt Branch Chief) 761
MALCOMSON, Dennis (Ofc of
   Persnl Mgmt Chief) 763
MCCUTCHEON, Dianne E.
   (Systs Libn) 801
MEHNERT, Robert B. (Chief) ... 821
MERCHANT, Barbara (Asst
   Adminstrv Ofcr) 825
MEREDITH, Pam (Ref Sect
   Acting Head) 825
PARASCANDOLA, John L.
   (Hist of Medcn Div Chief) 939
PEGRAM, Bryant (Adminstrv
   Ofcr) 954
PHILLIPS, Stanley J. (Deputy
   Executive Ofcr) 969
PINHO, Marie (Staff Asst) 974
RADA, Roy F. (Index Medicus
   Editor) 1002
RAWSTHORNE, Grace C.
   (Head of Monographs Unit II) 1011
ROBINSON, Arthur J. (EEO
   Ofcr) 1043
ROTARIU, Mark J. (Ofc of
   Financial Mgmt Chief) 1059
RUBEN, Patricia (Ofc of
   Adminstrv Mgmt Srvs Chief) 1064
SAVAGE, Allan G. (Assoc) 1085
SCHOOLMAN, Harold M.
   (Deputy Dir for Resrch &
   Educ) 1098
SCHULMAN, Jacque L. (Libn) . 1101
SCHUYLER, Peri L. (Biogph
   Srvs Div Deputy Chief) 1103
SEIGEL, Sidney (Chief) 1112
SIEGEL, Elliot R. (Actg Assoc
   Dir) 1136
SILVERSTEIN, Bernard
   (Devlpmnt Branch Chief) ... 1139
SINN, Sally (Technl Srvs Div
   Deputy Chief) 1144
SLATER, Susan B. (Deputy
   Asst Dir, Plng & Evaluation) . 1148
SMITH, Kent A. (Deputy Dir) ... 1156
SPANN, Melvin L. (Biomedical
   Info Srvs Sect) 1171
SWANSON, Brenda R.
   (Selection & Acqs Sect
   Head) 1213
THOMA, George R. (Chief) 1235
TILLEY, Carolyn N. (Medlard
   Mgmt Sect Head) 1245
UNGER, Carol P. (Spcl Project
   Ofcr, Preservation) 1269
VASTA, Bruno M. (Chief of
   Biomedical Files) 1279
WALLINGFORD, Karen T.
   (Libn, Index Sect) 1298
WEST, Richard T. (Chief, Prog
   Plng & Evaluation) 1326
WILLIAMS, Patricia D.
   (Adminstrv Ofcr) 1346
WILLMERING, William J. (Serial
   Records Sect Head) 1348
WOODSMALL, Rose M. (Prog
   Analyst) 1367
WORTHINGTON, Randall (Prog
   Ofcr) 1369
WRIGHT, Nancy D. (Index Sect
   Head) 1372

National Lib Relocations Inc (NY)
National Live Stock & Meat Board (IL)
MILLER, Scott W. (Pres) 842
SIARNY, William D. (Industry
   Info Ctr Dir) 1134

National Multiple Sclerosis
Society (NY)
    CALVANO, Margaret (Info &
      Profsnl Educ Dir) 174
    LAMANN, Amber N. (Med Info
      Spclst) 689

National Museum of American
History (DC)
    HASSE, John E. (Cur of Amer
      Music) 511

National Museum of
Communications Inc (TX)
    BRAGG, William J. (Executive
      Cur & Founder) 127

National Museum of Women in the
Arts (DC)
    WASSERMAN, Krystyna (Libn) . 1308

National Museums of Canada (ON)
    BLACK, Jane L. (Head of
      Catlgng) 101
    BOJIN, Minda A. (Museology
      Libn) 111

National Oceanic & Atmospheric
Admin (MD)
    MCKEAN, Joan M. (Supervisory
      Libn) 810

National Opinion Research
Center (IL)
    BOVA, Patrick (Libn) 120

National Optical Astronomy
Observatories (AZ)
    VANATTA, Cathaleen E. (Libn) . 1272

National Park Service (NJ)
    BURT, Leah (Cur) 164

National Park Service (WA)
    AROKSAAR, Richard D. (Asst
      Regnl Libn) 34

National Park Service (WV)
    HERIOT, Ruthanne (Spcl Cols
      Libn) 531
    NATHANSON, David (Ofc of Lib
      & Archvl Srvs Chief) 889

National Planning Data Corp (NY)
    SALTER, Douglas C. (Pres) ... 1077

National Press Club (DC)
    VANDEGRIFT, Barbara P. (Libn
      & Archvst) 1273

National Pub Radio (DC)
    MCGANN, Margot (Head Libn) .. 805
    ROBINSON, Robert C. (Ref
      Libn) 1044

National Radio Astronomy
Observatory (VA)
    BOUTON, Ellen N. (Libn) 119

National Railroad Museum (WI)
    MUSICH, Gerald D. (Exec Dir) .. 883

National Research Council of
Canada (ON)
    LEONARDO, Joan M. (Ref Libn) . 717
    LOW, Mary (Libn) 743
    PARKKARI, John (Head Acqs) .. 943
    SCHMIDT, Diana M. (Ref Libn) . 1095
    VEEKEN, Mary L. (Biomedical
      Info Spclst) 1280
    WALLACE, Kathryn M. (Asst
      Head of Ref Dept) 1297

National Research Council of
Canada (SK)
    CHEN, Flora F. (Branch Head) .. 205

National Research Council of the
US (DC)
    BROWNE, Lynda S. (Assoc
      Libn) 148
    LUKE, Lisbeth L. (Libn) 747

National Restaurant Association (DC)
    SMALLEY, Ann W. (Info Srvs &
      Lib Mgr) 1151

National Safety Council (IL)
    HALASZ, Marilynn J. (Libn
      Indxr) 484
    MARECEK, Robert J. (Mgr) 770
    MORTON, Laura (Catlgr &
      Indxr) 870

National Security Agency (MD)
    MEYER, William P. (Info Sci
      Analyst) 830

National Semiconductor (CA)
    HOLLAND, Mary (Mgr) 551

National Severe Storms
Laboratory (OK)
    MEACHAM, Mary (Libn) 819

National Solar Observatory (NM)
    CORNETT, John L. (Technl
      Dir) 247

National Standards Association (MD)
    GILBERT, Mattana (Acqs
      Supvsr) 433

National Taiwan Univ (TAI)
    HU, James S. (Prof Chairman &
      Dir) 567
    HUANG, Jack K. 568
    LEE, Lucy T. (Prof) 710
    SENG, Harris B. (Prof) 1115
    SHAW, Shiow J. (Instr) 1124

National Technical Information
Service (VA)
    FINCH, Walter 377
    KANE, Astor V. (Info Srvs Div
      Mgr) 624
    LAWALL, Marie (Product Mgr) .. 704
    ROSENBERG, Kenyon C.
      (Assoc Dir) 1056
    SMITH, Ruth S. (Dir of Ofc of
      Customer Srvs) 1160

National Technical Institute for
Deaf (NY)
    RITTER, Audrey L. (Resrc
      Spclst) 1036

National Theatre Corp (DC)
    SHOREBIRD, Thomas S.
      (Archvst) 1132

National Treasury Employment
Union (DC)
    STATTON, Thomas M. (Lib
      Mgr) 1183

National Univ (CA)
    KELLY, Myla S. (Lib Mgr) 638
    LINDBERG, Susan J.
      (Automation/Technl Srvs
      Libn) 729
    NICKELSON-DEARIE, Tammy
      A. (Head of Reader Srvs) 902
    LEVY, Sharon J. (Libn) 722

National Wildlife Federation (VA)

Native American Rights Fund (CO)
    HARRAGARRA WATERS,
      Deana J. (Law Libn) 503

Natural History Musm of Los Angeles
Cnty (CA)
    DONAHUE, Katharine E. (Musm
      Libn) 310
    EDWARDS, Jennifer L. (Sci
      Libn) 337

Navajo Community Coll (NM)
    JASSAL, Raghbir S. (Lib Srvs &
      Lrng Resrcs Ctr Dir) 595

Naval Aerospace Medical
Institute (FL)
    ROGERS, Ruth T. (Adminstrv
      Libn) 1050

Naval Dental Research Institute (IL)
    DIEHL, Mark 302

Naval Education & Training
Center (RI)
    AYLWARD, James F.
      (Adminstr) 42

Naval Education & Training
Program (FL)
    HOMEYARD, Marjorie A.
      (Acting Head, Naval Gen Lib
      Prog) 555

Naval Education & Training Support
Ctr (VA)
    BREWER, Helen L. (Naval
      Regional Libn) 134

Naval EOD Technology Ctr (MD)
    OMARA, Marie T. (Libn &
      Database Adminstr) 923

Naval Medical Research
Institute (MD)
    COSKEY, Rosemary B. (Head
      of Info Srvs Branch Div) 248

Naval Ocean Systems Center (CA)
    WRIGHT, Kathleen J. (Bayside
      Lib Supvsr) 1372

Naval Ordnance Station (MD)
    GALLAGHER, Charles F.
      (Supvsr Libn) 413

Naval Postgraduate Sch (CA)
    CLINE, Margery C. (Libn) 222
    MARTIN, Roger M. (Reader
      Srvs Libn) 778
    SPINKS, Paul (Prof/Dir of Libs) . 1175

Naval Research Laboratory (DC)
    KECK, Bruce L. (Deputy Libn) ... 633
    STACKPOLE, Laurie E. (Chief
      Libn) 1178

Naval Underwater Systems
Center (CT)
    CAMPBELL, Barbara A. (Sci &
      Tech Libn) 176

Naval War Coll (RI)
    CHERPAK, Evelyn M. (Naval
      Histl Col Head) 206

Nazarene Theological Seminary (MO)
    MILLER, William C. (Libn & Prof
      of Theol Bibl) 843

Nazareth Coll of Rochester (NY)
    MATZEK, Richard A. (Lib Dir) ... 786
    TUOHEY, Jeanne D. (Serials &
      Ref Libn) 1263

NdS Information Consultants (CT)
    DOUVILLE, Judith A. (Owner &
      Pres) 314

Neal-Schuman Publishers Inc (NY)
    PEDOLSKY, Andrea D.
      (Managing Editor) 954
    SCHUMAN, Patricia G. (Pres) .. 1103

Nebraska Legislative Council (NE)
    SLOAN, Patricia K. (Legislative
      Ref Libn) 1149

Nebraska Lib Commission (NE)
ALLEN, Richard H. (Lib Srvs Coordntr) 16
KOPISCHKE, John (Dir) 671
MUNDELL, Jacqueline L. (Supvsr, Interloan & Info Srvs) 878
NAUGLE, Gretchen R. (Supvsr Techni AV Srvs) 889
WAGNER, Rod G. (Deputy Dir) . 1292

Nebraska State Historical Society (NE)
DANIELS, Sherrill F. (Ref Srvs Dir) 273
PAUL, Andrea I. (Actg State Archvst) 949

Nebraska Wesleyan Univ (NE)
LU, Janet C. (Pub Srvs Head & Assoc Prof) 745

Nedbook International BV (NET)
OVEREYNDER, Rombout E. (Dir) 931

Neenah Pub Lib (WI)
FLYNN, Kathryn J. (Dir of Lib Srvs) 386

Negaunee Pub Schs (MI)
PAULIN, Mary A. (Sch Lib Media Spclst) 950

NELINET Inc (MA)
BOLAND, Mary J. (Mem Srvs Libn) 111
CUNNINGHAM, Robert L. (Bibliographic Srvs Mgr) 265
MOCKUS, Laima 851

Nelson-Atkins Museum of Art (MO)
HESS, Stanley W. (Libn) 534
MEIZNER, Karen L. (Assoc Libn) 822

Nelsonville Pub Lib (OH)
KURZ, David B. (Head of Main Branch) 685

Nemaha Valley Schools (KS)
PHILBRICK, Marcia (Libn & Media Coordntr) 967

Neosho County Community Coll (KS)
VIERGEVER, Dan W. (Lib Dir) . 1284

NERAC Inc (CT)
SENKUS, Linda J. (Srch Spclst) . 1115
WILDE, Daniel U. (Pres) 1338

Nestle Foods (NY)
REED, Catherine A. (Resrch Libn) 1015

Network for Continuing Medical Educ (NJ)
CONNICK, Kathleen D. (Network Affairs Regnl Mgr) .. 237

Network of Alabama Academic Libs (AL)
MEDINA, Sue O. (Dir) 820

Neuman Williams Anderson & Olson (IL)
JACOBSON, William R. (Libn) .. 590

Neumann Coll (PA)
MUDRICK, Kristine E. (Dir of Lib Srvs) 875
TOMAN, Jocelyn B. (Lib Srvs Dir) 1249

Neumann Monson PC (IA)
NEUMANN, Roy C. (Pres) 897

Neumann Prep High Sch (NJ)
KLOZA, Paula P. (Media Spclst) . 662

Neurofibrometusis Institute Inc (TX)
RICCARDI, Vincent M. (Dir) ... 1026

Neuropsychiatric Institute (ND)
NORDENG, Diane (Med Libn) ... 908

Neurosciences Institute (NY)
NARDUCCI, Frances (Biblgphr) .. 888

Neuse Regional Pub Lib (NC)
CAWLEY, Marianne (Ref Libn) .. 195
EARL, Susan R. (Asst Ref Dept Head) 332
JONES, John W. (Libs Dir) 613

Nevada Bell (NV)
BANTZ, K J. (Accounting Dir) 55
COWARD, J P. (External Affairs Dir) 252
DAVID, B J. (Gen Mgr, Operations/Engineer) 276
EPIFANI, R I. (Dir Mktg & External Affairs) 351
HANSEN, E G. (Finance Dir) 497
HILL, D L. (Mktg & Regulartory Dir) 539
HOPKINS, Lloyd T. (Financial Accounting Dir) 558
MATHSON, L J. (Mktg Dir) 784
MITCHELL, R G. (Attorney) 849
ORIEN, C G. (Info Systs Dir) 925
PIERSON, S M. (Gen Mgr, Operations & Engrng) 972
STEWART, J W. (District Mgr of Operations) 1192
VAN ALLEN, R K. (Pres & Chief Exec Ofcr) 1271

Nevada County Lib (CA)
BAILEY, Darlene L. (Chlds Coordntr) 46
HELLING, Madelyn (Nevada County Libn) 524
TORKELSON, Jon A. (Libn II) .. 1251

Nevada Sch of Law of Old Coll (NV)
MCNEAL, Betty (Law Lib Dir) ... 816

Nevada State Lib & Archives (NV)
KERSCHNER, Joan G. (State Libn) 644

Nevada State Museum & Historical Society (NV)
CAROLLO, Michael T. (Actg Dir) 184

Nevada Supreme Court (NV)
DION, Kathleen L. (Asst Libn) ... 305
SOUTHWICK, Susan A. (Law Libn) 1170

Nevins Memorial Lib (MA)
WILLS, Lynda J. (Dir) 1349

New Amberola Phonograph Co (VT)
BRYAN, Martin F. (Publshr & Edit) 151

New Brunswick Museum (NB)
ROSEVEAR, E C. (Head) 1057

New Canaan Lib (CT)
BLALOCK, Louise (Dir) 103
BUSCH, Kathleen M. (Dept Head, Chlds Srvs) 165

New Canaan Pub Schools (CT)
SENATOR, Rochelle B. (K-12 Lib Dept Chair & Libn) ... 1115

New Carlisle Bethel Schs (OH)
ROGERS, Cassandra J. (Lib Media Coordntr) 1049

New Castle County Lib Services (DE)
BEAMER, Lisa M. (Chlds Libn) ... 69
PUFFER, Yvonne L. (Libn) 997
SIMMONS, Elizabeth M. (Youth Srvs Libn) 1139

New Castle-Henry County Pub Lib (IN)
JOHNSON, Marjorie J. (Dir) 607

New Castle Pub Lib (DE)
BROWN, Sarah C. (Dir) 147

New Castle Pub Lib (PA)
GRAHAM, Anne M. (Youth Srvs Coordntr) 456

New City Lib (NY)
O'CONNELL, Susan (Admin & Ref Libn) 915
SIMON, Patricia B. (Adult Srvs Supvsr) 1140

New Cumberland Pub Lib (PA)
DILLEN, Judith A. (Dir) 303

The New England (MA)
KORMAN, Adrienne S. (Corprt Lib Mgr) 671

New England Baptist Hospital (MA)
WOODARD, Paul E. (Med Libn) 1366

New England Coll of Optometry (MA)
EPSTEIN, Lynne S. (Head Libn) . 351

New England Conservatory of Music (MA)
PRISTASH, Kenneth (Audio Libn) 993

New England Historic Genealogical Socty (MA)
HERMAN, Douglas C. (Techni Srvs Libn) 531
RUPERT, Mary A. (Conf Mgr) .. 1068

New England Lib Association (NH)
ACTON, Anne M. (Asst Libn) 4

New England Sch of Law (MA)
STEARNS, Barry T. (Ref Libn) . 1183
TATELMAN, Susan D. (Reader Srvs Libn) 1225

New England Wild Flower Society Inc (MA)
WALKER, Mary M. (Botanical Libn) 1296

New Hampshire State Lib (NH)
HIGGINS, Matthew J. (State Libn) 538
JOHNSON, Jean G. (Pub Lib Consult) 605
MCDONOUGH, Kathleen C. (LSCA Coordntr) 803
PALMATIER, Susan M. (Lib Consult) 936
RINDEN, Constance T. (Law Libn) 1035
RYAN, Clare E. (Dir, Techni Srvs) 1070
WHITTIER, Ruth E. (Retired) ... 1334

New Hampshire Technical Institute (NH)
HARE, William J. (Lrng Resrcs Coordntr) 501

New Hampshire Vocational Techni Coll (NH)
COMEAU, Reginald A. (Lrng Resrcs Dir) 234

New Hanover County Pub Lib (NC)
BEECH, Vivian W. (Extension Srvs Libn) 74

New Haven Colony Historical Society (CT)
KOEL, Maria O. (Libn & Cur of Mss) 667

New Haven Free Pub Lib (CT)
CLENDINNING, David (Ref Libn) 221
ENSEL, Ellen H. (Ref Libn) 350
KRITEMEYER, Ann C. (Libn II) . . 679
ROSS, Carole L. (Technl Srvs Supvsr) 1058

New Holland Community lib (PA)
SNELGROVE, Pamela S. (Pub Libn) 1163

New Hope-Solebury Sch District (PA)
ACKLER, Susan (Jr & Sr High Sch Libn) 4

New Jersey Bell Telephone (NJ)
FOSKO, Maureen E. (Law Libn) . 392

New Jersey Department of Education (NJ)
GOLDSMITH, Maxine K. (Libn) . . 446
MADDEN, Doreitha R. (Lib Literacy Progs Dir) 758
ROUMFORT, Susan B. (Head, Law & Ref Srvs) 1061
VOSS, Anne E. (Coordntr) 1289
WEAVER, Barbara F. (State Libn & Asst Commissioner) . 1312

New Jersey Dept of Law & Pub Safety (NJ)
ASSENHEIMER, Judy (Law Libn) 37

New Jersey Education Association (NJ)
VAN BUSKIRK, Elisabeth L. (Assoc Dir) 1272

New Jersey Historical Society (NJ)
COLLINS, Sarah F. (Lib Dir) 233
MEYERS, Elsa M. (Catlgr) 831

New Jersey Institute of Technology (NJ)
CALLANAN, Ellen M. (Circ & Ref Libn) 173
VAN FLEET, James A. (Perdcls/Ref Libn) 1275

New Jersey Lib Association (NJ)
MCDONOUGH, Roger H. (Govt Relations Consult) 803
STUDDIFORD, Abigail M. (Exec Dir) 1204

New Jersey Office of Legislative Srvs (NJ)
MAZZEI, Peter J. (Asst Libn) . . . 791

New Jersey State Lib (NJ)
BREEDLOVE, Elizabeth A. (Head of Bureau of Technl Lib Srvs) 131
CRAWFORD, Nola N. (Law Libn) 257
GORDON, Kaye B. (Law Libn) . . 451
LEE, J S. (Libn II) 710
RAILSBACK, Beverly D. (US Docums Libn) 1003
RAZZANO, Barbara W. (Asst Coordntr, Local Lib Srvs Sect) 1012

New Lenox Sch District 122 (IL)
STARK, Colette G. (Instrcl Media Ctr Dir) 1181

New London Board of Education (CT)
MCKISSICK, Mabel F. (Lib Media Spclst) 812

New Mexico Dept of Health & Environment (NM)
HAYNES, Douglas E. (Chief Libn) 516

New Mexico Military Institute (NM)
KLOPFER, Jerome J. (Lib Automated Systs Coordntr) . . . 662
MCLAREN, M B. (Dir, LRC/ITV) . 813

New Mexico Records Center & Archives (NM)
MILLER, Bryan M. (State Archvst & Records Adminstr) . 836

New Mexico State Univ at Alamogordo (NM)
RUCKMAN, Stanley N. (Lib Dir) 1065

New Mexico State Univ at Las Cruces (NM)
BARBER, Helen M. (Asst Ref Libn) 55
CHEN, Laura F. (Asst Catlg Libn) 205
DAVIS, Hiram L. (Dean of Univ Libs) 279
DUHRSEN, Lowell R. (Assoc Dean of Libs) 324
MOORER, Jenny R. (Asst Catlg Libn) 862

New Mexico Supreme Court (NM)
LANCASTER, Kevin M. (Assoc Libn) 692

New Milford Pub Lib (NJ)
WALSH, Carol J. (Ref Libn) . . . 1299

New Mills Law Lib (CA)
KOFF, Jacob (Lib Dir) 668

New Museum of Contemporary Art (NY)
FERGUSON, Russell (Libn) 372

New Orleans Baptist Theological Seminary (LA)
GERICKE, Paul W. (Lib Dir) 428
PONG, Connie K. (Head of Technl Srvs) 982

New Orleans Pub Lib (LA)
COADY, Reginald P. (Asst City Libn) 224
WILKINS, Marilyn W. (Music Speclst) 1340
WILSON, C D. (Dir) 1350

New Orleans Symphony (LA)
STRICKLAND, William C. (Libn) 1202

New Rochelle Pub Lib (NY)
GIORDANO, Frederick S. (Asst Dir) 438
ZINMAN, Sandra (Chlds Libn) . . 1389

New School for Social Research (NY)
SETTANNI, Joseph A. (Records Mgr) 1117

New South Wales Parliamentary Lib (AUS)
TILLOTSON, Greig S. (Sr Libn of Ref & Info Sect) 1245

New Trier High Sch (IL)
COBB, Marilyn R. (High Sch Media Spclst) 225
DUNN, Lucia S. (Libn/Archvst) . . 327
FISHER, Lois F. (Dir of Lib Srvs) . 381

New World Services Inc (FL)
RAPETTI, Vincent A. (Proj Mgr & Chief Libn) 1008

New York Academy of Medicine (NY)
BALKEMA, John B. (Head of Circ) 52
CLARE, Richard W. (Adminstrv Systs Libn) 216
KIRKPATRICK, Brett A. (Libn) . 655
PERRY, Claudia A. (Ref Dept Head) 960
RICHARDSON, Emma G. (Retired) 1029
WOLFE, N J. (Resrc Sharing Coordntr) 1361

New York Chiropractic Coll (NY)
HELLER, Jacqueline R. (Media Libn) 524
STERN, Marilyn (Lib Dir) 1189

New York City Board of Education (NY)
ARKHURST, Joyce C. (Sch Libn) 31
DE CUENCA, Pilar A. (Lib Tchr) . 286
DONNELLY, Mary E. (Sch Lib Media Spclst) 311
KLEIMAN, Rhoda E. (Libn) 659
MORRIS, Irving (Tchr of Lib Media) 866
PEARLMUTTER, Regina S. (Sch Libn) 952
PRUITT, Brenda F. (Sch Lib) . . . 996
SINGER, Phyllis Z. (Libn) 1143
WONSEVER, Eithne C. (Lib Media Spclst) 1363

New York City Bureau of Building Design (NY)
LEE, Sang C. (Proj Mgr & Comp Coordntr) 711

New York City Criminal Court (NY)
ROONEY, Mary T. (Law Libn) . . 1053

New York City Dept of Records & Info Srv (NY)
BUTLER, Tyrone G. (Deputy Dir) 167
KIRWAN, Kathleen (Exhibit Cur) . 656
TAYLOR, Patricia A. (Dir) 1228

New York City Health & Hospitals Corp (NY)
GALVIN, Jeanne D. (Libn) 415

New York City Human Resources Admin (NY)
BENSON, Harold W. (Head Libn) 83
PETTOLINA, Anthony M. (Analyst) 965

New York City Sch Lib System (NY)
KENNEDY BRIGHT, Sandra (Coordntr) 641

New York County Board of Education (NY)
RABIN, Alan H. (Sec Sch Libn) . 1001

New York County Lawyers Association (NY)

New York Daily News (NY)

NY Division of Equalization & Assessment (NY)

NY Genealogical & Biographical Society (NY)

New York Historical Society (NY)

New York Hospital (NY)

New York Infirmary (NY)

New York Law Sch (NY)

New York Lib Association (NY)

NY Metropolitan Ref & Resrch Lib Agency (NY)

New York Post (NY)

New York Power Authority (NY)

New York Psychoanalytic Inst & Socty (NY)

New York Pub Lib (NY)

GALGAN, Mary N. (Catlgr) 413
TANZER, Barbara (Asst Libn) . . 1223
BROWNE, Scott M. (Asst Libn) . . 148
ROSENTHAL, Faigi (Head Libn) 1057

BEVERLEY, Barbara S. (Dir) 93

POHL, Gunther E. (Trustee & Libn) 979
BARR, Jeffrey A. (Catlgr) 58
CAPRIELIAN, Arevig (Rare Bk Catlgr) 180
GOERNER, Tatiana (Rare Bk Catlgr) 443
MOONEY, James E. (Libn) 858
REMECZKI, Paul W. (Catlgr) . . 1022
LERNER, Adele A. 717
LEYDEN, Annette (Med Lib Dir) . 724
KELLER, Katarina S. (Catlgr, Govt Docums Libn) 635
MASTRANGELO, Paul J. (Technl Srvs Coordntr) 783
MOLINARI, Joseph G. (Pub Srvs Head) 853
NEWMAN, Marie S. (Lawyer & Libn) 899
SHAPIRO, Fred R. (Asst Libn for Pub Srvs) . . . 1121
YIRKA, Carl A. (Assoc Libn) . . . 1380
LIAN, Nancy W. (Exec Dir) 725

GOODMAN, Rhonna A. (Asst Coordntr of Progs & Srvs) . . . 449
MANBECK, Virginia B. (Asst Dir & Coordntr of Lib Srvs) 764
NEUMANN, Joan (Dir) 897
BOWEN, Christopher E. (Asst Head Libn) 120
SHERR, Merrill F. (Head Libn) . . 1129
SPARER, Saretta (Info Ctr Mgr) 1171

ROSS, David J. (Lib Dir) 1058
ALICEA, Ismael (Bronx Borough Community Spclst) 13
BAKER, John P. (Asst Preservation Dir) 48
BEHRMANN, Christine A. (Supvsng Chld's Matrls Spclst) 75
BOURKE, Thomas A. (Chief of Microforms Div) 119
BOWERS, Sherri (Record Libn) . . 121
BOZIWICK, George E. (Music Libn) 124
BROWAR, Lisa M. (Asst Dir) . . . 141
BUCK, Richard M. (Asst Chief) . . 154
BUELOW, Mary E. (Libn) 155
CAMPAGNA, Roxane R. (Sr Chlds Libn) 175
CASSEL, Susan D. (First Asst Branch Libn) 193
CASTRO, Julio E. (Adminstrv Assoc) 194
CHRISTENSON, Janet S. (Asst Docums Libn) 211
CIOPPA, Lawrence (Supvsng Drama & Film Libn) 214
CLAYPOOL, Richard D. (Music Catlgr) 220
COHEN, Renee G. (Libn II) 229
CORWIN, Betty L. (Theatre on Film & Tape Archv Dir) 248
DECANDIDO, Robert L. 285
DE GENNARO, Richard (Dir) . . . 287
D'ONOFRIO, Erminio (Docums Libn) 311
DOTSON, Mildred E. (Ofc of Spcl Srvs Coordntr) 313
EBER, Beryl E. (Supvsng Libn) . . 334

New York Pub Lib (NY)

FASANA, Paul J. (Andrew W Mellon Dir) 366
FIGUEREDO, Danilo H. (Asst Chief) 376
FRIEDMAN, Barbara S. (Controller & Asst Treas) 403
FRIEDMAN, Estelle Y. (Supvsng Branch Libn) 403
GREGORIAN, Vartan (Pres) 466
GRUTCHFIELD, Walter (Systs Devlpmnt Mgr) 475
GUBERT, Betty K. (Head of Gen Resrch & Ref Cols) 475
HARDISH, Patrick M. (Music Catlgr) 500
HOLMGREN, Edwin S. (Dir of the Branch Libs) 553
HSU, Karen M. (Head of Serial Catlgng Sect) 567
HUDSON, Alice C. (Div Chief) . . 569
JACKSON, Richard H. (Head of Americana Col) 588
JOHNSON, Patrelle E. (Libn) . . . 608
JUHL, M E. (Libn I) 619
KARATNYTSKY, Christine A. (Scripts Libn) 627
KENSELAAR, Robert (Asst Chief) 642
KLEIN, Stephen C. (Sr Principal Libn) 659
KOROLIK, Margarita N. (Libn) . . . 672
LACHATANERE, Diana (Asst Archvst) 686
LADUE, Annette S. (Libn) 687
LEE, Lolly P. (Libn) 710
LEFKOWITZ, Mona (Libn Trainee) 712
LEVIN, Peggy S. (Chlds Libn) . . . 720
LUTZ, Alexandra (Libn) 750
LYNCH, Richard C. (Asst Theatre Col Cur) 752
MACK, Phyllis G. (Regnl Sr Principal Libn) 756
MARTIN, Brian G. (Literary Site Adviser) 775
MULIA, Gusti (Head, Srchg & Catlgng Sect) 876
MYERS, Paul (Retired) 884
NATHAN, Frances E. (Legislative Relations Ofcr) . . . 889
OCKENE, David L. (Supvsng Libn) 915
O'CONNELL, Brian E. (Conservation Asst) 915
O'KEEFE, Laura K. (Archvst) . . . 919
OSTROWSKY, Edith (Supvsng Libn) 929
PASION, Betty D. (Branch Libn) . 946
PASSOFF, Barbara F. (Libn) 946
PATRI, Daniel 947
PERCELLI, Irene M. (Serials & Spcls Projs Coordntr) 958
PURCELL, Marcia L. (Sr Principal Regnl Libn) 998
QUARTELL, Robert J. (Libn) 999
RAPPAPORT, Susan E. (Technl Advisor) 1008
RIVERA, Gregorio (Dir, Microcomputer Srvs) 1037
ROHMANN, Gloria P. (Sci & Tech Div Asst Chief) 1050
SALTUS, Winifred T. (Supervising Ref Libn) 1077
SHUMAN, Kristen K. (Supervising Music Libn) . . . 1134
SOMMER, Susan T. (Asst Chief of Music Div) 1167
SPERLING, Robert B. (Chair) . . 1173

New York Pub Lib (NY)

SPYROS, Marsha L. (Adult
Programming Spclst) 1177
SWERDLOVE, Dorothy L. (Cur) 1215
VAN DYKE, Stehpen H.
(Supvsng Libn) 1275
VELEZ, Sara B. (Libn) 1281
WENDT, Mary E. (Bronx
Borough Coordntr) 1324
WERTSMAN, Vladimir F. (Sr
Libn) 1325
WILLIAMS, Richard C. (Catlgng
Asst Dir) 1346
WILLNER, Channan P. (Music
Libn) 1348
WOESTHOFF, Catherine F.
(Libn II) 1359
WOOD, Thor E. (Chief of
Performing Arts Resrch Ctr) . 1365
ZEIGLER, Susan A. (Chlds
Libn) 1387

New York Pulse (NY) EISBERG, Jeffrey L. (Pres &
Gen Mgr) 340

New York State (NY) BOTTA, Jean C. (Law Lib
Coordntr) 118
DUNN, Mary B. (Law Libn) 327
DWORKIN, Victoria G. (Ref
Libn) 330
GILSON, Robert (Alcoholism
Prog Spclst III) 437
LODATO, James J. (Principal
Law Libn) 736
STORMS, Kate (Resrc
Coordntr) 1198
WESTHUIS, Judith A. (Chief of
Law Lib Srvs) 1327

New York State Archives (NY) COX, Richard J. (Assoc Archvst
for External Progs) 253
DEARSTYNE, Bruce W.
(Principal Archvst) 284
WARD, Christine W.
(Preservation Adminstr) 1303

New York State Coll of Ceramics (NY) CONNOLLY, Bruce E. (Lib Dir) .. 237
CULLEY, Paul T. (Sr Asst Libn) . 263
FREEMAN, Carla C. (Visual
Resrcs Libn) 400
GULACSY, Elizabeth (Ref Libn) . 477

**New York State Department of
Corrections** (NY) SHERWIG, Mary J. (Sr Libn) .. 1129

**New York State Department of
Health** (NY) YOCHYM, Cynthia M. (Asst
Libn) 1380

**New York State Department of
Labor** (NY) WEINRICH, Gloria (Sr Libn) ... 1318

**New York State Department of
Law** (NY) KOUO, Lily W. (Sr Law Libn) ... 673
REEPMEYER, Marie C. (Asst
Libn) 1016
SHEINWALD, Franette (Sr Law
Libn) 1125

**New York State Education
Department** (NY) BARRON, Robert E. (Bureau of
Sch Lib Media Prog Chief) 60
BURKETT, Donald E. (Asst
Libn) 161
HACKMAN, Larry J. (Archvst &
Hist Records Coordntr) 481
MATTIE, Joseph J. (Lib Srvs
Assoc) 786
ROSCELLO, Frances R. (Assoc
in Sch Lib Srv) 1054
SHUBERT, Joseph F. (State
Libn/Asst Commisioner for
Lib) 1133
SHUMAN, Susan E. (Sch Lib
Srv Asst) 1134
SIMON, Anne E. (Lib Srvs Asst) 1140
SMITH, Frederick E. (Assoc in
Lib Srvs) 1155

**New York State Education
Department** (NY)

SOMERS, Betty J. (NY State
Lib for the Blind Dir) 1166
SWARTZELL, Ann G. (Assoc
Libn) 1214
WEBSTER, Patricia B. (Sch Lib
Srvs Asst) 1315

New York State Legislature (NY) BRESLIN, Ellen R. (Ref Libn) ... 133
MURRAY, Elizabeth F. (Info
Syst Libn) 881

New York State Lib (NY) BAIN, Christine A. (Assoc Libn) ... 47
CADE, Roberta G. (Lib
Devlpmnt Dir) 170
CHAPERO, Alicia (Asst Libn) ... 201
CORSARO, James (Sr Libn) 248
DESCH, Carol A. (Asst to the
Dir) 294
ESPOSITO, Michael A. (Sr Ref
Libn) 354
HOLT, Lisa A. (Asst Libn) 554
JUDD, J V. (Principal Libn) 619
NICHOLS-RANDALL, Barbara
L. (Assoc Libn) 902
PASTERNACK, Marcia A. (Asst
Libn) 946
SMITH, Audrey J. (Sr Libn) 1152
SMITH, Dorothy C. (Assoc in
Lib Srvs) 1154
STANTON, Lee W. (Principal
Libn for Ref) 1181
YAVARKOVSKY, Jerome (Lib
Dir) 1378

**New York State Nurses
Association** (NY) HAWKES, Warren G. (Lib Dir) .. 513

**New York State Office of Court
Admin** (NY) PILLAI, Karlye A. (Law Libn) 973

**New York State Office of Mental
Health** (NY) ABDULLAH, Bilquis (Sr Libn) 2
DANIELS, Pam (Mental Hlth
Libs & Info Srvs Dir) 273
MACINICK, James W. (Sr Libn) . 755

New York State Senate (NY) VANNORTWICK, Barbara L.
(Dir, Com on Interstate
Cooprtn) 1276

New York State Supreme Court (NY) BADERTSCHER, David G.
(Principal Law Libn) 44
GARA, Otto G. (Principal Libn) .. 416
GICK, Julie (Sr Law Libn) 432
LAUER, Judy (Law Libn) 702
PENICH, Sonia S. (Asst
Principal Law Libn) 956
SAHLEM, James R. (Principal
Law Libn) 1075

New York Stock Exchange Inc (NY) HALEY, Thomas E. (Mktg Data
Srv VP) 486

New York Times (NY) GREENGRASS, Alan R. (Spcl
Projs Mgr) 464
HAYES, Jude T. (Researcher &
Libn) 516
HOLMES, Harvey L. (Asst Dir of
Index Srvs) 553
ROTHMAN, John (Dir of Archs) 1060

New York Unified Court System (NY) FRALEY, Ruth A. (Chief Libn) ... 395

New York Univ (NY) BIDDEN, Julia E. (Head of
Acqs) 94
BOORMAN, Stanley H. (Dir, Ctr
for Early Music) 115
BRODY, Elaine (Prof of Music) .. 139
BROWN, Ronald L. (Resrch &
Ref Libn) 147
CARRENO, Angela M. (Ref Libn
for Latin Am Std) 186
CHEN, Ching F. (Assoc Cur) 205
DEDONATO, Ree (Gen &
Humanities Ref Ctr Head) 286
EARLY, Caroline L. (Acqs
Head) 332
FRUSCIANO, Thomas J. (Univ
Archvst) 406

New York Univ (NY)

GHALI, Raouf S. (Assoc Prof, Assoc Libn) 430
HENRY, Mary K. (Humanities Biblgphr) 529
HIGGINS, Steven (Performing Arts Libn) 538
IOANID, Aurora S. (Catlgr) 583
KASTNER, Arno A. (Catlg Dept Head) 629
KRANICH, Nancy C. (Pub & Adminstrv Srvs Dir) 676
KRONISH, Priscilla T. (Physical Scis Libn) 680
LEWIS, Margaret S. (Head Libn) . 723
LOMONACO, Martha S. (Archvst, Performing Arts Col) 738
MIHRAM, Danielle (Ref Libn) . . . 834
MILLER, Michael D. (Dept Head) 841
MONROE, William S. (Ref Libn for World Hist) 855
MYERS, Maria P. (Adminstr) 884
PERSKY, Gail M. (Assoc Dir of Technl Srvs for AP) 961
PETTIT, Marilyn H. (Asst Dir, Prog in Arch Mgmt) 965
ROCHELL, Carlton C. (Dean of Libs) 1046
SAGER, Naomi (Resrch Prof) . . 1074
SALVAGE, Barbara A. (Head, Catlg Maintenance) 1078
SHIROMA, Susan G. (Govt Docums Libn) 1131
SHUMAN, Jay A. (Ref Libn) . . . 1134
SINGLETON, Christine M. (Resrch Libn) 1143
SOLOMON, Geri E. (Asst Archvst) 1166
SPORE, Stuart (Catlgng Head) . 1175
SULLIVAN, Cecil G. (Assoc Cur Emeritus) 1207
SWANSON, Dorothy T. (Assoc Cur) 1213
TANNENBAUM, Robin L. (Asst Ref Libn) 1222
VINCENT-DAVISS, Diana (Law Libn & Prof of Law) 1284
WISE, Matthew W. (Lib Assoc) . 1357
YUCHT, Donald J. (Sci Ref Libn) 1384

New York Zoological Society (NY)
JOHNSON, Steven P. (Supvsng Libn & Archvst) 609

Newark Academy (NJ)
MALLALIEU, Robert K. (Head Libn) 763

Newark Pub Lib (NJ)
BEIMAN, Frances M. (Principal Libn, Educ Div) 75
BETANCOURT, Ingrid T. (Hispanic Srvs Coordntr) 92
CUMMINGS, Charles F. (Asst Chief Libn) 264
DANE, William J. (Art & Music Dept Mgr) 272
HAWLEY, George S. (Principal Libn of US Docum) 514
KAHN, Leslie A. (Gen Ref & Cols Libn) 622
KNIGHT, Shirley D. (Dir) 664
MILLER, Charles W. (Music Libn) 836
REDLICH, Barry (Ref Libn) 1014
RUPPRECHT, Leslie P. (Supvsg Ref Libn) 1068
SCHWARTZ, Lawrence C. (Head, Interlib Srvs) 1104
SHEARIN, Cynthia E. (Branch Libn) 1124

Newberry Coll (SC)
DENNIS, Everett J. (Dir of Lib and Media Srvs) 292

Newberry Lib (IL)

Newburgh Free Lib (NY)

Newfane Central Sch District (NY)

Newfoundland Pub Libs Board (NF)

Newman & Holtzinger P C (DC)
Newman Schlau Fitch & Burns P C (NY)
Newport Beach Pub Lib (CA)

Newport Pub Lib (RI)
The News & Observer Publishing Co (NC)

News Bank Inc (CT)

News-Gazette (IL)
News Journal Co (DE)

News Sentinel (IN)
News/Sun-Sentinel Co (FL)
NewsBank Inc (CT)

Newsday Inc (NY)

Newsday Videotex Services (NY)
Newsnet Inc (PA)

Newspaper Printing Corp (OK)
Newsweek Inc (DC)
Newsweek Inc (NY)

Newton Falls Pub Lib (OH)

Newton Free Lib (MA)

Newton Pub Lib (KS)
Newton Pub Schools (MA)

Newtown Friends Sch (PA)
NFAIS (PA)
NHPRC (MI)

Niagara Coll of Applied Arts & Tech (ON)

Niagara County Community Coll (NY)
Niagara-on-the-Lake Pub Lib Board (ON)

BURROWS, Thomas W. (Rare Book Catlgr) 163
CULLEN, Charles T. (Pres & Libn) 263
MARSHALL, Jerilyn A. (Ref Srvs Supvsr) 774
MICKELBERRY, Mark B. (Lib Automation Coor) 833
WYLY, Mary P. (Dir of Lib Srvs) 1375
HALPIN, James R. (Ref Srvs Head) 490
VONDERHEIDE, Scott T. (Sch Media Spclst) 1288
CAMERON, H C. (Asst Head) . . . 174
MORTON, Elaine (Books by Mail Libn) 870
PENNEY, Pearce J. (Chief Provincial Libn) 957
NEWTON, Stephanne K. (Libn) . . 900

COLE, Charles D. (Attorney) 230
EASTMAN, Franklin R. (Branch Libn) 333
JUNG, Soon J. (Actg Sect Mgr) . 620
POARCH, Margaret E. (Chlds Srvs Coordntr) 979
WATERS, Shirley V. (Asst Libn) 1309

LEONARD, Teresa G. (Resrch Libn) 717
ANDREWS, Chris C. (Dir of Product Devlpmnt) 26
VANCE, Carolyn J. (Chief Libn) 1272
WALKER, Charlotte J. (Chief Libn) 1295
MARTIN, Jody S. (Lib Supvsr) . . 776
ISAACS, Bob (Lib Srvs Mgr) 584
DYER, Carolyn A. (Vice Pres of Mktg) 330
HOFFMAN, David M. (Chief Libn) 547
RAYNOR, Julie M. (Dir of Plng) 1011
BUHSMER, John H. (Pres) 156
ELSTON, Andrew S. (Executive VP) 346
HUGHES, Marilyn A. (VP of Customer Relations) 572
REIBSAMEN, Gary G. 1018
FARLEY, Austin G. (Head Libn) . 364
FINE, Sandra R. (Bureau Libn) . . 377
PIDALA, Veronica C. (Advertising Resrc Ctr Mgr) . . 971
SALBER, Cecilia T. (Sr Ref Libn) 1076
SALBER, Peter J. (Asst Lib Dir) 1076
SLATE, Ted (Lib Dir) 1148
SOUDERS, Marilyn N. (Head of Acqs Sect) 1169
STEVENSON, Mata (Ref Libn) . 1191
TYLER, David M. (Ref Libn) . . . 1266
MC CLEAF-NESPECA, Sue E. (Asst Dir) 796
RASKIN, Susan R. (Chlds Srvs Supvsr) 1009
EBERHARD, Neysa C. (Dir) 334
SLATTERY, Carole C. (Sch Libn) 1148
OGLETREE, Elizabeth H. (Libn) . . 918
UNRUH, Betty 1269
SIEBERS, Bruce L. (Archvst Processor) 1135

BOWMAN, Robert J. (Coordntr, Lib Technician Prog) 122
HEWITT, Heather O. (Tchg Master) 535
FARRELL, Michele A. (Ref Libn) . 365

MOLSON, Gerda A. (Chief Exec Ofcr) 853

Niagara Univ (NY)

BUDGE, William D. (Coordntr of Pub Srvs) 155
CONEY, Kim C. (Ref Libn) 236
MORRIS, Leslie R. (Libs Dir) 867

Nicholas D Humez Publishers' Services (ME)

HUMEZ, Nicholas D. (Proprietor) . 573

Nicholls State Univ (LA)

DESSINO, Jacquelyn A. (Ref Libn) 296
MIDDLETON, Francine K. (Microforms Libn) 833

Nichols Lib (IL)

FIELDING, Susan K. (Chief Catlgr) 376

Nichols Sch (NY)

JOHNSON, Guy M. (Dir of Libs) . 605
RYBARCZYK, Barclay S. (Libn) 1071

Nicolet Coll (WI)

BRANT, Susan L. (Ref and Col Devlpmnt Libn) 129

NIDEP (NJ)

BARATTA, Maria (Lib Dir) 55

Nielsen Engineering & Research Inc (CA)

FALTZ, Judy A. (Libn) 363

Niesar Kregstein & Cecchini (CA)

JONES, Michael D. (Libn) 614

Nigerian Baptist Theological Seminary (NGR)

OKPARA, Ibiba M. (Assoc Libn) . 920
TARPLEY, Margaret J. (Assoc Libn) 1224

Niles Barton & Wilmer (MD)

HOLDEN, Nancy K. (Law Libn) . . 550

Niles City Schs (OH)

THOMAS, Saraalice F. (Elem Lib Media Spclst) 1238

Niles Pub Lib District (IL)

KALRA, Bhupinder S. (Ref Libn) . 623
MCKENZIE, Duncan J. (Adminstr) 811

NILS Publishing Co (CA)

BOOTH, Barbara A. (Database Devlpmnt Dir) 116

92 St Young Men's & Women's Hebrew Assn (NY)

SIEGEL, Steven W. (Lib Dir & Archvst) 1136

Ninth Circuit Court of Appeals (AZ)

DANIELS, Delores E. (Head Satellite Libn) 273
MAYNARD, Deo D. (Asst Libn) . . 790

NIOGA Lib System (NY)

KLIMEK, Chester R. (Devlpmnt Ofcr) 661

NKC Hospitals Inc (KY)

BUCHANAN, Holly S. (Corprt Info Resrcs Dir) 153

NLP Center of Texas (TX)

HASKELL, Peter C. (Dir) 510

NMC Children's Hospital (DC)

KNOBLOCH, Shirley S. (Med Libn & Info Spclst) 665

NOAA NESDIS/NCDC (NC)

SNODGRASS, Rex J. (Deputy Dir of NCDC/NOAA) 1163

Noble Communications (MO)

CARTER, Steva L. (Dir of Info Srvs) 190

Nobles County (MN)

SPILLERS, Roger E. (Lib Dir) . . 1174

Noblesville-Southeastern Pub Lib (IN)

COOPER, David L. (Lib Dir) 242
MAXWELL, Donald W. (Ref Libn) 788

Nola Regional Lib System (OH)

YANCURA, Ann J. (Dir) 1377

Noranda Minerals Inc (ON)

GOODINGS, Sally A. (Libn) 449

Norcliff Thayer Inc (MO)

ALDRIDGE, Gloria J. (Libn) 11

Norfolk Pub Lib (CT)

SCHIMMEL, Louise S. (Dir) . . . 1093

Norfolk Pub Lib (NE)

HANWAY, Wayne E. (Lib Dir) . . . 499

Norfolk Pub Lib (VA)

DRYE, Jerry L. (Head) 321
GRIFFLER, Carl W. (Branch Libn) 469
LEGO, Jane B. (Dept Head) 712
MAYER-HENNELLY, Mary B. (Comunty Srvs & Programming Coordntr) 789
NICHOLSON, Myreen M. (Asst Fiction Head) 902
PARKER, John A. (Gen Ref Head) 942

Norfolk State Univ (VA)

JONES-TRENT, Bernice R. (Lib Dir) 616

Norman Pub Sch System (OK)

PARKER, Eleanor V. (Lib Media Spclst) 941
MCKNIGHT, Michelynn (Libn) . . . 812

Norman Regional Hospital (OK)

REIERSON, Pamela M. (Media Spclst) 1019

Normandale Community Coll (MN)

COURTNEY, Marjorie S. (Libn) . . 251

Normandy Sch District (MO)

DEFALCO, Joseph (Vice Pres) . . 287

Norstar Data Services (NY)

North American Baptist Conference (SD)

DUNGER, George A. (Archvst) . . 326

North Arkansas Regional Lib (AR)

HAMBY, Tracy A. (Asst Regnl Libn) 491
VAN ARSDALE, Dennis G. (Regional Libn) 1272

North Babylon Union Free Sch District (NY)

RING, Constance B. (Sch Media Spclst) 1035

North Bay Cooperative Lib System (CA)

BATES, Henry E. (Acting Adminstr) 64

North Bay Pub Lib (ON)

NORRGARD, Don K. (AV and Ref Supvsr) 909

North Berwyn Sch Dist 98 (IL)

KRAUSE, Roberta A. (Coordntr of Info Srvs) 676

North Brunswick Township (NJ)

THONER, Jane T. (Jr Libn) 1242

North California Lib (CA)

MCLEAN, Janice A. (Coordntr) . . 814

North Carolina A & T State Univ (NC)

YOUNG, Tommie M. (Instrcl Srvs Dir) 1383

North Carolina A&T State Univ (NC)

JARRELL, James R. (Technl Srvs Div Head) 594

North Carolina Biotechnology Center (NC)

BRUCE, Nancy G. (Info Spclst) . . 149

North Carolina Central Univ (NC)

BALLARD, Robert M. (Lib & Info Sci Prof) 53
BOMARC, M D. (Assoc Libn & Asst Prof) 113
BRACY, Pauletta B. 125
BURGIN, Robert E. (Lectr) 159
HAZEL, Debora E. (Head of Ref) 517
LAWTON, Patrecia J. (Head of Catlgng Dept) 705
RICHMOND, Alice S. (Libn) . . . 1030
SHEARER, Kenneth D. (Prof) . . 1124
SPELLER, Benjamin F. (Dean) . 1172

North Carolina Dept of Cultural Resource (NC)

KAN, Irene E. (Acqs Libn) 624
MCGINN, Howard F. (Asst State Libn) 806
SMITH, Catherine (Chief Consult, Lib Devlpmnt) 1153
WILLIAMS, M J. (State Libn) . . 1345

NC Department of Cultural Resources (NC)

WILLIAMS, Gene J. (State Agency Records Archvst) . . . 1343
WILLIAMS, Mildred J. (State Libn) 1345

North Carolina Dept of Pub Instruction (NC)

BOWMAN, Gloria M. (Coordntr & Soc Resrch Asst) 121
BRUMBACK, Elsie (Asst State Superintendent) 150
TUGWELL, Helen M. (Regnl Sch Media Progs Coordntr) . . 1262

North Carolina Division of State Lib (NC)

DRUM, Eunice P. (Chief, Technl Srvs Sect) 321
WELCH, John T. (Grants Adminstr) 1321

North Carolina Foreign Language Center (NC)

CHAN, Moses C. (Foreign Languages Libn) 199

North Carolina Hospital Association (NC)

SPENCER, Linda A. (Libn) 1173

North Carolina Lib Association (NC)

MYRICK, Paulino F. (Pres) 885

North Carolina Maritime Museum (NC)

BUMGARNER, John L. (Hist Musm Spclst) 157

North Carolina School of the Arts (NC)

VAN HOVEN, William D. (Head Libn) 1276

North Carolina State Government (NC)

OLSON, David J. (State Archvst) 922

North Carolina State Lib (NC)

IRVING, Ophelia M. (Asst Chief Info Srvs) 584

North Carolina State Univ (NC)

BEST-NICHOLS, Barbara J. (Head Libn) 92
BROWN, Kathleen R. (Asst Head) 145

North Carolina State Univ (NC)

CARSTENS, Timothy V. (Asst Catlg Libn) 188
DAVIS, Jinnie Y. (Asst to the Dir for Plng) 279
FLOYD, Rebecca M. (Serials Libn) 386
GEBBIE, Janet L. (Catlg Libn) . . . 424
HIGH, Walter M. (Monographic Catlgng Dept Head) 538
HUNT, Margaret R. (Head, Col Devlpmnt & Acqs) 575
KING, Ebba K. (Ref Libn) 650
LEVINE, Cynthia R. (Ref Libn) . . . 720
LINK, Margaret A. (Coordntr & Libn) 730
LITTLETON, Isaac T. (Libs Dir) . . 734
MCGEACHY, John A. (Docums Libn) 805
NUTTER, Susan K. (Dir of Libs) . 912
OSEGUEDA, Laura M. (Agriculture & Life Scis Ref Libn) 927
PORTER, Jean M. 985
POZO, Frank J. (Ref Libn) 989
PURYEAR, Pamela E. (Dir, Tobacco Lit Srv) 998
ULMSCHNEIDER, John E. (Lib Systs Head) 1268
WALTNER, Nellie L. (Asst Dir for Technl Srvs) 1301

North Carolina Supreme Court (NC) HALL, Frances H. (Lib) 487
North Carolina Wesleyan Coll (NC) WILGUS, Anne B. (Lib Dir) 1339
North Castle Pub Lib (NY) DEVERS, Charlotte M. (Lib Dir) . . 297
STARK, Li S. (Chlds/Young Adult Libn) 1181
North Central Bible Coll (MN) SHIRK, John C. (Libn) 1131
North Central Bronx Hospital (NY) CHITTAMPALLI, Padma S. (Med Lib Dir) 209
North Central Coll (IL) MEACHEN, Edward W. (Lib Dir) . 819
North Central Lib Cooperative (OH) KARRE, David J. (Dir) 628
North Central Regional Lib System (IA) SWANSON, P A. (Adminstr) . . . 1213
North Coast Instruments (OH) IRWIN, James W. (Pres) 584
North Columbia Elem Sch (GA) WARNER, Wayne G. (Media Spclst) 1305
North Dade Regional Lib (FL) KINNEY, Molly S. (Head of Chlds Srvs) 653
North Dakota State Historical Society (ND) GRAY, David P. (Deputy State Archvst) 459
North Dakota State Lib (ND) HARRIS, Patricia L. (State Libn) . 505
HENDRICKS, Thom (Interlib Loan Head) 527
MOREHOUSE, Valerie J. (Consult for Lib Automation) . . 863
North Dakota State Univ (ND) BIRDSALL, Douglas G. (Head of Pub Srvs) 98
BLUE, Margaret R. (Technl Srvs Head) 107
BRKIC, Beverly T. (Catlg Dept Head) 138
NELSON, David N. (Catlg Libn) . 893
SORENSON, Lillian R. (Libn) . . 1168
North Detroit General Hospital (MI) BURSON, Barbara A. (Med Libn) 163
North East Independent Sch District (TX) HAAS, Ruth M. (Head Libn) 480
MCBURNEY, Lynnea R. (Libn) . . 792
North East Kansas Lib System (KS) PLAISTED, Glen L. (Dir) 977
North Edison Pub Lib (NJ) CULLUM, Carolyn N. (Chlds Libn) 263
North Florida Junior Coll (FL) HISS, Sheila M. (AV Libn) 544
North Georgia Coll (GA) MALCOLM, Carol L. (Ref & Govt Docums Libn) 762
North Greenville Coll (SC) BAKER, Steven L. (Ref Libn) 49
North Harris County Coll (TX) PEYTON, Janice L. (Pub Srvs Consult) 966
PORTER, Exa L. (Ref Libn) 984

North Hills Passavant Hospital (PA) TREVANION, Margaret U. (Med Libn) 1255
North Humboldt Unified Sch District (CA) MARVEL, Frances J. (Libn) 780
North Hunterdon High Sch Dist (NJ) HONTZ, M E. (Libn) 556
North Kansas City Pub Lib (MO) HARTMETZ, Walter J. (Lib Dir) . . 508
North Kansas City Sch District (MO) HAWKINS, Marilyn J. (Sch Lib Media Spclst) 514
North Memorial Medical Center (MN) BARBOUR-TALLEY, Donna L. (Mgr, Med Lib) 55
North Olympic Library Systems (WA) DAVIES, Jo (Dir) 277
North Park Coll (IL) BODI, Sonia E. (Head Ref Libn & Assoc Prof) 109
GROSS, Dorothy E. (Lib Dir) 472
JOHNSON, Timothy J. (Archs Dir) 609
KARSTEN, Eileen S. (Technl Srvs Head) 628
PEARSON, Karen L. (Ref and Serials Libn) 952
North Park Sch District (CO) SWEET, Sally K. (Lib Media Spclst K-12) 1215
North Pennsylvania School District (PA) NOLAN, Joan (Dept Head, Lib & Media Srvs) 907
North Providence Union Free Lib (RI) BIERDEN, Margaret W. (Chlds Libn) 95
North Richland Hills Pub Lib (TX) HALLAM, Arlita W. (Lib Dir) 489
MACFARLANE, Francis X. (Chlds & Young Adult Srvs Head) 755
STATTON, Alison H. (Chlds Libn) 1183
North Riverside Pub Lib (IL) DAVIS, Carol L. (Youth Srvs Libn) 278
North Royalton City Schs (OH) WEST, Loretta G. (Elem Sch Libn) 1326
North Seattle Community Coll (WA) CHASE, Dale L. (Ref Libn) 203
North Shore Community Coll (MA) GAGNON, Ronald A. (Automated Systs/Technl Srv Coordntr) 412
North Shore Country Day Sch (IL) LUNDQUIST, Marie A. (Media Coordntr) 748
North Shore Univ Hospital (NY) EISENBERG, Debra (Med Lib Dir) 340
NAPOLITANO, Joan A. (Assoc Med Libn) 887
North State Cooperative Lib System (CA) ALLENSWORTH, James H. (Ref Libn) 16
North Suburban Lib System (IL) GRODINSKY, Deborah (Ref Libn) 471
KANNER, Elliott E. (Resrcs Coordntr) 625
MCCLARREN, Robert R. (Syst Dir) 796
ROOSE, Tina (Dir of Ref) 1053
North Texas State Univ (TX) ALMQUIST, Sharon G. (Asst Monographs Catlgr, Music & AV) 17
CARROLL, Dewey E. (Prof) 187
CVELJO, Katherine (Prof) 268
FERSTL, Kenneth L. (Asst Prof) . 374
FOLLET, Robert E. (Asst Music Libn) 388
GALLOWAY, Margaret E. (Assoc Dir of Libs) 415
HIMMEL, Richard L. (Univ Archvst) 542
HOGAN, Sarah T. (Head of Biblgph Ctl Dept) 549
JONES, Lois S. (Art Prof & Art Hist Coordntr) 613
LAVENDER, Kenneth (Biblgphr) . 703
MITCHELL, George D. (Media Lib Dir) 848
POPE, Betty F. (Assoc Libn) 983
SASSEN, Catherine J. (Asst Catlg Libn, Monographs) . . . 1083
TOTTEN, Herman L. (Prof) 1252

North Texas State Univ (TX)
VONDRAN, Raymond F. (Dean) 1288

North View Elementary Sch (IL)
SULLIVAN, Geraldine M. (Lib
Media Ctr Dir) 1207

North York Board of Education (ON)
GREAVES, H P. (Coordntr,
Resrc Srvs) 461
MOORE, May E. (Head Libn) ... 860

North York Pub Lib Board (ON)
BURNETT, Wayne C. (Trustee) . 162
WILLIAMS, Lorraine O.
(Vice-Chairman & Board
Mem) 1344

Northampton Area Sch District (PA)
PAGOTTO, Sarah L. (Elem Sch
Libn) 934

Northbrook Pub Lib (IL)
NICKELS, Judith L. (Ref Libn) ... 902
REIMER, Elizabeth A. (Technl
Srvs Dept Head) 1020
REISNER, Susan (Head, Youth
Services) 1021
WESTON, Ann B. (Ref Libn) ... 1327

Northeast Louisiana Univ (LA)
LARASON, Larry (Lib Dir) 697

Northeast Missouri State Univ (MO)
ELLEBRACHT, Eleanor V. (Ref
Libn) 343
LOCKHART, Carol A. (Ref Libn) . 736
OFSTAD, Odessa L. (Spcl Cols
Libn and Archvst) 917

Northeast State Univ (OK)
VEITH, Charles R. (Instr, Math
Sci Tech Resrc Coordntr) ... 1281

**Northeast Technical Community
Coll** (NE)
WARNER, Karen R. (Coordntr
of Lib Srvs) 1305

Northeast Texas Lib System (TX)
MURRAY, Margaret A. (Col
Devlpmnt Libn) 882
QUEYROUZE, Mary E.
(Automation Consult) 999

Northeast Utilities Service Co (CT)
JOHNSON, Doris E. (Info
Spclst) 603

Northeastern Illinois Univ (IL)
ALTHAGE, Celia J. (Educ Libn) .. 18
HIGGINBOTHAM, Richard C.
(Instrc and Extension Srvs
Libn) 537
HILBURGER, Mary J. (Ref Libn) . 538
KISTNER, Glen A. (Circ Libn) ... 657
MCGREGOR, James W. (Spcl
Projs Libn) 808
MISTARAS, Evangeline (Head
Ref Libn) 848
REED, Virginia R. (Assoc Prof) . 1015
SCOTT, Sharon E. (Ctr for Inner
City Std Head Libn) 1108
VILARO, Annette B. (Head Educ
Libn) 1284

**Northeastern Ohio Univ Coll of
Medicine** (OH)
BREWER, Karen L. (Dir of
Ocasek Regnl Med Info Ctr) .. 134
OSTERFIELD, George T.
(Archvst, Catlgr, & Records
Ofcr) 928
PORTER, Marlene A. (Ref Libn
& Educ Coordntr) 985
UNGER, Monica A. (Systs Libn) 1269

**Northeastern Oklahoma State
Univ** (OK)
CHEATHAM, Gary L. (Ref Libn
& Resrc Coordntr for Bus) ... 204

**Northeastern Ontario Oncology
Program** (ON)
GOSS, Alison M. (Oncology
Libn) 453

Northeastern State Univ (OK)
BRICK, Sarah E. (Ref & Resrc
Coordntr, Lib Sci Instr) 134
HILL, Helen K. (Access Srvs
Libn) 540
MADAUS, J R. (Dean of Lib &
Lrng Resrcs) 758
MCQUITTY, Jeanette N. (User
Srvs Dir) 817
PATTERSON, Lotsee (Assoc
Prof & Lib Media Prog Chair) . 948
SUMNER, Delores T. (Spcl Cols
Libn) 1209

Northeastern Univ (MA)
BENENFELD, Alan R. (Univ
Libs Dean) 80
CAHALAN, Thomas H. (Asst
Libn) 171
CIANFARINI, Margaret (Acqs &
Catlgng Libn) 214
HANSSEN, Nancy E. (Head of
Serials Dept) 499
LEAHY, Lynda C. (User Srvs &
Col Devlpmnt Assoc Dean) ... 706
SCHALOW, John M. (Catlg
Dept Head) 1089
STEINBERG, Marilyn H. (Lib
Head) 1185

Northern Arizona Univ (AZ)
AWE, Susan C. (Bus Ref Libn) ... 42
EGAN, Terence W. (Media Ctr
Lib Asst III) 338
HASSELL, Robert H. (Head Ref
Libn) 511
JOHNSON, Harlan R. (Assoc
Prof of Lib Sci & Educ) 605
MULLANE, William H. (Spcl
Cols Libn) 877

**Northern California Health
Center** (CA)
DURSO, Angeline M. (Lib Dir) ... 329

Northern Illinois Lib System (IL)
ANDERSON, Nancy E. (Ref
Libn) 24
HUTCHINS, Mary J. (Multitype
Consult) 579
SCHOLTZ, James C. (Multitype
Consultant/AV Srvs) 1098
WELCH, Steven J. (Multitype
Consultant) 1321

Northern Illinois Univ (IL)
ABBOTT, Craig S. (Prof of Engl) ... 1
ALEXANDER, Liz C. (Asst Prof
& Govt Pubns Libn) 12
ANDERSON, Byron P. (Libn) 21
AUSTIN, John R. (Pub Srvs
Libn & Asst Prof) 40
DEQUIN, Henry C. (Prof) 293
DUTTON, Lee S. (Hart Col Libn) . 329
GILDEMEISTER, Glen A. (Dir,
Regnl Hist Ctr) 434
GRAHAM, Robert W. (Field Rep
& Archvst) 456
GROSCH, Mary F. (Bus & Econ
Libn) 472
HAMILTON, David A. (Catlgr) ... 491
HOLZBERLEIN, Deanne B.
(Assoc Prof) 555
HORST, Stanley E. (Assoc Dir) .. 561
HUANG, Samuel T.
(Coordntr/Comp Ref Srvs) ... 568
HURYCH, Jitka M. (Head of Sci
& Engrng Dept) 578
JONES, Dorothy E. (Asst Prof &
Lib Srvs Coordntr) 612
KAUFFMAN, S B. (Law Lib Dir) . 631
KIES, Cosette N. (Chair & Prof) .. 647
KISSINGER, Patricia A. (Soc
Sci Libn & Educ Subject
Spclst) 656
LANIER, Donald L. (Head of
Spcl Col & Area Std) 696
LARSEN, John C. (Assoc Prof) .. 698
MILLER, Doris A. (Gen Ref Dept
Head) 837
NAIMAN, Sandra M. (Subject
Spclst, Engl & Am Lit) 886
OSORIO, Nestor L. (Sci/Engrng
Subject Spclst) 928
RASMUSSEN, Gordon E. (Circ
Libn) 1009
RAST, Elaine K. (Head, Catlgng
& Automated Records) 1009
RENSHAW, Marita (Rare Bks
Catlgr) 1023
RIDER, Philip R. (Pubns Editor) . 1032

Northern Illinois Univ (IL)
RIDINGER, Robert B.
(Anthropology & Soclgy
Spclst) 1032
ROYLE, Maryanne (Serials &
Docums Libn) 1063
SCHORMANN, Victor (Gifts &
Exchange Libn) 1099
SCHREIBER, Robert E. (Gen
Ref Libn) 1099
SHAVIT, David (Assoc Prof) . . . 1123
SMITH, Lester K. (Hum & Soc
Scis Dept Head) 1157
STUDWELL, William E.
(Principal Catlgr) 1204
SULLIVAN, Peggy A. (Dean) . . 1208
TITUS, Elizabeth M. (Asst Dir for
Pub Srvs) 1247
TOROK, Andrew G. (Assoc Prof
of Lib & Info Std) 1251
VANDER MEER, Gary L.
(Technl Srvs Libn) 1274
VARNER, Carroll H. (Technl
Srvs Asst Dir) 1278
WELCH, Theodore F. (Dir of
Libs) 1321
WRIGHT, H S. (Music Libn) . . . 1371

Northern Inyo Hospital (CA)
KRATZ, Gale G. (Med Libn) 676
Northern Kentucky Univ (KY)
BENNETT, Donna S. (Head of
Technl Srvs) 81
BRATCHER, Perry R. (Catlgng
Libn) 129
BREDEMEYER, Carol (Pub Srvs
Head) 131
SCHULTZ, Lois E. (Technl Srvs
Head) 1102
STURM, Rebecca R. (Head of
Pub Srvs) 1205
WHITTLE, Ann H. (Secy to Lib
Dir) 1334

Northern Lights Lib Network (MN)
LARSON, Joan B. (Coordntr) . . . 699
Northern Michigan Univ (MI)
PETERS, Stephen H. (Assoc
Prof & Catlgr) 962
WAGAR, Joanna M. (Technl
Srvs Head) 1291

Northern Research & Engineering
Corp (MA)
BARRINGER, Nancy F. (Libn) 59
Northern State Coll (SD)
LUGER, Mary J. (Ref, Curr
Libn) 747
Northern States Power Co (MN)
SOLSETH, Gwenn M. (Info
Analyst) 1166
Northern Telecom Inc (NH)
NELSON, David W. (Quality
Software Engineer) 893
Northern Telecom Inc (TN)
PILCHER, Annette S. 973
Northern Virginia Community
Coll (VA)
BERNHARDT, Frances (Lib
Srvs Coordntr) 89
ENGLAND, Ellen M. (Libn) 349
JORDAN, Katherine H. (Ref
Libn and Asst Prof) 616
TERWILLIGER, Gloria P. (Lrng
Resrcs Dir) 1232
Northern Waters Lib Service (WI)
PAULI, David N. (Dir) 950
Northern Westchester Hospital
Center (NY)
WILLOUGHBY, Nona C. (Hlth
Scis Lib Dir) 1349
Northfield Mount Herman Sch (MA)
LANGE, Clare M. (Media Dir) . . . 695
Northfield Pub Lib (MN)
YOUNG, Lynne M. (Dir) 1382
Northland Coll (WI)
FENNESSEY, Mary D. (Head
Libn) 371
Northland Lib Cooperative (MI)
WILLIAMS, Susan S. (Dir) 1346
Northland Pioneer Coll (AZ)
ROTHLISBERG, Allen P. (Head
Libn) 1060
Northland Pub Lib (PA)
SMITH, Mary M. (Chld's Srvs
Coordntr) 1158
Northrop Corp (CA)
KILLIAN, Sandra L. (Info Resrch
Ctr Mgr) 648
MOLLETT, Mike M. (Info
Analyst) 853
PRINTZ, Naomi J. (Technl Libn) . 993

Northrop Corp (CA)
SALM, Kay E. (Sr Info Resrchr) 1077
SUGRANES, Maria R. (Mgr,
Corprt Resrch Lib) 1207
WILLIS, Joan K. (Libn) 1348
Northrop Corp (IL)
KONISHI, Sue S. (Technl Libn) . . 670
Northrop Corp (MA)
DELTANO, Pauline T. (Sr Bus
Info Coordntr) 290
Northrop Sch District (IL)
CAREY, Kevin J. (Data Analyst
Libn) 181
Northrop Univ (CA)
HALPIN, Jerome H. (Dir of Lib) . . 490
Northside Hospital (GA)
PAYNE-BUTTON, Linda (Hlth
Scis Libn) 951
Northside Independent Sch
District (TX)
FRIEDMAN, Tevia L. (Elem Sch
Libn) 404
Northwest Community Coll (AK)
ROSS, Rosemary E. (Lrng
Resrc Ctr Coordntr) 1058
Northwest Community Hospital (IL)
LIANG, Ching C. (Hospital Libn) . 725
Northwest Educational
Cooperative (IL)
PEISER, Richard H. (Libn) 955
Northwest General Hospital (WI)
MARKS, Coralyn (Med Lib Dir) . . 771
Northwest IN Area Lib Services
Authority (IN)
SNOWDEN, Deanna (Adminstr) 1164
Northwest Junior High Sch (IA)
LANGHORNE, Mary J. (Lib
Media Spclst) 696
Northwest Kansas Lib System (KS)
BUMBALOUGH, Bruce L. (Syst
Libn) 157
Northwest Missouri State Univ (MO)
HANKS, Nancy C. (Lib Dir) 496
MURPHY, Kathryn L. (Head of
Lib Automated Srvs) 880
Northwest Nazarene Coll (ID)
LANCASTER, Edith E. (Lib Dir) . . 691
RAMBO, Helen M. (Catlgr &
Catlg Libn) 1005
SIMMONS, Randall C. (Dir) . . . 1140
Northwest Regional Lib System (FL)
DANNECKER, Joyce H. (Asst
Lib Dir) 274
Northwest Regional Lib System (IA)
PLUEMER, Bonnie J. (Consult) . . 978
Northwestern Bell (NE)
BARTON, Laurel (Corprt
Strategy & Resrch Dir) 62
Northwestern Coll (WI)
GOSDECK, David M. (Lib Dir) . . 452
Northwestern Mutual Life Insurance
Co (WI)
BARLOGA, Carolyn J. (Info
Srvs Assoc) 57
HALL, Deborah A. (Adminstr) . . 487
MURPHY, Virginia A. (Resrch
Analyst) 881
Northwestern Oklahoma State
Univ (OK)
LAU, Ray D. (Lib Dir & Lib Sci
Dept Chair) 702
Northwestern Regional Lib (NC)
MACPHAIL, Jessica (Dir) 758
Northwestern State Univ of
Louisiana (LA)
BUCHANAN, William C. (Dir) . . . 153
HUSSEY, Sandra R. (Ref Libn) . . 578
JARRED, Ada D. (Dir of Libs) . . . 594
LANDRY, Abbie V. (Ref Div
Head) 693
MAYEAUX, Thurlow M. (Ref,
Govt Docums Libn, Instr) 789
MCCORMICK, Dorcas M.
(Shreveport Div Head) 798
YOUNG, Amanda M. (Div Head
& Asst Prof) 1381
Northwestern Univ (IL)
AAGAARD, James S. (Info
Systs Devlpmnt Dir) 1
BALL, Mary A. (User Srvs Libn) . . 52
BEATTY, William K. (Prof of
Med Bibl) 70
BENNETT, Scott B. (Asst Univ
Libn for Col Mgmt) 82
BERKEY, Irene (Foreign & Intl
Law Libn) 87
BJORNCRANTZ, Leslie B.
(Curr Libn & Educ Biblgphr) . . 100
BOELKE, Joanne H. (Dept
Head) 110
BRADY, Mary M. (Asst Acqs
Dept Head) 127
CAMPANA, Deborah A. (Music
Pub Srvs Libn) 175

Northwestern Univ (IL)

CLOUD, Patricia D. (Asst Univ Archvst) 223

DAVIDSON, Lloyd A. (Life Sci Libn & User Srvs Head) 276

ELSTEIN, Rochelle S. (Art Biblgphr) 346

FINEMAN, Charles S. (Hum Biblgphr) 377

FRIEDER, Richard D. (Preservation Libn) 403

GRISCOM, Richard W. (Music Techni Srvs Libn) 471

HILL, Janet S. (Catlg Dept Head) 540

HORNY, Karen L. (Asst Univ Libn for Techni Srvs) 560

KREINBRING, Mary (Head of Techni Srvs) 677

LEONARD, Kevin B. (Assoc Univ Archvst) 716

LOWMAN, Judith T. (Asst Curator) 744

MAYLONE, R R. (Cur) 790

MCCARTHY, Mary C. (Asst Head, Ref Dept) 794

MCGOWAN, John P. (Univ Libn) 807

MCHENRY, Renee E. (Info Srvs & Catlg Libn) 808

MCHUGH, William A. (Ref Libn) . 809

MICHAELSON, Robert C. (Head Sci & Engrng Lib) 832

NIELSEN, Brian (Ref Dept Head & Coordntr of Resrch) 903

OLSON, Anton J. (Head, Techni Srvs) 922

PANOFSKY, Hans E. (Curator) . . 938

PRENDERGAST, Kathleen M. (Mgr, Info Systs) 990

QUERY, Lance D. (Plng & Persnl Asst Univ Libn) 999

QUINN, Patrick M. (Univ Archvst) 1000

RAMM, Dorothy V. (Perdcls & Ref Libn) 1005

ROBERTS, Donald L. (Head Music Libn) 1039

ROBERTS, Sally M. (NUL CAIS Coordntr) 1041

SCHWERIN, Kurt (Prof of Law & Law Libn Emeritus) 1106

SHAYNE, Mette H. (Biblgphr & Ref Libn) 1124

SHEDLOCK, James (Head of Pub Srvs) 1124

SHERMAN, Sarah (Govt Docums Libn) 1128

STAMM, Andrea L. (Africana Catlgng Head) 1179

STRANGE, Michele M. (Asst Govt Pubns Libn) 1200

STRAWN, Gary L. (Authority Libn) 1201

STUTZ, Patricia A. (Asst Interlib Loan Libn) 1206

TAWYEA, Edward W. (Assoc Dir) 1225

WARD, Shirlene A. (Recorded Sound Srvs Libn) 1304

WILLIAMS, Charles M. (Retrospective Conversion Project As) 1342

YOON, Choong N. (Head of Catlgng Dept) 1380

Northwood Institute (ME) FRIDLEY, Russell W. (Dir) 403

Northwood Institute (MI) CHEN, Catherine W. (Dir of Libs) 205

Norton Christensen Inc (UT) LIU, Kitty P. (Info Spclst) 734

Norton Co (MA)

Norton Co (NY)

Norwalk Board of Education (CT)

Norwalk Community Coll (CT)

Norwalk Pub Lib (CT)

Norwalk Pub Lib (OH)
Norwell Pub Lib (MA)
Norwich Eaton Pharmaceuticals (NY)

Norwich Univ (VT)

Norwood Hospital (MA)
NOTIS Northwestern Univ (IL)

NOTIS Systems Inc (IL)

Notre Dame Academy (CA)

Notre Dame High Sch (CA)
Notre Dame High Sch (NY)

Notre Dame High Sch for Boys (IL)
Nova Scotia Attorney General Dept (NS)
Nova Scotia Legislative Lib (NS)
Nova Scotia Provincial Lib (NS)

Nova Univ (FL)

Novacor Chemicals Ltd (AB)

Novato United Sch District (CA)

Novatron Information Corp (NS)

Novi Community Schs (MI)
Novi Pub Lib (MI)

Novo Laboratories Inc (CT)

Novotny Associates (WI)

Nueva Learning Ctr (CA)
Nuodex Inc (NJ)

Nursing Heritage Foundation (MO)
NUS Corp (PA)
Nyack Coll & Alliance Theological Sem (NY)

Nyack Pub Lib (NY)

Nyack Pub Schs (NY)

NYNEX Corp (NY)

SILVERBERG, Mary E. (Techni Info Spclst) 1138

SUTHERLAND-NEHRING, Laurie A. (Info Spclst) 1211

KNOPP, Marie L. (Lib Media Spclst) 665

LAPOLT, Margaret B. (Lib Media Spclst) 697

SELVERSTONE, Harriet S. (Dist Coordntr of Sec Sch Libns) . 1114

BAYLES, Carmen L. (Dir of the Lrng Resrcs Ctr) 67

PIKUL, Diane M. (Automation & Instrcl Srvs Libn) 973

VAN DYKE, Aase S. (Chlds Srvs Div Chief) 1275

DRAPP, Laureen (Dir) 318

KADANOFF, Diane G. (Dir) 621

WINDSOR, Donald A. (Info Scientist) 1354

WORTHEN, Dennis B. (Formularies & Reimbursement Mgr) 1369

LINDBERG, Sandra (Techni Srvs Libn) 728

FOXMAN, Carole J. (Med Libn) . 395

MILLER, Bruce A. (Sr Systs Analyst) 836

DREWETT, William O. (Pgmr) . . . 319

MCGINN, Thomas P. (User Srvs Libn) 806

SCHAPIRO, Benjamin H. (User Srvs Libn) 1090

JAIN, Celeste C. (High Sch Libn) 591

EGAN, Janet M. (Libn) 338

STRANC, Mary C. (Lib & Media Ctr Libn) 1200

SCHMID, Judith L. (Libn) 1095

DEYOUNG, Marie (Libn) 298

GURAYA, Harinder (Ref Lib) 478

MORASH, Claire E. (Sr Ref Libn) 862

HEMPHILL, Lia S. (Acqs Libn) . . 525

KEMPER, Marlyn J. (Assoc Dir of Info Scis) 639

TAYSOM, Daniel B. (Comp & Media Srvs Head) 1229

JENKINS-PENDER, Maureen (Corporate Libn) 597

HIRABAYASHI, Joanne (Coorndtr of Lib & Instrcl Mtrls Ctr) 543

POTTER, Daniel 987

THORSTEINSON, William A. (Techni Operations Mgr) 1243

KIEFER, Marilyn V. (Libn) 647

DRUSCHEL, Pauline H. (Outreach Libn) 321

CARNEGLIA, Anna L. (Asst Libn) 183

SAMUELS, Lois A. (Info Spclst) 1079

NOVOTNY, Lynn E. (Info Spclst) 911

ABILOCK, Debbie (Libn) 2

CARNAHAN, Joan A. (Info Srvs Mgr) 183

LINEBACH, Laura M. (Dir) 730

STERLING, Alida B. (Libn) 1189

BRIGHAM, Jeffrey L. (Interim Dir of Libs) 136

GROTT, Joan (Dir) 473

SVIBRUCK, Jonathan (Head Libn) 1212

BREGMAN, Joan R. (Pgmr) 131

ECKENRODE, Robert J. 334

FOGARTY, Patricia C. (Exec Dir) 387

NYNEX Corp (NY)

MCGARVEY, Eileen B. (Info
    Spclst & Ref) 805
MUSKUS, Elizabeth A. (Staff
    Mgr) 883
SCHARF, Davida (Staff Dir) ... 1090
TIBBETTS, David W. (Staff Dir) 1243

O

**Oak Creek-Franklin Joint Sch
District** (WI)   MORROW, Kathryn M. (Libn) ... 869
Oak Creek Pub Lib (WI)   TALIS, Ross M. (Asst City Libn) 1221
    UTZINGER, Crchard L. (Chlds
    Srvs Dir) 1270
Oak Harbor Junior High (WA)   MERWINE, Glenda M. (Head
    Libn) 827
Oak Lawn Pub Lib (IL)   DOBREZ, Cynthia K. (Youth
    Srvs Libn) 307
    MCMAHON, Judith L. (Youth
    Srvs Dept Head) 814
    MOORMAN, John A. (Dir) 862
**Oak Park Elementary Sch District
97** (IL)   VOTH, Mary S. (Media Spclst) . 1289
Oak Park Pub Lib (IL)   STEVENSON, Sheila M. (Adult
    Srvs Head) 1191
Oak Park Pub Lib (MI)   BRANZBURG, Marian G.
    (Youth Srvs Coordntr) 129
    WASSERMAN, Sherry T. (Asst
    to Dir, Head of Adult Srvs) .. 1308
Oak Ridge Associated Univs (TN)   BURN, Harry T. (Libn & Sr Info
    Spclst) 161
    YALCINTAS, Rana (Med Lib
    Dir) 1376
Oak Ridge National Laboratory (TN)   CATON, Gloria M. 195
    EWBANK, W B. 359
    JONES, Kendra A. (Technl Libn) . 613
    MUNRO, Nancy B. (Technl Info
    Spclst) 879
    PFUDERER, Helen A. (Environ
    Info Dir) 966
Oakland Community Coll (MI)   WILLIAMS, Calvin (Libn) 1342
Oakland County Reference Lib (MI)   JOSE, Phyllis A. (Ref Lib Dir &
    Cnty Libn) 617
Oakland Pub Lib (CA)   BIBEL, Barbara M. (Ref Libn) 94
    CONMY, Peter T. (Libn
    Emeritus) 236
    GILDEN, Susanna C. (Supvsng
    Libn) 434
    LAMBREV, Garrett I. (Branch
    Libn) 691
    MILLER, Elissa R. (Branch Libn) . 837
    MULL, Richard G. (Dist Supvsr) . 876
    OSTROUMOV, Tatiana (Sr
    Catlgng Libn) 929
    PAGE, Kathryn (Ref Adminstr) .. 934
    SWANSON, Clara M. (Supvsng
    Libn) 1213
    WHITE, Lelia C. (Lib Srvs Dir) .. 1331
Oakland Pub Lib (NJ)   HANNON, Patricia A. (Dir) 497
Oakland Schs (MI)   CROSS, Jennie B. (Asst Eductnl
    Resrc Ctr Dir) 260
Oakland Univ (MI)   BLATT, Gloria T. (Assoc Prof) ... 104
    DAVID, Indra M. (Assoc Dean,
    Lib) 276
    FRANKIE, Suzanne O. (Dean of
    Libs) 397
    GAYLOR, Robert G. (Assoc
    Prof) 423
    HILDEBRAND, Linda L. (Ref
    Srvs Coordntr) 538
    KROMPART, Janet A.
    (Academic Libn) 679
Oaklawn Pub Lib (IL)   MCELROY, Beth A. (Trustee) ... 804
Oaklyn Memorial Lib (NJ)   WILINSKI, Grant W. (Dir) 1339
Oakridge Sch District (OR)   MCCOY, Joanne (Libn) 799

Oakton Community Coll (IL)   BOROWSKI, Joseph F. (Dir of
    Lrng Resrcs) 117
    HAWLEY, Marsha S. (Part-Time
    Faculty) 514
Oakwood Board of Education (OH)   BALL, Diane A. (Media Spclst) ... 52
Oakwood Secondary Sch (CA)   KYROPOULOS, Mary S. (Libn) .. 685
OAO Corp (MD)   AUSTIN, Rhea C. (Corprt Libn) ... 40
Ober Kaler Grimes & Shriver (MD)   HINSON, Karen C. (Law Libn) . 543
Oberlin Coll (OH)   BAUMANN, Roland M.
    (Archivist & Dept Head) 66
    BOYD, Alan D. (Head of
    Catlgng & Lib Systs) 122
    CARPENTER, Eric J. (Col
    Devlpmnt Libn) 184
    COMER, Cynthia H. (Assoc Ref
    Head) 234
    ENGLISH, Raymond A. (Assoc
    Dir, Ref Head) 350
    GOULD, Allison L. (Head of
    Circ) 454
    KNAPP, David (Cnsrvtry) 663
    MOFFETT, William A. (Libs Dir) . 852
    RICKER, Alison S. (Sci Libn) .. 1031
    SCHOONMAKER, Dina B. (Cur
    of Spcl Cols, Preservation
    Ofcr) 1098
    WEIDMAN, Jeffrey (Art Libn) .. 1316
    ZAGER, Daniel A.
    (Conservatory Libn) 1385
Oblate Sch of Theology (TX)   MANEY, James W. (Lib Dir) 765
**Oblong Community Unit Sch District
4** (IL)   HEYDUCK, Marilyn J. (Media
    Dir) 535
O'Brien-Atkins Association (NC)   RICE, Patricia A. (Info Ctr Mgr) . 1027
Occidental Chemical Corp (NY)   WAGNER, A B. (Assoc Info
    Scientst) 1291
Occidental Coll (CA)   MORRIS, Jacquelyn M. (Coll
    Libn) 866
Occidental Oil & Gas Corp (OK)   STAIR, Fred (Libn) 1178
**Occupational Health Services
Inc** (TN)   BRANSFORD, John S. (Pres) ... 129
Ocean City Free Pub Lib (NJ)   MASON, Michael L. (Ref Libn,
    Asst Lib Dir) 781
Ocean County Coll (NJ)   GARELICK, Alexander L. (Lib
    Srv Coordntr) 418
Ocean County Lib (NJ)   BELVIN, Carolyn J. (Sr Libn) ... 78
    JAROSLOW, Sylvia W. (Media
    Srvs Coordntr) 594
    KERN, Stella V. (Coordntr of
    Comunty Srvs) 643
    ROYCE, Carolyn S. (Branch
    Srvs Principal Libn) 1063
    SORRENTINO, Robert L. (Jr
    Libn) 1169
    WOLPERT, Scott L. (Ref Libn) ... 1362
Oceanside Pub Lib (CA)   ARNOLD, Donna W. (Comp
    Operations Coordntr) 33
    CAPPADONNA, Mary S. (Libn
    II Technl Prcsng) 180
    WAZNIS, Betty (Ref Libn) 1311
**OCLC Online Computer Lib
Center** (CA)   IVERSON, Diann S. (Sr
    Coordntr) 585
    PRESLAN, Bruce H. (Assoc Dir) . 991
    THELIN, Sonya R. (Coordntr) .. 1234
**OCLC Online Computer Lib
Center** (NY)   HANE, Paula J. (Editor) 495
**OCLC Online Computer Lib
Center** (OH)   BLANCHARD, Mark A. (Pub
    Srvs Mgr) 103
    BROWN, Rowland C. (Pres &
    Chief Exec Ofcr) 147
    BROWNELL, Barbara A.
    (Technl Prcsng Spclst) 148
    CALL, J R. (Mgr) 173
    CONNELL, Christopher J.
    (Documtn Libn) 237
    DAVIS, Carol C. (Mgr, Online
    Data Quality Control) 277
    DAVIS, Linda M. (Mktg Spclst) .. 280

OCLC Online Computer Lib Center (OH)

DILLON, Martin (Ofc of Resrch Dir) 303
DRONE, Jeanette M. (Post-Doctoral Resrch Fellow) 320
GRABENSTATTER, Christine N. (Technl Srvs Mgr) 455
HAYNES, Kathleen J. (Local Systs Proj Mgr) 516
HURLEY, Geraldine C. (Support & Trng Spclst) 577
JACOB, Mary E. (Lib Plng Vice Pres) 589
KILGOUR, Frederick G. (Founder Trustee) 648
KISER, Betsy N. (Mgr, EIDOS Devlpmnt) 656
LENSENMAYER, Nancy F. 715
MARSHALL, Mary E. (Mktg Mgr) 774
OLSZEWSKI, Lawrence J. (Mgr) 923
O'NEIL, Rosanna M. (Lib Liaison Ofcr) 924
PAK, Moo J. (CJK User Srvs Spclst) 935
PATTON, Glenn E. (Support & Training Spclst) 949
PRABHA, Chandra G. (Resrch Scitst) 989
SCHUITEMA, Joan E. (Syst Support & Trng Spclst) 1101
SHALOIKO, John L. (Liaison Ofcr) 1119
SHARP, Linda C. (Support & Trng Spclst) 1122
SHREWSBURY, Lynn D. (Local Systs Consult) 1133
TAVENNER, Deborah A. (Ref Libn) 1225
THOMAS, James M. (Local Syts Div Devlpmnt Dept Mgr) 1237
VIZINE-GOETZ, Diane (Resrch Scitst) 1286
WALBRIDGE, Sharon L. (Spcl Asst to the Pres) 1293
WALTERS, Clarence R. (Prog Dir for State & Pub Libs) . . . 1301
WEITZ, Jay N. (Quality Ctl Libn) 1320

OCLC Online Computer Lib Center (OR)
BOES, Rachel M. (Coordntr) 110
Ocmulgee Regional Lib System (GA)
WILSON, David C. (Dir) 1350
Oconee County Lib (SC)
CHANDLER, Dorothy S. (Lib Dir) 199
O'Connor & Associates (IL)
LONGMAN, Judith J. (Resrch Libn) 740
O'Connor Hospital (CA)
HAYES, Linda J. (Med Libn) 516
O'Connor Ranch Book & Historical Project (TX)
WAYLAND, Terry T. (Photographic Archvst) 1311
Oconomowoc Area Sch District (WI)
KILANDER, Ann H. (Libn) 647
Odin Feldman & Pittleman (VA)
FIENCKE, Elaine L. (Law Libn) . . 376
TOSIANO, Barbara A. (Libn) . . . 1252
Oerlibon Aerospace Inc (PQ)
JOBA, Judith C. (Info Spclst) 601
Office for the Handicapped of Quebec (PQ)
JANIK, Sophie (Documentalist) . . 593
Office of County Superintendent of Schs (CA)
DAY, Bettie B. (Lib & Resrcs Ctr Srvs Coordntr) 282
Office of Court Administration (NY)
ANTHONY, Mary M. (Law Libn) . . 28
Office of Legislative Services (PR)
NEGRON-GAZTAMBIDE, Olguita (Legal Libn IV) 892
Office of Management Studies (DC)
GARDNER, Jeffrey J. (Assoc Dir) 418
Office of the Auditor General (IL)
ETTER, Constance L. (Libn & Freedom of Info Ofcr) 355
Office of the Auditor General (ON)
RAY, Cathy J. (Catlg Libn) 1011

Office of the Comptroller of Currency (DC)
KLEIN, Kristine J. (Asst Libn) . . . 659
Office of the French Language (PQ)
ROBINSON, Chantal (Lib Chief) 1043
Office of the Secretary of State (GA)
WELDON, Edward (Dir) 1321
Office of the Secretary of State (LA)
LEMIEUX, Donald J. (State Archvst & Dir) 715
Office of the Secretary of State (MO)
BEAHAN, Gary W. (Actg Dir) 68
Office of the Secretary of State (WA)
MCAPLIN, Sidney (State Archvst) 792
Office of the State Lib (LA)
MCKANN, Michael R. (Deputy State Libn) 809
Official Airline Guides (IL)
JOHNSON, Carol (Sales & Mktg Mgr) 602
OGREN, Mark S. (Gen Mgr, Circ Sales) 918
Ogden Projects Inc (NJ)
COLLISHAW, Jackie J. (Libn) . . . 233
Ogdensburg Pub Lib (NY)
FRANZ, David A. (Dir) 398
Ogilvy & Mather Advertising Agency (NY)
PODWOL, Sharon L. (Interactive Media Production Mgr) 979
HORAH, Richard H. (Lib Spclst) . 558
Oglethorpe Power Corp (GA)
OSTHUS, Mary J. (Head Libn) . . 928
O'Gorman High Sch (SD)
COWELL, Judy M. (Lib & Media Ctr Dir) 252
Ohio Coll of Podiatric Medicine (OH)
KALLAY, Ernest R. (Dir) 623
Ohio County Pub Lib (WV)
BUTLER, Christina (Chair) 166
Ohio Dominican Coll (OH)
MALUMPHY, Sharon M. (Corprt Libn) 764
Ohio Edison Co (OH)
MOGREN, Diane A. (Asst Libn) . . 852
Ohio Historical Center (OH)
BAGBY, Ross F. (Volunteer Resrchr) 45
Ohio Historical Society (OH)
ARNOLD, Gary J. (Head of Resrch Srvs) 33
EAST, Dennis (State Archvst & Div Chief) 332
GAIECK, Frederick W. (OH Newspaper Proj Catlgr) 412
LINCK, Bonnie J. 728
VIOL, Robert W. (Acqs Archvst) 1285
Ohio Lib Foundation (OH)
PARSONS, Augustine C. (Exec Vice Pres) 944
Ohio Northern Univ (OH)
LEONARD, James (Asst Prof of Law & Dir of Law Lib) 716
Ohio Roots (OH)
RUGG, John D. (Dir of Resrch) . 1066
Ohio State Lib (OH)
MEAD, Catherine S. (Ref & Info Srvs Head) 819
Ohio State Univ (OH)
BAYER, Bernard I. (Assoc Prof) . . 67
BEYNEN, Gijsbertus K. (Assoc Prof) 93
BLOCK, Bernard A. (Ref & Docums Libn) 106
BLOMQUIST, Laura G. (Lib Head) 106
BOOMGAARDEN, Wesley L. (Preservation Ofcr) 115
BRADIGAN, Pamela S. (Ref Dept Head) 125
BRANSCOMB, Lewis C. (Prof Emeritus) 129
BRITTON, Constance J. (Libn) . . 137
CENTING, Richard R. (Head of Engl, Theatre & Comm Lib) . . 196
CHANG, Tony H. (Chinese Catlgr) 201
CLEAVER, Betty P. (Dir) 220
COUCH, Nena L. (Cur) 250
CROWE, William J. (Asst Dir for Technl Srvs) 261
DALRYMPLE, Tamsen (Info Srvs Dept Head) 271
GAUNT, Sandra L. (Borror Lab of Bioacoustics Cur) 423
GODWIN, Eva D. (Interlib Loan Head) 443
GOERLER, Raimund E. (Univ Archvst) 443
GOLDING, Alfred S. (Prof, Emeritus Dir) 445

Ohio State Univ (OH)

HAMILTON, Marsha J.
(Monograph Acq Div Head) . . 492
HECK, Thomas F. (Head of
Music & Dance Lib) 519
HOLOCH, S A. (Dir) 553
IBEN, Glenn A. (Asst Prof of
Family Medcn) 581
IVES, Jean E. (Libn) 586
JACKSON, George R. (Ref
Libn) 587
JAMISON, Martin P. (Ref & Circ
Libn) 593
KRUMM, Carol R. (Asst Prof &
Catlgr) 680
LINCOVE, David A. (Coord,
Online Searching, Ref Libn) . . 728
LOGAN, Susan J. (Coordntr of
Lib Automation) 737
LUDY, Lorene E. (Catlg Plng
Libn) 747
MERCADO, Heidi (Mathematics
Lib Head) 825
MIXTER, Keith E. (Prof of
Music) 850
MULARSKI, Carol A. (Online
Srvs & Users Educ Coordntr) . 876
MURPHY, James L. (Gen & Sci
Catlgr) 880
O'HANLON, Nancyanne (Ref &
Automated Srvs Head) 919
POPOVICH, Charles J. (Head of
Bus Lib) 984
POST, Phyllis C. (Head of
Catlgng) 986
PRONEVITZ, Gregory (Copy
Catlgng Head) 995
ROGERS, Sally A. (Spcl
Assignments Catlgr) 1050
ROMARY, Michael P. (Ref &
Biblgph Instrc Libn) 1052
SANDERS, Nancy P. (Head) . . 1080
SAWYERS, Elizabeth J. (Dir) . . 1086
STRALEY, Dona S. (Middle
East Libn) 1200
STUDER, William J. (Dir) 1204
VANBRIMMER, Barbara A.
(Technl Srvs & Ref Libn) . . . 1272
WALDEN, Graham R. (Ref Libn
& Info Spclst) 1294
WANG, Anna M. (Serials Catlgr) 1302
WOODS, Alan L. (Dir & Assoc
Prof) 1366
YAGELLO, Virginia E. (Head of
Chem Lib) 1376

Ohio Supreme Court (OH)

WEILANT, Edward (Pub Srvs
Libn) 1317

Ohio Univ (OH)

BAIN, George W. 47
BETCHER, William M. (Assoc
Dir of Libs for Srvs) 92
COHEN, Steven J. (Catlgr) 229
CONLIFFE, Bobbi L. (Curr
Resrcs Coordntr) 236
HOUDEK, G R. (Asst Ref Libn) . . 562
LEE, Hwa W. (Dir of Libs &
Prof) 710
MCCAULEY, Hannah V. (Dir) . . . 795
MILLER, David A. (Latin Am
Biblgphr) 836
MULLINER, Kent (Asst to the
Dir of Libs) 878
NOBLE, Susan E. (Dir of Lib) . . . 906
OBERLE, Holly E. (Music &
Dance Libn) 914
PLANTON, Stanley P. (Head
Libn) 977
ROBERTS, Sallie H. (Curr &
Instrc Asst Prof) 1041
ROGERS, William F. (Assoc Dir
of Libs for Admin) 1050

Ohio Univ (OH)

SMITH, Timothy D. (Instrcl Libn) 1161
WEI, Yin M. (Prof of Comp Sci) . 1316
WEINBERG, Wanda J. (Asst
Ref Libn) 1318
WILLIAMS, Karen J. (OVAL
Libn) 1344

Ohio Valley Area Libs (OH)

ANDERSON, Eric S. (Extension
Consult) 22

Ohio Wesleyan Univ (OH)

COHEN, Susan J. (Assoc Cur) . . 229
HARPER, Lucy B. (Pub Srvs
Libn & Ref Coordntr) 503
SCHLICHTING, Catherine N.
(Histl Col Cur) 1094
WHITAKER, Constance C.
(Govt Pubns Consult) 1329

OHIONET (OH)

DIENER, Ronald E. (Executive
Dir) 302
KENT, Joel S. (Deputy
Executive Dir) 642
KIE, Kathleen M. (Mem Srvs
Coordntr) 646
MLYNAR, Mary (Netwk
Coordntr) 850
SNIDER, Sondra L. (TLM
Project Mgr) 1163

Ohoopee Regional Lib (GA)

HARTZ, Frederic R. (Technl
Srvs Libn) 509

Ojai Unified Sch Dist (CA)

MOORE, Phyllis C. (Lib Supvsr) . 861

Ojala Associates (KS)

OJALA, Marydee P. (Info
Consultant) 919

Okaloosa-Walton Junior Coll (FL)

VINSON, B J. (Catlgng Libn) . . . 1285

**Okefenokee Regional Lib
System** (GA)

STANBERY, Nancy M. (Libn) . . 1179

Okemos Pub Schs (MI)

TREGLOAN, Donald C. (Instrcl
Media Ctrs Coordntr) 1255

Okey Research Inc (IN)

OKEY, Susan T. (Pres) 920

Oklahoma Arts Institute (OK)

DOBBERTEEN, Sara J. (Dir of
Adult Insts & Outreach
Progs) 307

Oklahoma Baptist Univ (OK)

ALDRIDGE, Betsy B. (Dir) 11
COBB, Sylvia R. (Serials and
Docums) 225

Oklahoma City Univ (OK)

NASH, Helen B. (Govt Docums
Libn) 888

Oklahoma City Zoo (OK)

WEISS, Catharine H. (Libn) 1320

**OK Coll of Osteopathic Medcn &
Surgery** (OK)

ROBERTS, Linda L. (Coll Libn) . 1041

Oklahoma Department of Libs (OK)

BELEU, Steve (US Docums
Regnl Libn) 76
BITTLE, Christine M. (Records
Mgr) 100
CLARK, Robert L. (Dir) 218
JONES, Beverly A. (Chief Plng
Ofcr) 611
LOWELL, Howard P. (Administr) . 744
MCVEY, Susan C. (Libn III,
Legislative Ref) 818
SKVARLA, Donna J. (Adult
Progs Consult) 1147
VESELY, Marilyn L. (Pub Info
Ofcr) 1283

**OK Dept of Vocational & Technical
Educ** (OK)

MURPHY, Peggy A. (Libn &
Resrc Ctr Mgr) 881

Oklahoma Junior Coll (OK)

BISHOP, Donna M. (Lrng
Resrcs Dir) 99

Oklahoma Lib Association (OK)

BOIES, Kay A. (Executive Secy) . 111

Oklahoma Osteopathic Hospital (OK)

COOPER, Sylvia J. (Lib Dir) 243

**Oklahoma State Department of
Education** (OK)

COWEN, Linda L. (Coordntr) 253
ROADS, Clarice D. (Asst
Adminstr) 1038

Oklahoma State Univ (OK)

BAUER, Carolyn J. (Prof) 65
BLEDSOE, Kathleen E. (Asst
Ref Libn) 105
CAROL, Barbara B. (Sr Catlgr) . . 184
DAVIS, Joyce N. (Asst Dir for
Automated Systs) 279
GAGE, Marilyn K. (Asst Libn) . . . 412

Oklahoma State Univ (OK)
HILKER, Emerson W. (Head, Physical Scis & Engrng) 539
HOLMES, Jill M. (Educ Libn) 553
JOHNSON, Edward R. (Univ Libn) 604
KIRKBRIDE, Rebecca M. (Libn) . 654
MORRIS, Karen T. (Asst Prof and Ref & Instrc Libn) 867
NELSON, Norman L. (Asst Univ Libn) 895
ROUSE, Roscoe (Dean of Lib Srvs) 1061
WOLFF, Cynthia J. (Instr & Asst Ref Libn) 1361

Oktibbeha County Pub Libs Syst (MS) NETTLES, Jess (Dir) 896
Olan Mills Portrait Studios (NE) SCHUSTER, Mary F. (Salesperson) 1103
Olathe Sch Dist (KS) GOODRICH PETERSON, Marilyn (Lib Media Spclst) . . 450
Old Dominion Univ (VA) DUNCAN, Cynthia B. (Univ Libn) 325
ERICKSON, Lynda L. (Acqs Libn) 352
LIU, Albert C. (Asst Univ Libn) . . 734
MCCART, Vernon A. (Ref Libn) . 794
MILLER, Ellen L. (Asst Prof) 837
SWAINE, Cynthia W. (Lib Instrc Libn) 1212
Old Greenwich Elementary Sch (CT) THORNBURG, Joan S. (Media Spclst) 1242
Old Sturbridge Village (MA) ALLEN, Joan C. (Asst Libn) 15
PERCY, Theresa R. (Dir of Resrch Lib) 958
Olde Tyme Music Scene (NJ) DONAHUE, Louise (Owner) 310
Oldham County High Sch (KY) DIAMOND, Shela W. (Sch Media Libn) 299
Olin Corp (CT) CAMPO, Lynn D. (Lib & Report Systs Supvsr) 177
STANYON, Kelly (Lit Resrch Coordntr) 1181
Olin E Teague Veterans Center (TX) HEMPEL, Ruth M. (Med Libn) . . . 525
Olivet Coll (MI) COOPER, B L. (Acad Vice Pres & Dean of Coll) 242
EVANS, Kathy J. (Govt Docums Libn) 357
STEVENS, Marjorie (Dir of Libs) 1190
Olivet Nazarene Univ (IL) KINNERSLEY, Ruth T. (Ref libn) . 653
Omaha Pub Lib (NE) BIALAC, Verda H. (Supvsr, Technl Srvs) 93
KUBICK, Dan P. (Libn I) 682
PHIPPS, Michael C. (Dir) 969
STEPHENS, Ann E. (Info Dept Head) 1187
Omaha Pub Schs (NE) CRAWFORD-ROSE, Kathleen J. (Media Spclst) 257
LITTLE, Nina M. (Lib Media Srvs Supvsr) 733
SJURSON, Gail M. (Lib Media Spclst) 1145
Omaha World-Herald (NE) PARISOT, Beverly J. (Chief Libn) 940
OMEC International Inc (DC) RADER, Ronald A. (Mgr, Info Srvs) 1002
O'Melveny & Meyers (CA) SMITH, Catherine M. (Ref Libn) 1153
WANG, Connie (Catlg Libn) . . . 1302
O'Melveny & Meyers (DC) OAKS, Robert K. (Ref & Legislative Libn) 913
Omnifacts Information Bureau Inc (NJ) ROSENSTEIN, Susan J. (Pres) . 1057
On-Line Research (WA) CARVER, Sue A. (Owner, Mgr) . 191
On-Line Software International (NJ) HUTCHINS, Pearl G. (Libn) 579
Onan Corp (MN) NELSON, Catherine G. (Lib Info Spclst) 893
ROHRER, Valera E. 1051
One World Publishing (IN) KIANG, C K. (Pres) 646
Oneida Tribe of Indians of Wisconsin (WI) CORNELIUS, Charlene E. (Records Mgr & Program Dir) . 246
Online Access Publishing Group (IL) CRIM, Elias F. (Editor) 258

Online Computer Systems Inc (MD) ALBRIGHT, John B. (Sr Lib Systs Analyst) 10
BATOR, Eileen F. (Lib Systs Mgr) 64
MILLER, Kenda (Mktg Asst) 839
Online Connection Inc (FL) CORCORAN, Maureen 246
Online Inc (CT) PEMBERTON, Jeffery K. (Pres & Publshr) 956
Online Inc (IN) GORDON, Helen A. (Edit of ONLINE) 451
Online Inc (KY) GARMAN, Nancy J. (Edit, DATABASE) 419
Onodaga-Cortland-Madison BOCFS (NY) FUNK, Nancy J. (Shared Tchr & Elem Libn) 410
Onondaga-Cortland-Madison BOCES (NY) ROSS, Kathleen A. (Sch Lib Syst Dir) 1058
Onondaga County Pub Lib (NY) CLEMINSHAW, Barbara B. (Libn II) 221
DEMARCO, Elizabeth A. (Adult Srvs Libn) 291
DEVENISH-CASSEL, Ann W. (Local Hist & Spcl Cols Dept Head) 297
GAWLER, Ann C. (Adult Srv Libn) 423
KINCHEN, Robert P. (Dir) 650
LOMICKA, Janet (Technl Srvs Head) 738
NAGLE, Ann (Pub Info Spclst) . . 886
NOTTINGHAM, Sharon E. (Community Srvs Consult) . . . 910
PFOHL, Theodore E. (Libn II) . . . 966
Onslow County Pub Lib (NC) VEITCH, Carol J. (Lib Dir) 1281
Ontario Bible Coll (ON) BELDAN, A C. (Technl Srvs Libn) 76
JOHNSON, James R. (Head Libn) 605
Ontario Cad/Cam Center (ON) LARSON, Anna M. (Info Srvs Supvst) 699
Ontario Cancer Institute (ON) MORRISON, Carol A. (Libn) 868
VAN ORDER, Mary J. (Database Spclst) 1276
Ontario Cancer Treatment & Resrch Fndtn (ON) FORKES, David (Libn) 390
Ontario Centre for Farm Machinery (ON) KEARNS, Mary J. (Info Analyst) . 633
MCNAUGHT, Hugh W. (Info Srvs Mgr) 816
Ontario City Lib (CA) GRAUE, Luz B. (Consulting Archvst & Lib Asst) 458
Ontario Hospital Association (ON) TAGG, John T. (Supvsr, Lib Srvs) 1219
Ontario Hydro (ON) BELLEFONTAINE, Gillian (Info Srvs Unit Head) 78
HENDERSON, Deborah A. (Info Analyst) 526
MCCLYMONT, Karen A. (Consultng Libn) 797
Ontario Institute for Studies (ON) BREGZIS, Ilze (Head, Technl Srvs) 131
BULAONG, Grace F. (Chief Libn) 156
BURTON, Donna M. (Info & Ref Libn) 164
Ontario Legislative Assembly (ON) DICKERSON, Mary E. (Deputy Executive Dir) 300
POWELL, Wyley L. (Exec Asst to the Exec Dir) 989
SMITH, Cynthia M. (Chief of Legislative Resrch Srv) 1153
Ontario Lib Association (ON) MCKEE, Penelope (Pres) 810
MOORE, Lawrence A. (Executive Dir) 860
Ontario Lib Service of Nipigon (ON) HSU, Peter T. (Lib Consult) 567
Ontario Lib Service of Rideau (ON) ARONSON, Marcia L. 34
Ontario Lib Service of Thames (ON) SKRZESZEWSKI, Stan E. (Chief Executive Ofcr) 1147

Ontario Lib Service of Trent (ON)
HARRISON, Karen A. (Field Srvs Coordntr) 507
GREENWOOD, Jan (Lib Srvs Mgr) 465

Ontario Medical Association (ON)

Ontario Ministry (ON)
BONGARD, Nancy D. (Libn) 114

Ontario Ministry of Agriculture & Food (ON)
GINSLER, Mindy F. (Lib Srvs Mgr) 438

Ontario Ministry of Citizenship/Culture (ON)
GRODSKI, Renata (Coordntr) . . . 471
WIERUCKI, Karen A. (Community Info Srvs Mgr) . . 1337

Ontario Ministry of Education (ON)
SHIP, Martin I. (Supvsr, Ref & Resrch) 1131

Ontario Ministry of Health (ON)
STANDING, Doris A. (Libn) . . . 1179

Ontario Ministry of Housing (ON)
BREZINA, Jennifer R. (Asst Libn) 134

Ontario Ministry of Industry (ON)
SERMAT-HARDING, Kaili I. (Mgr) 1116

Ontario Ministry of Labour (ON)
GOLD, Sandra (Ref Libn) 444
MORRISON, Brian H. (Ref Libn) . 867
WALSH, Sandra A. (Mgr) 1300

Ontario Ministry of Natural Resources (ON)
LOUET, Sandra (Mgr of Natural Resrcs Libs) 742

Ontario Ministry of Revenue (ON)
CRAIG, Wendy E. (Lib Srvs Mgr) 254

Ontario Ministry of the Environment (ON)
TIPLER, Stephen B. (Catlgr) . . . 1246

Ontario Ministry of Transportation, Comm (ON)
PAVLIN, Stefanie A. (Lib Srvs Coordntr) 951
ZVEJNIEKS, Laila R. (Technl Srvs Libn) 1391

Ontario Ministry of Treasury & Economics (ON)
WEATHERHEAD, Barbara A. (Lib Srvs Mgr) 1312

Ontario Mncpl Employees Retirement Syst (ON)
FAIR, Linda A. (Libn) 361

Ontario Police Commission (ON)
MERRYWEATHER, J M. (Libn) . 827

Ontario Research Foundation (ON)
WEI, Carl K. (Chief Libn) 1316

OPL Resources Ltd (NY)
ST. CLAIR, Guy (Pres) 1075

Oppenheimer & Co Inc (NY)
CRAWFORD, Carter (VP & Info Ctr Mgr) 256

Oppenheimer Wolff & Donnelly (MN)
HAASE, Gretchen E. (Libn) 480

Options & Choices Inc (MD)
POMERANTZ, Karyn L. (Info Spclst and Unit Coordntr) 982

Oral Hist Inst (VT)
MORRISSEY, Charles T. (Dir) . . . 869

Oral Roberts Univ (OK)
JUDKINS, Timothy C. (Dir, Hlth Scis Lib) 619
MOORE, Maxwell L. (Lib Tech & Comp Srvs Dir) 860

Orange County Community Coll (NY)
BAUM, Christina D. (Lrng Resrcs Dir) 66

Orange County Lib System (FL)
BROOMALL, Susan G. (Soc Sci Dept Head) 141
BUFKIN, Anne G. (Extension Head) 155
MARTIN, John H. (Head of Arts & Lit) 776
PETERSON, Carolyn S. (Chlds Dept Head) 963

Orange County Pub Lib (CA)
DENECOUR, Mary D. (Branch Libn) 291
EVANS, Rina A. (Lib Spclst) 358
HOUSEL, Mary B. (Sr Adminstrv Libn) 563
JOHNSON, Mary L. (Dir of Spcl Srvs) 607
MCSPARREN, Christine L. (Regnl Adminstr) 818
PENDLETON, Lynne G. (Ref Libn) 956
SMITH, Elizabeth M. (County Libn) 1154

Orange County Pub Lib (VA)
HOLLOWAY, Johnna H. (Libn) . . 552

Orange County Register (CA)
OSTMANN, Sharon G. (Lib Dir) . 929

Orange County Transit District (CA)
MASTERS, Robin J. (Resrc Spclst) 782

Orange County Transportation Commission (CA)
CHRISTNER, Deborah S. (Adminstrv Srvs Consult) 212

Orange North Supervisory Union (VT)
BATTEY, Jean D. (Coordntr of Elem Sch Lib Srvs) 64

Orange Pub Lib (NJ)
LIN, Fumei C. (Ref Libn) 727

Orangeburg County Lib (SC)
ALLEN, Debra C. (Extension Libn) 14
PAUL, Paula F. (Lib Dir) 949

Orbit Search Service (CA)
LONGO, Margaret K. (Mktg Comms Mgr) 740

Orchard Park Pub Lib (NY)
MAGUDA, Joyce M. (Chlds & Young Adult's Libn) 760

Ordered Word (CA)
RIGGS, Judith M. (Dir) 1034
SLOAN, Maureen G. (Libn) 1149

Oregon Graduate Center (OR)

Oregon Health Sciences Univ (OR)
CABLE, Leslie G. (Ref Libn) 170
JOHNSON, Millard F. (Assoc Dir of Libs) 607
JUDKINS, Dolores Z. (Dental Libn) 619
MORGAN, James E. (Dir of Libs) 864
O'DONOVAN, Patricia A. (Head, Serials/Acqs) 917
TEICH, Steven (OR Hlth Info Netwk Coordntr) 1230

Oregon Historical Society (OR)
WINROTH, Elizabeth C. (Maps Libn) 1355

Oregon Institute of Technology (OR)
CHASE, Judith H. (Ref & Govt Docums Libn) 203
PETERSON, Karen L. (Acq & Serials Libn) 964

Oregon Judicial Department (OR)
ANDRUS, Roger D. (Law Libn) . . . 27

Oregon State Lib (OR)
DOAK, Wesley A. (State Libn) . . 306
FORCIER, Peggy C. (Project Dir) 389
GINNANE, Mary J. (Rural & Small Lib Devlpmnt Consult) . . 437
MCHARG, Kathleen M. (Adminstr) 808
MOBERG, F A. (Ref Consult) . . . 851
WEBB, John (Deputy State Libn) 1313

Oregon State Univ (OR)
FILSON, Laurie (Univ Archvst) . . 377
GEORGE, Melvin R. (Dir of Libs) . 427
KINCH, Michael P. (Asst Head) . . 649
LAWRENCE, Robert E. (Head, Science/Technology Div) 705
MANNARINO, Elizabeth R. (Biological Scis Libn) 766
OSHEROFF, Shiela K. (Serials Catlgr) 928
PERRY, Joanne M. (Map Libn & Asst Prof) 960
REEVES, Marjorie A. (Assoc Dir) 1017
ST. CLAIR, Gloriana S. (Asst Dir for Tech Srvs) 1075
WILLIAMS, Janet L. (Serials Catlgr) 1344

Oregon Supreme Court (OR)
BAUER, Marilyn A. (Chief Justice Judicial Asst) 65

Organ Historical Society Inc (VA)
PINEL, Stephen L. (Archvst) 974

Organization of American States (DC)
FIGUERAS, Myriam (Ref & Info Srvs Libn) 376
WELCH, Thomas L. (Dir) 1321

ORI Inc (MD)
BRANDHORST, Ted (Info Systs Dir) 128
BRANDHORST, Wesley T. (ERIC Prcsng and Ref Facility Dir) 128
MISSAR, Charles D. (Sr Edit) . . . 847

Orillia Pub Lib (ON)
MCKINNON, Katherine D. (Chief Executive Ofcr) 812

Orion Township Pub Lib (MI)
SICKLES, Linda C. (Dir) 1135

Orland Park Pub Lib (IL)
KRAMER, Ruth M. (Head of Ref Srv) 675

Orleans Parish School Board (LA)
KLEIN, Victor C. (Libn) 659

Orrick Herrington et al (CA)
PAPERMASTER, Cynthia L. (Law Libn) 939

Ortho Pharmaceutical Canada
  Ltd (ON)   BODNAR, Marta (Part-Time
                                      Libn) 109
Ortho Pharmaceutical Corp (NJ)   BENTE, June E. (Lib Srvs Mgr) . . . 83
Oryx Press (AZ)   DEBACHER, Richard D. (Asst to
                                      the Pres) 284
                                  SLESINGER, Susan G. (Vice
                                      Pres, Editrl) 1148
                                  STECKLER, Phyllis B. (Pres) . . 1183
                                  THOMPSON, Anne E. (Sr
                                      Editor) 1238
                                  WASCHLER, Merl E. (VP of
                                      Finance) 1307
Oryx Press (NY)   BERKNER, Dimity S. (New Bus
                                      & Market Devlpmnt VP) 87
Oscar Mayer Foods Corp (WI)   WHITEMARSH, Thomas R.
                                      (Libn) 1333
Oshawa Pub Lib Board (ON)   BROOKING, Ruth P. (Chief
                                      Exec Ofcr) 140
Ossining Pub Lib (NY)   DOW, Sally R. (Chlds Srvs
                                      Head) 315
Ossining Union Free Schs (NY)   SPIN-WEINSTEIN, Ellen (Lib
                                      Media Spclst) 1175
Osterhout Free Lib (PA)   VAN DE CASTLE, Raymond M.
                                      (Ref Libn) 1273
Oswego BOCES (NY)   MAUTINO, Patricia H. (Instrcl
                                      Support Dir) 787
Oswego Pub Lib District (IL)   FEATHER, Pamela P. (Lib Dir) . . 367
                                  PORTER, Carol (Adult Srvs
                                      Libn) 984
Ottawa Board of Education (ON)   PERRY, William B. (Head Libn) . . 961
                                  WILLIAMS, Shelagh C. (Head
                                      Libn) 1346
Ottawa Citizen (ON)   PROULX, Steven D. (Chief Libn) . 996
Ottawa Civic Hospital (ON)   BROWN, Mabel (Lib Srvs Dir) . . . 145
Ottawa Pub Lib (ON)   CORDUKES, Laura L. (Chlds
                                      Libn) 246
                                  FRAPPIER, Gilles (Dir) 399
                                  MATTE, Suzanne (Branch
                                      Head) 785
                                  MUTCH, Donald G. (Asst Head,
                                      Ref Dept) 883
                                  SPRY, Patricia (Asst Head) 1176
Ottawa Pub Lib (PQ)   DUHAMEL, Louis (Lib Branch
                                      Head) 324
Ottawa Regional Cancer Centre (ON) LEBRUN, Anne (Libn, Info
                                      Spclst) 708
Ottawa Roman Cath Separate Sch
  Bd (ON)   DEVOE, Dan L. (Tchr Libn
                                      Consult) 297
Otterbein Coll (OH)   MACKENZIE, Alberta E. (Lib
                                      Dir) 756
                                  SALT, Elizabeth A. (Catlg Libn) . 1077
Ottumwa Pub Lib (IA)   GEIB, Jerry H. (Dir) 425
Ouachita Baptist Univ (AR)   CHILDRESS, Schelley H.
                                      (Techn Prcsng Head) 208
                                  RICK, Jean A. (Ref & Circ Libn) 1031
Ouachita Parish Pub Lib (LA)   BURNS, Ollie H. (Lib Trustee) . . . 162
                                  GODWIN, Tom P. (Trustee) 443
                                  KONTROVITZ, Eileen R. (Main
                                      Branch Libn) 671
Our Lady of Lourdes Hospital (NY) BRETSCHER, Susan M.
                                      (Hospital Libn) 134
Our Lady of Lourdes Medical
  Center (NJ)   KAFES, Frederick W. (Lib Mgr) . . 621
Our Lady of Mercy High Sch (NY)   CARSTATER, Mary E. (Libn) . . . 188
Our Lady of Mercy Sch (LA)   BARTON, Miriam V. (Sch Libn) . . . 62
Our Lady of Mercy Sch (NY)   SCHMIDTMANN, Nancy K.
                                      (Sch Media Spclst) 1096
Our Lady of Sorrows Sch (MO)   WINKLER, Carol A. (Sch Libn) . 1355
Our Lady of the Lake Regional Med
  Center (LA)   WHITED, Diane D. (Lib Dir) . . . 1332
Our Lady of the Lake Univ (TX)   SHAPIRO, Lenore M. (Serials,
                                      Ref Libn) 1121
Our Lady Star of The Sea High (MI) PARTHUM, John W. (Libn) 945
Our Mother of Sorrows Elementary
  Sch (PA)   DALY, Sally A. (Elem Sch Libn) . 271
Our Sunday Visitor Inc (IN)   ISCA, Joseph J. (Mktg Mgr) . . . 585
Out There Productions Inc (NY)   LESNIAK, Rose (Pres &
                                      Producer) 718

Overlake Sch (WA)   GARRETSON, Laurie J. (Libn) . . 420
Overlook Hospital (NJ)   MOELLER, Kathleen A. (Dir of
                                      Lib Srvs) 851
Overseas Development Council (DC) BOYLE, James E. (Libn) 123
Ovid Bell Press Inc (MO)   BELL, Ovid H. (Pres) 77
Owatonna Pub Lib (MN)   HOSLETT, Andrea E. (Asst Dir) . 561
Owens-Corning Fiberglas Corp (OH) CHRISTY, Patricia A. (Legal
                                      Asst) 212
                                  LEMON, Nancy A. (Resrch Lib
                                      Supvsr) 715
Owens Technical Coll (OH)   EMRICK, Nancy J. (Dir, Lrng
                                      Resrcs Media Ctr) 348
Owl Mountain Associates (WA)   EULENBERG, Julia N. (Consult
                                      & Eductr) 356
Oxbridge Communications (NY)   HAGOOD, Patricia C. (Pres) 483
Oxford County Lib (ON)   WEBB, Mary J. (Chief Libn) . . . 1313
Oxford Pub Lib (MI)   DOUBLESTEIN, Judith A. (Dir) . . 313
Ozark Christian Coll (MO)   ABERNATHY, William F. (Lib
                                      Dir) 2

P

PACCAR Defense Systems (WA)   CAMOZZI-EKBERG, Patricia L.
                                      (Libn) 175
PACCAR Technical Center (WA)   WARD, Maryanne
                                      (Documentalist) 1304
Pace Univ (NY)   BIRNBAUM, Henry (Univ Libn) . . . 98
                                  MURDOCK, William J. (Lib Dir) . . 880
                                  PIDGEON, Alice C. (Acqs Libn) . 971
                                  TRIFFIN, Nicholas (Law Lib Dir) 1256
Pacific Bell (CA)   MOYER, Barbara A. (Proj Dir) . . . 874
                                  RICHARDS, Jeff B. (Project
                                      Mgr) 1028
                                  VENTURA, Dan L. (Mktg VP) . . 1282
Pacific Biological Station (BC)   MILLER, Gordon (Head of Lib
                                      Srvs) 838
Pacific Book Co (OR)   BUSHMAN, James L.
                                      (Antiquarian Bookseller) 165
Pacific Energy & Resources
  Center (CA)   RADEMACHER, Kurt A. (Exec
                                      Dir) 1002
Pacific Gas & Electric Co (CA)   BERCIK, Mary E. (Info Spclst) 84
                                  MERRITT, Betty A. (Asst Law
                                      Libn) 827
                                  STROMME, Gary L. (Law Libn) . 1203
                                  WALLEN, Jody H. (Info Spclst) . 1298
Pacific Info Inc (CA)   PLATE, Kenneth H. (Pres) 977
Pacific Lutheran Univ (WA)   GILCHRIST, Debra L. (Ref Libn) . 434
Pacific Medical Center (WA)   SONG, Seungja Y. (Med Lib
                                      Mgr) 1167
Pacific Naval Educ & Trng Support
  Ctr (CA)   BUSCH, Barbara (Naval Regnl
                                      Libn) 165
Pacific Northwest Bell (WA)   BOLEN, Sheila (Mktg Analysis
                                      Mgr) 112
Pacific Oaks Coll (CA)   GRANGER, Dorothy J. (Head
                                      Libn) 457
Pacific Presbyterian Medical
  Center (CA)   COLALILLO, Robert M. (Asst
                                      Libn) 230
                                  GIBSON, Harold R. (Lib Dir) 432
Pacific Press Ltd (BC)   MOONEY, Shirley E. (Editrl Srvs
                                      Mgr) 858
Pacific Research Associates (CA) SCHRIBER, James E. (Pres) . . . 1100
Pacific Telesis Corp (CA)   CHANDLER, James (Bus
                                      Devlpmnt Mgr) 200
                                  MILLER, Ralph D. (Resrch
                                      Assoc) 841
                                  TYERMAN, Vernon H. (Bus
                                      Plng Dir) 1266
Pacific Union Coll (CA)   RUHL, Taylor D. (Dir of Lib
                                      Srvs) 1066
Pacific Univ (OR)   HUFFINE, Lucinda J. (Psy Libn) . 571
Packaging Corp of America (IL)   TRUE, Jacqueline J. (Info
                                      Spclst) 1259
Packard Press Corp (DC)   ARNSDORF, Dennis A. (Vice
                                      Pres) 34
Packard Press Corp (PA)   SCULLIN, Frank E. (Sr VP) 1109

Packer Engineering Associates Inc (IL) — VAUGHAN, Ruth M. (Technl Info Srvs Dir) 1280

Pactel Properties (CA) — MULLIN, Jack A. (Chief Finance Ofcr) 878

Pactel Publishing (CA) — OJALA, Rebecca A. (Plng & Corprt Devlpmnt Dir) 919

Paducah Pub Lib (KY) — SUTHERLAND, Thomas A. (Dir) 1211

Paine Webber (NY) — CAGAN, Penny M. (Asst Mgr and Ref Coordntr) 170
FACKLER, June M. (Libn) 360
FODY, Barbara A. (Asst Vice Pres & Lib Mgr) 387
MINKOFF, Jerry R. (Data Processing Libn) 846
NESTA, Frederick N. (Technl Srvs Libn) 896
NOBLE, James K. (First Vice Pres) 906
SLUSSER, W P. (Managing Dir & Mergers & Aqcs Head) . . . 1150
WOLF, Catharine D. (Sch Libn) . 1360

Pal-Mac Central Sch (NY) —

Palatine Pub Lib District (IL) — BOURKE, Jacqueline K. (Catlgr) . 119
BURNS, Mary F. (Assoc Libn & Head of Ref) 162
MAGNUSSEN, Ruth A. (Branch Head) 760

Palestine Independent Sch District (TX) — WILLIAMSON, Lanelle S. (Libn) 1347

Palestine Pub Lib (TX) — SELWYN, Laurie (Dir) 1114

PALINET (PA) — SCHOENUNG, James G. 1098
SILVERMAN, Karen S. (Coordntr of Network Srvs) . . 1138

Palisades Park Free Pub Lib (NJ) — CHELARIU, Ana R. (Dir) 204
RANIERI, Bernice A. (Chld's Libn) 1007

Pall Corp (NY) — LETTIS, Lucy B. (Mgr of Lib Srvs) 719

Palm Bay Pub Lib (FL) — BOGGUS, Tamara K. (Libn) . . . 110

Palm Beach County (FL) — BROWNLEE, Jerry W. (Lib Dir) . 148

Palm Beach County Pub Lib (FL) — ALLEN, Linda G. (Technl Srvs Div Head) 15
SNODGRASSE, Elaine (Libn I) . 1163

Palm Beach County Sch Board (FL) — CONOVER, Kathryn H. (Media Spclst) 238
TAFFEL, Bobbe H. (Media Spclst) 1219
TERWILLEGAR, Jane C. (Media Spclst) 1232

Palm Beach Junior Coll (FL) — RICHARDSON, Margaret B. (Ref Libn) 1029

Palm Harbor Lib (FL) — RHODES, Debra S. (Lib Dir) . . . 1026

Palmer & Dodge (MA) — LEONARD, Sharen C. (Head Libn) 717

Palmer Coll of Chiropractic (CA) — HAZEKAMP, Phyllis W. (Dir of the Lib) 517

Palmer Coll of Chiropractic (IA) — BUDREW, John (Lib Dept Dir) . . 155
PETERSON, Dennis R. (Pub Srvs Libn) 963
STOUT, Robert J. (Pub Srvs Libn) 1199
WIESE, Glenda C. (Technl Srvs Libn) 1337

Palmer Pub Lib (MA) — HOLMBERG, Olga S. (Dir) 553

Palmerton Lib Association (PA) — DEFASSIO, Sharon L. (Lib Dir) . . 287

Palo Alto Pub Lib (CA) — DRIVER, Linda A. (Supvsr of Catlgng) 320
LEVY, Mary J. (Dir of Libs) 722
OLSON, Sharon L. (Sr Libn) 923
MURPHY, Patricia A. (Dir) 881

Palo Verde Valley Dist Lib (CA) —

Palomar Coll (CA) — CATER, Judy J. (Dir of Lib & Media Ctr) 194
ROTTER, Virginia B. (Catlg Libn, Head of Catlg Dept) . . . 1061

Palos Verdes Lib District (CA) — ELLIOTT, Linda P. (Dir) 344
TSENG, Joan L. (Catlgng Srvs Supvsr) 1260
UEBELE, Dorothy B. (Lib Dir) . . 1268

Pan American Univ (TX) — GAUSE, George R. (Spcl Cols Libn) 423
HAYNIE, Altie V. (Catlg Lib Head) 517
MYCUE, David J. (Ref Libn) 884
SHABOWICH, Stanley A. (Acqs Libn) 1118
TINSMAN, William A. (Docums Libn) 1246

Pan American World Airways (NY) — CHIU, Liwa J. (Libn) 209

Panama Canal Coll (FL) — KANE, Joseph P. (Libn) 624

PanCanadian Petroleum Ltd (AB) — KENNEDY, Marcia G. (Corprt Libn) 641

Panel Publishers Inc (NY) — SIMMONDS, Ruth E. (Pres) . . . 1139

The Pantagraph (IL) — MILLER, Diane C. (Lib Dir) 837

Paoli Lib (PA) — LANG, Anna M. (Libn) 695

Papazian Associates (NJ) — PAPAZIAN, Pierre (Owner) 939

Paper Chaser (CA) — MUSICK, Nancy W. (Owner & Libn) 883

Papillion-La Vista High Sch (NE) — ZANARINI, Linda S. (Media Spclst) 1386

Papy Poole Weissenborn & Papy (FL) — MILLER, Jewell J. (Firm Libn & Resrch Spclst) 839

Paramax Electronics Inc (PQ) — RICHARDS, Stella (Program Control Coordntr Software) . . 1028

Paramus Pub Lib (NJ) — WELLSMAN, Jennifer A. (Ref Libn) 1323

Parapsychology Foundation Inc (NY) — NORMAN, Wayne R. (Libn) 909

Paris Union Sch District 95 (IL) — GERLACH, Gretchen J. (Lib Media Spclst) 429

Park Coll (MO) — SMITH, Harold F. (Lib Dir) 1155

Park Forest Pub Lib (IL) — MURRAY, Theresa A. (Technl Srvs Dir) 882

Park Hill K-5 Sch District (MO) — GARDNER, Laura L. (Non-Print Lib Media Spclst) 418

Park Nicollet Medical Foundation (MN) — LATTA, Barbara K. (Dir) 702

Park Ridge Pub Lib (IL) — BRICKMAN, Sally F. (Ref Libn) . . 135
MCCULLY, William C. (Executive Libn) 801

Park Ridge Sch District 64 (IL) — BOUMA, Ray H. (Libn) 119

Parke-Davis (MI) — COAN, La V. (Lit Scientist) 224
CYGAN, Rose M. (Lit Srvs Supvsr) 268

Parker Coulter Daley & White (MA) — ROFF, Jill R. (Law Libn) 1049

Parker Management Associates (ON) — PARKER, Arthur D. (Pres & Owner) 941

Parkland Regional Lib (SK) — CALEF, Daniel C. (Head Libn) . . . 172

Parkview Episcopal Medical Center (CO) — WILLIAMS, Alma (Lib Coordntr) 1341

Parkway Sch District (MO) — MERRELL, Sheila J. (Libn) 826
NOBLE, Barbara N. (Lib Media Dir) 906

Parkwood Hospital (ON) — SINGER, Eleanore M. (Lib Srvs Dir) 1143

Parliament of Canada (ON) — SPICER, Erik J. (Parliamentary Libn) 1174

Parlin-Ingersoll Lib (IL) — WILSON, W R. (Dir) 1353

Parmly Billings Lib (MT) — NEWBERG, Ellen J. (Dir) 898

Pars Information Design (IL) — SHENASSA, Daryoosh (Special Projects Mgr) 1126

Parsippany Troy Hills Board of Education (NJ) — MARTINEZ, Jane A. (Eductnl Media Spclst) 779

Parsippany Troy Hills Pub Lib (NJ) — WEINSTEIN, Judith L. (Branch Head) 1318

Parsons Brinckerhoff Quade & Douglas Inc (NY) — EARLE, Marcia H. (Info Mgr) 332
ETTLINGER, Sandra E. (Info Coordntr) 356

Parsons Pub Lib (KS) — MAST, Jane E. (Head Libn) 782

Pasadena Pub Lib (CA) — BISHOFF, Lizbeth J. (Principal Libn for Support Srvs) 99
CAIN, Anne H. (Ref Srvs Principal Libn) 171
GARNER, Carolyn L. (Libn II, Pasadena Hist Spclst) 419
POSTER, Susan E. (Libn) 986

Pascack Valley Hospital (NJ) — MICHAELS, Debbie D. (Med Lib Dir) 832

Pasco County Lib System (FL)
Passaic Board of Education (NJ)

Passaic Pub Lib (NJ)
Passavant Area Hospital (IL)
Passionist Monastery (NY)
Pat Guida Associates (NJ)
Patchogue-Medford Lib (NY)

Paterson Free Pub Lib (NJ)
Path Services Inc (MD)
Pathfinder Lib Syst (CO)
Pathfinder Productions Inc (CT)
Pathways Consultants (NC)
Patient Care (NJ)

Patrick Air Force Base (FL)
Patrick B Harris Psychiatric
  Hospital (SC)
Patterson Lib (NY)

Patton Museum of Cavalry &
  Armor (KY)
Patton State Hospital (CA)

Paul Pratt Memorial Lib (MA)
Paul Quinn Coll (TX)

Paul Sawyier Pub Lib (KY)
Paul Smith's Coll (NY)

Paul Weiss Rifkind Wharton &
  Garrison (NY)

Paw Paw Pub Lib (MI)
Payne Assn (TX)

PB-KBB Inc (TX)

Peabody Institute Lib (MA)
Peabody Museum of Salem (MA)

Peace Corp (MAL)
Peat Marwick Main & Co (CA)

Peat Marwick Main & Co (IL)

Peat Marwick Main & Co (MA)
Peat Marwick Main & Co (NJ)

Peat Marwick Main & Co (NY)
Peat Marwick Main & Co (TX)

Peat Marwick Mitchell (CA)
Peat Marwick Mitchell (DC)

MCKENNA, Gerald M. (Dir) 811
LOTZ, Marilyn R. (Elem Sch
  Libn) 742
SCHEAR, Thomas W. (Lib Dir) . 1090
KNIGHT, Dorothy H. (Libn) 664
JOHNSON, James G. (Libn) 605
GUIDA, Pat (Pres) 476
GIBBARD, Judith R. (Head of
  Technl Srvs & Automation) . . . 431
HOFFMAN, Barbara E. (AV
  Young Adult Dept Head) 547
HRYVNIAK, Joseph T. (Media
  Libn) 567
PAGELS, Helen H. (Catlgng
  Libn) 934
BROWN, Linda M. (Sr Libn) . . . 145
BEATTY, Samuel B. (Pres) 70
CAMPBELL, John D. (Dir) 176
ECKRICH, Herman J. (Owner) . 335
ISACCO, Jeanne M. (Partner) . . 584
O'CONNOR, Christine T. (Med
  Libn) 916
CURRY, John W. (Pubns Libn) . . 266

REIMER, Mary S. (Lib Srvs Dir) 1021
NYERGES, Michael S. (Dir) . . . 912

HOLT, David A. (Libn) 554
STUMBERG, Mary S. (Staff
  Libn) 1205
HAYES, Richard E. (Dir) 516
KEATTS, Rowena W. (Dir of
  Technl Srvs) 633
DOUTHITT, Rita C. (Lib Dir) . . . 314
MACK, Theodore D. (Head
  Libn) 756

BERGER, Paula E. (Legal Ref
  Libn) 86
PANELLA, Deborah S. (Chief
  Libn) 938
SMITH, Mark J. (Head of Technl
  Srvs) 1158
STEIN, Marsha (Asst Libn) 1185
PRITCHARD, Mildred H. (Dir) . . . 994
PAYNE, John R. (Appraiser &
  Lib Consult) 951
HACKNEY, Judith G. (Supvsr &
  Libn) 481
TRICARICO, Mary A. (Dir) 1256
TRINKAUS-RANDALL, Gregor
  (Libn & Archvst) 1257
SNYDER, Lisa A. (Libn) 1165
LEE, Diane T. (Info Srvs Supvsr) . 709
MANN, Thomas (Mgr, Natl Lib
  Consult Practice) 766
MAYERS, Karen A. (Libn &
  Records Supvsr) 789
GROFT, Mary L. (Info Srvs
  Supvsr) 471
WONG, Mabel K. (Sr Info
  Spclst) 1363
RAMSAY, Dorothy M. (Sr Info
  Spclst) 1005
BILES, Mark J. (Resrch Consult) . . 96
BRAIMON, Margie S. (Consult) . 127
LAUB, Barbara J. (Mgr) 702
SULLIVAN, Patrick F. 1208
EMERSON, Beth A. (Info
  Spclst) 347
KOHRS, Charlotte A. (Info Srvs
  Supvsr) 669
MCCLURE, Margaret R. (Dir,
  Info Srvs) 797
SHAW, Peggy (Asst Libn) 1123
CHAO, Yuan T. (Consult) 201
FRANKLIN, Brinley R. (Sr
  Consult & Mgr) 397

Peat Marwick Mitchell (NY)

Peat Marwick Mitchell (PA)
Peat Marwick Mitchell (TX)

Peat Marwick Mitchell (AB)

Peat Marwick Mitchell (ON)
Peck Research Group (FL)

PEI Associated (OH)

Pekin Pub Lib (IL)
Pellston Pub Schs (MI)

Pemberton Houston Willoughby Bell,
  et al (BC)
Pembroke Coll (ENG)
Pembroke Hill Sch (MO)
Pembroke Pub Lib (ON)

Pen Kem Inc (NY)

Pend Oreille County Lib (WA)
Pender County Lib (NC)
Penfield Pub Lib (NY)

Peninsula General Hospital Medical
  Ctr (MD)
Peninsula Hospital Center (NY)

Peninsula Lib and Historical
  Society (OH)

Peninsula Lib System (CA)

Penn Central Corporation (CT)

Penn Hills Sch District (PA)
Penn Yan Pub Lib (NY)
Pennie & Edmonds (NY)

Pennsylvania Academy of the Fine
  Arts (PA)

Pennsylvania Coll of Optometry (PA)
Pennsylvania Department of
  Education (PA)

Pennsylvania Economy League (PA)

Pennsylvania Histl & Museum
  Commission (PA)

Pennsylvania Institute of
  Technology (PA)
Pennsylvania Lib Association (PA)
Pennsylvania State Correctional
  Instn (PA)

Pennsylvania State Pub Welfare
  Dept (PA)
Pennsylvania State Univ (PA)

FORD, George H. (Resrch Libn) . 389
LIEBERFELD, Lawrence
  (Consulting Assoc) 726
FISHMAN, Lee H. (Info Spclst) . . 381
HARRISON, Karen M. (Info
  Spclst) 507
WHITTLESEY, Jane M. (Info
  Spclst) 1334
OAKE, Rhena E. (Resrc Ctr
  Mgr) 913
BELL, Hope A. (Resrc Ctr Mgr) . . . 77
PECK, Brian T. (Sr Resrch
  Analyst) 953
LE BLANC, Judith E. (Tech
  Libn) 708
WEISS, Paula K. (Dir) 1320
SMALLWOOD, Carol A. (High
  Sch Libn) 1151

BONIN, Denise R. (Libn) 114
WINSHIP, Michael 1355
ERICKSON, Anne E. (Sch Libn) . 352
MEHTA, Subbash C. (Chief Libn
  & Chief Exec Ofcr) 821
GOETZ, Helen L. (Info Srvs
  Mgr) 443
REMINGTON, David G. (Dir) . . . 1022
TAYLOR, Michael Y. (Lib Dir) . . 1228
O'NEIL, Margaret M. (Adult Srvs
  Libn) 924
SALUZZO, Mary S. (Chld's
  Libn) 1078

OGLE, Mary H. (Med Libn) 918
RUBINSTEIN, Edith (Dir, Med
  Lib) 1065

BERGDORF, Randolph S.
  (Achvst) 85
CROWE, Linda D. (Syst Dir) . . . 261
KERSHNER, Lois M. (Project
  Dir) 644
ZYGMONT, Carolyn A. (Lib
  Srvs Supvsr) 1392
MURPHY, Diana G. (Sch Libn) . . 880
OVERGAARD, Lynn H. (Dir) . . . 931
BURKEY, Lynne (Asst Libn) . . . 161
GILLIGAN, Mary A. (Libn) 436

BUSHNELL, Marietta P. (Libn) . . 165
LEIBOLD, Cheryl A. (Archvst) . . 713
KRIVDA, Marita J. (Lib Dir) 679

BEDDOES, Thomas P. (Gen Ref
  Head) 73
RICHVALSKY, Neil F. (Sch Lib
  Devlpmnt Adv) 1031
SPRANKLE, Vicki S. (Catlgr) . . 1176
WOZNIAK, Grace I. (Ref Libn) . 1369
BRENNAN, Ellen (Libn) 132
EVES, Judith A. (Libn/Resrch
  Assoc) 359

STAYER, Jonathan R. (Ref
  Archvst) 1183
TALLMAN, Carol W. (Libn) 1221

BURGESS, Rita N. (Libn) 159
BAUER, Margaret D. (Exec Dir) . . . 65

HOSTRANDER, Craig D. (Libn
  I) 562

LIEM, Frieda (Libn) 726
ATTIG, John C. (Catlgr) 38
BISSELL, Joann S. (Ref Libn &
  Sr Asst Libn) 100
BONTA, Bruce D. (Head, Gen
  Ref) 114
BURKHARDT, Marlene (Libn) . . . 161

Pennsylvania State Univ (PA)

CARR. Caryn J. (Asst Libn) 185
CARSON, M S. (Lib Systs & Stans Spclst) 188
CHAMBERLAIN, Carol E. (Acqs Dept Head) 197
CLINE, Nancy M. (Asst Dean & Head, Biblgph Resrcs) 222
CONKLING, Thomas W. (Engrng Lib Head) 236
DOLE, Wanda V. (Head Libn) ... 309
EMMER, Barbara L. (Head Libn) . 348
EZELL, Johanna V. (Head Libn) . 360
FERRAINOLO, John J. (Sr Asst Libn) 373
FERRIN, Eric G. (Technl Dir) 373
FISHER, Kim N. (Acqs Libn) 381
FORTH, Stuart (Dean of Univ Libs) 391
FREIVALDS, Dace I. (Lib Syst Spclst) 402
GARNER, Diane L. (Govt Docums Libn) 419
GERHART, Catherine A. (Catlg Libn) 428
GRUBER, Linda R. (Asst Engrng Libn & Engrng Catlgr) 474
HENSHAW, Rod (Access Srvs Dept Head) 529
HERRON, Nancy L. (Head Libn) . 533
JAMISON, Carolyn C. (Documents Libn/Soc Scis Catlgr) 593
JEAN, Lorraine A. (Gen Ref Libn) 596
KAISER, John R. (Col Devlpmnt Coordntr) 622
KALIN, Sarah G. (Ref Libn & LIAS Coordntr) 623
KELLERMAN, Lydia S. (Asst Libn) 636
LARSON, Mary E. (Sr Asst Libn, Gen Ref) 699
LINGLE, Virginia A. (Asst Ref Libn) 730
LODER, Michael W. (Campus Libn) 736
MALCOM, Dorothy L. (Asst Libn) 763
MANN, Charles W. (Rare Bks & Spcl Cols Lib Chief) 766
MARTIN, Noelene P. (Interlib Loan Sect Head) 777
MCCOMB, Ralph W. (Univ Libn Emeritus) 797
MCKOWN, Cornelius J. (Physical Sci Lib Head) 812
MORGANTI, Deena J. (Ref Libn) 864
MURPHY, Charles G. (Sr Asst Libn) 880
NADESKI, Karen L. (Sr Asst Libn) 886
NEAL, James G. (Asst Dean & Head of Ref) 890
OGBURN, Joyce L. (Acqs Libn) . 918
PASTER, Amy L. (Life Scis Catlgr & Ref Libn) 946
PIERCE, Miriam D. (Math Lib Head) 971
PIERCE, William S. (Facilities Plng Ofcr) 972
RAJPAR, Shamin H. (Ref Libn) . 1004
RAWLINS, Gordon W. (Asst Dean of Libs) 1010
RICE, Patricia O. (Acqs Libn, Serials) 1027
ROE, Eunice M. (Info Analyst) .. 1048
SALINGER, Florence A. (Technl Srvs Coordntr) 1076

Pennsylvania State Univ (PA)

SAMET, Janet S. (Serials Receiving Libn) 1078
SEEDS, Robert S. (Hlth Sci Libn) 1111
SEPP, Frederick C. (Sr Asst Libn) 1115
SMALL, Sally S. (Assoc & Head Libn) 1151
SMITH, Barbara J. (Asst Dean of Univ Libs) 1153
SMITH, Diane H. (Head, Docums & Maps Sect) 1154
SMITH, Elizabeth J. (Arts & Architecture Libn) 1154
STANLEY, Nancy M. (Catlg & Ref Libn) 1180
STOUT, Leon J. (Spcl Cols Univ Archvst & Libns) 1198
STRIEDIECK, Suzanne S. (Biblgph Operations Chief) .. 1202
SULZER, John H. (Sr Asst State & Local Docums Libn) . 1209
SWEENEY, Del (Resrch Assoc) 1215
SWINTON, Cordelia W. (Head, Lending Srvs) 1216
TOWNLEY, Charles T. (Div Head) 1253
TYCE, Richard (Lib Dir) 1266
ULINCY, Loretta D. (Ref Libn) .. 1268
WESTERMAN, Melvin E. (Assoc Libn) 1327
WHITTINGTON, Christine A. (Ref Libn) 1334
WOOD, M S. (Head of Ref) ... 1364
ZABEL, Diane M. (Soc Sci Ref Libn & Asst Libn) 1385
ZAGON, Eileen (Sr Asst Libn) .. 1385

Pennwalt (NY)
SCARFIA, Angela M. (Resrch Libn) 1087

Pennwalt (PA)
DONOVAN, Kathryn M. (Info Srvs Mgr) 312

Penrose Hospital (CO)
JANES, Nina (Dir of Libs) 593
WATERS, W R. (Med Libn) ... 1309

Pensacola Christian Coll (FL)
BROWN, Lyn S. (Libn) 145
TERNAK, Armand T. (Assoc Lib Dir) 1232

Pensacola Junior Coll (FL)
BOWER, Beverly L. (Lrng Resrc Srvs Dir) 120

Pentagon Lib (DC)
MINTER, Lyle 846
Penton Publishing (OH)
KEATING, Michael F. (Sr Mktg Analyst Resrch Mgr) 633

People's Lib (PA)
STICHA, Denise S. (Lib Dir) ... 1193
Peoria Pub Lib (IL)
GIBBS, Margareth (Dir) 431
KOSCIELSKI, Roberta L. (Branch Libn) 672
NELSON, Maggie E. (Pub Relations Coordntr) 894
SWORSKY, Felicia G. (Head of Automation) 1217

Pepper Hamilton & Scheetz (MI)
STAJNIAK, Elizabeth T. (Lib Mgr) 1178

Pepper Hamilton & Scheetz (PA)
BEYER, Robyn L. (Lib Srvs Dir) .. 93
LEVY, Anne W. (Asst Libn) 721

Pepperdine Univ (CA)
FRASHIER, Anne E. (Technl Processing Libn) 399
HEATHER, Joleen (Acqs Libn) .. 519
HOLLAND, Harold E. (Dir of Libs) 550
LEUNG, Terry S. (Libn) 719
SANDERS, Robert L. (Univ Archvst) 1080
STAHL, Ramona J. (Asst Ref Libn, Circ) 1178

Pepsi Cola USA (NY)
BURROWS, Shirley (Mktg Info Libn) 163

PEPSICO (NY)
FALCONE, Elena C. (Assoc Info Scientist) 362

Pequot Lib (CT)
KEMP, Thomas J. (Asst Dir) 639

PergaBase (VA)

BRIGGUM, Joan (Chem Info
   Spclst) 136

Pergamon Infoline Inc (NY)

GIBBINS, P J. (Technical Dir) . . . 431

Pergamon Infoline Inc (VA)

JONES, Michael W. (Mktg Mgr) . 614

POOL, Madlyn K. (Vice Pres,
   Mktg) 982

TERRAGNO, P J. (Pres) 1232

WINIARSKI, Marilee E.
   (Customer Srvs Mgr) 1355

Pergamon Microforms
   International (NY)

RITTER, Sally K. (Libn & Info
   Systs Mgr) 1037

Pergamon Press (NY)

SMITH-GREENWOLD, Kathryn
   R. (Consult) 1162

Perkins Cole (WA)

SMEWART, Jane (Head Libn) . . 1192

Perry County Sch District 32 (MO)

TUCKER, Phillip H. (Lrng
   Resrcs Prog Coordntr) 1262

Perry Dean Rogers & Partners,
   Architects (MA)

FOOTE, Steven M. (Principal) . . . 388

Perry Roe & Associates (MA)

ROE, Georgeanne T. (Consult &
   Info Broker) 1048

Pertamina (CA)

MASWAN, Yurita (Econ & Tech
   Dept Mgr) 783

Petaluma Secondary Sch
   District (CA)

GORDON, Ruth I. (Libn) 452

Petawawa National Forestry
   Institute (ON)

MITCHELL, Mary H. (Libn) 849

Peterborough Town Lib (NH)

GEISEL, Ann M. (Dir) 425

TIERNAN, Linda M. (Catlgr) . . . 1244

Peters Technology Transfer Inc (AR)

LANEY-SHEEHAN, Susan
   (Supervising Libn) 695

Petersburg Pub Lib (VA)

FRENCH, Randy A. (Branch
   Libn) 402

Petervin Press & Petervin Info
   Assocs (CA)

IRELAND, Laverne H. (Owner) . . 583

Petro-Canada Products (ON)

DAVIS, Wendy A. (Libn) 281

NEILSON, Ann (Libn) 892

Petroleum Industry Research
   Associates (NY)

KAGAN, Ilse E. (Info Spclst) 621

Petroleum Information Corp (CO)

KELLER, Michael (Sr VP) 635

STARK, Philip H. (Exec Vice
   Pres Intl) 1182

Petroleum Recovery Inst (AB)

JANJUA, Zaytoon (Libn) 593

Pfizer Canada Inc (PQ)

HAYWARD, Miriam C.
   (Scientific Info Ofcr) 517

Pharmacia P-L Biochemicals Inc (WI)

MENITOVE, Symie D. (Resrch
   Libn) 824

Pharr Memorial Lib (TX)

LIU, David T. (Lib Dir) 734

Philadelphia Board of
   Education (PA)

MARNET, Carole M. (Reading
   Tchr) 772

Philadelphia Coll of Bible (PA)

BLACK, Dorothy M. (Asst Libn
   and Music Libn) 101

Philadelphia Coll of Pharmacy &
   Science (PA)

ADAMS, Mignon S. (Dir of Lib
   Srvs) 5

BRIZUELA, B S. (Interlibrary
   Loan Ref Libn) 138

HESP, Judith A. (Biblgph Instrc
   Coordntr) 534

RAINEY, Nancy B. (Pub Srvs
   Head) 1004

SMINK, Marjorie M. (Ref &
   Serials Libn) 1152

ZOGOTT, Joyce (Head of Lrng
   Resrc Ctr) 1390

Philadelphia Coll of Textiles &
   Science (PA)

PHALAN, Mary A. (Technl Srvs
   Head) 967

Philadelphia Coll of the Arts (PA)

CALDWELL, John M. (Slide
   Coordntr & Music Lib Asst) . . 172

HALL, Martha H. (Head of Pub
   Srvs) 488

Philadelphia Flyers (PA)

LINN, Mott R. (Archvst) 731

Philadelphia Geriatric Center (PA)

POST, Joyce A. (Libn) 986

Philadelphia Jewish Archives
   Center (PA)

GRACE, William M. (Asst
   Archvst) 455

Philadelphia Museum of Art (PA)

Philadelphia Orchestra (PA)

Philadelphia Rare Books &
   Manuscripts Co (PA)

Philander Smith Coll (AR)

Philbrook Art Center (OK)

Phildelphia Print Shop Ltd (PA)

Philhaven Hospital (PA)

Philip Morris USA (VA)

Philippine Normal Coll (PHP)

Philips International B V (TN)

Philips Research Laboratories (CA)

Philips Subsystems (NY)

Phillips Corp (DC)

Phillips County Lib (AR)

Phillips Exeter Academy (NH)

Phillips Graduate Seminary (OK)

Phillips Petroleum Co (OK)

Phillips Publishing Inc (MD)

Phillips Univ (OK)

Phillipsburg Board of Education (NJ)

Phillipsburg Free Pub Lib (NJ)

Philo Township Pub Lib (IL)

Phoenix Art Museum (AZ)

Phoenix Newspapers Inc (AZ)

Phoenix Pub Lib (AZ)

Photographic Conservation Assoc
   Ltd (IL)

Photosearch Inc (NY)

Piano Research Association (NJ)

Pickens County Sch District (SC)

Pickwick Publications (PA)

Piedmont Regional Lib (GA)

Piedmont Virginia Community
   Coll (VA)

Pierce Coll (WA)

ERDREICH, Gina B. (Resrch &
   Ref Libn) 352

SEVY, Barbara S. (Libn) 1117

GROSSMAN, Robert M. (Asst
   Libn) 473

NIEWEG, Clinton F. (Principal
   Libn) 904

MERZ, Lawrie H. (Rare Bk
   Catlgr) 827

WILSON, Janora E. (Libn) 1351

YOUNG, Thomas E. (Libn) 1383

CRESSWELL, Donald H.
   (Owner) 258

DOLL, Harriet A. (Libn) 309

DEBARDELEBEN, Marian Z.
   (Assoc Sr Scientist, Info Ctr
   Leader) 284

ROSENBERG, Murray D. (Sect
   Leader) 1056

SOUTHWICK, Margaret A. (Info
   Chemist) 1170

DE CASTRO, Elinore H. (Lib Sci
   Prof Head of Grad Sch Lib) . . 285

GALL, Bert A. (Product Mktg
   Mgr CD-I) 413

TURK, Sally (Libn) 1263

MESSERSCHMITT, John C.
   (Pres) 828

SCHNEIDER, Karen (Libn) 1097

THOMAS, Cornel W. (Lib Dir) . . 1236

THOMAS, Jacquelyn H.
   (Academy Libn) 1236

HAMBURGER, Roberta L.
   (Seminarian Libn) 491

ROBIN, Annabeth (Lib Supvsr) . 1043

KIMMEL, Mark R. (Pubns Dir) . . 649

MESHINSKY, Jeff M. (Edit/Asst
   Edit) 827

SAYRE, John L. (Dir of Univ
   Libs) 1087

ROMBERGER, Alice J. (Sch
   Libn) 1052

HESS, Jayne L. (Lib Dir) 534

HIGHSMITH, June C. (Libn) . . . 538

KIRKING, Clayton C. (Libn) 655

LESHY, Dede (Ref Libn) 718

STEVENS, Paula F. (Libn) 1190

ALABASTER, Carol (Col
   Devlpmnt Coordntr) 9

CHUNG, Catherine L. (Catlgng
   Srvs Libn) 213

EDWARDS, Ralph M. (City
   Libn) 337

FARNHAM, Shera M. (Bus &
   Sci Head) 365

MEYERS, Kathleen H. (Ref
   Libn) 831

NORMAN, Nita V. (Branch
   Head) 909

ROATCH, Mary A. (Spcl Needs
   Ctr Supvsr) 1038

MATTENSON, Murray M. (Pres
   & Chief Conservator) 785

POLSTER, Joanne (Picture
   Resrchr) 982

YRIGOYEN, Robert P. 1384

DUSENBERRY, Mary D. (Media
   Spclst) 329

HADIDIAN, Dikran Y. (Dir &
   Gen Edit) 482

HOLMES, Nancy M. (Extension
   Srvs Coordntr) 553

EISENBERG, Phyllis B. (Libn) . . . 340

GRANITZ, Adrienne D. (Circ
   Supvsr) 457

HAMMOND, Mary W. (Ref Libn) . 494

Pierce County Rural Lib (WA)

KRUZIC, Evelyn D. (Asst Systs Expansion Mgr) 681
THOMPSON, Diane M. (Syst Expansion Prog Mgr) 1239

Pierian Press (MI)

REGAN, Lesley E. (Managing Editor) 1017

Pierpont Morgan Lib (NY)

CAHOON, Herbert (Robert H Taylor Autograph Mss Cur) .. 171
DUPONT, Inge (Supvsr of the Reading Room) 327
MAYO, Hope (Assoc Cur of Printed Bks) 790
WEINBERG, Valerie A. (Catlgr) . 1318
WILSON, Fredric W. (Cur) 1351

Pierson Semmes & Finley (DC)

WARRICK, Thomas S. (Partner) 1307

Pikes Peak Lib District (CO)

DOWLIN, Kenneth E. (Dir) 316
MAGRATH, Lynn L. (Deputy Dir) 760
MALYSHEV, Nina A. (Head of Info Srvs & Ref) 764
MITCHELL, Carolyn (Ref & Yng Adult Srvs Libn) 848
RITTEN, Karla J. (Libn I) 1036
WERNE, Kenneth L. (Ref Libn) . 1324

Pillsbury Co (MN)

PEDERSEN, Dennis C. (Info Scientist) 954
SCHUMACHER, Patricia C. (Technl Srvs Libn) 1103

Pima Community Coll (AZ)

ALURI, Rao (Assoc Faculty) 19
HOLLEMAN, Margaret (Lib Srvs Coordntr) 551
NAMSICK, Lynn J. (Rsv Spclst) . 887

Pima County (AZ)

MATTY, Paul D. (Libn) 786

Pinehurst-Kingston Free Lib District (ID)

BREIDT, Cheryll K. (Dir) 132

Pinellas County Board of Education (FL)

JONES, Winona N. (Dept Chair & Lib Media Spclst) 615
PASSARELLO, Nancy H. (Media Spclst) 946

The Pioneer Group Inc (MA)

DODSON, Nancy C. (Libn) 308

Pioneer Hi-Bred International Inc (IA)

BEVERIDGE, Mary I. (Info Resrcs Adminstr) 93
GOERS, Willona G. (Commercial Database Mgr) .. 443
HOEVEN, Helen D. (Resrch Lib Coordntr) 547

Pioneer Multi-County Lib System (OK)

DICKSON, Theresa J. (Lib Adminstr) 301
GOLDSBERRY, Maureen E. (Adult Srvs Libn) 446
JORDAN, Linda K. (Info Srvs Libn) 616
PETERS, Lloyd A. (Automation Coordntr) 962
SHERMAN, Mary A. (Dir) 1128

Piper & Marbury (DC)

GEHRINGER, Susanne E. (Head Libn) 425

Piper & Marbury (MD)

NIXON, Judith A. (Asst Libn) 906
RASCHKA, Katherine E. (Head Libn) 1008

Piscataway Board of Education (NJ)

MENINGALL, Evelyn L. (Eductnl Media Spclst) 824

Piscataway Pub Lib (NJ)

DEL GUIDICE, M R. (Head, Chlds Srvs) 289
SERPICO, Margaret A. (Chlds Libn) 1116

Pitman Board of Education (NJ)

PELLETIER, Karen E. (Media Dir) 955

Pitman-Moore Inc (IN)

BAUMGARTNER, Kurt O. (Sr Assoc Info Scientist) 66

Pitt-Des Moines Inc (PA)

FRANZ, N L. (Libn) 398

Pittsburg State Univ (KS)

COFFEE, Kathleen C. (Head of Technl Srvs) 226
DEGRUSON, Eugene H. (Spcl Cols Libn) 288
LEE, Earl W. (Catlgr & Col Devlpmnt Libn) 709

Pittsburg State Univ (KS)

VOLLEN, Gene E. (Chairman, Dept of Music) 1287

Pittsburgh Post-Gazette (PA)

KANE, Angelika R. (Head Libn) .. 624

Pittsburgh Pub Schs (PA)

MIZIK, Judy G. (Dir, Lib & Media Srvs) 850
PASHEL, Susan M. (Substitute Tchr) 945

Pittsburgh Regional Lib Center (PA)

ANDERSON, Elizabeth M. (Network Srvs Mgr) 22
BROADBENT, H E. (Exec Dir) .. 138

Pittsfield Middle High Sch (NH)

DRUKE-STICKLER, Janet A. (Libn) 320

Pittsford Central Sch District (NY)

RICHARDSON, Constance H. (Sch Lib Media Spclst) 1029
SOUTHCOMBE, Patricia A. (Sch Lib Media Spclst) 1169

Pittsford Community Lib (NY)

DEMALLIE, Marjorie W. (Chlds Srvs Libn) 291
SUMMERS, Ruth O. (Lib Dir) .. 1209

Pizer Archives Music Lib (NY)

PIZER, Charles R. (Pres) 977
PIZER, Elizabeth F. (Executive Dir) 977

Placer Union High Sch District (CA)

FROST, Shirley E. (Lib Media Spclst) 406

Plager Hasting & Krug Ltd (IL)

FREY, Roxanne C. (Paralegal) . 403

Plain Dealer Newspaper (OH)

PARCH, Grace D. (Lib Dir) ... 939

Plainedge Pub Lib (NY)

EISNER, Joseph (Lib Dir) 341

Plainfield Pub Lib (IN)

CARTER, Susan M. (Histl Libn, Adminstrv Asst) 190
MCMILLAN, Mary M. (Dir) .. 815

Plainfield Pub Lib (NJ)

TUTWILER, Dorothea F. (Ref Dept Head) 1266

Plainfield Sch Dist 202 (IL)

DIERCKS, Eileen K. (Eductnl Media Coordntr) 302

Plains & Peaks Regional Lib Service Syst (CO)

OWEN, Mary J. (Dir) 932

Plainsboro Free Pub Lib (NJ)

KAMEN, Francine B. (Ref Libn) .. 623

Plainview Old Bethpage Pub Lib (NY)

ROSEN, Wendy L. (Ref Libn) .. 1055

Plainview Old Bethpage Sch District (NY)

WOLFE, Barbara M. (Lib Coordntr) 1360

Plainwell High Sch (MI)

PARR, Michael P. (Sch Lib Media Spclst) 944

Planned Parenthood (DC)

FORREST, Phyllis E. (Resrce Ctr Coordntr) 391

Planned Parenthood (NY)

ROBERTS, Gloria A. (Head Libn) 1040

Planning Analysis Corp (KS)

POSTLEWAIT, Cheryl A. (Technl Libn) 986

Planning Research Corp (VA)

TRAVIS, Irene L. (Assoc Mem of Sr Technl Staff) 1254

Plano Pub Lib System (TX)

BONNELL, Pamela G. (Lib Mgr) . 114
DEILY, Carole C. (Sr Ref Libn) .. 288

Plaspec (NY)

VONHASSELL, Agostino (Gen Mrg) 1288

Platte River Power Authority (CO)

FELDMAN, Rosalie M. (Records Adminstr Libn) 369

Plattsburgh Pub Lib (NY)

RICKETSON, Karen F. (Lib Asst & Chld's Dept Head) 1032

The Players (NY)

RACHOW, Louis A. (Cur) 1001

Plenum Publishing Corp (NY)

MEAGHER, Anne E. (Managing Edit, Info Sci Abstracts) 819

Plum Creek Lib Syst (MN)

SCOTT, Thomas L. (Syst Dir) .. 1108

Plunkett & Cooney (MI)

KONDAK, Ann (Head Libn) 670

Plymouth Congregational United Church (DC)

PINKARD, Ophelia T. (Church Archvst) 974

Plymouth District Lib (MI)

RAWLINSON, Pamela (Deputy Dir) 1011

Plymouth Magistrates' Court (ENG)

PENGELLY, Joe (Court Official) . 956

Plymouth Pub Lib (MA)

LEWIS, David D. (Dir) 722

Plymouth Salem High Sch (MI)

WEST, Marian S. (Lib Media Spclst) 1326

Plymouth State Coll (NH)

FITZPATRICK, Robert E. (Ref & Instrc Libn) 383
KIETZMAN, William D. (Asst Libn for Pub Srv) 647

Pocatello Pub Lib (ID)

DOWNEY, Howard R. (Lib Dir) .. 316

Point Loma Nazarene Coll (CA)

POSEY, Vernell W. (Catlg Libn) . 985

Polaroid Corp (MA)
LINGHAM, Laurie W. (Analyst for Sec Resrch) 730
PRITCHARD, Robert W. (Adminstrv Spclst) 994

Polk County Sch Board (FL)
PAULSON, Mary E. (Sch Media Spclst) 950

Polly's Book Repair (AK)
KALLENBERG, Mary E. (Owner) 623

Polo Sch District 22 (IL)
WOOD, Jonette E. (Media Spclst) 1364

Polsinelli White Vardeman & Sheldon (MO)
KLEBBA, Lisa A. (Libn) 658

Poly Prep Country Day Sch (NY)
PERSON, Diane G. (Middle Sch Libn) 961

Polyclinic Medical Center (PA)
SHULTZ, Suzanne M. (Med Libn) 1133

Polysar (OH)
VARA, Margaret E. (Technl Writer & Edit) 1278

Polysar (ON)
O'DONNELL, Rosemary F. (Group Leader, Info Ctr) 917

Polytechnic Preparatory Country Day Sch (NY)
KAHN, Laura (Head Libn) 622

Polytechnic Univ (NY)
ROGERS, Jonathan B. (Senior Clerk) 1049
SCHEIN, Lorraine S. (Lib Mgr) . 1091
SWEENEY, Richard T. (Libs & Info Systs Dean) 1215
TURIEL, David (Technl Srvs Div Head) 1263

Pomona Pub Lib (CA)
SHAPTON, Gregory B. (Principal Libn) 1122
STREETER, David (Special Col Supvsr) 1201

Pomona Unified Sch Dist (CA)
REMKIEWICZ, Frank L. (Dir) .. 1022

Pomona Valley Community Hospital (CA)
KLEIN, Deborah S. (Med Libn) .. 659

Pompano Beach City Lib (FL)
GALLAHAR, Christine M. (Libn I & Branch Mgr) 414

Pontiac General Hospital (MI)
SAHYOUN, Naim K. (Dir of Media Srvs) 1075

Pontiac Pub Lib (IL)
HAMILTON, Patricia A. (Lib Dir) . 492

Popkin & Stern (MO)
COSTELLO, Elaine (Libn) 249

Poplar Bluff Pub Lib (MO)
BECKEMEIER, Dewayne R. (Dir) 72

Poplar Creek Pub Lib District (IL)
DEUEL, Marlene R. (Adminstrv Libn) 296
KLOCKENGA, Gary R. (Govt Docums Dept Head) 662

Population Council Lib (NY)
ZIMMERMAN, Hugh N. (Libn) .. 1389

Poquette & Associates (MN)
POQUETTE, Mary L. (Pres) 984

Port Arkansas Independent Sch District (TX)
DAVIS, Joan C. (Dist Libn) 279

Port Authority of New York & New Jersey (NY)
JANIAK, Jane M. (Chief Libn) ... 593
MARKER, Rhonda J. (Assoc Chief Libn for Catlgng) 771
SCIATTARA, Diane M. (Staff Libn) 1106

Port Chester Pub Lib (NY)
LAROSA, Thomas J. (Asst to Ref Libn) 698
LETTIERI, Robin M. (Dir) 719

Port Jervis Free Lib (NY)
CARRINGTON, Ruth (Dir) 186

Portage County District Lib (OH)
FINAN, Patrick E. (Lib Dir) 377
SPEAR, Linda A. (Head, Extension Srvs) 1172

Portage County Pub Lib (WI)
SWIFT, Leonard W. (Dir) 1216

Portage Free Lib (WI)
JENSEN, Hans W. (Dir) 598

Portage Pub Lib (MI)
HAENICKE, Carol A. (Adult Srvs Libn) 482
HEMPHILL, Frank A. (City Libn) . 525

Portage Township Schs (IN)
DUHAMELL, Lynnette H. (Dept Coordntr) 324
KRAMER, Arlene H. (Sch Lib Media Spclst) 675

Porter Memorial Hospital (CO)
BRITAIN, Karla K. (Med Lib Dir) . 137
VERCIO, Roseanne (Asst Med Libn) 1282

Porter Pub Lib (OH)
ADAMS, Liese A. (Asst Dir) 5
DOMBEY, Kathryn W. (Adult & Yng Srvs Libn) 310

Porter Wright Morris & Arthur (OH)
CHRISTIAN, Patricia A. (Law Libn) 211
SCHAEFGEN, Susan M. (Law Libn) 1089

Porterville Coll (CA)
NAUMER, Janet N. (Dir of Lib Media Ctr) 889

Portland Cement Assn (IL)
SPIGELMAN, Cynthia A. (Libn) . 1174

Portland General Electric (OR)
SHAVER, Donna B. (Supvsr, Lib Resrcs) 1123
WEBER, Robert F. (Technl Libn) 1314

Portland Pub Schs (OR)
ANDERSON, C L. (Libn Media Spclst) 21
JONES, Mary C. (Libn, Media Spclst) 614
PIERRE, Zenata W. (Lib Media Spclst) 972

Portland Sch of Art (ME)
WAXMAN, Joanne (Head Libn) . 1311

Portland State Univ (OR)
BRUSEAU, Laurence L. (Catlgr) . 151
GREEY, Kathleen M. (Educ Libn) 465
POWELL, Faye 988
SOOHOO, Terry A. (Technl Srvs Dept Head) 1167
TAMBLYN, Eldon W. (Head Catlgr) 1221
WRIGHT, Janet K. (Arts & Hum Libn) 1371

Portledge Sch (NY)
LAPIDUS, Lois E. (Lower Sch Libn) 697

Portsmouth Psychiatric Center (VA)
KERSTETTER, Virginia M. (Med Libn) 644

Portsmouth Pub Lib (NH)
LE BLANC, Charles A. (Technl Srvs Libn) 708
MCCANN, Susan F. (Asst Dir) .. 794

Portsmouth Pub Lib (OH)
COOK, Charles T. (Dir) 239

Portsmouth Pub Lib (VA)
BROWN, William A. (Asst Lib Dir) 148
BURGESS, Dean (Dir) 159
TURNER, Virginia S. (Supvsr of Libs) 1265

Post Falls Pub Lib (ID)
JONES-LITTEER, Corene A. (Lib Dir) 616

Post Foundation (MO)
SIMPSON, Leslie T. (Lib Dir) .. 1142

Post Oak Quarters (TX)
PHILLIPS, Ray S. (Asst Mgr) ... 969

The Post-Register (ID)
VERHOFF, Patricia A. (Editrl Libn) 1282

Potsdam Coll (NY)
FINCH, Frances (Ref Libn) 377
SUBRAMANIAN, Jane M. (Perdcls Coordntr) 1206

Pottstown Memorial Medical Center (PA)
CHAPIS, Marilyn D. (Med Staff Libn) 201

Pottsville Free Pub Lib (PA)
SAXMAN, Susan E. (Ref Libn) . 1086
TOWLE, Jean A. (Dist Conslt) .. 1252

Pottsville Hospital & Warne Clinic (PA)
LEINHEISER, Diane R. (Libn) ... 714

Poudre R-1 Sch Dist (CO)
LIRA, Judith A. (Media Spclst) .. 732

Powell Goldstein Frazer & Murphy (GA)
FULLER, Ruth V. (Operations Libn) 409
SCHEIN, Julia R. (Catlgr) 1091

Poynter Institute for Media Studies (FL)
CATES, Jo A. (Chief Libn) 194

PPG Industries (OH)
OBERLANDER, Deborah K. (Libn) 914

PPG Industries (PA)
FIDOTEN, Robert E. (Info Tech & Admin Dir) 375

Prairie Bible Institute (AB)
BRADLEY, Harold K. (Dir of Media Srvs) 126
JORDAHL, Ronald I. (Head Libn) 616

Prairie Information & Research Services (ND)
HOLDEN, Douglas H. (Info Spclst) 550

Prairie State Coll (IL)
BAYER, Susan P. (Catlgr & Ref Libn) 67

Prairie Trails Pub Lib District (IL)
WEST, Barbara G. (Lib Dir) ... 1326

Prairie View A&M Univ (TX)

ADAMS, Elaine P.
(Vice-President for Student
Affairs) 4
KUJOORY, Parvin (Asst Prof of
Instrcl Media & Tech) 683
WACHTER-NELSON, Ruth M.
(Univ Archvst, Spcl Cols
Libn) 1290
YEH, Helen S. (Asst Dir for
Technl Srvs) 1379

Pratt & Whitney (CT)   MOON, Mary G. (Libn) 857
Pratt Institute (NY)   CHICKERING, F W. (Multi
Media Srvs Dir) 208
GREENBERG, Roberta D.
(Coordntr of Architecture
Resrc Ctr) 463
HUMPHRY, James (Prof,
Adjunct) 574
KEAVENEY, Sydney S. (Prof) . . 633
MALINCONICO, S M. (Dean) . . 763
MATTA, Seoud M. (Prof) 785
MCSWEENEY, Josephine (Prof
& Ref Libn) 818

Praxis Biologics (NY)   HELBERS, Catherine A. (Info
Spclst) 523
Predicasts (CA)   HEDDEN, Judy A. (Online Srvs,
Mgr of Wester Region) 520
Predicasts (OH)   HARRIS, Richard (Pres) 506
HECHT, Joseph A. (Bus Info
Spclst) 519
OWEN, Paul E. 932
RICHARDSON, Ulrike L. 1030
Premark International (IL)   HAMILTON, Meredith L. (Law
Libn) 492
**Prentice Hall Information
Services** (DC)   FATTIBENE, James F. (Dir of
Washington Operations) 366
**Prentice Hall Information
Services** (NJ)   SATTIBENE, James (Govt
Procurement Dir) 1084
**Prentice Hall Information
Services** (NY)   SPEYER, Thomas W. (Dir of
Plng & Devlpmnt) 1174
Presbyterian Historical Society (PA) HAAS, John O. (Lib Asst) 480
Presbyterian Hospital (NC)   BERRY, Mary W. (Lrng Resrc
Ctr Dir) 90
Presbyterian Hospital (NY)   MOUNT, Albertina F. (Libn &
Supvsr) 873
Presbyterian Univ Hospital (PA) HESZ, Bianka M. (Med Libn) . . . 534
**Presbyterian Univ of
Pennsylvania** (PA)   ROEDELL, Ray F. (Libn) 1048
**Presbyterian Univ of Santa
Barbara** (CA)   ANDERSON, John F. (Exec
Presbyter & Stated Clerk) 23
Prescott Unified Sch Dist 1 (AZ) ELLIS, Caryl A. (Instrcl Mtrls Ctr
Dir) 344
Presentations (NY)   ROGINSKI, James W.
(Freelance Dirctry Complr) . . 1050
President's Committee (DC)   BROWN, Dale S. (Employment
Advisor) 143
The Press Democrat (CA)   CANT, Elaine N. (Head libn) 179
Preston High Sch (NY)   MCCANN, Kathleen (Libn) 794
**Preston Thorgrimson Ellis &
Holman** (DC)   ASMUTH, Gretchen W. (Libn) 36
**Preston Thorgrimson Ellis &
Holman** (WA)   JACKSON, Cleta L. (Asst Libn) . . 587
Prevention Research Center (CA) FISHER, Leslie R. (Assoc Libn) . . 381
YANEZ, Elva K. (Libn) 1377
Price City (UT)   SOWER, Marjorie T. (Libn) 1170
Price Waterhouse (CA)   BLUM, Linda C. (Info Spclst) . . . 107
VEASLEY, Mignon M. (Info
Spclst) 1280
VEENKER, Linda J. (Mgr) 1281
Price Waterhouse (DC)   SHEERAN, Carole A. (Libn) . . . 1125
WATERS, Susan S. (Info
Spclst) 1309
Price Waterhouse (FL)   TEW, Robin L. (Info Spclst) 1233
Price Waterhouse (MA)   BUSCH, Joseph A. (Mgr) 165
SCANLAN, Jean M. (Info Ctr
Dir) 1087

Price Waterhouse (NY)   CROFT, Elizabeth G. (Info
Spclst & Asst Adminstr) 260
FLEISHMAN, Lauren Z. (Ref
Libn) 384
SOSTACK, Maura (Info Spclst) . 1169
ZIPPER, Masha (Natl Info Ctr
Dir) 1390
Price Waterhouse (OH)   SPEECE, Yvonne M. (Libn) 1172
Price Waterhouse (TX)   PENDRAK, Eileen (Info Spclst) . . 956
SMITH, Kraleen S. (Info Spclst) . 1156
Price Waterhouse (WA)   FROST, Roxanna (Info Spclst) . . . 406
Price Waterhouse (ON)   SEDGWICK, Dorothy L. (Lib &
Info Srvs Mgr) 1111
WELLS, Nancy E. (Asst Libn) . . 1322
WILLIAMS, Gwendolyn (Dir) . . . 1343
YALLER, Loretta O. (Law Libn) . 1376
Prichard Pub Lib Board (AL)
Prickett Jones Elliott Kristol et al (DE) LEDWELL, Bill (Pres) 709
**Prince Edward Island Prfsnl Libns
Assn** (PE)   NICHOLSON, Dianne L. (Head
Prince George Pub Lib (BC)   of Support Srvs) 902
**Prince George's Community
Coll** (MD)   NEKRITZ, Leah K. (Assoc Dean
of Lrng Resrcs) 893
**Prince George's County Board of
Educ** (MD)   GERRING, Cheryl B. (Lib Media
Spclst) 429
**Prince George's County Memorial
Lib** (MD)   BURGESS, Eileen E. (Selection
Ofcr-Young Adult) 159
COOPER, Judith C. (Adminstrv
Asst) 243
GOODLETT, Doris R. (Area
Mgr) 449
GORDON, William R. (Dir) 452
HALL, Mary A. (Asst Dir of Pub
Srvs) 488
HARGROVE, Marion H. (Yng
Adult Libn) 501
LEVINE, Susan H. (Substitute
Libn) 721
LOSINSKI, Julia M. (Coordntr) . 742
MOORE, Craig P. (Libn II) 859
ROBINSON, Mark L. (Online
Database Searcher) 1044
SHIH, Walter D. (Asst Dir of
Datamation) 1130
WOODY, Jacqueline B. (Branch
Mgr) 1368
**Prince George's County Pub
Schs** (MD)   ASHFORD, Richard K. (Lib
Media Spclst) 36
BARTH, Edward W.
(Coordinating Supvsr) 61
CAMPA, Josephine (Lib Media
Spclst) 175
MATHEWS, Mary P. (Lib Media
Spclst) 784
MURRAY, Bruce C. (Lib Media
Spclst) 881
**Prince George's County Pub
Schs** (VA)   JACKSON, F C. (Lib Media
Spclst) 587
**Prince George's County Sch
Board** (VA)   TUGGLE, Pamela C. (Media
Coordntr) 1262
Prince George's Hospital Center (MD) KLEMAN, Eleanor L. (Med Libn) . 660
**Prince of Wales Northern Heritage
Centre** (NT)   KOBELKA, Carolynn L. (Libn) . . . 666
Prince William County Pub Schs (VA) GAUDET, Jean A. (Sch Libn &
Media Spclst) 422
HOSKINS, Sylvia H. (Libn) 561
KILLEEN, Erlene B. (Elem Sch
Libn) 648
ZIMMERMAN, Nancy P. (Lib
Media Spclst) 1389
Prince William Pub Lib System (VA) BARKALOW, Irene M. (Regnl
Adminstr) 56
BREEN, Catherine H.
(Libn-on-Call) 131

Prince William Pub Lib System (VA)

CHRISTOLON, Blair B. (Ref
Libn) 212
GARBELMAN, Alicia D. (Chlds
Libn) 417
MURPHY, Richard W. (Lib Dir) . 881

Princeton City Sch District (OH)

WOLFORD, Betty K. (Media
Spclst) 1361

Princeton Pub Lib (NJ)

BARZELATTO, Elba G. (Ref
Libn) 62
CARLSON, Dudley B. (Chlds
Dept Head) 182
GREENFELDT, Eric W. (Info
Srvs Head) 464
ROCK, Sue W. (Asst Dir) 1046
STRATTON, Elizabeth G. (Ref
Libn) 1200
THRESHER, Jacquelyn E. (Dir) . 1243

Princeton Theological Seminary (NJ)

IRVINE, James S. (Assoc Libn
for Technl Srvs) 584
TAYLOR, Sharon A. (Asst to the
Libn) 1228

Princeton Univ (NJ)

BELCHER, Emily M.
(Afro-American Selector &
Ref Libn) 76
BIELAWSKI, Marvin F. (Systs
Planner & Coordntr) 95
BLACK, William R. (Asst Order
Libn) 102
CARLISLE, Scott G. (Rare Bk
Catlgr) 182
CHAIKIN, Mary C. (Psy Libn) . . . 197
CINLAR, Anne (Slide Cur) 214
COE, D W. (Anglo-Am Biblgphr) . 226
CZIFFRA, Peter (Math, Physics
& Statistics Libn) 269
FARRELL, Mark R. (Robert H
Taylor Col Cur) 365
FERGUSON, Stephen (Cur of
Rare Bks) 372
GEORGE, Mary W. (Head of
Gen Ref Div) 427
HAJDAS, Susan A. (Asst
Serials Libn) 484
HENNEMAN, John B. (Hist
Biblgphr) 528
HIRSCH, David G. (Catlgr) 543
HOELLE, Dolores M. (Engrng
Libn) 547
JENSEN, Mary A. (Cur) 599
JOYCE, William L. (Rare Books
& Spcl Cols Assoc Libn) 618
KLATH, Nancy S. (Assoc Univ
Libn for Technl Srvs) 657
KOEPP, Donald W. (Univ Libn) . . 668
LITTLE, Rosemary A. (Pub
Admin, Politics and Law Libn) . 734
MCARTHUR, Anne (Asst Libn) . . 792
MONTGOMERY, Michael S.
(Gen, Hum Ref Libn) 856
MORGAN, Paula M. (Music
Libn) 864
NASE, Lois M. (Asst Engrng
Libn) 888
NEWHOUSE, Brian G. (Catlgr) . . 899
NEWMAN, Lisa A. (Asst Libn) . . 899
ODELL, Glendon T. (Deputy
Univ Libn) 916
PASTER, Luisa R. (Database
Mgmt Libn) 946
PHILLIPS, Richard F. (Leader,
European Languages
Catlgng) 969
PRESTON, Jean F. (Cur of
Mss) 991
ROTH, Stacy F. (Archvst) 1059
SCHMIDT, Mary M. (Libn) 1095
TOMPKINS, Louise (Asst Univ
Libn) 1250

Principia Coll (IL)

Principia Coll (MO)

Priscilla Kirshbaum Associates (CO)

Private Consult (MA)

Private Satellite Network Inc (NY)

Procter & Gamble Co (OH)

Proctor & Redfern Group (ON)

Proctor Junior-Senior High Sch (VT)

Proel Tecnologie ISC (ITL)

Professional Books & Services (OH)

**Professional Information
Resources** (AK)

Professional Lib Consultants (IL)

Professional Lib Services Inc (LA)

Professional Media Service Corp (CA)

Professional Sch of Psychology (CA)

**Program for Appropriate Tech in
Health** (WA)

Project Completers Inc (CA)

Project HOPE (VA)

Prolepsis Inc (MA)

**Proskauer Rose Goetz &
Mendelsohn** (CA)

**Proskauer Rose Goetz &
Mendelsohn** (NY)

Prospect Heights Pub Lib District (IL)

The Providence Athenaeum (RI)

**Providence Ctr, Counseling &
Psychiatric** (RI)

Providence Coll (RI)

Providence Hospital (DC)

Providence Hospital (MI)

Providence Hospital (OH)

Providence Hospital (WA)

Providence Journal Co (RI)

Providence Pub Lib (RI)

Providence Pub Schs (RI)

**Providence-St Margaret Health
Center** (KS)

Province House (NS)

BURRUSS, Marsha A. (Asst Dir
for Pub Srvs) 163
FABIAN, William M. (Head Libn) . 360
KIRSHBAUM, Priscilla J.
(Resrch Consult) 655
JAFFARIAN, Sara (Retired) 591
KNICKLE, James P. (Bus
Devlpmnt Dir) 664
WILSON, Sharon L. (Info Ctr
Secy) 1353
SPARK, Catherine L. (Libn) . . . 1171
SHERMAN, Madeline R. (Sch
Libn) 1128
FORRESTER, John H. (Asst
Prog Mgr) 391
MAYL, Gene (Owner) 790

PINNELL-STEPHENS, June A.
(Principal) 975
STOFFEL, Lester L. (Lib
Consult) 1196
SMOTHERS, Alyce A. (Owner) . 1162
HANSEN, Linda L. (Technl Srvs
Head) 497
JACOBS, Peter J. (Pres) 590
DUZAK, Sandra J. (Libn) 330

WOOD-LIM, Eileen K. (Libn) . . . 1366
BURNS, Nancy R. (Info Mgmt
Consultant) 162
NYBERG, Lelia J. (Consult) 912
BISCHOFF, Frances A. (Dir of
Educ) 99
WARPHEA, Rita C. (Lib Mgr) . . 1306
PLUNKET, Joy H. (Independent
Consult) 978

MULLER, Malinda S. (Libn) 877

JOHNSON, David J. (Libn) 603
RAUCH, Anne (Ref Libn) 1010
ROSEN, Nathan A. (Asst Dir of
Lib) 1055
MORGAN, Miriam M. (Head of
Youth Srvs) 864
ROZANSKI, Barbara (Adminstrv
Libn) 1064
DUPLAIX, Sally T. (Dir and
Libn) 327

VIGORITO, Patricia M. (Libn) . . 1284
DESMARAIS, Norman P. (Acqs
Libn) 295
DOHERTY, Joseph H. (Dir) 309
LEONE, Rosemarie G. (Hlth
Scis Lib Dir) 717
GILBERT, Carole M. (Lib Srvs
Dir) 433
EMANI, Nirupama (Libn) 347
CAMPBELL, Mary E. (Dir) 177
HENDERSON, Linda L. (Asst
Libn) 526
MEHR, Joseph O. (Lib Dir) 821
BUNDY, Annalee M. (Dir) 157
COOPER, Jacquelyn B. (Branch
Libn) 243
JOHNSEN-HARRIS, Amy (Ref
Libn) 602
MCKEE, Virginia W. (Chlds Srvs
Chief) 810
WADDINGTON, Susan R. (Dept
Head) 1290
MICHAEL, Richard T. (Eductnl
Tech Adminstr) 831

HOLLINGSHEAD, Mary A.
(Med Libn) 552
MURPHY, Margaret F.
(Legislative Libn) 881

Province of Manitoba (MB)
MACLOWICK, Frederick B.
(Head of Info Srvs) 757

Province of Quebec (PQ)
KLOK, Buddhi (Dir) 662

Province of St Joseph of Capuchin Order (MI)
WIEST, Donald H. (Provincial Archvst) 1337

Province of Saskatchewan (SK)
RUSSELL, Fraser (Libn) 1069

Provincial Lib (PE)
SCOTT, Donald (Provincial Libn) 1107

Prudential Bache (NY)
BUZZANGA, Heidi S. (Ref Libn) . 168

Prudential Bache Securities (NY)
PRAVER, Robin I. (Database Spclst) 990
SCHLUCKEBIER, Leslie F. (Ref Libn) 1094

Prudential Property & Casualty Insurance (NJ)
HENRY, Mary B. (Corpte Libn) . . 529

Prussian Cultural Heritage Foundation (WGR)
ELSTE, R O. (Cur) 346
KREH, Fritz (Adminstrv Libn II) . . 677
WALTER, Raimund E. (Head of Law Sect) 1300

Pryor City Schs (OK)
BARRETT, Lenna M. (Libn) 59

Psychological Service of Pittsburgh (PA)
FULMER, Dina J. (Libn) 409

Pub Affairs Information Service (NY)
PRESCHEL, Barbara M. (Executive Dir) 991
SEKELY, Maryann (Asst Edit) . . 1113
WOODS, Lawrence J. (Asst Exec Dir) 1367

Pub Archives of Canada (ON)
BATCHELDER, Robert 63
BIRRELL, Andrew (Photography Col Dir) 99
STONE, Gerald K. (Custodian of Photographs) 1197
VOSIKOVSKA, Jana (Film, Television, Sound Archs Chief) 1289

Pub Authority for Applied & Training (KWT)
ALTURKAIT, Adela A. (Dept of Libs Dir) 19

Pub Libs of Saginaw (MI)
O'CONNELL, Catherine A. (Dir) . 915
REINKE, Carol R. (Branch Head) 1021
RODGER, Eleanor J. (Exec Dir) . 1047

Pub Lib Association (IL)

Pub Lib of Brookline (MA)
STEINFELD, Michael (Dir) 1186

Pub Lib of Charlotte & Mecklenburg Cnty (NC)
AULD, Hampton M. (Branch Mgr) 39
CANNON, Robert E. (Dir of Libs) 179
GUENTHER, Christine G. (Branch Mgr) 475
MCCORMICK, Emily S. (Adult Srvs Libn) 798
MOYER, James M. (Branch Ref Libn) 874
MYERS, Carol B. (Technl Srvs Dir) 884
SUTTON, Judith K. (Deputy Dir of Libs) 1211

Pub Lib of Cincinnati & Hamilton County (OH)
ABRAMS, Roger E. (Subject Catlgr) 3
DAHMANN, Rosemary G. (Head, Sci & Tech Dept) 270
FERGUSON, George E. (Ref Libn) 372
HETTINGER, Susan F. (Educ & Religion Dept Head) 534
HORTON, Anna J. (Ref Libn) . . . 561
HUDZIK, Robert T. (Head, Films & Recordings Ctr) 570
HUGE, Sharon A. (Libn III & Grants Supvsr) 571
HUNT, James R. (Dir) 575
JOHNS, John E. (Asst Dept Head) 601
KRAMER, Sally J. (Subj Catlgr) . 675
LEE, Sooncha A. (Serials Dept Head) 711

Pub Lib of Cincinnati & Hamilton County (OH)
MCCOY, Betty J. (Technl Srvs Head) 799
POCKROSE, Sheryl R. (Fine Arts Libn) 979
RYAN, Richard A. (Libn II) 1071
SMITH, Maureen M. (Libn) 1158
STONESTREET, R D. (Assoc Dir & Clerk-Treasurer) 1198
WIEHE, Janet C. (Fiction & Yng Adult Srvs Head) 1336

Pub Lib of Columbus & Franklin County (OH)
BLACK, Larry D. (Executive Dir) . 101
HOWARTH, Meribah G. (Dir) . . 565
KYLES, Rubye R. (Asst Dir) . . . 685
MCWILLIAM, Deborah A. (Bus & Tech Mgr) 818
SCHROEDER, Donna L. (Libn II) 1100

Pub Lib of Des Moines (IA)
BOGNANNI, Kathleen J. (Branch Libn) 111
BROGDEN, Stephen R. (Head of Fine Arts Dept) 139
CLAYBURN, Marginell P. (Supvsng Libn) 220
ESTES, Elaine G. (Lib Dir) 355
GERSTENBERGER, Martha F. (Fine Arts Dept Music Spclst) . 429
SHISLER, Shirley M. (Ref Dept Head) 1131
STICK, Dorothy J. (Adminstrv Asst to the Dir) 1193
TRUCK, Lorna R. (Extension Srvs Coordntr) 1259

Pub Lib of Naperville (IL)
PEARSON, Roger L. (Lib Dir) . . . 953

Pub Lib of Nashville (TN)
HEARNE, Mary L. (The Nashville Room Dir) 518

Pub Lib of Steubenville (OH)
HALL, Alan C. (Dir) 486

Pub Lib of Youngstown & Mahoning County (OH)
DONAHUGH, Robert H. (Dir) . . . 310
TRUCKSIS, Theresa A. (Asst Lib Dir) 1259

Pub Records Division (KY)
BELLARDO, Lewis J. (State Archvst & Records Administr) . . 78

Pub Sch 49 Queens (NY)
WIENER, Sylvia B. (Lib Media Spclst) 1336

Pub Schs of Brookline Massachusetts (MA)
ZEIGER, Hanna B. (Sch Libn & Media Spclst) 1387

Pub Schs of Muskegon (MI)
PRETZER, Dale H. (Dir of Lib) . . 992

Pub Service Electric & Gas Co (NJ)
KRUSE, Theodore H. (Acq & Circ Adminstr) 681

Pub Services Co of Oklahoma (OK)
HAYHURST, Carol A. (Corprt Ref Ctr Supvsr) 516

Pub Services Electric & Gas Co (NJ)
HUNT, Florine E. (Libs & Info Resrcs Mgr) 575

Pub Technology Inc (DC)
JOHNSON, Elaine B. (Info Spclst) 604

Pub Utility Commission of Texas (TX)
WILLIAMS, Suzi (Libn) 1346

Publications Technical International (BRA)

Publishers Data Service Corp (CA)
GROSSMANN, Pierre (Dir Pres) . 473
SQUIRE, Diane (Mktg Devlpmnt Dir) 1177

PUDOC (NET)
KOSTER, Lieuwien M. (Info Ofcr) 673

Pueblo Community Coll (CO)
GARDNER, W J. (Lrng Resrvs Ctr Dir) 418

Pueblo County Sch District 70 (CO)
DIRKSEN, Phyllis A. (Media Dir) . 305

Pueblo Lib District (CO)
BATES, Charles E. (Dir) 63

Puerto Rico Attorney General (PR)
NADAL, Antonio (Law Lib Dir) . . 885

Puerto Rico Legal Services (PR)
CASTRO, Maritza (Asst Head Dir) 194

Puget Sound Power & Light (WA)
BALL, Susan C. (Libn) 52

Pulaski County Special Sch District (AR)
HENSON, Aleene E. (Media Spclst) 529
JONES, Wanda F. (Lib Media Spclst) 615

Pulaski County Special Sch District (AR)

MCKINNEY, Barbara J. (Media Spclst) 812

Pulp & Paper Research Institute, Canada (PQ)

FINNEMORE, Mary A. (User Srvs Libn) 378
STAHL, Hella (Mgr, Technl Info Sect) 1178

Purcell Marian High Sch (OH)

RIFFEY, Robin S. (Libn) 1033

Purdue Frederick Co (CT)

WALSH, Kathryn A. (Mgr of Lib Srvs) 1299

Purdue Univ (IN)

ANDREWS, Theodora A. (Prof of Lib Sci & Libn) 27
BAILEY, Martha J. (Lif Scis Libn) 46
BAXTER, Pam M. (Psy Soc Sci Libn) 67
BONHOMME, Mary S. (Asst Dir) 114
BRACKEN, James K. (Hum Biblgphr, Asst Prof of Lib Sci) . 124
BRANDT, Daryl S. (Libn) 128
CANGANELLI, Patrick W. (Info Systems Spclst) 178
COLLINS, Mary E. (Asst Prof & Ref Libn) 233
CORYA, William L. (Asst Dir Technl Srvs) 248
DAGNESE, Joseph M. (Dir of Libs) 269
ERDMANN, Charlotte A. (Asst Engrng Libn) 352
FUNKHOUSER, Richard L. (Sci Libn) 410
GOLOVIN, Naomi E. (Serials Libn) 447
HEWISON, Nancy S. (Asst Life Scis Libn) 535
HOLICKY, Bernard H. (Dir of Lib & AV Srvs & Prof) 550
LAW, Gordon T. (Mgmt & Econ Lib Head) 704
MARKEE, Katherine M. (Assoc Prof of Lib & Sci) 771
MARTINO, Sharon C. (Profsnl Libn) 779
MCKOWEN, Dorothy K. (Serials Catlgr) 812
MOBLEY, Emily R. (Assoc Dir) .. 851
MURDOCK, J L. (Docums Coordntr & Ref Libn) 879
NEVILLE, Ellen P. (Catlgr) 898
NIXON, Judith M. (Asst Prof) ... 906
OGLES, Lynn C. (Profsnl Libn) .. 918
PASK, Judith M. (Ref Libn & Assoc Prof of Lib Sci) 946
POLIT, Carlos E. (Foreign Langs Biblgphr & Ref Libn) 980
STEPHENS, Gretchen (Libn & Assoc Prof of Lib Sci) 1188
TUCKER, John M. (Sr Ref Libn) 1261
YOUNGEN, Gregory K. (Asst Engrng Libn) 1383

Purvin & Gertz Inc (TX)

KERWIN, Camillus A. (Info Systs Mgr) 644

Putnam County District Lib (OH)

JONES, Robert M. (Dir) 614

Putnam County Pub Lib (IL)

PITCHFORD, Martha K. (Lib Dir) 976

Putnam County Pub Lib (IN)
Putnam Hayes & Bartlett Inc (MA)

SEDLACK, Ellen M. (Dir) 1111
HONESS, Mary E. (Info Spclst & Technl Srvs) 555

Putnam-Northern Westchester BOCES (NY)

MORRISON, George J. (Coordntr of Eductnl Comms) . 868

Puyallup Sch District (WA)

BAZE, Mary P. (Jr High Sch Libn) 68

PWS-KENT Publishing Co (MA)

BARCOMB, Wayne A. (Pres) 55

Q

Quaker Chemical Corp (PA)
Quaker Oats Co (IL)
Quality Books Inc (IL)
Quantum Computer Service Inc (VA)
Quarles & Brady (WI)
Quebec Safety League (PQ)
Quebec Secretary of State (PQ)
Quebec Univs (PQ)
Queen Elizabeth Hospital (PE)
Queen of Holy Rosary Coll (CA)
Queen of Peace Church (NJ)
Queens Borough Pub Lib (NY)

Queens Coll of the City Univ of New York (NY)

MORROW, Ellen B. (Info Resrcs Ctr Mgr) 869
ROBSON, Amy K. (Info Srvs Libn) 1045
LEISNER, Anthony B. (Vice Pres) 714
CASE, Stephen M. (Mktg VP) ... 192
JANKOWSKI, Susan H. (Libn) .. 593
BISSON, Jacques (Documtn Technician) 100
MONDOU, Cecile (Libn) 854
DUPUIS, Onil (Resrch Ofcr) ... 327
KIELLY, Marion J. (Libn) 647
VANDERBECK, Maria (Head Libn) 1273
CASEY, Mary A. (Libn) 192
ALVAREZ, Ronald (Libn) 19
BENZ, Lieselotte (Branch Lib Mgr) 84
BORRESS, Lewis R. (Asst Head of Catlgng) 117
BREEN, Karen B. (Chlds Srvs Consul) 131
COOKE, Constance B. (Dir) 241
DICKERSON, D J. (Regnl Mgr) .. 300
FONTAINE, Sue (Pub Relations Dir) 388
HARWOOD, Vern (Persnl Dir) ... 510
HSU, Elizabeth L. (Info & Referral Mgr) 567
KRAMER, Mollie W. (Sr Libn) ... 675
KUGLER, Sharon (Ref Libn) 682
LIU, Carol F. (Centl Lib Asst Mgr) 734
MCMORRAN, Charles E. (Automated Systs Div Mgr) ... 815
RIECHEL, Rosemarie (Head, Info & Telephone Ref Div) .. 1033
RUBINSTEIN, Roslyn (Yng Adult Div Head) 1065
SHAPIRO, Martin P. (Libn) 1121
SIAHPOOSH, Farideh T. (Asst Branch Lib Mgr) 1134
SIMON, Anna E. (Principal Libn) 1140
SIVULICH, Kenneth G. (Deputy Dir) 1145
SPENSLEY, Malcolm C. (Info & Ref Div Asst Head) 1173
TANG, Grace L. (Branch Lib Mgr) 1222
VENER, Lucille (Ref Libn) 1282
WASSERMAN, Ricki F. (Asst Head of Adult Lrng Ctr) 1308

COHEN, David (Adjunct Prof of Lib Sci) 228
COHEN, Jackson B. (Head of Sci Lib & Assoc Prof) 228
COLBY, Robert A. (Prof Emeritus) 230
COOPER, Marianne (Asst Prof) .. 243
HARTMAN, Anne M. (Perdcls, Microforms, Docum Coordntr) . 508
HYMAN, Richard J. (Prof Emeritus) 580
KOSTER, Gregory E. (Law Lib Dir) 673
MACOMBER, Nancy (Ref & Docums Libn) 758
NORDSTROM, Virginia (Head of Educ Lib) 908
OHLE, William P. (Microform Asst) 919
PENCHANSKY, Mimi B. (Head of Gen Ref & Online Srch Srv) 956
REMUSAT, Suzanne L. (Interlib Loan & Circ Libn) 1023

Queens Coll of the City Univ of New York (NY)

RONNERMANN, Gail (Sci Ref & Bibl) 1053
RORICK, William C. (Music Ref Libn) 1054
SCOTT, Bettie H. (Assoc Dir) . . 1106
SURPRENANT, Thomas T. (Grad Sch of Lib & Info Std Dir) 1210
THOMAS, Lucille C. (Adjunct Prof) 1237
WALL, Richard L. (Ref Div Asst Prof) 1297

Queens Lib (NY)

AXLER, Judith A. (Chlds Libn) . . 42
LOUISDHON-WALTER, Marie L. (Chlds Libn) 742

Queen's Univ (ON)

MACDERMAID, Anne (Univ Archvst) 754
MCBURNEY, Margot B. (Chief Libn) 792
MOON, Jeffrey D. (Docums Libn) 857
SKEITH, Mary E. (Assoc Libn) . 1145

Queen's Univ (NIR)

LINTON, William D. (Libn) 731

Queensborough Coll, City Univ of NY (NY)

DAVILA, Daniel (Prof & Chief Libn) 277

Queensborough Coll of CUNY (NY)

NOVIK, Sandra P. (Instrcl Resrcs Dir) 911

Queensborough Pub Lib (NY)

BISSESSAR, Carmen T. (Chlds Libn) 100

Queensland Dept of Educ (AUS)

GOODELL, Paulette M. (Libn) . . . 448

Queensland Institute of Technology (AUS)

COCHRANE, Thomas G. (Chief Libn) 226
GOODELL, John S. (Lectr) 448

Quest Advisory Corp (NY)

GAYNOR, Joann T. (Libn) 424

Quest Information Services (NY)

FARAONE, Maria B. (Dir & Owner) 363

Quest Research Corp (VA)

SCHAEFER, Mary E. (Technl Edit) 1089

Quigley High Sch (PA)

JABLONOWSKI, Mary D. (Libn) . 586

Quigley Preparatory Seminary North (IL)

NORTON, Margaret W. (Libn) . . . 910

Quill & Quire (ON)

DOWDING, Martin R. (Lib News Edit) 315

Quillen-Dishner College of Medicine (TN)

MCLEAN, Martha L. (Media Libn) 814

Quincy Coll (IL)

KINGERY, Victor P. (Lib Dir) 652
WEE, Lily K. (Asst Libn) 1315

Quincy Junior Coll (MA)

NIELSEN, Sonja M. (Lib Dir) . . . 903

Quincy Pub Lib (IL)

CONROY, Margaret M. (Head of Catlg Srvs) 238
DECKER, Judy J. (Bookmobile Srvs Head) 286
MCKIERNAN, Lester I. (Administrv Libn) 811

Quinnipiac Coll (CT)

LANG, Norma F. (Instrcl Resrcs Ctr Dir) 695

Quinn's Records Management Service (MD)

QUINN, Sidney (Pres) 1000

Quinsigamond Community Coll (MA)

SHIH, Jenny (Coordntr) 1130

Quotron Systems Inc (CA)

GRANT, George K. (Dir of Plng) . 458

QVC Network (PA)

RUTKOWSKI, Hollace A. (Dir) . 1070

R

R J Reynolds Tobacco Co (NC)

CHUNG, Helen S. (Sr Resrch & Devlpmnt Lit Scitst) 213
MILLER, Barry K. (Mktg Devlpmnt Intelligence Ctr Mgr) 836
RALPH, Randy D. (Sr Resrch & Devlpmnt Lit Scitst) 1004

R M B Productions (IN)

BEATTY, R M. (Executive Dir) . . . 70

R R Bowker Co (NY)

AVALLONE, Susan (Lib Jnl Managing Edit) 41
BROOKS, Martin (Exec Edit) . . . 140
BUCENEC, Nancy L. (Production Edit) 153
CHEATHAM, Bertha M. (Managing Edit) 204
DECANDIDO, Graceanne A. (Asst Editor) 285
DE MAIO, M C. (Sr Legal Editor) 291
DIETLE, Craig I. (Technl Devlpmnt Mgr) 302
FERRARO, Tony (VP, Electronic Publshg) 373
HAVENS, Shirley E. (Contribtng Editor) 513
KOLTAY, Emery I. (Dir) 670
MACFARLAND, Scott D. (Dir, Serials & Media Publshg Group) 755
MEYER, Andrew W. (Sr Vice Pres, Finance & Operations) . . 829
NYREN, Karl (Editor, Lib Hotline) 913
PETERS, Jean R. (Info Resrcs Mgr) 962
REDEL, Judy A. (Directories Managing Edit) 1014
SADER, Marion (Exec Editor) . . 1073
SIMON, Peter E. (Vice Pres) . . . 1140
SPIER, Margaret M. (Executive Edit) 1174
TOPEL, Iris N. (Editing Supvsr) . 1251
WILBUR, Helen L. (CD-ROM Sales Mgr) 1338
YUSTER, Leigh C. (Exec Edit) . . 1385

R R Donnelley (IL)
R R Donnelly & Sons Co (IL)

MILLER, Thomas R. (Bus Mgr) . . 843
HAMILTON, Dawn J. (Bus Info Spclst) 492

R W Beck & Associates (WA)
R W Smith--Bookseller (CT)

SLIVKA, Enid M. (Libn) 1149
SMITH, Raymond W. (Bookseller) 1159

R Walton and Associates (TX)

TAYLOR, Nancy L. (Automation Consult) 1228

R&D Associates (CA)
Rabbit Press Ltd (ENG)
Racine Pub Lib (WI)

KATZ, Janet R. (Sr Asst Libn) . . . 630
GREEN, Jeffrey P. (Publshr) . . . 462
PATANE, John R. (Head of Extension Srvs Dept) 946
SCHINK, Sandra C. (Sr Profsnl Substitute) 1093

Radcliffe Coll (MA)

ENGELHART, Anne D. (Asst Cur of Mss) 349
KING, Patricia M. (Lib Dir) 652
MOSELEY, Eva S. (Manuscripts Cur) 870

Radford Univ (VA)

BRAINARD, Blair (Instrc & Ref Libn) 127
GIBSON, Robert S. (Lib Sci Prog Coordntr) 432
TURNER, Robert L. (Pub Srvs Asst Lib Dir) 1265
WILLIAMS, Greta A. (Periodicals Libn) 1343

Radian Corp (CA)

SCHEIBEL, Susan (Libn) 1091

Radiation Effects Research Foundation (JAP)

YORIOKA, Jimmie Y. (Libn) . . . 1380

Radio Free Europe/Radio Liberty Inc (NY)

DUTIKOW, Irene V. (Head Libn) . 329

Radio Station WQXR (NY)

JELLINEK, George (Broadcaster & Music Critic) 596

RAFAEL (ISR)

BLOCH, Uri (Chief Engineer for Info & Documtn) 105

Rahway Pub Lib (NJ)

SUDALL, Arthur D. (Dir) 1206

Rainier National Bank (WA)

BURKE, Vivienne C. (AVP & Mgr) 160

Ralston Purina Co (MO)
Ramapo Catskill Lib System (NY)

SUTTER, Mary A. (Libn) 1211
ANGLIN, Richard V. (Adult Srvs & Outreach Coordntr) 28
NELSON, James B. (Dir) 894

Ramapo Coll of New Jersey (NJ) — HEISE, George F. (Ref & Syst Analyst Libn) 522
YUEH, Norma N. (Prof & Dir of Lib Srvs) 1384

Ramapo Indian Hills Board of Education (NJ) — GOLLA, Viola K. (Eductnl Media Spclst) 447

Rampart Regional Lib District (CO) — LEITNER, Lavonne (Dir) 714

Ramsey County Pub Lib (MN) — CLARKE, Charlotte C. (Libn II) .. 218
GADE, Rachel P. (Ref Libn II) ... 411
JONES, Mary A. (Libn) 614
MICHEL, William D. (Coordntr, Branch Ref Srvs) 832
VINNES, Norman M. (Lib Dir) .. 1285

Ramsey Free Pub Lib (NJ) — SCARPELLINO, Rebecca A. (Young People's Libn) 1088

Rancho Santiago College (CA) — HOFFMAN, Herbert H. (Libn) ... 548

Rand Corp (CA) — BROPHY, Mary J. (Assoc Lib Dir) 141
GILL, Elizabeth D. 435
HELFER, Doris S. (Technl Srvs Head) 523
JOHNSON, Mary E. (Catlg Libn) . 607
SHANMAN, Roberta (Head Ref Srvs) 1120

Rand McNally & Co (IL) — GROSSMAN, David G. (Bus Devlpmnt Mgr) 473

Randolph & Co (CA) — RANDOLPH, Kevin H. (Pres) ... 1007

Randolph County Pub Schs (NC) — CHANDRA, Jane H. (Media Coordntr) 200
CLARK, Patty C. (Media Coordntr) 217
FREEMAN, Evangeline M. (High Sch Media Coordntr) 400
SPENCER, Sue R. (Instrcl Media Dir) 1173

Randolph-Macon Coll (VA) — BEDSOLE, Dan T. (Lib Dir) 73

Randolph-Macon Woman's Coll (VA) — DEMARS, Patricia (AV Libn) 291
JOHNSON, Jan (Col Devlpmnt Libn) 605

Randolph Pub Lib (NC) — BRENNER, Nancy F. (Dir) 133

Randolph Technical Coll (NC) — SMITH, Merrill F. (Dean of Lrng Resrcs Ctr) 1158

Random Corp (OH) — GROSVENOR, Philip G. 473

Rapides Parish Lib (LA) — LEBLANC, Donna P. (Branch Mgr) 708

Rappahannock Community Coll (VA) — ROGERS, Dean C. (Coll Libn) 1049

The Ratcliff Architects (CA) — HUNT, Judy L. (Libn) 575

Rauthem Co (RI) — BALDWIN, Mark F. (Technl Info Ctr Mgr) 52

Ravenna City Schs (OH) — WISE, Martha K. (Libn) 1357

Ravenstree Corp (AZ) — STUART, Gerard W. (Pres) ... 1204

Rawle & Henderson (PA) — HARVAN, Christine C. (Libn) ... 509

Raychem Corp (CA) — HOFFKNECHT, Carmen L. (Photography Suprvsr & Libn) 547

Raymond M Holt & Associates (CA) — HOLT, Raymond M. (Lib Consult) 554

Raytheon Co (MA) — MAXANT, Vicary (Head Libn) ... 787
O'CONNOR, Jerry (Bus Info Ctr Mgr) 916
PORTSCH-SNOW, Joanne (Technl Info Ctr Mgr) 985
REILLY, Dayle A. (Sr Libn) 1020

RCA Corp (MA) — HSU, Veronica 567

RCA Corp (NJ) — ARROWOOD, Nina R. (Lib Resrcs Mgr) 35
KAN, Halina S. (Libn) 624

RCA Corp (PQ) — WALKER, Elizabeth A. (Libn & Documtn Clerk) 1295

RDA/LOGICON (CA) — ANDERSON, Christine (Classified Docum Control Suprvsr) 22

RDC Associates (MA) — LAROSA, Sharon M. (Mktg & Info Consult) 698

READ Ltd (IL) — HILDRETH, Charles R. (Chief Consltng Sci) 539

Reader's Digest Magazines Ltd (NY) — FRASENE, Joanne R. (Head Libn) 399
MANNING, Jo A. (Libn) 766
VELARDI, Adrienne B. (Index Editor) 1281

Reader's Digest Magazines Ltd (PQ) — NISHIZAKI, Colette (Libn) 905

Readex Inc (VT) — BOCK, Thomas A. (Vice Pres) ... 109

Readex Microprint Corp (CT) — JONES, Daniel S. (Pres) 612

Readex Microprint Corp (OK) — LARSEN, Nancy E. (Managing Edit Landmarks of Sci) 698

Reading Alloys Inc (PA) — SCHLOTT, Florenceann (Libn) . 1094

Reading Pub Lib (MA) — FLANNERY, Susan M. (Dir) 383
FLANNERY, Susan M. (Dir) 384

Reading Pub Lib (PA) — COURTNEY, June M. (Asst Ref & Govt Docums Libn) 251
WEIHERER, Patricia D. (Ref Libn) 1317
YU, Lorraine L. (AV Libn) 1384

Readmore Publications (NY) — NASON, Stanley J. (Vice Pres of Mktg & Sales) 888
TONKERY, Thomas D. (Chief Executive Ofcr) 1250

Real Decisions Corp (CT) — COOKE, E P. (VP) 241

Real Estate Data Inc (FL) — JENKINS, George A. (Dir Electronic Publshg) 597

Reavis & McGrath (NY) — LASTRES, Steven A. (Head Libn) 701

Reboul MacMurray Hewitt Maynar & Kristol (NY) — MEHL, Cathy A. (Head Libn) 821

Record Collections Inc (MD) — LAZZARONI, Philip S. (Pres) ... 706

Record Collector's Monthly (NJ) — MENNIE, Don (Self-employed Edit) 824

Record Data Inc TRW (OH) — FELDER, Bruce B. (Pres & Co-Chief Exec Ofcr) 369

Record Lists (CA) — CHANDLER, Thomas V. (Owner) 200

Record-Rama Sound Archives (PA) — MAWHINNEY, Paul C. (Cur & Owner) 787

Recording for the Blind Inc (NJ) — KELLY, John P. (Mgr of Lib Srvs) 638

Records Revisited (NY) — SAVADA, Morton J. (Operator & Owner) 1085

Red Deer Coll (AB) — ARMSTRONG, Mary L. (Ref Libn) 32
BOULTBEE, Paul G. (Technl Srvs Libn) 119
BUCKLEY, Joanna 154

Red Deer Regional Hospital Centre (AB) — KAVANAGH, Elizabeth G. (Libn) . 631

Red River Community Coll (MB) — FOWLER, Margaret A. (Coordntr & Lib Tech) 394
PORTER, Patricia K. (Lib Srvs Dir) 985

Redding Museum & Art Center (CA) — BARNARD, Sandra K. (Docent Musm Libn) 57

Reddy Communications Inc (NM) — KLOS, Ann M. 662

Redeemer Coll (ON) — SAVAGE, Daniel A. (Chief Libn) 1085

Reditec (CSR) — MIRABELLI, Gerardo (Executive Dir) 847

Redstone Arsenal (AL) — FOREMAN, Anne P. 390

Redstone Scientific Informaton Center (AL) — KITCHENS, Philips H. (Govt Docum Ref Libn) 657

Redwood City Pub Lib (CA) — BANGE, Stephanie D. (Chlds Srvs Libn) 54
HIMMEL, Ned A. (Adlut Srvs Suprvsr) 542
LIGHT, Jane E. (Lib Dir) 726

Reed & Carnrick Pharmaceuticals (NJ) — DUTKA, Jeanne L. (Resrch Libn) 329

Reed Coll (OR) — SAYRE, Samuel R. (Ref/Interlib Loan Libn) 1087

Reed Inc (ON) — DRAKE, James B. 318

Reed Publishing USA (MA) — URBACH, Peter F. (Electronic Publshg Vice Pres) 1269

Reed Smith Shaw & McClay (PA) — MINES, Denise C. (Libn) 846
STEWART, Barbara R. (Head Libn) 1192

Reference Service Press (CA) — SCHLACHTER, Gail A. (Pres) . 1093

Reference Technology Inc (CA) ALCOCK, Anthony J. (Sales
                                    Dir) 11
Reference Technology Inc (CO) BARR, Arlene E. (Sales
                                    Communication Adminstr) 58
                                 BEFELER, Mike (Vice Pres,
                                    Strategic Mktg) 74
                                 MAIERHOFER, Ronald P. (Mktg
                                    & Sales VP) 761
                                 SMITH, Stephen S. (Pres &
                                    Chief Exec Ofcr) 1161
Reference Technology Inc (TX) RUBIN, Lenard H. (Vice Pres of
                                    Commercial Sales) 1064
Reflectone Inc (FL)   KING, Elizabeth (Engrng Libn) . . . 650
Reformed Presbyterian Theological
  Sem (PA)   GEORGE, Rachel (Libn) 428
Reformed Theological Seminary (MS) REID, Thomas G. (Lib Dir) 1019
Regie Intermunicipale des
  Bibliotheques (PQ)   BROSSEAU, Lise (Animation &
                                    Reference Lib) 141
Regina High Sch (MD)   BEAULIEU, Yvette E. (Libn) 70
Regina Pub Lib (SK)   DIRKSEN, Jean (Head of Adult
                                    Srvs) 305
                                 FIELDEN, Janet (Automated
                                    Srvs Coordntr) 376
                                 GAGNON, Andre (Head, Chlds
                                    Srvs Dept) 412
                                 GRAYBIEL, Luisa (Adult Prog
                                    Coordntr) 460
                                 JENSEN, Ken (Asst Chief Libn) . . 599
                                 VANDER LAAN, Lubbert (Ref
                                    Libn) 1274
Region Five Lib Cooperative (NJ) HIEBING, Dottie (Dir) 537
Region One Cooperating Lib Service
  Unit (CT)   FLANAGAN, Leo N. (Regnl
                                    Coordntr) 383
                                 LOW, Jocelyn L. (Prog Srvs
                                    Supvsr) 743
Regional Medical Lib Program (TX) LEE, Regina H. (Assoc Dir) 711
Regional Sch District 10 (CT) REILLY, Maureen E. (Libn) 1020
Regis Coll (MA)   KEENAN, Elizabeth L. (Lib Dir) . . 634
Regis High Sch (IA)   DAVIS, Deanna S. (Instrcl
                                    Media Ctr Dir) 278
Regis High Sch (WI)   NASSET, M J. (Libn) 889
Registered Nurses Association of
  BC (BC)   AUFIERO, Joan I. (Head Libn) . . . 39
Registered Nurses Association of
  Ontario (ON)   BOITE, Mary E. (Libn) 111
Rehabilitation Institute of
  Chicago (IL)   KALUZSA, Karen L. (Lrng
                                    Resrcs Ctr Coordntr) 623
                                 ZOROWITZ, Richard D.
                                    (Resident Physician) 1390
Reilly Tar & Chemical Corp (IN) GALOW, Donald G. (Chemical
                                    Resrch Libn) 415
Reinhart Boerner Van Deuren et
  al (WI)   BANNEN, Carol A. (Head Libn) . . 54
Reliance Grove Holdings (NY)   RUBIN, Ellen R. (Info Spclst) . . 1064
Religions of Jesus and Mary (MD) RHEAUME, Irene M. (Archvst) . 1025
Religious Sisters of Mercy (LA) MULDREY, Mary H. (Archvst,
                                    Libn, & Histn) 876
REMAC Info Corp (VA)   ALEXANDER, Carol G. (Project
                                    Mgr) 12
Reno Gazette-Journal (NV)   SPINA, Nan H. (Newspaper
                                    Libn) 1175
Rensselaer Polytechnic Institute (NY) KENNICK, Sylvia B. (Proj
                                    Archvst) 642
                                 LOCKETT, Barbara A. (Libs Dir) . 736
                                 MOLHOLT, Pat (Assoc Dir of
                                    Libs) 852
Research Libs Group Inc (CA)   ALIPRAND, Joan M. (Lib Systs
                                    Analyst) 13
                                 BALES, F K. (Syst Analysis &
                                    Design Mgr) 52
                                 CRAWFORD, Walt (Principal
                                    Analyst for Spcl Projects) 257
                                 GLAZIER, Ed (Biblgph Quality
                                    Assurance Spclst) 440
                                 JURIST, Susan (Asst to the Dir
                                    of RLIN) 620
                                 SCHMIDT, C J. (Vice Pres) . . . 1095

Research Libs Group Inc (CA)
                                 STOVEL, Madeleine D. (Lib
                                    Systs Analyst) 1199
Research Publications (CT)   BOGENSCHNEIDER, Duane R.
                                    (Editrl & Devlpmnt VP) 110
                                 DEL CERVO, Diane M.
                                    (Executive Edit) 289
                                 GREENWAY, Helen B. (VP of
                                    Mktg) 465
                                 KRAMER, Sheldon I. (Chairman
                                    & Chief Exec Ofcr) 675
Research Publications (IL)   DICK, John H. (VP & Publshr) . . 300
Research Publications (VA)   MEREK, Charles J. (Vice Pres) . . 825
Researcher's Data Bank (MO)   MARCHANT, Thomas O. (Pres) . 768
Residence
  Notre-Dame-de-la-Trinite (PQ) GAULIN, S D. (Chief Libn) 422
The Resource Center (MD)   MENNELLA, Dona M. (Dir) 824
Resource Planning Inc (MD)   PAUL, Rameshwar N. (Pres) . . . 949
ResourceNets
  Telecommunications (MA)   MAZUR, Ronald M. (Owner &
                                    Pres) 791
Resources Inc (VA)   MURPHY, Robert D. (Dir of
                                    Legal Info Srvs) 881
Response Analysis Corp (NJ)   FRIHART, Anne R. (Libn) 404
Reston Regional Lib (VA)   SINWELL, Carol A. (Asst
                                    Branch Mgr) 1144
Resurrection High Sch (IL)   LOCKWOOD, Sally S. (Libn &
                                    AV Coordntr) 736
Resurrection Hospital (IL)   WIMMER, Laura M. (Lib Srvs
                                    Dir) 1354
Reteaco Inc (ON)   LESLIE, Nathan (VP of Sales &
                                    Mktg) 718
                                 LOWRY, Douglas B. (Chief
                                    Scitst) 745
                                 LOWRY, John D. (Pres & Chief
                                    Exec Ofcr) 745
Reuben Hoar Pub Lib (MA)   DUNN, Jocelyn A. (Asst Libn) . . . 327
Revenue Canada Customs &
  Excise (ON)   PARSONAGE, Dianne L.
                                    (Departmental Libn) 944
Revenue Canada Taxation (PQ)   ROY, Christine (Libn) 1063
Revere Pub Lib (MA)   DYGERT, Michael H. (Dir) 331
Revlon Resrch Ctr (NJ)   TANEN, Lee J. (Lib & Info Srvs
                                    Mgr) 1222
Rex Hospital (NC)   MCCALLUM, Dorothy T. (Libn) . . 793
Reynaldo G Garga Sch of Law (TX) CORBIN, John (Dir of Lib & Prof
                                    of Law) 245
Reynold Electrical & Engineering Co
  Inc (NV)   ORTIZ, Cynthia (Technl Libn II) . . 927
Reynolda Manor Branch Lib (NC) THOMPSON, Barbara F. (Head) 1239
Reynolds & Reynolds Interactive (OH) POWELL, Lane P. (Mktg
                                    Consult) 988
Reynolds Metals Co (TX)   PHEGAN, Dolores M. (Technl
                                    Info Spclst) 967
Reynolds Metals Co (VA)   GREGORY, Carla L. (Adminstr,
                                    Info & Copier Srvs) 466
Reynoldsburg City Schs (OH)   MEESE, Jane E. (Sch Lib Media
                                    Spclst) 821
RHC-Spacemaster (IL)   TRELEASE, Robert J. (Sales
                                    Mgr) 1255
Rhode Island & Providence
  Plantations (RI)   WAGNER, Albin (Pub Records
                                    Adminstr) 1291
Rhode Island Coll (RI)   BRENNAN, Patricia B. (Asst
                                    Prof & Ref Libn) 133
                                 HRYCIW-WING, Carol A. (Head
                                    of Technl Srvs) 566
                                 OLSEN, Richard A. (Dir) 921
                                 SIBULKIN, Lucille (Asst Prof,
                                    Technl Srvs) 1135
Rhode Island Department of State
  Lib Srv (RI)   DANIELS, Bruce E. (Actg Dir) . . . 273
                                 SHEA, Margaret (Supvsr of
                                    Adult Srvs) 1124
                                 WILSON, Barbara L. (Chief) . . . 1350
Rhode Island Historical Society (RI) LAMAR, Christine L. (Ref Head) . 689
Rhode Island Hospital (RI)   LATHROP, Irene M. (Dir of Lib
                                    Srvs) 701

Rhode Island Sch of Design (RI) — AVERILL, Laurie J. (Readers Srvs Libn) 41
BRAUNSTEIN, Mark M. (Head of Slide & Photograph Col) . . . 130
TERRY, Carol S. (Dir of Lib Srvs) 1232

Rhode Island State Archives (RI) — SILVA, Phyllis C. (State Archvst) 1138

Rhode Island State Lib (RI) — PERRY, Beth I. (State Libn) 960
Rhode Island Supreme Court (RI) — SVENGALIS, Kendall F. (State Law Libn) 1212

Rhodes Coll (TN) — BLAIR, Lynne M. (Dir) 102
SHORT, William M. (Head, Info Srvs) 1132

Rhone-Poulenc Ag Co (NC) — LAVOY, Constance J. (Lib Srvs Supvsr) 704

Rice Lake Area Sch District (WI) — HOLLE, Arthur J. (Libn) 551
REINAGLE, Carol M. (Elem Media Spclst) 1021

Rice Memorial Hospital (MN) — CONRADI, Carol A. (Libn) 238
Rice Univ (TX) — BABER, Elizabeth A. (Principal Catlgr & Authorities Libn) 43
BAGHAL-KAR, Vali E. (Interlib Loan Dir) 45
BOOTHE, Nancy L. (Spcl Cols Dir) 116
CARRINGTON, Samuel M. (Univ Libn & Prof of French) . . 186
CRIST, Lynda L. (Papers of Jefferson Davis Edit) 259
FORD, Margaret C. (Spcl Projects Libn) 389
GOURLAY, Una M. (Comunty Srvs Dir) 454
HOLIBAUGH, Ralph W. (Assoc Univ Libn) 550
HUNTER, John H. (Libn) 576
HYMAN, Ferne B. (Asst Univ Libn for Col Mgmt) 580
KECK, Kerry A. (Asst Libn) 633
SCHWARTZ, Charles A. (Soc Sciences Libn) 1104
SUDENGA, Sara A. (Ref, Col Devlpmnt Libn) 1206

Ricerca Inc (OH) — BRANCHICK, Susan E. (Supvsr Corprt Lib Chem Info Syst) . . . 127
DUANE, Carol A. (Mgr, Info Srvs) 321

Rich Inc (IL) — MURPHY, Therese B. (Market Resrch Analyst) 881

Rich May Bilodeau & Flaherty (MA) — SWANN, Thomas E. (Legal Libn) 1213

Richard Bland Coll (VA) — HUETER, Eike (Lib Dir) 570
Richard Cady-Rare Books (IL) — CADY, Richard H. (Owner) 170
Richard de Boo Publishers (ON) — HALPIN, Gerard B. (Pres) 490
Richard E Wolf and Associates (VA) — WOLF, Richard E. (Gen Mgr) . . 1360
Richard Macnutt Ltd (ENG) — MACNUTT, Richard P. (Chairman) 758

Richards Lauton & Finger (DE) — WINSTEAD, Jean D. (Law Libn) 1356
Richards O'Neil & Allegaert (NY) — HODGES, Phyllis (Asst Libn) 546
Richards Piano Service (TX) — RICHARDS, James H. (Owner) . . 1028
Richards Watson & Gershon (CA) — BIRNIE, Elizabeth B. (Law Libn) . . 98
Richardson Independent Sch District (TX) — BELL, Jo A. (Lib Srvs Dir) 77
GRAY, Gloria M. (Libn) 460
SILVERMAN, Susanne J. (Libn) . . 1139
WEISS, Barbara M. (Principal Info Scitst) 1319

Richardson-Vicks Inc (CT) — CLEMENTS, Cynthia L. (Col Devlpmnt/Acqs Libn) 221
JESER-SKAGGS, Sharlee A. (Lib Instr & Ref Libn) 600

Richland Coll (TX) — BERGER, Sidney E. (Prof of Eng & Comms) 86

Richland Community Coll (IL) —

Richland County Pub Lib (SC) — FRIEDMAN, Amy G. (Newspaper Indxr) 403
KAHN, Gerda M. (Extension Srvs Chief) 622
RAWLINSON, Helen A. (Deputy Dir) 1011

Richland County Pub Lib (SC) — WARREN, Charles D. (Dir) 1306

Richland County Sch District One (SC) — NORRIS, Gale K. (Sch Libn) 909
Richland Northeast High Sch (SC) — KING, Evlyn J. (Lib Media Spclst) 651

Richland Pub Lib (WA) — FOLEY, Katherine E. (Lib Supvsr) 387

Richland Sch District 1 (SC) — BASS, Carolyn M. (Media Spclst) 63

Richland Sch District 400 (WA) — CARRIGAN, Marietta R. (Head Libn) 186

Richmond County Board of Education (GA) — WILLIAMS, Anita (Libn & Media Spclst) 1342

Richmond Hill Pub Lib (ON) — ABRAM, Persis R. (Catlgr) 3
LLOYD, Mary E. (Canadiana & Local Hist Sect Head) 735

Richmond Pub Lib (CA) — HOLTZMAN, Douglas A. (Ref Libn) 555

Richmond Pub Lib (VA) — DECAMPS, Alice L. (Bus, Sci & Tech Dept Head) 285

Richmond Pub Lib (BC) — KELNER, Gregory H. (Adult Srvs Libn) 638
WILLISON, Maureen I. (Adult Srvs Coordntr) 1348

Richmond Pub Schs (VA) — BAGAN, Beverly S. (Adminstr of Lib Media Srvs) 45
PRETLOW, Delores Z. (Media Srvs Supvsr) 992

Richmond R-XVI Sch District (MO) — WALKER, Patricia A. (Media Spclst) 1296

Richmond Unified Sch District (CA) — RYUS, Phyllis K. (Libn) 1072
Richter Productions (NY) — RICHTER, Robert (Independent Documentary Producer) 1031

Richton Park Pub Lib District (IL) — NEVINS, Patrick F. (Head Libn) . . 898
Rick Richmond Information Systems (CO) — RICHMOND, Rick (Consult) . . . 1030
Riddell Williams Bullitt & Walkinshaw (WA) — ZIKE, Ruth D. (Law Libn) 1388
Rider Coll (NJ) — MONTAVON, Victoria A. (Assoc Dir) 855
STEPHEN, Ross G. (Dir of Lib Srvs) 1187
TILLMAN, Hope N. (Coordntr of Info Srvs) 1245

Ridge High Sch (NJ) — MCNALLY, Mary J. (Media Spclst) 815

Ridgefield Board of Education (CT) — SULLI, Gerard C. (Sch Media Spclst Libn) 1207

Ridgefield Park Pub Lib (NJ) — ROSENTHAL, Phyllis T. (Lib Dir) 1057
SCHACHER, Betty C. (Dir) 1088

Ridgewood New Jersey Board of Education (NJ) — LATHAM, Candace (Libn & Media Spclst) 701
ROSS, Robert D. (Lib Dir) 1058

Ridgewood Pub Lib (NJ) — SAUNDERS, Vinette A. (Sr Documtn Libn) 1085
Riggs National Bank (DC) —

Riker Danzig Scherer Hyland & Perretti (NJ) — BRUNNER, Karen B. (Libn) 151
Riley Stoker Corp (MA) — MILLIGAN, Jane M. (Info Spclst) 843

Ringgold Management Systems Inc (OR) — SHOFFNER, Ralph M. (Pres) . . 1132
Ripon Coll (WI) — BURR, Charlotte A. (Assoc Libn, Readers Srvs) 163
MCGOWAN, Sarah M. (Lib Dir) . 807

Rittenhouse Book Distributors (PA) — PUALWAN, Emily (Lib Mktg Mgr) 996

River Bend Lib System (IL) — MCKAY, Robert W. (Lib Dir) 810
River East Sch Division 9 (MB) — GUILBERT, N P. (Matrl Resrcs Dir) 476

Riverhead Free Lib (NY) — RICHTER, Kathleen A. (Asst Dir & AV Srvs Head) 1031

Riverside City & County Pub Lib (CA) — JOHNSON, Thomas L. (Technl Srvs Head) 609
SWAFFORD, William M. (Libn I) 1212
WOOD, Linda M. (Dir) 1364

Riverside Community Coll (CA) PROSSER, Michael J. (Lrng
Resrcs Asst) 995
Riverside County Law Lib (CA) WEBB, Gayle E. (Dir) 1313
Riverside Hospital (OH) MALUCHNIK, Kathryn K. (Libn) . 764
Riverside Osteopathic Hospital (MI) SKOGLUND, Susan E. (Dir of
Lib Srvs) 1147
Riverside Presbyterian Day Sch (FL) PILLANS, Judith H. (Media
Spclst) 973
Riverside Pub Lib (IL) OLDERR, Steven (Dir) 920
Riverside Unified Sch District (CA) NEBEL, Jean C. (District Media
Spclst) 891
RUSSELL, Sandra W. (Libn) . . 1069
Rivkin Radler Dunne & Bayh (NY) CARTAFALSA, Joan C. (Asst
Libn) 188
MONACO, Ralph A. (Law Libn) . . 854
RMG Consultants Inc (CA) WOODS, Lawrence A. (Sr
Consult) 1367
RMG Consultants Inc (IL) IDDINGS, Daniel H. (Consult) . . . 581
MCCLINTOCK, Patrick J.
(Consultant) 797
MCGEE, Rob (Pres) 805
RMS Associates (MD) FOURNIER, Susan K.
(Automated Systs Libn) 393
GENUARDI, Michael T. (Chief
Analyst, Abstctng, Indexing) . . 427
SILVESTER, June P. (Project
Dir & Lexicographer) 1139
RMS Technologies Inc (NJ) SANDERS, Mary C. (Sr Technl
Libn) 1080
RMT Inc (WI) KAYES, Mary J. (Libn,) 632
Roanoke Bible Coll (NC) GRIFFIN, Patricia S. (Libn) 469
Roanoke Catholic Sch (VA) BANE, Madelyn R. (Dir of
Devlpmnt) 54
Roanoke Coll (VA) UMBERGER, Stan (Lib Dir) 1268
Roanoke County Pub Lib (VA) GARRETSON, George D. (Lib
Dir) 420
UMBERGER, Sheila S. (Head of
Catlgng) 1268
Roanoke County Pub Schs (VA) CHAMBERLAIN, M J. (Lib &
Media Spclst) 197
SPRENGER, Suzanne F. (Lib
Media Spclst) 1176
Roanoke Law Lib (VA) CALHOUN, Clayne M. (Law
Libn) 172
Roanoke Memorial Hospitals (VA) GLENN, Lucy D. (Chief Med
Libn) 441
Roanoke Rapids Pub Lib (NC) MITCHELL, Joyce L. (Dir) 849
Roanoke Times & World-News (VA) HARRIS, Belinda J. (Libn) 504
Roath & Brega (CO) NORBIE, Dorothy E. (Law Libn) . . 908
Robbinsdale Independent District
281 (MN) SCHEU, Jean W. (Media Spclst) 1092
Robert H Riley & Assocs (NJ) RILEY, Robert H. (Pres) 1034
Robert Louis Stevenson Sch (CA) ANDRUS, Eloise A. (Head Libn) . . 27
Robert Morris Coll (PA) MILLER, Mary C. (Lib Dir) 840
PIETZAK, Stephen D. (Pub Srvs
Libn) 972
SKOVIRA, Robert J. (Asst Prof) 1147
Robert R Walsh and Associates (NY) WALSH, Robert R. (Lib Plng
Consult) 1300
Robert W Mueller Rare Books (IL) MUELLER, Robert W.
(Proprietor) 875
Robert Wood Johnson
Foundation (NJ) GALLAGHER, Philip J. (Libn) . . . 414
Roberts Wesleyan Coll (NY) KROBER, Alfred C. (Lib Srvs
Dir) 679
Robinson & Cole (CT) MATTHEWSON, David S. (Law
Libn) 786
Robinson Information Service (CA) ROBINSON, Betty J. (Info
Spclst) 1043
Robinson Siverman Pearce
Aronsohn & Berm (NY) HENDERSON, Janice E. (Law
Libn) 526
Robinson Wayne Levin Riccio & La
Sala (NJ) FISHER, Scott L. (Law Libn) 381
Rochester Area Schs (MN) BENSON, Laurel D. (Media Srvs
Coordntr) 83
Rochester City Sch District (NY) STEVENS, Elizabeth B. (Sch Lib
Media Spclst) 1190
Rochester General Hospital (NY) POND, Frederick C. (Sr Circuit
Libn) 982

Rochester Hills Pub Lib (MI) BRAGLIA, Nancy L. (Head,
Chlds Srvs) 127
HAGE, Christine C. (Asst Dir) . . . 482
HOWARTH, Mary K. (Adult
Srvs Libn) 565
SATTERTHWAITE, Diane A.
(Ref Libn) 1084
WILSON, Patricia L. (Lib Dir) . . 1352
Rochester Institute of
Technology (NY) CAREN, Loretta (Head of Ref) . . 181
CHURCH, Virginia K. (Asst Dir
for Technl Srvs) 213
DEGOLYER, Christine C.
(Science Libn) 288
GRAY, Shirley M. (Supvsr,
Media Resrc Ctr) 460
LUNT, Ruth B. (Ref Libn &
Biblgphr) 749
TAYLOR, Gladys M. (Archvst) . 1226
TOTH, Gregory M. (Humanities,
Biblgph Instrc Ref Libn) 1252
Rochester Pub Lib (MN) GODSEY, James M. (Deputy
Dir) 443
Rochester Pub Lib (NY) BARNES, Robert W. (Head of
Reynolds AV Dept) 57
EAMES, Robert W. (Ref Srv
Spclst) 332
HUNT, Suellyn (Persnl & Trng
Consult) 575
KATZ, Jacqueline E. (Libn J) . . . 630
LINDSAY, Jean S. (Libn) 729
MCCLURE, Jean M. (Branch
Dir) 797
PERRY, Rodney B. (Assoc Dir) . . 961
ROSENBERG-NUGENT, Nanci
B. (Adult & Yng Adult Libn) . 1056
SHIPPEY, Susan S. (Libn) 1131
SULOUFF, Patricia T. (Libn) . . . 1208
Rockaway Township Free Pub
Lib (NJ) BOWERS, Alyce J. (Lib Dir) 120
Rockbridge Regional Lib (VA) KRANTZ, Linda L. (Lib Dir) 676
Rockdale County Schs (GA) DURAND, Joyce J. (Media
Coordntr) 328
Rockdale Independent Sch
District (TX) WORTHY, Annie B. (Dir of Lib
Srvs) 1369
Rockefeller Univ (NY) HESS, James W. (Assoc Dir,
Rockefeller Arch Ctr) 534
OAKHILL, Harold W. (Archvst) . . 913
STAPLETON, Darwin H. (Dir) . . 1181
Rockford Board of Education (IL) WINTER, Bernadette G.
(Supvsr, Lib Srvs) 1356
Rockford Memorial Hospital (IL) NATHAN, Phyllis (Lib Srvs
Coordntr) 889
Rockford Pub Lib (IL) LONG, Judith N. (Head & Sr
Libn for Extension Srvs) 739
NORWOOD, Pamela Z. (Ref
Libn) 910
PRESSING, Kirk L. (Mgr of
Adult Srvs) 991
ROSENFELD, Joel C. (Exec Dir) 1056
Rockford Research Inc (MA) MOOERS, Calvin N. (Proprietor) . 857
Rockford Sch District 205 (IL) LINDGREN, Beverly P. (Libn) . . . 729
Rockhurst Coll (MO) HUBBLE, Gerald B. (Dir) 568
Rockhurst High Sch (MO) DEACON, William W. (Libn) 283
Rockingham County Pub Lib (NC) DAVIDSON, Laura B.
(Automation Coordntr) 276
WRIGHT, Linda D. (Outreach
Coordntr) 1372
Rockingham County Pub Schs (NC) PENN, Lea M. (Media Coordntr) . 957
Rockingham County Pub Schs (VA) SOLES, Elizabeth S. (Libn &
Media Dir) 1166
Rockingham County Sch Board (VA) WAMPLER, Dorris M. (Media
Spclst) 1302
Rockingham Pub Lib (VA) FANNON, Elizabeth L. (Asst Ref
Libn) 363
Rockland County BOCES (NY) LEVINSON, Barbara (Sch Lib
Syst Dir) 721
Rockville Centre Pub Lib (NY) FRIEDLAND, Rhoda W. (Lib
Dir) 403

Rockway Township Free Pub Lib (NJ) COHN, Jeanette (Asst Dir) 229
Rockwell Hanford Operations (WA) KING, Betty J. (Analyst, Libn & Resrchr) 650
Rockwell International (CA) CRANFORD, Theodore N. (Coordntr AJO1) 255
HORACEK, Paula B. (Systs Analyst) 558
PAIK, Nan H. (Technl Info Ctr Supvsr) 935
RAINEY, Laura J. (Secy) 1004
Rockwell International (CO) MOOMEY, Margaret M. (Libn) ... 857
Rockwell International (IA) BLISS, David H. (High Frequency Tech Mgr) 105
LEAVITT, Judith A. (Info Ctr Supvsr) 707
Rockwell International (TX) COTTER, Stacy L. (Sr Resrch Libn) 250
Rocky River Board of Education (OH) SLANE, Barbara A. (Libn) 1147
Rocky River Pub lib (OH) GARRISON, Michael G. (Dir) 420
Roddenberry Memorial Lib (GA) DEENEY, Marian A. (Ref Libn) ... 286
Roddey Carpenter & White PA (SC) LUPPINO, Julie B. (Libn) 749
Rodey Dickason Sloan Akin & Robb PA (NM) MORLEY, Sarah K. (Asst Libn) .. 865
Rodman Pub Lib (OH) CLEM, Harriet M. (Dir) 220
HAYS, George W. (Head of Adult Dept) 517
Roger Williams Coll (RI) TRINKAUS, Tanya (Biblgph Ctl Libn) 1256
Rogers & Wells Esq (NY) NICOL, Margaret W. (Asst Libn) . 903
PELLETIER, Daniel J. (Law Libn) 955
Rogers-Hough Memorial Lib (AR) LANGSAM, Christine E. (Chlds Libn) 696
Rogers Memorial Lib (NY) BERKEBILE, Sue A. (Ref Libn) ... 87
Rogers Pub Sch System (AR) COLCLASURE, Marian S. (Tchr) 230
Rogovin & Lenzner PC (DC) NEVIN, Barbara B. (Libn) 898
Rohm & Haas Co (PA) DOTTERRER, Ellen C. 313
HOSTETTER, Sandra F. (Libn) . 562
OWENS, Frederick H. (Mgr Info Srvs) 932
STRONG, Darrell G. (Sr Chemist) 1203
WOOD, Barbara G. (Resrch Lib Mgr) 1363
Rohr Industries Inc (CA) TOMMEY, Richard J. (Sr Technl Libn) 1250
Rolf Jensen & Associates Ltd (IL) KIENE, Andrea L. (Info Spclst) .. 647
Rolf Werner Rosenthal (NY) LEE, Judy A. (Lib Srvs Dir) 710
Rolling Hills Consolidated Lib (MO) HUMEL, Joyce A. (Dir) 573
Rolling Meadows Pub Lib (IL) HEMENWAY, Patti J. (Ref Libn, Adult Srvs) 525
SVENSSON, C G. (Head, Adult Srvs) 1212
Rolling Prairie Lib System (IL) HICKS, Frederick M. (Syst Devlpmnt Ofcr) 537
WUNDERLICH, Nina M. (Conslltng Srvs Dir) 1374
Rollins Burdick Hunter Inc (WI) DETWILER, Eve N. (Adminstrv Asst) 296
Rollins Coll (FL) BLOODWORTH, Velda J. (Ref Libn) 106
GRANT, George C. (Lib Srvs Dir) 458
MCCLELLAN, Edna S. (Head, Catlgng) 796
SEBRIGHT, Terence F. (Technl Srvs Dir) 1110
Rolls-Royce Inc (GA) BELL, Karen L. (Info Mgr) 77
Roman Catholic Sch Board (NF) MARTINEZ, Helen (Tchr & Libn) . 779
Rome City Sch District (NY) BUSH, Dianne (Libn) 165
Romeo District Lib (MI) KRUSE, Marina B. (Dir) 681
Ronald L Henderson Association (MD) HENDERSON, Ronald L. (Pres) . 527
Rooks Pitts & Poust (IL) HENRY, Nancy J. (Head Libn) . 529
Roosevelt Univ (IL) BYRE, Calvin S. (Ref Libn) ... 169
JONES, Adrian (Libs Dir) 610
MORSI, Pamela A. (Libn) 869
Roper Hospital Inc (SC) TRUBEY, Cornelia (Libn) 1258
Ropes & Gray (MA) SHANNON, Jerry B. (Libn) 1120
Ropes Independent Sch District (TX)

Rorer Group Inc (PA) HESLIN, Catherine M. (Info Spclst) 534
Rosary Coll (IL) BLACK, Kenneth L. (Ref Libn, Archvst) 101
DAVIS, Richard A. (Assoc Prof & Asst Dean) 280
FENSKE, Ruth E. (Asst Prof) ... 371
LI, Richard T. (Dean & Prof) 725
NOONAN, Eileen F. (Prof Emerita) 908
TZE-CHUNG, Li (Dean & Prof) . 1267
Rose-Hulman Institute of Technology (IN) ROBSON, John M. (Lib Dir) ... 1045
Rose Medical Center (CO) SIMON, Nancy L. (Med Libn) .. 1140
Rose State Coll (OK) HUST, Carolyn R. (Lib Technl Srvs Coordntr) 578
SAULMON, Sharon A. (Ref, Spcl Projs Libn) 1084
Roseburg Sch District 4 (OR) GAULKE, Mary F. (Resrc & Lib Supvsr) 423
Roselle Free Pub Lib (NJ) OLSON, Evelyn N. (Dir) 922
Roselle Park Veterans Memorial Lib (NJ) BRIANT, Susan (Dir) 134
Rosemont Coll (PA) LYNCH, Mary D. (Lib Srvs Dir) . 752
Rosemount Inc (MN) WELDON, Barbara J. (Libn) ... 1321
Rosemount Sch Dist 196 (MN) SKELLY, Laurie J. (K-12 Media Generalist) 1146
Rosenbach Museum & Lib (PA) FULLER, Elizabeth E. (Manuscript Catlgr) 408
MORRIS, Leslie A. (Hist & Bibl Cur) 867
Rosenberg Lib (TX) HYATT, John D. (Exec Dir) 580
KENAMORE, Jane A. (Spcl Cols Head) 640
SHEPHERD, Antoinette (Head, Extension Srvs Dept) 1127
Rosenman & Colin (NY) LILLY, Elise M. (Asst Libn) 727
Rosenthal & Schanfield (IL) EMRE, Serpil A. (Law Libn) ... 348
Roseville Communtiy Schs (MI) TOLMAN, Bonnie B. (Tchr & Libn) 1249
Roseville Pub Lib (MI) KOLLMORGEN, Rose M. (Lib Dir) 669
Rosholt Pub Schs (WI) ADAMS, Helen R. (High Sch Libn, AV Dir) 5
Ross McDonald Co (CA) MCDONALD, Barbara J. (Owner, Mgr) 802
Rossford Pub Lib (OH) BURKE, Saretta K. (Adult Srvs) .. 160
FRENCH, Michael (Dir) 402
Roswell Independent Sch District (NM) KALER, Dorothy C. (High Sch Media Spclst) 623
Roswell Park Memorial Institute (NY) ABLOVE, Gayle J. (Sr Libn) 2
FRANKE, Gail E. (Sr Libn) 397
HUTCHINSON, Ann P. (Lib Dir) . 579
Rotary International (IL) HUNT, Janis E. (Donations-In-Kind Info Network) 575
Rothchild Consultants (CA) CARSCH, Ruth E. (Info Spclst) .. 187
Round Rock Independent Sch District (TX) SPAULDING, Nancy J. (Dir of Media) 1172
Round Rock Pub Lib (TX) JOHNSTON, L J. (Chlds Libn) . 610
The Rouse Co (MD) SEMKO, Melanie J. (Resrch Libn) 1115
Routt High Sch (IL) MILLER, Stella M. (Libn) 842
Rowan County Board of Education (KY) WHITAKER, Sharon N. (Libn) .. 1329
Rowan County Pub Lib (NC) BARTON, Phillip K. (Lib Dir) ... 62
CARPENTER, Jennifer K. (Ref Libn) 184
LYTLE, Marian M. (Chlds Srvs Libn) 753
Rowan Pub Lib (NC) MOXLEY, Melody A. (Circ Srvs Libn) 874
Roxborough Memorial Hospital (PA) BERNOFF, Barbara D. (Libn) 89
Roy F Weston Inc (DC) DOENGES, John C. (Tech Info Ctr Mgr) 308
Roy F Weston Inc (PA) DINNIMAN, Margo P. (Corprt Info Ctr Dir) 305

Royal Bank of Canada (ON)

DANCE, Barbara L. (Sr Info Spclst) 272

DYSART, Jane I. (Info Resrcs Mgr) 331

GRIMES, Deirdre E. (Technl Info Spclst) 470

KEALEY, Catherine M. (Technl Info Spclst) 632

Royal Bank of Canada (PQ)

O'SHAUGHNESSY, John M. (Technl Syst Spclst) 928

RABCHUK, Gordon K. (Corprt Archvst) 1001

Royal Canadian Mounted Police (ON) WALDRON, Nerine R. (Libn) . . 1294

Royal Ontario Museum (ON) WILBURN, Gene (Computer Systs Head) 1338

Royal Trust (ON) MITCHELL, Faye F. (Ref Libn) . . 848

Rubin Consulting (CA) RUBIN, Rhea J. (Dir) 1064

Rulon-Miller Books (MN) RULON-MILLER, Robert (Pres) 1067

Rural Lib Training Project (AB) MING, Marilyn (Proj Coordntr) . . . 846

Rush-Presbyterian St Luke's Medical Ctr (IL)

BOLEF, Doris (Dir) 112

DI MAURO, Paul (Col Devlpmnt Libn) 304

GARDNER, Trudy A. (Asst Dir) . 418

Rush Univ (IL)

MARSHALL, Maggie L. (Circ Libn) 774

SPARKS, Joanne L. (Ref Libn) . 1171

Rushmore National Health System (SD)

HAMILTON, Patricia J. (Hlth Scis Lib Dir) 492

Russell & Du Moulin (BC) INSELBERG, Diana E. (Libn) . . . 583

Russell County Board of Education (KY)

FOLEY, Mary D. (High Sch Libn) 387

Russell Lib (CT) FERRO, Frank J. (Head, Technl Srvs) 374

HERMAN, Felicia G. (Ref Libn) . . 531

PORTER, Stuart T. (Dir) 985

Russell Reynolds Associates Inc (CT) GAMBER, Deborah D. (Resrch Assoc) 416

Russell Reynolds Associates Inc (DC) MEADOWS, Beth W. (Resrch Asst) 819

Russell Reynolds Associates Inc (IL) DOLMON, Barbara N. (Resrch Assoc) 310

Russell Sage Coll (NY) RYAN, Donald L. (Dir of Libs) . . 1070

Russell Sage Foundation (NY) ROTHSTEIN, Pauline M. (Dir of Info Srvs) 1060

RUST International Corp Lib (AL) ATKINSON, Calberta O. (Libn) . . . 38

Rutgers Univ (NJ) ANDERSON, James D. (Assoc Dean & Prof) 23

ANSELMO, Edith H. (Spcl Srvs Asst Prof, Asst Dir) 28

AU, Ka N. (Bus Ref Libn) 38

AXEL-LUTE, Paul (Col Devlpmnt Libn) 42

BARTZ, Stephanie (Part-time Ref Libn) 62

BECK, Susan J. (Pub Srvs Head & Asst Prof) 72

BECKER, Ronald L. (Cur of Manuscripts) 72

BEEDE, Benjamin R. (Col Devlpmnt Libn, Libn I) 74

BEETHAM, Donald W. (Slide Cur) 74

BLASINGAME, Ralph (Prof Emeritus) 104

BOYLE, Jeanne E. (Assoc Dir for Pub Srvs) 124

CALHOUN, Ellen (Govt Docums Libn) 172

CAPARROS, Ilona S. (Acting Head) 179

CASSEL, Jeris F. (Online Srvs Coordntr & Ref Libn) 193

CHAO, Gloria F. (Libn II) 201

CHEN, Chiou S. (Serials Acqs Libn) 205

COFFEY, James R. (Ref Libn & Head of Circ) 227

Rutgers Univ (NJ)

CRESCENZI, Jean D. (Col Devlpmnt & Technl Srvs Libn) 258

DESS, Howard M. (Physical Scis Resrcs Libn) 295

DYKEMAN, Amy (Asst Dir of Techl Srvs) 331

EDELMAN, Hendrik (Prof) 335

ESPOSITO, Margaret (Actg Dir of NIVERC Lib) 354

EUSTER, Joanne R. (Univ Libn) . 356

FETZER, Mary K. (Govt Pubns Coordntr) 374

GRAHAM, Peter S. (Assoc Univ Libn) 456

GREENBERG, Evelyn (Asst Univ Libn for Pub Srvs) 463

GUSTAFSON, Ruth (Grad Asst & Sci Ref Spclst) 478

HALL, Homer J. (Visiting Prof) . . . 488

HARDGROVE, David J. (Original Catlgr) 499

HOFFMAN, Helen B. (Libn) 548

KING, Donald R. (Assoc Prof) . . . 650

KUHLTHAU, Carol C. (Asst Prof, Dir Eductnl Media Prog) . 682

LANGSCHIELD, Linda S. (Coordntr, Online Retrieval Srvs) 696

LI, Marjorie H. (Technl Srvs Libn) 724

MAMAN, Marie (Ref Libn in Life Scis) 764

MILLER, Lynn F. (Media Libn) . . . 840

MILLER, Sarah J. (Asst Prof, Lib & Info Std) 842

MOTT, Thomas H. (Prof II) 872

MULLINS, Lynn S. (Lib Dir) 878

NASH, Stanley D. (Info Srvs Libn) 888

NIGRIN, Albert G. (Lib Assoc & Film & Media Spclst) 904

NIPP, Deanna (Agriculture Resrcs Libn) 904

OTA, Leslie H. (Info Srvs Libn) . . 930

PAGE, Penny B. (Head of Lib) . . 934

PIERMATTI, Patricia A. (Pharmaceutical Scis Libn) . . . 972

POLACH, Frank (Deputy Univ Libn) 980

PROFETA, Patricia C. (Circ, Ref & Govt Docums Libn) 995

PUNIELLO, Francoise S. (Acting Dir) 997

REELING, Patricia G. (Chairperson) 1016

RICHARDS, Pamela S. (Assoc Prof) 1028

RUBEN, Brent D. (Prof & Dir, PhD Prog) 1064

SARACEVIC, Tefko (Prof) 1082

SCHRIEK, Robert W. (Ref Libn) 1100

SIMMONS, Ruth J. (Univ Archvst & Head of Spcl Cols) 1140

SMITH, Beryl K. (Art Libn) 1153

SWARTZ, Betty J. (Ref Libn) . . 1214

SWARTZBURG, Susan G. (Preservation Libn & Spclst) . 1214

TIPTON, Roberta L. (Bus Ref Libn) 1247

TUROCK, Betty J. (Assoc Prof) 1265

VANDERGRIFT, Kay E. (Asst Prof) 1274

VARLEJS, Jana (Dir of Profsnl Devlpmnt Std) 1278

WATSON, Marjorie O. (Acting Libn) 1310

WEGLARZ, Catherine R. (Alcohol Std Biblgphr) 1316

Rutgers Univ (NJ)

WEISBROD, David L. (Teaching Asst) 1319
WILSON, Myoung C. (Info Srvs Libn) 1352

Rutherford B Hayes Presidential Center (OH)

SMITH, Thomas A. (Chief Archvst & Head of Resrch) . . 1161

Ruthland Hospital (VT)
STANLEY, Donald E. (Med Dir) . 1180

Rutland Free Lib (VT)
SHERMAN, Jacob R. (Catlgr & Ref Libn) 1128

Ryder System Inc (FL)
OSWALD, Edward E. (Info Retrieval Spclst) 929

Rye Free Reading Room (NY)
GREENFIELD, Judith C. (Chlds Libn) 464
READ, Jean B. (Adult Srvs Libn) 1012

Ryerson Polytechnical Institute (ON)
KENDALL, Sandra A. (Sci & Tech Libn) 640
KING, Olive E. (Bus Mgmt Libn) . 652
NORTH, John A. (Lrng Resrc Ctr Dir) 909
PHELAN, Daniel F. (Libn) 967
TUDOR, Dean F. (Prof, Sch of Jnlsm) 1262

Ryley Carlock & Applewhite (AZ)
HOUK, Douglas J. (Libn) 563

S

S C Johnson & Son Inc (WI)
FREY, Luanne C. (Assoc Info Scientist) 402
TERANIS, Mara (Sr Info Sci) . . 1231

S M Detwiler & Associates (IN)
DETWILER, Susan M. (Principal) 296

Saatchi & Saatchi Compton (NY)
DAMON, Shirley J. (Head Libn) . . 272
MELITO, Joyce A. (Resrch Libn) . 822

Sabine Parish Lib (LA)
PICKETT, Joanne H. (Admnstrv Libn) 970

Sachem Pub Lib (NY)
ROMANELLI, Catherine A. (Lib Dir) 1052

Sacramento City Unified Sch District (CA)
JACKSON, Gloria D. (Dist Libn) . 587

Sacramento Pub Lib (CA)
EITZEN, Judy (Staff Devlpmnt Dir) 341
FERDUN, Georgenne M. (Libn) . . 372
JURGENS, Lann (Dir of Financial Devlpmnt) 620
KILLIAN, Richard M. (Lib Dir) . . . 648
LARSON, Janet E. (Deputy Dir of Pub Srvs) 699
O'NEILL, Diane J. (Ref Libn) 924
RICHARD, Robert J. (Dir) 1028
SHUMAKER, Lois (Technl Srvs Dir) 1134

Sacred Heart General Hospital (OR)
GRAHAM, Deborah L. (Lib Srvs Dir) 456
TYLER, Kim E. (Med Ref Libn) . 1266

Sacred Heart Medical Ctr (PA)
SOLLENBERGER, Wesley L. (Hlth Scis Libn) 1166

Sacred Heart Seminary (DC)
MAGRO, Emanuel P. 760

Sacred Heart Seminary (MI)
RZEPECKI, Arnold M. (Libn) . . . 1072

Sacred Heart Univ (CT)
KIJANKA, Dorothy M. (Dir) 647
ROGERS, Mary E. (Head of Pub Srvs) 1050

Sacred Heart Univ (PR)
BARRERAS, Dolly M. (Catlgr) 59

Saddleback Community Coll (CA)
GORDON, Wendy R. (Ref & Biogph Instrc Libn) 452
TASH, Steven J. (Libn) 1224

Saddleback Hospital and Health Center (CA)
KOPAN, Ellen K. (Med Libn) 671

Sadlon's Ltd (WI)
SADLON, Ramona J. (Pres) . . . 1074

Saginaw Cooperative Hospitals Inc (MI)
JOHN, Stephanie C. (Dir) 601

Saginaw Pub Lib (MI)
SCHULTZ, Christine K. (Substitute Libn) 1102

Saginaw Valley State Coll (MI)
JONES, Clifton H. (Dir) 612
KOSCHIK, Douglas R. (Technl Srvs & Systs Head) 672

St Agnes Academy (TX)
GOTHIA, Blanche (Media Coordntr) 453

St Agnes Hospital (MD)
SULLIVAN, Joanne L. (Dir, Hlth Sci Lib) 1207

St Albans Sch (DC)
MOORE, Patsy H. (Asst Libn) . . . 861

St Albert Pub Lib Board (AB)
KISSAU, Arlene M. (Chlds Srvs Libn) 656

St Alexis Hospital Medical Center (OH)
JOHNSON, Stephen C. (Dir of Lib Srvs) 609

St Alphonsus Regional Medical Center (ID)
STOLZ, Marty R. (Libn) 1196

St Alphonsus Sch (WI)
SCHULTE, Teresa M. (Libn) . . . 1101

St Ambrose Univ (IA)
OHRLUND, Bruce L. (Head of Technl Srvs) 919
POTTER, Corinne J. (Dir) 987

St Andrews Coll (NC)
HOLMES, Elizabeth A. (Lib Dir) . 553

St Andrews - Sewanee Sch (TN)
KENT, Candace D. (Libn) 642

St Ann Sch (OH)
REESE, Kathleen A. (Sch Libn) . 1016

St Anselm's Abbey Sch (DC)
NAVE, Greer G. (Libn) 890

St Anselms Coll (NH)
BERTHIAUME, Dennis A. (Asst Ref Libn) 90
MYHRE, Char (Libn) 885

St Ansgar Hospital (MN)
BROWN, Barbara B. (Elem Sch Libn) 142

St Anthony Elementary & Junior High Sch (VA)
CADY, Ruth A. (Libn & Media Spclst) 170

St Anthony High Sch (CA)
DALE, Nancy (Med Libn) 270

Saint Anthony Medical Center (IL)
DOYLE, James J. (Head Libn) . 317

St Anthony-on-Hudson Theological Sem (NY)
KLEIN, Penny (Dir) 659

St Barnabas Hospital (NY)
ORZEL, Dolores (Eductnl Media Srvs Dir) 927

Saint Basil Academy (PA)
TOWNSEND, Rita M. (Elem Sch Libn) 1253

St Bede Sch (PA)
MCMANAMON, Mary J. (Dir) . . . 814

St Bede's Publications (MA)
BLATZ, Imogene (Archvst) 104

St Benedict's Convent (MN)
MEYER, Albert (Libn) 829

St Bernard's Sch (NY)
SCHUBERT, Donald F. (Libn, Media Ctr Dir, Pub Libn) . . . 1101

St Bonaventure Academy (NM)
COPELAND, Mildred A. (Media Spclst) 244

St Brendan High Sch (FL)
DENNEHY, Margaret (Sch Libn) . 292

St Brigid Sch (NY)
TIPANE, Josephine (Libn, K-12) 1246

St Camillus Academy (KY)
WILLIAMSEN, Audrey M. (Lib Dir) 1347

St Catharine Coll (KY)
ARMBRUST, Susan P. (Hlth Scis Libn) 31

St Catherine's General Hospital (ON)
GLEASON, Ruth I. (Media Coordntr) 440

St Charles Borromeo Sch (IN)
ANTHONY, Rose M. (Lib Dir) . . . 29

St Charles Borromeo Sch (WI)
BOYLAN, Lorena A. (Dir of Libs) 123

St Charles Borromeo Seminary (PA)

St Charles City-County Lib District (MO)
HICKS, James M. (Bus Srvs Libn) 537
RADGINSKI, Martha E. (Branch Mgr & Chlds Srvs Libn) 1002
SANDSTEDT, Carl R. (Dir) 1081

St Charles City-County Lib System (MO)
DILLARD, Bonita D. (Ref Libn) . . 303

St Charles Community Coll (MO)
SANDERS, John B. (Lib Adminstr) 1080

St Charles Hospital (OH)
JOHNSON, Debbie L. (Hospital Libn) 603

St Charles Parish (LA)
MIGUEZ, Betsy B. (East Regnl Libn) 833
STROTHER, Garland (Dir) 1203

St Charles Pub Lib (IL)
BROWN, Diana M. (Dir) 143
HAULE, Laura M. (Info Srvs Libn) 512

St Clair County Community Coll (MI)
YAEK, Larry A. (Technl Srvs Coordntr) 1376

St Clair County Lib System (MI)
ARNETT, Stanley K. (Head of Adult Srvs) 33
WU, Harry P. (Lib Dir) 1373

St Clair Hospital (PA)
HO, Carol T. (Med Libn) 545

Saint Clair Shores Pub Lib (MI)
WALKER, Joe L. (Libn II) 1295
WOODFORD, Arthur M. (Dir) . . . 1366

St Cloud Hospital (MN)
HEETER, Judith A. (Hlth Sci Libn) 520

St Cloud State Univ (MN)   BERLING, John G. (Lrng Resrcs Srvs Dean) 88
CLARKE, Norman F. (Bus & MN Info Spclst) 219
SCHULZETENBERG, Anthony C. (Prof Emeritus) 1102
WESTBY, Jerry L. (Col Devlpmnt) 1326

St Daniel Catholic Church Lib (MI)   HIBLER, James P. (Libn) 536
St Edward's Univ (TX)   FELSTED, Carla M. (Ref Libn) . 370
SPRUG, Joseph W. (Sr Libn) .. 1176
St Elizabeth Hospital (IL)   VAIL, Evelyn J. (Med Libn & CME Prog Coordntr) 1270
St Elizabeth Hospital (OH)   ROSENTHAL, Barbara G. (Med Lib Dir) 1057
St Elizabeth Hospital (WI)   BAYORGEON, Mary M. (Dir of Lib Srvs) 68
St Elizabeth's Hospital (IL)   CORDONI, Earl C. (Trustee) 246
St Elizabeth's Hospital (MA)   BRAUN, Robin E. (Dir) 130
St Frances Sch (TX)   MACBETH, Helen L. (Libn) ... 754
St Francis Coll (NY)   TAN, Wendy W. (Technl Srvs Libn) 1222
TORRONE, Joan M. (Dir) 1251
St Francis Coll (PA)   BRUSH, Cassandra (Technl Srvs Coordntr) 151
NEGHERBON, Vincent R. (Devlpmnt Dir) 892
St Francis Convent (MN)   MARTHALER, Margaret K. (Dir) . 775
St Francis Episcopal Day Sch (TX)   KOBAYASHI, Lee P. (Head Libn) 666
St Francis Health System (PA)   MCCULLOCH, Elizabeth A. (Libn) 801
St Francis High Sch (CA)   SCHAFFER, Eamon (Libn) 1089
St Francis High Sch (NY)   PFEIFFER, Mary A. (Libn) 966
Saint Francis Hospital (CT)   WILCOX, Carolyn G. (Asst Dir) . 1338
St Francis Hospital (FL)   GROVER, Wilma S. (Med Libn) .. 474
Saint Francis Hospital (IL)   GIBSON, Patricia M. (Libn) 432
VAN DYKE, Mary C. (Dir, Med Lib) 1275
St Francis Hospital (NY)   WEINSTEIN, Judith K. (Libn) .. 1318
St Francis Hospital & Medical Center (KS)   KINZIE, Lenora A. (Med Libn) ... 653
St Francis Medical Center (HI)   SIROIS, Julie J. (Med Libn) 1144
Saint Francis Memorial Hospital (CA)   ZAREMSKA, Maryann (Dir of Lib Srvs) 1386
St Francis Prep Sch Lib (NY)   PERGOLA, Desales 958
St Francis Pub Lib (WI)   HACHMEISTER, Helen M. (Lib Dir) 481
St Francis Regional Medical Center (KS)   MATTOX, Rosemary S. (Asst Libn) 786
St Francis Seminary Sch (WI)   ZIRBES, Colette M. (Assoc Dir) 1390
St Gabriel's Church (CA)   DOLLEN, Charles J. (Pastor) ... 310
St George Hospital (AUS)   NGUYEN, Michael V. (Asst Med Libn) 900
St Gertrude Sch (OH)   BAKER, Carol J. (Libn & Media Spclst) 48
St Gregory the Great Elementary Sch (OH)   GEORGE, Linda H. (Sch Libn) .. 427
St Hedwig High Sch (MI)   FORSYTH, Karen R. (Head Libn, Tchr) 391
St Helens Sch District 502 (OR)   BARNETT, Donald E. (AV Educ Media Spclst) 57
St James Mercy Hospital (NY)   SMITH, Brian D. (Libn) 1153
St James Sch (OH)   MULLER, Madeline A. (Libn) 877
St James/Seton Elementary Sch (NE)   BENDA, Constance M. (Elem Sch Libn) 79
St Jeanne de Lestonnac Sch (CA)   YOUNG, Eleanor C. (Lib Media Spclst) 1381
St John & West Shore Hospital (OH)   GALLANT, Jennifer J. (Dir of Media Ctr) 414
St John Bosco High Sch (CA)   PESTUN, Aloysius J. (Libn) 961
St John Hospital (MI)   O'DONNELL, Ellen E. (Dir, Med Lib) 917
WAYLAND, Marilyn T. (Dir, Clinical Resrch & Curr Plng) . 1311
St John Hospital (OH)   HOLCZER, Lolita B. (Med Libn) .. 550
St John Medical Center (OK)   DONOVAN, James M. (Libn) ... 312

Saint John Regional Lib (NB)   COGSWELL, Howard L. (Branch Supvsr) 227
COWAN, Barbara M. (Adult Srvs Libn) 252
KISSICK, Barbara J. (Branch Mgr) 656
St John the Baptist High Sch (NY)   JOYCE, Therese (Lib Media Spclst) 618
REIMAN, Anthony C. (AV Coordntr) 1020
St John the Baptist Parish Pub Lib (LA)   DESOTO, Randy A. (Adminstrv Libn) 295
St John the Evangelist Sch (MD)   FITZGERALD, M A. (Libn) ... 382
St John Ursuline High Sch (CA)   SEGUNDO, Fe P. (Libn) 1112
St John's Coll (MD)   KINZER, Kathryn (Libn) 653
St John's Episcopal Day Sch (FL)   FOSTER, Candice L. (Libn) 392
St John's High Sch (MA)   O'BRIEN, John F. (High Sch Libn) 914
St John's Hospital (IL)   WRIGLEY, Kathryn J. (Hlth Scis Lib Dir) 1373
St John's Hospital (MN)   COVER, Teresa A. (Lib Srvs Dir) 252
Saint Johns Hospital & Health Center (CA)   PINCKNEY, Cathey L. (Dir, Med Lib) 974
St John's Med Coll and Hospital (IND)   KITTUR, Krishna N. (Libn) 657
St John's Mercy Medical Center (MO)   BRENNER, Saundra H. (Dir Med Ctr Lib) 133
St John's Prep Sch (NY)   GORMAN, Mary B. (Dir of Lib) .. 452
St John's Regional Health Center (MO)   CRABTREE, Anna B. (Med Lib Srvs Dir) 254
St John's Regional Medical Center (CA)   KENNEDY, Joanne (Libn) 641
St Johns River Water Management District (FL)   HUNTER, Judith G. (Libn) 576
St John's Sch (TX)   MCGOWN, Sue W. (Head Libn) . 807
St John's Seminary (CA)   RAMIREZ, Anthony L. (Libn) ... 1005
St John's Seminary (MI)   CARLEN, Claudia (Archvst) 181
DE BEAR, Estelle G. (Libn) 284
MCGARTY, Jean R. (Lib Dir) .. 805
St John's Univ (NY)   BENSON, James A. (Assoc Prof) 83
CLARK, Philip M. (Acting Dir) ... 218
CORRY, Emmett (Assoc Prof) ... 247
DOYAL, Patricia A. (Manuscript Libn) 317
GRANT, Mary A. (Hlth Educ Resrc Ctr Dir) 458
HABER, Mark N. (Libn) 481
HECKMAN, Lucy T. (Ref Libn) .. 519
LANG, Jovian P. (Assoc Prof) ... 695
LINDGREN, Arla M. (Head of Acqs Dept & Assoc Prof) 729
MARKE, Julius J. (Law Prof & Law Libn) 771
MELTON RSM, Marie F. (Dir of Univ Libs) 823
NOLAN, John A. (Assoc Prof & Interlib Loan Div Head) 907
PARR, Mary Y. (Asst Dir for Technl Srvs) 944
POWIS, Katherine E. (Asst Sci Libn) 989
SZMUK, Szilvia E. (Spcl Cols Libn) 1218
TURLEY, Harriet M. (Gen Ref, Interlib Libn Srvs) 1264
WEINBERG, Bella H. (Assoc Prof) 1317
St Johnsbury Academy (VT)   THOMPSON, Judith H. (Libn) .. 1240
St Joseph Central High Sch (MA)   BOSTLEY, Jean R. (Libn) 117
St Joseph High Sch (HI)   EPIL, Charlene M. (High Sch Libn) 351
St Joseph Hospital (CA)   BROWN, Elizabeth E. (Med Libn) 143
RYAN, Ann (Med Libn) 1070
SMITH, Julie L. (Dir of Lib Srvs) 1156

St Joseph Hospital (CT)
LIEBERMAN, Lucille N. (Hlth Scis Lib Dir) 726

St Joseph Hospital (MO)
SHIEH, Monica W. (Hlth Sci Libn) 1129

St Joseph Hospital (NH)
NOFTLE, Dorothy B. (Dir, Lib Srv) 907

Saint Joseph Hospital (PA)
IZZO, Kathleen A. (Libn) 586
MOREY, Carol M. (Asst Libn) ... 863

St Joseph Hospital (TN)
IRBY, Patricia P. (Med Libn) 583

St Joseph Hospital & Health Care Center (IL)
WIMMER, Katherine P. (Lib Srvs Dir) 1354

St Joseph Medical Center (IN)
SHEETS, Michael T. (Med Info Ctr Dir) 1125

St Joseph Mercy Hospital (MI)
LYNCH, Mollie S. (Lib Mgr) 752

Saint Joseph Pub Lib (MO)
ELLIOTT, Dorothy G. (Dir) 344

St Joseph Sch (AL)
CLAVER, M P. (Libn) 219

Saint Joseph's Coll (IN)
VIGEANT, Robert J. (Head Libn) 1284

St Joseph's Health Centre of London (ON)
LIN, Louise (Lib Srvs Mgr) 727
PARR, John R. (Clinical Coordntr) 943

St Joseph's Hospital (GA)
WAVERCHAK, Gail A. (Hlth Scis Libn) 1311

St Joseph's Hospital (WI)
ALLEN, Margaret A. (Libn) 15
SHAIKH, Sunja L. (Med Libn) .. 1119

St Joseph's Hospital & Medical Center (AZ)
WELLIK, Kay E. (Lib Srvs Mgr) . 1321

St Joseph's Hospital Health Center (NY)
SHRIER, Helene F. (Asst Libn) . 1133

St Joseph's Seminary (NY)
GAFFNEY, Ellen E. (Lib Dir) 412

St Joseph's Univ (PA)
ANDRILLI, Ene M. (Ref Libn) 27
PENROSE, Anna M. (Libn) 957
RATHBONE, Marjorie A. (Technl Srvs Libn) 1009
REILLY, Rebecca S. (Ref & Interlib Loan Libn) 1020
THOMAS, Deborah A. (Pub Srvs Coordntr) 1236

St Jude Children's Research Hospital (TN)
WALKER, Mary E. (Med Libn) . 1296

St Lawrence College (ON)
LOVE, Barbara (Ref Libn) 743

St Lawrence Hospital (MI)
CLAYTOR, Jane B. (Med Libn) .. 220

St Lawrence Univ (NY)
LARSEN, Joan A. (Ref & Docums Libn) 698

Saint Leo Coll (FL)
NEUHOFE, M D. (Lib Dir) 897

St Leo Coll (VA)
VERNON, Christie D. (Assoc Prof & Libn) 1283

St Louis Art Museum (MO)
BETH, Dana L. (Asst Libn) 92
SIGALA, Stephanie C. (Head Libn) 1137

St Louis Board of Education (MO)
DOSS, Mamie (Libn, Tchr) 313

St Louis County Lib (MO)
DELIVUK, John A. (Circ and Ref) 289
GAERTNER, Donell J. (Dir) 411
JANKU, Margaret M. (Asst Supvsr) 593
SCHRAMM, Betty V. (Asst Dir) . 1099

St Louis Metropolitan Police Dept (MO)
MIKSICEK, Barbara L. (Libn) ... 834

St Louis Post-Dispatch (MO)
BROWN, Gerald D. (Lib Dir) 144

St Louis Preparatory Seminary North (MO)
LAWS, Janet E. (Head Libn) 705

St Louis Pub Lib (MO)
GANYARD, Margaret E. (Popular Lib Supvsr) 416
LYONS, A J. (Adult Educ Coordntr) 753
MCKAY, Micheal W. (Bus Mgr) .. 810
REINHOLD, Edna J. (Dept Head, Hum & Soc Scis) 1021
ROBERTS, Jean A. (Branch Libn) 1040
SMITH, Nancy M. (Pub Srvs Dir) 1159
WATTS, Anne (Readers Srvs & Docums Supvsr) 1310

St Louis Regional Lib Network (MO)
TAYLOR, Arthur R. (Netwk Adminstr) 1226

St Louis Univ (IL)
ANTHONY, Paul L. (Dir of Instrcl Resrcs) 29

St Louis Univ (MO)
AGUILAR, Barbara S. (Media Coordntr) 8
AMELUNG, Richard C. (Head of Technl Srvs) 19
ELAM, Kristy L. (Asst Law Libn) . 341
GALLAGHER, Kathy E. (Ref Libn) 414
HEISER, W C. (Libn) 523
JOSEPH, Miriam E. (Ref Libn) ... 617
MCKENZIE, Elizabeth M. (Reader Srv Libn) 811
MESSERLE, Judith R. (Dir) 828
MILLES, James G. (Legal Resrch Biblgphr & Instr) 843
MOODY, Carol L. (Docums Libn) 857
NORTH, Daniel L. (Acqs Head) . 909
PLUTCHAK, T S. (Assoc Dir) ... 979
SEARLS, Eileen H. (Law Libn, Prof of Law) 1110
TAYLOR, Carolyn L. (Spcl Projs Libn) 1226

St Louise Sch (WA)
BIANCHI, Karen F. (Sch Libn) 93

St Lucie Board of County Commissioners (FL)

St Lucie County Lib System (FL)
HENEHAN, Alva D. (Dir) 528
BROOM, Susan E. (Asst Dir) ... 141
MITTLEMAN, Marilyn (Pub Srvs Supvsr) 850
POMERLEAU, Suzanne M. (Youth Srvs Supvsr) 982

St Luke Lutheran Church (IN)
SMITH, Robert E. (Pastor) 1160

St Luke's Hospital (IA)
POHNL, Donald R. (Dir) 980

St Luke's Hospital (MA)
WILDES, Elizabeth S. (Lib Srvs Dir) 1339

St Luke's Memorial Hospital (WI)
GRONHOLM, Shirley A. (Libn) .. 472

St Luke's Regional Medical Center (ID)
SPICKELMIER, Pamela S. (Med Lib Dir) 1174

St Luke's/Roosevelt Hospital Center (NY)
PANELLA, Nancy M. (Libn) 938

St Margaret Memorial Hospital (PA)
ARJONA, Sandra K. (Med Lib Dir) 31

St Mark's Hospital (UT)
SKIDMORE, Kerry F. 1146

St Martins Coll (WA)
WIEMAN, Jean M. (Continuing Educ/Comp Inservice Dir) ... 1336

Saint Mary Coll (KS)
FINK, Madonna (Ref & Periodicals) 378
HANNE, Anna R. (Head Libn) ... 497
POJMAN, Paul E. (Libn) 980
RECKS, Dorcas E. (Libn) 1013

St Mary Elementary Sch (OH)
BATTAGLIA, Mary H. (Libn) ... 64

St Mary Hospital (IL)
ATTARIAN, Lorraine B. (Med Lib Mgr) 38

St Mary Jacqueline Tarrant (MS)

St Mary Medical Center (CA)
MACKO, Lucinda M. (Med Libn) . 757

St Mary Medical Center (IN)
KEENAN, Mary T. (Med Libn) ... 634

St Mary of Nazareth Hospital Center (IL)

St Mary of the Plains Coll (KS)
COOKE, Bette L. (Lib Dir & Prof of Lib Sci) 241
DONNELLY, Lela M. (Assoc Engl Prof & Archvst) 311
NEAU, Philip F. (Libn) 891

St Mary Parish Sch Board (LA)
GOODMAN, L D. (Archvst & Emeritus Lib Dir) 440

St Mary's Coll (CA)
O'CONNOR, Thomas F. (Info Srvs Libn) 916
SEEKAMP, Linda W. (Info Srvs Libn) 1111

Saint Mary's Coll (IN)
HOHL, Robert J. (Ref & Instrc Libn) 550
HOLLENHORST, Bernice M. (Lib Dir) 551
JONES, Marjorie (Catlgr) 614

St Mary's Coll (MD)
BRITTEN, William A. (Online Srvs Coordntr) 137
REPENNING, Julie A. (Biblgph Instrc Coordntr) 1023
WILLIAMSON, John G. (Dir of Lib) 1347

St Mary's Coll (MI)   IRWIN, Lawrence L. (Dir of
St Mary's Coll (MN)   Technl Srvs) 584
                                       MOXNESS, Mary J. (Ref Libn &
St Mary's General Hospital (ME)   Asst Prof) 874
                                       GREENLAW, Evelyn A. (Hlth
St Mary's Hospital (IL)   Scis Libn) 465
St Mary's Hospital (MI)   FLANIGAN, Anne J. (Libn) 383
                                       HANSON, Mary A. (Head Libn) .. 498
St Mary's Hospital (MO)   MATHIS, Yvonne L. (Asst Libn) . 784
St Mary's Hospital (NV)   SERLING, Kitty (Hospital Libn) . 1116
Saint Mary's Hospital (NY)   PRATT, Kathleen L. (Libn) 990
St Mary's Hospital (SD)   CLUM, Audna T. (Libn) 223
St Mary's Hospital (VA)   HILMOE, Deann D. (Libn) 541
                                       PARHAM, Sandra H. (Hlth Scis
St Mary's Hospital & Medical   Libn) 940
   Center (CA)   BENELISHA, Eleanor (Lib Srvs
                                          Dir) 80
St Mary's Hospital & Medical
   Center (CO)   PAINE, Joan E. (Libn) 935
St Mary's Medical Center (IN)   SALTZMAN, E J. (Lib Srvs
                                          Mgr) 1077
St Mary's Medical Center (TN)   CLARK, Glenda C. (Med Libn) .. 217
St Mary's of the Lake Hospital (ON)   LEVI, Penelope G. (Dir of Lib,
                                          Archvl Srvs) 720
St Mary's Sch (IL)   MADAY, Geraldine (Libn) 758
St Mary's Seminary & Univ (MD)   CAREY, John T. (Technl Srvs
                                          Libn) 181
St Mary's Univ (TX)   GOERDT, Arthur L. (Assoc Prof
                                          of Engl) 443
                                       HENRICKS, Duane E. (Docums
                                          Libn) 529
                                       HICKEY, Lady J. (Catlgr) 536
Saint Mary's Univ (NS)   SMITH, Arthur M. (Head of
                                          Catlgng) 1152
                                       TAYYEB, Rashid (Technl Srvs
                                          Head) 1229
St Matthias' Episcopal Church (NY)   GUINN, Patricia L. (Volunteer
                                          Church Libn) 477
St Meinrad Coll and Sch of
   Theology (IN)   DALY, Simeon (Libn) 271
St Michael Hospital (WI)   SCHLUGE, Vicki L. (Lib Srvs
                                          Dir) 1094
St Michael's Hospital (ON)   WONG, Anita (Dir) 1362
St Michael's in the Hills Church (OH) HANNAFORD, Claudia L. (Lib
                                          Dir) 496
St Norbert Coll (WI)   PIETERS, Donald L. (Head of
                                          Readers Srvs) 972
St Olaf Coll (MN)   CHRISTENSEN, Beth E. (Music
                                          & Ref Libn) 211
                                       DITTMANN, Chrisma S. (Catlg
                                          Libn) 306
                                       HUBER, Kristina R. (Ref & Circ
                                          Libn & Asst Prof) 569
St Patrick's Catholic Church (NY)   DAVIS, Francis R. (Pastor) 279
St Patrick's Episcopal Day Sch (MD)   PECK, Ann D. (Libn) 953
St Paul Pioneer Press Dispatch (MN)   KATZUNG, Judith (Chief Libn) .. 630
St Paul Pub Lib (MN)   GALT, Francis E. (Branch Libs
                                          Pub Srvs Mgr) 415
                                       HLAVSA, Larry B. (Libn II) 544
                                       JACOB, Rosamond T. (Govt
                                          Docums Libn) 589
                                       REHNBERG, Marilyn J. (Soc
                                          Sci & Lit Libn) 1017
St Paul Pub Schs (MN)   KAISER, Sally A. (Elem Sch
                                          Libn) 622
Saint Paul Univ (ON)   HICKS, Barbara A. (Chief Libn) .. 536
St Paul's Episcopal Day Sch (MO)   AYLWARD, Judith A. (Sch Libn) .. 43
St Paul's Indian Grade Sch (MT)   HARTMANN, M C. (Tchr &
                                          Libn) 508
St Paul's Sch for Girls (MD)   KELLY, Carol N. (Libn) 637
St Peter Claver Church (MN)   JACKSON, Mildred E.
                                          (Volunteer) 588
St Peter's Coll (NJ)   ROMANKO, Karen A. (Head of
                                          Technl Srvs) 1052
                                       SCHUT, Grace W. (Libs Dir) ... 1103
St Peter's Hospital (NY)   MIYAUCHI, Phyllis J. (Lib Dir) ... 850

St Petersburg Junior Coll (FL)   DALLMAN, Glenn R. (Lib Srvs
                                          Dir) 270
                                       GOSS, Theresa C. (Lib Dir) 453
                                       LICHTENFELS, David D. (Libn) .. 725
St Petersburg Times (FL)   ALZOFON, Sammy R. (Asst
                                          Libn) 19
                                       SCOFIELD, James S. (News
                                          Resrch Coordntr) 1106
St Philip the Apostle Sch (MD)   MC HALE, Mary M. (Libn) 808
St Rita Sch for the Deaf (OH)   DINNESEN, Peter H. (Media
                                          Spclst) 305
St Rose Academy (CA)   KAUN, Thomas T. (Lib Dir) 631
St Rose of Lima Sch (NJ)   SCHUMACHER, Nancy C.
                                          (Libn) 1102
St Symphorosa Elementary Sch (IL)   GLEESON, Joyce M. (Libn Elem
                                          (K-8)) 441
St Tammany Parish Lib (LA)   SOTO, Donna G. (Juvenile Srvs
                                          Coordntr) 1169
                                       TAYLOR, Rebecca A. (Branch
                                          Libn) 1228
St Tammany Parish Sch Board (LA)   HOLLEY, Rebecca M. (Lib
                                          Media Dir) 551
St Thomas Aquinas Coll (NY)   BARTH, John E. (Catlg & Ref
                                          Libn) 61
St Thomas Aquinas High Sch (CT)   ANDRONIK, Catherine M. (Libn) .. 27
St Thomas Department of
   Education (VI)   MACLEAN, Ellen G. (Dist Libn) .. 757
                                       MILLS, Fiolina B. (State Dir) ... 844
St Thomas Episcopal Sch (FL)   LOPEZ, Silvia P. (Libn) 741
Saint Thomas Hospital (TN)   FORBES, Evelyn H. (Ref Libn) . 388
                                       FULTON, Dixie W. (Lib Srvs Dir) . 409
St Thomas Pub Lib (ON)   RHYNAS, Don M. (Semi-Profsnl
                                          Libn, Adult Srvs) 1026
St Thomas Theological
   Seminary (CO)   GERMOVNIK, Francis I. (Asst
                                          Libn) 429
                                       WHITE, Joyce L. (Lib Dir) 1331
St Thomas Univ (FL)   WOLFE, Bardie C. (Prof of Law
                                          & Law Libn) 1360
Saint Vincent Coll (PA)   BENYO, John C. (Asst Libn) 84
                                       HILL, Lawrence H. (Perdcls &
                                          Ref Libn) 540
                                       MACEY, John F. (Technl Srvs &
                                          Interlib Loan Head) 755
St Vincent de Paul High Sch (VA)   CARTER, Ann M. (Media
                                          Spclst) 189
St Vincent de Paul Sch (TN)   KILPATRICK, Barbara A.
                                          (Medial Spclst) 648
St Vincent Ferrer Sch (IL)   SCHAEFER, Elizabeth K. (Libn) 1088
St Vincent Hospital (MA)   DAVITT, Theresa B. (Hospital
                                          Libn) 281
St Vincent Hospital & Health Care
   Center (IN)   DURKIN, Virginia M. (Mgr, Lib
                                          Srvs) 328
St Vincent Hospital & Medical
   Center (OR)   JACOBS, Patt (Med Info Systs
                                          Coordntr) 590
St Vincent Medical Center (CA)   GELMAN-KMEC, Marsha (Hlth
                                          Sci Libn) 426
St Vincent's Hospital (AL)   SIMS, Joyce W. (Lib Mgr) 1142
St Vincent's Hospital & Medical
   Center (NY)   FRANK, Agnes T. (Med Lib Dir) . 396
Saint Vincent's Medical Center (CT)   GOERIG, Janet (Lib Srvs Dir) .. 443
St Vincent's Medical Center of
   Richmond (NY)   DIMATTEO, Lucy A. (Med Lib
                                          Dir) 304
Saints Peter & Paul Schs (VI)   STEIN, Josephine M. (Libn) ... 1185
Salem Community Coll (NJ)   BRANAN, Julia D. (Eductnl Srvs
                                          Dir) 127
Salem School District 57 (NH)   GRAZIER, Dorothy W. (Media
                                          Generalist & Sch Libn) 460
Salem State Coll (MA)   ANDREWS, Margaret (Libn I) 27
Salina Pub Lib (KS)   MCKENZIE, Joe M.
                                          (Interdepartmental Libn) 811
Salina Unified Sch District 305 (KS)   REED, Mary J. (Media Srvs Dir) 1015
Salinas Pub Lib (CA)   GAMBLE, Mary J. (Archvst) 416
Saline County Library (AR)   ASHCRAFT, Carolyn A.
                                          (Director/Librarian) 35
Salomon Brothers Inc (NY)   DI MEGLEO, Arthur J. (Resrch
                                          Assoc) 304

Salpointe Catholic High Sch (AZ)	MCBRIDE, Patricia A. (Libn)	792
Salt Lake City Pub Lib (UT)	DAY, J D. (Dir)	282
	EDMUNDSON, Margaret B. (Fine Arts & AV Dept Head) . .	336
	GIAUGUE, James A. (Bd of Dir) .	431
	GOFORTH, Allene M. (Asst Agency Head)	444
Salt Lake City Sch District (UT)	BURKS, C J. (Lib Media Coordntr)	161
	KARPISEK, Marian E. (Supvsr, Lib Media Srvs)	628
	OLSEN, Katherine M. (Sch Lib, Media Spclst)	921
	PETERSON, Francine (Media Coordntr)	963
Salt Lake Community Coll (UT)	STECKER, Alexander T. (Dir of Libs & Media Srvs)	1183
Salt Lake County Lib System (UT)	ELLEFSEN, David (Info Spclst) .	343
	FUJIMOTO, Jan D. (Ref Libn) . . .	408
	KITE, Yvonne D. (Asst Libn)	657
	MARCHANT, Cathy (Ref Libn) .	768
	SCHUURMAN, Guy (Lib Dir) . .	1103
	TALBERT, Dorothy R. (Libn) . . .	1220
Salt River Project (AZ)	KLASSEN, Bonnie	657
Salvation Army (NY)	JOHNSON, Judith (Archvst) . .	606
	WILSTED, Thomas P. (Archvst, Adminstr)	1353
Sam Houston State Univ (TX)	BAILEY, William G. (Ref Libn)	47
	BURKS, Paula (Head of Catlgng)	161
	BURT, Lesta N. (Sch of Lib Sci Prof)	164
	CARTER, Betty B. (Lectr)	189
	CULP, Paul M. (Spcl Cols Libn) .	264
	HARNSBERGER, R S. (Ref Libn & Biblgphr)	503
	HOFFMAN, Frank W. (Asst Prof)	548
	KIM, David U. (Libs Actg Dir) . . .	648
	PARIS, Janelle A. (Prof of Lib Sci)	940
	PICHETTE, William H. (Prof)	970
	THORNE, Bonnie B. (Actg Dir, Sch of Lib Sci)	1242
	WILSON, Craig A. (Col Devlpmnt Libn)	1350
Samaritan Hospital (NY)	SMITH, Annie J. (Lib Clerk) . .	1152
Samford Univ (AL)	CARTER, Selina J. (Hlth Lrng Resrc Coordntr & Lib Dir)	190
	CLAPP, Laurel R. (Law Libn/Prof of Law)	216
	JONES, Linda G. (Acqs Libn)	613
	NELSON, William N. (Dir)	895
	TAYLOR, Carol P. (Catlg Libn) .	1226
San Antonio Coll (TX)	BALCOM, Karen S. (Systs Libn & Asst Prof)	51
	DRUMMOND, Donald R. (Assoc Prof)	321
San Antonio Pub Lib (TX)	BENSON, Joyce (Libn)	83
San Bernardino Community Hospital (CA)	NOUROK, Marlene E. (Med Lib Dir)	910
San Bernardino County Lib (CA)	WATTS, Richard S. (Technl Prcsng Dept Coordntr)	1310
San Bernardino County Medical Center (CA)	WAKEFIELD, Jacqueline M. (Med Libn)	1293
San Diego Community Coll (CA)	KAYE, Karen (Pub Relations, Ref Libn)	632
San Diego County Law Lib (CA)	CH'NG, Saw K. (Ref Libn)	209
	DERSHEM, Larry D. (Catlgng & Interlib Loan Dept Head)	294
	DYER, Charles R. (Dir)	330
	EWING, Florence E. (Ref Libn) . .	359
	JOHNSRUD, Thomas E. (Ref Libn)	609

San Diego County Lib (CA)	CLINE, Cheryl L. (Acqs Libn) . . .	222
	ESQUEVIN, Christian R. (Comunty Libs Dir)	354
	HESS, M S. (Outreach Div Coordntr)	534
	LOOMIS, Barbara L. (Principal Libn)	740
	TRIVISON, Margaret A. (Libn III)	1257
	ZYROFF, Ellen S. (Principal Libn of Technl Srvs)	1392
San Diego County Office of Education (CA)	NIEMEYER, Kay M. (Sch Lib Resrcs Coordntr)	903
San Diego County Pub Lib System (CA)	SUBLER, Joyce A. (Ref Libn) . .	1206
San Diego Pub Lib (CA)	BOYLLS, Virginia W. (Sr Libn) . .	124
	FARMER, Marguerite E. (Libn) . .	364
	KATKA, Patricia P. (Branch Libn)	629
	MARC-AURELE, Heidi L. (Chlds Libn)	768
	MARTINEZ, Anna M. (Deputy Dir & Branch Libn)	779
	QUEEN, Margaret E. (Supvsr Libn, Ref Srvs)	999
	SANNWALD, William W. (City Libn)	1081
	SCHECTER, Fred (Deputy Dir of Technl Srvs)	1090
	SCLAR, Marta L. (Chlds Outreach)	1106
	SHERWOOD, Judith (Sr Libn) . .	1129
	STANLEY, Sydney J. (Sr Libn) .	1180
San Diego State Univ (CA)	BOSSEAU, Don L. (Univ Libn) . .	117
	CHAN, Lillian L. (Head, Sci Div) .	199
	DINTRONE, Charles V. (Head of Govt Pubns Div)	305
	LEERHOFF, Ruth E. (Spcl Cols Libn)	712
	MCNALLY, Ruth C. (Ref Libn) . .	816
	PEASE, William J. (Head of Col Devlpmnt)	953
	PERKINS, Michael J. (Bus Libn) .	959
	STRICKLAND, Muriel (Map Cur)	1202
	WHITE, Phillip M. (Ref Libn) . . .	1332
	WILSON, Carole F. (Head of Circulation Srvs)	1350
San Diego Supercomputer Center (CA)	MAISEL, Merry W. (Documtn Coordntr, Lib Sci Writer)	762
San Diego Unified Sch District (CA)	WYBORNEY, Charles E. (Lib Resrch Asst)	1374
San Domenico Sch (CA)	FARMER, Lesley S. (Lib Dir)	364
San Francisco Art Institute (CA)	GUNDERSON, Jeffery R. (Lib Srvs Dir)	477
San Francisco Bay Socty for Adlerian Psy (CA)	KAHN, Paul J. (Libn)	622
San Francisco Chronicle (CA)	CASTER, Suzanne (Head Libn) . .	194
	GEIGER, Richard G. (Lib Dir) . . .	425
	KIBBEE, Sally (Libn)	646
San Francisco Examiner (CA)	CANTER, Judy A. (Chief Libn) . .	179
San Francisco Municipal Railway (CA)	HOFSTADTER, Marc E. (Libn) . .	549
San Francisco Museum of Modern Art (CA)	CANDAU, Eugenie (Libn)	178
	ERVITI, Debra L. (Slide Libn) . . .	353
San Francisco Planning & Urban Research (CA)	HURLBERT, Roger W. (Land Info Systs Cur)	577
San Francisco Pub Lib (CA)	CADY, Steven R. (Ref Libn)	170
	COAKLEY, Dorothy J. (Chlds Srvs Libn)	224
	COLBY, Michael D. (Libn I, Catlg)	230
	FRANTZ, John C. (Dir)	398
	GOLDMACHER, Sheila L. (Adult Ref Libn)	445
	HUDSON, Jane (Libn)	569

San Francisco Pub Lib (CA)
KAVANAGH, Margaret M. (Branch Head) 631
KINCAID, Anne E. (Coordntr of Adult Srvs) 649
LANDGRAF, Mary N. (Head, Cir Syst Srvs) 692
LEWANDOWSKI, Joseph J. (Libn I) 722
MURTHA, Edward J. (Libn I) 883
NICHOLS, Elizabeth D. (Chief Libn for Technl Srvs) 901
NYHAN, Catherine W. (Chlds Libn) 912
RAMIREZ, William L. (Centl Lib Dir) 1005
REGNER-HYATT, Anne L. (Libn I) 1017
REILLY, James H. (Acqs Head) 1020
SCHNEIDER, Marcia G. (Bk Buddies Libn) 1097
TURITZ, Mitch L. (Serials Catlgr, Libn I) 1263

San Francisco State Univ (CA)
AVENEY, Brian H. (Systs Libn) . . . 41
BONFIELD, Lynn A. (Dir, Labor Archs & Resrch Ctr) 114
GERSTLE, Steven M. (Asst Libn) 429
HAIKALIS, Peter D. (Asst Dir, Reader Srvs) 484
JACOBSEN, Lavonne (Govt Pubns Coordntr) 590
JAMES, Olive C. (Lib Dir) 592
MCQUOWN, Eloise (Admin Srvs Asst Dir) 817
TREGGIARI, Arnaldo (Sr Asst Libn) 1255
WHITSON, Helene (Spcl Cols Libn & Archvst) 1334

San Jacinto Coll (TX)
CRENSHAW, Jan C. (Libn) 258
San Jacinto Museum of History Assn (TX)
ATKINS, Winston (Libn & Edit of Pubns) 38
San Joaquin County Office of Education (CA)
DEAN, Martha L. (Instcl Media Ctr Dir) 283
San Joaquin Delta Coll (CA)
CLARKE, Tobin D. (Lrng Resrcs Dir) 219
MOORE, Evia B. (Perdcls & Ref Libn) 859
San Joaquin Memorial High Sch (CA) LATIMER, Mary A. (Libn) 701
San Jose Bible Coll (CA) LLOVIO, Kay M. (Lib Dir) 735
San Jose Coll (PR) ALSTON, Jane C. (Libn) 18
San Jose Pub Lib (CA) ABNEY, Timothy A. (Ref Libn) 2
FOWLER, Brian R. (Libn I) 393
JESSUP, Carrie (Ref Libn) 600
RENDLER, Richard E. (Deputy Dir) 1023
ROSS, Ruth K. (Sr Resrch Libn) 1058
SULLIVAN, Anne L. (Branch Mgr) 1207
San Jose State Univ (CA) BELANGER, Sandra E. (Assoc Ref Libn) 75
BRUNDAGE, Christina A. (Ref Libn) 150
CEPPOS, Karen F. (Asst Prof) . . 196
COOVER, Robert W. (Libn) 244
CROWLEY, Terence (Prof of Lib and Info Sci) 262
ELLIOTT, Patricia G. (Cur) 344
EMMICK, Nancy J. (Ref Libn) . . . 348
HARMON, Robert B. (Ref Libn) . . 502
HEALEY, James S. (Lib & Info Sci Dir) 518
JOHNSON, Clifford R. (Catlgr & Sr Asst Libn) 603
LEONARD, Barbara G. (Budget & Plng Ofcr) 716
LIU, Susanna J. (Ref Libn & Spcl Srvs Coordntr) 734

San Jose State Univ (CA)
MAIN, Linda Y. (Asst Prof) 761
MARTIN, Rebecca R. (Asst Dir, User Srvs & Col Devlpmnt) . . 778
MULLEN, Cecilia P. (Engrng Ref Libn) 877
PAUL, Jeff H. (Media Dept & Chicano Lib Coordntr) 949
REDFERN, Bernice I. (Ref Libn) 1014
REYNOLDS, Judith L. (Bibliographic Instrc Coordntr) 1025
ROSEN, Elizabeth M. (Assoc Prof) 1055
SMITH, Edith (Archvst, Hist Dept) 1154
WHITLATCH, Jo B. (Asst Dir & Access Div) 1333
San Juan Coll (NM) RICHARD, Harris M. (Lib Dir, Lrng Resrc Ctr Coordntr) . . . 1027
San Luis Obispo County Law Lib (CA) BORRACCINO, Jean H. (Law Libn) 117
San Marcos Pub Lib (TX) RODE, Shelley J. (Pub Srvs Supvsr) 1047
San Mateo County Community Coll District (CA)
ENGELBRECHT, Mary E. (Substitute Libn) 349
San Mateo County Lib (CA) BOWLES, Carol A. (Technl Srvs Coordntr) 121
San Mateo County Office of Education (CA) LATHROP, Ann (Lib Coordntr) . . 701
San Mateo County Superintendent of Schs (CA)
MAY, Frank C. (Adminstr-Media & Lib Srvs) 788
San Rafael Pub Lib (CA) TRZECIAK, William J. (Ref Libn I) 1260
SandCastles Inc (CA) LEE, Judith C. (Managing Edit) . . 710
Sanders Associates (NH) BERLIN, Arthur E. (Lib Srvs Mgr) 87
Sandhill Regional Lib System (NC) WALTERS, Carol G. (Pub Srvs Libn) 1301
Sandhills Community Coll (NC) WILKINS, Alice L. (Head Libn) . 1340
Sandia National Laboratories (NM) PASTERCZYK, Catherine E. (Technl Info Spclst) 946
PRUETT, Nancy J. (Syst Analyst) 996
ZAMORA, Gloria J. (Mgmt Info Resrchr) 1386
Sandoz Canada Inc (PQ) BOISVERT, Diane (Info Srvs Supvsr) 111
BOLSVERT, Diane B. (Info Srvs Supvsr) 113
Sandoz Pharmaceuticals (NJ) KOELLE, Joyce G. (Med Comm & Info Srv Asst Dir) 667
Sandra H Hurd Consultants (MA) HURD, Sandra H. (Owner) 577
Sandusky Lib (OH) BRAUTIGAM, Faith J. (Head of Chlds' Srvs) 130
Sandwich Township Pub Lib (IL) JOHNSON, Joanne D. (Head Libn) 606
Sangamon State Univ (IL) ALLEY, Brian (Dean of Lib Srvs) . . 16
ROBERTSON, Ina N. (Instrcl Srvs Libn) 1042
SHACKLETON, Suzanne M. (Libn) 1118
Santa Ana Pub Lib (CA) MINICK, Donna J. (Supvsr, Ref/Info Section) 846
Santa Ana Unified Sch District (CA) PINCOCK, Rulon D. (Libn) 974
Santa Barbara Botanic Garden (CA) HAWVER, Nancy (Libn) 515
Santa Barbara County Law Lib (CA) MACGREGOR, Raymond (Law Libn) 755
Santa Barbara High Sch District (CA) MARR, Charles A. (Lib Media Spclst) 773
Santa Barbara Pub Lib System (CA) HERZIG, Stella J. (Ref Libn) . . . 534
RICHARDSON, Bill 1029
Santa Barbara Research Center (CA) GENTRY, Susan K. (Sr Libn) . . . 427
Santa Clara County Lib (CA) COLBY, Diana C. (Chlds Libn) . . 230
CONDIT, Larry D. (Libn, Young Adult Srvs) 235

Santa Clara Univ (CA)	BAZAN, Lorraine R. (Bus Libn) . . 68	Saskatoon Pub Lib (SK)	BARLOW, Elizabeth A. (Info
	EARHART, Marilyn N. (Acqs		Srvs Head) 57
	Libn) 332		RUSSELL, Vija (Serials Libn) . 1069
	FRIEDRICH, Barbara J. (Pub		TOMCHYSHYN, Theresa M.
	Srvs Libn) 404		(Legal Srvs Libn) 1249
	GOODWATER, Leanna K.	Saul Ewing Remick & Saul (PA)	ABRISS, Judith W. (Law Libn) 3
	(Coordntr of Col Devlpmnt) . . . 450	Savage Information Services (CA)	GIFFORD, Becky J. (Vice-Pres) . 433
	HOOD, Mary D. (Assoc Law		SAVAGE, Gretchen S. (Pres) . 1085
	Libn) 556		TUNG, Sandra J. (Div Dir) 1263
	JOHNSON, Linda B. (Docums		
	Libn) 607	Savannah-Chatham County Board of	BURKE, Grace W. (Adminstrv
	OKEEFE, Julia C. (Univ Archvst) . 919	Educ (GA)	Coordntr for Media Srvs) 160
	SALZER, Elizabeth M. (Univ	Save the Children (CT)	FAESY, Nancy N. (Libn) 361
	Libn) 1078	Sawtelle Goode Davidson &	
Santa Clara Valley Medical		Troilo (TX)	SPRINGER, Michelle M. (Libn) . 1176
Center (CA)	WILSON, Barbara A. (Lib Dir) . . 1350	Sayreville Board of Education (NJ)	WEISBURG, Hilda K. (High Sch
Santa Cruz City County Lib			Libn) 1319
System (CA)	ELGIN, Susan R. (Pub Srvs	Scarborough Pub Lib (ON)	SOLTYS, Amy (Dist Libn) 1166
	Libn) 342	Scarborough Pub Lib Board (ON)	BASSNETT, Peter J. (Chief
	SOUZA, Margaret A. (Head,		Exec Ofcr & Secy-Treas) 63
	Technl Srvs) 1170		MULLERBECK, Aino (Branch
	TURNER, Anne M. (Dir of Libs) . 1264		Head) 877
Santa Fe Community Coll (FL)	LITTLER, June D. (Ref Libn) 734		O'NEILL, Louise N. (Online Govt
Santa Fe Indian Sch (NM)	PIERSON, Robert M. (Catlgr) . . . 972		Docums Libn) 924
Santa Fe International Corp (CA)	KRAMER, Helen A. (Libn) 675	Scarecrow Press (NJ)	DAUB, Albert W. (Pres) 275
Santa Fe Minerals (TX)	DILLARD, Lois A. (Records		HORROCKS, Norman (Vice-
	Supvsr) 303		Pres, Editrl) 561
Santa Fe Pub Lib (NM)	BENNETT, Deborah L. (Young	Scarsdale Board of Education (NY)	FERRERO, Lucia N. (Libn) 373
	Adult Srvs Libn) 81	Scarsdale Junior High Sch (NY)	LEWIS, Marjorie (Libn) 723
Santa Fe Pub Schs (NM)	LOPEZ, Kathryn P. (Libn) 741	Scarsdale Pub Lib (NY)	NICHOLS, Joyce N. (Dir) 901
Santa Fe Railway (IL)	DREAZEN, Elizabeth P.	Scarsdale Sch System (NY)	RABBAN, Elana (Lib Media &
	(Coordntr) 318		AV Srv Coordntr) 1001
Santa Fe Southern Pacific Corp (IL)	ALFONSI-GIN, Mary A. (Law	Schaumburg Township Pub Lib (IL)	BRADLEY, Anne (Ref Libn &
	Dept Libn) 13		Online Scrchr) 125
Santa Gertrudis Independent Sch			MADDEN, Michael J. (Dir) 758
District (TX)	HUNTER, Cecilia A. (Libn) 576		SEAMAN, Sally G. (Ref Libn) . 1109
Santa Monica Hospital Medical		Schenectady County Community	
Center (CA)	ORFIRER, Lenore F. (Libn) 925	Coll (NY)	HELLER, Nancy M. (Dir, Lib
Santa Monica Pub Lib (CA)	FISHER, Alice J. (Ref Libn) 380		Srvs) 524
	GRIFFITH, Virginia M. (Chlds		SCOTT, Frances Y. (Pub Srvs
	Libn) 469		Libn) 1107
	SIMAS, Therese C. (Libn I) 1139	Schenectady County Pub Lib (NY)	ADAMS, Bruce A. (Ref Libn) 4
Santa Rosa Junior Coll (CA)	PETTAS, William A. (Lrng		HODGES, Lois F. (Coorndtr of
	Resrcs Dir) 965		Chlds Srvs) 546
Santa Rosa Memorial Hospital (CA)	HARRIS, Vallena D. (Hlth Lib		OCHS, Phyllis E. (Libn) 915
	Coordntr) 506		SULLIVAN, Robert G. (Ref Libn) 1208
SAR Academy (NY)	HERTZ, Cynthia L. (Lrng Resrc	Schenectady Gazette (NY)	DAZE, Colleen J. (Lib Mgr) 283
	Ctr Dir) 533	Schering-Plough Corp (NJ)	BLUMENTHAL, Sidney L. (Lib
Sarah Bush Lincoln Health			Info Ctr Mgr) 107
Center (IL)	CLAYTON, Nina A. (Med Libn) . . 220		NOCKA, Jean A. (Lit
Sarah Lawrence Coll (NY)	BURSTEIN, Rose A. (Lib Dir) . . 164		Dissemination Supvsr) 906
	ZIESELMAN, Paula M. (Libn) . . 1388	Schertz Cibolo Universal City ISD (TX)	YOUNG, Marjie D. (Libn) 1382
Sarasota County (FL)	HOPKINS, Joan A. (Lib Dir) 558	Schick Shadel Hospital (WA)	MILES, Pamela W. (Med Libn) . . 834
	PIKE, Nancy M. (Pub Srvs Libn) . 973	Schiff Hardin & Waite (DC)	KELMAN, Rosalind S. (Law
	PINTOZZI, Chestalene		Libn) 638
	(Enviromental Libn) 975	Schiff Hardin & Waite (IL)	MICKEY, Melissa B. (Database
Sarasota Opera Association Inc (FL)	PETRIE, Mildred M. (Chairman) . 965		Spclst) 833
Sargent Sch District (CO)	LUDWIG, Deborah M. (K-12 Lib		PATTERSON, Patricia A. (Dir,
	Media Dir) 746		Legal Info Srvs) 948
Sarris Bookmarketing Service (NY)	SARRIS, Shirley C. (Full Srv Bk	Schiller International Univ (FRN)	DEROODE, Clifford H. (Libn) 294
	Publshg Consult) 1083	Schiller Park Elementary Sch District	
Sartomer Co (PA)	GILLEN, Bonnie J. (Market	81 (IL)	EFFERTZ, Rose (Media Dir) 338
	Analyst) 435	Schlow Memorial Lib (PA)	LINDSAY, Ann M. (Technl Srvs
SK Alcohol & Drug Abuse			Head) 729
Commission (SK)	KING, Karen P. (Libn) 651	Schlumberger Doll Research (OT)	DANKS, Mary E. (Supvsr) 54
Saskatchewan Archives Board (SK)	HANDE, D A. (Acting Dir) 494	Schnader Harrison Segal &	
Saskatchewan Education (SK)	DUPERREAULT, Marilyn J.	Lewis (DC)	SIKKEMA, Fern C. (Libn) 1137
	(Spcl Srvs Coordntr) 327	Schnader Harrison Segal &	
Saskatchewan Highways &		Lewis (PA)	GLOECKNER, Paul B. (Chief
Transportation (SK)	BASLER, Ellen L. (Libn) 63		Libn) 441
Saskatchewan Legislative Lib (SK)	POWELL, Marian 988	Schneider Services International (TN)	BOYD, Effie W. (Technl Libn) . . . 122
Saskatchewan Lib (SK)	CAMPBELL, Joylene E. (Dir) . . . 177	Scholastic Inc (NY)	MASON, H J. (Lib & Bookstore
	IVANOCHKO, Robert W. (Ref		Promotion Mgr) 781
	Unit Supvsr) 585	Scholl Coll of Podiatric Medicine (IL)	NAGOLSKI, Donald J. (Assoc
Saskatchewan			Dir for Lib Srvs) 886
Telecommunications (SK)	POGUE, Basil G. (Corprt	Sch Administrative Unit 57 (NH)	BLESH, Tamara E. (Dir of Media
	Practices & Libs Mgr) 979		Srvs) 105
		Sch Board of Broward County (FL)	KLASING, Jane P. (Dir) 657
		School Board of Putnam County (FL)	MORGAN, Ina K. (Media Dir &
			Head Libn) 864

Sch Board of Saint Lucie County (FL)	HARRIS, Martha J. (Head Media Spclsts) 505	
Sch Board Sarasota County (FL)	DANIEL, Marianne M. (Media Consult) 272	
Sch District of Greenville County (SC)	SCALES, Pat R. (Lib Media Spclst) 1087	
Sch District of Lancaster (PA)	FRANCOS, Alexis (Tchr) 396	
	WALKER, Sue A. (Prog Coordntr for Lib Media Srvs) 1296	
Sch District of New London (WI)	DIEHL, Carol L. (Lib Media Srvs & Instrcl Tech Dir) 301	
Sch District of Philadelphia (PA)	BENDER, Evelyn (Libn) 79	
	BUCK, Patricia K. (Asst Libn) . . . 154	
	POLITIS, John V. (Libn) 981	
	STEINBERG, Eileen (Middle Sch Libn) 1185	
	USES, Ann K. (Libn) 1270	
School District of Pickens County (SC)	BLAIR, Sharon K. (Sch Libn & Media Spclst) 103	
Sch District of Platteville (WI)	KRENTZ, Roger F. (Dist Media Dir) 677	
Sch District of Rhinelander (WI)	SLYGH, Gyneth (Lrng Resrc Srvs Dir) 1151	
Sch District of Superior (WI)	AXT, Randolph W. (Spcl Capacity) 42	
Sch District of the City of St Charles (MO)	TERRY, Virginia W. (Elem Lib Supvsr) 1232	
Sch District of Waukesha (WI)	ROOZEN, Nancy L. (Chair, Lib-Media Dept) 1054	
Sch District of Wisconsin Rapids (WI)	LINDSAY, Jane A. (Elem Sch Libn) 729	
Sch District 1 Laramie County (WY)	MIDDLETON, Dorothy J. (Libn) . . 833	
Sch District 105 of La Grange (IL)	FERRO-NYALKA, Ruth R. (Lib Lrng Ctr Dir) 374	
Sch District 208 (IL)	HELLER, Dawn H. (Media Srvs Coordntr) 524	
Sch District 30 (IL)	WEISMAN, Kathryn M. (Dir) . . . 1319	
Sch District 38 (BC)	WEESE, Dwain W. (Tchr & Libn) 1316	
Sch Lib Journal (NY)	JONES, Trevelyn E. (Bk Rvw Edit) 615	
School of Aerospace Medicine (TX)	FRANZELLO, Joseph J. (Srch Analyst & Romance Lang Libn) 398	
Sch of Theology at Claremont (CA)	COBB, Jean L. (Ref Libn) 224	
	FREUDENBERGER, Elsie L. (Catlgng Dept Head) 402	
Sch Sisters of Notre Dame (WI)	GENIN, M S. (Archvst) 427	
Sch Sisters of St Francis (WI)	MISNER, Barbara (Archvst) 847	
Schoolcraft Coll (MI)	NUFFER, Roy A. (Libn, Info Srvs) 912	
Schs of the Sacred Heart (CA)	HAWKINS, Nina L. (Lib Adminstr) 514	
	LESH, Jane G. (Lib Dir) 718	
Schottenstein Zox & Dunn LPA (OH)	D'AMORE, Denice M. (Head Libn) 272	
Schroeder Editorial Services (IL)	SCHROEDER, Sandra J. (Pres) 1100	
Schumpert Medical Center (LA)	WILLIS, Marilyn (Dir of Med Lib) 1348	
Schuyler-Chemung-Tioga BOCES (NY)	LAPIER, Cynthia B. (Dir) 697	
Schwab Goldberg Price & Dannay (NY)	GOLDBERG, Morton D. 444	
Schwabe Williamson Wyatt (OR)	DAVID, Kay O. (Libn) 276	
Schwartz Kelm Warren & Rubenstein (OH)	HUNE, Mary G. (Coordntr of Info Srvs) 574	
Science Applications International Corp (CA)	GIBSON, Joanne (Archvst & Manuscript Cur) 432	
Science Applications International Corp (VA)	HAHN, Margaret M. (Info Srvs Dir) 483	
	MOORE, Penelope F. (Info Resrcs Spclst) 861	
Science Associates/International Inc (NY)	LYONS, Ivan (Publshr) 753	
Sci-Tech Information Services (NJ)	JOHNSON, Minnie L. (Info Broker) 607	

Scientific Management Associates Inc (MD)	OMAR, Elizabeth A. (Technl Libn) 923	
Scott Air Force Base (IL)	GORDON, Diane M. (Libn) 451	
Scott & White Memorial Hospital (TX)	WORLEY, Merry P. (Dir) 1369	
Scott City Elementary Sch (KS)	BARTLETT, Gwenell J. (Elem Libn) 61	
Scott Foresman & Co (IL)	HARRIS, Jane F. (Asst Libn) 504	
	ROBERTSON, S D. (Head Libn) 1042	
Scott Hulse Marshall Feuille et al (TX)	MCDONALD, Brenda D. (Libn) . . 802	
Scott Sebastian Regnl Lib (AR)	CLEVENGER, Judy B. (Lib Dir) . . 221	
Scottsbluff Pub Lib (NE)	OLTMANNS, Judith A. (Libn, Technl Srvs) 923	
Scottsboro Board of Education (AL)	ANDERSON, Ruby N. (Lib Media Spclst) 25	
Scottsdale Community Coll (AZ)	BIGLIN, Karen E. (Technl Srvs Libn) 96	
Scottsdale Pub Lib (AZ)	COLE, Christopher H. (Technl Srvs Coordntr) 230	
	COLE, Mitzi M. (Ref Libn) 231	
	GOEBEL, Heather L. (Ref Coordntr) 443	
	KLIMIADES, Mario N. (Southwest Libn) 661	
	PILLOW, William H. (Civic Cntr Lib Mgr) 973	
Scripps Clinic and Research Foundation (CA)	NEELY, Jesse G. (Head Med Libn) 892	
Scripps Clinic Medical Group Inc (CA)	DITO, William R. (Div of Lab Medcn Head) 305	
Scripps Coll (CA)	DRAKE, Dorothy M. (Retired Coll Libn & Prof) 318	
SDC Information Services (CA)	BROOKS, Kristina M. 140	
	SCHWARTZ, A (Gen Mgr) 1104	
SDSM & T (SD)	SCHWARTZ, James M. (Edit, Resrch Word Prcsng Nwsltr) 1104	
Seaford Pub Lib (NY)	FLUCKIGER, Adrienne N. (Dir) . . 386	
Seaforth Coll of Technl & Further Educ (AUS)	TANNER, Elizabeth (Libn in charge) 1222	
Seagate Associates (NJ)	GENTNER, Claudia A. (Sr VP) . . 427	
Searchline Associates Inc (MA)	SOVNER-RIBBLER, Judith (Pres) 1170	
Searchquest (MA)	COPPOLA, Peter A. (Mgr, Resrch & Ref) 245	
Sears Roebuck & Co (IL)	SYED, Mariam A. (Libn) 1217	
	WARNER, Claudette S. (Corprt Info Ctr Mgr) 1305	
Seattle Country Day Sch (WA)	MOCKETT, Sara H. 851	
Seattle First National Bank (WA)	PRIVAT, Jeannette M. (Asst VP & Mgr) 994	
Seattle Pacific Univ (WA)	HILL, Ann M. (Asst Dir of Pub Srv) 539	
	MCDONOUGH, George E. (Engl Prof & Univ Libn) 803	
	REED, Marcia E. (Biblgph Spclst) 1015	
Seattle Pub Lib (WA)	CHEN, Yvonne (Col Devlpmnt Coordntr) 205	
	COLDWELL, Charles P. (Managing Art & Music Libn) . 230	
	FOX, Howard A. (Libn) 394	
	HAMILTON, Darlene E. (Genealogy Libn) 491	
	LEONARD, Gloria J. (Managing Libn) 716	
	MEYER, Laura M. (Chlds Libn) . . 830	
	MILLER, G D. (Sr Asst Managing Libn) 837	
	MYERS, Antoinette B. (Chlds Srvs Libn) 884	
	PUDERBAUGH, Velma E. (Pub Srv Libn) 997	
	TAYLOR, James B. (Managing Libn, Hist/Lit/Quick Info) 1227	
	YEE, J E. (Adult Programming Libn) 1379	
Seattle Trust and Savings Bank (WA)	HUGHES, Dorothy S. (Libn) 571	

Seattle Univ (WA)
JENNERICH, Edward J. (Grad Dean) 598
THOMAS, Lawrence E. (Libn) . . 1237

Secretary of Pub Education (MEX)
MAGALONI, Ana M. (Gen Dir of Libs) 759

SEC ONLINE Inc (NY)
BARRETT, Michael D. (Pres) . . . 59

Securities Data Corp (NY)
WATKINS, Dorothy (Vice Pres) . 1309

Security Life Insurance Co of Denver (CO)
BENDER, Ruth (Corpte Libn) 79

Security Pacific National Bank (CA)
SHEA, Ann W. (Resrch Ofcr) . . 1124

Security Pacific Realty Advisory Srvs (NY)
LEVINE, Linda A. (Resrch Assoc) 720

The Sedbergh Sch (PQ)
WENK, Arthur B. (Math Tchr & Dir of Music) 1324

Sedgwick Deturt Moran & Arnold (CA)
BORKIN, Ann M. (Libn) 116

Sedgwick Tomenson Inc (ON)
CHOUDHURI, Kabita (Mgr) 211

Seek Information Service (CA)
ECKLUND, Lynn M. (VP) 335
GRENIER, Myra T. (Pres) 467

Selby Botanical Gardens (FL)
ALLEN, Francis P. (Libn) 15

Selby Pub Lib (FL)
JULIEN, Dorothy C. (Ref Libn) . 619
STRADER, Helen B. (AV Libn) . 1199

Selective Dissemination of Information (GA)
LETT, Rosalind K. (Info Broker) . . 719

Selkirk Coll (BC)
DEON, Judy S. (Asst Libn, Catgng) 293
MANSBRIDGE, John (Coll Lib Dir) 767
REID, Marion I. (Head Libn) . . . 1019

Selkirk Community Lib (MB)

Semiconductor Equipment & Materials Inst (CA)
SHERMAN, Roger S. (Libn) . . . 1128

Seminole Community Coll (FL)
LINSLEY, Laurie S. (Head of Catlgng) 731

Seminole County Pub Lib System (FL)
RHEIN, Jean F. (Dir of Lib Srvs) 1025

Seminole Pub Lib (OK)
RYAN, Kathleen M. (Dir) 1071

Semmes Bowen & Semmes (MD)
HARRIS, Helen Y. (Libn) 504

Senate of Pennsylvania (PA)
DUSZAK, Thomas J. (Senate Libn) 329
ODOM, Jane H. (Archvst) 917

Senator Lloyd Bentsen (DC)
SEIK, Jo E. (Info Spclst) 1112

Senco Products (OH)

Seneca Coll of Applied Arts & Technology (ON)
DAVIDSON-ARNOTT, Frances E. (Coordntr, Lib Techniques Prog) 277

Seneca Nation of Indians (NY)
BRAY, Ethel E. (Lib Dir) 130

Seneca Pub Lib (IL)
HOGAN, Louise G. (Dir & Libn) . . 549

SENMED (OH)
BAKER, Carole A. (Decision Support Srvs Adminstr) 48

Sentinel Communications Co (FL)
GRIMSLEY, Judy L. (Info Resrcs Mgr) 470

Sentry Insurance A Mutual Co (WI)
WHELIHAN, Annette S. (Asst Libn) 1329

Sequoia Hospital (CA)
HOUGHTON, Barbara H. (Med Libn) 562

Sergent Hauskins & Beckwith Engineers (AZ)
JEROME, Susanne M. (Libn) . . . 599

Service de Recherche Documentaire DSI (PQ)
DUVAL, Marc (Owner) 329

Servio Logic Corp (OR)
SUDDUTH, Susan F. (Corprt Info Ctr Mgr) 1206

Servite High Sch (CA)
RICHARDSON, Helen R. (Libn & Media Spclst) 1029

Seton Hall Univ (NJ)
FIELD, William N. (Libn Emeritus & Raro Bko Cur) 370
HERRERA, Deborah D. (Law Lib Dir) 532
TALAR, Anita (Ref Libn/Asst Prof) 1220

Seton High Sch (MD)
RODDY, Ruth (Libn) 1047

Seton Hill Coll (PA)
PAWLIK, Deborah A. (Lib Dir) . . 951

Seventh Circuit Court of Appeals (IN)
PIASECKI, Patricia S. (Asst Libn - Satellite) 970

Severn Sch (MD)
TITCOMB, Anne S. (Head Libn) 1247

Severy Inc (CA)
BARTH, Nancy L. (Libn) 61

Seward & Kissel (NY)
DAVIS, Robert J. (Chief Law Libn) 280

Seward County Community Coll (KS)
BROWN, Mary A. (Dir, Lrng Resrc Ctr) 146

Sewell & Riggs (TX)

Seyfarth Shaw Fairweather & Geraldson (DC)

Seyfarth Shaw Fairweather & Geraldson (NY)

Seymour Pub Lib (IN)

Shadduck & Sullivan Information Spclst (MN)

Shady Grove Adventist Hospital (MD)

Shadyside Hospital (PA)

Shaker Heights Board of Education (OH)

Shaker Heights Pub Lib (OH)

Shaler North Hills Lib (PA)

Shamokin & Coal Township Pub Lib (PA)

Shand Morahan & Co Inc (IL)

Shane-Armstrong Information Systems (AR)

Shanley High Sch (ND)

Shared Medical Systems (PA)

Sharp Memorial Hospital (CA)

Shasta County Lib (CA)

Shaughnessy Hospital (BC)

Shaw Univ (NC)

Shawnee High School (NJ)

Shawnee Lib System (IL)

Shawnee Local Schs (OH)

Shea & Gould (NY)

Shearman & Sterling (NY)

Shearson Lehman Brothers (NY)

Sheehan Phinney Bass & Green (NH)

Shelby County Pub Lib & Info Center (TN)

Shelby County Sch System (TN)

Sheldon Jackson Coll (AK)

Shelfmark Original Cataloging (CA)

Shell Canada Limited (AB)

Shell Development Co (TX)

Shell Oil Co (TX)

Shell Research Ltd (ENG)

Shelter Rock Pub Lib (NY)

Shenandoah County Lib (VA)

Shenandoah Pub Lib (IA)

Shenendehowa Central Sch (NY)

MAULSBY, Tommie L. (Libn) . . . 787
WILSON, Ann Q. (Libn) 1349

QUINN, Susan (Law Libn) 1000

INGLIS, Catherine A. (Law Libn) . 582
OZINGA, Connie J. (Dir) 933

SHADDUCK, Gregg S. 1118

HERIN, Nancy J. (Med Libn) 531

FETKOVICH, Malinda M. (Hlth Scis Lib Dir) 374

KAPLAN, Lois J. (Libn) 626
JACOBER, Sheryl A. (Asst Dir) . . 589
GRAHAM, Marilyn L. (Chlds Libn) 456
HAHN, Maureen (Adult Srvs) . . . 484
YATES, Diane G. (Lib Dir) 1378

LOWE, Mary E. (Head Libn) 744

FIELD, Connie N. (Libn) 375

SHANE, Charlotte J. (Partner) . . 1120

SORNSIN, Kathleen R. (Libn, Media Spclst) 1168

YOUNG, Dorothy E. (Lib Info Spclst) 1381

WORTHINGTON, A P. (Lib Srvs Dir) 1369

BIEK, David E. (Asst Dir) 95

JONSSON, Ellenor A. (Patients' Libn) 616

TOOMER, Clarence (Lib Dir) . . . 1251

DOMINESKE, Alice M. (Media Spclst) 310

UBEL, James A. (Dir) 1267

MCDANIEL, Deanna J. (Elem Lib Media Spclst) 801

KUMAR, C S. (Asst Libn) 684
O'GRADY, Jean P. (Legal Info Srvs Dir) 918
STRAM, Lynn R. (Systs Libn) . . 1200

ELLENBERGER, Jack S. (Dir of Libs) 343
HAND, Sally C. (Asst Libn) 494
MERKIN, David (Asst Ref Libn) . . 826

RODDEN, Stephanie L. (Asst Vice Pres) 1047

LIZOTTE, Jeanette S. (Libn) 735

LEVINE, Fay E. (Head Catlgr) . . . 720
WUJCIK, Dennis S. (Music Catlgr) 1374

CONLEY, Janis E. (High Sch Libn) 236
WILSON, Donna R. (Sch Libn) . 1350

BOEHMER, Elaine (Assoc Libn) . 109

FELDMAN, Irwin (Pres) 369

ZUBA, Elizabeth J. (Sr Libn) . . . 1390

BRUNNER, A M. (Info Technologist) 151

BAADE, Harley D. (Sr Srvs Rep) 43
CALDWELL, Marlene (Info Analyst) 172
COTE, Carolee T. (Law Libn) . . . 249
DORSETT, Anita W. (Sr Info Analyst) 313
HOWE, Paula E. (Tax Law Libn) . 565
KORKMAS, Carolyn C. (Asst Law Libn) 671
LYDEN, Edward W. (Sr Info Techgst) 750

THORP, Raymond G. (Info Scientist) 1242

CONRAD, Frances M. (Lib Dir) . . 238

STEINBERG, David L. (Dir) 1185

JENSEN, Janet L. (Dir) 598

RATZER, Mary B. (Libn) 1010

Shepherd Coll (WV) — GAUMOND, George R. (Lib Dir) . 423

WATSON, Carolyn R. (Info Srvs Libn) 1309

Sheppard-Pratt Hospital (MD) — FREDENBURG, Anne M. (Med Lib Dir) 399

Sheridan Coll (WY) — IVERSON, Deborah P. (Lib Dir/IRC Chair) 585

Sheridan Coll (ON) — MACKENZIE, Shirley A. (Campus Libn) 756

WILBURN, Marion T. (Lib Techniques Prog Coordntr) . . 1338

Sherman Coll of Straight Chiropractic (SC) — BOWLES, David M. (Lib Dir) 121

Sherwin-Williams Co (IL) — CIBULSKIS, Elizabeth R. (Info Srvs Dir) 214

Sherwin-Williams Co (OH) — HSU, Helena S. (Technl Info Spclst) 567

Shippensburg Univ (PA) — CROWE, Virginia M. (Dir of Libs) 261

CULBERTSON, Judith D. (Asst Prof) 263

HANSON, Eugene R. (Dept of Lib Sci Chairman) 498

SHONTZ, Marilyn L. (Assoc Prof) 1132

Ship's Haven Environmental Info Srvs (MA) — FELICETTI, Barbara W. (Owner) . 370

Shiraz Univ (IRN) — MEHRAD, Jafar (Asst Prof & Head) 821

Shlaes & Co (IL) — MACKEY, Denise R. (Data Base Mgr, Libn Resrchr) 756

Shodair Children's Hospital (MT) — HOLT, Suzy (Info Spclst) 554

Shook Hardy & Bacon (KS) — WITMER, Tonya C. (Info Analyst) 1358

Shook Hardy & Bacon (MO) — HIBBELER, Sara J. (Ref Libn) . . . 536

HUNT, Lori A. (Dir of Lib and Info Srvs) 575

Shoreham-Wading River Sch District (NY) — BENNETT, James F. (Lib Media Spclst) 81

WRIGHT-HESS, Anne H. (Lib Media Spclst) 1373

Shorewood Pub Lib (WI) — WEISMAN, Suzy (Libn) 1319

Shorewood-Troy Lib (IL) — POTENZIANI, Jo A. (Dir) 986

Shorter Coll (GA) — MOSLEY, Mary M. (Lib Srvs Dir) 871

Shreve Memorial Lib (LA) — COLON, Carlos W. (Ref and Reader's Advisory Supvsr) . . . 234

SALTER, Jeffrey L. (Asst Dir) . . 1077

Shubert Foundation (NY) — CHACH, Maryann (Archvst) 196

KUEPPERS, Brigitte (Archvst) . . . 682

Shumaker Loop & Kendrick (OH) — ESBIN, Martha P. (Law Libn) . . . 354

SICA Innovation Consultants Ltd (IRE) — SWEENEY, Gerald P. (Managing Dir) 1215

Sichuan Univ (CHI) — ZHU, Xiaofeng (Asst Libn) 1387

Sidley & Austin (CA) — LAMARTINE, Elisabeth A. (Head Libn) 689

Sidley & Austin (DC) — PACIFICI, Sabrina I. (Libn) 933

Sidley & Austin (NY) — KASPAR, Eileen (Head Law Libn) 629

Sidney Kramer Books/Lib Wholesale Srvs (DC) — KRAMER, William J. (Pres) 675

Siena Heights Coll (MI) — BAKER, Jean S. (Pub Srvs Libn) 48

DOMBROWSKI, Mark A. (Instnl Srvs Dir) 310

Sierra Club (CA) — PRESBY, Richard A. (Libn) 990

Sigma Theta Tau International (IN) — SPARKS, Marie C. (Dir, Lib & Info Srvs) 1171

Silver Platter Information Inc (MA) — CIUFFETTI, Peter D. (Mgr of Devlpmnt) 215

HAMILTON, Fae K. (Customer Support) 492

HATVANY, Bela R. (Gen Mgr & Pres) 512

POOLEY, Christopher G. (Sales Mgr) 983

RIETDYK, Ron J. (Vice pres) . . 1033

Silverado Museum (CA) — SHAFFER, Ellen (Cur) 1119

Simmons Coll (MA) — ANDERSON, A J. (Prof) 21

BAUGHMAN, James C. (Prof) . . . 66

BUSH, Margaret A. (Asst Prof) . . 165

CHEN, Ching C. (Prof & Assoc Dean) 205

DANIELLS, Lorna M. (Instr) . . . 273

HEINS, Ethel L. (Adjunct Prof) . . 522

HERNON, Peter (Prof) 532

INTNER, Sheila S. (Assoc Prof) . 583

LEONARD, Ruth S. (Assoc Prof Emeritus) 717

MATARAZZO, James M. (Assoc Dean & Prof) 783

MCKIRDY, Pamela R. (Asst Prof) 812

SCHWARTZ, Candy S. (Assoc Prof) 1104

SHARE, Donald S. (Catlgr) 1122

SNIFFIN-MARINO, Megan G. (Coll Archvst) 1163

STUEART, Robert D. (Dean & Prof) 1205

Simon Fraser Univ (BC) — FERJUC, Joan A. (Sr Libn) 372

GROVES, Percilla E. (Ref Libn & Fine Arts Libn) 474

MALINSKI, Richard M. (Ref Div Head) 763

Simon Greenleaf Sch of Law (CA) — MONTGOMERY, John W. (Lib Dean & Dir) 856

Simpson Thacher Bartlett (NY) — MARSH, John S. 773

Simsbury Board of Education (CT) — MICHAUD, Noreen R. (Dir of Lib & Media Srvs) 832

Singer Co (NY) — CARPENTER, Dale (Info Spclst) . 184

HAMLIN, Eileen M. (Info Ctr Mgr) 493

VALLIANT, Robert B. (Info Systs Spclst) 1271

Sioux Center Pub Lib (IA) — SIEBERSMA, Lois R. (Dir) 1135

Sioux City Pub Lib (IA) — HUNTING, Susan K. (Head of Info Srvs) 576

SCHEETZ, George H. (Dir) 1090

THOMPSON, Betsy J. (Asst Dir) 1239

Sioux Falls Pub Lib (SD) — CRANMER, Donna C. (Head of Technl Srvs) 255

ST. AUBIN, Kendra J. (Technl Libn) 1075

Sippican Inc (MA) — STILMAN, Ruth (Libn) 1194

Sir Mortimer B Davis Jewish Gen Hospital (PQ) —

SIRCO International (DC) — PFLEIDERER, Stephen D. (Pres) 966

Sirote Permutt McDermott Slepian et al (AL) — LEVINE, Patricia M. (Libn) 720

Sisters of Charity of Seton Hall (PA) — REILLY, Sara L. (Archvst) 1020

Sisters of Divine Providence (MA) — HIRSCH, Elizabeth (Elem Sch Libn) 543

Sisters of Mercy (RI) — LITTLE, Eleanor (Archvst) 733

Sisters of Mercy of Brooklyn (NY) — SULLIVAN, Majella M. (Archvst) 1208

Sisters of Mercy of Pittsburgh (PA) — CASLIN, Adele (Head Archvst) . . 193

Sisters of Mercy of St Louis (MO) — DEMUTH, Elizabeth J. (Archvst) . 291

Sisters of Mercy of the Omaha Providence (NE) — TURNER, Dorothea (Archvst) . . 1264

Sisters of Notre Dame de Namur (CA) — STARK, Anne C. (CA Province Archvst) 1181

Sisters of St Dominic-Amityville (NY) — MURTAGH, Mary B. (Lib Media Chairperson) 882

Sisters of St Dorothy (RI) — SANTILLO, Mary E. (Tchr & Libn) 1082

Sisters of St Francis Holy Name Province (NY) — SERBACKI, Mary (Province Archvst) 1116

Sisters of St Joseph (KS) — THOMAS, Evangeline M. (Dir of Ofc of Histl Std) 1236

Sisters of St Joseph (WI) — GUZMAN, Mary C. (Archvst) . . . 479

Sisters of St Joseph of Carondelet (MO) — DEUTSCH, N E. (Archvst) 297

KELLY, Patricia J. (St Louis Province Archvst) 638

Sisters of St Joseph of Peace (WA) — PATTERSON, Mary E. (Archvst) . 948

Sisters of St Joseph of Wichita (KS) — HESCHMEYER, Laura (Archvst) . 534

Sisters of St Mary of Namur (NY)   HEFNER, Xavier M. (Libn & Archvst) 520
Sisters of the Divine Savior (WI)   KINZER, Ferdinelle M. (Asst Archvst) 653
Sisters of the Holy Names (OR)   GIMPL, Caroline A. (Archvst) . . . 437
Sisters of the Presentation (IA)   OFFERMAN, Mary C. (Lib Coordntr) 917
Sisters of the Sorrowful Mother (OK)   UHL, M C. (Archvst) 1268
Sisters, Servant of Mary of
   Ladysmith (WI)   HENKE, Alice M. (Archvst) 528
Sitka Pub Schs (AK)   MCCLAIN, Harriet V. (Elem Sch Libn) 795
Sixty South Market Law Lib (CA)   DUNCAN, Rebecca (Lib Adminstr) 325
Skadden Arps Slate Meagher &
   Flom (CA)
Skadden Arps Slate Meagher &   KUCZMA, Michelle (Law Libn) . . 682
   Flom (IL)
Skadden Arps Slate Meagher &   MORRIS, Ann (Libn) 866
   Flom (NY)   LOCHER, Cornelia E. (Assoc Libn) 736
Skidmore Coll (NY)   DOE, Lynn M. (Coll Secy) 308
                                        EYMAN, David H. (Head Libn) . . 359
                                        LEWIS, Gillian H. (Head of Technl Srvs) 723
                                        SMITH, Barbara E. (Soc Scis & Govt Docums Libn) 1152
Skidmore Owings & Merrill (NY)   GRETES, Frances C. (Info Srvs Dir) 467
Ski's Market Inc (PA)   CHERESNOWSKI, Linda M. (Secy & Treas) 206
Skokie Pub Lib (IL)   ANTHONY, Carolyn A. (Lib Dir) . . 28
                                        CLELAND, Camille S. (Asst Dir for Technl Srvs, Coordntr) . . . 220
                                        GINSBURG, Coralie S. (Interlib Loan Coordntr) 438
                                        JACOB, Merle L. (Col Devlpmnt Coordntr) 589
                                        PALMORE, Sandra N. (Comunty Srvs Coordntr) 937
                                        SORENSON, Liene S. (Accessible Lib Srvs Mgr) . . 1168
SKP Associates (NY)   PAUL, Sandra K. (Pres) 949
Slippery Rock Univ (PA)   BACK, Andrew W. (Assoc Prof of Lib Sci) 43
                                        JOSEPH, Elizabeth T. (Asst Prof) 617
                                        JOSEPH, Patricia A. (Asst Prof) . 617
Smathers Thompson (FL)   KASKEY, Sid 629
Smith Anderson Blount Dorsett et
   al (NC)   MATZEN, Constance M. (Libn) . . 786
Smith Coll (MA)   BOZONE, Billie R. (Coll Libn) . . . 124
                                        DAVIS, Charles R. (Biblgphr) . . . 278
                                        GRIGG, Susan (Dir) 470
                                        KURKUL, Donna L. (Adminstrv Asst & Stack Supvsr) 684
                                        MORTIMER, Ruth (Cur of Rare Bks & Asst Libn) 870
                                        POIRRIER, Sherry (Visual Resrcs Cur) 980
                                        SCOTT, Alison M. (Asst Cur of Rare Bks) 1106
                                        SLY, Margery N. (Coll Archvst) . 1150
Smith Currie & Hancock (GA)   BAUSCH, Donna K. (Law Libn) . . . 67
                                        HEITZ, Kathleen R. (Law Libn) . . 523
Smith Haughey Rice & Roegge (MI)   RANSOM-BERGSTROM, Janette F. (Law Libn) 1008
Smith Helms Mulliss & Moore (NC)   DUVAL, Barbara C. (Libn) 329
                                        WASHBURN, Anne C. (Libn) . . 1307
Smith Kline & French
   Laboratories (PA)   ANTOS, Brian F. (Sr Info Scientist) 29
                                        PRITCHARD, Barbara (Info Scitst) 994
                                        SHALLEY, Doris P. (Libn) 1119
                                        YOUNG, K P. (Libn) 1382
Smith Kline Bio-Science
   Laboratories (CA)   MACKEY, Lois M. (Libn) 756

Smithsonian Institution (DC)   ADAMS, Robert (Secy) 6
                                        AVERA, Victoria E. (Chief, Automated Biblgph Control) . . . 41
                                        BROOKE, Anna (Chief Libn) 140
                                        CANICK, Maureen L. (Mgr) 178
                                        CHILD, Margaret S. (Asst Dir for Resrch Srvs) 208
                                        CHIN, Cecilia H. (Chief Libn) 208
                                        DAVIES, Mary K. (Libn) 277
                                        DERBYSHIRE, Richard (Arch Coordntr) 294
                                        FINK, Eleanor E. (Chief) 378
                                        FLECKNER, John A. (Archvst) . . 384
                                        GRAY, Mary C. (Chief of Centl Ref Srvs) 460
                                        HARDING, Robert S. (Manuscript Cols Head) 500
                                        HEISS, Harry G. (Archivist) 523
                                        HENNESSEY, Christine (Coordntr) 528
                                        HOBBINS, James M. (Exec Asst to the Secy) 545
                                        JUNEAU, Ann (Natural Hist Libn) 620
                                        KECSKES, Lily C. (Head Libn) . . 633
                                        KENYON, Kay A. (Chief Libn) . . . 643
                                        LEVIN, Amy E. (Libn) 720
                                        LUSKEY, Judith (Archvst & Cur of Photographic Cols) 749
                                        LYNAGH, Patricia M. (Asst Libn) 751
                                        MALOY, Robert (Dir) 764
                                        MAXWELL, Ted A. (Dir) 788
                                        MOSS, William W. (Archs Dir) . . 872
                                        NEFF, William B. (Head of Monographs Sect & Acqs Srvs) 892
                                        NIELSEN, Elizabeth A. (Musm Spclst in Geol) 903
                                        PIETROPAOLI, Frank A. (Libn) . . 972
                                        PRESLOCK, Karen (Chief Libn) . 991
                                        RATNER, Rhoda S. (Chief Libn) 1010
                                        REED, Patricia A. (Cols Info Syst Data Coordntr) 1015
                                        ROBINSON, Margaret L. (Exec Producer) 1044
                                        ROSENFELD, Mary A. (Adminstrv Libn) 1056
                                        SCHALLERT, Ruth F. (Botany Libn, Asst Natural Hist Libn) . 1089
                                        SCOTT, Catherine D. (Chief Libn) 1107
                                        SEITZ, Phillip R. (Proj Asst) . . . 1113
                                        SKARR, Robert J. (Ref Libn) . . . 1145
                                        STANLEY, Janet L. (Chief Libn) 1180
                                        SZARY, Richard V. (Syst Adminstr) 1218
                                        VIOLA, Herman J. (Dir, Quincentenary Progs) 1285
                                        VOGT-O'CONNOR, Diane L. (AV Archvst) 1287
                                        WELLS, Ellen B. (Spcl Cols Chief) 1322
                                        WILLIAMS, Martin T. (Acqs Edit) 1345
Smithsonian Institution (MA)   REY, Joyce (Libn) 1024
Smithsonian Institution (MD)   HAGGINS, Angela N. (Environmental Resrch Ctr Chief) 483
Smithsonian Institution (NY)   MARTINEZ, Katharine (Chief Libn) 779
Smithtown Central Sch District (NY)   ROSAR, Virginia W. (Lib Media Spclst) 1054
Smithtown Township (NY)   SHAPIRO, Barbara S. (Ref Libn) 1121
Smolian Sound Studios (MD)   SMOLIAN, Steven J. (Owner) . . 1162
Snap-on Tools Corp (WI)   HALL, Elizabeth L. (Engng Libn) . 487

Sno-Isle Regional Lib System (WA)
BETZ-ZALL, Jonathan R. (Ref Libn) 92
BUCKINGHAM, Rebecca M. (East Area Supvsr) 154
KAPLAN, Lesly A. (Chlds Libn) . . 626
SCOTT-MILLER, Gwen (Comunty Libn) 1108
STRONG, Sunny A. (Chlds & Yng Adult Srvs Coordntr) . . . 1203
TURNER, Kathleen G. (Libn) . . . 1264
WILSON, Evie (Asst Youth Srvs Coordntr) 1350

Snohomish County Law Lib (WA) SCOTT, Betty Z. (Libn) 1106

Social Issues Resources Series Inc (FL) HARDT, James R. (Regnl Rep) . . 500

Social Law Lib (MA)
FRANZEK, Karyn (Head of Technl Srvs) 398
HAPIJ, Maria S. (Col Devlpmnt Libn) 499
TAVARES, Cecelia M. (Head Catlgng Libn) 1225
TURKALO, David M. (Asst Head Catlgr) 1263

Social Policy Research Group Inc (MA)
RUTTER, Nancy R. (Dir of Info Systs) 1070

Social Sciences Research Council (NY)
RICHIUSO, John P. (Project Archvst) 1030

Social Security Administration (MD)
BREWER, Christina A. (Data Admin Spclst) 134
SMITH, Kathleen A. (Med Lib Technician) 1156

Societe Radio-Canada (PQ)
BACHAND, Michelle (Chief Libn) 43

Society of Actuaries (IL) CHAPA, Joan I. (Resrch Libn) . . . 201
Society of American Archivists (IL)
NEAL, Donn C. (Exec Dir) 890
WEBER, Lisa B. (Automation Prog Ofcr) 1314

Society of Automotive Engineers (PA) HAUGH, Amy J. (Technl Info Spclst) 512

Society of Manufactruing Engineers (MI) GROEN, Paulette E. (Lib Mgr) . . . 471
Sociological Abstracts Inc (CA) CHALL, Miriam (Operations VP) . 197
Socorro Independent Sch District (TX) NORTH, Yvonne M. (Sch Libn) . . 910
Sodarcan Inc (PQ) DUMONT, Monique (Mgr of Documtn Ctr & Info Srvs) 325
Sodus Central Sch (NY) BUTLER, Rebekah O. (Lib Media Spclst) 167
SofTech Inc (OH) O'GORMAN, Jack (Info Spclst) . . 918
Software Engineering Institute (PA) FUCHS, Karola M. (Info Spclst & Libn) 408
Software Smithy (OH) MARSH, Elizabeth C. (Consult) . . 773
Solano County Lib (CA)
CONDRA, Darrel A. (Col Devlpmnt Libn) 236
GOLD, Anne M. (Dir of Lib Srvs) . 444
MCCORMACK, Carolyn (Lib Asst III) 798

Solar Energy Research Institute (CO)
CHERVENAK, Joseph F. (Sect Mgr) 206
MADDOCK, Jerome T. (Lib & Info Srv Mgr) 759

Soldiers and Sailors Memorial Hospital (PA)
PATTERSON, Charlean P. (Dir of Lib and Visual Communication) 948

Solliciteur General du Canada (PQ) MARION, Guylaine (Info Agent) . . 770
Solomon R Guggenheim Museum (NY) WOLF, Marion (Asst Libn) 1360
Solomon Schechter Academy (TX) GREMONT, Joan C. (Sch Libn) . 467
Solon City Schs (OH) RODDA, Donna S. (Lib Coordntr & Media Spclst) 1047
Solution Associates Inc (CA) HUTCHESON, Don S. (Pres) . . . 578
Solutions by Design (VA) LEONARD, Lucinda E. (Sr Consult) 716

Somerset County Board of Education (MD)
SNYDER, Denny L. (Media Spclst) 1164

Somerset County Law Lib (NJ) GENNETT, Robert G. (Law Libn) 427
Somerset County Lib (NJ)
ADAMS, June B. (Dir) 5
WHITING, Elaine M. (Branch Head) 1333
KLINE, Eve P. 661
PLASO, Kathy A. (Libn) 977

Somerset State Hospital (PA)

Somerville Pub Lib (MA) MINTON, Alix M. (Ref Libn) 846
Sonoma County Law Lib (CA) WATSON, Benjamin (Asst Law Libn) 1309
Sonoma County Lib (CA)
HARRIS, Roger L. (Branch Mgr) . 506
MORRISON, Deborah L. (Libn) . . 868
PETTEY, Brent (Ref Libn II) 965
ROSASCHI, Jim P. (Principal Libn Extension Srvs) 1054
SABSAY, David (Dir) 1073
SIMONS, Maurice M. (Asst Coordntr, Adult Srvs) 1141
STRIBLING, Lorraine R. (Project Dir) 1202

Sonoma County Office of Education (CA) LEE, Mildred C. (Libn & Consult) . 711
Sonoma County Pub Lib (CA) WALSH, Donamarie F. (Ref Libn) 1299
Sonoma Developmental Center (CA) MOSIER, Eric M. (Sr Libn) . . . 871
Sonoma State Univ (CA)
HARRIS, Susan C. (Dir of the Lib) 506
WOLLTER, Patricia M. (Ref Libn) 1361

Sonoma Valley Unified Sch District (CA)
LUNARDI, Albert A. (Libn) 748
Sookmyung Women's Univ (SKO) KIM, Soon C. (Assoc Prof) 649
Sophienburg Museum & Archives (TX) SCHUMANN, Iris T. (Archs Chairperson & Coordntr) . . . 1103
Sorokin & Sorokin PC (CT) BARNUM, Deborah C. (Law Libn) 58
Sound View Press (CT) FALK, Peter H. (Resrch Dir) . . . 362
Source Telecomputing Corp (VA)
BUSSMANN, Steve (Mktg Devlpmnt Mgr) 166
EDWARDS, Wilmoth O. (Mgr) . . . 338
FILIPPONE, Anne (VP, Sales & Mktg) 377
KELLER, Jay (Pres) 635
LITTLE, William (Software Mktg Dir) 734
LOVETT, Bruce (Market Devlpmnt Mgr) 743
MAJOR, Skip (Product Devlpmnt Dir) 762
NEWLAND, Barbara (VP, Prod Devlpmnt) 899
RINALDI, Roberta (Mktg Dir) . . . 1035
RYAN, Maureen (Sales Dir) . . . 1071
STRATT, Randy (Mktg Devlpmnt Dir) 1200

Sources Pub Lib (PQ) GOLDEN, Helene (Lib Dir) 445
South Australian Coll of Advanced Educ (AUS) BEATTIE, Kathleen M. (Lecturer) 70
South Australian Institute of Technology (AUS) FOSKETT, Antony C. (Prof & Head of Sch) 392
South Baltimore General Hospital (MD) LAY, Shirley (Med Libn) 705
South Bay Family Practice (CA) FIEDLER, Albert E. (Physician) . . 375
South Bend Pub Lib (IN)
FUTA, Debra D. (Automated Srvs Systs Coordntr) 411
GUTSCHENRITTER, Victoria M. (Libn) 479
OSTROWSKI, Lawrence C. (AV Srvs Head) 929
PIANE, Mimi (Programming & Publicity Coordntr) 969
WARREN, Hugh P. (Persnl Srvs Adminstr) 1306

South Burlington Community Lib (VT) KNEELAND, Marjorie H. (Dir) . . . 664
South Carolina Dept of Archs & History (SC) HELSLEY, Alexia J. (Supvsr) . . . 525

South Carolina Department of Education (SC)
EHRHARDT, Margaret W. (Lib Media Consult) 339

South Carolina Dept of Health & Envirom (SC)
KRONENFELD, Michael R. (Eductnl Resrcs Ctr Dir) 679

South Carolina Electric & Gas Co (SC)
MOSS, Patsy G. (Libn) 872

South Carolina Historical Society (SC)
MOLTKE-HANSEN, David (Dir) . 853

South Carolina Lib Association (SC)
MAXIM, Virginia (Exec Secy) ... 787

South Carolina State Coll (SC)
JOHNSON, Minnie M. (Asst Prof & Ref & Info Spclst) 607
SMALLS, Mary L. (Coordntr, Col Organz) 1151
TAPLEY, Bridgette M. (Ref & Info Spclst) 1223
WILLIAMS-JENKINS, Barbara J. (Lib Dir & Prof) 1347

South Carolina State Lib (SC)
CALLAHAM, Betty E. (State Lib Dir) 173
FREEMAN, Larry S. (Field Srv Libn) 401
HERRON, Margie E. (Field Srvs Dir) 533
LANDRUM, John H. (Deputy Dir) 693
LAW, Aileen E. (Field Srv Libn) .. 704
MAZUR, Marjorie A. (Technl Srvs Dir) 791
MCGREGOR, Jane A. (Chld's Srvs Consult) 808
NOLTE, Alice I. (Field Srv Libn) . 908
WILLIAMS, Guynell (Sr Ref Libn) 1343

South Carolina Supreme Court (SC)
BARDIN, Angela D. (Libn) 56

South Central Kansas Lib System (KS)
GATTIN, Leroy M. (Dir) 422
HAWKINS, Paul J. (Asst Dir) ... 514

South Central Lib System (WI)
DAVIS, Phyllis B. (Automation Coordntr) 280
LUND, Patricia A. (Mutitype & Interloan Consult) 748
MCCONNELL, Shirley M. (Adult Srvs Consult) 798

South Central Regnl Medical Lib Program (TX)
CAMACHO, Nancy S. (Prog Devplmnt Coordntr) 174

South Central Research Lib Council (NY)
PACKARD, Joan L. (Asst Spcl Projects Dir) 933
STEINER, Janet E. (Exec Dir) .. 1186

South Chicago Community Hospital (IL)
RAYMAN, Ronald A. (Dir of Lib Srvs) 1011

South Community Hospital (OK)
JORSKI, Sharon D. (Med Libn) .. 617

South Dakota Sch of Mines and Technology (SD)
MORGAN, Bradford A. (Editor & Assoc Prof) 863

South Dakota State Archives (SD)
SOMMER, Linda M. (State Archvst) 1167

South Dakota State Lib (SD)
DAGANAAR, Mark L. (Catlgr) ... 269
GILLILAND, Donna E. (Sch Lib & Media Coordntr) 430

South Dakota State Univ (SD)
BRONSON, Mark C. (Circ Libn) . 140
BROWN, Philip L. (Dept Head) .. 146
CASPERS, Mary E. (Asst Ref Libn) 193
HALLMAN, Clark N. (Ref Head) . 489
HUDSON, Gary A. (Acqs Libn) .. 569
LISTER, Lisa F. (Asst Ref Libn & Intern) 732
RANEY, Leon (Dean of Libs) ... 1007
RICHARDS, Susan L. (Serials Libn & Asst Prof) 1028

South Florida Community Coll (FL)
APPELQUIST, Donald L. (Prof of Biology) 30
MOSLEY, Madison M. (Lib Dir) .. 871

South Florida Water Management Dist (FL)
PLOCKELMAN, Cynthia H. (Dir, Ref Systs) 978

South Georgia Neurological Institute (GA)
CLARKE, Elba C. (Adminstr) 218

South Hills Health System (PA)
KISH, Veronica R. (Dir of Med Record Srvs) 656

South Holland Pub Lib (IL)
NELSON, Barbara L. (Ref Libn) . 893

South Huron Hospital (ON)
WILCOX, Linda M. (Shared Lib Srvs Dir) 1338

South Jersey Regional Film Lib (NJ)
SCHALK-GREENE, Katherine (Exec Dir) 1089

South Jersey Regional Lib Cooperative (NJ)
HYMAN, Karen D. (Exec Dir) ... 580

South Lyon Public Lib (MI)
NIETHAMMER, Leslee (Dir) 904

South Miami Hospital (FL)
STEINBERG, Celia L. (Head Med Libn) 1185

South Mississippi Regional Lib System (MS)
SMITH, Judy S. (Libn) 1156

South Park Township (PA)
SALVAYON, Connie (Dir) 1078

South Plains Coll (TX)
STRICKLAND, Jimmy R. (Dir of Libs) 1202

South Salem Lib (NY)
FOGLESONG, Marilee (Dir) ... 387

South San Francisco Unified Sch District (CA)
NIEBOLT, Henry C. (Libn) 903

South Shore Printers Inc (IL)
MITZIGA, Walter J. (Libn) 850

South Shore Regional Lib (NS)
HIMMELMAN, Pauline 542

South Texas Coll of Law (TX)
LANGSTON, Sally J. (Pub Srvs Libn) 696
SCHWERBEL, Jeannette E. 1105
THOMPSON, Frances H. (Lib Dir) 1239

South Wayne Junior High Sch (IN)
STEVENS, Deborah L. (Media Spclst) 1190

South-Western Publishing Co (OH)
SMITH, C L. (Pres & Chief Exec Ofcr) 1153

Southam Communications Limited (ON)
MAYNARD, John C. (Vice Pres) . 790
WISE, Eileen M. (Libn) 1356
WISE, Sunny 1357

Southcentral Minnesota Interlib Exchange (MN)
LOWRY, Lucy J. (Coordntr) 745
TOHAL, Kate J. (Dir) 1248

Southeast Area Health Education Center (KY)
TURNER, Ray (Med Libn) 1265

Southeast Arkansas Regnl Lib (AR)
LAWSON, Martha G. (Regnl Dir) 705

Southeast Asia Information & Resrch Ctr (PQ)
CAN, Hung V. (Pres) 177

Southeast Missouri State Univ (MO)
BUIS, Edmund L. (Col Devplmnt Libn) 156

Southeastern Baptist Theological Sem (NC)
MCLEOD, Herbert E. (Libn & Professor of Bibliography) 814
PHILBECK, Jo S. (Ref Libn) 967

Southeastern Coll the Assemblies of God (FL)
JONES, Linda L. (Lib Dir) 613

Southeastern Connecticut Lib Association (CT)
BENN, James R. (Dir) 81
HOLLOWAY, Patricia W. (Asst Dir) 552

Southeastern Indiana Area Lib (IN)
SCHLESINGER, Louise D. (Ref Prog Dir) 1094

Southeastern Lib Association (GA)
MEDORI, Claudia (Exec Secy) .. 820

Southeastern Lib Network (GA)
BAUGHMAN, Steven A. (Mgr, Mem Srvs) 66
GRISHAM, Frank P. (Executive Dir) 471
ROBERTS, Lisa G. (Proj Leader) 1041
WILSON, Lesley P. (Mgr) 1351

Southeastern Lib Srvs (IA)
NAVARRE, Emily L. (Adminstr) .. 889

Southeastern Louisiana Univ (LA)
CAIN, Charlene C. (Govt Docums Libn) 171
GREAVES, F L. (Lib Dir) 461
PETERS, William W. (Ref Libn) .. 962

Southeastern Massachusetts Univ (MA)
DACE, Tish (Engl Prof) 269
GIBBS, Paige (Ref Libn) 431

Southeastern New York Lib (NY)

CRAWFORD-OPPENHIEMER, Christine (Interlibrary Loan Coordntr) 257
LAWRENCE, Thomas A. (Asst Dir) 705

Southeastern Oklahoma State Univ (OK)

PARHAM, Kay B. (Lib Dir) 940

Southeastern Pub Lib System (OK)

SIMON, Bradley A. (Exec Dir) . . 1140

Southeastern Univ at Washington (DC)

MUSSEHL, Allan A. (Lib Dir) 883
RISHWORTH, Susan K. (Dir of the Lib) 1036

Southeastern WI Health Systems Agency (WI)

FLETCHER, Nancy S. (Dir of Info and Data Srvs) 384

Southeastern WI Regnl Plng Commission (WI)

KLAUSMEIER, Arno M. (Libn) . . 658

Southen Connecticut Lib Council (CT)

HUPP, Sharon W. (Dir) 577

Southern Alabama Junior Coll (AL)

HARRIS, Jay (Libn) 504

Southern Alberta Institute of Technology (AB)

MATHEZER, Pauline B. (Lib & Info Tech Instr) 784

Southern Baptist Convention (TN)

SUMNERS, Bill F. (Archvst) . . . 1209

Southern Baptist Convention (NGR)

GUNN, Shirley A. (Head Libn) . . . 477

Southern Baptist Sunday Sch Board (TN)

SKELTON, William E. (Buyer) . . 1146

Southern Baptist Theological Seminary (KY)

DEBUSMAN, Paul M. (Ref Libn) . 285
DEERING, Ronald F. (Libn) 287
GERON, Cary A. (Interlib Loan Libn) 429
MAZUK, Melody (Technl Srvs Libn) 791
POWELL, Martha C. (Music Libn) 988
ROBINSON, Nancy D. (Catlg Libn) 1044

Southern California Edison Co (CA)

SCULLY, Patrick F. (Adminstr) . 1109

Southern California Gas Co (CA)

SANDVIKEN, Gordon L. (Info Spclst) 1081

Southern California Rapid Transit Dist (CA)

DEGOOD, S K. (Dist Libn) 288

Southern Coll of Seventh-Day Adventists (TN)

BENNETT, Peg E. (Dir of Libs) . . 82
GRACE, Loranne J. (Technl Srvs Dir) 455

Southern Connecticut State Univ (CT)

CLARIE, Thomas C. (Head Ref Libn) 216
HEINRITZ, Fred J. (Prof of Lib Sci) 522
HILL, John R. (Catlgng Head) . . . 540
HOLMER, Paul L. (Ref/Interlib Loan Libn) 553
HUGHES, Frances M. (Microforms Libn) 571
KUSACK, James M. (Asst Prof) . 685
PROSTANO, Emanuel T. (Dean) 995
STODDARD, Charles E. (Pub Srvs Libn) 1196
TRIOLO, Victor A. (Assoc Prof) . 1257
WALTER, Kenneth G. (Lib Srvs Dir) 1300

Southern Illinois Univ (IL)

MCCOY, Ralph E. (Emeritus Dean of Lib Affairs) 799

Southern Illinois Univ at Carbondale (IL)

BAUNER, Ruth E. (Educ & Psy Libn) 67
BEDIENT, Douglas (Dir Lrng Rescrs Svr) 73
BORUZKOWSKI, Lilly A. (Asst Prof) 117
COHN, Alan M. (Humanities Libn & Engl Prof) 229
COOK, Margaret K. (Asst Educ Libn) 240
COX, Shelley M. (Rare Bk Libn) . 253
CRANE, Lilly E. (Asst Catlgng Libn) 255

Southern Illinois Univ at Carbondale (IL)

DALE, Doris C. (Prof) 270
HARWOOD, Judith A. (Undergraduate Libn) 510
HOUDEK, Frank G. (Law Lib Dir & Assoc Law Prof) 562
JENKINS, Darrell L. (Dir of Lib Srvs) 597
KILPATRICK, Thomas L. (Interlib Loan Head) 648
KOCH, David V. (Spcl Cols Cur, Univ Archvst) 667
MATTHEWS, Elizabeth W. (Law Libn & Prof) 785
PALMER, Carole L. (Asst Humanities Libn) 936
PERSON, Roland C. (Assoc Prof, Asst Undergraduate Libn) 961
PETERSON, Kenneth G. (Dean of Lib Affairs) 964
POTEET, Susan S. (Catlgng Dept Head) 986
RYAN, Sheila (Manuscripts Cur) 1071
STARRATT, Joseph A. (Lib Srvs Asst Dir) 1182
WILSON, Betty R. (Asst Catlgng Libn) 1350
WITHEE, Jane S. (Preservation Lib) 1358

Southern Illinois Univ at Edwardsville (IL)

ABBOTT, John C. (Spcl & Resrch Cols Libn) 1
CALCAGNO, Philip M. (Biblgph Ctl Head) 172
JOHNSON, Charlotte L. (User Srvs Head) 603
MCFARLAND, Mary A. (Sci/Nursing Libn) 805
MOORE, Milton C. (Sr Catlgr & Rare Bk Libn) 860

Southern Illinois Univ Sch of Medicine (IL)

BERK, Robert A. (Lib Dir) 87
DILLEY, Richard A. (Head of Technl Srvs) 303
HITCHCOCK, Gail A. (Head of Catlgng) 544
HORNEY, Joyce C. (Head of Access Srvs) 560
KELLEY, Rhona S. (Head of Ref & Educ Srvs) 636
KLESTINSKI, Martha A. (Ref & Spcl Cols Instr) 661

Southern Maryland Regional Lib (MD)

HURREY, Katharine C. (Dir) 577
TARAN, Nadia P. (Assoc Dir for Regnl Srvs) 1223
WILSEY, Charlotte A. (Regnl Ref Spclst) 1349

Southern Methodist Univ (TX)

BAILEY, Anne M. (Perdcls Libn) . . 46
CASEY, Carol A. (Music Catlg Libn) 192
DOMA, Tshering (Serials Catlgr) . 310
FARMER, David (Head) 364
HEIZER, Carolyn H. (Oost Col Libn) 523
HOLLEMAN, Curt (Libn for Col Mgmt & Devlpmnt) 551
JORDAN, Travis E. (Media Srvs Dir) 617
KACENA, Carolyn (Dir of Lib Automation) 621
LATTIMORE, Clare I. (Serials Dept Head) 702
LETSON, Dawn E. (Cur of Mss & Photographs) 719
LOYD, Roger L. (Assoc Libn) . . . 745
MCTYRE, Ruthann B. (Asst to Music Libn) 818

Southern Methodist Univ (TX)

MONGOLD, Alice D. (Perdcls
Libn) 854
MUCK, Bruce E. (Sr Ref Libn) . . . 874
MURPHY, Kristine L. (Head,
Order Dept) 881
ORAM, Robert W. (Dir) 925
RANDALL, Laura H. (Sr Catlg
Libn) 1006
SKINNER, Robert G. (Music &
Fine Arts Libn) 1146
SNODGRASS, Wilson D.
(Assoc Dir) 1163
SZARKA, Tamara J. (Catlgr) . . 1218
THOMAS, Page A. (Assoc Libn) 1238
TOLMAN, Kimberly S. (Sr Ref
Libn) 1249
UMOH, Linda K. (Catlg Libn) . . 1268

Southern Nazarene Univ (OK)

COCHENOUR, Donnice K. (Dir
of Media) 225
FLINNER, Beatrice E. (Pub Srvs
Coordntr) 385
PELLEY, Shirley N. (Exec Dir) . . . 955
REINBOLD, Janice K. (Coordntr
of Online Srvs) 1021

**Southern New England
Telecommunications** (CT)

HARRISON, Burgess A.
(Account Mgr) 506

**Southern New England Telephone
Co** (CT)

MACDOUGAL, Gary N. (Div
Mgr) 754
STRAKA, Kathy M. (Libn) 1199

Southern Ohio Coll (OH)   MORRIS, Trisha A. (Dir) 867
Southern Oregon State Coll (OR)   BURKHOLDER, Sue A. (Lib Dir) . 161
OTNES, Harold M. (Acqs & Map
Libn) 930
Southern Prairie AEA 15 (IA)   BRANDT, Garnet J. (Media
Spclst) 128
Southern Progress Corp (AL)   NATHEWS, Ann (Libn & Photo
Libn) 889
Southern Univ and A&M Coll (LA)   POUNCY, Mitchell L. (Coordntr
of Technl Srvs) 987
Southern Univ of Baton Rouge (LA)   ROCHE, Alvin A. (Assoc Libn) . 1045
SMITH, Ledell B. (Archvst) 1157
Southern Univ of New Orleans (LA)   GROSS, Mary D. (Head, Technl
Srvs) 472
Southern Univ of Shreveport (LA)   BRAZILE, Orella R. (Head Libn) . 130
Southern Ute Indian Tribe (CO)   FROST, Debra R. (Records
Mgr) 406
Southfield Pub Lib (MI)   BENSON, Carol T. (Adult Srvs
Libn) 83
HORN, Anna E. (Adult Pub Srvs
Coordntr) 559
SMOLER, Shelly (Adult Srvs
Libn) 1162
VERGE, Colleen R. (Support
Srvs Coordntr) 1282
ZYSKOWSKI, Douglas A. (City
Libn) 1392
Southfield Pub Schools (MI)   MOSKOWITZ, May K. (Sch
Libn) 871
Southgate Pub Schools (KY)   FOX, Estella E. (Volunteer Elem
Sch Libn) 394
SouthNet (CA)   KING, Kitty G. (Ref Libn) 651
Southside Hospital (NY)   TRAVERS, Jane E. (Med Libn) . 1254
**Southside Regional Medical
Center** (VA)   POLLARD, Joan B. (Med Libn) . . 981
**Southwest Arkansas Regional
Lib** (AR)   TROMATER, Raymond B. (Dir) . 1257
Southwest Baptist Univ (MO)   VAN BLAIR, Betty A. (Dir of Lib
Srvs) 1272
**Southwest FL Water Management
District** (FL)   TORNABENE, Charles (Libn) . . 1251
Southwest Foundation (TX)   BROOKS, Ruth H. (Asst Libn) . . . 140
**SW Georgia Health Scis Lib
Consortium** (GA)   STATOM, Susan T. (Circuit
Med Libn) 1183
Southwest Georgia Regional Lib (GA)   MULCAHY, Bryan L.
(Reference-Genealogy Libn) . . 876

Southwest Missouri State Univ (MO)

COOMBS, James A. (Map Libn) . 241
FREEMAN, C L. (Coordntr of
CARDS) 400
GREEN, Walter H. (Music Lib
Head, Assoc Prof Lib Sci) . . . 463
HOWELLS, Joyce W. (Head of
Catlgng) 565
KOTAMRAJU, Sarada (Catlgr) . . 673
MACKEY, Neosha A. (Ref
Head) 756
MALTBY, Florence H. (Dept of
Lib Sci Assoc Prof) 764
MCCROSKEY, Marilyn J. (AV
Catlgr & Asst Prof) 800
MEADOR, John M. (Dean of Lib
Srvs) 819
STEWART, Byron (Govt
Docums Libn) 1192
Southwest Regional Lib (MO)   KAISER, Patricia L. (Dir) 622
Southwest Research Institute (TX)   LANG, Anita E. (Asst Libn) 695
Southwest Texas Junior Coll (TX)   KINGSBERY, Evelyn B. (Lib Dir) . 652
**Southwest Texas Methodist
Hospital** (TX)   HOUKE, Billy P. (Med Libn) 563
Southwest Texas State Univ (TX)   CAINE, William C. (Nonprint
Catlgr) 171
HUSTON, Susan S. (Catlg
Mgmt Libn) 578
MEARS, William F. (Dir of Lrng
Resrc Ctr) 820
RILEY, Richard K. (Head
Adminstrv Srvs Libn) 1034
WEATHERS, Jerry D. (Comp
Assisted Ref Srvs Libn) 1312
**Southwest Washington
Hospitals** (WA)   MACWILLIAMS, Sylvia E.
(Libn) 758
Southwest Wisconsin Lib System (WI)   DAWSON, Lawrence (Dir) 282
**Southwestern Baptist Theological
Sem** (TX)

PHILLIPS, Robert L. (Asst Dir
for Pub Srvs & Ref Libn) 969
RUSSELL, Barbara J. (Catlg
Libn) 1068
SIMS, Phillip W. (Music Libn &
Assoc Prof) 1142
WROTENBERY, Carl R. (Dir of
Libs) 1373
Southwestern Bell Corp (MO)   FORD, Gary E. (Mgr) 389
MASHBURN, Ray (Div Mgr) 780
Southwestern Coll (KS)   DECKER, Ralph W. (Registrar) . . 286
ZUCK, Gregory J. (Lib Dir) 1391
Southwestern Ohio Rural Libs (OH)   JOHNSON, Corinne E. (Dir) 603
**Southwestern Oregon Community
Coll** (OR)   TASHJIAN, Sharon A. (Libn) . . 1224
**Southwestern Univ of
Georgetown** (TX)   BIGLEY, John E. (Dir of Circ) 96
SWARTZ, Jon D. (Libs & Lrng
Resrcs Assoc Dean) 1214
**Southwestern Univ of Los
Angeles** (CA)

MORRIS, George H. (Adminstrv
Asst & Biblgphr) 866
STREIKER, Susan L. (Ref &
Media Libn) 1201
WEINER, Carole B. (Circ Libn) . 1318
WHISMAN, Linda A. (Dir of the
Law Lib, Assoc Prof, Law) . . 1329
Sovran Financial Corp (VA)   REEVES, Lois H. (Corprt Libn) . 1017
Soyatech Inc (ME)   GOLBITZ, Peter (Pres) 444
GOTTLIEB, Robert A. (Dir of
Pubns) 453
KINGMA, Sharyn L. (Vice Pres) . 652
**Space Telescope Science
Institute** (MD)   STEVENS-RAYBURN, Sarah L.
(Libn) 1191
Spalding Univ (KY)   CREAMER, Mary M. (Univ
Archvst) 257
FRANCK, Ilona G. (Technl Srvs
Libn) 396
HUFF, James E. (Rare Bks
Libn) 570

Spalding Univ (KY)

Spar Aerospace Ltd (PQ)

Sparta Area Schs (WI)

Sparta High Sch (NJ)

Spartanburg County Pub Lib (SC)

Spartanburg County Sch District Three (SC)

Spartanburg Regional Medical Center (SC)

Spearfish Sch District 40-2 (SD)

Special Information Services Inc (MD)

Special Libs Association (DC)

Special Lib Service (FL)
Spectator Magazine (NC)

Spectra Inc (NH)

Spectrum Emergency Care (MO)
Spence Sch (NY)

Spencerport Central Schs (NY)

Spertus Coll of Judaica (IL)
Spillman Pub Lib (WI)

Spilman Thomas Battle & Kloster Meyer (WV)
Spinning Hills Middle Sch (OH)

Spirit Lake Community Sch (IA)
Spokane Community Coll (WA)

Spokane County Lib District (WA)

Spokane Pub Lib (WA)

STROHECKER, Edwin C. (Lib Sci Prof) 1202
GROSS, Margaret B. (Lib Adminstr) 472
HAUG, Pauline C. (Lib Media Ctr Dir) 512
THOMAS, Carren A. (Eductnl Media Spclst) 1236
BRUCE, Dennis L. (Dir) 149
GRIMLEY, Susan M. (Extension Libn) 470
SMITH, Stephen C. (Ref Libn) . . 1161

WHITE, Ann T. (Dir of Media and Pub Info Srvs) 1330

CAMP, Mary A. (Dir of Lib Srvs) . 175
ASLESEN, Rosalie V. (High Sch Libn) 36

VELLUCCI, Matthew J. (Pres & Consult) 1282
BATTAGLIA, Richard D. (Asst Exec Dir) 64
BENDER, David R. (Executive Dir) 79
BRIMSEK, Tobi A. (Info Resrcs Mgr) 136
DOLAN, Beth C. (Asst Exec Dir, Admin) 309
HILL, Elaine (Asst Edit) 539
MORTON, Sandy (Dir) 870
PALANIJIAN, Barbara (Conf & Exhibits Mgr) 935
RODRIGUEZ, Ruth (Supvsr) . . . 1048
WARYE, Kathy (Dir) 1307
WELLINGTON, Carole E. (Support Srvs Mgr) 1322
EVERLOVE, Nora J. (Owner) . . . 359
LAMBERT, John W. (Classical Music Critic) 690
LERNER, Frederick A. (Technl Info Srvs Head) 717
MUETH, Elizabeth C. (Libn) 875
CORSON, Cornelia M. (Head Libn) 248
GOODRICH, Carolyn B. (Lower Sch Libn) 449
HARRINGTON, Judith F. (Lib Media Spclst) 504
SALTZMAN, Robbin R. (Libn) . . 1077
HANAMAN, Nancy J. (Chlds Libn) 494

ORLANDO, Karen T. (Law Libn) . 926
ARK, Connie E. (Eductnl Lib Media Spclst) 31
KOEPP, Sara H. (Media Dir) 668
REHMS, Jane C. (Instrcl Designer & Media Srv Supvsr) 1017
DEDAS, Madelyn W. (Asst Dir for Pub Srvs) 286
ICE, Priscilla T. (Managing Libn) . 581
WIRT, Michael J. (Dir) 1356
BENDER, Betty W. (Lib Dir) 79
FREDRICKSON, Dennis C. (Info Srvs Head) 400
JONES, Charlotte W. (Mgr, Neighborhood Srvs) 611
LANE, Steven P. (Educ & Job Info Ctr Libn) 694
TYSON, Christy (Young Adult Srvs Coordntr) 1267
WEBER, Joan L. (Neighborhood Srvs Libn) 1314
WOLFE, Lisa A. (Pub Info Coordntr) 1361

The Sporting News (MO)

Sprague Electric Co (MA)
Spring Arbor Coll (MI)

Spring Branch Independent Sch District (TX)
Spring Hill Coll (AL)

Spring Lake Township (MI)
Springdale Sch District (AR)

Springer-Verlag New York Inc (NY)
Springfield City Lib (MA)

Springfield Coll (MA)

Springfield-Greene County Lib (MO)

Springfield Lib & Museums Association (MA)

Springfield Pub Sch System (MA)

Springfield Technical Community Coll (MA)

Springfield Township Lib (PA)
SPS Technologies Inc (PA)

SRI International (CA)

SSC&B Inc (NY)
Stamford High Sch (CT)

Stamford Hospital (CT)
Standard & Poor's Compustat Services Inc (CO)

Standard & Poor's Corp (MA)
Standard & Poor's Corp (NY)

Standard Educational Corp (IL)
Standard Oil Co (OH)

GIETSCHIER, Steven P. (Histl Records Dir) 433
COGHLAN, Jill M. (Resrch Libn) . 227
BURNS, David J. (Technl Srvs Head) 162

MEADOR, Cornie M. (Libn) 819
PEARSON, Peter E. (Ref Libn) . . 953
SELLEN, Mary K. (Lib Dir) 1114
SHERIDAN, Clare A. (Lib Dir) . . 1127
GREESON, Janet S. (Lib Media Spclst) 465
FUGLE, Mary E. (Sales Mgr) 408
LAPIERRE, Barbe (Catlgr) 697
MCLAIN, Guy A. (Archvst) 813
STEVENS, Michael L. (Technl Prcsng Supvsr) 1190
TAUPIER, Andrea S. (Sr Ref Libn) 1225
DROSS, Polly C. (Online Info Srvs Libn) 320
DUCKWORTH, Paul M. (Ref Dept Mgr) 322
GLEASON, Virginia L. (Chlds Supvsr) 440
GLENN, Michael D. (Local Hist Libn) 441
LEITLE, Barbara K. (Branch Mgr and Chlds Libn) 714
SANDERS, Jan W. (Mgr, Brentwood Branch Lib) 1080
SMITH, Jewell (Dir) 1156

SKIPTON, Iris E. (Branch Supvsr) 1146
ERICKSON, Norma J. (Teacher-Librarian) 352

WURTZEL, Barbara S. (Ref Libn) 1374
NAISMITH, Patricia A. (Dir) 887
WOODLOCK, Stephanie (Corprt Technl Libn) 1366
DENNETT, Stephen C. (Pubns Mgr) 292
KLEINER, Donna H. (Sr Info Spclst) 660
MYERS, Nancy J. (Sr Ref Libn) . 884
REDFIELD, Elizabeth (Netwk Info Ctr Lib Srvs Mgr) 1014
ROLEN, Helen T. (Supvsr, Technl Srvs) 1051
STEELMAN, Lucille A. (Resrc Coordntr) 1184
CONNELLY, Marie 237
SERGEL, Carol K. (Lib Media Dept Head) 1116
FARADAY, Joanna (Lib Dir) 363

HAMBRIC, Donna R. (VP, Operations) 491
MCENTIRE, James E. (Group Vice Pres) 804
COOPER, J P. (Exec Vice Pres) . 243
HERENSTEIN, Ira (Pres) 530
JENSEN, Dennis F. (Lib Mgr) . . . 598
KIESER, Scott P. (Proj Dir) 647
MEYER, Garry S. (Vice Pres, Rating Data Mgmt) 830
O'CONOR, William C. (Proj Dir) . 916
PAYNE, Linda C. (Ref Libn) 951
REINGOLD, Celeste S. (Electronic Srvs Mgr) 1021
KING, David E. (Libn & Sr Edit) . . 650
FELL, Sally B. 370
JANKOWSKI, Dorothy A. (Mgr, Corporate Records & Info Srvs) 593
TURNER, Freya A. (Libn) 1264
YANCEY, Marianne (Info Spclst) 1377

Standard Oil Production Co (TX)

Stanford Medical Center (CA)
Stanford Telecommunications Inc (CA)
Stanford Univ (CA)

Stanislaus County Free Lib (CA)

DAVIS, Connie J. (Libn) 278
KLEIN, Mindy F. (Technl Info
  Srvs Supvsr) 659
METIVIER, Donna M. (Technl
  Libn) 828
YAU, Linda S. (Pub Srvs Asst) . 1378
NELSON, Alice R. (Lib Mgr) 893
ANDERES, Susan M. (Technl
  Srvs Libn) 21
ARROWOOD, Donna J. (Asst to
  Dirs Admin Srvs Technl
  Srvs) 34
BALDRIDGE, Alan (Head Libn &
  Biblgphr) 51
BRIDGMAN, David L. (Ref Libn) . 135
CLAEYS, Luisa T. (Ref Srvs
  Spclst) 215
CROCKETT, Darla J. (Asst
  Chief Libn for Access Srvs) . . 259
DERKSEN, Charlotte R. (Libn &
  Biblgphr) 294
DIBLE, Joan B. (Sci & Tech
  Catlgr) 299
DIMUNATION, Mark G. (Rare
  Bks Libn) 304
FORTSON, Judith (Conservation
  Ofcr) 392
FRANK, Peter R. (Cur for
  Germanic Cols) 397
GRIEDER, Elmer M. (Emeritus) . . 467
HOGAN, Eddy (Data & Info Srvs
  Libn) 549
ITNYRE, Jacqueline H. (GCRC
  Computing Systs Mgr) 585
JOHNSON, Peter A. (Ref Srvs
  Div Head) 608
KRASNER, Joan K. (Chief of
  Access Srvs) 676
LEGER, Norissa (Records Mgr) . . 712
MCELROY, Neil J. (Head of
  Readers' Srvs) 804
MCPHERON, William (Engl &
  Am Lit Cols Cur) 817
MIELKE, Marsha K. (Info
  Consult & Libn) 833
MILFORD, Charles C. (Head) . . . 835
MILLER, Dick R. (Systs Libn &
  Technl Srvs Head) 837
MUSEN, Mark A. (Clinical Instr) . 883
PAI, Herman H. (Acad Assoc
  Libn) 934
PALM, Miriam W. (Asst Chief,
  Serials Dept) 935
REICH, Victoria A. (Chief Libn of
  Serials Dept) 1018
ROSS, Alexander D. (Head Art
  Libn) 1057
SLOCUM, Hannah R. (Head Ref
  Libn) 1150
STANGL, Peter (Dir) 1180
SWEENEY, Suzanne (Head
  Catlgng Libn) 1215
THOMAS, Vivian (Catlg Libn) . . 1238
TRUJILLO, Roberto G. (Chief) . 1259
VADEBONCOEUR, Elizabeth J.
  (Info Consult & Libn) 1270
WARD, Sandra N. (Libn,
  Coordntr of Lib Instrc) 1304
WEBER, David C. (Univ Lib Dir) 1314
WIBLE, Joseph G. (Head Libn,
  Biblgphr for Biol Sci) 1335
WILSON, Karen A. (Head Pub
  Srvs Libn) 1351
WU, Harriet (Catlg Libn) 1373
YEH, Irene K. (Employment
  Coordntr) 1379
ZALEWSKI, Wojciech (Cur for
  Slavic & E European Cols) . . 1385
MOORE, Mary L. (Branch Head) . 860

Stanly County Pub Lib (NC)

Staples High Sch (MN)

Star-Kist Foods Inc (CA)

Stark County District Lib (OH)

Starved Rock Lib System (IL)
State College Area Sch District (PA)

State Farm Insurance Companies (IL)

State Historical Society of Iowa (IA)
State Historical Society of Missouri (MO)
State Historical Society of North Dakota (ND)

State Historical Society of Wisconsin (WI)

State Journal-Register (IL)
State Law Lib of Montana (MT)

State Lib of Florida (FL)

State Library of Georgia (GA)

State Lib of Iowa (IA)

State Lib of Louisiana (LA)

State Lib of Massachusetts (MA)

ESTES, Elizabeth W. (Asst Dir) . . 355
PARRISH, Nancy B. (Info Srvs
  Libn) 944
PRESTEBAK, Jane R. (High
  Sch Libn) 991
JADWIN, Rochelle J. (Mgmt
  Info Systs Libn) 591
CLARK, Kay S. (Online
  Coordntr) 217
GREEN, Gary A. (Technl Srvs
  Coordntr) 461
PLUMMER, Karen A. (Libn II) . . . 978
WILLSON, Richard E. (Exec Dir) 1349
WOLFE, Mary S. (Elem Sch
  Libn) 1361
JUSTICE, Sylvia H. (Asst Corp
  Libn) 620
WORK, Dawn E. (Catlgr) 1369

TUCKWOOD, Jo A. (Acq Libn) . 1262

NEWBORG, Gerald G. (State
  Archvst) 898
VYZRALEK, Dolores E. (Chief
  Libn) 1290

DANKY, James P. (Newspapers
  and Periodicals Libn) 274
EDMONDS, Michael (Supvsr) . . . 336
MULLER, H N. (Dir) 877
VANCE, Sandra L. (Editrl Libn) . 1273
GRASMICK, Brenda (Technl
  Srvs Libn) 458
MEADOWS, Judith A. (State
  Law Libn) 819
BYRD, Beverly P. (FL Col Libn) . 168
MAYO, Kathleen O. (Lib
  Consult) 790
MILLER, Betty D. (Youth Srvs
  Coordntr) 836
MOUNCE, Marvin W. (Interlib
  Cooprtn Consult) 873
PRATT, Darnell D. (Acqs Dept
  Head) 990
SUMMERS, Lorraine S. (Asst
  State Libn) 1209
WILKINS, Barratt (State Libn &
  Div Dir) 1340
HALL, Richard B. (Lib Building
  Consult) 488
COCHRAN, William M. (Lib
  Consult & LSCA Prog
  Coordntr) 225
DAGLEY, Helen J. (AV Srvs
  Head) 269
NICKELSBURG, Marilyn M.
  (Youth Srvs Consult) 902
REES, Pamela C. (Head of Info
  Srvs Bureau) 1016
ROBERTSON, Linda L. (Dir, Ofc
  of Lib Devlpmnt) 1042
BRADLEY, Jared W. (Serials
  Sect Head) 126
FERGUSON, Anna S. (Asst
  Coordntr) 372
FERGUSON, Gary L. (Asst
  Head of Ref Dept) 372
JAQUES, Thomas F. (State
  Libn) 594
SMITH, Richard J. (Spcl Srvs
  Dir) 1160
BEARDEN, Eithne C. (Pub Srvs
  69
NASON, Jennifer L. (Docums
  Libn) 888
SIEGEL, Bette L. (Asst Docums
  Libn) 1136

State Lib of Ohio (OH) — BETCHER, Melissa A. (Systs & Netwk Consult) 92
CHESKI, Richard M. (State Libn) 207
HEARD, Jeffrey L. (Catlgng Sect Head) 518
HORDUSKY, Clyde W. (Docums Spclst & Head of Govt Docums) 559
PHILIP, John J. (Head, Field Operations) 967
SMITH, Ellen A. (Ref Libn) . . . 1154
WILKS, Cheri L. (Ref Libn II) . 1341

State Lib of Pennsylvania (PA) — BROWN, Donald R. (Col Mgmt Prog Coordntr) 143
BRYSON, Susan A. (Catlgr) 152
CAHILL, Colleen R. (Libn II & Catlgr) 171
FELIX, Sally T. (Advsy Srvs & Contng Educ Coordntr) 370
FUNK, Elizabeth A. (Lib Devlpmnt Advisor) 410
HOFFMAN, David R. (Lib Srvs Dir) 547
INGRAHAM, Alice L. (Ref & Info Srvs Coordntr) 582
MALLINGER, Stephen M. (Lib Devlpmnt Adv) 763
SONDEN, Mary L. (Lib Asst II) . 1167
TENOR, Randell B. (Law Sect Ref Libn) 1231

State Network Services (MD) — CUNNINGHAM, Barbara M. (Chief) 265

State of Arizona (AZ) — SHABERLY, Leanna J. (Film Libn) 1118
TEVIS, Raymond H. (Asst Resrch Div Dir) 1233

State of California (CA) — BURNS, John F. (State Archvst) . 162
MARTINEZ, Barbara A. (Sr Libn) 779
STEVENSON, Marilyn E. (CA Lib Srvs Bd Mem) 1191

State of Colorado (CO) — CAMPBELL, Frances D. 176
State of Connecticut (CT) — TRAVER, Julia M. (Libn II, Hlth Scis Lib) 1254

State of Delaware (DE) — TRYON, Roy H. (State Archvst & Records Adminstr) 1260
WYCHE, Louise E. (Dir & State Libn) 1374

State of Hawaii (HI) — ELDREDGE, Jeffrey R. (Libn III) . 342
FREITAS-OBREGON, Brenda J. (Yng Adult Libn) 401
KAN, Katharine L. (Libn III) 624
MORGAN, Sally W. (Head Libn) . 864
USHIRODA, Christine H. (Sch Libn) 1270
VAN NIEL, Eloise S. (Performing Arts Spclst) 1276

State of Illinois (IL) — DALY, John E. (Dir) 271
EFIRD, Frank K. (Archvst) 338

State of Kentucky (KY) — BARRISH, Alan S. (Info Spclst) . . . 60
GILMER, Wesley (State Law Libn) 437

State of Maine (ME) — PIERCE, Ann E. (State Court Lib Supvsr) 971

State of Maryland (MD) — COLBORN, Robert J. (Adminstr) . 230
PAPENFUSE, Edward C. (State Archvst) 939

State of Michigan (MI) — CALLARD, Carole (Spcl Cols Libn) 173
FRY, James W. (State Libn) 406
SCHOLFIELD, Caroline A. (Ref Libn) 1098
SEFCIK, Delphine M. (Med Libn) 1111

State of Minnesota (MN) — WRIGHT, Myrna F. (Head Libn) . 1372
State of Nevada (NV) — ROCHA, Guy L. (Archvst) 1045
State of New Hampshire (NH) — MEVERS, Frank C. (State Archvst and Dir of Div) 829

State of New Jersey (NJ) — CONLEY, Gail D. (Catlgr) 236
STRONG, Moira O. (Resrch Srvs Chief) 1203
TOMAR, Jeanne (Catlgr) 1249

State of New Mexico (NM) — HENDLEY, Virginia (State Libn) . . 527
State of North Carolina (NC) — TABORY, Maxim (Dir, Lrng Resrc Ctr) 1219

State of Oregon (OR) — TURNBAUGH, Roy C. (State Archvst) 1264

State of Rhode Island (RI) — QUINN, Karen H. (Legislative Ref Libn) 1000
ZIPKOWITZ, Fay (Dept of State Lib Srvs Dir) 1389

State of South Dakota (SD) — KOLBE, Jane (State Libn) 669
State of Tennessee (TN) — HUGHES, Marylin B. (Sr Archvst) 572

State of Utah (UT) — SCOTT, Patricia L. (Local Govt Records Archvst) 1107

State of Vermont (VT) — KLINCK, Patricia E. (State Libn) . 661
State of Wisconsin (WI) — MATTHEWS, Geraldine M. (Dir of Human Srvs Info Ctr) 785

State of Wyoming (WY) — MCGOWAN, Anne W. (Lib Mgr) . 807
MENDOZA, Anthanett C. (Libn) . 824

State Records Center & Archives (NM) — GRAINTO, Mary (Deputy Adminstr) 457

State Street Research & Management Co (MA) — LYNCH, Jacqueline (Libn) 751
State Times Morning Advocate (LA) — LANDRY, Denise C. (Libn) 693
State Transportation Lib (MA) — MATIS, Lynn (Law Libn) 784
State Univ of New York at Albany (NY) — ANDERSON, Carol L. (Access Srvs Asst Dir) 22
BENEDICT, Marjorie A. (Biblgphr & Assoc Libn) 80
BONK, Sharon C. (Asst Dir) 114
HALSEY, Richard S. (Dean) 490
KATZ, William A. (Prof) 630
KLEMPNER, Irving M. (Prof) 660
KNAPP, Sara D. (Comp Srch Srv Coordntr) 663
KNEE, Michael (Scis Biblgphr & Ref Libn) 663
LENZ, Millicent A. (Sch of Info Sci & Policy Asst Prof) 716
LIPETZ, Ben A. (Prof) 732
MCCOMBS, Gillian M. (Head of Catlg Maintenance Dept) 797
MILLER, Heather S. (Acqs Dept Head) 838
MOREHEAD, Joe (Prof) 863
NITECKI, Joseph Z. (Lib Dir) 905
ROBERTS, Anne F. (Libn) 1039
SAFFADY, William (Assoc Prof) 1074
SHAFFER, Kay L. (Slavic Biblgphr & Catlgr) 1119
SMIRENSKY, Helen K. (Asst Libn) 1152
VIA, Barbara J. (Ref Libn & Biblgphr) 1283
WALKER, M G. (Asst Prof) 1296
WELLS, Gladysann (Lib Adminstrv Ofcr) 1322
WHALEN, Lucille (Assoc Dean & Prof) 1328
WING, Judith G. (Sr Asst Libn) . 1354

State Univ of New York at Alfred (NY) — LASH, David B. (Lib Dir) 700
State Univ of New York at Binghamton (NY) — BURNETTE, Michaelyn (Sr Asst Libn) 162
CHAMBERLAIN, Erna B. (Ref & Life Scis Biblgphr) 197
FINN, Margaret M. (Actg Asst Dir) 378
GERACI, Diane (Soc Sci Biblgphr) 428
LINCOLN, Betty W. (Assoc Libn) 728
LINCOLN, Harry B. (Distinguised Srv Prof of Music) 728

State Univ of New York at Binghamton (NY)

MCKEE, George D. (Fine Arts Biblgphr) 810

State Univ of New York at Brockport (NY)

FRASER, Charlotte R. (Sr Asst Libn) 399
MADAN, Raj (Dir of Lib Srvs) . . 758
RAKSHI, Sri R. (Assoc Prof of Theatre) 1004

State Univ of New York at Brooklyn (NY)

COOMBS, Ronald L. (Technl Srvs Div Asst Head) 241
DOHERTY, Mary C. (Sr Asst Libn, Ref Dept) 309
GAFFNEY, Denis C. (Sr Asst Libn) 412
POONITHARA, Pradee P. (Asst Libn) 983
SEMKOW, Julie L. (Head of Lib AV Dept) 1115

State Univ of New York at Buffalo (NY)

ALLERTON, Ellen M. (Asst Libn) 16
BERTUCA, David J. (Serials Mgmt Section Head) 91
BOBINSKI, George S. (Dean and Prof) 108
BRADLEY, Carol J. (Assoc Dir) . 125
BUSH, Renee B. (Asst Libn) 165
CHAPMAN, Renee D. (Technl Srvs Head) 202
CIPOLLA, Wilma R. (Lib Dir) 215
COOVER, James B. (Ziegle Prof of Music & Lib Dir) 244
DAVIS, Susan A. (Head, Serial Records) 281
DECKER, Jean S. 285
DENSMORE, Christopher (Assoc Archvst) 293
DIBARTOLO, Amy L. (Asst Libn & Microforms Libn) 299
DONG, Alvin L. (Student Edit) . . . 311
EDENS, John A. (Dir, Centl Tech Srvs) 336
ELLISON, John W. (Assoc Prof) . 345
GARLAND, Kathleen (Asst Prof, Sch of Info & Lib Std) 419
GIBSON, Ellen M. (Law Lib Dir) . 432
HAAS, Marilyn L. (Ref Libn) 480
HARDY, Gayle J. (Sr Asst Libn) . 500
HEPFER, Cynthia K. (Serials Dept Head) 530
HEPFER, William E. (Serials Dept Head) 530
HERMAN, Edward (Asst Docums Libn) 531
HOPKINS, Judith (Technl Srvs Resrch & Analysis Ofcr) 558
HUANG, C K. (Lib Dir & Adjunct Prof) 568
JONES, Martin J. (Archs & Spcl Cols Assoc Libn) 614
KELLER, Sharon A. (Info Srvs Dept Head) 635
LYMAN, Helen H. (Adjunct Prof) . 751
MCGRATH, Ellen T. (Catlgr) 807
MILLER, Mary F. (Acqs Libn) . . . 840
NEUMEISTER, Susan M. (Sr Asst Libn) 897
NEWMAN, George C. (Lib Dir) . . 899
NUZZO, David J. (Acqs Dept Head) 912
NUZZO, Nancy B. (Record Catlgr & Ref Libn) 912
ROSE, Pamela M. (Technl Asst for Acqs) 1055
SCHUTT, Dedre A. (Serials Catlgng Asst Libn) 1103

State Univ of New York at Buffalo (NY)

SENTZ, Lilli (Hist of Medcn Libn) 1115
SHIELDS, Gerald R. (Asst Dean) 1130
SMITH, Karen F. (Docums & Microforms Dept Head) 1156
STIEVATER, Susan M. (Ref Libn) 1194
VON WAHLDE, Barbara (Univ Lib Dir) 1288
WEBSTER, James K. (Mgr, Info Srvs) 1314
WELLS, Margaret R. (Head of Biblgph Instrc) 1322
YERKEY, A N. (Assoc Prof) . . . 1380
ZUBROW, Marcia L. (Head Ref Libn) 1391

State Univ of New York at Cobleskill (NY)

GALASSO, Nancy (Head of Technl Srvs) 412
NELSON, Winifred S. (Head of Access Srvs) 895

State Univ of New York at Cortland (NY)

HEARN, Stephen S. (Sr Asst Libn) 518
RITCHIE, David G. (Order Libn & AV Catlgr) 1036
SCHAFFER, D J. (Slide Cur) . . 1089
SCHROEDER, Eileen E. (Tchg Mtrls Ref Libn & Biblgphr) . . 1100

State Univ of New York at Fredonia (NY)

BESEMER, Susan P. (Dir of Lib Srvs) 91

State Univ of New York at Geneseo (NY)

MACLEAN, Paul (Managing Libn) 757
NEESE, Janet A. (Assoc for Col, Devlpmnt, and Admin) 892
QUICK, Richard C. (Dir of the Coll Libs) 999
WEAS, Andrea T. (Sr Asst Libn & Catlgr) 1311

State Univ of New York at Morrisville (NY)

DREW, Wilfred E. (Pub Srvs Libn) 319

State Univ of New York at New Paltz (NY)

CONNORS, William E. (Dir of the Lib) 238
LEE, Chui C. (Coordntr) 709
NYQUIST, Corinne E. (Interlib Loan & Regnl Lending Head) . 913

State Univ of New York at Old Westbury (NY)

COLLANTES, Lourdes Y. (Assoc Libn) 232
JUNG, Norman O. (Dir of Lib & Media Ctr) 620

State Univ of New York at Oneonta (NY)

ARNOLD, Linda A. (Head, Catlgng Dept) 34
BENSEN, Mary L. (Ref Libn) 83
BULSON, Christine (Head of Ref & Assoc Libn) 156
CLARK, Diane A. (Spcl Cols Libn) 216
CROWLEY, John V. (Assoc Dir of Libs) 261
DOWNING, Elaine L. (Head of Acqs & Access) 316
FRANCIS, Barbara B. (Sr Asst Ref Libn) 396
FRANCO, Kathryn C. (Ref Libn) . 396
GERBERG, Andrea F. (Asst Libn) 428
ICE, Diana C. (Asst Head of Catlgng) 581
JOHNSON, Richard D. (Dir of Libs) 608
POTTER, Janet L. 987

State Univ of New York at Oneonta (NY)

QUINN, Sharon E. (Asst Libn) . . 1000
ROUGEUX, Debora A. (Sr Asst
   Libn) 1061
SORGEN, Herbert J. (Libn) 1168

State Univ of New York at Oswego (NY)

CHU, Sylvia (Catlgr Libn) 213
DIAL, Ron (Circ Libn) 299
JUDD, Blanche E. (Libn &
   Coordntr of Ref Srvs) 618
OSBORNE, Nancy S. (Assoc
   Libn) 927
RYAN, Constance V. (Asst Dir) . 1070
SMILEY, Marilynn J.
   (Distinguished Tchr Prof) . . . 1151

State Univ of New York at Plattsburgh (NY)

BURTON, Robert E. (Dir of Libs) . 164

State Univ of New York at Potsdam (NY)

FOSTER, Selma V. (OCLC
   Coordntr, Head of Technl
   Srvs) 392

State Univ of New York at Purchase (NY)

EVANS, Robert W. (Dir of Lib) . . 358
FREIDES, Thelma (Head,
   Readers Srvs) 401
GARRETT, Margaret S. (Technl
   Srvs Head) 420
HAIMOVSKY, Kira A. (Art
   Slides Cur) 484
LIE, David W. (Catlgr) 725

State Univ of New York at Stony Brook (NY)

BAUM, Nathan (Head, Ref Dept) . 66
BLOHM, Laura A. (Catlgr) 106
HUFFORD, Jon R. (Microforms
   Libn) 571
KAUFMAN, Judith L. (Spcl Asst
   to the Dir) 631
KENDRICK, Curtis L. (Circ Dept
   Head) 640
KENEFICK, Colleen M. (Senior
   Asst Libn) 640
KING, Christine E. (Sr Asst
   Libn) 650
KINNEY, Daniel W. (Music Lib
   Asst Head & Music Catlgr) . . . 653
PANDIT, Jyoti P. (Head of
   Docums Sect) 937
SALINERO, Amelia (Catlgr &
   Asst Libn) 1076
SEWELL, Robert G. (Asst Dir
   for Col Mgmt and Devlpmnt) . 1117
SIMPSON, Charles W. (Asst Dir
   of Libs for Technl Srvs) 1141
SMITH, John B. (Dir of
   Libs/Dean of Lib Srvs) 1156
VOLAT-SHAPIRO, Helene M.
   (Humanities Biblgphr) 1287
WALCOTT, Rosalind (Earth &
   Space Scis Libn) 1294
WIENER, Paul B. (Film & Video
   Libn) 1336
WILLIAMS, Doris C. (Bio Libn) . 1343

State Univ of New York at Suffern (NY)

GLEASON, Robert W. (Dir &
   Prof of Lib Srvs) 440
PATTERSON, Grace L. (Asst
   Prof) 948

State Univ of New York at Syracuse (NY)

HULBERT, Linda A. (Assoc Libn
   Col Devlpmnt) 572
JUCHIMEK, Dianne M.
   (Coordntr, Col Devlpmnt
   Dept) 618
MURRAY, Suzanne H. (Interim
   Dir) 882
ONSI, Patricia W. (Technl Srvs
   Libn) 924
UVA, Peter A. (Assoc Libn for
   Pub Srvs) 1270

State Univ of New York at Utica (NY)

State Univ System of Florida (FL)

Staten Island Historical Society (NY)

Staten Island Institute of Arts & Scis (NY)

States News Service (DC)

Statesboro Regional Lib (GA)

Statistics Canada (ON)

Stauffer Chemical Co (CA)

Stauffer Chemical Co (CT)

Stauffer Chemical Co (NY)

Staunton Pub Lib (VA)

Stearns County Historical Society (MN)

Steele Memorial Lib Syst (NY)

Stein Roe & Farnham Inc (IL)

Steinmann Grayson Smylie (CA)

Stepan Co (IL)

Stephen F Austin State Univ (TX)

Stephen S Wise Temple (CA)

Steptoe & Johnson (DC)

Sterling & Francine Clark Art Institute (MA)

Sterling Coll (VT)

Sterling Drugs Inc (NY)

Sterling Heights Pub Lib (MI)

Sterling-Winthrop Research Institute (NY)

Stetson Lib (GA)

Stetson Univ (FL)

Stevens Institute of Technology (NJ)

Stevens Memorial Hospital (WA)

Stickney-Forest View Lib District (IL)

Stillwater Pub Schs (OK)

Stinson Mag & Fizzell (MO)

SCHABERT, Daniel R. (Instrcl
   Resrcs Ctr Dir) 1088

COREY, James F. (Dir of FL Ctr
   for Lib Automation) 246

BARTO, Stephen C. (Archvst) 61

HOGAN, Kristine K. (Archvst,
   Libn) 549
SCHWARTZ, Leland (Edit) 1104
PATON, John C. (Ref Libn) 947
ROYAL, Henrietta (Circ Libn &
   Genealogy Libn) 1063
WALKER, Terri L. (Extension
   Srvs Libn) 1296

BILLINGSLEY, Andrew G.
   (Mktg Coordntn Mgr) 96
COURNOYER, Joanne (Docum
   Delivery Libn) 251
JENSEN, L B. (Systems Libn) . . . 599
CHU, Insoo L. (Sr Technl Info
   Spclst) 212
PETERSON, Gretchen N. (Sr
   Technl Info Spclst) 963
SAYLOR, Linda (Supvsr, Info
   Srvs) 1086
EICKENHORST, Joanna W.
   (Info Srvs Supvsr) 339
HASSAN, Mohammad Z. (Sr
   Technl Info Spclst) 511
KOUTNIK, Charles J. (Technl
   Srvs Head) 673

DECKER, John W. (Archvst) 286
WEIDEMANN, Margaret A. (Pub
   Relations Coordntr) 1316
JANNUSCH, Celeste K. (Asst
   Libn) 593
MARANO, Nancy H. (Libn) 768
MERRIFIELD, Thomas C. (Dir) . . 826
BROWN, Patricia L. (Technl Info
   Srvs Mgr) 146
CAGE, Alvin C. (Dir of Libs) . . . 170
MUCKLEROY, Sue A. (Biogph
   Control Libn) 875
SCAMMAN, Carol J. (Hum
   Libn) 1087
LEFF, Barbara Y. (Lib Dir) 712
FLEMING, Thomas B. (Libn) 384
FOWLIE, Linda K. (Asst Libn) . . . 394
KAHN, Victoria (Ref Libn) 622

GIBSON, Sarah S. (Head Libn) . . 432
PATERSON, Elizabeth N. (Libn) . 947
ASTIFIDIS, Maria (Libn) 37
BROWN, Cynthia D. (Info Scitst) . 142
CURTIS, Kathleen W.
   (Substitute Libn) 267

WEIS, Ann M. (Supvsr, Lib
   Srvs) 1319
HAMMOND, Elizabeth D. (Libn) . 493
EVERETT, David D. (Ref Srvs
   Head) 358
JOHNSON, Betty D. (Head of
   Technl Srvs) 602
WATERS, Sally G. (Ref Libn &
   Adjunct Prof) 1308
WOODARD, Joseph L. (Law
   Libn, Prof of Law) 1365
LUXNER, Dick (Devlpmnt
   Resrch Ofcr) 750
DICKERSON, Bea (Libn) 300
WAGNER, Robin O. (Chlds
   Libn, Circ Dept Supvsr) 1292
ROUSE, Charlie L. (Libn) 1061
VIGLIATURO, Kristy (Libn) 1284

Stockton-San Joaquin County Pub Lib (CA)
BROWN, Donna M. (Asst Dir of Lib Srvs) 143
COLE, Gayle (Youth Srv Coordntr) 230
FRANCISCO, Marylynn (Order Libn) 396

Stockton State Coll (NJ)
GARZILLO, Robert R. (Media Catlgr) 421
MOLL, Joy K. (Prof of Info Sci) .. 853

Stoel Rives Boley Fraser & Wyse (OR)
PIPER, Larry W. (Libn) 975

Stone & Webster Engineering Corp (MA)
PELLINI, Nancy M. (Div Mgr) ... 955

Stone & Webster Mgmt Consultants Inc (NY)
ROBICHAUD, Marcel J. (Libn) . 1042

Stone Hills Area Lib Services Authority (IN)
LAUGHLIN, Sara G. (Coordntr) .. 703

Stone Mountain Regional Lib System (GA)
MANCINI, Donna D. (Asst Dir) .. 764
MOELLER, Edward R. (Lib Systs Analyst) 851
SKELLIE, Karen S. (Chlds Libn) 1145
WOLF, Melinda J. (Branch Mgr) 1360

Stonehill Coll (MA)
BOUCHARD-HALL, Robert W. (Catlg Dept Head) 118
PEARCE, Jean K. (Circ Head) .. 952

Stony Brook Sch (NY)
MASH, S D. (Lib Dir) 780

Strand Book Store (NY)
MONDLIN, Marvin (Vice Pres) .. 854

Strategic Developments Limited (ENG)
BUNCE, George D. (Managing Dir) 157

Strategic Intelligence Systems Inc (NY)
BARTLETT, Jay P. (Sr Consult) .. 61
KENDRIC, Marisa A. (Consult) .. 640
RUBINSTEIN, Ed (Proj Dir) 1065
STANAT, Ruth E. (Pres) 1179

Strategic Planning Associates Inc (DC)
CARDWELL, Diane O. (Ref Spclst) 181

Stratford Lib Association (CT)
JACOB, William (Head of Technl Srvs) 589

Stratford Pub Lib Board (ON)
KIRKPATRICK, Jane E. (Chief Exec Ofcr) 655

Strathcona County Board of Education (AB)
SCHMIDT, Raymond J. (Dir, Lrng Resrcs) 1095

Strathy Archibald & Seagram (ON)
COLVIN, Alison J. (Libn) 234

Straub Clinic & Hospital (HI)
MAZZOLA, Patricia R. (Asst Libn) 791
SMITH, Frances P. (Chief Libn) . 1155

Strawser & Allen (OH)
ALLEN, Cameron (Partner) 14

Strayer Coll (DC)
MOULTON, David A. (Dir of Libs) 873

Streetsboro Senior High (OH)
MCKEE, Barbara J. (Media Dir & Dist & Sr High Libn) 810

Streich Lang Weeks & Cardon (AZ)
EDWARDS, Winifred (Libn) 338

Strongsville City Schools (OH)
CUCCIARRE, Barbara L. (AV Media Spclst) 263

Stroud Booksellers (WV)
STROUD, John N. (Owner) 1203

Strybing Arboretum Society (CA)
GATES, Jane P. (Head Libn) 421

Stryker Tams & Dill (NJ)
SKYZINSKI, Susan E. (Libn) ... 1147

Stuart Country Day Sch of Sacred Heart (NJ)
HAYASHI, Chigusa (Head Libn) . 515

Stuart Pharmaceuticals (DE)
DANIEL, Alfred I. (Investigational Mtrls Coordntr) 272
DRUKKER, Alexander E. (Pharmaceutical Info Mgr) 320
JOHNSON, Hilary C. (Sr Resrch Info Scientist) 605

Sturgis Pub Schs (MI)
BERKLUND, Nancy J. (Middle Sch Libn & Media Spclst) 87

Subiaco Abbey & Academy (AR)
PIRRERA, Aaron C. (Libn) 975

Suburban Lib System (IL)
AMELING, Linda S. (Ref Libn) .. 19
EGAN, Elizabeth M. (Ref Libn) .. 338
GOULDING, Mary A. (Dir of Ref Srv) 454
HUSLIG, Dennis M. (Asst Dir) .. 578
MUELLER, Elizabeth (Consltng Srv Dir) 875
ROCHE, Richard G. (Ref Libn) . 1046

Suburban Lib System (IL)
SPENCER, Joan M. (Automation Syst Mgr) 1173

Sudbury Board of Education (ON)
BERTRAND, Doreen M. (Eductnl Media Coordntr) 91

Suffolk Community Coll (NY)
KUUSKMAE, Mati (Lib Dir) 685
PETERMAN, Kevin (Asst Prof of AV Srvs) 962

Suffolk Cooperative Lib System (NY)
CANTWELL, Mickey A. (Statscl Analyst) 179
EIDELMAN, Diane L. (Docums Libn) 340
KLAUBER, Julie B. (Outreach Srvs Adminstr) 658
LEVERING, Philip (AV Consult) .. 719
MULLER, Claudya B. (Dir) 877
PLUMER, F I. (Ref & Interlib Loan Libn) 978
RICHARDSON, John A. (Technl Srvs Coordntr) 1029
ROTHENBERG, Mark H. (Ref Spclst) 1060

Suffolk County Community Coll (NY)
KANIA, Antoinette M. (Libs Dean) 625
QUINN, David J. (Campus Head Libn) 1000

Suffolk Univ (MA)
BANDER, Edward J. (Law Libn) .. 54
COLEMAN, James R. (Asst Dir) . 231
HAMANN, Edmund G. (Lib Dir) .. 490
MAIO, Kathleen L. (Ref Libn) ... 762
SPEARS, Norman L. (Lrng Resrcs Dir) 1172

Sul Ross State Univ (TX)
ELDER, Nancy J. (Media Spclst) . 342

Sullivan Community Unit Schs Dist 300 (IL)
HASBROUCK, Clara H. (Media Srvs Dir) 510

Sullivan County Department of Education (TN)
TILSON, Koleta B. (Libn 9-12) . 1245

Sullivan County Sch (TN)
Sullivan High Sch (LA)
SANTA, Elizabeth C. (High Sch Libn) 1082

Summer Institute of Linguistics (AZ)
HARRIS, Mary J. (Linguist & Bible Translator) 505

Summer Institute of Linguistics (PHP)
COOK, Marjorie L. (Head Libn) .. 240

Summit Free Pub Lib (NJ)
ELENAUSKY, Edward V. (Dir) ... 342

Sumner County Board of Education (TN)
MILLS, Wanda R. (Head Libn) .. 844

Sumter County Lib (SC)
LINE, Faith A. (Dir) 730

Sumter County Sch District 2 (SC)
MILTON, Brenda R. (Chapter 1 Math Tchr) 845
SHIRLEY, Iris C. (Libn & Media Spclst) 1131

Sun Co (PA)
MORPHET, Norman D. (Sect Chief of Sun Lib) 865

Sun Herald Gulf Publishing Co (MS)
PUSTAY, Marilyn J. (Libn) 998

Sun Life Assurance Co of Canada (ON)
CARVALHO, Sarah V. (Libn) ... 191
GIBSON, Elizabeth A. (Mgr, Toronto Lib) 432
LUCIANI, Ellie (Lib Technician) .. 746

Sun Newspapers (IL)
KAGANN, Laurie K. (Newspaper Libn) 621

Sun Prairie Pub Lib (WI)
REANDEAU, Walter E. (Lib Dir) 1013

Sundstrand Aviation (IL)
HAMILTON, D A. (Info Spclst) .. 491

Sundstrand Data Control Inc (WA)
SMART, Doris M. (Engrng Resrch Libn) 1151

Sunflower County Lib (MS)
POWELL, Anice C. (Dir) 988

SunHealth Inc (NC)
BACKMAN, Carroll H. (Resrc Spclst) 44

Sunkist Growers Inc (CA)
NEMETH, Martha C. (Technl Libn) 895

Sunny von Bulow Natl Victim Advocacy Ctr (TX)
ARBELBIDE, Cindy L. (Libn) 30

Sunnybrook Medical Center (ON)
ARMSTRONG, Jennifer E. (Ref Libn) 32

Sunnyvale Pub Lib (CA)
CANNON, Eleanor (Ref Libn) ... 179

Sunset Mesa Schs Inc (NM)
MATTER, Kathy L. (Libn) 785

SunTrust Service Corp (GA)
BOZE, Lucy G. (Operations Ofcr & Libn) 124

Suomi Coll (MI)
PENTI, Marsha E. (Archs Dir) ... 957

Super Valu Stores (MN) — CANFIELD, Linda N. 178
Superior Court of Arizona (AZ) — EVANS, Iris I. (Catlgr) 357
Supreme Court of Canada (ON) — MURRAY-LACHAPELLE, Rosemary F. (Head of Technl Srvs & Systs) 882
Supreme Court of Illinois (IL) — BRADLEY, Catherine (Law Libn) . 125
Supreme Court of Ohio (OH) — FU, Paul S. (Law Libn) 407
Supreme Court of the United States (DC) — JENSEN, Doris J. (Resrch Libn) . 598
Supreme Court of Virginia (VA) — LONG, Elizabeth T. (Asst Libn) . . 739
WARREN, Gail (State Law Libn) 1306
Surrey Pub Lib (BC) — ASHCROFT, Susan M. (Branch Mgr) 35
GUTTERIDGE, Paul (Mgr of Technl Srvs and Col Devlpmnt) 479
HAABNIIT, Ene (Branch Mgr) . . . 480
SMITH, Stan (Chief Libn) 1161
Surry County Schs (NC) — STRICKLAND, Mary L. (Media Coordntr) 1202
Susan Baerg Epstein Ltd (CA) — EPSTEIN, Susan B. (Pres) 351
Susan Keats & Associates (MA) — KEATS, Susan E. (Pres) 633
Sussex County Lib System (NJ) — RAFFERTY, Stephen P. (Ref Libn) 1003
Sutin Thayer & Browne (NM) — MCGOEY, Richard P. (Libn) 807
Suwannee River Regional Lib (FL) — HALES, John D. (Dir of Libs) 486
Swarthmore Academy (PA) — JONES, Annabel B. (Libn) 611
Swarthmore Coll (PA) — FULLER, Edward H. (Spcl Cols Libn) 408
HUBER, George K. (Music Libn) . 569
LEHMANN, Stephen R. (Humanities Libn) 713
WILLIAMSON, Susan G. (Soc Scis Libn) 1348
Swarthmore Pub Lib (PA) — LICHTENBERG, Elsa R. (Dir) . . . 725
Swedish National Radio Corp (SWE) — CNATTINGIUS, Claes M. (Gramophone Dept Dir) 224
Swedlow Inc (CA) — FORD, Marjorie F. (Info Spclst) . . 389
Sweet Briar Coll (VA) — JAFFE, John G. (Dir of Libs) 591
Sweetwater County Lib System (WY) — HIGBY, Helen E. (Dir) 537
Sydney Dataproducts Inc (CA) — CHASE, Jan (Mktg Rep) 203
SANDELL, Judy L. (Sales Mgr) . . 1079
Sydney Wolf Cohen Inc (NY) — ABEND, Jody U. (Free-lance Bk Indxr) 2
Syncrude Canada Ltd (AB) — SLOAN, Stephen M. (Lib & Info Spclst) 1150
Synergen Inc (CO) — HOFFMAN, Ann M. (Libn & Proj Adminstr) 547
Syntactic Analyzer Inc (MN) — SCHULTZ, Arnold J. (Pres) . . . 1101
Syntex USA Inc (CA) — TRIMBLE, Kathy W. (Sr Info Spclst) 1256
Syosset Pub Lib (NY) — GOLDENKOFF, Isabel M. (Ref Libn) 445
KRISTIAN, Alice (Head Libn of Adult Srvs) 679
Syracuse Univ (NY) — ABBOTT, George L. (Head of Media Srvs) 1
BRAUN, Carl F. (Bus & Econ Libn) 129
COCHRANE, Pauline A. (Prof Emeritus) 226
EISENBERG, Michael B. (Asst Prof) 340
ELY, Donald P. (Dir of ERIC Clearinghouse) 347
FROEHLICH, Thomas J. (Asst Prof) 405
HORRELL, Jeffrey L. (Asst to the Univ Libn for Plng) 560
JOHNSON, Nancy B. (Adjunct Faculty) 608
KATZER, Jeffrey (Prof) 630
LANTZY, M L. (Assoc Libn) 697
MARCHAND, Donald A. (Dean) . 768
MARTIN, Thomas H. (Assoc Prof) 778
MCCLURE, Charles R. (Prof) . . . 797
MCLAUGHLIN, Pamela W. (User Srvs Coordntr) 813

Syracuse Univ (NY) — MINOR, Barbara B. (Pubns Coordntr) 846
MULLEN, Marion L. (Ref Dept Head) 877
NAYLOR, David L. (Assoc Law Libn) 890
PARKE, Carol R. (Assoc Univ Lib, Pub Srvs) 941
PRICE, Susan W. (Ref Libn) 992
PRINS, Johanna W. (Slide Cur) . 993
SEIBERT, Donald C. (Music Libn) 1112
STAM, David H. (Univ Lib) 1179
STAM, Deirdre C. (Asst Prof) . . 1179
UCHTORFF, Barbara J. (Acqs Libn) 1267
WALTZ, Mary A. (Geography & Map Libn) 1302
WASYLENKO, Lydia W. (Spcl Cols Catlg Libn) 1308
WU, Painan R. (Dir of Lib) 1373
Syscon Corp (RI) — COHEN, Barbara S. (Lib Operations & Automation Mgr) 228
System Development Corporation (CA) — GILHEANY, Stephen J. (Sr Systs Engineer) 435
System Planning Corp (VA) — MERCURY, Nicholas E. 825
Systems & Encoding Corp (NY) — MEDINA, Ildefonso M. (Pres) . . 820
Systems Engineering Associates Inc (OH) — RICHARDSON, Katherine A. (Lib Technician) 1029
Systems Planning (MD) — TONEY, Stephen R. (Pres) 1250

T

T O R Franciscans (OH) — BURKE, Ambrose L. (Archvst) . . . 160
T U Electric (TX) — MIDGETT, Ann S. (Corporate Libn) 833
Tabbert Cremer & Capehart (IN) — ANDREWS, Sylvia L. (Law Libn) 27
Tabor Coll (KS) — JOHNSON, Georgina (Libn & Archvst) 604
Tacoma Family Medicine (WA) — MENDELSON, Martin (Clinical Assoc Prof) 823
Tacoma News Tribune (WA) — BRITTON, Pilaivan H. (Libn) 137
Tacoma Pub Lib (WA) — HAGAN, Dalia L. (Technl Srvs Head) 482
REESE, Gary F. (Managing Spcl Cols Libn) 1016
Tacoma Sch District (WA) — BUELER, Roy D. (Instrcl Resrcs Coordntr) 155
Tacoma Sch District 10 (WA) — THORNDILL, Christine M. (Sch Lib Media Spclst) 1242
TAD Technical Services (FL) — FAHNERT, Elizabeth K. (Head Libn) 361
Taipei American Sch (TAI) — BRAUNGER, Patricia M. (Libn) . . 130
Tallahassee Community Coll (FL) — GIBLON, Charles B. (Technl Srvs Head) 431
Tallapossa County Board of Education (AL) — CANADY, Iris (Libn) 177
Tamaqua Area Sch District (PA) — TUZINSKI, Jean H. 1266
Tamarack Federation of Libs (MT) — SCHMIDT, Theodore A. (Dir & Coordntr) 1096
Tamkang Univ (TAI) — HUANG, Shih H. (Prof & Dir) . . . 568
Tampa Bay Lib Consortium Inc (FL) — MARTIN, Robert A. (Exec Dir) . . . 778
Tampa Bay Regional Planning Council (FL) — NOL, Maryke E. (Libn) 907
Tampa-Hillsborough County Pub Lib System (FL) — APPELBAUM, Sara B. (Head of Central Lib) 29
BRYAN, Michael G. (Chlds Libn) 151
CHALLENER, Marcee M. (Branch Libn) 197
CONKLIN, Candace V. (Libn I) . 236
FIORE, Carole D. (Head, Youth Srvs) 379

Tampa-Hillsborough County Pub Lib System (FL)

HAWK, Susan P. 513
LOSEY, Doris C. (Branch Libn & Youth Spclst) 742
NICHTER, Alan (Adult Matrls Coordntr) 902
RUDER, Clarice M. (Branch Libn) 1065
STINES, Joe R. (Branch Head) . 1194
STORCK, Bernadette R. (Head, Branches & Extension) 1198

Tandem Computers (CA)
DIFFERDING, Jane B. (Info Spclst) 302

Tandem Computers (TX)
WISE, Olga B. (Lib Mgr) 1357

Tantalus Inc (OH)
KANTOR, Paul B. (Pres) 626

TAPPI (GA)
STAHL, D G. (Info Resrcs Coordntr) 1178

Tarleton State Univ (TX)
TEVEBAUGH, Joyce E. (Asst Ref Libn & Libn I) 1233

Tarlton Law Lib (TX)
PRATTER, Jonathan (Intl & Comparative Law Libn) 990

Tarrant County (TX)
HOWINGTON, Tad C. (Records and Microfilm Srvs Dir) 566
WAYLAND, Sharon L. (Asst Libn) 1311

Tarrant County Junior Coll (TX)
FITE, Vicki A. (Dist Catlgr) 382
MCCRACKEN, Barbara L. (Dir) . 799

Tarrant County Law Lib (TX)
PERRY, Frances (Libn) 960

Tax Analysts (MD)
AMATRUDA, William T. (Indxr & Libn) 19

Tax Foundation Inc (DC)
MARSHALL, Marion B. (Libn) . . . 774

Taylor & Associates (CA)
TAYLOR, Kathryn E. (Lib Mgmt Consult) 1227

Taylor-Carlisle Booksellers Inc (NY)
FAST, Barry (Pres) 366

Taylor County Junior High Sch (FL)
GROSS, James B. (Media Spclst) 472

Taylor Univ (IN)
WOLCOTT, Laurie J. (Technl Srvs Libn) 1359

Taylorville Pub Lib (IL)
PODESCHI, Gwen (Lib Dir) 979

Teamsearch (CA)
NEWAY, Julie M. (Info Scitst) . . . 898

Teaneck Pub Lib (NJ)
WILEN, Rosamond L. (Libn) . . . 1339

Technl Assn of the Pulp & Paper Industry (GA)
BIBBY, Elizabeth A. (Info Resrcs Adminstr) 94

Technical Data International (MA)
MILLS, Andrew G. (Pres & Chief Operating Ofcr) 843

Technical Lib Consultancy (TRN)
MCCONNIE, Mary (Spcl Libs Consult) 798

Technical Lib Service Inc (NY)
HAAS, Elaine H. (President) 480

Technical Services Group (ON)
WEIHS, Jean (Lib Conslting Firm Principal) 1317

Technical Univ of Braunschweig (WGR)
EVERSBERG, Bernhard (Technl Srvs & Automation Dir) 359

Technomic Publishing Co Inc (PA)
DUNN, Richard L. (Vice Pres) . . . 327

Techsouth Inc (GA)
CRIM, Dewey H. (Pres) 258

Techworld (DC)
BOGATAY, Alan 110

Tecumseh Pub Lib (MI)
REASONER, Mary B. (Chlds Libn & Lib Asst) 1013

Ted Bates Advertising (NY)
BEALER, Jane A. (Libn) 68

Tektronix Inc (OR)
SOUCIE, Yan Y. (Libn) 1169
THOMAS, Sandra L. (Mgr) 1238

Tel Aviv Univ (ISR)
ERES, Beth K. (Sci & Info Policy Div Head) 352

The TELCO Report (CA)
PAEN, Alexander L. (Publshr) . . . 934

Telebase Systems Inc (PA)
HORWITZ, Seth (User Srvs Dir) . 561
KOLLIN, Richard P. (Pres) 669
NEUFELD, Lynne M. (Vice Pres) 897
GROHN, Susan M. 471

Telecom Canada (ON)
DOWDELL, Marlene S. (Sr Adminstr for Lib & Docum Ctl) 315

Teledyne Cae (OH)

Teledyne Engineering Services (MA)
FINGERMAN, Susan M. (Mgr of Info Srvs) 378

Telenet Communications Corp (VA)
ADAMS, Judith A. (Info Srvs Mgr) 5
COOK, Charlaine C. (Info Spclst) 239

Telenet Communications Corp (VA)
HARRISTON, Victoria R. (Supvsr of Ref & Info Retrieval) 507
HUFF, Patricia M. (Records Spclst) 570
MATHISON, Stuart (Spcl Project VP) 784
MCCLAIN, Deborah C. (Info Spclst) 795

Telephone & Data Systems Inc (IL)
KAPLAN, Rosalyn L. (Corprt Libn) 626

Telerate Systems Inc (NY)
COWLES, Richard J. 253

Telesat Canada (ON)
FOSTER, Eileen F. (Corp Libn) . . 392

Televents Corp (NJ)
GREEN, Donald T. (Executive Producer) 461

Television Information Office (NY)
POTEAT, James B. (Resrch Srvs Mgr) 986
SLOCUM, Leslie E. (Libn) 1150

Tell City-Perry County Pub Lib (IN)
HOLMAN, Mary J. (Dir) 553

Tempe Pub Lib (AZ)
PARK, Yong H. (Ref Libn) 941

Temple Barker & Sloane (MA)
PRUSAK, Laurence (Info Srvs Dir) 996

Temple Beth American Lib (FL)
BERMAN, Margot 88

Temple Beth El (FL)
KURLAND, Roslyn S. (Libn) 684

Temple Sch (MO)
HALLIER, Sara J. (Libn) 489

Temple Univ (ME)
HAMLIN, Arthur T. (Dir of Lib & Prof Emeritus) 492

Temple Univ (PA)
BOISCLAIR, Regina A. (Adjunct Faculty) 111
BURSTEIN, Karen (Ref Libn) . . . 164
CARINO, Leopoldo C. (Acqs Dept Head) 181
DURIS, Richard M. (Music Catlgr & Biblgphr) 328
ELSHAMI, Ahmed M. (Ref Libn) . 346
GRZESIAK, Margaret M. (Catlgr, Serials Libn) 475
JACOBS, Mark D. (Actg Head of Ref & Info Srvs) 589
JACOBY, Beth E. (Catlgr) 590
MCDONNELL, Janice M. (Head of Catlgng Dept) 803
MILLER, Fredric M. (Urban Archs Ctr Cur) 837
MYERS, James N. (Lib Dir) 884
PATTELA, Rao R. (Assoc Law Libn) 947
SWAN, Christine H. (Ref Law Libn) 1213
TUCKER, Cornelia A. (Head, Acqs & Prcsng Dept) 1261
WEINBERG, David M. (Asst Cur of Urban Archvs) 1317
WRIGHT, Barbara C. (Bus Libn) 1370

Tempo Enterprises Inc (GA)
WILLIAMS, Fred (Data Sales Mgr) 1343

Tenafly Pub Lib (NJ)
WECHTLER, Stephen R. (Lib Dir) 1315

Tenneco Inc (TX)
BAILEY, Linda S. (Sr Libn) 46
MULLINS, James R. (Assoc Law Libn) 878

Tennessean (TN)
MORRISON, Annette T. (Head Libn) 867

Tennessee Lib Association (TN)
NANCE, Betty (Exec Secy) 887

Tennessee State Lib & Archives (TN)
FANCHER, Evelyn P. (Dir of Libs & Media Resrcs) 363
GLEAVES, Edwin S. (State Libn and Archvst) 441
HARRELL, Neal (Libn) 503
HOM, Sharon L. (Asst Docums & Serials Libn) 555
THWEATT, John H. (Dir of Technl Srvs) 1243
WASH, Melba W. (Dir) 1307

Tennessee State Univ (TN)
ARMONTROUT, Brian A. (Ref Libn) 32
CHEN, Helen M. (Spcl Projs Libn) 205

Tennessee State Univ (TN)

HUDSON, Earline H. (Head of Acqs) 569
STEPHENS, Alonzo T. (Prof Emeritus) 1187

Tennessee Technological Univ (TN) JONES, Christine S. (TN & Ref Libn) 611
JONES, Roger G. (Col Devlpmnt Coordntr) 615
KOHUT, David R. (Soc Scis Ref Libn) 669
LAFEVER, Susan (Coordntr of Biblgph Control) 687
ROBERTS, Marica L. (Perdcls Head & Gifts Exchange Libn) 1041
TABACHNICK, Sharon (Sci & Engrng Libn) 1219
WALDEN, Winston A. (Lib Srvs Dir) 1294

Tennessee Valley Authority (AL) CLARK, Wendolyn H. (Resrch Libn) 218
GAMBRELL, Drucilla S. (Resrch Libn) 416
MONTGOMERY, Kimberly K. (Resrch Libn) 856
NICHOLS, Shirley G. (Lib Mgr) . 901

Tennessee Valley Authority (TN) BEST, Edwin J. (Supvsr of Srvs) .. 92
BULL, Margaret J. (Chief Libn) .. 156
KNIGHTLY, John J. (Nuclear Evaluator) 664
MILLS, Debra D. (Libn) 844
MYERS, William F. (Ref Libn) ... 885
NOONAN, Patricia K. (Libn) 908

Teradyne Inc (MA) BERNARD, Bobbi (Resrch Libn) .. 88
Terra Firma (NY) FABRIZIO, Timothy C. (Owner) .. 360
Terre Haute Medical Education Foundation (IN) KYKER, Penelope R. (Med Libn Cnsrtm Coordntr) 685
Terrebonne Parish Pub Lib (LA) COSPER, Mary F. (Asst Dir) 249
SHAFFER, Margaret M. (Dir) .. 1119
Territory of American Samoa (AS) MCDONNELL, Robert W. (Territorial Archvst) 803
Testa Hurwitz & Thibeault (MA) DRISCOLL, Kathleen 320
Teton County Lib (WY) EFFINGER, Nancy E. (Dir) 338
Tetra Tech Inc (WA) FIELDING, Carol J. (Libn) 376
Texaco Canada Resources (AB) DURIE, Debbie L. (Libn) 328
Texaco Inc (LA) FLEURY, Mary E. (Info Spclst) .. 385
Texaco Inc (NY) ROCQUE, Bernice L. (Trng & Devlpmnt Area Coordntr) ... 1046

Texas A&M Univ (TX) BROWN-WEBB, Deborah D. (Resrch Libn) 149
BUTKOVICH, Nancy J. (Sci Ref Libn) 166
CLARK, Charlene K. (Devlpmnt & Promotion Coordntr) 216
COOK, C C. (Circ Head, Lib Automation Coord) 239
FACKLER, Naomi P. (Technl Srvs Libn) 360
GYESZLY, Suzanne D. (Actg Head of Circ Div) 479
HALL, Halbert W. (Spcl Formats Div Head) 487
HALVERSON, Jacquelyn A. (Head, Interlib Srvs) 490
HAMBRIC, Jacqueline B. (Ref Libn, Asst Head, Biblgph Srvs) 491
HOADLEY, Irene B. (Dir) 545
KELLOUGH, Jean L. (Docums Libn) 637
KELLOUGH, Patrick H. (Original Caltgr, Spcl Cols) 637
PAYNE, Leila M. (Head of Prcsng Div) 951
RABINS, Joan W. (Asst Dir, Ctr for Histrc Resrcs) 1001
RHOLES, Julia M. (Microtext & Maps Dept Head) 1026

Texas A&M Univ (TX)

SCHMIDT, Sherrie (Asst Dir for Col & Biblgph Srvs) 1096
SCHULTZ, Charles R. (Univ Archvst) 1101
SHIPMAN, Natalie W. (Lib Dir) . 1131
SMITH, Charles R. (Resrc Devlpmnt Libn) 1153
THOMAS, Barbara C. (LS2000 Circ and Rsv Coodntr) 1236
THOMPSON, Christine E. (Head, Original Catlgng Dept) 1239

Texas Allergy Research Foundation (TX) MCGOVERN, John P. 807
Texas Christian Univ (TX) DUBIEL, Laura R. (Lib Asst & Archvst) 321
ECHT, Sandy A. (Database Srvs Libn) 334
FREEMAN, John P. (Cur & Asst Prof) 401
KARGES, Joann (Col Mgmt Libn) 627
MACDONALD, Hugh (Chief Ref Libn) 754
OLSEN, Robert A. (Libn) 921

Texas Coll of Osteopathic Medicine (TX) CARTER, Bobby R. (Lib Srvs Dir) 189
ELAM, Craig S. (Assoc Dir for Technl Srvs) 341
MASON, Timothy D. (Technl Srvs Libn) 781
WOOD, Richard C. (Assoc Dir for Pub Srvs) 1365
Texas Eastern Corp (TX) KIRTNER, R R. (Libn) 655
LUECKENHOFF, Anne F. (Acqs Libn) 747
Texas Education Agency (TX) KAHLER, June (Educ Spclst II) .. 621
Texas General Land Office (TX) HOOKS, Michael Q. (Dir of Archs) 556
Texas Instruments Inc (TX) ANDERSON, Margaret (Internal Technl Info Mgr) 24
ARNOLD, Gaye C. (Mgr, Training & Devlpmnt) 33
BARRUS, Phyl (Libn) 60
BELL, Charise F. (Libn) 76
HULSE, Phyllis (Info Analyst) .. 573
LUTZ, Linda A. (Mgr, Info Acq Sect) 750
MANNING, Helen M. (Coordntr, Semiconductor Group Libs) .. 766
MURPHY, Pency G. (Acqs Libn) . 881
POPE, Hermon L. (Sr Mem Tech Staff) 983
SHARP, Charlotte J. (Info Analyst) 1122
WALDEN, Millicent F. (Catlgng Spclst) 1294
WEBB, Sue E. (Libn) 1313
Texas Lib Association (TX) HOWARD, Ada M. (Exec Dir) ... 563
Texas Lutheran Coll (TX) HSU, Patrick K. (Lib Dir) 567
KOOPMAN, Frances A. (Reader Srvs Libn) 671
Texas Oil & Gas Corp (TX) MALCOLM, Jane B. (Corprt Libn) 762
Texas Panhandle Lib System (TX) WELLS, Mary K. (Syst Coordntr) 1322
Texas Scottish Rite Hospital (TX) PETERS, Mary N. (Med Libn) ... 962
Texas Southern Univ (TX) BEAN, Norma P. (Assoc Dir) 69
BUTLER, Marguerite L. (Assoc Law Libn) 166
CHAMPION, Walter T. (Law Lib Dir & Asst Prof) 198
VAUGHN, Frances A. (Dir of Lib) 1280
Texas Southmost Coll (TX) HAMBLETON, James E. (Dir) ... 490
Texas State Law Lib (TX) HARLOW, Sally S. (Law Libn) .. 502
SCHLUETER, Kay (Dir) 1094

Texas State Lib (TX)

BLACK, J A. (Archvst) 101
BRIDGE, Frank R. (Automation Consult) 135
CARTER, Janet K. (Supvsr, Genealogy Col) 189
HOLLAND, Michael E. (Asst Dir) . 551
MATHIS, Rama F. (Acqs Supvsr) 784
SCHAADT, Robert L. (Dir & Archvst) 1088
SCOTT, Paul R. (Records Consult) 1108
SEIDENBERG, Edward (Mgr) . . 1112
WALTON, Robert A. (Dir, Data Prcsng) 1301

Texas Tech Regnl Academic Hlth Ctr (TX)

NEELEY, Dana M. (Assoc Dir) . . 891

Texas Tech Univ (TX)

ANDREWS, Virginia L. (Automation Coordntr) 27
CARGILL, Jennifer S. (Assoc Dir) 181
CASELLA, Roberta L. (Libn, Friends Coordtn & Devlpmnt) 192
CLUFF, E D. (Dir of Libs) 223
DUFFY, Suzanne (Libn) 324
KELLEY, Carol M. (Acqs Head) . . 636
KNOTT, Teresa L. (Assoc Dir) . . 665
LINDSEY, Thomas K. (Docums Ref Coordntr) 730
LUIKART, Nancy B. (Info Access Libn) 747
MARLEY, Judith L. (Ref and Fine Arts Libn) 772
MARX, Patricia C. (Mtrls Prcsng Head) 780
OLM, Jane G. (Law Lib Dir) 921
PEDERSEN, Judy K. (Ref Libn/Faculty Assoc) 954
SARGENT, Charles W. (Dir of Libs) 1082
TROST, Theresa K. (User Instrc Coordntr) 1258
VAN SCHAIK, Jo A. (Media Libn) 1277
VUGRIN, Margaret Y. (Ref Libn) 1289
WARD, Deborah H. (Assoc Dir, Info Srvs) 1303
WEBB, Gisela M. (Lib for Admin Srvs Asst Dir) 1313

Texas Trans-Pecos Lib System (TX)

DAVIS, Joyce (Coordntr) 279

Texas Wesleyan Coll (TX)

CAGE, Willa F. (Head of Circ) . . . 171
CORLEY, Carol W. (Serials Libn) 246
FERRIER, Douglas M. (Lib Dir) . . 373

Texas Woman's Univ (TX)

CALIMANO, Ivan E. (Coordntr) . . 173
PEDEN, Rita Y. (Ref Libn) 954
SCHLESSINGER, Bernard S. (Prof & Assoc Dean) 1094
SHELDON, Brooke E. (Dean and Prof) 1125
SNAPP, Elizabeth M. (Dir of Libs) 1162
SWIGGER, Keith (Assoc Prof) . 1216
THOMAS, James L. (Assoc Prof) 1237
TURNER, Frank L. (Prof, Sch of Lib & Info Std) 1264
WAN, William W. (Coordntr for Acqs and Serials) 1302

Thacher Proffitt Wood (NY)

OHMAN, Elisabeth T. (Libn) 919

Theatre Lib Association (NY)

PALLY, Alan J. (Edit of Broadside) 935

THEATRICANA (GA)

KAHAN, Gerald (Owner, Bk Seller Spclst) 621

Thelen Marrin Johnson & Bridges (CA)

HARMON, Marlene K. (Libn) 502
ZWEIFLER, Lynn A. (Law Libn) 1392

Theodon Books Inc (CA)

BOWEN, Theodora (Owner & Pres) 120

Theodore F Jenkins Memorial Law Lib (PA)

PIECHNICK, Katarzyna M. (Catlgr) 971
SCHAEFER, John A. (Ref Libn) 1089
SPIVACK, Amy D. (Ref Libn) . . 1175
WEINGRAM, Ida (Ref Libn) . . . 1318

Theresa M Burke Employment Agency Inc (NY)

MCMEEN, Frances E. (Persnl Consult) 815

Think Small Computers Inc (CO)

COSTA, Betty L. (Lib Media Spclst & Consult) 249

Third Judicial Court (UT)

CHENG, Nancy H. (Law Libn) . . . 206

Third Point Systems (CA)

COLLINS, Thomas F. 233

13D Research Inc (NY)

YURO, David A. (Mgr of Info Srvs) 1384

Thomas Braniyan Memorial Lib (NM)

ATKINS, Gene D. (Technl Srvs Head) 37

Thomas Consulting Inc (MI)

THOMAS, Margaret J. (Bus Info Consul) 1237

Thomas Hackney Braswell Memorial Lib (NC)

HUGHES, Donna J. (Youth Srvs Libn) 571

Thomas Jefferson Lib System (MO)

ATHY, Doris J. (Dir) 37
READING, Barbara A. (Chlds Libn) 1012

Thomas Jefferson Univ (PA)

ARMISTEAD, Henry T. (Col Devlpmnt Libn) 32
DAVIS, Samuel A. (Spcl Cols Libn) 281
DEVLIN, Margaret K. (Access Srvs Libn) 297
MIKITA, Elizabeth G. (Catlg Libn) 834
RISSINGER, Michael (Reclass Technician) 1036
TIMOUR, John A. (Univ Libn) . . 1246
WARNER, Elizabeth R. (Ref Libn & User Educ Coordntr) . 1305

Thomas M Cooley Law Sch (MI)

BONGE, Barbara M. (Acting Lib Dir) 114
LUCAS, Ann (Acqs & Serials Libn) 745
MICHAUD, John C. (Evening Ref Libn) 832

Thomas More Coll (KY)

ALBERT, Stephen G. (Dir of the Lib) 10

Thomas Newcomen Memorial Lib & Museum (PA)

ARNOLD, Nancy K. (Lib, Cur) . . . 34

Thomas Publishing Co (NY)

ANDERSEN, Robert J. (Vice Pres of Plng) 21
LEE, Douglas E. (Spcl Publications Editor) 709
SAFRAN, Scott A. (Online Srvs Edit) 1074

Thompson & Mitchell (MO)

HOLSTEN, Terri L. (Libn) 554

Thompson Hine & Flory (OH)

FISHER, Jo A. (Libn) 381

Thompson Medical Co Inc (NY)

HOYT, Henry M. (Info Coordtr) . . 566

Thomson & Thomson (MA)

FERNALD, Anne C. (VP of Mktg & Sales) 373

Thomson Components-Mostek (TX)

OGDEN, William S. (Libn & Mgr) 918

Thorne Ernst & Whinney (AB)

DEGINNUS, Roxie (Libn) 287

Thorne Ernst & Whinney (ON)

JOHNSON, John E. (Info Srvs Mgr) 606

Thornton Township High Sch District 205 (IL)

GIBBS, Mary E. (Libn) 431
SHANNON, Kathleen L. (Libn) . 1120

Thousand Oaks Lib (CA)

BROOKS, Mary A. (Libn) 140
HOCKEL, Kathleen N. (Ref Libn) 545
SULLIVAN, Kathleen A. (Principal Libn) 1207

Thousand Trails (WA)

SCHUTTE, Raymond R. (Operations Mgr) 1103

3M (MN)

ANDERSON, Rebekah E. (Ref Libn) 25
BOYD, Cheryl J. (Ref Libn) 122
DUELTGEN, Ronald R. (Info Spclst) 323
FOLLMER, Diane E. 388

3M (MN)

HUPPERT, Ramona R. 577
LESLIE, Donald S. (Market
   Supvsr) 718

3M (TX)   MITTAG, Erika (Sr Libn) 850
3M Canada Inc (ON)   STEPHENSON, Cheryl E.
   (Technl Libn) 1188
Three Village Historical Society (NY) PACKARD, Agnes K. (Consult
   Archvst) 933
Ticonderoga Central Sch (NY) DAVIS, Bonnie V. (Sch Libn) . . . 277
Tidewater Community Coll (VA) BILLERT, Julia A. (Ref Libn &
   Catlgr) 96
   LIN, John T. (Coordntr of Lib
   Srvs) 727
Tiffin City Board of Education (OH) LEWIS, Gwen C. (Sch Lib
   Media Spclst) 723
Tilleke & Gibbins ROP (THA) RUNGSANG, Rebecca J. (Libn
   and Resrch Asst) 1067
Timberland Regional Lib (WA) CHRISTIANSEN, Claire B. (Sr
   Community Libn) 211
   DICKERSON, Lon R. (Lib Dir) . . . 300
   GREENWOOD, Alma I. (Ref
   Coordntr) 465
   LOKEN, Sarah F. (Asst Dir,
   Centl Srvs) 738
   SHAFFER, Maryann (Asst Dir of
   Pub Srvs) 1119
Time Inc (NY)   GOTTFRIED, Erika D. (Ref Libn) . 453
   RHODES, Deborah L. (Resrch
   Libn) 1026
   ZARCONE, Beth B. (Picture Col
   Chief) 1386
Time Sensitive Delivery Guide (CT) SHARPE, Murem S. 1122
Times Herald Record (NY) SCARANO, Lisa C. (Libn) 1087
Times Journal Co (VA) WHITE-WILLIAMS, Patricia
   (Editrl Rsrch Lib Dir) 1333
Times Mirror (CA) HOLLY, James H. (Pres of TMP
   Publshg Inc) 552
Times Mirror (NY) RUBIN, James S. (Group
   Vice-Pres) 1064
Times Mirror (PA) DONCEVIC, Lois A. (Lib Srvs
   Dir) 311
Tippecanoe County Pub Lib (IN) MITCHELL, Cynthia E. (Head of
   Ref) 848
   THOMAS, Victoria K. (Libn) . . . 1238
Tippecanoe Sch Corp (IN) TROUTNER, Joanne J. (Lib
   Media Spclst) 1258
TMS Inc (OK) BENGE, Bruce (Mgr) 80
   PHILLIPS, J R. (Pres) 968
Tobacco Institute (DC) PICCIANO, Laura (Libn) 970
**Todd Hood Information Means
Business** (NY) HOOD, Katherine T. (Proprietor) . 556
TOGG Films Inc (NY) GURIEVITCH, Grania B. (Pres) . . 478
Tohoku Univ (JAP) HARADA, Ryukichi (Assoc Dir) . . 499
Tokyo Gakugei Univ (JAP) TETSUYA, Inoue (Circ & Ref
   Chief) 1233
Tokyo Medical Coll (JAP) SUGA, Toshinobu (Prof) 1206
**Tokyo National Univ of Fine Arts &
Music** (JAP) KISHIMOTO, Hiroko (Lecturer) . . 656
Toledo Blade (OH) REDDINGTON, Mary E. (Head
   Libn) 1013
Toledo Hospital (OH) TILLMAN, Linda M. (Dir) 1245
Toledo Law Association (OH) WOODRUFF, Brenda B. (Dir,
   Law Libn) 1366
Toledo-Lucas County Pub Lib (OH) AVERY, Galen V. (Bus Ref
   Libn) 41
   BAKER, Paula J. (Dept Head,
   Fine Arts) 49
   CLARK, Marilyn L. (Chld's &
   Yng Adult Srvs) 217
   DANZIGER, Margaret (Asst Dir) . 274
   EASTERLY-POTTER, Anne P.
   (Chlds Libn) 333
   KUCINSKI, B J. (Ref
   Libn/Reader's Adv) 682
   LOCKE-GAGNON, Rebecca A.
   (Visual Srvs Libn) 736
   SCOLES, Clyde S. (Dir) 1106
Toledo Museum of Art (OH) MORRIS, Anne O. (Head Libn) . . 866
   SCOTT, Sharon A. (Catlgr) 1108

Toledo Pub Schs (OH) SHEPARD, Jon R. (Libn &
   Media Spclst) 1127
**Tom Green County Pub Lib
System** (TX) LACY, Yvonne M. (Ref Libn) . . . 687
Tomifobia Vallee Hi-Tech (PQ) GRENIER, Serge (Pres) 467
Tompkins County (NY) MCGINNIES, Nancy L. (Asst
   Dir) 806
Topeka Pub Lib (KS) MARVIN, James C. (Dir) 780
   MUTH, Thomas J. (Asst Libn) . . 883
   RUSTMAN, Mark M. (Music
   Libn) 1070
Toronto Dominion Bank (ON) PULLEYBLANK, Mildred C.
   (Corprt Archvst) 997
   SMITH, Ruth P. (Libn) 1160
   SMITHIES, Roger 1162
Toronto East General Hospital (ON) BAYNE, Jennifer M. (Chief Libn) . . 67
Toronto General Hospital (ON)
**Toronto Institute of Medical
Technology** (ON) LADD, Kenneth F. (Libn) 687
Toronto Jewish Congress (ON) SPEISMAN, Stephen A. (Dir) . . 1172
Toronto Pub Lib (ON) CHAN, Arlene S. (Branch Head,
   Traveling Branch) 199
   DE RONDE, Paula D. (Comunty
   Srvs Coordntr) 294
   FOWLIE, Les (Chief Libn) 394
   KRYGSMAN, Nancy T. (Asst
   Chief Libn) 681
   RODGER, Elizabeth A. (Asst
   Branch head) 1047
Toronto Stock Exchange (ON) JUOZAPAVICIUS, Danguole T.
   (Mgr) 620
Toronto Sun Publishing Co (ON) KIRSH, Julie (Chief Libn) 655
Toronto Western Hospital (ON) REID, Elizabeth A. (Dir, Hlth Sci
   Lib) 1018
**Torrance Memorial Hospital Medical
Ctr** (CA) KLECKER, Anita N. (Med Libn) . . 658
Torrance Pub Lib (CA) BEEBE, Richard J. (Sr Libn) 74
   BUCKLEY, James W. (City
   Libn) 154
   DOWNEY, Christine D. (AV
   Libn) 316
   REEDER, Norman L. (Prog
   Adminstr) 1015
   SIEGEL, Jacquelin B. (Catlgr) . . 1136
Torrance Unified Sch District (CA) MOORE, Richard K. (Libn) 861
**Tory Tory DesLauriers &
Binnington** (ON) DARBY, Janet M. (Libn) 274
Total Information (NY) GIGLIOTTI, Mary J. (Info
   Broker) 433
Touche Ross & Co (CA) TICE, Kathleen A. (Head Libn) . 1244
Touche Ross & Co (IL) GIAMBRONE, Richard J. (Libn) . 430
Touche Ross & Co (NY) BERNTSEN, Robert M. (Lib Dir) . . 90
   CONNER, Norma (Central Files
   Libn) 237
Touche Ross & Co (TX) SCHIELACK, Tricia J. (Libn) . . . 1092
Touro Coll (NY) KINYATTI, Njoki W. (Chief Libn) . 653
   MARGALITH, Helen M.
   (Coordntr of Ref Srvs) 770
   MARKOWITZ, Lois (Technl
   Srvs Head) 771
Towanda Area Sch District (PA) BURLINGAME, Connie (Libn) . . . 161
Tower Hill Sch (DE) MCCARTHY, Carrol B. (Libn) . . . 794
   MINNICH, Nancy P. (Lib Dir) . . . 846
Towers Perrin Forster & Crosby (GA) BATTEN, Henry R. (Asst Libn) . . 64
   BAUER, Leslie L. (Lib Asst) 65
Towers Perrin Forster & Crosby (NY) BORBELY, Jack (Info Srvs Dir) . . 116
   FIORILLO, Barbara A.
   (Database Indxr & Adminstr) . . 379
   HINKSON, Colin S. (Info Srvs
   Asst) 542
Towers Perrin Forster & Crosby (PQ) CHIPPS, Heather D. (Info
   Spclst) 209
Town of Amherst (NY) TAMMARO, James M. (Records
   Mgr) 1221
Town of Belchertown (MA) PECK, Ruth M. (Sch Lib Media
   Spclst) 953
Town of Brattleboro (VT) MORRISON, Meris E. (Dir) 868
Town of Brookline (MA) ABRAHAM, Deborah V. (Head
   of Ref Dept) 2
Town of Brossard (PQ) LACROIX, Yvon A. (Dir) 687
Town of Colonie (NY) NAYLOR, Richard J. (Asst Dir) . . 890

Town of Cromwell (CT)
BRANCIFORTE, Eileen G. (Lib Dir) 127

Town of Dedham (MA)
MCDONALD, Murray F. (Lib Dir) 803

Town of East Longmeadow (MA)
CARVER, Gloria C. (Dir) 191

Town of Foxborough (MA)
MILLER, Barbara J. (Educ Asst) . 835

Town of Gates (NY)
MACKNIGHT, Judith M. (Adult Srvs Programming Libn) 757

Town of Greenwich (CT)
BIHLER, Charles H. (Media Coordntr) 96

Town of Highland Park (TX)
CASE, Bonnie N. (Lib Dir) 191

Town of Holden (MA)
BAKER, Janet R. (Lib Dir) 48

Town of Lexington (MA)
KELLSTEDT, Jenny (Branch Libn) 637

Town of Littleton (MA)
WILLIAMS, Carole C. (Dir) 1342

Town of Marblehead (MA)
DYER, Victor E. (Asst Dir) 330

Town of Markham Pub Libs (ON)
HARE, Judith E. (Chief Exec Ofcr) 501

Town of Natick (MA)
FEEN, Anne B. (Lib Dir) 368

Town of Newmarket (ON)
READ-STARK, Marilyn A. (Chlds Srvs Head) 1012

Town of North Andover (MA)
REEVE, Russell J. (Dir) 1016

Town of North Haven (CT)
BALDINI, Lois D. (Dir of Lib Srvs) 51
GLICK, Kenneth W. (Circ Libn) . . 441

Town of Oakville (ON)
LA CHAPELLE, Jennifer R. (Records Mgr) 686

Town of Old Saybrook (CT)
NOVAK, Elaine L. (Dir) 910

Town of Perry (NY)
PARKER, Margaret S. (Lib Dir) . . 942

Town of Pickering Pub Lib (ON)
LINTON, Linda J. (Project Mgr) . 731

Town of Pittsfield (ME)
NICHOLSON, Carol C. (Libn) . . . 902

Town of Plymouth (MA)
BIBEAU, Janet A. (Media Spclst) 94

Town of San Anselmo (CA)
WINGATE, Eliza C. (Libn) 1354

Town of Shrewsbury (MA)
CHANG, Isabelle E. (Media Coordntr) 200

Town of Smithtown (NY)
GRAVITZ, Ina A. (Ref & Yng Adult Libn) 459

Town of Springfield (VT)
MOORE, Russell S. (Lib Dir) 861

Town of Stoughton (MA)
ANDERSON, Cheryl M. (K-12 Lib Srvs Dir) 22
BIRCH, Grace M. (Dir) 97

Town of Trumbull (CT)
HOLLEY, James L. (Dir) 551

Town of Vestal (NY)
PILLSBURY, Mary J. (Dir) 973

Town of Wareham (MA)
STILES, Muriel H. (Lib Dir) 1194

Town of West Boylston (MA)
WEEKS, Beverly J. (High Sch Libn) 1315

Town of West Springfield (MA)
DOUGLAS, Alice W. (Dir) 314

Town of Weston (MA)
KELLOGG, Joanne T. (Lib Dir) . . 637

Town of Windham (ME)
STEWART, Betty F. (Lib Dir) . . . 1192

Town of Yorktown (NY)
EVERHART, Paul R. (Media Chairman) 358

Township High Sch District 211 (IL)
HOLBROCK, Mary A. (Libn) 550

Township High Sch District 214 (IL)
LUEHS, Jeanne M. (Dir) 747

Township of Cedar Grove (NJ)
MEYER, Mary L. (Dir) 830

Township of Hamilton (NJ)
BUTLER, Patricia M. (Chlds Srvs Coordntr) 167

Township of Irvington (NJ)
KNAPP, Mabel J. (Head Libn) . . . 663

Township of Lower Merion (PA)
PULLER, Maryam W. (Dir) 997

Township of South Orange Village (NJ)
FAWCETT-BRANDON, Pamela S. (Sr Libn & Technl Srvs Head) 367

Township of Union (NJ)
WALSH, Florence C. (Lib Dir) . . 1299

Towson State Univ (MD)
CHEEKS, Cellestine (Asst Prof) . . 204
GERHARDT, Edwin L. (Volunteer Cur) 428
HARER, John B. (Head, Circ) . . . 501
HOFSTETTER, Eleanore O. (Asst Dir) 549
KALTENBORN, Helen P. (Assoc Dir for Tech Srvs) 623

Toyota Central R & D Lab Inc (JAP)
SANO, Hikomaro (Mgr) 1081

TPF&C Limited (ON)
BERCOVITCH, Sari (Info Srvs Supvsr) 84

TPF&C/Tillinghast (GA)
REYNOLDS, Carol C. (Libn) . . . 1025

Tracy-Locke Inc (TX)
SHAPLEY, Ellen M. (Vice Pres & Mgr) 1122

Tracy School Dist (CA)
WOBBE, Jean (Dist Libn) 1359

Tradenet (NY)
KOENIG, Michael E. (Data Design & Info Retrieval Dir) . . 668

Trans-World Visions (MA)
ALASTI, Aryt (Owner) 9

Transcom Electronics (RI)
HAMPTON, Sylvia S. (Engrng Libn) 494

Transition Management (TX)
RYDESKY, Mary M. (Sole Proprietor) 1071

Transnational Commerce Corp (NY)
NEWMAN, Jerald C. (Pres) 899

Transnational Publishers Inc (NY)
FENTON, Heike (Pres) 371

Transport Canada (ON)
ZIMMERMAN, Suzan E. (Info Ofcr) 1389

TRANSTECH International Corp (MA)
WANG, Gary Y. (Pres) 1302

Transylvania Univ (KY)
BRYSON, Kathleen C. (Lib Dir) . . 152
LEE, Soon H. (Info Spclst) 711

Travel Labs (IL)
ORLOSKE, Margaret Q. (Asst Dir) 926

The Travelers Insurance Cos (CT)
WORSTER, Carol L. (Technl Info Resrc Ctrs Supvsr) 1369

Travenol Laboratories Inc (IL)
KULIBERT, Marie M. (Ref Libn) . 683

Traverse Area District Lib (MI)
SCHAUB, Theresa F. (Chlds Libn) 1090

Traverse des Sioux Lib System (MN)
CHRISTENSON, John D. (Exec Dir) 211

Travis County (TX)
KESHISHIAN, Maria L. (Records Spclst) 644

Treasure Valley Community Coll (OR)
AMSBERRY, Dan F. (Asst Libn) . . 20

Trebizond Rare Books (CT)
BENEDICT, Williston R. (Proprietor) 80

Tredyffrin Pub Lib (PA)
STEVENS, Marian A. (Dir) 1190

Trent Univ (ON)
GENOE, Murray W. (Univ Libn) . . 427
WISEMAN, John A. (Cols Libn) 1357

Trenton State Coll (NJ)
BRODOWSKI, Joyce H. (Assoc Dir for Lib Srvs) 139
BUTCHER, Patricia S. (Asst Dir for Readers Srvs) 166
CORWIN, Dean W. (Music and Listening Srvs Libn) 248
DU BOIS, Paul Z. (Lib Dir) 322
MCCULLOUGH, Jack W. (Chairman) 801
WOODLEY, Robert H. (Humanities & Instruction Libn) 1366

Trey Foerster Ink Inc (WI)
FOERSTER, Trey (Publshg Consult) 387

Tri-County Dental Health Council (MI)
BINDSCHADLER, Valerie V. (Resrc Coordntr) 97

Tri-Meridian Inc (NJ)
DUDLEY, Debbra C. (VP & Gen Mgr MIS) 323

Tri-Met (OR)
KAWABATA, Julie (Libn) 632

Tri Star Publishing (PA)
NICKEL, R S. (Rep) 902
STEPHENSON, Jon R. (Vice Pres of Mktg) 1188

Tri-Tech Data Solutions Inc (TX)
ZYSK, John T. (Pres & Chief Executive Ofcr) 1392

Tri-Township Lib (IL)
HOLMES, Norman W. (Head Libn) 553

Triadvocates Associated (PA)
KLETZIEN, S D. (Exec Edit) 661

Trial Court-Law Libs (MA)
LINDHEIMER, Sandra K. (Lib Dir) 729

Triangle Research Libs Network (NC)
BENNETT, David B. (Systs Libn) 81
HANRAHAN, Geane (Mktg Dir) . . 497
STRYKER, Charles W. (Pres & CEO) 1203

Trinity Bible Coll (ND)
ZINK, Esther L. (Libn) 1389

Trinity Christian Coll (IL)
SLIEKERS, Hendrik (Lib Srvs Dir) 1149

Trinity Coll (CT)
BUNKER, Patricia J. (Ref Libn) . . 157
KAIMOWITZ, Jeffery H. (Cur) . . . 622
KNAPP, Peter J. (Ref Head & Coll Archvst) 663
MCKINNEY, Linda R. (Ref Libn) . 812
TALIT, Lynn (Film & Video Coordntr) 1221
WARZALA, Allison B. (Catlg Libn) 1307

Trinity Coll (DC)
LEIDER, Karen S. (Libn) 713

Trinity Coll (VT)
YERBURGH, Mark R. (Lib Dir & Assoc Prof of Hist) 1379

Trinity Coll (ON) CORMAN, Linda W. (Libn) 246
Trinity Coll (IRE) FOX, Peter K. (Univ Libn) 395
Trinity Episcopal School for Ministry (PA) MUNDAY, Robert S. (Admin Dean & Lib Dir) 878
Trinity Evangelical Divinty Sch (IL) OSWALT, Karen K. (Asst Ref Libn) 929
PORCELLA, Brewster (Libn) 984
WELLS, Keith P. (Ref Libn) 1322
Trinity Lutheran Seminary (OH) HUBER, Donald L. (Libn) 569
Trinity Univ (TX) BADING, Kathryn E. (Catlg Maintenance Libn) 44
BARRINGER, Sallie H. (Sci Libn) 60
CARMACK, Norma J. (Docums Libn) 183
CLARKSON, Mary C. (Circ Head) 219
FORD, Barbara J. (Assoc Dir) ... 389
HOOD, Elizabeth (Serials Catlg Libn & Asst Prof) 556
LIKNESS, Craig S. (Humamities Libn & Head Biblgphr) 727
NOLAN, Christopher W. (Ref Srvs Libn) 907
WERKING, Richard H. (Dir of Libs & Assoc Prof of Hist) .. 1324
Trintex (NY) SMITH, Harry E. (VP, Production & Commercial Dev) 1155
VALANDRA, Kent T. 1271
Triodyne Inc (IL) HAMILTON, Beth A. (Sr Info Scientist) 491
HANSEN, Cheryl A. (Engrng Ref Libn) 497
Trocaire Coll (NY) MULDOON, Jane K. (Lib Dir) ... 876
Troup County Archives (GA) LANNING, E K. (Dir) 696
Troup-Harris-Coweta Regional Lib (GA) BECHAM, Gerald C. (Dir) 71
Troy City Schs (OH) MILLER, John E. (Tech & Instrcl Resrcs Dir) 839
Troy-Miami County Pub Lib (OH) CRAM, Mary E. (Extension Coordntr) 255
TUCKER, Mary C. (Chlds Coordntr) 1262
Troy Pub Lib (NY) EVELAND, Ruth A. (Dir) 358
GINSBURG, Joanne R. (Community Relations Coordntr) 438
JANOWSKY, Cara A. (Adult Srvs Head) 593
Troy Sch District (MI) COREY, Glenn M. (Tchr) 246
Troy State Univ (AL) SMITH, Julia L. (Acq/Catlgng Libn) 1156
SOUTER, Thomas A. (Dean of the Lib) 1169
Truckee Meadows Community Coll (NV) COONEY, Mata M. (Pub Srvs Libn) 242
Truett-McConnell Coll (GA) WILSON, Janice E. (Libn) 1351
Truman Coll (IL) SKIDMORE, Gail (Techn Srvs Libn) 1146
Truman Medical Center East (MO) DALTON, Richard R. (Clinical Libn/Dir of Lib Srvs) 271
Truro Pub Libs (MA) BRAINARD, Elsie K. (Dir) 127
Truth or Consequences Pub Lib (NM) SAMPSON, Ellanie S. (Libn) .. 1078
TRW Defense Systems Group (CO) QUINN, Candy L. (Technl Libn) . 1000
TRW Federal Systems Group (VA) ROBINSON, David F. (Defense Data Spclst) 1043
TRW Information Systems Group (CA) ADAMS, Linda L. (Bus Info Analyst) 5
HIATT, Jack (Plng & Devlpmnt Dir) 536
MARCHIANO, Marilyn C. (Sr Data Mgmt Systs Analyst) ... 768
Tsuda Coll (JAP) KATO, Hisae (Catlgng Libn) 629
The Tucker Co (NH) TUCKER, Richard B. (President) 1262
Tucker Flyer Sanger & Lewis (DC) MOTEN, Derryn E. (Libn) 872
Tucson Medical Center (AZ) KING, Christee (Lib Srvs Mgr) .. 650
Tucson Planning Department (AZ) CROWE, Gloria J. (Plng Libn) ... 261

Tucson Pub Lib (AZ) BIERMAN, Kenneth J. (Asst Dir) .. 95
GOODRICH, Nita K. (Pub Info Ofcr) 449
HAMILTON, Rita (Adminstrv Asst) 492
LEWIS, Jean R. (Adult & Yng Adult Srvs Libn) 723
MCLACHLAN, Ross W. (Principal Catlgr) 812
STOUT, Mary A. (Catlgng Mgr) . 1199
TYMCIURAK, Olya T. (Branch Mgr) 1266
Tufts Univ (MA) BOYCE, Barbara S. (Assoc Libn) 122
EATON, Elizabeth K. (Hlth Sci Lib Dir) 333
FELDT, Candice K. (Music Catlgr & Asst Libn) 369
GOLDMAN, Brenda C. (Assoc Libn, Music) 445
JONES, Frederick S. (Assoc Libn, Col Devlpmnt & Finance) 613
KRUPANSKI, Pamela M. (Slide Cur) 680
MARTIN, Murray S. (Univ Libn) .. 777
MCDONALD, Ellen J. (Ref Libn) . 802
MCKIRDY, Colin (Assoc Univ Libn) 812
PAISTE, Marsha S. (Catlgr) 935
SAFFER-MARCHAND, Melinda (Lib Dir) 1074
SCHATZ, Natalie M. (Lib Dir) .. 1090
STAACK, Katherine A. (Assoc Libn, Spcl Projects) 1177
STEARNS, Norman S. 1183
WALSH, Jim (Govt Pubns and Maps Libn) 1299
Tulane Univ (LA) BARON, John H. (Prof of Music) .. 58
CARTEE, Lewis D. (Systs Libn) .. 188
COMBE, David A. (Law Libn & Prof of Law) 234
COPELAND, Patricia S. (Chief of Pub Srvs) 244
CURTIS, Robert L. (Music Lib Head) 267
FLEURY, Bruce E. (Sci & Engineering Div Head) 385
GOLDSTEIN, Cynthia H. (Chief of Technl Srvs) 446
HAGEDORN, Dorothy L. (Assoc Univ Libn) 482
HALFORD, Mary B. (Asst Biblgphr for Hum & Fine Arts) 486
HAMORI, Annemarie R. (Libn) . 494
JERDE, Curtis D. (Cur) 599
JONES, Philip L. (Ref Libn) 614
LEINBACH, Philip E. (Univ Libn) . 714
MOORE, Mildred M. (Serials Libn) 860
NACHOD, Katherine B. (Govt Docums, Microforms Libn) ... 885
POSTELL, William D. (Dir) 986
RENNIE, Margaret C. (Monographs Libn) 1023
STAFFORD, Cecilia D. (Ref Libn) 1178
THOMPSON, Jeannette C. (Catlg, Music & AV) 1240
WELSCH, Melissa W. (Info Srvs Libn) 1323
ZULA, Floyd M. (Monographs & Acqs Head) 1391
Tulare County Department of Education (CA) EBY, James F. (Prog Mgr) 334
Tulare County Lib (CA) PILLING, George P. (Chlds Coordntr) 973
Tuloso-Midway Independent School Dist (TX) SILVERMAN, Barbara G. (Libn) 1138

Tulsa City-County Lib System (OK) BUTHOD, J C. (Chief of the Centl Lib) 166
GRAHAM, John (Info II Libn) . . . 456
JENNINGS, Kathryn L. (Head of Chlds Dept) 598
KEENE, Janis C. (Asst Dir, Non Pub Srvs) 634
MEADOR, Joan S. (Ref Dept Head) 819
SEARS, Robert W. (Bus Libn) . . 1110
STURDIVANT, Nan J. (Coordntr of Chlds Srvs) 1205
TAPPANA, Kathy A. (Hlth Info Libn) 1223
WOODRUM, Patricia A. (Dir) . . 1366

Tulsa Junior Coll (OK) HACKER, Connie J. (Catlgng Libn) 481
MANES, Estelle L. (Libn & Head Catlgr) 765
MCCALL, Patricia (Serials and Ref Libn) 793
NORTON, Paula T. (Libn) 910

Tulsa Pub Schs (OK) WRIGHT, Patricia Y. (Libn & Media Coordntr) 1372

Turner Free Lib (MA) MICHAUD, Charles A. (Lib Dir) . . 832
WEISCHEDEL, Elaine F. (Chlds Libn) 1319

Turner Subscriptions (NY) BASCH, N B. (Pres) 62
KOCHOFF, Stephen T. (Mktg Dir) 667

Tuscaloosa Pub Lib (AL) MCKINLEY, Beebe M. (Catlgr) . . 811
Tuscarawas County Pub Lib (OH) HAGLOCH, Susan B. (Dir) 483
Tuskegee Inst (AL) DAVIS, Frances F. (Libn) 279
TV Ontario (ON) VOLPATTI, Rechilde (Lib Srvs Supvsr) 1288

Twinsburg Pub Lib (OH) KAUER, Patricia M. (Adult Srvs Libn) 630

Two Rivers Lib Board (WI) HEITKEMPER, Elsie M. (Dir) 523
Tydings & Rosenberg (MD) THIES, Gail M. (Law Libn) 1235
Tyler Cooper & Alcorn (CT) LUBIN, Joan S. (Libn) 745
Tyler Independent Sch District (TX) LAMBERTH, Linda E. (Coor Lib Srvs) 690

Tyler Junior Coll (TX) KENNEDY, Johnnye (Dir of Lib Srvs) 641
WILSON, George N. (Dir, Instrcl Media Srvs) 1351

U

U C Hastings Law Lib (CA) PERITORE, Laura D. (Assoc Law Libn) 958

Ukrainian Cultural & Educational Centre (MB) CHOMENKO, Tamara L. (Libn) . . 210
Ulster County Board (NY) STAINO, Rocco A. (Dir) 1178
Umpqua Community Coll (OR) MUNGER, Freda R. (Dir of Lib Srvs) 879

Underwood-Memorial Hospital (NJ) TIEDRICH, Ellen K. (Med Libn) . 1244
Unification Theological Seminary (NY) NAVRATIL, Jean (Dir) 890
Unilever Research (ENG) HOWARD, Theresa M. (Info Ctr Mgr) 564
Union Carbide Corp (CT) CONNER, Shirley D. (Sr Info Spclst) 237
MARIANI, Carolyn A. (Info Srvs Mgr) 770
MCPHERSON, Mary A. (Ref Libn) 817
SHEA, Roseanne M. (Assoc Law Libn) 1124
Union Carbide Corp (NJ) KLEMM, Carol B. (Staff Coordntr) 660
Union Carbide Corp (NY) GALBRAITH, Barry E. (Technl Info Scientist) 413
Union Carbide Corp (OH) RIFFLE, Linda (Mgr) 1034
Union Carbide Corp (WV) BEHR, Alice S. (Lib Mgr) 75
Union Coll (NE) NESMITH, Edmund D. (Pub Srvs & Automation Libn) 896

Union Coll (NY)

Union County Pub Lib (NC)

Union Electric Co (MO)

Union Gas Ltd (ON)
Union Hospital (NJ)

Union Memorial Hospital (MD)

Union Memorial Lib (MD)

Union Pacific Railroad (NE)
Union Pacific Resources (TX)

Union Pub Schs (OK)

Union Texas Petroleum (TX)

Union Theological Seminary (NY)

Union Theological Seminary (VA)

Union Univ at Albany (NY)

Union Univ at Jackson (TN)

Uniondale Pub Lib (NY)
Uniroyal Chemical Co Inc (CT)
Uniroyal Goodrich Tire Co (OH)
Uniroyal Ltd (ON)

Unisys Corp (CA)

Unisys Corp (MI)

Unisys Corp (MN)

Unisys Corp (NY)

Unisys Corp (PA)
Unisys Corp (UT)
United Charities of Chicago (IL)

United Church of Christ (WI)
United Engineers & Constructors Inc (CO)

United Engineers & Constructors Inc (MA)

United Engineers & Constructors Inc (PA)
United Fresh Fruit & Vegetable Assn (VA)

United Health Services (NY)

United Hospital Fund of New York (NY)

EVANS, Ruth A. (Assoc Libn) . . . 358
RAHN, Suzanne M. (Catlg Libn) 1003
SEEMANN, Ann M. (Libn) 1111
SHEVIAK, Jean K. (Coordntr, Online Syst) 1129
ABBOTT, Chien N. (Lib Clerk III) 1
GATLIN, Patricia F. 422
VERBECK, Alison F. (Technl Libn) 1282
WHALEY, E M. (Catlgr) 1328
TANNENBAUM, Aileen Z. (Med Libn) 1222
ZIMMERMAN, Martha B. (Lib and Info Resrcs Dir) 1389
DAUGHERTY, Carolyn M. (Libn) 275
OYER, Kenneth E. (Head Libn) . . 932
MCCANN, Debra W. (Centl Files Supvsr) 794
UNDERHILL, Jan (Sch Libn, Media Spclst) 1268
WRIGHT, Craig W. (Records Systs Supvsr) 1371
KASTEN, Seth E. (Head of Reader Srvs) 629
AYCOCK, Martha 43
THOMASON, Dorothy G. (Head, Catlgng Dept) 1238
TROTTI, John B. (Libn) 1258
DUNCAN, Elizabeth C. (Head of Technl Srvs) 325
ROBERTSON, Billy O. (Dir of Lib) 1041
OPATOW, Judith (Ref Libn) 925
HARMON, Patricia A. (Libn) 502
GALLICCHIO, Virginia G. (Mgr) . 414
COLE, Lorna P. (Mgr of Info Srvs & Legal Liaison) 231
OLMSTEAD, Nancy L. (Sr Technl Libn) 921
SZABO, Carolyn J. (Chief Libn) 1218
CARUSO, Genevieve O. (Mgr, Info Liaison) 190
FEDER, Carol S. (Info Spclst) . . . 367
FRANTILLA, K A. (Archvst) 398
WHITE, Jane F. (Info Spclst) . . . 1331
ELFSTRAND, Stephen F. (Info Analyst) 342
RASMUSSEN, Mary L. (Group Mgr) 1009
VAN HORN, Virginia A. (Acqs Libn) 1275
MONTALBANO, James J. (Asst Libn) 855
HAHN, Susan H. (Technl Libn) . . 484
NOEL, Eileen V. (Technl Libn) . . . 907
BURNS, Marie T. (Libn, Records Mgr) 162
CORBLY, James E. (Lib Adv) . . . 245
MATTINGLY, Debra B. (Info Resrch Spclst) 786
OBERG, Judy M. (Info Spclst) . . . 914
PRESTON, Margaret P. (Head Libn) 992
KNUP, Marie S. (Head Libn) 666
MCLAUGHLIN, Elaine C. (Info Spclst) 813
EDSALL, Shirley A. (Mgr of Lrng Resrcs Dept) 336
WESTERFIELD, Marjorie C. (Hlth Sci Libn) 1327
WILLER, Kenneth H. (Ref Libn) . 1341

United Hospitals Medical Center (NJ) GILHEANY, Rosary S. (Dir of Lib Srvs) 434
NAGELE, Nancy C. (Profsnl Srvs Libn) 886
United Methodist Church (AL) PICKARD, Mary A. (Archvst) . . . 970
United Methodist Church (MN) BOEDER, Thelma B. (Archvst) . . 109
United Methodist Church (NM) ROLLER, Twila J. (Archvst) . . . 1051
United Methodist Publishing House (TN) LEWIS, Rosalyn (Libn) 724
United Nations (NY) DAVIES, Carol A. (Database Mgr) 277
ERLANDSSON, Alf M. (Archvst) . 353
FRIED, Suzanne C. (UN Docums Indexer) 403
GINES, Noriko (Assocd Libn) . . . 437
KJOLSTAD-ERLANDSSON, Britt S. (Legal Libn) 657
MARTINEZ-RIVERA, Ivette (Asst Libn) 779
MUTTER, Letitia N. (Info Syts Unit Libn) 883
WARD, Edith (Sr TNC Affairs Ofcr) 1303
United Nations (KEN) PILLET, Sylvaine M. (Sr Info Ofcr) 973
United Nations (TRN) ELLIOTT, Lirlyn J. (Centre Libn) . 344
United Nations/Central Am Pub Admin Inst (CSR) CROWTHER, Warren W. (Pub Mgmt Expert & Prof) 262
UNICEF (NY) CANNATA, Arleen (Consult) 178
UNESCO (FRN) COURRIER, Yves G. (Chief of Spclst and User Trng) 251
UN Food & Agriculture Organization (ITL) MENOU, Michel J. (Field Operations Ofcr) 824
United Paperworkers International Union (TN) GLAUS, Roberta I. (Libn) 440
United Services Automobile Association (TX) PHILLIPS, Sylvia E. (Mgr, Lib Srvs) 969
US Agency for Intl Devlpmnt, Lesotho (DC) BERGQUIST, Christine F. (Lib Consult) 87
US Air Force (AL) ADAMS, Emily J. (Catlgr) 4
GATLING, James L. (Technl Info Spclst) 422
GOODMAN, Anita S. (Editor) . . . 449
HARPER, Marie F. (Biblgphr) . . . 503
LANE, Robert B. (Air Univ Lib Dir) 694
LASETER, Ernest P. (Technl Lib Adminstr) 700
LASETER, Shirley B. (Automated Lib Systs Head) . . 700
MAYTON, Regina A. (Systs Div Chief) 791
WISE, Kenda C. (Biblgphr) 1357
US Air Force (AR) GODBEY, Esther R. (Libn) 442
US Air Force (AZ) KESSLER, Katheryn M. (Libn) . . . 645
US Air Force (CA) BALLOU, Eleanor F. (Chief Libn) 53
CROWTHER, Carol (Base Libn) . 262
HEINES, Rodney M. (Chief Libn) . 522
JACOBS, Nina F. (Libn) 589
MOSER, Jane W. (Database Mgr & Technl Info Spclst) . . . 870
PAMINTUAN, Celia (Base Libn) . 937
ZEBROWSKI, Cheryl K. (Head Libn) 1387
US Air Force (CO) EIDSON, Alreeta (Command Libn) 340
US Air Force (DC) MAYHEW, Eileen G. (Lib Technician) 790
ZELINKA, Mary A. (Med Libn in Charge) 1387
US Air Force (FL) ROSEN, Bettylou (Chief Libn) . . 1055
US Air Force (HI) HASSLER, William B. (Adminstrv Libn) 511
LUSTER, Arlene L. (Lib Dir & Command Libn) 750

US Air Force (IL) BURNSIDE, Diane B. (Airlift Operations Sch Libn) 163
KNUDTSON, Gail L. (Command Libn) 666
MARSHALL, Kathryn E. (Chief Libn) 774
PROVINCE, William R. (Lib Dir) . 996
US Air Force (MA) DUFFEK, Elizabeth A. (Acqs Libn) 323
GERKE, Ray (Base Libn) 428
MCLAUGHLIN, Lee R. (Acqs Unit Chief) 813
SEIDMAN, Ruth K. (Lib Dir) . . . 1112
US Air Force (MS) FREEDMAN, Jack A. (Physcal Scis & Engineering Libn) 400
US Air Force (NC) OLENDER, Karen L. (Base Libn) . 920
US Air Force (NE) SAUER, Mary L. (Dir of Strategic Air Command Libs) 1084
US Air Force (NH) HATHAWAY, Teresa M. (Libn) . . 512
US Air Force (NM) JOURDAIN, Janet M. (Libn) 618
US Air Force (NY) BURKE, Joseph A. (Base Libn) . . 160
GADBOIS, Frank W. (Base Libn) 411
HAAS, Eva L. (Dir of Libs) 480
LOMEN, Nancy L. (Base Lib Mgr) 738
ROWELL, Regina A. (Med Libn) 1062
US Air Force (OH) BOETTCHER, Barry J. (Reader Srvs Chief) 110
NAM, Wonki K. (Libn) 887
US Air Force (TX) BLACK, Katherine S. (Ref Libn) . 101
FRIDLEY, Bonnie J. (Pub Srvs Chief) 403
PENNER, Elaine C. (Head Libn) . 957
ST. JOHN, Louise (Base Libn) . 1075
TODD, Fred W. (Chief Libn) . . . 1248
US Air Force (VA) ROY, Alice R. (Tactical Air Command Libn) 1063
US Air Force (WGR) WHITEHILL, Margaret (Base Libn) 1332
US Air Force Academy (CO) BARRETT, Donald J. (Pub Srvs Asst Dir) 59
KYSELY, Elizabeth C. (Chief of Ref Branch) 685
NELSON, Marie L. (Chief) 894
STEWART, Anna C. (Lib Aid) . . 1192
US Air Force Institute of Technology (OH) CUPP, Christian M. (Chief of Reader Srvs) 265
HELLING, James T. (Dir) 524
PURSCH, Lenore D. (Catlgr) . . . 998
US Air Force Lib Service (NY) ANDREWS, Margaret D. (Base Libn) 27
US Air Force Sch of Aerospace Medicine (TX) BREWSTER, Olive N. (Technl Prcsng Chief) 134
US Air Force Weapons Laboratory (NM) NEWTON, Barbara I. (Technl Lib Chief) 900
US Amccom, ARDEC, CCAS (NY) MACKSEY, Susan A. (Scintfc & Technl Info Ofc Chief) 757
US Army (AK) CHANEY, A. V. (Libn) 200
RICKS, Bonnie B. (Adminstrv Libn) 1032
US Army (AL) AIDE, Kathryn S. (Lib Technician) 8
US Army (DC) KUBAL, Gene J. (Ref Sect Chief) 681
US Army (GA) DOOLEY, Shelly Q. (Technl Srvs Libn) 312
US Army (IL) BLAKE, Martha A. (Libn) 103
US Army (KY) RIVES, Lydia L. (Supervisory Libn) 1037
US Army (LA) JONES, Stephanie R. (Supvsr & Tech Srvs Libn) 615
US Army (MD) GIBBONS, Katherine Y. (Med Libn) 431
HADDEN, Robert L. (Physical Scis & Engrng Libn) 481
US Army (MN) SCHMIDT, Jean M. (Libn) 1095

US Army (MO) TIPSWORD, Thomas N. (Acting Chief) 1246

US Army (MS) ABLES, Timothy D. (Info Systs Mgmt Spclst) 2

US Army (NJ) MARCO, Guy A. (Chief of Lib Activities) 769
MICHAL, Judith A. (Technl Srvs Libn) 832
VARIEUR, Normand L. (Scintfc & Technl Info Branch Chief) . 1278

US Army (NM) SAUNDERS, Laurel B. (Technl Lib Chief) 1084

US Army (NY) LIN, Susan T. (Div Libn) 728

US Army (OK) RELPH, Martha H. (Libn) 1022

US Army (TX) ARNN, Judith A. (Staff Libn) . . . 33

US Army (VA) BONNETT, Mary B. (ADP & Networking Adminstrv Libn) . . 114
LUH, Lydia Y. (Senior Catlgr) . . . 747
SCHEITLE, Janet M. (Supervisory Libn/Intern Trng Supvsr) 1091

US Army (WA) COHEN, Jane L. (Ref Libn & Col Devlpmnt Libn) 228

US Army Air Defense Artillery Sch (TX) RAMSEY, Donna E. (Supervisory Libn, Tech Srvs) 1005

US Army Center of Military History (DC) ZEIDLICK, Hannah M. (Histl Resrcs Branch Chief) 1387

US Army Command & General Staff Coll (KS) SNOKE, Elizabeth R. (Technl Info Spclst, Soc Scis) 1163

US Army Corps of Engineers (IL) ADAMSHICK, Robert D. (Libn) 6

US Army Corps of Engineers (MS) BLACK, Bernice B. (Dir) 101
KIRBY, Donald J. (Ref Libn) 654

US Army Corps of Engineers (VA) GORDON, Martin K. (Histn & Archvst) 451

US Army Engineer District (CA) NEWTON, Deborah A. (Dist Libn) 900

US Army Environmental Hygiene Agency (MD) GOEL, Krishan S. (Chief) 443

US Army Headquarters Services (DC) CROSS, Dorothy A. (Dir, Pentagon Lib) 260

US Army in Berlin (NY) BLACKBURN, Clayton E. (Technl Srvs Libn) 102
CHICARELLA, Joseph T. (Lib Dir) 207

US Army in Europe (NY) HOUGH, Allen D. (Lib Network Coordntr) 562

US Army in Italy (DC) BURNS, Dean A. (Chief, Info Srvs) 162

US Army Intelligence Sch (MA) PENSYL, Ornella L. (Info Mgr) . . 957

US Army Lib System (NY) MORRISON, J M. (Adminstrv Libn) 868

US Army Military History Institute (PA) GILBERT, Nancy L. (Asst Dir for Lib Srvs) 434
WIWEL, Pamela S. (Serials Catlg Libn) 1359

US Army Military Police Sch (AL) PARKS, Bernice Z. (Libn) 943

US Army Missle Command (AL) WARD, Dorothy S. (Catlgng Libn) 1303

US Army Research Institute (VA) CASWELL, Mary C. (Lib Technician) 194

US Army Tradoc Analysis Command (NM) GIBSON, Julie A. (Chief, Technl Lib Div) 432

US Army Training & Doctrine Command (TX) WILBUR, Sharon F. (Adminstrv Libn) 1338

US Army Training & Doctrine Command (VA) BURGESS, Edwin B. (Acqs Libn) 159
BYRN, James H. (Lib & Info Network Dir, Trailnet) 169
DOYLE, Frances M. (Supervisory Libn) 317

US Attorney's Office (DC) STOCKTON, Sue T. (Head Libn) 1196

US Bureau of Land Management (CO)

US Bureau of the Census (DC)

US Claims Court (DC)

US Congress (DC)

US Consulate in Poland (POL)

US Copyright Office (DC)

US Court House (AL)

US Court of Appeals (AR)

US Court of Appeals (CA)

US Court of Appeals (DC)

US Court of Appeals (GA)

US Court of Appeals (LA)

US Court of Appeals (MA)

US Court of Appeals (MO)

US Court of Appeals (OH)

US Court of Appeals (OR)

US Court of Appeals (UT)

US Court of Appeals (VA)

US Court of Appeals (WA)

US Court of Appeals, Ninth Circuit (CA)

US Court of Appeals, Tenth Circuit (NM)

US Court of International Trade (NY)

US Courts (AZ)

US Courts (MO)

US Defense Communications Agency (DC)

US Defense Mapping Agency (DC)

US Dept, Defense Overseas Dependent Schs (NY)

US Department of Agriculture (CA)

US Department of Agriculture (DC)

US Department of Agriculture (LA)

US Department of Agriculture (MD)

BOWERS, Sandra L. (Chief, BLM Lib) 121

CHAPMAN, Elwynda K. (Spcl Proj Asst for Resrch) 202
THOMPSON, Johanna W. (Decisions Reporter) 1240

KLEIMAN, Gerald S. (Professional Staff Mem) 659

CHOJNACKA, Jadwiga (Libn) . . . 210

HALL, Forest A. (Acqs Libn) 487
KENDRICK, Brent L. (Copyright Trng Coordntr) 640

NICHOLS, Amy S. (Law Libn) . . . 901

MAYS, Allison P. (Branch Libn) . . 791

CELLE, Deborah A. (Technl Srvs Libn) 196
MOORE, Gregory B. (Asst Libn) . 859
LOCKWOOD, David J. (Asst Libn) 736
MCDERMOTT, Patricia M. (Libn) 802

FENTON, Elaine P. (Circuit Libn) 371
FISTE, David A. (Technl Srvs Libn) 382

DULEY, Kay E. (Deputy Circuit Libn) 324

MILLER, Kristen L. (Deputy Circuit Libn) 839
MOSS, Karen M. (Circuit Libn) . . 872
RANDALL, Kristie C. (Asst Libn) 1006

FESSENDEN, Ann T. (Circuit Libn) 374
JUNG, Mary K. (Deputy Circuit Libn) 620

VOELKER, James R. (Ref & CALR Libn) 1286
WELKER, Kathy J. (Circuit Libn) 1321

MCCURDY, Scott M. (Libn) 801

HUMMEL, Patricia A. (Branch Libn) 573

FREY, Peter A. (Circuit Libn) 402
WOODWARD, Elaine H. (Asst Libn) 1368

NORWOOD, Deborah A. (Branch Libn) 910

MAZZA, Joanne C. (Libn) 791

DEMPSEY, Pamela M. (Libn) . . . 291
KLECKNER, Simone M. (Law Libn) 658
LIDSKY, Ella (Asst Libn) 725
WIEBELHAUS, Richard J. (Asst Libn) 1336

GREGORY, Kirk (Ref Libn) 466

GUERRIERO, Donald A. (Lib Dir) 476

GEE, Janet G. 424

YANOFF, Marcy S. (Libn & Media Spclst) 1377

SCHONBRUN, Rena (Libn) . . . 1098
SYPERT, Clyde F. (Mgmt Analyst, GS-12/345) 1217

BILLINGS, Edward S. (Law Libn) 96
PARSONS, John W. (Info Resrcs Branch Chief) 945
SPARKS, Richard M. (Technl Info Spclst) 1171

FLORENT, Marguerite R. (Libn) . 385

ANDRE, Pamela Q. (Info Systs Div Chief) 26
DECKER, Leola M. (Ref Libn) . . . 286
DITXLER, Carol J. (Head of Lending Branch) 306

US Department of Agriculture (MD)

EDWARDS, Shirley J. (Indexing Branch Head) 338
FORBES, John B. (Ref Libn) 389
FRANK, Robyn C. (Head, Info Ctrs Branch) 397
HANFMAN, Deborah A. (Technl Info Spclst) 495
HOOD, Martha W. (Technl Info Spclst) 556
HOWARD, Joseph H. (Dir) 564
KREBS-SMITH, James J. (Food & Nutrition Info Ctr Coordntr) . 677
LARSON, Jean A. (Technl Info Spclst) 699
LEFEBVRE, Veronica A. (Asst Head of the Lending Branch) . 712
LONGENECKER, William H. (Technl Info Spclst) 740
MACLEAN, Jayne T. (Info Ctr Coordntr) 757
MANGIN, Julianne (Head of Interlib Borrowing Unit) 765
MASON, Pamela R. (Acqs & Serials Branch Libn) 781
PISA, Maria G. (Asst to Chief of Pub Srvs Div) 975
SCHNEIDER, Karl R. (Ref Libn) 1097
STRANSKY, Maria (Technl Info Spclst) 1200
THOMPSON, Michael E. (Head of Translations Prog) 1240

US Department of Agriculture (NY)
PERLMAN, Stephen E. (Libn, Biological & Phyical Scis) 959

US Department of Agriculture (VA)
DENGROVE, Richard A. (Ref Ctr Technician) 292

US Department of Agriculture (WI)
SCHARMER, Roger C. (Info Ctr Mgr) 1090

US Dept of Agriculture Forest Service (MD)
AYER, Carol A. (Libn) 42

US Dept of Agriculture Forest Service (UT)
CLOSE, Elizabeth G. (Technl Info Ofcr) 223

US Department of Commerce (CO)
BANKHEAD, Jean M. (Pub Srvs Head & Lib Srvs Asst Chief) . . . 54
WATTERSON, Jane L. (Pub Srvs Libn, Circ & Ref) 1310

US Department of Commerce (DC)
RANDOLPH, Susan E. (Resrch Resrcs Mgr) 1007
ROARK, Robin D. (Technl Info Spclst) 1038

US Department of Commerce (MA)
BROWNLOW, Judith (Libn) 148

US Department of Commerce (ND)
ROBERTSON, Pamela S. (Civil Srv) 1042

US Department of Commerce (VA)
ELSBREE, John J. (Ofc of Pubns & Biblgph Srvs Dir) . . . 346
LEHMANN, Edward J. (Dir, Ofc of Product Devlpmnt) 713

US Department of Commerce (WA)
THAYER, Martha B. (Libn) 1234

US Department of Defense (DC)
HOLLENBACH, Karen L. (Ref Libn) 551

US Department of Defense (FL)
MISSAVAGE, Leonard (Lib Div Chief) 848

US Department of Defense (MD)
WILLIAMS, Beth A. 1342

US Department of Defense (MN)
WITT, Kenneth W. (Data Transcriber) 1358

US Department of Defense (NY)
RIVERA, Antonio (Media Coordntr) 1037

US Department of Defense (SC)
ELLIS, Janet L. (Libn) 344

US Department of Defense (VA)
JACOBSON, Carol E. 590

US Department of Defense (WA)
WOOSTER, Linda I. (Ref Libn) . 1368

US Department of Defense Dependents Schs (FL)
STAHLMAN, Cherry S. (Media Spclst & Libn) 1178

US Department of Defense Dependents Schs (NY)
CUNNINGHAM, Mary A. (Media Spclst) 265
GRIFFIN, Cheryl J. (Media Spclst) 468

US Department of Education (DC)
BUCK, Dayna E. (Asst to the Dir) 153
CARTER, Yvonne B. (Adminstrv Libn) 190
FORK, Donald J. (Adminstrv Libn) 390
JONES, Milbrey L. (Chief, US Dept of Educ Resrch Lib) 614
KIRSCHENBAUM, Arthur S. (Prog Analyst for Educ & Libs) 655
KLASSEN, Robert L. (Pub Lib Support Staff Dir) 657
STEVENS, Frank A. (Lib Devlpmnt Div Dir) 1190

US Department of Energy (DC)
CUMMINGS, Helen H. (Jr Ref Libn) 264
KING, Hannah M. (Sr Ref Libn) . . 651

US Department of Energy (TN)
CARROLL, Bonnie C. (Info Srvs Deputy Asst Mgr) 187
COYNE, Joseph 254
HARDIN, Nancy E. (Techn Info Spclst) 500
RUSHING, Jessie W. (DOE Resrch-in-Progress Database Mgr) 1068
SPATH, Charles E. (Info Acqs & Appraisal Asst Mgr) 1171
STUBER, Charles E. 1204

US Department of Energy (WA)
FENKER, John A. (Branch Libn) . 371

US Department of Health & Human Services (DC)
HALPIN, Peter (Prog Analyst) . . . 490

US Department of Health & Human Services (MD)
BROWN, Carolyn P. (Chief Libn) 142
LYNN, Kenneth C. (Resrch Data & Mgmt Info Chief) 752

US Dept of Housing & Urban Development (DC)
CHAPMAN, Susan E. (Technl Srvs Head) 202
STALLINGS, Elizabeth A. (Mgmt Analyst, Govt Technl Rep) 1179

US Department of Interior (DC)
BARBEE, Norman N. (Libn, Col Devlpmnt Coordntr) 55

US Department of Interior (NJ)
BOWLING, Mary B. (Archvst) . . . 121

US Department of Interior (OR)
BROOKS, Harry F. (Libn) 140

US Department of Justice (DC)
LEVINE, Emil H. (Comp Spclst & Info Scitst) 720

US Department of Labor (DC)
RILEY, Eileen V. (Acqs Chief) . . 1034

US Department of State (DC)
CLEMMER, Dan O. (Chief, Reader Srvs Branch) 221
CONGER, Lucinda D. (Principal Ref Libn) 236
STEERE, Paul J. (Regnl Lib Consult, East & SE Asia) . . . 1184
VON PFEIL, Helena P. (Intl Law Libn & Law Lib Dir) 1288

US Department of the Interior (DC)
SLOCA, Sue E. (Info Products Branch Chief) 1150

US Department of the Interior (VA)
JENSEN, Raymond A. (Chief Water Resrcs Sci Info Ctr) . . . 599

US Department of the Treasury (DC)
KNAUFF, Elisabeth S. (Info Srvs Mgr) 663

US Department of Transportation (DC)
DOERNBERG, David G. (Technl Info Spclst) 308
LEONARD, Lawrence E. (Chief, Lib & Distribution Srvs Div) . . . 716
NORRIS, Loretta W. (Law Srvs Sect Chief) 909
POEHLMAN, Dorothy J. (Chief, Info Srvs Branch) 979
REILLY, Francis S. (Ref Libn) . . 1020

US Department's Div of Info Management (DC)
FRAULINO, Philip S. (Technl Info Spclst) 399

US District Court (CA)
LUNDSTROM, Lynn E. (Court Libn) 748
MURRAY, Roberta N. (Libn) 882

US District Court (WI)

US District 357 (KS)

US District 480 (KS)

OBERLA, Janet L. (Libn) 914

METTLING, Cora E. (Elem &
Middle Sch Libn) 828

JANTZ, Helen N. (Library/Media
Spclst) 594

US Drug Enforcement
Administration (DC)

DOLAN, Maura E. (Supervisory
Freedom of Info Spclst) 309

GOREN, Morton S. (Libn) 452

US Environmental Protection
Agency (CA)

CIRCIELLO, Jean M. (Chief of
Info Systs Sect) 215

US Environmental Protection
Agency (CO)

EDDY, Dolores D. (Regnl Libn) . . 335

US Environmental Protection
Agency (DC)

BLALOCK, Charlotte R.
(Chemist) 103

GAMSON, Arthur L. (Ref Libn) . 416

NOWAK, Geraldine D. (Technl
Info Spclst) 911

US Environmental Protection
Agency (MA)

NELSON, Margaret R. (Libn) 894

SARAVIS, Judith A. (Lib
Technician) 1082

US Environmental Protection
Agency (OR)

MCCAULEY, Betty P. (Libn) . . . 795

US Environmental Protection
Agency (PA)

LEVIN, Pauline G. (Regnl
Asbestos Coordntr) 720

MCCREARY, Diane M. 800

US Federal Courts (WY)

FERRALL, Bard R. (Asst Libn) . . 373

US Fish & Wildlife Service (MO)

MULTER, Ell P. (Technl Info
Spclst) 878

US Fish & Wildlife Service (ND)

ZIMMERMAN, Ann S. (Libn) . . . 1388

US Food & Drug Administration (CA)

SNELL, Charles E.
(Investigations Branch) 1163

US Food & Drug Administration (DC)

BERNSTEIN, Lee S. (Ref Libn) . . 89

CHATFIELD, Michele R. (Dir) . . . 203

US Food & Drug Administration (MD)

KRUSE, Kathryn W. (Chief, Lib
Srvs Branch) 681

US Forest Service (GA)

RUTHERFORD, Virginia L.
(Administrv Libn) 1070

US General Accounting Office (CA)

SHARP, Linda F. (Technl Info
Spclst) 1122

US General Accounting Office (DC)

PARMING, Marju R. (Spcl Asst
for Info Resrcs Mgmt) 943

RUGE, Audrey L. (Ref Libn) . . . 1066

US General Services
Administration (MO)

NESBITT, John R. (Exec Asst to
Regnl Adminstr) 896

US Geological Society (VA)

SELLIN, Jon B. (Ref Libn) 1114

US Geological Survey (CO)

BIER, Robert A. (Denver Lib
Chief) 95

SHIELDS, Caryl L. (Ref Libn,
Physical Sci) 1129

US Geological Survey (VA)

CHAPPELL, Barbara A. (Chief
of Ref & Circ Sect) 202

KARRER, Jonathan K. (Ref
Libn) 628

LEWIS, Diane M. (Serial
Records Libn) 723

LISZEWSKI, Edward H. (Assoc
Chief Libn) 733

MERRYMAN, Margaret M.
(Actg Head of Acqs Sect) 827

MESSICK, Carol H. (Ref Libn) . . 828

SINNOTT, Gertrude M. (Ref
Libn) 1144

WILTSHIRE, Denise A. (Technl
Info Spclst) 1354

US Golf Assn (NJ)

SEAGLE, Janet M. (Musm Cur,
Libn) 1109

US Government (DC)

LATHAM, Donald C. (Ass Secy
of Defense) 701

PETERSON, Trudy H. (Asst
Archvst) 964

US Government (IN)

BROWN, Judith L. (Employment
Examiner) 145

US Government (MT)

SPOTTED EAGLE, Joy
(Medical Transcriptionist) . . . 1175

US Government (NY)

IRONS, Florence E. (Libn) 584

US Government Printing Office (DC)

DANIELSON, Wilfred D. (Libn &
Catlgr) 273

GRUHL, Andrea M. (Catlgr Fed
Docums) 474

HOA, Quynh N. (Depository Lib
Inspector) 545

KANELY, Edna A. (Lib
Adminstr) 625

SCULLY, Mark F. (Lib Progs
Srv Dir) 1109

TANSEY, Francis J. (Catlgng
Sect Chief) 1223

WOODWARD, Lawrence W.
(Libn & Catlgr) 1368

US House of Representatives (DC)

OWENS, Major (Congressman) . . 932

US Information Agency (CA)

BOONE, Mary L. (Regnl Lib
Consult) 115

US Information Agency (DC)

BORYS, Cynthia A. (Regnl Lib
Consult) 117

CHANG, Frances M. (Libn,
Engl) 200

GRAY, Michael H. (Libn) 460

KUPERMAN, Agota M. (Regnl
Lib Consult) 684

LEE, Amy C. (Regnl Lib
Consult) 709

MANNING, Martin J. (Adminstv
Libn) 766

STONE, Marvin (Deputy Dir) . . . 1197

TAYLOR, Joan R. (Adminstrv
Libn) 1227

WICK, Charles Z. (Dir) 1335

US Information Agency (NY)

HAUSRATH, Donald C. (Regnl
Lib & Bk Ofcr, Eastern
Europe) 513

US Information Agency (TX)

MULLER, Mary M. (Country Lib
Dir) 877

US International Trade
Commission (DC)

KOVER, Steven J. (Head of Law
Lib) 674

PRUETT, Barbara J. (Lib Dir) . . . 996

US International Univ (CA)

TEUTSCH, Walter (Profsnl
Assoc in Music) 1233

US International Univ in
Europe (ENG)

SMITH, Margit J. (Bus Libn) . . . 1157

US League of Savings Institutions (IL)

ENGRAM, Sandra K. (Resrch
Libn) 350

STONER, Ronald P. (Lib Resrcs
Coordntr) 1198

WILSON, Charlotte A. (Lib Srvs
Mgr) 1350

US Marine Corps (GA)

TOOKES, Amos J. (Logistics
Base Libn) 1250

US Marine Corps (VA)

BROWN, David C. (Adminstrv
Libn) 143

US Merchant Marine Academy (NY)

BILLY, George J. (Chief Libn) . . . 97

BOVARNICK, Esther W.
(Reader Srvs Libn) 120

US Military Academy (NY)

AIMONE, Alan C. (Military
Affairs Libn) 8

BARTH, Joseph M. (Asst Libn
for Col Devlpmt) 61

RANDALL, Lawrence E. (Systs
Libn) 1006

US National Guard Assn (DC)

WEAVER, Thomas M. (Reschr
& Libn) 1312

US Naval Academy (MD)

CREIGHTON, Alice S. (Asst
Libn for Spcl Cols) 258

CUMMINGS, John P. (Assoc
Dir) 264

DICKSON, Katherine M. (Ref
Libn) 301

DURBIN, Ramona J. (Biblgph
Ctl Branch Head) 328

WAGNER, Susan C.
(Automation Coordntr) 1292

US Naval Air Station (MD)

SULLIVAN, Carol W. (Libn) . . . 1207

US Naval Hospital, Guam (CA)

HADLEY, Alice E. (Libn) 482

US Naval Ocean Systems Center (CA)   BUNTZEN, Joan L. (Head,
                                       Technl Libs Branch) 157
                                     SWEENEY, Urban J. (Systems
                                       Libn) 1215
US Naval Support Activity (NY)   JONES, Kevin R. (Libn) 613
US Naval War Coll (RI)   HALL, Ann H. (Head of Catlgng
                                       Branch) 487
                                     OTTAVIANO, Doris B. (Ref
                                       Branch Head) 930
US Navy (CA)   MAYES, Elizabeth A. (Syst
                                       Adminstr) 789
                                     THOMPSON, Bryan (Lib Dir) . . 1239
US Navy (CT)   WILLIAMS, Edwin E. (Naval
                                       Regnl Libn) 1343
US Navy (DC)   KALKUS, Stanley (Navy Dept
                                       Lib Dir) 623
US Navy (MS)   LOOMIS, Ann R. 740
US Navy (NY)   LANE, Elizabeth L. (Adminstrv
                                       Libn) 694
US Navy (VA)   ANDERSON, Marcia M. (Libn) . . 24
                                     HUGHES, J M. (Technl Lib
                                       Head) 571
                                     POLLOK, Karen E. (Libn) 981
                                     TEAL, Erika U. (Field Lib Sect
                                       Head) 1229
US Navy (WA)   BODKIN, Sharon C. (Adminstrv
                                       Libn) 109
US News & World Report (DC)   ATKINSON, Rose M. (Libn) 38
                                     DENNIE, David L. (Ref Libn) . . . 292
                                     TRIMBLE, Kathleen L. (Lib Dir) . 1256
US Nuclear Regulatory
  Commission (DC)   SHELBURNE, Elizabeth C.
                                       (Chief, Pub Docums Branch) 1125
US Patent & Trademark Office (DC)   CROCKETT, Martha L. (Technl
                                       Info Spclst) 259
                                     GROOMS, David W. 472
                                     MAYKRANTZ, William J. 790
                                     RADUAZO, Dorothy M. (Mgr,
                                       Online Trng) 1002
US Patent & Trademark Office (VA)   MELVIN, Kay H. (Chief,
                                       Scientific Lit Div) 823
US Pharmacopeial Convention (MD)   WOLLAM, Martha A. (Med Info
                                       Spclst) 1361
US Pharmacopeial Convention
  Inc (MD)   GRIFFITHS, Mary C. (Dir of
                                       Pubn Srvs) 469
US Postal Service (DC)   EAST, Catherine R. (Info Srvs
                                       Spclst) 332
                                     GERIG, Reginald R. (Catlg Syst
                                       Spclst) 428
US Public Health Service (AZ)   MEAD, Thomas L. (Adminstrv
                                       Libn) 819
US Satellite Broadcasting (MN)   HEINERSCHEID, Paul R. (Dir) . . 522
US Saudi Arabian Joint Economic
  Com (NY)   MEDEIROS, Joseph (Info Srvs
                                       Dept Deputy) 820
US Senate (DC)   HALEY, Roger K. (Libn of the
                                       Senate) 486
                                     PAUL, Karen D. (Archvst) 949
                                     PFUND, Leona I. (Head Catlgr) . 966
                                     WOMELDORF, Ann C. (Asst
                                       Libn) 1362
US Small Business
  Administration (DC)   LATEGOLO, Meldie A. (Law
                                       Libn) 701
US Sports Academy (AL)   DANCE, Betty A. (Head Libn) . . 272
US Sprint (VA)   GENNARO, John L. (Bus Plng
                                       Mgr) 427
US Steel (PA)   RICHARDSON, Joy A. (Assoc
                                       Info Spclst) 1029
US Supreme Court (DC)   BAILEY, Marian C. (Acqs Libn) . 46
                                     SHERWIN, Rosalie L. (Asst Libn
                                       for Technl Srvs) 1129
US Tax Court (DC)   BONYNGE, Jeanne R. (Libn) . . . 115
US Tobacco (TN)   BORRELLI, Barbara A. (Resrch
                                       & Devlpmnt Libn) 117
US Treasury Department (DC)   UPDEGROVE, Robert A.
                                       (Adminstrv Libn) 1269
US Treasury Department (SDA)   OSIER, Donald V. (Technl Srvs
                                       Libn) 928

US West Inc (CO)   BIZZUL, Ash R. (Mkt Dev Dir) . . . 100
                                     SMITH, Sally A. (Commercial
                                       Div Dir) 1160
                                     SPANGLER, Bruce (Info Spclst) 1171
US West Knowledge Engineering
  Inc (CO)   BOSTON, Mary T. (Persnl &
                                       Admin Mgr) 118
                                     HARRIS, Michael A. (Exec
                                       Sales Dir) 505
                                     KENLEY, Vernon F. (Strategic
                                       Plng Dir) 640
US WGST (CO)   HUGHES, Brad R. (Prod Mgr) . . . 571
United Technologies Corp (CT)   MILLBROOKE, Anne (Corporate
                                       Archvst) 835
                                     SMALLWOOD, James R. (Libn) 1151
                                     STEELE, Noreen O. (Sr Libn) . . 1184
                                     WENDELL, Florence P. (Sr
                                       Libn) 1323
United Technologies Corp (NY)   SLOAN, Carol L. (Info Spclst) . . 1149
United Technologies Research
  Center (CT)   SIROIS, Valerie M. (Catlgr) 1144
United Telecommunications Inc (KS)   MOBLEY, Kathleen S. (Mgr,
                                       Corporate Resrch Ctr) 851
United Theological Seminary (MN)   MERRILL, Arthur L. (Dir of Lib
                                       Srvs) 826
United Theological Seminary (OH)   BERG, Richard R. (Asst Libn) . . . 84
                                     O'BRIEN, Betty A. (Resrch Asst
                                       to the Pres) 914
                                     O'BRIEN, Elmer J. (Libn and
                                       Prof) 914
United Virginia Bank (VA)   WEEKS, Linda F. (Info Srvs
                                       Ofcr) 1315
United Way - Crusade of Mercy (IL)   BARNUM, Sally J. (Lib and
                                       Records Mgr) 58
Univelt Inc Publishers (CA)   JACOBS, Horace (Pres) 589
Universal Foods Corp (WI)   MUNDSTOCK, Aileen M.
                                       (Technl Info Spclst) 879
Universidad Central de
  Bayamon (PR)   MOMBILLE, Pedro (Dir) 854
Universite Libre de Bruxelles (BEL) DARIS, Claude (Serials Libn) . . 274
Univ Club Lib (DC)   HUDGINS, Peggy (Libn) 569
Univ Club Lib (NY)   BERNER, Andrew J. (Lib Dir) . . . 88
Univ Community Hospital (FL)   TIBBS, Jo A. (Med Ref Libn) . . 1244
                                     WALTERS, Gwen E. (Lib Dir) . . 1301
Univ Heights Pub Lib (OH)   BORCHERT, Catherine G.
                                       (Libn) 116
                                     JANES, Jodith (Libn) 593
Univ Hospitals of Cleveland (OH)   KUCHERENKO, Eugenia
                                       (Hospital Archvst &
                                       Adminstrv Libn) 682
Univ Manitoba (MB)   DIVAY, Gabriele (German Catlgr
                                       & Biblgphr) 306
Univ Medical Center of Southern
  Nevada (NV)   JONYNAS, Aldona I. (Lib Srvs
                                       Dir) 616
Univ Microfilms International (MI)   BILLICK, David J. (Mgr) 96
                                     BREITENWISCHER, Rosalyn E.
                                       (Serials Libn) 132
                                     FITZSIMMONS, Joseph J.
                                       (Pres & Chief Executive Ofcr) . 383
                                     FOWELLS, Fumi T. (Abstctr) . . . 393
                                     KING, Kenneth E. (Biblgph Ctl
                                       Coordntr) 651
                                     MALCOLM, J P. (Sr Vice Pres
                                       & Gen Mgr) 762
                                     MAXWELL, Bonnie J.
                                       (Operations Mgr) 788
                                     SMILLIE, Pauline A. (Distributed
                                       Databases Product Mgr) 1151
                                     WERLING, Anita L. (Vice Pres
                                       & Gen Mgr) 1324
                                     WILSON, Amy S. (Mktg Support
                                       Srvs Mgr) 1349
                                     WOOD, Richard T. (Sr Vice
                                       Pres) 1365
UMI Data Courier (KY)   ARNOLD, Stephen E. (Vice
                                       Pres) 34
                                     AULD, Dennis B. (Pres) 39
                                     BLACKBURN-FOSTER, Brenda
                                       (Trng Spclst) 102

UMI Data Courier (KY)

GASKINS, Betty (Lib Srvs Mgr) . 421
JAMES, Bonnie B. (Managing
    Edit, ABI Inform) 592
JAMIOLKOWSKI, Nancy J.
    (Managing Editor) 593
MACLEOD, Valerie R. (Client
    Srvs Mgr) 757
SKLODOSKI, Terrance E.
    (Admin Srvs Mgr) 1147

UMI Data Courier Inc (KY)

GORDON, Dena 451

Univ of Akron (OH)

BERRINGER, Virginia M.
    (Catlgr) 90
BOLEK, Ann D. (Physical Scis
    Biblgphr) 112
BRINK, David R. (Bus Biblgphr) . 136
DURBIN, Roger (Lib Syst &
    Plng Ofcr) 328
GEISEY, Barbara T. (Dir, Lrng
    Resrcs Cntr) 425
GUSS, Margaret B. (Soc Scis
    Biblgphr) 478
KLINGLER, Thomas E. (Ref
    Dept Head) 662
MCFARLAND, Anne S. (Assoc
    Law Libn) 804
POPPLESTONE, John A.
    (Archs Dir & Prof of Psy) . . 984
RICHERT, Paul (Law Libn) 1030

Univ of Alabama at Birmingham (AL)

BATTISTELLA, Maureen S.
    (Acqs and Cols Devlpmnt
    Libn) 65
BLEILER, Richard J. (Hum Ref
    Libn) 105
BRITT, Mary C. (Cur) 137
CLEMMONS, Nancy W. (Ref
    Srvs Head) 221
GRAMKA, Billie J. (Catlgng
    Libn) 457
HARRIS, Linda S. (Bus &
    Engrng Libn) 505
LAING, Susan J. (Coordntr of
    the Multi-Media) 688
LAUGHLIN, Steven G. (Head of
    Access Srvs) 703
MCGARITY, Marysue (Assoc
    Prof) 805
PFAU, Julia G. (Spcl Projects
    Libn) 966
SPENCE, Paul H. (Col Devlpmnt
    Libn) 1173
STEPHENS, Jerry W. (Libn &
    Dir) 1188
WEATHERLY, Cynthia D.
    (Docums Ref Biblgphr) 1312
WRIGHT, Amos J. (Clinical
    Libn) 1370

Univ of Alabama at Huntsville (AL)

KENDRICK, Aubrey W. (Bus
    Libn) 640
MCNAMARA, Jay (Docums &
    Ref Libn) 816
WILLIAMS, Delmus E. (Lib Dir) . 1342

Univ of Alabama at Tuscaloosa (AL)

ATKINSON, Joan L. (Assoc
    Prof) 38
BENHAM, Frances (Assoc
    Dean) 80
COLEMAN, J G. (Asst Prof) 231
FIELD, Kathy M. (Ref Libn) 375
HAMILTON, Ann H. (Head of
    Circ Dept) 491
KALYONCY, Adydan A. 623
KASKE, Neal K. (Prof) 628
LEE, Sulan I. (Supvsr, Interlib
    Loan) 711
LOWE, David (Comp Srvs Libn) . 743
MOORE, Emily C. (Cur &
    Archvst) 859
MUIR, Scott P. (Systs Ofcr) 876
NEAVILL, Gordon B. (Assoc
    Prof) 891

Univ of Alabama at Tuscaloosa (AL)

OSBURN, Charles B. (Dean of
    Libs) 927
PRUITT, Paul M. (Asst Law
    Libn, Acqs & Col Devlpmnt) . . 996
RAGSDALE, Kate W. (Actg
    Plng Ofcr) 1003
RAMER, James D. (Dean Grad
    Sch of Lib Srv) 1005
RUSSELL, Lisa R. (Chief Med
    Libn) 1069
STEPHENS, Annabel K. (Asst
    Prof) 1187
STEWART, Sharon L. (Assoc
    Prof & Sr Libn) 1193
STIEG, Margaret F. (Prof) 1193
VISSCHER, Helga B. (Ref Libn) 1285
WATSON, Linda S. (Ref Col
    Spclst) 1309
WATTERS, Annette J. (Asst
    Dir) 1310

Univ of Alaska at Anchorage (AK)

INNES-TAYLOR, Catherine E.
    (Acqs Libn) 583
LESH, Nancy L. (Assoc Dir in
    Charge of Tech Srvs) 718
SOKOLOV, Barbara J. (Sr
    Resrch Analyst) 1165

Univ of Alaska at Fairbanks (AK)

GALBRAITH, Betty J. (Libn) 413
GONIWIECHA, Mark C. (Asst
    Prof Lib Sci) 447
HALES, David A. (Assoc Prof of
    Lib Sci) 486
LAKE, Gretchen L. (Libn & Instr) . 688
PARHAM, Robert B. (Asst Prof,
    Lib Sci & Asst Archvst) 940
STEPHENS, Dennis J. (Col
    Devlpmnt Ofcr) 1187

Univ of Alaska at Juneau (AK)

NICOLSON, Mary C. (Technl
    Srvs Libn) 903

Univ of Alberta (AB)

ALLISON, Scott (Libn) 17
BERTRAM, Sheila K. 91
BOUCHER, Michel (Ref Libn) . . . 118
BRUNDIN, Robert E. (Prof) 150
BUSCH, B J. (Area Coordntr for
    Hum & Soc Scis) 165
CAMPBELL, Sandra M. (Ref
    Libn) 177
COOKE, Geraldine A. (Head
    Libn) 241
DANCIK, Deborah B. (Pub Srvs
    Coordntr, Hum & Soc Sci) . . . 272
DELONG, Kathleen M. (Ref and
    Info Srvs Head) 290
DE SCOSSA, Catriona (Assoc
    Prof) 295
FETTERMAN, Nelma I. (Asst
    Prof) 374
FREEMAN, Peter (Libn) 401
HEBDITCH, Suzan A. (Adminstv
    Libn) 519
HOBBS, Brian (Biblgph
    Verification Div Head) 545
HOWE, Ernest A. (Online Pub
    Access Catlg Libn) 565
JONES, David L. (Sci & Tech
    Area Col Coordntr) 612
KUJANSUU, Asko J. (Catlgr) . . . 683
LASKOWSKI, Seno (Head,
    Catlgng Div) 700
MACGOWN, Madge C. (Educ
    Area Coordntr) 755
OBERG, Dianne (Asst Prof) 913
OLSON, Hope A. (HSS Catlgr) . 922
REICHARDT, Randall P. (Ref
    Libn) 1018
ROONEY, Sieglinde E. (Acqs
    Head) 1053
SCHRADER, Alvin M. (Assoc
    Prof) 1099

Univ of Alberta (AB)

SHORES, Sandra J. (Pub Srvs
   Libn) 1132
SMITHERS, Anne B. (Sci
   Catlgr) 1162
STARR, Lea K. (Ref Coordntr) . 1182
STRATHERN, Gloria V. (Prof) . . 1200
TRAICHEL, Rudolf D. (Catlgr) . . 1253
WRIGHT, John G. (Dean,
   Faculty of Lib Sci) 1371
YOUNG, Margo 1382
ZIEGLER, Fred (Technl Srvs
   Libn) 1388

Univ of Arizona (AZ)

ALTMAN, Ellen (Prof) 18
BAILEY, Tuuli T. (Asst Libn) . . 47
BALDWIN, Charlene M. (Assoc
   Libn, Sci Engrng Libn) 51
BUXTON, David T. (Asst Univ
   Libn for Syst Plng) 168
CAMPBELL, Dierdre A. (Libn) . . . 176
CARTER, Judith A. (Sci Catlg
   Libn) 189
CHAPMAN, Jennalyn W. (Spcl
   Cols Coordntr) 202
D'ANTONIO, Lynn M. (Lib Asst
   III) 274
DICKINSON, Donald C. (Lib Sci
   Prof) 300
DICKSTEIN, Ruth H. (Ref Libn) . . 301
EAGLESON, Laurie E. (Music
   Catlg Libn) 331
ETTER, Patricia A. (Mss Libn) . . . 355
FAHY, Terry W. (Acqs Head &
   Col Devlpmnt Coordntr) 361
FIEGEN, Ann M. (Lib Asst IV) . . . 375
FORE, Janet S. (Sci Catlg & Ref
   Libn) 390
FRANK, Donald G. (Head,
   Science-Engineering Lib) 396
GILREATH, Charles L. (Centl
   Ref Dept Head) 437
GOTHBERG, Helen M. (Assoc
   Prof) 453
HAWBAKER, A C. (Centl Ref
   Libn, Asst Dept Head) 513
HEIDENREICH, Fred L. (Ref
   Srvs Head) 521
HEITSHU, Sara C. (Asst Univ
   Libn, Technl Srvs) 523
HENDERSON, Joyce C. (Slide
   Cur) 526
HIEB, Louis A. (Head Libn, Spcl
   Cols) 537
HOLSINGER, Katherine (Film
   Lib Mgr) 554
HOOPES, Maria S. (Ref Libn) . . . 557
HURT, Charlie D. (Dir) 578
JONES, Douglas E. (Asst Head,
   Ref Libn) 612
KELLOGG, Rebecca B. (Assoc
   Dean) 637
KNIGHT, Rita C. (Principal Catlg
   Libn) 664
LAIRD, W D. (Univ Libn) 688
LAKE, Mary S. (Info Spclst) 689
LEI, Polin P. (Ref Libn) 713
LONG, Carla J. (Bus Libn) 739
MAKUCH, Andrew L. (Biblgphr
   for Cols Devlpmnt) 762
MARSHALL, Thomas H. (Catlg
   Libn) 775
MAUTNER, Robert W. (Sci Ref
   Libn) 787
MAXWELL, Margaret F. (Prof) . . 788
MCCRAY, Jeanette C. (Assoc
   Dir) 800
MILLER, Edward P. (Sr Lectr) . . . 837
MILLS, Victoria A. (Head Catlg
   Libn) 844

Univ of Arizona (AZ)

MINTON, James O. (Head, Map
   Dept) 846
MOORE, Anne C. (Hum, Lit
   Catlgr) 858
MOORE, Susan M. (Soc Scis &
   Scis Catlg Libn) 861
MOUNT, Jack D. (Sci Ref Libn) . 873
MYERS, Roger (Manuscripts
   Libn & Archvst) 885
NEWBY, Jill (Sci Ref Libn) 898
OLSRUD, Lois C. (Centl Ref
   Libn) 923
O'NEIL, Mary A. (Lib Asst) 924
OWENS, Clayton S. (Study
   Coordntr) 932
PHIPPS, Shelley E. (Asst Univ
   Libn for Branch Srvs) 969
POWELL, Lawrence C. (Prof
   Emeritus) 988
RAWAN, Atifa R. (Near East
   Catlg Libn) 1010
REICHEL, Mary (Asst Univ Libn,
   Centl Srvs) 1018
RICE, Virginia E. (Ref Libn) 1027
RIISE, Milton B. (Catlg Libn) . . . 1034
ROBROCK, David P. (Spcl Cols
   Libn) 1045
RUSSELL, Carne (Serials
   Catlgr) 1068
SABOVIK, Pavel (Catlg Libn) . . 1073
SCOTT, Sharon K. (Sr Serials
   Catlg Libn) 1108
SMITH, Dorman H. (Music Libs
   Head) 1154
SORENSEN, Lee R. (Centl Ref
   Libn) 1168
TALLMAN, Karen D. (Serials
   Dept Head) 1221
TAYLOR, Patricia A. (Acqs
   Libn) 1228
TAYLOR, Trish A. (Acqs Libn) . 1229
WHITE, Edward H. (Pub Srvs
   Asst Libn) 1330
WHITLEY, Katherine M. (Sci
   Ref Libn) 1333
WILLIAMS, Karen B. (Cntl Ref
   Libn) 1344
WOLFSON, Catherine L. (Acqs
   Libn) 1361

Univ of Arkansas at Fayetteville (AR)

CALLAHAN, Patrick F. (Catlgng
   Head) 173
CHICK, Catherine P. (Asst Libn) . 208
CLINKSCALES, Joyce M. (Fine
   Arts Libn) 222
DABRISHUS, Michael J. (Head
   Spcl Cols Dept) 269
DEW, Stephen H. (Assoc Ref
   Libn) 297
EARNEST, Jeffrey D. (Music
   Catlgr & Recordings
   Selector) 332
HARRISON, John A. (Dir Univ
   Libs) 506
MCKEE, Elizabeth C. (Assoc
   Libn) 810
MILLER, Leon C. (Resrch Asst) . 839
YOUNG, Juana R. (Assoc Dir of
   Libs) 1382

Univ of Arkansas at Little Rock (AR)

BASKIN, Jeffrey L. (AV Libn) . . . 63
BRECK, Paul A. (Project
   Archvst) 131
CASTLEBERRY, Crata L.
   (Resrch Libn) 194
CLOUGHERTY, Leo P. (Ref,
   Biblgph Instr Libn) 223
FOSTER, Lynn (Law Lib Dir and
   Assoc Prof of Law) 392
GHIDOTTI, Pauline A. (Asst to
   the Dir, Circ Dept) 430

Univ of Arkansas at Little Rock (AR)

HAWKS, Mary S. (Monographs Libn) 514
KASALKO, Sally G. (Ref Div Head) 628
RINGER, Sarah A. (Col Devlpmnt Libn) 1035
ROSE, Donna K. (Catlg Libn) .. 1054
SANDERS, Kathryn A. (Interim Dir) 1080
SEDELOW, Sally Y. (Comp Sci Prof) 1110
SEDELOW, Walter A. (Prof of Comp Sci) 1110
STURGEON, Mary C. (Lib Sci Assoc Prof) 1205
WALLS, Edwina (Hist of Medcn Libn & Archvst) 1298
WOLD, Shelley T. (Govt Docums Libn) 1359

Univ of Auckland (NZD)

RICHARDS, Valerie (Fine Arts Libn) 1028

Univ of Bahrain (BRN)

ALI, Syed N. (Asst Prof & Head of Pub Srvs) 13

Univ of Baltimore (MD)

BEHLES, Patricia A. (Govt Docums Libn) 74
GREENBERG, Emily R. (Law Lib Dir) 463
KLEIN, Ilene R. (Circ & Ref Libn) 659
LABASH, Stephen P. (Ref/Coordntr Biblgph Instrc) .. 685
YEAGER, Gerry (Dir of Spc Cols) 1378

Univ of Barcelona (SPN)

VELA, Leonor G. (Bibliography Tchr) 1281

Univ of Bridgeport (CT)

DELUCIA, Christina (Ref Libn) .. 290
FU, Theresa L. (Asst Libn for Technl Srvs) 407
HAMMOND, Harold A. (Head of Technl Srvs Dept) 493
HUGHES, John M. (Asst Law Libn for Pub Srvs) 571
JOHNSON, Eric W. (Ref Srvs Head) 604
MCELHANEY, William E. (Biblgph Instr Prof) 804
PARISI, Judith A. (Resrc Libn) .. 940
SATTERLUND, Lisa L. (Ref Libn) 1084

Univ of British Columbia (BC)

BEWLEY, Lois M. (Prof) 93
CAMERON, Hazel M. (Libn) 175
CHAN, Diana L. (Admin Libn) ... 199
CROOKS, Sylvia A. (Instr & Admissions & Placement Ofcr) 260
DOBBIN, Geraldine F. (Systs and Info Srvs Libn) 307
DODSON, Suzanne C. (Head, Govt Pubns & Microforms) ... 308
DYKSTRA, Stephanie (Serials Libn) 331
EASTWOOD, Terence M. (Assoc Prof) 333
GONNAMI, Tsuneharu (Japanese Ref Libn) 447
HOPKINS, Richard L. (Asst Prof) 558
KREIDER, Janice A. (Physical Sci Biblgphr) 677
LEITH, Anna R. (Woodward Biomedical Lib Head) 714
LIGHTHALL, Lynne I. (Instr II) ... 727
MCINNES, Douglas N. (Univ Libn) 809
PITERNICK, Anne B. (Prof & Assoc Dean, Faculty of Arts) . 976
ROTHSTEIN, Samuel (Prof Emeritus) 1060

Univ of British Columbia (BC)

SAINT, Barbara J. (Head of Hlth Scis Lib) 1075
SALTMAN, Judith M. (Asst Prof) 1077
STEPHENSON, Mary S. (Asst Prof) 1188
STUART-STUBBS, Basil F. (Dir) 1204

Univ of Calgary (AB)

BOUEY, Elaine F. (Access Srvs Head) 119
BROWN, David K. (Curr Libn) ... 143
CARRIE, Judith A. 186
CRAMER, Eugene C. (Head of Music Dept) 255
DEBRUIJN, Deborah I. (Educ & Econ Libn) 285
GHENT, Gretchen K. (Head) 430
GOODWIN, C R. (Arctic Sci & Tech Info Syst Mgr) 450
HAYWARD, Edith C. (Asst to the Dir of Libs) 517
HERSCOVITCH, Pearl (Ref Libn, Catlgr) 533
HOGAN, Kathleen M. (Biblgph Srvs Arts & Hum Coordntr) .. 549
KING, Marjorie H. (Libn) 651
MACDONALD, Alan H. (Dir of Libs & Univ Press) 754
MOFFAT, N L. (Soc Scis Lib Asst Head) 852
NASSERDEN, Marilyn D. (Technl Srvs Libn) 889
NECHKA, Ada M. (Lending Srvs Coordntr) 891
ONN, Shirley A. (Lib Asst I) 924
ROBERTSON, Kathleen A. 1042
ROBINS, Nora D. (Humanities Div Head) 1043
STEELE, Apollonia L. (Spcl Cols Libn) 1184
STEVELMAN, Sharon R. (Libn) . 1190
TENER, Jean F. (Univ Archvst) . 1231
VINE, Rita F. (Music Libn) 1285

Univ of California at Berkeley (CA)

BARKER, Joseph W. (Head of Acq) 56
BASART, Ann P. (Ref Libn) 62
BECK, Diane J. (Assoc Libn) 71
BENGSTON, Carl E. (Circ & Technl Srvs Head) 80
BENIDIR, Samia (Info Spclst) ... 80
BERGER, Michael G. (Asst Dir, Plng & Production) 85
BERRING, Robert C. (Dean & Prof) 90
BESSER, Howard A. (Info Spclst) 91
BOUCHE, Nicole L. (Asst Manuscripts Div Head) 118
BRAUNSTEIN, Yale M. (Assoc Prof) 130
BROWN, Diane M. (Ref & Database Libn) 143
BROWNRIGG, Edwin B. (Dir) ... 149
BUCKLAND, Michael K. (Prof) .. 154
BYRNE, Elizabeth D. (Environmental Design Lib Head) 169
COOPER, William S. (Prof) 244
COYLE, Karen E. (Database Devlpmnt Mgr) 253
DANTON, J P. (Prof Emeritus) .. 274
DEAN, Terry J. (Libn) 284
DONLEY, Leigh M. (Serials Catlgr) 311
DUGGAN, Mary K. (Assoc Prof) . 324
ECKMAN, Charles D. (Technl Srvs Div Head) 335
ELNOR, Nancy G. (Lectr) 346

Univ of California at Berkeley (CA)

FALK, Candace S. (Edit & Dir,
  The Emma Goldman Papers) . 362
FREEMAN, Kevin A.
  (Temporary Ref Libn) 401
FULSAAS, Esther M. (Serials
  Catlgng Div Assoc Libn) 409
GERKEN, Ann E. (Data Archvst) . 429
GLENDENNING, Barbara J.
  (Ref Libn) 441
GOLDMAN, Nancy L. (Pacific
  Film Arch Lib Head) 445
GRIFFIN, Thomas E. (Catlgr) . . . 469
HANDMAN, Gary P. (Media
  Resrcs Ctr Head) 495
HANFF, Peter E. (Technl Srvs
  Coordntr) 495
HARDWICK, Bonnie S.
  (Manuscripts Div Head) 500
HARLAN, Robert D. (Prof) 502
HECKART, Ronald J. (Libn) 519
HOEHN, Philip (Map Libn) 547
HORWITZ, Steven F. (Resrch
  Spclst) 561
HOSEL, Harold V. (Lib Analyst) . . 561
HOWLAND, Joan S. (Law Lib
  Deputy Dir) 566
HUMPHREYS, Nancy K.
  (Women's Resrc Ctr Lib
  Coordntr) 574
JENSEN, Ann M. (Assoc Libn) . . 598
JONES, Maralyn (Asst Head) . . . 614
KATZ, Jeffrey P. (Syst Libn) 630
KENEFICK, Mary L. (Asst
  Editor, Index to Foreign
  Legal) 640
KIRESEN, Evelyn M. (Online
  Catlg Access Libn) 654
KISLITZIN, Elizabeth H. (Head,
  Col Devlpmnt & Ref Srvs
  Dept) 656
KLEIBER, Michael C. (Head
  Libn) 658
KLUGMAN, Simone (Soc Scis
  Libn) 662
KOBZINA, Norma G. (Assoc
  Libn, Natural Resrc Lib
  Head) 666
KOYAMA, Janice T. (Head
  Libn) 674
LARSON, Ray R. (Asst Prof) . . . 699
LAWRENCE, Gary S. (Dir of Lib
  Std & Resrch) 704
LEISTER, Jack (Head Libn) 714
LEVIN, Marc A. (Libn for
  Adminstrv and Support Srvs) . 720
LEVY, Judith B. (Hlth Scis Info
  Srv Dir) 721
MELTZER, Ellen J. (Head, Ref
  & Col Devlpmnt Sect) 823
MIKLOSVARY, Jozsef (Assoc
  Libn & Canon Law Catlgr) . . . 834
MITCHELL, Annmarie D. (Polish
  Cols Libn) 848
MONTGOMERY, Teresa L.
  (Pgmr & Analyst) 856
MORENO, Catherine H. (Catlgr
  & Libn) 863
NICHOLS, Gail M. (Actg Head
  of Govt Docums Dept) 901
NOVAK, Gloria J. (Lib Space
  Planner) 910
OGDEN, Barclay W.
  (Conservation Dept Head) . . . 918
OGDEN, Dunbar H. (Assoc Prof) . 918
OLIVARES, Jose A. (Database
  Group Head) 920
ORTOPAN, Leroy D. (Libn IV) . . 927
RHEE, Susan F. (Assoc Univ
  Libn) 1025

Univ of California at Berkeley (CA)

ROBERT, Berring C. (Sch of Lib
  & Info Std Dean) 1039
ROBERTS, John H. (Music Lib
  Head) 1040
ROSENTHAL, Joseph (Univ
  Libn) 1057
RYUS, Joseph E. (Catlg Libn) . . 1072
SCHRIEFER, Kent (Asst Law
  Libn & Catlgng Head) 1100
SIBLEY, Elizabeth A. (Assoc
  Libn) 1135
SNOW, Maryly A. (Libn) 1164
SO, Henry K. (Assoc Libn) 1165
SPOHRER, James H. (Libn for
  Germanic Cols) 1175
SVIHRA, S J. (Libn) 1212
TENNANT, Roy (Ref & Col
  Devlpmnt Libn) 1231
URBANIC, Allan J. (Libn for
  Slavic Cols) 1269
VANDERBERG, Patricia S.
  (Assoc Libn) 1273
VAN HOUSE, Nancy A. (Asst
  Prof) 1275
WANAT, Camille A. (Head,
  Physics Lib) 1302
WEEDMAN, Judith (Actg Asst
  Prof) 1315
WEIL, Beth T. (Head Libn) 1317
WHITSON, William L. (Assoc
  Libn) 1334
WILSON, Patrick (Prof) 1352
ZBORAY, Ronald J. (Microfilm
  Edit) 1386

Univ of California at Davis (CA)

ANDERSON, David C. (Technl
  Srvs Libn) 22
BLANCHARD, J R. (Emeritus
  Univ Libn) 103
BLANK, Karen L. (Access Srvs
  Head) 104
BOORKMAN, Jo A. (Actg Hlth
  Scis Libn) 115
CACCESE, Vincent (Libn) 170
CASEMENT, Susan D.
  (Agriculture Econ Head &
  Assoc Libn) 192
DAILEY, Kazuko M. (Assoc Univ
  Libn) 270
DAVIS, Rebecca A. (Asst Libn,
  Coordntr of Online Srvs) 280
ELDREDGE, Mary (Acqs Dept
  Asst Head) 342
ELLIOTT, C D. (Asst Univ Libn
  for Cols) 343
JESTES, Edward C. (Libn) 600
KNOWLES, Em C. (Coordntr of
  Biblgphc Instr) 665
LAMPRECHT, Sandra J.
  (Online Srvs Coordntr) 691
LARUSSA, Carol J. (Asst Libn) . . 700
LEWIS, Alfred J. (Assoc Law
  Libn) 722
LUNDQUIST, David A. (Maps &
  State and Local Docums
  Libn) 748
LUST, Vernon G. (Col Mgmt Ofc
  Head) 750
MALMGREN, Terri L. (Head
  Libn) 763
MAWDSLEY, Katherine F. (Asst
  Univ Lib, Pub Srvs) 787
PEATTIE, Noel (Hum Libn) 953
PIPER, Patricia L. (Assoc Law
  Libn, Technl Srvs) 975
POPA, Opritsa A. (Bus Econ &
  Slavic Libn) 983
ROCKE, Reve P. (Original
  Catlgr) 1046

Univ of California at Davis (CA)

ROSS, Johanna C. (Libn, chem, mathb and statistics) 1058
SEHR, Dena P. (Asst Libn) 1112
SHARROW, Marilyn J. (Univ Libn) 1122
SHERLOCK, John A. (Asst Libn) 1128
SHORT, Virginia (Ref Libn) 1132
SIBIA, Tejinder S. (Bio and Agricultural Scis Head) 1134
TEBO, Marlene 1229
UHLINGER, Eleanor S. (Lib Dir) 1268
WILLIS, Glee M. (Engrng Libn) . 1348
WINTER, Michael F. (Biblgphr for Behavioral Scis) 1356

Univ of California at Irvine (CA)

ARIEL, Joan (Women's Std Libn & Pubns Coordntr) 31
BOYER, Calvin J. (Univ Libn) 123
BROIDY, Ellen J. (Libn) 139
CLANCY, Stephen L. (Assoc Libn) 215
CLARY, Rochelle L. (Ref Dept Head) 219
FALK, Joyce D. (Data Srvs Coordntr) 362
FINEMAN, Michael (Biological Scis Libn) 377
FORBES, Fred R. (Assoc Libn) . . 389
FRANK, Anne E. (Assoc Libn) . . 396
GELFAND, Julia M. (Ref Libn & Biblgphr) 426
HAN, Kenneth P. (Assoc Libn) . 494
HIXON, Donald L. (Fine Arts Biblgphr, Catlgr) 544
HORN, Judy K. (Govt Pubns & Microforms Dept Head) 559
LEUNG, Shirley W. (Asst Univ Libn) 719
LEWALLEN, David D. (Bus Libn) 722
MYONG, Jae H. (Catlg Libn) 885
POOLE, Jay M. (Asst Univ Libn) . 983
PUGSLEY, Sharon G. (Univ Archvst & Regnl Hist Mss Libn) 997
TSANG, Daniel C. (Soc Scis Libn & Biblgphr) 1260
TSENG, Sally C. (Principal Serials Catlgr) 1260
WEINTRAUB, D K. (Principal Catlgr) 1318
WOOLDRIDGE, Steven M. (Media Libn) 1368
WYKLE, Helen H. (Musm Scitst) 1375

Univ of California at Livermore (CA)

GIRILL, T R. (Lead Edit, Online Documtn Group) 438

Univ of California at Los Angeles (CA)

ABRAMSON, Jenifer S. (Libn) 3
ADAN, Adrienne (Assoc Law Libn for Technl Srvs) 6
ANDERSON, Dorothy J. (Asst Dean) 22
ANDREWS, Karen L. (Ref Libn) . . 26
BATES, Marcia J. (Assoc Prof) . . . 64
BERMAN, Marsha (Assoc Music Libn) 88
BIDWELL, John (Ref & Acqs Libn) 95
BISOM, Diane B. (Systs Libn) 99
BORKO, Harold (Prof) 116
CARAVELLO, Patti S. (Ref Libn) 180
CASE, Donald O. (Asst Prof) 191
CHAMMOU, Eliezer (Middle East Catlgr) 198
CONTINI, Janice L. (Online Srvs Coordntr) 239
COSTELLO, M R. (Col Devlpmnt & Ref Libn) 249

Univ of California at Los Angeles (CA)

COYLE, Leslie P. (Asst to Univ Libn & Ref Libn) 253
DAVIS, James (Rare Bks Libn) . . 279
DEENEY, Kay E. (Ref Desk Srvs Coordntr) 286
EISENBACH, Elizabeth R. (Sr Lectr) 340
FISHER, William 381
FRY, Stephen M. (Music Libn) . . . 407
FRY, Thomas K. (Coll Libn) 407
GILMAN, Lelde B. (Head of Col Devlpmnt) 436
GLITZ, Beryl (Assoc Libn) 441
GOLDSMITH, Jan E. (Readers Srvs Libn) 446
GORAL, Miki (Ref Libn) 451
GRAHAM, Elaine (Assoc Dir) . . . 456
GRASSIAN, Esther S. (Ref, Instrc Libn) 458
GULLION, Susan L. (Head) 477
HALL, Anthony (Lib & Info Sci Biblgphr) 487
HAYES, Robert M. (Dean) 516
HINCKLEY, Ann T. (Head, Ref Dept) 542
INGEBRETSEN, Dorothy L. (Systs Instr & Libn) 582
JOHNSON, Jane D. (Catlgr) 605
KUNSELMAN, Joan D. (Fine Arts Libs Head) 684
KWAN, Julie K. (Head, Ref Div) . 685
LAWRENCE, John R. (Ref & Interlib Loan Libn) 704
LEE, Don A. (Ref Libn) 709
MAACK, Mary N. (Assoc Prof) . . 753
MARCUS, Sharon F. (Libn) 769
MCCORMICK, Mona (Libn) 798
MCGARRY, Dorothy (Catlgng Div Head) 805
MILLER, James G. (Adjunct Prof) 838
NOGA, Michael M. (Head of Geology & Geophysics Lib) . . 907
NYHAN, Constance W. (Grad Adv) 912
PELZ, Bruce E. (Ref & Col Devlpmnt) 955
PETERS, Marion C. (Head) 962
PORTILLA, Teresa M. (Ref Libn) 985
RAEDER, Aggi W. (Ref Libn) . . 1003
RANDALL, Michael H. (Asst Dept Head) 1006
RICHARDSON, John V. (Assoc Prof) 1029
ROSENBERG, Betty (Sr Lectr, Emerita) 1056
SCHERREI, Rita A. (Adminstrv Systs & Persnl Srvs Dir) 1092
SCHOTTLAENDER, Brian E. (Catlgng Div Asst Head) 1099
SEBO, Lorraine M. (Pub Affairs Srv Head) 1110
SHANK, Russell (Univ Libn & Prof) 1120
STERNHEIM, Karen (Ref & Pub Srvs Libn) 1189
SUBLETTE, Doris L. (Libn) 1206
SVENONIUS, Elaine (Prof) 1212
TIENHAARA, Kaarina I. (Interlib Srvs Head) 1244
TING, Eunice T. (Catlgr & Col Devlpmnt Libn) 1246
VOSPER, Robert (Univ Libn & Prof Emeritus) 1289
WATERS, Marie B. (Col Devlpmnt Div Head) 1308
WATSON, Janet L. 1309

Univ of California at Los Angeles (CA)

WELLS, Dorothy V. (Local &
Out-of-State Docums Libn) . . 1322
WERNER, Gloria (Assoc Univ
Libn for Technl Srvs) 1324
YEE, Martha M. (Catlgng
Supvsr) 1379
ZEIDBERG, David S. (Head,
Dept of Spcl Cols) 1387
ZIEGLER, Janet M. (Head of
Ref Srvs Div) 1388
ZUCKERMAN, Arline (Head of
Authority Sect) 1391

Univ of California at Oakland (CA)

PRICE, Bennett J. (Principal
Systs Analyst) 992

Univ of California at Richmond (CA)

RUBENS, Charlotte C. (Technl
Operations Head) 1064
STOCKTON, Gloria J. (Northern
Regnl Lib Facility Dir) 1196

Univ of California at Riverside (CA)

BRISCOE, Peter M. (Col
Devlpmnt Ofcr) 136
CHURUKIAN, Araxie P. (Spcl
Cols, Catlg Libn) 213
DOUGLAS, Nancy E. (Catlgng
Dept Head) 314
FLOWERS, Pat (Ref Srvs Head) . 386
FUSICH, Monica G. (Ref Libn &
Biblpgh Instrc Coordntr) 410
HUNTER, David C. (Asst Libn) . . 576
JORDAN, Joan A. (Catlgr) 616
JORGENSEN, Venita (Interlib
Loan Libn) 617
KOSHER, Helene J. (Cur of
Slides & Photographs) 672
MITCHELL, Steve (Ref Libn) 849
MOONEY, Margaret T. (Govt
Pubns Libn) 858
SELTH, Jefferson P.
(Humanities and the Arts
Biblgphr) 1114
SNYDER, Henry L. (Prof &
Catlg Dir) 1164
STALKER, Laura A. (Asst Dir) . 1178
TANNO, John W. (Assoc Univ
Libn) 1223
THOMPSON, James C. (Univ
Libn) 1240
VIERICH, Richard W. (Head
Libn, Physical Scis Lib) 1284

Univ of California at San Diego (CA)

ALLISON, Terry L. (Acqs Dept
Asst Head) 17
BOWLES, Garrett H. (Music
Libn) 121
BRUEGGEMAN, Peter L. (Head
of Pub Srvs) 149
COOLMAN, Jacqueline (Asst
Univ Libn, Personnel) 241
CREELY, Kathryn L.
(Melanesian Std Libn) 257
DAY, Deborah C. (Archvst) 282
FEENEY, Karen E. (Technl Srvs
Head) 368
FERGUSON, Chris D. (Head of
Undergraduate Lib) 372
FISHER, Edith M. (Ethnic Std
Col Devlpr) 380
GALLOWAY, Sue (Ref
Biblgphr) 415
GREGOR, Dorothy D. (Univ
Libn) 466
HURLBERT, Irene W. (Ref Libn
& Subject Biblgphr) 577
KANTER, Elliot J. (Ref
Libn/Biblgphr) 625
MARKWORTH, Lawrence L.
(Assoc Libn) 772
MILLER, R B. (Technl Srvs Asst
Univ Libn) 841

Univ of California at San Diego (CA)

MIRSKY, Phyllis S. (Assoc Univ
Libn) 847
PARCHUCK, Jill A. (Spcl Cols
Catlgr) 940
SCHILLER, Anita R. (Ref &
Biblgphr) 1093
SLATER, Barbara M. (Ref Libn) 1148
SMITH, Phillip A. (Ref Libn,
Biblgphr) 1159
SOETE, George J. (Assoc Univ
Libn for Cols) 1165
SPRAIN, Mara L. (Ref & Instrcl
Srvs Libn) 1176
STARR, Susan 1182
SWEEDLER, Ulla S. (Ref
Libn/Lit Biblgphr) 1214
TALBOT, Dawn E. (Info Mgr) . . 1220
TILLETT, Barbara B. (Technl
Srvs Head) 1245
VOIGT, Melvin J. (Univ Libn
Emeritus) 1287
WILLHITE, Sherry (Info Srv
Libn, Chem Spclst) 1341
WILSON, Marilyn J. (Acqs Dept
Head) 1352

Univ of California at San Francisco (CA)

BELL, R E. (Ref Libn) 77
COOPER, Richard S. (Assoc
Univ Libn) 243
DUNKEL, Lisa M. (Libn) 326
HENKE, Dan (Prof of Law & Dir
of Legal Info Ctr) 528
HOLLAND, Rebecca J. (Asst
Libn, Catlgng) 551
PERLMAN-STITES, Janice
(Libn) 959
ROBERTS, Justine T. (Lib Systs
Ofc Libn) 1040
TARCZY, Stephen I. (Head of
Technl Srvs) 1224
VANDEGRIFT, Glennda E.
(Serials Libn) 1273
WAKEFORD, Paul J. (Acqs &
Preservation Head) 1293
WILSON, Jacqueline B. (Col
Devlpmnt, Educ Ofcr) 1351
WINSON, Gail I. (Assoc Dir) . . . 1355
ZINN, Nancy W. (Spcl Cols Lib
Head) 1389

Univ of California at Santa Barbara (CA)

ANDERSON, Carol L. (Libn
Asst, Music Circ Desk
Supvsr) 22
BOISSE, Joseph A. (Univ Libn) . . 111
BULLARD, Sharon W. (Serial
Catlgng Sect Head) 156
CRITTENDEN, Robert R. (Ref
Libn) 259
DAVIDSON, Donald C. (Univ
Libn) 276
DOWELL, Connie V. (Head of
Lib Ref Dept) 315
GEBHARD, Patricia (Ref Libn &
Coordntr of Lib Instrc) 424
GIBBONS, Carolbeth (Asst
Head of Ref Dept) 431
GRAZIANO, Eugene
(Humanistic Psy Archvist,
Ref) 460
HUBER, Charles F. (Chem Ref
Libn) 568
JOHNSON, Diane D. (Intern
Asst Libn) 603
KORENIC, Lynette M. (Asst Art
Libn) 671
LINVILLE, Herbert (Head, Govt
Pubns Dept) 731
MARKHAM, James W. (Asst
Catlgng & Ref Libn) 771

Univ of California at Santa Barbara (CA)

SILVER, Martin A. (Music Libn) . 1138
TAI, Henry H. (Oreintal Libn) . . . 1220
WEIMER, Sally W. (Assoc Libn) 1317

Univ of California at Santa Cruz (CA)

ANDERSON, Clifford D.
    (Coordntr for Prospect
    Resrch) 22
AUGUSTINE, Rolf S. (Catlgr) 39
DYSON, Allan J. (Univ Libn) 331
GAREY, Anita I. (Soc Scis
    Biblgphr) 418
MARIE, Jacquelyn (Assoc Libn) . 770
MOKRZYCKI, Karen M.
    (Preservation Ofcr & Head of
    Acqs) 852
PAQUETTE, Judith (Biblgphr) . . . 939
RITCH, Alan W. (Coordntr of Lib
    Instrc) 1036
ROBINSON, Margaret G. (Head
    Ref Srvs) 1044
STEVENS, Stanley D. (Map
    Libn) 1191
TAYLOR, Marion E. (Head of
    Col Plng) 1227

Univ of Cape Town (SAF)

BARBEN, Tanya A. (Law Libn) . . . 55

Univ of Central Arkansas (AR)

DUDEK, Robert J. (Acqs Libn) . 323
HARDIN, Willie (Lib Dir) 500
MOORE, Gay G. (Technl Srvs
    Head) 859
MORRISON, Margaret L. (Pub
    Srvs Coordntr) 868
ROYAL, Selvin W. (Prof and
    Chir) 1063

Univ of Central Florida (FL)

ALLISON, Anne M. (Dir of Libs) . . 17
BAIN, Janice W. (Head, Access
    Srvs Dept) 47
BRIERTY, Carol A. (Comp
    Applications Libn) 135
CRENSHAW, Tena L. (Chief
    Libn) 258
CUBBERLEY, Carol W. (Head,
    Acqs & Col Devlpmnt) 263
HUDSON, Phyllis J. (Univ Ref
    Libn) 569
LABRAKE, Orlyn B. (Assoc Dir) . 686
MAHAN, Cheryl A. (Assoc Univ
    Libn) 760
PFARRER, Theodore R. (Assoc
    Libn) 966
STILLMAN, June S. (Head, Ref
    Dept) 1194

Univ of Charleston (WV)

BARNES, Jean S. (Catlg Libn &
    Instr) 57

Univ of Chicago (IL)

BEZIRGAN, Basima (Middle
    East Catlgr, Arabic Spclst) 93
BIBLO, Mary (Head Libn) 94
BLOSS, Alexander B. (Actg
    Head Serials Libn) 106
BOOKSTEIN, Abraham (Prof) . . . 115
CLARK, Gerald L. (Mgr) 217
CORSARO, Julie A. (Chlds
    Libn) 248
DEERWESTER, Scott C. (Asst
    Prof) 287
DILLON, Howard (Pub Srvs
    Assoc Dir) 303
HALIBEY, Areta V. (Catlgr) 486
HURD, Julie M. (Dean of
    Students) 577
LENNEBERG, Hans H. (Music
    Libn & Prof of Music) 715
MEYER, Daniel (Asst Cur for
    Manuscripts & Archs) 830
MUNOFF, Gerald J. (Asst Dir) . . . 879
NOWAK, Ildiko D. (Hed, Natl
    Translations Ctr) 911
NYE, James H. (Biblgphr for
    Southern Asia) 912
OWNES, Dorothy J. (Catlgr) 932

Univ of Chicago (IL)

RADER, Jennette S. (Bus &
    Econ Libn) 1002
RUNKLE, Martin D. (Lib Dir) . . . 1067
SCHNOOR, Harriet E. (Sci Ref
    Libn) 1098
SINHA, Vaswati R. (Catlgr of
    Southern Asia Col) 1143
SUTHERLAND, Zena B. (Prof
    Emerita) 1211
SWANSON, Don R. (Prof) 1213
SWANSON, Patricia K. (Asst
    Dir for Sci Libs) 1213
VITOLINS, Ilga (Catlgr & Head
    of Original Catlgng) 1286
WINGER, Howard W.
    (Managing Edit, Lib
    Quarterly) 1355
WRIGHT, Judith M. (Law Libn) . 1372

Univ of Cincinnati (OH)

CAIN, Linda B. (Dean & Univ
    Libn) 171
CORNELL, Alice M. (Archs &
    Rare Books Dept) 246
DENHAM, Patricia K. (Acq Lib) . . 292
DESCHENE, Dorice (Head of
    Chem & Biology Lib) 294
FROMMEYER, L R. (Head,
    Acws, Monographs Dept) 405
GILLIAM, Susanne P. (Assoc
    Libn) 436
GILLILAND, Anne J. (Staff
    Archvst & Records Spclst) . . . 436
HEIDTMANN, Toby (Head of
    Binding & Conservation) 521
HEISHMAN, Eleanor L. (Assoc
    Univ Libn) 523
HUGHES, Marcelle E. (Ref Dept
    Assn Head) 572
JOHNS, Jean B.
    (Perdcls/Microform Libn) 601
JONES, Alice W. (Govt
    Docums, Microforms Libn) . . . 610
KONKEL, Mary S. (Head,
    Monograph Catlgng) 670
KOVACIC, Mark E. (Asst Head,
    Acq Dept) 673
LIPPERT, Margret G. (Engrng
    Ref Libn) 732
LORENZI, Nancy M. 741
NASRALLAH, Wahib T. (Bus &
    Econ Libn) 888
NEWMAN, Linda D. (Asst to the
    Dir of Lib Systs) 899
PALKOVIC, Mark A. (Record
    Libn) 935
PARR, Virginia H. (Head, Ref &
    Biogph Srvs) 944
PROPAS, Sharon W. (Biblgphr,
    Engl & Romance Languages) . 995
RILEY, Jacquelene W. 1034
ROMANOS, Vasso A. (Asst
    Prof) 1052
SANKOT, Janice M. (Evening
    Libn) 1081
THOMPSON, Ann M. (Assoc
    Univ Libn) 1238
TOLZMANN, Don H. (Sr Libn) . 1249
WELLINGTON, Jean S.
    (Classics Lib Head) 1322
WILSON, Lucy (Lib & Instrcl
    Media Tech Prog Dir) 1351
WOOD, Elizabeth B. (Ref Libn) . 1364

Univ of Colorado at Boulder (CO)

ANTHES, Susan H. (Asst Sci
    Libn & Map Cur) 28
BINTLIFF, Barbara A. (Assoc
    Dir) 97
BOUCHER, Virginia P. (Head of
    Interlib Cooperation) 118
BURKE, Marianne D. (Copy
    Catlgng Dept Head) 160

Univ of Colorado at Boulder (CO)

BYRNE, Timothy L. (Govt Pubns Lib Head) 169
CARTER, Nancy F. (Music Catlgr) 189
CHANAUD, Jo P. (Dir) 199
ELLSWORTH, Ralph E. (Lib Dir Emeritus) 345
FINK, Deborah (Instrcl Srvs Libn) 378
HENSLEY, Charlotta C. (Editor) .. 529
JOST, Richard M. (Ref, Govt Docums Libn) 618
KOHL, David F. (Asst Dir for Pub Srvs) 668
KRISMANN, Carol H. (Bus Lib Dept Head) 678
MASON, Ellsworth G. (Lib Consult) 781
MUELLER, Carolyn J. (Serials Dept Head) 875
QUINLAN, Nora J. (Spcl Cols Head) 1000
SANI, Martha J. (Asst Libn & Instr) 1081
WALTON, Clyde C. (Dir of Libs) 1301
WERTHEIMER, Marilyn L. (Ref Libn & Pol Sci Biblgphr) 1325
WYNNE, Allen (Math-Physics Branch Lib Dept Head) 1375

Univ of Colorado at Colorado Springs (CO)

MANNING, Leslie A. (Lib Dir) ... 766
WYLIE, Nethery A. (Sci & Engrng Ref Libn) 1375

Univ of Colorado at Denver (CO)

BOTHMER, A J. (Assoc Dir for Pub Srvs) 118
BREIVIK, Patricia S. (Dir) 132
ESKOZ, Patricia A. (Col & Automation Div Catlg Libn) ... 354
FORSMAN, Rick B. (Assoc Dir for Technl Systs) 391
GOODYEAR, Mary L. (Instrc & Resrch Srvs Asst Dir) 450
HEMPHILL, Jean F. (Assoc Dir) . 525
INGUI, Bettejean (Info Srvs Head) 583
MITCHELL, Marilyn J. (Asst Dir) . 849
SCHAFER, Jay G. (Deputy Asst Dir for Cols) 1089
WITTHUS, Rutherford W. (Archvs & Spcl Col Head, Hum Liaison) 1358

Univ of Connecticut at Farmington (CT)

ARCARI, Ralph D. (Asst VP for Academic Resrcs & Srvs) 30
RICHETELLE, Alberta L. (Healthnet Coordntr) 1030
WETMORE, Judith M. (Info Srvs Libn) 1328

Univ of Connecticut at Hartford (CT)

BENAMATI, Dennis C. (Head of Catlgng) 79
NORONHA, Marilyn S. (Ref Libn) 909
STONE, Dennis J. (Law Libn & Prof of Law) 1197

Univ of Connecticut at Storrs (CT)

BALMER, Mary (Technl Srvs Assoc Dir) 53
BOGNAR, Dorothy M. (Head Music Libn) 111
EMBARDO, Ellen E. (Spcl Cols Libn) 347
FORMAN, Camille L. (Libn III) ... 390
JAY, Hilda L. (Adjunct Faculty) .. 596
JENSEN, Joan W. (Ref Dept Head) 598
JIMERSON, Randall C. (Dir of Histl Manuscripts & Archs) ... 600
KAGAN, Alfred (Ref Biblgphr) ... 621
KLINE, Nancy M. (Instrcl Srvs and Orientation Head) 661

Univ of Connecticut at Storrs (CT)

MCDONALD, John P. (Dir of Lib Devlpmnt) 802
MERRILL-OLDHAM, Jan (Head, Preservation Dept) 827
ROLLIN, Marian B. (Head of Audio, Video & Microtext) ... 1051
SCHIMMELPFENG, Richard H. (Spcl Cols Dir) 1093
SCOTT, Joseph W. (Asst Music Libn) 1107
SCURA, Georgia A. (Dir of Pharmacy Lib) 1109
STEVENS, Norman D. (Dir of Univs Libs) 1190
SWIFT, Janet B. (Asst Dir) 1216

Univ of Connecticut at Waterbury (CT)

Univ of Connecticut at West Hartford (CT)

BRADBERRY, Richard P. (Lib Dir) 125
LI, Hong C. (Ref Libn) 724
MANNING, Beverley J. (Univ Libn III & Catlgr) 766

Univ of Connecticut Health Center (CT)

FREY, Barbara J. (Libn) 402
LEVINE, Marion H. (Assoc Dir) .. 720

Univ of Connicticut at Stamford (CT)

GILLIES, Nancy H. (Head of Catlgng) 436

Univ of Dallas (TX)

BAKER, Nettie L. (Lib Dir) 49
HAGLE, Claudette S. (Pub Srvs Dir & Ref Dept Head) 483
WHITE, Lely K. (Catlgng Dept Head) 1331
WORLEY, Larry J. (Head Acqs) 1369

Univ of Dayton (OH)

ARTZ, Theodora S. (Acqs Libn) .. 35
GARTEN, Edward D. (Dir of Univ Libs & Prof) 420
HANLEY, Thomas L. (Asst Prof & Dir of Law Lib) 496
HECHT, Judith N. (Mgr, Technl Info Srvs Ofc) 519
JENKINS, Fred W. (Catlg Spclst) 597
KRIEGER, Michael T. (Catlgr) ... 678
SIMONS, Linda K. (Coordntr of Info Srvs) 1141
WALKER, Mary A. (Lib Systs & Automation Coordntr) 1296
WERNERSBACH, Geraldine S. (Ref & Circ Libn, Dept Head) 1325

Univ of Delaware (DE)

BRYNTESON, Susan (Dir of Libs) 152
CASON, Maidel K. (Personnel Ofcr) 193
CHOU, Vivian M. (Biblgph Ctl Dept Catlgr) 210
CLAYTON, John M. (Univ Archvst & Dir of Records Mgmt) 220
EVERETT, Amy E. (Devlpmnt Resrch Mgr) 358
GLOGOFF, Stuart J. (Systs Dept Head) 441
HALL, Alice W. (Marine Std Libn) 486
KNIGHT, Rebecca C. (Ref Libn) . 664
PUFFER, Nathaniel H. (Asst Col Devlpmnt Dir) 997
ROBBINS, Rachel H. (Interlib Loans Asst Libn) 1039
RUDISELL, Carol A. (Black Std Ref Libn) 1065
SCHREYER, Alice D. (Lib Head) 1100
SHAW, Richard N. (Media Srv Dept Head) 1124
ULRICH, Sue (Technl Srvs Automation Asst Dir) 1268
WANG, Margaret K. (Coordntr of Original Catlgng) 1303
WOLFF, Stephen G. (Ref Libn) . 1361

Univ of Delaware (DE)

YOUNG, Kathryn A. (Govt Docums Maps Libn) 1382

Univ of Denver (CO)

ABRAMS, Jeanne E. (Archvst & Dir) 3
BARELA, Lori A. (Serials Catlg Libn) 56
COCO, Al (Prof of Law & Dir, Law Lib) 226
MOULTON, Suzanne L. (Music Libn/Instr) 873
RAINWATER, Barbara C. (Pub Srvs Libn) 1004
SMITH, Sallye W. (Ref Libn & Asst Prof) 1160

Univ of Detroit (MI)

AUER, Margaret E. (Dir of Libs) . . . 39
BLACK, Shirley R. (Instrcl Srvs Libn) 101
COOPER, Byron D. (Dir & Assoc Prof) 242
D'ELIA, Joseph G. (Branch Libn) 289
HOMANT, Sue J. (Instrcl Srvs Libn) 555
HUPP, Stephen L. (Pub Srv Libn) 577
SMITH, Peter A. (Asst Libn) . . . 1159

Univ of Dublin (IRE)

DUFFIN, Elizabeth A. (Deputy Libn) 323

Univ of Dubuque (IA)

KNEFEL, Mary A. (Ref Libn) . . . 664
ROBINSON, Vera L. (Catlgr) . . . 1045

Univ of Dubuque (WI)

FLIEGEL, Deborah A. (Pub Srvs & Ref Libn) 385

Univ of Evansville (IN)

MEEK, Janet E. (Biblgph Instrc Libn) 821

Univ of Florida at Gainesville (FL)

BADGER, Lynn C. (Lib Personnel Ofcr) 44
BALDWIN, Ruth M. (Libn) 52
BATTISTE, Anita L. (Assoc Univ Libn) 65
BENNETT, Richard F. (Chairman, Access Srvs Dept) 82
BROWN, M S. (Head of Coll of Educ Lib) 145
CANELAS, Dale B. (Dir of Univ Libs) 178
COVEY, William C. (Lib Systs Ofcr) 252
DRUM, Carol A. (Head) 320
FAIRBANKS, Deborah M. (Gift and Exchange Libn) 361
FELTZ, Carol (Asst Libn) 370
FRANCIS, Barbara W. (Visiting Asst Univ Libn) 396
HARRER, Gustave A. (Distinguished Srv Prof of Bibl) 503
HERBSMAN, Yael (Asst Libn) . . . 530
HOPE, Dorothy H. (Head, Automated Catlgng Unit) 557
HSU, Pi Y. (Online Srvs Coordntr) 567
IVES, Sidney E. (Univ Libn for Rare Bks & Mss) 586
KONOP, Bonnie M. (Docums Libn) 670
LEONARD, Louise F. (Assoc Univ Libn) 716
MALANCHUK, Iona R. (Assoc Univ Libn) 762
MALANCHUK, Peter P. (Chairman, Ref & Bibl Dept) . . 762
MCKAY, Peter Z. (Bus Libn) 810
ORSER, Frank W. (Asst Serials Chairman) 927
PRIMACK, Alice L. (Assoc Univ Libn) 993
SPENCER, Deirdre D. (Asst Univ Libn) 1173

Univ of Florida at Gainesville (FL)

TAYLOR, Betty W. (Legal Info Ctr Dir & Prof of Law) 1226
TEAGUE, Edward H. (Art/Architecture Biblgphr) . . 1229
WALTON, Carol G. (Latin American Monograph Catlgr) 1301
WILLIAMS, Nancy L. (Chair, Catlg Dept) 1345
WILLIAMS, Pamela D. (Head of Pub Srvs) 1345
WILLOCKS, Robert M. (Deputy Dir) 1349
WOODS, Susan E. (Info Spclst & Pubns Coordntr) 1367

Univ of Florida at Jacksonville (FL)

HALL, M C. (Dir) 488

Univ of Florida at Lake Alfred (FL)

RUSS, Pamela K. (Assoc Univ Libn) 1068

Univ of Florida at Tallahassee (FL)

AHMAD, Saiyed A. (Libn) 8

Univ of Geneva (SWZ)

JACQUESSON, Alain L. (Lib Srv Coordntn Chief) 591

Univ of Georgia (GA)

ANDERSON, Thomas G. (Systs Libn) 25
ANDREW, Paige G. (Map Catlgr Libn) 26
BAKER, Barry B. (Asst Technl Srvs Dir) 47
BERG, Elizabeth R. (Monograph Original Catlgr) 84
BISHOP, David F. (Libs Dir) 99
BROWN, Steven A. (Docum Delivery Head) 147
CAMPBELL, John L. (Online Srvs Coordntr) 176
CARPENTER, David E. (Ref Libn) 184
CLAYTON, William R. (Fine Arts & Media Depts Head) . . . 220
CLEMENS, Bonnie J. (Actg Dir of Libs) 220
COMPTON, Lawrence E. (Ref Libn) 235
COONIN, Bryna R. (Ref Libn) . . . 242
COSCARELLI, William F. (Music Biblgphr) 248
CURTIS, Susan C. (Head, Sci Ref Dept) 267
ELLIS, Marie C. (Engl & Am Lit Biblgphr) 345
GUBISTA, Kathryn R. (Sci Ref Libn & Online Srvs Coordntr) . 475
GULLEY, J L. (Georgia Newspaper Project Coordntr) . 477
HAAR, John M. (Biblgphr) 480
HUGHES, Martha T. (Monograph Original Catlgr) . . 572
HUGHES, Neil R. (Music Catlgr) . 572
KUHLMAN, James R. (Soc Scis Head) 682
LEDFORD, Carole L. (Libn) 708
LIBBEY, George H. (Admin Srvs Asst Dir) 725
LUCHSINGER, Arlene E. (Asst Dir for Branch Libs) 746
MASSEY, Katha D. (Catlgng Dept Head) 782
PADWA, David J. (Univ Prof in Mgmt) 934
PARK, Margaret K. (Comptng Admin & Plng Dir) 941
QUINLAN, Judy B. (Ref Head) . 1000
RIEMER, John J. (Head of Serials Catlgng) 1033
ROWLAND, Lucy M. (Med Resrcs Libn) 1062
RYSTROM, Barbara B. (Head of Interlib Loan Dept) 1072
SOMERS, Sally W. (Head, Acqs Dept) 1167

Univ of Georgia (GA)

SOUTHWICK, Mary L.
(Coordntr, Col Devlpmnt) ... 1170
SURRENCY, Erwin C. (Prof of
Law & Law Libn) 1210
SUTHERLAND, Johnnie D. (Cur
of Maps) 1211
VOGT, Sheryl B. (Dept Head) .. 1287
WALD, Marlena M. (Sci Ref
Libn) 1294
WHEELER, Carol L. (Govt
Docums Ref Libn) 1328
WHITEHEAD, James M. (Pub
Srvs Libn) 1332
WILLIAMS, Sara E. (Ref Libn) . 1346

Univ of Glasgow (SCT)

HEANEY, Henry J. (Libn &
Keeper of Hunterian Bk &
Mss) 518

Univ of Guam (GU)

DRIVER, Marjorie G. (Assoc
Prof) 320
UYEHARA, Harry Y. (Dean of
Lrng Resrcs) 1270

Univ of Guelph (ON)

BECKMAN, Margaret L. (Exec
Dir for Info Tech) 73
BLACK, John B. (Chief Libn) ... 101
GILLHAM, Virginia A. (Asst Dir) . 436
GOODGER-HILL, Carol (Catlgr) . 448
KATZ, Bernard M. (Hum & Soc
Sci Div Head) 630
PAL, Gabriel (Ref Libn) 935
PAWLEY, Carolyn P. (Interlib
Srvs and Orientation) 951
ROURKE, Lorna E. (Ref Libn) .. 1061

Univ of Hartford (CT)

MILLER, Jean J. (Art Libn) 838
PIERCE, Anne L. (Dir of Spcl
Projects) 971

Univ of Hawaii at Hilo (HI)

HERRICK, Kenneth R. (Dir of
Libs) 532

Univ of Hawaii at Honolulu (HI)

AUSTIN, Mary C. (Prof
Emeritus) 40
BARD, Therese B. (Assoc Prof) .. 56
COLEMAN, David E. (Libn) 231
EHRHORN, Jean H. (Assoc
Univ Libn) 339
FURUMOTO, Viola G. (Sci Tech
Ref Libn) 410
HAAK, John R. (Lib Dir) 480
JACKSON, Miles M. (Dean &
Prof) 588
LUNDEEN, Gerald W. (Prof) 748
NAHL-JAKOBOVITS, Diane
(Lectr) 886
POLANSKY, Patricia A.
(Russian Biblgphr) 980
SAKAI, Diane H. (Automation
Libn) 1076
SHELDEN, Patricia R. (Docums
Libn) 1125
SZILARD, Paula (Sci Ref Libn) . 1218
TAKAHASHI, Annabelle T.
(Humanities Ref Libn) 1220
TRAPIDO, Joel (Emeritus Prof,
Drama & Theatre) 1254
URAGO, Gail M. (Libn) 1269

Univ of Hawaii at Manoa (HI)

AYRAULT, Margaret W. (Prof
Emeritus) 43
ENOMOTO, Wanda H. (Catlg
Support Libn) 350
MATSUMORI, Donald M.
(Catlgr) 784
NAJ, Linda M. (Asst to Head of
Lib Systs) 887
NAKANO, Kimberly L. (Jr Lib
Spclst) 887
RIEDY, Allen J. (Jr Lib Spclst) .. 1033
STEVENS, Robert D. (Lectr and
Emeritus Prof) 1190
TRUETT, Carol A. (Assoc Prof) . 1259

Univ of Hong Kong (HKG)

LEE, Betty W. (Asst Libn) 709

Univ of Houston (TX)

Univ of Ibadan (NGR)

Univ of Idaho (ID)

Univ of Illinois at Chicago (IL)

ADDISON, Jane G. (Asst Catlg
Libn) 6
ALLEN, Virginia M. (Automation
Proj Coordntr) 16
BOWMAN, Laura M. (Chem
Libn) 122
CHANG, Robert H. (Dir of Lib
Srvs) 201
CORBIN, John (Automation &
Systs Asst Dir) 245
CRAIG, Marilyn J. (Catlgr Libn) .. 254
DOWNES, Robin N. (Dir) 316
FIELDING, Raymond E. (Dir &
Prof) 376
HALL, John D. (Catlgng Srvs
Head) 488
HOTVEDT, Eileen A. (Admnstr) . 562
KIMZEY, Ann C. (Technl Srvs
Assoc Dir) 649
LOPICCOLO, Cathy J. (Life
Scis Libn) 741
LYDERS, Josette A. (Asst Prof) . 750
WEISBAUM, Earl (Foreign & Intl
Law Libn) 1319
WELCH, C B. (Head of Instrcl &
Access Srvs Dept) 1321
WILSON, Thomas C. (Soc Scis
Ref Libn & Biblgphr) 1353
ABOYADE, Beatrice O. (Prof of
Lib Std) 2
ABRAHAM, Terry (Head, Spcl
Cols & Archs) 3
BAIRD, Dennis W. (Soc Sci
Libn) 47
BAIRD, Lynn N. (Head, Serials
Dept) 47
BECK, Richard J. (Assoc Dean
of Libs) 71
CURL, Margo W. (Catlg Libn) ... 265
ECKWRIGHT, Gail Z.
(Humanities Libn) 335
FORCE, Ronald W. (Humanities
Libn) 389
FUNABIKI, Ruth P. (Assoc Law
Libn for Technl Srvs) 409
HANSON, Donna M. (Sci Libn &
Assoc Prof) 498
HELLER, James S. (Dir of the
Law Lib, Assoc Prof) 524
PIKE, George H. (Assoc Law
Libn for Pub Srvs) 972
STEINHAGEN, Elizabeth N.
(Head, Serials Catlgng Sect) 1186
WAI, Lily C. (Docums Libn) 1292
AISTARS, Aivars (Catlgr) 9
BAMBERGER, Mary A. (Asst
Spcl Cols Libn) 53
BENGTSON, Marjorie C. (Asst
Docums Libn) 80
BLOOM, Stephen C. (Admnstrv
Srvs Libn) 106
CARPENTER, Kathryn H. (Acqs
Libn) 185
CARSON, James G. (Archs
Processor, Visiting Lectr) 188
COCHRANE, Kerry L. (Asst Ref
Libn) 225
CULLARS, John M. (Humanities
Biblgphr) 263
DAUGHERTY, Robert A. (Circ
Libn) 275
EASTERBROOK, David L.
(Principal Biblgphr) 333
EDWARDS, Dana S. (Asst Circ
Libn & Asst Prof) 337
FANG, Min L. (Catlgng Libn) 363
FRANKLIN, Annette E. (Ref Ctr
Dir) 397
GEROW, Sandra F. (Ref Libn) .. 429

Univ of Illinois at Chicago (IL)

HATTENDORF, Lynn C. (Asst Ref Libn, Asst Prof) 512
HOLLI, Melvin G. (Prof & Dir of Urban Histl Col) 552
JOHN, Nancy R. (Asst Univ Libn) 601
JOHNSON, Judith M. (Asst Acqs Libn) 606
JONES, William G. (Col Devlpmnt & Info Srvs Asst Libn) 615
KUKAC, Denise A. (Lib Intern) . . 683
LAMBRECHT, Jay H. (Catlg Libn) 691
LANDWIRTH, Trudy K. (Branch Libn) 694
LAUDERDALE, Diane S. (Asst Ref Libn) 702
LIMAYE, Asha A. (Libn) 727
LYNCH, Beverly P. (Univ Libn) . . 751
MALINOWSKY, H R. (Biblgphr for Sci & Engrng) 763
MAY, Ruby S. (Assoc Regnl Med Lib Dir) 789
MCCARTNEY, Elizabeth J. (Asst Circ Libn) 794
MOUW, James R. (Acqs Libn) . . 874
NAPSHA, Cheryl A. (Asst to the Univ Libn) 887
PAIETTA, Ann C. (Asst Univ Libn) 935
PIZER, Irwin H. (Univ Hlth Scis Libn) 977
RETTIG, James R. (Ref Dept Head) 1024
SCHULTHEISS, Louis A. (Budget & Plng Asst Univ Libn) 1101
SELMER, Marsha L. (Map Libn) 1114
STRAWN, Aimee W. (Asst Prof of Educ) 1201
TYLMAN, Wieslawa T. (Ref Libn & Asst Prof) 1266
VAN HOUTEN, Stephen (Catlg Dept Head) 1275
WESTON, E P. (Asst Ref Libn) . 1327
WHITE, Anne E. (Ref & Docums Libn) 1330
WIBERLEY, Stephen E. (Soc Scis Biblgphr) 1335
WILLIAMSON, Linda E. (Docums Dept Head & Docums Libn) 1347
WINNIKE, Mary E. (Libn) 1355
WARREN, Peggy A. (Ref) 1306

Univ of Illinois at Chicago (ON)
Univ of Illinois at Rockford (IL)

DALRYMPLE, Prudence W. (Hlth Scis Libn, Asst Prof) . . . 271

Univ of Illinois at Urbana-Champaign (IL)

AGGARWAL, Narindar K. (Assoc Asian Libn) 7
ALLEN, Walter C. (Assoc Prof Emeritus) 16
ANDERSON, Nancy D. (Math Libn & Asst Dir) 24
ATKINS, Stephen E. (Pol Sci Subject Spclst) 38
AULD, Lawrence W. (Asst Prof) . . 40
BINGHAM, Karen H. (Asst to Dir) 97
BOAST, Carol (Agricultural Libn & Prof) 108
BOPP, Richard E. (Ref Lib Head) 116
BRICHFORD, Maynard J. (Univ Archvst) 134
BROWN, Norman B. (Spcl Cols Asst Dir) 146
BURBANK, Richard D. (Music Catlg Coodntr & Asst Prof) . . . 158

Univ of Illinois at Urbana-Champaign (IL)

CAROTHERS, Diane F. (Comms Libn & Assoc Prof) . . 184
CHAPLAN, Margaret A. (Labor Libn) 201
CHOLDIN, Marianna T. (Head, Slavic & East European Lib) . . 210
CLARK, Barton M. (Dir of Deptmntl Lib Srvs) 216
CLARK, Sharon E. (Automated Srvs Libn) 218
CLOONAN, Michele V. (Instr) . . . 223
COBB, David A. (Map & Geography Libn) 224
DAVIS, Elisabeth B. (Bio Libn, Prof of Lib Admin) 278
DOWNS, Robert B. (Dean of Lib Admin Emeritus) 317
EDMONDS, M L. (Asst Prof) 336
ESTABROOK, Leigh S. (Dean & Prof) 355
FAIRCHILD, Constance A. (Asst Ref Libn) 361
FAYNZILBERG, Irina (Asst Slavic Libn) 367
FORREST, Charles G. (Asst Undergrad Libn/Media Coordntr) 390
GOLDHOR, Herbert (Dir, Lib Resrch Ctr) 445
GRIFFITHS, Suzanne N. (Classics Libn) 469
HENDERSON, Kathryn L. (Prof) . 526
HENDERSON, William T. (Preservation Libn) 527
HUETING, Gail P. (Asst Modern Lang Libn) 570
KIBBEE, Josephine Z. (Ref Libn & User Educ Coordntr) 646
KLINGBERG, Susan (Educ & Soc Sci Libn) 661
KOH, Siew B. (Grad Asst) 668
KRUMMEL, Donald W. (Grad Sch of Lib & Info Sci Prof) . . . 680
LANCASTER, Frederick W. (Prof) 691
LANDIS, Martha (Sr Ref Libn) . . . 693
LEONG, Carol L. (Original Serials Catlgr) 717
LIM, Peck B. (Grad Asst) 727
LITTLEWOOD, John M. (Docums Libn) 734
LOHRER, Alice (Prof Emeritus) . . 737
LOOMIS, Barbara (Asst Engrng Libn) 740
MAHER, William J. (Asst Univ Archvst) 760
MAKINO, Yasuko (Assoc Prof of Lib Admin) 762
MANSFIELD, Fred (Law Biblgphr) 767
MCBRIDE, Ruth B. (Assoc Lib Admin Prof) 792
MCCANDLESS, Patricia A. (Applied Life Std Libn) 793
MCCLELLAN, William M. (Music Libn) 796
MCCULLOH, Judith M. (Exec Edit) 801
MONTANELLI, Dale S. (Dir of Adminstrv Srvs) 855
MOSBORG, Stella F. (Residence Halls Libn) 870
NASH, N F. (Rare Books Cur) . . 888
NOGUCHI, Sachie (Asst Japanese Libn) 907
NYBERG, Cheryl R. (Asst Law Libn for Docums & Ref) 912

**Univ of Illinois at
Urbana-Champaign (IL)**

O'BRIEN, Nancy P. (Asst Educ
& Soc Sci Libn) 915
PAUSCH, Lois M. (Asst Math
Libn) 950
PENKA, Carol B. (Ref Libn) 956
PORTA, Maria A. (Asst
Agriculture Libn) 984
RAVENHALL, Mary (Libn) 1010
RICHARDSON, Selma K.
(Assoc Prof) 1030
ROLSTAD, Gary O. (Asst Dean) 1052
RUBIN, Richard E. (Visiting Asst
Prof) 1065
SCHMIDT, Karen A. (Acqs Libn) 1095
SELF, David A. 1113
SHAW, Debora (Asst Prof) 1123
SIEGEL, Martin A. (Assoc Prof
& Asst Dir) 1136
SMITH, Linda C. (Assoc Prof of
Lib & Info Sci) 1157
SMITH, Richard G. (Asst Ref
Libn) 1160
STENSTROM, Patricia F. (Lib &
Info Sci Libn) 1187
STERN, David (Physics &
Astronomy Libn) 1189
STEVENS, Rolland E. (Prof
Emeritus) 1191
STUART, Mary P. (Ref Libn) . . . 1204
TEMPERLEY, Nicholas (Prof) . . 1230
WAJENBERG, Arnold S.
(Principal Catlgr) 1293
WATSON, Paula D. (Asst Dir
for Gen Srv) 1310
WEECH, Terry L. (Assoc Prof) . 1315
WEI, Karen T. (Asst Chinese
Libn) 1316
WERT, Lucille M. (Prof
Emeritus) 1325
WHEELER, Claudia J. (Visiting
Asst Educ & Soc Sci Libn) . . 1328
WILLIAMS, James W. (Asst
Educ, Soc Sci Libn) 1344
WILLIAMS, Martha E. (Prof) . . . 1345
WILLIAMS, Mitsuko (Asst Bio
Libn) 1345
WILSON, Lizabeth A.
(Undergraduate Libn) 1351
WONG, William S. (Gen Srvs
Asst Dir) 1363
WOODARD, Beth S. (Cntl Info
Srvs Libn) 1365
WRIGHT, Joyce C. (Coordntr of
Ref & Instrcl Srvs) 1372
YU, Priscilla C. (Asst Hist Libn) . 1384

Univ of Illinois Lab Sch (IL)
LAWSON, Mary L. (Visiting
Libn) 705

Univ of Illinois Press (IL)
DAVIS, Charles H. (Edit, Library
Trends) 278

Univ of Indianapolis (IN)
YOUNG, Philip H. (Dir) 1383
Univ of Indonesia (IDN)
ADITIRTO, Irma U. (Lectr) 6
Univ of Iowa (IA)
BAKER, Sharon L. (Asst Prof) . . . 49
BELGUM, Kathie G. (Executive
Law Libn) 76
BENTZ, Dale M. (Univ Lib
Emeritus) 84
BIERBAUM, Esther G. (Asst
Prof) 95
BLOESCH, Ethel B. (Asst to the
Dir & Lectr) 106
CRETH, Sheila D. (Univ Libn) . . 258
DEWEY, Barbara I. (Asst to the
Univ Libn) 298
EICHER, Thomas E. (Head Ref
Libn) 339
EIMAS, Richard (Hist of
Medicine Libn) 340

Univ of Iowa (IA)

EMDE, Susan J. (Govt Docums
Libn) 347
ENGER, Kathy B. (Info Spclst) . . 349
ERTL, Mary R. (Acqs Libn) 353
FALCONER, Joan O. (Music
Libn) 362
GIAQUINTA, C J. (Govt
Docums Libn) 431
GORMAN, Lawrence R.
(Selector for French Catlgr) . . 452
HAUSMAN, Julie (Cur of Visual
Mtrls) 513
HIRST, Donna L. (Proj Mgr, Lib
Automation) 543
HOWELL, John B. (Intl Std
Biblgphr) 565
JORDAN, Robert P. (Test
Resrcs Libn) 616
KELLEY, Ann C. (Catlgr) 636
KOHLER, Carolyn W. (Head,
Govt Pubns Dept) 668
KRANCH, Douglas A. (Resc
Asst & Tchg Asst) 676
LARSON, Catherine A. (Media
Bibl) 699
LITTLE, Margaret C. (Tchg
Asst) 733
LORKOVIC, Tatjana B. (Head,
Catlgng Dept) 741
MELROY, Virginia A. (Catlgr) . . . 823
NEUFELD, Sue E. (Ref Libn) . . . 897
ORGREN, Carl F. (Dir, Sch of
Lib Sci) 925
RAWLEY, Wayne (Asst Univ
Libn for Reader Srvs) 1010
RICE, James G. (Sch of Lib &
Info Sci Assoc Prof) 1027
ROBINSON, Caitlin M. (Technl
Srvs & Comp Systs Libn) . . . 1043
ROGERS, Earl M. (Cur of
Archs) 1049
RUMSEY, Eric T. (AV Ref Libn) 1067
SCHACHT, John N. (Libn) 1088
SHIPE, Timothy R. (Libn) 1131
WACHEL, Kathleen B. (Head of
Acqs Dept) 1290

Univ of Kansas at Lawrence (KS)
BURCHILL, Mary D. (Assoc Dir
for Automation & Admin) 158
CRAIG, Susan V. (Art &
Architecture Libn) 254
FRANKLIN, Janice C. (Asst Sci
Libn) 397
HAWKINS, Mary J. (Asst Dean
for Pub Srvs) 514
HITCHENS, Susan H. (Music
Libn) 544
HOWARD, Clinton N. (Technl
Srvs Asst Dean) 564
HOWE, Priscilla P. (Slavic
Catlgr & Exchange Libn) 565
JOHNSON, Ellen S. (Archs of
Recorded Sound Libn) 604
KOEPP, Donna P. (Head of
Govt Docums & Map Lib) 668
LUNG, Mon Y. (Technl Srvs
Head) 748
MASON, Alexandra (Spencer
Libn & Spcl Cols Head) 780
NEELEY, James D. (Ref Dept
Head) 891
NEELEY, Kathleen L. (Head of
the Sci Libs) 892
NEUGEBAUER, Rhonda L.
(Latin Am
Monographic/Serials Catlgr) . . 897
OTTO, Kathryn D. (Serials
Catlgr, Wilcox Project) 930
RANZ, James (Dean of Libs) . . 1008

Univ of Kansas at Lawrence (KS)

RHODES, Saralinda A. (Ref Lib & US Hist Biblgphr) 1026
SCHANCK, Peter C. (Lib Dir & Prof of Law) 1090
SEAVER, James E. (Prof of Hist) 1110
SNYDER, Fritz (Pub Srvs Assoc Dir) 1164
STUHR-ROMMEREIM, Rebecca A. (Libn I) 1205
TRONIER, Suzanne (Catlgng Libn) 1258
WELLER, Leann C. (Engrng Libn) 1321
WILLIAMS, Ann E. (Catlgr) 1342

Univ of Kansas at Overland Park (KS) BURICH, Nancy J. (Regents Ctr Libn) 160

Univ of Kansas Medical Center (KS) BINGHAM, James L. (Dir) 97
CARVER, Jane W. (Head of Interlib Loan) 191
FARLEY, Alfred E. (Spcl Asst) . 364
HATCHER, Marihelen (Head, Acq) 511

Univ of Kentucky (KY)

BIRDWHISTELL, Terry L. (Univ Archvst) 98
BOYARSKI, Jennie S. (Lib Srvs Coordntr) 122
CHAN, Lois M. (Prof) 199
CUNHA, George M. (Adjuct Prof of Conservation) 265
CZARSKI, Charles M. (Libn) 268
HILTON, Beverly A. (Audiovisual Libn) 541
JAMES, William (Law Lib Dir & Prof of Law) 592
KRESSE, Kerry L. (Head, Chemistry/Physics Lib) 678
MCANINCH, Sandra L. (Head, Govern Pubn/Maps Dept) 792
MESNER, Lillian R. (Catlgr & Ref Libn) 827
POLLARD, Richard 981
RIPLEY, Joseph M. (Chairman) . 1035
ROBINSON, Christie M. (Proj Archvst) 1043
ROGERS, Joann V. (Prof) 1049
SEXTON, Ebba J. (Technl Srvs Libn) 1118
SINEATH, Timothy W. (Coll of Lib & Info Sci Dean & Prof) . 1143
STEPHENSON, Judy A. (Ofc of Info Srvs Supvsr) 1188
THOMPSON, Ann B. (Libn) 1238
WALDHART, Thomas J. (Assoc Prof) 1294
WARTH, L T. (Rare Bks Catlgr) 1307
WILLIS, Paul A. (Dir of Libs) . . . 1348
WIZA, Judith M. (Bus Libn & Dept Head) 1359

Univ of La Verne (CA) HECKMAN, Marlin L. (Univ Lib) . 520
KINMAN, Gay T. (Law Libs Dir Asst Prof of Law) 652

Univ of Lethbridge (AB) DROESSLER, Judith B. (Ref & Cols Libn) 320
JONES, Winstan M. (Head of Catlgng) 615
SEYEDMAHMOUD, Donna A. (Pub Srvs Coordntr) 1118

Univ of Lib & Information Science (JAP) NOZOE, Atsutake (Assoc Prof) . . 911
TAKEUCHI, Satoru (Prof) 1220

Univ of Louisville (KY) ANDERSON, James C. (Photographic Archs Head) 23
ANDERSON, Patricia E. (Law Lib Dir) 25
BRINKMAN, Carol S. (Head) . . . 136
CAMMARATA, Paul J. (Asst Law Libn) 175
COATES, Ann S. (Cur of Slides) . 224

Univ of Louisville (KY)

DORR, Ralze W. (Dir, Ofc of Plng & Adminstrv Srvs) 313
EDDY, Leonard M. (Dir of Kornhauser Hlth Scis Lib) 335
GILBERT, Gail R. (Head) 433
GRAY, Dorothy A. (Ref Dept Head) 459
HODGSON, Janet B. (Assoc Archvst) 546
KEARNEY, Anna R. (Asst to the Univ Libn) 633
KORDA, Marion (Prof and Libn) . 671
MILLER, Robert H. (Prof & Dept of Engl Chairman) 842
MORISON, William J. (Univ Archs & Records Ctr Dir) 865
NEELY, Glenda S. (Prof & Bus Ref Libn) 892
NILES, Judith F. (Dir of Div of Technl Srvs) 904
OLMSTED, Elizabeth H. (Music Catlgr) 921
PRIOR, Barbara Q. (Instr & Ref Libn) 993
REDMON, Sherrill (Archvst & Univ Archs Assoc Archvst) . . 1014
SELMER, Sylvia A. (Technl Srvs Libn) 1114
TEITELBAUM, Gene W. (Assoc Law Libn & Law Prof) 1230
TEN HOOR, Joan M. (Ref Libn) . 1231
WILEY, Theresa K. (Lib Mgr) . . 1339

Univ of Louvain (BEL) WALCKIERS, Marc A. (Med Lib Dir) 1293

Univ of Lowell (MA) CAYLOR, Lawrence M. (Head of Acqs Dept) 195
DESROCHES, Richard A. (Syst Mgr) 295
FARAH, Barbara D. (Sci Engrng Libn, Info Srvs Coordntr) 363
FORTIER, Jan M. (Head of Pub Srv) 391
KARR, Ronald D. (Ref Coordntr) . 628
SLAPSYS, Richard M. (Ref & Music Libn) 1148

Univ of Maine at Farmington (ME) HOLMES, Richard C. (Dir of Lib Media Tech) 553
MCNAMARA, Shelley G. (Prof) . . 816

Univ of Maine at Machias (ME) ALLEY, Katherine S. (Asst Libn) . . 16
PHIPPS, Bert L. (Head Libn & Dir) 969

Univ of Maine at Orono (ME) ALBRIGHT, Elaine M. (Dir of Libs) 10
BILODEAU, Judith M. (Univ College Libn) 97
CASSERLY, Mary F. (Col Devlpmnt Libn) 193
GOODWIN, Bryan D. (Hum & Soc Scis Libn) 450
MCCALLISTER, Myrna J. (Col Devlpmnt & Acqs Libn) 793
THOR, Angela M. (Sci & Engrng Libn) 1242
WHITE, Lucinda M. (Soc Scis & Hums Ref Libn) 1331
WIHBEY, Francis R. (Dept Head) 1337

Univ of Maine at Portland (ME) MILLIGAN, Patricia M. (Sr Law Catlgr) 843

Univ of Maine at Presque Isle (ME) VIGLE, John B. (Dir of Lib & Lrng Resrc Ctr) 1284

Univ of Manitoba (MB) BUDNICK, Carol (Biblgphr) 155
FAWCETT, Patrick J. (Systs Coordntr) 367
FERGUSON, Earle C. (Dir of Libs) 372
GODAVARI, S N. (Head of Engrng Dept Lib) 442
HARPER, Judy A. (Libn) 503

Univ of Manitoba (MB)

KERR, Audrey M. (Prof & Med Lib Head) 644
LINCOLN, Robert S. (Head of Acqs) 728
MARSHALL, Denis S. 774
NICHOLLS, Pat (Coordntr, Technl Srvs) 901
ROUTLEDGE, Patricia A. (Ref Libn) 1062
SANTORO, Corrado A. (Asst Univ Archvst) 1082
TULLY, Sharon I. (Comp Srch Srvs Coordntr) 1262
WRIGHT, Patrick D. (St John's Coll Lib Head) 1372

Univ of Mary Hardin at Baylor (TX)
KERLEY, Izoro D. (Asst Libn) ... 643

Univ of Maryland (NY)
SOKOLOWSKI, Denise G. (Libn) 1166

Univ of Maryland at Baltimore (MD)
BRENNAN, Edward P. (Resrch Libn) 132
EPSTEIN, Robert S. (Chief Resident) 351
FREIBURGER, Gary A. (Asst Dir for Systs & Automation) .. 401
GONTRUM, Barbara S. (Law Lib Dir) 448
HINEGARDNER, Patricia G. (Info Spclst) 542
HUMPHRIES, Anne W. (Info Spclst) 574
PETERSON, William S. 965
RAND, Pamela S. (Catlgr & Info Spclst) 1006
SMITH, Barbara G. (Asst Dir for Technl Srvs) 1152
TEITELBAUM, Sandra D. (Head of Info Srvs) 1230
TOOEY, Mary J. (Info Mgmt Educ Head) 1250
WILLIAMS, Mary A. (Info Spclst) 1345
WILSON, Marjorie P. (Vice Dean) 1352

Univ of Maryland at Baltimore County (MD)
CREST, Sarah E. (Asst Ref Libn) 258
KULP, William A. (Catlg Libn) ... 683
LEBRETON, Jonathan A. (Adminstrv Srvs Asst Dir) 708
STERLING, Judith K. (Assoc Dir) 1189
WILKINSON, Billy R. (Lib Dir) .. 1340
WILT, Larry J. (Assoc Dir, Cols & Access Srvs) 1353

Univ of Maryland at College Park (MD)
CUNNINGHAM, William D. (Asst Prof) 265
CURTIS, Peter H. (Cur of Marylandia) 267
EBELING-KONING, Blanche T. (Cur of Rare Bks & Lit Manuscripts) 334
EVANS, Sylvia D. (Chem Ref Libn) 358
FARREN, Donald (Assoc Dir of Libs for Spcl Cols) 365
HARRAR, H J. (Dir) 503
HEILPRIN, Laurence B. (Prof Emeritus) 521
HEUTTE, Frederic A. (Music Libn) 535
JACKSON, Carleton (Ref Libn) .. 587
KLAIR, Arlene F. (Catlg Mgmt Dept Head) 657
KOBAYASHI, Michiko (Japanese Catlgr) 666
LARSEN, Lida L. (Asst Dir of Admissions) 698

Univ of Maryland at College Park (MD)
MARCHIONINI, Gary J. (Asst Prof) 769
MERIKANGAS, Robert J. (Head of Ref Srvs) 826
NITECKI, Danuta A. (Pub Srvs Assoc Dir) 905
PITT, William B. (Assoc Libn) ... 976
ROBERTSON, Jack (Assoc Art Libn) 1042
SHEETS, Robin R. (Music Catlgr) 1125
SHULMAN, Frank J. (Cur & Head) 1133
SIMS, Sally R. (Histrc Preservation Libn) 1142
SOERGEL, Dagobert (Prof) 1165
STIELOW, Frederick J. (Asst Prof & Hist & Lib Sci Coordntr) 1194
VAN CAMPEN, Rebecca J. (Instrcl Srvs Coordntr) 1272
WALSTON, Claude E. (Lib & Info Srv Dean) 1300
WELLISCH, Hans H. (Prof) 1322
WILLIAMS, Helen E. (Asst Prof) 1343
WILSON, William G. (Libn & Lectr) 1353

Univ of Maryland at Eastern Shore (MD)
DADSON, Theresa E. (Acqs Head & Coordntr of Col Dvlpmnt) 269
PANDA, Rosamond E. (Serials & Docums Libn) 937
SMITH, Jessie C. (Dir of Lib Srvs) 1156

Univ of Maryland at Fort Washington (MD)
PHILLIPS, Gary B. (Retrospective Conversion Catlgr) 968
HEIL, Kathleen A. (Prog Analyst) . 521

Univ of Maryland at Solomons (MD)
Univ of Massachusetts at Amherst (MA)
ADAMS, Leonard R. (Govt Docums Libn) 5
CHADWICK, Alena F. (Branch Ref Libn) 196
CRAIG, James L. (Biological Scis Libn) 254
DONOHUE, Joseph (Prof of Engl) 312
FELDMAN, Laurence M. (Branch Libn) 369
FELLER, Siegfried (Assoc Dir of Libs for Col Devlpmnt) 370
FRETWELL, Gordon E. (Assoc Dir for Pub Srvs) 402
HOLM, Edla K. (Head, Interlib Loan) 552
JUENGLING, Pamela K. (Music Libn) 619
KENDALL, John D. (Head of Spcl Cols & Rare Books) 640
KOCSIS, Jeanne (Soc Sci Biblgphr) 667
MERRIAM, Joyce (Asst Head of Ref Dept) 826
TALBOT, Richard J. (Dir of Libs) 1220
TAUSKY, Janice (Libn) 1225
WOOD, Ann L. (Ref Libn) 1363

Univ of Massachusetts at Boston (MA)
GROSE, B D. (Dir of Libs) 472
MAZURANIC, Joseph R. (Circ Dept Head) 791
O'TOOLE, James M. (Asst Prof of Archs & Hist) 930
SCHLESINGER, Frances C. (Docums Libn) 1094

Univ of Massachusetts at Boston (MA)

STIFFLEAR, Allan J. (Acqs Libn) 1194
TSENG, Louisa (Sr Catlgr) 1260

Univ of Massachusetts at Sunderland (MA)

MCINTOSH, Nadia (Catlgr) 809

Univ of Massachusetts Medical Sch (MA)

KANG, Wen (Ref Libn) 625

Univ of Medicine & Dentistry of NJ (NJ)

IRWIN, Barbara S. (Spcl Cols Libn & Archvst) 584
PLAZA, Joyce S. 978
RAINEY, Kathleen O. (Ref Libn) 1004
ROSENSTEIN, Philip (Dir of Libs & Univ Libn) 1057
SCHUBACK COHN, Judith (Lib Dir) 1101
SKICA, Janice K. (Libn) 1146
SMITH, Reginald W. (Assoc Dir) 1159
SPRUNG, George (Ref Supvsr) . 1176

Univ of Miami (FL)

BURROWS, Suzetta C. (Regnl Progs Vice-Chair & Assoc Dir) 163
SANCHEZ, Sara M. (Ref Libn Subject Spclst & Biblgphr) .. 1079
WILLIAMS, Thomas L. (Assoc Dir) 1347

Univ of Miami at Coral Gables (FL)

AHMAD, Carol F. (Asst Dir, Pub Srvs) 8
DANIELS, Westwell R. (Law Libn) 273
DE VARONA, Esperanza B. (Asst Head Libn) 297
GOLIAN, Linda M. (Serials Ctl Libn) 447
HALE, Kay K. (Libn) 485
KOBIALKA, Nancy C. (Music Libn) 666
LADNER, Sharyn J. (Bus Biblgphr & Ref Libn) 687
LOWELL, Felice K. (Asst Technl Srvs Libn) 744
MESTRITS, Leila (Catlgng Libn) . 828
PETIT, Michael J. (Acqs Libn) ... 965
RABKIN, Judith R. (Asst Head, Catlg Dept) 1001
ROBAR, Terri J. (Asst Ref Libn) 1038
ROBARTS, Phyllis G. (Circ Dept Head) 1038
RODGERS, Frank (Libs Dir) ... 1047
SEILER, Susan L. (Sci Ref Libn) 1112
WAXMAN, Jack (Consult) 1311

Univ of Michigan at Ann Arbor (MI)

ADLER, Robert J. (Data Libn) 7
ANDERSEN, H F. (Asst Obstetrics & Gynecology Prof) 21
BEAN, Margaret 69
BEAUBIEN, Anne K. (Head of Coop Access Srvs) 70
BERGEN, Kathleen M. (Head of Map Lib) 85
BIDLACK, Russell E. (Dean Emeritus) 95
BIGGS, Debra R. (Libn) 95
BJORKE, Wallace S. (Asst Head of Music Lib) 100
BLOUIN, Francis X. (Dir) 107
BOLES, Frank (Asst Archvst) ... 112
BUTZ, Helen S. (Rare Book Libn) 168
CRAWFORD, David E. (Assoc Dean) 256
CROOKS, James E. (Coordntr) .. 260
DAUB, Peggy E. (Lib Head) 275
DAVIS, Anne C. (Libn) 277
DIDIER, Elaine K. (Dir) 301
DOUGHERTY, Richard M. (Univ Lib Dir) 314

Univ of Michigan at Ann Arbor (MI)

DOWNES, Virginia C. (Actg Libn) 316
DURRANCE, Joan C. (Assoc Dean) 328
FINERMAN, Carol B. (Archvst) .. 378
FRIEDMAN, Bruce A. (Prof of Pathology) 403
GALIK, Barbara A. (Head, Slavic Progs & Area Coordntr) 413
GATTIS, R G. (Resrch Info & Pubns Assoc Coordntr) 422
GOSLING, William A. (Asst Technl Srvs Dir) 453
GRIMM, Ann C. (Resrch Info & Pubns Coordntr) 470
HALL, Jo A. (Libn) 488
HART, Patricia H. (Mgr, Biblgph Products) 507
JASPER, Richard P. (Col Devlpmnt Coordntr) 595
KARP, Nancy S. (Ref Libn) 628
KOCHEN, Manfred (Prof of Info Scis) 667
KUSNERZ, Peggy A. (Art & Architecture Libn) 685
LEARY, Margaret R. (Law Lib Dir) 707
LOUP, Jean L. (Head of Docums Ctr) 742
MAHONY, Doris D. (Assoc Libn, Ref & Info Dept) 761
MASLOW, Linda S. (Chief Ref Libn) 780
MATZO, Deborah J. (Head Libn, Oxford Lib) 786
MCDONALD, David R. (Asst Dir for Systs) 802
MOSEY, Jeanette (Asst Prof) ... 871
NICHOLS, Darlene P. (Asst Libn) 901
PAO, Miranda L. (Assoc Prof) .. 938
POOLEY, Beverly J. (Law Prof & Law Lib Assoc Dean) 983
ROENZWEIG, Merle (Asst Libn) 1048
ROSEN, Barbara (Assoc Libn) . 1055
SALZER, Melodie A. (Serials Spclst) 1078
SCHWARTZ, Diane G. (Actg Pub Srvs Coordntr) 1104
SCOTT, Melissa C. (Career Resrcs Libn) 1107
SIEVING, Pamela C. (Libn) 1136
SLAVENS, Thomas P. (Prof) ... 1148
STOFFLE, Carla J. (Deputy Dir & Assoc Dir of Pub Srv) 1196
TAYLOR, Margaret T. (Lectr) .. 1227
VANCE, Kenneth E. (Prof Emeritus) 1273
WAGMAN, Frederick H. (Emeritus Dir, Emeritus Prof) . 1291
WARNER, Robert M. (Sch of Info & Lib Std Dean) 1305
WESTBROOK, Jo L. (Coordntr, Ref & Biblgph Instr) 1326
WHEATON, Julie A. (Col Devlpmnt & Acqs Coordntr) . 1328
WISE, Virginia J. (Ref Libn & Adjunct Prof) 1357
YOCUM, Patricia B. (Natural Sci Libs Head) 1380
YORK, Grace A. (Fed Docums Libn) 1381

Univ of Michigan at Dearborn (MI)

BROWN-MAY, Patricia A. (Asst Ref Libn) 148
LUKASIEWICZ, Barbara (Head of Pub Srvs) 747
NUCKOLLS, Karen A. (Head, Technl Srvs Dept) 912

Univ of Michigan at Dearborn (MI)

SCHNEIDER, Janet M. (Ref Libn) 1097
STUCK, Judy K. (Asst Libn) ... 1204

Univ of Michigan at Flint (MI)

GIFFORD, Paul M. (Archvst) 433
HART, David J. (Assoc Libn) ... 507
PALMER, David W. (Lib Dir) 936

Univ of Milan (ITL)

CASIRAGHI, Edoardo (Prof of Med Informatics) 192

Univ of Minnesota at Duluth (MN)

EBRO, Diane C. (Dir, Hlth Sci Lib) 334
ENRICI, Pamela L. (Engrng Libn) 350
JOHNSON, Deborah S. (Sr Civil Srv Ref Libn) 603

Univ of Minnesota at Minneapolis (MN)

ALLISON, Brent (Head, Map Lib) 17
ARTH, Janet M. (Coordntr) 35
BAUM, Marsha L. (Asst Libn) 66
BEAVEN, Miranda J. (Biblgphr, Russian & E European Std) ... 71
BILEYDI, Lois G. (Lib Asst) 96
BRANIN, Joseph J. (Dir, Hum/Soc Sci Libs) 128
BROGAN, Martha L. (Asst to the VP) 139
CHRISTIANSON, Ellory J. (Asst to Univ Libn & Fiscal Ofcr) ... 212
COGSWELL, James A. (Head, Ref & Info Srvs Div) 227
COLLINS, Mary F. (Dir of Centl Technl Srvs) 233
D'ELIA, George P. (Assoc Prof) ... 289
FAGERLIE, Joan M. (Biblgphr) .. 361
FOREMAN, Gertrude E. (Head of Pub Srvs) 390
FULLER, Sherrilynne S. (Lib Dir) . 409
GANGL, Susan D. (Asst Ref Libn) 416
GASTON, Judith A. (Dir of Univ Film & Video) 421
GLASGOW, Vicki L. (Coordntr & Ref Biblgphr) 440
GROSCH, Audrey N. (Prof & Asst to Univ Libn) 472
HALES-MABRY, Celia E. (Ref Libn) 486
HALLEWELL, Laurence (Ibero-Am Biblgphr) 489
HOPP, Ralph H. (Prof Emeritus) . 558
IMMLER, Frank (Head of Cols Div) 582
JOHNSON, Donald C. (Cur) 603
KARON, Bernard L. (Chief Sci Catlgr) 627
KELLY, Richard J. (Biblgphr) 638
KLAASSEN, David J. (Archvst) .. 657
KROSCH, Penelope S. (Archvst) 680
LA BISSONIERE, William R. (Head, Govt Pubns Lib) 686
LATHROP, Alan K. (Manuscripts Cur) 701
LONG, John M. (Assoc Prof & Dir) 739
LORING, Christopher B. (Asst Libn, Head of Interlib Loan) ... 741
MARION, Donald J. (Col Devlpmnt Coordntr) 770
MONSON, Dianne L. (Prof of Educ) 855
MUELLER, Mary G. (Asst Prof & Ref Biblgphr) 875
NEVIN, Susanne (Catlgng Libn) .. 898
OBERMAN, Cerise G. (Pub Srvs Plng Ofcr) 914
OLSON, Lowell E. (Assoc Prof, Lib Sci & Subj Biblgphr) 923

Univ of Minnesota at Minneapolis (MN)

OVERMIER, Judith A. (Cur & Assoc Prof) 931
PANKAKE, Marcia J. (Biblgphr, Engl & Am Lit) 938
REES, Warren D. (Asst Law Libn) 1016
REISNER, Suzanne R. (Head of Monographs Prcsng Div) ... 1021
RUBENS, Donna J. (Coordntr ESTIS and Sci Ref Biograph) 1064
SANDNESS, John G. (Resrch Assoc) 1081
SCHERER, Herbert G. (Art Libn) 1092
SMITH, Eldred R. (Univ Libn) .. 1154
SPETLAND, Charles G. (Ref Libn) 1174
STEINKE, Cynthia A. (Dir) 1186
STOKES, Claire Z. (Head, Ref & Resrch Srvs) 1196
TIBLIN, Mariann E. (Scandinavian Area Std Biblgphr) 1244
TURNER, Patricia (Biblgphr) ... 1265
VAN CLEVE, Nancy J. (Serials Catlgng Sect Head) 1273
WALDEN, Barbara L. (Hist Biblgphr) 1294
WEEKS, John M. (Soc Scis Biblgphr) 1315
WEINBERG, Gail B. (Libn) 1317
YAHNKE, Robert E. (Assoc Prof) 1376

Univ of Minnesota at St Paul (MN)

CARLSON, Livija I. (Veterinary Med Libn) 182
DELOACH, Lynda J. (NHPRC Fellow) 290
JOHNSON, Margaret A. (Asst Dir) 607
LETNES, Louise M. (Libn) 718
MCCLASKEY, Marilyn H. (Head of Catlgng) 796
MCDIARMID, Errett W. (Prof Emeritus) 802
MOODY, Suzanna (Guide Project Dir) 857
SCHOLBERG, Henry (Prof Emeritus) 1098
WURL, Joel F. (Cur) 1374

Univ of Mississippi (MS)

BUTLER, James C. (Circ Libn) .. 166
COCHRAN, J W. (Law Libn & Asst Prof of Law) 225
FISHER, Benjamin F. (Engl Prof & Editor) 380
GRAVES, Gail T. (Head, Ref Dept) 459
HARPER, Laura G. (Head of Online Srch Srv) 503
SELTZER, Ada M. (Dir) 1114
STEEL, Suzanne F. (Libn & Asst Prof) 1183
TUCKER, Ellis E. (Pub Srvs Libn) 1261
VERICH, Thomas M. (Head, Spcl Cols) 1282
WHITE, Elaine R. (Blues Archive Catlgr & Instr) 1331

Univ of Missouri at Columbia (MO)

ALBRITTON, Rosie L. (Asst to the Dir) 10
ALLCORN, Mary E. (Jnlsm Libn) 14
ALMONY, Robert A. (Asst Dir of Libs for Adminstrv Srvs) 17
ARCHER, Stephen M. (Theatre Prof) 31
BARNES, Everett W. (Gen Ref/Docum Libn) 57
BHULLAR, Pushpajit D. (Biogph Instrc Coordntr) 93

Univ of Missouri at Columbia (MO)

BREWER, O. J. (Libn III) 134
CARROLL, C E. (Prof of Lib and Info Sci) 187
DEL CASTILLO, Mireya (Title II-C Catlgng Dir) 289
DEWEESE, June L. (Soc Sci Libn) 298
ELS, Nancy T. (Soc Sci Libn) . . . 346
FAIR, Norma J. (Catlgr) 361
GULSTAD, Wilma B. (Libn II & Catlgr) 477
HAVENER, Ralph S. (Dir of Archvs) 513
HOWELL, Margaret A. (Head, Spcl Cols) 565
HUFFMAN, Robert F. (Educ & Psy Libn) 571
JOHNSON, E D. (Head, Info Srvs) 604
KOPP, Kurt W. (Sr Comp Pgmr Analyst) 671
LENOX, Mary F. (Dean) 715
LUH, Ming (Interlib Loan Libn) . . 747
MACEWAN, Bonnie J. (Art, Archaeology & Music Libn) . . . 755
MCKININ, Emma J. (Asst Prof) . . 811
MITCHELL, Joyce A. (Dir) 849
MYERS, Victor C. (Catlgng Systs Libn) 885
PALLARDY, Judy S. (Online Srch Coordntr) 935
PARKER, Ralph H. (Dean Emeritus) 942
POWELL, Ronald R. (Assoc Prof) 988
RACINE, John D. (Asst Dir For Technl Srvs) 1001
RICKERSON, George T. (Dir) . 1031
RIKLI, Arthur E. (Prof Emeritus) . 1034
RILEY, Ruth A. (Info Srvs Libn) . 1034
SHAUGHNESSY, Thomas W. (Lib Dir) 1123
SHIRKY, Martha H. (Lang & Lit Libn) 1131
STEVENS, Robert R. (Newspaper Libn) 1191
STEVENSON, Marsha J. (Access Srvs Div Head) 1191
TIMBERLAKE, Patricia P. (Asst Head) 1245
WADE, D J. (Ref Spclst) 1290
WINJUM, Roberta J. (Asst Acqs Libn) 1355

Univ of Missouri at Kansas City (MO)

BECK, Susan E. (Hum Ref Libn) . . 71
COURT, Patricia (Reader Srvs Libn) 251
GERRITY, Marline R. (Med Libn) 429
HOHENSTEIN, Margaret L. (Technl Srvs Asst Law Libn) . . 549
LABUDDE, Kenneth J. (Porf Emeritus of Hist) 686
LONDRE, Felicia H. (Prof of Theatre) 738
SHELDON, Ted P. (Dir of Libs) . 1126
SHIPLEY, Ruth M. (Clinical Med Libn) 1131
SPALDING, Helen H. (Assoc Dir of Libs) 1171
SULLIVAN, Marilyn G. (Chief Libn) 1208

Univ of Missouri at Rolla (MO)

STAUTER, Mark C. (Assoc Dir) 1183
STEWART, J A. (Ref Libn) 1192

Univ of Missouri at St Louis (MO)

CANN, Cheryle J. (Head) 178
PERSHE, Frank F. (Part Time Biblgphr) 961

Univ of Moncton (NB)

Univ of Montana (MT)

Univ of Montevallo (AL)

Univ of Montreal (PQ)

Univ of Nebraska at Lincoln (NE)

ARSENAULT, Alban (Catlg Dept Head) 35
BOUDREAU, Berthe (Prof & Dir of Tchg Resrcs Ctr) 118
DIONNE, Charlotte A. (Libn) 305
LEBLANC, Amedee (Acqs & Col Devlpmnt Head) 708
CHANDLER, Devon (Instrcl Mtrls Srv Dir) 199
DRIESSEN, Karen C. (Media Libn/Assoc Prof) 320
OELZ, Erling R. (Dir of Pub Srvs) 917
PATRICK, Ruth J. (Dean of Lib Srvs) 947
SCHUSTER, Bonnie H. (Acqs Libn) 1103
VANHORNE, Geneva T. 1275
DUNMIRE, Raymond V. (Tech Srvs Head) 326
SCALES, Diann R. (Ref Libn) . . 1087
WILLIAMS, Pauline C. (Assoc Prof & Perdcls Ref Libn) 1346
ARAJ, Houda (Libn) 30
BEDARD, Bernard J. (Circ & Technl Srvs Dept Head) 73
BERNHARD, Paulette (Asst Prof) 89
BERTRAND-GASTALDY, Suzanne (Assoc Prof) 91
BOIVIN-OSTIGUY, Jocelyne (Documentalist) 111
BOUDREAU, Gerald E. (Acqs & Col Devlpmnt Head) 118
BROCHU, Frederick (Archvst) . . . 138
BULL, Jerry J. (Ref Libn) 156
DARBON, Ginette (Technl Srvs Dir) 274
DESCHATELETS, Gilles H. (Prof Agrege) 294
DESROCHERS, Monique (Documentalist) 295
FLUK, Louise R. (Catlgr) 386
GARDNER, Richard K. (Prof) . . . 418
GIRARD, Luc (Ref Libn) 438
GREENE, Richard L. (Dir) 464
HETU, Sylvie (Libn) 534
MAYRAND, Lise M. (Acqs & Ref Libn) 791
ROLLAND-THOMAS, Paule (Prof) 1051
SAVARD, Rejean (Assoc Prof) . 1085
VADNAIS, Martine (Libn) 1270
COOK, Anita I. (Gen Srvs Chair) . 239
FROBOM, Jerome B. (Head Govt Docums Depository) 405
HENDRICKSON, Kent H. (Dean of Libs) 527
HERZINGER, Sandra S. (Catlgng Dept Chairperson) . . 534
JOHNSON, Judy L. (Acqs Libn) . 606
LANE, Alice L. (Serials Catlgng Sect Head) 694
LEITER, Richard A. (Pub Srvs Libn, Asst Prof of Law Lib) . . . 714
LOGAN-PETERS, Kay E. (Architecture Libn) 737
SARTORI, Eva M. (Liaison Libn) 1083
STRIMAN, Brian D. (Technl Srvs Libn) 1202
TIBBITS, Edith J. (Music & Asian Langs Catlgr) 1243
WISE, Sally H. (Law Libn & Asst Prof of Law) 1357
WOMACK, Sharon K. (Assoc Prof) 1362
WOOL, Gregory J. (Serials Catlgr) 1368

Univ of Nebraska at Omaha (NE)

BOYER, Janice S. (Asst Adminstrv Srvs Dir) 123
BROWN, Helen A. (Online Srvs Coordntr) 144
DICKSON, Laura K. (Bus Ref Libn) 301
FAWCETT, Georgene E. (Serials Libn) 367
HASELWOOD, Eldon L. (Dept of Tch Educ Prof) 510
NEWCOMER, Audrey P. (Technl Srvs Assoc Dir) 898
REIDELBACH, John H. (Col Devlpmnt Chairperson) 1019
RUNYON, Robert S. (Lib Dir) .. 1067
TOLLMAN, Thomas A. (Ref Dept Chair) 1249
WILLIS, Dorothy B. (Regnl Devlpmnt Coordntr) 1348

Univ of Nevada at Las Vegas (NV)

CLARK, Camille S. (Ref Libn) ... 216
COVINGTON, Robert D. (Head of Pub Srvs) 252
CURLEY, Elmer F. (Ref, Biblgphr) 265
DEACON, Mary D. (Dir of Libs) .. 283
HEATON, Shelley J. (Online Srvs Libn) 519
POLSON, Billie M. (Catlg Libn) .. 982
SAUNDERS, Laverna M. (Head, Technl Srvs) 1084

Univ of Nevada at Reno (NV)

BLESSE, Robert E. (Spcl Cols Dept Head) 105
BUTLER, Barbara E. (Bus Ref Libn) 166
CONWAY, Susan L. (Instrcl Srvs Libn) 239
DONOVAN, Ruth H. (Assoc Lib Dir) 312
GREFRATH, Richard W. (Ref Libn) 465
NEWMAN, Linda P. (Mines & Map Libn) 899
OTERO-BOISVERT, Maria (Basque Std Libn) 930
PARKHURST, Carol A. (Head of Systs & Access Srvs) 942
RICE, Dorothy F. (Gifts & Devlpmnt Libn) 1027
ZENAN, Joan S. (Dir & Med Libn) 1387
ZINK, Steven D. (Head, Pub Srvs) 1389

Univ of New Brunswick at Fredericton (NB)

COLSON, Judith K. (Cols Devlpmnt Dept Head) 234
POPE, Andrew T. (Libn) 983
RAUCH, Doris E. (Cols Devlpmnt Libn) 1010

Univ of New Brunswick at Saint John (NB)

COLLINS, Susan H. (Serials Acqs Libn) 233

Univ of New England (ME)

GOLUB, Andrew J. (Lib & Media Srvs Dir) 447

Univ of New Hampshire (NH)

FINLAY, J A. (Asst Serials Libn) . 378
GRIFFITH, Joan C. (Serials Libn) 469
HENNESSEY, Barry J. 528
JACOBS, Gloria (Monographs Catlgr) 589
KAPOOR, Jagdish C. (Acqs Libn & Assoc Prof) 626
LANE, David M. (Bio Scis Branch Libn & Asst Prof) 694
REIK, Constance (Asst Ref Libn) 1020
TEBBETTS, Diane R. (Asst Dir & Online Srvs) 1229

Univ of New Mexico (NM)

ADAMS, Dena R. (Visiting Instr) ... 4
BEJNAR, Thaddeus P. (Legal Resrch Libn) 75
BERNSTEIN, Judith R. (Bus Lib Dir) 89
BROWN, Eulalie W. (Ref & Govt Pubns Head) 143
DODSON, Carolyn (Ref Libn) ... 308
DUCHARME, Judith C. (Info Srvs Libn) 322
ELDREDGE, Jonathan D. (Chief, Col & Info Resrcs Devlpmnt) . 342
GROTHEY, Mina J. (Ibero-American Ref Libn) ... 473
IVES, Peter B. (Asst Bus Libn) . 586
KEMPF, Jody L. (Ref Libn) 639
KRUG, Ruth A. (Serials Catlgng Team Leader) 680
LEWIS, Linda K. (Ref Libn, Col Devlpmnt Coordntr) 723
LOVE, Erika (Prof & Dir) 743
RASSAM, Cynthia K. (Asst Prof) 1009
REX, Heather (Lib Spclst IV) ... 1024
ROLLINS, Stephen J. (Access Srvs Head) 1051
SEISER, Virginia (Adminstrv Srvs Dept Head) 1113
SHELSTAD, Kirsten R. (Clinical and Hospital Srvs Libn) 1126
SOHN, Jeanne G. (Assoc Dean of Lib Srvs) 1165
SUGNET, Christopher L. (Monographic Catlgng Dept Head) 1206
THOMPSON, Janet A. (Asst Head Spcl Cols, Cur of Mss) 1240
THORSON, Connie C. (Assoc Prof) 1242
VASSALLO, Paul (Assoc VP) .. 1279

Univ of New Orleans (LA)

HANKEL, Marilyn L. (Bus Ref Libn) 496
HARDY, D C. (Archvst) 500
HARRIS, Karen H. (Lib Sci Prof) . 505
PHELPS, Connie L. (Gen Libn) .. 967
SERBAN, William M. (Grad Asst) 1116
TIMBERLAKE, Phoebe W. (Serials Libn) 1245

Univ of New South Wales (AUS)

RAYWARD, W B. (Prof & Sch of Libnshp Head) 1011
WILSON, Concepcion S. (Sr Lecturer) 1350

Univ of Newcastle (AUS)

Univ of North Alabama (AL)

NEAME, Roderick L. (Sr Lectr) .. 891
CARR, Charles E. (Dir of Lrng Resrcs Ctr) 185
O'NEAL, Kenneth W. (Col Devlpmnt Libn) 924
SLOAN, Tom W. (Asst Libn & Govt Pubns & Maps Head) .. 1150

Univ of North Carolina at Asheville (NC)

BUCHANAN, William E. (Ref Libn) 153

Univ of North Carolina at Chapel Hill (NC)

ASHEIM, Lester E. (Prof Emeritus) 35
BAILEY, Charles W. (Head, Systems & Resrch Srvs) 46
BALLENTINE, Rebecca S. (Libn) 53
BERGUP, Bernice (Humanities Ref Libn) 87
BROADUS, Robert N. (Prof) 138
BYRD, Gary D. (Assoc Dir) 168
CARPENTER, Raymond L. (Prof) 185
CHENAULT, Elizabeth A. (Rare Bk Col Libn for Pub Srv) 205
COGGINS, Timothy L. (Assoc Law Libn) 227

Univ of North Carolina at Chapel Hill (NC)

COTTEN, Alice R. 250
COTTEN, Jerry W.
(Photographic Archvist) 250
CRANDALL, Elisabeth G. (Med
Info Coordntr) 255
DANIEL, Evelyn H. (Dean) 272
DARLING, John B. (Zoology
Libn) 275
DEBRECZENY, Gillian M. (Circ
& Rsv Libn) 285
DICKERSON, Jimmy (Chem
Libn) 300
FARKAS, Doina C. (Acqs Libn) . 364
FEEHAN, Patricia E. (PhD Prof,
Tchng Asst, & Instr) 368
FLOWERS, Janet L. (Acqs
Head) 386
FRANK, Linda V. (Info Srvs
Libn) 397
GASAWAY, Laura N. (Law Libn
& Prof of Law) 421
GLEIM, David E. (Monographic
Catlg Head) 441
GLEIM, Sharon S. (Asst Head of
Serials Dept) 441
GOVAN, James F. (Univ Libn &
Prof of Lib Sci) 454
GRENDLER, Marcella (Assoc
Univ Libn for Spcl Cols) 467
HEWITT, Joe A. (Assoc Univ
Libn) 535
HOLLEY, Edward G. (Prof) 551
JONES, H G. (Dir) 613
KESSLER, Ridley R. (Federal
Docums Libn) 645
LANEY, Elizabeth J. (Libn) 695
LOSEE, Robert M. (Asst Prof) . . . 742
MATER, Dee A. (Info Srvs Libn) . 783
MCNAMARA, Charles B. (Rare
Bks Cur) 816
MEEHAN-BLACK, Elizabeth C.
(Biblgph Searching Head) 821
MORAN, Barbara B. (Assoc
Prof) 862
NEAL, Michelle H. (Interlib Loan
& Ref Libn) 890
NYE, Julie B. (Functional Design
Mgr) 912
OWEN, Willy (Technl Support
Ofcr) 932
PALO, Eric E. (Head, Circ Dept) . 937
PRILLAMAN, Susan M. (Media
Spclst) 993
RHINE, Cynthia (Systs Libn) . . . 1025
SAYE, Jerry D. (Asst Prof) 1086
SAYE, Terri O. (Catlg Libn) 1086
SCHELL, Nancy S. (Lib Netwk
Advisor) 1091
SEGAL, Jane D. (Info Srvs Libn) 1111
SEIBERT, Karen S. (Pub Srvs
Assoc Univ Libn) 1112
SLOCUM, Charlotte A. (City &
Regnl Plng Libn) 1150
STIGLEMAN, Sue E. (Systems
Libn) 1194
STRAUSS, Diane (Bus Admin
Head) 1201
SUTTON, Ellen D. (Soc Scis
Ref Libn) 1211
SWINDLER, Luke (Soc Scis
Biblgphr) 1216
TALBERT, David M. (Info Srvs
Libn) 1220
TAYLOR, David C.
(Undergraduate Libn) 1226
TUCKER, Mary E. (Libn) 1262
TUTTLE, Marcia L. (Head,
Serials Dept) 1266

Univ of North Carolina at Chapel Hill (NC)

WEBSTER, Deborah K. (Ref
Libn) 1314
WOOD, Judith B. (Asst Prof) . . . 1364

Univ of North Carolina at Charlotte (NC)

AVELEYRA, Luz M. (Slide Cur) . . 41
BRABHAM, Robert F. (Spcl
Cols Libn) 124
FRANKLE, Raymond A. (Dir of
the Lib) 397
HUDSON, Donna T. (Sci Ref,
Life Scis & Chem Libn) 569
PENNINGER, Randy
(Manuscript Cur & Archvst) . . 957
STAHL, Wilson M. (Assoc Lib
Dir) 1178
WALKER, Judith A. (Curr
Resrcs Libn) 1295

Univ of North Carolina at Greensboro (NC)

BOMAR, Cora P. (Interim Chair) . 113
CHILDRESS, Eric R. (Prcsng
Supvsr) 208
LEVINSON, Catherine K. (Asst
Ref Libn) 721
MILLER, Marilyn L. (Prof &
Chair) 840
MITCHELL, W B. (Head Circ
Libn) 849
MOORE, Kathryn L. (Biogph
Instn Coordntr) 860
PARROTT, Margaret S. (Assoc
Prof) 944
WRIGHT, Keith C. (Prof) 1372
WURSTEN, Richard B. (Music
Listening Ctr Dir) 1374

Univ of North Carolina at Pittsboro (NC)

WHITENER, Betty L. (Libn &
Resrch Asst) 1333

Univ of North Dakota (ND)

BOONE, Jon A. (Col Devlpmnt
& Acq Coordntr) 115
ETTL, Lorraine R. (Head, Pub
Srvs) 356
GARD, Betty A. (Pub Srvs
Coordntr) 417
GOTT, Gary D. (Asst Prof of
Law & Dir) 453
NIENOW, Beth M. (Pub Srvs
Libn) 904
PEDERSEN, Lila (Asst Dir) 954
PEDERSON, Randy L. (Pub
Srvs Libn) 954
STRAHAN, Michael F. (Comp
Srvs and Ref Libn) 1199

Univ of North Florida (FL)

COHEN, Kathleen F. (Ref Dept
Head) 228
FARKAS, Andrew (Libs Dir, Prof
of Lib Sci) 364
JONES, Robert P. (Head,
Operations, Systs Div) 614
KAZLAUSKAS, Diane W.
(Assoc Univ Libn, Media
Resrcs Head) 632
RANDTKE, Angela W. (Asst
Catlg Libn) 1007
SMITH, Linda L. (Head, Catlgng
Dept) 1157
URBANSKI, Verna P. (Catlgr) . . 1269

Univ of Northern Colorado (CO)

FOX, Lynne M. (Ref Libn) 395
HUGHES, Sondra K. (Lib Media
Spclst) 572
JARAMILLO, George R. (Pub
Srvs Dir) 594
PITKIN, Gary M. (Dir of Libs) . . . 976
ROBERTS, Francis X. (Ref
Libn) 1040
SAVIG, Norman I. (Music Libn) . 1086
SCHULZE, Suzanne S. (Archs
Libn) 1102

Univ of Northern Colorado (CO)

Univ of Northern Iowa (IA)

SCHWEERS, Lucy (Lib
Technician) 1105
ELIZABETH, Martin A. (Dept
Head) 343
HIEBER, Douglas M. (Head of
Circ) 537
HILAND, Leah F. (Asst Prof) 538
LETTOW, Lucille J. (Youth Col
Libn & Asst Prof) 719
MARSHALL, Jessica A. (Acqs
Head) 774
MARTIN, Elizabeth A. (Dept
Head) 776
RITCHIE, Verna F. (Art and
Music Libn) 1036
SHAW, James T. (Ref Libn) . . . 1123
WEEG, Barbara E. (Ref Libn,
Asst Prof) 1315
WILKINSON, Patrick J.
(Docums & Maps Libn) 1340

Univ of Notre Dame (IN)

AMES, Charlotte A. (Biblgphr,
Catholic Americana) 19
DOLAN, Robert T. (Acq Clerk) . . 309
FUDERER, Laura S. (Biblgphr) . . 408
GLEASON, Maureen L. (Asst
Dir for Col Devlpmnt) 440
HARLAN, John B. (Engrng Lib
Spclst) 502
HAVLIK, Robert J. (Engrng &
Architecture Libn) 513
HAYES, Stephen M. (Ref & Pub
Docums Libn) 516
JACOBS, Roger F. (Dir) 590
JORDAN, Louis E. (Cur) 616
KRIEGER, Alan D. (Theology &
Philosophy Biblgphr) 678
LYSY, Peter J. (Asst Archvst) . . . 753
MAXWELL, Jan C. (Asst Head
of Acqs Dept) 788
MILLER, Robert C. (Libs Dir) 841
MOON, Elizabeth A. (Catlgr) 857
PEC, Jean A. (Head of Original
Catlgng) 953
SLINGER, Michael J. (Pub Srvs
Assoc Dir) 1149
TANTOCO, Dolores W. (Libn) . . 1223
WITTORF, Robert H. (Lib Systs
Mgr) 1359
ZEUGNER, Lorenzo A. (Acqs
Head) 1387

Univ of Nuevo Leon (MEX)

ARTEAGA, Georgina (Regnl
Med Info Ctr Dir) 35

Univ of Oklahoma at Norman (OK)

BATT, Fred (Head, Ref Dept) 64
BENDER, Nathan E. (Libn) 79
CLARK, Harry (Prof Emeritus) . . . 217
COCHENOUR, John J. (Asst
Prof) 225
FAIBISOFF, Sylvia G. (Dir &
Prof) 361
FAW, Marc T. (Bibl Assoc Prof) . 366
GOODMAN, Marcia M. (Hist of
Sci Libn) 449
HARRINGTON, Sue A. (Lib
Technl Srvs Dir) 504
HOVDE, David M. (Soc Sci Ref
Libn & Instr of Bibl) 563
KANCHANAKPAN, Pongsak
(Serials Catlgr) 624
LATROBE, Kathy H. (Asst Prof) . 701
LAUGHLIN, Mildred A. (Prof) . . . 703
LEE, Sul H. (Dean, Univ Libs) . . . 711
MATHIS, Barbara B. (Libn) 784
POLAND, Jean A. (Engrng Libn) . 980
STOLT, Wilbur A. (Dir of Lib
Pub Srvs) 1196
VOGES, Mickie A. (Dir & Prof of
Law) 1287

Univ of Oklahoma at Norman (OK)

**Univ of Oklahoma at Oklahoma
City** (OK)

Univ of Oklahoma at Tulsa (OK)
Univ of Oregon (OR)

WEAVER-MEYERS, Pat L.
(Access Srvs Dept Head &
Assoc Prof) 1313
CALLARD, Joanne C. (Gen
Srvs Head) 173
SHROUT, Sally J. (Serials Srvs
Head) 1133
MINNERATH, Janet E. (Lib Dir) . 846
ALLEN, Alice J. (Head, Catlg
Dept) 14
BARNWELL, Jane L. (Ref Libn
& Soc Sci Subject Spclst) . . 58
BONAMICI, Andrew R. (Head,
Budget, Persnl & Plng) 113
BYNON, George E. (Asst Univ
Libn, Adminstrv Srvs) 168
CARMIN, James H.
(Architecture & Allied Arts
Ref Libn) 183
CLAYTON, Mary E. (Assoc Law
Libn) 220
CONNORS, Kathleen M. (Ref
Libn & Educ Subject Spclst) . . 238
CRUMB, Lawrence N. (Ref
Libn) 262
CUMMINGS, Hilary A. (Curator
of Manuscripts) 264
D'ANDRAIA, Dana D. (Acqs
Dept Head) 272
DUCKETT, Kenneth W. (Spcl
Cols Cur) 322
FARRIER, Kathy D. (Catlg Lign
Supvsr Copy Catlg Sect) 365
FRANTZ, Paul A. (Lib Instrc
Coordntr) 398
GRIFFIN, Karen D. (Asst Head
of Catlg Dept) 468
HADDERMAN, Margaret
(Visiting Ref Libn) 482
HALGREN, Joanne V. (Head,
Interlibrary Loan) 486
HEINZKILL, J R. (Ref Libn) 522
HOTELLING, Katsuko T.
(Japanese Libn) 562
KLOS, Sheila M. (Head
Architecture & Allied Arts
Lib) 662
MORRISON, Perry D. (Lib Prof
Emeritus) 868
PYATT, Timothy D. (Rare Book
Libn) 999
ROBERTSON, Howard W.
(Slavic Catlg Libn, Biblgphr) . 1042
SCHENCK, William Z. (Col
Devlpmnt Libn) 1091
SHAW, Elizabeth L. (Comptng
Ctr Libn) 1123
SHIPMAN, George W. (Univ
Libn) 1131
SHULER, John A. (Pub Affairs
Libn) 1133
SMITH, Terry M. (Catlgr) 1161
SOUTH, Ruth E. (Ref Libn) 1169
STARK, Peter L. (Head, Map
Lib) 1181
STIRLING, Isabel A. (Sci Lib
Head) 1195
SUNDT, Christine L. (Slide &
Photograph Cur) 1210
WALKER, Luise E. (Gen Duty) . 1295
WAND, Patricia A. (Asst Univ
Libn for Pub Srv) 1302
WANG, Hsiao G. (Orientalia
Catlg Libn) 1303
WATSON, Mark R. (Catlg Libn
& Copy Catlg Sect Supvsr) . 1310

Univ of Osteopathic Medicine & Hlth Scis (IA)

Univ of Ottawa (ON)
BANFILL, Christine (Catlgr) 54
DUHAMEL, Marie (Head of Spcl Srvs) 324
LEBLANC, Jean J. (Asst Libn) .. 708
OUIMET, Jacinthe (Catlgr) 930
RATSOY, Marye G. (Libn II) .. 1010
RICHER, Yvon (Chief Libn) 1030
ST. JACQUES, Suzanne L. (Ref Srvs , Soc Sci & Hum Head) 1075
SAURIOL, Guy L. (Catlgr) 1085
THIBAULT, Jean (Head Catlgr) . 1235
THOMSON, Dorothy F. (Asst Cols Libn) 1241
WARD, William D. (Cols Devlpr) 1304

Univ of Pennsylvania (PA)
ADELMAN, Jean S. (Head Libn of Musm Lib) 6
AZZOLINA, David S. (Ref Libn) .. 43
BATISTA, Emily J. (Ref Libn) 64
BELL, Steven J. (Ref Libn) 77
BERWICK, Mary C. (Online Srvs Head) 91
BRYANT, Lillian D. (Libn) 152
GAEBLER, Ralph F. (Ref Libn) .. 411
GREEN, Patricia L. (Coordntr, Canine Genetics Proj) 462
GRILIKHES, Sandra B. (Dir) 470
HALLER, Douglas M. (Musm Archvst) 489
HALPERIN, Michael (Head) 489
HOLMES, John H. (Sr Resrch Coordntr) 553
JACKSON, Mary E. (Interlib Loan Dept Head) 588
KEANE, John J. (Bus Adminstr for the Libs) 633
MORENO, Rafael (Ref Libn) 863
MYERS, Charles J. (Dir) 884
PAGELL, Ruth A. (Assoc Dir) .. 934
RIDGEWAY, Patricia M. (Ref Libn & B I Coordntr) 1032
ROHDY, Margaret A. (Head of Shared Catlgng Dept) 1050
RUGGERE, Christine A. (Spcl Cols Cur) 1066
SLYHOFF, Merle J. (Media Srvs/Ref Libn) 1151
TARNAWSKY, Marta (Foreign & Intl Law Libn) 1224
TRAISTER, Daniel H. (Asst Dir of Libs for Spcl Cols) 1253
VAUGHAN-STERLING, Judith A. (Catlg Libn) 1280
WICKEY, Colleen (Field Archvst) 1335
YOLTON, Jean S. (Catlgr) 1380
YOUNG, James B. (Music Technl Srvs Libn) 1382

Univ of Phoenix (CA)
DOWNS, Sandra P. (Lrng Resrc Spclst) 317
SEGAL, Naomi R. (Lrng Resrc Spclst) 1112

Univ of Pittsburgh (PA)
AL SADAT, Amira A. (Head, Technl Srvs) 17
BANDEMER, June E. (Asst Dir) .. 54
BEARMAN, Toni C. (Dean of Sch of Lib & Info Sci) ... 69
BRICE, Heather W. (Dir) 134
CARTER, Ruth C. (Technl Srvs Asst Dir) 190
COHEN, Laurie J. (Ref Libn) 228
DAILY, Jay E. (Prof Emeritus) ... 270
DEBONS, Anthony (Prof Emeritus) 285
DETLEFSEN, Ellen G. (Assoc Prof) 296
DIMMICK, Mary L. (Info Libn) ... 304
DUCK, Patricia M. (Head Libn) .. 322

Univ of Osteopathic Medicine & Hlth Scis (IA)
MARQUARDT, Larry D. (Lib Dir) 772

Univ of Pittsburgh (PA)
ENGLERT, Mary A. (Asst Catlgr) 350
FREEDMAN, Phyllis D. (Resrch Assoc) 400
GLABICKI, Paul (Assoc Prof of Art) 439
GREENE, Nancy S. (Newspaper Catlgr) 464
HALLOCK, Nancy L. (Hispanic & Latin Am Catlgr) 489
JOSEY, E J. (Prof of Lib Sci) ... 618
KENT, Allen (Distinguished Srv Prof) 642
KIMMEL, Margaret M. (Prof) 649
KIRCHER, Linda M. (Asst to the Chair) 654
KREITZBURG, Marilyn J. (Biblgph Instrc Ref & Resrch Head) 677
KRZYS, Richard A. (Prof & Dir of Intl Lib Info Ctr) 681
LEIBOWITZ, Faye R. (Lead Newspaper Catlgr) 713
LOCKE, Jill L. (PhD Candidate) .. 736
LYNESS, Ann L. (Dir) 752
METZLER, Douglas P. (Asst Prof) 829
MICHALAK, Jo A. (Asst Dir for Automation) 832
MILLER, Mary E. (Ref & Govt Pubns Libn) 840
MITTEN, Lisa A. (Soc Sci Biblgphr) 850
NASRI, William Z. (Assoc Prof) .. 888
PAUL, Suzanne (Lib Dir) 949
PIPER, Paula (Adminstrv Spclst) . 975
ROOT, Deane L. (Curator, Foster Hall Col) 1054
ROSS, Nina M. (Instr) 1058
SAUNDERS, Allene W. (Libn) .. 1084
SILVERMAN, Marc B. (Head of Pub Srvs) 1138
STEPHENS, Norris L. (Music Libn) 1188
SUOZZI, Patricia 1210
WEBRECK, Susan J. (Asst to the Dean) 1314
WESSEL, Charles B. (Ref Libn) 1325
WHITMORE, Marilyn P. (Coordntr) 1333
WILLIAMS, James G. (Prof) ... 1344
WOO, Lisa C. (Biblgphr & Catlgr) 1363
WOODSWORTH, Anne (Assoc Provost and Dir of Univ Libs) 1367
WOOLLS, Esther B. (Prof) 1368
WRAY, Wendell L. (Prof) 1370
ZABROSKY, Frank A. (Cur) ... 1385

Univ of Portland (OR)
BROWNE, Joseph P. (Lib Dir) ... 148
HORAN, Patricia F. (Docums & Ref Libn) 559

Univ of Prince Edward Island (PE)
MANOVILLE, Susanne (Circ Supvsr) 767

Univ of Puerto Rico (PR)
AYALA-ORTIZ, Orietta (Acq Dept Head) 42
BERNAL-ROSA, Emilia (Prof) 88
BULERIN-LUGO, Josefina (Circ and Rsv Dept Head) ... 156
CASAS DE FAUNCE, Maria (Prof) 191
COLLAZO, Maria L. (Libn) 232
CONCEPCION, Luis (Libn) 235
FIGUEROA, Almaluces (Chief Libn) 376
GARCIA-RUIZ, Maritza L. (Serials & Perdcls Dir) 417
GONZALEZ-VELEZ, Isaura (Libn in Charge of Puerto Rican Col) 448

Univ of Puerto Rico (PR)

JARAMILLO, Juana S. (Libn I) . . 594
LOPEZ, Elsa M. (Technl Srvs
Libn) 741
MARTINEZ-NAZARIO, Ronaldo
(Libn) 779
MAURA-SARDO, Mariano A.
(Info Sci Asst Prof) 787
MCCARTHY, Carmen H. (Lib
Dir) 794
MUNOZ-SOLA, Haydee (Lib
Syst Dir) 879
RIVERA-ALVAREZ, Miguel A.
(Libn II & Pub Srvs Supvsr) . 1037
RODRIGUEZ, Ketty (Libn) 1048
THOMPSON, Annie F. (Dir) . . . 1239
VALENTIN-MARTY, Jeannette
(Catlgr) 1271

Univ of Puetro Rico (PR)
MILLS, Rolland W. (Libn III) . . . 844

Univ of Puget Sound (WA)
BECKER, Roger V. (Syst
Planner) 72
GILDENHAR, Janet (Lib Dir) . . . 434
HARVEY, Suzanne
(Bibliographic Systs Libn) . . . 509
JONES, Faye E. (Asst Law
Libn) 613
MENANTEAUX, A R. (Info Srvs
Libn) 823
RICIGLIANO, Lorraine M.
(Head, Ref & Info Srvs) . . . 1031
SCHREINER, Suzanne M. (Asst
Ref Libn) 1100
TAYLOR, Desmond (Lib Dir) . . . 1226

Univ of Quebec (PQ)
ALAIN, Jean M. (Documtn Ctrs
Dir) 9
ALLARD, Serge (Lib Dir) 14
BEAUMIER, Renald (Dir) 70
BERGERON, Gilles I. (Pub Srvs
Libn) 86
BIELLE, Christian P. (Ref Libn) . . . 95
BOULET, Paul E. (Lib Dir) 119
CHENIER, Andre (Lib Dir) 206
COTE, Jean P. (Syst Libn &
Head of Technl Srvs) 249
DU BREUIL, Laval (Documtn &
Telecommunications Dir) 322
DUPUIS, Marcel (Ref Libn) 327
GARDNER, Lucie (Libn) 418
GELINAS, Michel R. (Profsnl
Libn) 426
LAFRENIERE, Myriam (Libn) . . . 688
LATOUR, Pierre (Libn) 701
MANSEAU, Edith (Documtn
Advisor) 767
MENARD, Francoise (Libn) 823
PARKER, Charles G. (Music
Libn) 941
ROUSSEAU, Denis
(Researcher) 1061

Univ of Queensland (AUS)
LAMBERTON, Donald M. (Econ
Prof) 690
ROUTH, Spencer (Principal
Libn, Col Devlpmnt) 1061

Univ of Redlands (CA)
HEARTH, Fred E. (Dir of Lib) . . . 519
NOLAND, Jon (Acess Srvs, Ref
Libn) 908

Univ of Regina (SK)
AFFLECK, Delburt E. (Educ
Branch Lib Head) 7
BROWNE, Berks G. (Catlgr) 148
FIELDEN, Stanley (Assoc
Support Srvs Libn) 376
HAMBLETON, Alixe E. (Prof) . . . 490
INGLES, Ernie B. (Dir of Libs) . . . 582
MACK, A Y. (Admin Soc Sci
Libn) 756
RESCH, Peter T. (Sci Libn) 1024
SWEENEY, Shelley T. (Univ
Archvst) 1215
THAUBERGER, Marianne T.
(Ref Srv Coordntr) 1234

Univ of Rhode Island (NY)
Univ of Rhode Island (RI)
BERGEN, Daniel P. (Prof) 85
BARNETT, Judith B. (Assoc
Prof & Catlgr) 57
CAMERON, Lucille W. (Soc
Scis Ref & Biblgphr) 175
DEVIN, Robin B. (Acqs Head) . . . 297
ETCHINGHAM, John B. (Bus
Ref Libn) 355
FUTAS, Elizabeth (Dir & Prof) . . . 411
GIEBLER, Albert C. (Emeritus
Prof of Music) 432
GIOVENALE, Sharon (Asst Prof
& Libn) 438
KEEFE, Margaret J. (Pub Srvs
Dept Chair) 634
KELLAND, John L. (Ref &
Biblgphr for Life Scis) 635
KRAUSSE, Sylvia C. (Assoc
Prof & Ref Lib & Biblgphr) . . . 676
MASLYN, David C. (Spcl Cols
Head) 780
SCHNEIDER, Stewart P. (Assoc
Prof) 1097
SHERIDAN, Jean (Dir) 1127
SIEBURTH, Janice F. (Assoc
Prof & Head, Ref Dept) 1135
SIITONEN, Leena M. (Asst Prof) 1137
TRYON, Jonathan S. (Assoc
Prof) 1259
TYRON, Jonathan 1267
VOCINO, Michael C. (Head of
Technl Srvs) 1286
YOUNG, Arthur P. (Univ Libs
Dean & Prof) 1381

Univ of Richmond (VA)
ENGLISH, Susan B. (Law Libn
& Prof of Law) 350
GWIN, James E. (Technl Srvs
Dir) 479
HALL, Bonlyn G. (Music & Catlg
Libn) 487
MAXWELL, Littleton M. (Libn) . . . 788
MCCULLEY, Lucretia (Ref Libn) . 800
TYSON, John C. (Univ Libn) . . . 1267
WILLIAMS, Lila E. (Catlg Libn) . 1344

Univ of Rochester (NY)
BUFF, Iva M. (Acqs & Col
Devlpmnt Head) 155
BURNS, Violanda O. (Head of
Mgmt Lib) 163
JUNION, Gail J. (Catlg Dept
Head) 620
KABELAC, Karl S. (Manuscripts
Libn) 620
KAPLAN, Isabel C. (Engrng
Libn) 626
LINDAHL, Charles E. (Ref Libn
& Resrch Coordntr) 728
MCGOWAN, Kathleen M. (Ref
Libn & Educ Biblgphr) 807
METZ, Ray E. (Head of Access
Srvs & Systs) 828
NESBIT, Kathryn W. (Ref &
Interlib Loan Libn) 896
PLAIN, Marilyn V. (Catlgr of
Music Manuscripts) 977
RAME, Mary E. (Libn II, Rare
Books, Spcl Cols Asst) 1005
RICKER, Shirley E. (Libn I) 1031
ROBERTSON, Michael A. (Lib
Microcomputer Srvs Mgr) . . . 1042
SOLLENBERGER, Julia F. (Info
& Access Srvs Head) 1166
SOMERVILLE, Arleen N. (Sci &
Engrng Head, Chem Libn) . . 1167
STRIFE, Mary L. (Libn) 1202
THYM, Jurgen (Musicology Dept
Chair) 1243
WATANABE, Ruth T. (Histn
Archvst) 1308
WYATT, James F. (Lib Dir) 1374

Univ of Saarlandes (WGR)

Univ of Sains Malaysia (MLY)

Univ of St Thomas (TX)

Univ of San Diego (CA)

Univ of San Francisco (CA)

Univ of Santa Clara (CA)

Univ of Sarasota (FL)

Univ of Saskatchewan (SK)

Univ of Scranton (PA)

Univ of Sherbrooke (PQ)

Univ of Shippagan (NB)

Univ of South Africa (SAF)

Univ of South Alabama (AL)

VON KEITZ, Wolfgang (Asst
Prof) 1288
LIM, Hucktee E. (Chief Libn) . . . 727
WALKER, Constance M. (Head
Libn) 1295
CARTER, Nancy C. (Law Lib
Dir & Prof of Law) 189
HERON, Susan J. (Technl Srvs
Head) 532
HOLLEMAN, Marian P. (Univ
Libn) 551
HYDE, Mary L. (Docums &
Microforms Libn) 580
RATHSWOHL, Eugene J. 1009
BIRKEL, Paul E. (Dean of the
Univ Lib) 98
EWEN, Eric P. (Head Catlg
Libn) 359
GITLER, Robert L. (Univ Libn,
Prof Emeritus) 438
KELSH, Virginia J. (Law Libn &
Assoc Prof of Law) 639
RUNYON, Steven C. (Dir, Mass
Media Srvs) 1067
SHOSTROM, Marian L. (Asst
Libn for Pub Svs) 1133
SONIN, Hille (Head, Acq Dept) . 1167
STEFANCIC, Jean A. (Acqs &
Serials Libn) 1185
BAILEY, Rolene M. (Ref Libn) 46
HOLT, Ethel F. (Lib Dir) 554
CANEVARI DE PAREDES,
Donna A. (Cols Libn) 178
CHEN, William Y. (Catlgr) 205
FRITZ, Linda (Coop Std Libn) . . . 405
HAMMEL, Philip J. (Prof) 493
HUBBERTZ, Andrew P. (Govt
Pubns, Maps & Microforms
Head) 568
KRISHAN, Kewal (Libn III) 678
LAKHANPAL, Sarv K.
(Orientation Coordntr &
Biblph Instr) 689
NELSON, Ian C. (Asst Dir of
Libs for Cols) 893
PAREDES-RUIZ, Eudoxio B.
(Head, Biblgph Control Dept) . 940
REID, Marianne E. (Catlgng
Libn) 1019
SALT, David P. (Sci & Engrng
Libn) 1077
WIENS, Paul (Univ Libn & Dir of
Libs) 1336
APPELBAUM, Judith P. (Editor
of Bk Resrch Qtrly) 29
CHASSE, Jules (Asst Dir for
Technl Srvs) 203
CHOUINARD, Germain (Dir) 211
SOKOV, Asta M. (Dir) 1166
TANGUAY, Guy (Head Law
Libn) 1222
GAUTHIER, Rose M. (Head
Libn) 423
WILLEMSE, John (Dir) 1341
BUSH, Nancy W. (Curr Lab Dir
& Lib Sci Prof) 165
DAMICO, James A. (Dir of Univ
Libs) 271
ENGEBRETSON, Mary E.
(Head of Ref Srvs) 348
FINLEY, Vera L. (Serials & AV
Catlgr) 378
IRBY, Geraldine A. (Assoc Libn
& Ref Libn Serials) 583
MILLER, Hannelore A. (Head
Catlg Libn) 838
PERESICH, Mary G. (Catlg
Libn) 958
RODGERS, Patricia M. (Technl
Srvs Coordntr) 1047

Univ of South Alabama (AL)

Univ of South Carolina (SC)

Univ of South Dakota (SD)

Univ of South Florida (FL)

SHEARER, Barbara S. (Pub
Srvs Coordntr) 1124
BAKER, Augusta
(Storyteller-in-Residence) 47
BARRON, Daniel D. (Assoc
Prof) 60
BILLINSKY, Christyn G. (Instr) . . . 96
CHOI, Jin M. (Asst Prof) 210
CROSS, Joseph R. (Pub Srvs
Head) 260
CUBBEDGE, Frankie H. (Dir) . . . 262
DRYDEN, Sherre H. (Libn) 321
EASTMAN, Caroline M. (Assoc
Prof) 333
GABLE, Sarah H. (Ref Libn) 411
GEOGHEGAN, Doris J. (Catlg
Libn) 427
GISSENDANNER, Cassandra
S. (Catlg Libn) 438
HOLLEY, E J. (Asst Ref Libn) . . . 551
HOWARD-HILL, Trevor (Engl
Prof) 564
LANGE, Elizabeth A. (Asst Dir
of Libs for Technl Srvs) 695
LAWSON, James F. (Grad Asst
Volunteer Archvst) 705
LUCAS, Linda S. (Prof) 746
MCQUILLAN, David C. (Map
Libn) 817
OSBALDISTON, Diana M.
(Head Catlg Libn) 927
PEAKE, Luise E. (Prof of Music) . 952
PERRIN, Robert A. (Dir of Lib) . . 959
PUKL, Joseph M. (Order Dept
Head) 997
RIDGE, Davy J. (Assoc Dir of
Libs) 1032
ROPER, Fred W. (Dean) 1054
SCHULZ, Constance B.
(Applied Hist MA Prog Asst
Dir) 1102
SMITH, Nancy (Systs Libn) 1158
TOOMBS, Kenneth E. (Dir of
Libs) 1251
TYLER, Carolyn S. (Educ Libn) . 1266
UPHAM, Lois N. (Asst Prof) . . . 1269
WARREN, Karen T. (Union List
Coordntr, Serials Libn) 1306
WASHINGTON, Nancy H. (Asst
Dir) 1307
WEATHERS, Virginia W. (Asst
Ref Libn) 1312
WILLIAMS, Robert V. (Assoc
Prof) 1346
DEAN, Leann F. (Libn) 283
EDELEN, Joseph R.
(Bibliographic Control Libn) . . . 335
HULKONEN, David A. (Dir) 572
JENSEN, Mary B. (Asst Law
Libn & Asst Prof of Law) 599
LEGET, Max (Ref Libn) 712
MYERS, Nancy L. (Acqs Libn) . . 884
SPRULES, Marcia L. (Lib Srvs
Dir) 1176
ABBOTT, Randy L. (Grad
Student) 1
CHRISMAN, Larry G. (Assoc
Univ Libn) 211
CRAIG, James P. (Dir) 254
EL-HADIDY, Bahaa (Assoc
Prof) 342
EVANS, Josephine K. (Asst
Univ Libn & Dept Head) 357
FUSTUKJIAN, Samuel Y. (Lib
Dir) 410
GATES, Jean K. (Prof) 422
GRIMES, Maxyne M. (Technl
Srvs Asst Dir) 470

Univ of South Florida (FL)

HARKNESS, Mary L. (Univ Libn) 501
JENKINS, Althea H. (Lib Dir) . . . 597
JOHNSTON, Judy F. (Pub Srvs Asst Dir) 610
KETCHERSID, Arthur L. (Assoc Dir of Technl Srvs) 645
LIANG, Diana F. (Univ Libn & Asst Dept Head) 725
MCCROSSAN, John A. (Dir and Prof) 800
MCRAE, Linda (Slide Cur) 818
MERCADO, Marilyn A. (Univ Libn & Asst Dept Head) 825
PFISTER, Fred C. (Prof) 966
SMITH, Alice G. (Prof) 1152

Univ of Southern California (CA)

BELL, Christina D. (Info Spclst) . . . 76
BENNION, Bruce C. (Head, Ref & Online Srvs) 82
BOAZ, Martha T. (Dean Emeritus, Prof Emeritus) 108
BRECHT, Albert O. (Prof of Law, Dir of Law Lib) 131
BROWN, Janis F. (Educ Resrcs Assoc Dir) 144
CHRISTOPHER, Paul (Univ Archvst) 212
CLINTWORTH, William A. (Info Srvs Assoc Dir) 222
CRAMPON, Jean E. (Head Libn) 255
GILMAN, Nelson J. (Lib Dir) 436
HAYES, Melinda K. (Technl Srvs Libn) 516
HOROWITZ, Roberta S. (Info Scitst) 560
JAFFE, Lee D. (User Srvs Libn) . 591
KARASICK, Alice W. (Libn & Circuit Libn Coordntr) 627
KAZLAUSKAS, Edward J. (Assoc Prof) 632
KIM, Joy H. (Catlgr) 649
KLEIN, Kenneth D. (East Asian Libn) 659
MANNING, Phil R. (Assoc Vice Pres for Htl Affairs) 767
MANTHEY, Teresa M. (Info Spclst) 767
MORSE, David H. (Assoc Dir for Col Resrcs) 869
REINHARDT, Alice L. (Dir, Med Ctr Libs) 1021
RICE, Ronald E. (Asst Prof) . . . 1027
RITCHESON, Charles R. (Univ Libn, Dean & Vice Provost) . 1036
SHERMAN, Judith E. (Med Libn) 1128
SORGENFREI, Robert K. (Acqs Libn) 1168
STAYNER, Delsie A. (Acqs Libn) 1183
THOMPSON, Don K. (Ref Dept Head) 1239
TOMPKINS, Philip (Deputy Univ Libn & Assoc Dean) 1250
TROTTA, Victoria K. (Law Lib Asst Dir) 1258
WETTS, Hazel H. (Engrng Libn) 1328
WILK, Wanda (Dir) 1339
WILLIAMS, Leonette M. (Technl Srvs Head) 1344
WINEBURGH-FREED, Margaret (Biogph Mgmt Sect Head) . . 1354
WISE, Leona L. (Dir of Exhibits) 1357
WOOD, Elizabeth H. (Info Spclst) 1364
WUERTZ, Eva L. (Ref Libn) . . . 1373
ZIAIAN, Monir (Head Libn) 1387

Univ of Southern Colorado (CO)

Univ of Southern Maine (ME)

Univ of Southern Mississippi (MS)

Univ of Southwestern Louisiana (LA)

Univ of Sydney (AUS)
Univ of Tampa (FL)

Univ of Tennessee at Chattanooga (TN)

Univ of Tennessee at Knoxville (TN)

GRATE, Jon F. (Asst Ref Libn) . . 458
MOFFEIT, Tony A. (Asst Dir for Lib Srvs) 852
MOORE, Beverly B. (Lib Dir) 858
DUVAL, Marjorie A. (Univ Archvst) 329
KNOWLTON, Suzanne L. (Assoc Univ Libn) 666
PARKS, George R. (Univ Libn) . . 943
PERRY-BOWDER, Libbie E. (Music Dept Libn & Lecturer in Music) 961
BECK, Allisa L. (Ref Libn II) 71
BOYD, Sandra E. (Asst Archvst) . 123
BOYD, William D. (Asst Prof) . . 123
CARNOVALE, A N. (Prof of Music) 184
DRAKE, Betty S. (Genealogy Ref) 318
GRESSITT, Alexandra S. (Asst Univ Archvst) 467
HARRIS, Ouida C. (Grad Student) 505
HAUTH, Allan C. (Pub Srvs Dir) . 513
JONES, Dolores B. (Cur) 612
KELLY, John M. (Univ Biblgphr) . 638
LATOUR, Terry S. (Dir, Spcl Cols & Univ Archvst) 701
LAUGHLIN, Cheryl H. (Docums Coordntr) 703
LAUGHLIN, Jeannine L. (Dir, Sch of Lib Srvs) 703
THOMPSON, Karolyn S. (Interlib Loan Coordntr) 1240
VAN MELER, Vandelia L. (Asst Prof) 1276
WILLIAMS, Eddie A. (Automated Srvs Dir) 1343
WILSON, Mary S. (Sch of Lib Srv Asst Prof) 1352
WILTSE, Elaine E. (Lib Dir) . . . 1353
WITTIG, Glenn R. (Asst Prof) . . 1358
YOUNG, Julia M. (Asst Prof) . . . 1382
CARSTENS, Jane E. (Prof of Lib Sci) 188
FOX, Willard (Asst Prof) 395
HAMSA, Charles F. (Col Devlpmnt Biblgphr) 494
HIMEL, Sandra M. (Gen Ref Libn) 542
KREAMER, Jean T. (Dir, Univ Media Ctr, Regnl Film Lib) . . . 677
RAGHAVAN, Vijay V. (Assoc Prof) 1003
SCHMIDT, Jean M. (Libn) 1095
SHAUGHNESSY, Megan (Humanities & Soc Scis Biblgphr) 1123
STEWART, Mary E. (Instrcl Mtrls Ctr Dir) 1193
TURNER, I B. (Head, Archs & Spcl Cols) 1264
RADFORD, Neil (Univ Libn) . . . 1002
ACOSTA, Lydia A. (Libn) 4
JOHNSON, Susan J. (Gen Libn) . 609
MATHEWS, Richard B. (Assoc Prof of Engl) 784
JACKSON, Joseph A. (Prof & Dean of Libs) 587
MURGAI, Sarla R. (Ref Libn & Assoc Prof) 880
NICOL, Jessie T. (Assoc Prof/Head Acqs) 902
BEINTEMA, William J. (Dir of the Law Lib) 75
BENGTSON, Betty G. (Assoc Dir for Technl Srvs) 80
BEST, Reba A. (Asst Law Libn & Asst Prof) 92

Univ of Tennessee at Knoxville (TN)

CROWTHER, Karmen N. (Bus
Libn) 262
ESTES, Glenn E. (Prof) 355
GARRETT, Stuart (Catlgr) 420
GRADY, Agnes M. (Head,
Catlgng Dept) 455
HEWLETT, Carol C. (Sr Resrc
Consult) 535
HILL, Ruth J. (Asst Law Libn for
Pub Srvs & Ref) 540
HUNT, Donald R. (Libs Dir) 575
JETT, Don W. (Lib Head) 600
KARRENBROCK, Marilyn H.
(Asst Prof) 628
LEACH, Sandra S. (Database
Searching Coordntr) 706
LLOYD, James B. (Spcl Cols
Libn) 735
MITCHELL, Aubrey H. (Assoc
Dir for Pub Srvs) 848
MYERS, Marcia J. (Assoc Dir of
Libs for Adminstrv Srv) 884
PEMBERTON, J M. (Assoc
Prof) 956
PHILLIPS, Linda L. (Sci & Tech
Srvs Head) 968
PICQUET, D C. (Assoc Law
Libn & Assoc Prof) 971
PONNAPPA, Biddanda P.
(Microforms. Govt Docums
Libn) 982
PRENTICE, Ann E. (Dir) 990
RADER, Joe C. (Circ Srvs
Head) 1002
ROBINSON, William C. (Assoc
Prof) 1045
SAMMATARO, Linda J. (Asst
Prof and Ref Libn) 1078
SILCOX, Tinsley E. (Head) 1137
SOLBERG, Judy L. (Ref Libn) . . 1166
VIERA, Ann R. (Engl Ref Libn) . 1284
WALLACE, Alan H. (Ref Libn) . 1297

Univ of Tennessee at Martin (TN)

SMITH, Lori D. (Pub Srvs Libn) . 1157
STOWERS, Joel A. (Lib Dir) . . . 1199

Univ of Tennessee at Memphis (TN)

BELLAMY, Lois M. (Systs Libn) . . 77
BUNTING, Anne C. (Head of
Technl Srvs) 157
COOPER, Ellen R. (Acqs &
Serials Libn) 242
GIVENS, Mary K. (Assoc Dir) . . 439
LASSLO, Andrew (Medicinal
Chem Dept Prof & Chairman) . 700
MARTIN, Jess A. (Hlth Sci Lib
Dir) 776
SELIG, Susan A. (Head,
Reader's & Eductnl Srvs) . . . 1113

Univ of Texas at Arlington (TX)

HULL, Mary M. (Adminstrv Asst) . 572
KONDRASKE, Linda N. (Comp
Srchng Libn) 670
LEWIS, John S. (Assoc Prof) . . . 723
LOWRY, Charles B. (Dir of Libs) . 745
MORRIS, Pamela A. (Head of
Govt Pubns & Maps Dept) . . . 867
SAMSON, Robert C. (Asst Dir
of Automation Srvs) 1079
SHEETS, Shirley H. (Asst Dir for
Technl Srvs) 1125
STOAN, Stephen K. (Asst Dir
for Pub Srvs) 1195
WELLVANG, James K. (Head,
Preservation Dept) 1323

Univ of Texas at Austin (TX)

AIRTH, Elizabeth J. (Ref Libn &
Biblgphr) 9
ARTHUR, Donald B. (Catlgr) 35
BARKAN, Steven M. (Assoc
Law Libn) 56
BECK, Alison M. (Asst Archvst) . . 71
BICHTELER, Julie H. (Assoc
Prof) 94

Univ of Texas at Austin (TX)

BILLINGS, Harold W. (Gen Libs
Dir) 96
BRENNAN, Mary H. (Asst for
Col Devlpmnt Progs) 132
BUCKNALL, Carolyn F. (Col
Devlpmnt Asst Dir) 154
BURCH, David R. (Legal Info
Spclst) 158
BURLINGHAM, Merry L. (South
Asia Libn) 161
BURT, Eugene C. (Asst Head) . . 164
CABLE, Carole L. (Head, Fine
Arts Lib) 170
CRONEIS, Karen S. (Head Libn) . 260
DALLAS, Larayne J. (Asst
Engrng Libn) 270
DAVIS, Donald G. (Lib & Info
Sci Prof) 278
EISENBEIS, Kathleen M. (Tchg
Asst, Grad Student) 340
ELDER, Nancy I. (Head Libn,
Sci Lib) 342
GARNER, Jane (Libn) 419
GOODWIN, Willard (Biblgphr) . . . 450
GOULD, Karen K. (Lectr &
Biblgph Consult) 454
GRACY, David B. (Prof in
Archvl Enterprise) 455
GUTIERREZ, Margo (Mexican
Am Std Libn) 479
HARMON, Glynn (Prof) 502
HARTNESS, Ann (Asst Head
Libn) 508
HELFER, Robert S. (Profsnl
Libn) 523
HENDERSON, Cathy (Resrch
Libn) 526
HERRING, Billie G. (Assoc Prof) . 533
IMMROTH, Barbara F. (Assoc
Prof) 582
JACKSON, William V. (Lib Sci
Prof) 588
LANDIS, Lawrence A.
(Photographs Archvst) 693
LEACH, Sally S. (Asst to the
Dir) 706
MARSHALL, Suzanne K. (Head
Libn, Circ Srvs) 775
MERSKY, Roy M. (Hyder
Centennial Law Prof) 827
MIKSA, Francis L. (Prof) 834
MILLER, Karl F. (Media Libn &
Cur of Histl Music Col) 839
PERRYMAN, Wayne R. (Head
Libn, Acqs & Serials Dept) . . . 961
POUND, Mary E. (Pubns
Coordntr) 987
ROY, Loriene (Instr) 1063
SCHWARTZ, Philip J. (Educ
Biblgphr and Ref Libn) 1105
SENG, Mary A. (Asst Dir
Facilities & Support Srvs) . . . 1115
TONGATE, John T. (Head Libn,
Ref) 1250
WYLLYS, Ronald E. (Dean &
Prof) 1375

Univ of Texas at Dallas (TX)

ALLEN, Joan W. (Serials Dept
Head) 15
BANDELIN, Janis M. (Spcl Projs
Libn) 53
HENEBRY, Carolyn L. (Ref
Libn) 528
KRATZ, Abby R. (Assoc Lib Dir
for Pub Srvs) 676
MILLER, Jean K. (Lib Dir) 838
NISONGER, Thomas E. (Assoc
Lib Dir for Col Devlpmnt) 905
OLSSON, Margaret G. (Ref, Lib
Instruction) 923

Univ of Texas at Dallas (TX)

SAFLEY, Ellen D. (Ref & Info
Srvs Head) 1074
SALL, Larry D. (Assoc Lib Dir
for Spcl Cols) 1076
SHEA, Kathleen (Corpte Info
Srvs Mgr) 1124
SOUTHARD, Ruth K. (Assoc
Lib Dir for Media Srvs) 1169
WILKERSON, Judith C. (Serials
Dept Head) 1339

Univ of Texas at El Paso (TX)
BROWN, Susan W. (Interlib
Loan Libn) 147
GOODWIN, Charles B. (Music
Lib Dir) 450
SEAL, Robert A. (Univ Libn) . . . 1109

Univ of Texas at Galveston (TX)
FREY, Emil F. (Dir) 402
PHILLIPS, Carol B. (Asst Dir of
Pub Srvs) 967
WYGANT, Alice C. (Info Mgmt
Corrdntr) 1375
WYGANT, Larry J. (Assoc Dir
for Pub Srvs) 1375

Univ of Texas at Houston (TX)
CHUANG, Felicia S. (Lib Dir) . . . 213
TEUN, Rebecca L.
(Programming Srvs Supvsr) . 1233
WILLIAMS, Ann T. (Asst Libn) . . 1342

Univ of Texas at San Antonio (TX)
CRINION, Jacquelyn A. (Acqs
Libn, Bus Biblgphr) 259
JOSEPH, Margaret A. (Asst Dir
for Pub Srvs) 617
KRONICK, David A. (Prof of
Med Bibl) 679
RAY, Joyce M. (Curator of Histl
Cols) 1011
SCHMELZIE, Joan C. (Ref Libn) 1094

Univ of Texas Health Science
Center (TX)
ARMES, Patti (Assoc Dir of the
Lib) 32
CRAIG, Thomas B. (Asst to the
Dir of Lib Srvs) 254
HANKS, Ellen T. (Col Devlpmnt
& Sr Info Srvs Libn) 496
JONES, Daniel H. (Head of Col
Mgmt) 612
MAYO, Helen G. (Head) 790
PEDERSEN, Wayne A. (Med
Libn III) 954

Univ of Texas of the Permian
Basin (TX)
GROVES, Helen G. (Coordntr
for User & Info Srvs) 474
KLEPPER, Bobbie J. (Spcl Srvs
Libn) 660
LINDSAY, Lorin H. (Dir of Lib
Srvs) 729

Univ of the District of Columbia (DC)
AUERBACH, Bob S. (Ref Libn) . . . 39
JORDAN, Robert T. (Prof) 617
PAGE, John S. (Lrng Resrcs Div
Deputy Dir) 934
SARANGAPANI, Chetluru (Ref
Libn) 1082
SHEN, I Y. (Faculty Libn III) . . . 1126
THOMPSON, Elizabeth M.
(Media Spclst) 1239

Univ of the Pacific (CA)
LEONHARDT, Thomas W.
(Dean of Univ Libs) 717
MILLER, Suzanne M. (Asst Libn
for Technl Srvs) 842
NUNEZ-SCHALDACH, Ruth
(Ref Libn & Biblgphr) 912
SWANN, Arthur W. (Sci Libn
Prof Emeritus) 1213

Univ of the Philippines (PHP)
PICACHE, Ursula D. (Prof of Lib
Sci) 970
VALLEJO, Rosa M. (Dean, Inst
of Lib Sci) 1271

Univ of the South (TN)

Univ of the South Pacific (FIJ)

Univ of the West Indies (JAM)

Univ of the West Indies (TRN)

Univ of the Western Cape (SAF)

Univ of Toledo (OH)

Univ of Toronto (ON)

CAMP, Thomas E. (Theology
Sch Libn & Asst Univ Libn) . . 175
HAYMES, Don (Pub Srvs Libn) . . 516
PHILLIPS, Patricia A. (Technl
Srvs Coordntr) 968
RAWNSLEY, Virgilia I. (Pub
Srvs Coordntr) 1011
WATSON, Tom G. (VP for Univ
Relations) 1310
WOODS, Richard F. (Asst Libn) 1367
DOUGLAS, Daphne R. (Head &
Prof, Dept of Lib Std) 314
MANSINGH, Laxmi (Libn II) 767
NANTON-COMISSIONG,
Barbara L. (Deputy Libn) 887
SEPTEMBER, Peter E.
(Lecturer) 1115
BALDWIN, Julia F. (Docums
Libn) 51
BITTER, Diane S. (Catlg Dept
Head) 100
CARY, Mary K. (Asst Dir & Bus
Spclst) 191
ERNST, Gordon E. (Media
Catlgr) 353
GREEN, Denise D. (Ref Libn &
Bibl Instr) 461
LERNER, Esther T. (Instr in
German) 717
ORAM, Richard W. (Dir, Ward
Canaday Ctr for Spcl Cols) . . . 925
VOIGT, Kathleen J. (Head, Ref
Dept) 1287
WEAVER, Alice O. (Asst Ref
Libn) 1312
ANNETT, Adele M. (Serials
Catlgng Sect Head) 28
BALL, John L. (Coll Libn) 52
BELLAMY, Patricia C. (Ref
Libn) 78
BREGMAN, Alvan M. (Exec
Asst to the Dean) 131
CHERRY, Joan M. (Asst Prof,
Lib & Info Sci) 206
COOK, C D. (Prof) 239
CUMMINS, Marlene (Libn) 264
DENIS, Laurent G. (Prof) 292
FASICK, Adele M. (Prof) 366
GARLOCK, Gayle N. (Assoc
Libn) 419
GRANATSTEIN, M E. (Head
Libn) 457
HAJNAL, Peter I. (Govt Pubns
Selector) 484
HEATON, Gwynneth T. (Lib
Head) 519
HODGINS, Imelda J. (Perdcls
Sect Lib Technician) 546
HORNE, Alan J. (Devlpmnt and
Pub Affairs Coordntr) 560
HORNE, Bonnie L. (Cols Libn) . . 560
JONES, B E. (Pub Srvs Libn) . . . 611
LANDON, Richard G. (Head) . . . 693
MARSHALL, Joanne G. 774
MCLEAN-LOWE, Dallas (Ref
Libn, Libn III) 814
MEADOW, Charles T. (Prof) 819
MELVILLE, Karen E. (Placement
& Pub Relations Dir) 823
MILLS, Judy E. (Libn) 844
MOORE, Carole I. (Chief Libn) . . 858
RAE, E A. (Law Libn) 1002
SCHABAS, Ann H. (Prof and
Dean) 1088
TURKO, Karen A. (Head of
Preservation Srvs) 1263
VERYHA, Wasyl (Head, Slavic
Unit, Catlg Dept) 1283
VUKOV, Vesna (Ref Libn) 1290
WILKINSON, John P. (Prof) . . . 1340

Univ of Toronto (ON)
WILLIAMSON, Nancy J. (Prof) . 1347

Univ of Tulsa (OK)
DUCEY, Richard E. (Law Lib
Dir) 322
HILL, Linda L. (Asst Dir, Editrl
Srvs) 540
HUGHES, Carol A. (Lib Dir) 571
HUTTNER, Sidney F. (Curator,
Spcl Cols) 579
KANE, Kathy (Pub Srvs Libn) . . . 625
KEARNS, Richard P. (Bus Mgr) . 633
MURRAY, James T. (Dir of
Duplicating Srvs) 882
NELSON, Melanie D. (Pub Srvs
& Circ Law Libn) 894
PATTERSON, Robert H. (Libs &
Univ Planning Dir) 948
SANDERS, Melodie (Asst Libn,
Catlgr) 1080
SARK, Sue (Asst Dir, Col
Devlpmnt) 1083
SMITH, Donald R. (Assoc Dir for
Pub Srv, Col Devlpmnt) 1154
SMITH, Peggy C. (Assoc Dean) 1159
TOOLEY, Katherine J. (Technl
Srvs Law Libn) 1250
WEAVER, Pamela J. (Mgr of
Education) 1312

Univ of Utah (UT)
ANGIER, Jennifer J. (Lib Head) . . . 27
BAILEY, Clint R. (Records Mgr) . . 46
DOGU, Hikmet S. (Head of Fine
Arts Dept) 309
HAGGERTY, Maxine R. (Docum
Libn) 483
HANSON, Roger K. (Dir of Libs) . 498
HINZ, Julianne P. (Head of
Docums Div) 543
HOLLEY, Robert P. (Asst Dir for
Technl Srvs) 551
KRANZ, Ralph (Head Audio
Visual Div) 676
MOGREN, Paul A. (Gen Ref
Head) 852
MORRISON, David L. (Docums
& Patents Libn) 868
PATTERSON, Myron B. (Music
Libn) 948
REDDICK, Mary J. (Ref Libn) . . 1013
RUHLIN, Michele T. (Intl
Docums Libn) 1066
STODDART, Joan M. (Pub Srvs
Asst Dir) 1196
THOMSON, Ralph D. (Emeritus
Dir of Libs) 1242
VAN ORDEN, Richard D. (Head
of Online Catlgng) 1276
ZEIDNER, Christine M. (Asst Dir
for Pub Srvs) 1387

Univ of Vermont (VT)
CASWELL, Jerry V. (Syst Libn) . 194
CROUCH, Milton H. (Asst Dir
for Reader Srvs) 261
DAY, Martha T. (Media Lib Mgr) . 282
DURFEE, Tamara (Med Ref
Libn) 328
EATON, Nancy L. (Dir of Libs &
Media Srvs) 334
GALLAGHER, Connell B. (Univ
Archvst & Cur of Mss) 413
LEE, Donna K. (Ref Libn) 709
REIT, Janet W. (Media Libn) . . . 1022
SEKERAK, Robert J. (Plng Libn) 1113
WEINSTOCK, Joanna S.
(Head) 1318

Univ of Victoria (BC)
EKLAND, Patricia A. (Ref Libn) . . 341
GIBB, Betty J. (Interlib Loans
Libn) 431
HALLIWELL, Dean W. (Univ
Libn) 489
HAMILTON, Donald E. (Acting
Head, Ref Div) 492

Univ of Victoria (BC)
KOMOROUS, Hana J. (Sr
Serials Libn) 670
MOEHR, Jochen R. (Full Prof) . . . 851
ROMANIUK, Elena (Serials
Libn) 1052
ROSE, Frances E. (Govt
Docums Libn) 1054
SALMOND, Margaret A.
(Catlgng Libn) 1077
SCOTT, Priscilla R. (Circ Div
Head) 1108
SIGNORI, Donna L. (European
Langs Biblgphr & Ref Libn) . . 1137
SLADE, Alexander L. (Extension
Libn) 1147
TAGGART, William R. (Cols Div
Head) 1220
WHITE, Donald J. (Ref &
Orientation Libn) 1330

Univ of Virginia (VA)
BADER, Susan G. (User Educ
Libn) 44
BADERTSCHER, David A.
(Serials Conversion Coordntr,
Catlgr) 44
BERKELEY, Edmund (Cur,
Manuscripts & Univ Archvst) . . 87
BRAUN, Mina H. (Biblgph
Records Srvs Dir) 129
CAMPBELL, James M. (North
Europe Biblgphr) 176
CHISHOLM, Clarence E. (Dir of
Lib Srvs) 209
COOPER, Jean L. (Technl Srvs
Libn) 243
DUNNIGAN, Mary C. (Libn) 327
FARMER, Frances (Prof
Emeritus) 364
FRANTZ, Ray W. (Univ Libn) . . . 398
HURD, Douglas P. (Docum
Delivery Coordntr) 577
IVES, Gary W. (Circ Libn) 585
JORDAN, Ervin L. (Technl Srvs
Archvst & Asst Prof) 616
KRAEHE, Mary A. (African
Biblgphr/Out of Print Libn) . . . 674
LESTER, Linda L. (Ref Srvs Dir) . 718
LINDEMANN, Richard H. (Asst
Univ Archvst) 729
MALMQUIST, Katherine E. (Circ
Libn) 763
PANCAKE, Edwina (Dir) 937
RODRIGUEZ, Robert D.
(Monographs, Post-Catlgng
Unit Head) 1048
SADOWSKI, Frank E. (Tech
Srvs Asst Dir) 1074
SELF, James R. (Lib Dir) 1113
SLEEMAN, Allison M. (Catlgng
Head) 1148
STUBBS, Kendon L. (Assoc
Univ Libn) 1204
STURGIS, Marylee C. (Engl
Catlgr) 1205
THORKILDSON, Terry A. (Med
Ctr Dir) 1242
WALKER, Diane P. (Music Libn) 1295
WHITE, Lynda S. (Asst Fine
Arts Libn) 1331
WYNNE, Joseph J. (Ref Libn) . . 1375

Univ of Washington (WA)
AUSTIN, Martha L. (Head of
Physics-Astronomy Lib) 40
BENNE, Mae M. (Prof) 81
BERNARD, Molly S. (Info Srvs
Libn/User Educ Coordntr) 88
BLASE, Nancy G. (Head,
Natural Sci Lib) 104
BOLLING, Thomas E. (Ref Libn) . 112
BOYLAN, Merle N. (Dir of Libs) . 123

Univ of Washington (WA)

BRADT, Elizabeth J. (Access Srvs Libn) 126
BURSON, Scott F. (Head of Ref) 163
CHADWICK, Leroy D. (Serials Libn) 197
CHISHOLM, Margaret (Grad Sch of Lib & Info Sci Dir) 209
DENFELD, Kay F. 291
DIBIASE, Linda P. (Asst Col Devlpmnt Libn) 299
ENGEMAN, Richard H. (Libn) . . . 349
FASSETT, William E. (Asst Prof of Pharmacy) 366
FIDEL, Raya (Assoc Prof) 374
FRALEY, David B. (Ref & User Educ Libn) 395
FUGATE, Cynthia S. (Docums Serials Libn) 408
GREEN, Carol C. (Head of Forest Resrcs Lib) 461
HAZELTON, Penelope A. (Law Libn & Prof of Law) 517
HENSLEY, Randall B. (User Educ Libn) 529
HIATT, Peter (Prof) 536
HILDEBRANDT, Darlene M. (Comptng Info Srvs Adminstr) 538
HILLER, Steven Z. (Head of Sci Dept) 541
JEWELL, Timothy D. (Online Ref Libn) 600
KETCHELL, Debra S. (WA Hlth Info Netwk Coordntr) 645
LIPTON, Laura E. (Horticultural Libn) 732
LOPEZ, Loretta K. (Ref & Educ Libn) 741
LORD, Charles R. (Engrng Libn) . 741
MAACK, David J. (Foreign & Intl Govt Pubns Libn) 753
MAHONEY, Laura E. (Head Catlg Libn) 761
MENGES, Gary L. (Div Head) . . . 824
MIDDLETON, Dale R. (Hlth Scis Lib & Info Ctr Assoc Dir) 833
MOFJELD, Pamela A. (Head) . . . 852
MURDOCH, Martha T. (Mathematics Resrch Lib Head) 879
PASSARELLI, Anne B. (Bus Admin Lib Head) 946
PRESS, Nancy O. (Educ Coordntr) 991
PRITCHARD, Jackie L. (Asst Natural Scis Libn) 994
REDALJE, Susanne J. (Chem Lib & Info Srvs Head) 1013
RICKERSON, Carla (Pacific Northwest Col Head) 1031
ROWBERG, Alan H. (Asst Prof) 1062
SCHUELLER, Janette H. (Spcl Projs Libn) 1101
SENN, Sharon L. (Student) 1115
SERCOMBE, Laurel (Ethnomusicology Archvst) . . 1116
SKELLEY, Grant T. (Assoc Prof) 1145
SOPER, Mary E. (Asst Prof) . . . 1168
STEVENS, Peter H. (Head) 1190
SY, Karen J. (Asst Prof) 1217
VAN MASON, Patricia M. (Serials Catlgr Half-Time) . . . 1276
WALKER, Paula B. (Libs for Undergrad Srvs Asst Dir) . . . 1296
WEAVER, Carolyn G. (Assoc Dir) 1312
WIREN, Harold N. (Engrng Lib & Info Srvs Head) 1356

Univ of Waterloo (ON)

BEGLO, Jo N. (Libn of Fine Arts & Architecture) 74
PARROTT, James R. (Ref Libn) . 944
SHEPHERD, Murray C. (Univ Libn) 1127

Univ of West Florida (FL)

DEBOLT, W D. (Spcl Cols Dir) . . 284
DOERRER, David H. (Asst Dir of Tech Prcsng) 308
JOHNSON, Theresa P. (Humanities & Interlib Loan Libn) 609
MOREIN, P G. (Lib Dir) 863
PERDUE, Robert W. (Ref Libn, Asst Dept Head) 958
TOIFEL, Peggy W. (Head, Ref Dept) 1248

Univ of West Los Angeles (CA)
Univ of Western Ontario (ON)

BRISTOL, Arlen A. (Univ Libn) . . 137
CLOUSTON, John S. (Cols Mgmt Dept Head) 223
CRAVEN, Timothy C. (Assoc Prof) 256
FYFE, Janet H. (Sch of Lib & Info Sci Prof) 411
GALSWORTHY, Peter R. (Libn) . 415
KATZER, Sylvia U. (Coordntr, Northern Outreach Lib Srv) . . 630
LAW, Jean M. (Info Ofcr) 704
LUTZ, Linda J. (Head of Acqs Dept) 750
MEERVELD, Bert (Head of Prcsng) 821
MILLER, Beth M. (Coop Work Study Prog Coordntr) 836
NEILL, Sam D. (Prof) 892
NELSON, Michael J. (Asst Prof) . 894
RIPLEY, Victoria E. (Academic Support Srvs Coordntr) 1035
SCHULTE-ALBERT, Hans G. (Sch of Lib & Info Sci Assoc Prof) 1101
SMITH, Louise (Cols Libn for Music) 1157
TAGUE, Jean M. (Dean) 1220
WHITE, Janette H. (Prof & Dean Asst) 1331

Univ of Windsor (ON)

SINGLETON, Cynthia B. (Reader Srvs Dept Head) . . . 1143
SOULES, Aline E. (Syst Dept Head) 1169
WOLFE, Martha K. (Libn, Reader Srv Dept) 1361

Univ of Winnipeg (MB)

CONVERSE, Wm R. (Chief Libn) 239
DELONG, Linwood R. (Ref Libn) . 290

Univ of Wisconsin at Eau Claire (WI)

ENGELDINGER, Eugene A. (Head of Pub Srvs) 349
FOSTER, Leslie A. (Govt Pubns Libn) 392
MARQUARDT, Steve R. (Libs Dir) 772
THOMPSON, Glenn J. (Dept Chairman) 1239

Univ of Wisconsin at Fon du Lac (WI)

EBERT, John J. (Asst Academic Libn) 334

Univ of Wisconsin at Fond du Lac (WI)
Univ of Wisconsin at La Crosse (WI)

FRICK, John W. (Asst Prof) 403
HILL, Edwin L. (Chair of Lib Dept & Spcl Cols Libn) 539
SECHREST, Sandra L. (Docum Libn) 1110

Univ of Wisconsin at Madison (WI)

ARNESON, Arne J. (Dir, Mills Music Lib) 33
ARNOLD, Barbara J. (Admissions Placement Counselor) 33
BLANKENBURG, Julie J. (Docums Asst) 104
BOLL, John J. (Prof) 112
BOYER, Ann T. (Lib Srvs Asst) . 123
BUNGE, Charles A. (Prof) 157

Univ of Wisconsin at Madison (WI)

CARR, Jo A. (Dir) 185
CENTER, Sue L. (Pub Srvs
Asst Dir) 196
CRAWFORD, Josephine
(Automation Mgr) 256
DAVIS, Sally A. (Lib Dir) 281
DEWEY, Gene L. (Head, Acqs
Dept) 298
DILLON, John B. (European
Hum Biblgphr) 303
DIXON, Edith M. (Automation
Libn) 306
GALNEDER, Mary H. (Map
Libn) 415
GAPEN, D K. (Gen Lib Syst Dir) . 416
GIEBEL, Thomas W. (Docums
Delivery) 432
HERMAN, Gertrude B. (Prof
Emeritus) 531
HOPKINS, Dianne M. (Asst
Prof) 557
HSIEH-YEE, Ingrid P. (Tchg
Asst) 567
JESUDASON, Melba (Pub Srvs
Libn) 600
KRIKELAS, James (Prof) 678
KRUSE, Ginny M. (Dir) 681
LIVNY, Efrat (Biotech Info
Resrcs Facility Dir) 735
MCCLEMENTS, Nancy A. (Pub
Srvs Libn) 796
MONROE, Margaret E. (Prof
Emeritus) 855
NEILL, Priscilla (Asst Dir for
Persnl & Comm) 892
PAUL, Nancy A. (Technl Srvs
Asst Dir) 949
POPE, Nolan F. (Assoc Dir for
Automation) 983
POPLAWSKY, Diane M. (Spcl
Libn) 983
REEB, Richard C. (Notis
Implementation Coordntr) . . . 1014
ROBBINS, Jane B. (Dir) 1038
ROSENSHIELD, Jill K. (Hum
Libn) 1057
ROUSE, Kendall G. (Chem Lib
Head) 1061
SCHULTZ, Ellen A. (Ref & Info
Srvs Div Libn) 1102
SEARING, Susan E. (Women's
Std Libn) 1109
SESSIONS, Robert 1117
THOMPSON, Jean T. (Asst Dir
for Ref & Info Srvs) 1240
WALKER, Richard D. (Prof) . . . 1296
WEINGAND, Darlene E. (Prof) . 1318
WELSCH, Erwin K. (European
Hist Libn) 1323
WHITCOMB, Dorothy V. (Histl
Col Cur & Ref Lib) 1330
WIEGAND, Wayne A. (Assoc
Prof) 1336
WILCOX, Patricia F. (Assoc
Acad Libn II) 1338
WILLETT, Holly G. (Asst Prof) . 1341
WILLIAMSON, William L. (Prof
Emeritus) 1348
XIA, Hong (Project Asst) 1376
YOUNGER, Jennifer A. (Asst
Dir of Centl Technl Srvs) . . . 1383
ZOLLER, R T. (Foreign Law
Libn) 1390
ZWEIZIG, Douglas L. (Prof) . . . 1392

Univ of Wisconsin at Marinette (WI)
SCOFIELD, Constance V. (Dir) . 1106

Univ of Wisconsin at Milwaukee (WI)

Univ of Wisconsin at Oshkosh (WI)

Univ of Wisconsin at Parkside (WI)

Univ of Wisconsin at Platteville (WI)

Univ of Wisconsin at River Falls (WI)

**Univ of Wisconsin at Stevens
Point (WI)**

Univ of Wisconsin at Stout (WI)

Univ of Wisconsin at Superior (WI)

AMAN, Mary J. (Ref Libn) 19
AMAN, Mohammed M. (Dean) . . . 19
BARUTH, Christopher M. 62
BJORKLUND, Edi (Rare Books
& Spcl Cols Libn) 100
BLUE, Richard I. (Sch of Lib &
Info Sci Asst Prof) 107
BOULANGER, Mary E. 119
FONG, Wilfred W. (Resrc Ctr
Mgr) 388
GREENE, Victor R. (Hist Prof) . . . 464
HAENSEL, Kathrine C. 482
HARTIG, Linda (Music Libn) 508
JONES, Richard E. (Acqs & Col
Mgmt Head) 614
KOVAN, Allan S. (Univ Archvst) . 673
LUECHT, Richard M. (Comp
Applications Spclst) 747
MARKOWETZ, Marianna C.
(Educ Libn) 771
MORITZ, William D. (Assoc Lib
Dir) 865
PESCHEL, Susan M. (Catlgr,
Ref Libn) 961
POPESCU, Constantin C.
(Assoc Libn) 983
RISTIC, Jovanka (Ref Libn,
Catlgr & Indxr) 1036
SABLE, Martin H. (Prof) 1072
SCHERDIN, Mary J. (Asst
Dean) 1092
STANTON, Vida C. (Asst Prof) . 1181
SWEETLAND, James H. (Asst
Prof) 1215
TOBIN, R J. (Ref Libn) 1247
FU, Tina C. (Assoc Prof) 407
JONES, Norma L. (Acting Exec
Dir) 614
KRUEGER, Gerald J. (Docums
Libn) 680
SHARMA, Ravindra N. (Asst Dir
for Pub Srvs) 1122
BARUTH, Barbara P. (Asst Dir
of Tech Srvs & Info Spclst) 62
PIELE, Linda J. (Assoc Dir) 971
TRUPIANO, Rose M. (Online
Srvs Coordntr) 1259
DANIELS, Jerome P. (Lib Dir) . . . 273
GERLACH, Donald E. (Asst
Prof) 429
SCHMITT, Madelaine M.
(Catlgng, Ref Libn) 1096
ADAM, Anthony J. (Col Mgr) 4
FORTIN, Clifford C. (Lib Sci &
Media Educ Prof) 391
STEINWALL, Susan D. (Dir of
Area Rsrch Ctr) 1186
GILLESBY, John D. (Head Ref
Libn) 435
PAUL, Patricia J. (Head of
Catlgng) 949
STRUPP, Sybil A. (Catlgr) 1203
GRAF, David L. (Prog Dir &
Chairperson) 455
JAX, John J. (Lib Dir & Asst
Dean for Lrng Resrcs) 595
OLSON, Dennis H. (Ref & EMC
Libn) 922
SAWIN, Philip Q. (Col Devlpmnt
Ofcr) 1086
CARMACK, Bob (Lib & Media
Resrcs Dir) 183
JOHNSON, Denise J. (Pub Srvs
Libn, Instr) 603
TORNQUIST, Kristi M. (Col
Devlpmnt and Bibl Instr) 1251

Univ of Wisconsin at Whitewater (WI)　MANDERNACK, Scott B. (Info & Instrc Libn) 765
PAYSON, Evelyn H. (Dir of Lib Automation) 951
SCHARFENBERG, George E. (Lib Srvs Asst) 1090
WESTON, Karen A. (Info & Instrc Libn) 1327

Univ of Wyoming (WY)　BALDWIN, David A. (Assoc Dir for Pub Srv) 51
BURMAN, Marilyn P. (Pub Srvs Libn) 161
CHATTON, Barbara A. (Asst Prof) 204
CHISUM, Emmett D. (Resrch Histn, Prof) 209
COLLIER, Carol A. (Head) 232
CORS, Paul B. (Catlg Libn) 248
COTTAM, Keith M. (Dir of Libs) . 250
EMERSON, Tamsen L. (Sr Asst Libn) 347
MACK, Bonnie R. (Coordntr Hlth Scis Info Network) 756
MEALEY, Catherine E. (Law Libn, Prof of Law) 820
NELSON, Michael L. (Soc Sci Ref Libn) 894
OSTRYE, Anne T. (Head, Ref Dept) 929
ROOS, Tedine J. (Sr Asst Libnb) 1053
SEEBAUM, Carol J. (Libn) 1111
STEWART, William L. (Assoc Dir) 1193
VANARSDALE, William O. (Col Devlpmnt Ofcr) 1272
WOODS, Janet R. (Support Srvs Head) 1367

Univ Publications of America (MD)　REINERSTEIN, Gail G. (Sales Representative) 1021

Univ Research Corp (MD)　MARTINEZ-GOLDMAN, Aline (Info Spclst) 779

Univ Sch of Nashville (TN)　EISENSTEIN, Jill M. (High Sch Libn) 341

Univ System of Georgia (GA)　HENDERSON, Mary E. (Lib Dir) . 526
Unocal Corp (CA)　OROSZ, Barbara J. (Head Libn) . 926
Unz & Co (NJ)　KAZIMIR, Edward O. (VP) 632
SCOTT, Daniel T. 1107
Updata Publications Inc (CA)　SCLAR, Herbert (Pres) 1106
The Upjohn Co (MI)　ALLRED, Paula M. (Lib Info Spclst) 17
EVERITT, Janet M. (Sr Lib Info Spclst III) 359
HOMAN, J M. (Info Srvs Head) .. 555
MACKSEY, Julie A. (Info Scitst) . 757
NOBLE, Valerie (Mgr) 906
POWELL, James R. (Sr Info Scitst) 988
SATTLER, Pauline (PIRSU Project Leader) 1084
SLACH, June E. (Info Scitst I) .. 1147
WORDEN, Diane D. (Sr Info Spclst) 1369
Upper Arlington City Schs (OH)　DRIESSEN, Diane (Sch Libn) ... 320
Upper Arlington Pub Lib (OH)　ANDERSON, Carl A. (Asst Dir) ... 21
Upper Columbia Academy (WA)　MOLLER, Steffen A. (Dir) 853
Upper Cumberland Regional Lib (TN)　NICHOLS, Dolores D. (Asst Dir) . 901
Upper Darby Township & Seller Memrl Lib (PA)　JUSHCHYSHYN, Caroline B. (Branch Libn) 620
Upper Merion Township (PA)　HELICHER, Karl W. (Dir) 524
Upper Saddle River Pub Lib (NJ)　NEWMARK-KRUGER, Barbara (Dir) 900
Upper Savannah Area Health Educ Cnsrtm (SC)　HILL, Thomas W. (Libn) 541
Urbach Kahn & Werlin PC (NY)　DENOTO, Dorothy E. (Info Spclst) 293
Urban Institute (DC)　MOTTA, Camille A. (Dir, Lib Archvs) 872

Urban Libs Council (IL)　LADENSON, Alex (Executive Dir) 687
Urbana Free Lib (IL)　EDSTROM, James A. (Archs Dir) 337
HOGAN, Mary R. (Ref Libn) ... 549
REPTA, Vada L. (Chlds Libn) .. 1024
SCHLIPF, Frederick A. (Exec Dir) 1094
URS Corp (CA)　PRELINGER, Polly (Info Systs Mgr) 990
URS Dalton (OH)　SPAHR, Cheryl L. (Resrc Ctr Mgr) 1170
URS International-Trans Asia (IDN)　STONE, Clarence W. (Consult) . 1197
Ursuline Academy High Sch (DE)　ASTORGA, Alicia M. (Head Libn) 37
RECHNITZ, Harriet L. (Lib & Media Spclst) 1013
Ursuline Coll (OH)　BELKIN, Betsey B. (Lib Dir) 76
Ursuline Motherhouse (KY)　HEINTZMAN, Justina (Storyteller) 522
Ursuline Sisters (KY)　WALLER, M C. (Archvst) 1298
USA ITAC (DC)　ROBB, Thomas W. (Comp Spclst) 1038
USAA Group (TX)　TODD, Leslie N. (Libn) 1248
USACO Corp (JAP)　YAMAKAWA, Takashi (Pres) .. 1376
User Education ISI (PA)　TEMOS, Barbara (Lectr) 1230
USI Chemicals Co (OH)　RUDY, Michelle M. (Techl Libn) 1066
USN EOD (MD)　DAVIS, Bonnie D. (Tech Lib Div Head) 277
USX Corp (PA)　BERGER, Lewis W. (Sr Info Spclst) 85
CANTRALL, Rebecca J. (Libn) .. 179
POLLIS, Angela R. (Staff Supvsr) 981
Utah International Inc (CA)　DEWOLF, Timothy B. (Info Spclst) 298
Utah State Archives & Records Service (UT)　HEFNER, Loretta L. (Bureau Mgr) 520
JOHNSON, Jeffery O. (Mgr, Ref Bureau) 606
MOORE, Gwen A. (Certified Records Mgr) 859
NASH, Cherie A. (Archvst) 888
WOOD, Steven R. (Prcsng Archvst) 1365
Utah State Government (UT)　JENSEN, Charla J. (Info Analyst) 598
Utah State Historical Society (UT)　EVANS, Max J. (Dir) 357
Utah State Lib (UT)　BUTTARS, Gerald A. (Prog Dir) . 167
DOWNEY REIDA, Linda K. (Continuing Educ & Catlgng Libn) 316
HINDMARSH, Douglas P. (Ref Srvs Dir) 542
OWEN, Amy (Deputy Dir) 931
Utah State Univ (UT)　ANDERSON, Janet A. (Serials & Current Perdcls Head) 23
HAYCOCK, Richard C. (Assoc Dean) 515
NIELSEN, Steven P. (Bus Mgr) .. 903
PIETTE, Mary I. (Ref Libn) 972
WEISS, Stephen C. (Docums & Gen Ref) 1320
Utica City Schs (NY)　SCHEU, Susan P. (Sch Lib Media Spclst) 1092
Utica Pub Lib (NY)　BROOKES, Barbara (Ref Lib) ... 140
MOUSTAFA, Theresa A. (Libn) .. 874
Utility Fuels Inc (TX)　PHILLIPS, Toni M. (Info Ctr Spclst) 969
Utlans International of Canada Inc (ON)　BROWNING, Linda A. 148
Utlas International of Canada Inc (ON)　FRITZ, Richard J. (Authority Ctl Libn) 405
TAYLOR, Karen E. (Account Mgr) 1227

Utlas International US Inc (CA)   LIGHTBOWN, Parke P. (VP) . . . 726
SPENCER, John T. (Systs
Devlpmnt) 1173
Utlas International US Inc (KS)   ALLEN, Norene F. (Natl Sales
Mgr) 15
ROTH, Sally (Proposal Analyst) . 1059
SEVIER, Susan G. (Bids Mgr) . . 1117
Utlas International US Inc (MO)   HANIFORD, K L. (Regnl Mgr) . . . 496
Utlas International US Inc (ON)   CURTIS, Alison J. (Local Systs
Mktg) 267

V

V B Cook Co Limited (ON)   SENNETT, Judith A. (Libn) 1115
Vacaville Unified Sch District (CA)   MATTHIES, Donna K. (Libn) . . . 786
Valdosta State Coll (GA)   CLARK, Tommy A. (Head of
User Srvs) 218
CRAWFORD, Sherrida J. (Circ
Libn) 257
MONTGOMERY, Denise L. (Ref
& Interlib Loan Libn) 856
PAULK, Betty D. (Technl Srvs
Head) 950
WRIGHT, Dianne H. (Ref Sect
Head) 1371
Valencia Community Coll (FL)   HENDERSON, Patricia A. (Libn) . 526
HUTCHINSON, Beck (Adjunct
Faculty) 579
Valentine Museum (VA)   KIMBALL, Gregg D. (Cur of Bks
& Mss) 649
Valerie Metzler Archivist &
Historian (IL)   METZLER, Valerie (Founder) . . . 829
Valhalla Pub Schs (NY)   HIGGINS, Judith H. (Lib Media
Spclst) 538
Valley Forge Christian Coll (PA)   REYNOLDS, Dorsey (Libn) 1025
Valley Hospital (NJ)   ALLOCCO, Claudia (Med Lib
Dir) 17
Valley National Bank of Arizona (AZ)   GORMAN, Judith F. (Libn) 452
Valley News Dispatch (PA)   LANG, Audrey H. (Lib Dir) 695
Valley Regional Lib Syst (GA)   BAKER, Rowena E. (Head,
Technl Srvs Dept) 49
Valley View Elementary Sch (TX)   GILLETTE, Robert S. (Lrng
Resrcs Spclst) 435
Valley View Sch District 365U (IL)   MUNN, Patty L. (Libn) 879
Valparaiso Univ (IN)   HOLTERHOFF, Sarah G.
(Docums Libn) 555
MEYER, Ellen R. (Ref Libn,
Coordntr of Biblgph Instr) 830
MILLS, Richard E. (Asst Law
Libn) 844
PERRY, Margaret (Dir of Libs) . . . 960
PERSYN, Mary G. (Law Libn &
Assoc Prof of Law) 961
WATTS, Tim J. (Pub Srvs Libn) 1310
Value Line Inc (NY)   CLANCY, Kathy (Head Libn &
Dept Mgr) 215
Van Buren County Lib (MI)   TATE, David L. (Dir) 1225
Van Camp Information
Associates (IN)   VAN CAMP, Ann J. 1272
Vance-Granville Community Coll (NC)   SINCLAIR, R F. (Libn & Instr) . . 1142
Vancouver Board of Trade (BC)   MAROTZ, Karen V. (Info Srvs
Mgr) 772
Vancouver Community Coll (BC)   ANASTASIOU, Joan D. (Lib
Technician Prog Coordntr) 21
APPLETON, Brenda F.
(Campus Libn) 30
CARTER, Charles R. (Coll
Resrcs Dir) 189
WIEBE, Frieda (Campus Libn) . . 1336
Vancouver General Hospital (BC)   TRIP, Barbara M. (Libn) 1257
Vancouver Island Regional Lib (BC)   MEADOWS, Donald F. (Dir) 819
Vancouver Pub Lib (BC)   BELL, Barbara (Ref Srvs Chief
Libn) 76
CAMPBELL, Brian G. (Systs
Libn) 176
CAPES, Judy L. (Chief Lending
Srvs Libn) 179
DURSTON, Corinne L. (Head,
Youth Dept) 329

Vancouver Pub Schs (WA)   ZALESKI, Mary A. (Media
Spclst) 1385
Vancouver Sch Board (BC)   HAYCOCK, Kenneth R. (Head
of Prog Srvs) 515
Vancouver Sch of Theology (BC)   HART, Elizabeth (Libn) 507
Vancouver Vocational Inst (BC)   DEVAKOS, Elizabeth R. (Pub
Srvs Libn) 297
Vanderbilt Medical Center (TN)   LEWIS, Carol E. (Ref Libn) 722
Vanderbilt Univ (TN)   BRANTIGAN-STOWELL,
Martha J. (Monographs
Catlgr) 129
BROSS, Valerie (Serials Catlgr) . 141
CHENEY, Frances N. (Prof
Emerita) 206
DAVIS, Susan W. (Preservation
Libn) 281
ELDRIDGE, Virginia L. (User
Srvs Libn) 342
GETZ, Malcolm (Assoc Provost
for Info Srvs & Tech) 430
GRAHAM, Sylvia R. (Asst Dir) . . 456
HARWELL, Sara J. (Archvst &
Libn) 509
HELGUERA, Byrd S. (Assoc Dir
& Asst Dir for Pub Srvs) 524
HODGES, Terence M. (Dir) 546
KAVASS, Igor I. (Prof of Law &
Legal Info Ctr Dir) 631
LASATER, Mary C.
(Monographs Libn) 700
LEE, Geoffrey J. (Asst for
Devlpmnt & Lib Relations) . . . 710
LEISERSON, Annabelle (Acqs
Libn) 714
LYNCH, Frances H. (Asst Dir for
Technl Srvs) 751
MANNING, Dale (Engl,
Linguistics & Drama Biblgphr) . 766
PARKS, Dorothy R. (Dir of the
Divinity Lib) 943
PILKINGTON, James P.
(Adminstr) 973
QUINN, Joan M. (Info Srvs Libn) 1000
RICHARDS, Timothy F. (Centl &
Sci Libs Dir) 1028
RIEKE, Judith L. (Serials Libn,
Med Ctr Lib) 1033
ROMANS, Lawrence M. (Ref &
Docums Libn) 1052
SHABB, Cynthia H. (Sci Libn) . . 1118
STEFFEY, Ramona J.
(Automation Proj Libn) 1185
TAYLOR, William R. (Info Srvs
Coordntr) 1229
WILBURN, Clouse R. (Assoc
Prof) 1338
WILSON, Florence J. (Asst Dir
of Systs) 1351
WOLFE, Marice (Univ Archvst,
Dept Head) 1361
Vanguard Technologies Corp (VA)   STEIN, Karen E. (Analyst & Info
Spclst) 1185
Vanier Coll (PQ)   RATNER, Sabina T. (Prof of
Music) 1010
Vanitch (DE)   HITCHENS, Howard B.
(Communications Consult) . . . 544
Varian Associates (CA)   FARMAR, Donna M. (Sr Libn) . . . 364
MURPHY, Joan F. (Technl Lib
Mgr) 880
Varix Corp (TX)   SACKETT-WILK, Susan A.
(Software Libn) 1073
Vassar Coll (NY)   DURNIAK, Barbara A. (Ref
Libn/Database Search
Coordntr) 328
HILL, Thomas E. (Art Libn) 541
JEANNENEY, Mary L. (Ref,
Circ & Rsvs Libn) 596
LACKS, Bernice K. (Readers
Srvs Head) 686

Vassar Coll (NY)

MACKECHNIE, Nancy S. (Asst Cur of Rare Bks & Mss) 756

MAUL, Shirley A. (Asst Head of ReaderS Srvs) 787

RANSOM, Sarah B. (Music Catlgr) 1007

WEISS, Sabrina L. (Music Libn) 1320

WILLIAMS, Esther L. (Sci Ref Libn) 1343

Vaughan Pub Libs (ON)

KOSTIAK, Adele E. (Branch Operations Adminstrv Libn) . . . 673

VCH Publishers Inc (NY)

GRAYSON, Martin (Pres) 460

Vector Biology & Control Project (VA)   AUSTON, Ione (Info Spclst) 40

Ventress Memorial Lib (MA)

CORCORAN, Dennis R. (Lib Dir) 245

Ventura County Lib Services Agency (CA)

ADENIRAN, Dixie D. (Lib Srvs Dir) 6

BRONARS, Lori A. (Sr Libn) 140

REDFIELD, Dale E. (Sr Libn) . . . 1014

Veracorp (NY)   DESMOND, Andrew R. (Edit) 295

Vermillion Pub Lib (SD)   LARSON, Jane A. (Dir) 699

Vermont Department of Libs (VT)

CASSELL, Marianne K. (Devlpmnt & Adult Srvs Consult) 193

GREENE, Grace W. (Chlds Srvs Consult) 464

WARD, Robert C. (Regnl Libn) . 1304

Vermont Technical Coll (VT)   LAMSON, Maria W. (Ref Libn) . . 691

PATTERSON, Dewey F. (Lib Dir) 948

Vernon Free Lib (VT)   EVANS, Nancy I. (Libn) 357

Vernon Sch District 22 (BC)   FUNK, Grace E. (Libn) 410

GRABINSKY, Warren B. (Supvsr of Instrc) 455

Verona Pub Lib (NJ)   TRAFTON, William M. (Technl Srvs Head) 1253

Veronis Suhler & Associates Inc (NY)   BODDORF, James E. (Exec VP) . 109

DRONZEK, Ronald (Resrch Dir) . 320

HADLEY, J M. (Sr VP) 482

HALE, Paul E. (VP) 485

HUNNEWELL, Walter (Assoc) . 574

LAMB, David C. (VP) 689

SCHULTE, Anthony M. (Exec VP) 1101

SHAPIRO, Marvin L. (Exec VP) . 1121

STEVENSON, Jeffery T. (Sr VP) 1191

SUHLER, John S. (Pres) 1207

VERONIS, John J. (Chairman) . . 1283

Verrill & Dana (ME)   REIMAN, Anne M. (Law Libn) . . 1020

Versailles Exempted Village Schs (OH)

MINNICH, Conrad H. (High Sch Lib Media Spclst) 846

Versatec (CA)   TYLER, Sharon R. (Technl Info Spclst) 1266

Vestal Pub Lib (NY)   LA SORTE, Antonia J. (Adult Srvs & Ref Libn) 700

Veterans Administration (PA)   FALGER, David E. (Chief of Lib Srv) 362

Veterans Administration Central Office (DC)   MASSAY, Mary K. (Ref Libn) . . . 782

Veterans Administration Hospital (NY)

LEHNOFF-ONGIRSKI, Hannelore (Psychiatrist Officer of the Day) 713

Veterans Administration Lakeside Med Ctr (IL)

KINNAIRD, Cheryl D. (Med Libn) 653

Veterans Administration Medical Center (AL)   WILLIAMS, Nelle T. (Med Libn) 1345

Veterans Administration Medical Center (AR)   ZUMWALT, George M. (Chief of Lib Srv) 1391

Veterans Administration Medical Center (CA)

BRUGUERA, Eva A. (Libn) 150

CONNOLLY, Betty F. (Lib Srvs Chief) 237

Veterans Administration Medical Center (CA)

CONNOR, Paul L. (Biomedical Libn) 238

GOUVEIA, Sara C. (Med Libn) . 454

HUCKINS, Barbara W. (Lib Srv Chief) 569

LEONARD, Jean E. 716

MAYERS, Deborah L. (Clinical Libn) 789

MEYER, Cynthia K. (Lib Srv Chief) 830

Veterans Administration Medical Center (CO)

BRAGDON, Lynn (Chief, Lib Srv) 127

Veterans Administration Medical Center (DC)   RENNINGER, Karen (Div Chief) 1023

Veterans Administration Medical Center (GA)

SCHNICK, Robert M. (Med Libn) 1097

Veterans Administration Medical Center (IA)

BROWN, Jeanine B. (Chief, Lib Srv) 144

KRAUS, Marilyn J. (Med Libn) . . 676

Veterans Administration Medical Center (IL)

TROFIMUK, Janette A. (Med Libn) 1257

Veterans Administration Medical Center (IN)

ALFRED, Judith C. (Lib Srv Chief) 13

Veterans Administration Medical Center (KS)

GOTTSHALL, Judith L. (Med Libn) 454

Veterans Administration Medical Center (KY)   BAUGH, E S. (Lib Technician) . . . 65

Veterans Administration Medical Center (LA)

JONES, Dixie A. (Libn, Med & Biog Scis) 612

NEVEU, Wilma B. (Lib Srvs Chief) 897

Veterans Administration Medical Center (MA)

DEWEY, Marjorie C. (Lib Srv Chief) 298

KERN, Donald C. (Assoc Dir) . . . 643

NOYES, Suzanne N. (Lib Srv Chief) 911

Veterans Administration Medical Center (MD)

SCHULTZ, Barbara A. (Chief Lib Srvs) 1101

STOUT, Deborah A. (Lib Srv Chief) 1198

Veterans Administration Medical Center (MI)

BURHANS, Barbara C. (Med Libn) 159

DURIVAGE, Mary J. (Med Libn) . 328

DUROCHER, Jeanne M. (Lib Srv Chief) 328

SMITH, Victoria A. (Lib Srv Actg Chief) 1161

Veterans Administration Medical Center (MN)

SINHA, Dorothy P. (Med Libn) . 1143

STANKE, Judith U. (Med Libn) . 1180

Veterans Administration Medical Center (MO)

REPETTO, Ann M. (Libn) 1023

SMITH, Valerie K. (Med Libn) . . 1161

WEITKEMPER, Larry D. (Lib Srv Chief) 1320

Veterans Administration Medical Center (NC)

LAMBREMONT, Jane A. (Lib Srv Chief) 691

OWSLEY, Lucile C. (Med Libn) . . 932

Veterans Administration Medical Center (NH)

MCGINNIS, Joan M. (Chief Libn) 806

Veterans Administration Medical Center (NM)

MYER, Nancy E. (Chief, Lib Srv) 884

Veterans Administration Medical Center (NY)
BLAKE-O'HOGAN, Kathleen E. (Asst Chief Libn) 103
HALL, Russell W. (Med Libn) ... 488
LISZCZYNSKYJ, Halyna A. (Med Libn) 733
SHER, Deborah M. (Chief of Lib Srv) 1127
WISEMAN, Karin M. (Med Libn) 1357

Veterans Administration Medical Center (OH)
NOURSE, Mary E. (Med Libn) ... 910
TESMER, Nancy (Lib Srv Chief) 1233

Veterans Administration Medical Center (OK)
GUTIERREZ, Carolyn A. (Libn) .. 479

Veterans Administration Medical Center (OR)
JORDAN, Cathryn M. (Lib Srv Chief) 616

Veterans Administration Medical Center (PA)
BURTON, Mary L. (Lib Srv Chief) 164
KAGER, Jeffrey F. (Chief, Lib Srv) 621

Veterans Administration Medical Center (RI)
LLOYD, Lynn A. (Chief, Lib Srv) . 735

Veterans Administration Medical Center (TN)
EUBANKS, Marie (Med Libn) ... 356
GAUDET, Susan E. (Med Libn) .. 422

Veterans Administration Medical Center (TX)
CAMPBELL, Shirley A. (Med Libn) 177

Veterans Administration Medical Center (WA)
HARBOLD, Mary J. (Admin Libn) 499
JONES, Ruth A. (Chief, Lib Srv) . 615
LEVI, Dennis L. (Chief, Lib Srv) .. 720

Veterans Administration W Los Angeles (CA)
DAVIS, Marianne W. (Hospital Planner) 280

Veterans Admin West Side Medical Center (IL)
MORRIS, Lynne D. (Lib Srv Chief) 867

Veterans General Hospital (TAI)
CHUO, Josephine Y. (Chief Libn) 213

Veterans Memorial Pub Lib (ND)
HILDEBRANT, Darrel D. (Prog Coordntr) 539
WALDERA, Katherine A. (Ref and Info Srvs) 1294

Via Le Monde Productions (PQ)
NAGY, Cecile (Indxr) 886

Via Rail Canada Inc (PQ)
DUSABLON-BOTTEGA, Nicole (Lib Analyst) 329

Victor Free Lib (NY)
KELLY, Patricia A. (Lib Dir) 638

Victoria Coll & Univ of Houston (TX)
MCCORD, Stanley J. (Lib Dir) ... 798

Victoria County Board of Education (ON)
DEKKER, Barbara A. (Tchr Libn) 288

Victoria Independent Sch District (TX)
FRANKSON, Marie S. (Asst Libn) 398

Victoria Univ (ON)
BRANDEIS, Robert C. 128

Videodial Inc (NY)
THOMAS, Hilary B. 1236

Videolog Communications (CT)
BRIGISH, Alan P. (Pres) 136

Vidionics International Database (CA)
DAVISSON, Darell D. (Owner & Mgr) 281

Vigo County Pub Lib (IN)
KASER, John A. (AV Dept Head) 628
RAWLES-HEISER, Carolyn (Adminstrv Coordntr) 1010
WERT, Alice L. (Technl Srvs Coordntr) 1325

Vigo County Sch Corp (IN)
BRETT, Lorraine E. (Catlgr) 134
HANKS, Gardner C. (Asst Dir) .. 496

Villa Duchesne Sch (MO)
BREIMEIER, Lois (Libn) 132

Villa Maria Coll (NY)
DOBRZYNSKI, Terenita (Lib Dir) 307

Villa Maria Coll (PA)
ONUFFER, Joachim (Dir Curr, Media Libn) 924

Villa Park Pub Lib (IL)

Village of Bronxville (NY)
Village of Endicott (NY)
Village of Glen Carbon (IL)
Village of Irvington (NY)
Village of Randolph (WI)
Village of Tuckahoe (NY)
Village of Whitefish Bay (WI)
Villanova Univ (PA)

Vincennes Univ (IN)

Vincentian Sisters of Charity (PA)

Vinson & Elkins (TX)
Vintage Jazz Inc (MA)

Vinton Community Schs (IA)

Virgin Islands Department of Education (VI)

Virgin Islands Department of Health (VI)

Virgin Islands Government (VI)
Virgin Islands Lib Association (VI)
Virginia Beach City Pub Schs (VA)
Virginia Beach Department of Pub Libs (VA)

Virginia Beach Pub Lib (VA)

Virginia Commonwealth Univ (VA)

BALCOM, William T. (Lib Adminstr) 51
RYAN, Marilyn P. (Asst Adminstr & Head of Adult Srvs) 1071
SELVAR, Jane C. (Lib Dir) 1114
LOCKE, Stanley J. (Lib Dir) 736
DAVISON, Carol A. (Libn) 281
PERILLO, Marie J. (Lib Dir) 958
DEICH, Ione L. (Dir) 288
STEIN, Arlene B. (Dir) 1185
EGGUM, Janet M. (Lib Dir) 339
ARMSTRONG, Nancy A. (Ref Libn) 32
BARTZ, Alice P. (Instr) 62
BENGALI, Zarin P. (Weekend & Evening Ref Libn) 80
CRIBBEN, Mary M. (Assoc Prof) 258
DREHER, Janet H. (Technl Srvs Head) 319
ERDT, Terrence (Assoc Prof) ... 352
GALLAGHER, Dennis J. (Univ Archvst) 414
GRIFFIN, Mary A. (Dir) 468
PENNELL, Charles (Head, Catlgng & Bibliographic Ctl) .. 957
QUINTILIANO, Barbara (Asst Ref Libn) 1000
WALSH, Carolyn C. (Lib Sci Libn) 1299
PIEPENBURG, Scott R. (Dir of Technl Srvs) 971
HLUHANY, Patricia (Comunty Libn & Elem Sch Consult) ... 544
GRUBEN, Karl T. (Libn) 474
BRADLEY, Jack (Owner & Retail Store Mgr) 126
SHEPHERD, Rex L. (Media Spclst) 1127

MILLER, Veronica E. (Libn & Media Spclst) 843
PHARES, Abner J. (Libn) 967

BRONSTEIN, Dorothy J. (Territorial Med Libn) 140
BARZELAY, Mary S. (Libn) 62
WILLIAMS, Wallace D. (Pres) .. 1347
OWENS, Martha A. (Head Libn) . 932

CALLAHAN, John J. (Lib Support Srvs Adminstr) 173
MILLER, Nancy M. (Col Mgmt Biblgphr) 841
SWAIN, Lillian A. (Area Libn) .. 1212
WHYTE, Sean (Sr Catlgng Libn) 1335
BACHMAN, Katherine H. (Lib Devlpmnt Ofcr) 43
CARTER-LOVEJOY, Steven H. (Automation Libn) 190
DUKE, John K. (Bibliographic Srvs Dept Head) 324
HUMMEL, Ray O. (Scholar-in-Residence) 573
JOHNSON, Jane W. (Soc Behavioral Sci Col Mgmt Lib) . 605
MURDEN, Steven H. (Asst Head) 879
REAM, Daniel L. (Ref Srvs Head) 1012
THOMAS, Mary E. (Assoc Prof & Ref Libn) 1237
TURMAN, Lynne U. (Ref Libn) . 1264
WHALEY, John H. (Head, Spcl Cols and Archs) 1328
WOODY, Janet C. (Head, Automation Srvs Dept) 1368

Virginia Department of Education (VA)
BARBER, Gloria K. (Supvsr of Sch Libs & Info Tech) 55

Virginia Dept of Information Technology (VA)
TERRELL, Jane A. (Mgr, Telecommunications Technl Lib) 1232

Virginia Historical Society (VA)
SARTAIN, Sara M. (Libn for Books & Serials) 1083
SHEPARD, E L. (Libn) 1126
WINFREE, Waverly K. (Cur of Mss) 1354

Virginia Intermont Coll (VA)
HANLON, Gloria L. (Technl Srvs Libn) 496

Virginia Lib Association (VA)
TROCCHI, Debbie (Exec Dir) .. 1257

Virginia Mason Medical Center (WA)
ROBERTSON, Ann (Dir of Lib Srvs) 1041

Virginia Military Institute (VA)
DAVIS, Wylma P. (Asst Head Libn & Lectr in Bibl) 281
DELONG, Edward J. (AV Libn) .. 290
FUN, Winnie W. (Technl Srvs Libn) 409
GAINES, James E. (Head Libn) .. 412
HOLLY, Janet S. (Asst Ref Libn) . 552
JACOB, Diane B. (Archvst) 589
PEARSON, Marilyn R. (Circ Libn) 953

Virginia Museum of Fine Arts (VA)
JACOBY, Mary M. (Photographic Srvs) 590
STACY, Betty A. (Head Libn) .. 1178

Virginia Polytechnic Inst & State Univ (VA)
BAER, Eberhard A. (Humanities Catlgr) 44
COCHRANE, Lynn S. (Head of User Srvs) 225
EASTMAN, Ann H. (Univ Faculty Bk Publshg Ofcr) 333
GLENNON, Irene F. (Head of Sci Catlgng Div) 441
HINKLE, Mary R. (Educ Libn) .. 542
KOK, Victoria T. (Veterinary Medicn, Animal Scis Libn) ... 669
KRIZ, Harry M. (Head) 679
LINN, Cynthia S. (Sci Catlgr) .. 731
NORSTEDT, Marilyn L. (Head of Catlgng Dept) 909
RASMUSSEN, Lane D. (Bus Libn) 1009
RICHARDSON, Linda B. (Soc Sci Ref Libn) 1029
SPAHR, Janet E. (Docums Libn) 1170
ROYAL, Linda G. (Info Spclst) .. 1063

Virginia Power (VA)
Virginia State Lib (VA)
CHAMBERLAIN, William R. (Dir of Gen Lib Div) 197
HUBBARD, William J. (Dir of Automated Systs & Networking) 568
MANARIN, Louis H. (State Archvst) 764
YATES, Ella G. (State Libn & Archvst) 1378

Virginia State Univ (VA)
BERGELT, Robert L. (Asst Catlgr) 85
CLAYMAN, Ida H. (Catlg Libn) .. 220

Virginia Tech (VA)
COSGRIFF, John C. (Sci Ref Libn) 248
ENGELBRECHT, Pamela N. (Ref Libn) 349
FOX, Edward A. (Asst Prof) 394
GHERMAN, Paul M. (Dir of Libs) 430
KENNEY, Donald J. (Ref Dept Head) 641
METZ, Paul D. (Ref Biblgphr) ... 828

Virginia Wesleyan Coll (VA)
PEREZ-LOPEZ, Rene (Dir of the Lib) 958

The Virginian-Pilot & Leadger-Star (VA)
BASNIGHT, Clara P. (Asst Libn) .. 63

Visiting Nurse Association Inc (CA)
SIEBENMORGEN, Ruth (Libn) . 1135

Viskase Corp (IL)
PUPIUS, Nijole K. (Libn) 998

Vista Chemical Co (TX)
Vitro Corp (MD)
MORRIS, Louis M. (Project Head) 867

Viva Tours USA (NY)
JANSEN, Guenter A. (VP & Gen Mgr) 593

VLS Inc (OH)
CHRISTIANSEN, Eric G. (President) 211

VMS Realty Partners (IL)
GAYNON, David B. (Records Mgr) 424

VNU Amvest Inc (DC)
NYKS, Johannes M. 912

Vp Electronic Info Srvs (ON)
FOSTER, Margaret A. (Publshr) . 392

VSI Chemicals Co (IL)
VOSS, Ingrid M. (Info Spclst) .. 1289

VTLS Inc (VA)
ESPLEY, John L. (User Support Coordntr) 354
LEE, Carl R. (Dir of User Srvs) .. 709

BOWDEN, Gail L. (Mgr, Lib Srvs) 120
WHITMAN, Mary L. (Customer Srv Mgr) 1333
WILLCOX, M C. (Supvsr) 1341
WILLMANN, Donna S. (Mktg Dir) 1348

VU/TEXT Information Services Inc (PA)

W

W B Doner and Co Advertising (MI)
LEB, Joan P. (Resrch Libn) 707

W B Farrar, DDS Periodontics (SC)
HUYGEN, Eva (Transcriptionist) . 580

W B Saunders Co (PA)
MITCHEM, M T. (Mktg Mgr) 849

W C Bradley Lib (GA)
SMITH, Matilda M. (Head, Fine Arts Dept) 1158

W E Upjohn Institute (MI)
CLEMENTS, Susan S. (Libn) ... 221

W G Hutchison Co (ON)
JAGIELLOWICZ, Jadzia (Resrch Coordntr) 591

W Gozdz Enterprises Info (FL)
GOZDZ, Wanda E. (Pres) 455

W H Brady Co (WI)
GRUEL, Janice L. (Technl Libn) . 474

W R Grace & Co (MA)
METCALF, Marjorie (Libn) 828

W R Grace & Co (SC)
EZELL, Margaret M. (Technl Libn) 360
MCCULLEY, P M. (Asst Libn of Technl Lib) 800

W R Grace & Co (TX)
MILLER, Rea R. (Libn, Supvsr Records) 841
FRYE, Larry J. (Head Libn) 407
RILE, B B. (Asst Libn) 1034

Wabash Coll (IN)

Wabash Valley Area Lib Srvs Authority (IN)
MARTHEY, Rebecca J. (Interlib Loan & Ref Libn) 775

Waco Independent Sch (TX)
CARPENTER, Charlotte L. (Sch Libn) 184

Waddell & Reed Investment Management Co (MO)
HOWERTON, Betty J. (Head Libn) 565

Wadhams Hall Seminary-Coll (NY)
MARTIN, Helen (Head Libn) 776

Wadleigh Memorial Lib (NH)
BRYAN, Arthur L. (Dir) 151

Wadsworth Atheneum (CT)
MCNULTY, Karen (Asst Libn) ... 817

Wadsworth Inc (CA)
NEEDHAM, Michael V. (Pres of Brooks/Cole Publshg) 891
THORNTON, Jack N. (Pres & Chief Executive Ofcr) 1242
WAGNER, A C. (Assoc Lib Dir) 1291

Wagner Coll (NY)
TUPPER, Bobbie (Youth Libn) .. 1263

Wailuku Pub Lib (HI)

Wake Area Health Education Center (NC)
RICHARDSON, Beverly S. (Assoc AHEC Dir, Lib & Info Srvs) 1029

Wake County Dept of Pub Libs (NC)
COUSINS, Gloria D. (Libn II, Lib Branch Dir) 252
HORTON, James T. (Adult Srv & Ref Libn) 561
MOORE, Thomas L. (Dir) 861
PARKER, Lanny C. (Support Srvs Libn) 942
REILLY, Carol H. (Info & Referral & Outreach Coordntr) 1020
VAN HOY, Catherine S. (Adult Srvs Libn I) 1276

Wake County Dept of Pub Libs (NC)
WASILICK, Michael J. (Adult Srvs Head) 1308

Wake County Sch District (NC)
TAYLOR, Christine M. (Sch Lib Media Spclst) 1226

Wake Forest Univ (NC)
AHLERS, Glen P. (Head of Pub Srvs) 8
ANDERSON, Sherry (Asst Prof & Assoc Dir) 25
BERTHRONG, Merrill G. (Dir of Libs) 91
COBB, Mary L. (Asst Dir for Technl Srvs & Admin) 225
FOLTZ, Faye D. (Serials Head) . . 388
GETCHELL, Charles M. (Head, Ref Dept) 430
MOORE, Maxine B. (Catlgr, Rare Books) 860
STEELE, Tom M. (Law Lib Srvs Dir & Assoc Law Prof) 1184
WOODARD, John R. (Dir, NC Baptist Histl Coll, Archvst) . . 1365

Wake Medical Center (NC)
GRANDAGE, Karen K. (Dir) . . 457

Wakulla County (FL)
JONES, Douglas M. (Dir) 612

Waldenbooks (WA)
ARBUCKLE, Marybeth M. (Bookseller) 30

Waldwick Board of Education (NJ)
SLOAN, Ruth C. (Libn) 1149

Walker Art Center (MN)
FURTAK, Rosemary (Libn) 410

Walker Coll (AL)
ELLIOTT, Riette B. (Head Libn) . . 344

Walker-Wassac Art Alliance (NV)
PIERCE, Mildred L. (Dir, Technl Info Srv) 971

Wall Street On-Line Publishing Co (NY)
YOUNG, Howard (Pres) 1382

Walla Walla Community Coll (WA)
BLACKABY, Sandra L. (Dir of Lib Srvs) 102

Walla Walla County Rural Lib District (WA)
BREIT, Anitra D. (Dir) 132

Walla Walla Pub Lib (WA)
HALEY, Anne E. (Lib Dir) 486

Wallingford Pub Lib (CT)
SCHERER, Leslie C. (Dir) 1092

Wallkill Central Sch District (NY)
RUBIN, Ellen B. (Libn) 1064

Walnut Ridge Pub Schs (AR)
ALLEN, Lucia W. (Librarian) 15

The Walrus Press (VA)
JOHNSON, Bryan R. (Owner & Proprietor) 602

Walsh Associates (MA)
WALSH, Joanna M. (Lib Consult) 1299

Walsh Coll (OH)
SUVAK, Daniel S. (Lib Dir) 1212

Walsh Coll of Accountancy & Bus Admin (MI)
ELLIS, Gloria B. (Lib Dir) 344

Walsingham Academy Upper Sch (VA)
SHANNON, Theresa M. (Libn) . 1121

The Walt Disney Co (CA)
SIGMAN, Paula M. (Asst Archvst) 1137

Walter Cecil Rawls Lib & Museum (VA)
JOHNSON, Kenneth P. (Dir) 606

Walter Conston Alexander & Green PC (NY)
MENZEL, William H. (Libn) 825

Walter Reed Army Institute of Research (DC)
CASSEDY, Barbara S. (Technl Srvs Chief) 193

Walters Art Gallery (MD)
KLEEBERGER, Patricia L. (Asst Libn, Slide Libn) 658
TOPPAN, Muriel L. (Libn) 1251

Walters Pub Schools (OK)
ZACHARY, Patricia A. (Sch Lib Media Spclst) 1385

Walton Central Sch (NY)
LEPINNET, Nancy M. (Lib Media Spclst) 717

Walworth-Seely Pub Lib (NY)
VAN RIPER, Joy C. (Dir) 1277

Wamego Pub Lib (KS)
LEONARD, Leanne N. (Head Libn) 716

WaNee Community Schs (IN)
MATHEWS, Rosemary S. (Media Spclst) 784

Wang Institute of Graduate Studies (MA)
DENTON, Francesca L. (Head Libn) 293

Wang Labs Inc (MA)
ARSENAULT, Patricia A. (Libn) . . 35

Wantagh Sch District (NY)
LOPATIN, Edith K. (Sch Lib Media Spclst) 740
SCHOENBAUM, Rhoda A. (Lib Media Spclst) 1098

Wapiti Regional Lib (SK)
LABUIK, Karen L. (Branch Supvsr) 686

Ward Howell International Inc (IL)
PEURYE, Lloyd M. (Dir of Resrch) 966

Ward Howell International Inc (NY)
TICKER, Susan L. (Libn & Info Srvs Mgr) 1244

Warder Libs of Springfield & Clark Cnty (OH)
MCCROSKY, Janet E. (Acqs Libn) 800

Wardlaw-Hartridge Sch (NJ)
KOLAYA, Margaret B. (Head Libn) 669

Waring Cox (TN)
BAILEY, Barbara G. (Libn & Supvsr) 46

Warminster General Hospital (PA)
GRAHAM, Betty R. (Libn) 456

Warner Brothers Music Publications Inc (NJ)
SULTANOF, Jeff B. (Creative Edit) 1208

Warnick Pub Lib (RI)
PEARCE, Douglas A. (Dir) 952

Warren Consolidated Schs (MI)
BAIRD, Patricia M. (Libn) 47

Warren County Board of Education (KY)
GRIFFIN, Charlene F. (Libn) 468
ZIMMER, Connie W. (Libn) 1388

Warren County Community Coll (NJ)
ANDERMAN, Lynea (Dir Lib Lrng Resrcs Ctr) 21

Warren County Genealogical Society (OH)
FOLEY, Harriet E. (Volunteer, Catlgng Libn) 387

Warren County-Vicksburg Pub Lib (MS)
MITCHELL, Deborah S. (Dir) 848

Warren-Trumbull County Pub Lib (OH)
BRIELL, Robert D. (Dir) 135
JONES, Judykay (Automation Libn & Syst Coordntr) 613
TYSON, Edith S. (Young Adult Srvs & General Ref) 1267

Warren Wilson Coll (NC)
COOPER, Ruth K. (Perdcls Libn) 243
HUTTON, Jean R. (Dir) 579
STOCKNER, Patricia G. (Dir) . . 1195

Warrenville Pub Lib District (IL)
DOKS, Vija (Libn) 309

Warshaw Burstein Cohen Schlesinger & Kuh (NY)
BECK, Marianne J. (Libn) 71

Wartburg Coll (IA)
HESS, Sandra K. (Ref Circ Libn) . 534

Wartburg Theological Seminary (IA)
LISTOVITCH, Denise A. (Head of Tech Srvs/Automated Syst) 733

Warwick Pub Lib (RI)

Warwick Sch Department (RI)
BRYAN, Susan M. (Libn & Media Spclst) 152

Wascana Institute of Applied Arts & Scis (SK)
VOHRA, Pran (Chief Libn) 1287

Washakie County School District 1 (WY)
HARRINGTON, Carolyn B. (Libn) 504

Washburn Univ (KS)
ENSIGN, David J. (Assoc Dir) . . . 350
MELICK, Cal G. (Catlg & Ref Libn) 822
REIMER, Sylvia D. (Access Srvs & Ref Libn) 1021
VUKAS, Rachel R. (Ref Srvs Libn) 1290

Washington Adventist Hospital (MD)
HINKEL, Jeannine M. (Libn) 542

Washington & Lee Univ (VA)
BISSETT, John P. (Catlgng Libn) 100
BROWN, Barbara J. (Univ Libn) . 142
DANFORD, Robert E. (Catlgr & Dir of AV Srvs) 272
GREFE, Richard F. (Ref & Pub Srvs Libn) 465
HAYS, Peggy W. (Pub Srvs, Ref & Docums Libn) 517
WIANT, Sarah K. (Dir of the Law Lib & Assoc Prof) 1335

Washington Assn of Realtors Inc (DC)
KITZMILLER, Virginia G. (Dir Mktg & Comm) 657

Washington Coll (MD)
HYMES, Judith I. (Technl Srvs Libn) 580

Washington County Cooperative Lib Srvs (OR)
SELLE, Donna M. (Coordntr) . . . 1113

Washington County Free Lib (MD)
LIZER, Bonnie S. (Adult Srvs Head) 735
MALLERY, Mary S. (Regnl Libn) . 763
SUTTON, Sharan D. (Asst Dir) . 1212

Washington County Free Lib (UT)
SHIRTS, Russell B. (Lib Dir) ... 1131

Washington County Hospital Association (MD)
BINAU, Myra I. (Lib Srvs Coordntr) 97

Washington County Lib System (MS)
SCHALAU, Robert D. (Dir) 1089

Washington County Pub Lib (OH)
BELL, Ellen (Lib Dir) 76

Washington County Pub Lib (VA)
JESSEE, Brenda J. (Dir) 600

Washington Hospital Center (DC)
COOK, Marilyn M. (Med Lib Dir) . 240
COOK, Mickey (Dir) 240

Washington National Insurance Co (IL)
BRYANT, Eugenia D. (Head Libn) 152
COX, Joyce M. (Law Libn) 253

The Washington Post (DC)
BELTON, Jennifer H. (Dir of Info Srvs) 78
HAMACHEK, Ross F. (Plng & Devlpmnt VP) 490

Washington Program & Annenberg Schs (DC)
DEHART, Odell (Libn) 288

Washington State Dept of Corrections (WA)
SIENDA, Madeline M. (Law Libn) 1136

Washington State Energy Office (WA)
ALEXANDER, Ginger H. (Libn) ... 12

Washington State Lib (WA)
ANDRESEN, David 26
DEBUSE, Judith S. (Head, Serials Sect) 285
HAMMOCK, Janice D. (Catlgng Mgr) 493
KREIMEYER, Vicki R. (Deputy State Libn) 677
MOORE, Mary Y. (Lib Plng & Devlpmnt Chief) 860
PEARSON, Barbara F. (Libn) ... 952
VAN DER VOORN, Neal P. (Libn & Module Supvsr) 1274
ZUSSY, Nancy L. (State Libn) . 1391

Washington State Univ (WA)
BRADY, Eileen E. (Libn II) 126
BREKKE, Elaine C. (Ref Libn) .. 132
CHISMAN, Janet K. (Ref Libn/Database Coordntr) 209
FISHER, Rita C. (Ref Libn & Intl Devlpmnt Liaison) 381
KEMP, Barbara E. (Humanities/Soc Scis Pub Srvs Head) 639
KOPP, Carol S. (Catlgr) 671
KOPP, James J. (Systs Libn) ... 671
MCCOOL, Donna L. (Asst Dir for Admins Srvs) 798
NOFSINGER, Mary M. (Libn III) . 907
PASTINE, Maureen D. (Dir of Libs) 946
PRINGLE, Robert M. (Head Libn) 993
ROBERTS, Elizabeth P. (Lib Head) 1039
VYHNANEK, Kay E. (Circ & Interlib Loan Head) 1290
VYHNANEK, Louis (Ref Libn) .. 1290
WIERUM, Ann R. (Hum Col Devlpmnt Libn & Head) 1337
ZIEGLER, Ronald M. (Head Ref) 1388

Washington Suburban Sanitary Commission (MD)
YUILLE, Willie K. (Adminstrv Resrch Libn) 1384

Washington Township Pub Lib (OH)
KLINCK, Cynthia A. (Dir) 661

Washington Univ (MO)
ALLEN, Ronald (Lib Dir) 16
ANDERSON, Paul G. (Assoc Dir & Archvst) 25
BALACHANDRAN, Sarojini (Sci & Engrng Srvs Head) 50
BECK, Sara R. (Head, Circ Srvs) 71
BURCKEL, Nicholas C. (Pub Srvs & Col Devlpmnt Dir) 158
CHAN, Jeanny T. (Asst Libn) ... 199

Washington Univ (MO)
CRAWFORD, Susan Y. (Prof and Dir) 257
EWING, Jerry L. (Docums Libn) . 359
FEDDERS, Cynthia S. (Catlg Coordntr) 367
FOX, Judith A. (Head of Catlgng & Classftn Srvs) 395
FRISSE, Mark E. (Asst Prof of Medicine) 405
GODT, Carol (Ref Libn) 443
HALBROOK, Barbara (Deputy Dir) 485
HALL, Holly (Spcl Cols Head) ... 487
HELMS, Mary E. (Philsom Coordntr) 525
HUESTIS, Jeffrey C. (Data Prcsng Srvs Head) 570
KANAFANI, Kyung C. (Data Prcsng Libn) 624
LEWIS, Ruth E. (Bio Libn) 724
MCDERMOTT, Margaret H. (Ref Libn) 802
MCFARLAND, Robert T. (Chem Libn) 805
NELSON, Mary A. (Assoc Dir) .. 894
REAMS, Bernard D. (Acting Dean of Lib Srvs) 1013

Washington-Warren-Hamilton-Essex BOCES (NY)
GRAMINSKI, Denise M. (Dir) ... 457

Washoe County Lib (NV)
GOULD, Martha B. (Lib Dir) ... 454
MANLEY, Charles W. (Asst Dir) . 765
OSSOLINSKI, Lynn (Libn) 928

Washoe County Sch District (NV)
ZINK, Lois C. (Libn) 1389

Wasserman-Diener Associates Inc (MD)
DIENER, Carol W. (Pres & Principal Consult) 302
DIENER, Richard A. (Info Mgmt Consult) 302

Watch & Clock Collectors Museum (PA)
SUMMAR, Donald J. (Libn) 1209

Waterbury Village Pub Lib (VT)
HIRSCH, Barbara S. (Libn) ... 543

Waterford Township Pub Lib (NJ)
MCADOO, Jannifer C. (Pub Lib Dir) 792

Waterloo Community Schs (IA)
DUTCHER, Terry R. (Media Spclst) 329
TALLEY, Loretta K. (Libn & Media Spclst) 1221

Waterloo Pub Lib (IA)
ALLING, M P. (Ref Libn) 16
BROWN, Darmae J. (Technl Srvs Head) 143
LIND, Beverly F. (Lib Dir) 728
RIESBERG, Eunice L. (Regional Info Srv Libn I) 1033

Watertown City Sch District (NY)
MARSTON, Hope I. (Lib Media Spclst) 775

Watertown Free Pub Lib (MA)
REDDY, Sigrid R. (Dir) 1014
TUCHMAN, Helene L. (Asst Dir) 1261

Watertown High Sch (CT)
COGLISER, Luann L. (Lib Media Spclst) 227

Watertown Pub Schs (MA)
CLARK, Elizabeth K. (Lib Media Spclst) 216
GROSE, Rosemary F. (Lib Media Spclst) 472
SPROUL, Barbara A. (Lib Media Spclst) 1176

Watkins Institute (TN)
SCOTT, Willodene A. (Dir of Libs) 1108

Watson Clinic Med Lib (FL)
DEE, Cheryl R. (Lib Dir) 286

Watts Griffis & McQuat Limited (ON)
STRACHAN, Pamela H. (Info Spclst) 1199

Wauconda Township Lib (IL)
HEITMAN, Lynn (Young People's Libn) 523

Waukegan East High School (IL)
STEWART, Joanne R. (Head Libn/AV Dir) 1192

Waukegan Pub Lib (IL)
CARNELLI, Sandra R. (Ref & Adult Srvs Libn) 183
LI, Grace Y. (Technl Srvs Dept Head) 724

Waukesha County Lib System (WI)
GOSZ, Kathleen M. (Dir) 453

Waukesha County Technical Institute (WI)

Waukesha Memorial Hospital (WI)

Waukesha South High Sch (WI)

Waupun Pub Lib (WI)

Wausau Hospital Center (WI)

Wausau Insurance Co (WI)

AHL, Ruth E. (Lib Dir) 8
ODDAN, Linda (Med Libn) 916
MCGHEE, Patricia L. (AV Dir) . . 806
GREEN, Thomas A. (Lib Dir) 462
LIBRO, Teresa M. (Lib Srvs Dir) . 725
NUERNBURG, Donna S. (Ref Spclst) 912

Wave Hill (NY)

FRANK, Mortimer H. (Cur, Toscanini Col at Wave Hill) . . 397

Waverly Community Schs (MI)

YARBROUGH, Joseph W. (Lib & Comp Srvs Coordntr) 1378

Waverly Pub Lib (IA)

COFFIE, Patricia R. (Dir) 227

Wayland Pub Lib (MA)

BROWN, Louise R. (Dir) 145

Wayne Board of Education (NJ)

FIRSCHEIN, Sylvia H. (Eductnl Media Spclst) 379
ONELLI, Patricia M. (Elem Sch Media Spclst) 924

Wayne County Pub Lib (NC)

ALLEN, Lynne B. (Subject Libn) . . 15
SHEARY, Edward J. (Dir) 1124

Wayne County Pub Lib (OH)

MARCONI, Joseph V. (Dir) 769
MORRIS, Glenna E. (Ref Libn) . . 866
MORGAN, Patricia L. (Libn) 864

Wayne-Oakland Lib Federation (MI)

MURATA, Mabel M. (Dir) 879
WEISER, Douglas E. (Asst Dir) . 1319

Wayne Pub Lib (NJ)

BURNS, John A. (Dir) 162
DICKER, Joan F. (Head of Ref) . . 300
PUNSHON, Bette (Asst Dir) 998

Wayne State Coll of Nebraska (NE)

EGBERS, Gail L. (Ref & Biblgph Instrc Libn) 339
KENDRA, William E. (Docums Libn) 640

Wayne State Univ (MI)

ALLEN, Nancy H. (Asst Dir for Srvs) 15
BARTKOWSKI, Patricia (Archvst) 61
BISSETT, Donald J. (Chlds Lit Ctr Head) 100
BOLLINGER, Robert O. (Asst Prof) 112
BRAITHWAITE, Heather J. (Ref & Database Coordntr) 127
BUGG, Louise M. (Asst Dir, Lib Syst) 155
CASEY, Genevieve M. (Prof Emerita) 192
CHURCHWELL, Charles (Visiting Prof, Lib Sci Prog) . . . 213
CLARK, Georgia A. (Law Libn) . . 217
EDWARDS, Willie M. (Coordntr of Pub Srv Cols) 338
ENGLE, Constance B. (Head of Catlgng) 349
GRAZIER, Margaret H. (Prof Emerita) 461
GUNN, Arthur C. (Asst Prof) 477
KAUL, Kanhya L. (Law Ref & Govt Docums Libn) 631
KIRKESY, Oliver M. (Intl Counselor) 655
LARONGE, Philip V. (Lib Asst) . . 698
MENDELSOHN, Loren D. (Sci Libn) 823
MIKA, Joseph J. (Dir of Lib Sci Prog) 834
PFLUG, Warner W. (Asst Dir) . . . 966
ROBBINS, Lora A. (Pub Srvs Libn) 1039
ROSENBAUM, David (Ref Libn) 1055
SELBERG, Janice K. 1113
SHUMAN, Bruce A. (Assoc Prof) 1134
SMITH, Michael O. (Archvst) . . . 1158
SPYERS-DURAN, Peter (Dean of Libs & Lib Sci) 1177
VAN TOLL, Faith (Dir) 1277
WILLIAMS, James F. (Assoc Dir of Libs) 1343

Wayne State Univ Press (MI)

WEST, Donald (Asst Acqs Editor) 1326

Wayne Township Lib (IN)
Waynesboro Pub Lib (VA)
Weatherford Public Lib (TX)
Webb Sch of Knoxville (TN)
Weber County Lib (UT)

Webster & Sheffield (NY)
Webster Groves Pub Lib (MO)

Webster Groves Sch District (MO)

Webster Parish Lib (LA)
Webster Parish Sch Board (LA)
Webster Univ (MO)
Wei T'o Associates Inc (IL)
Weil Gotshal & Manges (TX)

Weinzimmer Associates Inc (NY)

Weizmann Institute of Science (ISR)

Weld County Sch District 6 (CO)

Weldon City Schools (NC)

Welland Pub Lib (ON)

Wellesley Coll (MA)

Wellesley Free Lib (MA)

Wellesley Hospital (ON)
Wellesley Pub Schs (MA)

Wells Fargo Bank (CA)

Wentworth Institute of Technology (MA)

Wentworth Lib Board (ON)
Werthein Schroder & Co Inc (NY)
Weslaco Indiana Sch District (TX)

Wesley Long Community Hospital (NC)

Wesley Medical Center (KS)
Wesleyan Univ (CT)

West Allis Pub Lib (WI)
West Aurora High School (IL)

West Bloomfield Schs (MI)

West Bloomfield Township Pub Lib (MI)

West Caldwell Board of Education (NJ)

SMYTH, Carol B. (Dir) 1162
RUFE, Charles P. (Asst Libn) . . 1066
HEEZEN, Ronald R. (Lib Dir) 520
TUDOR, Betty A. (Libn) 1262
WILSON, Brenda J. (Asst Non-fiction Dept Head) 1350
ZEDNEY, Francis L. (Libn) 1387
COOPER, Jo E. (Ref Libn) 243
BLANKENSHIP, Phyllis E. (Adult Srvs Libn) 104
DOBRUNZ, Sally J. (Lib Media Spclst) 307
SMITH, Sharon M. (Sch Lib/Media Spclst) 1160
WEISENFELS, Marjorie A. (Libn) 1319
SLACK, Barbara E. (Dir) 1147
NOLES, Judy H. (Libn) 908
CARGAS, Harry J. (Prof) 181
SMITH, Richard D. (Pres) 1159
BLACK, Elizabeth A. (Legal Resrch Libn) 101
WEINZIMMER, William A. (Pres) 1318
WOLVSKY, Haya S. (Archvs Dir) 1362
SERIS, Eileen J. (High Sch Libn) 1116
JOYCE, Robert A. (Sch Media Coordntr) 618
HANNS, Stephen (Adult Srvs Head) 497
GUSTAFSON, Eleanor A. (Libn) . 478
HARDY, Eileen D. (Head of Acqs) 500
STOCKARD, Joan (Readers Srvs Libn) 1195
WOOD, Ross (Music Libn) 1365
KELEHER, Carolyn P. (Ref & Interlib Loan) 635
EMPEY, Verla (Lib Srvs Dir) 348
CAMPANELLA, Alice D. (Elem Sch Libn) 175
HUNSUCKER, Alice E. (Vice Pres & Mgr) 574
MERBACH, Peggy O. (Ref Libn) . 825
MANDEL, Debra H. (Media Srvs Libn) 764
PICCININO, Rocco (Assoc Dir) . . 970
SMITH, Ann M. (Dir of Libs & Cur of Spcl Cols) 1152
CALBICK, Ian M. (Chief Libn) . . . 172
SIMON, Beth J. (Head Libn) . . . 1140
JOHNSON, Patricia T. (Head Libn) 608
FURR, Margaret H. (Hospital Libn) 410
TANNER, Jane E. (Libn) 1223
ADAMS, J R. (Univ Libn) 5
FARRINGTON, James (Music Libn) 365
KONERDING, Erhard F. (Govt Docums Libn) 670
OSTROFF, Cynthia R. (Sci Libn) 929
WASICK, Mary A. (Libn) 1308
HOWREY, Mary M. (Libn & Career Info Spclst) 566
MADDEN, Terence J. (Media Consult) 759
FORD, Gale I. (Head, Chlds Srvs) 389
KULBERG, Gretchen S. (Dir) . . . 683
SMITH, Nancy J. (Deputy Dir) . . 1158
CARMER, Ann R. (Media Spclst & Libn) 183

West Chester Univ (PA) — BURNS-DUFFY, Mary A. (Docum & Map Libn) 163
HELMS, Frank Q. (Lib Srvs Dir) . 525
MCCAWLEY, Christina W. (Serials Libn) 795
TRUESDELL, Eugenia R. (Head, Regular Col Catlgng) 1259

West Chicago Community High Sch (IL) — OLSEN, Sarah G. (Libn) 922

West Chicago Pub Lib District (IL) — SANDERS, Charlene R. (Adminstrv Libn) 1079

West Des Moines Community Sch (IA) — KIRK, Mary L. (Media Spclst) . . 654

West Georgia Coll (GA) — BEARD, Charles E. (Prof and Dir of Libs) 69
BENNETT, Priscilla B. (Asst Prof) 82
FARMER, Nancy R. (Libn) 364
JOBSON, Betty S. (Assoc Libs Dir) 601

West Georgia Regional Lib (GA) — WILLIS, Roni M. (Asst Dir) 1348

West High Sch (KS) — SCHEUERMAN, Luanne J. (Head, Lib Media Spclst) . . . 1092

West Indies Coll (JAM) — BALDWIN, Robert D. (Lib Dir) 52

West Islip Pub Lib (NY) — CARTER, Darline L. (Lib Dir) . . . 189
KEATING, Faith (Asst Dir) 633

West Jersey Health System (NJ) — BELSTERLING, Jean I. (Med Libn) 78

West Liberty State Coll (WV) — LYLE, Heather A. (Acqs Libn) . . . 751

West Long Branch Pub Lib (NJ) — OGONEK, Donna L. (Lib Dir) . . . 918

West Milford Township (NJ) — COURTNEY, Aida N. (Chlds Libn) 251

West Orange City (NJ) — FICHTELBERG, Susan (Lib Dept Head) 374

West Palm Beach Pub Lib (FL) — BAILEY, Sara G. (Asst Lib Dir) . . . 47
MOJO, Anne Z. (Tchnl Srvs Head) 852

West Philadelphia Girls High Sch (PA) — COX, Carol A. (Sch Lib Media Spclst) 253

West Point Pepperell (AL) — DABBS, Mary L. (Info Srvs Supvsr) 269

West Professional Services (IL) — WEST, L P. (Owner) 1326

West Publishing Co (MN) — MCKEE, James E. (Legal Edit) . . 810

West Springfield Pub Lib (MA) — HELO, Martin (Asst Dir) 525
SMITH, Barbara A. (Head Catlgr) 1152

West Texas State Univ (TX) — RIEPMA, Helen J. (Assoc Libn for Resrc Mgmt) 1033

West Valley Coll (CA) — BONNET, Janice M. (Libn) 114

West Valley Nuclear Services Co Inc (NY) — CURRY, Lenora Y. (Technl Libn) 266

West Vancouver Memorial Lib (BC) — MOUNCE, Jack (Chief Libn) 873

West Virginia Dept of Culture & History (WV) — ARMSTRONG, Fredrick H. (Assoc Dir) 32

West Virginia Department of Education (WV) — MOELLENDICK, M J. (Lib, Media & Tech Coordntr) 851

West Virginia Lib Commission (WV) — COOPER, Candace S. (Govt Docums Libn) 242
GLAZER, Frederic J. (Dir) 440
PROSSER, Judith M. (Chief Lib Consult) 995

West Virginia Northern Community Coll (WV) — JULIAN, Charles A. (Head Libn) . 619

West Virginia State Coll (WV) — SCOBELL, Elizabeth H. (Ref Libn) 1106
SCOTT, John E. (Dir of Lib Resrcs) 1107

West Virginia Univ (WV) — CUTHBERT, John A. (Assoc Cur) 267
ESKRIDGE, Virginia C. (Pub Srvs Head) 354
GRAHAM, Robert J. (Dir, Comunty Hlth Resrc Srvs) . . . 456
HOWARD, Betty J. (Head Libn) . . 564
HOWARD, Elizabeth F. (Assoc Prof of Lib Sci) 564

West Virginia Univ (WV) — MCKEE, Jean A. (Technl Srvs Libn) 810
SHILL, Harold B. (Libn & Assoc Prof) 1130

West Virginia Wesleyan Coll (WV) — CRESSWELL, Stephen (Ref Libn) 258

West Warwick Pub Lib System (RI) — LAMOUREUX, Jacquelyn W. (Head of Chlds Srvs) 691

Westark Community Coll (AR) — PIERSON, Betty (Technl Srvs Libn) 972

Westat Inc (MD) — POTTER, Andrea K. (Libn) 987

Westbury Christian Sch (TX) — STUBBLEFIELD, J G. (Libn) 1204

Westbury Memorial Pub Lib (NY) — KRAMPITZ, Barbara E. (Ref Libn) 676

Westchester County (NY) — SIKORSKI, Charlene S. (Med Libn) 1137

Westchester Lib System (NY) — PARRAVANO, Ellen A. (Interlib Srvs Head) 944
TABEN, Eva M. (Spcl Srvs Consult) 1219

Westenville City Schs (OH) — GILBERT, Donna J. (Print Media Spclst) 433

Westerly Pub Lib (RI) — LIGHT, Karen M. (Technl Srvs Head) 726

Western Baptist Hospital (KY) — YOUNG, Stephanie O. (Med Libn) 1383

Western Carolina Univ (NC) — COHEN, Edward S. (Ref Dept Head) 228
DORR, Lorna B. (Ref Libn) 313
KIRWAN, William J. (Libn) 656
MILLER, Lewis R. (Spcl Cols & Maps Libn) 840
OSER, Anita K. (Map Libn) 928
STETSON, Keith R. (Asst Prof, Asst Head) 1190
YOUNG, Judith E. (Head of Pub Srvs) 1382

Western Connecticut State Univ (CT) — FOWLER, Louise D. (Assoc Prof & Libn III) 394
HURLEY, Trudy M. (Docums Pub Srv Libn) 577
LOOMIS, Mary K. (Bus Libn) . . . 740
SHOLTZ, Katherine J. (Dir of Lib Srvs) 1132
WARZALA, Martin L. (Acqs Libn) 1307

Western Costume Co (CA) — NELSON-HARB, Sally R. (Dir of Resrch) 895

Western Evangelical Seminary (OR) — METZENBACHER, Gary W. (Lib Dir) 828

Western Gas Marketing Limited (AB) — VARSEK, Elizabeth A. (Lib Srvs Supvsr) 1279

Western Illinois Lib System (IL) — KIRK, Sherwood (Executive Dir) . 654
WINNER, Ronald (Asst Dir) . . . 1355

Western Illinois Univ (IL) — CHANG, Roy T. (Catlgng Coordntr) 201
CHU, Felix T. (Automation Libn) . 212
GOUDY, Allie W. (Music Libn) . . 454
NOLLEN, Sheila H. (Asst Prof, Govt Pubns Libn) 908
TING, Lee H. (Prof) 1246
WAGNER, Ralph D. (Asst Dir) . 1292

Western Information Services (WI) — WESTERN, Eric D. (Pres) 1327

Western Kentucky Univ (KY) — COUTTS, Brian E. (Coordntr of Col Devlpmnt) 252
CUDD, John M. (Hum Ref Libn) . 263
MILLS, Constance A. (Ref Libn) . 844
MOORE, Elaine E. (Hlth & Earth Scis Ref Libn) 859
STONE, Sue L. (Manuscripts Libn) 1197
WHICKER, Gene A. (Docums & Law Libn) 1329

Western Lib Network (WA) — HOLLAND, Helen K. (Biblgph Products Libn) 550
MAIOLI, Jerry R. (Lib Syst Spclst) 762
PUZIAK, Kathleen M. (Microcomputer Spclst) 998

Western Maryland Coll (MD)

DENMAN-WEST, Margaret W.
(Educ Dept) 292
NEIKIRK, Harold D. (Lib Dir) 892
QUINN, Carol J. (Head,Ref,Govt
Docums& Interlib Loan) 1000
RICHWINE, Eleanor N. (Catlg
Libn) 1031

**Western Massachusetts Regional
Lib** (MA)

GAUDET, Dodie E. (Technl Srvs
Head) 422
RICH, Marcia A. (Lib Devlpmnt
Coordntr) 1027

Western Medical Center (CA)

SIMPSON, Evelyn L. (Med Lib
Dir) 1141

Western Michigan Univ (MI)

BLEIL, Leslie A. (Serial and
Monograph Catlgr) 105
BOURGEOIS, Ann M. (Docums
Coordntr) 119
BRUNHUMER, Sondra K. (Catlg
Libn) 150
CARROLL, Hardy (Assoc Prof) . . 187
DRISCOLL, Jacqueline (Soc
Scis Ref Libn) 320
ENGELKE, Hans (Assoc Dir of
Libs) 349
GROTZINGER, Laurel A. (Grad
Coll Dean) 473
HEGEDUS, Mary E. (Bus Ref
Libn & Asst Prof) 521
ISAACSON, David K. (Asst
Head of Ref & Humanities
Libn) 584
LOWRIE, Jean E. (Prof
Emeritus) 744
NETZ, David H. (Head) 896
PEREZ-STABLE, Maria A.
(Libn) 958
RING, Donna M. (Bus Libn) . . . 1035
RIZZO, John R. (Mgmt Prof) . . . 1037
ROSS, Mary E. (Catlgr) 1058
SICHEL, Beatrice (Head) 1135
SMITH, William K. (Assoc Dir) . 1161
VANDER MEER, Patricia F.
(Libn) 1274

Western New England Coll (MA)

ARCHAMBAUL, Christine (Catlg
Libn) 30
DUNN, Donald J. (Law Libn &
Prof of Law) 326
GARBER, Suzanne (Ref Libn) . . . 417
KONESKI-WHITE, Bonnie L.
(Assoc Law Libn) 670
STACK, May E. (Asst Dir &
Head of Pub Srvs) 1177
WELLS, Susan C. (Technl Srvs
Head) 1323

Western New Mexico Univ (NM)   LEON, Louise B. (Actg Lib Dir) . . 716

**Western New York Lib Resrcs
Council** (NY)

EVERINGHAM, Joyce D.
(Executive Dir) 358

**Western North Carolina Lib
Network** (NC)

GREGORY, Roderick F.
(Coordntr) 466

**Western Ohio Regional Lib Devlpmnt
Syst** (OH)   SCHNEIDER, J K. (Dir) 1097

Western Oregon State Coll (OR)

GORCHELS, Clarence C. (Dir of
Libs) 451
JENSEN, Gary D. (Dir of Lib
Srvs) 598

**Western Pennsylvania Sch for the
Deaf** (PA)   SCHAEFER, Mary A. (Libn) . . . 1089

**Western Psychiatric Institute &
Clinic** (PA)   EPSTEIN, Barbara A. (Lib Dir) . . 351

**Western Reserve Historical
Society** (OH)

GRABOWSKI, John J. (Cur of
Manuscripts) 455
PIKE, Kermit J. (Lib Dir) 972

Western Seminary (OR)   KRUPP, Robert A. (Lib Dir) 681

Western State Coll (CO)

LANDRUM, Margaret C. (Lib
Srvs Dir) 693

Western State Univ at Fullerton (CA)

BECKER, Carol J. (Catlg Libn) . . 72
PERKINS, Steven C. (Univ Libn) . 959
THOMPSON, James A. (Ref
Libn) 1240

Western State Univ at San Diego (CA)

CASTETTER, Karla M. (Prof &
Assoc Univ Libn) 194
SARRAINO, Kathleen A. (Ref
Libn) 1083

Western Theology Seminary (MI)

SMITH, Paul M. (Libn and Instr
in Theol Bibl) 1159

Western Washington Univ (WA)

EDMONDS, Susan M. (Spcl
Cols Mgr) 336
HAAG, Enid E. (Educ Libn) 480
HASELBAUER, Kathleen J. (Sci
Libn) 510
JOHNSON, Dana E. (Online Ref
Srvs Coordntr) 603
PACKER, Donna E. (Col
Devlpmnt & Acqs Head) 933
PARKER, Diane C. (Dir of Libs) . 941
RHOADS, James B. (Prog in
Archs & Records Mgmt Dir) . 1026
SAUTER, Sylvia E. (Systs
Analyst & Private Consult) . . 1085
SYMES, Dal S. (Humanities
Libn) 1217

**Western Wyoming Community
Coll** (WY)

KALABUS, Robert L. (Assoc
Libn, Technl Srvs) 622

Westerville Pub Lib (OH)

GARDNER, Frank D. (Asst Dir) . . 417
TUROCI, Esther M. (Supvsr) . . . 1265

Westfield Memorial Lib (NJ)

HURLEY, John (Asst Dir) 577
THIELE, Barbara J. (Dir) 1235
WILSON, Carol A. (Coordntr of
Chlds Srvs) 1350

Westfield State Coll (MA)

HANDY, Catherine H. (Ref Libn) . 495
UPPGARD, Jeannine
(Curriculum Libn) 1269

Westinghouse Electric Corp (CA)

GESCHKE, Nancy A. (Technl
Libn) 430

Westinghouse Electric Corp (PA)

HODGSON, Cynthia A. (Mgr of
Info Resrcs) 546
KLEIN, Joanne S. (Ofc Srvs
Mgr) 659
MARLOW, Kathryn E. (Sr Info
Spclst) 772
NATHANSON, Esther M. (Sr
Info Spclst) 889
REICHERT, Richard E. (Systs
Analyst) 1018
SPIEGELMAN, Barbara M. (Sr
Info Spclst) 1174
VASILAKIS, Mary (Mgr, Info &
Communication Srvs) 1279

Westinghouse Hanford Co (WA)

TRAUB, Teresa L. (Pub Info
Spclst) 1254

Westlake Community Hospital (IL)

STRAUSS, Carol D. (Libn) 1201

Westlaw (MN)   MCLEOD, T J. (Asst Mgr) 814

Westminster Choir Coll (NJ)

BENTON, Mary A. (Acqs Libn) . . 84
VELLUCCI, Sherry L. (Lib &
Media Srvs Dir) 1282

Westminster Coll (PA)

BOLGER, Dorita F.
(Reference/Interlibrary Loan
Libn) 112
BRAUTIGAM, David K. (Acqs
Librarian) 130
SPINNEY, Molly P. (Libn &
Assoc Prof) 1175

Westminster Schs (GA)

DAYTON, Diane (Carlyle Fraser
Lib Head Libn) 283
MCCLELLAND, Katherine L.
(Libn) 796

**Westminster Theological
Seminary** (PA)   MUETHER, John R. (Lib Dir) 875

Westmont Coll (CA)

BILYEU, David D. (Asst Dir, Col
Devlpmnt) 97

Westmont Pub Lib (IL)   MANNING, Mary J. (Ref Libn) . . 766

Westmoreland County Community Coll (PA)
SCHEEREN, Judith A. (Asst Prof) 1090
SHEFFO, Belinda M. (Media Spclst) 1125

Westmoreland Hospital Association (PA)
PETRAK, Janet C. (Med Libn) .. 965

Westmount Pub Lib (PQ)
LYDON, Rosemary E. (Chief Libn) 751

Weston Pub Lib (OH)
FLOWER, Eileen D. (Dir) 386

Weston Pub Schs (MA)
GOZEMBA, Frances E. (AV Media Spclst) 455

Weston Research Centre (ON)
WONG, Lusi (Info Resrc Ctr Mgr) 1363

Westport Board of Education (CT)
FISHER, Margery M. (Sch Lib Media Spclst) 381

Westport Pub Lib (CT)
BOHRER, Karen M. (Adult Srvs Libn) 111
FADER, Ellen G. (Head of Chlds Srvs) 360
GORDON, Thelma S. (Head of AV Srvs) 452
POUNDSTONE, Sally H. (Dir) ... 987
WAGNER, George L. (Asst dir & Info Srvs Head) 1291

The Westport Publishing Group (CT)
RIBAROFF, Margaret F. (Owner) 1026

Westport Research Group (CT)
REISMAN, Sydelle S. (Consult & Info Broker) 1021

Westvaco Corp (SC)
RUST, Roxy J. (Libn) 1070

Westwood High Sch (AZ)
MAIN, Isabelle G. (Asst Libn) .. 761

Wethersfield Board of Education (CT)
MEUCCI, Victoria F. (Libn & Media Spclst) 829

Wethersfield Pub Lib (CT)
KIRKPATRICK, Elizabeth M. (Circ) 655

Weyerhaeuser Co (WA)
MARTINEZ, Linda W. (Technl Info Srvs Mgr) 779
MOHOLT, Megan L. (Archvst) ... 852

Whatcom Community Coll (WA)
GROVER, Iva S. (Lrng Resrcs Coordntr) 474

Whatcom County Lib System (WA)
HALLIDAY, John (Dir) 489

Wheatland Regional Lib (SK)
CAMERON, Bruce (Exec Dir) ... 174

Wheaton Coll (IL)
ERICKSEN, Paul A. (Archvst) ... 352
SHUSTER, Robert D. (Dir of Billy Graham Ctr Archives) .. 1134

Wheaton Coll (MA)
HOVORKA, Marjorie J. (Reader's Srvs Libn) 563
STICKNEY, Zephorene L. (Coll Archvst and Spc Cols Cur) .. 1193

Wheeler Basin Regional Lib (AL)
LAND, Edward P. (Dir) 692

Whirlpool Corp (MI)
HEILEMAN, Gene C. (Sr Info Spclst) 521

Whisler-Patri Architecture & Planning (CA)
CALDWELL, Kenneth R. (Head Libn) 172

Whismmon Sch District (CA)
ALBUM, Bernie (Dist Libn for Primary Grades) 11

White & Case (DC)
TOWELL, Jane M. (Libn) 1252

White & Case (NY)
ALIFANO, Alison F. (Sr Ref Libn) 13
REID, Pauline (Tax Libn) 1019
WAGSCHAL, Sara G. (Asst Law Libn) 1292

White & Janssen Inc (IL)
WHITE, Matthew H. (Chief Exec Ofcr & Publshr) 1331

White Memorial Medical Center (CA)
MARSON, Joyce (Dir) 775

White Pine County Pub Lib (NV)
GRAY, Robert G. (Dir) 460

White Pines Coll (NH)
GAVRISH, Diane L. (Assoc Libn) 423

White Plains Hospital Medical Center (NY)
GIORDANO, Joan (Med Lib Mgr) 438

White Plains Pub Lib (NY)
BUSH, Joyce (Ref Libn) 165
SIVULICH, Sandra S. (Chlds Libn) 1145

Whiteford Taylor & Preston (MD)
SPIVEY, Lynne G. (Libn) 1175

Whitehall Laboratories (NY)
ARAYA, Rose M. (Scintfc Affairs Assoc) 30

Whitehorse Department of Education (YT)

Whitfield County Board of Education (GA)

Whitman & Howard Inc (MA)

Whitman Coll (WA)

Whitman County Lib (WA)

Whittier Coll (CA)

Whitworth Coll (WA)

Wichita Art Museum (KS)

Wichita Eagle-Beacon Newspaper (KS)

Wichita Falls Pub Schs (TX)

Wichita Falls State Hospital (TX)

Wichita Pub Lib (KS)

Wichita Pub Schs (KS)

Wichita State Univ (KS)

Wicomico County Free Lib (MD)

Widener Univ (PA)

Wiggs Middle Sch (TX)

WILDCARD * RESOURCES (WI)

Wildman Harrold Allen & Dixon (IL)

Wilfrid Laurier Univ (ON)

Wilkes-Barre General Hospital (PA)

Wilkes Coll (PA)

HISCOCK, Audrey M. (Resrcs Srvs Coordntr) 544

SPENCE, Rethia C. (Media Spclst) 1173
FEIDLER, Anita J. (Info Spclst) .. 368
CARR, Carol L. (Catlg Libn) 185
YAPLE, Henry M. (Lib Dir) 1377
WARNER, Gail P. (Dir) 1305
DMOHOWSKI, Joseph F. (Sci & Spcl Cols Libn) 306
GOWAN, Christa I. (Serials Libn) 455
HAYTHORN, Joseph D. (Law Lib Dir & Law Prof) 517
KRIKORIAN, Rosanne (Asst Law Lib Dir & Instr of Law) ... 678
NOE, Christopher J. (Ref & Circ Libn) 906
O'BRIEN, Philip M. (Coll Libn) ... 915
THAKER, Virbala M. (Govt Docums Libn) 1234
WILLIAMS, Lisa B. (Dir of Major Gifts & Resrch) 1344
BYNAGLE, Hans E. (Lib Dir) 168
CRANE, Lois F. (Libn) 255

TANNER, Allan B. (Asst Libn) .. 1222
MCCULLEY, Lois P. (Head Libn) 800
ROBERTS, Ernest J. (Libn) 1040
MESSINEO, Leonard L. (Dir of Arts & Music Div) 828
RADEMACHER, Richard J. (Dir of Libs) 1002
FORFIA, Linda S. (Substitute Teacher/Librarian) 390
MEANS, E P. (Coordntr) 820
MEYERS, Judith K. (Lib Media Srvs Dir) 831
GERMANN, Malcolm P. (Asst Prof, Biomedical Libn) 429
IZBICKI, Thomas M. (Histl & Pol Std Libn) 586
MYERS, Marilyn (Coordntr of Col Devlpmnt) 884
MYERS, Robert C. (Soc Sci Subject Spclst) 885
SCHAD, Jasper G. (Dean of Libs) 1088
TAGGART, Thoburn (Asst Prof & Interlib Loan Libn) 1219
WILKE, Janet S. (Educ Subject Spclst) 1339
WILLIAMS, Brian W. (Bus Libn and Asst Prof) 1342
GOETZ, Arthur H. (Lib Adminstr) 443
HOMAN, Frances M. (Chlds Libn) 555
CARTULARO, Teresa C. (Ref Libn) 190
DIXON, Rebecca D. (Asst Dir) .. 306
FIDISHUN, Dolores (AV Srvs Head) 375
O'NEILL, Philip M. (Asst Libn, Ref & Archvst) 924
TABORSKY, Theresa (Lib Dir) . 1219
WELLS, Frances D. (Head Libn) 1322
BEHNKE, Charles (Owner, Info Spclst) 75
KRUPKA, Karen K. (Asst Libn) .. 680
SKELTON, Brooke (Head Catlgr) 1146
TAYLOR, Rosemarie K. (Lib & Comms Dir) 1228
ERDICK, Joseph W. (Info Srvs Libn) 352
PAUSTIAN, P R. (Lib Dir) 950

Wilkinsburg Pub Lib (PA)   THOMPSON, Marian A. (Chlds
                                      Libn) 1240
Will County Law Lib (IL)   MOEN, Art J. (Law Libn) 851
Willamette Falls Hospital (OR)   VONSEGEN, Ann M. (Med
                                      Libn) 1288
Willamsburg Regional Lib (VA)   VAZQUEZ, Martha W. (Dir) . . . 1280
Willard Lib (IN)   BAKER, Donald E. (Dir) 48
                                    ELLIOTT, Joan M. (Spcl Cols
                                      Libn) 344
William Beaumont Hospital (MI)   EMAHISER, Joan A. (Assoc
                                      Med Libn) 347
William Brinks Olds Hofer Gilson &
  Lions (IL)   HU, Robert T. (Law Libn) 568
William F Laman Pub Lib (AR)   PACK, Nancy C. (Dir) 933
William Floyd Sch District (NY)   SUDA, Rullie A. (Lib & Media
                                      Spclst) 1206
William Jewell Coll (MO)   KNAUSS, Bonnie S. (Ref &
                                      Spcl Cols Libn) 663
William M Mercer Limited (ON)   CHIU, Lily F. (Libn) 209
William M Mercer Meidinger Hansen
  Inc (IL)   FUKAI, Eiko (Info Resrch Ctr
                                      Mgr) 408
William Mitchell Coll of Law (MN)   ANDERSON, E A. (Acqs Libn) . . . 22
                                    CHERRY, Anna M. (Ref Libn) . . . 206
                                    MARION, Phyllis C. (Asst Dir &
                                      Technl Srvs Head) 770
                                    SATZER, Patricia A. (Catlgr) . . . 1084
William P Wreden Books &
  Manuscripts (CA)   WREDEN, William P.
                                      (Antiquarian Bookseller) 1370
William Paterson Coll (NJ)   HEGG, Judith L. (Head) 521
                                    JOB, Amy G. (Libn I) 601
                                    MCCLEAN, Vernon E. (Prof of
                                      African and African-Am Std) . . 796
William Rainey Harper Coll (IL)   FISHER, Marshall (Ref Libn) 381
William Reese Co (CT)   REESE, William S. (Pres) 1016
William S Hall Psychiatric
  Institute (SC)   SHAH, Neeta N. (Chief Med
                                      Libn) 1119
William W Gaunt & Sons Inc (FL)   GAUNT, James R. (Vice Pres) . . 423
William Wrigley Jr Co (IL)   HANRATH, Linda C. (Corp
                                      Libn) 497
                                    KOSMAN, Joyce E. (Info
                                      Techn) 672
Williams Coll (MA)   GOLDBERG, Steven R. (Technl
                                      Srvs Libn) 444
                                    HAMMOND, Wayne G. (Asst
                                      Libn) 494
                                    SUDDUTH, William E. (Docums
                                      Libn/Catlgr) 1206
Williamsburg Regional Lib (VA)   PAISLEY, Anna S. (Chlds Libn) . 935
Williamsport Area Community
  Coll (PA)   HICKEY, Kate D. (Dir of Lrng
                                      Resrcs Ctr) 536
Williamsville East High Sch (NY)   ORGREN, Sally C. (Sch Lib
                                      Media Spclst) 925
Williard Lib (IN)   SABA, Bettye M. (Head
                                      Libn/Retired) 1072
Willis Monie Books (NY)   MONIE, Willis J. (Antiquarian
                                      Bookseller) 855
Williston Northampton Sch (MA)   MELNICK, Ralph (Lib Dir) 823
Willkie Farr & Gallagher (DC)   CILIBERTI, Nancy A. (Libn) 214
Willkie Farr & Gallagher (NY)   O'DONNELL, Maryann T.
                                      (Technl Srvs Libn) 917
Willmar Pub Sch District 347 (MN)   PAULEY, Charles W. (Sch
                                      Media Spclst) 950
Willowbrook Pub Lib District (IL)   SCHACHT, Lenore A. (Lib Dir) . 1088
Wilmer Cutler & Pickering (DC)   MITCHELL, Elaine M. (Info Srvs
                                      Dir) 848
Wilmette Pub Lib District (IL)   THOMPSON, Richard E. (Dir) . . 1241
Wilmington Area Health Education
  Center (NC)   SEXTON, Spencer K. (Med Lib
                                      Dir) 1118
Wilmington Coll (OH)   NICHOLS, James T. (Lib Dir) . . . 901
                                    TOEDTMAN, Janet J. (Technl
                                      Srvs Libn) 1248
The Wilmington Institute (DE)   BURDASH, David H. (Dir) 158
Wilmington Institute Lib (DE)   MANUEL, Larry L. (Syst
                                      Coordntr) 767

Wilmington Lib (DE)   TITUS, Barbara K. (Coordntr of
                                      Adult, AV & Chlds Srvs) 1247
Wilmington Pub Lib of Clinton
  County (OH)   NOVAK, Mary S. (Lib Dir) 911
Wilmington Unit Sch District
  209-U (IL)   HANNON, Bobbie A. (Dist Libn) . 497
Wilson & McLane Inc (CT)   MCLANE, John F. (Partner) 813
Wilson Coll (PA)   SENECAL, Kristin S. (Ref Libn) . 1115
Wilson County Board of
  Education (TN)   HAMLIN, Lisa K. (Sch Lib
                                      Media Spclst) 493
Wilson County Pub Lib (NC)   VALENTINE, Patrick M. (Dir) . . 1271
Wilson Memorial Hospital (NC)   EDWARDS, Rosa C. (Asst Mgr) . 338
Wilson Sonsini Goodrich &
  Rosati (CA)   WILLIAMS, Donna S. (Ref Libn) 1342
Wilton Lib Association Inc (CT)   GOLRICK, Michael A. (Lib Dir) . . 447
Winchester House (IL)   RING, Anne M. (Nursing Home
                                      Libn) 1035
Winchester Industries Inc (MA)   PILE, Deborah R. (Dir of Lib
                                      Srvs) 973
Winchester Pub Schs (MA)   JOHNSON, Jean L. (Libn) 606
Windsor Locks Public Lib Inc (CT)   HUBBS, Ronald B. (Head Libn) . 568
Windsor Pub Lib Board (ON)   ISRAEL, Fred C. (Dir) 585
                                    ISRAEL, Kathleen (Pub Srvs
                                      Coordntr) 585
The Windsor Star Southam Inc (ON)   HANDY, Mary J. (Libn) 495
Windward Community Coll (HI)   STEPHENS, Diana C. (Libn) . . . 1188
                                    WILSON, Deetta C. (Head Libn) 1350
Wingate Coll (NC)   ABBOTT, Kent H. (Catlg Libn) 1
                                    HEUBERGER, Karen W. (Ref
                                      Libn) 535
                                    LACROIX, Michael J. (Lib Srvs
                                      Dir) 686
Winguth Schweichler Associates (CA) GERSH, Barbara S. (Resrch Dir) . 429
Winkler Filion & Wakely (ON)   MASEN, Naunihal S. (Libn) 780
Winn Parish Lib (LA)   STANDEFER, Steven R. (Dir) . . 1179
Winneconne Community Schs (WI)   TERESINSKI, Sally S. (Libn) . . . 1231
Winnefox Lib System (WI)   SCHWARZ, Joy L. (Interlib
                                      Loan Libn) 1105
Winnetka Pub Schs (IL)   TURCHI, Marilyn L. (Resrc Ctr
                                      Dir) 1263
Winnipeg Pub Lib (MB)   EGAN, Bessie C. (Coordntr of
                                      Chlds Srvs) 338
Winnipeg Sch Division 1 (MB)   BROWN, Gerald R. (Chief Libn) . 144
Winona Memorial Hospital (IN)   MONROE, Donald H. (Med
                                      Libn) 855
Winstead McGuire Sechrest &
  Minick (TX)   COOKSEY, Martha L. (Ref Libn) . 241
                                    DERMODY, Rita R. (Law Libn) . . 294
Winston & Strawn (AZ)   KLATT, Dixie K. (Law Libn) 657
Winston & Strawn (DC)   BAXTER, Janet G. (Libn) 67
Winston & Strawn (IL)   BURGH, Scott G. (Ref Libn) 159
Winston-Salem/Forsyth County
  Schs (NC)   CHAPMAN, Peggy H. (Coordntr
                                      of Media Srvs) 202
Winston-Salem Journal (NC)   ROLLINS, Marilyn H. (Ref Dept
                                      Mgr) 1051
Winston-Salem State Univ (NC)   RODNEY, Mae L. (Lib Srvs Dir) 1048
Winter Park Pub Lib (FL)   ANDREWS, Janet C. (Asst
                                      Technl Srvs Libn) 26
                                    BENNETT, Renae M. (Head of
                                      Technl Srvs) 82
                                    ELDER, Jane D. (Ref Libn) 342
The Winters Group (NY)   BERKMAN, Robert I. (Dir of Info
                                      Srvs Devlpmnt) 87
                                    KASE-MCLAREN, Karen A.
                                      (Resrch Analyst) 628
Winterthur Museum (DE)   MCKENNEY, Kathryn K. (Libn
                                      in Charge of Slides and
                                      Photos) 811
                                    THOMPSON, Neville M. (Libn) . 1241
Winthrop Coll (SC)   CHOPESIUK, Ronald J. (Spcl
                                      Cols Head) 210
                                    DAVIDSON, Nancy M. (Ref Libn
                                      & Biblgph Instrc Coordntr) . . . 276
                                    KELLEY, Gloria (Asst Technl
                                      Srvs Head) 636
                                    MITLIN, Laurance R. (Asst
                                      Dean of Lib Srvs) 850

Winthrop Coll (SC)
SILVERMAN, Susan M. (Head of Ref) 1139
TARLTON, Shirley M. (Dean of Lib Srvs) 1224

Winthrop Group Inc (MA)
EDGERLY, Linda (Consltg Archvst) 336

Winthrop Stimson Putnam & Roberts (NY)
GOLD, Hilary G. (Asst Law Libn) . 444

Winthrop-Univ Hospital (NY)
COOK, Virginia I. (Med Lib Dir) . . 240

Wisconsin Department of Justice (WI)
BEMIS, Michael F. (Law Libn) 79
PAUL, Sara J. (Asst Law Libn) . . 949

Wisconsin Dept of Natural Resources (WI)
HYNUM, Jill A. (Mgmt Info Technician) 580
PARSONS, Patricia S. (Libn) . . . 945

Wisconsin Department of Pub Instruction (WI)
DAHLGREN, Anders C. (Consult Pub Lib Construction & Plng) 269
LAMB, Donald K. (Pub Lib Admin & Funding Consult) . . . 689
NIX, Larry T. (Dir of Lib Devlpmnt) 905
SHIRES, Leslyn (Adminstr) . . . 1131
SORENSEN, Richard J. (Sch Lib Media Consult) 1168

Wisconsin Gas Company (WI)
SIMPSON, Carolyn A. (Supvsr, Info Resrcs) 1141

Wisconsin Interlibrary Services (WI)
MICHAELIS, Kathryn S. (Dir) . . 831

Wisconsin Lib Association (WI)
MIRACLE, Faith (Adminstr) 847

Wisconsin Lutheran Coll (WI)
SIEGMANN, Starla C. (Dir) 1136

Wisconsin State Cartographer's Office (WI)
REINHARD, Christine M. (Asst State Cartographer) 1021

Wisconsin Supreme Court (WI)
KOSLOV, Marcia J. (State Law Libn) 672

Wisconsin Valley Lib Service (WI)
ELDRED, Heather A. (Dir) 342
ORCUTT, Linda S. (Multitype Lib Consult) 925

Wissahickon Sch District (PA)
LYTLE, Marguerite S. (Libn) . . 753
PARSONS, Muriel W. (Libn) . . . 945
SACHS, Kathie B. (Sch Libn) . . 1073

Wissahickon Valley Pub Lib (PA)
MULLEN, Francis X. (Dir) 877

Witco Corp (NJ)
SMITH, Jo T. (Technl Info Ctr Mgr) 1156

Wittenberg Univ (OH)
MONTAG, John (Lib Dir) 855

Wixom Pub Lib (MI)
GOLDSTEIN, Doris R. (Lib Dir) . . 446

WLN Bibliographic Center (WA)
NEWELL, Rick K. (Biblgphc Libn) 898

WNYC-FM (NY)
GLASFORD, G R. (Lib Dir) 440

Wolf Creek Local Sch District (OH)
TEPE, Ann S. (Instrcl Resrcs Supvsr) 1231

Wolfeboro Pub Lib (NH)
GEHMAN, Louise A. (Lib Dir) . . 425

Womanhood Media (CA)
WHEELER, Helen R. (Owner) . . 1329

Woman's Missionary Union (AL)
BENTLEY, Elna J. (Archvst) 83
HURTT, Betty D. (Libn) 578

Womble Carlyle Sandridge & Rice (NC)
BOERINGER, Margaret J. (Foreign Lang Attorney) 110

Women's History Research Center (CA)
X, Laura (Exec Dir) 1376

Women's Occupational Health Resource Ctr (NY)
HOMMEL, Claudia (Archvl Consultant) 555

Wood County (OH)
GILL, Judith L. (Law Libn) 435

Wood Lib (NY)
CUMMINS, A B. (Dir) 264

Woodard Bay Co (WA)
DEBUSE, Raymond (Sr Consult) . 285

Woodbridge Free Pub Lib (NJ)
MADERE, Sue E. (Ref Libn) 759

Woodbridge Township (NJ)
TAYLOR, Anne C. (Branch Head) 1226

Woodbury County Bar Association (IA)
DUNN, Susan M. (Law Libn) 327

Woodbury Univ (CA)
MOORE, Everett L. (Lib Srvs Dir) 859

Woodlands Lib Cooperative (MI)
JENNINGS, Martha F. (Coop Dir) 598

Woodmen Accident & Life Co (NE)
SLOAN, Virgene K. (Libn) 1150

Woodridge Pub Lib (IL)

Woodrow Wilson Natl Fellowship Fndtn (NJ)

Woods Hole Data Base Inc (MA)

Woods Hole Oceanographic Instn (MA)

Woodstock Foundation (VT)

Woodstock Pub Lib (ON)

Woodstock Sch (IND)

Woodstock Theological Center (DC)

Woodstock Union High Sch (VT)

Woodward-Clyde Consultants (CA)

Woodward-Clyde Consultants (NJ)

Woonsocket Education Department (RI)

Woonsocket Harris Pub Lib (RI)

Woonsocket Hospital (RI)

Worcester Art Museum (MA)

Worcester City Hospital (MA)

Worcester County Lib (MD)

Worcester Memorial Hospital (MA)

Worcester Pub Lib (MA)

Word Hoard Author's Consulting Services (WA)

Worden Co (MI)

Words on Music Ltd (WI)

Work in America Institute Inc (NY)

World Affairs Council (CA)

World Almanac Education (OH)

The World & I (DC)

The World Bank (DC)

World Book Inc (IL)

World Coll of Journalism (TAI)

World Development Group Inc (MD)

World Health Organization (SWZ)

World Methodist Historical Society (VA)

World Resources Institute (DC)

World Wildlife Fund/Conservation Fndtn (DC)

World Zionist Organization (NY)

GREIN, Mary L. (Asst Head of Adult Srvs) 466
KELLER, Steven W. (Adult Srvs Head) 636

COUPER, Richard W. (Pres) 251

SHEPHARD, Frank C. (Chief Executive Ofcr) 1127

WINN, Carolyn P. (Resrch Libn) 1355
SWIFT, Esther M. (Lib Dir) 1216
JONES, Nancy P. (Chief Libn) . 614
EUSEBIUS, Nima V. (Libn) 356
ROONEY, Eugene M. (Libn) . . 1053
DICENSO, Jacquelyn C. (Jr, Sr High Sch Libn) 300
CRAWFORD, Margaret P. (Libn) 257
ELLIOTT, Valerie E. (Head Libn) . 344
WALLACE, Wendy L. (Corprt Libn) 1298

IMONDI, Lenore R. (Media Spclst) 582
LEVEILLEE, Louis R. (Media Srvs Dir) 719
MCDONOUGH, Douglas M. (Dir) 803
GILDEA, Ruthann (Libn) 434
BOLSHAW, Cynthia L. (Slide Libn) 112
RIVARD, Timothy D. (Med Libn) 1037
WELLS, Stewart L. (Dir) 1323
SIMEONE, Therese A. (Libn) . . 1139
JOHNSON, Dorothy A. (Govtl Docums Libn) 603
JOHNSON, Penelope B. (Assoc Libn) 608
MUSSER, Egbert G. (Head of Technl & Bldg Srv) 883
NOAH, Carolyn B. (Chlds Srvs Coordntr) 906
PARSONS, Duncan A. (GL II, Ref and Readers' Srvs) 945

BRZUSTOWICZ, Richard J. 152
GRANT, Robert S. (Dir of Sales) . 458
GRENDYSA, Peter A. (Dir) 467
ROWAN, Diane M. (Libn & Info Spclst) 1062
RUBINO, Cynthia C. (Info Srvs Mgr) 1065
BEESON, Lone C. (Head Libn) . . 74
RARESHEID, Cynthia L. (Dir) . . 1008
FALK, Diane M. (Managing Libn) 362
GEHRINGER, Michael E. (Lib Dir) 425
NEWTON, Robert C. (External Relations Libn) 900
ROBERTS, Lesley A. (Info Spclst) 1040
TRIPP-MELBY, Pamela (Libn) . . 1257
WONG, Ming K. (Catlgr) 1363
KAYAIAN, Mary S. (Lib Srvs Head) 632
NAULT, William H. (Publshr) . . . 889
LIN, Chih F. (Head, Dept of Lib & Info Sci) 727
GOLDSCHMIDT, Peter G. (Pres) 446
FAGERLUND, M L. (Records Mgmt Ofcr) 361
CALKIN, Homer L. 173
TERRY, Susan N. (Resrch Libn) 1232
RODES, Barbara K. (Resrch Libn) 1047
GOLDSTEIN, Alicia P. (Libn) . . . 446

Worthington Pub Lib (OH)
BRANCH, Susan (Ref Libn) 127
SHAW, Debra S. (Supvsr for
Ref Srvs) 1123
WILSON, Leigh K. (Ref Libn) .. 1351

Wren Systems (CO)
NICKEL, Edgar B. (Owner) 902
The Wright Consultants Inc (HI)
WRIGHT, John C. (Pres) 1371
Wright Database Services (CT)
CONNOLLY, John F. (Data Srv
Executive) 237

Wright Institute (CA)
PARKS, Mary L. (Libn) 943
Wright State Univ (OH)
BAKER, Narcissa L. (Catlg Libn) .. 49
BOX, Krista J. (Ref Libn) 122
MCNEER, Elizabeth J. (Asst
Univ Libn) 816
NOLAN, Patrick B. (Head of
Archs & Spcl Cols) 907
THOMAS, Ritchie D. (Univ Libn) 1238
WEHMEYER, Jeffrey M. (Libn) . 1316

WVIZ-TV 25 (OH)
SHELLENBARGER, Linda K.
(Libn and Info Spclst) 1126

WWGP & WFJA Broadcasting
Corp (NC)
MURCHISON, Margaret B.
(News & Pub Affairs Dir) 879
The Wyatt Co (DC)
MILLER, Herbert A. (Libn) 838
Wyatt Tarrant & Combs (KY)
WOOD, Linda H. (Head Libn) .. 1364
Wyckoff Pub Lib (NJ)
NELSON, Louise H. (Dir) 894
SCHMITT, Judy (Ref Libn) 1096
Wycoff Heights Hospital (NY)
BLOKH, Basheva (Med Lib Dir) .. 106
Wyeth Laboratories (PA)
CHU, John S. (Info Srvs Sect
Mgr) 212
TAYLOR, Larry D. (Lib Srvs
Supvsr) 1227
Wylie Independent Sch District (TX)
WEISLAK, Susan L. (Lib Media
Spclst) 1319

Wyman Bautzer Christensen Kuchel
Silbert (CA)
TAYLOR, Susan E. (Libn) 1228
Wyoming Correctional Facility (NY)
BARTLE, Matthew W. (Asst
Libn) 61
Wyoming Lib Association (WY)
ANDERSON, Lynnette (Pres) 24
NORD, Kay (Exec Secy) 908
Wyoming State (WY)
WALTERS, Corky (Continuing
Educ & Col Devlpmnt Ofcr) . 1301

WY State Archives Museums & Histl
Dept (WY)
HALLBERG, Carl V. (Archvst
Histn) 489
Wyoming State Hospital (WY)
MATCHINSKI, William L.
(Principal Libn) 783
Wyoming State Lib (WY)
JOHNSON, Wayne H. (State
Libn) 609
Wyoming Supreme Court (WY)
RAO, Dittakavi N. (Asst Law
Libn) 1008
Wytheville Community Coll (VA)
MATTIS, George E. (Asst Libn) .. 786

X

X Press Information Services (CO)
BENNINGTON, Gerald E. (Pres) .. 82
Xavier High Sch (CT)
SAVAGE, Judith G. (Libn) 1085
Xavier High Sch (NY)
AMISON, Mary V. (Sch Media
Spclst) 20
Xavier High Sch for Girls (AZ)
HEINTZ, Mary L. (Libn) 522
Xavier Univ (OH)
PRESNELL, Jenny L. (Ref, Circ
Libn) 991
Xavier Univ of Louisiana (LA)
SARKODIE-MENSAH, Kwasi
(Head, Pub Srvs) 1083
SKINNER, Robert E. (Lib Srvs
Dir) 1146
Xerox Corp (CA)
FELLER, Amy I. (Technl Info
Spclst) 370
LEWARK, Kathryn W. (Info Ctr
Coordntr) 722
Xerox Corp (CT)
ORRICO, James T. (Strategic
Plng & Devlpmnt Dir) 926
Xerox Corp (NY)
BELLI, Frank G. (Mgr of
Database & Indexing Srvs) 78
MUELLER, Leta A. (Technl Info
Spclst) 875
RICE, Cecelia E. (Mgr, Pub
Srvs, Technl Info Ctr) 1027
TUCKER, Laura R. (Supvsr
Interlib Loan) 1262

Xerox Research Center of
Canada (ON)
XMCO Inc (VA)

Y

Yaba Coll of Technology (NGR)

Yakima Valley Regional Lib (WA)
Yale Center for British Art (CT)
Yale Law Sch (CT)

Yale Univ (CT)

BASSETT, Betty A. (Technl Info
Srvs Mgr) 63
SCOTT, Mona L. (Libn) 1107

AFOLAYAN, Matthew A. (Asst
Chief Libn) 7
OSTRANDER, Richard E. (Dir) .. 929
FRIEDMAN, Joan M. 404
COHEN, Morris L. (Law Libn &
Prof of Law) 228
ABELL, Millicent D. (Univ Libn) 2
ARAKAWA, Steven R. (Supvsr,
LC Source Div) 30
BERSON, Bella Z. (Assoc Univ
Libn & Med Lib Dir) 90
BOLLIER, John A. (Asst Divinity
Libn) 112
BROOKS, Robert E. (Ref Dept
Head) 140
BROWN, William E. (Head
Technl Srvs) 148
COLLIER, Bonnie (Ref Libn) 232
CROOKER, Cynthia L. (Catlg
Libn) 260
DEVINE, Marie E. (Libn) 297
FERGUSON, Elizabeth E. (Ref
Libn) 372
FERNANDEZ, Nenita (Head
Catlg Libn) 373
FRANKLIN, Ralph W. (Assoc
Univ Libn & Dir) 398
FRYER, Regina K. (Head Ref
Libn) 407
HAHN, Boksoon (Head Catlgr) .. 483
HELENIUS, Majlen (Sr Ref Libn) . 523
HUNENKO, Maria P. (Principal
Catlg Libn) 574
IANNUZZI, Patricia A. (Access
Srvs Head) 581
ICHINOSE, Mitsuko (East Asian
Col Catlg & Ref Libn) 581
JARAMILLO, Ellen M. (Sr Catlg
Libn) 594
KANEKO, Hideo (Curator) 625
KAPLAN, Diane E. 626
KELLER, Michael A. (Assoc
Univ Libn for Col Devlpmnt) .. 635
KELSEY, Mary J. (Asst Law
Libn, Technl Srvs) 639
KILLHEFFER, Robert E. (Srchng
Div Head) 648
KOEL, Ake I. (Assoc Univ Libn
for Plng) 667
LAEUCHLI, Ann J. (Assoc Law
Libn) 687
LA FOGG, Mary C. (Archvst for
Adminstrv Srvs) 688
LAWRENCE, Carol A. (Head,
Technl Srvs & Col Devlpmnt) . 704
LOWELL, Gerald R. (Assoc
Univ Libn for Technl Srvs) ... 744
MANDOUR, Cecile A. (Asst
Libn for Original Catlgng) 765
MCCORKLE, Barbara B. (Map
Cur and Ref Libn) 798
MONTEE, Monty L. (Catlg Dept
Head Libn) 856
PARKS, Stephen (Cur & Edit) ... 943
PELTIER, Karen V. (Archvst) ... 955
PETERSON, Sandra K. (Govt
Docums Libn) 964
PETERSON, Stephen L. (Dir,
Yale Divinity Sch Lib) 964
ROBERTS, Susanne F.
(Humanities Biblgphr) 1041

Yale Univ (CT)

ROGERS, Rutherford D. (Libn
Emeritus) 1050
SAMUEL, Harold E. (Music Libn
& Music Prof) 1079
SIGGINS, Jack A. (Deputy Univ
Libn) 1137
SILVERSTEIN, Louis H.
(Principal Catlg Libn) 1139
SPURGEON, Kathy R. (Govt
Docums Ref Libn) 1176
STEVENS, Hannah M. (Asst to
Assoc Univ Libn) 1190
STUEHRENBERG, Paul F.
(Monographs Libn) 1205
SULLIVAN, Maureen (Head, Lib
Persnl) 1208
TIRRO, Frank P. (Dean) 1247
TRAINER, Karin A. (Assoc Univ
Libn) 1253
WALKER, Robin G. (Cur &
Preservation Dept Head Libn) 1296
WARREN, Richard (Cur) 1306
WOODS, Frances B. (Catlg
Dept Head) 1367

Yankee Atomic Electric Co (MA)
HUGGINS, Dean A. (Docum
Control Ctr Supvsr) 571

Yankee Book Peddler (NH)
DUCHIN, Douglas (VP) 322
NARDINI, Robert F. (Head
Biblgphr) 888

Yardstick Associates (PA)
WALL, H D. (Dir of Std) 1297

Yeshiva Univ (NY)
BRICKER, Naomi S. (Ref &
Perdcls Libn) 135
FEIGER, Cherie S. (Pub Srvs
Libn) 368
KOHN, Roger S. (Archs Dir) . . . 668
LUBETSKI, Edith E. (Head Libn) . 745
WISHART, H L. (Law Libn) 1357

Yesteryear Museum (NJ)
MUNSICK, Lee R. (Exec Dir) . . . 879

Yivo Inst for Jewish Research (NY)
BAKER, Zachary M. (Head
Libn) 50

Yolo County (CA)
WEBBER, Steven L. (Archvst) . 1313

Yonkers Pub Lib (NY)
AMICK, Charles W. (Chlds Dept
Head) 20
MILLER, Jacqueline E. (Lib Dir) . . 838
ROGERS, Irene (Asst Lib Dir) . . 1049
SCHWARZMANN, Diane D.
(Asst Lib Dir) 1105

Yorba Linda Pub Lib (CA)
VAN BAUCOM, Charles (Dir) . . 1272

York Coll (NE)
CAMPBELL, Susan M. (Lib Dir) . 177

York Coll of Pennsylvania (PA)
COLTON, Norma W. (Libn) 234

York County (VA)
LYON, David A. (Dir) 752

York County Lib (SC)
KAKOSCHKE, Mona S.
(Coordntr) 622

York-Finch General Hospital (ON)
EVITTS, Beth A. (Asst Libn) . . . 359

York Hospital (PA)
SHIRINIAN, George N. (Technl
Srvs Coordntr) 1131

York Pub Lib (ON)

York Region Board of Education (ON)
MCCRACKEN, Ronald W. (Lib
Dir) 799

York Regional Library Board (NB)
LE BUTT, Katherine L. (Dir) 708

York Univ (ON)
HOFFMANN, Ellen J. (Dir of
Libs) 548
MONTY, Vivienne (Head of
Govt and Bus Lib) 857
QUIXLEY, James V. (Govt
Docums Libn) 1001
STEVENS, Mary (Asst Dir for
Lib Systs) 1190
VARMA, Divakara K. (Adminstrv
Std Libn) 1278
WYMAN, Kathleen M. (Map
Libn) 1375

Young & Associates (MD)
YOUNG, Jean (Pres) 1382

Young & Rubicam (NY)
FEBLES, Mary T. (Chief Ref
Libn) 367
PINE, Maureen A. (Asst Dir of
Lib Srvs) 974

YWCA of the City of New York (NY)
DOUET, Madeleine J. (Dir) 313

Youngstown City Schs (OH)
GROHL, Arlene P. (High Sch
Lib Media Spclst) 471

Youngstown State Univ (OH)
GENAWAY, David C. (Libn) 426
JACOBSON, Susan D. (Head
Acq Libn) 590
LUTTRELL, Jeffrey R. (Catlg
Libn) 750
ROUTH, Sheila J. (Coordntr,
Mtrls Ctr) 1061
VARMA, Valsamani (Resrch
Libn) 1278
WALL, Carol (Pub Srvs
Librarian) 1297

Ypsilanti District Lib (MI)
LINDSTROM, Susan C. (Libn II) . 730

Ypsilanti Public Schools (MI)
TRIM, Kathryn (Head Media, Lib
Spclst) 1256

Ysleta Independent Sch District (TX)
BASS, Martha L. (Sch Libn) 63

Yukon-Kuskokwim Health Corp (AK)
EMMONS, Mary E. (Secy) 348

Z

Zia Cine Inc (NM)
WILLIAMS, Carroll W. (Co-Dir) . 1342

Ziff Corp (NY)
GREENFIELD, Stanley R. (Vice
Pres, Consult) 464

Zift Davis Publishing (CA)
VARKENTINE, Aganita
(Indexing Supvsr) 1278

Zipporah Films Inc (MA)
KONICEK, Karen B. (Distribution
Dir) 670

Zoetrope Studios (CA)
NAZARIAN, Anahid (Libn) 890

Zoological Society of San Diego (CA)
ROBINSON, Michaele M. (Mgr,
Lib Srvs) 1044

**Zurich-American Insurance
Group** (IL)
HORTON, Kathy L. (Market
Resrch Libn) 561

Consulting/Freelance Index

Professionals, with their phone numbers, are indexed by their consulting/freelance availability, arranged by state (Canadian province or country) and city. The state, city, and phone listed are the ones provided to be used for consulting/freelance purposes.

Consulting/Freelance areas appearing in this index are:

Abstracter	Indexer	Researcher
Academic Library Consultant	Library Automation Consultant	Reviewer
Archivist	Library Building Consultant	Speaker (free)
Bibliographer	Online Searcher	Speaker (honorarium)
Cataloger	Proofreader	Special Library Consultant
Collection Development/	Public Library Consultant	Staff Development Consultant
Evaluation Consultant	Public Relations Consultant	Trainer
Database/Systems Consultant	Records Management	Translator (by language)
General Library/Information	Consultant	Writer/Editor
Consultant		

ABSTRACTER

ALABAMA
Auburn	JONES, Allen W.	(205)826-4360	610
	STRAITON, T H.	(205)826-4500	1199
	ZLATOS, Christy L.	(205)826-3429	1390
Birmingham	VENABLE, Douglas R.	(205)871-3318	1282
Florence	MONTGOMERY, Kimberly K.	(205)764-5392	856
Huntsville	MCNAMARA, Jay	(205)895-6526	816
Maxwell AFB	HARPER, Marie F.	(205)293-5042	503
Montgomery	BREEDLOVE, Michael A.	(205)262-6172	131
	FRANKS, Janice	(205)271-6277	398
Oneonta	WEAVER, Clifton W.	(205)274-9111	1312

ALASKA
Anchorage	BRAUND-ALLEN, Julianna E.	(907)243-5947	130
	KRAFT, Gwen L.		675
Chugiak	PUTZ, Paul D.	(907)688-4894	998
Fairbanks	LAKE, Gretchen L.	(907)452-6751	688
	PARHAM, Robert B.	(907)479-5966	940

ARIZONA
Mesa	MEAD, Thomas L.	(602)892-3764	819
Tucson	OWENS, Clayton S.		932
	WILLIAMS, Karen B.	(602)621-4866	1344

ARKANSAS
Mountain View	MCNEIL, William K.	(501)269-3851	816

CALIFORNIA
Alhambra	PORTILLA, Teresa M.		985
Anaheim	WRIGHT, Betty A.	(714)998-1127	1370
Aptos	WYKLE, Helen H.	(408)662-3228	1375
Belmont	MEGLIO, Delores D.	(415)591-2333	821
Berkeley	ARONER, Miriam D.	(415)849-2711	34
	ZBORAY, Ronald J.		1386
Burlingame	SHERMAN, Roger S.	(415)344-1213	1128
Chico	POWER, Colleen J.	(916)895-4058	989
Chula Vista	GAGNON, Donna M.	(619)426-4527	412
Cypress	MOSER, Jane W.	(213)643-0322	870
Davis	KNOWLES, Em C.	(916)752-1126	665
	ROBINSON, Betty J.	(916)756-2187	1043
Del Mar	HOLLEMAN, Marian P.	(619)755-4253	551
East Palo Alto	FROST, Michelle	(415)321-4017	406
Emeryville	POKLAR, Mary J.	(415)420-1346	980
Fallbrook	COMPTON, Joan C.	(619)723-2860	235
Fullerton	MASTERS, Robin J.	(714)524-9696	782
Glendale	PRIME, Eugenie E.	(818)243-5707	993
Huntington Beach	MACKINTOSH, Mary L.	(714)896-4639	757
Inglewood	GOUDELOCK, Carol V.	(213)672-2543	454
Irvine	BLADEN, Marguerite	(714)551-6489	102
	PUGSLEY, Sharon G.	(714)856-7193	997
Isla Vista	GALLERY, M C.	(805)968-6842	414
Jamul	SERDZIAK, Edward J.	(619)426-2253	1116

ABSTRACTER (Cont'd)
CALIFORNIA (Cont'd)
Lafayette	SVIHRA, S J.	(415)933-9549	1212
Lake View Terrace	TASHIMA, Marie		1224
Long Beach	BENSON-TALLEY, Lois I.	(213)494-7817	83
	SINCLAIR, Lorelei P.	(213)423-6399	1142
Los Altos	FILES, Patricia T.		376
Los Angeles	CAMPBELL, Bill W.	(213)398-8992	176
	DONALDSON, Maryanne T.	(213)617-7070	311
	DOUGLAS, Carolyn T.	(213)472-5287	314
	GRIGST, Denise J.	(213)651-3643	470
	HASSAN, Abe H.	(213)649-2846	511
	LEE, Hee J.	(213)391-4226	710
	MICHEL, Dee A.	(213)478-7660	832
	NEMCHEK, Lee R.	(213)621-9484	895
	SVENONIUS, Elaine	(213)825-4352	1212
Malibu	CLARK, David L.	(818)888-9305	216
Menlo Park	REDFIELD, Elizabeth	(415)859-6187	1014
Monterey	SPINKS, Paul	(408)646-2341	1175
Mountain View	SPIGAI, Fran	(415)961-2880	1174
Novato	HOTZ, Sharon M.	(415)892-0821	562
Palo Alto	LEE, Judith C.	(415)494-0395	710
	MAIN, Linda Y.	(415)328-4865	761
	PEARSON, Judith G.	(415)856-2853	952
Pasadena	HOFFBERG, Judith A.	(818)797-0514	547
	LONGO, Margaret K.	(818)793-7682	740
	WONG, Maida L.	(818)795-1255	1363
Pleasant Hill	FOWELLS, Fumi T.	(415)689-0754	393
Pomona	ADAMSON, Danette	(714)869-3109	6
San Diego	HOWARD, Pamela F.		564
	JACOBS, Horace	(619)746-4005	589
	TABORN, Kym M.	(619)232-3320	1219
San Francisco	COLALILLO, Robert M.	(415)664-2264	230
	CONLEY, Linda A.	(415)285-6835	236
	DONOVAN, Diane C.	(415)587-7009	312
	GUNDERSON, Jeffery R.	(415)929-1472	477
	HUNG, Joanne Y.	(415)221-7325	574
	LEWANDOWSKI, Joseph J.	(415)626-3755	722
	LONDON, Glenn S.	(415)928-4277	738
	MOORE, Gregory B.	(415)753-2645	859
	REGNER-HYATT, Anne L.	(415)864-1154	1017
	SCHMIDT, Robert R.	(415)821-7762	1096
San Jose	MULLEN, Cecilia P.	(408)265-8799	877
San Luis Obispo	ROCKMAN, Ilene F.	(805)756-2273	1046
San Mateo	RAZE, Nasus B.	(415)345-9684	1012
Santa Barbara	HERZIG, Stella J.	(805)966-9764	534
	MAHAFFEY, Susan M.	(805)964-4978	760
Santa Monica	DIRLAM, Dona M.	(213)452-1897	305
Stanford	HOMNACK, Mark	(415)323-2244	555
Upland	GRAUE, Luz B.	(714)982-7574	458
Van Nuys	BALABAN, Robin M.	(818)781-6952	50
Woodland Hills	REIFMAN, Deborah S.		1019

ABSTRACTER (Cont'd)

COLORADO
Aurora	HARRIS, Michael A.	(303)694-4200	505
Boulder	KRISMANN, Carol H.	(303)499-2977	678
Denver	KAVANAGH, Janette R.	(303)777-8971	631
	LUEVANE, Marsha A.	(303)989-1036	747
	SHARP, Alice L.	(303)866-4682	1122
	WHITE, Joyce L.	(303)722-4687	1331
Englewood	OTTOSON, Robin D.	(303)761-2482	930
Fort Collins	NEWMAN, John	(303)491-1844	899
Lafayette	MACARTHUR, Marit S.	(303)665-8237	754
Littleton	ALSOP, Robyn J.	(303)779-1925	18
	WHITBY, Thomas J.	(303)798-7049	1330

CONNECTICUT
Bristol	CALLAHAN, Helen H.	(203)584-7787	173
	SENKUS, Linda J.	(203)589-1298	1115
Collinsville	EICKENHORST, Joanna W.	(203)693-4315	339
Danbury	FOWLER, Louise D.	(203)797-4478	394
Hartford	MCNULTY, Karen	(203)278-2670	817
	SHORE, Julia M.	(203)537-4910	1132
Middletown	DOUVILLE, Judith A.	(203)344-1880	314
New Britain	KASCUS, Marie A.	(203)827-7565	628
New Haven	HEINRITZ, Fred J.	(203)397-4530	522
	TRIOLO, Victor A.	(203)397-4520	1257
New London	JOHNSON, Carolyn A.	(203)447-7535	602
	SORENSEN, Pamela	(203)447-7622	1168
Storrs	BOGNAR, Dorothy M.		111
	ROLLIN, Marian B.	(203)429-4187	1051
Wallingford	MCGREGOR, M C.	(203)284-6000	808
Waterbury	JOY, Patricia L.	(203)757-6203	618
West Hartford	PIERCE, Anne L.	(203)243-4849	971
Westport	MUTTER, Letitia N.	(203)227-1992	883
	SELVERSTONE, Harriet S.	(203)226-6236	1114

DELAWARE
New Castle	BROWN, Sarah C.	(307)328-3447	147
Newark	DANIEL, Alfred I.	(302)731-9723	272
Wilmington	JOHNSON, Hilary C.	(302)994-2870	605

DISTRICT OF COLUMBIA
Washington	BOHANAN, Robert D.	(202)523-3214	111
	CHASE, Linda S.	(202)885-3238	203
	DAWSON, Barbara J.	(202)785-3330	282
	GAMSON, Arthur L.	(202)382-5921	416
	GREENE, Danielle L.	(202)543-6461	463
	HAITH, Dorothy M.	(202)484-4941	484
	HUDGINS, Peggy	(202)862-8800	569
	JAMES, Olive C.	(202)547-2157	592
	KIMBERLIN, Robert L.	(202)626-7493	649
	LANE, Elizabeth S.		694
	MCCOY-LARSON, Sandra	(202)544-5520	799
	MISSAR, Charles D.	(202)363-2751	847
	REITH, Louis J.	(202)686-0131	1022
	ROMEO, Sheryl R.	(202)626-7491	1052
	SAUVE, Deborah A.	(202)546-8770	1085
	SCHNEIDER, Hennie R.	(202)523-0013	1097
	VON PFEIL, Helena P.		1288
	WELCH, Thomas L.	(202)232-1706	1321
	YASUMATSU, Janet R.		1378

FLORIDA
Bunnell	MCKNIGHT, Jesse H.	(904)437-4151	812
Clearwater	POTTER, Robert E.	(813)442-9061	987
Daytona Beach	MINOR, Dorothy C.	(904)253-6627	846
De Land	EVERETT, David D.	(904)734-4121	358
Fort Lauderdale	MILLER, Margaret R.	(305)791-1278	840
Gainesville	LEONARD, Louise F.	(904)373-2705	716
	TEAGUE, Edward H.	(904)392-0222	1229
Key Biscayne	KIRBY, Diana G.	(305)361-3678	654
Key West	SOULE, Maria J.	(305)296-9081	1169
North Lauderdale	BRESLAUER, Lester M.	(305)721-5181	133
Oakland Park	WILLIAMS, Alexander	(305)565-2990	1341
Palm Coast	FRAZER, Ruth F.	(904)445-5409	399
Seminole	WEISS, Susan		1320
Tallahassee	DEENEY, Marian A.	(904)562-3246	286
	TOOLE, Gregor K.		1250
Tampa	EVERLOVE, Nora J.	(813)839-4868	359
	WOOD, James F.	(813)232-5221	1364

ABSTRACTER (Cont'd)

FLORIDA (Cont'd)
Winter Park	AHLIN, Nancy	(305)644-6424	8
	HUTCHINSON, Beck	(305)645-3608	579
Winter Springs	THOMAN, Nancy L.		1236

GEORGIA
Athens	CARPENTER, David E.	(404)542-8460	184
	GUBISTA, Kathryn R.	(404)546-8153	475
	LIBBEY, George H.	(404)542-2716	725
	SOUTHWICK, Mary L.	(404)542-6643	1170
Atlanta	DEES, Leslie M.	(404)894-4523	287
	FEINBERG, Hilda W.	(404)875-0077	368
	MILLER, Anthony G.	(404)688-4636	835
	MISRA, Jayasri T.	(404)524-5320	847
	THAXTON, Lyn	(404)292-6767	1234
Augusta	BUSTOS, Roxann R.	(404)737-1748	166
Columbus	CLEMENTS, Betty H.	(404)327-3399	221
Decatur	OVERBECK, James A.	(404)378-8821	931
Kennesaw	GRIFFIN, Martha R.	(404)422-9921	468

GUAM
Agana	WEINGARTH, Darlene	(671)472-1750	1318

HAWAII
Honolulu	CHAFE, Douglas A.	(808)537-8375	197
	NAJ, Linda M.	(808)946-5359	887
Kailua-Kona	KOLMAN, Roberta F.		669
Makawao	TUPPER, Bobbie	(808)572-1629	1263

IDAHO
Boise	WELLS, Merle W.	(208)334-3356	1322
Moscow	WAI, Lily C.	(208)882-0506	1292

ILLINOIS
Abbott Park	SWANSON, Ruth M.	(312)937-6959	1213
Aurora	MCKEARN, Anne B.	(312)892-4811	810
Berwyn	FEDECZKO, Joyce L.	(312)795-3089	367
Bethany	SYFERT, Samuel R.	(217)665-3063	1217
Carbondale	KILPATRICK, Thomas L.	(618)453-3374	648
	KOCH, David V.	(618)453-2516	667
	RYAN, Sheila	(618)549-7029	1071
Champaign	CHAPLAN, Margaret A.	(217)333-7993	201
	HEISTER, Carla G.	(217)333-6892	523
	MCCLELLAN, William M.	(217)352-1893	796
	REPTA, Vada L.	(217)398-5728	1024
Chicago	BREEN, Joanell C.	(312)929-1445	131
	BROWN, Patricia B.	(312)775-1515	146
	CICHON, Marilyn T.	(312)648-1155	214
	COATSWORTH, Patricia A.	(312)947-2160	224
	CURRY, John A.	(314)528-0870	266
	HOFFMANN, Maurine L.	(312)951-0599	548
	HOTIMLANSKA, Leah D.	(312)248-2013	562
	JOHNSON, Judith M.	(312)996-8988	606
	KINNAIRD, Cheryl D.	(312)508-5465	653
	KOBASA, Paul A.	(312)944-6780	666
	KOWITZ, Aletha A.	(312)440-2642	674
	LENNEBERG, Hans H.		715
	MANCUYAS, Natividad D.	(312)995-2284	764
	MOORE, Annie M.	(312)995-2254	858
	MOULTON, James C.	(312)525-7185	873
	MUELLER, Julie M.	(312)645-4839	875
	PERTELL, Grace M.	(312)286-5698	961
	POSNER, Frances A.	(312)334-7484	985
	SKIDMORE, Gail	(312)989-3965	1146
	WICKREMERATNE, Swarna	(312)493-0936	1335
Cicero	MALLER, Mark P.	(312)652-8084	763
De Kalb	RIDER, Philip R.	(815)758-2181	1032
	RIDINGER, Robert B.	(815)758-5070	1032
	TOROK, Andrew G.	(815)753-1734	1251
Downers Grove	MIFFLIN, Michael J.	(312)963-9285	833
Elmhurst	WATSON, Robert E.	(312)941-0892	1310
Evanston	BARNUM, Sally J.	(312)869-2976	58
	CLOUD, Patricia D.	(312)491-3136	223
	FIELD, Connie N.	(312)866-2800	375
	HURD, Albert E.	(312)866-7235	577
	PALMORE, Sandra N.	(312)328-5329	937
	PANOFSKY, Hans E.	(312)491-7684	938
Grayslake	KIENE, Andrea L.	(312)740-0620	647
Gurnee	MANDEL, Douglas J.	(312)336-7637	765

ABSTRACTER (Cont'd)
ILLINOIS (Cont'd)

Highland Park	JANES, Virginia		593
Hinsdale	HALASZ, Marilynn J.	(312)325-0819	484
Hoffman Estates	CHAPA, Joan I.	(312)934-7032	201
Homewood	MARKHAM, Robert P.	(312)799-4677	771
Joliet	STEVENSON, Katherine	(815)723-7846	1191
Lake Bluff	BROSK, Carol A.	(312)234-6752	141
Lincolnwood	BENNETT, Laura B.	(312)679-2327	82
Normal	DELOACH, Marva L.	(309)438-7463	290
	GOWDY, Laura E.	(309)438-7450	455
Northbrook	NICKELS, Judith L.	(312)272-6224	902
Oak Park	HALIBEY, Areta V.	(312)524-0023	486
	REDDY, Michael B.	(312)848-1754	1013
Park Forest	BUCKLEY, Ja A.	(312)748-2536	154
Park Ridge	KNARZER, Arlene	(312)692-9550	663
	LOFTHOUSE, Patricia A.	(312)698-9731	737
River Forest	DAVIS, Richard A.	(312)366-7383	280
Rockford	LONG, Judith N.	(815)229-7604	739
Round Lake	TAN, Elizabeth L.	(312)546-6311	1222
Springfield	SORENSEN, Mark W.	(217)782-1082	1168
Urbana	BURBANK, Richard D.	(217)333-2713	158
	KIBBEE, Josephine Z.	(217)333-2290	646
Westmont	MANNING, Mary J.	(312)964-3549	766
Wheaton	WALSH, Deborah T.	(312)653-1115	1299
Wheeling	LAMB, Sara G.	(312)541-8114	690
Wilmette	SPIGELMAN, Cynthia A.	(312)251-4892	1174
Woodridge	WHITT, Diane M.		1334

INDIANA

Anderson	KENDALL, Charles T.	(317)649-5039	640
Bloomington	HENSON, Jane E.	(812)336-8288	529
	READ, Glenn F.	(812)336-5984	1012
	ZIMMERMAN, Brenda M.		1388
Bluffton	ELLIOTT, Barbara J.	(219)824-2315	343
Fort Wayne	CLEGG, Michael B.		220
Indianapolis	DOLAN-HEITLINGER, Eileen	(317)269-1764	309
	DURKIN, Virginia M.	(317)871-2095	328
Muncie	KUO, Ming M.	(317)289-3123	684
	WILLIAMS, Nyal Z.	(317)285-5065	1345
Noblesville	WILLIAMS, Maudine	(317)773-1763	1345
Notre Dame	HAVLIK, Robert J.	(219)239-6665	513
West Lafayette	ANDREWS, Theodora A.	(317)463-6093	27
Winamac	SMITH, Robert E.	(219)946-6255	1160

IOWA

Cedar Rapids	LEAVITT, Judith A.	(319)390-3109	707
Iowa City	BROWN, Jeanine B.		144
	EIMAS, Richard	(319)337-5538	340
	ENGER, Kathy B.	(319)335-4123	349
	SNIDER, Jacqueline I.	(319)337-0660	1163
Manchester	CRAWFORD, Daniel R.		256
Marshalltown	TRAVILLIAN, Mary W.	(515)752-1578	1254
Ottumwa	BRANDT, Garnet J.	(515)682-6677	128

KANSAS

Alma	BIRNEY, Ann E.	(913)765-2370	98
Lawrence	BURCHILL, Mary D.	(913)864-3025	158
Manhattan	WEISENBURGER, Patricia J.	(913)532-5968	1319
Shawnee	STRAUSE, Robert C.	(913)268-9875	1200
Wichita	MEYERS, Judith K.	(316)832-1211	831
	TANNER, Jane E.	(316)682-4485	1223

KENTUCKY

Bowling Green	ZIMMER, Connie W.	(502)781-4165	1388
Wilmore	BUNDY, David D.	(606)858-3581	157

LOUISIANA

Baton Rouge	BOYCE, Bert R.	(504)388-1461	122
	FERGUSON, Anna S.	(504)272-3833	372
	MILLER, Susan E.	(504)388-8264	842
	SCULL, Roberta A.		1108
New Orleans	DAVIS, Margo	(504)488-1193	280
Ruston	MCFADDEN, Sue J.	(318)257-4357	804
Zachary	JACKSON, Audrey N.	(504)654-5491	586

MAINE

Orono	MCCALLISTER, Myrna J.		793
	THOR, Angela M.	(207)581-1678	1242

ABSTRACTER (Cont'd)
MARYLAND

Aberdeen	HADDEN, Robert L.	(301)272-1858	481
Annapolis	PRIMER, Ben	(301)974-3914	993
Baltimore	GENUARDI, Michael T.	(301)235-1168	427
	GERHARDT, Edwin L.	(301)242-0328	428
	HUMPHRIES, Anne W.	(301)328-7373	574
	SHAPIRO, Burton J.	(301)653-2757	1121
	THIES, Gail M.	(301)597-8918	1235
Bethesda	HENDERSON, Madeline M.	(301)530-6478	526
	HORAN, Meredith L.	(301)496-5497	559
	KUNZ, Margarett N.	(301)496-3541	684
	LAKSHMAN, Malathi K.	(301)229-9287	689
	LAZAROW-STETTEN, Jane K.	(301)656-5471	706
Brookeville	ROBERTS, Lesley A.	(301)774-4471	1040
Chevy Chase	SEARS, Jonathan R.	(301)656-2306	1110
College Park	TIBBO, Helen R.	(301)454-5441	1244
	WELLISCH, Hans H.	(301)345-3477	1322
Columbia	RUSS, Kennetta P.	(301)381-0579	1068
Damascus	JOHNSON, Susan W.	(301)253-2759	609
Fallston	SACK, Jean C.	(301)877-2825	1073
Flintstone	RAFATS, Jerome M.		1003
Fort Meade	KNICKERBOCKER, Wendy	(301)672-3057	664
Frederick	GIBBONS, Katherine Y.	(301)663-2720	431
Garrett Park	PRATT, Laura C.	(301)942-1764	990
Greenbelt	BYERLY, Imogene J.		168
	KOBAYASHI, Michiko		666
Laurel	GOLDENBERG, Joan M.	(301)953-9253	445
Mt Rainier	STRANSKY, Maria	(301)779-1627	1200
Rockville	MARTINEZ-GOLDMAN, Aline		779
Silver Spring	AGEE, Victoria V.	(301)434-7073	7
	AMATRUDA, William T.	(301)585-3570	19
	ARANDA-COODOU, Patricio	(301)946-7859	30
	BASA, Eniko M.	(301)384-4657	62
	FRAULINO, Philip S.	(301)495-5636	399
	LARSON, Jean A.	(301)890-2210	699
	MEIKAMP, Kathie D.	(301)593-0029	822
	OVERTON, Kathryn R.	(301)236-9754	931
	PICKETT, Olivia K.	(301)434-7503	971
	TAYLOR, Marcia E.	(301)942-6704	1227
	THURONYI, Geza T.	(301)593-1722	1243
	WAGNER, Lloyd F.		1292
	WALSH, Barclay		1299
Upper Marlboro	DICKSON, Katherine M.	(301)350-4035	301

MASSACHUSETTS

Amherst	ADAMS, Leonard R.	(413)545-2765	5
	CHADWICK, Alena F.	(413)545-2674	196
Arlington	ENGLISH, Cynthia J.	(617)227-0270	350
	LUKOS, Geraldine F.	(617)646-3439	748
	PLUNKET, Linda	(617)646-7825	979
Belmont	PHELAN, Mary C.		967
Boston	BLAKE, Michael R.	(617)572-3127	103
	BRITE, Agnes	(617)267-0369	137
	KOLCZYNSKI, Charlotte A.	(617)536-5400	669
	LEVINSON, Gail	(617)437-1600	721
	NESS, Arthur J.	(617)277-1776	896
	PLUNKET, Joy H.	(617)327-5175	978
	ROGAN, Michael J.	(617)536-5400	1049
	STIFFLEAR, Allan J.	(617)929-7640	1194
Brockton	UMANA, Christine J.	(617)586-6994	1268
Brookline	DONG, Tina	(617)731-3514	311
Cambridge	DAVY, Edgar W.	(617)253-5670	281
Concord	LEWONTIN, Amy	(017)369-9106	724
	NESS, Pamela M.	(617)369-7174	896
Farmingham	KING, Laurie L.	(617)877-3512	651
Framingham	KRIER, Mary M.	(617)879-7594	678
Hanscom AFB	DUFFEK, Elizabeth A.	(617)377-4768	323
Lexington	ROSENTHAL, Marylu C.	(617)862-8167	1057
Lincoln	COHEN, Martha J.	(413)259-9500	228
Medford	HARRIS, John C.	(617)396-9250	504
Needham	PAPADEMETRIOU, George C.	(617)444-8941	938
North Falmouth	FOSTER, Joan		392
North Quincy	NIELSEN, Sonja M.	(617)328-8306	903
Randolph	OAKLEY, Adeline D.	(617)963-7999	913
Salem	PANGALLO, Karen L.		938
Springfield	CLOUGH, Linda F.	(413)788-8411	223
Waban	CHERNIN, David A.	(617)731-6760	206

ABSTRACTER (Cont'd)

MASSACHUSETTS (Cont'd)

West Springfield	SMITH, Barbara A.	(413)736-4561	1152
Westford	NATOLI, Dorothy L.	(617)692-7192	889
Woods Hole	SHEPHARD, Frank C.	(617)548-2743	1127
Worcester	ANDREWS, Peter J.		27

MICHIGAN

Ann Arbor	BILLICK, David J.	(313)761-4700	96
	BOWEN, Jennifer B.	(313)663-6164	120
	DAVIDSEN, Susanna L.	(313)995-7352	276
	GATTIS, R G.	(313)936-1073	422
	MOUZON, Margaret W.	(313)662-9227	874
	REGAN, Lesley E.	(313)434-5530	1017
Cheboygan	SMALLWOOD, Carol A.	(616)627-2308	1151
Detroit	BRAITHWAITE, Heather J.	(313)577-3925	127
	CARUSO, Genevieve O.	(313)972-7000	190
	STAJNIAK, Elizabeth T.	(313)259-7110	1178
	THOMAS, Laverne J.	(313)849-2776	1237
East Lansing	RIVERA, Diana H.	(517)353-4593	1037
Flint	ARNOLD, Peggy	(313)744-4040	34
Grosse Pointe Woods	REID, Bette C.	(313)884-0884	1018
	STRATELAK, Nadia A.	(313)886-1043	1200
Jackson	SMITH, Catherine A.	(517)784-7025	1153
Kalamazoo	NETZ, David H.	(616)383-1666	896
	PEREZ-STABLE, Maria A.	(616)383-1666	958
	VANDER MEER, Patricia F.	(616)383-1666	1274
Lincoln Park	HECK-RABI, Louise E.	(313)928-3967	520
Mt Pleasant	MULLIGAN, William H.	(517)773-1374	877
Novi	COREY, Marjorie	(313)344-1770	246
Parchment	BOURGEOIS, Ann M.	(616)344-9097	119
Rochester	HILDEBRAND, Linda L.	(313)370-2483	538
	KROMPART, Janet A.	(313)651-4738	679
Taylor	MATZKE, Ellen S.	(313)291-9480	786
Utica	HORNE, Ernest L.	(313)731-4374	560
Warren	VAN ALLEN, Neil K.	(313)696-9508	1271
West Bloomfield	FEDER, Carol S.	(313)851-5822	367
Ypsilanti	MCGARTY, Jean R.	(313)572-1453	805
	YEE, Sandra G.	(313)487-2220	1379

MINNESOTA

Hopkins	YOUNG, Margaret L.	(612)933-5062	1382
Mankato	FARNER, Susan G.	(507)389-5957	365
Minneapolis	GASTON, Judith A.	(612)627-4277	421
	KARON, Bernard L.	(612)625-5050	627
	RAFTER, Susan	(618)870-1935	1003
Northfield	SANFORD, Carolyn C.	(507)663-4266	1081
St Paul	MCKEE, James E.	(612)228-2500	810
	OZOLINS, Karl L.	(612)645-2999	933
	SCHMIDT, Jean M.		1095
Woodbury	WELYGAN, Sylvia M.	(612)459-0764	1323

MISSISSIPPI

Biloxi	FREEDMAN, Jack A.	(601)388-2318	400
Jackson	BELL, Bernice	(601)366-8786	76
	SANDERS, Lou H.	(601)982-7094	1080

MISSOURI

Boonville	JOB, Rose A.		601
Chesterfield	GOLDMAN, Teri B.		446
Fenton	DEKEN, Jean M.	(314)827-1717	288
Florissant	ANTHONY, Paul L.	(314)921-6158	29
	BLANKENSHIP, Phyllis E.	(314)839-3966	104
Kansas City	CARSON, Bonnie L.		188
	DRAYSON, Pamela K.	(816)753-7600	318
	MEIZNER, Karen L.	(816)561-4000	822
	ROTH, Sally	(816)842-0984	1059
	RUBY, Carolyn M.		1065
Nevada	KIEL, Becky	(417)667-8181	647
St Louis	GELINNE, Michael S.	(314)694-4748	426
	MCDERMOTT, Margaret H.	(314)889-6443	802
	PERSHE, Frank F.		961
	SIGALA, Stephanie C.	(314)721-0067	1137
	STELLING, Dwight D.	(314)351-2419	1186

NEBRASKA

Lincoln	WOOL, Gregory J.	(402)475-0391	1368

ABSTRACTER (Cont'd)

NEVADA

Henderson	HARRISON, Susan E.		507
Las Vegas	VOIT, Irene E.	(702)361-5475	1287
Reno	RICE, Dorothy F.	(702)747-2849	1027

NEW HAMPSHIRE

Hampton	KORBER, Nancy	(603)926-6005	671
Keene	MADDEN, Robert J.	(603)352-1909	758
Merrimack	DENTON, Francesca L.	(603)424-8621	293
Nashua	BARRETT, Beth R.	(603)880-3542	59
	FERRIGNO, Helen F.	(603)889-3042	373
Portsmouth	JACOBS, Gloria	(603)431-9346	589
Rindge	STEARNS, Melissa M.	(603)899-5111	1183
Windham	CUNNIFFE, Charlene M.	(603)434-1847	265

NEW JERSEY

Bergenfield	HEISE, George F.	(201)385-9741	522
Bloomfield	LUSTIG, Joanne	(201)743-8777	750
Branchville	RAFFERTY, Stephen P.	(201)948-6380	1003
Bridgewater	DESS, Howard M.	(201)526-1981	295
Caldwell	SKIDANOW, Helene	(201)226-4458	1146
Chatham	SZE, Melanie C.	(201)635-4633	1218
Cherry Hill	GLATT, Carol R.		440
Chester	MANY, Florence L.	(201)879-5167	767
Columbus	ALITO, Martha A.	(609)298-5848	13
Cranford	HALL, Homer J.	(201)276-4311	488
Florham Park	BARRETT, Joyce C.	(201)765-1523	59
Fort Lee	THIRD, Bettie J.	(201)461-6511	1235
Hoboken	PAULSON, Barbara A.	(201)420-8017	950
Leonia	CIMBALA, Diane J.	(201)585-1921	214
Little Ferry	BOTKIN, Karen R.		118
Madison	EDWARDS, Melanie G.	(201)822-1309	337
Mendham	MANTHEY, Carolyn M.	(201)543-2129	767
Millburn	URKEN, Madeline	(201)379-2306	1270
Montclair	BROWN, Cynthia D.	(201)783-6420	142
New Brunswick	MAMAN, Marie	(201)932-9407	764
Newark	CUMMINGS, Charles F.	(201)733-7776	264
	PROFETA, Patricia C.	(201)648-5911	995
Ocean City	MASON, Michael L.	(609)398-0969	781
Perth Amboy	HARDISH, Patrick M.	(201)826-5298	500
Piscataway	CASSEL, Jeris F.	(201)752-0528	193
Pompton Lakes	MENZUL, Faina	(201)839-6885	825
Princeton	JOHNSON, David K.	(609)924-2870	603
	NEWHOUSE, Brian G.	(609)921-8803	899
	SCHMIDT, Mary M.	(609)452-5860	1095
Somerset	GREENBERG, Linda	(201)846-8497	463
Somerville	GABRIEL, Linda	(201)874-8061	411
	KUSHINKA, Kerry L.	(201)526-7323	685
Stanhope	ELIASON, Elisabetha S.	(201)347-8215	342
Summit	JOHNSON, Minnie L.	(201)273-4952	607
Sussex	SMITH, Jo T.	(201)875-3621	1156
Trenton	CONLEY, Gail D.	(609)771-6911	236
	HALPERN, Marilyn	(609)882-2450	489
	MCCULLOUGH, Jack W.	(609)771-2106	801
	WOODLEY, Robert H.	(609)771-2441	1366
Union	AMRON, Irving	(201)688-4980	20
Upper Montclair	O'CONNOR, Christine T.	(201)783-7995	916
Wayne	BIDDEN, Julia E.	(201)831-7801	94
Westfield	SEADER, Jane M.		1109
Whitehouse Station	HOYT, Henry M.	(201)689-7717	566
Woodbridge	DE WITT, Benjamin L.	(201)634-1316	298

NEW MEXICO

Albuquerque	KALE, Shirley W.	(505)298-5980	623
Kirtland AFB	JOURDAIN, Janet M.	(505)844-1768	618
Los Alamos	COMSTOCK, Daniel L.	(505)662-7668	235
Los Lunas	HAYNES, Douglas E.	(505)841-5318	516
Portales	SCHOTT, Mark E.	(505)356-8735	1099

NEW YORK

Albany	KNEE, Michael	(518)442-3586	663
	PINSLEY, Lauren J.	(518)445-2342	975
Alfred	CULLEY, Paul T.	(607)871-2492	263
	FREEMAN, Carla C.	(607)871-2492	400
Amherst	MAYER, Erich J.	(716)691-5554	789
Astoria	FISHER, Maureen C.	(718)204-0631	381
Bayside	BAKISH, David J.	(718)225-0475	50
	SINGER, Phyllis Z.	(718)279-2182	1143
Beechhurst	CARVER, Mary		191

ABSTRACTER (Cont'd)
NEW YORK (Cont'd)

Binghamton	CHAMBERLAIN, Erna B.	(607)723-4064	197
Brockport	RAKSHI, Sri R.	(716)395-5262	1004
Bronx	BARNETT, Philip	(212)549-5359	58
	HOWARD, Joyce M.	(212)588-8400	564
	IOANID, Aurora S.	(212)220-0543	583
	LAMPORT, Bernard	(212)430-3747	691
	ROY, Diptimoy	(914)668-1840	1063
	SHANNON, Michael O.	(212)960-7775	1120
Brooklyn	HOFFMAN, Allen	(718)736-8306	547
	KERR, Virginia M.	(718)789-5410	644
	KRAMER, Allan F.	(718)857-7825	675
	MARSHAK, Bonnie L.	(718)638-6821	773
	ROBBINS, Sara E.	(718)780-7980	1039
	WAHLERT, George A.	(718)833-1899	1292
	WENGER, Milton B.	(718)252-5019	1324
Buffalo	BUSH, Renee B.	(716)832-3081	165
	KASE-MCLAREN, Karen A.	(716)838-6610	628
	PERONE, Karen L.	(716)883-7000	959
	WOLFE, Theresa L.	(716)632-4491	1361
Cohoes	PINGITORE, Patricia E.		974
Dobbs Ferry	HASSAN, Mohammad Z.	(914)693-2031	511
East Aurora	UTTS, Janet R.	(716)655-0031	1270
Fairport	SULOUFF, Patricia T.	(716)223-6844	1208
Flushing	SAFRAN, Scott A.	(718)445-6752	1074
Forest Hills	NERBOSO, Donna L.	(718)897-9826	895
FPO New York	GAMAL, Sandra H.		416
Freeport	VOLLONO, Millicent D.	(516)223-0838	1288
Hamilton	WASHBURN, Keith E.	(315)824-3008	1307
Hastings on Hudson	PATTERSON, Kathleen J.	(914)478-0881	948
Hempstead	ANDREWS, Charles R.	(516)560-5940	26
Hicksville	HOLMES, Harvey L.	(516)935-4813	553
	TRAVERS, Jane E.		1254
Hudson	MARTIN, Lyn M.	(518)828-1465	777
Hyde Park	GRIFFITH, Sheryl	(914)229-8114	469
Islip Terrace	KLATT, Wilma F.	(516)581-5933	658
Ithaca	CASSARO, James P.	(607)255-7046	193
	COONS, William W.	(607)255-7959	242
	HICKEY, John T.	(607)273-1944	536
	STEWART, Linda G.	(607)255-7959	1192
Jackson Heights	RANHAND, Jori L.	(718)469-4728	1007
Nassau	CARABATEAS, Clarissa D.		180
New Paltz	O'CONNELL, Susan	(914)255-5987	915
New Rochelle	SWANSON, Mary A.	(914)633-3954	1213
New York	BALKEMA, John B.	(212)876-8200	52
	BEALER, Jane A.	(212)355-0083	68
	BERNAL, Rose M.	(212)674-6525	88
	BOZIWICK, George E.	(212)870-1675	124
	BRISTAH, Pamela J.	(212)749-2802	137
	COOPER, Jo E.	(212)808-6515	243
	CURTIS, James A.	(212)222-9638	267
	DERRICKSON, Margaret	(212)620-4230	294
	DEVERA, Rosalinda M.	(212)557-2570	297
	FENTON, Joan T.	(212)682-2500	371
	FLEISHMAN, Lauren Z.	(212)371-2000	384
	FRIED, Suzanne C.	(212)963-0508	403
	GOLLOP, Sandra G.	(212)770-7911	447
	GOODSELL, Joan W.	(212)210-7044	450
	GRANDE, Paula G.	(212)536-3229	457
	GRETES, Frances C.	(212)309-9634	467
	GROTE, Janet H.	(212)627-1500	473
	GUILER, Paula J.	(212)689-3341	476
	HERMAN, Marsha	(212)679-6105	531
	HYMAN, Richard J.	(212)865-7962	580
	KAIN, Joan P.	(212)850-0768	622
	KELLEY, Dennis L.	(212)210-7043	636
	KEMPE, Deborah A.	(212)595-6583	639
	KENSELAAR, Robert	(212)870-1661	642
	KING, Trina E.	(212)427-1023	652
	MOTIHAR, Kamla	(212)838-8400	872
	MOUNIR, Khalil A.	(212)373-5640	873
	PALMER, Paul R.	(212)865-5781	936
	PISTILLI, Susan A.	(212)621-1580	976
	REDEL, Judy A.	(212)337-7043	1014
	REMECZKI, Paul W.	(212)873-3400	1022
	RUBINSTEIN, Ed	(212)725-4550	1065
	SEGAL, Judith	(212)222-3699	1112
	SHAPIRO, Barbara G.	(212)621-1582	1121

ABSTRACTER (Cont'd)
NEW YORK (Cont'd)

New York	SWANSON, Dorothy T.	(212)998-2630	1213
	THURSTON, Ethel H.	(212)989-8073	1243
	VAUGHN, Susan J.	(212)260-2544	1280
	WEATHERFORD, Elizabeth	(212)925-4682	1311
	WOSH, Peter J.	(212)581-7400	1369
	WRIGHT, Sylvia H.	(212)222-6148	1373
North Syracuse	AUSTIN, Ralph A.	(315)457-1799	40
Norwich	WINDSOR, Donald A.	(607)336-4628	1354
Ogdensburg	FRANZ, David A.	(315)393-2950	398
Oneonta	CROWLEY, John V.	(607)431-2725	261
Palisades	WARD, Edith	(914)359-2081	1303
Pearl River	BRISFJORD, Inez S.	(914)735-1567	136
	SPERR BRISFJORD, Inez L.	(914)735-1567	1173
Rochester	BUFF, Iva M.	(716)244-7762	155
	CHURCH, Virginia K.	(716)475-2558	213
	HELBERS, Catherine A.	(716)594-9652	523
	ISGANITIS, Jamie C.	(716)461-1943	585
	REITANO, Maimie V.	(716)722-7067	1022
	RITTER, Audrey L.	(716)475-6823	1036
	SEASE, Sandra A.	(716)724-6783	1110
Roslyn	WEINSTEIN, Judith K.	(516)627-6200	1318
Scarsdale	ABEND, Jody U.	(914)723-1360	2
Schenectady	HOLT, Lisa A.	(518)370-1811	554
Shrub Oak	TIFFEAULT, Alice A.	(914)528-4048	1244
Syosset	CALVANO, Margaret	(516)921-1674	174
Syracuse	MCLAUGHLIN, Pamela W.	(315)476-7359	813
	MINOR, Barbara A.	(315)425-9348	846
	PRINS, Johanna W.	(315)475-5534	993
	WASYLENKO, Lydia W.	(315)423-2585	1308
White Plains	MCELHANEY, William E.	(914)949-3270	804
	MCGARVEY, Eileen B.	(914)683-2794	805
Williamsville	SCHUTT, Dedre A.	(716)633-6384	1103
Yorktown Heights	LEE, Douglas E.	(914)245-8978	709
	RUBINO, Cynthia C.	(914)962-4518	1065

NORTH CAROLINA

Beaufort	BUMGARNER, John L.	(919)728-5530	157
Chapel Hill	TALBERT, David M.	(919)962-0700	1220
	TUCKER, Mary E.	(919)933-8982	1262
Charlotte	HOWARD, Susanna J.	(704)364-7987	564
Durham	BALLARD, Robert M.	(919)489-6358	53
	CARRINGTON, Bessie M.	(919)684-2373	186
	LAVINE, Marcia M.	(919)684-2011	703
	SPARKS, Martha E.	(919)489-6012	1171
Greensboro	MITCHELL, W B.	(919)334-5452	849
	WRIGHT, Keith C.	(919)282-3712	1372
Greenville	SHIRES, Nancy P.	(919)758-8252	1131
Mebane	MINEIRO, Barbara E.	(919)578-4299	845
Reidsville	PENN, Lea M.		957
Sanford	BEAGLE, Donald R.	(919)776-8372	68
Winston-Salem	HICKS, Michael	(919)788-4084	537

NORTH DAKOTA

Minot	ROBERTSON, Pamela S.	(701)838-6080	1042

OHIO

Akron	GUSS, Margaret B.	(216)375-7224	478
Bay Village	BUTCHER, Sharon L.	(216)871-0913	166
Bedford	PARCH, Grace D.		939
Bowling Green	ENDRES, Maureen D.	(419)352-9213	348
Brunswick	HAMBLEY, Susan L.	(216)225-0436	490
Canfield	LITTLE, Dean K.	(216)533-6703	733
Chardon	KLINGER, William E.	(216)564-9340	661
Chillicothe	PLANTON, Stanley P.	(614)775-9500	977
Cincinnati	ALBERT, Stephen G.	(513)541-9119	10
	POCKROSE, Sheryl R.	(513)369-6954	979
	SCHUTZ, Robert S.	(513)948-7518	1103
	WELLINGTON, Jean S.	(513)475-6724	1322
Cleveland	FELDER, Bruce B.	(216)696-2100	369
	PETIT, J M.	(216)749-5052	965
	SANTAVICCA, Edmund F.	(216)687-2365	1082
Cleveland Heights	LANTZ, Elizabeth A.	(216)541-2905	697
Columbus	BOOMGAARDEN, Wesley L.	(614)447-0524	115
	BRANDT, Michael H.	(614)863-2814	128
	GOERLER, Raimund E.	(614)292-2409	443
	HEARD, Jeffrey L.		518
	MILLER, Dennis P.	(614)888-1886	837

ABSTRACTER (Cont'd)
OHIO (Cont'd)
Columbus

	PLATAU, Gerard O.	(614)457-1687	977
	RATLIFF, Priscilla	(614)488-1622	1009
	SANDERS, Nancy P.		1080
	STOBAUGH, Robert E.	(614)451-3271	1195
	STRALEY, Dona S.	(614)292-3362	1200
	WALDEN, Graham R.	(614)292-0938	1294
Dayton	HECHT, Judith N.	(513)229-3024	519
Fairview Park	HYSLOP, Marjorie R.	(216)333-8645	580
Huron	CURRIE, William W.	(419)433-5560	266
Lakewood	TAYLOR, Patricia L.	(216)226-8275	1228
Mayfield Heights	RASKIN, Rosa S.	(216)442-3009	1009
Sidney	WILSON, Memory A.	(513)492-1315	1352
Yellow Springs	NEWMAN, Marianne L.		899

OKLAHOMA

Ardmore	KIMBLE, Valerie F.	(405)226-3980	649
Norman	HOVDE, David M.	(405)325-4231	563
	POLAND, Jean A.	(405)360-7095	980
Oklahoma City	JONES, Charles E.	(405)751-0574	611
Stillwater	ROUSE, Roscoe	(405)377-1651	1061
Tahlequah	HILL, Helen K.		540

OREGON

Corvallis	MURRAY, Lucia M.		882
Eugene	HADDERMAN, Margaret	(503)342-5457	482
	ROBERTSON, Howard W.	(503)686-3064	1042
	WALKER, Luise E.	(503)686-3023	1295
Manzanita	LARSON, Signe E.	(503)368-6990	700
Portland	DAVID, Kay O.	(503)222-9981	276
	EDWARDS, Susan E.	(506)224-6812	338

PENNSYLVANIA

Allentown	WAGNER, Darla L.	(215)264-8203	1291
Blue Bell	LAUTENSCHLAG, Elisabeth C.		703
Clarion	HARTSOCK, Ralph M.	(814)226-2000	508
Coraopolis	KASPERKO, Jean M.		629
Easton	CRAWFORD, Gregory A.	(215)253-9459	256
Erie	KAGER, Jeffrey F.	(814)825-3066	621
Franklin Center	HOWLEY, Deborah H.	(215)459-7049	566
Gladwyne	FISHER, Daphne V.	(215)525-6628	380
Glenside	LOCKETT, Cheryl L.		736
Harrisburg	SHULTZ, Suzanne M.	(717)782-4292	1133
Jenkintown	SEVY, Barbara S.	(215)884-8275	1117
Kennerdell	CHERESNOWSKI, Linda M.	(814)385-6896	206
Lehigh Valley	WEBER, A C.	(215)837-9615	1313
Malvern	YOUNG, Dorothy E.	(215)647-7449	1381
McKeesport	KISH, Veronica R.	(412)678-1749	656
Meadville	STALLARD, Kathryn E.	(814)333-4363	1179
Millersville	JUDGE, Joseph M.	(717)872-7590	619
	LOTLIKAR, Sarojini D.		742
Monroeville	BERGER, Lewis W.	(412)825-2284	85
New Castle	FUSCO, Marilyn A.		410
Norristown	CATHEY, Gail L.	(215)278-5100	195
Philadelphia	AUGUST, Sidney	(215)985-2872	39
	BOISCLAIR, Regina A.	(215)438-0173	111
	COOPER, Linda	(215)625-4719	243
	CUTRONA, Cheryl	(215)844-9027	268
	GREEN, Patricia L.	(215)724-5715	462
	HOLMES, John H.	(215)592-1841	553
	KING, Eleanor M.		650
	LEVIN, Pauline G.	(215)561-5831	720
	MEREDITH, Phyllis C.	(609)757-4640	825
	SCHAEFFER, Judith E.	(215)843-8840	1089
	ZIPF, Elizabeth M.	(215)587-4815	1389
Pittsburgh	BROSKY, Catherine M.	(412)682-0837	141
	HARTNER, Elizabeth P.		508
	LAMMERT, Diana P.	(412)621-6941	691
	MITTEN, Lisa A.	(412)521-4462	850
	RAO, Rama K.	(412)429-0543	1008
	WRIGHT, Nancy M.	(412)237-5948	1372
Reading	SMALL, Sally S.	(215)320-4823	1151
	STILLMAN, Mary E.	(215)921-2381	1194
Sanatoga	NIPPERT, Carolyn C.	(215)323-4829	904
Sarver	LIVENGOOD, Candice C.		734
Shenandoah	USES, Ann K.	(717)462-0076	1270
State College	STOUT, Leon J.	(814)238-4855	1198

ABSTRACTER (Cont'd)
PENNSYLVANIA (Cont'd)

University Park	CARSON, M S.	(814)865-1818	188
	SULZER, John H.	(814)865-4861	1209
	ZABEL, Diane M.	(814)863-2898	1385
Upper Darby	MORGAN, Dorothy H.	(215)789-9727	863
Wilkes-Barre	TYCE, Richard	(717)826-1148	1266

PUERTO RICO

Caparra Heights	FERNANDEZ, Josefina L.	(809)782-2618	373

RHODE ISLAND

Kingston	SCHNEIDER, Stewart P.	(401)792-2878	1097

SOUTH CAROLINA

Charleston	PARKER, Mary A.	(803)556-9454	942
Clemson	TAYLOR, Dennis S.	(803)656-3031	1226
Columbia	CHOI, Jin M.	(803)799-8786	210
	MILTON, Brenda R.	(803)452-5454	845
	MOSS, Patsy G.	(803)799-4349	872
Greenwood	HARE, Ann T.	(803)229-8365	501

SOUTH DAKOTA

Brookings	BROWN, Philip L.	(605)692-7735	146
Sioux Falls	LANG, Elizabeth A.		695

TENNESSEE

Bristol	HERRING, Mark Y.	(615)968-9449	533
Clarksville	RIVES, Lydia L.	(615)647-9484	1037
Cookeville	TABACHNICK, Sharon	(615)372-3958	1219
Germantown	RONDESTVEDT, Helen F.	(901)756-5470	1053
Knoxville	CROWTHER, Karmen N.	(615)974-4171	262
	HASTINGS, Constance M.	(615)690-0368	511
Memphis	PERRY, Glenda L.	(901)527-4348	960
	VILES, Elza A.	(901)454-4412	1284
Nashville	ARMONTROUT, Brian A.	(615)320-3678	32
	PILKINGTON, James P.	(615)322-2927	973
Oak Ridge	SNYDER, Cathrine E.	(615)483-1228	1164
Palmyra	FOWLER, James W.	(615)647-4172	393

TEXAS

Abilene	ANDERSON, Madeleine J.	(915)674-2344	24
Austin	BURLINGHAM, Merry L.		161
	BURT, Eugene C.	(512)471-4777	164
	CABLE, Carole L.	(512)327-2158	170
	DIVELY, Reddy	(512)288-3371	306
	HELFER, Robert S.	(512)929-3086	523
	JACKSON, Eugene B.	(512)345-1653	587
	JACKSON, Ruth L.	(512)345-1653	588
	MCCANN, Charlotte P.		793
	RODE, Shelley J.		1047
	TAYLOR, Nancy L.	(512)346-1426	1228
	WESTBROOK, Jo L.		1326
	WILLIAMS, Suzi	(512)451-3482	1346
Bedford	PETERS, Mary N.	(817)283-3739	962
Brownfield	HAMILTON, Betty D.	(806)637-4213	491
College Station	ST. CLAIR, Gloriana S.	(409)696-8982	1075
Cooper	ALBRIGHT, Susie K.		10
Cypress	KUJOORY, Parvin	(713)890-7542	683
Denton	SCHLESSINGER, Bernard S.	(817)898-2617	1094
Evless	STATTON, Alison H.	(214)283-0802	1183
Fort Worth	WESTBROOK, Brenda S.	(817)831-7232	1326
	WOOD, Richard C.	(517)927-5389	1365
Houston	BAGHAL-KAR, Vali E.	(213)667-4336	45
	BRUNNER, A M.	(713)463-0416	151
	CEBRUN, Mary J.	(713)965-4045	196
	TRAFFORD, Susan M.	(713)271-5610	1253
Huntsville	YOUNG, J A.	(409)295-8766	1382
Irving	AYRES, Edwin M.	(214)254-4108	43
	COCHRAN, Carolyn	(214)258-6767	225
Lubbock	MARLEY, Judith L.	(806)799-3299	772
McAllen	MYCUE, David J.		884
San Angelo	PENNER, Elaine C.	(915)658-4534	957
San Antonio	CHANCE, Truett L.		199
	HEWINS, Elizabeth H.	(512)655-4672	535
	HOOD, Elizabeth	(512)736-7292	556
Waco	GEARY, Gregg S.		424
	RICHARDS, James H.	(817)756-0602	1028
Wimberley	SHAW, Ben B.	(512)847-2776	1123

ABSTRACTER (Cont'd)

UTAH
Bountiful	SANDERS, William D.	(801)292-4429	1080
Provo	NIELSON, Paula I.	(801)375-9241	903
Salt Lake City	REDDICK, Mary J.	(801)581-7024	1013

VERMONT
Burlington	YERBURGH, Mark R.	(802)658-0337	1379
Essex Junction	LAPIDOW, Amy R.	(802)878-2665	697
Middlebury	POST, Jennifer C.	(802)388-6252	986
Northfield	WARD, Robert C.	(802)485-7344	1304
Rutland	MCCULLOUGH, Doreen J.	(802)773-5900	801

VIRGINIA
Alexandria	AUSTON, Ione	(703)549-4325	40
	ROBERTSON, Jack	(703)549-3260	1042
Arlington	ASHKENAS, Bruce F.	(301)763-7410	36
	CALKIN, Homer L.	(703)920-4910	173
	CLARKE, Robert F.		219
	DESSAINT, Alain Y.	(703)247-7750	295
	WOLF, Richard E.	(703)276-0270	1360
Charlottesville	COOPER, Jean L.	(804)978-4363	243
	LINDEMANN, Richard H.	(804)924-3025	729
	RODRIGUEZ, Robert D.		1048
	WALKER, Diane P.	(804)924-7041	1295
Falls Church	HARRIS, Virginia B.	(703)698-6968	506
Herndon	GUERRIERO, Donald A.	(703)860-1058	476
Luray	GRIEVE, Karen R.		468
Lynchburg	KAWAGUCHI, Miyako	(804)239-3071	632
McLean	MACEWEN, Virginia B.		755
Reston	JENSEN, Raymond A.	(703)648-6820	599
	KARRER, Jonathan K.	(703)648-4302	628
	MCLANE, Kathleen	(703)620-3660	813
Richmond	GWIN, James E.	(804)288-7602	479
	HALL, Bonlyn G.	(804)359-0409	487
	VAN SICKLEN, Lindsay L.	(804)320-9691	1277
	WILLS, Luella G.	(804)233-7616	1349
Roanoke	COLLINS, Mitzi L.		233
Vienna	SCHAEFER, Mary E.	(703)759-6339	1089
Virginia Beach	BILLERT, Julia A.	(804)427-7150	96

WASHINGTON
Bellingham	SYMES, Dal S.		1217
Bothell	YEE, J E.	(206)625-4870	1379
Cheney	ALKIRE, Leland G.	(509)235-4669	13
Kirkland	SUGGS, John K.	(206)823-6754	1206
Renton	SIENDA, Madeline M.		1136
Seattle	CRANDALL, Michael D.	(206)633-2530	255
	GRIPPO, Christopher F.		471
	HARMALA, Amy A.	(206)632-8338	502
	KREPS, Lise E.	(206)527-2817	678
	SCOTT-MILLER, Gwen	(206)783-8687	1108
	SILVA, Mary E.		1138
Steilacoom	COHEN, Jane L.		228

WEST VIRGINIA
Charleston	HUMPHRIES, Joy D.		574
Wheeling	JULIAN, Charles A.	(304)233-5900	619

WISCONSIN
Appleton	KLAVER, Timothy J.	(414)735-0463	658
	NADZIEJKA, David E.	(414)731-8904	886
Lake Geneva	CIBOCH, Lorraine A.	(414)245-5806	214
Madison	CLARK, Peter W.	(608)257-4861	217
	ROSENSHIELD, Jill K.	(608)233-2518	1057
Menomonie	JAX, John J.	(715)232-1184	595
Mequon	NOVOTNY, Lynn E.	(414)241-8957	911
Milwaukee	SAGER, Lynn S.	(414)964-5940	1074
	SMITH-GREENWOLD, Kathryn R.	(414)445-3586	1162
Racine	SCHINK, Sandra C.	(414)634-1495	1093
Sheboygan	TOBIN, R J.	(414)459-7606	1247

CANADA

ALBERTA
Athabasca	DWORACZEK, Marian	(403)675-6261	330
Calgary	ONN, Shirley A.	(403)282-5311	924
	ROBINS, Nora D.	(403)274-8837	1043
	VINE, Rita F.	(403)247-6524	1285

ABSTRACTER (Cont'd)

ALBERTA (Cont'd)
Edmonton	COOKE, Geraldine A.	(403)439-5879	241
	ROONEY, Sieglinde E.	(403)432-3793	1053
Lethbridge	DROESSLER, Judith B.	(403)381-2285	320
Tofield	LEE, Diana W.	(403)662-3607	709

BRITISH COLUMBIA
Vancouver	DEVAKOS, Elizabeth R.	(604)255-6636	297
	GONNAMI, Tsuneharu	(604)224-4296	447
	HART, Elizabeth	(604)228-9031	507
Victoria	EKLAND, Patricia A.	(604)721-8275	341
	ROMANIUK, Elena	(604)592-8819	1052

MANITOBA
Winnipeg	MARSHALL, Kenneth E.	(204)269-3243	774

NOVA SCOTIA
Halifax	MACLENNAN, Oriel C.	(902)454-0697	757

ONTARIO
Bowmanville	MOON, Jeffrey D.	(416)263-8504	857
Brampton	CHAN, Bruce A.	(416)793-4636	199
Brockville	WARREN, Peggy A.	(613)342-6352	1306
Downsview	ZVEJNIEKS, Laila R.	(416)235-4545	1391
Guelph	PAL, Gabriel	(519)824-4120	935
	ROURKE, Lorna E.	(519)824-4120	1061
Mississauga	ATHA, Shirley A.	(416)822-5704	37
Nepean	KAYE, Barbara J.	(613)225-9920	632
Oakville	LUCIANI, Ellie	(416)842-4484	746
Ottawa	ARONSON, Marcia L.		34
	BRIERE, Jean M.	(613)996-3817	135
	GUILBERT, Manon M.	(613)233-8012	476
	LEUNG, Frank F.	(613)994-6920	719
	MASON-WARD, Lesley	(613)726-1314	781
	MCKEEN, C E.	(613)996-7388	810
Scarborough	BALL, John L.	(416)284-3245	52
Toronto	BREGMAN, Alvan M.	(416)767-3625	131
	CHIU, Lily F.	(416)868-2909	209
	DOWDING, Martin R.	(416)925-7593	315
	FRIEDLAND, Frances K.	(416)789-0741	403
	NIXON, Audrey I.	(416)531-0830	906
	OLSHEN, Toni	(416)488-5321	922
	SMITH, Anne C.	(416)423-9826	1152
	TIPLER, Stephen B.	(416)654-5617	1246
	TUDOR, Dean F.	(416)767-1340	1262

QUEBEC
Blainville	JETTE, Monika E.	(514)430-4945	600
Boischatel	LUSSIER, Richard	(418)822-1904	749
Chicoutimi	GAUDREAU, Louis	(418)549-9520	422
Hampstead	FLUK, Louise R.	(514)488-3187	386
Hull	MAILLOUX, Jean Y.	(819)997-5365	761
Montreal	BERARDINUCCI, Heather R.	(514)255-2445	84
	BERNHARD, Paulette	(514)343-7408	89
	BISSON, Jacques	(514)482-9110	100
	CAN, Hung V.	(514)521-8201	177
	CHAGNON, Danielle G.		197
	DESROCHERS, Monique	(514)733-0846	295
	DUCHESNEAU, Pierre	(514)281-6166	322
	DUMONT, Monique	(514)288-0100	325
	GAULIN, S D.	(514)645-9444	422
	GIRARD, Luc	(514)343-7445	438
	GONZALEZ, Paloma	(514)735-1977	448
	LATOUR, Pierre	(514)729-4165	701
	MOHAMMED, Selima	(514)398-4780	852
	NAGY, Cecile		886
	ORLANDO, Richard P.	(514)877-1470	926
	PARKER, Charles G.	(514)282-3934	941
	PELLETIER, Rosaire	(514)382-0895	955
	THACH, Phat V.	(514)727-6817	1233
Montreal Oest	MORRISON, H D.	(514)488-9279	868
Quebec	DENIGER, Constant	(418)692-4369	292
	GELINAS, Michel R.	(418)522-7203	426
Rosemere	LAPIERRE, France	(514)621-8507	697
St-Leonard	LAFRENIERE, Myriam	(514)322-6818	688
Sherbrooke	SOKOV, Asta M.	(819)821-7566	1166
Sillery	LALIBERTE, Madeleine A.	(418)687-9260	689
Touraine	MURRAY-LACHAPELLE, Rosemary F.	(819)568-0282	882

ABSTRACTER (Cont'd)
QUEBEC (Cont'd)
Westmount   WADE, C A.   1290

SASKATCHEWAN
Regina   BROWNE, Berks G.   (306)584-8247   148

AUSTRALIA
Queensland   GOODELL, John S.   448
Toowong   GOODELL, Paulette M.   448

CUBA
Havana   ASIS, Moises   36

HONG KONG
Fanling   WU, Edith Y.   1373
The Peak   SANDFELDER, Paula M.   1080

INDIA
Hyderabad   SATYANARAYANA, Vadhri V.   (260)586-0000   1084

ITALY
Milan   CASIRAGHI, Edoardo   192
Rome   HUEMER, Christina G.   570

JAPAN
Aichi-ken   SANO, Hikomaro   1081

NETHERLANDS
Rotterdam   SCHUURSMA, Ann B.   1103

NIGERIA
Lagos   AFOLAYAN, Matthew A.   (018)001-6040   7

PHILIPPINES
Quezon City   OREJANA, Rebecca D.   925

SAUDI ARABIA
Riyadh   BUTT, Abdul W.   167

ACADEMIC LIBRARY CONSULTANT

ALABAMA
Birmingham   SCALES, Diann R.   (205)322-8458   1087
    SPENCE, Paul H.   (205)934-6360   1173
    STEPHENS, Jerry W.   (209)363-6000   1188
Brewton   BIGGS-WILLIAMS, Evelyn A.   (205)867-2445   95
Helena   NELSON, William N.   (205)663-9251   895
Huntsville   KENDRICK, Aubrey W.   (205)837-7597   640
    WILLIAMS, Delmus E.   (205)895-6540   1342
Mobile   DAMICO, James A.   (205)460-7021   271
    PARSLEY, Brantley H.   (205)675-5990   944
Montgomery   GREGORY, Vicki L.   (205)277-1759   466
    LANE, Robert B.   (205)288-8122   694
    MCCRANK, Lawrence J.   (205)244-9202   800
Tuscaloosa   OSBURN, Charles B.   (205)348-7561   927

ALASKA
Anchorage   LESH, Nancy L.   (907)786-1877   718
Juneau   SCHORR, Alan E.   (907)586-6014   1099

ARIZONA
Chandler   MCGORRAY, John J.   (602)961-8016   807
Flagstaff   EGAN, Terence W.   (602)523-6819   338
Phoenix   BOROVANSKY, Vladimir T.   117
    HEINTZ, Mary L.   (602)277-3772   522
    MCCOLGIN, Michael A.   (602)255-4890   797
Scottsdale   POTTER, William G.   (602)991-5578   987
Tempe   OETTING, Edward C.   (602)345-7636   917
    RIGGS, Donald E.   (602)965-3950   1034
    STEEL, Virginia   (602)965-3282   1183
    STEWART, Douglas J.   (602)897-7191   1192
Tucson   BUXTON, David T.   (602)621-2101   168
    DICKINSON, Donald C.   (602)621-3565   300
    FRANK, Donald G.   (602)742-9688   396
    HEIDENREICH, Fred L.   (602)626-7724   521
    HEITSHU, Sara C.   (602)621-2101   523
    HURT, Charlie D.   (602)621-3566   578

ACADEMIC LIBRARY CONSULTANT (Cont'd)
ARIZONA (Cont'd)
Tucson   JOHNSON, Robert K.   (602)323-0418   608
    LAIRD, W D.   (602)621-2101   688
    MILLER, Edward P.   837
    MYERS, Roger   (602)792-3452   885
    PHIPPS, Shelley E.   (602)621-2101   969
    REICHEL, Mary   (602)621-2101   1018

ARKANSAS
Batesville   WATSON, Ellen I.   (501)793-9813   1309
Fayetteville   EARNEST, Jeffrey D.   (501)521-8388   332
    HARRISON, John A.   (501)443-4403   506
Fort Smith   PIERSON, Betty   (501)785-7135   972
Little Rock   BRECK, Paul A.   (501)569-3121   131
    SANDERS, Kathryn A.   (501)227-5581   1080
Mountain View   MCNEIL, William K.   (501)269-3851   816
Searcy   BEARD, Craig W.   (501)268-6161   69

CALIFORNIA
Alameda   HOSEL, Harold V.   (415)522-5875   561
Albany   EWEN, Eric P.   (415)527-0894   359
Aptos   HERON, David W.   (408)688-6994   532
Arcata   CROSBY-MUILENBURG, Corryn   260
    OYLER, David K.   (707)826-3441   932
Bakersfield   KIRKLAND, Janice J.   655
Benicia   MILLER, Davic C.   (707)746-6728   836
Berkeley   BARKER, Joseph W.   (415)642-0590   56
    BERGER, Michael G.   (415)642-9485   85
    BERRING, Robert C.   (415)642-9980   90
    CASTRO, Rafaela G.   (415)526-0815   194
    CLARENCE, Judy   (415)649-2400   216
    GALLOWAY, R D.   415
    HANDMAN, Gary P.   (415)524-9728   495
    KOBZINA, Norma G.   (415)643-6475   666
    LEVIN, Marc A.   (415)642-1472   720
    RHEE, Susan F.   (415)540-7150   1025
    ROBERT, Berring C.   (415)642-9980   1039
    SALMON, Stephen R.   (415)549-3394   1077
    SCHRIEFER, Kent   (415)642-8038   1100
    STOCKTON, Gloria J.   (415)843-8550   1196
    VAN HOUSE, Nancy A.   (415)642-0855   1275
    WHEELER, Helen R.   (415)549-2970   1329
Beverly Hills   CHAMMOU, Eliezer   (213)273-1395   198
    RUNYON, Judith A.   (213)859-5102   1067
Carmichael   PARSONS, Jerry L.   (916)966-2086   945
Castro Valley   CASTAGNOZZI, Carol A.   (415)581-6034   194
Chico   SESSIONS, Judith A.   (916)895-5862   1117
Claremont   ALLEN, Susan M.   16
Costa Mesa   EPSTEIN, Susan B.   (714)754-1559   351
Davis   BENOIT, Gerald   82
    BLANCHARD, J R.   (916)753-5126   103
    BLANK, Karen L.   (916)752-2110   104
    ELLIOTT, C D.   (916)752-2110   343
Del Mar   HOLT, Raymond M.   (619)755-7878   554
El Cerrito   KIRESEN, Evelyn M.   (415)526-6718   654
    MACAULEY, C C.   (415)524-2762   754
Fallbrook   MCNALLY, Ruth C.   816
Fullerton   BRIL, Patricia L.   (714)773-3852   136
Goleta   GRAZIANO, Eugene   (805)968-2281   460
Hayward   ROSE, Melissa M.   (415)881-3664   1055
    SASSE, Margo   (415)482-2770   1083
Irvine   FINEMAN, Michael   (714)856-8160   377
    POOLE, Jay M.   (714)856-6377   983
    SCHLACKS, Charles   (714)559-6184   1093
    SHAWL, Janice H.   (714)854-7413   1124
    TASH, Steven J.   (714)786-7857   1224
    TSENG, Sally C.   (714)856-6832   1260
    WOODS, Lawrence A.   (714)786-3507   1367
Kensington   LAWRENCE, Gary S.   (415)642-2370   704
La Jolla   ALLISON, Terry L.   (619)534-1256   17
    BOWLES, Garrett H.   (619)534-2759   121
    CASTETTER, Karla M.   (619)459-5369   194
    GALLOWAY, Sue   (619)534-6443   415
    HURLBERT, Irene W.   (619)534-1261   577
    MILLER, R B.   (619)534-3064   841
    MIRSKY, Phyllis S.   (619)534-1234   847
    SCHILLER, Anita R.   (619)534-3337   1093

ACADEMIC LIBRARY CONSULTANT (Cont'd)
CALIFORNIA (Cont'd)

Lomita	BOWLING, Lance C.	(213)831-1322	121
Long Beach	AYALA, John L.	(213)599-8028	42
	BRITTON, Helen H.	(213)498-4047	137
	SCEPANSKI, Jordan M.	(213)498-4047	1088
	SMITH, Gordon W.	(213)590-5542	1155
	WELLS, H L.	(213)598-3549	1322
Los Altos Hills	MCDONALD, Marilyn M.	(415)960-4390	803
Los Angeles	ANDREWS, Karen L.	(213)825-2649	26
	DALY, Eudice	(213)474-6080	271
	GRASSIAN, Esther S.	(213)825-2138	458
	HAYTHORN, Joseph D.	(213)938-3621	517
	HOFFMAN, Irene M.	(213)839-5722	548
	KHATTAB, Hosneya M.	(213)733-1196	646
	KUNSELMAN, Joan D.	(213)825-1204	684
	LEE, Don A.	(213)650-4946	709
	LEUNG, Terry S.	(213)306-5686	719
	MERRIFIELD, Thomas C.	(213)390-4717	826
	MORRIS, Jacquelyn M.	(213)259-2671	866
	RITCHESON, Charles R.	(213)743-2543	1036
	RONEY, Raymond G.	(213)532-3670	1053
	SCHERREI, Rita A.	(213)825-1201	1092
	SCHOTTLAENDER, Brian E.	(213)825-7785	1099
	STREIKER, Susan L.	(213)738-6727	1201
	TERZIAN, Shohig S.	(213)478-5193	1232
	TOMPKINS, Philip	(213)743-2543	1250
	WALTERS, Mary D.	(213)224-2215	1301
	WATERS, Marie B.	(213)825-1693	1308
	WILKINSON, David W.	(213)224-2251	1340
	WONG, Cecilia	(213)736-1139	1362
	ZEIDBERG, David S.	(213)825-4879	1387
Marina del Rey	SHANK, Russell	(213)823-6123	1120
Menlo Park	FRANK, Peter R.	(415)329-1173	397
	TRUJILLO, Roberto G.	(415)329-0227	1259
Mill Valley	WHITE, Cecil R.	(415)388-8080	1330
Northridge	DAVIS, Douglas A.	(818)885-2261	278
	DURAN, Karin J.	(818)885-2501	328
	ECKLUND, Kristin A.	(818)349-6115	335
Oakland	BENNETT, Celestine C.	(415)893-9645	81
	COOPER, Richard S.	(415)530-8080	243
	DANTON, J P.	(415)653-4802	274
	HOWATT, Helen C.	(415)433-1160	565
Palo Alto	KAHN, Paul J.	(415)327-3135	622
Pasadena	GOODSTEIN, Judith R.	(818)356-6433	450
Pomona	KUHNER, David A.	(714)593-2467	683
Poway	DOLLEN, Charles J.	(619)748-5348	310
Redwood City	SCHLACHTER, Gail A.	(415)594-0743	1093
Richmond	O'CONNOR, Brian C.	(415)237-6561	915
	VANDERBERG, Patricia S.	(415)237-1081	1273
Riverside	DUNN, Kathleen K.	(714)359-6420	327
	THOMPSON, James C.	(714)682-4549	1240
	VIERICH, Richard W.	(714)787-3511	1284
Sacramento	MARRIOTT, Lois I.	(916)455-8026	773
	MIRONENKO, Rimma	(916)355-4076	847
San Bernardino	JOHNSON, Paul A.	(714)883-3979	608
San Diego	BOSSEAU, Don L.	(619)229-2538	117
	DYER, Charles R.	(619)236-2292	330
	HOWARD, Pamela F.		564
	KAYE, Karen	(619)560-2695	632
	SOETE, George J.	(619)453-3538	1165
	VOIGT, Melvin J.		1287
San Francisco	CODER, Ann	(415)442-7000	226
	GITLER, Robert L.	(415)221-9216	438
	GUNDERSON, Jeffery R.	(415)929-1472	477
	HAIKALIS, Peter D.	(415)338-2188	484
	TREGGIARI, Arnaldo	(415)469-1649	1255
San Jose	BRIDGMAN, David L.	(408)997-3723	135
	EMMICK, Nancy J.	(408)277-3904	348
	LEONARD, Barbara G.	(408)277-3902	716
San Luis Obispo	ROCKMAN, Ilene F.	(805)756-2273	1046
	WALCH, David B.	(805)546-2345	1293
San Marcos	CATER, Judy J.	(619)744-1150	194
San Mateo	ATKINS, Gregg T.	(415)574-6100	38
San Rafael	PLOTKIN, Nathan	(415)479-7018	978
Santa Barbara	GIBBONS, Carolbeth	(805)961-3320	431
	RUDD, Janet K.	(805)682-9560	1065
Santa Cruz	COOPER, Susan C.	(408)426-2841	243
	DYSON, Allan J.	(408)429-2076	331
Santa Monica	HALL, Anthony	(213)827-1707	487

ACADEMIC LIBRARY CONSULTANT (Cont'd)
CALIFORNIA (Cont'd)

Santa Rosa	PETTAS, William A.	(707)527-4392	965
Saratoga	BONNET, Janice M.	(408)867-4561	114
Simi Valley	WONG, Clark C.	(805)522-5233	1362
Stanford	CARSON, Susan A.	(415)723-2092	188
	PAI, Herman H.	(415)723-6585	934
	SCHMIDT, C J.	(415)493-5280	1095
	STANGL, Peter		1180
Stockton	CLARKE, Tobin D.	(209)477-5952	219
	LEONHARDT, Thomas W.	(209)946-2434	717
	MOORE, Evia B.	(209)474-7029	859
Truckee	BLESSE, Robert E.	(916)587-3172	105
Turlock	AMRHEIN, John K.	(209)667-3607	20
Ukiah	FELDMAN, Irwin	(707)468-8163	369
Vacaville	ELDREDGE, Mary		342
Venice	EDELSTEIN, J M.	(213)827-8984	335
Ventura	BENNETT, Carson W.		81
Walnut Creek	SMITH, Susan A.	(415)944-1603	1161
Yucaipa	BUTLER, Randall R.	(714)797-3859	167

COLORADO

Boulder	FINK, Deborah	(303)492-8302	378
	KOHL, David F.	(303)492-6897	668
	WERTHEIMER, Marilyn L.	(303)442-5583	1325
Colorado Springs	BARRETT, Donald J.	(303)598-3163	59
	MANNING, Leslie A.	(303)593-3115	766
	SHERIDAN, John B.	(303)473-2233	1127
Denver	BREIVIK, Patricia S.	(303)556-2805	132
	GOODYEAR, Mary L.	(303)556-2683	450
	KIRSHBAUM, Priscilla J.	(313)756-1827	655
	MITCHELL, Marilyn J.	(303)556-2835	849
	SHAW, Ward	(303)861-5319	1124
	VERCIO, Roseanne	(303)778-5656	1282
Fort Collins	ANDERSON, Lemoyne W.	(303)484-7319	24
	BURNS, Robert W.	(303)491-1830	163
	CHAMBERS, Joan L.	(303)491-1833	198
Golden	LARSGAARD, Mary L.	(303)279-8243	698
	PHINNEY, Hartley K.	(303)273-3690	969
Grand Junction	RICHMOND, Rick	(303)241-4358	1030
Greeley	PITKIN, Gary M.	(303)339-2237	976
Gunnison	LANDRUM, Margaret C.		693
Littleton	WYNAR, Bohdan S.		1375

CONNECTICUT

Ansonia	MARTIN, Walter F.	(203)736-2601	779
Branford	KILLHEFFER, Robert E.	(203)432-1704	648
Fairfield	KIJANKA, Dorothy M.	(203)371-7700	647
Hamden	KANEKO, Hideo	(203)281-3586	625
	LANG, Norma F.	(203)288-5251	695
	NEWHALL, Ann C.	(203)288-8180	898
	SAMUEL, Harold E.	(203)432-0495	1079
	SMITH, Nolan E.	(203)776-3558	1159
Hartford	KAIMOWITZ, Jeffery H.	(203)527-3151	622
	STONE, Dennis J.	(203)241-4617	1197
Lakeville	CARVER, Jane C.	(203)435-9329	191
Middletown	BALAY, Robert E.	(203)347-6933	50
New Britain	KASCUS, Marie A.	(203)827-7565	628
	WARZALA, Martin L.		1307
New Canaan	LOKETS BEISCHROT, Dina		738
New Haven	KELLER, Michael A.	(203)389-2212	635
	KOEL, Ake I.	(203)432-1825	667
	LOWELL, Gerald R.	(203)773-3709	744
	PETERSON, Stephen L.	(203)432-5292	964
	SIGGINS, Jack A.	(203)776-3808	1137
	SULLIVAN, Maureen	(203)776-3808	1208
	TRAINER, Karin A.	(203)432-1818	1253
Storrs	MCDONALD, John P.	(203)429-5620	802
	ROLLIN, Marian B.	(203)429-4187	1051
	STEVENS, Norman D.	(203)429-7051	1190
West Hartford	BRADBERRY, Richard P.	(203)241-4704	125
	HORAK, Ellen B.	(203)233-3164	558
Willimantic	EMBARDO, Ellen E.	(203)456-1952	347
Windsor	NATALE, Barbara G.	(203)688-4467	889

DELAWARE

Dover	COONS, Daniel E.	(302)736-5111	242
Newark	ULRICH, Sue	(302)451-2231	1268
	WOLFF, Stephen G.	(302)451-2432	1361
Wilmington	TOMAN, Jocelyn B.		1249

ACADEMIC LIBRARY CONSULTANT (Cont'd)
DISTRICT OF COLUMBIA

Washington	BELLEFONTAINE, Arnold G.	(202)287-6587	78
	BERGQUIST, Christine F.		87
	BERWICK, Philip C.	(202)543-3369	91
	CHANG, Helen S.	(202)651-5214	200
	COOPER, David J.	(202)544-3653	242
	DAY, John M.	(202)651-5220	282
	GARLICK, Karen	(202)287-5634	419
	HEAD, Anita K.	(202)994-7336	518
	JAMES, Olive C.	(202)547-2157	592
	JUROW, Susan R.	(202)232-8656	620
	KNOWLTON, John D.	(202)362-8911	665
	LASNER, Mark S.	(202)745-1927	700
	LEONARD, Angela M.	(202)636-7926	716
	LISOWSKI, Andrew H.	(202)287-5491	732
	MILEVSKI, Robert J.	(202)287-5634	834
	MORIARTY, Ann	(202)333-9087	865
	MUSSEHL, Allan A.	(202)488-8162	883
	ROGERS, Sharon J.	(202)994-6455	1050
	SOLOMON, Arnold D.	(202)287-8786	1166
	STEWART, Ruth A.	(202)287-6587	1193
	SULLIVAN, Robert C.	(202)287-5330	1208
	SUNG, Carolyn H.	(202)287-5543	1210
	TSUNEISHI, Warren M.	(202)287-5543	1260
	TURTELL, Neal T.	(202)842-6506	1265

FLORIDA

Captiva	WALTON, Terence M.	(813)454-0410	1302
Clearwater	DALLMAN, Glenn R.	(813)791-2616	270
Coconut Grove	DEWAR, Jo E.	(305)858-8787	298
Coral Gables	AHMAD, Carol F.	(305)284-3551	8
Dade City	SPENCER, Albert F.		1173
De Land	JOHNSON, Betty D.	(904)734-7630	602
Englewood	GHALI, Raouf S.	(813)474-9436	430
Fort Myers	HUGHES, Joyce M.	(813)489-9464	572
Gainesville	BROWN, Pia T.	(904)375-6302	147
	GOGGIN, Margaret K.	(904)378-8144	444
	WILLETT, Charles	(904)378-1661	1341
	WILLOCKS, Robert M.	(904)392-0342	1349
Howey in the Hills	COHN, William L.	(904)324-2701	229
Jacksonville	GUNN, Thomas H.	(904)744-3950	477
	MCMICHAEL, Sandra C.	(904)731-8380	815
	SMITH, Linda L.	(904)731-1065	1157
Marianna	STABLER, William H.	(904)482-3474	1177
Melbourne	HENSON, Llewellyn L.	(305)768-8000	529
Miami	BYRD, Susan G.	(305)347-2068	169
	DANIELS, Westwell R.	(305)235-9484	273
	HALE, Kay K.	(305)271-3678	485
	MCNEAL, Archie L.		816
	MILLER, Laurence A.	(305)554-2461	839
	SEILER, Susan L.	(305)279-0545	1112
Naples	O'CONNOR, Mary A.	(813)598-9269	916
Orlando	HUDSON, Phyllis J.	(305)275-2584	569
Pensacola	BOWER, Beverly L.	(904)476-5410	120
	DEBOLT, W D.	(904)474-2213	284
	MOREIN, P G.	(904)474-2492	863
	TERNAK, Armand T.	(904)479-7835	1232
Plant City	PINGS, Vern M.	(813)752-3884	974
St Petersburg	FUSTUKJIAN, Samuel Y.	(813)893-9125	410
	GOSS, Theresa C.	(813)341-4732	453
	HARDESTY, Larry L.	(813)867-1166	499
San Antonio	NEUHOFE, M D.	(904)588-8320	897
Sarasota	JENKINS, Althea H.	(813)355-5003	597
Tallahassee	DE PEW, John N.	(904)644-5775	293
	MARTIN, James R.	(904)893-7306	776
	MILLER, Charles E.	(904)644-5211	836
Tampa	EVANS, Josephine K.	(813)974-4471	357
	HARKNESS, Mary L.	(813)961-7200	501
Thonotosassa	TABOR, Curtis H.	(813)986-3636	1219
Winter Park	ALLISON, Anne M.	(305)677-6372	17
	PFARRER, Theodore R.	(305)647-3294	966

GEORGIA

Americus	MCLAUGHLIN, Laverne L.	(912)924-9426	813
Athens	BAKER, Barry B.	(404)542-2534	47
	KAHAN, Gerald	(404)548-2514	621
	LIBBEY, George H.	(404)542-2716	725
	QUINLAN, Judy B.	(404)542-0654	1000
	RIEMER, John J.	(404)542-0591	1033

ACADEMIC LIBRARY CONSULTANT (Cont'd)
GEORGIA (Cont'd)

Athens	SUTHERLAND, Johnnie D.	(404)542-0690	1211
Atlanta	CRAFT, Guy C.	(404)522-8980	254
	FISTE, David A.		382
	JOHNSON, Herbert F.	(404)727-6861	605
	LUTHER, M J.	(404)325-4120	750
	PRESLEY, Roger L.	(404)658-2176	991
	RAQUET, Jacqueline R.	(404)320-9727	1008
	ROBISON, Carolyn L.	(404)658-2172	1045
	RUSSELL, Ralph E.	(404)658-2172	1069
Carrollton	BEARD, Charles E.	(404)832-9458	69
Decatur	CHAMBERS, Shirley M.	(404)289-6517	198
	OVERBECK, James A.	(404)378-8821	931
La Grange	LEWIS, Frank R.	(404)882-2911	723
Macon	HOWARD, Mary R.	(912)744-2960	564
Milledgeville	FENNELL, Janice C.	(912)453-4047	371
	SCOTT, Rupert N.	(912)453-5573	1108
Sylvester	MEREY-KADAR, Ervin R.	(912)776-0723	825

HAWAII

Honolulu	BREINICH, John A.	(808)536-9302	132
	CAMPBELL, R A.	(808)955-8822	177
	DILUCIA, Samuel J.	(808)955-1500	303
	HAAK, John R.	(808)948-7205	480
	JACKSON, Miles M.	(808)948-7321	588

IDAHO

Boise	TAYLOR, Adrien P.	(208)385-1621	1225
Moscow	ABRAHAM, Terry		3
Nampa	LANCASTER, Edith E.	(208)466-1011	691
	SIMMONS, Randall C.	(208)467-8609	1140
Pocatello	WATSON, Peter G.	(208)236-2997	1310
Rexburg	HART, Eldon C.	(208)356-4447	507

ILLINOIS

Cahokia	BEAN, Bobby G.	(618)875-6915	69
Carbondale	MCCOY, Ralph E.	(618)457-8707	799
	PETERSON, Kenneth G.	(618)529-1197	964
	RAY, Jean M.	(618)549-1290	1011
	STARRATT, Joseph A.	(618)453-2683	1182
Champaign	WERT, Lucille M.	(217)356-6600	1325
Charleston	LUQUIRE, Wilson	(217)581-6061	749
	RAO, Paladugu V.	(217)581-6061	1008
Chicago	BOLEF, Doris	(312)942-2271	112
	BOLT, Janice A.	(312)233-9399	113
	BOURDON, Cathleen J.	(312)944-6780	119
	BROWN, Doris R.	(312)341-8066	143
	BYRE, Calvin S.	(312)341-3643	169
	CARLSON, Robert P.	(312)944-6780	182
	DOWELL, David R.	(312)567-6844	315
	DUFF, John B.	(312)269-2984	323
	FANG, Min L.	(317)842-0321	363
	GARDNER, Trudy A.	(312)942-8735	418
	HIGGINBOTHAM, Richard C.	(312)549-6146	537
	HOLZENBERG, Eric J.	(312)248-3494	555
	IDDINGS, Daniel H.	(312)321-0432	581
	JOHN, Nancy R.	(312)996-2716	601
	LENNEBERG, Hans H.		715
	MALINOWSKY, H R.	(312)329-1549	763
	MATTENSON, Murray M.	(312)262-8282	785
	MCCARTNEY, Elizabeth J.	(312)666-8262	794
	MOCH, Mary I.	(312)539-2328	851
	MOUW, James R.	(312)996-2706	874
	MUNOFF, Gerald J.	(312)702-8749	879
	PIZER, Irwin H.	(312)996-8974	977
	SEGAL, Joan S.	(312)944-6780	1111
	VANCURA, Joyce B.	(312)822-0422	1273
	VEIT, Fritz	(312)363-2197	1281
	WAITE, Ellen J.	(312)508-2641	1293
	WELLS, James M.	(312)782-1172	1322
	WILLIAMSON, Linda E.	(312)996-2738	1347
Darien	BOWDEN, Philip L.	(312)887-1620	120
De Kalb	DUTTON, Lee S.	(815)753-1808	329
	RAST, Elaine K.	(815)758-5234	1009
	TITUS, Elizabeth M.	(815)753-1094	1247
	WELCH, Theodore F.	(815)758-6858	1321
Decatur	HALE, Charles E.	(217)864-5755	485
Dow	HOLZBERLEIN, Deanne B.	(618)466-3015	555

ACADEMIC LIBRARY CONSULTANT (Cont'd)
ILLINOIS (Cont'd)

East Peoria	LINDGREN, William D.	(309)694-5462	729
Edwardsville	JOHNSON, Charlotte L.	(618)656-5743	603
Elmhurst	KLATT, Melvin J.	(312)279-4100	658
Evanston	DAVIDSON, Lloyd A.	(312)491-2906	276
	GROSS, Dorothy E.	(312)583-2700	472
	HORNY, Karen L.	(312)491-7662	560
	NIELSEN, Brian	(312)491-2170	903
	PANOFSKY, Hans E.	(312)491-7684	938
	QUERY, Lance D.	(312)491-2882	999
	QUINN, Patrick M.	(312)869-2861	1000
	WHITE, Matthew H.	(312)328-2221	1331
Freeport	WELCH, Eric C.	(815)235-6121	1321
Glen Ellyn	FRADKIN, Bernard	(312)416-1199	395
	PEISER, Richard H.	(312)790-3293	955
Glenview	HAFNER, Arthur W.	(312)291-1022	482
Kenilworth	JONES, William G.	(312)251-3112	615
La Grange	SCHULTHEISS, Louis A.	(312)354-6958	1101
Lake Forest	MILLER, Arthur H.	(312)234-9247	835
Matteson	SMITH, Richard D.	(312)747-6660	1159
Normal	PETERSON, Fred M.	(309)438-3481	963
Oak Lawn	KELLY, Raymond T.		638
Palos Hills	HESSLER, Nancy R.	(312)974-4300	534
Riverdale	PATEL, Jashu	(312)849-3959	947
Rock Island	OHRLUND, Bruce L.	(309)786-0698	919
Sun City	STUHLMAN, Daniel D.	(312)262-8959	1205
Sycamore	BERRY, John W.	(815)895-4225	90
Urbana	ANDERSON, Nancy D.	(217)333-2884	24
	BINGHAM, Karen H.	(217)333-0317	97
	BOAST, Carol		108
	BRICHFORD, Maynard J.	(217)367-7072	134
	CLARK, Barton M.	(217)333-0317	216
	DAVIS, Elisabeth B.	(217)333-3654	278
	ESTABROOK, Leigh S.	(217)333-3280	355
	KLINGBERG, Susan	(217)333-2408	661
	MAKINO, Yasuko	(217)244-2048	762
	MONTANELLI, Dale S.	(217)333-0792	855
	SCHMIDT, Karen A.	(217)333-1054	1095
	WATSON, Paula D.	(217)333-1116	1310
	WILSON, Lizabeth A.	(217)333-3489	1351
Wauconda	SHENASSA, Daryoosh	(312)526-9123	1126
Wilmette	JONES, Adrian	(312)256-6202	610
Winnetka	THOMPSON, Richard E.	(312)446-7975	1241

INDIANA

Bloomington	BRISTOW, Ann	(812)335-8028	137
	FARRELL, David	(812)335-3403	365
	FRY, Bernard M.	(812)339-3571	406
	KUDRYK, Oleg	(812)332-1773	682
	LEE, Thomas H.	(812)331-7485	711
	READ, Glenn F.	(812)336-5984	1012
	SLOAN, Elaine F.	(812)335-3403	1149
	SNYDER, Carolyn A.	(812)335-3403	1164
Crawfordsville	FRYE, Larry J.	(317)364-4327	407
Fort Wayne	SIEVERS, Arlene M.	(219)493-7017	1136
Gary	MORAN, Robert F.	(219)980-6580	862
Hammond	HOLICKY, Bernard H.	(219)989-2249	550
Hanover	MORRILL, Walter D.	(812)866-2151	866
Indianapolis	BONNER, Robert J.	(317)283-7362	114
	FISCHLER, Barbara B.	(317)274-0462	380
	FRANCQ, Carole	(317)274-1411	396
	GALBRAITH, Leslie R.	(317)924-1331	413
	HEHMAN, Jennifer L.	(317)271-8595	521
	KONDELIK, John P.	(317)283-9226	670
	SIMON, Ralph C.	(317)875-5336	1141
	YOUNG, Philip H.	(317)788-3399	1383
Lafayette	LAW, Gordon T.	(317)447-2484	704
	MCKOWEN, Dorothy K.	(317)564-4585	812
Marion	BOYCE, Harold W.	(317)674-5211	122
Muncie	KUO, Ming M.	(317)289-3123	684
	MOORE, Thomas J.	(317)285-1307	861
	WOOD, Michael B.	(317)289-5417	1364
Notre Dame	HAYES, Stephen M.	(219)239-5268	516
	MILLER, Robert C.	(219)239-7790	841
South Bend	DOLAN, Robert T.	(219)289-1172	309
	HOHL, Robert J.	(219)289-8160	550
	MULLINS, James L.	(219)237-4449	878
	PEC, Jean A.	(219)277-3703	953
	TUCKER, Dennis C.		1261

ACADEMIC LIBRARY CONSULTANT (Cont'd)
INDIANA (Cont'd)

Terre Haute	LAMB, Robert S.	(812)237-2545	690
	LEACH, Ronald G.	(812)237-3700	706
Valparaiso	PERSYN, Mary G.	(219)465-7838	961
West Lafayette	FUNKHOUSER, Richard L.	(317)494-2855	410
	POLIT, Carlos E.	(317)463-6404	980

IOWA

Ames	KUHN, Warren B.	(515)294-1442	682
	MADISON, Olivia M.	(515)294-3669	759
Davenport	PETERSON, Dennis R.	(319)391-3877	963
Decorah	FENSTERMANN, Duane W.	(319)387-1164	371
Des Moines	FLICK, Frances J.	(515)277-2089	385
	STOPPEL, William A.	(515)255-5366	1198
Dubuque	KNEFEL, Mary A.	(319)589-3215	664
	OFFERMAN, Mary C.		917
Grinnell	MCKEE, Christopher	(515)269-3351	810
Iowa City	CRETH, Sheila D.	(319)335-5868	258
	DUNLAP, Leslie W.		326
	HOWELL, John B.	(319)335-5885	565
	LORKOVIC, Tatjana B.	(318)351-5304	741
	RICE, James G.	(319)335-5716	1027
	RUMSEY, Eric T.	(319)335-9151	1067

KANSAS

Emporia	STEWART, Henry R.	(316)343-1200	1192
Lawrence	HOWARD, Clinton N.	(913)864-3601	564
	KOEPP, Donna P.	(913)864-4880	668
Manhattan	GRASS, Charlene G.	(913)532-6516	458
McPherson	OLSEN, Rowena J.	(316)241-0731	921
Wichita	SCHAD, Jasper G.	(316)685-6588	1088

KENTUCKY

Berea	KIRK, Thomas G.	(606)986-9341	654
Bowling Green	COSSEY, M E.	(502)843-6560	249
Horse Cave	STROHECKER, Edwin C.	(502)453-3059	1202
Lexington	SINEATH, Timothy W.	(606)257-8876	1143
	WALDHART, Thomas J.	(606)257-3771	1294
Louisville	DEERING, Ronald F.	(502)897-4807	287
	HUFF, James E.	(502)585-9911	570
	KEARNEY, Anna R.	(502)588-6744	633
	NILES, Judith F.	(502)588-6756	904
	SCHLENE, Vickie J.	(502)935-9840	1094
Owensboro	YATES, Dudley V.	(502)526-3111	1378
Paducah	BOYARSKI, Jennie S.	(502)442-6131	122
Richmond	BARKSDALE, Milton K.	(606)622-1787	57
Wilmore	BUNDY, David D.	(606)858-3581	157

LOUISIANA

Alexandria	JARRED, Ada D.	(312)445-5230	594
Baton Rouge	HAMAKER, Charles A.	(504)388-8537	490
	HOGAN, Sharon A.	(504)388-2217	549
	MARTIN, Robert S.	(504)767-7167	778
	PHILLIPS, Faye	(504)388-6569	968
	REID, Marion T.	(504)388-2217	1019
	SHIFLETT, Orvin L.	(504)388-1462	1130
Hammond	GREAVES, F L.	(504)549-2234	461
Lafayette	FOX, Willard		395
Marrero	FAVORITE, Grealdine J.	(504)348-0234	366
Natchitoches	BUCHANAN, William C.	(318)357-4403	153
New Orleans	HAGEDORN, Dorothy L.	(504)865-5131	482
	LEINBACH, Philip E.	(504)865-5131	714
Ruston	BYERS, Cora M.	(318)257-3555	168
	WICKER, W W.	(318)257-2577	1335
Shreveport	BRAZILE, Orella R.	(318)674-3400	130

MAINE

Orono	ALBRIGHT, Elaine M.	(207)581-1661	10
	WIHBEY, Francis R.	(207)581-1681	1337
Westbrook	PARKS, George R.	(207)854-0355	943

MARYLAND

Adelphi	NITECKI, Danuta A.	(301)937-4791	905
Annapolis	MCKAY, Eleanor	(301)263-6526	809
	MENEGAUX, Edmond A.	(301)268-6741	824
	RICE, Rosamond H.	(301)263-0670	1027

ACADEMIC LIBRARY CONSULTANT (Cont'd)
MARYLAND (Cont'd)

Baltimore	BOURKOFF, Vivienne R.	(301)338-8914	119
	FRYER, Philip	(301)532-8787	407
	HSIEH, Rebecca T.	(301)522-1481	567
	LEBRETON, Jonathan A.	(301)455-2356	708
	LUCIER, Richard E.	(301)955-3411	746
	MATHESON, Nina W.	(301)837-1120	783
	PAPENFUSE, Edward C.	(301)467-6137	939
	WILSON, Marjorie P.	(301)328-3970	1352
Bethesda	BOEHR, Diane L.	(301)986-8560	109
	COSTABILE, Salvatore L.	(301)986-8560	249
	HIRTLE, Peter B.	(301)496-5963	544
	LORENZ, John G.	(301)320-4651	741
	SMINK, Anna R.	(301)365-5300	1152
Catonsville	WILT, Larry J.	(301)455-2341	1353
Churchton	TONEY, Stephen R.	(301)261-5650	1250
College Park	STIELOW, Frederick J.	(301)454-5790	1194
Columbia	DAHLEN, Roger W.	(301)964-9098	269
	KOSMIN, Linda J.	(301)997-8954	672
Ellicott City	MARTIN, Susan K.	(301)988-9893	778
Frostburg	GILLESPIE, David M.	(301)689-2701	435
Gambrills	YOUNG, Peter R.	(301)923-2902	1383
Germantown	ALBRIGHT, John B.	(301)428-3700	10
Gibson Island	ROVELSTAD, Howard		1062
Greenbelt	BYERLY, Imogene J.		168
Largo	NEKRITZ, Leah K.	(301)322-0462	893
Mount Airy	WETZBARGER, Cecilia G.	(301)829-0826	1328
Pikesville	JENG, Helene W.	(301)225-4450	596
Pocomoke City	SMITH, Jessie C.	(301)957-3320	1156
Potomac	HO, James K.		545
Rockville	LEWIS, Robert J.	(301)460-9145	724
	OAKLEY, Robert L.	(301)279-9103	913
Silver Spring	BASA, Eniko M.	(301)384-4657	62
	MERIKANGAS, Robert J.	(301)384-3449	826
	THOMAS, Sarah E.	(301)585-9446	1238
	VAN CAMPEN, Rebecca J.	(301)890-8588	1272
	VOGT-O'CONNOR, Diane L.	(301)681-7615	1287
	WAGNER, Lloyd F.		1292
Takoma Park	HICKERSON, Joseph C.	(301)270-1107	536
	WRIGHT, Arthuree M.	(301)445-1220	1370
Thurmont	FITZPATRICK, Kelly	(301)271-4109	383
Towson	HARER, John B.	(301)321-2456	501
Westminster	NEIKIRK, Harold D.	(301)848-7000	892

MASSACHUSETTS

Amherst	BRIDEGAM, Willis E.	(413)542-2212	135
Arlington	FORTIER, Jan M.	(617)646-5856	391
Boston	BEGG, Karin E.		74
	BENENFELD, Alan R.	(617)437-2350	80
	HAMANN, Edmund G.	(617)573-8536	490
	HERNON, Peter	(617)738-2223	532
	HILL, Barbara M.	(617)732-2808	539
	HOPKINS, Benjamin	(617)232-1555	557
	MATARAZZO, James M.	(617)738-2220	783
	MCKIRDY, Pamela R.	(617)738-2223	812
	MOSKOWITZ, Michael A.	(617)578-8670	871
	STIFFLEAR, Allan J.	(617)929-7640	1194
	STUEART, Robert D.	(617)738-2225	1205
	WEINSCHENK, Andrea	(617)353-9319	1318
Brockton	UMANA, Christine J.	(617)586-6994	1268
Cambridge	COLLINS, John W.	(617)495-4225	232
	DAVY, Edgar W.	(617)253-5670	281
	DUNKLY, James W.	(617)868-3450	326
	JACKSON, Arlyne A.	(617)492-0355	586
	OCHS, Michael	(617)495-2794	915
	PARKER, Susan E.	(617)495-3455	942
Charlestown	DOWLER, Lawrence E.		315
Chestnut Hill	CHANNING, Rhoda K.	(617)552-4470	201
	FENG, Yen T.		371
	SEEGRABER, Frank J.		1111
Concord	JACKSON, Patience K.	(617)369-0586	588
East Longmeadow	STACK, May E.	(413)525-6350	1177
Framingham	HANSSEN, Nancy E.	(617)875-0382	499
	MCDONALD, Stanley M.	(617)626-4651	803
Franklin	DACHS, Jerald K.	(617)528-9100	269
Heath	HOWLAND, Margaret E.	(413)337-4980	566
Ipswich	GRAY, Carolyn M.	(617)356-0773	459

ACADEMIC LIBRARY CONSULTANT (Cont'd)
MASSACHUSETTS (Cont'd)

Lexington	BERNSTEIN, D S.	(617)863-1284	89
	LUCKER, Jay K.	(617)862-4558	746
	WALSH, Joanna M.	(617)863-1275	1299
	WARNER, Alice S.	(617)862-9278	1305
Littleton	BUCKLAND, Lawrence F.	(617)899-1086	154
Lowell	KARR, Ronald D.	(617)452-5000	628
Medford	MARTIN, Murray S.	(617)776-3599	777
	SCHATZ, Natalie M.	(617)381-3273	1090
Milton	HOVORKA, Marjorie J.	(617)333-4902	563
	KEYS, Marshall	(617)333-0500	645
Needham	PAPADEMETRIOU, George C.	(617)444-8941	938
Newton Center	CARPENTER, Kenneth E.	(617)244-2117	185
Quincy	WHEALAN, Ronald E.	(617)479-3297	1328
Tyngsboro	FUNG, Margaret C.	(617)256-3090	409
Wellesley	HARDY, Eileen D.	(617)235-0320	500
West Newton	CHEN, Ching C.	(617)738-2224	205
Weston	KEENAN, Elizabeth L.	(617)893-1820	634
Westport	GIBBS, Paige	(617)674-6712	431
Westwood	CLAPPER, Mary E.	(617)329-3350	216
Williamstown	SUDDUTH, William E.	(413)597-2514	1206
	WIKANDER, Lawrence E.	(413)458-3888	1338
Winchester	JOHNSON, Jean L.	(617)721-7020	606
	SCHROCK, Nancy C.	(617)721-1229	1100
	SMITH, Ann M.	(617)729-7169	1152

MICHIGAN

Adrian	DOMBROWSKI, Mark A.	(517)263-0731	310
Albion	OBERG, Larry R.	(517)629-7297	914
Alma	DOLLARD, Peter A.	(512)463-7227	309
Ann Arbor	BERGEN, Kathleen M.	(313)936-3814	85
	BIGGS, Debra R.	(313)763-7080	95
	DAVIDSEN, Susanna L.	(313)995-7352	276
	DOUGHERTY, Richard M.	(313)764-9356	314
	GOSLING, William A.	(313)973-6325	453
	MCDONALD, David R.	(313)764-0412	802
	STOFFLE, Carla J.	(313)764-9356	1196
	WAGMAN, Frederick H.	(313)662-1214	1291
	YOCUM, Patricia B.	(313)995-4644	1380
Bloomfield Hills	DAVID, Indra M.	(313)338-3929	276
	FRANKIE, Suzanne O.	(313)855-6149	397
Dearborn	VINT, Patricia A.	(313)591-5073	1285
Detroit	GUNN, Arthur C.	(313)831-9707	477
	MIKA, Joseph J.	(313)577-1825	834
	PORTER, Jean F.	(313)961-5040	984
	RZEPECKI, Arnold M.	(313)868-2700	1072
	SPYERS-DURAN, Peter	(313)577-4048	1177
	WILLIAMS, James F.	(313)577-4021	1343
East Lansing	HAKA, Clifford H.	(517)353-5317	484
	MEAHL, D D.	(517)355-7641	819
	SHAPIRO, Beth J.	(517)355-2343	1121
	WIEMERS, Eugene L.	(517)355-2340	1336
Flint	PALMER, David W.	(313)238-0166	936
Grand Rapids	BURINSKI, Walter W.	(616)454-9635	160
	SIEBERS, Bruce L.	(616)774-2167	1135
Kalamazoo	NETZ, David H.	(616)383-1666	896
	RIZZO, John R.	(616)381-1323	1037
Midland	CHEN, Catherine W.	(517)631-9724	205
Mt Pleasant	WEATHERFORD, John W.	(517)772-3861	1311
Plymouth	DE BEAR, Richard S.	(313)459-5000	284
University Center	JONES, Clifton H.	(517)790-4236	612
Ypsilanti	BEAL, Sarell W.	(313)483-7729	68
	BOONE, Morell D.	(313)484-4384	115
	GLIKIN, Ronda	(313)487-2288	441
	KIRKENDALL, Carolyn A.	(313)482-7041	654
	MARSHALL, Albert P.		773
	YEE, Sandra G.	(313)487-2220	1379

MINNESOTA

Mankato	CARRISON, Dale K.	(507)389-5062	187
	PEISCHL, Thomas P.	(507)389-5953	955
Marine on St Croix	FULLER, Sherrilynne S.	(612)433-3893	409
Minneapolis	BEAVEN, Miranda J.	(612)624-5860	71
	BRANIN, Joseph J.	(612)624-5518	128
	COGSWELL, James A.	(612)624-5518	227
	STEINKE, Cynthia A.	(612)624-9500	1186
Northfield	GREENE, Mark A.	(507)663-4270	464
	METZ, T J.	(507)663-4267	828

ACADEMIC LIBRARY CONSULTANT (Cont'd)

MINNESOTA (Cont'd)

Rochester	BEYNEN, Gijsbertus K.		93
	KEYS, Thomas E.		645
St Louis Park	RINE, Joseph L.	(612)542-9631	1035
St Paul	HALES-MABRY, Celia E.	(612)645-2850	486
	HARWOOD, Karen L.	(612)690-6653	510
	KING, Jack B.	(612)641-2373	651
	KINNEY, Janet S.	(612)690-6650	653
	SCHERER, Herbert G.	(612)699-6165	1092
	SMITH, Eldred R.	(612)698-2362	1154
St Peter	HAEUSER, Michael J.	(507)931-7556	482
	HERVEY, Norma J.	(507)931-7563	533

MISSISSIPPI

Boyle	BAHR, Edward R.	(601)846-4607	45
Clinton	MYRICK, Judy C.	(601)924-6092	885
Columbus	PAYNE, David L.	(601)328-7565	951
Jackson	PARKS, James F.	(601)354-5201	943
	REID, Thomas G.	(601)922-4988	1019
	WEST, Carol C.	(601)944-1970	1326
Liberty	BURKS, Alvin L.	(601)657-8920	161
Oxford	HARPER, Laura G.	(601)234-1812	503
Raymond	WALL, Norma F.	(601)857-3253	1297
Ridgeland	RICE, Joyce I.	(601)856-5400	1027
University	COCHRAN, J W.	(601)232-7361	225
	FISHER, Benjamin F.		380
	GRAVES, Gail T.	(601)232-5875	459

MISSOURI

Ballwin	BUHR, Rosemary E.		156
Columbia	BARNES, Everett W.	(314)882-4581	57
	CARROLL, C E.	(314)443-8303	187
	PARKER, Ralph H.	(314)442-4631	942
	POWELL, Ronald R.	(314)882-9545	988
	SHAUGHNESSY, Thomas W.	(314)882-4701	1123
	TIMBERLAKE, Patricia P.	(314)882-4581	1245
Joplin	ABERNATHY, William F.	(417)624-2518	2
	KEMP, Charles H.	(417)625-9386	639
Kansas City	LABUDDE, Kenneth J.	(816)531-0770	686
	MARTIN, Louis E.	(816)363-4600	777
	MILLER, William C.	(816)333-6254	843
	SPALDING, Helen H.	(816)276-1531	1171
Kirksville	ELLEBRACHT, Eleanor V.	(816)665-6158	343
Maryville	HANKS, Nancy C.	(816)562-1590	496
	MURPHY, Kathryn L.	(816)582-4768	880
O'Fallon	SANDERS, John B.		1080
Parkville	SMITH, Harold F.	(816)741-6085	1155
St Louis	AMELUNG, Richard C.	(314)658-2754	19
	BECK, Sara R.	(314)889-5483	71
	BURCKEL, Nicholas C.	(314)889-5400	158
	CRAWFORD, Susan Y.	(314)362-7080	257
	PAGE, Jacqueline M.	(314)781-6352	934
Springfield	MACKEY, Neosha A.	(417)836-4537	756
	MEADOR, John M.	(417)882-8032	819

MONTANA

Bozeman	ALLDREDGE, Noreen S.	(406)587-4877	14
	MORTON, Bruce	(406)994-5313	870
Missoula	DRIESSEN, Karen C.	(406)243-4070	320

NEBRASKA

Fremont	BOYLE, Thomas E.	(402)721-5480	124
	PETERSON, Vivian A.	(402)721-9119	964
Kearney	MAYESKI, John K.	(308)234-8535	790
Lincoln	HENDRICKSON, Kent H.	(402)472-2526	527
	SARTORI, Eva M.		1083
	TIBBITS, Edith J.	(402)472-3545	1243
	WISE, Sally H.	(402)472-5737	1357
Omaha	MEANS, Raymond B.	(402)280-2705	820
	RUNYON, Robert S.	(402)393-3320	1067

NEVADA

Incline	OSSOLINSKI, Lynn	(702)831-2936	928
Las Vegas	CURLEY, Elmer F.		265

NEW HAMPSHIRE

Concord	HARE, William J.	(603)225-2012	501
Fremont	FARAH, Barbara D.		363
Hanover	CRONENWETT, Philip N.	(603)646-2037	260

ACADEMIC LIBRARY CONSULTANT (Cont'd)

NEW JERSEY

Bridgewater	STEVENS, Sharon G.	(201)218-3819	1191
	STUDDIFORD, Abigail M.	(201)725-5616	1204
Caldwell	HODGE, Patricia A.	(201)288-4424	546
Camden	CHAO, Gloria F.	(609)757-6172	201
Cherry Hill	BECK, Susan J.	(609)354-7638	72
Clifton	PIERMATTI, Patricia A.	(201)473-2454	972
East Orange	MATHAI, Aleyamma	(201)266-5613	783
Highland Park	MILLER, Lynn F.	(201)572-6563	840
Lakehurst	KUHN, Martin A.	(201)657-4270	682
Lawrenceville	STEPHEN, Ross G.	(609)896-5111	1187
Madison	COUGHLIN, Caroline M.	(201)377-3000	250
	JONES, Arthur E.	(201)377-6525	611
	SNELSON, Pamela	(201)377-3000	1163
Mahwah	YUEH, Norma N.	(201)529-7578	1384
Maplewood	STAHL, Wilson M.	(800)262-0070	1178
Neptune	EBELING, Elinor H.	(201)774-0793	334
New Brunswick	EDELMAN, Hendrik	(201)932-7836	335
	EUSTER, Joanne R.	(201)932-7505	356
	GRAHAM, Peter S.	(201)932-7505	456
	GREENBERG, Evelyn	(201)932-7505	463
	NASH, Stanley D.	(201)932-7014	888
	REELING, Patricia G.	(201)932-7917	1016
	SIMMONS, Ruth J.	(201)932-7006	1140
Ocean	VLOYANETES, Jeanne M.	(201)493-9007	1286
Paramus	MENTHE, Melissa		825
Princeton	BERKNER, Dimity S.	(609)924-3891	87
	BUTCHER, Patricia S.	(609)921-6203	166
	SCHMIDT, Mary M.	(609)452-5860	1095
Ridgewood	JONES, Anita M.	(201)444-7273	610
Rockaway	COHN, John M.	(201)627-8512	229
	KELSEY, Ann L.	(201)627-8512	639
Sewell	CROCKER, Jane L.	(609)468-5000	259
Somerdale	DALE, Charles F.	(609)346-4629	270
South Orange	FIELD, William N.	(201)761-1926	376
Trenton	BRODOWSKI, Joyce H.	(609)771-2343	139
Turnersville	SZILASSY, Sandor	(609)589-7193	1218
Upper Montclair	PARR, Mary Y.	(201)746-0352	944
Wayne	LEE, Minja P.		711
Willingboro	PELLETIER, Karen E.		955

NEW MEXICO

Alamogordo	RUCKMAN, Stanley N.	(505)434-3398	1065
Albuquerque	BEJNAR, Thaddeus P.	(505)277-0932	75
	BERNSTEIN, Judith R.	(505)262-2320	89
	SPURLOCK, Sandra E.	(505)828-5378	1177
	THOMPSON, Janet A.	(505)277-7172	1240
	VASSALLO, Paul	(505)277-8125	1279
Farmington	JASSAL, Raghbir S.	(505)327-7813	595
Hobbs	TUBESING, Richard L.	(505)393-6528	1261
Las Cruces	DAVIS, Hiram L.	(505)646-1509	279
	RICHARDS, James H.	(505)524-0281	1028
Los Lunas	HAYNES, Douglas E.	(505)841-5318	516
Santa Fe	PIERSON, Robert M.	(505)982-0371	972
Thoreau	SCHUBERT, Donald F.	(505)862-7465	1101
Toadlena	MCCAULEY, Elfrieda B.	(505)789-3205	795

NEW YORK

Albany	ANDERSON, Carol L.	(518)434-4802	22
	LOCKETT, Barbara A.	(518)456-0135	736
	MCCOMBS, Gillian M.	(518)442-3633	797
	NITECKI, Joseph Z.	(518)442-3568	905
	ROBERTS, Anne F.	(518)438-0607	1039
	WALSH, Daniel P.	(518)489-7968	1299
	YAVARKOVSKY, Jerome	(518)473-1189	1378
Alfred	BROWN, June E.	(607)587-9203	145
Amawalk	HANE, Paula J.	(914)962-2933	495
APO New York	GADBOIS, Frank W.		411
Auburn	MICHAEL, Douglas O.	(315)252-2247	831
Bayside	BILLY, George J.		97
	SINGER, Phyllis Z.	(718)279-2182	1143
Bellerose	GATNER, Elliott S.		422
Binghamton	MCKEE, George D.	(607)729-5490	810
Brewster	SHOLTZ, Katherine J.	(914)278-9078	1132
Bronx	FOLTER, Siegrun H.	(212)960-8831	388
	REIMAN, Donald H.	(212)549-4890	1020
Bronxville	BURSTEIN, Rose A.	(914)337-0700	164

ACADEMIC LIBRARY CONSULTANT (Cont'd)
NEW YORK (Cont'd)

City	Name	Phone	Page
Brooklyn	BRANDEAU, John H.	(718)852-8700	128
	BRAUCH, Patricia O.	(718)780-5581	129
	CHICKERING, F W.	(718)636-3456	208
	CLUNE, John R.	(718)680-7578	223
	KERR, Virginia M.	(718)789-5410	644
	MALINCONICO, S M.	(718)627-0558	763
	ROBBINS, Sara E.	(718)780-7980	1039
	SWIESZKOWSK, L S.	(718)383-8480	1216
Buffalo	BOBINSKI, George S.	(716)636-2412	108
	ELLISON, John W.	(716)636-3069	345
	HUANG, C K.	(716)831-3402	568
	NEWMAN, George C.	(716)886-8132	899
	PALMIERI, Lucien E.	(716)882-9275	937
	VON WAHLDE, Barbara	(716)636-2967	1288
Clinton	ANTHONY, Donald C.	(315)737-8347	28
Cobleskill	GALASSO, Nancy	(518)234-5841	412
Cornwall on Hudson	WEISS, Egon A.	(914)534-9467	1320
Croton-on-Hudson	COHEN, Aaron	(914)271-8170	227
Delhi	SORGEN, Herbert J.	(607)746-4107	1168
Dobbs Ferry	BONE, Larry E.	(914)693-4500	113
Flushing	KOSTER, Gregory E.	(718)575-4264	673
	RORICK, William C.	(718)520-7345	1054
	SURPRENANT, Thomas T.	(718)520-7194	1210
Freeport	NOTARSTEFANO, Vincent C.	(516)379-3245	910
Garden City	DOCTOROW, Erica	(516)663-1042	307
	FRIEDMAN, Arthur L.	(516)222-7406	403
Geneseo	CAREN, Loretta	(716)243-0438	181
Glens Falls	SMITH, Frederick E.	(518)792-8214	1155
Greenvale	YUKAWA, Masako	(516)299-2142	1384
Hamilton	GREEN, Judith G.	(315)824-3253	462
Hempstead	ANDREWS, Charles R.	(516)560-5940	26
Houghton	LAUER, Anita D.	(716)567-2211	702
Huntington	FOLCARELLI, Ralph J.	(516)271-0634	387
Ithaca	HAMMOND, Jane L.	(607)255-5857	493
	LIPPINCOTT, Joan K.	(607)255-7731	732
	MILLER, J G.	(607)272-1576	838
Jackson Heights	WALSH, Robert R.	(718)639-3188	1300
Larchmont	LANDMAN, Lillian L.	(914)834-3225	693
Long Island City	LOW, Frederick E.	(718)482-5424	743
Lynbrook	FIEGAS, Barbara E.	(516)593-1195	375
Manlius	WU, Painan R.	(315)682-2472	1373
Maryknoll	O'HALLORAN, James V.	(914)941-7590	918
McLean	DREW, Wilfred E.	(607)753-8180	319
Mt Kisco	NELSON, Nancy M.	(914)666-3394	894
Nesconset	GRUNDT, Leonard	(516)361-8987	475
New Hyde Park	LANG, Jovian P.	(516)352-1666	695
New Paltz	CONNORS, William E.	(914)257-2203	238
New Rochelle	HUMPHRY, James	(914)834-6941	574
	LARKIN, Patrick J.	(914)633-2350	698
New York	ALLENTUCK, Marcia E.		16
	ARMSTRONG, Joanne D.	(212)280-3743	32
	BIDDLE, Stanton F.	(212)725-3032	94
	BIRNBAUM, Henry	(212)473-3769	98
	BRAUDE, Robert M.	(212)472-5919	129
	BREWER, Joseph	(212)744-3828	134
	BROUDE, Ronald	(212)242-7001	141
	CLINE, Herman H.	(212)777-4575	222
	DALTON, Jack		271
	D'ANGELO, Paul P.	(212)760-1600	272
	DARLING, Pamela W.	(212)206-7031	275
	DEDONATO, Ree	(212)998-2510	286
	DE GENNARO, Richard	(212)930-0769	287
	FASANA, Paul J.	(212)930-0708	366
	GILLESPIE, John T.	(212)861-9294	435
	GOSSAGE, Wayne	(212)869-3348	453
	GREENFIELD, Stanley R.		464
	GRUENBERG, Michael L.	(212)732-5964	474
	HAEFLIGER, Kathleen A.	(212)663-7857	482
	HARVEY, John F.	(215)509-2612	509
	HIGGINBOTHAM, Barbra B.	(212)533-2173	537
	HUDSON, Alice C.	(212)222-2835	569
	KANIA, Antoinette M.		625
	KRANICH, Nancy C.	(212)998-2447	676
	KUHNER, Robert A.	(212)663-3360	683
	LAMANN, Amber N.	(212)677-4102	689
	LEE, Sang C.	(212)669-7961	711
	LIEBERFELD, Lawrence	(212)348-8499	726

ACADEMIC LIBRARY CONSULTANT (Cont'd)
NEW YORK (Cont'd)

City	Name	Phone	Page
New York	LUBETSKI, Edith E.	(212)340-7720	745
	MARGALITH, Helen M.	(212)575-0190	770
	MATTA, Seoud M.	(212)686-7532	785
	MCSWEENEY, Josephine	(212)254-6338	818
	MIHRAM, Danielle	(212)998-2515	834
	MILLER, Michael D.		841
	MILLER, Sarah J.		842
	MILLER-KUMMERFELD, Elizabeth	(212)751-0830	843
	MOLINARI, Joseph G.	(212)431-2382	853
	MOSES, Julian M.	(212)688-8426	871
	NESTA, Frederick N.	(212)982-9672	896
	PAUL, Sandra K.	(212)675-7804	949
	RESCIGNO, Dolores S.	(212)530-5969	1024
	RODERER, Nancy K.	(212)305-6302	1047
	ROTHSTEIN, Pauline M.	(212)750-6008	1060
	SHAPIRO, Fred R.	(203)432-1600	1121
	SOMMER, Susan T.	(212)870-1648	1167
	TRACY, Janet R.	(212)222-1157	1253
	VAJDA, Elizabeth A.	(212)254-6300	1271
	VAUGHN, Susan J.	(212)260-2544	1280
	VINCENT-DAVISS, Diana	(212)598-2367	1284
	WISHART, H L.	(212)790-0222	1357
Niagara University	MORRIS, Leslie R.	(716)285-1212	867
Oakdale	BEAUDRIE, Ronald A.	(516)244-3284	70
	GUY, Wendell A.	(516)244-3059	479
Oneonta	CROWLEY, John V.	(607)431-2725	261
	JOHNSON, Richard D.	(607)432-0131	608
Ossining	FRANCK, Jane P.	(914)762-6073	396
Oswego	JUDD, Blanche E.	(315)341-4267	618
Plattsburgh	BURTON, Robert E.	(518)561-1613	164
Potsdam	FOSTER, Selma V.	(315)267-2477	392
Poughkeepsie	JEANNENEY, Mary L.	(914)452-7000	596
Purchase	FREIDES, Thelma	(914)253-5096	401
Riverdale	CLANCY, Kathy	(212)796-2057	215
Rochester	KANSFIELD, Norman J.	(716)271-1320	625
	MATZEK, Richard A.	(716)586-2525	786
Saratoga Springs	DOE, Lynn M.	(518)584-5000	308
	EYMAN, David H.	(518)584-5000	359
Schenectady	HALSEY, Richard S.	(518)370-0902	490
	SHEVIAK, Jean K.	(518)370-6294	1129
Southampton	KETCHAM, Susan E.	(516)283-4000	645
Sparkill	BARRIE, John L.	(914)359-7200	59
	ZUBARIK, Therese	(914)359-7200	1390
Staten Island	KRIEGER, Tillie		678
	SCHUT, Grace W.	(718)442-5659	1103
Stony Brook	SMITH, John B.	(516)632-7100	1156
	VOLAT-SHAPIRO, Helene M.	(516)632-7100	1287
Suffern	GLEASON, Robert W.	(914)356-4650	440
Syracuse	HORRELL, Jeffrey L.	(315)423-2585	560
	MCCLURE, Charles R.	(315)423-2911	797
	PRICE, Susan W.	(315)423-2093	992
	SIMONIS, James J.	(315)445-4321	1141
Troy	BLANDY, Susan G.	(518)274-2098	104
	MOLHOLT, Pat	(518)276-8300	852
West Point	RANDALL, Lawrence E.	(914)938-4789	1006
Youngstown	TELATNIK, George M.		1230

NORTH CAROLINA

City	Name	Phone	Page
Albemarle	LACROIX, Michael J.	(704)982-1036	686
Boone	BARKER, Richard T.	(704)264-3621	56
Chapel Hill	BYRD, Gary D.	(919)966-2111	168
	DANIEL, Evelyn H.	(919)962-8366	272
	GASAWAY, Laura N.	(919)962-1321	421
	GOVAN, James F.	(919)962-1301	454
	GRENDLER, Marcella	(919)962-0114	467
	HIGH, Walter M.	(919)968-1468	538
	HOLLEY, Edward G.		551
	MORAN, Barbara B.	(919)962-8363	862
	NEAL, Michelle H.	(919)962-0077	890
	PALO, Eric E.	(919)493-7230	937
	SEVERANCE, Robert W.	(919)967-5021	1117
	TAYLOR, David C.	(919)962-1355	1226
Charlotte	FRANKLE, Raymond A.	(704)547-2221	397
Davidson	PARK, Leland M.	(704)892-1837	941

ACADEMIC LIBRARY CONSULTANT (Cont'd)
NORTH CAROLINA (Cont'd)

Durham	CAMPBELL, Jerry D.	(919)684-2034	176
	HEWITT, Joe A.	(919)489-9875	535
	KLINE, Lawrence O.	(919)684-6396	661
	LUBANS, John	(919)684-2034	745
	TOOMER, Clarence	(919)682-0238	1251
Elon College	JONES, Plummer A.	(919)584-2338	614
	SHEPHERD, Gay W.	(919)584-1112	1127
Greensboro	HANHAN, Leila M.	(919)292-1115	495
	JARRELL, James R.	(919)273-7061	594
	YOUNG, Tommie M.	(909)621-0032	1383
Greenville	BRILEY, Anne S.		136
	SCOTT, Ralph L.	(919)830-0522	1108
High Point	GAUGHAN, Thomas M.	(919)841-9215	422
Jacksonville	MARTIN, Richard T.	(919)455-1221	778
Lexington	THOMAS, John B.	(704)249-8186	1237
Pinehurst	WILKINS, Alice L.	(919)692-6185	1340
Raleigh	BROWN, Kathleen R.	(919)737-2603	145
Reidsville	KING, Willard B.	(919)349-6192	652
Winston-Salem	AHLERS, Glen P.	(919)761-5438	8
	RODNEY, Mae L.	(919)924-6992	1048
	STEELE, Tom M.	(919)761-5440	1184

NORTH DAKOTA

Ellendale	ZINK, Esther L.	(701)349-3609	1389
Fargo	BIRDSALL, Douglas G.	(701)237-8878	98

OHIO

Akron	BRINK, David R.	(216)375-7224	136
	DURBIN, Roger	(216)794-9706	328
Athens	BETCHER, William M.	(614)593-2701	92
	LEE, Hwa W.	(614)592-5194	710
	MULLINER, Kent	(614)593-2707	878
Berea	MACIUSZKO, Jerzy J.	(216)234-9206	755
Bowling Green	BURLINGAME, Dwight F.	(419)372-2708	161
	MCCALLUM, Brenda W.		793
	MILLER, Ruth G.	(419)352-0817	842
	MILLER, William	(419)372-2857	843
	REPP, Joan M.		1024
	ZAPOROZHETZ, Laurene E.	(419)354-2101	1386
Canfield	GENAWAY, David C.	(216)533-2194	426
Cincinnati	ALBRECHT, Cheryl C.	(513)871-0969	10
	HEISHMAN, Eleanor L.	(513)475-2218	523
Cleveland	CHESHIER, Robert G.	(216)368-3427	206
	LUPONE, George	(216)687-2475	749
	PEARMAN, Sara J.	(211)421-7340	952
	RADER, Hannelore B.	(216)687-2475	1002
	STANLEY, Jean B.	(216)368-6596	1180
Cleveland Heights	PIETY, John S.	(216)321-8121	972
	TRAMDACK, Philip J.	(216)371-3445	1254
Columbus	ALTAN, Susan B.	(614)252-0781	18
	BAYER, Bernard I.	(614)292-7895	67
	BOOMGAARDEN, Wesley L.	(614)447-0524	115
	CROWE, William J.	(614)261-1502	261
	DALRYMPLE, Tamsen	(614)486-2109	271
	HAMILTON, Marsha J.	(614)292-6314	492
	HECK, Thomas F.	(614)292-2310	519
	HUBER, Donald L.	(614)235-4136	569
	MIXTER, Keith E.	(614)263-7204	850
	POPOVICH, Charles J.	(614)292-2136	984
	STUDER, William J.	(614)292-4241	1204
	VANBRIMMER, Barbara A.	(614)292-9810	1272
Dayton	KNASIAK, Theresa J.	(513)254-1433	663
	MCNEER, Elizabeth J.	(513)873-2686	816
	NOLAN, Patrick B.	(513)274-3424	907
	PURSCH, Lenore D.	(513)434-7064	998
	THOMAS, Ritchie D.	(513)873-2380	1238
	WALKER, Mary A.	(513)229-3551	1296
Dublin	JACOB, Mary E.	(614)764-6063	589
	PAK, Moo J.	(514)761-2174	935
Hiram	DUFFETT, Gorman L.	(216)569-5353	323
Kent	WYNAR, Lubomyr R.		1375
Middletown	PALMER, Virginia E.	(513)424-4263	937
Oberlin	CARPENTER, Eric J.	(216)775-2546	184
	MOFFETT, William A.	(216)775-8285	852
Oxford	WORTMAN, William A.	(513)529-3936	1369
Shaker Heights	BELKIN, Betsey B.		76
Springfield	MONTAG, John	(513)327-7019	855

ACADEMIC LIBRARY CONSULTANT (Cont'd)
OHIO (Cont'd)

Toledo	AVERY, Galen V.	(419)475-8551	41
	CARY, Mary K.	(419)537-2833	191
	WEILANT, Edward		1317
Wilmington	NICHOLS, James T.	(513)382-6661	901
Wooster	ESHELMAN, William R.	(216)345-8708	354
Wright Patterson AFB	HELLING, James T.	(513)255-5894	524

OKLAHOMA

Ada	COULTER, Cynthia M.	(405)332-8000	251
Enid	SAYRE, John L.	(405)237-4433	1087
Norman	BATT, Fred	(405)325-4231	64
	CALLARD, Joanne C.	(405)364-0667	173
	LEE, Sul H.	(405)325-2611	711
Shawnee	ALDRIDGE, Betsy B.		11
Stillwater	HILKER, Emerson W.	(405)624-6305	539
	JOHNSON, Edward R.	(405)372-2637	604
	ROUSE, Roscoe	(405)377-1651	1061
Tahlequah	MADAUS, J R.		758
Tishomingo	KENNEDY, James W.	(405)371-2528	641
Tulsa	DUCEY, Richard E.	(918)592-6000	322
	PATTERSON, Robert H.	(918)585-3009	948
	SMITH, Donald R.	(918)592-6000	1154

OREGON

Beaverton	SHOFFNER, Ralph M.	(503)645-3502	1132
Corvallis	GEORGE, Melvin R.	(503)754-3411	427
Eugene	MORRISON, Perry D.	(503)342-2361	868
	SHIPMAN, George W.	(503)683-8262	1131
	SHULER, John A.	(503)686-3048	1133
	WAND, Patricia A.	(503)686-3056	1302
Monmouth	GORCHELS, Clarence C.	(503)838-1274	451
	JENSEN, Gary D.	(503)838-1220	598
Portland	FERGUSON, Douglas K.	(503)228-5512	372
	INGRAHAM-SWETS, Leonoor	(503)222-2608	582
	METZENBACHER, Gary W.	(503)654-5182	828
	WRIGHT, Janet K.	(503)464-4097	1371

PENNSYLVANIA

Ambridge	MUNDAY, Robert S.	(412)266-3838	878
Bethlehem	CADY, Susan A.	(215)758-4645	170
	JARVIS, William E.	(215)758-3035	595
	METZGER, Philip A.	(215)866-1257	829
Bloomsburg	VANN, John D.	(717)784-4283	1276
Bryn Mawr	BILLS, Linda G.	(215)645-5294	96
	MARKSON, Eileen	(215)645-5087	771
California	BECK, William L.	(412)938-4096	72
	CARUSO, Nicholas C.	(412)938-9166	190
Center Valley	MCCABE, James P.	(215)282-1100	793
	WELLE, Jacob P.	(215)282-1100	1321
Clarion	MCCABE, Gerard B.	(814)226-2343	792
	PERSON, Ruth J.	(814)226-5341	961
East Stroudsburg	SUMMERS, George V.	(717)424-3151	1209
Elizabethtown	BARD, Nelson P.	(717)367-1151	56
Gettysburg	HEDRICK, David T.	(717)334-8741	520
Glen Rock	LIEBERMAN, Ronald	(717)235-2134	726
Harrisburg	FOUST, Judith M.	(717)787-8007	393
Haverford	FREEMAN, Michael S.	(215)896-1272	401
	ROBERTSON, Robert B.	(215)896-1273	1042
Huntingdon	WILSON, Martin P.	(814)643-2808	1352
Indiana	KROAH, Larry A.	(412)463-2055	679
Jeannette	PAWLIK, Deborah A.		951
Jenkintown	MONTOYA, Leopoldo	(215)886-2299	856
Kingston	PAUSTIAN, P R.	(717)283-2651	950
Lancaster	BROWN, Charlotte B.	(717)291-4225	142
Loretto	NEGHERBON, Vincent R.	(814)472-7000	892
Mars	JOSEPH, Patricia A.	(412)776-9249	617
McKeesport	HERRON, Nancy L.	(412)675-9111	533
Middletown	RAMBLER, Linda K.	(412)349-4621	1005
	TOWNLEY, Charles T.	(717)948-6079	1253
New Kingstown	HANSON, Eugene R.	(717)243-0973	498
New Milford	MAASS, Eleanor A.	(717)465-3054	753
Philadelphia	ADAMS, Mignon S.	(215)596-8790	5
	AUGUST, Sidney	(215)985-2872	39
	BUTLER, Evelyn		166
	CRESSWELL, Donald H.	(215)242-4750	258
	DEVLIN, Margaret K.	(215)928-6994	297

ACADEMIC LIBRARY CONSULTANT (Cont'd)
PENNSYLVANIA (Cont'd)

Philadelphia	FUSELER-MCDOWELL,		
	Elizabeth A.	(215)423-9294	410
	GRILIKHES, Sandra B.	(215)898-7027	470
	HORNIG-ROHAN, James E.	(215)848-0554	560
	KOHN, Roger S.	(215)438-5635	668
	MARVIN, Stephen G.	(215)895-1874	780
	MCDONALD, Joseph A.	(215)637-5829	802
	MEREDITH, Phyllis C.	(609)757-4640	825
	MICIKAS, Lynda L.	(215)637-7700	832
	MONTAVON, Victoria A.	(215)557-6921	855
	PAGELL, Ruth A.	(215)898-5922	934
	ROHDY, Margaret A.	(215)387-5768	1050
	SAUNDERS, William B.	(215)224-0235	1085
	VAN HORNE, John C.	(215)546-3181	1275
	WALL, H D.	(215)438-1205	1297
	YOUNG, James B.	(215)898-6715	1382
Phoenixville	SAUER, James L.	(215)933-2236	1084
Pittsburgh	EVANS, Nancy H.	(412)268-2114	357
	FITZGERALD, Patricia A.	(412)268-2428	382
	FORD, Sylverna V.	(412)268-2446	390
	JOSEY, E J.	(412)624-9451	618
	MITCHELL, Joan M.	(412)578-6137	849
	NASRI, William Z.	(412)276-3234	888
	SILVERMAN, Marc B.	(412)648-1376	1138
	WEBRECK, Susan J.	(412)624-5230	1314
	WOODSWORTH, Anne		1367
Reading	HANNAFORD, William E.	(802)468-5611	496
	SMALL, Sally S.	(215)320-4823	1151
	STILLMAN, Mary E.	(215)921-2381	1194
Rosemont	LYNCH, Mary D.	(215)527-0200	752
Scranton	CAMPION, Carol M.	(717)348-0538	177
	SPEIRS, Gilmary	(717)348-6266	1172
Shippensburg	CROWE, Virginia M.	(717)532-1463	261
State College	CHANG, Shirley L.	(717)893-2312	201
	PIERCE, Miriam D.	(814)237-7004	971
	PIERCE, William S.	(814)237-7004	972
University Park	CARSON, M S.	(814)865-1818	188
	CLINE, Nancy M.	(814)865-1858	222
	FORTH, Stuart	(814)865-0401	391
	GERHART, Catherine A.	(814)865-1755	428
	GRUBER, Linda R.	(814)865-3451	474
	NEAL, James G.	(814)865-0401	890
	RICE, Patricia O.	(814)865-1858	1027
	SMITH, Barbara J.	(814)865-0401	1153
	SMITH, Diane H.	(814)865-4861	1154
	STRIEDIECK, Suzanne S.	(814)865-1755	1202
	SULZER, John H.	(814)865-4861	1209
	WESTERMAN, Melvin E.	(814)863-2898	1327
Upper Darby	SILVERMAN, Scott H.	(215)734-0146	1138
Villanova	DREHER, Janet H.		319
	GRIFFIN, Mary A.	(215)645-4290	468
West Chester	MCCAWLEY, Christina W.	(215)436-0720	795
Yardley	DU BOIS, Paul Z.	(215)493-6882	322

PUERTO RICO

Guaynabo	MOMBILLE, Pedro	(809)783-8622	854
Hormiguerow	MARTINEZ-NAZARIO,		
	Ronaldo		779
Ponce	PADUA, Flores N.	(809)844-4150	934
Rio Piedras	MUNOZ-SOLA, Haydee	(809)764-0000	879
San Juan	HAMEL, Eleanor C.	(809)765-4426	491
San Sebastian	JARAMILLO, Juana S.	(809)896-1389	594
Santurce	RIVERA-ALVAREZ, Miguel A.	(809)728-4191	1037

RHODE ISLAND

Kingston	DEVIN, Robin B.	(401)792-2662	297
	KRAUSSE, Sylvia C.	(401)789-6882	676
	VOCINO, Michael C.	(401)789-9357	1286
Providence	DOHERTY, Joseph H.	(401)865-2244	309
	FARK, Ronald K.	(401)941-0086	364
	LYNDEN, Frederick C.	(401)863-2946	752
	TAYLOR, Merrily E.	(401)863-2162	1227

ACADEMIC LIBRARY CONSULTANT (Cont'd)
SOUTH CAROLINA

Charleston	ROSS, Gary M.	(803)792-5530	1058
	SAWYER, Warren A.	(803)792-2374	1086
	SEAMAN, Sheila L.	(803)795-4416	1109
	WOOD, Richard J.	(803)763-8532	1365
Clemson	HIPPS, Gary M.	(803)654-3934	543
Columbia	TOOMBS, Kenneth E.	(803)776-0431	1251
Denmark	BOOK, Imogene I.	(803)793-3660	115
Florence	DOVE, Herbert P.	(803)661-1300	314
Newberry	HAMILTON, Ben	(803)276-6870	491
Orangeburg	SMALLS, Mary L.	(803)536-8852	1151
	WILLIAMS-JENKINS, Barbara		
	J.	(803)536-7045	1347
Spartanburg	BOWLES, David M.	(803)578-1472	121
Sumter	GORDON, Clara B.	(803)773-4041	451

SOUTH DAKOTA

Rapid City	MC CAULEY, Philip F.	(605)348-5124	795
Sioux Falls	THOMPSON, Ronelle K.	(605)336-4921	1241
Vermillion	EDELEN, Joseph R.	(605)677-6082	335

TENNESSEE

Bartlett	HAIR, William B.	(901)377-5434	484
Bristol	HERRING, Mark Y.	(615)968-9449	533
Clarksville	BERWIND, Anne M.		91
Cleveland	NICOL, Jessie T.		902
Dayton	WRIGHT, David A.	(615)775-2041	1371
Dowelltown	EASTERLY, Ambrose	(615)597-1390	333
Harriman	OVERTON, Margaret C.		931
Johnson City	BORCHUCK, Fred P.	(615)929-4337	116
	NORRIS, Carol B.	(615)929-5345	909
Knoxville	BENGTSON, Betty G.	(615)974-6640	80
	HUNT, Donald R.	(615)974-4127	575
	JETT, Don W.	(615)922-2548	600
	LLOYD, James B.	(615)974-4480	735
	MYERS, Marcia J.	(615)974-4465	884
	PEMBERTON, J M.	(615)690-5598	956
	PHILLIPS, Linda L.	(615)687-6734	968
	PONNAPPA, Biddanda P.	(615)675-4545	982
	RADER, Joe C.	(615)523-6937	1002
Maryville	WORLEY, Joan H.	(615)982-6412	1369
Memphis	HUGGINS, Annelle R.	(901)323-1525	571
	LINDENFELD, Joseph F.	(901)528-6743	729
	MABBOTT, Deborah D.	(901)388-1096	753
	RUDOLPH, N J.	(901)454-2208	1066
Murfreesboro	CRAIG, James D.	(615)896-9097	254
Nashville	CHEN, Helen M.	(612)251-1417	205
	FANCHER, Evelyn P.	(615)255-8033	363
	GOODALE, Adebonojo L.	(615)327-6728	448
	RICHARDS, Timothy F.	(615)385-1858	1028
Oak Ridge	DAVIS, Inez W.	(615)482-9619	279
Sewanee	WATSON, Tom G.	(615)598-1213	1310

TEXAS

Abilene	DAHLSTROM, Joe F.		269
Alpine	SPEARS, Norman L.	(915)837-8121	1172
Arlington	LOWRY, Charles B.	(817)273-3391	745
	YOUNKIN, C G.	(817)429-2674	1383
Austin	BILLINGS, Harold W.	(512)442-8597	96
	BUCKNALL, Carolyn F.	(512)478-5129	154
	HISLE, W L.	(512)495-7148	544
	MCADAMS, Nancy R.	(512)453-7177	792
	PAYNE, John R.	(512)478-7724	951
Beaumont	SPARKMAN, Mickey M.	(409)880-8118	1171
Buchanoan Dam	JONES, C L.	(512)793-6118	611
Cleburne	CARDENAS, Martha L.	(817)641-6641	180
College Station	GYESZLY, Suzanne D.	(409)845-3731	479
	PAYNE, Leila M.	(409)845-8157	951
Dallas	FARMER, David	(214)692-3231	364
	JAGOE, Katherine P.	(214)931-8938	591
	ORAM, Robert W.	(214)739-1310	925
	SWEARINGEN, Wilba S.	(214)380-0731	1214
	UDENYL, Evelyn U.		1267
	WATERS, Richard L.	(214)826-6981	1308
	WETHERBEE, Louella V.	(214)750-6130	1327
Denton	CARROLL, Dewey E.	(817)565-2445	187
	GALLOWAY, Margaret E.	(817)565-3024	415
	KHADER, Majed J.		645
	MITCHELL, George D.	(817)565-2489	848

ACADEMIC LIBRARY CONSULTANT (Cont'd)
TEXAS (Cont'd)
Denton

	SHELDON, Brooke E.	(817)898-2602	1125
	SNAPP, Elizabeth M.	(817)387-3980	1162
	TOTTEN, Herman L.	(817)383-1902	1252
	TURNER, Frank L.	(817)898-2603	1264
Edinburg	SHABOWICH, Stanley A.	(512)383-0441	1118
El Paso	RAMSEY, Donna E.	(915)855-1218	1005
Fort Worth	CARTER, Bobby R.	(817)735-2380	189
	WOOD, Richard C.	(517)927-5389	1365
Harlingen	CORBIN, John	(512)428-5475	245
Houston	ADAMS, Elaine P.	(713)785-8703	4
	BUTLER, Marguerite L.	(713)726-9244	166
	CARRINGTON, Samuel M.	(713)527-4022	186
	CHANG, Robert H.	(713)221-8181	201
	FIELDING, Raymond E.	(713)749-7444	376
	GOTHIA, Blanche	(713)266-5106	453
	HALL, John D.	(713)749-4762	488
	HOLIBAUGH, Ralph W.		550
	KLAPPERSACK, Dennis	(713)630-1130	657
	MORRISSEY, Charles T.	(713)799-4510	869
	PORTER, Exa L.	(713)443-5491	984
	WILLIAMS, Ann T.	(713)792-4094	1342
Huntsville	BAILEY, William G.	(409)294-1614	47
Irving	COCHRAN, Carolyn	(214)258-6767	225
	HAGLE, Claudette S.	(214)986-2343	483
	WHITE, Lely K.	(214)721-5310	1331
Kilgore	CLAER, Joycelyn H.	(214)983-8238	215
Laredo	BRESIE, Mayellen	(512)722-8001	133
Lubbock	CARGILL, Jennifer S.	(806)792-2349	181
	OLM, Jane G.	(806)742-3794	921
	SARGENT, Charles W.	(806)792-0754	1082
	WEBB, Gisela M.	(806)794-7359	1313
Marshall	MAGRILL, Rose M.	(214)935-7963	760
Mesquite	DUMONT, Paul E.	(214)324-7786	325
Midland	MIRANDA, Cecilia	(915)685-4557	847
Nacogdoches	CAGE, Alvin C.	(409)568-4101	170
Odessa	LINDSAY, Lorin H.	(915)367-2318	729
Richardson	KRATZ, Abby R.	(214)690-2960	676
San Antonio	BALCOM, Karen S.	(512)344-8654	51
	FORD, Barbara J.	(512)736-8121	389
	HENRICKS, Duane E.	(512)436-3435	529
	KRONICK, David A.	(512)344-5796	679
	LIKNESS, Craig S.	(512)736-7344	727
	MANEY, James W.	(512)341-1366	765
	MANEY, Lana E.	(512)496-7754	765
	PEDERSEN, Wayne A.	(512)641-4561	954
	VELA-CREIXELL, Mary I.	(512)733-7109	1281
	WERKING, Richard H.	(512)736-8161	1324
San Marcos	MEARS, William F.		820
Seguin	HSU, Patrick K.	(512)372-3868	567
The Woodlands	FRAMEL, Phyllis M.	(713)367-9522	395
Uvalde	KINGSBERY, Evelyn B.	(512)278-4401	652

UTAH
Logan	NIELSEN, Steven P.	(801)750-3166	903
	WEISS, Stephen C.		1320
Provo	GOULD, Douglas A.	(801)226-1469	454
	MARCHANT, Maurice P.	(801)378-2976	768
	ROWLEY, Edward D.	(801)378-6372	1063
	WIGGINS, Marvin E.	(801)378-6346	1337
Salt Lake City	HANSON, Roger K.	(801)581-8558	498
	HOLLEY, Robert P.	(801)581-7741	551
	KRANZ, Ralph	(801)581-7995	676

VERMONT
Middlebury	RUCKER, Ronald E.	(802)388-3711	1065

VIRGIN ISLANDS
St Thomas	CHANG, Henry C.	(809)774-3407	200

VIRGINIA
Alexandria	BROWN, Dale W.	(703)751-3236	143
	CARTLEDGE, Connie L.	(703)960-6020	190
	GOLDBERG, Jolande E.	(703)765-4521	444
	JORDAN, Robert T.		617
	MICHAELS, Andrea A.	(703)360-1297	831
	ROSENBERG, Kenyon C.	(703)642-5480	1056
	TERWILLIGER, Gloria P.	(703)845-6254	1232

ACADEMIC LIBRARY CONSULTANT (Cont'd)
VIRGINIA (Cont'd)
Annandale	CHOBOT, Mary C.	(703)323-9402	210
Arlington	CLARKE, Robert F.		219
	HARRIS, Linda S.	(703)521-2541	505
	HIGBEE, Joan F.	(703)524-5844	537
	LEATHER, Deborah J.	(703)522-5600	707
Ashland	BEDSOLE, Dan T.	(804)752-7256	73
Blacksburg	COCHRANE, Lynn S.		225
Burke	STEPHENSON, Richard W.	(703)323-7721	1188
Charlottesville	BRAUN, Mina H.	(804)924-4957	129
	GORDON, Vesta L.	(804)295-5586	452
Chesapeake	LEHMAN, Lois J.	(804)367-3709	713
	THOMAS, Nell M.		1238
Emory	JENNERICH, Elaine Z.	(703)944-3121	598
Fairfax	CONIGLIO, Jamie W.	(703)323-2877	236
	HURT, Charlene S.	(703)323-2616	577
Falls Church	HARRIS, Virginia B.	(703)698-6968	506
Fredericksburg	MULVANEY, John P.	(703)899-4666	878
Hampden Sydney	NORDEN, David J.	(804)223-4381	908
Hampton	DENDY, Adele S.	(804)727-5371	291
Harrisonburg	HABAN, Mary F.	(703)433-2183	480
	PALMER, Forrest C.	(703)568-6929	936
	ROBISON, Dennis E.	(703)568-6578	1045
Langley AFB	VERNON, Christie D.	(804)766-1468	1283
Lexington	DELONG, Edward J.	(703)463-0567	290
Lynchburg	KAWAGUCHI, Miyako	(804)239-3071	632
McLean	CHEVERIE, Joan F.	(703)893-3889	207
	GATTONE, Dean R.	(703)790-5694	422
	WANG, Chi	(703)893-3016	1302
Norfolk	DUNCAN, Cynthia B.	(804)583-0903	325
	JONES-TRENT, Bernice R.	(804)632-8873	616
Radford	TURNER, Robert L.	(703)731-1835	1265
Reston	LISZEWSKI, Edward H.	(301)648-4306	733
Richmond	HUBBARD, William J.	(804)786-2331	568
	MIAH, Abdul J.	(804)786-5638	831
	REAM, Daniel L.	(804)257-6545	1012
	TROTTI, John B.	(804)358-8956	1258
	TYSON, John C.	(804)289-8456	1267
Springfield	ALBIN, Michael W.	(703)978-3022	10
Sweet Briar	JAFFE, John G.	(804)381-6138	591
Williamsburg	GROVE, Pearce S.	(804)220-2477	473
	HEYMAN, Berna L.	(804)253-4029	536
	MARSHALL, Nancy H.	(804)253-4408	775
Wise	BENKE, Robin P.	(703)328-2431	81

WASHINGTON
Bellingham	PARKER, Diane C.	(206)676-3051	941
Custer	HASELBAUER, Kathleen J.	(206)366-5063	510
Ellensburg	DOI, Makiko	(509)963-2101	309
	SCHNEIDER, Frank A.	(509)963-1901	1097
Lacey	DEBUSE, Raymond	(206)491-7498	285
Longview	BAKER, Robert K.	(206)577-0756	49
Olympia	KREIMEYER, Vicki R.	(206)753-2916	677
	MOORE, Mary Y.	(206)866-8272	860
Pullman	KEMP, Barbara E.	(509)334-5809	639
	KOPP, James J.	(509)335-9133	671
	MCCOOL, Donna L.	(509)335-4557	798
Seattle	AUSTIN, Martha L.	(206)543-2988	40
	BOYLAN, Merle N.	(206)543-1760	123
	HAZELTON, Penelope A.	(206)543-4089	517
	HILL, Ann M.	(206)626-4212	539
	JENNERICH, Edward J.	(206)626-6320	598
	MAACK, David J.	(206)527-1112	753
	THOMAS, Lawrence E.	(206)626-6325	1237
	TWENEY, George H.	(206)243-8243	1266
Spangle	MOLLER, Steffen A.	(509)245-3610	853
Spokane	PRINGLE, Robert M.	(509)325-6139	993
Tacoma	BECKER, Roger V.	(206)591-2703	72
	SELING, Kathy A.	(206)756-5571	1113

WEST VIRGINIA
Barboursville	DZIERZAK, Edward M.		331
Institute	SCOTT, John E.	(304)766-3116	1107
Morgantown	ESKRIDGE, Virginia C.	(304)293-5300	354
	SHILL, Harold B.	(304)292-3762	1130
Salem	LANGER, Frank A.	(304)782-1007	695

ACADEMIC LIBRARY CONSULTANT (Cont'd)

WISCONSIN

Eau Claire	MARQUARDT, Steve R.	(715)834-5390	772
Grafton	MORITZ, William D.	(414)377-6695	865
Kenosha	BARUTH, Barbara P.	(414)553-2167	62
La Crosse	HILL, Edwin L.	(608)782-1753	539
Madison	ANDERSON, Axel R.	(608)233-0659	21
	BUNGE, Charles A.	(608)263-2900	157
	GAPEN, D K.	(608)262-2600	416
	JESUDASON, Melba	(608)263-7464	600
	WILCOX, Patricia F.	(608)263-4414	1338
	WILLIAMSON, William L.	(608)238-0770	1348
Marshfield	ALLEN, Margaret A.	(715)387-7271	15
Menomonie	JAX, John J.	(715)232-1184	595
	SAWIN, Philip Q.		1086
Mequon	AMAN, Mary J.	(414)242-9031	19
Milwaukee	AMAN, Mohammed M.	(414)239-4709	19
	BRENNEN, Patrick W.	(414)257-8323	133
	JONES, Richard E.	(414)229-6457	614
	LYNCH, Beverly P.	(414)774-1008	751
	SIEGMANN, Starla C.	(414)774-8620	1136
	SWEETLAND, James H.	(414)963-9996	1215
Oshkosh	CORBLY, James E.	(414)231-4768	245
	SHARMA, Ravindra N.	(414)424-0139	1122
Platteville	GERLACH, Donald E.	(608)348-6677	429
Ripon	MCGOWAN, Sarah M.	(414)748-8330	807

WYOMING

Laramie	COTTAM, Keith M.	(307)766-3279	250
Sheridan	IVERSON, Deborah P.	(307)674-7797	585

CANADA

ALBERTA

Calgary	BOUEY, Elaine F.	(403)284-4418	119
	CRAMER, Eugene C.	(403)220-5376	255
	MACDONALD, Alan H.	(403)220-5953	754
	VINE, Rita F.	(403)247-6524	1285
Edmonton	BUSCH, B J.	(403)432-3794	165
	STARR, Lea K.	(403)432-5154	1182
	ZIEGLER, Fred	(403)432-5972	1388

BRITISH COLUMBIA

Kamloops	LEVESQUE, Nancy B.	(604)374-0123	719
North Vancouver	DODSON, Suzanne C.	(604)988-4567	308
	ELROD, J M.	(604)929-3966	346
Vancouver	HAYCOCK, Kenneth R.	(604)731-1131	515
	LEITH, Anna R.	(604)228-2762	714
	MCINNES, Douglas N.	(604)736-5235	809
	STUART-STUBBS, Basil F.	(604)731-1978	1204
Victoria	SLADE, Alexander L.	(604)721-8221	1147

MANITOBA

Winnipeg	ROUTLEDGE, Patricia A.	(204)474-9445	1062

NEW BRUNSWICK

Riverview	ENNS, Carol F.	(506)386-1084	350

NEWFOUNDLAND

St John's	WOOD, Alberta A.	(709)753-3805	1363

NOVA SCOTIA

Halifax	TAYYEB, Rashid	(902)422-4684	1229

ONTARIO

Ancaster	SAVAGE, Daniel A.	(416)648-2131	1085
Downsview	KATZ, Bernard M.	(416)638-7695	630
Guelph	BLACK, John B.	(519)821-2565	101
	GILLHAM, Virginia A.	(519)824-4120	436
Haliburton	HOBBS, Kathleen M.		545
Hamilton	FLEMMING, Tom	(416)525-9140	384
Kingston	MCBURNEY, Margot B.	(613)544-7967	792
Kitchener	SHEPHERD, Murray C.		1127
North York	HOFFMANN, Ellen J.	(416)736-2100	548
	VARMA, Divakara K.	(416)736-5139	1278
Ottawa	ROSSMAN, Linda	(613)564-2653	1059
Scarborough	BULAONG, Grace F.	(416)283-5732	156

ACADEMIC LIBRARY CONSULTANT (Cont'd)

ONTARIO (Cont'd)

Toronto	BEAUMONT, Jane	(416)922-9364	70
	DAVIDSON-ARNOTT, Frances E.	(416)486-6488	277
	DENIS, Laurent G.	(416)978-3111	292
	HAJNAL, Peter I.	(416)533-7338	484
	MCCANN, Judith B.	(416)429-1247	794
	MOORE, Carole I.	(416)978-2292	858
	VEANER, Allen B.	(416)486-0239	1280
	WILKINSON, John P.	(416)978-3167	1340
Waterloo	BECKMAN, Margaret L.	(519)824-4120	73
	BEGLO, Jo N.	(519)885-1211	74
Windsor	SINGLETON, Cynthia B.	(519)253-4232	1143

QUEBEC

Boucherville	THERIAULT, Carmelle	(514)655-2665	1234
Drummondville Nord	HEON, Gerard	(819)472-4347	530
Hull	CHENIER, Andre	(819)595-3810	206
Montreal	BAZINET, Jeanne	(514)482-7188	68
	BISSON, Jacques	(514)482-9110	100
	CRAWFORD, David S.	(514)398-4723	256
	DARBON, Ginette	(514)343-7687	274
	GARNETT, Joyce C.	(514)398-4763	419
	GREENE, Richard L.	(514)343-7424	464
	GROEN, Frances K.	(514)845-2090	471
	HOBBINS, Alan J.	(514)398-4773	545
	HOWARD, Helen A.	(514)933-0893	564
	ORMSBY, Eric	(514)398-4677	926
	RATNER, Sabina T.		1010
	ROUSSEAU, Denis	(514)843-3214	1061
Quebec	BONNELLY, Claude	(418)656-2008	114
	PAGEAU, Denise	(418)688-8310	934
	TESSIER, Yves	(418)872-4304	1233
Sainte-Foy	PETRYK, Louise O.	(418)656-6921	965
Sherbrooke	CHASSE, Jules	(819)821-7550	203
Ste Anne de Bellevue	DOUGLAS-BONNELL, Eileen	(514)457-9487	314
	GRAINGER, Bruce	(514)398-7879	457
Trois-Rivieres	SIMARD, Denis	(819)376-1721	1139

SASKATCHEWAN

Regina	INGLES, Ernie B.	(306)584-4132	582
	MACK, A Y.	(306)543-6981	756

ARGENTINA

Entre Rios	HAMMERLY, Hernan D.		493

AUSTRALIA

Canberra	STEELE, Colin R.		1184
Turramurra	WILKINSON, Eoin H.		1340
Victoria	POWNALL, David E.	(033)418-2990	989

BAHRAIN

Al Manamah	ALI, Syed N.		13

BELGIUM

Kraainem	WALCKIERS, Marc A.		1293

COSTA RICA

San Jose	CROWTHER, Warren W.		262

EGYPT

Cairo	EL-DUWEINI, Aadel K.	(027)197-7200	342

ENGLAND

Harrogate	LINE, Maurice B.		730
Oxford	BISHOP, John		99

FEDERAL REPUBLIC OF CHINA

Taipei	HUANG, Shih H.		568

FEDERAL REPUBLIC OF GERMANY

Berlin	KREH, Fritz		677

GUATAMALA

Guatamala City	MARBAN, Ricio		768

ACADEMIC LIBRARY CONSULTANT (Cont'd)

HONG KONG

Kowloon	POON, Paul W.	983
Shatin	YEN, David S.	1379

HUNGARY

Budapest	LAZAR, Peter	706

INDIA

New Delhi	AGRAWAL, Surendra P.	7

IRAN

Shiraz	MEHRAD, Jafar	821

IRELAND

Dublin	FOX, Peter K.	395

ISRAEL

Birzeit	HADDAD, Aida N.	481

JAPAN

Aichi	TOGUCHI, Eiko		1248
Sendai Miyagi	HARADA, Ryukichi		499
Tokyo	KISHIMOTO, Hiroko		656
	URATA, Kazuo	(034)331-1110	1269

KENYA

Nairobi	BOWEN, Dorothy N.	120
	IRURIA, Daniel M.	584

KUWAIT

Khalidiah	HAMDY, Mohamed N.	491

MEXICO

Los Mochis	LAU, Jesus G.	702
Naucalpan	OROZCO-TENORIO, Jose M.	926
Nuevo Leon	ARTEAGA, Georgina	35

NETHERLANDS

Wageningen	KOSTER, Lieuwien M.	673

NIGERIA

Kano	AJIBERO, Matthew I.		9
Lagos	AFOLAYAN, Matthew A.	(018)001-6040	7
Ogbomoso	OKPARA, Ibiba M.		920

NORTHERN IRELAND

Belfast	LINTON, William D.	731

PAKISTAN

Lahore	TRAINER, Leslie F.	1253

PHILIPPINES

Makati	MORAN, Teresita C.	862
Manila	DE CASTRO, Elinore H.	285
Quezon City	PICACHE, Ursula D.	970

PORTUGAL

Lisbon	DE MACEDO, Maria L.	290

SAUDI ARABIA

Jeddah	KHAN, Mohammed A.	646

SCOTLAND

Glasgow	HEANEY, Henry J.	518

SOUTH AFRICA

Belhar Cape Province	SEPTEMBER, Peter E.	1115
Pretoria	WILLEMSE, John	1341

TRINIDAD

Valsayn	NANTON-COMISSIONG, Barbara L.	887

UGANDA

Mukono	MUKUNGU, Frederick N.	876

ARCHIVIST

ALABAMA

Montgomery	MCCRANK, Lawrence J.	(205)244-9202	800

ALASKA

Juneau	KINNEY, John M.	(907)586-1857	653

ARKANSAS

Fayetteville	MILLER, Leon C.	(501)575-5577	839

CALIFORNIA

Fullerton	STEPHENSON, Shirley E.	(714)773-3580	1189
Jamul	SERDZIAK, Edward J.	(619)426-2253	1116
Los Angeles	SORGENFREI, Robert K.	(213)743-6103	1168
Moreno Valley	SWAFFORD, William M.	(714)242-7719	1212
Santa Paula	CHRISTOPHER, Paul	(805)525-8092	212
Yucaipa	BUTLER, Randall R.	(714)797-3859	167

COLORADO

Denver	WHITE, Joyce L.	(303)722-4687	1331

CONNECTICUT

New Haven	BROWN, William E.	(203)432-1749	148

DELAWARE

Newark	RUDISELL, Carol A.	1065

DISTRICT OF COLUMBIA

Washington	LUSKEY, Judith	(202)357-4654	749
	MCCOY-LARSON, Sandra	(202)544-5520	799

ILLINOIS

Chicago	EVANS, Linda J.	(312)642-4600	357
	GAYNON, David B.	(312)399-5662	424
Elmhurst	STEWART, Virginia R.	(312)833-7090	1193
Evanston	METZLER, Valerie	(312)869-5992	829
Urbana	BRICHFORD, Maynard J.	(217)367-7072	134

IOWA

Ames	KLINE, Laura S.	(515)294-6672	661

MARYLAND

Annapolis	THAPAR, Shashi P.	(301)974-3015	1234
Bowie	EVANS, Frank B.	(301)464-8829	357
Rockville	MERZ, Nancy M.	(301)770-1170	827

MASSACHUSETTS

Boston	O'TOOLE, James M.	(617)929-8110	930
Northampton	SLY, Margery N.	(413)584-2700	1150
Wakefield	CHAPDELAINE, Susan A.	(617)246-5200	201

MICHIGAN

Ann Arbor	CONWAY, Paul L.	(313)668-2218	239
Detroit	WEST, Donald	(313)577-2525	1326
East Lansing	HONHART, Frederick L.	(517)355-2330	556
Galesburg	MOSHER, Robin A.	(616)665-4409	871
Lansing	FRYE, Dorothy T.	(517)393-7608	407

MINNESOTA

Minneapolis	BRUEMMER, Bruce H.	(612)624-5050	149
St Paul	JESSEE, W S.	(612)647-1329	600

MISSISSIPPI

Biloxi	FREEDMAN, Jack A.	(601)388-2318	400

MISSOURI

St Louis	GIETSCHIER, Steven P.	(314)993-7787	433
	RILEY, Martha J.	(314)577-5158	1034

NEW JERSEY

Morristown	DENSKY, Lois R.	(201)539-0407	293
North Arlington	CASEY, Mary A.	(201)997-2141	192
Princeton	ROTH, Stacy F.		1059
	SARETZKY, Gary D.	(609)734-5744	1082
Westfield	WILSTED, Thomas P.	(201)789-9147	1353

ARCHIVIST (Cont'd)

NEW YORK

Brooklyn	DINDAYAL, Joyce S.	(718)647-1624	304
	HOMMEL, Claudia	(718)237-0028	555
New York	HUNTER, Gregory S.	(212)940-1690	576
	MENT, David M.	(212)678-4104	824
	SIEGEL, Steven W.	(212)427-5395	1136
Stattsburg	LAFEVER, C R.	(914)889-8418	687
Wantagh	NOVITSKY, Edward G.		911

NORTH CAROLINA

Greenville	BOCCACCIO, Mary A.	(919)757-6671	108
Winston-Salem	WOODARD, John R.	(919)761-5089	1365

OHIO

Cincinnati	GILLILAND, Anne J.	(513)475-6459	436
Columbus	BRANDT, Michael H.	(614)863-2814	128
Delaware	COHEN, Susan J.	(614)363-9433	229

OREGON

Medford	THELEN, Richard L.	(503)776-7040	1234
Salem	FILSON, Laurie	(503)364-4162	377

PENNSYLVANIA

Glenside	NIEWEG, Clinton F.	(215)884-5878	904
Philadelphia	HALLER, Douglas M.	(215)898-8304	489
	KING, Eleanor M.		650
Pittsburgh	STIEBER, Michael T.	(412)268-2437	1193

SOUTH CAROLINA

Columbia	HELSLEY, Alexia J.	(803)781-8477	525

SOUTH DAKOTA

Sioux Falls	THOMPSON, Harry F.	(605)336-4007	1239

TENNESSEE

Nashville	RATKIN, Annette L.	(615)352-2000	1009

TEXAS

Austin	GRACY, David B.	(512)471-3821	455
	LANDIS, Lawrence A.	(512)451-3214	693
Dallas	BENGE, Joy L.	(214)528-4157	80
Houston	BOOTHE, Nancy L.	(713)667-1916	116
	LANGSTON, Sally J.	(713)659-8040	696
San Antonio	RAY, Joyce M.	(512)567-2470	1011

UTAH

Provo	ROWLEY, Edward D.	(801)378-6372	1063

VIRGINIA

Alexandria	CALMES, Alan R.	(202)523-5496	174
	CARTLEDGE, Connie L.	(703)960-6020	190
	CASSEDY, James G.	(703)768-2070	193
Charlottesville	BERKELEY, Edmund		87
Fairfax	PFEIFFER, David A.	(703)425-4685	966
	WALCH, Victoria I.	(703)273-3260	1293

WASHINGTON

Seattle	EULENBERG, Julia N.	(206)324-2605	356
	STIRLING, Dale A.	(206)367-2728	1195
	STORDAHL, Beth A.	(206)322-7411	1198

WISCONSIN

Fond Du Lac	EBERT, John J.	(414)929-3616	334
Madison	BEHRND-KLODT, Menzi L.	(608)238-3966	75
Milwaukee	KOVAN, Allan S.	(414)963-5402	673

CANADA

ALBERTA

Calgary	KLUMPENHOUWER, Richard	(403)237-6052	662

MANITOBA

Winnipeg	SANTORO, Corrado A.	(204)474-8243	1082

ONTARIO

Toronto	ARDERN, Christine M.		31

BIBLIOGRAPHER

ALABAMA

Auburn	COLSON, Harold G.	(205)826-4500	234
	PEDERSOLI, Heleni M.	(207)821-7168	954
	STRAITON, T H.	(205)826-4500	1199
	ZLATOS, Christy L.	(205)826-3429	1390
Birmingham	ATKINSON, Calberta O.	(205)787-3767	38
	BLEILER, Richard J.	(205)934-6364	105
	SCALES, Diann R.	(205)322-8458	1087
	WEATHERLY, Cynthia D.	(205)939-0120	1312
Helena	GOODWYN, Betty R.	(205)988-0896	450
Huntsville	MCNAMARA, Jay	(205)895-6526	816
Irondale	FEENKER, Cherie D.	(205)956-4544	368
Montgomery	FELDER, Jimmie R.	(205)265-2012	369
Oneonta	WEAVER, Clifton W.	(205)274-9111	1312
Pelham	WRIGHT, Amos J.	(205)663-3403	1370
Tuscaloosa	NEAVILL, Gordon B.	(205)348-1520	891
	OSBURN, Charles B.	(205)348-7561	927
	WATSON, Linda S.	(205)553-0826	1309

ALASKA

Anchorage	EGGLESTON, Phyllis A.	(907)337-0051	339
	LESH, Nancy L.	(907)786-1877	718
	LUDWIG, J D.	(907)333-8917	746
	SOKOLOV, Barbara J.	(907)346-2480	1165
Fairbanks	LAKE, Gretchen L.	(907)452-6751	688
	MUDD, Isabelle G.	(907)479-4522	875
	PARHAM, Robert B.	(907)479-5966	940

ARIZONA

Phoenix	BOROVANSKY, Vladimir T.		117
	GOEBEL, Heather L.	(602)994-2471	443
Scottsdale	KLIMIADES, Mario N.	(602)994-2471	661
Tempe	LESHY, Dede	(602)946-8090	718
	MULVIHILL, Joann	(602)965-5167	878
	SCHON, Isabel	(602)965-2996	1098
	STEWART, Douglas J.	(602)897-7191	1192
	WU, Ai H.	(602)965-3354	1373
Tucson	BALDWIN, Charlene M.	(602)327-2385	51
	CAMPBELL, Dierdre A.	(602)621-7897	176
	DICKINSON, Donald C.	(602)621-3565	300
	ETTER, Patricia A.	(602)299-5199	355
	HAWBAKER, A C.	(602)621-4869	513
	HIEB, Louis A.	(602)621-6077	537
	LAIRD, W D.	(602)621-2101	688
	MAKUCH, Andrew L.	(602)622-8572	762
	MARSHALL, Thomas H.	(602)621-6452	775
	MYERS, Roger	(602)792-3452	885
	RIISE, Milton B.	(602)325-1348	1034
	ROBROCK, David P.	(602)743-7072	1045
	RULE, Amy E.	(602)621-6273	1067
	SABOVIK, Pavel	(602)885-9923	1073
	SMITH, Dorman H.	(602)296-3760	1154
	SORENSEN, Lee R.	(602)621-4868	1168
	WHITE, Edward H.	(602)621-5455	1330
	WOLF, Noel C.	(602)746-7637	1360
Yuma	STUART, Gerard W.	(602)783-6742	1204

ARKANSAS

Conway	GREEN, Douglas A.	(501)327-5611	461
Fayetteville	EARNEST, Jeffrey D.	(501)521-8388	332
Little Rock	BRECK, Paul A.	(501)569-3121	131
	RAZER, Robert L.	(501)663-0789	1012
	WRIGHT, Jacqueline S.	(501)371-2147	1371
Mountain View	MCNEIL, William K.	(501)269-3851	816

CALIFORNIA

Aptos	WYKLE, Helen H.	(408)662-3228	1375
Arcata	KENYON, Sharmon H.	(707)826-3416	643
Belmont	GUEDON, Mary S.	(415)593-1600	475
Berkeley	BASART, Ann P.	(415)848-7805	62
	BENIDIR, Samia	(415)644-1129	80
	CANDAU, Eugenie	(415)849-4844	178
	DUGGAN, Mary K.	(415)642-5764	324
	FISHER, Leslie R.	(415)548-3542	381
	GAREY, Anita I.	(415)841-8414	418
	HANFF, Peter E.	(415)642-8172	495
	HUMPHREYS, Nancy K.	(415)642-4786	574
	KOBZINA, Norma G.	(415)643-6475	666

BIBLIOGRAPHER (Cont'd)
CALIFORNIA (Cont'd)

Berkeley			
	PARKS, Mary L.	(415)644-3401	943
	RAFAEL, Ruth K.	(415)849-2710	1003
	RIGGS, Judith M.	(415)654-2809	1034
Beverly Hills	JEROME, Michael S.	(213)550-6100	599
Canyon Country	CRUM, Norman J.	(805)252-9053	262
Carlsbad	KENNEDY, Charlene F.	(619)434-2871	640
Chico	BROWN, Carol G.	(916)861-2762	142
	LO, Henrietta W.	(916)895-6406	735
Claremont	ALLEN, Susan M.		16
	WRIGLEY, Elizabeth S.	(714)624-6305	1373
Corona del Mar	DOSER, Virginia A.	(714)760-0148	313
Costa Mesa	HAN, Kenneth P.	(714)557-4648	494
	POARCH, Margaret E.	(714)662-1867	979
Culver City	PATTEN, Frederick W.	(213)827-3335	947
Cupertino	JAJKO, Edward A.	(408)446-1306	592
Davis	BENOIT, Gerald		82
	ELLIOTT, C D.	(916)752-2110	343
	JESTES, Edward C.	(916)752-0519	600
	KNOWLES, Em C.	(916)752-1126	665
	LAMPRECHT, Sandra J.	(916)752-1126	691
	SHORT, Virginia	(916)752-1126	1132
	TEBO, Jay D.	(916)758-8256	1229
	WINTER, Michael F.	(916)752-1126	1356
Del Mar	HOLLEMAN, Marian P.	(619)755-4253	551
East Palo Alto	DERKSEN, Charlotte R.	(415)323-5386	294
	FROST, Michelle	(415)321-4017	406
Encino	GHAZARIAN, Salpi H.	(818)789-5041	430
Eureka	BROWN, Elizabeth E.	(707)443-8051	143
Fremont	TSAI, Sheh G.	(415)656-7097	1260
Fullerton	STEPHENSON, Shirley E.	(714)773-3580	1189
Garden Grove	HIXON, Donald L.	(714)638-9379	544
Goleta	MUSICK, Nancy W.	(805)964-8484	883
Huntington Beach	OPPENHEIM, Michael R.	(714)842-1548	925
Irvine	ARIEL, Joan	(714)856-4970	31
	FINEMAN, Michael	(714)856-8160	377
	FORBES, Fred R.	(714)856-4974	389
	GELFAND, Julia M.	(714)856-4971	426
	PUGSLEY, Sharon G.	(714)856-7193	997
	TSANG, Daniel C.	(714)856-4978	1260
	YOUNG, Eleanor C.	(714)552-5803	1381
La Canada-Flintridge	DUNKLEE, Joanna E.	(818)790-3518	326
La Jolla	FISHER, Edith M.	(619)534-1258	380
	HURLBERT, Irene W.	(619)534-1261	577
	SMITH, Phillip A.	(619)534-1266	1159
La Mirada	ANJOU-DURAZZO, Martel T.	(213)944-5981	28
Lafayette	SVIHRA, S J.	(415)933-9549	1212
Lake View Terrace	TASHIMA, Marie		1224
Livermore	PALLONE, Kitty J.	(415)447-2376	935
Long Beach	SINCLAIR, Lorelei P.	(213)423-6399	1142
	WILLIAMS, Valencia	(213)434-9151	1347
Los Angeles	BEVERAGE, Stephanie L.	(213)612-3242	93
	CHAMPLIN, Peggy	(213)472-4991	198
	HASSAN, Abe H.	(213)649-2846	511
	KHATTAB, Hosneya M.	(213)733-1196	646
	KUNSELMAN, Joan D.	(213)825-1204	684
	LEE, Hee J.	(213)391-4226	710
	MANTHEY, Teresa M.	(213)224-7234	767
	POPOVITCH-KREKIC, Ruzica	(213)476-2237	984
	SANDVIKEN, Gordon L.	(818)307-2872	1081
	SATER, Analya	(213)277-1969	1083
	SORGENFREI, Robert K.	(213)743-6103	1168
	STREIKER, Susan L.	(213)738-6727	1201
	TROTTA, Victoria K.	(213)743-6487	1258
	WUERTZ, Eva L.	(213)743-2540	1373
Los Gatos	BAILEY, Rolene M.	(408)356-9645	46
Menlo Park	FRANK, Peter R.	(415)329-1173	397
	NEWMARK, Laura C.	(415)321-2128	900
	REDFIELD, Elizabeth	(415)859-6187	1014
	TRUJILLO, Roberto G.	(415)329-0227	1259
Mill Valley	ASHLEY, Elizabeth	(415)388-8080	36
	WHITE, Cecil R.	(415)388-8080	1330
Moraga	RUDOLPH, Anne L.	(415)631-0926	1066
Northridge	DURAN, Karin J.	(818)885-2501	328
Oakland	BENNETT, Celestine C.	(415)893-9645	81
	BYRNE, Elizabeth D.	(415)658-6996	169
	WONG, Patricia M.	(415)834-2742	1363

BIBLIOGRAPHER (Cont'd)
CALIFORNIA (Cont'd)

Orange	WILSON, Wayne V.	(714)997-6912	1353
Palo Alto	HAMILTON, David M.	(415)853-0197	491
	KAHN, Paul J.	(415)327-3135	622
	WREDEN, William P.	(415)325-6851	1370
Pasadena	HOFFBERG, Judith A.	(818)797-0514	547
Ridgecrest	FRIEDMAN, Sandra M.	(619)375-8825	404
Riverside	HUNTER, David C.	(714)787-5841	576
	MITCHELL, Steve		849
	SELTH, Jefferson P.	(714)787-3703	1114
	STALKER, Laura A.	(714)787-5841	1178
Sacramento	KONG, Leslie M.	(916)278-5664	670
	MARTINEZ, Barbara A.	(916)429-1107	779
Salinas	COLLINS, Judith A.		232
San Bernardino	DEMENT, Alice R.	(714)883-6772	291
	MINDEMAN, George A.	(714)887-9753	845
San Diego	BUSCH, Barbara	(619)224-8412	165
	HESS, M S.	(619)565-5875	534
	JACOBS, Horace	(619)746-4005	589
	TABORN, Kym M.	(619)232-3320	1219
San Francisco	CONLEY, Linda A.	(415)285-6835	236
	DURSO, Angeline M.	(415)750-6072	329
	ECKMAN, Charles D.	(415)334-8449	335
	GRIFFIN, Michael D.	(415)664-2835	468
	HENKE, Dan	(415)565-4758	528
	LEWANDOWSKI, Joseph J.	(415)626-3755	722
	MOORE, Gregory B.	(415)753-2645	859
	REGNER-HYATT, Anne L.	(415)864-1154	1017
	STEFANCIC, Jean A.	(415)666-6678	1185
San Jose	BRIDGMAN, David L.	(408)997-3723	135
	ELLIOTT, Patricia G.	(408)277-9243	344
	HARMON, Robert B.	(408)297-2810	502
San Leandro	WENDROFF, Catriona	(415)569-3491	1323
San Marino	ZALL, Elisabeth W.	(818)405-2188	1386
San Rafael	PLOTKIN, Nathan	(415)479-7018	978
Santa Barbara	KINNELL, Susan K.	(805)965-1294	653
	KORENIC, Lynette M.	(805)961-3613	671
	MAHAFFEY, Susan M.	(805)964-4978	760
	TAI, Henry H.	(805)961-2365	1220
Santa Clara	BAZAN, Lorraine R.	(408)554-4658	68
Santa Cruz	LOMBARDI, Mary L.	(408)476-1131	738
Santa Monica	BERMAN, Marsha	(213)399-3674	88
	HALL, Anthony	(213)827-1707	487
	KARR, Linda		628
Santa Paula	CHRISTOPHER, Paul	(805)525-8092	212
Sebastopol	SIMONS, Maurice M.	(707)823-9275	1141
Sherman Oaks	MILLER, Margaret S.	(818)783-5264	840
Stanford	KRAKAUER, Elizabeth	(408)733-4611	675
Sunland	CLARK, Patricia A.	(818)353-6820	217
Turlock	PARKER, John C.	(209)634-9473	942
Vacaville	ELDREDGE, Mary		342
Van Nuys	DAVIS, L C.	(818)994-3044	280
Venice	EDELSTEIN, J M.	(213)827-8984	335
Westlake Village	TISE, Barbara L.	(818)991-0047	1247
Woodland Hills	REIFMAN, Deborah S.		1019

COLORADO

Boulder	CARTER, Nancy F.	(303)492-3928	189
	SANI, Martha J.	(303)492-8367	1081
	WERTHEIMER, Marilyn L.	(303)442-5583	1325
	WYNNE, Allen	(303)499-5616	1375
Colorado Springs	WATERS, W R.	(303)630-5288	1309
Denver	GOODRICH, Margaret	(303)320-6054	449
	MARSCHNER, Robyn J.	(303)321-2547	773
	MOULTON, Suzanne L.	(303)871-6427	873
	ZOOK, Ruth A.	(303)388-6809	1390
Englewood	OTTOSON, Robin D.	(303)761-2482	930
Fort Collins	ERNEST, Douglas J.	(303)491-1861	353
	NEWMAN, John	(303)491-1844	899
	SCHMIDT, Fred C.	(303)491-1881	1095
Greeley	SAVIG, Norman I.	(303)351-2251	1086
Littleton	GREALY, Deborah J.	(303)795-3156	461
	WHITBY, Thomas J.	(303)798-7049	1330
	WYNAR, Bohdan S.		1375

BIBLIOGRAPHER (Cont'd)
CONNECTICUT

Ansonia	MARTIN, Walter F.	(203)736-2601	779
Bethany	ASH, Lee M.	(203)393-2723	35
Branford	ADAMO, Clare	(203)488-1474	4
Bridgeport	FU, Theresa L.	(203)576-4236	407
	HUGHES, John M.	(203)576-4392	571
Bristol	SENKUS, Linda J.	(203)589-1298	1115
Columbia	PENN, Elinor K.	(203)228-9614	957
East Canaan	BYERS, Laura T.	(203)824-5971	168
East Hartford	SIROIS, Valerie M.	(203)565-7121	1144
Farmington	DEVINE, Marie E.	(203)677-2140	297
Hartford	WAIT, Gary E.	(236)236-5621	1293
Lakeville	RESTOUT, Denise T.	(203)435-9308	1024
Middletown	FARRINGTON, James	(203)347-9411	365
New Britain	WARZALA, Martin L.		1307
New Haven	COHEN, Morris L.	(203)432-1600	228
	HEINRITZ, Fred J.	(203)397-4530	522
	HILL, John R.	(203)397-4509	540
	ICHINOSE, Mitsuko	(203)432-1794	581
	KELLER, Michael A.	(203)389-2212	635
	KOEL, Ake I.	(203)432-1825	667
	LUBIN, Joan S.	(203)397-5154	745
	ROBERTS, Susanne F.	(203)432-1762	1041
	SILVERSTEIN, Louis H.	(203)624-6424	1139
	SPURGEON, Kathy R.		1176
Ridgefield	FARADAY, Joanna	(203)431-0062	363
	SWIFT, Janet B.	(203)438-5937	1216
Stamford	LIEBERMAN, Lucille N.	(203)353-2095	726
Storrs	FORMAN, Camille L.	(203)486-2526	390
	KAGAN, Alfred	(203)429-6565	621
Suffield	SCHMIDT, Alesandra M.		1095
Waterbury	JOY, Patricia L.	(203)757-6203	618
West Hartford	BRADBERRY, Richard P.	(203)241-4704	125
	LI, Hong C.	(203)523-5948	724
	NORONHA, Marilyn S.	(203)523-9765	909
	PIERCE, Anne L.	(203)243-4849	971
Westport	MUTTER, Letitia N.	(203)227-1992	883
Wilton	TRIFFIN, Nicholas	(914)681-4275	1256
Woodbridge	BOGENSCHNEIDER, Duane R.	(203)397-2600	110

DELAWARE

Newark	MYERS, Victoria B.	(302)454-2098	885
Winterthur	THOMPSON, Neville M.	(302)656-8591	1241

DISTRICT OF COLUMBIA

Washington	ACKERMAN, F C.	(202)398-1842	3
	BOHANAN, Robert D.	(202)523-3214	111
	BROOKE, Anna	(202)357-3222	140
	CARLSON, Julia F.	(202)225-2571	182
	CHAMBERS, Bettye T.	(202)625-4997	198
	CHIN, Cecilia H.	(202)543-3824	208
	COLETTI, Jeannette D.	(202)362-1664	231
	COOPER, David J.	(202)544-3653	242
	DEUTSCH, James I.	(202)342-6175	296
	DOUMATO, Lamia		314
	HAITH, Dorothy M.	(202)484-4941	484
	HANFORD, Sally		495
	JOHNSON, Gary M.		604
	JOHNSON, Lucy C.		607
	KENDRICK, Brent L.	(202)543-7031	640
	KOSTINKO, Gail A.	(202)483-4118	673
	LASNER, Mark S.	(202)745-1927	700
	LEFFALL, Dolores C.	(202)723-7645	712
	LEONARD, Angela M.	(202)636-7926	716
	MANNING, Martin J.	(202)485-6187	766
	MCCRAY, Maceo E.	(202)829-7737	800
	MCGILL, Theodora	(202)566-8320	806
	MCGOWAN, Anna T.	(202)245-1235	807
	MISSAR, Charles D.	(202)363-2751	847
	MISSAR, Margaret M.	(202)363-2751	847
	MODLIN, Marilyn J.	(202)452-4460	851
	MORRIS, Timothy J.	(202)462-8209	867
	NOWAK, Geraldine D.	(202)475-9419	911
	PETERSON, Charles B.		963
	PRUETT, Barbara J.	(202)362-1345	996
	REITH, Louis J.	(202)686-0131	1022
	RICHARDSON, Deborra A.		1029
	ROSENBERG, Jane A.	(202)786-0358	1056

BIBLIOGRAPHER (Cont'd)
DISTRICT OF COLUMBIA (Cont'd)

Washington			
	SANCHEZ, Jose L.	(202)387-7396	1079
	SCOTT, Catherine D.	(202)357-3101	1107
	SIPKOV, Ivan	(202)287-9850	1144
	THOMPSON, Elizabeth M.	(202)333-2108	1239
	VAN NIMMEN, Jane	(202)363-3664	1276
	VON PFEIL, Helena P.		1288
	WELCH, Thomas L.	(202)232-1706	1321
	YASUMATSU, Janet R.		1378

FLORIDA

Boca Raton	PELLEN, Rita M.	(305)395-6369	955
Clearwater	POTTER, Robert E.	(813)442-9061	987
Coral Gables	AHMAD, Carol F.	(305)284-3551	8
	KOBIALKA, Nancy C.	(305)284-2429	666
Coral Springs	KORNITSKY, Judith M.	(305)753-7081	672
De Land	EVERETT, David D.	(904)734-4121	358
Fort Lauderdale	HARTON, Pamela J.	(305)357-7454	508
Gainesville	BROWN, M S.	(904)392-0707	145
	BROWN, Pia T.	(904)375-6302	147
	LEONARD, Louise F.	(904)373-2705	716
	MALANCHUK, Peter P.	(904)392-0364	762
	TEAGUE, Edward H.	(904)392-0222	1229
	WILLETT, Charles	(904)378-1661	1341
Howey in the Hills	COHN, William L.	(904)324-2701	229
Jacksonville	FAHNERT, Elizabeth K.	(904)641-8649	361
	FARKAS, Andrew	(904)646-2554	364
Key Biscayne	KIRBY, Diana G.	(305)361-3678	654
Key West	SOULE, Maria J.	(305)296-9081	1169
Lauderhill	HURTES, Reva	(305)735-8655	578
Miami	BYRD, Susan G.	(305)347-2068	169
	CHAVES, Francisco M.	(305)385-2301	204
	HALE, Kay K.	(305)271-3678	485
	PARISE, Marina P.		940
	PHILLIPS, Donald J.	(305)274-5724	968
	ROVIROSA, Dolores F.		1062
	SANCHEZ, Sara M.	(305)854-7752	1079
	SEILER, Susan L.	(305)279-0545	1112
Miami Beach	EFRON, Muriel C.	(305)672-0696	338
	GROVER, Wilma S.	(305)868-5000	474
	LYON, Bruce C.	(305)868-4451	752
	MIRANDA, Salvador	(305)532-6834	847
North Lauderdale	BRESLAUER, Lester M.	(305)721-5181	133
Oakland Park	WILLIAMS, Alexander	(305)565-2990	1341
Plant City	PINGS, Joan G.	(813)752-3884	974
Royal Palm Beach	TERWILLEGAR, Jane C.	(305)793-4590	1232
St Petersburg	CATES, Jo A.	(813)522-1550	194
	WATERS, Sally G.	(813)345-1335	1308
Sarasota	HOLT, Ethel F.	(813)371-7640	554
	MOON, Ilse	(813)355-1795	857
Seminole	BRYAN, Michael G.	(813)595-4521	151
Tallahassee	CLARKSON, Jane S.	(904)385-9671	219
	CONAWAY, Charles W.	(904)893-1482	235
	DEENEY, Marian A.	(904)562-3246	286
	GIBLON, Charles B.	(904)893-3851	431
	PRATT, Darnell D.	(904)487-2651	990
	TOOLE, Gregor K.		1250
Tampa	EVANS, Josephine K.	(813)974-4471	357
	GATES, Jean K.	(813)974-3520	422
	KING, Elizabeth	(813)885-7481	650
	LOSEY, Doris C.	(813)885-4500	742
	WOOD, James F.	(813)232-5221	1364
Venice	CARR, Mary L.	(813)497-0420	186
Winter Park	AHLIN, Nancy	(305)644-6424	8

GEORGIA

Athens	COMPTON, Lawrence E.	(404)542-8460	235
	GUBISTA, Kathryn R.	(404)546-8153	475
	HAAR, John M.	(404)549-7625	480
	SOUTHWICK, Mary L.	(404)542-6643	1170
	WILLIAMS, Sara E.	(408)548-7519	1346
Atlanta	BULLOCK, Penelope L.	(404)792-0775	156
	COFFMAN, Joseph W.	(404)681-0251	227
	DEES, Anthony R.	(404)355-0551	287
	MENEELY, William E.	(404)658-3800	824
	MISRA, Jayasri T.	(404)524-5320	847
	RAQUET, Jacqueline R.	(404)320-9727	1008
	STOWELL, Donald C.	(404)231-4414	1199

BIBLIOGRAPHER (Cont'd)
GEORGIA (Cont'd)
Atlanta

	THAXTON, Lyn	(404)292-6767	1234
	WHITE, Carol A.	(404)351-8991	1330
College Park	CANN, Sharon F.	(404)768-0970	178
Columbus	CLEMENTS, Betty H.	(404)327-3399	221
Decatur	BISHOP, Beverly D.	(404)371-8488	99
	HATCHER, Nolan C.	(404)378-8282	511
	HULLUM, Cheri J.	(404)987-7473	573
	WENDEROTH, Christine	(404)378-8821	1323
East Point	BAIN, Michael L.	(404)761-4346	47
Experiment	LEDFORD, Carole L.	(404)228-7238	708
Richmond Hill	GLISSON, Patricia A.	(912)727-2592	441
Valdosta	MONTGOMERY, Denise L.	(912)333-5867	856
Warner Robins	MERK, P E.		826

GUAM
Agana

	WEINGARTH, Darlene	(671)472-1750	1318

HAWAII
Honolulu

	CAMPBELL, R A.	(808)955-8822	177
	GOODY, Cheryl S.	(808)521-5361	450
	LUSTER, Arlene L.	(808)737-8876	750
	STEPHENS, Diana C.	(808)945-2837	1188
	SZILARD, Paula	(808)948-8263	1218
	TAKAHASHI, Annabelle T.	(808)948-7214	1220
	VAN NIEL, Eloise S.	(808)548-6283	1276
Kaneohe	ASHFORD, Marguerite K.	(808)247-6834	36
Pearl City	KAN, Katharine L.		624

IDAHO
Boise

	ROBERTSON, Naida	(208)384-4340	1042
Moscow	ABRAHAM, Terry		3
	BRADY, Eileen E.	(208)883-0817	126
	STEINHAGEN, Elizabeth N.	(208)885-6260	1186

ILLINOIS

Abbott Park	SWANSON, Ruth M.	(312)937-6959	1213
Aurora	MCKEARN, Anne B.	(312)892-4811	810
Bloomington	ALEXANDER, Lynetta L.	(309)828-6053	12
Carbondale	BLACK, George W.	(618)453-2700	101
	COX, Shelley M.	(618)457-8975	253
	KILPATRICK, Thomas L.	(618)453-3374	648
	KOCH, David V.	(618)453-2516	667
	MCCOY, Ralph E.	(618)457-8707	799
	RAY, Jean M.	(618)549-1290	1011
	WILSON, Betty R.	(618)529-3318	1350
Champaign	BERGER, Sidney E.	(217)351-8140	86
	CLOONAN, Michele V.	(217)351-8140	223
Charleston	KAPLAN, Sylvia Y.	(217)345-4228	626
Chicago	ADKINS, Marjorie R.	(312)468-2139	6
	BEZIRGAN, Basima	(312)667-5205	93
	BYRE, Calvin S.	(312)341-3643	169
	CADY, Richard H.	(312)944-0856	170
	COATSWORTH, Patricia A.	(312)947-2160	224
	COOPER, Rosemarie A.	(312)341-8085	243
	CORSARO, Julie A.		248
	DELANA, Genevieve A.	(312)670-2875	288
	EPP, Ronald H.	(203)347-6933	351
	EPSTEIN, Dena J.	(312)373-0522	351
	FEDERICI, Yolanda D.	(312)427-0052	368
	FEINER, Arlene M.	(312)348-8382	369
	FULTON, Tara L.	(312)508-2655	409
	HERNANDEZ, Hector R.	(312)523-2453	531
	HOLZENBERG, Eric J.	(312)248-3494	555
	HOTIMLANSKA, Leah D.	(312)248-2013	562
	JOHNSON, Judith M.	(312)996-8988	606
	JORDAN, Charles R.	(312)478-7205	616
	KARSTEN, Eileen S.	(312)583-2700	628
	KAYAIAN, Mary S.	(312)245-2810	632
	KIM, Chung S.	(312)588-3901	648
	KOWITZ, Aletha K.	(312)440-2642	674
	LENNEBERG, Hans H.		715
	LIMAYE, Asha A.	(312)996-8988	727
	MALINOWSKY, H R.	(312)329-1549	763
	MANCUYAS, Natividad D.	(312)995-2284	764
	MCCOY, Patricia S.	(312)274-0370	799
	MILUTINOVIC, Eunhee C.	(312)472-9843	845
	MOORE, Annie M.	(312)995-2254	858

BIBLIOGRAPHER (Cont'd)
ILLINOIS (Cont'd)
Chicago

	MOORE, John R.	(312)763-7811	860
	REITER, Richard R.	(312)922-4200	1022
	SCHROEDER, Anne M.	(312)528-7486	1100
	SCHUSTER, Adeline	(312)939-4975	1103
	SCHWERIN, Kurt	(312)275-6776	1106
	SCOTT, Sharon E.	(312)268-7500	1108
	SELMER, Marsha L.	(312)996-5277	1114
	SKIDMORE, Gail	(312)989-3965	1146
	STENGER, Brenda E.	(312)782-1442	1187
	STINCHCOMB, Maxine K.	(312)348-2866	1194
	STONER, Ronald P.	(312)644-3100	1198
	TIWANA, Shah J.	(312)743-5146	1247
	WELLS, James M.	(312)782-1172	1322
	WIBERLEY, Stephen E.	(312)996-2730	1335
	WICKREMERATNE, Swarna	(312)493-0936	1335
	WILLIAMSON, Linda E.	(312)996-2738	1347
	WINNIKE, Mary E.	(312)996-6595	1355
	WRIGHT, Helen K.	(312)944-6780	1371
Chillicothe	CROTZ, D K.	(312)485-7805	261
De Kalb	LANIER, Donald L.	(815)753-0255	696
	LARSEN, John C.	(815)753-6269	698
	RIDINGER, Robert B.	(815)758-5070	1032
Edwardsville	MCFARLAND, Mary A.	(618)692-3828	805
Evanston	BEATTY, William K.	(312)328-5473	70
	PALMORE, Sandra N.	(312)328-5329	937
	PIRON, Alice M.	(312)864-3175	975
	SENN, Mary S.	(312)328-3767	1115
	SHERMAN, Sarah	(312)864-3801	1128
Evergreen Park	SOBKOWIAK, Emily J.	(312)425-1886	1165
Hinsdale	HALASZ, Marilynn J.	(312)325-0819	484
Homewood	BAYER, Susan P.	(312)798-6496	67
Joliet	STEVENSON, Katherine	(815)723-7846	1191
La Grange Park	STALZER, Rita M.	(312)354-9200	1179
Lake Bluff	JEFFORDS, Rebecca J.	(312)234-8923	596
Lake Forest	DANOFF, Fran	(312)234-2350	274
Lisle	SHOTWELL, Richard T.	(312)665-9107	1133
Lombard	MARSHALL, Mary G.	(312)932-1455	774
Mascoutah	SCHAACK, Wilma J.	(618)566-7385	1088
Monticello	ARNTZEN, Etta M.	(217)762-7827	34
Morrisonville	PODESCHI, John B.	(217)526-3256	979
Normal	NOURIE, Alan R.	(309)438-3480	910
North Riverside	MUELLER, Robert W.	(312)447-6441	875
Oak Park	HALIBEY, Areta V.	(312)524-0023	486
Park Ridge	JACKSON, William V.	(312)825-4364	588
Quincy	EGGERS, Thomas D.		339
	KINGERY, Victor P.	(217)228-5345	652
River Forest	DAVIS, Richard A.	(312)366-7383	280
	HEYMAN, Jerome S.	(312)771-3030	536
Riverdale	PATEL, Jashu	(312)849-3959	947
Rock Island	OHRLUND, Ava L.	(309)786-0698	919
	WESTERBERG, Kermit B.	(309)794-7221	1326
St Joseph	DUCHOW, Sally	(217)469-2237	322
Skokie	GRODINSKY, Deborah	(312)679-1380	471
Springfield	BRADWAY, Becky J.	(217)753-4117	126
Sun City	STUHLMAN, Daniel D.	(312)262-8959	1205
Urbana	AGGARWAL, Narindar K.	(217)333-2492	7
	ANDERSON, Nancy D.	(217)333-2884	24
	ATKINS, Stephen E.	(217)244-1867	38
	DAVIS, Elisabeth B.	(217)333-3654	278
	DOWNS, Jane B.	(217)344-1714	317
	KRUMMEL, Donald W.	(217)344-6311	680
	LEONG, Carol L.	(217)333-3399	717
	MAKINO, Yasuko	(217)244-2048	762
	NASH, N F.	(217)384-6350	888
	TEMPERLEY, Nicholas	(217)333-8733	1230
	WRIGHT, Joyce C.	(217)333-1031	1372
Waukegan	LI, Grace Y.	(312)623-2041	724
Wheeling	LAMB, Sara G.	(312)541-8114	690
Wilmette	ELSTEIN, Rochelle S.	(312)256-8484	346
Wilmington	BOBAN, Carol A.	(815)458-3411	108
Woodridge	WHITT, Diane M.		1334

INDIANA
Bloomington

	FLING, Robert M.	(812)335-2970	385
	FRY, Bernard M.	(812)339-3571	406
	HALPORN, Barbara	(812)335-1446	490
	KUDRYK, Oleg	(812)332-1773	682

BIBLIOGRAPHER (Cont'd)
INDIANA (Cont'd)

Bloomington			
	LEE, Thomas H.	(812)331-7485	711
	MARTIN, Fenton S.	(812)335-3851	776
	NELSON, Brenda	(812)335-8631	893
	READ, Glenn F.	(812)336-5984	1012
	SHAABAN, Marian F.	(812)335-6924	1118
	SILVER, Joel B.	(812)335-2452	1138
	WESTFALL, Gloria D.	(812)335-6924	1327
	WIGGINS, Gary D.	(812)335-9452	1337
	ZIMMERMAN, Brenda M.		1388
Crawfordsville	DAY, Thomas L.	(317)362-2242	283
	THOMPSON, Donald E.	(317)362-6851	1239
Fort Wayne	WEICK, Robert J.	(219)478-1018	1316
Goshen	SPRINGER, Joe A.	(219)534-5357	1176
Indianapolis	EBERSHOFF-COLES, Susan V.	(317)269-1815	334
	GANN, Daniel H.	(317)299-9058	416
	LOGSDON, Robert L.	(317)888-6772	737
	STARKEY, Edward D.	(317)274-0467	1182
	STUSSY, Susan A.	(317)929-0343	1205
La Porte	GUNNELLS, Danny C.	(219)324-0422	477
Lafayette	LINEPENSEL, Kenneth C.	(317)474-0269	730
Muncie	KUO, Ming M.	(317)289-3123	684
	WILLIAMS, Nyal Z.	(317)285-5065	1345
Noblesville	WILLIAMS, Maudine	(317)773-1763	1345
Notre Dame	FUDERER, Laura S.	(219)239-5176	408
	SLINGER, Michael J.	(219)239-5664	1149
South Bend	HOHL, Robert J.	(219)289-8160	550
Terre Haute	VANCIL, David E.	(812)237-2610	1273
Valparaiso	MILLS, Richard E.	(219)465-7878	844
	RAYMAN, Ronald A.	(219)464-2060	1011
	WATTS, Tim J.	(219)465-7838	1310
Warsaw	DETWILER, Susan M.	(219)269-5254	296
West Lafayette	ANDREWS, Theodora A.	(317)463-6093	27
	BAILEY, Martha J.	(317)494-2910	46
	BAXTER, Pam M.	(317)494-2969	67
	ERDMANN, Charlotte A.	(317)494-2872	352
	KERKER, Ann E.		643
	POLIT, Carlos E.	(317)463-6404	980
	TUCKER, John M.	(317)494-2833	1261
	YOUNGEN, Gregory K.	(317)743-9893	1383
Winamac	SMITH, Robert E.	(219)946-6255	1160
Zionsville	OKEY, Susan T.	(317)873-3114	920

IOWA

Ames	TYCKOSON, David A.	(515)294-3642	1266
Bettendorf	POLK, Diana B.	(319)332-8119	981
Boone	ADAMS, Larry D.	(515)432-1931	5
Cedar Falls	KOLLASCH, Matthew A.	(319)277-6125	669
	MARSHALL, Jessica A.	(319)273-2801	774
Cedar Rapids	LEAVITT, Judith A.	(319)390-3109	707
Davenport	MONTGOMERY, David E.	(319)326-7832	856
	PETERSON, Dennis R.	(319)391-3877	963
	STOUT, Robert J.	(319)326-6237	1199
Des Moines	FLICK, Frances J.	(515)277-2089	385
Dubuque	OFFERMAN, Mary C.		917
Iowa City	EICHER, Thomas E.	(319)335-9038	339
	EIMAS, Richard	(319)337-5538	340
	GORMAN, Lawrence R.	(319)335-5884	452
	HOWELL, John B.	(319)335-5885	565
	JORDAN, Robert P.	(319)337-2708	616
	LORKOVIC, Tatjana B.	(318)351-5304	741
	SNIDER, Jacqueline I.	(319)337-0660	1163
Sioux City	PHILLIPS, Donna M.	(712)258-6981	968
West Branch	DENNIS, Mary R.	(319)643-2583	292

KANSAS

Emporia	BOGAN, Mary E.	(316)342-1394	110
	MEDER, Marylouise D.	(316)343-1200	820
Kansas City	FARLEY, Alfred E.	(913)588-7040	364
Lawrence	CRAIG, Susan V.	(913)864-3020	254
	HOWARD, Clinton N.	(913)864-3601	564
	RHODES, Saralinda A.		1026
	SNOKE, Elizabeth R.		1163
Leavenworth	LUNG, Mon Y.	(913)864-3025	748
Leawood	COFFEE, E G.	(913)539-1628	226
Manhattan	VANDER VELDE, John J.	(913)532-6516	1274
	WILLIAMS, Sara R.	(913)532-6516	1346

BIBLIOGRAPHER (Cont'd)
KANSAS (Cont'd)

Pittsburg	DEGRUSON, Eugene H.	(316)231-7000	288
	VOLLEN, Gene E.	(316)231-7000	1287
Shawnee	STRAUSE, Robert C.	(913)268-9875	1200
Topeka	MELICK, Cal G.	(913)295-6479	822
Wichita	MEYERS, Judith K.	(316)832-1211	831
	MYERS, Marilyn	(316)689-3591	884
	SINGH, Swarn L.	(316)722-3741	1143

KENTUCKY

Bowling Green	COSSEY, M E.	(502)843-6560	249
	CUDD, John M.	(502)842-0901	263
Highland Heights	BENNETT, Donna S.	(606)572-5715	81
Lexington	BIRCHFIELD, Martha J.	(606)257-6098	98
	LEVSTIK, Frank R.	(606)266-9196	721
Louisville	COALTER, Milton J.	(502)895-3411	224
	EDDY, Leonard M.	(502)245-8633	335
	GRAY, Dorothy A.	(502)367-4772	459
	HOUSE, Katherine L.	(502)459-2429	563
	NEELY, Glenda S.	(502)588-6747	892
	TEITELBAUM, Gene W.	(502)588-6392	1230
	WHITE, Ernest M.	(502)897-3557	1331

LOUISIANA

Baton Rouge	HAMAKER, Charles A.	(504)388-8537	490
	MILLER, Susan E.	(504)388-8264	842
	PERRAULT, Anna H.	(504)924-5790	959
	ROUNDTREE, Lynn P.	(504)336-1306	1061
	SMITH, Ledell B.		1157
Lafayette	FOX, Willard		395
	TURNER, I B.	(318)231-5702	1264
Leesville	HIGGINBOTHAM, Cecelia B.	(318)239-4188	537
Monroe	KONTROVITZ, Eileen R.		671
New Orleans	CUMLET, Harolyn S.	(504)943-3618	264
	DANKNER, Laura R.	(504)865-2367	273
	FLEURY, Bruce E.	(504)865-5682	385
	HAGEDORN, Dorothy L.	(504)865-5131	482
	HARDY, D C.	(504)895-3981	500
	JUMONVILLE, Florence M.	(504)523-4662	619
	KELLER, Nancy H.	(504)899-9511	635
	LEMMON, Alfred E.	(504)523-4662	715
	MCKNIGHT, Mark C.	(504)866-3394	812
	NOLAN-MITCHELL, Patricia	(504)568-6102	908
	SERBAN, William M.	(504)286-6455	1116
	SKINNER, Robert E.	(504)483-7304	1146
Ruston	MCFADDEN, Sue J.	(318)257-4357	804
Shreveport	KING, Anne M.	(318)797-5738	650
	MCCLEARY, William E.	(318)865-9813	796
	WILLIS, Marilyn	(318)227-4501	1348
Zachary	JACKSON, Audrey N.	(504)654-5491	586

MAINE

Brunswick	SAEGER, Edwin J.	(207)729-5720	1074
Farmington	MCNAMARA, Shelley G.	(207)778-3501	816
Gorham	PERRY-BOWDER, Libbie E.	(207)780-5265	961
Mechanic Falls	NOYES, Nicholas	(207)345-3245	911
Orono	MCCALLISTER, Myrna J.		793
Portland	O'BRIEN, Francis M.	(207)774-0931	914

MARYLAND

Annapolis	RICE, Rosamond H.	(301)263-0670	1027
Baltimore	DE LERMA, Dominique R.	(301)467-2578	289
	GERHARDT, Edwin L.	(301)242-0328	428
	GRAVES, Louise H.		459
	GROSSHANS, Maxine Z.	(301)532-8590	473
	HOFSTETTER, Eleanore O.	(301)321-2454	549
	KELLER, William B.	(301)367-0338	636
	LEDBETTER, Sherry H.	(301)358-0285	708
	LOWENS, Margery M.	(301)532-7422	744
	SHAPIRO, Burton J.	(301)653-2757	1121
	STEVENS-RAYBURN, Sarah L.	(301)338-4961	1191
	TOPPAN, Muriel L.	(301)837-9155	1251
Bethesda	DAVIS, Deta S.	(301)564-0150	278
	KIM, Sunnie I.	(301)496-8124	649
	TURNER, Ellis S.	(301)530-4178	1264
BWI Airport	BUCHAN, Ronald L.	(301)859-5300	153

BIBLIOGRAPHER (Cont'd)
MARYLAND (Cont'd)

Chevy Chase	HOLLOWAY, Johnna H.	(301)652-8491	552
	KENTON, Charlotte	(301)657-3855	642
	SHAW, Renata V.	(301)654-3560	1123
College Park	CUNNINGHAM, William D.	(301)454-2376	265
	SHEETS, Robin R.	(301)454-5368	1125
	SHULMAN, Frank J.	(301)935-5614	1133
	STIELOW, Frederick J.	(301)454-5790	1194
	WELLISCH, Hans H.	(301)345-3477	1322
Columbia	GORDON, Martin K.	(301)992-7626	451
	GRUHL, Andrea M.	(301)596-5460	474
	HOLLENBACH, Karen L.		551
	RUSS, Kennetta P.	(301)381-0579	1068
	WOLTER, John A.	(301)730-6692	1362
Easton	MOLTER, Maureen M.	(301)822-1658	853
Forestville	MOORE, Virginia B.	(301)568-8743	861
Frederick	FRYSER, Benjamin S.	(301)698-5846	407
Gaithersburg	HARTZ, Mary K.	(301)948-1855	509
Gamber	BOGAGE, Alan R.	(301)795-6167	110
Garrett Park	AGENBROAD, James E.	(301)946-7326	7
	PRATT, Laura C.	(301)942-1764	990
Glen Burnie	STEINHOFF, Cynthia K.	(301)787-1549	1186
Greenbelt	BYERLY, Imogene J.		168
	KOBAYASHI, Michiko		666
Hyattsville	LEVINE, Susan H.	(301)699-3500	721
Kensington	SMITH, Karen G.	(301)564-0765	1156
Mount Airy	WETZBARGER, Cecilia G.	(301)829-0826	1328
Mt Rainier	STRANSKY, Maria	(301)779-1627	1200
North East	DENNEY, Christine A.	(301)287-6060	292
Reisterstown	BRADLEY, Wanda L.		126
Riverdale	PITT, William B.	(301)699-5739	976
Rockville	BLANDAMER, Ann W.	(301)340-8904	103
	COSMIDES, George J.	(301)762-5428	249
	DOWD, Frank B.	(301)279-1098	315
	LASER, Debra L.	(301)770-5470	700
Savage	FILBY, P W.	(301)792-7051	376
Silver Spring	AGEE, Victoria V.	(301)434-7073	7
	AMATRUDA, William T.	(301)585-3570	19
	BASA, Eniko M.	(301)384-4657	62
	FRAULINO, Philip S.	(301)495-5636	399
	KNOBBE, Mary L.	(301)681-6332	665
	MARKS, Cicely P.	(301)649-7200	771
	MEIKAMP, Kathie D.	(301)593-0029	822
	MYERS, R D.	(301)681-3967	885
	POMERANTZ, Karyn L.	(301)445-6204	982
	PRITCHARD, Sarah M.	(301)588-8624	994
	QUINN, Sidney	(301)589-4461	1000
	RICHARD, Sheila A.	(301)438-4555	1028
	SPURLING, Norman K.	(301)495-9229	1177
	TATUM, George M.	(301)236-9179	1225
	THURONYI, Geza T.	(301)593-1722	1243
Takoma Park	SLOAN, Cheryl A.	(301)589-6815	1149
	WRIGHT, Arthuree M.	(301)445-1220	1370
Upper Marlboro	DICKSON, Katherine M.	(301)350-4035	301
	WOODY, Jacqueline B.		1368
Upperco	RAND, Pamela S.	(301)429-2958	1006
Waldorf	WOLFE, Susan J.	(301)645-4784	1361
Walkersville	SHORT, Eleanor P.	(301)845-8015	1132
Wheaton	MWALIMU, Charles	(301)933-4040	884

MASSACHUSETTS

Amherst	DONOHUE, Joseph	(413)545-0498	312
	FELDMAN, Laurence M.	(413)253-9404	369
Arlington	JUDD, Eleanor M.		618
	LUKOS, Geraldine F.	(617)646-3439	748
Belmont	PHELAN, Mary C.		967
Bolton	BOGART, Betty B.	(617)897-7870	110
Boston	BRITE, Agnes	(617)267-0369	137
	BUSH, Margaret A.	(617)262-2045	165
	CAIN, Susan H.	(617)338-6553	171
	CEDERHOLM, Theresa D.	(617)536-5400	196
	GRAMENZ, Francis L.	(617)353-3705	457
	HENRY, Susan L.	(617)436-8214	529
	NESS, Arthur J.	(617)277-1776	896
	STEVENSON, Michael I.	(617)495-6374	1191
	SWANN, Thomas E.	(617)482-1360	1213
	VOIGT, John F.	(617)266-1400	1287
Bridgewater	CHANDRASEKHAR, Ratna	(617)697-3648	200
Brockton	UMANA, Christine J.	(617)586-6994	1268

BIBLIOGRAPHER (Cont'd)
MASSACHUSETTS (Cont'd)

Brookline	DONG, Tina	(617)731-3514	311
Cambridge	BROW, Ellen H.	(603)926-7371	141
	DANIELLS, Lorna M.		273
	DAVY, Edgar W.	(617)253-5670	281
	EPPARD, Philip B.	(617)492-4157	351
	HANKAMER, Roberta A.		496
	PINSON, Mark	(617)492-1590	975
	STODDARD, Roger E.	(617)495-2441	1196
	WARRINGTON, David R.	(617)495-4550	1307
	WHITE, Chandlee	(617)576-9299	1330
	WUNDERLICH, Clifford S.		1374
Chestnut Hill	DESJARDINS, Andrea C.		295
	KHAN, Syed M.	(617)552-4450	646
	LIPPMAN, Anne F.	(617)552-4457	732
	SEEGRABER, Frank J.		1111
Concord	LEWONTIN, Amy	(617)369-9106	724
Deerfield	PROPER, David R.	(413)774-5581	995
Hanscom AFB	DUFFEK, Elizabeth A.	(617)377-4768	323
	SEIDMAN, Ruth K.	(617)377-4895	1112
Lexington	FREITAG, Wolfgang M.	(617)861-0444	401
	ROSENTHAL, Marylu C.	(617)862-8167	1057
Lincoln	COHEN, Martha J.	(413)259-9500	228
Lowell	KARR, Ronald D.	(617)452-5000	628
	SLAPSYS, Richard M.	(617)452-5000	1148
Marshfield	TU, Shu C.	(617)837-8607	1261
Needham	PAPADEMETRIOU, George C.	(617)444-8941	938
	TSENG, Louisa	(617)449-3630	1260
Newton	ALPERT, Hillel R.		17
	ROFF, Jill R.	(617)527-4389	1049
Newton Center	CARPENTER, Kenneth E.	(617)244-2117	185
North Dartmouth	DACE, Tish	(617)999-8304	269
Northampton	DAVIS, Charles R.	(413)584-2700	278
	SCOTT, Alison M.	(413)584-2700	1106
Orange	PROUTY, Sharman E.	(617)544-6743	996
Quincy	WHEALAN, Ronald E.	(617)479-3297	1328
Randolph	MICHAUD, Charles A.	(617)963-3000	832
	OAKLEY, Adeline D.	(617)963-7999	913
Salem	PANGALLO, Karen L.		938
Springfield	CLOUGH, Linda F.	(413)788-8411	223
	DELZELL, William R.	(413)737-7000	290
Walpole	ESTES, Pamela J.	(617)668-3076	355
Wellesley	HARDY, Eileen D.	(617)235-0320	500
	SHERER, Elaine R.	(617)237-1100	1127
Wendell	HOLMBERG, Olga S.	(617)544-2706	553
West Newton	ST. AUBIN, Arleen K.		1075
Weston	KEENAN, Elizabeth L.	(617)893-1820	634
Westwood	KRUKONIS, Perkunas P.	(617)329-3350	680
Williamsburg	LANCASTER, John	(413)268-7679	692
Williamstown	HAMMOND, Wayne G.	(413)597-2462	494
Winchester	DAY, Virginia M.	(617)729-6026	283
Woods Hole	BROWNLOW, Judith	(617)548-5123	148
	WINN, Carolyn P.	(617)548-7066	1355

MICHIGAN

Adrian	BAKER, Jean S.	(517)263-0731	48
Albion	OBERG, Larry R.	(517)629-7297	914
Ann Arbor	BILLICK, David J.	(313)761-4700	96
	DWOSKIN, Beth M.	(212)382-6727	330
	HALL, Jo A.	(313)936-0132	488
	MOUZON, Margaret W.	(313)662-9227	874
	RICHTER, John H.		1031
	ROENZWEIG, Merle	(313)769-1805	1048
	TAYLOR, Margaret T.	(313)747-3592	1227
Berkley	MARLOW, Cecilia A.	(313)547-3098	772
Cheboygan	SMALLWOOD, Carol A.	(616)627-2308	1151
Clarkston	MEDER, Stephen A.	(313)625-5611	820
Dearborn	BREWER, Annie M.	(313)562-6871	134
	FORSYTH, Karen R.	(313)562-8830	391
	VINT, Patricia A.	(313)591-5073	1285
Detroit	KAUL, Kanhya L.	(313)577-3926	631
	RZEPECKI, Arnold M.	(313)868-2700	1072
	THOMAS, Laverne J.	(313)849-2776	1237
	WARD, Nancy E.	(313)256-9596	1304
East Lansing	BLACK-SHIER, Mary L.	(517)353-4526	102
	WIEMERS, Eugene L.	(517)355-2340	1336
Grand Rapids	BURINSKI, Walter W.	(616)454-9635	160
	DE KLERK, Peter	(616)957-6303	288

BIBLIOGRAPHER (Cont'd)
MICHIGAN (Cont'd)

Grosse Pointe Farms	DRAPER, James P.	(313)881-4397	318
Kalamazoo	PEREZ-STABLE, Maria A.	(616)383-1666	958
Livonia	VOIGHT, Nancy R.	(313)464-2306	1287
Marquette	PAULIN, Mary A.	(906)228-6686	950
Parchment	BOURGEOIS, Ann M.	(616)344-9097	119
Rochester	HILDEBRAND, Linda L.	(313)370-2483	538
	SHEPARD, Margaret E.	(313)651-1636	1127
Springfield	BURHANS, Barbara C.	(616)965-4096	159
Sturgis	BERKLUND, Nancy J.	(616)651-9361	87
Utica	HORNE, Ernest L.	(313)731-4374	560
Warren	DOYLE, James M.	(313)445-7401	317
West Bloomfield	FEDER, Carol S.	(313)851-5822	367
Ypsilanti	BEAL, Sarell W.	(313)483-7729	68
	GLIKIN, Ronda	(313)487-2288	441
	MCGARTY, Jean R.	(313)572-1453	805

MINNESOTA

Duluth	ENRICI, Pamela L.	(218)726-8586	350
Kilkenny	HAMMARGREN, Betty L.	(507)595-2575	493
Mankato	FARNER, Susan G.	(507)389-5957	365
Minneapolis	BEAVEN, Miranda J.	(612)624-5860	71
	BRANIN, Joseph J.	(612)625-5518	128
	DODGE, Christopher N.	(612)541-8572	308
	FURTAK, Rosemary	(612)375-7680	410
	GASTON, Judith A.	(612)627-4277	421
	IMMLER, Frank	(612)624-0091	582
	KARON, Bernard L.	(612)625-5050	627
	KELLY, Richard J.	(612)624-5860	638
	MIRANDA, Esmeralda C.	(612)437-0245	847
	O'LEARY, Mary E.	(612)872-4399	920
	OLSON, Lowell E.	(612)626-0824	923
	OVERMIER, Judith A.	(612)626-6881	931
	PANKAKE, Marcia J.	(612)331-2551	938
	RAFTER, Susan	(618)870-1935	1003
	TIBLIN, Mariann E.	(612)624-5860	1244
	WALDEN, Barbara L.	(612)624-5860	1294
	WARPHEA, Rita C.	(612)588-6985	1306
	WEEKS, John M.	(612)624-6833	1315
Robbinsdale	OSIER, Donald V.	(612)533-5025	928
Rochester	HAWTHORNE, Dorothy M.	(507)284-8797	514
	KEYS, Thomas E.		645
St Louis Park	RINE, Joseph L.	(612)542-9631	1035
St Paul	BROGAN, Martha L.	(612)698-1186	139
	OLSON, Ray A.	(612)484-8391	923
	OZOLINS, Karl L.	(612)645-2999	933
	SCHERER, Herbert G.	(612)699-6165	1092
	SCHOLBERG, Henry	(612)633-6851	1098
St Peter	ESSLINGER, Guenter W.	(507)931-7569	355
	HERVEY, Norma J.	(507)931-7563	533
Waite Park	CLARKE, Norman F.	(612)253-2695	219

MISSISSIPPI

Biloxi	VANCE, Mary L.		1273
Hattiesburg	BOYD, William D.	(601)266-4232	123
	CARNOVALE, A N.	(601)264-5452	184
	JONES, Dolores B.	(601)266-4349	612
	KELLY, John M.	(601)268-1537	638
	THOMPSON, Karolyn S.	(601)266-4256	1240
	VAN MELER, Vandelia L.	(601)266-4243	1276
	WILLIAMS, Eddie A.	(601)266-4245	1343
	WITTIG, Glenn R.	(601)266-4236	1358
Jackson	BELL, Bernice	(601)366-8786	76
	SANDERS, Lou H.	(601)982-7094	1080
Meridian	JOHNSON, Scott R.	(601)483-8241	609
University	FISHER, Benjamin F.		380
Vicksburg	BLACK, Bernice B.	(601)636-1990	101

MISSOURI

Bolivar	KAISER, Patricia L.	(417)326-4531	622
Columbia	ARCHER, Stephen M.	(314)442-0611	31
	WATERS, Bill F.	(314)443-3161	1308
Fenton	CHAN, Jeanny T.	(314)343-0929	199
	DEKEN, Jean M.	(314)827-1717	288
Kansas City	CARSON, Bonnie L.		188
	HESS, Stanley W.	(816)561-4000	534
	HOHENSTEIN, Margaret L.	(816)363-5409	549
	MEIZNER, Karen L.	(816)561-4000	822

BIBLIOGRAPHER (Cont'd)
MISSOURI (Cont'd)

Kansas City	PETERSON, Paul A.	(816)363-5020	964
	RUBY, Carolyn M.		1065
Kirksville	ELLEBRACHT, Eleanor V.	(816)665-6158	343
St Louis	DELIVUK, John A.	(314)645-1324	289
	DRAPER, Linda J.		318
	GILTINAN, Celia E.	(314)962-9048	437
	MCDERMOTT, Margaret H.	(314)889-6443	802
	MILLES, James G.	(314)658-3991	843
	NELSON, Mary A.	(314)889-6459	894
	PERSHE, Frank F.		961
	SIGALA, Stephanie C.	(314)721-0067	1137
Springfield	KOTAMRAJU, Sarada	(417)883-8590	673
	MALTBY, Florence H.	(417)862-5119	764
	MEADOR, John M.	(417)882-8032	819
Sugar Creek	STEELE, Anitra T.	(816)836-4031	1184
Warrensburg	HUND, Flower L.	(816)429-4797	574
	SADLER, Philip A.	(816)747-8726	1073
	WALKER, Stephen R.	(816)429-4070	1296
	WHITE, D J.	(816)429-4425	1330

MONTANA

Bozeman	MORTON, Bruce	(406)994-5313	870
Butte	HUYGEN, Michaele L.	(406)782-8400	580
Great Falls	O'BRYANT, Alice A.		915
Havre	RITTER, Ann L.	(466)265-1308	1036

NEBRASKA

Lincoln	LU, Janet C.	(402)465-2400	745
	SARTORI, Eva M.		1083
	TIBBITS, Edith J.	(402)472-3545	1243
Offutt AFB	SAUER, Mary L.	(402)294-2367	1084
Omaha	HASELWOOD, Eldon L.	(402)554-2211	510

NEVADA

Henderson	HARRISON, Susan E.		507
Las Vegas	CAROLLO, Michael T.	(702)385-0115	184
	CLARK, Camille S.	(702)739-3280	216
	CURLEY, Elmer F.		265
	GARDNER, Jack I.	(702)382-3493	418
	ORTIZ, Cynthia		927
	ORTIZ, Diane	(702)388-6501	927
Reno	ZINK, Steven D.	(702)345-0659	1389

NEW HAMPSHIRE

Durham	GRIFFITH, Joan C.	(603)659-3783	469
	KAPOOR, Jagdish C.	(603)868-2504	626
Hanover	ROLETT, Virginia V.	(603)643-3593	1051
Keene	PERLUNGHER, Richard A.	(603)357-4209	959
Portsmouth	JACOBS, Gloria	(603)431-9346	589
Sunapee	TATE, Joanne D.	(603)763-9948	1225

NEW JERSEY

Belle Mead	ODERWALD, Sara M.	(201)359-8229	916
Bergenfield	HEISE, George F.	(201)385-9741	522
Berkeley Heights	MAZURKIEWICZ, Helen L.	(201)464-0096	791
Bloomfield	BETANCOURT, Ingrid T.	(201)743-9511	92
	SHEARIN, Cynthia E.	(201)338-6545	1124
Bogota	MACKESY, Eileen M.		756
Branchville	RAFFERTY, Stephen P.	(201)948-6380	1003
Butler	GARDNER, Sue A.	(201)838-3262	418
Califon	JONES, Deborah A.	(201)832-9413	612
Chester	MANY, Florence L.	(201)879-5167	767
Cinnaminson	CRESCENZI, Jean D.	(609)757-6038	258
Clifton	PIERMATTI, Patricia A.	(201)473-2454	972
Cranford	BEIMAN, Frances M.	(201)272-5840	75
	SAWYCKY, Roman A.	(201)276-3134	1086
Dover	CAUSLEY, Monroe S.	(201)361-4531	195
East Brunswick	MENINGALL, Evelyn L.	(201)254-6403	824
Elizabeth	SKRAMOUSKY, Mary C.	(201)351-2671	1147
Glassboro	KENNEDY, Kathleen A.	(609)863-5335	641
Glen Rock	PERCELLI, Irene M.	(201)445-5983	958
Hamilton	HOOKER, Joan M.	(609)587-9669	556
Highland Park	BARZELATTO, Elba G.	(201)247-6248	62
	PAGE, Penny B.	(201)247-9353	934
Hoboken	PAULSON, Barbara A.	(201)420-8017	950
	SOLOMON, Geri E.	(201)420-8364	1166

BIBLIOGRAPHER (Cont'd)
NEW JERSEY (Cont'd)

Indian Mills	SCHREIBER-COIA, Barbara J.		1099
Irvington	KNIGHT, Shirley D.	(201)371-9324	664
Jersey City	PANDELAKIS, Helene S.	(201)795-8265	937
Lawrenceville	TILLMAN, Hope N.	(609)896-5115	1245
Madison	BROCKMAN, William S.	(201)377-3000	138
Montclair	BROWN, Cynthia D.	(201)783-6420	142
Montvale	REDRICK, Miriam J.	(201)573-9000	1014
Mountain Lakes	STEEN, Carol N.	(201)334-4941	1184
Neptune	OGONEK, Donna L.	(201)922-4986	918
New Brunswick	ANDERSON, James D.	(201)846-1510	23
	ANSELMO, Edith H.	(201)247-5610	28
	FAVORS, Thelma L.		366
	PUNIELLO, Francoise S.	(201)932-9346	997
	SWARTZBURG, Susan G.	(201)932-8573	1214
Newark	CUMMINGS, Charles F.	(201)733-7776	264
	DANE, William J.	(201)733-7848	272
Nutley	GILHEANY, Rosary S.	(201)667-7013	434
Ocean City	MASON, Michael L.	(609)398-0969	781
Park Ridge	WERNER, Edward K.	(201)391-4934	1324
Perth Amboy	HARDISH, Patrick M.	(201)826-5298	500
Piscataway	CASSEL, Jeris F.	(201)752-0528	193
	FIGUEREDO, Danilo H.	(201)463-3725	376
Pompton Lakes	MENZUL, Faina	(201)839-6885	825
Princeton	BELCHER, Emily M.	(609)924-8947	76
	FERGUSON, Stephen	(609)452-3184	372
	HAYASHI, Chigusa	(609)921-2330	515
	HENNEMAN, John B.	(609)921-0757	528
	HIRSCH, David G.	(609)683-7502	543
	NEWHOUSE, Brian G.	(609)921-8803	899
	SCHMIDT, Mary M.	(609)452-5860	1095
Ridgewood	JONES, Anita M.	(201)444-7273	610
Short Hills	HENRY, Mary K.	(201)379-4082	529
Somerset	GREENBERG, Linda	(201)846-8497	463
South Orange	BROWN, Ronald L.		147
	FAWCETT-BRANDON, Pamela S.	(201)762-0230	367
Springfield	CHANG, Joseph I.	(201)467-2037	200
	GLADSTONE, Mark A.	(201)376-2055	439
Trenton	BRODOWSKI, Joyce H.	(609)771-2343	139
	MCCULLOUGH, Jack W.	(609)771-2106	801
	WOODLEY, Robert H.	(609)771-2441	1366
Wayne	LEE, Minja P.		711
	MCCLEAN, Vernon E.	(201)595-2579	796
Whitehouse Station	HOYT, Henry M.	(201)689-7717	566

NEW MEXICO

Albuquerque	GROTHEY, Mina J.	(505)277-7144	473
	HENDRICKSON, Linnea M.	(505)255-4707	527
	HSU, Grace S.		567
	IVES, Peter B.	(505)277-9243	586
	KALE, Shirley W.	(505)298-5980	623
	REX, Heather	(505)277-7182	1024
	SEISER, Virginia	(505)842-5156	1113
	SPURLOCK, Sandra E.	(505)828-5378	1177
	THORSON, Connie C.	(505)277-7201	1242
Clovis	MCBETH, Deborah E.	(505)762-7161	792
Los Alamos	COMSTOCK, Daniel L.	(505)662-7668	235
Sunspot	CORNETT, John L.	(505)434-1390	247

NEW YORK

Albany	KOUO, Lily W.	(518)474-3840	673
	LOCKETT, Barbara A.	(518)456-0135	736
	VIA, Barbara J.	(518)442-3688	1283
	WALSH, Daniel P.	(518)489-7968	1299
Alfred	CULLEY, Paul T.	(607)871-2492	263
APO New York	GADBOIS, Frank W.		411
Astoria	FISHER, Maureen C.	(718)204-0631	381
Bakers Mills	SULLIVAN, Linda R.		1208
Bayside	BAKISH, David J.	(718)225-0475	50
	DE CUENCA, Pilar A.		286
	SINGER, Phyllis Z.	(718)279-2182	1143
	WEINER, Carolynn N.		1318
Beechhurst	DESSER, Darrilyn	(718)767-6955	296
Binghamton	COHEN, Ann E.	(607)724-9597	227
	MCKEE, George D.	(607)729-5490	810
Bohemia	JENSEN, Patricia K.	(516)244-2115	599
Brockport	RAKSHI, Sri R.	(716)395-5262	1004

BIBLIOGRAPHER (Cont'd)
NEW YORK (Cont'd)

Bronx	FOLTER, Siegrun H.	(212)960-8831	388
	GEE, Ka C.	(212)960-7770	424
	GHOSH, Subhra	(212)588-8400	430
	IOANID, Aurora S.	(212)220-0543	583
	RUBEY, Daniel R.	(212)960-8580	1064
	SHANNON, Michael O.	(212)960-7775	1120
Brooklyn	BAKER, Zachary M.	(718)855-6318	50
	BLOKH, Basheva	(718)963-7198	106
	BRAUCH, Patricia O.	(718)780-5581	129
	CANDELMO, Emily		178
	CLUNE, John R.	(718)680-7578	223
	ESSIEN, Victor K.	(718)941-9020	354
	GARGAN, William M.	(718)780-5276	419
	GREENBERG, Roberta D.	(718)857-0146	463
	GUREWITSCH, Bonnie	(718)338-6494	478
	HORNE, Dorice L.	(718)859-1830	560
	KEAVENEY, Sydney S.	(718)636-3685	633
	KUPERMAN, Aaron W.	(718)854-8637	684
	MARSHAK, Bonnie L.	(718)638-6821	773
	MATTERA, Joseph J.	(718)935-1746	785
	MEYERS, Charles	(718)342-1144	830
	NARDUCCI, Frances	(718)743-6001	888
	TURIEL, David	(718)336-2668	1263
	WENGER, Milton B.	(718)252-5019	1324
Buffalo	PERONE, Karen L.	(716)883-7000	959
	STIEVATER, Susan M.	(716)878-6313	1194
	WOLFE, Theresa L.	(716)632-4491	1361
Cherry Plain	GILCHER, Edwin	(518)658-2429	434
Clarence Ctr	CHAPMAN, Renee D.	(716)741-9644	202
Corona	KINYATTI, Njoki W.	(718)592-4782	653
Delmar	KRAMER-GREENE, Judith	(518)439-7028	675
Dewitt	POPOVIC, Tanya V.	(315)446-7488	983
	SHRIER, Helene F.	(315)446-5971	1133
East Aurora	UTTS, Janet R.	(716)655-0031	1270
Eastchester	KOLTAY, Emery I.	(914)337-0300	670
Flushing	COHEN, David	(718)520-7194	228
	DUTIKOW, Irene V.	(718)939-7382	329
	PENCHANSKY, Mimi B.	(718)520-7248	956
	RORICK, William C.	(718)520-7345	1054
Forest Hills	NERBOSO, Donna L.	(718)897-9826	895
Fulton	REED, Catherine A.	(315)598-3435	1015
Garden City	DOCTOROW, Erica	(516)663-1042	307
Glen Cove	WINCKLER, Paul A.	(516)671-0928	1354
Governors Island	GODWIN, Mary J.	(212)809-4351	443
Great Neck	DAMON, Shirley J.	(516)482-1202	272
Hicksville	SCHMIDTMANN, Nancy K.	(516)433-7040	1096
	TRAVERS, Jane E.		1254
Highland	RANKIN, Carol A.	(914)691-2275	1007
Hornell	SMITH, Brian D.	(607)324-0841	1153
Ithaca	ASHMUN, Lawrence F.		36
	EDDY, Donald D.	(607)255-5281	335
	ERICSON, Margaret D.	(607)274-3882	353
	SLOCUM, Robert B.	(716)255-4247	1150
	WAWRO, Wanda T.	(607)255-9478	1311
Jackson Heights	RANHAND, Jori L.	(718)469-4728	1007
Jamaica	SHAPIRO, Martin P.	(718)990-0760	1121
Jamaica Estates	BARTENBACH, Wilhelm K.	(718)658-3878	60
Jamestown	MORRIS, Kim	(716)484-7135	867
Kenmore	RYBARCZYK, Barclay S.	(716)877-0605	1071
Kings Park	PANDIT, Jyoti P.	(516)269-1070	937
Lake Grove	GRAVITZ, Ina A.	(516)467-4116	459
Maine	GERACI, Diane	(607)728-3954	428
Maryknoll	O'HALLORAN, James V	(914)941-7500	918
Massapequa	REID, Richard C.	(516)795-0262	1019
Massapequa Park	GIANNATTASI, Gerard E.	(516)541-6584	430
Nesconset	GRUNDT, Leonard	(516)361-8987	475
New Paltz	LEE, Chui C.	(914)257-2202	709
	NYQUIST, Corinne E.	(914)255-2209	913
New Rochelle	SWANSON, Mary A.	(914)633-3954	1213
New York	ARAYA, Rose M.	(718)461-4799	30
	BALKEMA, John B.	(212)876-8200	52
	BOURKE, Thomas A.	(212)930-0838	119
	BRISTAH, Pamela J.	(212)749-2802	137
	BRODY, Catherine T.	(212)228-7863	139
	BURGALASSI, Anthony J.	(212)382-6668	159
	CAPRIELIAN, Arevig	(718)459-2757	180
	CHITTAMPALLI, Padma S.	(212)874-0141	209
	CHO-PARK, Jaung J.	(212)280-2293	210

BIBLIOGRAPHER (Cont'd)
NEW YORK (Cont'd)
New York

	CHRISTENSON, Janet S.	(212)930-0686	211
	COHEN, Jackson B.	(212)595-6981	228
	COLBY, Robert A.	(212)787-3062	230
	COOPER, Jo E.	(212)808-6515	243
	DAGATA, Marie	(212)546-2507	269
	DEMANDY, Claire	(212)960-8575	291
	DERRICKSON, Margaret	(212)620-4230	294
	DEVERA, Rosalinda M.	(212)557-2570	297
	DUNLAP, Barbara J.	(212)690-5367	326
	FOLTER, Roland	(212)687-4808	388
	GARDNER, Ralph D.	(212)877-6820	418
	GESKE, Aina S.		430
	GITNER, Fred J.	(212)355-6100	439
	GOTTLIEB, Jane E.	(212)362-8671	453
	GRECH, Anthony P.	(212)382-6740	461
	GRETES, Frances C.	(212)309-9634	467
	GUBERT, Betty K.	(212)362-4256	475
	HAEFLIGER, Kathleen A.	(212)663-7857	482
	HEUMAN, Rabbi F.	(212)505-2174	535
	HIGGINS, Steven	(212)674-2087	538
	HYMAN, Richard J.	(212)865-7962	580
	JACKSON, Richard H.	(212)870-1647	588
	JANIAK, Jane M.	(212)466-4060	593
	JONES, Roger A.	(212)777-2959	615
	JUHL, M E.	(212)930-0830	619
	JURIST, Janet	(212)737-8120	620
	KARATNYTSKY, Christine A.	(212)420-1436	627
	KENSELAAR, Robert	(212)870-1661	642
	KILBERG, Jacqueline L.	(212)536-3562	648
	KING, Trina E.	(212)427-1023	652
	KLECKNER, Simone M.	(212)877-2448	658
	LAWRENCE, Arthur P.	(212)505-7996	704
	LINDGREN, Arla M.	(212)662-6386	729
	LUBETSKI, Edith E.	(212)340-7720	745
	MARGOLIES, Alan	(212)489-5042	770
	MASTRANGELO, Paul J.	(212)431-2128	783
	MOONEY, James E.	(212)873-3400	858
	MOTIHAR, Kamla	(212)838-8400	872
	NELOMS, Karen H.	(212)582-9239	893
	OSTROWSKY, Edith	(212)340-0890	929
	OSTWALD, Mark F.		929
	PALMER, Paul R.	(212)865-5781	936
	PETERS, Jean R.	(212)663-8910	962
	PINES, Doralynn	(212)570-3969	974
	POTEAT, James B.	(212)759-6800	986
	PRAGER, George A.	(212)725-3083	989
	RAJEC, Elizabeth M.	(212)690-4151	1004
	RAUCH, Anne	(212)906-8794	1010
	RAUM, Tamar	(212)889-2156	1010
	ROSEN, Nathan A.	(212)873-1017	1055
	ROSIGNOLO, Beverly A.	(212)962-4111	1057
	SEGAL, Judith	(212)222-3699	1112
	SLOCUM, Leslie E.	(212)759-6800	1150
	STARR, Daniel A.	(212)708-9440	1182
	STOLLER, Michael E.	(212)280-4356	1196
	SWANSON, Dorothy T.	(212)998-2630	1213
	SZMUK, Szilvia E.	(212)787-2573	1218
	VAJDA, Elizabeth A.	(212)254-6300	1271
	VAN DYKE, Stehpen H.	(212)340-0872	1275
	WALKER, William B.	(212)595-7335	1296
	WALL, Richard L.	(212)586-4418	1297
	WEATHERFORD, Elizabeth	(212)925-4682	1311
Newburgh	AIMONE, Alan C.	(914)564-2419	8
North Syracuse	AUSTIN, Ralph A.	(315)457-1799	40
Norwich	WINDSOR, Donald A.	(607)336-4628	1354
Oakdale	BEAUDRIE, Ronald A.	(516)244-3284	70
Ogdensburg	SMITH, Nicholas N.	(315)393-1075	1159
Orchard Park	WILLET, Ruth J.	(716)662-3598	1341
Ossining	LEW, Susan	(914)762-1154	722
	STAPLETON, Darwin H.	(914)762-8921	1181
Oswego	CHU, Sylvia	(315)341-3210	213
Palisades	WARD, Edith	(914)359-2081	1303
Pelham	FERRIBY, Peter G.	(914)738-3712	373
Poughkeepsie	JEANNENEY, Mary L.	(914)452-7000	596
Queens Village	HECKMAN, Lucy T.	(718)776-6285	519

BIBLIOGRAPHER (Cont'd)
NEW YORK (Cont'd)

Rochester	DEGOLYER, Christine C.	(716)475-2520	288
	KATZ, Jacqueline E.	(716)254-7144	630
	MCGOWAN, Kathleen M.	(716)275-4437	807
	ROSENBERG-NUGENT, Nanci B.		1056
Roslyn	WEINSTEIN, Judith K.	(516)627-6200	1318
St James	WIENER, Paul B.	(516)862-8723	1336
Saratoga Springs	LEWIS, Gillian H.	(518)587-0374	723
Schenectady	HOLT, Lisa A.	(518)370-1811	554
Selden	SALINERO, Amelia	(516)732-1268	1076
Setauket	THOM, Janice E.	(516)751-1484	1235
Shrub Oak	TIFFEAULT, Alice A.	(914)528-4048	1244
Somers	RITTER, Sally K.	(914)232-7889	1037
Staten Island	HOGAN, Matthew	(718)273-6245	549
	MANNING, Jo A.	(718)981-0120	766
	SCHUT, Grace W.	(718)442-5659	1103
Stony Brook	KING, Christine E.	(516)632-7110	650
	MASH, S D.		780
	VOLAT-SHAPIRO, Helene M.	(516)632-7100	1287
Syracuse	BRAUN, Carl F.	(315)423-2091	129
	LANTZY, M L.	(315)423-2527	697
	PFOHL, Theodore E.	(315)473-4493	966
	REINSTEIN, Diana J.	(315)492-5500	1021
	STAM, Deirdre C.		1179
	WALTZ, Mary A.	(315)478-1265	1302
Utica	BROOKES, Barbara	(315)735-2279	140
Warwick	BATTOE, Melanie K.		65
White Plains	BAXTER, Paula A.	(914)946-3275	67
Wynantskill	CORSARO, James		248
Yorktown Heights	HAIMOVSKY, Kira A.	(914)962-5628	484

NORTH CAROLINA

Beulaville	FRAZELLE, Betty	(919)298-4658	399
Boone	WISE, Mintron S.	(704)262-2823	1357
Chapel Hill	MCNAMARA, Charles B.	(919)962-1143	816
	MEEHAN-BLACK, Elizabeth C.		821
	TUCKER, Mary E.	(919)933-8982	1262
	WILLIAMS, Wiley J.		1347
Durham	BASEFSKY, Stuart M.	(919)684-2380	62
	DRUESEDOW, John E.	(919)684-6449	320
	GARTRELL, Ellen G.	(919)493-3747	420
	HAZEL, Debora E.	(919)683-6473	517
	LAVINE, Marcia M.	(919)684-2011	703
	MIDDLETON, Beverly D.	(919)477-8497	833
	SOUTHERN, Mary A.	(919)684-8118	1170
	SPARKS, Martha E.	(919)489-6012	1171
Greensboro	FLOYD, Rebecca M.	(919)852-3592	386
	HANHAN, Leila M.	(919)292-1115	495
	HARDIE, Karen R.	(919)288-7210	499
	MOORE, Kathryn L.	(919)334-5419	860
Greenville	COTTER, Michael G.	(919)752-8854	250
Kinston	EARL, Susan R.	(919)522-4773	332
	MILLER, Sylvia G.		843
Mars Hill	PETERSON, Cynthia L.	(704)689-2380	963
Raleigh	HORTON, James T.		561
Reidsville	KING, Willard B.	(919)349-6192	652
Sanford	MATOCHIK, Michael J.	(919)776-5737	784
Winston-Salem	EKSTRAND, Nancy L.	(919)765-4817	341
	ROWLAND, Janet M.	(919)765-2081	1062

NORTH DAKOTA

Valley City	HOLDEN, Douglas H.	(701)845-4940	550

OHIO

Akron	BRINK, David R.	(216)375-7224	136
Albany	CONLIFFE, Bobbi L.	(614)698-3336	236
Ashland	RHOADES, Nancy L.	(419)289-3969	1025
Athens	BETCHER, William M.	(614)593-2701	92
	HOUDEK, G R.	(614)593-5444	562
	MILLER, David A.	(614)592-5692	836
	OBERLE, Holly E.		914
Bay Village	BUTCHER, Sharon L.	(216)871-0913	166
Bowling Green	FIDLER, Linda M.	(419)354-1450	375
	HARNER, James L.	(419)372-7553	503
	POVSIC, Frances F.	(419)372-2956	987
Chardon	KLINGER, William E.	(216)564-9340	661

BIBLIOGRAPHER (Cont'd)
OHIO (Cont'd)

Cincinnati	CLASPER, James W.	(513)871-0969	219
	CONNICK, Kathleen D.	(513)474-4975	237
	KATZ, Lawrence M.	(516)761-0203	630
	LE BLANC, Judith E.		708
	NASRALLAH, Wahib T.	(513)475-2411	888
	PALKOVIC, Mark A.	(513)475-4471	935
	PROPAS, Sharon W.	(513)475-2411	995
	THOMPSON, Ann M.	(513)474-1443	1238
Cleveland	ABID, Ann B.	(216)421-7340	2
	BOBICK, James E.	(216)368-2992	108
	DEAN, Winifred F.	(216)687-2373	284
	DZIEDZINA, Christine A.	(216)459-4313	331
	PETIT, J M.	(216)749-5052	965
	RAY, Laura E.	(216)844-3788	1011
	SANTAVICCA, Edmund F.	(216)687-2365	1082
Cleveland Heights	MEYER, Jimmy E.	(216)291-1948	830
Columbus	BETCHER, Melissa A.	(614)466-5511	92
	CHANG, Tony H.	(614)292-2664	201
	CHRISTENSON, Donald E.	(614)236-5959	211
	HEARD, Jeffrey L.		518
	HECK, Thomas F.	(614)292-2310	519
	MERCADO, Heidi	(614)292-2009	825
	MIXTER, Keith E.	(614)263-7204	850
	MLYNAR, Mary	(614)486-7980	850
	MURPHY, James L.	(614)292-2664	880
	OLSZEWSKI, Lawrence J.		923
	ORLANDO, Jacqueline M.	(614)262-6765	926
	POPOVICH, Charles J.	(614)292-2136	984
	ROBINSON, David A.	(614)488-7346	1043
	SMITH, Ellen A.	(614)462-7054	1154
	STRALEY, Dona S.	(614)292-3362	1200
	VANBRIMMER, Barbara A.	(614)292-9810	1272
	WALDEN, Graham R.	(614)292-0938	1294
	WARNER, Susan B.	(614)424-5676	1305
Cuyahoga Falls	OSTERFIELD, George T.	(216)929-9470	928
Dayton	EVANS, Stephen P.	(513)220-9506	358
Dublin	PAK, Moo J.	(514)761-2174	935
Hiram	WANSER, Jeffery C.	(216)569-5358	1303
Hubbard	GROHL, Arlene P.	(216)759-7800	471
Kent	BIRK, Nancy	(216)672-2270	98
	BOLEK, Ann D.	(216)678-9429	112
	GILDZEN, Alex J.	(216)672-2270	434
	WYNAR, Lubomyr R.		1375
Lima	MCDANIEL, Deanna J.	(419)991-6065	801
Middletown	PALMER, Virginia E.	(513)424-4263	937
Mogadore	SMITH, Cynthia A.	(216)678-0662	1153
North Ridgeville	FACINELLI, Jaclyn R.	(216)327-7079	360
Oberlin	CARPENTER, Eric J.	(216)775-2546	184
	WEIDMAN, Jeffrey	(216)775-8635	1316
Oxford	QUAY, Richard H.	(513)529-4145	999
	WORTMAN, William A.	(513)529-3936	1369
Rootstown	PORTER, Marlene A.	(216)325-2511	985
Sidney	WILSON, Memory A.	(513)492-1315	1352
Tallmadge	GEARY, James W.	(216)633-1238	424
Terrace Park	SEIK, Jo E.	(513)831-0780	1112
University Heights	TOTH, Georgina G.	(216)371-5832	1252
Wapakoneta	FREW, Martha G.	(419)738-8333	402
Warren	TYSON, Edith S.	(216)393-3098	1267
Wilmington	NICHOLS, James T.	(513)382-6661	901
Wooster	POWELL, Margaret S.	(216)263-2279	988
Yellow Springs	WESTNEAT, Helen C.	(513)767-1574	1327
Youngstown	WALL, Carol	(216)742-1717	1297

OKLAHOMA

Ardmore	KIMBLE, Valerie F.	(405)226-3980	649
Bethany	FLINNER, Beatrice E.	(405)789-6400	385
Midwest City	ROBERTSON, Retha M.	(405)733-1543	1042
Norman	CLARK, Harry	(405)321-0352	217
	GOODMAN, Marcia M.	(405)325-2741	449
	HOVDE, David M.	(405)325-4231	563
Oklahoma City	JONES, Charles E.	(405)751-0574	611
Stillwater	HILKER, Emerson W.	(405)624-6305	539
	WOLFF, Cynthia A.	(405)372-0511	1361
Tulsa	HACKER, Connie J.	(918)587-6561	481
	HUTTNER, Sidney F.	(918)592-6000	579

BIBLIOGRAPHER (Cont'd)
OREGON

Eugene	HEINZKILL, J R.	(503)686-3078	522
	MORRISON, Perry D.	(503)342-2361	868
	ROBERTSON, Howard W.	(503)686-3064	1042
	WALKER, Luise E.	(503)686-3023	1295
Hillsboro	VIXIE, Anne C.	(503)645-0527	1286
Manzanita	LARSON, Signe E.	(503)368-6990	700
Philomath	REEVES, Marjorie A.	(503)929-5354	1017
Portland	DAVID, Kay O.	(503)222-9981	276
	LEGER, Norissa	(503)246-2714	712
	WRIGHT, Janet K.	(503)464-4097	1371
Roseburg	JORDAN, Cathryn M.	(503)440-1000	616
Salem	BAUER, Marilyn A.	(503)581-4292	65

PENNSYLVANIA

Abington	BISSELL, Joann S.	(215)886-9409	100
Allison Park	HADIDIAN, Dikran Y.	(412)487-2159	482
Bryn Mawr	MARKSON, Eileen	(215)645-5087	771
	MERZ, Lawrie H.	(215)527-6858	827
Carbondale	MCNABB, Corrine R.	(717)282-3151	815
Carlisle	POE, Terrence C.	(717)245-1866	979
Center Square	SCHAEFER, John A.	(215)277-6386	1089
Center Valley	MCCABE, James P.	(215)282-1100	793
	WELLE, Jacob P.	(215)282-1100	1321
Cheltenham	ELSHAMI, Ahmed M.	(215)635-3823	346
Clarion	HARTSOCK, Ralph M.	(814)226-2000	508
	HORN, Janice H.	(814)226-7367	559
Easton	CRAWFORD, Gregory A.	(215)253-9459	256
Erie	LAURITO, Gerard P.	(814)871-7553	703
	RITTENHOUSE, Robert J.	(814)838-4124	1036
Glenshaw	YATES, Diane G.	(412)486-0211	1378
Greensburg	KREDEL, Stephen F.		677
Harleysville	HILLEGAS, Ferne E.		541
Harrisburg	SHULTZ, Suzanne M.	(717)782-4292	1133
Hatboro	BURNS, Richard K.	(215)675-6762	162
Hatfield	PAKALA, James C.	(215)368-5000	935
Haverford	CORRIGAN, John T.	(215)896-7458	247
Hershey	ULINCY, Loretta D.	(717)531-8634	1268
Indiana	CHAMBERLIN, Richard R.	(412)357-2349	198
	ELLIKER, Calvin	(412)357-2892	343
	RAHKONEN, Carl J.		1003
Jenkintown	MONTOYA, Leopoldo	(215)886-2299	856
Johnstown	KREITZBURG, Marilyn J.	(814)266-7386	677
Kennerdell	CHERESNOWSKI, Linda M.	(814)385-6896	206
Lancaster	FRANCOS, Alexis	(717)397-9655	396
Langhorne	BLACK, Dorothy M.	(215)752-5800	101
Lansdale	CLAYPOOL, Richard D.	(215)368-7439	220
	WEBER ROOCHVARG, Lynn E.	(215)368-8688	1314
Lewisburg	BOYTINCK, Paul	(717)524-2678	124
Mechanicsburg	TENOR, Randell B.	(717)763-1804	1231
Media	BURGESS, Rita N.	(215)565-7900	159
Millersville	LOTLIKAR, Sarojini D.		742
New Hope	WESOLOWSKI, Paul G.	(215)862-9734	1325
Norristown	CATHEY, Gail L.	(215)278-5100	195
Philadelphia	ANDRILLI, Ene M.	(215)725-3660	27
	AZZOLINA, David S.	(215)898-8118	43
	BAKY, John S.	(215)951-1290	50
	BENDER, Evelyn	(215)634-0357	79
	BUCK, Patricia K.	(215)247-7443	154
	CLEVELAND, Susan E.	(215)662-2577	221
	GREEN, James N.	(215)546-3181	462
	GREEN, Patricia L.	(215)724-5715	462
	HELLER, Patricia A.	(215)625-4720	524
	HOLMES, John H.	(215)592-1841	553
	HOLUB, Joseph C.	(215)843-6220	555
	MARCO, Guy A.		769
	MCKITTRICK, Bruce W.	(215)235-3209	812
	MORENO, Rafael	(215)898-7555	863
	MOWERY, Susan G.	(215)248-8206	874
	MUETHER, John R.	(215)887-5511	875
	POST, Jeremiah B.	(215)748-2701	986
	POST, Joyce A.	(215)456-2971	986
	SAUNDERS, William B.	(215)224-0235	1085
	TARNAWSKY, Marta	(215)898-7442	1224
	WALSH, James A.	(215)587-4877	1299
	WARTLUFT, David J.	(215)242-8746	1307
	WOLF, Edwin		1360
	YOLTON, Jean S.	(215)878-7548	1380

BIBLIOGRAPHER (Cont'd)
PENNSYLVANIA (Cont'd)

Philadelphia

	YOUNG, James B.	(215)898-6715	1382
Pittsburgh	BLAIR, William W.	(412)355-8071	103
	EVES, Judith A.	(412)471-1477	359
	MAWHINNEY, Paul C.	(412)367-7330	787
	MAZEFSKY, Gertrude T.	(412)361-7582	791
	MITTEN, Lisa A.	(412)521-4462	850
	PISCIOTTA, Henry A.	(412)268-2451	976
	RAO, Rama K.	(412)429-0543	1008
	STEPHENS, Norris L.	(412)624-4130	1188
	THOMPSON, Dorothea M.	(412)268-2453	1239
	WOO, Lisa C.	(512)648-8188	1363
Reading	HANNAFORD, William E.	(802)468-5611	496
	STILLMAN, Mary E.	(215)921-2381	1194
	WEIHERER, Patricia D.	(215)376-7660	1317
Revere	WOOLMER, J H.	(215)847-5074	1368
Sarver	LIVENGOOD, Candice C.		734
Scranton	CAMPION, Carol M.	(717)348-0538	177
Slippery Rock	BACK, Andrew W.	(412)794-7817	43
State College	CHANG, Shirley L.	(717)893-2312	201
Swarthmore	HAMILTON, Gloria R.	(215)544-1369	492
University Park	FISHER, Kim N.	(814)865-1858	381
	KAISER, John R.	(814)863-1561	622
	MARTIN, Noelene P.	(814)865-3489	777
	ROE, Eunice M.	(814)863-0140	1048
	ZABEL, Diane M.	(814)863-2898	1385
Upper Darby	SILVERMAN, Scott H.	(215)734-0146	1138
Upper Saint Clair	HURLEY, Doreen S.	(412)257-1814	577
Villanova	BUSHNELL, Marietta P.	(215)527-2377	165
West Chester	GUENTHER, Nancy A.	(215)436-4049	476
Wilkes-Barre	TYCE, Richard	(717)826-1148	1266

PUERTO RICO

Ensenada	MEJILL-VEGA, Gregorio	(809)821-4734	822
Guaynabo	MOMBILLE, Pedro	(809)783-8622	854
Hato Rey	NEGRON-GAZTAMBIDE, Olguita	(809)767-4192	892
Miramar	CASAS DE FAUNCE, Maria		191
	MCCARTHY, Carmen H.	(908)721-6574	794
Ponce	SANTIAGO, Maria	(809)844-4150	1082
Ramey	CONCEPCION, Luis	(809)890-2681	235
San Juan	TORRES-TAPI, Manual A.		1251
Trujillo Alto	SABATER-SOLA, Rigel		1072

RHODE ISLAND

Carolina	HULL, Catherine C.	(401)364-6100	572
Chepachet	DESJARLAIS-LUETH, Christine	(401)568-8614	295
Kingston	ETCHINGHAM, John B.	(401)792-4637	355
	KRAUSSE, Sylvia C.	(401)789-6882	676
	SCHNEIDER, Stewart P.	(401)792-2878	1097
	VOCINO, Michael C.	(401)789-9357	1286
Newport	CARSON, Josephine R.		188
North Kingstown	OTTAVIANO, Doris B.	(401)295-0361	930
Providence	ADAMS, Thomas R.	(401)863-2158	6
	BRENNAN, Patricia B.	(401)456-8125	133
	LANDIS, Dennis C.	(401)863-2725	693
	MONTEIRO, George	(401)863-3266	856
	WILMETH, Don B.	(401)863-3289	1349
Woonsocket	IMONDI, Lenore R.	(401)762-5165	582

SOUTH CAROLINA

Aiken	CUBBEDGE, Frankie H.	(803)648-6851	262
Charleston	PARKER, Mary A.	(803)556-9454	942
	SCHMITT, John P.	(803)792-8014	1096
Clemson	LYLE, Martha E.	(803)656-5185	751
Columbia	FRITZ, William R.		405
	HOWARD-HILL, Trevor	(803)777-6499	564
	MILTON, Brenda R.	(803)452-5454	845
	WASHINGTON, Nancy H.	(803)777-4206	1307
Irmo	BARDIN, Angela D.	(803)781-3138	56
Newberry	HAMILTON, Ben	(803)276-6870	491
Spartanburg	FAWVER, Darlene E.	(803)596-9074	367

SOUTH DAKOTA

Brookings	BROWN, Philip L.	(605)692-7735	146

BIBLIOGRAPHER (Cont'd)
TENNESSEE

Antioch	HAMLIN, Lisa K.	(615)833-7541	493
Bristol	HERRING, Mark Y.	(615)968-9449	533
Cleveland	NICOL, Jessie T.		902
Johnson City	CONVERY, Sukhont K.	(615)926-3717	239
Knoxville	CROWTHER, Karmen N.	(615)974-4171	262
	HILL, Ruth J.	(615)974-4381	540
	LLOYD, James B.	(615)974-4480	735
	PICQUET, D C.	(615)974-4381	971
Memphis	BANNERMAN-WILLIAMS, Cheryl F.	(901)785-7350	54
	BOAZ, Ruth L.	(901)682-0595	108
	PERRY, Glenda L.	(901)527-4348	960
	TERRY, Carol D.	(901)529-2782	1232
	VILES, Elza A.	(901)454-4412	1284
Mt Juliet	ROBERTSON, Sally A.	(615)758-5750	1042
Murfreesboro	MARSHALL, John D.	(615)893-2091	774
	YOUREE, Beverly B.	(615)896-4911	1384
Nashville	GMEINER, Timothy J.	(615)297-7958	442
	MANNING, Dale	(615)322-2407	766
	STEPHENS, Alonzo T.		1187
Niota	BURN, Harry T.	(615)745-8590	161
Oak Ridge	MCDONALD, Ethel Q.	(615)482-5011	802
	PFUDERER, Helen A.	(615)574-5350	966
Sewanee	HAYMES, Don		516

TEXAS

Abilene	ANDERSON, Madeleine J.	(915)674-2344	24
Arlington	SHIH, Chia C.	(817)860-5475	1130
Austin	BICHTELER, Julie H.	(512)471-3821	94
	BRENNAN, Mary H.	(512)471-5523	132
	BURLINGHAM, Merry L.		161
	BURT, Eugene C.	(512)471-4777	164
	CABLE, Carole L.	(512)327-2158	170
	DAVIS, Donald G.	(512)471-3821	278
	DIVELY, Reddy	(512)288-3371	306
	GOODWIN, Willard	(512)288-2373	450
	HELBURN, Judith D.	(512)454-7229	523
	JACKSON, Eugene B.	(512)345-1653	587
	PRATTER, Jonathan	(512)471-7726	990
	RODE, Shelley J.		1047
	WILLIAMS, Suzi	(512)451-3482	1346
Bangs	WEEKS, Patsy L.	(915)752-7315	1315
Beaumont	NISBY, Dora R.	(409)899-9972	904
	SPARKMAN, Mickey M.	(409)880-8118	1171
Bryan	RABINS, Joan W.	(409)776-0374	1001
College Station	RHOLES, Julia M.	(409)845-1952	1026
	SMITH, Charles R.	(409)845-8850	1153
Commerce	CONRAD, James H.	(214)886-5737	238
Cooper	ALBRIGHT, Susie K.		10
Corpus Christi	NEU, Margaret J.	(512)884-2011	896
Cypress	KUJOORY, Parvin	(713)890-7542	683
Dallas	BOCKSTRUCK, Lloyd D.	(214)670-1406	109
	BROWN, Muriel W.	(214)348-7861	146
	FOUDRAY, Rita C.	(214)824-1943	393
	METIVIER, Donna M.	(214)701-4222	828
	SMITH, Michael K.	(214)296-5187	1158
	SNODGRASS, Wilson D.	(214)692-2342	1163
	STONE, Marvin H.	(214)670-1444	1197
	TEMPLETON, Virginia E.	(214)754-4875	1231
	UDENYL, Evelyn U.		1267
Denton	CALIMANO, Ivan E.	(817)898-4016	173
	FOLLET, Robert E.	(817)382-0037	388
	LAVENDER, Kenneth	(817)565-2768	703
	SNAPP, Elizabeth M.	(817)387-3980	1162
Edinburg	GAUSE, George R.	(512)383-0811	423
	SHABOWICH, Stanley A.	(512)383-0441	1118
El Paso	MALLORY, Elizabeth J.	(915)593-1337	763
	ROBERTS, Glenda S.	(915)541-4770	1040
	TAYLOR, Anne E.	(915)757-5095	1226
Fort Worth	ELAM, Craig S.	(817)294-0817	341
	HUGHSTON, Milan R.	(817)738-1933	572
	LEWIS, John S.	(817)921-0984	723
	RICE, Ralph A.	(817)626-7995	1027
	SCHMIDT HACKER, Margaret H.	(817)334-5525	1096
	WESTBROOK, Brenda S.	(817)831-7232	1326
Galveston	RASCHE, Richard R.	(409)762-3139	1008
Glen Rose	KENDALL, Lyle H.	(817)897-4991	640

BIBLIOGRAPHER (Cont'd)
TEXAS (Cont'd)

Houston	ENDELMAN, Sharon B.	(713)247-3541	348
	HANDROW, Margaret M.	(713)524-9447	495
	HOLIBAUGH, Ralph W.		550
	HUNTER, John H.	(713)527-4800	576
	LANGSTON, Sally J.	(713)659-8040	696
	SUDENGA, Sara A.	(713)527-8101	1206
Huntsville	BAILEY, William G.	(409)294-1614	47
	THORNE, Bonnie B.		1242
Irving	COCHRAN, Carolyn	(214)258-6767	225
Longview	GROSS, Sally L.		472
Lubbock	MARLEY, Judith L.	(806)799-3299	772
McAllen	MYCUE, David J.		884
McKinney	CORREDOR, Javier	(214)548-9971	247
Miles	LACY, Yvonne M.	(915)468-2151	687
Palestine	SELWYN, Laurie	(214)723-1436	1114
Plano	THOMAS, Page A.	(214)867-2595	1238
San Angelo	PENNER, Elaine C.	(915)658-4534	957
San Antonio	CRINION, Jacquelyn A.	(512)691-4575	259
	GRUENBECK, Laurie	(512)434-8938	474
	HICKEY, Lady J.	(512)436-3435	536
	HURT, Nancy S.	(512)225-5500	578
	LANG, Anita E.	(512)684-5111	695
	LIKNESS, Craig S.	(512)736-7344	727
	MORTON, Diane E.	(502)821-6094	870
Seguin	HSU, Patrick K.	(512)372-3868	567
	KOOPMAN, Frances A.	(512)379-4161	671
Sherman	GARCIA, Lana C.	(214)893-4401	417
Spring	ATRI, Pushkala V.	(713)370-3673	38
Wimberley	FELSTED, Carla M.	(512)847-5277	370

UTAH

Bountiful	SANDERS, William D.	(801)292-4429	1080
Logan	WEISS, Stephen C.		1320
North Salt Lake	YANG, Basil P.	(801)295-0276	1377
Payson	GILLUM, Gary P.	(801)465-4527	436
Provo	MATHIESEN, Thomas J.	(801)378-3688	784
	NIELSON, Paula I.	(801)375-9241	903
Salt Lake City	CASADY, Richard L.	(801)533-9607	191
	MARCHANT, Cathy	(801)364-8399	768
	REDDICK, Mary J.	(801)581-7024	1013
	SCOTT, Patricia L.	(801)533-5250	1107

VERMONT

Bennington	PRICE, Michael L.	(802)442-9051	992
Burlington	SINGER, George C.	(802)863-3854	1143
	YERBURGH, Mark R.	(802)658-0337	1379
Middlebury	MCBRIDE, Jerry L.	(802)388-3711	792
	POST, Jennifer C.	(802)388-6252	986
Norwich	FINNEGAN, Gregory A.	(802)649-1194	378

VIRGIN ISLANDS

St Croix	VAUGHN, Robert V.	(809)778-8465	1280
St Thomas	MILLER, Veronica E.	(809)774-0059	843

VIRGINIA

Alexandria	AUSTON, Ione	(703)549-4325	40
	HARRISTON, Victoria R.	(203)642-5382	507
	JORDAN, Robert T.		617
	MCLAUGHLIN, Elaine C.	(703)765-5860	813
	ROBERTSON, Jack	(703)549-3260	1042
	VAROUTSOS, Mary A.	(703)836-0156	1279
	WOODWARD, Lawrence W.	(703)751-9426	1368
Annandale	MCGINN, Ellen T.	(703)280-5085	806
Arlington	CALKIN, Homer L.	(703)920-4910	173
	COSGROVE-DAVIES, Lisa A.	(703)536-9452	248
	DESSAINT, Alain Y.	(703)247-7750	295
	KNOBLOCH, Shirley S.	(703)532-2598	665
	LARMOUR, Rosamond E.	(703)247-7820	698
	SAUR, Cindy S.	(703)379-2575	1085
	STARR, Marian U.	(703)237-0285	1182
	WIENER, Theodore		1336
	WOLF, Richard E.	(703)276-0270	1360
Blacksburg	BAER, Eberhard A.	(703)951-3480	44
	ESPLEY, John L.	(703)961-5847	354
	HINKLE, Mary R.	(703)951-1657	542
	JOHNSON, Bryan R.	(703)552-0876	602
Burke	STEPHENSON, Richard W.	(703)323-7721	1188

BIBLIOGRAPHER (Cont'd)
VIRGINIA (Cont'd)

Charlottesville	GORDON, Vesta L.	(804)295-5586	452
	KRAEHE, Mary A.	(804)295-3097	674
Chesapeake	REID, Kendall M.	(804)547-6592	1018
Christiansburg	LINN, Cynthia S.	(703)961-5988	731
Fairfax	WALCH, Timothy G.	(703)273-3260	1293
Falls Church	BROWN, Barbara B.	(703)820-7450	142
	HABERLAND, Jody	(703)573-7279	481
	KAHLER, Mary E.		622
Farmville	STWODAH, M I.	(804)392-8925	1206
Gloucester Point	BARRICK, Susan O.	(804)642-7114	59
Lexington	GREFE, Richard F.	(703)463-8648	465
	HOLLY, Janet S.		552
Lynchburg	KAWAGUCHI, Miyako	(804)239-3071	632
	SIDDONS, James D.	(804)846-8129	1135
Martinsville	PEARL, Patricia D.	(703)632-9096	952
Norfolk	BERENT, Irwin M.	(804)855-1272	84
	NICULA, J G.	(804)444-5321	903
Reston	KARRER, Jonathan K.	(703)648-4302	628
	WILTSHIRE, Denise A.	(703)391-0505	1354
Richmond	GWIN, James E.	(804)288-7602	479
	HALL, Bonlyn G.	(804)359-0409	487
	JACOBY, Mary M.	(804)231-2545	590
	MACLEOD, James M.	(804)355-1395	757
	SARTAIN, Sara M.		1083
	STACY, Betty A.	(804)359-4283	1178
	TROTTI, John B.	(804)358-8956	1258
	WILLS, Luella G.	(804)233-7616	1349
Roanoke	DIERCKS, Thelma C.	(703)362-6233	302
Springfield	SCHAAF, Robert W.	(703)451-7916	1088
Williamsburg	GROVE, Pearce S.	(804)220-2477	473
	HASKELL, John D.	(804)253-4408	510
Wise	CHISHOLM, Clarence E.	(703)328-2431	209
Woodbridge	ENGLAND, Ellen M.	(703)670-2191	349

WASHINGTON

Bainbridge Island	SPEARMAN, Marie A.	(206)842-6636	1172
Cheney	ALKIRE, Leland G.	(509)235-4669	13
Custer	HASELBAUER, Kathleen J.	(206)366-5063	510
Longview	DOLBEY, Mary B.	(206)577-2780	309
Oak Harbor	MERWINE, Glenda M.	(206)679-5807	827
Pullman	VYHNANEK, Louis	(509)332-3723	1290
Seattle	CLINE, Robert S.	(206)523-7268	222
	GRIPPO, Christopher F.		471
	HARMALA, Amy A.	(206)632-8338	502
	KREPS, Lise E.	(206)527-2817	678
	MCFADDEN, Denyse I.	(206)284-6280	804
	SILVA, Mary E.		1138
	SONG, Seungja Y.	(206)527-8737	1167
	STIRLING, Dale A.	(206)367-2728	1195
	TWENEY, George H.	(206)243-8243	1266
Spokane	BYNAGLE, Hans E.	(509)466-3260	168
Tacoma	TAYLOR, Desmond	(206)756-3244	1226
Walla Walla	YAPLE, Henry M.	(509)527-5191	1377

WEST VIRGINIA

Letter Gap	RUSSELL, Richard A.	(302)462-5471	1069
Wheeling	JULIAN, Charles A.	(304)233-5900	619

WISCONSIN

Brookfield	CHRISTMAN, Inese R.	(414)786-6700	212
Eau Claire	CARROLL, Barbara T.		187
Madison	ARNESON, Arne J.	(608)833-1617	33
	CARR, Jo A.	(008)273-1020	185
	JESUDASON, Melba	(608)263-7464	600
	KRUSE, Ginny M.		681
	LAESSIG, Joan M.	(608)238-3705	687
	SEARING, Susan E.	(608)263-5754	1109
	WELSCH, Erwin K.	(608)262-3195	1323
	WHITCOMB, Dorothy V.	(608)262-2402	1330
Menasha	DIETZ, Kathryn A.	(414)725-3803	302
Mequon	NOVOTNY, Lynn E.	(414)241-8957	911
Milwaukee	FONG, Wilfred W.	(414)229-4707	388
	HORNUNG, Susan D.	(414)359-2111	560
	JONES, Richard E.	(414)229-6457	614
	MARCUS, Terry C.	(414)352-5695	769
	MCKILLIP, Rita J.	(414)347-1335	811
	POPESCU, Constantin C.	(414)332-5909	983
	RUNKEL, Phillip M.		1067

BIBLIOGRAPHER (Cont'd)
WISCONSIN (Cont'd)
Milwaukee

	SCHLUGE, Vicki L.	(414)527-8477	1094
Oshkosh	JONES, Norma L.	(414)231-5137	614
Platteville	GERLACH, Donald E.	(608)348-6677	429
Ripon	BURR, Charlotte A.	(414)748-3244	163
River Falls	ADAM, Anthony J.	(715)425-5383	4
Superior	JOHNSON, Denise J.	(715)394-8512	603
Waukesha	HARTIG, Linda	(414)544-6005	508
Whitefish Bay	LANK, Dannette H.	(414)225-2107	696

WYOMING
Cheyenne	MENDOZA, Anthanett C.	(307)778-8706	824
	RAO, Dittakavi N.	(307)777-7509	1008
	SCHELL, Catherine L.	(307)637-7504	1091
Laramie	OSTRYE, Anne T.	(307)766-5312	929
	VANARSDALE, William O.	(307)766-4296	1272

CANADA

ALBERTA
Athabasca	DWORACZEK, Marian	(403)675-6261	330
Calgary	CRAMER, Eugene C.	(403)220-5376	255
	ROBINS, Nora D.	(403)274-8837	1043
Edmonton	BATEMAN, Robert A.	(403)483-3432	63
	COOKE, Geraldine A.	(403)439-5879	241
	LAVKULICH, Joanne	(403)427-3530	704
	LOVENBURG, Susan L.	(403)435-0176	743
	STARR, Jane E.	(403)466-6004	1182
	STRATHERN, Gloria V.	(403)432-3934	1200
	TRAICHEL, Rudolf D.	(403)437-5718	1253
Fort McMurray	BRUCE, Marianne E.	(403)743-5094	149
Lethbridge	JONES, Winstan M.	(403)327-0765	615
Red Deer	ARMSTRONG, Mary L.	(403)346-4491	32
	BOULTBEE, Paul G.	(403)346-8937	119
Sherwood Pk	NOGA, Dolores A.	(403)467-4003	907

BRITISH COLUMBIA
North Vancouver	DODSON, Suzanne C.	(604)988-4567	308
Vancouver	CAMERON, Hazel M.	(604)224-8470	175
	CHAN, Diana L.	(604)224-8470	199
	DEVAKOS, Elizabeth R.	(604)255-6636	297
	GONNAMI, Tsuneharu	(604)224-4296	447
	HALE, Linda L.	(604)321-0932	485
	STOKES, Roy B.	(604)261-4082	1196
Victoria	FIELD, Kenneth C.		375
	SIGNORI, Donna L.	(604)721-8247	1137

MANITOBA
Brandon	JONES, June D.	(204)727-3303	613
	SIMUNDSSON, Elva D.	(204)728-7234	1142
Winnipeg	BUDNICK, Carol	(204)474-9844	155
	DIVAY, Gabriele	(204)474-8926	306
	TULLY, Sharon I.	(204)474-9844	1262

NEWFOUNDLAND
Mt Pearl	MORGAN, Pamela S.	(709)368-5926	864

NORTHWEST TERRITORIES
Yellowknife	ALBRIGHT, Donald A.	(403)873-8347	10

NOVA SCOTIA
Amherst	CAMPBELL, Margaret E.	(902)667-2888	177
Halifax	GLENISTER, Peter	(902)443-4450	441
	HUANG, Paul T.	(902)454-5911	568
	SMITH, Arthur M.	(902)420-5538	1152

ONTARIO
Brampton	CHAN, Bruce A.	(416)793-4636	199
Brockville	WARREN, Peggy A.	(613)342-6352	1306
Downsview	ZVEJNIEKS, Laila R.	(416)235-4545	1391
Fort Erie	PORTEUS, Andrew C.	(416)871-3814	985
Guelph	PAL, Gabriel	(519)824-4120	935
Kingston	MORLEY, William F.	(613)548-3432	865
London	CLOUSTON, John S.	(519)679-2111	223
	FYFE, Janet H.	(519)472-5201	411
	MILLER, Beth M.	(519)661-3542	836
	PARR, John R.	(519)439-3271	943

BIBLIOGRAPHER (Cont'd)
ONTARIO (Cont'd)
Mississauga	MASEN, Naunihal S.	(416)897-6269	780
	WEI, Carl K.	(416)822-4111	1316
North York	VARMA, Divakara K.	(416)736-5139	1278
Ottawa	ARONSON, Marcia L.		34
	AUBREY, Irene E.	(613)996-7774	38
	BRIERE, Jean M.	(613)996-3817	135
	CAMPBELL, Laurie G.	(613)596-9797	177
	DUPRE, Monique	(819)994-6855	327
	EVANS, Gwynneth	(613)995-3904	357
	FOX, Rosalie	(613)232-4358	395
	LOW, Mary	(613)235-1158	743
	MACDONALD, Patricia A.	(819)997-7066	754
	SCOTT, Judith W.	(613)232-0579	1107
Scarborough	BALL, John L.	(416)284-3245	52
	MULLERBECK, Aino	(416)284-8779	877
Toronto	BELLAMY, Patricia C.	(416)595-0300	78
	BOITE, Mary E.	(416)461-2274	111
	BREGMAN, Alvan M.	(416)767-3625	131
	DESOMOGYI, Aileen A.	(416)466-6572	295
	DOWDING, Martin R.	(416)925-7593	315
	FRIEDLAND, Frances K.	(416)789-0741	403
	GARLOCK, Gayle N.	(416)763-2718	419
	HAYES, Janice E.	(416)480-7545	516
	KOTIN, David B.	(416)531-2104	673
	LANDON, Richard G.	(416)978-6107	693
	MORRISON, Brian H.	(416)965-1641	867
	TIPLER, Stephen B.	(416)654-5617	1246
	WEIHS, Jean	(416)961-6027	1317
Waterloo	BEGLO, Jo N.	(519)885-1211	74

QUEBEC
Ancienne-Lorette	JULIEN, Guy	(418)877-1054	619
Beaconsfield	HIRON, Barbara A.	(514)695-3200	543
Chicoutimi Nord	SAUCIER, Danielle	(418)549-5474	1084
Chomedey	DUPLESSIS, Daniel		327
Drummondville	JANIK, Sophie	(819)477-7100	593
Hampstead	FLUK, Louise R.	(514)488-3187	386
Hull	MAILLOUX, Jean Y.	(819)997-5365	761
Laval	CHAUMONT, Elise	(514)667-5100	204
	TESSIER, Mario C.	(514)669-7878	1233
Lennoxville	SHEERAN, Ruth J.	(819)569-9551	1125
Montebello	WENK, Arthur B.		1324
Montreal	BAZINET, Jeanne	(514)482-7188	68
	BISSON, Jacques	(514)482-9110	100
	BRESING, Sheindel H.	(514)483-2121	133
	BUTLER, Patricia	(514)283-9046	167
	CHAGNON, Danielle G.		197
	CLARKE, Robert F.	(514)731-9211	219
	CORBEIL, Lizette	(514)332-9854	245
	DARLINGTON, Susan	(514)737-3387	275
	DE LUISE, Alexandra	(514)871-1418	290
	DUBEAU, Pierre		321
	DUMOULIN, Nicole L.	(514)733-8051	325
	FOWLES, Alison C.	(514)842-7680	394
	GARDNER, Richard K.	(514)343-6046	418
	GAULIN, S D.	(514)645-9444	422
	GONZALEZ, Paloma	(514)735-1977	448
	HETU, Sylvie	(514)343-6949	534
	JOBA, Judith C.	(514)489-0117	601
	LATOUR, Pierre	(514)729-4165	701
	MUKHERJEE, Yolande	(514)932-6161	876
	NGUYEN, Vy K.	(514)494-1480	901
	ORMSBY, Eric	(514)398-4677	926
	PELLETIER, Rosaire	(514)382-0895	955
	PICARD, Albert	(514)276-5797	970
	PROVOST, Paul E.	(514)598-5389	996
	ROBIN, Madeleine	(514)738-0433	1043
	STILMAN, Ruth	(514)340-8210	1194
	THACH, Phat V.	(514)727-6817	1233
	WERYHO, Jan W.	(514)392-5766	1325
Pointe Claire Dorval	FIORE, Francine	(514)694-2055	379
Quebec	GELINAS, Michel R.	(418)522-7203	426
	ROY, Christine	(418)649-3115	1063
Saint-Jerome	HOULE, Louis P.	(514)438-3593	563
St-Leonard	LAFRENIERE, Myriam	(514)322-6818	688
Sainte-Foy	GUILMETTE, Pierre	(418)658-0470	476
Sherbrooke	FONTAINE, Nicole	(819)569-2551	388

BIBLIOGRAPHER (Cont'd)
QUEBEC (Cont'd)

Sillery	LALIBERTE, Madeleine A. . . .	(418)687-9260	689
Ste Anne de Bellevue	DOUGLAS-BONNELL, Eileen	(514)457-9487	314
Touraine	MURRAY-LACHAPELLE, Rosemary F.	(819)568-0282	882
Verdun	VAILLANCOURT, Alain	(514)765-7507	1270
Westmount	WADE, C A.		1290

SASKATCHEWAN

Regina	BROWNE, Berks G.	(306)584-8247	148
	INGLES, Ernie B.	(306)584-4132	582
	VOHRA, Pran	(306)787-4321	1287

AUSTRALIA

Fisher	WANG, Sing W.		1303
Toowong	GOODELL, Paulette M.		448
Victoria	POWNALL, David E.	(033)418-2990	989

BAHAMAS

Grand Bahamas Island	BARTON, Barbara I.		61

EGYPT

Giza	EL-MASRY, Mohammed		345

ENGLAND

Warwickshire	CHANDLER, George		200

FEDERAL REPUBLIC OF CHINA

Taidzi	CHENG, Sheung O.		206
Taipei	WANG, Sin C.		1303

FEDERAL REPUBLIC OF GERMANY

Berlin	ULRICH, Paul S.		1268
	WALTER, Raimund E.		1300

FRANCE

Paris	GARRETA, J C.		420
	PILLET, Sylvaine M.		973

HONG KONG

The Peak	SANDFELDER, Paula M.		1080

INDIA

Andhra Pradesh	SINHA, Pramod K.		1143
New Delhi	AGRAWAL, Surendra P.		7

ISRAEL

Birzeit	HADDAD, Aida N.		481
Ramat Gan	SNYDER, Esther M.		1164

ITALY

Milan	PUSATERI, Liborio		998
Rome	HUEMER, Christina G.		570

JAMAICA

Kingston	ERDEL, Timothy P.	(809)925-6801	352
	MANSINGH, Laxmi	(809)927-2748	767

JAPAN

Kanagawa-ken	TETSUYA, Inoue		1233

KUWAIT

Khalidiah	HAMDY, Mohamed N.		491

MEXICO

Benito	MACIAS-CHAPULA, Cesar A.		755
Mexico City	BARBERENA, Elsa		55

NIGERIA

Ibadan	ABOYADE, Beatrice O.		2
Okigwe	OGBAA, Clara K.		918

PHILIPPINES

Quezon City	OREJANA, Rebecca D.		925
	PICACHE, Ursula D.		970
	VALLEJO, Rosa M.		1271

BIBLIOGRAPHER (Cont'd)
SAUDI ARABIA

Riyadh	KIRKWOOD, Brenda S.		655
	MANSFIELD, Jerry W.		767
	SMITH, Marilynn C.		1157

SOUTH AFRICA

Somerset West	LUSK, Betty M.		749

SPAIN

Barcelona	VELA, Leonor G.		1281

SWITZERLAND

Villars Ollon	BURDET, Michele C.		158

TRINIDAD

Saint Joseph	MCCONNIE, Mary		798
Valsayn	NANTON-COMISSIONG, Barbara L.		887

UGANDA

Mukono	MUKUNGU, Frederick N.		876

ZAMBIA

Chilanga	LUMANDE, Edward		748

CATALOGER

ALABAMA

Birmingham	MCGARITY, Marysue	(205)879-6128	805
Huntsville	LIAW, Barbara C.	(205)532-5976	725
Mobile	MILLER, Hannelore A.	(205)343-0000	838
Montevallo	DUNMIRE, Raymond V.	(205)665-6104	326
Montgomery	ADAMS, Emily J.	(205)293-7691	4
	COLEMAN, James M.		231
	FELDER, Jimmie R.	(205)265-2012	369
	MARTIN, John B.	(205)244-0577	776

ALASKA

Anchorage	LESH, Nancy L.	(907)786-1877	718
Chugiak	PUTZ, Paul D.	(907)688-4894	998
Fairbanks	MUDD, Isabelle G.	(907)479-4522	875
Juneau	MITCHELL, Micheal L.	(907)789-0302	849
Nome	ROSS, Rosemary E.	(907)443-2201	1058

ARIZONA

Holbrook	ROTHLISBERG, Allen P.	(602)524-2257	1060
Phoenix	EVANS, Iris I.	(602)995-1701	357
	FOX, Frances J.		394
Scottsdale	KLIMIADES, Mario N.	(602)994-2471	661
Tempe	KNEPP, Kenneth B.	(602)965-1692	664
	WU, Ai H.	(602)965-3354	1373
Tucson	CARTER, Judith A.		189
	D'ANTONIO, Lynn M.	(602)327-0715	274
	FORE, Janet S.	(602)621-6452	390
	KNIGHT, Rita C.	(602)621-6448	664
	MARSHALL, Thomas H.	(602)621-6452	775
	MAXWELL, Margaret F.	(602)621-3565	788
	MILLS, Victoria A.	(602)795-5299	844
	MOORE, Susan M.	(602)621-6452	861
	MYERS, Roger	(602)792-3452	885
	RIISE, Milton B.	(602)325-1348	1034
	ROBROCK, David P.	(602)743-7072	1045
	RUSSELL, Carne	(602)621-6422	1068
	SABOVIK, Pavel	(602)885-9923	1073
	SCOTT, Sharon K.		1108
Uma	SWANN, Arthur W.		1213

ARKANSAS

Fayetteville	CALLAHAN, Patrick F.	(501)575-5417	173
	CHICK, Catherine P.	(501)443-4606	208
	EARNEST, Jeffrey D.	(501)521-8388	332
Fort Smith	PIERSON, Betty	(501)785-7135	972
Hazen	JEFFCOAT, Phyllis C.	(501)255-4546	596
Little Rock	BASKIN, Jeffrey L.	(501)661-5428	63
	MITCHAM, Janet C.	(501)371-2303	848
	ROSE, Donna K.	(501)569-3120	1054
Prescott	WATSON, Merlyn		1310

CATALOGER (Cont'd)
CALIFORNIA

Location	Name	Phone	Page
Agoura	THOMAS, Yvonne		1238
Albany	EWEN, Eric P.	(415)527-0894	359
Aptos	WYKLE, Helen H.	(408)662-3228	1375
Bellflower	PESTUN, Aloysius J.	(213)920-1734	961
Berkeley	GRIFFIN, Thomas E.	(415)643-6196	469
	MIKLOSVARY, Jozsef	(415)549-2443	834
	ORTOPAN, Leroy D.	(415)642-3810	927
	PISANO, Vivian M.	(415)527-1959	975
	SWANSON, Clara M.	(415)845-7201	1213
Beverly Hills	CHAMMOU, Eliezer	(213)273-1395	198
Bridgeport	REVEAL, Arlene H.	(619)932-7031	1024
Campbell	HAZEKAMP, Phyllis W.	(408)379-1611	517
Chico	DWYER, James R.	(916)895-5837	330
Chula Vista	GAGNON, Donna M.	(619)426-4527	412
Costa Mesa	HAN, Kenneth P.	(714)557-4648	494
Culver City	PATTEN, Frederick W.	(213)827-3335	947
Cupertino	JAJKO, Edward A.	(408)446-1306	592
Davis	BENOIT, Gerald		82
	ROCKE, Reve P.	(916)752-0597	1046
Del Mar	HOLLEMAN, Marian P.	(619)755-4253	551
El Cerrito	BERLOWITZ, Sara B.	(415)524-7257	88
	DONLEY, Leigh M.	(415)524-3695	311
Eureka	BROWN, Elizabeth E.	(707)443-8051	143
Fairfax	DOWNEY, Lynn A.	(418)454-4290	316
Fremont	DIBLE, Joan B.	(415)792-8736	299
	TSAI, Sheh G.	(415)656-7097	1260
Fresno	NELSON, Iris N.	(209)442-3968	894
	RICHTER, Bertina		1031
	WARD, Penny T.	(209)268-2545	1304
Garden Grove	HIXON, Donald L.	(714)638-9379	544
Goleta	MUSICK, Nancy W.	(805)964-8484	883
Hayward	SASSE, Margo	(415)482-2770	1083
Huntington Beach	OPPENHEIM, Michael R.	(714)842-1548	925
Irvine	JUNG, Soon J.	(714)730-8133	620
	MYONG, Jae H.	(714)856-6658	885
	SHAWL, Janice H.	(714)854-7413	1124
	TSENG, Sally C.	(714)856-6832	1260
	WEINTRAUB, D K.	(714)856-6079	1318
	WOOLDRIDGE, Steven M.	(714)856-7368	1368
	YOUNG, Eleanor C.	(714)552-5803	1381
Jamul	SERDZIAK, Edward J.	(619)426-2253	1116
Kensington	ROOSHAN, Gertrude I.	(415)525-5640	1053
La Canada-Flintridge	DUNKLEE, Joanna E.	(818)790-3518	326
La Jolla	GABBERT, Gretchen W.	(619)456-4083	411
La Mirada	MARTUCCI, Louis U.	(714)994-2409	779
Lafayette	SVIHRA, S J.	(415)933-9549	1212
Loma Linda	WURANGIAN, Nelia C.	(714)824-4300	1374
Long Beach	BRITTON, Helen H.	(213)498-4047	137
Los Angeles	BARROW, Jerry	(818)447-2886	60
	CAMPBELL, Bill W.	(213)398-8992	176
	DOUGLAS, Carolyn T.	(213)472-5287	314
	GINSBURG, Helen W.	(213)485-5400	438
	KACZOROWSKI, Monice M.	(213)485-1234	621
	KHATTAB, Hosneya M.	(213)733-1196	646
	KIM, Joy H.	(213)337-0794	649
	LEE, Don A.	(213)650-4946	709
	LEE, Hee J.	(213)391-4226	710
	MCGARRY, Dorothy	(213)825-3438	805
	MICHEL, Dee A.	(213)478-7660	832
	MITTAN, Rhonda L.	(213)271-6823	850
	PRINTZ, Naomi J.	(213)306-3573	993
	ROH, Jae M.	(213)381-1453	1050
	SCHOTTLAENDER, Brian E.	(213)825-7785	1099
	STERLIN, Annette S.	(213)645-2406	1189
	SVENONIUS, Elaine	(213)825-4352	1212
	SZEGEDI, Laszlo	(213)469-7030	1218
	WINEBURGH-FREED, Margaret	(213)224-7413	1354
	WONG, Cecilia	(213)736-1139	1362
	YEE, Martha M.	(213)462-4921	1379
Los Gatos	BAILEY, Rolene M.	(408)356-9645	46
Malibu	CLARK, David L.	(818)888-9305	216
Manhattan Beach	PHILLIPS, Clifford R.	(213)545-4828	968
Marina del Rey	KATZ, Janet R.	(213)822-1715	630
Menlo Park	BALES, F K.	(415)854-0115	52
	DILORETO, Ann M.	(415)326-7370	303
	REDFIELD, Elizabeth	(415)859-6187	1014

CATALOGER (Cont'd)
CALIFORNIA (Cont'd)

Location	Name	Phone	Page
Mill Valley	ASHLEY, Elizabeth	(415)388-8080	36
Mission Viejo	CHWEH, Steven S.	(714)768-3459	214
Monterey Park	WANG, Connie	(818)288-5518	1302
Moraga	RUDOLPH, Anne L.	(415)631-0926	1066
Northridge	DURAN, Karin J.	(818)885-2501	328
Oxnard	SMITH, Heather	(805)984-4637	1155
Palo Alto	MARANGONI, Eugene G.	(415)858-4053	768
	THOMAS, Vivian	(415)324-3739	1238
	WREDEN, William P.	(415)325-6851	1370
Palos Verdes Estates	UEBELE, Dorothy B.	(213)541-2559	1268
Pasadena	OLMSTEAD, Nancy L.	(818)351-6551	921
	YEUNG, Esther Y.		1380
Pleasant Hill	BRUNTON, Angela	(415)671-4941	151
	FOWELLS, Fumi T.	(415)689-0754	393
Pomona	ADAMSON, Danette	(714)869-3109	6
	HSIA, Ting M.	(714)869-3107	567
	IVERSON, Diann S.	(714)624-4728	585
	LIM, Sue C.	(714)869-3083	727
Port Reyes Station	ALLEN, Doris L.	(415)663-1122	14
Rancho Cordova	GRANADOS, Rose A.	(916)363-0473	457
Richmond	RYUS, Joseph E.	(415)222-0846	1072
	TURITZ, Mitch L.	(415)527-5109	1263
	VANDERBERG, Patricia S.	(415)237-1081	1273
Riverside	CHURUKIAN, Araxie P.	(714)787-3233	213
	DOUGLAS, Nancy E.	(714)787-5051	314
	KOSHER, Helene J.	(714)787-4628	672
	STALKER, Laura A.	(714)787-5841	1178
Sacramento	SCRIBNER, Ruth B.		1108
San Bernardino	MINDEMAN, George A.	(714)887-9753	845
San Diego	DERSHEM, Larry D.	(619)236-2409	294
	HERON, Susan J.	(619)260-4800	532
	PEASE, William J.	(619)265-4448	953
	WORTHINGTON, A P.	(619)541-3242	1369
San Francisco	BROWN, Barbara L.	(415)894-9896	142
	COLALILLO, Robert M.	(415)664-2264	230
	COLBY, Michael D.	(415)558-4633	230
	CONLEY, Linda A.	(415)285-6835	236
	JANK, David A.	(415)751-9958	593
	KAUN, Thomas T.	(415)821-9303	631
	LAND, Barbara J.	(415)221-7707	692
	LEWANDOWSKI, Joseph J.	(415)626-3755	722
	MAH, Jeffery	(415)552-4733	760
	PAPERMASTER, Cynthia L.	(415)773-5831	939
	REGNER-HYATT, Anne L.	(415)864-1154	1017
	SHAPIRO, Leonard P.	(415)469-5893	1121
	STOCKFLETH, Craig G.	(415)387-6040	1195
	TARCZY, Stephen I.	(415)476-8415	1224
	TREGGIARI, Arnaldo	(415)469-1649	1255
San Jose	ELLIOTT, Patricia G.	(408)277-9243	344
	HAAS, Florence A.	(408)289-1756	480
San Luis Obispo	DOBB, Linda S.	(805)756-2389	307
	HANSEN, Phyllis J.	(805)756-2389	498
San Marino	MCLOONE, Harriet V.	(818)405-2207	814
	ZALL, Elisabeth W.	(818)405-2188	1386
San Pedro	SPRUNG, Lori L.	(213)832-0593	1176
Santa Ana	HOFFMAN, Herbert H.	(714)667-3451	548
Santa Barbara	MAHAFFEY, Susan M.	(805)964-4978	760
	TAI, Henry H.	(805)961-2365	1220
Santa Clara	CHESSMAN, Rebecca L.	(408)244-2775	207
	HAMBRIDGE, Sally L.	(408)378-8616	491
Santa Cruz	LOMBARDI, Mary L.	(408)476-1131	738
Santa Rosa	WATSON, Benjamin	(707)527-2668	1309
Sebastopol	STRIBLING, Lorraine R.	(707)823-1419	1202
Sonoma	LUNARDI, Albert A.	(707)935-6020	748
South Pasadena	BESTE, Ian R.		92
Stanford	PAI, Herman H.	(415)723-6585	934
	SWEENEY, Suzanne	(415)725-2005	1215
Sun Valley	VOTAW, Floyd M.	(818)909-5634	1289
Torrance	HANSEN, Linda L.		497
Ukiah	FELDMAN, Irwin	(707)468-8163	369
Upland	GRAUE, Luz B.	(714)982-7574	458
	MOSER, Judith E.	(714)982-8753	871
Valencia	HUSKEY, Janet S.	(805)259-0783	578
Vallejo	LANE, David R.	(707)648-4265	694
Van Nuys	LEE, Lydia H.	(818)989-6433	710
Westminster	JADWIN, Rochelle J.	(714)894-2126	591
Whittier	RODRIGUEZ, Ronald	(213)693-0585	1048

CATALOGER (Cont'd)

COLORADO

Boulder	CARTER, Nancy F.	(303)492-3928	189
Colorado Springs	STEWART, Anna C.	(303)472-0268	1192
Denver	BARELA, Lori A.	(303)871-3447	56
	BOYER, Carol C.	(303)892-9404	123
	FORSMAN, Rick B.	(303)394-5125	391
	GERMOVNIK, Francis I.	(303)722-4687	429
	GIGNAC, Solange G.	(303)575-3751	433
	SHARP, Alice L.	(303)866-4682	1122
Englewood	GARZA, Rosario		421
Fort Collins	LINDGREN, William F.	(303)484-4432	729
Greeley	SAVIG, Norman I.	(303)351-2251	1086
Lafayette	MACARTHUR, Marit S.	(303)665-8237	754
Lakewood	ROESCH, Gay E.	(303)986-6365	1049
Walden	SWEET, Sally K.	(303)723-8354	1215

CONNECTICUT

Ansonia	MARTIN, Walter F.	(203)736-2601	779
Ashford	MCCAUGHTRY, Dorothy H.	(203)429-7637	795
Bethany	ASH, Lee M.	(203)393-2723	35
Branford	KILLHEFFER, Robert E.	(203)432-1704	648
Bridgeport	FU, Theresa L.	(203)576-4236	407
	SLOMSKI, Monica J.	(203)576-7403	1150
Bristol	WARAKSA, Raymond P.	(203)584-7759	1303
Cheshire	BLACKER, George A.		102
Danbury	SHEA, Roseanne M.	(203)744-3711	1124
Danielson	WEIGEL, James S.	(203)774-7755	1316
East Canaan	BYERS, Laura T.	(203)824-5971	168
East Hartford	SIROIS, Valerie M.	(203)565-7121	1144
Hamden	FERNANDEZ, Nenita	(203)562-1756	373
	KOEL, Maria O.	(203)281-3265	667
Hartford	MCNULTY, Karen	(203)278-2670	817
	WAIT, Gary E.	(236)236-5621	1293
Lakeville	RESTOUT, Denise T.	(203)435-9308	1024
New Fairfield	DYKMAN, Elaine K.	(203)746-0765	331
New Haven	HAHN, Boksoon	(203)432-1794	483
	HILL, John R.	(203)397-4509	540
	JARAMILLO, Ellen M.	(203)432-1798	594
Southport	HEFZALLAH, Mona G.	(203)259-9926	521
Storrs	FORMAN, Camille L.	(203)486-2526	390
Torrington	BENAMATI, Dennis C.	(203)489-2990	79
Wallingford	MANDOUR, Cecile A.	(203)269-4718	765
Waterbury	JOY, Patricia L.	(203)757-6203	618
Watertown	COGLISER, Luann L.	(203)274-5411	227
West Hartford	MICHAUD, Noreen R.	(203)232-6560	832
Westport	SELVERSTONE, Harriet S.	(203)226-6236	1114
Willimantic	EMBARDO, Ellen E.	(203)456-1952	347
Windsor	GAGNE, Susan P.	(203)285-3288	412
Woodbridge	MILLER, Irene K.	(203)393-0458	838

DELAWARE

Newark	RUDISELL, Carol A.		1065
Wilmington	PAUL, Jacqueline R.	(302)478-3000	949

DISTRICT OF COLUMBIA

Washington	ALEXANDER, Virginia A.	(202)554-1365	12
	BEDARD, Laura A.	(202)662-9172	73
	BENJAMIN, Marilyn	(202)287-1010	81
	BERGQUIST, Christine F.		87
	CANNAN, Judith P.	(202)287-5263	178
	CASSEDY, Barbara S.	(202)576-3279	193
	DE ARMAN, Charles L.	(202)797-7169	284
	DEHART, Odell	(202)393-7100	288
	ELSASSER, Katharine K.	(202)544-0552	346
	FOX, Ann M.	(202)244-6355	394
	GILLESPIE, Veronica M.	(202)287-5262	435
	HANFORD, Sally		495
	HERRICK, Judith M.	(202)287-6328	532
	HOPPER, Mildry S.		558
	HORCHLER, Gabriel F.	(202)547-6792	559
	JOHANSON, Cynthia J.	(202)287-5261	601
	JOHNSON, Gary M.		604
	KELLY, Mark M.	(202)625-4175	638
	KLEIN, Kristine J.	(202)362-2816	659
	LEONARD, Angela M.	(202)636-7926	716
	LITTLEJOHN, Grace M.	(202)291-6920	734
	MANNING, Martin J.	(202)485-6187	766
	MARYNOWYCH, Roman V.	(202)529-7606	780
	MORRIS, Timothy J.	(202)462-8209	867

CATALOGER (Cont'd)

DISTRICT OF COLUMBIA (Cont'd)

Washington	PETERSON, Charles B.		963
	REITH, Louis J.	(202)686-0131	1022
	ROONEY, Eugene M.		1053
	RZECZKOWSKI, Eugene M.	(202)529-5300	1072
	STARCK, William L.	(202)234-6006	1181
	STARNER, James A.	(202)332-7043	1182
	STORM, Jill	(202)775-6174	1198
	THOMPSON, Laurie L.	(202)994-2853	1240
	TRIPP-MELBY, Pamela	(202)676-9418	1257
	TSCHERNY, Alexander	(202)723-5415	1260
	VANDEGRIFT, J R.	(202)529-5300	1273
	WIGGINS, Beacher J.	(202)398-3427	1337
	WILLSON, Elizabeth	(202)745-7722	1349
	YASUMATSU, Janet R.		1378

FLORIDA

Apopka	RIVERA, Antonio	(305)869-7168	1037
Atlantic Beach	URBANSKI, Verna P.	(904)246-3631	1269
Boca Raton	DONAHUE, Janice E.	(305)393-3774	310
	STORCH, Barbara J.	(305)395-1056	1198
Bunnell	MCKNIGHT, Jesse H.	(904)437-4151	812
Coral Gables	GOLIAN, Linda M.	(305)284-2250	447
	KOBIALKA, Nancy C.	(305)284-2429	666
	LOWELL, Felice K.	(305)284-2250	744
	RABKIN, Judith R.	(305)284-4726	1001
Crawfordville	TODD, Hal W.	(904)926-5656	1248
Englewood	GHALI, Raouf S.	(813)474-9436	430
Fort Lauderdale	TAYSOM, Daniel B.	(305)760-5771	1229
Fort Myers	HUGHES, Joyce M.	(813)489-9464	572
Gainesville	HOPE, Dorothy H.	(904)371-2795	557
	LEONARD, Louise F.	(904)373-2705	716
	WALTON, Carol G.	(904)392-0351	1301
Jacksonville	BONFILI, Barbara J.	(904)725-5822	114
	CORNELL, Sylvia C.	(904)630-1994	247
	FAHNERT, Elizabeth K.	(904)641-8649	361
	RANDTKE, Angela W.	(904)646-2550	1007
	SMITH, Linda C.	(904)731-1065	1157
Melbourne	SHIAU, Ian L.	(305)768-0973	1129
Miami	ADAMS, Gustav C.	(305)261-7031	4
	CHAVES, Francisco M.	(305)385-2301	204
	DONIO, Dorothy	(305)375-5015	311
	PHILLIPS, Donald J.	(305)274-5724	968
	ROVIROSA, Dolores F.		1062
Miami Beach	LYON, Bruce C.	(305)868-4451	752
Miami Shores	PINE, Nancy M.	(305)758-3392	974
Niceville	VINSON, B J.	(904)678-5111	1285
Orlando	CUBBERLEY, Carol W.	(305)275-2521	263
Palm Coast	FRAZER, Ruth F.	(904)445-5409	399
Pembroke Pines	MULLER, Charles W.	(305)431-5123	877
Pensacola	KIEFER, Rosemary M.	(904)438-2732	647
Plant City	PINGS, Joan G.	(813)752-3884	974
Royal Palm Beach	TERWILLEGAR, Jane C.	(305)793-4590	1232
St Petersburg	ALLEN, Douglas R.	(813)343-4013	14
	CORNWELL, Douglas W.	(813)541-7206	247
Sarasota	DANIEL, Marianne M.	(813)351-6583	272
	HOLT, Ethel F.	(813)371-7640	554
	RETZER, Elizabeth H.	(813)921-1741	1024
Tallahassee	CLARKSON, Jane S.	(904)385-9671	219
	GIBLON, Charles B.	(904)893-3851	431
Tampa	HAMRELL, Larry G.	(813)971-4143	494
	HARKNESS, Mary L.	(813)961-7200	501
	LIANG, Diana F.	(813)900-2400	725
Thonotosassa	TABOR, Curtis H.	(813)986-3636	1219
West Palm Beach	FOSTER, Helen M.	(305)686-1776	392
Winter Park	ANDREWS, Janet C.		26

GEORGIA

Americus	MCLAUGHLIN, Laverne L.	(912)924-9426	813
Athens	ANDREW, Paige G.	(404)353-1707	26
	CARPENTER, David E.	(404)542-8460	184
	RIEMER, John J.	(404)542-0591	1033
Atlanta	ANDERSON, David G.	(404)651-2180	22
	DAVIS, Joy V.	(404)634-3511	279
	DEES, Leslie M.	(404)894-4523	287
	DREW, Frances K.	(404)881-0917	319
	FISTE, David A.		382
	LOWERY, Phyllis C.	(404)525-6165	744

CATALOGER (Cont'd)
GEORGIA (Cont'd)
Atlanta

	MENEELY, William E.	(404)658-3800	824
	MISRA, Jayasri T.	(404)524-5320	847
	SCHEIN, Julia R.	(404)624-1162	1091
	SWANSON, Joe	(404)699-1415	1213
	TROUTMAN, Joseph E.	(404)522-8980	1258
	VIDOR, Ann B.	(404)894-4523	1283
	WILSON, Lesley P.	(404)892-0944	1351
Augusta	FLAVIN, Linda M.	(404)721-2250	384
Bainbridge	MULCAHY, Bryan L.	(912)246-3887	876
College Park	CANN, Sharon F.	(404)768-0970	178
	DOOLEY, Shelly Q.	(404)996-4738	312
Columbus	BAKER, Rowena E.	(404)327-0211	49
Decatur	CHAMBERS, Shirley M.	(404)289-6517	198
	HUGHES, Glenda J.	(404)636-0108	571
	LANDRAM, Christina L.	(404)321-0778	693
	MARONEY, Daryle M.	(404)373-0546	772
Doraville	DRAPER, James D.	(404)457-4858	318
East Point	ELTZROTH, Elsbeth L.	(404)767-3144	346
Mt Vernon	PHILLIPS, Don	(912)583-2241	968
Riverdale	HANSON, Kathy H.	(404)471-5053	498
Vidalia	HARTZ, Frederic R.	(912)537-0195	509

HAWAII
Aiea	TIMBERLAKE, Cynthia A.	(808)488-4507	1245
Honolulu	CAMPBELL, R A.	(808)955-8822	177
	KOTO, Ann S.	(808)829-5835	673
Kaneohe	ASHFORD, Marguerite K.	(808)247-6834	36

IDAHO
Boise	ROBERTSON, Naida	(208)384-4340	1042
Moscow	CURL, Margo W.	(208)885-6260	265
	STEINHAGEN, Elizabeth N.	(208)885-6260	1186
Post Falls	JONES-LITTEER, Corene A.	(208)773-1515	616

ILLINOIS
Arlington Heights	VONDRUSKA, Eloise M.	(312)392-7232	1288
Barrington	POLL, Diane R.	(312)382-1300	981
Belleville	KIRCHGRABER, Nancy B.	(618)234-0441	654
Carbondale	COX, Shelley M.	(618)457-8975	253
	DALE, Doris C.	(618)536-2441	270
	WILSON, Betty R.	(618)529-3318	1350
Champaign	CLOONAN, Michele V.	(217)351-8140	223
	MANSFIELD, Fred	(217)244-3047	767
Chicago	BAKER, Ethelyn J.	(312)421-6513	48
	BEZIRGAN, Basima	(312)667-5205	93
	BOLEF, Doris	(312)942-2271	112
	CADY, Richard H.	(312)944-0856	170
	EPSTEIN, Dena J.	(312)373-0522	351
	EVANS, Linda J.	(312)642-4600	357
	FANG, Min L.	(317)842-0321	363
	FEINER, Arlene M.	(312)348-8382	369
	FIEG, Eugene C.	(312)947-9640	375
	HELGE, Brian L.	(312)955-4545	524
	HOLZENBERG, Eric J.	(312)248-3494	555
	HOTIMLANSKA, Leah D.	(312)248-2013	562
	HUNT, Janis E.	(312)275-8439	575
	IDDINGS, Daniel H.	(312)321-0432	581
	JAGODZINSKI, Cecile M.	(312)645-4860	591
	JOHN, Nancy R.	(312)996-2716	601
	JOHNSON, Timothy J.	(312)478-2696	609
	KARSTEN, Eileen S.	(312)583-2700	628
	LADENSON, Alex	(312)661-1493	687
	LAMBRECHT, Jay H.	(312)996-2736	691
	MANCUYAS, Natividad D.	(312)995-2284	764
	MCCOY, Patricia S.	(312)274-0370	799
	MITZIGA, Walter J.	(312)375-4646	850
	MOCH, Mary I.	(312)539-2328	851
	MUELLER, Julie M.	(312)645-4839	875
	MULLER, Karen	(312)944-6780	877
	NAGOLSKI, Donald J.	(312)878-1171	886
	OSGOOD, James B.		928
	OWNES, Dorothy J.	(312)702-8899	932
	POSNER, Frances A.	(312)334-7484	985
	RANDALL, Sara L.		1006
	SCHROEDER, Anne M.	(312)528-7486	1100
	SKIDMORE, Gail	(312)989-3965	1146
	STEWART, Richard A.	(312)269-2930	1193

CATALOGER (Cont'd)
ILLINOIS (Cont'd)
Chicago

	STONER, Ronald P.	(312)644-3100	1198
	STRAIT, Constance J.		1199
	STRAWN, Gary L.	(312)327-4930	1201
	TIWANA, Shah J.	(312)743-5146	1247
	VISKOCHIL, Larry A.	(312)935-1071	1285
	WICKREMERATNE, Swarna	(312)493-0936	1335
Crystal Lake	MILLER, Randy S.	(815)455-4660	841
De Kalb	AUSTIN, John R.	(815)753-9492	40
	RAST, Elaine K.	(815)758-5234	1009
	VANDER MEER, Gary L.	(815)753-9495	1274
Deerfield	LEE, Soon H.	(312)948-3880	711
Dow	HOLZBERLEIN, Deanne B.	(618)466-3015	555
Downers Grove	ALLEN, Dorothy L.	(312)963-1056	14
	CULBERTSON, Lillian D.	(312)971-3309	263
Dwight	MCCLAREY, Catherine A.	(815)584-3703	796
Edwardsville	MOORE, Milton C.	(618)692-1638	860
Elmhurst	DARLING, Elizabeth A.	(312)279-4100	274
Evanston	BARNUM, Sally J.	(312)869-2976	58
	BRADY, Mary M.	(312)491-2929	127
	CLOUD, Patricia D.	(312)491-3136	223
	GRISCOM, Richard W.	(312)491-3487	471
	JACOBSON, William R.	(312)328-7584	590
	JAVONOVICH, Kenneth L.	(312)764-7713	595
Evergreen Park	SOBKOWIAK, Emily J.	(312)425-1886	1165
Galesburg	WINNER, Ronald	(309)343-2380	1355
Geneseo	GILBORNE, Jean E.	(309)944-4384	434
Glen Ellyn	PEISER, Richard H.	(312)790-3293	955
	TEMPLE, Harold L.	(312)858-2800	1230
Glenview	MOSS, Barbara J.	(312)729-7500	872
Grayslake	KIENE, Andrea L.	(312)740-0620	647
Gurnee	FUNK, Carla J.	(312)367-6213	409
Homewood	BAYER, Susan P.	(312)798-6496	67
Jacksonville	ZUIDERVELD, Sharon R.	(217)243-6945	1391
Joliet	HASSERT, Rita M.	(815)485-8397	511
Kingston	SCHREIBER, Robert E.	(815)784-2280	1099
Lake Bluff	BROSK, Carol A.	(312)234-6752	141
Lombard	MARSHALL, Mary G.	(312)932-1455	774
Makanda	CRANE, Lilly E.	(618)549-6259	255
Mascoutah	SCHAACK, Wilma J.	(618)566-7385	1088
Morrisonville	PODESCHI, John B.	(217)526-3256	979
Nashville	RUSIEWSKI, Charles B.	(618)327-8304	1068
Normal	MATTHEWS, Priscilla J.	(309)452-8514	785
North Riverside	MUELLER, Robert W.	(312)447-6441	875
Oak Park	HALIBEY, Areta V.	(312)524-0023	486
Palatine	BOURKE, Jacqueline K.	(312)991-9335	119
Park Forest	BUCKLEY, Ja A.	(312)748-2536	154
	GIBBS, Mary E.	(312)481-1512	431
	HAYES, Hazel I.		515
	SHANNON, Kathleen L.	(312)481-1891	1120
Pekin	WALTERS, Patsy M.	(309)353-5075	1301
Quincy	KINGERY, Victor P.	(217)228-5345	652
	MORRIS, Susan M.	(217)224-0042	867
	WEE, Lily K.	(217)228-5350	1315
Rock Island	CONWAY, Colleen M.	(309)794-7316	239
	OHRLUND, Bruce L.	(309)786-0698	919
St Joseph	PAUSCH, Lois M.	(217)469-7311	950
Springfield	ETTER, Constance L.	(217)546-5436	355
Sun City	STUHLMAN, Daniel D.	(312)262-8959	1205
Sycamore	STUDWELL, William E.	(815)895-9868	1204
Urbana	BURBANK, Richard D.	(217)333-2713	158
	FAYNZILBERG, Irina	(217)333-5745	367
	HUETING, Gail P.	(217)244-0481	570
	LEONG, Carol L.	(217)333-3399	717
	MAKINO, Yasuko	(217)244-2048	762
	WAJENBERG, Arnold S.	(217)333-6411	1293
	WEI, Karen T.	(217)344-5647	1316
	WILLIAMS, James W.	(217)333-2305	1344
Waukegan	LI, Grace Y.	(312)623-2041	724
West Chicago	OLSEN, Sarah G.	(312)451-3078	922
Wheaton	HU, Robert T.	(312)690-7969	568
	WALSH, Deborah T.	(312)653-1115	1299
Wheeling	HAMMER, Louise K.	(312)541-8149	493
	LAMB, Sara G.	(312)541-8114	690
Wilmington	BOBAN, Carol A.	(815)458-3411	108
Winnetka	LUNDQUIST, Marie A.	(312)441-3315	748
Woodridge	WHITT, Diane M.		1334
Woodstock	RICHARDSON, Vickie W.	(815)338-8885	1030

CATALOGER (Cont'd)

INDIANA

Bloomington	LAIR, Nancy C.	(812)335-5113	688
	LEE, Thomas H.	(812)331-7485	711
	MCCLOY, William B.	(812)335-9666	797
	MCCUNE, Lois M.	(812)339-0505	801
	NELSON, Brenda	(812)335-8631	893
	NIEKAMP, Dorothy R.	(812)332-4065	903
Bluffton	ELLIOTT, Barbara J.	(219)824-2315	343
East Chicago	BROTON, Cecilianne S.	(219)398-4625	141
Elkhart	MILLER, Junelle	(219)875-8668	839
Fort Wayne	WEICK, Robert J.	(219)478-1018	1316
Granger	LE GUERN, Charles A.	(219)272-3298	712
Greencastle	LATSHAW, Ruth N.	(317)653-2318	701
Indianapolis	ASHER, Richard E.		36
	CONRADS, Douglas L.	(317)232-3686	238
	GOODWIN, Vania M.	(317)274-0491	450
	GRIFFITTS, Joan K.	(317)297-3283	469
	JOHNTING, Wendell E.	(317)894-1150	610
La Porte	GUNNELLS, Danny C.	(219)324-0422	477
Lafayette	MCKOWEN, Dorothy K.	(317)564-4585	812
Muncie	KELLEY, Colleen L.	(317)289-7262	636
North Manchester	STEPHENSON, Doris F.	(219)982-2141	1188
Notre Dame	JORDAN, Louis E.	(219)239-7420	616
	MOON, Elizabeth A.	(219)239-6218	857
	TANTOCO, Dolores W.	(219)239-6904	1223
South Bend	PEC, Jean A.	(219)277-3703	953
	WARREN, Lois B.	(219)287-6481	1306
Upland	WOLCOTT, Laurie J.	(317)998-7549	1359
Valparaiso	MILLS, Richard E.	(219)465-7878	844
Vincennes	PIEPENBURG, Scott R.	(812)885-5807	971

IOWA

Ames	COLE, Jim E.	(515)294-0432	230
	SCHMIDT, Sandra L.	(515)292-1118	1096
	WORK, Dawn E.		1369
Coralville	PEPETONE, Diane S.	(319)351-3922	957
Dubuque	OFFERMAN, Mary C.		917
Forest City	PALMER, Joy J.	(515)582-3513	936
Iowa City	BIERBAUM, Esther G.	(319)354-8639	95
	BROWN, Jeanine B.		144
	GORMAN, Lawrence R.	(319)335-5884	452
	HARMON, Charles T.	(319)337-2140	502
	JORDAN, Robert P.	(319)337-2708	616
	KELLEY, Ann C.	(319)335-5884	636
	LORKOVIC, Tatjana B.	(318)351-5304	741
Marion	ALDERSON, Karen A.	(319)377-0666	11
Marshalltown	TRAVILLIAN, Mary W.	(515)752-1578	1254
Ottumwa	BRANDT, Garnet J.	(515)682-6677	128
Red Oak	PETERSON, Carroll E.	(712)623-3069	963
Sioux City	PHILLIPS, Donna M.	(712)258-6981	968
	SCHEETZ, Kathy D.	(712)277-2423	1091
West Branch	DENNIS, Mary R.	(319)643-2583	292
	MATHER, Mildred E.	(319)643-5301	783

KANSAS

Dodge City	COOKE, Bette L.	(316)225-7271	241
Emporia	KLOSTERMANN, Helen M.	(316)343-1200	662
Hillsboro	JOHNSON, Georgina	(316)947-3121	604
Kansas City	VAN SICKLE, Mary L.	(913)621-3073	1277
Lawrence	BURCHILL, Mary D.	(913)864-3025	158
	HOWE, Priscilla P.	(913)864-3957	565
	MAY, Cecilia J.	(913)841-0929	788
	NEUGEBAUER, Rhonda L.	(913)749-2610	897
	TRONIER, Suzanne	(913)864-3038	1258
Leawood	LUNG, Mon Y.	(913)864-3025	748
Manhattan	GRASS, Charlene G.	(913)532-6516	458
	PRENTICE, Margaret A.		990
Topeka	MELICK, Cal G.	(913)295-6479	822

KENTUCKY

Edgewood	REESE, Virginia D.	(606)261-8211	1016
Florence	BRATCHER, Perry R.	(606)371-5875	129
Fort Thomas	GILLIAM, Susanne P.	(606)441-9518	436
Germantown	TEEGARDEN, Maude B.	(606)728-2312	1229
Highland Heights	SCHULTZ, Lois E.	(606)572-5275	1102
Lexington	BIRCHFIELD, Martha J.	(606)257-6098	98
	CHAN, Lois M.	(606)257-5942	199
	MESNER, Lillian R.	(606)273-4990	827
Louisville	HOUSE, Katherine L.	(502)459-2429	563

CATALOGER (Cont'd)
KENTUCKY (Cont'd)

Morehead	HALL, Juanita J.	(606)783-2827	488
Murray	BUSER, Robin A.	(502)762-2393	165

LOUISIANA

Baton Rouge	BALL, Dannie J.	(504)388-3119	52
	BLOOMSTONE, Ajaye	(504)767-0847	106
	CARPENTER, Michael A.	(504)766-7385	185
	FERGUSON, Anna S.	(504)272-3833	372
	HASCHAK, Paul G.	(504)766-9986	510
	MERING, Margaret V.	(504)344-5863	826
	ROUNDTREE, Lynn P.	(504)336-1306	1061
Harvey	WASHINGTON, Idella A.	(504)367-8429	1307
Metairie	REPMAN, Denise C.		1023
New Orleans	CAFFAREL, Agnes	(504)524-4237	170
	DU CARMONT, M C.	(504)861-8161	322
	GROSS, Mary D.	(504)282-4401	472
	MCKNIGHT, Mark C.	(504)866-3394	812
	RUSHING, Darla H.	(504)891-1127	1068

MAINE

Bath	MCKAY, Ann	(207)443-5524	809
Brunswick	SAEGER, Edwin J.	(207)729-5720	1074
Gorham	PERRY-BOWDER, Libbie E.	(207)780-5265	961

MARYLAND

Aberdeen Proving Gnd	GOEL, Krishan S.		443
Annapolis	CARMAN, Carol A.	(301)841-3810	183
	THAPAR, Shashi P.	(301)974-3015	1234
	WAGNER, Susan C.	(301)268-2315	1292
Baltimore	BROADY, Jessie	(301)661-1781	138
	GERHARDT, Edwin L.	(301)242-0328	428
	KUAN, David A.	(301)256-9044	681
	LAY, Shirley	(301)347-3419	705
	LAZZARONI, Philip S.	(301)528-1616	706
	SHAPIRO, Burton J.	(301)653-2757	1121
	SMITH, Mary P.	(301)358-0356	1158
	TOPPAN, Muriel L.	(301)837-9155	1251
Beltsville	AYER, Carol A.	(301)344-1969	42
	COLLINS, Donna S.	(301)344-3728	232
	ESMAN, Michael D.	(301)344-3729	354
	PRICE, Harry H.	(301)572-7798	992
Bethesda	BOEHR, Diane L.	(301)986-8560	109
	COSTABILE, Salvatore L.	(301)986-8560	249
	DAVIS, Deta S.	(301)564-0150	278
	HORAN, Meredith L.	(301)496-5497	559
	KIM, Sunnie I.	(301)496-8124	649
	PHILLIPS, Lena M.	(301)986-8560	968
	SCHWARTZ, Marla J.	(301)656-0043	1105
	YU, Pei	(301)986-8560	1384
Bowie	MASTRANGELO, Marjorie J.	(301)464-8745	782
Clarksburg	SORENSON, Lynn K.	(301)972-2329	1168
College Park	SHEETS, Robin R.	(301)454-5368	1125
	WELLISCH, Hans H.	(301)345-3477	1322
Columbia	GRUHL, Andrea M.	(301)596-5460	474
	JOHNSON, Bruce C.	(202)287-1308	602
Frederick	FRYSER, Benjamin S.	(301)698-5846	407
	GIBBONS, Katherine Y.	(301)663-2720	431
Gaithersburg	SANDIQUE-OWENS, Amelia A.	(301)869-8625	1080
Garrett Park	AGENBROAD, James E.	(301)946-7326	7
Greenbelt	BYERLY, Imogene J.		168
	KODAYASHI, Michiko		666
Hillcrest Heights	CHAPMAN, Elwynda K.	(301)894-0963	202
Hyattsville	RHEAUME, Irene M.	(301)434-8805	1025
Kensington	ZIMMERMANN, Carole R.	(301)564-0658	1389
Laurel	BRUNER, Linda J.	(301)498-6980	150
Mt Rainier	NITZ, Andrew M.		905
Patuxent River	SULLIVAN, Carol W.	(301)863-1931	1207
Phoenix	KIM, Chung S.	(301)628-6024	648
Rockville	LASER, Debra L.	(301)770-5470	700
	NGUYEN, Michael V.	(301)468-9697	900
	WHITMAN, Jean A.	(301)736-6804	1333
Silver Spring	AGEE, Victoria V.	(301)434-7073	7
	BLIXRUD, Julia C.	(301)622-1904	105
	GILBERT, Mattana	(301)565-2894	433
	RAWSTHORNE, Grace C.	(301)949-0698	1011
	WISNIEWSKI, Julia L.	(301)649-1590	1357

CATALOGER (Cont'd)

MARYLAND (Cont'd)

Suitland	MC HALE, Mary M.	(301)735-3451	808
Takoma Park	CHALMERS, Lois M.	(301)495-0187	197
Upperco	RAND, Pamela S.	(301)429-2958	1006
Walkersville	SHORT, Eleanor P.	(301)845-8015	1132

MASSACHUSETTS

Acton	HURD, Sandra H.	(617)263-7574	577
Acushnet	TAVARES, Cecelia M.	(617)995-1327	1225
Ayer	WILLIAMS, Carole C.	(617)433-6747	1342
Beverly	GAGNON, Ronald A.	(617)922-6722	412
Boston	BEST, Eleanor L.	(617)552-4421	92
	FOX, Susan	(617)463-3178	395
	GRIFFIN, Fredericia	(617)268-8210	468
	HOSTAGE, John B.	(617)782-0910	562
	KORT, Richard L.	(617)266-3646	672
	LEASON, Jane		707
	PRISTASH, Kenneth	(617)262-1120	993
	SCHALOW, John M.	(617)437-4962	1089
	SESKIN, Ann H.	(617)353-3715	1116
	SHARE, Donald S.	(617)738-2242	1122
	VOIGT, John F.	(617)266-1400	1287
Brockton	RESSMEYER, Ellen H.	(617)584-8133	1024
Cambridge	ALTENBERGER, Alicja	(617)495-4285	18
	ASCHMANN, Althea	(617)495-5709	35
	CHILDERS, Martha P.	(617)547-7334	208
	DESIMONE, Dorothy H.	(617)495-2432	295
	EPPARD, Philip B.	(617)492-4157	351
	ISHIMOTO, Carol F.	(617)495-2431	585
	PANAGOPOULOS, Beata D.	(617)495-2446	937
	PAPALAMBROS, Rita G.	(617)497-2047	939
	POLLARD, Russell O.	(617)495-5910	981
	SKLAR, Hinda F.	(617)495-9164	1146
	WUNDERLICH, Clifford S.		1374
Charlestown	CURTIN-STEVENSON, Mary C.	(617)241-9664	266
Chestnut Hill	DESJARDINS, Andrea C.		295
Concord	NESS, Pamela M.	(617)369-7174	896
Deerfield	KELLY, Patricia M.	(413)774-4627	638
East Brookfield	BOLSHAW, Cynthia L.	(617)867-2605	112
East Longmeadow	STACK, May E.	(413)525-6350	1177
Fall River	BETTENCOURT, Ronald J.	(617)675-8124	92
Gloucester	RHINELANDER, Mary F.	(617)281-2439	1025
Hanscom AFB	DUFFEK, Elizabeth A.	(617)377-4768	323
Lexington	BERNSTEIN, D S.	(617)863-1284	89
Lincoln	SCHWANN, William J.	(617)259-8212	1104
Lowell	SLAPSYS, Richard M.	(617)452-5000	1148
Needham	TSENG, Louisa	(617)449-3630	1260
New Bedford	FINNI, John J.	(617)999-6034	379
Newton	BOLAND, Mary J.	(617)969-0400	111
	CUNNINGHAM, Robert L.	(617)969-0400	265
	LINSKY, Leonore K.	(617)527-3646	731
North Adams	GOLDBERG, Steven R.	(413)664-6246	444
Northampton	SCOTT, Alison M.	(413)584-2700	1106
Orange	PROUTY, Sharman E.	(617)544-6743	996
Peabody	CODAIR, Frederick R.	(617)531-8200	226
Plymouth	HORN, Joseph A.	(617)746-6172	559
Reading	DAMICO, Nancy B.	(617)944-9411	272
	MARCY, Henry O.	(617)944-2194	769
Sharon	FRAZIER, James A.	(617)784-5642	399
Shrewsbury	CHANG, Isabelle E.	(617)845-4641	200
Somerville	FELDT, Candice K.	(617)666-2745	369
Springfield	CLOUGH, Linda F.	(413)788-8411	223
	DELZELL, William R.	(413)737-7000	290
	LAPIERRE, Barbe	(413)739-3871	697
	STEVENS, Michael L.	(413)739-3871	1190
Sturbridge	ALLEN, Joan C.	(508)347-3362	15
Sunderland	MCINTOSH, Nadia	(413)545-2728	809
Swampscott	BRENNER, Lawrence	(617)598-0370	133
Walpole	ESTES, Pamela J.	(617)668-3076	355
Waltham	HORGAN, Laura A.	(617)647-0868	559
	STRAND, Bethany	(617)736-4645	1200
West Newton	ST. AUBIN, Arleen K.		1075
West Springfield	SMITH, Barbara A.	(413)736-4561	1152
Williamsburg	LANCASTER, John	(413)268-7679	692
Williamstown	SUDDUTH, William E.	(413)597-2514	1206
Worcester	ANDREWS, Peter J.		27
	GONNEVILLE, Priscilla R.	(617)752-5615	447

CATALOGER (Cont'd)

MICHIGAN

Alma	GERLACH, William P.	(517)463-7227	429
Ann Arbor	BOWEN, Jennifer B.	(313)663-6164	120
	DWOSKIN, Beth M.	(212)382-6727	330
	PONOMARENKO, Ella	(313)996-5267	982
	REGAN, Lesley E.	(313)434-5530	1017
	ROENZWEIG, Merle	(313)769-1805	1048
	SWEET, Robert E.	(313)246-6204	1215
Berrien Springs	WALLER, Elaine J.	(616)473-3651	1298
Birmingham	GOLDSTEIN, Doris R.	(313)626-9299	446
	IRWIN, Lawrence L.	(313)626-5339	584
	MARTIN, John E.	(313)647-1700	776
Clarkston	MEDER, Stephen A.	(313)625-5611	820
Dearborn	NUCKOLLS, Karen A.	(313)593-5400	912
Detroit	THOMAS, Laverne J.	(313)849-2776	1237
East Lansing	BLACK-SHIER, Mary L.	(517)353-4526	102
	JIZBA, Laurel	(517)353-4526	600
	THUNELL, Allen E.	(517)353-4525	1243
Ferndale	BORAM, Joan M.	(313)542-2523	116
Flint	HART, David J.	(313)762-3414	507
Galesburg	MOSHER, Robin A.	(616)665-4409	871
Grand Rapids	SIEBERS, Bruce L.	(616)774-2167	1135
	WEAVER, Clarence L.		1312
Harper Woods	TODD, Suzanne L.	(313)881-5328	1248
Holland	LIGHT, Lin	(616)335-2540	726
	MURRAY, Diane E.	(616)394-7792	881
Kalamazoo	BLEIL, Leslie A.	(616)383-4963	105
Lawton	ROSS, Mary E.	(616)624-6897	1058
Livonia	BERRY, Charlene	(315)591-5017	90
Mattawan	BRUNHUMER, Sondra K.	(616)668-2391	150
Mt Clemens	CUNNINGHAM, Tina Y.	(313)286-5750	265
Muskegon	MARSHALL, Betty J.	(616)728-4766	773
Plymouth	DE BEAR, Estelle G.	(313)453-0912	284
Port Huron	YAEK, Larry A.	(313)484-3881	1376
Richland	HOWLETT, Jacqueline L.	(616)629-5352	566
Southfield	SMOLER, Shelly	(313)354-9100	1162
	VERGE, Colleen R.	(313)354-9100	1282
Troy	BIELICH, Paul S.	(313)689-9381	95
Utica	HORNE, Ernest L.	(313)731-4374	560

MINNESOTA

Columbia Heights	VAUGHAN, Janet E.	(612)574-6505	1279
Duluth	ENRICI, Pamela L.	(218)726-8586	350
Eden Prairie	BILEYDI, Lois G.	(612)934-3576	96
Kilkenny	HAMMARGREN, Betty L.	(507)595-2575	493
Little Canada	LO, Maryanne H.	(612)481-9412	735
Marshall	FOSTER, Veo G.	(507)532-4072	393
Minneapolis	BEDOR, Kathleen M.	(612)823-3945	73
	DODGE, Christopher N.	(612)541-8572	308
	GALT, Judith A.	(612)825-1190	415
	HILL, Constance L.	(612)372-6628	539
	KARON, Bernard L.	(612)625-5050	627
	MANNING, Mary L.	(612)870-3291	766
	O'LEARY, Mary E.	(612)872-4399	920
	OVERMIER, Judith A.	(612)626-6881	931
	ROLONTZ, Linda	(612)337-1644	1051
	WARPHEA, Rita C.	(612)588-6985	1306
	WITT, Kenneth W.	(612)871-4262	1358
Minnetonka	DESIREY, Janice M.	(612)541-8569	295
St Cloud	PRETZER, Shari G.		992
St Paul	DAVIS, Emmett A.	(612)699-4367	279
	EPSTEIN, Rheda	(612)292-6392	351
	HARWOOD, Karen L.	(612)690-6653	510
	MCCLASKEY, Marilyn H.	(612)624-5333	796
	NEVIN, Susanne	(612)625-1898	898
St Peter	HERVEY, Norma J.	(507)931-7563	533
White Bear Lake	BURESH, Reggie F.	(612)426-5300	158

MISSISSIPPI

Biloxi	FREEDMAN, Jack A.	(601)388-2318	400
Clinton	MYRICK, Judy C.	(601)924-6092	885
Hattiesburg	BOYD, William D.	(601)266-4232	123
	JONES, Dolores B.	(601)266-4349	612
	VAN MELER, Vandelia L.	(601)266-4243	1276
Jackson	WILSON, Ruth W.	(601)969-1013	1352
Kosciusko	RODICH, Nancy A.	(601)289-6683	1048
Raymond	WALL, Norma F.	(601)857-3253	1297

CATALOGER (Cont'd)

MISSOURI

Boonville	JOB, Rose A.		601
Columbia	HYDE, E C.	(314)442-3774	580
	SHIRKY, Martha H.	(314)882-6324	1131
Fenton	CHAN, Jeanny T.	(314)343-0929	199
	DEKEN, Jean M.	(314)827-1717	288
Independence	VOSS, Kathryn J.	(816)836-8100	1289
Kansas City	HOHENSTEIN, Margaret L.	(816)363-5409	549
	MEIZNER, Karen L.	(816)561-4000	822
Marionville	MCCROSKEY, Marilyn J.	(417)463-7372	800
Republic	HOWELLS, Joyce W.	(417)732-1128	565
St Louis	AMELUNG, Richard C.	(314)658-2754	19
	BETH, Dana L.	(314)721-0067	92
	LAURENSTEIN, Ann G.	(314)577-2669	703
	MCKEE, Eugenia V.	(314)576-9509	810
	NYSTROM, Kathleen A.	(314)577-5159	913
	PAGE, Jacqueline M.	(314)781-6352	934
	PERSHE, Frank F.		961
	REHKOP, Barbara L.		1017
	RILEY, Martha J.	(314)577-5158	1034
	TIPSWORD, Thomas N.	(314)263-2345	1246
	TOLSON, Stephanie D.	(314)741-7844	1249
Springfield	COOMBS, James A.	(417)836-4534	241
	KOTAMRAJU, Sarada	(417)883-8590	673
	MALTBY, Florence H.	(417)862-5119	764
Warrensburg	NIEMEYER, Mollie M.	(816)429-4070	903
	WALKER, Stephen R.	(816)429-4070	1296

MONTANA

Billings	NERODA, Edward W.	(406)657-2320	895
Butte	HUYGEN, Michaele L.	(406)782-8400	580
Havre	RITTER, Ann L.	(466)265-1308	1036
Heart Butte	SPOTTED EAGLE, Joy	(406)338-2282	1175
Missoula	DRIESSEN, Karen C.	(406)243-4070	320

NEBRASKA

Lincoln	HERZINGER, Sandra S.	(402)472-3545	534
	TIBBITS, Edith J.	(402)472-3545	1243
	WOOL, Gregory J.	(402)475-0391	1368
Minatare	JOHNSON, Elizabeth L.	(308)783-2188	604
Omaha	HASELWOOD, Eldon L.	(402)554-2211	510
Scottsbluff	OLTMANNS, Judith A.	(308)635-7673	923
Seward	MEIER, Marjorie A.	(402)643-3348	821

NEVADA

Las Vegas	MORGAN, James E.	(702)384-4887	864
	ORTIZ, Cynthia		927
	ORTIZ, Diane	(702)388-6501	927
	POLSON, Billie M.	(702)739-3125	982
Reno	PRATT, Kathleen L.	(702)789-3108	990

NEW HAMPSHIRE

Chester	GAVRISH, Diane L.	(603)887-4401	423
Derry	BISSETT, Claudia K.	(603)434-7354	100
Milford	LISTOVITCH, Denise A.	(603)672-0899	733
Nashua	BARRETT, Beth R.	(603)880-3542	59
	FERRIGNO, Helen F.	(603)889-3042	373
Portsmouth	LE BLANC, Charles A.	(603)436-4866	708
Rindge	STEARNS, Melissa M.	(603)899-5111	1183
Washington	HAMILL, Martha L.	(603)495-3994	491

NEW JERSEY

Audubon	VAUGHAN-STERLING, Judith A.	(609)546-0652	1280
Bloomfield	HUGHES, Kathleen	(201)748-3064	572
Califon	CAPOOR, Asha	(201)832-9323	180
Cape May Court House	HSU, Hsiu H.	(609)465-4500	567
Cherry Hill	KUAN, Jenny W.	(609)667-0300	681
Chester	MANY, Florence L.	(201)879-5167	767
Cliffside Park	ROBERTSON, Betty M.	(201)894-0235	1041
Colts Neck	MICHAL, Judith A.	(201)946-4839	832
East Brunswick	MENINGALL, Evelyn L.	(201)254-6403	824
East Orange	STICKEL, William R.	(201)678-4289	1193
Elizabeth	SKRAMOUSKY, Mary C.	(201)351-2671	1147
Englewood	HALASZ, Etelka B.	(201)858-6970	484
Glen Rock	PERCELLI, Irene M.	(201)445-5983	958
Hackettstown	ACKROYD-KELLY, Elaine S.	(201)852-1400	4
Highland Lakes	LINNAMAA, Mari M.		731

CATALOGER (Cont'd)

NEW JERSEY (Cont'd)

Hoboken	PAULSON, Barbara A.	(201)420-8017	950
Jersey City	RUBIN, Myra P.	(201)963-6456	1064
Kearny	CASSIDY, Joni L.	(201)991-5868	193
Little Ferry	BOTKIN, Karen R.		118
Lodi	TAORMINA, Anthony P.	(201)365-4044	1223
Marlton	STRONG, Darrell G.	(609)983-1998	1203
Matawan	KEARNEY, Jeanne E.	(201)566-7532	633
Morristown	MONROE-SECHREST, Nancy H.		855
Mount Holly	CRAWFORD, Lynn D.	(609)267-9660	257
Neptune	EBELING, Elinor H.	(201)774-0793	334
New Brunswick	ANDERSON, James D.	(201)846-1510	23
Oakland	GOLLA, Viola K.	(201)337-0100	447
Oradell	SUMMERS, Robert A.	(201)262-2529	1209
Park Ridge	WERNER, Edward K.	(201)391-4934	1324
Passaic	RUIZ-VALERA, Phoebe L.	(201)471-1770	1067
Pine Hill	GODFREY, Florence L.	(609)435-2682	442
Plainfield	KRUSE, Theodore H.	(201)725-2294	681
Port Murray	YRIGOYEN, Robert P.	(201)689-7069	1384
Princeton	BIELAWSKI, Marvin F.	(609)452-5143	95
	HIRSCH, David G.	(609)683-7502	543
	IRVINE, James S.	(609)921-8092	584
	NEWHOUSE, Brian G.	(609)921-8803	899
	PASTER, Luisa R.	(609)452-5464	946
	PHILLIPS, Richard F.	(609)452-3251	969
	VELLUCCI, Sherry L.	(609)921-3658	1282
Red Bank	PACHMAN, Frederic C.	(201)530-7695	933
Somerset	MOONEY, Jennifer M.		858
South Orange	FAWCETT-BRANDON, Pamela S.	(201)762-0230	367
Spring Lake	GARVEY, Nancy G.	(201)449-4673	421
Springfield	CHANG, Joseph I.	(201)467-2037	200
Stanhope	ELIASON, Elisabetha S.	(201)347-8215	342
Trenton	CONLEY, Gail D.	(609)771-6911	236
	PORTER, Eva L.	(609)890-3460	984
Upper Montclair	LUNG, Chan S.	(201)746-6733	748
Wayne	LEE, Minja P.		711
West Milford	JOB, Amy G.	(201)595-2160	601
Westwood	GINES, Noriko	(201)666-7042	437
Williamstown	BOGIS, Nana E.	(609)728-0569	110
Willingboro	PELLETIER, Karen E.		955
Woodbridge	DE WITT, Benjamin L.	(201)634-1316	298
Wrightstown	DRECHSEL, Marcella J.		319

NEW MEXICO

Albuquerque	HSU, Grace S.		567
	KALE, Shirley W.	(505)298-5980	623
	KRUG, Ruth A.	(505)277-7213	680
	SUGNET, Christopher L.	(505)277-7162	1206
Clovis	MCBETH, Deborah E.	(505)762-7161	792
Kirtland AFB	JOURDAIN, Janet M.	(505)844-1768	618
Las Cruces	CHEN, Laura F.	(505)522-2049	205
	MOORER, Jenny R.	(505)522-5126	862
Los Alamos	COMSTOCK, Daniel L.	(505)662-7668	235
Santa Fe	LANCASTER, Kevin M.	(505)827-4854	692

NEW YORK

Albany	BURKETT, Donald E.	(518)473-0584	161
	KOUO, Lily W.	(518)474-3840	673
	MCCOMBS, Gillian M.	(518)442-3633	797
	MILLER, Heather S.	(518)442-3626	838
	NICHOLS-RANDALL, Barbara L.	(518)489-7649	902
	PINSLEY, Lauren J.	(518)445-2342	975
Alfred	CONNOLLY, Bruce E.	(607)871-2494	237
	CULLEY, Paul T.	(607)871-2492	263
Astoria	FISHER, Maureen C.	(718)204-0631	381
Ausable Forks	ROGERS, Elizabeth S.		1049
Baldwin	FREESE, Melanie L.	(516)223-8784	401
Batavia	STRANC, Mary C.	(716)343-2783	1200
Bayside	WEINER, Carolynn N.		1318
Beechhurst	DESSER, Darrilyn	(718)767-6955	296
Bellport	RICHARDSON, John A.	(516)286-1600	1029
Binghamton	LINCOLN, Betty W.	(607)777-2862	728
Brentwood	ADAMS, Grover C.	(516)842-4000	4
Brewster	VELARDI, Adrienne B.	(914)279-5022	1281
Briarwood	BORRESS, Lewis R.	(718)441-6328	117

CATALOGER (Cont'd)
NEW YORK (Cont'd)

Bronx			
	DEEBRAH, Grace J.	(212)588-8400	286
	FOLTER, Siegrun H.	(212)960-8831	388
	GEE, Ka C.	(212)960-7770	424
	IOANID, Aurora S.	(212)220-0543	583
	WAGSCHAL, Sara G.	(212)601-1723	1292
Bronxville	ZIESELMAN, Paula M.	(914)337-0700	1388
Brooklyn	CANDELMO, Emily		178
	COHEN, Renee G.	(718)531-2647	229
	CORRSIN, Stephen D.	(718)851-2317	247
	KUPERMAN, Aaron W.	(718)854-8637	684
	LISZCZYNSKYJ, Halyna A.	(718)680-0368	733
	ROBBINS, Sara E.	(718)780-7980	1039
	STRAM, Lynn R.	(718)434-7815	1200
	SULTANOF, Jeff B.	(718)768-1611	1208
	WAHLERT, George A.	(718)833-1899	1292
	WEINRICH, Gloria	(708)998-9116	1318
Brookville	MAILLET, Lucienne G.	(516)299-2855	761
Buffalo	BRADLEY, Carol J.	(716)636-2935	125
	DECKER, Jean S.	(716)636-2784	285
	PERONE, Karen L.	(716)883-7000	959
Chappaqua	DI BIANCO, Phyllis R.	(914)238-3911	299
	NOVICK, Ruth	(914)238-4249	911
Clarence Ctr	CHAPMAN, Renee D.	(716)741-9644	202
Cornwall on Hudson	KONDZELA, Jeanette M.	(914)534-8282	670
Cortland	HEARN, Stephen S.	(607)753-2506	518
	RITCHIE, David G.	(607)753-2818	1036
Delmar	GRAVLEE, Diane D.	(518)439-7983	459
Dewitt	POPOVIC, Tanya V.	(315)446-7488	983
	SHRIER, Helene F.	(315)446-5971	1133
East Patchogue	PLUMER, F I.	(516)289-3134	978
East Setauket	BLOHM, Laura A.	(516)444-3105	106
Eastchester	KOLTAY, Emery I.	(914)337-0300	670
Farmingdale	ARMSTRONG, Ruth C.		32
Flushing	RORICK, William C.	(718)520-7345	1054
FPO New York	GAMAL, Sandra H.		416
Freeport	NOTARSTEFANO, Vincent C.	(516)379-3245	910
	VOLLONO, Millicent D.	(516)223-0838	1288
Hempstead	GRAVES, Howard E.	(516)560-5949	459
Hewlett	WILLER, Kenneth H.		1341
Hudson	HENDRICKS, Elaine M.		527
	MARTIN, Lyn M.	(518)828-1465	777
Hyde Park	GRIFFITH, Sheryl	(914)229-8114	469
Islip Terrace	KLATT, Wilma F.	(516)581-5933	658
Ithaca	CASSARO, James P.	(607)255-7046	193
	ERICSON, Margaret D.	(607)274-3882	353
	HICKEY, John T.	(607)273-1944	536
	MORRIS, Jennifer D.	(607)273-4074	866
	SLOCUM, Robert B.	(716)255-4247	1150
Kenmore	HEFNER, Xavier M.	(716)875-4705	520
Kew Gardens	SALAZAR, Pamela R.	(718)441-2350	1076
Latham	MACKSEY, Susan A.	(518)783-7058	757
Lindenhurst	MILNES, Patricia C.	(516)957-7755	845
Long Island City	LOW, Frederick E.	(718)482-5424	743
Marlboro	BAKER, Marie A.	(914)236-4441	49
Mastic	MACINICK, James W.	(516)399-3281	755
Mineola	TISHLER, Amnon	(516)294-7224	1247
Monticello	DORN, Robert J.	(914)794-4660	313
Mt Sinai	COHEN, Rosemary C.	(516)473-8717	229
New York	BARR, Jeffrey A.	(212)691-2389	58
	BENSON, Harold W.	(212)420-7652	83
	BRAYTON, Roy S.		130
	BRISTAH, Pamela J.	(212)749-2802	137
	CAPRIELIAN, Arevig	(718)459-2757	180
	CHITTAMPALLI, Padma S.	(212)874-0141	209
	CHO-PARK, Jaung J.	(212)280-2293	210
	CROFT, Elizabeth G.	(212)371-2000	260
	DEMANDY, Claire	(212)960-8575	291
	DERRICKSON, Margaret	(212)620-4230	294
	DIFEDE, Robert F.	(212)715-6307	302
	DOOLING, Marie	(212)510-4375	312
	FASANA, Paul J.	(212)930-0708	366
	FLOERSHEIMER, Lee M.	(212)787-3727	385
	GALGAN, Mary N.	(212)267-6646	413
	GITNER, Fred J.	(212)355-6100	439
	GOERNER, Tatiana	(212)222-3490	443
	HOOGAKKER, David A.	(212)243-5150	556
	HSIAO, Shu Y.	(212)749-2873	567

CATALOGER (Cont'd)
NEW YORK (Cont'd)

New York			
	HSU, Karen M.	(212)930-0703	567
	HYMAN, Richard J.	(212)865-7962	580
	KASTNER, Arno A.	(212)998-2477	629
	KEMPE, Deborah A.	(212)595-6583	639
	KENSELAAR, Robert	(212)870-1661	642
	LIDSKY, Ella	(212)663-4949	725
	LIN, Tung F.	(212)669-5178	728
	MANDAL, Mina R.	(212)491-8266	764
	MARGOLIES, Alan	(212)489-5042	770
	MASTRANGELO, Paul J.	(212)431-2128	783
	MOTIHAR, Kamla	(212)838-8400	872
	MULIA, Gusti	(212)930-0701	876
	NESTA, Frederick N.	(212)982-9672	896
	OSTWALD, Mark F.		929
	PARRIS, Angela P.	(212)836-7640	944
	PERRY, Paula J.	(212)348-8817	960
	PRAGER, George A.	(212)725-3083	989
	RAJEC, Elizabeth M.	(212)690-4151	1004
	REMECZKI, Paul W.	(212)873-3400	1022
	RESCIGNO, Dolores S.	(212)530-5969	1024
	ROSIGNOLO, Beverly A.	(212)962-4111	1057
	ROZENE, Janette B.	(212)760-7265	1064
	SALVAGE, Barbara A.	(212)998-2463	1078
	SANCHEZ, Eliana P.	(212)254-8829	1079
	SAVADA, Morton J.	(212)695-7155	1085
	SHIH, Diana	(212)769-5413	1130
	STALKER, Dianne S.	(212)280-8484	1178
	SULLIVAN, Stephen W.		1208
	VAJDA, Elizabeth A.	(212)254-6300	1271
	WEINBERG, Valerie A.	(212)685-0008	1318
	WOLF, Marion	(212)360-3572	1360
	ZARCONE, Beth B.	(212)982-0055	1386
Old Brookville	HELLER, Jacqueline R.	(516)626-2700	524
Oneonta	CHIANG, Nancy	(607)432-4200	207
	ROUGEUX, Debora A.	(607)432-0290	1061
Ossining	LEW, Susan	(914)762-1154	722
Oswego	CHU, Sylvia	(315)341-3210	213
Patchogue	GIBBARD, Judith R.	(516)654-4700	431
Peekskill	FALCONE, Elena C.	(914)528-2820	362
Pelham	FERRIBY, Peter G.	(914)738-3712	373
Penfield	PARKE, Kathryn E.		941
Plainview	SYWAK, Myron	(516)935-7821	1217
Potsdam	FOSTER, Selma V.	(315)267-2477	392
Purchase	LIE, David W.	(914)253-5095	725
	NICKERSON, Donna L.	(914)694-2200	902
Rhinebeck	NAVRATIL, Jean		890
Ridge	KINNEY, Daniel W.	(516)924-7338	653
Rochester	BARNES, Robert W.	(716)428-7335	57
	CHURCH, Virginia K.	(716)475-2558	213
	GRAY, Shirley M.	(716)475-2010	460
	JUNION, Gail J.	(716)275-4496	620
	ROSENBERG-NUGENT, Nanci B.		1056
Saratoga Springs	LEWIS, Gillian H.	(518)587-0374	723
Sayville	PAGELS, Helen H.	(516)589-2908	934
Schenectady	HUMPHRY, John A.	(518)374-8944	574
	KING, Maryde F.	(518)374-7287	651
Selden	SALINERO, Amelia	(516)732-1268	1076
Setauket	PACKARD, Agnes K.		933
Southampton	KETCHAM, Susan E.	(516)283-4000	645
Sparkill	BARTH, John E.	(914)359-9500	61
Staten Island	DIMATTEO, Lucy A.	(718)698-7095	304
	KRIEGER, Tillie		678
Stillwater	REEPMEYER, Marie C.	(518)785-6949	1016
Suffern	GLEASON, Robert W.	(914)356-4650	440
Syracuse	PFOHL, Theodore E.	(315)473-4493	966
	WALTZ, Mary A.	(315)478-1265	1302
	WASYLENKO, Lydia W.	(315)423-2585	1308
Three Mile Bay	PIZER, Charles R.	(315)649-5086	977
	PIZER, Elizabeth F.	(315)649-5086	977
Tuckahoe	ANDERSON, Birgitta M.	(914)793-6830	21
Valley Stream	ENG, Mamie	(516)825-6422	348
Wantagh	NOVITSKY, Edward G.		911
West Islip	JOYCE, Therese	(516)587-8000	618
Westhampton	BARR, Janet L.	(516)288-5539	58
White Plains	MCGARVEY, Eileen B.	(914)683-2794	805
Williamsville	SCHUTT, Dedre A.	(716)633-6384	1103

CATALOGER (Cont'd)
NEW YORK (Cont'd)

Yorktown Heights	HAIMOVSKY, Kira A.	(914)962-5628	484

NORTH CAROLINA

Belmont	MAYES, Susan E.	(704)825-3711	789
Beulaville	FRAZELLE, Betty	(919)298-4658	399
Chapel Hill	GLEIM, David E.	(919)962-0153	441
	HIGH, Walter M.	(919)968-1468	538
	SAYE, Jerry D.	(919)962-8073	1086
	SAYE, Terri O.	(919)962-1211	1086
Charlotte	MILLER, Gloria	(704)394-6848	838
Durham	HINSON, Doris M.	(919)684-4138	543
	KLINE, Lawrence O.	(919)684-6396	661
	LAWTON, Patrecia J.	(919)596-6364	705
Elkin	MACPHAIL, Jessica		758
Fayetteville	ASPINALL, David L.	(919)483-0543	37
	CHAN, Moses C.	(919)483-5022	199
Greensboro	FLOYD, Rebecca M.	(919)852-3592	386
	WURSTEN, Richard R.	(919)292-5683	1374
High Point	TOMLINSON, Charles E.	(919)887-3006	1250
Kinston	MILLER, Sylvia G.		843
Raleigh	BROWN, Kathleen R.	(919)737-2603	145
Reidsville	KING, Willard B.	(919)349-6192	652
Research Triangle Pk	MCCONNELL, Judith J.	(919)248-4869	797
	TUTTLE, Walter A.	(919)549-0661	1266
Sanford	MURCHISON, Margaret B.	(919)258-3277	879
Swannanoa	ALLEN, Christina Y.	(704)298-4742	14
Wingate	ABBOTT, Kent H.	(704)233-8094	1
Winston-Salem	HICKS, Michael	(919)788-4084	537
	JOHNSTON, Rebecca M.	(919)748-2299	610

NORTH DAKOTA

Fargo	BLUE, Margaret R.	(701)235-5164	107
	BRKIC, Beverly T.	(701)237-5865	138
	NELSON, David N.	(701)237-8891	893
Minot	ROBERTSON, Pamela S.	(701)838-6080	1042

OHIO

Ashland	RHOADES, Nancy L.	(419)289-3969	1025
Athens	MILLER, David A.	(614)592-5692	836
	OBERLE, Holly E.		914
Bowling Green	SLOVASKY, Stephen	(419)372-2106	1150
Chardon	KLINGER, William E.	(216)564-9340	661
Cincinnati	ABRAMS, Roger E.	(513)821-5984	3
	HEFFRON, Sheila F.	(513)891-4200	520
	KONKEL, Mary S.	(513)681-2074	670
	KRAMER, Sally J.	(513)369-6085	675
	PALKOVIC, Mark A.	(513)475-4471	935
	PERRY, Rebecca A.	(513)721-3707	960
	RIFFEY, Robin S.	(513)871-3087	1033
	WELLINGTON, Jean S.	(513)475-6724	1322
Cleveland	BALCAS, Georgeana	(216)368-2403	50
	MICHNAY, Susan E.	(216)749-7400	832
	RICHMOND, Phyllis A.	(216)461-4948	1030
	ROBSON, Timothy D.	(216)696-4390	1045
	ROSENFELD, Joseph S.	(216)523-7323	1056
	TURNER, Freya A.	(216)581-6778	1264
Cleveland Heights	LANTZ, Elizabeth A.	(216)541-2905	697
	SPAHR, Cheryl L.	(216)382-7675	1170
	TRAMDACK, Philip J.	(216)371-3445	1254
Columbus	BRANN, Andrew R.	(614)221-4181	128
	CALL, J R.	(614)885-4926	173
	CHANG, Tony H.	(614)292-2664	201
	CHRISTENSON, Donald E.	(614)236-5959	211
	CONNELL, Christopher J.	(614)848-5193	237
	HEARD, Jeffrey L.		518
	KIE, Kathleen M.	(614)481-7640	646
	KRUMM, Carol R.	(614)846-1683	680
	LUDY, Lorene E.	(614)292-2664	747
	MIMNAUGH, Ellen N.	(614)486-7755	845
	O'NEIL, Rosanna M.	(614)761-5057	924
	POST, Phyllis C.	(614)292-6691	986
	ROGERS, Sally A.	(614)292-2664	1050
	STRALEY, Dona S.	(614)292-3362	1200
	WALBRIDGE, Sharon L.	(614)274-4081	1293
	WANG, Anna M.	(614)294-8035	1302
	WARNER, Susan B.	(614)424-5676	1305

CATALOGER (Cont'd)
OHIO (Cont'd)

Dayton	BERG, Richard R.	(513)276-5104	84
	BRUMIT, Nancy T.	(513)274-4677	150
	EVANS, Stephen P.	(513)220-9506	358
	PURSCH, Lenore D.	(513)434-7064	998
Defiance	SEDLCOK, Barbara J.	(419)784-4010	1111
Delaware	SAMPLES, Judith L.	(614)362-3861	1078
Dublin	HAYNES, Kathleen J.	(614)764-6000	516
	PAK, Moo J.	(514)761-2174	935
	SCHUITEMA, Joan E.	(614)761-8827	1101
Fairborn	BAKER, Narcissa L.	(573)879-3638	49
Gahanna	WEITZ, Jay N.	(614)476-5489	1320
Kent	GILDZEN, Alex J.	(216)672-2270	434
	KIRKBRIDE, Amey L.	(216)672-3764	654
Kenton	PETTY, Sue W.	(419)673-2278	965
Lakewood	KEATING, Michael F.	(216)221-0608	633
North Ridgeville	FACINELLI, Jaclyn R.	(216)327-7079	360
Oberlin	KNAPP, David	(216)775-8280	663
Oxford	ZASLOW, Barry J.	(513)523-3980	1386
Shaker Heights	ENGLANDER, Marlene S.	(216)491-9277	349
	MELTON, Vivian B.	(216)921-5803	823
Steubenville	BURKE, Ambrose L.	(614)283-3771	160
Strongsville	JUNEJA, Derry C.	(216)238-7585	620
Toledo	HANNAFORD, Claudia L.	(419)536-7539	496
Youngstown	LUTTRELL, Jeffrey R.	(216)742-3681	750

OKLAHOMA

Edmond	RYLANDER, Carolyn S.	(405)478-3098	1072
Norman	LARSEN, Nancy E.	(405)321-6795	698
Oklahoma City	HARGIS-LYTLE, Betty L.	(405)721-2134	501
	JONES, Beverly A.	(405)751-0574	611
Tahlequah	HILL, Helen K.		540
Tulsa	HACKER, Connie J.	(918)587-6561	481
	MANES, Estelle L.	(918)582-7426	765
	TOOLEY, Katherine J.	(918)494-8759	1250
	WRIGHT, Patricia Y.	(918)585-1997	1372

OREGON

Ashland	PURCELL, V N.	(503)482-2629	998
Corvallis	OSHEROFF, Shiela K.	(503)754-3181	928
Eugene	ALLEN, Alice J.	(503)686-3064	14
	GRIFFIN, Karen D.	(503)686-3064	468
	ROBERTSON, Howard W.	(503)686-3064	1042
	SMITH, Terry M.	(503)686-3064	1161
	WANG, Hsiao G.	(503)686-3064	1303
Milton-Freewater	SARGENT, Phyllis M.	(503)938-3724	1083
Portland	KENNEY, Ann J.	(503)297-1894	641

PENNSYLVANIA

Alcoa Center	MOUNTS, Earl L.	(412)337-2396	873
Berwyn	SCAMMAHORN, Lynne	(215)296-3430	1087
Bloomsburg	ROCKWOOD, Susan M.	(717)784-8456	1046
Blue Bell	MARTIN, Shelby A.	(215)641-6587	778
Boyertown	EMERICK, John L.	(215)369-7422	347
Bryn Mawr	MERZ, Lawrie H.	(215)527-6858	827
California	NOLF, Marsha L.	(412)938-4048	908
Carlisle	NEITZ, Cordelia M.		892
	WIWEL, Pamela S.		1359
Chester Springs	GREBEY, Betty H.	(215)469-9333	461
Clarion	HARTSOCK, Ralph M.	(814)226-2000	508
	HORN, Janice H.	(814)226-7367	559
Devon	PIECHNICK, Katarzyna M.	(215)964-9348	971
Dresher	FU, Clare S.	(215)641-1978	407
Ebensburg	DRUSH, Cassandra	(814)472-7338	151
Erie	ANDRICK, Annita A.	(814)455-8080	27
Fleetwood	EMERICK, Michael J.	(215)944-8486	347
Greensburg	DUCK, Patricia M.	(412)836-9689	322
	KREDEL, Stephen F.		677
Harleysville	HILLEGAS, Ferne E.		541
Harrisburg	WEBSTER, Connie L.	(717)545-9912	1314
Hatfield	PAKALA, Denise M.	(215)368-5000	935
Haverford	ROBERTSON, Robert B.	(215)896-1273	1042
Indiana	ELLIKER, Calvin	(412)357-2892	343
	RAHKONEN, Carl J.		1003
Jenkintown	MONTOYA, Leopoldo	(215)886-2299	856
	SEVY, Barbara S.	(215)884-8275	1117
Johnsonburg	NELSON, Wilburta B.	(814)965-4110	895
Kennett Square	MORSE, Alfred W.	(215)444-3444	869
Lancaster	ZEAGER, Lloyd	(717)393-9745	1387

CATALOGER (Cont'd)
PENNSYLVANIA (Cont'd)

Langhorne	BLACK, Dorothy M.	(215)752-5800	101
Lansdale	CLAYPOOL, Richard D.	(215)368-7439	220
Lehigh Valley	WEBER, A C.	(215)837-9615	1313
Lewisburg	BOYTINCK, Paul	(717)524-2678	124
	JENKS, Zoya E.	(717)524-3243	597
Lititz	GERLOTT, Eleanor L.	(717)627-0944	429
Lower Oxford	MUDRICK, Kristine E.		875
Mercer	ELY, Betty L.	(412)662-2543	347
Middletown	STANLEY, Nancy M.	(717)944-4049	1180
Millersville	GLASS, Catherine C.	(717)872-3777	440
	LOTLIKAR, Sarojini D.		742
Morrisville	TOMAR, Jeanne	(215)736-2177	1249
New Castle	FUSCO, Marilyn A.		410
New Hope	CROWN, Faith W.	(215)794-8932	262
New Kingstown	HANSON, Eugene R.	(717)243-0973	498
Norristown	CATHEY, Gail L.	(215)278-5100	195
	PRITCHARD, Barbara		994
	SORG, Elizabeth A.	(215)279-3871	1168
Philadelphia	BRADLEY, James S.	(215)242-6112	126
	BUCK, Patricia K.	(215)247-7443	154
	CALDWELL, John M.	(215)545-2809	172
	CLEVELAND, Susan E.	(215)662-2577	221
	GROSSMAN, Robert M.	(215)893-1954	473
	HINTON, Frances	(215)843-8706	543
	JACOBY, Beth E.	(215)787-8215	590
	LAVERTY, Bruce	(215)925-2688	703
	ROEDELL, Ray F.	(215)739-7739	1048
	ROHDY, Margaret A.	(215)387-5768	1050
	RUGGERE, Christine A.	(215)898-7088	1066
	SCHAEFFER, Judith E.	(215)843-8840	1089
	SMIRAGLIA, Richard P.	(215)662-5699	1152
	YOLTON, Jean S.	(215)878-7548	1380
	YOUNG, James B.	(215)898-6715	1382
Pittsburgh	AL SADAT, Amira A.	(412)421-9444	17
	ENGLERT, Mary A.	(412)795-1761	350
	EVES, Judith A.	(412)471-1477	359
	HLUHANY, Patricia	(412)364-3000	544
	LEIBOWITZ, Faye R.	(412)421-7974	713
	MAWHINNEY, Paul C.	(412)367-7330	787
	MITTEN, Lisa A.	(412)521-4462	850
	RAO, Rama K.	(412)429-0543	1008
	ROSS, Nina M.	(412)624-9475	1058
	SPIEGELMAN, Barbara M.	(412)824-2222	1174
	STEPHENS, Norris L.	(412)624-4130	1188
	WOO, Lisa C.	(512)648-8188	1363
	WRIGHT, Nancy M.	(412)237-5948	1372
Pocono Summit	ANDERMAN, Lynea	(717)839-9495	21
Shippenville	EMERICK, Kenneth F.	(814)226-5775	347
State College	CHANG, Shirley L.	(717)893-2312	201
	JAMISON, Carolyn C.	(814)234-4512	593
	LINDSAY, Ann M.	(814)237-0714	729
	NADESKI, Karen L.	(814)238-7890	886
Topton	SPRANKLE, Anita T.		1176
University Park	GERHART, Catherine A.	(814)865-1755	428
	GRUBER, Linda R.	(814)865-3451	474
	STRIEDIECK, Suzanne S.	(814)865-1755	1202
Upper Darby	SILVERMAN, Karen S.	(215)734-0146	1138
	SILVERMAN, Scott H.	(215)734-0146	1138
Villanova	LEWIS, Marjorie B.		724
Wayne	ANTOS, Brian F.	(215)254-0754	29
	LAZARUS, Joan M.	(215)964-0477	706
Waynesboro	POSEY, Sussann F.	(717)762-3047	985
West Chester	MCCAWLEY, Christina W.	(215)436-0720	795
	TRUESDELL, Eugenia R.	(215)436-2917	1259
West Point	MESSICK, Karen J.	(215)661-6026	828

PUERTO RICO

Ensenada	MEJILL-VEGA, Gregorio	(809)821-4734	822
Hormiguerow	MARTINEZ-NAZARIO, Ronaldo		779
Mayaguez	VALENTIN-MARTY, Jeannette		1271
Miramar	CASAS DE FAUNCE, Maria		191
Ramey	CONCEPCION, Luis	(809)890-2681	235
San Juan	TORRES-TAPI, Manual A.		1251
Santurce	BARRERAS, Dolly M.	(809)728-1515	59

CATALOGER (Cont'd)
RHODE ISLAND

Barrington	COULOMBE, Dominique C.	(401)245-4018	250
Newport	CARSON, Josephine R.		188
Providence	COOLIDGE, Arlan R.		241
Wakefield	BARNETT, Judith B.	(401)789-7435	57
Westerly	LIGHT, Karen M.	(401)596-2877	726

SOUTH CAROLINA

Charleston	NEVILLE, Robert F.	(803)792-8024	898
	ROSS, Gary M.	(803)792-5530	1058
	SMITH, Nancy	(803)792-7672	1158
Clemson	TOOMEY, Alice F.		1251
Columbia	HUYGEN, Eva		580
	UPHAM, Lois N.	(803)777-6938	1269
Conway	LOWRIMORE, R T.	(803)248-2967	745
Easley	BLAIR, Sharon K.	(803)855-0866	103
Greenville	AYARI, Kaye W.	(803)235-4883	42
Greenwood	GOING, Susan C.	(803)229-7448	444
Manning	GILBERT, Sybil M.	(803)435-8633	434
Newberry	HAMILTON, Ben	(803)276-6870	491
Orangeburg	SMALLS, Mary L.	(803)536-8852	1151
Spartanburg	BOWLES, David M.	(803)578-1472	121
Sumter	GORDON, Clara B.	(803)773-4041	451
Surfside Beach	KLEM, Marjorie R.	(803)238-0460	660
West Columbia	GISSENDANNER, Cassandra S.	(803)794-9363	438

SOUTH DAKOTA

Madison	COOK, Nancy E.	(605)256-4709	240
Spearfish	JONES, Dora A.	(605)642-4256	612
Vermillion	EDELEN, Joseph R.	(605)677-6082	335

TENNESSEE

Antioch	HAMLIN, Lisa K.	(615)833-7541	493
Cookeville	LAFEVER, Susan	(615)372-3210	687
Cordova	SMITH, Philip M.	(901)386-1003	1159
Dowelltown	EASTERLY, Ambrose	(615)597-1390	333
Johnson City	BROWN, Phyllis J.	(615)929-3111	147
	CONVERY, Sukhont K.	(615)926-3717	239
Knoxville	BENGTSON, Betty G.	(615)974-6640	80
	BULL, Margaret J.	(615)632-6173	156
	GRADY, Agnes M.	(615)637-0008	455
Memphis	CO, Francisca	(901)324-2453	224
	LEVINE, Fay E.	(901)725-8880	720
	WUJCIK, Dennis S.	(901)722-8753	1374
Mt Juliet	ROBERTSON, Sally A.	(615)758-5750	1042
Nashville	BRANTIGAN-STOWELL, Martha J.	(615)352-0787	129
	CHEN, Helen M.	(612)251-1417	205
	GMEINER, Timothy J.	(615)297-7958	442
	LASATER, Mary C.	(615)322-2199	700
Oak Ridge	MCDONALD, Ethel Q.	(615)482-5011	802
Sewanee	PHILLIPS, Patricia A.	(615)598-1389	968
Signal Mountain	JACKSON, Joseph A.	(615)886-1753	587

TEXAS

Abilene	CAMPBELL, Mary K.	(915)673-8042	177
Amarillo	RIEPMA, Helen J.	(806)352-7486	1033
Austin	GOODWIN, Willard	(512)288-2373	450
	HELFER, Robert S.	(512)929-3086	523
	JACKSON, Ruth L.	(512)345-1653	588
	SPRUG, Joseph W.	(512)448-8474	1176
	WILLIAMS, Suzi	(512)451-3482	1346
Beaumont	COKINOS, Elizabeth G.	(409)866-6043	229
	NISBY, Dora R.	(409)899-9972	904
Bedford	PETERS, Mary N.	(817)283-3739	962
Bellaire	HOPKINS, Joyce A.	(713)667-3760	558
College Station	GYESZLY, Suzanne D.	(409)845-3731	479
	PAYNE, Leila M.	(409)845-8157	951
	THOMPSON, Christine E.	(409)845-8157	1239
Dallas	DOMA, Tshering		310
	HAWLEY, Laurie J.	(214)907-2940	514
	SNODGRASS, Wilson D.	(214)692-2342	1163
Denton	ALMQUIST, Sharon G.	(817)387-1703	17
	CALIMANO, Ivan E.	(817)898-4016	173
	FERSTL, Kenneth L.	(817)383-3775	374
	FOLLET, Robert E.	(817)382-0037	388
	POPE, Betty F.	(817)565-2609	983
Edinburg	HAYNIE, Altie V.	(512)383-7760	517

CATALOGER (Cont'd)
TEXAS (Cont'd)

El Paso	LABODDA, Marsha J.	(915)859-1956	686
	MATHIS, Margaret H.		784
	ROBERTS, Glenda S.	(915)541-4770	1040
Fort Worth	RICE, Ralph A.	(817)626-7995	1027
	RUSSELL, Barbara J.	(817)735-9136	1068
	SCHMIDT HACKER, Margaret H.	(817)334-5525	1096
Galveston	RASCHE, Richard R.	(409)762-3139	1008
Houston	BABER, Elizabeth A.	(713)527-8101	43
	BRUNNER, A M.	(713)463-0416	151
	CRAIG, Marilyn J.	(713)749-4762	254
	DAVIS, Sara	(713)669-2426	281
	FORD, Margaret C.	(713)527-8101	389
	HALL, John D.	(713)749-4762	488
	KIMZEY, Ann C.	(713)488-9280	649
	NOBLE, Ann A.	(713)774-7661	906
	SIVARAM, Swaraj L.		1144
Huntsville	BURKS, Paula	(409)294-1498	161
	THORNE, Bonnie B.		1242
	YOUNG, J A.	(409)295-8766	1382
Irving	AYRES, Edwin M.	(214)254-4108	43
	COCHRAN, Carolyn	(214)258-6767	225
	WHITE, Lely K.	(214)721-5310	1331
Kilgore	CLAER, Joycelyn H.	(214)983-8238	215
Longview	GROSS, Sally L.		472
Lubbock	ANDREWS, Virginia L.	(806)799-0534	27
Mesquite	BYROM, Jeanne	(214)216-6220	170
Plano	PROKESH, Jane	(214)754-6461	995
	THOMAS, Page A.	(214)867-2595	1238
Prairie View	YEH, Helen S.	(409)857-3192	1379
Round Rock	RICKLEFS, Dale L.	(512)255-3939	1032
San Antonio	BADING, Kathryn E.	(512)655-4120	44
	GONZALEZ, Sharon M.		448
	HICKEY, Lady J.	(512)436-3435	536
	HOOD, Elizabeth	(512)736-7292	556
	LANG, Anita E.	(512)684-5111	695
	MANEY, Lana E.	(512)496-7754	765
San Marcos	HUSTON, Susan S.	(515)396-3374	578
Seguin	KOOPMAN, Frances A.	(512)379-4161	671
Temple	SPOEDE, Mary H.	(817)773-0436	1175
	TIME, Ming M.	(817)778-5556	1245
Victoria	ALLEN, Virginia M.	(512)573-5889	16
Waco	KEATTS, Rowena W.	(817)753-6415	633

UTAH

North Salt Lake	YANG, Basil P.	(801)295-0276	1377
Provo	NIELSON, Paula I.	(801)375-9241	903
	SWENSEN, Dale S.	(801)378-4407	1215
Salt Lake City	CASADY, Richard L.	(801)533-9607	191
	DOWNEY REIDA, Linda K.	(801)466-5888	316
	HOLLEY, Robert P.	(801)581-7741	551
	JOHNSON, Jeffery O.	(801)533-5250	606
	MARCHANT, Cathy	(801)364-8399	768
	REED, Vernon M.	(801)531-3377	1015

VERMONT

Barre	GRIFFIN, Marie E.	(802)479-2810	468
Rutland	MCCULLOUGH, Doreen J.	(802)773-5900	801
	SHERMAN, Jacob R.	(802)773-1860	1128
Woodstock	DICENSO, Jacquelyn C.	(802)457-1317	300

VIRGIN ISLANDS

St Thomas	MILLER, Veronica E.	(809)774-0059	843
	SOUFFRONT, Blanche L.	(809)774-3407	1169

VIRGINIA

Alexandria	FISHER, Carl D.	(703)836-7951	380
	GOLDBERG, Jolande E.	(703)765-4521	444
	OMARA, Marie T.	(703)960-3981	923
	ROBERTSON, Jack	(703)549-3260	1042
	WANG, Ann C.	(703)751-4536	1302
	WOODWARD, Lawrence W.	(703)751-9426	1368
Annandale	MATON, Joanne J.	(703)256-2288	784
	TYSINGER, Barbara R.	(703)354-8688	1267
Arlington	COSGROVE-DAVIES, Lisa A.	(703)536-9452	248
	JOACHIM, Robert J.	(703)920-7721	600
	KECSKES, Lily C.	(703)528-0730	633
	PYKE, Carol J.	(703)241-7731	999

CATALOGER (Cont'd)
VIRGINIA (Cont'd)

Arlington	SWICEGOOD, Mary R.	(703)538-1087	1216
	WIENER, Theodore		1336
	WOLF, Richard E.	(703)276-0270	1360
Blacksburg	BAER, Eberhard A.	(703)951-3480	44
	ESPLEY, John L.	(703)961-5847	354
	JOHNSON, Bryan R.	(703)552-0876	602
	NORSTEDT, Marilyn L.	(703)961-4610	909
Charlottesville	BRAUN, Mina H.	(804)924-4957	129
	GORDON, Vesta L.	(804)295-5586	452
	RODRIGUEZ, Robert D.		1048
	STURGIS, Marylee C.	(804)924-3206	1205
Chesterfield	DUNAWAY, Carolyn D.	(804)748-1763	325
Christiansburg	LINN, Cynthia S.	(703)961-5988	731
Falls Church	HABERLAND, Jody	(703)573-7279	481
Fort Monroe	LUH, Lydia Y.	(804)727-4292	747
Grottoes	BUCCO, Louise F.	(703)249-5424	153
Hollins College	BECKER, Charlotte B.	(703)362-6235	72
Lexington	BISSETT, John P.	(703)463-8546	100
	DANFORD, Robert E.	(703)463-8657	272
Lynchburg	KAWAGUCHI, Miyako	(804)239-3071	632
Norfolk	LIU, Albert C.	(804)440-4141	734
Petersburg	BERGELT, Robert L.	(804)520-6112	85
	FRENCH, Randy A.	(804)861-4447	402
Quantico	BROWN, David C.	(703)221-1586	143
Reston	LEWIS, Diane M.	(703)860-4475	723
Richmond	GWIN, James E.	(804)288-7602	479
	HALL, Bonlyn G.	(804)359-0409	487
	MACLEOD, James M.	(804)355-1395	757
	MURPHY, Robert D.	(804)741-1311	881
	OWEN, Karen V.	(804)649-6132	931
	SARTAIN, Sara M.		1083
	WINFREE, Waverly K.	(804)271-4163	1354
	WOODWARD, Elaine H.	(804)771-2219	1368
Roanoke	COLLINS, Mitzi L.		233
Salem	GLENNON, Irene F.	(703)380-3552	441
Springfield	CASWELL, Mary C.	(703)642-0340	194
	KANE, Astor V.	(703)487-4696	624
Vienna	SCHAEFER, Mary E.	(703)759-6339	1089
Virginia Beach	BILLERT, Julia A.	(804)427-7150	96
	CARR, Jeanette A.	(804)481-6096	185
	WHYTE, Sean	(804)481-6096	1335
Williamsburg	SCHEITLE, Janet M.	(804)220-3104	1091

WASHINGTON

Auburn	GOLDSTEIN, Cynthia N.	(206)931-3018	446
Bothell	DECOSTER, Barbara L.	(206)488-7537	286
Edmonds	HALEY, Marguerite R.	(206)546-6561	486
Ellensburg	YEH, Thomas Y.	(509)925-9257	1379
Fall City	AROKSAAR, Richard D.	(206)442-5203	34
Federal Way	WILSON, Anthony M.	(206)839-0496	1349
Kirkland	SUGGS, John K.	(206)823-6754	1206
Richland	CARVER, Sue A.	(509)943-5478	191
Seattle	GRIPPO, Christopher F.		471
	HARMALA, Amy A.	(206)632-8338	502
	SOPER, Mary E.	(206)543-1887	1168
	STEERE, Paul J.	(206)367-0328	1184
	YONGMAN, Zhang	(206)522-6701	1380
Spokane	WYNN, Debra D.	(509)328-4220	1375
Tacoma	HAGAN, Dalia L.	(206)565-9669	482
Woodinville	GARRETSON, Laurie J.	(206)483-6213	420
Yakima	JORDAN, Sharon L.	(509)248-4522	617

WEST VIRGINIA

Charleston	HUMPHRIES, Joy D.		574
Glenville	VERMA, Prem V.	(304)462-5303	1282
Letter Gap	RUSSELL, Richard A.	(302)462-5471	1069
Salem	LANGER, Frank A.	(304)782-1007	695

WISCONSIN

Brookfield	CASEY, Jean M.	(414)781-2545	192
Caledonia	GRENDYSA, Peter A.	(414)764-3676	467
De Forest	SAYRS, Judith A.	(608)846-9363	1087
Eagle Heights	HSIEH, Cynthia C.	(608)238-7655	567
Eau Claire	BUGHER, Kathryn M.	(715)834-8104	155
	THOMPSON, Glenn J.	(715)836-5831	1239
Green Bay	CORNELIUS, Charlene E.	(414)869-2370	246
	JOBELIUS, Nancy L.	(414)497-7508	601

CATALOGER (Cont'd)
WISCONSIN (Cont'd)

Madison	BEHNKE, Charles	(608)244-3253	75
	BLANKENBURG, Julie J.		104
	LAESSIG, Joan M.	(608)238-3705	687
	ROSENSHIELD, Jill K.	(608)233-2518	1057
	XIA, Hong	(608)263-5624	1376
	YOUNGER, Jennifer A.	(608)262-4907	1383
Menasha	DIETZ, Kathryn A.	(414)725-3803	302
Mequon	NOVOTNY, Lynn E.	(414)241-8957	911
Milwaukee	MENITOVE, Symie D.	(414)225-2601	824
	POPESCU, Constantin C.	(414)332-5909	983
	WATERSTREET, Darlene E.	(414)964-2377	1309
Oshkosh	CORBLY, James E.	(414)231-4768	245
Platteville	SCHMITT, Madelaine M.	(608)342-1667	1096
St Francis	WESTERN, Eric D.	(414)769-0110	1327
Sheboygan	VAN STRATEN, Daniel G.	(414)459-3400	1277
Shorewood	POLLARD, Margaret E.	(414)332-7451	981
Waukesha	HARTIG, Linda	(414)544-6005	508
	MILLER, Julia E.	(414)548-0448	839
Wausau	CLARK, Margaret E.	(715)845-5097	217
Whitewater	SCHARFENBERG, George E.	(414)473-4246	1090

WYOMING

Worland	HARRINGTON, Carolyn B.	(307)347-4490	504

CANADA

ALBERTA

Athabasca	DWORACZEK, Marian	(403)675-6261	330
Calgary	LANE, Barbara K.	(403)283-9998	694
	LEESMENT, Helgi	(403)251-2221	712
Edmonton	BATEMAN, Robert A.	(403)483-3432	63
	HU, Shih S.	(403)436-9716	568
	JORDAN, Peter A.	(403)469-9473	616
	KUJANSUU, Asko J.	(403)435-1563	683
	LOVENBURG, Susan L.	(403)435-0176	743
	OLSON, Hope A.	(403)433-1537	922
	STARR, Jane E.	(403)466-6004	1182
	TRAICHEL, Rudolf D.	(403)437-5718	1253
Lethbridge	JONES, Winstan M.	(403)327-0765	615
Red Deer	BOULTBEE, Paul G.	(403)346-8937	119

BRITISH COLUMBIA

North Vancouver	ELROD, J M.	(604)929-3966	346
Vancouver	LIGHTHALL, Lynne I.	(604)228-1480	727
Victoria	FIELD, Kenneth C.		375

MANITOBA

Brandon	JONES, June D.	(204)727-3303	613
Winnipeg	SMITH, John R.	(204)986-6485	1156

NEWFOUNDLAND

Mt Pearl	MORGAN, Pamela S.	(709)368-5926	864
St John's	DENNIS, Christopher J.	(709)722-0981	292

NOVA SCOTIA

Halifax	GLENISTER, Peter	(902)443-4450	441
	HSIUNG, Lai Y.	(902)424-3645	567
	HUANG, Paul T.	(902)454-5911	568
	SMITH, Arthur M.	(902)420-5538	1152

ONTARIO

Arnprior	BARKE, Judith P.	(613)623-5411	56
Brampton	CHAN, Bruce A.	(416)793-4636	199
Deep River	ALBURGER, Thomas P.		11
Don Mills	FAIRLEY, Craig R.	(416)447-5336	361
Downsview	ZVEJNIEKS, Laila R.	(416)235-4545	1391
Fort Erie	PORTEUS, Andrew C.	(416)871-3814	985
Mississauga	MASEN, Naunihal S.	(416)897-6269	780
Nepean	KAYE, Barbara J.	(613)225-9920	632
Oakville	LUCIANI, Ellie	(416)842-4484	746
Ottawa	ARONSON, Marcia L.		34
	BANFILL, Christine	(613)235-8569	54
	BLACK, Jane L.	(613)234-5006	101
	DUPRE, Monique	(819)994-6855	327
	DURANCE, Cynthia J.	(613)728-8763	328
	DUSSIAUME, Robert	(613)234-2824	329
	GOODMAN, Julia M.	(613)722-8072	449
	HOUSTON, Louise B.	(519)993-7699	563

CATALOGER (Cont'd)
ONTARIO (Cont'd)

Ottawa	KIRKWOOD, Francis T.	(613)233-7592	655
	LOW, Mary	(613)235-1158	743
	VALENTINE, Scott	(819)994-6946	1271
	VEEKEN, Mary L.	(613)523-2169	1280
Pembroke	MEHTA, Subbash C.	(613)732-2914	821
Richmond Hill	ABRAM, Persis R.	(416)884-9288	3
St Thomas	RHYNAS, Don M.	(519)631-6050	1026
Scarborough	BULAONG, Grace F.	(416)283-5732	156
Shelburne	LA CHAPELLE, Jennifer R.	(519)925-2672	686
Sudbury	SLATER, Ronald J.	(705)522-3578	1148
Toronto	DESOMOGYI, Aileen A.	(416)466-6572	295
	FRIEDLAND, Frances K.	(416)789-0741	403
	FRITZ, Richard J.	(416)923-0890	405
	LAVERTY, Corinne Y.	(416)393-7024	703
	NIXON, Audrey I.	(416)531-0830	906
	PULLEYBLANK, Mildred C.	(416)982-8848	997
	SABLJIC, John A.	(416)782-6754	1072
	SMITH, Anne C.	(416)423-9826	1152
	TIPLER, Stephen B.	(416)654-5617	1246
	WEIHS, Jean	(416)961-6027	1317
	WILLIAMSON, Nancy J.		1347
	YANCHINSKI, Roma N.	(416)767-6781	1377

QUEBEC

Ancienne-Lorette	JULIEN, Guy	(418)877-1054	619
Bellefeuille	DANIS, Rolland J.	(514)432-6116	273
Hampstead	FLUK, Louise R.	(514)488-3187	386
Hull	MAILLOUX, Jean Y.	(819)997-5365	761
	TESSIER, Richard	(819)595-0910	1233
Laval	CHAUMONT, Elise	(514)667-5100	204
	FORTIN, Jean		391
Laval-des-Rapides	VONKA, Stephanie	(514)667-1947	1288
Lennoxville	SHEERAN, Ruth J.	(819)569-9551	1125
Montreal	BERARDINUCCI, Heather R.	(514)255-2445	84
	BUTLER, Patricia	(514)283-9046	167
	CAN, Hung V.	(514)521-8201	177
	DUMOULIN, Nicole L.	(514)733-8051	325
	DUSABLON-BOTTEGA, Nicole	(514)871-6442	329
	FOWLES, Alison C.	(514)842-7680	394
	GAULIN, S D.	(514)645-9444	422
	MOHAMMED, Selima	(514)398-4780	852
	MUKHERJEE, Yolande	(514)932-6161	876
	OUELLET, Louise M.		930
	PARKER, Charles G.	(514)282-3934	941
	ROLLAND-THOMAS, Paule	(514)343-6046	1051
	STILMAN, Ruth	(514)340-8210	1194
	THACH, Phat V.	(514)727-6817	1233
	TREVICK, Selma D.	(514)487-3367	1255
	WERYHO, Jan W.	(514)392-5766	1325
Quebec	CANTIN, Gemma	(418)656-5070	179
Rouyn-Noranda	TREMBLAY, Levis	(819)762-0931	1255
St-Felicien	LAMBERT, Yvan	(418)679-5412	690
Saint-Jerome	HOULE, Louis P.	(514)438-3593	563
Sainte-Foy	PETRYK, Louise O.	(418)656-6921	965
Sherbrooke	CHASSE, Jules	(819)821-7550	203
Sillery	LALIBERTE, Madeleine A.	(418)687-9260	689

SASKATCHEWAN

Regina	BROWNE, Berks G.	(306)584-8247	148
Saskatoon	KRISHAN, Kewal	(306)966-5954	678

AUSTRALIA

Magill	BEATTIE, Kathleen M.		70
Queensland	GOODELL, John S.		448
Toowong	GOODELL, Paulette M.		448
Victoria	SMITH, Lindsay L.		1157

COSTA RICA

Alajuela	MOSS, Loretta E.		872

EGYPT

Giza	EL-MASRY, Mohammed		345

ENGLAND

Bushey	SMITH, Margit J.		1157
Cambridge	HARKINS, Diane G.		501

CATALOGER (Cont'd)

FEDERAL REPUBLIC OF CHINA
Taipei	CHOU, Nancy O.		210

FEDERAL REPUBLIC OF GERMANY
Heidelberg	SOKOLOWSKI, Denise G.		1166

HONG KONG
Jardine's Lookout	LEE, Betty W.		709
Kowloon	FU, Ting W.		407

INDIA
Hyderabad	SATYANARAYANA, Vadhri V.	(260)586-0000	1084

INDONESIA
Jakarta	ADITIRTO, Irma U.		6

ISRAEL
Birzeit	HADDAD, Aida N.		481

ITALY
Milan	PUSATERI, Liborio		998

JAMAICA
Kingston	DOUGLAS, Daphne R.		314

JAPAN
Kanagawa-ken	TETSUYA, Inoue		1233

KUWAIT
Khalidiah	HAMDY, Mohamed N.		491

NEW ZEALAND
Auckland	TWEEDALE, Dellene M.		1266

NIGERIA
Lagos	AFOLAYAN, Matthew A.	(018)001-6040	7
Ogbomoso	OKPARA, Ibiba M.		920

PHILIPPINES
Makati	MORAN, Teresita C.		862
Manila	COOK, Marjorie L.		240
Quezon City	OREJANA, Rebecca D.		925
	PICACHE, Ursula D.		970

SAUDI ARABIA
Jeddah	KHAN, Mohammed A.		646
Riyadh	BROWN, Biraj L.		142
	BUTT, Abdul W.		167
	MARTIN, Nannette		777

SOUTH AFRICA
Somerset West	LUSK, Betty M.		749

SOUTH KOREA
Seoul	KIM, Soon C.		649

TRINIDAD
Saint Joseph	MCCONNIE, Mary		798

UGANDA
Mukono	MUKUNGU, Frederick N.		876

ZAMBIA
Chilanga	LUMANDE, Edward		748

COLLECTION DEVELOPMENT/EVALUATION CONSULTANT

ALABAMA
Auburn	ADAMS, Judith A.	(205)826-4500	5
	PEDERSOLI, Heleni M.	(207)821-7168	954
	ZLATOS, Christy L.	(205)826-3429	1390
Birmingham	BATTISTELLA, Maureen S.	(205)939-0581	65
	MCGARITY, Marysue	(205)879-6128	805
	OLIVE, J F.	(205)967-8481	921
	PENNINGTON, Walter W.	(205)226-4744	957
	ROGERS, Nancy H.	(205)991-6600	1050
	SIMS, Joyce W.	(205)939-7830	1142

COLLECTION DEVELOPMENT/EVALUATION CONSULTANT (Cont'd)

ALABAMA (Cont'd)
Daphne	ROBINSON, Gayle N.	(205)626-2345	1044
Huntsville	KENDRICK, Aubrey W.	(205)837-7597	640
Irondale	FEENKER, Cherie D.	(205)956-4544	368
Mobile	BUSH, Nancy W.	(205)343-8121	165
	JEFFERY, Phyllis D.	(205)434-7084	596
	PARSLEY, Brantley H.	(205)675-5990	944
Montevallo	WILLIAMS, Pauline C.	(205)665-4329	1346
Montgomery	FELDER, Jimmie R.	(205)265-2012	369
	FRANKS, Janice	(205)271-6277	398
	GREGORY, Vicki L.	(205)277-1759	466
	MCCRANK, Lawrence J.	(205)244-9202	800
	MEDINA, Sue O.	(205)269-2700	820
Prichard	WILLIAMS, Gwendolyn	(205)452-4395	1343
Tuscaloosa	OSBURN, Charles B.	(205)348-7561	927
	PRUITT, Paul M.	(205)348-1107	996

ALASKA
Anchorage	INNES-TAYLOR, Catherine E.	(907)786-1875	583
	SOKOLOV, Barbara J.	(907)346-2480	1165
Delta Junction	JENKS, Arlene I.	(907)895-4253	597
Fairbanks	STEPHENS, Dennis J.	(907)479-5826	1187
Juneau	NICOLSON, Mary C.	(907)789-4568	903
	SCHORR, Alan E.	(907)586-6014	1099
Sitka	MCCLAIN, Harriet V.	(907)747-8160	795

ARIZONA
Phoenix	ALABASTER, Carol	(602)262-7360	9
	BERK, Nancy G.	(602)971-9264	87
	GOEBEL, Heather L.	(602)994-2471	443
	GORMAN, Judith F.	(602)279-9741	452
	NIXON, Arless B.	(602)246-9196	906
Sells	CULL, Roberta	(602)383-2601	263
Tempe	ALCORN, Marianne S.	(602)965-4868	11
	LESHY, Dede	(602)946-8090	718
	OETTING, Edward C.	(602)345-7636	917
	SCHON, Isabel	(602)965-2996	1098
	STEWART, Douglas J.	(602)897-7191	1192
	WU, Ai H.	(602)965-3354	1373
Tucson	FAHY, Terry W.	(602)621-6446	361
	FRANK, Donald G.	(602)742-9688	396
	HENDERSON, Joyce C.	(602)621-1202	526
	HIEB, Louis A.	(602)621-6077	537
	HOLSINGER, Katherine	(602)621-3282	554
	JOHNSON, Robert K.	(602)323-0418	608
	LAIRD, W D.	(602)621-2101	688
	MAKUCH, Andrew L.	(602)622-8572	762
	MAUTNER, Robert W.	(602)621-6386	787
	MCCRACKEN, John R.	(602)327-4056	799
	MILLER, Edward P.		837
	MINTON, James O.	(602)792-9450	846
	NICHOLS, Margaret M.		901
	SMITH, Dorman H.	(602)296-3760	1154
	SORENSEN, Lee R.	(602)621-4868	1168
	WOLFSON, Catherine L.	(602)884-8305	1361
Yuma	STUART, Gerard W.	(602)783-6742	1204

ARKANSAS
Arkadelphia	WOODS, L B.	(501)246-5511	1367
Conway	GREEN, Douglas A.	(501)327-5611	461
	HARDIN, Willie	(501)450-3129	500
Fayetteville	EARNEST, Jeffrey D.	(501)521-8388	332
	HARRISON, John A.	(501)443-4403	506
Fort Smith	PIERSON, Botty	(501)785-7135	972
Little Rock	BASKIN, Jeffrey L.	(501)661-5428	63
Magnolia	BRADLEY, Florene J.	(501)234-1991	125
Prescott	WATSON, Merlyn		1310

CALIFORNIA
Agoura	THOMAS, Yvonne		1238
Arcadia	PERRY, Edward C.		960
Bakersfield	WINTER, Eugenia B.	(805)833-3175	1356
Bellflower	PESTUN, Aloysius J.	(213)920-1734	961
Belmont	CROWE, Linda D.	(415)349-5538	261
	RAMSEY, Robert D.	(415)593-1601	1006
Berkeley	BASART, Ann P.	(415)848-7805	62
	FRANKEL, Kate M.	(415)525-1533	397
	KOBZINA, Norma G.	(415)643-6475	666
	ORTOPAN, Leroy D.	(415)642-3810	927

COLLECTION DEVELOPMENT/EVALUATION CONSULTANT (Cont'd)
CALIFORNIA (Cont'd)

Berkeley
RAFAEL, Ruth K. . . . . (415)849-2710 1003
WHEELER, Helen R. . . . . . . (415)549-2970 1329
WOODBURY, Marda . . . . . (415)654-4810 1366
Beverly Hills CHAMMOU, Eliezer . . . . (213)273-1395 198
RUNYON, Judith A. . . . . . . (213)859-5102 1067
Brea PERKINS, Steven C. . . . . . . (714)671-0778 959
Campbell HAZEKAMP, Phyllis W. . . . . (408)379-1611 517
Cardiff By The Sea SCHALIT, Michael . . . . . (619)944-3913 1089
Chatsworth TANIS, Norman E. . . . . . . (818)886-1318 1222
Chico LO, Henrietta W. . . . . . . (916)895-6406 735
POWER, Colleen J. . . . . . . (916)895-4058 989
Claremont ALLEN, Susan M. 16
WRIGLEY, Elizabeth S. . . . . . (714)624-6305 1373
Concord PUGH, Mary J. . . . . . . (415)685-2133 997
Corona del Mar DOSER, Virginia A. . . . . . (714)760-0148 313
Coronado ESQUEVIN, Christian R. . . . . (619)437-1135 354
Costa Mesa POARCH, Margaret E. . . . . . (714)662-1867 979
Covina AROS, Andrew A. . . . . . . (818)966-4709 34
Culver City FITZGERALD, Diana S. . . . . . (231)839-5982 382
Cupertino JAJKO, Edward A. . . . . . (408)446-1306 592
Davis COLLINS, William J. . . . . . (916)758-4989 233
ELLIOTT, C D. . . . . . . (916)752-2110 343
LEWIS, Alfred J. . . . . . . (916)752-3325 722
LUST, Vernon G. . . . . . . (916)756-1672 750
Eagle Rock CRAWFORD, Marilyn L. . . . . . (213)259-8938 257
East Palo Alto DERKSEN, Charlotte R. . . . . (415)323-5386 294
El Cerrito PRESSNALL, Patricia E. . . . . (415)525-5186 991
El Segundo FELLER, Amy I. . . . . . . (213)333-5222 370
Encino GHAZARIAN, Salpi H. . . . . . (818)789-5041 430
Fresno WARD, Penny T. . . . . . (209)268-2545 1304
Fullerton BRIL, Patricia L. . . . . . (714)773-3852 136
THOMPSON, James A. . . . . . (714)738-1000 1240
Garden Grove SIMPSON, Evelyn L. . . . . . (714)534-5033 1141
Glen Ellen SCARBOROUGH, Katharine
T. . . . . . . (707)996-7993 1087
Glendale BURNS, Nancy R. . . . . . (818)244-1994 162
Goleta MUSICK, Nancy W. . . . . . (805)964-8484 883
Guerneville BATES, Henry E. . . . . . (707)869-9383 64
Hacienda Hts SZETO, Dorcas C. . . . . . (818)336-1200 1218
Hillsborough ABILOCK, Debbie . . . . . (415)348-2272 2
Huntington Beach HAYDEN, Ronald L. . . . . . (714)960-8836 515
Irvine BLADEN, Marguerite . . . . . (714)551-6489 102
GELFAND, Julia M. . . . . . (714)856-4971 426
HORN, Judy K. 559
YOUNG, Eleanor C. . . . . . (714)552-5803 1381
La
Canada-Flintridge DUNKLEE, Joanna E. . . . . . (818)790-3518 326
La Jolla BOWLES, Garrett H. . . . . . (619)534-2759 121
CASTETTER, Karla M. . . . . . (619)459-5369 194
FISHER, Edith M. . . . . . (619)534-1258 380
MCGILVERY, Laurence . . . . . (619)454-4443 806
TOMMEY, Richard J. . . . . . (619)454-4873 1250
La Mirada ANJOU-DURAZZO, Martel T. . . (213)944-5981 28
Lafayette SVIHRA, S J. . . . . . (415)933-9549 1212
Lake View Terrace NAVARRO, Frank A. 889
Long Beach AYALA, John L. . . . . . (213)599-8028 42
Los Angeles AHLSTROM, Romaine . . . . . (213)254-6448 8
CONNOR, Billie M. . . . . . (213)660-6399 237
EVANS, G E. . . . . . (213)642-4593 357
FRY, Stephen M. . . . . . (213)825-4882 407
GELMAN-KMEC, Marsha . . . . (213)484-5530 426
GILMAN, Lelde B. . . . . . (213)825-6498 436
JAIN, Celeste C. . . . . . (213)665-7510 591
KHATTAB, Hosneya M. . . . . . (213)733-1196 646
KIEFFER, Jay 647
KUNSELMAN, Joan D. . . . . . (213)825-1204 684
MANTHEY, Teresa M. . . . . . (213)224-7234 767
MORSE, David H. . . . . . (213)224-7413 869
NEMCHEK, Lee R. . . . . . (213)621-9484 895
PASCAL, Barbara R. . . . . . (213)934-2205 945
POPOVITCH-KREKIC, Ruzica (213)476-2237 984
STERLIN, Annette S. . . . . . (213)645-2406 1189
TERZIAN, Shohig S. . . . . . (213)478-5193 1232
TOMPKINS, Philip . . . . . (213)743-2543 1250
WAGNER, Sharon L. . . . . . (213)931-4048 1292
WALTERS, Mary D. . . . . . (213)224-2215 1301
WATERS, Marie B. . . . . . (213)825-1693 1308

COLLECTION DEVELOPMENT/EVALUATION CONSULTANT (Cont'd)
CALIFORNIA (Cont'd)

Los Angeles
WILKINSON, David W. . . . . . (213)224-2251 1340
ZEIDBERG, David S. . . . . . (213)825-4879 1387
Los Gatos SZABO, Carolyn J. . . . . . (408)353-2502 1218
Menlo Park FRANK, Peter R. . . . . . (415)329-1173 397
NEWMAN, Mark J. . . . . . (415)326-2114 899
TRUJILLO, Roberto G. . . . . . (415)329-0227 1259
Mill Valley ASHLEY, Elizabeth . . . . . (415)388-8080 36
WHITE, Cecil R. . . . . . (415)388-8080 1330
Montebello GALLEGO, Bert H. . . . . . (213)721-5102 414
Mountain View POST, Linda C. . . . . . (415)968-3045 986
SLOCUM, Hannah R. . . . . . (415)969-8356 1150
Northridge DURAN, Karin J. . . . . . (818)885-2501 328
PERKINS, David L. . . . . . (818)885-2256 959
Novato HIRABAYASHI, Joanne . . . . . (415)897-4245 543
Oakland BYRNE, Elizabeth D. . . . . . (415)658-6996 169
DANTON, J P. . . . . . (415)653-4802 274
GLYNN, Jeannette E. . . . . . (415)654-3543 442
MORGAN, Linda M. . . . . . (415)536-3331 864
MULL, Richard G. . . . . . (415)841-2590 876
RUBIN, Rhea J. . . . . . (415)339-1274 1064
WONG, Patricia M. . . . . . (415)834-2742 1363
Orange WILSON, Wayne V. . . . . . (714)997-6912 1353
Oroville ALLENSWORTH, James H. . . . (916)538-7197 16
Palo Alto CRABTREE, Sandra A. . . . . . (415)858-4767 254
HAMILTON, David M. . . . . . (415)853-0197 491
KAHN, Paul J. . . . . . (415)327-3135 622
ROSS, Alexander D. . . . . . (415)494-7302 1057
Pasadena GOODSTEIN, Judith R. . . . . . (818)356-6433 450
HOFFBERG, Judith A. . . . . . (818)797-0514 547
ZEIND, Samir M. . . . . . (818)440-5161 1387
Pebble Beach ANDRUS, Eloise A. . . . . . (408)624-1257 27
Pleasant Hill SIEGEL, Ernest . . . . . (415)944-3423 1136
Porterville NAUMER, Janet N. . . . . . (209)539-3288 889
Rancho
Cacamonga CONNELL, William S. . . . . . (714)989-0506 237
Redondo Beach CLIFFORD, Susan G. . . . . . (213)378-3824 222
Richmond BENELISHA, Eleanor . . . . . (415)223-6417 80
Riverside VIERICH, Richard W. . . . . . (714)787-3511 1284
WEBB, Gayle E. . . . . . (714)787-2460 1313
Rolling Hills Estate SAVAGE, Gretchen S. . . . . . (213)377-5032 1085
Sacramento ANDERSEN, Thomas K. . . . . . (916)324-4863 21
JACKSON, Gloria D. . . . . . (916)427-1956 587
KONG, Leslie D. . . . . . (916)278-5664 670
MALMGREN, Terri L. . . . . . (916)453-3529 763
SEHR, Dena P. . . . . . (916)453-3529 1112
Salinas COLLINS, Judith A. 232
SERTIC, Kenneth J. . . . . . (408)443-6186 1116
San Bernardino JOHNSON, Paul A. . . . . . (714)883-3979 608
WEBB, Duncan C. . . . . . (714)387-4959 1313
San Clemente KOPAN, Ellen K. . . . . . (714)498-4309 671
San Diego BUSCH, Barbara . . . . . (619)224-8412 165
DERSHEM, Larry D. . . . . . (619)236-2409 294
FORMAN, Jack . . . . . (619)546-9250 390
PEASE, William J. . . . . . (619)265-4448 953
ROSS, Mary A. . . . . . (619)566-4733 1058
SOETE, George J. . . . . . (619)453-3538 1165
VEGA, Carolyn L. 1281
VOIGT, Melvin J. 1287
WORTHINGTON, A P. . . . . . (619)541-3242 1369
San Francisco BONFIELD, Lynn A. . . . . . (415)826-2109 114
DURSO, Angeline M. . . . . . (415)750-6072 329
ERVITI, Debra L. . . . . . (415)863-8800 353
GIBSON, Harold R. 432
GITLER, Robert L. . . . . . (415)221-9216 438
GUNDERSON, Jeffery R. . . . . . (415)929-1472 477
HAIKALIS, Peter D. . . . . . (415)338-2188 484
HENKE, Dan . . . . . (415)565-4758 528
KAUN, Thomas T. . . . . . (415)821-9303 631
KIRSHENBAUM, Sandra D. . . . (415)776-1530 655
KOFF, Jacob . . . . . (415)781-2665 668
LUTTRELL, Jordan D. . . . . . (415)346-1839 750
MANN, Thomas . . . . . (415)951-0100 766
MORRIS, Effie L. . . . . . (415)931-2733 866
PABST, Kahleen T. . . . . . (415)421-1750 933
PRESBY, Richard A. . . . . . (415)776-2211 990
SHAPIRO, Leonard P. . . . . . (415)469-5893 1121
WAKEFORD, Paul J. . . . . . (415)476-2533 1293

COLLECTION DEVELOPMENT/EVALUATION CONSULTANT (Cont'd)
CALIFORNIA (Cont'd)

San Francisco			
	WILSON, Jacqueline B.	(415)476-2534	1351
San Jose	EARHART, Marilyn N.	(408)554-4986	332
	EMMICK, Nancy J.	(408)277-3904	348
	LEONARD, Barbara G.	(408)277-3902	716
	MULLEN, Cecilia P.	(408)265-8799	877
	RODICH, Lorraine E.	(408)277-9788	1047
	ROSEN, Elizabeth M.	(408)277-2270	1055
San Leandro	WENDROFF, Catriona	(415)569-3491	1323
San Luis Obispo	FOURIE, Denise K.	(805)544-5427	393
San Marcos	CATER, Judy J.	(619)744-1150	194
Santa Ana	AUSTIN, Stephen	(714)540-9870	40
Santa Barbara	ANDERSON, Carol L.	(805)685-7585	22
	RUDD, Janet K.	(805)682-9560	1065
	SILVER, Martin A.	(805)687-4198	1138
	TAI, Henry H.	(805)961-2365	1220
Santa Clara	CHESSMAN, Rebecca L.	(408)244-2775	207
Santa Cruz	COOPER, Susan C.	(408)426-2841	243
	PAQUETTE, Judith	(408)429-2970	939
Santa Monica	HALL, Anthony	(213)827-1707	487
Santa Paula	CHRISTOPHER, Paul	(805)525-8092	212
Santa Rosa	LEE, Mildred C.	(707)538-3484	711
	PETTAS, William A.	(707)527-4392	965
Sebastopol	CANT, Elaine N.	(707)823-3214	179
Sherman Oaks	LEWIS, Cookie A.	(818)788-5280	722
	MILLER, Margaret S.	(818)783-5264	840
Stockton	CLARKE, Tobin D.	(209)477-5952	219
	LEONHARDT, Thomas W.	(209)946-2434	717
Sunland	CLARK, Patricia A.	(818)353-6820	217
Sunnyvale	TYSON, Betty B.	(408)742-5937	1267
Thousand Oaks	SULLIVAN, Kathleen A.	(805)497-6282	1207
Torrance	MOORE, Richard K.	(213)533-4386	861
Vacaville	ELDREDGE, Mary		342
Van Nuys	BALABAN, Robin M.	(818)781-6952	50
	DAVIS, L C.	(818)994-3044	280
Venice	EDELSTEIN, J M.	(213)827-8984	335
Walnut Creek	SMITH, Susan A.	(415)944-1603	1161
West Hollywood	BUTKIS, John F.	(213)000-0000	166
Westminster	JADWIN, Rochelle J.	(714)894-2126	591
Whittier	ASAWA, Edward E.	(213)698-4461	35
Woodland	WEBBER, Steven L.	(916)661-1242	1313

COLORADO

Alamosa	SHELDON, L S.	(303)589-6592	1126
Aurora	HARRIS, Michael A.	(303)694-4200	505
	MURRAY, William A.	(303)364-8208	882
Boulder	SANI, Martha J.	(303)492-8367	1081
	VOLC, Judith G.	(303)442-3578	1287
	WYNNE, Allen	(303)499-5616	1375
Colorado Springs	BARRETT, Donald J.	(303)598-3163	59
	SITTER, Clara M.	(303)570-4524	1144
Denver	BRITAIN, Karla K.	(303)733-0816	137
	COCO, Al	(303)871-6200	226
	DULAN, Peter A.	(303)692-9261	324
	FOLEY, Georgiana	(303)571-2172	387
	GEHRES, Eleanor M.	(303)571-2012	425
	GIGNAC, Solange G.	(303)575-3751	433
	MOULTON, Suzanne L.	(303)871-6427	873
	NORBIE, Dorothy E.	(303)691-5400	908
	SCHAFER, Jay G.	(303)556-8370	1089
Englewood	BRUNTON, David W.	(303)771-3197	151
Fort Collins	ANDERSON, Lemoyne W.	(303)484-7319	24
	LIRA, Judith A.	(303)226-5626	732
	NEWMAN, John	(303)491-1844	899
	SCHMIDT, Fred C.	(303)491-1881	1095
Golden	LARSGAARD, Mary L.	(303)279-8243	698
	PHINNEY, Hartley K.	(303)273-3690	969
Grand Junction	HENDRICKSON, Charles R.	(303)248-1862	527
	RICHMOND, Elizabeth B.	(303)241-4358	1030
Greeley	SCHULZE, Suzanne S.		1102
Littleton	LOERTSCHER, David V.	(303)770-1220	737
Montrose	CAMPBELL, John D.	(303)249-1078	176
Pueblo	JONES, Donna R.	(303)542-2156	612
Wellington	JOHNSON, K S.	(303)491-1876	606

COLLECTION DEVELOPMENT/EVALUATION CONSULTANT (Cont'd)
CONNECTICUT

Ashford	MCCAUGHTRY, Dorothy H.	(203)429-7637	795
Bethany	ASH, Lee M.	(203)393-2723	35
Branford	ADAMO, Clare	(203)488-1474	4
Bridgeport	MULAWKA, Chet	(203)576-7402	876
Danbury	BURKAT, Leonard	(203)743-2137	160
	MARIANI, Carolyn A.	(203)794-6389	770
Fairfield	WARGO, Peggy M.	(203)259-8267	1305
Greenwich	LUSHINGTON, Nolan	(203)655-3632	749
Groton	DAIGNEAULT, Audrey I.	(203)446-8431	270
Guilford	GAFFNEY, Maureen	(203)453-6533	412
Hamden	KANEKO, Hideo	(203)281-3586	625
	NEWHALL, Ann C.	(203)288-8180	898
	SAMUEL, Harold E.	(203)432-0495	1079
	SMITH, Nolan E.	(203)776-3558	1159
	STRAKA, Kathy M.	(203)771-8383	1199
Hartford	WEINSTEIN, Daniel L.	(203)275-2699	1318
	WILKIE, Everett C.	(203)236-5621	1340
Kent	CUSTER, Deborah P.	(203)927-3098	267
Middletown	ASBELL, Mildred S.	(203)344-2304	35
New Britain	WARZALA, Martin L.		1307
New Canaan	LOKETS BEISCHROT, Dina		738
New Fairfield	DYKMAN, Elaine K.	(203)746-0765	331
New Haven	ICHINOSE, Mitsuko	(203)432-1794	581
	KELLER, Michael A.	(203)389-2212	635
	PETERSON, Stephen L.	(203)432-5292	964
	REESE, William S.	(203)789-8081	1016
	ROBERTS, Susanne F.	(203)432-1762	1041
	SIGGINS, Jack A.	(203)776-3808	1137
	WALTER, Kenneth G.	(203)397-4526	1300
New London	VANDERLYKE, Barbara A.	(203)442-2889	1274
Old Lyme	DEAKYNE, William J.	(203)434-9294	283
Ridgefield	FARADAY, Joanna	(203)431-0062	363
Southport	WITTEN, Laurence	(203)255-3474	1358
Stamford	DIMATTIA, Susan S.	(203)322-9055	304
	GOLOMB, Katherine A.	(203)964-1000	447
	KEMP, Thomas J.	(203)323-2826	639
	SILVERMAN, Susanne		1139
Storrs	BOGNAR, Dorothy M.		111
	SCURA, Georgia A.	(203)486-2218	1109
Torrington	BENAMATI, Dennis C.	(203)489-2990	79
Washington	LEAB, Katharine K.	(203)868-7408	706
West Hartford	BRADBERRY, Richard P.	(203)241-4704	125
Westport	REISMAN, Sydelle S.	(203)227-8710	1021
	SCHWARZ, Shirlee	(203)226-6606	1105
Woodbridge	MILLER, Irene K.	(203)393-0458	838

DELAWARE

Bear	MANUEL, Larry L.	(302)834-5748	767
Lewes	HALL, Alice W.	(302)645-4293	486
New Castle	IRWIN, Ruth A.	(302)328-8560	584
Newark	THORNTON, Alice J.	(302)454-2239	1242

DISTRICT OF COLUMBIA

Washington	ACKERMAN, F C.	(202)398-1842	3
	ANDERSON, John M.	(202)287-8723	23
	BATTLE, Thomas C.	(202)636-7241	65
	BELLARDO, Trudi	(202)363-9614	78
	BERGQUIST, Christine F.		87
	BOHANAN, Robert D.	(202)523-3214	111
	BOYLE, James E.	(202)234-8701	123
	BRIDGE, Peter H.	(202)287-5243	135
	CARTER, Yvonne B.	(202)357-6315	190
	CHIN, Cecilia H.	(202)543-3824	208
	COOPER, David J.	(202)544-3653	242
	COUGHLAN, Margaret N.		250
	DAWSON, Barbara J.	(202)785-3330	282
	DOUMATO, Lamia		314
	DURAKO, Frances G.	(202)785-9700	328
	FARINA, Robert A.	(202)287-5298	363
	FLEMING, Thomas B.	(202)429-6429	384
	FREEMAN, Carla		400
	HAITH, Dorothy M.	(202)484-4941	484
	HARRIS, Marie	(202)767-8643	505
	HEAD, Anita K.	(202)994-7336	518
	KING, Kamla J.	(202)452-4470	651
	KNAUFF, Elisabeth S.		663
	KOSTINKO, Gail A.	(202)483-4118	673
	KUPERMAN, Agota M.		684

COLLECTION DEVELOPMENT/EVALUATION CONSULTANT (Cont'd)
DISTRICT OF COLUMBIA (Cont'd)
Washington

	LEFFALL, Dolores C.	(202)723-7645	712
	LEICH, Harold M.	(202)328-3917	713
	LITTLEJOHN, Grace M.	(202)291-6920	734
	LUSKEY, Judith	(202)357-4654	749
	MARTIN, Kathleen S.	(202)789-7100	777
	MCKEAN, Joan M.	(301)443-8358	810
	MISSAR, Charles D.	(202)363-2751	847
	MUSSEHL, Allan A.	(202)488-8162	883
	NOWAK, Geraldine D.	(202)475-9419	911
	OSTROW, Stephen E.	(202)287-5836	929
	PILGRIM, Auriel J.	(202)484-5373	973
	PORTER, Suzanne	(203)994-8906	985
	PRUETT, Barbara J.	(202)362-1345	996
	RADER, Ronald A.	(639)890-0000	1002
	ROONEY, Eugene M.		1053
	ROSENBERG, Jane A.	(202)786-0358	1056
	SERVERINO, Roberto	(202)625-4574	1116
	SHEELER, Harva L.	(202)879-3954	1125
	SMITH, Kathleen S.		1156
	STEBELMAN, Scott D.	(202)994-6049	1183
	STORM, Jill	(202)775-6174	1198
	SULLIVAN, Robert C.	(202)287-5330	1208
	SWEENEY, June D.	(202)427-1392	1215
	THOMPSON, Elizabeth M.	(202)333-2108	1239
	TOCH, Terryann	(202)393-6820	1248
	TRIPP-MELBY, Pamela	(202)676-9418	1257
	TSUNEISHI, Warren M.	(202)287-5543	1260
	TURTELL, Neal T.	(202)842-6506	1265
	VASLEF, Irene	(202)342-3240	1279
	VON PFEIL, Helena P.		1288
	YASUMATSU, Janet R.		1378

FLORIDA
Avon Park	APPELQUIST, Donald L.	(813)453-6661	30
Captiva	WALTON, Terence M.	(813)454-0410	1302
Clearwater	BROMBERG, Johanna	(813)535-2595	139
	DALLMAN, Glenn R.	(813)791-2616	270
	MIELKE, Linda	(813)462-6916	833
Coral Gables	WAXMAN, Jack	(305)284-2429	1311
Daytona Beach	BRANDON, Alfred N.	(904)677-5098	128
	CREERON, Carolyn E.	(909)255-1021	257
De Land	JOHNSON, Betty D.	(904)734-7630	602
Dunedin	FIORE, Carole D.	(813)733-2595	379
Fort Lauderdale	GOZDZ, Wanda E.	(305)741-3410	455
	HATFIELD, Frances S.	(305)463-5928	511
Fort Myers	HUGHES, Joyce M.	(813)489-9464	572
	PEGLER, Ross J.	(813)267-2995	954
Gainesville	BROWN, Pia T.	(904)375-6302	147
	GOGGIN, Margaret K.	(904)378-8144	444
	MALANCHUK, Peter P.	(904)392-0364	762
	TEAGUE, Edward H.	(904)392-0222	1229
	WILLETT, Charles	(904)378-1661	1341
Howey in the Hills	COHN, William L.	(904)324-2701	229
Jacksonville	BONFILI, Barbara J.	(904)725-5822	114
	COHEN, Kathleen F.	(904)646-2616	228
	GUNN, Thomas H.	(904)744-3950	477
	SMITH, Margaret N.	(904)630-1994	1157
Jensen Beach	HENNINGS, Leroy	(305)334-6134	528
Jupiter	MOJO, Anne Z.	(305)746-6353	852
Largo	CESANEK, Sylvia B.	(813)585-1403	196
Lauderhill	HOLLMANN, Pauline V.	(305)393-3774	552
Miami	BOLDRICK, Samuel J.	(305)443-2216	112
	CHAVES, Francisco M.	(305)385-2301	204
	DANIELS, Westwell R.	(305)235-9484	273
	ROVIROSA, Dolores F.		1062
	SANCHEZ, Sara M.	(305)854-7752	1079
	SEGOR, Phyllis L.	(305)940-6014	1112
	SEILER, Susan L.	(305)279-0545	1112
	SINTZ, Edward F.	(305)375-5026	1144
	STEINBERG, Celia L.	(305)661-4611	1185
Miami Beach	GROVER, Wilma S.	(305)868-5000	474
	LESNIAK, Rose	(305)673-6309	718
	MIRANDA, Salvador	(305)532-6834	847
North Lauderdale	BRESLAUER, Lester M.	(305)721-5181	133
Oakland Park	WILLIAMS, Alexander	(305)565-2990	1341
Orlando	CUBBERLEY, Carol W.	(305)275-2521	263
Panama City	DANNECKER, Joyce H.	(904)785-3457	274

COLLECTION DEVELOPMENT/EVALUATION CONSULTANT (Cont'd)
FLORIDA (Cont'd)
Pensacola	JOHNSON, Theresa P.	(904)474-2168	609
	TERNAK, Armand T.	(904)479-7835	1232
Safety Harbor	DE MEO, Mary A.	(813)725-4120	291
St Petersburg	CORNWELL, Douglas W.	(813)541-7206	247
	GOSS, Theresa C.	(813)341-4732	453
Sanibel	KLASING, Jane P.	(813)472-8391	657
Sarasota	DANIEL, Marianne M.	(813)351-6583	272
	MOON, Eric	(813)355-1795	857
Tallahassee	DE PEW, John N.	(904)644-5775	293
	HART, Thomas L.	(904)385-7550	507
	MILLER, Betty D.	(904)335-4405	836
	PRATT, Darnell D.	(904)487-2651	990
Tampa	CRAIG, James P.	(813)238-5514	254
	GRIMES, Maxyne M.	(813)974-2157	470
	HAMRELL, Larry G.	(813)971-4143	494
	LIANG, Diana F.	(813)988-2406	725
Wauchula	MAPP, Erwin E.	(813)773-9207	768
West Palm Beach	PRITCHARD, Teresa N.	(305)684-7349	994

GEORGIA
Acworth	STAHL, D G.	(404)924-8505	1178
Americus	MCLAUGHLIN, Laverne L.	(912)924-9426	813
Appling	WARNER, Wayne G.	(404)868-7412	1305
Athens	HAAR, John M.	(404)549-7625	480
	KAHAN, Gerald	(404)548-2514	621
	SUTHERLAND, Johnnie D.	(404)542-0690	1211
Atlanta	COOPER, Glenn	(404)676-2096	243
	CRAFT, Guy C.	(404)522-8980	254
	DAVIS, Joy V.	(404)634-3511	279
	DEES, Anthony R.	(404)355-0551	287
	KLOPPER, Susan M.	(404)658-1776	662
	LAWSON, Venable A.	(404)377-1142	705
	LEE, Lauren K.	(404)588-1390	710
	MENEELY, William E.	(404)658-3800	824
	MISRA, Jayasri T.	(404)524-5320	847
	ROSS, Theodosia B.	(404)696-2355	1059
	RUSSELL, Ralph E.	(404)658-2172	1069
	STOWELL, Donald C.	(404)231-4414	1199
	STROUGAL, Patricia G.	(404)355-5497	1203
	THAXTON, Lyn	(404)292-6767	1234
	TROUTMAN, Joseph E.	(404)522-8980	1258
Augusta	SCHLATTER, M W.	(404)721-2992	1093
Bainbridge	MARSHALL, Ruth T.	(912)246-3887	775
Cartersville	HOWINGTON, Lee R.	(404)382-4203	566
Columbus	CLEMENTS, Betty H.	(404)327-3399	221
Decatur	ALLEN, William R.	(404)284-2981	16
	BUDLONG, Thomas F.	(404)289-0583	155
	HATCHER, Nolan C.	(404)378-8282	511
Experiment	LEDFORD, Carole L.	(404)228-7238	708
Griffin	WILKINSON, Evalyn S.	(404)227-8532	1340
Hartwell	BISSO, Arthur J.	(404)376-4655	100
Kennesaw	GRIFFIN, Martha R.	(404)422-9921	468
La Grange	LEWIS, Frank R.	(404)882-2911	723
Macon	CHANIN, Leah F.	(912)744-2665	201
Richmond Hill	GLISSON, Patricia A.	(912)727-2592	441
Stone Mountain	O'NEILL, Patricia E.	(404)292-6693	924
Vidalia	HARTZ, Frederic R.	(912)537-0195	509

HAWAII
Aiea	TIMBERLAKE, Cynthia A.	(808)488-4507	1245
Honolulu	CAMPBELL, R A.	(808)955-8822	177
	DILUCIA, Samuel J.	(808)955-1500	303
	SHELDEN, Patricia R.	(808)538-6430	1125
	URAGO, Gail M.	(808)949-6496	1269
	VAN NIEL, Eloise S.	(808)548-6283	1276

IDAHO
Boise	TAYLOR, Adrien P.	(208)385-1621	1225
Meridian	DENNY, Mary C.	(208)888-2924	293
Moscow	HANSON, Donna M.	(208)885-6235	498
Nampa	LANCASTER, Edith E.	(208)466-1011	691
	SIMMONS, Randall C.	(208)467-8609	1140

COLLECTION DEVELOPMENT/EVALUATION CONSULTANT (Cont'd)
ILLINOIS

City	Name	Phone	Page
Addison	WRIGHT, Deborah L.	(312)628-3338	1371
Cahokia	BEAN, Bobby G.	(618)875-6915	69
Carbondale	DALE, Doris C.	(618)536-2441	270
	HARWOOD, Judith A.	(618)453-2818	510
	MCCOY, Ralph E.	(618)457-8707	799
Carterville	UBEL, James A.	(618)985-3711	1267
Champaign	MCCLELLAN, William M.	(217)352-1893	796
	PENKA, Carol B.	(217)351-6026	956
Charleston	KAPLAN, Sylvia Y.	(217)345-4228	626
Chicago	ALTHAGE, Celia J.		18
	BROWN, Doris R.	(312)341-8066	143
	CADY, Richard H.	(312)944-0856	170
	CHANG, Sookang H.	(312)995-2240	201
	CLAPP, David F.	(312)465-0324	215
	COLLINS, Janet	(312)642-2136	232
	DI MAURO, Paul	(312)871-8235	304
	FEINER, Arlene M.	(312)348-8382	369
	FRANKLIN, Annette E.	(312)996-3447	397
	GENESEN, Judith L.		427
	GERDES, Neil W.	(312)753-3196	428
	GOMEZ, Martin J.		447
	HERNANDEZ, Hector R.	(312)523-2453	531
	HOLLI, Melvin G.	(312)996-3141	552
	HOLZENBERG, Eric J.	(312)248-3494	555
	JOHNSON, Judith M.	(312)996-8988	606
	KAYAIAN, Mary S.	(312)245-2810	632
	KIM, Chung S.	(312)588-3901	648
	KINNAIRD, Cheryl D.	(312)508-5465	653
	KOWITZ, Aletha A.	(312)440-2642	674
	LEWIS, Sherman L.		724
	LIMAYE, Asha A.	(312)996-8988	727
	MALINOWSKY, H R.	(312)329-1549	763
	MANCUYAS, Natividad D.	(312)995-2284	764
	MARTIN, Bennie E.	(312)443-5423	775
	MATTENSON, Murray M.	(312)262-8282	785
	MENZIES, Pamela C.	(312)924-8301	825
	MITZIGA, Walter J.	(312)375-4646	850
	MOCH, Mary I.	(312)539-2328	851
	MOORE, John R.	(312)763-7811	860
	MOULTON, James C.	(312)525-7185	873
	OTT, Bill	(312)944-6780	930
	PALMER, Raymond A.	(312)266-2456	936
	PETERSON, Randall T.	(312)427-2737	964
	POSNER, Frances A.	(312)334-7484	985
	RICHMOND, Diane A.	(312)269-2864	1030
	ROMAN, Susan	(312)944-6780	1052
	SCHUSTER, Adeline	(312)939-4975	1103
	SCOTT, Alice H.	(312)493-2451	1106
	SIARNY, William D.	(312)467-5520	1134
	STEELE, Leah J.	(312)631-2701	1184
	STINCHCOMB, Maxine K.	(312)348-2866	1194
	STRAIT, Constance J.		1199
	VISKOCHIL, Larry A.	(312)935-1071	1285
	WELLS, James M.	(312)782-1172	1322
	WIBERLEY, Stephen E.	(312)996-2730	1335
	WILLIAMSON, Linda E.	(312)996-2738	1347
Cicero	MALLER, Mark P.	(312)652-8084	763
Crystal Lake	MILLER, Randy S.	(815)455-4660	841
Darien	BOWDEN, Philip L.	(312)887-1620	120
De Kalb	DUTTON, Lee S.	(815)753-1808	329
	GRAHAM, Robert W.	(815)753-1779	456
	HORST, Stanley E.	(815)753-9497	561
	LANIER, Donald I	(815)753-0255	698
	OSORIO, Nestor L.	(815)753-9837	928
Decatur	HALE, Charles E.	(217)864-5755	485
Deerfield	CALLAGHAN, Linda W.	(312)945-3311	173
	LEE, Soon H.	(312)948-3880	711
Downers Grove	CULBERTSON, Lillian D.	(312)971-3309	263
Dwight	MCCLAREY, Catherine A.	(815)584-3703	796
East Peoria	WILFORD, Valerie J.	(309)694-4389	1339
Edwardsville	JOHNSON, Charlotte L.	(618)656-5743	603
Elk Grove Village	KALRA, Bhupinder S.	(312)529-8607	623
Evanston	BJORNCRANTZ, Leslie B.	(312)866-9112	100
	FINEMAN, Charles S.	(312)866-7428	377
	MICHAELSON, Robert C.	(312)491-3057	832
	PANOFSKY, Hans E.	(312)491-7684	938
	PIRON, Alice M.	(312)864-3175	975
	SMITH, Newland F.	(312)328-9300	1159

COLLECTION DEVELOPMENT/EVALUATION CONSULTANT (Cont'd)
ILLINOIS (Cont'd)

City	Name	Phone	Page
Evanston			
	WHITE, Matthew H.	(312)328-2221	1331
	WRIGHT, Donald E.	(312)866-0312	1371
Flossmoor	LOCKE, John W.	(312)798-3671	736
Galesburg	BABANOURY, Betty G.	(309)343-6118	43
Glenview	MARTINAZZI, Toni	(657)775-6000	779
Gurnee	ROBIEN, Eleanor K.	(312)223-8621	1043
Hinsdale	HALASZ, Marilynn J.	(312)325-0819	484
	MUELLER, Elizabeth	(312)323-8054	875
Kenilworth	PETERSON, Scott W.	(312)666-1404	964
La Grange	HUSLIG, Dennis M.	(312)352-7671	578
	MARTIN, John W.	(312)352-8115	776
La Grange Park	STALZER, Rita M.	(312)354-9200	1179
Lake Bluff	BROSK, Carol A.	(312)234-6752	141
	LEISNER, Anthony B.	(312)295-2010	714
Lisle	SHOTWELL, Richard T.	(312)665-9107	1133
Lombard	MARSHALL, Mary G.	(312)932-1455	774
Mascoutah	GORDON, Diane M.	(618)566-4981	451
	SCHAACK, Wilma J.	(618)566-7385	1088
Matteson	SMITH, Richard D.	(312)747-6660	1159
Moline	KRAMER, Pamela K.	(309)797-5117	675
Monticello	ARNTZEN, Etta M.	(217)762-7827	34
Morrisonville	PODESCHI, John B.	(217)526-3256	979
Naperville	ROWE, Dorothy B.	(312)355-9221	1062
Nashville	RUSIEWSKI, Charles B.	(618)327-8304	1068
Normal	NOURIE, Alan R.	(309)438-3480	910
North Aurora	HOWREY, Mary M.	(312)896-5837	566
North Riverside	MUELLER, Robert W.	(312)447-6441	875
Oak Park	BALCOM, William T.	(312)383-6824	51
	HALIBEY, Areta V.	(312)524-0023	486
	MARSHALL, Maggie L.	(312)848-4432	774
	STEVENSON, Sheila M.	(312)848-3637	1191
Ottawa	WILLSON, Richard E.	(815)434-7075	1349
Palatine	BOURKE, Jacqueline K.	(312)991-9335	119
	BURNS, Mary F.	(312)358-0137	162
	EVERHART, Paul R.	(312)991-2600	358
Palos Hills	TEO, Elizabeth A.	(312)974-4300	1231
Park Ridge	JACKSON, William V.	(312)825-4364	588
Paxton	PACEY, Brenda M.	(217)379-3517	933
Riverdale	PATEL, Jashu	(312)849-3959	947
Rock Island	OHRLUND, Ava L.	(309)786-0698	919
Rockford	CHITWOOD, Julius R.	(815)962-4409	209
	PRESSING, Kirk L.	(815)962-5569	991
Rolling Meadows	HEMENWAY, Patti J.	(312)255-6197	525
Skokie	GRODINSKY, Deborah	(312)679-1380	471
	JACOB, Merle L.		589
	SORENSON, Liene S.	(312)673-7774	1168
Springfield	SIVAK, Marie R.	(217)782-2826	1144
Urbana	AGGARWAL, Narindar K.	(217)333-2492	7
	ATKINS, Stephen E.	(217)244-1867	38
	BALACHANDRAN, Sarojini	(217)328-3577	50
	BRICHFORD, Maynard J.	(217)367-7072	134
	CHOLDIN, Marianna T.	(217)333-5739	210
	CLARK, Barton M.	(217)333-0317	216
	DAVIS, Elisabeth B.	(217)333-3654	278
	EDMONDS, M L.	(217)333-2008	336
	FAIRCHILD, Constance A.	(217)333-1900	361
	KIBBEE, Josephine Z.	(217)333-2290	646
	LANCASTER, Frederick W.	(217)384-7798	691
	NASH, N F.	(217)384-6350	888
	STENSTROM, Patricia F.	(217)333-4456	1187
	WEECH, Terry L.	(217)367 7111	1015
	WILLIAMS, James W.	(217)333-2305	1344
Wheaton	EMBAR, Indrani M.	(312)668-1742	347
Wheeling	HAMMER, Louise K.	(312)541-8149	493
	KANNER, Elliott E.	(312)459-1300	625
Williamsville	KELLERSTRASS, Amy L.	(217)566-3517	636
Wilmette	JONES, Adrian	(312)256-6202	610

INDIANA

City	Name	Phone	Page
Anderson	KENDALL, Charles T.	(317)649-5039	640
Bloomington	CALLISON, Daniel J.	(812)335-5113	174
	FARRELL, David	(812)335-3403	365
	FLING, Robert M.	(812)335-2970	385
	HALPORN, Barbara	(812)335-1446	490
	HEISER, Lois	(812)335-7170	523
	HENN, Barbara J.	(812)335-1666	528
	KUDRYK, Oleg	(812)332-1773	682

COLLECTION DEVELOPMENT/EVALUATION CONSULTANT (Cont'd)
INDIANA (Cont'd)
Bloomington

	LAIR, Nancy C.	(812)335-5113	688
	LEE, Thomas H.	(812)331-7485	711
	MARTIN, Fenton S.	(812)335-3851	776
	MURPHY, Marcy	(812)335-5113	881
	READ, Glenn F.	(812)336-5984	1012
	SHAABAN, Marian F.	(812)335-6924	1118
	SOWELL, Steven L.	(812)335-9792	1170
	WIGGINS, Gary D.	(812)335-9452	1337
Columbus	MEREDITH, Meri	(812)372-3482	825
Crawfordsville	DAY, Thomas L.	(317)362-2242	283
Fort Wayne	SHEETS, Michael T.	(219)483-2854	1125
	WEICK, Robert J.	(219)478-1018	1316
Franklin	FALLON, Marianna L.	(317)736-8441	362
Gary	GUYDON, Janet H.	(219)938-3376	479
Indianapolis	ALLEN, Joyce S.	(317)929-8021	15
	DURKIN, Virginia M.	(317)871-2095	328
	FISCHLER, Barbara B.	(317)274-0462	380
	GALBRAITH, Leslie R.	(317)924-1331	413
	HEHMAN, Jennifer L.	(317)271-8595	521
	KONDELIK, John P.	(317)283-9226	670
	KRASEAN, Thomas K.	(317)232-1882	676
	MATTS, Constance	(317)274-1928	786
	SIMON, Ralph C.	(317)875-5336	1141
Jeffersonville	HODGSON, Janet B.		546
La Porte	GUNNELLS, Danny C.	(219)324-0422	477
Logansport	SHIH, Philip C.	(219)753-6383	1130
Mishawaka	EISEN, David J.	(219)259-5277	340
Muncie	HODGE, Stanley P.	(317)285-8033	546
	KUO, Ming M.	(317)289-3123	684
Munster	MOGLE, Dawn E.	(219)923-8059	852
Notre Dame	FUDERER, Laura S.	(219)239-5176	408
	JORDAN, Louis E.	(219)239-7420	616
	MILLER, Robert C.	(219)239-7790	841
Richmond	FARBER, Evan I.	(317)966-2422	363
Rochester	LASHER, Esther L.	(219)223-8407	700
South Bend	OSTROWSKI, Lawrence C.	(219)282-4608	929
	WARREN, Lois B.	(219)287-6481	1306
	YATES, Donald N.	(219)289-3405	1378
Terre Haute	LEACH, Ronald G.	(812)237-3700	706
	VANCIL, David E.	(812)237-2610	1273
West Lafayette	BAILEY, Martha J.	(317)494-2910	46
	FUNKHOUSER, Richard L.	(317)494-2855	410
	KERKER, Ann E.		643
	POLIT, Carlos E.	(317)463-6404	980

IOWA

Ames	DOBSON, Cynthia	(515)294-5451	307
Atlantic	CRAVER, Susan J.	(712)243-5359	256
Cedar Falls	ELIZABETH, Martin A.	(319)273-2006	343
	MARTIN, Elizabeth A.	(319)273-2578	776
Davenport	BUDREW, John	(319)326-9895	155
	JONSON, Laurence F.	(319)323-9213	616
	PETERSON, Dennis R.	(319)391-3877	963
Denver	DUTCHER, Terry R.	(319)984-6120	329
Des Moines	GRIFFIN, Kathryn A.	(515)269-3351	468
Grinnell	MCKEE, Christopher	(515)269-3351	810
Iowa City	BAKER, Sharon L.	(319)335-5707	49
	DUNLAP, Leslie W.		326
	EGGERS, Lolly P.	(319)356-5206	339
	EICHER, Thomas E.	(319)335-9038	339
	EIMAS, Richard	(319)337-5538	340
	HARMON, Charles T.	(319)337-2140	502
	HOWELL, John B.	(319)335-5885	565
	JORDAN, Robert P.	(319)337-2708	616
	SCHACHT, John N.	(319)335-5299	1088
Marion	ALDERSON, Karen A.	(319)377-0666	11
	DAVIS, Deanna S.	(319)377-7135	278
Muscatine	MATHER, Becky R.	(319)263-9049	783
Ottumwa	BRANDT, Garnet J.	(515)682-6677	128
Sioux City	PHILLIPS, Donna M.	(712)258-6981	968
Vinton	SHEPHERD, Rex L.	(319)472-4721	1127

KANSAS

Alma	BIRNEY, Ann E.	(913)765-2370	98
Chanute	DRUSE, Judith A.	(316)431-3020	321
Emporia	MEDER, Marylouise D.	(316)343-1200	820
Hillsboro	JOHNSON, Georgina	(316)947-3121	604

COLLECTION DEVELOPMENT/EVALUATION CONSULTANT (Cont'd)
KANSAS (Cont'd)

Kansas City	WITMER, Tonya C.	(913)362-5327	1358
Lawrence	CRAIG, Susan V.	(913)864-3020	254
	HOWARD, Clinton N.	(913)864-3601	564
	JOHNSON, Ellen S.	(913)864-3496	604
	KOEPP, Donna P.	(913)864-4880	668
	MAY, Cecilia J.	(913)841-0929	788
	SEAVER, James E.	(913)864-3569	1110
	SNYDER, Fritz	(913)864-3025	1164
Lenexa	MCLEOD, Debra A.	(913)492-4512	814
Manhattan	COFFEE, E G.	(913)539-1628	226
	STUBBAN, Vanessa L.		1204
Topeka	BRAND, Alice A.	(913)273-7500	127
	JOHNSON, Duane F.	(913)296-3296	603
	LYNN, Barbara A.	(913)233-4252	752
	VOSS, Ernestine D.	(913)269-3296	1289
Wichita	BRADEN, Jan	(316)686-5954	125
	GERMANN, Malcolm P.	(316)689-3591	429
	MEYERS, Judith K.	(316)832-1211	831
	MYERS, Marilyn	(316)689-3591	884
	MYERS, Robert C.	(316)689-3591	885
	SCHAD, Jasper G.	(316)685-6588	1088
	SCHEUERMAN, Luanne J.	(316)684-0624	1092
	SINGH, Swarn L.	(316)722-3741	1143

KENTUCKY

Bowling Green	COUTTS, Brian E.	(502)745-6339	252
Cynthiana	DOAN, Janice K.	(606)441-1180	307
Edgewood	REESE, Virginia D.	(606)261-8211	1016
Lexington	BARRISH, Alan S.	(606)278-1933	60
Louisville	ANDERSON, James C.	(502)588-6752	23
	AULD, Dennis B.		39
	COATES, Ann S.	(502)588-5917	224
	HUFF, James E.	(502)585-9911	570
	JOHNSON, Garry B.	(502)897-8100	604
	REDMON, Sherrill	(502)451-5907	1014
	ROBY, B D.	(502)561-8638	1045
	SCHLENE, Vickie J.	(502)935-9840	1094
	TEITELBAUM, Gene W.	(502)588-6392	1230
	WHITE, Ernest M.	(502)897-3557	1331
Maple Mount	BUSAM, Emma C.	(502)229-4103	164
Richmond	BARKSDALE, Milton K.	(606)622-1787	57
Whitesburg	OLIVER, Scot	(606)633-0108	921
Wilmore	BUNDY, David D.	(606)858-3581	157

LOUISIANA

Alexandria	JARRED, Ada D.	(312)445-5230	594
Baton Rouge	BINGHAM, Elizabeth E.	(504)292-1038	97
	HAMAKER, Charles A.	(504)388-8537	490
	LOUBIERE, Sue	(504)346-3172	742
	MILLER, Susan E.	(504)388-8264	842
	PASKOFF, Beth M.	(504)388-1480	946
	PERRAULT, Anna H.	(504)924-5790	959
	PHILLIPS, Faye	(504)388-6569	968
	SHIFLETT, Orvin L.	(504)388-1462	1130
	SMITH, Ledell B.		1157
Harvey	WASHINGTON, Idella A.	(504)367-8429	1307
Lafayette	FOX, Willard		395
	HAMSA, Charles F.	(318)984-9305	494
	STEWART, Mary E.	(318)984-4139	1193
	TURNER, I B.	(318)231-5702	1264
Metairie	GOLDSTEIN, Cynthia H.	(504)885-5296	446
	SALVATORE, Gayle E.	(504)456-2660	1078
Monroe	KONTROVITZ, Eileen R.		671
Natchitoches	BUCHANAN, William C.	(318)357-4403	153
	HARRINGTON, Charles W.	(318)357-0813	504
New Orleans	CUMLET, Harolyn S.	(504)943-3618	264
	HAGEDORN, Dorothy L.	(504)865-5131	482
	HARDY, D C.	(504)895-3981	500
	JERDE, Curtis D.	(504)865-5688	599
	MCKNIGHT, Mark C.	(504)866-3394	812
	MCREYNOLDS, Rosalee	(504)866-9820	818
Ruston	WICKER, W W.	(318)257-2577	1335

MAINE

Bangor	WOODWARD, Robert C.	(207)942-4760	1368
East Sebago	AIREY, Martha R.	(207)787-2817	9
Orono	CASSERLY, Mary F.	(207)581-1675	193
	MCCALLISTER, Myrna J.		793

COLLECTION DEVELOPMENT/EVALUATION CONSULTANT (Cont'd)
MAINE (Cont'd)
Portland	SMITH, Barbara J.	(207)761-2932	1153

MARYLAND
Aberdeen	HADDEN, Robert L.	(301)272-1858	481
Annapolis	LIVELY, Nancy J.	(301)268-0530	734
	MENEGAUX, Edmond A.	(301)268-6741	824
	MOTEN, Derryn E.	(301)757-3846	872
	RICE, Rosamond H.	(301)263-0670	1027
Baldwin	WASIELEWSKI, Eleanor B.	(301)557-7293	1308
Baltimore	BLANK, Annette C.	(301)396-5350	104
	FLORANCE, Valerie	(301)383-9436	385
	FREDENBURG, Anne M.	(301)377-9080	399
	GENUARDI, Michael T.	(301)235-1168	427
	HOFSTETTER, Eleanore O.	(301)321-2454	549
	KELLER, William B.	(301)367-0338	636
	LAPIDES, Linda F.	(301)396-5356	697
	LEDBETTER, Sherry H.	(301)358-0285	708
	MCADAM, Paul E.	(301)747-5030	791
	MONTGOMERY, Paula K.	(301)685-8621	856
	PAPENFUSE, Edward C.	(301)467-6137	939
	SHAPIRO, Burton J.	(301)653-2757	1121
	SILVER, Marcy L.		1138
	SZCZCPANIAK, Adam S.	(301)539-0872	1218
Bel Air	SEDNEY, Frances V.	(301)838-7484	1111
Bethesda	CONGER, Lucinda D.	(301)229-7716	236
	COSTABILE, Salvatore L.	(301)986-8560	249
	FISHBEIN, Meyer H.	(301)530-5391	380
	GAUJARD, Pierre G.	(301)652-0034	422
	JOHNSON, Carol A.	(301)251-5378	602
	KUNZ, Margarett N.	(301)496-3541	684
	LORENZ, John G.	(301)320-4651	741
	PHILLIPS, Lena M.	(301)986-8560	968
	THOMAS, Patricia A.	(301)229-4194	1238
	TURNER, Ellis S.	(301)530-4178	1264
Catonsville	WILT, Larry J.	(301)455-2341	1353
Chevy Chase	CHARTRAND, Robert L.		203
	HOLLOWAY, Johnna H.	(301)652-8491	552
	KENTON, Charlotte	(301)657-3855	642
	NAINIS, Linda	(301)654-0335	886
	SHAW, Renata V.	(301)654-3560	1123
College Park	STIELOW, Frederick J.	(301)454-5790	1194
	WILSON, William G.	(301)454-6003	1353
Columbia	JOHNSON, Elaine B.	(301)992-5502	604
	KOSMIN, Linda J.	(301)997-8954	672
	RUSS, Kennetta P.	(301)381-0579	1068
	WOLTER, John A.	(301)730-6692	1362
Easton	MOLTER, Maureen M.	(301)822-1658	853
Ellicott City	DUCHAC, Kenneth F.	(301)531-3389	322
Fallston	SACK, Jean C.	(301)877-2825	1073
Frederick	BANKS, Jane L.	(301)695-6726	54
	NATHANSON, David	(301)662-4499	889
Frostburg	GILLESPIE, David M.	(301)689-2701	435
Glen Burnie	HACKMAN, Mary H.	(301)768-2569	481
	STEINHOFF, Cynthia K.	(301)787-1549	1186
Greenbelt	BYERLY, Imogene J.		168
	KOBAYASHI, Michiko		666
Hyattsville	BURGESS, Eileen E.	(301)864-7223	159
Kensington	WILLMERING, William J.	(301)946-2753	1348
La Plata	WILLIAMS, J L.	(301)932-6768	1343
Landover	BARTH, Edward W.	(301)773-9790	61
Laurel	OMAR, Elizabeth A.	(301)490-3871	923
Mount Airy	WETZBARGER, Cecilia G.	(301)829-0826	1328
New Carrollton	WILLIAMS, Helen E.	(301)454-6068	1343
Now Market	WILSON, Susan W.	(301)831-6118	1353
Pikesville	JENG, Helene W.	(301)225-4450	596
Potomac	CHANG, Frances M.	(301)258-0772	200
	HO, James K.		545
	SMOLIAN, Steven J.	(301)299-2764	1162
Rockville	BARALOTO, R A.	(301)279-3271	55
	BYRD, Harvey C.	(301)251-5481	169
	CANTELON, Philip L.	(301)770-1170	179
	CHIANG, Ahushun	(301)251-5486	207
	DEAN, Frances C.	(301)424-9289	283
	DOWD, Frank B.	(301)279-1098	315
	FREEDMAN, Lynn P.	(301)468-2600	400
Salisbury	CUNNINGHAM, Barbara M.	(301)742-1537	265
	DADSON, Theresa E.	(301)546-6950	269
	STRANGE, Elizabeth B.	(301)543-8360	1200

COLLECTION DEVELOPMENT/EVALUATION CONSULTANT (Cont'd)
MARYLAND (Cont'd)
Silver Spring	ARANDA-COODOU, Patricio	(301)946-7859	30
	BASA, Eniko M.	(301)384-4657	62
	FEINBERG, Beryl L.	(301)946-3282	368
	GILBERT, Mattana	(301)565-2894	433
	MARKS, Cicely P.	(301)649-7200	771
	TATUM, George M.	(301)236-9179	1225
	VOGT-O'CONNOR, Diane L.	(301)681-7615	1287
	WAGNER, Lloyd F.		1292
Solomons	HEIL, Kathleen A.	(301)326-2967	521
Takoma Park	SLOAN, Cheryl A.	(301)589-6815	1149
	WRIGHT, Arthuree M.	(301)445-1220	1370
Thurmont	FITZPATRICK, Kelly	(301)271-4109	383
Towson	DRACH, Marian C.	(301)825-8877	317
Upper Marlboro	WOODY, Jacqueline B.		1368
Waldorf	WOLFE, Susan J.	(301)645-4784	1361
Westminster	NEIKIRK, Harold D.	(301)848-7000	892

MASSACHUSETTS
Amherst	FELDMAN, Laurence M.	(413)253-9404	369
Andover	GREENE, Cathy C.	(617)470-0902	463
Arlington	ENGLISH, Cynthia J.	(617)227-0270	350
	FORTIER, Jan M.	(617)646-5856	391
	JUDD, Eleanor M.		618
Assonet	MEDEIROS, Joseph	(617)624-4094	820
Auburndale	TUCHMAN, Maurice S.	(617)969-9791	1261
Belmont	LABREE, Rosanne	(617)855-2460	686
Boston	ALCORN, Cynthia W.	(617)578-8675	11
	CHRISTOPHER, Irene	(617)267-2876	212
	CURLEY, Arthur	(617)536-5400	265
	FRYDRYK, Teresa E.	(617)482-9485	407
	GRAMENZ, Francis L.	(617)353-3705	457
	HAYES, Alison M.	(617)482-1776	515
	HEINS, Ethel L.	(617)527-2736	522
	HERNON, Peter	(617)738-2223	532
	HILL, Barbara M.	(617)732-2808	539
	MATIS, Lynn	(617)973-8000	784
	MOSKOWITZ, Michael A.	(617)578-8670	871
	O'TOOLE, James M.	(617)929-8110	930
	PEARLSTEIN, Toby	(617)973-8000	952
	PICCININO, Rocco	(617)442-9010	970
	SCANLAN, Jean M.	(617)439-7412	1087
	SHARE, Donald S.	(617)738-2242	1122
	STIFFLEAR, Allan J.	(617)929-7640	1194
	STUEART, Robert D.	(617)738-2225	1205
	SWANN, Thomas E.	(617)482-1360	1213
	TRIPP, Maureen A.	(617)578-8676	1257
	VOIGT, John F.	(617)266-1400	1287
Bridgewater	CHANDRASEKHAR, Ratna	(617)697-3648	200
Brockton	UMANA, Christine J.	(617)586-6994	1268
Brookline	LEAHY, Lynda C.	(617)731-5237	706
	STEINFELD, Michael	(617)730-2360	1186
Cambridge	BROW, Ellen H.	(603)926-7371	141
	DANIELLS, Lorna M.		273
	DUNKLY, James W.	(617)868-3450	326
	GROVE, Shari T.	(617)864-3563	474
	JACKSON, Arlyne A.	(617)492-0355	586
	OCHS, Michael	(617)495-2794	915
	STODDARD, Roger E.	(617)495-2441	1196
	WARRINGTON, David R.	(617)495-4550	1307
Carver	NEUBAUER, Richard A.	(617)866-5186	896
Charlestown	CURTIN-STEVENSON, Mary C.	(617)241-9664	266
Chestnut Hill	CHANNING, Rhoda K.	(617)552-4470	201
	FENG, Yen T.		371
	KHAN, Syed M.	(617)552-4450	646
	LIPPMAN, Anne F.	(617)552-4457	732
Concord	BANDER, Edward J.		54
	BENDER, Elizabeth H.	(617)369-4222	79
	JACKSON, Patience K.	(617)369-0586	588
Dedham	LOSCALZO, Anita B.	(617)329-3964	741
Deerfield	PROPER, David R.	(413)774-5581	995
	VON KRIES, Beverley A.	(413)772-0241	1288
East Brookfield	BOLSHAW, Cynthia L.	(617)867-2605	112
Eastham	ELDRIDGE, Jane A.	(617)255-3070	342
Fitchburg	WALSH, Jim	(617)342-9078	1299
Gloucester	RHINELANDER, Mary F.	(617)281-2439	1025
Hanscom AFB	SEIDMAN, Ruth K.	(617)377-4895	1112
Haverhill	JAFFARIAN, Sara	(617)373-5922	591

COLLECTION DEVELOPMENT/EVALUATION CONSULTANT (Cont'd)

MASSACHUSETTS (Cont'd)

Heath	HOWLAND, Margaret E.	(413)337-4980	566
Holbrook	MEAGHER, Janet H.	(617)767-3644	819
Lexington	FREITAG, Wolfgang M.	(617)861-0444	401
	PRUSAK, Laurence	(617)861-7580	996
Longmeadow	MCGARRY, Marie L.	(413)567-0001	805
Lowell	CAYLOR, Lawrence M.	(617)452-5000	195
Medford	JONES, Frederick S.	(617)381-3345	613
	MARTIN, Murray S.	(617)776-3599	777
	SCHATZ, Natalie M.	(617)381-3273	1090
Milton	HOVORKA, Marjorie J.	(617)333-4902	563
	OPPENHEIM, Roberta A.	(617)698-6268	925
Monterey	INTNER, Sheila J.	(413)528-2698	583
Needham	CABEZAS, Sue A.	(617)449-3965	170
	MARKUSON, Carolyn A.	(617)449-6299	772
Newton Highlands	FOX, Elyse H.	(617)443-4798	394
North Grafton	SAFFER-MARCHAND, Melinda	(617)839-5302	1074
Northampton	DAVIS, Charles R.	(413)584-2700	278
Pelham	FELLER, Siegfried	(413)253-3115	370
Quincy	WHEALAN, Ronald E.	(617)479-3297	1328
Randolph	MICHAUD, Charles A.	(617)963-3000	832
Reading	SARAIDARIDIS, Susan B.		1082
Salem	CLOHERTY, Lauretta M.		223
South Deerfield	CRAIG, James L.	(413)665-2041	254
Springfield	CLOUGH, Linda F.	(413)788-8411	223
	DUNN, Donald J.	(413)782-1454	326
Sturbridge	PERCY, Theresa R.	(617)347-3362	958
Swampscott	BRENNER, Lawrence	(617)598-0370	133
Tyngsboro	FUNG, Margaret C.	(617)256-3090	409
Wareham	PILLSBURY, Mary J.	(617)295-2343	973
Wellesley	HARDY, Eileen D.	(617)235-0320	500
West Newton	ST. AUBIN, Arleen K.		1075
West Springfield	PECK, Ruth M.	(413)736-0989	953
Weston	REED-SCOTT, Jutta R.	(617)736-4734	1015
Westport	GIBBS, Paige	(617)674-6712	431
Williamsburg	O'BRIEN, Marjorie S.	(413)268-7131	914
Winchester	JOHNSON, Jean L.	(617)721-7020	606
	KEATS, Susan E.	(617)729-9317	633
Woods Hole	WINN, Carolyn P.	(617)548-7066	1355
Worcester	STANKUS, Tony	(617)793-2643	1180
Yarmouthport	STEEVES, Henry A.		1184

MICHIGAN

Albion	OBERG, Larry R.	(517)629-7297	914
Ann Arbor	BLOUIN, Francis X.	(313)764-3482	107
	COFFEY, Dorothy A.	(313)994-2350	227
	EDWARDS, Willie M.	(313)994-6513	338
	HOUGH, Carolyn A.	(313)665-0537	562
	JASPER, Richard P.	(313)973-0747	595
	SLAVENS, Thomas P.	(313)665-6663	1148
	WEST, Marian S.	(313)663-5907	1326
	YOCUM, Patricia B.	(313)995-4644	1380
Auburn Hills	WILLIAMS, Calvin	(313)853-4226	1342
Belleville	STARESINA, Lois J.	(313)699-7549	1181
Berrien Springs	FITZGERALD, Ruth F.	(616)471-7725	382
Birmingham	ORMOND, Sarah C.	(313)647-1700	926
Bloomfield Hills	SIDEN, Harriet F.	(313)258-8532	1135
Canton	BRYANT, Barton B.	(313)397-3660	152
Clarkston	D'ELIA, Joseph G.	(313)625-8274	289
	MEDER, Stephen A.	(313)625-5611	820
Dearborn	CRAWFORD, Geraldine H.	(313)271-2184	256
Detroit	ALLEN, Nancy H.	(313)577-4033	15
	BRUNK, Thomas W.	(313)331-4930	150
	GIGLIO, Linda M.	(313)872-4311	433
	PFLUG, Warner W.	(313)577-4024	966
	WARD, Nancy E.	(313)256-9596	1304
	WEST, Donald	(313)577-2525	1326
East Lansing	SHAPIRO, Beth J.	(517)355-2343	1121
	WIEMERS, Eugene L.	(517)355-2340	1336
Farmington Hills	RENKIEWICZ, Frank A.	(313)478-4506	1023
Flint	HERTZ, Sylvia	(313)733-5074	533
	MORELAND, Patricia L.	(313)762-2141	863
	PALMER, David W.	(313)238-0166	936
Grand Blanc	KINGSTON, Jo A.	(313)694-7323	652
Grand Rapids	BOSE, Deborah L.	(616)453-1900	117
	BURINSKI, Walter W.	(616)454-9635	160
	SIEBERS, Bruce L.	(616)774-2167	1135
Highland Park	NDENGA, Viola W.	(313)868-5986	890

COLLECTION DEVELOPMENT/EVALUATION CONSULTANT (Cont'd)

MICHIGAN (Cont'd)

Kalamazoo	APPS, Michelle L.	(616)375-3611	30
	CARROLL, Hardy	(616)383-1926	187
	WILLIAMS, S J.	(616)384-0100	1346
Lansing	CALLARD, Carole	(517)373-1593	173
Livonia	CHAKLOSH, Cynthia L.		197
	VOIGHT, Nancy R.	(313)464-2306	1287
Midland	CHEN, Catherine W.	(517)631-9724	205
Monroe	MARGOLIS, Bernard A.	(313)243-5213	770
Mt Clemens	CUNNINGHAM, Tina Y.	(313)286-5750	265
	LUFT, William	(313)791-3418	747
Mt Pleasant	MULLIGAN, William H.	(517)773-1374	877
Muskegon	MARSHALL, Betty J.	(616)728-4766	773
Northville	FIELD, Judith J.	(313)349-1953	375
	ROCKALL, Diane M.	(313)349-9005	1046
Novi	KIEFER, Marilyn V.	(313)344-8300	647
Okemos	TREGLOAN, Donald C.	(517)349-7767	1255
Petoskey	KELLY, Kay	(616)348-4500	638
Sault Sainte Marie	NAIRN, Charles E.	(906)635-2402	886
Sturgis	BERKLUND, Nancy J.	(616)651-9361	87
Traverse City	SICILIANO, Peg P.	(616)947-1480	1135
Trenton	GREEN, Katherine A.		462
Troy	BIELICH, Paul S.	(313)689-9381	95
Ypsilanti	BEAL, Sarell W.	(313)483-7729	68
	MARSHALL, Albert P.		773

MINNESOTA

Bloomington	NAUEN, Lindsay B.	(612)854-2879	889
Columbia Heights	VAUGHAN, Janet E.	(612)574-6505	1279
Duluth	ENRICI, Pamela L.	(218)726-8586	350
Embarrass	ESALA, Lillian H.	(218)741-3434	354
Hopkins	SMITH, David R.	(612)933-0199	1154
Minneapolis	ALLISON, Brent	(612)624-4549	17
	BEAVEN, Miranda J.	(612)624-5860	71
	BEDOR, Kathleen M.	(612)823-3945	73
	BRANIN, Joseph J.	(612)624-5518	128
	BRUEMMER, Bruce H.	(612)624-5050	149
	CARLSON, Stan W.	(612)571-2046	182
	FURTAK, Rosemary	(612)375-7680	410
	GASTON, Judith A.	(612)627-4277	421
	IMMLER, Frank	(612)624-0091	582
	JOHNSON, Donald C.		603
	LATHROP, Alan K.	(612)789-4046	701
	OVERMIER, Judith A.	(612)626-6881	931
	PANKAKE, Marcia J.	(612)331-2551	938
	TIBLIN, Mariann E.	(612)624-5860	1244
	WALDEN, Barbara L.	(612)624-5860	1294
	WARPHEA, Rita C.	(612)588-6985	1306
	WEEKS, John M.	(612)624-6833	1315
Minnetonka	HUTTNER, Marian A.	(612)545-2338	579
Mound	GELINAS, Jeanne L.	(612)472-4046	426
Owatonna	HOSLETT, Andrea E.	(507)451-0312	561
Robbinsdale	OSIER, Donald V.	(612)533-5025	928
Rochester	KEY, Jack D.	(507)284-2068	645
	KEYS, Thomas E.		645
St Louis Park	RINE, Joseph L.	(612)542-9631	1035
St Paul	BROGAN, Martha L.	(612)698-1186	139
	CARLSON, Livija I.	(612)624-3078	182
	DELOACH, Lynda J.	(612)627-4208	290
	HARWOOD, Karen L.	(612)690-6653	510
	KING, Jack B.	(612)641-2373	651
	OZOLINS, Karl L.	(612)645-2999	933
	WURL, Joel F.	(612)627-4208	1374
Waite Park	CLARKE, Norman F.	(612)253-2695	219
Worthington	SCOTT, Thomas L.	(507)376-5803	1108
	SPILLERS, Roger E.	(507)372-2981	1174

MISSISSIPPI

Biloxi	FREEDMAN, Jack A.	(601)388-2318	400
Clinton	BUCHANAN, Gerald	(601)924-7511	153
Columbus	PAYNE, David L.	(601)328-7565	951
Hattiesburg	BOYD, William D.	(601)266-4232	123
	KELLY, John M.	(601)268-1537	638
	LATOUR, Terry S.	(601)266-4345	701
	VAN MELER, Vandelia L.	(601)266-4243	1276
Itta Bena	BOWEN, Ethel B.	(601)254-9041	120
Jackson	REID, Thomas G.	(601)922-4988	1019
Liberty	BURKS, Alvin L.	(601)657-8920	161

COLLECTION DEVELOPMENT/EVALUATION CONSULTANT (Cont'd)

MISSISSIPPI (Cont'd)

City	Name	Phone	Page
Meridian	JOHNSON, Scott R.	(601)483-8241	609
	MACNEILL, Daniel S.	(601)693-6771	758
Oxford	HARPER, Laura G.	(601)234-1812	503
Raymond	WALL, Norma F.	(601)857-3253	1297
University	FISHER, Benjamin F.		380
	GRAVES, Gail T.	(601)232-5875	459

MISSOURI

City	Name	Phone	Page
Ballwin	BUHR, Rosemary E.		156
Butler	FISHER, Georgeann	(816)679-6121	381
Columbia	POWELL, Ronald R.	(314)882-9545	988
	SHAUGHNESSY, Thomas W.	(314)882-4701	1123
Fenton	CHAN, Jeanny T.	(314)343-0929	199
Florissant	BLANKENSHIP, Phyllis E.	(314)839-3966	104
Independence	MEYERS, Martha L.	(816)833-1472	831
	VOSS, Kathryn J.	(816)836-8100	1289
Joplin	ABERNATHY, William F.	(417)624-2518	2
Kansas City	BRADBURY, Daniel J.	(816)221-3203	125
	HAMMOND, John J.	(816)221-2695	493
	HAWKINS, Marilyn J.	(816)436-1400	514
	HESS, Stanley W.	(816)561-4000	534
	JENKINS, Harold R.	(816)444-2590	597
	KARNS, Kermit B.	(816)453-1294	627
	LABUDDE, Kenneth J.	(816)531-0770	686
	SERLING, Kitty	(816)753-5700	1116
Kirksville	ELLEBRACHT, Eleanor V.	(816)665-6158	343
Liberty	HOOVER, Jonnette L.	(816)781-7812	557
O'Fallon	SANDERS, John B.		1080
St Louis	BAERWALD, Susan M.	(314)772-1364	45
	GILTINAN, Celia E.	(314)962-9048	437
	HELMS, Mary E.	(314)362-2787	525
	HUESTIS, Jeffrey C.	(314)889-5409	570
	LEWIS, Ruth E.	(314)889-5405	724
	NOBLE, Barbara N.	(314)367-6324	906
	SMITH, Nancy M.	(314)241-2288	1159
	SUELFLOW, August R.	(314)721-5934	1206
	TIPSWORD, Thomas N.	(314)263-2345	1246
	VOLLMAR, William J.	(314)577-2279	1288
Springfield	MACKEY, Neosha A.	(417)836-4537	756
	MEADOR, John M.	(417)882-8032	819

MONTANA

City	Name	Phone	Page
Bozeman	ALLDREDGE, Noreen S.	(406)587-4877	14
	BRUWELHEIDE, Janis H.	(406)587-0405	151
	MORTON, Bruce	(406)994-5313	870
Heart Butte	SPOTTED EAGLE, Joy	(406)338-2282	1175
Helena	CLARK, Robert M.	(406)444-4787	218
	MORROW, Delores J.	(406)444-4714	869
	PARKER, Sara A.	(406)444-3115	942
Missoula	CHANDLER, Devon	(406)243-4072	199
	SCHMIDT, Theodore A.	(406)721-2811	1096

NEBRASKA

City	Name	Phone	Page
Lincoln	SARTORI, Eva M.		1083
	WOMACK, Sharon K.		1362
Omaha	HASELWOOD, Eldon L.	(402)554-2211	510
	LITTLE, Nina M.	(402)554-6282	733
	PHIPPS, Michael C.	(402)444-4834	969
Ralston	OYER, Kenneth E.	(402)331-8843	932

NEVADA

City	Name	Phone	Page
Boulder City	LANGEVIN, Ann T.	(702)293-3168	695
Carson City	DION, Kathleen L.	(702)885-5140	305
Las Vegas	CAROLLO, Michael T.	(702)385-0115	184
	CURLEY, Elmer F.		265
	MORGAN, James E.	(702)384-4887	864
	ORTIZ, Diane	(702)388-6501	927

NEW HAMPSHIRE

City	Name	Phone	Page
Amherst	SHERWOOD, Janet R.	(603)673-9242	1129
Concord	MEVERS, Frank C.	(603)224-3896	829
Durham	KAPOOR, Jagdish C.	(603)868-2504	626
Hanover	CRONENWETT, Philip N.	(603)646-2037	260
Manchester	BERTHIAUME, Dennis A.	(603)669-1030	90
	THOMPSON, Debra J.	(603)669-1048	1239
Nashua	WARREN, Ann R.	(603)883-4141	1306
Sunapee	TATE, Joanne D.	(603)763-9948	1225
Washington	HAMILL, Martha L.	(603)495-3994	491

COLLECTION DEVELOPMENT/EVALUATION CONSULTANT (Cont'd)

NEW JERSEY

City	Name	Phone	Page
Basking Ridge	THOMPSON, Melia M.	(201)953-3326	1240
Belle Mead	LEE, J S.	(201)359-5845	710
Bergenfield	HEISE, George F.	(201)385-9741	522
	HILL, George R.	(201)384-4034	539
Bloomfield	BETANCOURT, Ingrid T.	(201)743-9511	92
Bridgewater	ROMANASKY, Marcia C.	(201)218-0400	1052
	STEVENS, Sharon G.	(201)218-3819	1191
	STUDDIFORD, Abigail M.	(201)725-5616	1204
Caldwell	HODGE, Patricia A.	(201)288-4424	546
Califon	CAPOOR, Asha	(201)832-9323	180
Cherry Hill	ARROWOOD, Nina R.	(609)667-7653	35
Cinnaminson	CRESCENZI, Jean D.	(609)757-6038	258
Clifton	PIERMATTI, Patricia A.	(201)473-2454	972
	TROJAN, Judith L.	(201)472-3868	1257
Colts Neck	MICHAL, Judith A.	(201)946-4839	832
Columbus	ALITO, Martha A.	(609)298-5848	13
Cranford	WOLFE, N J.	(201)279-9563	1361
Demarest	MCDERMOTT, Ellen	(201)767-1618	801
Denville	VARIEUR, Normand L.		1278
Dover	RYAN, Mary E.	(201)989-3079	1071
East Orange	GORMAN, Audrey J.	(201)676-2472	452
Elizabeth	LATINI, Samuel A.	(201)354-6060	701
Hamilton	HOOKER, Joan M.	(609)587-9669	556
Highland Park	NIGRIN, Albert G.		904
	PAGE, Penny B.	(201)247-9353	934
Irvington	KNIGHT, Shirley D.	(201)371-9324	664
Kearny	HAWLEY, George S.	(201)997-5299	514
Leonia	SCHARF, Davida	(201)947-6839	1090
Linden	PISKORIK, Elizabeth	(201)486-3888	976
Madison	CONNORS, Linda E.	(201)377-3000	238
	JONES, Arthur E.	(201)377-6525	611
	LONG, Joanna R.	(201)377-2376	739
Mahwah	YUEH, Norma N.	(201)529-7578	1384
Maplewood	AUSTIN, Fay A.		40
	BRYANT, David S.	(201)763-9294	152
	KRUPP, Robert G.	(201)763-8436	681
Marlton	RICHIE, Mark L.	(609)985-0436	1030
Metuchen	BECKER, Ronald L.	(201)494-6447	72
Montclair	HOROWITZ, Marjorie B.	(201)744-8697	560
Morristown	BRUNNER, Karen B.	(201)538-0800	151
	MONROE-SECHREST, Nancy H.		855
Mt Laurel	O'CONNOR, Elizabeth W.	(609)235-5003	916
Mountain Lakes	STEEN, Carol N.	(201)334-4941	1184
Mountainside	LINGELBACH, Lorene N.	(201)654-7694	730
Murray Hill	BROWN, Ina A.	(201)582-2417	144
New Brunswick	EDELMAN, Hendrik	(201)932-7836	335
	SWARTZBURG, Susan G.	(201)932-8573	1214
New Providence	GERBER, Warren C.		428
Newark	SCHWARTZ, Lawrence C.		1104
Ocean City	MASON, Michael L.	(609)398-0969	781
Passaic	SCHEAR, Thomas W.	(201)777-6146	1090
Patterson	SAWYER, Miriam		1086
Pequannock	SUSSMAN, Valerie J.	(201)696-9655	1210
Perth Amboy	HARDISH, Patrick M.	(201)826-5298	500
Phillipsburg	HESS, Jayne L.	(201)454-3712	534
Piscataway	FIGUEREDO, Danilo H.	(201)463-3725	376
	KAPLAN, Susan J.	(201)699-4327	626
	MENZEL, John P.	(201)463-0634	825
Plainfield	KRUSE, Theodore H.	(201)725-2294	681
	MCCOY, W K.	(201)753-0618	799
Point Pleasant	GREENE, Ellin P.	(201)899-2270	464
Port Murray	YRIGOYEN, Robert P.	(201)689-7069	1384
Princeton	BELCHER, Emily M.	(609)924-8947	76
	BERKNER, Dimity S.	(609)924-3891	87
	CHAIKIN, Mary C.	(609)452-6084	197
	FERGUSON, Stephen	(609)452-3184	372
	HAYASHI, Chigusa	(609)921-2330	515
	HOELLE, Dolores M.	(609)452-3201	547
	NASE, Lois M.	(609)452-3237	888
	SCHMIDT, Mary M.	(609)452-5860	1095
Rahway	SUDALL, Arthur D.	(201)388-0761	1206
Ridgewood	KOONTZ, John	(201)652-0185	671
Rockaway	BOWERS, Alyce J.	(201)627-2344	120
Short Hills	HENRY, Mary K.	(201)379-4082	529
Somerville	MOYER, Holley M.	(201)725-1600	874
South Orange	FIELD, William N.	(201)761-1926	376
Sparta	GUIDA, Pat	(201)729-8176	476

COLLECTION DEVELOPMENT/EVALUATION CONSULTANT (Cont'd)
NEW JERSEY (Cont'd)

Springfield	CHANG, Joseph I.	(201)467-2037	200
	GLADSTONE, Mark A.	(201)376-2055	439
	SCOTT, Miranda D.	(201)467-7010	1107
Stanhope	KUTTEROFF, Ethel C.	(201)347-7600	685
Sussex	SMITH, Jo T.	(201)875-3621	1156
Teaneck	MOUNT, Ellis	(201)836-1137	873
Trenton	BRODOWSKI, Joyce H.	(609)771-2343	139
Turnersville	SZILASSY, Sandor	(609)589-7193	1218
Upper Montclair	LUNG, Chan S.	(201)746-6733	748
Upper Saddle River	MICHAELS, Debbie D.	(201)327-5006	832
Vineland	GREENBLATT, Ruth	(609)794-4243	463
Washington Township	MAYNES, Kathleen R.	(201)358-0209	790
Wayne	COHEN, Adrea G.	(201)696-8948	227
	FIRSCHEIN, Sylvia H.	(201)694-8600	379
	HEGG, Judith L.	(201)595-2346	521
	LEE, Minja P.		711
West Long Branch	PALMISANO-DRUCKER, Elsalyn	(201)870-9194	937
West Milford	COURTNEY, Aida N.	(201)728-2823	251
Willingboro	PELLETIER, Karen E.		955
Woodbridge	SPANGLER, William N.	(201)634-4450	1171
Wrightstown	DRECHSEL, Marcella J.		319

NEW MEXICO

Albuquerque	BEJNAR, Thaddeus P.	(505)277-0932	75
	CARLSON, Kathleen A.	(505)883-1924	182
	ELDREDGE, Jonathan D.	(505)277-0654	342
	FREEMAN, Patricia E.		401
	HLAVA, Marjorie M.	(505)265-3591	544
	SOHN, Jeanne G.	(505)277-6401	1165
	SPURLOCK, Sandra E.	(505)828-5378	1177
	THORSON, Connie C.	(505)277-7201	1242
Farmington	JASSAL, Raghbir S.	(505)327-7813	595
Hobbs	TUBESING, Richard L.	(505)393-6528	1261
Las Cruces	RICHARDS, James H.	(505)524-0281	1028

NEW YORK

Albany	GILLESPIE, Gerald V.	(518)449-3380	435
	KNEE, Michael	(518)442-3586	663
	LOCKETT, Barbara A.	(518)456-0135	736
	SEVERINGHAUS, Ethel L.	(518)456-2110	1117
	WALSH, Daniel P.	(518)489-7968	1299
Alfred	BROWN, June E.	(607)587-9203	145
	CULLEY, Paul T.	(607)871-2492	263
	LASH, David B.	(607)587-4313	700
Amherst	ROSENFELD, Jane D.	(716)691-8454	1056
APO New York	GADBOIS, Frank W.		411
Ausable Forks	ROGERS, Elizabeth S.		1049
Bakers Mills	SULLIVAN, Linda R.		1208
Ballston Lake	EGAN, Mary J.	(518)399-5151	338
Batavia	STRANC, Mary C.	(716)343-2783	1200
Bay Shore	HEINTZELMAN, Susan K.	(516)666-0177	522
Bayside	SINGER, Phyllis Z.	(718)279-2182	1143
Beechhurst	DESSER, Darrilyn	(718)767-6955	296
Bellerose	GATNER, Elliott S.		422
Bergen	FABRIZIO, Timothy C.	(716)494-2264	360
Bethpage	BURDEN, John	(516)575-3912	158
Binghamton	CARPENTER, Dale	(607)797-0176	184
	COHEN, Ann E.	(607)724-9597	227
	MCKEE, George D.	(607)729-5490	810
	WILLIAMS, Deborah H.	(607)723-6457	1342
Briarcliff Manor	FARKAS, Charles R.	(914)941-7672	364
Broadalbin	ANDERSON, Pauline H.	(518)883-3771	25
Bronx	FOLTER, Siegrun H.	(212)960-8831	388
	ROY, Diptimoy	(914)668-1840	1063
	RUBEY, Daniel R.	(212)960-8580	1064
	WAGSCHAL, Sara G.	(212)601-1723	1292
Brooklyn	CANDELMO, Emily		178
	CHICKERING, F W.	(718)636-3456	208
	CLUNE, John R.	(718)680-7578	223
	DINDAYAL, Joyce S.	(718)677-1624	304
	ESSIEN, Victor K.	(718)941-9020	354
	GENCO, Barbara A.	(718)499-8750	426
	HORNE, Dorice L.	(718)859-1830	560
	KITT, Sandra E.		657
	KUPERMAN, Aaron W.	(718)854-8637	684
	MARTINEZ-RIVERA, Ivette	(718)854-5176	779

COLLECTION DEVELOPMENT/EVALUATION CONSULTANT (Cont'd)
NEW YORK (Cont'd)

Brooklyn	MATTERA, Joseph J.	(718)935-1746	785
	MEYERS, Charles	(718)342-1144	830
	PERSON, Diane G.	(718)596-2345	961
	RUBINSTEIN, Roslyn	(718)834-8779	1065
	SEMKOW, Julie L.	(718)624-3189	1115
	SWIESZKOWSK, L S.	(718)383-8480	1216
	TUDIVER, Lillian	(718)789-7220	1262
	TURIEL, David	(718)336-2668	1263
	WOFSE, Joy G.	(718)788-5360	1359
Buffalo	BREEN, M F.	(716)881-6264	131
	GARLAND, Kathleen	(716)636-3068	419
	KARCH, Linda S.	(716)827-2323	627
	PALMIERI, Lucien E.	(716)882-9275	937
Cheektowaga	WITT, Susan T.	(716)686-3620	1358
Clarence Ctr	CHAPMAN, Renee D.	(716)741-9644	202
Cold Spring	BARNHART, David K.	(914)265-2822	58
Commack	SCHRIFT, Leonard B.	(516)543-5600	1100
Cornwall on Hudson	WEISS, Egon A.	(914)534-9467	1320
Corona	KINYATTI, Njoki W.	(718)592-4782	653
Delhi	SEN, Joyce H.	(607)746-7350	1115
Delmar	BRESLIN, Ellen R.	(518)439-7568	133
Dobbs Ferry	BONE, Larry E.	(914)693-4500	113
East Meadow	MCCARTNEY, Margaret M.	(516)489-8136	794
Eastchester	KOLTAY, Emery I.	(914)337-0300	670
Elmhurst	SALEY, Stacey		1076
Elmsford	TRUDELL, Robert J.	(914)993-1608	1259
Farmingdale	ARMSTRONG, Ruth C.		32
Flushing	RATZABI, Arlene	(718)479-7238	1010
	RORICK, William C.	(718)520-7345	1054
Forest Hills	WIENER, Sylvia B.	(718)263-9469	1336
FPO New York	GAMAL, Sandra H.		416
Freeport	NOTARSTEFANO, Vincent C.	(516)379-3245	910
Garden City	BANICK, Albert N.		54
	DOCTOROW, Erica	(516)663-1042	307
	FRIEDMAN, Arthur L.	(516)222-7406	403
Glenmont	SACCO, Gail A.	(518)439-8549	1073
Great Neck	DAMON, Shirley J.	(516)482-1202	272
Greenvale	YUKAWA, Masako	(516)299-2142	1384
Hempstead	BARTEN, Sharon S.		60
Holbrook	ROMANELLI, Catherine A.	(516)588-5171	1052
Huntington	FOLCARELLI, Ralph J.	(516)271-0634	387
	JASSIN, Raymond M.	(516)266-1093	595
	WOLFE, Barbara M.	(516)423-2495	1360
Huntington Station	ROSS, David J.	(516)385-4951	1058
Islip Terrace	KLATT, Wilma F.	(516)581-5933	658
Ithaca	CHIANG, Katherine S.	(607)272-3086	207
	ERICSON, Margaret D.	(607)274-3882	353
	OLSEN, Wallace C.	(607)255-2551	922
	PARKHURST, Kathleen A.	(607)273-4073	942
Jamaica	BREEN, Karen B.	(718)990-0716	131
	MANSBACH, Carolyn	(718)657-1800	767
Johnstown	BAILIE, Donna L.	(518)762-4633	47
Kew Gardens	SALAZAR, Pamela R.	(718)441-2350	1076
Kings Park	PANDIT, Jyoti P.	(516)269-1070	937
Larchmont	SETON, Charles B.	(914)834-0598	1117
Lindenhurst	WARD, Peter K.	(516)957-6678	1304
Long Island City	MARTIN, Brian G.	(718)726-5885	775
Mamaroneck	O'CONOR, William C.	(914)698-4741	916
Manlius	WU, Painan R.	(315)682-2472	1373
Maryknoll	O'HALLORAN, James V.	(914)941-7590	918
Massapequa Park	AKS, Gloria	(516)795-7297	9
	GIANNATTASI, Gerard E.	(516)541-6584	430
McLean	DREW, Wilfred E.	(607)753-8180	319
Menands	GILSON, Robert	(518)463-4181	437
Miller Place	TODOSOW, Helen K.	(516)928-7174	1248
Mt Sinai	COHEN, Rosemary C.	(516)473-8717	229
Mt Vernon	OCKENE, David L.	(914)699-0949	915
	ROSSWURM, K M.	(914)667-6836	1059
New City	SIMON, Patricia B.	(914)634-4998	1140
New Hyde Park	LANG, Jovian P.	(516)352-1666	695
New Rochelle	HUMPHRY, James	(914)834-6941	574
New York	ALICEA, Ismael	(212)220-6582	13
	AMISON, Mary V.	(212)666-9645	20
	BANKS-ISZARD, Kimberly K.	(212)280-5658	54
	BEHRMANN, Christine A.	(212)568-6349	75
	BENSON, Harold W.	(212)420-7652	83

COLLECTION DEVELOPMENT/EVALUATION CONSULTANT (Cont'd)
NEW YORK (Cont'd)
New York

	BERNER, Andrew J.	(212)515-5299	88
	BRAUN, Robert L.		130
	BREWER, Joseph	(212)744-3828	134
	BROUDE, Ronald	(212)242-7001	141
	CASSELL, Kay A.	(212)614-6551	193
	CHITTAMPALLI, Padma S.	(212)874-0141	209
	COHEN, Frederick S.	(212)594-9880	228
	COHEN, Jackson B.	(212)595-6981	228
	COHEN, Rochelle F.	(212)577-3333	229
	COLBY, Robert A.	(212)787-3062	230
	COPLEN, Ron	(212)869-3348	244
	CROCKER, Susan O.	(212)777-8900	259
	CURTIS, James A.	(212)222-9638	267
	DEVERA, Rosalinda M.	(212)557-2570	297
	DOUET, Madeleine J.	(212)755-4500	313
	FEBLES, Mary T.	(212)210-3983	367
	FISHER, Carolyn H.	(212)873-0844	380
	FODY, Barbara A.	(212)713-3673	387
	FOLTER, Roland	(212)687-4808	388
	FRIEDMAN, Judy B.		404
	GINSBURG, Carol L.	(212)850-1440	438
	GOSSAGE, Wayne	(212)869-3348	453
	GOTTLIEB, Jane E.	(212)362-8671	453
	GRECH, Anthony P.	(212)382-6740	461
	GRETES, Frances C.	(212)309-9634	467
	HARRIS, Carolyn L.	(212)280-2223	504
	HAYNES, Patricia	(212)371-3200	516
	HEWITT, Vivian D.		535
	HUDSON, Alice C.	(212)222-2835	569
	HUTSON, Jean B.	(212)368-1515	579
	JONES, Roger A.	(212)777-2959	615
	KANIA, Antoinette M.		625
	KAPNICK, Laura B.	(212)975-2917	626
	KLECKNER, Simone M.	(212)877-2448	658
	KOLATA, Judith	(212)902-0080	669
	LEWIS, Margaret S.	(212)420-5090	723
	LIN, Tung F.	(212)669-5178	728
	LINDGREN, Arla M.	(212)662-6386	729
	LUBETSKI, Edith E.	(212)340-7720	745
	MACK, Phyllis G.	(212)926-2479	756
	MANDAL, Mina R.	(212)491-8266	764
	MASYR, Caryl L.	(212)777-9271	783
	MAYER, George L.	(212)724-8057	789
	MCSWEENEY, Josephine	(212)254-6338	818
	MERKIN, David	(212)837-6588	826
	MILLER, Ellen L.	(212)406-3186	837
	MILLER, Michael D.		841
	MILLER-KUMMERFELD, Elizabeth	(212)751-0830	843
	MOUNT, Albertina F.	(212)305-2916	873
	NELOMS, Karen H.	(212)582-9239	893
	NESTA, Frederick N.	(212)982-9672	896
	OSTROWSKY, Edith	(212)340-0890	929
	OSTWALD, Mark F.		929
	PALMER, Paul R.	(212)865-5781	936
	PANELLA, Nancy M.		938
	PAVLAKIS, Christopher		950
	PELLOWSKI, Anne	(212)316-1170	955
	PETTOLINA, Anthony M.	(212)790-2888	965
	PHILLPOT, Clive J.	(212)708-9431	969
	PINES, Doralynn	(212)570-3969	974
	PRAGER, George A.	(212)725-3083	989
	RACHOW, Louis A.	(212)228-7610	1001
	RAJEC, Elizabeth M.	(212)690-4151	1004
	RAUM, Tamar	(212)889-2156	1010
	RICHARDS, Daniel T.	(212)678-0908	1028
	ROTHMAN, John	(212)645-3008	1060
	ROTHSTEIN, Pauline M.	(212)750-6008	1060
	ST. CLAIR, Guy	(212)515-5299	1075
	SCHUMAN, Patricia G.	(212)925-8650	1103
	SEGAL, Judith	(212)222-3699	1112
	SLOAN, William J.	(212)708-9530	1150
	SOMMER, Susan T.	(212)870-1648	1167
	STOLLER, Michael E.	(212)280-4356	1196
	SWANSON, Dorothy T.	(212)998-2630	1213
	TAYLOR, Robert N.	(212)664-9021	1228
	TICE, Margaret E.		1244

COLLECTION DEVELOPMENT/EVALUATION CONSULTANT (Cont'd)
NEW YORK (Cont'd)
New York

	VAJDA, Elizabeth A.	(212)254-6300	1271
	VAN DYKE, Stehpen H.	(212)340-0872	1275
	VINCENT-DAVISS, Diana	(212)598-2367	1284
	WALKER, William B.	(212)595-7335	1296
	WARNER, Elaine	(212)477-9517	1305
	WEATHERFORD, Elizabeth	(212)925-4682	1311
	WERTSMAN, Vladimir F.	(212)246-8176	1325
	WRIGHT, Sylvia H.	(212)222-6148	1373
	YAKEL, Elizabeth	(212)581-7400	1376
	ZARCONE, Beth B.	(212)982-0055	1386
Newburgh	AIMONE, Alan C.	(914)564-2419	8
North Bellmore	SHERWOOD, Nancy	(516)781-5063	1129
Old Westbury	COLLANTES, Lourdes Y.	(516)876-3154	232
Oneonta	CHIANG, Nancy	(607)432-4200	207
	CROWLEY, John V.	(607)431-2725	261
Orchard Park	WILLET, Ruth J.	(716)662-3598	1341
Ossining	FRANCK, Jane P.	(914)762-6073	396
	LEW, Susan	(914)762-1154	722
Oswego	CHU, Sylvia	(315)341-3210	213
Patchogue	BOROCK, Freddie	(516)654-7774	116
Peekskill	HALLINAN, Patricia R.	(914)739-2268	489
	SALUSTRI, Madeline	(914)739-2823	1077
Plattsburgh	BURTON, Robert E.	(518)561-1613	164
Port Chester	LETTIERI, Robin M.	(914)939-6710	719
Port Washington	BRENNER, Everett H.	(516)767-2728	133
Poughkeepsie	SEEBER, Frances M.	(914)452-8122	1111
	WIGG, Ristiina M.	(914)471-6060	1337
Purchase	EVANS, Robert W.	(914)253-5085	358
Rochester	BALKIN, Ruth G.	(716)482-1506	52
	BARNES, Robert W.	(716)428-7335	57
	BLUM, Elaine G.	(716)423-1611	107
	BUFF, Iva M.	(716)244-7762	155
	CUSEO, Allan A.	(716)325-4264	267
	GLASER, June E.	(716)275-5010	439
	RITTER, Audrey L.	(716)475-6823	1036
	ROBBINS, Diane D.	(716)473-2200	1038
	ROSENBERG-NUGENT, Nanci B.		1056
Rockville Centre	FRIEDLAND, Rhoda W.	(516)766-6387	403
Roslyn	SIAHPOOSH, Farideh T.	(516)627-1919	1134
St James	WIENER, Paul B.	(516)862-8723	1336
Saratoga Springs	DOE, Lynn M.	(518)584-5000	308
	KEARNEY, Robert D.	(518)587-7470	633
Scarsdale	COAN, Mary L.	(914)723-5325	224
Schenectady	HODGES, Lois F.	(518)377-7738	546
	HUMPHRY, John A.	(518)374-8944	574
	KING, Maryde F.	(518)374-7287	651
	KLEMPNER, Irving M.	(518)393-5983	660
Seaford	FLUCKIGER, Adrienne N.	(516)221-1334	386
Setauket	PACKARD, Agnes K.		933
Somers	BURROWS, Shirley	(914)767-7337	163
	RITTER, Sally K.	(914)232-7889	1037
Sparkill	BARRIE, John L.	(914)359-7200	59
Staten Island	HOGAN, Matthew	(718)273-6245	549
	SCHUT, Grace W.	(718)442-5659	1103
Stony Brook	SEWELL, Robert G.	(516)632-7100	1117
Sunnyside	WOOD, Sallie B.	(718)565-5490	1365
Syracuse	HORRELL, Jeffrey L.	(315)423-2585	560
	HULBERT, Linda A.	(315)473-4257	572
	LANTZY, M L.	(315)423-2527	697
	PRINS, Johanna W.	(315)475-5534	993
	SHELANDER, Frances R.	(315)469-8068	1125
	STAM, Deirdre C.		1179
Three Mile Bay	PIZER, Charles R.	(315)649-5086	977
	PIZER, Elizabeth F.	(315)649-5086	977
Troy	BLANDY, Susan G.	(518)274-2098	104
Voorheesville	BARRON, Robert E.		60
Wallkill	RUBIN, Ellen B.	(914)565-5620	1064
Wantagh	LOMONACO, Martha S.	(516)783-9051	738
Water Mill	GROSSMAN, Adrian J.	(516)537-3623	473
West Islip	JOYCE, Therese	(516)587-8000	618
West Nyack	SIVULICH, Sandra S.	(914)358-9298	1145
White Plains	HIGGINS, Judith H.	(914)949-2175	538
	LEWIS, Marjorie	(914)428-5759	723
Williamsville	BOBINSKI, Mary F.	(716)688-4919	108
Wynantskill	CORSARO, James		248
Yonkers	GAFFNEY, Ellen E.	(914)968-6200	412

COLLECTION DEVELOPMENT/EVALUATION CONSULTANT (Cont'd)
NEW YORK (Cont'd)

Yorktown Heights	YURO, David A.	(914)962-5200	1384

NORTH CAROLINA

Albemarle	LACROIX, Michael J.	(704)982-1036	686
Asheville	BUTSON, Linda C.	(704)254-2932	167
Bahama	STINE, Roy S.	(719)471-8853	1194
Beulaville	FRAZELLE, Betty	(919)298-4658	399
Boone	HATHAWAY, Milton G.	(704)262-5113	512
Cary	OLSON, David J.	(919)469-8176	922
Chapel Hill	BROADUS, Robert N.	(919)962-8063	138
	COGGINS, Timothy L.	(919)962-6202	227
	DICKERSON, Jimmy	(919)962-1188	300
	GRENDLER, Marcella	(919)962-0114	467
	MCNAMARA, Charles B.	(919)962-1143	816
	OWEN, Willy	(919)962-1301	932
	PEACOCK, Helen M.		951
	PRILLAMAN, Susan M.	(919)962-3791	993
	SWINDLER, Luke	(919)962-8045	1216
	WILLIAMS, Wiley J.		1347
Charlotte	MYERS, Carol B.	(704)523-1260	884
	WALKER, Judith A.	(704)547-2559	1295
Cullowhee	LESUEUR, Joan K.	(704)456-3396	718
Dallas	HUNSUCKER, David L.	(704)922-8041	575
Durham	BRUCE, Nancy G.	(919)490-0069	149
	HAZEL, Debora E.	(919)683-6473	517
	SOUTHERN, Mary A.	(919)684-8118	1170
	STRAUSS, Diane	(919)286-7895	1201
	TOOMER, Clarence	(919)682-0238	1251
	WOODBURN, Judy I.	(919)684-5987	1366
Fayetteville	BEATTIE, Barbara C.	(919)867-5143	70
	DEVITO, Robert M.	(919)483-7727	297
	KRIEGER, Lee A.	(919)864-9349	678
Greensboro	HANHAN, Leila M.	(919)292-1115	495
	PARROTT, Margaret S.	(919)294-2087	944
	RANCER, Susan P.	(919)288-2160	1006
	TUGWELL, Helen M.	(919)334-5764	1262
	WINKEL, Lois	(919)275-4935	1355
Greenville	CHENG, Chao S.	(929)756-4543	206
	LANIER, Gene D.	(919)757-6627	696
	SCOTT, Ralph L.	(919)830-0522	1108
	YORK, Maurice C.	(919)752-5260	1381
Kinston	EARL, Susan R.	(919)522-4773	332
Kittrell	SHAFFER, Nancy R.	(919)492-9684	1119
Montreat	BROOKS, Jerrold L.	(704)669-7661	140
	FERM, Lois R.	(704)669-5550	373
	FOREMAN, Kenneth J.	(704)669-2782	390
Morganton	BUSH, Mary E.	(704)433-2303	165
Raleigh	BRADBURN, Frances B.	(919)878-4497	125
	SMITH, Catherine	(919)851-4703	1153
Reidsville	GUNN, Shirley A.	(919)342-0951	477
	KING, Willard B.	(919)349-6192	652
Rocky Mount	WILGUS, Anne B.	(919)442-2662	1339
Sanford	MATOCHIK, Michael J.	(919)776-5737	784
Spring Hope	LANEY, Elizabeth J.	(919)478-3836	695
Winston-Salem	CHAPMAN, Peggy H.	(919)727-2373	202
	RODNEY, Mae L.	(919)924-6992	1048
	SIBLEY, Shawn C.	(919)777-3020	1135
	STEELE, Tom M.	(919)761-5440	1184

NORTH DAKOTA

Bismarck	GRAY, David P.	(701)224-2668	459
Ellendale	ZINK, Esther L.	(701)349-3609	1389
Fargo	SIBLEY, Carol H.	(701)235-0664	1134
Grand Forks	BOONE, Jon A.	(701)777-4637	115

OHIO

Akron	BRINK, David R.	(216)375-7224	136
Ashland	RHOADES, Nancy L.	(419)289-3969	1025
Athens	HOUDEK, G R.	(614)593-5444	562
	OBERLE, Holly E.		914
Bowling Green	HARNER, James L.	(419)372-7553	503
	MILLER, William	(419)372-2857	843
Centerville	GARTEN, Edward D.		420
Chardon	KLINGER, William E.	(216)564-9340	661
Cincinnati	DAVIS, Yvonne M.	(513)221-7699	281
	FERGUSON, George E.	(513)559-9908	372
	HILAND, Gerard P.	(513)231-0810	538
	LEWIS, Betty J.		722

COLLECTION DEVELOPMENT/EVALUATION CONSULTANT (Cont'd)
OHIO (Cont'd)

Cincinnati	MC NAIR, Marian B.	(513)369-4750	815
	NASRALLAH, Wahib T.	(513)475-2411	888
	PATIENCE, Alice	(513)841-8589	947
	PROPAS, Sharon W.	(513)475-2411	995
	THOMPSON, Ann M.	(513)474-1443	1238
	WELKER, Kathy J.	(513)684-2678	1321
Cleveland	BOBICK, James E.	(216)368-2992	108
	DRACH, Priscilla L.		318
	EAGLEN, Audrey B.	(216)398-1800	331
	GILLMORE, Salley G.	(216)442-2200	436
	JARABEK, Leona T.	(216)433-5767	594
	MICHNAY, Susan E.	(216)749-7400	832
	ORR, Cynthia	(216)449-2049	926
	PEARMAN, Sara J.	(211)421-7340	952
	RAY, Laura E.	(216)844-3788	1011
	SANTAVICCA, Edmund F.	(216)687-2365	1082
	STANLEY, Jean B.	(216)368-6596	1180
Cleveland Heights	PIETY, John S.	(216)321-8121	972
	SPAHR, Cheryl L.	(216)382-7675	1170
Columbus	BLOUGH, Keith A.	(614)221-4181	106
	BOOMGAARDEN, Wesley L.	(614)447-0524	115
	BRANN, Andrew R.	(614)221-4181	128
	CANTWELL, Mary L.	(614)459-1704	179
	CENTING, Richard R.	(614)292-6175	196
	FU, Paul S.	(614)466-2044	407
	GOLDING, Alfred S.		445
	HADDOCK, Mable	(614)258-9052	482
	HUBER, Donald L.	(614)235-4136	569
	IRELAND, Clara R.	(614)486-9891	583
	MCWILLIAM, Deborah A.	(614)222-7165	818
	MIXTER, Keith E.	(614)263-7204	850
	ORLANDO, Jacqueline M.	(614)262-6765	926
	SANDERS, Nancy P.		1080
	STRALEY, Dona S.	(614)292-3362	1200
	TANNEHILL, Robert S.	(614)488-7587	1222
	WALDEN, Graham R.	(614)292-0938	1294
	WOODS, Alan L.	(614)292-8251	1366
Dayton	EVANS, Stephen P.	(513)220-9506	358
	MCNEER, Elizabeth J.	(513)873-2686	816
	PURSCH, Lenore D.	(513)434-7064	998
	QUINTEN, Rebecca G.	(513)277-3598	1000
	TRIVEDI, Harish S.	(513)225-2201	1257
	VANGROV, Helene R.	(513)274-5622	1275
Delaware	GILBERT, Donna J.	(614)369-7705	433
Elyria	RUSSO, Stephen A.		1070
Fairborn	BAKER, Narcissa L.	(573)879-3638	49
Findlay	DICKINSON, Luren E.	(419)423-4934	301
Gambier	WILT, Charles F.	(614)427-5681	1353
Georgetown	TOMLIN, Marsha A.	(513)378-3154	1250
Greenbrier Commons	BINA, Marcella A.	(216)884-2313	97
Highland Heights	JENKINS, Glen P.	(216)442-1475	597
Hubbard	GROHL, Arlene P.	(216)759-7800	471
Kent	WYNAR, Lubomyr R.		1375
Lakewood	JANES, Jodith	(216)221-0437	593
Mansfield	BENISHEK, Kristine K.	(419)526-8515	81
Mogadore	SMITH, Cynthia A.	(216)678-0662	1153
New Philadelphia	KOBULNICKY, Michael	(216)339-3391	666
Oberlin	CARPENTER, Eric J.	(216)775-2546	184
Oxford	QUAY, Richard H.	(513)529-4145	999
	WORTMAN, William A.	(513)529-3936	1369
Parma	ROBINSON, Doris J.	(216)888-3462	1043
Perrysburg	LOCKE-GAGNON, Rebecca A.	(419)874-1725	736
Rootstown	BREWER, Karen L.	(216)325-2511	134
Shaker Heights	MELTON, Vivian B.	(216)921-5803	823
	RODDA, Donna S.	(216)283-1064	1047
South Euclid	BENSING, Karen M.	(216)932-0186	83
Steubenville	HALL, Alan C.	(614)264-4410	486
Toledo	BAKER, Paula J.	(419)472-0204	49
	HANNAFORD, Claudia L.	(419)536-7539	496
Walton Hills	POJMAN, Paul E.	(216)232-0527	980
Wapakoneta	FREW, Martha G.	(419)738-8333	402
Warrensville	GORDON, Shirlee J.		452
Westlake	CHARVAT, Catherine T.	(216)871-6391	203
Wilmington	NICHOLS, James T.	(513)382-6661	901
Worthington	EAST, Dennis	(614)888-9923	332

COLLECTION DEVELOPMENT/EVALUATION CONSULTANT (Cont'd)
OHIO (Cont'd)

Xenia	OVERTON, Julie M.	(513)376-4952	931
	WALDER, Antoinette L.	(513)376-2995	1294
Youngstown	DONAHUGH, Robert H.	(216)788-6950	310
	YANCURA, Ann J.	(216)746-7042	1377

OKLAHOMA

Edmond	ALSWORTH, Frances W.	(405)341-2980	18
	ROADS, Clarice D.	(405)341-3660	1038
McAlester	SIMON, Bradley A.	(918)423-3468	1140
Midwest City	PETERSON, Denise D.		963
Norman	CALLARD, Joanne C.	(405)364-0667	173
	MCKNIGHT, Michelynn	(405)360-2080	812
Oklahoma City	CORLEE, Lisa	(405)235-0571	246
	CORNEIL, Charlotte E.	(405)235-7763	246
	JONES, Charles E.	(405)751-0574	611
	LITTLE, Paul L.	(405)789-9400	733
Stillwater	HILKER, Emerson W.	(405)624-6305	539
Tishomingo	KENNEDY, James W.	(405)371-2528	641
Tulsa	SMITH, Donald R.	(918)592-6000	1154

OREGON

Albany	FELLA, Sarah C.	(503)928-2361	370
Ashland	OTNES, Harold M.	(503)482-6445	930
Bend	BYRNE, Helen E.	(503)382-1621	169
Corvallis	MURRAY, Lucia M.		882
Eugene	EMMENS, Thomas A.	(503)345-6439	348
	HADDERMAN, Margaret	(503)342-5457	482
	HEINZKILL, J R.	(503)686-3078	522
	KNIEVEL, Helen A.	(503)345-2032	664
	ROBERTSON, Howard W.	(503)686-3064	1042
	STIRLING, Isabel A.	(503)686-3075	1195
Monmouth	GORCHELS, Clarence C.	(503)838-1274	451
Newport	KRABBE, Natalie	(503)336-2546	674
Portland	DAVID, Kay O.	(503)222-9981	276
	FERGUSON, Douglas K.	(503)228-5512	372
	INGRAHAM-SWETS, Leonoor	(503)222-2608	582
	JONES, Mary C.	(503)228-7016	614
	KENNEY, Ann J.	(503)297-1894	641
	METZENBACHER, Gary W.	(503)654-5182	828
	PIPER, Larry W.	(503)232-1781	975
	TEICH, Steven	(503)225-8026	1230
Salem	BUSHMAN, James L.	(503)585-9121	165
	DOAK, Wesley A.	(503)581-4292	306
Tolovanna Park	NAKATA, Yuri		887

PENNSYLVANIA

Abington	DOLE, Wanda V.	(215)886-9400	309
Alcoa Center	MOUNTS, Earl L.	(412)337-2396	873
Allison Park	HADIDIAN, Dikran Y.	(412)487-2159	482
Ambler	MORROW, Ellen B.	(215)646-1755	869
Ambridge	MUNDAY, Robert S.	(412)266-3838	878
Bala Cynwyd	KREMER, Jill L.	(215)667-6787	677
Berwyn	MACBETH, Eileen M.	(215)296-3430	754
	SCAMMAHORN, Lynne	(215)296-3430	1087
Bethel Park	MCGINNESS, Mary B.	(412)835-2207	806
Bethlehem	JARVIS, William E.	(215)758-3035	595
Bloomsburg	ROCKWOOD, Susan M.	(717)784-8456	1046
	VANN, John D.	(717)784-4283	1276
Blue Bell	TERRY, Terese M.	(215)641-6594	1232
Broomall	CLINTON, Janet C.	(215)356-1927	222
California	BECK, William L.	(412)938-4096	72
Camp Hill	ALBRECHT, Lois K.	(717)737-6111	10
Chester Heights	OWENS, Irene E.		932
Chester Springs	GREBEY, Betty H.	(215)469-9333	461
Clarion	MCCABE, Gerard B.	(814)226-2343	792
Coatesville	SILVER, Diane L.	(215)384-7648	1138
Danielsville	PAGOTTO, Sarah L.	(215)767-3055	934
Drexel Hill	MULLEN, Francis X.	(215)623-7045	877
Eagleville	PECK, Marian B.	(215)631-1129	953
Erie	GALLIVAN, Marion F.	(814)452-2333	414
	RITTENHOUSE, Robert J.	(814)838-4124	1036
Glen Rock	LIEBERMAN, Ronald	(717)235-2134	726
Harrisburg	MALLINGER, Stephen M.	(717)783-5737	763
Hatboro	BURNS, Richard K.	(215)675-6762	162
Haverford	ROBERTSON, Robert B.	(215)896-1273	1042
Holsopple	SLICK, Myrna H.	(814)479-7148	1149
Indiana	ELLIKER, Calvin	(412)357-2892	343
	KROAH, Larry A.	(412)463-2055	679

COLLECTION DEVELOPMENT/EVALUATION CONSULTANT (Cont'd)
PENNSYLVANIA (Cont'd)

Johnstown	BRICE, Heather W.	(814)539-8153	134
	WILSON, Fred L.	(814)288-3363	1351
Kutztown	MACK, Sara R.		756
Lansdale	BLAUERT, Mary A.	(215)822-2929	105
Lewisburg	JENKS, George M.	(717)524-3250	597
Lionville	MCSWAIN, Christy A.	(215)269-7672	818
McKeesport	HERRON, Nancy L.	(412)675-9111	533
Media	BURGESS, Rita N.	(215)565-7900	159
	ELLISON, J T.	(215)566-1699	345
Middletown	BARRY, James W.		60
	RAMBLER, Linda K.	(412)349-4621	1005
Millersville	JUDGE, Joseph M.	(717)872-7590	619
Miquon	MANCALL, Jacqueline C.	(215)828-4410	764
Monroeville	MURPHY, Diana G.	(412)327-5976	880
Narberth	SOKOLOFF, Michele	(215)664-2117	1165
New Kensington	TEOLIS, Marilyn G.	(412)339-0255	1231
New Kingstown	HANSON, Eugene R.	(717)243-0973	498
New Milford	MAASS, Eleanor A.	(717)465-3054	753
New Wilmington	BRAUTIGAM, David K.	(412)946-7330	130
North Wales	MAXIN, Jacqueline A.	(215)855-5675	787
Philadelphia	AZZOLINA, David S.	(215)898-8118	43
	BAKY, John S.	(215)951-1290	50
	BARR, Marilyn P.	(215)844-2036	58
	BAUMGARTNER, Barbara W.	(215)686-5418	66
	BRADLEY, James S.	(215)242-6112	126
	BUTLER, Evelyn		166
	CLEVELAND, Susan E.	(215)662-2577	221
	CRESSWELL, Donald H.	(215)242-4750	258
	FIELD, Carolyn W.	(215)438-4086	375
	FUSELER-MCDOWELL, Elizabeth A.	(215)423-9294	410
	GRAY, Priscilla M.	(215)386-6276	460
	GRIFFITH, Belver C.	(215)895-2474	469
	GRILIKHES, Sandra B.	(215)898-7027	470
	GROSSMAN, Robert M.	(215)893-1954	473
	HOLUB, Joseph C.	(215)843-6220	555
	HORNIG-ROHAN, James E.	(215)848-0554	560
	MADER, Marion C.	(215)342-0760	759
	MARCO, Guy A.		769
	MCKITTRICK, Bruce W.	(215)235-3209	812
	MEREDITH, Phyllis C.	(609)757-4640	825
	MICIKAS, Lynda L.	(215)637-7700	832
	MOWERY, Susan G.	(215)248-8206	874
	MYERS, Charles J.	(215)898-7267	884
	PARKER, Peter J.	(215)732-6200	942
	POST, Jeremiah B.	(215)748-2701	986
	ROEDELL, Ray F.	(215)739-7739	1048
	RUGGERE, Christine A.	(215)898-7088	1066
	SAUNDERS, William B.	(215)224-0235	1085
	SNOWTEN, Renee Y.	(215)557-8295	1164
	SOULTOUKIS, Donna Z.	(215)922-5460	1169
	SOWICZ, Eugenia V.	(215)354-2110	1170
	TERRY, Joseph D.	(215)686-5348	1232
	WALSH, James A.	(215)587-4877	1299
	WARTLUFT, David J.	(215)242-8746	1307
Phoenixville	SAUER, James L.	(215)933-2236	1084
Pittsburgh	BLAIR, William W.	(412)355-8071	103
	DETLEFSEN, Ellen G.	(412)624-9444	296
	DILWORTH, Kirby D.	(412)622-3105	303
	GREEN, Joyce M.	(412)234-5039	462
	KIRCHER, Linda M.	(412)624-9444	654
	KRZYS, Richard A.	(412)624-9459	681
	MAWHINNEY, Paul C.	(412)367-7330	787
	PARADISE, Don M.	(412)929-9800	939
	PISCIOTTA, Henry A.	(412)268-2451	976
	RAO, Rama K.	(412)429-0543	1008
	RICHARDS, Barbara G.	(412)268-2448	1028
	ROOT, Deane L.	(412)624-4100	1054
	SCHUMACHER, Carolyn S.	(412)363-0190	1102
	SPIEGELMAN, Barbara M.	(412)824-2222	1174
	STEPHENS, Norris L.	(412)624-4130	1188
	STERLING, Alida B.	(412)323-1430	1189
	TINSLEY, Geraldine L.	(412)268-2427	1246
	WESSEL, Charles B.	(412)731-8800	1325
	WRAY, Wendell L.	(412)363-0251	1370
	ZABROSKY, Frank A.	(412)648-8197	1385
Reading	HANNAFORD, William E.	(802)468-5611	496
	STILLMAN, Mary E.	(215)921-2381	1194

COLLECTION DEVELOPMENT/EVALUATION CONSULTANT (Cont'd)

PENNSYLVANIA (Cont'd)

Revere	WOOLMER, J H.	(215)847-5074	1368
Scranton	CAMPION, Carol M.	(717)348-0538	177
	SPEIRS, Gilmary	(717)348-6266	1172
Shenandoah	USES, Ann K.	(717)462-0076	1270
Shippensburg	SHONTZ, Marilyn L.	(717)532-1472	1132
State College	CARR, Caryn J.	(814)234-4203	185
Swarthmore	LEHMANN, Stephen R.	(215)328-8492	713
Tamaqua	TUZINSKI, Jean H.	(717)668-2970	1266
Topton	SPRANKLE, Anita T.		1176
University Park	CONKLING, Thomas W.	(814)865-3451	236
	KAISER, John R.	(814)863-1561	622
	ROE, Eunice M.	(814)863-0140	1048
Villanova	BUSHNELL, Marietta P.	(215)527-2377	165
	DREHER, Janet H.		319
	LEWIS, Marjorie B.		724
	WEINER, Betty	(215)688-6950	1318
West Chester	AMICONE, Janice L.	(215)692-6889	20
	CHAFF, Sandra L.	(215)524-0547	197
	MILES, Donald D.	(215)431-7685	834
West Point	MESSICK, Karen J.	(215)661-6026	828

PUERTO RICO

Ensenada	MEJILL-VEGA, Gregorio	(809)821-4734	822
Guaynabo	LEON, Carmencita H.	(809)792-7873	716
	MOMBILLE, Pedro	(809)783-8622	854
Miramar	CASAS DE FAUNCE, Maria		191
Ponce	PADUA, Flores N.	(809)844-4150	934
	SANTIAGO, Maria	(809)844-4150	1082
Rio Piedras	MUNOZ-SOLA, Haydee	(809)764-0000	879
San German	ALSTON, Jane C.	(809)892-3523	18
San Juan	HAMEL, Eleanor C.	(809)765-4426	491
	NADAL, Antonio	(809)724-6869	885
San Sebastian	JARAMILLO, Juana S.	(809)896-1389	594

RHODE ISLAND

Carolina	HULL, Catherine C.	(401)364-6100	572
Chepachet	DESJARLAIS-LUETH, Christine	(401)568-8614	295
Kingston	FUTAS, Elizabeth	(401)792-2947	411
	VOCINO, Michael C.	(401)789-9357	1286
Lincoln	DESMARAIS, Norman P.	(401)333-3275	295
Newport	CARSON, Josephine R.		188
Portsmouth	AYLWARD, James F.	(401)683-1889	42
Providence	DOHERTY, Joseph H.	(401)865-2244	309
	LATHROP, Irene M.	(401)277-8070	701
	LYNDEN, Frederick C.	(401)863-2946	752
	MARSH, Corrie V.	(401)863-2954	773
	MICHAEL, Richard T.	(401)456-9314	831
	WILMETH, Don B.	(401)863-3289	1349
Westerly	LIGHT, Karen M.	(401)596-2877	726
Woonsocket	LEVEILLEE, Louis R.	(401)762-4440	719

SOUTH CAROLINA

Aiken	JACOBS, Mildred H.		589
Cayce	FREEMAN, Larry S.	(803)794-5370	401
Charleston	MOLTKE-HANSEN, David	(803)723-3225	853
	STRAUCH, Katina P.	(803)723-3536	1200
Clemson	DIXON, Linda A.		306
Columbia	BARRON, Daniel D.	(803)777-4825	60
	CHOI, Jin M.	(803)799-8786	210
	HOWARD-HILL, Trevor	(803)777-6499	564
	VASSALLO, John A.	(803)776-7286	1279
Glendale	WHITE, Ann T.	(803)579-3330	1330
Greenville	SCALES, Pat R.	(803)232-1271	1087
	TOWELL, Fay J.	(803)232-2941	1252
McCormick	TOWNSEND, Catherine M.	(803)465-3185	1253
Newberry	HAMILTON, Ben	(803)276-6870	491
Rock Hill	KELLEY, Gloria	(803)325-2131	636
Sumter	GORDON, Clara B.	(803)773-4041	451
Surfside Beach	KLEM, Marjorie R.	(803)238-0460	660

SOUTH DAKOTA

Brookings	BROWN, Philip L.	(605)692-7735	146
Pierre	GILLILAND, Donna E.	(605)224-1358	436
Sioux Falls	DUNGER, George A.	(605)336-6588	326

COLLECTION DEVELOPMENT/EVALUATION CONSULTANT (Cont'd)

TENNESSEE

Bartlett	HAIR, William B.	(901)377-5434	484
Bristol	HERRING, Mark Y.	(615)968-9449	533
Cookeville	JONES, Roger G.	(615)526-5557	615
	TABACHNICK, Sharon	(615)372-3958	1219
Dowelltown	EASTERLY, Ambrose	(615)597-1390	333
Germantown	COOPER, Ellen R.	(901)755-7411	242
Jackson	ROBERTSON, Billy O.	(901)668-1818	1041
Knoxville	ROBINSON, William C.	(615)974-2148	1045
Memphis	BANNERMAN-WILLIAMS, Cheryl F.	(901)785-7350	54
	BOAZ, Ruth L.	(901)682-0595	108
	BUNTING, Anne C.	(901)528-5635	157
	EVANS, David H.	(901)454-3317	356
	LINDENFELD, Joseph F.	(901)528-6743	729
	MABBOTT, Deborah D.	(901)388-1096	753
Murfreesboro	MARSHALL, John D.	(615)893-2091	774
Nashville	FANCHER, Evelyn P.	(615)255-8033	363
	GLEAVES, Edwin S.	(615)741-3666	441
	GMEINER, Timothy J.	(615)297-7958	442
	HARWELL, Sara J.	(615)322-2807	509
	PATTERSON, Jennifer J.	(615)383-4251	948
	SHOCKLEY, Ann A.	(615)353-0771	1132
	STEPHENS, Alonzo T.		1187
Oak Ridge	EKKEBUS, Allen E.	(615)574-5485	341
Old Hickory	MCHOLLIN, Mattie L.	(615)754-5411	809
Signal Mountain	JACKSON, Joseph A.	(615)886-1753	587

TEXAS

Alpine	SPEARS, Norman L.	(915)837-8121	1172
Amarillo	WELLS, Mary K.	(806)381-2435	1322
Angelton	BROWN, Steven L.	(409)849-5711	147
Arlington	MACFARLANE, Francis X.	(817)265-8309	755
	WILKERSON, Judith C.	(817)795-6555	1339
Austin	ARTHUR, Donald B.	(512)471-5523	35
	BICHTELER, Julie H.	(512)471-3821	94
	BIERI, Sandra J.	(512)458-5551	95
	BILLINGS, Harold W.	(512)442-8597	96
	BRENNAN, Mary H.	(512)471-5523	132
	BUCKNALL, Carolyn F.	(512)478-5129	154
	BURLINGHAM, Merry L.		161
	CABLE, Carole L.	(512)327-2158	170
	CARTER, Janet K.	(512)463-5463	189
	DAVIS, Donald G.	(512)471-3821	278
	DAYO, Ayo	(512)472-8980	283
	HARMON, Jacqueline B.	(512)343-0978	502
	HOOKS, Michael Q.	(512)250-1419	556
	KAHLER, June	(512)463-9660	621
	MIDDLETON, Robert K.	(512)454-1888	833
	PARKER, David F.	(512)450-1931	941
	PAYNE, John R.	(512)478-7724	951
	PRATTER, Jonathan	(512)471-7726	990
	ROY, Loriene	(512)471-6316	1063
	WISE, Olga B.	(512)244-8330	1357
Bangs	WEEKS, Patsy L.	(915)752-7315	1315
Beaumont	NISBY, Dora R.	(409)899-9972	904
	POOL, Jeraldine B.	(409)753-3180	982
	SPARKMAN, Mickey M.	(409)880-8118	1171
Bellaire	HOLAB-ABELMAN, Robin S.		550
Bryan	RABINS, Joan W.	(409)776-0374	1001
Buda	TISSING, Robert W.	(512)295-4834	1247
Burkville	TEDDER, Dorothy L.	(409)565-2201	1229
Cleburne	CARDENAS, Martha L.	(817)641-6641	180
College Station	GYESZLY, Suzanne D.	(409)845-3731	479
	KELLOUGH, Jean L.	(409)845-2551	637
Dallas	BOCKSTRUCK, Lloyd D.	(214)670-1406	109
	BROWN, Muriel W.	(214)348-7861	146
	CLEMENTS, Cynthia L.	(214)238-6153	221
	CRABB, Elizabeth A.	(214)233-4382	254
	CROW, Rebecca N.	(214)749-4285	261
	FARMER, David	(214)692-3231	364
	FOUTS, Judith F.	(214)341-3961	393
	HOLLEMAN, Curt	(214)692-2324	551
	JONES, Lois S.	(214)528-2732	613
	JORDAN, Travis E.	(214)692-3199	617
	LEVINE, Harriet L.	(214)521-7165	720
	MENDRO, Donna C.		824
	METIVIER, Donna M.	(214)701-4222	828
	MIDGETT, Ann S.	(214)954-5966	833

COLLECTION DEVELOPMENT/EVALUATION CONSULTANT (Cont'd)
TEXAS (Cont'd)
Dallas

	MITCHE, Cynthia R.	(214)692-6767	848
	MITCHELL, Cynthia R.	(214)692-6767	848
	ORAM, Robert W.	(214)739-1310	925
	SMITH, Michael K.	(214)296-5187	1158
	WETHERBEE, Louella V.	(214)750-6130	1327
Denton	CARROLL, Dewey E.	(817)565-2445	187
	FERSTL, Kenneth L.	(817)383-3775	374
	FOLLET, Robert E.	(817)382-0037	388
	KHADER, Majed J.		645
	LAVENDER, Kenneth	(817)565-2768	703
	SCHLESSINGER, Bernard S.	(817)898-2617	1094
	SNAPP, Elizabeth M.	(817)387-3980	1162
	TOTTEN, Herman L.	(817)383-1902	1252
Edinburg	SHABOWICH, Stanley A.	(512)383-0441	1118
El Paso	FISCHER, Beverly J.	(915)595-0442	379
	GOODMAN, Helen C.	(915)584-4509	449
Fort Worth	ARBELBIDE, Cindy L.	(817)877-3355	30
	BRACEY, Ann E.	(817)738-9940	124
	CRAIGHEAD, Alice A.	(817)292-6571	254
	ELAM, Craig S.	(817)294-0817	341
	RICE, Ralph A.	(817)626-7995	1027
	ROARK, Carol E.	(817)926-4212	1038
	WROTENBERY, Carl R.	(817)923-1921	1373
Fredericksburg	YOUNG, Marjie D.	(512)997-2253	1382
Garland	MURRAY, Margaret A.	(214)494-7192	882
Houston	ALESSI, Dana L.	(713)669-0419	11
	BEDARD, Evelyn M.		73
	BUTLER, Marguerite L.	(713)726-9244	166
	CHANG, Robert H.	(713)221-8181	201
	ENDELMAN, Sharon B.	(713)247-3541	348
	FIELDING, Raymond E.	(713)749-7444	376
	GOLEY, Elaine P.	(713)467-5784	447
	HENINGTON, David M.	(713)247-2700	528
	HYMAN, Ferne B.	(713)527-8101	580
	JOITY, Donna M.	(713)583-7160	610
	LANGSTON, Sally J.	(713)659-8040	696
	LYDERS, Josette A.	(713)728-3893	750
	MAGNER, Mary F.	(713)870-7011	759
	MORRISSEY, Charles T.	(713)799-4510	869
	PORTER, Exa L.	(713)443-5491	984
	REIFEL, Louie E.		1019
	STUBBLEFIELD, J G.		1204
	SUDENGA, Sara A.	(713)527-8101	1206
Huntsville	BAILEY, William G.	(409)294-1614	47
	HOFFMAN, Frank W.	(409)294-1152	548
	PICHETTE, William H.	(409)291-2994	970
	THORNE, Bonnie B.		1242
Irving	COCHRAN, Carolyn	(214)258-6767	225
	LANKFORD, Mary D.	(214)579-7818	696
Kingsville	MERCHANT, Cheryl N.	(512)592-9684	825
Lewisville	TALLEY, Pat L.	(214)434-2545	1221
Lubbock	OLM, Jane G.	(806)742-3794	921
	SARGENT, Charles W.	(806)792-0754	1082
Marshall	MAGRILL, Rose M.	(214)935-7963	760
McKinney	CORREDOR, Javier	(214)548-9971	247
Midland	MIRANDA, Cecilia	(915)685-4557	847
Odessa	GROVES, Helen G.	(915)363-9604	474
Overton	HANES, Fred W.		495
Palacios	WOLL, Christina B.	(512)972-2166	1361
Pharr	LIU, David T.	(512)787-1491	734
Plano	DEILY, Carole C.	(214)578-7175	288
Richardson	HENEBRY, Carolyn L.	(214)690-2914	528
	KRATZ, Abby R.	(214)690-2960	676
	NISONGER, Thomas E.	(214)690-2961	905
San Antonio	CRINION, Jacquelyn A.	(512)691-4575	259
	HOLLOWAY, Geraldine B.	(512)531-3335	552
	HURT, Nancy S.	(512)225-5500	578
	KRONICK, David A.	(512)344-5796	679
	LANG, Anita E.	(512)684-5111	695
	LIKNESS, Craig S.	(512)736-7344	727
	MANEY, James W.	(512)341-1366	765
	PEDERSEN, Wayne A.	(512)641-4561	954
	TODD, Fred W.	(512)826-8121	1248
	WERKING, Richard H.	(512)736-8161	1324
Seguin	HSU, Patrick K.	(512)372-3868	567
Sherman	GARCIA, Lana C.	(214)893-4401	417
Spring	RIEMANN, Frederick A.	(713)288-3960	1033

COLLECTION DEVELOPMENT/EVALUATION CONSULTANT (Cont'd)
TEXAS (Cont'd)

The Woodlands	PEYTON, Janice L.	(713)292-4441	966
Uvalde	KINGSBERY, Evelyn B.	(512)278-4401	652
Waco	KEATTS, Rowena W.	(817)753-6415	633
	PHILLIPS, Luouida V.		968
Weatherford	HEEZEN, Ronald R.	(817)599-0833	520
Wichita Falls	HARVILL, Melba S.	(817)692-6611	509
Wimberley	SHAW, Ben B.	(512)847-2776	1123
	WAYLAND, Terry T.	(512)847-9295	1311

UTAH

Farmington	POLLARD, Louise	(801)451-5282	981
Logan	WEISS, Stephen C.		1320
North Salt Lake	YANG, Basil P.	(801)295-0276	1377
Ogden	WILSON, Brenda J.	(801)479-1407	1350
Provo	HALL, Blaine H.	(801)378-6117	487
	NIELSON, Paula I.	(801)375-9241	903
Salt Lake City	HEYER, Terry L.	(801)321-1054	535
	HOLLEY, Robert P.	(801)581-7741	551
	MCMURRIN, Jean A.	(801)322-1586	815
	PARTRIDGE, Cathleen F.	(801)277-3486	945
	PATTERSON, Myron B.	(801)581-7265	948
	SKIDMORE, Kerry F.		1146
	SPERRY, Kip	(801)255-9615	1174
Springville	PETERSON, Douglas L.	(801)489-5248	963

VERMONT

Burlington	SINGER, George C.	(802)863-3854	1143
	YERBURGH, Mark R.	(802)658-0337	1379
Chelsea	BATTEY, Jean D.	(802)276-3086	64
Richmond	REIT, Janet W.	(802)482-2352	1022
South Royalton	SWIFT, Esther M.	(802)763-7163	1216

VIRGIN ISLANDS

St Thomas	MILLS, Fiolina B.	(809)776-8396	844

VIRGINIA

Alexandria	AUSTON, Ione	(703)549-4325	40
	BROWN, Dale W.	(703)751-3236	143
	CALMES, Alan R.	(202)523-5496	174
	GOLDBERG, Jolande E.	(703)765-4521	444
	HARRISTON, Victoria R.	(203)642-5382	507
	HASSE, John E.		511
	JONES, Frank	(703)820-6283	613
	JORDAN, Robert T.		617
	KUHL, Danuta	(703)461-0234	682
Arlington	ALEXANDER, Carol G.		12
	BARRINGER, George M.	(703)920-2541	59
	COSGROVE-DAVIES, Lisa A.	(703)536-9452	248
	DESSAINT, Alain Y.	(703)247-7750	295
	GOLDBERG, Lisbeth S.	(703)243-0796	444
	HARRIS, Linda S.	(703)521-2541	505
	HIGBEE, Joan F.	(703)524-5844	537
	KECSKES, Lily C.	(703)528-0730	633
	LEATHER, Deborah J.	(703)522-5600	707
	WOODALL, Nancy C.	(703)528-5128	1365
Blacksburg	BAER, Eberhard A.	(703)951-3480	44
	JOHNSON, Bryan R.	(703)552-0876	602
	KOK, Victoria T.	(703)951-3203	669
Burke	STEPHENSON, Richard W.	(703)323-7721	1188
Charlottesville	CAMPBELL, James M.	(804)924-4985	176
	GORDON, Vesta L.	(804)295-5586	452
	JORDAN, Ervin L.	(804)924-4975	616
	KRAEHE, Mary A.	(804)295-3097	674
Chesterfield	WAGENKNECHT, Robert E.	(804)748-1601	1291
Fairfax	CRAWFORD, Elva B.	(703)425-6974	256
	GOODWIN, Jane G.	(703)246-5847	450
	WALCH, Timothy G.	(703)273-3260	1293
Falls Church	BEAM, Christopher M.	(703)356-4908	69
	KAHLER, Mary E.		622
Fredericksburg	BULLEY, Joan S.	(703)899-1597	156
	MULVANEY, John P.	(703)899-4666	878
Gloucester Point	BARRICK, Susan O.	(804)642-7114	59
Great Falls	CYLKE, Frank K.	(703)759-2031	268
Hampden Sydney	NORDEN, David J.	(804)223-4381	908
Hampton	BIGELOW, Therese G.	(804)727-6234	95
	DENDY, Adele S.	(804)727-5371	291

COLLECTION DEVELOPMENT/EVALUATION CONSULTANT (Cont'd)
VIRGINIA (Cont'd)

Harrisonburg	BLANKENBURG, Judith B.	(703)568-6792	104
	GILL, Gerald L.	(703)568-6898	435
	HABAN, Mary F.	(703)433-2183	480
	STEINBERG, David L.	(703)433-1572	1185
Lynchburg	KAWAGUCHI, Miyako	(804)239-3071	632
	SIDDONS, James D.	(804)846-8129	1135
	YOUNGER, Melinda M.	(804)384-2369	1383
Manassas	KILLEEN, Erlene B.	(703)369-7193	648
McLean	FURR, Susan H.	(703)893-4089	410
	WANG, Chi	(703)893-3016	1302
Norfolk	BREWER, Helen L.	(804)444-7951	134
	NICHOLSON, Myreen M.	(804)627-6281	902
Portsmouth	LIN, John T.	(804)484-2121	727
Reston	LISZEWSKI, Edward H.	(301)648-4306	733
Richmond	BAGAN, Beverly S.	(804)780-7691	45
	JOHNSON, Jane W.	(804)257-1112	605
	LIGGAN, Mary K.	(804)355-2509	726
	MOSER, Emily F.	(804)355-3348	870
	MURPHY, Robert D.	(804)741-1311	881
	REMICK, Katherine G.	(804)288-2665	1022
	SARTAIN, Sara M.		1083
	SMITH, Walter H.	(804)264-0539	1161
	SNAIR, Dale S.	(804)786-1489	1162
	TROTTI, John B.	(804)358-8956	1258
	WHALEY, John H.	(804)257-1108	1328
	ZANG, Patricia J.	(804)226-5712	1386
Roanoke	CHAMBERLAIN, M J.	(703)772-7556	197
Springfield	ALBIN, Michael W.	(703)978-3022	10
Sweet Briar	JAFFE, John G.	(804)381-6138	591
Triangle	GAUDET, Jean A.	(703)221-6434	422
Virginia Beach	CAYWOOD, Carolyn A.	(804)464-9320	195
	WISECARVER, Betty A.	(804)463-6666	1357
Williamsburg	PAISLEY, Anna S.	(804)229-7326	935
	SCHEITLE, Janet M.	(804)220-3104	1091
Wise	CHISHOLM, Clarence E.	(703)328-2431	209
Woodbridge	MELVIN, Kay H.	(703)491-2055	823
Wytheville	PRESGRAVES, Jim	(703)686-5813	991

WASHINGTON

Bellingham	PACKER, Donna E.	(206)676-3061	933
Blaine	BACON, Carey H.	(206)332-6045	44
Bothell	YEE, J E.	(206)625-4870	1379
East Wenatchee	BELT, Jane		78
Edmonds	HALEY, Marguerite R.	(206)546-6561	486
	STRONG, Sunny A.	(206)778-3804	1203
Ellensburg	DOI, Makiko	(509)963-2101	309
	SCHNEIDER, Frank A.	(509)963-1901	1097
Kenmore	TAYLOR, James B.	(206)483-2954	1227
Kennewick	KNOLL, Betty A.	(509)735-2173	665
Kirkland	ROBERTSON, Ann	(206)821-0506	1041
	SUGGS, John K.	(206)823-6754	1206
Lacey	WIEMAN, Jean M.	(206)491-4700	1336
Longview	DOLBEY, Mary B.	(206)577-2780	309
Olympia	KREIMEYER, Vicki R.	(206)753-2916	677
Pullman	FISHER, Rita C.	(509)335-2671	381
Richland	CARRIGAN, Marietta R.	(509)375-9671	186
	FOLEY, Katherine E.	(509)943-9117	387
Seattle	AUSTIN, Martha L.	(206)543-2988	40
	BOYLAN, Merle N.	(206)543-1760	123
	CHEN, Yvonne	(206)625-5523	205
	CLINE, Robert S.	(206)523-7268	222
	JOHNSON, Carolynn K.	(206)684-6681	603
	MCFADDEN, Denyse I.	(206)284-6280	804
	PASSARELLI, Anne B.	(206)543-4360	946
	POLISHUK, Bernard	(206)524-8676	980
	SONG, Seungja Y.	(206)527-8737	1167
	THOMAS, Lawrence E.	(206)626-6325	1237
	TOLLIVER, Barbara J.	(206)684-6615	1248
	TURNER, Tamara A.	(216)325-9481	1265
	TWENEY, George H.	(206)243-8243	1266
Spokane	LANE, Steven P.	(509)838-4728	694
	PRINGLE, Robert M.	(509)325-6139	993
Steilacoom	PARR, Loraine E.	(206)582-7557	943
Tacoma	BUELER, Roy D.	(206)593-6860	155
	GILDENHAR, Janet		434
	MENANTEAUX, A R.	(206)591-2973	823
Vancouver	HUTTON, Emily A.	(206)695-1566	579
Walla Walla	YAPLE, Henry M.	(509)527-5191	1377

COLLECTION DEVELOPMENT/EVALUATION CONSULTANT (Cont'd)
WEST VIRGINIA

Charleston	HUMPHRIES, Joy D.		574
	MARTIN, June R.	(304)343-4646	777
Fairmont	POWELL, Ruth A.	(304)367-4734	988
Huntington	FIDLER, Leah J.	(304)522-2744	375
Philippi	SIZEMORE, William C.		1145
St Albans	PALMER, Marguerite C.	(304)722-6349	936
Williamsburg	STROUD, John N.	(304)645-7169	1203

WISCONSIN

Appleton	PENNINGTON, Jerome G.	(414)735-6167	957
Burlington	PROCES, Stephen L.	(414)763-7623	994
De Pere	SADLON, Ramona J.	(414)336-6665	1074
Eau Claire	BUGHER, Kathryn M.	(715)834-8104	155
Green Bay	CORNELIUS, Charlene E.	(414)869-2370	246
	GORSEGNER, Betty D.	(414)465-1529	452
	MUSICH, Gerald D.	(414)437-7623	883
Greenfield	MEERDINK, Richard E.	(414)282-2229	821
Janesville	KRUEGER, Karen J.	(608)755-2800	680
La Crosse	CIMPL, Kathleen A.	(608)785-0530	214
	HILL, Edwin L.	(608)782-1753	539
Madison	BEHRND-KLODT, Menzi L.	(608)238-3966	75
	DRESANG, Eliza T.	(608)267-9357	319
	HOWDEN, Regis	(608)257-1023	565
	KRUSE, Ginny M.		681
	MCCONNELL, Shirley M.	(608)274-7222	798
	SEARING, Susan E.	(608)263-5754	1109
	WELSCH, Erwin K.	(608)262-3195	1323
	WHITCOMB, Dorothy V.	(608)262-2402	1330
	WILLIAMSON, William L.	(608)238-0770	1348
	WISEMAN, Mary J.		1357
Menasha	LOCH-WOUTERS, Marge	(414)724-5165	736
Menomonie	SAWIN, Philip Q.		1086
Mequon	NOVOTNY, Lynn E.	(414)241-8957	911
Milton	HAY, Mary K.	(608)868-7260	515
Milwaukee	ALTMANN, Thomas F.	(414)278-3000	18
	BRENNEN, Patrick W.	(414)257-8323	133
	JONES, Richard E.	(414)229-6457	614
	MARCUS, Terry C.	(414)352-5695	769
	MARKOWETZ, Marianna C.	(414)963-4074	771
	MCKILLIP, Rita J.	(414)347-1335	811
	MURPHY, Virginia E.	(414)271-1444	881
	SWEETLAND, James H.	(414)963-9996	1215
	WATERSTREET, Darlene E.	(414)964-2377	1309
New London	DIEHL, Carol L.	(414)982-5040	301
Oak Creek	TASNADI, Deborah L.	(414)764-9725	1224
Oshkosh	JONES, Norma L.	(414)231-5137	614
	PARKS, Dennis H.	(414)426-4800	943
Sheboygan	TOBIN, R J.	(414)459-7606	1247
Wauwatosa	BOCHTE, Terrence C.	(414)259-1414	109
Whitewater	SCHARFENBERG, George E.	(414)473-4246	1090

WYOMING

Cheyenne	BYERS, Edward W.	(307)635-1032	168
	RAO, Dittakavi N.	(307)777-7509	1008
Laramie	VANARSDALE, William O.	(307)766-4296	1272
Worland	HARRINGTON, Carolyn B.	(307)347-4490	504

CANADA

ALBERTA

Calgary	ANDERSON, Gail	(403)260-2646	23
	CRAMER, Eugene C.	(403)220-5376	255
	MACRAE, Lorne G.	(403)294-8538	758
	WHITE, Valerie L.	(403)255-6419	1332
Canmore	LUTHY, Jean M.	(403)678-5883	750
Edmonton	BERNARD, Marie L.	(403)455-2436	88
	BRUNDIN, Robert E.	(403)432-3930	150
	HU, Shih S.	(403)436-9716	568
	JONES, David L.	(403)481-3209	612
	LAVKULICH, Joanne	(403)427-3530	704
	MCLAUGHLIN, W K.	(403)427-3567	813
	RICHARDS, Vincent P.	(403)429-9814	1029
	ZIEGLER, Fred	(403)432-5972	1388
Sherwood Park	SCHMIDT, Raymond J.	(403)464-8234	1095

COLLECTION DEVELOPMENT/EVALUATION CONSULTANT (Cont'd)
BRITISH COLUMBIA

Castlegar	MANSBRIDGE, John	(604)365-6448	767
Clearbrook	VIIERANS, Mary E.	(604)859-7814	1284
North Vancouver	ASHCROFT, Susan M.	(604)984-8004	35
	DODSON, Suzanne C.	(604)988-4567	308
Richmond	ELLIS, Kathy M.	(604)272-5389	344
	WEESE, Dwain W.		1316
Vancouver	CAMERON, Hazel M.	(604)224-8470	175
	CHAN, Diana L.	(604)224-8470	199
	DEVAKOS, Elizabeth R.	(604)255-6636	297
	GONNAMI, Tsuneharu	(604)224-4296	447
Victoria	SIGNORI, Donna L.	(604)721-8247	1137

MANITOBA

Brandon	JONES, June D.	(204)727-3303	613
Winnipeg	BROWN, Gerald R.	(204)772-2474	144
	BUDNICK, Carol	(204)474-9844	155
	DIVAY, Gabriele	(204)474-8926	306
	TULLY, Sharon I.	(204)474-9844	1262

NEWFOUNDLAND

St John's	MARTINEZ, Helen	(709)753-6210	779
	MILNE, Dorothy J.	(709)737-8270	845

NOVA SCOTIA

Cleveland	MACRURY, Mary E.	(902)625-1016	758
Halifax	AMEY, Lorne J.	(902)422-8639	20
	GURAYA, Harinder	(902)423-8868	478
	HUANG, Paul T.	(902)454-5911	568

ONTARIO

Ancaster	SAVAGE, Daniel A.	(416)648-2131	1085
Brampton	CHAN, Bruce A.	(416)793-4636	199
Don Mills	FAIRLEY, Craig R.	(416)447-5336	361
Go-Home Bay	CAMPBELL, Harry	(705)756-1878	176
Guelph	PAL, Gabriel	(519)824-4120	935
Haliburton	HOBBS, Kathleen M.		545
Kingston	FLOWER, M A.	(613)645-6122	386
	MORLEY, Mae L.	(613)546-1101	865
Kitchener	SHEPHERD, Murray C.		1127
London	CLOUSTON, John S.	(519)679-2111	223
	LIN, Louise	(519)439-3271	727
Mississauga	DAVIS, Virginia K.	(416)673-2644	281
	DINEEN, Diane M.	(416)279-7002	304
North Bay	NORRGARD, Don K.	(705)474-3332	909
North York	VARMA, Divakara K.	(416)736-5139	1278
Ottawa	AUBREY, Irene E.	(613)996-7774	38
	BLACK, Jane L.	(613)234-5006	101
	BURROWS, Sandra	(613)996-1342	163
	CAMPBELL, Laurie G.	(613)596-9797	177
	DUPRE, Monique	(819)994-6855	327
	GORDON, Robert S.	(613)233-2452	451
	KAVANAGH, Susan E.	(819)997-7059	631
	MACDONALD, Patricia A.	(819)997-7066	754
	PARE, Richard	(613)733-8391	940
	SCHRYER, Michel J.	(819)994-6827	1100
	SPRY, Patricia		1176
	TSAI, Shaopan		1260
	WARD, William D.	(613)225-7557	1304
Pembroke	MEHTA, Subbash C.	(613)732-2914	821
Shelburne	LA CHAPELLE, Jennifer R.	(519)925-2672	686
Stratford	KIRKPATRICK, Jane E.		655
Thornhill	SPEISMAN, Stephen A.	(416)886-2508	1172
Toronto	BAYNE, Jennifer M.	(416)595-3429	67
	BOITE, Mary E.	(416)461-2274	111
	FASICK, Adele M.	(416)978-7074	366
	GARLOCK, Gayle N.	(416)763-2718	419
	GRANATSTEIN, M E.	(416)978-6654	457
	HAJNAL, Peter I.	(416)533-7338	484
	KENDALL, Sandra A.		640
	KING, Olive E.	(416)979-5081	652
	KOTIN, David B.	(416)531-2104	673
	LANDON, Richard G.	(416)978-6107	693
	MILANICH, Melanie M.	(416)393-7180	834
	SMITH, Anne C.	(416)423-9826	1152
Waterloo	BEGLO, Jo N.	(519)885-1211	74
Whitby	LINTON, Linda J.	(416)831-6265	731
Willowdale	JOHNSON, James R.	(416)226-6380	605

COLLECTION DEVELOPMENT/EVALUATION CONSULTANT (Cont'd)
ONTARIO (Cont'd)

Windsor	SINGLETON, Cynthia B.	(519)253-4232	1143
	WALSH, G M.	(519)253-7817	1299

QUEBEC

Baie d'Urfe	KLOK, Buddhi	(514)457-2757	662
Beaconsfield	HIRON, Barbara A.	(514)695-3200	543
Bellefeuille	DANIS, Rolland J.	(514)432-6116	273
Blainville	JETTE, Monika E.	(514)430-4945	600
Boucherville	NADEAU, Johan	(514)655-4858	885
Chambly	ASSUNCAO, Isabel	(514)658-3882	37
Hull	DUHAMEL, Louis	(819)771-4453	324
Jonquiere	HARVEY, Serge	(418)548-7821	509
Lennoxville	SHEERAN, Ruth J.	(819)569-9551	1125
Longueuil	OUIMET, Yves	(514)646-8615	930
Montreal	BAZINET, Jeanne	(514)482-7188	68
	BISSON, Jacques	(514)482-9110	100
	BOIVIN-OSTIGUY, Jocelyne	(514)343-6193	111
	COURTEMANCHE, Pierre O.		251
	CRAWFORD, David S.	(514)398-4723	256
	DUSABLON-BOTTEGA, Nicole	(514)871-6442	329
	GARDNER, Lucie	(514)845-7814	418
	GARDNER, Richard K.	(514)343-6046	418
	GAULIN, S D.	(514)645-9444	422
	GREENE, Richard L.	(514)343-7424	464
	GROEN, Frances K.	(514)845-2090	471
	MAYRAND, Lise M.	(514)343-6765	791
	MOLLER, Hans	(514)398-4740	853
	MOLLER, Hans	(514)398-4740	853
	ORMSBY, Eric	(514)398-4677	926
	PARKER, Charles G.	(514)282-3934	941
	PICARD, Albert	(514)276-5797	970
	ROBIN, Madeleine	(514)738-0433	1043
	ROUSSEAU, Denis	(514)843-3214	1061
	SYKES, Stephanie L.	(514)870-7088	1217
Outremont	LACROIX, Yvon A.	(514)273-7423	687
Quebec	BERNIER, Gaston	(418)643-4032	89
	TAILLON, Yolande A.	(418)656-5781	1220
St-Bruno	LECOMPTE, Louis L.	(514)653-7290	708
St-Laurent	DJEVALIKIAN, Sonia	(514)744-7315	306
Sainte-Foy	GUILMETTE, Pierre	(418)658-0470	476
Sherbrooke	FONTAINE, Nicole	(819)569-2551	388
Trois-Rivieres	BAILLARGEON, Daniele	(819)376-1721	47

SASKATCHEWAN

Regina	GAGNON, Andre	(306)569-7567	412
	MACK, A Y.	(306)543-6981	756
	VOHRA, Pran	(306)787-4321	1287
Saskatoon	CANEVARI DE PAREDES, Donna A.	(306)966-5972	178
	FRITZ, Linda	(306)934-3785	405

AUSTRALIA

Canberra	STEELE, Colin R.		1184
Fisher	WANG, Sing W.		1303
Victoria	POWNALL, David E.	(033)418-2990	989
	SMITH, Lindsay L.		1157

BAHRAIN

Al Manamah	ALI, Syed N.		13

BELGIUM

St Niklaas	VAN GARSSE, Yvan		1275

COSTA RICA

San Jose	SMITH, Sharon		1160

ENGLAND

Essex	GAGE, Laurie E.		412
Harrogate	LINE, Maurice B.		730
Withyham	MACNUTT, Richard P.		758

FEDERAL REPUBLIC OF CHINA

Taipei	LIN, Chih F.		727

FEDERAL REPUBLIC OF GERMANY

Berlin	KREH, Fritz		677
Bonn	LOTZ, Rainer E.		742

COLLECTION DEVELOPMENT/EVALUATION CONSULTANT (Cont'd)

FRANCE

Paris	PILLET, Sylvaine M.	973

HONG KONG

Kowloon	FU, Ting W.	407
	POON, Paul W.	983
Shatin	YEN, David S.	1379

INDIA

Bangalore	KITTUR, Krishna N.	657
Hyderabad	SATYANARAYANA, Vadhri V. (260)586-0000	1084

INDONESIA

Jakarta	ADITIRTO, Irma U.	6

IRELAND

Dublin	ASTON, Jennefer	37
	LAMBKIN, Anthony	690

ISRAEL

Jerusalem	DIAMANT, Betsy	299

ITALY

Milan	FABRE DE MORLHON, Christiane	360

JAMAICA

Kingston	ERDEL, Timothy P. (809)925-6801	352

JAPAN

Tokyo	YAMAZAKI, Shigeaki (034)331-1110	1377

KENYA

Nairobi	IRURIA, Daniel M.	584

KUWAIT

Khalidiah	HAMDY, Mohamed N.	491
Salmiyah	ABDEL-MOTEY, Yaser Y.	2

MEXICO

Mexico City	BARBERENA, Elsa	55
	MAGALONI, Ana M.	759
Naucalpan	OROZCO-TENORIO, Jose M.	926

NIGERIA

Ogbomoso	OKPARA, Ibiba M.	920

NORTHERN IRELAND

Belfast	LINTON, William D.	731

PHILIPPINES

Makati	MORAN, Teresita C.	862

POLAND

Poznan	CHOJNACKA, Jadwiga	210

SAUDI ARABIA

Jeddah	KHAN, Mohammed A.	646
Riyadh	ALI, Farooq M. (467)615-7000	13
	BROWN, Biraj L.	142
	MARTIN, Nannette	777

SCOTLAND

Glasgow	HEANEY, Henry J.	518

TRINIDAD

Valsayn	NANTON-COMISSIONG, Barbara L.	887

UGANDA

Mukono	MUKUNGU, Frederick N.	876

DATABASE/SYSTEMS CONSULTANT

ALABAMA

Birmingham	STEPHENS, Jerry W.	(209)363-6000	1188
Gadsden	BUCKNER, Rebecca S.	(205)543-8849	154
Huntsville	MCCANLESS, Christel L.	(205)536-3458	793
Mobile	NICHOLS, Amy S.	(205)694-3895	901

ALASKA

Fairbanks	GALBRAITH, William B.	(907)479-5196	413
Sitka	MCCLAIN, Harriet V.	(907)747-8160	795

ARIZONA

Chandler	MCGORRAY, John J.	(602)961-8016	807
Mesa	MEAD, Thomas L.	(602)892-3764	819
Phoenix	EWING, Alison L.	(602)256-0454	359
Scottsdale	COLE, Christopher H.	(602)994-7959	230
	KLIMIADES, Mario N.	(602)994-2471	661
	POTTER, William G.	(602)991-5578	987
Tempe	HAWKOS, Lise J.	(602)965-6163	514
	MACHOVEC, George S.	(602)965-5889	755
	STEWART, Douglas J.	(602)897-7191	1192
Tucson	ALURI, Rao	(602)722-5678	19
	BIERMAN, Kenneth J.	(602)887-4631	95
	BUXTON, David T.	(602)621-2101	168
	FAHY, Terry W.	(602)621-6446	361
	LEI, Polin P.		713

ARKANSAS

Fayetteville	MILLER, Leon C.	(501)575-5577	839
Harrison	VAN ARSDALE, Dennis G.	(501)741-8029	1272
Heber Springs	SEDELOW, Sally Y.	(501)362-3476	1110
	SEDELOW, Walter A.		1110
Little Rock	KASALKO, Sally G.	(501)661-5980	628

CALIFORNIA

Albany	BLITZ, Ruth R.	(415)525-4186	105
Anaheim	KOGA, James S.	(714)630-0618	668
Anaheim Hills	JOHNSON, Thomas L.	(714)998-4347	609
Belmont	MEGLIO, Delores D.	(415)591-2333	821
Benicia	HUTCHESON, Don S.	(707)746-8021	578
	RANDOLPH, Kevin H.	(707)745-9388	1007
Berkeley	BENIDIR, Samia	(415)644-1129	80
	BERGER, Michael G.	(415)642-9485	85
	BESSER, Howard A.	(415)643-8641	91
	BROWN, Diane M.	(415)642-3532	143
	BROWNRIGG, Edwin B.		149
	FALANGA, Rosemarie E.	(415)524-5501	361
	GRIFFIN, Thomas E.	(415)643-6196	469
	HUNT, Judy L.	(415)849-2708	575
	KOOLISH, Ruth K.	(415)525-6220	671
	LARSON, Ray R.	(415)642-6046	699
	MCCARTHY, John L.	(415)486-5307	794
	PISANO, Vivian M.	(415)527-1959	975
	SILBERSTEIN, Stephen M.	(415)644-3600	1137
	SPENCER, John T.	(415)341-9442	1173
	ZBORAY, Ronald J.		1386
Beverly Hills	CHAMMOU, Eliezer	(213)273-1395	198
Burbank	ELMAN, Stanley A.	(818)351-8245	345
Cardiff By The Sea	MARKWORTH, Lawrence L.	(619)943-1197	772
Carlsbad	KENNEDY, Charlene F.	(619)434-2871	640
	TILLETT, Barbara B.		1245
Carmichael	PARSONS, Jerry L.	(916)966-2086	945
Carson	KENNY-SLOAN, Linda		642
Castro Valley	CASTAGNOZZI, Carol A.	(415)581-6034	194
Chico	DWYER, James R.	(916)895-5837	330
	SESSIONS, Judith A.	(916)895-5862	1117
Claremont	PRESLAN, Bruce H.	(714)621-9998	991
	ROSE, David L.	(714)624-9041	1054
Costa Mesa	EPSTEIN, Susan B.	(714)754-1559	351
	MARLOR, Hugh T.	(714)631-5637	772
	PETERMAN, Claudia A.	(714)650-9014	962
Culver City	ANDRADE, Rebecca	(213)837-5448	26
Cupertino	KERSHNER, Lois M.	(408)255-2719	644
	MILLER, Ronald F.	(408)257-9162	842
Cypress	MOSER, Jane W.	(213)643-0322	870
Danville	CREW-NOBLE, Sara M.	(415)837-1399	258
Davis	BLANK, Karen L.	(916)752-2110	104
Eagle Rock	CRAWFORD, Marilyn L.	(213)259-8938	257

DATABASE/SYSTEMS CONSULTANT (Cont'd)
CALIFORNIA (Cont'd)

El Cerrito	DONLEY, Leigh M.	(415)524-3695	311
	KATZ, Jeffrey P.		630
Encinitas	PIERCE, Patricia J.	(619)436-5055	971
Fallbrook	COMPTON, Joan C.	(619)723-2860	235
Fremont	TSAI, Sheh G.	(415)656-7097	1260
Fresno	WARD, Penny T.	(209)268-2545	1304
Goleta	MUSICK, Nancy W.	(805)964-8484	883
Inglewood	GOUDELOCK, Carol V.	(213)672-2543	454
Irvine	CLANCY, Stephen L.	(714)856-7309	215
	CLARY, Rochelle L.	(714)856-6531	219
	FINEMAN, Michael	(714)856-8160	377
	SHAWL, Janice H.	(714)854-7413	1124
	TASH, Steven J.	(714)786-7857	1224
	WEINTRAUB, D K.	(714)856-6079	1318
La Honda	HOLLAND, Mary	(415)747-0511	551
La Jolla	BOWLES, Garrett H.	(619)534-2759	121
	DITO, William R.	(619)457-8559	305
	GABBERT, Gretchen W.	(619)456-4083	411
	MILLER, R B.	(619)534-3064	841
	TALBOT, Dawn E.	(619)534-6213	1220
Lafayette	NEWAY, Julie M.	(415)283-1862	898
Laguna Beach	KOUNTZ, John C.	(714)494-8783	673
Livermore	BURTON, Hilary D.	(415)423-8063	164
	HUNT, Richard K.	(415)443-5525	575
Long Beach	ADAMS, Linda L.	(213)590-7639	5
Los Altos	GESCHKE, Nancy A.	(415)969-7737	430
Los Altos Hills	MCDONALD, Marilyn M.	(415)960-4390	803
Los Angeles	BISOM, Diane B.	(213)825-7557	99
	CAMPBELL, Bill W.	(213)398-8992	176
	CASE, Donald O.	(213)825-1379	191
	DEENEY, Kay E.	(213)479-6672	286
	GELMAN-KMEC, Marsha	(213)484-5530	426
	HADLEY, Peter H.	(213)879-1834	482
	HAYTHORN, Joseph D.	(213)938-3621	517
	JAFFE, Lee D.	(213)935-6770	591
	KING, Joseph T.	(213)660-3530	651
	LEE, Diane T.	(213)972-4000	709
	MANTHEY, Teresa M.	(213)224-7234	767
	MICHEL, Dee A.	(213)478-7660	832
	MORSE, David H.	(213)224-7413	869
	NEWCOMER, Susan N.	(213)224-5978	898
	PRINTZ, Naomi J.	(213)306-3573	993
	PRUHS, Sharon	(213)974-7780	996
	RAEDER, Aggi W.	(213)825-2649	1003
	ROSE, Steven C.	(213)668-0444	1055
	SCLAR, Herbert	(213)474-5900	1106
	STREIKER, Susan L.	(213)738-6727	1201
	SUGRANES, Maria R.	(213)201-3507	1207
	VILLERE, Dawn N.	(213)290-2989	1284
	WILKINSON, David W.	(213)224-2251	1340
Malibu	CLARK, David L.	(818)888-9305	216
Menlo Park	DENNETT, Stephen C.		292
	DILORETO, Ann M.	(415)326-7370	303
	NEWMAN, Mark J.	(415)326-2114	899
	REDFIELD, Elizabeth	(415)859-6187	1014
Mill Valley	ROBERTS, Justine T.		1040
Mission Viejo	CHWEH, Steven S.	(714)768-3459	214
Modesto	SHAMS, Kamruddin	(209)576-8585	1120
Mountain View	BUTLER, Matilda J.	(415)969-0606	167
	SLOCUM, Hannah R.	(415)969-8356	1150
	SPIGAI, Fran	(415)961-2880	1174
Northridge	SHERMAN, Judith E.	(818)366-8100	1128
Novato	HOTZ, Sharon M.	(415)892-0821	562
Oakland	GLYNN, Jeannette E.	(415)654-3543	442
	NEWCOMBE, Barbara T.	(415)763-4406	898
	SYPERT, Clyde F.	(415)763-6046	1217
Orange	JOHNSON, Mary L.	(714)634-7708	607
	LA BORDE, Charlotte A.	(714)385-4454	686
Oroville	ALLENSWORTH, James H.	(916)538-7197	16
Pacific Grove	HAY, Wayne M.	(408)646-9858	515
Pacific Palisades	SCHRIBER, James E.	(213)459-1825	1100
Palo Alto	ANDREWS, Chris C.		26
	ELLSWORTH, Dianne J.	(415)321-2253	345
	GREEN-MALONEY, Nancy	(415)858-3816	465
	ITNYRE, Jacqueline H.	(415)329-1880	585
	MAIN, Linda Y.	(415)328-4865	761
	PRESTON, Cecilia M.	(415)327-5364	991
	SUMMIT, Roger K.	(415)858-3777	1209

DATABASE/SYSTEMS CONSULTANT (Cont'd)
CALIFORNIA (Cont'd)

Palo Alto	TRIMBLE, Kathy W.	(415)855-5493	1256
Pasadena	CARD, Sandra E.	(818)356-6775	180
	CHICK, Cynthia L.	(818)796-8194	208
	HOROWITZ, Roberta S.	(213)681-3032	560
	KALVINSKAS, Louanne A.	(818)797-9890	623
Pleasant Hill	FOWELLS, Fumi T.	(415)689-0754	393
Pomona	IVERSON, Diann S.	(714)624-4728	585
	MORGAN, Ferrell	(714)625-7190	864
	REMKIEWICZ, Frank L.	(714)623-5251	1022
	SHAPTON, Gregory B.	(714)623-5672	1122
Rancho Cacamonga	CONNELL, William S.	(714)989-0506	237
Rancho Palos Verdes	KATTLOVE, Rose W.	(213)544-0061	630
Redondo Beach	CLIFFORD, Susan G.	(213)378-3824	222
Redwood City	TAOKA, Wesley M.	(415)365-3317	1223
Ridgecrest	MAYES, Elizabeth A.	(619)446-6862	789
Riverside	DUNN, Kathleen K.	(714)359-8429	327
	MOONEY, Margaret T.	(714)787-3226	858
Rolling Hills Estate	SAVAGE, Gretchen S.	(213)377-5032	1085
	TUNG, Sandra J.	(213)377-5032	1263
Sacramento	KAST, Gloria E.	(916)483-6765	629
	MILLER, Suzanne M.	(916)739-7010	842
	MIRONENKO, Rimma	(916)355-4076	847
San Bernardino	NOUROK, Marlene E.	(714)887-6333	910
	WEBB, Duncan C.	(714)387-4959	1313
San Diego	BUSCH, Barbara	(619)224-8412	165
	DAVISSON, Darell D.	(619)458-1544	281
	GIBSON, Joanne	(619)450-0333	432
	KANJI, Zainab J.	(619)231-8381	625
San Francisco	AVENEY, Brian H.	(415)338-2956	41
	DEWOLF, Timothy B.	(415)774-2454	298
	GEIGER, Richard G.	(415)777-1111	425
	GERSH, Barbara S.	(415)346-7882	429
	HENKE, Dan	(415)565-4758	528
	JANK, David A.	(415)751-9958	593
	MANN, Thomas	(415)951-0100	766
	MORITZ, Thomas D.	(415)750-7102	865
	MOYER, Barbara A.	(415)386-6297	874
	PAPERMASTER, Cynthia L.	(415)773-5831	939
	SHEW, Anne L.	(415)565-6352	1129
	SULLIVAN, Edward A.	(415)752-6671	1207
	TARTER, Blodwen	(415)346-8199	1224
	TREGGIARI, Arnaldo	(415)469-1649	1255
San Jose	BERCIK, Mary E.	(408)288-9798	84
	DUNCAN, Rebecca	(408)971-9060	325
San Mateo	RAZE, Nasus B.	(415)345-9684	1012
San Pedro	SCULLY, Patrick F.	(213)832-6526	1109
	SPRUNG, Lori A.	(213)832-0593	1176
San Rafael	PLOTKIN, Nathan	(415)479-7018	978
	ROSENBERGER, Diane C.	(415)472-7667	1056
Santa Ana	AUSTIN, Stephen	(714)540-9870	40
	HOFFMAN, Herbert H.	(714)667-3451	548
Santa Barbara	GIBBONS, Carolbeth	(805)961-3320	431
Santa Clara	HAMBRIDGE, Sally L.	(408)378-8616	491
Santa Cruz	ANDERSON, Clifford D.	(408)429-2501	22
Santa Monica	HALL, Anthony	(213)827-1707	487
	QUINT, Barbara E.	(213)451-0252	1000
	SLEETER, Ellen L.	(213)829-4832	1148
	WITTMANN, Cecelia V.	(213)454-8300	1358
Sebastopol	CANT, Elaine N.	(707)823-3214	179
	STRIBLING, Lorraine R.	(707)823-1419	1202
Sherman Oaks	KWAN, Julie K.	(818)784-8606	685
	LEWIS, Cookie A.	(818)788-5280	722
Stanford	CARSON, Susan A.	(415)723-2092	188
	MUSEN, Mark A.	(415)723-6979	883
	WIBLE, Joseph G.	(415)723-1110	1335
Studio City	PLATE, Kenneth H.	(818)797-7654	977
Thousand Oaks	SOY, Susan K.	(805)523-7288	1170
Vacaville	KERNS, John T.	(207)448-4459	644
Van Nuys	DAVIS, Becky C.	(818)764-3732	277
Woodland Hills	HORACEK, Paula B.	(818)704-6460	558
	REIFMAN, Deborah S.		1019

DATABASE/SYSTEMS CONSULTANT (Cont'd)
COLORADO

Arvada	PRESTON, Lawrence N.	(303)423-8729	991
Aurora	HARRIS, Michael A.	(303)694-4200	505
	HUGHES, Brad R.	(305)699-6248	571
Boulder	CHANAUD, Jo P.	(303)449-0849	199
	COLLARD, R M.	(303)444-1355	232
Colorado Springs	MALYSHEV, Nina A.	(303)531-6333	764
	SHERIDAN, John B.	(303)473-2233	1127
Denver	BOWERS, Sandra L.	(303)236-6649	121
	BRUNELL, David H.	(303)691-0550	150
	DULAN, Peter A.	(303)692-9261	324
	FORSMAN, Rick B.	(303)394-5125	391
	GUTH, Karen K.	(303)869-2395	478
	HENSINGER, James S.	(303)691-0550	529
	INGUI, Bettejean	(303)394-5158	583
	KAVANAGH, Janette R.	(303)777-8971	631
	LUEVANE, Marsha A.	(303)989-1036	747
	NORBIE, Dorothy E.	(303)691-5400	908
	SHAW, Ward	(303)861-5319	1124
	SMITH, Randolph R.	(303)744-8764	1159
Englewood	THOMASSON, George O.	(303)779-0550	1238
	WHITE, Suellen S.	(303)790-0600	1332
Fort Collins	SJOGREN, Mack D.		1145
Golden	GRAHAM, Su D.	(303)642-7802	456
	KENNEY, Brigitte L.	(303)278-8482	641
Grand Junction	RICHMOND, Rick	(303)241-4358	1030
Greeley	CUTTS, William B.	(303)353-1551	268
Littleton	SPANGLER, Bruce	(303)797-1300	1171
	STARK, Philip H.	(305)740-7100	1182
Montrose	CAMPBELL, John D.	(303)249-1078	176
Pueblo	JANES, Nina	(303)542-4591	593

CONNECTICUT

Bloomfield	BROQUE, Suzanne	(203)242-3473	141
Bristol	WARAKSA, Raymond P.	(203)584-7759	1303
Danbury	HORRIGAN, John J.	(203)797-2731	560
Farmington	WETMORE, Judith M.	(203)679-2942	1328
Greenwich	MCLANE, John F.	(203)629-9200	813
Hartford	CORCORAN, Virginia H.	(203)524-2230	246
	KLEMARCZYK, Laurice D.	(203)547-3099	660
	STONE, Dennis J.	(203)241-4617	1197
	WEINSTEIN, Daniel L.	(203)275-2699	1318
Madison	HARRISON, Burgess A.	(203)421-4098	506
Middletown	DOUVILLE, Judith A.	(203)344-1880	314
	SABOSIK, Patricia E.	(203)347-6933	1073
New Haven	FRYER, Regina K.	(203)785-4356	407
	LOWELL, Gerald R.	(203)773-3709	744
	PRATT, Allan D.	(203)389-0183	989
	TRIOLO, Victor A.	(203)397-4520	1257
Ridgefield	MILSTEAD, Jessica L.	(203)431-8175	845
	SUPEAU, Cynthia	(203)798-5154	1210
Stamford	BERLIET, Nathalie B.	(203)359-9359	87
	BREGMAN, Joan R.		131
	KEMP, Thomas J.	(203)323-2826	639
	MEYER, Garry S.	(203)348-3028	830
	ORRICO, James T.	(203)968-3280	926
	TIBBETTS, David W.	(203)329-2824	1243
Tollard	WILDE, Daniel U.	(203)872-7000	1338
Wallingford	MCGREGOR, M C.	(203)284-6000	808
Warren	HENTZ, Margaret B.	(203)868-9178	530
West Hartford	CHICHESTER, Gerald C.	(203)674-0888	208
	MICHAUD, Noreen R.	(203)232-6560	832
	PIERCE, Anne L.	(203)243-4849	971
Westport	LOWE, Ida B.	(203)255-8780	743
Windsor	PARKS, Amy N.	(203)549-0404	943

DELAWARE

Bear	MANUEL, Larry L.	(302)834-5748	767
Newark	EVERETT, Amy E.	(302)451-2104	358
	ULRICH, Sue	(302)451-2231	1268
	WOLFF, Stephen G.	(302)451-2432	1361
Wilmington	BRETON, Ernest J.		133
	MINNICH, Nancy P.	(302)478-5291	846

DISTRICT OF COLUMBIA

Washington	ANGLE, Joanne G.	(202)682-1698	28
	ASMUTH, Gretchen W.	(202)628-1700	36
	BARTLEY, Linda K.	(202)362-7837	61
	DAWSON, Barbara J.	(202)785-3330	282

DATABASE/SYSTEMS CONSULTANT (Cont'd)
DISTRICT OF COLUMBIA (Cont'd)

Washington			
	DAY, Melvin S.	(202)363-1890	283
	DE ARMAN, Charles L.	(202)797-7169	284
	DEHART, Odell	(202)393-7100	288
	DOUMATO, Lamia		314
	FLEMING, Thomas B.	(202)429-6429	384
	FRIERSON, Eleanor G.	(202)623-7000	404
	HALEY, Roger K.	(202)224-2976	486
	HEARTY, John A.	(202)872-4533	519
	HERRICK, Judith M.	(202)287-6328	532
	HORTON, Forest W.		561
	JOHANSON, Cynthia J.	(202)287-5261	601
	KEHOE, Patrick E.	(202)885-2674	634
	KLEIMAN, Gerald S.	(202)224-5950	659
	KOSTINKO, Gail A.	(202)483-4118	673
	LANE, Elizabeth S.		694
	LOO, Shirley	(202)546-1196	740
	LUNIN, Lois F.	(202)965-3924	749
	LUSKEY, Judith	(202)357-4654	749
	MCRAE, Alexander D.	(202)686-1788	818
	MORRIS, Timothy J.	(202)462-8209	867
	PACIFICI, Sabrina I.	(202)429-4094	933
	RADER, Ronald A.	(639)890-0000	1002
	REYNOLDS, Dennis J.	(202)745-7722	1025
	SARANGAPANI, Chetluru	(202)282-3091	1082
	SAUVE, Deborah A.	(202)546-8770	1085
	SHELBURNE, Elizabeth C.	(202)966-0738	1125
	SONNEMANN, Gail J.	(202)543-4536	1167
	STOCKTON, Ken R.	(202)293-7070	1196
	YARNALL, James L.	(202)234-6293	1378

FLORIDA

Avon Park	APPELQUIST, Donald L.	(813)453-6661	30
Bunnell	MCKNIGHT, Jesse H.	(904)437-4151	812
Captiva	WALTON, Terence M.	(813)454-0410	1302
Clearwater	SCHMID, Cynthia M.	(813)462-7889	1094
Coral Gables	LADNER, Sharyn J.	(305)443-1122	687
	LOWELL, Felice K.	(305)284-2250	744
Crawfordville	TODD, Hal W.	(904)926-5656	1248
Fort Lauderdale	TAYSOM, Daniel B.	(305)760-5771	1229
Fort Myers	PEGLER, Ross J.	(813)267-2995	954
Freeport	DAVIS, Bonnie D.	(904)835-4432	277
Gainesville	WILLOCKS, Robert M.	(904)392-0342	1349
Jacksonville	JENKIN, Michael A.		596
	JONES, Robert P.	(904)646-2615	614
Lauderhill	HOLLMANN, Pauline V.	(305)393-3774	552
Melbourne	SHIAU, Ian L.	(305)768-0973	1129
Miami	PAUL, Nora M.	(305)376-3402	949
	PHILLIPS, Donald J.	(305)274-5724	968
	STEINBERG, Celia L.	(305)661-4611	1185
	WRIGHT, Joseph F.	(305)379-3105	1372
Orlando	GRIMSLEY, Judy L.	(305)896-2535	470
Pembroke Pines	MULLER, Charles W.	(305)431-5123	877
Pompano Beach	WHITESIDE, Lee A.	(305)782-0194	1333
Tallahassee	CONAWAY, Charles W.	(904)893-1482	235
	LOGAN, Elisabeth L.		737
Tampa	JOHNSTON, Judy F.	(813)974-2162	610
	MARTIN, Robert A.	(813)253-3333	778
West Palm Beach	PRITCHARD, Teresa N.	(305)684-7349	994
Winter Park	ANDREWS, Janet C.		26
	PFARRER, Theodore R.	(305)647-3294	966
	SEBRIGHT, Terence F.	(305)678-8846	1110

GEORGIA

Acworth	STAHL, D G.	(404)924-8505	1178
Athens	ANDERSON, Thomas G.	(404)542-0598	25
	PARK, Margaret K.	(404)549-8382	941
Atlanta	BARNETT, Becky L.	(404)529-3886	57
	BRYANT, Nancy J.	(404)955-9550	152
	DEEMER, Selden S.	(404)727-0271	286
	FISTE, David A.		382
	KRONE, Judith P.	(404)581-5275	679
	LONG, Linda E.	(404)521-4210	739
	MENEELY, William E.	(404)658-3800	824
	PRESLEY, Roger L.	(404)658-2176	991
	ROAN, Tattie W.	(404)320-9376	1038
	SCHEIN, Julia R.	(404)624-1162	1091
	WILLIAMS, Fred	(404)432-2723	1343

DATABASE/SYSTEMS CONSULTANT (Cont'd)

GEORGIA (Cont'd)

Atlanta			
	WILTSE, Helen C.	(404)451-4260	1353
Decatur	AMMERMAN, Jackie W.	(404)377-0207	20
Doerun	BOWEN, Louise E.	(912)782-5408	120
East Point	ELTZROTH, Elsbeth L.	(404)767-3144	346
Marietta	LISI, Susan C.	(404)955-1375	732
Red Oak	LETT, Rosalind K.		719
Watkinsville	WHITEHEAD, James M.	(404)769-8917	1332

GUAM

Agana	WEINGARTH, Darlene	(671)472-1750	1318

HAWAII

Honolulu	GOODY, Cheryl S.	(808)521-5361	450
	LUNDEEN, Gerald W.	(808)948-7321	748
	SMITH, Frances P.	(808)523-2311	1155
	UCHIDA, Deborah K.	(808)548-7915	1267
Waiaulua	VEATCH, Laurie L.	(808)237-8411	1280

IDAHO

Rexburg	HART, Eldon C.	(208)356-4447	507

ILLINOIS

Beardstown	WEST, L P.	(217)323-5788	1326
Berwyn	FEDECZKO, Joyce L.	(312)795-3089	367
Carol Stream	SONDALLE, Barbara J.	(312)653-7000	1167
Champaign	DESSOUKY, Ibtesam	(217)333-4956	296
	FREDERICK, Sidney C.	(217)352-0048	399
	JOHNSON, Jane S.		605
	PENKA, Carol B.	(217)351-6026	956
Charleston	RAO, Paladugu V.	(217)581-6061	1008
Chicago	BOLEF, Doris	(312)942-2271	112
	BREEN, Joanell C.	(312)929-1445	131
	CARLSON, Robert P.	(312)944-6780	182
	CHUNG, Alison L.	(312)222-9350	213
	CLARK, Gerald L.	(312)924-4362	217
	COLLINS, Janet	(312)642-2136	232
	CORNICK, Ron	(312)282-6579	247
	CURRY, John A.	(314)528-0870	266
	DONAHUE, Karin V.		310
	EVANS, Linda J.	(312)642-4600	357
	FOUSER, Jane G.	(312)477-4712	393
	GARDNER, Trudy A.	(312)942-8735	418
	GIANGRANDE, Mark G.		430
	HARRIS, Jeanne G.	(312)580-0069	504
	IDDINGS, Daniel H.	(312)321-0432	581
	JOHN, Nancy R.	(312)996-2716	601
	LEE, Joel M.	(312)944-6780	710
	MACKEY, Denise R.	(312)467-1000	756
	MCCLINTOCK, Patrick J.		797
	MICHAEL, Ann B.	(312)399-8354	831
	MILLER, Robert	(312)488-7195	841
	MILLER, Thomas R.	(312)769-6159	843
	MILUTINOVIC, Eunhee C.	(312)472-9843	845
	MOCH, Mary I.	(312)539-2328	851
	MOTTRAM, Geoffrey	(312)642-8655	873
	MOULTON, James C.	(312)525-7185	873
	MOUW, James R.	(312)996-2706	874
	RANDALL, Sara L.		1006
	REMEIKIS, Lois A.	(312)782-1442	1022
	SPARKS, Joanne L.	(312)728-5510	1171
	STRAIT, Constance J.		1199
	STRAWN, Gary L.	(312)327-4930	1201
	TYI MAN, Wieelawa T.	(312)666-7193	1266
	VISKOCHIL, Larry A.	(312)935-1071	1285
De Kalb	GILDEMEISTER, Glen A.	(815)753-9392	434
	TOROK, Andrew G.	(815)753-1734	1251
Deerfield	LEE, Soon H.	(312)948-3880	711
Downers Grove	MIFFLIN, Michael J.	(312)963-9285	833
Edwardsville	JOHNSON, Charlotte L.	(618)656-5743	603
Elgin	GORDON, Lewis H.	(312)695-1455	451
Elmhurst	KRUSS, Daniel M.	(312)941-0090	681
Evanston	DAVIDSON, Lloyd A.	(312)491-2906	276
	GRISCOM, Richard W.	(312)491-3487	471
	HURD, Albert E.	(312)866-7235	577
	JACOBSON, William R.	(312)328-7584	590
Evergreen Park	GARCIA-RUIZ, Maritza L.	(312)425-6104	417
Forest Park	VAN HOUTEN, Stephen		1275

DATABASE/SYSTEMS CONSULTANT (Cont'd)

ILLINOIS (Cont'd)

Freeport	WELCH, Eric C.	(815)235-6121	1321
Grayslake	DEPKE, Robert W.		293
	DIEHL, Mark	(312)680-5119	302
Gurnee	FUNK, Carla J.	(312)367-6213	409
Harvey	FOLEY, Donna H.	(312)333-2300	387
Hinsdale	GREGORY, Melissa R.	(312)325-2807	466
Homewood	MARKHAM, Robert P.	(312)799-4677	771
Joliet	JOHNSTON, James R.	(815)729-3481	610
La Grange	PROBST, Virginia M.		994
Lake Bluff	DICK, John H.	(312)234-1220	300
Lake Forest	MARSHALL, Deborah M.	(312)234-9220	774
Lincolnwood	BENNETT, Laura B.	(312)679-2327	82
Lisle	STUNKARD, Gilbert L.	(312)969-5426	1205
Lombard	EGAN, Elizabeth M.	(312)627-7130	338
	SCHIPMA, Peter B.	(312)627-0550	1093
Makanda	CRANE, Lilly E.	(618)549-6259	255
North Aurora	HOWREY, Mary M.	(312)896-5837	566
Oak Park	CAREY, Kevin J.	(312)848-0682	181
	PAPPALARDO, Marcia J.	(312)848-5035	939
Palatine	BROWN, Patricia L.	(312)991-1278	146
Park Ridge	KNARZER, Arlene	(312)692-9550	663
Rock Island	OHRLUND, Bruce L.	(309)786-0698	919
Rolling Meadows	LOWELL, Brian V.	(312)981-6950	744
Skokie	GROSSMAN, David G.	(312)673-9100	473
	MITCHELL, Joyce P.	(312)676-1714	849
Springfield	HILDRETH, Charles R.		539
	LARISON, Brenda	(217)529-9233	697
Urbana	SHAW, Debora	(217)333-1666	1123
	WILLIAMS, James W.	(217)333-2305	1344
	WILLIAMS, Martha E.	(217)333-1074	1345
	WILLIAMS, Mitsuko	(217)333-3654	1345
Villa Park	ELL, Elizabeth L.	(312)279-6456	343
Waukegan	KOZAK, Marlene G.	(312)473-3000	674
West Chicago	KOSMAN, Joyce E.	(312)231-0774	672
Wheaton	HU, Robert T.	(312)690-7969	568
	RUSSELL, Janet	(312)653-1115	1069
Wheeling	HAMMER, Donald P.	(312)541-8149	493
Wilmette	GRIES, James P.	(312)256-7000	468
Winnetka	BLACKBURN, Joy M.	(312)446-8697	102

INDIANA

Anderson	SACZAWA, Rosemary	(317)778-2254	1073
Bloomington	COPLER, Judith A.	(812)335-9255	244
	HENSON, Jane E.	(812)336-8288	529
	MORGAN, James J.	(812)332-8709	864
	WALLACE, Danny P.	(812)335-2848	1297
	ZHU, Xiaofeng	(812)335-2666	1387
	ZIMMERMAN, Brenda M.		1388
Columbus	POOR, William E.	(812)377-7201	983
Crawfordsville	DAY, Thomas L.	(317)362-2242	283
Fort Wayne	CLEGG, Michael B.		220
	SHEETS, Michael T.	(219)483-2854	1125
	STANLEY, Luana K.	(219)432-3287	1180
Indianapolis	ANDREWS, Sylvia L.	(317)844-8538	27
	HOYT, Lester H.	(317)849-0620	566
	MASON, Dorothy L.	(317)845-3684	781
	SPARKS, Marie C.	(317)255-6932	1171
Lafayette	NIXON, Judith M.		906
	TROUTNER, Joanne J.	(317)477-7306	1258
Mishawaka	WITTORF, Robert H.	(219)259-4112	1359
Muncie	KROEHLER, Beth A.	(314)284-1841	679
	RANSIL, M M	(317)285-8032	1007
South Bend	DOLAN, Robert T.	(219)289-1172	309
Terre Haute	BAUMGARTNER, Kurt O.	(812)234-4818	66
	SHANE, T C.	(812)299-5289	1120
West Lafayette	BRANDT, Daryl S.		128
	CANGANELLI, Patrick W.	(317)494-2768	178

IOWA

Bettendorf	POLK, Diana B.	(319)332-8119	981
Cedar Rapids	NELSON, Donald A.	(319)369-7393	893
Coralville	PEPETONE, Diane S.	(319)351-3922	957
Iowa City	EICHER, Thomas E.	(319)335-9038	339
	ENGER, Kathy B.	(319)335-4123	349
	HAUSMAN, Julie	(319)337-1786	513
	HOWELL, John B.	(319)335-5885	565
Marshalltown	BURGESS, Barbara J.	(515)752-4812	159

DATABASE/SYSTEMS CONSULTANT (Cont'd)

KANSAS

Derby	MATTOX, Rosemary S.	(316)268-5979	786
Kansas City	WITMER, Tonya C.	(913)362-5327	1358
Manhattan	COFFEE, E G.	(913)539-1628	226
Overland Park	ALLEN, Norene F.	(800)338-8527	15
Winfield	ZUCK, Gregory J.	(316)221-4150	1391

KENTUCKY

Fort Thomas	NEWMAN, Linda D.	(606)441-0899	899
Lexington	SIMS, Edward N.	(606)252-2291	1142
Louisville	AULD, Dennis B.		39
	DIESING, Arthur C.	(502)568-7976	302
	JOHNSON, Garry B.	(502)897-8100	604
	MACLEOD, Valerie R.	(502)637-6026	757

LOUISIANA

Baton Rouge	BOYCE, Bert R.	(504)388-1461	122
	SMITH, Richard J.	(504)342-4942	1160
Lafayette	DOMBOURIAN, Sona J.	(318)261-5775	310
	RAGHAVAN, Vijay V.	(318)231-6603	1003
	RAMAKRISHNAN, T	(318)989-9333	1004
Marrero	FAVORITE, Grealdine J.	(504)348-0234	366
Ruston	DICARLO, Michael A.	(318)257-3594	300
Slidell	HOLLEY, Rebecca M.	(504)641-0198	551

MAINE

Alfred	ANDERSON, Marjorie E.	(207)324-6915	24
Bangor	BEISER, Karl A.	(207)947-4876	75
Boothbay	SEELEY, Catherine R.		1111
Georgetown	LUDGIN, Donald H.	(207)371-2221	746
Winthrop	KING, Alan S.	(207)377-2879	650

MARYLAND

Adamstown	LIGHTBOWN, Parke P.		726
Annapolis	CARMAN, Carol A.	(301)841-3810	183
	MENEGAUX, Edmond A.	(301)268-6741	824
	MOTEN, Derryn E.	(301)757-3846	872
	WAGNER, Susan C.	(301)268-2315	1292
Arnold	OLSON, Christine A.	(301)647-6708	922
Baltimore	BLUTE, Mary R.	(301)889-4080	107
	BOURKOFF, Vivienne R.	(301)338-8914	119
	CONNOR, Elizabeth	(301)828-8646	237
	FLORANCE, Valerie	(301)383-9436	385
	FREIBURGER, Gary A.	(301)328-7547	401
	HILDITCH, Bonny M.	(301)675-4333	539
	JENSEN, Joseph E.	(301)539-0872	599
	LAZZARONI, Philip S.	(301)528-1616	706
	MATHESON, Nina W.	(301)837-1120	783
	MEYER, Alan H.	(301)484-5594	829
	PAPENFUSE, Edward C.	(301)467-6137	939
	PUGH, W J.	(301)955-5819	997
	SATTERTHWAITE, Rebecca K.	(301)955-3410	1084
	SZARY, Richard V.	(301)358-2064	1218
	WOODS, Catharine C.	(301)323-8319	1366
	ZIMMERMAN, Martha B.	(301)668-5744	1389
Beltsville	MCCONE, Gary K.	(301)344-3813	797
Bethesda	ANDERSON, John E.	(301)496-1351	23
	BEATTY, Samuel B.	(301)654-8500	70
	CONGER, Lucinda D.	(301)229-7716	236
	GAUJARD, Pierre G.	(301)652-0034	422
	GOLDSCHMIDT, Peter G.	(301)656-5070	446
	HAWK, Susan A.	(301)897-8367	513
	HENDERSON, Madeline M.	(301)530-6478	526
	HSIEH, Richard K.	(301)496-6481	567
	JOHNSON, Carol A.	(301)251-5378	602
	MCCUTCHEON, Dianne E.	(301)496-1218	801
	MENNELLA, Dona M.	(301)652-0106	824
	MOBLEY, Arthur B.	(301)530-0081	851
	OSTROW, Dianne G.	(301)496-7391	929
	RADA, Roy F.	(301)654-6210	1002
	SHOCKLEY, Cynthia W.	(301)320-2000	1132
	THOMA, George R.	(301)496-4496	1235
	TURNER, Susan A.	(301)229-0508	1265
Brooksville	BASCOM, James F.	(301)774-3175	62
Catonsville	STERLING, Judith K.	(301)455-3468	1189
Chevy Chase	MESHINSKY, Jeff M.	(301)652-4740	827
	SEARS, Jonathan R.	(301)656-2306	1110
Churchton	TONEY, Stephen R.	(301)261-5650	1250

DATABASE/SYSTEMS CONSULTANT (Cont'd)

MARYLAND (Cont'd)

College Hts Estates	PARMING, Marju R.	(301)277-5210	943
College Park	ASSOUAD, Carol S.	(301)935-5631	37
	KLAIR, Arlene F.	(301)454-5066	657
	MARCHIONINI, Gary J.	(301)454-3235	769
	SOERGEL, Dagobert	(301)454-5451	1165
Columbia	DIENER, Carol W.	(301)381-2525	302
	DIENER, Richard A.	(301)381-2525	302
	JOHNSON, Bruce C.	(202)287-1308	602
	NEWMAN, Wilda B.	(301)730-7583	900
	SCHWARTZ, Betsy J.	(301)381-5028	1104
Ellicott City	LEVY, Sandra R.	(301)461-2409	722
	MARTIN, Susan K.	(301)988-9893	778
Gaithersburg	BENNETT, Harry D.	(301)840-1467	81
	GROCKI, Daniel J.	(301)253-6044	471
	PAUL, Rameshwar N.	(301)258-0768	949
	SAYER, John S.	(301)948-7278	1086
	VAN BRUNT, Virginia	(301)762-6701	1272
Gambrills	YOUNG, Peter R.	(301)923-2902	1383
Garrett Park	AGENBROAD, James E.	(301)946-7326	7
Germantown	ALBRIGHT, John B.	(301)428-3700	10
	MCQUEEN, Judith D.	(301)428-3400	817
	MOLINE, Judi A.	(301)972-5708	853
Grasonville	SCHNEIDER, Karl R.	(301)827-9339	1097
Hillcrest Heights	CHAPMAN, Elwynda K.	(301)894-0963	202
Kensington	CHAPUT, Linda J.	(703)683-8184	202
	WILLMERING, William J.	(301)946-2753	1348
Lanham	HUFFER, Mary A.	(301)577-3640	570
Laurel	GOLDENBERG, Joan M.	(301)953-9253	445
	LEVINE, Emil H.	(301)776-3062	720
	SAWYER, Edmond J.	(301)725-4750	1086
Mount Airy	LISTON, David M.	(301)831-3008	732
	WETZBARGER, Cecilia G.	(301)829-0826	1328
Phoenix	KIM, Chung S.	(301)628-6024	648
Potomac	HO, James K.		545
	LYNN, Kenneth C.	(301)424-7642	752
	PATRICIU, Florin S.	(301)983-9579	947
Riverdale	PITT, William B.	(301)699-5739	976
Rockville	BERUL, Lawrence H.	(301)984-9400	91
	BRANDHORST, Wesley T.	(301)460-6932	128
	BYRD, Harvey C.	(301)251-5481	169
	CHIANG, Ahushun	(301)251-5486	207
	COSMIDES, George J.	(301)762-5428	249
	DEXTER, Patrick J.	(301)424-2000	298
	DICKINSON, Patricia C.	(301)251-1173	301
	GRIFFITHS, Jose M.	(301)881-6766	469
	JONES, Gerry U.	(301)493-9438	613
	MARTINEZ-GOLDMAN, Aline		779
	MERZ, Nancy M.	(301)770-1170	827
	UNGER, Carol P.	(301)460-8375	1269
	WALL, Eugene	(301)881-4990	1297
	WHITMAN, Jean A.	(301)736-6804	1333
	ZAHARKO, Nancy W.	(301)460-1419	1385
Severn	JACK, Robert F.	(301)859-5300	586
Silver Spring	BATTY, Charles D.	(301)593-8901	65
	BLIXRUD, Julia C.	(301)622-1904	105
	FELMY, John C.	(301)681-9069	370
	FRAULINO, Philip S.	(301)495-5636	399
	HARBISON, John H.	(801)589-4223	499
	HENDERSON, Ronald L.	(301)588-2844	527
	KADEC, Sarah T.	(301)598-7694	621
	LEVITAN, Karen B.	(301)588-8139	721
	PEMPE, Ruta	(301)587-3846	956
	STERN, Michael P.	(301)495-9413	1189
	VOGT-O'CONNOR, Diane L.	(301)681-7615	1287
Suitland	BROWN, Maxine M.	(301)899-6289	146

MASSACHUSETTS

Acton	SAUNDERS, Leslie E.	(617)263-3639	1084
Amherst	DONOHUE, Joseph	(413)545-0498	312
	FELDMAN, Laurence M.	(413)253-9404	369
Arlington	PLUNKET, Linda	(617)646-7825	979
Beverly	GAGNON, Ronald A.	(617)922-6722	412
Boston	BLAKE, Michael R.	(617)572-3127	103
	BYRN, William H.	(617)542-7440	169
	HAYES, Alison M.	(617)482-1776	515
	KERN, Donald C.	(617)638-8030	643
	MCKIRDY, Pamela R.	(617)738-2223	812
	PLUNKET, Joy H.	(617)327-5175	978

DATABASE/SYSTEMS CONSULTANT (Cont'd)
MASSACHUSETTS (Cont'd)
Boston

	WESTLING, Ellen R.	(617)726-8600	1327
Brookline	SOVNER-RIBBLER, Judith	(617)277-2991	1170
Cambridge	CLIFT, Scott B.	(617)661-1869	222
	COLLINS, John W.	(617)495-4225	232
	FERNALD, Anne C.	(617)491-4077	373
	GROVE, Shari T.	(617)864-3563	474
	JACKSON, Arlyne A.	(617)492-0355	586
	KNAACK, Linda M.	(617)253-8462	663
	MARCUS, Richard S.	(617)253-2340	769
	MOFFITT, Michael D.	(617)864-5770	852
	PAPALAMBROS, Rita G.	(617)497-2047	939
	WHITE, Chandlee	(617)576-9299	1330
Carlisle	HAMILTON, Fae K.	(617)369-1981	492
Chestnut Hill	LIPPMAN, Anne F.	(617)552-4457	732
Framingham	KUKLINSKI, Joan L.	(617)879-8575	683
Ipswich	GRAY, Carolyn M.	(617)356-0773	459
Lexington	BROWN, George F.	(617)863-5100	144
	PRUSAK, Laurence	(617)861-7580	996
	ROSENTHAL, Marylu C.	(617)862-8167	1057
	TAUBER, Stephen J.	(617)861-6295	1225
Littleton	BUCKLAND, Lawrence F.	(617)899-1086	154
Lowell	DESROCHES, Richard A.	(617)452-5000	295
	KARR, Ronald D.	(617)452-5000	628
Marlborough	FERGUSON, Roberta J.	(617)481-5866	372
Marshfield	TU, Shu C.	(617)837-8607	1261
Medford	PELLEGRINI, Deborah A.	(617)396-5457	955
Millis	PERRY, Guest	(617)376-8459	960
Milton	OPPENHEIM, Roberta A.	(617)698-6268	925
Natick	WANG, Gary Y.	(617)237-7715	1302
New Bedford	FINNI, John J.	(617)999-6034	379
Newton	ALPERT, Hillel R.		17
	CUNNINGHAM, Robert L.	(617)969-0400	265
	LINSKY, Leonore K.	(617)527-3646	731
	WALLAS, Philip R.	(617)527-1762	1298
North Abington	LAROSA, Sharon M.	(617)871-6288	698
North Adams	GOLDBERG, Steven R.	(413)664-6246	444
North Andover	HOLMES, Lyndon S.	(617)689-9334	553
	REEVE, Russell J.	(617)682-6260	1016
North Grafton	SAFFER-MARCHAND, Melinda	(617)839-5302	1074
Northampton	MAZUR, Ronald M.	(413)586-5980	791
Norton	MANGION, Barbara E.	(617)226-3122	765
Reading	DAMICO, Nancy B.	(617)944-9411	272
Somerville	HUSSEY, Laurie L.	(617)776-2614	578
Waban	CHERNIN, David A.	(617)731-6760	206
West Newton	CHEN, Ching C.	(617)738-2224	205
West Roxbury	HARZBECKER, Joseph J.	(617)323-1372	510
Westford	NATOLI, Dorothy L.	(617)692-7192	889
Westwood	CLAPPER, Mary E.	(617)329-3350	216
Woods Hole	SHEPHARD, Frank C.	(617)548-2743	1127
Worcester	ANDREWS, Peter J.		27
	ROCHELEAU, Kathleen D.	(617)793-7319	1046

MICHIGAN
Ann Arbor

	ADLER, Robert J.	(313)995-5808	7
	ANDERSEN, H F.	(313)936-7573	21
	DAVIS, Anne C.	(313)668-0385	277
	GATTIS, R G.	(313)936-1073	422
	KELLER, Karen A.	(313)769-4315	635
	KOCHEN, Manfred	(313)764-2585	667
	LANSDALE, Metta T.		696
	MCDONALD, David R.	(313)764-0412	802
	MOSEY, Jeanette	(313)973-8607	871
	PAO, Miranda L.	(313)747-3611	938
	SMILLIE, Pauline A.	(313)665-8821	1151
	TERWILLIGER, Doris H.	(313)761-3912	1232
	WERLING, Anita L.	(313)761-4700	1324
Belleville	STARESINA, Lois J.	(313)699-7549	1181
Birmingham	MARTIN, John E.	(313)647-1700	776
Canton	BRYANT, Barton B.	(313)397-3660	152
Dearborn	REID, Valerie L.	(313)278-1307	1019
Detroit	BRAITHWAITE, Heather J.	(313)577-3925	127
	COIR, Mark A.	(313)837-3643	229
	LABEAU, Dennis	(313)393-5411	685
	MORROW, Blaine V.	(313)893-1746	869
	SELBERG, Janice K.	(313)577-6175	1113
	SHUMAN, Bruce A.	(313)577-1825	1134

DATABASE/SYSTEMS CONSULTANT (Cont'd)
MICHIGAN (Cont'd)
Detroit

	WILLIAMS, James F.	(313)577-4021	1343
East Lansing	ACKERMAN, Katherine K.	(517)332-6818	4
	MAYERS, Henry L.	(517)332-3442	789
	MEAHL, D D.	(517)355-7641	819
	YARBROUGH, Joseph W.	(517)337-0693	1378
Farmington Hills	BEICHMAN, John C.	(313)553-5600	75
Flint	MORELAND, Patricia L.	(313)762-2141	863
Grand Rapids	FITZPATRICK, Nancy C.	(616)676-1568	383
Grosse Pointe Park	BOLLINGER, Robert O.		112
	TOLMAN, Bonnie B.	(313)885-0764	1249
Grosse Pointe Woods	WAYLAND, Marilyn T.		1311
Holland	LIGHT, Lin	(616)335-2540	726
Kalamazoo	CARROLL, Hardy	(616)383-1926	187
Lansing	HEINLEN, Bethany A.	(517)377-8389	522
Okemos	TREGLOAN, Donald C.	(517)349-7767	1255
Rochester	SHEPARD, Margaret E.	(313)651-1636	1127
Southfield	KAPUR, Geraldine P.	(313)559-3087	626
West Bloomfield	ABRAMSON, Lawrence J.	(313)626-8126	3

MINNESOTA

Bemidji	KISHEL, Deane A.	(218)751-3709	656
Eden Prairie	GROSCH, Audrey N.	(612)937-2345	472
Edina	LONG, John M.	(612)942-0140	739
Mankato	PEISCHL, Thomas P.	(507)389-5953	955
Minneapolis	BARRETT, Darryl D.	(612)370-0869	59
	BRUTON, Robert T.	(612)540-1084	151
	ELFSTRAND, Stephen F.	(612)722-9952	342
	OLSEN, Stephen	(612)333-9307	922
	POQUETTE, Mary L.	(612)377-6691	984
	SANDNESS, John G.	(612)866-7033	1081
	WEINBERG, Gail B.	(612)624-6492	1317
New Brighton	KEIM, Robert	(612)633-3393	635
Plymouth	VETH, Terry R.	(612)559-2179	1283
Robbinsdale	HERTHER, Nancy K.	(612)529-0115	533
Roseville	TALLY, Roy D.	(612)488-2028	1221
St Paul	BALDWIN, Jerome C.	(612)297-4532	51
	DAVIS, Emmett A.	(612)699-4367	279
	EPSTEIN, Rheda	(612)292-6392	351
	KING, Jack B.	(612)641-2373	651
	LEHMAN, Tom	(612)292-9947	713
	RASMUSSEN, Mary L.	(612)644-0685	1009
	STOKES, Claire Z.	(612)642-0120	1196
Worthington	SCOTT, Thomas L.	(507)376-5803	1108

MISSISSIPPI

Brandon	SELTZER, Ada M.		1114
Hattiesburg	WILLIAMS, Eddie A.	(601)266-4245	1343
Liberty	BURKS, Alvin L.	(601)657-8920	161

MISSOURI

Butler	FISHER, Georgeann	(816)679-6121	381
Columbia	ANDREWS, Mark J.	(314)875-0154	27
	BARNES, Everett W.	(314)882-4581	57
	KOPP, Kurt W.	(314)449-0185	671
	MITCHELL, Joyce A.	(314)882-6966	849
	MULTER, Ell P.		878
	RAITHEL, Frederick J.	(314)875-0026	1004
	RICKERSON, George T.	(314)445-1493	1031
	TIMBERLAKE, Patricia P.	(314)882-4581	1245
Independence	BRILEY, Carol A	(816)833-1400	136
Kansas City	HAMMOND, John J.	(816)221-2695	493
	LINSE, Mary M.	(816)765-0831	731
	MARCHANT, Thomas O.	(816)761-8873	768
	POSTLEWAIT, Cheryl A.	(913)384-0197	986
Maryville	MURPHY, Kathryn L.	(816)582-4768	880
Perryville	TUCKER, Phillip H.	(314)547-7433	1262
St Charles	MUETH, Elizabeth C.	(314)447-5116	875
St Louis	GELINNE, Michael S.	(314)694-4748	426
	GODT, Carol	(314)966-4976	443
	HELMS, Mary E.	(314)362-2787	525
	HUESTIS, Jeffrey C.	(314)889-5409	570

MONTANA

Bozeman	STACK, Laurie A.	(406)994-5310	1177
Butte	HUYGEN, Michaele L.	(406)782-8400	580

DATABASE/SYSTEMS CONSULTANT (Cont'd)

NEBRASKA
Lincoln	WAGNER, Rod G.	(402)423-7476	1292
Omaha	EARLEY, Dorothy A.	(402)333-5734	332

NEVADA
Carson City	STURM, H P.	(702)882-1361	1205
Henderson	HARRISON, Susan E.		507
Reno	PARKHURST, Carol A.	(702)784-6566	942

NEW HAMPSHIRE
Concord	DRUKE-STICKLER, Janet A.	(603)224-1865	320
	NELSON, David W.	(603)224-8286	893
Fremont	FARAH, Barbara D.		363
Hampton	KORBER, Nancy	(603)926-6005	671
Manchester	MESMER, Frank B.	(603)668-1593	827
Merrimack	DENTON, Francesca L.	(603)424-8621	293
Milford	LISTOVITCH, Denise A.	(603)672-0899	733

NEW JERSEY
Annandale	MURO, Ernest A.	(201)735-9633	880
Bergenfield	HILL, George R.	(201)384-4034	539
Bogota	MACKESY, Eileen M.		756
Caldwell	SKIDANOW, Helene	(201)226-4458	1146
Califon	CAPOOR, Asha	(201)832-9323	180
Chatham	ETTLINGER, Sandra E.	(201)635-6407	356
Cherry Hill	BECK, Susan J.	(609)354-7638	72
	BENSON, James A.	(609)354-7638	83
Clifton	PIERMATTI, Patricia A.	(201)473-2454	972
Creamridge	GEORGE, Muriel S.	(609)758-3198	428
Delanco	WOLFORD, Larry E.	(609)461-5667	1361
Denville	THOMAS, Hilary B.	(201)625-8136	1236
East Brunswick	KING, Donald R.	(201)828-2752	650
Florham Park	BARRETT, Joyce C.	(201)765-1523	59
	CHAPMAN, Janet L.	(201)765-2451	202
	SWINBURNE, Ralph E.	(201)377-8390	1216
Green Village	KEON, Edward F.	(201)822-0062	643
Highland Park	CLARK, Philip M.	(201)572-5414	218
	LI, Marjorie H.	(201)828-8730	724
Indian Mills	SCHREIBER-COIA, Barbara J.		1099
Iselin	FRANTS, Valery	(212)579-2496	398
	SILVA, Nelly H.	(201)321-0683	1138
Jersey City	RUBIN, Myra P.	(201)963-6456	1064
Lawrenceville	TILLMAN, Hope N.	(609)896-5115	1245
Leonia	SCHARF, Davida	(201)947-6839	1090
	TUCKER, Mary E.	(201)592-1451	1262
Little Ferry	BOTKIN, Karen R.		118
Madison	EDWARDS, Melanie G.	(201)822-1309	337
	SNELSON, Pamela	(201)377-3000	1163
Mahwah	MAYDET, Steven I.		789
Maplewood	D'ALLEYRAND, Marc R.	(201)761-1028	270
	LAUB, Barbara J.	(201)763-8379	702
Matawan	KEARNEY, Jeanne E.	(201)566-7532	633
Middletown	RILEY, Robert H.	(201)615-0900	1034
Montclair	BROWN, Cynthia D.	(201)783-6420	142
Mountain Lakes	CLARK, Rick	(201)299-0181	218
	HANEY, Kevin M.	(201)299-0181	495
New Brunswick	ANDERSON, James D.	(201)846-1510	23
	GRAHAM, Peter S.	(201)932-7505	456
	NASH, Stanley D.	(201)932-7014	888
	SARACEVIC, Tefko	(201)932-7447	1082
Oceanport	WAITE, William F.	(201)542-7216	1293
Paramus	WHITE, Robert W.	(201)652-6772	1332
Parsippany	VOGT, Herwart C.	(201)263-5669	1287
Pomona	MOLL, Joy K.	(609)652-1776	853
Pompton Lakes	MENZUL, Faina	(201)839-6885	825
Princeton	FRIHART, Anne R.	(609)921-3333	404
Princeton Junction	CHU, Wendy N.	(609)799-0814	213
Randolph	PAVELY, Richard W.	(201)989-0229	950
Ridgewood	JONES, Anita M.	(201)444-7273	610
Rockaway	COHN, John M.	(201)627-8512	229
	KELSEY, Ann L.	(201)627-8512	639
Rocky Hill	MOTT, Thomas H.	(609)924-8623	872
Roseland	MARTINEZ, Jane A.	(201)228-2172	779
Rutherford	RAPPAPORT, Susan E.		1008
Saddle Brook	AUGHEY, Kathleen M.		39
Secaucus	COVILL, Bruce	(201)902-1951	252
Short Hills	GOLDSMITH, Carol C.	(201)376-0216	446
Somerset	GREENBERG, Linda	(201)846-8497	463

DATABASE/SYSTEMS CONSULTANT (Cont'd)

NEW JERSEY (Cont'd)
Somerville	GABRIEL, Linda	(201)874-8061	411
Stanhope	ELIASON, Elisabetha S.	(201)347-8215	342
Tenafly	KORNFELD, Carol E.	(201)568-2231	672
Trenton	BREEDLOVE, Elizabeth A.	(609)292-9623	131
Union	AMRON, Irving	(201)688-4980	20
West Milford	JOB, Amy G.	(201)595-2160	601
West New York	BRITTON, Jeffrey W.	(201)868-2029	137

NEW MEXICO
Albuquerque	BEJNAR, Thaddeus P.	(505)277-0932	75
	HLAVA, Marjorie M.	(505)265-3591	544
	HSU, Grace S.		567
	ROLLINS, Stephen J.	(505)277-5057	1051
	SUGNET, Christopher L.	(505)277-7162	1206
Los Alamos	COMSTOCK, Daniel L.	(505)662-7668	235
Portales	DOWLIN, C E.	(505)562-2624	316
Roswell	KLOPFER, Jerome J.	(505)622-6250	662
Sunspot	CORNETT, John L.	(505)434-1390	247

NEW YORK
Albany	MCCOMBS, Gillian M.	(518)442-3633	797
	RUBIN, David S.	(518)471-5173	1064
Amherst	ROSENFELD, Jane D.	(716)691-8454	1056
Bellport	RICHARDSON, John A.	(516)286-1600	1029
Brewster	VELARDI, Adrienne B.	(914)279-5022	1281
Briarwood	BORRESS, Lewis R.	(718)441-6328	117
Brighton	RAHN, Erwin P.	(716)442-8980	1003
Bronx	CANNATA, Arleen	(212)295-5910	178
	GAROOGIAN, Rhoda	(212)588-2266	420
	PERSKY, Gail M.	(212)548-6007	961
	WEINBERG, Bella H.	(212)547-5159	1317
Brooklyn	LANDOLFI, Lisa M.	(718)853-7871	693
	MALINCONICO, S M.	(718)627-0558	763
	MARTINEZ-RIVERA, Ivette	(718)854-5176	779
	SKROBELA, Katherine C.	(718)462-6749	1147
	STRAM, Lynn R.	(718)434-7815	1200
	TANNER, Ellen B.	(718)780-3195	1222
Buffalo	COTY, Patricia A.	(716)636-3377	250
	GARLAND, Kathleen	(716)636-3068	419
	KASE-MCLAREN, Karen A.	(716)838-6610	628
	SAHLEM, James R.	(716)852-0712	1075
	STELZLE, James J.	(716)832-6066	1186
	YERKEY, A N.	(716)636-3069	1380
Cobleskill	GALASSO, Nancy	(518)234-5841	412
Dewitt	ELY, Donald P.	(315)446-0259	347
Dobbs Ferry	HASSAN, Mohammad Z.	(914)693-2031	511
East Aurora	UTTS, Janet R.	(716)655-0031	1270
East Northport	DAVIDSON, Steven I.	(516)368-0841	276
East Patchogue	CANTWELL, Mickey A.	(516)475-7007	179
East Setauket	ALBERTUS, Donna M.		10
	BLOHM, Laura A.	(516)444-3105	106
Eastchester	KOLTAY, Emery I.	(914)337-0300	670
Elmhurst	HSU, Elizabeth L.	(718)271-6623	567
Elmira	LAPIER, Cynthia B.	(607)739-3581	697
Farmingdale	ARMSTRONG, Ruth C.		32
Flushing	KOSTER, Gregory E.	(718)575-4264	673
	MCMORRAN, Charles E.	(718)358-4526	815
	MEDINA, Ildefonso M.	(718)359-3306	820
	SAFRAN, Scott A.	(718)445-6752	1074
Forest Hills	VAN BRUNT, Amy S.	(718)261-0313	1272
Glen Falls	GRAMINSKI, Denise M.	(518)793-2927	457
Glens Falls	SMITH, Frederick E.	(518)792-8214	1155
Hicksville	TRAVERS, Jane E.		1254
Highland	LAWRENCE, Thomas A.	(914)691-2734	705
Huntington	WESTERLING, Mary L.	(516)549-9441	1327
Huntington Station	MAUTER, George A.	(516)421-9291	787
	ROSS, David J.	(516)385-4951	1058
Ithaca	CHIANG, Katherine S.	(607)272-3086	207
	MORRIS, Jennifer D.	(607)273-4074	866
	OLSEN, Wallace C.	(607)255-2551	922
Jamaica Estates	BARTENBACH, Wilhelm K.	(718)658-3878	60
Kew Gardens	SALAZAR, Pamela R.	(718)441-2350	1076
Lackawanna	BEDNAR, Sheila	(716)822-0840	73
Latham	BRUNELLE, Bette S.	(518)783-1161	150
	VEGTER, Amy H.	(518)783-1161	1281
	ZIRPOLO, Frank	(212)247-7770	1390
Long Island City	LOW, Frederick E.	(718)482-5424	743
Lynbrook	FIEGAS, Barbara E.	(516)593-1195	375

DATABASE/SYSTEMS CONSULTANT (Cont'd)
NEW YORK (Cont'd)

Mamaroneck	O'CONOR, William C.	(914)698-4741	916
Middletown	ANGLIN, Richard V.	(914)343-1131	28
Mt Vernon	EARLE, Marcia H.		332
Nanuet	MOLLO, Terry	(914)623-0531	853
Nassau	LIPETZ, Ben A.	(518)766-3014	732
New York	ALLEN, Robert R.	(212)337-6991	16
	BADERTSCHER, David G.	(212)374-5615	44
	BANKS-ISZARD, Kimberly K.	(212)280-5658	54
	BERGFELD, C D.	(212)496-2668	86
	BING, Robert H.	(212)627-1921	97
	BROWN-SPRUILL, Debra K.		149
	COVERT, Nadine	(212)988-4876	252
	CROFT, Elizabeth G.	(212)371-2000	260
	DAVIS, Robert J.	(212)412-4270	280
	DENNIS, Anne R.	(212)645-4500	292
	DOOLING, Marie	(212)510-4375	312
	ESPO, Hal	(212)682-4630	354
	ETZI, Richard		356
	FRUSCIANO, Thomas J.	(212)998-2644	406
	GREENFIELD, Stanley R.		464
	GROSS, Gretchen		472
	GROTE, Janet H.	(212)627-1500	473
	HALL, Alix M.	(212)536-3598	486
	HENDERSON, Brad	(212)666-2674	526
	JOHNSON, Judith	(212)337-7428	606
	JONES, Anne	(212)903-8183	611
	KELLEY, Dennis L.	(212)210-7043	636
	KILBERG, Jacqueline L.	(212)536-3562	648
	KOENIG, Michael E.	(212)867-0489	668
	LAMANN, Amber N.	(212)677-4102	689
	LANDAU, Herbert B.	(212)705-7600	692
	LAWSON, George F.	(212)703-4121	705
	LEE, Sang C.	(212)669-7961	711
	MARKERT, Patricia B.	(212)925-4939	771
	MIHRAM, Danielle	(212)998-2515	834
	MILLER, Elien L.	(212)406-3186	837
	MILLER-KUMMERFELD, Elizabeth	(212)751-0830	843
	MONACO, James	(212)254-8235	854
	MOUNIR, Khalil A.	(212)373-5640	873
	NESTA, Frederick N.	(212)982-9672	896
	O'GRADY, Jean P.	(212)370-8690	918
	OSTROW, Rona	(212)691-1672	929
	PAUL, Sandra K.	(212)675-7804	949
	PETTOLINA, Anthony M.	(212)790-2888	965
	POWELL, Timothy W.	(212)807-7083	989
	PRAVER, Robin I.	(212)214-1720	990
	PRESCHEL, Barbara M.	(212)753-8458	991
	PRONIN, Monica		995
	RAUM, Tamar	(212)889-2156	1010
	RODERER, Nancy K.	(212)305-6302	1047
	ROTHMAN, John	(212)645-3008	1060
	RUBINSTEIN, Ed	(212)725-4550	1065
	SMITH, David F.	(212)243-1753	1154
	SMITH, Mark J.	(212)373-2401	1158
	SOLOMON, Samuel H.	(212)208-1200	1166
	STANAT, Ruth E.	(212)725-4550	1179
	THOMAS, Dorothy	(212)799-0970	1236
	VAUGHAN, John	(212)924-3729	1279
	WATKINS, Dorothy	(212)668-0940	1309
	WOODS, Lawrence J.	(212)736-6629	1367
	WRIGHT, Bernell	(212)866-3042	1370
	YUSTER, Leigh C.	(212)337-7131	1385
Palisades	WARD, Edith	(914)359-2081	1303
Peekskill	CLARE, Richard W.		216
	HALLINAN, Patricia R.	(914)739-2268	489
Plattsburgh	BURTON, Robert E.	(518)561-1613	164
Port Washington	BRENNER, Everett H.	(516)767-2728	133
Potsdam	FOSTER, Selma V.	(315)267-2477	392
Poughkeepsie	STAINO, Rocco A.		1178
Rhinebeck	MCCLELLAND, Bruce A.	(914)876-2230	796
Rochester	ISGANITIS, Jamie C.	(716)461-1943	585
	SEASE, Sandra A.	(716)724-6783	1110
Roslyn Harbor	CARTAFALSA, Joan C.	(516)671-7411	188
Rouses Point	CURRAN, George L.		266
Schenectady	KING, Maryde F.	(518)374-7287	651
	SHEVIAK, Jean K.	(518)370-6294	1129
Scotia	HENDRICKSON, Maria F.	(518)374-6209	527

DATABASE/SYSTEMS CONSULTANT (Cont'd)
NEW YORK (Cont'd)

Setauket	THOM, Janice E.	(516)751-1484	1235
Staten Island	SVENNINGSEN, Karen L.	(718)987-1168	1212
Syracuse	ABBOTT, George L.	(315)445-0484	1
	EISENBERG, Michael B.	(315)423-4549	340
	FROEHLICH, Thomas J.	(315)425-9080	405
	MARTIN, Thomas H.	(315)423-3840	778
	SIMONIS, James J.	(315)445-4321	1141
	STAM, Deirdre C.		1179
Troy	MOLHOLT, Pat	(518)276-8300	852
Tuckahoe	ZOTTOLI, Danny A.	(914)961-6294	1390
Uniondale	BARTENBACH, Martha A.	(516)292-8920	60
Voorheesville	BARRON, Robert E.		60
Wantagh	WESTERMANN, Mary L.	(516)679-8842	1327
Water Mill	GROSSMAN, Adrian J.	(516)537-3623	473
Webster	DESMOND, Andrew R.	(716)671-7657	295
West Point	RANDALL, Lawrence E.	(914)938-4789	1006
White Plains	DAVIES, Carol A.	(212)754-7438	277
	HOUGHTON, Joan I.	(914)335-7839	562
Woodhaven	VAZQUEZ, Edward	(718)296-2280	1280

NORTH CAROLINA

Asheville	BUTSON, Linda C.	(704)254-2932	167
Bahama	STINE, Roy S.	(719)471-8853	1194
Cary	BURCSU, James E.	(919)469-2731	158
Cedar Grove	WRIGHT, Larry L.		1372
Chapel Hill	BENNETT, David B.	(919)962-8022	81
	DANIEL, Evelyn H.	(919)962-8366	272
	DICKERSON, Jimmy	(919)962-1188	300
	KISER, Anita H.	(919)968-3946	656
	LOSEE, Robert M.	(919)962-8366	742
	MATER, Dee A.	(919)962-0700	783
	ROBERTSON, W D.	(919)933-6894	1042
	SCHELL, Nancy S.		1091
	TELFER, Margaret E.	(919)933-7563	1230
Charlotte	MYERS, Carol B.	(704)523-1260	884
Durham	BRUCE, Nancy G.	(919)490-0069	149
	FEINGLOS, Susan J.	(919)493-2904	369
	NYE, Julie B.	(919)471-1833	912
Greensboro	O'CONNOR, Sandra L.	(919)273-1914	916
	RANCER, Susan P.	(919)288-2160	1006
Greenville	GLUCK, Myke H.	(919)757-6514	442
	SPEER, Susan C.	(919)757-2212	1172
Raleigh	OSEGUEDA, Laura M.	(919)834-1024	927
	SMITH, Catherine	(919)851-4703	1153
Research Triangle Pk	MENDELL, Stefanie	(919)248-1842	823
	THOMPSON, Reubin C.	(919)248-4147	1241
Winston-Salem	RALPH, Randy D.	(919)788-4591	1004

NORTH DAKOTA

Bismarck	MOREHOUSE, Valerie J.	(701)224-4658	863

OHIO

Bay Village	BACON, Agnes K.		44
Canfield	GENAWAY, David C.	(216)533-2194	426
Cincinnati	BAKER, Carole A.	(513)871-2042	48
	CLASPER, James W.	(513)871-0969	219
	DOBBS, David L.	(513)271-4827	307
	GILLILAND, Anne J.	(513)475-6459	436
	LIPPERT, Margret G.	(513)821-8733	732
	LONG, Clare S.	(513)721-8565	739
	MC CORMICK, Lisa L.	(513)369-2540	798
	PATIENCE, Alice	(513)841-8589	947
Cleveland	BAUMGARTNER, Robert M.		66
	JOHNSON, Stephen C.	(216)429-8245	609
	KANTOR, Paul B.	(216)321-7713	626
	MCSPADDEN, Robert M.	(216)229-5900	818
	PEARMAN, Sara J.	(211)421-7340	952
Cleveland Heights	BOWIE, Angela B.	(216)291-5588	121
	DONNELLY, Kathleen	(216)381-9017	311
	PAUSLEY, Barbara H.	(216)932-2448	950
	PIETY, John S.	(216)321-8121	972
Columbus	ANDERSON, Carl A.	(614)486-9100	21
	BAYER, Bernard I.	(614)292-7895	67
	CALL, J R.	(614)885-4926	173
	CONNELL, Christopher J.	(614)848-5193	237
	FU, Paul S.	(614)466-2044	407
	HUNE, Mary G.	(614)224-3168	574

DATABASE/SYSTEMS CONSULTANT (Cont'd)
OHIO (Cont'd)
Columbus

Columbus	HUNTER, James J.	(614)461-5039	576
	KNOBLAUCH, Carol J.	(614)299-4020	665
	MLYNAR, Mary	(614)486-7980	850
	PLATAU, Gerard O.	(614)457-1687	977
	POPOVICH, Charles J.	(614)292-2136	984
Dayton	MAXWELL, Marjo V.	(513)848-4069	788
	PRICKETT, Dan S.	(513)294-5586	993
Delaware	GILBERT, Donna J.	(614)369-7705	433
Dublin	MARSH, Elizabeth C.	(614)488-1942	773
	SHREWSBURY, Lynn D.	(614)764-6403	1133
Fairfield	LUCAS, Jean M.	(513)829-5227	746
Grafton	DIAL, David E.	(216)926-3317	299
Lakewood	SEELY, Edward	(216)221-3453	1111
	TRIVISON, Donna	(216)221-9401	1257
London	DIENER, Ronald E.		302
Mansfield	KARRE, David J.	(419)526-1337	628
Mayfield Heights	RASKIN, Rosa S.	(216)442-3009	1009
Mentor	DUANE, Carol A.	(216)255-3323	321
New Albany	HERB, Elizabeth D.	(614)855-7441	530
Powell	RUSH, James E.	(614)881-5949	1068
Shaker Heights	LANDAU, Lucille	(216)283-6109	692
	MCCONNELL, Pamela J.	(216)921-7457	798
Uniontown	CREELAN, Marilee M.	(216)699-4454	257
Westlake	CHAMIS, Alice Y.	(216)777-2198	198
Youngstown	YANCURA, Ann J.	(216)746-7042	1377

OKLAHOMA

McAlester	SIMON, Bradley A.	(918)423-3468	1140
Midwest City	MOSLEY, Thomas E.	(405)733-0922	872
Oklahoma City	BOOTENHOFF, Rebecca J.	(405)728-7072	116
	CORNEIL, Charlotte E.	(405)235-7763	246
	JONES, Beverly A.	(405)751-0574	611
	PASCHAL, John M.	(405)751-6400	945
	ROACH, Eddie D.	(405)751-6400	1037
Stillwater	BENGE, Bruce	(405)377-0880	80
	DAVIS, Joyce N.	(405)377-8326	279
Tulsa	HILL, Linda L.	(918)584-0891	540

OREGON

Beaverton	SHOFFNER, Ralph M.	(503)645-3502	1132
Eugene	GRAHAM, Deborah L.		456
	SUNDT, Christine L.	(503)686-3052	1210
Hillsboro	VIXIE, Anne C.	(503)645-0527	1286
Portland	FERGUSON, Douglas K.	(503)228-5512	372
	SIMON, Dale	(503)227-7617	1140
	VAN HORN, Neal F.	(503)796-7717	1275
Roseburg	GAULKE, Mary F.	(503)440-4036	423
Salem	DOAK, Wesley A.	(503)581-4292	306
	WEBB, John	(503)378-4246	1313

PENNSYLVANIA

Allentown	BURYLO, Michelle A.	(215)481-7991	164
Ambler	SYEN, Sarah	(215)542-9967	1217
Bala Cynwyd	BOWERS, Paul A.	(215)664-9644	120
	CORVESE, Lisa A.	(215)668-4930	248
Belle Vernon	KLEIN, Joanne S.	(412)929-8290	659
Bensalem	CHU, John S.	(215)639-0768	212
Bloomsburg	ROCKWOOD, Susan M.	(717)784-8456	1046
Bryn Mawr	BILLS, Linda G.	(215)645-5294	96
California	BARREAU, Deborah K.	(412)938-5772	58
Carlisle	WIWEL, Pamela S.		1359
Chambersburg	MARLOW, Kathryn E.	(717)264-2382	772
Cheltenham	ELSHAMI, Ahmed M.	(215)635-3823	346
Coatesville	BURTON, Mary L.	(215)383-0245	164
Coraopolis	SKOVIRA, Robert J.	(412)262-8257	1147
Erie	RITTENHOUSE, Robert J.	(814)838-4124	1036
Friedens	KLINE, Eve P.	(814)443-2903	661
Greensburg	BALAS, Janet L.	(412)836-4849	50
King of Prussia	RICH, Denise A.	(215)935-7054	1027
Lionville	MCSWAIN, Christy A.	(215)269-7672	818
Lititz	GERLOTT, Eleanor L.	(717)627-0944	429
Mars	JOSEPH, Patricia A.	(412)776-9249	617
McKeesport	KISH, Veronica R.	(412)678-1749	656
Middletown	RAMBLER, Linda K.	(412)349-4621	1005
Mt Lebanon	WEISFIELD, Cynthia F.	(412)831-8225	1319
Narberth	SOKOLOFF, Michele	(215)664-2117	1165
North Wales	MAXIN, Jacqueline A.	(215)855-5675	787

DATABASE/SYSTEMS CONSULTANT (Cont'd)
PENNSYLVANIA (Cont'd)

Philadelphia	BOWDEN, Gail L.	(215)574-4417	120
	BRADLEY, James S.	(215)242-6112	126
	CUTRONA, Cheryl	(215)844-9027	268
	FENICHEL, Carol H.	(215)448-7185	371
	GRIFFITH, Belver C.	(215)895-2474	469
	HARRISON, Susan B.	(215)848-9164	507
	HOLMES, John H.	(215)592-1841	553
	HORNIG-ROHAN, James E.	(215)848-0554	560
	KREULEN, Thomas	(215)893-2495	678
	LYTLE, Richard H.	(215)895-2475	753
	MYERS, Charles J.	(215)898-7267	884
	POST, Joyce A.	(215)456-2971	986
	RUTKOWSKI, Hollace A.		1070
Pittsburgh	ARJONA, Sandra K.	(412)821-2263	31
	BEARMAN, David A.	(412)421-4638	69
	EPSTEIN, Barbara A.	(412)624-2378	351
	EVANS, Nancy H.	(412)268-2114	357
	FIDOTEN, Robert E.	(412)963-8785	375
	HODGSON, Cynthia A.	(412)374-4816	546
	MAWHINNEY, Paul C.	(412)367-7330	787
	METZLER, Douglas P.	(412)624-9414	829
	MICCO, Helen M.	(412)665-0412	831
	PAUL, Suzanne	(412)624-0418	949
	PISCIOTTA, Henry A.	(412)268-2451	976
	RICHARDS, Barbara G.	(412)268-2448	1028
	ROSS, Nina M.	(412)624-9475	1058
	VASILAKIS, Mary	(412)422-5694	1279
	WILLIAMS, James G.	(412)624-9418	1344
Radnor	KELLER, Kate V.	(215)688-6989	635
Somerset	PLASO, Kathy A.	(814)445-6501	977
Springfield	MAIN, Annette Z.		761
	SCULLIN, Frank E.		1109
State College	JAMISON, Carolyn C.	(814)234-4512	593
	PHILLIPS, Janet C.	(814)238-0254	968
	STOUT, Leon J.	(814)238-4855	1198
Unityville	VEDDER, Harvey B.	(717)482-3541	1280
University Park	FERRIN, Eric G.	(814)865-1818	373
	RAWLINS, Gordon W.	(814)865-1818	1010
Upland	BARON, Herman	(215)499-7415	58
Villanova	ERDT, Terrence	(215)645-4670	352
Warminster	BECKER, Linda C.	(215)443-7008	72
Wayne	ANTOS, Brian F.	(215)254-0754	29
	DRIEHAUS, Rosemary H.		320
Wescosville	FISLER, Charlotte D.	(215)395-6400	382
West Chester	DINNIMAN, Margo P.	(215)430-3080	305
	FIDISHUN, Dolores	(215)692-6806	375
	MILES, Donald D.	(215)431-7685	834
Wilkes-Barre	ERDICK, Joseph W.	(717)824-3725	352

RHODE ISLAND

Providence	BOWLBY, Raynna M.	(401)274-7224	121
	LLOYD, Lynn A.	(401)457-3001	735
	MARSH, Corrie V.	(401)863-2954	773
	WAGNER, Albin	(401)277-2283	1291

SOUTH CAROLINA

Charleston	ROSS, Gary M.	(803)792-5530	1058
Columbia	CHOI, Jin M.	(803)799-8786	210
Conway	LOWRIMORE, R T.	(803)248-2967	745
Spartanburg	BOWLES, David M.	(803)578-1472	121
Sumter	COOK, Galen B.	(803)469-9180	240

SOUTH DAKOTA

Rapid City	SCHWARTZ, James M.	(605)394-1246	1104
Vermillion	JENSEN, Mary B.	(605)677-5259	599

TENNESSEE

Clarksville	CARLIN, Don	(615)648-2095	182
Clinton	SPATH, Charles E.	(615)457-8616	1171
Cordova	SMITH, Philip M.	(901)386-1003	1159
Knoxville	BULL, Margaret J.	(615)632-6173	156
	HASTINGS, Constance M.	(615)690-0368	511
	PONNAPPA, Biddanda P.	(615)675-4545	982
Memphis	GIVENS, Mary K.	(901)528-5166	439
Murfreesboro	NEAL, James H.	(615)895-1383	890

DATABASE/SYSTEMS CONSULTANT (Cont'd)

TENNESSEE (Cont'd)

Nashville	GAUDET, Susan E.	(615)327-4751	422
	GMEINER, Timothy J.	(615)297-7958	442
	HARWELL, Sara J.	(615)322-2807	509
	MARTIN, Laquita V.	(615)383-0953	777
	PATTERSON, Jennifer J.	(615)383-4251	948
	WILBURN, Clouse R.	(615)322-8050	1338
Niota	BURN, Harry T.	(615)745-8590	161
Oak Ridge	CARROLL, Bonnie C.	(615)482-3230	187
	PFUDERER, Helen A.	(615)574-5350	966
	SNYDER, Cathrine E.	(615)483-1228	1164
	YALCINTAS, Rana	(615)482-9397	1376
Palmyra	FOWLER, James W.	(615)647-4172	393
Sewanee	PHILLIPS, Patricia A.	(615)598-1389	968
Signal Mountain	JACKSON, Joseph A.	(615)886-1753	587

TEXAS

Abilene	ANDERSON, Madeleine J.	(915)674-2344	24
Amarillo	RUDDY, Mary K.	(806)353-1534	1065
Arlington	MCCLURE, Margaret R.	(817)275-6594	797
Austin	AIROLDI, Melissa	(512)476-8049	9
	BICHTELER, Julie H.	(512)471-3821	94
	BRIDGE, Frank R.	(512)328-6006	135
	DIVELY, Reddy	(512)288-3371	306
	HELFER, Robert S.	(512)929-3086	523
	JUERGENS, Bonnie	(512)288-2072	619
	MARTIN, Jean K.	(512)346-2973	776
	MIDDLETON, Robert K.	(512)454-1888	833
	STANDIFER, Hugh A.	(512)288-2072	1179
	TAYLOR, Nancy L.	(512)346-1426	1228
	WALTON, Robert A.	(512)346-1426	1301
	WYLLYS, Ronald E.	(512)471-3821	1375
College Station	COOK, C C.	(409)845-3731	239
Dallas	BIRD, H C.	(214)553-5995	98
	HAWLEY, Laurie J.	(214)907-2940	514
	HOPKINS, Terry F.	(214)969-8499	558
	JAGOE, Katherine P.	(214)931-8938	591
	KLEIN, Mindy F.	(214)701-4116	659
	MITCHE, Cynthia R.	(214)692-6767	848
	MITCHELL, Cynthia R.	(214)692-6767	848
	PEDEN, Robert M.	(214)746-3646	954
	SACKETT-WILK, Susan A.	(214)307-1304	1073
Denton	ALMQUIST, Sharon G.	(817)387-1703	17
Edinburg	HAYNIE, Altie V.	(512)383-7760	517
Fort Worth	RUSSELL, Barbara J.	(817)735-9136	1068
	VERNON, James R.	(817)923-4901	1283
Garland	QUEYROUZE, Mary E.	(214)494-2112	999
Groves	MCCONNELL, Karen S.	(409)963-1481	797
Houston	CALDWELL, Marlene	(713)661-5787	172
	CAMP, Joyce H.	(713)789-9810	175
	CARTER, Daniel H.	(713)665-5150	189
	LYDEN, Edward W.	(713)777-8212	750
	MCCANN, Debra W.	(713)691-0148	794
	MULLINS, James R.	(713)522-8131	878
	RAMBO, Neil H.	(713)797-1230	1005
	RICCARDI, Vincent M.	(713)558-9907	1026
	TEUN, Rebecca L.	(713)792-6630	1233
	WEGMANN, Pamela A.	(713)655-3400	1316
Katy	POWELL, Alan D.	(713)392-9340	987
Lewisville	MCCOY, Judy I.	(214)221-9251	799
Lubbock	SARGENT, Charles W.	(806)792-0754	1082
Mesquite	GIBSON, Timothy T.	(214)289-2479	432
Midland	MIRANDA, Cecilia	(915)685-4557	847
Prairie View	YEH, Helen S.	(409)857-3192	1379
San Antonio	BALCOM, Karen S.	(512)344-8654	51
	HEWINS, Elizabeth H.	(512)655-4672	535
	LEATHERBURY, Maurice C.	(512)829-7033	707
	O'DONOGHUE, Patrice	(512)681-1207	917
Sugar Land	JOHNSON, Pat M.	(713)980-5350	608
Temple	TIME, Ming M.	(817)778-5556	1245
Wichita Falls	ROBERTS, Ernest J.	(817)855-2390	1040

DATABASE/SYSTEMS CONSULTANT (Cont'd)

UTAH

Logan	NIELSEN, Steven P.	(801)750-3166	903
Provo	GOULD, Douglas A.	(801)226-1469	454
	LAMB, Connie	(801)378-5627	689
Salt Lake City	CUMMINGS, Christopher H.	(801)534-1669	264
	JAMES, Brent C.	(801)533-3730	592
	JENSEN, Charla J.	(801)533-5250	598
	MARCHANT, Cathy	(801)364-8399	768
	REED, Vernon M.	(801)531-3377	1015
	SKIDMORE, Kerry F.		1146

VERMONT

Barre	GRIFFIN, Marie E.	(802)479-2810	468
Burlington	CASWELL, Jerry V.	(802)656-3321	194
Milton	SEKERAK, Robert J.		1113
Northfield	WARD, Robert C.	(802)485-7344	1304
Putney	THOMPSON, Jane K.	(802)387-4767	1240
South Royalton	SWIFT, Esther M.	(802)763-7163	1216

VIRGINIA

Alexandria	AUSTON, Ione	(703)549-4325	40
	BERGMAN, Rita F.	(703)836-5200	86
	DAVIDSON, Dero H.	(703)998-2976	276
	DRUMMOND, Louis E.		321
	GALE, John C.	(703)548-4320	413
	JONES, Frank	(703)820-6283	613
	KAISER, Donald W.	(703)836-0225	622
	OLIVETTI, L J.	(703)683-8190	921
	ROBERTSON, Jack	(703)549-3260	1042
	ROSENBERG, Kenyon C.	(703)642-5480	1056
	SEVERTSON, Susan M.	(703)683-4890	1117
	STEIN, Karen E.	(703)354-3154	1185
Arlington	CAPUTO, Anne S.	(703)534-3433	180
	CAPUTO, Richard P.	(703)553-8455	180
	CIPRIANI, Debra A.	(703)769-7736	215
	DORNER, Steven J.	(703)841-8400	313
	GREEN, Randall N.	(703)243-5631	462
	HELMINSKI, James C.	(703)525-1324	525
	HENDERSON, Susanne	(703)931-8433	527
	JOACHIM, Robert J.	(703)920-7721	600
	MOORE, Penelope F.	(703)979-5900	861
	PRICE, Joseph W.	(703)241-0447	992
	WELLS, Christine		1322
	YODER, William M.	(703)527-7225	1380
Burke	GOUDREAU, Ronald A.	(703)569-0994	454
	TOSIANO, Barbara A.		1252
Charlottesville	BRAUN, Mina H.	(804)924-4957	129
Fairfax	FESSLER, Vera F.	(703)352-7200	374
	ROBINSON, David F.	(703)273-6139	1043
	SCOTT, Mona L.	(703)378-8027	1107
	SULLIVAN, Michael M.	(703)876-2000	1208
Falls Church	BUCK, Dayna E.	(703)847-0271	153
	CHUNG, Catherine A.	(703)534-3114	213
	LEONARD, Lucinda E.	(703)536-2373	716
	PARSONS, John W.	(703)671-7756	945
	REID, Judith P.	(703)379-0739	1018
	SEGEL, Bernard J.	(703)532-7287	1112
Farmville	STWODAH, M I.	(804)392-8925	1206
Herndon	GUERRIERO, Donald A.	(703)860-1058	476
	PAVEK, C C.	(703)481-0711	950
Leesburg	GRIMES, Judith E.	(703)777-9441	470
McLean	FURR, Susan H.	(703)893-4089	410
	NIGAM, Alok C.	(703)883-6751	904
	SCHULMAN, Jacque L.	(703)527-2627	1101
Newport News	HAMMOND, Theresa M.	(804)595-8179	494
Norfolk	LIU, Albert C.	(804)440-4141	734
Reston	GENNARO, John L.	(703)689-5616	427
	JENSEN, Raymond A.	(703)648-6820	599
	MCLANE, Kathleen	(703)620-3660	813
	WILTSHIRE, Denise A.	(703)391-0505	1354
Richmond	CARNEY, Marillyn L.	(804)254-2447	183
	DEBARDELEBEN, Marian Z.	(804)274-2876	284
	KANE, Dorothea S.		624
	MOSER, Emily F.	(804)355-3348	870
	ROSENBERG, Murray D.	(804)740-0019	1056
	SOUTHWICK, Margaret A.	(804)274-2661	1170
	WILLS, Luella G.	(804)233-7616	1349
Salem	GLENNON, Irene F.	(703)380-3552	441

DATABASE/SYSTEMS CONSULTANT (Cont'd)
VIRGINIA (Cont'd)

Springfield	FOURNIER, Susan K.	(703)569-9468	393
	KANE, Astor V.	(703)487-4696	624
	ROARK, Robin D.	(703)644-7372	1038
Vienna	COCHRANE, Maryjane S.	(703)938-2037	226
Virginia Beach	CARR, Jeanette A.	(804)481-6096	185

WASHINGTON

Auburn	GOLDSTEIN, Cynthia N.	(206)931-3018	446
Bellingham	JOHNSON, Dana E.	(206)734-3941	603
Kenmore	TAYLOR, James B.	(206)483-2954	1227
Kent	CHAPMAN, Kathleen A.	(206)630-0538	202
Lacey	DEBUSE, Raymond	(206)491-7498	285
	PUZIAK, Kathleen M.	(206)491-0347	998
Pullman	KOPP, James J.	(509)335-9133	671
	VYHNANEK, Kay E.	(509)335-9671	1290
Richland	SAMPLE, Charles R.	(509)376-1506	1078
Seattle	BOYLAN, Merle N.	(206)543-1760	123
	CHASE, Dale L.	(206)525-0795	203
	CRANDALL, Michael D.	(206)633-2530	255
	EIPERT, Susan L.	(206)522-3174	340
	ERICKSON, Randall D.	(206)523-9356	352
	FASSETT, William E.	(206)545-2272	366
	GRIPPO, Christopher F.		471
	JEWELL, Timothy D.	(206)524-8820	600
	JOHNSON, Carolynn K.	(206)684-6681	603
	KREPS, Lise E.	(206)527-2817	678
	MCFADDEN, Denyse I.	(206)284-6280	804
	MILLER, Carmen L.	(206)285-4248	836
	ROWBERG, Alan H.	(206)548-6250	1062
	SCHUELLER, Janette H.	(206)543-8262	1101
	SONG, Seungja Y.	(206)527-8737	1167
	STOCK, Carole G.	(206)325-8364	1195
	SY, Karen J.	(206)545-2873	1217
Tacoma	BECKER, Roger V.	(206)591-2703	72
	HAGAN, Dalia L.	(206)565-9669	482
	KRUZIC, Evelyn D.	(206)752-9156	681
	MENDELSON, Martin	(206)383-5855	823
Vancouver	CONABLE, Irene H.	(206)694-0604	235
Yakima	JORDAN, Sharon L.	(509)248-4522	617

WEST VIRGINIA

Barboursville	DZIERZAK, Edward M.		331
Charleston	PROSSER, Judith M.	(304)344-8583	995
Clarksburg	GREATHOUSE, Brenda J.	(304)624-9649	461
Huntington	REENSTJERNA, Frederick R.	(304)523-9651	1016
Point Pleasant	WILLIAMSON, Judy D.	(304)675-4350	1347

WISCONSIN

Appleton	BOOHER, Craig S.	(414)738-3384	115
	KLAVER, Timothy J.	(414)735-0463	658
	PENNINGTON, Jerome G.	(414)735-6167	957
Grafton	MORITZ, William D.	(414)377-6695	865
Kenosha	BARUTH, Barbara P.	(414)553-2167	62
La Crosse	CIMPL, Kathleen A.	(608)785-0530	214
Madison	ANDERSON, Axel R.	(608)233-0659	21
	BEHNKE, Charles	(608)244-3253	75
	CRAWFORD, Josephine	(608)274-7984	256
	GAPEN, D K.	(608)262-2600	416
	JEFFCOTT, Janet B.	(608)246-6633	596
	WILCOX, Patricia F.	(608)263-4414	1338
Mequon	AMAN, Mary J.	(414)242-9031	19
Milwaukee	BLUE, Richard I.	(414)963-4707	107
	DETWILER, Eve N.	(414)332-3367	296
North Fond Du Lac	GIEBEL, Thomas W.	(414)921-8348	432
Oshkosh	PARKS, Dennis H.	(414)426-4800	943
St Francis	WESTERN, Eric D.	(414)769-0110	1327
Wauwatosa	CHAPLOCK, Sharon K.	(414)778-2167	201
West Allis	LUECHT, Richard M.	(414)321-3152	747
Whitefish Bay	LANK, Dannette H.	(414)225-2107	696
Wisconsin Rapids	WILSON, William J.	(715)424-4272	1353

WYOMING

Cheyenne	SCHELL, Catherine L.	(307)637-7504	1091

DATABASE/SYSTEMS CONSULTANT (Cont'd)
CANADA

ALBERTA

Calgary	GASHUS, Karin C.	(403)237-4508	421
	GUNSON, Murray J.	(403)256-7327	478
Edmonton	BATEMAN, Robert A.	(403)483-3432	63
	STARR, Lea K.	(4C3)432-5154	1182
Red Deer	GISHLER, John R.	(304)340-3922	438

BRITISH COLUMBIA

Richmond	ELLIS, Kathy M.	(604)272-5389	344
Vancouver	CAMPBELL, Brian G.	(604)665-3579	176
	CHAN, Diana L.	(604)224-8470	199
	HALE, Linda L.	(604)321-0932	485
	NICHOL, Kathleen M.	(604)263-7081	901
	PEPPER, David A.	(604)664-4311	958
	WARREN, Lois M.	(604)687-1072	1306
Victoria	MOEHR, Jochen R.	(604)721-8581	851
	TRUBKIN, Loene	(604)386-4140	1259

MANITOBA

Winnipeg	COVVEY, H D.	(204)942-5335	252
	LINCOLN, Robert S.	(204)786-2387	728
	MARSHALL, Kenneth E.	(204)269-3243	774

NEW BRUNSWICK

Riverview	ENNS, Carol F.	(506)386-1084	350

NEWFOUNDLAND

Mt Pearl	MORGAN, Pamela S.	(709)368-5926	864

NORTHWEST TERRITORIES

Yellowknife	O'KEEFE, Kevin T.	(403)873-5715	919

NOVA SCOTIA

Halifax	DYKSTRA, Mary E.	(902)424-3656	331
	HSIUNG, Lai Y.	(902)424-3645	567
	SIEGERT, Lindy E.	(902)424-3656	1136
	TAYYEB, Rashid	(902)422-4684	1229

ONTARIO

Bowmanville	MOON, Jeffrey D.	(416)263-8504	857
Deep River	LEWIS, Leslie	(613)584-2605	723
Downsview	BERNSTEIN, Elaine S.	(416)638-1962	89
	JONES, B E.	(416)244-3621	611
	STEVENS, Mary		1190
Go-Home Bay	CAMPBELL, Harry	(705)756-1878	176
Guelph	BLACK, John B.	(519)821-2565	101
Haliburton	HOBBS, Kathleen M.		545
Hamilton	BROWNRIDGE, James R.	(416)572-2981	149
	FLEMMING, Tom	(416)525-9140	384
Kingston	FORKES, David	(613)544-2630	390
London	RUTHERFORD, Frederick S.	(519)471-4867	1070
	TAGUE, Jean M.	(519)471-1311	1220
Markham	MORTON, Robert E.	(416)475-0525	870
Mississauga	OLMSTEAD, Marcia E.	(416)848-9403	921
	WEI, Carl K.	(416)822-4111	1316
North York	HEATON, Gwynneth T.	(416)225-4859	519
Ottawa	BRODIE, Nancy E.	(613)996-7391	139
	KNOPPERS, Jake V.		665
	LEUNG, Frank F.	(613)994-6920	719
	MACDONALD, Marcia H.	(819)994-6947	754
	MACLELLAND, Margaret A.	(819)994-6832	757
	PARE, Richard	(613)733-8391	940
	PROULX, Steven D.	(613)596-3746	996
	VALENTINE, Scott	(819)994-6946	1271
Sault Ste Marie	BAZILLION, Richard J.	(705)949-4352	68
Scarborough	O'NEILL, Louise N.	(416)431-2222	924
Toronto	ATTINGER, Monique L.	(416)699-2530	38
	BEAUMONT, Jane	(416)922-9364	70
	CAMPBELL, Bonnie	(416)323-3566	176
	CHIU, Lily F.	(416)868-2909	209
	DAVEY, Dorothy M.	(416)485-0377	276
	DYSART, Jane I.	(416)974-2780	331
	FRITZ, Richard J.	(416)923-0890	405
	LA MARCHE, David L.	(416)766-5289	689
	MARSHALL, Joanne G.	(416)978-7111	774
	MEADOW, Charles T.	(416)530-4934	819
	MERILEES, Bobbie	(416)485-4177	826

DATABASE/SYSTEMS CONSULTANT (Cont'd)

ONTARIO (Cont'd)

Toronto

	NORTH, John A.	(416)979-5142	909
	ODHO, Marc	(416)596-2682	917
	OLSHEN, Toni	(416)488-5321	922
	PARKER, Arthur D.	(416)967-5525	941
	SABLJIC, John A.	(416)782-6754	1072
	TAYLOR, Karen E.	(416)923-0890	1227
	THODY, Susan I.	(416)762-1690	1235
	VAN ORDER, Mary J.	(416)924-0671	1276
	YANCHINSKI, Roma N.	(416)767-6781	1377
	ZURBRIGG, Lyn E.	(416)961-9323	1391
Willowdale	BELDAN, A C.	(416)226-6380	76

QUEBEC

Boischatel	LUSSIER, Richard	(418)822-1904	749
Boucherville	THERIAULT, Carmelle	(514)655-2665	1234
Chambly	ASSUNCAO, Isabel	(514)658-3882	37
Greenfield Park	RICHARDS, Stella	(514)672-1008	1028
Jonquiere	HARVEY, Serge	(418)548-7821	509
Laval	AUGER, Bernard	(514)687-9730	39
Montreal	ALLARD, Andre	(514)256-2522	14
	ARAJ, Houda	(514)343-7095	30
	DUCHESNEAU, Pierre	(514)281-6166	322
	DUSABLON-BOTTEGA, Nicole	(514)871-6442	329
	GARDNER, Lucie	(514)845-7814	418
	GONZALEZ, Paloma	(514)735-1977	448
	LESAGE, Jacques	(514)648-8461	717
	MARCIL, Louise	(514)333-6621	769
	MCINTOSH, Julia E.	(514)283-3639	809
	NAGY, Cecile		886
	PIGGOTT, Sylvia E.	(514)877-9383	972
	PROVOST, Paul E.	(514)598-5389	996
	TOUCHETTE, Francois G.	(514)524-7878	1252
Pointe Claire	MACFARLANE, Judy A.	(514)697-9572	755
Quebec	DENIGER, Constant	(418)692-4369	292
	GELINAS, Michel R.	(418)522-7203	426
	TESSIER, Yves	(418)872-4304	1233
Repentigny	MERCIER, Diane	(514)582-3920	825
Rouyn-Noranda	TREMBLAY, Levis	(819)762-0931	1255
Sherbrooke	CHOUINARD, Germain	(819)564-5297	211
	GOODFELLOW, Marjorie E.	(819)562-1694	448
	SOKOV, Asta M.	(819)821-7566	1166
Stanstead	GRENIER, Serge	(819)876-2981	467
Trois-Rivieres	BAILLARGEON, Daniele	(819)376-1721	47
Verdun	DIMITRESCU, Ioana	(514)765-8219	304
	VAILLANCOURT, Alain	(514)765-7507	1270
Westmount	LEDOUX, Marc A.	(514)484-5951	708

AUSTRALIA

East Hawthorn	BENNETT, David M.		81
Kensington	WILSON, Concepcion S.		1350
Newcastle	NEAME, Roderick L.		891

BELGIUM

Beerse	PEETERS, Marc D.		954
Brussels	VAN SLYPE, Georges		1277

COSTA RICA

San Jose	MIRABELLI, Gerardo	(506)315-0540	847

ENGLAND

Cheshire	HOWARD, Theresa M.		564
Letchworth Herts	AITCHISON, Thomas M.		9
London	BUNCE, George D.		157
Oxford	BISHOP, John		99
Reading	WOODWARD, Anthony M.		1367
Surrey	NOERR, Kathleen T.		907

FEDERAL REPUBLIC OF GERMANY

Berlin	ULRICH, Paul S.		1268
	WERSIG, Gernot		1325
Bremerhaven	GOMEZ, Michael J.		447
Saarbrucken	VON KEITZ, Wolfgang		1288
Taufkirchen	ADENEY, Carol D.		6

FIJI

Suva	WOODS, Richard F.		1367

DATABASE/SYSTEMS CONSULTANT (Cont'd)

FRANCE

Paris	CHAUMIER, Jacques		204
	PILLET, Sylvaine M.		973

GUATAMALA

Guatamala City	MARBAN, Ricio		768

HONG KONG

The Peak	SANDFELDER, Paula M.		1080

INDIA

Andhra Pradesh	SINHA, Pramod K.		1143

IRAN

Shiraz	MEHRAD, Jafar		821

ISRAEL

Brak	CAREL, Rafael S.		181
Haifa	BEAVERS, Janet W.		71
	BLOCH, Uri		105
Jerusalem	LANGERMAN, Shoshana P.		695
Tel-Aviv	HOFFMANN, Eliahu W.		548

ITALY

Florence	FORRESTER, John H.		391
Milan	FABRE DE MORLHON, Christiane		360
Rome	MENOU, Michel J.		824

JAPAN

Chiba-ken	NASU, Yukio		889
Ibaraki-ken	NOZOE, Atsutake		911
Tokyo	KATAOKA, Yoko		629
	MIWA, Makiko		850
	YAMAZAKI, Hisamichi		1377
Tokyo 105	YAMAKAWA, Takashi		1376

LUXEMBOURG

Helmsange	CORNELIUS, Peter K.		246

MEXICO

Benito	MACIAS-CHAPULA, Cesar A.		755

NETHERLANDS

The Haag	RAITT, David I.	(311)719-8301	1004

NEW ZEALAND

Auckland	TWEEDALE, Dellene M.		1266

SOUTH AFRICA

Tygerberg	ROSSOUW, Steve F.		1059

SWEDEN

Jarfalla	SHELTON, Anita L.		1126

SWITZERLAND

Geneva	OHLMAN, Herbert		919

TRINIDAD

Saint Joseph	MCCONNIE, Mary		798

GENERAL LIBRARY/INFORMATION CONSULTANT

ALABAMA

Auburn	JONES, Allen W.	(205)826-4360	610
	VEENSTRA, Robert J.	(205)826-4780	1281
Birmingham	ATKINSON, Calberta O.	(205)787-3767	38
	DAY, Janeth N.	(205)226-3614	282
	GRIFFITH, Ethel T.	(205)254-2982	469
	HARRIS, Jay	(205)251-2821	504
	MCCARTHY, Sherri L.	(205)226-3630	794
	MCGARITY, Marysue	(205)879-6128	805
	OLIVE, J F.	(205)967-8481	921
	SCALES, Diann R.	(205)322-8458	1087
	STEPHENS, Jerry W.	(205)363-6000	1188
Brewton	BIGGS-WILLIAMS, Evelyn A.	(205)867-2445	95
Decatur	MORRIS, Betty J.	(205)773-6262	866

GENERAL LIBRARY/INFORMATION CONSULTANT (Cont'd)

ALABAMA (Cont'd)

Florence	CARR, Charles E.	(205)767-2310	185
Helena	GOODWYN, Betty R.	(205)988-0896	450
Huntsville	KENDRICK, Aubrey W.	(205)837-7597	640
Jasper	ELLIOTT, Riette B.	(205)387-0511	344
Mobile	BUSH, Nancy W.	(205)343-8121	165
	JEFFERY, Phyllis D.	(205)434-7084	596
	MCWHORTER, Jimmie M.	(205)342-5336	818
	NICHOLS, Amy S.	(205)694-3895	901
	PARSLEY, Brantley H.	(205)675-5990	944
Montevallo	WILLIAMS, Pauline C.	(205)665-4329	1346
Montgomery	BIVINS, Hulen E.	(205)272-1700	100
	DESSY, Blane K.	(205)277-7330	296
	FELDER, Jimmie R.	(205)265-2012	369
	LANE, Robert B.	(205)288-8122	694
Phenix City	KLUESNER, Marvin P.	(205)298-6371	662
Prichard	WILLIAMS, Gwendolyn	(205)452-4395	1343
Tuscaloosa	RAMER, James D.	(205)348-1516	1005
Tuskegee Institute	CLAVER, M P.	(205)727-0620	219

ALASKA

Anchorage	EGGLESTON, Phyllis A.	(907)337-0051	339
	LUDWIG, J D.	(907)333-8917	746
	PIERCE, Linda I.	(907)338-6421	971
	SOKOLOV, Barbara J.	(907)346-2480	1165
Bethel	EMMONS, Mary E.	(907)543-3682	348
College	GALBRAITH, Betty J.	(903)479-5196	413
Delta Junction	JENKS, Arlene I.	(907)895-4253	597
Fairbanks	GALBRAITH, William B.	(907)479-5196	413
	LAKE, Gretchen L.	(907)452-6751	688
	MUDD, Isabelle G.	(907)479-4522	875
	PINNELL-STEPHENS, June A.	(907)479-5826	975
Juneau	CRANE, Karen R.	(907)456-2910	255
	KOLB, Audrey P.	(907)452-2999	669
	MITCHELL, Micheal L.	(907)789-0302	849
	SMITH, George V.	(907)789-2559	1155
Nome	ROSS, Rosemary E.	(907)443-2201	1058
Sitka	MCCLAIN, Harriet V.	(907)747-8160	795

ARIZONA

Flagstaff	BAUM, Ester B.	(602)774-8878	66
	EGAN, Terence W.	(602)523-6819	338
	HASSELL, Robert H.	(602)523-2171	511
	JOHNSON, Harlan R.	(602)523-4408	605
Mesa	MAIN, Isabelle G.	(602)962-4310	761
Phoenix	ALABASTER, Carol	(602)262-7360	9
	BOROVANSKY, Vladimir T.		117
	DOHERTY, Walter E.	(602)262-5303	309
	EVANS, Iris I.	(602)995-1701	357
	GOEBEL, Heather L.	(602)994-2471	443
	GORMAN, Judith F.	(602)279-9741	452
	NIXON, Arless B.	(602)246-9196	906
	ROATCH, Mary A.	(602)254-7678	1038
	STEPHENS, Stefanie N.	(602)257-9234	1188
	WELLIK, Kay E.	(602)285-3299	1321
Scottsdale	PILLOW, William H.	(602)994-2691	973
Sedona	CHICOREL, Marietta S.	(601)602-2826	208
Sells	CULL, Roberta	(602)383-2601	263
Tempe	LESHY, Dede	(602)946-8090	718
	RIGGS, Donald E.	(602)965-3950	1034
	STEEL, Virginia	(602)965-3282	1183
Tucson	BALDWIN, Charlene M.	(602)327-2385	51
	HURT, Charlie D.	(602)621-3566	578
	LEI, Polin P.		713
	MCBRIDE, Patricia A.	(602)327-6581	792
	MCCRACKEN, John R.	(602)327-4056	799
	MILLER, Edward P.		837
	NICHOLS, Margaret M.		901
	OLSRUD, Lois C.	(602)621-2297	923
	TALLMAN, Karen D.	(602)577-3317	1221
	WHITE, Edward H.	(602)621-5455	1330

ARKANSAS

Arkadelphia	WOODS, L B.	(501)246-5511	1367
Batesville	WATSON, Ellen I.	(501)793-9813	1309
Conway	HARDIN, Willie	(501)450-3129	500
Eureka Springs	STOWE, Jean E.	(501)253-8754	1199
Fayetteville	HARRISON, John A.	(501)443-4403	506

GENERAL LIBRARY/INFORMATION CONSULTANT (Cont'd)

ARKANSAS (Cont'd)

Fort Smith	PIERSON, Betty	(501)785-7135	972
Greenwood	CLEVENGER, Judy B.	(501)996-2856	221
Hazen	JEFFCOAT, Phyllis C.	(501)255-4546	596
Heber Springs	SEDELOW, Sally Y.	(501)362-3476	1110
	SEDELOW, Walter A.		1110
Hot Springs	MILLS, Peggy	(501)767-9371	844
Little Rock	HALL, John J.	(501)221-2912	488
	MULKEY, Jack C.	(501)225-2246	876
Magnolia	BRADLEY, Florene J.	(501)234-1991	125
North Little Rock	FOOS, Donald D.	(501)758-5112	388
Prescott	WATSON, Merlyn		1310
Roland	PATRICK, Retta B.	(501)868-5740	947

CALIFORNIA

Agoura	THOMAS, Yvonne		1238
Alameda	HOSEL, Harold V.	(415)522-5875	561
Anaheim	ADAMS, Joyce A.	(714)637-8385	5
	WRIGHT, Betty A.	(714)998-1127	1370
APO San Francisco	HEINES, Rodney M.		522
Aptos	HERON, David W.	(408)688-6994	532
Arcata	KENYON, Sharmon H.	(707)826-3416	643
	OYLER, David K.	(707)826-3441	932
Bellflower	PESTUN, Aloysius J.	(213)920-1734	961
Benicia	MILLER, Davic C.	(707)746-6728	836
Berkeley	BENIDIR, Samia	(415)644-1129	80
	BERGER, Michael G.	(415)642-9485	85
	BROWNRIGG, Edwin B.		149
	DUGGAN, Mary K.	(415)642-5764	324
	FLUM, Judith G.	(415)486-0378	386
	HANDMAN, Gary P.	(415)524-9728	495
	MINUDRI, Regina U.	(415)843-7242	847
	RHEE, Susan F.	(415)540-7150	1025
	SPENCER, John T.	(415)341-9442	1173
	STOCKTON, Gloria J.	(415)843-8550	1196
	VAN HOUSE, Nancy A.	(415)642-0855	1275
	WOODBURY, Marda	(415)654-4810	1366
Beverly Hills	ANNETT, Susan E.	(213)550-4720	28
Burlingame	PERLMAN-STITES, Janice	(415)579-7660	959
Callahan	FARRIER, George F.	(916)467-3334	365
Cardiff By The Sea	MARKWORTH, Lawrence L.	(619)943-1197	772
	SCHALIT, Michael	(619)944-3913	1089
Carmichael	PARSONS, Jerry L.	(916)966-2086	945
	STRONG, Gary E.	(916)966-2037	1203
Carson	KENNY-SLOAN, Linda		642
Castro Valley	CASTAGNOZZI, Carol A.	(415)581-6034	194
Cerritos	ZEIDLER, Patricia L.	(213)926-1101	1387
Chatsworth	TAYLOR, Susan E.	(818)882-9729	1228
Chico	HUANG, George W.	(916)891-3455	568
	SESSIONS, Judith A.	(916)895-5862	1117
Chula Vista	GAGNON, Donna M.	(619)426-4527	412
Claremont	PRESLAN, Bruce H.	(714)621-9998	991
Concord	LAMANNA, Joan M.	(415)825-0418	689
	REYES, Helen M.	(415)000-0000	1024
Corona del Mar	DOSER, Virginia A.	(714)760-0148	313
Coronado	ESQUEVIN, Christian R.	(619)437-1135	354
Corte Madera	FARMER, Lesley S.	(415)924-6633	364
Costa Mesa	EPSTEIN, Susan B.	(714)754-1559	351
	MARLOR, Hugh T.	(714)631-5637	772
	PETERMAN, Claudia A.	(714)650-9014	962
Culver City	FITZGERALD, Diana S.	(231)839-5982	382
	KIRBY, Barbara L.	(213)839-1009	653
Cupertino	MILLER, Ronald F.	(408)257-9162	842
Daly City	NIEBOLT, Henry C.	(415)992-3911	903
Davis	DAILEY, Kazuko M.	(916)752-2110	270
Dobbins	LE DORR, Lillian E.	(916)692-1659	708
El Cerrito	KIRESEN, Evelyn M.	(415)526-6718	654
Encinitas	SCLAR, Marta L.	(619)944-3963	1106
Encino	GHAZARIAN, Salpi H.	(818)789-5041	430
Escondido	NING, Mary J.		904
Fairfield	GOLD, Anne M.	(707)429-6601	444
Fallbrook	MCNALLY, Ruth C.		816
Foster City	LEE, Doreen H.	(415)345-5292	709
FPO San Francisco	HADLEY, Alice E.	(671)344-9250	482
Fremont	TSAI, Sheh G.	(415)656-7097	1260
Fresno	CARLSON, Alan C.	(209)445-0828	182
	COBB, Karen B.	(209)488-3438	225
Fullerton	THOMPSON, James A.	(714)738-1000	1240

GENERAL LIBRARY/INFORMATION CONSULTANT (Cont'd)
CALIFORNIA (Cont'd)

Garden Grove	SIMPSON, Evelyn L.	(714)534-5033	1141
Glendale	BURNS, Nancy R.	(818)244-1994	162
	ECKLUND, Lynn M.	(818)242-2793	335
	NYBERG, Lelia J.	(818)244-1994	912
Goleta	GRAZIANO, Eugene	(805)968-2281	460
	MUSICK, Nancy W.	(805)964-8484	883
Hayward	ARROWOOD, Donna J.	(415)881-2791	34
	ROSE, Melissa M.	(415)881-3664	1055
Huntington Beach	HAYDEN, Ronald L.	(714)960-8836	515
	RIGGS, Quentin T.	(714)536-2823	1034
Irvine	POOLE, Jay M.	(714)856-6377	983
	TASH, Steven J.	(714)786-7857	1224
	TSENG, Sally C.	(714)856-6832	1260
	WOODS, Lawrence A.	(714)786-3507	1367
	YOUNG, Eleanor C.	(714)552-5803	1381
Kensington	ROOSHAN, Gertrude I.	(415)525-5640	1053
La Jolla	GABBERT, Gretchen W.	(619)456-4083	411
	NEELY, Jesse G.	(619)455-8705	892
	ZYROFF, Ellen S.	(619)459-1513	1392
Long Beach	ATTARIAN, Lorraine B.	(213)491-9295	38
	AYALA, John L.	(213)599-8028	42
	BRITTON, Helen H.	(213)498-4047	137
	HOUSEL, Mary B.	(213)595-4154	563
Los Altos	GESCHKE, Nancy A.	(415)969-7737	430
Los Altos Hills	MCDONALD, Marilyn M.	(415)960-4390	803
Los Angeles	ALFORD, Thomas E.	(213)612-3333	13
	BIRNIE, Elizabeth B.	(213)626-8484	98
	COSTELLO, M R.	(213)825-3047	249
	CREWS, Kenneth D.	(213)397-1518	258
	CROSS, Claudette S.	(213)256-2123	260
	DALY, Eudice	(213)474-6080	271
	ENYINGI, Peter	(213)629-3531	351
	EVANS, G E.	(213)642-4593	357
	GELMAN-KMEC, Marsha	(213)484-5530	426
	GINSBURG, Helen W.	(213)485-5400	438
	GRAY, Tomysena F.	(213)753-7541	460
	GREEN, Ellen W.	(213)855-3751	461
	HALE, Kaycee	(213)204-0793	485
	HAYES, Melinda K.	(213)743-0480	516
	HAYTHORN, Joseph D.	(213)938-3621	517
	KAPLAN, Robin	(213)851-2480	626
	KARASICK, Alice W.	(213)224-7411	627
	KUCZMA, Michelle	(213)687-5000	682
	KUNSELMAN, Joan D.	(213)825-1204	684
	LEE, Don A.	(213)650-4946	709
	MAACK, Mary N.	(213)475-7962	753
	MANTHEY, Teresa M.	(213)224-7234	767
	MICHEL, Dee A.	(213)478-7660	832
	MULLER, Malinda S.	(213)557-2900	877
	NEMCHEK, Lee R.	(213)621-9484	895
	REYNOLDS, Diane C.	(213)629-3531	1025
	RONEY, Raymond G.	(213)532-3670	1053
	SANDVIKEN, Gordon L.	(818)307-2872	1081
	SCHERREI, Rita A.	(213)825-1201	1092
	SMITH, Catherine M.	(213)669-6523	1153
	STERLIN, Annette S.	(213)645-2406	1189
	TOMPKINS, Philip	(213)743-2543	1250
	TREISTER, Cyril C.	(213)227-1604	1255
	VEASLEY, Mignon M.	(213)236-3515	1280
	VILLERE, Dawn N.	(213)290-2989	1284
	WATERS, Marie B.	(213)825-1693	1308
	WONG, Cecilia	(213)736-1139	1362
Los Gatos	SZABO, Carolyn J.	(408)353-2502	1218
Manhattan Beach	MORRISEY, Locke J.	(213)318-3923	867
	PHILLIPS, Clifford R.	(213)545-4828	968
Marina del Rey	SHANK, Russell	(213)823-6123	1120
Menlo Park	BALES, F K.	(415)854-0115	52
	HALL, Elede T.	(415)366-2937	487
	NEWMAN, Mark J.	(415)326-2114	899
Mission Viejo	WIERZBA, Heidemarie B.	(714)859-5193	1337
Montclair	CARRIGAN, John L.	(714)621-5225	186
Montebello	GALLEGO, Bert H.	(213)721-5102	414
Mountain View	ALBUM, Bernie	(415)967-5593	11
	DAWSON, Debra A.	(415)948-2756	282
	PORTER-ROTH, Anne	(415)965-7799	985
	POST, Linda C.	(415)968-3045	986
	SLOCUM, Hannah R.	(415)969-8356	1150
	SPIGAI, Fran	(415)961-2880	1174

GENERAL LIBRARY/INFORMATION CONSULTANT (Cont'd)
CALIFORNIA (Cont'd)

Napa	VANVUREN, Darcy D.		1277
Nevada City	BISHOP, Diane		99
Northridge	DURAN, Karin J.	(818)885-2501	328
	ECKLUND, Kristin A.	(818)349-6115	335
Oakland	BENNETT, Celestine C.	(415)893-9645	81
	CHESTER, Claudia J.	(415)835-4692	207
	HOWATT, Helen C.	(415)433-1160	565
	MORGAN, Linda M.	(415)536-3331	864
	SYPERT, Clyde F.	(415)763-6046	1217
Oceanside	NELSON, Helen M.	(619)439-7330	893
Orange	RYAN, Ann	(714)771-8291	1070
	SMITH, Elizabeth M.	(714)634-7809	1154
Oroville	ALLENSWORTH, James H.	(916)538-7197	16
Oxnard	SMITH, Heather	(805)984-4637	1155
Pacific Palisades	HILLIS, Patricia K.	(213)454-0611	541
	SCHRIBER, James E.	(213)459-1825	1100
Palo Alto	CRABTREE, Sandra A.	(415)858-4767	254
	ELLSWORTH, Dianne J.	(415)321-2253	345
	HAMILTON, David M.	(415)853-0197	491
	HEMINGWAY, Beverly L.	(415)328-1884	525
	MARANGONI, Eugene G.	(415)858-4053	768
	PRESTON, Cecilia M.	(415)327-5364	991
Palos Verdes Estates	STEVENSON, Marilyn E.	(213)377-7563	1191
	UEBELE, Dorothy B.	(213)541-2559	1268
Pasadena	CHICK, Cynthia L.	(818)796-8194	208
	CHOUDHURY, Lori B.	(818)449-9468	211
	YEUNG, Esther Y.		1380
Pebble Beach	ANDRUS, Eloise A.	(408)624-1257	27
Pinole	YANEZ, Elva K.	(415)724-2914	1377
Placentia	CHRISTNER, Deborah S.	(714)996-2749	212
Pleasant Hill	SIEGEL, Ernest	(415)944-3423	1136
Pomona	REMKIEWICZ, Frank L.	(714)623-5251	1022
Poway	DOLLEN, Charles J.	(619)748-5348	310
Rancho Cacamonga	CONNELL, William S.	(714)989-0506	237
Rancho Cordova	GRANADOS, Rose A.	(916)363-0473	457
Rancho Palos Verdes	KATTLOVE, Rose W.	(213)544-0061	630
Redondo Beach	CLIFFORD, Susan G.	(213)378-3824	222
Redwood City	TAOKA, Wesley M.	(415)365-3317	1223
Reseda	STEINMANN, Lois S.	(818)343-8262	1186
Richmond	BENELISHA, Eleanor	(415)223-6417	80
	O'CONNOR, Brian C.	(415)237-6561	915
	VANDERBERG, Patricia S.	(415)237-1081	1273
Ridgecrest	MAYES, Elizabeth A.	(619)446-6862	789
Riverside	MITCHELL, Steve		849
	WEBB, Gayle E.	(714)787-2460	1313
Rolling Hills Estate	SAVAGE, Gretchen S.	(213)377-5032	1085
	TUNG, Sandra J.	(213)377-5032	1263
Rowland Heights	SIGLER, Ronald F.	(818)965-9917	1137
Sacramento	AKEY, Sharon A.	(916)445-7356	9
	ANDERSEN, Thomas K.	(916)324-4863	21
	BENNETT, Michael W.	(916)927-9181	82
	BURNS, John F.	(916)445-4293	162
	FERRELL, Mary S.	(916)447-8541	373
	JACKSON, Gloria D.	(916)427-1956	587
	KAST, Gloria E.	(916)483-6765	629
	MCGOVERN, Gail J.	(916)446-2411	807
	MIRONENKO, Rimma	(916)355-4076	847
	RUBY, Carmela M.	(916)453-1174	1065
	SEHR, Dena P.	(916)453-3529	1112
Salinas	COLLINS, Judith A.		232
San Bernardino	NOUROK, Marlene E.	(714)887-6333	910
	WEBB, Duncan C.	(714)387-4959	1313
San Clemente	KOPAN, Ellen K.	(714)498-4309	671
San Diego	DERSHEM, Larry D.	(619)236-2409	294
	FORMAN, Jack	(619)546-9250	390
	HOWARD, Pamela F.		564
	LOOMIS, Barbara L.	(619)565-3172	740
	MONROE, Shula H.	(619)222-1206	855
	MORRISON, Patricia	(619)292-2859	868
	ROSS, Mary A.	(619)566-4733	1058
	SANNWALD, William W.	(619)236-5870	1081
	SOETE, George J.	(619)453-3538	1165
	VEGA, Carolyn L.		1281

GENERAL LIBRARY/INFORMATION CONSULTANT (Cont'd)
CALIFORNIA (Cont'd)

San Francisco	CARSCH, Ruth E.	(415)641-5014	187
	DURSO, Angeline M.	(415)750-6072	329
	GIBSON, Harold R.		432
	GITLER, Robert L.	(415)221-9216	438
	GRIFFIN, Michael D.	(415)664-2835	468
	HUNSUCKER, Alice E.	(415)396-7909	574
	LESH, Jane G.	(415)563-2900	718
	MANN, Thomas	(415)951-0100	766
	MCNAMEE, Gilbert W.	(415)474-3636	816
	MERRITT, Betty A.	(415)972-4294	827
	MORITZ, Thomas D.	(415)750-7102	865
	PAPERMASTER, Cynthia L.	(415)773-5831	939
	RAMIREZ, William L.	(415)564-5637	1005
	SEGUNDO, Fe P.	(415)586-6333	1112
	SULLIVAN, Edward A.	(415)752-6671	1207
	TAYLOR, Kathryn E.	(415)391-9170	1227
	WILSON, Jacqueline B.	(415)476-2534	1351
San Jose	CEPPOS, Karen F.	(408)277-2280	196
	DUNCAN, Rebecca	(408)971-9060	325
	EMMICK, Nancy J.	(408)277-3904	348
San Luis Obispo	FOURIE, Denise K.	(805)544-5427	393
San Pedro	SCULLY, Patrick F.	(213)832-6526	1109
San Rafael	HAMMER, Sharon A.	(415)499-6051	493
	PLOTKIN, Nathan	(415)479-7018	978
San Ramon	O'HEARN, Sarah A.	(415)842-0306	919
Santa Ana	AUSTIN, Stephen	(714)540-9870	40
	PINCOCK, Rulon D.	(714)558-5811	974
Santa Barbara	FAY, Evelyn V.	(805)569-7240	367
	GEBHARD, Patricia	(805)969-1031	424
	GIBBONS, Carolbeth	(805)961-3320	431
	MACGREGOR, Raymond	(805)682-5654	755
	MAHAFFEY, Susan M.	(805)964-4978	760
	RUDD, Janet K.	(805)682-9560	1065
Santa Monica	ANDERSON, Dorothy J.	(213)394-1899	22
	BECKER, Joseph	(213)829-6866	72
	KARR, Linda		628
	WITTMANN, Cecelia V.	(213)454-8300	1358
Santa Rosa	LEE, Mildred C.	(707)538-3484	711
	WALSH, Donamarie F.		1299
Sebastopol	SIMONS, Maurice M.	(707)823-9275	1141
Sherman Oaks	LEWIS, Cookie A.	(818)788-5280	722
Simi Valley	WONG, Clark C.	(805)522-5233	1362
Sonoma	LUNARDI, Albert A.	(707)935-6020	748
Stanford	KRAKAUER, Elizabeth	(408)733-4611	675
	PAI, Herman H.	(415)723-6585	934
Stockton	MOORE, Evia B.	(209)474-7029	859
Studio City	KAZLAUSKAS, Edward J.	(818)797-7654	632
Suisun	CISLER, Stephen A.	(707)422-5089	215
Sunnyvale	TYSON, Betty B.	(408)742-5937	1267
	VAN VELZER, Verna J.	(408)738-2888	1277
Thousand Oaks	SMITH, Marvin E.	(805)497-6282	1158
Torrance	DOWNEY, Christine D.	(213)618-5962	316
	KLECKER, Anita N.	(213)517-4720	658
Ukiah	MCGREEVY, Kathleen T.	(707)468-3053	808
Valencia	CURZON, Susan C.	(805)259-8946	267
	HUSKEY, Janet S.	(805)259-0783	578
Vallejo	WONG, Carol Y.	(707)646-2532	1362
Van Nuys	BALABAN, Robin M.	(818)781-6952	50
	DAVIS, Becky C.	(818)764-3732	277
Venice	WALTER, Virginia A.	(213)392-7627	1300
Ventura	BENNETT, Carson W.		81
Vista	KELLY, Myla S.	(619)945-6180	638
Woodland	WEBBER, Steven L.	(916)661-1242	1313
Woodland Hills	REIFMAN, Deborah S.		1019

COLORADO

Aurora	MURRAY, William A.	(303)364-8208	882
Boulder	BANKHEAD, Jean M.	(303)497-5566	54
	CHANAUD, Jo P.	(303)449-0849	199
	COLLARD, R M.	(303)444-1355	232
	KOHL, David F.	(303)492-6897	668
	ROTHMAN, Marilyn R.	(303)447-9938	1060
Colorado Springs	SITTER, Clara M.	(303)570-4524	1144
	WATERS, W R.	(303)630-5288	1309
Denver	ASHTON, Rick J.	(303)745-9883	36
	BARELA, Lori A.	(303)871-3447	56
	BROCK, Laurie N.	(303)333-2772	138
	BRUNELL, David H.	(303)691-0550	150

GENERAL LIBRARY/INFORMATION CONSULTANT (Cont'd)
COLORADO (Cont'd)

Denver	COCO, Al	(303)871-6200	226
	FOLEY, Georgiana	(303)571-2172	387
	GEHRES, Eleanor M.	(303)571-2012	425
	GORAL, Barbara J.	(303)866-2081	451
	GUTH, Karen K.	(303)869-2395	478
	KIRSHBAUM, Priscilla J.	(313)756-1827	655
	MILLER, Charles G.	(303)761-1764	836
	MITCHELL, Marilyn J.	(303)556-2835	849
	NORBIE, Dorothy E.	(303)691-5400	908
	SHARP, Alice L.	(303)866-4682	1122
	SHAW, Ward	(303)861-5319	1124
	VERCIO, Roseanne	(303)778-5656	1282
	WAGNER, Barbara L.	(303)297-3611	1291
	WHITE, Joyce L.	(303)722-4687	1331
Fort Collins	AMAN, Ann L.	(303)484-9205	19
	ANDERSON, Lemoyne W.	(303)484-7319	24
	CHAMBERS, Joan L.	(303)491-1833	198
Golden	GRAHAM, Su D.	(303)642-7802	456
	KENNEY, Brigitte L.	(303)278-8482	641
	MADDOCK, Jerome T.	(303)231-1367	759
Grand Junction	NICKELS, Anita B.		902
	RICHMOND, Elizabeth B.	(303)241-4358	1030
	RICHMOND, Rick	(303)241-4358	1030
Greeley	KNEPEL, Nancy	(303)356-4357	664
	PITKIN, Gary M.	(303)339-2237	976
Hayden	COSTA, Betty L.	(303)276-4345	249
Lafayette	MACARTHUR, Marit S.	(303)665-8237	754
Lakewood	HOLTON, Janet E.	(303)232-6800	555
Lamar	BURNETT, James H.	(303)336-4632	161
Littleton	BETTENCOURT, Nancy J.	(303)771-0968	92
	GREALY, Deborah J.	(303)795-3156	461
	SALLE, Ellen M.	(303)794-2641	1076
	SZABO, Kathleen S.	(303)796-9718	1218
Meeker	NICKEL, Edgar B.	(303)878-3209	902
Montrose	CAMPBELL, John D.	(303)249-1078	176
Pueblo	GARDNER, W J.	(303)549-3308	418
	JANES, Nina	(303)542-4591	593
	JONES, Donna R.	(303)542-2156	612

CONNECTICUT

Ashford	MCCAUGHTRY, Dorothy H.	(203)429-7637	795
Bloomfield	BROQUE, Suzanne	(203)242-3473	141
Branford	KILLHEFFER, Robert E.	(203)432-1704	648
Bridgeport	MINERVINO, Louise	(203)576-7779	846
Bristol	LEAHY, Michael D.	(203)582-0608	707
Danbury	SHEA, Roseanne M.	(203)744-3711	1124
Darien	GAMBER, Deborah D.	(203)655-6869	416
Derby	FINNUCAN, Louise A.	(203)732-7399	379
Farmington	LEVINE, Marion H.	(203)679-3323	720
Greenwich	LUSHINGTON, Nolan	(203)655-3632	749
Guilford	WALDEN, Katherine G.	(203)453-5645	1294
Hamden	KAPLAN, Diane E.	(203)248-8319	626
	ROGERS, Rutherford D.	(203)777-1682	1050
	SMITH, Nolan E.	(203)776-3558	1159
Hartford	NEUFELD, Irving H.	(203)278-3202	897
	PORTER, Kathryn W.	(203)727-4321	985
Middletown	DOUVILLE, Judith A.	(203)344-1880	314
Moosup	KASPER, Barbara	(203)564-4303	629
New Britain	LAWRENCE, Scott W.	(203)677-1659	705
New Canaan	LOKETS BEISCHROT, Dina		738
New Fairfield	DYKMAN, Elaine K.	(203)746-0765	331
New Hartford	GIBSON, Barbara H.	(203)379-3548	431
New Haven	FRYER, Regina K.	(203)785-4356	407
	KOEL, Ake I.	(203)432-1825	667
	LOWELL, Gerald R.	(203)773-3709	744
	PRATT, Allan D.	(203)389-0183	989
	PROSTANO, Emanuel T.	(203)397-4532	995
	SPURGEON, Kathy R.		1176
	TRAINER, Karin A.	(203)432-1818	1253
New London	VANDERLYKE, Barbara A.	(203)442-2889	1274
Niantic	BENN, James R.	(203)445-5577	81
Norwalk	BOHRER, Karen M.	(203)854-5275	111
Ridgefield	SAMUELS, Lois A.	(203)431-3342	1079
Stamford	BERLIET, Nathalie B.	(203)359-9359	87
	DIMATTIA, Ernest A.	(203)322-9055	304
	GOLOMB, Katherine A.	(203)964-1000	447
	KEMP, Thomas J.	(203)323-2826	639

GENERAL LIBRARY/INFORMATION CONSULTANT (Cont'd)
CONNECTICUT (Cont'd)

Stamford
ORRICO, James T.	(203)968-3280	926
PALMER, Shirley	(203)325-3500	937
SILVERMAN, Susanne		1139
TIBBETTS, David W.	(203)329-2824	1243
WILLIAMS, Judy R.	(203)964-1000	1344

Stonington	WILLIAMS, Edwin E.	(203)535-0720	1343
Storrs	LAMB, Gertrude		690
Wallingford	EBINGER, Meada G.	(203)269-5114	334
Warren	HENTZ, Margaret B.	(203)868-9178	530
Waterbury	CARRINGTON, Virginia F.	(203)574-4702	186
	FLANAGAN, Leo N.	(203)756-6149	383
	YOUNG, Marianne F.	(203)574-8216	1382
West Hartford	BRADBERRY, Richard P.	(203)241-4704	125
	BURGER, Leslie B.	(203)233-0478	159
	MICHAUD, Noreen R.	(203)232-6560	832
Westport	MECKLER, Alan M.	(203)226-6967	820
	REISMAN, Sydelle S.	(203)227-8710	1021
	SCHWARZ, Shirlee	(203)226-6606	1105
Wethersfield	DONOHUE, Christine N.	(203)529-2938	311
Willimantic	EMBARDO, Ellen E.	(203)456-1952	347
Wilton	TRIFFIN, Nicholas	(914)681-4275	1256
Windsor	SIMON, William H.		1141
Windsor Locks	MASTERS, Fred N.	(203)623-9801	782

DELAWARE

Bear	MANUEL, Larry L.	(302)834-5748	767
New Castle	IRWIN, Ruth A.	(302)328-8560	584
Newark	CHASTAIN-WARHEIT, Christine C.	(302)733-1116	203
	MYERS, Victoria B.	(302)454-2098	885
	RUDISELL, Carol A.		1065
	THORNTON, Alice J.	(302)454-2239	1242
	WOLFF, Stephen G.	(302)451-2432	1361
Wilmington	BROWN, Atlanta T.	(302)998-0803	142
	BURDASH, David H.	(302)571-7402	158
	GRILLO, Anthony L.	(302)774-6603	470
	TITUS, H M.	(302)656-1722	1247

DISTRICT OF COLUMBIA

APO Washington	BURNS, Dean A.	(202)863-3547	162
Washington	ACKERMAN, F C.	(202)398-1842	3
	ANGLE, Joanne G.	(202)682-1698	28
	ATKINSON, Rose M.	(202)955-2139	38
	BARTLEY, Linda K.	(202)362-7837	61
	BECKERMAN, George	(202)775-9022	72
	BERGQUIST, Christine F.		87
	BISHOP, Sarah G.	(202)244-6841	99
	CARTER, Yvonne B.	(202)357-6315	190
	CHANG, Helen S.	(202)651-5214	200
	CILIBERTI, Nancy A.	(202)328-8000	214
	COLETTI, Jeannette D.	(202)362-1664	231
	DAWSON, Barbara J.	(202)785-3330	282
	DAY, Melvin S.	(202)363-1890	283
	DE ARMAN, Charles L.	(202)797-7169	284
	DICKSON, Constance P.	(202)955-8566	301
	DOUMATO, Lamia		314
	FALK, Diane M.	(202)291-3821	362
	FARINA, Robert A.	(202)287-5298	363
	FORREST, Phyllis E.		391
	FRANKLIN, Brinley R.	(202)223-9525	397
	FRANKLIN, Hardy R.	(202)727-1101	397
	FREEMAN, Carla		400
	FRIERSON, Eleanor G.	(202)623-7000	404
	GAMSON, Arthur L.	(202)382-5921	416
	GILLESPIE, Veronica M.	(202)287-5262	435
	HAITH, Dorothy M.	(202)484-4941	484
	HALEY, Roger K.	(202)224-2976	486
	HARRIS, Marie	(202)767-8643	505
	JOHANSON, Cynthia J.	(202)287-5261	601
	JOHNSON, Lucy C.		607
	KUPERMAN, Agota M.		684
	LEE, Amy C.	(202)546-5539	709
	LEFFALL, Dolores C.	(202)723-7645	712
	LEONARD, Angela M.	(202)636-7926	716
	LITTLEJOHN, Grace M.	(202)291-6920	734
	LUNIN, Lois F.	(202)965-3924	749
	MARTIN, Kathleen S.	(202)789-7100	777

GENERAL LIBRARY/INFORMATION CONSULTANT (Cont'd)
DISTRICT OF COLUMBIA (Cont'd)

Washington
MARYNOWYCH, Roman V.	(202)529-7606	780
MCCRAY, Maceo E.	(202)829-7737	800
MCRAE, Alexander D.	(202)686-1788	818
MISSAR, Charles D.	(202)363-2751	847
MITCHELL, Elaine M.	(202)663-6761	848
MUSSEHL, Allan A.	(202)488-8162	883
NOWAK, Geraldine D.	(202)475-9419	911
O'BRIEN, Kathleen	(202)331-8400	914
PACIFICI, Sabrina I.	(202)429-4094	933
PAGE, John S.	(202)554-0486	934
PERELLA, Susanne B.	(202)326-2379	958
PRICE, Mary S.	(202)287-5137	992
PRUETT, Barbara J.	(202)362-1345	996
PULVER, Thomas B.	(202)293-0500	997
RADER, Ronald A.	(639)890-0000	1002
REIFSNYDER, Betsy S.	(202)287-7984	1020
RENNINGER, Karen	(202)233-2711	1023
ROSENFELD, Mary A.	(202)357-1940	1056
RZECZKOWSKI, Eugene M.	(202)529-5300	1072
SARANGAPANI, Chetluru	(202)282-3091	1082
SAUVE, Deborah A.	(202)546-8770	1085
SHEELER, Harva L.	(202)879-3954	1125
SHEERAN, Carole A.	(202)296-0800	1125
SMITH, Kathleen S.		1156
SOLOMON, Arnold D.	(202)287-8786	1166
STORM, Jill	(202)775-6174	1198
SULLIVAN, Robert C.	(202)287-5330	1208
SWEENEY, June D.	(202)427-1392	1215
TERRY, Susan N.	(202)332-7120	1232
TOCH, Terryann	(202)393-6820	1248
TRIPP-MELBY, Pamela	(202)676-9418	1257
TSCHERNY, Elena	(202)727-1183	1260
TSUNEISHI, Warren M.	(202)287-5543	1260
WEBB, Barbara A.	(202)797-8909	1313
WELSH, William J.	(202)287-5215	1323

FLORIDA

APO Miami	KANE, Joseph P.		624
Apopka	BLOODWORTH, Velda J.	(305)862-1208	106
	RIVERA, Antonio	(305)869-7168	1037
Bradenton	PLACE, Philip A.	(813)746-1358	977
Brooksville	TORNABENE, Charles	(904)686-9318	1251
Clearwater	DALLMAN, Glenn R.	(813)791-2616	270
	MIELKE, Linda	(813)462-6916	833
	TIBBS, Jo A.	(813)447-7157	1244
Cooper City	JACKSON, Nancy I.	(305)434-8724	588
De Land	JOHNSON, Betty D.	(904)734-7630	602
Dunedin	TEW, Robin L.	(813)734-5634	1233
Fort Lauderdale	ALGAZE, Selma B.	(305)357-7501	13
	HATFIELD, Frances S.	(305)463-5928	511
	MCCLAIN, Mary P.	(305)771-8000	796
Fort Myers	PEGLER, Ross J.	(813)267-2995	954
	SCHWENN, Janet M.	(813)489-9505	1105
Freeport	DAVIS, Bonnie D.	(904)835-4432	277
Gainesville	BROWN, Pia T.	(904)375-6302	147
	MALANCHUK, Peter P.	(904)392-0364	762
Gulf Breeze	COBLE, Gerald M.	(904)932-4849	225
Howey in the Hills	COHN, William L.	(904)324-2701	229
Jacksonville	BONFILI, Barbara J.	(904)725-5822	114
	GUNN, Thomas H.	(904)744-3950	477
	JONES, Robert P.	(904)646-2615	614
	MARION, Gail E.	(904)633-2088	770
	MCMICHAEL, Sandra C.	(904)731-8380	815
	SUGDEN, Martin D.	(904)634-1626	1206
Jensen Beach	HENNINGS, Leroy	(305)334-6134	528
Jupiter	MOJO, Anne Z.	(305)746-6353	852
Key West	SOULE, Maria J.	(305)296-9081	1169
Largo	CESANEK, Sylvia B.	(813)585-1403	196
Lauderhill	HOLLMANN, Pauline V.	(305)393-3774	552
Live Oak	HISS, Sheila M.	(904)362-6936	544
Marianna	STABLER, William H.	(904)482-3474	1177
Melbourne	HENSON, Llewellyn L.	(305)768-8000	529
Miami	ADAMS, Gustav C.	(305)261-7031	4
	BYRD, Susan G.	(305)347-2068	169
	CARDEN, Marguerite	(305)375-5005	180
	CHAVES, Francisco M.	(305)385-2301	204
	KASKEY, Sid		629

GENERAL LIBRARY/INFORMATION CONSULTANT (Cont'd)
FLORIDA (Cont'd)

Miami	MCNEAL, Archie L.		816
	PAUL, Nora M.	(305)376-3402	949
	STEINBERG, Celia L.	(305)661-4611	1185
Miami Beach	LYON, Bruce C.	(305)868-4451	752
Miami Shores	PINE, Nancy M.	(305)758-3392	974
Naples	BOULA, Lillian Y.		119
Orlando	CRENSHAW, Tena L.	(305)646-5637	258
	DAVIDOFF, Marcia	(305)894-5508	276
	GEBET, Russell W.	(305)849-0300	424
	LABRAKE, Orlyn B.	(305)275-4564	686
	SESSA, Frank B.		1116
Pensacola	BOWER, Beverly L.	(904)476-5410	120
	JOHNSON, Theresa P.	(904)474-2168	609
	RAMEY, Linda K.		1005
	TERNAK, Armand T.	(904)479-7835	1232
Plant City	PINGS, Vern M.	(813)752-3884	974
Pompano Beach	GULLETTE, Irene		477
Ponte Vedra Beach	PECK, Brian T.	(904)246-1400	953
Royal Palm Beach	TERWILLEGAR, Jane C.	(305)793-4590	1232
St Petersburg	GOSS, Theresa C.	(813)341-4732	453
	HARDESTY, Larry L.	(813)867-1166	499
San Antonio	NEUHOFE, M D.	(904)588-8320	897
Sanibel	KLASING, Jane P.	(813)472-8391	657
Sarasota	DANIEL, Marianne M.	(813)351-6583	272
	HOLT, Ethel F.	(813)371-7640	554
	HOPKINS, Joan A.	(813)951-5502	558
	JENKINS, Althea H.	(813)355-5003	597
	MOON, Ilse	(813)355-1795	857
Seminole	WEISS, Susan		1320
Tallahassee	CONAWAY, Charles W.	(904)893-1482	235
	FLEMING, Lois D.		384
	GIBLON, Charles B.	(904)893-3851	431
	HART, Thomas L.	(904)385-7550	507
	MILLER, Betty D.	(904)335-4405	836
	MOUNCE, Marvin W.	(904)487-2651	873
	PRATT, Darnell D.	(904)487-2651	990
	SUMMERS, F W.	(904)644-5775	1209
	TREZZA, Alphonse F.	(904)878-5551	1256
Tampa	ABBOTT, Randy L.	(813)988-7912	1
	EL-HADIDY, Bahaa	(813)974-3520	342
	LOSEY, Doris C.	(813)885-4500	742
	WOOD, James F.	(813)232-5221	1364
Tarpon Springs	O'BRIEN, Elizabeth M.	(813)942-3291	914
Wauchula	MAPP, Erwin E.	(813)773-9207	768
West Palm Beach	PRITCHARD, Teresa N.	(305)684-7349	994
Winter Park	ALLISON, Anne M.	(305)677-6372	17
	PFARRER, Theodore R.	(305)647-3294	966
Winter Springs	THOMAN, Nancy L.		1236

GEORGIA

Acworth	STAHL, D G.	(404)924-8505	1178
Albany	TOOKES, Amos J.	(912)439-5242	1250
Americus	MCLAUGHLIN, Laverne L.	(912)924-9426	813
	PASCHAL, Eloise R.	(912)924-3168	945
Athens	ANDERSON, Thomas G.	(404)542-0598	25
	ANDREW, Paige G.	(404)353-1707	26
	BISHOP, David F.	(404)542-0621	99
	QUINLAN, Judy B.	(404)542-0654	1000
Atlanta	BRADLEY, Gail P.	(404)872-9472	125
	BRYANT, Nancy J.	(404)955-9550	152
	CLEMONS, John E.	(404)727-6840	221
	CRAFT, Guy C.	(404)522-8980	254
	DAVIS, Joy V.	(404)634-3511	279
	DRAKE, Miriam A.	(404)894-4501	318
	ENGLER, June L.	(404)727-6405	350
	FISTE, David A.		382
	FORSEE, Joe B.	(404)656-2461	391
	GASKINS, Stephen D.		421
	HEID, Gregory G.	(404)688-4636	521
	JAMES, Stephen E.	(404)681-0251	592
	JOHNSON, Herbert F.	(404)727-6861	605
	LAWSON, A V.	(404)377-1142	705
	LAWSON, Venable A.	(404)377-1142	705
	LOWERY, Phyllis C.	(404)525-6165	744
	MCDAVID, Michael W.	(404)885-8320	801
	PRESLEY, Roger L.	(404)658-2176	991
	ROAN, Tattie W.	(404)320-9376	1038

GENERAL LIBRARY/INFORMATION CONSULTANT (Cont'd)
GEORGIA (Cont'd)

Atlanta	ROSS, Theodosia B.	(404)696-2355	1059
	SEARCY, David L.	(404)525-8802	1109
	SLOAN, Mary J.	(404)874-6224	1149
	SWANSON, Joe	(404)699-1415	1213
Augusta	BASLER, Thomas G.	(404)828-2856	63
	MCCANN, Jett C.	(404)828-3491	794
	SCHLATTER, M W.	(404)721-2992	1093
Bainbridge	MARSHALL, Ruth T.	(912)246-3887	775
	MULCAHY, Bryan L.	(912)246-3887	876
College Park	CANN, Sharon F.	(404)768-0970	178
Columbus	SELF, Sharon W.	(404)323-5520	1113
Decatur	BUDLONG, Thomas F.	(404)289-0583	155
	CHAMBERS, Shirley M.	(404)289-6517	198
	GRELL, Holly J.	(404)378-5948	467
	LANDRAM, Christina L.	(404)321-0778	693
Doerun	BOWEN, Louise E.	(912)782-5408	120
Duluth	SHELTON, John L.	(404)381-8060	1126
Eastman	WILSON, David C.	(912)374-4711	1350
Fitzgerald	HEFFINGTON, Carl O.	(912)423-3642	520
Jonesboro	BAKER, Gordon N.	(404)961-9824	48
La Grange	GIBSON, Ricky S.	(404)884-3757	432
Macon	RANKIN, Jocelyn A.	(912)744-2515	1007
Milledgeville	SCOTT, Rupert N.	(912)453-5573	1108
Norcross	DEWBERRY, Claire D.	(404)564-1634	298
Riverdale	HANSON, Kathy H.	(404)471-5053	498
Stone Mountain	O'NEILL, Patricia E.	(404)292-6693	924
	SULLIVAN, Mary A.	(404)469-0395	1208
Valdosta	CLARK, Tommy A.	(912)244-6124	218
	WRIGHT, Dianne H.	(912)244-6872	1371
Watkinsville	WHITEHEAD, James M.	(404)769-8917	1332
Waycross	STANBERY, Nancy M.	(912)283-3126	1179
Winder	HOLMES, Nancy M.	(404)867-2762	553

HAWAII

Honolulu	BARD, Therese B.	(808)948-7321	56
	BREINICH, John A.	(808)536-9302	132
	GOVERNS, Molly K.		454
	JACKSON, Miles M.	(808)948-7321	588
	KANE, Bartholomew A.	(808)524-8344	624
	KOTO, Ann S.	(808)829-5835	673
	LINVILLE, Marcia L.	(808)737-2511	731
	MATSUMORI, Donald M.	(805)737-6260	784
	SMITH, Frances P.	(808)523-2311	1155
	TOM, Chow L.	(808)537-9321	1249
	URAGO, Gail M.	(808)949-6496	1269
Kailua	WRIGHT, John C.	(808)261-3714	1371
Pearl City	FUJINO, Amy H.	(808)455-9023	408

IDAHO

Boise	ROBERTSON, Naida	(208)384-4340	1042
	TAYLOR, Adrien P.	(208)385-1621	1225
Cambridge	HAWKINS, Nina L.	(208)257-3541	514
Idaho Falls	HOLLAND, Paul E.	(208)529-1450	551
	WINWARD, Coleen C.	(208)529-6077	1356
Meridian	DENNY, Mary C.	(208)888-2924	293
Moscow	ABRAHAM, Terry		3
	BAIRD, Lynn N.	(208)885-6713	47
	WAI, Lily C.	(208)882-0506	1292
Nampa	LANCASTER, Edith E.	(208)466-1011	691
	SIMMONS, Randall C.	(208)467-8609	1140
Pocatello	DOWNEY, Howard R.	(208)232-1263	316
	WATSON, Peter G.	(208)236-2997	1310

ILLINOIS

Abbott Park	SWANSON, Ruth M.	(312)937-6959	1213
Argonne	DAVIDOFF, Gary N.	(312)972-4224	276
Arlington Heights	GIANNINI, Evelyn L.	(312)398-3142	431
Aurora	BEAN, Janet R.	(312)859-2222	69
Belleville	KIRCHGRABER, Nancy B.	(618)234-0441	654
Berwyn	FEDECZKO, Joyce L.	(312)795-3089	367
Bloomington	HUFFMAN, Carol P.	(309)829-2271	571
	STROYAN, Susan E.	(309)827-4321	1203
Blue Island	WOZNY, Jay	(312)388-1078	1370
Bolingbrook	IFFLAND, Carol D.	(312)739-6398	581
Cahokia	BEAN, Bobby D.	(618)875-6915	69
Carbondale	HARWOOD, Judith A.	(618)453-2818	510
	JENKINS, Darrell L.	(618)549-8053	597

GENERAL LIBRARY/INFORMATION CONSULTANT (Cont'd)
ILLINOIS (Cont'd)

Carterville	BARRETTE, Linda J.	(618)549-7335	59
Champaign	DESSOUKY, Ibtesam	(217)333-4956	296
	GOLDHOR, Herbert	(217)359-5636	445
	JOHNSON, Jane S.		605
	PENKA, Carol B.	(217)351-6026	956
	WERT, Lucille M.	(217)356-6600	1325
Charleston	LUQUIRE, Wilson	(217)581-6061	749
Chicago	ADAMSHICK, Robert D.	(312)353-1157	6
	ALTHAGE, Celia J.		18
	BAKER, Ethelyn J.	(312)421-6513	48
	BOLEF, Doris	(312)942-2271	112
	BOLT, Janice A.	(312)233-9399	113
	BREEN, Joanell C.	(312)929-1445	131
	CHANG, Sookang H.	(312)995-2240	201
	CLAPP, David F.	(312)465-0324	215
	COLLINS, Janet	(312)642-2136	232
	COTILLAS, Therese G.	(312)856-8341	250
	CURRY, John A.	(314)528-0870	266
	DI MAURO, Paul	(312)871-8235	304
	DRAKE, Francis L.	(312)876-7170	318
	DREAZEN, Elizabeth P.	(312)347-2057	318
	FANG, Min L.	(317)842-0321	363
	FEINER, Arlene M.	(312)348-8382	369
	FOUSER, Jane G.	(312)477-4712	393
	GENESEN, Judith L.		427
	GLANZ, Lenore M.	(312)528-7817	439
	GODLEWSKI, Susan G.	(312)443-3936	442
	GOMEZ, Martin J.		447
	GUSS, Emily R.	(312)268-4377	478
	HARRIS, Jeanne G.	(312)580-0069	504
	HELGE, Brian L.	(312)955-4545	524
	JAGODZINSKI, Cecile M.	(312)645-4860	591
	KALUZSA, Karen L.	(312)908-2859	623
	KAYAIAN, Mary S.	(312)245-2810	632
	KIM, Chung S.	(312)588-3901	648
	KOBASA, Paul A.	(312)944-6780	666
	LANDRY, Ronald	(312)943-3282	694
	LYNCH, Mary J.	(312)944-6780	752
	MARTIN, Bennie E.	(312)443-5423	775
	MCCLINTOCK, Patrick J.		797
	MCNEILL, Janice M.	(312)642-4600	816
	MENZIES, Pamela C.	(312)924-8301	825
	MEYER, Barbara G.	(312)829-2033	829
	MOCH, Mary I.	(312)539-2328	851
	MOORE, Annie M.	(312)995-2254	858
	MORRISON, Samuel F.	(312)269-3053	868
	MUNOFF, Gerald J.	(312)702-8749	879
	PETERSON, Randall T.	(312)427-2737	964
	RABAI, Terezia		1001
	REILLY, Jane A.	(312)764-2413	1020
	ROMAN, Susan	(312)944-6780	1052
	SCOTT, Alice H.	(312)493-2451	1106
	SHAEVEL, Evelyn F.	(312)944-6780	1118
	SIARNY, William D.	(312)467-5520	1134
	SIMPSON, Donald B.	(312)955-4545	1141
	VANCURA, Joyce B.	(312)822-0422	1273
	VIRGO, Julie A.	(312)751-1454	1285
	WICKREMERATNE, Swarna	(312)493-0936	1335
Chicago Ridge	LOTZ, Marsha A.	(312)423-7753	742
Coal Valley	WALKER, Laura L.	(309)234-5483	1295
Columbia	SUTTER, Mary A.	(618)281-7734	1211
Crystal Lake	MITCHELL, Martha M.	(815)455-5165	849
Darien	BOWDEN, Philip L.	(312)887-1620	120
De Kalb	TITUS, Elizabeth M.	(815)753-1094	1247
Decatur	HALE, Charles E.	(217)864-5755	485
Des Plaines	BOROWSKI, Joseph F.	(312)635-1640	117
	BURNS, Marie E.	(312)635-4732	162
Downers Grove	CULBERTSON, Lillian D.	(312)971-3309	263
	STOFFEL, Lester L.	(312)964-2541	1196
East Peoria	LINDGREN, William D.	(309)694-5462	729
	WILFORD, Valerie J.	(309)694-4389	1339
Edwardsville	JOHNSON, Charlotte L.	(618)656-5743	603
Elgin	JUERGENSMEYER, John E.	(312)695-9800	619
Elmhurst	MASON, John A.		781
	WATSON, Robert E.	(312)941-0892	1310

GENERAL LIBRARY/INFORMATION CONSULTANT (Cont'd)
ILLINOIS (Cont'd)

Evanston	ANTON, Tess	(312)869-8219	29
	BARNUM, Sally J.	(312)869-2976	58
	METZLER, Valerie	(312)869-5992	829
	NIELSEN, Brian	(312)491-2170	903
	QUERY, Lance D.	(312)491-2882	999
	WHITE, Matthew H.	(312)328-2221	1331
Evergreen Park	GARCIA-RUIZ, Maritza L.	(312)425-6104	417
	SOBKOWIAK, Emily J.	(312)425-1886	1165
Flora	DOCKINS, Glenn	(618)662-2679	307
	HARRIS, Thomas J.	(618)662-2679	506
Galesburg	WINNER, Ronald	(309)343-2380	1355
Geneseo	GILBORNE, Jean E.	(309)944-3384	434
	REDINGTON, Deirdre E.	(309)944-3311	1014
Geneva	SHURMAN, Richard L.	(312)232-8457	1134
Glen Ellyn	GEYER, Robert I.	(312)858-2800	430
Glencoe	WEISMAN, Kathryn M.	(312)835-4122	1319
Glenview	HAFNER, Arthur W.	(312)291-1022	482
	MARTINAZZI, Toni	(657)775-6000	779
Gurnee	FUNK, Carla J.	(312)367-6213	409
	ROBIEN, Eleanor K.	(312)223-8621	1043
Highland Park	SHERRY, Diane H.	(312)433-3968	1129
Hinsdale	GREGORY, Melissa R.	(312)325-2807	466
	MUELLER, Elizabeth	(312)323-8054	875
Hoffman Estates	CHAPA, Joan I.	(312)934-7032	201
Homewood	BAYER, Susan P.	(312)798-6496	67
Itasca	HOGAN, Patricia M.	(312)773-1699	549
Joliet	JOHNSTON, James R.	(815)729-3481	610
Kewanee	HARRIET, Conklin W.	(309)853-4993	503
La Grange	HELLER, Dawn H.	(312)579-0903	524
Lockport	TROY, Shannon M.	(312)534-5000	1258
Lombard	EGAN, Elizabeth M.	(312)627-7130	338
	SCHIPMA, Peter B.	(312)627-0550	1093
Mascoutah	GORDON, Diane M.	(618)566-4981	451
	SCHAACK, Wilma J.	(618)566-7385	1088
McLean	VAN HOORN, Audra G.	(309)874-2291	1275
Naperville	FURLONG, Robert E.	(312)979-2550	410
	ROWE, Dorothy B.	(312)355-9221	1062
Nashville	RUSIEWSKI, Charles B.	(618)327-8304	1068
Niles	CARTER, Ida	(312)647-9000	189
Normal	DELOACH, Marva L.	(309)438-7463	290
	MEISELS, Henry R.	(309)452-4485	822
North Aurora	HOWREY, Mary M.	(312)896-5837	566
Northfield	ANDERSON, Charles R.	(312)446-8259	22
Oak Lawn	MOORMAN, John A.	(312)422-4990	862
Oak Park	BALCOM, William T.	(312)383-6824	51
	DICK, Ellen A.	(312)386-9385	300
	MARSHALL, Maggie L.	(312)848-4432	774
O'Fallon	KNUDTSON, Gail L.	(618)624-2719	666
Ottawa	WILLSON, Richard E.	(815)434-7075	1349
Palatine	BURNS, Mary F.	(312)358-0137	162
	EVERHART, Paul R.	(312)991-2600	358
Palos Hills	HESSLER, Nancy R.	(312)974-4300	534
Park Forest	GIBBS, Mary E.	(312)481-1512	431
	HAYES, Hazel I.		515
	SHANNON, Kathleen L.	(312)481-1891	1120
Park Ridge	KNARZER, Arlene	(312)692-9550	663
Paxton	PACEY, Brenda M.	(217)379-3517	933
Pekin	WALTERS, Patsy M.	(309)353-5075	1301
Quincy	TYER, Travis E.	(217)223-5024	1266
River Forest	LI, Richard T.	(312)366-2490	725
Rock Island	OHRLUND, Ava L.	(309)786-0698	919
Rockford	CHITWOOD, Julius R.	(815)962-4409	209
	HUTCHINS, Mary J.	(815)229-0330	579
	ROSENFELD, Joel C.	(815)965-6731	1056
	SCHOLTZ, James C.	(815)229-0330	1098
Rolling Meadows	HEMENWAY, Patti J.	(312)255-6197	525
St Charles	MORRISON, Carol J.	(312)377-2499	868
Springfield	BERK, Robert A.	(217)782-2658	87
	ETTER, Constance L.	(217)546-5436	355
	LAMONT, Bridget L.	(217)787-2299	691
	SIVAK, Marie R.	(217)782-2826	1144
Sycamore	BERRY, John W.	(815)895-4225	90
Taylorville	PODESCHI, Gwen	(217)824-5695	979
Urbana	BALACHANDRAN, Sarojini	(217)328-3577	50
	BINGHAM, Karen H.	(217)333-0317	97
	DOWNS, Jane B.	(217)344-1714	317
	EDMONDS, M L.	(217)333-2306	336
	ESTABROOK, Leigh S.	(217)333-3280	355

GENERAL LIBRARY/INFORMATION CONSULTANT (Cont'd)
ILLINOIS (Cont'd)

Urbana

	FORREST, Charles G.	(217)244-3770	390
	LANCASTER, Frederick W.	(217)384-7798	691
	SIEGEL, Martin A.	(217)333-3247	1136
	WEECH, Terry L.	(217)367-7111	1315
	WEI, Karen T.	(217)344-5647	1316
	WRIGHT, Joyce C.	(217)333-1031	1372
Villa Park	ELL, Elizabeth L.	(312)279-6456	343
	POINTON, Louis R.	(312)833-6555	980
Washington	WOOLARD, Wilma L.	(309)444-2845	1368
Waukegan	CARNELLI, Sandra R.	(312)623-2041	183
West Chicago	KOSMAN, Joyce E.	(312)231-0774	672
Wheaton	BERGER, Carol A.	(312)653-1115	85
	EMBAR, Indrani M.	(312)668-1742	347
	HU, Robert T.	(312)690-7969	568
	RUSSELL, Janet	(312)653-1115	1069
	WALSH, Deborah T.	(312)653-1115	1299
Wheeling	HAMMER, Donald P.	(312)541-8149	493
	KANNER, Elliott E.	(312)459-1300	625
	MCCLARREN, Robert R.	(312)459-1300	796
Williamsville	KELLERSTRASS, Amy L.	(217)566-3517	636
Wilmette	JONES, Adrian	(312)256-6202	610
Winnetka	LUNDQUIST, Marie A.	(312)441-3315	748
Woodridge	KELLER, Steven W.	(312)964-7899	636

INDIANA

Bloomington	FRY, Bernard M.	(812)339-3571	406
	HEISER, Lois	(812)335-7170	523
	MURPHY, Marcy	(812)335-5113	881
	PUNGITORE, Verna L.	(812)335-5113	997
	STEELE, Patricia A.	(812)335-1619	1184
	WHITE, Herbert S.	(812)335-2848	1331
Carmel	NIEMEYER, Karen K.	(317)844-8961	903
Chesterton	DUHAMELL, Lynnette H.	(219)926-3743	324
Columbus	MEREDITH, Meri	(812)372-3482	825
	POOR, William E.	(812)377-7201	983
Evansville	WINSLOW, Carol M.	(812)867-2146	1355
Fort Wayne	LISTON, Karen A.	(219)424-6664	733
	SHEETS, Michael T.	(219)483-2854	1125
	WEICK, Robert J.	(219)478-1018	1316
Gary	MILLENDER, Dharathola	(219)882-4050	835
Hammond	HOLICKY, Bernard H.	(219)989-2249	550
	MEYERS, Arthur S.	(219)931-5100	830
Highland	ENGELBERT, Peter J.	(219)923-2173	348
Indianapolis	ALLEN, Joyce S.	(317)929-8021	15
	ANDREWS, Sylvia L.	(317)844-8538	27
	DURKIN, Virginia M.	(317)871-2095	328
	FISCHLER, Barbara B.	(317)274-0462	380
	GRIFFITTS, Joan K.	(317)297-3283	469
	MASON, Dorothy L.	(317)845-3684	781
	MATTS, Constance	(317)274-1928	786
	WOODARD, Marcia S.	(317)297-1803	1366
La Porte	GUNNELLS, Danny C.	(219)324-0422	477
Lafayette	BONHOMME, Mary S.	(317)448-1251	114
	MCKOWEN, Dorothy K.	(317)564-4585	812
Marion	BOYCE, Harold W.	(317)674-5211	122
Michigan City	DEYOUNG, Charles D.	(219)879-4561	298
Mishawaka	EISEN, David J.	(219)259-5277	340
Muncie	KROEHLER, Beth A.	(314)284-1841	679
	MOORE, Thomas J.	(317)285-1307	861
	WOOD, Michael B.	(317)289-5417	1364
Notre Dame	DOELLMAN, Michael A.	(219)232-0778	308
Richmond	FARBER, Evan I.	(317)966-2422	363
Rochester	LASHER, Esther L.	(219)223-8407	700
South Bend	BEATTY, R M.	(219)232-2349	70
	HOHL, Robert J.	(219)289-8160	550
	OSTROWSKI, Lawrence C.	(219)282-4608	929
	TUCKER, Dennis C.		1261
Terre Haute	LEACH, Ronald G.	(812)237-3700	706
	LITTLE, Robert D.	(812)237-2488	733
	NORMAN, Orval G.	(812)232-6120	909
	SHANE, T C.	(812)299-5289	1120
Valparaiso	MEYER, Ellen R.	(219)464-5360	830
West Lafayette	CANGANELLI, Patrick W.	(317)494-2768	178
	MOBLEY, Emily R.	(317)494-2900	851

GENERAL LIBRARY/INFORMATION CONSULTANT (Cont'd)
IOWA

Ames	MATHEWS, Eleanor R.	(515)294-3642	784
Bettendorf	MEIER, Patricia L.	(319)355-3895	821
	POLK, Diana B.	(319)332-8119	981
Cedar Rapids	BLISS, David H.	(319)393-5892	105
Davenport	NAVARRE, Emily L.	(319)324-5140	889
Decorah	FENSTERMANN, Duane W.	(319)387-1164	371
Des Moines	DAGLEY, Helen J.	(515)281-3063	269
	ELLIOTT, Kay M.	(515)281-6033	344
	GEORGE, Shirley H.	(515)281-4105	428
	GRIFFIN, Kathryn A.		468
	JOHNSON, Nancy E.	(515)262-6714	608
	KERN, Sharon P.	(515)243-2300	643
	ROBERTSON, Linda L.	(515)281-7572	1042
Dubuque	OFFERMAN, Mary C.		917
Iowa City	BELGUM, Kathie G.	(319)335-9016	76
	CRETH, Sheila D.	(319)335-5868	258
	DEWEY, Barbara I.	(319)335-5867	298
	FALK, Mark F.	(319)354-7474	362
	NICKELSBURG, Marilyn M.	(319)351-2072	902
	RICE, James G.	(319)335-5716	1027
Marion	ALDERSON, Karen A.	(319)377-0666	11
	DAVIS, Deanna S.	(319)377-7135	278
Marshalltown	BURGESS, Barbara J.	(515)752-4812	159
	TRAVILLIAN, Mary W.	(515)752-1578	1254
Ottumwa	BRANDT, Garnet J.	(515)682-6677	128
Sioux City	PHILLIPS, Donna M.	(712)258-6981	968
	PLUEMER, Bonnie J.	(712)279-6186	978
	SCHEETZ, Kathy D.	(712)277-2423	1091
Vinton	SHEPHERD, Rex L.	(319)472-4721	1127
West Branch	MATHER, Mildred E.	(319)643-5301	783
	MAYER, Dale C.	(319)643-5301	789

KANSAS

Alma	BIRNEY, Ann E.	(913)765-2370	98
Atchison	BURBACH, Jude	(913)367-5340	158
Coffeyville	BUFFINGTON, Karyl L.	(316)251-1370	155
	HENDERSON, Rosemary	(316)251-2158	527
Dodge City	COOKE, Bette L.	(316)225-7271	241
Emporia	STEWART, Henry R.	(316)343-1200	1192
Hesston	EICHELBERGER, Marianne	(316)327-4666	339
Kansas City	RIDDLE, Raymond E.	(913)621-3073	1032
Lawrence	MAY, Cecilia J.	(913)841-0929	788
Manhattan	COFFEE, E G.	(913)539-1628	226
Miltonvale	BRADLEY, Susanne A.	(913)427-2228	126
Newton	EBERHARD, Neysa C.	(316)283-2890	334
Salina	REED, Mary J.	(913)823-2246	1015
	WHITE, George R.	(913)825-2101	1331
Topeka	KINZIE, Lenora A.	(913)295-8247	653
	LYNN, Barbara A.	(913)233-4252	752
	MARVIN, James C.	(913)233-2040	780
	VOSS, Ernestine D.	(913)269-3296	1289
Westwood	KLEBBA, Lisa A.		658
Wichita	BERARD, Sue A.	(316)267-6371	84
	BRADEN, Jan	(316)686-5954	125
	GERMANN, Malcolm P.	(316)689-3591	429
	MEYERS, Judith K.	(316)832-1211	831
	SHARMA, Shirley K.	(316)744-1448	1122
	SINGH, Swarn L.	(316)722-3741	1143

KENTUCKY

Bowling Green	COSSEY, M E.	(502)843-6560	249
Covington	GARMAN, Nancy J.	(606)331-6345	419
Cynthiana	DOAN, Janice K.	(606)441-1180	307
Edgewood	REESE, Virginia D.	(606)261-8211	1016
Florence	BROWN, Lucinda A.	(606)371-6222	145
Frankfort	COOPER, Judy L.	(502)564-2672	243
	HELLARD, Ellen G.	(502)875-7000	524
	KLEE, Edward L.	(502)875-7000	658
	NELSON, James A.	(502)875-7000	894
Germantown	TEEGARDEN, Maude B.	(606)728-2312	1229
Highland Heights	SCHULTZ, Lois E.	(606)572-5275	1102
	STURM, Rebecca R.	(606)572-5636	1205
Lexington	BARRISH, Alan S.	(606)278-1933	60
	SINEATH, Timothy W.	(606)257-8876	1143
	STEENSLAND, Ronald P.		1184
	WALDHART, Thomas J.	(606)257-3771	1294
	WILLIS, Paul A.	(606)257-3801	1348
	YOUNG, Sandra C.	(606)268-7677	1383

GENERAL LIBRARY/INFORMATION CONSULTANT (Cont'd)
KENTUCKY (Cont'd)

Louisville	BRINKMAN, Carol S.	(502)588-6297	136
	COATES, Ann S.	(502)588-5917	224
	DIESING, Arthur C.	(502)568-7976	302
	EDDY, Leonard M.	(502)245-8633	335
	JOHNSON, Garry B.	(502)897-8100	604
	KEARNEY, Anna R.	(502)588-6744	633
	SCHLENE, Vickie J.	(502)935-9840	1094
Murray	BUSER, Robin A.	(502)762-2393	165
	WALL, Celia J.	(502)762-4990	1297
Owensboro	YATES, Dudley V.	(502)526-3111	1378
Paducah	SUTHERLAND, Thomas A.	(502)443-2664	1211
Richmond	BARKSDALE, Milton K.	(606)622-1787	57
	MARTIN, June H.	(606)622-6176	777

LOUISIANA

Alexandria	JARRED, Ada D.	(312)445-5230	594
Baton Rouge	BINGHAM, Elizabeth E.	(504)292-1038	97
	CARPENTER, Michael A.	(504)766-7385	185
	COE, Miriam M.		226
	LOUBIERE, Sue	(504)346-3172	742
	PERRY, Emma B.	(504)928-3622	960
	SMITH, Ledell B.		1157
Bossier City	BROWN, Sue S.	(318)746-9593	147
Charenton	NEAU, Philip F.	(318)923-7261	891
Harvey	WASHINGTON, Idella A.	(504)367-8429	1307
Heflin	NOLES, Judy H.	(318)377-8582	908
Iberville	ROBINSON, Joyce W.	(504)642-5301	1044
Lake Charles	CUROL, Helen B.	(318)477-1780	266
Marrero	FAVORITE, Grealdine J.	(504)348-0234	366
Metairie	SALVATORE, Gayle E.	(504)456-2660	1078
Monroe	KONTROVITZ, Eileen R.		671
	MEINEL, Nancy T.	(318)343-3399	822
Natchitoches	HARRINGTON, Charles W.	(318)357-0813	504
New Orleans	FISHER, Collette J.	(504)581-3333	380
	GROSS, Mary D.	(504)282-4401	472
	MARIX, Mary L.	(504)488-4286	770
	WILSON, C D.	(504)596-2600	1350
Ruston	BYERS, Cora M.	(318)257-3555	168
	LOWE, Joy L.	(318)255-4379	744
Shreveport	BRAZILE, Orella R.	(318)674-3400	130
	MOSLEY, Mattie J.	(318)797-5100	871
Slidell	HOLLEY, Rebecca M.	(504)641-0198	551

MAINE

Augusta	TARANKO, Walter J.	(207)289-5628	1223
Bangor	WOODWARD, Robert C.	(207)942-4760	1368
Bar Harbor	BAKER, Alison	(207)288-3371	47
Bath	MCKAY, Ann	(207)443-5524	809
Mechanic Falls	NOYES, Nicholas	(207)345-3245	911
Orono	ALBRIGHT, Elaine M.	(207)581-1661	10
Waterville	DAMON, Cora M.	(207)872-1224	272

MARYLAND

Abingdon	ANDERSON, Della L.	(301)679-5720	22
Adelphi	NITECKI, Danuta A.	(301)937-4791	905
Annapolis	CARMAN, Carol A.	(301)841-3810	183
	RICE, Rosamond H.	(301)263-0670	1027
	THAPAR, Shashi P.	(301)974-3015	1234
Arnold	OLSON, Christine A.	(301)647-6708	922
Baltimore	BLUTE, Mary R.	(301)889-4080	107
	BOURKOFF, Vivienne R.	(301)338-8914	119
	CONNOR, Elizabeth	(301)828-8646	237
	FINNEY, Lance C.	(301)685-0074	379
	GRAVES, Louise H.		459
	HSIEH, Rebecca T.	(301)522-1481	567
	LANDRY, Mary E.	(301)235-8067	693
	LEDBETTER, Sherry H.	(301)358-0285	708
	MCADAM, Paul E.	(301)747-5030	791
	MOLLENKOPF, Carolyn M.	(301)866-3156	853
	NIXON, Judith A.	(301)576-1927	906
	PAPENFUSE, Edward C.	(301)467-6137	939
	PARTRIDGE, James C.	(301)664-4301	945
	RASCHKA, Katherine E.	(301)539-2530	1008
	STEPHAN, Sandra S.	(301)333-2118	1187
	SZCZCPANIAK, Adam S.	(301)539-0872	1218
	THOMAS, Fannette H.	(301)435-4409	1236
	ZIMMERMAN, Martha B.	(301)668-5744	1389

GENERAL LIBRARY/INFORMATION CONSULTANT (Cont'd)
MARYLAND (Cont'd)

Beltsville	AYER, Carol A.	(301)344-1969	42
	CHEN, John H.		205
Bethesda	BEATTY, Samuel B.	(301)654-8500	70
	BOEHR, Diane L.	(301)986-8560	109
	BOHLEN, Jeanne L.	(301)897-9823	111
	BROWN, Carolyn P.	(301)496-2447	142
	CONGER, Lucinda D.	(301)229-7716	236
	COSTABILE, Salvatore L.	(301)986-8560	249
	FISHBEIN, Meyer H.	(301)530-5391	380
	GLOCK, Martha H.	(301)496-5511	441
	HORAN, Meredith L.	(301)496-5497	559
	JOHNSON, Carol A.	(301)251-5378	602
	LAKSHMAN, Malathi K.	(301)229-9287	689
	LAZAROW-STETTEN, Jane K.	(301)656-5471	706
	LORENZ, John G.	(301)320-4651	741
	MENNELLA, Dona M.	(301)652-0106	824
	MOBLEY, Arthur B.	(301)530-0081	851
	PEARSE, Nancy J.	(301)564-1967	952
	PHILLIPS, Lena M.	(301)986-8560	968
	THOMAS, Patricia A.	(301)229-4194	1238
	TURNER, Ellis S.	(301)530-4178	1264
Bowie	GIGANTE, Vickilyn M.	(301)249-2609	433
Brookeville	ROBERTS, Lesley A.	(301)774-4471	1040
Cabin John	ROBINSON, Barbara M.	(301)320-6011	1043
	SEWELL, Winifred	(301)229-5008	1118
Cambridge	DEL SORDO, Jean S.	(301)228-7331	290
Catonsville	WILT, Larry J.	(301)455-2341	1353
Chevy Chase	CHARTRAND, Robert L.		203
	ERLICK, Louise S.		353
	SHAW, Renata V.	(301)654-3560	1123
Churchton	TONEY, Stephen R.	(301)261-5650	1250
College Hts Estates	PARMING, Marju R.	(301)277-5210	943
College Park	APPLEBAUM, Edmond L.	(301)474-7322	30
	ASSOUAD, Carol S.	(301)935-5631	37
	STIELOW, Frederick J.	(301)454-5790	1194
	TIBBO, Helen R.	(301)454-5441	1244
	WILSON, William G.	(301)454-6003	1353
Columbia	AVERSA, Elizabeth S.	(301)992-3711	41
	DAHLEN, Roger W.	(301)964-9098	269
	DIENER, Carol W.	(301)381-2525	302
	DIENER, Richard A.	(301)381-2525	302
	DOVE, Samuel	(301)964-4189	315
	HILL, Norma L.	(301)997-8000	540
	JOHNSON, Elaine B.	(301)992-5502	604
	YUILLE, Willie K.		1384
Damascus	JOHNSON, Susan W.	(301)253-2759	609
Edgewater	KROST, Mary G.		680
Ellicott City	DUCHAC, Kenneth F.	(301)531-3389	322
	MARTIN, Susan K.	(301)988-9893	778
Fallston	CLARK, David S.	(301)838-0223	216
Fort Washington	KALKUS, Stanley	(301)839-5729	623
Frederick	BANKS, Jane L.	(301)695-6726	54
	NATHANSON, David	(301)662-4499	889
Gaithersburg	GRIFFEN, Agnes M.	(301)340-3378	468
	GROCKI, Daniel J.	(301)253-6044	471
	HARTZ, Mary K.	(301)948-1855	509
	PAUL, Rameshwar N.	(301)258-0768	949
	SHELAR, James W.	(301)809-8445	1125
	YOUNG, Peter R.	(301)923-2902	1383
Gambrills	KING, Hannah M.	(301)540-0282	651
Germantown	MCQUEEN, Judith D.	(301)428-3400	817
Glen Burnie	HACKMAN, Mary H.	(301)768-2569	481
	STEINHOFF, Cynthia K.	(301)787-1549	1186
Greenbelt	ASHFORD, Richard K.	(301)982-5074	36
	AUSTIN, Rhea C.	(301)345-0750	40
	BOGGESS, John J.		110
	BYERLY, Imogene J.		168
	HENEKS, Julia A.	(301)345-2548	528
Hyattsville	LOSINSKI, Julia M.	(301)699-3500	742
Kensington	PRICE, Douglas S.	(301)942-2091	992
Landover	BARTH, Edward W.	(301)773-9790	61
Lanham	HUFFER, Mary A.	(301)577-3640	570
Largo	NEKRITZ, Leah K.	(301)322-0462	893
Laurel	BARKER, Lillian H.	(301)776-2260	56
	OMAR, Elizabeth A.	(301)490-3871	923
	SAWYER, Edmond J.	(301)725-4750	1086
Mount Airy	LISTON, David M.	(301)831-3008	732

GENERAL LIBRARY/INFORMATION CONSULTANT (Cont'd)
MARYLAND (Cont'd)

New Market	WILSON, Susan W.	(301)831-6118	1353
Olneg	WATERS, Susan S.	(301)774-3439	1309
Patuxent River	SULLIVAN, Carol W.	(301)863-1931	1207
Pikesville	JENG, Helene W.	(301)225-4450	596
Pocomoke City	SMITH, Jessie C.	(301)957-3320	1156
Potomac	CHANG, Frances M.	(301)258-0772	200
Reisterstown	BRADLEY, Wanda L.		126
Rockville	BYRD, Harvey C.	(301)251-5481	169
	CHIANG, Ahushun	(301)251-5486	207
	DEAN, Frances C.	(301)424-9289	283
	DEXTER, Patrick J.	(301)424-2000	298
	FREEDMAN, Lynn P.	(301)468-2600	400
	GRIFFITHS, Jose M.	(301)881-6766	469
	KING, Donald W.	(301)881-6766	650
	LEWIS, Robert J.	(301)460-9145	724
	MARTINEZ-GOLDMAN, Aline		779
	NGUYEN, Michael V.	(301)468-9697	900
	OAKLEY, Robert L.	(301)279-9103	913
	PEDAK-KARI, Maria	(301)279-1940	954
	WALL, Eugene	(301)881-4990	1297
Salisbury	CUNNINGHAM, Barbara M.	(301)742-1537	265
Seabrook	LARSEN, Lida L.	(301)459-3931	698
Silver Spring	ARANDA-COODOU, Patricio	(301)946-7859	30
	BATTY, Charles D.	(301)593-8901	65
	FEINBERG, Beryl L.	(301)946-3282	368
	HARBISON, John H.	(801)589-4223	499
	JACKSON, Carleton	(301)890-8594	587
	KADEC, Sarah T.	(301)598-7694	621
	KNOBBE, Mary L.	(301)681-6332	665
	LEVITAN, Karen B.	(301)588-8139	721
	MYERS, R D.	(301)681-3967	885
	STERN, Michael P.	(301)495-9413	1189
Solomons	HEIL, Kathleen A.	(301)326-2967	521
Takoma Park	NITZBERG, Dale B.	(301)587-5789	905
Towson	DRACH, Marian C.	(301)825-8877	317
	HARER, John B.	(301)321-2456	501
Upper Marlboro	HARBERT, Cathy E.	(301)868-9280	499
	WOODY, Jacqueline B.		1368
Waldorf	WOLFE, Susan J.	(301)645-4784	1361
Westminster	MCCARTY, Emily H.	(301)848-1825	795
Wheaton	MWALIMU, Charles	(301)933-4040	884

MASSACHUSETTS

Acton	HURD, Sandra H.	(617)263-7574	577
Amherst	FELDMAN, Laurence M.	(413)253-9404	369
Arlington	FORTIER, Jan M.	(617)646-5856	391
	PLUNKET, Linda	(617)646-7825	979
	TRINKAUS-RANDALL, Gregor	(617)641-1273	1257
Assonet	MEDEIROS, Joseph	(617)624-4094	820
Attleboro	PREVE, Roberta J.	(617)222-7035	992
Auburndale	TUCHMAN, Maurice S.	(617)969-9791	1261
Belmont	PHELAN, Mary C.		967
Bolton	BOGART, Betty B.	(617)897-7870	110
Boston	BUSH, Margaret A.	(617)262-2045	165
	CAIN, Susan H.	(617)338-6553	171
	CHRISTOPHER, Irene	(617)267-2876	212
	CURLEY, Arthur	(617)536-5400	265
	EATON, Elizabeth K.	(617)523-7415	333
	FRYDRYK, Teresa E.	(617)482-9485	407
	HAYES, Alison M.	(617)482-1776	515
	HERNON, Peter	(617)738-2223	532
	MCCARTHY, Germaine A.	(617)742-3958	794
	MOSKOWITZ, Michael A.	(617)578-8670	871
	MURRAY, Lynn T.	(617)330-9000	882
	PEARLSTEIN, Toby	(617)973-8000	952
	PRESTON, Margaret P.	(617)338-6000	992
	SHANNON, Marcia A.	(617)267-9400	1120
	SHARE, Donald S.	(617)738-2242	1122
	STEVENSON, Michael I.	(617)495-6374	1191
Bridgewater	CHANDRASEKHAR, Ratna	(617)697-3648	200
Brockton	NOYES, Suzanne N.	(617)583-4500	911
	UMANA, Christine J.	(617)586-6994	1268
Brookline	BLESH, Tamara E.	(617)739-0523	105
	PAPADEMETRIOU, Athanasia	(617)731-3500	938
	SOVNER-RIBBLER, Judith	(617)277-2991	1170
	STEINFELD, Michael	(617)730-2360	1186
Burlington	MCLAUGHLIN, Lee R.	(617)272-5772	813

GENERAL LIBRARY/INFORMATION CONSULTANT (Cont'd)
MASSACHUSETTS (Cont'd)

Byfield	BERNIER, Esta S.	(617)462-9809	89
Cambridge	CLIFT, Scott B.	(617)661-1869	222
	COLLINS, John W.	(617)495-4225	232
	ISHIMOTO, Carol F.	(617)495-2431	585
	MANDEL, Debra H.	(617)497-0929	764
	PINSON, Mark	(617)492-1590	975
	POLLARD, Russell O.	(617)495-5910	981
	WOLPERT, Ann J.	(617)864-5770	1362
Charlestown	DOWLER, Lawrence E.		315
Chestnut Hill	SEEGRABER, Frank J.		1111
Concord	BENDER, Elizabeth H.	(617)369-4222	79
Deerfield	KELLY, Patricia M.	(413)774-4627	638
Douglas	COPPOLA, H P.	(617)476-2975	245
Dover	WINQUIST, Elaine W.	(617)785-0816	1355
Dracut	ARSENAULT, Patricia A.	(617)459-4648	35
East Brookfield	BOLSHAW, Cynthia L.	(617)867-2605	112
Easthampton	MELNICK, Ralph	(413)527-3036	823
Farmingham	KING, Laurie L.	(617)877-3512	651
Hanscom AFB	SEIDMAN, Ruth K.	(617)377-4895	1112
Heath	HOWLAND, Margaret E.	(413)337-4980	566
Holbrook	MEAGHER, Janet H.	(617)767-3644	819
Holyoke	DUTCHER, Henry D.	(413)538-7000	329
Ipswich	GRAY, Carolyn M.	(617)356-0773	459
Leverett	ZIPKOWITZ, Fay	(413)367-9573	1389
Lexington	BERNSTEIN, D S.	(617)863-1284	89
	BROWN, George F.	(617)863-5100	144
	HARTMAN, David G.	(617)860-6668	508
	PRUSAK, Laurence	(617)861-7580	996
	STANTON, Martha	(617)861-0905	1181
	WARNER, Alice S.	(617)862-9278	1305
Littleton	BUCKLAND, Lawrence F.	(617)899-1086	154
Longmeadow	MCGARRY, Marie L.	(413)567-0001	805
Marlborough	FERGUSON, Roberta J.	(617)481-5866	372
Medford	JONES, Frederick S.	(617)381-3345	613
	MARTIN, Murray S.	(617)776-3599	777
	MCDONALD, Ellen J.	(617)381-3273	802
	PELLEGRINI, Deborah A.	(617)396-5457	955
	SCHATZ, Natalie M.	(617)381-3273	1090
Millis	ROE, Georgeanne T.	(617)376-8459	1048
Milton	HOVORKA, Marjorie J.	(617)333-4902	563
Natick	DLOTT, Nancy B.	(617)655-9163	306
Needham	ABRAHAM, Deborah V.	(617)444-8453	2
	MARKUSON, Carolyn A.	(617)449-6299	772
Newburyport	JACQUES, Donna M.	(617)462-7105	591
North Attleboro	VIGORITO, Patricia M.	(617)699-2342	1284
North Falmouth	FOSTER, Joan		392
North Grafton	SAFFER-MARCHAND, Melinda	(617)839-5302	1074
Peabody	CODAIR, Frederick R.	(617)531-8200	226
Pembroke	ROBINSON, Phyllis A.	(617)293-2193	1044
Quincy	BARNHART, Arlene C.	(617)770-3000	58
Reading	MARCY, Henry O.	(617)944-2194	769
Sagamore	OLIANSKY, Joseph D.	(617)888-6189	920
Salem	PANGALLO, Karen L.		938
	SCHWALLER, Marian C.	(617)744-0076	1104
	WHITNEY, Howard F.	(617)744-1769	1334
Sharon	AVERILL, Laurie J.	(617)784-7329	41
Shrewsbury	CHANG, Isabelle E.	(617)845-4641	200
Somerville	HUSSEY, Laurie L.	(617)776-2614	578
Springfield	KEOUGH, Francis P.	(413)739-1837	643
	LAPIERRE, Barbe	(413)739-3871	697
Stoughton	ANDERSON, Cheryl M.	(617)344-4000	22
Stow	GIULIANO, Lillian C.	(617)485-0494	439
Tyngsboro	FUNG, Margaret C.	(617)256-3090	409
Uxbridge	LEWIS, Thomas F.		724
West Springfield	HELO, Martin	(413)736-4561	525
Westford	NATOLI, Dorothy L.	(617)692-7192	889
Weston	KEENAN, Elizabeth L.	(617)893-1820	634
Westwood	CLAPPER, Mary E.	(617)329-3350	216
Williamstown	SUDDUTH, William E.	(413)597-2514	1206
Winchester	JOHNSON, Jean L.	(617)721-7020	606
Woods Hole	BROWNLOW, Judith	(617)548-5123	148
Worcester	MILLIGAN, Jane M.	(617)852-7100	843
	ROCHELEAU, Kathleen D.	(617)793-7319	1046
Yarmouthport	STEEVES, Henry A.		1184

GENERAL LIBRARY/INFORMATION CONSULTANT (Cont'd)
MICHIGAN

Albion	JENNINGS, Martha F.	(517)629-9469	598
Alpena	WILLIAMS, Susan S.	(517)356-1622	1346
Ann Arbor	BEAUBIEN, Anne K.	(313)763-5060	70
	COFFEY, Dorothy A.	(313)994-2350	227
	DIDIER, Elaine K.	(313)763-0378	301
	DOUGHERTY, Richard M.	(313)764-9356	314
	DURRANCE, Joan C.	(313)763-1569	328
	HALL, Jo A.	(313)936-0132	488
	KOCHEN, Manfred	(313)764-2585	667
	LANSDALE, Metta T.		696
	SLAVENS, Thomas P.	(313)665-6663	1148
	STOFFLE, Carla J.	(313)764-9356	1196
	WERLING, Anita L.	(313)761-4700	1324
	WEST, Marian S.	(313)663-5907	1326
	YOCUM, Patricia B.	(313)995-4644	1380
	YORK, Grace A.	(313)971-4732	1381
Auburn Hills	WILLIAMS, Calvin	(313)853-4226	1342
Bay City	KORMELINK, Barbara A.	(517)894-3782	671
Belleville	STARESINA, Lois J.	(313)699-7549	1181
Birmingham	ORMOND, Sarah C.	(313)647-1700	926
Bloomfield Hills	BRISTOR, Patricia R.	(313)852-0206	137
	DAVID, Indra M.	(313)338-3929	276
	FRANKIE, Suzanne O.	(313)855-6149	397
	SIDEN, Harriet F.	(313)258-8532	1135
Canton	BRYANT, Barton B.	(313)397-3660	152
Clarkston	MEDER, Stephen A.	(313)625-5611	820
Dearborn	VINT, Patricia A.	(313)591-5073	1285
Decatur	TATE, David L.	(616)423-4771	1225
Detroit	ALLEN, Nancy H.	(313)577-4033	15
	CARUSO, Genevieve O.	(313)972-7000	190
	COIR, Mark A.	(313)837-3643	229
	GIGLIO, Linda M.	(313)872-4311	433
	KAUL, Kanhya L.	(313)577-3926	631
	KLEIN, Michele S.		659
	LILLEY, Barbara A.	(313)222-3020	727
	MA, Helen Y.	(313)833-1016	753
	MIKA, Joseph J.	(313)577-1825	834
	PORTER, Jean F.	(313)961-5040	984
	RUFFNER, Frederick G.	(313)961-2242	1066
	SHUMAN, Bruce A.	(313)577-1825	1134
	STAJNIAK, Elizabeth T.	(313)259-7110	1178
	THOMAS, Laverne J.	(313)849-2776	1237
	TSAI, Fu M.	(313)876-0133	1260
	WARD, Nancy E.	(313)256-9596	1304
East Lansing	ACKERMAN, Katherine K.	(517)332-6818	4
	MEAHL, D D.	(517)355-7641	819
	WOODARD, Beth E.	(517)355-5774	1365
Eaton Rapids	FLAHERTY, Kevin C.	(517)663-2362	383
Farmington Hills	PAPAI, Beverly D.	(313)553-0300	938
	RENKIEWICZ, Frank A.	(313)478-4506	1023
Ferndale	BORAM, Joan M.	(313)542-2523	116
Flint	ARNOLD, Peggy	(313)744-4040	34
	HERTZ, Sylvia	(313)733-5074	533
Galesburg	MOSHER, Robin A.	(616)665-4409	871
Grand Haven	BROOKS, Burton H.	(616)842-2586	140
Grand Rapids	BERGIN, Karen S.	(616)458-0098	86
	SIEBERS, Bruce L.	(616)774-2167	1135
	WEAVER, Clarence L.		1312
Grosse Pointe	CASEY, Genevieve M.		192
Grosse Pointe Farms	DRAPER, James P.	(313)881-4397	318
Grosse Pointe Woods	REID, Bette C.	(313)884-0884	1018
Harper Woods	TODD, Suzanne L.	(313)881-5328	1248
Highland Park	NDENGA, Viola W.	(313)868-5986	890
Holland	GRANT, Robert S.	(616)396-1875	458
	LIGHT, Lin	(616)335-2540	726
	YETMAN, Nancy J.	(616)394-2363	1380
Holt	KEDDLE, David G.	(517)694-2746	634
Jenison	VELTEMA, John H.	(616)457-3400	1282
Kalamazoo	APPS, Michelle L.	(616)375-3611	30
Lansing	DUKELOW, Ruth H.	(517)373-1593	324
	HEINLEN, Bethany A.	(517)377-8389	522
	RADEMACHER, Matthew J.	(517)483-1644	1002
Lapeer	VOELZ, Laura D.	(313)667-9583	1286
Marquette	PAULIN, Mary A.	(906)228-6686	950
Midland	CHEN, Catherine W.	(517)631-9724	205
Muskegon	MARSHALL, Betty J.	(616)728-4766	773

GENERAL LIBRARY/INFORMATION CONSULTANT (Cont'd)
MICHIGAN (Cont'd)

Northville	FIELD, Judith J.	(313)349-1953	375
Novi	COREY, Marjorie	(313)344-1770	246
	KIEFER, Marilyn V.	(313)344-8300	647
	KING, Kenneth	(313)478-4963	651
Okemos	TREGLOAN, Donald C.	(517)349-7767	1255
Pontiac	LYNCH, Mollie S.	(313)858-3495	752
Port Huron	ARNETT, Stanley K.	(313)987-7323	33
	WU, Harry P.	(313)982-2765	1373
Portage	POWELL, James R.	(616)327-9540	988
Rochester	HAGE, Christine C.	(313)375-1038	482
Romeo	NOWICKE, Carole E.	(313)752-6664	911
Saginaw	JOHN, Stephanie C.	(517)771-6846	601
Southfield	THOMAS, Margaret J.	(313)357-4952	1237
Spring Lake	PRETZER, Dale H.	(616)846-8967	992
Sterling Heights	SAHYOUN, Naim K.	(313)939-6425	1075
Sturgis	BERKLUND, Nancy J.	(616)651-9361	87
	VANZUILEN, Darlene A.	(616)467-7836	1278
Trenton	GREEN, Katherine A.		462
Troy	STEPHENS, Karen L.	(313)879-6856	1188
West Bloomfield	SMITH, Nancy J.	(313)682-2120	1158
Ypsilanti	BOONE, Morell D.	(313)484-4384	115
	YEE, Sandra G.	(313)487-2220	1379

MINNESOTA

Bloomington	NAUEN, Lindsay B.	(612)854-2879	889
Columbia Heights	VAUGHAN, Janet E.	(612)574-6505	1279
Embarrass	ESALA, Lillian H.	(218)741-3434	354
Fergus Falls	BERG, David C.		84
Hopkins	SMITH, David R.	(612)933-0199	1154
Kilkenny	HAMMARGREN, Betty L.	(507)595-2575	493
Little Canada	LO, Maryanne H.	(612)481-9412	735
Mankato	CARRISON, Dale K.	(507)389-5062	187
	PEISCHL, Thomas P.	(507)389-5953	955
Minneapolis	ASPNES, Grieg G.	(612)926-1749	37
	BARRETT, Darryl D.	(612)370-0869	59
	CARLSON, Stan W.	(612)571-2046	182
	GALT, Judith A.	(612)825-1190	415
	JOHNSON, Donald C.		603
	OLSON, Lowell E.	(612)626-0824	923
	ROHLF, Robert H.	(612)926-6105	1050
	ROSSMAN, Muriel J.	(612)624-4002	1059
	SKELLY, Laurie J.	(612)823-2556	1146
	SOLSETH, Gwenn M.	(612)330-6936	1166
	SPETLAND, Charles G.	(612)624-8060	1174
	WARPHEA, Rita C.	(612)588-6985	1306
Minnetonka	JENSEN, Wilma M.	(612)473-5965	599
Mound	GELINAS, Jeanne L.	(612)472-4046	426
Northfield	BRUCE, Robert K.	(507)645-9279	149
Pine River	O'BRIEN, Marlys H.	(218)587-2171	915
Red Wing	SWEEN, Roger	(612)388-5723	1214
Robbinsdale	OSIER, Donald V.	(612)533-5025	928
Rochester	KEY, Jack D.	(507)284-2068	645
St Louis Park	RINE, Joseph L.	(612)542-9631	1035
St Paul	BALDWIN, Jerome C.	(612)297-4532	51
	BLUMBERG-MCKEE, Hazel	(612)292-1680	107
	CLARKE, Charlotte C.	(612)645-7359	218
	DOLAN, Mary M.	(612)296-7719	309
	GADE, Rachel P.	(612)631-0494	411
	HALES-MABRY, Celia E.	(612)645-2850	486
	KINNEY, Janet S.	(612)690-6650	653
	MCCLASKEY, Marilyn H.	(612)624-5333	706
	MINOR, Barbara G.	(612)698-4978	846
	RICCI, Patricia L.	(612)771-4764	1026
	SCHMIDT, Jean M.		1095
St Peter	HAEUSER, Michael J.	(507)931-7556	482
Scandia	HANSEN, Kathelen L.	(612)433-5477	497
Waite Park	CLARKE, Norman F.	(612)253-2695	219
White Bear Lake	LEWIS, Alan D.	(612)429-2508	722
Winona	MOXNESS, Mary J.	(507)452-5177	874
Worthington	SCOTT, Thomas L.	(507)376-5803	1108
	SPILLERS, Roger E.	(507)372-2981	1174

MISSISSIPPI

Biloxi	FREEDMAN, Jack A.	(601)388-2318	400
Clinton	BUCHANAN, Gerald	(601)924-7511	153
	MYRICK, Judy C.	(601)924-6092	885
Columbus	PAYNE, David L.	(601)328-7565	951

GENERAL LIBRARY/INFORMATION CONSULTANT (Cont'd)
MISSISSIPPI (Cont'd)

Hattiesburg	DUNCAN, Bettye M.	(601)264-6849	325
	HAUTH, Allan C.	(601)266-4126	513
	WILSON, Mary S.	(601)266-4240	1352
Itta Bena	BOWEN, Ethel B.	(601)254-9041	120
Jackson	BELL, Bernice	(601)366-8786	76
Liberty	BURKS, Alvin L.	(601)657-8920	161
Meridian	MACNEILL, Daniel S.	(601)693-6771	758
Natchez	RANDAZZO, Corinne O.	(601)445-2848	1006
Ridgeland	RICE, Joyce I.	(601)856-5400	1027
Starkville	ELLSBURY, Susan H.	(601)324-1475	345
Vicksburg	BLACK, Bernice B.	(601)636-1990	101

MISSOURI

Ballwin	BUHR, Rosemary E.		156
	TAYLOR, Arthur R.	(314)394-9973	1226
Bolivar	VAN BLAIR, Betty A.	(417)326-5281	1272
Butler	FISHER, Georgeann	(816)679-6121	381
Cape Girardeau	STIEGEMEYER, Nancy H.	(314)334-3674	1193
Columbia	BELCHER, Nancy S.	(314)443-3161	76
	MARTIN, Mason G.	(314)449-5798	777
	RAITHEL, Frederick J.	(314)875-0026	1004
	TIMBERLAKE, Patricia P.	(314)882-4581	1245
	YOUNG, Virginia G.	(314)443-8413	1383
Creve Coeur	GAFFEY, Mary V.	(314)432-7726	411
Harrisonville	FRANKLIN, Jill S.	(816)884-6223	397
Joplin	KEMP, Charles H.	(417)625-9386	639
Kansas City	BRADBURY, Daniel J.	(816)221-3203	125
	GIBSON, Patricia A.	(816)333-9700	432
	JENKINS, Harold R.	(816)444-2590	597
	LINSE, Mary M.	(816)765-0831	731
	MARCHANT, Thomas O.	(816)761-8873	768
	RUBY, Carolyn M.		1065
Kirksville	ELLEBRACHT, Eleanor V.	(816)665-6158	343
	ONSAGER, Lawrence W.	(816)665-4283	924
Kirkwood	SNYDER, Elizabeth A.	(314)965-7421	1164
Lexington	ROSS, Shirley D.	(816)259-3694	1059
Liberty	HOOVER, Jonnette L.	(816)781-7812	557
Maryville	MURPHY, Kathryn L.	(816)582-4768	880
O'Fallon	SANDERS, John B.		1080
Parkville	SMITH, Harold F.	(816)741-6085	1155
Saint Joseph	HUGHES, Joan L.	(816)271-6000	571
St Louis	BECK, Sara R.	(314)889-5483	71
	GELINNE, Michael S.	(314)694-4748	426
	LYONS, A J.	(314)241-2288	753
	MESSERLE, Judith R.	(314)577-8607	828
	PAGE, Jacqueline M.	(314)781-6352	934
	REHKOP, Barbara L.		1017
	ROBERTS, Jean A.	(314)664-0939	1040
	SMITH, Nancy M.	(314)241-2288	1159
	STELLING, Dwight D.	(314)351-2419	1186
	TIPSWORD, Thomas N.	(314)263-2345	1246
St Peters	HICKS, James D.	(314)441-0522	537
Shelbyville	MASON, Laura L.	(816)762-4285	781
Springfield	MALTBY, Florence H.	(417)862-5119	764
	SINCLAIR, Regina A.	(417)865-8731	1143

MONTANA

Bozeman	ALLDREDGE, Noreen S.	(406)587-4877	14
	MORTON, Bruce	(406)994-5313	870
Butte	HUYGEN, Michaele L.	(406)782-8400	580
Great Falls	O'BRYANT, Alice A.		915
Havre	RITTER, Ann L.	(466)265-1308	1036
Heart Butte	SPOTTED EAGLE, Joy	(406)338-2282	1175
Helena	PARKER, Sara A.	(406)444-3115	942
	SCHLESINGER, Deborah L.	(406)442-2373	1094

NEBRASKA

Beatrice	DUX-IDEUS, Sherrie L.	(402)223-4581	330
Bellevue	JACKA, David C.	(402)293-3157	586
Fremont	PETERSON, Vivian A.	(402)721-9119	964
Lincoln	ALLEN, Richard H.	(402)435-4052	16
	COOK, Anita I.	(402)466-3981	239
	LU, Janet C.	(402)465-2400	745
	NESMITH, Edmund D.	(402)486-2514	896
	WAGNER, Rod G.	(402)423-7476	1292
Minatare	JOHNSON, Elizabeth L.	(308)783-2188	604

GENERAL LIBRARY/INFORMATION CONSULTANT (Cont'd)
NEBRASKA (Cont'd)

Omaha	DICKSON, Laura K.	(402)554-2217	301
	EARLEY, Dorothy A.	(402)333-5734	332
	HASELWOOD, Eldon L.	(402)554-2211	510
	LITTLE, Nina M.	(402)554-6282	733
	WILLIS, Dorothy B.	(402)556-3431	1348
Ralston	OYER, Kenneth E.	(402)331-8843	932

NEVADA

Boulder City	LANGEVIN, Ann T.	(702)293-3168	695
Carson City	KERSCHNER, Joan G.	(702)887-2615	644
Dayton	STURM, Danna G.	(702)246-0250	1205
Incline	OSSOLINSKI, Lynn	(702)831-2936	928
Las Vegas	CURLEY, Elmer F.		265
	DALTON, Phyllis I.	(702)732-4793	271
	DAVENPORT, Marilyn G.	(702)453-5606	275
	GARDNER, Jack I.	(702)382-3493	418
	ORTIZ, Cynthia		927
	SAUNDERS, Laverna M.	(702)739-3069	1084
	WELLS, David B.	(702)733-3641	1322
Reno	MCNEAL, Betty	(702)325-5859	816

NEW HAMPSHIRE

Amherst	SHERWOOD, Janet R.	(603)673-9242	1129
Chester	GAVRISH, Diane L.	(603)887-4401	423
Concord	DRUKE-STICKLER, Janet A.	(603)224-1865	320
	HARE, William J.	(603)225-2012	501
Durham	GRIFFITH, Joan C.	(603)659-3783	469
	LANE, David M.	(603)862-3718	694
Exeter	THOMAS, Jacquelyn H.	(603)772-4311	1236
Hampton	KORBER, Nancy	(603)926-6005	671
Hancock	BRYAN, Arthur L.	(603)525-6614	151
Keene	PERLUNGHER, Richard A.	(603)357-4209	959
Manchester	BERTHIAUME, Dennis A.	(603)669-1030	90
	KENT, Jeffrey A.	(603)622-4408	642
	THOMPSON, Debra J.	(603)669-1048	1239
Nashua	BERLIN, Arthur E.	(603)885-4674	87
Twin Mountain	PALMATIER, Susan M.	(603)846-2239	936
Windham	CUNNIFFE, Charlene M.	(603)434-1847	265

NEW JERSEY

Annandale	MURO, Ernest A.	(201)735-9633	880
Basking Ridge	JIULIANO, Margaret C.	(201)204-3031	600
	THOMPSON, Melia M.	(201)953-3326	1240
Bergenfield	CHELARIU, Ana R.	(201)384-8302	204
	HEISE, George F.	(201)385-9741	522
Berkeley Heights	MAZURKIEWICZ, Helen L.	(201)464-0096	791
Bernardsville	BURDEN, Geraldine R.	(201)766-0118	158
Bloomfield	PICCIANO, Jacqueline L.	(201)743-9661	970
Bridgewater	STUDDIFORD, Abigail M.	(201)725-5616	1204
Califon	CAPOOR, Asha	(201)832-9323	180
	ROSENBERG, Gail L.		1056
Cherry Hill	ARROWOOD, Nina R.	(609)667-7653	35
	BECK, Susan J.	(609)354-7638	72
	BROWN, Anita P.	(609)663-2247	142
	ROBERTSON, Betty M.	(201)894-0235	1041
Cliffside Park	EDWARDS, Susan M.	(201)842-7679	338
Colts Neck	ALITO, Martha A.	(609)298-5848	13
Columbus	BEIMAN, Frances M.	(201)272-5840	75
Cranford	WOLFE, N J.	(201)279-9563	1361
Creamridge	GEORGE, Muriel S.	(609)758-3198	428
Dayton	LAMBKIN, Claire A.	(201)329-0648	691
Delanco	WOLFORD, Larry E.	(609)461-5667	1361
Demarest	MCDERMOTT, Ellen	(201)767-1618	801
Denville	VARIEUR, Normand L.		1278
Dover	RYAN, Mary E.	(201)989-3079	1071
East Brunswick	KHEEL, Susan T.	(201)390-6764	646
	TANG, Grace L.		1222
Edison	DINERMAN, Gloria	(201)906-1777	304
	FERRERE, Cathy M.	(201)819-8924	373
Elizabeth	BOSS, Catherine M.	(201)558-8092	117
	LATINI, Samuel A.	(201)354-6060	701
	MILLER, Virginia L.	(201)351-3288	843
Florham Park	SWINBURNE, Ralph E.	(201)377-8390	1216
Forked River	ROYCE, Carolyn S.	(609)971-0665	1063
Green Brook	SINGER, Susan A.	(201)968-1157	1143
Green Village	KEON, Edward F.	(201)822-0062	643
Haddonfield	SWARTZ, Betty J.	(609)429-8498	1214
Highland Lakes	LINNAMAA, Mari M.		731

GENERAL LIBRARY/INFORMATION CONSULTANT (Cont'd)
NEW JERSEY (Cont'd)

Highland Park	BARZELATTO, Elba G.	(201)247-6248	62
	PARAS, Lucille P.		939
	YUCHT, Donald J.	(201)572-0173	1384
Hoboken	LIN, Fumei C.	(201)795-5066	727
Hopewell	BENTE, June E.	(201)218-7436	83
Irvington	KNIGHT, Shirley D.	(201)371-9324	664
Iselin	FRANTS, Valery	(212)579-2496	398
	SILVA, Nelly H.	(201)321-0683	1138
Jersey City	PANDELAKIS, Helene S.	(201)795-8265	937
Lawrenceville	STEPHEN, Ross G.	(609)896-5111	1187
Leonia	DAIN, Phyllis	(212)280-4032	270
	SCHARF, Davida	(201)947-6839	1090
	TUCKER, Mary E.	(201)592-1451	1262
Linden	PISKORIK, Elizabeth	(201)486-3888	976
Little Ferry	BOTKIN, Karen R.		118
Lodi	KARETZKY, Stephen	(201)778-1190	627
	TAORMINA, Anthony P.	(201)365-4044	1223
Mahwah	YUEH, Norma N.	(201)529-7578	1384
Maplewood	D'ALLEYRAND, Marc R.	(201)761-1028	270
	KRUPP, Robert G.	(201)763-8436	681
	STAHL, Wilson M.	(800)262-0070	1178
Marlton	KALDENBERG, Katherine A.	(609)983-1444	622
Mendham	MANTHEY, Carolyn M.	(201)543-2129	767
Montvale	REDRICK, Miriam J.	(201)573-9000	1014
Moorestown	LADOF, Nina S.	(609)235-1570	687
	SCHEPP, Brad J.	(609)778-1975	1091
Morristown	BRUNNER, Karen B.	(201)538-0800	151
	BUCK, Anne M.	(201)829-5111	153
Mount Holly	ALTERMAN, Deborah H.	(609)261-3458	18
	RILEY, Marie R.		1034
Mountain Lakes	STEEN, Carol N.	(201)334-4941	1184
Neshanic	VANDERGRIFT, Kay E.	(201)369-8685	1274
New Brunswick	ANDERSON, James D.	(201)846-1510	23
	ANSELMO, Edith H.	(201)247-5610	28
	GRAHAM, Peter S.	(201)932-7505	456
	SARACEVIC, Tefko	(201)932-7447	1082
Ocean	VLOYANETES, Jeanne M.	(201)493-9007	1286
Oceanport	WAITE, William F.	(201)542-7216	1293
Peapack	WHITING, Elaine M.	(201)234-0598	1333
Pequannock	SUSSMAN, Valerie J.	(201)696-9655	1210
Phillipsburg	HESS, Jayne L.	(201)454-3712	534
Piscataway	MENZEL, John P.	(201)463-0634	825
	SPAULDING, Frank H.	(201)463-0158	1172
Pomona	MOLL, Joy K.	(609)652-1776	853
Princeton	BLASINGAME, Ralph	(609)987-0273	104
	CHAIKIN, Mary C.	(609)452-6084	197
	CRITCHLOW, Therese E.	(609)924-9529	259
	HAYASHI, Chigusa	(609)921-2330	515
	IRVINE, James S.	(609)921-8092	584
	THRESHER, Jacquelyn E.	(609)924-9529	1243
	VELLUCCI, Sherry L.	(609)921-3658	1282
Princeton Junction	CHU, Wendy N.	(609)799-0814	213
Rahway	SUDALL, Arthur D.	(201)388-0761	1206
Red Bank	PACHMAN, Frederic C.	(201)530-7695	933
Ridgewood	ROSS, Robert D.	(201)652-4836	1058
Riverdale	LINNAVUORI, Julie R.	(201)839-3909	731
Rockaway	COHN, John M.	(201)627-8512	229
	KELSEY, Ann L.	(201)627-8512	639
Roselle	GAINES, Irene A.	(201)245-8277	412
Roselle Park	MAGEE, Patricia A.	(201)245-1963	759
Saddle Brook	AUGHEY, Kathleen M.		39
Sewell	CROCKER, Jane L.	(609)468-5000	259
Short Hills	TALCOTT, Ann W.	(201)379-6721	1221
Somerdale	DALE, Charles F.	(609)346-4629	270
Somerset	JONES, Sandra K.	(201)249-5783	615
Somerville	KAN, Halina S.	(201)685-6017	624
Sparta	GUIDA, Pat	(201)729-8176	476
Spring Lake	GARVEY, Nancy G.	(201)449-4673	421
Springfield	GLADSTONE, Mark A.	(201)376-2055	439
	SCOTT, Miranda D.	(201)467-7010	1107
Stanhope	ELIASON, Elisabetha S.	(201)347-8215	342
	KUTTEROFF, Ethel C.	(201)347-7600	685
Stratford	AVENICK, Karen	(609)784-8977	41
Sussex	SMITH, Jo T.	(201)875-3621	1156
Tenafly	KORNFELD, Carol E.	(201)568-2231	672
Trenton	BRODOWSKI, Joyce H.	(609)771-2343	139
	HALPERN, Marilyn	(609)882-2450	489
	MADDEN, Doreitha R.		758

GENERAL LIBRARY/INFORMATION CONSULTANT (Cont'd)
NEW JERSEY (Cont'd)

Upper Montclair	PARR, Mary Y.	(201)746-0352	944
Upper Saddle River	DUDLEY, Debbra C.	(201)327-4006	323
	MICHAELS, Debbie D.	(201)327-5006	832
Vineland	GREENBLATT, Ruth	(609)794-4243	463
Warren	WEIL, Ben H.	(201)647-0892	1317
Washington Township	MAYNES, Kathleen R.	(201)358-0209	790
Wayne	DICKER, Joan F.	(201)694-4272	300
	LEE, Minja P.		711
	MCCLEAN, Vernon E.	(201)595-2579	796
West Caldwell	CARMER, Ann R.	(201)228-6981	183
West Long Branch	FISHER, Scott L.	(201)229-9222	381
	PALMISANO-DRUCKER, Elsalyn	(201)870-9194	937
Williamstown	BOGIS, Nana E.	(609)728-0569	110
Willingboro	PELLETIER, Karen E.		955
Woodcliff Lake	SPOHN, Veronica G.	(201)391-6873	1175
Wrightstown	DRECHSEL, Marcella J.		319

NEW MEXICO

Alamogordo	RUCKMAN, Stanley N.	(505)434-3398	1065
Albuquerque	BERNSTEIN, Judith R.	(505)262-2320	89
	LOVE, Erika	(505)277-2548	743
	STRUB, Jeane E.	(505)262-7158	1203
Farmington	JASSAL, Raghbir S.	(505)327-7813	595
Las Cruces	DAVIS, Hiram L.	(505)646-1509	279
	DRESP, Donald F.	(505)522-3627	319
Portales	DOWLIN, C E.	(505)562-2624	316
	SCHOTT, Mark E.	(505)356-8735	1099
Roswell	KLOPFER, Jerome J.	(505)622-6250	662
	MCLAREN, M B.	(505)622-6250	813
Silver City	KEIST, Sandra H.	(505)538-2663	635
Sunspot	CORNETT, John L.	(505)434-1390	247
White Sands	BANICKI, Cynthia A.	(505)678-5820	54

NEW YORK

Albany	ANDERSON, Carol L.	(518)434-4802	22
	DENOTO, Dorothy E.	(518)449-3166	293
	GILLESPIE, Gerald V.	(518)449-3380	435
	NITECKI, Joseph Z.	(518)442-3568	905
	ROBERTS, Anne F.	(518)438-0607	1039
	SEVERINGHAUS, Ethel L.	(518)456-2110	1117
	SHUBERT, Joseph F.	(518)474-5930	1133
	SMITH, Audrey J.	(518)438-4316	1152
	WALSH, Daniel P.	(518)489-7968	1299
APO New York	CHICARELLA, Joseph T.		207
	GRIFFIN, Cheryl J.		468
	PRINZ, Jane A.		993
Auburn	MICHAEL, Douglas O.	(315)252-2247	831
Babylon	CORRY, Emmett	(516)587-2585	247
Bakers Mills	SULLIVAN, Linda R.		1208
Batavia	STRANC, Mary C.	(716)343-2783	1200
Bay Shore	HEINTZELMAN, Susan K.	(516)666-0177	522
Bayside	BILLY, George J.		97
	NOVIK, Sandra P.	(718)631-6271	911
	SINGER, Phyllis Z.	(718)279-2182	1143
Bethpage	BURDEN, John	(516)575-3912	158
Binghamton	CARPENTER, Dale	(607)797-0176	184
	COHEN, Ann E.	(607)724-9597	227
	HILL, Malcolm K.	(607)723-8236	540
	JENSEN, Patricia K.	(516)244-2115	599
Bohemia	ADAMS, Grover C.	(516)842-4000	4
Brentwood	RAHN, Erwin P.	(716)442-8980	1003
Brighton	CANNATA, Arleen	(212)295-5910	178
Bronx	CLAYBORNE, Jon L.	(212)588-8400	219
	COONEY, Martha D.	(212)543-8357	242
	DECANDIDO, Graceanne A.		285
	PATRYCH, Joseph		947
	WAGSCHAL, Sara G.	(212)601-1723	1292
Brooklundy	HAMILTON, Reatha B.		492
Brooklyn	ARMEIT, Marilyn	(718)209-1718	32
	BLAKE-O'HOGAN, Kathleen E.	(718)625-2829	103
	CLUNE, John R.	(718)680-7578	223
	DEFALCO, Joseph	(718)693-8377	287
	JOHNSON, Sheila A.	(718)780-7744	609
	KLEIMAN, Allan M.	(718)645-2396	658
	LANDOLFI, Lisa M.	(718)853-7871	693

GENERAL LIBRARY/INFORMATION CONSULTANT (Cont'd)
NEW YORK (Cont'd)

Brooklyn

	MALINCONICO, S M.	(718)627-0558	763
	MANBECK, Virginia B.	(718)253-9413	764
	MARTINEZ-RIVERA, Ivette	(718)854-5176	779
	NARDUCCI, Frances	(718)743-6001	888
	NEUBERG, Karen S.	(718)627-9796	897
	ORR, Coleridge W.	(718)934-5971	926
	ROMALIS, Carl		1052
	SCHWABACHER, Sara A.	(718)388-0023	1104
	STRAM, Lynn R.	(718)434-7815	1200
	TANNER, Ellen B.	(718)780-3195	1222
	TURIEL, David	(718)336-2668	1263
	WAHLERT, George A.	(718)833-1899	1292
	WILLNER, Richard A.	(718)596-9573	1349
Brookville	MAILLET, Lucienne G.	(516)299-2855	761
Buffalo	BOBINSKI, George S.	(716)636-2412	108
	BREEN, M F.	(716)881-6264	131
	ELLISON, John W.	(716)636-3069	345
	EVERINGHAM, Joyce D.	(716)852-3844	358
	HUANG, C K.	(716)831-3402	568
	HUTCHINSON, Ann P.	(716)845-5966	579
	KARCH, Linda S.	(716)827-2323	627
	NEWMAN, George C.	(716)886-8132	899
	STIEVATER, Susan M.	(716)878-6313	1194
	SZEMRAJ, Edward R.	(716)895-7675	1218
	VON WAHLDE, Barbara	(716)636-2967	1288
	WAGNER, Stephen K.	(716)837-1563	1292
	WELLS, Margaret R.	(716)636-2943	1322
Campbell	EDSALL, Shirley A.	(607)770-6030	336
Chappaqua	CHEATHAM, Bertha M.	(914)238-3586	204
Cheektowaga	WITT, Susan T.	(716)686-3620	1358
Circleville	NELSON, James B.	(914)361-2415	894
Clinton	ANTHONY, Donald C.	(315)737-8347	28
Cobleskill	GALASSO, Nancy	(518)234-5841	412
Cohoes	PINGITORE, Patricia E.		974
Commack	ROFES, William L.	(516)499-4370	1049
	SCHRIFT, Leonard B.	(516)543-5600	1100
Cornwall on Hudson	WEISS, Egon A.	(914)534-9467	1320
Corona	KINYATTI, Njoki W.	(718)592-4782	653
Cortland	RITCHIE, David G.	(607)753-2818	1036
Delmar	BRESLIN, Ellen R.	(518)439-7568	133
	POLAND, Ursula H.	(518)439-6872	980
Dobbs Ferry	HASSAN, Mohammad Z.	(914)693-2031	511
East Meadow	FRANZEN, John F.	(516)794-2570	398
East Northport	MILLER, Scott W.	(516)543-2821	842
East Patchogue	CANTWELL, Mickey A.	(516)475-7007	179
	PLUMER, F I.	(516)289-3134	978
East Setauket	BLOHM, Laura A.	(516)444-3105	106
Eastchester	KOLTAY, Emery I.	(914)337-0300	670
Elmhurst	HSU, Elizabeth L.	(718)271-6623	567
	SALEY, Stacey		1076
Fishkill	SHERWIG, Mary J.	(914)831-6600	1129
Flushing	COOPER, Marianne	(718)520-7194	243
	DUTIKOW, Irene V.	(718)939-7382	329
	RATZABI, Arlene	(718)479-7238	1010
	SURPRENANT, Thomas T.	(718)520-7194	1210
Forest Hills	VAN BRUNT, Amy S.	(718)261-0313	1272
Freeport	NOTARSTEFANO, Vincent C.	(516)379-3245	910
Fulton	REED, Catherine A.	(315)598-3435	1015
Glendale	SOSTACK, Maura	(718)417-8242	1169
Grand Island	WATERS, Betsy M.		1308
Greenvale	YUKAWA, Masako	(516)299-2142	1384
Hamilton	BERGEN, Daniel P.	(315)824-2381	85
	WASHBURN, Keith E.	(315)824-3008	1307
Harrison	WOOD, Arline L.	(914)835-3300	1363
Hewlett	WILLER, Kenneth H.		1341
Highland	LAWRENCE, Thomas A.	(914)691-2734	705
	RANKIN, Carol A.	(914)691-2275	1007
Holbrook	ROMANELLI, Catherine A.	(516)588-5171	1052
Huntington	FOLCARELLI, Ralph J.	(516)271-0634	387
	JASSIN, Raymond M.	(516)266-1093	595
	NEWMAN, Eileen M.	(516)673-2023	899
	WOLFE, Barbara M.	(516)423-2495	1360
Huntington Station	ROSS, David J.	(516)385-4951	1058
Ithaca	MILLER, J G.	(607)272-1576	838
	OLSEN, Wallace C.	(607)255-2551	922
	PARKHURST, Kathleen A.	(607)273-4073	942

GENERAL LIBRARY/INFORMATION CONSULTANT (Cont'd)
NEW YORK (Cont'd)

Jamaica	GRANT, Mary A.	(718)990-6161	458
	MARKE, Julius J.	(718)990-6759	771
	VENER, Lucille	(718)990-0761	1282
Johnstown	BAILIE, Donna L.	(518)762-4633	47
Kenmore	HEFNER, Xavier M.	(716)875-4705	520
Lackawanna	BEDNAR, Sheila	(716)822-0840	73
Lake Success	TRINKOFF, Elaine	(516)466-9148	1257
Larchmont	LANDMAN, Lillian L.	(914)834-3225	693
Lindenhurst	ROECKEL, Alan G.	(516)884-0832	1048
	WARD, Peter K.	(516)957-6678	1304
Liverpool	ROSSOFF, Judith H.	(315)457-0310	1059
Manlius	WU, Painan R.	(315)682-2472	1373
Marlboro	BAKER, Marie A.	(914)236-4441	49
Maryknoll	O'HALLORAN, James V.	(914)941-7590	918
Massapequa	EISNER, Joseph	(516)735-4133	341
Massapequa Park	AKS, Gloria	(516)795-7297	9
Mastic	MACINICK, James W.	(516)399-3281	755
McLean	DREW, Wilfred E.	(607)753-8180	319
Menands	GILSON, Robert	(518)463-4181	437
Mexico	MAUTINO, Patricia H.	(315)963-7251	787
Middle Island	NARBY, Ann E.	(516)345-2718	888
Miller Place	TODOSOW, Helen K.	(516)928-7174	1248
Monticello	DORN, Robert J.	(914)794-4660	313
Mt Kisco	NELSON, Nancy M.	(914)666-3394	894
Mt Sinai	COHEN, Rosemary C.	(516)473-8717	229
Mt Vernon	OCKENE, David L.	(914)699-0949	915
	SHERRILL, Jocelyn T.	(914)667-4190	1129
Nassau	LIPETZ, Ben A.	(518)766-3014	732
	VANNORTWICK, Barbara L.	(518)766-4190	1276
Nesconset	GRUNDT, Leonard	(516)361-8987	475
New City	SIMON, Patricia B.	(914)634-4998	1140
New Hyde Park	LANG, Jovian P.	(516)352-1666	695
New Paltz	NYQUIST, Corinne E.	(914)255-2209	913
New Rochelle	KONOVALOFF, Maria S.		670
New York	ALICEA, Ismael	(212)220-6582	13
	BADERTSCHER, David G.	(212)374-5615	44
	BAKER, John P.	(212)255-7267	48
	BERGFELD, C D.	(212)496-2668	86
	BERNER, Andrew J.	(212)515-5299	88
	BOCKMAN, Eugene J.	(212)566-5398	109
	BONACORDA, James J.	(212)982-8358	113
	BONADIA, Roseann	(212)422-3000	113
	BORBELY, Jack		116
	BOWKER, Scott W.	(212)683-8261	121
	BOWLEY, Craig	(212)239-0827	121
	BURGALASSI, Anthony J.	(212)382-6668	159
	BUSSEY, Holly J.	(212)708-5181	165
	CHITTAMPALLI, Padma S.	(212)874-0141	209
	CLINE, Herman H.	(212)777-4575	222
	COOPER, Carol D.	(212)982-1302	242
	COPLEN, Ron	(212)869-3348	244
	D'ANGELO, Paul P.	(212)760-1600	272
	DAVILA, Daniel	(212)989-1732	277
	DEDONATO, Ree	(212)998-2510	286
	DENNIS, Anne R.	(212)645-4500	292
	DOOLING, Marie	(212)510-4375	312
	DOUET, Madeleine J.	(212)755-4500	313
	DYER, Esther R.	(212)777-9064	330
	ELLIS, Peter K.	(212)222-3274	345
	FASANA, Paul J.	(212)930-0708	366
	FODY, Barbara A.	(212)713-3673	387
	GILLESPIE, John T.	(212)861-9294	435
	GINSBURG, Carol L.	(212)850-1440	438
	GITNER, Fred J.	(212)355-6100	439
	GLASFORD, G R.	(212)669-3336	440
	GOSSAGE, Wayne	(212)869-3348	453
	GRETES, Frances C.	(212)309-9634	467
	GROSS, Gretchen		472
	HARVEY, John F.	(215)509-2612	509
	HAYWARD, Diane J.	(212)757-2200	517
	HENDERSON, Janice E.	(212)687-0400	526
	HERBERT, Annette F.	(212)371-6220	530
	HEWITT, Vivian D.		535
	HOLTZE, Sally H.	(212)674-6973	555
	HUTSON, Jean B.	(212)368-1515	579
	JANIAK, Jane M.	(212)466-4060	593
	KENDRICK, Alice M.	(212)532-6350	640
	KILBERG, Jacqueline L.	(212)536-3562	648

GENERAL LIBRARY/INFORMATION CONSULTANT (Cont'd)
NEW YORK (Cont'd)
New York

	KLEIMAN, Rhoda E.	(212)247-2650	659
	KOENIG, Michael E.	(212)867-0489	668
	KOLATA, Judith	(212)902-0080	669
	KRANICH, Nancy C.	(212)998-2447	676
	KUHNER, Robert A.	(212)663-3360	683
	LANDAU, Herbert B.	(212)705-7600	692
	LEWIS, Anne	(212)906-1200	722
	LIDSKY, Ella	(212)663-4949	725
	LIEBERFELD, Lawrence	(212)348-8499	726
	LIN, Tung F.	(212)669-5178	728
	LUBETSKI, Edith E.	(212)340-7720	745
	MACK, Phyllis G.	(212)926-2479	756
	MANDAL, Mina R.	(212)491-8266	764
	MANDEL, Carol A.	(212)280-2226	764
	MASSIS, Bruce E.	(212)595-2000	782
	MASYR, Caryl L.	(212)777-9271	783
	MATTA, Seoud M.	(212)686-7532	785
	MCSWEENEY, Josephine	(212)254-6338	818
	MIHRAM, Danielle	(212)998-2515	834
	MILLER, Sarah J.		842
	MILLER-KUMMERFELD, Elizabeth	(212)751-0830	843
	MOONEY, James E.	(212)873-3400	858
	MORRIS, Irving	(718)728-4078	866
	MORRIS, Margaret J.	(212)682-2500	867
	MOUNIR, Khalil A.	(212)373-5640	873
	OSTROWSKY, Edith	(212)340-0890	929
	PALMER, Julia R.	(212)744-7202	936
	PALMER, Paul R.	(212)865-5781	936
	PANELLA, Nancy M.		938
	PAUL, Sandra K.	(212)675-7804	949
	PEARCE, Karla J.	(212)280-3353	952
	PINEDA, Conchita J.	(212)371-5188	974
	POLLARD, Bobbie T.	(212)725-7648	981
	POTEAT, James B.	(212)759-6800	986
	PRAVER, Robin I.	(212)214-1720	990
	PURCELL, Marcia L.	(212)982-3786	998
	RAUM, Tamar	(212)889-2156	1010
	REGAN, Muriel	(212)869-3348	1017
	RHODES, Deborah L.		1026
	RICHARDSON, Emma G.		1029
	RIPIN, Laura G.	(212)480-6649	1035
	RODERER, Nancy K.	(212)305-6302	1047
	ROJAS, Alexandra A.	(212)489-9500	1051
	ROTH, Claire J.	(212)755-6710	1059
	ROTHMAN, John	(212)645-3008	1060
	ROTHSTEIN, Pauline M.	(212)750-6008	1060
	ST. CLAIR, Guy	(212)515-5299	1075
	SALBER, Peter J.	(212)350-4680	1076
	SALY, Alan J.	(212)475-5400	1078
	SANCHEZ, Eliana P.	(212)254-8829	1079
	SCHUMAN, Patricia G.	(212)925-8650	1103
	SHAPIRO, Fred R.	(203)432-1600	1121
	SLATE, Ted	(212)350-4682	1148
	SMITH, Mark J.	(212)373-2401	1158
	SOROBAY, Roman T.	(212)878-9314	1169
	STRINGFELLOW, William T.	(212)586-2000	1202
	SULLIVAN, Stephen W.		1208
	TAYLOR, Patricia A.	(212)566-4285	1228
	TAYLOR, Robert N.	(212)664-9021	1228
	TYLER, David M.	(212)350-4679	1266
	VELEZ, Sara B.	(212)870-1661	1281
	WALKER, William B.	(212)595-7335	1296
	WEATHERFORD, Elizabeth	(212)925-4682	1311
	WEINZIMMER, William A.	(212)421-1950	1318
	WOODS, Lawrence J.	(212)736-6629	1367
	WOOTEN, Jean A.	(212)720-8289	1368
	WRIGHT, Bernell	(212)866-3042	1370
	WRIGHT, Sylvia H.	(212)222-6148	1373
	WYDEN, Elaine S.	(212)753-9229	1374
Newburgh	HALPIN, James E.	(914)561-1836	490
Oakdale	BEAUDRIE, Ronald A.	(516)244-3284	70
Oceanside	ROGGENKAMP, Alice M.	(516)766-1397	1050
Ogdensburg	FRANZ, David A.	(315)393-2950	398
Old Westbury	COLLANTES, Lourdes Y.	(516)876-3154	232
Oswego	CHU, Sylvia	(315)341-3210	213
Patchogue	NEUFELD, Judith B.	(516)289-6813	897

GENERAL LIBRARY/INFORMATION CONSULTANT (Cont'd)
NEW YORK (Cont'd)

Pearl River	BRISFJORD, Inez S.	(914)735-1567	136
Peekskill	HALLINAN, Patricia R.	(914)739-2268	489
	SALUSTRI, Madeline	(914)739-2823	1077
Plattsburgh	RANSOM, Stanley A.	(518)563-5719	1007
Port Chester	LETTIERI, Robin M.	(914)939-6710	719
Port Washington	BRENNER, Everett H.	(516)767-2728	133
Poughkeepsie	WIGG, Ristiina M.	(914)471-6060	1337
Richmond Hill	BISSESSAR, Carmen T.	(718)835-6514	100
Riverdale	CLANCY, Kathy	(212)796-2057	215
	POMRENZE, Seymour J.		982
Rochester	BARRETT, Lizabeth A.	(716)272-1905	59
	BERKMAN, Robert I.	(716)461-3206	87
	BLUM, Elaine G.	(716)423-1611	107
	CUSEO, Allan A.	(716)325-4264	267
	GIGLIOTTI, Mary J.	(716)254-0621	433
	GLASER, June E.	(716)275-5010	439
	HELBERS, Catherine A.	(716)594-9652	523
	HUNT, Suellyn	(716)428-6981	575
	LINDSAY, Jean S.	(716)428-7300	729
	PERRY, Rodney B.	(716)482-6478	961
Rockville Centre	FRIEDLAND, Rhoda W.	(516)766-6387	403
Ronkonkoma	SHERIDAN, Robert N.	(516)981-5739	1128
Roslyn	SIAHPOOSH, Farideh T.	(516)627-1919	1134
Saratoga Springs	EYMAN, David H.	(518)584-5000	359
	RATZER, Mary B.		1010
Sayville	PAGELS, Helen H.	(516)589-2908	934
Scarborough	HOPKINS, Lee B.	(914)941-5810	558
Scarsdale	SEULOWITZ, Lois	(914)472-4097	1117
Schenectady	HALSEY, Richard S.	(518)370-0902	490
	HOLT, Lisa A.	(518)370-1811	554
	HUMPHRY, John A.	(518)374-8944	574
	KING, Maryde F.	(518)374-7287	651
	KLEMPNER, Irving M.	(518)393-5983	660
	SEEMANN, Ann M.	(518)370-6277	1111
Setauket	COOK, Jeannine S.	(516)941-4090	240
	NICHOLS, Gerald D.	(516)689-7071	901
	VERBESEY, J R.	(516)751-6913	1282
Sparkill	BARRIE, John L.	(914)359-7200	59
Staten Island	BARTO, Stephen C.	(718)727-8940	61
	DIMATTEO, Lucy A.	(718)698-7095	304
	HOGAN, Matthew	(718)273-6245	549
	KRIEGER, Tillie		678
	MANNING, Jo A.	(718)981-0120	766
	SCHUT, Grace W.	(718)442-5659	1103
	SVENNINGSEN, Karen L.	(718)987-1168	1212
Stillwater	REEPMEYER, Marie C.	(518)785-6949	1016
Stony Brook	MASH, S D.		780
Syracuse	ABBOTT, George L.	(315)445-0484	1
	EISENBERG, Michael B.	(315)423-4549	340
	FUNK, Nancy J.	(315)423-2627	410
	GRANKA, Bernard D.	(315)463-0875	457
	HORRELL, Jeffrey L.	(315)423-2585	560
	PRICE, Susan W.	(315)423-2093	992
	SHELANDER, Frances R.	(315)469-8068	1125
Troy	SUTHERLAND-NEHRING, Laurie A.	(518)273-0100	1211
Tuckahoe	ZOTTOLI, Danny A.	(914)961-6294	1390
Upper Nyack	POUNDSTONE, Sally H.	(914)358-9294	987
Utica	BROOKES, Barbara	(315)735-2279	140
Voorheesville	BARRON, Robert E.		60
Wallkill	RUBIN, Ellen B.	(914)565-5620	1064
Wantagh	NOVITSKY, Edward G.		911
West Hempstead	MASCIA, Regina B.	(516)489-9261	780
West Islip	JOYCE, Therese	(516)587-8000	618
West Point	RANDALL, Lawrence E.	(914)938-4789	1006
Westhampton Beach	KIRSCH, Anne S.	(516)288-2492	655
White Plains	DAVIES, Carol A.	(212)754-7438	277
	HIGGINS, Judith H.	(914)949-2175	538
	HOUGHTON, Joan I.	(914)335-7839	562
	MCELHANEY, William E.	(914)949-3270	804
	MCGARVEY, Eileen B.	(914)683-2794	805
	MCLAUGHLIN, Denis F.	(914)948-3666	813
	MOSLANDER, Charlotte D.	(914)428-1533	871
	ROCQUE, Bernice L.	(914)253-4307	1046
	TREFRY, Mary G.	(914)761-5478	1255
Whitestone	RIECHEL, Rosemarie	(718)990-0714	1033
Williamsville	BOBINSKI, Mary F.	(716)688-4919	108

GENERAL LIBRARY/INFORMATION CONSULTANT (Cont'd)
NEW YORK (Cont'd)

Willow	LOWE, Mildred	(914)679-6222	744
Woodhaven	PAYNE, Linda C.	(718)849-1320	951
Yonkers	BERGER, Paula E.	(914)968-7906	86
	SIKORSKI, Charlene S.	(914)968-2674	1137
Yorktown Heights	YURO, David A.	(914)962-5200	1384

NORTH CAROLINA

Angier	FISH, Paula H.	(919)639-4331	380
Asheville	BUTSON, Linda C.	(704)254-2932	167
	THIBODEAU, Patricia L.	(704)257-4448	1235
Beulaville	FRAZELLE, Betty	(919)298-4658	399
Boone	BARKER, Richard T.	(704)264-3621	56
	WORRELL, Diane F.		1369
Cary	BRUMBACK, Elsie	(919)467-6697	150
	BURCSU, James E.	(919)469-2731	158
Cedar Grove	WRIGHT, Larry L.		1372
Chapel Hill	DANIEL, Evelyn H.	(919)962-8366	272
	DICKERSON, Jimmy	(919)962-1188	300
	GOVAN, James F.	(919)962-1301	454
	HOLLEY, Edward G.		551
	MEEHAN-BLACK, Elizabeth C.		821
	PALO, Eric E.	(919)493-7230	937
	TELFER, Margaret E.	(919)933-7563	1230
Charlotte	BERRY, Mary W.	(704)371-4258	90
	FRANKLE, Raymond A.	(704)547-2221	397
	MILLER, Gloria	(704)394-6848	838
	MOORE, Patricia R.	(704)332-0092	860
Dallas	HUNSUCKER, David L.	(704)922-8041	575
Davidson	PARK, Leland M.	(704)892-1837	941
Durham	BARROWS, William D.	(919)549-0517	60
	BOMARC, M D.	(919)683-6244	113
	BRUCE, Nancy G.	(919)490-0069	149
	CARRINGTON, Bessie M.	(919)684-2373	186
	HAZEL, Debora E.	(919)683-6473	517
	HEWITT, Joe A.	(919)489-9875	535
	SPELLER, Benjamin F.	(919)683-6485	1172
	VARGHA, Rebecca B.	(919)544-6045	1278
Fayetteville	HANSEL, Patsy J.	(919)484-7096	497
Garner	RICHARDSON, Beverly S.		1029
Greensboro	FLOYD, Rebecca M.	(919)852-3592	386
	JARRELL, James R.	(919)273-7061	594
	LEVINSON, Catherine K.	(919)334-5419	721
	MCZORN, Bonita A.	(919)273-4886	819
	MILLER, Marilyn L.	(919)334-5100	840
	O'CONNOR, Sandra L.	(919)273-1914	916
	TUGWELL, Helen M.	(919)334-5764	1262
Hickory	PRITCHARD, John A.	(704)294-0326	994
High Point	GAUGHAN, Thomas M.	(919)841-9215	422
Jacksonville	MARTIN, Richard T.	(919)455-1221	778
Jefferson	FRANKLIN, Robert M.	(919)246-4460	398
Kinston	MILLER, Sylvia G.		843
	SOUTHERLAND, Carol A.	(919)523-0819	1169
Lewisville	BROWN, Merrikay E.	(919)945-3786	146
Montreat	FERM, Lois R.	(704)669-5550	373
Morganton	BUSH, Mary E.	(704)433-2303	165
New Bern	KEE, Walter A.		634
Raleigh	HORTON, James T.		561
	ISACCO, Jeanne M.	(919)851-4703	584
	MURPHY, Malinda M.	(919)821-2072	881
	PURYEAR, Pamela E.	(919)737-2836	998
	RATHGEBER, Jo F.	(919)872-3323	1009
	SMITH, Catherine	(919)851-4703	1153
	TAYLOR, Raymond M.	(919)787-7824	1228
Reidsville	KING, Willard B.	(919)349-6192	652
Research Triangle Pk	BEST-NICHOLS, Barbara J.	(919)544-3808	92
	TUTTLE, Walter A.	(919)549-0661	1266
Roanoke Rapids	JOYCE, Robert A.	(919)537-1324	618
Rocky Mount	FINCH, Lynette	(919)443-4011	377
Salisbury	ALDRICH, Willie L.	(704)636-1158	11
Sanford	MCGINN, Howard F.	(919)776-2335	806
	MURCHISON, Margaret B.	(919)258-3277	879
Spring Hope	LANEY, Elizabeth J.	(919)478-3836	695
Swannanoa	ALLEN, Christina Y.	(704)298-4742	14
Washington	TIMOUR, John A.	(919)975-3355	1246

GENERAL LIBRARY/INFORMATION CONSULTANT (Cont'd)
NORTH CAROLINA (Cont'd)

Winston-Salem	CHAPMAN, Peggy H.	(919)727-2373	202
	RALPH, Randy D.	(919)788-4591	1004
	SIBLEY, Shawn C.	(919)777-3020	1135

NORTH DAKOTA

Bismarck	HENDRICKS, Thom	(701)627-4635	527
Ellendale	ZINK, Esther L.	(701)349-3609	1389
Fargo	BIRDSALL, Douglas G.	(701)237-8878	98
	JANZEN, Deborah K.	(701)277-1865	594
	YLINIEMI, Hazel A.	(701)293-8074	1380
Valley City	HOLDEN, Douglas H.	(701)845-4940	550

OHIO

Akron	GUSS, Margaret B.	(216)375-7224	478
	RICHERT, Paul	(216)375-7447	1030
Albany	CONLIFFE, Bobbi L.	(614)698-3336	236
Athens	BETCHER, William M.	(614)593-2701	92
	LEE, Hwa W.	(614)592-5194	710
	MULLINER, Kent	(614)593-2707	878
Barnesville	THOMPSON, Myra D.	(614)425-3617	1240
Bay Village	BUTCHER, Sharon L.	(216)871-0913	166
Bowling Green	BURLINGAME, Dwight F.	(419)372-2708	161
	FIDLER, Linda M.	(419)354-1450	375
	MILLER, Ruth G.	(419)352-0817	842
	MILLER, William	(419)372-2857	843
Canfield	GENAWAY, David C.	(216)533-2194	426
	LITTLE, Dean K.	(216)533-6703	733
Centerville	GARTEN, Edward D.		420
Cincinnati	ALBRECHT, Cheryl C.	(513)871-0969	10
	CLASPER, James W.	(513)871-0969	219
	DAVIS, Yvonne M.	(513)221-7699	281
	FERGUSON, George E.	(513)559-9908	372
	HEFFRON, Sheila F.	(513)891-4200	520
	HEISHMAN, Eleanor L.	(513)475-2218	523
	HUGE, Sharon A.	(513)369-6940	571
	KUEHNLE, Emery C.	(513)421-4142	682
	LEWIS, Betty J.		722
	MCCOY, Betty J.	(513)369-6980	799
	ROSENTHAL, Francine C.	(513)825-4143	1057
	SHIVERDECKER, Darlene J.	(513)281-3760	1132
	SUHRE, Carol A.	(513)732-7109	1207
	WELKER, Kathy J.	(513)684-2678	1321
	WILSON, Lucy	(513)745-4313	1351
Cleveland	CHESHIER, Robert G.	(216)368-3427	206
	DZIEDZINA, Christine A.	(216)459-4313	331
	GRAY, Elisabeth M.	(216)831-0430	459
	KANTOR, Paul B.	(216)321-7713	626
	MICHNAY, Susan E.	(216)749-7400	832
	RAY, Laura E.	(216)844-3788	1011
	SILVER, Linda R.	(216)398-1800	1138
	STANLEY, Jean B.	(216)368-6596	1180
	VICTORY, Karen M.	(216)696-1313	1283
Cleveland Heights	GRABOWSKI, John J.	(216)932-8805	455
	SPAHR, Cheryl L.	(216)382-7675	1170
	TRAMDACK, Philip J.	(216)371-3445	1254
Columbus	BAYER, Bernard I.	(614)292-7895	67
	BRANCH, Susan	(614)267-3805	127
	CHESKI, Richard M.	(614)462-6843	207
	DALRYMPLE, Tamsen	(614)486-2109	271
	D'AMORE, Denice M.	(614)221-3211	272
	ELWELL, Pamela M.		347
	EVANS, Shirley A.	(614)860-2496	358
	HEARD, Jeffrey L.		518
	HOLOCH, S A.	(614)292-6691	553
	HUNE, Mary G.	(614)224-3168	574
	IRELAND, Clara R.	(614)486-9891	583
	LINCOVE, David A.	(614)292-3480	728
	MERCADO, Heidi	(614)292-2009	825
	MULARSKI, Carol A.	(614)292-9810	876
	PARSONS, Augustine C.	(614)895-3201	944
	ROBINSON, David A.	(614)488-7346	1043
	SMITH, Ellen A.	(614)462-7054	1154
	SMITH, Noralee W.	(614)299-0453	1159
	TANNEHILL, Robert S.	(614)488-7587	1222
	WALBRIDGE, Sharon L.	(614)274-4081	1293
	WALDEN, Graham R.	(614)292-0938	1294

GENERAL LIBRARY/INFORMATION CONSULTANT (Cont'd)
OHIO (Cont'd)

Dayton	EVANS, Stephen P.	(513)220-9506	358
	KNASIAK, Theresa J.	(513)254-1433	663
	MARSHALL, Mary E.	(513)461-1548	774
	QUINTEN, Rebecca G.	(513)277-3598	1000
	ROHMILLER, Ellen L.	(513)298-4508	1051
	TRIVEDI, Harish S.	(513)225-2201	1257
	VANGROV, Helene R.	(513)274-5622	1275
Delaware	GILBERT, Donna J.	(614)369-7705	433
Dublin	HAYNES, Kathleen J.	(614)764-6000	516
	JACOB, Mary E.	(614)764-6063	589
	PAK, Moo J.	(514)761-2174	935
	SHREWSBURY, Lynn D.	(614)764-6403	1133
	SPEECE, Yvonne M.	(614)764-9555	1172
Fairfield	LUCAS, Jean M.	(513)829-5227	746
Findlay	DUDLEY, Durand S.	(419)423-1113	323
	JANKY, Donna L.	(419)422-3211	593
Gahanna	WEITZ, Jay N.	(614)476-5489	1320
Gambier	WILT, Charles F.	(614)427-5681	1353
Georgetown	TOMLIN, Marsha A.	(513)378-3154	1250
Granville	LEMON, Nancy A.	(614)587-7265	715
Hubbard	GROHL, Arlene P.	(216)759-7800	471
Huron	CURRIE, William W.	(419)433-5560	266
Kent	DU MONT, Rosemary R.	(216)672-2782	325
Kettering	ROHMILLER, Thomas D.	(513)259-4543	1051
Mansfield	BENISHEK, Kristine K.	(419)526-8515	81
	KARRE, David J.	(419)526-1337	628
	ROMARY, Michael P.	(419)755-4321	1052
Mentor	DUANE, Carol A.	(216)255-3323	321
North Ridgeville	FACINELLI, Jaclyn R.	(216)327-7079	360
Oregon	JOHNSON, Debbie L.	(419)698-7318	603
Oxford	SCHMALBERG, Aaron	(513)529-3747	1094
Painesville	BRANCHICK, Susan E.	(216)357-3462	127
Portsmouth	COOK, Charles T.	(614)354-5688	239
Powell	RUSH, James E.	(614)881-5949	1068
Richmond Heights	SIESS, Judith A.	(216)486-7443	1136
Rootstown	BREWER, Karen L.	(216)325-2511	134
Shaker Heights	BELKIN, Betsey B.		76
	LANDAU, Lucille	(216)283-6109	692
	NISSENBAUM, Robert J.	(216)561-8168	905
	RODDA, Donna S.	(216)283-1064	1047
Springfield	ARK, Connie E.	(513)324-8470	31
Steubenville	BURKE, Ambrose L.	(614)283-3771	160
Sylvania	DOWDELL, Marlene S.	(419)882-6974	315
Toledo	ELLENBOGEN, Barbara R.	(419)536-4538	343
	SCOLES, Clyde S.	(419)255-7055	1106
	SHEPARD, Jon R.	(419)726-9402	1127
Troy	CRAM, Mary E.	(513)334-5067	255
	MILLER, John E.	(513)335-8801	839
Uniontown	CREELAN, Marilee M.	(216)699-4454	257
Upper Arlington	BROWN, Rowland C.	(614)488-6329	147
Versailles	MINNICH, Conrad H.	(513)526-4427	846
Warren	BRIELL, Robert D.	(216)399-8807	135
Westerville	WILSON, Leigh K.	(614)898-3953	1351
Westlake	CHARVAT, Catherine T.	(216)871-6391	203
Wooster	BRITTON, Constance J.	(216)264-8649	137
Wright Patterson AFB	HELLING, James T.	(513)255-5894	524
Xenia	WALDER, Antoinette L.	(513)376-2995	1294
Yellow Springs	WESTNEAT, Helen C.	(513)767-1574	1327
Youngstown	YANCURA, Ann J.	(216)746-7042	1377

OKLAHOMA

Ada	COULTER, Cynthia M.	(405)332-8000	251
Bartlesville	ROBIN, Annabeth	(918)336-7240	1043
Edmond	ROADS, Clarice D.	(405)341-3660	1038
McAlester	SIMON, Bradley A.	(918)423-3468	1140
	WRIGHT, Carolyn R.	(918)423-4746	1370
Norman	JORDAN, Linda K.	(405)321-1481	616
	LOWELL, Howard P.	(405)366-7719	744
	SHERMAN, Mary A.	(405)321-1481	1128
Oklahoma City	BOOTENHOFF, Rebecca J.	(405)728-7072	116
	BRAWNER, Lee B.	(405)947-1109	130
	CLARK, Robert L.	(405)521-2502	218
	DAVIS, Denyvetta	(405)424-2106	278
	JORSKI, Sharon D.	(405)636-7087	617
	WEISS, Catharine H.	(405)424-3344	1320
Shawnee	ALDRIDGE, Betsy B.		11

GENERAL LIBRARY/INFORMATION CONSULTANT (Cont'd)
OKLAHOMA (Cont'd)

Stillwater	HILKER, Emerson W.	(405)624-6305	539
	ROUSE, Charlie L.	(405)372-4651	1061
Tishomingo	KENNEDY, James W.	(405)371-2528	641
Tulsa	HUGHES, Carol A.	(918)585-8228	571
	MANES, Estelle L.	(918)582-7426	765
	WOODRUM, Patricia A.	(918)592-7897	1366

OREGON

Beaverton	POND, Patricia B.	(503)641-5524	982
	SHOFFNER, Ralph M.	(503)645-3502	1132
Coos Bay	TASHJIAN, Sharon A.	(503)267-5605	1224
Eugene	GRAHAM, Deborah L.		456
	MORRISON, Perry D.	(503)342-2361	868
	SHIPMAN, George W.	(503)683-8262	1131
Grants Pass	MCCOY, Joanne	(503)474-1739	799
Hillsboro	VIXIE, Anne C.	(503)645-0527	1286
Milton-Freewater	SARGENT, Phyllis M.	(503)938-3724	1083
Monmouth	JENSEN, Gary D.	(503)838-1220	598
Newport	KRABBE, Natalie	(503)336-2546	674
Portland	DAVID, Kay O.	(503)222-9981	276
	FERGUSON, Douglas K.	(503)228-5512	372
	FLYNN, Lauri R.	(503)244-1181	387
	JONES, Mary C.	(503)228-7016	614
	JUDKINS, Dolores Z.	(503)236-6743	619
	KENNEY, Ann J.	(503)297-1894	641
	KRUPP, Robert A.	(503)233-8561	681
	SUDDUTH, Susan F.		1206
	WRIGHT, Janet K.	(503)464-4097	1371
Roseburg	COOK, Sybilla A.	(503)673-0504	240
	GAULKE, Mary F.	(503)440-4036	423
Salem	MOBERG, F A.	(503)581-5244	851

PENNSYLVANIA

Allentown	ANDEL, June	(215)395-5168	21
	MOSES, Lynn M.		871
	WAGNER, Darla L.	(215)264-8203	1291
Ambler	MORROW, Ellen B.	(215)646-1755	869
Ardmore	PULLER, Maryam W.	(215)642-5187	997
Baden	JABLONOWSKI, Mary D.	(412)869-2188	586
Bala Cynwyd	CORVESE, Lisa A.	(215)668-4930	248
Belle Vernon	KLEIN, Joanne S.	(412)929-8290	659
Bensalem	CHU, John S.	(215)639-0768	212
Berwyn	BROWN, David E.	(215)644-5241	143
Bethel Park	MCGINNESS, Mary B.	(412)835-2207	806
Bethlehem	BERK, Jack M.	(215)867-3761	87
Boyertown	EMERICK, John L.	(215)369-7422	347
Bristol	WOOD, Barbara G.	(215)785-8055	1363
Bryn Mawr	HILL, Judith L.	(215)526-1305	540
California	CARUSO, Nicholas C.	(412)938-9166	190
	NOLF, Marsha L.	(412)938-4048	908
Camp Hill	ALBRECHT, Lois K.	(717)737-6111	10
Carlisle	NEITZ, Cordelia M.		892
	WIWEL, Pamela S.		1359
Carnegie	DEBONS, Anthony	(412)279-6170	285
Catasauqua	SIMONE-HOHE, M J.	(215)262-1596	1141
Chester Heights	OWENS, Irene E.		932
Clarion	MCCABE, Gerard B.	(814)226-2343	792
	PERSON, Ruth J.	(814)226-5341	961
Coatesville	KELLEY, John F.	(215)383-8147	636
Danielsville	PAGOTTO, Sarah L.	(215)767-3055	934
East Stroudsburg	RIEBEL, Ellis F.	(717)421-3038	1033
Elkins Park	NEMEYER, Carol A.		895
Erie	GALLIVAN, Marion F.	(814)452-2333	414
	LAURITO, Gerard P.	(814)871-7553	703
	RITTENHOUSE, Robert J.	(814)838-4124	1036
Fleetwood	EMERICK, Michael J.	(215)944-8486	347
Friedens	KLINE, Eve P.	(814)443-2903	661
Gettysburg	CHIESA, Adele M.	(717)334-1651	208
Gladwyne	FISHER, Daphne V.	(215)525-6628	380
Glen Rock	LIEBERMAN, Ronald	(717)235-2134	726
Gwynedd Valley	CRESCENT, Victoria L.	(215)646-7300	258
Harrisburg	BAUER, Margaret D.	(717)233-3113	65
	LINGLE, Virginia A.	(717)652-1950	730
	MALLINGER, Stephen M.	(717)783-5737	763
Hatboro	BURNS, Richard K.	(215)675-6762	162
Haverford	CORRIGAN, John T.	(215)649-5251	247
	FREEMAN, Michael S.	(215)896-1272	401
Hershey	WOODRUFF, William M.	(717)534-5106	1366

GENERAL LIBRARY/INFORMATION CONSULTANT (Cont'd)
PENNSYLVANIA (Cont'd)

Huntingdon	SWIGART, William E.	(814)643-3000	1216
Jeffersonville	GRIFFITH, Dorothy A.	(215)539-1205	469
Jenkintown	BARTZ, Alice P.	(215)887-4338	62
	SEVY, Barbara S.	(215)884-8275	1117
Johnsonburg	NELSON, Wilburta B.	(814)965-4110	895
Johnstown	WILSON, Fred L.	(814)288-3363	1351
Kennerdell	CHERESNOWSKI, Linda M.	(814)385-6896	206
Kingston	PAUSTIAN, P R.	(717)283-2651	950
Langhorne	BLACK, Dorothy M.	(215)752-5800	101
Lansdale	BLAUERT, Mary A.	(215)822-2929	105
	NOLAN, Joan	(215)368-9800	907
Lebanon	HABER, Walter H.		481
Lehigh Valley	WEBER, A C.	(215)837-9615	1313
Lewisburg	DE KLERK, Ann M.	(717)524-1557	288
Library	SALVAYON, Connie	(412)833-5585	1078
Lionville	MCSWAIN, Christy A.	(215)269-7672	818
Loretto	NEGHERBON, Vincent R.	(814)472-7000	892
Lower Oxford	MUDRICK, Kristine E.		875
Malvern	YOUNG, Dorothy E.	(215)647-7449	1381
McKeesport	HERRON, Nancy L.	(412)675-9111	533
	HORVATH, Robert T.	(412)672-0625	561
Media	COURTRIGHT, Harry R.	(215)891-5190	252
	LARSON, Phyllis S.	(215)566-2809	699
Millersville	JUDGE, Joseph M.	(717)872-7590	619
	LOTLIKAR, Sarojini D.		742
Miquon	MANCALL, Jacqueline C.	(215)828-4410	764
Monroeville	MURPHY, Diana G.	(412)327-5976	880
Mt Lebanon	WEISFIELD, Cynthia F.	(412)831-8225	1319
Narberth	SOKOLOFF, Michele	(215)664-2117	1165
New Kensington	TEOLIS, Marilyn G.	(412)339-0255	1231
New Kingstown	HANSON, Eugene R.	(717)243-0973	498
New Milford	MAASS, Eleanor A.	(717)465-3054	753
Pennsylvania Furnace	SAMET, Janet S.	(814)237-1555	1078
Philadelphia	ADELMAN, Jean S.	(215)545-4446	6
	AXAM, John A.	(215)549-6485	42
	BARR, Marilyn P.	(215)844-2036	58
	BENDER, Evelyn	(215)634-0357	79
	CHILDERS, Thomas A.	(215)895-2479	208
	DEVLIN, Margaret K.	(215)928-6994	297
	DEWANE, Kathleen M.	(215)546-5600	298
	DONOVAN, Judith G.	(215)928-0577	312
	FISHER, Douglas A.	(215)587-4915	380
	FUSELER-MCDOWELL, Elizabeth A.	(215)423-9294	410
	GARRISON, Guy G.	(215)895-2474	420
	GRAY, Priscilla M.	(215)386-6276	460
	GRIFFITH, Belver C.	(215)895-2474	469
	GROSSMAN, Robert M.	(215)893-1954	473
	HELLER, Patricia A.	(215)625-4720	524
	ICKES, Barbara J.	(215)745-9767	581
	MARCO, Guy A.		769
	MONTAVON, Victoria A.	(215)557-6921	855
	MYERS, James N.	(215)787-8231	884
	NAISMITH, Patricia A.	(215)235-0256	887
	PAGELL, Ruth A.	(215)898-5922	934
	PARKER, Peter J.	(215)732-6200	942
	PATTELA, Rao R.	(215)787-4534	947
	POSES, June A.	(215)564-1350	985
	PROMOS, Marianne	(215)686-5351	995
	ROACH, Linda	(215)238-0904	1038
	ROEDELL, Ray F.	(215)739-7739	1048
	RUOCCHIO, James P.	(215)289-5700	1068
	RUTKOWSKI, Hollace A.		1070
	SHELKROT, Elliot J.	(215)686-5300	1126
	SNOWTEN, Renee Y.	(215)557-8295	1164
	SOWICZ, Eugenia V.	(215)354-2110	1170
	WALKER, Charlotte J.	(215)877-3470	1295
Pittsburgh	BLAIR, William W.	(412)355-8071	103
	BROADBENT, H E.	(412)441-6409	138
	BROSKY, Catherine M.	(412)682-0837	141
	CRONEBERGER, Robert B.	(412)622-3100	260
	DETLEFSEN, Ellen G.	(412)624-9444	296
	DOW, Elizabeth H.		315
	FIDOTEN, Robert E.	(412)963-8785	375
	GREEN, Joyce M.	(412)234-5039	462
	HLUHANY, Patricia	(412)364-3000	544
	HODGSON, Cynthia A.	(412)374-4816	546

GENERAL LIBRARY/INFORMATION CONSULTANT (Cont'd)
PENNSYLVANIA (Cont'd)

Pittsburgh	JOSEY, E J.	(412)624-9451	618
	KERCHOF, Kathryn K.	(412)434-6000	643
	KING, Mimi	(412)237-2593	652
	KRZYS, Richard A.	(412)624-9459	681
	MAZEFSKY, Gertrude T.	(412)361-7582	791
	MCCULLOCH, Elizabeth A.	(412)931-6931	801
	NASRI, William Z.	(412)276-3234	888
	PARADISE, Don M.	(412)929-9800	939
	PIETZAK, Stephen D.	(412)227-6839	972
	ROSEN, Gloria K.	(412)363-8423	1055
	SHAPERA, Gladys S.	(412)243-8723	1121
	VASILAKIS, Mary	(412)422-5694	1279
	WESSEL, Charles B.	(412)731-8800	1325
	WILLIAMS, James G.	(412)624-9418	1344
	WOODSWORTH, Anne		1367
	WOOLLS, Esther B.	(412)624-9435	1368
	WRIGHT, Nancy M.	(412)237-5948	1372
Reading	STILLMAN, Mary E.	(215)921-2381	1194
	WEIHERER, Patricia D.	(215)376-7660	1317
	YU, Lorraine L.	(215)374-4548	1384
Rosemont	LYNCH, Mary D.	(215)527-0200	752
Sanatoga	NIPPERT, Carolyn C.	(215)323-4829	904
Scranton	CAMPION, Carol M.	(717)348-0538	177
Shenandoah	USES, Ann K.	(717)462-0076	1270
Shippensburg	SHONTZ, Marilyn L.	(717)532-1472	1132
Slippery Rock	BACK, Andrew W.	(412)794-7817	43
Somerset	PLASO, Kathy A.	(814)445-6501	977
Springfield	MAIN, Annette Z.		761
State College	CARR, Caryn J.	(814)234-4203	185
	CHANG, Shirley L.	(717)893-2312	201
	LINDSAY, Ann M.	(814)237-0714	729
	MURPHY, Charles G.	(814)865-6621	880
	PIERCE, Miriam D.	(814)237-7004	971
Trafford	FETKOVICH, Malinda M.	(412)373-0799	374
University Park	CLINE, Nancy M.	(814)865-1858	222
	PASTER, Amy L.	(814)865-7056	946
	RICE, Patricia O.	(814)865-1858	1027
	SULZER, John H.	(814)865-4861	1209
Upland	BARON, Herman	(215)499-7415	58
Upper Darby	SILVERMAN, Karen S.	(215)734-0146	1138
	SILVERMAN, Scott H.	(215)734-0146	1138
Villanova	ERDT, Terrence	(215)645-4670	352
	GRIFFIN, Mary A.	(215)645-4290	468
	LEWIS, Marjorie B.		724
	WEINER, Betty	(215)688-6950	1318
Warminster	BECKER, Linda C.	(215)443-7008	72
Wayne	DRIEHAUS, Rosemary H.		320
Wescosville	FISLER, Charlotte D.	(215)395-6400	382
West Chester	AMICONE, Janice L.	(215)692-6889	20
	ASTORGA, Alicia M.	(215)793-2417	37
	DINNIMAN, Margo P.	(215)430-3080	305
	FIDISHUN, Dolores	(215)692-6806	375
West Point	MESSICK, Karen J.	(215)661-6026	828
Wyomissing	MORGANTI, Deena J.	(215)320-4849	864
Yardley	BARATTA, Maria	(215)321-3289	55

PUERTO RICO

Ensenada	MEJILL-VEGA, Gregorio	(809)821-4734	822
Guaynabo	LEON, Carmencita H.	(809)792-7873	716
Hato Rey	NEGRON-GAZTAMBIDE, Olguita	(809)767-4192	892
Hormiguerow	MARTINEZ-NAZARIO, Ronaldo		779
Miramar	MCCARTHY, Carmen H.	(908)721-6574	794
Ponce	PADUA, Flores N.	(809)844-4150	934
	SANTIAGO, Maria	(809)844-4150	1082
San Juan	HAMEL, Eleanor C.	(809)765-4426	491
	NADAL, Antonio	(809)724-6869	885
San Sebastian	JARAMILLO, Juana S.	(809)896-1389	594
Santurce	RIVERA-ALVAREZ, Miguel A.	(809)728-4191	1037

GENERAL LIBRARY/INFORMATION CONSULTANT (Cont'd)
RHODE ISLAND

Barrington	BUNDY, Annalee M.	(401)245-2232	157
Chepachet	DESJARLAIS-LUETH, Christine	(401)568-8614	295
Kingston	KRAUSSE, Sylvia C.	(401)789-6882	676
	SIITONEN, Leena M.	(401)792-2878	1137
	VOCINO, Michael C.	(401)789-9357	1286
Pawtucket	MILLS, Catherine H.	(401)728-9112	843
Portsmouth	AYLWARD, James F.	(401)683-1889	42
Providence	DOHERTY, Joseph H.	(401)865-2244	309
	FARK, Ronald K.	(401)941-0086	364
	LATHROP, Irene M.	(401)277-8070	701
	MARSH, Corrie V.	(401)863-2954	773
	RUSSELL, Elizabeth		1068
	SILVA, Phyllis C.	(401)277-2353	1138
	TAYLOR, Merrily E.	(401)863-2162	1227
Saunderstown	BRENNAN, Deborah B.	(401)294-3175	132
Warwick	BRYAN, Susan M.	(401)737-3300	152
Westerly	LIGHT, Karen M.	(401)596-2877	726

SOUTH CAROLINA

Aiken	CUBBEDGE, Frankie H.	(803)648-6851	262
Cayce	FREEMAN, Larry S.	(803)794-5370	401
Charleston	ROSS, Gary M.	(803)792-5530	1058
	SEAMAN, Sheila L.	(803)795-4416	1109
	WOOD, Richard J.	(803)763-8532	1365
Clemson	MCCULLEY, P M.	(803)654-8753	800
Columbia	BARRON, Daniel D.	(803)777-4825	60
	CALLAHAM, Betty E.	(803)772-3788	173
	EASTMAN, Caroline M.	(803)777-8103	333
	HOLLEY, E J.	(803)774-4866	551
	LAW, Aileen E.	(803)734-8666	704
	WARREN, Charles D.	(803)782-4219	1306
	WILLIAMS, Robert V.	(803)799-2324	1346
Glendale	WHITE, Ann T.	(803)579-3330	1330
Greenville	SCALES, Pat R.	(803)232-1271	1087
Greenwood	HILL, Thomas W.	(803)227-4851	541
Liberty	DUSENBERRY, Mary D.	(803)843-8225	329
Mountain Rest	CHANDLER, Dorothy S.	(803)638-2487	199
Orangeburg	WILLIAMS-JENKINS, Barbara J.	(803)536-7045	1347
Sumter	GORDON, Clara B.	(803)773-4041	451
Surfside Beach	KLEM, Marjorie R.	(803)238-0460	660
West Columbia	HARDIN, Sue H.	(803)791-5000	500

SOUTH DAKOTA

Aberdeen	LUGER, Mary J.	(605)622-2645	747
Rapid City	MC CAULEY, Philip F.	(605)348-5124	795
Sioux Falls	DUNGER, George A.	(605)336-6588	326
	OSTHUS, Mary J.	(605)336-3644	928
Vermillion	EDELEN, Joseph R.	(605)677-6082	335

TENNESSEE

Antioch	HAMLIN, Lisa K.	(615)833-7541	493
Brentwood	NORTON, Tedgina	(615)371-0090	910
Cleveland	NICOL, Jessie T.		902
Clinton	GREESON, Judy G.	(615)457-0931	465
	SPATH, Charles E.	(615)457-8616	1171
Cookeville	JONES, Roger G.	(615)526-5557	615
Dowelltown	EASTERLY, Ambrose	(615)597-1390	333
Gallatin	COLLIER, Virginia S.		232
Germantown	COOPER, Ellen R.	(901)755-7411	242
Harriman	OVERTON, Margaret C.		931
Kingsport	ERWIN, Mary J.	(615)378-5273	353
	PRESLAR, M G.	(615)229-6117	991
Knoxville	BEAL, Gretchen F.	(615)521-2500	68
	BEINTEMA, William J.	(615)974-4381	75
	HILL, Ruth J.	(615)974-4381	540
	JETT, Don W.	(615)922-2548	600
	KNIGHTLY, John J.	(615)691-7996	664
	MYERS, Marcia J.	(615)974-4465	884
	PEMBERTON, J M.	(615)690-5598	956
	PHILLIPS, Linda L.	(615)687-6734	968
	PONNAPPA, Biddanda P.	(615)675-4545	982
	PRENTICE, Ann E.	(615)974-2148	990
	RADER, Joe C.	(615)523-6937	1002
Maryville	WORLEY, Joan H.	(615)982-6412	1369

GENERAL LIBRARY/INFORMATION CONSULTANT (Cont'd)
TENNESSEE (Cont'd)

Memphis	BANNERMAN-WILLIAMS, Cheryl F.	(901)785-7350	54
	BOAZ, Ruth L.	(901)682-0595	108
	DRESCHER, Judith A.	(901)276-0104	319
	HALE, Relda D.		485
	LINDENFELD, Joseph F.	(901)528-6743	729
	MABBOTT, Deborah D.	(901)388-1096	753
	MARTIN, Jess A.	(901)528-5636	776
	MCDONELL, W E.	(901)278-0330	803
	POURCIAU, Lester J.	(901)454-2201	987
	RUDOLPH, N J.	(901)454-2208	1066
	SMITH, Robert F.	(901)725-8872	1160
Murfreesboro	CRAIG, James D.	(615)896-9097	254
Nashville	HODGES, Terence M.	(615)322-2299	546
	MARTIN, Laquita V.	(615)383-0953	777
	MOON, Fletcher F.	(615)833-1125	857
	PATTERSON, Jennifer J.	(615)383-4251	948
	SKELTON, William E.	(615)833-0195	1146
Oak Ridge	CARROLL, Bonnie C.	(615)482-3230	187
	DAVIS, Inez W.	(615)482-9619	279
	NORTON, Nancy P.	(615)574-7159	910
	VEACH, Lynn H.	(615)574-1240	1280
	YALCINTAS, Rana	(615)482-9397	1376
Sewanee	WATSON, Tom G.	(615)598-1213	1310

TEXAS

Abilene	DAHLSTROM, Joe F.		269
Alpine	SPEARS, Norman L.	(915)837-8121	1172
Amarillo	NEELEY, Dana M.	(806)354-5447	891
	SNELL, Marykay H.	(806)353-5329	1163
	WELLS, Mary K.	(806)381-2435	1322
Arlington	LOWRY, Charles B.	(817)273-3391	745
	MCCLURE, Margaret R.	(817)275-6594	797
	WILKERSON, Judith C.	(817)795-6555	1339
Austin	BIERI, Sandra J.	(512)458-5551	95
	BILLINGS, Harold W.	(512)442-8597	96
	DAVIS, Donald G.	(512)471-3821	278
	DAYO, Ayo	(512)472-8980	283
	GAMEZ, Juanita L.	(512)837-6247	416
	HARTNESS, Ann	(512)471-3818	508
	HISLE, W L.	(512)495-7148	544
	JACKSON, Ruth L.	(512)345-1653	588
	KAHLER, June	(512)463-9660	621
	MARTIN, Jean K.	(512)346-2973	776
	MIDDLETON, Robert K.	(512)454-1888	833
	MIKSA, Francis L.	(572)346-6769	834
	PARKER, David F.	(512)450-1931	941
	RODE, Shelley J.		1047
	ROY, Loriene	(512)471-6316	1063
	SEIDENBERG, Edward	(512)463-5459	1112
	SKINNER, Vicki F.	(512)892-3997	1146
Beaumont	POOL, Jeraldine B.	(409)753-3180	982
Bellaire	HOLAB-ABELMAN, Robin S.		550
Big Spring	BRADBERRY, Anna L.	(915)263-1468	125
Boerne	HANKS, Ellen T.	(512)249-9670	496
Brazoria	RASKA, Ginny	(409)798-1628	1009
Cleburne	CARDENAS, Martha L.	(817)641-6641	180
Conroe	BALDWIN, Joe M.	(409)756-4484	51
Corpus Christi	NEU, Margaret J.	(512)884-2011	896
Cypress	KUJOORY, Parvin	(713)890-7542	683
Dallas	ARMES, Patti	(214)341-6675	32
	BIRD, H C.	(214)553-5995	98
	CAMPBELL, Shirley A.	(214)330-0027	177
	CLEMENTS, Cynthia L.	(214)238-6153	221
	CRABB, Elizabeth A.	(214)233-4382	254
	CROW, Rebecca N.	(214)749-4285	261
	DOBSON, Christine B.	(214)746-3646	307
	EATENSON, Ervin T.	(214)521-4839	333
	EWUNES, Ernest L.	(214)376-4102	359
	FOUTS, Judith F.	(214)341-3961	393
	HAWLEY, Laurie J.	(214)907-2940	514
	JAGOE, Katherine P.	(214)931-8938	591
	KLEIN, Mindy F.	(214)701-4116	659
	LEVINE, Harriet L.	(214)521-7165	720
	MASON, Florence M.	(214)358-5755	781
	METIVIER, Donna M.	(214)701-4222	828
	MITCHE, Cynthia R.	(214)692-6767	848
	MITCHELL, Cynthia R.	(214)692-6767	848

GENERAL LIBRARY/INFORMATION CONSULTANT (Cont'd)
TEXAS (Cont'd)

Dallas			
	RYDESKY, Mary M.	(214)339-3349	1071
	SHAPLEY, Ellen M.	(214)692-6407	1122
	SMITH, Kraleen S.	(214)754-7985	1156
	SWEARINGEN, Wilba S.	(214)380-0731	1214
	UDENYL, Evelyn U.		1267
	WATERS, Richard L.	(214)826-6981	1308
	WETHERBEE, Louella V.	(214)750-6130	1327
	WHISENNAND, Cynthia S.	(214)253-1428	1329
Denton	CVELJO, Katherine	(817)565-2445	268
	GALLOWAY, Margaret E.	(817)565-3024	415
	SCHLESSINGER, Bernard S.	(817)898-2617	1094
	SHELDON, Brooke E.	(817)898-2602	1125
	TOTTEN, Herman L.	(817)383-1902	1252
El Paso	BROWN, Susan W.	(915)747-5678	147
	GOODMAN, Helen C.	(915)584-4509	449
	KNOTT, Teresa L.	(915)533-3020	665
	RAMSEY, Donna E.	(915)855-1218	1005
	TAYLOR, Anne E.	(915)757-5095	1226
Fort Worth	ALLMAND, Linda F.	(817)870-7709	17
	ARBELBIDE, Cindy L.	(817)877-3355	30
	ARD, Harold J.	(817)293-5474	31
	BRACEY, Ann E.	(817)738-9940	124
	CARTER, Bobby R.	(817)735-2380	189
	DE TONNANCOUR, P R.	(817)763-1790	296
	DUNCAN, Donna P.	(817)237-9828	325
	MACDONALD, Hugh	(817)921-7117	754
Fredericksburg	YOUNG, Marjie D.	(512)997-2253	1382
Freeport	TYLER-WHITE, Patricia G.		1266
Galveston	FREY, Emil F.	(409)761-2371	402
	RASCHE, Richard R.	(409)762-3139	1008
Garland	LARSON, Jeanette C.	(214)240-0661	699
	MURRAY, Margaret A.	(214)494-7192	882
Groves	MCCONNELL, Karen S.	(409)963-1481	797
Harlingen	CORBIN, John	(512)428-5475	245
Houston	BEDARD, Evelyn M.		73
	CARRINGTON, Samuel M.	(713)527-4022	186
	CARTER, Daniel H.	(713)665-5150	189
	CRENSHAW, Jan C.	(713)459-7116	258
	FIELDING, Raymond E.	(713)749-7444	376
	FLESHMAN, Nancy A.	(713)552-2000	384
	GIROUARD, J L.	(713)520-6835	438
	GOTHIA, Blanche	(713)266-5106	453
	HACKNEY, Judith G.	(713)496-5590	481
	HASKELL, Peter C.	(713)529-6681	510
	HENINGTON, David M.	(713)247-2700	528
	HOLIBAUGH, Ralph W.		550
	KIRTNER, R R.	(713)759-3535	655
	LYDERS, Josette A.	(713)728-3893	750
	MILES, Ruby A.	(713)522-4219	834
	MOORE, Guusje Z.	(713)680-0715	859
	PHILLIPS, Ray S.	(713)622-9686	969
	POWELL, Patricia K.	(713)488-5017	988
	RAMBO, Neil H.	(713)797-1230	1005
	REIFEL, Louie E.		1019
	SINCLAIR, Rose P.	(713)452-5555	1143
	WELCH, C B.	(713)749-4245	1321
Huntsville	THORNE, Bonnie B.		1242
Irving	LANKFORD, Mary D.	(214)579-7818	696
Katy	POWELL, Alan D.	(713)392-9340	987
Kilgore	CLAER, Joycelyn H.	(214)983-8238	215
Kingsville	MERCHANT, Cheryl N.	(512)592-9684	825
Leander	BIGLEY, John E.		96
Lubbock	CARGILL, Jennifer S.	(806)792-2349	181
	HARP, Marlene M.		503
	OLM, Jane G.	(806)742-3794	921
	WEBB, Gisela M.	(806)794-7359	1313
McAllen	MITTELSTAEDT, Gerard E.	(512)686-3029	850
McKinney	CORREDOR, Javier	(214)548-9971	247
	DOYLE, Patricia L.	(214)542-4461	317
Miles	LACY, Yvonne M.	(915)468-2151	687
Mineral Wells	CHESHER, Joyce A.	(817)325-7801	206
North Richland Hills	HALLAM, Arlita W.	(817)281-0041	489
Odessa	LINDSAY, Lorin H.	(915)367-2318	729
Palestine	SELWYN, Laurie	(214)723-1436	1114
Pharr	LIU, David T.	(512)787-1491	734
Plano	ANDERSON, Margaret	(214)424-2813	24
Prairie View	YEH, Helen S.	(409)857-3192	1379

GENERAL LIBRARY/INFORMATION CONSULTANT (Cont'd)
TEXAS (Cont'd)

Richardson	KRATZ, Abby R.	(214)690-2960	676
	SHEA, Kathleen	(214)690-2960	1124
Round Rock	RICKLEFS, Dale L.	(512)255-3939	1032
San Antonio	BELL, Joy A.	(512)496-2057	77
	HENRICKS, Duane E.	(512)436-3435	529
	HEWINS, Elizabeth H.	(512)655-4672	535
	HOLLOWAY, Geraldine B.	(512)531-3335	552
	HURT, Nancy S.	(512)225-5500	578
	MANEY, Lana E.	(512)496-7754	765
	PEDERSEN, Wayne A.	(512)641-4561	954
	TODD, Fred W.	(512)826-8121	1248
	WALLACE, James O.	(512)924-4338	1297
San Juan	SIEMENS, Bessie M.		1136
San Marcos	MEARS, William F.		820
Seguin	KOOPMAN, Frances A.	(512)379-4161	671
Sherman	GARCIA, Lana C.	(214)893-4401	417
Spring	ATRI, Pushkala V.	(713)370-3673	38
	RIEMANN, Frederick A.	(713)288-3960	1033
The Woodlands	FRAMEL, Phyllis M.	(713)367-9522	395
Waco	KEATTS, Rowena W.	(817)753-6415	633
	PHILLIPS, Luouida V.		968
Wichita Falls	ROBERTS, Ernest J.	(817)855-2390	1040

UTAH

Farmington	POLLARD, Louise	(801)451-5282	981
North Salt Lake	YANG, Basil P.	(801)295-0276	1377
Ogden	WILSON, Brenda J.	(801)479-1407	1350
Pleasant Grove	STECKER, Alexander T.	(801)785-2761	1183
St George	SHIRTS, Russell B.	(801)673-5895	1131
Salt Lake City	DAY, J D.	(801)363-5733	282
	HANSON, Roger K.	(801)581-8558	498
	HEYER, Terry L.	(801)321-1054	535
	HINDMARSH, Douglas P.	(801)328-2609	542
	MARCHANT, Cathy	(801)364-8399	768
	MCMURRIN, Jean A.	(801)322-1586	815
	OWEN, Amy	(801)466-5888	931

VERMONT

Bennington	PRICE, Michael L.	(802)442-9051	992
Milton	SEKERAK, Robert J.		1113
Montpelier	KLINCK, Patricia E.	(802)828-3265	661
Richmond	REIT, Janet W.	(802)482-2352	1022
St Johnsbury	BRYAN, Martin F.	(802)748-9264	151

VIRGIN ISLANDS

St Croix	VAUGHN, Robert V.	(809)778-8465	1280
St Thomas	CHANG, Henry C.	(809)774-3407	200
	MILLER, Veronica E.	(809)774-0059	843
	MILLS, Fiolina B.	(809)776-8396	844

VIRGINIA

Alexandria	BERGMAN, Rita F.	(703)836-5200	86
	DAVIDSON, Dero H.	(703)998-2976	276
	HARRISTON, Victoria R.	(203)642-5382	507
	JORDAN, Robert T.		617
	KUHL, Danuta	(703)461-0234	682
	OMARA, Marie T.	(703)960-3981	923
	OSIA, Ruby R.	(703)549-3048	928
	QUINN, Susan		1000
	ROSENBERG, Kenyon C.	(703)642-5480	1056
	SMITH, Thomas E.		1161
	STEIN, Karen E.	(703)354-3154	1185
	STEVENS, Roberta A.	(703)960-0464	1191
	WALDE, Norma J.	(703)642-4178	1294
Annandale	CHOBOT, Mary C.	(703)323-9402	210
	MATON, Joanne T.	(703)256-2288	784
Arlington	ARDEN, Caroline	(703)532-1548	31
	BETTS, Ardith M.	(703)524-8384	92
	CIPRIANI, Debra A.	(703)769-7736	215
	COSGROVE-DAVIES, Lisa A.	(703)536-9452	248
	GOLDBERG, Lisbeth S.	(703)243-0796	444
	HARRIS, Linda S.	(703)521-2541	505
	POEHLMAN, Dorothy J.		979
	PRICE, Joseph W.	(703)241-0447	992
	SAUR, Cindy S.	(703)379-2575	1085
	STARR, Marian U.	(703)237-0285	1182
	STEVENS, Frank A.		1190
	WELLS, Christine		1322

GENERAL LIBRARY/INFORMATION CONSULTANT (Cont'd)
VIRGINIA (Cont'd)

Blacksburg	KENNEY, Donald J.	(703)961-5069	641
Charlottesville	EVERINGHAM, Neil G.	(804)979-7151	358
	FRANKLIN, Robert D.	(804)973-3238	398
Chesapeake	FOREHAND, Margaret P.	(804)547-6579	390
	KERSTETTER, Virginia M.	(804)483-6544	644
	LEHMAN, Lois J.	(804)367-3709	713
	THOMAS, Nell M.		1238
Christiansburg	LINN, Cynthia S.	(703)961-5988	731
Dumfries	HOSKINS, Sylvia H.	(203)670-2885	561
Fairfax	FESSLER, Vera F.	(703)352-7200	374
	GOODWIN, Jane G.	(703)246-5847	450
	SCOTT, Mona L.	(703)378-8027	1107
Falls Church	HARRIS, Virginia B.	(703)698-6968	506
	REID, Judith A.	(703)379-0739	1018
Fort Monroe	BYRN, James H.	(804)727-4491	169
Fredericksburg	BULLEY, Joan S.	(703)899-1597	156
	HUGHES, J M.		571
	MULVANEY, John P.	(703)899-4666	878
Gloucester Point	BARRICK, Susan O.	(804)642-7114	59
Great Falls	CYLKE, Frank K.	(703)759-2031	268
Hampden Sydney	NORDEN, David J.	(804)223-4381	908
Hampton	LANKES, J B.	(804)722-7821	696
Harrisonburg	GILL, Gerald L.	(703)568-6898	435
	RAMSEY, Inez L.	(703)568-6791	1006
Herndon	GUERRIERO, Donald A.	(703)860-1058	476
	PAVEK, C C.	(703)481-0711	950
	SINWELL, Carol A.	(703)689-0086	1144
Lynchburg	YOUNGER, Melinda M.	(804)384-2369	1383
Manassas	CHRISTOLON, Blair B.	(703)369-3535	212
	KILLEEN, Erlene B.	(703)369-7193	648
McLean	ADAMS, Judith A.	(703)241-0973	5
	CHEVERIE, Joan F.	(703)893-3889	207
	GATTONE, Dean R.	(703)790-5694	422
	MORRISON, M C.	(703)356-1797	868
Mechanicsville	GEORGE, Melba R.	(804)798-5239	427
Melian	BELTON, Jennifer H.		78
Newport News	HAMMOND, Theresa M.	(804)595-8179	494
Norfolk	BREWER, Helen L.	(804)444-7951	134
	DUNCAN, Cynthia B.	(804)583-0903	325
	JONES-TRENT, Bernice R.	(804)632-8873	616
	NICULA, J G.	(804)444-5321	903
	SWAINE, Cynthia W.	(804)627-1115	1212
North Springfield	AINES, Andrew A.	(703)569-4872	8
Portsmouth	LIN, John T.	(804)484-2121	727
Reston	BROERING, Naomi C.	(703)860-1871	139
	LEWIS, Diane M.	(703)860-4475	723
	LISZEWSKI, Edward H.	(301)648-4306	733
	MCCLAIN, Deborah C.	(703)689-5194	795
	MONTGOMERY, Suzanne L.	(703)435-1974	856
Richmond	BAGAN, Beverly S.	(804)780-7691	45
	CARNEY, Marilyn L.	(804)254-2447	183
	GWIN, James E.	(804)288-7602	479
	JACOBY, Mary M.	(804)231-2545	590
	MIAH, Abdul J.	(804)786-5638	831
	ROSENBERG, Murray D.	(804)740-0019	1056
	SADLER, Graham H.	(804)222-1643	1073
	SNAIR, Dale S.	(804)786-1489	1162
	TROTTI, John B.	(804)358-8956	1258
	WARD, Brenda H.	(804)697-1200	1303
	WOODWARD, Elaine H.	(804)771-2219	1368
	YATES, Ella G	(804)786-2332	1378
	ZANG, Patricia J.	(804)226-5712	1386
Springfield	ALBIN, Michael W.	(703)978-3022	10
	FOURNIER, Susan K.	(703)569-9468	393
	GEHRINGER, Michael E.	(703)451-0334	425
	KANE, Astor V.	(703)487-4696	624
	LEONARD, Lawrence E.	(703)569-1541	716
	SCHAAF, Robert W.	(703)451-7916	1088
Triangle	GAUDET, Jean A.	(703)221-6434	422
Vienna	KUNEY, Joseph H.	(703)938-3889	684
Williamsburg	SCHEITLE, Janet M.	(804)220-3104	1091
Wise	BENKE, Robin P.	(703)328-2431	81
Woodbridge	ENGLAND, Ellen M.	(703)670-2191	349
	MELVIN, Kay H.	(703)491-2055	823

GENERAL LIBRARY/INFORMATION CONSULTANT (Cont'd)
WASHINGTON

Bainbridge Island	SPEARMAN, Marie A.	(206)842-6636	1172
Bellevue	SKELLEY, Cornelia A.	(206)747-6473	1145
	SMART, Doris M.	(206)822-8435	1151
Bellingham	GROVER, Iva S.	(206)671-3643	474
Blaine	BACON, Carey H.	(206)332-6045	44
Bothell	DECOSTER, Barbara L.	(206)488-7537	286
Bremerton	KANNEL, Selma	(206)377-3911	625
East Wenatchee	BELT, Jane		78
Edmonds	HALEY, Marguerite R.	(206)546-6561	486
	TURNER, Kathleen G.	(206)771-1933	1264
Kirkland	SUGGS, John K.	(206)823-6754	1206
Lacey	DEBUSE, Raymond	(206)491-7498	285
Marysville	WILSON, Evie		1350
Mercer Island	FIELDING, Carol J.	(206)232-8988	376
Mt Vernon	JONES, Sally L.	(206)428-6164	615
	SAUTER, Sylvia E.	(206)336-2604	1085
Newport	REMINGTON, David G.	(509)447-2636	1022
Oak Harbor	MERWINE, Glenda M.	(206)679-5807	827
Olympia	KREIMEYER, Vicki R.	(206)753-2916	677
	MOORE, Mary Y.	(206)866-8272	860
	SHAFFER, Maryann	(206)943-5001	1119
	ZUSSY, Nancy L.	(206)786-9647	1391
Pullman	FISHER, Rita C.	(509)335-2671	381
	MCCOOL, Donna L.	(509)335-4557	798
	ROBERTS, Elizabeth P.	(509)335-2671	1039
Richland	CARRIGAN, Marietta R.	(509)375-9671	186
Seattle	BOYLAN, Merle N.	(206)543-1760	123
	BRZUSTOWICZ, Richard J.	(206)527-9357	152
	BURKE, Vivienne C.	(206)522-0478	160
	CHASE, Dale L.	(206)525-0795	203
	CHISHOLM, Margaret	(206)543-1794	209
	EIPERT, Susan L.	(206)522-3174	340
	ERICKSON, Jane	(206)938-0846	352
	JENNERICH, Edward J.	(206)626-6320	598
	LEONARD, Gloria J.	(206)722-4828	716
	LOPEZ, Loretta K.	(206)526-1728	741
	MAACK, David J.	(206)527-1112	753
	MAIOLI, Jerry R.	(206)459-6518	762
	POLISHUK, Bernard	(206)524-8676	980
	SONG, Seungja Y.	(206)527-8737	1167
	STEERE, Paul J.	(206)367-0328	1184
	SY, Karen J.	(206)545-2873	1217
	TURNER, Tamara A.	(216)325-9481	1265
	WEAVER, Carolyn G.	(206)543-5530	1312
Seguim	DAVIES, Jo	(206)683-5229	277
Spokane	LANE, Steven P.	(509)838-4728	694
	WADDEN, Emily E.	(509)455-9555	1290
	WEBER, Joan L.	(509)489-6959	1314
Steilacoom	PARR, Loraine E.	(206)582-7557	943
Tacoma	BUELER, Roy D.	(206)593-6860	155
	HAGAN, Dalia L.	(206)565-9669	482
	MENANTEAUX, A R.	(206)591-2973	823
	RICIGLIANO, Lorraine M.		1031
	SELING, Kathy A.	(206)756-5571	1113
Vancouver	HUTTON, Emily A.	(206)695-1566	579
Yakima	JORDAN, Sharon L.	(509)248-4522	617

WEST VIRGINIA

Barboursville	DZIERZAK, Edward M.		331
Bluefield	DYE, Luella I.	(304)487-2037	330
Cross Lanes	COOPER, Candace S.	(304)776-5945	242
Fairmont	POWELL, Ruth A.	(304)367-4734	988
Glenville	VERMA, Prem V.	(304)462-5303	1282
Institute	SCOBELL, Elizabeth H.	(304)727-3314	1106
Philippi	SIZEMORE, William C.		1145
Spencer	RADER, H J.	(304)927-1770	1002
Welch	MULLER, William A.	(304)436-3070	877

WISCONSIN

Appleton	BAYORGEON, Mary M.	(414)738-2325	68
	PENNINGTON, Jerome G.	(414)735-6167	957
	VIGNOVICH, Ray L.	(414)735-1290	1284
Brookfield	CASEY, Jean M.	(414)781-2545	192
	CHRISTMAN, Inese R.	(414)786-6700	212
Cedarburg	PITEL, Vonna J.	(414)377-6030	976
Eau Claire	THOMPSON, Glenn J.	(715)836-5831	1239
Grafton	MORITZ, William D.	(414)377-6695	865

GENERAL LIBRARY/INFORMATION CONSULTANT (Cont'd)
WISCONSIN (Cont'd)

Janesville	HARFST, Linda L.	(608)754-3201	501
	KRUEGER, Karen J.	(608)755-2800	680
Kenosha	TRUPIANO, Rose M.	(414)553-2143	1259
La Crosse	ACCARDI, Joseph J.	(608)784-5755	3
	CIMPL, Kathleen A.	(608)785-0530	214
Madison	ANDERSON, Axel R.	(608)233-0659	21
	BUNGE, Charles A.	(608)263-2900	157
	CLARK, Peter W.	(608)257-4861	217
	DRESANG, Eliza T.	(608)267-9357	319
	GAPEN, D K.	(608)262-2600	416
	HOWDEN, Regis	(608)257-1023	565
	KRIKELAS, James	(608)263-2900	678
	LAESSIG, Joan M.	(608)238-3705	687
	MCCONNELL, Shirley M.	(608)274-7222	798
	ROBBINS, Jane B.	(608)263-2908	1038
	SORENSEN, Richard J.	(608)266-1924	1168
	WALKER, Richard D.	(608)257-5574	1296
	WILLIAMSON, William L.	(608)238-0770	1348
Marshfield	ZIMMERMANN, Albert J.	(715)387-2418	1389
Menasha	DIETZ, Kathryn A.	(414)725-3803	302
Menomonee Falls	SEUSS, Herbert J.	(414)251-7674	1117
Menomonie	JAX, John J.	(715)232-1184	595
	SAWIN, Philip Q.		1086
Mequon	MADSEN, Joyce	(414)242-5403	759
Middleton	ZWEIZIG, Douglas L.	(608)831-4364	1392
Milwaukee	AMAN, Mohammed M.	(414)239-4709	19
	BRENNEN, Patrick W.	(414)257-8323	133
	HORNUNG, Susan D.	(414)359-2111	560
	MCKINNEY, Venora	(414)278-3025	812
	MURPHY, Virginia A.	(414)271-1444	881
	REITMAN, Jo	(414)224-2376	1022
	SCHLUGE, Vicki L.	(414)527-8477	1094
	SHUTKIN, Sara A.	(414)332-3321	1134
	SMITH-GREENWOLD, Kathryn R.	(414)445-3586	1162
	ZIRBES, Colette M.	(414)483-1979	1390
Neenah	LAMB, Cheryl M.	(414)729-8169	689
New London	DIEHL, Carol L.	(414)982-5040	301
Oak Creek	TASNADI, Deborah L.	(414)764-9725	1224
Oshkosh	JONES, Norma L.	(414)231-5137	614
	PARKS, Dennis H.	(414)426-4800	943
Platteville	GERLACH, Donald E.	(608)348-6677	429
St Francis	WESTERN, Eric D.	(414)769-0110	1327
Sheboygan	CONDON, John J.	(414)458-8711	236
Stevens Point	SWIFT, Leonard W.	(715)346-1550	1216
Twin Lakes	OPEM, John D.	(414)877-9539	925
Verona	KNODLE, Shirley M.	(608)845-7180	665
Waukesha	ROOZEN, Nancy L.	(414)521-8868	1054
Wausau	ELDRED, Heather A.	(715)847-5535	342

WYOMING

Cheyenne	JOHNSON, Wayne H.	(307)777-7283	609
	MENDOZA, Anthanett C.	(307)778-8706	824
	RAO, Dittakavi N.	(307)777-7509	1008
	SCHELL, Catherine L.	(307)637-7504	1091
Rawlins	HOFF, Vickie J.	(307)324-7220	547
Sheridan	IVERSON, Deborah P.	(307)674-7797	585
Worland	HARRINGTON, Carolyn B.	(307)347-4490	504

CANADA

ALBERTA

Calgary	GOODMAN, Henry J.	(403)220-6296	449
	GUNSON, Murray J.	(403)256-7327	478
	LANE, Barbara K.	(403)283-9998	694
	LEESMENT, Helgi	(403)251-2221	712
	MACRAE, Lorne G.	(403)294-8538	758
Edmonton	COOKE, Geraldine A.	(403)439-5879	241
	HU, Shih S.	(403)436-9716	568
	JONES, David L.	(403)481-3209	612
	JORDAN, Peter A.	(403)469-9473	616
	LAVKULICH, Joanne	(403)427-3530	704
	LOVENBURG, Susan L.	(403)435-0176	743
	RICHARDS, Vincent P.	(403)429-9814	1029
	STARR, Lea K.	(403)432-5154	1182
Red Deer	GISHLER, John R.	(304)340-3922	438
Sherwood Pk	NOGA, Dolores A.	(403)467-4003	907
	SCHMIDT, Raymond J.	(403)464-8234	1095

GENERAL LIBRARY/INFORMATION CONSULTANT (Cont'd)
ALBERTA (Cont'd)

Strathmore	LUNN, Rowena F.	(403)934-5334	749
Tofield	LEE, Diana W.	(403)662-3607	709

BRITISH COLUMBIA

Abbotsford	HARRIS, Winifred E.	(604)853-7441	506
Burnaby	GOW, Susan P.	(604)439-0931	454
Clearbrook	HUDSON, Susan P.	(604)859-7814	570
	SEARCY HOWARD, Linda M.	(604)859-7814	1109
	VIIERANS, Mary E.	(604)859-7814	1284
Cranbrook	WHITELEY, Catherine M.	(604)489-2751	1333
Kamloops	LEVESQUE, Nancy B.	(604)374-0123	719
Prince George	MAYFIELD, Betty L.	(604)562-1929	790
Richmond	ELLIS, Kathy M.	(604)272-5389	344
Vancouver	BROOME, Diana M.	(604)684-5986	141
	HAYCOCK, Kenneth R.	(604)731-1131	515
	PEPPER, David A.	(604)664-4311	958
	ROBERTSON, Guy M.	(604)689-8494	1041
	STUART-STUBBS, Basil F.	(604)731-1978	1204
	WARREN, Lois M.	(604)687-1072	1306
Victoria	VAN REENEN, Johannes A.	(604)595-9612	1277

MANITOBA

Winnipeg	BROWN, Gerald R.	(204)772-2474	144
	BUDNICK, Carol	(204)474-9844	155
	FAWCETT, Patrick J.	(204)474-9908	367
	FOWLER, Margaret A.	(204)884-6593	394
	REEDMAN, M R.	(204)983-3437	1015
	TULLY, Sharon I.	(204)474-9844	1262

NEW BRUNSWICK

Moncton	AMIS, Terence K.	(506)372-4717	20

NEWFOUNDLAND

St John's	WOOD, Alberta A.	(709)753-3805	1363

NORTHWEST TERRITORIES

Yellowknife	O'KEEFE, Kevin T.	(403)873-5715	919

NOVA SCOTIA

Amherst	CAMPBELL, Margaret E.	(902)667-2888	177
Cleveland	MACRURY, Mary E.	(902)625-1016	758
Halifax	DYKSTRA, Mary E.	(902)424-3656	331
	HUANG, Paul T.	(902)454-5911	568
Sydney	MACINTOSH, Ian R.	(902)562-1115	755

ONTARIO

Cambridge	SKELTON, W M.	(519)621-0460	1146
Don Mills	FAIRLEY, Craig R.	(416)447-5336	361
	TEMPLIN, Dorothy	(416)447-2380	1231
Downsview	BERNSTEIN, Elaine S.	(416)638-1962	89
	JONES, B E.	(416)244-3621	611
	KATZ, Bernard M.	(416)638-7695	630
Exeter	WILCOX, Linda M.	(519)235-2700	1338
Fort Erie	PORTEUS, Andrew C.	(416)871-3814	985
Gloucester	KENT, Charles D.		642
Gormley	RHYDWEN, David A.	(416)887-9552	1026
Guelph	PAWLEY, Carolyn P.	(519)824-4120	951
Hamilton	FLEMMING, Tom	(416)525-9140	384
Kingston	FORKES, David	(613)544-2630	390
London	LIN, Louise	(519)439-3271	727
	RUTHERFORD, Frederick S.	(519)471-4867	1070
Markham	MORTON, Robert E.	(416)475-0525	870
Mississauga	DINEEN, Diane M.	(416)279-7002	304
	WEI, Carl K.	(416)822-4111	1316
North Bay	NORRGARD, Don K.	(705)474-3332	909
North York	HEATON, Gwynneth T.	(416)225-4859	519
	MURDOCH, Arthur W.	(416)221-1795	879
Ottawa	BLACK, Jane L.	(613)234-5006	101
	CAMPBELL, Laurie G.	(613)596-9797	177
	COONEY, Jane	(613)232-9625	241
	DURANCE, Cynthia J.	(613)728-8763	328
	DUSSIAUME, Robert	(613)234-2824	329
	GUILBERT, Manon M.	(613)233-8012	476
	JESKE, Margo	(613)995-1118	600
	KANNEL, Ene	(819)994-7966	625
	KIRKWOOD, Francis T.	(613)233-7592	655
	KNOPPERS, Jake V.		665
	MACDONALD, Marcia H.	(819)994-6947	754

GENERAL LIBRARY/INFORMATION CONSULTANT (Cont'd)
ONTARIO (Cont'd)

Ottawa

	MCCALLUM, David L.	(613)237-4586	793
	SCHRYER, Michel J.	(819)994-6827	1100
	SPICER, Erik J.	(613)995-1166	1174
	VEEKEN, Mary L.	(613)523-2169	1280
Scarborough	BALL, John L.	(416)284-3245	52
	BASSNETT, Peter J.	(416)298-0614	63
Sudbury	GOSS, Alison M.	(705)522-2883	453
Thunder Bay	HSU, Peter T.	(807)623-2794	567
Toronto	BAYNE, Jennifer M.	(416)595-3429	67
	BEAUMONT, Jane	(416)922-9364	70
	BOITE, Mary E.	(416)461-2274	111
	DAVEY, Dorothy M.	(416)485-0377	276
	DAVIDSON-ARNOTT, Frances E.	(416)486-6488	277
	DENIS, Laurent G.	(416)978-3111	292
	DYSART, Jane I.	(416)974-2780	331
	GIBSON, Elizabeth A.	(416)595-7894	432
	GOLD, Sandra	(416)782-7236	444
	GREENWOOD, Jan	(416)963-9383	465
	HARRISON, Karen A.	(416)462-1550	507
	HAYES, Janice E.	(416)480-7545	516
	JOHNSON, John E.	(416)423-6979	606
	KENDALL, Sandra A.		640
	KLEMENT, Susan P.	(416)486-0239	660
	LAND, Reginald B.	(416)965-3742	692
	LORENTOWICZ, Genia	(416)393-7018	741
	LOUET, Sandra	(416)965-6319	742
	MCCANN, Judith B.	(416)429-1247	794
	MERILEES, Bobbie	(416)485-4177	826
	MOORE, Carole I.	(416)978-2292	858
	MOORE, Lawrence A.	(416)363-3388	860
	MOORE, May E.	(416)787-4988	860
	NORTH, John A.	(416)979-5142	909
	ODHO, Marc	(416)596-2682	917
	PARKER, Arthur D.	(416)967-5525	941
	SELLERS, Alexander G.	(416)489-4908	1114
	SMITH, Anne C.	(416)423-9826	1152
	WEIHS, Jean	(416)961-6027	1317
	WILKINSON, John P.	(416)978-3167	1340
	WONG, Lusi	(416)922-5100	1363
Waterloo	BECKMAN, Margaret L.	(519)824-4120	73
Whitby	LINTON, Linda J.	(416)831-6265	731
Willowdale	MCLEAN, Paulette A.	(416)636-4877	814
Windsor	SINGLETON, Cynthia B.	(519)253-4232	1143

QUEBEC

Baie d'Urfe	KLOK, Buddhi	(514)457-2757	662
Beaconsfield	HIRON, Barbara A.	(514)695-3200	543
Bellefeuille	DANIS, Rolland J.	(514)432-6116	273
Boucherville	DUVAL, Marc	(514)655-3709	329
	NADEAU, Johan	(514)655-4858	885
	THERIAULT, Carmelle	(514)655-2665	1234
Chambly	ASSUNCAO, Isabel	(514)658-3882	37
Chicoutimi	GAUDREAU, Louis	(418)549-9520	422
Gatineau	ST. AMANT, Robert	(819)561-4988	1075
Hull	CHENIER, Andre	(819)595-3810	206
	CHEVRIER, Francine	(819)777-4341	207
	DUHAMEL, Louis	(819)771-4453	324
Jonquiere	HARVEY, Serge	(418)548-7821	509
Laval	SHANEFIELD, Irene D.	(514)688-9550	1120
	TESSIER, Mario C.	(514)669-7878	1233
Laval-des-Rapides	VONKA, Stephanie	(514)667-1947	1288
Montreal	APPLEBY, Judith A.	(514)848-7759	30
	BERNHARD, Paulette	(514)343-7408	89
	BRESING, Sheindel H.	(514)483-2121	133
	BUTLER, Patricia	(514)283-9046	167
	CHALIFOUX, Jean P.	(514)285-7007	197
	CLARKE, Robert F.	(514)731-9211	219
	CORBEIL, Lizette	(514)332-9854	245
	COURTEMANCHE, Pierre O.		251
	CRAWFORD, David S.	(514)398-4723	256
	CURRAN, William M.	(514)392-4939	266
	DARBON, Ginette	(514)343-7687	274
	DAUNAIS, Marie J.	(514)633-4170	275
	DUCHESNEAU, Pierre	(514)281-6166	322
	DUSABLON-BOTTEGA, Nicole	(514)871-6442	329

GENERAL LIBRARY/INFORMATION CONSULTANT (Cont'd)
QUEBEC (Cont'd)

Montreal

	FOWLES, Alison C.	(514)842-7680	394
	GARDNER, Lucie	(514)845-7814	418
	GONZALEZ, Paloma	(514)735-1977	448
	HOWARD, Helen A.	(514)933-0893	564
	JOBA, Judith C.	(514)489-0117	601
	LALONDE, Diane	(514)767-3490	689
	LEIDE, John E.	(514)398-4204	713
	MARCIL, Louise	(514)333-6621	769
	MCINTOSH, Julia E.	(514)283-3639	809
	NAGY, Cecile		886
	PICARD, Albert	(514)276-5797	970
	PIGGOTT, Sylvia E.	(514)877-9383	972
	RABCHUK, Gordon K.	(514)874-2104	1001
	ROBINSON, Chantal	(514)873-2997	1043
	SYKES, Stephanie L.	(514)870-7088	1217
	WALUZYNIEC, Hanna	(514)398-4759	1302
Outremont	LACROIX, Yvon A.	(514)273-7423	687
Quebec	BERNIER, Gaston	(418)643-4032	89
	CYR, Solange	(418)643-7095	268
St-Bruno	LECOMPTE, Louis L.	(514)653-7290	708
St-Janvier	GRITZKA, Gerda M.	(514)437-3400	471
St Laurent D'Orleans	SIMON, Marie L.	(514)744-7315	1140
Sainte-Foy	AUGER, Claudette	(418)654-4676	39
	FLORIAN, Trudel	(418)652-2210	385
	PETRYK, Louise O.	(418)656-6921	965
Sherbrooke	CHASSE, Jules	(819)821-7550	203
	CHOUINARD, Germain	(819)564-5297	211
	GOODFELLOW, Marjorie E.	(819)562-1694	448
Ste Anne de Bellevue	DOUGLAS-BONNELL, Eileen	(514)457-9487	314
	GRAINGER, Bruce	(514)398-7879	457
Touraine	MURRAY-LACHAPELLE, Rosemary F.	(819)568-0282	882
Val D'Or	MARCHAND, Jacques	(819)825-4670	768
Verdun	DIMITRESCU, Ioana	(514)765-8219	304
Westmount	LEDOUX, Marc A.	(514)484-5951	708
	WADE, C A.		1290

SASKATCHEWAN

Regina	BALON, Brett J.	(306)586-1990	53
	BASLER, Ellen L.	(306)949-5431	63
	MACK, A Y.	(306)543-6981	756
	POGUE, Basil G.	(306)586-6846	979
	TURNBULL, Keith	(306)757-8915	1264
	VOHRA, Pran	(306)787-4321	1287
Saskatoon	CAMERON, Bruce	(306)684-1648	174
	HAMMEL, Philip J.	(306)966-7657	493

AUSTRALIA

Brisbane	COCHRANE, Thomas G.	226
Canberra	STEELE, Colin R.	1184
Kensington	RAYWARD, W B.	1011
Marrickville	TILLOTSON, Greig S.	1245
Queensland	GOODELL, John S.	448
Turramurra	WILKINSON, Eoin H.	1340
Victoria	SMITH, Lindsay L.	1157

BAHAMAS

Grand Bahamas Island	BARTON, Barbara I.	61

BAHRAIN

Al Manamah	ALI, Syed N.	13

BELGIUM

Brussels	VAN SLYPE, Georges	1277
Kraainem	WALCKIERS, Marc A.	1293

COSTA RICA

San Jose	CROWTHER, Warren W.	262

EGYPT

Giza	MAHOUD ALY, Usama E.	761

GENERAL LIBRARY/INFORMATION CONSULTANT (Cont'd)

ENGLAND
Harrogate	LINE, Maurice B.	730
Letchworth Herts	AITCHISON, Thomas M.	9
London	BUNCE, George D.	157
Reading	WOODWARD, Anthony M.	1367
Warwickshire	CHANDLER, George	200

FEDERAL REPUBLIC OF CHINA
Taipei	CHOU, Nancy O.	210
	HU, James S.	567
	LEE, Lucy T.	710

FEDERAL REPUBLIC OF GERMANY
Bonn	LOTZ, Rainer E.	742
Bremen	MORRISON, J M.	868

FRANCE
Guyancourt	COURRIER, Yves G.	251
Paris	CHAUMIER, Jacques	204
	DEROODE, Clifford H.	294
	GRATTAN, Robert	458
	ROBERTS, Kenneth H.	1040
	STONE, Toby G.	1197
	WACHTER, Margery C.	1290

HONG KONG
Kowloon	POON, Paul W.	983

HUNGARY
Budapest	LAZAR, Peter	706

INDIA
Hyderabad	SATYANARAYANA, Vadhri V. ..... (260)586-0000	1084

INDONESIA
Jakarta	ADITIRTO, Irma U.	6
	STONE, Clarence W.	1197

IRELAND
Dublin	ASTON, Jennefer	37
	SLINEY, Marjory T.	1149

ISRAEL
Haifa	BLOCH, Uri	105
Jerusalem	BORCK, Liba	116

ITALY
Milan	FABRE DE MORLHON, Christiane	360
Rome	JOLING, Carole G.	610
	MENOU, Michel J.	824

JAMAICA
Kingston	DOUGLAS, Daphne R.	314
	MANSINGH, Laxmi ..... (809)927-2748	767

JAPAN
Chiba-ken	NASU, Yukio	889
Tokyo	HOSONO, Kimio	562
	KAWASHIMA, Hiroko	632
	URATA, Kazuo ..... (034)331-1110	1269
	YAMAZAKI, Hisamichi	1377
Tokyo 105	YAMAKAWA, Takashi	1376

KUWAIT
Khalidiah	HAMDY, Mohamed N.	491
Salmiyah	ABDEL-MOTEY, Yaser Y.	2

MEXICO
Naucalpan	OROZCO-TENORIO, Jose M.	926

NETHERLANDS
Amersfoort	VAN HALM, Johan	1275
The Haag	RAITT, David I. ..... (311)719-8301	1004

NIGERIA
Akure	ONONOGBO, Raphael U.	924
Ogbomoso	OKPARA, Ibiba M.	920

GENERAL LIBRARY/INFORMATION CONSULTANT (Cont'd)

NORTHERN IRELAND
Belfast	LINTON, William D.	731

PHILIPPINES
Manila	COOK, Marjorie L.	240

POLAND
Poznan	CHOJNACKA, Jadwiga	210

SAUDI ARABIA
Jeddah	KHAN, Mohammed A.	646
Riyadh	ALI, Farooq M. ..... (467)615-7000	13
	BUTT, Abdul W.	167
	KIRKWOOD, Brenda S.	655
	MARTIN, Nannette	777

SOUTH AFRICA
Belhar Cape Province	SEPTEMBER, Peter E.	1115

SOUTH KOREA
Seoul	KIM, Soon C.	649

SPAIN
Barcelona	VELA, Leonor G.	1281

SWEDEN
Jarfalla	SHELTON, Anita L.	1126

SWITZERLAND
Geneva	OHLMAN, Herbert	919

TRINIDAD
Valsayn	NANTON-COMISSIONG, Barbara L.	887

UGANDA
Mukono	MUKUNGU, Frederick N.	876

ZAMBIA
Chilanga	LUMANDE, Edward	748

INDEXER

ALABAMA
Auburn	NELSON, Barbara K.	(205)826-4500	893
	STRAITON, T H.	(205)826-4500	1199
Birmingham	LAUGHLIN, Steven G.	(205)934-2379	703
	VENABLE, Douglas R.	(205)871-3318	1282
Maxwell AFB	GOODMAN, Anita S.	(205)293-2504	449
	HARPER, Marie F.	(205)293-5042	503
Mobile	SHEARER, Barbara S.	(205)471-7855	1124
Montevallo	WILLIAMS, Pauline C.	(205)665-4329	1346
Montgomery	ADAMS, Emily J.	(205)293-7691	4
	BEST, Rickey D.	(205)244-9212	92
	FRANKS, Janice	(205)271-6277	398
	MCCRANK, Lawrence J.	(205)244-9202	800
Oneonta	WEAVER, Clifton W.	(205)274-9111	1312

ALASKA
Anchorage	BRAUND-ALLEN, Julianna E.	(907)243-5947	130
	LESH, Nancy L.	(907)786-1877	718
	LUDWIG, J D.	(907)333-8917	746
	PIERCE, Linda I.	(907)338-6421	971
Fairbanks	GALBRAITH, William B.	(907)479-5196	413
	LAKE, Gretchen L.	(907)452-6751	688
	PINNELL-STEPHENS, June A.	(907)479-5826	975

ARIZONA
Chandler	VATHIS, Alma C.	(602)899-7147	1279
Flagstaff	BAUM, Ester B.	(602)774-8878	66
	JOHNSON, Harlan R.	(602)523-4408	605
Kingman	BURNHAM-KIDWELL, Debbie	(602)565-3796	162
Phoenix	MEYERS, Kathleen H.	(602)262-8667	831
Scottsdale	FERRALL, J E.	(602)965-5167	373

INDEXER (Cont'd)
ARIZONA (Cont'd)

Tucson	CAMPBELL, Dierdre A.	(602)621-7897	176
	CARTER, Judith A.		189
	ETTER, Patricia A.	(602)299-5199	355
	MARSHALL, Thomas H.	(602)621-6452	775
	MCCRAY, Jeanette C.	(602)626-6143	800
	MILLS, Victoria A.	(602)795-5299	844
	MYERS, Roger	(602)792-3452	885
	RULE, Amy E.	(602)621-6273	1067
	WILLIAMS, Karen B.	(602)621-4866	1344
	WOLF, Noel C.	(602)746-7637	1360

ARKANSAS

Conway	GREEN, Douglas A.	(501)327-5611	461
Fayetteville	MCKEE, Elizabeth C.	(501)442-5002	810
	SHANE, Charlotte J.	(501)521-8657	1120
Searcy	BEARD, Craig W.	(501)268-6161	69

CALIFORNIA

Alhambra	PORTILLA, Teresa M.		985
Bakersfield	COOPER, William E.	(805)861-2136	244
	WINTER, Eugenia C.	(805)833-3175	1356
Berkeley	BROWNRIGG, Edwin B.		149
	FISHER, Leslie R.	(415)548-3542	381
	GOLDMAN, Nancy L.	(415)642-0366	445
	HUMPHREYS, Nancy K.	(415)642-4786	574
	PARKS, Mary L.	(415)644-3401	943
	RIGGS, Judith M.	(415)654-2809	1034
	VANYOUNG, Sayre	(415)848-2229	1278
	WOODBURY, Marda	(415)654-4810	1366
	ZBORAY, Ronald J.		1386
Burbank	BROWNE, Jeri A.	(818)953-8770	148
Canyon Country	CRUM, Norman J.	(805)252-9053	262
Carmichael	O'NEILL, Diane J.	(916)965-0935	924
Carson	KENNY-SLOAN, Linda		642
Cerritos	ZEIDLER, Patricia L.	(213)926-1101	1387
Chula Vista	GAGNON, Donna M.	(619)426-4527	412
Concord	REYES, Helen M.	(415)000-0000	1024
Culver City	ANDRADE, Rebecca	(213)837-5448	26
	KIRBY, Barbara L.	(213)839-1009	653
	PATTEN, Frederick W.	(213)827-3335	947
Davis	JESTES, Edward C.	(916)752-0519	600
	KNOWLES, Em C.	(916)752-1126	665
	ROBINSON, Betty J.	(916)756-2187	1043
	TEBO, Jay D.	(916)758-8256	1229
Del Mar	HOLLEMAN, Marian P.	(619)755-4253	551
Dobbins	LE DORR, Lillian E.	(916)692-1659	708
East Palo Alto	FROST, Michelle	(415)321-4017	406
El Cerrito	MACAULEY, C C.	(415)524-2762	754
Emeryville	POKLAR, Mary J.	(415)420-1346	980
Encino	GHAZARIAN, Salpi H.	(818)789-5041	430
Foster City	LEE, Doreen H.	(415)345-5292	709
FPO San Francisco	HADLEY, Alice E.	(671)344-9250	482
Fremont	DIBLE, Joan B.	(415)792-8736	299
Fullerton	MASTERS, Robin J.	(714)524-9696	782
	STEPHENSON, Shirley E.	(714)773-3580	1189
Garden Grove	HIXON, Donald L.	(714)638-9379	544
Hayward	ARROWOOD, Donna J.	(415)881-2791	34
Huntington Beach	MACKINTOSH, Mary L.	(714)896-4639	757
Irvine	HORN, Judy K.		559
	JUNG, Soon J.	(714)730-8133	620
	TSANG, Daniel C.	(714)856-4978	1260
	WEINTRAUB, D K.	(714)856-6079	1318
Isla Vista	GALLERY, M C.	(805)968-6842	414
Jamul	SERDZIAK, Edward J.	(619)426-2253	1116
Kensington	MULVANY, Nancy	(415)524-4498	878
La Jolla	BRIDGMAN, Amy R.	(619)587-1306	135
Lake View Terrace	TASHIMA, Marie		1224
Livermore	LOVE, Sandra R.	(415)422-7310	743
Long Beach	ADAMS, Linda L.	(213)590-7639	5
	BENSON-TALLEY, Lois I.	(213)494-7817	83
	SINCLAIR, Lorelei P.	(213)423-6399	1142
Los Altos	FILES, Patricia T.		376
Los Angeles	BENNION, Bruce C.	(213)743-2118	82
	CAMPBELL, Bill W.	(213)398-8992	176
	DONALDSON, Maryanne T.	(213)617-7070	311
	ELLISON, Bettye H.	(213)666-5433	345
	ENYINGI, Peter	(213)629-3531	351
	GINSBURG, Helen W.	(213)485-5400	438

INDEXER (Cont'd)
CALIFORNIA (Cont'd)

Los Angeles	GLITZ, Beryl	(213)206-8016	441
	HASSAN, Abe H.	(213)649-2846	511
	HOFFMAN, Irene M.	(213)839-5722	548
	KACZOROWSKI, Monice M.	(213)485-1234	621
	KIM, Joy H.	(213)337-0794	649
	MICHEL, Dee A.	(213)478-7660	832
	PASCAL, Barbara R.	(213)934-2205	945
	REYNOLDS, Diane C.	(213)629-3531	1025
	SATER, Analya	(213)277-1969	1083
	STERNHEIM, Karen	(213)825-3047	1189
	SVENONIUS, Elaine	(213)825-4352	1212
	THOMPSON, Don K.	(213)743-2540	1239
	TREISTER, Cyril C.	(213)227-1604	1255
	TROTTA, Victoria K.	(213)743-6487	1258
Los Gatos	BAILEY, Rolene M.	(408)356-9645	46
Montclair	CARRIGAN, John L.	(714)621-5225	186
Monterey	SPINKS, Paul	(408)646-2341	1175
Mountain View	SPIGAI, Fran	(415)961-2880	1174
Napa	CHAMBERLIN, Leslie A.	(707)253-1071	198
Northridge	DURAN, Karin J.	(818)885-2501	328
Novato	HOTZ, Sharon M.	(415)892-0821	562
Oakland	NEWCOMBE, Barbara T.	(415)763-4406	898
Orange	LA BORDE, Charlotte A.	(714)385-4454	686
Palo Alto	KAHN, Paul J.	(415)327-3135	622
	LEE, Judith C.	(415)494-0395	710
	MAIN, Linda Y.	(415)328-4865	761
	THOMAS, Vivian	(415)324-3739	1238
	TRIMBLE, Kathy W.	(415)855-5493	1256
	VARKENTINE, Aganita	(415)493-8853	1278
Pasadena	POSTER, Susan E.	(818)398-8897	986
	WONG, Maida L.	(818)795-1255	1363
Pinole	YANEZ, Elva K.	(415)724-2914	1377
Pleasant Hill	FOWELLS, Fumi T.	(415)689-0754	393
Pomona	ADAMSON, Danette	(714)869-3109	6
	STREETER, David	(714)620-2026	1201
Poway	DOLLEN, Charles J.	(619)748-5348	310
Rancho Palos Verdes	KATTLOVE, Rose W.	(213)544-0061	630
Redondo Beach	CASTONGUAY, Russell	(213)372-6281	194
Redwood City	SCHLACHTER, Gail A.	(415)594-0743	1093
Ridgecrest	FRIEDMAN, Sandra M.	(619)375-8825	404
Sacramento	KAST, Gloria E.	(916)483-6765	629
	MARTINEZ, Barbara A.	(916)429-1107	779
	SEHR, Dena P.	(916)453-3529	1112
Salinas	COLLINS, Judith A.		232
San Anselmo	LEACH, Elizabeth A.	(415)485-5571	706
San Diego	ELLIOTT, Valerie E.	(619)224-2911	344
	JACOBS, Horace	(619)746-4005	589
San Francisco	CANTER, Judy A.	(415)777-7845	179
	COLALILLO, Robert M.	(415)664-2264	230
	CONLEY, Linda A.	(415)285-6835	236
	DURSO, Angeline M.	(415)750-6072	329
	GIBSON, Harold R.		432
	GRIFFIN, Michael D.	(415)664-2835	468
	LEWANDOWSKI, Joseph J.	(415)626-3755	722
	LONDON, Glenn S.	(415)928-4277	738
	REGNER-HYATT, Anne L.	(415)864-1154	1017
	ROOS, Barbara J.	(415)567-0460	1053
	SCHMIDT, Robert R.	(415)821-7762	1096
	SEGUNDO, Fe P.	(415)586-6333	1112
San Jose	HARMON, Robert B.	(408)297-2810	502
	JESSUP, Carrie	(408)629-3403	600
	MULLEN, Cecilia P.	(408)265-8799	877
	RODICH, Lorraine E.	(408)277-9788	1047
San Marino	ZALL, Elisabeth W.	(818)405-2188	1386
San Pedro	SPRUNG, Lori L.	(213)832-0593	1176
Santa Ana	AUSTIN, Stephen	(714)540-9870	40
	HOFFMAN, Herbert H.	(714)667-3451	548
Santa Barbara	KINNELL, Susan K.	(805)965-1294	653
	MAHAFFEY, Susan M.	(805)964-4978	760
Santa Clara	HAMBRIDGE, Sally L.	(408)378-8616	491
Santa Cruz	LOMBARDI, Mary L.	(408)476-1131	738
	MARIE, Jacquelyn	(408)429-2802	770
Santa Monica	DIRLAM, Dona M.	(213)452-1897	305
	WITTMANN, Cecelia V.	(213)454-8300	1358
Sherman Oaks	KYROPOULOS, Mary S.	(818)789-6022	685
Sierra Madre	KNUDSEN, Helen Z.		666

INDEXER (Cont'd)
CALIFORNIA (Cont'd)

Sun Valley	VOTAW, Floyd M.	(818)909-5634	1289
Thousand Oaks	HOCKEL, Kathleen N.		545
Turlock	PARKER, John C.	(209)634-9473	942
Ukiah	FELDMAN, Irwin	(707)468-8163	369
	LINDHEIMER, Elinor	(707)468-0464	729
Van Nuys	BALABAN, Robin M.	(818)781-6952	50
	LEE, Lydia H.	(818)989-6433	710
Westlake Village	TISE, Barbara L.	(818)991-0047	1247
Whittier	RODRIGUEZ, Ronald	(213)693-0585	1048
Woodland Hills	NELSON-HARB, Sally R.		895

COLORADO

Aurora	HARRIS, Michael A.	(303)694-4200	505
	MOOMEY, Margaret M.	(303)690-1478	857
Boulder	CARTER, Nancy F.	(303)492-3928	189
	PORPA, Edythe C.	(303)442-2847	984
Colorado Springs	GREEN, Nancy W.	(303)591-1177	462
Denver	GILBERT, Ruth E.	(303)757-3622	434
	INGUI, Bettejean	(303)394-5158	583
	KAVANAGH, Janette R.	(303)777-8971	631
	LUEVANE, Marsha A.	(303)989-1036	747
Englewood	BRUNTON, David W.	(303)771-3197	151
	OTTOSON, Robin D.	(303)761-2482	930
Fort Collins	LINDGREN, William F.	(303)484-4432	729
	NEWMAN, John	(303)491-1844	899
Greeley	SCHULZE, Suzanne S.		1102
Lamar	BURNETT, James H.	(303)336-4632	161
Littleton	ALSOP, Robyn J.	(303)779-1925	18
	HALLER, Robin M.	(303)220-1031	489
	SPANGLER, Bruce	(303)797-1300	1171
	SZABO, Kathleen S.	(303)796-9718	1218
	WHITBY, Thomas J.	(303)798-7049	1330

CONNECTICUT

Avon	BLOTNER, Linda S.	(203)677-0286	106
Bristol	SENKUS, Linda J.	(203)589-1298	1115
Brookfield	SLONE, Eugenia F.	(203)775-4583	1150
Collinsville	EICKENHORST, Joanna W.	(203)693-4315	339
East Canaan	BYERS, Laura T.	(203)824-5971	168
East Hartford	SIROIS, Valerie M.	(203)565-7121	1144
Farmington	DEVINE, Marie E.	(203)677-2140	297
	LEVINE, Marion H.	(203)679-3323	720
Hamden	FERNANDEZ, Nenita	(203)562-1756	373
Hartford	SHORE, Julia M.	(203)537-4910	1132
	WAIT, Gary E.	(236)236-5621	1293
Middletown	ASBELL, Mildred S.	(203)344-2304	35
	DOUVILLE, Judith A.	(203)344-1880	314
	FARRINGTON, James	(203)347-9411	365
Milford	BARGAR, Arthur W.	(203)783-3290	56
New Britain	KASCUS, Marie A.	(203)827-7565	628
New Canaan	KUHR, Patricia S.	(203)966-7235	683
New Haven	COLLIER, Bonnie	(203)432-1783	232
	HEINRITZ, Fred J.	(203)397-4530	522
	HILL, John R.	(203)397-4509	540
	LUBIN, Joan S.	(203)397-5154	745
	PELTIER, Karen V.	(203)432-4794	955
	TRIOLO, Victor A.	(203)397-4520	1257
Ridgefield	FARADAY, Joanna	(203)431-0062	363
Southport	HEFZALLAH, Mona G.	(203)259-9926	521
Stamford	KNOPP, Marie L.	(203)348-1173	665
Stratford	ROTH, Alison C.	(203)378-8700	1059
Wallingford	MCGREGOR, M C.	(203)284-6000	808
Warren	HENTZ, Margaret B.	(203)868-9178	530
Waterbury	JOY, Patricia L.	(203)757-6203	618
Westport	MUTTER, Letitia N.	(203)227-1992	883
	SELVERSTONE, Harriet S.	(203)226-6236	1114
Wilton	TRIFFIN, Nicholas	(914)681-4275	1256

DELAWARE

Odessa	JAMISON, Susan C.	(302)378-2158	593
Wilmington	BRETON, Ernest J.		133
	JOHNSON, Hilary C.	(302)994-2870	605
Winterthur	THOMPSON, Neville M.	(302)656-8591	1241

INDEXER (Cont'd)
DISTRICT OF COLUMBIA

Washington	ALEXANDER, Virginia A.	(202)554-1365	12
	BLOZIS, Jolene M.	(202)857-7056	107
	BLUMER, Thomas J.	(202)543-7031	107
	BOYLE, James E.	(202)234-8701	123
	CARLSON, Julia F.	(202)225-2571	182
	CHIN, Cecilia H.	(202)543-3824	208
	DAWSON, Barbara J.	(202)785-3330	282
	DEHART, Odell	(202)393-7100	288
	FALK, Diane M.	(202)291-3821	362
	GAMSON, Arthur L.	(202)382-5921	416
	GREENE, Danielle L.	(202)543-6461	463
	HAITH, Dorothy M.	(202)484-4941	484
	HANFORD, Sally		495
	HAUCK, Janice B.	(202)362-5052	512
	HUDGINS, Peggy	(202)862-8800	569
	JAMES, Olive G.	(202)547-2157	592
	KIMBERLIN, Robert L.	(202)626-7493	649
	KLEIMAN, Helen M.	(202)452-4301	659
	LANE, Elizabeth S.		694
	LEFFALL, Dolores C.	(202)723-7645	712
	MANNING, Martin J.	(202)485-6187	766
	MARSHALL, David L.	(202)625-4171	774
	MISSAR, Margaret M.	(202)363-2751	847
	NEWTON, Robert C.	(202)477-8350	900
	PETERSON, Charles B.		963
	REIFSNYDER, Betsy S.	(202)287-7984	1020
	ROMEO, Sheryl R.	(202)626-7491	1052
	RUSH, Candace M.	(202)393-4695	1068
	SAUVE, Deborah A.	(202)546-8770	1085
	SCHNEIDER, Hennie R.	(202)523-0013	1097
	SCOTT, Catherine D.	(202)357-3101	1107
	STANN, Patsy H.	(202)387-8706	1180
	SWANBERG, Lisa A.	(202)965-1036	1213
	TERRY, Susan N.	(202)332-7120	1232
	WELCH, Thomas L.	(202)232-1706	1321
	YASUMATSU, Janet R.		1378

FLORIDA

Apopka	RIVERA, Antonio	(305)869-7168	1037
Atlantic Beach	URBANSKI, Verna P.	(904)246-3631	1269
Boca Raton	SKALLERUP, Amy G.		1145
Bradenton	MORR, Lynell A.	(813)747-4319	866
Bunnell	MCKNIGHT, Jesse H.	(904)437-4151	812
Coral Gables	GOLIAN, Linda M.	(305)284-2250	447
De Land	EVERETT, David D.	(904)734-4121	358
Fort Lauderdale	MILLER, Margaret R.	(305)791-1278	840
Fort Myers	HUGHES, Joyce M.	(813)489-9464	572
Gainesville	TEAGUE, Edward H.	(904)392-0222	1229
	WALTON, Carol G.	(904)392-0351	1301
Jacksonville	RANDTKE, Angela W.	(904)646-2550	1007
Key Biscayne	KIRBY, Diana G.	(305)361-3678	654
Lake Worth	MOFFETT, Martha L.	(305)964-7044	852
Miami	BOLDRICK, Samuel J.	(305)443-2216	112
	SANCHEZ, Sara M.	(305)854-7752	1079
Miami Beach	LYON, Bruce C.	(305)868-4451	752
Niceville	VINSON, B J.	(904)678-5111	1285
Orlando	CUBBERLEY, Carol W.	(305)275-2521	263
	GEBET, Russell W.	(305)849-0300	424
Palm Coast	FRAZER, Ruth F.	(904)445-5409	399
Palm Harbor	HO, Paul J.	(813)785-1874	545
Pensacola	DEBOLT, W D.	(904)474-2213	284
Ponte Vedra Beach	PECK, Brian T.	(904)246-1400	953
St Petersburg	CORNWELL, Douglas W.	(813)541-7206	247
	WOODARD, Joseph L.	(813)345-1335	1365
Sanford	LINSLEY, Laurie S.	(305)323-1450	731
Tallahassee	DALLET, Jane L.	(904)222-5286	270
	DEENEY, Marian A.	(904)562-3246	286
	TOOLE, Gregor K.		1250
Tampa	WOOD, James F.	(813)232-5221	1364
Thonotosassa	TABOR, Curtis H.	(813)986-3636	1219
Winter Park	ANDREWS, Janet C.		26
Winter Springs	THOMAN, Nancy L.		1236

INDEXER (Cont'd)
GEORGIA

Athens	CARPENTER, David E.	(404)542-8460	184
	GUBISTA, Kathryn R.	(404)546-8153	475
	SOUTHWICK, Mary L.	(404)542-6643	1170
Atlanta	BULLOCK, Penelope L.	(404)792-0775	156
	DEES, Anthony R.	(404)355-0551	287
	DEES, Leslie M.	(404)894-4523	287
	DREW, Frances K.	(404)881-0917	319
	FEINBERG, Hilda W.	(404)875-0077	368
	LONG, Linda E.	(404)521-4210	739
	MCDAVID, Michael W.	(404)885-8320	801
	MISRA, Jayasri T.	(404)524-5320	847
	REYNOLDS, Carol C.	(404)843-9327	1025
	SCHEIN, Julia R.	(404)624-1162	1091
	SIMMONS, Hal	(404)451-0331	1140
	TROUTMAN, Joseph E.	(404)522-8980	1258
Decatur	ALLEN, William R.	(404)284-2981	16
	AMMERMAN, Jackie W.	(404)377-0207	20
	HULLUM, Cheri J.	(404)987-7473	573
	MARONEY, Daryle M.	(404)373-0546	772
East Point	ELTZROTH, Elsbeth L.	(404)767-3144	346
Kennesaw	GRIFFIN, Martha R.	(404)422-9921	468
La Grange	GIBSON, Ricky S.	(404)884-3757	432
Marietta	LISI, Susan C.	(404)955-1375	732
Morrow	HENDERSON, Laurel E.	(404)961-7753	526
Statesboro	JOHNSON, Jane G.	(912)681-1609	605
Valdosta	MONTGOMERY, Denise L.	(912)333-5867	856
Watkinsville	CURTIS, Susan C.	(404)542-0705	267

GUAM

Agana	WEINGARTH, Darlene	(671)472-1750	1318

HAWAII

Aiea	TIMBERLAKE, Cynthia A.	(808)488-4507	1245
Honolulu	CHAFE, Douglas A.	(808)537-8375	197
	GOVERNS, Molly K.		454
	HORIE, Ruth H.		559
	NAJ, Linda M.	(808)946-5359	887
	SCHULTZ, Elaine V.	(808)395-1801	1102
	SZILARD, Paula	(808)948-8263	1218
Kailua-Kona	KOLMAN, Roberta F.		669
Kaneohe	ASHFORD, Marguerite K.	(808)247-6834	36
Makawao	TUPPER, Bobbie	(808)572-1629	1263
Pearl City	KAN, Katharine L.		624

IDAHO

Boise	GREEN, Carol A.	(208)345-0482	461
	WELLS, Merle W.	(208)334-3356	1322
Moscow	WAI, Lily C.	(208)882-0506	1292

ILLINOIS

Abbott Park	SWANSON, Ruth M.	(312)937-6959	1213
Aurora	MCKEARN, Anne B.	(312)892-4811	810
Bloomington	ALEXANDER, Lynetta L.	(309)828-6053	12
Champaign	BERGER, Sidney E.	(217)351-8140	86
	HEISTER, Carla G.	(217)333-6892	523
	REPTA, Vada L.	(217)398-5728	1024
Chicago	CICHON, Marilyn T.	(312)648-1155	214
	COATSWORTH, Patricia A.	(312)947-2160	224
	CULLEN, Charles T.	(312)943-9090	263
	DOYLE, Francis R.	(312)670-2950	317
	EBERHART, George M.	(312)944-6780	334
	FEDERICI, Yolanda D.	(312)427-0052	368
	HERNANDEZ, Hector R.	(312)523-2453	531
	HOTIMLANSKA, Leah D.	(312)248-2013	562
	JOHNSON, Judith M.	(312)996-8988	606
	JORDAN, Charles R.	(312)478-7205	616
	KOWITZ, Aletha A.	(312)440-2642	674
	MELTON, Emily I.	(312)944-6780	823
	MICHAEL, Ann B.	(312)399-8354	831
	MOORE, John R.	(312)763-7811	860
	MOULTON, James C.	(312)525-7185	873
	MUELLER, Julie M.	(312)645-4839	875
	PERTELL, Grace M.	(312)286-5698	961
	PILARSKI, James P.	(312)769-2714	973
	POFELSKI, David	(312)768-9228	979
	POSNER, Frances A.	(312)334-7484	985
	SCHRAMM, Mary T.	(312)248-7934	1099
	SCHROEDER, Anne M.	(312)528-7486	1100

INDEXER (Cont'd)
ILLINOIS (Cont'd)

Chicago	SIARNY, William D.	(312)467-5520	1134
	SKIDMORE, Gail	(312)989-3965	1146
	SLAWNIAK, Patricia M.	(312)338-7589	1148
	STENGER, Brenda E.	(312)782-1442	1187
	STONER, Ronald P.	(312)644-3100	1198
	WICKREMERATNE, Swarna	(312)493-0936	1335
De Kalb	HAMILTON, David A.	(815)753-9857	491
	RIDER, Philip R.	(815)758-2181	1032
	RIDINGER, Robert B.	(815)758-5070	1032
	TOROK, Andrew G.	(815)753-1734	1251
Deerfield	LEE, Soon H.	(312)948-3880	711
Des Plaines	BURNS, Marie T.	(312)635-4732	162
Dwight	MCCLAREY, Catherine A.	(815)584-3703	796
Elk Grove Village	HOLBROCK, Mary A.	(312)439-4800	550
Evanston	BAUGH, L S.	(312)328-0243	65
	FIELD, Connie N.	(312)866-2800	375
	HURD, Albert E.	(312)866-7235	577
	JACOBSON, William R.	(312)328-7584	590
	PALMORE, Sandra N.	(312)328-5329	937
	PANOFSKY, Hans E.	(312)491-7684	938
	QUERY, Lance D.	(312)491-2882	999
	SENN, Mary S.	(312)328-3767	1115
Forest Park	VAN HOUTEN, Stephen		1275
Grayslake	KIENE, Andrea L.	(312)740-0620	647
Gurnee	FUNK, Carla J.	(312)367-6213	409
	MANDEL, Douglas J.	(312)336-7637	765
Hinsdale	HALASZ, Marilynn J.	(312)325-0819	484
Homewood	BAYER, Susan P.	(312)798-6496	67
	MARKHAM, Robert P.	(312)799-4677	771
Joliet	STEVENSON, Katherine	(815)723-7846	1191
Kingston	SCHREIBER, Robert E.	(815)784-2280	1099
Lake Bluff	BROSK, Carol A.	(312)234-6752	141
Lincolnwood	BENNETT, Laura B.	(312)679-2327	82
Makanda	CRANE, Lilly E.	(618)549-6259	255
Normal	DELOACH, Marva L.	(309)438-7463	290
	GOWDY, Laura E.	(309)438-7450	455
	MATTHEWS, Priscilla J.	(309)452-8514	785
North Aurora	HOWREY, Mary M.	(312)896-5837	566
Northbrook	NICKELS, Judith L.	(312)272-6224	902
Northfield	ANDERSON, Charles R.	(312)446-8259	22
Oak Park	DICK, Ellen A.	(312)386-9385	300
	HALIBEY, Areta V.	(312)524-0023	486
	KELM, Carol R.	(312)386-8752	638
	OLDERR, Steven	(312)383-8176	920
Palatine	BURNS, Mary F.	(312)358-0137	162
Park Forest	BUCKLEY, Ja A.	(312)748-2536	154
	HAYES, Hazel I.		515
Park Ridge	LOFTHOUSE, Patricia A.	(312)698-9731	737
Pekin	WALTERS, Patsy M.	(309)353-5075	1301
Quincy	KINGERY, Victor P.	(217)228-5345	652
	WEE, Lily K.	(217)228-5350	1315
River Forest	DAVIS, Richard A.	(312)366-7383	280
	HEYMAN, Jerome S.	(312)771-3030	536
Rolling Meadows	SCHROEDER, Sandra J.	(312)303-0989	1100
Round Lake	TAN, Elizabeth L.	(312)546-6311	1222
South Barrington	JUSTIE, Julie H.	(312)551-2093	620
Springfield	BRADWAY, Becky J.	(217)753-4117	126
Sycamore	SULLIVAN, Peggy A.	(815)753-6155	1208
Urbana	DOWNS, Jane B.	(217)344-1714	317
	GUSHEE, Marion S.	(217)367-9610	478
	KIRREE, Josephino Z.	(217)333-2290	646
	SHAW, Debora	(217)333-1666	1123
Wheaton	RUSSELL, Janet	(312)653-1115	1069
Wheeling	LAMB, Sara G.	(312)541-8114	690
Wilmette	SPIGELMAN, Cynthia A.	(312)251-4892	1174
Woodridge	WHITT, Diane M.		1334

INDIANA

Anderson	KENDALL, Charles T.	(317)649-5039	640
Bloomington	HEISER, Lois	(812)335-7170	523
	HENSON, Jane E.	(812)336-8288	529
	NELSON, Brenda	(812)335-8631	893
	NEUMANN, Mary G.	(812)333-6189	897
	NIEKAMP, Dorothy R.	(812)332-4065	903
	ZIMMERMAN, Brenda M.		1388
Evansville	WINSLOW, Carol M.	(812)867-2146	1355

INDEXER (Cont'd)
INDIANA (Cont'd)

Fort Wayne	BUDD, Anne D.	(219)424-6111	155
	CLEGG, Michael B.		220
	SANDSTROM, Pamela E.	(219)424-7241	1081
Greencastle	LATSHAW, Ruth N.	(317)653-2318	701
Hobart	CHRISTIANSON, Elin B.	(219)942-5536	212
Indianapolis	ELLSWORTH, Marlene A.	(317)274-7185	345
	YOUNG, Philip H.	(317)788-3399	1383
Lafayette	NIXON, Judith M.		906
Mishawaka	EISEN, David J.	(219)259-5277	340
Muncie	KUO, Ming M.	(317)289-3123	684
Upland	WOLCOTT, Laurie J.	(317)998-7549	1359
Valparaiso	MEYER, Ellen R.	(219)464-5360	830
West Lafayette	ANDREWS, Theodora A.	(317)463-6093	27
Westfield	VAN CAMP, Ann J.	(317)896-3537	1272

IOWA

Ames	KLINE, Laura S.	(515)294-6672	661
Cedar Falls	KOLLASCH, Matthew A.	(319)277-6125	669
Cedar Rapids	LEAVITT, Judith A.	(319)390-3109	707
Davenport	PETERSON, Dennis R.	(319)391-3877	963
Iowa City	BIERBAUM, Esther G.	(319)354-8639	95
	BROWN, Jeanine B.		144
	ENGER, Kathy B.	(319)335-4123	349
	SNIDER, Jacqueline I.	(319)337-0660	1163
Manchester	CRAWFORD, Daniel R.		256
Marion	ALDERSON, Karen A.	(319)377-0666	11
	DAVIS, Deanna S.	(319)377-7135	278
Oxford	LARSON, Catherine A.	(319)645-2674	699
Red Oak	PETERSON, Carroll E.	(712)623-3069	963
Rock Rapids	KOHRT, Ruth D.		669
Sioux City	PHILLIPS, Donna M.	(712)258-6981	968
West Branch	DENNIS, Mary R.	(319)643-2583	292
	MATHER, Mildred E.	(319)643-5301	783

KANSAS

Kansas City	FARLEY, Alfred E.	(913)588-7040	364
Lawrence	BURCHILL, Mary D.	(913)864-3025	158
	TRONIER, Suzanne	(913)864-3038	1258
Manhattan	COFFEE, E G.	(913)539-1628	226
	VANDER VELDE, John J.	(913)532-6516	1274
	WEISENBURGER, Patricia J.	(913)532-5968	1319
Shawnee	STRAUSE, Robert C.	(913)268-9875	1200
Topeka	MELICK, Cal G.	(913)295-6479	822
Wichita	MYERS, Robert C.	(316)689-3591	885
	STRECK, Helen T.	(316)942-2201	1201
	TANNER, Jane E.	(316)682-4485	1223

KENTUCKY

Bowling Green	COSSEY, M E.	(502)843-6560	249
	ZIMMER, Connie W.	(502)781-4165	1388
Highland Heights	BENNETT, Donna S.	(606)572-5715	81
Lexington	CHAN, Lois M.	(606)257-5942	199
	MESNER, Lillian R.	(606)273-4990	827
	PICKENS, Nancy C.	(606)299-9638	970
Louisville	GRAY, Dorothy A.	(502)367-4772	459
	MAZUK, Melody	(502)897-4807	791
	ROBY, B D.	(502)561-8638	1045

LOUISIANA

Baton Rouge	BLOOMSTONE, Ajaye	(504)767-0847	106
	BOYCE, Bert R.	(504)388-1461	122
	BRADLEY, Jared W.	(504)766-9375	126
	FERGUSON, Anna S.	(504)272-3833	372
	MILLER, Susan E.	(504)388-8264	842
	SMITH, Ledell B.		1157
Bossier City	BROWN, Sue S.	(318)746-9593	147
Houma	COSPER, Mary F.	(504)879-4243	249
Lafayette	HIMEL, Sandra M.		542
	SCHMIDT, Jean M.	(318)231-6031	1095
Metairie	REPMAN, Denise C.		1023
Natchitoches	HARRINGTON, Charles W.	(318)357-0813	504
	HUSSEY, Sandra R.	(318)352-2996	578
New Orleans	DAVIS, Margo	(504)488-1193	280
	SERBAN, William M.	(504)286-6455	1116
	WELSCH, Melissa W.	(504)584-2403	1323
Ruston	MCFADDEN, Sue J.	(318)257-4357	804
Shreveport	MCCLEARY, William E.	(318)865-9813	796
	WILLIS, Marilyn	(318)227-4501	1348

INDEXER (Cont'd)
LOUISIANA (Cont'd)

Zachary	JACKSON, Audrey N.	(504)654-5491	586

MAINE

Bath	MCKAY, Ann	(207)443-5524	809
Boothbay	SEELEY, Catherine R.		1111
Georgetown	LUDGIN, Donald H.	(207)371-2221	746
Orono	THOR, Angela M.	(207)581-1678	1242
Portland	HUMEZ, Nicholas D.	(207)773-3405	573

MARYLAND

Aberdeen	HADDEN, Robert L.	(301)272-1858	481
Annapolis	PRIMER, Ben	(301)974-3914	993
Baltimore	CONNOR, Elizabeth	(301)828-8646	237
	FORSHAW, William S.	(301)727-3100	391
	GENUARDI, Michael T.	(301)235-1168	427
	HUMPHRIES, Anne W.	(301)328-7373	574
	LABASH, Stephen P.	(301)625-3133	685
	SLEEMAN, William E.	(301)346-5430	1148
	TOPPAN, Muriel L.	(301)837-9155	1251
Beltsville	EDWARDS, Shirley J.	(301)344-3829	338
	ESMAN, Michael D.	(301)344-3729	354
Bethesda	HORAN, Meredith L.	(301)496-5497	559
	KIGER, Anne F.	(301)496-3294	647
	LAZAROW-STETTEN, Jane K.	(301)656-5471	706
	TURNER, Ellis S.	(301)530-4178	1264
Bowie	GIGANTE, Vickilyn M.	(301)249-2609	433
	MATHEWS, Mary P.	(301)262-0732	784
BWI Airport	BUCHAN, Ronald L.	(301)859-5300	153
Cheverly	SILVESTER, June P.	(301)773-0407	1139
Chevy Chase	ERLICK, Louise S.		353
	SEARS, Jonathan R.	(301)656-2306	1110
College Park	WELLISCH, Hans H.	(301)345-3477	1322
Columbia	GRUHL, Andrea M.	(301)596-5460	474
	HOLLENBACH, Karen L.		551
	WENGEL, Linda	(301)995-1469	1324
Damascus	JOHNSON, Susan W.	(301)253-2759	609
Ellicott City	DUCHAC, Kenneth F.	(301)531-3389	322
Flintstone	RAFATS, Jerome M.		1003
Fort Meade	KNICKERBOCKER, Wendy	(301)672-3057	664
Frederick	FRYSER, Benjamin S.	(301)698-5846	407
	GIBBONS, Katherine Y.	(301)663-2720	431
Frostburg	GILLESPIE, David M.	(301)689-2701	435
Gaithersburg	PAUL, Rameshwar N.	(301)258-0768	949
Green Meadows	MILL, Rodney H.	(301)422-1437	835
Greenbelt	KOBAYASHI, Michiko		666
Laurel	DEANE, Roxanna	(301)776-6942	284
	GOLDENBERG, Joan M.	(301)953-9253	445
Mt Rainier	STRANSKY, Maria	(301)779-1627	1200
Perry Point	SCHULTZ, Barbara A.	(301)642-2411	1101
Potomac	CHANG, Frances M.	(301)258-0772	200
Riverdale	PITT, William B.	(301)699-5739	976
Rockville	BLANDAMER, Ann W.	(301)340-8904	103
	LASER, Debra L.	(301)770-5470	700
	MICHAELS, Carolyn L.	(301)564-0509	831
	WHITMAN, Jean A.	(301)736-6804	1333
Salisbury	DADSON, Theresa E.	(301)546-6950	269
Silver Spring	AGEE, Victoria V.	(301)434-7073	7
	AMATRUDA, William T.	(301)585-3570	19
	GILBERT, Mattana	(301)565-2894	433
	LARSON, Jean A.	(301)890-2210	699
	MEIKAMP, Kathie D.	(301)593-0029	822
	OVERTON, Kathryn R.	(301)236-9754	931
	PICKETT, Olivia K.	(301)434-7503	971
	QUINN, Sidney	(301)589-4461	1000
	RICHARD, Sheila A.	(301)438-4555	1028
	SPURLING, Norman K.	(301)495-9229	1177
	TAYLOR, Marcia E.	(301)942-6704	1227
	WALSH, Barclay		1299
Takoma Park	IBACH, Marilyn	(301)270-8950	581
Upper Marlboro	DICKSON, Katherine M.	(301)350-4035	301
Walkersville	SHORT, Eleanor P.	(301)845-8015	1132
Wheaton	KAESSINGER, Carla S.	(301)949-1477	621

INDEXER (Cont'd)
MASSACHUSETTS

Acton	HURD, Sandra H.	(617)263-7574	577
Amherst	ADAMS, Leonard R.	(413)545-2765	5
Belmont	PHELAN, Mary C.		967
Billerica	REID, Angea S.	(617)663-3455	1018
Boston	BRITE, Agnes	(617)267-0369	137
	KOLCZYNSKI, Charlotte A.	(617)536-5400	669
	LEASON, Jane		707
	LEIGHTON, Helene L.	(617)726-8600	714
	ROGAN, Michael J.	(617)536-5400	1049
	SCHWARTZ, Candy S.	(617)738-2223	1104
	STIFFLEAR, Allan J.	(617)929-7640	1194
Brookline	DONG, Tina	(617)731-3514	311
Cambridge	BRUMM, Gordon L.	(617)547-5673	150
	BURG, Barbara A.	(617)547-4762	159
	DESIMONE, Dorothy H.	(617)495-2432	295
	GROVE, Shari T.	(617)864-3563	474
	JOBE, Shirley A.	(617)868-0079	601
	PAPALAMBROS, Rita G.	(617)497-2047	939
Charlestown	CURTIN-STEVENSON, Mary C.	(617)241-9664	266
Chestnut Hill	DESJARDINS, Andrea C.		295
Concord	BANDER, Edward J.		54
	NESS, Pamela M.	(617)369-7174	896
Dedham	LOSCALZO, Anita B.	(617)329-3964	741
Deerfield	KELLY, Patricia M.	(413)774-4627	638
Framingham	KRIER, Mary M.	(617)879-7594	678
Hanscom AFB	DUFFEK, Elizabeth A.	(617)377-4768	323
Lexington	ROSENTHAL, Marylu C.	(617)862-8167	1057
Lincoln	COHEN, Martha J.	(413)259-9500	228
	SCHWANN, William J.	(617)259-8212	1104
Longmeadow	MCGARRY, Marie L.	(413)567-0001	805
Marblehead	LYNCH, Jacqueline	(617)631-0624	751
Needham	TSENG, Louisa	(617)449-3630	1260
Newton Highlands	FOX, Elyse H.	(617)443-4798	394
North Quincy	NIELSEN, Sonja M.	(617)328-8306	903
Northampton	SCOTT, Alison M.	(413)584-2700	1106
Peabody	CODAIR, Frederick R.	(617)531-8200	226
Petersham	MCMANAMON, Mary J.	(617)724-3407	814
Reading	SARAIDARIDIS, Susan B.		1082
Roybury	SUTTON, Joyce A.	(617)427-4941	1211
Salem	PANGALLO, Karen L.		938
Springfield	LAPIERRE, Barbe	(413)739-3871	697
	TAUPIER, Andrea S.	(413)788-3315	1225
Waban	CHERNIN, David A.	(617)731-6760	206
Watertown	TUCHMAN, Helene L.	(617)924-5391	1261
West Springfield	SMITH, Barbara A.	(413)736-4561	1152
Westford	NATOLI, Dorothy L.	(617)692-7192	889
Williamsburg	LANCASTER, John	(413)268-7679	692
Winchester	DAY, Virginia M.	(617)729-6026	283
Woods Hole	SHEPHARD, Frank C.	(617)548-2743	1127
Worcester	ANDREWS, Peter J.		27
	KANG, Wen	(617)856-2511	625

MICHIGAN

Adrian	BAKER, Jean S.	(517)263-0731	48
Ann Arbor	BILLICK, David J.	(313)761-4700	96
	BOWEN, Jennifer B.	(313)663-6164	120
	DAVIDSEN, Susanna L.	(313)995-7352	276
	FINERMAN, Carol B.	(313)995-4485	378
	HALL, Jo A.	(313)936-0132	488
	HOUGH, Carolyn A.	(313)665-0537	562
	NICHOLS, Darlene P.	(313)764-4479	901
	PAO, Miranda L.	(313)747-3611	938
	RICHTER, John H.		1031
	ROENZWEIG, Merle	(313)769-1805	1048
	TERWILLIGER, Doris H.	(313)761-3912	1232
Berkley	MARLOW, Cecilia A.	(313)547-3098	772
Birmingham	IRWIN, Lawrence L.	(313)626-5339	584
Detroit	BRAITHWAITE, Heather J.	(313)577-3925	127
	FRANTILLA, K A.	(313)972-0318	398
	OLDENBURG, Joseph F.	(313)833-4027	920
	RUNCHOCK, Rita M.	(313)961-2242	1067
	RZEPECKI, Arnold M.	(313)868-2700	1072
	STREETER, Linda D.		1201
East Lansing	RIVERA, Diana H.	(517)353-4593	1037
	SCOTT, Randall W.	(517)353-4526	1108
Flint	ARNOLD, Peggy	(313)744-4040	34
Grand Rapids	WEAVER, Clarence L.		1312

INDEXER (Cont'd)
MICHIGAN (Cont'd)

Grosse Pointe Woods	STRATELAK, Nadia A.	(313)886-1043	1200
Harper Woods	TODD, Suzanne L.	(313)881-5328	1248
Jackson	SMITH, Catherine A.	(517)784-7025	1153
Kalamazoo	APPS, Michelle L.	(616)375-3611	30
	CARROLL, Hardy	(616)383-1926	187
	NETZ, David H.	(616)383-1666	896
	PEREZ-STABLE, Maria A.	(616)383-1666	958
	VANDER MEER, Patricia F.	(616)383-1666	1274
Lansing	FRYE, Dorothy T.	(517)393-7608	407
Lapeer	VOELZ, Laura D.	(313)667-9583	1286
Lincoln Park	HECK-RABI, Louise E.	(313)928-3967	520
Parchment	BOURGEOIS, Ann M.	(616)344-9097	119
Rochester	HILDEBRAND, Linda L.	(313)370-2483	538
	KROMPART, Janet A.	(313)651-4738	679
Sault Sainte Marie	NAIRN, Charles E.	(906)635-2402	886
Springfield	BURHANS, Barbara C.	(616)965-4096	159
Taylor	MATZKE, Ellen S.	(313)291-9480	786
Troy	BIELICH, Paul S.	(313)689-9381	95
Utica	HORNE, Ernest L.	(313)731-4374	560
Vicksburg	HEGEDUS, Mary E.	(616)679-5396	521
Warren	VAN ALLEN, Neil K.	(313)696-9508	1271
Ypsilanti	MCGARTY, Jean R.	(313)572-1453	805

MINNESOTA

Braham	MCGRIFF, Ronald I.	(612)396-3957	808
Eden Prairie	BILEYDI, Lois G.	(612)934-3576	96
Embarrass	ESALA, Lillian N.	(218)741-3434	354
Hopkins	YOUNG, Margaret L.	(612)933-5062	1382
Little Canada	LO, Maryanne H.	(612)481-9412	735
Mankato	FARNER, Susan G.	(507)389-5957	365
Marshall	FOSTER, Veo G.	(507)532-4072	393
Minneapolis	GASTON, Judith A.	(612)627-4277	421
	HALLEWELL, Laurence	(612)724-6565	489
	MIRANDA, Esmeralda C.	(612)437-0245	847
	O'LEARY, Mary E.	(612)872-4399	920
	RAFTER, Susan	(618)870-1935	1003
	REHNBERG, Marilyn J.	(612)722-3234	1017
	ROLONTZ, Linda	(612)337-1644	1051
	TERTELL, Susan M.	(612)372-6658	1232
	WEEKS, John M.	(612)624-6833	1315
Northfield	NILES, Ann A.	(507)663-4268	904
	YOUNG, Lynne M.	(507)645-5778	1382
Red Wing	SWEEN, Roger	(612)388-5723	1214
Roseville	KAUFENBERG, Jane M.	(612)642-9221	630
St Paul	BLUMBERG-MCKEE, Hazel	(612)292-1680	107
	HLAVSA, Larry B.	(612)699-7198	544
	OZOLINS, Karl L.	(612)645-2999	933
	SCHMIDT, Jean M.		1095
	SCHOLBERG, Henry	(612)633-6851	1098
	TURNER, Ann S.	(612)291-9340	1264
Shoreview	MOODY, Suzanna	(612)481-7275	857
Waite Park	CLARKE, Norman F.	(612)253-2695	219
Woodbury	WELYGAN, Sylvia M.	(612)459-0764	1323

MISSISSIPPI

Biloxi	FREEDMAN, Jack A.	(601)388-2318	400
	VANCE, Mary L.		1273
Hattiesburg	CARNOVALE, A N.	(601)264-5452	184
	DRAKE, Betty S.	(601)266-5077	318
	JONES, Dolores B.	(601)266-4349	612
	WILLIAMS, Eddie A.	(601)266-4245	1343
Itta Bena	BOWEN, Ethel B.	(601)254-9041	120
Jackson	BELL, Bernice	(601)366-8786	76

MISSOURI

Bolivar	KAISER, Patricia L.	(417)326-4531	622
	VAN BLAIR, Betty A.	(417)326-5281	1272
Chesterfield	GOLDMAN, Teri B.		446
Columbia	STEVENS, Robert R.	(314)445-5320	1191
Florissant	ANTHONY, Paul L.	(314)921-6158	29
	BLANKENSHIP, Phyllis E.	(314)839-3966	104
Harrisonville	FRANKLIN, Jill S.	(816)884-6223	397
Kansas City	DRAYSON, Pamela K.	(816)753-7600	318
	GERRITY, Marline R.	(816)276-1893	429
	JENKINS, Harold R.	(816)444-2590	597
	KARNS, Kermit B.	(816)453-1294	627
	MEIZNER, Karen L.	(816)561-4000	822

INDEXER (Cont'd)
MISSOURI (Cont'd)
Kansas City

ROTH, Sally . . . . (816)842-0984   1059
SULLIVAN, Marilyn G. . . . . . (816)276-1871   1208

St Louis
DRAPER, Linda J.   318
GELINNE, Michael S. . . . . . (314)694-4748   426
MCDERMOTT, Margaret H. . . (314)889-6443   802
PLUTCHAK, T S. . . . . (314)577-8605   979
WEAVER, Nancy B. . . . . (314)821-1338   1312

MONTANA
Havre   RITTER, Ann L. . . . . (466)265-1308   1036
Heart Butte   SPOTTED EAGLE, Joy . . . . . (406)338-2282   1175

NEBRASKA
Lincoln
FROBOM, Jerome B. . . . . . . (402)483-7129   405
JOHNSON, Judy L. . . . . (402)472-3938   606
WOOL, Gregory J. . . . . (402)475-0391   1368

NEVADA
Las Vegas   GARDNER, Jack I. . . . . (702)382-3493   418
Reno   MANLEY, Charles W. . . . . . (702)785-4012   765
               RICE, Dorothy F. . . . . (702)747-2849   1027

NEW HAMPSHIRE
Amherst   SHERWOOD, Janet R. . . . . . (603)673-9242   1129
Concord   HARE, William J. . . . . (603)225-2012   501
Contoocook   RINDEN, Constance T. . . . . (603)225-5232   1035
Franconia   BJORNER, Susan N. . . . . . . (603)823-8838   100
Nashua   FERRIGNO, Helen F. . . . . . (603)889-3042   373
Portsmouth   JACOBS, Gloria . . . . (603)431-9346   589
Rindge   STEARNS, Melissa M. . . . . . (603)899-5111   1183
Windham   CUNNIFFE, Charlene M. . . . . (603)434-1847   265

NEW JERSEY
Belleville   JACKRELL, Thomas L. . . . . . (201)759-5318   586
Bergenfield   CHELARIU, Ana R. . . . . (201)384-8302   204
               HEISE, George F. . . . . (201)385-9741   522
Berkeley Heights MAZURKIEWICZ, Helen L. . . (201)464-0096   791
Bloomfield   LUSTIG, Joanne . . . . (201)743-8777   750
               PICCIANO, Jacqueline L. . . . (201)743-9661   970
Bogota   MACKESY, Eileen M.   756
Bridgewater   DESS, Howard M. . . . . (201)526-1981   295
Caldwell   SKIDANOW, Helene . . . . (201)226-4458   1146
Cherry Hill   WALSH, Sharon T. . . . . (609)243-1500   1300
Chester   MANY, Florence L. . . . . (201)879-5167   767
Cliffside Park ROBERTSON, Betty M. . . . . . (201)894-0235   1041
               SEKELY, Maryann . . . . (201)943-4117   1113
Colts Neck   MICHAL, Judith A. . . . . (201)946-4839   832
Cranford   SAWYCKY, Roman A. . . . . . . (201)276-3134   1086
Florham Park   BARRETT, Joyce C. . . . . . . (201)765-1523   59
Fort Lee   THIRD, Bettie J. . . . . (201)461-6511   1235
Hamilton   HOOKER, Joan M. . . . . (609)587-9669   556
Highland Park LI, Marjorie H. . . . . (201)828-8730   724
Hoboken   LIN, Fumei C. . . . . (201)795-5066   727
               SOLOMON, Geri E. . . . . (201)420-8364   1166
Indian Mills   SCHREIBER-COIA, Barbara
               J.   1099
Irvington   KNIGHT, Shirley D. . . . . . . (201)371-9324   664
Jersey City   PANDELAKIS, Helene S. . . . . (201)795-8265   937
               RUBIN, Myra P. . . . . (201)963-6456   1064
Little Ferry   BOTKIN, Karen R. . . . . (201)542-7216   118
Madison   EDWARDS, Melanie G. . . . . . (201)822-1309   337
               JONES, Arthur E. . . . . (201)377-6525   611
Mendham   MANTHEY, Carolyn M. . . . . . (201)543-2129   767
Millburn   URKEN, Madeline . . . . (201)379-2306   1270
Morristown   DENSKY, Lois R. . . . . (201)539-0407   293
Mountainside   LINGELBACH, Lorene N. . . . . (201)654-7694   730
New Brunswick ANDERSON, James D. . . . . . (201)846-1510   23
               FAVORS, Thelma L.   366
               MAZZEI, Peter J. . . . . (201)249-4120   791
Newark   CUMMINGS, Charles F. . . . . . (201)733-7776   264
               PROFETA, Patricia C. . . . . . (201)648-5911   995
               SCHWARTZ, Lawrence C.   1104
Oceanport   WAITE, William F. . . . . . . (201)542-7216   1293
Park Ridge   LUXNER, Dick . . . . (201)391-5935   750
Pine Hill   GODFREY, Florence L. . . . . . (609)435-2682   442
Piscataway   CASSEL, Jeris F. . . . . (201)752-0528   193
Plainfield   KRUSE, Theodore H. . . . . . . (201)725-2294   681

INDEXER (Cont'd)
NEW JERSEY (Cont'd)
Pompton Lakes MENZUL, Faina . . . . (201)839-6885   825
Princeton   BELCHER, Emily M. . . . . . . (609)924-8947   76
               CRITCHLOW, Therese E. . . . . (609)924-9529   259
               JOHNSON, David K. . . . . . . (609)924-2870   603
               MOSS, Susan K. . . . . (609)452-1212   872
               NASE, Lois M. . . . . (609)452-3237   888
               SCHMIDT, Mary M. . . . . (609)452-5860   1095
               THRESHER, Jacquelyn E. . . . . (609)924-9529   1243
Saddle Brook   AUGHEY, Kathleen M.   39
Short Hills   GOLDSMITH, Carol C. . . . . . (201)376-0216   446
Somerset   GREENBERG, Linda . . . . (201)846-8497   463
Somerville   KUSHINKA, Kerry L. . . . . . . (201)526-7323   685
Springfield   GLADSTONE, Mark A. . . . . . (201)376-2055   439
Stanhope   ELIASON, Elisabetha S. . . . . (201)347-8215   342
Sussex   SMITH, Jo T. . . . . (201)875-3621   1156
Teaneck   MOUNT, Ellis . . . . (201)836-1137   873
Trenton   CONLEY, Gail D. . . . . (609)771-6911   236
               HALPERN, Marilyn . . . . (609)882-2450   489
               WOODLEY, Robert H. . . . . . . (609)771-2441   1366
Union   AMRON, Irving . . . . (201)688-4980   20
Upper Montclair O'CONNOR, Christine T. . . . (201)783-7995   916
Wayne   BIDDEN, Julia E. . . . . (201)831-7801   94
Westfield   SEADER, Jane M.   1109
Westwood   GINES, Noriko . . . . (201)666-7042   437
Whitehouse Station HOYT, Henry M. . . . . . . (201)689-7717   566

NEW MEXICO
Albuquerque
GROTHEY, Mina J. . . . . (505)277-7144   473
KALE, Shirley W. . . . . (505)298-5980   623
KRUG, Ruth A. . . . . (505)277-7213   680
MILLER, Hester M. . . . . . . (505)821-4782   838
SEISER, Virginia . . . . (505)842-5156   1113
SUGNET, Christopher L. . . . . (505)277-7162   1206
Clovis   HUMPHREY, Thomas W. . . . . . (505)769-2811   573
               MCBETH, Deborah E. . . . . . . (505)762-7161   792
Kirtland AFB   JOURDAIN, Janet M. . . . . . . (505)844-1768   618
Los Alamos   COMSTOCK, Daniel L. . . . . . (505)662-7668   235
Portales   SCHOTT, Mark E. . . . . (505)356-8735   1099
Silver City   KEIST, Sandra H. . . . . (505)538-2663   635

NEW YORK
Albany   KNEE, Michael . . . . (518)442-3586   663
               MILLER, Heather S. . . . . . . (518)442-3626   838
               PINSLEY, Lauren J. . . . . . . (518)445-2342   975
               VAILLANCOURT, Pauline M. . . . (518)489-6207   1271
               WALKER, M G. . . . . (518)436-1975   1296
Alfred   FREEMAN, Carla C. . . . . . . (607)871-2492   400
APO New York   NEUWILLER, Charlene   897
Armonk   DEVERS, Charlotte M. . . . . . (914)273-3887   297
Astoria   FISHER, Maureen C. . . . . . . (718)204-0631   381
Bayside   SINGER, Phyllis Z. . . . . . . (718)279-2182   1143
               WEINER, Carolynn N.   1318
Beechhurst   CARVER, Mary   191
               DESSER, Darrilyn . . . . (718)767-6955   296
Belfast   GULACSY, Elizabeth . . . . . . (716)466-7117   477
Binghamton   CHAMBERLAIN, Erna B. . . . . . (607)723-4064   197
               LINCOLN, Betty W. . . . . . . (607)777-2862   728
               LINCOLN, Harry B. . . . . . . (607)777-6738   728
Brewster   VELARDI, Adrienne B. . . . . . (914)279-5022   1281
Brockport   RAKSHI, Sri R. . . . . (716)395-5262   1004
Bronx   BARNETT, Philip . . . . (212)549-5359   58
               DEEBRAH, Grace J. . . . . . . (212)588-8400   286
               GHOSH, Subhra . . . . (212)588-8400   430
               HOWARD, Joyce M. . . . . (212)588-8400   564
               IOANID, Aurora S. . . . . . . (212)220-0543   583
               JOHNSON, Steven P. . . . . . . (212)220-6874   609
               LAMPORT, Bernard . . . . (212)430-3747   691
               ROY, Diptimoy . . . . (914)668-1840   1063
               WEINBERG, Bella H. . . . . . . (212)547-5159   1317
Brooklyn   BRISTOW, Barbara A. . . . . . (718)596-1275   137
               GREENBERG, Roberta D. . . . . (718)857-0146   463
               HOMMEL, Claudia . . . . (718)237-0028   555
               JAROSEK, Joan E. . . . . (718)237-2147   594
               KERR, Virginia M. . . . . . . (718)789-5410   644
               KRAMER, Allan F. . . . . (718)857-7825   675
               MARSHAK, Bonnie L. . . . . . . (718)638-6821   773
               MARTINEZ-RIVERA, Ivette . . (718)854-5176   779
               MEYERS, Charles . . . . (718)342-1144   830

INDEXER (Cont'd)
NEW YORK (Cont'd)
Brooklyn

	NARDUCCI, Frances	(718)743-6001	888
	PEDALINO, M C.	(718)768-3889	954
	ROBBINS, Sara E.	(718)780-7980	1039
	TUDIVER, Lillian	(718)789-7220	1262
	WEINRICH, Gloria	(708)998-9116	1318
	WENGER, Milton B.	(718)252-5019	1324
	WILD, Judith W.	(718)780-5347	1338
	ZOLNERZAK, Robert	(718)522-0591	1390
Buffalo	BUSH, Renee B.	(716)832-3081	165
	DIBARTOLO, Amy L.	(716)878-6309	299
	PERONE, Karen L.	(716)883-7000	959
	SCHENK, Kathryn L.	(716)886-0413	1091
	STELZLE, James J.	(716)832-6066	1186
	STIEVATER, Susan M.	(716)878-6313	1194
	WOLFE, Theresa L.	(716)632-4491	1361
	YERKEY, A N.	(716)636-3069	1380
Canton	FINCH, Frances	(315)267-2487	377
Cherry Plain	GILCHER, Edwin	(518)658-2429	434
Clinton	ANTHONY, Mary M.	(315)737-8347	28
Cobleskill	GALASSO, Nancy	(518)234-5841	412
Delmar	GRAVLEE, Diane D.	(518)439-7983	459
Dewitt	SHRIER, Helene F.	(315)446-5971	1133
Dobbs Ferry	HASSAN, Mohammad Z.	(914)693-2031	511
	ROSHON, Nina C.	(914)693-9251	1057
East Aurora	UTTS, Janet R.	(716)655-0031	1270
Fairport	SULOUFF, Patricia T.	(716)223-6844	1208
Flushing	LINZER, Elliot	(718)353-1261	732
	SAFRAN, Scott A.	(718)445-6752	1074
	SMITH, Sweetman R.	(718)939-8068	1161
FPO New York	GAMAL, Sandra H.		416
	LANE, Elizabeth L.		694
Freeport	VOLLONO, Millicent D.	(516)223-0838	1288
Fulton	REED, Catherine A.	(315)598-3435	1015
Great Neck	DAMON, Shirley J.	(516)482-1202	272
Hastings on Hudson	PATTERSON, Kathleen J.	(914)478-0881	948
Hicksville	HOLMES, Harvey L.	(516)935-4813	553
Hudson	MARTIN, Lyn M.	(518)828-1465	777
Hyde Park	GRIFFITH, Sheryl	(914)229-8114	469
Islip Terrace	KLATT, Wilma F.	(516)581-5933	658
Ithaca	ERICSON, Margaret D.	(607)274-3882	353
	HICKEY, John T.	(607)273-1944	536
	SLOCUM, Robert B.	(716)255-4247	1150
	STEWART, Linda G.	(607)255-7959	1192
Jackson Heights	RANHAND, Jori L.	(718)469-4728	1007
Jamaica Estates	BARTENBACH, Wilhelm K.	(718)658-3878	60
Jamestown	LEE, Sylvia	(716)483-5415	711
Kew Gardens	TANNENBAUM, Robin L.	(718)793-0372	1222
Long Island City	HEWITT, Mary L.	(718)721-1862	535
Lynbrook	HESSLEIN, Shirley B.	(516)887-5071	534
Mattituck	PERLMAN, Stephen E.	(516)298-4335	959
Mt Vernon	SHERRILL, Jocelyn T.	(914)667-4190	1129
Nassau	CARABATEAS, Clarissa D.		180
	LIPETZ, Ben A.	(518)766-3014	732
New Hyde Park	FLANZRAICH, Gerri	(516)741-2831	384
New Rochelle	SWANSON, Mary A.	(914)633-3954	1213
New York	APPEL, Marsha C.	(212)682-2500	29
	ARAYA, Rose M.	(718)461-4799	30
	BEALER, Jane A.	(212)355-0083	68
	BERNAL, Rose M.	(212)674-6525	88
	BOWEN, Christopher E.	(212)815-8200	120
	BOZIWICK, George E.	(212)870-1675	124
	CAPRIELIAN, Arevig	(718)459-2757	180
	DEVERA, Rosalinda M.	(212)557-2570	297
	ELLENBERGER, Jack S.	(212)837-6583	343
	EPPES, William D.	(212)675-2070	351
	FLEISHMAN, Lauren Z.	(212)371-2000	384
	FREIFELD, Roberta I.	(212)777-9271	401
	FRIED, Suzanne C.	(212)963-0508	403
	GOLLOP, Sandra G.	(212)770-7911	447
	GOODMAN, Edward C.	(212)280-8407	449
	GOODSELL, Joan W.	(212)210-7044	450
	GRANDE, Paula G.	(212)536-3229	457
	GROTE, Janet H.	(212)627-1500	473
	GUILER, Paula J.	(212)689-3341	476
	HERMAN, Marsha	(212)679-6105	531
	HOLTZE, Sally H.	(212)674-6973	555

INDEXER (Cont'd)
NEW YORK (Cont'd)
New York

	HSIAO, Shu Y.	(212)749-2873	567
	HUTSON, Jean B.	(212)368-1515	579
	HYMAN, Richard J.	(212)865-7962	580
	JONES, Roger A.	(212)777-2959	615
	JURIST, Janet	(212)737-8120	620
	KAIN, Joan P.	(212)850-0768	622
	KELLEY, Dennis L.	(212)210-7043	636
	KEMPE, Deborah A.	(212)595-6583	639
	KING, Trina E.	(212)427-1023	652
	KOEHNLEIN, Bill	(212)674-9145	667
	LASKOWITZ, Roberta G.	(212)684-2089	700
	LILLY, Elise M.	(212)940-8596	727
	MASTRANGELO, Paul J.	(212)431-2128	783
	MEAGHER, Anne E.	(212)620-8462	819
	MEYER, Albert	(212)254-7031	829
	MOTIHAR, Kamla	(212)838-8400	872
	MOUNIR, Khalil A.	(212)373-5640	873
	MULIA, Gusti	(212)930-0701	876
	NELOMS, Karen H.	(212)582-9239	893
	OSTWALD, Mark F.		929
	PALMER, Paul R.	(212)865-5781	936
	PEHE, Jana	(718)278-0630	954
	PINEDA, Conchita J.	(212)371-5188	974
	PISTILLI, Susan A.	(212)621-1580	976
	POLSTER, Joanne	(212)564-7640	982
	PRESCHEL, Barbara M.	(212)753-8458	991
	REDEL, Judy A.	(212)337-7043	1014
	ROHMANN, Gloria P.	(212)930-0576	1050
	RONNBERG, Annmari	(212)697-3480	1053
	ROSIGNOLO, Beverly A.	(212)962-4111	1057
	SEGAL, Judith	(212)222-3699	1112
	SETTANNI, Joseph A.	(212)289-9059	1117
	SHAPIRO, Barbara G.	(212)621-1582	1121
	SLOCUM, Leslie E.	(212)759-6800	1150
	SWANSON, Dorothy T.	(212)998-2630	1213
	TERLIZZI, Joseph M.	(212)587-9689	1232
	THOMAS, Dorothy	(212)799-0970	1236
	VAUGHN, Susan J.	(212)260-2544	1280
	VELEZ, Sara B.	(212)870-1661	1281
	WOLF, Marion	(212)360-3572	1360
	WOO, Janice	(212)662-3534	1363
	WOODS, Lawrence J.	(212)736-6629	1367
Newark	GARCIA, Kathleen J.	(315)331-4070	417
North Syracuse	AUSTIN, Ralph A.	(315)457-1799	40
North Tonawanda	HODGSON, Elizabeth A.	(716)694-8364	546
Norwich	WINDSOR, Donald A.	(607)336-4628	1354
Oceanside	ROGGENKAMP, Alice M.	(516)766-1397	1050
Ogdensburg	FRANZ, David A.	(315)393-2950	398
Oswego	CHU, Sylvia	(315)341-3210	213
Palisades	WARD, Edith	(914)359-2081	1303
Patchogue	NEUFELD, Judith B.	(516)289-6813	897
Pomona	HONOR, Naomi G.		556
Rochester	BARNES, Robert W.	(716)428-7335	57
	CHURCH, Virginia K.	(716)475-2558	213
	GIGLIOTTI, Mary J.	(716)254-0621	433
	HELBERS, Catherine A.	(716)594-9652	523
	ISGANITIS, Jamie C.	(716)461-1943	585
	KARNEZIS, Kristine C.	(716)482-3221	627
	REITANO, Maimie V.	(716)722-7067	1022
	RITTER, Audrey L.	(716)475-6823	1036
	ROSENBERG-NUGENT, Nanci B.		1056
	STOSS, Frederick W.	(716)436-8719	1198
	STRIFE, Mary L.	(716)334-0091	1202
Roslyn	WEINSTEIN, Judith K.	(516)627-6200	1318
Saratoga Springs	LEWIS, Gillian H.	(518)587-0374	723
Scarsdale	ABEND, Jody U.	(914)723-1360	2
Shrub Oak	TIFFEAULT, Alice A.	(914)528-4048	1244
Staten Island	HOGAN, Kristine K.	(718)727-1135	604
	SCHUT, Grace W.	(718)442-5659	1103
Stillwater	REEPMEYER, Marie C.	(518)785-6949	1016
Syosset	JENSEN, Dennis F.	(516)921-0418	598
Syracuse	MCLAUGHLIN, Pamela W.	(315)476-7359	813
	PRINS, Johanna W.	(315)475-5534	993
	REINSTEIN, Diana J.	(315)492-5500	1021
Utica	BROOKES, Barbara	(315)735-2279	140
Valley Stream	KUGLER, Sharon	(516)791-9385	682

INDEXER (Cont'd)
NEW YORK (Cont'd)

Warwick	BATTOE, Melanie K.		65
White Plains	HESS, James W.	(914)592-4342	534
	MOSLANDER, Charlotte D.	(914)428-1533	871
Williamsville	SCHUTT, Dedre A.	(716)633-6384	1103
Woodstock	LISS, Gail	(914)679-7173	732
Wynantskill	CORSARO, James		248
Yorktown Heights	LEE, Douglas E.	(914)245-8978	709
	RUBINO, Cynthia C.	(914)962-4518	1065

NORTH CAROLINA

Boone	WORRELL, Diane F.		1369
Chapel Hill	DEBRECZENY, Gillian M.	(919)929-5282	285
	TALBERT, David M.	(919)962-0700	1220
	TUCKER, Mary E.	(919)933-8982	1262
Charlotte	HOWARD, Susanna J.	(704)364-7987	564
Durham	BARROWS, William D.	(919)549-0517	60
	SEMONCHE, Barbara P.	(919)489-7247	1115
	SPARKS, Martha E.	(919)489-6012	1171
	WHITTINGTON, Erma P.	(919)489-9689	1334
Greensboro	HARDIE, Karen R.	(919)288-7210	499
	WRIGHT, Keith C.	(919)282-3712	1372
Greenville	SHIRES, Nancy P.	(919)758-8252	1131
Hendersonville	THICKITT, Lisa		1235
High Point	TOMLINSON, Charles E.	(919)887-3006	1250
Mars Hill	PETERSON, Cynthia L.	(704)689-2380	963
Matthews	BACKMAN, Carroll H.	(704)847-6055	44
Research Triangle Pk	LAVOY, Constance J.	(919)549-2649	704
	THOMPSON, Reubin C.	(919)248-4147	1241
Spruce Pine	AUSTIN, Mary C.		40
Wilmington	SEXTON, Spencer K.	(919)799-0177	1118
Winston-Salem	WOODARD, John R.	(919)761-5089	1365

NORTH DAKOTA

Bismarck	VYZRALEK, Dolores E.	(701)223-1857	1290
	WEZELMAN, Joy L.	(701)222-0271	1328
Devil's Lake	EVENSEN, Sharon L.	(701)662-4691	358
Fargo	JANZEN, Deborah K.	(701)277-1865	594

OHIO

Akron	GUSS, Margaret B.	(216)375-7224	478
Athens	HOUDEK, G R.	(614)593-5444	562
Bowling Green	POVSIC, Frances F.	(419)372-2956	987
Brunswick	HAMBLEY, Susan L.	(216)225-0436	490
Canfield	LITTLE, Dean K.	(216)533-6703	733
Canton	TERHUNE, R S.	(216)489-0800	1231
Cincinnati	ALBERT, Stephen G.	(513)541-9119	10
	PALKOVIC, Mark A.	(513)475-4471	935
	RIFFEY, Robin S.	(513)871-3087	1033
	WELLINGTON, Jean S.	(513)475-6724	1322
Cleveland	SANTAVICCA, Edmund F.	(216)687-2365	1082
Cleveland Heights	MCMAHON, Melody L.	(216)371-5744	814
Columbus	BRANCH, Susan A.	(614)267-3805	127
	BRANDT, Michael H.	(614)863-2814	128
	CHRISTENSON, Donald E.	(614)236-5959	211
	HEARD, Jeffrey L.		518
	HECK, Thomas F.	(614)292-2310	519
	HUNTER, James J.	(614)461-5039	576
	KRUMM, Carol R.	(614)846-1683	680
	MERCADO, Heidi	(614)292-2009	825
	MILLER, Dennis P.	(614)888-1886	837
	MIMNAUGH, Ellen N.	(614)486-7755	845
	MLYNAR, Mary	(614)486-7980	850
	PLATAU, Gerard O.	(614)457-1687	977
	SANDERS, Nancy P.		1080
	SMITH, Ellen A.	(614)462-7054	1154
	WARNER, Susan B.	(614)424-5676	1305
Dayton	BRUMIT, Nancy T.	(513)274-4677	150
	EVANS, Stephen P.	(513)220-9506	358
	HECHT, Judith N.	(513)229-3024	519
	O'BRIEN, Betty A.	(513)433-5420	914
	QUINTEN, Rebecca G.	(513)277-3598	1000
	SEXTON, Sally V.	(513)890-1421	1118
	TRIVEDI, Harish S.	(513)225-2201	1257
Fairborn	BAKER, Narcissa L.	(573)879-3638	49
Fairview Park	HYSLOP, Marjorie R.	(216)333-8645	580
Granville	RUGG, John D.		1066
Hiram	WANSER, Jeffery C.	(216)569-5358	1303

INDEXER (Cont'd)
OHIO (Cont'd)

Huron	CURRIE, William W.	(419)433-5560	266
Kent	MORRIS, Trisha A.	(216)673-3464	867
Lima	MCDANIEL, Deanna J.	(419)991-6065	801
Mayfield Heights	RASKIN, Rosa S.	(216)442-3009	1009
Mogadore	SMITH, Cynthia A.	(216)678-0662	1153
Reynoldsburg	WULKER, Clare	(614)866-5963	1374
Steubenville	BURKE, Ambrose L.	(614)283-3771	160
Terrace Park	SEIK, Jo E.	(513)831-0780	1112
Toledo	ELLENBOGEN, Barbara R.	(419)536-4538	343
Wilmington	NICHOLS, James T.	(513)382-6661	901
Youngstown	WALL, Carol	(216)742-1717	1297

OKLAHOMA

Ardmore	KIMBLE, Valerie F.	(405)226-3980	649
Moore	GOLDSBERRY, Maureen E.	(405)799-3326	446
Muskogee	CHEATHAM, Gary L.	(918)683-2475	204
	GUTIERREZ, Carolyn A.	(918)687-6479	479
Norman	HOVDE, David M.	(405)325-4231	563
	MEACHAM, Mary	(405)321-8444	819
	PETERS, Lloyd A.		962
	POLAND, Jean A.	(405)360-7095	980
Oklahoma City	BOOTENHOFF, Rebecca J.	(405)728-7072	116
	DOBBERTEEN, Sara J.	(405)842-0890	307
	HARGIS-LYTLE, Betty L.	(405)721-2134	501
Tahlequah	HILL, Helen K.		540
Tulsa	HILL, Linda L.	(918)584-0891	540
	SMITH, Donald R.	(918)592-6000	1154

OREGON

Corvallis	MURRAY, Lucia M.		882
Eugene	HEINZKILL, J R.	(503)686-3078	522
	MCDANIELS, Patricia R.	(503)343-4728	801
Manzanita	LARSON, Signe E.	(503)368-6990	700
Marylhurst	GIMPL, Caroline A.	(503)636-8105	437
Philomath	REEVES, Marjorie A.	(503)929-5354	1017
Portland	EDWARDS, Susan E.	(506)224-6812	338
	KAWABATA, Julie	(503)238-4814	632
Salem	MOBERG, F A.	(503)581-5244	851

PENNSYLVANIA

Allentown	ANDEL, June	(215)395-5168	21
	SWARTZ, Patrice B.	(215)797-5696	1214
Ambler	MORROW, Ellen B.	(215)646-1755	869
Appollo	RICHARDSON, Joy A.	(412)733-1081	1029
Blue Bell	LAUTENSCHLAG, Elisabeth C.		703
Broomall	CLINTON, Janet C.	(215)356-1927	222
Carlisle	NEITZ, Cordelia M.		892
Center Valley	WELLE, Jacob P.	(215)282-1100	1321
Cheltenham	ELSHAMI, Ahmed M.	(215)635-3823	346
Clarion	DINGLE, Susan	(814)226-2271	304
Coatesville	SILVER, Diane L.	(215)384-7648	1138
Colwyn	THOMAS, Deborah A.	(215)522-1786	1236
Coraopolis	KASPERKO, Jean M.		629
Franklin Center	HOWLEY, Deborah H.	(215)459-7049	566
Gettysburg	CHIESA, Adele M.	(717)334-1651	208
Glenside	LOCKETT, Cheryl L.		736
Harrisburg	SALINGER, Florence A.	(717)545-1874	1076
Indiana	KROAH, Larry A.	(412)463-2055	679
King of Prussia	RICH, Denise A.	(215)935-7054	1027
Lancaster	FRANCOS, Alexis	(717)397-9655	396
Lansdale	CLAYPOOL, Richard D.	(215)368-7439	220
Lehigh Valley	WEBER, A C.	(215)837-9615	1313
Malvern	HOLSTON, Kim R.	(215)644-2100	554
	YOUNG, Dorothy E.	(215)647-7449	1381
Millersville	LOTLIKAR, Sarojini D.		742
Monroeville	BERGER, Lewis W.	(412)825-2284	85
Natrona Heights	HAUGH, Amy J.	(412)224-5004	512
New Holland	MCGEE, Yvonne M.		806
Norristown	CATHEY, Gail L.	(215)278-5100	195
	SORG, Elizabeth A.	(215)279-3871	1168
Philadelphia	ALDRIDGE, Carol J.	(215)893-9613	11
	CALDWELL, John M.	(215)545-2809	172
	COOPER, Linda	(215)625-4719	243
	CUTRONA, Cheryl	(215)844-9027	268
	DONOVAN, Judith G.	(215)928-0577	312
	HOLMES, John H.	(215)592-1841	553
	LAVERTY, Bruce	(215)925-2688	703

INDEXER (Cont'd)
PENNSYLVANIA (Cont'd)
Philadelphia

	LEVIN, Pauline G.	(215)561-5831	720
	MUETHER, John R.	(215)887-5511	875
	POST, Joyce A.	(215)456-2971	986
	SCHAEFFER, Judith E.	(215)843-8840	1089
	SHUPAK, Harris J.	(215)438-5064	1134
	WALSH, James A.	(215)587-4877	1299
	WARTLUFT, David J.	(215)242-8746	1307
	ZIPF, Elizabeth M.	(215)587-4815	1389
Pittsburgh	BROSKY, Catherine M.	(412)682-0837	141
	DILWORTH, Kirby D.	(412)622-3105	303
	EPSTEIN, Barbara A.	(412)624-2378	351
	HARTNER, Elizabeth P.		508
	PIETZAK, Stephen D.	(412)227-6839	972
	SPIEGELMAN, Barbara M.	(412)824-2222	1174
	WEIR, Alexandra L.	(412)247-0207	1319
	WRIGHT, Nancy M.	(412)237-5948	1372
Radnor	KELLER, Kate V.	(215)688-6989	635
Reading	IZZO, Kathleen A.	(215)373-2981	586
	SMALL, Sally S.	(215)320-4823	1151
	STILLMAN, Mary E.	(215)921-2381	1194
	WEIHERER, Patricia D.	(215)376-7660	1317
	YU, Lorraine L.	(215)374-4548	1384
Sarver	LIVENGOOD, Candice C.		734
Scranton	VAN DE CASTLE, Raymond M.	(717)342-4603	1273
Spring House	WICKS, Pamela J.	(215)628-5632	1335
Swarthmore	HAMILTON, Gloria R.	(215)544-1369	492
University Park	CARSON, M S.	(814)865-1818	188
	RICE, Patricia O.	(814)865-1858	1027
Upland	BARON, Herman	(215)499-7415	58
Upper Darby	MORGAN, Dorothy H.	(215)789-9727	863
West Chester	CASSAR, Ann	(215)459-2380	193
	CHAFF, Sandra L.	(215)524-0547	197
	GUENTHER, Nancy A.	(215)436-4049	476
Wilkes-Barre	TYCE, Richard	(717)826-1148	1266
Yardley	BARATTA, Maria	(215)321-3289	55

PUERTO RICO

Caparra Heights	FERNANDEZ, Josefina L.	(809)782-2618	373
Ensenada	MEJILL-VEGA, Gregorio	(809)821-4734	822
Miramar	MCCARTHY, Carmen H.	(908)721-6574	794
San Juan	COLLAZO, Maria L.		232
	RODRIGUEZ, Ketty		1048

RHODE ISLAND

Kingston	FUTAS, Elizabeth	(401)792-2947	411
Providence	BRAUNSTEIN, Mark M.	(401)521-4771	130
Wakefield	BARNETT, Judith B.	(401)789-7435	57

SOUTH CAROLINA

Aiken	CUBBEDGE, Frankie H.	(803)648-6851	262
Charleston	PARKER, Mary A.	(803)556-9454	942
	SINDEL, Amy C.	(803)766-1282	1143
Clemson	LYLE, Martha E.	(803)656-5185	751
Columbia	CHOI, Jin M.	(803)799-8786	210
	MILTON, Brenda R.	(803)452-5042	845
	MOSS, Patsy G.	(803)799-4349	872
Greenwood	FECKO, Marybeth	(803)223-1810	367
	HARE, Ann T.	(803)229-8365	501
Irmo	BARDIN, Angela D.	(803)781-3138	56
Spartanburg	SMITH, Stephen C.	(803)596-3505	1161

SOUTH DAKOTA

Beresford	MYERS, Nancy L.	(605)763-5364	884
Brookings	HALLMAN, Clark N.	(605)688-5572	489
Sioux Falls	LANG, Elizabeth A.		695
Volga	LISTER, Lisa F.	(605)627-9409	732

TENNESSEE

Cookeville	TABACHNICK, Sharon	(615)372-3958	1219
Dayton	WRIGHT, David A.	(615)775-2041	1371
Germantown	RONDESTVEDT, Helen F.	(901)756-5470	1053
Knoxville	GRADY, Agnes M.	(615)637-0008	455
	HILL, Ruth J.	(615)974-4381	540
	PICQUET, D C.	(615)974-4381	971

INDEXER (Cont'd)
TENNESSEE (Cont'd)

Memphis	BAKER, Bonnie U.	(901)324-6536	48
	BOAZ, Ruth L.	(901)682-0595	108
	CO, Francisca	(901)324-2453	224
	PERRY, Glenda L.	(901)527-4348	960
	VILES, Elza A.	(901)454-4412	1284
Nashville	ARMONTROUT, Brian A.	(615)320-3678	32
	MARTIN, Laquita V.	(615)383-0953	777
	PILKINGTON, James P.	(615)322-2927	973
	SKELTON, William E.	(615)833-0195	1146
	WHITEHEAD, Jane		1332
Oak Ridge	ALDERFER, Jane B.	(615)482-2215	11
	DAVIS, Inez W.	(615)482-9619	279
	MCDONALD, Ethel Q.	(615)482-5011	802
Palmyra	FOWLER, James W.	(615)647-4172	393
Sewanee	HAYMES, Don		516

TEXAS

Abilene	ANDERSON, Madeleine J.	(915)674-2344	24
Amarillo	SNELL, Marykay H.	(806)353-5329	1163
Arlington	WILKERSON, Judith C.	(817)795-6555	1339
Austin	BECK, Alison M.	(512)263-5502	71
	BURLINGHAM, Merry L.		161
	BURT, Eugene C.	(512)471-4777	164
	DIVELY, Reddy	(512)288-3371	306
	GRACY, David B.	(512)471-3821	455
	JACKSON, Eugene B.	(512)345-1653	587
	JACKSON, Ruth L.	(512)345-1653	588
	SPRUG, Joseph W.	(512)448-8474	1176
	WEBSTER, Linda	(512)458-1852	1314
	WILLIAMS, Suzi	(512)451-3482	1346
	WISE, Olga B.	(512)244-8330	1357
Beaumont	HOLLAND, Mary M.	(409)892-8885	551
Bedford	PETERS, Mary N.	(817)283-3739	962
Boerne	HANKS, Ellen T.	(512)249-9670	496
Brownfield	HAMILTON, Betty D.	(806)637-4213	491
Bryan	HALL, Halbert W.	(409)846-0798	487
	HAMBRIC, Jacqueline B.	(409)846-0831	491
College Station	SMITH, Charles M.	(409)845-8850	1153
Cooper	ALBRIGHT, Susie K.		10
Corpus Christi	NEU, Margaret J.	(512)884-2011	896
Dallas	FOUDRAY, Rita C.	(214)824-1943	393
	HEIZER, Carolyn H.	(214)363-5148	523
	LOVELL, Bonnie A.	(214)826-1924	743
	METIVIER, Donna M.	(214)701-4222	828
	SALL, Larry D.	(214)385-8528	1076
	SMITH, Michael K.	(214)296-5187	1158
Denton	CALIMANO, Ivan E.	(817)898-4016	173
	SCHLESSINGER, Bernard S.	(817)898-2617	1094
Edinburg	GAUSE, George R.	(512)383-0811	423
El Paso	MATHIS, Margaret H.		784
	TAYLOR, Anne E.	(915)757-5095	1226
Evless	STATTON, Alison H.	(214)283-0802	1183
Flower Mound	SVEINSSON, Joan L.	(214)539-9308	1212
Fort Worth	ROARK, Carol E.	(817)926-4212	1038
Freeport	TYLER-WHITE, Patricia G.		1266
Galveston	NEALE, Marilee	(409)765-5575	891
Garland	DUREN, Norman	(214)686-1409	328
Houston	ANDERSON, Eliane G.	(713)229-7276	22
	BAGHAL-KAR, Vali E.	(213)667-4336	45
	CEBRUN, Mary J.	(713)965-4045	196
	CRENSHAW, Jan C.	(713)459-7116	258
	CRIST, Lynda L.	(713)527-4000	259
	EMERSON, Beth A.	(713)224-4262	347
	FORD, Margaret C.	(713)527-8101	389
	GILBERT, Barry	(713)629-6600	433
	HANDROW, Margaret M.	(713)524-9447	495
	MCCANN, Debra W.	(713)691-0148	794
	SCHWERBEL, Jeannette E.	(713)861-1373	1105
	TRAFFORD, Susan M.	(713)271-5610	1253
	WORCHEL, Harris M.	(713)956-7361	1368
Irving	AYRES, Edwin M.	(214)254-4108	43
	HAGLE, Claudette S.	(214)986-2343	483
	WHITE, Lely K.	(214)721-5310	1331
Longview	GROSS, Sally L.		472
Lubbock	LINDSEY, Thomas K.	(806)791-4770	730
McKinney	BALCOMBE, Judith A.	(214)548-4430	51
Mineral Wells	CHESHER, Joyce A.	(817)325-7801	206
Palestine	SELWYN, Laurie	(214)723-1436	1114

INDEXER (Cont'd)
TEXAS (Cont'd)

San Antonio	HEWINS, Elizabeth H.	(512)655-4672	535
	HICKEY, Lady J.	(512)436-3435	536
	HOOD, Elizabeth	(512)736-7292	556
	HURT, Nancy S.	(512)225-5500	578
	LANG, Anita E.	(512)684-5111	695
	MANEY, James W.	(512)341-1366	765
	MORTON, Diane E.	(502)821-6094	870
Sherman	GARCIA, Lana C.	(214)893-4401	417
Spring	ATRI, Pushkala V.	(713)370-3673	38
Victoria	ALLEN, Virginia M.	(512)573-5889	16
Waco	SHARP, Avery T.	(817)755-1366	1122

UTAH

Bountiful	SANDERS, William D.	(801)292-4429	1080
Payson	GILLUM, Gary P.	(801)465-4527	436
Provo	NIELSON, Paula I.	(801)375-9241	903
Salt Lake City	NOEL, Eileen V.	(801)594-6182	907
	REDDICK, Mary J.	(801)581-7024	1013

VERMONT

Middlebury	RAUM, Hans L.	(802)388-3711	1010
South Burlington	JULIANELLE, Shelley M.	(802)658-0103	619

VIRGIN ISLANDS

St Croix	VAUGHN, Robert V.	(809)778-8465	1280

VIRGINIA

Alexandria	DAVIDSON, Dero H.	(703)998-2976	276
	KOSLOSKE, Verleah B.	(703)931-1423	672
	MCLAUGHLIN, Elaine C.	(703)765-5860	813
	ROBERTSON, Jack	(703)549-3260	1042
Arlington	ASHKENAS, Bruce F.	(301)763-7410	36
	CLARKE, Robert F.		219
	DENNIE, David L.	(703)685-0208	292
	KNIGHT, Nancy H.	(703)522-2604	664
	LARMOUR, Rosamond E.	(703)247-7820	698
	WOLF, Richard E.	(703)276-0270	1360
Blacksburg	JOHNSON, Bryan R.	(703)552-0876	602
	KOK, Victoria T.	(703)951-3203	669
Charlottesville	MORRIS, Karen L.	(804)293-2475	867
	RODRIGUEZ, Robert D.		1048
	WALKER, Diane P.	(804)924-7041	1295
	WHITE, William		1332
Chesterfield	DUNAWAY, Carolyn D.	(804)748-1763	325
Christiansburg	LINN, Cynthia S.	(703)961-5988	731
Fairfax	CONIGLIO, Jamie W.	(703)323-2877	236
	FIENCKE, Elaine L.	(703)385-7700	376
Gloucester Point	BARRICK, Susan O.	(804)642-7114	59
Grottoes	BUCCO, Louise F.	(703)249-5424	153
Hampton	JORDAN, Caroline D.	(804)727-6234	616
Lexington	GREFE, Richard F.	(703)463-8648	465
Luray	GRIEVE, Karen R.		468
McLean	MACEWEN, Virginia B.		755
Norfolk	NICULA, J G.	(804)444-5321	903
Reston	JENSEN, Raymond A.	(703)648-6820	599
	JOSLYN, Camille	(703)471-1641	618
	KARRER, Jonathan K.	(703)648-4302	628
	MCLANE, Kathleen	(703)620-3660	813
Richmond	CLEMANS, Margaret H.	(804)358-9379	220
	HALL, Bonlyn G.	(804)359-0409	487
	VAN SICKLEN, Lindsay L.	(804)320-9691	1277
	WILLS, Luella G.	(804)233-7616	1349
	WINFREE, Waverly K.	(804)271-4163	1354
	YATES, Ella G.	(804)786-2332	1378
Roanoke	COLLINS, Mitzi L.		233
Salem	GLENNON, Irene F.	(703)380-3552	441
Springfield	FOURNIER, Susan K.	(703)569-9468	393
	LEONARD, Lawrence E.	(703)569-1541	716
Vienna	SCHAEFER, Mary E.	(703)759-6339	1089

WASHINGTON

Bainbridge Island	SPEARMAN, Marie A.	(206)842-6636	1172
Bothell	DECOSTER, Barbara L.	(206)488-7537	286
	YEE, J E.	(206)625-4870	1379
Ellensburg	DOI, Makiko	(509)963-2101	309
Mt Vernon	SAUTER, Sylvia E.	(206)336-2604	1085
Renton	SIENDA, Madeline M.		1136
Richland	CARVER, Sue A.	(509)943-5478	191

INDEXER (Cont'd)
WASHINGTON (Cont'd)

Seattle	BRZUSTOWICZ, Richard J.	(206)527-9357	152
	BURSON, Scott F.	(206)543-6794	163
	CHASE, Dale L.	(206)525-0795	203
	CRANDALL, Michael D.	(206)633-2530	255
	GRIPPO, Christopher F.		471
	HARMALA, Amy A.	(206)632-8338	502
	HILDEBRANDT, Darlene M.	(206)543-5818	538
	KREPS, Lise E.	(206)527-2817	678
	LIPTON, Laura E.	(206)543-8616	732
	SCOTT-MILLER, Gwen	(206)783-8687	1108
	SILVA, Mary E.		1138
	STIRLING, Dale A.	(206)367-2728	1195
Walla Walla	BREIT, Anitra D.		132

WEST VIRGINIA

Charleston	HUMPHRIES, Joy D.		574
Institute	SCOBELL, Elizabeth H.	(304)727-3314	1106
St Albans	PALMER, Marguerite C.	(304)722-6349	936

WISCONSIN

Appleton	KLAVER, Timothy J.	(414)735-0463	658
	NADZIEJKA, David E.	(414)731-8904	886
Caledonia	GRENDYSA, Peter A.	(414)764-3676	467
De Forest	SAYRS, Judith A.	(608)846-9363	1087
Eagle Heights	HSIEH, Cynthia C.	(608)238-7655	567
Green Bay	JOBELIUS, Nancy L.	(414)497-7508	601
Lake Geneva	CIBOCH, Lorraine A.	(414)245-5806	214
Madison	ARNESON, Arne J.	(608)833-1617	33
	HUMPHRIES, Lajean	(608)233-5540	574
	JESUDASON, Melba	(608)263-7464	600
	ROSENSHIELD, Jill K.	(608)233-2518	1057
	SHAFTMAN, Sarah	(608)241-7153	1119
Mequon	MADSEN, Joyce	(414)242-5403	759
Milwaukee	BJORKLUND, Edi		100
	COONEY, Charles W.	(414)444-6130	241
	FONG, Wilfred W.	(414)229-4707	388
	GEISAR, Barbara J.	(414)482-4948	425
	HORNUNG, Susan D.	(414)359-2111	560
	MARCUS, Terry C.	(414)352-5695	769
	PETERSON, Christine E.	(414)466-4817	963
	RISTIC, Jovanka	(414)229-6282	1036
	SAGER, Lynn S.	(414)964-5940	1074
	SCHLUGE, Vicki L.	(414)527-8477	1094
	WATERSTREET, Darlene E.	(414)964-2377	1309
North Fond Du Lac	GIEBEL, Thomas W.	(414)921-8348	432
Oshkosh	PARKS, Dennis H.	(414)426-4800	943
	TERESINSKI, Sally S.	(414)582-4324	1231
Racine	SCHINK, Sandra C.	(414)634-1495	1093
	TERANIS, Mara	(414)631-4144	1231
Sheboygan	TOBIN, R J.	(414)459-7606	1247

WYOMING

Cheyenne	KLEIN, Barbara L.	(307)635-3270	659
	MENDOZA, Anthanett C.	(307)778-8706	824
Laramie	EMERSON, Tamsen L.	(307)442-8643	347

CANADA

ALBERTA

Athabasca	DWORACZEK, Marian	(403)675-6261	330
Calgary	LANE, Barbara K.	(403)283-9998	694
	LEESMENT, Helgi	(403)251-2221	712
	ONN, Shirley A.	(403)282-5311	924
Edmonton	BATEMAN, Robert A.	(403)483-3432	63
	BAYRAK, Bettie	(403)478-8062	68
	COOKE, Geraldine A.	(403)439-5879	241
	DELONG, Kathleen M.	(403)432-5951	290
	SINCLAIR, John M.	(403)488-2646	1142
	STARR, Jane E.	(403)466-6004	1182
Lethbridge	DROESSLER, Judith B.	(403)381-2285	320
Tofield	LEE, Diana W.	(403)662-3607	709

INDEXER (Cont'd)

BRITISH COLUMBIA
North Vancouver	ASHCROFT, Susan M.	(604)984-8004	35
Prince George	PLETT, Katherine	(604)562-2131	978
Richmond	WEESE, Dwain W.		1316
Vancouver	DEVAKOS, Elizabeth R.	(604)255-6636	297
	GONNAMI, Tsuneharu	(604)224-4296	447
	ROBERTSON, Guy M.	(604)689-8494	1041
Victoria	ROMANIUK, Elena	(604)592-8819	1052

MANITOBA
| Winnipeg | MARSHALL, Kenneth E. | (204)269-3243 | 774 |

NEWFOUNDLAND
Mt Pearl	MORGAN, Pamela S.	(709)368-5926	864
St John's	DENNIS, Christopher J.	(709)722-0981	292
	MILNE, Dorothy J.	(709)737-8270	845

NOVA SCOTIA
| Amherst | CAMPBELL, Margaret E. | (902)667-2888 | 177 |
| Halifax | MACLENNAN, Oriel C. | (902)454-0697 | 757 |

ONTARIO
Brampton	CHAN, Bruce A.	(416)793-4636	199
Deep River	ALBURGER, Thomas P.		11
	LEWIS, Leslie	(613)584-2605	723
Don Mills	TEMPLIN, Dorothy	(416)447-2380	1231
Guelph	PAL, Gabriel	(519)824-4120	935
Kingston	FORKES, David	(613)544-2630	390
	MORLEY, William F.	(613)548-3432	865
Mississauga	MASEN, Naunihal S.	(416)897-6269	780
	MCLEAN-LOWE, Dallas	(416)828-5232	814
	WEI, Carl K.	(416)822-4111	1316
Nepean	KAYE, Barbara J.	(613)225-9920	632
Oakville	LUCIANI, Ellie	(416)842-4484	746
Ottawa	ARONSON, Marcia L.		34
	BRIERE, Jean M.	(613)996-3817	135
	GUILBERT, Manon M.	(613)233-8012	476
	HOUSTON, Louise B.	(519)993-7699	563
	MASON-WARD, Lesley	(613)726-1314	781
	VEEKEN, Mary L.	(613)523-2169	1280
Richmond Hill	ABRAM, Persis R.	(416)884-9288	3
St Thomas	RHYNAS, Don M.	(519)631-6050	1026
Toronto	BELLAMY, Patricia C.	(416)595-0300	78
	BREGMAN, Alvan M.	(416)767-3625	131
	CHIU, Lily F.	(416)868-2909	209
	DAVEY, Dorothy M.	(416)485-0377	276
	FRIEDLAND, Frances K.	(416)789-0741	403
	GIBSON, Elizabeth A.	(416)595-7894	432
	KHAN, Asma S.	(416)364-0321	646
	KLEMENT, Susan P.	(416)486-0239	660
	MCCANN, Judith B.	(416)429-1247	794
	MORRISON, Brian H.	(416)965-1641	867
	MORRISON, Carol A.	(416)967-3796	868
	NIXON, Audrey I.	(416)531-0830	906
	OLSHEN, Toni	(416)488-5321	922
	SABLJIC, John A.	(416)782-6754	1072
	SMITH, Anne C.	(416)423-9826	1152
	TIPLER, Stephen B.	(416)654-5617	1246
	TUDOR, Dean F.	(416)767-1340	1262
	WEIHS, Jean	(416)961-6027	1317
	WILLIAMSON, Nancy J.		1347
Willowdale	MARSHALL, Alexandra P.	(416)225-8193	773

PRINCE EDWARD ISLAND
| Brackley Beach | MANOVILLE, Susanne | (902)672-2714 | 767 |

QUEBEC
Ancienne-Lorette	JULIEN, Guy	(418)877-1054	619
Blainville	JETTE, Monika E.	(514)430-4945	600
Boischatel	LUSSIER, Richard	(418)822-1904	749
Boucherville	THERIAULT, Carmelle	(514)655-2665	1234
Bromont	RICHARD, Marie F.	(514)534-2321	1028
Chicoutimi	GAUDREAU, Louis	(418)549-9520	422
Chicoutimi Nord	SAUCIER, Danielle	(418)549-5474	1084
Drummondville	JANIK, Sophie	(819)477-7100	593
Hampstead	FLUK, Louise R.	(514)488-3187	386
Hull	MAILLOUX, Jean Y.	(819)997-5365	761
	TESSIER, Richard	(819)595-0910	1233
Laval	FORTIN, Jean		391

INDEXER (Cont'd)

QUEBEC (Cont'd)
Lennoxville	SHEERAN, Ruth J.	(819)569-9551	1125
Montreal	BERARDINUCCI, Heather R.	(514)255-2445	84
	BOIVIN-OSTIGUY, Jocelyne	(514)343-6193	111
	BUTLER, Patricia	(514)283-9046	167
	CAN, Hung V.	(514)521-8201	177
	CHAGNON, Danielle G.		197
	DESROCHERS, Monique	(514)733-0846	295
	DUCHESNEAU, Pierre	(514)281-6166	322
	DUMONT, Monique	(514)288-0100	325
	DUMOULIN, Nicole L.	(514)733-8051	325
	FOWLES, Alison C.	(514)842-7680	394
	GAULIN, S D.	(514)645-9444	422
	LALONDE, Diane	(514)767-3490	689
	LATOUR, Pierre	(514)729-4165	701
	MCFARLANE, Agnes	(514)282-2774	805
	MOHAMMED, Selima	(514)398-4780	852
	MUKHERJEE, Yolande	(514)932-6161	876
	NAGY, Cecile		886
	PELLETIER, Rosaire	(514)382-0895	955
	RABCHUK, Gordon K.	(514)874-2104	1001
	TEES, Miriam H.	(514)392-3362	1229
	THACH, Phat V.	(514)727-6817	1233
	TREVICK, Selma D.	(514)487-3367	1255
Montreal Oest	MORRISON, H D.	(514)488-9279	868
Pointe Claire			
Dorval	FIORE, Francine	(514)694-2055	379
Quebec	BERNIER, Gaston	(418)643-4032	89
	CANTIN, Gemma	(418)656-5070	179
	DENIGER, Constant	(418)692-4369	292
	GELINAS, Michel R.	(418)522-7203	426
Rouyn-Noranda	TREMBLAY, Levis	(819)762-0931	1255
St Lambert De			
Levis	HERLINGER, Peggy	(514)672-7360	531
St-Leonard	LAFRENIERE, Myriam	(514)322-6818	688
Sainte-Foy	ALAIN, Jean M.	(418)657-2485	9
	PETRYK, Louise O.	(418)656-6921	965
Sherbrooke	SOKOV, Asta M.	(819)821-7566	1166
Sillery	LALIBERTE, Madeleine A.	(418)687-9260	689
Westmount	LEDOUX, Marc A.	(514)484-5951	708

SASKATCHEWAN
Regina	BASLER, Ellen L.	(306)949-5431	63
	BROWNE, Berks G.	(306)584-8247	148
	THAUBERGER, Marianne T.	(306)757-9589	1234

AUSTRALIA
Kensington	WILSON, Concepcion S.		1350
Queensland	GOODELL, John S.		448
Toowong	GOODELL, Paulette M.		448

BAHAMAS
| Grand Bahamas | | | |
| Island | BARTON, Barbara I. | | 61 |

EGYPT
| Giza | EL-MASRY, Mohammed | | 345 |

ENGLAND
| Cambridge | HARKINS, Diane G. | | 501 |

FEDERAL REPUBLIC OF CHINA
Taidzi	CHENG, Sheung O.		200
Taipei	HUANG, Shih H.		568
	WANG, Sin C.		1303

FEDERAL REPUBLIC OF GERMANY
| Berlin | ULRICH, Paul S. | | 1268 |
| Heidelberg | SOKOLOWSKI, Denise G. | | 1166 |

FRANCE
| Guyancourt | COURRIER, Yves G. | | 251 |

GUATAMALA
| Guatamala City | MARBAN, Ricio | | 768 |

HONG KONG
| Fanling | WU, Edith Y. | | 1373 |
| The Peak | SANDFELDER, Paula M. | | 1080 |

INDEXER (Cont'd)
INDIA
Andhra Pradesh	SINHA, Pramod K.		1143
Bangalore	KITTUR, Krishna N.		657
Hyderabad	SATYANARAYANA, Vadhri V.	(260)586-0000	1084

INDONESIA
Jakarta	ADITIRTO, Irma U.		6

IRELAND
Banger	DUFFIN, Elizabeth A.		323

ISRAEL
Haifa	BEAVERS, Janet W.		71
Jerusalem	LANGERMAN, Shoshana P.		695

ITALY
Milan	PUSATERI, Liborio		998

JAMAICA
Kingston	MANSINGH, Laxmi	(809)927-2748	767

JAPAN
Ibaraki-ken	NOZOE, Atsutake		911

KENYA
Nairobi	IRURIA, Daniel M.		584

MEXICO
Benito	MACIAS-CHAPULA, Cesar A.		755
Mexico City	BARBERENA, Elsa		55
	RODRIGUEZ, Serafin L.		1048

NETHERLANDS
Rotterdam	SCHUURSMA, Ann B.		1103

NEW ZEALAND
Auckland	RICHARDS, Valerie		1028
	TWEEDALE, Dellene M.		1266

NIGERIA
Lagos	AFOLAYAN, Matthew A.	(018)001-6040	7
Okigwe	OGBAA, Clara K.		918

PHILIPPINES
Quezon City	OREJANA, Rebecca D.		925

SAUDI ARABIA
Riyadh	BUTT, Abdul W.		167
	KIRKWOOD, Brenda S.		655
	SMITH, Marilynn C.		1157

ZAMBIA
Chilanga	LUMANDE, Edward		748

LIBRARY AUTOMATION CONSULTANT

ALABAMA
Birmingham	BATTISTELLA, Maureen S.	(205)939-0581	65
	DAY, Janeth N.	(205)226-3614	282
	STEPHENS, Jerry W.	(209)363-6000	1188
	VANDERPOORTEN, Mary B.	(205)991-1368	1274
Decatur	MORRIS, Betty J.	(205)773-6262	866
Jasper	ELLIOTT, Riette B.	(205)387-0511	344
Mobile	DAMICO, James A.	(205)460-7021	271
Montgomery	LANE, Robert B.	(205)288-8122	694
Tuscaloosa	KASKE, Neal K.	(205)348-1521	628
	LEE, Sulan I.	(205)752-6008	711
	MUIR, Scott P.	(205)348-2299	876

ALASKA
Fairbanks	GALBRAITH, William B.	(907)479-5196	413

LIBRARY AUTOMATION CONSULTANT (Cont'd)
ARIZONA
Chandler	MCGORRAY, John J.	(602)961-8016	807
Flagstaff	EGAN, Terence W.	(602)523-6819	338
Glendale	MOSLEY, Shelley E.	(602)939-5469	872
Phoenix	DOHERTY, Walter E.	(602)262-5303	309
Scottsdale	COLE, Christopher H.	(602)994-7959	230
	POTTER, William G.	(602)991-5578	987
Sells	CULL, Roberta	(602)383-2601	263
Tempe	MACHOVEC, George S.	(602)965-5889	755
	RIGGS, Donald E.	(602)965-3950	1034
Tucson	ALURI, Rao	(602)722-5678	19
	BIERMAN, Kenneth J.	(602)887-4631	95
	BUXTON, David T.	(602)621-2101	168
	HURT, Charlie D.	(602)621-3566	578
	LEI, Polin P.		713

ARKANSAS
Fort Smith	PIERSON, Betty	(501)785-7135	972
Heber Springs	SEDELOW, Sally Y.	(501)362-3476	1110
	SEDELOW, Walter A.		1110

CALIFORNIA
Anaheim Hills	JOHNSON, Thomas L.	(714)998-4347	609
Bakersfield	KIRKLAND, Janice J.		655
Belmont	MEGLIO, Delores D.	(415)591-2333	821
Berkeley	BENGSTON, Carl E.	(415)642-5071	80
	BERGER, Michael G.	(415)642-9485	85
	BROWNRIGG, Edwin B.		149
	FALANGA, Rosemarie E.	(415)524-5501	361
	FROHMBERG, Katherine A.	(415)644-3600	405
	GRIFFIN, Hillis L.	(415)486-7499	468
	LARSON, Ray R.	(415)642-6046	699
	PARKS, Mary L.	(415)644-3401	943
	SALMON, Stephen R.	(415)549-3394	1077
	SILBERSTEIN, Stephen M.	(415)644-3600	1137
	SPENCER, John T.	(415)341-9442	1173
	WILLIAMS, Mary S.	(415)649-2520	1345
	ZBORAY, Ronald J.		1386
Burbank	ELMAN, Stanley A.	(818)351-8245	345
Camarillo	GILHEANY, Stephen J.	(805)987-6811	435
Cardiff By The Sea	MARKWORTH, Lawrence L.	(619)943-1197	772
Carmichael	PARSONS, Jerry L.	(916)966-2086	945
Carphell	ALIX, Cleta M.	(408)371-3294	13
Carson	KENNY-SLOAN, Linda		642
Chico	HUANG, George W.	(916)891-3455	568
	RYAN, Frederick W.	(916)895-5862	1071
	SESSIONS, Judith A.	(916)895-5862	1117
Claremont	PRESLAN, Bruce H.	(714)621-9998	991
	ROSE, David L.	(714)624-9041	1054
Concord	SKAPURA, Robert J.	(415)945-7268	1145
Costa Mesa	EPSTEIN, Susan B.	(714)754-1559	351
	MARLOR, Hugh T.	(714)631-5637	772
Culver City	ANDRADE, Rebecca	(213)837-5448	26
Cupertino	ALIPRAND, Joan M.	(408)253-0249	13
	KERSHNER, Lois M.	(408)255-2719	644
	MILLER, Ronald F.	(408)257-9162	842
Cypress	MOSER, Jane W.	(213)643-0322	870
Danville	CREW-NOBLE, Sara M.	(415)837-1399	258
Davis	BLANK, Karen L.	(916)752-2110	104
	IRELAND, Laverne H.	(916)756-1105	583
Eagle Rock	CRAWFORD, Marilyn L.	(213)259-8938	257
El Cerrito	KATZ, Jeffrey P.		630
Encinitas	PIERCE, Patricia J.	(619)436-5055	971
Fallbrook	MCNALLY, Ruth C.		816
Hayward	SASSE, Margo	(415)482-2770	1083
Inglewood	GOUDELOCK, Carol V.	(213)672-2543	454
Irvine	TSENG, Sally C.	(714)856-6832	1260
	WOODS, Lawrence A.	(714)786-3507	1367
Kensington	LAWRENCE, Gary S.	(415)642-2370	704
La Canada-Flintridge	DUNKLEE, Joanna E.	(818)790-3518	326
La Honda	HOLLAND, Mary	(415)747-0511	551
La Jolla	BOWLES, Garrett H.	(619)534-2759	121
	GABBERT, Gretchen W.	(619)456-4083	411
	MILLER, R B.	(619)534-3064	841
	TOMMEY, Richard J.	(619)454-4873	1250
Laguna Beach	KOUNTZ, John C.	(714)494-8783	673
Livermore	BURTON, Hilary D.	(415)423-8063	164
	PALLONE, Kitty J.	(415)447-2376	935

LIBRARY AUTOMATION CONSULTANT (Cont'd)
CALIFORNIA (Cont'd)

Long Beach	HECKLINGER, Ellen L.		519
Los Altos	BUTLER, Brett B.	(415)948-1064	166
Los Altos Hills	MCDONALD, Marilyn M.	(415)960-4390	803
Los Angeles	BISOM, Diane B.	(213)825-7557	99
	GRIGST, Denise J.	(213)651-3643	470
	JAFFE, Lee D.	(213)935-6770	591
	LEE, Diane T.	(213)972-4000	709
	MORRIS, Jacquelyn M.	(213)259-2671	866
	PRUHS, Sharon	(213)974-7780	996
	SCHOTTLAENDER, Brian E.	(213)825-7785	1099
	SUGRANES, Maria R.	(213)201-3507	1207
Malibu	CLARK, David L.	(818)888-9305	216
Menlo Park	BALES, F K.	(415)854-0115	52
	DENNETT, Stephen C.		292
	DILORETO, Ann M.	(415)326-7370	303
Mission Viejo	CHWEH, Steven S.	(714)768-3459	214
	WIERZBA, Heidemarie B.	(714)859-5193	1337
Modesto	SHAMS, Kamruddin	(209)576-8585	1120
Northridge	DAVIS, Douglas A.	(818)885-2261	278
Oakland	PRICE, Bennett J.	(415)642-9485	992
Orange	JOHNSON, Mary L.	(714)634-7708	607
Pacific Grove	HAY, Wayne M.	(408)646-9858	515
Pacific Palisades	HILLIS, Patricia K.	(213)454-0611	541
Palo Alto	MAIN, Linda Y.	(415)328-4865	761
	PRESTON, Cecilia M.	(415)327-5364	991
	TRIMBLE, Kathy W.	(415)855-5493	1256
Pasadena	CARD, Sandra E.	(818)356-6775	180
	KALVINSKAS, Louanne A.	(818)797-9890	623
Pleasant Hill	FOWELLS, Fumi C.	(415)689-0754	393
Pomona	LAMONTAGNE, Therese	(714)623-2716	691
	MORGAN, Ferrell	(714)625-7190	864
Port Reyes Station	ALLEN, Doris L.	(415)663-1122	14
Porterville	NAUMER, Janet N.	(209)539-3288	889
Rancho Cacamonga	CONNELL, William S.	(714)989-0506	237
Rancho Palos Verdes	WORMINGTON, Peggie		1369
Redondo Beach	CLIFFORD, Susan G.	(213)378-3824	222
Richmond	TURITZ, Mitch L.	(415)527-5109	1263
Ridgecrest	MAYES, Elizabeth A.	(619)446-6862	789
Riverside	MOONEY, Margaret T.	(714)787-3226	858
	THOMPSON, James C.	(714)682-4549	1240
Rolling Hills Estate	SAVAGE, Gretchen S.	(213)377-5032	1085
	TUNG, Sandra J.	(213)377-5032	1263
Sacramento	KAST, Gloria E.	(916)483-6765	629
	SEHR, Dena P.	(916)453-3529	1112
Salinas	SERTIC, Kenneth J.	(408)443-6186	1116
San Bernardino	DEMENT, Alice R.	(714)883-6772	291
	MILLS, Denise Y.		844
	WEBB, Duncan C.	(714)387-4959	1313
San Diego	BOSSEAU, Don L.	(619)229-2538	117
	HERON, Susan J.	(619)260-4800	532
	KAYE, Karen	(619)560-2695	632
San Francisco	AVENEY, Brian H.	(415)338-2956	41
	CHAO, Yuan T.	(415)981-8230	201
	JANK, David A.	(415)751-9958	593
	KOFF, Jacob	(415)781-2665	668
	MANN, Thomas	(415)951-0100	766
San Jose	EARHART, Marilyn N.	(408)554-4986	332
San Rafael	PLOTKIN, Nathan	(415)479-7018	978
Santa Ana	HOFFMAN, Herbert H.	(714)667-3451	548
	PINCOCK, Rulon D.	(714)558-5811	974
Santa Clara	HAMBRIDGE, Sally L.	(408)378-8616	401
Santa Cruz	ANDERSON, Clifford D.	(408)429-2501	22
Santa Monica	BECKER, Joseph	(213)829-6866	72
	HALL, Anthony	(213)827-1707	487
	SLEETER, Ellen L.	(213)829-4832	1148
Sebastopol	STRIBLING, Lorraine R.	(707)823-1419	1202
Sherman Oaks	LEWIS, Cookie A.	(818)788-5280	722
Sonoma	WINSON, Gail I.	(707)935-1546	1355
Stanford	CARSON, Susan A.	(415)723-2092	188
	CRAWFORD, Walt	(415)329-3551	257
	SCHMIDT, C J.	(415)493-5280	1095
Stockton	NICHOLS, Elizabeth D.	(209)943-2484	901
Studio City	KAZLAUSKAS, Edward J.	(818)797-7654	632
	PLATE, Kenneth H.	(818)797-7654	977
Thousand Oaks	SOY, Susan K.	(805)523-7288	1170
Vacaville	KERNS, John T.	(207)448-4459	644

LIBRARY AUTOMATION CONSULTANT (Cont'd)
CALIFORNIA (Cont'd)

West Covina	HOFFMAN, William J.	(818)919-5222	548

COLORADO

Arvada	PRESTON, Lawrence N.	(303)423-8729	991
Aurora	HUGHES, Brad R.	(305)699-6248	571
Boulder	KOHL, David F.	(303)492-6897	668
Colorado Springs	MALYSHEV, Nina A.	(303)531-6333	764
	SHERIDAN, John B.	(303)473-2233	1127
Denver	BOWERS, Sandra L.	(303)236-6649	121
	BRUNELL, David H.	(303)691-0550	150
	COCO, Al	(303)871-6200	226
	DULAN, Peter A.	(303)692-9261	324
	FORSMAN, Rick B.	(303)394-5125	391
	GOODYEAR, Mary L.	(303)556-2683	450
	HENSINGER, James S.	(303)691-0550	529
	ROSE, Phillip E.	(303)538-4276	1055
	SHAW, Ward	(303)861-5319	1124
	SMITH, Randolph R.	(303)744-8764	1159
Englewood	GARZA, Rosario		421
Evergreen	SHARER, E J.	(303)292-4458	1122
Fort Collins	SJOGREN, Mack D.		1145
Golden	KENNEY, Brigitte L.	(303)278-8482	641
	MADDOCK, Jerome T.	(303)231-1367	759
	PHINNEY, Hartley K.	(303)273-3690	969
Grand Junction	RICHMOND, Rick	(303)241-4358	1030
Greeley	PITKIN, Gary M.	(303)339-2237	976
Hayden	COSTA, Betty L.	(303)276-4345	249
Lakewood	ROESCH, Gay E.	(303)986-6365	1049
Littleton	LOERTSCHER, David V.	(303)770-1220	737
Meeker	NICKEL, Edgar B.	(303)878-3209	902
Montrose	CAMPBELL, John D.	(303)249-1078	176
Pueblo	JANES, Nina	(303)542-4591	593

CONNECTICUT

Danbury	BANKS, Mary E.	(203)792-0028	54
	SHEA, Roseanne M.	(203)744-3711	1124
Fairfield	COOMBS, Elisabeth G.	(203)254-4044	241
Greenwich	LUSHINGTON, Nolan	(203)655-3632	749
Hartford	CORCORAN, Virginia H.	(203)524-2230	246
	STONE, Dennis J.	(203)241-4617	1197
New Britain	WARZALA, Martin L.		1307
New Haven	HAHN, Boksoon	(203)432-1794	483
	KELLER, Michael A.	(203)389-2212	635
	LOWELL, Gerald R.	(203)773-3709	744
	TRAINER, Karin A.	(203)432-1818	1253
	TRIOLO, Victor A.	(203)397-4520	1257
	WEISBROD, David L.	(203)776-4043	1319
New London	SORENSEN, Pamela	(203)447-7622	1168
Stamford	BREGMAN, Joan R.		131
	KEMP, Thomas J.	(203)323-2826	639
	MEYER, Garry S.	(203)348-3028	830
Waterbury	FLANAGAN, Leo N.	(203)756-6149	383
	YOUNG, Marianne F.	(203)574-8216	1382
West Hartford	BRADBERRY, Richard P.	(203)241-4704	125
	MICHAUD, Noreen P.	(203)232-6560	832
Wethersfield	DONOHUE, Christine N.	(203)529-2938	311
Windsor	PARKS, Amy N.	(203)549-0404	943
Windsor Locks	MASTERS, Fred N.	(203)623-9801	782

DELAWARE

Bear	MANUEL, Larry L.	(302)834-5748	767
Newark	GLOGOFF, Stuart J.	(302)451-2234	441
	ULRICH, Sue	(302)451-2231	1268
Wilmington	BURDASH, David H.	(302)571-7402	158
	MINNICH, Nancy P.	(302)478-5291	846

DISTRICT OF COLUMBIA

Washington	BOHANAN, Robert D.	(202)523-3214	111
	CORTEZ, Edwin M.	(202)234-0388	248
	DEHART, Odell	(202)393-7100	288
	DENHAM, Maryanne H.	(202)662-9198	292
	FRANKLIN, Brinley R.	(202)223-9525	397
	FRIERSON, Eleanor G.	(202)623-7000	404
	GILLESPIE, Veronica M.	(202)287-5262	435
	HALEY, Roger K.	(202)224-2976	486
	KEHOE, Patrick E.	(202)885-2674	634
	LISOWSKI, Andrew H.	(202)287-5491	732
	LOO, Shirley	(202)546-1196	740

LIBRARY AUTOMATION CONSULTANT (Cont'd)
DISTRICT OF COLUMBIA (Cont'd)
Washington

	PACIFICI, Sabrina I.	(202)429-4094	933
	PAGE, John S.	(202)554-0486	934
	PRICE, Mary S.	(202)287-5137	992
	REYNOLDS, Dennis J.	(202)745-7722	1025
	SARANGAPANI, Chetluru	(202)282-3091	1082
	TURTELL, Neal T.	(202)842-6506	1265

FLORIDA
Avon Park	APPELQUIST, Donald L.	(813)453-6661	30
Captiva	WALTON, Terence M.	(813)454-0410	1302
Coconut Grove	DEWAR, Jo E.	(305)858-8787	298
Cooper City	JACKSON, Nancy I.	(305)434-8724	588
Coral Gables	LOWELL, Felice K.	(305)284-2250	744
	ROBAR, Terri J.	(305)284-4706	1038
Crawfordville	TODD, Hal W.	(904)926-5656	1248
Fort Lauderdale	HATFIELD, Frances S.	(305)463-5928	511
	KEMPER, Marlyn S.	(305)475-7047	639
	TAYSOM, Daniel B.	(305)760-5771	1229
Freeport	DAVIS, Bonnie D.	(904)835-4432	277
Gainesville	COREY, James F.	(904)372-2747	246
	TAYLOR, Betty W.	(904)372-0716	1226
	WILLOCKS, Robert M.	(904)392-0342	1349
Jacksonville	CORNELL, Sylvia C.	(904)630-1994	247
	JONES, Robert P.	(904)646-2615	614
Jensen Beach	HENNINGS, Leroy	(305)334-6134	528
Lakeland	DEE, Cheryl R.		286
Marianna	STABLER, William H.	(904)482-3474	1177
Melbourne	HENSON, Llewellyn L.	(305)768-8000	529
	SHIAU, Ian L.	(305)768-0973	1129
Miami	PAUL, Nora M.	(305)376-3402	949
	WILLIAMS, Thomas L.	(305)547-5782	1347
	WRIGHT, Joseph F.	(305)379-3105	1372
North Lauderdale	BRESLAUER, Lester M.	(305)721-5181	133
Orlando	GRIMSLEY, Judy L.	(305)896-2535	470
	LABRAKE, Orlyn B.	(305)275-4564	686
Pembroke Pines	MULLER, Charles W.	(305)431-5123	877
St Petersburg	CORNWELL, Douglas C.	(813)541-7206	247
Tallahassee	CONAWAY, Charles W.	(904)893-1482	235
	HART, Thomas L.	(904)385-7550	507
	LOGAN, Elisabeth L.		737
Tampa	CRAIG, James P.	(813)238-5514	254
	MARTIN, Robert A.	(813)253-3333	778
Tarpon Springs	O'BRIEN, Elizabeth M.	(813)942-3291	914
Thonotosassa	TABOR, Curtis H.	(813)986-3636	1219
West Palm Beach	PRITCHARD, Teresa N.	(305)684-7349	994
Winter Park	SEBRIGHT, Terence F.	(305)678-8846	1110
Winter Springs	THOMAN, Nancy L.		1236

GEORGIA
Athens	ANDERSON, Thomas G.	(404)542-0598	25
	BAKER, Barry B.	(404)542-2534	47
	BISHOP, David F.	(404)542-0621	99
Atlanta	COOPER, Glenn	(404)676-2096	243
	DEEMER, Selden S.	(404)727-0271	286
	DRAKE, Miriam A.	(404)894-4501	318
	FISTE, David A.		382
	HENDRIX, Linda S.	(404)252-5745	527
	JOHNSON, Herbert F.	(404)727-6861	605
	LONG, Linda E.	(404)521-4210	739
	PRESLEY, Roger L.	(404)658-2176	991
	ROAN, Tattie W.	(404)320-9376	1038
	WILSON, Lesley P.	(404)892-0944	1351
	WILTSE, Helen C.	(404)451-4260	1353
Decatur	CHAMBERS, Shirley M.	(404)289-6517	198
	LANDRAM, Christina L.	(404)321-0778	693
	MOELLER, Edward R.	(404)294-6641	851
Duluth	SHELTON, John L.	(404)381-8060	1126
Griffin	WILKINSON, Evalyn S.	(404)227-8532	1340
Jonesboro	BAKER, Gordon N.	(404)961-9824	48
Macon	HOWARD, Mary R.	(912)744-2960	564
	RANKIN, Jocelyn A.	(912)744-2515	1007
Marietta	LISI, Susan C.	(404)955-1375	732
Red Oak	LETT, Rosalind K.		719
Watkinsville	WHITEHEAD, James M.	(404)769-8917	1332

LIBRARY AUTOMATION CONSULTANT (Cont'd)
HAWAII
Honolulu

	CHAFE, Douglas A.	(808)537-8375	197
	HAAK, John R.	(808)948-7205	480
	KANE, Bartholomew A.	(808)524-8344	624
	LUNDEEN, Gerald W.	(808)948-7321	748
	UCHIDA, Deborah K.	(808)548-7915	1267

IDAHO
Cambridge	HAWKINS, Nina L.	(208)257-3541	514
Menan	COVINGTON, Eddis E.	(208)754-4183	252
Moscow	BAIRD, Lynn N.	(208)885-6713	47
	FORCE, Ronald W.	(208)885-6584	389
Pocatello	WATSON, Peter G.	(208)236-2997	1310
Post Falls	JONES-LITTEER, Corene A.	(208)773-1515	616

ILLINOIS
Addison	WRIGHT, Deborah L.	(312)628-3338	1371
Arlington Heights	VONDRUSKA, Eloise M.	(312)392-7232	1288
Berwyn	FEDECZKO, Joyce L.	(312)795-3089	367
Carol Stream	SONDALLE, Barbara J.	(312)653-7000	1167
Champaign	DESSOUKY, Ibtesam	(217)333-4956	296
	JOHNSON, Jane S.		605
Charleston	RAO, Paladugu V.	(217)581-6061	1008
Chicago	BREEN, Joanell C.	(312)929-1445	131
	CARLSON, Robert P.	(312)944-6780	182
	CARSON, James G.	(312)996-2742	188
	CLARK, Gerald L.	(312)924-4362	217
	DOWELL, David R.	(312)567-6844	315
	DREWETT, William O.	(312)281-3651	319
	EVANS, Linda J.	(312)642-4600	357
	FOUSER, Jane G.	(312)477-4712	393
	FRANKLIN, Annette E.	(312)996-3447	397
	GARDNER, Trudy A.	(312)942-8735	418
	GIANGRANDE, Mark G.		430
	GROFT, Mary L.	(312)477-7065	471
	IDDINGS, Daniel H.	(312)321-0432	581
	JOHN, Nancy R.	(312)996-2716	601
	KLEINMUNTZ, Dalia S.	(312)883-3580	660
	MCCARTNEY, Elizabeth J.	(312)666-8262	794
	MCCLINTOCK, Patrick J.		797
	MCGEE, Rob	(312)321-0432	805
	MILLER, Robert	(312)488-7195	841
	MOUW, James R.	(312)996-2706	874
	MULLER, Karen	(312)944-6780	877
	PETERSON, Randall T.	(312)427-2737	964
	PIZER, Irwin H.	(312)996-8974	977
	RANDALL, Sara L.		1006
	REED, Virginia R.	(312)477-6836	1015
	RICHMOND, Diane A.	(312)269-2864	1030
	SCOTT, Alice H.	(312)493-2451	1106
	SIMPSON, Donald B.	(312)955-4545	1141
	STRAWN, Gary L.	(312)327-4930	1201
	VISKOCHIL, Larry A.	(312)935-1071	1285
	WAITE, Ellen J.	(312)508-2641	1293
Crystal Lake	MILLER, Randy S.	(815)455-4660	841
Darien	BOWDEN, Philip L.	(312)887-1620	120
De Kalb	RAST, Elaine K.	(815)758-5234	1009
	TOROK, Andrew G.	(815)753-1734	1251
	VARNER, Carroll H.	(815)753-1094	1278
Des Plaines	MCKENZIE, Duncan J.	(312)967-8554	811
East Peoria	LINDGREN, William D.	(309)694-5462	729
Elgin	GORDON, Lewis A.	(312)695-1455	451
Evanston	CLOUD, Patricia D.	(312)491-3136	223
	GRISCOM, Richard W.	(312)491-3487	471
	HORNY, Karen L.	(312)491-7662	560
	JACOBSON, William R.	(312)328-7584	590
	NIELSEN, Brian	(312)491-2170	903
	SCHAPIRO, Benjamin H.	(312)491-5186	1090
Evergreen Park	GARCIA-RUIZ, Maritza L.	(312)425-6104	417
Flora	HARRIS, Thomas J.	(618)662-2679	506
Forest Park	VAN HOUTEN, Stephen		1275
Freeport	WELCH, Eric C.	(815)235-6121	1321
Geneva	SHURMAN, Richard L.	(312)232-8457	1134
Glenview	MOSS, Barbara J.	(312)729-7500	872
Gurnee	FUNK, Carla J.	(312)367-6213	409
Highland Park	SHERRY, Diane H.	(312)433-3968	1129
Joliet	JOHNSTON, James R.	(815)729-3481	610
La Grange	SCHULTHEISS, Louis A.	(312)354-6958	1101
Lisle	STUNKARD, Gilbert L.	(312)969-5426	1205

LIBRARY AUTOMATION CONSULTANT (Cont'd)
ILLINOIS (Cont'd)

Mascoutah	GORDON, Diane M.	(618)566-4981	451
Maywood	LUDWIG, Logan T.	(312)531-3192	747
Normal	DELOACH, Marva L.	(309)438-7463	290
Oak Park	BEN-SHIR, Rya H.	(312)386-5444	83
	MARSHALL, Maggie L.	(312)848-4432	774
Pearl City	DAWSON, Lawrence	(815)443-2856	282
Peoria	SWORSKY, Felicia G.	(309)672-8885	1217
Rock Island	CONWAY, Colleen M.	(309)794-7316	239
	OHRLUND, Bruce L.	(309)786-0698	919
Skokie	MITCHELL, Joyce P.	(312)676-1714	849
Springfield	HILDRETH, Charles R.		539
	LARISON, Brenda	(217)529-9233	697
	SHACKLETON, Suzanne M.	(217)786-6375	1118
Sullivan	ELDER, Nancy J.	(217)728-4832	342
Sun City	STUHLMAN, Daniel D.	(312)262-8959	1205
Sycamore	BERRY, John W.	(815)895-4225	90
Taylorville	PODESCHI, Gwen	(217)824-5695	979
Urbana	MAHER, William J.	(217)333-0798	760
	SHAW, Debora	(217)333-1666	1123
	SIEGEL, Martin A.	(217)333-3247	1136
	WEI, Karen T.	(217)344-5647	1316
Wauconda	SHENASSA, Daryoosh	(312)526-9123	1126
West Chicago	KOSMAN, Joyce E.	(312)231-0774	672
Wheaton	BERGER, Carol A.	(312)653-1115	85
	EMBAR, Indrani M.	(312)668-1742	347
	HU, Robert T.	(312)690-7969	568
	RUSSELL, Janet	(312)653-1115	1069
Wheeling	HAMMER, Donald P.	(312)541-8149	493
Wilmette	MCGINN, Thomas P.	(312)256-5596	806
Winnetka	LUNDQUIST, Marie A.	(312)441-3315	748

INDIANA

Anderson	SACZAWA, Rosemary	(317)778-2254	1073
Bloomington	MORGAN, James J.	(812)332-8709	864
	WALLACE, Danny P.	(812)335-2848	1297
	ZHU, Xiaofeng	(812)335-2666	1387
Columbus	MEREDITH, Meri	(812)372-3482	825
	POOR, William E.	(812)377-7201	983
Fort Wayne	KRULL, Jeffrey R.	(219)424-7241	680
	SHEETS, Michael T.	(219)483-2854	1125
	STANLEY, Luana K.	(219)432-3287	1180
Indianapolis	EBERSHOFF-COLES, Susan V.	(317)269-1815	334
	FRANCQ, Carole	(317)274-1411	396
Logansport	SHIH, Philip C.	(219)753-6383	1130
Marion	BOYCE, Harold W.	(317)674-5211	122
Mishawaka	WITTORF, Robert H.	(219)259-4112	1359
Muncie	RANSIL, M M.	(317)285-8032	1007
	WOOD, Michael B.	(317)289-5417	1364
South Bend	DOLAN, Robert T.	(219)289-1172	309
Terre Haute	BAUMGARTNER, Kurt O.	(812)234-4818	66
	GALE, Sarah E.	(812)237-2529	413
	LEACH, Ronald G.	(812)237-3700	706
	SHANE, T C.	(812)299-5289	1120
West Lafayette	CANGANELLI, Patrick W.	(317)494-2768	178

IOWA

Ames	MORRIS, Dilys E.	(515)294-8186	866
	SCHMIDT, Sandra L.	(515)292-1118	1096
Cedar Rapids	BLISS, David H.	(319)393-5892	105
Coralville	PEPETONE, Diane S.	(319)351-3922	957
Iowa City	BROWN, Jeanine B.		144
	ENGER, Kathy B.	(319)335-4123	349
	HARMON, Charles T.	(319)337-2140	502
	ROBINSON, Caitlin M.	(319)335-9049	1043
Marshalltown	TRAVILLIAN, Mary W.	(515)752-1578	1254

KANSAS

Hesston	EICHELBERGER, Marianne	(316)327-4666	339
Lawrence	JOHNSON, Ellen S.	(913)864-3496	604
Manhattan	GRASS, Charlene G.	(913)532-6516	458
	MORELAND, Rachel S.	(913)539-8713	863
Overland Park	ALLEN, Norene F.	(800)338-8527	15
	SEVIER, Susan G.	(913)451-3111	1117
Topeka	CARROLL, James K.	(913)273-9156	187
Wichita	MEYERS, Judith K.	(316)832-1211	831
Winfield	ZUCK, Gregory J.	(316)221-4150	1391

LIBRARY AUTOMATION CONSULTANT (Cont'd)
KENTUCKY

Fort Thomas	NEWMAN, Linda D.	(606)441-0899	899
Highland Heights	SCHULTZ, Lois E.	(606)572-5275	1102
Lexington	STEENSLAND, Ronald P.		1184
Louisville	BING, Dorothy A.	(502)448-4607	97
	HUFF, James E.	(502)585-9911	570
	NILES, Judith F.	(502)588-6756	904

LOUISIANA

Baton Rouge	SCULL, Roberta A.		1108
	SMITH, Richard J.	(504)342-4942	1160
Lafayette	RAGHAVAN, Vijay V.	(318)231-6603	1003
Marrero	FAVORITE, Grealdine J.	(504)348-0234	366
Metairie	GOLDSTEIN, Cynthia H.	(504)885-5296	446
	SALVATORE, Gayle E.	(504)456-2660	1078
New Orleans	CARTEE, Lewis D.	(504)865-5131	188
Ruston	DICARLO, Michael A.	(318)257-3594	300
Saint Amant	HILL, Sue A.		540
Slidell	HOLLEY, Rebecca M.	(504)641-0198	551

MAINE

Alfred	ANDERSON, Marjorie E.	(207)324-6915	24
Bangor	BEISER, Karl A.	(207)947-4876	75
Orono	ALBRIGHT, Elaine M.	(207)581-1661	10

MARYLAND

Adamstown	LIGHTBOWN, Parke P.		726
Annapolis	MENEGAUX, Edmond A.	(301)268-6741	824
	WAGNER, Susan C.	(301)268-2315	1292
Baltimore	ARRINGTON, Susan J.	(301)396-4042	34
	BLUTE, Mary R.	(301)889-4080	107
	BROADY, Jessie	(301)661-1781	138
	FREIBURGER, Gary A.	(301)328-7547	401
	LUCIER, Richard E.	(301)955-3411	746
	MEYER, Alan H.	(301)484-5594	829
	SMITH, Mary P.	(301)358-0356	1158
	SZARY, Richard V.	(301)358-2064	1218
	WOODS, Catharine C.	(301)323-8319	1366
Bethesda	HENDERSON, Madeline M.	(301)530-6478	526
	JOHNSON, Carol A.	(301)251-5378	602
	MCCUTCHEON, Dianne E.	(301)496-1218	801
	SHOCKLEY, Cynthia W.	(301)320-2000	1132
	TURNER, Susan A.	(301)229-0508	1265
Catonsville	WILT, Larry J.	(301)455-2341	1353
Churchton	TONEY, Stephen R.	(301)261-5650	1250
College Park	ASSOUAD, Carol S.	(301)935-5631	37
	KLAIR, Arlene F.	(301)454-5066	657
Columbia	DIENER, Carol W.	(301)381-2525	302
	DOVE, Samuel	(301)964-4189	315
	NEWMAN, Wilda B.	(301)730-7583	900
	SCHWARTZ, Betsy J.	(301)381-5028	1104
Damascus	JOHNSON, Susan W.	(301)253-2759	609
Ellicott City	MARTIN, Susan K.	(301)988-9893	778
Gaithersburg	BENNETT, Harry D.	(301)840-1467	81
	VAN BRUNT, Virginia	(301)762-6701	1272
Gambrills	YOUNG, Peter R.	(301)923-2902	1383
Germantown	ALBRIGHT, John B.	(301)428-3700	10
	MCQUEEN, Judith D.	(301)428-3400	817
Hillcrest Heights	CHAPMAN, Elwynda K.	(301)894-0963	202
Kensington	WILLMERING, William J.	(301)946-2753	1348
Lanham	HUFFER, Mary A.	(301)577-3640	570
Laurel	SAWYER, Edmond J.	(301)725-4750	1086
Mount Airy	LISTON, David M.	(301)831-3000	732
Potomac	CHANG, Frances M.	(301)258-0772	200
	PATRICIU, Florin S.	(301)983-9579	947
Rockville	BERUL, Lawrence H.	(301)984-9400	91
	BYRD, Harvey C.	(301)251-5481	169
	GRIFFITHS, Jose M.	(301)881-6766	469
	MARTINEZ-GOLDMAN, Aline		779
	WALL, Eugene	(301)881-4990	1297
Salisbury	CUNNINGHAM, Barbara M.	(301)742-1537	265
Silver Spring	BATTY, Charles D.	(301)593-8901	65
	HARBISON, John H.	(801)589-4223	499
	HENDERSON, Ronald L.	(301)588-2844	527
	KADEC, Sarah T.	(301)598-7694	621
	MARKS, Cicely P.	(301)649-7200	771
	MCDONALD, Michael L.	(301)946-0278	803
	PEMPE, Ruta	(301)587-3846	956
	QUINN, Sidney	(301)589-4461	1000

LIBRARY AUTOMATION CONSULTANT (Cont'd)
MARYLAND (Cont'd)
Silver Spring

	STERN, Michael P.	(301)495-9413	1189
Takoma Park	MCNELLIS, Claudia H.	(301)270-8950	817
Upper Marlboro	HARBERT, Cathy E.	(301)868-9280	499
Welcome	DUDLEY, Robyn A.	(301)934-4602	323
Wheaton	MWALIMU, Charles	(301)933-4040	884

MASSACHUSETTS
Acton	HURD, Sandra H.	(617)263-7574	577
Bedford	MAIER, Robert C.	(617)275-9440	761
Belmont	PHELAN, Mary C.		967
Beverly	GAGNON, Ronald A.	(617)922-6722	412
Boston	BEGG, Karin E.		74
	HAYES, Alison M.	(617)482-1776	515
	KERN, Donald C.	(617)638-8030	643
	MCKIRDY, Pamela R.	(617)738-2223	812
	PLUNKET, Joy H.	(617)327-5175	978
	SCHWARTZ, Frederick E.	(617)522-0234	1104
	SHARE, Donald S.	(617)738-2242	1122
Bridgewater	CHANDRASEKHAR, Ratna	(617)697-3648	200
Cambridge	COLLINS, John W.	(617)495-4225	232
	DEARBORN, Susan C.	(617)576-3205	284
	KNAACK, Linda M.	(617)253-8462	663
	MOFFITT, Michael D.	(617)864-5770	852
	PAPALAMBROS, Rita G.	(617)497-2047	939
Carlisle	HAMILTON, Fae K.	(617)369-1981	492
Chelmsford	DONOVAN, Paul	(617)250-7270	312
Chestnut Hill	CHANNING, Rhoda K.	(617)552-4470	201
East Longmeadow	STACK, May E.	(413)525-6350	1177
Framingham	KUKLINSKI, Joan L.	(617)879-8575	683
Ipswich	GRAY, Carolyn M.	(617)356-0773	459
Lexington	LUCKER, Jay K.	(617)862-4558	746
	MAXANT, Vicary		787
	WALSH, Joanna M.	(617)863-1275	1299
Littleton	BUCKLAND, Lawrence F.	(617)899-1086	154
Lowell	DESROCHES, Richard A.	(617)452-5000	295
	KARR, Ronald D.	(617)452-5000	628
Medford	MCKIRDY, Colin	(617)381-3345	812
	PELLEGRINI, Deborah A.	(617)396-5457	955
Millis	PERRY, Guest	(617)376-8459	960
Monterey	INTNER, Sheila S.	(413)528-2698	583
Natick	WANG, Gary Y.	(617)237-7715	1302
Needham	MARKUSON, Carolyn A.	(617)449-6299	772
New Bedford	FINNI, John J.	(617)999-6034	379
Newton	CUNNINGHAM, Robert L.	(617)969-0400	265
	LINSKY, Leonore K.	(617)527-3646	731
Newtonville	INGERSOLL, Diane S.	(612)438-3978	582
North Adams	GOLDBERG, Steven R.	(413)664-6246	444
North Andover	HOLMES, Lyndon S.	(617)689-9334	553
	REEVE, Russell J.	(617)682-6260	1016
Peabody	TRICARICO, Mary A.	(617)531-0100	1256
Reading	DAMICO, Nancy B.	(617)944-9411	272
	MARCY, Henry O.	(617)944-2194	769
	O'CONNOR, Jerry	(617)944-6452	916
Roybury	SUTTON, Joyce A.	(617)427-4941	1211
Springfield	STEVENS, Michael L.	(413)739-3871	1190
Stoughton	ANDERSON, Cheryl M.	(617)344-4000	22
Waltham	CHATTERTON, Leigh A.	(617)893-4807	204
	HORGAN, Laura A.	(617)647-0868	559
West Newton	CHEN, Ching C.	(617)738-2224	205
West Springfield	HELO, Martin	(413)736-4561	525
Westwood	CLAPPER, Mary E.	(617)329-3350	216
Worcester	CHAMBERLAIN, Ruth B.	(617)244-3612	197

MICHIGAN
Ann Arbor	DOUGHERTY, Richard M.	(313)764-9356	314
	LANSDALE, Metta T.		696
	MCDONALD, David R.	(313)764-0412	802
	MOSEY, Jeanette	(313)973-8607	871
Belleville	STARESINA, Lois J.	(313)699-7549	1181
Birmingham	MARTIN, John E.	(313)647-1700	776
Dearborn	LUKASIEWICZ, Barbara	(313)593-5400	747
	NUCKOLLS, Karen A.	(313)593-5400	912
Detroit	MA, Helen Y.	(313)833-1016	753
	MORROW, Blaine V.	(313)893-1746	869
	SHUMAN, Bruce A.	(313)577-1825	1134
	SPYERS-DURAN, Peter	(313)577-4048	1177
	WILLIAMS, James F.	(313)577-4021	1343

LIBRARY AUTOMATION CONSULTANT (Cont'd)
MICHIGAN (Cont'd)
East Lansing	MEAHL, D D.	(517)355-7641	819
	YARBROUGH, Joseph W.	(517)337-0693	1378
Eaton Rapids	FLAHERTY, Kevin C.	(517)663-2362	383
Grand Rapids	FITZPATRICK, Nancy C.	(616)676-1568	383
Holland	LIGHT, Lin	(616)335-2540	726
	MURRAY, Diane E.	(616)394-7792	881
Lansing	FRY, James W.	(517)373-1593	406
Northville	FIELD, Judith J.	(313)349-1953	375
Novi	KIEFER, Marilyn V.	(313)344-8300	647
Okemos	TREGLOAN, Donald C.	(517)349-7767	1255
Pontiac	LYNCH, Mollie S.	(313)858-3495	752
Portage	HEMPHILL, Frank A.	(616)323-2627	525
Southfield	SUMMERS, Sheryl H.	(313)357-0404	1209
Spring Lake	PRETZER, Dale H.	(616)846-8967	992
University Center	JONES, Clifton H.	(517)790-4236	612

MINNESOTA
Eden Prairie	GROSCH, Audrey N.	(612)937-2345	472
Mankato	CARRISON, Dale K.	(507)389-5062	187
	MOORE, Barbara N.	(507)389-5957	858
	PEISCHL, Thomas P.	(507)389-5953	955
	READY, Sandra K.	(507)388-4003	1012
Minneapolis	BARRETT, Darryl D.	(612)370-0869	59
	BRUEMMER, Bruce H.	(612)624-5050	149
	COGSWELL, James A.	(612)624-5518	227
Minnetonka	HUTTNER, Marian A.	(612)545-2338	579
New Brighton	KEIM, Robert	(612)633-3393	635
Pine Island	BENSON, Laurel D.	(507)356-8515	83
Plymouth	VETH, Terry R.	(612)559-2179	1283
Red Wing	SWEEN, Roger	(612)388-5723	1214
Roseville	TALLY, Roy D.	(612)488-2028	1221
St Paul	EPSTEIN, Rheda	(612)292-6392	351
	KING, Jack B.	(612)641-2373	651
	RASMUSSEN, Mary L.	(612)644-0685	1009

MISSISSIPPI
Clinton	MYRICK, Judy C.	(601)924-6092	885
Pascagoula	MAJURE, William D.	(601)769-7149	762
University	COCHRAN, J W.	(601)232-7361	225

MISSOURI
Boonville	JOB, Rose A.		601
Columbia	ANDREWS, Mark J.	(314)875-0154	27
	BARNES, Everett W.	(314)882-4581	57
	KOPP, Kurt W.	(314)449-0185	671
	PARKER, Ralph H.	(314)442-4631	942
	RAITHEL, Frederick J.	(314)875-0026	1004
	RICKERSON, George T.	(314)445-1493	1031
Fenton	CHAN, Jeanny T.	(314)343-0929	199
Joplin	KEMP, Charles H.	(417)625-9386	639
Kansas City	HAMMOND, John J.	(816)221-2695	493
	LINSE, Mary M.	(816)765-0831	731
Kirksville	ONSAGER, Lawrence W.	(816)665-4283	924
Kirkwood	SHALLENBERGER, Anna F.	(314)821-4169	1119
Maryville	HANKS, Nancy C.	(816)562-1590	496
	MURPHY, Kathryn L.	(816)582-4768	880
Perryville	TUCKER, Phillip H.	(314)547-7433	1262
St Charles	MUETH, Elizabeth C.	(314)447-5116	875
St Louis	FABIAN, William M.	(314)275-3582	360
	HALBROOK, Barbara	(314)362-2786	485
	HELMS, Mary E.	(314)362-2787	525
	HUESTIS, Jeffrey C.	(314)889-5409	570
	NOBLE, Barbara N.	(314)367-6324	906
	WILKINSON, William A.	(314)997-3585	1340
Springfield	MEADOR, John M.	(417)882-8032	819

MONTANA
Bozeman	ALLDREDGE, Noreen S.	(406)587-4877	14
	STACK, Laurie A.	(406)994-5310	1177

NEBRASKA
Beatrice	FINDLING, Carol A.	(402)223-4595	377
Bellevue	JACKA, David C.	(402)293-3157	586
Lincoln	COOK, Anita I.	(402)466-3981	239
	NESMITH, Edmund D.	(402)486-2514	896
	WAGNER, Rod G.	(402)423-7476	1292
Omaha	LITTLE, Nina M.	(402)554-6282	733
Ralston	OYER, Kenneth E.	(402)331-8843	932

LIBRARY AUTOMATION CONSULTANT (Cont'd)

NEVADA

Carson City	KERSCHNER, Joan G.	(702)887-2615	644
Henderson	HARRISON, Susan E.		507
Las Vegas	HUNSBERGER, Charles W.	(702)733-7810	574
Reno	PARKHURST, Carol A.	(702)784-6566	942

NEW HAMPSHIRE

Concord	DRUKE-STICKLER, Janet A.	(603)224-1865	320
Durham	KAPOOR, Jagdish C.	(603)868-2504	626
Manchester	COMEAU, Reginald A.	(603)668-6706	234
	KENT, Jeffrey A.	(603)622-4408	642
Merrimack	DENTON, Francesca L.	(603)424-8621	293
Milford	LISTOVITCH, Denise A.	(603)672-0899	733
Washington	HAMILL, Martha L.	(603)495-3994	491

NEW JERSEY

Califon	CAPOOR, Asha	(201)832-9323	180
Camden	CHAO, Gloria F.	(609)757-6172	201
Cedar Knolls	MILLINGTON, Kathleen A.	(201)540-8700	843
Creamridge	GEORGE, Muriel S.	(609)758-3198	428
Delanco	WOLFORD, Larry E.	(609)461-5667	1361
Denville	VARIEUR, Normand L.		1278
East Brunswick	KING, Donald R.	(201)828-2752	650
Glen Rock	PERCELLI, Irene M.	(201)445-5983	958
Haddonfield	WILLIAMSON, Carol L.	(609)354-6213	1347
Highland Park	BEETHAM, Donald W.	(201)249-3268	74
	CLARK, Philip M.	(201)572-5414	218
	LI, Marjorie H.	(201)828-8730	724
	PARAS, Lucille P.		939
Hopewell	BENTE, June E.	(201)218-7436	83
Iselin	SILVA, Nelly H.	(201)321-0683	1138
Jersey City	RUBIN, Myra P.	(201)963-6456	1064
Lawrenceville	STEPHEN, Ross G.	(609)896-5111	1187
Leonia	SCHARF, Davida	(201)947-6839	1090
Madison	SNELSON, Pamela	(201)377-3000	1163
Maplewood	D'ALLEYRAND, Marc R.	(201)761-1028	270
	STAHL, Wilson M.	(800)262-0070	1178
Matawan	KEARNEY, Jeanne E.	(201)566-7532	633
Middletown	RILEY, Robert H.	(201)615-0900	1034
Neptune	EBELING, Elinor H.	(201)774-0793	334
New Brunswick	GRAHAM, Peter S.	(201)932-7505	456
Paramus	WHITE, Robert W.	(201)652-6772	1332
Parsippany	VOGT, Herwart C.	(201)263-5669	1287
Princeton	BIELAWSKI, Marvin F.	(609)452-5143	95
	ROCK, Sue W.	(609)921-3927	1046
Princeton Junction	CHU, Wendy N.	(609)799-0814	213
Randolph	PAVELY, Richard W.	(201)989-0229	950
Rockaway	BOWERS, Alyce J.	(201)627-2344	120
	COHN, John M.	(201)627-8512	229
	KELSEY, Ann L.	(201)627-8512	639
Rocky Hill	MOTT, Thomas H.	(609)924-8623	872
Roselle	GAINES, Irene A.	(201)245-8277	412
Roselle Park	MAGEE, Patricia A.	(201)245-1963	759
Rutherford	RAPPAPORT, Susan E.		1008
Somerville	GABRIEL, Linda	(201)874-8061	411
Teaneck	FORCE, Stephen	(201)836-1698	389
	MOUNT, Ellis	(201)836-1137	873
Tenafly	KORNFELD, Carol E.	(201)568-2231	672
Trenton	BREEDLOVE, Elizabeth A.	(609)292-9623	131
Wayne	LEE, Minja P.		711
Williamstown	BOGIS, Nana E.	(609)728-0569	110

NEW MEXICO

Albuquerque	HLAVA, Marjorie M.	(505)265-3501	544
	HSU, Grace S.		567
	ROLLINS, Stephen J.	(505)277-5057	1051
	SUGNET, Christopher L.	(505)277-7162	1206
	VASSALLO, Paul	(505)277-8125	1279
Roswell	KLOPFER, Jerome J.	(505)622-6250	662
	MCLAREN, M B.	(505)622-6250	813
White Sands	BANICKI, Cynthia A.	(505)678-5820	54

NEW YORK

Albany	JUDD, J V.	(518)474-5955	619
	MATTURRO, Richard C.	(518)454-5734	786
	MCCOMBS, Gillian M.	(518)442-3633	797
	NICHOLS-RANDALL, Barbara L.	(518)489-7649	902
	YAVARKOVSKY, Jerome	(518)473-1189	1378

LIBRARY AUTOMATION CONSULTANT (Cont'd)

NEW YORK (Cont'd)

APO New York	NEUWILLER, Charlene		897
Bellport	RICHARDSON, John A.	(516)286-1600	1029
Binghamton	HILL, Malcolm K.	(607)723-8236	540
Briarwood	BORRESS, Lewis R.	(718)441-6328	117
Brighton	RAHN, Erwin P.	(716)442-8980	1003
Bronx	PERSKY, Gail M.	(212)548-6007	961
Brooklyn	DEFALCO, Joseph	(718)693-8377	287
	GARA, Otto G.	(718)875-1300	416
	LANDOLFI, Lisa M.	(718)853-7871	693
	MALINCONICO, S M.	(718)627-0558	763
	MARTINEZ-RIVERA, Ivette	(718)854-5176	779
	STRAM, Lynn M.	(718)434-7815	1200
	SWEENEY, Richard T.	(718)643-4446	1215
	WOFSE, Joy G.	(718)788-5360	1359
Buffalo	ROSE, Pamela M.	(716)837-7175	1055
	STELZLE, James J.	(716)832-6066	1186
	YERKEY, A N.	(716)636-3069	1380
Carle Place	HABER, Elinor L.	(516)877-1190	480
Circleville	NELSON, James B.	(914)361-2415	894
Delmar	SAFFADY, William	(518)439-2469	1074
East Meadow	FRANZEN, John F.	(516)794-2570	398
East Northport	DAVIDSON, Steven I.	(516)368-0841	276
East Setauket	ALBERTUS, Donna M.		10
	BLOHM, Laura A.	(516)444-3105	106
Elmhurst	HSU, Elizabeth L.	(718)271-6623	567
Elmira	LAPIER, Cynthia B.	(607)739-3581	697
Farmingdale	ARMSTRONG, Ruth C.		32
Flushing	KOSTER, Gregory E.	(718)575-4264	673
	MCMORRAN, Charles E.	(718)358-4526	815
Glen Falls	GRAMINSKI, Denise M.	(518)793-2927	457
Glens Falls	SMITH, Frederick E.	(518)792-8214	1155
Grand Island	WATERS, Betsy M.		1308
Hamilton	GREEN, Judith G.	(315)824-3253	462
Harrison	WOOD, Arline L.	(914)835-3300	1363
Hempstead	GRAVES, Howard E.	(516)560-5949	459
	STEFANI, Carolyn R.	(516)481-6990	1185
Highland	LAWRENCE, Thomas A.	(914)691-2734	705
Ithaca	HAMMOND, Jane L.	(607)255-5857	493
	MILLER, J G.	(607)272-1576	838
	MORRIS, Jennifer D.	(607)273-4074	866
	PARKHURST, Kathleen A.	(607)273-4073	942
Jacksonville	HILLMANN, Diane I.	(602)387-9207	541
Jamestown	LEE, Sylvia	(716)483-5415	711
Kew Gardens	SALAZAR, Pamela R.	(718)441-2350	1076
Lackawanna	BEDNAR, Sheila	(716)822-0840	73
Loudonville	NAYLOR, Richard J.	(518)458-9274	890
Lynbrook	FIEGAS, Barbara E.	(516)593-1195	375
Massapequa Park	AKS, Gloria	(516)795-7297	9
Middletown	ANGLIN, Richard V.	(914)343-1131	28
Mt Kisco	FREEDMAN, Maurice J.	(914)592-8214	400
	NELSON, Nancy M.	(914)666-3394	894
New Paltz	LEE, Chui C.	(914)257-2202	709
New Rochelle	MITTELGLUCK, Eugene L.	(914)834-8739	850
New York	ALLEN, Robert R.	(212)337-6991	16
	CROFT, Elizabeth G.	(212)371-2000	260
	DAVILA, Daniel	(212)989-1732	277
	DE GENNARO, Richard	(212)930-0769	287
	ETZI, Richard		356
	FASANA, Paul J.	(212)930-0708	366
	FRUSCIANO, Thomas J.	(212)998-2644	406
	GROSS, Gretchen		472
	HAND, Sally C.	(212)040-0100	494
	HENDERSON, Janice E.	(212)687-0400	526
	HOOVER, James L.	(212)280-3737	557
	JANIAK, Jane M.	(212)466-4060	593
	KASTNER, Arno A.	(212)998-2477	629
	KELLEY, Dennis L.	(212)210-7043	636
	KOENIG, Michael E.	(212)867-0489	668
	KUHNER, Robert A.	(212)663-3360	683
	LAMANN, Amber N.	(212)677-4102	689
	LANDAU, Herbert B.	(212)705-7600	692
	LEE, Sang C.	(212)669-7961	711
	MANDEL, Carol A.	(212)280-2226	764
	MATTA, Seoud M.	(212)686-7532	785
	MILLER, Ellen L.	(212)406-3186	837
	MILLER, Michael D.		841
	MILLER-KUMMERFELD, Elizabeth	(212)751-0830	843

LIBRARY AUTOMATION CONSULTANT (Cont'd)
NEW YORK (Cont'd)
New York

	PARRIS, Angela P.	(212)836-7640	944
	PAUL, Sandra K.	(212)675-7804	949
	PRAVER, Robin I.	(212)214-1720	990
	RESCIGNO, Dolores S.	(212)530-5969	1024
	RODERER, Nancy K.	(212)305-6302	1047
	ROZENE, Janette B.	(212)760-7265	1064
	RUBINSTEIN, Ed	(212)725-4550	1065
	SMITH, David F.	(212)243-1753	1154
	SMITH, Mark J.	(212)373-2401	1158
	SOROBAY, Roman T.	(212)878-9314	1169
	VAUGHAN, John	(212)924-3729	1279
Niagara University	MORRIS, Leslie R.	(716)285-1212	867
North Bellmore	SHERWOOD, Nancy	(516)781-5063	1129
Oneonta	CHIANG, Nancy	(607)432-4200	207
Patchogue	GIBBARD, Judith R.	(516)654-4700	431
Peekskill	CLARE, Richard W.		216
Plattsburgh	BURTON, Robert E.	(518)561-1613	164
Potsdam	FOSTER, Selma V.	(315)267-2477	392
Rensselaerville	STORMS, Kate	(518)797-5154	1198
Riverdale	CLANCY, Kathy	(212)796-2057	215
Rochester	ISGANITIS, Jamie C.	(716)461-1943	585
	MATZEK, Richard A.	(716)586-2525	786
	MOUREY, Deborah A.	(716)724-6819	874
	PERRY, Rodney B.	(716)482-6478	961
Roslyn Harbor	CARTAFALSA, Joan C.	(516)671-7411	188
Rouses Point	CURRAN, George L.		266
Schenectady	KLEMPNER, Irving M.	(518)393-5983	660
	SHEVIAK, Jean K.	(518)370-6294	1129
Setauket	NICHOLS, Gerald D.	(516)689-7071	901
Southampton	KETCHAM, Susan E.	(516)283-4000	645
Syracuse	MARTIN, Thomas H.	(315)423-3840	778
Troy	MOLHOLT, Pat	(518)276-8300	852
Uniondale	BARTENBACH, Martha A.	(516)292-8920	60
Wantagh	WESTERMANN, Mary L.	(516)679-8842	1327
West Islip	JOYCE, Therese	(516)587-8000	618
West Point	RANDALL, Lawrence E.	(914)938-4789	1006
White Plains	DAVIES, Carol A.	(212)754-7438	277
	HOUGHTON, Joan I.	(914)335-7839	562
	ROCQUE, Bernice L.	(914)253-4307	1046

NORTH CAROLINA

Belmont	MAYES, Susan E.	(704)825-3711	789
Boone	GREGORY, Roderick F.	(704)262-3956	466
Chapel Hill	BAILEY, Charles W.	(919)962-0600	46
	KISER, Anita H.	(919)968-3946	656
	LOSEE, Robert M.	(919)962-8366	742
	OWEN, Willy	(919)962-1301	932
	PALO, Eric E.	(919)493-7230	937
	ROBERTSON, W D.	(919)933-6894	1042
	SCHELL, Nancy S.		1091
	TELFER, Margaret E.	(919)933-7563	1230
Durham	BURGIN, Robert E.	(919)683-6485	159
	CAMPBELL, Jerry D.	(919)684-2034	176
	MOORE, Scott L.	(919)684-3372	861
	SEMONCHE, Barbara P.	(919)489-7247	1115
	SPELLER, Benjamin F.	(919)683-6485	1172
Elkin	MACPHAIL, Jessica		758
Greensboro	O'CONNOR, Sandra L.	(919)273-1914	916
Greenville	GLUCK, Myke H.	(919)757-6514	442
	SCOTT, Ralph L.	(919)830-0522	1108
	SPEER, Susan C.	(919)757-2212	1172
Hickory	PRITCHARD, John A.	(704)294-0326	994
High Point	MORRIS, R P.	(919)887-3006	867
Kinston	JONES, John W.	(919)527-7066	613
New Bern	KEE, Walter A.		634
Raleigh	ISACCO, Jeanne M.	(919)851-4703	584
Roanoke Rapids	JOYCE, Robert A.	(919)537-1324	618
Rocky Mount	FINCH, Lynette	(919)443-4011	377
Sanford	BEAGLE, Donald R.	(919)776-8372	68
	MCGINN, Howard F.	(919)776-2335	806
Winston-Salem	ANDERSON, Sherry	(919)748-2305	25
	RALPH, Randy D.	(919)788-4591	1004
	STEELE, Tom M.	(919)761-5440	1184

NORTH DAKOTA

Bismarck	MOREHOUSE, Valerie J.	(701)224-4658	863

LIBRARY AUTOMATION CONSULTANT (Cont'd)
OHIO

Akron	DURBIN, Roger	(216)794-9706	328
Athens	LEE, Hwa W.	(614)592-5194	710
	MULLINER, Kent	(614)593-2707	878
Bay Village	BACON, Agnes K.		44
Burton	DONALDSON, Timothy P.	(216)834-4466	311
	VARGA, Carol C.	(216)834-4466	1278
Canfield	GENAWAY, David C.	(216)533-2194	426
Canton	GREEN, Gary A.	(216)452-0665	461
Chillicothe	PLANTON, Stanley P.	(614)775-9500	977
Cincinnati	MCCOY, Betty J.	(513)369-6980	799
	SHIVERDECKER, Darlene J.	(513)281-3760	1132
Cleveland	LOWELL, Virginia L.	(216)398-1800	744
	MCSPADDEN, Robert M.	(216)229-5900	818
	ORR, Cynthia	(216)449-2049	926
	PEARMAN, Sara J.	(211)421-7340	952
	VENABLE, Andrew A.	(216)541-4128	1282
Cleveland Heights	PIETY, John S.	(216)321-8121	972
Columbus	ANDERSON, Carl A.	(614)486-9100	21
	BAYER, Bernard I.	(614)292-7895	67
	CALL, J R.	(614)885-4926	173
	DAVIS, Linda M.	(614)294-5429	280
	FU, Paul S.	(614)466-2044	407
	HEARD, Jeffrey L.		518
	HOLOCH, S A.	(614)292-6691	553
	KIE, Kathleen M.	(614)481-7640	646
	KNOBLAUCH, Carol J.	(614)299-4020	665
	STUDER, William J.	(614)292-4241	1204
	TANNEHILL, Robert S.	(614)488-7587	1222
	WALBRIDGE, Sharon L.	(614)274-4081	1293
	WANG, Anna M.	(614)294-8035	1302
Dayton	MARSHALL, Mary E.	(513)461-1548	774
	TRIVEDI, Harish S.	(513)225-2201	1257
	WALKER, Mary A.	(513)229-3551	1296
Dublin	DITMARS, David W.	(614)761-7303	305
	HAYNES, Kathleen J.	(614)764-6000	516
	JACOB, Mary E.	(614)764-6063	589
	MARSH, Elizabeth C.	(614)488-1942	773
	PAK, Moo J.	(514)761-2174	935
	SHREWSBURY, Lynn D.	(614)764-6403	1133
Englewood	CUPP, Christian M.	(513)832-0136	265
Fairfield	LUCAS, Jean M.	(513)829-5227	746
Findlay	JANKY, Donna L.	(419)422-3211	593
Jackson	ANDERSON, Eric S.	(614)286-6685	22
Lakewood	MULLER, Madeline A.	(216)221-8088	877
	SEELY, Edward	(216)221-3453	1111
London	DIENER, Ronald E.		302
Mansfield	KARRE, David J.	(419)526-1337	628
Medina	SMITH, Robert S.	(216)725-0588	1160
New Albany	HERB, Elizabeth D.	(614)855-7441	530
Niles	STOUT, Chester B.	(216)652-1704	1198
Powell	RUSH, James E.	(614)881-5949	1068
Shaker Heights	LANDAU, Lucille	(216)283-6109	692
	MCCONNELL, Pamela J.	(216)921-7457	798
Toledo	ELLENBOGEN, Barbara R.	(419)536-4538	343
Uniontown	CREELAN, Marilee M.	(216)699-4454	257
Upper Arlington	BROWN, Rowland C.	(614)488-6329	147
Warren	BRIELL, Robert D.	(216)399-8807	135
Westlake	CHAMIS, Alice Y.	(216)777-2198	198

OKLAHOMA

Edmond	CURTIS, Ronald A.	(405)341-2980	267
	ROADS, Clarice D.	(405)341-3660	1038
McAlester	SIMON, Bradley A.	(918)423-3468	1140
Norman	PETERS, Lloyd A.		962
	WEAVER-MEYERS, Pat L.	(405)325-3341	1313
Oklahoma City	JONES, Beverly A.	(405)751-0574	611
	PASCHAL, John M.	(405)751-6400	945
Stillwater	DAVIS, Joyce N.	(405)377-8326	279
	HILKER, Emerson W.	(405)624-6305	539
Tahlequah	HILL, Helen K.		540
	MADAUS, J R.		758
Tulsa	BUTHOD, J C.	(918)592-7894	166
	HILL, Linda L.	(918)584-0891	540
	HUGHES, Carol A.	(918)585-8228	571
	UNDERHILL, Jan	(918)663-3646	1268

LIBRARY AUTOMATION CONSULTANT (Cont'd)

OREGON

Beaverton	SHOFFNER, Ralph M.	(503)645-3502	1132
Eugene	FEUERHELM, Jill A.	(503)345-6498	374
	GRAHAM, Deborah L.		456
	SHIPMAN, George W.	(503)683-8262	1131
Milton-Freewater	SARGENT, Phyllis M.	(503)938-3724	1083
Portland	KENNEY, Ann J.	(503)297-1894	641
	SELLE, Donna M.	(503)629-5886	1113
	VAN HORN, Neal F.	(503)796-7717	1275
Roseburg	GAULKE, Mary F.	(503)440-4036	423
Salem	DOAK, Wesley A.	(503)581-4292	306
	WEBB, John	(503)378-4246	1313

PENNSYLVANIA

Allentown	IOBST, Barbara J.	(215)778-2263	583
Ardmore	PULLER, Maryam W.	(215)642-5187	997
Bethlehem	CADY, Susan A.	(215)758-4645	170
Bloomsburg	VANN, John D.	(717)784-4283	1276
Bristol	WOOD, Barbara G.	(215)785-8055	1363
Bryn Mawr	BILLS, Linda G.	(215)645-5294	96
California	BARREAU, Deborah K.	(412)938-5772	58
Carlisle	WIWEL, Pamela S.		1359
Catasauqua	SIMONE-HOHE, M J.	(215)262-1596	1141
Coatesville	BURTON, Mary L.	(215)383-0245	164
Easton	SHINER, Sharon L.	(215)258-8390	1130
Ebensburg	BRUSH, Cassandra	(814)472-7338	151
Fleetwood	EMERICK, Michael J.	(215)944-8486	347
Hershey	WOODRUFF, William M.	(717)534-5106	1366
Huntingdon	WILSON, Martin P.	(814)643-2808	1352
Lewisburg	DE KLERK, Ann M.	(717)524-1557	288
Macungie	BAHR, Alice H.	(215)821-1255	45
Media	COURTRIGHT, Harry R.	(215)891-5190	252
Middletown	RAMBLER, Linda K.	(412)349-4621	1005
	STANLEY, Nancy M.	(717)944-4049	1180
	TOWNLEY, Charles T.	(717)948-6079	1253
Muncy	SHEAFFER, Marc L.	(717)546-8491	1124
Narberth	SOKOLOFF, Michele	(215)664-2117	1165
Philadelphia	BOWDEN, Gail R.	(215)574-4417	120
	FISHER, Douglas A.	(215)587-4915	380
	HARRISON, Susan B.	(215)848-9164	507
	MCDONALD, Joseph A.	(215)637-5829	802
	WALL, H D.	(215)438-1205	1297
	WEINBERG, David M.	(215)787-8257	1317
Pittsburgh	BEARMAN, David A.	(412)421-4638	69
	BROADBENT, H E.	(412)441-6409	138
	DOW, Elizabeth H.		315
	FITZGERALD, Patricia A.	(412)268-2428	382
	GREEN, Joyce M.	(412)234-5039	462
	HODGSON, Cynthia A.	(412)374-4816	546
	KING, Mimi	(412)237-2593	652
	MICCO, Helen M.	(412)665-0412	831
	MICHALAK, Jo A.	(412)648-7710	832
	MITCHELL, Joan M.	(412)578-6137	849
	PISCIOTTA, Henry A.	(412)268-2451	976
	RICHARDS, Barbara G.	(412)268-2448	1028
	WILLIAMS, James G.	(412)624-9418	1344
	WRIGHT, Nancy M.	(412)237-5948	1372
Springfield	MAIN, Annette Z.		761
State College	JAMISON, Carolyn C.	(814)234-4512	593
Tamaqua	TUZINSKI, Jean H.	(717)668-2970	1266
Unityville	VEDDER, Harvey B.	(717)482-3541	1280
University Park	CARSON, M S.	(814)865-1818	188
	CHAMBERLAIN, Carol E.	(814)865-1858	197
	CLINE, Nancy M.	(814)865-1858	222
	FERRIN, Eric G.	(814)865-1818	373
	FORTH, Stuart	(814)865-0401	391
	GERHART, Catherine A.	(814)865-1755	428
	KALIN, Sarah G.	(814)863-2898	623
	NEAL, James G.	(814)865-0401	890
	RAWLINS, Gordon W.	(814)865-1818	1010
	STRIEDIECK, Suzanne S.	(814)865-1755	1202
Upper Darby	SILVERMAN, Karen S.	(215)734-0146	1138
Villanova	GRIFFIN, Mary A.	(215)645-4290	468
Warminster	BECKER, Linda C.	(215)443-7008	72
Wescosville	FISLER, Charlotte D.	(215)395-6400	382
West Chester	MCCAWLEY, Christina W.	(215)436-0720	795

LIBRARY AUTOMATION CONSULTANT (Cont'd)

PUERTO RICO

Miramar	CASAS DE FAUNCE, Maria		191
San Juan	MAURA-SARDO, Mariano A.	(809)764-0000	787
	RODRIGUEZ, Ketty		1048

RHODE ISLAND

Barrington	BUNDY, Annalee M.	(401)245-2232	157
Providence	BOWLBY, Raynna M.	(401)274-7224	121
	FARK, Ronald K.	(401)941-0086	364
	LATHROP, Irene M.	(401)277-8070	701
	LYNDEN, Frederick C.	(401)863-2946	752
	TAYLOR, Merrily E.	(401)863-2162	1227

SOUTH CAROLINA

Aiken	JACOBS, Mildred H.		589
Charleston	ROSS, Gary M.	(803)792-5530	1058
	SMITH, Nancy	(803)792-7672	1158
	WOOD, Richard J.	(803)763-8532	1365
Clemson	MEYER, Richard W.	(803)656-3026	830
Columbia	BILLINSKY, Christyn G.	(803)777-3858	96
	UPHAM, Lois N.	(803)777-6938	1269
Conway	LOWRIMORE, R T.	(803)248-2967	745
Florence	MARTIN, Neal A.	(803)661-1310	777
McCormick	TOWNSEND, Catherine M.	(803)465-3185	1253
North Myrtle Beach	BELL, David B.	(803)272-1624	76
Rock Hill	KELLEY, Gloria	(803)325-2131	636
	MITLIN, Laurance R.	(803)329-5716	850
Sumter	GORDON, Clara B.	(803)773-4041	451

SOUTH DAKOTA

Madison	COOK, Nancy E.	(605)256-4709	240
Vermillion	EDELEN, Joseph R.	(605)677-6082	335
	JENSEN, Mary B.	(605)677-5259	599

TENNESSEE

Clarksville	CARLIN, Don	(615)648-2095	182
Cordova	SMITH, Philip M.	(901)386-1003	1159
Knoxville	BENGTSON, Betty G.	(615)974-6640	80
	LLOYD, James B.	(615)974-4480	735
Memphis	CO, Francisca	(901)324-2453	224
Murfreesboro	HUNTER, Joy W.	(615)893-1360	576
Nashville	WILBURN, Clouse R.	(615)322-8050	1338
Oak Ridge	NORTON, Nancy P.	(615)574-7159	910
	YALCINTAS, Rana	(615)482-9397	1376
Palmyra	FOWLER, James W.	(615)647-4172	393
Signal Mountain	JACKSON, Joseph A.	(615)886-1753	587

TEXAS

Amarillo	RIEPMA, Helen J.	(806)352-7486	1033
	RUDDY, Mary K.	(806)353-1534	1065
	SNELL, Marykay H.	(806)353-5329	1163
Arlington	MCCLURE, Margaret R.	(817)275-6594	797
	SAMSON, Robert C.	(817)273-3391	1079
Austin	AIROLDI, Melissa	(512)476-8049	9
	BILLINGS, Harold W.	(512)442-8597	96
	BRIDGE, Frank R.	(512)328-6006	135
	HARMON, Jacqueline B.	(512)343-0978	502
	HELFER, Robert S.	(512)929-3086	523
	HISLE, W L.	(512)495-7148	544
	JUERGENS, Bonnie	(512)288-2072	619
	MARTIN, Jean K.	(512)346-2973	776
	PELOQUIN, Margaret I.		955
	SEIDENBERG, Edward	(512)463-5459	1112
	SKINNER, Vicki F.	(512)892-3997	1146
	STANDIFER, Hugh A.	(512)288-2072	1179
	TAYLOR, Nancy L.	(512)346-1426	1228
	WALTON, Robert A.	(512)346-1426	1301
Brownsville	VAUGHN, Frances A.	(512)544-8220	1280
Bryan	HALL, Halbert W.	(409)846-0798	487
College Station	COOK, C C.	(409)845-3731	239
	GYESZLY, Suzanne D.	(409)845-3731	479
Conroe	BALDWIN, Joe M.	(409)756-4484	51
Dallas	ARMES, Patti	(214)341-6675	32
	KACENA, Carolyn	(214)361-9254	621
	KANE, Deborah A.	(214)247-1952	624
	PEDEN, Robert M.	(214)746-3646	954
	WETHERBEE, Louella V.	(214)750-6130	1327
Denton	ALMQUIST, Sharon G.	(817)387-1703	17

LIBRARY AUTOMATION CONSULTANT (Cont'd)
TEXAS (Cont'd)

Fort Worth	DIXON, Catherine A.	(817)870-7708	306
	RUSSELL, Barbara J.	(817)735-9136	1068
	WOOD, Richard C.	(517)927-5389	1365
Galveston	FREY, Emil F.	(409)761-2371	402
Garland	QUEYROUZE, Mary E.	(214)494-2112	999
Groves	MCCONNELL, Karen S.	(409)963-1481	797
Houston	CALDWELL, Marlene	(713)661-5787	172
	CARTER, Daniel H.	(713)665-5150	189
	CLARK, Jay B.	(713)247-1631	217
	CORBIN, John	(713)749-4241	245
	KIMZEY, Ann C.	(713)488-9280	649
	MCCANN, Debra W.	(713)691-0148	794
	MULLINS, James R.	(713)522-8131	878
	PHILLIPS, Ray S.	(713)622-9686	969
	RAMBO, Neil H.	(713)797-1230	1005
	WILSON, Thomas C.	(713)995-8401	1353
Lubbock	ANDREWS, Virginia L.	(806)799-0534	27
	SARGENT, Charles W.	(806)792-0754	1082
Mesquite	DUMONT, Paul E.	(214)324-7786	325
Odessa	LINDSAY, Lorin H.	(915)367-2318	729
Prairie View	YEH, Helen S.	(409)857-3192	1379
Round Rock	RICKLEFS, Dale L.	(512)255-3939	1032
San Antonio	BALCOM, Karen S.	(512)344-8654	51
	LEATHERBURY, Maurice C.	(512)829-7033	707
	MANEY, Lana E.	(512)496-7754	765
Seguin	KOOPMAN, Frances A.	(512)379-4161	671
Sugar Land	JOHNSON, Pat M.	(713)980-5350	608

UTAH

Logan	NIELSEN, Steven P.	(801)750-3166	903
Provo	GOULD, Douglas A.	(801)226-1469	454
	ROWLEY, Edward D.	(801)378-6372	1063
	WILSON, D K.	(801)375-2770	1350
Salt Lake City	CUMMINGS, Christopher H.	(801)534-1669	264
	JENSEN, Charla J.	(801)533-5250	598
	KRANZ, Ralph	(801)581-7995	676
	NOEL, Eileen V.	(801)594-6182	907
	REED, Vernon M.	(801)531-3377	1015
	SKIDMORE, Kerry F.		1146
	VAN ORDEN, Richard D.	(801)485-1075	1276
Springville	PETERSON, Douglas L.	(801)489-5248	963

VERMONT

Burlington	CASWELL, Jerry V.	(802)656-3321	194
Montpelier	KLINCK, Patricia E.	(802)828-3265	661
Northfield	WARD, Robert C.	(802)485-7344	1304

VIRGINIA

Alexandria	DAVIDSON, Dero H.	(703)998-2976	276
	DRUMMOND, Louis E.		321
	FISHER, Carl D.	(703)836-7951	380
	HARTT, Richard W.	(703)960-8741	509
	KAISER, Donald W.	(703)836-0225	622
	REYNOLDS, Jon K.	(703)548-2860	1025
	SEVERTSON, Susan M.	(703)683-4890	1117
Arlington	ALEXANDER, Carol G.		12
	GOLDBERG, Lisbeth S.	(703)243-0796	444
	HENDERSON, Susanne	(703)931-8433	527
	JOACHIM, Robert J.	(703)920-7721	600
	MOORE, Penelope F.	(703)979-5900	861
	PRICE, Joseph W.	(703)241-0447	992
	WEIST, Melody S.		1320
	YODER, William M.	(703)527-7225	1380
Blacksburg	ESPLEY, John L.	(703)961-5847	354
	KOK, Victoria T.	(703)951-3203	669
	KRIZ, Harry M.	(703)951-7007	679
	NORSTEDT, Marilyn L.	(703)961-4610	909
Burke	GOUDREAU, Ronald A.	(703)569-0994	454
Charlottesville	BRAUN, Mina H.	(804)924-4957	129
Chesapeake	FOREHAND, Margaret P.	(804)547-6579	390
Fairfax	FESSLER, Vera F.	(703)352-7200	374
	SCOTT, Mona L.	(703)378-8027	1107
Falls Church	BUCK, Dayna E.	(703)847-0271	153
	LEONARD, Lucinda E.	(703)536-2373	716
	PARSONS, John W.	(703)671-7756	945
	REID, Judith P.	(703)379-0739	1018
	SEGEL, Bernard J.	(703)532-7287	1112
Farmville	STWODAH, M I.	(804)392-8925	1206

LIBRARY AUTOMATION CONSULTANT (Cont'd)
VIRGINIA (Cont'd)

Fredericksburg	HUGHES, J M.		571
Hampton	SMITH, David A.	(804)827-8129	1153
Herndon	GUERRIERO, Donald A.	(703)860-1058	476
Leesburg	GRIMES, Judith E.	(703)777-9441	470
McLean	FURR, Susan H.	(703)893-4089	410
	GATTONE, Dean R.	(703)790-5694	422
Norfolk	DUNCAN, Cynthia B.	(804)583-0903	325
	LIU, Albert C.	(804)440-4141	734
Petersburg	CARTER, Ann M.	(804)732-6517	189
Portsmouth	BURGESS, Dean	(804)393-8501	159
Radford	TURNER, Robert L.	(703)731-1835	1265
Reston	BROERING, Naomi C.	(703)860-1871	139
	LISZEWSKI, Edward H.	(301)648-4306	733
Richmond	BAGAN, Beverly S.	(804)780-7691	45
	CARNEY, Marillyn L.	(804)254-2447	183
	DEBARDELEBEN, Marian Z.	(804)274-2876	284
	HUBBARD, William J.	(804)786-2331	568
	KANE, Dorothea S.		624
	MACLEOD, James M.	(804)355-1395	757
Roanoke	SPRENGER, Suzanne F.	(703)989-4949	1176
Sweet Briar	JAFFE, John G.	(804)381-6138	591
Triangle	GAUDET, Jean A.	(703)221-6434	422
Virginia Beach	CARR, Jeanette A.	(804)481-6096	185
Williamsburg	HEYMAN, Berna L.	(804)253-4029	536

WASHINGTON

Bothell	DECOSTER, Barbara L.	(206)488-7537	286
Ellensburg	YEH, Thomas Y.	(509)925-9257	1379
Fall City	AROKSAAR, Richard D.	(206)442-5203	34
Kenmore	TAYLOR, James B.	(206)483-2954	1227
Lacey	DEBUSE, Raymond	(206)491-7498	285
	PUZIAK, Kathleen M.	(206)491-0347	998
Longview	BAKER, Robert K.	(206)577-0756	49
Newport	REMINGTON, David G.	(509)447-2636	1022
Pullman	KOPP, James J.	(509)335-9133	671
	VYHNANEK, Kay E.	(509)335-9671	1290
Seattle	BOYLAN, Merle N.	(206)543-1760	123
	CHASE, Dale L.	(206)525-0795	203
	ERICKSON, Randall D.	(206)523-9356	352
	KETCHELL, Debra S.	(206)543-5530	645
	LEONARD, Gloria J.	(206)722-4828	716
	MAIOLI, Jerry R.	(206)459-6518	762
	MCCORMICK, Jack M.	(206)526-6107	798
	MCFADDEN, Denyse I.	(206)284-6280	804
	SONG, Seungja Y.	(206)527-8737	1167
	SY, Karen J.	(206)545-2873	1217
Spangle	MOLLER, Steffen A.	(509)245-3610	853
Spokane	LANE, Steven P.	(509)838-4728	694
	MURRAY, James M.	(509)838-3680	882
	PRINGLE, Robert M.	(509)325-6139	993
Tacoma	BECKER, Roger V.	(206)591-2703	72
	HAGAN, Dalia L.	(206)565-9669	482
	MENDELSON, Martin	(206)383-5855	823
Vancouver	CONABLE, Irene H.	(206)694-0604	235
Yakima	JORDAN, Sharon L.	(509)248-4522	617

WEST VIRGINIA

Athens	BROWN, Thomas M.	(304)384-3115	148
Barboursville	DZIERZAK, Edward M.		331
Charleston	PROSSER, Judith M.	(304)344-8583	995
Glenville	VERMA, Prem V.	(304)462-5303	1282
Point Pleasant	WILLIAMSON, Judy D.	(304)675-4350	1347
Spencer	RADER, H J.	(304)927-1770	1002
Welch	MULLER, William A.	(304)436-3070	877

WISCONSIN

Appleton	BOOHER, Craig S.	(414)738-3384	115
	PENNINGTON, Jerome G.	(414)735-6167	957
Brookfield	CASEY, Jean M.	(414)781-2545	192
Eau Claire	MARQUARDT, Steve R.	(715)834-5390	772
Kenosha	BARUTH, Barbara P.	(414)553-2167	62
La Crosse	ACCARDI, Joseph J.	(608)784-5755	3
Madison	CRAWFORD, Josephine	(608)274-7984	256
	EPSTEIN, Hank	(608)255-4800	351
	JEFFCOTT, Janet B.	(608)246-6633	596

LIBRARY AUTOMATION CONSULTANT (Cont'd)

WISCONSIN (Cont'd)

Milwaukee	AMAN, Mohammed M.	(414)239-4709	19
	BLUE, Richard I.	(414)963-4707	107
	FONG, Wilfred W.	(414)229-4707	388
	SAGER, Donald J.	(414)278-3020	1074
Oshkosh	CORBLY, James E.	(414)231-4768	245
Rhinelander	SLYGH, Gyneth	(715)362-3465	1151
St Francis	WESTERN, Eric D.	(414)769-0110	1327
Superior	TORNQUIST, Kristi M.	(715)394-8359	1251
Wisconsin Rapids	WILSON, William J.	(715)424-4272	1353

CANADA

ALBERTA

Calgary	GUNSON, Murray J.	(403)256-7327	478
Edmonton	BATEMAN, Robert A.	(403)483-3432	63
	LAVKULICH, Joanne	(403)427-3530	704
	RICHARDS, Vincent P.	(403)429-9814	1029
Red Deer	GISHLER, John R.	(304)340-3922	438

BRITISH COLUMBIA

Kamloops	LEVESQUE, Nancy B.	(604)374-0123	719
North Vancouver	ELROD, J M.	(604)929-3966	346
Prince George	MAYFIELD, Betty L.	(604)562-1929	790
Vancouver	CAMERON, Hazel M.	(604)224-8470	175
	LIGHTHALL, Lynne I.	(604)228-1480	727
	PEPPER, David A.	(604)664-4311	958

MANITOBA

FlinFlon	HOBBS, Henry C.	(204)687-6647	545
Winnipeg	FAWCETT, Patrick J.	(204)474-9908	367
	LINCOLN, Robert S.	(204)786-2387	728

NEW BRUNSWICK

Riverview	ENNS, Carol F.	(506)386-1084	350

NOVA SCOTIA

Halifax	BIANCHINI, Lucian	(902)445-2987	94
	HSIUNG, Lai Y.	(902)424-3645	567
	TAYYEB, Rashid	(902)422-4684	1229

ONTARIO

Bowmanville	MOON, Jeffrey D.	(416)263-8504	857
Cambridge	SKELTON, W M.	(519)621-0460	1146
Deep River	LEWIS, Leslie	(613)584-2605	723
Downsview	BERNSTEIN, Elaine S.	(416)638-1962	89
	STEVENS, Mary		1190
Gormley	RHYDWEN, David A.	(416)887-9552	1026
Guelph	BLACK, John B.	(519)821-2565	101
Kingston	FORKES, David	(613)544-2630	390
	MCBURNEY, Margot B.	(613)544-7967	792
Kitchener	SHEPHERD, Murray C.		1127
London	RUTHERFORD, Frederick S.	(519)471-4867	1070
Markham	MORTON, Robert E.	(416)475-0525	870
Ottawa	BLACK, Jane L.	(613)234-5006	101
	BUCHANAN, Zoe A.	(613)526-3287	153
	DURANCE, Cynthia J.	(613)728-8763	328
	KANNEL, Ene	(819)994-7966	625
	KARCICH, Grant J.	(416)723-6068	627
	LEUNG, Frank F.	(613)994-6920	719
	MACDONALD, Marcia H.	(819)994-6947	754
	MACLELLAND, Margaret A.	(819)994-6832	757
	MCCALLUM, David L.	(613)237-4586	793
	PARE, Richard	(613)733-8391	940
	ROSSMAN, Linda	(613)564-2653	1059
Scarborough	BASSNETT, Peter J.	(416)298-0614	63
	BULAONG, Grace F.	(416)283-5732	156
	MILLER, Ann M.	(416)694-3897	835
Shelburne	LA CHAPELLE, Jennifer R.	(519)925-2672	686
Sudbury	SLATER, Ronald J.	(705)522-3578	1148
Toronto	ATTINGER, Monique L.	(416)699-2530	38
	BEAUMONT, Jane	(416)922-9364	70
	CAMPBELL, Bonnie	(416)323-3566	176
	CHIU, Lily F.	(416)868-2909	209
	DAVEY, Dorothy M.	(416)485-0377	276
	DYSART, Jane I.	(416)974-2780	331
	FRITZ, Richard J.	(416)923-0890	405
	LADD, Kenneth F.	(416)596-3124	687
	MERILEES, Bobbie	(416)485-4177	826

LIBRARY AUTOMATION CONSULTANT (Cont'd)

ONTARIO (Cont'd)

Toronto	NORTH, John A.	(416)979-5142	909
	PARKER, Arthur D.	(416)967-5525	941
	TAYLOR, Karen E.	(416)923-0890	1227
	THODY, Susan I.	(416)762-1690	1235
	VAN ORDER, Mary J.	(416)924-0671	1276
	VEANER, Allen B.	(416)486-0239	1280
Waterloo	BECKMAN, Margaret L.	(519)824-4120	73
Willowdale	BELDAN, A C.	(416)226-6380	76
Windsor	HANDY, Mary J.	(519)256-3250	495

QUEBEC

Chambly	ASSUNCAO, Isabel	(514)658-3882	37
Greenfield Park	RICHARDS, Stella	(514)672-1008	1028
Hull	MAILLOUX, Jean Y.	(819)997-5365	761
Jonquiere	HARVEY, Serge	(418)548-7821	509
Laval	AUGER, Bernard	(514)687-9730	39
Montreal	ALLARD, Andre	(514)256-2522	14
	DAUNAIS, Marie J.	(514)633-4170	275
	GONZALEZ, Paloma	(514)735-1977	448
	NAGY, Cecile		886
	PIGGOTT, Sylvia E.	(514)877-9383	972
	PROVOST, Paul E.	(514)598-5389	996
	SYKES, Stephanie L.	(514)870-7088	1217
	VADNAIS, Martine		1270
Pointe Claire	MACFARLANE, Judy A.	(514)697-9572	755
Pointe Claire Dorval	STAHL, Hella	(514)630-4100	1178
Quebec	TESSIER, Yves	(418)872-4304	1233
Repentigny	MERCIER, Diane	(514)582-3920	825
Rouyn-Noranda	TREMBLAY, Levis	(819)762-0931	1255
St-Bruno	LECOMPTE, Louis L.	(514)653-7290	708
St-Laurent	DJEVALIKIAN, Sonia	(514)744-7315	306
St-Nicolas E	GELINAS, Rene	(418)831-1659	426
Sainte-Foy	TRUDEL, Florian	(418)652-2210	1259
Sherbrooke	CHASSE, Jules	(819)821-7550	203
Trois-Rivieres	SIMARD, Denis	(819)376-1721	1139
Verdun	DIMITRESCU, Ioana	(514)765-8219	304
	VAILLANCOURT, Alain	(514)765-7507	1270

SASKATCHEWAN

Regina	FIELDEN, Stanley	(306)584-4291	376

BELGIUM

Brussels	VAN SLYPE, Georges		1277
Kraainem	WALCKIERS, Marc A.		1293

EGYPT

Giza	MAHOUD ALY, Usama E.		761

ENGLAND

Surrey	NOERR, Kathleen T.		907

FEDERAL REPUBLIC OF CHINA

Taipei	CHOU, Nancy O.		210
	HUANG, Shih H.		568
	LEE, Lucy T.		710

FEDERAL REPUBLIC OF GERMANY

Berlin	ULRICH, Paul S.		1268
Bremerhaven	GOMEZ, Michael J.		447

FIJI

Suva	WOODS, Richard F.		1367

FRANCE

Paris	CHAUMIER, Jacques		204
	GRATTAN, Robert		458
	WACHTER, Margery C.		1290

GUATAMALA

Guatamala City	MARBAN, Ricio		768

HONG KONG

Kowloon	FU, Ting W.		407
Shatin	YEN, David S.		1379

LIBRARY AUTOMATION CONSULTANT (Cont'd)

INDIA
Andhra Pradesh	SINHA, Pramod K.	1143
Bangalore	KITTUR, Krishna N.	657

ISRAEL
Haifa	BLOCH, Uri	105

ITALY
Milan	FABRE DE MORLHON, Christiane	360

MALAYSIA
Penang	LIM, Hucktee E.	727

MEXICO
Nuevo Leon	ARTEAGA, Georgina	35

NETHERLANDS
Amersfoort	VAN HALM, Johan	1275

NEW ZEALAND
Auckland	TWEEDALE, Dellene M.	1266

NIGERIA
Kano	AJIBERO, Matthew I.	9

SOUTH AFRICA
Bedfordview	ARMSTRONG, Denise M.	32

LIBRARY BUILDING CONSULTANT

ALABAMA
Birmingham	DAY, Janeth N.	(205)226-3614	282
	PENNINGTON, Walter W.	(205)226-4744	957
	SPENCE, Paul H.	(205)934-6360	1173
	STEPHENS, Jerry W.	(209)363-6000	1188
	STEWART, George R.	(205)226-3611	1192
Hoover	ANDREWS, Linda R.	(205)978-5528	26
Huntsville	KENDRICK, Aubrey W.	(205)837-7597	640
Mobile	DAMICO, James A.	(205)460-7021	271
Montevallo	DUNMIRE, Raymond V.	(205)665-6104	326
Montgomery	BIVINS, Hulen E.	(205)272-1700	100
	LANE, Robert B.	(205)288-8122	694
Troy	SOUTER, Thomas A.	(205)566-3000	1169

ALASKA
Anchorage	WILLIAMS, Robert C.	(907)261-2970	1346

ARIZONA
Glendale	MOSLEY, Shelley E.	(602)939-5469	872
Mesa	ANDERSON, Herschel V.	(602)839-2742	23
Phoenix	BOROVANSKY, Vladimir T.		117
Tempe	RIGGS, Donald E.	(602)965-3950	1034
Tucson	HIEB, Louis A.	(602)621-6077	537
	LAIRD, W D.	(602)621-2101	688
Uma	SWANN, Arthur W.		1213

ARKANSAS
Fayetteville	HARRISON, John A.	(501)443-4403	506
Fort Smith	LARSON, Larry	(501)783-0229	699
Little Rock	BASKIN, Jeffrey L.	(501)661-5428	63
	MULKEY, Jack C.	(501)225-2246	876
Roland	PATRICK, Retta B.	(501)868-5740	947

CALIFORNIA
Altadena	GREGORY, Timothy P.	(818)798-1268	466
APO San Francisco	HEINES, Rodney M.		522
Aptos	HERON, David W.	(408)688-6994	532
Arcadia	PERRY, Edward C.		960
Arcata	OYLER, David K.	(707)826-3441	932
Berkeley	HANFF, Peter E.	(415)642-8172	495
	OGDEN, Barclay W.	(415)642-4946	918
	SILVER, Cy H.	(415)524-5501	1138
	STOCKTON, Gloria J.	(415)843-8550	1196
Bridgeport	REVEAL, Arlene H.	(619)932-7031	1024
Callahan	FARRIER, George F.	(916)467-3334	365
Campbell	HAZEKAMP, Phyllis W.	(408)379-1611	517

LIBRARY BUILDING CONSULTANT (Cont'd)

CALIFORNIA (Cont'd)
Chatsworth	TANIS, Norman E.	(818)886-1318	1222
Concord	REYES, Helen M.	(415)000-0000	1024
Culver City	ANDRADE, Rebecca	(213)837-5448	26
Davis	BLANK, Karen L.	(916)752-2110	104
Del Mar	HOLT, Raymond M.	(619)755-7878	554
Eagle Rock	CRAWFORD, Marilyn L.	(213)259-8938	257
Goleta	DAVIDSON, Donald C.		276
	GRAZIANO, Eugene	(805)968-2281	460
Irvine	POOLE, Jay M.	(714)856-6377	983
La Jolla	MIRSKY, Phyllis S.	(619)534-1234	847
Laguna Beach	KOUNTZ, John C.	(714)494-8783	673
Lake View Terrace	TASHIMA, Marie		1224
Long Beach	AYALA, John L.	(213)599-8028	42
	CONNOLLY, Betty F.	(213)494-5465	237
Los Angeles	ALFORD, Thomas E.	(213)612-3333	13
	EVANS, G E.	(213)642-4593	357
	HAYTHORN, Joseph D.	(213)938-3621	517
	JAIN, Celeste C.	(213)665-7510	591
	JONES, Wyman	(213)612-3332	615
	MERRIFIELD, Thomas C.	(213)390-4717	826
	RITCHESON, Charles R.	(213)743-2543	1036
	TOMPKINS, Philip	(213)743-2543	1250
	VEASLEY, Mignon M.	(213)236-3515	1280
Menlo Park	NEWMAN, Mark J.	(415)326-2114	899
Mill Valley	WHITE, Cecil R.	(415)388-8080	1330
Northridge	DAVIS, Douglas A.	(818)885-2261	278
Oakland	COOPER, Richard S.	(415)530-8080	243
	NOVAK, Gloria J.	(415)658-9458	910
	PRICE, Bennett J.	(415)642-9485	992
Oceanside	NELSON, Helen M.	(619)439-7330	893
Orange	SMITH, Elizabeth M.	(714)634-7809	1154
Pasadena	CHICK, Cynthia L.	(818)796-8194	208
Pleasanton	LUCAS, Linda L.		746
Pomona	KUHNER, David A.	(714)593-2467	683
Riverside	VIERICH, Richard W.	(714)787-3511	1284
Rowland Heights	SIGLER, Ronald F.	(818)965-9917	1137
Sacramento	BURNS, John F.	(916)445-4293	162
	KAST, Gloria E.	(916)483-6765	629
	KILLIAN, Richard M.	(916)440-5926	648
San Bernardino	WEBB, Duncan C.	(714)387-4959	1313
San Clemente	KOPAN, Ellen K.	(714)498-4309	671
San Diego	BOSSEAU, Don L.	(619)229-2538	117
	KAYE, Karen	(619)560-2695	632
	LOOMIS, Barbara L.	(619)565-3172	740
	SANNWALD, William W.	(619)236-5870	1081
	VOIGT, Melvin J.		1287
San Francisco	CARSCH, Ruth E.	(415)641-5014	187
	CODER, Ann	(415)442-7000	226
	FOX, Marylou P.	(415)546-8466	395
	GITLER, Robert L.	(415)221-9216	438
	HENKE, Dan	(415)565-4758	528
San Jose	CEPPOS, Karen F.	(408)277-2280	196
Santa Ana	PINCOCK, Rulon D.	(714)558-5811	974
Santa Barbara	ANDERSON, Carol L.	(805)685-7585	22
Santa Monica	BECKER, Joseph	(213)829-6866	72
	HALL, Anthony	(213)827-1707	487
Santa Paula	CHRISTOPHER, Paul	(805)525-8092	212
Santa Rosa	PETTAS, William A.	(707)527-4392	965
Sebastopol	SABSAY, David	(707)545-0831	1073
Simi Valley	WONG, Clark C.	(805)522-5233	1362
Sonoma	LUNARDI, Albert A.	(707)935-6020	748
Stanford	SCHMIDT, C J.	(415)493-5280	1095
Thousand Oaks	SMITH, Marvin E.	(805)497-6282	1158
Turlock	AMRHEIN, John K.	(209)667-3607	20
Ventura	BENNETT, Carson W.		81
Walnut Creek	HELLUM-BERMAN, Bertha D.	(415)935-6516	524
	MORRIS, John	(415)933-3365	866
West Covina	HOFFMAN, William J.	(818)919-5222	548
Woodland	KELLUM-ROSE, Nancy P.	(916)662-6616	637
Yucaipa	BUTLER, Randall R.	(714)797-3859	167

COLORADO
Boulder	ELLSWORTH, Ralph E.		345
Colorado Springs	BARRETT, Donald J.	(303)598-3163	59
	MAGRATH, Lynn L.	(303)473-2080	760
Denver	COCO, Al	(303)871-6200	226
	HEMPSTEAD, John	(303)866-6730	525
	SCHAFER, Jay G.	(303)556-8370	1089

LIBRARY BUILDING CONSULTANT (Cont'd)
COLORADO (Cont'd)

Fort Collins	ANDERSON, Lemoyne W.	(303)484-7319	24
	BURNS, Robert W.	(303)491-1830	163
Golden	PHINNEY, Hartley K.	(303)273-3690	969
Grand Lake	ARMITAGE, Constance	(303)328-5293	32
Leadville	PARRY, David R.	(303)486-2626	944
New Castle	GARYPIE, Renwick	(303)984-2346	421
Pueblo	GARDNER, W J.	(303)549-3308	418

CONNECTICUT

Greenwich	LUSHINGTON, Nolan	(203)655-3632	749
Hamden	ROGERS, Rutherford D.	(203)777-1682	1050
	SMITH, Nolan E.	(203)776-3558	1159
Hartford	PORTER, Kathryn W.	(203)727-4321	985
	STONE, Dennis J.	(203)241-4617	1197
	WILKIE, Everett C.	(203)236-5621	1340
Kensington	RIBNICKY, Karen F.	(203)828-6537	1026
Middletown	ADAMS, J R.	(203)347-9411	5
New Hartford	GIBSON, Barbara H.	(203)379-3548	431
New Haven	COHEN, Morris L.	(203)432-1600	228
	KELLER, Michael A.	(203)389-2212	635
	PETERSON, Stephen L.	(203)432-5292	964
	SIGGINS, Jack A.	(203)776-3808	1137
Old Lyme	DEAKYNE, William J.	(203)434-9294	283
Stamford	DIMATTIA, Ernest A.	(203)322-9055	304
	GOLOMB, Katherine A.	(203)964-1000	447
	LIEBERMAN, Lucille N.	(203)353-2095	726
Storrs	MCDONALD, John P.	(203)429-5620	802
Torrington	BENAMATI, Dennis C.	(203)489-2990	79
Wallingford	SCHERER, Leslie C.	(203)265-6754	1092
Westport	SCHWARZ, Shirlee	(203)226-6606	1105
Wilton	TRIFFIN, Nicholas	(914)681-4275	1256
Windsor	SIMON, William H.		1141

DELAWARE

Dover	COONS, Daniel E.	(302)736-5111	242
Wilmington	TITUS, H M.	(302)656-1722	1247

DISTRICT OF COLUMBIA

Washington	BERWICK, Philip C.	(202)543-3369	91
	FLEMING, Thomas B.	(202)429-6429	384
	HEAD, Anita K.	(202)994-7336	518
	KEHOE, Patrick E.	(202)885-2674	634
	MILEVSKI, Robert J.	(202)287-5634	834
	O'BRIEN, Kathleen	(202)331-8400	914
	ROSENFELD, Mary A.	(202)357-1940	1056
	SHEELER, Harva L.	(202)879-3954	1125
	VANDEGRIFT, Barbara P.	(202)662-7523	1273

FLORIDA

Boynton Beach	FARACE, Virginia K.	(305)732-2624	363
Bradenton	PLACE, Philip A.	(813)746-1358	977
Chattahoochee	BEASLEY, Clarence W.		69
Clearwater	MIELKE, Linda	(813)462-6916	833
Coconut Grove	DEWAR, Jo E.	(305)858-8787	298
Daytona Beach	BRANDON, Alfred N.	(904)677-5098	128
Fort Lauderdale	HATFIELD, Frances S.	(305)463-5928	511
Gainesville	BECKER, Josephine M.	(904)371-3808	72
	DRUM, Carol A.	(904)335-8501	320
	TAYLOR, Betty W.	(904)372-0716	1226
	WILLOCKS, Robert M.	(904)392-0342	1349
Jacksonville	FARKAS, Andrew	(904)646-2554	364
	JONES, Robert P.	(904)646-2615	614
Jensen Beach	HENNINGS, Leroy	(305)334-6134	528
Lauderhill	HURTES, Reva	(305)735-8655	578
Marianna	STABLER, William H.	(904)482-3474	1177
Melbourne	HENSON, Llewellyn L.	(305)768-8000	529
Miami	DANIELS, Westwell R.	(305)235-9484	273
	MCNEAL, Archie L.		816
	MILLER, Laurence A.	(305)554-2461	839
	SINTZ, Edward F.	(305)375-5026	1144
Orlando	LABRAKE, Orlyn B.	(305)275-4564	686
	SESSA, Frank B.		1116
Pembroke Pines	MULLER, Charles W.	(305)431-5123	877
Pensacola	MOREIN, P G.	(904)474-2492	863
Plant City	PINGS, Vern M.	(813)752-3884	974
Pompano Beach	GULLETTE, Irene		477
St Petersburg	FUSTUKJIAN, Samuel Y.	(813)893-9125	410
	WOODARD, Joseph L.	(813)345-1335	1365

LIBRARY BUILDING CONSULTANT (Cont'd)
FLORIDA (Cont'd)

San Antonio	NEUHOFE, M D.	(904)588-8320	897
Sanibel	KLASING, Jane P.	(813)472-8391	657
Sarasota	DANIEL, Marianne M.	(813)351-6583	272
	JENKINS, Althea H.	(813)355-5003	597
Tallahassee	BUSTETTER, Stanley R.	(904)487-2667	166
	HART, Thomas L.	(904)385-7550	507
	MARTIN, James R.	(904)893-7306	776
	MILLER, Charles E.	(904)644-5211	836
	SCHROEDER, Edwin M.	(904)644-4578	1100
	TREZZA, Alphonse F.	(904)878-5551	1256
Tampa	CRAIG, James P.	(813)238-5514	254
	EVERLOVE, Nora J.	(813)839-4868	359
Tarpon Springs	O'BRIEN, Elizabeth M.	(813)942-3291	914
Wauchula	MAPP, Erwin E.	(813)773-9207	768
West Palm Beach	BROWNLEE, Jerry W.	(305)686-0895	148
	FOSTER, Helen M.	(305)686-1776	392
Winter Park	SEBRIGHT, Terence F.	(305)678-8846	1110

GEORGIA

Atlanta	BATTEN, Henry R.	(404)876-3657	64
	FORSEE, Joe B.	(404)656-2461	391
	SLOAN, Mary J.	(404)874-6224	1149
	SWANSON, Joe	(404)699-1415	1213
	WILTSE, Helen C.	(404)451-4260	1353
Augusta	BASLER, Thomas G.	(404)828-2856	63
Cartersville	HOWINGTON, Lee R.	(404)382-4203	566
Decatur	HULLUM, Cheri J.	(404)987-7473	573
Doraville	DRAPER, James D.	(404)457-4858	318
Eastman	WILSON, David C.	(912)374-4711	1350
Hartwell	BISSO, Arthur J.	(404)376-4655	100
Jonesboro	STEWART, Carol J.	(404)478-7120	1192
Richmond Hill	GLISSON, Patricia A.	(912)727-2592	441
Watkinsville	WHITEHEAD, James M.	(404)769-8917	1332

HAWAII

Honolulu	BREINICH, John A.	(808)536-9302	132
	DILUCIA, Samuel J.	(808)955-1500	303
	HORNE, Norman P.	(808)524-8094	560
	KANE, Bartholomew A.	(808)524-8344	624

IDAHO

Idaho Falls	WINWARD, Coleen C.	(208)529-6077	1356
Menan	COVINGTON, Eddis E.	(208)754-4183	252
Post Falls	JONES-LITTEER, Corene A.	(208)773-1515	616
Rexburg	HART, Eldon C.	(208)356-4447	507

ILLINOIS

Bolingbrook	TODD, Alexander W.	(312)759-2102	1248
Carterville	UBEL, James A.	(618)985-3711	1267
Champaign	ALLEN, Walter C.	(217)586-3882	16
	MCCLELLAN, William M.	(217)352-1893	796
Chicago	AHN, Hyonah K.	(312)728-8652	8
	DAVIS, Glenn G.	(312)943-2911	279
	DOWELL, David R.	(312)567-6844	315
	DOYLE, Francis R.	(312)670-2950	317
	MORRISON, Samuel F.	(312)269-3053	868
	PAIETTA, Ann C.	(312)996-2716	935
	PALMER, Raymond A.	(312)266-2456	936
	PETERSON, Randall T.	(312)427-2737	964
	PIZER, Irwin H.	(312)996-8974	977
	SIMPSON, Donald B.	(312)955-4545	1141
	STEFL, Leah J.	(312)031-2701	1184
De Kalb	TITUS, Elizabeth M.	(815)753-1094	1247
Downers Grove	STOFFEL, Lester L.	(312)964-2541	1196
East Peoria	LINDGREN, William D.	(309)694-5462	729
Flora	DOCKINS, Glenn	(618)662-2679	307
Glen Ellyn	FRADKIN, Bernard	(312)416-1199	395
Grayslake	DEPKE, Robert W.		293
Gurnee	FUNK, Carla J.	(312)367-6213	409
Highland Park	SHERRY, Diane H.	(312)433-3968	1129
Joliet	JOHNSTON, James R.	(815)729-3481	610
Kenilworth	JONES, William G.	(312)251-3112	615
La Grange	SCHULTHEISS, Louis A.	(312)354-6958	1101
Manteno	MC LAUGHLIN, Terry L.	(815)468-6424	813
Mascoutah	GORDON, Diane M.	(618)566-4981	451
Maywood	LUDWIG, Logan T.	(312)531-3192	747
Melrose Park	TRELEASE, Robert J.	(312)345-2500	1255
Monmouth	KINNEY, M R.		653

LIBRARY BUILDING CONSULTANT (Cont'd)
ILLINOIS (Cont'd)

Naperville	PEARSON, Roger L.	(312)355-1540	953
	ROWE, Dorothy B.	(312)355-9221	1062
	YOUNG, Nancy J.	(312)357-2392	1382
Nashville	RUSIEWISKI, Charles B.	(618)327-8304	1068
Normal	MEISELS, Henry R.	(309)452-4485	822
Oak Lawn	MOORMAN, John A.	(312)422-4990	862
Oak Park	BEN-SHIR, Rya H.	(312)386-5444	83
	MARSHALL, Maggie L.	(312)848-4432	774
Palatine	BURNS, Mary F.	(312)358-0137	162
Park Forest	HAYES, Hazel I.		515
Park Ridge	CRISPEN, Joanne	(312)696-6594	259
Peoria	JACKSON, Susan M.	(309)674-2008	588
Riverdale	ZENKE, Mary H.	(312)849-0879	1387
Rockford	CHITWOOD, Julius R.	(815)962-4409	209
St Charles	BROWN, Diana M.		143
Streamwood	DEUEL, Marlene R.	(312)837-8242	296
Wauconda	LUEDER, Dianne B.	(312)526-6075	747
	SHENASSA, Daryoosh	(312)526-9123	1126
Wheeling	MCCLARREN, Robert R.	(312)459-1300	796
Wilmington	BOBAN, Carol A.	(815)458-3411	108
Winnetka	LUNDQUIST, Marie A.	(312)441-3315	748
	THOMPSON, Richard E.	(312)446-7975	1241

INDIANA

Bloomington	CALLISON, Daniel J.	(812)335-5113	174
	FARRELL, David	(812)335-3403	365
	IRVINE, Betty J.	(812)335-3403	584
	KASER, David	(812)335-5113	628
	RABER, Nevin W.	(812)336-4522	1001
Fort Wayne	CLEGG, Michael B.		220
	KRULL, Jeffrey R.	(219)424-7241	680
Hanover	MORRILL, Walter D.	(812)866-2151	866
Indianapolis	GALBRAITH, Leslie R.	(317)924-1331	413
Mishawaka	EISEN, David J.	(219)259-5277	340
Muncie	MOORE, Thomas J.	(317)285-1307	861
	WOOD, Michael B.	(317)289-5417	1364
Noblesville	COOPER, David L.	(317)773-1384	242
Richmond	FARBER, Evan I.	(317)966-2422	363
South Bend	MULLINS, James L.	(219)237-4449	878

IOWA

Ames	KUHN, Warren B.	(515)294-1442	682
Bellevue	KIEFFER, Marian L.	(319)872-4991	647
Davenport	JONSON, Laurence F.	(319)323-9213	616
Decorah	FENSTERMANN, Duane W.	(319)387-1164	371
Grinnell	MCKEE, Christopher	(515)269-3351	810
Iowa City	DUNLAP, Leslie W.		326
	EGGERS, Lolly P.	(319)356-5206	339

KANSAS

Coffeyville	HENDERSON, Rosemary	(316)251-2158	527
Hesston	EICHELBERGER, Marianne	(316)327-4666	339
Hutchinson	HAWKINS, Paul J.	(316)663-5441	514
Lawrence	JOHNSON, Ellen S.	(913)864-3496	604
McPherson	OLSEN, Rowena J.	(316)241-0731	921
Topeka	JOHNSON, Duane F.	(913)296-3296	603
	MARVIN, James C.	(913)233-2040	780

KENTUCKY

Edgewood	REESE, Virginia D.	(606)261-8211	1016
Frankfort	COOPER, Judy L.	(502)564-2672	243
	HELLARD, Ellen G.	(502)875-7000	524
Horse Cave	STROHECKER, Edwin C.	(502)453-3059	1202
Lexington	CUNHA, George M.	(606)257-8876	265
	SCHABEL, Donald J.	(606)223-4017	1088
	STEENSLAND, Ronald P.		1184
	WRIGHT, Paul L.	(606)525-6324	1372
Louisville	ANDERSON, James C.	(502)588-6752	23
	DORR, Ralze W.	(502)588-6745	313
	TEITELBAUM, Gene W.	(502)588-6392	1230
Owensboro	YATES, Dudley V.	(502)526-3111	1378
Paducah	SUTHERLAND, Thomas A.	(502)443-2664	1211

LOUISIANA

Baton Rouge	CARPENTER, Michael A.	(504)766-7385	185
	MARTIN, Robert S.	(504)767-7167	778
	PERRY, Emma B.	(504)928-3622	960
	ROCHE, Alvin A.	(504)771-4900	1045

LIBRARY BUILDING CONSULTANT (Cont'd)
LOUISIANA (Cont'd)

Hammond	GREAVES, F L.	(504)549-2234	461
Metairie	BENOIT, Anthony H.	(504)888-5379	82
Natchitoches	BUCHANAN, William C.	(318)357-4403	153
New Orleans	WILSON, C D.	(504)596-2600	1350
Ruston	BYERS, Cora M.	(318)257-3555	168
	WICKER, W W.	(318)257-2577	1335

MAINE

Augusta	TARANKO, Walter J.	(207)289-5628	1223
Bangor	WOODWARD, Robert C.	(207)942-4760	1368
Lewiston	GROSS, Richard F.	(207)782-3958	472
Machias	PHIPPS, Bert L.	(207)255-3313	969
Portland	REIMAN, Anne M.	(207)774-4000	1020
Westbrook	PARKS, George R.	(207)854-0355	943

MARYLAND

Baltimore	FINNEY, Lance C.	(301)685-0074	379
	LEBRETON, Jonathan A.	(301)455-2356	708
	PAPENFUSE, Edward C.	(301)467-6137	939
Bethesda	SMINK, Anna R.	(301)365-5300	1152
Bowie	EVANS, Frank B.	(301)464-8829	357
College Park	WELLISCH, Hans H.	(301)345-3477	1322
Columbia	HILL, Norma L.	(301)997-8000	540
Cumberland	NEAL, Robert L.	(301)777-7738	890
Fort Washington	KALKUS, Stanley	(301)839-5729	623
Gibson Island	ROVELSTAD, Howard		1062
Greenbelt	BOGGESS, John J.		110
Hagerstown	BINAU, Myra I.	(301)824-8801	97
Landover	BARTH, Edward W.	(301)773-9790	61
Largo	NEKRITZ, Leah K.	(301)322-0462	893
Rockville	OAKLEY, Robert L.	(301)279-9103	913
Silver Spring	VOGT-O'CONNOR, Diane L.	(301)681-7615	1287
Solomons	HEIL, Kathleen A.	(301)326-2967	521
Westminster	NEIKIRK, Harold D.	(301)848-7000	892

MASSACHUSETTS

Amherst	BRIDEGAM, Willis E.	(413)542-2212	135
	KURKUL, Donna L.	(413)253-5975	684
Andover	JACOBSON, Nancy C.	(617)475-6960	590
Ashburnham	KISSNER, Arthur J.	(617)827-4507	656
Boston	CURLEY, Arthur	(617)536-5400	265
	EATON, Elizabeth K.	(617)523-7415	333
	HAMANN, Edmund G.	(617)573-8536	490
	MOSKOWITZ, Michael A.	(617)578-8670	871
	NIMS, Judith C.	(617)573-3196	904
Brighton	BRAUN, Robin E.	(617)789-2177	130
Brookline	LEAHY, Lynda C.	(617)731-5237	706
Cambridge	DUNKLY, James W.	(617)868-3450	326
	SAKEY, Joseph G.	(617)498-9000	1076
Carver	NEUBAUER, Richard A.	(617)866-5186	896
Charlestown	DOWLER, Lawrence E.		315
Chestnut Hill	CHANNING, Rhoda K.	(617)552-4470	201
Concord	JACKSON, Patience K.	(617)369-0586	588
East Boston	SCHLAFF, Donna G.	(617)561-0153	1093
Eastham	ELDRIDGE, Jane A.	(617)255-3070	342
Framingham	MCDONALD, Stanley M.	(617)626-4651	803
Leverett	ZIPKOWITZ, Fay	(413)367-9573	1389
Lexington	BERNSTEIN, D S.	(617)863-1284	89
	HILTON, Robert C.	(617)862-6288	541
	LUCKER, Jay K.	(617)862-4558	746
Medford	JONES, Frederick S.	(617)381-3345	613
North Andover	REEVE, Russell J.	(617)682-6260	1016
Northampton	BOZONE, Billie R.	(413)584-2700	124
Springfield	DUNN, Donald J.	(413)782-1454	326
	KEOUGH, Francis P.	(413)739-1837	643
Stoughton	ANDERSON, Cheryl M.	(617)344-4000	22
Uxbridge	LEWIS, Thomas F.		724
Waltham	GILROY, Rupert E.	(617)736-4912	437
Wareham	PILLSBURY, Mary J.	(617)295-2343	973
Watertown	REDDY, Sigrid M.	(617)924-3282	1014
Wayland	BROWN, Louise R.	(617)358-4220	145
Williamsburg	O'BRIEN, Marjorie S.	(413)268-7131	914
Winchester	KEATS, Susan E.	(617)729-9317	633
Worcester	CHAMBERLAIN, Ruth B.	(617)244-3612	197
	JOHNSON, Penelope B.	(617)799-1653	608
	STANKUS, Tony	(617)793-2643	1180

LIBRARY BUILDING CONSULTANT (Cont'd)

MICHIGAN
City	Name	Phone	No.
Ann Arbor	DALY, Kathleen E.	(313)662-7631	271
	DIDIER, Elaine K.	(313)763-0378	301
	DOUGHERTY, Richard M.	(313)764-9356	314
	LANSDALE, Metta T.		696
	LEARY, Margaret R.	(313)663-7324	707
	WAGMAN, Frederick H.	(313)662-1214	1291
	WARNER, Robert M.	(313)763-2281	1305
Birmingham	SWEENEY, Thomas F.	(313)964-0030	1215
Bloomfield Hills	FRANKIE, Suzanne O.	(313)855-6149	397
Detroit	GUNN, Arthur C.	(313)831-9707	477
	PFLUG, Warner W.	(313)577-4024	966
	SPYERS-DURAN, Peter	(313)577-4048	1177
East Lansing	CHAPIN, Richard E.	(517)355-2341	201
	HAKA, Clifford H.	(517)353-5317	484
Flint	PALMER, David W.	(313)238-0166	936
Grosse Pointe Farms	HANSON, Charles D.	(313)882-3627	498
Jackson	LEAMON, David L.	(517)788-4199	707
Jenison	VELTEMA, John H.	(616)457-3400	1282
Lansing	FRY, James W.	(517)373-1593	406
Mt Pleasant	KRUUT, Evald	(517)773-5184	681
Northville	FIELD, Judith J.	(313)349-1953	375
Plainwell	PARR, Michael P.	(616)685-9554	944
Plymouth	DE BEAR, Richard S.	(313)459-5000	284
Pontiac	LYNCH, Mollie S.	(313)858-3495	752
Port Huron	WU, Harry P.	(313)982-2765	1373
Southfield	GILBERT, Carole M.	(313)424-3294	433
Spring Lake	PRETZER, Dale H.	(616)846-8967	992

MINNESOTA
City	Name	Phone	No.
Bloomington	NAUEN, Lindsay B.	(612)854-2879	889
Braham	MCGRIFF, Ronald I.	(612)396-3957	808
Circle Pines	YOUNG, Jerry F.	(612)786-5689	1382
Hopkins	SMITH, David R.	(612)933-0199	1154
Minneapolis	HOPP, Ralph H.		558
	ROHLF, Robert H.	(612)926-6105	1050
Minnetonka	HUTTNER, Marian A.	(612)545-2338	579
Northfield	METZ, T J.	(507)663-4267	828
Pine Island	BENSON, Laurel D.	(507)356-8515	83
Roseville	VINNES, Norman M.	(612)483-1103	1285
St Paul	CLEMMER, Joel G.	(612)696-6345	221
	FEYE-STUKAS, Janice	(612)296-2821	374
	WENTE, Norman G.	(612)641-3224	1324
White Bear Lake	LEWIS, Alan D.	(612)429-2508	722

MISSISSIPPI
City	Name	Phone	No.
Hattiesburg	WILSON, Mary S.	(601)266-4240	1352
Hernando	ANDERSON, James F.	(601)368-4439	23
Meridian	JOHNSON, Scott R.	(601)483-8241	609
Natchez	RANDAZZO, Corinne O.	(601)445-2848	1006
Pascagoula	MAJURE, William D.	(601)769-7149	762
Sunflower	POWELL, Anice C.	(601)569-3663	988
University	COCHRAN, J W.	(601)232-7361	225

MISSOURI
City	Name	Phone	No.
Ballwin	BUHR, Rosemary E.		156
Columbia	MARTIN, Mason G.	(314)449-5798	777
Harrisonville	FRANKLIN, Jill S.	(816)884-6223	397
Joplin	KEMP, Charles H.	(417)625-9386	639
Kansas City	HAMMOND, John J.	(816)221-2695	493
	MARTIN, Louis E.	(816)363-4600	777
	NESBITT, John R.	(813)926-7616	896
Kirksville	ONSAGER, Lawrence W.	(816)665-4283	924
St Louis	HALBROOK, Barbara	(314)362-2786	485
	HUESTIS, Jeffrey C.	(314)889-5409	570
	JOSEPH, Miriam E.	(314)965-4372	617
	SCHRAMM, Betty V.	(314)994-3300	1099
	SUELFLOW, August R.	(314)721-5934	1206
	WEITKEMPER, Larry D.	(314)353-6757	1320
St Peters	SANDSTEDT, Carl R.	(314)441-2300	1081

NEBRASKA
City	Name	Phone	No.
Bellevue	JACKA, David C.	(402)293-3157	586
Kearney	MAYESKI, John K.	(308)234-8535	790
Lincoln	WAGNER, Rod G.	(402)423-7476	1292
Omaha	MEANS, Raymond B.	(402)280-2705	820
	PHIPPS, Michael C.	(402)444-4834	969

LIBRARY BUILDING CONSULTANT (Cont'd)

NEVADA
City	Name	Phone	No.
Las Vegas	HUNSBERGER, Charles W.	(702)733-7810	574

NEW HAMPSHIRE
City	Name	Phone	No.
Concord	HIGGINS, Matthew J.	(603)228-3127	538
Exeter	THOMAS, Jacquelyn H.	(603)772-4311	1236
Fremont	FARAH, Barbara D.		363
Hancock	BRYAN, Arthur L.	(603)525-6614	151
Manchester	COMEAU, Reginald A.	(603)668-6706	234
	KENT, Jeffrey A.	(603)622-4408	642
Portsmouth	PRIDHAM, Sherman C.	(603)431-2000	993
Twin Mountain	PALMATIER, Susan M.	(603)846-2239	936

NEW JERSEY
City	Name	Phone	No.
Delanco	WOLFORD, Larry E.	(609)461-5667	1361
East Brunswick	STONE, Jason R.	(201)390-6775	1197
Florham Park	SWINBURNE, Ralph E.	(201)377-8390	1216
Glen Rock	PERCELLI, Irene M.	(201)445-5983	958
Haddonfield	WILLIAMSON, Carol L.	(609)354-6213	1347
Iselin	SILVA, Nelly H.	(201)321-0683	1138
Madison	COUGHLIN, Caroline M.	(201)377-3000	250
	JONES, Arthur E.	(201)377-6525	611
Maplewood	D'ALLEYRAND, Marc R.	(201)761-1028	270
Marlton	RICHIE, Mark L.	(609)985-0436	1030
Montclair	HOROWITZ, Marjorie B.	(201)744-8697	560
	MCPHERSON, Kenneth F.	(201)543-2278	817
Moorestown	LADOF, Nina S.	(609)235-1570	687
Newark	ROSENSTEIN, Philip	(201)456-4353	1057
Nutley	GILHEANY, Rosary S.	(201)667-7013	434
Patterson	SAWYER, Miriam		1086
Pennington	PRIESING, Patricia L.	(609)737-1411	993
Princeton	HOELLE, Dolores M.	(609)452-3201	547
Rahway	SUDALL, Arthur D.	(201)388-0761	1206
Sewell	COUMBE, Robert E.	(609)589-2000	251
	CROCKER, Jane L.	(609)468-5000	259
Short Hills	TALCOTT, Ann W.	(201)379-6721	1221
Somerville	MOYER, Holley M.	(201)725-1600	874
Springfield	APPEL MOSESOF, Rhoda S.	(201)379-3556	29
	GLADSTONE, Mark A.	(201)376-2055	439
Stratford	SCHUBACK COHN, Judith	(609)346-6800	1101
Sussex	SMITH, Jo T.	(201)875-3621	1156
Teaneck	MOUNT, Ellis	(201)836-1137	873
Trenton	STRONG, Moira O.	(609)292-4958	1203
Turnersville	SZILASSY, Sandor	(609)589-7193	1218
Williamstown	BOGIS, Nana E.	(609)728-0569	110
Woodbridge	BECKERMAN, Edwin P.	(609)634-4450	72

NEW MEXICO
City	Name	Phone	No.
Albuquerque	BERNSTEIN, Judith R.	(505)262-2320	89
	HSU, Grace S.		567
	RASSAM, Cynthia K.	(505)277-4203	1009
	SPURLOCK, Sandra E.	(505)828-5378	1177
	VASSALLO, Paul	(505)277-8125	1279
Las Cruces	DAVIS, Hiram L.	(505)646-1509	279
	DRESP, Donald F.	(505)522-3627	319
	RICHARDS, James H.	(505)524-0281	1028
Roswell	MCLAREN, M B.	(505)622-6250	813
Toadlena	MCCAULEY, Elfrieda B.	(505)789-3205	795

NEW YORK
City	Name	Phone	No.
Albany	ANDERSON, Carol L.	(518)434-4802	22
	SEVERINGHAUS, Ethel L.	(518)456-2110	1117
Alfred	LASH, David B.	(607)587-4313	700
APO New York	HAAS, Eva L.		480
Ballston Lake	FRALEY, Ruth A.	(518)399-9542	395
Bellerose	GATNER, Elliott S.		422
Bellport	JANSEN, Guenter A.	(516)286-2626	593
Brighton	RAHN, Erwin P.	(716)442-8980	1003
Broadalbin	ANDERSON, Pauline H.	(518)883-3771	25
Brooklyn	SEMKOW, Julie L.	(718)624-3189	1115
	SWEENEY, Richard T.	(718)643-4446	1215
Buffalo	BREEN, M F.	(716)881-6264	131
	HUANG, C K.	(716)831-3402	568
	NEWMAN, George C.	(716)886-8132	899
	PALMIERI, Lucien E.	(716)882-9275	937
	ROUNDS, Joseph B.	(716)846-8904	1061
Circleville	NELSON, James B.	(914)361-2415	894
Clinton	ANTHONY, Donald C.	(315)737-8347	28

LIBRARY BUILDING CONSULTANT (Cont'd)
NEW YORK (Cont'd)

Cornwall on Hudson	WEISS, Egon A.	(914)534-9467	1320
Croton-on-Hudson	COHEN, Aaron	(914)271-8170	227
Delhi	SORGEN, Herbert J.	(607)746-4107	1168
Delmar	SHUMAN, Susan E.	(518)475-1202	1134
East Meadow	FRANZEN, John F.	(516)794-2570	398
East Northport	MILLER, Scott W.	(516)543-2821	842
Flushing	KOSTER, Gregory E.	(718)575-4264	673
Freeport	MORIN, Wilfred L.	(516)368-6242	865
Garrison	BALDWIN, Geraldine S.	(914)424-3020	51
Glendale	SOSTACK, Maura	(718)417-8242	1169
Holbrook	ROMANELLI, Catherine A.	(516)588-5171	1052
Ithaca	CASSARO, James P.	(607)255-7046	193
	HAMMOND, Jane L.	(607)255-5857	493
Jackson Heights	WALSH, Robert R.	(718)639-3188	1300
Jamaica	JOHNSON, James G.	(718)739-6503	605
	MARKE, Julius J.	(718)990-6759	771
Manlius	WU, Painan R.	(315)682-2472	1373
New Paltz	CONNORS, William E.	(914)257-2203	238
New Rochelle	HUMPHRY, James	(914)834-6941	574
	LARKIN, Patrick J.	(914)633-2350	698
	MITTELGLUCK, Eugene L.	(914)834-8739	850
New York	BUSSEY, Holly J.	(212)708-5181	165
	D'ANGELO, Paul P.	(212)760-1600	272
	DE GENNARO, Richard	(212)930-0769	287
	ELLENBERGER, Jack S.	(212)837-6583	343
	HARRIS, Carolyn L.	(212)280-2223	504
	HOOVER, James L.	(212)280-3737	557
	KUHNER, Robert A.	(212)663-3360	683
	LEE, Sang C.	(212)669-7961	711
	LIEBERFELD, Lawrence	(212)348-8499	726
	MASYR, Caryl L.	(212)777-9271	783
	MILLER, Michael D.		841
	MOONEY, James E.	(212)873-3400	858
	RUBINSTEIN, Ed	(212)725-4550	1065
	VINCENT-DAVISS, Diana	(212)598-2367	1284
	WARNER, Elaine	(212)477-9517	1305
	WEINZIMMER, William A.	(212)421-1950	1318
Niagara University	MORRIS, Leslie R.	(716)285-1212	867
Ossining	FRANCK, Jane P.	(914)762-6073	396
Plattsburgh	RANSOM, Stanley A.	(518)563-5719	1007
Port Jervis	HOFMANN, Susan M.	(914)856-1513	548
Rochester	BALKIN, Ruth G.	(716)482-1506	52
	KANSFIELD, Norman J.	(716)271-1320	625
	SHAPIRO, June R.	(716)461-5929	1121
	SOMERVILLE, Arleen N.	(716)275-4495	1167
Schenectady	HUMPHRY, John A.	(518)374-8944	574
	KING, Maryde F.	(518)374-7287	651
Setauket	COOK, Jeannine S.	(516)941-4090	240
Smithtown	BENNETT, James F.	(516)265-2037	81
Syracuse	FUNK, Nancy J.	(315)433-2627	410
	KINCHEN, Robert P.	(315)473-2702	650
Uniondale	GREEN, Joseph H.	(516)292-8920	462
Williamsville	BOBINSKI, Mary F.	(716)688-4919	108
Youngstown	TELATNIK, George M.		1230

NORTH CAROLINA

Asheboro	SMITH, Merrill F.	(919)629-1471	1158
Boone	GREGORY, Roderick F.	(704)262-3956	466
	HATHAWAY, Milton G.	(704)262-5113	512
Chapel Hill	BROADUS, Robert N.	(919)962-8063	138
	GOVAN, James F.	(919)962-1301	454
	PRILLAMAN, Susan M.	(919)962-3791	993
	SEVERANCE, Robert W.	(919)967-5021	1117
Charlotte	GALVIN, Hoyt R.	(704)366-4335	415
	MOYER, James M.	(704)568-3151	874
Dallas	HUNSUCKER, David L.	(704)922-8041	575
Davidson	PARK, Leland M.	(704)892-1837	941
Durham	BIRD, Warren P.	(919)684-2092	98
	BURGIN, Robert E.	(919)683-6485	159
Fayetteville	HANSEL, Patsy J.	(919)484-7096	497
	THRASHER, Jerry A.	(919)483-1580	1243
Greensboro	TUGWELL, Helen M.	(919)334-5764	1262
Hickory	PRITCHARD, John A.	(704)294-0326	994
High Point	GAUGHAN, Thomas M.	(919)841-9215	422
Kinston	JONES, John W.	(919)527-7066	613
Lexington	THOMAS, John B.	(704)249-8186	1237
Matthews	CANNON, Robert E.	(704)847-0394	179

LIBRARY BUILDING CONSULTANT (Cont'd)
NORTH CAROLINA (Cont'd)

Montreat	BROOKS, Jerrold L.	(704)669-7661	140
	FOREMAN, Kenneth J.	(704)669-2782	390
Pinehurst	WILKINS, Alice L.	(919)692-6185	1340
Raleigh	ISACCO, Jeanne M.	(919)851-4703	584
	MURPHY, Malinda M.	(919)821-2072	881
	WELCH, John T.	(919)872-0552	1321
Research Triangle Pk	BEST-NICHOLS, Barbara J.	(919)544-3808	92
Robbinsville	LARSON, Josephine	(704)479-8192	699
Winston-Salem	ROBERTS, William H.	(919)727-2556	1041
	RODNEY, Mae L.	(919)924-6992	1048
	STEELE, Tom M.	(919)761-5440	1184

NORTH DAKOTA

Bismarck	HARRIS, Patricia L.	(701)224-8112	505
	NEWBORG, Gerald G.	(701)224-2668	898
Fargo	YLINIEMI, Hazel A.	(701)293-8074	1380

OHIO

Athens	LEE, Hwa W.	(614)592-5194	710
Bowling Green	BURLINGAME, Dwight F.	(419)372-2708	161
	FIDLER, Linda M.	(419)354-1450	375
Burton	VARGA, Carol C.	(216)834-4466	1278
Chesterland	CORBUS, Lawrence J.	(216)286-8941	245
Cincinnati	HUNT, James R.	(513)369-6972	575
	WELKER, Kathy J.	(513)684-2678	1321
	ZAFREN, Herbert C.	(513)221-4712	1385
Cleveland	KOZLOWSKI, Ronald S.	(216)398-1800	674
	PIKE, Kermit J.	(216)721-5722	972
	VENABLE, Andrew A.	(216)541-4128	1282
Cleveland Heights	GRABOWSKI, John J.	(216)932-8805	455
	SPAHR, Cheryl L.	(216)382-7675	1170
Columbus	CHESKI, Richard M.	(614)462-6843	207
	FU, Paul S.	(614)466-2044	407
	HOLOCH, S A.	(614)292-6691	553
	PARSONS, Augustine C.	(614)895-3201	944
	STUDER, William J.	(614)292-4241	1204
Dayton	KNASIAK, Theresa J.	(513)254-1433	663
	THOMAS, Ritchie D.	(513)873-2380	1238
	WALLACH, John S.	(513)227-9500	1298
Englewood	CUPP, Christian M.	(513)832-0136	265
Findlay	DICKINSON, Luren E.	(419)423-4934	301
Garrettsville	FINAN, Patrick E.	(216)569-7665	377
Georgetown	TOMLIN, Marsha A.	(513)378-3154	1250
Mansfield	KARRE, David J.	(419)526-1337	628
New Philadelphia	KOBULNICKY, Michael	(216)339-3391	666
Norwalk	DRAPP, Laureen	(419)668-6063	318
Rootstown	BREWER, Karen L.	(216)325-2511	134
Steubenville	HALL, Alan C.	(614)264-4410	486
Toledo	SCOLES, Clyde S.	(419)255-7055	1106
Warren	BRIELL, Robert D.	(216)399-8807	135
Westerville	GARDNER, Frank D.	(614)882-0221	417
Wickliffe	JOHNSON, Ruth E.	(216)943-1317	608
Wilmington	NICHOLS, James T.	(513)382-6661	901
Wooster	ESHELMAN, William R.	(216)345-8708	354
Worthington	EAST, Dennis	(614)888-9923	332
Wright Patterson AFB	HELLING, James T.	(513)255-5894	524

OKLAHOMA

Ardmore	ROBINSON, Joel M.	(405)223-3164	1044
McAlester	SIMON, Bradley A.	(918)423-3468	1140
Norman	LEE, Sul H.	(405)325-2611	711
	LOWELL, Howard P.	(405)366-7719	744
Oklahoma City	BRAWNER, Lee B.	(405)947-1109	130
	LITTLE, Paul L.	(405)789-9400	733
Stillwater	ROUSE, Roscoe	(405)377-1651	1061
Tahlequah	MADAUS, J R.		758
Tulsa	WOODRUM, Patricia A.	(918)592-7897	1366

OREGON

Beaverton	SHOFFNER, Ralph M.	(503)645-3502	1132
Corvallis	GEORGE, Melvin R.	(503)754-3411	427
Eugene	SHIPMAN, George W.	(503)683-8262	1131
	WAND, Patricia A.	(503)686-3056	1302
Portland	METZENBACHER, Gary W.	(503)654-5182	828
	TEICH, Steven	(503)225-8026	1230
Salem	DOAK, Wesley A.	(503)581-4292	306

LIBRARY BUILDING CONSULTANT (Cont'd)

PENNSYLVANIA

Bala Cynwyd	KREMER, Jill L.	(215)667-6787	677
Bloomsburg	FROST, Rebecca H.	(717)784-6856	406
	VANN, John D.	(717)784-4283	1276
Boyertown	EMERICK, John L.	(215)369-7422	347
California	BECK, William L.	(412)938-4096	72
Carlisle	FOX, James R.	(717)243-4611	394
Center Valley	MCCABE, James P.	(215)282-1100	793
Clarion	MCCABE, Gerard B.	(814)226-2343	792
Danielsville	PAGOTTO, Sarah L.	(215)767-3055	934
Drexel Hill	MULLEN, Francis X.	(215)623-7045	877
East Stroudsburg	SUMMERS, George V.	(717)424-3151	1209
Gettysburg	HEDRICK, David T.	(717)334-8741	520
Glenshaw	YATES, Diane G.	(412)486-0211	1378
Jeannette	PAWLIK, Deborah A.		951
Jenkintown	BARTZ, Alice P.	(215)887-4338	62
Lebanon	HABER, Walter H.		481
Lewisburg	DE KLERK, Ann M.	(717)524-1557	288
Lititz	GERLOTT, Eleanor L.	(717)627-0944	429
Loretto	NEGHERBON, Vincent R.	(814)472-7000	892
McKeesport	HORVATH, Robert T.	(412)672-0625	561
Media	COURTRIGHT, Harry R.	(215)891-5190	252
Middletown	BARRY, James W.		60
Philadelphia	BUTLER, Evelyn		166
	CLEVELAND, Susan E.	(215)662-2577	221
	GARRISON, Guy G.	(215)895-2474	420
	GILBERT, Thomas F.	(215)645-9319	434
	WALL, H D.	(215)438-1205	1297
Pittsburgh	FALGIONE, Joseph F.	(412)622-3127	362
	GREEN, Joyce M.	(412)234-5039	462
	WRIGHT, Nancy M.	(412)237-5948	1372
Springfield	MAIN, Annette Z.		761
State College	PIERCE, William S.	(814)237-7004	972
Wilkes-Barre	ERDICK, Joseph W.	(717)824-3725	352
York	CAMPBELL, Susan M.	(717)846-7788	177

PUERTO RICO

Santurce	RIVERA-ALVAREZ, Miguel A.	(809)728-4191	1037

RHODE ISLAND

Barrington	BUNDY, Annalee M.	(401)245-2232	157
Providence	LATHROP, Irene M.	(401)277-8070	701
	TAYLOR, Merrily E.	(401)863-2162	1227
	WAGNER, Albin	(401)277-2283	1291
Woonsocket	LEVEILLEE, Louis R.	(401)762-4440	719

SOUTH CAROLINA

Charleston	SAWYER, Warren A.	(803)792-2374	1086
Columbia	TOOMBS, Kenneth E.	(803)776-0431	1251
	WARREN, Charles D.	(803)782-4219	1306
Florence	DOVE, Herbert P.	(803)661-1300	314
Glendale	WHITE, Ann T.	(803)579-3330	1330
Hilton Head Island	CHAIT, William	(803)671-3720	197
Summerville	MAY, Robert E.	(803)871-2201	789
Sumter	GORDON, Clara B.	(803)773-4041	451

SOUTH DAKOTA

Rapid City	MC CAULEY, Philip F.	(605)348-5124	795

TENNESSEE

Bartlett	HAIR, William B.	(901)377-5434	484
Brentwood	NORTON, Tedgina	(615)371-0090	910
Cookeville	WALDEN, Winston A.	(615)372-3408	1294
Gallatin	COLLIER, Virginia S.		232
Knoxville	HUNT, Donald R.	(615)974-4127	575
	JETT, Don W.	(615)922-2548	600
	MYERS, Marcia J.	(615)974-4465	884
	PEMBERTON, J M.	(615)690-5598	956
Memphis	BANNERMAN-WILLIAMS, Cheryl F.	(901)785-7350	54
	MARTIN, Jess A.	(901)528-5636	776
	SMITH, Robert F.	(901)725-8872	1160
Nashville	MARTIN, Laquita V.	(615)383-0953	777
Sewanee	WATSON, Tom G.	(615)598-1213	1310
Signal Mountain	JACKSON, Joseph A.	(615)886-1753	587

LIBRARY BUILDING CONSULTANT (Cont'd)

TEXAS

Amarillo	WELLS, Mary K.	(806)381-2435	1322
Austin	BIERI, Sandra J.	(512)458-5551	95
	HISLE, W L.	(512)495-7148	544
	MCADAMS, Nancy R.	(512)453-7177	792
	MIDDLETON, Robert K.	(512)454-1888	833
	SENG, Mary A.	(512)444-5148	1115
Bangs	WEEKS, Patsy L.	(915)752-7315	1315
Beaumont	SPARKMAN, Mickey M.	(409)880-8118	1171
Buchanoan Dam	JONES, C L.	(512)793-6118	611
Cleburne	CARDENAS, Martha L.	(817)641-6641	180
College Station	SMITH, Charles R.	(409)845-8850	1153
Conroe	BALDWIN, Joe M.	(409)756-4484	51
Dallas	IBACH, Robert D.	(214)824-3094	581
	MASON, Florence M.	(214)358-5755	781
	WATERS, Richard L.	(214)826-6981	1308
Denton	CARROLL, Dewey E.	(817)565-2445	187
	MITCHELL, George D.	(817)565-2489	848
	SNAPP, Elizabeth M.	(817)387-3980	1162
El Paso	GEARY, Kathleen A.	(915)533-5777	424
Flower Mound	SVEINSSON, Joan L.	(214)539-9308	1212
Fort Worth	ALLMAND, Linda F.	(817)870-7706	17
	ARD, Harold J.	(817)293-5474	31
	CARTER, Bobby R.	(817)735-2380	189
	WROTENBERY, Carl R.	(817)923-1921	1373
Fredericksburg	YOUNG, Marjie D.	(512)997-2253	1382
Galveston	FREY, Emil F.	(409)761-2371	402
Houston	ADAMS, Elaine P.	(713)785-8703	4
	BROWN, Carol J.	(713)247-2227	142
	CHANG, Robert H.	(713)221-8181	201
	EICHSTADT, John R.	(713)221-5183	339
	GOTHIA, Blanche	(713)266-5106	453
	HENINGTON, David M.	(713)247-2700	528
	PHILLIPS, Ray S.	(713)622-9686	969
	RADOFF, Leonard I.	(713)692-1952	1002
	SINCLAIR, Rose P.	(713)452-5555	1143
Huntsville	PICHETTE, William H.	(409)291-2994	970
Irving	LANKFORD, Mary D.	(214)579-7818	696
McKinney	DOYLE, Patricia L.	(214)542-4461	317
North Richland Hills	HALLAM, Arlita W.	(817)281-0041	489
Overton	HANES, Fred W.		495
San Antonio	KRONICK, David A.	(512)344-5796	679
	TODD, Fred W.	(512)826-8121	1248
San Marcos	MEARS, William F.		820
Waco	PHILLIPS, Luouida V.		968
Weatherford	HEEZEN, Ronald R.	(817)599-0833	520
Wichita Falls	HARVILL, Melba S.	(817)692-6611	509
	ROBERTS, Ernest J.	(817)855-2390	1040

UTAH

Provo	GOULD, Douglas A.	(801)226-1469	454
St George	SHIRTS, Russell B.	(801)673-5895	1131
Salt Lake City	DAY, J D.	(801)363-5733	282
	HAYMOND, Jay M.	(801)533-5808	516

VERMONT

Brattleboro	HAY, Linda A.	(802)254-5595	515
Burlington	YERBURGH, Mark R.	(802)658-0337	1379
Middlebury	REHBACH, Jeffrey R.	(802)388-3711	1017

VIRGIN ISLANDS

St Thomas	CHANG, Henry C.	(809)774-3407	200

VIRGINIA

Alexandria	BROWN, Dale W.	(703)751-3236	143
	GRAY, Dorothy L.	(703)684-8244	459
	HINDMAN, Pamela J.	(703)836-9168	542
	MICHAELS, Andrea A.	(703)360-1297	831
	MICHAELS, David L.	(703)360-1297	832
Arlington	ALEXANDER, Carol G.		12
	BROWN, Charles M.	(703)284-8174	142
Ashland	BEDSOLE, Dan T.	(804)752-7256	73
Charlottesville	FRANKLIN, Robert D.	(804)973-3238	398
Chesapeake	LEHMAN, Lois J.	(804)367-3709	713
Chesterfield	WAGENKNECHT, Robert E.	(804)748-1601	1291
Fairfax	WALCH, Timothy G.	(703)273-3260	1293
Great Falls	CYLKE, Frank K.	(703)759-2031	268
Hampden Sydney	NORDEN, David J.	(804)223-4381	908
Harrisonburg	HABAN, Mary F.	(703)433-2183	480

LIBRARY BUILDING CONSULTANT (Cont'd)
VIRGINIA (Cont'd)

Manassas	MURPHY, Richard W.	(703)361-8211	881
Mclean	WANG, Chi	(703)893-3016	1302
Norfolk	DUNCAN, Cynthia B.	(804)583-0903	325
	PEREZ-LOPEZ, Rene	(804)423-7655	958
Reston	LISZEWSKI, Edward H.	(301)648-4306	733
Richmond	COSTA, Robert N.	(804)233-6274	249
	LIGGAN, Mary K.	(804)355-2509	726
	MIAH, Abdul J.	(804)786-5638	831
	MURPHY, Robert D.	(804)741-1311	881
	YATES, Ella G.	(804)786-2332	1378
Virginia Beach	BARKLEY, Carolyn L.	(804)431-3070	56
	STEWART, John D.	(804)486-0893	1192
Williamsburg	GROVE, Pearce S.	(804)220-2477	473

WASHINGTON

Bellevue	MUTSCHLER, Herbert F.	(206)746-3952	883
East Wenatchee	BELT, Jane		78
Edmonds	TURNER, Kathleen G.	(206)771-1933	1264
Kennewick	KNOLL, Betty A.	(509)735-2173	665
Olympia	SHAFFER, Maryann	(206)943-5001	1119
Pullman	ROBERTS, Elizabeth P.	(509)335-2671	1039
Seattle	BOYLAN, Merle N.	(206)543-1760	123
	JENNERICH, Edward J.	(206)626-6320	598
	SONG, Seungja Y.	(206)527-8737	1167
	STEERE, Paul J.	(206)367-0328	1184
	WALTERS, Daniel L.	(206)684-6683	1301
Seguim	DAVIES, Jo	(206)683-5229	277
Spokane	REHMS, Jane C.	(509)536-7049	1017
Tacoma	BECKER, Roger V.	(206)591-2703	72
	KRUZIC, Evelyn D.	(206)752-9156	681
	TAYLOR, Desmond	(206)756-3244	1226
Vancouver	CONABLE, Gordon M.	(206)694-0604	235
Yakima	JORDAN, Sharon L.	(509)248-4522	617

WEST VIRGINIA

Bluefield	DYE, Luella I.	(304)487-2037	330
Glenville	VERMA, Prem V.	(304)462-5303	1282
Philippi	SIZEMORE, William C.		1145
Welch	MULLER, William A.	(304)436-3070	877

WISCONSIN

Ashland	PAULI, David N.	(705)682-2365	950
Brookfield	CHRISTMAN, Inese R.	(414)786-6700	212
Franklin	BELLIN, Bernard E.	(414)461-1484	78
Grafton	MORITZ, William D.	(414)377-6695	865
Kewaunee	ECKERT, Daniel L.	(414)388-2176	335
La Crosse	WHITE, James W.	(608)784-8623	1331
Madison	DAHLGREN, Anders C.	(608)271-9148	269
	JEFFCOTT, Janet B.	(608)246-6633	596
	SORENSEN, Richard J.	(608)266-1924	1168
Menomonie	JAX, John J.	(715)232-1184	595
Middleton	NIX, Larry T.	(608)836-5616	905
Milwaukee	SAGER, Donald J.	(414)278-3020	1074
	SIEGMANN, Starla C.	(414)774-8620	1136
Stevens Point	SWIFT, Leonard W.	(715)346-1550	1216

CANADA

ALBERTA

Edmonton	BRUNDIN, Robert E.	(403)432-3930	150
	JONES, David L.	(403)481-3209	612
Red Deer	GISHLER, John R.	(304)340-3922	438

BRITISH COLUMBIA

Abbotsford	HARRIS, Winifred E.	(604)853-7441	506
	RAY, Gordon L.	(604)859-7141	1011
Vancouver	BEWLEY, Lois M.	(604)228-4250	93
	LEITH, Anna R.	(604)228-2762	714

NOVA SCOTIA

Dartmouth	LOGAN, Penelope A.	(902)434-6664	737
Halifax	BIANCHINI, Lucian	(902)445-2987	94

ONTARIO

Cambridge	SKELTON, W M.	(519)621-0460	1146
Gloucester	KENT, Charles D.		642
Guelph	BLACK, John B.	(519)821-2565	101
Keswick	MCCRACKEN, Ronald W.	(416)476-5556	799

LIBRARY BUILDING CONSULTANT (Cont'd)
ONTARIO (Cont'd)

Kingston	FLOWER, M A.	(613)645-6122	386
Kitchener	SHEPHERD, Murray C.		1127
London	CADA, Elizabeth J.	(519)661-5136	170
Mississauga	RYAN, Noel	(416)826-3782	1071
North York	HEATON, Gwynneth T.	(416)225-4859	519
	MURDOCH, Arthur W.	(416)221-1795	879
Scarborough	BALL, John L.	(416)284-3245	52
	BASSNETT, Peter J.	(416)298-0614	63
Thornhill	SPEISMAN, Stephen A.	(416)886-2508	1172
Toronto	HARRISON, Karen A.	(416)462-1550	507
	RAE, E A.	(416)486-9419	1002
	SCHWENGER, Frances S.	(416)393-7215	1105
	THODY, Susan I.	(416)762-1690	1235
	VEANER, Allen B.	(416)486-0239	1280
Waterloo	BECKMAN, Margaret L.	(519)824-4120	73
Windsor	WALSH, G M.	(519)253-7817	1299

QUEBEC

Aylmer	MACKEY, Laurette	(819)684-0410	756
Boucherville	DUBOIS, Florian	(514)655-3131	322
	NADEAU, Johan	(514)655-4858	885
Jonquiere	HARVEY, Serge	(418)548-7821	509
Montreal	GREENE, Richard L.	(514)343-7424	464
	LAPLANTE, Carole	(514)721-3093	697
	ROBIN, Madeleine	(514)738-0433	1043
Outremont	LACROIX, Yvon A.	(514)273-7423	687
St-Bruno	LECOMPTE, Louis L.	(514)653-7290	708
Trois-Rivieres	SIMARD, Denis	(819)376-1721	1139

SASKATCHEWAN

Saskatoon	SALT, David P.	(306)966-5978	1077

ARGENTINA

Entre Rios	HAMMERLY, Hernan D.		493

AUSTRALIA

Turramurra	WILKINSON, Eoin H.		1340
Victoria	POWNALL, David E.	(033)418-2990	989

BELGIUM

Kraainem	WALCKIERS, Marc A.		1293

ENGLAND

Warwickshire	CHANDLER, George		200

FEDERAL REPUBLIC OF CHINA

Taipei	HUANG, Shih H.		568
	LIN, Chih F.		727

FRANCE

Paris	PILLET, Sylvaine M.		973

HONG KONG

Shatin	YEN, David S.		1379

INDIA

Bangalore	KITTUR, Krishna N.		657

IRAN

Shiraz	MEHRAD, Jafar		821

IRELAND

Banger	DUFFIN, Elizabeth A.		323

ISRAEL

Birzeit	HADDAD, Aida N.		481
Ramat Gan	SNYDER, Esther M.		1164

JAPAN

Sendai Miyagi	HARADA, Ryukichi		499

KUWAIT

Salmiyah	ABDEL-MOTEY, Yaser Y.		2

MEXICO

Naucalpan	OROZCO-TENORIO, Jose M.		926

LIBRARY BUILDING CONSULTANT (Cont'd)

NORTHERN IRELAND
Belfast	LINTON, William D.		731

PORTUGAL
Lisbon	DE MACEDO, Maria L.		290

SCOTLAND
Glasgow	HEANEY, Henry J.		518

SOUTH AFRICA
Pretoria	WILLEMSE, John		1341

TRINIDAD
Saint Joseph	MCCONNIE, Mary		798
Valsayn	NANTON-COMISSIONG, Barbara L.		887

ONLINE SEARCHER

ALABAMA
Birmingham	ATKINSON, Calberta O.	(205)787-3767	38
	HARRIS, Linda S.	(205)934-6364	505
	LAUGHLIN, Steven G.	(205)934-2379	703
	MCCARTHY, Sherri L.	(205)226-3630	794
	SIMS, Joyce W.	(205)939-7830	1142
Florence	CARR, Charles E.	(205)767-2310	185
	MONTGOMERY, Kimberly K.	(205)764-5392	856
Gadsden	BUCKNER, Rebecca S.	(205)543-8849	154
Irondale	FEENKER, Cherie D.	(205)956-4544	368
Jacksonville	TAYLOR, Douglas M.	(205)231-5781	1226
Jasper	ELLIOTT, Riette B.	(205)387-0511	344
Mobile	NICHOLS, Amy S.	(205)694-3895	901
	SHEARER, Barbara S.	(205)471-7855	1124
Montevallo	WILLIAMS, Pauline C.	(205)665-4329	1346

ALASKA
Anchorage	EGGLESTON, Phyllis A.	(907)337-0051	339
	LUDWIG, J D.	(907)333-8917	746
	WILLIAMS, Robert C.	(907)261-2970	1346
College	GALBRAITH, Betty J.	(903)479-5196	413
Fairbanks	PINNELL-STEPHENS, June A.	(907)479-5826	975

ARIZONA
Chandler	MCGORRAY, John J.	(602)961-8016	807
	VATHIS, Alma C.	(602)899-7147	1279
Flagstaff	AWE, Susan C.	(602)523-6808	42
	BAUM, Ester B.	(602)774-8878	66
	EGAN, Terence W.	(602)523-6819	338
	HASSELL, Robert H.	(602)523-2171	511
Mesa	JOSEPHINE, Helen B.	(602)983-0237	617
	MEAD, Thomas L.	(602)892-3764	819
Phoenix	BERK, Nancy G.	(602)971-9264	87
	BOROVANSKY, Vladimir T.		117
	DOHERTY, Walter E.	(602)262-5303	309
	GORMAN, Judith F.	(602)279-9741	452
	JEROME, Susanne M.	(602)272-6848	599
	WELLIK, Kay E.	(602)285-3299	1321
Scottsdale	FERRALL, J E.	(602)965-5167	373
Tempe	LESHY, Dede	(602)946-8090	718
	MACHOVEC, George S.	(602)965-5889	755
	MULVIHILL, Joann	(602)965-5167	878
	STEEL, Virginia	(602)965-3282	1183
	STEWART, Douglas J.	(602)897-7191	1192
Tucson	BALDWIN, Charlene M.	(602)327-2385	51
	DICKSTEIN, Ruth H.	(602)886-0386	301
	FORE, Janet S.	(602)621-6452	390
	FRANK, Donald G.	(602)742-9688	396
	GILREATH, Charles L.	(602)621-4865	437
	HAWBAKER, A C.	(602)621-4869	513
	HEIDENREICH, Fred L.	(602)626-7724	521
	LEI, Polin P.		713
	MAUTNER, Robert W.	(602)621-6386	787
	MCCRAY, Jeanette C.	(602)626-6143	800
	OLSRUD, Lois C.	(602)621-2297	923
	WHITLEY, Katherine M.	(602)621-6375	1333
	WILLIAMS, Karen B.	(602)621-4866	1344

ONLINE SEARCHER (Cont'd)

ARKANSAS
Fayetteville	MCKEE, Elizabeth C.	(501)442-5002	810
Little Rock	KASALKO, Sally G.	(501)661-5980	628
	SANDERS, Kathryn A.	(501)227-5581	1080
Searcy	BEARD, Craig W.	(501)268-6161	69

CALIFORNIA
Alameda	HUNT, Deborah S.	(415)523-6518	575
Albany	BLITZ, Ruth R.	(415)525-4186	105
Anaheim	ADAMS, Joyce A.	(714)637-8385	5
	KOGA, James S.	(714)630-0618	668
	WRIGHT, Betty A.	(714)998-1127	1370
APO San Francisco	HEINES, Rodney M.		522
Aptos	HERON, David W.	(408)688-6994	532
Arcata	KENYON, Sharmon H.	(707)826-3416	643
Belmont	LEWIS, Gretchen S.	(415)591-4336	723
Berkeley	BENIDIR, Samia	(415)644-1129	80
	BROWN, Diane M.	(415)642-3532	143
	CLARENCE, Judy	(415)649-2400	216
	DUGGAN, Mary K.	(415)642-5764	324
	KOBZINA, Norma G.	(415)643-6475	666
	MARKS, Larry	(415)644-2111	771
	MAXWELL, Christine Y.	(415)644-4500	788
	MITCHELL, Andrea L.	(415)642-5208	848
	PARKS, Mary L.	(415)644-3401	943
	WEEDMAN, Judith	(415)642-9980	1315
Beverly Hills	JEROME, Michael S.	(213)550-6100	599
	RUNYON, Judith A.	(213)859-5102	1067
Bishop	KRATZ, Gale G.	(619)873-3007	676
Burlingame	PERLMAN-STITES, Janice	(415)579-7660	959
	SHERMAN, Roger S.	(415)344-1213	1128
Canyon Country	CRUM, Norman J.	(805)252-9053	262
Cardiff By The Sea	MARKWORTH, Lawrence L.	(619)943-1197	772
	SCHALIT, Michael	(619)944-3913	1089
Carlsbad	KENNEDY, Charlene F.	(619)434-2871	640
Carmichael	O'NEILL, Diane J.	(916)965-0935	924
Carphell	ALIX, Cleta M.	(408)371-3294	13
Carson	KENNY-SLOAN, Linda		642
Castro Valley	CASTAGNOZZI, Carol A.	(415)581-6034	194
Cerritos	ZEIDLER, Patricia L.	(213)926-1101	1387
Chatsworth	TAYLOR, Susan E.	(818)882-9729	1228
Chico	ARIARATNAM, Lakshmi V.	(916)895-6406	31
Concord	LAMANNA, Joan M.	(415)825-0418	689
	REYES, Helen M.	(415)000-0000	1024
Costa Mesa	PETERMAN, Claudia A.	(714)650-9014	962
Culver City	ANDRADE, Rebecca	(213)837-5448	26
	FITZGERALD, Diana S.	(231)839-5982	382
Cypress	MOSER, Jane W.	(213)643-0322	870
Danville	CREW-NOBLE, Sara M.	(415)837-1399	258
Davis	CACCESE, Vincent	(916)752-3052	170
	DAVIS, Rebecca A.	(916)752-6204	280
	IRELAND, Laverne H.	(916)756-1105	583
	LAMPRECHT, Sandra J.	(916)752-1126	691
	ROBINSON, Betty J.	(916)756-2187	1043
	ROSS, Johanna C.		1058
	TEBO, Jay D.	(916)758-8256	1229
Downey	PAIK, Nan H.	(213)922-4648	935
Eagle Rock	CRAWFORD, Marilyn L.	(213)259-8938	257
East Palo Alto	DERKSEN, Charlotte R.	(415)323-5386	294
El Cerrito	DONLEY, Leigh M.	(415)524-3695	311
	KIRESEN, Evelyn M.	(415)526-6718	654
El Segundo	FELLER, Amy I.	(213)333-5222	370
Emeryville	POKLAR, Mary J.	(415)420-1346	980
Encinitas	PIERCE, Patricia J.	(619)436-5055	971
Encino	GHAZARIAN, Salpi H.	(818)789-5041	430
Escondido	NING, Mary J.		904
Eureka	BROWN, Elizabeth E.	(707)443-8051	143
Fallbrook	MCNALLY, Ruth C.		816
Fremont	TSAI, Sheh G.	(415)656-7097	1260
Fresno	CONNOR, Paul L.	(209)225-6100	238
	KAUFFMAN, Inge S.	(209)486-8424	631
	NELSON, Iris N.	(209)442-3968	894
	WARD, Penny T.	(209)268-2545	1304
Fullerton	ANDERSEN, Leslie N.		21
Garden Grove	SIMPSON, Evelyn L.	(714)534-5033	1141
Glendale	ECKLUND, Lynn M.	(818)242-2793	335
	WAY, Kathy A.		1311
Goleta	GRAZIANO, Eugene	(805)968-2281	460

ONLINE SEARCHER (Cont'd)
CALIFORNIA (Cont'd)

Huntington Beach	OPPENHEIM, Michael R.	(714)842-1548	925
Irvine	ARIEL, Joan	(714)856-4970	31
	BLADEN, Marguerite	(714)551-6489	102
	CLANCY, Stephen L.	(714)856-7309	215
	CLARY, Rochelle L.	(714)856-6531	219
	FINEMAN, Michael	(714)856-8160	377
	FORBES, Fred R.	(714)856-4974	389
	JUNG, Soon J.	(714)730-8133	620
	NOVACK, Dona A.	(714)752-4854	910
	SHAWL, Janice H.	(714)854-7413	1124
	TASH, Steven J.	(714)786-7857	1224
Kensington	ROOSHAN, Gertrude I.	(415)525-5640	1053
La Honda	HOLLAND, Mary	(415)747-0511	551
La Jolla	BRIDGMAN, Amy R.	(619)587-1306	135
	NEELY, Jesse G.	(619)455-8705	892
	TALBOT, Dawn E.	(619)534-6213	1220
	TOMMEY, Richard J.	(619)454-4873	1250
	ZYROFF, Ellen S.	(619)459-1513	1392
Lafayette	NEWAY, Julie M.	(415)283-1862	898
Livermore	HUNT, Richard K.	(415)443-5525	575
	LOVE, Sandra R.	(415)422-7310	743
Loma Linda	MAYERS, Deborah L.	(714)825-7084	789
Long Beach	ADAMS, Linda L.	(213)590-7639	5
	ATTARIAN, Lorraine B.	(213)491-9295	38
	BENSON-TALLEY, Lois I.	(213)494-7817	83
	SIMS, Sidney B.	(213)437-3937	1142
	SINCLAIR, Lorelei P.	(213)423-6399	1142
Los Angeles	BENNION, Bruce C.	(213)743-2118	82
	BEVERAGE, Stephanie L.	(213)612-3242	93
	CHAMPLIN, Peggy	(213)472-4991	198
	COSTELLO, M R.	(213)825-3047	249
	DALY, Eudice	(213)474-6080	271
	DAVIS, Marianne W.	(213)397-7904	280
	DEENEY, Kay E.	(213)479-6672	286
	GELMAN-KMEC, Marsha	(213)484-5530	426
	GORAL, Miki	(213)825-1544	451
	GRANGER, Dorothy J.	(818)795-9161	457
	GRIGST, Denise J.	(213)651-3643	470
	HADLEY, Peter H.	(213)879-1834	482
	HAYTHORN, Joseph D.	(213)938-3621	517
	HOLLINGSWORTH, Dena M.	(213)229-7217	552
	KAPLAN, Robin	(213)851-2480	626
	KARASICK, Alice W.	(213)224-7411	627
	KING, Joseph T.	(213)660-3530	651
	LEE, Diane T.	(213)972-4000	709
	LEE, Hee J.	(213)391-4226	710
	LEUNG, Terry S.	(213)306-5686	719
	MANTHEY, Teresa M.	(213)224-7234	767
	MULLER, Malinda S.	(213)557-2900	877
	NEMCHEK, Lee R.	(213)621-9484	895
	NEWCOMER, Susan N.	(213)224-5978	898
	PRUHS, Sharon	(213)974-7780	996
	RAEDER, Aggi W.	(213)825-2649	1003
	ROSE, Steven C.	(213)668-0444	1055
	SANDVIKEN, Gordon L.	(818)307-2872	1081
	SMITH, Catherine M.	(213)669-6523	1153
	STERNHEIM, Karen	(213)825-3047	1189
	STREIKER, Susan L.	(213)738-6727	1201
	SUGRANES, Maria R.	(213)201-3601	1207
	SZEGEDI, Laszlo	(213)469-7030	1218
	TREISTER, Cyril C.	(213)227-1604	1255
	VEASLEY, Mignon M.	(213)236-3515	1280
	WILKINSON, David W.	(213)224-2251	1340
	WOOD, Elizabeth H.	(213)224-7234	1364
Los Gatos	SZABO, Carolyn J.	(408)353-2502	1218
Manhattan Beach	BALDWIN, Claudia A.	(213)372-1987	51
	MORRISEY, Locke J.	(213)318-3923	867
Menlo Park	HALL, Elede T.	(415)366-2937	487
	KLEINER, Donna H.	(415)859-5983	660
	NEWMAN, Mark J.	(415)326-2114	899
	NEWMARK, Laura C.	(415)321-2128	900
	REDFIELD, Elizabeth	(415)859-6187	1014
Mission Viejo	CHWEH, Steven S.	(714)768-3459	214
Montclair	CARRIGAN, John L.	(714)621-5225	186
Moraga	RUDOLPH, Anne L.	(415)631-0926	1066
Mountain View	DAWSON, Debra A.	(415)948-2756	282
	POST, Linda C.	(415)968-3045	986
National City	FIEDLER, Albert E.	(619)267-9190	375

ONLINE SEARCHER (Cont'd)
CALIFORNIA (Cont'd)

Newport Beach	SCHULTZ, Ute M.	(714)760-2308	1102
Oakland	GLYNN, Jeannette E.	(415)654-3543	442
	MULL, Richard G.	(415)841-2590	876
Orange	LA BORDE, Charlotte A.	(714)385-4454	686
	SMITH, Julie L.	(714)771-8291	1156
	WILSON, Wayne V.	(714)997-6912	1353
Oroville	ALLENSWORTH, James H.	(916)538-7197	16
Pacific Grove	HAY, Wayne M.	(408)646-9858	515
Pacific Palisades	SCHRIBER, James E.	(213)459-1825	1100
Palo Alto	CORCHADO, Veronica A.	(415)858-3828	245
	GREEN-MALONEY, Nancy	(415)858-3816	465
	HEMINGWAY, Beverly L.	(415)328-1884	525
	LEE, Judith C.	(415)494-0395	710
	MAIN, Linda Y.	(415)328-4865	761
	MARANGONI, Eugene G.	(415)858-4053	768
	PEARSON, Judith G.	(415)856-2853	952
	PRESTON, Cecilia M.	(415)327-5364	991
	SUMMIT, Roger K.	(415)858-3777	1209
	TRIMBLE, Kathy W.	(415)855-5493	1256
	VUGRINECZ, Anna E.	(415)857-6626	1289
Pasadena	CHOUDHURY, Lori B.	(818)449-9468	211
	KALVINSKAS, Louanne A.	(818)797-9890	623
	LONGO, Margaret K.	(818)793-7682	740
	ROTH, Dana L.	(818)356-6423	1059
	STANLEY, Dale R.	(818)793-2131	1180
	YEUNG, Esther Y.		1380
	ZEIND, Samir M.	(818)440-5161	1387
Pinole	YANEZ, Elva K.	(415)724-2914	1377
Pleasanton	WALLEN, Jody H.		1298
Pomona	MORGAN, Ferrell	(714)625-7190	864
Port Reyes Station	ALLEN, Doris L.	(415)663-1122	14
Portola Valley	ENGELBRECHT, Mary E.	(415)851-3352	349
	ERTEL, Monica	(415)851-1007	353
Rancho Palos Verdes	DAVENPORT, Constance B.		275
	KATTLOVE, Rose W.	(213)544-0061	630
	WORMINGTON, Peggie		1369
Redondo Beach	CLIFFORD, Susan G.	(213)378-3824	222
Redwood City	HOUGHTON, Barbara H.	(415)369-5811	562
	LEWARK, Kathryn W.	(415)364-1764	722
	TAOKA, Wesley M.	(415)365-3317	1223
Richmond	LAMBERT, Nancy	(415)620-3161	690
Riverside	CUEVAS, John R.	(714)684-4636	263
	MITCHELL, Steve		849
	MOONEY, Margaret T.	(714)787-3226	858
Rolling Hills Estate	TUNG, Sandra J.	(213)377-5032	1263
Sacramento	BENNETT, Michael W.	(916)927-9181	82
	KONG, Leslie M.	(916)278-5664	670
	MALMGREN, Terri L.	(916)453-3529	763
	MIRONENKO, Rimma	(916)355-4076	847
	SEHR, Dena P.	(916)453-3529	1112
Salinas	COLLINS, Judith A.		232
San Bernardino	NOUROK, Marlene E.	(714)887-6333	910
San Clemente	KOPAN, Ellen K.	(714)498-4309	671
San Diego	BUSCH, Barbara	(619)224-8412	165
	DERSHEM, Larry D.	(619)236-2409	294
	KANJI, Zainab J.	(619)231-8381	625
	PLOTSKY, Andrea G.	(619)695-1132	978
	ROBINSON, Michaele M.	(619)231-1515	1044
	ROSS, Mary A.	(619)566-4733	1058
	VEGA, Carolyn L.		1281
	WEBB, Ty	(619)487-3204	1313
	WHITE, Phillip M.	(619)265-6742	1332
	WILSON, Carole F.	(619)229-2269	1350
San Francisco	COLALILLO, Robert M.	(415)664-2264	230
	CONLEY, Linda A.	(415)285-6835	236
	DURSO, Angeline M.	(415)750-6072	329
	DUZAK, Sandra J.	(415)563-2277	330
	ECKMAN, Charles D.	(415)334-8449	335
	ELNOR, Nancy G.	(415)929-1948	346
	GEIGER, Richard G.	(415)777-1111	425
	GERSH, Barbara S.	(415)346-7882	429
	HUNG, Joanne Y.	(415)221-7325	574
	JANK, David A.	(415)751-9958	593
	KRAEMER, Linda L.	(415)981-0250	674
	LEWANDOWSKI, Joseph J.	(415)626-3755	722
	LONDON, Glenn S.	(415)928-4277	738
	MAH, Jeffery	(415)552-4733	760

ONLINE SEARCHER (Cont'd)
CALIFORNIA (Cont'd)
San Francisco

	MCDEVITT-PARKS, Kathryn B.	(415)759-8018	802
	MOORE, Gregory B.	(415)753-2645	859
	MORITZ, Thomas D.	(415)750-7102	865
	PAPERMASTER, Cynthia L.	(415)773-5831	939
	SHAPIRO, Leonard P.	(415)469-5893	1121
	SHEW, Anne L.	(415)565-6352	1129
	SULLIVAN, Edward A.	(415)752-6671	1207
	TREGGIARI, Arnaldo	(415)469-1649	1255
San Jose	BERCIK, Mary E.	(408)288-9798	84
	EMMICK, Nancy J.	(408)277-3904	348
	GROOT, Elizabeth N.		472
	HARMON, Robert B.	(408)297-2810	502
	JESSUP, Carrie	(408)629-3403	600
	MULLEN, Cecilia P.	(408)265-8799	877
	RODICH, Lorraine E.	(408)277-9788	1047
San Leandro	WENDROFF, Catriona	(415)569-3491	1323
San Lorenzo	CARR, Richard D.	(415)276-9345	186
San Luis Obispo	ROCKMAN, Ilene F.	(805)756-2273	1046
San Mateo	RAZE, Nasus B.	(415)345-9684	1012
Santa Barbara	FALK, Joyce D.	(805)687-7283	362
	GEBHARD, Patricia	(805)969-1031	424
	GIBBONS, Carolbeth	(805)961-3320	431
	KINNELL, Susan K.	(805)965-1294	653
	KORENIC, Lynette M.	(805)961-3613	671
	MAHAFFEY, Susan M.	(805)964-4978	760
Santa Clara	BAZAN, Lorraine R.	(408)554-4658	68
Santa Cruz	ANDERSON, Clifford D.	(408)429-2501	22
Santa Monica	DIRLAM, Dona M.	(213)452-1897	305
	KARR, Linda		628
	QUINT, Barbara E.	(213)451-0252	1000
Santa Rosa	BALOGH, Leeni I.	(707)539-8955	53
	HARRIS, Vallena D.		506
	WATSON, Benjamin	(707)527-2668	1309
Sebastopol	SIMONS, Maurice M.	(707)823-9275	1141
Sherman Oaks	LEWIS, Cookie A.	(818)788-5280	722
Sierra Madre	KNUDSEN, Helen Z.		666
Sonoma	WINSON, Gail I.	(707)935-1546	1355
Stanford	HOGAN, Eddy	(415)725-1054	549
	WIBLE, Joseph G.	(415)723-1110	1335
Thousand Oaks	HOCKEL, Kathleen N.		545
Torrance	KLECKER, Anita N.	(213)517-4720	658
Upland	THELIN, Sonya R.	(714)982-2336	1234
Valencia	HUSKEY, Janet S.	(805)259-0783	578
Vallejo	WONG, Carol Y.	(707)646-2532	1362
Van Nuys	LEE, Lydia H.	(818)989-6433	710
Venice	CHARBONNEAU, Ronald P.	(213)396-5441	202
Vista	KELLY, Myla S.	(619)945-6180	638
Walnut Creek	BECK, Diane J.	(415)939-9129	71

COLORADO

Arvada	PRESTON, Lawrence N.	(303)423-8729	991
Aurora	MOOMEY, Margaret M.	(303)690-1478	857
Boulder	BANKHEAD, Jean M.	(303)497-5566	54
	CHANAUD, Jo P.	(303)449-0849	199
	COLLARD, R M.	(303)444-1355	232
	KRISMANN, Carol H.	(303)499-2977	678
	SANI, Martha J.	(303)492-8367	1081
Colorado Springs	LAZARUS, Josephine G.	(303)528-7609	706
	MALYSHEV, Nina A.	(303)531-6333	764
	WATERS, W R.	(303)630-5288	1309
	WYLIE, Nethery A.	(606)593-3290	1375
Denver	BOTHMER, A J.	(303)394-5125	118
	BOWERS, Sandra L.	(303)236-6649	121
	BRITAIN, Karla K.	(303)733-0816	137
	BRUNER, Robert B.	(303)744-1138	150
	GILBERT, Ruth E.	(303)757-3622	434
	GUTH, Karen K.	(303)869-2395	478
	INGUI, Bettejean	(303)394-5158	583
	KAVANAGH, Janette R.	(303)777-8971	631
	LUEVANE, Marsha A.	(303)989-1036	747
	MARSCHNER, Robyn J.	(303)321-2547	773
	NORBIE, Dorothy E.	(303)691-5400	908
	RAINWATER, Barbara C.	(303)871-6206	1004
	ROSE, Phillip E.	(303)538-4276	1055
	SIMON, Nancy L.	(303)320-2160	1140
	WAGNER, Barbara L.	(303)297-3611	1291

ONLINE SEARCHER (Cont'd)
COLORADO (Cont'd)

Fort Collins	ERNEST, Douglas J.	(303)491-1861	353
	LIRA, Judith A.	(303)226-5626	732
Grand Junction	NICKELS, Anita B.		902
Greeley	CUTTS, William B.	(303)353-1551	268
	SAVIG, Norman I.	(303)351-2251	1086
Lakewood	HOLTON, Janet E.	(303)232-6800	555
	ROESCH, Gay E.	(303)986-6365	1049
	SMITH, Catherine C.	(303)987-2815	1153
Littleton	ALSOP, Robyn J.	(303)779-1925	18
	GREALY, Deborah J.	(303)795-3156	461
	SZABO, Kathleen S.	(303)796-9718	1218
Pueblo	GRATE, Jon F.	(303)549-2362	458
	JANES, Nina	(303)542-4591	593
Wellington	JOHNSON, K S.	(303)491-1876	606

CONNECTICUT

Branford	ADAMO, Clare	(203)488-1474	4
Bridgeport	BARNES, Denise M.	(203)372-5434	57
	ESCARILLA, Jose G.	(203)366-0684	354
	HUGHES, John M.	(203)576-4392	571
	STEMMER, Katherine R.	(203)384-3254	1186
Bristol	SENKUS, Linda J.	(203)589-1298	1115
Danbury	BANKS, Mary E.	(203)792-0028	54
East Canaan	BYERS, Laura T.	(203)824-5971	168
Farmington	WETMORE, Judith M.	(203)679-2942	1328
Greenwich	MUSKUS, Elizabeth A.	(203)661-7058	883
Guilford	HELENIUS, Majlen	(203)453-1744	523
Hamden	STRAKA, Kathy M.	(203)771-8383	1199
Hartford	CORCORAN, Virginia H.	(203)524-2230	246
	KLEMARCZYK, Laurice D.	(203)547-3099	660
	MCNULTY, Karen	(203)278-2670	817
	WEINSTEIN, Daniel L.	(203)275-2699	1318
Middletown	BRECK, Evelyn M.	(203)344-6286	131
	DOUVILLE, Judith A.	(203)344-1880	314
New Britain	UBYSZ, Priscilla M.	(203)229-9917	1267
New Canaan	KUHR, Patricia S.	(203)966-7235	683
	LOKETS BEISCHROT, Dina		738
New Fairfield	DYKMAN, Elaine K.	(203)746-0765	331
New Haven	CLARIE, Thomas C.	(203)397-4511	216
	FRYER, Regina K.	(203)785-4356	407
	HERMAN, Felicia G.	(203)776-6244	531
	IANNUZZI, Patricia A.	(203)432-1785	581
	KRITEMEYER, Ann C.		679
	LUBIN, Joan S.	(203)397-5154	745
	SPURGEON, Kathy R.		1176
	TRIOLO, Victor A.	(203)397-4520	1257
	WALES, Patricia L.	(203)789-3330	1294
Newington	LERITZ, M K.	(203)278-1280	717
Norwalk	BOHRER, Karen M.	(203)854-5275	111
Ridgefield	FARADAY, Joanna	(203)431-0062	363
	MCMASTER, Deborah L.	(203)798-5574	815
	SAMUELS, Lois A.	(203)431-3342	1079
	SUPEAU, Cynthia	(203)798-5154	1210
Stamford	BERLIET, Nathalie B.	(203)359-9359	87
	MASTERS, Kathy B.	(203)967-6749	782
	O'BRIEN, Doris J.	(203)359-1114	914
Stratford	WEISS, Barbara M.	(203)378-0022	1319
Unionville	MOON, Peter S.	(203)675-6675	858
Wallingford	MCGREGOR, M C.	(203)284-6000	808
Warren	HENTZ, Margaret B.	(203)868-9178	530
West Hartford	HORAK, Ellen B.	(203)233-3164	558
Westport	LOWE, Ida B.	(203)255-8780	743
	MUTTER, Letitia N.	(203)227-1992	883
	REISMAN, Sydelle S.	(203)227-8710	1021
Wilton	DENMAN, Monica K.	(203)762-8957	292
Windsor	GAGNE, Susan P.	(203)285-3288	412
	NATALE, Barbara G.	(203)688-4467	889
Windsor Locks	MASTERS, Fred N.	(203)623-9801	782
Woodbridge	SHERMAN, Dottie	(203)393-1167	1128

DELAWARE

Bear	MANUEL, Larry L.	(302)834-5748	767
Lewes	HALL, Alice W.	(302)645-4293	486
New Castle	IRWIN, Ruth A.	(302)328-8560	584
Newark	CHASTAIN-WARHEIT, Christine C.	(302)733-1116	203
	EVERETT, Amy E.	(302)451-2104	358
	THORNTON, Alice J.	(302)454-2239	1242

ONLINE SEARCHER (Cont'd)
DELAWARE (Cont'd)
Newark

	TRUMBORE, Jean F.	(302)368-3241	1259
Wilmington	DRUKKER, Alexander E.	(302)478-1746	320
	JOHNSON, Hilary C.	(302)994-2870	605
	MINNICH, Nancy P.	(302)478-5291	846
	PIFALO, Victoria	(302)656-1629	972

DISTRICT OF COLUMBIA

Washington	ACKERMAN, F C.	(202)398-1842	3
	ASMUTH, Gretchen W.	(202)628-1700	36
	ATKINSON, Rose M.	(202)955-2139	38
	AUSTIN, Monique C.	(202)546-7236	40
	BATES, Mary E.	(202)887-3132	64
	BELLARDO, Trudi	(202)363-9614	78
	CARLSON, Julia F.	(202)225-2571	182
	CHASE, Linda S.	(202)885-3238	203
	CILIBERTI, Nancy A.	(202)328-8000	214
	COLETTI, Jeannette D.	(202)362-1664	231
	DOUMATO, Lamia		314
	DURAKO, Frances G.	(202)785-9700	328
	ELLIOT, Hugh	(202)333-8312	343
	FALK, Diane M.	(202)291-3821	362
	GILLESPIE, Veronica M.	(202)287-5262	435
	HUDGINS, Peggy	(202)862-8800	569
	HUGGENS, Gary D.	(202)328-9248	571
	JOHNSON, Jacqueline B.	(202)635-7498	605
	KAHN, Victoria	(202)543-0752	622
	KENDRICK, Brent L.	(202)543-7031	640
	LANE, Elizabeth S.		694
	LARSEN, Lynda L.	(202)328-5150	698
	LEVIN, Amy E.	(202)357-3133	720
	MARTIN, Kathleen S.	(202)789-7100	777
	MCCRAY, Maceo E.	(202)829-7737	800
	MCGOWAN, Anna T.	(202)245-1235	807
	MILLER, William S.	(202)775-4080	843
	MISSAR, Charles D.	(202)363-2751	847
	MODLIN, Marilyn J.	(202)452-4460	851
	MORRIS, Timothy J.	(202)462-8209	867
	NOWAK, Geraldine D.	(202)475-9419	911
	O'BRIEN, Kathleen	(202)331-8400	914
	PACIFICI, Sabrina I.	(202)429-4094	933
	PULVER, Thomas B.	(202)293-0500	997
	REIFSNYDER, Betsy S.	(202)287-7984	1020
	SANCHEZ, Jose L.	(202)387-7396	1079
	SARANGAPANI, Chetluru	(202)282-3091	1082
	SCHNEIDER, Hennie R.	(202)523-0013	1097
	STREHL, Susan J.	(202)287-1658	1201
	TSCHERNY, Alexander	(202)723-5415	1260
	VANDEGRIFT, Barbara P.	(202)662-7523	1273
	WEAVER, Thomas M.	(202)526-4262	1312

FLORIDA

Avon Park	APPELQUIST, Donald L.	(813)453-6661	30
Boca Raton	PELLEN, Rita M.	(305)395-6369	955
	STORCH, Barbara J.	(305)395-1056	1198
Clearwater	SCHMID, Cynthia M.	(813)462-7889	1094
	TIBBS, Jo A.	(813)447-7157	1244
De Land	EVERETT, David D.	(904)734-4121	358
Dunedin	TEW, Robin L.	(813)734-5634	1233
Fort Lauderdale	BROWN, Jeanette L.	(305)523-9145	144
	GALLAHAR, Christine M.		414
	HAYES, L S.	(305)587-2900	516
	TAYSOM, Daniel B.	(305)760-5771	1229
Gainesville	BADGER, Lynn C.	(904)392-0342	44
	BROWN, M S.	(904)392-0707	145
	FRANCIS, Barbara W.	(904)375-0633	396
	PROCTOR, Dixie L.	(904)377-3442	994
	WOODS, Susan E.	(904)392-4018	1367
Jacksonville	COHEN, Kathleen F.	(904)646-2616	228
	FAHNERT, Elizabeth K.	(904)641-8649	361
	RANDTKE, Angela W.	(904)646-2550	1007
Key Biscayne	KIRBY, Diana G.	(305)361-3678	654
Lake Alfred	RUSS, Pamela K.	(813)956-1151	1068
Largo	CESANEK, Sylvia B.	(813)585-1403	196
Lauderhill	HOLLMANN, Pauline V.	(305)393-3774	552
Lutz	WALTERS, Gwen E.	(813)949-6992	1301

ONLINE SEARCHER (Cont'd)
FLORIDA (Cont'd)

Miami	ADAMS, Gustav C.	(305)261-7031	4
	CARR, Sallyann	(305)592-0081	186
	HALE, Kay K.	(305)271-3678	485
	KASKEY, Sid		629
	MILLER, Jewell J.	(305)662-4212	839
	PAUL, Nora M.	(305)376-3402	949
	REAM, Diane F.	(305)596-6506	1013
	SEILER, Susan L.	(305)279-0545	1112
	STEINBERG, Celia L.	(305)661-4611	1185
	WRIGHT, Joseph F.	(305)379-3105	1372
Miami Beach	EFRON, Muriel C.	(305)672-0696	338
Miami Shores	PINE, Nancy M.	(305)758-3392	974
Milton	PERDUE, Robert W.	(904)994-7640	958
North Lauderdale	BRESLAUER, Lester M.	(305)721-5181	133
Oakland Park	WILLIAMS, Alexander	(305)565-2990	1341
Orlando	GEBET, Russell W.	(305)849-0300	424
	HUDSON, Phyllis J.	(305)275-2584	569
Pensacola	JOHNSON, Theresa P.	(904)474-2168	609
	KIEFER, Rosemary M.	(904)438-2732	647
Pompano Beach	WHITESIDE, Lee A.	(305)782-0194	1333
Ponte Vedra Beach	PECK, Brian T.	(904)246-1400	953
St Petersburg	CORNWELL, Douglas W.	(813)541-7206	247
Sanford	LINSLEY, Laurie S.	(305)323-1450	731
Sarasota	DANIEL, Marianne M.	(813)351-6583	272
Seminole	WEISS, Susan		1320
Tallahassee	BILAL, Dania M.	(904)575-5793	96
	CLARKSON, Jane S.	(904)385-9671	219
	CONAWAY, Charles W.	(904)893-1482	235
	PATTON, Linda L.	(904)644-5019	949
Tampa	EL-HADIDY, Bahaa	(813)974-3520	342
	EVERLOVE, Nora J.	(813)839-4868	359
	JOHNSTON, Judy F.	(813)974-2162	610
	KING, Elizabeth	(813)885-7481	650
West Palm Beach	PRITCHARD, Teresa N.	(305)684-7349	994
Winter Park	PFARRER, Theodore R.	(305)647-3294	966

GEORGIA

Acworth	STAHL, D G.	(404)924-8505	1178
Americus	MCLAUGHLIN, Laverne L.	(912)924-9426	813
Athens	CARPENTER, David E.	(404)542-8460	184
	GUBISTA, Kathryn R.	(404)546-8153	475
	HAAR, John M.	(404)549-7625	480
	RIEMER, John J.	(404)542-0591	1033
	ROWLAND, Lucy M.	(404)543-3690	1062
	WILLIAMS, Sara E.	(408)548-7519	1346
Atlanta	BATTEN, Henry R.	(404)876-3657	64
	BROWN, Carolyn M.	(404)727-5813	142
	BRYANT, Nancy J.	(404)955-9550	152
	COFFMAN, Joseph W.	(404)681-0251	227
	DICKENS, Rosa L.	(404)261-1837	300
	FULLER, Ruth V.		409
	KLOPPER, Susan M.	(404)658-1776	662
	MCDAVID, Michael W.	(404)885-8320	801
	MENEELY, William E.	(404)658-3800	824
	MILLER, Jack E.	(404)892-3600	838
	RAQUET, Jacqueline R.	(404)320-9727	1008
	ROAN, Tattie W.	(404)320-9376	1038
	ROSS, Theodosia B.	(404)696-2355	1059
	SCHEIN, Julia R.	(404)624-1162	1091
	THAXTON, Lyn	(404)292-6767	1234
College Park	CANN, Sharon F.	(404)768-0970	178
Columbus	SELF, Sharon W.	(404)323-5520	1113
Decatur	ALLEN, William R.	(404)284-2981	16
	GRELL, Holly J.	(404)378-5948	467
	MARONEY, Daryle M.	(404)373-0546	772
Experiment	LEDFORD, Carole L.	(404)228-7238	708
Fitzgerald	PAULK, Sara L.	(912)423-5531	950
Hartwell	BISSO, Arthur J.	(404)376-4655	100
Red Oak	LETT, Rosalind K.		719
Stone Mountain	O'NEILL, Patricia E.	(404)292-6693	924
Tucker	LEIGHTON, Victoria C.	(404)491-0464	714
Valdosta	WRIGHT, Dianne H.	(912)244-6872	1371
Watkinsville	CURTIS, Susan C.	(404)542-0705	267

GUAM

Agana	WEINGARTH, Darlene	(671)472-1750	1318

ONLINE SEARCHER (Cont'd)

HAWAII

Honolulu	CHAFE, Douglas A.	(808)537-8375	197
	GOVERNS, Molly K.		454
	SCHULTZ, Elaine V.	(808)395-1801	1102
	SMITH, Frances P.	(808)523-2311	1155
	STEPHENS, Diana C.	(808)945-2837	1188
	UCHIDA, Deborah K.	(808)548-7915	1267
Kailua-Kona	KOLMAN, Roberta F.		669
Waiaulua	VEATCH, Laurie L.	(808)237-8411	1280

IDAHO

Idaho Falls	LOOP, Jacqueline N.	(208)523-1787	740
	VERHOFF, Patricia A.	(208)523-9601	1282
Moscow	FORCE, Ronald W.	(208)885-6584	389
	HANSON, Donna M.	(208)885-6235	498
	WAI, Lily C.	(208)882-0506	1292
Nampa	BALCERZAK, Judy A.	(208)467-1171	50
Rexburg	NELSON, Kathy J.	(208)356-3691	894

ILLINOIS

Abbott Park	SWANSON, Ruth M.	(312)937-6959	1213
Addison	WRIGHT, Deborah L.	(312)628-3338	1371
Argonne	DAVIDOFF, Gary N.	(312)972-4224	276
Arlington Heights	FINNERTY, James L.	(312)259-3496	379
Aurora	BEAN, Janet R.	(312)859-2222	69
Beardstown	WEST, L P.	(217)323-5788	1326
Berwyn	FEDECZKO, Joyce L.	(312)795-3089	367
Bloomington	STROYAN, Susan E.	(309)827-4321	1203
Carol Stream	SONDALLE, Barbara J.	(312)653-7000	1167
Champaign	CHAPLAN, Margaret A.	(217)333-7993	201
	HEISTER, Carla G.	(217)333-6892	523
	PENKA, Carol B.	(217)351-6026	956
	WERT, Lucille M.	(217)356-6600	1325
Chicago	ACKER, Robert L.	(312)341-8085	3
	BROWN, Patricia B.	(312)775-1515	146
	BURGH, Scott G.	(312)558-5740	159
	CICHON, Marilyn T.	(312)648-1155	214
	CLAGGETT, Laura K.	(312)661-0222	215
	COTILLAS, Therese G.	(312)856-8341	250
	CURRY, John A.	(314)528-0870	266
	DELANA, Genevieve A.	(312)670-2875	288
	DONAHUE, Karin V.		310
	DUJSIK, Gerald	(312)225-1700	324
	FOUSER, Jane G.	(312)477-4712	393
	GARDNER, Trudy A.	(312)942-8735	418
	GRAVES, Karen J.	(312)348-0930	459
	GROFT, Mary L.	(312)477-7065	471
	GUINEE, Andrea M.	(312)528-5792	476
	HILBURGER, Mary J.	(312)794-2614	538
	HOFFMANN, Maurine L.	(312)951-0599	548
	HOTIMLANSKA, Leah D.	(312)248-2013	562
	JOHNSON, Timothy J.	(312)478-2696	609
	JORDAN, Charles R.	(312)478-7205	616
	KALUZSA, Karen L.	(312)908-2859	623
	KEARNEY, Sharon M.	(312)549-3148	633
	KINNAIRD, Cheryl D.	(312)508-5465	653
	KIRKLAND, Kenneth L.	(312)341-8165	655
	KLEINMUNTZ, Dalia S.	(312)883-3580	660
	KOVITZ, Nancy R.	(312)938-3434	674
	LANDRY, Ronald	(312)943-3282	694
	LEWIS, Sherman L.		724
	MEEKER, Robert B.	(312)995-2235	821
	MICKEY, Melissa B.	(312)324-8583	833
	MILUTINOVIC, Eunhee C	(312)472-0840	845
	MOORE, John R.	(312)763-7811	860
	MOORHEAD, John D.	(312)944-4020	862
	MORRIS, Ann	(312)764-8064	866
	MOULTON, James C.	(312)525-7185	873
	MUELLER, Julie M.	(312)645-4839	875
	NAGOLSKI, Donald J.	(312)878-1171	886
	OSGOOD, James B.		928
	OWNES, Dorothy J.	(312)702-8899	932
	RABAI, Terezia		1001
	REMEIKIS, Lois A.	(312)782-1442	1022
	SCHRAMM, Mary T.	(312)248-7934	1099
	SCHROEDER, Anne M.	(312)528-7486	1100
	SHEDLOCK, James	(312)908-8109	1124
	SIARNY, William D.	(312)467-5520	1134
	SLAWNIAK, Patricia M.	(312)338-7589	1148

ONLINE SEARCHER (Cont'd)

ILLINOIS (Cont'd)

Chicago			
	SPARKS, Joanne L.	(312)728-5510	1171
	STENGER, Brenda E.	(312)782-1442	1187
	STONER, Ronald P.	(312)644-3100	1198
	TIWANA, Shah J.	(312)743-5146	1247
	TYLMAN, Wieslawa T.	(312)666-7193	1266
	WESTON, E P.	(312)996-2728	1327
	WICKREMERATNE, Swarna	(312)493-0936	1335
	WINNIKE, Mary E.	(312)996-6595	1355
	WONG, Mabel K.	(312)938-1000	1363
Chicago Ridge	LOTZ, Marsha A.	(312)423-7753	742
Columbia	SUTTER, Mary A.	(618)281-7734	1211
Crystal Lake	MILLER, Randy S.	(815)455-4660	841
	MITCHELL, Martha M.	(815)455-5165	849
De Kalb	AUSTIN, John R.	(815)753-9492	40
	HUANG, Samuel T.	(815)756-2296	568
	HURYCH, Jitka M.	(815)753-1947	578
	OSORIO, Nestor L.	(815)753-9837	928
Deerfield	LEE, Soon H.	(312)948-3880	711
Downers Grove	MIFFLIN, Michael J.	(312)963-9285	833
Edwardsville	JOHNSON, Charlotte L.	(618)656-5743	603
Elk Grove Village	KALRA, Bhupinder S.	(312)529-8607	623
Elmhurst	WATSON, Robert E.	(312)941-0892	1310
Evanston	FIELD, Connie N.	(312)866-2800	375
	JACOBSON, William R.	(312)328-7584	590
	PALMORE, Sandra N.	(312)328-5329	937
	PRENDERGAST, Kathleen M.	(312)491-7298	990
	SCHAPIRO, Benjamin H.	(312)491-5186	1090
	SENN, Mary S.	(312)328-3767	1115
	VAN DYKE, Mary C.	(312)492-2459	1275
Evergreen Park	GARCIA-RUIZ, Maritza L.	(312)425-6104	417
Freeport	WELCH, Eric C.	(815)235-6121	1321
Galesburg	BABANOURY, Betty G.	(309)343-6118	43
Grayslake	DEPKE, Robert W.		293
Gurnee	MANDEL, Douglas J.	(312)336-7637	765
Harvey	FOLEY, Donna H.	(312)333-2300	387
Highland Park	JANES, Virginia		593
Kingston	SCHREIBER, Robert E.	(815)784-2280	1099
La Grange	HATTENDORF, Lynn C.	(312)579-0873	512
	PROBST, Virginia M.		994
La Grange Park	STALZER, Rita M.	(312)354-9200	1179
Lincolnwood	BENNETT, Laura B.	(312)679-2327	82
Lisle	STUNKARD, Gilbert L.	(312)969-5426	1205
Lombard	EGAN, Elizabeth M.	(312)627-7130	338
	SCHIPMA, Peter B.	(312)627-0550	1093
Makanda	CRANE, Lilly E.	(618)549-6259	255
Moline	HAGBERG, Betty S.	(309)752-4881	482
Mt Prospect	MURPHY, Therese B.	(312)439-6911	881
Niles	CARTER, Ida	(312)647-9000	189
Northfield	ANDERSON, Charles R.	(312)446-8259	22
Oak Lawn	KELLY, Janice E.	(312)857-5127	637
	ROCHE, Richard G.	(312)423-7110	1046
Oak Park	BEN-SHIR, Rya H.	(312)386-5444	83
	CAREY, Kevin J.	(312)848-0682	181
	MORRIS, Lynne D.	(312)848-6230	867
	REDDY, Michael B.	(312)848-1754	1013
Palatine	BROWN, Patricia L.	(312)991-1278	146
Palos Hills	SODOWSKY, Kay M.	(312)430-2164	1165
Park Ridge	LOFTHOUSE, Patricia A.	(312)698-9731	737
Pekin	WALTERS, Patsy M.	(309)353-5075	1301
Quincy	EGGERS, Thomas D.		339
	WEE, Lily K.	(217)228-5360	1315
River Forest	LI, Richard T.	(312)366-2490	725
Rock Island	OHRLUND, Bruce L.	(309)786-0698	919
Rockford	HUTCHINS, Richard G.	(815)968-0756	579
Round Lake	TAN, Elizabeth L.	(312)546-6311	1222
St Charles	MORRISON, Carol J.	(312)377-2499	868
Skokie	GRODINSKY, Deborah	(312)679-1380	471
	GROSSMAN, David G.	(312)673-9100	473
Springfield	HILDRETH, Charles R.		539
	KELLEY, Rhona S.	(217)782-2658	636
	LARISON, Brenda	(217)529-9233	697
	WRIGLEY, Kathryn J.	(217)544-6464	1373
Sycamore	SULLIVAN, Peggy A.	(815)753-6155	1208
Urbana	BALACHANDRAN, Sarojini	(217)328-3577	50
	BURBANK, Richard D.	(217)333-2713	158
	DAVIS, Elisabeth B.	(217)333-3654	278
	JOHNSON, Anita D.	(217)367-0647	602

ONLINE SEARCHER (Cont'd)
ILLINOIS (Cont'd)

City	Name	Phone	No.
Urbana	KIBBEE, Josephine Z.	(217)333-2290	646
	LEONG, Carol L.	(217)333-3399	717
	SMITH, Linda C.	(217)333-7742	1157
	WILLIAMS, James W.	(217)333-2305	1344
	WILLIAMS, Mitsuko	(217)333-3654	1345
	WRIGHT, Joyce C.	(217)333-1031	1372
Villa Park	ELL, Elizabeth L.	(312)279-6456	343
	POINTON, Louis R.	(312)833-6555	980
Waukegan	CARNELLI, Sandra R.	(312)623-2041	183
Westmont	MANNING, Mary J.	(312)964-3549	766
Wheaton	HU, Robert T.	(312)690-7969	568
Winnetka	BLACKBURN, Joy M.	(312)446-8697	102
Woodridge	KELLER, Steven W.	(312)964-7899	636
	WHITT, Diane M.		1334

INDIANA

City	Name	Phone	No.
Bloomington	BRISTOW, Ann	(812)335-8028	137
	COPLER, Judith A.	(812)335-9255	244
	HEISER, Lois	(812)335-7170	523
	HENSON, Jane E.	(812)336-8288	529
	MILLER, Constance R.	(812)335-5729	836
	SMITH, Lary		1156
	SOWELL, Steven L.	(812)335-9792	1170
	WALLACE, Danny P.	(812)335-2848	1297
	WIGGINS, Gary D.	(812)335-9452	1337
	ZHU, Xiaofeng	(812)335-2666	1387
	ZIMMERMAN, Brenda M.		1388
Bluffton	ELLIOTT, Barbara J.	(219)824-2315	343
Carmel	DANIELS, Ann A.	(317)846-7721	273
Columbus	MEREDITH, Meri	(812)372-3482	825
	POOR, William E.	(812)377-7201	983
Crawfordsville	DAY, Thomas L.	(317)362-2242	283
Elkhart	SAARI, David S.	(219)295-8090	1072
Evansville	MEEK, Janet E.	(812)479-2487	821
Fort Wayne	DEANE, Paul D.	(219)424-7241	284
	LISTON, Karen A.	(219)424-6664	733
	MARTIN, Jody S.	(219)461-8468	776
	SHEETS, Michael T.	(219)483-2854	1125
Granger	LE GUERN, Charles A.	(219)272-3298	712
Greenfield	WEHLACZ, Joseph T.	(317)467-4330	1316
Indianapolis	BRAHMI, Frances A.	(317)274-1401	127
	CORBETT, Ann L.	(317)274-7185	245
	DURKIN, Virginia M.	(317)871-2095	328
	GRIFFITTS, Joan K.	(317)297-3283	469
	HOOK-SHELTON, Sara A.	(317)274-7204	556
	MASON, Dorothy L.	(317)845-3684	781
	RIES, Steven T.	(317)251-2420	1033
Lafayette	COLLINS, Mary E.		233
	LINEPENSEL, Kenneth C.	(317)474-0269	730
	MITCHELL, Cynthia E.	(317)423-2602	848
	NIXON, Judith M.		906
Muncie	DOLAK, Frank J.	(317)285-5141	309
Notre Dame	HAVLIK, Robert J.	(219)239-6665	513
South Bend	DOLAN, Robert T.	(219)289-1172	309
	MILLER, Jeanne L.	(219)284-7491	839
Terre Haute	BAUMGARTNER, Kurt O.	(812)234-4818	66
	ENSOR, Pat L.	(812)237-2580	350
	KYKER, Penelope R.	(812)237-2540	685
	SHANE, T C.	(812)299-5289	1120
Upland	WOLCOTT, Laurie J.	(317)998-7549	1359
Valparaiso	WATTS, Tim J.	(219)465-7838	1310
Warsaw	DETWILER, Susan M.	(219)269-5254	296
West Lafayette	BAXTER, Pam M.	(317)494-2969	67
	CANGANELLI, Patrick W.	(317)494-2768	178
	HEWISON, Nancy S.	(317)463-0904	535
	OGLES, Lynn C.	(317)494-2853	918
	PASK, Judith M.	(317)494-6735	946
	YOUNGEN, Gregory K.	(317)743-9893	1383
Westfield	VAN CAMP, Ann J.	(317)896-3537	1272
Zionsville	OKEY, Susan T.	(317)873-3114	920

IOWA

City	Name	Phone	No.
Ames	MATHEWS, Eleanor R.	(515)294-3642	784
	TYCKOSON, David A.	(515)294-3642	1266
	WORK, Dawn E.		1369
Bettendorf	POLK, Diana B.	(319)332-8119	981

ONLINE SEARCHER (Cont'd)
IOWA (Cont'd)

City	Name	Phone	No.
Cedar Falls	HILAND, Leah F.	(319)273-2299	538
	KOLLASCH, Matthew A.	(319)277-6125	669
Cedar Rapids	BLISS, David H.	(319)393-5892	105
	NELSON, Donald A.	(319)369-7393	893
Davenport	STOUT, Robert J.	(319)326-6237	1199
Des Moines	KROMMINGA, Patricia G.	(515)263-5181	679
Dubuque	KNEFEL, Mary A.	(319)589-3215	664
Grinnell	ENGEL, Kevin R.	(515)269-3354	348
Iowa City	BROWN, Jeanine B.		144
	EIMAS, Richard	(319)337-5538	340
	ENGER, Kathy B.	(319)335-4123	349
	NEUFELD, Sue E.	(319)335-9871	897
	RUMSEY, Eric T.	(319)335-9151	1067
Sioux City	SCHEETZ, Kathy D.	(712)277-2423	1091

KANSAS

City	Name	Phone	No.
Derby	MATTOX, Rosemary S.	(316)268-5979	786
Fairway	CARVER, Jane W.	(913)236-8688	191
Leavenworth	GOTTSHALL, Judith L.		454
Leawood	GINGRICH, Linda K.	(913)491-4215	437
Manhattan	COFFEE, E G.	(913)539-1628	226
	STUBBAN, Vanessa L.		1204
Overland Park	KEMPF, Andrea C.	(913)469-8500	639
	OJALA, Marydee P.		919
Shawnee Mission	WAY, Harold E.	(913)831-1550	1311
Topeka	CARROLL, James K.	(913)273-9156	187
	KINZIE, Lenora A.	(913)295-8247	653
	VUKAS, Rachel R.	(913)295-6479	1290
Wichita	BRADEN, Jan	(316)686-5954	125
	GERMANN, Malcolm P.	(316)689-3591	429
	MYERS, Robert C.	(316)689-3591	885
	TANNER, Jane E.	(316)682-4485	1223
Winfield	ZUCK, Gregory J.	(316)221-4150	1391

KENTUCKY

City	Name	Phone	No.
Covington	GARMAN, Nancy J.	(606)331-6345	419
Lexington	BARRISH, Alan S.	(606)278-1933	60
	MESNER, Lillian R.	(606)273-4990	827
Louisville	BLACKBURN-FOSTER, Brenda	(502)582-4111	102
	BRINKMAN, Carol S.	(502)588-6297	136
	GRAY, Dorothy A.	(502)367-4772	459
	JOHNSON, Garry B.	(502)897-8100	604
	LINCOLN, Carol S.	(502)568-7683	728
	MACLEOD, Valerie R.	(502)637-6026	757
	NEELY, Glenda S.	(502)588-6747	892
	PRIOR, Barbara Q.	(502)588-6747	993
Morehead	WILLIAMS, Helen E.	(606)783-2828	1343
Murray	WALL, Celia J.	(502)762-4990	1297

LOUISIANA

City	Name	Phone	No.
Baton Rouge	BALL, Dannie J.	(504)388-3119	52
	BLOOMSTONE, Ajaye	(504)767-0847	106
	BOYCE, Bert R.	(504)388-1461	122
	HASCHAK, Paul G.	(504)766-9986	510
	KLEINER, Janellyn P.	(504)928-1960	660
	MATTMILLER, C F.	(504)344-8074	786
	MILLER, Susan E.	(504)388-8264	842
	STANLEY, Eileen H.	(504)388-4395	1180
Metairie	REPMAN, Denise C.		1023
Natchitoches	HUSSEY, Sandra R.	(318)352-2996	578
New Orleans	FISHER, Collette J.	(504)581-3333	380
	FLEURY, Bruce E.	(504)865-5682	385
	HANKEL, Marilyn L.	(504)286-7276	496
	KELLER, Nancy H.	(504)899-9511	635
	MARIX, Mary L.	(504)488-4286	770
	NOLAN-MITCHELL, Patricia	(504)568-6102	908
	SARKODIE-MENSAH, Kwasi	(504)483-7306	1083
	WELSCH, Melissa W.	(504)584-2403	1323
Ruston	DICARLO, Michael A.	(318)257-3594	300
Shreveport	KING, Anne M.	(318)797-5738	650

MAINE

City	Name	Phone	No.
Bar Harbor	BAKER, Alison	(207)288-3371	47
Boothbay	SEELEY, Catherine R.		1111
East Sebago	AIREY, Martha R.	(207)787-2817	9
Mechanic Falls	NOYES, Nicholas	(207)345-3245	911

ONLINE SEARCHER (Cont'd)
MAINE (Cont'd)

Orono	THOR, Angela M.	(207)581-1678	1242
	WHITE, Lucinda M.	(207)581-1674	1331
Scarborough	SPIEGEL, Nancy C.	(207)883-4131	1174
Veazie	JAGELS, Suellen T.	(207)947-0608	591
Winthrop	KING, Alan S.	(207)377-2879	650

MARYLAND

Aberdeen	HADDEN, Robert L.	(301)272-1858	481
Abingdon	ANDERSON, Della L.	(301)679-5720	22
Annapolis	LIVELY, Nancy J.	(301)268-0530	734
	MOTEN, Derryn E.	(301)757-3846	872
Baltimore	ARRINGTON, Susan J.	(301)396-4042	34
	BLUTE, Mary R.	(301)889-4080	107
	BOURKOFF, Vivienne R.	(301)338-8914	119
	BRENNAN, Edward P.	(301)675-8835	132
	BROADY, Jessie	(301)661-1781	138
	CONNOR, Elizabeth	(301)828-8646	237
	GENUARDI, Michael T.	(301)235-1168	427
	GROSSHANS, Maxine Z.	(301)532-8590	473
	HILDITCH, Bonny M.	(301)675-4333	539
	HIRSCH, Dorothy K.	(304)655-7280	543
	HOOFNAGLE, Bettea J.	(301)522-5447	556
	HUMPHRIES, Anne W.	(301)328-7373	574
	KUAN, David A.	(301)256-9044	681
	LAY, Shirley	(301)347-3419	705
	LAZZARONI, Philip S.	(301)528-1616	706
	LEDBETTER, Sherry H.	(301)358-0285	708
	MOLLENKOPF, Carolyn M.	(301)866-3156	853
	NIXON, Judith A.	(301)576-1927	906
	PERKINS, Earle R.	(301)338-8540	959
	PUGH, W J.	(301)955-5819	997
	RASCHKA, Katherine E.	(301)539-2530	1008
	SATTERTHWAITE, Rebecca K.	(301)955-3410	1084
	SZCZCPANIAK, Adam S.	(301)539-0872	1218
	THIES, Gail M.	(301)597-8918	1235
	WILLIAMS, Mary A.	(301)328-7373	1345
	ZIMMERMAN, Martha B.	(301)668-5744	1389
Beltsville	AYER, Carol A.	(301)344-1969	42
	EVANS, Sylvia D.	(301)937-0328	358
	KREBS-SMITH, James J.	(301)344-3719	677
Bethesda	BACKUS, Joyce E.	(301)496-6097	44
	CONGER, Lucinda D.	(301)229-7716	236
	GLOCK, Martha H.	(301)496-5511	441
	HAWK, Susan A.	(301)897-8367	513
	HORAN, Meredith L.	(301)496-5497	559
	KIM, Sunnie I.	(301)496-8124	649
	LAKSHMAN, Malathi K.	(301)229-9287	689
	LAZAROW-STETTEN, Jane K.	(301)656-5471	706
	MENNELLA, Dona M.	(301)652-0106	824
	MOBLEY, Arthur B.	(301)530-0081	851
	PEARSE, Nancy J.	(301)564-1967	952
	PHILLIPS, Lena M.	(301)986-8560	968
	TIFFT, Jeanne D.	(301)229-7415	1244
	YU, Pei	(301)986-8560	1384
Bowie	GIGANTE, Vickilyn M.	(301)249-2609	433
	MASTRANGELO, Marjorie J.	(301)464-8745	782
BWI Airport	BUCHAN, Ronald L.	(301)859-5300	153
Cabin John	SEWELL, Winifred	(301)229-5008	1118
Chevy Chase	FINE, Sandra D.	(301)951-3453	377
	KENTON, Charlotte	(301)657-3855	642
	MESHINSKY, Jeff M.	(301)652-4740	827
	SEARS, Jonathan R.	(301)656-2306	1110
Clinton	CHEEKS, Cellestine S.	(301)868-5048	204
Columbia	AVERSA, Elizabeth S.	(301)992-3711	41
	HOLLENBACH, Karen L.		551
	JOHNSON, Elaine B.	(301)992-5502	604
	KOSMIN, Linda J.	(301)997-8954	672
	SCHWARTZ, Betsy J.	(301)381-5028	1104
Damascus	JOHNSON, Susan W.	(301)253-2759	609
Davidsonville	SKARR, Robert J.	(301)261-4383	1145
Easton	MOLTER, Maureen M.	(301)822-1658	853
Edgewater	KROST, Mary G.		680
Flintstone	RAFATS, Jerome M.		1003

ONLINE SEARCHER (Cont'd)
MARYLAND (Cont'd)

Frederick	BANKS, Jane L.	(301)695-6726	54
	GIBBONS, Katherine Y.	(301)663-2720	431
	KINNA, Dorothy H.	(301)898-5212	652
	NATHANSON, David	(301)662-4499	889
Gaithersburg	GROCKI, Daniel J.	(301)253-6044	471
	HARTZ, Mary K.	(301)948-1855	509
	SHELAR, James W.	(301)809-8445	1125
	VAN BRUNT, Virginia	(301)762-6701	1272
Gamber	BOGAGE, Alan R.	(301)795-6167	110
Garrett Park	PRATT, Laura C.	(301)942-1764	990
Germantown	KING, Hannah M.	(301)540-0282	651
	PERRONE, Jeanne M.	(301)428-1810	960
Glen Burnie	STEINHOFF, Cynthia K.	(301)787-1549	1186
Grasonville	SCHNEIDER, Karl R.	(301)827-9339	1097
Hillcrest Heights	CHAPMAN, Elwynda K.	(301)894-0963	202
Kensington	SMITH, Karen G.	(301)564-0765	1156
	ZIMMERMANN, Carole R.	(301)564-0658	1389
Laurel	LEVINE, Emil H.	(301)776-3062	720
	OMAR, Elizabeth A.	(301)490-3871	923
	SWEETLAND, Loraine F.	(801)490-8231	1215
Mt Rainier	NITZ, Andrew M.		905
New Market	WILSON, Susan W.	(301)831-6118	1353
North East	DENNEY, Christine A.	(301)287-6060	292
Olney	WATERS, Susan S.	(301)774-3439	1309
Patuxent River	SULLIVAN, Carol W.	(301)863-1931	1207
Potomac	CHANG, Frances M.	(301)258-0772	200
Reisterstown	BRADLEY, Wanda L.		126
Riverdale	PITT, William B.	(301)699-5739	976
Rockville	BRANDHORST, Wesley T.	(301)460-6932	128
	CHIANG, Ahushun	(301)251-5486	207
	DEXTER, Patrick J.	(301)424-2000	298
	DICKINSON, Patricia C.	(301)251-1173	301
	KRUSE, Kathryn W.	(301)443-3180	681
	NGUYEN, Michael V.	(301)468-9697	900
	PHIFER, Kenneth O.	(301)770-0498	967
	WHITMAN, Jean A.	(301)736-6804	1333
	ZAHARKO, Nancy W.	(301)460-1419	1385
St Marys City	BRITTEN, William A.		137
Salisbury	DADSON, Theresa E.	(301)546-6950	269
Severn	JACK, Robert F.	(301)859-5300	586
Silver Spring	AMATRUDA, William T.	(301)585-3570	19
	FRAULINO, Philip S.	(301)495-5636	399
	HARBISON, John H.	(801)589-4223	499
	JACKSON, Carleton	(301)890-8594	587
	MCDONALD, Michael L.	(301)946-0278	803
	OVERTON, Kathryn R.	(301)236-9754	931
	POMERANTZ, Karyn L.	(301)445-6204	982
	RICHARD, Sheila A.	(301)438-4555	1028
	SPURLING, Norman K.	(301)495-9229	1177
	WALSH, Barclay		1299
	WISNIEWSKI, Julia L.	(301)649-1590	1357
Takoma Park	SLOAN, Cheryl A.	(301)589-6815	1149
Upper Marlboro	HARBERT, Cathy E.	(301)868-9280	499
Upperco	RAND, Pamela S.	(301)429-2958	1006
Wheaton	MWALIMU, Charles	(301)933-4040	884

MASSACHUSETTS

Acton	FINGERMAN, Susan M.	(617)263-1881	378
Amherst	FELDMAN, Laurence M.	(413)253-9404	369
Arlington	GRIGORIS, Lygia	(617)648-2290	470
	PLUNKET, Linda	(617)646-7825	979
Attleboro	PREVE, Roberta J.	(617)222-7036	992
Bedford	BERGIN, Dorothy O.	(617)275-7071	86
	MAIER, Robert C.	(617)275-9440	761
Belmont	LABREE, Rosanne	(617)855-2460	686
Billerica	REID, Angea S.	(617)663-3455	1018
Bolton	BOGART, Betty B.	(617)897-7870	110
Boston	BERNARD, Bobbi	(617)353-1568	88
	BLAKE, Michael R.	(617)572-3127	103
	CAIN, Susan H.	(617)338-6553	171
	CARROLL, Virginia L.	(617)742-5151	187
	FOX, Susan	(617)463-3178	395
	HAYES, Alison M.	(617)482-1776	515
	HOLT, June C.	(617)727-1140	554
	KORT, Richard L.	(617)266-3646	672
	LEIGHTON, Helene L.	(617)726-8600	714
	MACIVER, Linda B.		756
	PICCININO, Rocco	(617)442-9010	970

ONLINE SEARCHER (Cont'd)
MASSACHUSETTS (Cont'd)

Boston

	PLUNKET, Joy H.	(617)327-5175	978
	PRESTON, Margaret P.	(617)338-6000	992
	PRISTASH, Kenneth	(617)262-1120	993
	SCHATZ, Cindy A.	(617)732-2134	1090
	STEVENSON, Michael I.	(617)495-6374	1191
	WEINSCHENK, Andrea	(617)353-9319	1318
	WESTLING, Ellen R.	(617)726-8600	1327
Bridgewater	CHANDRASEKHAR, Ratna	(617)697-3648	200
Brighton	BRAUN, Robin E.	(617)789-2177	130
Brookline	DONG, Tina	(617)731-3514	311
	SOVNER-RIBBLER, Judith	(617)277-2991	1170
Cambridge	ALTENBERGER, Alicja	(617)495-4285	18
	COLLINS, John W.	(617)495-4225	232
	DAVY, Edgar W.	(617)253-5670	281
	HEACOCK, Pamela P.	(617)661-1330	518
	JACKSON, Arlyne A.	(617)492-0355	586
	KNAACK, Linda M.	(617)253-8462	663
	PINSON, Mark	(617)492-1590	975
	WHITE, Chandlee	(617)576-9299	1330
Canton	EDWARDS, Betty	(617)364-2000	337
Chelmsford	MATTHEWS, Charles E.	(617)256-6600	785
Chestnut Hill	LIPPMAN, Anne F.	(617)552-4457	732
Concord	BENDER, Elizabeth H.	(617)369-4222	79
	LEWONTIN, Amy	(617)369-9106	724
Dedham	LOSCALZO, Anita B.	(617)329-3964	741
Deerfield	KELLY, Patricia M.	(413)774-4627	638
Douglas	COPPOLA, H P.	(617)476-2975	245
	COPPOLA, Peter A.	(617)476-2975	245
Dover	WINQUIST, Elaine W.	(617)785-0816	1355
Dracut	ARSENAULT, Patricia A.	(617)459-4648	35
Farmingham	KING, Laurie L.	(617)877-3512	651
Hanscom AFB	GERKE, Ray	(617)377-2177	428
Jamaica Plain	WHELAN, Julia S.	(617)522-3064	1329
Lexington	BROWN, George F.	(617)863-5100	144
	KATES, Jacqueline R.	(617)862-1919	629
	WAKS, Jane B.	(617)863-2000	1293
Lincoln	COHEN, Martha J.	(413)259-9500	228
Marlborough	FERGUSON, Roberta J.	(617)481-5866	372
Marshfield	TU, Shu C.	(617)837-8607	1261
Medford	HARRIS, John C.	(617)396-9250	504
	MCDONALD, Ellen J.	(617)381-3273	802
	PELLEGRINI, Deborah A.	(617)396-5457	955
Millis	PERRY, Guest	(617)376-8459	960
	ROE, Georgeanne T.	(617)376-8459	1048
Milton	OPPENHEIM, Roberta A.	(617)698-6268	925
Natick	DLOTT, Nancy E.	(617)655-9163	306
Needham	TSENG, Louisa	(617)449-3630	1260
Needham Heights	ORENSTEIN, Ruth M.		925
New Bedford	FINNI, John J.	(617)999-6034	379
Newburyport	JACQUES, Donna M.	(617)462-7105	591
Newton	ALPERT, Hillel R.		17
	SARAVIS, Judith A.	(617)969-6852	1082
	WALLAS, Philip R.	(617)527-1762	1298
North Abington	LAROSA, Sharon M.	(617)871-6288	698
North Grafton	SAFFER-MARCHAND, Melinda	(617)839-5302	1074
Norwood	DELTANO, Pauline T.	(617)762-5300	290
Randolph	HALL, Robert G.	(617)963-8549	488
Reading	O'CONNOR, Jerry	(617)944-6452	916
	SARAIDARIDIS, Susan B.		1082
Revere	MOORE, Catherine I.	(617)289-4595	859
Roybury	SUTTON, Joyce A.	(617)427-4941	1211
Sagamore	OLIANSKY, Joseph D.	(617)888-6189	920
Salem	SCHWALLER, Marian C.	(617)744-0076	1104
Shrewsbury	CHANG, Isabelle E.	(617)845-4641	200
Springfield	DELZELL, William R.	(413)737-7000	290
	TAUPIER, Andrea S.	(413)788-3315	1225
Stockbridge	LINTON, Helen W.	(413)298-5511	731
Taunton	TURKALO, David M.	(617)824-8769	1263
Walpole	ESTES, Pamela J.	(617)668-3076	355
Wellesley Hills	KENNEDY, Amy J.	(617)237-4013	640
West Roxbury	HARZBECKER, Joseph J.	(617)323-1372	510
Williamsburg	O'BRIEN, Marjorie S.	(413)268-7131	914
Williamstown	SUDDUTH, William E.	(413)597-2514	1206
Winchester	DAY, Virginia M.	(617)729-6026	283
Woods Hole	WINN, Carolyn P.	(617)548-7066	1355

ONLINE SEARCHER (Cont'd)
MASSACHUSETTS (Cont'd)

Worcester	ANDREWS, Peter J.		27
	GONNEVILLE, Priscilla R.	(617)752-5615	447
	KANG, Wen	(617)856-2511	625
	RIVARD, Timothy D.	(617)799-8186	1037
	ROCHELEAU, Kathleen D.	(617)793-7319	1046
Yarmouthport	STEEVES, Henry A.		1184

MICHIGAN

Ann Arbor	BEAUBIEN, Anne K.	(313)763-5060	70
	BENNETT, Christine H.	(313)769-8500	81
	BENSON, Peggy	(313)665-0651	83
	BIGGS, Debra R.	(313)763-7080	95
	CROOKS, James E.	(313)936-2408	260
	DAVIDSEN, Susanna L.	(313)995-7352	276
	DAVIS, Anne C.	(313)668-0385	277
	DWOSKIN, Beth M.	(212)382-6727	330
	HALL, Jo A.	(313)936-0132	488
	LANSDALE, Metta T.		696
	MAHONY, Doris D.	(313)764-1210	761
	MARTIN, Patricia W.	(313)665-3776	777
	MOUZON, Margaret W.	(313)662-9227	874
	PAO, Miranda L.	(313)747-3611	938
	SCHWARTZ, Diane G.	(313)763-2037	1104
	SIEVING, Pamela C.	(313)761-1418	1136
	SMILLIE, Pauline A.	(313)665-8821	1151
	TERWILLIGER, Doris H.	(313)761-3912	1232
	WILSON, Amy S.	(313)761-4700	1349
Auburn Hills	WILLIAMS, Calvin	(313)853-4226	1342
Augusta	AEBLI, Carol L.	(616)731-5587	7
Bay City	KORMELINK, Barbara A.	(517)894-3782	671
Bloomfield Hills	BRISTOR, Patricia R.	(313)852-0206	137
	HERBST, Linda R.	(313)642-5800	530
	KELLEY, Barbara C.	(313)646-8086	636
Canton	BRYANT, Barton B.	(313)397-3660	152
Cedar Springs	RANSOM-BERGSTROM, Janette F.	(616)696-3428	1008
Dearborn	LUKASIEWICZ, Barbara	(313)593-5400	747
	REID, Valerie L.	(313)278-1307	1019
Detroit	BRAITHWAITE, Heather J.	(313)577-3925	127
	BRENNAN, Jean M.	(313)745-7178	132
	CARUSO, Genevieve O.	(313)972-7000	190
	KLEIN, Michele S.		659
	MENDELSOHN, Loren D.	(313)577-6317	823
	SELBERG, Janice K.	(313)577-6175	1113
	SHUMAN, Bruce A.	(313)577-1825	1134
	STAJNIAK, Elizabeth T.	(313)259-7110	1178
	WARD, Nancy E.	(313)256-9596	1304
East Lansing	ACKERMAN, Katherine K.	(517)332-6818	4
	COURTOIS, Martin P.	(517)355-8494	251
	WOODARD, Beth E.	(517)355-5774	1365
	YARBROUGH, Joseph W.	(517)337-0693	1378
Farmington Hills	PAPAI, Beverly D.	(313)553-0300	938
	ROBBINS, Lora A.	(313)661-6957	1039
Flint	HART, David J.	(313)762-3414	507
	MORELAND, Patricia L.	(313)762-2141	863
Grand Blanc	SCHAAFSMA, Roberta A.	(313)695-5571	1088
Grand Rapids	BRACKETT, Norman S.	(616)241-7467	124
	BURINSKI, Walter W.	(616)454-9635	160
	FITZPATRICK, Nancy C.	(616)676-1568	383
	KING, Kathryn L.		651
Grosse Pointe Park	TOLMAN, Bonnie B.	(313)885-0764	1249
Grosse Pointe Woods	STRATELAK, Nadia A.	(313)886-1043	1200
Harper Woods	TODD, Suzanne L.	(313)881-5328	1248
Haslett	OLIVER, James W.	(517)339-0846	921
Holland	YETMAN, Nancy J.	(616)394-2363	1380
Holt	KEDDLE, David G.	(517)694-2746	634
Kalamazoo	CARROLL, Hardy	(616)383-1926	187
	RING, Donna M.	(616)375-8350	1035
	VANDER MEER, Patricia F.	(616)383-1666	1274
Lansing	CALLARD, Carole	(517)373-1593	173
	CONWAY, Michael J.		239
	HEINLEN, Bethany A.	(517)377-8389	522
	RADEMACHER, Matthew J.	(517)483-1644	1002
Midland	DYKHUIS, Randy	(517)835-5227	331
Muskegon	MARSHALL, Betty J.	(616)728-4766	773
Novi	COREY, Marjorie	(313)344-1770	246
Oak Park	PERECMAN, Carol J.	(313)968-8719	958

ONLINE SEARCHER (Cont'd)

MICHIGAN (Cont'd)

Okemos	TREGLOAN, Donald C.	(517)349-7767	1255
Petoskey	KELLY, Kay	(616)348-4500	638
Rochester	SHEPARD, Margaret E.	(313)651-1636	1127
Saint Clair Shores	AMES, Kay L.	(313)773-7054	20
Saint Joseph	WOJCIKIEWICZ, Carol A.	(616)429-8618	1359
Southfield	GILBERT, Carole M.	(313)424-3294	433
	VERGE, Colleen R.	(313)354-9100	1282
Springfield	BURHANS, Barbara C.	(616)965-4096	159
Sterling Heights	SAHYOUN, Naim K.	(313)939-6425	1075
Troy	STEPHENS, Karen L.	(313)879-6856	1188
Utica	HORNE, Ernest L.	(313)731-4374	560
Warren	DOYLE, James M.	(313)445-7401	317
West Bloomfield	ABRAMSON, Lawrence J.	(313)626-8126	3
	FEDER, Carol S.	(313)851-5822	367

MINNESOTA

Duluth	ENRICI, Pamela L.	(218)726-8586	350
Eagan	BOYD, Cheryl J.	(612)454-8254	122
Little Canada	LO, Maryanne H.	(612)481-9412	735
Mankato	HITT, Charles J.	(507)625-4834	544
Minneapolis	BARRETT, Darryl D.	(612)370-0869	59
	BEDOR, Kathleen M.	(612)823-3945	73
	ELFSTRAND, Stephen F.	(612)722-9952	342
	GALT, Judith A.	(612)825-1190	415
	GLASGOW, Vicki L.	(612)626-5808	440
	OLSEN, Stephen	(612)333-9307	922
	POQUETTE, Mary L.	(612)377-6691	984
	ROLONTZ, Linda	(612)337-1644	1051
	ROSSMAN, Muriel J.	(612)624-4002	1059
	SANDNESS, John G.	(612)866-7033	1081
	SPETLAND, Charles G.	(612)624-8060	1174
	STANKE, Judith U.	(612)725-6767	1180
	TERTELL, Susan M.	(612)372-6658	1232
	WEINBERG, Gail B.	(612)624-6492	1317
North Oaks	HONEBRINK, Andrea C.	(612)481-0968	555
Northfield	SANFORD, Carolyn C.	(507)663-4266	1081
Red Wing	SWEEN, Roger	(612)388-5723	1214
Robbinsdale	HERTHER, Nancy K.	(612)529-0115	533
Rochester	ERWIN, Patricia J.	(507)288-8560	353
	HAWTHORNE, Dorothy M.	(507)284-8797	514
St Cloud	HEETER, Judith A.	(612)251-2700	520
St Paul	ANDERSON, Rebekah E.	(612)733-9057	25
	BALDWIN, Jerome C.	(612)297-4532	51
	CARLSON, Livija I.	(612)624-3078	182
	CATHCART, Marilyn S.	(612)646-0254	195
	GADE, Rachel P.	(612)631-0494	411
	HLAVSA, Larry B.	(612)699-7198	544
	HOLT, Constance W.	(612)690-6599	554
	KINNEY, Janet S.	(612)690-6650	653
	MINOR, Barbara G.	(612)698-4978	846
	OLSON, Carol A.	(612)484-8391	922
	OLSON, Ray A.	(612)484-8391	923
	RICCI, Patricia L.	(612)771-4764	1026
	SCHMIDT, Jean M.		1095
	TURNER, Ann S.	(612)291-9340	1264
Scandia	HANSEN, Kathelen L.	(612)433-5477	497
Winona	MOXNESS, Mary J.	(507)452-5177	874

MISSISSIPPI

Brandon	SELTZER, Ada M.		1114
Hattiesburg	DUNCAN, Bettye M.	(601)264-6849	325
	THOMPSON, Karolyn S.	(601)266-4256	1240
	WILLIAMS, Eddie A.	(601)266-4245	1043
	WITTIG, Glenn R.	(601)266-4236	1358
Jackson	SANDERS, Lou H.	(601)982-7094	1080
Oxford	HARPER, Laura G.	(601)234-1812	503
Starkville	ELLSBURY, Susan H.	(601)324-1475	345

MISSOURI

Ballwin	BRENNER, Saundra H.	(314)256-3936	133
Chesterfield	GOLDMAN, Teri B.		446
Columbia	ANDREWS, Mark J.	(314)875-0154	27
	BARNES, Everett W.	(314)882-4581	57
	LUH, Ming		747
	MCKININ, Emma J.	(314)442-4419	811
	MULTER, Eli P.		878
	PALLARDY, Judy S.	(314)882-4692	935
	STEVENS, Robert R.	(314)445-5320	1191

ONLINE SEARCHER (Cont'd)

MISSOURI (Cont'd)

Columbia			
	WATERS, Bill F.	(314)443-3161	1308
Creve Coeur	GAFFEY, Mary V.	(314)432-7726	411
Florissant	ANTHONY, Paul L.	(314)921-6158	29
Independence	VOSS, Kathryn J.	(816)836-8100	1289
Joplin	KEMP, Charles H.	(417)625-9386	639
	REIMAN, David A.	(417)625-9362	1020
Kansas City	CARSON, Bonnie L.		188
	DRAYSON, Pamela K.	(816)753-7600	318
	GARDNER, Laura L.	(816)741-4070	418
	GIBSON, Patricia A.	(816)333-9700	432
	GINDRA, Janice J.	(816)842-3600	437
	HUBBLE, Gerald B.	(816)926-4144	568
	MARCHANT, Thomas O.	(816)761-8873	768
	POSTLEWAIT, Cheryl A.	(913)384-0197	986
	ROTH, Sally	(816)842-0984	1059
	RUBY, Carolyn M.		1065
Kirksville	ONSAGER, Lawrence W.	(816)665-4283	924
Kirkwood	SHALLENBERGER, Anna F.	(314)821-4169	1119
Nevada	KIEL, Becky	(417)667-8181	647
Parkville	SMITH, Harold F.	(816)741-6085	1155
Richmond	WALKER, Patricia A.	(816)776-2226	1296
Rolla	STEWART, J A.	(314)341-4007	1192
Saint Joseph	HUGHES, Joan L.	(816)271-6000	571
St Louis	BECK, Sara R.	(314)889-5483	71
	ELAM, Kristy L.	(314)658-2759	341
	GELINNE, Michael S.	(314)694-4748	426
	GIBSON, Marianne	(314)432-1600	432
	GODT, Carol	(314)966-4976	443
	IGLAUER, Carol	(314)768-3137	581
	LEWIS, Ruth E.	(314)889-5405	724
	MCDERMOTT, Margaret H.	(314)889-6443	802
	PERSHE, Frank F.		961
	REHKOP, Barbara L.		1017
	TOLSON, Stephanie D.	(314)741-7844	1249
	WHITE, Cheryl L.	(314)367-0741	1330
St Peters	HICKS, James M.	(314)441-0522	537
Springfield	CARTER, Steva L.	(417)882-5050	190
	CRABTREE, Anna B.	(417)887-1531	254
	FREEMAN, C L.	(417)836-4536	400
	KOTAMRAJU, Sarada	(417)883-8590	673

MONTANA

Bozeman	BREMER, Thomas A.	(406)994-5295	132
Butte	HUYGEN, Michaele L.	(406)782-8400	580
Helena	BERGERON, Cheri Y.	(406)443-4333	86

NEBRASKA

Bellevue	JACKA, David C.	(402)293-3157	586
Lincoln	LU, Janet C.	(402)465-2400	745
	NESMITH, Edmund D.	(402)486-2514	896
	TIBBITS, Edith J.	(402)472-3545	1243
	WOMACK, Sharon K.		1362
Omaha	BROWN, Helen A.	(402)559-4326	144
	EARLEY, Dorothy A.	(402)333-5734	332
	GENDLER, Carol J.	(402)444-7174	426
	LEBEAU, Chris	(402)280-2219	707
Ralston	OYER, Kenneth E.	(402)331-8843	932

NEVADA

Carson City	DION, Kathleen L.	(702)885-5140	305
	SOUTHWICK, Susan A.	(702)885-5140	1170
	STURM, H P.	(702)882-1361	1205
Dayton	STURM, Danna G.	(702)246-0250	1205
Las Vegas	HEATON, Shelley J.	(702)739-3512	519
	ORTIZ, Cynthia		927
	POLSON, Billie M.	(702)739-3125	982
	WELLS, David B.	(702)733-3641	1322
Reno	ORCUTT, Roberta K.	(702)747-4388	925
	PRATT, Kathleen L.	(702)789-3108	990

NEW HAMPSHIRE

Franconia	BJORNER, Susan N.	(603)823-8838	100
Fremont	FARAH, Barbara D.		363
Hampton	KORBER, Nancy	(603)926-6005	671
Manchester	BERTHIAUME, Dennis A.	(603)669-1030	90
	MCGINNIS, Joan M.	(603)624-4366	806
	REINGOLD, Judith S.	(603)669-5300	1021

ONLINE SEARCHER (Cont'd)

NEW HAMPSHIRE (Cont'd)

Merrimack	DENTON, Francesca L.	(603)424-8621	293
Nashua	FERRIGNO, Helen F.	(603)889-3042	373
Portsmouth	LE BLANC, Charles A.	(603)436-4866	708

NEW JERSEY

Allenwood	ERBE, Evalina S.	(201)223-9388	352
Atlantic City	CROSS, Roberta A.	(609)345-2269	261
Belle Mead	LEE, J S.	(201)359-5845	710
	ODERWALD, Sara M.	(201)359-8229	916
Boontown	HOVER, Leila M.	(201)335-7434	563
Bridgewater	DESS, Howard M.	(201)526-1981	295
Butler	GARDNER, Sue A.	(201)838-3262	418
Caldwell	SKIDANOW, Helene	(201)226-4458	1146
Cape May Court House	HSU, Hsiu H.	(609)465-4500	567
Cedar Knolls	MILLINGTON, Kathleen A.	(201)540-8700	843
Chatham	SZE, Melanie C.	(201)635-4633	1218
Cherry Hill	ARROWOOD, Nina R.	(609)667-7653	35
	BECK, Susan J.	(609)354-7638	72
	BENSON, James A.	(609)354-7638	83
Chester	MANY, Florence L.	(201)879-5167	767
Cliffside Park	PAWSON, Robert D.	(201)943-3228	951
	SEKELY, Maryann	(201)943-4117	1113
Columbus	ALITO, Martha A.	(609)298-5848	13
Cranford	WOLFE, N J.	(201)279-9563	1361
Creamridge	GEORGE, Muriel S.	(609)758-3198	428
Demarest	MCDERMOTT, Ellen	(201)767-1618	801
East Orange	MATHAI, Aleyamma	(201)266-5613	783
	STICKEL, William R.	(201)678-4289	1193
Edison	LEICHTMAN, Anne B.	(201)572-1982	713
Elizabeth	BOSS, Catherine M.	(201)558-8092	117
	MILLER, Virginia L.	(201)351-3288	843
Glassboro	GARRABRANT, William A.	(609)863-6111	420
Haddonfield	SWARTZ, Betty J.	(609)429-8498	1214
	WILLIAMSON, Carol L.	(609)354-6213	1347
Highland Park	BARZELATTO, Elba G.	(201)247-6248	62
	PARAS, Lucille P.		939
	YUCHT, Donald J.	(201)572-0173	1384
Hoboken	LIN, Fumei C.	(201)795-5066	727
	SOLOMON, Geri E.	(201)420-8364	1166
Indian Mills	SCHREIBER-COIA, Barbara J.		1099
Iselin	FRANTS, Valery	(212)579-2496	398
Jersey City	PANDELAKIS, Helene S.	(201)795-8265	937
	RUBIN, Myra P.	(201)963-6456	1064
Kearny	CASSIDY, Joni L.	(201)991-5868	193
Lawrenceville	TILLMAN, Hope N.	(609)896-5115	1245
Lincroft	REESE, Carol H.	(201)842-1900	1016
Madison	SNELSON, Pamela	(201)377-3000	1163
Maplewood	AUSTIN, Fay A.		40
	LAUB, Barbara J.	(201)763-8379	702
Matawan	KEARNEY, Jeanne E.	(201)566-7532	633
Millburn	URKEN, Madeline	(201)379-2306	1270
Montclair	BROWN, Cynthia D.	(201)783-6420	142
Moorestown	SCHEPP, Brad J.	(609)778-1975	1091
Mount Holly	RILEY, Marie R.		1034
Mt Laurel	O'CONNOR, Elizabeth W.	(609)235-5003	916
Mountainside	LINGELBACH, Lorene N.	(201)654-7694	730
Murray Hill	LEWIS, Dale E.	(201)582-5021	722
New Brunswick	MAZZEI, Peter J.	(201)249-4120	791
	NASH, Stanley D.	(201)932-7014	888
	SARACEVIC, Tefko	(201)932-7447	1082
Nutley	GILHEANY, Rosary S.	(201)667-7013	434
Paramus	CESARD, Mary A.	(201)444-4389	196
Passaic	RUIZ-VALERA, Phoebe L.	(201)471-1770	1067
Piscataway	CASSEL, Jeris F.	(201)752-0528	193
	KAPLAN, Susan J.	(201)699-4327	626
Pompton Lakes	MENZUL, Faina	(201)839-6885	825
Princeton	CHAIKIN, Mary C.	(609)452-6084	197
	FRIHART, Anne R.	(609)921-3333	404
	HIRSCH, David G.	(609)683-7502	543
	HOELLE, Dolores M.	(609)452-3201	547
	NASE, Lois M.	(609)452-3237	888
Ridgewood	JONES, Anita M.	(201)444-7273	610
Roselle Park	MAGEE, Patricia A.	(201)245-1963	759
Saddle Brook	AUGHEY, Kathleen M.		39
Short Hills	LEVEROCK, Lisa A.	(201)379-4800	719
Shrewsbury	KRANIS, Janet C.	(201)842-5995	676

ONLINE SEARCHER (Cont'd)

NEW JERSEY (Cont'd)

Somerville	GABRIEL, Linda	(201)874-8061	411
	KAN, Halina S.	(201)685-6017	624
	KUSHINKA, Kerry L.	(201)526-7323	685
South Orange	TALAR, Anita	(201)761-9434	1220
	VITART, Jane A.	(201)763-2181	1286
Sparta	GUIDA, Pat	(201)729-8176	476
Spring Lake	GARVEY, Nancy G.	(201)449-4673	421
Springfield	CHANG, Joseph I.	(201)467-2037	200
	SCOTT, Miranda D.	(201)467-7010	1107
Summit	JOHNSON, Minnie L.	(201)273-4952	607
Sussex	SMITH, Jo T.	(201)875-3621	1156
Teaneck	ROSENSTEIN, Susan J.	(201)836-7719	1057
Tenafly	KORNFELD, Carol E.	(201)568-2231	672
Union	AMRON, Irving	(201)688-4980	20
Upper Montclair	O'CONNOR, Christine T.	(201)783-7995	916
Upper Saddle River	DUDLEY, Debbra C.	(201)327-4006	323
	MICHAELS, Debbie D.	(201)327-5006	832
Washington Township	MAYNES, Kathleen R.	(201)358-0209	790
Westfield	REGENBERG, Patricia B.	(201)232-4870	1017
Westwood	GINES, Noriko	(201)666-7042	437
Whitehouse Station	HOYT, Henry M.	(201)689-7717	566
Woodbridge	DE WITT, Benjamin L.	(201)634-1316	298

NEW MEXICO

Albuquerque	BERNSTEIN, Judith R.	(505)262-2320	89
	HLAVA, Marjorie M.	(505)265-3591	544
	KALE, Shirley W.	(505)298-5980	623
	KEMPF, Jody L.	(505)277-6202	639
	ROLLINS, Stephen J.	(505)277-5057	1051
	SPURLOCK, Sandra E.	(505)828-5378	1177
	STRUB, Jeane E.	(505)262-7158	1203
Farmington	RICHARD, Harris M.	(509)326-2936	1027
Kirtland AFB	JOURDAIN, Janet M.	(505)844-1768	618
Los Alamos	COMSTOCK, Daniel L.	(505)662-7668	235
Portales	SCHOTT, Mark E.	(505)356-8735	1099
Sunspot	CORNETT, John L.	(505)434-1390	247

NEW YORK

Albany	DENOTO, Dorothy E.	(518)449-3166	293
	KNEE, Michael	(518)442-3586	663
	VIA, Barbara J.	(518)442-3688	1283
	WALKER, M G.	(518)436-1975	1296
	WALSH, Daniel P.	(518)489-7968	1299
Alfred	CULLEY, Paul T.	(607)871-2492	263
Amawalk	HANE, Paula J.	(914)962-2933	495
Amherst	MAYER, Erich J.	(716)691-5554	789
APO New York	NEUWILLER, Charlene		897
	RUDA, Donna R.		1065
Astoria	FISHER, Maureen C.	(718)204-0631	381
Bayside	SHER, Deborah M.	(718)225-3435	1127
Bethpage	BURDEN, John	(516)575-3912	158
Binghamton	CARPENTER, Dale	(607)797-0176	184
Brewster	VELARDI, Adrienne B.	(914)279-5022	1281
Bronx	BARNETT, Philip	(212)549-5359	58
	CANNATA, Arleen	(212)295-5910	178
	CLAYBORNE, Jon L.	(212)588-8400	219
	GAROOGIAN, Rhoda	(212)588-2266	420
	GEE, Ka C.	(212)960-7770	424
	GHOSH, Subhra	(212)588-8400	430
	IOANID, Aurora S.	(212)220-0543	583
	JOHNSON, Steven P.	(212)220-6874	609
	LIEBER, Ellen C.	(212)920-4666	726
	LOCASCIO, Aline M.	(212)588-8400	735
	RUBEY, Daniel R.	(212)960-8580	1064
Brooklyn	COHEN, Renee G.	(718)531-2647	229
	DIMARTINO, Diane J.	(718)783-8205	303
	DINDAYAL, Joyce S.	(718)647-1624	304
	HORNE, Dorice L.	(718)859-1830	560
	JAROSEK, Joan E.	(718)237-2147	594
	KRAUSS, Susan E.	(718)230-4752	676
	LANDOLFI, Lisa M.	(718)853-7871	693
	MARSHAK, Bonnie L.	(718)638-6821	773
	MARTINEZ-RIVERA, Ivette	(718)854-5176	779
	MATTERA, Joseph J.	(718)935-1746	785
	NARDUCCI, Frances	(718)743-6001	888
	NEUBERG, Karen S.	(718)627-9796	897
	NICOL, Margaret W.	(718)768-2890	903

ONLINE SEARCHER (Cont'd)
NEW YORK (Cont'd)

Brooklyn

	SCHWARTZ, Dorothy D.	(718)857-4069	1104
	STANKIEWICZ, Carol A.	(718)858-5580	1180
	STRAM, Lynn R.	(718)434-7815	1200
	TANNER, Ellen B.	(718)780-3195	1222
	TURIEL, David	(718)336-2668	1263
	WAHLERT, George A.	(718)833-1899	1292
	WOFSE, Joy G.	(718)788-5360	1359
Buffalo	BUSH, Renee B.	(716)832-3081	165
	COTY, Patricia A.	(716)636-3377	250
	HALL, Russell W.	(716)834-9200	488
	KASE-MCLAREN, Karen A.	(716)838-6610	628
	SAHLEM, James R.	(716)852-0712	1075
	STELZLE, James J.	(716)832-6066	1186
	STIEVATER, Susan M.	(716)878-6313	1194
	WAGNER, Stephen K.	(716)837-1563	1292
	WELLS, Margaret R.	(716)636-2943	1322
Centerport	COOPER, Catherine M.	(516)754-9262	242
Chappaqua	DI BIANCO, Phyllis R.	(914)238-3911	299
	NOVICK, Ruth	(914)238-4249	911
Clarence Ctr	CHAPMAN, Renee D.	(716)741-9644	202
Cohoes	PINGITORE, Patricia E.		974
Cold Spring	BARNHART, David K.	(914)265-2822	58
Cold Spring Harbor	FARAONE, Maria B.	(516)271-1771	363
	MACCALLUM, Barbara B.		754
Corona	KINYATTI, Njoki W.	(718)592-4782	653
Croton-on-Hudson	TUCKERMAN, Susan	(914)271-5723	1262
Dansville	MINEMIER, Betty M.	(716)335-6258	845
Delhi	SEN, Joyce H.	(607)746-7350	1115
Delmar	BRESLIN, Ellen R.	(518)439-7568	133
Dobbs Ferry	HASSAN, Mohammad Z.	(914)693-2031	511
East Aurora	UTTS, Janet R.	(716)655-0031	1270
East Patchogue	PLUMER, F I.	(516)289-3134	978
East Setauket	ALBERTUS, Donna M.		10
Eastchester	KOLTAY, Emery I.	(914)337-0300	670
Elmhurst	HSU, Elizabeth L.	(718)271-6623	567
	NOLAN, John A.	(718)565-1627	907
Elmira	LAPIER, Cynthia B.	(607)739-3581	697
Fairport	SULOUFF, Patricia T.	(716)223-6844	1208
Farmingdale	ARMSTRONG, Ruth C.		32
Flushing	PENCHANSKY, Mimi B.	(718)520-7248	956
	SAFRAN, Scott A.	(718)445-6752	1074
Forest Hills	NERBOSO, Donna L.	(718)897-9826	895
Fresh Meadows	MULCAHY, Brian J.	(718)454-2157	876
Fulton	REED, Catherine A.	(315)598-3435	1015
Geneseo	CAREN, Loretta	(716)243-0438	181
Glendale	SOSTACK, Maura	(718)417-8242	1169
Grand Island	WATERS, Betsy M.		1308
Hempstead	BARTEN, Sharon S.		60
	LOUISDHON-WALTER, Marie L.	(718)990-0767	742
Hewlett	WILLER, Kenneth H.		1341
Hicksville	EDWARDS, Harriet M.		337
	TRAVERS, Jane E.		1254
Highland	LAWRENCE, Thomas A.	(914)691-2734	705
	RANKIN, Carol A.	(914)691-2275	1007
Houghton	LAUER, Jonathan D.	(716)567-2211	702
Huntington	CLOWE, Isabel B.	(516)385-9012	223
	FALVEY, Genemary H.	(516)673-0015	363
	JASSIN, Raymond M.	(516)266-1093	595
	WESTERLING, Mary L.	(516)549-9441	1327
Huntington Station	MAUTER, George A.	(516)421-9291	787
	ROSS, David J.	(516)385-4951	1058
Islip Terrace	KLATT, Wilma F.	(516)581-5933	658
Ithaca	COONS, William W.	(607)255-7959	242
	POWELL, Jill H.	(607)255-3925	988
	SCHNEDEKER, Donald W.	(607)255-3389	1096
	STEWART, Linda G.	(607)255-7959	1192
Jamaica	GRANT, Mary A.	(718)990-6161	458
	SHAPIRO, Martin P.	(718)990-0760	1121
	VENER, Lucille	(718)990-0761	1282
Jamaica Estates	BARTENBACH, Wilhelm K.	(718)658-3878	60
Kew Gardens	THAU, Richard	(718)847-7736	1234
Larchmont	LANDMAN, Lillian L.	(914)834-3225	693
Latham	MACKSEY, Susan A.	(518)783-7058	757
	VEGTER, Amy H.	(518)783-1161	1281
Lindenhurst	MONTALBANO, James J.	(516)884-8670	855
	WARD, Peter K.	(516)957-6678	1304

ONLINE SEARCHER (Cont'd)
NEW YORK (Cont'd)

Maine	GERACI, Diane	(607)728-3954	428
Mamaroneck	O'CONOR, William C.	(914)698-4741	916
Manhasset	NAPOLITANO, Joan A.	(516)562-4324	887
Massapequa Park	AKS, Gloria	(516)795-7297	9
Mattituck	PERLMAN, Stephen E.	(516)298-4335	959
Medina	TUOHEY, Jeanne D.	(716)798-2285	1263
Miller Place	TODOSOW, Helen K.	(516)928-7174	1248
Mineola	KRATZ, Charles E.		676
	TISHLER, Amnon	(516)294-7224	1247
Mt Sinai	COHEN, Rosemary C.	(516)473-8717	229
Nassau	CARABATEAS, Clarissa D.		180
New City	GROSS, Elinor L.	(914)634-1373	472
New Rochelle	SWANSON, Mary A.	(914)633-3954	1213
New York	ARAYA, Rose M.	(718)461-4799	30
	ARTHUR, Christine	(212)732-5964	35
	AVERILL, M S.	(212)677-2331	41
	BADERTSCHER, David G.	(212)374-5615	44
	BANKS-ISZARD, Kimberly K.	(212)280-5658	54
	BATES, Ellen	(212)503-8007	63
	BEALER, Jane A.	(212)355-0083	68
	BENNIN, Cheryl S.	(212)685-5885	82
	BENSON, Harold W.	(212)420-7652	83
	BERGFELD, C D.	(212)496-2668	86
	BONACORDA, James J.	(212)982-8358	113
	BUSSEY, Holly J.	(212)708-5181	165
	CHITTAMPALLI, Padma S.	(212)874-0141	209
	CURTIS, James A.	(212)222-9638	267
	DAGATA, Marie	(212)546-2507	269
	DARNOWSKI, Christina M.	(212)750-5749	275
	DAVIS, Robert J.	(212)412-4270	280
	DEDONATO, Ree	(212)998-2510	286
	DEMANDY, Claire	(212)960-8575	291
	DENNIS, Anne R.	(212)645-4500	292
	ENGLER, Gretchen	(212)703-4127	349
	GESKE, Aina S.		430
	GILLIGAN, Mary A.	(212)790-9090	436
	GINSBURG, Carol L.	(212)850-1440	438
	GOLLOP, Sandra G.	(212)770-7911	447
	GOODMAN, Edward C.	(212)280-8407	449
	GOODSELL, Joan W.	(212)210-7044	450
	GROSS, Gretchen		472
	GROTE, Janet H.	(212)627-1500	473
	HAYWARD, Diane J.	(212)757-2200	517
	HERMAN, Marsha	(212)679-6105	531
	HIGGINS, Steven	(212)674-2087	538
	HSIAO, Shu Y.	(212)749-2873	567
	KAPNICK, Laura B.	(212)975-2917	626
	KEMPE, Deborah A.	(212)595-6583	639
	KILBERG, Jacqueline L.	(212)536-3562	648
	KLEIMAN, Rhoda E.	(212)247-2650	659
	KOLATA, Judith	(212)902-0080	669
	LAMANN, Amber N.	(212)677-4102	689
	LASTRES, Steven A.	(212)486-9500	701
	LEWIS, Anne	(212)906-1200	722
	LIDSKY, Ella	(212)663-4949	725
	LILLY, Elise M.	(212)940-8596	727
	MARKERT, Patricia B.	(212)925-4939	771
	MINTZ, Anne P.	(212)620-2499	847
	MULIA, Gusti	(212)930-0701	876
	NARCISO, Susan D.	(212)260-0718	888
	O'GRADY, Jean P.	(212)370-8690	918
	OSTROW, Rona	(212)601-1072	929
	OSTWALD, Mark F.		929
	PERRY, Claudia A.	(212)876-8200	960
	PINEDA, Conchita J.	(212)371-5188	974
	POLLARD, Bobbie T.	(212)725-7648	981
	POWELL, Timothy W.	(212)807-7083	989
	PRAGER, George A.	(212)725-3083	989
	PRAVER, Robin I.	(212)214-1720	990
	QUAIN, Julie R.		999
	RABER, Steven	(212)839-7161	1001
	RAUCH, Anne	(212)906-8794	1010
	RAUM, Tamar	(212)889-2156	1010
	REDEL, Judy A.	(212)337-7043	1014
	REID, Carolyn A.	(212)472-5919	1018
	ROHMANN, Gloria P.	(212)930-0576	1050
	ROSEN, Nathan A.	(212)873-1017	1055
	ROTHSTEIN, Pauline M.	(212)750-6008	1060

ONLINE SEARCHER (Cont'd)
NEW YORK (Cont'd)
New York

	ROZENE, Janette B.	(212)760-7265	1064
	RUBINSTEIN, Ed	(212)725-4550	1065
	SAYWARD, Nick H.	(212)573-4798	1087
	SCIOLINO, Elaine T.	(212)371-5900	1106
	SEGAL, Judith	(212)222-3699	1112
	SHAPIRO, Barbara G.	(212)621-1582	1121
	SHAPIRO, Fred R.	(203)432-1600	1121
	SMITH, Mark J.	(212)373-2401	1158
	SOROBAY, Roman T.	(212)878-9314	1169
	STEIN, Pamela H.	(212)586-0152	1185
	STEVENSON, Mata	(212)759-9883	1191
	TICKER, Susan L.	(212)787-2780	1244
	TOMASULO, Patricia A.	(212)472-6442	1249
	TYLER, David M.	(212)350-4679	1266
	VAN DYKE, Stephen H.	(212)340-0872	1275
	VELEZ, Sara B.	(212)870-1661	1281
	WITSENHAUSEN, Helen A.	(212)850-6050	1358
	WOO, Janice	(212)662-3534	1363
	WOODS, Lawrence J.	(212)736-6629	1367
Niagara University	BUDGE, William D.	(716)285-1212	155
North White Plains	SHADE, Ronald H.	(914)285-9583	1118
Oakdale	BEAUDRIE, Ronald A.	(516)244-3284	70
Old Brookville	HELLER, Jacqueline R.	(516)626-2700	524
Oneonta	ROUGEUX, Debora A.	(607)432-0290	1061
Patchogue	NEUFELD, Judith B.	(516)289-6813	897
Peekskill	FALCONE, Elena C.	(914)528-2820	362
Plattsburgh	RANSOM, Christina R.	(518)563-5719	1007
Pomona	HONOR, Naomi G.		556
Poughkeepsie	LEE, Judy A.	(914)473-3719	710
Queens	BUSTAMANTE, Corazon R.	(718)361-0887	166
Queens Village	HECKMAN, Lucy T.	(718)776-6285	519
Rensselaerville	STORMS, Kate	(518)797-5154	1198
Rochester	BLUM, Elaine G.	(716)423-1611	107
	DEGOLYER, Christine C.	(716)475-2520	288
	GIGLIOTTI, Mary J.	(716)254-0621	433
	GLASER, June E.	(716)275-5010	439
	HOOD, Katherine T.	(716)454-5293	556
	KATZ, Jacqueline E.	(716)254-7144	630
	MATZEK, Richard A.	(716)586-2525	786
	MCGOWAN, Kathleen M.	(716)275-4437	807
	REITANO, Maimie V.	(716)722-7067	1022
	ROSENBERG-NUGENT, Nanci B.		1056
	SOMERVILLE, Arleen N.	(716)275-4495	1167
	STOSS, Frederick W.	(716)436-8719	1198
Roslyn	WEINSTEIN, Judith K.	(516)627-6200	1318
Roslyn Harbor	CARTAFALSA, Joan C.	(516)671-7411	188
Rouses Point	CURRAN, George L.		266
Scarsdale	ABEND, Jody U.	(914)723-1360	2
	BERGER, Pam P.	(914)723-3156	86
	COAN, Mary L.	(914)723-5325	224
	SEULOWITZ, Lois	(914)472-4097	1117
Schenectady	HOLT, Lisa A.	(518)370-1811	554
Setauket	THOM, Janice E.	(516)751-1484	1235
Shrub Oak	TIFFEAULT, Alice A.	(914)528-4048	1244
Smithtown	BENNETT, James F.	(516)265-2037	81
Somers	BURROWS, Shirley	(914)767-7337	163
Sparkill	BARTH, John E.	(914)359-9500	61
	ZUBARIK, Therese	(914)359-7200	1390
Staten Island	DIMATTEO, Lucy A.	(718)698-7095	304
	KRIEGER, Tillie		678
	MANNING, Jo A.	(718)981-0120	766
	SVENNINGSEN, Karen L.	(718)987-1168	1212
Stony Brook	BAUM, Nathan J.	(516)632-7110	66
	WILLIAMS, Doris C.	(516)632-7152	1343
Syracuse	ABBOTT, George L.	(315)445-0484	1
	MCLAUGHLIN, Pamela W.	(315)476-7359	813
	PRICE, Susan W.	(315)423-2093	992
	REINSTEIN, Diana J.	(315)492-5500	1021
Troy	SUTHERLAND-NEHRING, Laurie A.	(518)273-0100	1211
Uniondale	BARTENBACH, Martha A.	(516)292-8920	60
Wantagh	SCHOENBAUM, Rhoda A.	(516)781-8000	1098
	WESTERMANN, Mary L.	(516)679-8842	1327
Webster	DESMOND, Andrew R.	(716)671-7657	295
	MUELLER, Leta A.	(716)422-3444	875
West Nyack	RIGNEY, Shirley A.	(914)578-7101	1034

ONLINE SEARCHER (Cont'd)
NEW YORK (Cont'd)

West Valley	CURRY, Lenora Y.	(716)942-4362	266
Westhampton	BARR, Janet L.	(516)288-5539	58
White Plains	DAVIES, Carol A.	(212)754-7438	277
	HOUGHTON, Joan I.	(914)335-7839	562
	MCELHANEY, William E.	(914)949-3270	804
	MCGARVEY, Eileen B.	(914)683-2794	805
Whitestone	RIECHEL, Rosemarie	(718)990-0714	1033
Williamsville	SCHUTT, Dedre A.	(716)633-6384	1103
Woodhaven	PAYNE, Linda C.	(718)849-1320	951
	VAZQUEZ, Edward	(718)296-2280	1280
Yonkers	BERGER, Paula E.	(914)968-7906	86

NORTH CAROLINA

Asheville	BUTSON, Linda C.	(704)254-2932	167
Belmont	MAYES, Susan E.	(704)825-3711	789
Boone	BUSBIN, O M.	(704)264-7141	164
	WISE, Mintron S.	(704)262-2823	1357
	WORRELL, Diane F.		1369
Broadway	CRANDALL, Elisabeth G.	(919)258-3553	255
Carrboro	DICKINSON, Gail K.		301
Cedar Grove	WRIGHT, Larry L.		1372
Chapel Hill	DICKERSON, Jimmy	(919)962-1188	300
	MATER, Dee A.	(919)962-0700	783
	MEEHAN-BLACK, Elizabeth C.		821
	METZGER, Eva C.	(919)929-4870	829
	TALBERT, David M.	(919)962-0700	1220
	TELFER, Margaret E.	(919)933-7563	1230
Charlotte	SUMMERFORD, Steven L.	(704)378-1032	1209
Cullowhee	DORR, Lorna B.		313
Durham	BARROWS, William D.	(919)549-0517	60
	BASEFSKY, Stuart M.	(919)684-2380	62
	BRUCE, Nancy G.	(919)490-0069	149
	CARRINGTON, Bessie M.	(919)684-2373	186
	FARKAS, Doina C.	(919)493-1890	364
	FEINGLOS, Susan J.	(919)493-2904	369
	HEBERT, Robert A.	(919)684-4087	519
	LAWTON, Patricia J.	(919)596-6364	705
	MIDDLETON, Beverly D.	(919)477-8497	833
	NYE, Julie B.	(919)471-1833	912
	PORTER, Katherine R.	(919)684-3004	985
	VARGHA, Rebecca B.	(919)544-6045	1278
Garner	RICHARDSON, Beverly S.		1029
Greensboro	LEVINSON, Catherine K.	(919)334-5419	721
	MOORE, Kathryn L.	(919)334-5419	860
	O'CONNOR, Sandra L.	(919)273-1914	916
	WRIGHT, Keith C.	(919)282-3712	1372
Greenville	DALTON, Lisa K.	(919)727-6533	271
	GLUCK, Myke H.	(919)757-6514	442
	SCOTT, Ralph L.	(919)830-0522	1108
Mebane	MINEIRO, Barbara E.	(919)578-4299	845
Raleigh	MURPHY, Malinda M.	(919)821-2072	881
	OSEGUEDA, Laura M.	(919)834-1024	927
	PURYEAR, Pamela E.	(919)737-2836	998
Research Triangle Pk	LAVOY, Constance J.	(919)549-2649	704
	THOMAS, Katharine S.	(919)541-8500	1237
Washington	TIMOUR, John A.	(919)975-3355	1246
Winston-Salem	EKSTRAND, Nancy L.	(919)765-4817	341
	MILLER, Barry K.	(919)777-5597	836
	RALPH, Randy D.	(919)788-4591	1004
	SIBLEY, Shawn C.	(919)777-3020	1135

NORTH DAKOTA

Bismarck	MOREHOUSE, Valerie J.	(701)224-4658	863
Valley City	HOLDEN, Douglas H.	(701)845-4940	550

OHIO

Akron	BRINK, David R.	(216)375-7224	136
	GUSS, Margaret B.	(216)375-7224	478
	HOLLIS, William F.	(216)798-4082	552
Ashland	ROEPKE, David E.		1048
Athens	HOUDEK, G R.	(614)593-5444	562
	KURZ, David B.	(614)593-8505	685
Bay Village	BUTCHER, Sharon L.	(216)871-0913	166
Bowling Green	ENDRES, Maureen D.	(419)352-9213	348
	ZAPOROZHETZ, Laurene E.	(419)354-2101	1386

ONLINE SEARCHER (Cont'd)
OHIO (Cont'd)

City	Name	Phone	No.
Canton	CLARK, Kay S.	(216)452-0665	217
	TERHUNE, R S.	(216)489-0800	1231
Cincinnati	ABRAMS, Roger E.	(513)821-5984	3
	BAKER, Carole A.	(513)871-2042	48
	CLASPER, James W.	(513)871-0969	219
	DAVIS, Yvonne M.	(513)221-7699	281
	DOBBS, David L.	(513)271-4827	307
	KRAMER, Sally J.	(513)369-6085	675
	LE BLANC, Judith E.		708
	LIPPERT, Margret G.	(513)821-8733	732
	ROSENTHAL, Francine C.	(513)825-4143	1057
	WILSON, Lucy	(513)745-4313	1351
Cleveland	BORUCKI, Jennifer A.	(216)696-1313	117
	DEAN, Winifred F.	(216)687-2373	284
	DORNER, Marian T.	(216)444-5697	313
	DZIEDZINA, Christine A.	(216)459-4313	331
	FINET, Scott	(216)687-2250	378
	JARABEK, Leona T.	(216)433-5767	594
	JOHNSON, Stephen C.	(216)429-8245	609
	MAHOVLIC, Leanne M.	(216)368-3646	761
	PETIT, J M.	(216)749-5052	965
	PRYSZLAK, Lydia M.	(216)459-2043	996
	SKUTNIK, John S.	(216)241-2141	1147
	STANLEY, Jean B.	(216)368-6596	1180
	TURNER, Freya A.	(216)581-6778	1264
	VICTORY, Karen M.	(216)696-1313	1283
Cleveland Heights	BOWIE, Angela B.	(216)291-5588	121
	DONNELLY, Kathleen	(216)381-9017	311
	PAUSLEY, Barbara H.	(216)932-2448	950
Columbus	BLOUGH, Keith A.	(614)221-4181	106
	BRANDT, Michael H.	(614)863-2814	128
	CHANG, Tony H.	(614)292-2664	201
	DALRYMPLE, Tamsen	(614)486-2109	271
	DAVIS, Linda M.	(614)294-5429	280
	ELWELL, Pamela M.		347
	EVANS, Shirley A.	(614)860-2496	358
	HODGES, Pauline R.	(614)421-3600	546
	HUNE, Mary G.	(614)224-3168	574
	HUNTER, James J.	(614)461-5039	576
	LINCOVE, David A.	(614)292-3480	728
	MCDOWELL, Judith H.	(614)771-0273	804
	MERCADO, Heidi	(614)292-2009	825
	MILLER, Dennis P.	(614)888-1886	837
	MIMNAUGH, Ellen N.	(614)486-7755	845
	MLYNAR, Mary	(614)486-7980	850
	MULARSKI, Carol A.	(614)292-9810	876
	OLSZEWSKI, Lawrence J.		923
	POPOVICH, Charles J.	(614)292-2136	984
	RATLIFF, Priscilla	(614)488-1622	1009
	SMITH, Ellen A.	(614)462-7054	1154
	SMITH, Noralee W.	(614)299-0453	1159
	WAGNER, Judith O.	(614)451-7471	1292
	WALDEN, Graham R.	(614)292-0938	1294
	WARNER, Susan B.	(614)424-5676	1305
	WILKS, Cheri L.	(614)253-3507	1341
Cuyahoga Falls	KLINGLER, Thomas E.	(216)923-5504	662
	OSTERFIELD, George T.	(216)929-9470	928
	WAGNER, Louis F.	(216)922-0681	1292
Dayton	MAXWELL, Marjo V.	(513)848-4069	788
	ROHMILLER, Ellen L.	(513)298-4508	1051
	SEXTON, Sally V.	(513)890-1421	1118
	TRIVEDI, Harish S.	(513)226-2201	1257
	WALKER, Mary A.	(513)229-3551	1296
Delaware	GILBERT, Donna J.	(614)369-7705	433
Dublin	BLANCHARD, Mark A.	(614)764-6000	103
	HURLEY, Geraldine C.	(614)764-6108	577
	MARSH, Elizabeth C.	(614)488-1942	773
Englewood	CUPP, Christian M.	(513)832-0136	265
Fairborn	BAKER, Narcissa L.	(573)879-3638	49
Findlay	DUDLEY, Durand S.	(419)423-1113	323
	LUST, Jeanette M.	(419)424-5739	749
Gahanna	WEITZ, Jay N.	(614)476-5489	1320
Granville	LEMON, Nancy A.	(614)587-7265	715
Kent	BOLEK, Ann D.	(216)678-9429	112
	GALLICCHIO, Virginia G.	(216)373-5608	414
Kettering	ROHMILLER, Thomas D.	(513)259-4543	1051

ONLINE SEARCHER (Cont'd)
OHIO (Cont'd)

City	Name	Phone	No.
Lakewood	JANES, Jodith	(216)221-0437	593
	KEATING, Michael F.	(216)221-0608	633
	TRIVISON, Donna	(216)221-9401	1257
Mansfield	BENISHEK, Kristine K.	(419)526-8515	81
Mayfield Heights	RASKIN, Rosa S.	(216)442-3009	1009
New Albany	HERB, Elizabeth D.	(614)855-7441	530
New Philadelphia	KOBULNICKY, Michael	(216)339-3391	666
Oberlin	GOULD, Allison L.	(216)775-8285	454
	RICKER, Alison S.	(216)775-8310	1031
Painesville	BRANCHICK, Susan E.	(216)357-3462	127
Richmond Heights	SIESS, Judith A.	(216)486-7443	1136
Rootstown	PORTER, Marlene A.	(216)325-2511	985
Shaker Heights	ENGLANDER, Marlene S.	(216)491-9277	349
	LANDAU, Lucille	(216)283-6109	692
	MCCONNELL, Pamela J.	(216)921-7457	798
South Euclid	BENSING, Karen M.	(216)932-0166	83
Springfield	MONTAG, John	(513)327-7019	855
Terrace Park	SEIK, Jo E.	(513)831-0780	1112
Toledo	WEILANT, Edward		1317
Troy	BAKER, Martha A.	(513)335-6397	49
Uniontown	CREELAN, Marilee M.	(216)699-4454	257
University Heights	HECHT, Joseph A.	(216)291-5506	519
Westchester	EMANI, Nirupama	(513)777-5264	347
Westerville	WILSON, Leigh K.	(614)898-3953	1351
Westlake	CHAMIS, Alice Y.	(216)777-2198	198
	GALLANT, Jennifer J.	(216)835-6020	414
Wooster	BRITTON, Constance J.	(216)264-8649	137
Yellow Springs	NEWMAN, Marianne L.		899

OKLAHOMA

City	Name	Phone	No.
Bartlesville	ROBIN, Annabeth	(918)336-7240	1043
Midwest City	MOSLEY, Thomas E.	(405)733-0922	872
Muskogee	GUTIERREZ, Carolyn A.	(918)687-6479	479
Norman	BATT, Fred	(405)325-4231	64
	POLAND, Jean A.	(405)360-7095	980
Oklahoma City	BOOTENHOFF, Rebecca J.	(405)728-7072	116
	CORNEIL, Charlotte E.	(405)235-7763	246
	JORSKI, Sharon D.	(405)636-7087	617
	ROACH, Eddie D.	(405)751-6400	1037
Shawnee	ALDRIDGE, Betsy B.		11
Stillwater	HILKER, Emerson W.	(405)624-6305	539
	HOLMES, Jill M.	(405)624-6542	553
Tahlequah	VEITH, Charles R.	(918)456-5511	1281
Tulsa	HACKER, Connie J.	(918)587-6561	481
	HILL, Linda L.	(918)584-0891	540
	MANES, Estelle L.	(918)582-7426	765
	SMITH, Donald R.	(918)592-6000	1154

OREGON

City	Name	Phone	No.
Beaverton	SLOAN, Maureen G.	(503)690-1060	1149
Eugene	FRANTZ, Paul A.	(503)342-5759	398
	GRAHAM, Deborah L.		456
	MCDANIELS, Patricia R.	(503)343-4728	801
Hillsboro	VIXIE, Anne C.	(503)645-0527	1286
Manzanita	LARSON, Signe E.	(503)368-6990	700
Milton-Freewater	SARGENT, Phyllis M.	(503)938-3724	1083
Portland	DAVID, Kay O.	(503)222-9981	276
	EDWARDS, Susan E.	(506)224-6812	338
	JUDKINS, Dolores Z.	(503)236-6743	619
	KENNEY, Ann J.	(503)297-1894	641
	OLSON-URLIE, Carolyn T.	(503)233-3242	923
	SHAVER, Donna B.	(503)226-8695	1123
	SIMON, Dale	(503)227-7617	1140
	SUDDUTH, Susan F.		1206
	WRIGHT, Janet K.	(503)464-4097	1371
Roseburg	JORDAN, Cathryn M.	(503)440-1000	616

PENNSYLVANIA

City	Name	Phone	No.
Alcoa Center	MOUNTS, Earl L.	(412)337-2396	873
Allentown	ANDEL, June	(215)395-5168	21
	BURYLO, Michelle A.	(215)481-7991	164
	IOBST, Barbara J.	(215)778-2263	583
	SWARTZ, Patrice B.	(215)797-5696	1214
Bala Cynwyd	BOWERS, Paul A.	(215)664-9644	120
Belle Vernon	KLEIN, Joanne S.	(412)929-8290	659
Bensalem	CHU, John S.	(215)639-0768	212
Bloomsburg	ROCKWOOD, Susan M.	(717)784-8456	1046

ONLINE SEARCHER (Cont'd)
PENNSYLVANIA (Cont'd)

Blue Bell	LAUTENSCHLAG, Elisabeth		
	C.		703
Broomall	CLINTON, Janet C.	(215)356-1927	222
California	CARUSO, Nicholas C.	(412)938-9166	190
Carbondale	MCNABB, Corrine R.	(717)282-3151	815
Carlisle	POE, Terrence C.	(717)245-1866	979
Center Square	SCHAEFER, John A.	(215)277-6386	1089
Center Valley	MCCABE, James P.	(215)282-1100	793
Chambersburg	MARLOW, Kathryn E.	(717)264-2382	772
Cheltenham	ELSHAMI, Ahmed M.	(215)635-3823	346
Chester	GOLDMAN, Richard	(215)876-7292	446
Clarion	DINGLE, Susan	(814)226-2271	304
Clifton Heights	WHITMAN, Mary L.		1333
Coatesville	BURTON, Mary L.	(215)383-0245	164
	KELLEY, John F.	(215)383-8147	636
Colwyn	THOMAS, Deborah A.	(215)522-1786	1236
Coraopolis	KASPERKO, Jean M.		629
Dalton	THOMAS, Scott E.	(717)563-2014	1238
Devon	PIECHNICK, Katarzyna M.	(215)964-9348	971
Dresher	FU, Clare S.	(215)641-1978	407
Easton	CRAWFORD, Gregory A.	(215)253-9459	256
Erie	HOWARD, Dianne D.	(814)868-3611	564
	LAURITO, Gerard P.	(814)871-7553	703
	RITTENHOUSE, Robert J.	(814)838-4124	1036
Franklin Center	CUTLER, Judith	(215)459-6932	268
	HOWLEY, Deborah H.	(215)459-7049	566
Friedens	KLINE, Eve P.	(814)443-2903	661
Gladwyne	FISHER, Daphne V.	(215)525-6628	380
Greensburg	BALAS, Janet L.	(412)836-4849	50
Harrisburg	CAPITANI, Cheryl A.	(717)782-5511	180
	LINGLE, Virginia A.	(717)652-1950	730
Hershey	ULINCY, Loretta D.	(717)531-8634	1268
	WOOD, M S.	(717)531-8630	1364
	WOODRUFF, William M.	(717)534-5106	1366
Jenkintown	SEVY, Barbara S.	(215)884-8275	1117
Johnstown	BRICE, Heather W.	(814)539-8153	134
	WILSON, Fred L.	(814)288-3363	1351
Kennerdell	CHERESNOWSKI, Linda M.	(814)385-6896	206
King of Prussia	RICH, Denise A.	(215)935-7054	1027
Langhorne	BLACK, Dorothy M.	(215)752-5800	101
Lansdale	BLAUERT, Mary A.	(215)822-2929	105
	NOLAN, Joan	(215)368-9800	907
Lehigh Valley	WEBER, A C.	(215)837-9615	1313
Malvern	QUINTILIANO, Barbara		1000
Mars	JOSEPH, Patricia A.	(412)776-9249	617
Marysville	RICHARDSON, Alice W.	(717)957-3808	1029
McKeesport	HERRON, Nancy L.	(412)675-9111	533
Mechanicsburg	TENOR, Randell B.	(717)763-1804	1231
Mercer	ELY, Betty L.	(412)662-2543	347
Merion	HAAS, Carol C.	(215)664-1689	480
Millersville	JUDGE, Joseph M.	(717)872-7590	619
Monroeville	BERGER, Lewis W.	(412)825-2284	85
Natrona Heights	HAUGH, Amy J.	(412)224-5004	512
New Holland	MCGEE, Yvonne M.		806
New Kensington	TEOLIS, Marilyn G.	(412)339-0255	1231
Philadelphia	AZZOLINA, David S.	(215)898-8118	43
	BERWICK, Mary C.	(215)898-4112	91
	BOWDEN, Gail L.	(215)574-4417	120
	CLEVELAND, Susan E.	(215)662-2577	221
	COOPER, Linda	(215)625-4719	243
	DONOVAN, Judith G.	(215)928-0577	312
	EVEY, Patricia G.	(215)848-3016	359
	FISHMAN, Lee H.	(215)564-3521	381
	GREEN, Patricia L.	(215)724-5715	462
	HELLER, Patricia A.	(215)625-4720	524
	HOLMES, John H.	(215)592-1841	553
	HOLUB, Joseph C.	(215)843-6220	555
	HORNIG-ROHAN, James E.	(215)848-0554	560
	LEVIN, Pauline G.	(215)561-5831	720
	LIGHTNER, Karen J.	(215)387-8663	727
	MARVIN, Stephen G.	(215)895-1874	780
	MEREDITH, Phyllis C.	(609)757-4640	825
	MOWERY, Susan G.	(215)248-8206	874
	MYERS, Charles J.	(215)898-7267	884
	NISTA, Ann S.	(215)728-2711	905
	PITCHON, Cindy A.	(215)235-4486	976
	PROCTOR, David J.	(215)893-5128	994
	RAINEY, Nancy B.	(215)596-8967	1004

ONLINE SEARCHER (Cont'd)
PENNSYLVANIA (Cont'd)

Philadelphia	ROEDELL, Ray F.	(215)739-7739	1048
	SCHAEFFER, Judith E.	(215)843-8840	1089
	SMITH, Linda D.	(215)963-3670	1157
	YERGER, George A.	(215)587-4887	1379
Pittsburgh	AL SADAT, Amira A.	(412)421-9444	17
	ARJONA, Sandra K.	(412)821-2263	31
	BOUTWELL, Barbara J.	(412)967-3131	119
	DOW, Elizabeth H.		315
	EPSTEIN, Barbara A.	(412)624-2378	351
	FITZGERALD, Patricia A.	(412)268-2428	382
	FUCHS, Karola M.		408
	HODGSON, Cynthia A.	(412)374-4816	546
	JOHNSTON, Bruce A.	(412)731-8800	610
	KERCHOF, Kathryn K.	(412)434-6000	643
	KIRCHER, Linda M.	(412)624-9444	654
	PAUL, Suzanne	(412)624-0418	949
	ROSEN, Gloria K.	(412)363-8423	1055
	ROSS, Nina M.	(412)624-9475	1058
	STERLING, Alida B.	(412)323-1430	1189
	WESSEL, Charles B.	(412)731-8800	1325
Reading	IZZO, Kathleen A.	(215)373-2981	586
Sanatoga	NIPPERT, Carolyn C.	(215)323-4829	904
Sarver	LIVENGOOD, Candice C.		734
Scranton	BABISH, Jo A.	(717)963-2145	43
	CAMPION, Carol M.	(717)348-0538	177
Shenandoah	USES, Ann K.	(717)462-0076	1270
Shippensburg	SHONTZ, Marilyn L.	(717)532-1472	1132
Somerset	PLASO, Kathy A.	(814)445-6501	977
Spring House	WICKS, Pamela J.	(215)628-5632	1335
Springfield	STESIS, Karen R.	(215)328-8749	1189
State College	CARR, Caryn J.	(814)234-4203	185
	MURPHY, Charles G.	(814)865-6621	880
	PIERCE, Miriam D.	(814)237-7004	971
Tamaqua	EVERHART, Nancy L.	(717)668-3334	358
University Park	CONKLING, Thomas W.	(814)865-3451	236
	SULZER, John H.	(814)865-4861	1209
	SWEENEY, Del	(814)863-3952	1215
	WESTERMAN, Melvin E.	(814)863-2898	1327
Villanova	WEINER, Betty	(215)688-6950	1318
Wayne	ANTOS, Brian F.	(215)254-0754	29
	CRAUMER, Patricia A.	(215)687-6777	255
	DRIEHAUS, Rosemary H.		320
Waynesboro	POSEY, Sussann F.	(717)762-3047	985
Wescosville	FISLER, Charlotte D.	(215)395-6400	382
West Chester	DINNIMAN, Margo P.	(215)430-3080	305
	MILES, Donald D.	(215)431-7685	834
West Point	MESSICK, Karen J.	(215)661-6026	828
Wilkes-Barre	ERDICK, Joseph W.	(717)824-3725	352
	TYCE, Richard	(717)826-1148	1266
Wyomissing	MORGANTI, Deena J.	(215)320-4849	864

PUERTO RICO

Hato Rey	NEGRON-GAZTAMBIDE,		
	Olguita	(809)767-4192	892
Hormiguerow	MARTINEZ-NAZARIO,		
	Ronaldo		779
Ponce	GUILLEMARD DE COLON,		
	Teresita		476
San Juan	MAURA-SARDO, Mariano A.	(809)764-0000	787
	RODRIGUEZ, Ketty		1048
Santurce	RIVERA-ALVAREZ, Miguel A.	(809)728-4191	1037
Trujillo Alto	SABATER-SOLA, Rigel		1072

RHODE ISLAND

Kingston	ETCHINGHAM, John B.	(401)792-4637	355
	KRAUSSE, Sylvia C.	(401)789-6882	676
	SCHNEIDER, Stewart P.	(401)792-2878	1097
	SIEBURTH, Janice F.	(401)792-2640	1135
	SIITONEN, Leena M.	(401)792-2878	1137
North Kingstown	OTTAVIANO, Doris B.	(401)295-0361	930
Pawtucket	MILLS, Catherine H.	(401)728-9112	843
Providence	BRENNAN, Patricia B.	(401)456-8125	133
	FARK, Ronald K.	(401)941-0086	364
	HENDERSON, Linda L.	(401)277-7887	526
	LLOYD, Lynn A.	(401)457-3001	735
	SHERIDAN, Jean	(401)277-3818	1127
Smithfield	CAMERON, Constance B.	(401)232-6299	174

ONLINE SEARCHER (Cont'd)

SOUTH CAROLINA

Charleston	ANDERSON, Marcia	(803)792-2371	24
	SCHMITT, John P.	(803)792-8014	1096
Clemson	HIPPS, Gary M.	(803)654-3934	543
	LYLE, Martha E.	(803)656-5185	751
	MCCULLEY, P M.	(803)654-8753	800
Columbia	CHOI, Jin M.	(803)799-8786	210
	CROSS, Joseph R.	(803)777-3365	260
	GABLE, Sarah H.	(803)733-3344	411
	HOLLEY, E J.	(803)774-4866	551
	KINTNER, Susan B.	(803)771-4077	653
	KRONENFELD, Michael R.	(803)734-4769	679
Florence	MARTIN, Neal A.	(803)661-1310	777
Greenville	TOWELL, Fay J.	(803)232-2941	1252
Greenwood	HILL, Thomas W.	(803)227-4851	541
Rock Hill	SILVERMAN, Susan M.	(803)323-2131	1139

SOUTH DAKOTA

Brookings	HALLMAN, Clark N.	(605)688-5572	489
Madison	COOK, Nancy E.	(605)256-4709	240
	SMITH, Rise L.	(605)256-5319	1160
Pierre	HILMOE, Deann D.	(605)224-3178	541
Rapid City	HAMILTON, Patricia J.	(605)341-7101	492
Vermillion	JENSEN, Mary B.	(605)677-5259	599
	SPRULES, Marcia L.	(605)624-6764	1176

TENNESSEE

Antioch	HAMLIN, Lisa K.	(615)833-7541	493
Bristol	HERRING, Mark Y.	(615)968-9449	533
Clarksville	CARLIN, Don	(615)648-2095	182
Germantown	COOPER, Ellen R.	(901)755-7411	242
	RONDESTVEDT, Helen F.	(901)756-5470	1053
Johnson City	CONVERY, Sukhont K.	(615)926-3717	239
	NORRIS, Carol B.	(615)929-5345	909
Kingsport	ERWIN, Mary J.	(615)378-5273	353
	PRESLAR, M G.	(615)229-6117	991
Knoxville	CROWTHER, Karmen N.	(615)974-4171	262
	HILL, Ruth J.	(615)974-4381	540
	LEACH, Sandra S.	(615)579-1315	706
	PONNAPPA, Biddanda P.	(615)675-4545	982
	SAMMATARO, Linda J.	(615)521-7750	1078
	VIERA, Ann R.	(615)974-4171	1284
Memphis	BAKER, Bonnie U.	(901)324-6536	48
	BELLAMY, Lois M.	(901)528-5155	77
	BOAZ, Ruth L.	(901)682-0595	108
	GIVENS, Mary K.	(901)528-5166	439
	MABBOTT, Deborah D.	(901)388-1096	753
	MADER, Sharon B.	(901)454-2208	759
	PARK, Elizabeth H.	(901)454-2208	941
Nashville	ARMONTROUT, Brian A.	(615)320-3678	32
	BORRELLI, Barbara A.	(615)244-5270	117
	CHEN, Helen M.	(612)251-1417	205
	MOON, Fletcher F.	(615)833-1125	857
	PATTERSON, Jennifer J.	(615)383-4251	948
	STEFFEY, Ramona J.	(615)662-0438	1185
	WATTS, Adalyn	(615)321-1332	1310
	WILBURN, Clouse R.	(615)322-8050	1338
Oak Ridge	EKKEBUS, Allen E.	(615)574-5485	341
	MCDONALD, Ethel Q.	(615)482-5011	802
	YALCINTAS, Rana	(615)482-9397	1376
Palmyra	FOWLER, James W.	(615)647-4172	393

TEXAS

Abilene	ANDERSON, Madeleine J.	(915)674-2344	24
	SPECHT, Alice W.	(915)677-7281	1172
Alpine	SPEARS, Norman L.	(915)837-8121	1172
Amarillo	NEELEY, Dana M.	(806)354-5447	891
Arlington	MCCLURE, Margaret R.	(817)275-6594	797
	WILKERSON, Judith C.	(817)795-6555	1339
Austin	HARMON, Jacqueline B.	(512)343-0978	502
	MCCANN, Charlotte P.		793
	PARKER, David F.	(512)450-1931	941
	PELOQUIN, Margaret I.		955
	TRANFAGLIA, Twyla L.	(512)472-8800	1254
	WILLIAMS, Suzi	(512)451-3482	1346
Baytown	NEWMAN, Robert M.	(713)425-2475	899
Bellaire	HOLAB-ABELMAN, Robin S.		550
	HOPKINS, Joyce A.	(713)667-3760	558
Boerne	HANKS, Ellen T.	(512)249-9670	496

ONLINE SEARCHER (Cont'd)

TEXAS (Cont'd)

Brownsville	VAUGHN, Frances A.	(512)544-8220	1280
Bryan	THOMAS, Barbara C.	(409)774-1273	1236
Cedar Park	MITTAG, Erika	(512)259-0569	850
College Station	BROWN-WEBB, Deborah D.	(409)845-1636	149
	RHOLES, Julia M.	(409)845-1952	1026
Corpus Christi	HOUSTON, Barbara B.	(512)889-8517	563
Cypress	KUJOORY, Parvin	(713)890-7542	683
Dallas	BARRETT, Carol A.	(214)969-8499	59
	CAMPBELL, Shirley A.	(214)330-0027	177
	CLEE, June E.	(214)941-3375	220
	COMPTON, Erlinda R.	(214)506-3601	235
	DOBSON, Christine B.	(214)746-3646	307
	GALBRAITH, Paula L.	(214)680-3782	413
	HAWLEY, Laurie J.	(214)907-2940	514
	HOPKINS, Terry F.	(214)969-8499	558
	JARVIS, Mary E.	(214)337-2615	595
	KANE, Deborah A.	(214)247-1952	624
	KERWIN, Camillus A.	(214)742-7201	644
	MALCOLM, Jane B.	(214)307-8355	762
	METIVIER, Donna M.	(214)701-4222	828
	MITCHE, Cynthia R.	(214)692-6767	848
	MITCHELL, Cynthia R.	(214)692-6767	848
	SHAPLEY, Ellen M.	(214)692-6407	1122
	UDENYL, Evelyn U.		1267
Edinburg	TINSMAN, William A.	(512)383-2008	1246
El Paso	BROWN, Susan W.	(915)747-5678	147
	KNOTT, Teresa L.	(915)533-3020	665
	LABODDA, Marsha J.	(915)859-1956	686
Fort Worth	RICE, Ralph A.	(817)626-7995	1027
	WESTBROOK, Brenda S.	(817)831-7232	1326
Freeport	TYLER-WHITE, Patricia G.		1266
Galveston	WYGANT, Alice C.		1375
Groves	MCCONNELL, Karen S.	(409)963-1481	797
Houston	BAGHAL-KAR, Vali E.	(213)667-4336	45
	BEAN, Norma P.	(713)527-7147	69
	BRUNNER, A M.	(713)463-0416	151
	BUTLER, Marguerite L.	(713)726-9244	166
	CALDWELL, Marlene	(713)661-5787	172
	CEBRUN, Mary J.	(713)945-4045	196
	DAVIS, Sara	(713)669-2426	281
	FLESHMAN, Nancy A.	(713)552-2000	384
	FORD, Margaret C.	(713)527-8101	389
	HUNTER, John H.	(713)527-4800	576
	LYDEN, Edward W.	(713)777-8212	750
	MAGNER, Mary F.	(713)870-7011	759
	MCCANN, Debra W.	(713)691-0148	794
	MULLINS, James R.	(713)522-8131	878
	SUDENGA, Sara A.	(713)527-8101	1206
	WEGMANN, Pamela A.	(713)655-3400	1316
	WILSON, Thomas C.	(713)995-8401	1353
	WORCHEL, Harris M.	(713)956-7361	1368
Huntsville	HOFFMAN, Frank W.	(409)294-1152	548
Irving	OGDEN, William S.	(214)255-3470	918
	WHITE, Lely K.	(214)721-5310	1331
Katy	POWELL, Alan D.	(713)392-9340	987
Lewisville	TALLEY, Pat L.	(214)434-2545	1221
Lubbock	MARLEY, Judith L.	(806)799-3299	772
	WARD, Deborah H.	(806)743-2209	1303
Mesquite	GIBSON, Timothy T.	(214)289-2479	432
Midland	MIRANDA, Cecilia	(915)685-4557	847
Miles	LACY, Yvonne M.	(915)468-2151	687
Plano	ANDERSON, Margaret	(214)424-2013	24
	PROKESH, Jane	(214)754-6461	995
Richardson	HENEBRY, Carolyn L.	(214)690-2914	528
	MARTIN, Irmgarde D.	(214)231-6121	776
	SCHRAEDER, Diana C.	(214)386-6164	1099
	SHEA, Kathleen	(214)690-2960	1124
Rockwall	HULSE, Phyllis	(214)722-4598	573
San Antonio	BELL, Joy A.	(512)496-2057	77
	HEWINS, Elizabeth H.	(512)655-4672	535
	HOLLOWAY, Geraldine B.	(512)531-3335	552
	LANG, Anita E.	(512)684-5111	695
	NOLAN, Christopher W.	(512)736-7429	907
	O'DONOGHUE, Patrice	(512)681-1207	917
	PEDERSEN, Wayne A.	(512)641-4561	954
Spring	ATRI, Pushkala V.	(713)370-3673	38
Temple	TIME, Ming M.	(817)778-5556	1245
The Woodlands	WEST, Deborah C.	(713)367-6201	1326

ONLINE SEARCHER (Cont'd)
TEXAS (Cont'd)

Tyler	LAMBERTH, Linda E.	(214)595-3481	690
Universal City	FRIDLEY, Bonnie J.	(512)658-8473	403
Waco	SHARP, Avery T.	(817)755-1366	1122
Wichita Falls	GRIMES, John F.	(817)855-0463	470
Wimberley	FELSTED, Carla M.	(512)847-5277	370
	SHAW, Ben B.	(512)847-2776	1123

UTAH

Farmington	POLLARD, Louise	(801)451-5282	981
North Salt Lake	YANG, Basil P.	(801)295-0276	1377
Provo	LAMB, Connie	(801)378-5627	689
Salt Lake City	ELLEFSEN, David	(801)943-4636	343
	HEYER, Terry L.	(801)321-1054	535
	HINDMARSH, Douglas P.	(801)328-2609	542
	JENSEN, Charla J.	(801)533-5250	598
	MARCHANT, Cathy	(801)364-8399	768
	NOEL, Eileen V.	(801)594-6182	907
	PARTRIDGE, Cathleen F.	(801)277-3486	945
	PATTERSON, Myron B.	(801)581-7265	948
	REED, Vernon M.	(801)531-3377	1015
	SKIDMORE, Kerry F.		1146
	STODDART, Joan M.	(801)272-2749	1196

VERMONT

Bennington	PRICE, Michael L.	(802)442-9051	992
Burlington	ABAZARNIA, Diane B.	(802)864-5751	1
	WEINSTOCK, Joanna S.	(802)656-4376	1318
Essex Junction	LAPIDOW, Amy R.	(802)878-2665	697
Milton	SEKERAK, Robert J.		1113
Northfield	WARD, Robert C.	(802)485-7344	1304
Woodstock	DICENSO, Jacquelyn C.	(802)457-1317	300

VIRGIN ISLANDS

St Thomas	MILLER, Veronica E.	(809)774-0059	843

VIRGINIA

Alexandria	AUSTON, Ione	(703)549-4325	40
	DRUMMOND, Louis E.		321
	HARRISTON, Victoria R.	(203)642-5382	507
	OMARA, Marie T.	(703)960-3981	923
	STEIN, Karen E.	(703)354-3154	1185
	VAROUTSOS, Mary A.	(703)836-0156	1279
	WANG, Ann C.	(703)751-4536	1302
	WOODWARD, Lawrence W.	(703)751-9426	1368
Annandale	MCGINN, Ellen T.	(703)280-5085	806
Arlington	BETTS, Ardith M.	(703)524-8384	92
	CAPUTO, Anne S.	(703)534-3433	180
	CAPUTO, Richard P.	(703)553-8455	180
	COSKEY, Rosemary B.		248
	DENNIE, David L.	(703)685-0208	292
	JOACHIM, Robert J.	(703)920-7721	600
	KNOBLOCH, Shirley S.	(703)532-2598	665
	LARMOUR, Rosamond E.	(703)247-7820	698
	MCKENNEY, Linda S.	(703)247-7829	811
	SAUR, Cindy S.	(703)379-2575	1085
	STARR, Marian U.	(703)237-0285	1182
Blacksburg	HINKLE, Mary R.	(703)951-1657	542
	KOK, Victoria T.	(703)951-3203	669
Burke	GOUDREAU, Ronald A.	(703)569-0994	454
	TOSIANO, Barbara A.		1252
Charlottesville	BADER, Susan G.	(804)973-2397	44
	CAHILL, Linda J.	(804)296-5676	171
	HURD, Douglas P.	(804)293-7358	577
	LOY, Dennis C.	(804)973-3410	745
Chesapeake	KERSTETTER, Virginia M.	(804)483-6544	644
Christiansburg	LINN, Cynthia S.	(703)961-5988	731
Dale City	MARTIN, Elaine R.	(703)680-0164	776
Falls Church	BROWN, Barbara B.	(703)820-7450	142
	CHUNG, Catherine A.	(703)534-3114	213
	REID, Judith P.	(703)379-0739	1018
Harrisonburg	GILL, Gerald L.	(703)568-6898	435
	RAMSEY, Inez L.	(703)568-6791	1006
Herndon	PAVEK, C C.	(703)481-0711	950
	SINWELL, Carol A.	(703)689-0086	1144
Lexington	DANFORD, Robert E.	(703)463-8657	272
	GREFE, Richard F.	(703)463-8648	465
	HOLLY, Janet S.		552
Manassas	CHRISTOLON, Blair B.	(703)369-3535	212

ONLINE SEARCHER (Cont'd)
VIRGINIA (Cont'd)

McLean	CHEVERIE, Joan F.	(703)893-3889	207
	MACEWEN, Virginia B.		755
	MORISSEAU, Anne L.	(703)821-9171	865
	WINIARSKI, Marilee E.	(800)421-7229	1355
Melian	BELTON, Jennifer H.		78
Newport News	DANIEL, Mary H.	(804)599-7245	272
	HAMMOND, Theresa M.	(804)595-8179	494
Norfolk	JONES-TRENT, Bernice R.	(804)632-8873	616
Reston	JENSEN, Raymond A.	(703)648-6820	599
	KARRER, Jonathan K.	(703)648-4302	628
	MCCLAIN, Deborah C.	(703)689-5194	795
	MCLANE, Kathleen	(703)620-3660	813
	WARD, Carol T.	(703)860-5664	1303
	WILTSHIRE, Denise A.	(703)391-0505	1354
Richmond	CLEMANS, Margaret H.	(804)358-9379	220
	DEBARDELEBEN, Marian Z.	(804)274-2876	284
	GREGORY, Carla L.	(804)281-2804	466
	JOHNSON, Jane W.	(804)257-1112	605
	MOSER, Emily F.	(804)355-3348	870
	SARTAIN, Sara M.		1083
	SOUTHWICK, Margaret A.	(804)274-2661	1170
	THOMAS, Mary E.	(804)786-0823	1237
	VAN SICKLEN, Lindsay L.	(804)320-9691	1277
	WILLS, Luella G.	(804)233-7616	1349
	ZANG, Patricia J.	(804)226-5712	1386
Roanoke	CALHOUN, Clayne M.	(703)981-2268	172
	SEAMANS, Nancy H.	(703)985-8508	1109
Springfield	FOURNIER, Susan K.	(703)569-9468	393
	ROARK, Robin D.	(703)644-7372	1038
Vienna	COCHRANE, Maryjane S.	(703)938-2037	226
Virginia Beach	WELSH, Eric L.	(804)424-7000	1323

WASHINGTON

Auburn	GOLDSTEIN, Cynthia N.	(206)931-3018	446
Bainbridge Island	SPEARMAN, Marie A.	(206)842-6636	1172
Bellevue	SMART, Doris M.	(206)822-8435	1151
Bellingham	ANDERSEN, Eileen	(206)676-6481	21
	GROVER, Iva S.	(206)671-3643	474
	JOHNSON, Dana E.	(206)734-3941	603
	SYMES, Dal S.		1217
Bremerton	KANNEL, Selma	(206)377-3911	625
Custer	HASELBAUER, Kathleen J.	(206)366-5063	510
East Wenatchee	BELT, Jane		78
Everett	VAN DYKE, Ruth L.	(206)335-2406	1275
Federal Way	WILSON, Anthony M.	(206)839-0496	1349
Kirkland	ROBERTSON, Ann	(206)821-0506	1041
Lacey	WIEMAN, Jean M.	(206)491-4700	1336
Pullman	FISHER, Rita C.	(509)335-2671	381
	NOFSINGER, Mary M.	(509)335-8950	907
	VYHNANEK, Louis	(509)332-3723	1290
Richland	CARVER, Sue A.	(509)943-5478	191
	FOLEY, Katherine M.	(509)943-9117	387
	SAMPLE, Charles R.	(509)376-1506	1078
Seattle	AUSTIN, Martha L.	(206)543-2988	40
	BURKE, Vivienne C.	(206)522-0478	160
	BURSON, Scott F.	(206)543-6794	163
	CRANDALL, Michael D.	(206)633-2530	255
	EIPERT, Susan L.	(206)522-3174	340
	GRIPPO, Christopher F.		471
	HARMALA, Amy A.	(206)632-8338	502
	HAZELTON, Penelope A.	(206)543-4089	517
	HENSLEY, Randall B.	(206)543-2060	529
	JEWELL, Timothy D.	(206)524-8820	600
	KREPS, Lise E.	(206)527-2817	678
	LIPTON, Laura E.	(206)543-8616	732
	LOPEZ, Loretta K.	(206)526-1728	741
	MAIOLI, Jerry R.	(206)459-6518	762
	MCFADDEN, Denyse I.	(206)284-6280	804
	PRESS, Nancy O.	(206)367-6568	991
	PRESTON, Deirdre R.	(206)283-0754	991
	REDALJE, Susanne J.	(206)543-2070	1013
	ROWBERG, Alan H.	(206)548-6250	1062
	SCHUELLER, Janette H.	(206)543-8262	1101
	SLIVKA, Enid M.	(206)723-4846	1149
	STOCK, Carole G.	(206)325-8364	1195
	TURNER, Tamara A.	(216)325-9481	1265
Spokane	PRINGLE, Robert M.	(509)325-6139	993

ONLINE SEARCHER (Cont'd)

WASHINGTON (Cont'd)

Tacoma	GILDENHAR, Janet		434
	JONES, Faye E.	(206)564-9254	613
	MENANTEAUX, A R.	(206)591-2973	823
	RICIGLIANO, Lorraine M.		1031
Walla Walla	BREIT, Anitra D.		132
Yakima	JORDAN, Sharon L.	(509)248-4522	617

WEST VIRGINIA

Charleston	BEHR, Alice S.		75
Clarksburg	GREATHOUSE, Brenda J.	(304)624-9649	461
Cross Lanes	COOPER, Candace S.	(304)776-5945	242
Glenville	VERMA, Prem V.	(304)462-5303	1282
Huntington	REENSTJERNA, Frederick R.	(304)523-9651	1016
Morgantown	ESKRIDGE, Virginia C.	(304)293-5300	354
	SHILL, Harold B.	(304)292-3762	1130

WISCONSIN

Appleton	BAYORGEON, Mary M.	(414)738-2325	68
	DAWSON, Terry P.	(414)735-6168	282
Beloit	THOM, Pat A.	(608)365-3311	1235
Green Bay	JOBELIUS, Nancy L.	(414)497-7508	601
Hales Corners	BARLOGA, Carolyn J.	(414)425-0355	57
Kenosha	TRUPIANO, Rose M.	(414)553-2143	1259
Kewaunee	ECKERT, Daniel L.	(414)388-2176	335
La Crosse	ACCARDI, Joseph J.	(608)784-5755	3
	CIMPL, Kathleen A.	(608)785-0530	214
Lake Geneva	CIBOCH, Lorraine A.	(414)245-5806	214
Madison	BEHNKE, Charles	(608)244-3253	75
	CONNER, P Z.	(608)256-4440	237
	JEFFCOTT, Janet B.	(608)246-6633	596
	LAESSIG, Joan M.	(608)238-3705	687
	MCCLEMENTS, Nancy A.	(608)263-4934	796
	SCHARMER, Roger C.	(608)264-5711	1090
	WHITEMARSH, Thomas R.	(608)222-3478	1333
	WILCOX, Patricia F.	(608)263-4414	1338
	XIA, Hong	(608)263-5624	1376
Marshfield	ZIMMERMANN, Albert J.	(715)387-2418	1389
Menasha	DIETZ, Kathryn A.	(414)725-2803	302
Mequon	AMAN, Mary J.	(414)242-9031	19
	NOVOTNY, Lynn E.	(414)241-8957	911
Milwaukee	DETWILER, Eve N.	(414)332-3367	296
	EUKEY, Jim O.		356
	FONG, Wilfred W.	(414)229-4707	388
	GILLETTE, Meredith	(414)351-3501	435
	MENITOVE, Symie D.	(414)225-2601	824
	MURPHY, Virginia A.	(414)271-1444	881
	SCHLUGE, Vicki L.	(414)527-8477	1094
	SMITH-GREENWOLD, Kathryn R.	(414)445-3586	1162
	STRUBE, Kathleen	(414)257-8326	1203
	SWEETLAND, James H.	(414)963-9996	1215
Oshkosh	PARKS, Dennis H.	(414)426-4800	943
Racine	TERANIS, Mara	(414)631-4144	1231
Ripon	BURR, Charlotte A.	(414)748-3244	163
River Falls	ADAM, Anthony J.	(715)425-5383	4
Whitewater	MANDERNACK, Scott B.	(414)473-4341	765

WYOMING

Cheyenne	SCHELL, Catherine L.	(307)637-7504	1091
Lander	HEUER, Jane T.	(307)332-3793	535
Laramie	JACKSON, Sue H.	(307)742-2141	588

CANADA

ALBERTA

Airdrie	WAUGH, Alan L.	(403)948-7921	1310
Calgary	GUNSON, Murray J.	(403)256-7327	478
	LANE, Barbara K.	(403)283-9998	694
	STEVELMAN, Sharon R.	(403)271-0134	1190
Edmonton	DELONG, Kathleen M.	(403)432-5951	290
	FETTERMAN, Nelma I.	(403)432-3813	374
	JORDAN, Peter A.	(403)469-9473	616
	KUJANSUU, Sylvia S.	(403)435-1563	683
	LAVKULICH, Joanne	(403)427-3530	704
	STARR, Lea K.	(403)432-5154	1182
Lethbridge	DROESSLER, Judith B.	(403)381-2285	320
Red Deer	ARMSTRONG, Mary L.	(403)346-4491	32
Sherwood Pk	NOGA, Dolores A.	(403)467-4003	907

ONLINE SEARCHER (Cont'd)

ALBERTA (Cont'd)

| Tofield | LEE, Diana W. | (403)662-3607 | 709 |

BRITISH COLUMBIA

Vancouver	AUFIERO, Joan I.	(604)325-2317	39
	CHAN, Diana L.	(604)224-8470	199
	PEPPER, David A.	(604)664-4311	958
	WARREN, Lois M.	(604)687-1072	1306
Victoria	ROMANIUK, Elena	(604)592-8819	1052
	VAN REENEN, Johannes A.	(604)595-9612	1277

MANITOBA

Winnipeg	COVVEY, H D.	(204)942-5335	252
	FOWLER, Margaret A.	(204)884-6593	394
	MARSHALL, Kenneth E.	(204)269-3243	774
	ROUTLEDGE, Patricia A.	(204)474-9445	1062
	TULLY, Sharon I.	(204)474-9844	1262

NEW BRUNSWICK

| Riverview | ENNS, Carol F. | (506)386-1084 | 350 |

NOVA SCOTIA

Halifax	BANFIELD, Eilzabeth S.	(902)421-4570	54
	HUANG, Paul T.	(902)454-5911	568
	PARIS, Terrence L.	(902)443-4450	940

ONTARIO

Aqimeont	JAGIELLOWICZ, Jadzia	(410)492-8341	591
Deep River	LEWIS, Leslie	(613)584-2605	723
Downsview	BERNSTEIN, Elaine S.	(416)638-1962	89
	JONES, B E.	(416)244-3621	611
Fort Erie	PORTEUS, Andrew C.	(416)871-3814	985
Guelph	PAL, Gabriel	(519)824-4120	935
Haliburton	HOBBS, Kathleen M.		545
Hamilton	BROWNRIDGE, James R.	(416)572-2981	149
	FLEMMING, Tom	(416)525-9140	384
Kingston	FORKES, David	(613)544-2630	390
London	LIN, Louise	(519)439-3271	727
	PARR, John R.	(519)439-3271	943
	RUTHERFORD, Frederick S.	(519)471-4867	1070
Mississauga	ATHA, Shirley A.	(416)822-5704	37
	GALTON, Gwen	(416)823-9040	415
	WEI, Carl K.	(416)822-4111	1316
North York	CROXFORD, Agnes M.	(416)493-4188	262
Ottawa	ARONSON, Marcia L.		34
	BREGAINT, Bernard J.	(613)741-0242	131
	FOX, Rosalie	(613)232-4358	395
	JESKE, Margo	(613)995-1118	600
	KANNEL, Ene	(819)994-7966	625
	KARCICH, Grant J.	(416)723-6068	627
	LEBRUN, Anne	(613)725-6277	708
	LEUNG, Frank F.	(613)994-6920	719
	MACDONALD, Marcia H.	(819)994-6947	754
	MACDONALD, Patricia A.	(819)997-7066	754
	SCHNEIDER, Tatiana	(613)564-2640	1097
	SCHRYER, Michel J.	(819)994-6827	1100
	TAYLOR, Margaret P.	(613)232-6172	1227
	VEEKEN, Mary L.	(613)523-2169	1280
Sault Ste Marie	BAZILLION, Richard J.	(705)949-4352	68
Shelburne	LA CHAPELLE, Jennifer R.	(519)925-2672	686
Sudbury	GOSS, Alison M.	(705)522-2883	453
Toronto	ARMSTRONG, Jennifer E.	(416)466-8089	32
	DAVEY, Dorothy M.	(416)486-0377	276
	DYSART, Jane I.	(416)974-2780	331
	FAIR, Linda A.	(416)369-2438	361
	FRIEDLAND, Frances K.	(416)789-0741	403
	FRITZ, Richard J.	(416)923-0890	405
	GOLD, Sandra	(416)782-7236	444
	GRANATSTEIN, M E.	(416)978-6654	457
	JOHNSON, John E.	(416)423-6979	606
	MARSHALL, Joanne G.	(416)978-7111	774
	MORRISON, Carol A.	(416)967-3796	868
	OLSHEN, Toni	(416)488-5321	922
	THODY, Susan I.	(416)762-1690	1235
	TIPLER, Stephen B.	(416)654-5617	1246
	WONG, Lusi	(416)922-5100	1363
	ZURBRIGG, Lyn E.	(416)961-9323	1391
Willowdale	DANIEL, Eileen	(416)223-2495	272
Windsor	HANDY, Mary J.	(519)256-3250	495

ONLINE SEARCHER (Cont'd)
QUEBEC

Ancienne-Lorette	JULIEN, Guy	(418)877-1054	619
Beaconsfield	KAMICHAITIS, Penelope H.	(574)697-1634	624
Bellefeuille	DANIS, Rolland J.	(514)432-6116	273
Boucherville	DESCHATELETS, Gilles H.	(514)655-9400	294
Chomedey	DUPLESSIS, Daniel		327
Dorval	MAHARAJ, Diana J.	(514)631-1972	760
Drummondville	JANIK, Sophie	(819)477-7100	593
Laval	CHAUMONT, Elise	(514)667-5100	204
	TESSIER, Mario C.	(514)669-7878	1233
Laval-des-Rapides	VONKA, Stephanie	(514)667-1947	1288
Montreal	ALLARD, Andre	(514)256-2522	14
	ARAJ, Houda	(514)343-7095	30
	CHAGNON, Danielle G.		197
	CLARKE, Robert F.	(514)731-9211	219
	CORBEIL, Lizette	(514)332-9854	245
	DARLINGTON, Susan	(514)737-3387	275
	DUBEAU, Pierre		321
	DUCHESNEAU, Pierre	(514)281-6166	322
	DUSABLON-BOTTEGA, Nicole	(514)871-6442	329
	FOWLES, Alison C.	(514)842-7680	394
	GARDNER, Lucie	(514)845-7814	418
	GARNETT, Joyce C.	(514)398-4763	419
	HETU, Sylvie	(514)343-6949	534
	JOBA, Judith C.	(514)489-0117	601
	LALONDE, Diane	(514)767-3490	689
	LAMBROU, Angella	(514)398-4757	691
	LAPLANTE, Carole	(514)721-3093	697
	LATOUR, Pierre	(514)729-4165	701
	MARCIL, Louise	(514)333-6621	769
	MCINTOSH, Julia E.	(514)283-3639	809
	NAGY, Cecile		886
	PIGGOTT, Sylvia E.	(514)877-9383	972
	PROVOST, Paul E.	(514)598-5389	996
	ROBINSON, Chantal	(514)873-2997	1043
	SCHEPPER, Josee H.	(514)496-6119	1091
	SHLIONSKY, Anatoly	(514)861-1411	1132
	STILMAN, Ruth	(514)340-8210	1194
	THACH, Phat V.	(514)727-6817	1233
	VADNAIS, Martine		1270
Pointe Claire Dorval	FIORE, Francine	(514)694-2055	379
	STAHL, Hella	(514)630-4100	1178
Quebec	DENIGER, Constant	(418)692-4369	292
	GELINAS, Michel R.	(418)522-7203	426
	ROY, Christine	(418)649-3115	1063
	TAILLON, Yolande A.	(418)656-5781	1220
Repentigny	MERCIER, Diane	(514)582-3920	825
Rouyn-Noranda	TREMBLAY, Levis	(819)762-0931	1255
Sainte-Foy	FLORIAN, Trudel	(418)652-2210	385
	GUILMETTE, Pierre	(418)658-0470	476
	TRUDEL, Florian	(418)652-2210	1259
Sherbrooke	CHOUINARD, Germain	(819)564-5297	211
	SOKOV, Asta M.	(819)821-7566	1166
Ste Anne De Bellevue	GRAINGER, Bruce	(514)398-7879	457
Verdun	DIMITRESCU, Ioana	(514)765-8219	304
Westmount	WADE, C A.		1290

SASKATCHEWAN

Regina	MACK, A Y.	(306)543-6981	756
	POGUE, Basil G.	(306)586-6846	979
	THAUBERGER, Marianne T.	(306)757-9589	1234
Saskatoon	SALT, David P.	(306)966-5978	1077

AUSTRALIA

Kensington	WILSON, Concepcion S.		1350

BAHRAIN

Al Manamah	ALI, Syed N.		13

BRAZIL

Pelotas	CASTAGNO, Lucio A.		194

COSTA RICA

San Jose	MIRABELLI, Gerardo	(506)315-0540	847
	SMITH, Sharon		1160

ONLINE SEARCHER (Cont'd)
ENGLAND

Cheshire	HOWARD, Theresa M.	564

FEDERAL REPUBLIC OF CHINA

Taipei	HUANG, Shih H.	568

FEDERAL REPUBLIC OF GERMANY

Berlin	KREH, Fritz	677
Bremerhaven	GOMEZ, Michael J.	447

GUATAMALA

Guatamala City	MARBAN, Ricio	768

HONG KONG

Jardine's Lookout	LEE, Betty W.	709
Kowloon	FU, Ting W.	407
The Peak	SANDFELDER, Paula M.	1080

INDIA

Andhra Pradesh	SINHA, Pramod K.	1143
Bangalore	KITTUR, Krishna N.	657

ISRAEL

Jerusalem	BORCK, Liba	116
Ramat Gan	SNYDER, Esther M.	1164

JAPAN

Aichi-ken	SANO, Hikomaro	1081
Chiba-ken	NASU, Yukio	889
Tokyo	KATAOKA, Yoko	629
	KAWASHIMA, Hiroko	632
	MIWA, Makiko	850
	YAMAZAKI, Hisamichi	1377
Tokyo 105	YAMAKAWA, Takashi	1376

LUXEMBOURG

Helmsange	CORNELIUS, Peter K.	246

MEXICO

Benito	MACIAS-CHAPULA, Cesar A.	755

NEW ZEALAND

Auckland	TWEEDALE, Dellene M.	1266

NIGERIA

Lagos	AFOLAYAN, Matthew A.	(018)001-6040	7
Ogbomoso	OKPARA, Ibiba M.		920

SAUDI ARABIA

Jeddah	KHAN, Mohammed A.	646
Riyadh	BROWN, Biraj L.	142
	MARTIN, Nannette	777
	SMITH, Marilynn C.	1157

SOUTH AFRICA

Bedfordview	ARMSTRONG, Denise M.	32
Tygerberg	ROSSOUW, Steve F.	1059

SWEDEN

Jarfalla	SHELTON, Anita L.	1126

SWITZERLAND

Geneva	OHLMAN, Herbert	919

PROOFREADER
ALABAMA

Auburn	NELSON, Barbara K.	(205)826-4500	893
Birmingham	BLEILER, Richard J.	(205)934-6364	105
	HARRIS, Jay	(205)251-2821	504
	OLIVE, J F.	(205)967-8481	921
	VENABLE, Douglas R.	(205)871-3318	1282
Daphne	ROBINSON, Gayle N.	(205)626-2345	1044
Dothan	SMITH, Julia L.	(205)677-5367	1156
Florence	CARR, Charles E.	(205)767-2310	185
Helena	NELSON, William N.	(205)663-9251	895

PROOFREADER (Cont'd)

ALABAMA (Cont'd)

Maxwell AFB	GOODMAN, Anita S.	(205)293-2504	449
	HARPER, Marie F.	(205)293-5042	503
Mobile	MILLER, Hannelore A.	(205)343-0000	838
Montgomery	BEST, Rickey D.	(205)244-9212	92
	BREEDLOVE, Michael A.	(205)262-6172	131
	FELDER, Jimmie R.	(205)265-2012	369
Northport	HAMILTON, Ann H.	(205)752-3830	491
Tuscaloosa	PRUITT, Paul M.	(205)348-1107	996
	WATTERS, Annette J.	(205)348-6191	1310

ALASKA

Anchorage	EGGLESTON, Phyllis A.	(907)337-0051	339
	KRAFT, Gwen L.		675
Bethel	EMMONS, Mary E.	(907)543-3682	348
Valdez	LEAHY, M J.	(907)835-2801	706

ARIZONA

Apache Junction	WHORTON, Pamela J.	(602)982-1110	1334
Chandler	VATHIS, Alma C.	(602)899-7147	1279
Flagstaff	JOHNSON, Harlan R.	(602)523-4408	605
	MULLANE, William H.	(602)523-6501	877
Holbrook	ROTHLISBERG, Allen P.	(602)524-2257	1060
Phoenix	BERK, Nancy G.	(602)971-9264	87
	SLESINGER, Susan G.	(602)254-6156	1148
	TEVIS, Raymond H.	(602)255-4590	1233
Tempe	STEEL, Virginia	(602)965-3282	1183
Tucson	D'ANTONIO, Lynn M.	(602)327-0715	274
	HOOPES, Maria S.		557
	MCCRAY, Jeanette C.	(602)626-6143	800
	NAMSICK, Lynn J.	(602)624-0063	887
	OWENS, Clayton S.		932
	TAYLOR, Patricia A.	(602)621-1548	1228
	TAYLOR, Trish A.	(602)621-1548	1229
	WOLF, Noel C.	(602)746-7637	1360
	WOLFSON, Catherine L.	(602)884-8305	1361

ARKANSAS

Eureka Springs	STOWE, Jean E.	(501)253-8754	1199
Fayetteville	CHICK, Catherine P.	(501)443-4606	208
Greenwood	CLEVENGER, Judy B.	(501)996-2856	221
Harrison	HAMBY, Tracy A.	(501)743-1203	491
Hope	TROMATER, Raymond B.	(501)777-3361	1257
Little Rock	BRECK, Paul A.	(501)569-3121	131
	RAZER, Robert L.	(501)663-0789	1012
	RINGER, Sarah A.	(501)569-3121	1035
	SANDERS, Kathryn A.	(501)227-5581	1080
Mountain View	MCNEIL, William K.	(501)269-3851	816
Prescott	WATSON, Merlyn		1310
Searcy	BEARD, Craig W.	(501)268-6161	69

CALIFORNIA

Alameda	HUNT, Deborah S.	(415)523-6518	575
Altadena	GREGORY, Timothy P.	(818)798-1268	466
Anaheim	WRIGHT, Betty A.	(714)998-1127	1370
Aptos	WYKLE, Helen H.	(408)662-3228	1375
Bakersfield	WINTER, Eugenia B.	(805)833-3175	1356
Belmont	MEGLIO, Delores D.	(415)591-2333	821
Berkeley	CLARENCE, Judy	(415)649-2400	216
	HANDMAN, Gary P.	(415)524-9728	495
	HUNT, Judy L.	(415)849-2708	575
	MAXWELL, Christine Y.	(415)644-4500	788
	VANYOUNG, Sayre	(415)848-2229	1278
Blytho	MURPHY, Patricia A.	(619)922-5371	881
Cardiff By The Sea	SCHALIT, Michael	(619)944-3913	1089
Carmichael	O'NEILL, Diane J.	(916)965-0935	924
Carpinteria	ALLABACK, Patricia G.	(805)684-4127	13
Cerritos	ZEIDLER, Patricia L.	(213)926-1101	1387
Chico	BROWN, Carol G.	(916)861-2762	142
Chula Vista	GAGNON, Donna M.	(619)426-4527	412
Culver City	NG, Carol S.	(213)202-6523	900
	PATTEN, Frederick W.	(213)827-3335	947
Davis	KNOWLES, Em C.	(916)752-1126	665
	ROBINSON, Betty J.	(916)756-2187	1043
	SHORT, Virginia	(916)752-1126	1132
El Cajon	LEVINE, Beryl	(619)465-1700	720
El Cerrito	PRESSNALL, Patricia E.	(415)525-5186	991
Encino	WOOD, Raymund F.		1364
Fremont	DIBLE, Joan B.	(415)792-8736	299

PROOFREADER (Cont'd)

CALIFORNIA (Cont'd)

Fresno	WARD, Penny T.	(209)268-2545	1304
Fullerton	BRIL, Patricia L.	(714)773-3852	136
	STEPHENSON, Shirley E.	(714)773-3580	1189
Garden Grove	HIXON, Donald L.	(714)638-9379	544
Glen Ellen	SCARBOROUGH, Katharine T.	(707)996-7993	1087
Glendale	BURNS, Nancy R.	(818)244-1994	162
Grand Terrace	MARCHIANO, Marilyn C.	(714)382-2353	768
Hayward	ARROWOOD, Donna J.	(415)881-2791	34
Irvine	JUNG, Soon J.	(714)730-8133	620
	WOOLDRIDGE, Steven M.	(714)856-7368	1368
Isla Vista	GALLERY, M C.	(805)968-6842	414
La Verne	HECKMAN, Marlin L.	(714)593-8680	520
Livermore	PALLONE, Kitty J.	(415)447-2376	935
Long Beach	BENSON-TALLEY, Lois I.	(213)494-7817	83
	WILLIAMS, Valencia	(213)434-9151	1347
Los Angeles	COSTELLO, M R.	(213)825-3047	249
	DOUGLAS, Carolyn T.	(213)472-5287	314
	GINSBURG, Helen W.	(213)485-5400	438
	GOWAN, Christa I.		455
	GRANGER, Dorothy J.	(818)795-9161	457
	HASSAN, Abe H.	(213)649-2846	511
	HOFFMAN, Irene M.	(213)839-5722	548
	KACZOROWSKI, Monice M.	(213)485-1234	621
	NEMCHEK, Lee R.	(213)621-9484	895
	PANSKI, Saul J.	(213)655-1415	938
	ROLLING, George M.	(213)224-2251	1051
	STERLIN, Annette S.	(213)645-2406	1189
	STERN, Teena B.	(213)680-2525	1189
	WAGNER, Sharon L.	(213)931-4048	1292
	WOOD, Elizabeth H.	(213)224-7234	1364
Los Gatos	BAILEY, Rolene M.	(408)356-9645	46
Menlo Park	BOYE, Inger	(415)325-8077	123
Mill Valley	ASHLEY, Elizabeth	(415)388-8080	36
Modesto	MORAN, Irene E.	(209)576-2740	862
Napa	CHAMBERLIN, Leslie A.	(707)253-1071	198
Nevada City	BISHOP, Diane		99
Northridge	ECKLUND, Kristin A.	(818)349-6115	335
Oakland	MULL, Richard G.	(415)841-2590	876
	WONG, Patricia M.	(415)834-2742	1363
Ojai	MOORE, Phyllis C.	(805)646-8592	861
Oxnard	SMITH, Heather	(805)984-4637	1155
Palo Alto	GREEN-MALONEY, Nancy	(415)858-3816	465
	LEE, Judith C.	(415)494-0395	710
	VARKENTINE, Aganita	(415)493-8853	1278
Pasadena	CHOUDHURY, Lori B.	(818)449-9468	211
	HICKS, Cynthia S.	(818)792-6830	536
	LONGO, Margaret K.	(818)793-7682	740
	WONG, Maida L.	(818)795-1255	1363
Pebble Beach	ANDRUS, Eloise A.	(408)624-1257	27
Pleasant Hill	BRUNTON, Angela	(415)671-4941	151
Pleasanton	LUCAS, Linda L.		746
Pomona	ADAMSON, Danette	(714)869-3109	6
Redwood City	BANGE, Stephanie D.	(415)369-6251	54
Richmond	BENELISHA, Eleanor	(415)223-6417	80
	LAMBERT, Nancy	(415)620-3161	690
	RYUS, Joseph E.	(415)222-0846	1072
Riverside	STALKER, Laura A.	(714)787-5841	1178
Roseville	NICKERSON, Susan L.	(916)781-0221	902
Sacramento	AKEY, Sharon A.	(916)445-7356	9
	HICKS, Mary F.	(916)925-3115	537
	MARTINEZ, Barbara A.	(916)429-1107	779
	MILLER, Suzanne M.	(916)739-7010	842
	SCHEIBEL, Susan	(916)392-9461	1091
	SCRIBNER, Ruth B.		1108
San Diego	PLOTSKY, Andrea G.	(619)695-1132	978
	ROBINSON, Michaele M.	(619)231-1515	1044
	TABORN, Kym M.	(619)232-3320	1219
San Francisco	BROWN, Barbara L.	(415)894-9896	142
	COLALILLO, Robert M.	(415)664-2264	230
	DURSO, Angeline M.	(415)750-6072	329
	ECKMAN, Charles D.	(415)334-8449	335
	MOYER, Barbara A.	(415)386-6297	874
	RUNYON, Steven C.	(415)386-5873	1067
	SCHMIDT, Robert R.	(415)821-7762	1096
	SEGUNDO, Fe P.	(415)586-6333	1112
	STOCKFLETH, Craig G.	(415)387-6040	1195
San Lorenzo	CARR, Richard D.	(415)276-9345	186

PROOFREADER (Cont'd)
CALIFORNIA (Cont'd)

San Mateo	CROCKETT, Darla J.	(415)573-0494	259
Santa Rosa	WALSH, Donamarie F.		1299
Sherman Oaks	MILLER, Margaret S.	(818)783-5264	840
Sierra Madre	KNUDSEN, Helen Z.		666
South Pasadena	WISE, Leona L.	(213)257-4020	1357
Stockton	MOORE, Evia B.	(209)474-7029	859
Sunland	CLARK, Patricia A.	(818)353-6820	217
Thousand Oaks	HOCKEL, Kathleen N.		545
Torrance	BEEBE, Richard J.	(213)323-7200	74
	HANSEN, Linda L.		497
Vallejo	WONG, Carol Y.	(707)646-2532	1362
Van Nuys	BALABAN, Robin M.	(818)781-6952	50
Venice	CHARBONNEAU, Ronald P.	(213)396-5441	202
Walnut Creek	SMITH, Susan A.	(415)944-1603	1161
West Hollywood	BUTKIS, John F.	(213)000-0000	166
Westlake Village	TISE, Barbara L.	(818)991-0047	1247
Woodland Hills	RUBEN, Jacquelen S.		1064

COLORADO

Boulder	CHANAUD, Jo P.	(303)449-0849	199
	FINK, Deborah	(303)492-8302	378
	MEYER, Andrea P.		829
	PORPA, Edythe C.	(303)442-2847	984
Colorado Springs	STEWART, Anna C.	(303)472-0268	1192
Denver	BOYER, Carol C.	(303)892-9404	123
	GIGNAC, Solange G.	(303)575-3751	433
	GILBERT, Ruth E.	(303)757-3622	434
	GOODRICH, Margaret	(303)320-6054	449
	INGUI, Bettejean	(303)394-5158	583
	KATSH, Sara	(303)773-8729	630
	RAINWATER, Barbara C.	(303)871-6206	1004
	VOLZ, Edward J.	(303)571-2033	1288
Englewood	BRUNTON, David W.	(303)771-3197	151
Fort Collins	AMAN, Ann L.	(303)484-9205	19
	BURNS, Robert W.	(303)491-1830	163
	LINDGREN, William F.	(303)484-4432	729
Greeley	CUTTS, William B.	(303)353-1551	268
	SAVIG, Norman I.	(303)351-2251	1086
Lakewood	ROESCH, Gay E.	(303)986-6365	1049
Littleton	HALLER, Robin M.	(303)220-1031	489
	SZABO, Kathleen S.	(303)796-9718	1218

CONNECTICUT

Avon	BLOTNER, Linda S.	(203)677-0286	106
Branford	KILLHEFFER, Robert E.	(203)432-1704	648
Bridgeport	BARNES, Denise M.	(203)372-5434	57
Danbury	FOWLER, Louise D.	(203)797-4478	394
Derby	FINNUCAN, Louise A.	(203)732-7399	379
East Canaan	BYERS, Laura T.	(203)824-5971	168
Farmington	LEVINE, Marion H.	(203)679-3323	720
	WETMORE, Judith M.	(203)679-2942	1328
Hamden	DEL CERVO, Diane M.	(203)248-4815	289
	KOEL, Maria O.	(203)281-3265	667
	STRAKA, Kathy M.	(203)771-8383	1199
Hartford	MCNULTY, Karen	(203)278-2670	817
Kent	CUSTER, Deborah P.	(203)927-3098	267
Milford	BARGAR, Arthur W.	(203)783-3290	56
New Haven	ENSEL, Ellen H.	(203)782-2525	350
	HILL, John R.	(203)397-4509	540
	LUBIN, Joan S.	(203)397-5154	745
	PELTIER, Karen V.	(203)432-4794	955
New London	ROGERS, Brian D.	(203)447-7622	1049
Northford	SAVAGE, Judith G.	(203)484-2175	1085
Ridgefield	SWIFT, Janet B.	(203)438-5937	1216
Stratford	ROTH, Alison C.	(203)378-8700	1059
Wallingford	EBINGER, Meada G.	(203)269-5114	334
Warren	HENTZ, Margaret B.	(203)868-9178	530
Waterbury	JOY, Patricia L.	(203)757-6203	618
	LOW, Jocelyn L.	(203)756-6149	743
	YOUNG, Marianne F.	(203)574-8216	1382
Westport	SELVERSTONE, Harriet S.	(203)226-6236	1114
Willimantic	EMBARDO, Ellen E.	(203)456-1952	347

DELAWARE

Newark	DANIEL, Alfred I.	(302)731-9723	272
Wilmington	DRUKKER, Alexander E.	(302)478-1746	320
	GRILLO, Anthony L.	(302)774-6603	470
	PAUL, Jacqueline R.	(302)478-3000	949

PROOFREADER (Cont'd)
DISTRICT OF COLUMBIA

Washington	BALL, Alice D.	(202)362-6047	52
	BATTLE, Thomas C.	(202)636-7241	65
	CANNAN, Judith P.	(202)287-5263	178
	CARLSON, Julia F.	(202)225-2571	182
	CASSEDY, Barbara S.	(202)576-3279	193
	CHESTNUT, Paul I.	(202)462-3280	207
	DE ARMAN, Charles L.	(202)797-7169	284
	ELLIOT, Hugh	(202)333-8312	343
	FALK, Diane M.	(202)291-3821	362
	FARINA, Robert A.	(202)287-5298	363
	GILLESPIE, Veronica M.	(202)287-5262	435
	HAUCK, Janice B.	(202)362-5052	512
	JENKINS, Lydia E.	(202)673-7263	597
	JOHNSON, Gary M.		604
	JOHNSON, Jacqueline B.	(202)635-7498	605
	JOHNSON, Lucy C.		607
	KENDRICK, Brent L.	(202)543-7031	640
	KIMBERLIN, Robert L.	(202)626-7493	649
	LATEGOLO, Meldie A.		701
	LEFFALL, Dolores C.	(202)723-7645	712
	MANNING, Martin J.	(202)485-6187	766
	MCGILL, Theodora	(202)566-8320	806
	MEADOWS, Beth W.	(202)628-2150	819
	MISSAR, Margaret M.	(202)363-2751	847
	MORIARTY, Ann	(202)333-9087	865
	PAGE, John S.	(202)554-0486	934
	PETERSON, Charles B.		963
	PURDY, Virginia C.	(202)523-3105	998
	RICHARDSON, Deborra A.		1029
	SERVERINO, Roberto	(202)625-4574	1116
	STARCK, William L.	(202)234-6006	1181
	WIGGINS, Beacher J.	(202)398-3427	1337
	YARNALL, James L.	(202)554-0486	1378
	YASUMATSU, Janet R.	(202)234-6293	1378

FLORIDA

Atlantic Beach	URBANSKI, Verna P.	(904)246-3631	1269
Boca Raton	DONAHUE, Janice E.	(305)393-3774	310
	GOLDMAN, Ava R.	(305)487-1891	445
	SKALLERUP, Amy G.		1145
	STORCH, Barbara J.	(305)395-1056	1198
Bonifay	HOWELL, Wanda H.	(904)547-3631	565
Bradenton	JULIEN, Dorothy C.	(813)792-7899	619
	MORR, Lynell A.	(813)747-4319	866
Bunnell	MCKNIGHT, Jesse H.	(904)437-4151	812
Casselberry	BARAGER, Wendy A.	(305)699-6657	55
Clearwater	POTTER, Robert E.	(813)442-9061	987
Coral Springs	KORNITSKY, Judith M.	(305)753-7081	672
Fort Lauderdale	GALLAHAR, Christine M.		414
	HARTON, Pamela J.	(305)357-7454	508
Gainesville	WALTON, Carol G.	(904)392-0351	1301
Indialantic	MELNICOVE, Annette R.		823
Jacksonville	MARION, Gail E.	(904)633-2088	770
	SMITH, Linda L.	(904)731-1065	1157
Key West	SOULE, Maria J.	(305)296-9081	1169
Lake Worth	MOFFETT, Martha L.	(305)964-7044	852
Lauderhill	HURTES, Reva	(305)735-8655	578
Miami	MILLER, Jewell J.	(305)662-4212	839
	PARISE, Marina P.		940
	PHILLIPS, Donald J.	(305)274-5724	968
Miami Beach	EFRON, Muriel C.	(305)672-0696	338
Naples	O'CONNOR, Mary A.	(813)598-9269	916
North Miami	MCCAMMON, Leslie V.	(305)940-5716	793
North Miami Beach	KAPLAN, Tiby	(305)944-2697	626
Orlando	ARMSTRONG, Ruth C.	(305)422-7218	32
	CUBBERLEY, Carol W.	(305)275-2521	263
	DAVIDOFF, Marcia	(305)894-5508	276
	GEBET, Russell W.	(305)849-0300	424
Palatka	HUNTER, Judith G.	(904)325-1532	576
Palm Bay	TIPPLE, Roberta L.	(904)984-2891	1246
Palm Coast	FRAZER, Ruth F.	(904)445-5409	399
Palm Harbor	HO, Paul J.	(813)785-1874	545
	PASSARELLO, Nancy H.	(813)733-7986	946
Pensacola	BOWER, Beverly L.	(904)476-5410	120
	BROWN, Lyn S.	(904)478-8480	145
	KIEFER, Rosemary M.	(904)438-2732	647
Pompano Beach	WHITESIDE, Lee A.	(305)782-0194	1333
Port Charlotte	HOLSTINE, Lesa G.	(813)697-3365	554

PROOFREADER (Cont'd)
FLORIDA (Cont'd)
St Petersburg	WATERS, Sally G.	(813)345-1335	1308
Sanford	LINSLEY, Laurie S.	(305)323-1450	731
Tallahassee	CLARKSON, Jane S.	(904)385-9671	219
	HUNT, Mary A.	(904)644-5775	575
Tampa	HAWK, Susan P.	(813)239-3268	513
	MATHEWS, Richard B.	(813)253-3333	784
Vero Beach	KISER, Mary D.	(305)567-4111	656

GEORGIA
Acworth	STAHL, D G.	(404)924-8505	1178
Americus	MCLAUGHLIN, Laverne L.	(912)924-9426	813
Athens	ANDREW, Paige G.	(404)353-1707	26
	MASSEY, Katha D.	(404)542-2534	782
	RIEMER, John J.	(404)542-0591	1033
	SOUTHWICK, Mary L.	(404)542-6643	1170
	WILLIAMS, Sara E.	(408)548-7519	1346
Atlanta	BULLOCK, Penelope L.	(404)792-0775	156
	CAMP, John F.	(404)875-4373	175
	DAVIS, Joy V.	(404)634-3511	279
	DEES, Leslie M.	(404)894-4523	287
	DREW, Frances K.	(404)881-0917	319
	FEINBERG, Hilda W.	(404)875-0077	368
	FISTE, David A.		382
	JAMES, Stephen E.	(404)681-0251	592
	MCIVER, Stephanie P.	(404)688-4636	809
	MILLER, Anthony G.	(404)688-4636	835
	REYNOLDS, Carol C.	(404)843-9327	1025
	ROSS, Theodosia B.	(404)696-2355	1059
	THAXTON, Lyn	(404)292-6767	1234
	TOMAJKO, Kathy L.	(404)894-4511	1249
	TROUTMAN, Joseph E.	(404)522-8980	1258
	WHITE, Carol A.	(404)351-8991	1330
Augusta	BUSTOS, Roxann R.	(404)737-1748	166
Bremen	BROCK, Kathy T.	(404)537-4960	138
Cartersville	HOWINGTON, Lee R.	(404)382-4203	566
Columbus	CLEMENTS, Betty H.	(404)327-3399	221
Decatur	CHAMBERS, Shirley M.	(404)289-6517	198
	HATCHER, Nolan C.	(404)378-8282	511
	WENDEROTH, Christine	(404)378-8821	1323
Gainesville	VAUGHAN, Elinor F.	(404)534-6120	1279
Griffin	WILKINSON, Evalyn S.	(404)227-8532	1340
Richmond Hill	GLISSON, Patricia A.	(912)727-2592	441
Riverdale	HANSON, Kathy H.	(404)471-5053	498
Statesboro	JOHNSON, Jane G.	(912)681-1609	605
Stone Mountain	ENGERRAND, Steven W.	(404)469-5066	349
Winder	HOLMES, Nancy M.	(404)867-2762	553

HAWAII
Honolulu	SCHULTZ, Elaine V.	(808)395-1801	1102
	URAGO, Gail M.	(808)949-6496	1269
Kailua	WRIGHT, John C.	(808)261-3714	1371
Kaneohe	ASHFORD, Marguerite K.	(808)247-6834	36

IDAHO
Boise	SCHIFF, Margaret M.	(208)344-9349	1092
Idaho Falls	VERHOFF, Patricia A.	(208)523-9601	1282
Nampa	LANCASTER, Edith E.	(208)466-1011	691
	RAMBO, Helen M.	(208)467-8608	1005

ILLINOIS
Argonne	DAVIDOFF, Gary N.	(312)972-4224	276
Aurora	MCKEARN, Anne B.	(312)892-4811	810
Belleville	DOMESCIK, Carol J.	(618)235-2565	310
Bethany	SYFERT, Samuel R.	(217)665-3063	1217
Brookfield	IRONS, Carol A.	(312)485-3503	584
Cahokia	BEAN, Bobby G.	(618)875-6915	69
Carbondale	BORUZKOWSKI, Lilly A.	(618)453-2365	117
	PERSON, Roland C.	(618)453-2818	961
	RYAN, Sheila	(618)549-7029	1071
	WILSON, Betty R.	(618)529-3318	1350
Champaign	BERGER, Sidney E.	(217)351-8140	86
	MCCLELLAN, William M.	(217)352-1893	796
Chicago	ADKINS, Marjorie R.	(312)468-2139	6
	EPP, Ronald H.	(203)347-6933	351
	GLANZ, Lenore M.	(312)528-7817	439
	HANSEN, Roland C.	(312)443-3748	498
	HARRINGTON, Margaret V.	(312)472-6543	504
	HERNANDEZ, Hector R.	(312)523-2453	531

PROOFREADER (Cont'd)
ILLINOIS (Cont'd)
Chicago	HOFFMANN, Maurine L.	(312)951-0599	548
	HOTIMLANSKA, Leah D.	(312)248-2013	562
	HUNT, Janis E.	(312)275-8439	575
	JAGODZINSKI, Cecile M.	(312)645-4860	591
	KOBASA, Paul A.	(312)944-6780	666
	MACKEY, Denise R.	(312)467-1000	756
	MARSHALL, Jerilyn A.		774
	MARTIN, Bennie E.	(312)443-5423	775
	MCCOY, Patricia S.	(312)274-0370	799
	MCELWAIN, William	(312)248-5564	804
	MELTON, Emily I.	(312)944-6780	823
	MITZIGA, Walter J.	(312)375-4646	850
	MOORE, Annie M.	(312)995-2254	858
	MORRISON, Samuel F.	(312)269-3053	868
	OWNES, Dorothy J.	(312)702-8899	932
	PILARSKI, James P.	(312)769-2714	973
	POSNER, Frances A.	(312)334-7484	985
	SCHRAMM, Mary T.	(312)248-7934	1099
	SCHROEDER, Anne M.	(312)528-7486	1100
	STEWART, Richard A.	(312)269-2930	1193
	SUTHERLAND, Zena B.	(312)702-8293	1211
	TAYLOR, Terry S.	(312)372-2000	1229
	WILLIAMS, Charles M.	(312)275-2004	1342
	WINGER, Howard W.	(312)748-1129	1355
	WINNIKE, Mary E.	(312)996-6595	1355
	WRIGHT, Helen K.	(312)944-6780	1371
	ZVIRIN, Stephanie H.	(312)944-6780	1392
Dawson	CHESLEY, Thea B.		207
De Kalb	RIDER, Philip R.	(815)758-2181	1032
	RIDINGER, Robert B.	(815)758-5070	1032
Downers Grove	ALLEN, Dorothy L.	(312)963-1056	14
Dwight	MCCLAREY, Catherine A.	(815)584-3703	796
Edwardsville	MCFARLAND, Mary A.	(618)692-3828	805
Elk Grove Village	HOLBROCK, Mary A.	(312)439-4800	550
Evanston	BARNUM, Sally J.	(312)869-2976	58
	BRADY, Mary M.	(312)491-2929	127
	FINEMAN, Charles S.	(312)866-7428	377
	STUTZ, Patricia A.	(312)491-7630	1206
	SUNDELL, Elizabeth B.	(312)866-0310	1210
	WRIGHT, Donald E.	(312)866-0312	1371
Glen Ellyn	PEISER, Richard H.	(312)790-3293	955
	TEMPLE, Harold L.	(312)858-2800	1230
Gurnee	MANDEL, Douglas J.	(312)336-7637	765
Hoffman Estates	CHAPA, Joan I.	(312)934-7032	201
Kingston	SCHREIBER, Robert E.	(815)784-2280	1099
Lake Forest	DANOFF, Fran	(312)234-2350	274
Makanda	CRANE, Lilly E.	(618)549-6259	255
Moline	KRAMER, Pamela K.	(309)797-5117	675
Normal	GOWDY, Laura E.	(309)438-7450	455
	MATTHEWS, Priscilla J.	(309)452-8514	785
Oak Lawn	KELLY, Raymond T.		638
Oak Park	REDDY, Michael B.	(312)848-1754	1013
Palatine	HORTON, Kathy L.	(312)934-3794	561
Park Forest	BUCKLEY, Ja A.	(312)748-2536	154
	HAYES, Hazel I.		515
Park Ridge	OSERMAN, Stuart	(312)696-5060	928
Peoria	SWORSKY, Felicia G.	(309)672-8885	1217
Quincy	MORRIS, Susan M.	(217)224-0042	867
River Forest	HEYMAN, Jerome S.	(312)771-3030	536
Rock Island	CONWAY, Colleen M.	(309)794-7316	239
	MASON, Marjorie L.	(300)708-7217	781
	OHRLUND, Ava L.	(309)786-0698	919
Rockford	HAMILTON, D A.	(815)226-6752	491
St Joseph	DUCHOW, Sally	(217)469-2237	322
Silvis	SWATOS, Priscilla L.	(309)792-3306	1214
Springfield	BRADWAY, Becky J.	(217)753-4117	126
	SHACKLETON, Suzanne M.	(217)786-6375	1118
Sullivan	ELDER, Nancy J.	(217)728-4832	342
Urbana	BINGHAM, Karen H.	(217)333-0317	97
	BURBANK, Richard D.	(217)333-2713	158
	DOWNS, Jane B.	(217)344-1714	317
	GUSHEE, Marion S.	(217)367-9610	478
	LOOMIS, Barbara	(217)333-7496	740
	ROLSTAD, Gary O.	(217)333-3280	1052
	SCHMIDT, Karen A.	(217)333-1054	1095
	SMITH, Linda C.	(217)333-7742	1157
Westmont	MANNING, Mary J.	(312)964-3549	766

PROOFREADER (Cont'd)
ILLINOIS (Cont'd)

Wheaton	WALSH, Deborah T.	(312)653-1115	1299
Wheeling	LAMB, Sara G.	(312)541-8114	690
Wilmette	REIF, Lenore S.	(312)156-1100	1019
	SPIGELMAN, Cynthia A.	(312)251-4892	1174

INDIANA

Anderson	KENDALL, Charles T.	(317)649-5039	640
Bloomington	HENSON, Jane E.	(812)336-8288	529
	MCCLOY, William B.	(812)335-9666	797
	MCCUNE, Lois M.	(812)339-0505	801
	NEUMANN, Mary G.	(812)333-6189	897
Bluffton	ELLIOTT, Barbara J.	(219)824-2315	343
Charlestown	WHALEY, Janie B.	(812)256-6363	1328
Chesterton	BECKING, Mara S.	(219)926-5618	73
Evansville	BAKER, Donald E.	(812)425-4309	48
Fort Wayne	SANDSTROM, Pamela E.	(219)424-7241	1081
	STANLEY, Luana K.	(219)432-3287	1180
Gary	GUYDON, Janet H.	(219)938-3376	479
	MACKO, Lucinda M.	(219)882-9411	757
	MCSHANE, Stephen G.	(219)980-6628	818
Goshen	SPRINGER, Joe A.	(219)534-5357	1176
Greencastle	LATSHAW, Ruth N.	(317)653-2318	701
Hanover	MORRILL, Walter D.	(812)866-2151	866
Indianapolis	AUTRY, Carolyn	(317)291-9866	41
	ELLSWORTH, Marlene A.	(317)274-7185	345
	MASON, Dorothy L.	(317)845-3684	781
	TIMKO, Patricia A.		1246
	WOODARD, Marcia S.	(317)297-1803	1366
	YOUNG, Philip H.	(317)788-3399	1383
La Porte	GUNNELLS, Danny C.	(219)324-0422	477
Lafayette	BONHOMME, Mary S.	(317)448-1251	114
Muncie	WILLIAMS, Nyal Z.	(317)285-5065	1345
Notre Dame	MAXWELL, Jan C.	(219)239-6188	788
Plainfield	MILLER, Ida M.	(317)839-6883	838
South Bend	HARLAN, John B.	(219)288-0693	502
	WARREN, Lois B.	(219)287-6481	1306
Terre Haute	MILLER, Marsha A.	(812)237-2605	840
Upland	WOLCOTT, Laurie J.	(317)998-7549	1359
Valparaiso	HOLTERHOFF, Sarah G.	(219)465-7866	555
	RAYMAN, Ronald A.	(219)464-2060	1011
	WATTS, Tim J.	(219)465-7838	1310
West Lafayette	ANDERSON, Marilyn M.	(317)583-2586	24
	BAXTER, Pam M.	(317)494-2969	67
	OGLES, Lynn C.	(317)494-2853	918
	POLIT, Carlos E.	(317)463-6404	980
	TUCKER, John M.	(317)494-2833	1261

IOWA

Ames	SCHMIDT, Sandra L.	(515)292-1118	1096
Atlantic	CRAVER, Susan J.	(712)243-5359	256
Cedar Falls	KOLLASCH, Matthew A.	(319)277-6125	669
Cedar Rapids	JANUS, Bridget M.	(319)365-5055	594
Denver	DUTCHER, Terry R.	(319)984-6120	329
Des Moines	DAGLEY, Helen J.	(515)281-3063	269
	ELLIOTT, Kay M.	(515)281-6033	344
	FLICK, Frances J.	(515)277-2089	385
Forest City	PALMER, Joy J.	(515)582-3513	936
Iowa City	KELLEY, Ann C.	(319)335-5884	636
	KOHLER, Carolyn W.	(319)337-9839	668
	SCHERUBEL, Melody	(319)351-6264	1092
Manchester	CRAWFORD, Daniel R.		256
Marion	DAVIS, Deanna S.	(319)377-7135	278
Marshalltown	BURGESS, Barbara J.	(515)752-4812	159
	TRAVILLIAN, Mary W.	(515)752-1578	1254
Muscatine	SORENSON, Debra J.	(319)263-1670	1168
Rock Rapids	KOHRT, Ruth D.		669
Sioux City	CUMMINGS, Kevin	(712)258-4962	264
	DUNN, Susan M.		327
	SCHEETZ, Kathy D.	(712)277-2423	1091
Vinton	SHEPHERD, Rex L.	(319)472-4721	1127
Waterloo	ALLING, M P.	(319)291-4476	16
West Branch	MATHER, Mildred E.	(319)643-5301	783

PROOFREADER (Cont'd)
KANSAS

Alma	BIRNEY, Ann E.	(913)765-2370	98
Cimarron	CROTTS, Carolyn D.	(316)855-3641	261
Coffeyville	BUFFINGTON, Karyl L.	(316)251-1370	155
Emporia	BOGAN, Mary E.	(316)342-1394	110
	STEWART, Henry R.	(316)343-1200	1192
Kansas City	BENNETT, Samuel J.	(913)831-2242	82
	FARLEY, Alfred E.	(913)588-7040	364
Lawrence	HOWE, Priscilla P.	(913)864-3957	565
	RHODES, Saralinda A.		1026
Leavenworth	SNOKE, Elizabeth R.		1163
Leawood	LUNG, Mon Y.	(913)864-3025	748
Manhattan	TALAB, Rosemary S.	(913)532-5550	1220
	WILLIAMS, Sara R.	(913)532-6516	1346
McPherson	EIS, Myrna M.	(316)241-3713	340
Overland Park	SEVIER, Susan G.	(913)451-3111	1117
Pittsburg	DEGRUSON, Eugene H.	(316)231-7000	288
Shawnee	STRAUSE, Robert C.	(913)268-9875	1200
Wichita	STRECK, Helen T.	(316)942-2201	1201

KENTUCKY

Berea	HAWLEY, Mary B.	(606)986-1638	514
Bowling Green	COSSEY, M E.	(502)843-6560	249
Frankfort	COOPER, Judy L.	(502)564-2672	243
Horse Cave	STROHECKER, Edwin C.	(502)453-3059	1202
Lexington	MCANINCH, Sandra L.	(606)231-9279	792
Louisville	ANDERSON, Patricia E.	(502)588-6392	25
	MAZUK, Melody	(502)897-4807	791
	WHITE, Ernest M.	(502)897-3557	1331
Morehead	WILLIAMS, Helen E.	(606)783-2828	1343
Murray	BUSER, Robin A.	(502)762-2393	165
	WALL, Celia J.	(502)762-4990	1297
Owensboro	YATES, Dudley V.	(502)526-3111	1378
Richmond	MARTIN, June H.	(606)622-6176	777
Southgate	FOX, Estella E.	(606)441-0743	394

LOUISIANA

Baton Rouge	BLOOMSTONE, Ajaye	(504)767-0847	106
	BRADLEY, Jared W.	(504)766-9375	126
	COE, Miriam M.		226
	HASCHAK, Paul G.	(504)766-9986	510
	MERING, Margaret V.	(504)344-5863	826
	ROUNDTREE, Lynn P.	(504)336-1306	1061
	SMITH, Ledell B.		1157
Houma	COSPER, Mary F.	(504)879-4243	249
Lafayette	SCHMIDT, Jean M.	(318)231-6031	1095
Metairie	KLEIN, Victor C.	(504)861-0488	659
Monroe	KONTROVITZ, Eileen R.		671
Natchitoches	HUSSEY, Sandra R.	(318)352-2996	578
New Orleans	CUMLET, Harolyn S.	(504)943-3618	264
	DAVIS, Margo	(504)488-1193	280
	DRAUGHON, Ralph B.	(504)891-1921	318
	JERDE, Curtis D.	(504)865-5688	599
	MARIX, Mary L.	(504)488-4286	770
	NOLAN-MITCHELL, Patricia	(504)568-6102	908
	RENNIE, Margaret C.	(504)587-2062	1023
	RUSHING, Darla H.	(504)891-1127	1068
Shreveport	BRAZILE, Orella R.	(318)674-3400	130
	KING, Anne M.	(318)797-5738	650
	MCCLEARY, William E.	(318)865-9813	796
	WILLIS, Marilyn	(318)227-4501	1348

MAINE

Bar Harbor	BAKER, Alison	(207)288-3371	47
Baritarbon	GOTTLIEB, Robert A.	(207)288-9574	453
Bath	MCKAY, Ann	(207)443-5524	809
Brunswick	SAEGER, Edwin J.	(207)729-5720	1074
Georgetown	LUDGIN, Donald H.	(207)371-2221	746
Gorham	PERRY-BOWDER, Libbie E.	(207)780-5265	961
North Anson	LYONS, Dean E.	(207)566-0511	753
Orono	THOR, Angela M.	(207)581-1678	1242
Portland	HUMEZ, Nicholas D.	(207)773-3405	573

MARYLAND

Abingdon	ANDERSON, Della L.	(301)679-5720	22
Annapolis	LIVELY, Nancy J.	(301)268-0530	734
	MCKAY, Eleanor	(301)263-6526	809
	PRIMER, Ben	(301)974-3914	993

PROOFREADER (Cont'd)
MARYLAND (Cont'd)

Baltimore	BLUTE, Mary R.	(301)889-4080	107
	CONNOR, Elizabeth	(301)828-8646	237
	DAVISH, William	(301)323-1010	281
	GRAVES, Louise H.		459
	HIRSCH, Dorothy K.	(304)655-7280	543
	HUMPHRIES, Anne W.	(301)328-7373	574
	KLEIN, Ilene R.		659
	LEBRETON, Jonathan A.	(301)455-2356	708
	LOWENS, Margery M.	(301)532-7422	744
	STEVENS-RAYBURN, Sarah L.	(301)338-4961	1191
	THOMAS, Fannette H.	(301)435-4409	1236
	TOPPAN, Muriel L.	(301)837-9155	1251
	ZIMMERMAN, Martha B.	(301)668-5744	1389
Bethesda	HORAN, Meredith L.	(301)496-5497	559
	LAZAROW-STETTEN, Jane K.	(301)656-5471	706
Bowie	GERRING, Cheryl B.	(301)464-0910	429
	MATHEWS, Mary P.	(301)262-0732	784
Brookeville	ROBERTS, Lesley A.	(301)774-4471	1040
Chevy Chase	MESHINSKY, Jeff M.	(301)652-4740	827
Columbia	HOLLENBACH, Karen L.		551
Fort Meade	KNICKERBOCKER, Wendy	(301)672-3057	664
Frederick	FRYSER, Benjamin S.	(301)698-5846	407
Gaithersburg	HARTZ, Mary K.	(301)948-1855	509
Glenn Dale	MURRAY, Bruce C.	(301)464-1278	881
Green Meadows	MILL, Rodney H.	(301)422-1437	835
Hyattsville	RHEAUME, Irene M.	(301)434-8805	1025
Rockville	PHIFER, Kenneth O.	(301)770-0498	967
St Marys City	REPENNING, Julie A.	(301)862-0267	1023
Salisbury	OGLE, Mary H.	(301)543-7094	918
Seabrook	LARSEN, Lida L.	(301)459-3931	698
Silver Spring	KIMMEL, Mark R.	(301)340-2100	649
	MARKS, Cicely P.	(301)649-7200	771
	MEIKAMP, Kathie D.	(301)593-0029	822
	MYERS, R D.	(301)681-3967	885
	POMERANTZ, Karyn L.	(301)445-6204	982
	RAWSTHORNE, Grace C.	(301)949-0698	1011
	TAYLOR, Marcia E.	(301)942-6704	1227
	WISNIEWSKI, Julia L.	(301)649-1590	1357
Takoma Park	CHALMERS, Lois M.	(301)495-0187	197
	IBACH, Marilyn	(301)270-8950	581
	WRIGHT, Authuree M.	(301)445-1220	1370
Thurmont	FITZPATRICK, Kelly	(301)271-4109	383
Timonium	STUART, Karen A.	(301)561-4446	1204
Upperco	RAND, Pamela S.	(301)429-2958	1006
Welcome	DUDLEY, Robyn A.	(301)934-4602	323

MASSACHUSETTS

Amherst	ADAMS, Leonard R.	(413)545-2765	5
Arlington	ENGLISH, Cynthia J.	(617)227-0270	350
	LUKOS, Geraldine F.	(617)646-3439	748
Bedford	BERGIN, Dorothy O.	(617)275-7071	86
	HALE, Janice L.	(617)275-0377	485
Bolton	BOGART, Betty B.	(617)897-7870	110
Boston	FOX, Susan	(617)463-3178	395
	FRYDRYK, Teresa E.	(617)482-9485	407
	HUENNEKE, Judith A.	(617)282-1553	570
	KORT, Richard L.	(617)266-3646	672
	MURRAY, Lynn T.	(617)330-9000	882
	PRISTASH, Kenneth	(617)262-1120	993
	ROGAN, Michael J.	(617)536-5400	1049
	STIFFLEAR, Allan J.	(617)929-7640	1194
Cambridge	BURG, Barbara A.	(617)547-4762	159
	HEACOCK, Pamela P.	(617)661-1330	518
	JOBE, Shirley A.	(617)868-0079	601
Chestnut Hill	DESJARDINS, Andrea C.		295
Concord	BANDER, Edward J.		54
Deerfield	KELLY, Patricia M.	(413)774-4627	638
Dover	WINQUIST, Elaine W.	(617)785-0816	1355
Dracut	ARSENAULT, Patricia A.	(617)459-4648	35
Easthampton	MELNICK, Ralph	(413)527-3036	823
Framingham	KRIER, Mary M.	(617)879-7594	678
Heath	HOWLAND, Margaret E.	(413)337-4980	566
Lexington	ROSENTHAL, Marylu C.	(617)862-8167	1057
	WAKS, Jane B.	(617)863-2000	1293
Lowell	CAYLOR, Lawrence M.	(617)452-5000	195
Melrose	MURPHY, Eva B.	(617)665-7572	880

PROOFREADER (Cont'd)
MASSACHUSETTS (Cont'd)

Newton	ALPERT, Hillel R.		17
	SARAVIS, Judith A.	(617)969-6852	1082
Northampton	MORTIMER, Ruth	(413)584-2700	870
	SCOTT, Alison M.	(413)584-2700	1106
Orange	PROUTY, Sharman E.	(617)544-6743	996
Peabody	CODAIR, Frederick R.	(617)531-8200	226
Pembroke	ROBINSON, Phyllis A.	(617)293-2193	1044
Petersham	MCMANAMON, Mary J.	(617)724-3407	814
Pittsfield	BOSTLEY, Jean R.	(413)447-9121	117
Reading	O'CONNOR, Jerry	(617)944-6452	916
Sharon	FRAZIER, James A.	(617)784-5642	399
Shrewsbury	CHANG, Isabelle E.	(617)845-4641	200
Somerville	FELDT, Candice K.	(617)666-2745	369
	STAACK, Katherine A.	(617)623-1147	1177
South Deerfield	CRAIG, James L.	(413)665-2041	254
Springfield	CLOUGH, Linda F.	(413)788-8411	223
Stoughton	ANDERSON, Cheryl M.	(617)344-4000	22
Sturbridge	ALLEN, Joan C.	(508)347-3362	15
Sudbury	KOVED, Ruth B.	(617)443-3591	674
Swampscott	BRENNER, Lawrence	(617)598-0370	133
Wellesley Hills	KENNEDY, Amy J.	(617)237-4013	640
Wendell	HOLMBERG, Olga S.	(617)544-2706	553
West Roxbury	HARZBECKER, Joseph J.	(617)323-1372	510
West Springfield	SMITH, Barbara A.	(413)736-4561	1152
Westwood	KNAPP, Leslie C.	(617)329-3350	663
Williamstown	HAMMOND, Wayne G.	(413)597-2462	494
Winchester	SMITH, Ann M.	(617)729-7169	1152
Worcester	GONNEVILLE, Priscilla R.	(617)752-5615	447

MICHIGAN

Adrian	BAKER, Jean S.	(517)263-0731	48
Ann Arbor	BENSON, Peggy	(313)665-0651	83
	HALL, Jo A.	(313)936-0132	488
	JASPER, Richard P.	(313)973-0747	595
	MARTIN, Patricia W.	(313)665-3776	777
	PONOMARENKO, Ella	(313)996-5267	982
	SCOTT, Melissa C.	(313)764-7460	1107
	WEST, Marian S.	(313)663-5907	1326
Auburn Hills	EL MOUCHI, Joan S.	(313)370-9466	346
Bay City	KORMELINK, Barbara A.	(517)894-3782	671
Berkley	MARLOW, Cecilia A.	(313)547-3098	772
Berrien Springs	WALLER, Elaine J.	(616)473-3651	1298
	WILDMAN, Linda	(801)471-9764	1339
Birmingham	GOLDSTEIN, Doris R.	(313)626-9299	446
	JERYAN, Christine B.	(313)645-6268	600
	ROSE, Sharon G.	(313)647-4148	1055
Cedar Springs	RANSOM-BERGSTROM, Janette F.	(616)696-3428	1008
Cheboygan	SMALLWOOD, Carol A.	(616)627-2308	1151
Dearborn	FORSYTH, Karen R.	(313)562-8830	391
	LIMBACHER, James L.	(313)565-9687	727
	NUCKOLLS, Karen A.	(313)593-5400	912
Detroit	GUNN, Arthur C.	(313)831-9707	477
	PORTER, Jean F.	(313)961-5040	984
	RUNCHOCK, Rita M.	(313)961-2242	1067
	RZEPECKI, Arnold M.	(313)868-2700	1072
	SKONIECZNY, Jill	(313)927-7073	1147
	THOMAS, Laverne J.	(313)849-2776	1237
East Lansing	BLACK-SHIER, Mary L.	(517)353-4526	102
	RIVERA, Diana H.	(517)353-4593	1037
Flint	ARNOLD, Peggy	(313)744-4040	34
Grand Blanc	KINGSTON, Jo A.	(313)694-7323	652
Grand Rapids	BURINSKI, Walter W.	(616)454-9635	160
	DE KLERK, Peter	(616)957-6303	288
	MATTESON, James S.	(616)245-9368	785
	WEAVER, Clarence L.		1312
Grosse Pointe Woods	REID, Bette C.	(313)884-0884	1018
Harper Woods	TODD, Suzanne L.	(313)881-5328	1248
Highland Park	NDENGA, Viola W.	(313)868-5986	890
Huntington Woods	BINDSCHADLER, Valerie V.	(313)547-2962	97
Jackson	SMITH, Catherine A.	(517)784-7025	1153
Kalamazoo	GROTZINGER, Laurel A.	(616)381-1865	473
	ISAACSON, David K.	(616)383-1562	584
	NESBURG, Janet A.	(616)349-7775	896
	PEREZ-STABLE, Maria A.	(616)383-1666	958
Lansing	RADEMACHER, Matthew J.	(517)483-1644	1002
Livonia	CHAKLOSH, Cynthia L.		197

PROOFREADER (Cont'd)

MICHIGAN (Cont'd)
Parchment	BOURGEOIS, Ann M.	(616)344-9097	119
Port Huron	YAEK, Larry A.	(313)484-3881	1376
Richland	HOWLETT, Jacqueline L.	(616)629-5352	566
Rochester	HILDEBRAND, Linda L.	(313)370-2483	538
Southfield	COCOZZOLI, Gary R.	(313)443-8905	226
Sturgis	VANZUILEN, Darlene A.	(616)467-7836	1278
Taylor	MATZKE, Ellen S.	(313)291-9480	786
Warren	DOYLE, James M.	(313)445-7401	317
Wayne	WEISER, Douglas E.	(313)326-8910	1319
Ypsilanti	MCGARTY, Jean R.	(313)572-1453	805

MINNESOTA
Eden Prairie	BILEYDI, Lois G.	(612)934-3576	96
Embarrass	ESALA, Lillian H.	(218)741-3434	354
Hopkins	YOUNG, Margaret L.	(612)933-5062	1382
Mankato	FARNER, Susan G.	(507)389-5957	365
Minneapolis	BOEDER, Thelma B.	(612)870-3657	109
	GUNTHER, Paul B.	(612)371-5622	478
	OLSEN, Stephen	(612)333-9307	922
	REHNBERG, Marilyn J.	(612)722-3234	1017
	SPETLAND, Charles G.	(612)624-8060	1174
	TIBLIN, Mariann E.	(612)624-5860	1244
	WITT, Kenneth W.	(612)871-4262	1358
Northfield	SANFORD, Carolyn C.	(507)663-4266	1081
	YOUNG, Lynne M.	(507)645-5778	1382
Roseville	KAUFENBERG, Jane M.	(612)642-9221	630
St Paul	BLUMBERG-MCKEE, Hazel	(612)292-1680	107
	COLOKATHIS, Jane	(612)297-4969	234
	DELOACH, Lynda J.	(612)627-4208	290
	JACKSON, Mildred E.	(612)222-5593	588
	TURNER, Ann S.	(612)291-9340	1264

MISSISSIPPI
Biloxi	VANCE, Mary L.		1273
Cleveland	STEWART, Jeanne E.	(601)843-2774	1192
Columbus	ZUMBERGE, Gloria A.	(601)434-7762	1391
Hattiesburg	CARNOVALE, A N.	(601)264-5452	184
	JONES, Dolores B.	(601)266-4349	612
	VAN MELER, Vandelia L.	(601)266-4243	1276
Jackson	SANDERS, Lou H.	(601)982-7094	1080
Mount Olive	BOYD, Sandra E.	(601)797-3334	123
Prentiss	SMITH, Judy S.		1156
Starkville	NETTLES, Jess	(601)323-5558	896
University	FISHER, Benjamin F.		380
	TUCKER, Ellis E.	(601)232-7361	1261
Vicksburg	ABLES, Timothy D.	(601)636-8088	2
	BLACK, Bernice B.	(601)636-1990	101

MISSOURI
Bolivar	KAISER, Patricia L.	(417)326-4531	622
Chesterfield	GOLDMAN, Teri B.		446
Columbia	BELCHER, Nancy S.	(314)443-3161	76
	ELS, Nancy T.	(314)882-9162	346
	O'DELL, Charles A.	(314)445-6467	916
	SHIRKY, Martha H.	(314)882-6324	1131
	STEVENS, Robert R.	(314)445-5320	1191
Independence	VOSS, Kathryn J.	(816)836-8100	1289
Jefferson City	TORDOFF, Brian G.	(314)893-3147	1251
Kansas City	GERRITY, Marline R.	(816)276-1893	429
	GINDRA, Janice J.	(816)842-3600	437
	HUDSON, Rosetta A.	(816)459-6606	570
	INGERSOL, Robert S.	(816)333-7000	582
	MARCHANT, Thomas O.	(816)761-8873	768
	PETERSON, Paul A.	(816)363-5020	964
	ROTH, Sally	(816)842-0984	1059
	SPALDING, Helen H.	(816)276-1531	1171
	SULLIVAN, Marilyn G.	(816)276-1871	1208
Kirksville	ELLEBRACHT, Eleanor V.	(816)665-6158	343
Marionville	MCCROSKEY, Marilyn J.	(417)463-7372	800
Nevada	KIEL, Becky	(417)667-8181	647
Republic	HOWELLS, Joyce W.	(417)732-1128	565
Rolla	STEWART, J A.	(314)341-4007	1192
St Charles	MUETH, Elizabeth C.	(314)447-5116	875
Saint Joseph	HUGHES, Joan L.	(816)271-6000	571
St Louis	BECK, Sara R.	(314)889-5483	71
	DRAPER, Linda J.		318
	IGLAUER, Carol	(314)768-3137	581
	JOSEPH, Miriam E.	(314)965-4372	617

PROOFREADER (Cont'd)

MISSOURI (Cont'd)
St Louis	MCDERMOTT, Margaret H.	(314)889-6443	802
	NORTH, Daniel L.	(314)658-3093	909
	SMITH, Nancy M.	(314)241-2288	1159
	STELLING, Dwight D.	(314)351-2419	1186
	WHITE, Cheryl L.	(314)367-0741	1330
Springfield	CRABTREE, Anna B.	(417)887-1531	254
	KOTAMRAJU, Sarada	(417)883-8590	673
	MALTBY, Florence H.	(417)862-5119	764
	SINCLAIR, Regina A.	(417)865-8731	1143
Warrensburg	SADLER, Philip A.	(816)747-8726	1073

MONTANA
Havre	RITTER, Ann L.	(466)265-1308	1036
Missoula	DRIESSEN, Karen C.	(406)243-4070	320

NEBRASKA
Beatrice	FINDLING, Carol A.	(402)223-4595	377
Lincoln	FROBOM, Jerome B.	(402)483-7129	405
Minatare	JOHNSON, Elizabeth L.	(308)783-2188	604
Omaha	HOOVER, Clara G.	(402)895-3605	557
	WILLIS, Dorothy B.	(402)556-3431	1348

NEVADA
Las Vegas	MASTALIR, Janet K.	(702)648-7461	782
	SAUNDERS, Laverna M.	(702)739-3069	1084
	VOIT, Irene E.	(702)361-5475	1287
Reno	MANLEY, Charles W.	(702)785-4012	765

NEW HAMPSHIRE
Amherst	SHERWOOD, Janet R.	(603)673-9242	1129
Concord	HARE, William J.	(603)225-2012	501
	HIGGINS, Matthew J.	(603)228-3127	538
Derry	HARDSOG, Ellen L.	(603)432-6140	500
Hanover	BROWN, Stanley W.	(603)646-2037	147
Keene	MADDEN, Robert J.	(603)352-1909	758
Manchester	REINGOLD, Judith S.	(603)669-5300	1021
	THOMPSON, Debra J.	(603)669-1048	1239
Nashua	BARRETT, Beth R.	(603)880-3542	59
Portsmouth	JACOBS, Gloria	(603)431-9346	589
Rindge	STEARNS, Melissa M.	(603)899-5111	1183
Sunapee	TATE, Joanne D.	(603)763-9948	1225
Twin Mountain	PALMATIER, Susan M.	(603)846-2239	936

NEW JERSEY
Bloomfield	SHEARIN, Cynthia E.	(201)338-6545	1124
Cliffside Park	PAWSON, Robert D.	(201)943-3228	951
	SEKELY, Maryann	(201)943-4117	1113
Clifton	TROJAN, Judith L.	(201)472-3868	1257
Colts Neck	EDWARDS, Susan M.	(201)842-7679	338
Denville	VARIEUR, Normand L.		1278
Dover	RYAN, Mary E.	(201)989-3079	1071
Elizabeth	MILLER, Virginia L.	(201)351-3288	843
	SKRAMOUSKY, Mary C.	(201)351-2671	1147
Englewood	HALASZ, Etelka B.	(201)858-6970	484
Florham Park	BARRETT, Joyce C.	(201)765-1523	59
Glassboro	GARRABRANT, William A.	(609)863-6111	420
Hopatcong	FEAKINS, Lois S.	(201)398-8800	367
Linden	CANAVAN, Roberta N.	(201)486-3888	178
	PISKORIK, Elizabeth	(201)486-3888	976
Little Falls	RANDALL, Lynn E.	(201)278-5400	1006
Long Branch	HENKEL, Grace E.	(201)229-5721	528
Manalapan	FIELD, Jack	(201)431-7226	375
Matawan	KEARNEY, Jeanne E.	(201)566-7532	633
Metuchen	HIGGINS, Marilyn E.	(201)321-8745	538
Montvale	REDRICK, Miriam J.	(201)573-9000	1014
Morristown	DENSKY, Lois R.	(201)539-0407	293
Mount Holly	ALTERMAN, Deborah H.	(609)261-3458	18
	CARR, Charles E.	(609)267-9660	185
	CRAWFORD, Lynn D.	(609)267-9660	257
Neptune	EBELING, Elinor R.	(201)774-0793	334
	OGONEK, Donna L.	(201)922-4986	918
New Brunswick	FAVORS, Thelma L.		366
	MAZZEI, Peter J.	(201)249-4120	791
Newark	PROFETA, Patricia C.	(201)648-5911	995
North Arlington	CASEY, Mary A.	(201)997-2141	192
Oceanport	REISLER, Reina	(201)222-8182	1021
Paterson	ROTSAERT, Stefanie C.	(201)279-8044	1060

PROOFREADER (Cont'd)
NEW JERSEY (Cont'd)

Pennington	KAZIMIR, Edward O.	(609)737-3582	632
Piscataway	KAPLAN, Susan J.	(201)699-4327	626
Princeton	FARRELL, Mark R.		365
	HOELLE, Dolores M.	(609)452-3201	547
	IRVINE, James S.	(609)921-8092	584
	MOSS, Susan K.	(609)452-1212	872
Ridgewood	JONES, Anita M.	(201)444-7273	610
Roselle Park	BRIANT, Susan	(201)245-2456	134
South Orange	FAWCETT-BRANDON, Pamela S.	(201)762-0230	367
	VITART, Jane A.	(201)763-2181	1286
Springfield	CHANG, Joseph I.	(201)467-2037	200
Summit	SOMMER, Ursula M.	(201)593-8526	1167
Tenafly	VAN BIEMA, Mary E.	(201)567-3841	1272
Trenton	CONLEY, Gail D.	(609)771-6911	236
	WOODLEY, Robert H.	(609)771-2441	1366
Wayne	BIDDEN, Julia E.	(201)831-7801	94
	COHEN, Adrea G.	(201)696-8948	227
	FIRSCHEIN, Sylvia H.	(201)694-8600	379
Westwood	GINES, Noriko	(201)666-7042	437
Whippany	MUNSICK, Lee R.	(201)386-1920	879
Woodbridge	SPANGLER, William N.	(201)634-4450	1171

NEW MEXICO

Albuquerque	FREEMAN, Patricia E.		401
	ROLLER, Twila J.	(505)884-7871	1051
Clovis	MCBETH, Deborah E.	(505)762-7161	792
Las Cruces	MOORER, Jenny R.	(505)522-5126	862
Los Alamos	GODFREY, Lois E.	(505)662-7381	442
Santa Fe	LOPEZ, Kathryn P.	(505)982-5683	741

NEW YORK

Albany	LEWIS, Frances R.	(518)869-9317	723
	MILLER, Heather S.	(518)442-3626	838
	PINSLEY, Lauren J.	(518)445-2342	975
	SEVERINGHAUS, Ethel L.	(518)456-2110	1117
	VIA, Barbara J.	(518)442-3688	1283
Alfred	CONNOLLY, Bruce E.	(607)871-2494	237
	CULLEY, Paul T.	(607)871-2492	263
Amherst	MAYER, Erich J.	(716)691-5554	789
Bayside	BAKISH, David J.	(718)225-0475	50
	WEINER, Carolynn N.		1318
Bayville	SPIRT, Diana L.	(516)628-8341	1175
Bellerose	GATNER, Elliott S.		422
Binghamton	CHAMBERLAIN, Erna B.	(607)723-4064	197
Bohemia	JENSEN, Patricia K.	(516)244-2115	599
Briarwood	BORRESS, Lewis R.	(718)441-6328	117
Bronx	FRIEDMAN, Estelle Y.	(212)543-9060	403
	GEE, Ka C.	(212)960-7770	424
	GHOSH, Subhra	(212)588-8400	430
	GOLDBERG, Judy W.	(212)588-8400	444
	IOANID, Aurora S.	(212)220-0543	583
	LIEBER, Ellen C.	(212)920-4666	726
	MARK, Linda R.	(212)588-8400	770
	SOPELAK, Mary J.	(212)588-2266	1168
Bronxville	HUEBNER, Mary A.	(914)337-9300	570
Brooklyn	BRISTOW, Barbara A.	(718)596-1275	137
	GOTTFRIED, Erika D.	(713)852-5435	453
	KRAMER, Allan F.	(718)857-7825	675
	MANBECK, Virginia B.	(718)253-9413	764
	MEYERS, Charles	(718)342-1144	830
	NYREN, Dorothy E.	(718)780-7799	913
	PRUITT, Brenda F.	(718)287-1681	996
	ROGINSKI, James W.	(718)499-4850	1050
	WEINRICH, Gloria	(708)998-9116	1318
Buffalo	BUSH, Renee B.	(716)832-3081	165
	DECKER, Jean S.	(716)636-2784	285
	DIBARTOLO, Amy L.	(716)878-6309	299
	HALL, Russell W.	(716)834-9200	488
	NUZZO, Nancy B.	(716)636-2924	912
	SZEMRAJ, Edward R.	(716)895-7675	1218
	WELLS, Margaret R.	(716)636-2943	1322
Carle Place	HABER, Elinor L.	(516)877-1190	480
Chappaqua	CHEATHAM, Bertha M.	(914)238-3586	204
	DI BIANCO, Phyllis R.	(914)238-3911	299
Cheektowaga	WITT, Susan T.	(716)686-3620	1358
Cherry Plain	GILCHER, Edwin	(518)658-2429	434
Cold Spring	BARNHART, David K.	(914)265-2822	58

PROOFREADER (Cont'd)
NEW YORK (Cont'd)

Commack	SHAPIRO, Barbara S.	(516)368-4143	1121
Cortland	HEARN, Stephen S.	(607)753-2506	518
Croton-on-Hudson	CLARKE, Elizabeth S.	(914)271-3729	218
Dobbs Ferry	HASSAN, Mohammad Z.	(914)693-2031	511
	ROSHON, Nina C.	(914)693-9251	1057
East Northport	O'KEEFE, Laura K.		919
East Patchogue	PLUMER, F I.	(516)289-3134	978
Elmira	WEIDEMANN, Margaret A.	(607)733-8609	1316
Farmingdale	SALITA, Christine T.		1076
Fishkill	WINSOR, Kathleen	(914)896-6898	1356
FPO New York	LANE, Elizabeth L.		694
Garden City	DOCTOROW, Erica	(516)663-1042	307
	PIRODSKY, Nancy E.	(516)742-8405	975
Garrison	BALDWIN, Geraldine S.	(914)424-3020	51
Glen Falls	GRAMINSKI, Denise M.	(518)793-2927	457
Governors Island	GODWIN, Mary J.	(212)809-4351	443
Hamilton	WASHBURN, Keith E.	(315)824-3008	1307
Hempstead	ANDREWS, Charles R.	(516)560-5940	26
Hicksville	EDWARDS, Harriet M.		337
	HOLMES, Harvey L.	(516)935-4813	553
	SCHMIDTMANN, Nancy K.	(516)433-7040	1096
	TRAVERS, Jane E.		1254
Highland	LAWRENCE, Thomas A.	(914)691-2734	705
Hollis Hills	GOLD, Renee L.	(718)479-9534	444
Hornell	SMITH, Brian D.	(607)324-0841	1153
Hudson	HENDRICKS, Elaine M.		527
	MARTIN, Lyn M.	(518)828-1465	777
Huntington	FALVEY, Genemary H.	(516)673-0015	363
	ROSAR, Virginia W.	(516)549-4576	1054
	WOLFE, Barbara M.	(516)423-2495	1360
Jamestown	LEE, Sylvia	(716)483-5415	711
Long Beach	WASSERMAN, Ricki F.		1308
Long Island City	GORMAN, Mary B.	(718)392-2248	452
	HEWITT, Mary L.	(718)721-1862	535
Manhasset	DEE, Camille C.		286
Mattituck	PERLMAN, Stephen E.	(516)298-4335	959
Medina	TUOHEY, Jeanne D.	(716)798-2285	1263
Mt Vernon	O'DELL, Lorraine I.		916
	SHERRILL, Jocelyn T.	(914)667-4190	1129
New Rochelle	KONOVALOFF, Maria S.		670
New York	AMISON, Mary V.	(212)666-9645	20
	AUFSES, Harriet W.	(212)410-6056	39
	BERNAL, Rose M.	(212)674-6525	88
	BOWEN, Christopher E.	(212)815-8200	120
	BOZIWICK, George E.	(212)870-1675	124
	BRODY, Catherine T.	(212)228-7863	139
	BROWAR, Lisa M.	(212)930-0556	141
	BRUGNOLOTTI, Phyllis T.	(212)873-0677	150
	BUCENEC, Nancy L.	(212)337-6987	153
	CAMBRIA, Roberto		174
	CHRISTENSON, Janet S.	(212)930-0686	211
	CLINE, Herman H.	(212)777-4575	222
	COHEN, Rochelle F.	(212)577-3333	229
	COVERT, Nadine	(212)988-4876	252
	ENGLER, Gretchen	(212)703-4127	349
	FEBLES, Mary T.	(212)210-3983	367
	FLOERSHEIMER, Lee M.	(212)787-3727	385
	GITNER, Fred J.	(212)355-6100	439
	GOLD, Hilary G.	(212)242-2180	444
	GOLLOP, Sandra G.	(212)770-7911	447
	GRAY, Karen	(212)758-9663	460
	GRETES, Frances C.	(212)309-9034	467
	HAVENS, Shirley E.	(212)463-6804	513
	HAYNES, Patricia	(212)371-3200	516
	HENDERSON, Brad	(212)666-2674	526
	HERMAN, Marsha	(212)679-6105	531
	HOLTZE, Sally H.	(212)674-6973	555
	HOWELL, Josephine T.	(212)702-4255	565
	HSIAO, Shu Y.	(212)749-2873	567
	KAGAN, Ilse E.	(212)867-0174	621
	KAPNICK, Laura B.	(212)975-2917	626
	KARATNYTSKY, Christine A.	(212)420-1436	627
	KEMPE, Deborah A.	(212)595-6583	639
	LIDSKY, Ella	(212)663-4949	725
	MARGALITH, Helen M.	(212)575-0190	770
	MARTIN, Jean F.	(212)928-4231	776
	MEAGHER, Anne E.	(212)620-8462	819
	MOONEY, James E.	(212)873-3400	858

PROOFREADER (Cont'd)
NEW YORK (Cont'd)
New York

	MOTIHAR, Kamla	(212)838-8400	872
	MYERS, Maria P.	(212)473-6673	884
	PALMER, Paul R.	(212)865-5781	936
	POLSTER, Joanne	(212)564-7640	982
	PRAGER, George A.	(212)725-3083	989
	REMECZKI, Paul W.	(212)873-3400	1022
	ROSIGNOLO, Beverly A.	(212)962-4111	1057
	ROZENE, Janette B.	(212)760-7265	1064
	RUBINSTEIN, Ed	(212)725-4550	1065
	SAUNDERS, Dorette	(212)371-4800	1084
	SAYWARD, Nick H.	(212)573-4798	1087
	STOLLER, Michael E.	(212)280-4356	1196
	SULLIVAN, Stephen W.		1208
	SZMUK, Szilvia E.	(212)787-2573	1218
	TOMASULO, Patricia A.	(212)472-6442	1249
	TOPEL, Iris N.	(212)337-6988	1251
	TYLER, David M.	(212)350-4679	1266
	VELEZ, Sara B.	(212)870-1661	1281
North Tonawanda	HODGSON, Elizabeth A.	(716)694-8364	546
Oceanside	ROGGENKAMP, Alice M.	(516)766-1397	1050
Ossining	DOW, Sally R.	(914)941-2416	315
	LEW, Susan	(914)762-1154	722
Patchogue	NEUFELD, Judith B.	(516)289-6813	897
Peekskill	FALCONE, Elena C.	(914)528-2820	362
Penfield	PARKE, Kathryn E.		941
Pomona	HONOR, Naomi G.		556
Port Jervis	HOFMANN, Susan M.	(914)856-1513	548
Poughkeepsie	JEANNENEY, Mary L.	(914)452-7000	596
Riverdale	CLANCY, Kathy	(212)796-2057	215
Rochester	GRAY, Shirley M.	(716)475-2010	460
	HELBERS, Catherine A.	(716)594-9652	523
	ISGANITIS, Jamie C.	(716)461-1943	585
	LINDSAY, Jean S.	(716)428-7300	729
	MCGOWAN, Kathleen M.	(716)275-4437	807
	PLAIN, Marilyn V.	(716)275-8210	977
	SEASE, Sandra A.	(716)724-6783	1110
	STRIFE, Mary L.	(716)334-0091	1202
Saratoga Springs	ROBINSON, Jolene A.	(518)583-0208	1044
Scarsdale	ABEND, Jody U.	(914)723-1360	2
Schenectady	HODGES, Lois F.	(518)377-7738	546
	SEEMANN, Ann M.	(518)370-6277	1111
Selden	SALINERO, Amelia	(516)732-1268	1076
Sparkill	BARRIE, John L.	(914)359-7200	59
Stillwater	REEPMEYER, Marie C.	(518)785-6949	1016
Stony Brook	MASH, S D.		780
Sunnyside	WOOD, Sallie B.	(718)565-5490	1365
Syosset	JENSEN, Dennis F.	(516)921-0418	598
Syracuse	GRANKA, Bernard D.	(315)463-0875	457
	MINOR, Barbara B.	(315)425-9348	846
	PFOHL, Theodore E.	(315)473-4493	966
	REINSTEIN, Diana J.	(315)492-5500	1021
	SHELANDER, Frances R.	(315)469-8068	1125
Upton	LANE, Sandra G.	(516)282-7159	694
Utica	BROOKES, Barbara	(315)735-2279	140
Valley Stream	KUGLER, Sharon	(516)791-9385	682
Wallkill	RUBIN, Ellen B.	(914)565-5620	1064
Warwick	BATTOE, Melanie K.		65
West Hempstead	MASCIA, Regina B.	(516)489-9261	780
Westhampton Beach	KIRSCH, Anne S.	(516)288-2492	655
White Plains	HESS, James W.	(914)592-4342	534
Yonkers	BERGER, Paula E.	(914)968-7906	86
	GAFFNEY, Ellen E.	(914)968-6200	412
Yorktown Heights	LEE, Douglas E.	(914)245-8978	709

NORTH CAROLINA

Beaufort	BUMGARNER, John L.	(919)728-5530	157
Beulaville	FRAZELLE, Betty	(919)298-4658	399
Boone	BARKER, Richard T.	(704)264-3621	56
	BUSBIN, O M.	(704)264-7141	164
	WORRELL, Diane F.		1369
Chapel Hill	CARMICHAEL, James V.		183
	EATON, Elizabeth G.	(919)967-7966	333
	PEACOCK, Helen M.		951
	TALBERT, David M.	(919)962-0700	1220
Charlotte	BERRY, Mary W.	(704)371-4258	90

PROOFREADER (Cont'd)
NORTH CAROLINA (Cont'd)

Durham	CLEMONS, Kenneth L.	(919)688-2361	221
	EZZELL, Joline R.	(919)684-2034	360
	HAZEL, Debora E.	(919)683-6473	517
	MIDDLETON, Beverly D.	(919)477-8497	833
	WHITTINGTON, Erma P.	(919)489-9689	1334
Greensboro	JARRELL, James R.	(919)273-7061	594
	MCZORN, Bonita A.	(919)273-4886	819
	WURSTEN, Richard B.	(919)292-5683	1374
Greenville	COTTER, Michael G.	(919)752-8854	250
	DALTON, Lisa K.	(919)727-6533	271
	SHIRES, Nancy P.	(919)758-8252	1131
Jacksonville	VEITCH, Carol J.	(919)455-7350	1281
Kinston	EARL, Susan R.	(919)522-4773	332
Matthews	BACKMAN, Carroll H.	(704)847-6055	44
Montreat	FOREMAN, Kenneth J.	(704)669-2782	390
Newell	PENNINGER, Randy	(704)597-9248	957
Raleigh	PURYEAR, Pamela E.	(919)737-2836	998
	TAYLOR, Christine M.	(919)755-6870	1226
Reidsville	GUNN, Shirley A.	(919)342-0951	477
	PENN, Lea M.		957
Rocky Mount	WILGUS, Anne B.	(919)442-2662	1339
Sanford	MATOCHIK, Michael J.	(919)776-5737	784
	MURCHISON, Margaret B.	(919)258-3277	879
Wilmington	SEXTON, Spencer K.	(919)799-0177	1118
Winston-Salem	EKSTRAND, Nancy L.	(919)765-4817	341
	FOLTZ, Faye D.	(919)748-2295	388

NORTH DAKOTA

Bismarck	VYZRALEK, Dolores E.	(701)223-1857	1290
	WEZELMAN, Joy L.	(701)222-0271	1328
Fargo	BRKIC, Beverly T.	(701)237-5865	138
Minot	BOARDMAN, Edna M.	(701)839-7424	108
	ROBERTSON, Pamela S.	(701)838-6080	1042

OHIO

Akron	GUSS, Margaret B.	(216)375-7224	478
Albany	CONLIFFE, Bobbi L.	(614)698-3336	236
Ashland	ROEPKE, David E.		1048
Bay Village	DOMBEY, Kathryn W.	(216)871-5024	310
Bedford	PARCH, Grace D.		939
Bowling Green	COLLINS, Evron S.	(419)372-7905	232
Cincinnati	ABRAMS, Roger E.	(513)821-5984	3
	CONNICK, Kathleen D.	(513)474-4975	237
	DINNESEN, Peter H.	(513)771-7600	305
	FROMMEYER, L R.	(513)475-3627	405
	HALIBEY-BILYK, Christine M.	(513)559-4320	486
	KENT, Rose M.		642
	LE BLANC, Judith E.		708
	LEIBOLD, Cynthia K.		713
	PALKOVIC, Mark A.	(513)475-4471	935
	POCKROSE, Sheryl R.	(513)369-6954	979
	RIFFEY, Robin S.	(513)871-3087	1033
	SMITH, Maureen M.	(513)369-6917	1158
Cleveland	PETIT, J M.	(216)749-5052	965
Cleveland Heights	BORCHERT, Catherine G.	(216)932-8324	116
	SPAHR, Cheryl L.	(216)382-7675	1170
Columbus	BETCHER, Melissa A.	(614)466-5511	92
	BRANCH, Susan	(614)267-3805	127
	BRANDT, Michael H.	(614)863-2814	128
	MCDOWELL, Judith H.	(614)771-0273	804
	MULARSKI, Carol A.	(614)292-9810	876
	ORLANDO, Jacqueline M.	(614)262-6765	926
	RATLIFF, Priscilla	(614)488-1622	1009
	SANDERS, Nancy P.		1080
	STOBAUGH, Robert E.	(614)451-3271	1195
Dayton	EVANS, Stephen P.	(513)220-9506	358
Hubbard	GROHL, Arlene P.	(216)759-7800	471
Kalida	MILLER, Marian A.		840
Kent	BOLEK, Ann D.	(216)678-9429	112
Lakewood	KEATING, Michael F.	(216)221-0608	633
Lima	MCDANIEL, Deanna J.	(419)991-6065	801
Maple Heights	KATONA, Florence C.		629
Marion	GERWIN, Barbara L.	(614)387-0992	430
Massillon	LESLIE, Camille J.	(216)832-9831	718
	PLUMMER, Karen A.	(216)477-1447	978
Oregon	JOHNSON, Debbie L.	(419)698-7318	603
Oxford	ZASLOW, Barry J.	(513)523-3980	1386

Perrysburg	LOCKE-GAGNON, Rebecca		
	A.	(419)874-1725	736
Reynoldsburg	WULKER, Clare	(614)866-5963	1374
Shaker Heights	RODDA, Donna S.	(216)283-1064	1047
Sidney	WILSON, Memory A.	(513)492-1315	1352
South Euclid	BENSING, Karen M.	(216)932-0186	83
Springfield	ARK, Connie E.	(513)324-8470	31
Terrace Park	SEIK, Jo E.	(513)831-0780	1112
Toledo	LERNER, Esther T.	(419)531-2269	717
Troy	BAKER, Martha A.	(513)335-6397	49
University Heights	HECHT, Joseph A.	(216)291-5506	519
Wapakoneta	FREW, Martha G.	(419)738-8333	402
Westlake	CHARVAT, Catherine T.	(216)871-6391	203
Worthington	BLOCK, Bernard A.	(614)436-7140	106
Yellow Springs	NEWMAN, Marianne L.		899
Youngstown	JACOBSON, Susan D.	(216)742-3679	590
	LUTTRELL, Jeffrey R.	(216)742-3681	750

OKLAHOMA

Ardmore	KIMBLE, Valerie F.	(405)226-3980	649
Bethany	FLINNER, Beatrice E.	(405)789-6400	385
Midwest City	ROBERTSON, Retha M.	(405)733-1543	1042
Muskogee	GUTIERREZ, Carolyn A.	(918)687-6479	479
Norman	MEACHAM, Mary	(405)321-8444	819
Oklahoma City	BOOTENHOFF, Rebecca J.	(405)728-7072	116
	DOBBERTEEN, Sara J.	(405)842-0890	307
	MEYERS, Duane H.	(405)946-2488	830
	NASH, Helen B.	(405)525-7504	888
Tahlequah	HILL, Helen K.		540
Tulsa	HACKER, Connie J.	(918)587-6561	481
	MURPHY, Peggy A.	(918)743-7177	881
	TOOLEY, Katherine J.	(918)494-8759	1250
	WEAVER, Pamela J.	(918)592-6000	1312
Walters	ZACHARY, Patricia A.	(405)875-3071	1385

OREGON

Eugene	ALLEN, Alice J.	(503)686-3064	14
	EMMENS, Thomas A.	(503)345-6439	348
	MCDANIELS, Patricia R.	(503)343-4728	801
	SHULER, John A.	(503)686-3048	1133
	WAND, Patricia A.	(503)686-3056	1302
Forest Grove	FALZON, Judith A.	(503)357-3023	363
Grants Pass	MCCOY, Joanne	(503)474-1739	799
Hillsboro	VIXIE, Anne C.	(503)645-0527	1286
Marylhurst	GIMPL, Caroline A.	(503)636-8105	437
Portland	EDWARDS, Susan E.	(506)224-6812	338
	LEGER, Norissa	(503)246-2714	712
Salem	BAUER, Marilyn A.	(503)581-4292	65

PENNSYLVANIA

Allison Park	HADIDIAN, Dikran Y.	(412)487-2159	482
Altoona	SHERIDAN, Margaret G.	(814)942-2565	1127
Blue Bell	LAUTENSCHLAG, Elisabeth		
	C.		703
Boyertown	EMERICK, John L.	(215)369-7422	347
Braddock	SHAPIRO, Ruth T.	(412)636-5030	1121
Bryn Mawr	MERZ, Lawrie H.	(215)527-6858	827
Center Valley	WELLE, Jacob P.	(215)282-1100	1321
Chambersburg	EZELL, Johanna V.	(717)264-2269	360
Chester Heights	OWENS, Irene E.		932
Clarion	DINGLE, Susan	(814)226-2271	304
	HORN, Janice H.	(814)226-7367	559
Coatesville	SILVER, Diane L.	(215)384-7648	1138
Gettysburg	CHIESA, Adele M.	(717)334-1651	208
Glenmoore	VOURVOULIAS, Sabrina M.	(215)942-3421	1289
Glenside	NIEWEG, Clinton F.	(215)884-5878	904
Harleysville	HILLEGAS, Ferne E.		541
Harrisburg	SHULTZ, Suzanne M.	(717)782-4292	1133
Hatfield	RITTER, Ralph E.	(215)368-5000	1037
Haverford	CORRIGAN, John T.	(215)896-7458	247
Holsopple	SLICK, Myrna H.	(814)479-7148	1149
Indiana	KROAH, Larry A.	(412)463-2055	679
Jenkintown	BARTZ, Alice P.	(215)887-4338	62
Johnstown	BRICE, Heather W.	(814)539-8153	134
	KREITZBURG, Marilyn J.	(814)266-7386	677
Kingston	PAUSTIAN, P R.	(717)283-2651	950
Lancaster	ZEAGER, Lloyd	(717)393-9745	1387
Langhorne	BURSK, Mary A.	(215)752-5101	163

Lock Haven	PALMA, Nancy C.	(717)748-1049	935
Malvern	QUINTILIANO, Barbara		1000
Meadville	STALLARD, Kathryn E.	(814)333-4363	1179
Media	BURGESS, Rita N.	(215)565-7900	159
	ELLISON, J T.	(215)566-1699	345
Merion	HAAS, Carol C.	(215)664-1689	480
Morrisville	TOMAR, Jeanne	(215)736-2177	1249
New Castle	FUSCO, Marilyn A.		410
New Holland	MCGEE, Yvonne M.		806
New Kensington	TEOLIS, Marilyn G.	(412)339-0255	1231
New Oxford	FOX, Merle U.		395
New Wilmington	BRAUTIGAM, David K.	(412)946-7330	130
Norristown	CATHEY, Gail L.	(215)278-5100	195
Philadelphia	ADELMAN, Jean S.	(215)545-4446	6
	ALDRIDGE, Carol J.	(215)893-9613	11
	CALDWELL, John M.	(215)545-2809	172
	COX, Carol A.		253
	CUTRONA, Cheryl	(215)844-9027	268
	GRACE, William M.	(215)925-8090	455
	GRAY, Priscilla M.	(215)386-6276	460
	GREEN, Rose B.	(215)828-7029	462
	GROSSMAN, Robert M.	(215)893-1954	473
	HORNIG-ROHAN, James E.	(215)848-0554	560
	ICKES, Barbara J.	(215)745-9767	581
	JACOBY, Beth E.	(215)787-8215	590
	KOHN, Roger S.	(215)438-5635	668
	MADER, Marion C.	(215)342-0760	759
	MORRIS, Leslie A.	(215)985-4384	867
	NIGHTINGALE, Daniel	(215)288-1151	904
	SCARPATO, Loann C.	(215)438-1911	1088
	SMITH, Linda D.	(215)963-3670	1157
	SOWICZ, Eugenia V.	(215)354-2110	1170
	SPAWN, Carol M.	(215)299-1093	1172
	TANNER, Anne B.	(215)895-2483	1222
	WOLF, Edwin		1360
	YERGER, George A.	(215)587-4887	1379
	YOLTON, Jean S.	(215)878-7548	1380
	ZIPF, Elizabeth M.	(215)587-4815	1389
Pittsburgh	AL SADAT, Amira A.	(412)421-9444	17
	BLEIER, Carol S.	(412)563-2712	105
	ENGLERT, Mary A.	(412)795-1761	350
	EVES, Judith A.	(412)471-1477	359
	FREEDMAN, Phyllis D.	(412)784-8599	400
	JOHNSTON, Bruce A.	(412)731-8800	610
	KRZYS, Richard A.	(412)624-9459	681
	MITTEN, Lisa A.	(412)521-4462	850
	ROOT, Deane L.	(412)624-4100	1054
	ROSS, Nina M.	(412)624-9475	1058
Pocono Summit	ANDERMAN, Lynea	(717)839-9495	21
Point Pleasant	GENNETT, Robert G.		427
Scranton	BABISH, Jo A.	(717)963-2145	43
Shippenville	EMERICK, Kenneth F.	(814)226-5775	347
South Williamsport	HICKEY, Kate D.	(717)322-2733	536
State College	CHANG, Shirley L.	(717)893-2312	201
	LINDSAY, Ann M.	(814)237-0714	729
	NADESKI, Karen L.	(814)238-7890	886
	PHILLIPS, Janet C.	(814)238-0254	968
Swarthmore	HAMILTON, Gloria R.	(215)544-1369	492
University Park	CARSON, M S.	(814)865-1818	188
	GARNER, Diane L.	(814)865-4861	419
	ZABEL, Diane M.	(814)863-2898	1385
Upper Darby	MORGAN, Dorothy H.	(215)789-9727	863
	REILLY, Rebecca S.		1020
	SILVERMAN, Karen S.	(215)734-0146	1138
Upper Saint Clair	FULMER, Dina J.	(412)831-8664	409
Warminster	BECKER, Linda C.	(215)443-7008	72
West Chester	ASTORGA, Alicia M.	(215)793-2417	37
	MCCAWLEY, Christina W.	(215)436-0720	795
Yardley	ROSE, Dianne E.	(215)493-2311	1054

PUERTO RICO

Caparra Heights	FERNANDEZ, Josefina L.	(809)782-2618	373
Ponce	GUILLEMARD DE COLON,		
	Teresita		476
San Juan	COLLAZO, Maria L.		232
	HAMEL, Eleanor C.	(809)765-4426	491
	NADAL, Antonio	(809)724-6869	885
San Sebastian	JARAMILLO, Juana S.	(809)896-1389	594

PROOFREADER (Cont'd)
PUERTO RICO (Cont'd)

Trujillo Alto	SABATER-SOLA, Rigel		1072

RHODE ISLAND

Kingston	SCHNEIDER, Stewart P.	(401)792-2878	1097
Lincoln	DESMARAIS, Norman P.	(401)333-3275	295
Providence	BRAUNSTEIN, Mark M.	(401)521-4771	130
	CASHMAN, Norine D.	(401)863-3218	192
	QUINN, Karen H.	(401)277-2473	1000
	WILSON, Barbara L.	(401)277-2726	1350

SOUTH CAROLINA

Charleston	PARKER, Mary A.	(803)556-9454	942
Clemson	TAYLOR, Dennis S.	(803)656-3031	1226
Columbia	FRITZ, William R.		405
	GEOGHEGAN, Doris J.	(803)777-4206	427
	MILTON, Brenda R.	(803)452-5454	845
	MOSS, Patsy G.	(803)799-4349	872
Denmark	BOOK, Imogene I.	(803)793-3660	115
Easley	BLAIR, Sharon K.	(803)855-0866	103
Greenville	SLIFE, Joye D.	(803)271-7281	1149
Greenwood	FECKO, Marybeth	(803)223-1810	367
	HARE, Ann T.	(803)229-8365	501
	HILL, Thomas W.	(803)227-4851	541
Irmo	BARDIN, Angela D.	(803)781-3138	56
Liberty	DUSENBERRY, Mary D.	(803)843-8225	329
Orangeburg	SMALLS, Mary L.	(803)536-8852	1151
Spartanburg	FAWVER, Darlene E.	(803)596-9074	367
Surfside Beach	SALMON, Robin R.	(803)238-4655	1077

SOUTH DAKOTA

Brookings	BROWN, Philip L.	(605)692-7735	146
Pierre	HILMOE, Deann D.	(605)224-3178	541
Sioux Falls	LANG, Elizabeth A.		695

TENNESSEE

Brentwood	NORTON, Tedgina	(615)371-0090	910
Bristol	HERRING, Mark Y.	(615)968-9449	533
Chattanooga	REARDON, Elizabeth M.		1013
Clarksville	RIVES, Lydia L.	(615)647-9484	1037
Cleveland	NICOL, Jessie T.		902
Cookeville	LAFEVER, Susan	(615)372-3210	687
Dowelltown	EASTERLY, Ambrose	(615)597-1390	333
Germantown	RONDESTVEDT, Helen F.	(901)756-5470	1053
Kingsport	FANSLOW, Malinda C.	(645)246-7171	363
Knoxville	BEAL, Gretchen F.	(615)521-2500	68
	CLELAND, Nancy D.	(615)588-5406	220
	HASTINGS, Constance M.	(615)690-0368	511
	HILL, Ruth J.	(615)974-4381	540
	LOCKWOOD, Bonnie J.	(615)687-5221	736
	PICQUET, D C.	(615)974-4381	971
	RADER, Joe C.	(615)523-6937	1002
Memphis	BAER, Ellen H.	(901)725-8853	45
	BAKER, Bonnie U.	(901)324-6536	48
	PERRY, Glenda L.	(901)527-4348	960
Murfreesboro	YOUREE, Beverly B.	(615)896-4911	1384
Nashville	ARMONTROUT, Brian A.	(615)320-3678	32
	FANCHER, Evelyn P.	(615)255-8033	363
	GMEINER, Timothy J.	(615)297-7958	442
	HEARNE, Mary G.	(615)383-8989	518
	HODGES, Terence M.	(615)322-2299	546
	LEWIS, Carol E.	(615)322-2291	722
	STEPHENS, Alonzo T.		1187
	WATTS, Adalyn	(615)321-1332	1310
	WHITEHEAD, Jane		1332
Oak Ridge	DAVIS, Inez W.	(615)482-9619	279
Sewanee	CAMP, Thomas E.	(616)598-5931	175
	HAYMES, Don		516
	WATSON, Gail H.	(615)598-0120	1309

TEXAS

Abilene	BRADLEY, C D.	(915)677-7281	125
Amarillo	GROSS, Iva H.	(806)378-3000	472
	SNELL, Marykay H.	(806)353-5329	1163
Arlington	MACFARLANE, Francis X.	(817)265-8309	755
Austin	PARKER, David F.	(512)450-1931	941
	SPRUG, Joseph W.	(512)448-8474	1176
	TAYLOR, Nancy L.	(512)346-1426	1228
	WASSENICH, Red	(512)495-7151	1308

PROOFREADER (Cont'd)
TEXAS (Cont'd)

Beaumont	HOLLAND, Mary M.	(409)892-8885	551
	NISBY, Dora R.	(409)899-9972	904
Bedford	PETERS, Mary N.	(817)283-3739	962
Big Spring	BRADBERRY, Anna L.	(915)263-1468	125
Brownfield	HAMILTON, Betty D.	(806)637-4213	491
Bryan	MOUNCE, Clara B.	(409)779-1736	873
	RABINS, Joan W.	(409)776-0374	1001
College Station	ST. CLAIR, Gloriana S.	(409)696-8982	1075
	THOMPSON, Christine E.	(409)845-8157	1239
Dallas	CAMPBELL, Shirley A.	(214)330-0027	177
	CLEE, June E.	(214)941-3375	220
	CLEMENTS, Cynthia L.	(214)238-6153	221
	DOMA, Tshering		310
	FOUDRAY, Rita C.	(214)824-1943	393
	HEIZER, Carolyn H.	(214)363-5148	523
	KANE, Deborah A.	(214)247-1952	624
	LEVINE, Harriet L.	(214)521-7165	720
	LOVELL, Bonnie A.	(214)826-1924	743
	MENDRO, Donna C.		824
	SACKETT-WILK, Susan A.	(214)307-1304	1073
	SNODGRASS, Wilson D.	(214)692-2342	1163
El Paso	ANDERSON, Mark	(915)858-0905	24
	BROWN, Susan W.	(915)747-5678	147
	GEARY, Kathleen A.	(915)533-5777	424
	KNOTT, Teresa L.	(915)533-3020	665
	MALLORY, Elizabeth J.	(915)593-1337	763
	RAMSEY, Donna E.	(915)855-1218	1005
	ROBERTS, Glenda S.	(915)541-4770	1040
Flower Mound	SVEINSSON, Joan L.	(214)539-9308	1212
Fort Worth	DE TONNANCOUR, P R.	(817)763-1790	296
	MONGOLD, Alice D.	(817)457-9080	854
	MUELLER, Peggy	(817)870-7701	875
	WESTBROOK, Brenda S.	(817)831-7232	1326
	WROTENBERY, Carl R.	(817)923-1921	1373
Galveston	NEALE, Marilee	(409)765-5575	891
	RASCHE, Richard R.	(409)762-3139	1008
Glen Rose	KENDALL, Lyle H.	(817)897-4991	640
Harlingen	MILLS, Helen L.		844
Houston	BEDARD, Evelyn M.		73
	CRIST, Lynda L.	(713)527-4990	259
	FLESHMAN, Nancy A.	(713)552-2000	384
	FORD, Margaret C.	(713)527-8101	389
	HACKNEY, Judith G.	(713)496-5590	481
	MOORE, Sheryl R.	(713)271-1092	861
	SCHWERBEL, Jeannette E.	(713)861-1373	1105
	STUBBLEFIELD, J G.		1204
	TEUN, Rebecca L.	(713)792-6630	1233
	WELCH, C B.	(713)749-4245	1321
Huntsville	CULP, Paul M.	(409)294-1619	264
Irving	AYRES, Edwin M.	(214)254-4108	43
La Porte	ATKINS, Winston	(713)479-2421	38
Lake Jackson	RICE, Margaret R.	(409)297-2897	1027
Leander	BIGLEY, John E.		96
Lewisville	TALLEY, Pat L.	(214)434-2545	1221
Lockhart	HOLLAND, Deborah K.	(512)398-4665	550
Lubbock	HARP, Marlene M.		503
	LUIKART, Nancy B.	(806)799-5471	747
	VAN SCHAIK, Jo A.	(806)743-2213	1277
McAllen	MYCUE, David J.		884
McKinney	CORREDOR, Javier	(214)548-9971	247
San Angelo	PENNER, Elaine C.	(915)658-4534	957
San Antonio	BADING, Kathryn E.	(512)655-4120	44
	BELL, Joy A.	(512)496-2057	77
	CHANCE, Truett L.		199
	DUNCAN, Lucy E.	(512)828-1261	325
	GONZALEZ, Sharon M.		448
	LOCH, Edward J.	(512)734-2620	735
	MANEY, James W.	(512)341-1366	765
	PHILLIPS, Sylvia E.	(512)333-2598	969
Spring	ATRI, Pushkala V.	(713)370-3673	38
The Woodlands	PEYTON, Janice L.	(713)292-4441	966
Uvalde	KINGSBERY, Evelyn B.	(512)278-4401	652
Waco	COLEY, Betty A.	(817)754-6114	231
Wichita Falls	ROBERTS, Ernest J.	(817)855-2390	1040

PROOFREADER (Cont'd)
UTAH
Farmington	POLLARD, Louise	(801)451-5282	981
Logan	PIETTE, Mary I.	(801)753-6878	972
Magna	GOFORTH, Allene M.	(801)250-7507	444
Ogden	WILSON, Brenda J.	(801)479-1407	1350
Payson	GILLUM, Gary P.	(801)465-4527	436
Provo	LAMB, Connie	(801)378-5627	689
	LYMAN, Lovisa	(801)378-3297	751
Salt Lake City	HINDMARSH, Douglas P.	(801)328-2609	542
	MARCHANT, Cathy	(801)364-8399	768
	PATTERSON, Myron B.	(801)581-7265	948

VERMONT
Burlington	DAY, Martha T.	(802)863-0506	282
Putney	THOMPSON, Jane K.	(802)387-4767	1240
Rutland	MCCULLOUGH, Doreen J.	(802)773-5900	801
	SHERMAN, Jacob R.	(802)773-1860	1128

VIRGIN ISLANDS
Charlotte Amalie	BARZELAY, Mary S.	(809)774-4838	62

VIRGINIA
Alexandria	HALL, Forest A.	(703)548-6367	487
	OMARA, Marie T.	(703)960-3981	923
	OSIA, Ruby R.	(703)549-3048	928
	SMITH, Thomas E.		1161
	STEVENS, Roberta A.	(703)960-0464	1191
	VAROUTSOS, Mary A.	(703)836-0156	1279
	WOODWARD, Lawrence W.	(703)751-9426	1368
Amelia	SMITH, Adeline M.		1152
Annandale	TYSINGER, Barbara R.	(703)354-8688	1267
Arlington	ASHKENAS, Bruce F.	(301)763-7410	36
	BROWN, Charles M.	(703)284-8174	142
	CARR, Timothy B.		186
	DENNIE, David L.	(703)685-0208	292
	KECSKES, Lily C.	(703)528-0730	633
	KNIGHT, Nancy H.	(703)522-2604	664
	LARMOUR, Rosamond E.	(703)247-7820	698
Burke	GOUDREAU, Ronald A.	(703)569-0994	454
Charlottesville	COOPER, Jean L.	(804)978-4363	243
	MORRIS, Karen L.	(804)293-2475	867
	WHITE, William		1332
Chesterfield	DUNAWAY, Carolyn D.	(804)748-1763	325
Fairfax	PFEIFFER, David A.	(703)425-4685	966
Falls Church	HABERLAND, Jody	(703)573-7279	481
Fredericksburg	VANDERBERG, E S.	(703)371-3311	1273
Hampton	JORDAN, Caroline D.	(804)727-6234	616
Hollins College	BECKER, Charlotte B.	(703)362-6235	72
Lexington	DELONG, Edward J.	(703)463-0567	290
McLean	CHEVERIE, Joan F.	(703)893-3889	207
Norfolk	NICULA, J G.	(804)444-5321	903
	SWAINE, Cynthia W.	(804)627-1115	1212
Reston	JOSLYN, Camille	(703)471-1641	618
	KARRER, Jonathan K.	(703)648-4302	628
	MONTGOMERY, Suzanne L.	(703)435-1974	856
Richmond	LIGGAN, Mary K.	(804)355-2509	726
	OWEN, Karen V.	(804)649-6132	931
	SHEPARD, E L.	(804)358-4901	1126
	WOODWARD, Elaine H.	(804)771-2219	1368
Roanoke	COLLINS, Mitzi L.		233
	OBRIST, Cynthia W.	(703)362-6235	915
Springfield	CASWELL, Mary C.	(703)642-0340	194
Virginia Beach	BILLERT, Julia A.	(804)427-7150	96
Waynesboro	RUFE, Charles P.	(703)949-6173	1066
Wise	CHISHOLM, Clarence E.	(703)328-2431	209
Woodbridge	ENGLAND, Ellen M.	(703)670-2191	349
	MELVIN, Kay H.	(703)491-2055	823

WASHINGTON
Bainbridge Island	SPEARMAN, Marie A.	(206)842-6636	1172
Bellingham	ANDERSEN, Eileen	(206)676-6481	21
	BLUME, Scott	(206)671-8960	107
Bothell	DECOSTER, Barbara L.	(206)488-7537	286
	YEE, J E.	(206)625-4870	1379
Edmonds	HALEY, Marguerite R.	(206)546-6561	486
Everett	GRINSTEAD, Beth K.	(206)258-1951	471
Longview	DOLBEY, Mary B.	(206)577-2780	309
Ocean Park	EASLEY, Janet T.	(206)665-5580	332

PROOFREADER (Cont'd)
WASHINGTON (Cont'd)
Seattle	BAGG, Deborah L.	(206)621-7896	45
	BRZUSTOWICZ, Richard J.	(206)527-9357	152
	ERICKSON, Jane	(206)938-0846	352
	HILL, Ann M.	(206)525-4212	539
	LIPTON, Laura E.	(206)543-8616	732
	PRESS, Nancy O.	(206)367-6568	991
	SILVA, Mary E.		1138
	TURNER, Tamara A.	(216)325-9481	1265
Walla Walla	CARR, Carol L.	(509)527-5191	185
Woodinville	GARRETSON, Laurie J.	(206)483-6213	420

WEST VIRGINIA
Huntington	STARKEY, Bonnie F.	(303)523-3109	1182
Morgantown	ESKRIDGE, Virginia C.	(304)293-5300	354
St Albans	PALMER, Marguerite C.	(304)722-6349	936
Wheeling	JULIAN, Charles A.	(304)233-5900	619

WISCONSIN
Appleton	VIGNOVICH, Ray L.	(414)735-1290	1284
Beloit	THOM, Pat A.	(608)365-3311	1235
Brookfield	CASEY, Jean M.	(414)781-2545	192
Cudahy	KLAUSMEIER, Arno M.	(414)744-0268	658
Eau Claire	BUGHER, Kathryn M.	(715)834-8104	155
	CARROLL, Barbara T.		187
Franklin	SANCHEZ, Alexander J.	(414)425-8214	1079
Green Bay	MUSICH, Gerald D.	(414)437-7623	883
Madison	CONNER, P Z.	(608)256-4440	237
	HOWDEN, Regis	(608)257-1023	565
	JESUDASON, Melba	(608)263-7464	600
	LAESSIG, Joan M.	(608)238-3705	687
	ROSENSHIELD, Jill K.	(608)233-2518	1057
	SHAFTMAN, Sarah	(608)241-7153	1119
	WISEMAN, Mary J.		1357
Menomonie	GRAF, David L.	(715)232-1202	455
Mequon	AMAN, Mary J.	(414)242-9031	19
	MADSEN, Joyce	(414)242-5403	759
Milwaukee	BJORKLUND, Edi		100
	COONEY, Charles W.	(414)444-6130	241
	GILL, Norman N.	(414)352-1545	435
	MCKILLIP, Rita J.	(414)347-1335	811
	MISNER, Barbara	(414)384-6535	847
	MURPHY, Virginia A.	(414)271-1444	881
	POPESCU, Constantin C.	(414)332-5909	983
	RISTIC, Jovanka	(414)229-6282	1036
	SCHLUGE, Vicki L.	(414)527-8477	1094
	SHUTKIN, Sara A.	(414)332-3321	1134
Montello	TANNER, Linda L.	(608)297-2228	1223
Oak Creek	TASNADI, Deborah L.	(414)764-9725	1224
Oshkosh	CORBLY, James E.	(414)231-4768	245
	TERESINSKI, Sally S.	(414)582-4324	1231
Platteville	SCHMITT, Madelaine M.	(608)342-1667	1096
Reedsville	OHLEMACHER, Janet H.	(414)754-4831	919
Rhinelander	SLYGH, Gyneth	(715)362-3465	1151
River Falls	ADAM, Anthony J.	(715)425-5383	4
Waukesha	ROOZEN, Nancy L.	(414)521-8868	1054
	TREBBY, Janis G.	(414)548-0261	1255
West Allis	GRUEL, Janice L.	(414)541-5222	474

WYOMING
Cheyenne	HALLBERG, Carl V.	(307)778-8577	489
	KLEIN, Barbara L.	(307)635-3270	659
	MCGOWAN, Anne W.	(307)777-6430	807
	RAU, Dittakavi N.	(307)777-7509	1008
Lander	HEUER, Jane T.	(307)332-3793	535
Laramie	OSTRYE, Anne T.	(307)766-5312	929
Worland	HARRINGTON, Carolyn B.	(307)347-4490	504

CANADA

ALBERTA
Airdrie	WAUGH, Alan L.	(403)948-7921	1310
Calgary	ONN, Shirley A.	(403)282-5311	924
	ROBINS, Nora D.	(403)274-8837	1043
	STEVELMAN, Sharon R.	(403)271-0134	1190
Edmonton	BAYRAK, Bettie	(403)478-8062	68
	COOKE, Geraldine A.	(403)439-5879	241
	RIDGE, Alan D.		1032
	ROONEY, Sieglinde E.	(403)432-3793	1053

PROOFREADER (Cont'd)
ALBERTA (Cont'd)
Edmonton

	TRAICHEL, Rudolf D.	(403)437-5718	1253
Fort McMurray	BRUCE, Marianne E.	(403)743-5094	149
Spirit River	ZUK, Donna R.	(403)864-3503	1391

BRITISH COLUMBIA
Burnaby	GOW, Susan P.	(604)439-0931	454
Clearbrook	HUDSON, Susan P.	(604)859-7814	570
	VIIERANS, Mary E.	(604)859-7814	1284
North Vancouver	ASHCROFT, Susan M.	(604)984-8004	35
Vancouver	HART, Elizabeth	(604)228-9031	507

MANITOBA
Brandon	SIMUNDSSON, Elva D.	(204)728-7234	1142
FlinFlon	HOBBS, Henry C.	(204)687-6647	545
Winnipeg	REEDMAN, M R.	(204)983-3437	1015

NEWFOUNDLAND
St John's	MARTINEZ, Helen	(709)753-6210	779

NOVA SCOTIA
Amherst	CAMPBELL, Margaret E.	(902)667-2888	177
Dartmouth	LOGAN, Penelope A.	(902)434-6664	737
Halifax	GLENISTER, Peter	(902)443-4450	441
	MACLENNAN, Oriel C.	(902)454-0697	757

ONTARIO
Barrie	ADDY, Kathryn J.	(705)726-8693	6
Deep River	ALBURGER, Thomas P.		11
Guelph	PAWLEY, Carolyn P.	(519)824-4120	951
	ROURKE, Lorna E.	(519)824-4120	1061
Kingston	MORLEY, William F.	(613)548-3432	865
London	PARR, John R.	(519)439-3271	943
Ottawa	BLACK, Jane L.	(613)234-5006	101
	BREGAINT, Bernard J.	(613)741-0242	131
	BRIERE, Jean M.	(613)996-3817	135
	COOK, Terry G.	(613)996-7726	240
	REILLY, Brian O.	(613)993-9225	1020
	SPRY, Patricia		1176
	VEEKEN, Mary L.	(613)523-2169	1280
	WARD, William D.	(613)225-7557	1304
Richmond Hill	ABRAM, Persis R.	(416)884-9288	3
St Thomas	RHYNAS, Don M.	(519)631-6050	1026
Scarborough	KEYS, Sandra A.		645
Sudbury	GOSS, Alison M.	(705)522-2883	453
Toronto	BOITE, Mary E.	(416)461-2274	111
	DESOMOGYI, Aileen A.	(416)466-6572	295
	DOWDING, Martin R.	(416)925-7593	315
	FAIR, Linda A.	(416)369-2438	361
	LAVERTY, Corinne Y.	(416)393-7024	703
	MILANICH, Melanie M.	(416)393-7180	834
	MORRISON, Carol A.	(416)967-3796	868
	NIXON, Audrey I.	(416)531-0830	906
	NORTH, John A.	(416)979-5142	909
	POWELL, Wyley L.	(416)965-3906	989
	THODY, Susan I.	(416)762-1690	1235
	VAN ORDER, Mary J.	(416)924-0671	1276
	WEIHS, Jean	(416)961-6027	1317
Willowdale	MCLEAN, Paulette A.	(416)636-4877	814
Windsor	HANDY, Mary J.	(519)256-3250	495

QUEBEC
Blainville	JETTE, Monika E.	(514)430-4945	600
Hull	MAILLOUX, Jean Y.	(819)997-5365	761
Laval	AUGER, Bernard	(514)687-9730	39
Montebello	WENK, Arthur B.		1324
Montreal	AUBIN, Robert	(514)323-7260	38
	BERARDINUCCI, Heather R.	(514)255-2445	84
	BUTLER, Patricia	(514)283-9046	167
	CLARKE, Robert F.	(514)731-9211	219
	DUMONT, Monique	(514)288-0100	325
	FOWLES, Alison C.	(514)842-7680	394
	MOLLER, Hans	(514)398-4740	853
	ORLANDO, Richard P.	(514)877-1470	926
	PELLETIER, Rosaire	(514)382-0895	955
	ROUSSEAU, Denis	(514)843-3214	1061
	TREVICK, Selma D.	(514)487-3367	1255
	WINIARZ, Elizabeth	(514)848-7726	1355

PROOFREADER (Cont'd)
QUEBEC (Cont'd)
Montreal Oest	MORRISON, H D.	(514)488-9279	868
Pointe Claire	SMYTH, John	(514)697-3486	1162
Quebec	MCKENZIE, Donald R.	(418)691-6357	811
Rosemere	LAPIERRE, France	(514)621-8507	697
St-Bruno	LECOMPTE, Louis L.	(514)653-7290	708
Sainte-Foy	PETRYK, Louise O.	(418)656-6921	965

SASKATCHEWAN
Prince Albert	LABUIK, Karen L.	(306)764-0712	686
Regina	MACK, A Y.	(306)543-6981	756
Saskatoon	NELSON, Ian C.	(306)652-4934	893

BAHAMAS
Grand Bahamas Island	BARTON, Barbara I.		61

CUBA
Havana	ASIS, Moises		36

ENGLAND
Bushey	SMITH, Margit J.		1157

FEDERAL REPUBLIC OF GERMANY
Heidelberg	SOKOLOWSKI, Denise G.		1166

FRANCE
Paris	GARRETA, J C.		420

IRELAND
Dublin	ASTON, Jennefer		37

ISRAEL
Jerusalem	DIAMANT, Betsy		299

ITALY
Rome	HUEMER, Christina G.		570

KENYA
Nairobi	IRURIA, Daniel M.		584

MALAWI
Lilongwe	SNYDER, Lisa A.		1165

NIGERIA
Akure	ONONOGBO, Raphael U.		924
Ogbomoso	OKPARA, Ibiba M.		920
	TARPLEY, Margaret J.		1224

SOUTH AFRICA
Somerset West	LUSK, Betty M.		749

PUBLIC LIBRARY CONSULTANT

ALABAMA
Birmingham	DAY, Janeth N.	(205)226-3614	282
	MCCARTHY, Sherri L.	(205)226-3630	794
	STEWART, George R.	(205)226-3611	1192
Gadsden	BUCKNER, Rebecca S.	(205)543-8849	154
Montgomery	BIVINS, Hulen E.	(205)272-1700	100
	DESSY, Blane K.	(205)277-7330	296
	MEDINA, Sue O.	(205)269-2700	820
Prattville	LASETER, Ernest P.	(205)365-8549	700
Prichard	WILLIAMS, Gwendolyn	(205)452-4395	1343

ALASKA
Anchorage	PIERCE, Linda I.	(907)338-6421	971
	WILLIAMS, Robert C.	(907)261-2970	1346
Fairbanks	MUDD, Isabelle G.	(907)479-4522	875
Juneau	CRANE, Karen R.	(907)456-2910	255
	KOLB, Audrey P.	(907)452-2999	669
	SMITH, George V.	(907)789-2559	1155

PUBLIC LIBRARY CONSULTANT (Cont'd)

ARIZONA

Flagstaff	DOWNUM, Evelyn R.	(602)774-6059	317
Mesa	ANDERSON, Herschel V.	(602)839-2742	23
Phoenix	ALABASTER, Carol	(602)262-7360	9
	GOEBEL, Heather L.	(602)994-2471	443
	NIXON, Arless B.	(602)246-9196	906
	ROATCH, Mary A.	(602)254-7678	1038
Scottsdale	PILLOW, William H.	(602)994-2691	973
Tucson	BIERMAN, Kenneth J.	(602)887-4631	95
	DUFORE, Thomas H.	(602)296-3823	324
	GOLDBERG, Susan S.	(602)747-2663	445
	HURT, Charlie D.	(602)621-3566	578
	MCCRACKEN, John R.	(602)327-4056	799
	MILLER, Edward P.		837

ARKANSAS

Arkadelphia	WOODS, L B.	(501)246-5511	1367
El Dorado	ARN, Nancy L.	(501)862-3385	33
Eureka Springs	STOWE, Jean E.	(501)253-8754	1199
Fayetteville	EARNEST, Jeffrey D.	(501)521-8388	332
Fort Smith	LARSON, Larry	(501)783-0229	699
Greenwood	CLEVENGER, Judy B.	(501)996-2856	221
Hope	TROMATER, Raymond B.	(501)777-3361	1257
Little Rock	HALL, John J.	(501)221-2912	488
	MARTIN, Rosemary S.	(501)370-5954	778
	MULKEY, Jack C.	(501)225-2246	876
Magnolia	BRADLEY, Florene J.	(501)234-1991	125
North Little Rock	FOOS, Donald D.	(501)758-5112	388
	PACK, Nancy C.	(501)758-1720	933

CALIFORNIA

Anaheim Hills	JOHNSON, Thomas L.	(714)998-4347	609
APO San Francisco	HEINES, Rodney M.		522
Arcadia	PERRY, Edward C.		960
Bakersfield	WINTER, Eugenia B.	(805)833-3175	1356
Belmont	CROWE, Linda D.	(415)349-5538	261
Ben Lomond	CROWLEY, Terence	(408)336-5019	262
Berkeley	FLUM, Judith G.	(415)486-0378	386
	MINUDRI, Regina U.	(415)843-7242	847
	VAN HOUSE, Nancy A.	(415)642-0855	1275
Beverly Hills	ANNETT, Susan E.	(213)550-4720	28
Callahan	FARRIER, George F.	(916)467-3334	365
Carmichael	STRONG, Gary E.	(916)966-2037	1203
Castro Valley	OVERMYER, Elizabeth C.	(415)670-6281	931
Coronado	ESQUEVIN, Christian R.	(619)437-1135	354
Costa Mesa	EPSTEIN, Susan B.	(714)754-1559	351
	POARCH, Margaret E.	(714)662-1867	979
Culver City	KIRBY, Barbara L.	(213)839-1009	653
Del Mar	HOLT, Raymond M.	(619)755-7878	554
Fairfield	GOLD, Anne M.	(707)429-6601	444
FPO San Francisco	HADLEY, Alice E.	(671)344-9250	482
Fresno	COBB, Karen B.	(209)488-3438	225
Guerneville	BATES, Henry E.	(707)869-9383	64
Huntington Beach	HAYDEN, Ronald L.	(714)960-8836	515
Lake View Terrace	NAVARRO, Frank A.		889
Lomita	BOWLING, Lance C.	(213)831-1322	121
Long Beach	AYALA, John L.	(213)599-8028	42
Los Angeles	ALFORD, Thomas E.	(213)612-3333	13
	HENDERSON, Ellen B.	(213)480-1105	526
	JAIN, Celeste C.	(213)665-7510	591
	MERRIFIELD, Thomas C.	(213)390-4717	826
Manhattan Beach	MARKEY, Penny S.	(213)374-1838	771
	PHILLIPS, Clifford R.	(213)545-4828	968
Menlo Park	TRUJILLO, Roberto G.	(415)329-0227	1259
Mission Viejo	CHWEH, Steven S.	(714)768-3459	214
Mountain View	POST, Linda C.	(415)968-3045	986
Oakland	GLYNN, Jeannette E.	(415)654-3543	442
Ojai	MOORE, Phyllis C.	(805)646-8592	861
Orange	SMITH, Elizabeth M.	(714)634-7809	1154
Oroville	ALLENSWORTH, James H.	(916)538-7197	16
Palos Verdes Estates	STEVENSON, Marilyn E.	(213)377-7563	1191
	UEBELE, Dorothy B.	(213)541-2559	1268
Pasadena	KLINE, Victoria E.	(818)405-2100	661
	TEMA, William J.	(818)798-9270	1230
Pleasant Hill	SIEGEL, Ernest	(415)944-3423	1136
Pomona	MORGAN, Ferrell	(714)625-7190	864
Redwood City	BANGE, Stephanie D.	(415)369-6251	54

PUBLIC LIBRARY CONSULTANT (Cont'd)

CALIFORNIA (Cont'd)

Richmond	VANDERBERG, Patricia S.	(415)237-1081	1273
Ridgecrest	MAYES, Elizabeth A.	(619)446-6862	789
Rowland Heights	SIGLER, Ronald F.	(818)965-9917	1137
Sacramento	KILLIAN, Richard M.	(916)440-5926	648
	MCGOVERN, Gail J.	(916)446-2411	807
	RUBY, Carmela M.	(916)453-1174	1065
San Diego	FORMAN, Jack	(619)546-9250	390
	LOOMIS, Barbara L.	(619)565-3172	740
	MONROE, Shula H.	(619)222-1206	855
	SANNWALD, William W.	(619)236-5870	1081
	THORNE, Marco G.		1242
	TRIVISON, Margaret A.	(619)452-7338	1257
San Francisco	MANN, Thomas	(415)951-0100	766
	MCNAMEE, Gilbert W.	(415)474-3636	816
	MORRIS, Effie L.	(415)931-2733	866
	RAMIREZ, William L.	(415)564-5637	1005
San Rafael	HAMMER, Sharon A.	(415)499-6051	493
Santa Clara	CHESSMAN, Rebecca L.	(408)244-2775	207
Santa Cruz	TURNER, Anne M.	(408)429-3532	1264
Sebastopol	SABSAY, David	(707)545-0831	1073
	SIMONS, Maurice M.	(707)823-9275	1141
Torrance	BEEBE, Richard J.	(213)323-7200	74
	DOWNEY, Christine D.	(213)618-5962	316
Ukiah	FELDMAN, Irwin	(707)468-8163	369
Valencia	CURZON, Susan C.	(805)259-8946	267
Venice	WALTER, Virginia A.	(213)392-7627	1300
Walnut Creek	HELLUM-BERMAN, Bertha D.	(415)935-6516	524
Whittier	RODRIGUEZ, Ronald	(213)693-0585	1048
Woodland	KELLUM-ROSE, Nancy P.	(916)662-6616	637

COLORADO

Boulder	COLLARD, R M.	(303)444-1355	232
	GRALAPP, Marcelee G.		457
	VARNES, Richard S.	(303)444-8051	1279
Brighton	KELVER, Ann E.	(303)659-1799	639
Colorado Springs	DOWLIN, Kenneth E.	(303)635-2236	316
	MAGRATH, Lynn L.	(303)473-2080	760
Denver	ASHTON, Rick J.	(303)745-9883	36
	BOLT, Nancy M.	(303)866-6732	113
	ROSE, Phillip E.	(303)538-4276	1055
	VOLZ, Edward J.	(303)571-2033	1288
Englewood	BRUNTON, David W.	(303)771-3197	151
Grand Junction	RICHMOND, Rick	(303)241-4358	1030
Grand Lake	ARMITAGE, Constance	(303)328-5293	32
Greeley	KNEPEL, Nancy	(303)356-4357	664
Lamar	BURNETT, James H.	(303)336-4632	161
Leadville	PARRY, David R.	(303)486-2626	944
Littleton	BETTENCOURT, Nancy J.	(303)771-0968	92
Meeker	NICKEL, Robbie L.	(303)878-3209	902
Montrose	CAMPBELL, John D.	(303)249-1078	176
New Castle	GARYPIE, Renwick	(303)984-2346	421
Pueblo	JONES, Donna R.	(303)542-2156	612

CONNECTICUT

Ansonia	MARTIN, Walter F.	(203)736-2601	779
Avery Point	HOLLOWAY, Patricia W.	(203)445-5577	552
Bridgeport	MINERVINO, Louise	(203)576-7779	846
	MULAWKA, Chet	(203)576-7402	876
Danbury	HORRIGAN, John J.	(203)797-2731	560
Danielson	WEIGEL, James H.	(203)774-7755	1316
Darien	BERRY, Louise P.	(203)655-2568	90
Fairfield	WARGO, Peggy M.	(203)259-8267	1305
Glastonbury	SCHUTT, Cheryl M.	(203)633-0427	1103
Greenwich	LUSHINGTON, Nolan	(203)655-3632	749
Guilford	GAFFNEY, Maureen	(203)453-6533	412
Hartford	BURGAN, John S.	(203)724-0297	159
Moosup	KASPER, Barbara	(203)564-4303	629
New Hartford	GIBSON, Barbara H.	(203)379-3548	431
New London	VANDERLYKE, Barbara A.	(203)442-2889	1274
Niantic	BENN, James R.	(203)445-5577	81
Norwalk	BOHRER, Karen M.	(203)854-5275	111
Stamford	DIMATTIA, Ernest A.	(203)322-9055	304
	DIMATTIA, Susan S.	(203)322-9055	304
	GOLOMB, Katherine A.	(203)964-1000	447
Stonington	WILLIAMS, Edwin E.	(203)535-0720	1343
Wallingford	SCHERER, Leslie C.	(203)265-6754	1092
Waterbury	CARRINGTON, Virginia F.	(203)574-4702	186
West Hartford	BURGER, Leslie B.	(203)233-0478	159

PUBLIC LIBRARY CONSULTANT (Cont'd)

CONNECTICUT (Cont'd)

Westport	REISMAN, Sydelle S.	(203)227-8710	1021
	SCHWARZ, Shirlee	(203)226-6606	1105

DELAWARE

Bear	MANUEL, Larry L.	(302)834-5748	767
New Castle	BROWN, Sarah C.	(307)328-3447	147
Wilmington	BURDASH, David H.	(302)571-7402	158
	TITUS, H M.	(302)656-1722	1247

DISTRICT OF COLUMBIA

Washington	BERGQUIST, Christine F.		87
	FRANKLIN, Hardy R.	(202)727-1101	397
	HAGEMEYER, Alice L.	(202)727-2255	483
	KNOWLTON, John D.	(202)362-8911	665
	PHELPS, Thomas C.	(202)786-0271	967
	SOLOMON, Arnold D.	(202)287-8786	1166
	SWEENEY, June D.	(202)427-1392	1215
	TSCHERNY, Elena	(202)727-1183	1260
	WEBB, Barbara A.	(202)797-8909	1313

FLORIDA

Bradenton	PLACE, Philip A.	(813)746-1358	977
Captiva	WALTON, Terence M.	(813)454-0410	1302
Chattahoochee	BEASLEY, Clarence W.		69
Clearwater	BROMBERG, Johanna	(813)535-2595	139
	MIELKE, Linda	(813)462-6916	833
Crawfordville	TODD, Hal W.	(904)926-5656	1248
Dunedin	FIORE, Carole D.	(813)733-2595	379
	SHINN, Sydniciel	(813)733-4115	1131
Fort Lauderdale	ALGAZE, Selma B.	(305)357-7501	13
Gainesville	BECKER, Josephine M.	(904)371-3808	72
	HOLE, Carol C.	(904)378-0270	550
	WILLOCKS, Robert M.	(904)392-0342	1349
Howey in the Hills	COHN, William L.	(904)324-2701	229
Jacksonville	MARION, Gail E.	(904)633-2088	770
Jensen Beach	HENNINGS, Leroy	(305)334-6134	528
Miami	CARDEN, Marguerite	(305)375-5005	180
	SINTZ, Edward F.	(305)375-5026	1144
Orlando	PETERSON, Carolyn S.	(305)425-4694	963
	SESSA, Frank B.		1116
Panama City	DANNECKER, Joyce H.	(904)785-3457	274
Sarasota	HOPKINS, Joan A.	(813)951-5502	558
Tallahassee	BUSTETTER, Stanley R.	(904)487-2667	166
	FLEMING, Lois D.		384
	MILLER, Betty D.	(904)335-4405	836
	MOUNCE, Marvin W.	(904)487-2651	873
	SUMMERS, F W.	(904)644-5775	1209
	TREZZA, Alphonse F.	(904)878-5551	1256
Tampa	LOSEY, Doris C.	(813)885-4500	742
	MCCROSSAN, John A.	(813)974-3520	800
Wauchula	MAPP, Erwin E.	(813)773-9207	768
West Palm Beach	BROWNLEE, Jerry W.	(305)686-0895	148

GEORGIA

Atlanta	BRADLEY, Gail P.	(404)872-9472	125
	COFFMAN, Joseph W.	(404)681-0251	227
	ENGLER, June L.	(404)727-6405	350
	FORSEE, Joe B.	(404)656-2461	391
	HEID, Gregory G.	(404)688-4636	521
	JAMES, Stephen E.	(404)681-0251	592
	LAWSON, A V.	(404)377-1142	705
	LAWSON, Venable A.	(404)377-1142	705
	SEARCY, David L.	(404)525-8802	1109
	TOPE, Diana R.	(404)656-2461	1251
Bainbridge	MARSHALL, Ruth T.	(912)246-3887	775
Decatur	BUDLONG, Thomas F.	(404)289-0583	155
	COHRS, Joyce S.	(404)377-3744	229
Duluth	SHELTON, John L.	(404)381-8060	1126
Eastman	WILSON, David C.	(912)374-4711	1350
Fitzgerald	HEFFINGTON, Carl O.	(912)423-3642	520
Hartwell	BISSO, Arthur J.	(404)376-4655	100
	BISSO, Arthur J.	(404)376-4655	100
Jonesboro	STEWART, Carol J.	(404)478-7120	1192
Waycross	STANBERY, Nancy M.	(912)283-3126	1179

PUBLIC LIBRARY CONSULTANT (Cont'd)

HAWAII

Honolulu	CAMPBELL, R A.	(808)955-8822	177
	HORNE, Norman P.	(808)524-8094	560
	KANE, Bartholomew A.	(808)524-8344	624
	LINVILLE, Marcia L.	(808)737-2511	731
	SPENCER, Caroline P.	(808)735-2822	1173

IDAHO

Boise	ROBERTSON, Naida	(208)384-4340	1042
Idaho Falls	HOLLAND, Paul E.	(208)529-1450	551
Moscow	BRADY, Eileen E.	(208)883-0817	126
Post Falls	JONES-LITTEER, Corene A.	(208)773-1515	616

ILLINOIS

Algonquin	VLCEK, Randall	(312)658-4343	1286
Bloomington	HUFFMAN, Carol P.	(309)829-2271	571
	KELLEY, H N.	(309)828-3128	636
Blue Island	WOZNY, Jay	(312)388-1078	1370
Bolingbrook	IFFLAND, Carol D.	(312)739-6398	581
	TODD, Alexander W.	(312)759-2102	1248
Carbondale	CAMPBELL, Ray	(618)457-0354	177
	DALE, Doris C.	(618)536-2441	270
Carterville	UBEL, James A.	(618)985-3711	1267
Champaign	GOLDHOR, Herbert	(217)359-5636	445
	MCCABE, Ronald B.	(217)352-8317	793
Chicago	ADKINS, Marjorie R.	(312)468-2139	6
	CLAPP, David F.	(312)465-0324	215
	DAVIS, Glenn G.	(312)943-2911	279
	DEMPSEY, Frank J.	(312)327-6955	291
	DOLNICK, Sandy F.	(312)944-6780	310
	DUFF, John B.	(312)269-2984	323
	FEDERICI, Yolanda D.	(312)427-0052	368
	GOMEZ, Martin J.		447
	GUSS, Emily R.	(312)268-4377	478
	HAAS, Carolyn B.	(312)822-0809	480
	HOFFMANN, Maurine L.	(312)951-0599	548
	IDDINGS, Daniel H.	(312)321-0432	581
	KIM, Chung S.	(312)588-3901	648
	LENNEBERG, Hans H.		715
	MANN, Vijai S.	(312)443-5423	766
	MATTENSON, Murray M.	(312)262-8282	785
	MCCLINTOCK, Patrick J.		797
	MCELWAIN, William	(312)248-5564	804
	MILLER, Robert	(312)488-7195	841
	MORRISON, Samuel F.	(312)269-3053	868
	OAKS, Claire	(312)271-1207	913
	REILLY, Jane A.	(312)764-2413	1020
	RICHMOND, Diane A.	(312)269-2864	1030
	ROMAN, Susan	(312)944-6780	1052
	SCOTT, Alice H.	(312)493-2451	1106
	SHAEVEL, Evelyn F.	(312)944-6780	1118
	STEELE, Leah J.	(312)631-2701	1184
	STINCHCOMB, Maxine K.	(312)348-2866	1194
	STRAIT, Constance J.		1199
	VIRGO, Julie A.	(312)751-1454	1285
Chicago Ridge	LOTZ, Marsha A.	(312)423-7753	742
Cicero	MALLER, Mark P.	(312)652-8084	763
Crystal Lake	MILLER, Randy S.	(815)455-4660	841
De Kalb	KIES, Cosette N.	(815)753-1735	647
	SHAVIT, David	(815)753-6271	1123
Downers Grove	BALCOM, Kathleen M.	(312)960-1200	51
	STOFFEL, Lester L.	(312)964-2541	1196
Elgin	JUERGENSMEYER, John E.	(312)695-9800	619
Elk Grove Village	KALRA, Bhupinder S.	(312)529-8607	623
Evanston	RODGER, Eleanor J.		1047
	WHITE, Matthew H.	(312)328-2221	1331
	WRIGHT, Donald E.	(312)866-0312	1371
Flora	DOCKINS, Glenn	(618)662-2679	307
	HARRIS, Thomas J.	(618)662-2679	506
Flossmoor	LOCKE, John W.	(312)798-3671	736
Galesburg	WINNER, Ronald	(309)343-2380	1355
Geneseo	REDINGTON, Deirdre E.	(309)944-3311	1014
Geneva	SHURMAN, Richard L.	(312)232-8457	1134
Glendale Heights	VOJTECH, Kathryn	(312)260-1550	1287
Highland Park	GREENFIELD, Jane W.	(312)432-0216	464
Hinsdale	MUELLER, Elizabeth	(312)323-8054	875
Hoffman Estates	MILLER, Deborah	(312)882-3698	837
Itasca	HOGAN, Patricia M.	(312)773-1699	549
Kewanee	HARRIET, Conklin W.	(309)853-4993	503

PUBLIC LIBRARY CONSULTANT (Cont'd)

ILLINOIS (Cont'd)

La Grange	HUSLIG, Dennis M.	(312)352-7671	578
Lake Bluff	LEISNER, Anthony B.	(312)295-2010	714
Mascoutah	SCHAACK, Wilma J.	(618)566-7385	1088
Matteson	SMITH, Richard D.	(312)747-6660	1159
Mt Prospect	MCCULLY, William C.	(312)635-9811	801
Normal	MEISELS, Henry R.	(309)452-4485	822
Oak Lawn	IHRIG, Alice B.		581
	MOORMAN, John A.	(312)422-4990	862
Oak Park	BALCOM, William T.	(312)383-6824	51
	HARRIS, Robert A.	(312)524-8849	506
	OLDERR, Steven	(312)383-8176	920
O'Fallon	KNUDTSON, Gail L.	(618)624-2719	666
Ottawa	WILLSON, Richard E.	(815)434-7075	1349
Park Forest	HAYES, Hazel I.		515
	OCHSNER, Renata E.	(312)748-5374	915
Paxton	PACEY, Brenda M.	(217)379-3517	933
Payson	ALBSMEYER, Betty J.	(217)656-3679	11
Pearl City	DAWSON, Lawrence	(815)443-2856	282
Peoria	GIBBS, Margareth	(309)672-8840	431
	JACKSON, Susan M.	(309)674-2008	588
Quincy	TYER, Travis E.	(217)223-5024	1266
Richton Park	NEVINS, Patrick F.	(312)481-5333	898
Riverdale	ZENKE, Mary H.	(312)849-0879	1387
Rock Island	OHRLUND, Ava L.	(309)786-0698	919
Rockford	CHITWOOD, Julius R.	(815)962-4409	209
	HUTCHINS, Mary J.	(815)229-0330	579
	LONG, Judith N.	(815)229-7604	739
	ROSENFELD, Joel C.	(815)965-6731	1056
	WELCH, Steven J.	(815)963-5133	1321
Rolling Meadows	HEMENWAY, Patti J.	(312)255-6197	525
St Charles	BROWN, Diana M.		143
Skokie	ANTHONY, Carolyn A.	(312)673-7774	28
	JACOB, Merle L.		589
	KAPLAN, Paul M.		626
Springfield	LAMONT, Bridget L.	(217)787-2299	691
Streamwood	DEUEL, Marlene R.	(312)837-8242	296
Sycamore	SULLIVAN, Peggy A.	(815)753-6155	1208
Taylorville	PODESCHI, Gwen	(217)824-5695	979
Urbana	BINGHAM, Karen H.	(217)333-0317	97
	EDMONDS, M L.	(217)333-2306	336
	ESTABROOK, Leigh S.	(217)333-3280	355
	ROLSTAD, Gary O.	(217)333-3280	1052
	RUBIN, Richard E.	(217)333-3280	1065
	SCHLIPF, Frederick A.	(217)367-4057	1094
	WEECH, Terry L.	(217)367-7111	1315
Wauconda	LUEDER, Dianne B.	(312)526-6075	747
	SHENASSA, Daryoosh	(312)526-9123	1126
Wheeling	MCCLARREN, Robert R.	(312)459-1300	796
Williamsville	KELLERSTRASS, Amy L.	(217)566-3517	636
Winnetka	THOMPSON, Richard E.	(312)446-7975	1241

INDIANA

Bloomington	FARLEY, Janice S.	(812)339-2271	364
	JACKSON, Susan M.	(812)334-7049	588
	PUNGITORE, Verna L.	(812)335-5113	997
East Chicago	MILLER, Marcia M.	(219)397-1072	840
Fort Wayne	CLEGG, Michael B.		220
	DEANE, Paul D.	(219)424-7241	284
	KRULL, Jeffrey R.	(219)424-7241	680
Frankfort	CADDELL, Claude W.	(317)654-7038	170
Gary	GUYDON, Janet H.	(219)938-3376	479
	MILLENDER, Dharathola	(219)882-4050	835
Greencastle	LATSHAW, Ruth N.	(317)653-2318	701
Hammond	MEYERS, Arthur S.	(219)931-5100	830
Huntington	ISCA, Joseph J.	(219)672-8194	585
Indianapolis	BRIDGE, Stephen W.	(317)359-7260	135
	BROWN, Judith L.		145
	DOLAN-HEITLINGER, Eileen	(317)269-1764	309
	GANN, Daniel H.	(317)299-9058	416
	THOMPSON, Anna M.		1238
	WOODARD, Marcia S.	(317)297-1803	1366
La Porte	GUNNELLS, Danny C.	(219)324-0422	477
Michigan City	DEYOUNG, Charles D.	(219)879-4561	298
Muncie	BEILKE, Patricia F.	(317)284-2457	75
Munster	MOGLE, Dawn E.	(219)923-8059	852
Noblesville	COOPER, David L.	(317)773-1384	242
Notre Dame	DOELLMAN, Michael A.	(219)232-0778	308
Rochester	LASHER, Esther L.	(219)223-8407	700

PUBLIC LIBRARY CONSULTANT (Cont'd)

IOWA

Charles City	STARK, Ted	(515)228-5532	1182
Davenport	NAVARRE, Emily L.	(319)324-5140	889
Des Moines	DAGLEY, Helen J.	(515)281-3063	269
	ESTES, Elaine G.	(515)283-4152	355
	GEORGE, Shirley H.	(515)281-4105	428
	JOHNSON, Nancy E.	(515)262-6714	608
	ROBERTSON, Linda L.	(515)281-7572	1042
Dubuque	MINTER, Elizabeth D.	(319)556-7553	846
Iowa City	BAKER, Sharon L.	(319)335-5707	49
	EGGERS, Lolly P.	(319)356-5206	339
	NICKELSBURG, Marilyn M.	(319)351-2072	902
Mason City	SWANSON, P A.	(515)423-6917	1213
Sioux City	PLUEMER, Bonnie J.	(712)279-6186	978

KANSAS

Coffeyville	BUFFINGTON, Karyl L.	(316)251-1370	155
Emporia	BODART-TALBOT, Joni	(316)343-1200	109
	HALE, Martha L.		485
Great Bend	SWAN, James A.	(316)792-4865	1213
Hays	MILLER, Melanie A.	(913)625-9014	841
Hesston	EICHELBERGER, Marianne	(316)327-4666	339
Hutchinson	GATTIN, Leroy M.	(316)663-5441	422
	HAWKINS, Paul J.	(316)663-5441	514
Kansas City	RIDDLE, Raymond E.	(913)621-3073	1032
Lawrence	KOEPP, Donna P.	(913)864-4880	668
	MAY, Cecilia J.	(913)841-0929	788
Newton	EBERHARD, Neysa C.	(316)283-2890	334
Salina	MCKENZIE, Joe M.	(913)825-4624	811
Shawnee Mission	WAY, Harold E.	(913)831-1550	1311
Topeka	JOHNSON, Duane F.	(913)296-3296	603
	VOSS, Ernestine D.	(913)269-3296	1289

KENTUCKY

Florence	BROWN, Lucinda A.	(606)371-6222	145
Frankfort	HELLARD, Ellen G.	(502)875-7000	524
	KLEE, Edward L.	(502)875-7000	658
Germantown	TEEGARDEN, Maude B.	(606)728-2312	1229
Lexington	SCHABEL, Donald J.	(606)223-4017	1088
	SINEATH, Timothy W.	(606)257-8876	1143
	STEENSLAND, Ronald P.		1184
	WRIGHT, Paul L.	(606)525-6324	1372
Louisville	ROBY, B D.	(502)561-8638	1045
	SOMERVILLE, Mary R.	(502)893-8451	1167
	VOYLES, James R.	(502)589-4440	1289

LOUISIANA

Baton Rouge	BINGHAM, Elizabeth E.	(504)292-1038	97
	HEIM, Kathleen M.	(504)388-3158	521
	PERRY, Emma D.	(504)928-3622	960
	PHENIX, Katharine J.	(504)388-3158	967
	SMITH, Richard J.	(504)342-4942	1160
Harvey	WASHINGTON, Idella A.	(504)367-8429	1307
Lafayette	DOMBOURIAN, Sona J.	(318)261-5775	310
Metairie	BENOIT, Anthony H.	(504)888-5379	82
New Orleans	COADY, Reginald P.	(504)596-2601	224
	WILSON, C D.	(504)596-2600	1350
Oakdale	LYNCH, Minnie L.	(318)335-3442	752
Ruston	AVANT, Julia K.	(318)255-1920	41
Shreveport	SALTER, Jeffrey L.	(318)226-5871	1077

MAINE

Auburn	HILYARD, Nann B.	(207)782-3191	542
Bangor	WOODWARD, Robert C.	(207)942-4760	1368
Lewiston	GROSS, Richard F.	(207)782-3958	472
Orono	ALBRIGHT, Elaine M.	(207)581-1661	10
Paris	MOTT, Schuyler L.	(207)743-6216	872
Portland	O'BRIEN, Francis M.	(207)774-0931	914
	SMITH, Barbara J.	(207)761-2932	1153

MARYLAND

Baltimore	CURRY, Anna A.	(301)396-5430	266
	CYR, Helen W.	(301)235-8719	268
	FINNEY, Lance C.	(301)685-0074	379
	GRAVES, Louise H.		459
	HEISER, Jane C.	(301)396-5470	523
	HIRSCH, Dorothy K.	(304)655-7280	543
	LAPIDES, Linda F.	(301)396-5356	697
	LEDBETTER, Sherry H.	(301)358-0285	708

PUBLIC LIBRARY CONSULTANT (Cont'd)
MARYLAND (Cont'd)

Baltimore			
	MCADAM, Paul E.	(301)747-5030	791
	PARTRIDGE, James C.	(301)664-4301	945
	SONDHEIM, John W.	(301)396-5429	1167
	STEPHAN, Sandra S.	(301)333-2118	1187
Bel Air	MASSEY, James E.	(301)838-7484	782
	SEDNEY, Frances V.	(301)838-7484	1111
Cabin John	ROBINSON, Barbara M.	(301)320-6011	1043
Cambridge	DEL SORDO, Jean S.	(301)228-7331	290
Churchton	TONEY, Stephen R.	(301)261-5650	1250
College Park	CUNNINGHAM, William D.	(301)454-2376	265
	STIELOW, Frederick J.	(301)454-5790	1194
Columbia	AVERSA, Elizabeth S.	(301)992-3711	41
	HILL, Norma L.	(301)997-8000	540
Denton	SANDS, George A.	(301)479-1343	1081
Ellicott City	DUCHAC, Kenneth F.	(301)531-3389	322
Fallston	CLARK, David S.	(301)838-0223	216
Gaithersburg	GRIFFEN, Agnes M.	(301)340-3378	468
Glen Burnie	SUMLER, Claudia B.	(301)768-4320	1209
Hyattsville	COOPER, Judith C.	(301)699-3500	243
	LOSINSKI, Julia M.	(301)699-3500	742
Port Republik	HURREY, Katharine C.		577
Rockville	DOWD, Frank B.	(301)279-1098	315
	GRIFFITHS, Jose M.	(301)881-6766	469
	KING, Donald W.	(301)881-6766	650
Salisbury	CUNNINGHAM, Barbara M.	(301)742-1537	265
Silver Spring	BATTY, Charles D.	(301)593-8901	65
	FEINBERG, Beryl L.	(301)946-3282	368
Solomons	HEIL, Kathleen A.	(301)326-2967	521
Takoma Park	NITZBERG, Dale B.	(301)587-5789	905
Towson	ROBINSON, Charles W.	(301)296-8500	1043
Westminster	MCCARTY, Emily H.	(301)848-1825	795

MASSACHUSETTS

Acton	HURD, Sandra H.	(617)263-7574	577
Boston	BUSH, Margaret A.	(617)262-2045	165
	CURLEY, Arthur	(617)536-5400	265
	MCCARTHY, Germaine A.	(617)742-3958	794
	MCKIRDY, Pamela R.	(617)738-2223	812
	SHANNON, Marcia A.	(617)267-9400	1120
Brockton	UMANA, Christine J.	(617)586-6994	1268
Brookline	STEINFELD, Michael	(617)730-2360	1186
Cambridge	SAKEY, Joseph G.	(617)498-9000	1076
Carver	NEUBAUER, Richard A.	(617)866-5186	896
Concord	JACKSON, Patience K.	(617)369-0586	588
Dracut	ARSENAULT, Patricia A.	(617)459-4648	35
East Boston	SCHLAFF, Donna G.	(617)561-0153	1093
Hanover	FRIEDMAN, Fred T.	(617)826-2972	403
Holbrook	MEAGHER, Janet H.	(617)767-3644	819
Jamaica Plain	ALASTI, Aryt	(617)524-0411	9
Lexington	HILTON, Robert C.	(617)862-6288	541
	WALSH, Joanna M.	(617)863-1275	1299
	WARNER, Alice S.	(617)862-9278	1305
Millis	ROE, Georgeanne T.	(617)376-8459	1048
Monterey	INTNER, Sheila S.	(413)528-2698	583
New Bedford	FINNI, John J.	(617)999-6034	379
North Andover	REEVE, Russell J.	(617)682-6260	1016
North Falmouth	FOSTER, Joan		392
Norwell	KADANOFF, Diane G.	(617)659-2015	621
Palmer	BERNAT, Mary A.		88
Peabody	TRICARICO, Mary A.	(617)531-0100	1256
Reading	FLANNERY, Susan M.	(617)944-0840	383
	FLANNERY, Susan M.	(617)944-0840	384
Salem	WHITNEY, Howard F.	(617)744-1769	1334
Springfield	CLOUGH, Linda F.	(413)788-8411	223
	KEOUGH, Francis P.	(413)739-1837	643
Stoughton	ANDERSON, Cheryl M.	(617)344-4000	22
Stow	GIULIANO, Lillian C.	(617)485-0494	439
Uxbridge	LEWIS, Thomas F.		724
Wareham	PILLSBURY, Mary J.	(617)295-2343	973
Watertown	REDDY, Sigrid R.	(617)924-3282	1014
Wayland	BROWN, Louise R.	(617)358-4220	145
Wendell	HOLMBERG, Olga S.	(617)544-2706	553
West Springfield	HELO, Martin	(413)736-4561	525
	PECK, Ruth M.	(413)736-0989	953
	SMITH, Barbara A.	(413)736-4561	1152
Worcester	CHAMBERLAIN, Ruth B.	(617)244-3612	197
	JOHNSON, Penelope B.	(617)799-1653	608

PUBLIC LIBRARY CONSULTANT (Cont'd)
MICHIGAN

Albion	JENNINGS, Martha F.	(517)629-9469	598
Alpena	WILLIAMS, Susan S.	(517)356-1622	1346
Ann Arbor	DURRANCE, Joan C.	(313)763-1569	328
Auburn Hills	WILLIAMS, Calvin	(313)853-4226	1342
Birmingham	GOLDSTEIN, Doris R.	(313)626-9299	446
	ORMOND, Sarah C.	(313)647-1700	926
	SWEENEY, Thomas F.	(313)964-0030	1215
Dearborn	MCCARTY, Linda A.	(313)582-7867	795
Decatur	TATE, David L.	(616)423-4771	1225
Detroit	JOHNSON, Veronica A.	(313)532-6715	609
	MA, Helen Y.	(313)833-1016	753
	MORROW, Blaine V.	(313)893-1746	869
	OLDENBURG, Joseph F.	(313)833-4027	920
	PORTER, Jean F.	(313)961-5040	984
	SHUMAN, Bruce A.	(313)577-1825	1134
	TSAI, Fu M.	(313)876-0133	1260
Farmington Hills	PAPAI, Beverly D.	(313)553-0300	938
Fenton	SCHERBA, Sandra A.	(313)629-0812	1092
Grand Blanc	KINGSTON, Jo A.	(313)694-7323	652
Grand Rapids	RAZ, Robert E.	(616)791-9496	1012
Grosse Pointe	CASEY, Genevieve M.		192
Grosse Pointe Farms	HANSON, Charles D.	(313)882-3627	498
Grosse Pointe Woods	REID, Bette C.	(313)884-0884	1018
Harper Woods	ARRIVEE, Sally D.	(313)343-2575	34
Highland Park	NDENGA, Viola W.	(313)868-5986	890
Holland	LIGHT, Lin	(616)335-2540	726
Jackson	LEAMON, David L.	(517)788-4199	707
Kalamazoo	RIFE, Mary C.	(616)342-9837	1033
	RIZZO, John R.	(616)381-1323	1037
Lansing	DUKELOW, Ruth H.	(517)373-1593	324
	EZELL, Charlaine L.	(517)485-8019	360
Lincoln Park	HECK-RABI, Louise E.	(313)928-3967	520
Livonia	VOIGHT, Nancy R.	(313)464-2306	1287
Monroe	MARGOLIS, Bernard A.	(313)243-5213	770
Mt Pleasant	KRUUT, Evald	(517)773-5184	681
Northville	FIELD, Judith J.	(313)349-1953	375
Novi	KING, Kenneth	(313)478-4963	651
Otsego	PARK, Janice R.	(616)694-4546	941
Plymouth	DE BEAR, Richard S.	(313)459-5000	284
	GAREN, Robert J.	(313)455-5771	418
Port Huron	ARNETT, Stanley K.	(313)987-7323	33
Portage	HEMPHILL, Frank A.	(616)323-2627	525
Saginaw	O'CONNELL, Catherine A.	(517)792-6852	915
Troy	ZARYCZNY, Wlodzimierz A.	(313)879-7217	1386
West Bloomfield	SMITH, Nancy J.	(313)682-2120	1158

MINNESOTA

Bloomington	NAUEN, Lindsay B.	(612)854-2879	889
Braham	MCGRIFF, Ronald I.	(612)396-3957	808
Circle Pines	YOUNG, Jerry F.	(612)786-5689	1382
Embarrass	ESALA, Lillian H.	(218)741-3434	354
Golden Valley	COLE, Jack W.		230
Grand Rapids	VALANCE, Marsha J.	(218)327-2336	1271
Hopkins	SMITH, David R.	(612)933-0199	1154
Mankato	CHRISTENSON, John D.	(507)625-6169	211
Minneapolis	ROHLF, Robert H.	(612)926-6105	1050
Minnetonka	HUTTNER, Marian A.	(612)545-2338	579
Mound	GELINAS, Jeanne L.	(612)472-4046	426
Northfield	BRUCE, Robert K.	(507)645-9279	149
Pine River	O'BRIEN, Marlys H.	(218)587-2171	915
Roseville	VINNES, Norman M.	(612)483-1103	1285
St Paul	CLARKE, Charlotte C.	(612)645-7359	218
	FEYE-STUKAS, Janice	(612)296-2821	374
White Bear Lake	LEWIS, Alan D.	(612)429-2508	722
Worthington	SCOTT, Thomas L.	(507)376-5803	1108
	SPILLERS, Roger E.	(507)372-2981	1174

MISSISSIPPI

Clarksdale	GRAVES, Sid F.	(601)627-2322	459
Cleveland	WISE, Ronnie W.	(601)846-7266	1357
Clinton	BUCHANAN, Gerald	(601)924-7511	153
Hernando	ANDERSON, James F.	(601)368-4439	23
Kosciusko	RODICH, Nancy A.	(601)289-6683	1048
Pascagoula	MAJURE, William D.	(601)769-7149	762
Plantersville	TOWERY, Margaret G.		1252
Starkville	NETTLES, Jess	(601)323-5558	896

PUBLIC LIBRARY CONSULTANT (Cont'd)
MISSISSIPPI (Cont'd)

Sunflower	POWELL, Anice C.	(601)569-3663	988

MISSOURI

Cape Girardeau	STIEGEMEYER, Nancy H.	(314)334-3674	1193
Columbia	MARTIN, Mason G.	(314)449-5798	777
	MILLSAP, Gina J.	(314)443-3161	844
	YOUNG, Virginia G.	(314)443-8413	1383
Harrisonville	FRANKLIN, Jill S.	(816)884-6223	397
Kansas City	BRADBURY, Daniel J.	(816)221-3203	125
	HAMMOND, John J.	(816)221-2695	493
	JENKINS, Harold R.	(816)444-2590	597
	SERLING, Kitty	(816)753-5700	1116
Saint Joseph	ELLIOTT, Dorothy G.	(816)232-7729	344
St Louis	ELSESSER, Lionelle H.	(314)725-4722	346
	ROBERTS, Jean A.	(314)664-0939	1040
	SCHRAMM, Betty V.	(314)994-3300	1099
	SMITH, Nancy M.	(314)241-2288	1159
St Peters	HICKS, James M.	(314)441-0522	537
	SANDSTEDT, Carl R.	(314)441-2300	1081

MONTANA

Helena	SCHLESINGER, Deborah L.	(406)442-2373	1094
Missoula	SCHMIDT, Theodore A.	(406)721-2811	1096

NEBRASKA

Beatrice	DUX-IDEUS, Sherrie L.	(402)223-4581	330
Bellevue	JACKA, David C.	(402)293-3157	586
Hastings	REA, Linda M.	(402)461-2346	1012
Kearney	NORMAN, Ronald V.	(308)237-5133	909
Lincoln	ALLEN, Richard H.	(402)435-4052	16
Omaha	HASELWOOD, Eldon L.	(402)554-2211	510
	PHIPPS, Michael C.	(402)444-4834	969

NEVADA

Henderson	TRASATTI, Margaret S.	(702)733-3613	1254
Las Vegas	CAROLLO, Michael T.	(702)385-0115	184
	DALTON, Phyllis I.	(702)732-4793	271
	DAVENPORT, Marilyn G.	(702)453-5606	275
	HUNSBERGER, Charles W.	(702)733-7810	574
Reno	GOULD, Martha B.	(702)785-4518	454

NEW HAMPSHIRE

Concord	HIGGINS, Matthew J.	(603)228-3127	538
	JOHNSON, Jean G.	(603)271-2429	605
Hancock	BRYAN, Arthur L.	(603)525-6614	151
Keene	LESSER, Charlotte B.	(603)357-1086	718
Milford	LISTOVITCH, Denise A.	(603)672-0899	733
Mirror Lake	SARLES, Christie V.	(603)569-4932	1083
Twin Mountain	PALMATIER, Susan M.	(603)846-2239	936
Washington	HAMILL, Martha L.	(603)495-3994	491

NEW JERSEY

Bergenfield	CHELARIU, Ana R.	(201)384-8302	204
Bernardsville	BURDEN, Geraldine R.	(201)766-0118	158
Bloomfield	BETANCOURT, Ingrid T.	(201)743-9511	92
Califon	CAPOOR, Asha	(201)832-9323	180
	ROSENBERG, Gail L.		1056
Cranford	BEIMAN, Frances M.	(201)272-5840	75
East Orange	GORMAN, Audrey J.	(201)676-2472	452
	MATHAI, Aleyamma	(201)266-5613	783
Elizabeth	LATINI, Samuel A.	(201)354-6060	701
Florham Park	BYOUK, Nancy K.	(201)377-2694	168
Forked River	ROYCE, Carolyn S.	(609)971-0665	1063
Hamilton	HOOKER, Joan M.	(609)587-9669	556
Highland Park	CLARK, Philip M.	(201)572-5414	218
Linden	PISKORIK, Elizabeth	(201)486-3888	976
Lodi	TAORMINA, Anthony P.	(201)365-4044	1223
Maplewood	BRYANT, David S.	(201)763-9294	152
Marlton	KALDENBERG, Katherine A.	(609)983-1444	622
Montclair	TUROCK, Betty J.	(201)744-3354	1265
Moorestown	LADOF, Nina S.	(609)235-1570	687
Morristown	MONROE-SECHREST, Nancy H.		855
Mount Holly	CARR, Charles E.	(609)267-9660	185
Neshanic	VANDERGRIFT, Kay E.	(201)369-8685	1274
New Brunswick	VARLEJS, Jana	(201)932-7169	1278
Newark	CUMMINGS, Charles F.	(201)733-7776	264
	DANE, William J.	(201)733-7848	272

PUBLIC LIBRARY CONSULTANT (Cont'd)
NEW JERSEY (Cont'd)

Paramus	WHITE, Robert W.	(201)652-6772	1332
Passaic	SCHEAR, Thomas W.	(201)777-6146	1090
Patterson	SAWYER, Miriam		1086
Peapack	WHITING, Elaine M.	(201)234-0598	1333
Phillipsburg	HESS, Jayne L.	(201)454-3712	534
Piscataway	MENZEL, John P.	(201)463-0634	825
Point Pleasant	GREENE, Ellin P.	(201)899-2270	464
Princeton	BLASINGAME, Ralph	(609)987-0273	104
	THRESHER, Jacquelyn E.	(609)924-9529	1243
Rahway	SUDALL, Arthur D.	(201)388-0761	1206
Red Bank	PACHMAN, Frederic C.	(201)530-7695	933
Ridgewood	ROSS, Robert D.	(201)652-4836	1058
Riverdale	LINNAVUORI, Julie R.	(201)839-3909	731
Rockaway	COHN, John M.	(201)627-8512	229
	KELSEY, Ann L.	(201)627-8512	639
Shrewsbury	KRANIS, Janet C.	(201)842-5995	676
Stratford	AVENICK, Karen	(609)784-8977	41
Tenafly	WECHTLER, Stephen R.	(201)568-8680	1315
Toms River	WOLPERT, Scott L.	(201)349-6200	1362
Trenton	MADDEN, Doreitha R.		758
	RAZZANO, Barbara W.	(609)984-7608	1012
Upper Montclair	LUNG, Chan S.	(201)746-6733	748
	PARR, Mary Y.	(201)746-0352	944
Voorhees	ROMISHER, Sivya S.	(609)772-1636	1053
Williamstown	BOGIS, Nana E.	(609)728-0569	110
Woodbridge	BECKERMAN, Edwin P.	(609)634-4450	72

NEW MEXICO

Las Cruces	DRESP, Donald F.	(505)522-3627	319
Los Alamos	SAYRE, Edward C.	(505)662-6889	1087
Thoreau	SCHUBERT, Donald F.	(505)862-7465	1101

NEW YORK

Albany	GILLESPIE, Gerald V.	(518)449-3380	435
	SHUBERT, Joseph F.	(518)474-5930	1133
APO New York	GADBOIS, Frank W.		411
	HAAS, Eva L.		480
Armonk	DEVERS, Charlotte M.	(914)273-3887	297
Ausable Forks	ROGERS, Elizabeth S.		1049
Bay Shore	HEINTZELMAN, Susan K.	(516)666-0177	522
Bayside	IPPOLITO, Andrew V.	(718)224-9484	583
Bayville	SPIRT, Diana L.	(516)628-8341	1175
Bellport	JANSEN, Guenter A.	(516)286-2626	593
	KLAUBER, Julie B.	(516)286-1600	658
	LEVERING, Philip	(516)286-1600	719
	RICHARDSON, John A.	(516)286-1600	1029
Binghamton	HILL, Malcolm K.	(607)723-8236	540
	SEARS, Carlton A.	(607)723-6475	1110
Bohemia	JENSEN, Patricia K.	(516)244-2115	599
Briarcliff Manor	FARKAS, Charles R.	(914)941-7672	364
Bronx	FRIEDMAN, Estelle Y.	(212)543-9060	403
	WENDT, Mary E.	(212)220-6560	1324
Brooklyn	GENCO, Barbara A.	(718)499-8750	426
	JOHNSON, Sheila A.	(718)780-7744	609
	KLEIMAN, Allan M.	(718)645-2396	658
	MALINCONICO, S M.	(718)627-0558	763
	SCHWABACHER, Sara A.	(718)388-0023	1104
	SWIESZKOWSK, L S.	(718)383-8480	1216
Buffalo	CHRISMAN, Diane J.	(716)846-7189	211
	GURN, Robert M.	(716)846-7187	478
	ROUNDS, Joseph B.	(716)846-8904	1061
Canadaigua	CUMMINS, A B.	(716)394-1381	204
Centereach	HEINEMAN, Stephanie R.	(516)585-9393	522
Circleville	NELSON, James B.	(914)361-2415	894
Croton-on-Hudson	COHEN, Aaron	(914)271-8170	227
Delanson	SOMERS, Betty J.	(518)864-5235	1166
Dewitt	ELY, Donald P.	(315)446-0259	347
Dobbs Ferry	BONE, Larry E.	(914)693-4500	113
East Amherst	CLOUDSLEY, Donald H.	(716)689-6162	223
East Meadow	FRANZEN, John F.	(516)794-2570	398
Elmsford	TRUDELL, Robert J.	(914)993-1608	1259
Freeport	MORIN, Wilfred L.	(516)368-6242	865
Highland	RANKIN, Carol A.	(914)691-2275	1007
Holbrook	ROMANELLI, Catherine A.	(516)588-5171	1052
Ithaca	MORRIS, Jennifer D.	(607)273-4074	866
	PANZ, Richard A.	(607)273-4074	938
	PARKHURST, Kathleen A.	(607)273-4073	942
Jackson Heights	SPYROS, Marsha L.	(718)424-7849	1177

PUBLIC LIBRARY CONSULTANT (Cont'd)
NEW YORK (Cont'd)

Jamaica	VENER, Lucille	(718)990-0761	1282
Lindenhurst	ROECKEL, Alan G.	(516)884-0832	1048
Liverpool	ROSSOFF, Judith H.	(315)457-0310	1059
Long Island City	MARTIN, Brian G.	(718)726-5885	775
Loudonville	NAYLOR, Richard J.	(518)458-9274	890
Massapequa	EISNER, Joseph	(516)735-4133	341
Menands	GILSON, Robert	(518)463-4181	437
Mt Vernon	OCKENE, David L.	(914)699-0949	915
	O'DELL, Lorraine I.		916
New Rochelle	MITTELGLUCK, Eugene L.	(914)834-8739	850
New York	BOCKMAN, Eugene J.	(212)566-5398	109
	CASSELL, Kay A.	(212)614-6551	193
	COHEN, Jackson B.	(212)595-6981	228
	CORWIN, Betty L.	(212)870-1641	248
	GLASER, Gloria T.	(212)753-8694	439
	GOSSAGE, Wayne	(212)869-3348	453
	GRUENBERG, Michael L.	(212)732-5964	474
	HUDSON, Alice C.	(212)222-2835	569
	LEE, Sang C.	(212)669-7961	711
	LIEBERFELD, Lawrence	(212)348-8499	726
	MACK, Phyllis G.	(212)926-2479	756
	MATTA, Seoud M.	(212)686-7532	785
	MILLER, Michael D.		841
	MOUNIR, Khalil A.	(212)373-5640	873
	NATHAN, Frances E.	(212)876-0269	889
	PALMER, Julia R.	(212)744-7202	936
	PAUL, Sandra K.	(212)675-7804	949
	PELLOWSKI, Anne	(212)316-1170	955
	PURCELL, Marcia L.	(212)982-3786	998
	RODERER, Nancy K.	(212)305-6302	1047
	TICE, Margaret E.		1244
	VAN DYKE, Stehpen H.	(212)340-0872	1275
	WYDEN, Elaine S.	(212)753-9229	1374
Newburgh	HALPIN, James R.	(914)561-1836	490
Niagara Falls	SHIELDS, Gerald R.	(716)284-2928	1130
North Bellmore	SHERWOOD, Nancy	(516)781-5063	1129
Orchard Park	LYMAN, Helen H.	(716)662-3525	751
Plattsburgh	RANSOM, Stanley A.	(518)563-5719	1007
Pomona	GUBITS, Helen S.	(914)354-1340	475
Port Chester	LETTIERI, Robin M.	(914)939-6710	719
Poughkeepsie	WIGG, Ristiina M.	(914)471-6060	1337
Richmond Hill	BISSESSAR, Carmen T.	(718)835-6514	100
Rochester	CUMMINS, Julie A.	(716)428-7366	264
	HOPE, Thomas W.	(716)458-4250	557
	HUNT, Suellyn	(716)428-6981	575
	PERRY, Rodney B.	(716)482-6478	961
	SHAPIRO, June R.	(716)461-5929	1121
	SWANTON, Susan I.	(716)247-0142	1214
Rockville Centre	FRIEDLAND, Rhoda W.	(516)766-6387	403
Ronkonkoma	SHERIDAN, Robert N.	(516)981-5739	1128
Roslyn	SIAHPOOSH, Farideh T.	(516)627-1919	1134
Sayville	PAGELS, Helen R.	(516)589-2908	934
Schenectady	HUMPHRY, John A.	(518)374-8944	574
Seaford	FLUCKIGER, Adrienne N.	(516)221-1334	386
Setauket	COOK, Jeannine S.	(516)941-4090	240
	NICHOLS, Gerald D.	(516)689-7071	901
	VERBESEY, J R.	(516)751-6913	1282
Syracuse	CASEY, Daniel W.	(315)468-0176	192
	JOHNSON, Nancy B.	(315)423-2911	608
	KINCHEN, Robert P.	(315)473-2702	650
	MCCLURE, Charles R.	(315)423-2911	797
	PRINS, Johanna W.	(315)475-5534	993
Troy	EVELAND, Ruth A.	(518)274-2389	358
Uniondale	GREEN, Joseph H.	(516)292-8920	462
Upper Nyack	POUNDSTONE, Sally H.	(914)358-9294	987
Valley Stream	ENG, Mamie	(516)825-6422	348
Vestal	HOLLEY, James L.	(607)754-4243	551
West Nyack	SIVULICH, Sandra S.	(914)358-9298	1145
White Plains	MOSLANDER, Charlotte D.	(914)428-1533	871
	TREFRY, Mary G.	(914)761-5478	1255
Williamsville	BOBINSKI, Mary F.	(716)688-4919	108

NORTH CAROLINA

Asheville	PERRY, Douglas F.	(704)252-8703	960
Chapel Hill	DANIEL, Evelyn A.	(919)962-8366	272
	FEEHAN, Patricia E.	(919)962-8366	368
Charlotte	MYERS, Carol B.	(704)523-1260	884

PUBLIC LIBRARY CONSULTANT (Cont'd)
NORTH CAROLINA (Cont'd)

Durham	BOMARC, M D.	(919)683-6244	113
	BURGIN, Robert E.	(919)683-6485	159
	SHEARER, Kenneth D.	(919)683-6485	1124
Elkin	MACPHAIL, Jessica		758
Fayetteville	HANSEL, Patsy J.	(919)484-7096	497
	THRASHER, Jerry A.	(919)483-1580	1243
Garner	RICHARDSON, Beverly S.		1029
Greensboro	VIELE, George B.	(919)373-2474	1283
Greenville	YORK, Maurice C.	(919)752-5260	1381
Hickory	PRITCHARD, John A.	(704)294-0326	994
Jacksonville	VEITCH, Carol J.	(919)455-7350	1281
Kittrell	SHAFFER, Nancy R.	(919)492-9684	1119
Lewisville	BROWN, Merrikay E.	(919)945-3786	146
Matthews	CANNON, Robert E.	(704)847-0394	179
Raleigh	SMITH, Catherine	(919)851-4703	1153
	WELCH, John T.	(919)872-0552	1321
Spring Hope	LANEY, Elizabeth J.	(919)478-3836	695
Wilmington	BEECH, Vivian W.	(919)763-3303	74
	VON OESEN, Elaine		1288
Wilson	VALENTINE, Patrick M.	(919)237-5355	1271
Winston-Salem	ROBERTS, William H.	(919)727-2556	1041
Yanceyville	MASSEY, Nancy O.	(919)968-0852	782

NORTH DAKOTA

Bismarck	HARRIS, Patricia L.	(701)224-8112	505
	HENDRICKS, Thom	(701)627-4635	527
	HILDEBRANT, Darrel D.	(701)222-6410	539
	MOREHOUSE, Valerie J.	(701)224-4658	863
Fargo	JANZEN, Deborah K.	(701)277-1865	594

OHIO

Bay Village	DOMBEY, Kathryn W.	(216)871-5024	310
Burton	VARGA, Carol C.	(216)834-4466	1278
Chesterland	CORBUS, Lawrence J.	(216)286-8941	245
Cincinnati	DICKMAN, Emmajane H.		301
	HUNT, James R.	(513)369-6972	575
Cleveland	KOZLOWSKI, Ronald S.	(216)398-1800	674
	SILVER, Linda R.	(216)398-1800	1138
	VENABLE, Andrew A.	(216)541-4128	1282
Columbus	DALRYMPLE, Tamsen	(614)486-2109	271
	DRIESSEN, Diane	(614)486-0621	320
	PARSONS, Augustine C.	(614)895-3201	944
	PHILIP, John J.	(614)462-7061	967
	VANBRIMMER, Barbara A.	(614)292-9810	1272
Cuyahoga Falls	BERRY, Diana M.	(216)929-1948	90
Dayton	BANTA, Gratia J.	(513)277-4444	55
	BUCK, Jeremy R.	(513)227-9500	153
	KLINCK, Cynthia A.	(513)435-7375	661
	PURSCH, Lenore D.	(513)434-7064	998
Euclid	COLEMAN, Judith	(216)261-5300	231
Findlay	DICKINSON, Luren E.	(419)423-4934	301
	JANKY, Donna L.	(419)422-3211	593
Greenbrier Commons	BINA, Marcella A.	(216)884-2313	97
Lakewood	SEELY, Edward	(216)221-3453	1111
Mansfield	KARRE, David J.	(419)526-1337	628
Medina	SMITH, Robert S.	(216)725-0588	1160
New Philadelphia	HAGLOCH, Susan B.	(216)364-4474	483
Norwalk	DRAPP, Laureen	(419)668-6063	318
Parma	ROBINSON, Doris J.	(216)888-3462	1043
Portsmouth	COOK, Charles T.	(614)354-5688	239
Sidney	BELVIN, Robert J.	(513)492-6851	78
Steubenville	HALL, Alan C.	(614)264-4410	486
Toledo	AVERY, Galen V.	(419)475-8551	41
	SCOLES, Clyde S.	(419)255-7055	1106
Warren	BRIELL, Robert D.	(216)399-8807	135
Waynesville	JOHNSON, Corinne E.	(513)897-2343	603
Westerville	GARDNER, Frank D.	(614)882-0221	417
	LOVEJOY, Eunice G.	(614)882-4791	743
Westlake	CHAMIS, Alice Y.	(216)777-2198	198
	CHARVAT, Catherine T.	(216)871-6391	203
Wickliffe	JOHNSON, Ruth E.	(216)943-1317	608
Willow Wood	REID, Margaret B.	(614)643-2925	1018
Xenia	WALDER, Antoinette L.	(513)376-2995	1294
Youngstown	DONAHUGH, Robert H.	(216)788-6950	310
	YANCURA, Ann J.	(216)746-7042	1377

PUBLIC LIBRARY CONSULTANT (Cont'd)

OKLAHOMA

Midwest City	PETERSON, Denise D.		963
Moore	GOLDSBERRY, Maureen E.	(405)799-3326	446
Norman	JORDAN, Linda K.	(405)321-1481	616
	SHERMAN, Mary A.	(405)321-1481	1128
Oklahoma City	BRAWNER, Lee B.	(405)947-1109	130
	CLARK, Robert L.	(405)521-2502	218
	DAVIS, Denyvetta	(405)424-2106	278
	LITTLE, Paul L.	(405)789-9400	733
	MEYERS, Duane H.	(405)946-2488	830
	SAULMON, Sharon A.	(405)634-3181	1084
Tulsa	BUTHOD, J C.	(918)592-7894	166
	WOODRUM, Patricia A.	(918)592-7897	1366

OREGON

Beaverton	SHOFFNER, Ralph M.	(503)645-3502	1132
Bend	BYRNE, Helen E.	(503)382-1621	169
Eugene	HILDEBRAND, Carol I.	(503)344-4267	538
	KNIEVEL, Helen A.	(503)345-2032	664
	MEEKS, James D.	(503)687-5454	821
Jacksonville	GORDON, Patricia H.	(503)899-7438	451
Milton-Freewater	SARGENT, Phyllis M.	(503)938-3724	1083
Portland	LONG, Sarah A.	(503)221-7731	740
	SELLE, Donna M.	(503)629-5886	1113
Salem	DOAK, Wesley A.	(503)581-4292	306

PENNSYLVANIA

Abington	POSEL, Nancy R.	(215)885-5181	985
Allentown	MOSES, Lynn M.		871
Allison Park	SMITH, Mary M.	(412)487-2883	1158
Ardmore	PULLER, Maryam W.	(215)642-5187	997
Bellefonte	WOLFE, Gary D.	(814)355-1516	1360
Bryn Mawr	BILLS, Linda G.	(215)645-5294	96
Camp Hill	ALBRECHT, Lois K.	(717)737-6111	10
Clarion	MCCABE, Gerard B.	(814)226-2343	792
Doylestown	WHITTAKER, Edward L.	(215)348-0332	1334
Drexel Hill	MULLEN, Francis X.	(215)623-7045	877
Eagleville	PECK, Marian B.	(215)631-1129	953
Emmaus	STEPHANOFF, Kathryn	(215)797-8838	1187
Erie	GALLIVAN, Marion F.	(814)452-2333	414
Glenshaw	YATES, Diane G.	(412)486-0211	1378
Harrisburg	BAUER, Margaret D.	(717)233-3113	65
	FOUST, Judith M.	(717)787-8007	393
Lansdale	BLAUERT, Mary A.	(215)822-2929	105
Lebanon	HABER, Walter H.		481
Library	SALVAYON, Connie	(412)833-5585	1078
McKeesport	HORVATH, Robert T.	(412)672-0625	561
Media	COURTRIGHT, Harry R.	(215)891-5190	252
	LARSON, Phyllis S.	(215)566-2809	699
Norristown	CATHEY, Gail L.	(215)278-5100	195
Philadelphia	AXAM, John A.	(215)549-6485	42
	BARR, Marilyn P.	(215)844-2036	58
	BAUMGARTNER, Barbara W.	(215)686-5418	66
	BRICKER, Will S.	(215)548-3033	135
	CHILDERS, Thomas A.	(215)895-2479	208
	GARRISON, Guy G.	(215)895-2474	420
	GREEN, Rose B.	(215)828-7029	462
	MARCO, Guy A.		769
	MARVIN, Stephen G.	(215)895-1874	780
	MOODY, Marilyn D.	(215)686-5310	857
	NAISMITH, Patricia A.	(215)235-0256	887
	NEWCOMBE, Jack A.	(215)934-7240	898
	ORSBURN, Elizabeth C.	(215)686-5367	927
	PROMOS, Marianne	(215)686-5351	995
	SHELKROT, Elliot L.	(215)686-5300	1126
	SNOWTEN, Renee Y.	(215)557-8295	1164
	WRIGHT, Irene R.	(215)923-1726	1371
Pittsburgh	CRONEBERGER, Robert B.	(412)622-3100	260
	DILWORTH, Kirby D.	(412)622-3105	303
	FALGIONE, Joseph F.	(412)622-3127	362
	JOSEY, E J.	(412)624-9451	618
	LEONARD, Peter C.	(414)422-5815	716
	LOCKE, Jill L.	(412)624-9435	736
	WOODSWORTH, Anne		1367
	WRAY, Wendell L.	(412)363-0251	1370
Slippery Rock	BACK, Andrew W.	(412)794-7817	43
State College	PIERCE, William S.	(814)237-7004	972
Williamsport	FOGAL, Annabel E.	(717)326-2461	387
Yardley	BARATTA, Maria	(215)321-3289	55

PUBLIC LIBRARY CONSULTANT (Cont'd)

RHODE ISLAND

Barrington	BUNDY, Annalee M.	(401)245-2232	157
	BURKE, Lauri K.	(401)245-3741	160
East Providence	CAIRNS, Roberta A.	(401)433-0159	171
Portsmouth	AYLWARD, James F.	(401)683-1889	42
Providence	DANIELS, Bruce E.	(401)277-2726	273
	MCKEE, Virginia W.	(401)467-8435	810
Saunderstown	BRENNAN, Deborah B.	(401)294-3175	132
Warwick	PEARCE, Douglas A.	(401)739-5440	952
Westerly	LIGHT, Karen M.	(401)596-2877	726

SOUTH CAROLINA

Cayce	FREEMAN, Larry S.	(803)794-5370	401
Columbia	CALLAHAM, Betty E.	(803)772-3788	173
	CROSS, Joseph R.	(803)777-3365	260
	LAW, Aileen E.	(803)734-8666	704
	WARREN, Charles D.	(803)782-4219	1306
Greenville	AYARI, Kaye W.	(803)235-4883	42
Greer	MESSINEO, Anthony	(803)268-7267	828
Hilton Head Island	CHAIT, William	(803)671-3720	197
Manning	GILBERT, Sybil M.	(803)435-8633	434
Spartanburg	BRUCE, Dennis L.	(803)596-3507	149
Summerville	MAY, Robert E.	(803)871-2201	789

SOUTH DAKOTA

Aberdeen	RAVE, David A.	(605)622-7097	1010
Sioux Falls	DERTIEN, James L.	(605)339-7115	294

TENNESSEE

Brentwood	NORTON, Tedgina	(615)371-0090	910
Clinton	GREESON, Judy G.	(615)457-0931	465
Gallatin	COLLIER, Virginia S.		232
Harriman	OVERTON, Margaret C.		931
Jackson	AUD, Thomas L.	(901)668-2896	39
Memphis	DRESCHER, Judith A.	(901)276-0104	319
	HALE, Relda D.		485
	SMITH, Robert F.	(901)725-8872	1160
Nashville	GLEAVES, Edwin S.	(615)741-3666	441

TEXAS

Amarillo	WELLS, Mary K.	(806)381-2435	1322
Arlington	MACFARLANE, Francis X.	(817)265-8309	755
Austin	BRIDGE, Frank R.	(512)328-6006	135
	DAYO, Ayo	(512)472-8980	283
	DEGRUYTER, M L.	(512)929-3086	288
	JUERGENS, Bonnie	(512)288-2072	619
	PAYNE, John R.	(512)478-7724	951
	ROY, Loriene	(512)471-6316	1063
	SEIDENBERG, Edward	(512)463-5459	1112
	SKINNER, Vicki F.	(512)892-3997	1146
	STANDIFER, Hugh A.	(512)288-2072	1179
Brazoria	RASKA, Ginny	(409)798-1628	1009
Conroe	BALDWIN, Joe M.	(409)756-4484	51
Corpus Christi	NEU, Margaret J.	(512)884-2011	896
Dallas	BOCKSTRUCK, Lloyd D.	(214)670-1406	109
	CRABB, Elizabeth A.	(214)233-4382	254
	CROW, Rebecca N.	(214)749-4285	261
	EATENSON, Ervin T.	(214)521-4839	333
	EWUNES, Ernest L.	(214)376-4102	359
	FOUTS, Judith F.	(214)341-3961	393
	JAGOE, Katherine P.	(214)931-8938	591
	LEVINE, Harriet L.	(214)521-7165	720
	MASON, Florence M.	(214)358-5755	781
	MENDRO, Donna C.		824
	MOLTZAN, Janet R.	(214)691-3267	854
	WATERS, Richard L.	(214)826-6981	1308
Denton	FERSTL, Kenneth L.	(817)383-3775	374
	SHELDON, Brooke E.	(817)898-2602	1125
	TOURAINE, Linda S.	(817)382-2954	1252
El Paso	ANDERSON, Mark	(915)858-0905	24
	GEARY, Kathleen A.	(915)533-5777	424
Flower Mound	SVEINSSON, Joan L.	(214)539-9308	1212
Fort Worth	ALLMAND, Linda F.	(817)870-7706	17
	ARBELBIDE, Cindy L.	(817)877-3355	30
	ARD, Harold J.	(817)293-5474	31
	BRACEY, Ann E.	(817)738-9940	124
	DIXON, Catherine A.	(817)870-7708	306
Galveston	RASCHE, Richard R.	(409)762-3139	1008

PUBLIC LIBRARY CONSULTANT (Cont'd)
TEXAS (Cont'd)

Garland	LARSON, Jeanette C.	(214)240-0661	699
	MURRAY, Margaret A.	(214)494-7192	882
Harlingen	CORBIN, John	(512)428-5475	245
	MILLS, Helen L.		844
Houston	BROWN, Carol J.	(713)247-2227	142
	BROWN, Freddiemae E.	(713)227-9177	144
	CARTER, Daniel H.	(713)665-5150	189
	GOLDBERG, Rhoda L.	(713)522-4079	444
	GOLEY, Elaine P.	(713)467-5784	447
	HENINGTON, David M.	(713)247-2700	528
	LANDINGHAM, Alpha M.	(713)522-9091	692
	MILES, Ruby A.	(713)522-4219	834
	PHILLIPS, Ray S.	(713)622-9686	969
	RADOFF, Leonard I.	(713)692-1952	1002
Huntsville	HOFFMAN, Frank W.	(409)294-1152	548
McAllen	MITTELSTAEDT, Gerard E.	(512)686-3029	850
McKinney	DOYLE, Patricia L.	(214)542-4461	317
North Richland Hills	HALLAM, Arlita W.	(817)281-0041	489
Palestine	SELLERS, Wayne C.	(214)729-4829	1114
Pasadena	CATES, Susan W.	(713)487-1714	195
Round Rock	RICKLEFS, Dale L.	(512)255-3939	1032
San Antonio	VELA-CREIXELL, Mary I.	(512)733-7109	1281
Weatherford	HEEZEN, Ronald R.	(817)599-0833	520

UTAH

American Fork	TOMLIN, Celia K.	(801)756-4681	1250
Ogden	WILSON, Brenda J.	(801)479-1407	1350
Provo	MARCHANT, Maurice P.	(801)378-2976	768
St George	SHIRTS, Russell B.	(801)673-5895	1131
Salt Lake City	DAY, J D.	(801)363-5733	282
	DOWNEY REIDA, Linda K.	(801)466-5888	316
	GIACOMA, Pete J.	(801)364-2624	430
	HINDMARSH, Douglas P.	(801)328-2609	542
	OWEN, Amy	(801)466-5888	931
Springville	PETERSON, Douglas L.	(801)489-5248	963

VERMONT

Bennington	PRICE, Michael L.	(802)442-9051	992
Brattleboro	HAY, Linda A.	(802)254-5595	515
	MORRISON, Meris E.	(802)257-0725	868
Colchester	KNEELAND, Marjorie H.	(802)655-0279	664
Montpelier	CASSELL, Marianne K.	(802)223-5653	193
	GREENE, Grace W.	(802)828-3261	464
	KLINCK, Patricia E.	(802)828-3265	661

VIRGINIA

Alexandria	HINDMAN, Pamela J.	(703)836-9168	542
	MICHAELS, Andrea A.	(703)360-1297	831
	PLITT, Jeanne G.	(703)838-4558	978
	STEVENS, Roberta A.	(703)960-0464	1191
Arlington	BROWN, Charles M.	(703)284-8174	142
	GOLDBERG, Lisbeth S.	(703)243-0796	444
	HIGBEE, Joan F.	(703)524-5844	537
Charlottesville	EVERINGHAM, Neil G.	(804)979-7151	358
	FRANKLIN, Robert D.	(804)973-3238	398
Chesapeake	FOREHAND, Margaret P.	(804)547-6579	390
Chesterfield	WAGENKNECHT, Robert E.	(804)748-1601	1291
Fairfax	GOODWIN, Jane G.	(703)246-5847	450
Falls Church	PARSONS, John W.	(703)671-7756	945
Fredericksburg	VANDERBERG, E S.	(703)371-3311	1273
Hampton	LANKES, J B.	(804)722-7821	696
Harrisonburg	STEINBERG, David L.	(703)433-1572	1185
Herndon	SINWELL, Carol A.	(703)689-0086	1144
Manassas	CHRISTOLON, Blair B.	(703)369-3535	212
	MURPHY, Richard W.	(703)361-8211	881
Mclean	WANG, Chi	(703)893-3016	1302
Norfolk	NICHOLSON, Myreen M.	(804)627-6281	902
Portsmouth	BROWN, William A.	(804)483-2195	148
	BURGESS, Dean	(804)393-8501	159
Richmond	COSTA, Robert N.	(804)233-6274	249
	SADLER, Graham H.	(804)222-1643	1073
	SNAIR, Dale S.	(804)786-1489	1162
	YATES, Ella G.	(804)786-2332	1378
Virginia Beach	BARKLEY, Carolyn L.	(804)431-3070	56
	CAYWOOD, Carolyn A.	(804)464-9320	195
Winchester	BISCHOFF, Frances A.	(703)667-5350	99

PUBLIC LIBRARY CONSULTANT (Cont'd)
WASHINGTON

Bellevue	MUTSCHLER, Herbert F.	(206)746-3952	883
Bothell	YEE, J E.	(206)625-4870	1379
Cheney	BENDER, Betty W.	(509)838-4283	79
Edmonds	STRONG, Sunny A.	(206)778-3804	1203
	TURNER, Kathleen G.	(206)771-1933	1264
Kenmore	TAYLOR, James B.	(206)483-2954	1227
Kingston	HENINGER, Irene C.	(206)297-3002	528
Lacey	DEBUSE, Raymond	(206)491-7498	285
Marysville	WILSON, Evie		1350
Newport	REMINGTON, David G.	(509)447-2636	1022
Olympia	CHRISTIANSEN, Claire B.	(206)459-7420	211
	DICKERSON, Lon R.	(206)943-5001	300
	MOORE, Mary Y.	(206)866-8272	860
	SHAFFER, Maryann	(206)943-5001	1119
	ZUSSY, Nancy L.	(206)786-9647	1391
Seattle	BETZ-ZALL, Jonathan R.	(206)782-9305	92
	GREGGS, Elizabeth M.	(206)242-6044	465
	JOHNSON, Carolynn K.	(206)684-6681	603
	LEONARD, Gloria J.	(206)722-4828	716
	MADDEN, Susan B.	(206)684-6626	758
	POLISHUK, Bernard	(206)524-8676	980
	RICKELTON, Esther G.	(206)684-6617	1031
	WALTERS, Daniel L.	(206)684-6683	1301
Seguim	DAVIES, Jo	(206)683-5229	277
Spokane	LANE, Steven P.	(509)838-4728	694
	SHIDELER, John C.	(509)838-5242	1129
	TYSON, Christy	(509)624-9744	1267
	WEBER, Joan L.	(509)489-6959	1314
Vancouver	CONABLE, Gordon M.	(206)694-0604	235
	HUTTON, Emily A.	(206)695-1566	579
Walla Walla	HALEY, Anne E.	(509)527-4388	486

WEST VIRGINIA

Bluefield	DYE, Luella I.	(304)487-2037	330
Huntington	REENSTJERNA, Frederick R.	(304)523-9651	1016
Martinsburg	BEALL, C E.	(304)263-3871	68
Point Pleasant	WILLIAMSON, Judy D.	(304)675-4350	1347
St Albans	PALMER, Marguerite C.	(304)722-6349	936
Salem	LANGER, Frank A.	(304)782-1007	695
Welch	MULLER, William A.	(304)436-3070	877

WISCONSIN

Appleton	DAWSON, Terry P.	(414)735-6168	282
	PENNINGTON, Jerome G.	(414)735-6167	957
	VIGNOVICH, Ray L.	(414)735-1290	1284
Ashland	PAULI, David N.	(705)682-2365	950
Burlington	PROCES, Stephen L.	(414)763-7623	994
Eau Claire	MERRIAM, Louise A.	(715)839-5003	826
Franklin	BELLIN, Bernard E.	(414)461-1484	78
Janesville	HARFST, Linda L.	(608)754-3201	501
	KRUEGER, Karen J.	(608)755-2800	680
Kenosha	BAKER, Douglas	(414)656-8058	48
Kewaunee	ECKERT, Daniel L.	(414)388-2176	335
La Crosse	ACCARDI, Joseph J.	(608)784-5755	3
	WHITE, James W.	(608)784-8623	1331
Madison	BUNGE, Charles A.	(608)263-2900	157
	DAHLGREN, Anders C.	(608)271-9148	269
	MCCONNELL, Shirley M.	(608)274-7222	798
	MONROE, Margaret E.	(608)263-2900	855
	ROBBINS, Jane B.	(608)263-2908	1038
	WAITY, Gloria J.	(608)222-7783	1293
	WEINGAND, Darlene E.	(608)262-8952	1318
	WILLETT, Holly G.	(608)251-0633	1341
Middleton	NIX, Larry T.	(608)836-5616	905
	ZWEIZIG, Douglas L.	(608)831-4364	1392
Milwaukee	BOTHAM, Jane	(414)278-3078	118
	MCKINNEY, Venora	(414)278-3025	812
	SAGER, Donald J.	(414)278-3020	1074
	SAGER, Lynn S.	(414)964-1402	1074
Stevens Point	SWIFT, Leonard W.	(715)346-1550	1216
Stoughton	LUND, Patricia A.	(608)873-9446	748
Verona	KNODLE, Shirley M.	(608)845-7180	665
Waukesha	GOSZ, Kathleen M.	(414)548-7997	453
Wisconsin Rapids	WILSON, William J.	(715)424-4272	1353

PUBLIC LIBRARY CONSULTANT (Cont'd)

WYOMING

Cheyenne	BYERS, Edward W.	(307)635-1032	168
	JOHNSON, Wayne H.	(307)777-7283	609
Gillette	SIEBERSMA, Dan	(307)686-0786	1135
Green River	HIGBY, Helen E.	(307)875-3615	537
Lander	HEUER, William J.	(307)332-3793	535
Laramie	CHATTON, Barbara A.	(307)766-2167	204

CANADA

ALBERTA

Airdrie	EVANS, Patricia D.		357
Calgary	ANDERSON, Gail	(403)260-2646	23
	MANSON, Bill B.	(403)260-2620	767
Canmore	LUTHY, Jean M.	(403)678-5883	750
Edmonton	RICHARDS, Vincent P.	(403)429-9814	1029
Red Deer	GISHLER, John R.	(304)340-3922	438
Strathmore	LUNN, Rowena F.	(403)934-5334	749

BRITISH COLUMBIA

Abbotsford	RAY, Gordon L.	(604)859-7141	1011
Burnaby	GOW, Susan P.	(604)439-0931	454
Clearbrook	VIIERANS, Mary E.	(604)859-7814	1284
Nanaimo	MEADOWS, Donald F.	(604)753-3662	819
Vancouver	BEWLEY, Lois M.	(604)228-4250	93

NOVA SCOTIA

Halifax	AMEY, Lorne J.	(902)422-8639	20

ONTARIO

Arnprior	BARKE, Judith P.	(613)623-5411	56
Belfountain	DE RONDE, Paula D.	(519)927-5156	294
Cambridge	SKELTON, W M.	(519)621-0460	1146
Don Mills	TEMPLIN, Dorothy	(416)447-2380	1231
Gloucester	KENT, Charles D.		642
Keswick	MCCRACKEN, Ronald W.	(416)476-5556	799
London	CADA, Elizabeth J.	(519)661-5136	170
Mississauga	DINEEN, Diane M.	(416)279-7002	304
Ottawa	BLACK, Jane L.	(613)234-5006	101
Pembroke	MEHTA, Subbash C.	(613)732-2914	821
Scarborough	BASSNETT, Peter J.	(416)298-0614	63
Stratford	KIRKPATRICK, Jane E.		655
Thornhill	HARE, Judith E.	(416)881-4804	501
Thunder Bay	HSU, Peter T.	(807)623-2794	567
Toronto	BEAUMONT, Jane	(416)922-9364	70
	CAMPBELL, Bonnie	(416)323-3566	176
	DENIS, Laurent G.	(416)978-3111	292
	FASICK, Adele M.	(416)978-7074	366
	LORENTOWICZ, Genia	(416)393-7018	741
	MCCANN, Judith B.	(416)429-1247	794
	PARKER, Arthur D.	(416)967-5525	941
	SCHWENGER, Frances S.	(416)393-7215	1105
Waterloo	BECKMAN, Margaret L.	(519)824-4120	73

QUEBEC

Aylmer	MACKEY, Laurette	(819)684-0410	756
Baie d'Urfe	KLOK, Buddhi	(514)457-2757	662
Beaconsfield	HIRON, Barbara A.	(514)695-3200	543
Boucherville	DUBOIS, Florian	(514)655-3131	322
	NADEAU, Johan	(514)655-4858	885
Hull	BOYER, Denis P.	(819)771-1189	123
	DUHAMEL, Louis	(819)771-4453	324
Levis	LAMOUREUX, Michele	(418)833-8144	691
Longueuil	OUIMET, Yves	(514)646-8615	930
Mascouche	ALLARD, Diane	(514)474-4150	14
Montreal	CORBEIL, Lizette	(514)332-9854	245
	COURTEMANCHE, Pierre O.		251
	DAUNAIS, Marie J.	(514)633-4170	275
	DUMOULIN, Nicole L.	(514)733-8051	325
	MITTERMEYER, Diane	(514)398-4204	850
	PICARD, Albert	(514)276-5797	970
	SAVARD, Rejean	(514)343-6044	1085
	WALSH, Mary A.	(514)937-6633	1300
Outremont	LACROIX, Yvon A.	(514)273-7423	687
Pointe Claire			
Dorval	COTE, Claire	(514)630-1218	249
Quebec	FOERTIN, Yves P.	(418)649-0811	387
Saint-Eustache	KHOUZAM, Monique	(514)472-4440	646

PUBLIC LIBRARY CONSULTANT (Cont'd)

QUEBEC (Cont'd)

St Laurent			
D'Orleans	SIMON, Marie L.	(514)744-7315	1140
Shawinigan-Sud	MATTE, Pierre V.	(819)536-3519	785

SASKATCHEWAN

Prince Albert	LABUIK, Karen L.	(306)764-0712	686
Regina	TURNBULL, Keith	(306)757-8915	1264

AUSTRALIA

Kensington	RAYWARD, W B.		1011

ENGLAND

Warwickshire	CHANDLER, George		200

FEDERAL REPUBLIC OF CHINA

Taipei	LIN, Chih F.		727

ISRAEL

Haifa	WASERMAN, Barbara		1307
Jerusalem	DIAMANT, Betsy		299

JAPAN

Ibaraki-ken	TAKEUCHI, Satoru		1220
Sendai Miyagi	HARADA, Ryukichi		499

MEXICO

Mexico City	MAGALONI, Ana M.		759

NIGERIA

Ibadan	ABOYADE, Beatrice O.		2

POLAND

Poznan	CHOJNACKA, Jadwiga		210

PUBLIC RELATIONS CONSULTANT

ALABAMA

Birmingham	SCALES, Diann R.	(205)322-8458	1087
	VANDERPOORTEN, Mary B.	(205)991-1368	1274
Daphne	ROBINSON, Gayle N.	(205)626-2345	1044
Gadsden	BUCKNER, Rebecca S.	(205)543-8849	154
Mobile	BUSH, Nancy W.	(205)343-8121	165

ALASKA

Bethel	EMMONS, Mary E.	(907)543-3682	348
Central	OAKES, Patricia A.		913
Fairbanks	MUDD, Isabelle G.	(907)479-4522	875
Valdez	LEAHY, M J.	(907)835-2801	706

ARIZONA

Holbrook	ROTHLISBERG, Allen P.	(602)524-2257	1060
Phoenix	NIXON, Arless B.	(602)246-9196	906
Sells	CULL, Roberta	(602)383-2601	263
Tucson	FRANK, Donald G.	(602)742-9688	396
	GOLDBERG, Susan S.	(602)747-2663	445
	GOODRICH, Nita K.	(602)791-4168	449
	GOTHBERG, Helen M.	(602)887-2262	453
	HIEB, Louis A.	(602)621-6077	537
	RIISE, Milton B.	(602)325-1348	1034

ARKANSAS

Arkadelphia	WOODS, L B.	(501)246-5511	1367
Magnolia	BRADLEY, Florene J.	(501)234-1991	125

CALIFORNIA

Berkeley	FLUM, Judith G.	(415)486-0378	386
Beverly Hills	RUNYON, Judith A.	(213)859-5102	1067
Callahan	FARRIER, George F.	(916)467-3334	365
Carmichael	STRONG, Gary E.	(916)966-2037	1203
Carphell	ALIX, Cleta M.	(408)371-3294	13
Encinitas	PIERCE, Patricia J.	(619)436-5055	971
Fresno	CARLSON, Alan C.	(209)445-0828	182
Glen Ellen	SCARBOROUGH, Katharine T.	(707)996-7993	1087
Half Moon Bay	MALONEY, James J.	(415)726-9317	764
Hayward	ARROWOOD, Donna J.	(415)881-2791	34
Irvine	ARIEL, Joan	(714)856-4970	31

PUBLIC RELATIONS CONSULTANT (Cont'd)
CALIFORNIA (Cont'd)

Long Beach	BRITTON, Helen H.	(213)498-4047	137
Los Angeles	CROSS, Claudette S.	(213)256-2123	260
	HALE, Kaycee	(213)204-0793	485
	HOFFMAN, Irene M.	(213)839-5722	548
	JAIN, Celeste C.	(213)665-7510	591
	POPOVITCH-KREKIC, Ruzica	(213)476-2237	984
	REAGAN, Bob	(213)612-3320	1012
	RITCHESON, Charles R.	(213)743-2543	1036
	TERZIAN, Shohig S.	(213)478-5193	1232
	VILLERE, Dawn N.	(213)290-2989	1284
Manhattan Beach	MARKEY, Penny S.	(213)374-1838	771
Modesto	MORAN, Irene E.	(209)576-2740	862
Mountain View	DAWSON, Debra A.	(415)948-2756	282
Ojai	MOORE, Phyllis C.	(805)646-8592	861
Orange	ERLICH, Martin		353
	SMITH, Elizabeth M.	(714)634-7809	1154
Palo Alto	ELLSWORTH, Dianne J.	(415)321-2253	345
	HAMILTON, David M.	(415)853-0197	491
Petaluma	GORDON, Ruth I.	(707)778-4719	452
Pleasanton	BUTLER, David W.	(415)846-3308	166
Sacramento	BURNS, John F.	(916)445-4293	162
	KAST, Gloria E.	(916)483-6765	629
	MCGOVERN, Gail J.	(916)446-2411	807
	RUDDOCK, Velda I.	(916)921-0521	1065
San Diego	KAYE, Karen	(619)560-2695	632
	LAGIES, Meinhart J.	(619)283-0608	688
San Francisco	FOX, Marylou P.	(415)546-8466	395
	GERSH, Barbara S.	(415)346-7882	429
	MOYER, Barbara A.	(415)386-6297	874
	RUNYON, Steven C.	(415)386-5873	1067
	SCHNEIDER, Marcia G.	(415)584-8228	1097
	TARTER, Blodwen	(415)346-8199	1224
Santa Barbara	MACGREGOR, Raymond	(805)682-5654	755
Santa Clara	SMOKEY, Sheila C.	(408)289-3490	1162
Santa Monica	ANDERSON, Dorothy J.	(213)394-1899	22
South Gate	BUBOLTZ, Dale D.	(213)567-1431	152
South Pasadena	WISE, Leona L.	(213)257-4020	1357
Suisun	CISLER, Stephen A.	(707)422-5089	215
Travis AFB	JACOBS, Nina F.	(707)438-5254	589
Upland	MORRIS, George H.	(714)982-9858	866
Whittier	WILLIAMS, Lisa B.	(213)693-0771	1344
Woodland Hills	CLIFTON, Joe A.	(818)716-3171	222

COLORADO

Aurora	LAMBERT, Shirley A.	(303)770-1220	690
	MURRAY, William A.	(303)364-8208	882
Boulder	VARNES, Richard S.	(303)444-8051	1279
Denver	WAGNER, Barbara L.	(303)297-3611	1291
Grand Lake	ARMITAGE, Constance	(303)328-5293	32
Littleton	BETTENCOURT, Nancy J.	(303)771-0968	92
Pueblo	JONES, Donna R.	(303)542-2156	612

CONNECTICUT

Ashford	MCCAUGHTRY, Dorothy H.	(203)429-7637	795
Derby	FINNUCAN, Louise A.	(203)732-7399	379
Hartford	STONE, Dennis J.	(203)241-4617	1197
Middletown	BECK, Arthur R.	(203)347-1387	71
	BRECK, Evelyn M.	(203)344-6286	131
New Britain	LAWRENCE, Scott W.	(203)677-1659	705
Ridgefield	NORTON, Alice	(203)438-4064	910
Stamford	DIMATTIA, Ernest A.	(203)322-9055	304
	SERGEL, Carol K.	(203)977-4256	1116
Waterbury	FLANAGAN, Leo N.	(203)756-6149	383
West Hartford	HORAK, Ellen B.	(203)233-3164	558
	PIERCE, Anne L.	(203)243-4849	971
	TALIT, Lynn	(203)233-7793	1221
Westport	MECKLER, Alan M.	(203)226-6967	820
Wethersfield	DONOHUE, Christine N.	(203)529-2938	311

DELAWARE

Frankford	HITCHENS, Howard B.	(302)539-2420	544
New Castle	IRWIN, Ruth A.	(302)328-8560	584
Newark	DANIEL, Alfred I.	(302)731-9723	272
Wilmington	BURDASH, David H.	(302)571-7402	158

PUBLIC RELATIONS CONSULTANT (Cont'd)
DISTRICT OF COLUMBIA

Washington	ATKIN, Michael I.	(202)539-8252	37
	BELLEFONTAINE, Arnold G.	(202)287-6587	78
	HAGEMEYER, Alice L.	(202)727-2255	483
	JOHNSON, Lucy C.		607
	JONES, Elin D.		612
	KITZMILLER, Virginia G.		657
	KUPERMAN, Agota M.		684
	LAWTON, Bethany L.	(202)651-5220	705
	LEONARD, Angela M.	(202)636-7926	716
	LITTLEJOHN, Grace M.	(202)291-6920	734
	LUNIN, Lois F.	(202)965-3924	749
	PHELPS, Thomas C.	(202)786-0271	967
	SIPKOV, Ivan	(202)287-9850	1144
	STEWART, Ruth A.	(202)287-6587	1193
	STONE, Elizabeth W.	(202)338-5574	1197
	TSCHERNY, Elena	(202)727-1183	1260
	WEBB, Barbara A.	(202)797-8909	1313
	WILLIAMS, Martin T.	(202)287-3759	1345

FLORIDA

Gainesville	BECKER, Josephine M.	(904)371-3808	72
Miami	CARDEN, Marguerite	(305)375-5005	180
	WULF, Karlinne V.	(305)856-6022	1374
Miami Beach	GROVER, Wilma S.	(305)868-5000	474
	LESNIAK, Rose	(305)673-6309	718
Orlando	CRENSHAW, Tena L.	(305)646-5637	258
St Petersburg	FUSTUKJIAN, Samuel Y.	(813)893-9125	410
Tallahassee	FLEMING, Lois D.		384
	MILLER, Betty D.	(904)335-4405	836
Tampa	CRAIG, James P.	(813)238-5514	254
	JOHNSTON, Judy F.	(813)974-2162	610
	LIANG, Diana F.	(813)988-2406	725
	MCCROSSAN, John A.	(813)974-3520	800
	STORCK, Bernadette R.	(813)223-8860	1198
	WOOD, James F.	(813)232-5221	1364
Winter Park	ALLISON, Anne M.	(305)677-6372	17

GEORGIA

Atlanta	QUINLIN, Margaret M.	(404)874-1589	1000
	SLOAN, Mary J.	(404)874-6224	1149
Bainbridge	MARSHALL, Ruth T.	(912)246-3887	775
Cartersville	HOWINGTON, Lee R.	(404)382-4203	566
Doraville	DRAPER, James D.	(404)457-4858	318
Eastman	WILSON, David C.	(912)374-4711	1350
Fitzgerald	HEFFINGTON, Carl O.	(912)423-3642	520
Kennesaw	GRIFFIN, Martha R.	(404)422-9921	468
Sylvester	MEREY-KADAR, Ervin R.	(912)776-0723	825
Valdosta	CLARK, Tommy A.	(912)244-6124	218

HAWAII

Honolulu	LUSTER, Arlene L.	(808)737-8876	750

IDAHO

Boise	ROBERTSON, Naida	(208)384-4340	1042

ILLINOIS

Arlington Heights	SHUMAN, Marilyn J.	(312)253-7752	1134
Carbondale	STARRATT, Joseph A.	(618)453-2683	1182
Champaign	MCCABE, Ronald B.	(217)352-8317	793
Chicago	BRICKMAN, Sally F.		135
	DEMPSEY, Frank J.	(312)327-6955	291
	FRISBIE, Richard	(312)332-3984	405
	GERDES, Neil W.	(312)753-3196	428
	GOMEZ, Martin J.		447
	KUSZMAUL, Marcia J.	(312)929-7537	685
	OAKS, Claire	(312)271-1207	913
	PERTELL, Grace M.	(312)286-5698	961
	ROBLING, John S.	(312)620-9600	1045
	VIRGO, Julie A.	(312)751-1454	1285
De Kalb	KIES, Cosette N.	(815)753-1735	647
	WELCH, Theodore F.	(815)758-6858	1321
Edwardsville	JOHNSON, Charlotte L.	(618)656-5743	603
Evanston	QUINN, Patrick M.	(312)869-2861	1000
Flora	DOCKINS, Glenn	(618)662-2679	307
Glendale Heights	VOJTECH, Kathryn	(312)260-1550	1287
Hinsdale	MUELLER, Elizabeth	(312)323-8054	875
Hoffman Estates	MILLER, Deborah	(312)882-3698	837

PUBLIC RELATIONS CONSULTANT (Cont'd)
ILLINOIS (Cont'd)

La Grange	HELLER, Dawn H.	(312)579-0903	524
	TUGGLE, Ann M.	(312)627-9250	1262
Oak Lawn	IHRIG, Alice B.		581
	MCELROY, Beth A.	(312)425-1616	804
Oak Park	BALCOM, William T.	(312)383-6824	51
	PAPPALARDO, Marcia J.	(312)848-5035	939
Park Forest	SHANNON, Kathleen L.	(312)481-1891	1120
Peoria	NELSON, Maggie E.	(309)672-8841	894
	NIEHAUS, Barbara J.	(309)697-3798	903
Rolling Meadows	HEMENWAY, Patti J.	(312)255-6197	525
St Charles	MORRISON, Carol J.	(312)377-2499	868
Skokie	KAPLAN, Paul M.		626
Springfield	BRADWAY, Becky J.	(217)753-4117	126
	ETTER, Constance L.	(217)546-5436	355
	FRISCH, Corrine A.	(217)753-4925	405
	SIVAK, Marie R.	(217)782-2826	1144
	SORENSEN, Mark W.	(217)782-1082	1168
Urbana	FAYNZILBERG, Irina	(217)333-5745	367
	WRIGHT, Joyce C.	(217)333-1031	1372
Williamsville	KELLERSTRASS, Amy L.	(217)566-3517	636

INDIANA

Bloomington	CALLISON, Daniel J.	(812)335-5113	174
	WHITE, Herbert S.	(812)335-2848	1331
Evansville	TEUBERT, Lola H.	(812)428-8229	1233
Frankfort	CADDELL, Claude W.	(317)654-7038	170
Indianapolis	BROWN, Judith L.		145
	FISCHLER, Barbara B.	(317)274-0462	380
	GILL, John H.	(317)872-2045	435
	WOODARD, Marcia S.	(317)297-1803	1366
Michigan City	DEYOUNG, Charles D.	(219)879-4561	298
Muncie	MOORE, Thomas J.	(317)285-1307	861
Noblesville	COOPER, David L.	(317)773-1384	242
South Bend	BEATTY, R M.	(219)232-2349	70
	HARLAN, John B.	(219)288-0693	502
	PEC, Jean A.	(219)277-3703	953
	YATES, Donald N.	(219)289-3405	1378
Terre Haute	NORMAN, Orval G.	(812)232-6120	909

IOWA

Ames	KUHN, Warren B.	(515)294-1442	682
Des Moines	ROBERTSON, Linda L.	(515)281-7572	1042

KANSAS

Chanute	DRUSE, Judith A.	(316)431-3020	321
Emporia	BODART-TALBOT, Joni	(316)343-1200	109
Great Bend	SWAN, James A.	(316)792-4865	1213
Manhattan	QUIRING, Virginia M.	(913)532-5693	1000
Miltonvale	BRADLEY, Susanne A.	(913)427-2228	126
Overland Park	OJALA, Marydee P.		919
Salina	MCKENZIE, Joe M.	(913)825-4624	811
	THOMAS, Evangeline M.	(913)827-1604	1236
Wichita	MEYERS, Judith K.	(316)832-1211	831

KENTUCKY

Frankfort	KLEE, Edward L.	(502)875-7000	658
Germantown	TEEGARDEN, Maude B.	(606)728-2312	1229
Lexington	RIPLEY, Joseph M.	(606)257-4243	1035
Louisville	SOMERVILLE, Mary R.	(502)893-8451	1167
Murray	WALL, Celia J.	(502)762-4990	1297
Paducah	BOYARSKI, Jennie S.	(502)442-6131	122

LOUISIANA

Baton Rouge	BINGHAM, Elizabeth E.	(504)292-1038	97
	KLEINER, Janellyn P.	(504)928-1960	660
	MCKANN, Michael R.	(504)342-4922	809
	SCULL, Roberta A.		1108
Harvey	WASHINGTON, Idella A.	(504)367-8429	1307
Metairie	KLEIN, Victor C.	(504)861-0488	659
Oakdale	LYNCH, Minnie L.	(318)335-3442	752
Ruston	AVANT, Julia K.	(318)255-1920	41

MAINE

Bar Harbor	GOLBITZ, Peter	(207)288-4969	444
	KINGMA, Sharyn L.	(207)288-4969	652
Baritarbon	GOTTLIEB, Robert A.	(207)288-9574	453
Bath	MCKAY, Ann	(207)443-5524	809
Brunswick	HEISER, Nancy E.	(207)725-4253	523

PUBLIC RELATIONS CONSULTANT (Cont'd)
MAINE (Cont'd)

Winthrop	KING, Alan S.	(207)377-2879	650

MARYLAND

Arnold	OLSON, Christine A.	(301)647-6708	922
Baltimore	BOURKOFF, Vivienne R.	(301)338-8914	119
	CHELTON, Mary K.	(301)355-0906	204
	COPLAN, Kate M.		244
	COX, Irvin E.	(301)396-3734	253
	FORSHAW, William S.	(301)727-3100	391
	LEBRETON, Jonathan A.	(301)455-2356	708
Bethesda	BALL, Thomas W.	(301)493-5184	52
	MILLENSON, Roy H.		835
Brookeville	ROBERTS, Lesley A.	(301)774-4471	1040
Cambridge	DEL SORDO, Jean S.	(301)228-7331	290
Chevy Chase	CHARTRAND, Robert L.		203
	GOLDSBERG, Elizabeth D.		446
	MESHINSKY, Jeff M.	(301)652-4740	827
College Park	JOHNSON, Emily P.	(301)935-5382	604
Columbia	AVERSA, Elizabeth S.	(301)992-3711	41
	HILL, Norma L.	(301)997-8000	540
Forestville	MOORE, Virginia B.	(301)568-8743	861
Fort Washington	KALKUS, Stanley	(301)839-5729	623
Fulton	FRANK, Robyn C.	(301)490-5898	397
Hagerstown	BINAU, Myra I.	(301)824-8801	97
Hyattsville	BURGESS, Eileen E.	(301)864-7223	159
La Plata	WILLIAMS, J L.	(301)932-6768	1343
Port Republik	HURREY, Katharine C.		577
Rockville	COSMIDES, George J.	(301)762-5428	249
	PEDAK-KARI, Maria	(301)279-1940	954
Silver Spring	FEINBERG, Beryl L.	(301)946-3282	368
	NORRIS, Loretta W.	(301)587-3470	909
Towson	DRACH, Marian C.	(301)825-8877	317

MASSACHUSETTS

Belmont	PHELAN, Mary C.		967
Boston	VOIGT, John F.	(617)266-1400	1287
	WESTLING, Ellen R.	(617)726-8600	1327
Brighton	BRAUN, Robin E.	(617)789-2177	130
Burlington	MCLAUGHLIN, Lee R.	(617)272-5772	813
Cambridge	SAKEY, Joseph G.	(617)498-9000	1076
Charlestown	CURTIN-STEVENSON, Mary C.	(617)241-9664	266
Concord	BENDER, Elizabeth H.	(617)369-4222	79
Millis	PERRY, Guest	(617)376-8459	960
Needham	CABEZAS, Sue A.	(617)449-3965	170
North Abington	LAROSA, Sharon M.	(617)871-6288	698
North Falmouth	FOSTER, Joan		392
Sagamore	OLIANSKY, Joseph D.	(617)888-6189	920
Salem	SCHWALLER, Marian C.	(617)744-0076	1104
	WHITNEY, Howard F.	(617)744-1769	1334
Uxbridge	LEWIS, Thomas F.		724
Williamstown	SUDDUTH, William E.	(413)597-2514	1206
Winchester	KEATS, Susan E.	(617)729-9317	633
Worcester	ROCHELEAU, Kathleen D.	(617)793-7319	1046

MICHIGAN

Alpena	WILLIAMS, Susan S.	(517)356-1622	1346
Ann Arbor	DIDIER, Elaine K.	(313)763-0378	301
	WARNER, Robert M.	(313)763-2281	1305
	WERLING, Anita L.	(313)761-4700	1324
Bloomfield Hills	ST. AMAND, Norma P.	(313)644-1878	1075
Dearborn	MCCARTY, Linda A.	(313)582-7867	795
Decatur	TATE, David L.	(616)423-4771	1225
Detroit	GIGLIO, Linda M.	(313)872-4311	433
	JOHNSON, Veronica A.	(313)532-6715	609
Eaton Rapids	FLAHERTY, Kevin C.	(517)663-2362	383
Farmington Hills	PAPAI, Beverly D.	(313)553-0300	938
Fenton	SCHERBA, Sandra A.	(313)629-0812	1092
Flint	MORELAND, Patricia L.	(313)762-2141	863
Grand Haven	BROOKS, Burton H.	(616)842-2586	140
Jackson	LEAMON, David L.	(517)788-4199	707
Kalamazoo	APPS, Michelle L.	(616)375-3611	30
	NOBLE, Valerie	(616)323-6352	906
Lansing	EZELL, Charlaine L.	(517)485-8019	360
Marcellus	TATE, Carole A.	(616)646-5081	1225
Monroe	MARGOLIS, Bernard A.	(313)243-5213	770
Mt Pleasant	KRUUT, Evald	(517)773-5184	681
Northville	ROCKALL, Diane M.	(313)349-9005	1046

PUBLIC RELATIONS CONSULTANT (Cont'd)

MICHIGAN (Cont'd)

Okemos	TREGLOAN, Donald C.	(517)349-7767	1255
Plymouth	GAREN, Robert J.	(313)455-5771	418
Saginaw	JOHN, Stephanie C.	(517)771-6846	601
Spring Lake	PRETZER, Dale H.	(616)846-8967	992
Wayne	WEISER, Douglas E.	(313)326-8910	1319

MINNESOTA

Grand Rapids	VALANCE, Marsha J.	(218)327-2336	1271
Mankato	ALLAN, David W.	(507)947-3936	14
	HITT, Charles J.	(507)625-4834	544
	TOHAL, Kate J.	(507)389-5963	1248
Minneapolis	CARLSON, Stan W.	(612)571-2046	182
	SKELLY, Laurie J.	(612)823-2556	1146
Minnetonka	JENSEN, Wilma M.	(612)473-5965	599
St Peter	HAEUSER, Michael J.	(507)931-7556	482

MISSISSIPPI

Clarksdale	GRAVES, Sid F.	(601)627-2322	459
Hattiesburg	WILSON, Mary S.	(601)266-4240	1352
Hernando	ANDERSON, James F.	(601)368-4439	23
Liberty	BURKS, Alvin L.	(601)657-8920	161
Starkville	NETTLES, Jess	(601)323-5558	896

MISSOURI

Ballwin	FORD, Gary E.	(314)225-6723	389
	TAYLOR, Arthur R.	(314)394-9973	1226
Cape Girardeau	MAXWELL, Martha A.	(314)334-6549	788
	STIEGEMEYER, Nancy H.	(314)334-3674	1193
Columbia	YOUNG, Virginia G.	(314)443-8413	1383
Independence	MORALES, Milton F.	(816)836-5200	862
Kansas City	NESBITT, John R.	(813)926-7616	896
	PETERSON, Paul A.	(816)363-5020	964
St Charles	MUETH, Elizabeth C.	(314)447-5116	875
Saint Joseph	ELLIOTT, Dorothy G.	(816)232-7729	344
St Louis	MESSERLE, Judith R.	(314)577-8607	828
	ROBERTS, Jean A.	(314)664-0939	1040

MONTANA

Bozeman	ALLDREDGE, Noreen S.	(406)587-4877	14
	BRUWELHEIDE, Janis H.	(406)587-0405	151
Great Falls	WARDEN, Margaret S.		1304
Missoula	SCHMIDT, Theodore A.	(406)721-2811	1096

NEBRASKA

Lincoln	LU, Janet C.	(402)465-2400	745
Omaha	BROWN, Helen A.	(402)559-4326	144
	LITTLE, Nina M.	(402)554-6282	733

NEVADA

Henderson	TRASATTI, Margaret S.	(702)733-3613	1254
Incline	OSSOLINSKI, Lynn	(702)831-2936	928
Las Vegas	DAVENPORT, Marilyn G.	(702)453-5606	275
	HUNSBERGER, Charles W.	(702)733-7810	574
Reno	GOULD, Martha B.	(702)785-4518	454
	MCNEAL, Betty	(702)325-5859	816

NEW HAMPSHIRE

Exeter	THOMAS, Jacquelyn H.	(603)772-4311	1236
Mirror Lake	SARLES, Christie V.	(603)569-4932	1083
Nashua	BERLIN, Arthur E.	(603)885-4674	87

NEW JERSEY

Caldwell	EDELSON, Ken		335
Clifton	TROJAN, Judith L.	(201)472-3868	1257
Dumont	PAPAZIAN, Pierre	(201)385-8225	939
East Brunswick	MENINGALL, Evelyn L.	(201)254-6403	824
Edison	DINERMAN, Gloria	(201)906-1777	304
	FERRERE, Cathy M.	(201)819-8924	373
Florham Park	SWINBURNE, Ralph E.	(201)377-8390	1216
Forked River	ROYCE, Carolyn S.	(609)971-0665	1063
Green Village	KEON, Edward F.	(201)822-0062	643
Highland Park	LI, Marjorie H.	(201)828-8730	724
Maplewood	BRYANT, David S.	(201)763-9294	152
Marlton	RICHIE, Mark L.	(609)985-0436	1030
Middletown	RILEY, Robert H.	(201)615-0900	1034
New Brunswick	EDELMAN, Hendrik	(201)932-7836	335
	RUBEN, Brent D.	(201)932-7447	1064
Paramus	CESARD, Mary A.	(201)444-4389	196

PUBLIC RELATIONS CONSULTANT (Cont'd)

NEW JERSEY (Cont'd)

Peapack	WHITING, Elaine M.	(201)234-0598	1333
Red Bank	PACHMAN, Frederic C.	(201)530-7695	933
Ridgewood	ROSS, Robert D.	(201)652-4836	1058
Tenafly	WECHTLER, Stephen R.	(201)568-8680	1315
Wayne	COHEN, Adrea G.	(201)696-8948	227
West Long Branch	FISHER, Scott L.	(201)229-9222	381
	PALMISANO-DRUCKER, Elsalyn	(201)870-9194	937
Whippany	MUNSICK, Lee R.	(201)386-1920	879

NEW MEXICO

Albuquerque	ELDREDGE, Jonathan D.	(505)277-0654	342
	RASSAM, Cynthia K.	(505)277-4203	1009
Las Cruces	DRESP, Donald F.	(505)522-3627	319
Roswell	MCLAREN, M B.	(505)622-6250	813
Thoreau	SCHUBERT, Donald F.	(505)862-7465	1101

NEW YORK

Albany	LEWIS, Frances R.	(518)869-9317	723
	MATTIE, Joseph J.	(518)474-4970	786
	MOORE, Rue I.	(518)445-5197	861
	ROBERTS, Anne F.	(518)438-0607	1039
	VAILLANCOURT, Pauline M.	(518)489-6207	1271
Ballston Lake	EGAN, Mary J.	(518)399-5151	338
Bayside	NOVIK, Sandra P.	(718)631-6271	911
Beechhurst	CARVER, Mary		191
Brentwood	PETERMAN, Kevin	(516)434-6742	962
Bronx	CLAYBORNE, Jon L.	(212)588-8400	219
Brooklyn	GARA, Otto G.	(718)875-1300	416
	KLEIMAN, Allan M.	(718)645-2396	658
	ROGINSKI, James W.	(718)499-4850	1050
	WAHLERT, George A.	(718)833-1899	1292
Buffalo	ELLISON, John W.	(716)636-3069	345
	KARCH, Linda S.	(716)827-2323	627
	NEWMAN, George C.	(716)886-8132	899
Carle Place	HABER, Elinor L.	(516)877-1190	480
Chappaqua	CHEATHAM, Bertha M.	(914)238-3586	204
Cheektowaga	WITT, Susan T.	(716)686-3620	1358
Clarence	ALLERTON, Ellen M.	(716)759-2893	16
Cornwall on Hudson	WEISS, Egon A.	(914)534-9467	1320
Delmar	SHUMAN, Susan E.	(518)475-1202	1134
East Meadow	MCCARTNEY, Margaret M.	(516)489-8136	794
Elmira	WEIDEMANN, Margaret A.	(607)733-8609	1316
Freeport	MORIN, Wilfred L.	(516)368-6242	865
Governors Island	GODWIN, Mary J.	(212)809-4351	443
Hempstead	STERN, Marc J.	(516)560-5975	1189
Hewlett	WILLER, Kenneth H.		1341
Hicksville	SCHMIDTMANN, Nancy K.	(516)433-7040	1096
Highland	RANKIN, Carol A.	(914)691-2275	1007
Hornell	SMITH, Brian D.	(607)324-0841	1153
Huntington Station	MAUTER, George A.	(516)421-9291	787
Larchmont	GILLIGAN, Julie		436
Lindenhurst	WARD, Peter K.	(516)957-6678	1304
Little Neck	EDWARDS, Barnett A.	(718)425-2576	337
Lockport	KLIMEK, Chester R.	(716)434-6167	661
Manlius	NAGLE, Ann	(315)682-8160	886
Massapequa	EISNER, Joseph	(516)735-4133	341
Mastic	MACINICK, James W.	(516)399-3281	755
Menands	GILSON, Robert	(518)463-4181	437
Mt Kisco	NELSON, Nancy M.	(914)666-3394	894
Mt Vernon	SEITZ, Robert J.	(914)699-6917	1113
New Windsor	SANKER, Paul N.	(914)562-0470	1081
New York	BERNER, Andrew J.	(212)515-5299	88
	CASSELL, Kay A.	(212)614-6551	193
	CROCKER, Susan O.	(212)777-8900	259
	DYER, Esther R.	(212)777-9064	330
	FONTAINE, Sue	(212)533-7226	388
	GARDNER, Ralph D.	(212)877-6820	418
	GESKE, Aina S.		430
	HENDERSON, Brad	(212)666-2674	526
	HEWITT, Vivian D.		535
	KENDRIC, Marisa A.	(212)725-4550	640
	KOCHOFF, Stephen T.	(212)254-4454	667
	KRANICH, Nancy C.	(212)998-2447	676
	MASON, H J.	(212)505-3560	781
	MILLER-KUMMERFELD, Elizabeth	(212)751-0830	843

PUBLIC RELATIONS CONSULTANT (Cont'd)
NEW YORK (Cont'd)
New York

	PETTOLINA, Anthony M.	(212)790-2888	965
	ST. CLAIR, Guy	(212)515-5299	1075
	SARRIS, Shirley C.	(212)473-2990	1083
	SLATE, Ted	(212)350-4682	1148
	STILLMAN, Stanley W.		1194
	STRINGFELLOW, William T.	(212)586-2000	1202
	THOMAS, Dorothy	(212)799-0970	1236
	WOLFE, Allis	(212)496-0008	1360
North Chatham	WELLS, Gladysann		1322
Pearl River	SPERR BRISFJORD, Inez L.	(914)735-1567	1173
Port Chester	LETTIERI, Robin M.	(914)939-6710	719
Rensselaerville	STORMS, Kate	(518)797-5154	1198
Rochester	HOPE, Thomas W.	(716)458-4250	557
	LINDSAY, Jean S.	(716)428-7300	729
	LOCKE, William G.	(716)288-5422	736
	MOUREY, Deborah A.	(716)724-6819	874
Saratoga Springs	DOE, Lynn M.	(518)584-5000	308
Scarborough	HOPKINS, Lee B.	(914)941-5810	558
Scarsdale	BERGER, Pam P.	(914)723-3156	86
Setauket	COOK, Jeannine S.	(516)941-4090	240
Syracuse	CASEY, Daniel W.	(315)468-0176	192
	HORRELL, Jeffrey L.	(315)423-2585	560
	KINCHEN, Robert P.	(315)473-2702	650
Troy	BLANDY, Susan G.	(518)274-2098	104
	EVELAND, Ruth A.	(518)274-2389	358
	GINSBURG, Joanne R.	(518)274-7071	438
Wallkill	RUBIN, Ellen B.	(914)565-5620	1064
White Plains	BOWLES, Edmund A.	(914)696-1900	121
Williamsville	BOBINSKI, Mary F.	(716)688-4919	108
Yonkers	BERGER, Paula E.	(914)968-7906	86

NORTH CAROLINA

Asheville	BUCHANAN, William E.	(704)251-6436	153
Bahama	STINE, Roy S.	(719)471-8853	1194
Chapel Hill	COGGINS, Timothy L.	(919)962-6202	227
	FEEHAN, Patricia E.	(919)962-8366	368
Durham	CAMPBELL, Jerry D.	(919)684-2034	176
	HAZEL, Debora E.	(919)683-6473	517
Greensboro	JARRELL, James R.	(919)273-7061	594
	RANCER, Susan P.	(919)288-2160	1006
Jefferson	FRANKLIN, Robert M.	(919)246-4460	398
Kinston	JONES, John W.	(919)527-7066	613
	SOUTHERLAND, Carol A.	(919)523-0819	1169
Matthews	CANNON, Robert E.	(704)847-0394	179
Montreat	BROOKS, Jerrold L.	(704)669-7661	140
Morganton	BUSH, Mary E.	(704)433-2303	165
Raleigh	HORTON, James T.		561
	TAYLOR, Raymond M.	(919)787-7824	1228
Research Triangle Pk	BEST-NICHOLS, Barbara J.	(919)544-3808	92
Robbinsville	LARSON, Josephine	(704)479-8192	699
Salisbury	ALDRICH, Willie L.	(704)636-1158	11
Sanford	MCGINN, Howard F.	(919)776-2335	806
Troy	WALTERS, Carol G.	(919)572-1311	1301
Wilmington	BEECH, Vivian W.	(919)763-3303	74

NORTH DAKOTA

Bismarck	HENDRICKS, Thom	(701)627-4635	527
	HILDEBRANT, Darrel D.	(701)222-6410	539
Fargo	OLSON, Chris D.	(701)282-8973	922

OHIO

Akron	LATSHAW, Patricia H.	(216)762-7621	701
Chesterland	CORBUS, Lawrence J.	(216)286-8941	245
Cincinnati	FERGUSON, George E.	(513)559-9908	372
	GROSVENOR, Philip G.	(513)683-0315	473
	HILAND, Gerard P.	(513)231-0810	538
	SHIVERDECKER, Darlene J.	(513)281-3760	1132
Cleveland	KOZLOWSKI, Ronald S.	(216)398-1800	674
	STANLEY, Jean B.	(216)368-6596	1180
Columbus	HECK, Thomas F.	(614)292-2310	519
	PLATAU, Gerard D.	(614)457-1687	977
	TANNEHILL, Robert S.	(614)488-7587	1222
	WALBRIDGE, Sharon L.	(614)274-4081	1293

PUBLIC RELATIONS CONSULTANT (Cont'd)
OHIO (Cont'd)
Dayton

	BALL, Diane A.	(513)293-7339	52
	BANTA, Gratia J.	(513)277-4444	55
	COYLE, Christopher B.	(513)865-6882	253
	PEAKE, Sharon K.	(513)865-6958	952
Euclid	COLEMAN, Judith	(216)261-5300	231
Findlay	DICKINSON, Luren E.	(419)423-4934	301
Georgetown	TOMLIN, Marsha A.	(513)378-3154	1250
Grafton	DIAL, David E.	(216)926-3317	299
Granville	RUGG, John D.		1066
Kent	MORRIS, Trisha A.	(216)673-3464	867
Lakewood	KEATING, Michael F.	(216)221-0608	633
Lisbon	MCPEAK, James J.	(216)424-3117	817
Medina	SMITH, Robert S.	(216)725-0588	1160
Mentor	DUANE, Carol A.	(216)255-3323	321
New Philadelphia	HAGLOCH, Susan B.	(216)364-4474	483
Toledo	SCOLES, Clyde S.	(419)255-7055	1106
Troy	MILLER, John E.	(513)335-8801	839
Willow Wood	REID, Margaret B.	(614)643-2925	1018
Youngstown	DONAHUGH, Robert H.	(216)788-6950	310

OKLAHOMA

Ada	ROBBINS, Louise S.	(405)436-0642	1039
McAlester	SIMON, Bradley A.	(918)423-3468	1140
Norman	LEE, Sul H.	(405)325-2611	711
Oklahoma City	CLARK, Robert L.	(405)521-2502	218
	DAVIS, Denyvetta	(405)424-2106	278
	DOBBERTEEN, Sara J.	(405)842-0890	307
	MEYERS, Duane H.	(405)946-2488	830
	SAULMON, Sharon A.	(405)634-3181	1084
	VESELY, Marilyn L.		1283

OREGON

Eugene	KNIEVEL, Helen A.	(503)345-2032	664
	MEEKS, James D.	(503)687-5454	821
	SHIPMAN, George W.	(503)683-8262	1131
Portland	FERGUSON, Douglas K.	(503)228-5512	372
	LONG, Sarah A.	(503)221-7731	740
	THENELL, Janice C.	(503)221-7726	1234

PENNSYLVANIA

Allentown	MOSES, Lynn M.		871
Bethlehem	BERK, Jack M.	(215)867-3761	87
Broomall	WASERSTEIN, Gina S.	(215)353-0776	1307
Catasauqua	SIMONE-HOHE, M J.	(215)262-1596	1141
Eagleville	PECK, Marian B.	(215)631-1129	953
Elkins Park	NEMEYER, Carol A.		895
Friedens	KLINE, Eve P.	(814)443-2903	661
Harrisburg	BAUER, Margaret D.	(717)233-3113	65
	FOUST, Judith M.	(717)787-8007	393
Haverford	CORRIGAN, John T.	(215)896-7458	247
Huntingdon	SWIGART, William B.	(814)643-3000	1216
Jeannette	PAWLIK, Deborah A.		951
Lansdowne	BATISTA, Emily J.	(215)626-3567	64
Philadelphia	FARREN, Ann L.	(215)848-8146	365
	HALE, Carolyn R.	(215)843-9805	485
	MITCHEM, M T.		849
	NAISMITH, Patricia A.	(215)235-0256	887
	POSES, June A.	(215)564-1350	985
	SNOWTEN, Renee Y.	(215)557-8295	1164
	TANNER, Anne B.	(215)895-2483	1222
	WILLMANN, Donna S.		1040
Pittsburgh	BLEIER, Carol S.	(412)563-2712	105
	MAZEFSKY, Gertrude T.	(412)361-7582	791
	SPIEGELMAN, Barbara M.	(412)824-2222	1174
Scranton	FADDEN, Donald M.	(412)621-8802	360
Slippery Rock	JOSEPH, Elizabeth T.	(412)794-4623	617
Springfield	STESIS, Karen R.	(215)328-8749	1189
University Park	SMITH, Barbara J.	(814)865-0401	1153
West Chester	AMICONE, Janice L.	(215)692-6889	20
	DINNIMAN, Margo P.	(215)430-3080	305
Yardley	BARATTA, Maria	(215)321-3289	55
	DU BOIS, Paul Z.	(215)493-6882	322

PUERTO RICO

Hato Rey	NEGRON-GAZTAMBIDE, Olguita	(809)767-4192	892
Santurce	RIVERA-ALVAREZ, Miguel A.	(809)728-4191	1037

PUBLIC RELATIONS CONSULTANT (Cont'd)

RHODE ISLAND

Barrington	BURKE, Lauri K.	(401)245-3741	160
East Providence	CAIRNS, Roberta A.	(401)433-0159	171
Providence	REEVES, Joan R.	(401)272-7745	1016

SOUTH CAROLINA

Charleston	STRAUCH, Katina P.	(803)723-3536	1200
Clemson	MCCULLEY, P M.	(803)654-8753	800
Columbia	WARREN, Charles D.	(803)782-4219	1306
Glendale	WHITE, Ann T.	(803)579-3330	1330
Greer	MESSINEO, Anthony	(803)268-7267	828

SOUTH DAKOTA

Rapid City	SCHWARTZ, James M.	(605)394-1246	1104

TENNESSEE

Brentwood	NORTON, Tedgina	(615)371-0090	910
Cookeville	TABACHNICK, Sharon	(615)372-3958	1219
Germantown	COOPER, Ellen R.	(901)755-7411	242
Harriman	OVERTON, Margaret C.		931
Maryville	WORLEY, Joan H.	(615)982-6412	1369
Memphis	BAER, Ellen H.	(901)725-8853	45
	BANNERMAN-WILLIAMS, Cheryl F.	(901)785-7350	54
	DRESCHER, Judith A.	(901)276-0104	319
	POURCIAU, Lester J.	(901)454-2201	• 987
Nashville	GOODALE, Adebonojo L.	(615)327-6728	448
	LEE, Geoffrey J.	(615)322-7390	710
	MOON, Fletcher F.	(615)833-1125	857
	SWIFT, David L.	(615)352-0308	1216
Oak Ridge	CARROLL, Bonnie C.	(615)482-3230	187

TEXAS

Amarillo	SNELL, Marykay H.	(806)353-5329	1163
Arlington	MACFARLANE, Francis X.	(817)265-8309	755
	MCCLURE, Margaret R.	(817)275-6594	797
Austin	DAYO, Ayo	(512)472-8980	283
	GAMEZ, Juanita L.	(512)837-6247	416
Bryan	CLARK, Charlene K.	(409)822-7263	216
Buda	TISSING, Robert W.	(512)295-4834	1247
Cleburne	CARDENAS, Martha L.	(817)641-6641	180
Dallas	CRABB, Elizabeth A.	(214)233-4382	254
	EATENSON, Ervin T.	(214)521-4839	333
	RYDESKY, Mary M.	(214)339-3349	1071
	SHAPLEY, Ellen M.	(214)692-6407	1122
Denton	TOTTEN, Herman L.	(817)383-1902	1252
Edinburg	SHABOWICH, Stanley A.	(512)383-0441	1118
El Paso	GEARY, Kathleen A.	(915)533-5777	424
	TAYLOR, Anne E.	(915)757-5095	1226
Fredericksburg	YOUNG, Marjie D.	(512)997-2253	1382
Houston	BROWN, Carol J.	(713)247-2227	142
	CHANG, Robert H.	(713)221-8181	201
	GIROUARD, J L.	(713)520-6835	438
	HENINGTON, David M.	(713)247-2700	528
	LYDEN, Edward W.	(713)777-8212	750
	PHILLIPS, Ray S.	(713)622-9686	969
	WEGMANN, Pamela A.	(713)655-3400	1316
	WILLIAMS, Ann T.	(713)792-4094	1342
Huntsville	PICHETTE, William H.	(409)291-2994	970
Irving	BRAGG, William J.	(214)556-1234	127
	LANKFORD, Mary D.	(214)579-7818	696
Palestine	SELLERS, Wayne C.	(214)729-4829	1114
Tyler	LAMBERTH, Linda E.	(214)595-3481	690
Weatherford	HEEZEN, Ronald R.	(817)599-0833	520

UTAH

Ogden	WILSON, Brenda J.	(801)479-1407	1350
Pleasant Grove	STECKER, Alexander T.	(801)785-2761	1183
Salt Lake City	BURKS, C J.	(801)466-2183	161
West Jordan	KARPISEK, Marian E.	(801)561-4676	628

VIRGINIA

Alexandria	KUHL, Danuta	(703)461-0234	682
	OSIA, Ruby R.	(703)549-3048	928
	RUSH, James S.	(703)765-3557	1068
	STEIN, Karen E.	(703)354-3154	1185
Arlington	DORNER, Steven J.	(703)841-8400	313
	WOODALL, Nancy C.	(703)528-5128	1365
Blacksburg	EASTMAN, Ann H.	(703)951-4770	333

PUBLIC RELATIONS CONSULTANT (Cont'd)

VIRGINIA (Cont'd)

Charlottesville	EVERINGHAM, Neil G.	(804)979-7151	358
	FRANKLIN, Robert D.	(804)973-3238	398
	WHITE, William		1332
Farmville	STWODAH, M I.	(804)392-8925	1206
Herndon	PAVEK, C C.	(703)481-0711	950
Langley AFB	VERNON, Christie D.	(804)766-1468	1283
Lexington	HAYS, Peggy W.	(703)463-8643	517
Norfolk	BERENT, Irwin M.	(804)855-1272	84
	NICHOLSON, Myreen M.	(804)627-6281	902
	SWAINE, Cynthia W.	(804)627-1115	1212
Portsmouth	BURGESS, Dean	(804)393-8501	159
Richmond	REAM, Daniel L.	(804)257-6545	1012
Roanoke	BANE, Madelyn R.	(703)345-2435	54
Virginia Beach	OWENS, Martha A.	(804)481-1738	932

WASHINGTON

Bothell	YEE, J E.	(206)625-4870	1379
Mt Vernon	SAUTER, Sylvia E.	(206)336-2604	1085
Newport	REMINGTON, David G.	(509)447-2636	1022
Seattle	HILL, Ann M.	(206)525-4212	539
	MAIOLI, Jerry R.	(206)459-6518	762
	STEERE, Paul J.	(206)367-0328	1184
	THORSEN, Jeanne M.	(206)684-6606	1242

WEST VIRGINIA

Charleston	BRYAN, Carol L.	(304)345-2378	151
	MOELLENDICK, M J.	(304)348-2691	851
Clarksburg	GREATHOUSE, Brenda J.	(304)624-9649	461
Morgantown	ESKRIDGE, Virginia C.	(304)293-5300	354
Philippi	SIZEMORE, William C.		1145
Welch	MULLER, William A.	(304)436-3070	877

WISCONSIN

Cedarburg	PITEL, Vonna J.	(414)377-6030	976
Iola	FOERSTER, Trey	(715)445-3838	387
La Crosse	ACCARDI, Joseph J.	(608)784-5755	3
Madison	MATTHEWS, Geraldine M.	(608)266-1164	785
Milton	HAY, Mary K.	(608)868-7260	515
Milwaukee	LOCKETT, Sandra B.	(414)278-3090	736
	SAGER, Lynn S.	(414)964-5940	1074
New London	DIEHL, Carol L.	(414)982-5040	301
Oak Creek	TASNADI, Deborah L.	(414)764-9725	1224
Reedsville	OHLEMACHER, Janet H.	(414)754-4831	919
Rhinelander	SLYGH, Gyneth	(715)362-3465	1151
Superior	AXT, Randolph W.	(715)398-6767	42
Twin Lakes	OPEM, John D.	(414)877-9539	925

WYOMING

Lander	HEUER, William J.	(307)332-3793	535

CANADA

ALBERTA

Calgary	BAILEY, Madeleine J.	(403)240-6134	46

BRITISH COLUMBIA

Clearbrook	VIIERANS, Mary E.	(604)859-7814	1284
Vancouver	HALE, Linda L.	(604)321-0932	485

ONTARIO

Gloucester	KENT, Charles D.		642
Keswick	MCCRACKEN, Ronald W.	(416)476-5556	799
Ottawa	EVANS, Gwynneth	(613)995-3904	357
	MCCALLUM, David L.	(613)237-4586	793
Stratford	KIRKPATRICK, Jane E.		655
Toronto	HARRISON, Karen A.	(416)462-1550	507
Windsor	WALSH, G M.	(519)253-7817	1299

QUEBEC

Jonquiere	HARVEY, Serge	(418)548-7821	509
Montreal	CURRAN, William M.	(514)392-4939	266
	DUPUIS, Onil	(514)288-8524	327
	DUSABLON-BOTTEGA, Nicole	(514)871-6442	329
	MITTERMEYER, Diane	(514)398-4204	850
	PICARD, Albert	(514)276-5797	970
	RABCHUK, Gordon K.	(514)874-2104	1001
	SAVARD, Rejean	(514)343-6044	1085

PUBLIC RELATIONS CONSULTANT (Cont'd)
QUEBEC (Cont'd)
Montreal

	SYKES, Stephanie L.	(514)870-7088	1217
	TOUCHETTE, Francois G.	(514)524-7878	1252
	WALUZYNIEC, Hanna	(514)398-4759	1302
Outremont	LACROIX, Yvon A.	(514)273-7423	687
Ste Anne de Bellevue	DOUGLAS-BONNELL, Eileen	(514)457-9487	314
Westmount	GLASS, Gerald	(514)931-4625	440

SASKATCHEWAN
Prince Albert	LABUIK, Karen L.	(306)764-0712	686
Regina	TURNBULL, Keith	(306)757-8915	1264

EGYPT
Cairo	EL-DUWEINI, Aadel K.	(027)197-7200	342

ENGLAND
London NW8ONP	BRILL, Kathryn R.		136

FEDERAL REPUBLIC OF CHINA
Taipei	LIN, Chih F.		727

FEDERAL REPUBLIC OF GERMANY
Berlin	WERSIG, Gernot		1325

FRANCE
Paris	GRATTAN, Robert		458

HONG KONG
Shatin	YEN, David S.		1379

ITALY
Rome	JOLING, Carole G.		610

KENYA
Nairobi	IRURIA, Daniel M.		584

MALAWI
Lilongwe	SNYDER, Lisa A.		1165

MEXICO
Mexico City	RODRIGUEZ, Serafin L.		1048
Nuevo Leon	ARTEAGA, Georgina		35

NIGERIA
Kano	AJIBERO, Matthew I.		9

RECORDS MANAGEMENT CONSULTANT

CALIFORNIA
Berkeley	HUNT, Judy L.	(415)849-2708	575
Chula Vista	GAGNON, Donna M.	(619)426-4527	412
Rolling Hills Estate	TUNG, Sandra J.	(213)377-5032	1263

COLORADO
Golden	GRAHAM, Su D.	(303)642-7802	456

CONNECTICUT
Danbury	MARIANI, Carolyn A.	(203)794-6389	770
New Haven	BROWN, William E.	(203)432-1749	148

FLORIDA
West Palm Beach	FOSTER, Helen M.	(305)686-1776	392

ILLINOIS
Chicago	EVANS, Linda J.	(312)642-4600	357
	GAYNON, David B.	(312)399-5662	424
Des Plaines	BURNS, Marie T.	(312)635-4732	162
Springfield	SORENSEN, Mark W.	(217)782-1082	1168
Urbana	BRICHFORD, Maynard J.	(217)367-7072	134

IOWA
Ames	KLINE, Laura S.	(515)294-6672	661

KENTUCKY
Lexington	LEVSTIK, Frank R.	(606)266-9196	721

RECORDS MANAGEMENT CONSULTANT (Cont'd)
MARYLAND
Bowie	EVANS, Frank B.	(301)464-8829	357
Rockville	MERZ, Nancy M.	(301)770-1170	827

MASSACHUSETTS
Boston	HUENNEKE, Judith A.	(617)282-1553	570
Wakefield	CHAPDELAINE, Susan A.	(617)246-5200	201

MICHIGAN
Detroit	WEST, Donald	(313)577-2525	1326

MISSOURI
Kansas City	LINSE, Mary M.	(816)765-0831	731

NEVADA
Las Vegas	ORTIZ, Diane	(702)388-6501	927

NEW JERSEY
Cliffside Park	ROBERTSON, Betty M.	(201)894-0235	1041
Creamridge	GEORGE, Muriel S.	(609)758-3198	428
New Brunswick	MAZZEI, Peter J.	(201)249-4120	791

NEW YORK
Brooklyn	DINDAYAL, Joyce S.	(718)647-1624	304
Grand Island	WATERS, Betsy M.		1308
New York	FREIFELD, Roberta I.	(212)777-9271	401
	HERBERT, Annette F.	(212)371-6220	530
	HUNTER, Gregory S.	(212)940-1690	576
	LAMANN, Amber N.	(212)677-4102	689
	PIDALA, Veronica C.		971
Stattsburg	LAFEVER, C R.	(914)889-8418	687

OHIO
Canton	ERWIN, Nancy S.	(216)477-7309	353
Cincinnati	GILLILAND, Anne J.	(513)475-6459	436
Cleveland Heights	SPAHR, Cheryl L.	(216)382-7675	1170
Delaware	COHEN, Susan J.	(614)363-9433	229

OKLAHOMA
Oklahoma City	JORSKI, Sharon D.	(405)636-7087	617
Tulsa	MANES, Estelle L.	(918)582-7426	765

OREGON
Medford	THELEN, Richard L.	(503)776-7040	1234
Salem	FILSON, Laurie	(503)364-4162	377

PENNSYLVANIA
Hershey	WOODRUFF, William M.	(717)534-5106	1366

TEXAS
Dallas	BENGE, Joy L.	(214)528-4157	80

VIRGINIA
Alexandria	CARTLEDGE, Connie L.	(703)960-6020	190
	CASSEDY, James G.	(703)768-2070	193
Charlottesville	BERKELEY, Edmund		87

WASHINGTON
Seattle	EULENBERG, Julia N.	(200)324-2605	356
	PRESTON, Deirdre R.	(206)283-0754	991
	STIRLING, Dale A.	(206)367-2728	1195

WISCONSIN
Fond Du Lac	EBERT, John J.	(414)929-3616	334

CANADA

MANITOBA
Winnipeg	SANTORO, Corrado A.	(204)474-8243	1082

ONTARIO
Toronto	ARDERN, Christine M.		31
	ATTINGER, Monique L.	(416)699-2530	38
Windsor	HANDY, Mary J.	(519)256-3250	495

RESEARCHER

ALABAMA

Auburn	ADAMS, Judith A.	(205)826-4500	5
	COLSON, Harold G.	(205)826-4500	234
	JONES, Allen W.	(205)826-4360	610
Birmingham	ATKINSON, Calberta O.	(205)787-3767	38
	BENTLEY, Elna J.	(205)969-2326	83
	GRIFFITH, Ethel T.	(205)254-2982	469
	HARRIS, Linda S.	(205)934-6364	505
	OLIVE, J F.	(205)967-8481	921
	SCALES, Diann R.	(205)322-8458	1087
	WEATHERLY, Cynthia D.	(205)939-0120	1312
Decatur	MORRIS, Betty J.	(205)773-6262	866
Florence	MONTGOMERY, Kimberly K.	(205)764-5392	856
Helena	GOODWYN, Betty R.	(205)988-0896	450
Huntsville	KITCHENS, Philips H.		657
	MCNAMARA, Jay	(205)895-6526	816
Irondale	FEENKER, Cherie D.	(205)956-4544	368
Mobile	BUSH, Nancy W.	(205)343-8121	165
	MILLER, Hannelore A.	(205)343-0000	838
	SHEARER, Barbara S.	(205)471-7855	1124
Montgomery	BREEDLOVE, Michael A.	(205)262-6172	131
Oneonta	WEAVER, Clifton W.	(205)274-9111	1312
Pelham	WRIGHT, Amos J.	(205)663-3403	1370
Tuscaloosa	KASKE, Neal K.	(205)348-1521	628
	LEE, Sulan I.	(205)752-6008	711
	PRUITT, Paul M.	(205)348-1107	996
	WATSON, Linda S.	(205)553-0826	1309
	WATTERS, Annette J.	(205)348-6191	1310

ALASKA

Anchorage	BRAUND-ALLEN, Julianna E.	(907)243-5947	130
	EGGLESTON, Phyllis A.	(907)337-0051	339
	KRAFT, Gwen L.		675
	PIERCE, Linda I.	(907)338-6421	971
	SOKOLOV, Barbara J.	(907)346-2480	1165
Central	OAKES, Patricia A.		913
Chugiak	KALLENBERG, Mary E.	(907)688-2919	623
College	GALBRAITH, Betty J.	(903)479-5196	413
Fairbanks	GALBRAITH, William B.	(907)479-5196	413
	LAKE, Gretchen L.	(907)452-6751	688
	PARHAM, Robert B.	(907)479-5966	940
	PINNELL-STEPHENS, June A.	(907)479-5826	975
Juneau	KINNEY, John M.	(907)586-1857	653
	NEWTON, Virginia A.	(907)586-4029	900
Valdez	LEAHY, M J.	(907)835-2801	706

ARIZONA

Chandler	VATHIS, Alma C.	(602)899-7147	1279
Flagstaff	AWE, Susan C.	(602)523-6808	42
	EGAN, Terence W.	(602)523-6819	338
Mesa	JOSEPHINE, Helen B.	(602)983-0237	617
	MAIN, Isabelle G.	(602)962-4310	761
	MEAD, Thomas L.	(602)892-3764	819
Phoenix	DANIELS, Delores E.	(602)261-3879	273
	JEROME, Susanne M.	(602)272-6848	599
	TEVIS, Raymond H.	(602)255-4590	1233
Scottsdale	FERRALL, J E.	(602)965-5167	373
	KLIMIADES, Mario N.	(602)994-2471	661
Tempe	ALCORN, Marianne E.	(602)965-4868	11
	LESHY, Dede	(602)946-8090	718
	MACHOVEC, George S.	(602)965-5889	755
	SCHON, Isabel	(602)965-2996	1098
	STEEL, Virginia	(602)965-3282	1183
Tucson	ALURI, Rao	(602)722-5678	19
	CAMPBELL, Dierdre A.	(602)621-7897	176
	D'ANTONIO, Lynn M.	(602)327-0715	274
	ETTER, Patricia A.	(602)299-5199	355
	FRANK, Donald G.	(602)742-9688	396
	GOTHBERG, Helen M.	(602)887-2262	453
	HAMILTON, Rita	(602)791-4391	492
	HAWBAKER, A C.	(602)621-4869	513
	HOLSINGER, Katherine	(602)621-3282	554
	HURT, Charlie D.	(602)621-3566	578
	LEI, Polin P.		713
	LONG, Carla J.	(602)621-4869	739
	MAKUCH, Andrew L.	(602)622-8572	762
	MCCRAY, Jeanette C.	(602)626-6143	800

ARIZONA (Cont'd)

Tucson	NAMSICK, Lynn J.	(602)624-0063	887
	NICHOLS, Margaret M.		901
	OLSRUD, Lois C.	(602)621-2297	923
	OWENS, Clayton S.		932
	RIISE, Milton B.	(602)325-1348	1034
	ROBROCK, David P.	(602)743-7072	1045
	RULE, Amy E.	(602)621-6273	1067
	WHITE, Edward H.	(602)621-5455	1330
	WOLF, Noel C.	(602)746-7637	1360
Uma	SWANN, Arthur W.		1213

ARKANSAS

Eureka Springs	STOWE, Jean E.	(501)253-8754	1199
Hazen	JEFFCOAT, Phyllis C.	(501)255-4546	596
Heber Springs	SEDELOW, Sally Y.	(501)362-3476	1110
	SEDELOW, Walter A.		1110
Little Rock	BRECK, Paul A.	(501)569-3121	131
	RAZER, Robert L.	(501)663-0789	1012
Prescott	WATSON, Merlyn		1310

CALIFORNIA

Agoura	THOMAS, Yvonne		1238
Alameda	HOSEL, Harold V.	(415)522-5875	561
Albany	BLITZ, Ruth R.	(415)525-4186	105
Altadena	GREGORY, Timothy P.	(818)798-1268	466
Anaheim	ADAMS, Joyce A.	(714)637-8385	5
	RICHARDSON, Helen R.	(714)774-7575	1029
	WRIGHT, Betty A.	(714)998-1127	1370
APO San Francisco	HEINES, Rodney M.		522
Aptos	WYKLE, Helen H.	(408)662-3228	1375
Bakersfield	KIRKLAND, Janice J.		655
Belmont	LEWIS, Gretchen S.	(415)591-4336	723
	RAMSEY, Robert D.	(415)593-1601	1006
Ben Lomond	CROWLEY, Terence	(408)336-5019	262
Benicia	MILLER, Davic C.	(707)746-6728	836
Berkeley	BENIDIR, Samia	(415)644-1129	80
	BIBEL, Barbara M.	(415)525-2628	94
	CASTRO, Rafaela G.	(415)526-0815	194
	FALK, Candace S.	(415)526-9591	362
	FISHER, Leslie R.	(415)548-3542	381
	GLENDENNING, Barbara J.	(415)642-2531	441
	GOLDMAN, Nancy L.	(415)642-0366	445
	HANDMAN, Gary P.	(415)524-9728	495
	HUMPHREYS, Nancy K.	(415)642-4786	574
	HUNT, Judy L.	(415)849-2708	575
	LARSON, Ray R.	(415)642-6046	699
	MARKS, Larry	(415)644-2111	771
	MAXWELL, Christine Y.	(415)644-4500	788
	PARKS, Mary L.	(415)644-3401	943
	RAFAEL, Ruth K.	(415)849-2710	1003
	ROBERT, Berring C.	(415)642-9980	1039
	VAN HOUSE, Nancy A.	(415)642-0855	1275
	VANYOUNG, Sayre	(415)848-2229	1278
	WEEDMAN, Judith	(415)642-9980	1315
	WHEELER, Helen R.	(415)549-2970	1329
	WOODBURY, Marda	(415)654-4810	1366
	X, Laura	(415)548-1770	1376
Beverly Hills	ANNETT, Susan E.	(213)550-4720	28
	CHAMMOU, Eliezer	(213)273-1395	198
	JEROME, Michael S.	(213)550-6100	599
	RUNYON, Judith A.	(213)859-5102	1067
Bishop	KRATZ, Gale G.	(619)873-3007	676
Burbank	BROWNE, Jeri A.	(818)953-8770	148
Burlingame	PERLMAN-STITES, Janice	(415)579-7660	959
	SHERMAN, Roger S.	(415)344-1213	1128
Canyon Country	CRUM, Norman J.	(805)252-9053	262
Cardiff By The Sea	MARKWORTH, Lawrence L.	(619)943-1197	772
Carlsbad	KENNEDY, Charlene F.	(619)434-2871	640
	TILLETT, Barbara B.		1245
Carmichael	O'NEILL, Diane J.	(916)965-0935	924
Castro Valley	CASTAGNOZZI, Carol A.	(415)581-6034	194
Cerritos	ZEIDLER, Patricia L.	(213)926-1101	1387
Chatsworth	TAYLOR, Susan E.	(818)882-9729	1228
Chico	HUANG, George W.	(916)891-3455	568
	LO, Henrietta W.	(916)895-6406	735
Claremont	WRIGLEY, Elizabeth S.	(714)624-6305	1373

RESEARCHER (Cont'd)
CALIFORNIA (Cont'd)

Concord	LAMANNA, Joan M.	(415)825-0418	689
Corona del Mar	DOSER, Virginia A.	(714)760-0148	313
Corte Madera	FARMER, Lesley S.	(415)924-6633	364
Costa Mesa	PETERMAN, Claudia A.	(714)650-9014	962
Culver City	KIRBY, Barbara L.	(213)839-1009	653
	NG, Carol S.	(213)202-6523	900
	PATTEN, Frederick W.	(213)827-3335	947
Cupertino	JAJKO, Edward A.	(408)446-1306	592
Davis	BENOIT, Gerald		82
	COLLINS, William J.	(916)758-4989	233
	ROBINSON, Betty J.	(916)756-2187	1043
	SHORT, Virginia	(916)752-1126	1132
	TEBO, Jay D.	(916)758-8256	1229
Del Mar	HOLLEMAN, Marian P.	(619)755-4253	551
Dobbins	LE DORR, Lillian E.	(916)692-1659	708
Downey	PAIK, Nan H.	(213)922-4648	935
	SHEA, Ann W.		1124
Eagle Rock	CRAWFORD, Marilyn L.	(213)259-8938	257
El Cerrito	DONLEY, Leigh M.	(415)524-3695	311
	MACAULEY, C C.	(415)524-2762	754
	PRESSNALL, Patricia E.	(415)525-5186	991
El Segundo	FELLER, Amy I.	(213)333-5222	370
Escondido	NING, Mary J.		904
Fair Oaks	HILL, Kristin E.	(916)966-6024	540
Fairfax	DOWNEY, Lynn A.	(418)454-4290	316
Fallbrook	COMPTON, Joan C.	(619)723-2860	235
	MCNALLY, Ruth C.		816
Fresno	KAUFFMAN, Inge S.	(209)486-8424	631
Fullerton	ANDERSEN, Leslie N.		21
	MASTERS, Robin J.	(714)524-9696	782
	STEPHENSON, Shirley E.	(714)773-3580	1189
	THOMPSON, James A.	(714)738-1000	1240
Glen Ellen	SCARBOROUGH, Katharine T.	(707)996-7993	1087
Glendale	BURNS, Nancy R.	(818)244-1994	162
	WAY, Kathy A.		1311
Goleta	GRAZIANO, Eugene	(805)968-2281	460
	MUSICK, Nancy W.	(805)964-8484	883
Huntington Beach	OPPENHEIM, Michael R.	(714)842-1548	925
	RIGGS, Quentin T.	(714)536-2823	1034
Inglewood	GOUDELOCK, Carol V.	(213)672-2543	454
Irvine	ARIEL, Joan	(714)856-4970	31
	BLADEN, Marguerite	(714)551-6489	102
	CLANCY, Stephen L.	(714)856-7309	215
	FINEMAN, Michael	(714)856-8160	377
	GELFAND, Julia M.	(714)856-4971	426
	HORN, Judy K.		559
	NOVACK, Dona A.	(714)752-4854	910
	PUGSLEY, Sharon G.	(714)856-7193	997
	TASH, Steven J.	(714)786-7857	1224
	TSANG, Daniel C.	(714)856-4978	1260
Jamul	SERDZIAK, Edward J.	(619)426-2253	1116
Kensington	LAWRENCE, Gary S.	(415)642-2370	704
	ROOSHAN, Gertrude I.	(415)525-5640	1053
La Canada-Flintridge	MORAN, William R.	(818)790-1529	862
La Crescenta	BUTTERWORTH, Linda M.		167
La Jolla	ALLISON, Terry L.	(619)534-1256	17
	BRIDGMAN, Amy R.	(619)587-1306	135
	FISHER, Edith M.	(619)534-1258	380
	SCHILLER, Anita R.	(619)534-3337	1093
	TOMMEY, Richard J.	(610)464-4073	1250
	ZYROFF, Ellen S.	(619)459-1513	1392
La Mirada	ANJOU-DURAZZO, Martel T.	(213)944-5981	28
	MARTUCCI, Louis U.	(714)994-2409	779
La Verne	HECKMAN, Marlin L.	(714)593-8680	520
Lafayette	SVIHRA, S J.	(415)933-9549	1212
Livermore	BURTON, Hilary D.	(415)423-8063	164
	GIRILL, T R.	(415)422-0146	438
	HUNT, Richard K.	(415)443-5525	575
	LOVE, Sandra R.	(415)422-7310	743
	PALLONE, Kitty J.	(415)447-2376	935
Lomita	BOWLING, Lance C.	(213)831-1322	121
Long Beach	ADAMS, Linda L.	(213)590-7639	5
	ATTARIAN, Lorraine B.	(213)491-9295	38
	BENSON-TALLEY, Lois I.	(213)494-7817	83
	HECKLINGER, Ellen L.		519

RESEARCHER (Cont'd)
CALIFORNIA (Cont'd)

Los Angeles	BATES, Marcia J.	(213)825-4352	64
	BENNION, Bruce C.	(213)743-2118	82
	BEVERAGE, Stephanie L.	(213)612-3242	93
	BIRNIE, Elizabeth B.	(213)626-8484	98
	CASE, Donald O.	(213)825-1379	191
	CHAMPLIN, Peggy	(213)472-4991	198
	COLLINS, Richard H.	(213)398-7017	233
	CREWS, Kenneth D.	(213)397-1518	258
	CROSS, Claudette S.	(213)256-2123	260
	DALY, Eudice	(213)474-6080	271
	DONALDSON, Maryanne T.	(213)617-7070	311
	DOUGLAS, Carolyn T.	(213)472-5287	314
	ELLISON, Bettye H.	(213)666-5323	345
	GINSBURG, Helen W.	(213)485-5400	438
	GRANGER, Dorothy J.	(818)795-9161	457
	GRIGST, Denise J.	(213)651-3643	470
	HASSAN, Abe H.	(213)649-2846	511
	HOFFMAN, Irene M.	(213)839-5722	548
	HOLLINGSWORTH, Dena M.	(213)229-7217	552
	HORIGAN, Evelyn A.	(213)665-2039	559
	JAIN, Celeste C.	(213)665-7510	591
	KAPLAN, Robin	(213)851-2480	626
	LEE, Don A.	(213)650-4946	709
	LEE, Hee J.	(213)391-4226	710
	MCCORMICK, Mona	(213)825-1693	798
	MERRIFIELD, Thomas C.	(213)390-4717	826
	MULLER, Malinda S.	(213)557-2900	877
	PANSKI, Saul J.	(213)655-1415	938
	POPOVITCH-KREKIC, Ruzica	(213)476-2237	984
	PRUHS, Sharon	(213)974-7780	996
	REYNOLDS, Diane C.	(213)629-3531	1025
	RICHARDSON, John V.	(213)825-4352	1029
	RITCHESON, Charles R.	(213)743-2543	1036
	ROLLING, George M.	(213)224-2251	1051
	SANDVIKEN, Gordon L.	(818)307-2872	1081
	SATER, Analya	(213)277-1969	1083
	SMITH, Catherine M.	(213)669-6523	1153
	STERN, Teena B.	(213)680-2525	1189
	STERNHEIM, Karen	(213)825-3047	1189
	STREIKER, Susan L.	(213)738-6727	1201
	TREISTER, Cyril C.	(213)227-1604	1255
	VEASLEY, Mignon M.	(213)236-3515	1280
	VILLERE, Dawn N.	(213)290-2989	1284
	WAGNER, Sharon L.	(213)931-4048	1292
	WATERS, Marie B.	(213)825-1693	1308
	WEISBAUM, Earl		1319
Los Gatos	BAILEY, Rolene M.	(408)356-9645	46
	SZABO, Carolyn J.	(408)353-2502	1218
Malibu	CLARK, David L.	(818)888-9305	216
Manhattan Beach	BALDWIN, Claudia A.	(213)372-1987	51
	MORRISEY, Locke J.	(213)318-3923	867
	PHILLIPS, Clifford R.	(213)545-4828	968
Menlo Park	BOYE, Inger	(415)325-8077	123
	FRANK, Peter R.	(415)329-1173	397
	HALL, Elede T.	(415)366-2937	487
	NEWMAN, Mark J.	(415)326-2114	899
Mill Valley	ASHLEY, Elizabeth	(415)388-8080	36
	LAPERRIERE, Renee J.	(415)488-9232	697
Mission Viejo	CHWEH, Steven J.	(714)768-3459	214
Montclair	CARRIGAN, John L.	(714)621-5225	186
Moreno Valley	SWAFFORD, William M	(714)242-7719	1212
Mountain View	ALBUM, Bernie	(415)967-5593	11
	POST, Linda C.	(415)968-3045	986
	SLOCUM, Hannah R.	(415)969-8356	1150
	STANEK, Suzanne	(415)969-9225	1179
Nevada City	BISHOP, Diane		99
North Hollywood	PLUMB, Carolyn G.	(818)763-2017	978
Norton AFB	CROWTHER, Carol	(714)382-7119	262
Novato	HOTZ, Sharon M.	(415)892-0821	562
Oakland	BENNETT, Celestine C.	(415)893-9645	81
	DANTON, J P.	(415)653-4802	274
	GLYNN, Jeannette E.	(415)654-3543	442
	MULL, Richard G.	(415)841-2590	876
	NEWCOMBE, Barbara T.	(415)763-4406	898
	RUBIN, Rhea J.	(415)339-1274	1064
	SYPERT, Clyde F.	(415)763-6046	1217
Orange	RYAN, Ann	(714)771-8291	1070

RESEARCHER (Cont'd)
  CALIFORNIA (Cont'd)

Palo Alto	COOK, Sherry M.	(415)858-4296	240
	CRABTREE, Sandra A.	(415)858-4767	254
	HEMINGWAY, Beverly L.	(415)328-1884	525
	KAHN, Paul J.	(415)327-3135	622
	LEE, Judith C.	(415)494-0395	710
	MARANGONI, Eugene G.	(415)858-4053	768
	PEARSON, Judith G.	(415)856-2853	952
	PRESTON, Cecilia M.	(415)327-5364	991
	VARKENTINE, Aganita	(415)493-8853	1278
	VUGRINECZ, Anna E.	(415)857-6626	1289
Pasadena	CHOUDHURY, Lori B.	(818)449-9468	211
	HOFFBERG, Judith A.	(818)797-0514	547
	HOROWITZ, Roberta S.	(213)681-3032	560
	KLINE, Victoria E.	(818)405-2100	661
	LONGO, Margaret K.	(818)793-7682	740
Pebble Beach	ANDRUS, Eloise A.	(408)624-1257	27
Pleasant Hill	BRUNTON, Angela	(415)671-4941	151
Pleasanton	WALLEN, Jody H.		1298
Pomona	HSIA, Ting M.	(714)869-3107	567
Rancho Cordova	GRANADOS, Rose A.	(916)363-0473	457
Rancho Palos Verdes	DAVENPORT, Constance B.		275
	WORMINGTON, Peggie		1369
Redwood City	SCHLACHTER, Gail A.	(415)594-0743	1093
Reseda	STEINMANN, Lois S.	(818)343-8262	1186
Richmond	BENELISHA, Eleanor	(415)223-6417	80
	O'CONNOR, Brian C.	(415)237-6561	915
Ridgecrest	FRIEDMAN, Sandra M.	(619)375-8825	404
	MAYES, Elizabeth A.	(619)446-6862	789
Riverside	CUEVAS, John R.	(714)684-4636	263
	DUNN, Kathleen K.	(714)359-8429	327
	HUNTER, David C.	(714)787-5841	576
	MITCHELL, Steve		849
Rowland Heights	SIGLER, Ronald F.	(818)965-9917	1137
Rutherford	NAZARIAN, Anahid	(707)963-9451	890
Sacramento	AKEY, Sharon A.	(916)445-7356	9
	ANDREW, Karen L.	(916)278-6291	26
	KONG, Leslie M.	(916)278-5664	670
	MARTINEZ, Barbara A.	(916)429-1107	779
	MILLER, Suzanne M.	(916)739-7010	842
	SCHEIBEL, Susan	(916)392-9461	1091
	TESTA, Elizabeth M.	(916)322-8031	1233
Salinas	COLLINS, Judith A.		232
San Bernardino	DEMENT, Alice R.	(714)883-6772	291
	JOHNSON, Paul A.	(714)883-3979	608
	NOUROK, Marlene E.	(714)887-6333	910
San Diego	CARTER, Nancy C.		189
	DYER, Charles R.	(619)236-2292	330
	GIBSON, Joanne	(619)450-0333	432
	HOWARD, Pamela F.		564
	KANJI, Zainab J.	(619)231-8381	625
	LAGIES, Meinhart J.	(619)283-0608	688
	MORRISON, Patricia	(619)292-2859	868
	PLOTSKY, Andrea G.	(619)695-1132	978
	ROBINSON, Michaele M.	(619)231-1515	1044
	ROSS, Mary A.	(619)566-4733	1058
	TABORN, Kym M.	(619)232-3320	1219
San Francisco	BROWN, Barbara L.	(415)894-9896	142
	CANTER, Judy A.	(415)777-7845	179
	CARSCH, Ruth E.	(415)641-5014	187
	CASTER, Suzanne	(415)387-9528	194
	CONLEY, Linda A.	(415)285-6835	236
	ECKMAN, Charles D.	(415)334-8449	335
	ELNOR, Nancy G.	(415)929-1948	346
	ERVITI, Debra L.	(415)863-8800	353
	GOLDMACHER, Sheila L.	(415)824-2810	445
	GRIFFIN, Michael D.	(415)664-2835	468
	GUNDERSON, Jeffery R.	(415)929-1472	477
	HUNG, Joanne Y.	(415)221-7325	574
	HUNSUCKER, Alice E.	(415)396-7909	574
	KRAEMER, Linda L.	(415)981-0250	674
	LAND, Barbara J.	(415)221-7707	692
	LEWANDOWSKI, Joseph J.	(415)626-3755	722
	MACKLER, Mark E.	(415)954-4452	757
	MAH, Jeffery	(415)552-4733	760
	MCDEVITT-PARKS, Kathryn B.	(415)759-8018	802
	MOORE, Gregory B.	(415)753-2645	859

RESEARCHER (Cont'd)
  CALIFORNIA (Cont'd)

San Francisco	STEFANIC, Jean A.	(415)666-6678	1185
	VANSLYKE, Lisa M.	(415)431-0717	1277
San Jose	BERCIK, Mary E.	(408)288-9798	84
	BRIDGMAN, David L.	(408)997-3723	135
	ELLIOTT, Patricia G.	(408)277-9243	344
	HARMON, Robert B.	(408)297-2810	502
	JESSUP, Carrie	(408)629-3403	600
	MULLEN, Cecilia P.	(408)265-8799	877
	RODICH, Lorraine E.	(408)277-9788	1047
	ROSEN, Elizabeth M.	(408)277-2270	1055
San Leandro	WENDROFF, Catriona	(415)569-3491	1323
San Luis Obispo	ROCKMAN, Ilene F.	(805)756-2273	1046
San Marino	MCLOONE, Harriet V.	(818)405-2207	814
	ZALL, Elisabeth W.	(818)405-2188	1386
San Mateo	RAZE, Nasus B.	(415)345-9684	1012
Santa Barbara	FALK, Joyce D.	(805)687-7283	362
	GEBHARD, Patricia	(805)969-1031	424
	KINNELL, Susan K.	(805)965-1294	653
	RUDD, Janet K.	(805)682-9560	1065
Santa Clara	BAZAN, Lorraine R.	(408)554-4658	68
Santa Cruz	ANDERSON, Clifford D.	(408)429-2501	22
	MARIE, Jacquelyn	(408)429-2802	770
	STEVENS, Stanley D.	(408)475-9172	1191
Santa Monica	BECKER, Joseph	(213)829-6866	72
	BERMAN, Marsha	(213)399-3674	88
	DIRLAM, Dona M.	(213)452-1897	305
	FISHER, Alice J.	(213)459-0414	380
	KARR, Linda		628
	WITTMANN, Cecelia V.	(213)454-8300	1358
Santa Paula	CHRISTOPHER, Paul	(805)525-8092	212
Santa Rosa	WALSH, Donamarie F.		1299
	WATSON, Benjamin	(707)527-2668	1309
Saratoga	CLAEYS, Luisa T.	(408)741-5426	215
Sebastopol	CANT, Elaine N.	(707)823-3214	179
	SIMONS, Maurice M.	(707)823-9275	1141
	STRIBLING, Lorraine R.	(707)823-1419	1202
Sherman Oaks	KYROPOULOS, Mary S.	(818)789-6022	685
	LEWIS, Cookie A.	(818)788-5280	722
Sierra Madre	KNUDSEN, Helen Z.		666
Stanford	CARSON, Susan A.	(415)723-2092	188
	KRAKAUER, Elizabeth	(408)733-4611	675
Stockton	BOYER, Laura M.		123
Sunland	CLARK, Patricia A.	(818)353-6820	217
Sunnyvale	VAN VELZER, Verna J.	(408)738-2888	1277
	WARNOCK, Patric F.	(408)245-0146	1305
Thousand Oaks	HOCKEL, Kathleen N.		545
Upland	GRAUE, Luz B.	(714)982-7574	458
	THELIN, Sonya R.	(714)982-2336	1234
Van Nuys	LEE, Lydia H.	(818)989-6433	710
Venice	CHARBONNEAU, Ronald P.	(213)396-5441	202
	WALTER, Virginia A.	(213)392-7627	1300
Ventura	WEIMER, Sally W.	(805)659-0374	1317
Walnut Creek	SMITH, Susan A.	(415)944-1603	1161
West Covina	RINGWALT, Arthur	(818)965-2598	1035
West Hollywood	BUTKIS, John F.	(213)000-0000	166
Westlake Village	LARSON, Donald A.	(818)706-5023	699
Woodland	STALLARD, Thomas W.	(916)666-1917	1179
Woodland Hills	HORACEK, Paula B.	(818)704-6460	558
	NELSON-HARB, Sally R.		895
	REIFMAN, Deborah S.		1019

COLORADO

Arvada	PRESTON, Lawrence N.	(303)423-8729	991
Aurora	MOOMEY, Margaret M.	(303)690-1478	857
Boulder	CHANAUD, Jo P.	(303)449-0849	199
	FINK, Deborah	(303)492-8302	378
	KOHL, David F.	(303)492-6897	668
	KRISMANN, Carol H.	(303)499-2977	678
	MEYER, Andrea P.		829
	ROTHMAN, Marilyn R.	(303)447-9938	1060
	SANI, Martha J.	(303)492-8367	1081
Colorado Springs	GREEN, Nancy W.	(303)591-1177	462
	LAZARUS, Josephine G.	(303)528-7609	706
	WATERS, W R.	(303)630-5288	1309
	WYLIE, Nethery A.	(606)593-3290	1375

RESEARCHER (Cont'd)
COLORADO (Cont'd)

Denver	ABRAMS, Jeanne E.	(303)871-2961	3
	BROCK, Laurie N.	(303)333-2772	138
	BRUNER, Robert B.	(303)744-1138	150
	BURNS, Linda L.	(303)892-7300	162
	GIGNAC, Solange G.	(303)575-3751	433
	GILBERT, Ruth E.	(303)757-3622	434
	GUTH, Karen K.	(303)869-2395	478
	INGUI, Bettejean	(303)394-5158	583
	KIRSHBAUM, Priscilla J.	(313)756-1827	655
	LANCE, Keith C.	(303)866-6737	692
	LUEVANE, Marsha A.	(303)989-1036	747
	MARSCHNER, Robyn J.	(303)321-2547	773
	NORBIE, Dorothy E.	(303)691-5400	908
	RAINWATER, Barbara C.	(303)871-6206	1004
	SHARP, Alice L.	(303)866-4682	1122
	VOLZ, Edward J.	(303)571-2033	1288
	WHITE, Joyce L.	(303)722-4687	1331
Englewood	WHITE, Suellen S.	(303)790-0600	1332
Evergreen	SHARER, E J.	(303)292-4458	1122
Fort Collins	AMAN, Ann L.	(303)484-9205	19
	CHRISTENSEN, Erin S.	(303)224-4588	211
	SCHMIDT, Fred C.	(303)491-1881	1095
Golden	BOND, Mary J.	(303)277-3506	113
	KENNEY, Brigitte L.	(303)278-8482	641
	MADDOCK, Jerome T.	(303)231-1367	759
Grand Junction	NICKELS, Anita B.		902
	RICHMOND, Elizabeth B.	(303)241-4358	1030
Greeley	SAVIG, Norman I.	(303)351-2251	1086
Lafayette	MACARTHUR, Marit S.	(303)665-8237	754
Littleton	ALSOP, Robyn J.	(303)779-1925	18
	GREALY, Deborah J.	(303)795-3156	461
	LOERTSCHER, David V.	(303)770-1220	737
	SPANGLER, Bruce	(303)797-1300	1171
	WHITBY, Thomas J.	(303)798-7049	1330
	WYNAR, Bohdan S.		1375
Pueblo	GRATE, Jon F.	(303)549-2362	458
Walden	SWEET, Sally K.	(303)723-8354	1215

CONNECTICUT

Ashford	MCCAUGHTRY, Dorothy H.	(203)429-7637	795
Avon	BLOTNER, Linda S.	(203)677-0286	106
Branford	ADAMO, Clare	(203)488-1474	4
Bridgeport	BARNES, Denise M.	(203)372-5434	57
	ESCARILLA, Jose G.	(203)366-0684	354
	HUGHES, John M.	(203)576-4392	571
Colchester	CONRAD, Celia B.	(203)537-2241	238
Danbury	SHEA, Roseanne M.	(203)744-3711	1124
Darien	GAMBER, Deborah D.	(203)655-6869	416
East Hartford	SIROIS, Valerie M.	(203)565-7121	1144
Farmington	DEVINE, Marie E.	(203)677-2140	297
Greenwich	MUSKUS, Elizabeth A.	(203)661-7058	883
Hamden	KOEL, Maria O.	(203)281-3265	667
	NEWHALL, Ann C.	(203)288-8180	898
	SAMUEL, Harold E.	(203)432-0495	1079
	SMITH, Nolan E.	(203)776-3558	1159
	STRAKA, Kathy M.	(203)771-8383	1199
Hartford	KLEMARCZYK, Laurice D.	(203)547-3099	660
	MCNULTY, Karen	(203)278-2670	817
	SHORE, Julia M.	(203)537-4910	1132
	WEINSTEIN, Daniel L.	(203)275-2699	1318
Madison	FALK, Peter H.	(203)245-2246	362
Middletown	FARRINGTON, James	(203)347-9411	365
New Britain	KASCUS, Marie A.	(203)827-7565	628
	UBYSZ, Priscilla M.	(203)229-9917	1267
	WARZALA, Martin L.		1307
New Canaan	KUHR, Patricia S.	(203)966-7235	683
	LOKETS BEISCHROT, Dina		738
New Fairfield	DYKMAN, Elaine K.	(203)746-0765	331
New Haven	COLLIER, Bonnie	(203)432-1783	232
	ENSEL, Ellen H.	(203)782-2525	350
	HERMAN, Felicia G.	(203)776-6244	531
	KOEL, Ake I.	(203)432-1825	667
	KRITEMEYER, Ann C.		679
	LUBIN, Joan S.	(203)397-5154	745
	PELTIER, Karen V.	(203)432-4794	955
	SPURGEON, Kathy R.		1176
	TRIOLO, Victor A.	(203)397-4520	1257
New London	TARANOW, Gerda	(203)447-1991	1223

RESEARCHER (Cont'd)
CONNECTICUT (Cont'd)

Newington	LERITZ, M K.	(203)278-1280	717
Newtown	STANYON, Kelly	(203)426-1674	1181
Norwalk	BOHRER, Karen M.	(203)854-5275	111
Ridgefield	FARADAY, Joanna	(203)431-0062	363
	SAMUELS, Lois A.	(203)431-3342	1079
Stamford	MASTERS, Kathy B.	(203)967-6749	782
	O'BRIEN, Doris J.	(203)359-1114	914
	PALMER, Shirley	(203)325-3500	937
Stonington	WILLIAMS, Edwin E.	(203)535-0720	1343
Storrs	JIMERSON, Randall C.	(203)486-2893	600
	KAGAN, Alfred	(203)429-6565	621
Stratford	ROTH, Alison C.	(203)378-8700	1059
Suffield	CHEESEMAN, Bruce S.	(203)668-6273	204
	SCHMIDT, Alesandra M.		1095
Torrington	BENAMATI, Dennis C.	(203)489-2990	79
Waterbury	JOY, Patricia L.	(203)757-6203	618
West Hartford	BRADBERRY, Richard P.	(203)241-4704	125
	HORAK, Ellen B.	(203)233-3164	558
Westport	GORDON, Thelma S.	(203)227-2732	452
	REISMAN, Sydelle S.	(203)227-8710	1021
	SELVERSTONE, Harriet S.	(203)226-6236	1114
Willimantic	EMBARDO, Ellen E.	(203)456-1952	347
Windsor	GAGNE, Susan P.	(203)285-3288	412
Windsor Locks	MASTERS, Fred N.	(203)623-9801	782
Woodbridge	BOGENSCHNEIDER, Duane R.	(203)397-2600	110
	MILLER, Irene K.	(203)393-0458	838

DELAWARE

New Castle	IRWIN, Ruth A.	(302)328-8560	584
Newark	CHASTAIN-WARHEIT, Christine C.	(302)733-1116	203
	EVERETT, Amy E.	(302)451-2104	358
	WOLFF, Stephen G.	(302)451-2432	1361
Wilmington	GRILLO, Anthony L.	(302)774-6603	470
	TOMAN, Jocelyn B.		1249
Winterthur	ADAMS, Barbara M.	(302)656-8591	4
	THOMPSON, Neville M.	(302)656-8591	1241

DISTRICT OF COLUMBIA

Washington	ANDERSON, John M.	(202)287-8723	23
	ATKINSON, Rose M.	(202)955-2139	38
	AUSTIN, Monique C.	(202)546-7236	40
	BALL, Alice D.	(202)362-6047	52
	BECKERMAN, George	(202)775-9022	72
	BEDARD, Laura A.	(202)662-9172	73
	BELLARDO, Trudi	(202)363-9614	78
	BERWICK, Philip C.	(202)543-3369	91
	BISHOP, Sarah G.	(202)244-6841	99
	BLOZIS, Jolene M.	(202)857-7056	107
	BLUMER, Thomas J.	(202)543-7031	107
	BOHANAN, Robert D.	(202)523-3214	111
	BOYLE, James E.	(202)234-8701	123
	BROOKE, Anna	(202)357-3222	140
	CALLINAN, Ellen M.	(202)624-2838	173
	CHANG, Helen S.	(202)651-5214	200
	CHESTNUT, Paul I.	(202)462-3280	207
	CHIN, Cecilia H.	(202)543-3824	208
	COLETTI, Jeannette D.	(202)362-1664	231
	COUGHLAN, Margaret N.		250
	DAWSON, Barbara J.	(202)785-3330	282
	DE ARMAN, Charles L.	(202)707-7109	284
	DEUTSCH, James I.	(202)342-6175	296
	DOUMATO, Lamia		314
	DURAKO, Frances G.	(202)785-9700	328
	ELLIOT, Hugh	(202)333-8312	343
	FALK, Diane M.	(202)291-3821	362
	FARINA, Robert A.	(202)287-5298	363
	FLYNN, Richard M.	(202)638-1956	387
	FORREST, Phyllis E.		391
	GAMSON, Arthur L.	(202)382-5921	416
	GRAY, Michael H.	(202)755-4799	460
	GREENE, Danielle L.	(202)543-6461	463
	GRIMES, A R.	(202)663-7600	470
	HANFORD, Sally		495
	HARDING, Robert S.	(202)357-1789	500
	HARWOOD, James L.	(202)523-3281	510
	HAUCK, Janice B.	(202)362-5052	512

RESEARCHER (Cont'd)
DISTRICT OF COLUMBIA (Cont'd)
Washington

	HOPPER, Mildry S.		558
	HORCHLER, Gabriel F.	(202)547-6792	559
	HORTON, Forest W.		561
	HUDGINS, Peggy	(202)862-8800	569
	HUGGENS, Gary D.	(202)328-9248	571
	JEMIOLA, Nancy E.	(202)475-1948	596
	JENKINS, Lydia E.	(202)673-7263	597
	JOHNSON, Gary M.		604
	JOHNSON, Jacqueline B.	(202)635-7498	605
	JOHNSON, Lucy C.		607
	JONES, Elin D.		612
	KAHN, Victoria	(202)543-0752	622
	KENDRICK, Brent L.	(202)543-7031	640
	KIMBERLIN, Robert L.	(202)626-7493	649
	KLEIN, Kristine J.	(202)362-2816	659
	KOSTINKO, Gail A.	(202)483-4118	673
	LANE, Elizabeth S.		694
	LARSEN, Lynda L.	(202)328-5150	698
	LEFFALL, Dolores C.	(202)723-7645	712
	LEONARD, Angela M.	(202)636-7926	716
	LEVIN, Amy E.	(202)357-3133	720
	LITTLEJOHN, Grace M.	(202)291-6920	734
	LUNIN, Lois F.	(202)965-3924	749
	LUSKEY, Judith	(202)357-4654	749
	MANNING, Martin J.	(202)485-6187	766
	MARTIN, Kathleen S.	(202)789-7100	777
	MCCRAY, Maceo E.	(202)829-7737	800
	MCGILL, Theodora	(202)566-8320	806
	MCGUIRE, Brian		808
	MCKEAN, Joan M.	(301)443-8358	810
	MEADOWS, Beth W.	(202)628-2150	819
	MILEVSKI, Sandra N.	(202)543-7145	835
	MILLER, William S.	(202)775-4080	843
	MISSAR, Margaret M.	(202)363-2751	847
	MORRIS, Timothy J.	(202)462-8209	867
	O'BRIEN, Kathleen	(202)331-8400	914
	PILGRIM, Auriel J.	(202)484-5373	973
	PINKETT, Harold T.	(202)363-2742	974
	PORTER, Suzanne	(203)994-8906	985
	PRICE, Mary S.	(202)287-5137	992
	PRUETT, Barbara J.	(202)362-1345	996
	PULVER, Thomas B.	(202)293-0500	997
	PURDY, Virginia C.	(202)523-3105	998
	RADER, Ronald A.	(639)890-0000	1002
	RICHARDSON, Deborra A.		1029
	ROMEO, Sheryl R.	(202)626-7491	1052
	ROONEY, Eugene M.		1053
	ROSS, Rodney A.	(202)554-2272	1058
	SANCHEZ, Jose L.	(202)387-7396	1079
	SCHNEIDER, Hennie R.	(202)523-0013	1097
	SCOTT, Catherine D.	(202)357-3101	1107
	SCUKA, Aletta N.	(202)965-5678	1108
	SERVERINO, Roberto	(202)625-4574	1116
	SHEERAN, Carole A.	(202)296-0800	1125
	SIPKOV, Ivan	(202)287-9850	1144
	SMITH, Clara M.	(202)686-6684	1153
	SOLOMON, Arnold D.	(202)287-8786	1166
	STOCKTON, Ken R.	(202)293-7070	1196
	STONE, Elizabeth W.	(202)338-5574	1197
	STORM, Jill	(202)775-6174	1198
	SULLIVAN, Robert C.	(202)287-5330	1208
	SUNG, Carolyn H.	(202)287-5543	1210
	THOMPSON, Elizabeth M.	(202)333-2108	1239
	TSCHERNY, Alexander	(202)723-5415	1260
	VANDEGRIFT, Barbara P.	(202)662-7523	1273
	VASLEF, Irene	(202)342-3240	1279
	VON PFEIL, Helena P.		1288
	WALLACE, Michael T.	(202)562-1879	1298
	WASSERMAN, Krystyna	(202)783-5000	1308
	WEAVER, Thomas M.	(202)526-4262	1312
	YARNALL, James L.	(202)234-6293	1378

FLORIDA

Boca Raton	GOLDMAN, Ava R.	(305)487-1891	445
	PELLEN, Rita M.	(305)395-6369	955
Bonifay	HOWELL, Wanda H.	(904)547-3631	565
Bradenton	MORR, Lynell A.	(813)747-4319	866

RESEARCHER (Cont'd)
FLORIDA (Cont'd)

Clearwater	BROMBERG, Johanna	(813)535-2595	139
Coral Gables	AHMAD, Carol F.	(305)284-3551	8
	PEREZ, Maria L.	(305)553-1134	958
Dade City	SPENCER, Albert F.		1173
De Land	EVERETT, David D.	(904)734-4121	358
Fort Lauderdale	HARTON, Pamela J.	(305)357-7454	508
Fort Myers	PEGLER, Ross J.	(813)267-2995	954
Gainesville	BROWN, Pia T.	(904)375-6302	147
	LEONARD, Louise F.	(904)373-2705	716
	MALANCHUK, Peter P.	(904)392-0364	762
	PRIMACK, Alice L.	(904)335-8525	993
	PROCTOR, Dixie L.	(904)377-3442	994
	WILLETT, Charles	(904)378-1661	1341
	WOODS, Susan E.	(904)392-4018	1367
Jacksonville	COHEN, Kathleen F.	(904)646-2616	228
	FAHNERT, Elizabeth K.	(904)641-8649	361
	MARION, Gail E.	(904)633-2088	770
	RANDTKE, Angela W.	(904)646-2550	1007
Key Biscayne	KIRBY, Diana G.	(305)361-3678	654
Lake Worth	MOFFETT, Martha L.	(305)964-7044	852
Live Oak	HISS, Sheila M.	(904)362-6936	544
Miami	ADAMS, Gustav C.	(305)261-7031	4
	BOLDRICK, Samuel J.	(305)443-2216	112
	CARR, Sallyann	(305)592-0081	186
	KASKEY, Sid		629
	LEHMAN, Douglas K.	(305)279-5770	712
	MILLER, Jewell J.	(305)662-4212	839
	PAUL, Nora M.	(305)376-3402	949
	PHILLIPS, Donald J.	(305)274-5724	968
	ROVIROSA, Dolores F.		1062
	SANCHEZ, Sara M.	(305)854-7752	1079
	SEILER, Susan L.	(305)279-0545	1112
	WRIGHT, Joseph F.	(305)379-3105	1372
Miami Beach	EFRON, Muriel C.	(305)672-0696	338
	GROVER, Wilma S.	(305)868-5000	474
	LYON, Bruce C.	(305)868-4451	752
Miami Shores	PINE, Nancy M.	(305)758-3392	974
Milton	PERDUE, Robert W.	(904)994-7640	958
Naples	O'CONNOR, Mary A.	(813)598-9269	916
Oakland Park	WILLIAMS, Alexander	(305)565-2990	1341
Orlando	DAVIDOFF, Marcia	(305)894-5508	276
	GEBET, Russell W.	(305)849-0300	424
Palm Coast	FRAZER, Ruth F.	(904)445-5409	399
Palm Harbor	HO, Paul J.	(813)785-1874	545
Pensacola	DEBOLT, W D.	(904)474-2213	284
Plant City	PINGS, Vern M.	(813)752-3884	974
Pompano Beach	WHITESIDE, Lee A.	(305)782-0194	1333
Ponte Vedra Beach	PECK, Brian T.	(904)246-1400	953
St Petersburg	ALLEN, Douglas R.	(813)343-4013	14
	CATES, Jo A.	(813)522-1550	194
	WATERS, Sally G.	(813)345-1335	1308
Sarasota	MOON, Ilse	(813)355-1795	857
Seminole	WEISS, Susan		1320
Tallahassee	BILAL, Dania M.	(904)575-5793	96
	CLARKSON, Jane S.	(904)385-9671	219
	CONAWAY, Charles W.	(904)893-1482	235
	DEENEY, Marian A.	(904)562-3246	286
	DE PEW, John N.	(904)644-5775	293
	PATTON, Linda L.	(904)644-5019	949
	TOOLE, Gregor K.		1250
Tampa	ABBOTT, Randy L.	(813)988-7912	1
	EL-HADIDY, Bahaa	(813)974-3520	342
	EVANS, Josephine K.	(813)974-4471	357
	EYLES, Heberle H.	(813)837-3896	359
	GATES, Jean K.	(813)974-3520	422
	HAWK, Susan P.	(813)239-3268	513
	KING, Elizabeth	(813)885-7481	650
	MCCROSSAN, John A.	(813)974-3520	800
	MCRAE, Linda	(813)974-2360	818
	PFISTER, Fred C.	(813)971-0755	966
	WOOD, James F.	(813)232-5221	1364
Venice	CARR, Mary L.	(813)497-0420	186
Vero Beach	KISER, Mary D.	(305)567-4111	656
Winter Park	AHLIN, Nancy	(305)644-6424	8

RESEARCHER (Cont'd)
GEORGIA

Athens	CARPENTER, David E.	(404)542-8460	184
	GUBISTA, Kathryn R.	(404)546-8153	475
	RIEMER, John J.	(404)542-0591	1033
	ROWLAND, Lucy M.	(404)543-3690	1062
	SOUTHWICK, Mary L.	(404)542-6643	1170
	WALD, Marlena M.	(404)549-5501	1294
	WILLIAMS, Sara E.	(408)548-7519	1346
Atlanta	BRYANT, Nancy J.	(404)955-9550	152
	BULLOCK, Penelope L.	(404)792-0775	156
	CAMP, John F.	(404)875-4373	175
	COOPER, Glenn	(404)676-2096	243
	CORRELL, Emily N.	(404)633-3320	247
	COURSEY, W T.	(404)264-0714	251
	DICKENS, Rosa L.	(404)261-1837	300
	ELAM, Joice B.	(404)727-6824	341
	FEINBERG, Hilda W.	(404)875-0077	368
	FRENCH, Melodee J.	(404)658-9117	402
	FULLER, Ruth V.		409
	GASKINS, Stephen D.		421
	JAMES, Stephen E.	(404)681-0251	592
	MILLER, Jack E.	(404)892-3600	838
	RAQUET, Jacqueline R.	(404)320-9727	1008
	ROSS, Theodosia B.	(404)696-2355	1059
	SIMMONS, Hal	(404)451-0331	1140
	STOWELL, Donald C.	(404)231-4414	1199
	TEMPLETON, Mary E.	(404)727-6875	1231
	THAXTON, Lyn	(404)292-6767	1234
	TROUTMAN, Joseph E.	(404)522-8980	1258
	WHITE, Carol A.	(404)351-8991	1330
Augusta	BUSTOS, Roxann R.	(404)737-1748	166
Bainbridge	MULCAHY, Bryan L.	(912)246-3887	876
Bremen	BROCK, Kathy T.	(404)537-4960	138
College Park	CANN, Sharon F.	(404)768-0970	178
Dalton	LARY, Marilyn S.	(404)272-4527	700
Decatur	ALLEN, William R.	(404)284-2981	16
	BISHOP, Beverly D.	(404)371-8488	99
	GRELL, Holly J.	(404)378-5948	467
	HATCHER, Nolan C.	(404)378-8282	511
	HUGHES, Glenda J.	(404)636-0108	571
	MARONEY, Daryle M.	(404)373-0546	772
	OVERBECK, James A.	(404)378-8821	931
Doerun	BOWEN, Louise E.	(912)782-5408	120
East Point	ELTZROTH, Elsbeth L.	(404)767-3144	346
Fitzgerald	PAULK, Sara L.	(912)423-5531	950
Hartwell	BISSO, Arthur J.	(404)376-4655	100
Kennesaw	GRIFFIN, Martha R.	(404)422-9921	468
La Grange	GIBSON, Ricky S.	(404)884-3757	432
Lilburn	HOUGH, Leslie S.	(404)979-0270	562
Milledgeville	SCOTT, Rupert N.	(912)453-5573	1108
Norcross	DEWBERRY, Claire D.	(404)564-1634	298
Red Oak	LETT, Rosalind K.		719
Roswell	MARTIN, Clarece	(404)993-0625	775
Stone Mountain	ENGERRAND, Steven W.	(404)469-5066	349
Sylvester	MEREY-KADAR, Ervin R.	(912)776-0723	825
Tucker	LEIGHTON, Victoria C.	(404)491-0464	714
Valdosta	MONTGOMERY, Denise L.	(912)333-5867	856
Vidalia	HARTZ, Frederic R.	(912)537-0195	509
Winder	HOLMES, Nancy M.	(404)867-2762	553

GUAM

Agana	WEINGARTH, Darlene	(671)472-1750	1318

HAWAII

Aiea	TIMBERLAKE, Cynthia A.	(808)488-4507	1245
Honolulu	DILUCIA, Samuel J.	(808)955-1500	303
	GOODY, Cheryl S.	(808)521-5361	450
	HORIE, Ruth H.		559
	KOTO, Ann S.	(808)829-5835	673
	SCHULTZ, Elaine V.	(808)395-1801	1102
	SHELDEN, Patricia M.	(808)538-6430	1125
	TAKAHASHI, Annabelle T.	(808)948-7214	1220
	TOM, Chow L.	(808)537-9321	1249
	TRAPIDO, Joel	(808)988-2068	1254
	UCHIDA, Deborah K.	(808)548-7915	1267
	VAN NIEL, Eloise S.	(808)548-6283	1276
Kailua	NAHL-JAKOBOVITS, Diane	(808)261-2382	886
	WRIGHT, John C.	(808)261-3714	1371
Kaneohe	ASHFORD, Marguerite K.	(808)247-6834	36

RESEARCHER (Cont'd)
HAWAII (Cont'd)

Waiaulua	VEATCH, Laurie L.	(808)237-8411	1280

IDAHO

Boise	ROBERTSON, Naida	(208)384-4340	1042
	TAYLOR, Adrien P.	(208)385-1621	1225
	WELLS, Merle W.	(208)334-3356	1322
Moscow	BRADY, Eileen E.	(208)883-0817	126
	WAI, Lily C.	(208)882-0506	1292

ILLINOIS

Addison	WRIGHT, Deborah L.	(312)628-3338	1371
Arlington Heights	FINNERTY, James L.	(312)259-3496	379
	GIANNINI, Evelyn L.	(312)398-3142	431
Aurora	BEAN, Janet R.	(312)859-2222	69
	MCKEARN, Anne B.	(312)892-4811	810
Beardstown	WEST, L P.	(217)323-5788	1326
Brookfield	IRONS, Carol A.	(312)485-3503	584
Cahokia	BEAN, Bobby G.	(618)875-6915	69
Carbondale	BORUZKOWSKI, Lilly A.	(618)453-2365	117
	COX, Shelley M.	(618)457-8975	253
	DALE, Doris C.	(618)536-2441	270
	RAY, Jean M.	(618)549-1290	1011
	RYAN, Sheila	(618)549-7029	1071
	WILSON, Betty R.	(618)529-3318	1350
Champaign	CLOONAN, Michele V.	(217)351-8140	223
	GOLDHOR, Herbert	(217)359-5636	445
	HEISTER, Carla G.	(217)333-6892	523
	PENKA, Carol B.	(217)351-6026	956
	REPTA, Vada L.	(217)398-5728	1024
	WERT, Lucille M.	(217)356-6600	1325
Charleston	NESBIT, Angus B.	(217)345-7293	896
Chicago	ADAMSHICK, Robert D.	(312)353-1157	6
	ADKINS, Marjorie R.	(312)468-2139	6
	BAMBERGER, Mary A.	(312)996-2742	53
	BOOKSTEIN, Abraham	(312)762-8268	115
	BREEN, Joanell C.	(312)929-1445	131
	BRICKMAN, Sally F.		135
	BROWN, Patricia B.	(312)775-1515	146
	BURGH, Scott G.	(312)558-5740	159
	BYRE, Calvin S.	(312)341-3643	169
	CICHON, Marilyn T.	(312)648-1155	214
	CLAPP, David F.	(312)465-0324	215
	COATSWORTH, Patricia A.	(312)947-2160	224
	CORSARO, Julie A.		248
	COTILLAS, Therese G.	(312)856-8341	250
	DONAHUE, Karin V.		310
	DUFF, John B.	(312)269-2984	323
	EMRE, Serpil A.	(312)236-5622	348
	EPP, Ronald H.	(203)347-6933	351
	EPSTEIN, Dena J.	(312)373-0522	351
	FANG, Min L.	(317)842-0321	363
	FEDERICI, Yolanda D.	(312)427-0052	368
	GARDNER, Trudy A.	(312)942-8735	418
	GERDES, Neil W.	(312)753-3196	428
	GLANZ, Lenore M.	(312)528-7817	439
	GROFT, Mary L.	(312)477-7065	471
	GUINEE, Andrea M.	(312)528-5792	476
	HILBURGER, Mary J.	(312)794-2614	538
	HOFFMANN, Maurine L.	(312)951-0599	548
	HUNT, Janis E.	(312)275-8439	575
	JORDAN, Charles R.	(312)478-7205	616
	KALUZSA, Karen L.	(312)008 2859	623
	KAYAIAN, Mary S.	(312)245-2810	632
	KEARNEY, Sharon M.	(312)549-3148	633
	KOVITZ, Nancy R.	(312)938-3434	674
	LANDRY, Ronald	(312)943-3282	694
	LEWIS, Sherman L.		724
	LYNCH, Mary J.	(312)944-6780	752
	MACKEY, Denise R.	(312)467-1000	756
	MANCUYAS, Natividad D.	(312)995-2284	764
	MANN, Vijai S.	(312)443-5423	766
	MARANO, Nancy H.	(312)368-7777	768
	MARSHALL, Jerilyn A.		774
	MARTIN, Bennie E.	(312)443-5423	775
	MELTON, Emily I.	(312)944-6780	823
	MENZIES, Pamela C.	(312)924-8301	825
	MILLER, Robert	(312)488-7195	841
	MILUTINOVIC, Eunhee C.	(312)472-9843	845

RESEARCHER (Cont'd)
ILLINOIS (Cont'd)
Chicago

MITZIGA, Walter J.	(312)375-4646	850
MOORHEAD, John D.	(312)944-4020	862
MORRIS, Ann	(312)764-8064	866
MORRISON, Samuel F.	(312)269-3053	868
MOULTON, James C.	(312)525-7185	873
MUELLER, Julie M.	(312)645-4839	875
O'HEARON, Doris M.	(312)221-0570	919
OSBORN, Walter	(312)329-4140	927
OWNES, Dorothy J.	(312)702-8899	932
PARK, Chung I.	(312)942-3000	940
REILLY, Jane A.	(312)764-2413	1020
REITER, Richard R.	(312)922-4200	1022
REMEIKIS, Lois A.	(312)782-1442	1022
SCHRAMM, Mary T.	(312)248-7934	1099
SCHROEDER, Anne M.	(312)528-7486	1100
SCHWERIN, Kurt	(312)275-6776	1106
SCOTT, Sharon E.	(312)268-7500	1108
SHAW, Joyce M.	(312)294-4640	1123
SIARNY, William D.	(312)467-5520	1134
SLAWNIAK, Patricia M.	(312)338-7589	1148
SMITH, Denis J.		1154
SPARKS, Joanne L.	(312)728-5510	1171
STENGER, Brenda E.	(312)782-1442	1187
STONER, Ronald P.	(312)644-3100	1198
WELLS, James M.	(312)782-1172	1322
WIBERLEY, Stephen E.	(312)996-2730	1335
WILLIAMSON, Linda E.	(312)996-2738	1347
WINNIKE, Mary E.	(312)996-6595	1355
WRIGHT, Helen K.	(312)944-6780	1371

Chicago Ridge	LOTZ, Marsha A.	(312)423-7753	742
Chillicothe	CROTZ, D K.	(312)485-1903	261
Cicero	MALLER, Mark P.	(312)652-8084	763
De Kalb	AUSTIN, John R.	(815)753-9492	40
	KIES, Cosette N.	(815)753-1735	647
	OSORIO, Nestor L.	(815)753-9837	928
	RAST, Elaine K.	(815)758-5234	1009
	SHAVIT, David	(815)753-6271	1123
	TITUS. Elizabeth M.	(815)753-1094	1247
	TOROK, Andrew G.	(815)753-1734	1251
Deerfield	CALLAGHAN, Linda W.	(312)945-3311	173
	LEE, Soon H.	(312)948-3880	711
Des Plaines	BURNS, Marie T.	(312)635-4732	162
Downers Grove	MIFFLIN, Michael J.	(312)963-9285	833
Edwardsville	MCFARLAND, Mary A.	(618)692-3828	805
	MOORE, Milton C.	(618)692-1638	860
Elk Grove Village	HOLBROCK, Mary A.	(312)439-4800	550
Elmhurst	DARLING, Elizabeth A.	(312)279-4100	274
Evanston	BAUGH, L S.	(312)328-0243	65
	BJORNCRANTZ, Leslie B.	(312)866-9112	100
	BRADY, Mary M.	(312)491-2929	127
	DAVIDSON, Lloyd A.	(312)491-2906	276
	HURD, Albert E.	(312)866-7235	577
	KAPLAN, Rosalyn L.	(312)869-1035	626
	METZLER, Valerie	(312)869-5992	829
	NIELSEN, Brian	(312)491-2170	903
	PIRON, Alice M.	(312)864-3175	975
	SENN, Mary S.	(312)328-3767	1115
	SHERMAN, Sarah	(312)864-3801	1128
	STEWART, Donald E.	(312)475-5529	1192
	WHITELEY, Sandra M.	(312)475-7931	1333
Evergreen Park	SOBKOWIAK, Emily J.	(312)425-1886	1165
Geneseo	REDINGTON, Deirdre E.	(309)944-3311	1014
Glenview	HAFNER, Arthur W.	(312)291-1022	482
	HAMILTON, Beth A.	(312)998-6567	491
Grayslake	DEPKE, Robert W.		293
	KIENE, Andrea L.	(312)740-0620	647
Harvey	FOLEY, Donna H.	(312)333-2300	387
Highland Park	JANES, Virginia		593
Hinsdale	HALASZ, Marilynn J.	(312)325-0819	484
Hoffman Estates	CHAPA, Joan I.	(312)934-7032	201
	MILLER, Deborah	(312)882-3698	837
Itasca	HOGAN, Patricia M.	(312)773-1699	549
Kenilworth	PETERSON, Scott W.	(312)666-1404	964
La Grange	HATTENDORF, Lynn C.	(312)579-0873	512
	PROBST, Virginia M.		994
Lake Bluff	BROSK, Carol A.	(312)234-6752	141
	JEFFORDS, Rebecca J.	(312)234-8923	596

RESEARCHER (Cont'd)
ILLINOIS (Cont'd)

Lake Forest	DANOFF, Fran	(312)234-2350	274
	MARSHALL, Deborah M.	(312)234-9220	774
Lena	FREY, Roxanne C.	(815)369-5372	403
Libertyville	BRIGGS, Martha T.		135
Lincolnwood	BENNETT, Laura B.	(312)679-2327	82
Lisle	SHOTWELL, Richard T.	(312)665-9107	1133
Lockport	TROY, Shannon M.	(312)534-5000	1258
Lombard	EGAN, Elizabeth M.	(312)627-7130	338
	MARSHALL, Mary G.	(312)932-1455	774
	SCHIPMA, Peter B.	(312)627-0550	1093
Macomb	TING, Lee H.	(309)298-1770	1246
Mascoutah	SCHAACK, Wilma J.	(618)566-7385	1088
Maywood	LUDWIG, Logan T.	(312)531-3192	747
Naperville	MEACHEN, Edward W.	(312)420-3425	819
Nashville	RUSIEWSKI, Charles B.	(618)327-8304	1068
Niles	CARTER, Ida	(312)647-9000	189
	HANSEN, Cheryl A.	(312)677-4730	497
North Aurora	HOWREY, Mary M.	(312)896-5837	566
Oak Park	DICK, Ellen A.	(312)386-9385	300
	FENSKE, Ruth E.	(312)383-0966	371
	HALIBEY, Areta V.	(312)524-0023	486
	MARSHALL, Maggie L.	(312)848-4432	774
	PAPPALARDO, Marcia J.	(312)848-5035	939
	REDDY, Michael B.	(312)848-1754	1013
Ottawa	WILLSON, Richard E.	(815)434-7075	1349
Palatine	BROWN, Patricia L.	(312)991-1278	146
	BURNS, Mary F.	(312)358-0137	162
	HORTON, Kathy L.	(312)934-3794	561
Palos Hills	SODOWSKY, Kay M.	(312)430-2164	1165
Park Forest	BUCKLEY, Ja A.	(312)748-2536	154
Park Ridge	JACKSON, William V.	(312)825-4364	588
	KNARZER, Arlene	(312)692-9550	663
	LOFTHOUSE, Patricia A.	(312)698-9731	737
Pekin	WALTERS, Patsy M.	(309)353-5075	1301
Quincy	EGGERS, Thomas D.		339
	KINGERY, Victor P.	(217)228-5345	652
River Forest	HEYMAN, Jerome S.	(312)771-3030	536
	LI, Richard T.	(312)366-2490	725
Riverdale	PATEL, Jashu	(312)849-3959	947
Rock Island	MASON, Marjorie L.	(309)788-7217	781
	WESTERBERG, Kermit B.	(309)794-7221	1326
Rockford	DALRYMPLE, Prudence W.	(815)968-9111	271
	HUTCHINS, Richard G.	(815)398-0756	579
St Joseph	DUCHOW, Sally	(217)469-2237	322
Skokie	GRODINSKY, Deborah	(312)679-1380	471
	JACOB, Merle L.		589
South Barrington	JUSTIE, Julie H.	(312)551-2093	620
Springfield	ALLEY, Brian	(217)522-8970	16
	BERK, Robert A.	(217)782-2658	87
	BRADWAY, Becky J.	(217)753-4117	126
	EFIRD, Frank K.	(217)523-0579	338
	HILDRETH, Charles R.		539
	LARISON, Brenda	(217)529-9233	697
	SIVAK, Marie R.	(217)782-2826	1144
	TEMPLE, Wayne C.	(217)528-6330	1230
Sun City	STUHLMAN, Daniel D.	(312)262-8959	1205
Urbana	ATKINS, Stephen E.	(217)244-1867	38
	BALACHANDRAN, Sarojini	(217)328-3577	50
	BRICHFORD, Maynard J.	(217)367-7072	134
	BURBANK, Richard D.	(217)333-2713	158
	DAVIS, Elisabeth B.	(217)333-3654	278
	EDMONDS, M L.	(217)333-2306	336
	ESTABROOK, Leigh S.	(217)333-3280	355
	FAIRCHILD, Constance A.	(217)333-1900	361
	FORREST, Charles G.	(217)244-3770	390
	GUSHEE, Marion S.	(217)367-9610	478
	JOHNSON, Anita D.	(217)367-0647	602
	KRUMMEL, Donald W.	(217)344-6311	680
	LANCASTER, Frederick W.	(217)384-7798	691
	LEONG, Carol L.	(217)333-3399	717
	MONTANELLI, Dale S.	(217)333-0792	855
	ROLSTAD, Gary O.	(217)333-3280	1052
	SCHMIDT, Karen A.	(217)333-1054	1095
	SMITH, Linda C.	(217)333-7742	1157
	WEECH, Terry L.	(217)367-7111	1315
	WEI, Karen T.	(217)344-5647	1316
	WILLIAMS, Martha E.	(217)333-1074	1345
	WILSON, Lizabeth A.	(217)333-3489	1351

RESEARCHER (Cont'd)
ILLINOIS (Cont'd)

Villa Park	POINTON, Louis R.	(312)833-6555	980
Wauconda	FERME, Paul H.	(312)526-9123	373
Waukegan	CARNELLI, Sandra R.	(312)623-2041	183
Westmont	MANNING, Mary J.	(312)964-3549	766
Wilmette	ELSTEIN, Rochelle S.	(312)256-8484	346
Winnetka	BLACKBURN, Joy M.	(312)446-8697	102
Woodridge	WHITT, Diane M.		1334

INDIANA

Bloomington	FRY, Bernard M.	(812)339-3571	406
	JACKSON, Susan M.	(812)334-7049	588
	MILLER, Constance R.	(812)335-5729	836
	MURPHY, Marcy	(812)335-5113	881
	NELSON, Brenda	(812)335-8631	893
	POPP, Mary F.	(812)335-9857	984
	SHAABAN, Marian F.	(812)335-6924	1118
	SILVER, Joel B.	(812)335-2452	1138
	TALALAY, Kathryn M.	(812)335-2970	1220
	WALLACE, Danny P.	(812)335-2848	1297
	ZHU, Xiaofeng	(812)335-2666	1387
Chesterton	BECKING, Mara S.	(219)926-5618	73
Crawfordsville	THOMPSON, Donald E.	(317)362-6851	1239
Elkhart	SAARI, David S.	(219)295-8090	1072
Evansville	BAKER, Donald E.	(812)425-4309	48
	WINSLOW, Carol M.	(812)867-2146	1355
Fort Wayne	BUDD, Anne D.	(219)424-6111	155
	LISTON, Karen A.	(219)424-6664	733
Frankfort	MUNDELL, Eric L.	(317)659-2027	878
Gary	MILLENDER, Dharathola	(219)882-4050	835
Hammond	MEYERS, Arthur S.	(219)931-5100	830
Highland	ENGELBERT, Peter J.	(219)923-2173	348
Indianapolis	ANDREWS, Sylvia L.	(317)844-8538	27
	AUTRY, Carolyn	(317)291-9866	41
	DURKIN, Virginia M.	(317)871-2095	328
	ELLSWORTH, Marlene A.	(317)274-7185	345
	GANN, Daniel H.	(317)299-9058	416
	GRIFFITTS, Joan K.	(317)297-3283	469
	HEHMAN, Jennifer L.	(317)271-8595	521
	JOHNTING, Wendell E.	(317)894-1150	610
	LOGSDON, Robert L.	(317)888-6772	737
	MASON, Dorothy L.	(317)845-3684	781
	MATTHEW, Jeannette M.	(317)283-1053	785
	MATTS, Constance	(317)274-1928	786
	RIES, Steven T.	(317)251-2420	1033
	SIMON, Ralph C.	(317)875-5336	1141
	STUSSY, Susan A.	(317)929-0343	1205
	YOUNG, Noraleen A.	(317)786-4561	1382
Jeffersonville	HODGSON, Janet B.		546
La Porte	SMYERS, Richard P.	(219)324-2186	1162
Muncie	BEILKE, Patricia F.	(317)284-2457	75
Noblesville	WILLIAMS, Maudine	(317)773-1763	1345
Notre Dame	HAVLIK, Robert J.	(219)239-6665	513
	HAYES, Stephen M.	(219)239-5268	516
	LYSY, Peter J.	(219)259-9158	753
Plainfield	MILLER, Ida M.	(317)839-6883	838
Rochester	LASHER, Esther L.	(219)223-8407	700
South Bend	BEATTY, R M.	(219)232-2349	70
	HOHL, Robert J.	(219)289-8160	550
	WARREN, Lois B.	(219)287-6481	1306
Terre Haute	SHANE, T C.	(812)299-5289	1120
Upland	WOLCOTT, Laurie J.	(317)998-7549	1359
Valparaiso	HOLTERHOFF, Sarah G.	(219)465-7866	555
	MEYER, Ellen R.	(219)464-5360	830
	RAYMAN, Ronald A.	(219)464-2060	1011
Warsaw	DETWILER, Susan M.	(219)269-5254	296
West Lafayette	ANDERSON, Marilyn M.	(317)583-2586	24
	ERDMANN, Charlotte A.	(317)494-2872	352
	HEWISON, Nancy S.	(317)463-0904	535
	PASK, Judith M.	(317)494-6735	946
	TUCKER, John M.	(317)494-2833	1261
	YOUNGEN, Gregory K.	(317)743-9893	1383
Westfield	VAN CAMP, Ann J.	(317)896-3537	1272
Winamac	SMITH, Robert E.	(219)946-6255	1160
Zionsville	OKEY, Susan T.	(317)873-3114	920

RESEARCHER (Cont'd)
IOWA

Ames	DOBSON, Cynthia	(515)294-5451	307
	WORK, Dawn E.		1369
Bettendorf	MEIER, Patricia L.	(319)355-3895	821
	POLK, Diana B.	(319)332-8119	981
Boone	ADAMS, Larry D.	(515)432-1931	5
Cedar Falls	KOLLASCH, Matthew A.	(319)277-6125	669
	RITCHIE, Verna F.	(319)273-6257	1036
Cedar Rapids	BLISS, David H.	(319)393-5892	105
Davenport	JONSON, Laurence F.	(319)323-9213	616
	MONTGOMERY, David E.	(319)326-7832	856
	STOUT, Robert J.	(319)326-6237	1199
Dubuque	KNEFEL, Mary A.	(319)589-3215	664
Iowa City	BAKER, Sharon L.	(319)335-5707	49
	EICHER, Thomas E.	(319)335-9038	339
	FALK, Mark F.	(319)354-7474	362
	NEUFELD, Sue E.	(319)335-9871	897
	SCHERUBEL, Melody	(319)351-6264	1092
	SNIDER, Jacqueline I.	(319)337-0660	1163
Manchester	CRAWFORD, Daniel R.		256
Marion	ALDERSON, Karen A.	(319)377-0666	11
Sioux City	SCHEETZ, Kathy D.	(712)277-2423	1091
West Branch	DENNIS, Mary R.	(319)643-2583	292
	MATHER, Mildred E.	(319)643-5301	783
	MAYER, Dale C.	(319)643-5301	789
West Des Moines	MARQUARDT, Larry D.	(515)224-9278	772

KANSAS

Emporia	BOGAN, Mary E.	(316)342-1394	110
	STEWART, Henry R.	(316)343-1200	1192
Fairway	CARVER, Jane W.	(913)236-8688	191
Kansas City	RUSSELL, Marilyn L.	(913)299-1540	1069
	WITMER, Tonya C.	(913)362-5327	1358
Lawrence	MAY, Cecilia J.	(913)841-0929	788
	RHODES, Saralinda A.		1026
	SEAVER, James E.	(913)864-3569	1110
Manhattan	CRAWFORD, Anthony R.	(913)532-6516	256
	TALAB, Rosemary S.	(913)532-5550	1220
	WEISENBURGER, Patricia J.	(913)532-5968	1319
North Newton	HAURY, David A.	(316)283-2500	512
Overland Park	OJALA, Marydee P.		919
	SEVIER, Susan G.	(913)451-3111	1117
Pittsburg	DEGRUSON, Eugene H.	(316)231-7000	288
Salina	THOMAS, Evangeline M.	(913)827-1604	1236
Shawnee	STRAUSE, Robert C.	(913)268-9875	1200
Topeka	KINZIE, Lenora A.	(913)295-8247	653
	MELICK, Cal G.	(913)295-6479	822
	RICHMOND, Robert W.	(913)234-4704	1031
Valley Center	MEANS, E P.	(316)755-0414	820
Westwood	KLEBBA, Lisa A.		658
Wichita	BERARD, Sue A.	(316)267-6371	84
	BRADEN, Jan	(316)686-5954	125
	IZBICKI, Thomas M.	(316)683-8157	586
	MYERS, Robert C.	(316)689-3591	885
	SINGH, Swarn L.	(316)722-3741	1143
	STRECK, Helen T.	(316)942-2201	1201
	TANNER, Jane E.	(316)682-4485	1223
Winfield	ZUCK, Gregory J.	(316)221-4150	1391

KENTUCKY

Bowling Green	COSSEY, M E.	(502)843-6560	249
	CUDD, John M.	(502)842-0901	263
	MOORE, Elaine F.	(502)745-6114	859
	ZIMMER, Connie W.	(502)781-4165	1388
Covington	GARMAN, Nancy J.	(606)331-6345	419
Edgewood	REESE, Virginia D.	(606)261-8211	1016
Elizabethtown	HOLT, David A.	(502)737-1473	554
Lexington	BARRISH, Alan S.	(606)278-1933	60
	DARE, Philip N.	(606)252-0361	274
	LEVSTIK, Frank R.	(606)266-9196	721
	RIPLEY, Joseph M.	(606)257-4243	1035
	ROGERS, Joann V.	(606)278-6246	1049
	WALDHART, Thomas J.	(606)257-3771	1294
Louisville	ANDERSON, Patricia E.	(502)588-6392	25
	CAMMARATA, Paul J.	(502)588-6392	175
	CONNOR, Lynn S.	(502)589-4200	238
	HOUSE, Katherine L.	(502)459-2429	563
	MAZUK, Melody	(502)897-4807	791
	NEELY, Glenda S.	(502)588-6747	892

RESEARCHER (Cont'd)
KENTUCKY (Cont'd)
Louisville

	PRIOR, Barbara Q.	(502)588-6747	993
	REDMON, Sherrill	(502)451-5907	1014
	SCHLENE, Vickie J.	(502)935-9840	1094
Murray	HEIM, Keith M.	(502)762-6152	521
	WALL, Celia J.	(502)762-4990	1297
Richmond	HAY, Charles C.	(606)622-2820	515
	MARTIN, June H.	(606)622-6176	777
Wilmore	BUNDY, David D.	(606)858-3581	157

LOUISIANA

Baton Rouge	BOYCE, Bert R.	(504)388-1461	122
	BRADLEY, Jared W.	(504)766-9375	126
	COE, Miriam M.		226
	HASCHAK, Paul G.	(504)766-9986	510
	KRAFT, Donald H.	(504)388-1495	674
	MATTMILLER, C F.	(504)344-8074	786
	MCENANY, Arthur E.	(504)342-2415	804
	MERING, Margaret V.	(504)344-5863	826
	PASKOFF, Beth M.	(504)388-1480	946
	ROCHE, Alvin A.	(504)771-4900	1045
	ROUNDTREE, Lynn P.	(504)336-1306	1061
	SCULL, Roberta A.		1108
	SHIFLETT, Orvin L.	(504)388-1462	1130
	SMITH, Ledell B.		1157
	STANLEY, Eileen H.	(504)388-4395	1180
Lafayette	FOX, Willard		395
	KREAMER, Jean T.	(318)231-6780	677
	RAGHAVAN, Vijay V.	(318)231-6603	1003
	RAMAKRISHNAN, T	(318)989-9333	1004
	SCHMIDT, Jean M.	(318)231-6031	1095
	TURNER, I B.	(318)231-5702	1264
Lake Charles	CAGLE, Robert B.	(318)437-5740	171
	CUROL, Helen B.	(318)477-1780	266
Leesville	HIGGINBOTHAM, Cecelia B.	(318)239-4188	537
Metairie	KLEIN, Victor C.	(504)861-0488	659
Natchitoches	HARRINGTON, Charles W.	(318)357-0813	504
	HUSSEY, Sandra R.	(318)352-2996	578
New Orleans	DAVIS, Margo	(504)488-1193	280
	DRAUGHON, Ralph B.	(504)891-1921	318
	FISHER, Collette J.	(504)581-3333	380
	FLEURY, Bruce E.	(504)865-5682	385
	HANKEL, Marilyn L.	(504)286-7276	496
	HARDY, D C.	(504)895-3981	500
	JUMONVILLE, Florence M.	(504)523-4662	619
	LEMMON, Alfred E.	(504)523-4662	715
	MARIX, Mary L.	(504)488-4286	770
	MCKNIGHT, Mark C.	(504)866-3394	812
	NOLAN-MITCHELL, Patricia	(504)568-6102	908
	SARKODIE-MENSAH, Kwasi	(504)483-7306	1083
	SERBAN, William M.	(504)286-6455	1116
	WELSCH, Melissa W.	(504)584-2403	1323
Plaquemines	MCCRAY, Evelina W.	(504)659-2541	800
Ruston	MCFADDEN, Sue J.	(318)257-4357	804
Shreveport	KING, Anne M.	(318)797-5738	650
	MCCLEARY, William E.	(318)865-9813	796
	WOOD, Julienne L.		1364
Zachary	JACKSON, Audrey N.	(504)654-5491	586

MAINE

Alfred	ANDERSON, Marjorie E.	(207)324-6915	24
Bangor	WOODWARD, Robert C.	(207)942-4760	1368
Bar Harbor	GOLBITZ, Peter	(207)288-4969	444
	KINGMA, Sharyn L.	(207)288-4969	652
Boothbay	LENTHALL, Franklyn	(207)633-4536	715
Brunswick	HEISER, Nancy E.	(207)725-4253	523
	SAEGER, Edwin J.	(207)729-5720	1074
East Sebago	AIREY, Martha R.	(207)787-2817	9
Farmington	MCNAMARA, Shelley G.	(207)778-3501	816
Georgetown	LUDGIN, Donald H.	(207)371-2221	746
Mechanic Falls	NOYES, Nicholas	(207)345-3245	911
Orono	THOR, Angela M.	(207)581-1678	1242
Portland	HUMEZ, Nicholas D.	(207)773-3405	573

RESEARCHER (Cont'd)
MARYLAND

Annapolis	LIVELY, Nancy J.	(301)268-0530	734
	MCKAY, Eleanor	(301)263-6526	809
	MOTEN, Derryn E.	(301)757-3846	872
	PRIMER, Ben	(301)974-3914	993
Baltimore	ARRINGTON, Susan J.	(301)396-4042	34
	BRENNAN, Edward P.	(301)675-8835	132
	DE LERMA, Dominique R.	(301)467-2578	289
	EPSTEIN, Robert S.	(301)328-3928	351
	FLORANCE, Valerie	(301)383-9436	385
	GERHARDT, Edwin L.	(301)242-0328	428
	GROSSHANS, Maxine Z.	(301)532-8590	473
	HILDITCH, Bonny M.	(301)675-4333	539
	KLEEBERGER, Patricia L.	(301)547-9000	658
	KLEIN, Ilene R.		659
	LANDRY, Mary E.	(301)235-8067	693
	LAY, Shirley	(301)347-3419	705
	LOWENS, Margery M.	(301)532-7422	744
	MOLLENKOPF, Carolyn M.	(301)866-3156	853
	SHAPIRO, Burton J.	(301)653-2757	1121
	SILVER, Marcy L.		1138
	THIES, Gail M.	(301)597-8918	1235
	TOPPAN, Muriel L.	(301)837-9155	1251
	VARGA, Nicholas	(301)323-1010	1278
Beltsville	ESMAN, Michael D.	(301)344-3729	354
Bethesda	DAVIS, Deta S.	(301)564-0150	278
	FISHBEIN, Meyer H.	(301)530-5391	380
	GAUJARD, Pierre G.	(301)652-0034	422
	GOLDSCHMIDT, Peter G.	(301)656-5070	446
	HSIEH, Richard K.	(301)496-6481	567
	KIM, Sunnie I.	(301)496-8124	649
	MENNELLA, Dona M.	(301)652-0106	824
	MOBLEY, Arthur B.	(301)530-0081	851
	PEARSE, Nancy J.	(301)564-1967	952
	RADA, Roy F.	(301)654-6210	1002
	TIFFT, Jeanne D.	(301)229-7415	1244
	TURNER, Ellis S.	(301)530-4178	1264
Bowie	GIGANTE, Vickilyn M.	(301)249-2609	433
Brooksville	BASCOM, James F.	(301)774-3175	62
Cabin John	ROBINSON, Barbara M.	(301)320-6011	1043
Cambridge	DEL SORDO, Jean S.	(301)228-7331	290
Chevy Chase	ERLICK, Louise S.		353
	FINE, Sandra R.	(301)951-3453	377
	KENTON, Charlotte	(301)657-3855	642
	MESHINSKY, Jeff M.	(301)652-4740	827
	SEARS, Jonathan R.	(301)656-2306	1110
	SHAW, Renata V.	(301)654-3560	1123
Clinton	CHEEKS, Cellestine	(301)868-5048	204
College Park	CUNNINGHAM, William D.	(301)454-2376	265
	MARCHIONINI, Gary J.	(301)454-3235	769
	SOERGEL, Dagobert	(301)454-5451	1165
	TIBBO, Helen R.	(301)454-5441	1244
	WILSON, William G.	(301)454-6003	1353
Columbia	AVERSA, Elizabeth S.	(301)992-3711	41
	DAHLEN, Roger W.	(301)964-9098	269
	DIENER, Richard A.	(301)381-2525	302
	DOVE, Samuel	(301)964-4189	315
	HOLLENBACH, Karen L.		551
	JOHNSON, Elaine B.	(301)992-5502	604
	RUSS, Kennetta P.	(301)381-0579	1068
	SEMKO, Melanie J.	(301)992-6342	1115
	WOLTER, John A.	(301)730-6692	1362
	YUILLE, Willie K.		1384
Dundalk	MILLER, Everett G.	(301)522-5785	837
Easton	MOLTER, Maureen M.	(301)822-1658	853
Fallston	SACK, Jean C.	(301)877-2825	1073
Flintstone	RAFATS, Jerome M.		1003
Forestville	MOORE, Virginia B.	(301)568-8743	861
Frederick	FRYSER, Benjamin S.	(301)698-5846	407
	NATHANSON, David	(301)662-4499	889
Frostburg	WILLIAMS, Pamela S.		1346
Gaithersburg	GROCKI, Daniel J.	(301)253-6044	471
	HARTZ, Mary K.	(301)948-1855	509
	VAN BRUNT, Virginia	(301)762-6701	1272
Gamber	BOGAGE, Alan R.	(301)795-6167	110
Gambrills	YOUNG, Peter R.	(301)923-2902	1383
Garrett Park	PRATT, Laura C.	(301)942-1764	990
Germantown	ALBRIGHT, John B.	(301)428-3700	10
	MOLINE, Judi A.	(301)972-5708	853

RESEARCHER (Cont'd)
MARYLAND (Cont'd)

Grasonville	SCHNEIDER, Karl R.	(301)827-9339	1097
Green Meadows	MILL, Rodney H.	(301)422-1437	835
Greenbelt	BOGGESS, John J.		110
Hillcrest Heights	CHAPMAN, Elwynda K.	(301)894-0963	202
Hyattsville	RHEAUME, Irene M.	(301)434-8805	1025
Hydes	LANTZ, Louise K.	(301)592-2232	697
Kensington	CHAPUT, Linda J.	(703)683-8184	202
	SMITH, Karen G.	(301)564-0765	1156
Lanham	HUFFER, Mary A.	(301)577-3640	570
Laurel	DEANE, Roxanna	(301)776-6942	284
	LEVINE, Emil H.	(301)776-3062	720
	OMAR, Elizabeth A.	(301)490-3871	923
Mt Rainier	NITZ, Andrew M.		905
	STRANSKY, Maria	(301)779-1627	1200
Olneg	WATERS, Susan S.	(301)774-3439	1309
Potomac	HO, James K.		545
Reisterstown	BRADLEY, Wanda L.		126
Rockville	BLANDAMER, Ann W.	(301)340-8904	103
	CANTELON, Philip L.	(301)770-1170	179
	CHIANG, Ahushun	(301)251-5486	207
	COSMIDES, George J.	(301)762-5428	249
	DICKINSON, Patricia C.	(301)251-1173	301
	FREEDMAN, Lynn P.	(301)468-2600	400
	HERIN, Nancy J.	(301)279-6101	531
	JONES, Gerry U.	(301)493-9438	613
	KING, Donald W.	(301)881-6766	650
	LEWIS, Robert J.	(301)460-9145	724
	MICHAELS, Carolyn L.	(301)564-0509	831
St Marys City	BRITTEN, William A.		137
Silver Spring	AMATRUDA, William T.	(301)585-3570	19
	ARANDA-COODOU, Patricio	(301)946-7859	30
	FEINBERG, Beryl L.	(301)946-3282	368
	FELMY, John C.	(301)681-9069	370
	FRAULINO, Philip S.	(301)495-5636	399
	KIMMEL, Mark R.	(301)340-2100	649
	KNOBBE, Mary L.	(301)681-6332	665
	LEVITAN, Karen B.	(301)588-8139	721
	MCDONALD, Michael L.	(301)946-0278	803
	MERINGOLO, Joseph A.	(202)872-7689	826
	MYERS, R D.	(301)681-3967	885
	NORRIS, Loretta W.	(301)587-3470	909
	PICKETT, Olivia K.	(301)434-7503	971
	PRITCHARD, Sarah M.	(301)588-8624	994
	SCHEIPS, Paul J.		1091
	TATUM, George M.	(301)236-9179	1225
	TAYLOR, Marcia E.	(301)942-6704	1227
	VAN CAMPEN, Rebecca J.	(301)890-8588	1272
	WAGNER, Lloyd F.		1292
	WALSH, Barclay		1299
Takoma Park	HICKERSON, Joseph C.	(301)270-1107	536
	IBACH, Marilyn	(301)270-8950	581
	SLOAN, Cheryl A.	(301)589-6815	1149
	WRIGHT, Arthuree M.	(301)445-1220	1370
Upper Marlboro	DICKSON, Katherine M.	(301)350-4035	301
Upperco	RAND, Pamela S.	(301)429-2958	1006
Waldorf	WOLFE, Susan J.	(301)645-4784	1361
Wheaton	KAESSINGER, Carla S.	(301)949-1477	621
	MWALIMU, Charles	(301)933-4040	884

MASSACHUSETTS

Acton	FINGERMAN, Susan M.	(617)263-1881	378
Acushnet	TAVARES, Cecelia M.	(617)995-1327	1225
Amherst	DONOHUE, Joseph	(413)545-0498	312
	FELDMAN, Laurence M.	(413)253-9404	369
Arlington	ENGLISH, Cynthia J.	(617)227-0270	350
	GRIGORIS, Lygia	(617)648-2290	470
	LUKOS, Geraldine F.	(617)646-3439	748
	PLUNKET, Linda	(617)646-7825	979
Assonet	MEDEIROS, Joseph	(617)624-4094	820
Attleboro	PREVE, Roberta J.	(617)222-7035	992
Bedford	BERGIN, Dorothy O.	(617)275-7071	86
Billerica	REID, Angea S.	(617)663-3455	1018
Bolton	BOGART, Betty B.	(617)897-7870	110
Boston	BERNARD, Bobbi	(617)353-1568	88
	BRITE, Agnes	(617)267-0369	137
	CAIN, Susan H.	(617)338-6553	171
	FOX, Susan	(617)463-3178	395
	FRYDRYK, Teresa E.	(617)482-9485	407

RESEARCHER (Cont'd)
MASSACHUSETTS (Cont'd)

Boston			
	GRAMENZ, Francis L.	(617)353-3705	457
	HAYES, Alison M.	(617)482-1776	515
	HENRY, Susan L.	(617)436-8214	529
	HERNON, Peter	(617)738-2223	532
	HUENNEKE, Judith A.	(617)282-1553	570
	KOLCZYNSKI, Charlotte A.	(617)536-5400	669
	LEASON, Jane		707
	LEVINSON, Gail	(617)437-1600	721
	MACIVER, Linda B.		756
	MATIS, Lynn	(617)973-8000	784
	MURRAY, Lynn T.	(617)330-9000	882
	NESS, Arthur J.	(617)277-1776	896
	PIGGFORD, Roland	(617)267-9400	972
	PLUNKET, Joy H.	(617)327-5175	978
	SCHATZ, Cindy A.	(617)732-2134	1090
	SHARE, Donald S.	(617)738-2242	1122
	SNIFFIN-MARINO, Megan G.	(617)738-3141	1163
	STEVENSON, Michael I.	(617)495-6374	1191
	SWANN, Thomas E.	(617)482-1360	1213
Bridgewater	CHANDRASEKHAR, Ratna	(617)697-3648	200
Brockton	RESSMEYER, Ellen H.	(617)584-8133	1024
Brookline	DONG, Tina	(617)731-3514	311
	SOVNER-RIBBLER, Judith	(617)277-2991	1170
Cambridge	ASCHMANN, Althea	(617)495-5709	35
	BURG, Barbara A.	(617)547-4762	159
	COLLINS, John W.	(617)495-4225	232
	DUCKETT, Joan	(617)495-4516	322
	EPPARD, Philip B.	(617)492-4157	351
	GROVE, Shari T.	(617)864-3563	474
	HANKAMER, Roberta A.		496
	HEACOCK, Pamela P.	(617)661-1330	518
	JACKSON, Arlyne A.	(617)492-0355	586
	KNAACK, Linda M.	(617)253-8462	663
	MARCUS, Richard S.	(617)253-2340	769
	PARKER, Susan E.	(617)495-3455	942
	PINSON, Mark	(617)492-1590	975
	WHITE, Chandlee	(617)576-9299	1330
Charlestown	CURTIN-STEVENSON, Mary C.	(617)241-9664	266
	DOWLER, Lawrence E.		315
Chelmsford	DONOVAN, Paul	(617)250-7270	312
Chestnut Hill	SEEGRABER, Frank J.		1111
Concord	BENDER, Elizabeth H.	(617)369-4222	79
	LEWONTIN, Amy	(617)369-9106	724
Dedham	LOSCALZO, Anita B.	(617)329-3964	741
Deerfield	PROPER, David R.	(413)774-5581	995
Douglas	COPPOLA, Peter A.	(617)476-2975	245
Dover	WINQUIST, Elaine W.	(617)785-0816	1355
Easthampton	MELNICK, Ralph	(413)527-3036	823
Farmingham	KING, Laurie L.	(617)877-3512	651
Fitchburg	LAMBERT, Lyn D.	(617)345-6726	690
Framingham	KRIER, Mary M.	(617)879-7594	678
Gardner	COOLIDGE, Christina L.	(617)632-6600	241
Gloucester	RHINELANDER, Mary F.	(617)281-2439	1025
Greenfield	LEE, Marilyn M.	(413)773-8477	710
Hanover	FRIEDMAN, Fred T.	(617)826-2972	403
Hanscom AFB	DUFFEK, Elizabeth A.	(617)377-4768	323
Holyoke	DUTCHER, Henry D.	(413)538-7000	329
Ipswich	DRAKE, Robert E.	(617)356-7752	318
Jamaica Plain	ALASTI, Aryt	(617)524-0411	9
	WHELAN, Julia E.	(617)522-3064	1329
Kingston	FELICETTI, Barbara W.	(617)585-5662	370
Lexington	BROWN, George F.	(617)863-5100	144
	CARTER, Walter F.	(617)860-6739	190
	HARTMAN, David G.	(617)860-6668	508
	PRUSAK, Laurence	(617)861-7580	996
	ROSENTHAL, Marylu C.	(617)862-8167	1057
Lincoln	SCHWANN, William J.	(617)259-8212	1104
Longmeadow	MCGARRY, Marie L.	(413)567-0001	805
Lowell	SLAPSYS, Richard M.	(617)452-5000	1148
Marblehead	LYNCH, Jacqueline	(617)631-0624	751
Marlborough	FERGUSON, Roberta J.	(617)481-5866	372
Medford	JONES, Frederick S.	(617)381-3345	613
Melrose	MURPHY, Eva B.	(617)665-7572	880
Millis	PERRY, Guest	(617)376-8459	960
	ROE, Georgeanne T.	(617)376-8459	1048
Milton	OPPENHEIM, Roberta A.	(617)698-6268	925

RESEARCHER (Cont'd)
MASSACHUSETTS (Cont'd)

Natick	DLOTT, Nancy B.	(617)655-9163	306
Needham	FRIEND, Ann S.	(617)449-1592	404
	TSENG, Louisa	(617)449-3630	1260
Needham Heights	ORENSTEIN, Ruth M.		925
Newton	ALPERT, Hillel R.		17
	ROFF, Jill R.	(617)527-4389	1049
	SARAVIS, Judith A.	(617)969-6852	1082
North Abington	LAROSA, Sharon M.	(617)871-6288	698
North Attleboro	VIGORITO, Patricia M.	(617)699-2342	1284
North Falmouth	FOSTER, Joan		392
North Quincy	NIELSEN, Sonja M.	(617)328-8306	903
Norwood	DELTANO, Pauline T.	(617)762-5300	290
Orange	PROUTY, Sharman E.	(617)544-6743	996
Palmer	BERNAT, Mary A.		88
Quincy	WHEALAN, Ronald E.	(617)479-3297	1328
Randolph	HALL, Robert G.	(617)963-8549	488
Reading	DAMICO, Nancy B.	(617)944-9411	272
	SARAIDARIDIS, Susan B.		1082
Revere	TATELMAN, Susan D.	(617)284-0154	1225
Roybury	SUTTON, Joyce A.	(617)427-4941	1211
Sagamore	OLIANSKY, Joseph D.	(617)888-6189	920
Salem	PANGALLO, Karen L.		938
	SCHWALLER, Marian C.	(617)744-0076	1104
	WHITNEY, Howard F.	(617)744-1769	1334
Sharon	AVERILL, Laurie J.	(617)784-7329	41
	FRAZIER, James A.	(617)784-5642	399
Somerville	STAACK, Katherine A.	(617)623-1147	1177
Springfield	DELZELL, William R.	(413)737-7000	290
	LAPIERRE, Barbe	(413)739-3871	697
	TAUPIER, Andrea S.	(413)788-3315	1225
Sudbury	KOVED, Ruth B.	(617)443-3591	674
Swampscott	BRENNER, Lawrence	(617)598-0370	133
Taunton	TURKALO, David M.	(617)824-8769	1263
Waban	CHERNIN, David A.	(617)731-6760	206
Wakefield	BOZOIAN, Paula	(617)438-0779	124
Walpole	ESTES, Pamela J.	(617)668-3076	355
Watertown	BAKST, Shelley D.	(617)872-8200	50
Wellesley	SHERER, Elaine R.	(617)237-1100	1127
West Groton	BARRINGER, Nancy F.	(617)448-2125	59
West Newton	CHEN, Ching C.	(617)738-2224	205
West Springfield	PECK, Ruth M.	(413)736-0989	953
Westhampton	LOMBARDO, Daniel J.	(413)527-1796	738
Weston	KEENAN, Elizabeth L.	(617)893-1820	634
Westport	GIBBS, Paige	(617)674-6712	431
Westwood	KNAPP, Leslie C.	(617)329-3350	663
	KRUKONIS, Perkunas P.	(617)329-3350	680
Winchester	DAY, Virginia M.	(617)729-6026	283
Woods Hole	BROWNLOW, Judith	(617)548-5123	148
Worcester	ANDREWS, Peter J.		27
	KASPERSON, Jeanne X.	(617)793-7133	629
	ROCHELEAU, Kathleen D.	(617)793-7319	1046
Yarmouthport	STEEVES, Henry A.		1184

MICHIGAN

Adrian	BAKER, Jean S.	(517)263-0731	48
Ann Arbor	ANDERSEN, H F.	(313)936-7573	21
	BENNETT, Christine H.	(313)769-8500	81
	BENSON, Peggy	(313)665-0651	83
	BIGGS, Debra R.	(313)763-7080	95
	BOWEN, Jennifer B.	(313)663-6164	120
	CONWAY, Paul L.	(313)668-2218	239
	DAVIDSEN, Susanna L.	(313)995-7352	276
	DURRANCE, Joan C.	(313)763-1569	328
	DWOSKIN, Beth M.	(212)382-6727	330
	FINERMAN, Carol B.	(313)995-4485	378
	HALL, Jo A.	(313)936-0132	488
	KOCHEN, Manfred	(313)764-2585	667
	LEARY, Margaret R.	(313)663-7324	707
	NICHOLS, Darlene P.	(313)764-4479	901
	PAO, Miranda L.	(313)747-3611	938
	SCHWARTZ, Diane G.	(313)763-2037	1104
	SLAVENS, Thomas P.	(313)665-6663	1148
	SMILLIE, Pauline A.	(313)665-8821	1151
	SWEET, Robert E.	(313)246-6204	1215
	TAYLOR, Margaret T.	(313)747-3592	1227
	TERWILLIGER, Doris H.	(313)761-3912	1232
	WARNER, Robert M.	(313)763-2281	1305
	WISE, Virginia J.	(313)663-5674	1357

RESEARCHER (Cont'd)
MICHIGAN (Cont'd)

Ann Arbor	YORK, Grace A.	(313)971-4732	1381
Auburn Hills	WILLIAMS, Calvin	(313)853-4226	1342
Belleville	STARESINA, Lois J.	(313)699-7549	1181
Berkley	MARLOW, Cecilia A.	(313)547-3098	772
Birmingham	GOLDSTEIN, Doris R.	(313)626-9299	446
	IRWIN, Lawrence L.	(313)626-5339	584
	ROSE, Sharon G.	(313)647-4148	1055
Bloomfield Hills	HERBST, Linda R.	(313)642-5800	530
	KELLEY, Barbara C.	(313)646-8086	636
Canton	BRYANT, Barton B.	(313)397-3660	152
Cedar Springs	RANSOM-BERGSTROM, Janette F.	(616)696-3428	1008
Cheboygan	SMALLWOOD, Carol A.	(616)627-2308	1151
Clarkston	MEDER, Stephen A.	(313)625-5611	820
Dearborn	BREWER, Annie M.	(313)562-6871	134
	CRAWFORD, Geraldine H.	(313)271-2184	256
	FORSYTH, Karen R.	(313)562-8830	391
	LIMBACHER, James L.	(313)565-9687	727
	NUCKOLLS, Karen A.	(313)593-5400	912
	VINT, Patricia A.	(313)591-5073	1285
Dearborn Heights	KIRKESY, Oliver M.	(313)278-4670	655
Decatur	TATE, David L.	(616)423-4771	1225
Detroit	BARTKOWSKI, Patricia	(313)577-4024	61
	BISSETT, Donald J.	(313)577-1615	100
	BRAITHWAITE, Heather J.	(313)577-3925	127
	BRUNK, Thomas W.	(313)331-4930	150
	FRANTILLA, K A.	(313)972-0318	398
	GIGLIO, Linda M.	(313)872-4311	433
	HAUSMAN, Lisa M.	(313)833-1444	513
	HEINEN, Margaret A.	(313)256-7516	522
	LILLEY, Barbara A.	(313)222-3020	727
	MENDELSOHN, Loren D.	(313)577-6317	823
	OLDENBURG, Joseph F.	(313)833-4027	920
	PORTER, Jean F.	(313)961-5040	984
	RUNCHOCK, Rita M.	(313)961-2242	1067
	RZEPECKI, Arnold M.	(313)868-2700	1072
	SMITH, Michael O.	(313)577-4024	1158
	STAJNIAK, Elizabeth T.	(313)259-7110	1178
	STREETER, Linda D.		1201
	THOMAS, Laverne J.	(313)849-2776	1237
East Lansing	BLATT, Gloria T.	(313)332-6817	104
	MAYERS, Henry L.	(517)332-3442	789
	SANFORD, John D.	(517)355-2330	1081
	WOODARD, Beth E.	(517)355-5774	1365
Farmington Hills	RENKIEWICZ, Frank A.	(313)478-4506	1023
	ROBBINS, Lora A.	(313)661-6957	1039
Ferndale	BORAM, Joan M.	(313)542-2523	116
Flint	HERTZ, Sylvia	(313)733-5074	533
	MORELAND, Patricia L.	(313)762-2141	863
Grand Blanc	SCHAAFSMA, Roberta A.	(313)695-5571	1088
Grand Rapids	BRACKETT, Norman S.	(616)241-7467	124
	BURINSKI, Walter W.	(616)454-9635	160
	DE KLERK, Peter	(616)957-6303	288
	FITZPATRICK, Nancy C.	(616)676-1568	383
	KING, Kathryn L.		651
	MATTESON, James S.	(616)245-9368	785
	SIEBERS, Bruce L.	(616)774-2167	1135
	WEAVER, Clarence L.		1312
Grosse Pointe Woods	STRATELAK, Nadia A.	(313)886-1043	1200
	WAYLAND, Marilyn T.		1311
Hancock	PENTI, Marsha E.	(906)482-5300	957
Haslett	OLIVER, James W.	(517)339-0846	921
Jackson	SMITH, Catherine A.	(517)784-7025	1153
Kalamazoo	GROTZINGER, Laurel A.	(616)381-1865	473
La Salle	KULL, Christine L.	(313)243-0691	683
Lansing	FRYE, Dorothy T.	(517)393-7608	407
Lincoln Park	HECK-RABI, Louise E.	(313)928-3967	520
Mt Clemens	LUFT, William	(313)791-3418	747
Mt Pleasant	TIMBERS, Jill G.		1245
Novi	COREY, Marjorie	(313)344-1770	246
Oak Park	PERECMAN, Carol J.	(313)968-8719	958
Olivet	COOPER, B L.	(616)749-7618	242
	EVANS, Kathy J.	(616)749-9431	357
Parchment	BOURGEOIS, Ann M.	(616)344-9097	119
Port Huron	ARNETT, Stanley K.	(313)987-7323	33
	WU, Harry P.	(313)982-2765	1373

RESEARCHER (Cont'd)
MICHIGAN (Cont'd)

Rochester	HILDEBRAND, Linda L.	(313)370-2483	538
Romeo	NOWICKE, Carole E.	(313)752-6664	911
Saint Clair Shores	AMES, Kay L.	(313)773-7054	20
Saint Joseph	WOJCIKIEWICZ, Carol A.	(616)429-8618	1359
Springfield	BURHANS, Barbara C.	(616)965-4096	159
Traverse City	SICILIANO, Peg P.	(616)947-1480	1135
Trenton	GREEN, Katherine A.		462
Troy	COREY, Glenn M.	(313)689-0600	246
	STEPHENS, Karen L.	(313)879-6856	1188
Utica	HORNE, Ernest L.	(313)731-4374	560
Warren	DOYLE, James M.	(313)445-7401	317
	HENSON, Ruby P.	(313)751-4331	530
West Bloomfield	FEDER, Carol S.	(313)851-5822	367
	WREN, James A.	(313)682-6310	1370
Westland	SHAFER, Steven I.		1119
Ypsilanti	BEAL, Sarell W.	(313)483-7729	68
	YEE, Sandra G.	(313)487-2220	1379

MINNESOTA

Bloomington	NAUEN, Lindsay B.	(612)854-2879	889
Duluth	ENRICI, Pamela L.	(218)726-8586	350
Embarrass	ESALA, Lillian H.	(218)741-3434	354
Hopkins	YOUNG, Margaret L.	(612)933-5062	1382
Kilkenny	HAMMARGREN, Betty L.	(507)595-2575	493
Mankato	FARNER, Susan G.	(507)389-5957	365
	HITT, Charles J.	(507)625-4834	544
Marine on St Croix	FULLER, Sherrilynne S.	(612)433-3893	409
Minneapolis	ABELES, Tom		2
	ASPNES, Grieg G.	(612)926-1749	37
	BARRETT, Darryl D.	(612)370-0869	59
	BEDOR, Kathleen M.	(612)823-3945	73
	BRUEMMER, Bruce H.	(612)624-5050	149
	BRUTON, Robert T.	(612)540-1084	151
	CARLSON, Stan W.	(612)571-2046	182
	CORCORAN, Nancy L.	(612)623-1086	246
	JOHNSON, Donald C.		603
	LATHROP, Alan K.	(612)789-4046	701
	MIRANDA, Esmeralda C.	(612)437-0245	847
	O'LEARY, Mary E.	(612)872-4399	920
	OLSEN, Stephen	(612)333-9307	922
	OLSON, Lowell E.	(612)626-0824	923
	POQUETTE, Mary L.	(612)377-6691	984
	RAFTER, Susan	(618)870-1935	1003
	REES, Warren D.	(612)625-4309	1016
	ROSSMAN, Muriel J.	(612)624-4002	1059
	RUBENS, Donna J.	(612)624-7082	1064
	SKELLY, Laurie J.	(612)823-2556	1146
	SOLSETH, Gwenn M.	(612)330-6936	1166
	TERTELL, Susan M.	(612)372-6658	1232
	WALDEN, Barbara L.	(612)624-5860	1294
	WARPHEA, Rita C.	(612)588-6985	1306
	WEEKS, John M.	(612)624-6833	1315
	WITT, Kenneth W.	(612)871-4262	1358
	YAHNKE, Robert E.	(612)625-0504	1376
Minnetonka	HUTTNER, Marian A.	(612)545-2338	579
Northfield	SANFORD, Carolyn C.	(507)663-4266	1081
Red Wing	SWEEN, Roger	(612)388-5723	1214
Robbinsdale	OSIER, Donald V.	(612)533-5025	928
Rochester	ERWIN, Patricia J.	(507)288-8560	353
	KEY, Jack D.	(507)284-2068	645
Roseville	KAUFENBERG, Jane M.	(612)642-9221	630
St Paul	ANDERSON, Rebekah E.	(612)733-9057	25
	BLUMBERG-MCKEE, Hazel	(612)292-1680	107
	BROGAN, Martha L.	(612)698-1186	139
	CATHCART, Marilyn S.	(612)646-0254	195
	COLOKATHIS, Jane	(612)297-4969	234
	DANIELS, Paul A.	(612)611-3205	273
	DELOACH, Lynda J.	(612)627-4208	290
	HALES-MABRY, Celia E.	(612)645-2850	486
	HOLT, Constance W.	(612)690-6599	554
	JESSEE, W S.	(612)647-1329	600
	MCKEE, James E.	(612)228-2500	810
	MINOR, Barbara G.	(612)698-4978	846
	NEVIN, Susanne	(612)625-1898	898
	OLSON, Carol A.	(612)484-8391	922
	OLSON, Ray A.	(612)484-8391	923
	RICCI, Patricia L.	(612)771-4764	1026
	SCHMIDT, Jean M.		1095

RESEARCHER (Cont'd)
MINNESOTA (Cont'd)

St Paul			
	TURNER, Ann S.	(612)291-9340	1264
	WALSTROM, Jon L.	(612)296-4543	1300
	WHITE, William T.	(612)227-9531	1332
St Peter	ESSLINGER, Guenter W.	(507)931-7569	355
Scandia	HANSEN, Kathelen L.	(612)433-5477	497
Waite Park	CLARKE, Norman F.	(612)253-2695	219

MISSISSIPPI

Biloxi	VANCE, Mary L.		1273
Cleveland	STEWART, Jeanne E.	(601)843-2774	1192
Hattiesburg	CARNOVALE, A N.	(601)264-5452	184
	HAUTH, Allan C.	(601)266-4126	513
	JONES, Dolores B.	(601)266-4349	612
Itta Bena	BOWEN, Ethel B.	(601)254-9041	120
Jackson	SANDERS, Lou H.	(601)982-7094	1080
Laurel	CLARK, Diane E.	(601)649-6374	216
Mississippi State	WELLS, Anne S.	(601)325-7679	1322
Mount Olive	BOYD, Sandra E.	(601)797-3334	123
Oxford	HARPER, Laura G.	(601)234-1812	503
University	FISHER, Benjamin F.		380
Vicksburg	BLACK, Bernice B.	(601)636-1990	101

MISSOURI

Afton	WOHLRABE, John C.	(314)843-8131	1359
Chesterfield	GOLDMAN, Teri B.		446
Columbia	ARCHER, Stephen M.	(314)442-0611	31
	BARNES, Everett W.	(314)882-4581	57
	ELS, Nancy T.	(314)882-9162	346
	HAVENER, Ralph S.	(314)882-4602	513
	HOWELL, Margaret A.	(314)882-7461	565
	MCKININ, Emma J.	(314)442-4419	811
	MITCHELL, Joyce A.	(314)882-6966	849
	MULTER, Ell P.		878
	POWELL, Ronald R.	(314)882-9545	988
	SHAUGHNESSY, Thomas W.	(314)882-4701	1123
	STEVENS, Robert R.	(314)445-5320	1191
	WADE, D J.	(314)449-5958	1290
	WATERS, Bill F.	(314)443-3161	1308
Creve Coeur	GAFFEY, Mary V.	(314)432-7726	411
Florissant	ANTHONY, Paul L.	(314)921-6158	29
	BLANKENSHIP, Phyllis E.	(314)839-3966	104
Independence	BRILEY, Carol A.	(816)833-1400	136
	MEYERS, Martha L.	(816)833-1472	831
	VOSS, Kathryn J.	(816)836-8100	1289
Kansas City	CARSON, Bonnie L.		188
	DRAYSON, Pamela K.	(816)753-7600	318
	GINDRA, Janice J.	(816)842-3600	437
	INGERSOL, Robert S.	(816)333-7000	582
	KARNS, Kermit B.	(816)453-1294	627
	LABUDDE, Kenneth J.	(816)531-0770	686
	LINEBACH, Laura M.	(816)361-7031	730
	PETERSON, Paul A.	(816)363-5020	964
	RUBY, Carolyn M.		1065
Kirksville	ELLEBRACHT, Eleanor V.	(816)665-6158	343
Kirkwood	SHALLENBERGER, Anna F.	(314)821-4169	1119
	SNYDER, Elizabeth A.	(314)965-7421	1164
Linn	PARKES, Darla J.		942
Ozark	WARNER, Wayne E.	(417)485-3972	1305
Parkville	SMITH, Harold F.	(816)741-6085	1155
St Louis	BAERWALD, Susan M.	(314)772-1364	45
	CRAWFORD, Susan Y.	(314)362-7080	257
	DELIVUK, John A.	(314)645-1324	289
	GELINNE, Michael S.	(314)694-4748	426
	GIETSCHIER, Steven P.	(314)993-7787	433
	GILTINAN, Celia E.	(314)962-9048	437
	JOSEPH, Miriam E.	(314)965-4372	617
	KISSANE, Mary K.	(314)727-8865	656
	MCDERMOTT, Margaret H.	(314)889-6443	802
	MILLES, James G.	(314)658-3991	843
	NORTH, Daniel L.	(314)658-3093	909
	PERSHE, Frank F.		961
	REHKOP, Barbara L.		1017
	REINHOLD, Edna J.	(314)231-2349	1021
	RILEY, Martha J.	(314)577-5158	1034
	SIGALA, Stephanie C.	(314)721-0067	1137
	STELLING, Dwight D.	(314)351-2419	1186
	SUELFLOW, August R.	(314)721-5934	1206

RESEARCHER (Cont'd)
MISSOURI (Cont'd)
St Louis

	TIPSWORD, Thomas N.	(314)263-2345	1246
	VOLLMAR, William J.	(314)577-2279	1288
	WHITE, Cheryl L.	(314)367-0741	1330
St Peters	HICKS, James M.	(314)441-0522	537
Shelbyville	MASON, Laura L.	(816)762-4285	781
Springfield	COOMBS, James A.	(417)836-4534	241
	MORROW, Paula J.	(417)887-8161	869
	SINCLAIR, Regina A.	(417)865-8731	1143
Warrensburg	WALKER, Stephen R.	(816)429-4070	1296

MONTANA

Billings	HAUSE, Aaron H.	(406)248-3802	512
Butte	HUYGEN, Michaele L.	(406)782-8400	580
Havre	RITTER, Ann L.	(466)265-1308	1036
Heart Butte	SPOTTED EAGLE, Joy	(406)338-2282	1175
Helena	JACKSON, George R.	(406)449-3935	587
	MORROW, Delores J.	(406)444-4714	869

NEBRASKA

Lincoln	SARTORI, Eva M.		1083
	TIBBITS, Edith J.	(402)472-3545	1243

NEVADA

Boulder City	KEENE, Roberta E.	(702)293-3568	634
Carson City	DION, Kathleen L.	(702)885-5140	305
	KERSCHNER, Joan G.	(702)887-2615	644
	ROCHA, Guy L.	(702)885-5210	1045
Henderson	HARRISON, Susan E.		507
Incline	OSSOLINSKI, Lynn	(702)831-2936	928
Las Vegas	CLARK, Camille S.	(702)739-3280	216
	GARDNER, Jack I.	(702)382-3493	418
	MASTALIR, Janet K.	(702)648-7461	782
	MOUJAES, Sylva S.	(702)454-0559	873
	ORTIZ, Cynthia		927
	ORTIZ, Diane	(702)388-6501	927
	VOIT, Irene E.	(702)361-5475	1287
Reno	MANLEY, Charles W.	(702)785-4012	765
	ORCUTT, Roberta K.	(702)747-4388	925
	ZINK, Steven D.	(702)345-0659	1389

NEW HAMPSHIRE

Concord	HARE, William J.	(603)225-2012	501
	HIGGINS, Matthew J.	(603)228-3127	538
Durham	GRIFFITH, Joan C.	(603)659-3783	469
	KAPOOR, Jagdish C.	(603)868-2504	626
Franconia	BJORNER, Susan N.	(603)823-8838	100
Fremont	FARAH, Barbara D.		363
Hampton	KORBER, Nancy	(603)926-6005	671
Hanover	REED, Barbara E.	(603)646-3831	1014
	ROLETT, Virginia V.	(603)643-3593	1051
Manchester	REINGOLD, Judith S.	(603)669-5300	1021
	THOMPSON, Debra J.	(603)669-1048	1239
Merrimack	DENTON, Francesca L.	(603)424-8621	293
Nashua	FERRIGNO, Helen F.	(603)889-3042	373
	KOZIKOWSKI, Derek M.	(603)881-1057	674
Peterborough	PERRON, Michelle M.	(603)924-9281	960
Portsmouth	JACOBS, Gloria	(603)431-9346	589
	LE BLANC, Charles A.	(603)436-4866	708
Rindge	STEARNS, Melissa M.	(603)899-5111	1183
Sunapee	TATE, Joanne D.	(603)763-9948	1225
Windham	CUNNIFFE, Charlene M.	(603)434-1847	265

NEW JERSEY

Allenwood	ERBE, Evalina S.	(201)223-9388	352
Atlantic City	CROSS, Roberta A.	(609)345-2269	261
Belle Mead	LEE, J S.	(201)359-5845	710
	ODERWALD, Sara M.	(201)359-8229	916
Bergenfield	HEISE, George F.	(201)385-9741	522
Berkeley Heights	MAZURKIEWICZ, Helen L.	(201)464-0096	791
Bloomfield	SHEARIN, Cynthia E.	(201)338-6545	1124
Branchville	RAFFERTY, Stephen P.	(201)948-6380	1003
Califon	JONES, Deborah A.	(201)832-9413	612
Cherry Hill	ARROWOOD, Nina R.	(609)667-7653	35
	BENSON, James A.	(609)354-7638	83
	BROWN, Anita P.	(609)663-2247	142
	GLATT, Carol R.		440
Chester	MANY, Florence L.	(201)879-5167	767

RESEARCHER (Cont'd)
NEW JERSEY (Cont'd)

Cliffside Park	PAWSON, Robert D.	(201)943-3228	951
	ROBERTSON, Betty M.	(201)894-0235	1041
Clifton	TROJAN, Judith L.	(201)472-3868	1257
Columbus	ALITO, Martha A.	(609)298-5848	13
Cranford	BEIMAN, Frances M.	(201)272-5840	75
	HALL, Homer J.	(201)276-4311	488
	SAWYCKY, Roman A.	(201)276-3134	1086
Dayton	LAMBKIN, Claire A.	(201)329-0648	691
Demarest	MCDERMOTT, Ellen	(201)767-1618	801
Dumont	PAPAZIAN, Pierre	(201)385-8225	939
East Orange	STICKEL, William R.	(201)678-4289	1193
East Windsor	PINEL, Stephen L.	(609)448-8427	974
Elizabeth	LATINI, Samuel A.	(201)354-6060	701
	MILLER, Virginia L.	(201)351-3288	843
	SKRAMOUSKY, Mary C.	(201)351-2671	1147
Far Hills	SEAGLE, Janet M.	(201)234-2300	1109
Flemington	MCGREGOR, Walter	(201)788-3025	808
Florham Park	BYOUK, Nancy K.	(201)377-2694	168
Highland Park	BARZELATTO, Elba G.	(201)247-6248	62
	CLARK, Philip M.	(201)572-5414	218
	LI, Marjorie H.	(201)828-8730	724
	PAGE, Penny B.	(201)247-9353	934
	YUCHT, Donald J.	(201)572-0173	1384
Hoboken	PAULSON, Barbara A.	(201)420-8017	950
	SOLOMON, Geri E.	(201)420-8364	1166
Indian Mills	SCHREIBER-COIA, Barbara J.		1099
Iselin	FEDORS, Maurica R.	(201)548-5287	368
	FRANTS, Valery	(212)579-2496	398
Jersey City	PANDELAKIS, Helene S.	(201)795-8265	937
	RUBIN, Myra P.	(201)963-6456	1064
Lincroft	REESE, Carol H.	(201)842-1900	1016
Little Ferry	BOTKIN, Karen R.		118
Livingston	LIND, Judith Y.	(201)740-8704	728
Lodi	KARETZKY, Stephen	(201)778-1190	627
Long Branch	HENKEL, Grace E.	(201)229-5721	528
Madison	CONNORS, Linda E.	(201)377-3000	238
Maplewood	AUSTIN, Fay A.		40
	BRYANT, David S.	(201)763-9294	152
	LAUB, Barbara J.	(201)763-8379	702
Marlton	STRONG, Darrell G.	(609)983-1998	1203
Mendham	MANTHEY, Carolyn M.	(201)543-2129	767
	MENNIE, Don	(201)543-9520	824
Metuchen	HIGGINS, Marilyn E.	(201)321-8745	538
Millburn	URKEN, Madeline	(201)379-2306	1270
Montclair	BROWN, Cynthia D.	(201)783-6420	142
	TUROCK, Betty J.	(201)744-3354	1265
Montvale	REDRICK, Miriam J.	(201)573-9000	1014
Moorestown	SCHEPP, Brad J.	(609)778-1975	1091
Morristown	DENSKY, Lois R.	(201)539-0407	293
Mount Holly	ALTERMAN, Deborah H.	(609)261-3458	18
Mountainside	LINGELBACH, Lorene N.	(201)654-7694	730
New Brunswick	ANSELMO, Edith H.	(201)247-5610	28
	FAVORS, Thelma L.		366
	MAZZEI, Peter J.	(201)249-4120	791
	NASH, Stanley D.	(201)932-7014	888
	PUNIELLO, Francoise S.	(201)932-9346	997
	REELING, Patricia G.	(201)932-7917	1016
	RICHARDS, Pamela S.		1028
	SARACEVIC, Tefko	(201)932-7447	1082
	SMITH, Beryl K.	(201)932-7739	1153
	SWARTZBURG, Susan G.	(201)932-8573	1214
New Providence	GERBER, Warren C.		428
Newark	CUMMINGS, Charles F.	(201)733-7776	264
Nutley	GILHEANY, Rosary S.	(201)667-7013	434
Ocean	VLOYANETES, Jeanne M.	(201)493-9007	1286
Ocean City	MASON, Michael L.	(609)398-0969	781
Oradell	SUMMERS, Robert A.	(201)262-2529	1209
Paramus	CESARD, Mary A.	(201)444-4389	196
	MENTHE, Melissa		825
Parsippany	VOGT, Herwart C.	(201)263-5669	1287
Passaic	RUIZ-VALERA, Phoebe L.	(201)471-1770	1067
Paterson	ROTSAERT, Stefanie C.	(201)279-8044	1060
Pennington	KAZIMIR, Edward O.	(609)737-3582	632
Perth Amboy	HARDISH, Patrick M.	(201)826-5298	500
Piscataway	CALHOUN, Ellen	(201)932-4363	172
	FIGUEREDO, Danilo H.	(201)463-3725	376
Plainfield	KRUSE, Theodore H.	(201)725-2294	681

RESEARCHER (Cont'd)
NEW JERSEY (Cont'd)

Pomona	MOLL, Joy K.	(609)652-1776	853
Pompton Lakes	MENZUL, Faina	(201)839-6885	825
Port Murray	YRIGOYEN, Robert P.	(201)689-7069	1384
Princeton	BELCHER, Emily M.	(609)924-8947	76
	FERGUSON, Stephen	(609)452-3184	372
	MOSS, Susan K.	(609)452-1212	872
	NASE, Lois M.	(609)452-3237	888
	NEWHOUSE, Brian G.	(609)921-8803	899
	ROCK, Sue W.	(609)921-3927	1046
	ROTH, Stacy F.		1059
	SCHMIDT, Mary M.	(609)452-5860	1095
Ridgewood	JONES, Anita M.	(201)444-7273	610
	KOONTZ, John	(201)652-0185	671
Rocky Hill	MOTT, Thomas H.	(609)924-8623	872
Roselle Park	MAGEE, Patricia A.	(201)245-1963	759
Short Hills	GOLDSMITH, Carol C.	(201)376-0216	446
	HENRY, Mary K.	(201)379-4082	529
Somerdale	DALE, Charles F.	(609)346-4629	270
Somerset	GREENBERG, Linda	(201)846-8497	463
Somerville	GABRIEL, Linda	(201)874-8061	411
South Orange	BROWN, Ronald L.		147
	FAWCETT-BRANDON, Pamela S.	(201)762-0230	367
	VITART, Jane A.	(201)763-2181	1286
Spring Lake	GARVEY, Nancy G.	(201)449-4673	421
Springfield	GLADSTONE, Mark A.	(201)376-2055	439
	SCOTT, Miranda D.	(201)467-7010	1107
Stanhope	ELIASON, Elisabetha S.	(201)347-8215	342
Stratford	AVENICK, Karen	(609)784-8977	41
Summit	JOHNSON, Minnie L.	(201)273-4952	607
	SOMMER, Ursula M.	(201)593-8526	1167
Teaneck	MOUNT, Ellis	(201)836-1137	873
	ROSENSTEIN, Susan J.	(201)836-7719	1057
	TORRONE, Joan M.	(201)836-5402	1251
Tenafly	KORNFELD, Carol E.	(201)568-2231	672
Toms River	WOLPERT, Scott L.	(201)349-6200	1362
Trenton	MCCULLOUGH, Jack W.	(609)771-2106	801
Turnersville	SZILASSY, Sandor	(609)589-7193	1218
Upper Saddle River	DUDLEY, Debbra C.	(201)327-4006	323
	MICHAELS, Debbie D.	(201)327-5006	832
Warren	WEIL, Ben H.	(201)647-0892	1317
Wayne	BIDDEN, Julia E.	(201)831-7801	94
	COHEN, Adrea G.	(201)696-8948	227
	HEGG, Judith L.	(201)595-2346	521
	MCCLEAN, Vernon E.	(201)595-2579	796
West Caldwell	CARMER, Ann R.	(201)228-6981	183
West Long Branch	FISHER, Scott L.	(201)229-9222	381
	PALMISANO-DRUCKER, Elsalyn	(201)870-9194	937
West Milford	COURTNEY, Aida N.	(201)728-2823	251
West Orange	MILGRIM, Martin S.	(201)669-0545	835
Westwood	GINES, Noriko	(201)666-7042	437
Willingboro	PELLETIER, Karen E.		955
Woodbridge	DE WITT, Benjamin L.	(201)634-1316	298

NEW MEXICO

Albuquerque	GROTHEY, Mina J.	(505)277-7144	473
	IVES, Peter B.	(505)277-9243	586
	KRUG, Ruth A.	(505)277-7213	680
	MILLER, Hester M.	(505)821-4782	838
	ROLLER, Twila J.	(505)884-7871	1051
	SPURLOCK, Sandra E.	(505)828-5378	1177
	THOMPSON, Janet A.	(505)277-7172	1240
Clovis	MCBETH, Deborah E.	(505)762-7161	792
Portales	SCHOTT, Mark E.	(505)356-8735	1099
Silver City	KEIST, Sandra H.	(505)538-2663	635
Sunspot	CORNETT, John L.	(505)434-1390	247

NEW YORK

Albany	BRISKA, Boniface	(518)465-5631	137
	DENOTO, Dorothy E.	(518)449-3166	293
	MOORE, Rue I.	(518)445-5197	861
	MOREHEAD, Joe	(518)442-5128	863
	NEAT, Charles M.	(518)482-0469	891
	NITECKI, Joseph Z.	(518)442-3568	905
	PINSLEY, Lauren J.	(518)445-2342	975
	ROBERTS, Anne F.	(518)438-0607	1039
	RUBIN, David S.	(518)471-5173	1064

RESEARCHER (Cont'd)
NEW YORK (Cont'd)

Albany			
	WALSH, Daniel P.	(518)489-7968	1299
Amherst	COOVER, James B.	(176)636-2935	244
APO New York	GADBOIS, Frank W.		411
	MEIGS, Carolyn R.		821
Astoria	DAVIS, Deborah G.	(718)726-7873	278
	FISHER, Maureen C.	(718)204-0631	381
	QUARTELL, Robert J.	(718)274-7568	999
	SPINA, Marie C.	(718)274-6136	1175
Bakers Mills	SULLIVAN, Linda R.		1208
Bayside	BAKISH, David J.	(718)225-0475	50
	SHER, Deborah M.	(718)225-3435	1127
Bayville	SPIRT, Diana L.	(516)628-8341	1175
Beechhurst	CARVER, Mary		191
	DESSER, Darrilyn	(718)767-6955	296
Bergen	FABRIZIO, Timothy C.	(716)494-2264	360
Bethpage	BURDEN, John	(516)575-3912	158
Binghamton	CARPENTER, Dale	(607)797-0176	184
	COHEN, Ann E.	(607)724-9597	227
Bohemia	JENSEN, Patricia K.	(516)244-2115	599
Brewster	VELARDI, Adrienne B.	(914)279-5022	1281
Bronx	BARNETT, Philip	(212)549-5359	58
	DAVIS, Mary B.	(212)829-7770	280
	FOLTER, Siegrun H.	(212)960-8831	388
	GAROOGIAN, Rhoda	(212)588-2266	420
	GEE, Ka C.	(212)960-7770	424
	GHOSH, Subhra	(212)588-8400	430
	PATRYCH, Joseph		947
	ROY, Diptimoy	(914)668-1840	1063
	RUBEY, Daniel R.	(212)960-8580	1064
	WEINBERG, Bella H.	(212)547-5159	1317
Bronxville	BURSTEIN, Rose A.	(914)337-0700	164
Brooklundy	HAMILTON, Reatha B.		492
Brooklyn	ARMEIT, Marilyn	(718)209-1718	32
	BAKER, Zachary M.	(718)855-6318	50
	CLUNE, John R.	(718)680-7578	223
	CORRSIN, Stephen D.	(718)851-2317	247
	DIMARTINO, Diane J.	(718)783-8205	303
	DINDAYAL, Joyce S.	(718)647-1624	304
	ESSIEN, Victor K.	(718)941-9020	354
	GOTTFRIED, Erika D.	(713)852-5435	453
	GREENBERG, Roberta D.	(718)857-0146	463
	GUREWITSCH, Bonnie	(718)338-6494	478
	JAROSEK, Joan E.	(718)237-2147	594
	JOHNSON, Sheila A.	(718)780-7744	609
	KEAVENEY, Sydney S.	(718)636-3685	633
	KITT, Sandra E.		657
	KRAMER, Allan F.	(718)857-7825	675
	KRAUSS, Susan E.	(718)230-4752	676
	KUPERMAN, Aaron W.	(718)854-8637	684
	LANDOLFI, Lisa M.	(718)853-7871	693
	MANBECK, Virginia B.	(718)253-9413	764
	MARSHAK, Bonnie L.	(718)638-6821	773
	MATTERA, Joseph J.	(718)935-1746	785
	MEYERS, Charles	(718)342-1144	830
	NARDUCCI, Frances	(718)743-6001	888
	NEUBERG, Karen S.	(718)627-9796	897
	ORR, Coleridge W.	(718)934-5971	926
	PRUITT, Brenda T.	(718)287-1681	996
	ROGINSKI, James W.	(718)499-4850	1050
	SCHWABACHER, Sara A.	(718)388-0023	1104
	STANKIEWICZ, Carol A.	(718)858-5580	1180
	SULTANOF, Jeff B.	(718)768-1611	1208
	TANNER, Ellen B.	(718)780-3195	1222
	TUDIVER, Lillian	(718)789-7220	1262
	WAHLERT, George A.	(718)833-1899	1292
	WENGER, Milton B.	(718)252-5019	1324
Buffalo	BOBINSKI, George S.	(716)636-2412	108
	BRADLEY, Carol J.	(716)636-2935	125
	COTY, Patricia A.	(716)636-3377	250
	DONG, Alvin L.	(716)636-2101	311
	GARLAND, Kathleen	(716)636-3068	419
	KARCH, Linda S.	(716)827-2323	627
	KASE-MCLAREN, Karen A.	(716)838-6610	628
	SZEMRAJ, Edward R.	(716)895-7675	1218
	WAGNER, Stephen K.	(716)837-1563	1292
	WELLS, Margaret R.	(716)636-2943	1322
	WOLFE, Theresa L.	(716)632-4491	1361

RESEARCHER (Cont'd)
NEW YORK (Cont'd)

Carle Place	HABER, Elinor L.	(516)877-1190	480
Centerport	COOPER, Catherine M.	(516)754-9262	242
Chappaqua	DI BIANCO, Phyllis R.	(914)238-3911	299
Clarence Ctr	CHAPMAN, Renee D.	(716)741-9644	202
Clinton	ANTHONY, Mary M.	(315)737-8347	28
Cohoes	PINGITORE, Patricia E.		974
Cold Spring	BARNHART, David K.	(914)265-2822	58
Cold Spring Harbor	FARAONE, Maria B.	(516)271-1771	363
	MACCALLUM, Barbara B.		754
Commack	SHAPIRO, Barbara S.	(516)368-4143	1121
Corning	HORNICK-LOCKARD, Barbara A.	(607)962-9251	560
Corona	KINYATTI, Njoki W.	(718)592-4782	653
Croton-on-Hudson	CLARKE, Elizabeth S.	(914)271-3729	218
	TUCKERMAN, Susan	(914)271-5723	1262
Delhi	SEN, Joyce H.	(607)746-7350	1115
Delmar	BRESLIN, Ellen R.	(518)439-7568	133
	GRAVLEE, Diane D.	(518)439-7983	459
	POLAND, Ursula H.	(518)439-6872	980
Dewitt	SHRIER, Helene F.	(315)446-5971	1133
East Aurora	UTTS, Janet R.	(716)655-0031	1270
East Meadow	MCCARTNEY, Margaret M.	(516)489-8136	794
East Northport	O'KEEFE, Laura K.		919
East Patchogue	CANTWELL, Mickey A.	(516)475-7007	179
	PLUMER, F I.	(516)289-3134	978
East Rockaway	WONSEVER, Eithne C.	(516)599-0812	1363
East Setauket	ALBERTUS, Donna M.		10
Elmhurst	HSU, Elizabeth L.	(718)271-6623	567
Flushing	COOPER, Marianne	(718)520-7194	243
	DUTIKOW, Irene V.	(718)939-7382	329
	MACOMBER, Nancy	(718)523-5707	758
	MATTHEOU, Antonia	(718)591-9342	785
	PENCHANSKY, Mimi B.	(718)520-7248	956
	RATZABI, Arlene	(718)479-7238	1010
	RORICK, William C.	(718)520-7345	1054
	SAFRAN, Scott A.	(718)445-6752	1074
	SURPRENANT, Thomas T.	(718)520-7194	1210
Forest Hills	GELLER, Lawrence D.		426
	NERBOSO, Donna L.	(718)897-9826	895
	REMUSAT, Suzanne L.	(718)263-2218	1023
	VAN BRUNT, Amy S.	(718)261-0313	1272
Freeport	NOTARSTEFANO, Vincent C.	(516)379-3245	910
Fulton	REED, Catherine A.	(315)598-3435	1015
Garden City	DOCTOROW, Erica	(516)663-1042	307
Getzville	DENSMORE, Christopher	(716)688-2001	293
Glen Cove	WINCKLER, Paul A.	(516)671-0928	1354
Glendale	SOSTACK, Maura	(718)417-8242	1169
Grand Island	WATERS, Betsy M.		1308
Great Neck	DAMON, Shirley J.	(516)482-1202	272
	POHL, Gunther E.	(516)482-6037	979
Hamilton	BERGEN, Daniel P.	(315)824-2381	85
Hempstead	LOUISDHON-WALTER, Marie L.	(718)990-0767	742
	STERN, Marc J.	(516)560-5975	1189
Hewlett	WILLER, Kenneth H.		1341
Hicksville	EDWARDS, Harriet M.		337
	SCHMIDTMANN, Nancy K.	(516)433-7040	1096
Highland	CRAWFORD-OPPENHIEME-R, Christine	(914)691-2734	257
	RANKIN, Carol A.	(914)691-2275	1007
Houghton	LAUER, Jonathan D.	(716)567-2211	702
Hudson	HENDRICKS, Elaine M.		527
Huntington	CLOWE, Isabel B.	(516)385-9012	223
	FALVEY, Genemary H.	(516)673-0015	363
	ROSAR, Virginia W.	(516)549-4576	1054
Huntington Station	ROSS, David J.	(516)385-4951	1058
Hyde Park	GRIFFITH, Sheryl	(914)229-8114	469
Islip Terrace	KLATT, Wilma F.	(516)581-5933	658
Ithaca	ASHMUN, Lawrence F.		36
	OLSEN, Wallace C.	(607)255-2551	922
	SALTON, Gerard	(607)255-4117	1077
	SCHNEDEKER, Donald W.	(607)255-3389	1096
	ZASLAW, Neal	(607)257-1052	1386
Jackson Heights	RANHAND, Jori L.	(718)469-4728	1007
	SPYROS, Marsha L.	(718)424-7849	1177

RESEARCHER (Cont'd)
NEW YORK (Cont'd)

Jamaica	HODGES, Phyllis	(718)949-3213	546
	JOHNSON, James G.	(718)739-6503	605
	MARKE, Julius J.	(718)990-6759	771
	SHAPIRO, Martin P.	(718)990-0760	1121
	VENER, Lucille	(718)990-0761	1282
Kenmore	RYBARCZYK, Barclay S.	(716)877-0605	1071
Kew Gardens	THAU, Richard	(718)847-7736	1234
Kings Park	PANDIT, Jyoti P.	(516)269-1070	937
Lake Success	TRINKOFF, Elaine	(516)466-9148	1257
Larchmont	LANDMAN, Lillian L.	(914)834-3225	693
Latham	BRUNELLE, Bette S.	(518)783-1161	150
Lindenhurst	MONTALBANO, James J.	(516)884-8670	855
Lynbrook	HAYES, Jude T.	(516)887-2493	516
Manhasset	DEE, Camille C.		286
Marlboro	BAKER, Marie A.	(914)236-4441	49
Massapequa	REID, Richard C.	(516)795-0262	1019
Massapequa Park	GIANNATTASI, Gerard E.	(516)541-6584	430
Mastic	MACINICK, James W.	(516)399-3281	755
Mattituck	PERLMAN, Stephen E.	(516)298-4335	959
Medina	TUOHEY, Jeanne D.	(716)798-2285	1263
Menands	LENZ, Millicent A.		716
Miller Place	TODOSOW, Helen K.	(516)928-7174	1248
Mineola	TISHLER, Amnon	(516)294-7224	1247
Monticello	DORN, Robert J.	(914)794-4660	313
Mt Sinai	COHEN, Rosemary C.	(516)473-8717	229
Mt Vernon	OCKENE, David L.	(914)699-0949	915
	ROSSWURM, K M.	(914)667-6836	1059
	SEITZ, Robert J.	(914)699-6917	1113
	SHERRILL, Jocelyn T.	(914)667-4190	1129
Nassau	CARABATEAS, Clarissa D.		180
	LIPETZ, Ben A.	(518)766-3014	732
	VANNORTWICK, Barbara L.	(518)766-4190	1276
Nesconset	GRUNDT, Leonard	(516)361-8987	475
New Hyde Park	FLANZRAICH, Gerri	(516)741-2831	384
New Paltz	O'CONNELL, Susan	(914)255-5987	915
New Rochelle	KONOVALOFF, Maria S.		670
	SWANSON, Mary A.	(914)633-3954	1213
New York	AMISON, Mary V.	(212)666-9645	20
	ARMSTRONG, Joanne D.	(212)280-3743	32
	AUFSES, Harriet W.	(212)410-6056	39
	BADERTSCHER, David G.	(212)374-5615	44
	BANKS-ISZARD, Kimberly K.	(212)280-5658	54
	BARR, Jeffrey A.	(212)691-2389	58
	BATES, Ellen	(212)503-8007	63
	BEALER, Jane A.	(212)355-0083	68
	BENNIN, Cheryl S.	(212)685-5885	82
	BERGFELD, C D.	(212)496-2668	86
	BERNSTEIN, Mark P.		89
	BIDDLE, Stanton F.	(212)725-3032	94
	BOURKE, Thomas A.	(212)930-0838	119
	BOWEN, Christopher E.	(212)815-8200	120
	BOWLEY, Craig	(212)239-0827	121
	BOZIWICK, George E.	(212)870-1675	124
	BRAYTON, Roy S.		130
	BRISTAH, Pamela J.	(212)749-2802	137
	BRODY, Catherine T.	(212)228-7863	139
	BRUGNOLOTTI, Phyllis T.	(212)873-0677	150
	BULLOCK, Frances E.	(212)666-9037	156
	BURROUGHS, Christine M.	(212)751-3122	163
	BUSSEY, Holly J.	(212)708-5181	165
	CAMBRIA, Roberto		174
	CAMPBELL, Francis D.	(212)234-3130	176
	CAPRIELIAN, Arevig	(718)459-2757	180
	CHITTAMPALLI, Padma S.	(212)874-0141	209
	CHO-PARK, Jaung J.	(212)280-2293	210
	CHRISTENSON, Janet S.	(212)930-0686	211
	CIOPPA, Lawrence	(212)677-5688	214
	COHEN, Frederick S.	(212)594-9880	228
	COOPER, Jo E.	(212)808-6515	243
	COPLEN, Ron	(212)869-3348	244
	COVERT, Nadine	(212)988-4876	252
	CURTIS, James A.	(212)222-9638	267
	DAGATA, Marie	(212)546-2507	269
	DARNOWSKI, Christina M.	(212)750-5749	275
	DEMANDY, Claire	(212)960-8575	291
	DEVERA, Rosalinda M.	(212)557-2570	297
	DISHON, Robert M.	(212)254-2257	305
	DOOLING, Marie	(212)510-4375	312

RESEARCHER (Cont'd)
NEW YORK (Cont'd)
New York

DUNLAP, Barbara J.	(212)690-5367	326
ENGLER, Gretchen	(212)703-4127	349
EPPES, William D.	(212)675-2070	351
FEBLES, Mary T.	(212)210-3983	367
FENTON, Joan T.	(212)682-2500	371
FLEISHMAN, Lauren Z.	(212)371-2000	384
FLOERSHEIMER, Lee M.	(212)787-3727	385
FOLTER, Roland	(212)687-4808	388
FRANKLIN, Linda C.	(212)679-6038	398
FRIEDMAN, Judy B.		404
FRUSCIANO, Thomas J.	(212)998-2644	406
GARDNER, Ralph D.	(212)877-6820	418
GESKE, Aina S.		430
GLASFORD, G R.	(212)669-3336	440
GOLD, Hilary G.	(212)242-2180	444
GOLLOP, Sandra G.	(212)770-7911	447
GOODMAN, Edward C.	(212)280-8407	449
GOTTLIEB, Jane E.	(212)362-8671	453
GRANDE, Paula G.	(212)536-3229	457
GRECH, Anthony P.	(212)382-6740	461
GRETES, Frances C.	(212)309-9634	467
GROTE, Janet H.	(212)627-1500	473
GUBERT, Betty K.	(212)362-4256	475
GUILER, Paula J.	(212)689-3341	476
HALL, Alix M.	(212)536-3598	486
HAND, Sally C.	(212)940-3100	494
HARVEY, John F.	(215)509-2612	509
HAVENS, Shirley E.	(212)463-6804	513
HENDERSON, Brad	(212)666-2674	526
HENDERSON, Janice E.	(212)687-0400	526
HERMAN, Marsha	(212)679-6105	531
HEUMAN, Rabbi F.	(212)505-2174	535
HIGGINS, Steven	(212)674-2087	538
JONES, Roger A.	(212)777-2959	615
JURIST, Janet	(212)737-8120	620
KAIN, Joan P.	(212)850-0768	622
KAPNICK, Laura B.	(212)975-2917	626
KARATNYTSKY, Christine A.	(212)420-1436	627
KEMPE, Deborah A.	(212)595-6583	639
KENSELAAR, Robert	(212)870-1661	642
KING, Trina E.	(212)427-1023	652
KLECKNER, Simone M.	(212)877-2448	658
KLEIMAN, Rhoda E.	(212)247-2650	659
KOLATA, Judith	(212)902-0080	669
KULLESEID, Eleanor R.	(212)666-6013	683
LAMBE, Michael	(212)371-9400	690
LAWRENCE, Arthur P.	(212)505-7996	704
LEE, Sang C.	(212)669-7961	711
LEVINSON, Debra J.		721
LEWIS, Anne	(212)906-1200	722
LILLY, Elise M.	(212)940-8596	727
LINDGREN, Arla M.	(212)662-6386	729
LUBETSKI, Edith E.	(212)340-7720	745
MACK, Phyllis G.	(212)926-2479	756
MARGALITH, Helen M.	(212)575-0190	770
MARGOLIES, Alan	(212)489-5042	770
MARTIN, Jean F.	(212)928-4231	776
MAYER, George L.	(212)724-8057	789
MERKIN, David	(212)837-6588	826
MIHRAM, Danielle	(212)998-2515	834
MINTZ, Anne P.	(212)620-2499	847
MOLZ, Redmond K.	(212)280-4787	854
MOONEY, James E.	(212)873-3400	858
MOORE, Sonia	(212)755-5120	861
MORRIS, Irving	(718)728-4078	866
MORRIS, Margaret J.	(212)682-2500	867
MOSES, Julian M.	(212)688-8426	871
MOTIHAR, Kamla	(212)838-8400	872
MOUNIR, Khalil A.	(212)373-5640	873
MOUNT, Albertina F.	(212)305-2916	873
MYERS, Maria P.	(212)473-6673	884
NARCISO, Susan D.	(212)260-0718	888
O'CONNELL, Brian E.	(212)873-5860	915
O'GRADY, Jean P.	(212)370-8690	918
OSTROW, Rona	(212)691-1672	929
OSTROWSKY, Edith	(212)340-0890	929
OSTWALD, Mark F.		929

RESEARCHER (Cont'd)
NEW YORK (Cont'd)
New York

	PALMER, Julia R.	(212)744-7202	936
	PETERS, Jean R.	(212)663-8910	962
	PETTOLINA, Anthony M.	(212)790-2888	965
	PIDALA, Veronica C.		971
	PINEDA, Conchita J.	(212)371-5188	974
	PINES, Doralynn	(212)570-3969	974
	PISTILLI, Susan A.	(212)621-1580	976
	POLLARD, Bobbie T.	(212)725-7648	981
	POLSTER, Joanne	(212)564-7640	982
	POTEAT, James B.	(212)759-6800	986
	RABER, Steven	(212)839-7161	1001
	RACHOW, Louis A.	(212)228-7610	1001
	RAUCH, Anne	(212)906-8794	1010
	RAUM, Tamar	(212)889-2156	1010
	REMECZKI, Paul W.	(212)873-3400	1022
	RHODES, Deborah L.		1026
	RIPIN, Laura G.	(212)480-6649	1035
	ROBERTS, Gloria A.	(212)535-2985	1040
	ROJAS, Alexandra A.	(212)489-9500	1051
	ROSEN, Nathan A.	(212)873-1017	1055
	SALBER, Peter J.	(212)350-4680	1076
	SALY, Alan J.	(212)475-5400	1078
	SARRIS, Shirley C.	(212)473-2990	1083
	SAVADA, Morton J.	(212)695-7155	1085
	SAYWARD, Nick H.	(212)573-4798	1087
	SETTANNI, Joseph A.	(212)289-9059	1117
	SHAPIRO, Barbara G.	(212)621-1582	1121
	SHAPIRO, Fred R.	(203)432-1600	1121
	SHERBY, Louise S.	(212)280-2241	1127
	SHIROMA, Susan G.	(212)998-2602	1131
	SLATE, Ted	(212)350-4682	1148
	SLOCUM, Leslie E.	(212)759-6800	1150
	SOROBAY, Roman T.	(212)878-9314	1169
	SPIER, Margaret M.	(212)337-6983	1174
	SPRUNG, George	(212)362-9389	1176
	STALKER, Dianne S.	(212)280-8484	1178
	STEVENSON, Mata	(212)759-9883	1191
	SULLIVAN, Stephen W.		1208
	SWANSON, Dorothy T.	(212)998-2630	1213
	SZMUK, Szilvia E.	(212)787-2573	1218
	TAYLOR, Robert N.	(212)664-9021	1228
	TICKER, Susan L.	(212)787-2780	1244
	TOMASULO, Patricia A.	(212)472-6442	1249
	TYLER, David M.	(212)350-4679	1266
	VAUGHN, Susan J.	(212)260-2544	1280
	VELEZ, Sara B.	(212)870-1661	1281
	WALL, Richard L.	(212)586-4418	1297
	WEATHERFORD, Elizabeth	(212)925-4682	1311
	WEINBERG, Valerie A.	(212)685-0008	1318
	WERTSMAN, Vladimir F.	(212)246-8176	1325
	WISHART, H L.	(212)790-0222	1357
	WOLF, Marion	(212)360-3572	1360
	WOLFE, Allis	(212)496-0008	1360
	WRIGHT, Bernell	(212)866-3042	1370
	WRIGHT, Sylvia H.	(212)222-6148	1373
North Chatham	WELLS, Gladysann		1322
North Syracuse	AUSTIN, Ralph A.	(315)457-1799	40
North White Plains	SHADE, Ronald H.	(914)285-9583	1118
Oakdale	BEAUDRIE, Ronald A.	(516)244-3284	70
Oceanside	ROGGENKAMP, Alice M.	(516)766-1397	1050
Ogdensburg	FRANZ, David A.	(315)393-2950	398
	SMITH, Nicholas N.	(315)393-1075	1159
Old Brookville	HELLER, Jacqueline R.	(516)626-2700	524
Oneonta	CROWLEY, John V.	(607)431-2725	261
Orchard Park	LYMAN, Helen H.	(716)662-3525	751
	WILLET, Ruth J.	(716)662-3598	1341
Oswego	CHU, Sylvia	(315)341-3210	213
Palisades	KLIMLEY, Susan	(914)359-2900	661
Pearl River	BRISFJORD, Inez S.	(914)735-1567	136
	SPERR BRISFJORD, Inez L.	(914)735-1567	1173
Peekskill	CLARE, Richard W.		216
	FALCONE, Elena C.	(914)528-2820	362
Pelham	FERRIBY, Peter G.	(914)738-3712	373
Pike	KING, Charles L.	(716)493-2783	650
Plainview	SYWAK, Myron	(516)935-7821	1217
Plattsburgh	BURTON, Robert E.	(518)561-1613	164
	RANSOM, Christina R.	(518)563-5719	1007

RESEARCHER (Cont'd)
NEW YORK (Cont'd)

Port Chester	LETTIERI, Robin M.	(914)939-6710	719
Port Jervis	HOFMANN, Susan M.	(914)856-1513	548
Port Washington	SCHREIBMAN, Fay C.	(516)767-0081	1099
Poughkeepsie	LEE, Judy A.	(914)473-3719	710
	SEEBER, Frances M.	(914)452-8122	1111
Queens	BUSTAMANTE, Corazon R.	(718)361-0887	166
Queens Village	HECKMAN, Lucy T.	(718)776-6285	519
Rensselaerville	STORMS, Kate	(518)797-5154	1198
Rhinebeck	NAVRATIL, Jean		890
Riverdale	CLANCY, Kathy	(212)796-2057	215
Rochester	BARRETT, Lizabeth A.	(716)272-1905	59
	BERKMAN, Robert I.	(716)461-3206	87
	BLUM, Elaine G.	(716)423-1611	107
	BUFF, Iva M.	(716)244-7762	155
	GIGLIOTTI, Mary J.	(716)254-0621	433
	HELBERS, Catherine A.	(716)594-9652	523
	HOOD, Katherine T.	(716)454-5293	556
	HOPE, Thomas W.	(716)458-4250	557
	KARNEZIS, Kristine C.	(716)482-3221	627
	KATZ, Jacqueline E.	(716)254-7144	630
	LINDSAY, Jean S.	(716)428-7300	729
	MCGOWAN, Kathleen M.	(716)275-4437	807
	MOUREY, Deborah A.	(716)724-6819	874
	PERRY, Rodney B.	(716)482-6478	961
	PLAIN, Marilyn V.	(716)275-8210	977
	REITANO, Maimie V.	(716)722-7067	1022
	SEASE, Sandra A.	(716)724-6783	1110
	SIMMONS, Rebecca A.	(706)271-3361	1140
	STRIFE, Mary L.	(716)334-0091	1202
Ronkonkoma	SHERIDAN, Robert N.	(516)981-5739	1128
Roslyn	WEINSTEIN, Judith K.	(516)627-6200	1318
Roslyn Harbor	CARTAFALSA, Joan C.	(516)671-7411	188
Roslyn Heights	HARRIS, Martha	(516)484-0792	505
St James	WIENER, Paul B.	(516)862-8723	1336
Saratoga Springs	LEWIS, Gillian H.	(518)587-0374	723
	ROBINSON, Jolene A.	(518)583-0208	1044
Sayville	PAGELS, Helen H.	(516)589-2908	934
Scarsdale	ABEND, Jody U.	(914)723-1360	2
	COAN, Mary L.	(914)723-5325	224
	SEULOWITZ, Lois	(914)472-4097	1117
Schenectady	HOLT, Lisa A.	(518)370-1811	554
	KING, Maryde F.	(518)374-7287	651
	KLEMPNER, Irving M.	(518)393-5983	660
	SCOTT, Frances Y.	(518)346-5052	1107
Sea Cliff	LETTIS, Lucy B.		719
Setauket	THOM, Janice E.	(516)751-1484	1235
Shrub Oak	TIFFEAULT, Alice A.	(914)528-4048	1244
Somers	RITTER, Sally K.	(914)232-7889	1037
Staten Island	BARTO, Stephen C.	(718)727-8940	61
	HOGAN, Kristine K.	(718)727-1135	549
	HOGAN, Matthew	(718)273-6245	549
	KLINGLE, Philip A.	(718)390-5291	662
	KRIEGER, Tillie		678
	MANNING, Jo A.	(718)981-0120	766
	SCHUT, Grace W.	(718)442-5659	1103
	SVENNINGSEN, Karen L.	(718)987-1168	1212
Sunnyside	WOOD, Sallie B.	(718)565-5490	1365
Syracuse	BOISSY, Robert W.	(315)428-8398	111
	FROEHLICH, Thomas J.	(315)425-9080	405
	GRANKA, Bernard D.	(315)463-0875	457
	JOHNSON, Nancy B.	(315)423-2911	608
	KATZER, Jeffrey	(315)423-2911	630
	MARCHAND, Donald A.	(315)423-2736	768
	MARTIN, Thomas H.	(315)423-3840	778
	MCCLURE, Charles R.	(315)423-2911	797
	MCLAUGHLIN, Pamela W.	(315)476-7359	813
	PFOHL, Theodore E.	(315)473-4493	966
	PFOHL, Theodore E.	(315)473-4493	966
	PRINS, Johanna W.	(315)475-5534	993
	WALTZ, Mary A.	(315)478-1265	1302
	WASYLENKO, Lydia W.	(315)423-2585	1308
Three Mile Bay	PIZER, Charles R.	(315)649-5086	977
	PIZER, Elizabeth F.	(315)649-5086	977
Upton	LANE, Sandra G.	(516)282-7159	694
Utica	BROOKES, Barbara	(315)735-2279	140
	WEBER, Jerome F.	(315)732-4747	1314

RESEARCHER (Cont'd)
NEW YORK (Cont'd)

Wantagh	LOMONACO, Martha S.	(516)783-9051	738
	NOVITSKY, Edward G.		911
	WESTERMANN, Mary L.	(516)679-8842	1327
Warwick	BATTOE, Melanie K.		65
Webster	DESMOND, Andrew R.	(716)671-7657	295
West Point	MARTIN, Janet L.	(914)446-4639	776
West Valley	CURRY, Lenora Y.	(716)942-4362	266
Westhampton	BARR, Janet L.	(516)288-5539	58
Westhampton Beach	KIRSCH, Anne S.	(516)288-2492	655
White Plains	BOWLES, Edmund A.	(914)696-1900	121
	HESS, James W.	(914)592-4342	534
	HIGGINS, Judith H.	(914)949-2175	538
	MCGARVEY, Eileen B.	(914)683-2794	805
Whitestone	RIECHEL, Rosemarie	(718)990-0714	1033
Woodhaven	PAYNE, Linda C.	(718)849-1320	951
	VAZQUEZ, Edward	(718)296-2280	1280
Wynantskill	CORSARO, James		248
Yonkers	BERGER, Paula E.	(914)968-7906	86
Yorktown Heights	HAIMOVSKY, Kira A.	(914)962-5628	484
	YURO, David A.	(914)962-5200	1384

NORTH CAROLINA

Angier	FISH, Paula H.	(919)639-4331	380
Bahama	STINE, Roy S.	(719)471-8853	1194
Beaufort	BUMGARNER, John L.	(919)728-5530	157
Belmont	MAYES, Susan E.	(704)825-3711	789
Boone	BUSBIN, O M.	(704)264-7141	164
	WISE, Mintron S.	(704)262-2823	1357
	WORRELL, Diane F.		1369
Chapel Hill	CARPENTER, Raymond L.	(919)962-8364	185
	HOLLEY, Edward G.		551
	LOSEE, Robert M.	(919)962-8366	742
	MORAN, Barbara B.	(919)962-8363	862
	TUCKER, Mary E.	(919)933-8982	1262
Charlotte	BERRY, Mary W.	(704)371-4258	90
	HOWARD, Susanna J.	(704)364-7987	564
Durham	BARROWS, William D.	(919)549-0517	60
	CLEMONS, Kenneth L.	(919)688-2361	221
	DUNN, Elizabeth B.	(919)684-2373	326
	GARTRELL, Ellen G.	(919)493-3747	420
	HAZEL, Debora E.	(919)683-6473	517
	HEWITT, Joe A.	(919)489-9875	535
	LAVINE, Marcia M.	(919)684-2011	703
	MIDDLETON, Beverly D.	(919)477-8497	833
	MOORE, Scott L.	(919)684-3372	861
	SPARKS, Martha E.	(919)489-6012	1171
Elon College	JONES, Plummer A.	(919)584-2338	614
Fayetteville	DEVITO, Robert M.	(919)483-7727	297
Greensboro	LEVINSON, Catherine K.	(919)334-5419	721
	MCZORN, Bonita A.	(919)273-4886	819
	MOORE, Kathryn L.	(919)334-5419	860
	YOUNG, Tommie M.	(909)621-0032	1383
Greenville	MELLON, Constance A.	(919)757-6870	822
	SHIRES, Nancy P.	(919)758-8252	1131
	YORK, Maurice C.	(919)752-5260	1381
Jacksonville	MARTIN, Richard T.	(919)455-1221	778
Kinston	EARL, Susan R.	(919)522-4773	332
	MILLER, Sylvia G.		843
Mars Hill	PETERSON, Cynthia L.	(704)689-2380	963
Morganton	BUSH, Mary E.	(704)433-2303	165
Mt Holly	TUCKER, Mae S.		1262
Raleigh	DAVIS, Jinnie Y.	(919)737-2680	279
	MURPHY, Malinda M.	(919)821-2072	881
	RATHGEBER, Jo F.	(919)872-3323	1009
	TAYLOR, Raymond M.	(919)787-7824	1228
Reidsville	KING, Willard B.	(919)349-6192	652
Research Triangle Pk	TUTTLE, Walter A.	(919)549-0661	1266
Sanford	BEAGLE, Donald R.	(919)776-8372	68
	MATOCHIK, Michael J.	(919)776-5737	784
Winston-Salem	AHLERS, Glen P.	(919)761-5438	8
	HICKS, Michael	(919)788-4084	537
	ROWLAND, Janet M.	(919)765-2081	1062
	WOODARD, John R.	(919)761-5089	1365

RESEARCHER (Cont'd)

NORTH DAKOTA

Bismarck	GRAY, David P.	(701)224-2668	459
	VYZRALEK, Dolores E.	(701)223-1857	1290
	WEZELMAN, Joy L.	(701)222-0271	1328
Fargo	JANZEN, Deborah K.	(701)277-1865	594
Minot	ROBERTSON, Pamela S.	(701)838-6080	1042
Valley City	HOLDEN, Douglas H.	(701)845-4940	550

OHIO

Akron	GUSS, Margaret B.	(216)375-7224	478
Ashland	ROEPKE, David E.		1048
Athens	KURZ, David B.	(614)593-8505	685
	MILLER, David A.	(614)592-5692	836
	MULLINER, Kent	(614)593-2707	878
Barberton	SWINEHART, Katharine J.	(216)745-1194	1216
Bay Village	BUTCHER, Sharon L.	(216)871-0913	166
	LORANTH, Alice N.	(216)871-9014	741
Bedford	PARCH, Grace D.		939
Bowling Green	KLOPFENSTEIN, Bruce C.	(419)372-2138	662
	POVSIC, Frances F.	(419)372-2956	987
	ZAPOROZHETZ, Laurene E.	(419)354-2101	1386
Canton	ERWIN, Nancy S.	(216)477-7309	353
Chardon	KLINGER, William E.	(216)564-9340	661
Cincinnati	ALBERT, Stephen G.	(513)541-9119	10
	CONNICK, Kathleen D.	(513)474-4975	237
	DAVIS, Yvonne M.	(513)221-7699	281
	DICKMAN, Emmajane H.		301
	GILNER, David J.	(513)221-1875	437
	HALIBEY-BILYK, Christine M.	(513)559-4320	486
	HEFFRON, Sheila F.	(513)891-4200	520
	HILAND, Gerard P.	(513)231-0810	538
	HUGE, Sharon A.	(513)369-6940	571
	KRAMER, Sally J.	(513)369-6085	675
	LE BLANC, Judith E.		708
	LEIBOLD, Cynthia K.		713
	LIPPERT, Margret G.	(513)821-8733	732
	RIFFEY, Robin S.	(513)871-3087	1033
Cleveland	BORUCKI, Jennifer A.	(216)696-1313	117
	FINET, Scott	(216)687-2250	378
	MAHOVLIC, Leanne M.	(216)368-3646	761
	MICHNAY, Susan E.	(216)749-7400	832
	PEARMAN, Sara J.	(211)421-7340	952
	PETIT, J M.	(216)749-5052	965
	PRYSZLAK, Lydia M.	(216)459-2043	996
	RAY, Laura E.	(216)844-3788	1011
	SANTAVICCA, Edmund F.	(216)687-2365	1082
	VICTORY, Karen M.	(216)696-1313	1283
Cleveland Heights	BOWIE, Angela B.	(216)291-5588	121
	GRABOWSKI, John J.	(216)932-8805	455
	LANTZ, Elizabeth A.	(216)541-2905	697
	MCMAHON, Melody L.	(216)371-5744	814
	MEYER, Jimmy E.	(216)291-1948	830
	PAUSLEY, Barbara H.	(216)932-2448	950
Columbus	ALLEN, Cameron	(614)237-1516	14
	BETCHER, Melissa A.	(614)466-5511	92
	BLOUGH, Keith A.	(614)221-4181	106
	BRANCH, Susan	(614)267-3805	127
	BRANDT, Michael H.	(614)863-2814	128
	CONNELL, Christopher J.	(614)848-5193	237
	EVANS, Shirley A.	(614)860-2496	358
	GOLDING, Alfred S.		445
	HAMILTON, Marsha J.	(614)292-6314	492
	HUNE, Mary G.	(614)224-3168	574
	HUNTER, James J.	(614)461-5039	576
	IRELAND, Clara R.	(614)480-9891	583
	LINCOVE, David A.	(614)292-3480	728
	MERCADO, Heidi	(614)292-2009	825
	MILLER, Dennis P.	(614)888-1886	837
	MIMNAUGH, Ellen N.	(614)486-7755	845
	MLYNAR, Mary	(614)486-7980	850
	NORMORE, Lorraine F.	(614)421-3600	909
	OLSZEWSKI, Lawrence J.		923
	ORLANDO, Jacqueline M.	(614)262-6765	926
	POPOVICH, Charles J.	(614)292-2136	984
	RATLIFF, Priscilla	(614)488-1622	1009
	ROBINSON, David A.	(614)488-7346	1043
	SANDERS, Nancy P.		1080
	SMITH, Ellen A.	(614)462-7054	1154
	STOBAUGH, Robert E.	(614)451-3271	1195

RESEARCHER (Cont'd)

OHIO (Cont'd)

Columbus	STRALEY, Dona S.	(614)292-3362	1200
	VANBRIMMER, Barbara A.	(614)292-9810	1272
	WARNER, Susan B.	(614)424-5676	1305
	WILKS, Cheri L.	(614)253-3507	1341
	WOODS, Alan L.	(614)292-8251	1366
Cuyahoga Falls	KLINGLER, Thomas E.	(216)923-5504	662
	OSTERFIELD, George T.	(216)929-9470	928
	WAGNER, Louis F.	(216)922-0681	1292
Dayton	NOLAN, Patrick B.	(513)274-3424	907
	O'BRIEN, Betty A.	(513)433-5420	914
	QUINTEN, Rebecca G.	(513)277-3598	1000
	SEXTON, Sally V.	(513)890-1421	1118
	TRIVEDI, Harish S.	(513)225-2201	1257
	VANGROV, Helene R.	(513)274-5622	1275
Delaware	COHEN, Susan J.	(614)363-9433	229
Dublin	HURLEY, Geraldine C.	(614)764-6108	577
	PRABHA, Chandra G.	(614)764-6086	989
	SPEECE, Yvonne M.	(614)764-9555	1172
Fairborn	BAKER, Narcissa L.	(573)879-3638	49
Fairview Park	MAYNARD, Elizabeth	(216)333-1463	790
Findlay	DICKINSON, Luren E.	(419)423-4934	301
	DUDLEY, Durand S.	(419)423-1113	323
	LUST, Jeanette M.	(419)424-5739	749
Granville	LEMON, Nancy A.	(614)587-7265	715
	RUGG, John D.		1066
Hiram	WANSER, Jeffery C.	(216)569-5358	1303
Hubbard	GROHL, Arlene P.	(216)759-7800	471
Huron	CURRIE, William W.	(419)433-5560	266
Kalida	MILLER, Marian A.		840
Kent	DU MONT, Rosemary R.	(216)672-2782	325
	GATTEN, Jeffrey N.	(216)672-2516	422
	MORRIS, Trisha A.	(216)673-3464	867
	WYNAR, Lubomyr R.		1375
Kettering	ROHMILLER, Thomas D.	(513)259-4543	1051
Lakewood	JANES, Jodith	(216)221-0437	593
	KEATING, Michael F.	(216)221-0608	633
Mansfield	ROMARY, Michael P.	(419)755-4321	1052
Massillon	PLUMMER, Karen A.	(216)477-1447	978
Mayfield Heights	RASKIN, Rosa S.	(216)442-3009	1009
North Olmsted	ADAMS, Liese A.	(216)777-7560	5
North Ridgeville	FACINELLI, Jaclyn R.	(216)327-7079	360
Oberlin	RICKER, Alison S.	(216)775-8310	1031
	WEIDMAN, Jeffrey	(216)775-8635	1316
Oxford	WORTMAN, William A.	(513)529-3936	1369
Painesville	ENGEL, Carl T.	(216)354-3359	348
Parma	OBLOY, Elaine C.	(216)885-5362	914
Shaker Heights	LANDAU, Lucille	(216)283-6109	692
	MCCONNELL, Pamela J.	(216)921-7457	798
Sidney	WILSON, Memory A.	(513)492-1315	1352
South Euclid	BENSING, Karen M.	(216)932-0186	83
Steubenville	BURKE, Ambrose L.	(614)283-3771	160
Terrace Park	SEIK, Jo E.	(513)831-0780	1112
Toledo	ELLENBOGEN, Barbara R.	(419)536-4538	343
	LERNER, Esther T.	(419)531-2269	717
	WEILANT, Edward		1317
Troy	BAKER, Martha A.	(513)335-6397	49
University Heights	HECHT, Joseph A.	(216)291-5506	519
	TOTH, Georgina G.	(216)371-5832	1252
Versailles	MINNICH, Conrad H.	(513)526-4427	846
Warrensville	GORDON, Shirlee J.		452
Westerville	WILSON, Leigh K.	(614)898-3953	1351
Wooster	POWELL, Margaret S.	(216)263-2279	988
Worthington	EAST, Dennis	(614)888-9923	332
Yellow Springs	WESTNEAT, Helen C.	(513)767-1574	1327
Youngstown	LUTTRELL, Jeffrey R.	(216)742-3681	750

OKLAHOMA

Ada	HUESMANN, James L.	(405)332-7632	570
Bartlesville	ROBIN, Annabeth	(918)336-7240	1043
Midwest City	MOSLEY, Thomas E.	(405)733-0922	872
	ROBERTSON, Retha M.	(405)733-1543	1042
Norman	BATT, Fred	(405)325-4231	64
	CLARK, Harry	(405)321-0352	217
	HOVDE, David M.	(405)325-4231	563
	POLAND, Jean A.	(405)360-7095	980
	WEAVER-MEYERS, Pat L.	(405)325-3341	1313

RESEARCHER (Cont'd)
OKLAHOMA (Cont'd)

Oklahoma City	BOOTENHOFF, Rebecca J.	(405)728-7072	116
	CORNEIL, Charlotte E.	(405)235-7763	246
	DAVIS, Denyvetta	(405)424-2106	278
	HARGIS-LYTLE, Betty L.	(405)721-2134	501
	JONES, Beverly A.	(405)751-0574	611
	JONES, Charles E.	(405)751-0574	611
	LITTLE, Paul L.	(405)789-9400	733
	WEISS, Catharine H.	(405)424-3344	1320
Stillwater	ROUSE, Charlie L.	(405)372-4651	1061
	ROUSE, Roscoe	(405)377-1651	1061
	WOLFF, Cynthia J.	(405)372-0511	1361
Tahlequah	HILL, Helen K.		540
	MCQUITTY, Jeanette N.	(918)456-5511	817
	VEITH, Charles R.	(918)456-5511	1281
Tulsa	MANES, Estelle L.	(918)582-7426	765
	SEARS, Robert W.	(918)593-7573	1110
	WRIGHT, Patricia Y.	(918)585-1997	1372

OREGON

Beaverton	POND, Patricia B.	(503)641-5524	982
Corvallis	MURRAY, Lucia M.		882
Eugene	EMMENS, Thomas A.	(503)345-6439	348
	HADDERMAN, Margaret	(503)342-5457	482
	KNIEVEL, Helen A.	(503)345-2032	664
	MCDANIELS, Patricia R.	(503)343-4728	801
	MORRISON, Perry D.	(503)342-2361	868
	SHULER, John A.	(503)686-3048	1133
	STIRLING, Isabel A.	(503)686-3075	1195
	WALKER, Luise E.	(503)686-3023	1295
Forest Grove	FALZON, Judith A.	(503)357-3023	363
Hillsboro	VIXIE, Anne C.	(503)645-0527	1286
Manzanita	LARSON, Signe E.	(503)368-6990	700
Marylhurst	GIMPL, Caroline A.	(503)636-8105	437
Monmouth	GORCHELS, Clarence C.	(503)838-1274	451
	JENSEN, Gary D.	(503)838-1220	598
Philomath	REEVES, Marjorie A.	(503)929-5354	1017
Portland	DAVID, Kay O.	(503)222-9981	276
	EDWARDS, Susan E.	(506)224-6812	338
	FELDMAN, Marianne L.	(503)292-2940	369
	JUDKINS, Dolores Z.	(503)236-6743	619
	KENNEY, Ann J.	(503)297-1894	641
	SIMON, Dale	(503)227-7617	1140
	SUDDUTH, Susan F.		1206
	WRIGHT, Janet K.	(503)464-4097	1371
Roseburg	GAULKE, Mary F.	(503)440-4036	423
Tolovanna Park	NAKATA, Yuri		887

PENNSYLVANIA

Abington	BISSELL, Joann S.	(215)886-9409	100
Alcoa Center	MOUNTS, Earl L.	(412)337-2396	873
Allentown	SWARTZ, Patrice B.	(215)797-5696	1214
	WAGNER, Darla L.	(215)264-8203	1291
Altoona	SHERIDAN, Margaret G.	(814)942-2565	1127
Ambler	MORROW, Ellen B.	(215)646-1755	869
Ardmore	VLADUTZ, George E.	(215)649-1148	1286
	VLEDUTS-STOKOLOV, Natalia	(215)649-1148	1286
Baden	JABLONOWSKI, Mary D.	(412)869-2188	586
Bala Cynwyd	BOWERS, Paul A.	(215)664-9644	120
	KREMER, Jill L.	(215)667-6787	677
Bethlehem	JARVIS, William E.	(215)758-3035	595
Blue Bell	LAUTENSCHLAG, Elisabeth C.		703
	TERRY, Terese M.	(215)641-6594	1232
Braddock	SHAPIRO, Ruth T.	(412)636-5030	1121
California	NOLF, Marsha L.	(412)938-4048	908
Carlisle	NEITZ, Cordelia M.		892
Carnegie	DEBONS, Anthony	(412)279-6170	285
Catasauqua	SIMONE-HOHE, M J.	(215)262-1596	1141
Center Valley	MCCABE, James P.	(215)282-1100	793
Coatesville	KELLEY, John F.	(215)383-8147	636
Colwyn	THOMAS, Deborah A.	(215)522-1786	1236
Coraopolis	KASPERKO, Jean M.		629
Danielsville	PAGOTTO, Sarah L.	(215)767-3055	934
Dresher	FU, Clare S.	(215)641-1978	407
East Stroudsburg	SUMMERS, George V.	(717)424-3151	1209
Easton	CRAWFORD, Gregory A.	(215)253-9459	256

RESEARCHER (Cont'd)
PENNSYLVANIA (Cont'd)

Erie	ANDRICK, Annita A.	(814)455-8080	27
	LAURITO, Gerard P.	(814)871-7553	703
	RITTENHOUSE, Robert J.	(814)838-4124	1036
	YAPLE, Deborah A.	(814)899-7574	1377
Franklin Center	CUTLER, Judith	(215)459-6932	268
	HOWLEY, Deborah H.	(215)459-7049	566
Gettysburg	CHIESA, Adele M.	(717)334-1651	208
Gladwyne	FISHER, Daphne V.	(215)525-6628	380
Glenmoore	VOURVOULIAS, Sabrina M.	(215)942-3421	1289
Glenside	LOCKETT, Cheryl L.		736
	NIEWEG, Clinton F.	(215)884-5878	904
Greensburg	KREDEL, Stephen F.		677
Harleysville	HILLEGAS, Ferne E.		541
	LINN, Mott R.	(215)464-4500	731
Harrisburg	CAPITANI, Cheryl L.	(717)782-5511	180
	MALLINGER, Stephen M.	(717)783-5737	763
	SHULTZ, Suzanne M.	(717)782-4292	1133
	STAYER, Jonathan R.	(717)787-2701	1183
Hatboro	BURNS, Richard K.	(215)675-6762	162
Indiana	ELLIKER, Calvin	(412)357-2892	343
	RAHKONEN, Carl J.		1003
Jeffersonville	GRIFFITH, Dorothy A.	(215)539-1205	469
Johnsonburg	NELSON, Wilburta B.	(814)965-4110	895
Kennerdell	CHERESNOWSKI, Linda M.	(814)385-6896	206
Kingston	PAUSTIAN, P R.	(717)283-2651	950
Lancaster	FRANCOS, Alexis	(717)397-9655	396
Langhorne	BLACK, Dorothy M.	(215)752-5800	101
Lansdale	BLAUERT, Mary A.	(215)822-2929	105
	CLAYPOOL, Richard D.	(215)368-7439	220
Lehigh Valley	WEBER, A C.	(215)837-9615	1313
Malvern	QUINTILIANO, Barbara		1000
	VANDOREN, Sandra S.	(215)640-9809	1275
	YOUNG, Dorothy E.	(215)647-7449	1381
Mars	JOSEPH, Patricia A.	(412)776-9249	617
Marysville	RICHARDSON, Alice W.	(717)957-3808	1029
McKeesport	HERRON, Nancy L.	(412)675-9111	533
	KISH, Veronica R.	(412)678-1749	656
Meadville	STALLARD, Kathryn E.	(814)333-4363	1179
Mechanicsburg	TENOR, Randell B.	(717)763-1804	1231
Media	BURGESS, Rita N.	(215)565-7900	159
	ELLISON, J T.	(215)566-1699	345
Merion	HAAS, Carol C.	(215)664-1689	480
Millersville	LOTLIKAR, Sarojini D.		742
Morrisville	TOMAR, Jeanne	(215)736-2177	1249
Natrona Heights	HAUGH, Amy J.	(412)224-5004	512
New Castle	FUSCO, Marilyn A.		410
New Holland	MCGEE, Yvonne M.		806
New Hope	WESOLOWSKI, Paul G.	(215)862-9734	1325
New Kensington	TEOLIS, Marilyn G.	(412)339-0255	1231
New Kingstown	HANSON, Eugene R.	(717)243-0973	498
New Milford	MAASS, Eleanor A.	(717)465-3054	753
New Oxford	FOX, Merle U.		395
Norristown	PRITCHARD, Barbara		994
	ZANAN, Arthur S.	(215)272-3515	1386
Old Forge	FANUCCI, Mary M.	(717)457-3613	363
Pennsylvania Furnace	SAMET, Janet S.	(814)237-1555	1078
Philadelphia	ALDRIDGE, Carol J.	(215)893-9613	11
	ANDRILLI, Ene M.	(215)725-3660	27
	AZZOLINA, David S.	(215)898-8118	43
	BAKY, John S.	(215)951-1290	50
	BENDER, Evelyn	(215)634-0357	79
	BOISCLAIR, Regina A.	(215)438-0173	111
	BOODIS, Maxine S.	(215)963-8200	115
	BUCK, Patricia K.	(215)247-7443	154
	CALDWELL, John M.	(215)545-2809	172
	CHILDERS, Thomas A.	(215)895-2479	208
	CLEVELAND, Susan E.	(215)662-2577	221
	COOPER, Linda	(215)625-4719	243
	CUTRONA, Cheryl	(215)844-9027	268
	DEWANE, Kathleen M.	(215)546-5600	298
	DUCLOW, Geradline		322
	EVEY, Patricia G.	(215)848-3016	359
	FENICHEL, Carol H.	(215)448-7185	371
	FISHMAN, Lee H.	(215)564-3521	381
	FLOOD, Barbara J.	(215)732-8543	385
	GRACE, William M.	(215)925-8090	455
	GRAY, Priscilla M.	(215)386-6276	460

RESEARCHER (Cont'd)
PENNSYLVANIA (Cont'd)

Philadelphia

	GREEN, Patricia L.	(215)724-5715	462
	HALLER, Douglas M.	(215)898-8304	489
	HELLER, Patricia A.	(215)625-4720	524
	HOLMES, John H.	(215)592-1841	553
	HOLUB, Joseph C.	(215)843-6220	555
	HORNIG-ROHAN, James E.	(215)848-0554	560
	KOHN, Roger S.	(215)438-5635	668
	KREULEN, Thomas	(215)893-2495	678
	LAVERTY, Bruce	(215)925-2688	703
	LEVIN, Pauline G.	(215)561-5831	720
	LEVITT, Martin L.	(215)627-0706	721
	LIGHTNER, Karen J.	(215)387-8663	727
	MCDONALD, Joseph A.	(215)637-5829	802
	MICIKAS, Lynda L.	(215)637-7700	832
	MORRIS, Leslie A.	(215)985-4384	867
	MYERS, Charles J.	(215)898-7267	884
	NIGHTINGALE, Daniel	(215)288-1151	904
	PANCOE, Deborra S.	(215)561-5900	937
	PARKER, Peter J.	(215)732-6200	942
	PITCHON, Cindy A.	(215)235-4486	976
	POST, Joyce A.	(215)456-2971	986
	PROCTOR, David J.	(215)893-5128	994
	PROMOS, Marianne	(215)686-5351	995
	RUTKOWSKI, Hollace A.		1070
	SAUNDERS, William B.	(215)224-0235	1085
	SCHAEFFER, Judith E.	(215)843-8840	1089
	SKILLIN, Glenn B.		1146
	SMIRAGLIA, Richard P.	(215)662-5699	1152
	SNYDER, Theresa	(215)732-6200	1165
	SOWICZ, Eugenia V.	(215)354-2110	1170
	WALKER, Charlotte J.	(215)877-3470	1295
	WRIGHT, Irene R.	(215)923-1726	1371
	YOLTON, Jean S.	(215)878-7548	1380
Phoenixville	SAUER, James L.	(215)933-2236	1084
Pittsburgh	AL SADAT, Amira A.	(412)421-9444	17
	ARJONA, Sandra K.	(412)821-2263	31
	BLEIER, Carol S.	(412)563-2712	105
	BROSKY, Catherine M.	(412)682-0837	141
	CASLIN, Adele	(412)687-7738	193
	DETLEFSEN, Ellen G.	(412)624-9444	296
	EVANS, Nancy H.	(412)268-2114	357
	EVES, Judith A.	(412)471-1477	359
	FIDOTEN, Robert E.	(412)963-8785	375
	GREEN, Joyce M.	(412)234-5039	462
	JOHNSTON, Bruce A.	(412)731-8800	610
	JOSEY, E J.	(412)624-9451	618
	KANE, Angelika R.	(412)263-1397	624
	KERCHOF, Kathryn K.	(412)434-6000	643
	KIRCHER, Linda M.	(412)624-9444	654
	KRZYS, Richard A.	(412)624-9459	681
	LEIBOWITZ, Faye R.	(412)421-7974	713
	MAWHINNEY, Paul C.	(412)367-7330	787
	MAZEFSKY, Gertrude T.	(412)361-7582	791
	METZLER, Douglas P.	(412)624-9414	829
	MICCO, Helen M.	(412)665-0412	831
	MITTEN, Lisa A.	(412)521-4462	850
	PARADISE, Don M.	(412)929-9800	939
	PIETZAK, Stephen D.	(412)227-6839	972
	RISHEL, Joseph F.	(412)885-3980	1035
	ROOT, Deane L.	(412)624-4100	1054
	ROSEN, Gloria K.	(412)363-8423	1055
	ROSS, Nina M.	(412)624-9475	1058
	SCHEETZ, Mary D.	(412)421-4297	1091
	SOUDER, Edith I.	(412)343-9325	1169
	STERLING, Alida B.	(412)323-1430	1189
	THOMPSON, Dorothea M.	(412)268-2453	1239
	WEBRECK, Susan J.	(412)624-5230	1314
	WOOLLS, Esther B.	(412)624-9435	1368
	ZABROSKY, Frank A.	(412)648-8197	1385
Point Pleasant	GENNETT, Robert G.		427
Radnor	KELLER, Kate V.	(215)688-6989	635
Reading	SMALL, Sally S.	(215)320-4823	1151
	WEIHERER, Patricia D.	(215)376-7660	1317
Sarver	LIVENGOOD, Candice C.		734
Scranton	CAMPION, Carol M.	(717)348-0538	177
State College	CHANG, Shirley L.	(717)893-2312	201
Swarthmore	HAMILTON, Gloria R.	(215)544-1369	492

RESEARCHER (Cont'd)
PENNSYLVANIA (Cont'd)

University Park	FISHER, Kim N.	(814)865-1858	381
	KAISER, John R.	(814)863-1561	622
	MARTIN, Noelene P.	(814)865-3489	777
	NEAL, James G.	(814)865-0401	890
	ROE, Eunice M.	(814)863-0140	1048
	SMITH, Diane H.	(814)865-4861	1154
	SWEENEY, Del	(814)863-3952	1215
	WESTERMAN, Melvin E.	(814)863-2898	1327
	ZABEL, Diane M.	(814)863-2898	1385
Upland	BARON, Herman	(215)499-7415	58
Upper Darby	MORGAN, Dorothy H.	(215)789-9727	863
	SILVERMAN, Scott H.	(215)734-0146	1138
Upper Saint Clair	FULMER, Dina J.	(412)831-8664	409
	HURLEY, Doreen S.	(412)257-1814	577
Villanova	BUSHNELL, Marietta P.	(215)527-2377	165
	ERDT, Terrence	(215)645-4670	352
Warminster	BECKER, Linda C.	(215)443-7008	72
Wayne	ANTOS, Brian F.	(215)254-0754	29
	DRIEHAUS, Rosemary H.		320
	LAZARUS, Karin	(215)964-0477	706
Waynesboro	POSEY, Sussann F.	(717)762-3047	985
Wescosville	FISLER, Charlotte D.	(215)395-6400	382
West Chester	CHAFF, Sandra L.	(215)524-0547	197
	DINNIMAN, Margo P.	(215)430-3080	305
Wilkes-Barre	ERDICK, Joseph W.	(717)824-3725	352
	TYCE, Richard	(717)826-1148	1266
Yardley	BARATTA, Maria	(215)321-3289	55
	DU BOIS, Paul Z.	(215)493-6882	322
	FOGARTY, Catherine B.	(215)968-4236	387

PUERTO RICO

Hato Rey	NEGRON-GAZTAMBIDE, Olguita	(809)767-4192	892
Hormiguerow	MARTINEZ-NAZARIO, Ronaldo		779
Miramar	MCCARTHY, Carmen H.	(908)721-6574	794
Ponce	GUILLEMARD DE COLON, Teresita		476
	SANTIAGO, Maria	(809)844-4150	1082
San German	ALSTON, Jane C.	(809)892-3523	18
San Juan	HAMEL, Eleanor C.	(809)765-4426	491
	TORRES-TAPI, Manual A.		1251
Trujillo Alto	SABATER-SOLA, Rigel		1072

RHODE ISLAND

Chepachet	DESJARLAIS-LUETH, Christine	(401)568-8614	295
Kingston	ETCHINGHAM, John B.	(401)792-4637	355
	SIITONEN, Leena M.	(401)792-2878	1137
Newport	CARSON, Josephine R.		188
North Kingstown	OTTAVIANO, Doris B.	(401)295-0361	930
Peace Dale	ALEXANDER, Jacqueline P.	(401)783-3408	12
Providence	BRAUNSTEIN, Mark M.	(401)521-4771	130
	BRENNAN, Patricia B.	(401)456-8125	133
	FARK, Ronald K.	(401)941-0086	364
	HENDERSON, Linda L.	(401)277-7887	526
	LAMAR, Christine L.	(401)331-8575	689
	LANDIS, Dennis C.	(401)863-2725	693
	LLOYD, Lynn A.	(401)457-3001	735
	MARSH, Corrie V.	(401)863-2954	773
	MONTEIRO, George	(401)863-3266	856
	QUINN, Karen H.	(401)277-2473	1000
	RAINWATER, Jean M.	(401)863-3723	1004
	SHERIDAN, Jean	(401)277-3818	1127
	SILVA, Phyllis C.	(401)277-2353	1138
	WAGNER, Albin	(401)277-2283	1291
Saunderstown	BRENNAN, Deborah B.	(401)294-3175	132
Warwick	BRYAN, Susan M.	(401)737-3300	152
Westerly	LIGHT, Karen M.	(401)596-2877	726
Woonsocket	IMONDI, Lenore R.	(401)762-5165	582

SOUTH CAROLINA

Charleston	MOLTKE-HANSEN, David	(803)723-3225	853
	PARKER, Mary A.	(803)556-9454	942
Chester	MURDOCK, Everlyne K.	(803)377-8145	879
Clemson	LYLE, Martha E.	(803)656-5185	751
	MCCULLEY, P M.	(803)654-8753	800
	TAYLOR, Dennis S.	(803)656-3031	1226

RESEARCHER (Cont'd)
SOUTH CAROLINA (Cont'd)

Columbia	CHOI, Jin M.	(803)799-8786	210
	FRITZ, William R.		405
	GEOGHEGAN, Doris J.	(803)777-4206	427
	HELSLEY, Alexia J.	(803)781-8477	525
	HOLLEY, E J.	(803)774-4866	551
	KRONENFELD, Michael R.	(803)734-4769	679
	MOSS, Patsy G.	(803)799-4349	872
	SCHULZ, Constance B.	(803)777-4854	1102
	TYLER, Carolyn S.	(803)256-8692	1266
	VASSALLO, John A.	(803)776-7286	1279
	WASHINGTON, Nancy H.	(803)777-4206	1307
	WILLIAMS, Robert V.	(803)799-2324	1346
Florence	HUX, Roger K.	(803)665-6121	579
Greenville	TOWELL, Fay J.	(803)232-2941	1252
Greenwood	FECKO, Marybeth	(803)223-1810	367
	HILL, Thomas W.	(803)227-4851	541
Rock Hill	CHOPESIUK, Ronald J.	(803)366-5440	210
	SILVERMAN, Susan M.	(803)323-2131	1139
Spartanburg	BOWLES, David M.	(803)578-1472	121

SOUTH DAKOTA

Sioux Falls	DUNGER, George A.	(605)336-6588	326
	LANG, Elizabeth A.		695
	THOMPSON, Harry F.	(605)336-4007	1239

TENNESSEE

Antioch	HAMLIN, Lisa K.	(615)833-7541	493
Clarksville	RIVES, Lydia L.	(615)647-9484	1037
	THWEATT, John H.	(615)647-0954	1243
Cleveland	NICOL, Jessie T.		902
Columbia	WAGGENER, Jean B.	(615)388-9282	1291
Johnson City	BROWN, Phyllis J.	(615)929-3111	147
Knoxville	CLELAND, Nancy D.	(615)588-5406	220
	HASTINGS, Constance M.	(615)690-0368	511
	HILL, Ruth J.	(615)974-4381	540
	KNIGHTLY, John J.	(615)691-7996	664
	LEACH, Sandra S.	(615)579-1315	706
	PHILLIPS, Linda L.	(615)687-6734	968
	PONNAPPA, Biddanda P.	(615)675-4545	982
	ROBINSON, William C.	(615)974-2148	1045
	VIERA, Ann R.	(615)974-4171	1284
Memphis	BOAZ, Ruth L.	(901)682-0595	108
	CO, Francisca	(901)324-2453	224
	GIVENS, Mary K.	(901)528-5166	439
	MABBOTT, Deborah D.	(901)388-1096	753
	PARK, Elizabeth H.	(901)454-2208	941
	PERRY, Glenda L.	(901)527-4348	960
Murfreesboro	NEAL, James H.	(615)895-1383	890
	WELLS, Paul F.	(615)898-2449	1323
Nashville	BORRELLI, Barbara A.	(615)244-5270	117
	BRANTIGAN-STOWELL, Martha J.	(615)352-0787	129
	CAMERON, Sam A.	(615)329-1163	175
	CHEN, Helen M.	(612)251-1417	205
	EISENSTEIN, Jill M.	(615)327-8158	341
	HEARNE, Mary G.	(615)383-8989	518
	MARTIN, Laquita V.	(615)383-0953	777
	MOON, Fletcher F.	(615)833-1125	857
	PATTERSON, Jennifer J.	(615)383-4251	948
	SEEMANN, Charles H.	(615)256-1639	1111
	STEFFEY, Ramona J.	(615)662-0438	1185
	STEPHENS, Alonzo T.		1187
	SUMNERS, Bill F.	(615)251-2126	1209
Oak Ridge	MCDONALD, Ethel Q.	(615)482-5011	802
	PFUDERER, Helen A.	(615)574-5350	966
	YALCINTAS, Rana	(615)482-9397	1376
Old Hickory	MCHOLLIN, Mattie L.	(615)754-5411	809
Sewanee	HAYMES, Don		516

TEXAS

Abilene	SPECHT, Alice W.	(915)677-7281	1172
Amarillo	GROSS, Iva H.	(806)378-3000	472
	SNELL, Marykay H.	(806)353-5329	1163
Arlington	KERBY, Ramona A.	(817)478-9829	643
	LEATHERMAN, Donald G.	(817)459-6910	707
	MCCLURE, Margaret R.	(817)275-6594	797
	SHIH, Chia C.	(817)860-5475	1130

RESEARCHER (Cont'd)
TEXAS (Cont'd)

Austin	BECK, Alison M.	(512)263-5502	71
	BIERI, Sandra J.	(512)458-5551	95
	BURCH, David R.	(512)471-7726	158
	BURLINGHAM, Merry L.		161
	BURT, Eugene C.	(512)471-4777	164
	CABLE, Carole L.	(512)327-2158	170
	DAYO, Ayo	(512)472-8980	283
	DEGRUYTER, M L.	(512)929-3086	288
	GAMEZ, Juanita L.	(512)837-6247	416
	GRACY, David B.	(512)471-3821	455
	HARMON, Jacqueline B.	(512)343-0978	502
	HELFER, Robert S.	(512)929-3086	523
	HOOKS, Michael Q.	(512)250-1419	556
	LANDIS, Lawrence A.	(512)451-3214	693
	LANDIS, Lawrence A.	(512)451-3214	693
	MCCANN, Charlotte P.		793
	MIKSA, Francis L.	(572)346-6769	834
	PARKER, David F.	(512)450-1931	941
	ROY, Loriene	(512)471-6316	1063
	SEIDENBERG, Edward	(512)463-5459	1112
	SPRUG, Joseph W.	(512)448-8474	1176
	TRANFAGLIA, Twyla L.	(512)472-8800	1254
	WALTON, Robert A.	(512)346-1426	1301
	WEBSTER, Linda	(512)458-1852	1314
	WESTBROOK, Jo L.		1326
Beaumont	HOLLAND, Mary M.	(409)892-8885	551
	NISBY, Dora R.	(409)899-9972	904
Bellaire	HOPKINS, Joyce A.	(713)667-3760	558
Big Spring	BRADBERRY, Anna L.	(915)263-1468	125
Boerne	HANKS, Ellen T.	(512)249-9670	496
Brazoria	RASKA, Ginny	(409)798-1628	1009
Brownsville	VAUGHN, Frances A.	(512)544-8220	1280
Bryan	RABINS, Joan W.	(409)776-0374	1001
Buda	TISSING, Robert W.	(512)295-4834	1247
College Station	COOK, C C.	(409)845-3731	239
	GYESZLY, Suzanne D.	(409)845-3731	479
	ST. CLAIR, Gloriana S.	(409)696-8982	1075
	THOMPSON, Christine E.	(409)845-8157	1239
Corpus Christi	NEU, Margaret J.	(512)884-2011	896
Cypress	KUJOORY, Parvin	(713)890-7542	683
Dallas	BOCKSTRUCK, Lloyd D.	(214)670-1406	109
	CLEE, June E.	(214)941-3375	220
	CLEMENTS, Cynthia L.	(214)238-6153	221
	COMPTON, Erlinda R.	(214)506-3601	235
	DILLARD, Lois A.	(214)701-7300	303
	EWUNES, Ernest L.	(214)376-4102	359
	FOUDRAY, Rita C.	(214)824-1943	393
	HOWINGTON, Tad C.	(214)337-7779	566
	JARVIS, Mary E.	(214)337-2615	595
	JONES, Lois S.	(214)528-2732	613
	KANE, Deborah A.	(214)247-1952	624
	KERWIN, Camillus A.	(214)742-7201	644
	LEVINE, Harriet L.	(214)521-7165	720
	LOVELL, Bonnie A.	(214)826-1924	743
	MALCOLM, Jane B.	(214)307-8355	762
	METIVIER, Donna M.	(214)701-4222	828
	MITCHE, Cynthia R.	(214)692-6767	848
	MITCHELL, Cynthia R.	(214)692-6767	848
	RYDESKY, Mary M.	(214)339-3349	1071
	SALL, Larry D.	(214)385-8528	1076
	SHAPLEY, Ellen M.	(214)692-6407	1122
	SMITH, Michael K.	(214)296-5187	1158
	TEMPLETON, Virginia E.	(214)754-4875	1231
	UDENYI, Evelyn U.		1267
Denton	CARROLL, Dewey E.	(817)565-2445	187
	CVELJO, Katherine	(817)565-2445	268
	GALLOWAY, Margaret E.	(817)565-3024	415
	KHADER, Majed J.		645
	LAVENDER, Kenneth	(817)565-2768	703
	SWIGGER, Keith	(817)898-2609	1216
Edinburg	TINSMAN, William A.	(512)383-2008	1246
El Paso	BROWN, Susan W.	(915)747-5678	147
	GEARY, Kathleen A.	(915)533-5777	424
	GOODMAN, Helen C.	(915)584-4509	449
	MALLORY, Elizabeth J.	(915)593-1337	763
	MATHIS, Margaret H.		784
	RAMSEY, Donna E.	(915)855-1218	1005
	TAYLOR, Anne E.	(915)757-5095	1226

RESEARCHER (Cont'd)
TEXAS (Cont'd)

Flint	RUSSELL, Paula V.	(214)561-1258	1069
Fort Worth	DE TONNANCOUR, P R.	(817)763-1790	296
	HUGHSTON, Milan R.	(817)738-1933	572
	HULL, Mary M.	(817)927-7735	572
	MONGOLD, Alice D.	(817)457-9080	854
	RICE, Ralph A.	(817)626-7995	1027
	ROARK, Carol E.	(817)926-4212	1038
	SCHMIDT HACKER, Margaret H.	(817)334-5525	1096
	WESTBROOK, Brenda S.	(817)831-7232	1326
Freeport	TYLER-WHITE, Patricia G.		1266
Galveston	FREY, Emil F.	(409)761-2371	402
	RASCHE, Richard R.	(409)762-3139	1008
	WYGANT, Alice C.		1375
Georgetown	SWARTZ, Jon D.	(512)863-1214	1214
Houston	ANDERSON, Eliane G.	(713)229-7276	22
	BEAN, Norma P.	(713)527-7147	69
	BEDARD, Evelyn M.		73
	BOOTHE, Nancy L.	(713)667-1916	116
	BRUNNER, A M.	(713)463-0416	151
	BUTLER, Marguerite L.	(713)726-9244	166
	CALDWELL, Marlene	(713)661-5787	172
	CHAMPION, Walter T.	(713)527-7125	198
	CRIST, Lynda L.	(713)527-4990	259
	FORD, Margaret C.	(713)527-8101	389
	HOLIBAUGH, Ralph W.		550
	LANGSTON, Sally J.	(713)659-8040	696
	MCCANN, Debra W.	(713)691-0148	794
	MOORE, Guusje Z.	(713)680-0715	859
	MOORE, Sheryl R.	(713)271-1092	861
	PENDRAK, Eileen	(713)654-4100	956
	RICCARDI, Vincent M.	(713)558-9907	1026
	ROBINSON, Kathleen M.		1044
	SCHWARTZ, Charles A.	(713)527-8101	1104
	SCHWERBEL, Jeannette E.	(713)861-1373	1105
	SINCLAIR, Rose P.	(713)452-5555	1143
	SIVARAM, Swaraj L.		1144
	SUDENGA, Sara A.	(713)527-8101	1206
	TRAFFORD, Susan M.	(713)271-5610	1253
	WEATHERS, Barbara H.	(713)468-8211	1312
	WILLIAMS, Ann T.	(713)792-4094	1342
	WILSON, Ann Q.	(713)871-0505	1349
	WORCHEL, Harris M.	(713)956-7361	1368
	WU, Jean	(713)921-3253	1373
Huntsville	BAILEY, William G.	(409)294-1614	47
	BURT, Lesta N.	(409)295-1001	164
	YOUNG, J A.	(409)295-8766	1382
Irving	COCHRAN, Carolyn	(214)258-6767	225
Katy	POWELL, Alan D.	(713)392-9340	987
Laredo	BRESIE, Mayellen	(512)722-8001	133
Lewisville	MCCOY, Judy I.	(214)221-9251	799
Lubbock	LINDSEY, Thomas K.	(806)791-4770	730
	MARLEY, Judith L.	(806)799-3299	772
	OLM, Jane G.	(806)742-3794	921
Marshall	MAGRILL, Rose M.	(214)935-7963	760
McAllen	MYCUE, David J.		884
McKinney	BALCOMBE, Judith A.	(214)548-4430	51
Mesquite	GIBSON, Timothy T.	(214)289-2479	432
New Braunfels	SCHUMANN, Iris T.	(512)625-5656	1103
Odessa	KLEPPER, Bobbie J.	(915)326-3654	660
Pharr	LIU, David T.	(512)787-1491	734
Richardson	KRATZ, Abby R.	(214)690-2960	676
	SCHRAEDER, Diana C.	(214)386-6164	1090
	SHEA, Kathleen	(214)690-2960	1124
Round Rock	RICKLEFS, Dale L.	(512)255-3939	1032
San Angelo	PENNER, Elaine C.	(915)658-4534	957
San Antonio	BELL, Joy A.	(512)496-2057	77
	FRIEDMAN, Tevia L.	(512)696-2211	404
	HENRICKS, Duane E.	(512)436-3435	529
	HEWINS, Elizabeth H.	(512)655-4672	535
	HICKEY, Lady J.	(512)436-3435	536
	HOOD, Elizabeth	(512)736-7292	556
	LEATHERBURY, Maurice C.	(512)829-7033	707
	MORTON, Diane E.	(502)821-6094	870
	O'DONOGHUE, Patrice	(512)681-1207	917
	PEDERSEN, Wayne A.	(512)641-4561	954
	WERKING, Richard H.	(512)736-8161	1324
San Juan	SIEMENS, Bessie M.		1136

RESEARCHER (Cont'd)
TEXAS (Cont'd)

Sherman	GARCIA, Lana C.	(214)893-4401	417
Spring	ATRI, Pushkala V.	(713)370-3673	38
Sugar Land	JOHNSON, Pat M.	(713)980-5350	608
Tyler	MILLER, Susan A.		842
Uvalde	KINGSBERY, Evelyn B.	(512)278-4401	652
Waco	COLEY, Betty A.	(817)754-6114	231
	GEARY, Gregg S.		424
	KEATTS, Rowena W.	(817)753-6415	633
	RICHARDS, James H.	(817)756-0602	1028
Wichita Falls	GRIMES, John F.	(817)855-0463	470
	ROBERTS, Ernest J.	(817)855-2390	1040
Wimberley	FELSTED, Carla M.	(512)847-5277	370
	SHAW, Ben B.	(512)847-2776	1123
	WAYLAND, Terry T.	(512)847-9295	1311

UTAH

Bountiful	SANDERS, William D.	(801)292-4429	1080
Farmington	POLLARD, Louise	(801)451-5282	981
Ogden	WILSON, Brenda J.	(801)479-1407	1350
Payson	GILLUM, Gary P.	(801)465-4527	436
Provo	CHANDLER, Jody A.	(801)373-2397	200
	LAMB, Connie	(801)378-5627	689
	MARCHANT, Maurice P.	(801)378-2976	768
	MATHIESEN, Thomas J.	(801)378-3688	784
	ROWLEY, Edward D.	(801)378-6372	1063
Salt Lake City	CASADY, Richard L.	(801)533-9607	191
	DOGU, Hikmet S.	(801)486-3238	309
	JENSEN, Charla J.	(801)533-5250	598
	JOHNSON, Jeffery O.	(801)533-5250	606
	MCMURRIN, Jean A.	(801)322-1586	815
	NASH, Cherie A.	(801)533-5250	888
	PATTERSON, Myron B.	(801)581-7265	948
	REDDICK, Mary J.	(801)581-7024	1013
	SCOTT, Patricia L.	(801)533-5250	1107
	STODDART, Joan M.	(801)272-2749	1196
	VAN ORDEN, Richard D.	(801)485-1075	1276
Sandy	KIESSLING, Mary S.	(801)561-4474	647

VERMONT

Burlington	ABAZARNIA, Diane B.	(802)864-5751	1
Essex Junction	LAPIDOW, Amy R.	(802)878-2665	697
Northfield	WARD, Robert C.	(802)485-7344	1304
Putney	THOMPSON, Jane K.	(802)387-4767	1240
Rutland	MCCULLOUGH, Doreen J.	(802)773-5900	801
St Johnsbury	BRYAN, Martin F.	(802)748-9264	151
South Burlington	JULIANELLE, Shelley M.	(802)658-0103	619

VIRGIN ISLANDS

St Croix	VAUGHN, Robert V.	(809)778-8465	1280
St Thomas	CHANG, Henry C.	(809)774-3407	200
	MILLER, Veronica E.	(809)774-0059	843
	MILLS, Fiolina B.	(809)776-8396	844

VIRGINIA

Alexandria	CARTLEDGE, Connie L.	(703)960-6020	190
	CASSEDY, James G.	(703)768-2070	193
	DAVIDSON, Dero H.	(703)998-2976	276
	GOLDBERG, Jolande E.	(703)765-4521	444
	HARRISTON, Victoria R.	(203)642-5382	507
	JORDAN, Robert T.		617
	MARA, Ruth M.	(703)765-0262	768
	OMARA, Marie T.	(703)960-3981	923
	OSIA, Ruby R.	(703)549-3048	928
	QUINN, Susan		1000
	ROTHSCHILD, M C.	(202)274-7206	1060
	RUSH, James S.	(703)765-3557	1068
	SMITH, Thomas E.		1161
	STEIN, Karen E.	(703)354-3154	1185
	VAROUTSOS, Mary A.	(703)836-0156	1279
	WALDE, Norma J.	(703)642-4178	1294
	WOODWARD, Lawrence W.	(703)751-9426	1368
Annandale	CHOBOT, Mary C.	(703)323-9402	210
	MCGINN, Ellen T.	(703)280-5085	806
	TYSINGER, Barbara R.	(703)354-8688	1267
Arlington	ARDEN, Caroline	(703)532-1548	31
	ASHKENAS, Bruce F.	(301)763-7410	36
	CALKIN, Homer L.	(703)920-4910	173
	CARR, Timothy B.		186

RESEARCHER (Cont'd)
VIRGINIA (Cont'd)

Arlington
CIPRIANI, Debra A.	(703)769-7736	215
COSGROVE-DAVIES, Lisa A.	(703)536-9452	248
DENNIE, David L.	(703)685-0208	292
DESSAINT, Alain Y.	(703)247-7750	295
GOLDBERG, Lisbeth S.	(703)243-0796	444
HELMINSKI, James C.	(703)525-1324	525
HIGBEE, Joan F.	(703)524-5844	537
HILL, Victoria C.		541
KECSKES, Lily C.	(703)528-0730	633
MEREK, Charles J.	(703)920-5050	825
POEHLMAN, Dorothy J.		979
PRICE, Joseph W.	(703)241-0447	992
SAUR, Cindy S.	(703)379-2575	1085
STARR, Marian U.	(703)237-0285	1182
WIENER, Theodore		1336
WOLF, Richard E.	(703)276-0270	1360

Blacksburg	FOX, Edward A.	(703)552-8667	394
Charlottesville	BADER, Susan G.	(804)973-2397	44
	CAHILL, Linda J.	(804)296-5676	171
	GORDON, Vesta L.	(804)295-5586	452
	JORDAN, Ervin L.	(804)924-4975	616
	MORRIS, Karen L.	(804)293-2475	867
Christiansburg	LINN, Cynthia S.	(703)961-5988	731
Fairfax	CRAWFORD, Elva B.	(703)425-6974	256
	FIENCKE, Elaine L.	(703)385-7700	376
	GOODWIN, Jane G.	(703)246-5847	450
	PFEIFFER, David A.	(703)425-4685	966
	ROBINSON, David F.	(703)273-6139	1043
	SCOTT, Mona L.	(703)378-8027	1107
	WALCH, Victoria I.	(703)273-3260	1293
Falls Church	BROWN, Barbara B.	(703)820-7450	142
	HARRIS, Virginia B.	(703)698-6968	506
	HELGERSON, Linda W.	(703)237-0682	524
	KAHLER, Mary E.		622
	VIOLA, Herman J.	(703)573-6211	1285
Fredericksburg	VANDERBERG, E S.	(703)371-3311	1273
Gloucester Point	BARRICK, Susan O.	(804)642-7114	59
Great Falls	KOVACS, Katherine M.	(703)759-4511	673
Harrisonburg	GILL, Gerald L.	(703)568-6898	435
	RAMSEY, Inez L.	(703)568-6791	1006
Herndon	GUERRIERO, Donald A.	(703)860-1058	476
	PAVEK, C C.	(703)481-0711	950
	SINWELL, Carol A.	(703)689-0086	1144
Lexington	GREFE, Richard F.	(703)463-8648	465
	HOLLY, Janet S.		552
Lynchburg	SIDDONS, James D.	(804)846-8129	1135
McLean	ADAMS, Judith A.	(703)241-0973	5
	CHEVERIE, Joan F.	(703)893-3889	207
	FURR, Susan H.	(703)893-4089	410
Norfolk	BERENT, Irwin M.	(804)855-1272	84
	BREWER, Helen L.	(804)444-7951	134
	JONES-TRENT, Bernice R.	(804)632-8873	616
	NICHOLSON, Myreen M.	(804)627-6281	902
	TRASK, Benjamin H.		1254
Quantico	BROWN, David C.	(703)221-1586	143
Reston	KARRER, Jonathan K.	(703)648-4302	628
	WARD, Carol T.	(703)860-5664	1303
Richmond	CLEMANS, Margaret H.	(804)358-9379	220
	JACOBY, Mary M.	(804)231-2545	590
	MOSER, Emily F.	(804)355-3348	870
	MURPHY, Robert D.	(804)741-1311	881
	OWEN, Karen V.	(804)649-6132	931
	SARTAIN, Sara M.		1083
	SHEPARD, E L.	(804)358-4901	1126
	SMITH, Walter H.	(804)264-0539	1161
	SNAIR, Dale S.	(804)786-1489	1162
	STACY, Betty A.	(804)359-4283	1178
	THOMAS, Mary E.	(804)786-0823	1237
	WINFREE, Waverly K.	(804)271-4163	1354
	WOODWARD, Elaine H.	(804)771-2219	1368
Roanoke	CALHOUN, Clayne M.	(703)981-2268	172
	SEAMANS, Nancy H.	(703)985-8508	1109
Springfield	ALBIN, Michael W.	(703)978-3022	10
	LEONARD, Lawrence E.	(703)569-1541	716
	ROARK, Robin D.	(703)644-7372	1038
	SCHAAF, Robert W.	(703)451-7916	1088

RESEARCHER (Cont'd)
VIRGINIA (Cont'd)

Vienna	COCHRANE, Maryjane S.	(703)938-2037	226
	DODSON, Whit	(703)938-2630	308
	SCHAEFER, Mary E.	(703)759-6339	1089
Virginia Beach	CICCONE, Amy N.	(808)481-9113	214
Williamsburg	BERG, Susan	(804)229-8799	85
	GROVE, Pearce S.	(804)220-2477	473
Woodbridge	ENGLAND, Ellen M.	(703)670-2191	349

WASHINGTON

Bainbridge Island	SPEARMAN, Marie A.	(206)842-6636	1172
Bellevue	SMART, Doris M.	(206)822-8435	1151
Bellingham	JOHNSON, Dana E.	(206)734-3941	603
	SYMES, Dal S.		1217
Bremerton	KANNEL, Selma	(206)377-3911	625
Cheney	ALKIRE, Leland G.	(509)235-4669	13
	MUTSCHLER, Charles V.	(509)235-2706	883
Custer	HASELBAUER, Kathleen J.	(206)366-5063	510
Everett	GRINSTEAD, Beth K.	(206)258-1951	471
Federal Way	WILSON, Anthony M.	(206)839-0496	1349
Kirkland	DIBIASE, Linda P.	(206)821-2863	299
Mt Vernon	SAUTER, Sylvia E.	(206)336-2604	1085
Oak Harbor	MERWINE, Glenda M.	(206)679-5807	827
Ocean Park	EASLEY, Janet T.	(206)665-5580	332
Pullman	KEMP, Barbara E.	(509)334-5809	639
Redmond	WALLS, Francine E.	(206)333-4815	1299
Renton	SIENDA, Madeline M.		1136
Richland	FOLEY, Katherine E.	(509)943-9117	387
Seattle	BETZ-ZALL, Jonathan R.	(206)782-9305	92
	BRZUSTOWICZ, Richard J.	(206)527-9357	152
	BURSON, Scott F.	(206)543-6794	163
	CHASE, Dale L.	(206)525-0795	203
	CLINE, Robert S.	(206)523-7268	222
	CRANDALL, Michael D.	(206)633-2530	255
	EIPERT, Susan L.	(206)522-3174	340
	EULENBERG, Julia N.	(206)324-2605	356
	HARBOLD, Mary J.	(206)764-2075	499
	HARMALA, Amy A.	(206)632-8338	502
	HAZELTON, Penelope A.	(206)543-4089	517
	KREPS, Lise E.	(206)527-2817	678
	LOPEZ, Loretta K.	(206)526-1728	741
	MCFADDEN, Denyse I.	(206)284-6280	804
	PRESTON, Deirdre R.	(206)283-0754	991
	RICKERSON, Carla	(206)543-1929	1031
	SHINN, Isabella E.	(206)527-2466	1130
	STOCK, Carole G.	(206)325-8364	1195
	SY, Karen J.	(206)545-2873	1217
	YONGMAN, Zhang	(206)522-6701	1380
Spokane	REHMS, Jane C.	(509)536-7049	1017
	SHIDELER, John C.	(509)838-5242	1129
	WYNN, Debra D.	(509)328-4220	1375
Steilacoom	COHEN, Jane L.		228
	PARR, Loraine E.	(206)582-7557	943
Tacoma	GILDENHAR, Janet		434
	JONES, Faye E.	(206)564-9254	613
	MENANTEAUX, A R.	(206)591-2973	823
	RICIGLIANO, Lorraine M.		1031
	SCHREINER, Suzanne M.	(206)756-3646	1100
Walla Walla	BREIT, Anitra D.		132

WEST VIRGINIA

Charleston	HUMPHRIES, Joy D.		574
Clarksburg	GREATHOUSE, Brenda J.	(304)624-9649	461
Cross Lanes	COOPER, Candace S.	(304)776-5945	242
Glenville	VERMA, Prem V.	(304)462-5303	1282
Huntington	REENSTJERNA, Frederick R.	(304)523-9651	1016
	STARKEY, Bonnie F.	(303)523-3109	1182
Morgantown	ESKRIDGE, Virginia C.	(304)293-5300	354
Wheeling	JULIAN, Charles A.	(304)233-5900	619

WISCONSIN

Brookfield	CHRISTMAN, Inese R.	(414)786-6700	212
Caledonia	GRENDYSA, Peter A.	(414)764-3676	467
Cudahy	KLAUSMEIER, Arno M.	(414)744-0268	658
Eau Claire	CARROLL, Barbara T.		187
	MERRIAM, Louise A.	(715)839-5003	826
	NASSET, M J.	(715)835-5141	889
Fond Du Lac	EBERT, John J.	(414)929-3616	334
Green Bay	JOBELIUS, Nancy L.	(414)497-7508	601

RESEARCHER (Cont'd)
WISCONSIN (Cont'd)

Iola	FOERSTER, Trey	(715)445-3838	387
La Crosse	HILL, Edwin L.	(608)782-1753	539
Lake Geneva	CIBOCH, Lorraine A.	(414)245-5806	214
Madison	BEHNKE, Charles	(608)244-3253	75
	BEHRND-KLODT, Menzi L.	(608)238-3966	75
	BLANKENBURG, Julie J.		104
	BOYER, Ann T.	(608)233-7252	123
	BUNGE, Charles A.	(608)263-2900	157
	JESUDASON, Melba	(608)263-7464	600
	KRIKELAS, James	(608)263-2900	678
	ROBBINS, Jane B.	(608)263-2908	1038
	ROSENSHIELD, Jill K.	(608)233-2518	1057
	SHAFTMAN, Sarah	(608)241-7153	1119
	WALKER, Richard D.	(608)257-5574	1296
	WILLETT, Holly G.	(608)251-0633	1341
	WILLIAMSON, William L.	(608)238-0770	1348
Menasha	DIETZ, Kathryn A.	(414)725-3803	302
Middleton	ZWEIZIG, Douglas L.	(608)831-4364	1392
Milwaukee	BLUE, Richard I.	(414)963-4707	107
	COONEY, Charles W.	(414)444-6130	241
	DETWILER, Eve N.	(414)332-3367	296
	EUKEY, Jim O.		356
	GILL, Norman N.	(414)352-1545	435
	GREENE, Victor R.	(414)963-7063	464
	LYNCH, Beverly P.	(414)774-1008	751
	MARCUS, Terry C.	(414)352-5695	769
	MCKILLIP, Rita J.	(414)347-1335	811
	MURPHY, Virginia A.	(414)271-1444	881
	PETERSON, Christine E.	(414)466-4817	963
	POPESCU, Constantin C.	(414)332-5909	983
	RISTIC, Jovanka	(414)229-6282	1036
	RUNKEL, Phillip M.		1067
	SHUTKIN, Sara A.	(414)332-3321	1134
	SMITH-GREENWOLD, Kathryn R.	(414)445-3586	1162
	WATERSTREET, Darlene E.	(414)964-2377	1309
	ZIRBES, Colette M.	(414)483-1979	1390
Oshkosh	FU, Tina C.	(414)424-2206	407
	JONES, Norma L.	(414)231-5137	614
	SHARMA, Ravindra N.	(414)424-0139	1122
Racine	SCHINK, Sandra C.	(414)634-1495	1093
Rhinelander	SLYGH, Gyneth	(715)362-3465	1151
Ripon	BURR, Charlotte A.	(414)748-3244	163
St Francis	WESTERN, Eric D.	(414)769-0110	1327
Sheboygan	TOBIN, R J.	(414)459-7606	1247
Stevens Point	WACHTER-NELSON, Ruth M.		1290
Stoughton	DANKY, James P.	(608)873-8722	274
	LUND, Patricia A.	(608)873-9446	748
Superior	AXT, Randolph W.	(715)398-6767	42
	JOHNSON, Denise J.	(715)394-8512	603
West Allis	LUECHT, Richard M.	(414)321-3152	747
Whitefish Bay	LANK, Dannette H.	(414)225-2107	696

WYOMING

Cheyenne	HALLBERG, Carl V.	(307)778-8577	489
	MCGOWAN, Anne W.	(307)777-6430	807
	MENDOZA, Anthanett C.	(307)778-8706	824
	SCHELL, Catherine L.	(307)637-7504	1091
Laramie	CHISUM, Emmett D.	(307)766-6385	209
	EMERSON, Tamsen L.	(307)442-8643	347
	OSTRYE, Anne T.	(307)766-5312	929
Worland	HARRINGTON, Carolyn B.	(307)347-4490	504

CANADA

ALBERTA

Airdrie	WAUGH, Alan L.	(403)948-7921	1310
Calgary	GOODMAN, Henry J.	(403)220-6296	449
	LANE, Barbara K.	(403)283-9998	694
	MING, Marilyn	(403)284-8072	846
	VINE, Rita F.	(403)247-6524	1285
Edmonton	BAYRAK, Bettie	(403)478-8062	68
	FETTERMAN, Nelma I.	(403)432-3813	374
	SCHRADER, Alvin M.	(403)432-4578	1099
	SINCLAIR, John M.	(403)488-2646	1142
	STRATHERN, Gloria V.	(403)432-3934	1200
	TRAICHEL, Rudolf D.	(403)437-5718	1253

RESEARCHER (Cont'd)
ALBERTA (Cont'd)

Lethbridge	DROESSLER, Judith B.	(403)381-2285	320
Sherwood Pk	NOGA, Dolores A.	(403)467-4003	907
	SCHMIDT, Raymond J.	(403)464-8234	1095

BRITISH COLUMBIA

Abbotsford	HARRIS, Winifred E.	(604)853-7441	506
Burnaby	GOW, Susan P.	(604)439-0931	454
North Vancouver	ASHCROFT, Susan M.	(604)984-8004	35
Richmond	WEESE, Dwain W.		1316
Vancouver	CAMERON, Hazel M.	(604)224-8470	175
	CHAN, Diana L.	(604)224-8470	199
	HALE, Linda L.	(604)321-0932	485
	HART, Elizabeth	(604)228-9031	507
	HOPKINS, Richard L.	(604)228-3184	558
	NICHOL, Kathleen M.	(604)263-7081	901
	PITERNICK, Anne B.	(604)228-3359	976
	ROBERTSON, Guy M.	(604)689-8494	1041
	STUART-STUBBS, Basil F.	(604)731-1978	1204
	WARREN, Lois M.	(604)687-1072	1306
Victoria	MOEHR, Jochen R.	(604)721-8581	851
	ROMANIUK, Elena	(604)592-8819	1052
	SIGNORI, Donna L.	(604)721-8247	1137
	TRUBKIN, Loene	(604)386-4140	1259
	VAN REENEN, Johannes A.	(604)595-9612	1277

MANITOBA

Winnipeg	COVVEY, H D.	(204)942-5335	252
	DIVAY, Gabriele	(204)474-8926	306
	FOWLER, Margaret A.	(204)884-6593	394
	SANTORO, Corrado A.	(204)474-8243	1082

NEWFOUNDLAND

Mt Pearl	MORGAN, Pamela S.	(709)368-5926	864
St John's	MILNE, Dorothy J.	(709)737-8270	845

NORTHWEST TERRITORIES

Yellowknife	O'KEEFE, Kevin T.	(403)873-5715	919

NOVA SCOTIA

Amherst	CAMPBELL, Margaret E.	(902)667-2888	177
Halifax	BANFIELD, Eilzabeth S.	(902)421-4570	54
	DEYOUNG, Marie	(902)424-7699	298
	DYKSTRA, Mary E.	(902)424-3656	331
Sydney	MACINTOSH, Ian R.	(902)562-1115	755

ONTARIO

Aqimeont	JAGIELLOWICZ, Jadzia	(410)492-8341	591
Bowmanville	MOON, Jeffrey D.	(416)263-8504	857
Brockville	WARREN, Peggy A.	(613)342-6352	1306
Cambridge	SKELTON, W M.	(519)621-0460	1146
Don Mills	TEMPLIN, Dorothy	(416)447-2380	1231
Downsview	BERNSTEIN, Elaine S.	(416)638-1962	89
	JONES, B E.	(416)244-3621	611
Fort Erie	PORTEUS, Andrew C.	(416)871-3814	985
Gloucester	KENT, Charles D.		642
Hamilton	BROWNRIDGE, James R.	(416)572-2981	149
Kingston	FLOWER, M A.	(613)645-6122	386
	MORLEY, Mae L.	(613)546-1101	865
London	FYFE, Janet H.	(519)472-5201	411
	NELSON, Michael J.	(519)661-3542	894
	PARR, John R.	(519)439-3271	943
	RUTHERFORD, Frederick S.	(519)471-4867	1070
	TAGUE, Jean M.	(519)471-1311	1220
Mississauga	ATHA, Shirley A.	(416)822-5704	37
	MASEN, Naunihal S.	(416)897-6269	780
	MCLEAN-LOWE, Dallas	(416)828-5232	814
Ottawa	ANDERSON, Beryl L.	(613)238-3734	21
	ARBEZ, Gilbert J.	(819)997-7990	30
	BANFILL, Christine	(613)235-8569	54
	BREGAINT, Bernard J.	(613)741-0242	131
	BRIERE, Jean M.	(613)996-3817	135
	BURROWS, Sandra	(613)996-1342	163
	CAMPBELL, Laurie G.	(613)596-9797	177
	FOX, Rosalie	(613)232-4358	395
	GUILBERT, Manon M.	(613)233-8012	476
	KARCICH, Grant J.	(416)723-6068	627
	KIRKWOOD, Francis T.	(613)233-7592	655
	KNOPPERS, Jake V.		665

RESEARCHER (Cont'd)
ONTARIO (Cont'd)
Ottawa

	LEBRUN, Anne	(613)725-6277	708
	MACLELLAND, Margaret A.	(819)994-6832	757
	SCOTT, Judith W.	(613)232-0579	1107
	TAYLOR, Margaret P.	(613)232-6172	1227
	TSAI, Shaopan		1260
Sarnia	O'DONNELL, Rosemary F.	(519)337-8251	917
Scarborough	BALL, John L.	(416)284-3245	52
	KEYS, Sandra A.		645
Thornhill	SPEISMAN, Stephen A.	(416)886-2508	1172
Toronto	ATTINGER, Monique L.	(416)699-2530	38
	BELLAMY, Patricia C.	(416)595-0300	78
	BOITE, Mary E.	(416)461-2274	111
	BREGMAN, Alvan M.	(416)767-3625	131
	CHERRY, Joan M.	(416)924-5257	206
	CHOUDHURI, Kabita	(416)484-0441	211
	DESOMOGYI, Aileen A.	(416)466-6572	295
	DOWDING, Martin R.	(416)925-7593	315
	DRAKE, James B.	(416)922-8907	318
	GIBSON, Elizabeth A.	(416)595-7894	432
	GOLD, Sandra	(416)782-7236	444
	HAJNAL, Peter I.	(416)533-7338	484
	JOHNSON, John E.	(416)423-6979	606
	KENDALL, Sandra A.		640
	KLEMENT, Susan P.	(416)486-0239	660
	KOTIN, David B.	(416)531-2104	673
	LADD, Kenneth F.	(416)596-3124	687
	LAVERTY, Corinne Y.	(416)393-7024	703
	MARSHALL, Joanne G.	(416)978-7111	774
	MCCANN, Judith B.	(416)429-1247	794
	MCCUBBIN, George M.	(416)487-8732	800
	MEADOW, Charles T.	(416)530-4934	819
	MILANICH, Melanie M.	(416)393-7180	834
	MORRISON, Brian H.	(416)965-1641	867
	MORRISON, Carol A.	(416)967-3796	868
	SMITH, Cynthia M.	(416)488-6117	1153
	TIPLER, Stephen B.	(416)654-5617	1246
	TUDOR, Dean F.	(416)767-1340	1262
	WEAVER, Maggie	(416)925-5478	1312
	WILKINSON, John P.	(416)978-3167	1340
	WILLIAMSON, Nancy J.		1347
	YANCHINSKI, Roma N.	(416)767-6781	1377
	ZURBRIGG, Lyn E.	(416)961-9323	1391
Waterloo	BEGLO, Jo N.	(519)885-1211	74
Willowdale	DANIEL, Eileen	(416)223-2495	272
	MCLEAN, Paulette A.	(416)636-4877	814

QUEBEC

Baie d'Urfe	KLOK, Buddhi	(514)457-2757	662
Beaconsfield	HIRON, Barbara A.	(514)695-3200	543
	KAMICHAITIS, Penelope H.	(574)697-1634	624
Boischatel	LUSSIER, Richard	(418)822-1904	749
Boucherville	NADEAU, Johan	(514)655-4858	885
Chicoutimi	GAUDREAU, Louis	(418)549-9520	422
Chomedey	DUPLESSIS, Daniel		327
Cote Saint-Luc	KATZ, Solomon B.	(514)488-7673	630
Drummondville	JANIK, Sophie	(819)477-7100	593
Gatineau	ST. AMANT, Robert	(819)561-4988	1075
Hampstead	FLUK, Louise R.	(514)488-3187	386
Hull	CHEVRIER, Francine	(819)777-4341	207
Laval	CHAUMONT, Elise	(514)667-5100	204
	TESSIER, Mario C.	(514)669-7878	1233
Laval-des-Rapides	VONKA, Stephanie	(514)667-1947	1288
Lennoxville	SHEERAN, Ruth J.	(819)569-9551	1125
Montebello	WENK, Arthur B.		1324
Montreal	ARAJ, Houda	(514)343-7095	30
	BAZINET, Jeanne	(514)482-7188	68
	BERARDINUCCI, Heather R.	(514)255-2445	84
	BERNHARD, Paulette	(514)343-7408	89
	BERTRAND-GASTALDY, Suzanne	(514)343-6048	91
	BISSON, Jacques	(514)482-9110	100
	BOUCHER, Lorna M.	(514)481-7430	118
	BROCHU, Frederick	(514)598-1947	138
	CAYA, Marcel	(514)398-7100	195
	CHAGNON, Danielle G.		197
	CHALIFOUX, Jean P.	(514)285-7007	197
	CLARKE, Robert F.	(514)731-9211	219

RESEARCHER (Cont'd)
QUEBEC (Cont'd)
Montreal

	CORBEIL, Lizette	(514)332-9854	245
	DARLINGTON, Susan	(514)737-3387	275
	DE LUISE, Alexandra	(514)871-1418	290
	DUBEAU, Pierre		321
	DUMOULIN, Nicole L.	(514)733-8051	325
	FINN, Julia P.	(514)487-9804	378
	GAULIN, S D.	(514)645-9444	422
	GIRARD, Luc	(514)343-7445	438
	JOBA, Judith C.	(514)489-0117	601
	LALONDE, Diane	(514)767-3490	689
	LEIDE, John E.	(514)398-4204	713
	MITTERMEYER, Diane	(514)398-4204	850
	ORLANDO, Richard P.	(514)877-1470	926
	ORMSBY, Eric	(514)398-4677	926
	OUELLET, Louise M.		930
	RABCHUK, Gordon K.	(514)874-2104	1001
	RATNER, Sabina T.		1010
	ROBIN, Madeleine	(514)738-0433	1043
	ROUSSEAU, Denis	(514)843-3214	1061
	TODD, Rose A.	(514)283-9045	1248
	TOUCHETTE, Francois G.	(514)524-7878	1252
	WERYHO, Jan W.	(514)392-5766	1325
Montreal Oest	MORRISON, H D.	(514)488-9279	868
Pointe Claire	SMYTH, John	(514)697-3486	1162
Pointe Claire Dorval	STAHL, Hella	(514)630-4100	1178
Quebec	DENIGER, Constant	(418)692-4369	292
	GUERETTE, Charlotte M.	(418)656-3017	476
	TESSIER, Yves	(418)872-4304	1233
Rosemere	LAPIERRE, France	(514)621-8507	697
St Laurent D'Orleans	BOLDUC, Yves		112
St-Leonard	LAFRENIERE, Myriam	(514)322-6818	688
Sherbrooke	GOODFELLOW, Marjorie E.	(819)562-1694	448
	SOKOV, Asta M.	(819)821-7566	1166
Stanstead	GRENIER, Serge	(819)876-2981	467
Touraine	MURRAY-LACHAPELLE, Rosemary F.	(819)568-0282	882
Verdun	DIMITRESCU, Ioana	(514)765-8219	304
	VAILLANCOURT, Alain	(514)765-7507	1270
Westmount	WADE, C A.		1290

SASKATCHEWAN

Regina	BALON, Brett J.	(306)586-1990	53
	BROWNE, Berks G.	(306)584-8247	148
	MACK, A Y.	(306)543-6981	756
	THAUBERGER, Marianne T.	(306)757-9589	1234
Saskatoon	HANDE, D A.	(306)653-5692	494

AUSTRALIA

Bedford Park	BROWN, Pauline		146
Kensington	WILSON, Concepcion S.		1350
Magill	BEATTIE, Kathleen M.		70
St Lucia	LAMBERTON, Donald M.		690
Toowong	GOODELL, Paulette M.		448
Victoria	POWNALL, David E.	(033)418-2990	989

BAHAMAS

Grand Bahamas Island	BARTON, Barbara I.		61

BAHRAIN

Al Manamah	ALI, Syed N.		13

BRAZIL

Pelotas	CASTAGNO, Lucio A.		194
Sao Paulo	GROSSMANN, Pierre	(011)255-3053	473

COSTA RICA

San Jose	CROWTHER, Warren W.		262
	SMITH, Sharon		1160

EGYPT

Cairo	EL-DUWEINI, Aadel K.	(027)197-7200	342
Giza	EL-MASRY, Mohammed		345
	MAHOUD ALY, Usama E.		761

RESEARCHER (Cont'd)
ENGLAND

Cambridge	HARKINS, Diane G.	501
Harrogate	LINE, Maurice B.	730
London	ELLIOTT, Pirkko E.	344
	PRITCHARD, Jane E.	994
Oxford	BISHOP, John	99
Plymouth	PENGELLY, Joe	956
Reading	WOODWARD, Anthony M.	1367
Sussex	GREEN, Jeffrey P.	462

FEDERAL REPUBLIC OF CHINA

Taidzi	CHENG, Sheung O.	206
Taipei	HU, James S.	567
	LEE, Lucy T.	710
	SENG, Harris B.	1115
	WANG, Sin C.	1303

FEDERAL REPUBLIC OF GERMANY

Berlin	ELSTE, R O.	346
	KREH, Fritz	677
	ULRICH, Paul S.	1268
	WERSIG, Gernot	1325
Bonn	LOTZ, Rainer E.	742
Heidelberg	SOKOLOWSKI, Denise G.	1166
Saarbrucken	VON KEITZ, Wolfgang	1288
Taufkirchen	ADENEY, Carol D.	6

FRANCE

Paris	GRATTAN, Robert	458
	ROBERTS, Kenneth H.	1040
	STONE, Toby G.	1197

HONG KONG

Kowloon	FU, Ting W.	407
	POON, Paul W.	983
The Peak	SANDFELDER, Paula M.	1080

INDONESIA

Jakarta	STONE, Clarence W.	1197

ISRAEL

Haifa	BLOCH, Uri	105
Jerusalem	DIAMANT, Betsy	299

ITALY

Florence	FORRESTER, John H.	391
Milan	CASIRAGHI, Edoardo	192
	PUSATERI, Liborio	998

JAMAICA

Kingston	DOUGLAS, Daphne R.	314
	MANSINGH, Laxmi .... (809)927-2748	767

JAPAN

Aichi	TOGUCHI, Eiko	1248
Chiba-ken	NASU, Yukio	889
Ibaraki-ken	NOZOE, Atsutake	911
	TAKEUCHI, Satoru	1220
Tokyo	HOSONO, Kimio	562
	KAWASHIMA, Hiroko	632
	YAMAZAKI, Hisamichi	1377
	YAMAZAKI, Shigeaki ... (034)331-1110	1377

KENYA

Nairobi	BOWEN, Dorothy N.	120

KUWAIT

Salmiyah	ABDEL-MOTEY, Yaser Y.	2

MALAWI

Lilongwe	SNYDER, Lisa A.	1165

MEXICO

Benito	MACIAS-CHAPULA, Cesar A.	755
Los Mochis	LAU, Jesus G.	702
Mexico City	BARBERENA, Elsa	55

RESEARCHER (Cont'd)
NEW ZEALAND

Auckland	TWEEDALE, Dellene M.	1266

NIGERIA

Akure	ONONOGBO, Raphael U.	924
Ibadan	ABOYADE, Beatrice O.	2
Kano	AJIBERO, Matthew I.	9
Okigwe	OGBAA, Clara K.	918

PHILIPPINES

Quezon City	PICACHE, Ursula D.	970

SAUDI ARABIA

Riyadh	BROWN, Biraj L.	142
	BUTT, Abdul W.	167
	KIRKWOOD, Brenda S.	655
	MANSFIELD, Jerry W.	767
	SMITH, Marilynn C.	1157

SOUTH AFRICA

Somerset West	LUSK, Betty M.	749

SPAIN

Barcelona	VELA, Leonor G.	1281

SWEDEN

Taeby	CNATTINGIUS, Claes M.	224

SWITZERLAND

Geneva	OHLMAN, Herbert	919

TRINIDAD

Valsayn	NANTON-COMISSIONG, Barbara L.	887

REVIEWER

ALABAMA

Auburn	ADAMS, Judith A.	(205)826-4500	5
	CANTRELL, Clyde H.	(205)826-4500	179
	FRIEDMAN, Richard E.	(205)826-4510	404
	PEDERSOLI, Heleni M.	(207)821-7168	954
	STRAITON, T H.	(205)826-4500	1199
	VEENSTRA, Robert J.	(205)826-4780	1281
	ZLATOS, Christy L.	(205)826-3429	1390
Birmingham	BLEILER, Richard J.	(205)934-6364	105
	GROOMS, Richard O.	(205)324-6142	472
	MCCARTHY, Sherri L.	(205)226-3630	794
	OLIVE, J F.	(205)967-8481	921
	SCALES, Diann R.	(205)322-8458	1087
	VENABLE, Douglas R.	(205)871-3318	1282
	WEED, Joe K.	(205)991-6600	1315
Brewton	BIGGS-WILLIAMS, Evelyn A.	(205)867-2445	95
Daphne	ROBINSON, Gayle N.	(205)626-2345	1044
Florence	CARR, Charles E.	(205)767-2310	185
Helena	GOODWYN, Betty R.	(205)988-0896	450
Huntsville	KENDRICK, Aubrey W.	(205)837-7597	640
	KITCHENS, Philips H.		657
Mobile	JEFFERY, Phyllis D.	(205)434-7084	596
	MCWHORTER, Jimmie M.	(205)342-5336	818
Montgomery	BEST, Rickey D.	(205)244-9212	92
	FELDER, Jimmie R.	(205)265-2012	369
	GREGORY, Vicki L.	(205)277-1759	466
Pelham	WRIGHT, Amos J.	(205)663-3403	1370
Tuscaloosa	COLEMAN, J G.	(205)348-1523	231
	NEAVILL, Gordon B.	(205)348-1520	891
	PRUITT, Paul M.	(205)348-1107	996

ALASKA

Anchorage	BRAUND-ALLEN, Julianna E.	(907)243-5947	130
	KRAFT, Gwen L.		675
	LESH, Nancy L.	(907)786-1877	718
Bethel	EMMONS, Mary E.	(907)543-3682	348
Central	OAKES, Patricia A.		913
Delta Junction	JENKS, Arlene I.	(907)895-4253	597
Fairbanks	LAKE, Gretchen L.	(907)452-6751	688
	PARHAM, Robert B.	(907)479-5966	940

REVIEWER (Cont'd)
ALASKA (Cont'd)

Juneau	SCHORR, Alan E.	(907)586-6014	1099
	SMITH, George V.	(907)789-2559	1155
Nome	ROSS, Rosemary E.	(907)443-2201	1058
Sitka	MCCLAIN, Harriet V.	(907)747-8160	795

ARIZONA

Apache Junction	WHORTON, Pamela J.	(602)982-1110	1334
Chandler	VATHIS, Alma C.	(602)899-7147	1279
Flagstaff	AWE, Susan C.	(602)523-6808	42
	EGAN, Terence W.	(602)523-6819	338
	HASSELL, Robert H.	(602)523-2171	511
	JOHNSON, Harlan R.	(602)523-4408	605
Glendale	MOSLEY, Shelley E.	(602)939-5469	872
Mesa	MAIN, Isabelle G.	(602)962-4310	761
Phoenix	ALABASTER, Carol	(602)262-7360	9
	TEVIS, Raymond H.	(602)255-4590	1233
Scottsdale	FERRALL, J E.	(602)965-5167	373
Tempe	MILLER, Rosanna	(602)965-3582	842
	SCHON, Isabel	(602)965-2996	1098
	STEWART, Douglas J.	(602)897-7191	1192
Tucson	ALURI, Rao	(602)722-5678	19
	BALDWIN, Charlene M.	(602)327-2385	51
	BUXTON, David T.	(602)621-2101	168
	DICKINSON, Donald C.	(602)621-3565	300
	ETTER, Patricia A.	(602)299-5199	355
	FORE, Janet S.	(602)621-6452	390
	GILREATH, Charles L.	(602)621-4865	437
	GOLDBERG, Susan S.	(602)747-2663	445
	HEIDENREICH, Fred L.	(602)626-7724	521
	HEITSHU, Sara C.	(602)621-2101	523
	HIEB, Louis A.	(602)621-6077	537
	HOLSINGER, Katherine	(602)621-3282	554
	HURT, Charlie D.	(602)621-3566	578
	HUSBAND, Susan M.	(602)624-3301	578
	LAIRD, W D.	(602)621-2101	688
	MAKUCH, Andrew L.	(602)622-8572	762
	MAUTNER, Robert W.	(602)621-6386	787
	MILLS, Victoria A.	(602)795-5299	844
	MINTON, James O.	(602)792-9450	846
	MOUNT, Jack D.	(602)621-6375	873
	MYERS, Roger	(602)792-3452	885
	NICHOLS, Margaret M.		901
	PHIPPS, Shelley E.	(602)621-2101	969
	RIISE, Milton B.	(602)325-1348	1034
	ROBROCK, David P.	(602)743-7072	1045
	RULE, Amy E.	(602)621-6273	1067
	SMITH, Dorman H.	(602)296-3760	1154
	SORENSEN, Lee R.	(602)621-4868	1168
	STOUT, Mary A.	(602)791-4368	1199
	WILLIAMS, Karen B.	(602)621-4866	1344
	WOLFSON, Catherine L.	(602)884-8305	1361

ARKANSAS

Fayetteville	CALLAHAN, Patrick F.	(501)575-5417	173
	DABRISHUS, Michael J.	(501)575-5577	269
	LANGSAM, Christine E.	(501)443-6402	696
	MILLER, Leon C.	(501)575-5577	839
Greenwood	CLEVENGER, Judy B.	(501)996-2856	221
Little Rock	BRECK, Paul A.	(501)569-3121	131
	HALL, John J.	(501)221-2912	488
	MARTIN, Rosemary S.	(501)370-5954	778
	RAZER, Robert L.	(501)663-0789	1012
	RINGER, Sarah A.	(501)569-3121	1035
	SANDERS, Kathryn A.	(501)227-5581	1080
Mountain View	MCNEIL, William K.	(501)269-3851	816
Searcy	BEARD, Craig W.	(501)268-6161	69
Springdale	GREESON, Janet S.	(501)751-4901	465

CALIFORNIA

Alameda	HOSEL, Harold V.	(415)522-5875	561
Alhambra	PORTILLA, Teresa M.		985
Anaheim Hills	JOHNSON, Thomas L.	(714)998-4347	609
APO San Francisco	HEINES, Rodney M.		522
Aptos	HERON, David W.	(408)688-6994	532

REVIEWER (Cont'd)
CALIFORNIA (Cont'd)

Bakersfield	COOPER, William E.	(805)861-2136	244
	KIRKLAND, Janice J.		655
	WADE, Sherry A.		1290
	WINTER, Eugenia B.	(805)833-3175	1356
Ben Lomond	CROWLEY, Terence	(408)336-5019	262
Benicia	MILLER, Davic C.	(707)746-6728	836
	RANDOLPH, Kevin H.	(707)745-9388	1007
Berkeley	ARONER, Miriam D.	(415)849-2711	34
	BARKER, Joseph W.	(415)642-0590	56
	BASART, Ann P.	(415)848-7805	62
	BROWN, Diane M.	(415)642-3532	143
	DUGGAN, Mary K.	(415)642-5764	324
	EASUN, M S.		333
	FALK, Candace S.	(415)526-9591	362
	GAREY, Anita I.	(415)841-8414	418
	GLENDENNING, Barbara J.	(415)642-2531	441
	GRIFFIN, Thomas E.	(415)643-6196	469
	HANDMAN, Gary P.	(415)524-9728	495
	KOBZINA, Norma G.	(415)643-6475	666
	LARSON, Ray R.	(415)642-6046	699
	MAXWELL, Christine Y.	(415)644-4500	788
	MITCHELL, Andrea L.	(415)642-5208	848
	PISANO, Vivian M.	(415)527-1959	975
	SALMON, Stephen R.	(415)549-3394	1077
	SCHNEIDER, Francisca M.	(415)644-6871	1097
	SIBLEY, Elizabeth A.	(415)642-5070	1135
	STOCKTON, Gloria J.	(415)843-8550	1196
	WEEDMAN, Judith	(415)642-9980	1315
	WHEELER, Helen R.	(415)549-2970	1329
	WILLIAMS, Mary S.	(415)649-2520	1345
	ZBORAY, Ronald J.		1386
Brea	PERKINS, Steven C.	(714)671-0778	959
Burlingame	SHERMAN, Roger S.	(415)344-1213	1128
Carlsbad	KENNEDY, Charlene F.	(619)434-2871	640
	TILLETT, Barbara B.		1245
Carphell	ALIX, Cleta M.	(408)371-3294	13
Carpinteria	ALLABACK, Patricia G.	(805)684-4127	13
Carson	SUNDSTRAND, Jacquelyn K.	(213)516-3700	1210
Cerritos	ZEIDLER, Patricia L.	(213)926-1101	1387
Chico	BROWN, Carol G.	(916)861-2762	142
	DWYER, James R.	(916)895-5837	330
	LO, Henrietta W.	(916)895-6406	735
	POWER, Colleen J.	(916)895-4058	989
	SESSIONS, Judith A.	(916)895-5862	1117
Claremont	ALLEN, Susan M.		16
Corona del Mar	DOSER, Virginia A.	(714)760-0148	313
Costa Mesa	POARCH, Margaret E.	(714)662-1867	979
Covina	AROS, Andrew A.	(818)966-4709	34
Culver City	KIRBY, Barbara L.	(213)839-1009	653
	NG, Carol S.	(213)202-6523	900
	PATTEN, Frederick W.	(213)827-3335	947
Cupertino	JAJKO, Edward A.	(408)446-1306	592
	MACEK, Rosanne M.	(408)973-3116	755
	MILLER, Ronald F.	(408)257-9162	842
Davis	CACCESE, Vincent	(916)752-3052	170
	COLLINS, William J.	(916)758-4989	233
	KNOWLES, Em C.	(916)752-1126	665
	LAMPRECHT, Sandra J.	(916)752-1126	691
	SHARROW, Marilyn J.	(916)752-2110	1122
Downey	PAIK, Nan H.	(213)922-4648	935
East Palo Alto	FROST, Michelle	(415)321-4017	406
El Cerrito	HARDWICK, Bonnie S.	(415)237-7011	500
	MACAULEY, C C.	(415)524-2762	754
	PRESSNALL, Patricia E.	(415)525-5186	991
Encino	WOOD, Raymund F.		1364
Fallbrook	COMPTON, Joan C.	(619)723-2860	235
Fremont	DIBLE, Joan A.	(415)792-8736	299
Fresno	KING, Cynthia		650
Fullerton	ANDERSEN, Leslie N.		21
	BRIL, Patricia L.	(714)773-3852	136
	MASTERS, Robin J.	(714)524-9696	782
Garden Grove	HIXON, Donald L.	(714)638-9379	544
Glen Ellen	SCARBOROUGH, Katharine T.	(707)996-7993	1087
Glendale	BURNS, Nancy R.	(818)244-1994	162
Grand Terrace	MARCHIANO, Marilyn C.	(714)382-2353	768
Hayward	ARROWOOD, Donna J.	(415)881-2791	34
Hillsborough	ABILOCK, Debbie	(415)348-2272	2

REVIEWER (Cont'd)
CALIFORNIA (Cont'd)

Huntington Beach	BAUER, Caroline F.	(714)969-2777	65
	MACKINTOSH, Mary L.	(714)896-4639	757
	OPPENHEIM, Michael R.	(714)842-1548	925
Inglewood	GOUDELOCK, Carol V.	(213)672-2543	454
Irvine	ARIEL, Joan	(714)856-4970	31
	FORBES, Fred R.	(714)856-4974	389
	GELFAND, Julia M.	(714)856-4971	426
	HORN, Judy K.		559
	POOLE, Jay M.	(714)856-6377	983
	PUGSLEY, Sharon G.	(714)856-7193	997
	TSANG, Daniel C.	(714)856-4978	1260
	WOODS, Lawrence A.	(714)786-3507	1367
	YOUNG, Eleanor C.	(714)552-5803	1381
Kensington	MULVANY, Nancy	(415)524-4195	878
La Canada-Flintridge	MORAN, William R.	(818)790-1529	862
La Crescenta	BUTTERWORTH, Linda M.		167
La Jolla	ALLISON, Terry L.	(619)534-1256	17
	BOWLES, Garrett H.	(619)534-2759	121
	CASTETTER, Karla M.	(619)459-5369	194
	HURLBERT, Irene W.	(619)534-1261	577
	MILLER, R B.	(619)534-3064	841
	SCHILLER, Anita R.	(619)534-3337	1093
	SMITH, Phillip A.	(619)534-1266	1159
La Mirada	ANJOU-DURAZZO, Martel T.	(213)944-5981	28
Lafayette	NEWAY, Julie M.	(415)283-1862	898
Lake View Terrace	NAVARRO, Frank A.		889
Lodi	YAMAMOTO, Conrad S.	(209)478-2533	1376
Long Beach	OSSEN, Virginia F.	(213)424-5415	928
	SINCLAIR, Lorelei P.	(213)423-6399	1142
	WILLIAMS, Valencia	(213)434-9151	1347
Los Altos	CONDIT, Larry D.	(415)948-7690	235
Los Angeles	ANDREWS, Karen L.	(213)825-2649	26
	BATES, Marcia J.	(213)825-4352	64
	BEVERAGE, Stephanie L.	(213)612-3242	93
	CAMPBELL, Patricia J.	(213)666-6967	177
	CASE, Donald O.	(213)825-1379	191
	CHAMPLIN, Peggy	(213)472-4991	198
	CONNOR, Anne C.	(213)312-8323	237
	CONNOR, Billie M.	(213)660-6399	237
	CREWS, Kenneth D.	(213)397-1518	258
	DEENEY, Kay E.	(213)479-6672	286
	DOUGLAS, Carolyn T.	(213)472-5287	314
	GLITZ, Beryl	(213)206-8016	441
	GRANGER, Dorothy J.	(818)795-9161	457
	GRASSIAN, Esther S.	(213)825-2138	458
	JAFFE, Lee D.	(213)935-6770	591
	KAPLAN, Robin	(213)851-2480	626
	KUNSELMAN, Joan D.	(213)825-1204	684
	LAWRENCE, John R.	(213)206-1223	704
	MITTAN, Rhonda L.	(213)271-6823	850
	MORSE, David H.	(213)224-7413	869
	PANSKI, Saul J.	(213)655-1415	938
	PASCAL, Barbara R.	(213)934-2205	945
	PATRON, Susan H.	(213)612-3285	947
	RICHARDSON, John V.	(213)825-4352	1029
	ROSENBERG, Melvin H.	(213)612-3242	1056
	SATER, Analya	(213)277-1969	1083
	SCHERREI, Rita A.	(213)825-1201	1092
	SCHOTTLAENDER, Brian E.	(213)825-7785	1099
	SMITH, Catherine M.	(213)669-6523	1153
	STERNHEIM, Karen	(213)825-3047	1189
	SUGRANES, Maria R.	(213)201-3507	1207
	THOMPSON, Don K.	(213)743-2540	1239
	TREISTER, Cyril C.	(213)227-1604	1255
	WAGNER, Sharon L.	(213)931-4048	1292
	WATERS, Marie B.	(213)825-1693	1308
	WEISBAUM, Earl		1319
	WOOD, Elizabeth H.	(213)224-7234	1364
	WUERTZ, Eva L.	(213)743-2540	1373
Manhattan Beach	BALDWIN, Claudia A.	(213)372-1987	51
Marina del Rey	SHANK, Russell	(213)823-6123	1120
Menlo Park	BOYE, Inger	(415)325-8077	123
	DENNETT, Stephen C.		292
	DILORETO, Ann M.	(415)326-7370	303
	MYERS, Nancy J.	(415)854-3591	884
Mill Valley	ROBERTS, Justine T.		1040
	WHITE, Cecil R.	(415)388-8080	1330

REVIEWER (Cont'd)
CALIFORNIA (Cont'd)

Mission Viejo	GORDON, Wendy R.	(714)582-4932	452
Monterey	BRUMAN, Janet L.		150
Moraga	RUDOLPH, Anne L.	(415)631-0926	1066
Moreno Valley	SWAFFORD, William M.	(714)242-7719	1212
Mountain View	BUTLER, Matilda L.	(415)969-0606	167
	PAISLEY, William J.	(415)969-0606	935
	STANEK, Suzanne	(415)969-9225	1179
Napa	CHAMBERLIN, Leslie A.	(707)253-1071	198
Nevada City	BISHOP, Diane		99
Northridge	ECKLUND, Kristin A.	(818)349-6115	335
Norton AFB	CROWTHER, Carol	(714)382-7119	262
Novato	HIRABAYASHI, Joanne	(415)897-4245	543
	HOTZ, Sharon M.	(415)892-0821	562
Oakland	BYRNE, Elizabeth D.	(415)658-6996	169
	CHESTER, Claudia J.	(415)835-4692	207
	DANTON, J P.	(415)653-4802	274
	MULL, Richard G.	(415)841-2590	876
	NEWCOMBE, Barbara T.	(415)763-4406	898
	RUBIN, Rhea J.	(415)339-1274	1064
	WONG, Patricia M.	(415)834-2742	1363
Ojai	MOORE, Phyllis C.	(805)646-8592	861
Palo Alto	GREEN-MALONEY, Nancy	(415)858-3816	465
	OLSON, Sharon L.	(415)329-2694	923
	ROSS, Alexander D.	(415)494-7302	1057
	SUMMIT, Roger K.	(415)858-3777	1209
	VARKENTINE, Aganita	(415)493-8853	1278
Pasadena	CHOUDHURY, Lori B.	(818)449-9468	211
	HICKS, Cynthia S.	(818)792-6830	536
	KLINE, Victoria E.	(818)405-2100	661
	LONGO, Margaret K.	(818)793-7682	740
	POSTER, Susan E.	(818)398-8897	986
	WONG, Maida L.	(818)795-1255	1363
Pebble Beach	ANDRUS, Eloise A.	(408)624-1257	27
Petaluma	GORDON, Ruth I.	(707)778-4719	452
Placentia	HAUSSMANN, Virginia D.		513
Pomona	ADAMSON, Danette	(714)869-3109	6
	HSIA, Ting M.	(714)869-3107	567
	IVERSON, Diann S.	(714)624-4728	585
	STREETER, David	(714)620-2026	1201
Portola Valley	ERTEL, Monica	(415)851-1007	353
Poway	D'ADOLF, Steven P.	(619)451-2130	269
	DOLLEN, Charles J.	(619)748-5348	310
Rancho Cacamonga	CONNELL, William S.	(714)989-0506	237
Redwood City	BANGE, Stephanie D.	(415)369-6251	54
	HIMMEL, Ned A.	(415)369-6251	542
	SCHLACHTER, Gail A.	(415)594-0743	1093
Richmond	TURITZ, Mitch L.	(415)527-5109	1263
Riverside	HUNTER, David C.	(714)787-5841	576
	KOSHER, Helene J.	(714)787-4628	672
	MITCHELL, Steve		849
	STALKER, Laura A.	(714)787-5841	1178
	THOMPSON, James C.	(714)682-4549	1240
	WEBB, Gayle E.	(714)787-2460	1313
Roseville	NICKERSON, Susan L.	(916)781-0221	902
Sacramento	ANDERSEN, Thomas K.	(916)324-4863	21
	JACKSON, Gloria D.	(916)427-1956	587
	KONG, Leslie M.	(916)278-5664	670
	LOW, Kathleen	(916)322-4570	743
	RUDDOCK, Velda I.	(916)921-0521	1065
	SCHEIBEL, Susan	(916)392-9461	1091
	WILLIAMS, Joan F.	(916)927-4953	1344
Saint Helena	STOCKWELL, Judith R.	(707)963-3533	1196
San Diego	BUSCH, Barbara	(619)224-8412	165
	FORMAN, Jack	(619)546-9250	390
	HERON, Susan J.	(619)260-4800	532
	JACOBS, Horace	(619)746-4005	589
	LAGIES, Meinhart J.	(619)283-0608	688
	TRIVISON, Margaret A.	(619)452-7338	1257
	VEGA, Carolyn L.		1281
San Francisco	AVENEY, Brian H.	(415)338-2956	41
	CARSCH, Ruth E.	(415)641-5014	187
	COLBY, Michael D.	(415)558-4633	230
	DONOVAN, Diane C.	(415)587-7009	312
	ECKMAN, Charles D.	(415)334-8449	335
	ELNOR, Nancy G.	(415)929-1948	346
	GRIFFIN, Michael D.	(415)664-2835	468
	GUNDERSON, Jeffery R.	(415)929-1472	477

REVIEWER (Cont'd)
CALIFORNIA (Cont'd)
San Francisco

	HUNG, Joanne Y.	(415)221-7325	574
	HUNSUCKER, Alice E.	(415)396-7909	574
	JANK, David A.	(415)751-9958	593
	KAUN, Thomas T.	(415)821-9303	631
	KIRSHENBAUM, Sandra D.	(415)776-1530	655
	LAND, Barbara J.	(415)221-7707	692
	MANN, Thomas	(415)951-0100	766
	MORITZ, Thomas D.	(415)750-7102	865
	MORRIS, Effie L.	(415)931-2733	866
	NYHAN, Catherine W.	(415)558-3510	912
	PABST, Kahleen T.	(415)421-1750	933
	REGNER-HYATT, Anne L.	(415)864-1154	1017
	RUNYON, Steven C.	(415)386-5873	1067
	STOCKFLETH, Craig G.	(415)387-6040	1195
	WILSON, Jacqueline B.	(415)476-2534	1351
San Jose	BRIDGMAN, David L.	(408)997-3723	135
	ELLIOTT, Patricia G.	(408)277-9243	344
	HARMON, Robert B.	(408)297-2810	502
	RODICH, Lorraine E.	(408)277-9788	1047
	ROSEN, Elizabeth M.	(408)277-2270	1055
San Leandro	WENDROFF, Catriona	(415)569-3491	1323
San Luis Obispo	ROCKMAN, Ilene F.	(805)756-2273	1046
San Marcos	CATER, Judy J.	(619)744-1150	194
San Marino	SPIRO GREEN, Becky A.	(818)405-2188	1175
San Rafael	TRZECIAK, William J.	(415)485-3319	1260
Santa Barbara	ANDERSON, Carol L.	(805)685-7585	22
	DAY, Bettie B.	(805)964-4711	282
	HERZIG, Stella J.	(805)966-9764	534
	MACGREGOR, Raymond	(805)682-5654	755
Santa Clara	CHESSMAN, Rebecca L.	(408)244-2775	207
Santa Cruz	COOPER, Susan C.	(408)426-2841	243
	LOMBARDI, Mary L.	(408)476-1131	738
	MARIE, Jacquelyn	(408)429-2802	770
	RITCH, Alan W.	(408)429-2802	1036
	STEVENS, Stanley D.	(408)475-9172	1191
Santa Monica	BERMAN, Marsha	(213)399-3674	88
Santa Paula	CHRISTOPHER, Paul	(805)525-8092	212
Santa Rosa	WALSH, Donamarie F.		1299
Sebastopol	SIMONS, Maurice M.	(707)823-9275	1141
Sherman Oaks	KWAN, Julie K.	(818)784-8606	685
	MILLER, Margaret S.	(818)783-5264	840
Sonoma	WINSON, Gail I.	(707)935-1546	1355
South Pasadena	BESTE, Ian R.		92
Stanford	CARSON, Susan A.	(415)723-2092	188
	CRAWFORD, Walt	(415)329-3551	257
	MUSEN, Mark A.	(415)723-6979	883
	SCHMIDT, C J.	(415)493-5280	1095
Stockton	LEONHARDT, Thomas W.	(209)946-2434	717
	MOORE, Evia B.	(209)474-7029	859
Sunland	CLARK, Patricia A.	(818)353-6820	217
Sunnyvale	VAN VELZER, Verna J.	(408)738-2888	1277
Torrance	DOWNEY, Christine D.	(213)618-5962	316
	HANSEN, Linda L.		497
	MOORE, Richard K.	(213)533-4386	861
Turlock	PARKER, John C.	(209)634-9473	942
Venice	CHARBONNEAU, Ronald P.	(213)396-5441	202
	EDELSTEIN, J M.	(213)827-8984	335
	WALTER, Virginia A.	(213)392-7627	1300
Walnut Creek	BECK, Diane J.	(415)939-9129	71
West Hollywood	BUTKIS, John F.	(213)000-0000	166
Westlake Village	TISE, Barbara L.	(818)991-0047	1247
Whittier	WILLIAMS, Lisa B.	(213)693-0771	1344
Winters	PEATTIE, Noel	(916)662-3364	953
Woodland	WEBBER, Steven L.	(916)661-1242	1313
Woodland Hills	CLIFTON, Joe A.	(818)716-3171	222
	NELSON-HARB, Sally R.		895
	RUBEN, Jacquelen S.		1064

COLORADO

Alamosa	SHELDON, L S.	(303)589-6592	1126
Boulder	FINK, Deborah	(303)492-8302	378
	KOHL, David F.	(303)492-6897	668
	KRISMANN, Carol H.	(303)499-2977	678
	MEYER, Andrea P.		829
	MUELLER, Carolyn J.	(313)492-6788	875
	VARNES, Richard S.	(303)444-8051	1279
	VOLC, Judith G.	(303)442-3578	1287

REVIEWER (Cont'd)
COLORADO (Cont'd)

Colorado Springs	NEILON, Barbara L.	(303)574-6167	892
	STEWART, Anna C.	(303)472-0268	1192
	WYLIE, Nethery A.	(606)593-3290	1375
Denver	ABRAMS, Jeanne E.	(303)871-2961	3
	ASHTON, Rick J.	(303)745-9883	36
	BROCK, Laurie N.	(303)333-2772	138
	ESTES, Mark E.	(303)861-7000	355
	FOLEY, Georgiana	(303)571-2172	387
	GIGNAC, Solange G.	(303)575-3751	433
	HENSINGER, James S.	(303)691-0550	529
	MOULTON, Suzanne L.	(303)871-6427	873
	SCHAFER, Jay G.	(303)556-8370	1089
	VOLZ, Edward J.	(303)571-2033	1288
Fort Collins	CHAMBERS, Joan L.	(303)491-1833	198
	CHRISTENSEN, Erin S.	(303)224-4588	211
	NEWMAN, John	(303)491-1844	899
	SCHMIDT, Fred C.	(303)491-1881	1095
Greeley	KNEPEL, Nancy	(303)356-4357	664
Littleton	ALSOP, Robyn J.	(303)779-1925	18
	GREALY, Deborah J.	(303)795-3156	461
	SALLE, Ellen M.	(303)794-2641	1076
	WHITBY, Thomas J.	(303)798-7049	1330
	WYNAR, Bohdan S.		1375

CONNECTICUT

Ansonia	MARTIN, Walter F.	(203)736-2601	779
Avery Point	HOLLOWAY, Patricia W.	(203)445-5577	552
Bethany	ASH, Lee M.	(203)393-2723	35
Bridgeport	HUGHES, John M.	(203)576-4392	571
	MULAWKA, Chet	(203)576-7402	876
	STEMMER, Katherine R.	(203)384-3254	1186
Bristol	CALLAHAN, Helen H.	(203)584-7787	173
Collinsville	EICKENHORST, Joanna W.	(203)693-4315	339
Danbury	BURKAT, Leonard	(203)743-2137	160
Danielson	WEIGEL, James S.	(203)774-7755	1316
Derby	FINNUCAN, Louise A.	(203)732-7399	379
Farmington	DEVINE, Marie E.	(203)677-2140	297
Glastonbury	SCHUTT, Cheryl M.	(203)633-0427	1103
Groton	DAIGNEAULT, Audrey I.	(203)446-8431	270
Hamden	NEWHALL, Ann C.	(203)288-8180	898
	SAMUEL, Harold E.	(203)432-0495	1079
Hartford	KAIMOWITZ, Jeffery H.	(203)527-3151	622
	NEUFELD, Irving H.	(203)278-3202	897
	SCHULTZE, Salvatrice G.	(203)525-9121	1102
Kent	CUSTER, Deborah P.	(203)927-3098	267
Lakeville	RESTOUT, Denise T.	(203)435-9308	1024
Middletown	BALAY, Robert E.	(203)347-6933	50
	BECK, Arthur R.	(203)347-1387	71
	FARRINGTON, James	(203)347-9411	365
	SABOSIK, Patricia E.	(203)347-6933	1073
Milford	BARGAR, Arthur W.	(203)783-3290	56
	WESTBROOK, Patricia C.	(203)878-3551	1326
New Britain	KASCUS, Marie A.	(203)827-7565	628
	LAWRENCE, Scott W.	(203)677-1659	705
	WARZALA, Martin L.		1307
New Canaan	ROCKMAN, Connie C.	(203)972-3731	1046
	SENATOR, Rochelle B.	(203)966-5645	1115
New Haven	BROWN, William E.	(203)432-1749	148
	CLARIE, Thomas C.	(203)397-4511	216
	COLLIER, Bonnie	(203)432-1783	232
	ENSEL, Ellen H.	(203)782-2525	350
	HEINRITZ, Fred J.	(203)397-4530	522
	HERMAN, Felicia G.	(203)776-6244	531
	HILL, John R.	(203)397-4509	540
	IANNUZZI, Patricia A.	(203)432-1785	581
	JOHNSON, Eric W.	(203)467-8721	604
	KRITEMEYER, Ann C.		679
	LAWRENCE, Carol A.	(203)785-4346	704
	ROBERTS, Susanne F.	(203)432-1762	1041
	SIGGINS, Jack A.	(203)776-3808	1137
New London	JOHNSON, Carolyn A.	(203)447-7535	602
	ROGERS, Brian D.	(203)447-7622	1049
	SORENSEN, Pamela	(203)447-7622	1168
Newington	LERITZ, M K.	(203)278-1280	717
Norwalk	BOHRER, Karen M.	(203)854-5275	111
Ridgefield	FARADAY, Joanna	(203)431-0062	363
	SWIFT, Janet B.	(203)438-5937	1216

REVIEWER (Cont'd)
CONNECTICUT (Cont'd)

Stamford	GOLOMB, Katherine A.	(203)964-1000	447
	KNOPP, Marie L.	(203)348-1173	665
	LIEBERMAN, Lucille N.	(203)353-2095	726
	WILLIAMS, Judy R.	(203)964-1000	1344
Stonington	WILLIAMS, Edwin E.	(203)535-0720	1343
Storrs	BOGNAR, Dorothy M.		111
	JENSEN, Joan W.	(203)486-2513	598
	KAGAN, Alfred	(203)429-6565	621
	ROLLIN, Marian B.	(203)429-4187	1051
	STEVENS, Norman D.	(203)429-7051	1190
Suffield	CHEESEMAN, Bruce S.	(203)668-6273	204
Tollard	WILDE, Daniel U.	(203)872-7000	1338
Torrington	BENAMATI, Dennis C.	(203)489-2990	79
Wallingford	MANDOUR, Cecile A.	(203)269-4718	765
Warren	HENTZ, Margaret B.	(203)868-9178	530
Waterbury	CARRINGTON, Virginia F.	(203)574-4702	186
Watertown	COGLISER, Luann L.	(203)274-5411	227
West Hartford	NORONHA, Marilyn S.	(203)523-9765	909
	TALIT, Lynn	(203)233-7793	1221
Weston	FADER, Ellen G.	(203)226-8403	360
Wilton	TRIFFIN, Nicholas	(914)681-4275	1256
Windsor	PARKS, Amy N.	(203)549-0404	943

DELAWARE

Dover	COONS, Daniel E.	(302)736-5111	242
	TRYON, Roy H.	(302)674-4522	1260
New Castle	BROWN, Sarah C.	(307)328-3447	147
Odessa	JAMISON, Susan C.	(302)378-2158	593
Wilmington	COE, Gloria M.	(302)998-8814	226
	DRUKKER, Alexander E.	(302)478-1746	320
	MINNICH, Nancy P.	(302)478-5291	846
	TITUS, H M.	(302)656-1722	1247
	TOMAN, Jocelyn B.		1249

DISTRICT OF COLUMBIA

Washington	BALL, Alice D.	(202)362-6047	52
	BATTLE, Thomas C.	(202)636-7241	65
	BECKERMAN, George	(202)775-9022	72
	BEDARD, Laura A.	(202)662-9172	73
	BEDARD, Laura A.	(202)662-9172	73
	BELLARDO, Trudi	(202)363-9614	78
	BERWICK, Philip C.	(202)543-3369	91
	BLOZIS, Jolene M.	(202)857-7056	107
	BLUMER, Thomas J.	(202)543-7031	107
	CHAMBERS, Bettye T.	(202)625-4997	198
	CHANG, Helen S.	(202)651-5214	200
	CHASE, Linda S.	(202)885-3238	203
	CHESTNUT, Paul I.	(202)462-3280	207
	CHILD, Margaret S.	(202)357-1521	208
	DE ARMAN, Charles L.	(202)797-7169	284
	DOWD, Mary J.	(202)523-3174	315
	DOWLING, Shelley L.	(202)662-9144	316
	ELSASSER, Katharine K.	(202)544-0552	346
	FLYNN, Richard M.	(202)638-1956	387
	FORREST, Phyllis E.		391
	FOX, Ann M.	(202)244-6355	394
	GAMSON, Arthur L.	(202)382-5921	416
	GARLICK, Karen	(202)287-5634	419
	GRAY, Michael H.	(202)755-4799	460
	HARWOOD, James L.	(202)523-3281	510
	HEARTY, John A.	(202)872-4533	519
	JONES, Catherine A.	(202)287-8935	611
	KEHOE, Patrick E.	(202)805-2074	634
	KENDRICK, Brent L.	(202)543-7031	640
	KITZMILLER, Virginia G.		657
	KLEIN, Kristine J.	(202)362-2816	659
	KNAUFF, Elisabeth S.		663
	LISOWSKI, Andrew H.	(202)287-5491	732
	MANNING, Martin J.	(202)485-6187	766
	MCCOY-LARSON, Sandra	(202)544-5520	799
	MCGUIRE, Brian		808
	MCNAMARA, Emma J.	(202)382-5922	816
	MILEVSKI, Robert J.	(202)287-5634	834
	MILEVSKI, Sandra N.	(202)543-7145	835
	MUSSEHL, Allan A.	(202)488-8162	883
	PACIFICO, Michele F.	(202)253-3214	933
	PAGE, John S.	(202)554-0486	934
	PEYTON, David	(202)544-1969	966

REVIEWER (Cont'd)
DISTRICT OF COLUMBIA (Cont'd)

Washington	PREER, Jean L.	(202)635-5085	990
	PRUETT, Barbara J.	(202)362-1345	996
	PURDY, Virginia C.	(202)523-3105	998
	REITH, Louis J.	(202)686-0131	1022
	ROMEO, Sheryl R.	(202)626-7491	1052
	ROONEY, Eugene M.		1053
	ROSENBERG, Jane A.	(202)786-0358	1056
	ROSENFELD, Mary A.	(202)357-1940	1056
	RUSH, Candace M.	(202)393-4695	1068
	SANCHEZ, Jose L.	(202)387-7396	1079
	SIPKOV, Ivan	(202)287-9850	1144
	STARCK, William L.	(202)234-6006	1181
	STEBELMAN, Scott D.	(202)994-6049	1183
	STEWART, Ruth A.	(202)287-6587	1193
	STONE, Elizabeth W.	(202)338-5574	1197
	TERRY, Susan N.	(202)332-7120	1232
	THOMPSON, Elizabeth M.	(202)333-2108	1239
	TURTELL, Neal T.	(202)842-6506	1265
	VASLEF, Irene	(202)342-3240	1279
	WALKER, Heather C.	(202)544-2443	1295
	WELCH, Thomas L.	(202)232-1706	1321
	YARNALL, James L.	(202)234-6293	1378

FLORIDA

Atlantic Beach	URBANSKI, Verna P.	(904)246-3631	1269
Belle Glade	SNODGRASSE, Elaine	(305)996-3453	1163
Bonifay	HOWELL, Wanda H.	(904)547-3631	565
Bradenton	MORR, Lynell A.	(813)747-4319	866
Clearwater	POTTER, Robert E.	(813)442-9061	987
	RITZ, Paul S.	(813)585-0985	1037
Coral Gables	ROBAR, Terri J.	(305)284-4706	1038
	WAXMAN, Jack	(305)284-2429	1311
Dade City	SPENCER, Albert F.		1173
Daytona Beach	MINOR, Dorothy C.	(904)253-6627	846
De Land	EVERETT, David D.	(904)734-4121	358
	JOHNSON, Betty D.	(904)734-7630	602
Dunedin	FIORE, Carole D.	(813)733-2595	379
	TEW, Robin L.	(813)734-5634	1233
Fort Lauderdale	MILLER, Margaret R.	(305)791-1278	840
Gainesville	COVEY, William C.	(904)392-0796	252
	LEONARD, Louise F.	(904)373-2705	716
	MALANCHUK, Peter P.	(904)392-0364	762
	TEAGUE, Edward H.	(904)392-0222	1229
	WILLETT, Charles	(904)378-1661	1341
	WOODS, Susan E.	(904)392-4018	1367
Howey in the Hills	COHN, William L.	(904)324-2701	229
Jacksonville	GUNN, Thomas H.	(904)744-3950	477
	SUGDEN, Martin D.	(904)634-1626	1206
Key West	SOULE, Maria J.	(305)296-9081	1169
Live Oak	HISS, Sheila M.	(904)362-6936	544
Miami	ADAMS, Gustav C.	(305)261-7031	4
	BYRD, Susan G.	(305)347-2068	169
	CHAVES, Francisco M.	(305)385-2301	204
	LEHMAN, Douglas K.	(305)279-5770	712
	LIANZI, Theresa L.	(305)375-5230	725
	LOPEZ, Silvia P.	(305)596-1695	741
	PARISE, Marina P.		940
	SANCHEZ, Sara M.	(305)854-7752	1079
	SEGOR, Phyllis L.	(305)940-6014	1112
	SEILER, Susan L.	(305)279-0545	1112
	WILLIAMS, Thomas L.	(305)547-5782	1347
	WULF, Karlinne V.	(305)856-6022	1374
Miami Beach	MIRANDA, Salvador	(305)532-6834	847
Naples	O'CONNOR, Mary A.	(813)598-9269	916
North Miami	MCCAMMON, Leslie V.	(305)940-5716	793
Orlando	BRIERTY, Carol A.	(305)275-2564	135
	CUBBERLEY, Carol W.	(305)275-2521	263
	HUDSON, Phyllis J.	(305)275-2584	569
	TREMBLAY, Gerald F.	(305)277-6944	1255
Palm Bay	TIPPLE, Roberta L.	(305)984-2891	1246
Palm Harbor	PASSARELLO, Nancy H.	(813)733-7986	946
Pensacola	BROWN, Lyn S.	(904)478-8480	145
	MOREIN, P. G.	(904)474-2492	863
	TERNAK, Armand T.	(904)479-7835	1232
Pompano Beach	GULLETTE, Irene		477
Port Charlotte	HOLSTINE, Lesa G.	(813)697-3365	554
Royal Palm Beach	TERWILLEGAR, Jane C.	(305)793-4590	1232

REVIEWER (Cont'd)
FLORIDA (Cont'd)

St Petersburg	CATES, Jo A.	(813)522-1550	194
	HARDESTY, Larry L.	(813)867-1166	499
	WATERS, Sally G.	(813)345-1335	1308
Sarasota	JENKINS, Althea H.	(813)355-5003	597
	MOON, Eric	(813)355-1795	857
	RETZER, Elizabeth H.	(813)921-1741	1024
	WEAVER, James B.	(813)378-1287	1312
Seminole	BRYAN, Michael G.	(813)595-4521	151
	WEISS, Susan		1320
Tallahassee	DE PEW, John N.	(904)644-5775	293
	MILLER, Betty D.	(904)335-4405	836
	MILLER, Charles E.	(904)644-5211	836
	SUMMERS, F W.	(904)644-5775	1209
	TOOLE, Gregor K.		1250
	VAN ORDEN, Phyllis J.	(904)385-1290	1276
Tampa	CRAIG, James P.	(813)238-5514	254
	EVANS, Josephine K.	(813)974-4471	357
	HAMRELL, Larry G.	(813)971-4143	494
	HAWK, Susan P.	(813)239-3268	513
	LOSEY, Doris C.	(813)885-4500	742
	MATHEWS, Richard B.	(813)253-3333	784
Venice	CARR, Mary L.	(813)497-0420	186
West Palm Beach	TAFFEL, Bobbe H.	(305)582-2539	1219

GEORGIA

Albany	TOOKES, Amos J.	(912)439-5242	1250
Athens	BAKER, Barry B.	(404)542-2534	47
	ELLIS, Marie C.	(404)548-7830	345
	GUBISTA, Kathryn R.	(404)546-8153	475
	LIBBEY, George H.	(404)542-2716	725
	QUINLAN, Judy B.	(404)542-0654	1000
	SUTHERLAND, Johnnie D.	(404)542-0690	1211
	WILLIAMS, Sara E.	(408)548-7519	1346
Atlanta	BAUSCH, Donna K.	(404)521-3800	67
	BERGMANN, Sue A.	(404)261-4719	87
	BIBBY, Elizabeth A.	(404)255-6840	94
	BRADLEY, Gail P.	(404)872-9472	125
	CAMP, John F.	(404)875-4373	175
	CORRELL, Emily N.	(404)633-3320	247
	COURSEY, W T.	(404)264-0714	251
	DEES, Leslie M.	(404)894-4523	287
	ELZY, Martin I.	(404)331-3942	347
	HEID, Gregory G.	(404)688-4636	521
	JAMES, Stephen E.	(404)681-0251	592
	JOHNSON, Herbert F.	(404)727-6861	605
	LAWSON, Venable A.	(404)377-1142	705
	LEE, Lauren K.	(404)588-1390	710
	MCDAVID, Sara J.	(404)395-1605	801
	MCIVER, Stephanie P.	(404)688-4636	809
	MILLER, Anthony G.	(404)688-4636	835
	MILLER, Jack E.	(404)892-3600	838
	NITSCHKE, Marie M.	(404)727-6875	905
	NIX, Kemie	(404)355-7421	905
	QUINLIN, Margaret M.	(404)874-1589	1000
	ROSS, Theodosia B.	(404)696-2355	1059
	SEARCY, David L.	(404)525-8802	1109
	TOMAJKO, Kathy L.	(404)894-4511	1249
	TROUTMAN, Joseph E.	(404)522-8980	1258
	WHITE, Carol A.	(404)351-8991	1330
	WILLIAMS, Nancy F.	(404)451-0331	1345
	WILTSE, Helen C.	(404)451-4260	1353
Augusta	BUSTOS, Roxann R.	(404)737-1748	166
	MCCANN, Jett C.	(404)828-3491	794
Cartersville	HOWINGTON, Lee R.	(404)382-4203	566
Columbus	CLEMENTS, Betty H.	(404)327-3399	221
	SELF, Sharon W.	(404)323-5520	1113
Dalton	LARY, Marilyn S.	(404)272-4527	700
Decatur	BUDLONG, Thomas F.	(404)289-0583	155
	HATCHER, Nolan C.	(404)378-8282	511
	HUGHES, Glenda J.	(404)636-0108	571
	OVERBECK, James A.	(404)378-8821	931
	WENDEROTH, Christine	(404)378-8821	1323
Doerun	BOWEN, Louise E.	(912)782-5408	120
East Point	BAIN, Michael L.	(404)761-4346	47
	ELTZROTH, Elsbeth L.	(404)767-3144	346
Experiment	LEDFORD, Carole L.	(404)228-7238	708
Griffin	WILKINSON, Evalyn S.	(404)227-8532	1340

REVIEWER (Cont'd)
GEORGIA (Cont'd)

La Grange	GIBSON, Ricky S.	(404)884-3757	432
	LEWIS, Frank R.	(404)882-2911	723
Lilburn	HOUGH, Leslie S.	(404)979-0270	562
Macon	HOWARD, Mary R.	(912)744-2960	564
Norcross	DEWBERRY, Claire D.	(404)564-1634	298
Statesboro	JOHNSON, Jane G.	(912)681-1609	605
Stone Mountain	ENGERRAND, Steven W.	(404)469-5066	349
Sylvester	MEREY-KADAR, Ervin R.	(912)776-0723	825
Thomasville	CLARKE, Elba C.	(912)228-4280	218
Valdosta	CLARK, Tommy A.	(912)244-6124	218

HAWAII

Aiea	TIMBERLAKE, Cynthia A.	(808)488-4507	1245
Honolulu	CAMPBELL, R A.	(808)955-8822	177
	DILUCIA, Samuel J.	(808)955-1500	303
	JACKSON, Miles M.	(808)948-7321	588
	LINVILLE, Marcia L.	(808)737-2511	731
	LUNDEEN, Gerald W.	(808)948-7321	748
	SZILARD, Paula	(808)948-8263	1218
	TRAPIDO, Joel	(808)988-2068	1254
	VAN NIEL, Eloise S.	(808)548-6283	1276
Kailua-Kona	KOLMAN, Roberta F.		669
Pearl City	KAN, Katharine L.		624

IDAHO

Boise	WELLS, Merle W.	(208)334-3356	1322
Idaho Falls	VERHOFF, Patricia A.	(208)523-9601	1282
Moscow	ABRAHAM, Terry		3
	CURL, Margo W.	(208)885-6260	265
Pocatello	DOWNEY, Howard R.	(208)232-1263	316
	WATSON, Peter G.	(208)236-2997	1310

ILLINOIS

Addison	WRIGHT, Deborah L.	(312)628-3338	1371
Arlington Heights	VONDRUSKA, Eloise M.	(312)392-7232	1288
Bloomington	ALEXANDER, Lynetta L.	(309)828-6053	12
Carbondale	BAUNER, Ruth E.	(618)457-5773	67
	BLACK, George W.	(618)453-2700	101
	BORUZKOWSKI, Lilly A.	(618)453-2365	117
	COX, Shelley M.	(618)457-8975	253
	DALE, Doris C.	(618)536-2441	270
	JENKINS, Darrell L.	(618)549-8053	597
	KILPATRICK, Thomas L.	(618)453-3374	648
	PERSON, Roland C.	(618)453-2818	961
	RYAN, Sheila	(618)549-7029	1071
	STARRATT, Joseph A.	(618)453-2683	1182
Champaign	ALLEN, Walter C.	(217)586-3882	16
	BERGER, Sidney E.	(217)351-8140	86
	CHAPLAN, Margaret A.	(217)333-7993	201
	CLOONAN, Michele V.	(217)351-8140	223
	MCCLELLAN, William M.	(217)352-1893	796
	REPTA, Vada L.	(217)398-5728	1024
	WERT, Lucille M.	(217)356-6600	1325
Charleston	KAPLAN, Sylvia Y.	(217)345-4228	626
	NESBIT, Angus B.	(217)345-7293	896
	POLLARD, Frances M.	(217)345-5610	981
Chicago	ALTHAGE, Celia J.		18
	BAMBERGER, Mary A.	(312)996-2742	53
	BEZIRGAN, Basima	(312)667-5205	93
	BOLEF, Doris	(312)942-2271	112
	BOLT, Janice A.	(312)233-9399	113
	BOOKSTEIN, Abraham	(312)762-8268	115
	BROWN, Doris R.	(312)341-8066	143
	CAPANO, Laura M.	(312)269-2835	179
	CLAGGETT, Laura K.	(312)661-0222	215
	CORSARO, Julie A.		248
	COX, James C.	(312)583-6932	253
	CURRY, John A.	(314)528-0870	266
	DEMPSEY, Frank J.	(312)327-6955	291
	DONOVAN, William A.	(312)947-9276	312
	DOWNES, Valerie	(312)871-7559	316
	EMRE, Serpil A.	(312)236-5622	348
	EPP, Ronald H.	(203)347-6933	351
	EPSTEIN, Dena J.	(312)373-0522	351
	EVANS, Linda J.	(312)642-4600	357
	FANG, Min L.	(317)842-0321	363
	FEDERICI, Yolanda D.	(312)427-0052	368
	FULTON, Tara L.	(312)508-2655	409

REVIEWER (Cont'd)
ILLINOIS (Cont'd)
Chicago

Name	Phone	No.
GODLEWSKI, Susan G.	(312)443-3936	442
HAAS, Carolyn B.	(312)822-0809	480
HERNANDEZ, Hector R.	(312)523-2453	531
HILBURGER, Mary J.	(312)794-2614	538
HOFFMANN, Maurine L.	(312)951-0599	548
HUNT, Janis E.	(312)275-8439	575
JACOBSEN, Teresa T.	(312)266-1265	590
JAGODZINSKI, Cecile M.	(312)645-4860	591
JOHN, Nancy R.	(312)996-2716	601
JORDAN, Charles R.	(312)478-7205	616
KAMINECKI, Ronald M.	(312)726-9206	624
KING, David E.	(312)346-7440	650
KNOBLAUCH, Mark G.	(312)549-5247	665
KOWITZ, Aletha A.	(312)440-2642	674
LENNEBERG, Hans H.		715
MALINOWSKY, H R.	(312)329-1549	763
MANCUYAS, Natividad D.	(312)995-2284	764
MARSHALL, Jerilyn A.		774
MAYFIELD, Maurice K.	(312)281-0510	790
MCCOY, Patricia S.	(312)274-0370	799
MCDERMOTT, Patrice	(312)944-6780	802
MCELWAIN, William	(312)248-5564	804
MCNEILL, Janice M.	(312)642-4600	816
MEYER, Barbara G.	(312)829-2033	829
MICKEY, Melissa B.	(312)324-8583	833
MITZIGA, Walter J.	(312)375-4646	850
MOORE, Annie M.	(312)995-2254	858
MOUW, James R.	(312)996-2706	874
MULLER, Karen	(312)944-6780	877
MUNOFF, Gerald J.	(312)702-8749	879
NEAL, Donn C.	(312)922-0140	890
O'HEARON, Doris M.	(312)221-0570	919
OTT, Bill	(312)944-6780	930
PARK, Chung I.	(312)942-3000	940
PATTERSON, Patricia A.	(312)876-1000	948
POSNER, Frances A.	(312)334-7484	985
REED, Virginia R.	(312)477-6836	1015
RETTIG, James R.	(312)996-2735	1024
ROMAN, Susan	(312)944-6780	1052
SCHRAMM, Mary T.	(312)248-7934	1099
SELMER, Marsha L.	(312)996-5277	1114
SHAW, Joyce M.	(312)294-4640	1123
SIMPSON, Donald B.	(312)955-4545	1141
SKIDMORE, Gail	(312)989-3965	1146
SPARKS, Joanne L.	(312)728-5510	1171
STRAWN, Aimee W.	(312)996-5628	1201
SUTHERLAND, Zena B.	(312)702-8293	1211
THORNHILL, Robert E.	(312)269-3097	1242
TIWANA, Shah J.	(312)743-5146	1247
VANCURA, Joyce B.	(312)822-0422	1273
VISKOCHIL, Larry A.	(312)935-1071	1285
WAITE, Ellen J.	(312)508-2641	1293
WILLIAMSON, Linda E.	(312)996-2738	1347
WILSON, Phillis M.	(312)944-6780	1352
WINGER, Howard W.	(312)748-1129	1355
WRIGHT, Helen K.	(312)944-6780	1371
WYLY, Mary P.	(312)477-5413	1375
ZVIRIN, Stephanie H.	(312)944-6780	1392

Place	Name	Phone	No.
Chillicothe	CROTZ, D K.	(312)485-7805	261
Cicero	MALLER, Mark P.	(312)652-8084	763
Clinton	ADCOCK, Betty L.	(217)935-3493	6
Crystal Lake	MILLER, Randy S.	(815)455-4660	841
Dawson	CHESLEY, Thea B.		207
De Kalb	ABBOTT, Craig S.	(815)753-6634	1
	DUTTON, Lee S.	(815)753-1808	329
	GRAHAM, Robert W.	(815)753-1779	456
	HORST, Stanley E.	(815)753-9497	561
	HUANG, Samuel T.	(815)756-2296	568
	HURYCH, Jitka M.	(815)753-1947	578
	KIES, Cosette N.	(815)753-1735	647
	LANIER, Donald L.	(815)753-0255	696
	LARSEN, John C.	(815)753-6269	698
	RAST, Elaine K.	(815)758-5234	1009
	RIDER, Philip R.	(815)758-2181	1032
Deerfield	CALLAGHAN, Linda W.	(312)945-3311	173
Downers Grove	MIFFLIN, Michael J.	(312)963-9285	833
Dwight	MCCLAREY, Catherine A.	(815)584-3703	796

REVIEWER (Cont'd)
ILLINOIS (Cont'd)

Place	Name	Phone	No.
Edwardsville	MCFARLAND, Mary A.	(618)692-3828	805
Elgin	GORDON, Lewis A.	(312)695-1455	451
Elk Grove Village	KALRA, Bhupinder S.	(312)529-8607	623
Elmhurst	CALTVEDT, Sarah C.	(312)833-0381	174
	DARLING, Elizabeth A.	(312)279-4100	274
	KLATT, Melvin J.	(312)279-4100	658
	WATSON, Robert E.	(312)941-0892	1310
Evanston	BEATTY, William K.	(312)328-5473	70
	BJORNCRANTZ, Leslie B.	(312)866-9112	100
	CLOUD, Patricia D.	(312)491-3136	223
	GOLDBERGER, Virginia F.	(312)492-7811	445
	GRISCOM, Richard W.	(312)491-3487	471
	GROSS, Dorothy E.	(312)583-2700	472
	HILL, Janet S.	(312)491-7587	540
	HORNY, Karen L.	(312)491-7662	560
	HURD, Albert E.	(312)866-7235	577
	JACOBSON, William R.	(312)328-7584	590
	KAPLAN, Rosalyn L.	(312)869-1035	626
	MICHAELSON, Robert C.	(312)491-3057	832
	PIRON, Alice M.	(312)864-3175	975
	QUERY, Lance D.	(312)491-2882	999
	QUINN, Patrick M.	(312)869-2861	1000
	SHAFER, Anne E.	(312)492-5940	1119
	SHERMAN, Sarah	(312)864-3801	1128
	SUNDELL, Elizabeth B.	(312)866-0310	1210
	WHITELEY, Sandra M.	(312)475-7931	1333
Fox River Grove	CORCORAN, Frances E.	(312)639-5306	245
Franklin Park	VOSS, Joyce M.	(312)678-1528	1289
Glen Ellyn	ADCOCK, Donald C.	(312)858-2734	6
Glencoe	WEISMAN, Kathryn M.	(312)835-4122	1319
Glenview	HAFNER, Arthur W.	(312)291-1022	482
Highland Park	BRACHMANN, Kathleen A.	(312)432-0216	124
Hinsdale	CZARNECKI, Cary J.	(312)986-1976	268
Itasca	HOGAN, Patricia M.	(312)773-1699	549
Jacksonville	ZUIDERVELD, Sharon R.	(217)243-6945	1391
Joliet	STEVENSON, Katherine	(815)723-7846	1191
Kingston	SCHREIBER, Robert E.	(815)784-2280	1099
La Grange	HATTENDORF, Lynn C.	(312)579-0873	512
	MARTIN, John W.	(312)352-8115	776
	SCHULTHEISS, Louis A.	(312)354-6958	1101
Lake Forest	DANOFF, Fran	(312)234-2350	274
	MIKOLYZK, Thomas A.	(312)295-6247	834
Lena	FREY, Roxanne C.	(815)369-5372	403
Libertyville	BRIGGS, Martha T.		135
Lincolnwood	BENNETT, Laura B.	(312)679-2327	82
Lisle	SHOTWELL, Richard T.	(312)665-9107	1133
Lombard	EGAN, Elizabeth M.	(312)627-7130	338
	SCHIPMA, Peter B.	(312)627-0550	1093
Macomb	TING, Lee H.	(309)298-1770	1246
Matteson	SMITH, Richard D.	(312)747-6660	1159
Moline	KRAMER, Pamela K.	(309)797-5117	675
Mt Prospect	MARABOTTI, Denise M.	(312)253-5675	768
	MCCULLY, William C.	(312)635-9811	801
Naperville	MEACHEN, Edward W.	(312)420-3425	819
Northfield	ANDERSON, Charles R.	(312)446-8259	22
Oak Lawn	DOBREZ, Cynthia K.	(312)422-4990	307
	KELLY, Raymond T.		638
	MOORMAN, John A.	(312)422-4990	862
Oak Park	BALCOM, William T.	(312)383-6824	51
	DICK, Ellen A.	(312)386-9385	300
	REDDY, Michael B.	(312)848-1754	1013
Palatine	HORTON, Kathy L.	(312)004-3794	561
	STRANGE, Michele M.	(312)359-8539	1200
Palos Hills	TEO, Elizabeth A.	(312)974-4300	1231
Park Forest	OCHSNER, Renata E.	(312)748-5374	915
	SHANNON, Kathleen L.	(312)481-1891	1120
Park Ridge	CRISPEN, Joanne	(312)696-6594	259
	JACKSON, William V.	(312)825-4364	588
Paxton	PACEY, Brenda M.	(217)379-3517	933
Peoria	SWORSKY, Felicia G.	(309)672-8885	1217
Quincy	TYER, Travis S.	(217)223-5024	1266
River Forest	HEYMAN, Jerome S.	(312)771-3030	536
	LI, Richard T.	(312)366-2490	725
	NOONAN, Eileen F.	(312)366-9346	908
Rock Island	CONWAY, Colleen M.	(309)794-7316	239
Rockford	DALRYMPLE, Prudence W.	(815)968-9110	271
	SCHOLTZ, James C.	(815)229-0330	1098
Round Lake	TAN, Elizabeth L.	(312)546-6311	1222

REVIEWER (Cont'd)
ILLINOIS (Cont'd)

St Joseph	DUCHOW, Sally	(217)469-2237	322
Silvis	SWATOS, Priscilla L.	(309)792-3306	1214
Skokie	JACOB, Merle L.		589
	KAPLAN, Paul M.		626
	SORENSON, Liene S.	(312)673-7774	1168
Springfield	ALLEY, Brian	(217)522-8970	16
	ETTER, Constance L.	(217)546-5436	355
	TEMPLE, Wayne C.	(217)528-6330	1230
Sullivan	ELDER, Nancy J.	(217)728-4832	342
Sycamore	SULLIVAN, Peggy A.	(815)753-6155	1208
Urbana	ANDERSON, Nancy D.	(217)333-2884	24
	ATKINS, Stephen E.	(217)244-1867	38
	CLARK, Barton M.	(217)333-0317	216
	DAVIS, Elisabeth B.	(217)333-3654	278
	DOWNS, Jane B.	(217)344-1714	317
	FAIRCHILD, Constance A.	(217)333-1900	361
	FORREST, Charles G.	(217)244-3770	390
	GUSHEE, Marion S.	(217)367-9610	478
	HUETING, Gail P.	(217)244-0481	570
	KIBBEE, Josephine Z.	(217)333-2290	646
	KRUMMEL, Donald W.	(217)344-6311	680
	MAHER, William J.	(217)333-0798	760
	MAKINO, Yasuko	(217)244-2048	762
	MONTANELLI, Dale S.	(217)333-0792	855
	O'BRIEN, Nancy P.	(217)333-2305	915
	ROLSTAD, Gary O.	(217)333-3280	1052
	RUBIN, Richard E.	(217)333-3280	1065
	SCHLIPF, Frederick A.	(217)367-4057	1094
	SHAW, Debora	(217)333-1666	1123
	SIEGEL, Martin A.	(217)333-3247	1136
	SMITH, Linda C.	(217)333-7742	1157
	STUART, Mary P.	(217)333-1900	1204
	TEMPERLEY, Nicholas	(217)333-8733	1230
	WEI, Karen T.	(217)344-5647	1316
	WILLIAMS, Mitsuko	(217)333-3654	1345
	WRIGHT, Joyce C.	(217)333-1031	1372
Villa Park	ELL, Elizabeth L.	(312)279-6456	343
	POINTON, Louis R.	(312)833-6555	980
Wauconda	HEITMAN, Lynn	(312)526-6225	523
Waukegan	KOZAK, Marlene G.	(312)473-3000	674
West Chicago	OLSEN, Sarah G.	(312)451-3078	922
Wheaton	RUSSELL, Janet	(312)653-1115	1069
Wheeling	KANNER, Elliott E.	(312)459-1300	625
	MCCLARREN, Robert R.	(312)459-1300	796
Wilmette	JONES, Adrian	(312)256-6202	610
	REIF, Lenore S.	(312)156-1100	1019
Wilmington	BOBAN, Carol A.	(815)458-3411	108
Winnetka	THOMPSON, Richard E.	(312)446-7975	1241

INDIANA

Anderson	KENDALL, Charles T.	(317)649-5039	640
Bloomington	CALLISON, Daniel J.	(812)335-5113	174
	COPLER, Judith A.	(812)335-9255	244
	FARRELL, David	(812)335-3403	365
	FLING, Robert M.	(812)335-2970	385
	FRY, Bernard M.	(812)339-3571	406
	HALPORN, Barbara	(812)335-1446	490
	MILLER, Constance R.	(812)335-5729	836
	MURPHY, Marcy	(812)335-5113	881
	NIEKAMP, Dorothy R.	(812)332-4065	903
	POPP, Mary F.	(812)335-9857	984
	PUNGITORE, Verna L.	(812)335-5113	997
	SELLBERG, Roxanne J.	(812)335-4626	1113
	SILVER, Joel B.	(812)335-2452	1138
	SMITH, Lary		1156
	SOWELL, Steven L.	(812)335-9792	1170
	STEELE, Patricia A.	(812)335-1619	1184
	WHITE, Herbert S.	(812)335-2848	1331
	ZIMMERMAN, Brenda M.		1388
Chesterton	BECKING, Mara S.	(219)926-5618	73
	DUHAMELL, Lynnette H.	(219)926-3743	324
Clinton	RAWLES-HEISER, Carolyn	(317)832-9969	1010
Elkhart	SAARI, David S.	(219)295-8090	1072
Evansville	BAKER, Donald E.	(812)425-4309	48
	WINSLOW, Carol M.	(812)867-2146	1355
Fort Wayne	MCCAFFERY, Laurabelle	(219)422-5245	793
	SANDSTROM, Pamela E.	(219)424-7241	1081

REVIEWER (Cont'd)
INDIANA (Cont'd)

Gary	GUYDON, Janet H.	(219)938-3376	479
	MCSHANE, Stephen G.	(219)980-6628	818
Goshen	SPRINGER, Joe A.	(219)534-5357	1176
Greencastle	LATSHAW, Ruth N.	(317)653-2318	701
Hammond	HOLICKY, Bernard H.	(219)989-2249	550
	MEYERS, Arthur S.	(219)931-5100	830
Highland	ENGELBERT, Peter J.	(219)923-2173	348
Hobart	CHRISTIANSON, Elin B.	(219)942-5536	212
Indianapolis	ASHER, Richard E.		36
	BRADLEY, Johanna	(317)751-3779	126
	BRAHMI, Frances A.	(317)274-1401	127
	EBERSHOFF-COLES, Susan V.	(317)269-1815	334
	ELLSWORTH, Marlene A.	(317)274-7185	345
	GALBRAITH, Leslie R.	(317)924-1331	413
	GANN, Daniel H.	(317)299-9058	416
	HOOK-SHELTON, Sara A.	(317)274-7204	556
	JONES, Thomas Q.		615
	KONDELIK, John P.	(317)283-9226	670
	KONDELIK, Marlene R.	(317)232-3732	670
	LOGSDON, Robert L.	(317)888-6772	737
	SCHMIDT, Steven J.	(317)274-0470	1096
	SIMON, Ralph C.	(317)875-5336	1141
	STUSSY, Susan A.	(317)929-0343	1205
	THOMPSON, Anna M.		1238
	YOUNG, Noraleen A.	(317)786-4561	1382
La Porte	SMYERS, Richard P.	(219)324-2186	1162
Lafayette	COLLINS, Mary E.		233
	LAW, Gordon T.	(317)447-2484	704
	NIXON, Judith M.		906
	TROUTNER, Joanne J.	(317)477-7306	1258
Marion	BOYCE, Harold W.	(317)674-5211	122
Michigan City	DEYOUNG, Charles D.	(219)879-4561	298
Muncie	DOLAK, Frank J.	(317)285-5141	309
	HODGE, Stanley P.	(317)285-8033	546
	KUO, Ming M.	(317)289-3123	684
	MOORE, Thomas J.	(317)285-1307	861
	WILLIAMS, Nyal Z.	(317)285-5065	1345
Noblesville	MAXWELL, Donald W.	(317)773-1384	788
	WILLIAMS, Maudine	(317)773-1763	1345
Notre Dame	CONNELLY, James T.	(219)233-9675	237
	FUDERER, Laura S.	(219)239-5176	408
	HAVLIK, Robert J.	(219)239-6665	513
	HAYES, Stephen M.	(219)239-5268	516
	JORDAN, Louis E.	(219)239-7420	616
	MILLER, Robert C.	(219)239-7790	841
	SLINGER, Michael J.	(219)239-5664	1149
Portage	KRAMER, Arlene H.	(219)762-6939	675
Richmond	FARBER, Evan I.	(317)966-2422	363
South Bend	BEATTY, R M.	(219)232-2349	70
	HOHL, Robert J.	(219)289-8160	550
	MULLINS, James L.	(219)237-4449	878
	OSTROWSKI, Lawrence C.	(219)282-4608	929
	PIANE, Mimi	(219)282-4649	969
	TUCKER, Dennis C.		1261
	YATES, Donald N.	(219)289-3405	1378
Terre Haute	ENSOR, Pat L.	(812)237-2580	350
	LITTLE, Robert D.	(812)237-2488	733
	MILLER, Marsha A.	(812)237-2605	840
	NORMAN, Orval G.	(812)232-6120	909
	VANCIL, David E.	(812)237-2610	1273
Valparaiso	HOLTERHOFF, Sarah G.	(219)465-7866	555
	RAYMAN, Ronald A.	(219)464-2060	1011
West Lafayette	ADDISON, Paul H.	(317)463-2511	6
	ANDREWS, Theodora A.	(317)463-6093	27
	BAILEY, Martha J.	(317)494-2910	46
	BAXTER, Pam M.	(317)494-2969	67
	BRANDT, Daryl S.		128
	CANGANELLI, Patrick W.	(317)494-2768	178
	HEWISON, Nancy S.	(317)463-0904	535
	MOBLEY, Emily R.	(317)494-2900	851
	PASK, Judith M.	(317)494-6735	946
	TUCKER, John M.	(317)494-2833	1261
Winamac	SMITH, Robert E.	(219)946-6255	1160
Zionsville	OKEY, Susan T.	(317)873-3114	920

REVIEWER (Cont'd)
IOWA

Ames	COLE, Jim E.	(515)294-0432	230
	MADISON, Olivia M.	(515)294-3669	759
	MATHEWS, Eleanor R.	(515)294-3642	784
	TYCKOSON, David A.	(515)294-3642	1266
Bettendorf	CLOW, Faye E.	(319)332-7427	223
	MEIER, Patricia L.	(319)355-3895	821
Burlington	JOHNSON, Anne C.	(319)753-1647	602
Cedar Falls	KOLLASCH, Matthew A.	(319)277-6125	669
	WILKINSON, Patrick J.	(319)273-6327	1340
Cedar Rapids	JANUS, Bridget M.	(319)365-5055	594
	LEAVITT, Judith A.	(319)390-3109	707
Davenport	PETERSON, Dennis R.	(319)391-3877	963
Denver	DUTCHER, Terry R.	(319)984-6120	329
Des Moines	CLAYBURN, Marginell P.	(515)279-6967	220
	DAGLEY, Helen J.	(515)281-3063	269
	JOHNSON, Nancy E.	(515)262-6714	608
Dubuque	KNEFEL, Mary A.	(319)589-3215	664
	OFFERMAN, Mary C.		917
Iowa City	DEWEY, Barbara I.	(319)335-5867	298
	EIMAS, Richard	(319)337-5538	340
	FALK, Mark F.	(319)354-7474	362
	HAUSMAN, Julie	(319)337-1786	513
	JORDAN, Robert P.	(319)337-2708	616
	KELLEY, Ann C.	(319)335-5884	636
	KOHLER, Carolyn W.	(319)337-9839	668
	SCHERUBEL, Melody	(319)351-6264	1092
	SNIDER, Jacqueline I.	(319)337-0660	1163
Le Grand	WOOD, Marilyn R.	(515)479-2785	1364
Manchester	CRAWFORD, Daniel R.		256
Marion	DAVIS, Deanna S.	(319)377-7135	278
Marshalltown	BURGESS, Barbara J.	(515)752-4812	159
Muscatine	MATHER, Becky R.	(319)263-9049	783
Rock Rapids	KOHRT, Ruth D.		669
Vinton	SHEPHERD, Rex L.	(319)472-4721	1127
West Branch	MAYER, Dale C.	(319)643-5301	789
West Des Moines	MARQUARDT, Larry D.	(515)224-9278	772

KANSAS

Chanute	DRUSE, Judith A.	(316)431-3020	321
Cimarron	CROTTS, Carolyn D.	(316)855-3641	261
Dodge City	COOKE, Bette L.	(316)225-7271	241
El Dorado	BEATTIE, Brian	(316)321-3363	70
Emporia	BODART-TALBOT, Joni	(316)343-1200	109
	BOGAN, Mary E.	(316)342-1394	110
Fairway	CARVER, Jane W.	(913)236-8688	191
Hays	MILLER, Melanie A.	(913)625-9014	841
Kansas City	BENNETT, Samuel J.	(913)831-2242	82
Lawrence	BURCHILL, Mary D.	(913)864-3025	158
	HOWARD, Clinton N.	(913)864-3601	564
	MAY, Cecilia J.	(913)841-0929	788
	RHODES, Saralinda A.		1026
	TRONIER, Suzanne	(913)864-3038	1258
Lenexa	MCLEOD, Debra A.	(913)492-4512	814
Manhattan	ATCHISON, Fres D.	(913)776-4741	37
	QUIRING, Virginia M.	(913)532-5693	1000
	TALAB, Rosemary S.	(913)532-5550	1220
	WEISENBURGER, Patricia J.	(913)532-5968	1319
	WILLIAMS, Sara R.	(913)532-6516	1346
McPherson	EIS, Myrna M.	(316)241-3713	340
	OLSEN, Rowena J.	(316)241-0731	921
Miltonvale	BRADLEY, Susanne A.	(913)427-2228	126
North Newton	HAURY, David A.	(316)283-2500	512
	SCHRAG, Dale R.	(316)283-2500	1099
Olathe	GOODRICH PETERSON, Marilyn	(913)897-3318	450
Overland Park	KEMPF, Andrea C.	(913)469-8500	639
Pittsburg	DEGRUSON, Eugene H.	(316)231-7000	288
	LEE, Earl W.	(316)231-7000	709
	VOLLEN, Gene E.	(316)231-7000	1287
Salina	THOMAS, Evangeline M.	(913)827-1604	1236
	WHITE, George R.	(913)825-2101	1331
Shawnee	STRAUSE, Robert C.	(913)268-9875	1200
Shawnee Mission	WAY, Harold E.	(913)831-1550	1311
Topeka	CARROLL, James K.	(913)273-9156	187
	LEVEL, M J.	(913)296-3434	719
	LYNN, Barbara A.	(913)233-4252	752
	RICHMOND, Robert W.	(913)234-4704	1031
Valley Center	MEANS, E P.	(316)755-0414	820

REVIEWER (Cont'd)
KANSAS (Cont'd)

Wichita	GERMANN, Malcolm P.	(316)689-3591	429
	IZBICKI, Thomas M.	(316)683-8157	586
	MYERS, Robert C.	(316)689-3591	885
	SINGH, Swarn L.	(316)722-3741	1143
	STRECK, Helen T.	(316)942-2201	1201
	TANNER, Jane E.	(316)682-4485	1223
Winfield	ZUCK, Gregory J.	(316)221-4150	1391

KENTUCKY

Bowling Green	COUTTS, Brian E.	(502)745-6339	252
	CUDD, John M.	(502)842-0901	263
	MOORE, Elaine E.	(502)745-6114	859
	ZIMMER, Connie W.	(502)781-4165	1388
Covington	DECKER, Charlotte J.	(606)581-7871	285
Cynthiana	DOAN, Janice K.	(606)441-1180	307
Elizabethtown	HOLT, David A.	(502)737-1473	554
Florence	BROWN, Lucinda A.	(606)371-6222	145
Frankfort	COOPER, Judy L.	(502)564-2672	243
Highland Heights	BENNETT, Donna S.	(606)572-5715	81
	STURM, Rebecca R.	(606)572-5636	1205
Lexington	BARRISH, Alan S.	(606)278-1933	60
	BIRCHFIELD, Martha J.	(606)257-6098	98
	LEVSTIK, Frank R.	(606)266-9196	721
	MCANINCH, Sandra L.	(606)231-9279	792
	RIPLEY, Joseph M.	(606)257-4243	1035
	ROGERS, Joann V.	(606)278-6246	1049
	SINEATH, Timothy W.	(606)257-8876	1143
Louisville	ANDERSON, Patricia E.	(502)588-6392	25
	BELL, Mary M.	(502)426-4732	77
	COALTER, Milton J.	(502)895-3411	224
	CONNOR, Lynn S.	(502)589-4200	238
	HOUSE, Katherine L.	(502)459-2429	563
	KEARNEY, Anna R.	(502)588-6744	633
	LINCOLN, Carol S.	(502)568-7683	728
	MAZUK, Melody	(502)897-4807	791
	REDMON, Sherrill	(502)451-5907	1014
	VOYLES, James R.	(502)589-4440	1289
Murray	BUSER, Robin A.	(502)762-2393	165
Owensboro	YATES, Dudley V.	(502)526-3111	1378
Richmond	BARKSDALE, Milton K.	(606)622-1787	57
	HAY, Charles C.	(606)622-2820	515
	MARTIN, June H.	(606)622-6176	777
Southgate	FOX, Estella E.	(606)441-0743	394
Whitesburg	OLIVER, Scot	(606)633-0108	921
Wilmore	BUNDY, David D.	(606)858-3581	157

LOUISIANA

Alexandria	JARRED, Ada D.	(312)445-5230	594
Baton Rouge	BALL, Dannie J.	(504)388-3119	52
	BINGHAM, Elizabeth E.	(504)292-1038	97
	BOYCE, Bert R.	(504)388-1461	122
	BRADLEY, Jared W.	(504)766-9375	126
	CARPENTER, Michael A.	(504)766-7385	185
	COE, Miriam M.		226
	HASCHAK, Paul G.	(504)766-9986	510
	HOGAN, Sharon A.	(504)388-2217	549
	KRAFT, Donald H.	(504)388-1495	674
	MCKANN, Michael R.	(504)342-4922	809
	MERING, Margaret V.	(504)344-5863	826
	PACKOFF, Beth M.	(504)388-1480	946
	PHILLIPS, Faye	(504)388-6569	968
	REID, Marion T.	(504)388-2217	1019
	SHIFLETT, Orvin L.	(504)388-1462	1130
Covington	SOTO, Donna G.	(504)892-0812	1169
Harvey	WASHINGTON, Idella A.	(504)367-8429	1307
Houma	COSPER, Mary F.	(504)879-4243	249
Lafayette	FOX, Willard		395
	HAMSA, Charles F.	(318)984-9305	494
	RAMAKRISHNAN, T	(318)989-9333	1004
	STEWART, Mary E.	(318)984-4139	1193
	TURNER, I B.	(318)231-5702	1264
Metairie	KLEIN, Victor C.	(504)861-0488	659
Monroe	MEINEL, Nancy T.	(318)343-3399	822
Natchitoches	HARRINGTON, Charles W.	(318)357-0813	504
	HUSSEY, Sandra R.	(318)352-2996	578

REVIEWER (Cont'd)
LOUISIANA (Cont'd)

New Orleans	CUMLET, Harolyn S.	(504)943-3618	264
	DANKNER, Laura R.	(504)865-2367	273
	DRAUGHON, Ralph B.	(504)891-1921	318
	FLEURY, Bruce E.	(504)865-5682	385
	FLEURY, Mary E.	(504)865-1851	385
	HALFORD, Mary B.	(504)865-6865	486
	HANKEL, Marilyn L.	(504)286-7276	496
	HARDY, D C.	(504)895-3981	500
	HARRIS, Karen H.	(504)286-7162	505
	JERDE, Curtis D.	(504)865-5688	599
	LEMMON, Alfred E.	(504)523-4662	715
	MCKNIGHT, Mark C.	(504)866-3394	812
	RUSHING, Darla H.	(504)891-1127	1068
	SKINNER, Robert E.	(504)483-7304	1146
	WILSON, C D.	(504)596-2600	1350
	ZULA, Floyd M.	(504)865-5693	1391
Ruston	DICARLO, Michael A.	(318)257-3594	300
	LOWE, Joy L.	(318)255-4379	744
Shreveport	KING, Anne M.	(318)797-5738	650
	MCCLEARY, William E.	(318)865-9813	796
	MOSLEY, Mattie J.	(318)797-5100	871
	SALTER, Jeffrey L.	(318)226-5871	1077

MAINE

Alfred	ANDERSON, Marjorie E.	(207)324-6915	24
Auburn	HILYARD, Nann B.	(207)782-3191	542
Augusta	TARANKO, Walter J.	(207)289-5628	1223
Bangor	WOODWARD, Robert C.	(207)942-4760	1368
Bar Harbor	BAKER, Alison	(207)288-3371	47
Boothbay	LENTHALL, Franklyn	(207)633-4536	715
Brunswick	HEISER, Nancy E.	(207)725-4253	523
	SAEGER, Edwin J.	(207)729-5720	1074
Farmington	MCNAMARA, Shelley G.	(207)778-3501	816
Kennebunkport	PEERS, Charles T.	(207)967-5764	954
Mechanic Falls	NOYES, Nicholas	(207)345-3245	911
North Anson	LYONS, Dean E.	(207)566-0511	753
Orono	GOODWIN, Bryan D.	(207)581-1674	450
	MCCALLISTER, Myrna J.		793
	WHITE, Lucinda M.	(207)581-1674	1331
Portland	HUMEZ, Nicholas D.	(207)773-3405	573
	O'BRIEN, Francis M.	(207)774-0931	914
Skowhegan	FRIDLEY, Russell W.	(207)474-7133	403

MARYLAND

Adamstown	LIGHTBOWN, Parke P.		726
Adelphi	NITECKI, Danuta A.	(301)937-4791	905
Annapolis	MCKAY, Eleanor	(301)263-6526	809
	PRIMER, Ben	(301)974-3914	993
Baldwin	WASIELEWSKI, Eleanor B.	(301)557-7293	1308
Baltimore	BLANK, Annette C.	(301)396-5350	104
	BRENNAN, Edward P.	(301)675-8835	132
	CHELTON, Mary K.	(301)355-0906	204
	CONNOR, Elizabeth	(301)828-8646	237
	DAVISH, William	(301)323-1010	281
	DE LERMA, Dominique R.	(301)467-2578	289
	FLORANCE, Valerie	(301)383-9436	385
	FREDENBURG, Anne M.	(301)377-9080	399
	GREENBERG, Emily R.	(301)625-3401	463
	HIRSCH, Dorothy K.	(304)655-7280	543
	HSIEH, Rebecca T.	(301)522-1481	567
	KLEEBERGER, Patricia L.	(301)547-9000	658
	LEBRETON, Jonathan A.	(301)455-2356	708
	LEDBETTER, Sherry H.	(301)358-0285	708
	LOWENS, Margery M.	(301)532-7422	744
	LUCIER, Richard E.	(301)955-3411	746
	MATHESON, Nina W.	(301)837-1120	783
	MCADAM, Paul E.	(301)747-5030	791
	PERKINS, Earle R.	(301)338-8540	959
	QUIST, Edwin A.	(301)659-8154	1001
	SHAPIRO, Burton J.	(301)653-2757	1121
	SZARY, Richard V.	(301)358-2064	1218
	THOMAS, Fannette H.	(301)435-4409	1236
	TOOEY, Mary J.	(301)744-0521	1250
	VARGA, Nicholas	(301)323-1010	1278
	ZIMMERMAN, Martha B.	(301)668-5744	1389
Bel Air	SEDNEY, Frances V.	(301)838-7484	1111

REVIEWER (Cont'd)
MARYLAND (Cont'd)

Beltsville	ANDRE, Pamela Q.	(301)344-3813	26
	COLLINS, Donna S.	(301)344-3728	232
	KREBS-SMITH, James J.	(301)344-3719	677
	MASON, Pamela R.	(301)344-3999	781
	RUSSELL, Keith W.	(301)344-3834	1069
Bethesda	BOHLEN, Jeanne L.	(301)897-9823	111
	BYRNES, Margaret M.	(301)496-0382	169
	FISHBEIN, Meyer H.	(301)530-5391	380
	GOLDSCHMIDT, Peter G.	(301)656-5070	446
	HENDERSON, Madeline M.	(301)530-6478	526
	LAKSHMAN, Malathi K.	(301)229-9287	689
	MOBLEY, Arthur B.	(301)530-0081	851
	SAVAGE, Allan G.	(301)496-4126	1085
	SCHWARTZ, Marla J.	(301)656-0043	1105
	SLATER, Susan B.	(301)496-2311	1148
Bowie	GERRING, Cheryl B.	(301)464-0910	429
	MASTRANGELO, Marjorie J.	(301)464-8745	782
	NELSEN, Alice R.	(301)262-2194	893
Brooksville	BASCOM, James F.	(301)774-3175	62
Cabin John	SEWELL, Winifred	(301)229-5008	1118
Catonsville	STERLING, Judith K.	(301)455-3468	1189
	WILT, Larry J.	(301)455-2341	1353
Chevy Chase	GOLDSBERG, Elizabeth D.		446
	HOLLOWAY, Johnna H.	(301)652-8491	552
Clinton	CHEEKS, Cellestine	(301)868-5048	204
College Park	JOHNSON, Emily P.	(301)935-5382	604
	O'DELL, M P.	(301)454-9341	916
	SOERGEL, Dagobert	(301)454-5451	1165
	TIBBO, Helen R.	(301)454-5441	1244
	WILSON, William G.	(301)454-6003	1353
Columbia	DAHLEN, Roger W.	(301)964-9098	269
	GORDON, Martin K.	(301)992-7626	451
	GRUHL, Andrea M.	(301)596-5460	474
	RUSS, Kennetta P.	(301)381-0579	1068
	WOLTER, John A.	(301)730-6692	1362
Dundalk	MILLER, Everett G.	(301)522-5785	837
Ellicott City	MARTIN, Susan K.	(301)988-9893	778
Fallston	SACK, Jean C.	(301)877-2825	1073
Forestville	MOORE, Virginia B.	(301)568-8743	861
Fort Washington	BRADSHER, James G.	(301)248-8884	126
Germantown	MOLINE, Judi A.	(301)972-5708	853
Glen Burnie	HACKMAN, Mary H.	(301)768-2569	481
Green Meadows	MILL, Rodney H.	(301)422-1437	835
Greenbelt	ASHFORD, Richard K.	(301)982-5074	36
	SIMS, Sally R.	(301)345-0619	1142
Hyattsville	BURGESS, Eileen E.	(301)864-7223	159
	LEVINE, Susan H.	(301)699-3500	721
	LOSINSKI, Julia M.	(301)699-3500	742
Kensington	PRICE, Douglas S.	(301)942-2091	992
La Plata	WILLIAMS, J L.	(301)932-6768	1343
Lanham	PUCCIO, Joseph A.	(301)459-0871	997
Laurel	GOLDENBERG, Joan M.	(301)953-9253	445
	SWEETLAND, Loraine F.	(801)490-8231	1215
Mount Airy	WETZBARGER, Cecilia G.	(301)829-0826	1328
New Carrollton	WILLIAMS, Helen E.	(301)454-6068	1343
Reisterstown	BRADLEY, Wanda L.		126
Rockville	BARALOTO, R A.	(301)279-3271	55
	BRANDHORST, Wesley T.	(301)460-6932	128
	DEAN, Frances C.	(301)424-9289	283
	DOWD, Frank B.	(301)279-1098	315
	HERIN, Nancy J.	(301)279-6101	531
	MEIZNER, Kathie L.	(301)279-1960	822
	MICHAELS, Carolyn L.	(301)564-0509	831
	PHIFER, Kenneth O.	(301)770-0498	967
	UNGER, Carol P.	(301)460-8375	1269
St Marys City	BRITTEN, William A.		137
	REPENNING, Julie A.	(301)862-0267	1023
Seabrook	LARSEN, Lida L.	(301)459-3931	698
Silver Spring	ARANDA-COODOU, Patricio	(301)946-7859	30
	BATTY, Charles D.	(301)593-8901	65
	FELMY, John C.	(301)681-9069	370
	KADEC, Sarah T.	(301)598-7694	621
	MERIKANGAS, Robert J.	(301)384-3449	826
	MYERS, R D.	(301)681-3967	885
	NORRIS, Loretta W.	(301)587-3470	909
	PRITCHARD, Sarah M.	(301)538-8624	994
	RAWSTHORNE, Grace C.	(301)949-0698	1011
	SCHEIPS, Paul J.		1091

REVIEWER (Cont'd)
MARYLAND (Cont'd)
Silver Spring

	VAN CAMPEN, Rebecca J.	(301)890-8588	1272
	WAGNER, Lloyd F.		1292
	WALSH, Barclay		1299
Thurmont	FITZPATRICK, Kelly	(301)271-4109	383
Timonium	STUART, Karen A.	(301)561-4446	1204
Towson	DRACH, Marian C.	(301)825-8877	317
Upper Marlboro	DICKSON, Katherine M.	(301)350-4035	301
	HARBERT, Cathy E.	(301)868-9280	499
	WOODY, Jacqueline B.		1368
Westminster	MCCARTY, Emily H.	(301)848-1825	795

MASSACHUSETTS
Acton	FINGERMAN, Susan M.	(617)263-1881	378
	YACOUBY, Ray S.	(617)263-6764	1376
Amherst	ADAMS, Leonard R.	(413)545-2765	5
	CHADWICK, Alena F.	(413)545-2674	196
	DONOHUE, Joseph	(413)545-0498	312
Andover	GREENE, Cathy C.	(617)470-0902	463
	JACOBSON, Nancy C.	(617)475-6960	590
Arlington	JUDD, Eleanor M.		618
Auburndale	TUCHMAN, Maurice S.	(617)969-9791	1261
Beverly	GAGNON, Ronald A.	(617)922-6722	412
Boston	ALCORN, Cynthia W.	(617)578-8675	11
	ANDERSON, A J.	(617)738-2230	21
	ANZALONE, Filippa M.		29
	BEGG, Karin E.		74
	BUSH, Margaret A.	(617)262-2045	165
	CAIN, Susan H.	(617)338-6553	171
	CEDERHOLM, Theresa D.	(617)536-5400	196
	CYPHERS, James E.	(617)727-2181	268
	GOODRICH, Allan B.	(617)929-4530	449
	HEINS, Ethel L.	(617)527-2736	522
	KERN, Donald C.	(617)638-8030	643
	KOLCZYNSKI, Charlotte A.	(617)536-5400	669
	MAIO, Kathleen L.	(617)573-8532	762
	MCCARTHY, Germaine A.	(617)742-3958	794
	MOSKOWITZ, Michael A.	(617)578-8670	871
	NESS, Arthur J.	(617)277-1776	896
	PEARLSTEIN, Toby	(617)973-8000	952
	ROGAN, Michael J.	(617)536-5400	1049
	SCHALOW, John M.	(617)437-4962	1089
	SCHWARTZ, Candy S.	(617)738-2223	1104
	SHANNON, Marcia A.	(617)267-9400	1120
	SHARE, Donald S.	(617)738-2242	1122
	SNIFFIN-MARINO, Megan G.	(617)738-3141	1163
	TRIPP, Maureen A.	(617)578-8676	1257
Brookline	LEAHY, Lynda C.	(617)731-5237	706
	ZEIGER, Hanna B.	(617)730-2586	1387
Cambridge	ALTENBERGER, Alicja	(617)495-4285	18
	ASCHMANN, Althea	(617)495-5709	35
	BURG, Barbara A.	(617)547-4762	159
	CRANE, Hugh M.	(617)498-9080	255
	DESIMONE, Dorothy H.	(617)495-2432	295
	EPPARD, Philip B.	(617)492-4157	351
	GROVE, Shari T.	(617)864-3563	474
	MANDEL, Debra H.	(617)497-0929	764
	MARCUS, Richard S.	(617)253-2340	769
	PARKER, Susan E.	(617)495-3455	942
	WUNDERLICH, Clifford S.		1374
Chestnut Hill	CHANNING, Rhoda K.	(617)552-4470	201
	CONSTANCE, Joseph W.	(617)552-3698	238
	MORNER, Claudia J.	(617)552-4489	865
Concord	LEWONTIN, Amy	(617)369-9106	724
	NESS, Pamela M.	(617)369-7174	896
Easthampton	MELNICK, Ralph	(413)527-3036	823
Fitchburg	LAMBERT, Lyn D.	(617)345-6726	690
	WALSH, Jim	(617)342-9078	1299
Framingham	KRIER, Mary M.	(617)879-7594	678
Hanover	FRIEDMAN, Fred T.	(617)826-2972	403
Hanscom AFB	GERKE, Ray	(617)377-2177	428
Jamaica Plain	WHELAN, Julia S.	(617)522-3064	1329
Leverett	ZIPKOWITZ, Fay	(413)367-9573	1389
Lexington	CARTER, Walter F.	(617)860-6739	190
	TAUBER, Stephen J.	(617)861-6295	1225
Lincoln	COHEN, Martha J.	(413)259-9500	228
Longmeadow	MCGARRY, Marie L.	(413)567-0001	805

REVIEWER (Cont'd)
MASSACHUSETTS (Cont'd)
Lowell	CAYLOR, Lawrence M.	(617)452-5000	195
	KARR, Ronald D.	(617)452-5000	628
	SLAPSYS, Richard M.	(617)452-5000	1148
Marion	ST. AUBIN, Kendra J.	(617)748-1160	1075
Medford	JONES, Frederick S.	(617)381-3345	613
	MARTIN, Murray S.	(617)776-3599	777
	MCDONALD, Ellen J.	(617)381-3273	802
Millis	ROE, Georgeanne T.	(617)376-8459	1048
Monterey	INTNER, Sheila S.	(413)528-2698	583
Nahant	DESTEFANO, Daniel A.	(617)596-1767	296
Needham	ABRAHAM, Deborah V.	(617)444-8453	2
	CABEZAS, Sue A.	(617)449-3965	170
Newton	ROFF, Jill R.	(617)527-4389	1049
Newton Highlands	FOX, Elyse H.	(617)443-4798	394
North Falmouth	FOSTER, Joan		392
Northampton	GRIGG, Susan	(413)584-2700	470
	SCOTT, Alison M.	(413)584-2700	1106
	SLY, Margery N.	(413)584-2700	1150
Norwell	KADANOFF, Diane G.	(617)659-2015	621
Orange	PROUTY, Sharman E.	(617)544-6743	996
Palmer	BERNAT, Mary A.		88
Pembroke	ROBINSON, Phyllis A.	(617)293-2193	1044
Petersham	MCMANAMON, Mary J.	(617)724-3407	814
Quincy	WHEALAN, Ronald E.	(617)479-3297	1328
Randolph	MICHAUD, Charles A.	(617)963-3000	832
	OAKLEY, Adeline D.	(617)963-7999	913
	WEISCHEDEL, Elaine F.	(617)963-2560	1319
Reading	DAMICO, Nancy B.	(617)944-9411	272
	FLANNERY, Susan M.	(617)944-0840	383
	FLANNERY, Susan M.	(617)944-0840	384
Roslindale	CLANCY, Catherine M.	(617)327-0013	215
Sagamore	OLIANSKY, Joseph D.	(617)888-6189	920
Salem	CLOHERTY, Lauretta M.		223
Shrewsbury	CHANG, Isabelle E.	(617)845-4641	200
South Hamilton	DVORAK, Robert	(617)468-7111	330
Springfield	TAUPIER, Andrea S.	(413)788-3315	1225
	WURTZEL, Barbara S.	(413)781-7822	1374
Stow	MOULTON, Lynda W.	(617)897-7163	873
Swampscott	BRENNER, Lawrence	(617)598-0370	133
Taunton	TURKALO, David M.	(617)824-8769	1263
Uxbridge	LEWIS, Thomas F.		724
Wareham	PILLSBURY, Mary J.	(617)295-2343	973
Watertown	LANDESMAN, Betty J.	(617)924-7182	692
	TASHJIAN, Virginia A.	(617)552-7151	1224
Wellesley	WOOD, Ross	(617)235-0323	1365
Wendell	HOLMBERG, Olga S.	(617)544-2706	553
West Roxbury	HARZBECKER, Joseph J.	(617)323-1372	510
Westfield	HANDY, Catherine H.	(413)568-3311	495
Westhampton	LOMBARDO, Daniel J.	(413)527-1796	738
Williamsburg	LANCASTER, John	(413)268-7679	692
Williamstown	HAMMOND, Wayne G.	(413)597-2462	494
Winchester	DAY, Virginia M.	(617)729-6026	283
	JOHNSON, Jean L.	(617)721-7020	606
Worcester	BARNHILL, Georgia B.	(617)755-5221	58
	GONNEVILLE, Priscilla R.	(617)752-5615	447
	NOAH, Carolyn B.	(617)799-1655	906

MICHIGAN
Albion	OBERG, Larry R.	(517)629-7297	914
Alma	DOLLARD, Peter A.	(512)463-7227	309
Ann Arbor	ANDERSEN, H F.	(313)936-7573	21
	BIGGS, Debra R.	(313)763-7080	95
	BOWEN, Jennifer B.	(313)663-6164	120
	CONWAY, Paul L.	(313)668-2218	239
	DWOSKIN, Beth M.	(212)382-6727	330
	EDWARDS, Willie M.	(313)994-6513	338
	HOUGH, Carolyn A.	(313)665-0537	562
	JASPER, Richard P.	(313)973-0747	595
	KOCHEN, Manfred	(313)764-2585	667
	KUSNERZ, Peggy A.		685
	LANSDALE, Metta T.		696
	LEARY, Margaret R.	(313)663-7324	707
	MAHONY, Doris D.	(313)764-1210	761
	MAXFIELD, David K.		787
	PAO, Miranda L.	(313)747-3611	938
	SCOTT, Melissa D.	(313)764-7460	1107
	SIEVING, Pamela C.	(313)761-1418	1136
	SMILLIE, Pauline A.	(313)665-8821	1151

REVIEWER (Cont'd)
MICHIGAN (Cont'd)

Ann Arbor			
	STOFFLE, Carla J.	(313)764-9356	1196
	WHEATON, Julie A.	(313)764-5746	1328
Auburn Hills	EL MOUCHI, Joan S.	(313)370-9466	346
Berkley	MARLOW, Cecilia A.	(313)547-3098	772
Berrien Springs	SOPER, Marley H.	(616)471-3379	1168
Birmingham	GOLDSTEIN, Doris R.	(313)626-9299	446
	IRWIN, Lawrence L.	(313)626-5339	584
	ORMOND, Sarah C.	(313)647-1700	926
	SICKLES, Linda C.	(313)335-3447	1135
Bloomfield Hills	FRANKIE, Suzanne O.	(313)855-6149	397
	RAFAL, Marian D.	(313)642-5800	1003
	SANDY, Marjorie M.	(313)642-5800	1081
Cedar Springs	RANSOM-BERGSTROM,		
	Janette F.	(616)696-3428	1008
Cheboygan	SMALLWOOD, Carol A.	(616)627-2308	1151
Clarkston	D'ELIA, Joseph G.	(313)625-8274	289
Dearborn	BREWER, Annie M.	(313)562-6871	134
	CRAWFORD, Geraldine H.	(313)271-2184	256
	FORSYTH, Karen R.	(313)562-8830	391
	LIMBACHER, James L.	(313)565-9687	727
Dearborn Heights	KIRKESY, Oliver M.	(313)278-4670	655
Detroit	BARTKOWSKI, Patricia	(313)577-4024	61
	BISSETT, Donald J.	(313)577-1615	100
	BRUNK, Thomas W.	(313)331-4930	150
	GRAZIER, Margaret H.	(313)862-7106	461
	GREGORY, Helen B.	(313)885-3437	466
	KNIFFEL, Leonard J.	(313)864-0982	664
	PFLUG, Warner W.	(313)577-4024	966
	RZEPECKI, Arnold M.	(313)868-2700	1072
	SHUMAN, Bruce A.	(313)577-1825	1134
	SMITH, Michael O.	(313)577-4024	1158
East Lansing	BLATT, Gloria T.	(313)332-6817	104
	CHAPIN, Richard E.	(517)355-2341	201
	JIZBA, Laurel	(517)353-4526	600
	WOODARD, Beth E.	(517)355-5774	1365
Eaton Rapids	FLAHERTY, Kevin C.	(517)663-2362	383
Farmington Hills	BEICHMAN, John C.	(313)553-5600	75
	RENKIEWICZ, Frank A.	(313)478-4506	1023
Flint	ARNOLD, Peggy	(313)744-4040	34
	PALMER, David W.	(313)238-0166	936
Grand Blanc	KINGSTON, Jo A.	(313)694-7323	652
Grand Haven	BROOKS, Burton H.	(616)842-2586	140
Grand Rapids	BOSE, Deborah L.	(616)453-1900	117
	KING, Kathryn L.		651
Grosse Pointe	CASEY, Genevieve M.		192
Grosse Pointe Farms	DRAPER, James P.	(313)881-4397	318
	HANSON, Charles D.	(313)882-3627	498
Grosse Pointe Woods	REID, Bette C.	(313)884-0884	1018
	STRATELAK, Nadia A.	(313)886-1043	1200
	WAYLAND, Marilyn T.		1311
Hancock	PENTI, Marsha E.	(906)482-5300	957
Kalamazoo	APPS, Michelle L.	(616)375-3611	30
	GROTZINGER, Laurel A.	(616)381-1865	473
	ISAACSON, David K.	(616)383-1562	584
	NETZ, David H.	(616)383-1666	896
	RIFE, Mary C.	(616)342-9837	1033
	VANDER MEER, Patricia F.	(616)383-1666	1274
Lansing	ARMSTRONG, Carole S.	(517)485-9813	32
	DUKELOW, Ruth H.	(517)373-1593	324
	FRYE, Dorothy T.	(517)393-7608	407
Livonia	CHAKLOSH, Cynthia L.		197
	VOIGHT, Nancy R.	(313)464-2306	1287
Marcellus	TATE, Carole A.	(616)646-5081	1225
Marquette	PAULIN, Mary A.	(906)228-6686	950
Midland	CHEN, Catherine W.	(517)631-9724	205
	DYKHUIS, Randy	(517)835-5227	331
Monroe	MARGOLIS, Bernard A.	(313)243-5213	770
Mt Pleasant	MULLIGAN, William H.	(517)773-1374	877
	TIMBERS, Jill G.		1245
	WEATHERFORD, John W.	(517)772-3861	1311
Novi	COREY, Marjorie	(313)344-1770	246
Olivet	COOPER, B L.	(616)749-7618	242
Plainwell	PARR, Michael P.	(616)685-9554	944
Port Huron	WU, Harry P.	(313)982-2765	1373
Rochester	KROMPART, Janet A.	(313)651-4738	679

REVIEWER (Cont'd)
MICHIGAN (Cont'd)

Sault Sainte Marie	NAIRN, Charles E.	(906)635-2402	886
Southfield	COCOZZOLI, Gary R.	(313)443-8905	226
	JOSE, Phyllis A.	(313)355-9282	617
	THOMAS, Margaret J.	(313)357-4952	1237
Spring Lake	PRETZER, Dale H.	(616)846-8967	992
Sturgis	BERKLUND, Nancy J.	(616)651-9361	87
Troy	BIELICH, Paul S.	(313)689-9381	95
	COREY, Glenn M.	(313)689-0600	246
West Bloomfield	WREN, James A.	(313)682-6310	1370
Westland	SHAFER, Steven I.		1119
Ypsilanti	BOONE, Morell D.	(313)484-4384	115
	MARSHALL, Albert P.		773
	YEE, Sandra G.	(313)487-2220	1379

MINNESOTA

Bemidji	ELLIOTT, Gwendolyn W.	(218)751-1041	344
Bloomington	NAUEN, Lindsay B.	(612)854-2879	889
Eagan	BOYD, Cheryl J.	(612)454-8254	122
Eden Prairie	GROSCH, Audrey N.	(612)937-2345	472
Fergus Falls	BERG, David C.		84
Grand Marais	GILLIS, Ruth J.		436
Grand Rapids	VALANCE, Marsha J.	(218)327-2336	1271
Mankato	FARNER, Susan G.	(507)389-5957	365
	PEISCHL, Thomas P.	(507)389-5953	955
	PIEHL, Kathleen K.	(507)389-5961	971
	READY, Sandra K.	(507)388-4003	1012
Minneapolis	ALLISON, Brent	(612)624-4549	17
	BEAVEN, Miranda J.	(612)624-5860	71
	BOEDER, Thelma B.	(612)870-3657	109
	BRANIN, Joseph J.	(612)624-5518	128
	BRUEMMER, Bruce H.	(612)624-5050	149
	BRUTON, Robert T.	(612)540-1084	151
	COGSWELL, James A.	(612)624-5518	227
	DODGE, Christopher N.	(612)541-8572	308
	GASTON, Judith A.	(612)627-4277	421
	HALLEWELL, Laurence	(612)724-6565	489
	IMMLER, Frank	(612)624-0091	582
	JOHNSON, Donald C.		603
	KELLY, Richard J.	(612)624-5860	638
	LATHROP, Alan K.	(612)789-4046	701
	OLSON, Lowell E.	(612)626-0824	923
	OVERMIER, Judith A.	(612)626-6881	931
	PANKAKE, Marcia J.	(612)331-2551	938
	REHNBERG, Marilyn J.	(612)722-3234	1017
	RUBENS, Donna J.	(612)624-7082	1064
	SANDNESS, John G.	(612)866-7033	1081
	SKELLY, Laurie J.	(612)823-2556	1146
	TERTELL, Susan M.	(612)372-6658	1232
	TIBLIN, Mariann E.	(612)624-5860	1244
	WALDEN, Barbara L.	(612)624-5860	1294
	WEEKS, John M.	(612)624-6833	1315
	WITT, Kenneth W.	(612)871-4262	1358
	YAHNKE, Robert E.	(612)625-0504	1376
Minnetonka	DESIREY, Janice M.	(612)541-8569	295
Mound	GELINAS, Jeanne L.	(612)472-4046	426
New Brighton	KEIM, Robert	(612)633-3393	635
Northfield	BRUCE, Robert K.	(507)645-9279	149
	SANFORD, Carolyn C.	(507)663-4266	1081
Owatonna	HOSLETT, Andrea E.	(507)451-0312	561
Pine River	O'BRIEN, Marlys H.	(218)587-2171	915
Rochester	BEYNEN, Gijsbertus K.		93
	HAWTHORNE, Dorothy M.	(507)284-8797	514
	KEY, Jack D.	(507)284-2068	645
	KEYS, Thomas E.		645
St Cloud	HEETER, Judith A.	(612)251-2700	520
Saint Joseph	HYNES, Arleen M.		580
St Louis Park	RINE, Joseph L.	(612)542-9631	1035
St Paul	BAKER, Tracey I.	(612)296-1273	50
	BROGAN, Martha L.	(612)698-1186	139
	CATHCART, Marilyn S.	(612)646-0254	195
	CLARKE, Charlotte C.	(612)645-7359	218
	CORNELL, Pamela J.	(612)296-1494	246
	DAVIS, Emmett A.	(612)699-4367	279
	HLAVSA, Larry B.	(612)699-7198	544
	JESSEE, W S.	(612)647-1329	600
	KING, Jack B.	(612)641-2373	651
	MARION, Donald J.	(612)624-6379	770
	NEVIN, Susanne	(612)625-1898	898

REVIEWER (Cont'd)
MINNESOTA (Cont'd)
St Paul

	OZOLINS, Karl L.	(612)645-2999	933
	SMITH, Eldred R.	(612)698-2362	1154
	STEINWALL, Susan D.	(612)690-5766	1186
	STOKES, Claire Z.	(612)642-0120	1196
	WALSTROM, Jon L.	(612)296-4543	1300
	WHITE, William T.	(612)227-9531	1332
St Peter	HAEUSER, Michael J.	(507)931-7556	482
	HERVEY, Norma J.	(507)931-7563	533
Warren	STEMME, Virginia L.	(218)745-4762	1186

MISSISSIPPI

Boyle	BAHR, Edward R.	(601)846-4607	45
Columbus	ZUMBERGE, Gloria A.	(601)434-7762	1391
Hattiesburg	BOYD, William D.	(601)266-4232	123
	CARNOVALE, A N.	(601)264-5452	184
	LATOUR, Terry S.	(601)266-4345	701
	VAN MELER, Vandelia L.	(601)266-4243	1276
	WITTIG, Glenn R.	(601)266-4236	1358
Itta Bena	BOWEN, Ethel B.	(601)254-9041	120
Jackson	BELL, Bernice	(601)366-8786	76
	PARKS, James F.	(601)354-5201	943
	SANDERS, Lou H.	(601)982-7094	1080
	WEST, Carol C.	(601)944-1970	1326
	WILSON, Ruth W.	(601)969-1013	1352
Mississippi State	WELLS, Anne S.	(601)325-7679	1322
Oxford	HARPER, Laura G.	(601)234-1812	503
Pontotoc	WILLIS, Jan L.	(601)489-3522	1348
Starkville	ELLSBURY, Susan H.	(601)324-1475	345

MISSOURI

Afton	WOHLRABE, John C.	(314)843-8131	1359
Ballwin	FORD, Gary E.	(314)225-6723	389
	TAYLOR, Arthur R.	(314)394-9973	1226
Cape Girardeau	STIEGEMEYER, Nancy H.	(314)334-3674	1193
Columbia	ANDREWS, Mark J.	(314)875-0154	27
	ARCHER, Stephen M.	(314)442-0611	31
	BELCHER, Nancy S.	(314)443-3161	76
	HAVENER, Ralph S.	(314)882-4602	513
	MCKININ, Emma J.	(314)442-4419	811
	MULTER, Ell P.		878
	STEVENS, Robert R.	(314)445-5320	1191
	TIMBERLAKE, Patricia P.	(314)882-4581	1245
	WATERS, Bill F.	(314)443-3161	1308
Florissant	ANTHONY, Paul L.	(314)921-6158	29
	BLANKENSHIP, Phyllis E.	(314)839-3966	104
Independence	BRILEY, Carol A.	(816)833-1400	136
Joplin	KEMP, Charles H.	(417)625-9386	639
	REIMAN, David A.	(417)625-9362	1020
Kansas City	COX, Bruce B.		253
	DRAYSON, Pamela K.	(816)753-7600	318
	GAMER, May L.	(816)361-8666	416
	GIBSON, Patricia A.	(816)333-9700	432
	HAMMOND, John J.	(816)221-2695	493
	HESS, Stanley W.	(816)561-4000	534
	LABUDDE, Kenneth J.	(816)531-0770	686
	LONDRE, Felicia H.	(816)444-1878	738
	MILLS, Elaine L.	(816)333-1245	844
	NESBITT, John R.	(813)926-7616	896
	SPALDING, Helen H.	(816)276-1531	1171
Marionville	MCCROSKEY, Marilyn J.	(417)463-7372	800
Maryville	HANKS, Nancy C.	(816)562-1590	496
Parkville	SMITH, Harold F.	(816)741-6085	1155
Saint Joseph	ELLIOTT, Dorothy G.	(816)232-7729	344
	HUGHES, Joan L.	(816)271-6000	571
St Louis	BECK, Sara R.	(314)889-5483	71
	BETH, Dana L.	(314)721-0067	92
	BURCKEL, Nicholas C.	(314)889-5400	158
	CRAWFORD, Susan Y.	(314)362-7080	257
	EIKEN, Mary A.	(314)385-8739	340
	GIETSCHIER, Steven P.	(314)993-7787	433
	GIETSCHIER, Steven P.	(314)993-7787	433
	LAURENSTEIN, Ann G.	(314)577-2669	703
	NELSON, Mary A.	(314)889-6459	894
	PAGE, Jacqueline M.	(314)781-6352	934
	SIGALA, Stephanie C.	(314)721-0067	1137
	STELLING, Dwight D.	(314)351-2419	1186
	VOLLMAR, William J.	(314)577-2279	1288

REVIEWER (Cont'd)
MISSOURI (Cont'd)
St Louis

	WILKINSON, William A.	(314)997-3585	1340
	WINKLER, Carol A.	(314)481-4753	1355
St Peters	HICKS, James M.	(314)441-0522	537
Shelbyville	MASON, Laura L.	(816)762-4285	781
Springfield	COOMBS, James A.	(417)836-4534	241
	DUCKWORTH, Paul M.	(417)866-6978	322
	KOTAMRAJU, Sarada	(417)883-8590	673
	LEITLE, Barbara K.	(417)865-5558	714
	MACKEY, Neosha A.	(417)836-4537	756
	MALTBY, Florence H.	(417)862-5119	764
	MORROW, Paula J.	(417)887-8161	869
	SINCLAIR, Regina A.	(417)865-8731	1143
Sugar Creek	STEELE, Anitra T.	(816)836-4031	1184
Warrensburg	NIEMEYER, Mollie M.	(816)429-4070	903
	SADLER, Philip A.	(816)747-8726	1073
	WALKER, Stephen R.	(816)429-4070	1296
	WHITE, D J.	(816)429-4425	1330

MONTANA

Billings	HAUSE, Aaron H.	(406)248-3802	512
	NERODA, Edward W.	(406)657-2320	895
Bozeman	BRUWELHEIDE, Janis H.	(406)587-0405	151
Great Falls	O'BRYANT, Alice A.		915
Helena	CLARK, Robert M.	(406)444-4787	218
	JACKSON, George R.	(406)449-3935	587
	MORROW, Delores J.	(406)444-4714	869
Missoula	SCHMIDT, Theodore A.	(406)721-2811	1096

NEBRASKA

Kearney	NORMAN, Ronald V.	(308)237-5133	909
Lincoln	ALLEN, Richard H.	(402)435-4052	16
	LEITER, Richard A.	(402)466-3468	714
	TIBBITS, Edith J.	(402)472-3545	1243
	WAGNER, Rod G.	(402)423-7476	1292
	WISE, Sally H.	(402)472-5737	1357
Minatare	JOHNSON, Elizabeth L.	(308)783-2188	604
Papillion	ZANARINI, Linda S.	(402)339-0405	1386

NEVADA

Carson City	ROCHA, Guy L.	(702)885-5210	1045
Incline	OSSOLINSKI, Lynn	(702)831-2936	928
Las Vegas	CAROLLO, Michael T.	(702)385-0115	184
	GARDNER, Jack I.	(702)382-3493	418
	GROSSHANS, Merilyn P.	(702)799-7855	473
	MORGAN, James E.	(702)384-4887	864
	VOIT, Irene E.	(702)361-5475	1287
Reno	GREFRATH, Richard W.		465
	MANLEY, Charles W.	(702)785-4012	765
	MCNEAL, Betty	(702)325-5859	816
	RICE, Dorothy F.	(702)747-2849	1027
	ZINK, Steven D.	(702)345-0659	1389

NEW HAMPSHIRE

Concord	HARE, William J.	(603)225-2012	501
	HIGGINS, Matthew J.	(603)228-3127	538
	MEVERS, Frank C.	(603)224-3896	829
	RYAN, Clare E.	(603)271-2316	1070
Franconia	BJORNER, Susan N.	(603)823-8838	100
Fremont	FARAH, Barbara D.		363
Hanover	CRONENWETT, Philip N.	(603)646-2037	260
	REED, Barbara E.	(603)646-3831	1014
	ROLETT, Virginia V.	(603)643-3593	1051
Keene	LESSER, Charlotte B.	(603)357-1086	718
	PERLUNGHER, Richard A.	(603)357-4209	959
	VINCENT, Charles P.	(603)352-1909	1284
Manchester	THOMPSON, Debra J.	(603)669-1048	1239
Milford	LISTOVITCH, Denise A.	(603)672-0899	733
Mirror Lake	SARLES, Christie V.	(603)569-4932	1083
Nashua	BARRETT, Beth R.	(603)880-3542	59
	KOZIKOWSKI, Derek M.	(603)881-1057	674
Portsmouth	JACOBS, Gloria	(603)431-9346	589
Sunapee	TATE, Joanne D.	(603)763-9948	1225
Windham	CUNNIFFE, Charlene M.	(603)434-1847	265

REVIEWER (Cont'd)
NEW JERSEY

Allenwood	ERBE, Evalina S.	(201)223-9388	352
Audubon	VAUGHAN-STERLING, Judith A.	(609)546-0652	1280
Belle Mead	LEE, J S.	(201)359-5845	710
Belleville	JACKRELL, Thomas L.	(201)759-5318	586
Bergenfield	HILL, George R.	(201)384-4034	539
Berkeley Heights	MAZURKIEWICZ, Helen L.	(201)464-0096	791
Bernardsville	BURDEN, Geraldine R.	(201)766-0118	158
Bloomfield	SHEARIN, Cynthia E.	(201)338-6545	1124
Branchville	RAFFERTY, Stephen P.	(201)948-6380	1003
Bridgewater	DESS, Howard M.	(201)526-1981	295
Butler	GARDNER, Sue A.	(201)838-3262	418
Caldwell	EDELSON, Ken		335
	HODGE, Patricia A.	(201)288-4424	546
Cherry Hill	BROWN, Anita P.	(609)663-2247	142
	GLATT, Carol R.		440
	KUAN, Jenny W.	(609)667-0300	681
	WALSH, Sharon T.	(609)243-1619	1300
Cliffside Park	PAWSON, Robert D.	(201)943-3228	951
Clifton	TROJAN, Judith L.	(201)472-3868	1257
Colts Neck	HIGGINS, Flora T.	(201)431-5656	537
Cranford	BEIMAN, Frances M.	(201)272-5840	75
	HALL, Homer J.	(201)276-4311	488
	SAWYCKY, Roman A.	(201)276-3134	1086
	WOLFE, N J.	(201)279-9563	1361
Dayton	LAMBKIN, Claire A.	(201)329-0648	691
East Brunswick	MENINGALL, Evelyn L.	(201)254-6403	824
East Orange	GORMAN, Audrey J.	(201)676-2472	452
East Windsor	PINEL, Stephen L.	(609)448-8427	974
Edison	FERRERE, Cathy M.	(201)819-8924	373
Elizabeth	RICE, Anna C.	(201)352-5328	1026
Englewood	HALASZ, Etelka B.	(201)858-6970	484
Flemington	MCGREGOR, Walter	(201)788-3025	808
Florham Park	BYOUK, Nancy K.	(201)377-2694	168
Glassboro	KENNEDY, Kathleen A.	(609)863-5335	641
Green Village	KEON, Edward F.	(201)822-0062	643
Haddonfield	SWARTZ, Betty J.	(609)429-8498	1214
Hamilton	HOOKER, Joan M.	(609)587-9669	556
Highland Park	BEETHAM, Donald W.	(201)249-3268	74
	JONES, Dorothy C.		612
	MILLER, Lynn F.	(201)572-6563	840
	PAGE, Penny B.	(201)247-9353	934
Irvington	KNIGHT, Shirley D.	(201)371-9324	664
Iselin	FRANTS, Valery	(212)579-2496	398
Kearny	HAWLEY, George S.	(201)997-5299	514
Kenilworth	FLICK, Susan E.	(201)276-2451	385
Lawrenceville	STEPHEN, Ross G.	(609)896-5111	1187
	TILLMAN, Hope N.	(609)896-5115	1245
Leonia	CIMBALA, Diane J.	(201)585-1921	214
	SCHARF, Davida	(201)947-6839	1090
	SHERMAN, Louise L.	(201)461-6137	1128
Linden	PISKORIK, Elizabeth	(201)486-3888	976
Little Falls	RANDALL, Lynn E.	(201)278-5400	1006
Livingston	LIND, Judith Y.	(201)740-8704	728
Lodi	KARETZKY, Stephen	(201)778-1190	627
Madison	BROCKMAN, William S.	(201)377-3000	138
	CONNORS, Linda E.	(201)377-3000	238
	COUGHLIN, Caroline M.	(201)377-3000	250
	JONES, Arthur E.	(201)377-6525	611
	LONG, Joanna R.	(201)377-2376	739
	SNELSON, Pamela	(201)377-3000	1163
Maplewood	KRUPP, Robert G.	(201)763-8436	681
Mendham	MANTHEY, Carolyn M.	(201)543-2129	767
Metuchen	BECKER, Ronald L.	(201)494-6447	72
	HIGGINS, Marilyn E.	(201)321-8745	538
Morristown	BUCK, Anne M.	(201)829-5111	153
Mount Holly	ALTERMAN, Deborah H.	(609)261-3458	18
	CARR, Charles E.	(609)267-9660	185
Mt Laurel	O'CONNOR, Elizabeth W.	(609)235-5003	916
Mountain Lakes	STEEN, Carol N.	(201)334-4941	1184
Mountainside	LINGELBACH, Lorene N.	(201)654-7694	730
Neptune	OGONEK, Donna L.	(201)922-4986	918
Neshanic	VANDERGRIFT, Kay E.	(201)369-8685	1274
New Brunswick	ANDERSON, James D.	(201)846-1510	23
	EUSTER, Joanne R.	(201)932-7505	356
	RICHARDS, Pamela S.		1028
	SWARTZBURG, Susan G.	(201)932-8573	1214
Newark	DANE, William J.	(201)733-7848	272

REVIEWER (Cont'd)
NEW JERSEY (Cont'd)

North Arlington	CASEY, Mary A.	(201)997-2141	192
Ocean	VLOYANETES, Jeanne M.	(201)493-9007	1286
Paramus	WHITE, Robert W.	(201)652-6772	1332
Park Ridge	LUXNER, Dick	(201)391-5935	750
Parsippany	VOGT, Herwart C.	(201)263-5669	1287
Paterson	ROTSAERT, Stefanie C.	(201)279-8044	1060
Patterson	SAWYER, Miriam		1086
Pennington	KAZIMIR, Edward O.	(609)737-3582	632
Pequannock	SUSSMAN, Valerie J.	(201)696-9655	1210
Piscataway	CASSEL, Jeris F.	(201)752-0528	193
	HOFFMAN, Helen B.	(201)932-3855	548
Plainfield	KRUSE, Theodore H.	(201)725-2294	681
	MCCOY, W K.	(201)753-0618	799
Plainsboro	BLACK, William R.	(609)275-9104	102
Point Pleasant	GREENE, Ellin P.	(201)899-2270	464
Princeton	BELCHER, Emily M.	(609)924-8947	76
	BENEDUCE, Ann K.	(609)921-6624	80
	BUTCHER, Patricia S.	(609)921-6203	166
	CARLSON, Dudley B.		182
	CRITCHLOW, Therese E.	(609)924-9529	259
	HENNEMAN, John B.	(609)921-0757	528
	HOELLE, Dolores M.	(609)452-3201	547
	JOHNSON, David K.	(609)924-2870	603
	LOGAN, Harold J.	(609)520-4066	737
	MORGAN, Paula M.	(609)452-3230	864
	NASE, Lois M.	(609)452-3237	888
	NEWHOUSE, Brian G.	(609)921-8803	899
	PASTER, Luisa R.	(609)452-5464	946
Ramsey	SCARPELLINO, Rebecca A.	(201)825-1297	1088
Red Bank	ANTCZAK, Janice	(201)741-0815	28
Ridgewood	KOONTZ, John	(201)652-0185	671
Rutherford	RAPPAPORT, Susan E.		1008
Sewell	CROCKER, Jane L.	(609)468-5000	259
Somerdale	DALE, Charles F.	(609)346-4629	270
South Orange	BROWN, Ronald L.		147
	FAWCETT-BRANDON, Pamela S.	(201)762-0230	367
	TALAR, Anita	(201)761-9434	1220
Sparta	GUIDA, Pat	(201)729-8176	476
Stanhope	KUTTEROFF, Ethel C.	(201)347-7600	685
Summit	SOMMER, Ursula M.	(201)593-8526	1167
Teaneck	JOHNSON, Patrelle E.	(201)833-1788	608
	TORRONE, Joan M.	(201)836-5402	1251
Trenton	MADDEN, Doreitha R.		758
	MCCULLOUGH, Jack W.	(609)771-2106	801
	RAZZANO, Barbara W.	(609)984-7608	1012
	WOODLEY, Robert H.	(609)771-2441	1366
Turnersville	SZILASSY, Sandor	(609)589-7193	1218
Upper Montclair	STOCK, Norman	(201)893-7151	1195
Warren	WEIL, Ben H.	(201)647-0892	1317
West Long Branch	FISHER, Scott L.	(201)229-9222	381
	PALMISANO-DRUCKER, Elsalyn	(201)870-9194	937
West Milford	COURTNEY, Aida N.	(201)728-2823	251
	JOB, Amy G.	(201)595-2160	601
West Orange	FICHTELBERG, Susan	(201)736-0198	374
Westfield	SEADER, Jane M.		1109
	WILSTED, Thomas P.	(201)789-9147	1353
Whippany	MUNSICK, Lee R.	(201)386-1920	879
Whitehouse Station	HOYT, Henry M.	(201)689-7717	566
Williamstown	BOGIS, Nana E.	(609)728-0569	110
Woodbridge	BOYLE, Jean E.	(201)634-3460	124
	DE WITT, Benjamin L.	(201)634-1316	298
	SPANGLER, William N.	(201)634-4450	1171

NEW MEXICO

Albuquerque	ELDREDGE, Jonathan D.	(505)277-0654	342
	FREEMAN, Patricia E.		401
	GROTHEY, Mina J.	(505)277-7144	473
	HLAVA, Marjorie M.	(505)265-3591	544
	IVES, Peter B.	(505)277-9243	586
	KRUG, Ruth A.	(505)277-7213	680
	PRUETT, Nancy J.		996
	REX, Heather	(505)277-7182	1024
	SEISER, Virginia	(505)842-5156	1113
	SUGNET, Christopher L.	(505)277-7162	1206
	THOMPSON, Janet A.	(505)277-7172	1240
	THORSON, Connie C.	(505)277-7201	1242

REVIEWER (Cont'd)
NEW MEXICO (Cont'd)
Albuquerque

	WHITLOW, Cherrill M.	(505)266-1472	1333
Clovis	MCBETH, Deborah E.	(505)762-7161	792
Las Cruces	ODENHEIM, Claire E.	(505)522-8814	916
	RICHARDS, James H.	(505)524-0281	1028
Los Alamos	KRAEMER, Mary P.	(505)662-7219	674
Portales	MCGUIRE, Laura H.	(505)356-8485	808
	SCHOTT, Mark E.	(505)356-8735	1099
Roswell	KLOPFER, Jerome J.	(505)622-6250	662
Santa Fe	LANCASTER, Kevin M.	(505)827-4854	692
	PIERSON, Robert M.	(505)982-0371	972
Thoreau	SCHUBERT, Donald F.	(505)862-7465	1101
Toadlena	MCCAULEY, Elfrieda B.	(505)789-3205	795

NEW YORK

Albany	COX, Richard J.	(518)486-4820	253
	KNAPP, Sara D.	(518)442-3539	663
	KNEE, Michael	(518)442-3586	663
	LEWIS, Frances R.	(518)869-9317	723
	MATTIE, Joseph J.	(518)474-4970	786
	MCCOMBS, Gillian M.	(518)442-3633	797
	MILLER, Heather S.	(518)442-3626	838
	MOREHEAD, Joe	(518)442-5128	863
	NEVETT, Micki S.	(518)459-2178	897
	NICHOLS-RANDALL, Barbara L.	(518)489-7649	902
	NITECKI, Joseph Z.	(518)442-3568	905
	ROBERTS, Anne F.	(518)438-0607	1039
	SEVERINGHAUS, Ethel L.	(518)456-2110	1117
	VIA, Barbara J.	(518)442-3688	1283
	WALKER, M G.	(518)436-1975	1296
	YAVARKOVSKY, Jerome	(518)473-1189	1378
Alfred	CONNOLLY, Bruce E.	(607)871-2494	237
Amawalk	HANE, Paula J.	(914)962-2933	495
Amherst	COOVER, James B.	(176)636-2935	244
	MAYER, Erich J.	(716)691-5554	789
APO New York	GADBOIS, Frank W.		411
	MEIGS, Carolyn R.		821
Astoria	QUARTELL, Robert J.	(718)274-7568	999
Ausable Forks	ROGERS, Elizabeth S.		1049
Ballston Lake	EGAN, Mary J.	(518)399-5151	338
Bayside	BAKISH, David J.	(718)225-0475	50
Bellerose	GATNER, Elliott S.		422
Bergen	FABRIZIO, Timothy C.	(716)494-2264	360
Binghamton	CHAMBERLAIN, Erna B.	(607)723-4064	197
	COHEN, Ann E.	(607)724-9597	227
	HILL, Malcolm K.	(607)723-8236	540
	MCKEE, George D.	(607)729-5490	810
	WILLIAMS, Deborah H.	(607)723-6457	1342
Brockport	RAKSHI, Sri R.	(716)395-5262	1004
Bronx	DAVIS, Mary B.	(212)829-7770	280
	DECANDIDO, Graceanne A.		285
	GAROOGIAN, Rhoda	(212)588-2266	420
	LAMPORT, Bernard	(212)430-3747	691
	LOCASCIO, Aline M.	(212)588-8400	735
	PATRYCH, Joseph		947
	REIMAN, Donald H.	(212)549-4890	1020
	RUBEY, Daniel R.	(212)960-8580	1064
	WEINBERG, Bella H.	(212)547-5159	1317
Bronxville	HUEBNER, Mary A.	(914)337-9300	570
Brooklundy	HAMILTON, Reatha B.		492
Brooklyn	BAKER, Zachary M.	(718)855-6318	50
	BRAUCH, Patricia O.	(718)780-5581	129
	CORRSIN, Stephen D.	(718)851-2317	247
	DOHERTY, Mary C.	(718)270-2106	309
	ELLIS, Kathleen V.	(718)287-4873	344
	GARGAN, William M.	(718)780-5276	419
	GENCO, Barbara A.	(718)499-8750	426
	GUREWITSCH, Bonnie	(718)338-6494	478
	HOMMEL, Claudia	(718)237-0028	555
	KALKHOFF, Ann L.	(708)622-4036	623
	KEAVENEY, Sydney S.	(718)636-3685	633
	KLEIMAN, Allan M.	(718)645-2396	658
	KRAMER, Allan F.	(718)857-7825	675
	KUPERMAN, Aaron W.	(718)854-8637	684
	MANBECK, Virginia B.	(718)253-9413	764
	MARSHAK, Bonnie L.	(718)638-6821	773
	MEYERS, Charles	(718)342-1144	830

REVIEWER (Cont'd)
NEW YORK (Cont'd)
Brooklyn

	NYREN, Dorothy E.	(718)780-7799	913
	PERSON, Diane G.	(718)596-2345	961
	PRUITT, Brenda F.	(718)287-1681	996
	ROBBINS, Sara E.	(718)780-7980	1039
	ROGINSKI, James W.	(718)499-4850	1050
	RUBINSTEIN, Roslyn	(718)834-8779	1065
	SCHNEIDER, Adele	(718)743-7172	1096
	SEMKOW, Julie L.	(718)624-3189	1115
	SULTANOF, Jeff B.	(718)768-1611	1208
	WENGER, Milton B.	(718)252-5019	1324
Buffalo	BOBINSKI, George S.	(716)636-2412	108
	BRADLEY, Carol J.	(716)636-2935	125
	BUSH, Renee B.	(716)832-3081	165
	DECKER, Jean S.	(716)636-2784	285
	HEPFER, Cynthia K.	(716)831-2139	530
	HEPFER, William E.	(716)636-2784	530
	KARCH, Linda S.	(716)827-2323	627
	SZEMRAJ, Edward R.	(716)895-7675	1218
	WAGNER, Stephen K.	(716)837-1563	1292
Centerport	COOPER, Catherine M.	(516)754-9262	242
Chappaqua	CHEATHAM, Bertha M.	(914)238-3586	204
Cheektowaga	WITT, Susan T.	(716)686-3620	1358
Cherry Plain	GILCHER, Edwin	(518)658-2429	434
Cold Spring	BARNHART, David K.	(914)265-2822	58
	FEICK, Christina L.	(914)265-2304	368
Cold Spring Harbor	FARAONE, Maria B.	(516)271-1771	363
Commack	ROFES, William L.	(516)499-4370	1049
Corning	HORNICK-LOCKARD, Barbara J.	(607)962-9251	560
Cornwall	HANSON, Jan E.	(914)534-3104	498
Cortland	HEARN, Stephen S.	(607)753-2506	518
Croton-on-Hudson	CLARKE, Elizabeth S.	(914)271-3729	218
Dansville	MINEMIER, Betty M.	(716)335-6258	845
Dewitt	POPOVIC, Tanya V.	(315)446-7488	983
Dobbs Ferry	BONE, Larry E.	(914)693-4500	113
East Setauket	ALBERTUS, Donna M.		10
	BLOHM, Laura A.	(516)444-3105	106
Elma	DRZEWIECKI, Iris M.	(716)683-0592	321
Elmhurst	NOLAN, John A.	(718)565-1627	907
Elmira	LAPIER, Cynthia B.	(607)739-3581	697
	WEIDEMANN, Margaret A.	(607)733-8609	1316
Fairport	WOLF, Catharine D.	(716)223-9284	1360
Flushing	COHEN, David	(718)520-7194	228
	COOPER, Marianne	(718)520-7194	243
	DUTIKOW, Irene V.	(718)939-7382	329
	MACOMBER, Nancy	(718)523-5707	758
	PENCHANSKY, Mimi B.	(718)520-7248	956
Forest Hills	NERBOSO, Donna L.	(718)897-9826	895
	VAN BRUNT, Amy S.	(718)261-0313	1272
Franklin Square	PILLA, Marianne L.	(516)775-4143	973
Freeport	MORIN, Wilfred L.	(516)368-6242	865
	VOLLONO, Millicent D.	(516)223-0838	1288
Garden City	FRIEDMAN, Arthur L.	(516)222-7406	403
	PIRODSKY, Nancy E.	(516)742-8405	975
Germantown	LINDSLEY, Barbara N.	(518)537-4114	730
Getzville	DENSMORE, Christopher	(716)688-2001	293
Glen Cove	WINCKLER, Paul A.	(516)671-0928	1354
Glens Falls	SMITH, Frederick E.	(518)792-8214	1155
Governors Island	GODWIN, Mary J.	(212)009-4351	443
Hamilton	DERGEN, Daniel P.	(315)824-2381	85
	WASHBURN, Keith E.	(315)824-3008	1307
Hastings on Hudson	JELLINEK, George	(914)478-1979	596
Hempstead	ANDREWS, Charles R.	(516)560-5940	26
	LOUISDHON-WALTER, Marie L.	(718)990-0767	742
Hicksville	EDWARDS, Harriet M.		337
Hollis Hills	GOLD, Renee L.	(718)479-9534	444
Horseheads	BROUSE, Ann G.	(607)562-8986	141
Houghton	LAUER, Jonathan D.	(716)567-2211	702
Huntington	FOLCARELLI, Ralph J.	(516)271-0634	387
	MARKOWITZ, Lois	(516)421-2244	771
	WOLFE, Barbara M.	(516)423-2495	1360
Huntington Station	ROSS, David J.	(516)385-4951	1058

Ithaca	ASHMUN, Lawrence F.		36
	CASSARO, James P.	(607)255-7046	193
	ERICSON, Margaret D.	(607)274-3882	353
	HICKEY, John T.	(607)273-1944	536
	POWELL, Jill H.	(607)255-3925	988
	SCHNEDEKER, Donald W.	(607)255-3389	1096
	STEWART, Linda G.	(607)255-7959	1192
	ZASLAW, Neal	(607)257-1052	1386
Jackson Heights	RANHAND, Jori L.	(718)469-4728	1007
	SPYROS, Marsha L.	(718)424-7849	1177
Jamaica	MARKE, Julius J.	(718)990-6759	771
	POWIS, Katherine E.	(718)990-6089	989
Jamestown	LEE, Sylvia	(716)483-5415	711
	MORRIS, Kim	(716)484-7135	867
Kenmore	RYBARCZYK, Barclay S.	(716)877-0605	1071
Kew Gardens	TANNENBAUM, Robin L.	(718)793-0372	1222
Kings Park	PANDIT, Jyoti P.	(516)269-1070	937
Lake Grove	GRAVITZ, Ina A.	(516)467-4116	459
Lake Success	TRINKOFF, Elaine	(516)466-9148	1257
Larchmont	LANDMAN, Lillian L.	(914)834-3225	693
Latham	BRUNELLE, Bette S.	(518)783-1161	150
Liverpool	POLLY, Jean A.	(315)457-0310	981
Long Beach	WASSERMAN, Ricki F.		1308
Long Island City	MARTIN, Brian G.	(718)726-5885	775
Loudonville	NAYLOR, Richard J.	(518)458-9274	890
Lynbrook	HESSLEIN, Shirley B.	(516)887-5071	534
Macedon	WEMETT, Lisa C.	(315)986-3949	1323
Mamaroneck	O'CONOR, William C.	(914)698-4741	916
Manhasset	DEE, Camille C.		286
Massapequa	REID, Richard C.	(516)795-0262	1019
Massapequa Park	GIANNATTASI, Gerard E.	(516)541-6584	430
McLean	DREW, Wilfred E.	(607)753-8180	319
Menands	GILSON, Robert	(518)463-4181	437
	LENZ, Millicent A.		716
Middletown	BAUM, Christina D.	(914)344-3615	66
Mineola	KRATZ, Charles E.		676
Monticello	DORN, Robert J.	(914)794-4660	313
Mt Sinai	COHEN, Rosemary C.	(516)473-8717	229
Mt Vernon	OCKENE, David L.	(914)699-0949	915
	O'DELL, Lorraine I.		916
	ROSSWURM, K M.	(914)667-6836	1059
Nassau	LIPETZ, Ben A.	(518)766-3014	732
	VANNORTWICK, Barbara L.	(518)766-4190	1276
Nesconset	GRUNDT, Leonard	(516)361-8987	475
New Hyde Park	LANG, Jovian P.	(516)352-1666	695
New Paltz	NYQUIST, Corinne E.	(914)255-2209	913
New Rochelle	KONOVALOFF, Maria S.		670
New York	ALLENTUCK, Marcia E.		16
	AMISON, Mary V.	(212)666-9645	20
	ARMSTRONG, Joanne D.	(212)280-3743	32
	AVALLONE, Susan	(212)315-4808	41
	BAKER, John P.	(212)255-7267	48
	BALKEMA, John B.	(212)876-8200	52
	BEALER, Jane A.	(212)355-0083	68
	BEHRMANN, Christine A.	(212)568-6349	75
	BERNER, Andrew J.	(212)515-5299	88
	BERNSTEIN, Mark P.		89
	BOCKMAN, Eugene J.	(212)566-5398	109
	BOURKE, Thomas A.	(212)930-0838	119
	BOZIWICK, George E.	(212)870-1675	124
	BRAUN, Robert L.		130
	BRODY, Catherine T.	(212)228-7863	139
	BROWAR, Lisa M.	(212)930-0556	141
	BRUGNOLOTTI, Phyllis T.	(212)873-0677	150
	BUCK, Richard M.		154
	BUTLER, Tyrone G.	(212)566-5367	167
	CAMBRIA, Roberto		174
	CASSELL, Kay A.	(212)614-6551	193
	COHEN, Frederick S.	(212)594-9880	228
	COLBY, Robert A.	(212)787-3062	230
	COMEAU, Amy R.	(212)341-7000	234
	COVERT, Nadine	(212)988-4876	252
	CURTIS, James A.	(212)222-9638	267
	DARNOWSKI, Christina M.	(212)750-5749	275
	DERRICKSON, Margaret	(212)620-4230	294
	DUNLAP, Barbara J.	(212)690-5367	326
	EBER, Beryl E.	(212)621-0635	334
	EPPES, William D.	(212)675-2070	351

	FISHER, Carolyn H.	(212)873-0844	380
	FLEISHMAN, Lauren Z.	(212)371-2000	384
	FODY, Barbara A.	(212)713-3673	387
	FRANKLIN, Linda C.	(212)679-6038	398
	FRIEDMAN, Judy B.		404
	FRUSCIANO, Thomas J.	(212)998-2644	406
	GARDNER, Ralph D.	(212)877-6820	418
	GERHARDT, Lillian N.	(212)463-6759	428
	GILLESPIE, John T.	(212)861-9294	435
	GLASFORD, G R.	(212)669-3336	440
	GOLD, Hilary G.	(212)242-2180	444
	GOTTLIEB, Jane E.	(212)362-8671	453
	GRAY, Karen	(212)758-9663	460
	GUBERT, Betty K.	(212)362-4256	475
	GUILER, Paula J.	(212)689-3341	476
	GURIEVITCH, Grania B.	(212)974-9507	478
	HAEFLIGER, Kathleen A.	(212)663-7857	482
	HAGSTROM, Jack W.	(212)491-1704	483
	HALL, Alix M.	(212)536-3598	486
	HARVEY, John F.	(215)509-2612	509
	HAVENS, Shirley E.	(212)463-6804	513
	HAYNES, Patricia	(212)371-3200	516
	HIGGINS, Steven	(212)674-2087	538
	HOLTZE, Sally H.	(212)674-6973	555
	HOWELL, Josephine T.	(212)702-4255	565
	HUDSON, Alice C.	(212)222-2835	569
	HUNTER, Gregory S.	(212)940-1690	576
	HUTSON, Jean B.	(212)368-1515	579
	JACKSON, Richard H.	(212)870-1647	588
	JENNINGS, Vincent		598
	JOHNSON, Judith	(212)337-7428	606
	JONES, Roger A.	(212)777-2959	615
	JURIST, Janet	(212)737-8120	620
	KAIN, Joan P.	(212)850-0768	622
	KARATNYTSKY, Christine A.	(212)420-1436	627
	KENSELAAR, Robert	(212)870-1661	642
	KRANICH, Nancy C.	(212)998-2447	676
	KUHNER, Robert A.	(212)663-3360	683
	LAWRENCE, Arthur P.	(212)505-7996	704
	LIEBERFELD, Lawrence	(212)348-8499	726
	LINDGREN, Arla M.	(212)662-6386	729
	MARGALITH, Helen M.	(212)575-0190	770
	MARGOLIES, Alan	(212)489-5042	770
	MARKERT, Patricia B.	(212)925-4939	771
	MARTIN, Jean F.	(212)928-4231	776
	MARTIN, Richard	(212)760-7970	778
	MASSIS, Bruce E.	(212)595-2000	782
	MAYER, George L.	(212)724-8057	789
	MCGLINCHEE, Claire	(212)737-1875	806
	MCSWEENEY, Josephine	(212)254-6338	818
	MEYER, Albert	(212)254-7031	829
	MIHRAM, Danielle	(212)998-2515	834
	MINTZ, Anne P.	(212)620-2499	847
	MOLZ, Redmond K.	(212)280-4787	854
	MOONEY, James E.	(212)873-3400	858
	MOSES, Julian M.	(212)688-8426	871
	MYERS, Maria P.	(212)473-6673	884
	OSTROW, Rona	(212)691-1672	929
	PASQUARIELLA, Susan K.	(212)781-0324	946
	PEARCE, Karla J.	(212)280-3353	952
	PERRY, Claudia A.	(212)876-8200	960
	PETTOLINA, Anthony M.	(212)790-2888	965
	POLSTER, Joanne	(212)564-7640	982
	POTEAT, James B.	(212)759-6800	986
	PRONIN, Monica		995
	PURCELL, Marcia L.	(212)982-3786	998
	RACHOW, Louis A.	(212)228-7610	1001
	REID, Carolyn A.	(212)472-5919	1018
	ROHMANN, Gloria P.	(212)930-0576	1050
	ROTHSTEIN, Pauline M.	(212)750-6008	1060
	SALBER, Peter J.	(212)350-4680	1076
	SCHUMAN, Patricia G.	(212)925-8650	1103
	SETTANNI, Joseph A.	(212)289-9059	1117
	SHAPIRO, Fred R.	(203)432-1600	1121
	SHERBY, Louise S.	(212)280-2241	1127
	SHIROMA, Susan G.	(212)998-2602	1131
	SOMMER, Susan T.	(212)870-1648	1167

REVIEWER (Cont'd)
NEW YORK (Cont'd)
New York

	SPRUNG, George	(212)362-9389	1176
	STALKER, Dianne S.	(212)280-8484	1178
	SWANSON, Dorothy T.	(212)998-2630	1213
	SZMUK, Szilvia E.	(212)787-2573	1218
	TAYLOR, Robert N.	(212)664-9021	1228
	TICE, Margaret E.		1244
	VAN DYKE, Stephen H.	(212)340-0872	1275
	VAUGHN, Susan J.	(212)260-2544	1280
	VINCENT-DAVISS, Diana	(212)598-2367	1284
	WILLNER, Channan P.	(212)870-1675	1348
	WOLFE, Allis	(212)496-0008	1360
	WOSH, Peter J.	(212)581-7400	1369
	YAKEL, Elizabeth	(212)581-7400	1376
Niagara Falls	SHIELDS, Gerald R.	(716)284-2928	1130
Ogdensburg	FRANZ, David A.	(315)393-2950	398
	SMITH, Nicholas N.	(315)393-1075	1159
Oneonta	BULSON, Christine	(607)431-2453	156
	CROWLEY, John V.	(607)431-2725	261
	JOHNSON, Richard D.	(607)432-0131	608
	POTTER, Janet L.		987
Ossining	DOW, Sally R.	(914)941-2416	315
	STAPLETON, Darwin H.	(914)762-8921	1181
Palisades	KLIMLEY, Susan	(914)359-2900	661
Patchogue	NEUFELD, Judith B.	(516)289-6813	897
Peekskill	FALCONE, Elena C.	(914)528-2820	362
Pelham	FERRIBY, Peter G.	(914)738-3712	373
Pittsford	RICHARDSON, Constance H.	(716)385-6750	1029
Plainview	SYWAK, Myron	(516)935-7821	1217
Plattsburgh	BURTON, Robert E.	(518)561-1613	164
Pomona	GUBITS, Helen S.	(914)354-1340	475
Port Jervis	HOFMANN, Susan M.	(914)856-1513	548
Port Washington	BRENNER, Everett H.	(516)767-2728	133
	SCHREIBMAN, Fay C.	(516)767-0081	1099
Potsdam	NOLTE, James S.	(315)268-2292	908
Poughkeepsie	SEEBER, Frances M.	(914)452-8122	1111
	WALSH, Robin S.	(914)462-7129	1300
Purchase	EVANS, Robert W.	(914)253-5085	358
	FREIDES, Thelma	(914)253-5096	401
Queens Village	HECKMAN, Lucy T.	(718)776-6285	519
Ridge	KINNEY, Daniel W.	(516)924-7338	653
Riverdale	KLEINBURD, Freda		659
Rochester	BERKMAN, Robert I.	(716)461-3206	87
	CUMMINS, Julie A.	(716)428-7366	264
	CUSEO, Allan A.	(716)325-4264	267
	JUNION, Gail J.	(716)275-4496	620
	KATZ, Jacqueline E.	(716)254-7144	630
	MATZEK, Richard A.	(716)586-2525	786
	MOUREY, Deborah A.	(716)724-6819	874
	SIMMONS, Rebecca A.	(706)271-3361	1140
	STOSS, Frederick W.	(716)436-8719	1198
Rye	GREENFIELD, Judith C.	(914)967-0480	464
St James	WIENER, Paul B.	(516)862-8723	1336
Saratoga Springs	RATZER, Mary B.		1010
Sayville	PAGELS, Helen H.	(516)589-2908	934
Scarborough	HOPKINS, Lee B.	(914)941-5810	558
Scarsdale	BERGER, Pam P.	(914)723-3156	86
Schenectady	HODGES, Lois F.	(518)377-7738	546
	SCOTT, Frances Y.	(518)346-5052	1107
Scotia	HENDRICKSON, Maria F.	(518)374-6209	527
Sea Cliff	LETTIS, Lucy B.		719
Setauket	NICHOLS, Gerald D.	(516)689-7071	901
Somers	RITTER, Sally K.	(914)232-7889	1037
	SHAPIRO, Lillian L.	(914)276-2269	1121
Staten Island	HOGAN, Matthew	(718)273-6245	549
	KLINGLE, Philip A.	(718)390-5291	662
	MANNING, Jo A.	(718)981-0120	766
Stillwater	REEPMEYER, Marie C.	(518)785-6949	1016
Stony Brook	KING, Christine E.	(516)632-7110	650
	MASH, S D.		780
	SEWELL, Robert G.	(516)632-7100	1117
	SIMPSON, Charles W.	(516)632-7100	1141
	WILLIAMS, Doris C.	(516)632-7152	1343
Syosset	CALVANO, Margaret	(516)921-1674	174
	JENSEN, Dennis F.	(516)921-0418	598

REVIEWER (Cont'd)
NEW YORK (Cont'd)

Syracuse	BOISSY, Robert W.	(315)428-8398	111
	FROEHLICH, Thomas J.	(315)425-9080	405
	GRANKA, Bernard D.	(315)463-0875	457
	HORRELL, Jeffrey L.	(315)423-2585	560
	JOHNSON, Nancy B.	(315)423-2911	608
	MARCHAND, Donald A.	(315)423-2736	768
	PFOHL, Theodore E.	(315)473-4493	966
	REINSTEIN, Diana J.	(315)492-5500	1021
	RYAN, Jenny L.	(315)422-9121	1071
	WALTZ, Mary A.	(315)478-1265	1302
	WASYLENKO, Lydia W.	(315)423-2585	1308
Three Mile Bay	PIZER, Elizabeth F.	(315)649-5086	977
Troy	BLANDY, Susan G.	(518)274-2098	104
	MOLHOLT, Pat	(518)276-8300	852
Uniondale	BARTENBACH, Martha A.	(516)292-8920	60
Upper Nyack	POUNDSTONE, Sally H.	(914)358-9294	987
Utica	WEBER, Jerome F.	(315)732-4747	1314
Valley Stream	KUGLER, Sharon	(516)791-9385	682
Vestal	HOLLEY, James L.	(607)754-4243	551
Wallkill	RUBIN, Ellen B.	(914)565-5620	1064
Wantagh	LOMONACO, Martha S.	(516)783-9051	738
	NOVITSKY, Edward G.		911
Water Mill	GROSSMAN, Adrian J.	(516)537-3623	473
Westhampton Beach	KIRSCH, Anne S.	(516)288-2492	655
White Plains	BAXTER, Paula A.	(914)946-3275	67
	HIGGINS, Judith H.	(914)949-2175	538
	LEWIS, Marjorie	(914)428-5759	723
	MOSLANDER, Charlotte D.	(914)428-1533	871
Yonkers	FRANK, Mortimer H.	(914)423-2304	397
	GAFFNEY, Ellen E.	(914)968-6200	412

NORTH CAROLINA

Albemarle	ESTES, Elizabeth W.	(704)983-7332	355
Asheville	BUCHANAN, William E.	(704)251-6436	153
Beaufort	BUMGARNER, John L.	(919)728-5530	157
Belmont	BAUMSTEIN, Paschal M.	(704)825-3711	66
Boone	BUSBIN, O M.	(704)264-7141	164
	HATHAWAY, Milton G.	(704)262-5113	512
	WISE, Mintron S.	(704)262-2823	1357
Carrboro	DICKINSON, Gail K.		301
Cedar Grove	WRIGHT, Larry L.		1372
Chapel Hill	ASHEIM, Lester E.	(919)967-1882	35
	BAILEY, Charles W.	(919)962-0600	46
	BROADUS, Robert N.	(919)962-8063	138
	CARMICHAEL, James V.		183
	EATON, Elizabeth G.	(919)967-7966	333
	GLEIM, David E.	(919)962-0153	441
	HOLLEY, Edward G.		551
	MCNAMARA, Charles B.	(919)962-1143	816
	MEEHAN-BLACK, Elizabeth C.		821
	PEACOCK, Helen M.		951
	PRILLAMAN, Susan M.	(919)962-3791	993
	SAYE, Jerry D.	(919)962-8073	1086
	SEIBERT, Karen S.	(919)962-1301	1112
	TAYLOR, David C.	(919)962-1355	1226
	WILLIAMS, Wiley J.		1347
Charlotte	MOORE, Patricia R.	(704)332-0092	860
	WALKER, Judith A.	(704)547-2559	1295
Concord	HULL, Laurence O.	(704)788-3167	572
Durham	BALLARD, Robert M.	(910)409-6358	53
	DASEFSKY, Stuart M.	(919)684-2380	62
	BERGER, Kenneth W.	(919)684-2373	85
	CARRINGTON, Bessie M.	(919)684-2373	186
	CLARK, Marie L.	(919)684-2380	217
	CLEMONS, Kenneth L.	(919)688-2361	221
	DRUESEDOW, John E.	(919)684-6449	320
	DUNN, Elizabeth B.	(919)684-2373	326
	FEINGLOS, Susan J.	(919)493-2904	369
	GARTRELL, Ellen G.	(919)493-3747	420
	GERMAIN, Claire M.	(919)684-6182	429
	HEBERT, Robert A.	(919)684-4087	519
	HEWITT, Joe A.	(919)489-9875	535
	KLINE, Lawrence O.	(919)684-6396	661
	NYE, Julie B.	(919)471-1833	912
	SPARKS, Martha E.	(919)489-6012	1171
	STRAUSS, Diane	(919)286-7895	1201

REVIEWER (Cont'd)
NORTH CAROLINA (Cont'd)

Eden	DAVIDSON, Laura B.	(919)627-1106	276
Elizabeth City	LEE, Charles D.	(919)335-0322	709
Elon College	JONES, Plummer A.	(919)584-2338	614
Fayetteville	FREEDMAN, Barbara G.	(919)868-1637	400
	HUNTER, Julie A.	(919)485-5496	576
Greensboro	HANHAN, Leila M.	(919)292-1115	495
	MITCHELL, W B.	(919)334-5452	849
	MOORE, Kathryn L.	(919)334-5419	860
	RANCER, Susan P.	(919)288-2160	1006
	TUGWELL, Helen M.	(919)334-5764	1262
	WASHBURN, Anne C.	(919)378-1450	1307
	WINKEL, Lois	(919)275-4935	1355
Greenville	BOCCACCIO, Mary A.	(919)757-6671	108
	CHENG, Chao S.	(929)756-4543	206
	COLLINS, Donald E.	(919)756-5469	232
	COTTER, Michael G.	(919)752-8854	250
	DALTON, Lisa K.	(919)727-6533	271
	GLUCK, Myke H.	(919)757-6514	442
	LANIER, Gene D.	(919)757-6627	696
	SCOTT, Ralph L.	(919)830-0522	1108
	SHIRES, Nancy P.	(919)758-8252	1131
	YORK, Maurice C.	(919)752-5260	1381
High Point	AUSTIN, Neal F.	(919)869-6260	40
	GAUGHAN, Thomas M.	(919)841-9215	422
Kinston	MILLER, Sylvia G.		843
	SOUTHERLAND, Carol A.	(919)523-0819	1169
	TABORY, Maxim	(919)522-3830	1219
Maiden	CARDENAS, Mary E.		180
Raleigh	BRADBURN, Frances B.	(919)878-4497	125
	DAVIS, Jinnie Y.	(919)737-2680	279
	KING, Ebba K.	(419)737-2935	650
	LAMBERT, John W.	(919)833-8937	690
	PRICE, William S.	(919)733-7305	993
	RATHGEBER, Jo F.	(919)872-3323	1009
	TAYLOR, Christine M.	(919)755-6870	1226
	WILLIAMS, Gene J.	(919)828-5063	1343
Reidsville	GUNN, Shirley A.	(919)342-0951	477
	PENN, Lea M.		957
Research Triangle Pk	MENDELL, Stefanie	(919)248-1842	823
	TUTTLE, Walter A.	(919)549-0661	1266
Riegelwood	KERESEY, Gayle	(919)669-2934	643
Robbinsville	LARSON, Josephine	(704)479-8192	699
Sanford	MATOCHIK, Michael J.	(919)776-5737	784
	MCGINN, Howard F.	(919)776-2335	806
Spruce Pine	AUSTIN, Mary C.		40
Swannanoa	ALLEN, Christina Y.	(704)298-4742	14
Wilmington	SEXTON, Spencer K.	(919)799-0177	1118
Winston-Salem	AHLERS, Glen P.	(919)761-5438	8
	FOLTZ, Faye D.	(919)748-2295	388
	HICKS, Michael	(919)788-4084	537
	ROWLAND, Janet M.	(919)765-2081	1062
Yanceyville	MASSEY, Nancy O.	(919)968-0852	782

NORTH DAKOTA

Devil's Lake	EVENSEN, Sharon L.	(701)662-4691	358
Fargo	BIRDSALL, Douglas G.	(701)237-8878	98
	BRKIC, Beverly T.	(701)237-5865	138
	NELSON, David N.	(701)237-8891	893
	SIBLEY, Carol H.	(701)235-0664	1134
	SORNSIN, Kathleen R.	(701)232-5788	1168
Grand Forks	GARD, Betty A.	(701)777-2617	417
Minot	BOARDMAN, Edna M.	(701)839-7424	108
	ROBERTSON, Pamela S.	(701)838-6080	1042
Valley City	HOLDEN, Douglas H.	(701)845-4940	550

OHIO

Akron	BERRINGER, Virginia M.	(216)375-6260	90
	LATSHAW, Patricia H.	(216)762-7621	701
	REED, Elizabeth M.	(216)724-3093	1015
Ashland	ROEPKE, David E.		1048
Ashtabula	WARREN, Dorothea C.		1306
Athens	HOUDEK, G R.	(614)593-5444	562
	LEE, Hwa W.	(614)592-5194	710
	MULLINER, Kent	(614)593-2707	878
Barberton	SWINEHART, Katharine J.	(216)745-1194	1216
Bay Village	DOMBEY, Kathryn W.	(216)871-5024	310
	LORANTH, Alice N.	(216)871-9014	741

REVIEWER (Cont'd)
OHIO (Cont'd)

Berea	MACIUSZKO, Jerzy J.	(216)234-9206	755
Bowling Green	BURLINGAME, Dwight F.	(419)372-2708	161
	MCCALLUM, Brenda W.		793
	POVSIC, Frances F.	(419)372-2956	987
	REPP, Joan M.		1024
Centerville	GARTEN, Edward D.		420
Chillicothe	PLANTON, Stanley P.	(614)775-9500	977
Cincinnati	ABRAMS, Roger E.	(513)821-5984	3
	DAVIS, Yvonne M.	(513)221-7699	281
	FROMMEYER, L R.	(513)475-3627	405
	GILLILAND, Anne J.	(513)475-6459	436
	HALIBEY-BILYK, Christine M.	(513)559-4320	486
	HEFFRON, Sheila F.	(513)891-4200	520
	HILAND, Gerard P.	(513)231-0810	538
	HUDZIK, Robert T.	(513)369-6924	570
	HUGE, Sharon A.	(513)369-6940	571
	KATZ, Lawrence M.	(516)761-0203	630
	KENT, Rose M.		642
	KONKEL, Mary S.	(513)681-2074	670
	LEIBOLD, Cynthia K.		713
	LIPPERT, Margret G.	(513)821-8733	732
	MC NAIR, Marian B.	(513)369-4750	815
	PRESNELL, Jenny L.	(513)745-3881	991
	PROPAS, Sharon W.	(513)475-2411	995
	RIFFEY, Robin S.	(513)871-3087	1033
	SIMMONS, Edlyn S.	(513)948-7829	1139
	SMITH, Maureen M.	(513)369-6917	1158
	WIEHE, Janet C.	(513)369-6918	1336
	ZAFREN, Herbert C.	(513)221-4712	1385
Cleveland	CALMER, Charles E.	(216)231-7300	174
	DEAN, Winifred F.	(216)687-2373	284
	DRACH, Priscilla L.		318
	DZIEDZINA, Christine A.	(216)459-4313	331
	FINET, Scott	(216)687-2250	378
	ORR, Cynthia	(216)449-2049	926
	RICHMOND, Phyllis A.	(216)461-4948	1030
	SANTAVICCA, Edmund F.	(216)687-2365	1082
Cleveland Heights	BORCHERT, Catherine G.	(216)932-8324	116
	LANTZ, Elizabeth A.	(216)541-2905	697
	MCMAHON, Melody L.	(216)371-5744	814
	MEYER, Jimmy E.	(216)291-1948	830
Columbus	ALLEN, Cameron	(614)237-1516	14
	BETCHER, Melissa A.	(614)466-5511	92
	BOOMGAARDEN, Wesley L.	(614)447-0524	115
	BRANCH, Susan	(614)267-3805	127
	BRANN, Andrew R.	(614)221-4181	128
	CHRISTENSON, Donald E.	(614)236-5959	211
	DALRYMPLE, Tamsen	(614)486-2109	271
	DRIESSEN, Diane	(614)486-0621	320
	GOERLER, Raimund E.	(614)292-2409	443
	HAMILTON, Marsha J.	(614)292-6314	492
	HOLOCH, S A.	(614)292-6691	553
	JAMISON, Martin P.	(614)895-8465	593
	MERCADO, Heidi	(614)292-2009	825
	MILLER, Dennis P.	(614)888-1886	837
	MURPHY, James L.	(614)292-2664	880
	NORMORE, Lorraine F.	(614)421-3600	909
	OLSZEWSKI, Lawrence J.		923
	O'NEIL, Rosanna M.	(614)761-5057	924
	ORLANDO, Jacqueline M.	(614)262-6765	926
	SANDERS, Nancy P.		1080
	STRALEY, Dona S.	(614)292-3362	1200
	VANBRIMMER, Barbara A.	(614)292-9810	1272
	WALDEN, Graham R.	(614)292-0938	1294
	WANG, Anna M.	(614)294-8035	1302
	WOODS, Alan L.	(614)292-8251	1366
Cuyahoga Falls	WAGNER, Louis F.	(216)922-0681	1292
Dayton	BALL, Diane A.	(513)293-7339	52
	BANTA, Gratia J.	(513)277-4444	55
	BRUMIT, Nancy T.	(513)274-4677	150
	COYLE, Christopher B.	(513)865-6882	253
	MCNEER, Elizabeth J.	(513)873-2686	816
	SEXTON, Sally V.	(513)890-1421	1118
	WYLLIE, Stanley C.	(513)252-8496	1375
Delaware	COHEN, Susan J.	(614)363-9433	229
	HARPER, Lucy B.	(614)369-4431	503

REVIEWER (Cont'd)
OHIO (Cont'd)

City	Name	Phone	Page
Dublin	BLANCHARD, Mark A.	(614)764-6000	103
	JACOB, Mary E.	(614)764-6063	589
	PRABHA, Chandra G.	(614)764-6086	989
Findlay	HARDESTY, Vicki H.	(419)422-6121	499
	LUST, Jeanette M.	(419)424-5739	749
Gahanna	WEITZ, Jay N.	(614)476-5489	1320
Gallipolis	GUTHRIE, Chab C.	(614)446-7323	479
Grafton	SCHMUHL, Gayle B.	(216)458-6607	1096
Highland Heights	JENKINS, Glen P.	(216)442-1475	597
Hiram	WANSER, Jeffery C.	(216)569-5358	1303
Huron	CURRIE, William W.	(419)433-5560	266
Jackson	ANDERSON, Eric S.	(614)286-6685	22
Kalida	MILLER, Marian A.		840
Kent	BOLEK, Ann D.	(216)678-9429	112
	KREYCHE, Michael R.	(216)672-3024	678
	MORRIS, Trisha A.	(216)673-3464	867
	WYNAR, Lubomyr R.		1375
Lakewood	JANES, Jodith	(216)221-0437	593
	TAYLOR, Patricia L.	(216)226-8275	1228
Lima	MCDANIEL, Deanna J.	(419)991-6065	801
Lisbon	MCPEAK, James J.	(216)424-3117	817
Marion	GERWIN, Barbara L.	(614)387-0992	430
Martins Ferry	STORCK, John W.	(614)633-0314	1198
Massillon	PLUMMER, Karen A.	(216)477-1447	978
Middletown	PALMER, Virginia E.	(513)424-4263	937
New Philadelphia	HAGLOCH, Susan B.	(216)364-4474	483
	KOBULNICKY, Michael	(216)339-3391	666
North Olmsted	ADAMS, Liese A.	(216)777-7560	5
North Ridgeville	FACINELLI, Jaclyn R.	(216)327-7079	360
Oberlin	CARPENTER, Eric J.	(216)775-2546	184
	GREENBERG, Eva M.	(216)774-1383	463
	RICKER, Alison S.	(216)775-8310	1031
	WEIDMAN, Jeffrey	(216)775-8635	1316
Oxford	QUAY, Richard H.	(513)529-4145	999
	WORTMAN, William A.	(513)529-3936	1369
Rootstown	PORTER, Marlene A.	(216)325-2511	985
Shaker Heights	KAPLAN, Lois J.	(216)921-1400	626
	LANDAU, Lucille	(216)283-6109	692
	RODDA, Donna S.	(216)283-1064	1047
Sidney	WILSON, Memory A.	(513)492-1315	1352
South Euclid	BENSING, Karen M.	(216)932-0186	83
Springfield	ARK, Connie E.	(513)324-8470	31
	MONTAG, John	(513)327-7019	855
Steubenville	HALL, Alan C.	(614)264-4410	486
Streetsboro	MCKEE, Barbara J.	(216)626-4902	810
Toledo	BAKER, Paula J.	(419)472-0204	49
	CARY, Mary K.	(419)537-2833	191
	CLARK, Marilyn L.	(419)255-7055	217
	ORAM, Richard W.	(419)537-2443	925
Troy	CRAM, Mary E.	(513)334-5067	255
	MILLER, John E.	(513)335-8801	839
Uniontown	MCCHESNEY, Kathryn M.	(216)672-2782	795
University Heights	SWEENY, Mary K.	(216)397-4234	1215
	TOTH, Georgiana G.	(216)371-5832	1252
Upper Arlington	GRIEVE, Shelley	(614)442-1073	468
Walton Hills	POJMAN, Paul E.	(216)232-0527	980
Wapakoneta	FREW, Martha G.	(419)738-8333	402
Warren	TYSON, Edith S.	(216)393-3098	1267
Westerville	SALT, Elizabeth A.	(614)898-1314	1077
Westlake	CHARVAT, Catherine T.	(216)871-6391	203
	GALLANT, Jennifer J.	(216)835-6020	414
Willow Wood	REID, Margaret B.	(614)643-2925	1018
Wooster	POWELL, Margaret S.	(216)263-2279	988
Worthington	BLOCK, Bernard A.	(014)436-7140	106
Xenia	WALDER, Antoinette L.	(513)376-2995	1294
Yellow Springs	NEWMAN, Marianne L.		899
Youngstown	LUTTRELL, Jeffrey R.	(216)742-3681	750

OKLAHOMA

City	Name	Phone	Page
Ada	COULTER, Cynthia M.	(405)332-8000	251
	HUESMANN, James L.	(405)332-7632	570
	ROBBINS, Louise S.	(405)436-0642	1039
Ardmore	KIMBLE, Valerie F.	(405)226-3980	649
Bethany	FLINNER, Beatrice E.	(405)789-6400	385
Edmond	ALSWORTH, Frances W.	(405)341-2980	18
	CURTIS, Ronald A.	(405)341-2980	267
	ROADS, Clarice D.	(405)341-3660	1038
Lawton	RABURN, Josephine R.	(405)581-2325	1001

REVIEWER (Cont'd)
OKLAHOMA (Cont'd)

City	Name	Phone	Page
Norman	BATT, Fred	(405)325-4231	64
	BENDER, Nathan E.	(405)325-2904	79
	CLARK, Harry	(405)321-0352	217
	HOVDE, David M.	(405)325-4231	563
	LATROBE, Kathy H.	(405)325-3921	701
	LAUGHLIN, Mildred A.	(405)325-3921	703
	MCKNIGHT, Michelynn	(405)360-2080	812
	PETERS, Lloyd A.		962
Oklahoma City	DOBBERTEEN, Sara J.	(405)842-0890	307
	JONES, Charles E.	(405)751-0574	611
	MEYERS, Duane H.	(405)946-2488	830
	WEISS, Catharine H.	(405)424-3344	1320
Shawnee	ALDRIDGE, Betsy B.		11
Tahlequah	MCQUITTY, Jeanette N.	(918)456-5511	817
	PATTERSON, Lotsee	(918)456-6882	948
	VEITH, Charles R.	(918)456-5511	1281
Tulsa	SMITH, Peggy C.	(918)592-6000	1159
	TOOLEY, Katherine J.	(918)494-8759	1250
	UNDERHILL, Jan	(918)663-3646	1268
Walters	ZACHARY, Patricia A.	(405)875-3071	1385

OREGON

City	Name	Phone	Page
Albany	FELLA, Sarah C.	(503)928-2361	370
Ashland	OTNES, Harold M.	(503)482-6445	930
	PURCELL, V N.	(503)482-2629	998
Bend	BYRNE, Helen E.	(503)382-1621	169
Corvallis	GEORGE, Melvin R.	(503)754-3411	427
	PERRY, Joanne M.	(503)754-2971	960
Eugene	ALLEN, Alice J.	(503)686-3064	14
	BONAMICI, Andrew R.	(503)683-5194	113
	CARMIN, James H.	(503)686-3637	183
	EMMENS, Thomas A.	(503)345-6439	348
	HADDERMAN, Margaret	(503)342-5457	482
	HEINZKILL, J R.	(503)686-3078	522
	KNIEVEL, Helen A.	(503)345-2032	664
	ROBERTSON, Howard W.	(503)686-3064	1042
	SHAW, Elizabeth L.	(503)343-9569	1123
	SHULER, John A.	(503)686-3048	1133
	WAND, Patricia A.	(503)686-3056	1302
Forest Grove	FALZON, Judith A.	(503)357-3023	363
Grants Pass	MCCOY, Joanne	(503)474-1739	799
Hillsboro	HERMENS, Dorothy M.		531
Milton-Freewater	SARGENT, Phyllis M.	(503)938-3724	1083
Monmouth	GORCHELS, Clarence C.	(503)838-1274	451
	JENSEN, Gary D.	(503)838-1220	598
Portland	ANDERSON, C L.	(503)280-5160	21
	KRUPP, Robert A.	(503)233-8561	681
	LEGER, Norissa	(503)246-2714	712
	SELLE, Donna M.	(503)629-5886	1113
	WRIGHT, Janet K.	(503)464-4097	1371
Roseburg	GAULKE, Mary F.	(503)440-4036	423
Salem	BAUER, Marilyn A.	(503)581-4292	65
West Linn	BARNETT, Jean D.	(503)636-8566	57

PENNSYLVANIA

City	Name	Phone	Page
Abington	BISSELL, Joann S.	(215)886-9409	100
Allison Park	SMITH, Mary M.	(412)487-2883	1158
Altoona	SHERIDAN, Margaret G.	(814)942-2565	1127
Ambridge	MUNDAY, Robert S.	(412)266-3838	878
Ardmore	PULLER, Maryam W.	(215)642-5187	997
Bala Cynwyd	CORVESE, Lisa A.	(215)668-4930	248
Berwyn	BROWN, David E.	(215)644-5241	143
Bethlehem	JARVIS, William E.	(215)758-3035	595
	METZGER, Philip A.	(215)866-1257	829
Boyertown	EMERICK, John L.	(215)369-7422	347
Braddock	SHAPIRO, Ruth T.	(412)636-5030	1121
Bryn Mawr	HILL, Judith L.	(215)526-1305	540
Carnegie	DEBONS, Anthony	(412)279-6170	285
Center Square	SCHAEFER, John A.	(215)277-6386	1089
Center Valley	WELLE, Jacob P.	(215)282-1100	1321
Chambersburg	EZELL, Johanna V.	(717)264-2269	360
	SENECAL, Kristin S.	(717)264-4141	1115
Chester	GOLDMAN, Richard	(215)876-7292	446
Chester Heights	OWENS, Irene E.		932
Clarion	HARTSOCK, Ralph M.	(814)226-2000	508
	HORN, Roger G.	(814)226-2490	559
Coraopolis	KASPERKO, Jean M.		629
	SKOVIRA, Robert J.	(412)262-8257	1147

REVIEWER (Cont'd)
PENNSYLVANIA (Cont'd)

Danielsville	PAGOTTO, Sarah L.	(215)767-3055	934
Drexel Hill	MULLEN, Francis X.	(215)623-7045	877
Du Bois	EMMER, Barbara L.	(814)371-2800	348
Easton	CRAWFORD, Gregory A.	(215)253-9459	256
Ebensburg	BRUSH, Cassandra	(814)472-7338	151
Elkins Park	NEMEYER, Carol A.		895
Erie	ANDRICK, Annita A.	(814)455-8080	27
	KAGER, Jeffrey F.	(814)825-3066	621
Fleetwood	EMERICK, Michael J.	(215)944-8486	347
Gladwyne	FISHER, Daphne V.	(215)525-6628	380
Glenshaw	YATES, Diane G.	(412)486-0211	1378
Glenside	LOCKETT, Cheryl L.		736
Greensburg	DUCK, Patricia M.	(412)836-9689	322
	SCHEEREN, William O.	(412)834-9000	1090
Harleysville	HILLEGAS, Ferne E.		541
	LINN, Mott R.	(215)464-4500	731
Harrisburg	LINGLE, Virginia A.	(717)652-1950	730
	WEBSTER, Connie L.	(717)545-9912	1314
Hatboro	BURNS, Richard K.	(215)675-6762	162
Hatfield	PAKALA, James C.	(215)368-5000	935
	RITTER, Ralph E.	(215)368-5000	1037
Haverford	CORRIGAN, John T.	(215)896-7458	247
	ROBERTSON, Robert B.	(215)896-1273	1042
Havertown	HOFFMAN, Elizabeth P.	(215)446-3082	547
Hershey	ULINCY, Loretta D.	(717)531-8634	1268
Huntingdon	TYNAN, Laurie F.	(814)643-6172	1267
Indiana	KROAH, Larry A.	(412)463-2055	679
	MILLER, Sheila K.		842
	RAHKONEN, Carl J.		1003
Jeffersonville	GRIFFITH, Dorothy A.	(215)539-1205	469
Jenkintown	BARTZ, Alice P.	(215)887-4338	62
	MONTOYA, Leopoldo	(215)886-2299	856
Johnstown	BRICE, Heather W.	(814)539-8153	134
Kennerdell	CHERESNOWSKI, Linda M.	(814)385-6896	206
Kingston	PAUSTIAN, P R.	(717)283-2651	950
Kutztown	MACK, Sara R.		756
Lancaster	FRANCOS, Alexis	(717)397-9655	396
	ZEAGER, Lloyd	(717)393-9745	1387
Langhorne	BURSK, Mary A.	(215)752-5101	163
Lock Haven	PALMA, Nancy C.	(717)748-1049	935
Loretto	NEGHERBON, Vincent R.	(814)472-7000	892
Lower Oxford	MUDRICK, Kristine E.		875
Macungie	BAHR, Alice H.	(215)821-1255	45
Malvern	VANDOREN, Sandra S.	(215)640-9809	1275
Mansfield	DOWLING, John	(717)662-4753	316
Mars	JOSEPH, Patricia A.	(412)776-9249	617
McKeesport	KISH, Veronica R.	(412)678-1749	656
Mechanicsburg	TENOR, Randell B.	(717)763-1804	1231
Merion	SILER, Marguerite S.	(215)604-8759	1138
Mt Lebanon	WEISFIELD, Cynthia F.	(412)831-8225	1319
Narberth	SOKOLOFF, Michele	(215)664-2117	1165
Natrona Heights	HAUGH, Amy J.	(412)224-5004	512
New Kensington	TEOLIS, Marilyn G.	(412)339-0255	1231
New Wilmington	BRAUTIGAM, David K.	(412)946-7330	130
Norristown	SORG, Elizabeth A.	(215)279-3871	1168
Philadelphia	ADAMS, Mignon S.	(215)596-8790	5
	ADELMAN, Jean S.	(215)545-4446	6
	ANDRILLI, Ene M.	(215)725-3660	27
	BAKY, John S.	(215)951-1290	50
	BENDER, Evelyn	(215)634-0357	79
	BOISCLAIR, Regina A.	(215)438-0173	111
	CALDWELL, John M.	(215)545-2809	172
	CRAWFORD, Miriam I.	(215)877-1250	257
	DIAZ, Magna M.	(215)686-1994	299
	DONOVAN, Judith G.	(215)928-0577	312
	EDWARDS, David M.	(215)386-0100	337
	EVEY, Patricia G.	(215)848-3016	359
	FENICHEL, Carol H.	(215)448-7185	371
	FLOOD, Barbara J.	(215)732-8543	385
	FREEDMAN, Bernadette	(215)332-6937	400
	GENDRON, Michele M.	(215)592-6211	426
	GREEN, Rose B.	(215)828-7029	462
	GRILIKHES, Sandra B.	(215)898-7027	470
	HALLER, Douglas M.	(215)898-8304	489
	HOLUB, Joseph C.	(215)843-6220	555
	ICKES, Barbara J.	(215)745-9767	581
	KING, Eleanor M.		650
	KOHN, Roger S.	(215)438-5635	668

REVIEWER (Cont'd)
PENNSYLVANIA (Cont'd)
Philadelphia

	KREULEN, Thomas	(215)893-2495	678
	LEVITT, Martin L.	(215)627-0706	721
	MADER, Marion C.	(215)342-0760	759
	MARVIN, Stephen G.	(215)895-1874	780
	MAYOVER, Steven J.	(215)686-5400	791
	MEYER, Kenton T.	(215)893-5265	830
	MORRIS, Leslie A.	(215)985-4384	867
	MOWERY, Susan G.	(215)248-8206	874
	MUETHER, John R.	(215)887-5511	875
	MYERS, Charles J.	(215)898-7267	884
	MYERS, James N.	(215)787-8231	884
	NAISMITH, Patricia A.	(215)235-0256	887
	ORSBURN, Elizabeth C.	(215)686-5367	927
	PANCOE, Deborra S.	(215)561-5900	937
	PARKER, Peter J.	(215)732-6200	942
	POST, Jeremiah B.	(215)748-2701	986
	PROMOS, Marianne	(215)686-5351	995
	ROHDY, Margaret A.	(215)387-5768	1050
	SKILLIN, Glenn B.		1146
	SMIRAGLIA, Richard P.	(215)662-5699	1152
	SNOW, Bonnie		1164
	TARNAWSKY, Marta	(215)898-7442	1224
	TERRY, Joseph D.	(215)686-5348	1232
	WALSH, James A.	(215)587-4877	1299
	WOLF, Edwin		1360
	WRIGHT, Irene R.	(215)923-1726	1371
	YOLTON, Jean S.	(215)878-7548	1380
	ZOGOTT, Joyce	(215)596-8994	1390
Phoenixville	SAUER, James L.	(215)933-2236	1084
Pittsburgh	BROADBENT, H E.	(412)441-6409	138
	DETLEFSEN, Ellen G.	(412)624-9444	296
	DOW, Elizabeth H.		315
	EPSTEIN, Barbara A.	(412)624-2378	351
	EVANS, Nancy H.	(412)268-2114	357
	FORD, Sylverna V.	(412)268-2446	390
	HARTNER, Elizabeth P.		508
	HODGSON, Cynthia A.	(412)374-4816	546
	HOWARD, Elizabeth F.	(412)441-3753	564
	KENT, Allen	(412)341-6095	642
	KING, Mimi	(412)237-2593	652
	KIRCHER, Linda M.	(412)624-9444	654
	KRZYS, Richard A.	(412)624-9459	681
	LEONARD, Peter C.	(414)422-5815	716
	METZLER, Douglas P.	(412)624-9414	829
	MITTEN, Lisa A.	(412)521-4462	850
	PARADISE, Don M.	(412)929-9800	939
	PASHEL, Susan M.	(412)481-4970	945
	PISCIOTTA, Henry A.	(412)268-2451	976
	RAO, Rama K.	(412)429-0543	1008
	RISHEL, Joseph F.	(412)885-3980	1035
	ROOT, Deane L.	(412)624-4100	1054
	SCHUMACHER, Carolyn S.	(412)363-0190	1102
	SCOTT, Lydia E.	(419)281-3753	1107
	STERLING, Alida B.	(412)323-1430	1189
	WEBRECK, Susan J.	(412)624-5230	1314
	WRAY, Wendell L.	(412)363-0251	1370
Point Pleasant	GENNETT, Robert G.		427
Reading	HANNAFORD, William E.	(802)468-5611	496
	IZZO, Kathleen A.	(215)373-2981	586
	MOREY, Carol M.	(215)378-2391	863
	SMALL, Sally S.	(215)320-4823	1151
Rosemont	LYNCH, Mary D.	(215)527-0200	752
	SCHWALB, Ann W.	(215)527-3131	1104
Scranton	MILLER, Mary E.	(717)348-6205	840
	SPEIRS, Gilmary	(717)348-6266	1172
	VAN DE CASTLE, Raymond M.	(717)342-4603	1273
Secane	CASINI, Barbara P.	(215)543-4309	192
Shenandoah	USES, Ann K.	(717)462-0076	1270
Shippensburg	SHONTZ, Marilyn L.	(717)532-1472	1132
Shippenville	EMERICK, Kenneth F.	(814)226-5775	347
Slippery Rock	BACK, Andrew W.	(412)794-7817	43
	JOSEPH, Elizabeth T.	(412)794-4623	617
State College	JAMISON, Carolyn C.	(814)234-4512	593
	NADESKI, Karen L.	(814)238-7890	886
	STOUT, Leon J.	(814)238-4855	1198
Swarthmore	LEHMANN, Stephen R.	(215)328-8492	713

REVIEWER (Cont'd)
PENNSYLVANIA (Cont'd)

Tamaqua	EVERHART, Nancy L.	(717)668-3334	358
	TUZINSKI, Jean H.	(717)668-2970	1266
University Park	CONKLING, Thomas W.	(814)865-3451	236
	FISHER, Kim N.	(814)865-1858	381
	FORTH, Stuart	(814)865-0401	391
	GARNER, Diane L.	(814)865-4861	419
	JEAN, Lorraine A.	(814)865-0670	596
	KALIN, Sarah G.	(814)863-2898	623
	NEAL, James G.	(814)865-0401	890
	RICE, Patricia O.	(814)865-1858	1027
	ROE, Eunice M.	(814)863-0140	1048
	SMITH, Diane H.	(814)865-4861	1154
	SULZER, John H.	(814)865-4861	1209
	SWEENEY, Del	(814)863-3952	1215
	WESTERMAN, Melvin E.	(814)863-2898	1327
	WHITTINGTON, Christine A.	(814)863-2898	1334
	ZABEL, Diane M.	(814)863-2898	1385
Upland	BARON, Herman	(215)499-7415	58
Upper Darby	REILLY, Rebecca S.		1020
	SILVERMAN, Karen S.	(215)734-0146	1138
	SILVERMAN, Scott H.	(215)734-0146	1138
Upper Saint Clair	HURLEY, Doreen S.	(412)257-1814	577
	JENKINS, Georgann K.	(412)885-7559	597
Villanova	ERDT, Terrence	(215)645-4670	352
	WEINER, Betty	(215)688-6950	1318
Wayne	CRAUMER, Patricia A.	(215)687-6777	255
	LAZARUS, Karin	(215)964-0477	706
West Chester	AMICONE, Janice L.	(215)692-6889	20
	CHAFF, Sandra L.	(215)524-0547	197
	MCCAWLEY, Christina W.	(215)436-0720	795
Wexford	CARTER, Ruth C.	(412)935-1752	190
Wilkes-Barre	TYCE, Richard	(717)826-1148	1266
Yardley	DU BOIS, Paul Z.	(215)493-6882	322
	FOGARTY, Catherine B.	(215)968-4236	387
Youngwood	SCHEEREN, Judith A.	(412)925-4126	1090

PUERTO RICO

Caparra Heights	FERNANDEZ, Josefina L.	(809)782-2618	373
Miramar	MCCARTHY, Carmen H.	(908)721-6574	794
Ponce	SANTIAGO, Maria	(809)844-4150	1082
San German	ALSTON, Jane C.	(809)892-3523	18
San Sebastian	JARAMILLO, Juana S.	(809)896-1389	594
Trujillo Alto	SABATER-SOLA, Rigel		1072

RHODE ISLAND

Barrington	BURKE, Lauri K.	(401)245-3741	160
Carolina	HULL, Catherine C.	(401)364-6100	572
Kingston	DEVIN, Robin B.	(401)792-2662	297
	FUTAS, Elizabeth	(401)792-2947	411
	MASLYN, David C.	(401)792-2594	780
	SCHNEIDER, Stewart P.	(401)792-2878	1097
	SIITONEN, Leena M.	(401)792-2878	1137
	TRYON, Jonathan S.	(401)792-2878	1259
	VOCINO, Michael C.	(401)789-9357	1286
	YOUNG, Arthur P.	(401)792-2666	1381
Lincoln	DESMARAIS, Norman P.	(401)333-3275	295
North Kingstown	OTTAVIANO, Doris B.	(401)295-0361	930
Providence	BRAUNSTEIN, Mark M.	(401)521-4771	130
	BRENNAN, Patricia B.	(401)456-8125	133
	HENDERSON, Linda L.	(401)277-7887	526
	ILACQUA, Anne K.		581
	LAMAR, Christine L.	(401)331-8575	689
	LANDIS, Dennis C.	(401)863-2725	693
	LYNDEN, Frederick C.	(401)863-2946	752
	MONTEIRO, George	(401)863-3266	856
	QUINN, Karen H.	(401)277-2473	1000
	RAINWATER, Jean M.	(401)863-3723	1004
	SVENGALIS, Kendall F.	(401)274-3196	1212
	WAGNER, Albin	(401)277-2283	1291
	WILMETH, Don B.	(401)863-3289	1349
Saunderstown	BRENNAN, Deborah B.	(401)294-3175	132
Woonsocket	IMONDI, Lenore R.	(401)762-5165	582
	LEVEILLEE, Louis R.	(401)762-4440	719

REVIEWER (Cont'd)
SOUTH CAROLINA

Aiken	CUBBEDGE, Frankie H.	(803)648-6851	262
Charleston	MOLTKE-HANSEN, David	(803)723-3225	853
	SCHMITT, John P.	(803)792-8014	1096
	STRAUCH, Katina P.	(803)723-3536	1200
Clemson	HIPPS, Gary M.	(803)654-3934	543
	JOHNSON, Steven D.	(803)654-3360	609
	KOHL, Michael F.	(803)656-5176	668
Columbia	CROSS, Joseph R.	(803)777-3365	260
	EASTMAN, Caroline M.	(803)777-8103	333
	HELSLEY, Alexia J.	(803)781-8477	525
	HOLLEY, E J.	(803)774-4866	551
	HOWARD-HILL, Trevor	(803)777-6499	564
	KRONENFELD, Michael R.	(803)734-4769	679
	NORRIS, Gale K.	(803)265-9920	909
	PEAKE, Luise E.	(803)777-3214	952
	SCHULZ, Constance B.	(803)777-4854	1102
	WASHINGTON, Nancy H.	(803)777-4206	1307
Easley	BLAIR, Sharon K.	(803)855-0866	103
Florence	HUX, Roger K.	(803)665-6121	579
Gaffney	EDEN, David E.	(803)489-4381	336
Greenville	SLIFE, Joye D.	(803)271-7281	1149
Greenwood	FECKO, Marybeth	(803)223-1810	367
	HARE, Ann T.	(803)229-8365	501
Greer	MESSINEO, Anthony	(803)268-7267	828
Irmo	BARDIN, Angela D.	(803)781-3138	56
McCormick	TOWNSEND, Catherine M.	(803)465-3185	1253
Mountain Rest	CHANDLER, Dorothy S.	(803)638-2487	199
North Myrtle Beach	BELL, David B.	(803)272-1624	76
Orangeburg	SMALLS, Mary L.	(803)536-8852	1151
Rock Hill	CHOPESIUK, Ronald J.	(803)366-5440	210
Spartanburg	SMITH, Stephen C.	(803)596-3505	1161

SOUTH DAKOTA

Brookings	BROWN, Philip L.	(605)692-7735	146
Pierre	HILMOE, Deann D.	(605)224-3178	541
Rapid City	MC CAULEY, Philip F.	(605)348-5124	795
	SCHWARTZ, James M.	(605)394-1246	1104
Sioux Falls	LANG, Elizabeth A.		695
	MODICA, Mary L.	(605)388-3701	851
	THOMPSON, Harry F.	(605)336-4007	1239
	THOMPSON, Ronelle K.	(605)336-4921	1241
Vermillion	JENSEN, Mary B.	(605)677-5259	599
	SPRULES, Marcia L.	(605)624-6764	1176

TENNESSEE

Bartlett	CONLEY, Janis E.	(901)386-2000	236
Chattanooga	BRUNER, Katharine E.	(615)266-0676	150
	REARDON, Elizabeth M.		1013
Clarksville	RIVES, Lydia L.	(615)647-9484	1037
	THWEATT, John H.	(615)647-0954	1243
Clinton	GREESON, Judy G.	(615)457-0931	465
Columbia	WAGGENER, Jean B.	(615)388-9282	1291
Cookeville	TABACHNICK, Sharon	(615)372-3958	1219
	WALDEN, Winston A.	(615)372-3408	1294
Dowelltown	EASTERLY, Ambrose	(615)597-1390	333
Jackson	AUD, Thomas L.	(901)668-2896	39
Kingsport	PRESLAR, M G.	(615)229-6117	991
Knoxville	CROWTHER, Karmen N.	(615)974-4171	262
	GRADY, Agnes M.	(615)637-0008	455
	LEACH, Sandra S.	(615)579-1315	706
	MYERS, Marcia J.	(615)974-4465	884
	PEMBERTON, J M.	(615)690-5598	956
	PHILLIPS, Linda L.	(615)687-6734	968
	PICQUET, D C.	(615)974-4381	971
	PRENTICE, Ann E.	(615)974-2148	990
	RADER, Joe C.	(615)523-6937	1002
	SAMMATARO, Linda J.	(615)521-7750	1078
	SOLBERG, Judy L.	(615)974-5011	1166
	WALLACE, Alan H.	(615)975-5011	1297
Maryville	WORLEY, Joan H.	(615)982-6412	1369
Memphis	BAKER, Bonnie U.	(901)324-6536	48
	HUGGINS, Annelle R.	(901)323-1525	571
	MABBOTT, Deborah D.	(901)388-1096	753
	MADER, Sharon B.	(901)454-2208	759
	PARK, Elizabeth H.	(901)454-2208	941
	RUDOLPH, N J.	(901)454-2208	1066
	VILES, Elza A.	(901)454-4412	1284
	WEDIG, Eric M.	(901)454-2206	1315

REVIEWER (Cont'd)
TENNESSEE (Cont'd)

Murfreesboro	MARSHALL, John D.	(615)893-2091	774
	NEAL, James H.	(615)895-1383	890
	YOUREE, Beverly B.	(615)896-4911	1384
Nashville	ARMONTROUT, Brian A.	(615)320-3678	32
	CHENEY, Frances N.		206
	EISENSTEIN, Jill M.	(615)327-8158	341
	FANCHER, Evelyn P.	(615)255-8033	363
	GLEAVES, Edwin S.	(615)741-3666	441
	HEARNE, Mary G.	(615)383-8989	518
	HELGUERA, Byrd S.	(615)322-2299	524
	HODGES, Terence M.	(615)322-2299	546
	MANNING, Dale	(615)322-2407	766
	RICHARDS, Timothy F.	(615)385-1858	1028
	SHOCKLEY, Ann A.	(615)353-0771	1132
	SKELTON, William E.	(615)833-0195	1146
	STEFFEY, Ramona J.	(615)662-0438	1185
	STEPHENS, Alonzo T.		1187
	SUMNERS, Bill F.	(615)251-2126	1209
Oak Ridge	CARROLL, Bonnie C.	(615)482-3230	187
	DAVIS, Inez W.	(615)482-9619	279
	EKKEBUS, Allen E.	(615)574-5485	341
	PFUDERER, Helen A.	(615)574-5350	966
	SNYDER, Cathrine E.	(615)483-1228	1164
Sewanee	HAYMES, Don		516

TEXAS

Amarillo	GROSS, Iva H.	(806)378-3000	472
Arlington	LOWRY, Charles B.	(817)273-3391	745
	MACFARLANE, Francis X.	(817)265-8309	755
	STOAN, Stephen K.	(817)273-3391	1195
Austin	ARTHUR, Donald B.	(512)471-5523	35
	BILLINGS, Harold W.	(512)442-8597	96
	BURLINGHAM, Merry L.		161
	BURT, Eugene C.	(512)471-4777	164
	CRONEIS, Karen S.	(512)834-9244	260
	DEGRUYTER, M L.	(512)929-3086	288
	GAMEZ, Juanita L.	(512)837-6247	416
	GOODWIN, Willard	(512)288-2373	450
	GOULD, Karen K.	(512)453-2602	454
	HARTNESS, Ann	(512)471-3818	508
	HOOKS, Michael Q.	(512)250-1419	556
	JACKSON, Eugene B.	(512)345-1653	587
	JACKSON, Ruth L.	(512)345-1653	588
	LANDIS, Lawrence A.	(512)451-3214	693
	MCCANN, Charlotte P.		793
	MIKSA, Francis L.	(572)346-6769	834
	PRATTER, Jonathan	(512)471-7726	990
	RODE, Shelley J.		1047
	SKINNER, Vicki F.	(512)892-3997	1146
	SPRUG, Joseph W.	(512)448-8474	1176
	WESTBROOK, Jo L.		1326
	WIDENER, Sarah A.	(512)328-4100	1335
	WISE, Olga B.	(512)244-8330	1357
Bangs	WEEKS, Patsy L.	(915)752-7315	1315
Beaumont	NISBY, Dora R.	(409)899-9972	904
Bellaire	HOPKINS, Joyce A.	(713)667-3760	558
Big Spring	BRADBERRY, Anna L.	(915)263-1468	125
Brazoria	RASKA, Ginny	(409)798-1628	1009
Brownfield	HAMILTON, Betty D.	(806)637-4213	491
Bryan	MOUNCE, Clara B.	(409)779-1736	873
	RABINS, Joan W.	(409)776-0374	1001
Buda	TISSING, Robert W.	(512)295-4834	1247
Burkville	TEDDER, Dorothy L.	(409)565-2201	1229
College Station	BROWN-WEBB, Deborah D.	(409)845-1636	149
	KELLOUGH, Jean L.	(409)845-2551	637
	SCHULTZ, Charles R.	(409)845-1815	1101
	SMITH, Charles R.	(409)845-8850	1153
	THOMPSON, Christine E.	(409)845-8157	1239
Cooper	ALBRIGHT, Susie K.		10
Corpus Christi	HOUSTON, Barbara B.	(512)889-8517	563
	SILVERMAN, Barbara G.	(512)887-9225	1138
Cypress	KUJOORY, Parvin	(713)890-7542	683
Dallas	BOCKSTRUCK, Lloyd D.	(214)670-1406	109
	DOBSON, Christine B.	(214)746-3646	307
	EATENSON, Ervin T.	(214)521-4839	333
	FOUDRAY, Rita C.	(214)824-1943	393
	GALBRAITH, Paula L.	(214)680-3782	413
	HEIZER, Carolyn H.	(214)363-5148	523

REVIEWER (Cont'd)
TEXAS (Cont'd)

Dallas	HOWINGTON, Tad C.	(214)337-7779	566
	IBACH, Robert D.	(214)824-3094	581
	JARVIS, Mary E.	(214)337-2615	595
	JOHNSON, Johanna H.	(214)670-1468	606
	JORDAN, Travis E.	(214)692-3199	617
	KRALISZ, Victor F.	(214)247-7944	675
	LOVELL, Bonnie A.	(214)826-1924	743
	MENDRO, Donna C.		824
	PEDEN, Robert M.	(214)746-3646	954
	SHUEY, Andrea L.		1133
	SMITH, Michael K.	(214)296-5187	1158
	STONE, Marvin H.	(214)670-1444	1197
	TEMPLETON, Virginia E.	(214)754-4875	1231
	WHISENNAND, Cynthia S.	(214)253-1428	1329
Denton	CARROLL, Dewey E.	(817)565-2445	187
	CVELJO, Katherine	(817)565-2445	268
	FERSTL, Kenneth L.	(817)383-3775	374
	FOLLET, Robert E.	(817)382-0037	388
	GALLOWAY, Margaret E.	(817)565-3024	415
	MITCHELL, George D.	(817)565-2489	848
	SNAPP, Elizabeth M.	(817)387-3980	1162
	TOTTEN, Herman L.	(817)383-1902	1252
	TURNER, Frank L.	(817)898-2603	1264
Dimmitt	AUTRY, Brick	(806)647-3666	41
Edinburg	SHABOWICH, Stanley A.	(512)383-0441	1118
El Paso	ANDERSON, Mark	(915)858-0905	24
	BROWN, Susan W.	(915)747-5678	147
	CAMERON, Dee B.	(915)566-1656	174
	FISCHER, Beverly J.	(915)595-0442	379
	KNOTT, Teresa L.	(915)533-3020	665
	NORTH, Yvonne M.	(915)592-4354	910
	TAYLOR, Anne E.	(915)757-5095	1226
Flint	RUSSELL, Paula V.	(214)561-1258	1069
Fort Worth	ARBELBIDE, Cindy L.	(817)877-3355	30
	CRAIGHEAD, Alice A.	(817)292-6571	254
	HULL, Mary M.	(817)927-7735	572
	MACDONALD, Hugh	(817)921-7117	754
	MONGOLD, Alice D.	(817)457-9080	854
	TANNER, Clarabel	(817)738-3718	1222
	VERNON, James R.	(817)923-4901	1283
	WOOD, Richard C.	(517)927-5389	1365
Galveston	WYGANT, Alice C.		1375
Garland	LARSON, Jeanette C.	(214)240-0661	699
Georgetown	SWARTZ, Jon D.	(512)863-1214	1214
Houston	ADAMS, Elaine P.	(713)785-8703	4
	ALESSI, Dana L.	(713)669-0419	11
	BAGHAL-KAR, Vali E.	(213)667-4336	45
	BEDARD, Evelyn M.		73
	CARTER, Betty B.	(713)467-0463	189
	CHAMPION, Walter T.	(713)527-7125	198
	CORBIN, John	(713)749-4241	245
	CRIST, Lynda L.	(713)527-4990	259
	ELLISOR, F L.	(713)782-7258	345
	ENDELMAN, Sharon B.	(713)247-3541	348
	FORD, Delores C.	(713)631-7730	389
	GOLEY, Elaine P.	(713)467-5784	447
	GOURLAY, Una M.	(713)528-3553	454
	HANDROW, Margaret M.	(713)524-9447	495
	HUNTER, John H.	(713)527-4800	576
	JOITY, Donna M.	(713)583-7160	610
	LANDINGHAM, Alpha M.	(713)522-9091	692
	LYDEN, Edward W.	(713)777-8212	750
	MAGNER, Mary F.	(713)870-7011	759
	MCGOWN, Sue W.	(713)850-0222	807
	MOORE, Guusje Z.	(713)680-0715	859
	MOORE, Sheryl D.	(713)271-1092	861
	REIFEL, Louie E.		1019
	SCHWARTZ, Charles A.	(713)527-8101	1104
	STUBBLEFIELD, J G.		1204
	WEATHERS, Barbara H.	(713)468-8211	1312
	WIKOFF, Ruth S.		1338
	WILSON, Thomas C.	(713)995-8401	1353
	ZWICK, Louise Y.	(713)680-1710	1392
Huntsville	BAILEY, William G.	(409)294-1614	47
	BURT, Lesta N.	(409)295-1001	164
	HOFFMAN, Frank W.	(409)294-1152	548
	YOUNG, J A.	(409)295-8766	1382

REVIEWER (Cont'd)
TEXAS (Cont'd)

Irving	AYRES, Edwin M.	(214)254-4108	43
Kingsville	MERCHANT, Cheryl N.	(512)592-9684	825
Laredo	MULLER, Mary M.	(905)211-0042	877
Leander	BIGLEY, John E.		96
Lewisville	MARMION, Daniel K.	(214)436-5125	772
Lockhart	HOLLAND, Deborah K.	(512)398-4665	550
Lubbock	HARP, Marlene M.		503
	LINDSEY, Thomas K.	(806)791-4770	730
	LUIKART, Nancy B.	(806)799-5471	747
	MARLEY, Judith L.	(806)799-3299	772
	OLM, Jane G.	(806)742-3794	921
Marshall	MAGRILL, Rose M.	(214)935-7963	760
McAllen	MYCUE, David J.		884
McKinney	BALCOMBE, Judith A.	(214)548-4430	51
Mesquite	MANN, Carol A.	(214)285-6258	765
Odessa	GROVES, Helen G.	(915)363-9604	474
	KLEPPER, Bobbie J.	(915)326-3654	660
Palacios	WOLL, Christina B.	(512)972-2166	1361
Palestine	SELWYN, Laurie	(214)723-1436	1114
Pasadena	CATES, Susan W.	(713)487-1714	195
Plano	DEILY, Carole C.	(214)578-7175	288
	PROKESH, Jane	(214)754-6461	995
Richardson	KRATZ, Abby R.	(214)690-2960	676
	NISONGER, Thomas E.	(214)690-2961	905
San Antonio	BADING, Kathryn E.	(512)655-4120	44
	BARRINGER, Sallie H.	(512)736-7343	60
	FORD, Barbara J.	(512)736-8121	389
	FRIEDMAN, Tevia L.	(512)696-2211	404
	HOOD, Elizabeth	(512)736-7292	556
	KRONICK, David A.	(512)344-5796	679
	LOCH, Edward J.	(512)734-2620	735
	MANEY, James W.	(512)341-1366	765
	NOLAN, Christopher W.	(512)736-7429	907
	RAY, Joyce M.	(512)567-2470	1011
	SCHMELZIE, Joan C.	(512)684-8430	1094
	TODD, Fred W.	(512)826-8121	1248
	VELA-CREIXELL, Mary I.	(512)733-7109	1281
	WERKING, Richard H.	(512)736-8161	1324
San Marcos	HUSTON, Susan S.	(515)396-3374	578
Seguin	HSU, Patrick K.	(512)372-3868	567
Texas City	MONCLA, Carolyn S.	(409)948-3111	854
The Woodlands	MILLER, Carol A.	(713)367-7500	836
	PEYTON, Janice L.	(713)292-4441	966
Tyler	LAMBERTH, Linda E.	(214)595-3481	690
Uvalde	KINGSBERY, Evelyn B.	(512)278-4401	652
Waco	CARPENTER, Charlotte L.	(817)772-4262	184
	COLEY, Betty A.	(817)754-6114	231
	GEARY, Gregg S.		424
	HILLMAN, Kathy R.	(817)755-2111	541
	PHILLIPS, Luouida V.		968
Wichita Falls	GRIMES, John F.	(817)855-0463	470
	HARVILL, Melba S.	(817)692-6611	509
Wimberley	FELSTED, Carla M.	(512)847-5277	370

UTAH

American Fork	TOMLIN, Celia K.	(801)756-4681	1250
Bountiful	SANDERS, William D.	(801)292-4429	1080
Logan	PIETTE, Mary I.	(801)753-6878	972
Provo	HALL, Blaine H.	(801)378-6117	487
	MATHIESEN, Thomas J.	(801)378-3688	784
	ROWLEY, Edward D.	(801)378-6372	1063
Salt Lake City	CASADY, Richard L.	(801)533-9607	191
	JOHNSON, Jeffery O.	(801)533-5250	606
	KRANZ, Ralph	(801)581-7995	676
	OLSEN, Katherine M.	(801)355-0301	921
	PATTERSON, Myron B.	(801)581-7265	948
	REDDICK, Mary J.	(801)581-7024	1013
	SPERRY, Kip	(801)255-9615	1174
Sandy	KIESSLING, Mary S.	(801)561-4474	647

VERMONT

Barre	GRIFFIN, Marie E.	(802)479-2810	468
Bennington	PRICE, Michael L.	(802)442-9051	992
Brattleboro	HAY, Linda A.	(802)254-5595	515
Burlington	SINGER, George C.	(802)863-3854	1143
	YERBURGH, Mark R.	(802)658-0337	1379
Chelsea	BATTEY, Jean D.	(802)276-3086	64
Colchester	KNEELAND, Marjorie H.	(802)655-0279	664

REVIEWER (Cont'd)
VERMONT (Cont'd)

Middlebury	MCBRIDE, Jerry L.	(802)388-3711	792
	POST, Jennifer C.	(802)388-6252	986
Montpelier	GREENE, Grace W.	(802)828-3261	464
Northfield	LINDBERG, Sandra	(802)485-2171	728
Norwich	FINNEGAN, Gregory A.	(802)649-1194	378
Putney	THOMPSON, Jane K.	(802)387-4767	1240
Rutland	MCCULLOUGH, Doreen J.	(802)773-5900	801
	SHERMAN, Jacob R.	(802)773-1860	1128
St Johnsbury	BRYAN, Martin F.	(802)748-9264	151
South Royalton	SWIFT, Esther M.	(802)763-7163	1216

VIRGIN ISLANDS

Charlotte Amalie	BARZELAY, Mary S.	(809)774-4838	62
St Croix	VAUGHN, Robert V.	(809)778-8465	1280
St Thomas	CHANG, Henry C.	(809)774-3407	200

VIRGINIA

Alexandria	BROWN, Dale W.	(703)751-3236	143
	CARTLEDGE, Connie L.	(703)960-6020	190
	CASSEDY, James G.	(703)768-2070	193
	JORDAN, Robert T.		617
	KAISER, Donald W.	(703)836-0225	622
	ROSENBERG, Kenyon C.	(703)642-5480	1056
	ROTHSCHILD, M C.	(202)274-7206	1060
	SMITH, Thomas E.		1161
	STEVENS, Roberta A.	(703)960-0464	1191
	WANG, Ann C.	(703)751-4536	1302
Annandale	MCGINN, Ellen T.	(703)280-5085	806
Arlington	ASHKENAS, Bruce F.	(301)763-7410	36
	CARR, Timothy B.		186
	DENNIE, David L.	(703)685-0208	292
	DESSAINT, Alain Y.	(703)247-7750	295
	KECSKES, Lily C.	(703)528-0730	633
	STARR, Marian U.	(703)237-0285	1182
	STEVENS, Frank A.		1190
	WEILERSTEIN, Deborah E.	(703)284-8181	1317
Blacksburg	EASTMAN, Ann H.	(703)951-4770	333
	ESPLEY, John L.	(703)961-5847	354
	JOHNSON, Bryan R.	(703)552-0876	602
	KENNEY, Donald J.	(703)961-5069	641
	KRIZ, Harry M.	(703)951-7007	679
	SPAHR, Janet E.	(703)961-6181	1170
Charlottesville	ANDERSON, Valerie J.	(804)296-5544	25
	BADER, Susan G.	(804)973-2397	44
	BERKELEY, Edmund		87
	CAMPBELL, James M.	(804)924-4985	176
	COOPER, Jean L.	(804)978-4363	243
	JORDAN, Ervin L.	(804)924-4975	616
	MORRIS, Karen L.	(804)293-2475	867
	RODRIGUEZ, Robert D.		1048
	WHITE, William		1332
Chesapeake	REID, Kendall M.	(804)547-6592	1018
Chesterfield	WAGENKNECHT, Robert E.	(804)748-1601	1291
Fairfax	CONIGLIO, Jamie W.	(703)323-2877	236
	CRAWFORD, Elva B.	(703)425-6974	256
Falls Church	BEAM, Christopher M.	(703)356-4908	69
	BROWN, Barbara B.	(703)820-7450	142
	HABERLAND, Jody	(703)573-7279	481
	HELGERSON, Linda W.	(703)237-0682	524
Fort Monroe	BURGESS, Edwin B.	(804)727-4291	159
	BYRN, James H.	(804)727-4491	169
Fredericksburg	HUGHES, J M.		571
	MULVANEY, John P.	(703)899-4666	878
	VANDERBERG, E S.	(703)371-3311	1273
Great Falls	CYLKE, Frank K.	(703)759-2031	268
Hampden Sydney	NORDEN, David J.	(804)223-4381	908
Hampton	BIGELOW, Therese G.	(804)727-6234	95
	JORDAN, Caroline D.	(804)727-6234	616
Harrisonburg	PALMER, Forrest C.	(703)568-6929	936
	RAMSEY, Inez L.	(703)568-6791	1006
	ROBISON, Dennis E.	(703)568-6578	1045
Langley AFB	VERNON, Christie D.	(804)766-1468	1283
Lexington	DANFORD, Robert E.	(703)463-8657	272
	HAYS, Peggy W.	(703)463-8643	517
Luray	GRIEVE, Karen R.		468
Lynchburg	YOUNGER, Melinda M.	(804)384-2369	1383

REVIEWER (Cont'd)
VIRGINIA (Cont'd)

Manassas	CHRISTOLON, Blair B.	(703)369-3535	212
	KILLEEN, Erlene B.	(703)369-7193	648
	MURPHY, Richard W.	(703)361-8211	881
Martinsville	PEARL, Patricia D.	(703)632-9096	952
McLean	SCHULMAN, Jacque L.	(703)527-2627	1101
	TRAVIS, Irene L.		1254
Melian	BELTON, Jennifer H.		78
Middleburg	MATTHEWS, Stephen L.	(703)687-5555	786
Newport News	HAMMOND, Theresa M.	(804)595-8179	494
Norfolk	GRIFFLER, Carl W.	(804)441-5332	469
	MAYER-HENNELLY, Mary B.	(804)441-2733	789
	MILLER, Ellen L.	(804)440-3283	837
	PEREZ-LOPEZ, Rene	(804)423-7655	958
	SWAINE, Cynthia W.	(804)627-1115	1212
	TRASK, Benjamin H.		1254
Portsmouth	BROWN, William A.	(804)483-2195	148
	BURGESS, Dean	(804)393-8501	159
Quantico	BROWN, David C.	(703)221-1586	143
Radford	TURNER, Robert L.	(703)731-1835	1265
Reston	JENSEN, Raymond A.	(703)648-6820	599
Richmond	GWIN, James E.	(804)288-7602	479
	HALL, Bonlyn G.	(804)359-0409	487
	KIMBALL, Gregg D.	(804)649-0711	649
	MACLEOD, James M.	(804)355-1395	757
	REAM, Daniel L.	(804)257-6545	1012
	REMICK, Katherine G.	(804)288-2665	1022
	SHEPARD, E L.	(804)358-4901	1126
	STACY, Betty A.	(804)359-4283	1178
	THOMAS, Mary E.	(804)786-0823	1237
	TROTTI, John B.	(804)358-8956	1258
	VAN SICKLEN, Lindsay L.	(804)320-9691	1277
	YATES, Ella G.	(804)786-2332	1378
Roanoke	DIERCKS, Thelma C.	(703)362-6233	302
Springfield	CASWELL, Mary C.	(703)642-0340	194
	LEONARD, Lawrence E.	(703)569-1541	716
	ROARK, Robin D.	(703)644-7372	1038
	SCHAAF, Robert W.	(703)451-7916	1088
Vienna	SCHAEFER, Mary E.	(703)759-6339	1089
Virginia Beach	BARKLEY, Carolyn L.	(804)431-3070	56
	CAYWOOD, Carolyn A.	(804)464-9320	195
Wise	CHISHOLM, Clarence E.	(703)328-2431	209
Woodbridge	ENGLAND, Ellen M.	(703)670-2191	349

WASHINGTON

Bellingham	BLUME, Scott	(206)671-8960	107
Camas	BRENNAN, Cindy L.	(206)834-4692	132
Cheney	ALKIRE, Leland G.	(509)235-4669	13
	MUTSCHLER, Charles V.	(509)235-2706	883
	TRACY, Joan I.	(509)359-7892	1253
Custer	HASELBAUER, Kathleen J.	(206)366-5063	510
Ellensburg	DOI, Makiko	(509)963-2101	309
Everett	GRINSTEAD, Beth K.	(206)258-1951	471
Kingston	HENINGER, Irene C.	(206)297-3002	528
Longview	DOLBEY, Mary B.	(206)577-2780	309
Marysville	WILSON, Evie		1350
Oak Harbor	MERWINE, Glenda M.	(206)679-5807	827
Pullman	KEMP, Barbara E.	(509)334-5809	639
	KOPP, James J.	(509)335-9133	671
	VYHNANEK, Louis	(509)332-3723	1290
Richland	FOLEY, Katherine E.	(509)943-9117	387
Seattle	AUSTIN, Martha L.	(206)543-2988	40
	BENNE, Mae M.	(206)789-4267	81
	BETZ-ZALL, Jonathan R.	(206)782-9305	92
	BURSON, Scott F.	(206)543-6794	163
	CHASE, Dale L.	(206)525-0795	203
	CLINE, Robert S.	(206)523-7268	222
	EULENBERG, Julia N.	(206)324-2605	356
	FASSETT, William E.	(206)545-2272	366
	GREGGS, Elizabeth M.	(206)242-6044	465
	HENSLEY, Randall B.	(206)543-2060	529
	HILL, Ann M.	(206)525-4212	539
	JEWELL, Timothy D.	(206)524-8820	600
	KETCHELL, Debra S.	(206)543-5530	645
	MADDEN, Susan B.	(206)684-6626	758
	MAIOLI, Jerry R.	(206)459-6518	762
	MEYER, Laura M.	(206)522-2162	830
	POLISHUK, Bernard	(206)524-8676	980
	PRESTON, Deirdre R.	(206)283-0754	991

REVIEWER (Cont'd)
WASHINGTON (Cont'd)

Seattle	ROWBERG, Alan H.	(206)548-6250	1062
	SCHUELLER, Janette H.	(206)543-8262	1101
	SHINN, Isabella E.	(206)527-2466	1130
	SILVA, Mary E.		1138
	STIRLING, Dale A.	(206)367-2728	1195
	SY, Karen J.	(206)545-2873	1217
	TWENEY, George H.	(206)243-8243	1266
Spokane	BYNAGLE, Hans E.	(509)466-3260	168
	LANE, Steven P.	(509)838-4728	694
	MURRAY, James M.	(509)838-3680	882
	TYSON, Christy	(509)624-9744	1267
	WYNN, Debra D.	(509)328-4220	1375
Steilacoom	COHEN, Jane L.		228
Tacoma	MENANTEAUX, A R.	(206)591-2973	823
	THORNDILL, Christine M.	(206)752-9623	1242
Vancouver	HUTTON, Emily A.	(206)695-1566	579
Walla Walla	BREIT, Anitra D.		132
	CARR, Carol L.	(509)527-5191	185
Woodinville	GARRETSON, Laurie J.	(206)483-6213	420

WEST VIRGINIA

Athens	BROWN, Thomas M.	(304)384-3115	148
Bluefield	DYE, Luella I.	(304)487-2037	330
Charleston	MARTIN, June R.	(304)343-4646	777
Cross Lanes	COOPER, Candace S.	(304)776-5945	242
Glenville	FAULKNER, Ronnie W.	(304)462-7361	366
Huntington	STARKEY, Bonnie F.	(303)523-3109	1182
Morgantown	CUTHBERT, John A.	(304)293-3536	267
Salem	LANGER, Frank A.	(304)782-1007	695
Wheeling	JULIAN, Charles A.	(304)233-5900	

WISCONSIN

Appleton	DAWSON, Terry P.	(414)735-6168	282
Ashland	PAULI, David N.	(705)682-2365	950
Brookfield	CASEY, Jean M.	(414)781-2545	192
	CHRISTMAN, Inese R.	(414)786-6700	212
Burlington	PROCES, Stephen L.	(414)763-7623	994
Caledonia	GRENDYSA, Peter A.	(414)764-3676	467
Cudahy	KLAUSMEIER, Arno M.	(414)744-0268	658
Eau Claire	CARROLL, Barbara T.		187
Green Bay	GORSEGNER, Betty D.	(414)465-1529	452
	MUSICH, Gerald D.	(414)437-7623	883
Iola	FOERSTER, Trey	(715)445-3838	387
Kewaunee	ECKERT, Daniel L.	(414)388-2176	335
La Crosse	ACCARDI, Joseph J.	(608)784-5755	3
	HILL, Edwin L.	(608)782-1753	539
Madison	ARNESON, Arne J.	(608)833-1617	33
	ARNOLD, Barbara J.	(608)263-2909	33
	BEHNKE, Charles	(608)244-3253	75
	CARR, Jo A.	(608)273-1620	185
	CONNER, P Z.	(608)256-4440	237
	DAHLGREN, Anders C.	(608)271-9148	269
	DRESANG, Eliza T.	(608)267-9357	319
	EDMONDS, Michael	(608)262-4672	336
	HERMAN, Gertrude B.		531
	HUMPHRIES, Lajean	(608)233-5540	574
	KRIKELAS, James	(608)263-2900	678
	KRUSE, Ginny M.		681
	PARSONS, Patricia S.		945
	SEARING, Susan E.	(608)263-5754	1109
	WAITY, Gloria J.	(608)222-7783	1293
	WALKER, Richard D.	(608)257-5574	1296
	WIEGAND, Wayne A.	(608)263-2914	1336
	WILLETT, Holly G.	(608)251-0633	1341
	WILLIAMSON, William L.	(608)238-0770	1348
	WISEMAN, Mary J.		1357
Mequon	AMAN, Mary J.	(414)242-9031	19
	MADSEN, Joyce	(414)242-5403	759
Milwaukee	BJORKLUND, Edi		100
	BOTHAM, Jane	(414)278-3078	118
	BOULANGER, Mary E.	(414)229-4659	119
	EUKEY, Jim O.		356
	FONG, Wilfred W.	(414)229-4707	388
	GILL, Norman N.	(414)352-1545	435
	GREENE, Victor R.	(414)963-7063	464
	HOOTKIN, Neil M.	(414)332-4953	557
	HORNUNG, Susan D.	(414)359-2111	560

REVIEWER (Cont'd)
WISCONSIN (Cont'd)
Milwaukee

	KOVAN, Allan S.	(414)963-5402	673
	MARCUS, Terry C.	(414)352-5695	769
	MARKOWETZ, Marianna C.	(414)963-4074	771
	MISNER, Barbara	(414)384-6535	847
	MURPHY, Virginia A.	(414)271-1444	881
	SAGER, Lynn S.	(414)964-5940	1074
	SHUTKIN, Sara A.	(414)332-3321	1134
	SMITH-GREENWOLD, Kathryn R.	(414)445-3586	1162
	SWEETLAND, James H.	(414)963-9996	1215
	ZIRBES, Colette M.	(414)483-1979	1390
Oak Creek	TASNADI, Deborah L.	(414)764-9725	1224
Oshkosh	CORBLY, James E.	(414)231-4768	245
	JONES, Norma L.	(414)231-5137	614
	PARKS, Dennis H.	(414)426-4800	943
	SHARMA, Ravindra N.	(414)424-0139	1122
Racine	SCHINK, Sandra C.	(414)634-1495	1093
Rhinelander	BRANT, Susan L.	(715)369-4429	129
Ripon	MCGOWAN, Sarah M.	(414)748-8330	807
River Falls	ADAM, Anthony J.	(715)425-5383	4
St Francis	WESTERN, Eric D.	(414)769-0110	1327
Sheboygan	TOBIN, R J.	(414)459-7606	1247
Stevens Point	WACHTER-NELSON, Ruth M.		1290
Stoughton	DANKY, James P.	(608)873-8722	274
	LUND, Patricia A.	(608)873-9446	748
Superior	AXT, Randolph W.	(715)398-6767	42
	JOHNSON, Denise J.	(715)394-8512	603
Wauwatosa	CHAPLOCK, Sharon K.	(414)778-2167	201
West Allis	GRUEL, Janice L.	(414)541-5222	474
	WASICK, Mary A.	(414)476-6550	1303
Whitefish Bay	LANK, Dannette H.	(414)225-2107	696

WYOMING

Cheyenne	HALLBERG, Carl V.	(307)778-8577	489
	RAO, Dittakavi N.	(307)777-7509	1008
Laramie	CHATTON, Barbara A.	(307)766-2167	204
	OSTRYE, Anne T.	(307)766-5312	929
	STAFFORD, Leva L.		1178
Rawlins	HOFF, Vickie J.	(307)324-7220	547
Worland	HARRINGTON, Carolyn B.	(307)347-4490	504

CANADA

ALBERTA

Airdrie	OTTOSEN, Charles F.	(403)948-5407	930
Calgary	BAILEY, Madeleine J.	(403)240-6134	46
	BROWN, David K.	(403)220-6295	143
	CRAMER, Eugene C.	(403)220-5376	255
	MACRAE, Lorne G.	(403)294-8538	758
	MANSON, Bill B.	(403)260-2620	767
	MING, Marilyn	(403)284-8072	846
	NECHKA, Ada M.	(403)220-3755	891
	ONN, Shirley A.	(403)282-5311	924
	ROBINS, Nora D.	(403)274-8837	1043
	STEVELMAN, Sharon R.	(403)271-0134	1190
	VINE, Rita F.	(403)247-6524	1285
	WHITE, Valerie L.	(403)255-6419	1332
Canmore	LUTHY, Jean M.	(403)678-5883	750
Edmonton	BERNARD, Marie L.	(403)455-2436	88
	BUSCH, J.	(403)432-3794	165
	COMPRI, Jeannine L.	(403)474-0577	235
	DELONG, Kathleen M.	(403)432-5951	290
	HU, Shih S.	(403)436-9716	568
	LOVENBURG, Susan L.	(403)435-0176	743
	SCHRADER, Alvin M.	(403)432-4578	1099
	STARR, Jane E.	(403)466-6004	1182
Lethbridge	DROESSLER, Judith B.	(403)381-2285	320
Red Deer	ARMSTRONG, Mary L.	(403)346-4491	32
	BOULTBEE, Paul G.	(403)346-8937	119
Three Hills	JORDAHL, Ronald I.	(403)443-5511	616

REVIEWER (Cont'd)
BRITISH COLUMBIA

Abbotsford	HARRIS, Winifred E.	(604)853-7441	506
Burnaby	GOW, Susan P.	(604)439-0931	454
Coquitlam	UTSUNOMIYA, Leslie D.	(604)937-0455	1270
North Vancouver	ASHCROFT, Susan M.	(604)984-8004	35
	DODSON, Suzanne C.	(604)988-4567	308
	ELROD, J M.	(604)929-3966	346
Richmond	WEESE, Dwain W.		1316
Vancouver	BEWLEY, Lois M.	(604)228-4250	93
	DEVAKOS, Elizabeth R.	(604)255-6636	297
	GONNAMI, Tsuneharu	(604)224-4296	447
	HART, Elizabeth	(604)228-9031	507
	NICHOL, Kathleen M.	(604)263-7081	901
	STOKES, Roy B.	(604)261-4082	1196
Vernon	FUNK, Grace E.	(604)542-5385	410
Victoria	EKLAND, Patricia A.	(604)721-8275	341
	MOEHR, Jochen R.	(604)721-8581	851
	ROMANIUK, Elena	(604)592-8819	1052

MANITOBA

Brandon	SIMUNDSSON, Elva D.	(204)728-7234	1142
Winnipeg	BLANCHARD, Jim	(204)949-3360	103
	BUDNICK, Carol	(204)474-9844	155
	COVVEY, H D.	(204)942-5335	252
	FOWLER, Margaret A.	(204)884-6593	394
	LINCOLN, Robert S.	(204)786-2387	728
	NIELSON, Paul F.	(204)945-7027	903
	SANTORO, Corrado A.	(204)474-8243	1082

NEWFOUNDLAND

Grand Falls	MORTON, Elaine	(709)489-5935	870
St John's	MARTINEZ, Helen	(709)753-6210	779
	WOOD, Alberta A.	(709)753-3805	1363

NORTHWEST TERRITORIES

Yellowknife	ALBRIGHT, Donald A.	(403)873-8347	10

NOVA SCOTIA

Halifax	AMEY, Lorne J.	(902)422-8639	20
	BANFIELD, Eilzabeth S.	(902)421-4570	54
	BIANCHINI, Lucian	(902)445-2987	94
	DYKSTRA, Mary E.	(902)424-3656	331
	GURAYA, Harinder	(902)423-8868	478
	PARIS, Terrence L.	(902)443-4450	940
	TAYYEB, Rashid	(902)422-4684	1229

ONTARIO

Arnprior	BARKE, Judith P.	(613)623-5411	56
Barrie	ADDY, Kathryn J.	(705)726-8693	6
Belfountain	DE RONDE, Paula D.	(519)927-5156	294
Bowmanville	MOON, Jeffrey D.	(416)263-8504	857
Brampton	CHAN, Bruce A.	(416)793-4636	199
Brockville	WARREN, Peggy A.	(613)342-6352	1306
Cambridge	SKELTON, W M.	(519)621-0460	1146
Downsview	KATZ, Bernard M.	(416)638-7695	630
	ZVEJNIEKS, Laila R.	(416)235-4545	1391
Etobicoke	DETERVILLE, Linda C.	(416)622-2840	296
Gloucester	KENT, Charles D.		642
	ST. JACQUES, Suzanne L.	(613)824-4232	1075
Guelph	GILLHAM, Virginia A.	(519)824-4120	436
	PAL, Gabriel	(519)824-4120	935
	ROURKE, Lorna E.	(519)824-4120	1061
Keswick	MCCRACKEN, Ronald W.	(416)476-5556	799
Kingston	MACDERMAID, Anne	(613)545-2378	754
	MORLEY, William F.	(613)548-3432	865
Leamington	NICHOLSON, Jill A.	(519)326-3441	902
London	FYFE, Janet H.	(519)472-5201	411
	MILLER, Beth M.	(519)661-3542	836
	NELSON, Michael J.	(519)661-3542	894
	PARR, John R.	(519)439-3271	943
	WHITE, Janette H.	(519)661-3542	1331
Mississauga	DAVIS, Virginia K.	(416)673-2644	281
	MCLEAN-LOWE, Dallas	(416)828-5232	814
Nepean	KAYE, Barbara J.	(613)225-9920	632
North York	VARMA, Divakara K.	(416)736-5139	1278
	WILLIAMS, Lorraine O.		1344

REVIEWER (Cont'd)
ONTARIO (Cont'd)

Ottawa	AUBREY, Irene E.	(613)996-7774	38
	BREGAINT, Bernard J.	(613)741-0242	131
	BRODIE, Nancy E.	(613)996-7391	139
	COOK, Terry G.	(613)996-7726	240
	EVANS, Gwynneth	(613)995-3904	357
	FOX, Rosalie	(613)232-4358	395
	GORDON, Robert S.	(613)233-2452	451
	GUILBERT, Manon M.	(613)233-8012	476
	JESKE, Margo	(613)995-1118	600
	KIDD, Betty H.	(613)996-7605	646
	MASON-WARD, Lesley	(613)726-1314	781
	MCKEEN, C E.	(613)996-7388	810
	OKUDA, Sachiko E.	(613)994-6898	920
	PARE, Richard	(613)733-8391	940
	REILLY, Brian O.	(613)993-9225	1020
	SCOLLIE, F B.	(613)996-0825	1106
	SCOTT, Judith W.	(613)232-0579	1107
	SPICER, Erik J.	(613)995-1166	1174
	SPRY, Patricia		1176
	TAYLOR, Margaret P.	(613)232-6172	1227
St Thomas	RHYNAS, Don M.	(519)631-6050	1026
Sault Ste Marie	BAZILLION, Richard J.	(705)949-4352	68
Scarborough	BALL, John L.	(416)284-3245	52
	MILLER, Ann M.	(416)694-3897	835
	MULLERBECK, Aino	(416)284-8779	877
Sudbury	GOSS, Alison M.	(705)522-2883	453
Toronto	ARDERN, Christine M.		31
	BREGMAN, Alvan M.	(416)767-3625	131
	CARVALHO, Sarah V.	(416)979-2824	191
	CURTIS, Alison J.	(416)923-0890	267
	DAVIDSON-ARNOTT, Frances E.	(416)486-6488	277
	DE STRICKER, Ulla	(416)593-5211	296
	FASICK, Adele M.	(416)978-7074	366
	GARLOCK, Gayle N.	(416)763-2718	419
	GUNDARA, Jaswinder	(416)483-7810	477
	HAJNAL, Peter I.	(416)533-7338	484
	KENDALL, Sandra A.		640
	LAND, Reginald B.	(416)965-3742	692
	MARSHALL, Joanne G.	(416)978-7111	774
	MCCANN, Judith B.	(416)429-1247	794
	MELVILLE, Karen E.	(416)978-3035	823
	MERRYWEATHER, J M.	(416)965-3281	827
	MILANICH, Melanie M.	(416)393-7180	834
	NORTH, John A.	(416)979-5142	909
	SABLJIC, John A.	(416)782-6754	1072
	SMITH, Cynthia M.	(416)488-6117	1153
	TUDOR, Dean F.	(416)767-1340	1262
	WILBURN, Gene	(416)586-5713	1338
	WILKINSON, John P.	(416)978-3167	1340
	WILLIAMSON, Nancy J.		1347
Waterloo	BEGLO, Jo N.	(519)885-1211	74
Willowdale	DANIEL, Eileen	(416)223-2495	272
	JOHNSON, James R.	(416)226-6380	605
	MCLEAN, Paulette A.	(416)636-4877	814
Windsor	HANDY, Mary J.	(519)256-3250	495
	SINGLETON, Cynthia B.	(519)253-4232	1143
	WALSH, G M.	(519)253-7817	1299

QUEBEC

Cote Saint-Luc	KATZ, Solomon B.	(514)488-7673	630
Hull	CHEVRIER, Francine	(819)777-4341	207
	TESSIER, Richard	(819)595-0910	1233
Laval	SHANEFIELD, Irene D.	(514)688-9550	1120
Lennoxville	SHEERAN, Ruth J.	(819)569-9551	1125
Montebello	WENK, Arthur B.		1324
Montreal	BERNHARD, Paulette	(514)343-7408	89
	BERTRAND-GASTALDY, Suzanne	(514)343-6048	91
	BROCHU, Frederick	(514)598-1947	138
	CAYA, Marcel	(514)398-7100	195
	DE LUISE, Alexandra	(514)871-1418	290
	DUMONT, Monique	(514)288-0100	325
	GARDNER, Richard K.	(514)343-6046	418
	GARNETT, Joyce C.	(514)398-4763	419
	GROEN, Frances K.	(514)845-2090	471
	HOBBINS, Alan J.	(514)398-4773	545
	HOWARD, Helen A.	(514)933-0893	564

REVIEWER (Cont'd)
QUEBEC (Cont'd)

Montreal	MITTERMEYER, Diane	(514)398-4204	850
	MOHAMMED, Selima	(514)398-4780	852
	MOLLER, Hans	(514)398-4740	853
	ORLANDO, Richard P.	(514)877-1470	926
	PARKER, Charles G.	(514)282-3934	941
	PELLETIER, Rosaire	(514)382-0895	955
	RATNER, Sabina T.		1010
	ROLLAND-THOMAS, Paule	(514)343-6046	1051
	WALSH, Mary A.	(514)937-6633	1300
	WALUZYNIEC, Hanna	(514)398-4759	1302
	WERYHO, Jan W.	(514)392-5766	1325
	WINIARZ, Elizabeth	(514)848-7726	1355
Quebec	BERNIER, Gaston	(418)643-4032	89
	COLLISTER, Edward A.	(418)643-1515	233
	GUERETTE, Charlotte M.	(418)656-3017	476
	MCKENZIE, Donald R.	(418)691-6357	811
	TESSIER, Yves	(418)872-4304	1233
St Lambert De Levis	HERLINGER, Peggy	(514)672-7360	531
Sillery	LALIBERTE, Madeleine A.	(418)687-9260	689
Stanstead	GRENIER, Serge	(819)876-2981	467
Ste Anne de Bellevue	DOUGLAS-BONNELL, Eileen	(514)457-9487	314
	GRAINGER, Bruce	(514)398-7879	457
Westmount	GLASS, Gerald	(514)931-4625	440

SASKATCHEWAN

North Battleford	RIDLER, Elizabeth A.		1032
Regina	BALON, Brett J.	(306)586-1990	53
	GAGNON, Andre	(306)569-7567	412
	POGUE, Basil G.	(306)586-6846	979
	VOHRA, Pran	(306)787-4321	1287
Saskatoon	FRITZ, Linda	(306)934-3785	405
	HAMMEL, Philip J.	(306)966-7657	493
	LAKHANPAL, Sarv K.	(306)966-5982	689
	NELSON, Ian C.	(306)652-4934	893
	SALT, David P.	(306)966-5978	1077

AUSTRALIA

Brisbane	COCHRANE, Thomas G.	226
Canberra	STEELE, Colin R.	1184
East Hawthorn	BENNETT, David M.	81
Fisher	WANG, Sing W.	1303
Magill	BEATTIE, Kathleen M.	70
Marrickville	TILLOTSON, Greig S.	1245
St Lucia	LAMBERTON, Donald M.	690
Seaforth	TANNER, Elizabeth	1222

BAHAMAS

Grand Bahamas Island	BARTON, Barbara I.	61

CUBA

Havana	ASIS, Moises	36

ENGLAND

Bushey	SMITH, Margit J.	1157
London	ELLIOTT, Pirkko E.	344
Plymouth	PENGELLY, Joe	956
Sussex	GREEN, Jeffrey P.	462

FEDERAL REPUBLIC OF CHINA

Taipei	HU, James S.	567

FEDERAL REPUBLIC OF GERMANY

Berlin	ELSTE, R O.	346
	WERSIG, Gernot	1325
Bonn	LOTZ, Rainer E.	742
Taufkirchen	ADENEY, Carol D.	6

FRANCE

Paris	GRATTAN, Robert	458

HONG KONG

Jardine's Lookout	LEE, Betty W.	709

REVIEWER (Cont'd)			
IRELAND			
Banger	DUFFIN, Elizabeth A.		323
Dublin	FOX, Peter K.		395
	LAMBKIN, Anthony		690
	SLINEY, Marjory T.		1149
ISRAEL			
Jerusalem	DIAMANT, Betsy		299
ITALY			
Milan	CASIRAGHI, Edoardo		192
Rome	HUEMER, Christina G.		570
JAMAICA			
Kingston	ERDEL, Timothy P.	(809)925-6801	352
JAPAN			
Tokyo	HOSONO, Kimio		562
	YAMAZAKI, Shigeaki	(034)331-1110	1377
NETHERLANDS			
Rotterdam	SCHUURSMA, Ann B.		1103
The Haag	RAITT, David I.	(311)719-8301	1004
NEW ZEALAND			
Auckland	RICHARDS, Valerie		1028
NORTHERN IRELAND			
Belfast	LINTON, William D.		731
PAKISTAN			
Lahore	TRAINER, Leslie F.		1253
PHILIPPINES			
Makati	MORAN, Teresita C.		862
Quezon City	OREJANA, Rebecca D.		925
SAUDI ARABIA			
Riyadh	MANSFIELD, Jerry W.		767
SWITZERLAND			
Geneva	FAGERLUND, M L.		361

SPEAKER (Free)

ALABAMA			
Auburn	ADAMS, Judith A.	(205)826-4500	5
	JONES, Allen W.	(205)826-4360	610
	VEENSTRA, Robert J.	(205)826-4780	1281
Birmingham	ROGERS, Nancy H.	(205)991-6600	1050
	VANDERPOORTEN, Mary B.	(205)991-1368	1274
	WEED, Joe K.	(205)991-6600	1315
Mobile	MCWHORTER, Jimmie M.	(205)342-5336	818
Montgomery	GREGORY, Vicki L.	(205)277-1759	466
Pelham	WRIGHT, Amos J.	(205)663-3403	1370
Prattville	LASETER, Ernest P.	(205)365-8549	700
Tuscaloosa	WATTERS, Annette J.	(205)348-6191	1310
ALASKA			
Anchorage	SOKOLOV, Barbara J.	(907)346-2480	1165
	WILLIAMS, Robert C.	(907)261-2970	1346
Fairbanks	STEPHENS, Dennis J.	(907)479-5826	1187
Juneau	CRANE, Karen R.	(907)456-2910	255
Sitka	MCCLAIN, Harriet V.	(907)747-8160	795
ARIZONA			
Flagstaff	DOWNUM, Evelyn R.	(602)774-6059	317
Glendale	MOSLEY, Shelley E.	(602)939-5469	872
Holbrook	ROTHLISBERG, Allen P.	(602)524-2257	1060
Mesa	JOSEPHINE, Helen B.	(602)983-0237	617
	MAIN, Isabelle G.	(602)962-4310	761
Phoenix	DEBACHER, Richard D.	(602)254-6156	284
	EVANS, Iris I.	(602)995-1701	357
	SCHNEIDER, Elizabeth K.	(602)261-7450	1097
Scottsdale	POTTER, William G.	(602)991-5578	987
Tempe	MILLER, Rosanna	(602)965-3582	842
	RIGGS, Donald E.	(602)965-3950	1034
	STEEL, Virginia	(602)965-3282	1183

SPEAKER (Free) (Cont'd)			
ARIZONA (Cont'd)			
Tucson	BUXTON, David T.	(602)621-2101	168
	DICKSTEIN, Ruth H.	(602)886-0386	301
	GILREATH, Charles L.	(602)621-4865	437
	GOODRICH, Nita K.	(602)791-4168	449
	HEITSHU, Sara C.	(602)621-2101	523
	HOLSINGER, Katherine	(602)621-3282	554
	MAKUCH, Andrew L.	(602)622-8572	762
	MAUTNER, Robert W.	(602)621-6386	787
	MILLS, Victoria A.	(602)795-5299	844
	REICHEL, Mary	(602)621-2101	1018
	ROBROCK, David P.	(602)743-7072	1045
	SMITH, Dorman H.	(602)296-3760	1154
	STRICKLAND, Ann T.	(602)881-6244	1202
ARKANSAS			
Arkadelphia	WOODS, L B.	(501)246-5511	1367
Conway	HARDIN, Willie	(501)450-3129	500
El Dorado	ARN, Nancy L.	(501)862-3385	33
Fayetteville	MILLER, Leon C.	(501)575-5577	839
Little Rock	MCKINNEY, Barbara J.	(501)227-6479	812
	MOORE, Bessie B.	(501)225-6914	858
	RAZER, Robert L.	(501)663-0789	1012
	SANDERS, Kathryn A.	(501)227-5581	1080
North Little Rock	JONES, Wanda F.	(501)835-7730	615
	PACK, Nancy C.	(501)758-1720	933
CALIFORNIA			
Anaheim	ADAMS, Joyce A.	(714)637-8385	5
	KOGA, James S.	(714)630-0618	668
Bakersfield	WINTER, Eugenia B.	(805)833-3175	1356
Belmont	LEWIS, Gretchen S.	(415)591-4336	723
Berkeley	BARKER, Joseph W.	(415)642-0590	56
	BERRING, Robert C.	(415)642-9980	90
	BESSER, Howard A.	(415)643-8641	91
	FALK, Candace V.	(415)526-9591	362
	FROHMBERG, Katherine A.	(415)644-3600	405
	GOLDMAN, Nancy L.	(415)642-0366	445
	LARSON, Ray R.	(415)642-6046	699
	MARKS, Larry	(415)644-2111	771
	MAXWELL, Christine Y.	(415)644-4500	788
	MONTGOMERY, Teresa L.	(415)642-1752	856
	SALMON, Stephen R.	(415)549-3394	1077
	STOCKTON, Gloria J.	(415)843-8550	1196
Beverly Hills	RUNYON, Judith A.	(213)859-5102	1067
	WALDOW, Mitch		1294
Buena Park	MUELLER, Jane L.	(714)527-8175	875
Burbank	BROWNE, Jeri A.	(818)953-8770	148
	ELMAN, Stanley A.	(818)351-8245	345
Callahan	FARRIER, George F.	(916)467-3334	365
Carlsbad	TILLETT, Barbara B.		1245
Carmichael	STRONG, Gary E.	(916)966-2037	1203
Castro Valley	OVERMYER, Elizabeth C.	(415)670-6281	931
Chico	LO, Henrietta W.	(916)895-6406	735
	SESSIONS, Judith A.	(916)895-5862	1117
Concord	SKAPURA, Robert J.	(415)945-7268	1145
Costa Mesa	PETERMAN, Claudia A.	(714)650-9014	962
Cupertino	MILLER, Ronald F.	(408)257-9162	842
Cypress	MOSER, Jane W.	(213)643-0322	870
Danville	CREW-NOBLE, Sara M.	(415)837-1399	258
Davis	LEWIS, Alfred J.	(916)752-3325	722
	SHARROW, Marilyn J.	(916)752-2110	1122
El Cerrito	HARDWICK, Bonnie S.	(415)237-7011	500
El Segundo	LOHNES, Richard B.	(213)772-2381	737
Encino	WOOD, Raymund F.		1364
Fairfax	DOWNEY, Lynn A.	(418)454-4290	316
Fairfield	GOLD, Anne M.	(707)429-6601	444
Fallbrook	MCNALLY, Ruth C.		816
Garden Grove	FRANK, Elizabeth W.	(714)892-3253	397
Glendale	ECKLUND, Lynn M.	(818)242-2793	335
	PRIME, Eugenie E.	(818)243-5707	993
Hillsborough	ABILOCK, Debbie	(415)348-2272	2
Irvine	HORN, Judy K.		559
	PUGSLEY, Sharon G.	(714)856-7193	997
	WEINTRAUB, D K.	(714)856-6079	1318
	WOODS, Lawrence A.	(714)786-3507	1367
Kensington	LAWRENCE, Gary S.	(415)642-2370	704
	MULVANY, Nancy	(415)524-4195	878

SPEAKER (Free) (Cont'd)
CALIFORNIA (Cont'd)

City	Name	Phone	No.
La Jolla	CASTETTER, Karla M.	(619)459-5369	194
	FISHER, Edith M.	(619)534-1258	380
	HURLBERT, Irene W.	(619)534-1261	577
La Verne	HECKMAN, Marlin L.	(714)593-8680	520
Long Beach	HECKLINGER, Ellen L.		519
	HOUSEL, Mary B.	(213)595-4154	563
	OSSEN, Virginia F.	(213)424-5415	928
	WELLS, H L.	(213)598-3549	1322
Los Altos Hills	MCDONALD, Marilyn M.	(415)960-4390	803
Los Angeles	ALFORD, Thomas E.	(213)612-3333	13
	BATES, Marcia J.	(213)825-4352	64
	CONNOR, Billie M.	(213)660-6399	237
	CROSS, Claudette S.	(213)256-2123	260
	GELMAN-KMEC, Marsha	(213)484-5530	426
	GLITZ, Beryl	(213)206-8016	441
	GRAY, Tomysena F.	(213)753-7541	460
	HAYTHORN, Joseph D.	(213)938-3621	517
	JAIN, Celeste C.	(213)665-7510	591
	KING, Joseph T.	(213)660-3530	651
	LEUNG, Terry S.	(213)306-5686	719
	PATRON, Susan H.	(213)612-3285	947
	SCHERREI, Rita A.	(213)825-1201	1092
	STERN, Teena B.	(213)680-2525	1189
	TROTTA, Victoria K.	(213)743-6487	1258
	VEASLEY, Mignon M.	(213)236-3515	1280
	VILLERE, Dawn N.	(213)290-2989	1284
	WALLACE, Marie G.	(213)485-1234	1297
	YEE, Martha M.	(213)462-4921	1379
Malibu	ROSENBERG, Betty	(213)456-2573	1056
Manhattan Beach	MARKEY, Penny S.	(213)374-1838	771
Menlo Park	BALES, F K.	(415)854-0115	52
	BOYE, Inger	(415)325-8077	123
Mill Valley	WHITE, Cecil R.	(415)388-8080	1330
Monterey	BRUMAN, Janet L.		150
Mountain View	ALBUM, Bernie	(415)967-5593	11
	BUTLER, Matilda L.	(415)969-0606	167
	PAISLEY, William J.	(415)969-0606	935
	PORTER-ROTH, Anne	(415)965-7799	985
Northridge	ECKLUND, Kristin A.	(818)349-6115	335
	PERKINS, David L.	(818)885-2256	959
Novato	HIRABAYASHI, Joanne	(415)897-4245	543
Oakland	BYRNE, Elizabeth D.	(415)658-6996	169
	CHESTER, Claudia J.	(415)835-4692	207
Orange	ERLICH, Martin		353
	JOHNSON, Mary L.	(714)634-7708	607
Palo Alto	ANDREWS, Chris C.		26
	LEVY, Mary J.	(415)325-9581	722
	LEWIS, Ralph W.	(415)446-9366	724
	WREDEN, William P.	(415)325-6851	1370
Palos Verdes Estates	STEVENSON, Marilyn E.	(213)377-7563	1191
	UEBELE, Dorothy B.	(213)541-2559	1268
Pasadena	CARD, Sandra E.	(818)356-6775	180
Pleasant Hill	SIEGEL, Ernest	(415)944-3423	1136
Pomona	REMKIEWICZ, Frank L.	(714)623-5251	1022
	STREETER, David	(714)620-2026	1201
Poway	D'ADOLF, Steven P.	(619)451-2130	269
Rancho Cacamonga	CONNELL, William S.	(714)989-0506	237
Redondo Beach	CLIFFORD, Susan G.	(213)378-3824	222
Redwood City	BANGE, Stephanie D.	(415)369-6251	54
Richmond	LAMBERT, Nancy	(415)620-3161	690
	O'CONNOR, Brian C.	(415)237-6561	915
	RYUS, Joseph E.	(415)222-0846	1072
Riverside	CHURUKIAN, Araxie P.	(714)787-3233	213
	CUEVAS, John R.	(714)684-4636	263
	DUNN, Kathleen K.	(714)359-8429	327
	SNYDER, Henry L.	(714)784-5806	1164
	STALKER, Laura A.	(714)787-5841	1178
	THOMPSON, James C.	(714)682-4549	1240
	WEBB, Gayle E.	(714)787-2460	1313
Rolling Hills Estate	SAVAGE, Gretchen S.	(213)377-5032	1085
Sacramento	JACKSON, Gloria D.	(916)427-1956	587
	KONG, Leslie M.	(916)278-5664	670
	LOW, Kathleen	(916)322-4570	743
	MILLER, Suzanne M.	(916)739-7010	842
	RUBY, Carmela M.	(916)453-1174	1065
San Bernardino	WEBB, Duncan C.	(714)387-4959	1313

SPEAKER (Free) (Cont'd)
CALIFORNIA (Cont'd)

City	Name	Phone	No.
San Diego	BOSSEAU, Don L.	(619)229-2538	117
	CARTER, Nancy C.		189
	DYER, Charles R.	(619)236-2292	330
	HOWARD, Pamela F.		564
	MONROE, Shula H.	(619)222-1206	855
	MORRISON, Patricia	(619)292-2859	868
	TABORN, Kym M.	(619)232-3320	1219
	TRIVISON, Margaret A.	(619)452-7338	1257
San Francisco	AVENEY, Brian H.	(415)338-2956	41
	FOX, Marylou P.	(415)546-8466	395
	GATES, Jane P.	(415)661-1514	421
	GERSH, Barbara S.	(415)346-7882	429
	GITLER, Robert L.	(415)221-9216	438
	GLOVER, Frank J.	(415)731-4477	442
	HAIKALIS, Peter D.	(415)338-2188	484
	HUNSUCKER, Alice E.	(415)396-7909	574
	MACKLER, Mark E.	(415)954-4452	757
	RAMIREZ, William L.	(415)564-5637	1005
	WILSON, Jacqueline B.	(415)476-2534	1351
San Jose	EMMICK, Nancy J.	(408)277-3904	348
San Mateo	ATKINS, Gregg T.	(415)574-6100	38
	RAZE, Nasus B.	(415)345-9684	1012
San Pedro	SCULLY, Patrick F.	(213)832-6526	1109
San Rafael	HAMMER, Sharon A.	(415)499-6051	493
	TRZECIAK, William J.	(415)485-3319	1260
Santa Barbara	GEBHARD, Patricia	(805)969-1031	424
Santa Clara	HAMBRIDGE, Sally L.	(408)378-8616	491
Santa Cruz	MARIE, Jacquelyn	(408)429-2802	770
	TURNER, Anne M.	(408)429-3532	1264
Simi Valley	WONG, Clark C.	(805)522-5233	1362
Sonoma	WINSON, Gail I.	(707)935-1546	1355
South Pasadena	WISE, Leona L.	(213)257-4020	1357
Stanford	CRAWFORD, Walt	(415)329-3551	257
	KRAKAUER, Elizabeth	(408)733-4611	675
	SWEENEY, Suzanne	(415)725-2005	1215
Stockton	LEONHARDT, Thomas W.	(209)946-2434	717
	NICHOLS, Elizabeth D.	(209)943-2484	901
Sunnyvale	DI MUCCIO, Mary J.	(408)733-8261	304
Thousand Oaks	SULLIVAN, Kathleen A.	(805)497-6282	1207
Torrance	BEEBE, Richard J.	(213)323-7200	74
Travis AFB	JACOBS, Nina F.	(707)438-5254	589
Turlock	PARKER, John C.	(209)634-9473	942
Upland	THELIN, Sonya R.	(714)982-2336	1234
Vacaville	KERNS, John T.	(207)448-4459	644
Whittier	RODRIGUEZ, Ronald	(213)693-0585	1048
	WILLIAMS, Lisa B.	(213)693-0771	1344
Winters	PEATTIE, Noel	(916)662-3364	953
Woodland	KELLUM-ROSE, Nancy P.	(916)662-6616	637
	STALLARD, Thomas W.	(916)666-1917	1179
	WEBBER, Steven L.	(916)661-1242	1313
Woodland Hills	CLIFTON, Joe A.	(818)716-3171	222
	NELSON-HARB, Sally R.		895
	RUBEN, Jacquelen S.		1064

COLORADO

City	Name	Phone	No.
Boulder	BINTLIFF, Barbara A.	(303)492-2708	97
	BOUCHER, Virginia P.	(303)492-6176	118
	CHANAUD, Jo P.	(303)449-0849	199
	FINK, Deborah	(303)492-8302	378
	MEYER, Andrea P.		829
Colorado Springs	MAGRATH, Lynn L.	(303)473-2080	760
	MANNING, Leslie A.	(303)593-3115	766
	NEILON, Barbara L.	(303)574-6167	892
Denver	ASHTON, Rick J.	(303)745-9883	36
	BREIVIK, Patricia S.	(303)556-2805	132
	BRUNER, Robert B.	(303)744-1138	150
	GORAL, Barbara J.	(303)866-2081	451
	KAVANAGH, Janette R.	(303)777-8971	631
	MITCHELL, Marilyn J.	(303)556-2835	849
	MOULTON, Suzanne L.	(303)871-6427	873
	SHAW, Ward	(303)861-5319	1124
	VOLZ, Edward J.	(303)571-2033	1288
Fort Collins	ANDERSON, Lemoyne W.	(303)484-7319	24
	CHAMBERS, Joan L.	(303)491-1833	198
	ERNEST, Douglas J.	(303)491-1861	353
Golden	GRAHAM, Su D.	(303)642-7802	456
	MADDOCK, Jerome T.	(303)231-1367	759
Grand Lake	ARMITAGE, Constance	(303)328-5293	32

SPEAKER (Free) (Cont'd)
COLORADO (Cont'd)

Greeley	KNEPEL, Nancy	(303)356-4357	664
	PITKIN, Gary M.	(303)339-2237	976
	SCHULZE, Suzanne S.		1102
Gunnison	LANDRUM, Margaret C.		693
Lamar	BURNETT, James H.	(303)336-4632	161
Pueblo	GARDNER, W J.	(303)549-3308	418

CONNECTICUT

Bridgeport	MINERVINO, Louise	(203)576-7779	846
Danbury	MARIANI, Carolyn A.	(203)794-6389	770
Danielson	WEIGEL, James S.	(203)774-7755	1316
Darien	BERRY, Louise P.	(203)655-2568	90
Greenwich	MCLANE, John F.	(203)629-9200	813
	MUSKUS, Elizabeth A.	(203)661-7058	883
Guilford	WALDEN, Katherine G.	(203)453-5645	1294
Hamden	NEWHALL, Ann C.	(203)288-8180	898
Hartford	BURGAN, John S.	(203)724-0297	159
	PORTER, Kathryn W.	(203)727-4321	985
	WEINSTEIN, Daniel L.	(203)275-2699	1318
	WILKIE, Everett C.	(203)236-5621	1340
Middletown	WHITE, Charles M.	(203)638-4110	1330
New Britain	LAWRENCE, Scott W.	(203)677-1659	705
New Canaan	SENATOR, Rochelle B.	(203)966-5645	1115
New Haven	BROWN, William E.	(203)432-1749	148
	KELLER, Michael A.	(203)389-2212	635
	PETERSON, Stephen L.	(203)432-5292	964
	PRATT, Allan D.	(203)389-0183	989
	SULLIVAN, Maureen	(203)776-3808	1208
	TRAINER, Karin A.	(203)432-1818	1253
	WALTER, Kenneth G.	(203)397-4526	1300
Ridgefield	MILSTEAD, Jessica L.	(203)431-8175	845
Southport	MOES, Robert T.	(203)255-9332	852
Stamford	CASE, Ann M.	(203)322-3383	191
	DIMATTIA, Ernest A.	(203)322-9055	304
	TIBBETTS, David W.	(203)329-2824	1243
	WILLIAMS, Judy R.	(203)964-1000	1344
Storrs	FORMAN, Camille L.	(203)486-2526	390
	JIMERSON, Randall C.	(203)486-2893	600
	LAMB, Gertrude		690
Waterbury	CARRINGTON, Virginia F.	(203)574-4702	186
	FLANAGAN, Leo N.	(203)756-6149	383
Westport	LOWE, Ida B.	(203)255-8780	743
	MECKLER, Alan M.	(203)226-6967	820
	RIBAROFF, Margaret F.	(203)849-0211	1026
Woodbridge	BOGENSCHNEIDER, Duane R.	(203)397-2600	110

DELAWARE

Milford	CARPENTER, Carole H.	(302)422-4290	184
Newark	GLOGOFF, Stuart J.	(302)451-2234	441
Wilmington	BRETON, Ernest J.		133
	BROWN, Atlanta T.	(302)998-0803	142
	BURDASH, David H.	(302)571-7402	158
	MINNICH, Nancy P.	(302)478-5291	846

DISTRICT OF COLUMBIA

Washington	ANDERSON, John M.	(202)287-8723	23
	BALL, Alice D.	(202)362-6047	52
	BATTLE, Thomas C.	(202)636-7241	65
	BECKERMAN, George	(202)775-9022	72
	BEDARD, Laura A.	(202)662-9172	73
	BEDARD, Laura A.	(202)662-9172	73
	BELLEFONTAINE, Arnold G.	(202)287-6587	78
	BLUMER, Thomas J.	(202)543-7031	107
	CANNAN, Judith P.	(202)287-5263	178
	CHILD, Margaret S.	(202)357-1521	208
	EDWARDS, Andrea Y.	(202)269-3449	337
	FLYNN, Richard M.	(202)638-1956	387
	GRAY, Michael H.	(202)755-4799	460
	HAGEMEYER, Alice L.	(202)727-2255	483
	HARWOOD, James L.	(202)523-3281	510
	HEARTY, John A.	(202)872-4533	519
	JOHANSON, Cynthia J.	(202)287-5261	601
	KEHOE, Patrick E.	(202)885-2674	634
	KINLEY, Jo H.	(202)822-4605	652
	KITZMILLER, Virginia G.		657
	LISOWSKI, Andrew H.	(202)287-5491	732
	MCCRAY, Maceo E.	(202)829-7737	800

SPEAKER (Free) (Cont'd)
DISTRICT OF COLUMBIA (Cont'd)

Washington			
	MCKEAN, Joan M.	(301)443-8358	810
	MIDDLETON, Carl H.	(202)628-3576	833
	MILEVSKI, Sandra N.	(202)543-7145	835
	MILLER, William S.	(202)775-4080	843
	OSTROW, Stephen E.	(202)287-5836	929
	PACIFICO, Michele F.	(202)253-3214	933
	PEYTON, David	(202)544-1969	966
	PHELPS, Thomas C.	(202)786-0271	967
	PREER, Jean L.	(202)635-5086	990
	PURDY, Virginia C.	(202)523-3105	998
	RENNINGER, Karen	(202)233-2711	1023
	RICHARDSON, Deborra A.		1029
	ROSENBERG, Jane A.	(202)786-0358	1056
	ROSENFELD, Mary A.	(202)357-1940	1056
	SCHNEIDER, Hennie R.	(202)523-0013	1097
	SCOTT, Catherine D.	(202)357-3101	1107
	SEELE, Ronald E.	(202)872-3970	1111
	STORM, Jill	(202)775-6174	1198
	STROUP, Elizabeth F.	(202)287-5543	1203
	TAFT, James R.	(202)966-7086	1219
	TRIPP-MELBY, Pamela	(202)676-9418	1257
	VANDEGRIFT, Barbara P.	(202)662-7523	1273
	WELSH, William J.	(202)287-5215	1323

FLORIDA

Belle Glade	SNODGRASSE, Elaine	(305)996-3453	1163
Brooksville	TORNABENE, Charles	(904)686-9318	1251
Chattahoochee	BEASLEY, Clarence W.		69
Coral Springs	KORNITSKY, Judith M.	(305)753-7081	672
Dunedin	FIORE, Carole D.	(813)733-2595	379
Fort Lauderdale	HEMPHILL, Lia S.	(305)760-5771	525
	MCCLAIN, Mary P.	(305)771-8000	796
Fort Myers	SCHWENN, Janet M.	(813)489-9505	1105
Freeport	DAVIS, Bonnie D.	(904)835-4432	277
Gainesville	BROWN, Pia T.	(904)375-6302	147
	TAYLOR, Betty W.	(904)372-0716	1226
Jacksonville	BROWN, G R.	(904)262-7644	144
	SUGDEN, Martin D.	(904)634-1626	1206
Miami	LIGHTERMAN, Mark	(305)279-5467	726
	MILLER, Laurence A.	(305)554-2461	839
	REAM, Diane F.	(305)596-6506	1013
	WILLIAMS, Thomas L.	(305)547-5782	1347
	WULF, Karlinne V.	(305)856-6022	1374
Naples	O'CONNOR, Mary A.	(813)598-9269	916
North Miami Beach	FRIEDMAN, Sylvia	(305)947-1435	404
Orlando	HUDSON, Phyllis J.	(305)275-2584	569
	SMITH, Mary D.	(305)843-7860	1158
	TREMBLAY, Gerald F.	(305)277-6944	1255
Pensacola	DEBOLT, W D.	(904)474-2213	284
St Petersburg	FUSTUKJIAN, Samuel Y.	(813)893-9125	410
	HARDESTY, Larry L.	(813)867-1166	499
	WOODARD, Joseph L.	(813)345-1335	1365
Sarasota	WEAVER, James B.	(813)378-1287	1312
Tallahassee	BUSTETTER, Stanley R.	(904)487-2667	166
	MILLER, Charles E.	(904)644-5211	836
	SUMMERS, F W.	(904)644-5775	1209
	TREZZA, Alphonse F.	(904)878-5551	1256
Tampa	EVERLOVE, Nora J.	(813)839-4868	359
	EYLES, Heberle H.	(813)837-3896	359
	LOSEY, Doris C.	(813)885-4500	742
	STORCK, Bernadette R.	(813)223-0000	1198
West Palm Beach	FOSTER, Helen M.	(305)686-1776	392
Winter Park	AHLIN, Nancy	(305)644-6424	8
	ANDREWS, Janet C.		26
	SEBRIGHT, Terence F.	(305)678-8846	1110

GEORGIA

Athens	BAKER, Barry B.	(404)542-2534	47
	BISHOP, David F.	(404)542-0621	99
	LIBBEY, George H.	(404)542-2716	725
	QUINLAN, Judy B.	(404)542-0654	1000
	ROWLAND, Lucy M.	(404)543-3690	1062
	SUTHERLAND, Johnnie D.	(404)542-0690	1211
Atlanta	BARNETT, Becky L.	(404)529-3886	57
	BIBBY, Elizabeth A.	(404)255-6840	94
	CORRELL, Emily N.	(404)633-3320	247
	ELZY, Martin I.	(404)331-3942	347

SPEAKER (Free) (Cont'd)
GEORGIA (Cont'd)
Atlanta

	ENGLER, June L.	(404)727-6405	350
	FORSEE, Joe B.	(404)656-2461	391
	NIX, Kemie	(404)355-7421	905
	PRESLEY, Roger L.	(404)658-2176	991
	QUINLIN, Margaret M.	(404)874-1589	1000
	RUSSELL, Ralph E.	(404)658-2172	1069
	SLOAN, Mary J.	(404)874-6224	1149
	SMITH, Jane B.	(205)271-5163	1155
	STOWELL, Donald C.	(404)231-4414	1199
	TOMAJKO, Kathy L.	(404)894-4511	1249
	WILLIAMS, Fred	(404)432-2723	1343
	WILTSE, Helen C.	(404)451-4260	1353
Augusta	MCCANN, Jett C.	(404)828-3491	794
Bainbridge	MARSHALL, Ruth T.	(912)246-3887	775
Carrollton	BEARD, Charles E.	(404)832-9458	69
Decatur	BISHOP, Beverly D.	(404)371-8488	99
	BUDLONG, Thomas F.	(404)289-0583	155
Fitzgerald	HEFFINGTON, Carl O.	(912)423-3642	520
Gainesville	VAUGHAN, Elinor F.	(404)534-6120	1279
La Grange	LEWIS, Frank R.	(404)882-2911	723
Macon	CHANIN, Leah F.	(912)744-2665	201
	HOWARD, Mary R.	(912)744-2960	564
Milledgeville	FENNELL, Janice C.	(912)453-4047	371
Norcross	DEWBERRY, Claire D.	(404)564-1634	298
Red Oak	LETT, Rosalind K.		719
Richmond Hill	GLISSON, Patricia A.	(912)727-2592	441
Stone Mountain	SULLIVAN, Mary A.	(404)469-0395	1208
Sylvester	MEREY-KADAR, Ervin R.	(912)776-0723	825
Valdosta	CLARK, Tommy A.	(912)244-6124	218
Watkinsville	WHITEHEAD, James M.	(404)769-8917	1332

HAWAII

Honolulu	JACKSON, Miles M.	(808)948-7321	588
	KANE, Bartholomew A.	(808)524-8344	624
Kailua	NAHL-JAKOBOVITS, Diane	(808)261-2382	886
Makawao	TUPPER, Bobbie	(808)572-1629	1263

IDAHO

Boise	WELLS, Merle W.	(208)334-3356	1322
Nampa	SIMMONS, Randall C.	(208)467-8609	1140
Pocatello	WATSON, Peter G.	(208)236-2997	1310

ILLINOIS

Barrington	KARON, Joyce E.	(312)381-1400	627
Bethany	SYFERT, Samuel R.	(217)665-3063	1217
Bloomington	KELLEY, H N.	(309)828-3128	636
Blue Island	WOZNY, Jay	(312)388-1078	1370
Bolingbrook	IFFLAND, Carol D.	(312)739-6398	581
Canton	WILSON, W R.	(309)647-0064	1353
Carbondale	JENKINS, Darrell L.	(618)549-8053	597
	KILPATRICK, Thomas L.	(618)453-3374	648
	MATTHEWS, Elizabeth W.	(618)536-7711	785
	RYAN, Sheila	(618)549-7029	1071
Champaign	CLOONAN, Michele V.	(217)351-8140	223
Charleston	KAPLAN, Sylvia Y.	(217)345-4228	626
	RAO, Paladugu V.	(217)581-6061	1008
Chicago	ALTHAGE, Celia J.		18
	BOLEF, Doris	(312)942-2271	112
	BOLT, Janice A.	(312)233-9399	113
	BROWN, Doris R.	(312)341-8066	143
	BURGH, Scott G.	(312)558-5740	159
	CARPENTER, Kathryn H.	(312)996-8988	185
	CURRY, John A.	(314)528-0870	266
	DAVIS, Glenn G.	(312)943-2911	279
	DEMPSEY, Frank J.	(312)327-6955	291
	DOLNICK, Sandy F.	(312)944-6780	310
	DOWNES, Valerie	(312)871-7559	316
	DUFF, John B.	(312)269-2984	323
	EMRE, Serpil A.	(312)236-5622	348
	EPP, Ronald H.	(203)347-6933	351
	FULTON, Tara L.	(312)508-2655	409
	GENESEN, Judith L.		427
	GODLEWSKI, Susan G.	(312)443-3936	442
	GOMEZ, Martin J.		447
	HAAS, Carolyn B.	(312)822-0809	480
	HARRIS, Jeanne G.	(312)580-0069	504
	HIGGINBOTHAM, Richard C.	(312)549-6146	537

SPEAKER (Free) (Cont'd)
ILLINOIS (Cont'd)
Chicago

	JACOBSEN, Teresa T.	(312)266-1265	590
	JOHN, Nancy R.	(312)996-2716	601
	KAMINECKI, Ronald M.	(312)726-9206	624
	KING, David E.	(312)346-7440	650
	MATTENSON, Murray M.	(312)262-8282	785
	MAYFIELD, Maurice K.	(312)281-0510	790
	MCCARTNEY, Elizabeth J.	(312)666-8262	794
	MCDERMOTT, Patrice	(312)944-6780	802
	MCELWAIN, William	(312)248-5564	804
	MCNEILL, Janice M.	(312)642-4600	816
	MELTON, Emily I.	(312)944-6780	823
	MILLER, Thomas R.	(312)769-6159	843
	MOORHEAD, John D.	(312)944-4020	862
	MOTLEY, Archie	(312)642-4600	872
	MOUW, James R.	(312)996-2706	874
	OAKS, Claire	(312)271-1207	913
	PARENT, Roger H.	(312)944-6780	940
	RANDALL, Sara L.		1006
	REMEIKIS, Lois A.	(312)782-1442	1022
	SHAEVEL, Evelyn F.	(312)944-6780	1118
	SIMPSON, Donald B.	(312)955-4545	1141
	STEWART, Richard A.	(312)269-2930	1193
	STRAIT, Constance J.		1199
	SVENSSON, C G.	(312)478-2939	1212
Dawson	CHESLEY, Thea B.		207
De Kalb	GILDEMEISTER, Glen A.	(815)753-9392	434
	HUANG, Samuel T.	(815)756-2296	568
	OSORIO, Nestor L.	(815)753-9837	928
	RAST, Elaine K.	(815)758-5234	1009
	TITUS, Elizabeth M.	(815)753-1094	1247
	WELCH, Theodore F.	(815)758-6858	1321
Dow	HOLZBERLEIN, Deanne B.	(618)466-3015	555
Edwardsville	MOORE, Milton C.	(618)692-1638	860
Elmhurst	MASON, John A.		781
Evanston	BJORNCRANTZ, Leslie B.	(312)866-9112	100
	CLOUD, Patricia D.	(312)491-3136	223
	DAVIDSON, Lloyd A.	(312)491-2906	276
	FRIEDER, Richard D.	(312)491-7599	403
	HILL, Janet S.	(312)491-7587	540
	HORNY, Karen L.	(312)491-7662	560
	METZLER, Valerie	(312)869-5992	829
	NIELSEN, Brian	(312)491-2170	903
	ROOSE, Tina	(312)491-0662	1053
	SHERMAN, Sarah	(312)864-3801	1128
Flora	HARRIS, Thomas J.	(618)662-2679	506
Franklin Park	VOSS, Joyce M.	(312)678-1528	1289
Hanover Park	KLOCKENGA, Gary R.	(312)830-8942	662
Highland Park	GREENFIELD, Jane W.	(312)432-0216	464
Hinsdale	CZARNECKI, Cary J.	(312)986-1976	268
	MUELLER, Elizabeth	(312)323-8054	875
Hoffman Estates	MILLER, Deborah	(312)882-3698	837
Homewood	MARKHAM, Robert P.	(312)799-4677	771
Itasca	HOGAN, Patricia M.	(312)773-1699	549
Joliet	JOHNSTON, James R.	(815)729-3481	610
La Grange	HATTENDORF, Lynn C.	(312)579-0873	512
	SCHULTHEISS, Louis A.	(312)354-6958	1101
Lake Bluff	LEISNER, Anthony B.	(312)295-2010	714
Lake Forest	MIKOLYZK, Thomas A.	(312)295-6247	834
Lombard	SCHIPMA, Peter B.	(312)627-0550	1093
Macomb	TING, Lee H.	(309)298-1770	1246
Manteno	MC LAUGHLIN, Terry L.	(815)468-6424	813
Matteson	SMITH, Richard D.	(312)747-6660	1159
Mt Morris	LONG, Roger J.	(815)734-4183	739
Mt Prospect	MCCULLY, William C.	(312)635-9811	801
Mundelein	RING, Anne M.	(312)566-0898	1035
Naperville	ROWE, Dorothy B.	(312)355-9221	1062
Niles	HANSEN, Cheryl A.	(312)677-4730	497
Normal	EASTON, William W.	(309)452-3105	333
	MATTHEWS, Priscilla J.	(309)452-8514	785
North Aurora	HOWREY, Mary M.	(312)896-5837	566
Northbrook	WICKS, Jerry R.	(312)272-6400	1335
Oak Lawn	DOBREZ, Cynthia K.	(312)422-4990	307
	MOORMAN, John A.	(312)422-4990	862
Oak Park	HARRIS, Robert A.	(312)524-8849	506
	PAPPALARDO, Marcia J.	(312)848-5035	939
Palatine	HORTON, Kathy L.	(312)934-3794	561
Park Ridge	OSERMAN, Stuart	(312)696-5060	928

SPEAKER (Free) (Cont'd)
ILLINOIS (Cont'd)

Paxton	PACEY, Brenda M.	(217)379-3517	933
Peoria	JACKSON, Susan M.	(309)674-2008	588
	NIEHAUS, Barbara J.	(309)697-3798	903
	SWORSKY, Felicia G.	(309)672-8885	1217
Quincy	TYER, Travis E.	(217)223-5024	1266
River Forest	LI, Richard T.	(312)366-2490	725
	NOONAN, Eileen F.	(312)366-9346	908
Rock Island	CONWAY, Colleen M.	(309)794-7316	239
	WESTERBERG, Kermit B.	(309)794-7221	1326
Rockford	LONG, Judith N.	(815)229-7604	739
St Charles	MORRISON, Carol J.	(312)377-2499	868
Skokie	GROSSMAN, David G.	(312)673-9100	473
	JACOB, Merle L.		589
	KAPLAN, Paul M.		626
	SORENSON, Liene S.	(312)673-7774	1168
Springfield	ALLEY, Brian	(217)522-8970	16
	SIVAK, Marie R.	(217)782-2826	1144
Urbana	ATKINS, Stephen E.	(217)244-1867	38
	CLARK, Barton M.	(217)333-0317	216
	FORREST, Charles G.	(217)244-3770	390
	KRUMMEL, Donald W.	(217)344-6311	680
	MAKINO, Yasuko	(217)244-2048	762
	SCHLIPF, Frederick A.	(217)367-4057	1094
	SHAW, Debora	(217)333-1666	1123
	SIEGEL, Martin A.	(217)333-3247	1136
	SMITH, Linda C.	(217)333-7742	1157
	WATSON, Paula D.	(217)333-1116	1310
	WILLIAMS, Mitsuko	(217)333-3654	1345
	WILSON, Lizabeth A.	(217)333-3489	1351
West Chicago	KOSMAN, Joyce E.	(312)231-0774	672
Wheaton	BERGER, Carol A.	(312)653-1115	85
Wheeling	KANNER, Elliott E.	(312)459-1300	625
	MCCLARREN, Robert R.	(312)459-1300	796
Wilmington	BOBAN, Carol A.	(815)458-3411	108
Winnetka	LUNDQUIST, Marie A.	(312)441-3315	748

INDIANA

Bloomington	BRISTOW, Ann	(812)335-8028	137
	FRY, Bernard M.	(812)339-3571	406
	HENN, Barbara J.	(812)335-1666	528
	POPP, Mary F.	(812)335-9857	984
	PUNGITORE, Verna L.	(812)335-5113	997
	READ, Glenn F.	(812)336-5984	1012
	SHAABAN, Marian F.	(812)335-6924	1118
	STEELE, Patricia A.	(812)335-1619	1184
	WHITE, Herbert S.	(812)335-2848	1331
Evansville	BAKER, Donald E.	(812)425-4309	48
	TEUBERT, Lola H.	(812)428-8229	1233
	WINSLOW, Carol M.	(812)867-2146	1355
Frankfort	CADDELL, Claude W.	(317)654-7038	170
Gary	MILLENDER, Dharathola	(219)882-4050	835
Hammond	MEYERS, Arthur S.	(219)931-5100	830
Indianapolis	BRIDGE, Stephen W.	(317)359-7260	135
	BROWN, Judith L.		145
	DOLAN-HEITLINGER, Eileen	(317)269-1764	309
	GOODWIN, Vania M.	(317)274-0491	450
	KONDELIK, John P.	(317)283-9226	670
	KRASEAN, Thomas K.	(317)232-1882	676
	MATTHEW, Jeannette M.	(317)283-1053	785
	STARKEY, Edward D.	(317)274-0467	1182
	THOMPSON, Anna M.		1238
Lafayette	BONHOMME, Mary S.	(317)448-1251	114
	MCKOWEN, Dorothy K.	(317)564-4585	812
	MITCHELL, Cynthia E.	(317)423-2602	848
Michigan City	DEYOUNG, Charles D.	(219)879-4561	298
Mishawaka	STRATTON, Martha G.	(219)255-5262	1200
Muncie	DOLAK, Frank J.	(317)285-5141	309
Munster	MOGLE, Dawn E.	(219)923-8059	852
Noblesville	COOPER, David L.	(317)773-1384	242
Notre Dame	CONNELLY, James T.	(219)233-9675	237
	FUDERER, Laura S.	(219)239-5176	408
	HAVLIK, Robert J.	(219)239-6665	513
	HAYES, Stephen M.	(219)239-5268	516
	SLINGER, Michael J.	(219)239-5664	1149
Richmond	FARBER, Evan I.	(317)966-2422	363
Rochester	LASHER, Esther L.	(219)223-8407	700

SPEAKER (Free) (Cont'd)
INDIANA (Cont'd)

South Bend	MILLER, Jeanne L.	(219)284-7491	839
	MULLINS, James L.	(219)237-4449	878
	PIANE, Mimi	(219)282-4649	969
	YATES, Donald N.	(219)289-3405	1378
Terre Haute	ENSOR, Pat L.	(812)237-2580	350
Valparaiso	PERRY, Margaret	(219)464-5364	960
Vincennes	PIEPENBURG, Scott R.	(812)885-5807	971
West Lafayette	BAILEY, Martha J.	(317)494-2910	46
	BAXTER, Pam M.	(317)494-2969	67

IOWA

Ames	COLE, Jim E.	(515)294-0432	230
	MADISON, Olivia M.	(515)294-3669	759
Boone	ADAMS, Larry D.	(515)432-1931	5
Cedar Falls	WILKINSON, Patrick J.	(319)273-6327	1340
Decorah	FENSTERMANN, Duane W.	(319)387-1164	371
Des Moines	EDWARDS, John D.	(515)271-2141	337
	ESTES, Elaine G.	(515)283-4152	355
	GEORGE, Shirley H.	(515)281-4105	428
	JOHNSON, Nancy E.	(515)262-6714	608
	KERN, Sharon P.	(515)243-2300	643
Iowa City	FALK, Mark F.	(319)354-7474	362
	LORKOVIC, Tatjana B.	(318)351-5304	741
Marshalltown	BURGESS, Barbara J.	(515)752-4812	159
Ottumwa	GEIB, Jerry H.	(515)682-7563	425
Sioux City	DUNN, Susan M.		327
West Branch	MAYER, Dale C.	(319)643-5301	789

KANSAS

Chanute	DRUSE, Judith A.	(316)431-3020	321
Coffeyville	HENDERSON, Rosemary	(316)251-2158	527
Hays	MILLER, Melanie A.	(913)625-9014	841
Kansas City	RUSSELL, Marilyn L.	(913)299-1540	1069
Lawrence	HOWARD, Clinton N.	(913)864-3601	564
	SNYDER, Fritz	(913)864-3025	1164
Leavenworth	SNOKE, Elizabeth R.		1163
Leawood	LUNG, Mon Y.	(913)864-3025	748
Lenexa	MCLEOD, Debra A.	(913)492-4512	814
Manhattan	GRASS, Charlene G.	(913)532-6516	458
	QUIRING, Virginia M.	(913)532-5693	1000
	TALAB, Rosemary S.	(913)532-5550	1220
Miltonvale	BRADLEY, Susanne A.	(913)427-2228	126
Newton	EBERHARD, Neysa C.	(316)283-2890	334
North Newton	SCHRAG, Dale R.	(316)283-2500	1099
Overland Park	ALLEN, Norene F.	(800)338-8527	15
Pittsburg	LEE, Earl W.	(316)231-7000	709
Salina	WHITE, George R.	(913)825-2101	1331
Topeka	LEVEL, M J.	(913)296-3434	719

KENTUCKY

Bowling Green	CUDD, John M.	(502)842-0901	263
Fort Thomas	NEWMAN, Linda D.	(606)441-0899	899
Highland Heights	BREDEMEYER, Carol	(606)572-5395	131
	SCHULTZ, Lois E.	(606)572-5275	1102
	STURM, Rebecca R.	(606)572-5636	1205
Lexington	SIMS, Edward N.	(606)252-2291	1142
Louisville	ANDERSON, James C.	(502)588-6752	23
	AULD, Dennis B.		39
	BLACKBURN-FOSTER, Brenda	(502)582-4111	102
	CONNOR, Lynn S.	(502)589-4200	238
	EDDY, Leonard M.	(502)245-8633	335
	HUFF, James E.	(502)585-9911	570
	NILES, Judith F.	(502)588-6756	904
	REDMON, Sherrill	(502)451-5907	1014
	SCHLENE, Vickie J.	(502)935-9840	1094
	VOYLES, James R.	(502)589-4440	1289
Owensboro	YATES, Dudley V.	(502)526-3111	1378
Paducah	BOYARSKI, Jennie S.	(502)442-6131	122
Richmond	BARKSDALE, Milton K.	(606)622-1787	57
Southgate	FOX, Estella E.	(606)441-0743	394

LOUISIANA

Baton Rouge	BRADLEY, Jared W.	(504)766-9375	126
	HAMAKER, Charles A.	(504)388-8537	490
	HEIM, Kathleen M.	(504)388-3158	521
	HOGAN, Sharon A.	(504)388-2217	549
	KLEINER, Janellyn P.	(504)928-1960	660

SPEAKER (Free) (Cont'd)
LOUISIANA (Cont'd)

Baton Rouge			
	KRAFT, Donald H.	(504)388-1495	674
	MCKANN, Michael R.	(504)342-4922	809
	PASKOFF, Beth M.	(504)388-1480	946
	PHENIX, Katharine J.	(504)388-3158	967
	REID, Marion T.	(504)388-2217	1019
Lafayette	RAMAKRISHNAN, T	(318)989-9333	1004
Lake Charles	CAGLE, Robert B.	(318)437-5740	171
Monroe	MEINEL, Nancy T.	(318)343-3399	822
Natchitoches	BUCHANAN, William C.	(318)357-4403	153
New Orleans	DRAUGHON, Ralph B.	(504)891-1921	318
	GERICKE, Paul W.	(504)282-4455	428
	HANKEL, Marilyn L.	(504)286-7276	496
	RUSHING, Darla H.	(504)891-1127	1068
	SARKODIE-MENSAH, Kwasi	(504)483-7306	1083
	SKINNER, Robert E.	(504)483-7304	1146
	WILSON, C D.	(504)596-2600	1350
Ruston	DICARLO, Michael A.	(318)257-3594	300
Shreveport	MOSLEY, Mattie J.	(318)797-5100	871
Slidell	HOLLEY, Rebecca M.	(504)641-0198	551

MAINE

Bar Harbor	GOLBITZ, Peter	(207)288-4969	444
Boothbay	SEELEY, Catherine R.		1111
Brunswick	HEISER, Nancy E.	(207)725-4253	523
Farmington	MCNAMARA, Shelley G.	(207)778-3501	816
North Anson	LYONS, Dean E.	(207)566-0511	753
Westbrook	PARKS, George R.	(207)854-0355	943

MARYLAND

Adamstown	LIGHTBOWN, Parke P.		726
Adelphi	NITECKI, Danuta A.	(301)937-4791	905
Annapolis	CARMAN, Carol A.	(301)841-3810	183
	MCKAY, Eleanor	(301)263-6526	809
	WAGNER, Susan C.	(301)268-2315	1292
Baltimore	ARRINGTON, Susan J.	(301)396-4042	34
	BLANK, Annette C.	(301)396-5350	104
	BRENNAN, Edward P.	(301)675-8835	132
	DAVISH, William	(301)323-1010	281
	HEINRICH, Lois M.	(301)686-8065	522
	HEISER, Jane C.	(301)396-5470	523
	LAPIDES, Linda F.	(301)396-5356	697
	MONTGOMERY, Paula K.	(301)685-8621	856
	PARTRIDGE, James C.	(301)664-4301	945
	RUFF, Martha R.	(301)367-2831	1066
	TOOEY, Mary J.	(301)744-0521	1250
Bel Air	SEDNEY, Frances V.	(301)838-7484	1111
Beltsville	ANDRE, Pamela Q.	(301)344-3813	26
	MCCONE, Gary K.	(301)344-3813	797
Bethesda	BALL, Thomas W.	(301)493-5184	52
	BYRNES, Margaret M.	(301)496-0382	169
	GAUJARD, Pierre G.	(301)652-0034	422
	HAWK, Susan A.	(301)897-8367	513
	JOHNSON, Carol A.	(301)251-5378	602
	MOBLEY, Arthur B.	(301)530-0081	851
	PARASCANDOLA, John L.	(301)496-5405	939
	SLATER, Susan B.	(301)496-2311	1148
	THOMAS, Patricia A.	(301)229-4194	1238
	WOODSMALL, Rose M.	(301)496-8834	1367
Bowie	EVANS, Frank B.	(301)464-8829	357
	NELSEN, Alice R.	(301)262-2194	893
Brooksville	BASCOM, James F.	(301)774-3175	62
Chevy Chase	HOLLOWAY, Johnna H.	(301)652-8491	552
	MESHINSKY, Jeff M.	(301)652-4740	827
	SHAW, Renata V.	(301)654-3560	1123
Clinton	CHEEKS, Cellestine	(301)868-5048	204
College Park	JOHNSON, Emily P.	(301)935-5382	604
	MARCHIONINI, Gary J.	(301)454-3235	769
	WILSON, William G.	(301)454-6003	1353
Columbia	DIENER, Carol W.	(301)381-2525	302
	GORDON, Martin K.	(301)992-7626	451
	NEWMAN, Wilda B.	(301)730-7583	900
Dundalk	MILLER, Everett G.	(301)522-5785	837
Fallston	SACK, Jean C.	(301)877-2825	1073
Fort Washington	BRADSHER, James G.	(301)248-8884	126
Frederick	BANKS, Jane L.	(301)695-6726	54
Fulton	FRANK, Robyn C.	(301)490-5898	397

SPEAKER (Free) (Cont'd)
MARYLAND (Cont'd)

Gaithersburg	BENNETT, Harry D.	(301)840-1467	81
	GRIFFEN, Agnes M.	(301)340-3378	468
Gamber	BOGAGE, Alan R.	(301)795-6167	110
Gambrills	YOUNG, Peter R.	(301)923-2902	1383
Grasonville	SCHNEIDER, Karl R.	(301)827-9339	1097
Hyattsville	BURGESS, Eileen E.	(301)864-7223	159
Lanham	HUFFER, Mary A.	(301)577-3640	570
Laurel	BARKER, Lillian H.	(301)776-2260	56
	SAWYER, Edmond J.	(301)725-4750	1086
Mt Rainier	NITZ, Andrew M.		905
New Carrollton	WILLIAMS, Helen E.	(301)454-6068	1343
Pocomoke City	SMITH, Jessie C.	(301)957-3320	1156
Rockville	BERUL, Lawrence H.	(301)984-9400	91
	CANTELON, Philip L.	(301)770-1170	179
	FREEDMAN, Lynn P.	(301)468-2600	400
St Marys City	REPENNING, Julie A.	(301)862-0267	1023
Silver Spring	AGEE, Victoria V.	(301)434-7073	7
	FELMY, John C.	(301)681-9069	370
	HENDERSON, Ronald L.	(301)588-2844	527
	LARSON, Jean A.	(301)890-2210	699
	MERINGOLO, Joseph A.	(202)872-7689	826
	PEMPE, Ruta	(301)587-3846	956
	PICKETT, Olivia K.	(301)434-7503	971
	PRITCHARD, Sarah M.	(301)588-8624	994
	THOMAS, Sarah E.	(301)585-9446	1238
	VAN CAMPEN, Rebecca J.	(301)890-8588	1272
	WAGNER, Lloyd F.		1292
Takoma Park	SLOAN, Cheryl A.	(301)589-6815	1149
Thurmont	FITZPATRICK, Kelly	(301)271-4109	383
Towson	ROBINSON, Charles W.	(301)296-8500	1043
Upper Marlboro	WOODY, Jacqueline B.		1368
Welcome	DUDLEY, Robyn A.	(301)934-4602	323
Wheaton	MWALIMU, Charles	(301)933-4040	884

MASSACHUSETTS

Andover	JACOBSON, Nancy C.	(617)475-6960	590
Boston	ANZALONE, Filippa M.		29
	BEGG, Karin E.		74
	CARROLL, Virginia L.	(617)742-5151	187
	HEINS, Ethel L.	(617)527-2736	522
	HUDSON, Robert E.	(617)353-3917	570
	KORT, Richard L.	(617)266-3646	672
	LEIGHTON, Helene L.	(617)726-8600	714
	MATIS, Lynn	(617)973-8000	784
	MCCARTHY, Germaine A.	(617)742-3958	794
	PEARLSTEIN, Toby	(617)973-8000	952
	SCHWARTZ, Candy S.	(617)738-2223	1104
	SCHWARTZ, Frederick E.	(617)522-0234	1104
	SNIFFIN-MARINO, Megan G.	(617)738-3141	1163
	WARNER, Marnie M.	(617)725-8733	1305
Brockton	NOYES, Suzanne N.	(617)583-4500	911
Burlington	MCLAUGHLIN, Lee R.	(617)272-5772	813
Cambridge	DEARBORN, Susan C.	(617)576-3205	284
	FERNALD, Anne C.	(617)491-4077	373
	MOFFITT, Michael D.	(617)864-5770	852
	PARKER, Susan E.	(617)495-3455	942
	PINSON, Mark	(617)492-1590	975
Chestnut Hill	CHANNING, Rhoda K.	(617)552-4470	201
East Boston	SCHLAFF, Donna G.	(617)561-0153	1093
Greenfield	LEE, Marilyn M.	(413)773-8477	710
Holyoke	DUTCHER, Henry D.	(413)538-7000	329
Ipswich	GRAY, Carolyn M.	(617)356-0773	459
Leverett	ZIPKOWITZ, Fay	(413)367-9573	1389
Lexington	LUCKER, Jay K.	(617)862-4558	746
	WYSS, David A.	(617)860-6751	1376
Littleton	BUCKLAND, Lawrence F.	(617)899-1086	154
Medford	SCHATZ, Natalie M.	(617)381-3273	1090
Milton	KEYS, Marshall	(617)333-0500	645
Nahant	DESTEFANO, Daniel A.	(617)596-1767	296
Newtonville	FRIEDMAN, Terri M.	(617)965-6310	404
	GLASSMAN, Penny L.	(617)965-6310	440
North Andover	REEVE, Russell J.	(617)682-6260	1016
Northampton	DAVIS, Charles R.	(413)584-2700	278
	SLY, Margery N.	(413)584-2700	1150
Norwell	KADANOFF, Diane G.	(617)659-2015	621
Pittsfield	BOSTLEY, Jean R.	(413)447-9121	117
Plymouth	HORN, Joseph A.	(617)746-6172	559
Randolph	OAKLEY, Adeline D.	(617)963-7999	913

Revere	TATELMAN, Susan D.	(617)284-0154	1225
Roslindale	CLANCY, Catherine M.	(617)327-0013	215
Salem	SCHWALLER, Marian C.	(617)744-0076	1104
Sharon	FRAZIER, James A.	(617)784-5642	399
South Hamilton	DVORAK, Robert	(617)468-7111	330
Springfield	MCLAIN, Guy A.	(413)739-3871	813
Sturbridge	PERCY, Theresa R.	(617)347-3362	958
Wakefield	CHAPDELAINE, Susan A.	(617)246-5200	201
Walpole	ESTES, Pamela J.	(617)668-3076	355
Waltham	CHATTERTON, Leigh A.	(617)893-4807	204
Watertown	LANDESMAN, Betty J.	(617)924-7182	692
Westwood	CLAPPER, Mary E.	(617)329-3350	216
Winchester	JOHNSON, Jean L.	(617)721-7020	606
Woods Hole	WINN, Carolyn P.	(617)548-7066	1355
Worcester	GONNEVILLE, Priscilla R.	(617)752-5615	447
	JOHNSON, Penelope B.	(617)799-1653	608
	NOAH, Carolyn B.	(617)799-1655	906

MICHIGAN

Albion	JENNINGS, Martha F.	(517)629-9469	598
Ann Arbor	BERGEN, Kathleen M.	(313)936-3814	85
	BIGGS, Debra R.	(313)763-7080	95
	DURRANCE, Joan C.	(313)763-1569	328
	KOCHEN, Manfred	(313)764-2585	667
	LEARY, Margaret R.	(313)663-7324	707
	STOFFLE, Carla J.	(313)764-9356	1196
	WILSON, Amy S.	(313)761-4700	1349
	YOCUM, Patricia B.	(313)995-4644	1380
Benton Harbor	KIRBY, Frederick J.	(616)926-1690	654
Berrien Springs	SOPER, Marley H.	(616)471-3379	1168
Birmingham	ORMOND, Sarah C.	(313)647-1700	926
Bloomfield Hills	DAVID, Indra M.	(313)338-3929	276
	ST. AMAND, Norma P.	(313)644-1878	1075
Canton	BRYANT, Barton B.	(313)397-3660	152
Dearborn Heights	KIRKESY, Oliver M.	(313)278-4670	655
Decatur	TATE, David L.	(616)423-4771	1225
Detroit	BARTKOWSKI, Patricia	(313)577-4024	61
	BISSETT, Donald J.	(313)577-1615	100
	GIGLIO, Linda M.	(313)872-4311	433
	JOHNSON, Veronica A.	(313)532-6715	609
	KAUL, Kanhya L.	(313)577-3926	631
	PFLUG, Warner W.	(313)577-4024	966
	SMITH, Michael O.	(313)577-4024	1158
East Lansing	CHAPIN, Richard E.	(517)355-2341	201
	HAKA, Clifford H.	(517)353-5317	484
	JIZBA, Laurel	(517)353-4526	600
	SANFORD, John D.	(517)355-2330	1081
Farmington Hills	PAPAI, Beverly D.	(313)553-0300	938
Ferndale	BORAM, Joan M.	(313)542-2523	116
Grand Haven	BROOKS, Burton H.	(616)842-2586	140
Grand Rapids	BRACKETT, Norman S.	(616)241-7467	124
Haslett	OLIVER, James W.	(517)339-0846	921
Highland Park	NDENGA, Viola W.	(313)868-5986	890
Iron Mountain	SILVER, Gary L.	(906)774-3005	1138
Jenison	VELTEMA, John H.	(616)457-3400	1282
Kalamazoo	GROTZINGER, Laurel A.	(616)381-1865	473
	ISAACSON, David K.	(616)383-1562	584
Lansing	DUKELOW, Ruth H.	(517)373-1593	324
	FRY, James W.	(517)373-1593	406
	FRYE, Dorothy T.	(517)393-7608	407
Livonia	OHAKLOSH, Cynthia L.		197
	VOIGHT, Nancy R.	(313)464-2306	1287
Northville	FIELD, Judith J.	(313)349-1953	375
Otsego	PARK, Janice R.	(616)694-4546	941
Petoskey	KELLY, Kay	(616)348-4500	638
Rochester	HAGE, Christine C.	(313)375-1038	482
Saginaw	JOHN, Stephanie C.	(517)771-6846	601
	O'CONNELL, Catherine A.	(517)792-6852	915
Southfield	SUMMERS, Sheryl H.	(313)357-0404	1209
Spring Lake	PRETZER, Dale H.	(616)846-8967	992
Troy	STEPHENS, Karen L.	(313)879-6856	1188
Vicksburg	HEGEDUS, Mary E.	(616)679-5396	521
West Bloomfield	SMITH, Nancy J.	(313)682-2120	1158
	WREN, James A.	(313)682-6310	1370
Ypsilanti	BOONE, Morell D.	(313)484-4384	115

Duluth	SCHROEDER, Janet K.	(218)723-3821	1100
Eden Prairie	GROSCH, Audrey N.	(612)937-2345	472
Edina	LONG, John M.	(612)942-0140	739
Mankato	CARRISON, Dale K.	(507)389-5062	187
	HITT, Charles J.	(507)625-4834	544
	PEISCHL, Thomas P.	(507)389-5953	955
Marine on St Croix	FULLER, Sherrilynne S.	(612)433-3893	409
Minneapolis	ASPNES, Grieg G.	(612)926-1749	37
	BOEDER, Thelma B.	(612)870-3657	109
	BRUTON, Robert T.	(612)540-1084	151
	DEJOHN, William T.	(612)624-2839	288
	GLASGOW, Vicki L.	(612)626-5808	440
	OLSON, Lowell E.	(612)626-0824	923
	PANKAKE, Marcia J.	(612)331-2551	938
	ROSSMAN, Muriel J.	(612)624-4002	1059
	ROTH, Alvin R.	(612)789-3879	1059
	SELANDER, Lucy M.	(612)729-5989	1113
Minnetonka	DESIREY, Janice M.	(612)541-8569	295
	JENSEN, Wilma M.	(612)473-5965	599
Moorhead	RUDIE, Helen M.	(218)233-6817	1065
New Brighton	KEIM, Robert	(612)633-3393	635
Northfield	METZ, T J.	(507)663-4267	828
Pine River	O'BRIEN, Marlys H.	(218)587-2171	915
Rochester	BEYNEN, Gijsbertus K.		93
	HAWTHORNE, Dorothy M.	(507)284-8797	514
	KEYS, Thomas E.		645
St Paul	CLARKE, Charlotte C.	(612)645-7359	218
	FEYE-STUKAS, Janice	(612)296-2821	374
	KING, Jack B.	(612)641-2373	651
	RICCI, Patricia L.	(612)771-4764	1026
	STOKES, Claire Z.	(612)642-0120	1196
St Peter	HERVEY, Norma J.	(507)931-7563	533

MISSISSIPPI

Hattiesburg	BOYD, William D.	(601)266-4232	123
	HAUTH, Allan C.	(601)266-4126	513
	LATOUR, Terry S.	(601)266-4345	701
Jackson	WEST, Carol C.	(601)944-1970	1326
Mississippi State	BRELAND, June M.	(601)325-1240	132
Starkville	NETTLES, Jess	(601)323-5558	896
Sunflower	POWELL, Anice C.	(601)569-3663	988
University	COCHRAN, J W.	(601)232-7361	225

MISSOURI

Afton	WOHLRABE, John C.	(314)843-8131	1359
Columbia	ALMONY, Robert A.	(314)882-4701	17
	CARROLL, C E.	(314)443-8303	187
	HAVENER, Ralph S.	(314)882-4602	513
	RICKERSON, George T.	(314)445-1493	1031
	WATERS, Bill F.	(314)443-3161	1308
Florissant	BLANKENSHIP, Phyllis E.	(314)839-3966	104
Harrisonville	FRANKLIN, Jill S.	(816)884-6223	397
Independence	BRILEY, Carol A.	(816)833-1400	136
	MORALES, Milton F.	(816)836-5200	862
Jefferson City	BEHLER, Patricia A.	(314)635-0608	74
Kansas City	GARDNER, Laura L.	(816)741-4070	418
	LINEBACH, Laura M.	(816)361-7031	730
	NESBITT, John R.	(813)926-7616	890
	SERLING, Kitty	(816)753-5700	1116
Liberty	HOOVER, Jonnette L.	(816)781-7812	557
Ozark	WARNER, Wayne E.	(417)485-3972	1305
Saint Joseph	ELLIOTT, Dorothy G.	(816)232-7729	344
	HUGHES, Joan L.	(816)271-6000	571
St Louis	ELAM, Kristy L.	(314)658-2759	341
	ELSESSER, Lionelle H.	(314)725-4722	346
	HELMS, Mary E.	(314)362-2787	525
	LYONS, A J.	(314)241-2288	753
	NELSON, Mary A.	(314)889-6459	894
	SIGALA, Stephanie C.	(314)721-0067	1137
	WINKLER, Carol A.	(314)481-4753	1355
St Peters	SANDSTEDT, Carl R.	(314)441-2300	1081
Springfield	COOMBS, James A.	(417)836-4534	241
	MEADOR, John M.	(417)882-8032	819
Sugar Creek	STEELE, Anitra T.	(816)836-4031	1184
Warrensburg	NIEMEYER, Mollie M.	(816)429-4070	903

SPEAKER (Free) (Cont'd)

MONTANA
Billings	NEWBERG, Ellen J.	(406)245-5483	898
Great Falls	WARDEN, Margaret S.		1304
Helena	PARKER, Sara A.	(406)444-3115	942

NEBRASKA
Beatrice	FINDLING, Carol A.	(402)223-4595	377
Lincoln	LEITER, Richard A.	(402)466-3468	714
	WISE, Sally H.	(402)472-5737	1357
Omaha	BROWN, Helen A.	(402)559-4326	144
	MEANS, Raymond B.	(402)280-2705	820
	RUNYON, Robert S.	(402)393-3320	1067

NEVADA
Carson City	KERSCHNER, Joan G.	(702)887-2615	644
	SOUTHWICK, Susan A.	(702)885-5140	1170
Incline	OSSOLINSKI, Lynn	(702)831-2936	928
Las Vegas	CAROLLO, Michael T.	(702)385-0115	184
	CUTLER, Marsha L.	(702)646-3932	268
	DALTON, Phyllis I.	(702)732-4793	271
	GROSSHANS, Merilyn P.	(702)799-7855	473
	HUNSBERGER, Charles W.	(702)733-7810	574
	SAUNDERS, Laverna M.	(702)739-3069	1084
Reno	CONWAY, Susan L.	(702)784-6508	239
	MANLEY, Charles W.	(702)785-4012	765

NEW HAMPSHIRE
Hanover	CRONENWETT, Philip N.	(603)646-2037	260
Keene	VINCENT, Charles P.	(603)352-1909	1284
Manchester	MESMER, Frank B.	(603)668-1593	827

NEW JERSEY
Bernardsville	BURDEN, Geraldine R.	(201)766-0118	158
Bloomfield	BETANCOURT, Ingrid T.	(201)743-9511	92
Bogota	MACKESY, Eileen M.		756
Bridgewater	ROMANASKY, Marcia C.	(201)218-0400	1052
	STUDDIFORD, Abigail M.	(201)725-5616	1204
Caldwell	EDELSON, Ken		335
Denville	THOMAS, Hilary B.	(201)625-8136	1236
Edison	DINERMAN, Gloria	(201)906-1777	304
	FERRERE, Cathy M.	(201)819-8924	373
Far Hills	SEAGLE, Janet M.	(201)234-2300	1109
Flemington	MCGREGOR, Walter	(201)788-3025	808
Glen Rock	PERCELLI, Irene M.	(201)445-5983	958
Haddonfield	SWARTZ, Betty J.	(609)429-8498	1214
Highland Park	CLARK, Philip M.	(201)572-5414	218
Hightstown	BRODMAN, Estelle	(609)443-8094	139
Lawrenceville	STEPHEN, Ross G.	(609)896-5111	1187
Leonia	CIMBALA, Diane J.	(201)585-1921	214
	SCHARF, Davida	(201)947-6839	1090
Madison	COUGHLIN, Caroline M.	(201)377-3000	250
	POVILAITIS, Leanna J.	(201)377-0722	987
Maplewood	LAUB, Barbara J.	(201)763-8379	702
Marlton	RICHIE, Mark L.	(609)985-0436	1030
Metuchen	BECKER, Ronald L.	(201)494-6447	72
Montclair	HOROWITZ, Marjorie B.	(201)744-8697	560
Morristown	BUCK, Anne M.	(201)829-5111	153
	CLARK, Joan	(201)644-1104	217
Mount Holly	CARR, Charles E.	(609)267-9660	185
Mountain Lakes	CLARK, Rick	(201)299-0181	218
Murray Hill	BROWN, Ina A.	(201)582-2417	144
New Brunswick	ANSELMO, Edith H.	(201)247-5610	28
	EUSTER, Joanne R.	(201)932-7505	356
	GRAHAM, Peter S.	(201)932-7505	456
	NASH, Stanley D.	(201)932-7014	888
	REELING, Patricia G.	(201)932-7917	1016
	SARACEVIC, Tefko	(201)932-7447	1082
Newark	DANE, William J.	(201)733-7848	272
North Arlington	CASEY, Mary A.	(201)997-2141	192
Parsippany	VOGT, Herwart C.	(201)263-5669	1287
Pequannock	SUSSMAN, Valerie J.	(201)696-9655	1210
Piscataway	CALHOUN, Ellen	(201)932-4363	172
	FIGUEREDO, Danilo H.	(201)463-3725	376
Princeton	BAKES, Floy L.	(609)520-4631	50
	BERKNER, Dimity S.	(609)924-3891	87
	CARLSON, Dudley B.		182
	FERGUSON, Stephen	(609)452-3184	372
	HOELLE, Dolores M.	(609)452-3201	547
	JOHNSON, David K.	(609)924-2870	603

SPEAKER (Free) (Cont'd)

NEW JERSEY (Cont'd)
Rahway	SUDALL, Arthur D.	(201)388-0761	1206
Ridgewood	SEER, Gitelle	(201)652-2595	1111
Rutherford	RAPPAPORT, Susan E.		1008
Sewell	COUMBE, Robert E.	(609)589-2000	251
Short Hills	TALCOTT, Ann W.	(201)379-6721	1221
Somerville	MOYER, Holley M.	(201)725-1600	874
Tenafly	WECHTLER, Stephen R.	(201)568-8680	1315
Trenton	BREEDLOVE, Elizabeth A.	(609)292-9623	131
Turnersville	SZILASSY, Sandor	(609)589-7193	1218
Upper Montclair	PARR, Mary Y.	(201)746-0352	944
Vineland	GREENBLATT, Ruth	(609)794-4243	463
Voorhees	ROMISHER, Sivya S.	(609)772-1636	1053
West Long Branch	HEDLUND, Dennis M.	(201)229-2343	520
West New York	BRITTON, Jeffrey W.	(201)868-2029	137
Westfield	WILSTED, Thomas P.	(201)789-9147	1353

NEW MEXICO
Albuquerque	ELDREDGE, Jonathan D.	(505)277-0654	342
	HLAVA, Marjorie M.	(505)265-3591	544
	IVES, Peter B.	(505)277-9243	586
	LOVE, Erika	(505)277-2548	743
	PRUETT, Nancy J.		996
	REX, Heather	(505)277-7182	1024
	ROLLINS, Stephen J.	(505)277-5057	1051
	THORSON, Connie C.	(505)277-7201	1242
	WHITLOW, Cherrill M.	(505)266-1472	1333
Las Cruces	DAVIS, Hiram L.	(505)646-1509	279
	DRESP, Donald F.	(505)522-3627	319
	RICHARDS, James H.	(505)524-0281	1028
Roswell	KLOPFER, Jerome J.	(505)622-6250	662
	MCLAREN, M B.	(505)622-6250	813
Santa Fe	LOPEZ, Kathryn P.	(505)982-5683	741
Thoreau	SCHUBERT, Donald F.	(505)862-7465	1101
White Sands	BANICKI, Cynthia A.	(505)678-5820	54

NEW YORK
Albany	BRISKA, Boniface	(518)465-5631	137
	COX, Richard J.	(518)486-4820	253
	KNAPP, Sara D.	(518)442-3539	663
	MATTIE, Joseph J.	(518)474-4970	786
	MOORE, Rue I.	(518)445-5197	861
	NICHOLS-RANDALL, Barbara L.	(518)489-7649	902
	PAULSON, Peter J.	(518)489-8549	950
	WALKER, M G.	(518)436-1975	1296
APO New York	HAUSRATH, Donald C.		513
Armonk	DEVERS, Charlotte M.	(914)273-3887	297
Bellport	KLAUBER, Julie B.	(516)286-1600	658
	MULLER, Claudya B.	(516)286-1600	877
Bethpage	BURDEN, John	(516)575-3912	158
Binghamton	HILL, Malcolm K.	(607)723-8236	540
Briarcliff Manor	SOLIN, Myron	(914)762-3838	1166
Bronx	BUCKWALD, Joel	(212)543-5911	155
	CANNATA, Arleen	(212)295-5910	178
	CLAYBORNE, Jon L.	(212)588-8400	219
	DAVIS, Mary B.	(212)829-7770	280
	GAROOGIAN, Rhoda	(212)588-2266	420
	LOCASCIO, Aline M.	(212)588-8400	735
	PERSKY, Gail M.	(212)548-6007	961
	SOPELAK, Mary J.	(212)588-2266	1168
Brooklyn	DEFALCO, Joseph	(718)693-8377	287
	GENCO, Barbara A.	(718)499-8750	426
	HORNE, Dorice L.	(718)859-1830	560
	JOHNSON, Sheila A.	(718)780-7744	609
	KUPERMAN, Aaron W.	(718)854-8637	684
	ROMALIS, Carl		1052
	TUDIVER, Lillian	(718)789-7220	1262
	WOFSE, Joy G.	(718)788-5360	1359
Buffalo	BOBINSKI, George S.	(716)636-2412	108
	BREEN, M F.	(716)881-6264	131
	DONG, Alvin L.	(716)636-2101	311
	FARRELL, Michele A.	(716)876-8549	365
	NEWMAN, George C.	(716)886-8132	899
	WOLFE, Theresa L.	(716)632-4491	1361
Cherry Plain	GILCHER, Edwin	(518)658-2429	434
Cold Spring	FEICK, Christina L.	(914)265-2304	368
Cold Spring Harbor	FARAONE, Maria B.	(516)271-1771	363
Commack	SCHRIFT, Leonard B.	(516)543-5600	1100

SPEAKER (Free) (Cont'd)
NEW YORK (Cont'd)

Coram	EIDELMAN, Diane L.	(516)331-8662	340
Corning	HORNICK-LOCKARD,		
	Barbara A.	(607)962-9251	560
Cornwall	HANSON, Jan E.	(914)534-3104	498
Dansville	MINEMIER, Betty M.	(716)335-6258	845
Delanson	SOMERS, Betty J.	(518)864-5235	1166
Delmar	SHUMAN, Susan E.	(518)475-1202	1134
Dewitt	ELY, Donald P.	(315)446-0259	347
East Meadow	CANDE, Lorraine N.	(516)794-1202	178
	MCCARTNEY, Margaret M.	(516)489-8136	794
Elmhurst	SALEY, Stacey		1076
Elmsford	TRUDELL, Robert J.	(914)993-1608	1259
Fairport	WOLF, Catharine D.	(716)223-9284	1360
Flushing	COOPER, Marianne	(718)520-7194	243
	MCMORRAN, Charles E.	(718)358-4526	815
Freeport	MORIN, Wilfred L.	(516)368-6242	865
Garden City	FRIEDMAN, Arthur L.	(516)222-7406	403
Germantown	LINDSLEY, Barbara N.	(518)537-4114	730
Getzville	DENSMORE, Christopher	(716)688-2001	293
Glenmont	SACCO, Gail A.	(518)439-8549	1073
Glens Falls	SMITH, Frederick E.	(518)792-8214	1155
Governors Island	GODWIN, Mary J.	(212)809-4351	443
Greenvale	YUKAWA, Masako	(516)299-2142	1384
Hamilton	BERGEN, Daniel P.	(315)824-2381	85
Hicksville	HOLMES, Harvey L.	(516)935-4813	553
Highland	LAWRENCE, Thomas A.	(914)691-2734	705
Hornell	SMITH, Brian D.	(607)324-0841	1153
Horseheads	BROUSE, Ann G.	(607)562-8986	141
Huntington Station	MAUTER, George A.	(516)421-9291	787
Ithaca	COONS, William W.	(607)255-7959	242
	LIPPINCOTT, Joan K.	(607)255-7731	732
	PANZ, Richard	(607)273-4074	938
	STEWART, Linda G.	(607)255-7959	1192
Jackson Heights	SPYROS, Marsha L.	(718)424-7849	1177
Jamaica Estates	BARTENBACH, Wilhelm K.	(718)658-3878	60
Jamestown	LEE, Sylvia	(716)483-5415	711
Johnstown	BAILIE, Donna L.	(518)762-4633	47
Kenmore	RYBARCZYK, Barclay S.	(716)877-0605	1071
Kew Gardens	SALAZAR, Pamela R.	(718)441-2350	1076
Lackawanna	BEDNAR, Sheila	(716)822-0840	73
Lake Success	TRINKOFF, Elaine	(516)466-9148	1257
Latham	BRUNELLE, Bette S.	(518)783-1161	150
Liverpool	GOLDEN, Fay A.	(315)451-5890	445
Long Beach	WASSERMAN, Ricki F.		1308
Macedon	WEMETT, Lisa C.	(315)986-3949	1323
Manlius	NAGLE, Ann	(315)682-8160	886
Menands	GILSON, Robert	(518)463-4181	437
Mt Vernon	SEITZ, Robert J.	(914)699-6917	1113
Nassau	VANNORTWICK, Barbara L.	(518)766-4190	1276
Nesconset	GRUNDT, Leonard	(516)361-8987	475
New Hyde Park	LANG, Jovian P.	(516)352-1666	695
New Paltz	CONNORS, William E.	(914)257-2203	238
	NYQUIST, Corinne E.	(914)255-2209	913
New York	ALLEN, Robert R.	(212)337-6991	16
	ARKHURST, Joyce C.	(212)368-1788	31
	ARTHUR, Christine	(212)732-5964	35
	BEHRMANN, Christine A.	(212)568-6349	75
	BINGHAM, Kathleen S.		97
	BOCKMAN, Eugene J.	(212)566-5398	109
	BROWAR, Lisa M.	(212)930-0556	141
	BRUGNOLOTTI, Phyllis T.	(212)873-0677	150
	BUTLER, Tyrone G.	(212)566-5367	167
	CIOPPA, Lawrence	(212)677-5688	214
	CLINE, Herman H.	(212)777-4575	222
	COHEN, Frederick S.	(212)594-9880	228
	COHEN, Rochelle F.	(212)577-3333	229
	COOPER, Carol D.	(212)982-1302	242
	DARNOWSKI, Christina M.	(212)750-5749	275
	DEDONATO, Ree	(212)998-2510	286
	DENNIS, Anne R.	(212)645-4500	292
	DERRICKSON, Margaret	(212)620-4230	294
	EBER, Beryl E.	(212)621-0635	334
	EPPES, William D.	(212)675-2070	351
	FERGUSON, Russell	(212)219-1222	372
	FODY, Barbara A.	(212)713-3673	387
	FREIFELD, Roberta I.	(212)777-9271	401
	GINSBURG, Carol L.	(212)850-1440	438
	GRECH, Anthony P.	(212)382-6740	461

SPEAKER (Free) (Cont'd)
NEW YORK (Cont'd)
New York

	GRUENBERG, Michael L.	(212)732-5964	474
	HALL, Alix M.	(212)536-3598	486
	HIGGINBOTHAM, Barbra B.	(212)533-2173	537
	HUNTER, Karen A.	(212)916-1265	576
	KOCHOFF, Stephen T.	(212)254-4454	667
	KRANICH, Nancy C.	(212)998-2447	676
	KULLESEID, Eleanor R.	(212)666-6013	683
	LAMBE, Michael	(212)371-9400	690
	LIEBERFELD, Lawrence	(212)348-8499	726
	MACINTYRE, Ronald R.	(212)227-5599	755
	MARGALITH, Helen M.	(212)575-0190	770
	MARTIN, Richard	(212)760-7970	778
	MASSIS, Bruce E.	(212)595-2000	782
	MASYR, Caryl L.	(212)777-9271	783
	MCSWEENEY, Josephine	(212)254-6338	818
	MELKIN, Audrey D.	(212)850-6705	822
	MILLER, Ellen L.	(212)406-3186	837
	MILLER, Sarah J.		842
	MINTZ, Anne P.	(212)620-2499	847
	MOLZ, Redmond K.	(212)280-4787	854
	MOORE, Sonia	(212)755-5120	861
	MORRIS, Irving	(718)728-4078	866
	NATHAN, Frances E.	(212)876-0269	889
	O'GRADY, Jean P.	(212)370-8690	918
	PETTOLINA, Anthony M.	(212)790-2888	965
	POWELL, Timothy W.	(212)807-7083	989
	PRESCHEL, Barbara M.	(212)753-8458	991
	REID, Carolyn A.	(212)472-5919	1018
	RICHARDS, Daniel T.	(212)678-0908	1028
	RIVERA, Gregorio	(212)340-0949	1037
	SEGAL, Judith	(212)222-3699	1112
	SETTANNI, Joseph A.	(212)289-9059	1117
	SOMMER, Susan T.	(212)870-1648	1167
	STALKER, Dianne S.	(212)280-8484	1178
	TAYLOR, Patricia A.	(212)566-4285	1228
	THOMAS, Dorothy	(212)799-0970	1236
	TICE, Margaret E.		1244
	VINCENT-DAVISS, Diana	(212)598-2367	1284
	WALKER, William B.	(212)595-7335	1296
	WALSH, Mark L.	(212)996-4168	1300
	WILLNER, Channan P.	(212)870-1675	1348
Oneonta	BULSON, Christine	(607)431-2453	156
Palisades	WARD, Edith	(914)359-2081	1303
Pelham	FERRIBY, Peter G.	(914)738-3712	373
Pittsford	RICHARDSON, Constance H.	(716)385-6750	1029
Plattsburgh	RANSOM, Stanley A.	(518)563-5719	1007
Port Chester	LETTIERI, Robin M.	(914)939-6710	719
Port Washington	SCHREIBMAN, Fay C.	(516)767-0081	1099
Poughkeepsie	JEANNENEY, Mary L.	(914)452-7000	596
	SEEBER, Frances M.	(914)452-8122	1111
	WALSH, Robin S.	(914)462-7129	1300
Purchase	FREIDES, Thelma	(914)253-5096	401
Rhinebeck	MCCLELLAND, Bruce A.	(914)876-2230	796
Rochester	BAILEY, Joe A.	(716)724-0212	46
	BERKMAN, Robert I.	(716)461-3206	87
	CUSEO, Allan A.	(716)325-4264	267
	SIMMONS, Rebecca A.	(706)271-3361	1140
	STOSS, Frederick W.	(716)436-8719	1198
	SWANTON, Susan I.	(716)247-0142	1214
Rouses Point	CURRAN, George L.		266
Rye	GREENFIELD, Judith C.	(914)967-0480	464
St James	WIENER, Paul B.	(516)862-8723	1336
Schenectady	SHEVIAK, Jean K.	(518)370-6294	1129
Staten Island	MANNING, Jo A.	(718)981-0120	766
Syosset	CALVANO, Margaret	(516)921-1674	174
Syracuse	CASEY, Daniel W.	(315)468-0176	192
	DUNN, Mary B.	(315)476-0402	327
	FROEHLICH, Thomas J.	(315)425-9080	405
	MARCHAND, Donald A.	(315)423-2736	768
	STAM, Deirdre C.		1179
Troy	BLANDY, Susan G.	(518)274-2098	104
	EVELAND, Ruth A.	(518)274-2389	358
	GINSBURG, Joanne R.	(518)274-7071	438
Tuckahoe	ZOTTOLI, Danny A.	(914)961-6294	1390
Uniondale	GREEN, Joseph H.	(516)292-8920	462
Upper Nyack	POUNDSTONE, Sally H.	(914)358-9294	987
Vestal	HOLLEY, James L.	(607)754-4243	551

SPEAKER (Free) (Cont'd)

NEW YORK (Cont'd)

Wallkill	RUBIN, Ellen B.	(914)565-5620	1064
Wantagh	WESTERMANN, Mary L.	(516)679-8842	1327
White Plains	BAXTER, Paula A.	(914)946-3275	67
	TREFRY, Mary G.	(914)761-5478	1255
Williamsville	TAMMARO, James M.	(716)631-7049	1221

NORTH CAROLINA

Boone	HATHAWAY, Milton G.	(704)262-5113	512
Cary	BURCSU, James E.	(919)469-2731	158
Chapel Hill	BAILEY, Charles W.	(919)962-0600	46
	DEBRECZENY, Gillian M.	(919)929-5282	285
	HOLLEY, Edward G.		551
	MEEHAN-BLACK, Elizabeth C.		821
	PEACOCK, Helen M.		951
	PRILLAMAN, Susan M.	(919)962-3791	993
	SCHELL, Nancy S.		1091
Charlotte	MOORE, Patricia R.	(704)332-0092	860
	MYERS, Carol B.	(704)523-1260	884
	WALKER, Judith A.	(704)547-2559	1295
Cullowhee	LESUEUR, Joan K.	(704)456-3396	718
Durham	BALLARD, Robert M.	(919)489-6358	53
	BASEFSKY, Stuart M.	(919)684-2380	62
	GARTRELL, Ellen G.	(919)493-3747	420
	HEWITT, Joe A.	(919)489-9875	535
	SHEARER, Kenneth D.	(919)683-6485	1124
	STRAUSS, Diane	(919)286-7895	1201
	VARGHA, Rebecca B.	(919)544-6045	1278
Elkin	MACPHAIL, Jessica		758
Fayetteville	HANSEL, Patsy J.	(919)484-7096	497
	KRIEGER, Lee A.	(919)864-9349	678
Greensboro	JACQUES, Eunice L.	(919)292-7100	591
	O'CONNOR, Sandra L.	(919)273-1914	916
	YOUNG, Tommie M.	(909)621-0032	1383
Greenville	CHENG, Chao S.	(929)756-4543	206
	GLUCK, Myke H.	(919)757-6514	442
Jefferson	FRANKLIN, Robert M.	(919)246-4460	398
Kinston	JONES, John W.	(919)527-7066	613
Maiden	CARDENAS, Mary E.		180
Matthews	CANNON, Robert E.	(704)847-0394	179
Mebane	MINEIRO, Barbara E.	(919)578-4299	845
Montreat	FERM, Lois R.	(704)669-5550	373
Morganton	BUSH, Mary E.	(704)433-2303	165
Raleigh	BRADBURN, Frances B.	(919)878-4497	125
	ISACCO, Jeanne M.	(919)851-4703	584
	KING, Ebba K.	(419)737-2935	650
	PURYEAR, Pamela E.	(919)737-2836	998
	WILLIAMS, Gene J.	(919)828-5063	1343
Reidsville	GUNN, Shirley A.	(919)342-0951	477
Research Triangle Pk	MENDELL, Stefanie	(919)248-1842	823
	TUTTLE, Walter A.	(919)549-0661	1266
Riegelwood	KERESEY, Gayle	(919)669-2934	643
Robbinsville	LARSON, Josephine	(704)479-8192	699
Salisbury	ALDRICH, Willie L.	(704)636-1158	11
Sanford	MCGINN, Howard F.	(919)776-2335	806
Washington	TIMOUR, John A.	(919)975-3355	1246
Winston-Salem	ROBERTS, William H.	(919)727-2556	1041
	STEELE, Tom M.	(919)761-5440	1184

NORTH DAKOTA

Bismarck	HILDEBRANT, Darrel D.	(701)222-6410	539
	NEWBORG, Gerald G.	(701)224-2668	898
Fargo	BIRDSALL, Douglas G.	(701)237-8878	98
	SCHULTZ, Gary J.	(701)241-1493	1102

OHIO

Akron	BERRINGER, Virginia M.	(216)375-6260	90
	NOWAK, Leslie A.	(216)836-1081	911
	REED, Elizabeth M.	(216)724-3093	1015
Albany	CONLIFFE, Bobbi L.	(614)698-3336	236
Bay Village	BACON, Agnes K.		44
	LORANTH, Alice N.	(216)871-9014	741
Bellaire	KNIESNER, John T.	(614)676-4620	664
Bowling Green	BURLINGAME, Dwight F.	(419)372-2708	161
	ENDRES, Maureen D.	(419)352-9213	348
	ZAPOROZHETZ, Laurene E.	(419)354-2101	1386
Chesterland	CORBUS, Lawrence J.	(216)286-8941	245

SPEAKER (Free) (Cont'd)

OHIO (Cont'd)

Chillicothe	PLANTON, Stanley P.	(614)775-9500	977
Cincinnati	FROMMEYER, L R.	(513)475-3627	405
	GILLILAND, Anne J.	(513)475-6459	436
	GROSVENOR, Philip G.	(513)683-0315	473
	HUGE, Sharon A.	(513)369-6940	571
	KATZ, Lawrence M.	(516)761-0203	630
	LONG, Clare S.	(513)721-8565	739
	SCHUTZ, Robert S.	(513)948-7518	1103
	SIMMONS, Edlyn S.	(513)948-7829	1139
	SMITH, Maureen M.	(513)369-6917	1158
	THOMPSON, Ann M.	(513)474-1443	1238
	WELKER, Kathy J.	(513)684-2678	1321
	WILSON, Lucy	(513)745-4313	1351
Cleveland	CHESHIER, Robert G.	(216)368-3427	206
	JOHNSON, Stephen C.	(216)429-8245	609
	ORR, Cynthia	(216)449-2049	926
	PASQUAL, Patricia E.	(216)861-1933	946
	ROBSON, Timothy D.	(216)696-4390	1045
Columbus	ALLEN, Cameron	(614)237-1516	14
	BOOMGAARDEN, Wesley L.	(614)447-0524	115
	DAVIS, Linda M.	(614)294-5429	280
	FU, Paul S.	(614)466-2044	407
	HAMILTON, Marsha J.	(614)292-6314	492
	HOLOCH, S A.	(614)292-6691	553
	HUNE, Mary G.	(614)224-3168	574
	KIE, Kathleen M.	(614)481-7640	646
	KNOBLAUCH, Carol J.	(614)299-4020	665
	MCDOWELL, Judith H.	(614)771-0273	804
	OLSZEWSKI, Lawrence J.		923
	PHILIP, John J.	(614)462-7061	967
	WANG, Anna M.	(614)294-8035	1302
Cuyahoga Falls	BERRY, Diana M.	(216)929-1948	90
	OSTERFIELD, George T.	(216)929-9470	928
Dayton	COYLE, Christopher B.	(513)865-6882	253
	MARSHALL, Mary E.	(513)461-1548	774
	NOLAN, Patrick B.	(513)274-3424	907
	PEAKE, Sharon K.	(513)865-6958	952
	TAYLOR, Orphus R.	(513)228-4198	1228
	WYLLIE, Stanley C.	(513)252-8496	1375
Delaware	GILBERT, Donna J.	(614)369-7705	433
Dublin	HAYNES, Kathleen J.	(614)764-6000	516
	HURLEY, Geraldine C.	(614)764-6108	577
	MOORE, Brian P.	(614)761-7229	858
	PRABHA, Chandra G.	(614)764-6086	989
East Cleveland	KEENON, Una H.	(216)932-5090	634
Findlay	HARDESTY, Vicki H.	(419)422-6121	499
	JANKY, Donna L.	(419)422-3211	593
	LUST, Jeanette M.	(419)424-5739	749
Grafton	DIAL, David E.	(216)926-3317	299
Highland Heights	JENKINS, Glen P.	(216)442-1475	597
Kent	BIRK, Nancy	(216)672-2270	98
Lancaster	MCCAULEY, Hannah V.	(614)654-6711	795
Lima	MCDANIEL, Deanna J.	(419)991-6065	801
Middlefield	GUMPPER, Mary F.	(216)632-1961	477
North Ridgeville	FACINELLI, Jaclyn R.	(216)327-7079	360
Oberlin	RICKER, Alison S.	(216)775-8310	1031
Parma	OBLOY, Elaine C.	(216)885-5362	914
Shaker Heights	RODDA, Donna S.	(216)283-1064	1047
Springfield	ARK, Connie E.	(513)324-8470	31
	MONTAG, John	(513)327-7019	855
Toledo	BAKER, Paula J.	(419)472-0204	49
	CARY, Mary K.	(419)537-2833	191
	HANNAFORD, Claudia L.	(419)536-7539	496
	SINK, Thomas R.	(419)259-1327	1143
Troy	CRAM, Mary E.	(513)334-5067	255
Uniontown	MCCHESNEY, Kathryn M.	(216)672-2782	795
Upper Arlington	BROWN, Rowland C.	(614)488-6329	147
Warren	TYSON, Edith S.	(216)393-3098	1267

OKLAHOMA

Ada	HUESMANN, James L.	(405)332-7632	570
Ardmore	KIMBLE, Valerie F.	(405)226-3980	649
	ROBINSON, Joel M.	(405)223-3164	1044
Norman	LOWELL, Howard P.	(405)366-7719	744
	MCKNIGHT, Michelynn	(405)360-2080	812

Oklahoma City	MELTON, Howard E.		823
	NASH, Helen B.	(405)525-7504	888
	PASCHAL, John M.	(405)751-6400	945
	VESELY, Marilyn L.		1283
Stillwater	JOHNSON, Edward R.	(405)372-2637	604
	ROUSE, Charlie L.	(405)372-4651	1061
	ROUSE, Roscoe	(405)377-1651	1061
Tulsa	BUTHOD, J C.	(918)592-7894	166
	SMITH, Peggy C.	(918)592-6000	1159

OREGON

Ashland	OTNES, Harold M.	(503)482-6445	930
	PURCELL, V N.	(503)482-2629	998
Beaverton	JACOBS, Patt	(503)646-6959	590
Corvallis	GEORGE, Melvin R.	(503)754-3411	427
Eugene	FEUERHELM, Jill A.	(503)345-6498	374
	HILDEBRAND, Carol I.	(503)344-4267	538
	STIRLING, Isabel A.	(503)686-3075	1195
	SUNDT, Christine L.	(503)686-3052	1210
	WAND, Patricia A.	(503)686-3056	1302
Portland	BURSON, Lorraine E.	(508)246-4097	163
	LONG, Sarah A.	(503)221-7731	740
	SHAVER, Donna B.	(503)226-8695	1123
	SIMON, Dale	(503)227-7617	1140
	THENELL, Janice C.	(503)221-7726	1234
Roseburg	COOK, Sybilla A.	(503)673-0504	240

PENNSYLVANIA

Abington	POSEL, Nancy R.	(215)885-5181	985
Allentown	MOSES, Lynn M.		871
	WAGNER, Darla L.	(215)264-8203	1291
Allison Park	SMITH, Mary M.	(412)487-2883	1158
Altoona	SHERIDAN, Margaret G.	(814)942-2565	1127
Bala Cynwyd	CORVESE, Lisa A.	(215)668-4930	248
Bensalem	CHU, John S.	(215)639-0768	212
Boyertown	EMERICK, John L.	(215)369-7422	347
Bryn Mawr	BILLS, Linda G.	(215)645-5294	96
	HILL, Judith L.	(215)526-1305	540
California	CARUSO, Nicholas C.	(412)938-9166	190
	NOLF, Marsha L.	(412)938-4048	908
Carlisle	WIWEL, Pamela S.		1359
Chambersburg	EZELL, Johanna V.	(717)264-2269	360
	MARLOW, Kathryn E.	(717)264-2382	772
Clarion	HORN, Roger G.	(814)226-2490	559
	PERSON, Ruth J.	(814)226-5341	961
Clifton Heights	WHITMAN, Mary L.		1333
Coatesville	BURTON, Mary L.	(215)383-0245	164
East Stroudsburg	SUMMERS, George V.	(717)424-3151	1209
Easton	SHINER, Sharon L.	(215)258-8390	1130
Elizabethtown	BARD, Nelson P.	(717)367-1151	56
Elkins Park	NEMEYER, Carol A.		895
Emmaus	STEPHANOFF, Kathryn	(215)797-8838	1187
Friedens	KLINE, Eve P.	(814)443-2903	661
Glen Rock	LIEBERMAN, Ronald	(717)235-2134	726
Greensburg	SCHEEREN, William O.	(412)834-9000	1090
Harleysville	LINN, Mott R.	(215)464-4500	731
Harrisburg	FOUST, Judith M.	(717)787-8007	393
	LINGLE, Virginia A.	(717)652-1950	730
	MALLINGER, Stephen M.	(717)783-5737	763
	STAYER, Jonathan R.	(717)787-2701	1183
Hatfield	RITTER, Ralph E.	(215)368-5000	1037
Haverford	CORRIGAN, John T.	(215)896-7458	247
	CORRINGAN, John T.	(215)649-5251	247
Hershey	WOODRUFF, William M.	(717)534-5106	1366
Huntingdon	SWIGART, William E.	(814)643-3000	1216
Indiana	ELLIKER, Calvin	(412)357-2892	343
Jeannette	PAWLIK, Deborah A.		951
Jenkintown	BARTZ, Alice P.	(215)887-4338	62
Lansdowne	BATISTA, Emily J.	(215)626-3567	64
Library	SALVAYON, Connie	(412)833-5585	1078
McKeesport	HORVATH, Robert T.	(412)672-0625	561
Mechanicsburg	TENOR, Randell B.	(717)763-1804	1231
Media	COURTRIGHT, Harry R.	(215)891-5190	252
Middletown	RAMBLER, Linda K.	(412)349-4621	1005
New Hope	CROWN, Faith W.	(215)794-8932	262

Philadelphia	AXAM, John A.	(215)549-6485	42
	AZZOLINA, David S.	(215)898-8118	43
	BUTLER, Evelyn		166
	COOPER, Linda	(215)625-4719	243
	CRAWFORD, Miriam I.	(215)877-1250	257
	DUCLOW, Geradline		322
	EDWARDS, David M.	(215)386-0100	337
	FISHER, Douglas A.	(215)587-4915	380
	FUSELER-MCDOWELL, Elizabeth A.	(215)423-9294	410
	GRACE, William M.	(215)925-8090	455
	GREEN, Rose B.	(215)828-7029	462
	GRIFFITH, Belver C.	(215)895-2474	469
	GROSSMAN, Robert M.	(215)893-1954	473
	HALLER, Douglas M.	(215)898-8304	489
	HINTON, Frances	(215)843-8706	543
	KENNEDY, H E.	(215)587-4800	641
	LYTLE, Richard H.	(215)895-2475	753
	MAYOVER, Steven J.	(215)686-5400	791
	MEREDITH, Phyllis C.	(609)757-4640	825
	MICIKAS, Lynda L.	(215)637-7700	832
	MYERS, Charles J.	(215)898-7267	884
	MYERS, James N.	(215)787-8231	884
	NAISMITH, Patricia A.	(215)235-0256	887
	PANCOE, Deborra S.	(215)561-5900	937
	POST, Jeremiah B.	(215)748-2701	986
	RIDGEWAY, Patricia M.	(215)898-7555	1032
	ROEDELL, Ray F.	(215)739-7739	1048
	WILLMANN, Donna S.		1348
	WRIGHT, Irene R.	(215)923-1726	1371
	YOUNG, James B.	(215)898-6715	1382
	ZIPF, Elizabeth M.	(215)587-4815	1389
Phoenixville	SAUER, James L.	(215)933-2236	1084
Pittsburgh	BROADBENT, H E.	(412)441-6409	138
	FITZGERALD, Patricia A.	(412)268-2428	382
	FORD, Sylverna V.	(412)268-2446	390
	LEIBOWITZ, Faye R.	(412)421-7974	713
	PISCIOTTA, Henry A.	(412)268-2451	976
	SILVERMAN, Marc B.	(412)648-1376	1138
	SOUDER, Edith I.	(412)343-9325	1169
	STERLING, Alida B.	(412)323-1430	1189
	WESSEL, Charles B.	(412)731-8800	1325
Reading	HANNAFORD, William E.	(802)468-5611	496
	SMALL, Sally S.	(215)320-4823	1151
Rosemont	WELSH, Barbara W.	(215)527-3976	1323
Sanatoga	NIPPERT, Carolyn C.	(215)323-4829	904
Scranton	MILLER, Mary E.	(717)348-6205	840
Secane	CASINI, Barbara P.	(215)543-4309	192
Shenandoah	USES, Ann K.	(717)462-0076	1270
Shippensburg	SHONTZ, Marilyn L.	(717)532-1472	1132
Springfield	SCULLIN, Frank E.		1109
State College	JAMISON, Carolyn C.	(814)234-4512	593
	PIERCE, Miriam D.	(814)237-7004	971
Trafford	FETKOVICH, Malinda M.	(412)373-0799	374
University Park	CHAMBERLAIN, Carol E.	(814)865-1858	197
	FORTH, Stuart	(814)865-0401	391
	KALIN, Sarah G.	(814)863-2898	623
	NEAL, James G.	(814)865-0401	890
Upland	BARON, Herman	(215)499-7415	58
Villanova	GRIFFIN, Mary A.	(215)645-4290	468
Wayne	CRAUMER, Patricia A.	(215)687-6777	255
	DRIEHAUS, Rosemary H.		320
Waynesboro	POSEY, Sussann F.	(717)762-3047	985
Wyomissing	MORGANTI, Deena J.	(215)320-4849	864
Youngwood	SCHEEREN, Judith A.	(412)925-4126	1090

PUERTO RICO

Guaynabo	LEON, Carmencita H.	(809)792-7873	716
	MOMBILLE, Pedro	(809)783-8622	854
San Sebastian	JARAMILLO, Juana S.	(809)896-1389	594
Santurce	RIVERA-ALVAREZ, Miguel A.	(809)728-4191	1037

SPEAKER (Free) (Cont'd)
RHODE ISLAND

Barrington	BUNDY, Annalee M.	(401)245-2232	157
Chepachet	DESJARLAIS-LUETH, Christine	(401)568-8614	295
Kingston	DEVIN, Robin B.	(401)792-2662	297
	ETCHINGHAM, John B.	(401)792-4637	355
	TRYON, Jonathan S.	(401)792-2878	1259
	YOUNG, Arthur P.	(401)792-2666	1381
Providence	LYNDEN, Frederick C.	(401)863-2946	752
	MARSH, Corrie V.	(401)863-2954	773
	REEVES, Joan R.	(401)272-7745	1016
	SILVA, Phyllis C.	(401)277-2353	1138
	SVENGALIS, Kendall F.	(401)274-3196	1212
	TAYLOR, Merrily E.	(401)863-2162	1227
	WILSON, Barbara L.	(401)277-2726	1350
Woonsocket	IMONDI, Lenore R.	(401)762-5165	582

SOUTH CAROLINA

Cayce	FREEMAN, Larry S.	(803)794-5370	401
Charleston	ROSS, Gary M.	(803)792-5530	1058
	STRAUCH, Katina P.	(803)723-3536	1200
Clemson	DIXON, Linda A.		306
	MEYER, Richard W.	(803)656-3026	830
Columbia	BARRON, Daniel D.	(803)777-4825	60
	CROSS, Joseph R.	(803)777-3365	260
	EASTMAN, Caroline M.	(803)777-8103	333
	HELSLEY, Alexia J.	(803)781-8477	525
	KRONENFELD, Michael R.	(803)734-4769	679
	LUCAS, Linda S.	(803)777-3858	746
	PEAKE, Luise E.	(803)777-3214	952
	TOOMBS, Kenneth E.	(803)776-0431	1251
	TYLER, Carolyn S.	(803)256-8692	1266
	WILLIAMS, Robert V.	(803)799-2324	1346
Denmark	BOOK, Imogene I.	(803)793-3660	115
Gaffney	EDEN, David E.	(803)489-4381	336
Greenwood	HILL, Thomas W.	(803)227-4851	541
Liberty	DUSENBERRY, Mary D.	(803)843-8225	329
McCormick	TOWNSEND, Catherine M.	(803)465-3185	1253
North Myrtle Beach	BELL, David B.	(803)272-1624	76
Orangeburg	SMALLS, Mary L.	(803)536-8852	1151
Sumter	COOK, Galen B.	(803)469-9180	240

SOUTH DAKOTA

| Rapid City | SCHWARTZ, James M. | (605)394-1246 | 1104 |
| Sioux Falls | DERTIEN, James L. | (605)339-7115 | 294 |

TENNESSEE

Chattanooga	REARDON, Elizabeth M.		1013
Clarksville	THWEATT, John H.	(615)647-0954	1243
Clinton	GREESON, Judy G.	(615)457-0931	465
	SPATH, Charles E.	(615)457-8616	1171
Columbia	WAGGENER, Jean B.	(615)388-9282	1291
Kingsport	TILSON, Koleta B.	(615)245-6572	1245
Knoxville	BENGTSON, Betty G.	(615)974-6640	80
	LEACH, Sandra S.	(615)579-1315	706
	PRENTICE, Ann E.	(615)974-2148	990
	RADER, Joe C.	(615)523-6937	1002
Memphis	CARD, Judy	(901)725-8851	180
	DRESCHER, Judith A.	(901)276-0104	319
	LINDENFELD, Joseph F.	(901)528-6743	729
	MADER, Sharon B.	(901)454-2208	759
	POURCIAU, Lester J.	(901)454-2201	987
	RUDOLPH, N J.	(901)454-2208	1066
	SMITH, Robert F.	(901)725-8872	1160
Murfreesboro	HUNTER, Joy W.	(615)893-1360	576
	MARSHALL, John D.	(615)893-2091	774
	YOUREE, Beverly B.	(615)896-4911	1384
Nashville	BRANSFORD, John S.	(615)292-1180	129
	CAMERON, Sam A.	(615)329-1163	175
	FANCHER, Evelyn P.	(615)255-8033	363
	GLEAVES, Edwin S.	(615)741-3666	441
	HARWELL, Sara J.	(615)322-2807	509
	HEARNE, Mary G.	(615)383-8989	518
	HODGES, Terence M.	(615)322-2299	546
	RICHARDS, Timothy F.	(615)385-1858	1028
	STEPHENS, Alonzo T.		1187
	SUMNERS, Bill F.	(615)251-2126	1209
	WATTS, Adalyn	(615)321-1332	1310
	WILBURN, Clouse R.	(615)322-8050	1338

SPEAKER (Free) (Cont'd)
TENNESSEE (Cont'd)

Norris	DYER, Barbara M.	(615)494-9555	330
Oak Ridge	CARROLL, Bonnie C.	(615)482-3230	187
	EKKEBUS, Allen E.	(615)574-5485	341
	NORTON, Nancy P.	(615)574-7159	910
	PFUDERER, Helen A.	(615)574-5350	966
	ROBBINS, Gordon D.	(615)574-7178	1038
	SNYDER, Cathrine E.	(615)483-1228	1164
Sewanee	WATSON, Tom G.	(615)598-1213	1310

TEXAS

Amarillo	RUDDY, Mary K.	(806)353-1534	1065
Arlington	KERBY, Ramona A.	(817)478-9829	643
	LEATHERMAN, Donald G.	(817)459-6910	707
	LOWRY, Charles B.	(817)273-3391	745
	STOAN, Stephen K.	(817)273-3391	1195
	YOUNKIN, C G.	(817)429-2674	1383
Austin	BRIDGE, Frank R.	(512)328-6006	135
	CARTER, Janet K.	(512)463-5463	189
	GAMEZ, Juanita L.	(512)837-6247	416
	GOULD, Karen K.	(512)453-2602	454
	HARMON, Jacqueline B.	(512)343-0978	502
	HELBURN, Judith D.	(512)454-7229	523
	HISLE, W L.	(512)495-7148	544
	KAHLER, June	(512)463-9660	621
	MIKSA, Francis L.	(572)346-6769	834
	SKINNER, Vicki F.	(512)892-3997	1146
	SMITH, Dorothy B.	(512)453-1384	1154
	SMITH, Nancy M.	(512)482-5137	1158
	WYLLYS, Ronald E.	(512)471-3821	1375
Beaumont	COKINOS, Elizabeth G.	(409)866-6043	229
Bellaire	HOLAB-ABELMAN, Robin S.		550
Brownsville	VAUGHN, Frances A.	(512)544-8220	1280
Buda	TISSING, Robert W.	(512)295-4834	1247
Cedar Park	MITTAG, Erika	(512)259-0569	850
College Station	COOK, C C.	(409)845-3731	239
	HOADLEY, Irene B.	(409)845-8111	545
	ST. CLAIR, Gloriana S.	(409)696-8982	1075
	SCHULTZ, Charles R.	(409)845-1815	1101
Conroe	BALDWIN, Joe M.	(409)756-4484	51
Corpus Christi	HOUSTON, Barbara B.	(512)889-8517	563
Dallas	ALLEN, Sarabeth	(214)670-1400	16
	ARMES, Patti	(214)341-6675	32
	BROWN, Muriel W.	(214)348-7861	146
	CAMPBELL, Shirley A.	(214)330-0027	177
	COMPTON, Erlinda R.	(214)506-3601	235
	CRABB, Elizabeth A.	(214)233-4382	254
	CROW, Rebecca N.	(214)749-4285	261
	GALBRAITH, Paula L.	(214)680-3782	413
	HOWINGTON, Tad C.	(214)337-7779	566
	KACENA, Carolyn	(214)361-9254	621
	MASON, Florence M.	(214)358-5755	781
	TEMPLETON, Virginia E.	(214)754-4875	1231
	WATERS, Richard L.	(214)826-6981	1308
Denton	FERSTL, Kenneth L.	(817)383-3775	374
	GALLOWAY, Margaret E.	(817)565-3024	415
	KHADER, Majed J.		645
	VONDRAN, Raymond F.	(817)565-2445	1288
Dimmitt	AUTRY, Brick	(806)647-3666	41
Edinburg	GAUSE, George R.	(512)383-0811	423
El Paso	BROWN, Susan W.	(915)747-5678	147
Fort Worth	DIXON, Catherine A.	(817)870-7708	306
	MUELLER, Peggy	(817)870-7701	875
	SCHMIDT HACKER, Margaret H.	(817)334-5525	1096
	WOOD, Richard C.	(517)927-5389	1365
	WYGANT, Alice C.		1375
Galveston	LARSON, Jeanette C.	(214)240-0661	699
Groves	MCCONNELL, Karen S.	(409)963-1481	797
Houston	ADAMS, Elaine P.	(713)785-8703	4
	ALESSI, Dana L.	(713)669-0419	11
	CAMP, Joyce H.	(713)789-9810	175
	CEBRUN, Mary J.	(713)965-4045	196
	CORBIN, John	(713)749-4241	245
	ELLISOR, F L.	(713)782-7258	345
	GOURLAY, Una M.	(713)528-3553	454
	LANDINGHAM, Alpha M.	(713)522-9091	692
	LYDEN, Edward W.	(713)777-8212	750
	MULLINS, James R.	(713)522-8131	878

SPEAKER (Free) (Cont'd)
TEXAS (Cont'd)
Houston

	REIFEL, Louie E.		1019
	SINCLAIR, Rose P.	(713)452-5555	1143
	WEGMANN, Pamela A.	(713)655-3400	1316
	WELCH, C B.	(713)749-4245	1321
Irving	BRAGG, William J.	(214)556-1234	127
Laredo	MULLER, Mary M.	(905)211-0042	877
Lewisville	MARMION, Daniel K.	(214)436-5125	772
Lubbock	CARGILL, Jennifer S.	(806)792-2349	181
	SARGENT, Charles W.	(806)792-0754	1082
	WEBB, Gisela M.	(806)794-7359	1313
McAllen	MITTELSTAEDT, Gerard E.	(512)686-3029	850
	MYCUE, David J.		884
Mesquite	GIBSON, Timothy T.	(214)289-2479	432
Miles	LACY, Yvonne M.	(915)468-2151	687
Palestine	SELLERS, Wayne C.	(214)729-4829	1114
Richardson	KRUSE, Luanne M.	(214)680-9677	681
San Antonio	FORD, Barbara J.	(512)736-8121	389
	HURT, Nancy S.	(512)225-5500	578
	JOSEPH, Margaret A.	(512)435-9568	617
	KRONICK, David A.	(512)344-5796	679
	LEATHERBURY, Maurice C.	(512)829-7033	707
	WERKING, Richard H.	(512)736-8161	1324
Seguin	KOOPMAN, Frances A.	(512)379-4161	671
Sugar Land	JOHNSON, Pat M.	(713)980-5350	608
Texas City	MONCLA, Carolyn S.	(409)948-3111	854
The Woodlands	FRAMEL, Phyllis M.	(713)367-9522	395
	PEYTON, Janice L.	(713)292-4441	966
Waco	GEARY, Gregg S.		424
	RICHARDS, James H.	(817)756-0602	1028
Wichita Falls	HARVILL, Melba S.	(817)692-6611	509

UTAH
American Fork	TOMLIN, Celia K.	(801)756-4681	1250
Logan	PIETTE, Mary I.	(801)753-6878	972
Pleasant Grove	STECKER, Alexander T.	(801)785-2761	1183
Provo	SMITH, Nathan M.	(801)378-2977	1159
	WILSON, D K.	(801)375-2770	1350
Salt Lake City	BUTTARS, Gerald A.	(801)466-6363	167
	DAY, J D.	(801)363-5733	282
	GIACOMA, Pete J.	(801)364-2624	430
	HANSON, Roger K.	(801)581-8558	498
	HEFNER, Loretta L.	(801)485-2005	520
	HOLLEY, Robert P.	(801)581-7741	551
	JOHNSON, Jeffery O.	(801)533-5250	606
	KRANZ, Ralph	(801)581-7995	676
	MCMURRIN, Jean A.	(801)322-1586	815
	OWEN, Amy	(801)466-5888	931

VERMONT
Barre	GRIFFIN, Marie E.	(802)479-2810	468
Brattleboro	HAY, Linda A.	(802)254-5595	515
Rutland	SHERMAN, Jacob R.	(802)773-1860	1128

VIRGINIA
Alexandria	CALMES, Alan R.	(202)523-5496	174
	CASSEDY, James G.	(703)768-2070	193
	DRUMMOND, Louis E.		321
	KAISER, Donald W.	(703)836-0225	622
	KUHL, Danuta	(703)461-0234	682
	ROTHSCHILD, M C.	(202)274-7206	1060
	RUSH, James S.	(703)705-3557	1068
Arlington	GREEN, Randall N.	(703)243-5631	462
	HARRIS, Linda S.	(703)521-2541	505
	HENDERSON, Susanne	(703)931-8433	527
	HIRONS, Jean L.	(703)243-9437	543
	MEREK, Charles J.	(703)920-5050	825
	STEVENS, Frank A.		1190
	WELLS, Christine		1322
	YODER, William M.	(703)527-7225	1380
Blacksburg	EASTMAN, Ann H.	(703)951-4770	333
	KENNEY, Donald J.	(703)961-5069	641
Charlottesville	JORDAN, Ervin L.	(804)924-4975	616
	WHITE, William		1332
Fairfax	GOODWIN, Jane G.	(703)246-5847	450
	SCOTT, Mona L.	(703)378-8027	1107

SPEAKER (Free) (Cont'd)
VIRGINIA (Cont'd)
Falls Church	BROWN, Barbara B.	(703)820-7450	142
	BUCK, Dayna E.	(703)847-0271	153
	CHUNG, Catherine A.	(703)534-3114	213
	HELGERSON, Linda W.	(703)237-0682	524
	PARSONS, John W.	(703)671-7756	945
	REID, Judith P.	(703)379-0739	1018
Fort Monroe	BYRN, James H.	(804)727-4491	169
Fredericksburg	VANDERBERG, E S.	(703)371-3311	1273
Great Falls	CYLKE, Frank K.	(703)759-2031	268
Hampton	BIGELOW, Therese G.	(804)727-6234	95
Harrisonburg	BLANKENBURG, Judith B.	(703)568-6792	104
	GILL, Gerald L.	(703)568-6898	435
	RAMSEY, Inez L.	(703)568-6791	1006
Langley AFB	VERNON, Christie D.	(804)766-1468	1283
Lexington	HAYS, Peggy W.	(703)463-8643	517
Manassas	KILLEEN, Erlene B.	(703)369-7193	648
	MURPHY, Richard W.	(703)361-8211	881
Martinsville	PEARL, Patricia D.	(703)632-9096	952
McLean	GATTONE, Dean R.	(703)790-5694	422
	MORISSEAU, Anne L.	(703)821-9171	865
	TRAVIS, Irene L.		1254
	WANG, Chi	(703)893-3016	1302
	WINIARSKI, Marilee E.	(800)421-7229	1355
Melian	BELTON, Jennifer H.		78
Norfolk	GRIFFLER, Carl W.	(804)441-5332	469
	LEGO, Jane B.	(804)461-4389	712
	MAYER-HENNELLY, Mary B.	(804)441-2733	789
	MILLER, Ellen L.	(804)440-3283	837
	TRASK, Benjamin H.		1254
North Springfield	AINES, Andrew A.	(703)569-4872	8
Reston	GENNARO, John L.	(703)689-5616	427
	WILTSHIRE, Denise A.	(703)391-0505	1354
Richmond	CARNEY, Marillyn L.	(804)254-2447	183
	DEBARDELEBEN, Marian Z.	(804)274-2876	284
	DUKE, John K.	(804)257-6539	324
	GREGORY, Carla L.	(804)281-2804	466
	KIMBALL, Gregg D.	(804)649-0711	649
	REAM, Daniel L.	(804)257-6545	1012
	WHALEY, John H.	(804)257-1108	1328
Springfield	CASWELL, Mary C.	(703)642-0340	194
	FOURNIER, Susan K.	(703)569-9468	393
	SCHAAF, Robert W.	(703)451-7916	1088
Vienna	COCHRANE, Maryjane S.	(703)938-2037	226
Virginia Beach	WISECARVER, Betty A.	(804)463-6666	1357
Waynesboro	RUFE, Charles P.	(703)949-6173	1066
Williamsburg	BERG, Susan	(804)229-8799	85
Wise	CHISHOLM, Clarence E.	(703)328-2431	209
Wytheville	PRESGRAVES, Jim	(703)686-5813	991

WASHINGTON
Bellevue	MUTSCHLER, Herbert F.	(206)746-3952	883
Bellingham	GROVER, Iva S.	(206)671-3643	474
Cheney	BENDER, Betty W.	(509)838-4283	79
	MUTSCHLER, Charles V.	(509)235-2706	883
	TRACY, Joan I.	(509)359-7892	1253
Clallam Bay	PEARSON, Barbara F.	(206)963-2369	952
East Wenatchee	BELT, Jane		78
Edmonds	TURNER, Kathleen G.	(206)771-1933	1264
Ellensburg	SCHNEIDER, Frank A.	(509)963-1901	1097
Everett	GRINSTEAD, Beth K.	(206)258-1951	471
Kingston	HENINGER, Irene C.	(206)297-3002	528
Kirkland	ROBERTSON, Ann	(206)821-0506	1041
Nowport	HEMINGTON, David G.	(509)447-2636	1022
Olympia	KREIMEYER, Vicki R.	(206)753-2916	677
	MOORE, Mary Y.	(206)866-8272	860
	ZUSSY, Nancy L.	(206)786-9647	1391
Pullman	KEMP, Barbara E.	(509)334-5809	639
	KOPP, James J.	(509)335-9133	671
	PASTINE, Maureen D.	(509)334-0255	946
Seattle	BURSON, Scott F.	(206)543-6794	163
	EDWARDS, Steven M.	(206)526-6501	338
	FASSETT, William E.	(206)545-2272	366
	FEATHERS, John E.	(206)282-3804	367
	HAZELTON, Penelope A.	(206)543-4089	517
	HENSLEY, Randall B.	(206)543-2060	529
	HILDEBRANDT, Darlene M.	(206)543-5818	538
	MAIOLI, Jerry R.	(206)459-6518	762
	MEYER, Laura M.	(206)522-2162	830

SPEAKER (Free) (Cont'd)
WASHINGTON (Cont'd)
Seattle

SCHUELLER, Janette H.	(206)543-8262	1101
THORSEN, Jeanne M.	(206)684-6606	1242
TOLLIVER, Barbara J.	(206)684-6615	1248
TURNER, Tamara A.	(216)325-9481	1265
WEAVER, Carolyn G.	(206)543-5530	1312

Spokane

LANE, Steven P.	(509)838-4728	694
TYSON, Christy	(509)624-9744	1267

Tacoma

BECKER, Roger V.	(206)591-2703	72
HAGAN, Dalia L.	(206)565-9669	482
MENANTEAUX, A R.	(206)591-2973	823
MENDELSON, Martin	(206)383-5855	823
SELING, Kathy A.	(206)756-5571	1113
THORNDILL, Christine M.	(206)752-9623	1242

Vancouver

CONABLE, Gordon M.	(206)694-0604	235
CONABLE, Irene H.	(206)694-0604	235

WEST VIRGINIA

Charleston	MOELLENDICK, M J.	(304)348-2691	851
Glenville	FAULKNER, Ronnie W.	(304)462-7361	366
Huntington	STARKEY, Bonnie F.	(303)523-3109	1182
Philippi	SIZEMORE, William C.		1145
Salem	LANGER, Frank A.	(304)782-1007	695

WISCONSIN

Appleton	DAWSON, Terry P.	(414)735-6168	282
	NADZIEJKA, David E.	(414)731-8904	886
Beloit	THOM, Pat A.	(608)365-3311	1235
Cedarburg	PITEL, Vonna J.	(414)377-6030	976
Eau Claire	MARQUARDT, Steve R.	(715)834-5390	772
Franklin	BELLIN, Bernard E.	(414)461-1484	78
Janesville	KRUEGER, Karen J.	(608)755-2800	680
La Crosse	CIMPL, Kathleen A.	(608)785-0530	214
Madison	CARR, Jo A.	(608)273-1620	185
	HERMAN, Gertrude B.		531
	HOPKINS, Dianne M.	(608)263-2900	557
	LAESSIG, Joan M.	(608)238-3705	687
Middleton	NIX, Larry T.	(608)836-5616	905
Milton	HAY, Mary K.	(608)868-7260	515
Milwaukee	BANNEN, Carol A.	(414)271-1190	54
	BLUE, Richard I.	(414)963-4707	107
	BOULANGER, Mary E.	(414)229-4659	119
	GILL, Norman N.	(414)352-1545	435
	GILLETTE, Meredith	(414)351-3501	435
	HOOTKIN, Neil M.	(414)332-4953	557
	JONES, Richard E.	(414)229-6457	614
	LOCKETT, Sandra B.	(414)278-3090	736
	MARKOWETZ, Marianna C.	(414)963-4074	771
	SAGER, Donald J.	(414)278-3020	1074
	SCHWARTZ, Virginia C.	(414)278-3216	1105
	THIEL, Mark G.	(414)224-7256	1235
Neenah	LAMB, Cheryl M.	(414)729-8169	689
Racine	TERANIS, Mara	(414)631-4144	1231
Rhinelander	BRANT, Susan L.	(715)369-4429	129
Sheboygan	CONDON, John J.	(414)458-8711	236
Stevens Point	SWIFT, Leonard W.	(715)346-1550	1216
Stoughton	DANKY, James P.	(608)873-8722	274
Superior	AXT, Randolph W.	(715)398-6767	42
West Allis	LUECHT, Richard M.	(414)321-3152	747
Wisconsin Rapids	WILSON, William J.	(715)424-4272	1353

WYOMING

Cheyenne	JOHNSON, Wayne H.	(307)777-7283	609
Gillette	SIEBERSMA, Dan	(307)686-0786	1135
Laramie	MACK, Bonnie R.	(307)766-6537	756

CANADA

ALBERTA

Airdrie	EVANS, Patricia D.		357
Calgary	BAILEY, Madeleine J.	(403)240-6134	46
	GOODMAN, Henry J.	(403)220-6296	449
	MACDONALD, Alan H.	(403)220-5953	754
	MACRAE, Lorne G.	(403)294-8538	758
Edmonton	BUSCH, B J.	(403)432-3794	165
	COMPRI, Jeannine L.	(403)474-0577	235
	RICHARDS, Vincent P.	(403)429-9814	1029
Three Hills	JORDAHL, Ronald I.	(403)443-5511	616

SPEAKER (Free) (Cont'd)
BRITISH COLUMBIA

Clearbrook	SEARCY HOWARD, Linda M.	(604)859-7814	1109
Nanaimo	MEADOWS, Donald F.	(604)753-3662	819
North Vancouver	DODSON, Suzanne C.	(604)988-4567	308
Richmond	ELLIS, Kathy M.	(604)272-5389	344
Vancouver	DEVAKOS, Elizabeth R.	(604)255-6636	297
	LIGHTHALL, Lynne I.	(604)228-1480	727
	PITERNICK, Anne B.	(604)228-3359	976
Victoria	EKLAND, Patricia A.	(604)721-8275	341
	MOEHR, Jochen R.	(604)721-8581	851

MANITOBA

FlinFlon	HOBBS, Henry C.	(204)687-6647	545
Winnipeg	BROWN, Gerald R.	(204)772-2474	144
	BUDNICK, Carol	(204)474-9844	155
	DIVAY, Gabriele	(204)474-8926	306
	MARSHALL, Kenneth E.	(204)269-3243	774
	NIELSON, Paul F.	(204)945-7027	903
	REEDMAN, M R.	(204)983-3437	1015
	SANTORO, Corrado A.	(204)474-8243	1082

NEWFOUNDLAND

St John's	MARTINEZ, Helen	(709)753-6210	779

NOVA SCOTIA

Halifax	AMEY, Lorne J.	(902)422-8639	20
	BIANCHINI, Lucian	(902)445-2987	94
	DEYOUNG, Marie	(902)424-7699	298

ONTARIO

Etobicoke	DETERVILLE, Linda C.	(416)622-2840	296
Gloucester	ST. JACQUES, Suzanne L.	(613)824-4232	1075
Gormley	RHYDWEN, David A.	(416)887-9552	1026
Guelph	BLACK, John B.	(519)821-2565	101
Kitchener	SHEPHERD, Murray C.		1127
London	CLOUSTON, John S.	(519)679-2111	223
	FYFE, Janet H.	(519)472-5201	411
North Bay	NORRGARD, Don K.	(705)474-3332	909
North York	HOFFMANN, Ellen J.	(416)736-2100	548
Ottawa	AUBREY, Irene E.	(613)996-7774	38
	BRODIE, Nancy E.	(613)996-7391	139
	COOK, Terry G.	(613)996-7726	240
	DUCHESNE, Roderick M.	(819)997-7991	322
	DURANCE, Cynthia J.	(613)728-8763	328
	EVANS, Gwynneth	(613)995-3904	357
	KIDD, Betty H.	(613)996-7605	646
	KNOPPERS, Jake V.		665
	LUNAU, Carrol D.	(613)996-7391	748
	PARE, Richard	(613)733-8391	940
	PROULX, Steven D.	(613)596-3746	996
	SPICER, Erik J.	(613)995-1166	1174
	SYLVESTRE, Guy	(613)521-8468	1217
	TAYLOR, Margaret P.	(613)232-6172	1227
	TSAI, Shaopan		1260
	WEIR, Leslie	(819)994-6943	1319
Scarborough	BULAONG, Grace F.	(416)283-5732	156
	MULLERBECK, Aino	(416)284-8779	877
Toronto	ARDERN, Christine M.		31
	BAYNE, Jennifer M.	(416)595-3429	67
	CURTIS, Alison J.	(416)923-0890	267
	DE STRICKER, Ulla	(416)593-5211	296
	DYSART, Jane I.	(416)974-2780	331
	FAST, Louise	(416)593-5211	366
	GARLOCK, Gayle N.	(416)763-2718	419
	KOTIN, David B.	(416)531-2104	673
	LESLIE, Nathan	(416)497-0579	718
	LOWRY, John D.	(416)497-0579	745
	MEADOW, Charles T.	(416)530-4934	819
	MERILEES, Bobbie	(416)485-4177	826
	ODHO, Marc	(416)596-2682	917
	SMITH, Cynthia M.	(416)488-6117	1153
	VANDERELST, Wil	(416)965-2696	1274
	WEAVER, Maggie	(416)925-5478	1312
	WILLIAMSON, Nancy J.		1347
	WONG, Lusi	(416)922-5100	1363
Willowdale	MARSHALL, Alexandra P.	(416)225-8193	773
Windsor	SINGLETON, Cynthia B.	(519)253-4232	1143

SPEAKER (Free) (Cont'd)
QUEBEC
Greenfield Park	RICHARDS, Stella	(514)672-1008	1028
Laval	AUGER, Bernard	(514)687-9730	39
	FORTIN, Jean		391
Montreal	BERTRAND-GASTALDY, Suzanne	(514)343-6048	91
	CURRAN, William M.	(514)392-4939	266
	DARLINGTON, Susan	(514)737-3387	275
	FINN, Julia P.	(514)487-9804	378
	GARNETT, Joyce C.	(514)398-4763	419
	GROEN, Frances K.	(514)845-2090	471
	HOBBINS, Alan J.	(514)398-4773	545
	MOLLER, Hans	(514)398-4740	853
	MOLLER, Hans	(514)398-4740	853
	PIGGOTT, Sylvia E.	(514)877-9383	972
	ROLLAND-THOMAS, Paule	(514)343-6046	1051
	WALSH, Mary A.	(514)937-6633	1300
Quebec	GUERETTE, Charlotte M.	(418)656-3017	476
	MCKENZIE, Donald R.	(418)691-6357	811
St Laurent D'Orleans	SIMON, Marie L.	(514)744-7315	1140
Sillery	LALIBERTE, Madeleine A.	(418)687-9260	689

SASKATCHEWAN
Regina	INGLES, Ernie B.	(306)584-4132	582
Saskatoon	HANDE, D A.	(306)653-5692	494

AUSTRALIA
Brisbane	COCHRANE, Thomas G.	226
Canberra	STEELE, Colin R.	1184
East Hawthorn	BENNETT, David M.	81
Queensland	GOODELL, John S.	448
St Lucia	LAMBERTON, Donald M.	690
Victoria	POWNALL, David E. (033)418-2990	989

BAHRAIN
Al Manamah	ALI, Syed N.	13

BRAZIL
Pelotas	CASTAGNO, Lucio A.	194

CUBA
Havana	ASIS, Moises	36

ENGLAND
London	BUNCE, George D.	157
Oxford	BISHOP, John	99
Plymouth	PENGELLY, Joe	956

FEDERAL REPUBLIC OF CHINA
Taipei	HU, James S.	567
	LIN, Chih F.	727
	SENG, Harris B.	1115

IRELAND
Banger	DUFFIN, Elizabeth A.	323
Dublin	FOX, Peter K.	395
	LAMBKIN, Anthony	690

ISRAEL
Haifa	BLOCH, Uri	105

JAPAN
Ibaraki-ken	TAKEUCHI, Satoru	1220
Tokyo 105	YAMAKAWA, Takashi	1376

KENYA
Nairobi	BROCKMAN, Norbert C.	138

MEXICO
Los Mochis	LAU, Jesus G.	702
Mexico City	ORTIZ MONASTERIO, Leonor	927

NETHERLANDS
The Haag	RAITT, David I.	(311)719-8301	1004

NEW ZEALAND
Auckland	RICHARDS, Valerie	1028

SPEAKER (Free) (Cont'd)
NIGERIA
Ogbomoso	TARPLEY, Margaret J.	1224

PHILIPPINES
Manila	DE CASTRO, Elinore H.	285
Quezon City	VALLEJO, Rosa M.	1271

SOUTH AFRICA
Tygerberg	ROSSOUW, Steve F.	1059

SPEAKER (Honorarium)

ALABAMA
Auburn	ADAMS, Judith A.	(205)826-4500	5
Birmingham	BRITT, Mary C.	(203)934-4475	137
	CLEMMONS, Nancy W.	(205)934-2230	221
	SIMS, Joyce W.	(205)939-7830	1142
	STEPHENS, Jerry W.	(209)363-6000	1188
	STEWART, George R.	(205)226-3611	1192
Decatur	MORRIS, Betty J.	(205)773-6262	866
Florence	CARR, Charles E.	(205)767-2310	185
Mobile	BUSH, Nancy W.	(205)343-8121	165
Montgomery	BIVINS, Hulen E.	(205)272-1700	100
	DESSY, Blane K.	(205)277-7330	296
	LANE, Robert B.	(205)288-8122	694
	MCCRANK, Lawrence J.	(205)244-9202	800
Pelham	WRIGHT, Amos J.	(205)663-3403	1370
Tuscaloosa	KASKE, Neal K.	(205)348-1521	628
	PRUITT, Paul M.	(205)348-1107	996

ALASKA
Anchorage	SOKOLOV, Barbara J.	(907)346-2480	1165
	WILLIAMS, Robert C.	(907)261-2970	1346
Central	OAKES, Patricia A.		913
Fairbanks	STEPHENS, Dennis J.	(907)479-5826	1187
Juneau	CRANE, Karen R.	(907)456-2910	255
	SCHORR, Alan E.	(907)586-6014	1099

ARIZONA
Flagstaff	DOWNUM, Evelyn R.	(602)774-6059	317
Glendale	MOSLEY, Shelley E.	(602)939-5469	872
Mesa	JOSEPHINE, Helen B.	(602)983-0237	617
Phoenix	EVANS, Iris I.	(602)995-1701	357
	MCCOLGIN, Michael A.	(602)255-4890	797
	NIXON, Arless B.	(602)246-9196	906
	NORMAN, Nita V.	(602)271-9216	909
	ROATCH, Mary A.	(602)254-7678	1038
Scottsdale	POTTER, William G.	(602)991-5578	987
Sedona	CHICOREL, Marietta S.	(601)602-2826	208
Sun City	BERNINGHAUSEN, David K.	(602)933-8439	89
Tempe	NILSEN, Alleen P.		904
	OETTING, Edward C.	(602)345-7636	917
	SCHON, Isabel	(602)965-2996	1098
Tucson	BALDWIN, Charlene M.	(602)327-2385	51
	CROWE, Gloria J.	(602)792-9450	261
	DICKSTEIN, Ruth H.	(602)886-0386	301
	GOLDBERG, Susan S.	(602)747-2663	445
	GOTHBERG, Helen M.	(602)887-2262	453
	HEITSHU, Sara C.	(602)621-2101	523
	KELLOGG, Rebecca B.	(602)621-3338	637
	MAKUCH, Andrew L.	(602)622-8572	762
	MILLER, Edward P.		837
	REICHEL, Mary	(602)621-2101	1018
	SORENSEN, Lee R.	(602)621-4868	1168
	TALLMAN, Karen D.	(602)577-3317	1221

ARKANSAS
Arkadelphia	WOODS, L B.	(501)246-5511	1367
Fort Smith	PIERSON, Betty	(501)785-7135	972
Heber Springs	SEDELOW, Sally Y.	(501)362-3476	1110
	SEDELOW, Walter A.		1110
Little Rock	BAKER, Russell P.	(501)371-2141	49
North Little Rock	FOOS, Donald D.	(501)758-5112	388
	JONES, Wanda F.	(501)835-7730	615
Springdale	GREESON, Janet S.	(501)751-4901	465

SPEAKER (Honorarium) (Cont'd)
CALIFORNIA

Alameda	HOSEL, Harold V.	(415)522-5875	561
Anaheim Hills	JOHNSON, Thomas L.	(714)998-4347	609
Belmont	LEWIS, Gretchen S.	(415)591-4336	723
	MEGLIO, Delores D.	(415)591-2333	821
	RAMSEY, Robert D.	(415)593-1601	1006
Ben Lomond	CROWLEY, Terence	(408)336-5019	262
Benicia	MILLER, Davic C.	(707)746-6728	836
	RANDOLPH, Kevin H.	(707)745-9388	1007
Berkeley	BERRING, Robert C.	(415)642-9980	90
	BESSER, Howard A.	(415)643-8641	91
	BROWNRIGG, Edwin B.		149
	DUGGAN, Mary K.	(415)642-5764	324
	FALANGA, Rosemarie E.	(415)524-5501	361
	FALK, Candace S.	(415)526-9591	362
	FLUM, Judith G.	(415)486-0378	386
	FROHMBERG, Katherine A.	(415)644-3600	405
	GOLDMAN, Nancy L.	(415)642-0366	445
	GRIFFIN, Hillis L.	(415)486-7499	468
	HANFF, Peter E.	(415)642-8172	495
	JONES, Maralyn	(415)642-4946	614
	LARSON, Ray R.	(415)642-6046	699
	MINUDRI, Regina U.	(415)843-7242	847
	OGDEN, Barclay W.	(415)642-4946	918
	RAFAEL, Ruth K.	(415)849-2710	1003
	ROBERT, Berring C.	(415)642-9980	1039
	SALMON, Stephen R.	(415)549-3394	1077
	STOCKTON, Gloria J.	(415)843-8550	1196
	WHEELER, Helen R.	(415)549-2970	1329
	X, Laura	(415)548-1770	1376
Buena Park	MUELLER, Jane L.	(714)527-8175	875
Burbank	ELMAN, Stanley A.	(818)351-8245	345
	SIGMAN, Paula M.	(818)840-5424	1137
Campbell	HAZEKAMP, Phyllis W.	(408)379-1611	517
Cardiff By The Sea	SCHALIT, Michael	(619)944-3913	1089
Carlsbad	TILLETT, Barbara B.		1245
Carmichael	STRONG, Gary E.	(916)966-2037	1203
Carphell	ALIX, Cleta M.	(408)371-3294	13
Castro Valley	OVERMYER, Elizabeth C.	(415)670-6281	931
Chatsworth	TANIS, Norman E.	(818)886-1318	1222
Chico	DWYER, James R.	(916)895-5837	330
Corte Madera	FARMER, Lesley S.	(415)924-6633	364
Costa Mesa	EPSTEIN, Susan B.	(714)754-1559	351
	POARCH, Margaret E.	(714)662-1867	979
Culver City	KIRBY, Barbara L.	(213)839-1009	653
Cupertino	KERSHNER, Lois M.	(408)255-2719	644
	MILLER, Ronald F.	(408)257-9162	842
Davis	BLANK, Karen L.	(916)752-2110	104
	COLLINS, William J.	(916)758-4989	233
	LEWIS, Alfred J.	(916)752-3325	722
	SHARROW, Marilyn J.	(916)752-2110	1122
El Cerrito	BLANK, Les	(415)525-0942	104
	HARDWICK, Bonnie S.	(415)237-7011	500
Encinitas	PIERCE, Patricia J.	(619)436-5055	971
Fairfield	GOLD, Anne M.	(707)429-6601	444
Fresno	CARLSON, Alan C.	(209)445-0828	182
	KING, Cynthia		650
Fullerton	STEPHENSON, Shirley E.	(714)773-3580	1189
Glendale	ECKLUND, Lynn M.	(818)242-2793	335
	PRIME, Eugenie E.	(818)243-5707	993
Granado Hills	SINOFSKY, Esther R.	(818)360-2146	1144
Hayward	SASSE, Margo	(415)482-2770	1083
Hillsborough	ABILOCK, Debbie	(415)348-2272	2
Huntington Beach	BAUER, Caroline F.	(714)969-2777	65
Inglewood	GOUDELOCK, Carol V.	(213)672-2543	454
Irvine	ARIEL, Joan	(714)856-4970	31
	HORN, Judy K.		559
	TASH, Steven J.	(714)786-7857	1224
	TSANG, Daniel C.	(714)856-4978	1260
	TSENG, Sally C.	(714)856-6832	1260
	WOODS, Lawrence A.	(714)786-3507	1367
	YOUNG, Eleanor C.	(714)552-5803	1381
Kensington	LAWRENCE, Gary S.	(415)642-2370	704
	MULVANY, Nancy	(415)524-4195	878
La Jolla	BOWLES, Garrett H.	(619)534-2759	121
	FISHER, Edith M.	(619)534-1258	380
	MILLER, R B.	(619)534-3064	841
	ZYROFF, Ellen S.	(619)459-1513	1392
La Verne	HECKMAN, Marlin L.	(714)593-8680	520

SPEAKER (Honorarium) (Cont'd)
CALIFORNIA (Cont'd)

Laguna Beach	KOUNTZ, John C.	(714)494-8783	673
Livermore	GIRILL, T R.	(415)422-0146	438
Lomita	BOWLING, Lance C.	(213)831-1322	121
Long Beach	WELLS, H L.	(213)598-3549	1322
Los Altos Hills	MCDONALD, Marilyn M.	(415)960-4390	803
Los Angeles	BATES, Marcia J.	(213)825-4352	64
	CAMPBELL, Patricia J.	(213)666-6967	177
	CASE, Donald O.	(213)825-1379	191
	CONNOR, Billie M.	(213)660-6399	237
	CREWS, Kenneth D.	(213)397-1518	258
	CROSS, Claudette S.	(213)256-2123	260
	DEENEY, Kay E.	(213)479-6672	286
	ENYINGI, Peter	(213)629-3531	351
	EVANS, G E.	(213)642-4593	357
	FRY, Stephen M.	(213)825-4882	407
	GRAY, Tomysena F.	(213)753-7541	460
	HALE, Kaycee	(213)204-0793	485
	KING, Joseph T.	(213)660-3530	651
	KUNSELMAN, Joan D.	(213)825-1204	684
	MAACK, Mary N.	(213)475-7962	753
	MERRIFIELD, Thomas C.	(213)390-4717	826
	PASCAL, Barbara R.	(213)934-2205	945
	PATRON, Susan H.	(213)612-3285	947
	PRINTZ, Naomi J.	(213)306-3573	993
	ROSENBERG, Melvin H.	(213)612-3242	1056
	SCHERREI, Rita A.	(213)825-1201	1092
	SCLAR, Herbert	(213)474-5900	1106
	STERN, Teena B.	(213)680-2525	1189
	TOMPKINS, Philip	(213)743-2543	1250
	TREISTER, Cyril C.	(213)227-1604	1255
	WALLACE, Marie G.	(213)485-1234	1297
	WATERS, Marie B.	(213)825-1693	1308
	WEISBAUM, Earl		1319
	YEE, Martha M.	(213)462-4921	1379
Malibu	ROSENBERG, Betty	(213)456-2573	1056
Manhattan Beach	MARKEY, Penny S.	(213)374-1838	771
Menlo Park	MURPHY, Joan F.	(415)323-3508	880
Modesto	SHAMS, Kamruddin	(209)576-8585	1120
Monterey	BRUMAN, Janet L.		150
Mountain View	ALBUM, Bernie	(415)967-5593	11
	BUTLER, Matilda L.	(415)969-0606	167
	PAISLEY, William J.	(415)969-0606	935
	PORTER-ROTH, Anne	(415)965-7799	985
	SLOCUM, Hannah R.	(415)969-8356	1150
	SPIGAI, Fran	(415)961-2880	1174
Napa	CHAMBERLIN, Leslie A.	(707)253-1071	198
	VANVUREN, Darcy D.		1277
Northridge	PERKINS, David L.	(818)885-2256	959
Novato	HIRABAYASHI, Joanne	(415)897-4245	543
Oakland	BYRNE, Elizabeth D.	(415)658-6996	169
	CHESTER, Claudia J.	(415)835-4692	207
	DANTON, J P.	(415)653-4802	274
	HOWATT, Helen C.	(415)433-1160	565
	NEWCOMBE, Barbara T.	(415)763-4406	898
	NOVAK, Gloria J.	(415)658-9458	910
	RUBIN, Rhea J.	(415)339-1274	1064
	SYPERT, Clyde F.	(415)763-6046	1217
	WONG, Patricia M.	(415)834-2742	1363
Orange	ERLICH, Martin		353
	SMITH, Elizabeth M.	(714)634-7809	1154
Palo Alto	ANDREWS, Chris C.		26
	HAMILTON, David M.	(415)853-0197	491
	LEVY, Mary J.	(415)325-9581	722
	SUMMIT, Roger K.	(415)858-3777	1209
Palos Verdes Estates	STEVENSON, Marilyn E.	(213)377-7563	1191
Pasadena	HOFFBERG, Judith A.	(818)797-0514	547
	KLINE, Victoria E.	(818)405-2100	661
	YEUNG, Esther Y.		1380
Petaluma	GORDON, Ruth I.	(707)778-4719	452
Pleasant Hill	SIEGEL, Ernest	(415)944-3423	1136
Pleasanton	BUTLER, David W.	(415)846-3308	166
Pomona	IVERSON, Diann S.	(714)624-4728	585
	STREETER, David	(714)620-2026	1201
Poway	D'ADOLF, Steven P.	(619)451-2130	269
Redwood City	BANGE, Stephanie D.	(415)369-6251	54
	SCHLACHTER, Gail A.	(415)594-0743	1093

SPEAKER (Honorarium) (Cont'd)
CALIFORNIA (Cont'd)

Richmond	LAMBERT, Nancy	(415)620-3161	690
	O'CONNOR, Brian C.	(415)237-6561	915
	RYUS, Joseph E.	(415)222-0846	1072
Riverside	DUNN, Kathleen K.	(714)359-8429	327
	SELTH, Jefferson P.	(714)787-3703	1114
	THOMPSON, James C.	(714)682-4549	1240
Sacramento	BURNS, John F.	(916)445-4293	162
	MCGOVERN, Gail J.	(916)446-2411	807
	MILLER, Suzanne M.	(916)739-7010	842
	RUBY, Carmela M.	(916)453-1174	1065
	WILLIAMS, Joan F.	(916)927-4953	1344
Salinas	SERTIC, Kenneth J.	(408)443-6186	1116
San Anselmo	BLUME, August G.	(415)457-0215	107
San Diego	BOSSEAU, Don L.	(619)229-2538	117
	CARTER, Nancy C.		189
	DERSHEM, Larry D.	(619)236-2409	294
	DYER, Charles R.	(619)236-2292	330
	FORMAN, Jack	(619)546-9250	390
	KAYE, Karen	(619)560-2695	632
	LAGIES, Meinhart J.	(619)283-0608	688
	MONROE, Shula M.	(619)222-1206	855
	TRIVISON, Margaret A.	(619)452-7338	1257
San Francisco	AVENEY, Brian H.	(415)338-2956	41
	CARSCH, Ruth E.	(415)641-5014	187
	GITLER, Robert L.	(415)221-9216	438
	GLOVER, Frank J.	(415)731-4477	442
	HAIKALIS, Peter D.	(415)338-2188	484
	HENKE, Dan	(415)565-4758	528
	HUNSUCKER, Alice E.	(415)396-7909	574
	HURLBERT, Roger W.	(415)221-0414	577
	KIRSHENBAUM, Sandra D.	(415)776-1530	655
	MACKLER, Mark E.	(415)954-4452	757
	MORRIS, Effie L.	(415)931-2733	866
	RAMIREZ, William L.	(415)564-5637	1005
	RUNYON, Steven C.	(415)386-5873	1067
	SHEW, Anne L.	(415)565-6352	1129
	STROMME, Gary L.	(415)972-4293	1203
	TARTER, Blodwen	(415)346-8199	1224
	TAYLOR, Kathryn E.	(415)391-9170	1227
	VANSLYKE, Lisa M.	(415)431-0717	1277
	WAKEFORD, Paul J.	(415)476-2533	1293
	WILSON, Jacqueline B.	(415)476-2534	1351
San Jose	CEPPOS, Karen F.	(408)277-2280	196
	EMMICK, Nancy J.	(408)277-3904	348
	ROSEN, Elizabeth M.	(408)277-2270	1055
San Luis Obispo	FOURIE, Denise K.	(805)544-5427	393
San Rafael	HAMMER, Sharon A.	(415)499-6051	493
	TRZECIAK, William J.	(415)485-3319	1260
Santa Barbara	FALK, Joyce D.	(805)687-7283	362
	GEBHARD, Patricia	(805)969-1031	424
Santa Clara	CHESSMAN, Rebecca L.	(408)244-2775	207
Santa Cruz	LOMBARDI, Mary L.	(408)476-1131	738
	MARIE, Jacquelyn	(408)429-2802	770
	RITCH, Alan W.	(408)429-2802	1036
	TURNER, Anne M.	(408)429-3532	1264
Santa Monica	ANDERSON, Dorothy J.	(213)394-1899	22
	BECKER, Joseph	(213)829-6866	72
	DIRLAM, Dona M.	(213)452-1897	305
	QUINT, Barbara E.	(213)451-0252	1000
Sherman Oaks	KWAN, Julie K.	(818)784-8606	685
	MILLER, Margaret S.	(818)783-5264	840
Simi Valley	WONG, Clark C.	(805)522-5233	1362
Stanford	CRAWFORD, Walt	(415)329-3551	257
	MUSEN, Mark A.	(415)723-0979	883
	SCHMIDT, C J.	(415)493-5280	1095
	WIBLE, Joseph G.	(415)723-1110	1335
Stockton	NICHOLS, Elizabeth D.	(209)943-2484	901
Studio City	KAZLAUSKAS, Edward J.	(818)797-7654	632
Sunnyvale	DI MUCCIO, Mary J.	(408)733-8261	304
Thousand Oaks	SOY, Susan K.	(805)523-7288	1170
	SULLIVAN, Kathleen A.	(805)497-6282	1207
Torrance	BEEBE, Richard J.	(213)323-7200	74
Turlock	PARKER, John C.	(209)634-9473	942
Vacaville	KERNS, John T.	(207)448-4459	644
Valencia	CURZON, Susan C.	(805)259-8946	267
Venice	EDELSTEIN, J M.	(213)827-8984	335
	WALTER, Virginia A.	(213)392-7627	1300
Walnut Creek	MORRIS, John	(415)933-3365	866

SPEAKER (Honorarium) (Cont'd)
CALIFORNIA (Cont'd)

Whittier	WILLIAMS, Lisa B.	(213)693-0771	1344
Woodland Hills	NELSON-HARB, Sally R.		895
Yucaipa	BUTLER, Randall R.	(714)797-3859	167

COLORADO

Aurora	MURRAY, William A.	(303)364-8208	882
Boulder	BINTLIFF, Barbara A.	(303)492-2708	97
	BOUCHER, Virginia P.	(303)492-6176	118
	MUELLER, Carolyn J.	(313)492-6788	875
	VARNES, Richard S.	(303)444-8051	1279
	VOLC, Judith D.	(303)442-3578	1287
	ZOELLICK, Bill		1390
Colorado Springs	DOWLIN, Kenneth E.	(303)635-2236	316
	MAGRATH, Lynn L.	(303)473-2080	760
	MALYSHEV, Nina A.	(303)531-6333	764
	NEILON, Barbara L.	(303)574-6167	892
Denver	ABRAMS, Jeanne E.	(303)871-2961	3
	ASHTON, Rick J.	(303)745-9883	36
	BREIVIK, Patricia S.	(303)556-2805	132
	BRUNELL, David H.	(303)691-0550	150
	BRUNER, Robert B.	(303)744-1138	150
	FORSMAN, Rick B.	(303)394-5125	391
	GEHRES, Eleanor M.	(303)571-2012	425
	GOODYEAR, Mary L.	(303)556-2683	450
	HENSINGER, James S.	(303)691-0550	529
	MOULTON, Suzanne L.	(303)871-6427	873
	RAINWATER, Barbara C.	(303)871-6206	1004
	ROSE, Phillip E.	(303)538-4276	1055
	SHAW, Ward	(303)861-5319	1124
	SMITH, Randolph R.	(303)744-8764	1159
	VOLZ, Edward J.	(303)571-2033	1288
	WAGNER, Barbara L.	(303)297-3611	1291
	WHITE, Joyce L.	(303)722-4687	1331
Englewood	THOMASSON, George O.	(303)779-0550	1238
Evergreen	SHARER, E J.	(303)292-4458	1122
Fort Collins	CHAMBERS, Joan L.	(303)491-1833	198
	NEWMAN, John	(303)491-1844	899
Golden	GRAHAM, Su D.	(303)642-7802	456
	KENNEY, Brigitte L.	(303)278-8482	641
	MADDOCK, Jerome T.	(303)231-1367	759
Grand Junction	HENDRICKSON, Charles R.	(303)248-1862	527
Greeley	KNEPEL, Nancy	(303)356-4357	664
	PITKIN, Gary M.	(303)339-2237	976
	SCHULZE, Suzanne S.		1102
Hayden	COSTA, Betty L.	(303)276-4345	249
Littleton	LOERTSCHER, David V.	(303)770-1220	737
	STARK, Philip H.	(305)740-7100	1182
Meeker	NICKEL, Edgar B.	(303)878-3209	902
Pueblo	GARDNER, W J.	(303)549-3308	418
	JONES, Donna R.	(303)542-2156	612
	MOFFEIT, Tony A.	(303)549-2751	852

CONNECTICUT

Bethany	ASH, Lee M.	(203)393-2723	35
Danbury	BURKAT, Leonard	(203)743-2137	160
	MARIANI, Carolyn A.	(203)794-6389	770
Danielson	WEIGEL, James S.	(203)774-7755	1316
Darien	BERRY, Louise P.	(203)655-2568	90
Guilford	GAFFNEY, Maureen	(203)453-6533	412
	WALDEN, Katherine G.	(203)453-5645	1294
Hamden	SAMUEL, Harold E.	(203)432-0495	1079
Hartford	CORCORAN, Virginia H.	(203)524-2230	246
	HALE, Robert G.	(205)566-4111	485
	KAIMOWITZ, Jeffery H.	(203)527-3151	622
	STONE, Dennis J.	(203)241-4617	1197
	WILKIE, Everett L.	(203)236-5621	1340
Lakeville	RESTOUT, Denise T.	(203)435-9308	1024
Madison	FALK, Peter H.	(203)245-2246	362
	HARRISON, Burgess A.	(203)421-4098	506
Middletown	BECK, Arthur R.	(203)347-1387	71
	SABOSIK, Patricia E.	(203)347-6933	1073
	WHITE, Charles R.	(203)638-4110	1330
Moosup	KASPER, Barbara	(203)564-4303	629
New Canaan	ROCKMAN, Connie C.	(203)972-3731	1046
	SENATOR, Rochelle B.	(203)966-5645	1115
New Hartford	GIBSON, Barbara H.	(203)379-3548	431

SPEAKER (Honorarium) (Cont'd)
  CONNECTICUT (Cont'd)

New Haven	BROWN, William E.	(203)432-1749	148
	PETERSON, Stephen L.	(203)432-5292	964
	ROBERTS, Susanne F.	(203)432-1762	1041
	SIGGINS, Jack A.	(203)776-3808	1137
	SULLIVAN, Maureen	(203)776-3808	1208
	TRAINER, Karin A.	(203)432-1818	1253
	WALTER, Kenneth G.	(203)397-4526	1300
New London	TARANOW, Gerda	(203)447-1991	1223
Niantic	BENN, James R.	(203)445-5577	81
Ridgefield	MCMASTER, Deborah L.	(203)798-5574	815
	MILSTEAD, Jessica L.	(203)431-8175	845
	NORTON, Alice	(203)438-4064	910
Stamford	DIMATTIA, Ernest A.	(203)322-9055	304
	LIEBERMAN, Lucille N.	(203)353-2095	726
	TIBBETTS, David W.	(203)329-2824	1243
	WILLIAMS, Judy R.	(203)964-1000	1344
Storrs	FORMAN, Camille L.	(203)486-2526	390
	JIMERSON, Randall C.	(203)486-2893	600
	LAMB, Gertrude		690
	ROLLIN, Marian B.	(203)429-4187	1051
	STEVENS, Norman D.	(203)429-7051	1190
Suffield	CHEESEMAN, Bruce S.	(203)668-6273	204
Washington	LEAB, Katharine K.	(203)868-7408	706
Waterbury	FLANAGAN, Leo N.	(203)756-6149	383
Waterford	MCDONALD, Lois E.	(203)443-0051	803
West Hartford	CHICHESTER, Gerald C.	(203)674-0888	208
	PIERCE, Anne L.	(203)243-4849	971
	TALIT, Lynn	(203)233-7793	1221
Weston	FADER, Ellen G.	(203)226-8403	360
Westport	MECKLER, Alan M.	(203)226-6967	820
	RIBAROFF, Margaret F.	(203)849-0211	1026
Wethersfield	DONOHUE, Christine N.	(203)529-2938	311
Windsor	URICCHIO, William J.	(203)549-0404	1269
Woodbridge	BOGENSCHNEIDER, Duane R.	(203)397-2600	110
	MILLER, Irene K.	(203)393-0458	838

DELAWARE

Dover	COONS, Daniel E.	(302)736-5111	242
	TRYON, Roy H.	(302)674-4522	1260
Frankford	HITCHENS, Howard B.	(302)539-2420	544
Milford	CARPENTER, Carole H.	(302)422-4290	184
Newark	ULRICH, Sue	(302)451-2231	1268
Wilmington	BROWN, Atlanta T.	(302)998-0803	142

DISTRICT OF COLUMBIA

Washington	ANDERSON, Gillian B.	(202)287-8451	23
	BATTLE, Thomas C.	(202)636-7241	65
	BECK, Douglas J.	(313)663-7600	71
	BECKERMAN, George	(202)775-9022	72
	BELLARDO, Trudi	(202)363-9614	78
	BERWICK, Philip C.	(202)543-3369	91
	BLUMER, Thomas J.	(202)543-7031	107
	BOHANAN, Robert D.	(202)523-3214	111
	CANNAN, Judith P.	(202)287-5263	178
	COOPER, David J.	(202)544-3653	242
	EDWARDS, Andrea Y.	(202)269-3449	337
	FLYNN, Richard M.	(202)638-1956	387
	FRANKLIN, Hardy R.	(202)727-1101	397
	FREEMAN, Carla		400
	GARLICK, Karen	(202)287-5634	419
	GRIMES, A R.	(202)663-7600	470
	HAGEMEYER, Alice L.	(202)727-2255	483
	HAITH, Dorothy M.	(202)484-4941	484
	HALEY, Roger K.	(202)224-2976	486
	HARRIS, Marie	(202)767-8643	505
	HEARTY, John A.	(202)872-4533	519
	HORTON, Forest W.		561
	JOHANSON, Cynthia J.	(202)287-5261	601
	JUROW, Susan R.	(202)232-8656	620
	KNOWLTON, John D.	(202)362-8911	665
	KUPERMAN, Agota M.		684
	LASNER, Mark S.	(202)745-1927	700
	LUNIN, Lois F.	(202)965-3924	749
	MCCRAY, Maceo E.	(202)829-7737	800
	MCKEAN, Joan M.	(301)443-8358	810
	MCRAE, Alexander D.	(202)686-1788	818
	MIDDLETON, Carl H.	(202)628-3576	833

SPEAKER (Honorarium) (Cont'd)
  DISTRICT OF COLUMBIA (Cont'd)

Washington	MILEVSKI, Robert J.	(202)287-5634	834
	MILEVSKI, Sandra N.	(202)543-7145	835
	MILLER, William S.	(202)775-4080	843
	OSTROW, Stephen E.	(202)287-5836	929
	PACIFICO, Michele F.	(202)253-3214	933
	PHELPS, Thomas C.	(202)786-0271	967
	PREER, Jean L.	(202)635-5085	990
	PULVER, Thomas B.	(202)293-0500	997
	REITH, Louis J.	(202)686-0131	1022
	RICHARDSON, Deborra A.		1029
	SAUVE, Deborah A.	(202)546-8770	1085
	SCHNEIDER, Hennie R.	(202)523-0013	1097
	SERVERINO, Roberto	(202)625-4574	1116
	STEWART, Ruth A.	(202)287-6587	1193
	STONE, Elizabeth W.	(202)338-5574	1197
	STORM, Jill	(202)775-6174	1198
	SWEENEY, June D.	(202)427-1392	1215
	TAFT, James R.	(202)966-7086	1219
	TSUNEISHI, Warren M.	(202)287-5543	1260
	VANDEGRIFT, Barbara P.	(202)662-7523	1273
	WEAVER, Thomas M.	(202)526-4262	1312
	WEBB, Barbara A.	(202)797-8909	1313
	WEITZENKORN, Laurie	(202)842-6604	1320
	WELSH, William J.	(202)287-5215	1323
	WILLIAMS, Martin T.	(202)287-3759	1345
	YARNALL, James L.	(202)234-6293	1378

FLORIDA

Atlantic Beach	URBANSKI, Verna P.	(904)246-3631	1269
Belle Glade	SNODGRASSE, Elaine	(305)996-3453	1163
Brooksville	TORNABENE, Charles	(904)686-9318	1251
Clearwater	POTTER, Robert E.	(813)442-9061	987
	RITZ, Paul S.	(813)585-0985	1037
Coral Springs	KORNITSKY, Judith M.	(305)753-7081	672
Daytona Beach	BRANDON, Alfred N.	(904)677-5098	128
Dunedin	FIORE, Carole D.	(813)733-2595	379
Fort Lauderdale	HATFIELD, Frances S.	(305)463-5928	511
	HAYES, L S.	(305)587-2900	516
	HEMPHILL, Lia S.	(305)760-5771	525
	KINNEY, Molly S.	(305)563-7842	653
Freeport	DAVIS, Bonnie D.	(904)835-4432	277
Gainesville	COVEY, William C.	(904)392-0796	252
	HOLE, Carol C.	(904)378-0270	550
	WILLOCKS, Robert M.	(904)392-0342	1349
Havana	MAYO, Kathleen O.	(904)539-6895	790
Jacksonville	FARKAS, Andrew	(904)646-2554	364
	SMITH, Linda L.	(904)731-1065	1157
Miami	BOLDRICK, Samuel J.	(305)443-2216	112
	REAM, Diane F.	(305)596-6506	1013
	RYAN, Audrey H.	(305)382-1625	1070
	WILLIAMS, Thomas L.	(305)547-5782	1347
	WULF, Karlinne V.	(305)856-6022	1374
Miami Beach	LESNIAK, Rose	(305)673-6309	718
Naples	O'CONNOR, Mary A.	(813)598-9269	916
Orlando	HUDSON, Phyllis J.	(305)275-2584	569
	PETERSON, Carolyn S.	(305)425-4694	963
	TREMBLAY, Gerald F.	(305)277-6944	1255
Pensacola	MOREIN, P G.	(904)474-2492	863
St Petersburg	CATES, Jo A.	(813)522-1550	194
	FUSTUKJIAN, Samuel Y.	(813)893-9125	410
	HARDESTY, Larry L.	(813)867-1166	499
Sanibel	KLASING, Jane P.	(813)472-8391	657
Sarasota	MOON, Eric	(813)355-1795	857
	WEAVER, James B.	(813)378-1287	1312
Tallahassee	BUSTETTER, Stanley R.	(904)487-2667	166
	DE PEW, John N.	(904)644-5775	293
	FLEMING, Lois D.		384
	HART, Thomas L.	(904)385-7550	507
	HUNT, Mary A.	(904)644-5775	575
	MILLER, Charles E.	(904)644-5211	836
	SUMMERS, F W.	(904)644-5775	1209
	TREZZA, Alphonse F.	(904)878-5551	1256
	VAN ORDEN, Phyllis J.	(904)385-1290	1276
Tampa	LOSEY, Doris C.	(813)885-4500	742
	MATHEWS, Richard B.	(813)253-3333	784
	MCCROSSAN, John A.	(813)974-3520	800
	STORCK, Bernadette R.	(813)223-8860	1198

SPEAKER (Honorarium) (Cont'd)
  FLORIDA (Cont'd)

West Palm Beach	BROWNLEE, Jerry W.	(305)686-0895	148
	PRITCHARD, Teresa N.	(305)684-7349	994
Winter Park	ALLISON, Anne M.	(305)677-6372	17
	PFARRER, Theodore R.	(305)647-3294	966
	SEBRIGHT, Terence F.	(305)678-8846	1110

GEORGIA

Appling	WARNER, Wayne G.	(404)868-7412	1305
Athens	BISHOP, David F.	(404)542-0621	99
	LIBBEY, George H.	(404)542-2716	725
	QUINLAN, Judy B.	(404)542-0654	1000
	ROWLAND, Lucy M.	(404)543-3690	1062
Atlanta	COURSEY, W T.	(404)264-0714	251
	DEES, Anthony R.	(404)355-0551	287
	DRAKE, Miriam A.	(404)894-4501	318
	ENGLER, June L.	(404)727-6405	350
	FORSEE, Joe B.	(404)656-2461	391
	HEID, Gregory G.	(404)688-4636	521
	JOHNSON, Herbert F.	(404)727-6861	605
	NIX, Kemie	(404)355-7421	905
	PRESLEY, Roger L.	(404)658-2176	991
	QUINLIN, Margaret M.	(404)874-1589	1000
	ROAN, Tattie W.	(404)320-9376	1038
	STOWELL, Donald C.	(404)231-4414	1199
	TEMPLETON, Mary E.	(404)727-6875	1231
	TOMAJKO, Kathy L.	(404)894-4511	1249
	WHITE, Carol A.	(404)351-8991	1330
Bainbridge	MARSHALL, Ruth T.	(912)246-3887	775
Carrollton	BEARD, Charles E.	(404)832-9458	69
Dalton	LARY, Marilyn S.	(404)272-4527	700
Decatur	BISHOP, Beverly D.	(404)371-8488	99
Doraville	DRAPER, James D.	(404)457-4858	318
Fitzgerald	HEFFINGTON, Carl O.	(912)423-3642	520
Gainesville	VAUGHAN, Elinor F.	(404)534-6120	1279
La Grange	LEWIS, Frank R.	(404)882-2911	723
Lilburn	HOUGH, Leslie S.	(404)979-0270	562
Macon	CHANIN, Leah F.	(912)744-2665	201
	HOWARD, Mary R.	(912)744-2960	564
Milledgeville	FENNELL, Janice C.	(912)453-4047	371
Norcross	DEWBERRY, Claire D.	(404)564-1634	298
Roswell	MARTIN, Clarece	(404)993-0625	775
Stone Mountain	SULLIVAN, Mary A.	(404)469-0395	1208
Vidalia	HARTZ, Frederic A.	(912)537-0195	509
Watkinsville	WHITEHEAD, James M.	(404)769-8917	1332

HAWAII

Honolulu	FREITAS-OBREGON, Brenda J.	(808)847-6486	401
	JACKSON, Miles M.	(808)948-7321	588
	KANE, Bartholomew A.	(808)524-8344	624
	LINVILLE, Marcia L.	(808)737-2511	731
	LUSTER, Arlene L.	(808)737-8876	750
Kailua	NAHL-JAKOBOVITS, Diane	(808)261-2382	886
Makawao	TUPPER, Bobbie	(808)572-1629	1263

IDAHO

Idaho Falls	HOLLAND, Paul E.	(208)529-1450	551
Moscow	ABRAHAM, Terry		3
Nampa	SIMMONS, Randall C.	(208)467-8609	1140
Pocatello	WATSON, Peter G.	(208)236-2997	1310
Rexburg	HART, Eldon C.	(208)356-4447	507

ILLINOIS

Barrington	KARON, Joyce E.	(312)381-1400	627
Beardstown	WEST, L P.	(217)323-5788	1326
Bloomington	KELLEY, H N.	(309)828-3128	636
Blue Island	WOZNY, Jay	(312)388-1078	1370
Bolingbrook	IFFLAND, Carol D.	(312)739-6398	581
Carbondale	BEDIENT, Douglas	(618)453-2258	73
	BORUZKOWSKI, Lilly A.	(618)453-2365	117
	JENKINS, Darrell L.	(618)549-8053	597
	WILSON, Betty R.	(618)529-3318	1350
Champaign	BERGER, Sidney E.	(217)351-8140	86
	CLOONAN, Michele V.	(217)351-8140	223
	MCCABE, Ronald B.	(217)352-8317	793
Charleston	RAO, Paladugu V.	(217)581-6061	1008

SPEAKER (Honorarium) (Cont'd)
  ILLINOIS (Cont'd)

Chicago	ALTHAGE, Celia J.		18
	BAMBERGER, Mary A.	(312)996-2742	53
	BOLT, Janice A.	(312)233-9399	113
	BOOKSTEIN, Abraham	(312)762-8268	115
	BROWN, Doris R.	(312)341-8066	143
	BURGH, Scott G.	(312)558-5740	159
	CARPENTER, Kathryn H.	(312)996-8988	185
	CORSARO, Julie A.		248
	CRIM, Elias F.	(312)922-9292	258
	DEMPSEY, Frank J.	(312)327-6955	291
	DOLNICK, Sandy F.	(312)944-6780	310
	DOWELL, David R.	(312)567-6844	315
	DOWNES, Valerie	(312)871-7559	316
	DUFF, John B.	(312)269-2984	323
	ELLEMAN, Barbara J.	(312)944-6780	343
	EPSTEIN, Dena J.	(312)373-0522	351
	ESTES, Sally C.	(312)944-6780	355
	FEDERICI, Yolanda D.	(312)427-0052	368
	GODLEWSKI, Susan G.	(312)443-3936	442
	GOMEZ, Martin J.		447
	HAAS, Carolyn B.	(312)822-0809	480
	HARRIS, Jeanne G.	(312)580-0069	504
	IDDINGS, Daniel H.	(312)321-0432	581
	JACOBSEN, Teresa T.	(312)266-1265	590
	JORDAN, Charles R.	(312)478-7205	616
	KAMINECKI, Ronald M.	(312)726-9206	624
	LANDRY, Ronald	(312)943-3282	694
	LEE, Joel M.	(312)944-6780	710
	LENNEBERG, Hans H.		715
	LYNCH, Mary J.	(312)944-6780	752
	MALINOWSKY, H R.	(312)329-1549	763
	MATTENSON, Murray M.	(312)262-8282	785
	MAYFIELD, Maurice K.	(312)281-0510	790
	MCDERMOTT, Patrice	(312)944-6780	802
	MCNEILL, Janice M.	(312)642-4600	816
	MITZIGA, Walter J.	(312)375-4646	850
	MOTLEY, Archie	(312)642-4600	872
	MUNOFF, Gerald J.	(312)702-8749	879
	NEAL, Donn C.	(312)922-0140	890
	OAKS, Claire	(312)271-1207	913
	OTT, Bill	(312)944-6780	930
	PLOTNIK, Arthur	(312)929-8985	978
	RANDALL, Sara L.		1006
	RETTIG, James R.	(312)996-2735	1024
	ROCHMAN, Hazel P.	(312)944-6780	1046
	ROMAN, Susan	(312)944-6780	1052
	RUMNEY, Leslie W.	(312)787-0820	1067
	SCOTT, Alice H.	(312)493-2451	1106
	SEGAL, Joan S.	(312)944-6780	1111
	SHAEVEL, Evelyn F.	(312)944-6780	1118
	SIARNY, William D.	(312)467-5520	1134
	STEWART, Richard A.	(312)269-2930	1193
	SVENSSON, C G.	(312)478-2939	1212
	VANCURA, Joyce B.	(312)822-0422	1273
	VIRGO, Julie A.	(312)751-1454	1285
	VISKOCHIL, Larry A.	(312)935-1071	1285
	WELLS, James M.	(312)782-1172	1322
	WILLIAMSON, Linda E.	(312)996-2738	1347
	WINGER, Howard W.	(312)748-1129	1355
Chillicothe	CROTZ, D K.	(312)485-7805	201
Clinton	ADCOCK, Betty L.	(217)935-3493	6
De Kalb	ABBOTT, Craig S.	(815)753-6634	1
	KIES, Cosette N.	(815)753-1735	647
	TITUS, Elizabeth M.	(815)753-1094	1247
	TOROK, Andrew G.	(815)753-1734	1251
	WELCH, Theodore F.	(815)758-6858	1321
Decatur	HALE, Charles E.	(217)864-5755	485
Deerfield	CALLAGHAN, Linda W.	(312)945-3311	173
Dow	HOLZBERLEIN, Deanne B.	(618)466-3015	555
Downers Grove	BALCOM, Kathleen M.	(312)960-1200	51
East Peoria	WILFORD, Valerie J.	(309)694-4389	1339
Edwardsville	MOORE, Milton C.	(618)692-1638	860
Elgin	FORD, Jennifer D.	(312)742-1040	389
	JUERGENSMEYER, John E.	(312)695-9800	619
Elk Grove Village	KALRA, Bhupinder S.	(312)529-8607	623
Elmhurst	STEWART, Virginia R.	(312)833-7090	1193

SPEAKER (Honorarium) (Cont'd)
ILLINOIS (Cont'd)

Evanston	BJORNCRANTZ, Leslie B.	(312)866-9112	100
	FRIEDER, Richard D.	(312)491-7599	403
	GROSS, Dorothy E.	(312)583-2700	472
	HILL, Janet S.	(312)491-7587	540
	HORNY, Karen L.	(312)491-7662	560
	METZLER, Valerie	(312)869-5992	829
	NIELSEN, Brian	(312)491-2170	903
	PALMORE, Sandra N.	(312)328-5329	937
	PIRON, Alice M.	(312)864-3175	975
	PRENDERGAST, Kathleen M.	(312)491-7298	990
	QUINN, Patrick M.	(312)869-2861	1000
	ROOSE, Tina	(312)491-0662	1053
	SHERMAN, Sarah	(312)864-3801	1128
	STEWART, Donald E.	(312)475-5529	1192
	WHITELEY, Sandra M.	(312)475-7931	1333
Flora	DOCKINS, Glenn	(618)662-2679	307
	HARRIS, Thomas J.	(618)662-2679	506
Fox River Grove	CORCORAN, Frances E.	(312)639-5306	245
Franklin Park	VOSS, Joyce M.	(312)678-1528	1289
Freeport	WELCH, Eric C.	(815)235-6121	1321
Glen Ellyn	TEMPLE, Harold L.	(312)858-2800	1230
Glenview	HAMILTON, Beth A.	(312)998-6567	491
Grayslake	DIEHL, Mark	(312)680-5119	302
	KIENE, Andrea L.	(312)740-0620	647
Hanover Park	KLOCKENGA, Gary R.	(312)830-8942	662
Hinsdale	CZARNECKI, Cary J.	(312)986-1976	268
Hoffman Estates	MILLER, Deborah	(312)882-3698	837
La Grange	HATTENDORF, Lynn C.	(312)579-0873	512
	HELLER, Dawn H.	(312)579-0903	524
	HUSLIG, Dennis M.	(312)352-7671	578
	TUGGLE, Ann M.	(312)627-9250	1262
Lake Bluff	DICK, John H.	(312)234-1220	300
	LEISNER, Anthony B.	(312)295-2010	714
Lombard	MARSHALL, Mary G.	(312)932-1455	774
Macomb	TING, Lee H.	(309)298-1770	1246
Manteno	MC LAUGHLIN, Terry L.	(815)468-6424	813
Matteson	SMITH, Richard D.	(312)747-6660	1159
Maywood	LUDWIG, Logan T.	(312)531-3192	747
Mundelein	RING, Anne M.	(312)566-0898	1035
Naperville	ROWE, Dorothy B.	(312)355-9221	1062
Normal	DELOACH, Marva L.	(309)438-7463	290
	EASTON, William W.	(309)452-3105	333
Northbrook	WICKS, Jerry R.	(312)272-6400	1335
Northfield	ANDERSON, Charles R.	(312)446-8259	22
Oak Lawn	DOBREZ, Cynthia K.	(312)422-4990	307
	IHRIG, Alice B.		581
Oak Park	ALFONSI-GIN, Mary A.	(312)383-4713	13
	BEN-SHIR, Rya H.	(312)386-5444	83
	DICK, Ellen A.	(312)386-9385	300
	PAPPALARDO, Marcia J.	(312)848-5035	939
	REDDY, Michael B.	(312)848-1754	1013
	STEVENSON, Sheila M.	(312)848-3637	1191
Palatine	HORTON, Kathy L.	(312)934-3794	561
Park Forest	OCHSNER, Renata E.	(312)748-5374	915
Park Ridge	JACKSON, William V.	(312)825-4364	588
Paxton	PACEY, Brenda M.	(217)379-3517	933
Peoria	JACKSON, Susan M.	(309)674-2008	588
River Forest	NOONAN, Eileen F.	(312)366-9346	908
Riverdale	PATEL, Jashu	(312)849-3959	947
	ZENKE, Mary H.	(312)849-0879	1387
Rock Island	WESTERBERG, Kermit B.	(309)794-7221	1326
Rockford	DALRYMPLE, Prudence W.	(815)968-9111	271
	ROSENFELD, Joel C.	(815)965-6731	1056
	WELCH, Steven J.	(815)963-5133	1321
Rolling Meadows	HEMENWAY, Patti J.	(312)255-6197	525
Skokie	ANTHONY, Carolyn A.	(312)673-7774	28
	JACOB, Merle L.		589
Springfield	BERK, Robert A.	(217)782-2658	87
	FRISCH, Corrine A.	(217)753-4925	405
	HILDRETH, Charles R.		539
	LAMONT, Bridget L.	(217)787-2299	691
	SHACKLETON, Suzanne M.	(217)786-6375	1118
	TEMPLE, Wayne C.	(217)528-6330	1230
Sun City	STUHLMAN, Daniel D.	(312)262-8959	1205
Sycamore	BERRY, John W.	(815)895-4225	90
	SULLIVAN, Peggy A.	(815)753-6155	1208

SPEAKER (Honorarium) (Cont'd)
ILLINOIS (Cont'd)

Urbana	BALACHANDRAN, Sarojini	(217)328-3577	50
	BRICHFORD, Maynard J.	(217)367-7072	134
	CHOLDIN, Marianna T.	(217)333-5739	210
	COBB, David A.	(217)333-0827	224
	EDMONDS, M L.	(217)333-2306	336
	ESTABROOK, Leigh S.	(217)333-3280	355
	FORREST, Charles G.	(217)244-3770	390
	KRUMMEL, Donald W.	(217)344-6311	680
	LANCASTER, Frederick W.	(217)384-7798	691
	O'BRIEN, Nancy P.	(217)333-2305	915
	ROLSTAD, Gary O.	(217)333-3280	1052
	RUBIN, Richard E.	(217)333-3280	1065
	SCHLIPF, Frederick A.	(217)367-4057	1094
	SIEGEL, Martin A.	(217)333-3247	1136
	SMITH, Linda C.	(217)333-7742	1157
	TEMPERLEY, Nicholas	(217)333-8733	1230
	WAJENBERG, Arnold S.	(217)333-6411	1293
	WEECH, Terry L.	(217)367-7111	1315
	WILLIAMS, Martha E.	(217)333-1074	1345
	WILSON, Lizabeth A.	(217)333-3489	1351
Waukegan	KOZAK, Marlene G.	(312)473-3000	674
Wheaton	EMBAR, Indrani M.	(312)668-1742	347
Wheeling	MCCLARREN, Robert R.	(312)459-1300	796
Wilmette	GRIES, James P.	(312)256-7000	468
	JONES, Adrian	(312)256-6202	610
Winnetka	THOMPSON, Richard E.	(312)446-7975	1241

INDIANA

Bloomington	BRISTOW, Ann	(812)335-8028	137
	CALLISON, Daniel J.	(812)335-5113	174
	COPLER, Judith A.	(812)335-9255	244
	FARRELL, David	(812)335-3403	365
	HENN, Barbara J.	(812)335-1666	528
	IRVINE, Betty J.	(812)335-3403	584
	PUNGITORE, Verna L.	(812)335-5113	997
	READ, Glenn F.	(812)336-5984	1012
	STEELE, Patricia A.	(812)335-1619	1184
	WHITE, Herbert S.	(812)335-2848	1331
Carmel	NIEMEYER, Karen K.	(317)844-8961	903
Evansville	BAKER, Donald E.	(812)425-4309	48
	TEUBERT, Lola H.	(812)428-8229	1233
Fort Wayne	BUDD, Anne D.	(219)424-6111	155
	CLEGG, Michael B.		220
	STANLEY, Luana K.	(219)432-3287	1180
	TRUESDELL, Cheryl B.	(219)481-6509	1259
Frankfort	CADDELL, Claude W.	(317)654-7038	170
Gary	GUYDON, Janet H.	(219)938-3376	479
	MCSHANE, Stephen G.	(219)980-6628	818
	MILLENDER, Dharathola	(219)882-4050	835
Hammond	MEYERS, Arthur S.	(219)931-5100	830
Indianapolis	ALLEN, Joyce S.	(317)929-8021	15
	BONNER, Robert J.	(317)283-7362	114
	BRADLEY, Johanna	(317)751-3779	126
	BRAHMI, Frances A.	(317)274-1401	127
	BRIDGE, Stephen W.	(317)359-7260	135
	CHAMPLIN, Constance J.	(317)845-9400	198
	DOLAN-HEITLINGER, Eileen	(317)269-1764	309
	FISCHLER, Barbara B.	(317)274-0462	380
	GANN, Daniel H.	(317)299-9058	416
	GILL, John H.	(317)872-2045	435
	KONDELIK, John P.	(317)283-9226	670
	MATTHEW, Jeannette M.	(317)283-1053	785
	SIMON, Ralph C.	(317)875-5336	1141
	STUSSY, Susan A.	(317)929-0343	1205
	WOODARD, Marcia S.	(317)297-1803	1366
La Porte	SMYERS, Richard P.	(219)324-2186	1162
Lafayette	BONHOMME, Mary S.	(317)448-1251	114
	LAW, Gordon T.	(317)447-2484	704
	MCKOWEN, Dorothy K.	(317)564-4585	812
	TROUTNER, Joanne J.	(317)477-7306	1258
Marion	BOYCE, Harold W.	(317)674-5211	122
Michigan City	DEYOUNG, Charles D.	(219)879-4561	298
Mishawaka	STRATTON, Martha G.	(219)255-5262	1200
Muncie	BEILKE, Patricia A.	(317)284-2457	75
	HODGE, Stanley P.	(317)285-8033	546
	WOOD, Michael B.	(317)289-5417	1364
Noblesville	COOPER, David L.	(317)773-1384	242

SPEAKER (Honorarium) (Cont'd)

INDIANA (Cont'd)

Notre Dame	CONNELLY, James T.	(219)233-9675	237
	DOELLMAN, Michael A.	(219)232-0778	308
	FUDERER, Laura S.	(219)239-5176	408
	HAYES, Stephen M.	(219)239-5268	516
	JORDAN, Louis E.	(219)239-7420	616
	MILLER, Robert C.	(219)239-7790	841
	SLINGER, Michael J.	(219)239-5664	1149
Plainfield	MILLER, Ida M.	(317)839-6883	838
Richmond	FARBER, Evan I.	(317)966-2422	363
South Bend	MULLINS, James L.	(219)237-4449	878
	TUCKER, Dennis C.		1261
	WARREN, Lois B.	(219)287-6481	1306
Terre Haute	LEACH, Ronald G.	(812)237-3700	706
Valparaiso	PERRY, Margaret	(219)464-5364	960
West Lafayette	BAILEY, Martha J.	(317)494-2910	46
	HEWISON, Nancy S.	(317)463-0904	535
	MOBLEY, Emily R.	(317)494-2900	851
	POLIT, Carlos E.	(317)463-6404	980
Westfield	VAN CAMP, Ann J.	(317)896-3537	1272
Winamac	SMITH, Robert E.	(219)946-6255	1160

IOWA

Ames	KUHN, Warren B.	(515)294-1442	682
	MADISON, Olivia M.	(515)294-3669	759
Bettendorf	CLOW, Faye E.	(319)332-7427	223
	MEIER, Patricia L.	(319)355-3895	821
Boone	ADAMS, Larry D.	(515)432-1931	5
Cedar Falls	WILKINSON, Patrick J.	(319)273-6327	1340
Cedar Rapids	LEAVITT, Judith A.	(319)390-3109	707
Coralville	PEPETONE, Diane S.	(319)351-3922	957
Davenport	JONSON, Laurence F.	(319)323-9213	616
Des Moines	EDWARDS, John D.	(515)271-2141	337
	GEORGE, Shirley H.	(515)281-4105	428
	KERN, Sharon P.	(515)243-2300	643
Dubuque	OFFERMAN, Mary C.		917
Iowa City	BAKER, Sharon L.	(319)335-5707	49
	DONHAM, Jean O.	(319)338-3685	311
	FALK, Mark F.	(319)354-7474	362
	HAUSMAN, Julie	(319)337-1786	513
	LORKOVIC, Tatjana B.	(318)351-5304	741
	RICE, James G.	(319)335-5716	1027
Marshalltown	BURGESS, Barbara J.	(515)752-4812	159
Waverly	COFFIE, Patricia R.	(319)352-1223	227
West Branch	MAYER, Dale C.	(319)643-5301	789

KANSAS

Alma	BIRNEY, Ann E.	(913)765-2370	98
Coffeyville	HENDERSON, Rosemary	(316)251-2158	527
El Dorado	BEATTIE, Brian	(316)321-3363	70
Emporia	BODART-TALBOT, Joni	(316)343-1200	109
	BOGAN, Mary E.	(316)342-1394	110
	HALE, Martha L.		485
Great Bend	SWAN, James A.	(316)792-4865	1213
Kansas City	RIDDLE, Raymond E.	(913)621-3073	1032
Lawrence	JOHNSON, Ellen S.	(913)864-3496	604
	SEAVER, James E.	(913)864-3569	1110
	SNYDER, Fritz	(913)864-3025	1164
Leavenworth	SNOKE, Elizabeth R.		1163
Lenexa	MCLEOD, Debra A.	(913)492-4512	814
Manhattan	QUIRING, Virginia M.	(913)532-5693	1000
North Newton	HAURY, David A.	(316)283-2500	512
	SCHRAG, Dale R.	(316)283-2500	1099
Olathe	GOODRICH PETERSON, Marilyn	(913)897-3318	450
Overland Park	KEMPF, Andrea C.	(913)469-8500	639
Pittsburg	DEGRUSON, Eugene H.	(316)231-7000	288
Shawnee Mission	WAY, Harold E.	(913)831-1550	1311
Topeka	BRAND, Alice A.	(913)273-7500	127
	LEVEL, M J.	(913)296-3434	719
	LYNN, Barbara A.	(913)233-4252	752
	RICHMOND, Robert W.	(913)234-4704	1031
Wakeeney	DIRKS, Martha W.	(913)743-6767	305
Wichita	WOOLF, Amy K.	(316)733-5730	1368

SPEAKER (Honorarium) (Cont'd)

KENTUCKY

Berea	KIRK, Thomas G.	(606)986-9341	654
Bowling Green	CUDD, John M.	(502)842-0901	263
Cynthiana	DOAN, Janice K.	(606)441-1180	307
Frankfort	COOPER, Judy L.	(502)564-2672	243
	NELSON, James A.	(502)875-7000	894
Highland Heights	BREDEMEYER, Carol	(606)572-5395	131
	STURM, Rebecca R.	(606)572-5636	1205
Horse Cave	STROHECKER, Edwin C.	(502)453-3059	1202
Lexington	CUNHA, George M.	(606)257-8876	265
	LEVSTIK, Frank R.	(606)266-9196	721
	RIPLEY, Joseph M.	(606)257-4243	1035
	ROGERS, Joann V.	(606)278-6246	1049
	SIMS, Edward N.	(606)252-2291	1142
	STEENSLAND, Ronald P.		1184
	WALDHART, Thomas J.	(606)257-3771	1294
Louisville	ANDERSON, James C.	(502)588-6752	23
	BELL, Mary M.	(502)426-4732	77
	BLACKBURN-FOSTER, Brenda	(502)582-4111	102
	COATES, Ann S.	(502)588-5917	224
	DEERING, Ronald F.	(502)897-4807	287
	SCHLENE, Vickie J.	(502)935-9840	1094
	SOMERVILLE, Mary R.	(502)893-8451	1167
	VOYLES, James R.	(502)589-4440	1289
Paducah	BOYARSKI, Jennie S.	(502)442-6131	122
Southgate	FOX, Estella E.	(606)441-0743	394

LOUISIANA

Alexandria	JARRED, Ada D.	(312)445-5230	594
Baton Rouge	BRADLEY, Jared W.	(504)766-9375	126
	HEIM, Kathleen M.	(504)388-3158	521
	HOGAN, Sharon A.	(504)388-2217	549
	MARTIN, Robert S.	(504)767-7167	778
	MCKANN, Michael R.	(504)342-4922	809
	PASKOFF, Beth M.	(504)388-1480	946
	PHENIX, Katharine J.	(504)388-3158	967
	PHILLIPS, Faye	(504)388-6569	968
	REID, Marion T.	(504)388-2217	1019
	SCULL, Roberta A.		1108
Lafayette	KREAMER, Jean T.	(318)231-6780	677
	RAMAKRISHNAN, T	(318)989-9333	1004
Lake Charles	CAGLE, Robert B.	(318)437-5740	171
	CUROL, Helen B.	(318)477-1780	266
Metairie	KLEIN, Victor C.	(504)861-0488	659
	SALVATORE, Gayle E.	(504)456-2660	1078
Natchitoches	BUCHANAN, William C.	(318)357-4403	153
New Orleans	BARON, John H.	(504)865-5271	58
	DRAUGHON, Ralph B.	(504)891-1921	318
	FLEURY, Bruce E.	(504)865-5682	385
	GERICKE, Paul W.	(504)282-4455	428
	HARDY, D C.	(504)895-3981	500
	HARRIS, Karen H.	(504)286-7162	505
	JERDE, Curtis D.	(504)865-5688	599
	LEMMON, Alfred E.	(504)523-4662	715
	MCREYNOLDS, Rosalee	(504)866-9820	818
	SARKODIE-MENSAH, Kwasi	(504)483-7306	1083
	SKINNER, Robert E.	(504)483-7304	1146
	WILSON, C D.	(504)596-2600	1350
Oakdale	LYNCH, Minnie L.	(318)335-3442	752
Ruston	LOWE, Joy L.	(318)255-4379	744
Shreveport	MOSLEY, Mattie J.	(310)797-5100	871
Slidell	HOLLEY, Rebecca M.	(504)641-0198	551

MAINE

Augusta	WISMER, Donald	(207)289-5600	1357
Bangor	BEISER, Karl A.	(207)947-4876	75
Boothbay	LENTHALL, Franklyn	(207)633-4536	715
	SEELEY, Catherine R.		1111
Brunswick	HEISER, Nancy E.	(207)725-4253	523
East Sebago	AIREY, Martha R.	(207)787-2817	9
Farmington	MCNAMARA, Shelley G.	(207)778-3501	816
Kennebunkport	PEERS, Charles T.	(207)967-5764	954
Lewiston	GROSS, Richard F.	(207)782-3958	472
Portland	HUMEZ, Nicholas D.	(207)773-3405	573
	O'BRIEN, Francis M.	(207)774-0931	914
	REIMAN, Anne M.	(207)774-4000	1020
Skowhegan	FRIDLEY, Russell W.	(207)474-7133	403

SPEAKER (Honorarium) (Cont'd)
MARYLAND

Adamstown	LIGHTBOWN, Parke P.		726
Adelphi	NITECKI, Danuta A.	(301)937-4791	905
	YOST, F D.	(301)439-8544	1381
Annapolis	CARMAN, Carol A.	(301)841-3810	183
	MENEGAUX, Edmond A.	(301)268-6741	824
Arnold	OLSON, Christine A.	(301)647-6708	922
Baltimore	BLANK, Annette C.	(301)396-5350	104
	CHELTON, Mary K.	(301)355-0906	204
	CYR, Helen W.	(301)235-8719	268
	DAVISH, William	(301)323-1010	281
	DE LERMA, Dominique R.	(301)467-2578	289
	EPSTEIN, Robert S.	(301)328-3928	351
	FREDENBURG, Anne M.	(301)377-9080	399
	HARDNETT, Carolyn J.	(301)332-6250	500
	HEISER, Jane C.	(301)396-5470	523
	KELLER, William B.	(301)367-0338	636
	LANDRY, Mary E.	(301)235-8067	693
	LUCIER, Richard E.	(301)955-3411	746
	MATHESON, Nina W.	(301)837-1120	783
	MONTGOMERY, Paula K.	(301)685-8621	856
	PAPENFUSE, Edward C.	(301)467-6137	939
	PARTRIDGE, James C.	(301)664-4301	945
	RUFF, Martha R.	(301)367-2831	1066
	THIES, Gail M.	(301)597-8918	1235
	TOOEY, Mary J.	(301)744-0521	1250
	VARGA, Nicholas	(301)323-1010	1278
Bel Air	MASSEY, James E.	(301)838-7484	782
Beltsville	ANDRE, Pamela Q.	(301)344-3813	26
Bethesda	BALL, Thomas W.	(301)493-5184	52
	BOHLEN, Jeanne L.	(301)897-9823	111
	BYRNES, Margaret M.	(301)496-0382	169
	CONGER, Lucinda D.	(301)229-7716	236
	FISHBEIN, Meyer H.	(301)530-5391	380
	GOLDSCHMIDT, Peter G.	(301)656-5070	446
	HAWK, Susan A.	(301)897-8367	513
	LAKSHMAN, Malathi K.	(301)229-9287	689
	MILLENSON, Roy H.		835
	SHOCKLEY, Cynthia W.	(301)320-2000	1132
	SMINK, Anna R.	(301)365-5300	1152
	THOMA, George R.	(301)496-4496	1235
	WOODSMALL, Rose M.	(301)496-8834	1367
Bowie	GIGANTE, Vickilyn M.	(301)249-2609	433
Brentwood	MOREY, Frederick L.	(301)864-8527	863
Cabin John	SEWELL, Winifred	(301)229-5008	1118
Chevy Chase	CHARTRAND, Robert L.		203
Clinton	CHEEKS, Cellestine	(301)868-5048	204
College Park	MARCHIONINI, Gary J.	(301)454-3235	769
	SHULMAN, Frank J.	(301)935-5614	1133
Columbia	DAHLEN, Roger W.	(301)964-9098	269
	DIENER, Richard A.	(301)381-2525	302
	GORDON, Martin K.	(301)992-7626	451
	GRUHL, Andrea M.	(301)596-5460	474
	KOSMIN, Linda J.	(301)997-8954	672
	NEWMAN, Wilda B.	(301)730-7583	900
	REIDER, William L.	(301)995-1639	1019
	WOLTER, John A.	(301)730-6692	1362
Dundalk	MILLER, Everett G.	(301)522-5785	837
Ellicott City	MARTIN, Susan K.	(301)988-9893	778
Forestville	MOORE, Virginia B.	(301)568-8743	861
Fulton	FRANK, Robyn C.	(301)490-5898	397
Gaithersburg	BENNETT, Harry D.	(301)840-1467	81
	GRIFFEN, Agnes M.	(301)340-3378	468
Gamber	BOGAGE, Alan R.	(301)795-6167	110
Glen Burnie	HACKMAN, Mary H.	(301)768-2569	481
Grasonville	SCHNEIDER, Karl R.	(301)827-9339	1097
Greenbelt	ASHFORD, Richard K.	(301)982-5074	36
	SIMS, Sally R.	(301)345-0619	1142
Hyattsville	BURGESS, Eileen E.	(301)864-7223	159
Kensington	PRICE, Douglas S.	(301)942-2091	992
Landover	BARTH, Edward W.	(301)773-9790	61
Laurel	BARKER, Lillian H.	(301)776-2260	56
Mount Airy	LISTON, David M.	(301)831-3008	732
New Carrollton	WILLIAMS, Helen E.	(301)454-6068	1343
Pocomoke City	SMITH, Jessie C.	(301)957-3320	1156
Potomac	PATRICIU, Florin S.	(301)983-9579	947

SPEAKER (Honorarium) (Cont'd)
MARYLAND (Cont'd)

Rockville	BARALOTO, R A.	(301)279-3271	55
	BERUL, Lawrence H.	(301)984-9400	91
	BRODERICK, John C.	(301)762-0504	138
	BYRD, Harvey C.	(301)251-5481	169
	CANTELON, Philip L.	(301)770-1170	179
	COSMIDES, George J.	(301)762-5428	249
	DEAN, Frances C.	(301)424-9289	283
	FREEDMAN, Lynn P.	(301)468-2600	400
	GRIFFITHS, Jose M.	(301)881-6766	469
	HERIN, Nancy J.	(301)279-6101	531
	KING, Donald W.	(301)881-6766	650
	MEIZNER, Kathie L.	(301)279-1960	822
	MICHAELS, Carolyn L.	(301)564-0509	831
	PEDAK-KARI, Maria	(301)279-1940	954
Savage	FILBY, P W.	(301)792-7051	376
Seabrook	LARSEN, Lida L.	(301)459-3931	698
Severn	JACK, Robert F.	(301)859-5300	586
Silver Spring	AGEE, Victoria V.	(301)434-7073	7
	BATTY, Charles D.	(301)593-8901	65
	FELMY, John C.	(301)681-9069	370
	GIBBS, Beatrice E.		431
	LARSON, Jean A.	(301)890-2210	699
	LEVITAN, Karen B.	(301)588-8139	721
	MARKS, Cicely P.	(301)649-7200	771
	MERIKANGAS, Robert J.	(301)384-3449	826
	MERINGOLO, Joseph A.	(202)872-7689	826
	PEMPE, Ruta	(301)587-3846	956
	RICHARD, Sheila A.	(301)438-4555	1028
	SCHEIPS, Paul J.		1091
	THOMAS, Sarah E.	(301)585-9446	1238
	VOGT-O'CONNOR, Diane L.	(301)681-7615	1287
Solomons	HEIL, Kathleen A.	(301)326-2967	521
Takoma Park	HICKERSON, Joseph C.	(301)270-1107	536
	SLOAN, Cheryl A.	(301)589-6815	1149
Thurmont	FITZPATRICK, Kelly	(301)271-4109	383
Towson	DRACH, Marian C.	(301)825-8877	317
	ROBINSON, Charles W.	(301)296-8500	1043
Westminster	MCCARTY, Emily H.	(301)848-1825	795

MASSACHUSETTS

Acton	HURD, Sandra H.	(617)263-7574	577
	YACOUBY, Ray S.	(617)263-6764	1376
Amherst	DONOHUE, Joseph	(413)545-0498	312
Andover	JACOBSON, Nancy C.	(617)475-6960	590
Arlington	FORTIER, Jan M.	(617)646-5856	391
	TRINKAUS-RANDALL, Gregor	(617)641-1273	1257
Auburndale	TUCHMAN, Maurice S.	(617)969-9791	1261
Boston	ANDERSON, A J.	(617)738-2230	21
	BUSH, Margaret A.	(617)262-2045	165
	CURLEY, Arthur	(617)536-5400	265
	EATON, Elizabeth K.	(617)523-7415	333
	ELAM, Barbara C.	(617)825-2658	341
	HEINS, Ethel L.	(617)527-2736	522
	HERNON, Peter	(617)738-2223	532
	KERN, Donald C.	(617)638-8030	643
	LEIGHTON, Helene L.	(617)726-8600	714
	MATARAZZO, James M.	(617)738-2220	783
	MONOSSON, Adolf S.	(617)267-2900	855
	MOSKOWITZ, Michael A.	(617)578-8670	871
	PEARLSTEIN, Toby	(617)973-8000	952
	SCHWARTZ, Candy S.	(617)738-2223	1104
	SNIFFIN-MARINO, Megan G.	(617)738-3141	1163
	STEVENSON, Michael I.	(617)495-6374	1191
	STUEART, Robert D.	(617)738-2225	1205
	WARNER, Marnie M.	(617)725-8733	1305
Brookline	ZEIGER, Hanna B.	(617)730-2586	1387
Burlington	MCLAUGHLIN, Lee R.	(617)272-5772	813
Cambridge	DUNKLY, James W.	(617)868-3450	326
	FERNALD, Anne C.	(617)491-4077	373
	PARKER, Susan E.	(617)495-3455	942
	STODDARD, Roger E.	(617)495-2441	1196
	WOLPERT, Ann J.	(617)864-5770	1362
Concord	BANDER, Edward J.		54
	NESS, Pamela M.	(617)369-7174	896
Deerfield	PROPER, David R.	(413)774-5581	995
East Boston	SCHLAFF, Donna G.	(617)561-0153	1093
Gloucester	RHINELANDER, Mary F.	(617)281-2439	1025

SPEAKER (Honorarium) (Cont'd)
MASSACHUSETTS (Cont'd)

Greenfield	LEE, Marilyn M.	(413)773-8477	710
Hanscom AFB	SEIDMAN, Ruth K.	(617)377-4895	1112
Kingston	FELICETTI, Barbara W.	(617)585-5662	370
Leverett	ZIPKOWITZ, Fay	(413)367-9573	1389
Lexington	CARTER, Walter F.	(617)860-6739	190
	CATON, Christopher N.	(617)860-6711	195
	COOPER, J P.	(617)860-6116	243
	HARTMAN, David G.	(617)860-6668	508
	LUCKER, Jay K.	(617)862-4558	746
	MAXANT, Vicary		787
	STANTON, Martha	(617)861-0905	1181
	WALSH, Joanna M.	(617)863-1275	1299
	WARNER, Alice S.	(617)862-9278	1305
	WYSS, David A.	(617)860-6751	1376
Medford	MARTIN, Murray S.	(617)776-3599	777
Milton	KEYS, Marshall	(617)333-0500	645
Monterey	INTNER, Sheila S.	(413)528-2698	583
Nahant	DESTEFANO, Daniel A.	(617)596-1767	296
Needham	MARKUSON, Carolyn A.	(617)449-6299	772
Newton Center	CARPENTER, Kenneth E.	(617)244-2117	185
Newtonville	GLASSMAN, Penny L.	(617)965-6310	440
Northampton	BOZONE, Billie R.	(413)584-2700	124
	DAVIS, Charles R.	(413)584-2700	278
Norwell	KADANOFF, Diane G.	(617)659-2015	621
Pelham	FELLER, Siegfried	(413)253-3115	370
Petersham	MCMANAMON, Mary J.	(617)724-3407	814
Pittsfield	BOSTLEY, Jean R.	(413)447-9121	117
Plymouth	HORN, Joseph A.	(617)746-6172	559
Reading	FLANNERY, Susan M.	(617)944-0840	383
	FLANNERY, Susan M.	(617)944-0840	384
Revere	TATELMAN, Susan D.	(617)284-0154	1225
Salem	SCHWALLER, Marian C.	(617)744-0076	1104
	WHITNEY, Howard F.	(617)744-1769	1334
Sharon	FRAZIER, James A.	(617)784-5642	399
Springfield	KEOUGH, Francis P.	(413)739-1837	643
	MCLAIN, Guy A.	(413)739-3871	813
Stow	MOULTON, Lynda W.	(617)897-7163	873
Sturbridge	PERCY, Theresa R.	(617)347-3362	958
Walpole	ESTES, Pamela J.	(617)668-3076	355
Waltham	CHATTERTON, Leigh A.	(617)893-4807	204
Watertown	BAKST, Shelley D.	(617)872-8200	50
	LANDESMAN, Betty J.	(617)924-7182	692
Wellesley	MARX, Peter	(617)237-9585	780
West Newton	CHEN, Ching C.	(617)738-2224	205
West Springfield	HELO, Martin	(413)736-4561	525
Westhampton	LOMBARDO, Daniel J.	(413)527-1796	738
Westwood	CLAPPER, Mary E.	(617)329-3350	216
Williamsburg	O'BRIEN, Marjorie S.	(413)268-7131	914
Williamstown	WIKANDER, Lawrence E.	(413)458-3888	1338
Winchester	JOHNSON, Jean L.	(617)721-7020	606
Worcester	BARNHILL, Georgia B.	(617)755-5221	58
	STANKUS, Tony	(617)793-2643	1180

MICHIGAN

Albion	JENNINGS, Martha F.	(517)629-9469	598
Alpena	WILLIAMS, Susan S.	(517)356-1622	1346
Ann Arbor	ANDERSEN, H F.	(313)936-7573	21
	BEAUBIEN, Anne K.	(313)763-5060	70
	BENSON, Peggy	(313)665-0651	83
	BERGEN, Kathleen M.	(313)936-3814	85
	BIGGS, Debra R.	(313)763-7080	95
	BLOUIN, Francis X.	(313)764-3482	107
	CROOKS, James E.	(313)936-2408	260
	DAVIS, Anne C.	(313)668-0385	277
	DIDIER, Elaine K.	(313)763-0378	301
	DOUGHERTY, Richard M.	(313)764-9356	314
	DURRANCE, Joan C.	(313)763-1569	328
	LEARY, Margaret R.	(313)663-7324	707
	MCDONALD, David R.	(313)764-0412	802
	SCHWARTZ, Diane G.	(313)763-2037	1104
	SLAVENS, Thomas P.	(313)665-6663	1148
	SMILLIE, Pauline A.	(313)665-8821	1151
	STOFFLE, Carla J.	(313)764-9356	1196
	WARNER, Robert M.	(313)763-2281	1305
	WERLING, Anita L.	(313)761-4700	1324
	WISE, Virginia J.	(313)663-5674	1357
	YOCUM, Patricia B.	(313)995-4644	1380
Bay City	KORMELINK, Barbara A.	(517)894-3782	671

SPEAKER (Honorarium) (Cont'd)
MICHIGAN (Cont'd)

Birmingham	SWEENEY, Thomas F.	(313)964-0030	1215
Bloomfield Hills	DAVID, Indra M.	(313)338-3929	276
	FRANKIE, Suzanne O.	(313)855-6149	397
Dearborn	BREWER, Annie M.	(313)562-6871	134
	LIMBACHER, James L.	(313)565-9687	727
	VINT, Patricia A.	(313)591-5073	1285
Dearborn Heights	KIRKESY, Oliver M.	(313)278-4670	655
Detroit	BARTKOWSKI, Patricia	(313)577-4024	61
	BISSETT, Donald J.	(313)577-1615	100
	BRUNK, Thomas W.	(313)331-4930	150
	COIR, Mark A.	(313)837-3643	229
	GREGORY, Helen B.	(313)885-3437	466
	GUNN, Arthur C.	(313)831-9707	477
	JOHNSON, Veronica A.	(313)532-6715	609
	KNIFFEL, Leonard J.	(313)864-0982	664
	MIKA, Joseph J.	(313)577-1825	834
	MORROW, Blaine V.	(313)893-1746	869
	PFLUG, Warner W.	(313)577-4024	966
	PORTER, Jean F.	(313)961-5040	984
East Lansing	ACKERMAN, Katherine K.	(517)332-6818	4
	BLATT, Gloria T.	(313)332-6817	104
	CHAPIN, Richard E.	(517)355-2341	201
	HAKA, Clifford H.	(517)353-5317	484
	WOODARD, Beth E.	(517)355-5774	1365
Farmington Hills	RENKIEWICZ, Frank A.	(313)478-4506	1023
Flint	PALMER, David W.	(313)238-0166	936
Grand Blanc	KINGSTON, Jo A.	(313)694-7323	652
Grand Haven	BROOKS, Burton H.	(616)842-2586	140
Grand Rapids	BOSE, Deborah L.	(616)453-1900	117
Grosse Pointe	CASEY, Genevieve M.		192
Hancock	PENTI, Marsha E.	(906)482-5300	957
Haslett	OLIVER, James W.	(517)339-0846	921
Highland Park	NDENGA, Viola W.	(313)868-5986	890
Holt	KEDDLE, David G.	(517)694-2746	634
Kalamazoo	GROTZINGER, Laurel A.	(616)381-1865	473
	ISAACSON, David K.	(616)383-1562	584
	RIZZO, John R.	(616)381-1323	1037
Lansing	CALLARD, Carole	(517)373-1593	173
	DUKELOW, Ruth H.	(517)373-1593	324
	EZELL, Charlaine L.	(517)485-8019	360
	FRY, James W.	(517)373-1593	406
Marquette	PAULIN, Mary A.	(906)228-6686	950
Monroe	MARGOLIS, Bernard A.	(313)243-5213	770
Mt Pleasant	MULLIGAN, William H.	(517)773-1374	877
	WEATHERFORD, John W.	(517)772-3861	1311
Northville	ROCKALL, Diane M.	(313)349-9005	1046
Olivet	COOPER, B L.	(616)749-7618	242
Plymouth	GAREN, Robert J.	(313)455-5771	418
Rochester	WILSON, Patricia L.	(313)656-2900	1352
Saginaw	JOHN, Stephanie C.	(517)771-6846	601
Sault Sainte Marie	NAIRN, Charles E.	(906)635-2402	886
Southfield	JOSE, Phyllis A.	(313)355-9282	617
Stevensville	BEDUNAH, Virginia M.	(616)429-9779	74
Sturgis	BERKLUND, Nancy J.	(616)651-9361	87
Troy	STEPHENS, Karen L.	(313)879-6856	1188
Vicksburg	HEGEDUS, Mary E.	(616)679-5396	521
Warren	DOYLE, James M.	(313)445-7401	317
West Bloomfield	WREN, James A.	(313)682-6310	1370
Ypsilanti	BOONE, Morell D.	(313)484-4384	115

MINNESOTA

Duluth	ENRICI, Pamela L.	(218)726-8586	350
	SCHROEDER, Janet K.	(218)723-3821	1100
Eden Prairie	GROSCH, Audrey N.	(612)937-2345	472
Edina	LONG, John M.	(612)942-0140	739
Grand Marais	GILLIS, Ruth J.		436
Grand Rapids	VALANCE, Marsha J.	(218)327-2336	1271
Hopkins	SMITH, David R.	(612)933-0199	1154
	YOUNG, Margaret L.	(612)933-5062	1382
Kilkenny	HAMMARGREN, Betty L.	(507)595-2575	493
Mankato	ALLAN, David W.	(507)947-3936	14
	BIRMINGHAM, Frank R.	(507)389-5210	98
	CARRISON, Dale K.	(507)389-5062	187
	CHRISTENSON, John D.	(507)625-6169	211
	HITT, Charles J.	(507)625-4834	544
	MCDONALD, Frances B.	(507)389-1965	802
	READY, Sandra K.	(507)388-4003	1012
	TOHAL, Kate J.	(507)389-5963	1248

SPEAKER (Honorarium) (Cont'd)
MINNESOTA (Cont'd)

Marine on St Croix	FULLER, Sherrilynne S.	(612)433-3893	409
Minneapolis	ABELES, Tom		2
	ALLISON, Brent	(612)624-4549	17
	ASPNES, Grieg G.	(612)926-1749	37
	BOEDER, Thelma B.	(612)870-3657	109
	BRANIN, Joseph J.	(612)624-5518	128
	BRUTON, Robert T.	(612)540-1084	151
	DEJOHN, William T.	(612)624-2839	288
	GLASGOW, Vicki L.	(612)626-5808	440
	KUKLA, Edward R.	(612)372-6522	683
	LACY, Lyn E.	(612)724-6110	687
	LATHROP, Alan K.	(612)789-4046	701
	OBERMAN, Cerise G.	(612)624-4520	914
	OVERMIER, Judith A.	(612)626-6881	931
	PANKAKE, Marcia J.	(612)331-2551	938
	ROSSMAN, Muriel J.	(612)624-4002	1059
	ROTH, Alvin R.	(612)789-3879	1059
	RUBENS, Donna J.	(612)624-7082	1064
	SANDNESS, John G.	(612)866-7033	1081
	YAHNKE, Robert E.	(612)625-0504	1376
Minnetonka	HUTTNER, Marian A.	(612)545-2338	579
	JENSEN, Wilma M.	(612)473-5965	599
Moorhead	RUDIE, Helen M.	(218)233-6817	1065
New Brighton	KEIM, Robert	(612)633-3393	635
Northfield	METZ, T J.	(507)663-4267	828
Robbinsdale	HERTHER, Nancy K.	(612)529-0115	533
Rochester	HAWTHORNE, Dorothy M.	(507)284-8797	514
	KEY, Jack D.	(507)284-2068	645
	KEYS, Thomas E.		645
Saint Joseph	HYNES, Arleen M.		580
St Louis Park	RINE, Joseph L.	(612)542-9631	1035
St Paul	DAVIS, Emmett A.	(612)699-4367	279
	FEYE-STUKAS, Janice	(612)296-2821	374
	HALES-MABRY, Celia E.	(612)645-2850	486
	HOLT, Constance W.	(612)690-6599	554
	RASMUSSEN, Mary L.	(612)644-0685	1009
	SCHERER, Herbert G.	(612)699-6165	1092
	SCHOLBERG, Henry	(612)633-6851	1098
	SMITH, Eldred R.	(612)698-2362	1154
	STOKES, Claire Z.	(612)642-0120	1196
	WALSTROM, Jon L.	(612)296-4543	1300
Scandia	HANSEN, Kathelen L.	(612)433-5477	497
Warren	STEMME, Virginia L.	(218)745-4762	1186
Worthington	SPILLERS, Roger E.	(507)372-2981	1174

MISSISSIPPI

Boyle	BAHR, Edward R.	(601)846-4607	45
Brandon	SELTZER, Ada M.		1114
Clarksdale	GRAVES, Sid F.	(601)627-2322	459
Clinton	BUCHANAN, Gerald	(601)924-7511	153
Hattiesburg	CARNOVALE, A N.	(601)264-5452	184
	HAUTH, Allan C.	(601)266-4126	513
	LATOUR, Terry S.	(601)266-4345	701
	WILSON, Mary S.	(601)266-4240	1352
Jackson	WEST, Carol C.	(601)944-1970	1326
Meridian	JOHNSON, Scott R.	(601)483-8241	609
Sunflower	POWELL, Anice C.	(601)569-3663	988
University	COCHRAN, J W.	(601)232-7361	225

MISSOURI

Afton	WOHLRABE, John C.	(314)843-8131	1359
Ballwin	BUHR, Rosemary E.		156
	TAYLOR, Arthur R.	(314)394-9973	1226
Blue Springs	CURTIS, George H.	(816)229-4799	267
Boonville	JOB, Rose A.		601
Cape Girardeau	STIEGEMEYER, Nancy H.	(314)334-3674	1193
Columbia	ARCHER, Stephen M.	(314)442-0611	31
	CARROLL, C E.	(314)443-8303	187
	HAVENER, Ralph S.	(314)882-4602	513
	LENOX, Mary F.	(314)882-4546	715
	RAITHEL, Frederick J.	(314)875-0026	1004
	SHAUGHNESSY, Thomas W.	(314)882-4701	1123
	WATERS, Bill F.	(314)443-3161	1308
	YOUNG, Virginia G.	(314)443-8413	1383
Fenton	DEKEN, Jean M.	(314)827-1717	288
Independence	BRILEY, Carol A.	(816)833-1400	136
	MEYERS, Martha L.	(816)833-1472	831
	MORALES, Milton F.	(816)836-5200	862

SPEAKER (Honorarium) (Cont'd)
MISSOURI (Cont'd)

Kansas City	BRADBURY, Daniel J.	(816)221-3203	125
	HESS, Stanley W.	(816)561-4000	534
	LINEBACH, Laura M.	(816)361-7031	730
	LONDRE, Felicia H.	(816)444-1878	738
	MILLS, Elaine L.	(816)333-1245	844
	PLUMB, Warren G.	(816)741-4824	978
	SERLING, Kitty	(816)753-5700	1116
	SPALDING, Helen H.	(816)276-1531	1171
Kirkwood	SHALLENBERGER, Anna F.	(314)821-4169	1119
Liberty	HOOVER, Jonnette L.	(816)781-7812	557
Maryville	HANKS, Nancy C.	(816)562-1590	496
Parkville	SMITH, Harold F.	(816)741-6085	1155
St Louis	BAERWALD, Susan M.	(314)772-1364	45
	CARGAS, Harry J.	(314)968-7014	181
	ELAM, Kristy L.	(314)658-2759	341
	ELSESSER, Lionelle H.	(314)725-4722	346
	GIETSCHIER, Steven P.	(314)993-7787	433
	LYONS, A J.	(314)241-2288	753
	NELSON, Mary A.	(314)889-6459	894
	ROBERTS, Jean A.	(314)664-0939	1040
	SUELFLOW, August R.	(314)721-5934	1206
	WINKLER, Carol A.	(314)481-4753	1355
St Peters	SANDSTEDT, Carl R.	(314)441-2300	1081
Springfield	COOMBS, James A.	(417)836-4534	241
	KOTAMRAJU, Sarada	(417)883-8590	673
Sugar Creek	STEELE, Anitra T.	(816)836-4031	1184
Warrensburg	NIEMEYER, Mollie M.	(816)429-4070	903
	SADLER, Philip A.	(816)747-8726	1073

MONTANA

Bozeman	ALLDREDGE, Noreen S.	(406)587-4877	14
	BREMER, Thomas A.	(406)994-5295	132
	BRUWELHEIDE, Janis H.	(406)587-0405	151
	MORTON, Bruce	(406)994-5313	870
Great Falls	O'BRYANT, Alice A.		915
	WARDEN, Margaret S.		1304
Helena	MORROW, Delores J.	(406)444-4714	869
	PARKER, Sara A.	(406)444-3115	942

NEBRASKA

Beatrice	DUX-IDEUS, Sherrie L.	(402)223-4581	330
Fremont	PETERSON, Vivian A.	(402)721-9119	964
Kearney	NORMAN, Ronald V.	(308)237-5133	909
Lincoln	BARRICK, Judy H.	(402)488-1668	59
	LEITER, Richard A.	(402)466-3468	714
Omaha	BROWN, Helen A.	(402)559-4326	144
	EARLEY, Dorothy A.	(402)333-5734	332
	LITTLE, Nina M.	(402)554-6282	733
	PHIPPS, Michael C.	(402)444-4834	969

NEVADA

Carson City	KERSCHNER, Joan G.	(702)887-2615	644
	ROCHA, Guy L.	(702)885-5210	1045
Henderson	TRASATTI, Margaret S.	(702)733-3613	1254
Las Vegas	BATSON, Darrell L.	(702)649-8845	64
	CUTLER, Marsha L.	(702)646-3932	268
	DALTON, Phyllis I.	(702)732-4793	271
	DAVENPORT, Marilyn A.	(702)453-5606	275
	GROSSHANS, Merilyn P.	(702)799-7855	473
	HUNSBERGER, Charles W.	(702)733-7810	574
Reno	GOULD, Martha B.	(702)785-4518	454
	MCNEAL, Betty	(702)325-5859	816
	ZINK, Steven D.	(702)345-0659	1389

NEW HAMPSHIRE

Concord	JOHNSON, Jean G.	(603)271-2429	605
	MEVERS, Frank C.	(603)224-3896	829
Hanover	ROLETT, Virginia V.	(603)643-3593	1051
Keene	LESSER, Charlotte B.	(603)357-1086	718
Manchester	COMEAU, Reginald A.	(603)668-6706	234
	KENT, Jeffrey A.	(603)622-4408	642
	MCGINNIS, Joan M.	(603)624-4366	806
Mirror Lake	SARLES, Christie V.	(603)569-4932	1083
Peterborough	BOND, George	(603)924-9281	113
Twin Mountain	PALMATIER, Susan M.	(603)846-2239	936

SPEAKER (Honorarium) (Cont'd)

NEW JERSEY

Aberdeen	WEISBURG, Hilda K.	(201)566-1995	1319
Annandale	MURO, Ernest A.	(201)735-9633	880
Bloomfield	BETANCOURT, Ingrid T.	(201)743-9511	92
Bogota	MACKESY, Eileen M.		756
Boontown	HOVER, Leila M.	(201)335-7434	563
Butler	GARDNER, Sue A.	(201)838-3262	418
Califon	ROSENBERG, Gail L.		1056
Cherry Hill	BECK, Susan J.	(609)354-7638	72
	GLATT, Carol R.		440
Cranford	BEIMAN, Frances M.	(201)272-5840	75
	HALL, Homer J.	(201)276-4311	488
	WOLFE, N J.	(201)279-9563	1361
Denville	THOMAS, Hilary B.	(201)625-8136	1236
	VARIEUR, Normand L.		1278
Dumont	PAPAZIAN, Pierre	(201)385-8225	939
East Brunswick	KING, Donald R.	(201)828-2752	650
East Orange	GORMAN, Audrey J.	(201)676-2472	452
	MATHAI, Aleyamma	(201)266-5613	783
Edison	DINERMAN, Gloria	(201)906-1777	304
Far Hills	SEAGLE, Janet M.	(201)234-2300	1109
Flemington	MCGREGOR, Walter	(201)788-3025	808
Fort Lee	ALTOMARA, Rita E.	(201)592-3614	18
Glen Rock	PERCELLI, Irene M.	(201)445-5983	958
Green Village	KEON, Edward F.	(201)822-0062	643
Haddonfield	SWARTZ, Betty J.	(609)429-8498	1214
Highland Park	CLARK, Philip M.	(201)572-5414	218
	LI, Marjorie H.	(201)828-8730	724
	MILLER, Lynn F.	(201)572-6563	840
	NIGRIN, Albert G.		904
	PAGE, Penny B.	(201)247-9353	934
Hightstown	BRODMAN, Estelle	(609)443-8094	139
Lakewood	HERBERT, Barbara R.	(201)364-2200	530
Lawrenceville	STEPHEN, Ross G.	(609)896-5111	1187
Leonia	DAIN, Phyllis	(212)280-4032	270
	SHERMAN, Louise L.	(201)461-6137	1128
Madison	COUGHLIN, Caroline M.	(201)377-3000	250
	LONG, Joanna R.	(201)377-2376	739
	SNELSON, Pamela	(201)377-3000	1163
Mahwah	YUEH, Norma N.	(201)529-7578	1384
Maplewood	BRYANT, David S.	(201)763-9294	152
	D'ALLEYRAND, Marc R.	(201)761-1028	270
Middletown	RILEY, Robert H.	(201)615-0900	1034
Montclair	HOROWITZ, Marjorie B.	(201)744-8697	560
	TUROCK, Betty J.	(201)744-3354	1265
Morristown	BUCK, Anne M.	(201)829-5111	153
Mount Holly	ALTERMAN, Deborah H.	(609)261-3458	18
	CARR, Charles E.	(609)267-9660	185
Neptune	WILSON, Fredric W.	(201)922-9491	1351
Neshanic	VANDERGRIFT, Kay E.	(201)369-8685	1274
New Brunswick	EUSTER, Joanne R.	(201)932-7505	356
	NASH, Stanley D.	(201)932-7014	888
	REELING, Patricia G.	(201)932-7917	1016
	RICHARDS, Pamela S.		1028
	SARACEVIC, Tefko	(201)932-7447	1082
	SIMMONS, Ruth J.	(201)932-7006	1140
	SWARTZBURG, Susan G.	(201)932-8573	1214
Newark	CUMMINGS, Charles F.	(201)733-7776	264
	HARVELL, Valeria G.		509
Ocean City	MASON, Michael L.	(609)398-0969	781
Oradell	SUMMERS, Robert A.	(201)262-2529	1209
Paramus	WHITE, Robert W.	(201)652-6772	1332
Park Ridge	WERNER, Edward K.	(201)391-4934	1324
Pequannock	SUSSMAN, Valerie J.	(201)696-9655	1210
Perth Amboy	HARDISH, Patrick M.	(201)826-5298	500
Piscataway	FIGUEREDO, Danilo H.	(201)463-3725	376
	SPAULDING, Frank H.	(201)463-0158	1172
Point Pleasant	GREENE, Ellin P.	(201)899-2270	464
Pomona	MOLL, Joy K.	(609)652-1776	853
Princeton	BERKNER, Dimity S.	(609)924-3891	87
	CARLSON, Dudley B.		182
	JOHNSON, David K.	(609)924-2870	603
	LOGAN, Harold J.	(609)520-4066	737
	THRESHER, Jacquelyn E.	(609)924-9529	1243
Red Bank	ANTCZAK, Janice	(201)741-0815	28
Ridgewood	SEER, Gitelle	(201)652-2595	1111
Rutherford	RAPPAPORT, Susan E.		1008
Sewell	CROCKER, Jane L.	(609)468-5000	259
Short Hills	TALCOTT, Ann W.	(201)379-6721	1221

SPEAKER (Honorarium) (Cont'd)

NEW JERSEY (Cont'd)

Somerville	MOYER, Holley M.	(201)725-1600	874
Sparta	GUIDA, Pat	(201)729-8176	476
Summit	SOMMER, Ursula M.	(201)593-8526	1167
Tenafly	WECHTLER, Stephen R.	(201)568-8680	1315
Trenton	MCCULLOUGH, Jack W.	(609)771-2106	801
	RAZZANO, Barbara W.	(609)984-7608	1012
Upper Montclair	PARR, Mary Y.	(201)746-0352	944
Wayne	COHEN, Adrea G.	(201)696-8948	227
West Long Branch	PALMISANO-DRUCKER, Elsalyn	(201)870-9194	937
West New York	BRITTON, Jeffrey W.	(201)868-2029	137
Westfield	WILSTED, Thomas P.	(201)789-9147	1353
Woodbridge	SPANGLER, William N.	(201)634-4450	1171

NEW MEXICO

Albuquerque	CARLSON, Kathleen A.	(505)883-1924	182
	ELDREDGE, Jonathan D.	(505)277-0654	342
	FALARDEAU, Ernest R.	(505)242-3462	361
	LOVE, Erika	(505)277-2548	743
	PRUETT, Nancy J.		996
	ROLLER, Twila J.	(505)884-7871	1051
	ROLLINS, Stephen J.	(505)277-5057	1051
	THOMPSON, Janet A.	(505)277-7172	1240
	WHITLOW, Cherrill M.	(505)266-1472	1333
Farmington	JASSAL, Raghbir S.	(505)327-7813	595
Hobbs	TUBESING, Richard L.	(505)393-6528	1261
Roswell	KLOPFER, Jerome J.	(505)622-6250	662
	MCLAREN, M B.	(505)622-6250	813

NEW YORK

Albany	COX, Richard J.	(518)486-4820	253
	DANIELS, Pam	(518)473-8177	273
	KNAPP, Sara D.	(518)442-3539	663
	LEWIS, Frances R.	(518)869-9317	723
	MATTIE, Joseph J.	(518)474-4970	786
	MOORE, Rue I.	(518)445-5197	861
	MOREHEAD, Joe	(518)442-5128	863
	NEVETT, Micki S.	(518)459-2178	897
	NICHOLS-RANDALL, Barbara L.	(518)489-7649	902
	PAULSON, Peter J.	(518)489-8549	950
	SMITH, Audrey J.	(518)438-4316	1152
	VAILLANCOURT, Pauline M.	(518)489-6207	1271
	WALKER, M G.	(518)436-1975	1296
Amawalk	HANE, Paula J.	(914)962-2933	495
APO New York	HAUSRATH, Donald C.		513
Astoria	SPINA, Marie C.	(718)274-6136	1175
Babylon	CORRY, Emmett	(516)587-2585	247
Ballston Lake	EGAN, Mary J.	(518)399-5151	338
Bayside	BILLY, George J.		97
Beechhurst	CARVER, Mary		191
Bellport	JANSEN, Guenter A.	(516)286-2626	593
	KLAUBER, Julie B.	(516)286-1600	658
	MULLER, Claudya B.	(516)286-1600	877
Bergen	FABRIZIO, Timothy C.	(716)494-2264	360
Binghamton	HILL, Malcolm K.	(607)723-8236	540
Black River	MARSTON, Hope I.	(315)773-5847	775
Bronx	BUCKWALD, Joel	(212)543-5911	155
	CANNATA, Arleen	(212)295-5910	178
	DAVIS, Mary B.	(212)829-7770	280
	DECANDIDO, Graceanne A.		285
	LOCASCIO, Aline M.	(212)588-8400	735
	PATRYCH, Joseph		947
	PERSKY, Gail M.	(212)548-6007	961
	REIMAN, Donald H.	(212)549-4890	1020
	SHANNON, Michael O.	(212)960-7775	1120
	SOPELAK, Mary J.	(212)588-2266	1168
	WEINBERG, Bella H.	(212)547-5159	1317
Brooklyn	BLAKE-O'HOGAN, Kathleen E.	(718)625-2829	103
	BRANDEAU, John H.	(718)852-8700	128
	CHICKERING, F W.	(718)636-3456	208
	GENCO, Barbara A.	(718)499-8750	426
	GUREWITSCH, Bonnie	(718)338-6494	478
	HOMMEL, Claudia	(718)237-0028	555
	HORNE, Dorice L.	(718)859-1830	560
	JOHNSON, Sheila A.	(718)780-7744	609
	KLEIMAN, Allan M.	(718)645-2396	658

SPEAKER (Honorarium) (Cont'd)
NEW YORK (Cont'd)
Brooklyn

	MALINCONICO, S M.	(718)627-0558	763
	PETTIT, Marilyn H.	(718)237-0672	965
	ROGINSKI, James W.	(718)499-4850	1050
	ROMALIS, Carl		1052
	RUBINSTEIN, Roslyn	(718)834-8779	1065
	SCHWABACHER, Sara A.	(718)388-0023	1104
	SEMKOW, Julie L.	(718)624-3189	1115
	SULTANOF, Jeff B.	(718)768-1611	1208
	SWEENEY, Richard T.	(718)643-4446	1215
	SWIESZKOWSK, L S.	(718)383-8480	1216
	THOMAS, Lucille C.	(718)778-1585	1237
	TUDIVER, Lillian	(718)789-7220	1262
	WOFSE, Joy G.	(718)788-5360	1359
Brookville	GRANT, Mary M.	(516)299-2832	458
	MAILLET, Lucienne G.	(516)299-2855	761
Buffalo	BOBINSKI, George S.	(716)636-2412	108
	ELLISON, John W.	(716)636-3069	345
	GURN, Robert M.	(716)846-7187	478
	KELLER, Sharon A.	(716)831-3337	635
	ROSE, Pamela M.	(716)837-7175	1055
	VON WAHLDE, Barbara	(716)636-2967	1288
	WAGNER, Stephen K.	(716)837-1563	1292
	WELLS, Margaret R.	(716)636-2943	1322
	WOLFE, Theresa L.	(716)632-4491	1361
Canadaigua	CUMMINS, A B.	(716)394-1381	264
Chappaqua	CHEATHAM, Bertha M.	(914)238-3586	204
Cherry Plain	GILCHER, Edwin	(518)658-2429	434
Circleville	NELSON, James B.	(914)361-2415	894
Cold Spring	BARNHART, David K.	(914)265-2822	58
	FEICK, Christina L.	(914)265-2304	368
Cold Spring Harbor	FARAONE, Maria B.	(516)271-1771	363
Commack	ROFES, William L.	(516)499-4370	1049
Coram	EIDELMAN, Diane L.	(516)331-8662	340
Cornwall	HANSON, Jan E.	(914)534-3104	498
Cornwall on			
Hudson	WEISS, Egon A.	(914)534-9467	1320
Croton-on-Hudson	COHEN, Aaron	(914)271-8170	227
Delanson	SOMERS, Betty J.	(518)864-5235	1166
Delhi	SORGEN, Herbert J.	(607)746-4107	1168
Delmar	SAFFADY, William	(518)439-2469	1074
	SHUMAN, Susan E.	(518)475-1202	1134
Dewitt	ELY, Donald P.	(315)446-0259	347
East Meadow	CANDE, Lorraine N.	(516)794-1202	178
	MCCARTNEY, Margaret M.	(516)489-8136	794
East Northport	DAVIDSON, Steven I.	(516)368-0841	276
Elma	DRZEWIECKI, Iris M.	(716)683-0592	321
Elmsford	TRUDELL, Robert J.	(914)993-1608	1259
Flushing	COHEN, David	(718)520-7194	228
	COOPER, Marianne	(718)520-7194	243
	MCMORRAN, Charles E.	(718)358-4526	815
	SURPRENANT, Thomas T.	(718)520-7194	1210
Forest Hills	GELLER, Lawrence D.		426
Franklin Square	PILLA, Marianne L.	(516)775-4143	973
Garden City	FRIEDMAN, Arthur L.	(516)222-7406	403
Garrison	BALDWIN, Geraldine S.	(914)424-3020	51
Geneseo	CAREN, Loretta	(716)243-0438	181
Getzville	DENSMORE, Christopher	(716)688-2001	293
Glen Falls	GRAMINSKI, Denise M.	(518)793-2927	457
Great Neck	LERNER, Arthur		717
Hamilton	BERGEN, Daniel P.	(315)824-2381	85
Hastings on			
Hudson	JELLINEK, George	(914)478-1979	596
Hempstead	ANDREWS, Charles R.	(516)560-5940	26
	STERN, Marc J.	(516)560-5975	1189
Hicksville	HOLMES, Harvey L.	(516)935-4813	553
Horseheads	BROUSE, Ann G.	(607)562-8986	141
Houghton	LAUER, Jonathan D.	(716)567-2211	702
Huntington	NEWMAN, Eileen M.	(516)673-2023	899
Ithaca	ASHMUN, Lawrence F.		36
	CHIANG, Katherine S.	(607)272-3086	207
	COONS, William W.	(607)255-7959	242
	EDDY, Donald D.	(607)255-5281	335
	LIPPINCOTT, Joan K.	(607)255-7731	732
	OLSEN, Wallace C.	(607)255-2551	922
	PANZ, Richard	(607)273-4074	938
	ZASLAW, Neal	(607)257-1052	1386

SPEAKER (Honorarium) (Cont'd)
NEW YORK (Cont'd)

Jackson Heights	RANHAND, Jori L.	(718)469-4728	1007
	WALSH, Robert R.	(718)639-3188	1300
Jacksonville	HILLMANN, Diane I.	(602)387-9207	541
Jamaica	MARKE, Julius J.	(718)990-6759	771
Lake Success	TRINKOFF, Elaine	(516)466-9148	1257
Larchmont	GILLIGAN, Julie		436
	SETON, Charles B.	(914)834-0598	1117
Latham	BRUNELLE, Bette S.	(518)783-1161	150
Little Neck	EDWARDS, Barnett A.	(718)425-2576	337
Liverpool	GOLDEN, Fay A.	(315)451-5890	445
	POLLY, Jean A.	(315)457-0310	981
Long Beach	WASSERMAN, Ricki F.		1308
Long Island City	MARTIN, Brian G.	(718)726-5885	775
Lynbrook	HESSLEIN, Shirley B.	(516)887-5071	534
Macedon	WEMETT, Lisa C.	(315)986-3949	1323
Manlius	NAGLE, Ann	(315)682-8160	886
Mastic	MACINICK, James W.	(516)399-3281	755
Mattituck	PERLMAN, Stephen E.	(516)298-4335	959
Menands	LENZ, Millicent A.		716
Mexico	MAUTINO, Patricia H.	(315)963-7251	787
Middletown	ANGLIN, Richard V.	(914)343-1131	28
	BAUM, Christina D.	(914)344-3615	66
Mt Kisco	NELSON, Nancy M.	(914)666-3394	894
Mt Vernon	SEITZ, Robert J.	(914)699-6917	1113
Nassau	VANNORTWICK, Barbara L.	(518)766-4190	1276
New Paltz	CONNORS, William E.	(914)257-2203	238
	NYQUIST, Corinne E.	(914)255-2209	913
New Windsor	SANKER, Paul N.	(914)562-0470	1081
New York	ALLEN, Robert R.	(212)337-6991	16
	ALLENTUCK, Marcia E.		16
	ARKHURST, Joyce C.	(212)368-1788	31
	BAKER, John P.	(212)255-7267	48
	BEHRMANN, Christine A.	(212)568-6349	75
	BERNER, Andrew J.	(212)515-5299	88
	BOCKMAN, Eugene J.	(212)566-5398	109
	BORBELY, Jack		116
	BOURKE, Thomas A.	(212)930-0838	119
	BOWLEY, Craig	(212)239-0827	121
	BRAUDE, Robert M.	(212)472-5919	129
	BRODY, Elaine	(212)535-9229	139
	BROWAR, Lisa M.	(212)930-0556	141
	BRUGNOLOTTI, Phyllis T.	(212)873-0677	150
	BUCK, Richard M.		154
	BUTLER, Tyrone G.	(212)566-5367	167
	CAMBRIA, Roberto		174
	CASSELL, Kay A.	(212)614-6551	193
	CIOPPA, Lawrence	(212)677-5688	214
	COHEN, Frederick	(212)431-3059	228
	COHEN, Frederick S.	(212)594-9880	228
	COPLEN, Ron	(212)869-3348	244
	DE GENNARO, Richard	(212)930-0769	287
	DENNIS, Anne R.	(212)645-4500	292
	DERRICKSON, Margaret	(212)620-4230	294
	DYER, Esther R.	(212)777-9064	330
	EBER, Beryl E.	(212)621-0635	334
	ETZI, Richard		356
	FERGUSON, Russell	(212)219-1222	372
	FOLTER, Roland	(212)687-4808	388
	FONTAINE, Sue	(212)533-7226	388
	FRANKLIN, Linda C.	(212)679-6038	398
	FREIFELD, Roberta I.	(212)777-9271	401
	FRUSCIANO, Thomas J.	(212)998-2644	406
	GARDNER, Ralph D.	(212)877-6820	418
	GERHARDT, Lillian N.	(212)463-6759	428
	GINSBURG, Carol L.	(212)850-1440	438
	GLASER, Gloria T.	(212)753-8694	439
	GRECH, Anthony P.	(212)382-6740	461
	GRELE, Ronald J.	(212)280-2273	467
	GURIEVITCH, Grania B.	(212)974-9507	478
	HARRIS, Carolyn L.	(212)280-2223	504
	HARVEY, John F.	(215)509-2612	509
	HEWITT, Vivian D.		535
	HIGGINBOTHAM, Barbra B.	(212)533-2173	537
	HOLTZE, Sally H.	(212)674-6973	555
	HUDSON, Alice C.	(212)222-2835	569
	HUNTER, Gregory S.	(212)940-1690	576
	HUTSON, Jean B.	(212)368-1515	579
	KAIN, Joan P.	(212)850-0768	622

SPEAKER (Honorarium) (Cont'd)
NEW YORK (Cont'd)
New York

	KARATNYTSKY, Christine A.	(212)420-1436	627
	KNAPPMAN, Edward W.	(212)683-2244	663
	KOENIG, Michael E.	(212)867-0489	668
	KRANICH, Nancy C.	(212)998-2447	676
	KUHNER, Robert A.	(212)663-3360	683
	KULLESEID, Eleanor R.	(212)666-6013	683
	LAMBE, Michael	(212)371-9400	690
	LANDAU, Herbert B.	(212)705-7600	692
	LUBETSKI, Edith E.	(212)340-7720	745
	MACINTYRE, Ronald R.	(212)227-5599	755
	MANDEL, Carol A.	(212)280-2226	764
	MARGOLIES, Alan	(212)489-5042	770
	MARTIN, Jean F.	(212)928-4231	776
	MARTIN, Richard	(212)760-7970	778
	MASSIS, Bruce E.	(212)595-2000	782
	MASYR, Caryl L.	(212)777-9271	783
	MELKIN, Audrey D.	(212)850-6705	822
	MIHRAM, Danielle	(212)998-2515	834
	MILLER, Ellen L.	(212)406-3186	837
	MILLER, Michael D.		841
	MILLER, Sarah J.		842
	MINTZ, Anne P.	(212)620-2499	847
	MOLZ, Redmond K.	(212)280-4787	854
	MONACO, James	(212)254-8235	854
	MONDLIN, Marvin	(212)982-8189	854
	MOORE, Sonia	(212)755-5120	861
	MOSES, Julian M.	(212)688-8426	871
	MYERS, Maria P.	(212)473-6673	884
	NELOMS, Karen H.	(212)582-9239	893
	O'GRADY, Jean P.	(212)370-8690	918
	OSTROW, Rona	(212)691-1672	929
	PALMER, Julia R.	(212)744-7202	936
	PAUL, Sandra K.	(212)675-7804	949
	PELLOWSKI, Anne	(212)316-1170	955
	PURCELL, Marcia L.	(212)982-3786	998
	QUAIN, Julie R.		999
	RAUCH, Anne	(212)906-8794	1010
	REGAN, Muriel	(212)869-3348	1017
	REID, Carolyn A.	(212)472-5919	1018
	RICHARDS, Daniel T.	(212)678-0908	1028
	RICHTER, Robert	(212)947-1395	1031
	ROSIGNOLO, Beverly A.	(212)962-4111	1057
	ROTHMAN, John	(212)645-3008	1060
	ST. CLAIR, Guy	(212)515-5299	1075
	SARRIS, Shirley C.	(212)473-2990	1083
	SCHUMAN, Patricia G.	(212)925-8650	1103
	SETTANNI, Joseph A.	(212)289-9059	1117
	SLATE, Ted	(212)350-4682	1148
	SOLOMON, Samuel H.	(212)208-1200	1166
	STANAT, Ruth E.	(212)725-4550	1179
	STILLMAN, Stanley W.		1194
	TAYLOR, Patricia A.	(212)566-4285	1228
	TAYLOR, Robert N.	(212)664-9021	1228
	TICE, Margaret E.		1244
	VAUGHAN, John	(212)924-3729	1279
	WALKER, William B.	(212)595-7335	1296
	WALSH, Mark L.	(212)996-4168	1300
	WEATHERFORD, Elizabeth	(212)925-4682	1311
	WERTSMAN, Vladimir F.	(212)246-8176	1325
	WILLNER, Channan P.	(212)870-1675	1348
	WOSH, Peter J.	(212)581-7400	1369
	WRIGHT, Bernell	(212)866-3042	1370
	WRIGHT, Sylvia H.	(212)222-6148	1373
Niagara Falls	SHIELDS, Gerald R.	(716)284-2928	1130
Oneonta	JOHNSON, Richard D.	(607)432-0131	608
Orchard Park	LYMAN, Helen H.	(716)662-3525	751
Ossining	STAPLETON, Darwin H.	(914)762-8921	1181
Palisades	WARD, Edith	(914)359-2081	1303
Pearl River	BRISFJORD, Inez S.	(914)735-1567	136
	SPERR BRISFJORD, Inez L.	(914)735-1567	1173
Plattsburgh	RANSOM, Stanley A.	(518)563-5719	1007
Port Washington	BRENNER, Everett H.	(516)767-2728	133
	EPSTEIN, Connie C.	(516)883-8177	351
	SCHREIBMAN, Fay C.	(516)767-0081	1099
Poughkeepsie	SEEBER, Frances M.	(914)452-8122	1111
	WALSH, Robin S.	(914)462-7129	1300
	WIGG, Ristiina M.	(914)471-6060	1337

SPEAKER (Honorarium) (Cont'd)
NEW YORK (Cont'd)

Purchase	FREIDES, Thelma	(914)253-5096	401
Rhinebeck	MCCLELLAND, Bruce A.	(914)876-2230	796
Riverdale	KLEINBURD, Freda		659
Rochester	BERKMAN, Robert I.	(716)461-3206	87
	CUMMINS, Julie A.	(716)428-7366	264
	CUSEO, Allan A.	(716)325-4264	267
	GLASER, June E.	(716)275-5010	439
	GRAUER, Sally M.	(716)461-4380	458
	HOPE, Thomas W.	(716)458-4250	557
	HUNT, Suellyn	(716)428-6981	575
	KANSFIELD, Norman J.	(716)271-1320	625
	SIMMONS, Rebecca A.	(706)271-3361	1140
	STOSS, Frederick W.	(716)436-8719	1198
Rockville Centre	FRIEDLAND, Rhoda W.	(516)766-6387	403
Rotterdam	SIMON, Anne E.	(518)355-8391	1140
Rouses Point	CURRAN, George L.		266
Rye	GREENFIELD, Judith C.	(914)967-0480	464
Saratoga Springs	RATZER, Mary B.		1010
Scarborough	HOPKINS, Lee B.	(914)941-5810	558
Scarsdale	BERGER, Pam P.	(914)723-3156	86
Schenectady	HALSEY, Richard S.	(518)370-0902	490
	KLEMPNER, Irving M.	(518)393-5983	660
	SHEVIAK, Jean K.	(518)370-6294	1129
Scotia	HENDRICKSON, Maria F.	(518)374-6209	527
Seaford	FLUCKIGER, Adrienne N.	(516)221-1334	386
Setauket	NICHOLS, Gerald D.	(516)689-7071	901
	VERBESEY, J R.	(516)751-6913	1282
Smithtown	BENNETT, James F.	(516)265-2037	81
Somers	SHAPIRO, Lillian L.	(914)276-2269	1121
Staten Island	KLINGLE, Philip A.	(718)390-5291	662
Sunnyside	WOOD, Sallie B.	(718)565-5490	1365
Syosset	CALVANO, Margaret	(516)921-1674	174
	JENSEN, Dennis F.	(516)921-0418	598
Syracuse	ABBOTT, George L.	(315)445-0484	1
	CASEY, Daniel W.	(315)468-0176	192
	EISENBERG, Michael B.	(315)423-4549	340
	FROEHLICH, Thomas J.	(315)425-9080	405
	HULBERT, Linda A.	(315)473-4257	572
	MARCHAND, Donald A.	(315)423-2736	768
	MARTIN, Thomas H.	(315)423-3840	778
	MCCLURE, Charles R.	(315)423-2911	797
	STAM, Deirdre C.		1179
Troy	GINSBURG, Joanne R.	(518)274-7071	438
	MOLHOLT, Pat	(518)276-8300	852
Uniondale	BARTENBACH, Martha A.	(516)292-8920	60
	GREEN, Joseph H.	(516)292-8920	462
Upper Nyack	POUNDSTONE, Sally H.	(914)358-9294	987
Utica	WEBER, Jerome F.	(315)732-4747	1314
Voorheesville	BARRON, Robert E.		60
Wantagh	WESTERMANN, Mary L.	(516)679-8842	1327
Water Mill	GROSSMAN, Adrian J.	(516)537-3623	473
West Nyack	SIVULICH, Sandra S.	(914)358-9298	1145
Westhampton	BARR, Janet L.	(516)288-5539	58
White Plains	BOWLES, Edmund A.	(914)696-1900	121
	HIGGINS, Judith H.	(914)949-2175	538
	ROCQUE, Bernice L.	(914)253-4307	1046
	TREFRY, Mary G.	(914)761-5478	1255
Whitestone	RIECHEL, Rosemarie	(718)990-0714	1033
Williamsville	BOBINSKI, Mary F.	(716)688-4919	108
Wynantskill	CORSARO, James		248
Yonkers	FRANK, Mortimer H.	(914)423-2304	397
	GAFFNEY, Ellen E.	(914)968-6200	412

NORTH CAROLINA

Bahama	STINE, Roy S.	(719)471-8853	1194
Belmont	BAUMSTEIN, Paschal M.	(704)825-3711	66
Boone	HATHAWAY, Milton G.	(704)262-5113	512
Cary	BRUMBACK, Elsie	(919)467-6697	150
	BURCSU, James E.	(919)469-2731	158
Chapel Hill	ASHEIM, Lester E.	(919)967-1882	35
	BROADUS, Robert N.	(919)962-8063	138
	DANIEL, Evelyn H.	(919)962-8366	272
	EATON, Elizabeth G.	(919)967-7966	333
	FEEHAN, Patricia E.	(919)962-8366	368
	GASAWAY, Laura N.	(919)962-1321	421
	HOLLEY, Edward G.		551
	KISER, Anita H.	(919)968-3946	656
	NEAL, Michelle H.	(919)962-0077	890

SPEAKER (Honorarium) (Cont'd)

NORTH CAROLINA (Cont'd)

Chapel Hill			
	SAYE, Jerry D.	(919)962-8073	1086
	SEIBERT, Karen S.	(919)962-1301	1112
Durham	BASEFSKY, Stuart M.	(919)684-2380	62
	BURGIN, Robert E.	(919)683-6485	159
	CAMPBELL, Jerry D.	(919)684-2034	176
	FEINGLOS, Susan J.	(919)493-2904	369
	GARTRELL, Ellen G.	(919)493-3747	420
	GERMAIN, Claire M.	(919)684-6182	429
	HEWITT, Joe A.	(919)489-9875	535
	SEMONCHE, Barbara P.	(919)489-7247	1115
	SHEARER, Kenneth D.	(919)683-6485	1124
	STRAUSS, Diane	(919)286-7895	1201
	TOOMER, Clarence	(919)682-0238	1251
Fayetteville	BEATTIE, Barbara C.	(919)867-5143	70
	KRIEGER, Lee A.	(919)864-9349	678
Greensboro	JARRELL, James R.	(919)273-7061	594
	MILLER, Marilyn L.	(919)334-5100	840
	O'CONNOR, Sandra L.	(919)273-1914	916
	WINKEL, Lois	(919)275-4935	1355
	YOUNG, Tommie M.	(909)621-0032	1383
Greenville	BOCCACCIO, Mary A.	(919)757-6671	108
	CHENG, Chao S.	(929)756-4543	206
	LANIER, Gene D.	(919)757-6627	696
	MELLON, Constance A.	(919)757-6870	822
	SCOTT, Ralph L.	(919)830-0522	1108
High Point	AUSTIN, Neal F.	(919)869-6260	40
Jacksonville	VEITCH, Carol J.	(919)455-7350	1281
Jefferson	FRANKLIN, Robert M.	(919)246-4460	398
Kinston	SOUTHERLAND, Carol A.	(919)523-0819	1169
	TABORY, Maxim	(919)522-3830	1219
Mebane	MINEIRO, Barbara E.	(919)578-4299	845
Montreat	BROOKS, Jerrold L.	(704)669-7661	140
	FOREMAN, Kenneth J.	(704)669-2782	390
Raleigh	BRADBURN, Frances B.	(919)878-4497	125
	ISACCO, Jeanne M.	(919)851-4703	584
	PRICE, William S.	(919)733-7305	993
	PURYEAR, Pamela E.	(919)737-2836	998
	TAYLOR, Raymond M.	(919)787-7824	1228
	WILLIAMS, Gene J.	(919)828-5063	1343
Reidsville	GUNN, Shirley A.	(919)342-0951	477
Research Triangle Pk	BEST-NICHOLS, Barbara J.	(919)544-3808	92
	MENDELL, Stefanie	(919)248-1842	823
Riegelwood	KERESEY, Gayle	(919)669-2934	643
Salisbury	ALDRICH, Willie L.	(704)636-1158	11
Sanford	MCGINN, Howard F.	(919)776-2335	806
	MURCHISON, Margaret B.	(919)258-3277	879
Spruce Pine	AUSTIN, Mary C.		40
Swannanoa	ALLEN, Christina Y.	(704)298-4742	14
Troy	WALTERS, Carol G.	(919)572-1311	1301
Washington	TIMOUR, John A.	(919)975-3355	1246
Wilson	VALENTINE, Patrick M.	(919)237-5355	1271
Winston-Salem	HAUPERT, Thomas J.	(919)722-1742	512
	WOODARD, John R.	(919)761-5089	1365
Yanceyville	MASSEY, Nancy O.	(919)968-0852	782

NORTH DAKOTA

Bismarck	MOREHOUSE, Valerie J.	(701)224-4658	863
	NEWBORG, Gerald G.	(701)224-2668	898
Ellendale	ZINK, Esther L.	(701)349-3609	1389
Fargo	BIRDSALL, Douglas G.	(701)237-8878	98
	SIBLEY, Carol H.	(701)235-0664	1134

OHIO

Akron	BERRINGER, Virginia M.	(216)375-6260	90
	DURBIN, Roger	(216)794-9706	328
	LATSHAW, Patricia H.	(216)762-7621	701
Albany	CONLIFFE, Bobbi L.	(614)698-3336	236
Barberton	SWINEHART, Katharine J.	(216)745-1194	1216
Bay Village	BACON, Agnes K.		44
	BUTCHER, Sharon L.	(216)871-0913	166
	DOMBEY, Kathryn W.	(216)871-5024	310
	LORANTH, Alice N.	(216)871-9014	741
Bedford	PARCH, Grace D.		939
Berea	MACIUSZKO, Jerzy J.	(216)234-9206	755

SPEAKER (Honorarium) (Cont'd)

OHIO (Cont'd)

Bowling Green	BURLINGAME, Dwight F.	(419)372-2708	161
	HARNER, James L.	(419)372-7553	503
	MCCALLUM, Brenda W.		793
	MILLER, Ruth G.	(419)352-0817	842
	MILLER, William	(419)372-2857	843
	REPP, Joan M.		1024
	ZAPOROZHETZ, Laurene E.	(419)354-2101	1386
Canfield	GENAWAY, David C.	(216)533-2194	426
Canton	ERWIN, Nancy S.	(216)477-7309	353
Centerville	GARTEN, Edward D.		420
Chesterland	CORBUS, Lawrence J.	(216)286-8941	245
Chillicothe	PLANTON, Stanley P.	(614)775-9500	977
Cincinnati	BAKER, Carole A.	(513)871-2042	48
	HILAND, Gerard P.	(513)231-0810	538
	HUGE, Sharon A.	(513)369-6940	571
	KONKEL, Mary S.	(513)681-2074	670
	POCKROSE, Sheryl R.	(513)369-6954	979
	SHIVERDECKER, Darlene J.	(513)281-3760	1132
	WELKER, Kathy J.	(513)684-2678	1321
	WILSON, Lucy	(513)745-4313	1351
Cleveland	CHESHIER, Robert G.	(216)368-3427	206
	DRACH, Priscilla L.		318
	EAGLEN, Audrey B.	(216)398-1800	331
	KANTOR, Paul B.	(216)321-7713	626
	MACIUSZKO, Kathleen L.	(216)826-2839	755
	MCSPADDEN, Robert M.	(216)229-5900	818
	ORR, Cynthia	(216)449-2049	926
	PEARMAN, Sara J.	(211)421-7340	952
	PIKE, Kermit J.	(216)721-5722	972
	RADER, Hannelore B.	(216)687-2475	1002
	RAY, Laura E.	(216)844-3788	1011
	ROBSON, Timothy D.	(216)696-4390	1045
	VENABLE, Andrew A.	(216)541-4128	1282
	WAREHAM, Nancy L.	(216)921-3900	1304
Cleveland Heights	BOWIE, Angela B.	(216)291-5588	121
	GRABOWSKI, John J.	(216)932-8805	455
Columbus	ALLEN, Cameron	(614)237-1516	14
	BOOMGAARDEN, Wesley L.	(614)447-0524	115
	BRANN, Andrew R.	(614)221-4181	128
	DAVIS, Linda M.	(614)294-5429	280
	DRIESSEN, Diane	(614)486-0621	320
	GOLDING, Alfred S.		445
	HADDOCK, Mable	(614)258-9052	482
	HAMILTON, Marsha J.	(614)292-6314	492
	HECK, Thomas F.	(614)292-2310	519
	IBEN, Glenn A.	(614)293-8925	581
	KNOBLAUCH, Carol J.	(614)299-4020	665
	MCDOWELL, Judith H.	(614)771-0273	804
	MCWILLIAM, Deborah A.	(614)222-7165	818
	MIXTER, Keith E.	(614)263-7204	850
	PARSONS, Augustine C.	(614)895-3201	944
	PHILIP, John J.	(614)462-7061	967
	WAGNER, Judith O.	(614)451-7471	1292
	WOODS, Alan L.	(614)292-8251	1366
Cuyahoga Falls	BERRY, Diana M.	(216)929-1948	90
	OSTERFIELD, George T.	(216)929-9470	928
	WAGNER, Louis F.	(216)922-0681	1292
Dayton	BALL, Diane A.	(513)293-7339	52
	BANTA, Gratia J.	(513)277-4444	55
	MARSHALL, Mary E.	(513)461-1548	774
	PEAKE, Sharon K.	(513)865-6958	952
Delaware	SAMPLES, Judith L.	(614)362-3861	1078
Dublin	HAYNES, Kathleen J.	(614)764-6000	516
	JACOB, Mary E.	(614)764-6063	589
Englewood	CUPP, Christian M.	(513)832-0136	265
Euclid	COLEMAN, Judith	(216)261-5300	231
Findlay	HARDESTY, Vicki H.	(419)422-6121	499
	LUST, Jeanette M.	(419)424-5739	749
Gallipolis	GUTHRIE, Chab C.	(614)446-7323	479
Georgetown	TOMLIN, Marsha A.	(513)378-3154	1250
Granville	RUGG, John D.		1066
Highland Heights	JENKINS, Glen P.	(216)442-1475	597
Jackson	ANDERSON, Eric S.	(614)286-6685	22
Kent	GILDZEN, Alex J.	(216)672-2270	434
	NELSON, Olga G.	(216)678-8236	895
Lancaster	MCCAULEY, Hannah V.	(614)654-6711	795
Lima	MCDANIEL, Deanna J.	(419)991-6065	801
Lisbon	MCPEAK, James J.	(216)424-3117	817

SPEAKER (Honorarium) (Cont'd)

OHIO (Cont'd)

London	DIENER, Ronald E.		302
Medina	SMITH, Robert S.	(216)725-0588	1160
New Albany	HERB, Elizabeth D.	(614)855-7441	530
Norwalk	DRAPP, Laureen	(419)668-6063	318
Oberlin	CARPENTER, Eric J.	(216)775-2546	184
	MOFFETT, William A.	(216)775-8285	852
	WEIDMAN, Jeffrey	(216)775-8635	1316
Piqua	OVERHOLT, Maria B.	(513)773-3640	931
Powell	RUSH, James E.	(614)881-5949	1068
Shaker Heights	NISSENBAUM, Robert J.	(216)561-8168	905
	RODDA, Donna S.	(216)283-1064	1047
Springfield	ARK, Connie E.	(513)324-8470	31
	MONTAG, John	(513)327-7019	855
Strongsville	JUNEJA, Derry C.	(216)238-7585	620
Toledo	BAKER, Paula J.	(419)472-0204	49
	CARY, Mary K.	(419)537-2833	191
Upper Arlington	BROWN, Rowland C.	(614)488-6329	147
Wapakoneta	FREW, Martha G.	(419)738-8333	402
Warren	TYSON, Edith S.	(216)393-3098	1267
Waterford	TEPE, Ann S.	(614)749-3007	1231
Westerville	LOVEJOY, Eunice G.	(614)882-4791	743
Westlake	CHAMIS, Alice Y.	(216)777-2198	198
	CHARVAT, Catherine T.	(216)871-6391	203
Willow Wood	REID, Margaret B.	(614)643-2925	1018
Worthington	EAST, Dennis	(614)888-9923	332
Xenia	OVERTON, Julie M.	(513)376-4952	931
Youngstown	DONAHUGH, Robert H.	(216)788-6950	310
	MC CLEAF-NESPECA, Sue E.	(216)792-4470	796
	YANCURA, Ann J.	(216)746-7042	1377

OKLAHOMA

Ardmore	ROBINSON, Joel M.	(405)223-3164	1044
Edmond	ROADS, Clarice D.	(405)341-3660	1038
Lawton	RABURN, Josephine R.	(405)581-2325	1001
Midwest City	MOSLEY, Thomas E.	(405)733-0922	872
Norman	CLARK, Harry	(405)321-0352	217
	LAUGHLIN, Mildred A.	(405)325-3921	703
	LOWELL, Howard P.	(405)366-7719	744
	MCKNIGHT, Michelynn	(405)360-2080	812
	SHERMAN, Mary A.	(405)321-1481	1128
	WEAVER-MEYERS, Pat L.	(405)325-3341	1313
Oklahoma City	BRAWNER, Lee B.	(405)947-1109	130
	CLARK, Robert L.	(405)521-2502	218
	LITTLE, Paul L.	(405)789-9400	733
	MEYERS, Duane H.	(405)946-2488	830
	NASH, Helen B.	(405)525-7504	888
	PASCHAL, John M.	(405)751-6400	945
	VESELY, Marilyn L.		1283
Shawnee	ALDRIDGE, Betsy B.		11
Stillwater	BAUER, Carolyn J.	(405)372-6584	65
Tahlequah	MADAUS, J R.		758
	PATTERSON, Lotsee	(918)456-6882	948
Tulsa	BUTHOD, J C.	(918)592-7894	166
	WOODRUM, Patricia A.	(918)592-7897	1366

OREGON

Ashland	OTNES, Harold M.	(503)482-6445	930
Beaverton	JACOBS, Patt	(503)646-6959	590
	POND, Patricia B.	(503)641-5524	982
Bend	BYRNE, Helen E.	(503)382-1621	169
Eugene	FEUERHELM, Jill A.	(503)345-6498	374
	GRAHAM, Deborah L.		456
	MEEKS, James D.	(503)687-5454	821
	SHULER, John A.	(503)686-3048	1133
	SUNDT, Christine L.	(503)686-3052	1210
Monmouth	GORCHELS, Clarence C.	(503)838-1274	451
	JENSEN, Gary D.	(503)838-1220	598
Newport	KRABBE, Natalie	(503)336-2546	674
Portland	ANDERSON, C L.	(503)280-5160	21
	BURSON, Lorraine E.	(508)246-4097	163
	LEGER, Norissa	(503)246-2714	712
	LONG, Sarah A.	(503)221-7731	740
	PIPER, Larry W.	(503)232-1781	975
	SHAVER, Donna B.	(503)226-8695	1123
	THENELL, Janice C.	(503)221-7726	1234
Roseburg	COOK, Sybilla A.	(503)673-0504	240
Salem	DOAK, Wesley A.	(503)581-4292	306

SPEAKER (Honorarium) (Cont'd)

PENNSYLVANIA

Allentown	MOSES, Lynn M.		871
Altoona	SHERIDAN, Margaret G.	(814)942-2565	1127
Ardmore	VLADUTZ, George E.	(215)649-1148	1286
Bala Cynwyd	KREMER, Jill L.	(215)667-6787	677
Berwyn	BROWN, David E.	(215)644-5241	143
Bethlehem	BERK, Jack M.	(215)867-3761	87
Bloomsburg	VANN, John D.	(717)784-4283	1276
Bryn Mawr	HILL, Judith L.	(215)526-1305	540
California	CARUSO, Nicholas C.	(412)938-9166	190
Camp Hill	ALBRECHT, Lois K.	(717)737-6111	10
Chambersburg	EZELL, Johanna V.	(717)264-2269	360
	MARLOW, Kathryn E.	(717)264-2382	772
Chester Heights	OWENS, Irene E.		932
Clarion	PERSON, Ruth J.	(814)226-5341	961
Coatesville	BURTON, Mary L.	(215)383-0245	164
Coraopolis	SKOVIRA, Robert J.	(412)262-8257	1147
Eagleville	PECK, Marian B.	(215)631-1129	953
Elizabethtown	BARD, Nelson P.	(717)367-1151	56
Emmaus	STEPHANOFF, Kathryn	(215)797-8838	1187
Erie	ANDRICK, Annita A.	(814)455-8080	27
Glen Rock	LIEBERMAN, Ronald	(717)235-2134	726
Glenside	NIEWEG, Clinton F.	(215)884-5878	904
Harleysville	LINN, Mott R.	(215)464-4500	731
Harrisburg	BAUER, Margaret D.	(717)233-3113	65
	LINGLE, Virginia A.	(717)652-1950	730
	STAYER, Jonathan R.	(717)787-2701	1183
Hatfield	RITTER, Ralph E.	(215)368-5000	1037
Haverford	FREEMAN, Michael S.	(215)896-1272	401
Havertown	HOFFMAN, Elizabeth P.	(215)446-3082	547
Honesdale	BROWN, Kent L.	(717)253-1080	145
Huntingdon	SWIGART, William E.	(814)643-3000	1216
Jeannette	PAWLIK, Deborah A.		951
Johnstown	KREITZBURG, Marilyn J.	(814)266-7386	677
Kutztown	MACK, Sara R.		756
Lancaster	BROWN, Charlotte B.	(717)291-4225	142
	FRANCOS, Alexis	(717)397-9655	396
Lansdale	WEBER ROOCHVARG, Lynn E.	(215)368-8688	1314
Library	SALVAYON, Connie	(412)833-5585	1078
Macungie	BAHR, Alice H.	(215)821-1256	45
Mansfield	DOWLING, John	(717)662-4753	316
McKeesport	HERRON, Nancy L.	(412)675-9111	533
	KISH, Veronica R.	(412)678-1749	656
Media	LARSON, Phyllis S.	(215)566-2809	699
Middletown	RAMBLER, Linda K.	(412)349-4621	1005
Monroeville	MURPHY, Diana G.	(412)327-5976	880
Mt Lebanon	WEISFIELD, Cynthia F.	(412)831-8225	1319
Narberth	SOKOLOFF, Michele	(215)664-2117	1165
Natrona Heights	HAUGH, Amy J.	(412)224-5004	512
New Hope	WESOLOWSKI, Paul G.	(215)862-9734	1325
New Kingstown	HANSON, Eugene R.	(717)243-0973	498
New Oxford	FOX, Merle U.		395
North Wales	MAXIN, Jacqueline A.	(215)855-5675	787
Pennsylvania Furnace	WOLFE, Mary S.	(814)234-5660	1361
Philadelphia	ADAMS, Mignon S.	(215)596-8790	5
	AXAM, John A.	(215)549-6485	42
	AZZOLINA, David S.	(215)898-8118	43
	BAUMGARTNER, Barbara W.	(215)686-5418	66
	BUTLER, Evelyn		166
	CHILDERS, Thomas A.	(215)895-2479	208
	CRAWFORD, Miriam I.	(215)877-1250	257
	CRESSWELL, Donald H.	(215)242-4750	258
	DUCLOW, Geradline		322
	FENICHEL, Carol H.	(215)448-7185	371
	FIELD, Carolyn W.	(215)438-4086	375
	FLOOD, Barbara J.	(215)732-8543	385
	FREEDMAN, Bernadette	(215)332-6937	400
	FUSELER-MCDOWELL, Elizabeth A.	(215)423-9294	410
	GARFIELD, Eugene	(215)386-0100	418
	GRIFFITH, Belver C.	(215)895-2474	469
	GRILIKHES, Sandra B.	(215)898-7027	470
	HALLER, Douglas M.	(215)898-8304	489
	HEANEY, Howell J.	(215)248-3454	518
	KENNEDY, H E.	(215)587-4800	641
	KING, Eleanor M.		650
	KOHN, Roger S.	(215)438-5635	668

SPEAKER (Honorarium) (Cont'd)
PENNSYLVANIA (Cont'd)
Philadelphia

	LYTLE, Richard H.	(215)895-2475	753
	MARVIN, Stephen G.	(215)895-1874	780
	MAYOVER, Steven J.	(215)686-5400	791
	MICIKAS, Lynda L.	(215)637-7700	832
	MILLER, Fredric M.	(213)787-8257	837
	MOSS, Roger W.	(215)925-2688	872
	MYERS, James N.	(215)787-8231	884
	PAGELL, Ruth A.	(215)898-5922	934
	PANCOE, Deborra S.	(215)561-5900	937
	PARKER, Peter J.	(215)732-6200	942
	POST, Jeremiah B.	(215)748-2701	986
	RIDGEWAY, Patricia M.	(215)898-7555	1032
	SHELKROT, Elliot L.	(215)686-5300	1126
	SMIRAGLIA, Richard P.	(215)662-5699	1152
	SNOW, Bonnie		1164
	WILLMANN, Donna S.		1348
	WOLF, Edwin		1360
	ZIPF, Elizabeth M.	(215)587-4815	1389
	ZOGOTT, Joyce	(215)596-8994	1390
Pittsburgh	BROADBENT, H E.	(412)441-6409	138
	DOW, Elizabeth H.		315
	EVANS, Nancy H.	(412)268-2114	357
	FIDOTEN, Robert E.	(412)963-8785	375
	FITZGERALD, Patricia A.	(412)268-2428	382
	GLABICKI, Paul	(412)521-6612	439
	HOWARD, Elizabeth F.	(412)441-3753	564
	JOSEY, E J.	(412)624-9451	618
	KIRCHER, Linda M.	(412)624-9444	654
	KURTIK, Frank J.	(412)687-3084	685
	LEIBOWITZ, Faye R.	(412)421-7974	713
	MAWHINNEY, Paul C.	(412)367-7330	787
	METZLER, Douglas P.	(412)624-9414	829
	MICCO, Helen M.	(412)665-0412	831
	NASRI, William Z.	(412)276-3234	888
	RAO, Rama K.	(412)429-0543	1008
	SCHUMACHER, Carolyn S.	(412)363-0190	1102
	WEBRECK, Susan J.	(412)624-5230	1314
	WESSEL, Charles B.	(412)731-8800	1325
	WOODSWORTH, Anne		1367
	WOOLLS, Esther B.	(412)624-9435	1368
	WRAY, Wendell L.	(412)363-0251	1370
Radnor	KELLER, Kate V.	(215)688-6989	635
Rosemont	LYNCH, Mary D.	(215)527-0200	752
	SCHWALB, Ann W.	(215)527-3131	1104
	WELSH, Barbara W.	(215)527-3976	1323
Scranton	APPELBAUM, Judith P.	(212)532-5280	29
	FADDEN, Donald M.	(412)621-8802	360
	MILLER, Mary E.	(717)348-6205	840
Secane	CASINI, Barbara P.	(215)543-4309	192
Shippensburg	SHONTZ, Marilyn L.	(717)532-1472	1132
Slippery Rock	JOSEPH, Elizabeth T.	(412)794-4623	617
Springfield	STESIS, Karen R.	(215)328-8749	1189
State College	JAMISON, Carolyn C.	(814)234-4512	593
	PIERCE, Miriam D.	(814)237-7004	971
	STOUT, Leon J.	(814)238-4855	1198
Tamaqua	EVERHART, Nancy L.	(717)668-3334	358
	TUZINSKI, Jean H.	(717)668-2970	1266
University Park	CLINE, Nancy M.	(814)865-1858	222
	FORTH, Stuart	(814)865-0401	391
	NEAL, James G.	(814)865-0401	890
	RICE, Patricia O.	(814)865-1858	1027
	SMITH, Diane H.	(814)865-4861	1154
	WESTERMAN, Melvin E.	(814)863-2898	1327
Villanova	ERDT, Terrence	(215)645-4670	352
	GRIFFIN, Mary A.	(215)645-4290	468
West Chester	CHAFF, Sandra L.	(215)524-0547	197
Wyomissing	MORGANTI, Deena J.	(215)320-4849	864

PUERTO RICO
Guaynabo

	LEON, Carmencita H.	(809)792-7873	716

RHODE ISLAND

Barrington	BUNDY, Annalee M.	(401)245-2232	157
	BURKE, Lauri K.	(401)245-3741	160
Chepachet	DESJARLAIS-LUETH, Christine	(401)568-8614	295
East Providence	CAIRNS, Roberta A.	(401)433-0159	171

SPEAKER (Honorarium) (Cont'd)
RHODE ISLAND (Cont'd)

Kingston	DEVIN, Robin B.	(401)792-2662	297
	ETCHINGHAM, John B.	(401)792-4637	355
	FUTAS, Elizabeth	(401)792-2947	411
	SIITONEN, Leena M.	(401)792-2878	1137
	TRYON, Jonathan S.	(401)792-2878	1259
	YOUNG, Arthur P.	(401)792-2666	1381
Lincoln	DESMARAIS, Norman P.	(401)333-3275	295
Newport	CHERPAK, Evelyn M.	(401)841-2435	206
Providence	DANIELS, Bruce E.	(401)277-2726	273
	LAMAR, Christine L.	(401)331-8575	689
	LYNDEN, Frederick C.	(401)863-2946	752
	MONTEIRO, George	(401)863-3266	856
	SVENGALIS, Kendall F.	(401)274-3196	1212
	TAYLOR, Merrily E.	(401)863-2162	1227
	WAGNER, Albin	(401)277-2283	1291
	WILMETH, Don B.	(401)863-3289	1349
Woonsocket	IMONDI, Lenore R.	(401)762-5165	582

SOUTH CAROLINA

Charleston	SEAMAN, Sheila L.	(803)795-4416	1109
	STRAUCH, Katina P.	(803)723-3536	1200
	WOOD, Richard J.	(803)763-8532	1365
Clemson	MEYER, Richard W.	(803)656-3026	830
Columbia	CROSS, Joseph R.	(803)777-3365	260
	EASTMAN, Caroline M.	(803)777-8103	333
	HELSLEY, Alexia J.	(803)781-8477	525
	HOWARD-HILL, Trevor	(803)777-6499	564
	SCHULZ, Constance B.	(803)777-4854	1102
	WILLIAMS, Robert V.	(803)799-2324	1346
Denmark	BOOK, Imogene I.	(803)793-3660	115
Glendale	WHITE, Ann T.	(803)579-3330	1330
Greenville	SCALES, Pat R.	(803)232-1271	1087
	TOWELL, Fay J.	(803)232-2941	1252
Orangeburg	SMALLS, Mary L.	(803)536-8852	1151
Summerville	MAY, Robert E.	(803)871-2201	789
Sumter	COOK, Galen B.	(803)469-9180	240

SOUTH DAKOTA

Rapid City	SCHWARTZ, James M.	(605)394-1246	1104
Sioux Falls	DERTIEN, James L.	(605)339-7115	294
	MODICA, Mary L.	(605)388-3701	851

TENNESSEE

Chattanooga	BRUNER, Katharine E.	(615)266-0676	150
Clarksville	THWEATT, John H.	(615)647-0954	1243
Clinton	GREESON, Judy G.	(615)457-0931	465
	SPATH, Charles E.	(615)457-8616	1171
Columbia	WAGGENER, Jean B.	(615)388-9282	1291
Johnson City	SPEARS, Ross	(615)926-8637	1172
Kingsport	TILSON, Koleta B.	(615)245-6572	1245
Knoxville	KNIGHTLY, John J.	(615)691-7996	664
	LEACH, Sandra S.	(615)579-1315	706
	MYERS, Marcia J.	(615)974-4465	884
	PEMBERTON, J M.	(615)690-5598	956
Maryville	WORLEY, Joan B.	(615)982-6412	1369
Memphis	DRESCHER, Judith A.	(901)276-0104	319
	EVANS, David H.	(901)454-3317	356
	LASSLO, Andrew	(901)528-6080	700
	LINDENFELD, Joseph F.	(901)528-6743	729
	MADER, Sharon B.	(901)454-2208	759
	POURCIAU, Lester J.	(901)454-2201	987
	WUJCIK, Dennis S.	(901)722-8753	1374
Murfreesboro	WELLS, Paul F.	(615)898-2449	1323
	YOUREE, Beverly B.	(615)896-4911	1384
Nashville	CAMERON, Sam A.	(615)329-1163	175
	FANCHER, Evelyn P.	(615)255-8033	363
	HARWELL, Sara J.	(615)322-2807	509
	HODGES, Terence M.	(615)322-2299	546
	MOON, Fletcher F.	(615)833-1125	857
	SEEMANN, Charles H.	(615)256-1639	1111
	SUMNERS, Bill F.	(615)251-2126	1209
	WILBURN, Clouse R.	(615)322-8050	1338
Norris	DYER, Barbara M.	(615)494-9555	330
Oak Ridge	CARROLL, Bonnie C.	(615)482-3230	187
	EKKEBUS, Allen E.	(615)574-5485	341
	NORTON, Nancy P.	(615)574-7159	910
	ROBBINS, Gordon D.	(615)574-7178	1038
Sewanee	WATSON, Tom G.	(615)598-1213	1310

SPEAKER (Honorarium) (Cont'd)
TEXAS

Abilene	GILLETTE, Robert S.	(915)677-5103	435
Amarillo	RUDDY, Mary K.	(806)353-1534	1065
	WELLS, Mary K.	(806)381-2435	1322
Arlington	KERBY, Ramona A.	(817)478-9829	643
	STOAN, Stephen K.	(817)273-3391	1195
	YOUNKIN, C G.	(817)429-2674	1383
Austin	CARTER, Janet K.	(512)463-5463	189
	DEGRUYTER, M L.	(512)929-3086	288
	GOULD, Karen K.	(512)453-2602	454
	GRACY, David B.	(512)471-3821	455
	HELBURN, Judith D.	(512)454-7229	523
	HOOKS, Michael Q.	(512)250-1419	556
	JUERGENS, Bonnie	(512)288-2072	619
	KAHLER, June	(512)463-9660	621
	MARTIN, Jean K.	(512)346-2973	776
	MATHIS, Rama F.	(512)343-7521	784
	MIKSA, Francis L.	(572)346-6769	834
	ROY, Loriene	(512)471-6316	1063
	SMITH, Dorothy B.	(512)453-1384	1154
	STANDIFER, Hugh A.	(512)288-2072	1179
	WALTON, Robert A.	(512)346-1426	1301
	WYLLYS, Ronald E.	(512)471-3821	1375
Bangs	WEEKS, Patsy L.	(915)752-7315	1315
Big Spring	BRADBERRY, Anna L.	(915)263-1468	125
Brazoria	RASKA, Ginny	(409)798-1628	1009
Brownsville	VAUGHN, Frances A.	(512)544-8220	1280
Bryan	HALL, Halbert W.	(409)846-0798	487
Buda	TISSING, Robert W.	(512)295-4834	1247
College Station	HOADLEY, Irene B.	(409)845-8111	545
	SCHULTZ, Charles R.	(409)845-1815	1101
Corpus Christi	HOUSTON, Barbara B.	(512)889-8517	563
Dallas	BOCKSTRUCK, Lloyd D.	(214)670-1406	109
	BROWN, Muriel W.	(214)348-7861	146
	CAMPBELL, Shirley A.	(214)330-0027	177
	COMPTON, Erlinda R.	(214)506-3601	235
	CROW, Rebecca N.	(214)749-4285	261
	DOBSON, Christine B.	(214)746-3646	307
	EWUNES, Ernest L.	(214)376-4102	359
	FARMER, David	(214)692-3231	364
	GALBRAITH, Paula L.	(214)680-3782	413
	HEIZER, Carolyn H.	(214)363-5148	523
	JAGOE, Katherine P.	(214)931-8938	591
	JONES, Lois S.	(214)528-2732	613
	KACENA, Carolyn	(214)361-9254	621
	KRALISZ, Victor F.	(214)247-7944	675
	MASON, Florence M.	(214)358-5755	781
	MCCASLIN, Cheryl A.	(214)490-8701	795
	MOLTZAN, Janet R.	(214)691-3267	854
	ORAM, Robert W.	(214)739-1310	925
	PEDEN, Robert M.	(214)746-3646	954
	RYDESKY, Mary M.	(214)339-3349	1071
	SALL, Larry D.	(214)385-8528	1076
	SHAPLEY, Ellen M.	(214)692-6407	1122
	TEMPLETON, Virginia L.	(214)754-4875	1231
	WETHERBEE, Louella V.	(214)750-6130	1327
Denton	ALMQUIST, Sharon G.	(817)387-1703	17
	CARROLL, Dewey E.	(817)565-2445	187
	CVELJO, Katherine	(817)565-2445	268
	FERSTL, Kenneth L.	(817)383-3775	374
	KHADER, Majed J.		645
	MITCHELL, George D.	(817)565-2489	848
	SHELDON, Brooke E.	(817)898-2602	1125
	THOMAS, James L.	(817)382-1697	1237
	VONDRAN, Raymond F.	(817)565-2445	1288
El Paso	GOODMAN, Helen C.	(915)584-4509	449
Flower Mound	SVEINSSON, Joan L.	(214)539-9308	1212
Fort Worth	ARBELBIDE, Cindy L.	(817)877-3355	30
	ARD, Harold J.	(817)293-5474	31
	TANNER, Clarabel	(817)738-3718	1222
	WOOD, Richard C.	(517)927-5389	1365
Galveston	WYGANT, Alice C.		1375
Garland	LARSON, Jeanette C.	(214)240-0661	699
Houston	ADAMS, Elaine P.	(713)785-8703	4
	ALESSI, Dana L.	(713)669-0419	11
	BROWN, Freddiemae E.	(713)227-9177	144
	CARTER, Betty B.	(713)467-0463	189
	CARTER, Daniel H.	(713)665-5150	189
	CEBRUN, Mary J.	(713)965-4045	196

SPEAKER (Honorarium) (Cont'd)
TEXAS (Cont'd)

Houston	CHAMPION, Walter T.	(713)527-7125	198
	CLARK, Jay B.	(713)247-1631	217
	CORBIN, John	(713)749-4241	245
	CRIST, Lynda L.	(713)527-4990	259
	EISENBEIS, Kathleen M.	(713)280-9780	340
	GILBERT, Barry	(713)629-6600	433
	GOLEY, Elaine P.	(713)467-5784	447
	GOURLAY, Una M.	(713)528-3553	454
	HASKELL, Peter C.	(713)529-6681	510
	HOLIBAUGH, Ralph W.		550
	MAGNER, Mary F.	(713)870-7011	759
	MORRISSEY, Charles T.	(713)799-4510	869
	MULLINS, James R.	(713)522-8131	878
	RICCARDI, Vincent M.	(713)558-9907	1026
	WELCH, C B.	(713)749-4245	1321
	WILSON, Thomas C.	(713)995-8401	1353
	ZWICK, Louise Y.	(713)680-1710	1392
Huntsville	BURT, Lesta N.	(409)295-1001	164
	PICHETTE, William H.	(409)291-2994	970
Irving	HAGLE, Claudette S.	(214)986-2343	483
	LANKFORD, Mary D.	(214)579-7818	696
Kilgore	CLAER, Joycelyn H.	(214)983-8238	215
Kingsville	MERCHANT, Cheryl N.	(512)592-9684	825
Laredo	MULLER, Mary M.	(905)211-0042	877
Lewisville	MARMION, Daniel K.	(214)436-5125	772
Liberty	SCHAADT, Robert L.	(409)336-7097	1088
Lubbock	CARGILL, Jennifer S.	(806)792-2349	181
	LINDSEY, Thomas K.	(806)791-4770	730
	WEBB, Gisela M.	(806)794-7359	1313
Mesquite	DUMONT, Paul E.	(214)324-7786	325
Odessa	KLEPPER, Bobbie J.	(915)326-3654	660
Palacios	WOLL, Christina B.	(512)972-2166	1361
Pharr	LIU, David T.	(512)787-1491	734
Richardson	KRUSE, Luanne M.	(214)680-9677	681
San Antonio	FORD, Barbara J.	(512)736-8121	389
	KRONICK, David A.	(512)344-5796	679
	MANEY, Lana E.	(512)496-7754	765
	VELA-CREIXELL, Mary I.	(512)733-7109	1281
	WERKING, Richard H.	(512)736-8161	1324
The Woodlands	FRAMEL, Phyllis M.	(713)367-9522	395
Waco	COLEY, Betty A.	(817)754-6114	231
	KEATTS, Rowena W.	(817)753-6415	633
	PHILLIPS, Luouida V.		968
	RICHARDS, James H.	(817)756-0602	1028
Wichita Falls	GRIMES, John F.	(817)855-0463	470

UTAH

Payson	GILLUM, Gary P.	(801)465-4527	436
Pleasant Grove	STECKER, Alexander T.	(801)785-2761	1183
Provo	MARCHANT, Maurice P.	(801)378-2976	768
	WIGGINS, Marvin E.	(801)378-6346	1337
Salt Lake City	BUTTARS, Gerald A.	(801)466-6363	167
	GIACOMA, Pete J.	(801)364-2624	430
	HANSON, Roger K.	(801)581-8558	498
	HEFNER, Loretta L.	(801)485-2005	520
	JAMES, Brent C.	(801)533-3730	592
	KRANZ, Ralph	(801)581-7995	676
	NASH, Cherie A.	(801)533-5250	888
	OLSEN, Katherine M.	(801)355-0301	921
	OWEN, Amy	(801)466-5888	931
	SCOTT, Patricia I.	(801)533-5250	1107
	SPERRY, Kip	(801)255-9615	1174
	VAN ORDEN, Richard D.	(801)485-1075	1276
West Jordan	KARPISEK, Marian E.	(801)561-4676	628

VERMONT

Barre	GRIFFIN, Marie E.	(802)479-2810	468
Bennington	PRICE, Michael L.	(802)442-9051	992
Brattleboro	HAY, Linda A.	(802)254-5595	515
Burlington	DAY, Martha T.	(802)863-0506	282
Chelsea	BATTEY, Jean D.	(802)276-3086	64
Colchester	KNEELAND, Marjorie H.	(802)655-0279	664
Milton	SEKERAK, Robert J.		1113
Montpelier	KLINCK, Patricia E.	(802)828-3265	661

VIRGIN ISLANDS

St Thomas	MILLS, Fiolina B.	(809)776-8396	844

SPEAKER (Honorarium) (Cont'd)

VIRGINIA

Alexandria	DRUMMOND, Louis E.		321
	GALE, John C.	(703)548-4320	413
	HASSE, John E.		511
	KAISER, Donald W.	(703)836-0225	622
	MARA, Ruth M.	(703)765-0262	768
	MICHAELS, Andrea A.	(703)360-1297	831
	MICHAELS, David L.	(703)360-1297	832
	OSIA, Ruby R.	(703)549-3048	928
	ROSENBERG, Kenyon C.	(703)642-5480	1056
	ROTHSCHILD, M C.	(202)274-7206	1060
	RUSH, James S.	(703)765-3557	1068
	STEVENS, Roberta A.	(703)960-0464	1191
Annandale	CHOBOT, Mary C.	(703)323-9402	210
Arlington	ALEXANDER, Carol G.		12
	ARDEN, Caroline	(703)532-1548	31
	BARRINGER, George M.	(703)920-2541	59
	CLARKE, Robert F.		219
	HENDERSON, Susanne	(703)931-8433	527
	HIGBEE, Joan F.	(703)524-5844	537
	HIRONS, Jean L.	(703)243-9437	543
	PRICE, Joseph W.	(703)241-0447	992
	WELLS, Christine		1322
	YODER, William M.	(703)527-7225	1380
Blacksburg	EASTMAN, Ann H.	(703)951-4770	333
	FOX, Edward A.	(703)552-8667	394
Burke	STEPHENSON, Richard W.	(703)323-7721	1188
Charlottesville	FRANKLIN, Robert D.	(804)973-3238	398
	JORDAN, Ervin L.	(804)924-4975	616
Chesterfield	WAGENKNECHT, Robert E.	(804)748-1601	1291
Emory	JENNERICH, Elaine Z.	(703)944-3121	598
Fairfax	GOODWIN, Jane G.	(703)246-5847	450
	WALCH, Timothy G.	(703)273-3260	1293
Falls Church	CHUNG, Catherine A.	(703)534-3114	213
	HELGERSON, Linda W.	(703)237-0682	524
	VIOLA, Herman J.	(703)573-6211	1285
Fort Monroe	BYRN, James H.	(804)727-4491	169
Hampton	BIGELOW, Therese G.	(804)727-6234	95
Harrisonburg	BLANKENBURG, Judith B.	(703)568-6792	104
	HABAN, Mary F.	(703)433-2183	480
	ROBISON, Dennis E.	(703)568-6578	1045
Herndon	PAVEK, C C.	(703)481-0711	950
Langley AFB	VERNON, Christie D.	(804)766-1468	1283
Lynchburg	SIDDONS, James D.	(804)846-8129	1135
Manassas	KILLEEN, Erlene B.	(703)369-7193	648
Mclean	WANG, Chi	(703)893-3016	1302
	WINIARSKI, Marilee E.	(800)421-7229	1355
Melian	BELTON, Jennifer H.		78
Norfolk	BERENT, Irwin M.	(804)855-1272	84
	DUNCAN, Cynthia B.	(804)583-0903	325
	MAYER-HENNELLY, Mary B.	(804)441-2733	789
	NICHOLSON, Myreen M.	(804)627-6281	902
	PEREZ-LOPEZ, Rene	(804)423-7655	958
North Springfield	AINES, Andrew A.	(703)569-4872	8
Portsmouth	BROWN, William A.	(804)483-2195	148
Reston	GENNARO, John L.	(703)689-5616	427
	MCLANE, Kathleen	(703)620-3660	813
Richmond	BAGAN, Beverly S.	(804)780-7691	45
	BARBER, Gloria K.	(804)225-2958	55
	DEBARDELEBEN, Marian Z.	(804)274-2876	284
	TYSON, John C.	(804)289-8456	1267
	VAN SICKLEN, Lindsay L.	(804)320-9691	1277
	YATES, Ella G.	(804)786-2332	1378
Roanoke	BANE, Madelyn R.	(703)345-2435	54
Springfield	ALBIN, Michael W.	(703)978-3022	10
	CASWELL, Mary C.	(703)642-0340	194
	GEHRINGER, Michael E.	(703)451-0334	425
Vienna	COCHRANE, Maryjane S.	(703)938-2037	226
	DODSON, Whit	(703)938-2630	308
Virginia Beach	CAYWOOD, Carolyn A.	(804)464-9320	195
Williamsburg	BERG, Susan	(804)229-8799	85

WASHINGTON

Bellingham	GROVER, Iva S.	(206)671-3643	474
Bothell	DECOSTER, Barbara L.	(206)488-7537	286
Cheney	ALKIRE, Leland G.	(509)235-4669	13
	BENDER, Betty W.	(509)838-4283	79
Clallam Bay	PEARSON, Barbara F.	(206)963-2369	952
Edmonds	STRONG, Sunny A.	(206)778-3804	1203

SPEAKER (Honorarium) (Cont'd)

WASHINGTON (Cont'd)

Ellensburg	DOI, Makiko	(509)963-2101	309
Friday Harbor	MILLER, Jerome K.	(206)378-5128	839
Kirkland	MACDONALD, Margaret R.	(206)486-8931	754
	ROBERTSON, Ann	(206)821-0506	1041
Marysville	WILSON, Evie		1350
Newport	REMINGTON, David G.	(509)447-2636	1022
Oak Harbor	MERWINE, Glenda M.	(206)679-5807	827
Olympia	KREIMEYER, Vicki R.	(206)753-2916	677
	SHAFFER, Maryann	(206)943-5001	1119
	ZUSSY, Nancy L.	(206)786-9647	1391
Pullman	KEMP, Barbara E.	(509)334-5809	639
Seattle	BETZ-ZALL, Jonathan R.	(206)782-9305	92
	BURSON, Scott F.	(206)543-6794	163
	CHISHOLM, Margaret	(206)543-1794	209
	CLINE, Robert S.	(206)523-7268	222
	EULENBERG, Julia V.	(206)324-2605	356
	FASSETT, William E.	(206)545-2272	366
	FEATHERS, John E.	(206)282-3804	367
	HAZELTON, Penelope A.	(206)543-4089	517
	HENSLEY, Randall B.	(206)543-2060	529
	HILDEBRANDT, Darlene M.	(206)543-5818	538
	JENNERICH, Edward J.	(206)626-6320	598
	JOHNSON, Carolynn K.	(206)684-6681	603
	KETCHELL, Debra S.	(206)543-5530	645
	LEONARD, Gloria J.	(206)722-4828	716
	MADDEN, Susan B.	(206)684-6626	758
	MEYER, Laura M.	(206)522-2162	830
	POLISHUK, Bernard	(206)524-8676	980
	PRESS, Nancy O.	(206)367-6568	991
	ROWBERG, Alan H.	(206)548-6250	1062
	SCHUELLER, Janette H.	(206)543-8262	1101
	THORSEN, Jeanne M.	(206)684-6606	1242
	TOLLIVER, Barbara J.	(206)684-6615	1248
	TURNER, Tamara A.	(216)325-9481	1265
	TWENEY, George H.	(206)243-8243	1266
Spokane	MURRAY, James M.	(509)838-3680	882
	WEBER, Joan L.	(509)489-6959	1314
Tacoma	MENDELSON, Martin	(206)383-5855	823
Vancouver	CONABLE, Gordon M.	(206)694-0604	235
	CONABLE, Irene H.	(206)694-0604	235
Walla Walla	BLACKABY, Sandra L.	(509)527-4292	102

WEST VIRGINIA

Bluefield	DYE, Luella I.	(304)487-2037	330
Charleston	PROSSER, Judith M.	(304)344-8583	995
Philippi	SIZEMORE, William C.		1145
Point Pleasant	WILLIAMSON, Judy D.	(304)675-4350	1347

WISCONSIN

Appleton	KLAVER, Timothy J.	(414)735-0463	658
Burlington	PROCES, Stephen L.	(414)763-7623	994
Cedarburg	PITEL, Vonna J.	(414)377-6030	976
Eau Claire	MARQUARDT, Steve R.	(715)834-5390	772
Green Bay	GORSEGNER, Betty D.	(414)465-1529	452
Hales Corners	BARLOGA, Carolyn J.	(414)425-0355	57
Janesville	KRUEGER, Karen J.	(608)755-2800	680
La Crosse	CIMPL, Kathleen A.	(608)785-0530	214
	HILL, Edwin L.	(608)782-1753	539
Madison	ARNOLD, Barbara J.	(608)263-2909	33
	BUNGE, Charles A.	(608)263-2900	157
	CAIN, Carolyn L.	(608)271-6198	171
	DAHLGREN, Anders C.	(608)271-9148	269
	DRESANG, Eliza T.	(608)267-9357	319
	GAPEN, D K.	(608)262-2600	416
	HERMAN, Gertrude B.		531
	HOPKINS, Dianne M.	(608)263-2900	557
	KRUSE, Ginny M.		681
	MCCONNELL, Shirley M.	(608)274-7222	798
	MONROE, Margaret E.	(608)263-2900	855
	MULLER, H N.	(608)262-7580	877
	ROBBINS, Jane B.	(608)263-2908	1038
	SEARING, Susan E.	(608)263-5754	1109
	SORENSEN, Richard J.	(608)266-1924	1168
	WAITY, Gloria J.	(608)222-7783	1293
	WEINGAND, Darlene E.	(608)262-8952	1318
	WELSCH, Erwin K.	(608)262-3195	1323
	WIEGAND, Wayne A.	(608)263-2914	1336
	WILLETT, Holly G.	(608)251-0633	1341

SPEAKER (Honorarium) (Cont'd)
WISCONSIN (Cont'd)
Madison

	WISEMAN, Mary J.		1357
	YOUNGER, Jennifer A.	(608)262-4907	1383
Marshfield	ALLEN, Margaret A.	(715)387-7271	15
Menomonie	GRAF, David L.	(715)232-1202	455
Middleton	ZWEIZIG, Douglas L.	(608)831-4364	1392
Milwaukee	AMAN, Mohammed M.	(414)239-4709	19
	ANTHONY, Rose M.	(414)384-6535	29
	BLUE, Richard I.	(414)963-4707	107
	BOTHAM, Jane	(414)278-3078	118
	BOULANGER, Mary E.	(414)229-4659	119
	GILL, Norman N.	(414)352-1545	435
	GREENE, Victor R.	(414)963-7063	464
	HOOTKIN, Neil M.	(414)332-4953	557
	JONES, Richard E.	(414)229-6457	614
	LYNCH, Beverly P.	(414)774-1008	751
	MISNER, Barbara	(414)384-6535	847
	SWEETLAND, James H.	(414)963-9996	1215
	THIEL, Mark G.	(414)224-7256	1235
Neenah	LAMB, Cheryl M.	(414)729-8169	689
New London	DIEHL, Carol L.	(414)982-5040	301
Oshkosh	CORBLY, James E.	(414)231-4768	245
	FU, Tina C.	(414)424-2206	407
	JONES, Norma L.	(414)231-5137	614
	SHARMA, Ravindra N.	(414)424-0139	1122
Racine	TERANIS, Mara	(414)631-4144	1231
Reedsville	OHLEMACHER, Janet H.	(414)754-4831	919
Rosholt	ADAMS, Helen R.	(715)592-4614	5
Stoughton	DANKY, James P.	(608)873-8722	274
Superior	AXT, Randolph W.	(715)398-6767	42
West Allis	LUECHT, Richard M.	(414)321-3152	747
Wisconsin Rapids	WILSON, William J.	(715)424-4272	1353

WYOMING

Cheyenne	JOHNSON, Wayne H.	(307)777-7283	609
	MCGOWAN, Anne W.	(307)777-6430	807
Gillette	SIEBERSMA, Dan	(307)686-0786	1135
Lander	HEUER, William J.	(307)332-3793	535
Laramie	CHATTON, Barbara A.	(307)766-2167	204
	COTTAM, Keith M.	(307)766-3279	250
	MACK, Bonnie R.	(307)766-6537	756

CANADA

ALBERTA

Airdrie	EVANS, Patricia D.		357
	WAUGH, Alan L.	(403)948-7921	1310
Calgary	GOODMAN, Henry J.	(403)220-6296	449
	MACDONALD, Alan H.	(403)220-5953	754
	ONN, Shirley A.	(403)282-5311	924
	WHITE, Valerie L.	(403)255-6419	1332
Edmonton	BERNARD, Marie L.	(403)455-2436	88
	COMPRI, Jeannine L.	(403)474-0577	235
	RICHARDS, Vincent P.	(403)429-9814	1029
Three Hills	JORDAHL, Ronald I.	(403)443-5511	616

BRITISH COLUMBIA

Clearbrook	VIIERANS, Mary E.	(604)859-7814	1284
North Vancouver	ELROD, J M.	(604)929-3966	346
Richmond	ELLIS, Kathy M.	(604)272-5389	344
Vancouver	HALE, Linda L.	(604)321-0932	485
	HAYCOCK, Carol A.	(604)734-0255	515
	HAYCOCK, Kenneth R.	(604)731-1131	515
	LIGHTHALL, Lynne I.	(604)228-1480	727
	NICHOL, Kathleen M.	(604)263-7081	901
	PEPPER, David A.	(604)664-4311	958
	PITERNICK, Anne B.	(604)228-3359	976
	ROBERTSON, Guy M.	(604)689-8494	1041
	SALTMAN, Judith M.	(604)228-2587	1077
	STOKES, Roy B.	(604)261-4082	1196
	STUART-STUBBS, Basil F.	(604)731-1978	1204
Victoria	GIBB, Betty J.	(604)721-8234	431
	HAMILTON, Donald E.	(604)721-7899	492
	MOEHR, Jochen R.	(604)721-8581	851

SPEAKER (Honorarium) (Cont'd)
MANITOBA

FlinFlon	HOBBS, Henry C.	(204)687-6647	545
Winnipeg	BLANCHARD, Jim	(204)949-3360	103
	BROWN, Gerald R.	(204)772-2474	144
	COVVEY, H D.	(204)942-5335	252
	REEDMAN, M R.	(204)983-3437	1015
	REINALDO DA SILVA, Joann T.	(204)237-4203	1021

NORTHWEST TERRITORIES

Yellowknife	ALBRIGHT, Donald A.	(403)873-8347	10

NOVA SCOTIA

Halifax	AMEY, Lorne J.	(902)422-8639	20
	DYKSTRA, Mary E.	(902)424-3656	331
	FRICK, Elizabeth A.	(902)424-3656	403
	TAYYEB, Rashid	(902)422-4684	1229

ONTARIO

Belfountain	DE RONDE, Paula D.	(519)927-5156	294
Don Mills	FAIRLEY, Craig R.	(416)447-5336	361
Downsview	JONES, B E.	(416)244-3621	611
	KATZ, Bernard M.	(416)638-7695	630
Etobicoke	DETERVILLE, Linda C.	(416)622-2840	296
Exeter	WILCOX, Linda M.	(519)235-2700	1338
Gloucester	ST. JACQUES, Suzanne L.	(613)824-4232	1075
Guelph	BLACK, John B.	(519)821-2565	101
Kingston	FLOWER, M A.	(613)645-6122	386
London	CLOUSTON, John S.	(519)679-2111	223
	FYFE, Janet H.	(519)472-5201	411
	MILLER, Beth M.	(519)661-3542	836
Mississauga	DAVIS, Virginia K.	(416)673-2644	281
North York	HEATON, Gwynneth T.	(416)225-4859	519
	WILLIAMS, Lorraine O.		1344
Ottawa	BURROWS, Sandra	(613)996-1342	163
	COOK, Terry G.	(613)996-7726	240
	COONEY, Jane	(613)232-9625	241
	DUCHESNE, Roderick M.	(819)997-7991	322
	DURANCE, Cynthia J.	(613)728-8763	328
	KIDD, Betty H.	(613)996-7605	646
	KIRKWOOD, Francis T.	(613)233-7592	655
	KNOPPERS, Jake V.		665
	MASON-WARD, Lesley	(613)726-1314	781
	SPICER, Erik J.	(613)995-1166	1174
	SYLVESTRE, Guy	(613)521-8468	1217
	TAYLOR, Margaret P.	(613)232-6172	1227
Scarborough	BASSNETT, Peter J.	(416)298-0614	63
Shelburne	LA CHAPELLE, Jennifer R.	(519)925-2672	686
Thornhill	SPEISMAN, Stephen A.	(416)886-2508	1172
Toronto	CAMPBELL, Bonnie	(416)323-3566	176
	CURTIS, Alison J.	(416)923-0890	267
	DE STRICKER, Ulla	(416)593-5211	296
	FASICK, Adele M.	(416)978-7074	366
	GREENWOOD, Jan	(416)963-9383	465
	HAJNAL, Peter I.	(416)533-7338	484
	KLEMENT, Susan P.	(416)486-0239	660
	KOTIN, David B.	(416)531-2104	673
	LANDON, Richard G.	(416)978-6107	693
	LAVERTY, Corinne Y.	(416)393-7024	703
	LESLIE, Nathan	(416)497-0579	718
	LORENTOWICZ, Genia	(416)393-7018	741
	LOWRY, Douglas B.	(416)497-0579	745
	LOWRY, John D.	(416)497-0579	745
	MEADOW, Charles T.	(416)530-4934	819
	MERILEES, Bobbie	(416)485-4177	826
	MERRYWEATHER, J M.	(416)965-3281	827
	ODHO, Marc	(416)596-2682	917
	PARKER, Arthur D.	(416)967-5525	941
	SMITH, Cynthia M.	(416)488-6117	1153
	VANDERELST, Wil	(416)965-2696	1274
	VEANER, Allen B.	(416)486-0239	1280
	WEIHS, Jean	(416)961-6027	1317
	WILKINSON, John P.	(416)978-3167	1340
	WONG, Lusi	(416)922-5100	1363
	ZURBRIGG, Lyn E.	(416)961-9323	1391
Waterloo	BECKMAN, Margaret L.	(519)824-4120	73
Windsor	HANDY, Mary J.	(519)256-3250	495
	WALSH, G M.	(519)253-7817	1299

SPEAKER (Honorarium) (Cont'd)

QUEBEC

Beaconsfield	HIRON, Barbara A.	(514)695-3200	543
Greenfield Park	RICHARDS, Stella	(514)672-1008	1028
Montebello	WENK, Arthur B.		1324
Montreal	CAYA, Marcel	(514)398-7100	195
	CURRAN, William M.	(514)392-4939	266
	GARNETT, Joyce C.	(514)398-4763	419
	HOBBINS, Alan J.	(514)398-4773	545
	LEIDE, John E.	(514)398-4204	713
	MCINTOSH, Julia E.	(514)283-3639	809
	MOLLER, Hans	(514)398-4740	853
	PARKER, Charles G.	(514)282-3934	941
	ROLLAND-THOMAS, Paule	(514)343-6046	1051
	SYKES, Stephanie L.	(514)870-7088	1217
	WALSH, Mary A.	(514)937-6633	1300
Quebec	FOERTIN, Yves P.	(418)649-0811	387
	GUERETTE, Charlotte M.	(418)656-3017	476
St Laurent D'Orleans	SIMON, Marie L.	(514)744-7315	1140
Sherbrooke	GOODFELLOW, Marjorie E.	(819)562-1694	448
Ste Anne de Bellevue	DOUGLAS-BONNELL, Eileen	(514)457-9487	314
Verdun	VAILLANCOURT, Alain	(514)765-7507	1270
Westmount	GLASS, Gerald	(514)931-4625	440
	LEDOUX, Marc A.	(514)484-5951	708

SASKATCHEWAN

Regina	BALON, Brett J.	(306)586-1990	53
	GAGNON, Andre	(306)569-7567	412
Saskatoon	FRITZ, Linda	(306)934-3785	405
	HAMMEL, Philip J.	(306)966-7657	493

AUSTRALIA

Canberra	STEELE, Colin R.	1184
East Hawthorn	BENNETT, David M.	81
Kensington	RAYWARD, W B.	1011
Magill	BEATTIE, Kathleen M.	70
St Lucia	LAMBERTON, Donald M.	690

BELGIUM

Beerse	PEETERS, Marc D.	954

ENGLAND

Essex	GAGE, Laurie E.	412
Harrogate	LINE, Maurice B.	730
London	BUNCE, George D.	157
	ELLIOTT, Pirkko E.	344
	PRITCHARD, Jane E.	994
	ROBERTSON, Stephen E.	1042
Sussex	GREEN, Jeffrey P.	462
Warwickshire	CHANDLER, George	200

FEDERAL REPUBLIC OF GERMANY

Berlin	ELSTE, R O.	346
	WERSIG, Gernot	1325
Bonn	LOTZ, Rainer E.	742
Taufkirchen	ADENEY, Carol D.	6

HONG KONG

Shatin	YEN, David S.	1379

INDONESIA

Jakarta	STONE, Clarence W.	1197

IRELAND

Banger	DUFFIN, Elizabeth A.	323
Dublin	FOX, Peter K.	395

ISRAEL

Jerusalem	DIAMANT, Betsy	299

ITALY

Rome	JOLING, Carole G.	610
	MENOU, Michel J.	824

SPEAKER (Honorarium) (Cont'd)

JAPAN

Chiba-ken	NASU, Yukio	889
Ibaraki-ken	NOZOE, Atsutake	911
	TAKEUCHI, Satoru	1220
Tokyo	HOSONO, Kimio	562

KENYA

Nairobi	BROCKMAN, Norbert C.	138
	IRURIA, Daniel M.	584

MEXICO

Mexico City	MAGALONI, Ana M.	759

NETHERLANDS

Amersfoort	VAN HALM, Johan	1275
Rotterdam	SCHUURSMA, Ann B.	1103
The Haag	RAITT, David I.	(311)719-8301	1004

NIGERIA

Ibadan	ABOYADE, Beatrice O.	2
Ogbomoso	TARPLEY, Margaret J.	1224

NORTHERN IRELAND

Belfast	LINTON, William D.	731

PAKISTAN

Lahore	TRAINER, Leslie F.	1253

PHILIPPINES

Makati	MORAN, Teresita C.	862
Manila	DE CASTRO, Elinore H.	285
Quezon City	PICACHE, Ursula D.	970
	VALLEJO, Rosa M.	1271

SWEDEN

Jarfalla	SHELTON, Anita L.	1126

SWITZERLAND

Geneva	FAGERLUND, M L.	361

SPECIAL LIBRARY CONSULTANT

ALABAMA

Birmingham	ATKINSON, Calberta O.	(205)787-3767	38
	BRITT, Mary C.	(203)934-4475	137
	SIMS, Joyce W.	(205)939-7830	1142
Gadsden	BUCKNER, Rebecca S.	(205)543-8849	154
Huntsville	MCCANLESS, Christel L.	(205)536-3458	793
Montgomery	BIVINS, Hulen E.	(205)272-1700	100
	LANE, Robert B.	(205)288-8122	694

ALASKA

Anchorage	LUDWIG, J D.	(907)333-8917	746
	WILLIAMS, Robert C.	(907)261-2970	1346
College	GALBRAITH, Betty J.	(903)479-5196	413
Juneau	KINNEY, John M.	(907)586-1857	653
	MITCHELL, Micheal L.	(907)789-0302	849
	NEWTON, Virginia A.	(907)586-4029	900

ARIZONA

Chandler	MCGORRAY, John J.	(602)961-8016	807
Mesa	MEAD, Thomas L.	(602)892-3764	819
Phoenix	BERK, Nancy G.	(602)971-9264	87
	DANIELS, Delores E.	(602)261-3879	273
	DOHERTY, Walter E.	(602)262-5303	309
	GORMAN, Judith F.	(602)279-9741	452
	KIRKING, Clayton C.	(602)257-1880	655
	ROATCH, Mary A.	(602)254-7678	1038
	SCHNEIDER, Elizabeth K.	(602)261-7450	1097
Tempe	ALCORN, Marianne S.	(602)965-4868	11
	OETTING, Edward C.	(602)345-7636	917
Tucson	BALDWIN, Charlene M.	(602)327-2385	51
	CROWE, Gloria J.	(602)792-9450	261
	HEIDENREICH, Fred L.	(602)626-7724	521
	HENDERSON, Joyce C.	(602)621-1202	526
	HIEB, Louis A.	(602)621-6077	537
	HUSBAND, Susan M.	(602)624-3301	578
	LEI, Polin P.		713

SPECIAL LIBRARY CONSULTANT (Cont'd)
ARIZONA (Cont'd)
Tucson

	MINTON, James O.	(602)792-9450	846
	MYERS, Roger	(602)792-3452	885
	STRICKLAND, Ann T.	(602)881-6244	1202

ARKANSAS
Fayetteville	DABRISHUS, Michael J.	(501)575-5577	269
	HARRISON, John A.	(501)443-4403	506
Heber Springs	SEDELOW, Walter A.		1110
Little Rock	FOSTER, Lynn	(501)371-1071	392

CALIFORNIA
Alameda	HUNT, Deborah S.	(415)523-6518	575
Albany	BLITZ, Ruth R.	(415)525-4186	105
Altadena	DEGOOD, S K.	(818)791-9859	288
Belmont	CROWE, Linda D.	(415)349-5538	261
	RAMSEY, Robert D.	(415)593-1601	1006
Berkeley	FALANGA, Rosemarie E.	(415)524-5501	361
	FRANKEL, Kate M.	(415)525-1533	397
	HUNT, Judy L.	(415)849-2708	575
	LEVIN, Marc A.	(415)642-1472	720
	MARKS, Larry	(415)644-2111	771
	MITCHELL, Andrea L.	(415)642-5208	848
	PARKS, Mary L.	(415)644-3401	943
	RAFAEL, Ruth K.	(415)849-2710	1003
	RIGGS, Judith M.	(415)654-2809	1034
	WOODBURY, Marda	(415)654-4810	1366
	X, Laura	(415)548-1770	1376
Beverly Hills	ANNETT, Susan E.	(213)550-4720	28
	CHAMMOU, Eliezer	(213)273-1395	198
	JEROME, Michael S.	(213)550-6100	599
Bishop	KRATZ, Gale G.	(619)873-3007	676
Brea	PERKINS, Steven C.	(714)671-0778	959
Burbank	ELMAN, Stanley A.	(818)351-8245	345
	SIGMAN, Paula M.	(818)840-5424	1137
Burlingame	PERLMAN-STITES, Janice	(415)579-7660	959
Campbell	HAZEKAMP, Phyllis W.	(408)379-1611	517
Cardiff By The Sea	MARKWORTH, Lawrence L.	(619)943-1197	772
	SCHALIT, Michael	(619)944-3913	1089
Carlsbad	TILLETT, Barbara B.		1245
Carson	SUNDSTRAND, Jacquelyn K.	(213)516-3700	1210
Concord	PUGH, Mary J.	(415)685-2133	997
	REYES, Helen M.	(415)000-0000	1024
Costa Mesa	MARLOR, Hugh T.	(714)631-5637	772
Culver City	ANDRADE, Rebecca	(213)837-5448	26
Danville	CREW-NOBLE, Sara M.	(415)837-1399	258
Davis	BENOIT, Gerald		82
	BLANCHARD, J R.	(916)753-5126	103
Downey	PAIK, Nan H.	(213)922-4648	935
El Cerrito	HARDWICK, Bonnie S.	(415)237-7011	500
	MACAULEY, C C.	(415)524-2762	754
	PRESSNALL, Patricia E.	(415)525-5186	991
Encinitas	PIERCE, Patricia J.	(619)436-5055	971
Foster City	LEE, Doreen H.	(415)345-5292	709
Fresno	KAUFFMAN, Inge S.	(209)486-8424	631
	WARD, Penny T.	(209)268-2545	1304
Fullerton	MASTERS, Robin J.	(714)524-9696	782
Glendale	WAY, Kathy A.		1311
Goleta	GRAZIANO, Eugene	(805)968-2281	460
Kensington	ROOSHAN, Gertrude I.	(415)525-5640	1053
La Canada-Flintridge	MORAN, William R.	(818)790-1529	862
La Honda	HOLLAND, Mary	(415)747-0511	551
La Jolla	BRIDGMAN, Amy R.	(619)587-1306	135
	CASTETTER, Karla M.	(619)459-5369	194
	GABBERT, Gretchen W.	(619)456-4083	411
	HUCKINS, Barbara W.	(619)453-7500	569
	MCGILVERY, Laurence	(619)454-4443	806
	MCPHAIL, Martha E.	(619)454-0411	817
	TALBOT, Dawn E.	(619)534-6213	1220
	TOMMEY, Richard J.	(619)454-4873	1250
La Mirada	ANJOU-DURAZZO, Martel T.	(213)944-5981	28
Lafayette	NEWAY, Julie M.	(415)283-1862	898
Lake View Terrace	TASHIMA, Marie		1224
Livermore	BURTON, Hilary D.	(415)423-8063	164
	HUNT, Richard K.	(415)443-5525	575
Long Beach	ADAMS, Linda L.	(213)590-7639	5
	ATTARIAN, Lorraine B.	(213)491-9295	38

SPECIAL LIBRARY CONSULTANT (Cont'd)
CALIFORNIA (Cont'd)
Los Altos	GESCHKE, Nancy A.	(415)969-7737	430
Los Angeles	BEN-ZVI, Hava	(213)852-1234	84
	CAMPBELL, Bill W.	(213)398-8992	176
	DALY, Eudice	(213)474-6080	271
	DEENEY, Kay E.	(213)479-6672	286
	DONALDSON, Maryanne T.	(213)617-7070	311
	ENYINGI, Peter	(213)629-3531	351
	FRY, Stephen M.	(213)825-4882	407
	GRAHAM, Elaine	(213)825-1200	456
	GREEN, Ellen W.	(213)855-3751	461
	HALE, Kaycee	(213)204-0793	485
	HORIGAN, Evelyn A.	(213)665-2039	559
	MERRIFIELD, Thomas C.	(213)390-4717	826
	PRINTZ, Naomi J.	(213)306-3573	993
	PRUHS, Sharon	(213)974-7780	996
	STERLIN, Annette S.	(213)645-2406	1189
	TERZIAN, Shohig S.	(213)478-5193	1232
	VEASLEY, Mignon M.	(213)236-3515	1280
	VILLERE, Dawn N.	(213)290-2989	1284
	WONG, Cecilia	(213)736-1139	1362
Los Gatos	BAILEY, Rolene M.	(408)356-9645	46
	SZABO, Carolyn J.	(408)353-2502	1218
Menlo Park	DILORETO, Ann M.	(415)326-7370	303
	HOFFKNECHT, Carmen L.	(415)361-6335	547
Mission Viejo	WIERZBA, Heidemarie B.	(714)859-5193	1337
Modesto	LUEBKE, Margaret F.	(209)578-1211	747
Montclair	CARRIGAN, John L.	(714)621-5225	186
Moraga	RUDOLPH, Anne L.	(415)631-0926	1066
Mountain View	PORTER-ROTH, Anne	(415)965-7799	985
	POST, Linda C.	(415)968-3045	986
	STANEK, Suzanne	(415)969-9225	1179
Newport Beach	SCHULTZ, Ute M.	(714)760-2308	1102
North Hollywood	PLUMB, Carolyn G.	(818)763-2017	978
Novato	HOTZ, Sharon M.	(415)892-0821	562
Oakland	BYRNE, Elizabeth D.	(415)658-6996	169
	CHESTER, Claudia J.	(415)835-4692	207
	NEWCOMBE, Barbara T.	(415)763-4406	898
	RUBIN, Rhea J.	(415)339-1274	1064
	WONG, Patricia M.	(415)834-2742	1363
Orange	LA BORDE, Charlotte A.	(714)385-4454	686
	SMITH, Julie L.	(714)771-8291	1156
	WILSON, Wayne V.	(714)997-6912	1353
Palo Alto	CRABTREE, Sandra A.	(415)858-4767	254
	LEWIS, Ralph W.	(415)446-9366	724
	VUGRINECZ, Anna E.	(415)857-6626	1289
Pasadena	OLMSTEAD, Nancy L.	(818)351-6551	921
	POSTER, Susan E.	(818)398-8897	986
Pinole	YANEZ, Elva K.	(415)724-2914	1377
Pomona	KUHNER, David A.	(714)593-2467	683
Portola Valley	ERTEL, Monica	(415)851-1007	353
Poway	DOLLEN, Charles J.	(619)748-5348	310
Rancho Cordova	GRANADOS, Rose A.	(916)363-0473	457
Rancho Palos Verdes	DAVENPORT, Constance B.		275
	KATTLOVE, Rose W.	(213)544-0061	630
	WORMINGTON, Peggie		1369
Redwood City	HOUGHTON, Barbara H.	(415)369-5811	562
Richmond	O'CONNOR, Brian C.	(415)237-6561	915
Ridgecrest	MAYES, Elizabeth A.	(619)446-6862	789
Rolling Hills Estate	SAVAGE, Gretchen S.	(213)377-5032	1085
	TUNG, Sandra J.	(213)377-5032	1263
Rutherford	NAZARIAN, Anahid	(707)963-0451	890
Sacramento	BURNS, John F.	(916)445-4293	162
	MALMGREN, Terri L.	(916)453-3529	763
	RUDDOCK, Velda I.	(916)921-0521	1065
	SCHEIBEL, Susan	(916)392-9461	1091
	SEHR, Dena P.	(916)453-3529	1112
	TESTA, Elizabeth M.	(916)322-8031	1233
San Bernardino	NOUROK, Marlene E.	(714)887-6333	910
San Clemente	KOPAN, Ellen K.	(714)498-4309	671
San Diego	BOSSEAU, Don L.	(619)229-2538	117
	CARTER, Nancy C.		189
	DYER, Charles R.	(619)236-2292	330
	ELLIOTT, Valerie E.	(619)224-2911	344
	MORRISON, Patricia	(619)292-2859	868
	ROSS, Mary A.	(619)566-4733	1058
	TRIVISON, Margaret A.	(619)452-7338	1257
	VEGA, Carolyn L.		1281

SPECIAL LIBRARY CONSULTANT (Cont'd)
CALIFORNIA (Cont'd)

San Diego			
	WEBB, Ty	(619)487-3204	1313
San Francisco	CARSCH, Ruth E.	(415)641-5014	187
	DEWOLF, Timothy B.	(415)774-2454	298
	FOX, Marylou P.	(415)546-8466	395
	GATES, Jane P.	(415)661-1514	421
	HUNSUCKER, Alice E.	(415)396-7909	574
	KRAEMER, Linda L.	(415)981-0250	674
	MAH, Jeffery	(415)552-4733	760
	PABST, Kahleen T.	(415)421-1750	933
	PAPERMASTER, Cynthia L.	(415)773-5831	939
	REGNER-HYATT, Anne L.	(415)864-1154	1017
	SHEW, Anne L.	(415)565-6352	1129
	TAYLOR, Kathryn E.	(415)391-9170	1227
	VANSLYKE, Lisa M.	(415)431-0717	1277
San Jose	BRIDGMAN, David L.	(408)997-3723	135
	CEPPOS, Karen F.	(408)277-2280	196
	DUNCAN, Rebecca	(408)971-9060	325
San Luis Obispo	FOURIE, Denise K.	(805)544-5427	393
San Ramon	O'HEARN, Sarah A.	(415)842-0306	919
Santa Barbara	RUDD, Janet K.	(805)682-9560	1065
Santa Clara	HAMBRIDGE, Sally L.	(408)378-8616	491
	SMOKEY, Sheila C.	(408)289-3490	1162
Santa Cruz	ANDERSON, Clifford D.	(408)429-2501	22
Santa Monica	KARR, Linda		628
Santa Rosa	HARRIS, Vallena D.		506
Seal Beach	FORD, Marjorie F.	(213)430-2150	389
Sebastopol	CANT, Elaine N.	(707)823-3214	179
Sherman Oaks	LEFF, Barbara Y.	(818)981-6920	712
Stanford	SWEENEY, Suzanne	(415)725-2005	1215
Studio City	KAZLAUSKAS, Edward J.	(818)797-7654	632
	PLATE, Kenneth H.	(818)797-7654	977
Sun Valley	VOTAW, Floyd M.	(818)909-5634	1289
Sunnyvale	VAN VELZER, Verna J.	(408)738-2888	1277
Truckee	BLESSE, Robert E.	(916)587-3172	105
Vacaville	KERNS, John T.	(207)448-4459	644
Van Nuys	BALABAN, Robin M.	(818)781-6952	50
Walnut Creek	SMITH, Susan A.	(415)944-1603	1161
Westminster	JADWIN, Rochelle J.	(714)894-2126	591
Whittier	WILLIAMS, Lisa B.	(213)693-0771	1344
Woodland Hills	CLIFTON, Joe A.	(818)716-3171	222
Yucaipa	BUTLER, Randall R.	(714)797-3859	167

COLORADO

Arvada	PRESTON, Lawrence N.	(303)423-8729	991
Boulder	BANKHEAD, Jean M.	(303)497-5566	54
	KRISMANN, Carol H.	(303)499-2977	678
	MEYER, Andrea P.		829
	ROTHMAN, Marilyn R.	(303)447-9938	1060
	SANI, Martha J.	(303)492-8367	1081
Colorado Springs	GREEN, Nancy W.	(303)591-1177	462
	LAZARUS, Josephine G.	(303)528-7609	706
Denver	ABRAMS, Jeanne E.	(303)871-2961	3
	BOTHMER, A J.	(303)394-5125	118
	BRITAIN, Karla K.	(303)733-0816	137
	DULAN, Peter A.	(303)692-9261	324
	GILBERT, Ruth E.	(303)757-3622	434
	GORAL, Barbara J.	(303)866-2081	451
	KIRSHBAUM, Priscilla J.	(313)756-1827	655
	MOULTON, Suzanne L.	(303)871-6427	873
	NORBIE, Dorothy E.	(303)691-5400	908
	ROSE, Phillip E.	(303)538-4276	1055
	SHARP, Alice L.	(303)866-4682	1122
	WAGNER, Barbara L.	(303)297-3611	1291
	ZOOK, Ruth A.	(303)388-6809	1390
Fort Collins	AMAN, Ann L.	(303)484-9205	19
Golden	GRAHAM, Su D.	(303)642-7802	456
	MADDOCK, Jerome T.	(303)231-1367	759
	PHINNEY, Hartley K.	(303)273-3690	969
Grand Junction	RICHMOND, Elizabeth B.	(303)241-4358	1030
	RICHMOND, Rick	(303)241-4358	1030
Lafayette	MACARTHUR, Marit S.	(303)665-8237	754
Lakewood	ROESCH, Gay E.	(303)986-6365	1049
	SMITH, Catherine C.	(303)987-2815	1153
Westminster	BOYD, Ruth E.	(303)450-4710	122

SPECIAL LIBRARY CONSULTANT (Cont'd)
CONNECTICUT

Ashford	MCCAUGHTRY, Dorothy H.	(203)429-7637	795
Avon	BLOTNER, Linda S.	(203)677-0286	106
Bloomfield	BROQUE, Suzanne	(203)242-3473	141
Branford	ADAMO, Clare	(203)488-1474	4
Bridgeport	BARNES, Denise M.	(203)372-5434	57
	ESCARILLA, Jose G.	(203)366-0684	354
Danbury	MARIANI, Carolyn A.	(203)794-6389	770
Fairfield	FROST, Mary K.	(203)259-6509	406
Greenwich	MUSKUS, Elizabeth A.	(203)661-7058	883
Guilford	GAFFNEY, Maureen	(203)453-6533	412
Hamden	KANEKO, Hideo	(203)281-3586	625
	NEWHALL, Ann C.	(203)288-8180	898
	SAMUEL, Harold E.	(203)432-0495	1079
	SMITH, Nolan E.	(203)776-3558	1159
	STRAKA, Kathy M.	(203)771-8383	1199
Hartford	NEUFELD, Irving H.	(203)278-3202	897
	WAIT, Gary E.	(236)236-5621	1293
Middletown	DOUVILLE, Judith A.	(203)344-1880	314
New Canaan	LOKETS BEISCHROT, Dina		738
New Fairfield	DYKMAN, Elaine K.	(203)746-0765	331
New Haven	COHEN, Morris L.	(203)432-1600	228
	REESE, William S.	(203)789-8081	1016
	WALES, Patricia L.	(203)789-3330	1294
Ridgefield	MILSTEAD, Jessica L.	(203)431-8175	845
	SAMUELS, Lois A.	(203)431-3342	1079
Southport	WITTEN, Laurence	(203)255-3474	1358
Stamford	DIMATTIA, Susan S.	(203)322-9055	304
	KEMP, Thomas J.	(203)323-2826	639
	LIEBERMAN, Lucille N.	(203)353-2095	726
	MASTERS, Kathy B.	(203)967-6749	782
	SILVERMAN, Susanne		1139
Stonington	WILLIAMS, Edwin E.	(203)535-0720	1343
Storrs	BOGNAR, Dorothy M.		111
	JIMERSON, Randall C.	(203)486-2893	600
	LAMB, Gertrude		690
Torrington	BENAMATI, Dennis C.	(203)489-2990	79
Vernon	MATTHEWSON, David S.		786
Washington	LEAB, Katharine K.	(203)868-7408	706
West Hartford	PIERCE, Anne L.	(203)243-4849	971
Westport	FAESY, Nancy N.	(203)226-7271	361
	MECKLER, Alan M.	(203)226-6967	820
	REISMAN, Sydelle S.	(203)227-8710	1021
	SCHWARZ, Shirlee	(203)226-6606	1105
Wethersfield	DONOHUE, Christine N.	(203)529-2938	311
Wilton	DENMAN, Monica K.	(203)762-8957	292
Windsor	SIMON, William H.		1141
Windsor Locks	MASTERS, Fred N.	(203)623-9801	782
Woodbridge	MILLER, Irene K.	(203)393-0458	838
	SHERMAN, Dottie	(203)393-1167	1128

DELAWARE

New Castle	IRWIN, Ruth A.	(302)328-8560	584
Newark	SELZER, Nancy S.	(302)366-5231	1114
	TEETER, Enola J.	(302)737-9621	1229
Wilmington	PIFALO, Victoria	(302)656-1629	972
Winterthur	ADAMS, Barbara M.	(302)656-8591	4

DISTRICT OF COLUMBIA

APO Washington	BURNS, Dean A.	(202)863-3547	162
Washington	ANGLE, Joanne G.	(202)682-1698	28
	ATKINSON, Rose M.	(202)955-2139	38
	BALL, Alice D.	(202)362-6047	52
	BERGQUIST, Christine F.		87
	COOK, Marilyn M.	(202)541-6221	240
	DATTALO, Elmo F.	(202)778-9160	275
	DICKSON, Constance P.	(202)955-8566	301
	DOWLING, Shelley L.	(202)662-9144	316
	DURAKO, Frances G.	(202)785-9700	328
	FARINA, Robert A.	(202)287-5298	363
	FREEMAN, Carla		400
	FRIERSON, Eleanor G.	(202)623-7000	404
	GARLICK, Karen	(202)287-5634	419
	GREENE, Danielle L.	(202)543-6461	463
	HALEY, Roger K.	(202)224-2976	486
	HEAD, Anita K.	(202)994-7336	518
	JOHNSON, Lucy C.		607
	JONES, Catherine A.	(202)287-8935	611
	KING, Kamla J.	(202)452-4470	651

SPECIAL LIBRARY CONSULTANT (Cont'd)
DISTRICT OF COLUMBIA (Cont'd)
Washington

KNAUFF, Elisabeth S.		663
KNOWLTON, John D.	(202)362-8911	665
LARSEN, Lynda L.	(202)328-5150	698
LASNER, Mark S.	(202)745-1927	700
LEE, Amy C.	(202)546-5539	709
LOO, Shirley	(202)546-1196	740
MCGANN, Margot	(202)822-2064	805
MCGUIRE, Brian		808
MCKEAN, Joan M.	(301)443-8358	810
MILLER, William S.	(202)775-4080	843
MISSAR, Charles D.	(202)363-2751	847
MUSSEHL, Allan A.	(202)488-8162	883
NOWAK, Geraldine D.	(202)475-9419	911
PILGRIM, Auriel J.	(202)484-5373	973
RADER, Ronald A.	(639)890-0000	1002
SCOTT, Catherine D.	(202)357-3101	1107
SEELE, Ronald E.	(202)872-3970	1111
SERVERINO, Roberto	(202)625-4574	1116
SHEELER, Harva L.	(202)879-3954	1125
SHELBURNE, Elizabeth C.	(202)966-0738	1125
SMITH, Kathleen S.		1156
SONNEMANN, Gail J.	(202)543-4536	1167
SPONDER, Dorothy R.		1175
TERRY, Susan N.	(202)332-7120	1232
TRIPP-MELBY, Pamela	(202)676-9418	1257
TURTELL, Neal T.	(202)842-6506	1265
VANDEGRIFT, Barbara P.	(202)662-7523	1273
VON PFEIL, Helena P.		1288
WELCH, Thomas L.	(202)232-1706	1321

FLORIDA

Belleair	JENNINGS, Patricia S.	(813)581-4820	598
Brooksville	TORNABENE, Charles	(904)686-9318	1251
Clearwater	TIBBS, Jo A.	(813)447-7157	1244
Coral Gables	LADNER, Sharyn J.	(305)443-1122	687
	ROBAR, Terri J.	(305)284-4706	1038
Daytona Beach	BRANDON, Alfred N.	(904)677-5098	128
Dunedin	TEW, Robin L.	(813)734-5634	1233
Fort Lauderdale	GOZDZ, Wanda E.	(305)741-3410	455
	ISAACS, Bob	(305)761-4060	584
Fort Myers	PEGLER, Ross J.	(813)267-2995	954
Gainesville	DRUM, Carol A.	(904)335-8501	320
	TAYLOR, Betty W.	(904)372-0716	1226
Lakeland	DEE, Cheryl R.		286
Miami	HALE, Kay K.	(305)271-3678	485
	LIGHTERMAN, Mark	(305)279-5467	726
	MILLER, Jewell J.	(305)662-4212	839
Miami Beach	EFRON, Muriel C.	(305)672-0696	338
	GROVER, Wilma S.	(305)868-5000	474
North Lauderdale	BRESLAUER, Lester M.	(305)721-5181	133
Orlando	CRENSHAW, Tena L.	(305)646-5637	258
	DAVIDOFF, Marcia	(305)894-5508	276
	GEBET, Russell W.	(305)849-0300	424
	GRIMSLEY, Judy L.	(305)896-2535	470
	SMITH, Mary D.	(305)843-7860	1158
Pensacola	DEBOLT, W D.	(904)474-2213	284
Pompano Beach	WHITESIDE, Lee A.	(305)782-0194	1333
Ponte Vedra Beach	PECK, Brian T.	(904)246-1400	953
St Petersburg	CATES, Jo A.	(013)522-1550	194
	CORNWELL, Douglas W.	(813)541-7206	247
	WOODARD, Joseph L.	(813)345-1335	1365
Sanibel	KLASING, Jane P.	(813)472-8391	657
Sarasota	PETRIE, Mildred M.	(813)366-8450	965
Tampa	EVANS, Josephine K.	(813)974-4471	357
	EVERLOVE, Nora J.	(813)839-4868	359
	EYLES, Heberle H.	(813)837-3896	359
	GRIMES, Maxyne M.	(813)974-2157	470
	MATHEWS, Richard B.	(813)253-3333	784
	MCRAE, Linda	(813)974-2360	818
West Palm Beach	FOSTER, Helen M.	(305)686-1776	392
	TAFFEL, Bobbe H.	(305)582-2539	1219
Winter Park	AHLIN, Nancy	(305)644-6424	8
Winter Springs	THOMAN, Nancy L.		1236

SPECIAL LIBRARY CONSULTANT (Cont'd)
GEORGIA

Athens	KAHAN, Gerald	(404)548-2514	621
	SUTHERLAND, Johnnie D.	(404)542-0690	1211
Atlanta	BIBBY, Elizabeth A.	(404)255-6840	94
	BOZE, Lucy G.	(404)874-6714	124
	BRYANT, Nancy J.	(404)955-9550	152
	DRAKE, Miriam A.	(404)894-4501	318
	DREW, Frances K.	(404)881-0917	319
	FEINBERG, Hilda W.	(404)875-0077	368
	KLOPPER, Susan M.	(404)658-1776	662
	MARKWELL, Linda G.	(404)589-3532	772
	MCDAVID, Sara J.	(404)395-1605	801
	MENEELY, William E.	(404)658-3800	824
	MILLER, Jack E.	(404)892-3600	838
	MISRA, Jayasri T.	(404)524-5320	847
	RAQUET, Jacqueline R.	(404)320-9727	1008
	ROAN, Tattie W.	(404)320-9376	1038
	STROUGAL, Patricia G.	(404)355-5497	1203
	TOMAJKO, Kathy L.	(404)894-4511	1249
Augusta	BASLER, Thomas G.	(404)828-2856	63
College Park	CANN, Sharon F.	(404)768-0970	178
Decatur	ALLEN, William R.	(404)284-2981	16
	CHAMBERS, Shirley M.	(404)289-6517	198
	COHRS, Joyce S.	(404)377-3744	229
	HUGHES, Glenda J.	(404)636-0108	571
	OVERBECK, James A.	(404)378-8821	931
Eastman	WILSON, David C.	(912)374-4711	1350
Lilburn	HOUGH, Leslie S.	(404)979-0270	562
Macon	RANKIN, Jocelyn A.	(912)744-2515	1007
Marietta	LISI, Susan C.	(404)955-1375	732
Norcross	DEWBERRY, Claire D.	(404)564-1634	298
Red Oak	LETT, Rosalind K.		719
Tucker	LEIGHTON, Victoria C.	(404)491-0464	714
Vidalia	HARTZ, Frederic R.	(912)537-0195	509

HAWAII

Honolulu	BREINICH, John A.	(808)536-9302	132
	COLEMAN, David E.	(808)947-4512	231
	GOODY, Cheryl S.	(808)521-5361	450
	GOVERNS, Molly K.		454
	SCHULTZ, Elaine V.	(808)395-1801	1102
	STEPHENS, Diana C.	(808)945-2837	1188
	URAGO, Gail M.	(808)949-6496	1269
Kailua	WRIGHT, John C.	(808)261-3714	1371

ILLINOIS

Aurora	BEAN, Janet R.	(312)859-2222	69
Bloomingdale	APOSTOLOPOULOS, Sophia S.	(312)893-1740	29
Bloomington	STROYAN, Susan E.	(309)827-4321	1203
Bolingbrook	IFFLAND, Carol D.	(312)739-6398	581
Brookfield	IRONS, Carol A.	(312)485-3503	584
Carbondale	MATTHEWS, Elizabeth W.	(618)536-7711	785
	RAY, Jean M.	(618)549-1290	1011
Champaign	CHAPLAN, Margaret A.	(217)333-7993	201
	DESSOUKY, Ibtesam	(217)333-4956	296
	HEISTER, Carla G.	(217)333-6892	523
	JOHNSON, Jane S.		605
Charleston	KAPLAN, Sylvia Y.	(217)345-4228	626
	LUQUIRE, Wilson	(217)581-6061	749
Chicago	BLOSS, Marjorie E.	(312)567-5265	106
	COATSWORTH, Patricia A.	(312)947-2160	224
	COLLINS, Janet	(312)642-2136	232
	DAVIS, Glenn G.	(312)943-2911	279
	DOLNICK, Sandy F.	(312)944-6780	310
	DONAHUE, Karin V.		310
	DOYLE, Francis R.	(312)670-2950	317
	DRAKE, Francis L.	(312)876-7170	318
	DREAZEN, Elizabeth P.	(312)347-2057	318
	DUFF, John B.	(312)269-2984	323
	FRANKLIN, Annette E.	(312)996-3447	397
	GENESEN, Judith L.		427
	GLANZ, Lenore M.	(312)528-7817	439
	GODLEWSKI, Susan G.	(312)443-3936	442
	GRAVES, Karen J.	(312)348-0930	459
	GROFT, Mary L.	(312)477-7065	471
	KAYAIAN, Mary S.	(312)245-2810	632
	KING, David E.	(312)346-7440	650
	KLEINMUNTZ, Dalia S.	(312)883-3580	660

SPECIAL LIBRARY CONSULTANT (Cont'd)
ILLINOIS (Cont'd)
Chicago

	KOVITZ, Nancy R.	(312)938-3434	674
	KOWITZ, Aletha A.	(312)440-2642	674
	LADENSON, Alex	(312)661-1493	687
	LANDRY, Ronald	(312)943-3282	694
	MANN, Vijai S.	(312)443-5423	766
	MARANO, Nancy H.	(312)368-7777	768
	MARTIN, Bennie E.	(312)443-5423	775
	MATTENSON, Murray M.	(312)262-8282	785
	MCNEILL, Janice M.	(312)642-4600	816
	MICHAEL, Ann B.	(312)399-8354	831
	MICKEY, Melissa B.	(312)324-8583	833
	MILLER, Robert	(312)488-7195	841
	MILUTINOVIC, Eunhee C.	(312)472-9843	845
	MOORE, John R.	(312)763-7811	860
	PIZER, Irwin H.	(312)996-8974	977
	REED, Virginia R.	(312)477-6836	1015
	REMEIKIS, Lois A.	(312)782-1442	1022
	SCHUSTER, Adeline	(312)939-4975	1103
	SHAW, Joyce M.	(312)294-4640	1123
	STRABLE, Edward G.	(314)947-8085	1199
	SUTHERLAND, Zena B.	(312)702-8293	1211
	TAWYEA, Edward W.	(312)908-8033	1225
	VIRGO, Julie A.	(312)751-1454	1285
	WARNER, Claudette S.	(312)875-7131	1305
	WERNETTE, Janice J.	(312)751-7000	1325
Chillicothe	CROTZ, D K.	(312)485-7805	261
Clarendon Hills	AMBROSE, Karen S.	(312)325-7964	19
Columbia	SUTTER, Mary A.	(618)281-7734	1211
Darien	BOWDEN, Philip L.	(312)887-1620	120
De Kalb	GILDEMEISTER, Glen A.	(815)753-9392	434
	GRAHAM, Robert W.	(815)753-1779	456
	HUANG, Samuel T.	(815)756-2296	568
	OSORIO, Nestor L.	(815)753-9837	928
Des Plaines	BURNS, Marie T.	(312)635-4732	162
Elgin	FORD, Jennifer D.	(312)742-1040	389
Elmhurst	STEWART, Virginia R.	(312)833-7090	1193
Evanston	FIELD, Connie N.	(312)866-2800	375
	KAPLAN, Rosalyn L.	(312)869-1035	626
	ROBERTS, Donald L.	(312)491-3434	1039
	WHITE, Matthew H.	(312)328-2221	1331
Evergreen Park	GARCIA-RUIZ, Maritza L.	(312)425-6104	417
Glenview	HAFNER, Arthur W.	(312)291-1022	482
	HAMILTON, Beth A.	(312)998-6567	491
Grayslake	KIENE, Andrea L.	(312)740-0620	647
Highland Park	SHERRY, Diane H.	(312)433-3968	1129
Hinsdale	GREGORY, Melissa R.	(312)325-2807	466
	HALASZ, Marilynn J.	(312)325-0819	484
La Grange	PROBST, Virginia M.		994
Lake Bluff	BROSK, Carol A.	(312)234-6752	141
Lisle	SHOTWELL, Richard T.	(312)665-9107	1133
Manteno	MC LAUGHLIN, Terry L.	(815)468-6424	813
Morrisonville	PODESCHI, John B.	(217)526-3256	979
Mundelein	RING, Anne M.	(312)566-0898	1035
Naperville	FURLONG, Robert E.	(312)979-2550	410
	ROWE, Dorothy B.	(312)355-9221	1062
Niles	CARTER, Ida	(312)647-9000	189
Oak Park	ALFONSI-GIN, Mary A.	(312)383-4713	13
	BEN-SHIR, Rya H.	(312)386-5444	83
Palatine	BROWN, Patricia L.	(312)991-1278	146
	HORTON, Kathy L.	(312)934-3794	561
Park Ridge	CRISPEN, Joanne	(312)696-6594	259
	KNARZER, Arlene	(312)692-9550	663
River Forest	DAVIS, Richard A.	(312)366-7383	280
Rock Island	OHRLUND, Bruce L.	(309)786-0698	919
Rockford	DALRYMPLE, Prudence W.	(815)968-9111	271
	HUTCHINS, Richard G.	(815)398-0756	579
	WELCH, Steven J.	(815)963-5133	1321
Springfield	BERK, Robert A.	(217)782-2658	87
	SHACKLETON, Suzanne M.	(217)786-6375	1118
Urbana	BOAST, Carol		108
	COBB, David A.	(217)333-0827	224
Villa Park	ELL, Elizabeth L.	(312)279-6456	343
Wauconda	SHENASSA, Daryoosh	(312)526-9123	1126
Waukegan	KOZAK, Marlene G.	(312)473-3000	674
Wheaton	BERGER, Carol A.	(312)653-1115	85
	EMBAR, Indrani M.	(312)668-1742	347
	ERICKSEN, Paul A.	(312)260-5910	352

SPECIAL LIBRARY CONSULTANT (Cont'd)
ILLINOIS (Cont'd)

Williamsville	KELLERSTRASS, Amy L.	(217)566-3517	636
Wilmette	SPIGELMAN, Cynthia A.	(312)251-4892	1174
Winnetka	BLACKBURN, Joy M.	(312)446-8697	102
	LUNDQUIST, Marie A.	(312)441-3315	748

INDIANA

Bloomington	RABER, Nevin W.	(812)336-4522	1001
	RUDOLPH, L C.	(812)335-1447	1066
	SOWELL, Steven L.	(812)335-9792	1170
	WHITE, Herbert S.	(812)335-2848	1331
Columbus	MEREDITH, Meri	(812)372-3482	825
	POOR, William E.	(812)377-7201	983
Fort Wayne	SHEETS, Michael T.	(219)483-2854	1125
	WEICK, Robert J.	(219)478-1018	1316
Highland	ENGELBERT, Peter J.	(219)923-2173	348
Hobart	CHRISTIANSON, Elin B.	(219)942-5536	212
Huntington	ISCA, Joseph J.	(219)672-8194	585
Indianapolis	ALLEN, Joyce S.	(317)929-8021	15
	GRIFFITTS, Joan K.	(317)297-3283	469
	HEHMAN, Jennifer L.	(317)271-8595	521
	SPARKS, Marie C.	(317)255-6932	1171
Lafayette	BONHOMME, Mary S.	(317)448-1251	114
Noblesville	WILLIAMS, Maudine	(317)773-1763	1345
Notre Dame	SLINGER, Michael J.	(219)239-5664	1149
South Bend	MILLER, Jeanne L.	(219)284-7491	839
Terre Haute	BAUMGARTNER, Kurt O.	(812)234-4818	66
	KYKER, Penelope R.	(812)237-2540	685
Valparaiso	WATTS, Tim J.	(219)465-7838	1310
West Lafayette	ANDREWS, Theodora A.	(317)463-6093	27
	KERKER, Ann E.		643
	MOBLEY, Emily R.	(317)494-2900	851

IOWA

Bettendorf	POLK, Diana B.	(319)332-8119	981
Boone	ADAMS, Larry D.	(515)432-1931	5
Cedar Rapids	BLISS, David H.	(319)393-5892	105
Des Moines	EDWARDS, John D.	(515)271-2141	337
	ELLIOTT, Kay M.	(515)281-6033	344
	FLICK, Frances J.	(515)277-2089	385
	GRIFFIN, Kathryn A.		468
	KROMMINGA, Patricia G.	(515)263-5181	679
Iowa City	BIERBAUM, Esther G.	(319)354-8639	95
	NICKELSBURG, Marilyn M.	(319)351-2072	902
Marion	ALDERSON, Karen A.	(319)377-0666	11
West Branch	MAYER, Dale C.	(319)643-5301	789

KANSAS

Kansas City	FARLEY, Alfred E.	(913)588-7040	364
	RUSSELL, Marilyn L.	(913)299-1540	1069
	WITMER, Tonya C.	(913)362-5327	1358
Lawrence	BURCHILL, Mary D.	(913)864-3025	158
	CRAIG, Susan V.	(913)864-3020	254
	SEAVER, James E.	(913)864-3569	1110
Manhattan	WEISENBURGER, Patricia J.	(913)532-5968	1319
North Newton	HAURY, David A.	(316)283-2500	512
Overland Park	OJALA, Marydee P.		919
Topeka	BRAND, Alice A.	(913)273-7500	127
	RICHMOND, Robert W.	(913)234-4704	1031
Wichita	BERARD, Sue A.	(316)267-6371	84
	BRADEN, Jan	(316)686-5954	125
	IZBICKI, Thomas M.	(316)683-8157	586

KENTUCKY

Bowling Green	MOORE, Elaine E.	(502)745-6114	859
Covington	GARMAN, Nancy J.	(606)331-6345	419
Danville	GILMER, Wesley	(606)236-1323	437
Fort Thomas	GILLIAM, Susanne P.	(606)441-9518	436
Lexington	BARRISH, Alan S.	(606)278-1933	60
	DARE, Philip N.	(606)252-0361	274
	WALDHART, Thomas J.	(606)257-3771	1294
	YOUNG, Sandra C.	(606)268-7677	1383
Louisville	ANDERSON, James C.	(502)588-6752	23
	BELL, Mary M.	(502)426-4732	77
	BRINKMAN, Carol S.	(502)588-6297	136
	BUCHANAN, Holly S.	(502)562-8128	153
	COATES, Ann S.	(502)588-5917	224
	DEERING, Ronald F.	(502)897-4807	287
	EDDY, Leonard M.	(502)245-8633	335

SPECIAL LIBRARY CONSULTANT (Cont'd)
KENTUCKY (Cont'd)
Louisville

	LINCOLN, Carol S.	(502)568-7683	728
	REDMON, Sherrill	(502)451-5907	1014
	TEITELBAUM, Gene W.	(502)588-6392	1230
	WHITE, Ernest M.	(502)897-3557	1331
Wilmore	BUNDY, David D.	(606)858-3581	157

LOUISIANA
Baton Rouge	LOUBIERE, Sue	(504)346-3172	742
	MATTMILLER, C F.	(504)344-8074	786
	PASKOFF, Beth M.	(504)388-1480	946
	PHILLIPS, Faye	(504)388-6569	968
	SCULL, Roberta A.		1108
Lafayette	STEWART, Mary E.	(318)984-4139	1193
	TURNER, I B.	(318)231-5702	1264
New Orleans	CAFFAREL, Agnes	(504)524-4237	170
	DANKNER, Laura R.	(504)865-2367	273
	MARIX, Mary L.	(504)488-4286	770
Shreveport	MCCORMICK, Dorcas M.	(318)677-3007	798

MAINE
Bar Harbor	BAKER, Alison	(207)288-3371	47
East Sebago	AIREY, Martha R.	(207)787-2817	9
Portland	O'BRIEN, Francis M.	(207)774-0931	914
Skowhegan	FRIDLEY, Russell W.	(207)474-7133	403
Winthrop	KING, Alan S.	(207)377-2879	650

MARYLAND
Aberdeen	HADDEN, Robert L.	(301)272-1858	481
Annapolis	CARMAN, Carol A.	(301)841-3810	183
	MENEGAUX, Edmond A.	(301)268-6741	824
Arnold	OLSON, Christine A.	(301)647-6708	922
Baltimore	ARRINGTON, Susan J.	(301)396-4042	34
	FREDENBURG, Anne M.	(301)377-9080	399
	GREENBERG, Emily R.	(301)625-3401	463
	HARDNETT, Carolyn J.	(301)332-6250	500
	HEISER, Jane C.	(301)396-5470	523
	HILDITCH, Bonny M.	(301)675-4333	539
	PARTRIDGE, James C.	(301)664-4301	945
	RASCHKA, Katherine E.	(301)539-2530	1008
	SILVER, Marcy L.		1138
	STEVENS-RAYBURN, Sarah L.	(301)338-4961	1191
	SZCZCPANIAK, Adam S.	(301)539-0872	1218
	THIES, Gail M.	(301)597-8918	1235
Bethesda	BOEHR, Diane L.	(301)986-8560	109
	BOHLEN, Jeanne L.	(301)897-9823	111
	BROWN, Carolyn P.	(301)496-2447	142
	COSTABILE, Salvatore L.	(301)986-8560	249
	JOHNSON, Carol A.	(301)251-5378	602
	MASTROIANNI, Richard L.	(301)657-6023	783
	MENNELLA, Dona M.	(301)652-0106	824
	PEARSE, Nancy J.	(301)564-1967	952
	PHILLIPS, Lena M.	(301)986-8560	968
Bowie	GIGANTE, Vickilyn M.	(301)249-2609	433
Chevy Chase	CHARTRAND, Robert L.		203
Churchton	TONEY, Stephen R.	(301)261-5650	1250
College Park	ASSOUAD, Carol S.	(301)935-5631	37
	STIELOW, Frederick J.	(301)454-5790	1194
Columbia	DAHLEN, Roger W.	(301)964-9098	269
	DOVE, Samuel	(301)964-4189	315
	GORDON, Martin K.	(301)992-7626	451
	JOHNSON, Elaine B.	(301)992-5502	604
	KOSMIN, Linda J.	(301)997-8954	672
	NEWMAN, Wilda B.	(301)730-7583	900
	WENGEL, Linda	(301)995-1469	1324
Davidsonville	SKARR, Robert J.	(301)261-4383	1145
Easton	MOLTER, Maureen M.	(301)822-1658	853
Edgewater	KROST, Mary G.		680
Fort Washington	KALKUS, Stanley	(301)839-5729	623
Frederick	BANKS, Jane L.	(301)695-6726	54
	NATHANSON, David	(301)662-4499	889
Fulton	FRANK, Robyn C.	(301)490-5898	397
Gaithersburg	PAUL, Rameshwar N.	(301)258-0768	949
	VAN BRUNT, Virginia	(301)762-6701	1272
Germantown	MOLINE, Judi A.	(301)972-5708	853
Gibson Island	ROVELSTAD, Howard		1062

SPECIAL LIBRARY CONSULTANT (Cont'd)
MARYLAND (Cont'd)
Greenbelt	AUSTIN, Rhea C.	(301)345-0750	40
	BOGGESS, John J.		110
Hydes	LANTZ, Louise K.	(301)592-2232	697
Lanham	HUFFER, Mary A.	(301)577-3640	570
Laurel	LEVINE, Emil H.	(301)776-3062	720
	SAWYER, Edmond J.	(301)725-4750	1086
	SWEETLAND, Loraine F.	(801)490-8231	1215
Lusby	HUMMEL, Janice A.	(301)586-2200	573
New Carrollton	SLOCA, Sue E.	(301)459-7106	1150
New Market	WILSON, Susan W.	(301)831-6118	1353
Rockville	BYRD, Harvey C.	(301)251-5481	169
	DEXTER, Patrick J.	(301)424-2000	298
	FREEDMAN, Lynn P.	(301)468-2600	400
	GRIFFITHS, Jose M.	(301)881-6766	469
	JONES, Gerry U.	(301)493-9438	613
	KING, Donald W.	(301)881-6766	650
	MICHAELS, Carolyn L.	(301)564-0509	831
	OAKLEY, Robert L.	(301)279-9103	913
	WALL, Eugene	(301)881-4990	1297
Salisbury	STRANGE, Elizabeth B.	(301)543-8360	1200
Silver Spring	HARBISON, John H.	(801)589-4223	499
	KADEC, Sarah T.	(301)598-7694	621
	KNOBBE, Mary L.	(301)681-6332	665
	MARKS, Cicely P.	(301)649-7200	771
	MERINGOLO, Joseph A.	(202)872-7689	826
	PICKETT, Olivia K.	(301)434-7503	971
	RICHARD, Sheila A.	(301)438-4555	1028
	STERN, Michael P.	(301)495-9413	1189
	VOGT-O'CONNOR, Diane L.	(301)681-7615	1287
Takoma Park	VELLUCCI, Matthew J.	(301)439-4481	1282
Upper Marlboro	HARBERT, Cathy E.	(301)868-9280	499
Waldorf	WOLFE, Susan J.	(301)645-4784	1361

MASSACHUSETTS
Acton	FINGERMAN, Susan M.	(617)263-1881	378
Arlington	GRIGORIS, Lygia	(617)648-2290	470
Assonet	MEDEIROS, Joseph	(617)624-4094	820
Auburndale	TUCHMAN, Maurice S.	(617)969-9791	1261
Belmont	LABREE, Rosanne	(617)855-2460	686
Bolton	BOGART, Betty B.	(617)897-7870	110
Boston	ALLEN, Nancy S.	(617)267-9300	15
	BERNARD, Bobbi	(617)353-1568	88
	BRITE, Agnes	(617)267-0369	137
	CARROLL, Virginia L.	(617)742-5151	187
	CHRISTOPHER, Irene	(617)267-2876	212
	EATON, Elizabeth K.	(617)523-7415	333
	FRYDRYK, Teresa E.	(617)482-9485	407
	GOODRICH, Allan B.	(617)929-4530	449
	GRAMENZ, Francis L.	(617)353-3705	457
	HOLT, June C.	(617)727-1140	554
	MACIVER, Linda B.		756
	MATARAZZO, James M.	(617)738-2220	783
	MOSS, Karen M.	(617)223-9044	872
	NESS, Arthur J.	(617)277-1776	896
	PEARLSTEIN, Toby	(617)973-8000	952
	PICCININO, Rocco	(617)442-9010	970
	PLUNKET, Joy H.	(617)327-5175	978
	PRESTON, Margaret P.	(617)338-6000	992
	SCANLAN, Jean M.	(617)439-7412	1087
	SCHATZ, Cindy A.	(617)732-2134	1090
	SWANN, Thomas E.	(617)482-1360	1213
	TRIPP, Maureen A.	(617)578-8676	1257
	WARNER, Marnie M.	(617)725-8733	1305
	ZIMPFER, William E.	(617)353-3034	1389
Brighton	BRAUN, Robin E.	(617)789-2177	130
Brockton	NOYES, Suzanne N.	(617)583-4500	911
Brookline	SOVNER-RIBBLER, Judith	(617)277-2991	1170
Cambridge	DAVY, Edgar W.	(617)253-5670	281
	DEARBORN, Susan C.	(617)576-3205	284
	HANKAMER, Roberta A.		496
	PINSON, Mark	(617)492-1590	975
	WARRINGTON, David R.	(617)495-4550	1307
Charlestown	DOWLER, Lawrence E.		315
Chelmsford	MATTHEWS, Charles E.	(617)256-6600	785
Chestnut Hill	DESJARDINS, Andrea C.		295
Concord	BENDER, Elizabeth H.	(617)369-4222	79
Dedham	LOSCALZO, Anita B.	(617)329-3964	741

SPECIAL LIBRARY CONSULTANT (Cont'd)
MASSACHUSETTS (Cont'd)

Douglas	COPPOLA, H P.	(617)476-2975	245
	COPPOLA, Peter A.	(617)476-2975	245
Dover	WINQUIST, Elaine W.	(617)785-0816	1355
Dracut	ARSENAULT, Patricia A.	(617)459-4648	35
Farmingham	KING, Laurie L.	(617)877-3512	651
Fitchburg	LAMBERT, Lyn D.	(617)345-6726	690
Hanscom AFB	SEIDMAN, Ruth K.	(617)377-4895	1112
Haverhill	JAFFARIAN, Sara	(617)373-5922	591
Heath	HOWLAND, Margaret E.	(413)337-4980	566
Ipswich	DRAKE, Robert E.	(617)356-7752	318
Jamaica Plain	ALASTI, Aryt	(617)524-0411	9
	WHELAN, Julia S.	(617)522-3064	1329
Kingston	FELICETTI, Barbara W.	(617)585-5662	370
Lawrence	FIRTH, Margaret A.		379
Lexington	BERNSTEIN, D S.	(617)863-1284	89
	FREITAG, Wolfgang M.	(617)861-0444	401
	KATES, Jacqueline R.	(617)862-1919	629
	LUCKER, Jay K.	(617)862-4558	746
	PRUSAK, Laurence	(617)861-7580	996
	WALSH, Joanna M.	(617)863-1275	1299
	WARNER, Alice S.	(617)862-9278	1305
Lincoln	SCHWANN, William J.	(617)259-8212	1104
Littleton	BUCKLAND, Lawrence F.	(617)899-1086	154
Marlborough	FERGUSON, Roberta J.	(617)481-5866	372
Medford	PELLEGRINI, Deborah A.	(617)396-5457	955
Millis	PERRY, Guest	(617)376-8459	960
	ROE, Georgeanne T.	(617)376-8459	1048
Milton	OPPENHEIM, Roberta A.	(617)698-6268	925
Nahant	DESTEFANO, Daniel A.	(617)596-1767	296
New Bedford	FINNI, John J.	(617)999-6034	379
Newburyport	JACQUES, Donna M.	(617)462-7105	591
Newton Highlands	FOX, Elyse H.	(617)443-4798	394
North Attleboro	VIGORITO, Patricia M.	(617)699-2342	1284
North Grafton	SAFFER-MARCHAND, Melinda	(617)839-5302	1074
North Quincy	NIELSEN, Sonja M.	(617)328-8306	903
Northampton	GRIGG, Susan	(413)584-2700	470
	SLY, Margery N.	(413)584-2700	1150
Petersham	MCMANAMON, Mary J.	(617)724-3407	814
Quincy	WHEALAN, Ronald E.	(617)479-3297	1328
Reading	DAMICO, Nancy B.	(617)944-9411	272
	O'CONNOR, Jerry	(617)944-6452	916
Revere	MOORE, Catherine I.	(617)289-4595	859
South Deerfield	CRAIG, James L.	(413)665-2041	254
Sturbridge	PERCY, Theresa R.	(617)347-3362	958
Uxbridge	LEWIS, Thomas F.		724
Waltham	STRAND, Bethany	(617)736-4645	1200
Wellesley	MARX, Peter	(617)237-9585	780
West Springfield	HELO, Martin	(413)736-4561	525
Williamsburg	O'BRIEN, Marjorie S.	(413)268-7131	914
Winchester	KEATS, Susan E.	(617)729-9317	633
Woods Hole	WINN, Carolyn P.	(617)548-7066	1355
Worcester	RIVARD, Timothy D.	(617)799-8186	1037
	STANKUS, Tony	(617)793-2643	1180
Yarmouthport	STEEVES, Henry A.		1184

MICHIGAN

Ann Arbor	BEAUBIEN, Anne K.	(313)763-5060	70
	BENSON, Peggy	(313)665-0651	83
	BERGEN, Kathleen M.	(313)936-3814	85
	BLOUIN, Francis X.	(313)764-3482	107
	HOUGH, Carolyn A.	(313)665-0537	562
	LEARY, Margaret R.	(313)663-7324	707
	SCOTT, Melissa C.	(313)764-7460	1107
	WERLING, Anita L.	(313)761-4700	1324
Augusta	AEBLI, Carol L.	(616)731-5587	7
Bay City	KORMELINK, Barbara A.	(517)894-3782	671
Belleville	STARESINA, Lois J.	(313)699-7549	1181
Detroit	BRUNK, Thomas M.	(313)331-4930	150
	HEINEN, Margaret A.	(313)256-7516	522
	JOHNSON, Veronica A.	(313)532-6715	609
	MENDELSOHN, Loren D.	(313)577-6317	823
	STAJNIAK, Elizabeth T.	(313)259-7110	1178
	WARD, Nancy E.	(313)256-9596	1304
Ferndale	BORAM, Joan M.	(313)542-2523	116
Flint	BROWN, Eve C.	(313)238-5651	144
	MORELAND, Patricia L.	(313)762-2141	863

SPECIAL LIBRARY CONSULTANT (Cont'd)
MICHIGAN (Cont'd)

Grand Rapids	BERGIN, Karen S.	(616)458-0098	86
	BRACKETT, Norman S.	(616)241-7467	124
	FITZPATRICK, Nancy C.	(616)676-1568	383
	SIEBERS, Bruce L.	(616)774-2167	1135
Holland	YETMAN, Nancy J.	(616)394-2363	1380
Holt	KEDDLE, David G.	(517)694-2746	634
Kalamazoo	CARROLL, Hardy	(616)383-1926	187
Lansing	CALLARD, Carole	(517)373-1593	173
	HEINLEN, Bethany A.	(517)377-8389	522
Lapeer	VOELZ, Laura D.	(313)667-9583	1286
Lathrup Village	COCHRAN, Catherine	(313)557-1635	225
Mt Pleasant	MULLIGAN, William H.	(517)773-1374	877
Northville	ROCKALL, Diane M.	(313)349-9005	1046
Petoskey	KELLY, Kay	(616)348-4500	638
Plymouth	DE BEAR, Richard S.	(313)459-5000	284
Pontiac	LYNCH, Mollie S.	(313)858-3495	752
Romeo	NOWICKE, Carole E.	(313)752-6664	911
Saginaw	JOHN, Stephanie C.	(517)771-6846	601
Saint Clair Shores	AMES, Kay L.	(313)773-7054	20
Southfield	JOSE, Phyllis A.	(313)355-9282	617
	SUMMERS, Sheryl H.	(313)357-0404	1209
	THOMAS, Margaret J.	(313)357-4952	1237
Troy	STEPHENS, Karen L.	(313)879-6856	1188
Warren	VAN ALLEN, Neil K.	(313)696-9508	1271

MINNESOTA

Eden Prairie	GROSCH, Audrey N.	(612)937-2345	472
Kilkenny	HAMMARGREN, Betty L.	(507)595-2575	493
Mankato	TOHAL, Kate J.	(507)389-5963	1248
Marine on St Croix	FULLER, Sherrilynne S.	(612)433-3893	409
Minneapolis	ASPNES, Grieg G.	(612)926-1749	37
	BEDOR, Kathleen M.	(612)823-3945	73
	BRUEMMER, Bruce H.	(612)624-5050	149
	CARLSON, Stan W.	(612)571-2046	182
	FURTAK, Rosemary	(612)375-7680	410
	GUNTHER, Paul B.	(612)371-5622	478
	MIRANDA, Esmeralda C.	(612)437-0245	847
	REHNBERG, Marilyn J.	(612)722-3234	1017
	RUBENS, Donna J.	(612)624-7082	1064
	SOLSETH, Gwenn M.	(612)330-6936	1166
	STANKE, Judith U.	(612)725-6767	1180
	WARPHEA, Rita C.	(612)588-6985	1306
Minnetonka	JENSEN, Wilma M.	(612)473-5965	599
North Oaks	HONEBRINK, Andrea C.	(612)481-0968	555
Robbinsdale	HERTHER, Nancy K.	(612)529-0115	533
Rochester	KEY, Jack D.	(507)284-2068	645
Roseville	KAUFENBERG, Jane M.	(612)642-9221	630
St Cloud	HEETER, Judith A.	(612)251-2700	520
St Paul	BALDWIN, Jerome C.	(612)297-4532	51
	CATHCART, Marilyn S.	(612)646-0254	195
	DAVIS, Emmett A.	(612)699-4367	279
	DOLAN, Mary M.	(612)296-7719	309
	NEVIN, Susanne	(612)625-1898	898
	RASMUSSEN, Mary L.	(612)644-0685	1009
	RICCI, Patricia L.	(612)771-4764	1026
	SCHOLBERG, Henry	(612)633-6851	1098
	WALSTROM, Jon L.	(612)296-4543	1300
	WURL, Joel F.	(612)627-4208	1374
St Peter	ESSLINGER, Guenter W.	(507)931-7569	355
Scandia	HANSEN, Kathelen L.	(612)433-5477	497

MISSISSIPPI

Hattiesburg	DRAKE, Betty S.	(601)266-5077	318
	DUNCAN, Bettye M.	(601)264-6849	325
	LATOUR, Terry S.	(601)266-4345	701
University	COCHRAN, J W.	(601)232-7361	225
Vicksburg	BLACK, Bernice B.	(601)636-1990	101

MISSOURI

Ballwin	BRENNER, Saundra H.	(314)256-3936	133
	BUHR, Rosemary E.		156
Boonville	JOB, Rose A.		601
Chesterfield	GOLDMAN, Teri B.		446
Columbia	TIMBERLAKE, Patricia P.	(314)882-4581	1245
Joplin	ABERNATHY, William F.	(417)624-2518	2

SPECIAL LIBRARY CONSULTANT (Cont'd)
MISSOURI (Cont'd)

Kansas City	COX, Bruce B.		253
	DALTON, Richard R.	(816)361-3295	271
	GAMER, May L.	(816)361-8666	416
	POSTLEWAIT, Cheryl A.	(913)384-0197	986
	SERLING, Kitty	(816)753-5700	1116
Kirksville	ONSAGER, Lawrence W.	(816)665-4283	924
St Louis	AMELUNG, Richard C.	(314)658-2754	19
	ANDERSON, Paul G.	(314)534-0643	25
	ELAM, Kristy L.	(314)658-2759	341
	ELSESSER, Lionelle H.	(314)725-4722	346
	GILTINAN, Celia E.	(314)962-9048	437
	HALBROOK, Barbara	(314)362-2786	485
	LAURENSTEIN, Ann G.	(314)577-2669	703
	MESSERLE, Judith R.	(314)577-8607	828
	PAGE, Jacqueline M.	(314)781-6352	934
	TIPSWORD, Thomas N.	(314)263-2345	1246
	WEITKEMPER, Larry D.	(314)353-6757	1320
	WILKINSON, William A.	(314)997-3585	1340
St Peters	HICKS, James M.	(314)441-0522	537
Springfield	CARTER, Steva L.	(417)882-5050	190
	COOMBS, James A.	(417)836-4534	241
	CRABTREE, Anna B.	(417)887-1531	254
	MORROW, Paula J.	(417)887-8161	869
Warrensburg	SADLER, Philip A.	(816)747-8726	1073

MONTANA
Missoula	CHANDLER, Devon	(406)243-4072	199

NEBRASKA
Beatrice	DUX-IDEUS, Sherrie L.	(402)223-4581	330
Lincoln	LEITER, Richard A.	(402)466-3468	714
	WISE, Sally H.	(402)472-5737	1357
Omaha	EARLEY, Dorothy A.	(402)333-5734	332
Ralston	OYER, Kenneth E.	(402)331-8843	932

NEVADA
Henderson	TRASATTI, Margaret S.	(702)733-3613	1254
Las Vegas	BATSON, Darrell L.	(702)649-8845	64
	DAVENPORT, Marilyn G.	(702)453-5606	275
	MORGAN, James E.	(702)384-4887	864
	ORTIZ, Cynthia		927
	ORTIZ, Diane	(702)388-6501	927

NEW HAMPSHIRE
Hanover	ROLETT, Virginia V.	(603)643-3593	1051
Nashua	EMOND, Kathleen A.		348
	KOZIKOWSKI, Derek M.	(603)881-1057	674
Windham	CUNNIFFE, Charlene M.	(603)434-1847	265

NEW JERSEY
Allenwood	ERBE, Evalina S.	(201)223-9388	352
Annandale	MURO, Ernest A.	(201)735-9633	880
Atlantic City	CROSS, Roberta A.	(609)345-2269	261
Basking Ridge	THOMPSON, Melia M.	(201)953-3326	1240
Bernardsville	BURDEN, Geraldine R.	(201)766-0118	158
Bloomfield	PICCIANO, Jacqueline L.	(201)743-9661	970
Chatham	SZE, Melanie C.	(201)635-4633	1218
Cherry Hill	ARROWOOD, Nina R.	(609)667-7653	35
	GLATT, Carol R.		440
Clifton	PIERMATTI, Patricia A.	(201)473-2454	972
	TROJAN, Judith L.	(201)472-3868	1257
Creamridge	GEORGE, Muriel S.	(609)758-3198	428
Dayton	LAMBKIN, Claire A.	(201)329-0648	691
Delanco	WOLFORD, Larry E.	(609)461-5667	1361
Denville	VARIEUR, Normand L.		1278
Edison	DINERMAN, Gloria	(201)906-1777	304
Florham Park	SWINBURNE, Ralph E.	(201)377-8390	1216
Forked River	ROYCE, Carolyn S.	(609)971-0665	1063
Haddonfield	WILLIAMSON, Carol L.	(609)354-6213	1347
Highland Park	BEETHAM, Donald W.	(201)249-3268	74
	NIGRIN, Albert G.		904
	PAGE, Penny B.	(201)247-9353	934
	PARAS, Lucille P.		939
Hightstown	BRODMAN, Estelle	(609)443-8094	139
Hoboken	PAULSON, Barbara A.	(201)420-8017	950
	SOLOMON, Geri E.	(201)420-8364	1166
Hopewell	BENTE, June E.	(201)218-7436	83
Iselin	SILVA, Nelly H.	(201)321-0683	1138

SPECIAL LIBRARY CONSULTANT (Cont'd)
NEW JERSEY (Cont'd)

Kearny	CASSIDY, Joni L.	(201)991-5868	193
Madison	JONES, Arthur E.	(201)377-6525	611
Maplewood	D'ALLEYRAND, Marc R.	(201)761-1028	270
	KRUPP, Robert G.	(201)763-8436	681
	LAUB, Barbara J.	(201)763-8379	702
	STAHL, Wilson M.	(800)262-0070	1178
Morristown	BRUNNER, Karen B.	(201)538-0800	151
	BUCK, Anne M.	(201)829-5111	153
Mt Laurel	O'CONNOR, Elizabeth W.	(609)235-5003	916
	O'CONNOR, Elizabeth W.	(609)235-5003	916
Mountainside	LINGELBACH, Lorene N.	(201)654-7694	730
Murray Hill	BROWN, Ina A.	(201)582-2417	144
Paramus	CESARD, Mary A.	(201)444-4389	196
Parsippany	VOGT, Herwart C.	(201)263-5669	1287
Perth Amboy	HARDISH, Patrick M.	(201)826-5298	500
Piscataway	CARNAHAN, Joan A.	(201)752-4731	183
	SPAULDING, Frank H.	(201)463-0158	1172
Plainsboro	QUINN, Ralph M.	(609)799-3072	1000
Princeton	BLASINGAME, Ralph	(609)987-0273	104
	CHAIKIN, Mary C.	(609)452-6084	197
	FRIHART, Anne R.	(609)921-3333	404
	MOSS, Susan K.	(609)452-1212	872
Red Bank	PACHMAN, Frederic C.	(201)530-7695	933
Ridgewood	SEER, Gitelle	(201)652-2595	1111
Rockaway	COHN, John M.	(201)627-8512	229
	KELSEY, Ann L.	(201)627-8512	639
Roselle	GAINES, Irene A.	(201)245-8277	412
Saddle Brook	AUGHEY, Kathleen M.		39
Short Hills	LEVEROCK, Lisa A.	(201)379-4800	719
	TALCOTT, Ann W.	(201)379-6721	1221
Somerville	GABRIEL, Linda	(201)874-8061	411
	KUSHINKA, Kerry L.	(201)526-7323	685
Springfield	SCOTT, Miranda D.	(201)467-7010	1107
Summit	JOHNSON, Minnie L.	(201)273-4952	607
Teaneck	MOUNT, Ellis	(201)836-1137	873
Tenafly	KORNFELD, Carol E.	(201)568-2231	672
Trenton	ROUMFORT, Susan B.	(609)292-6210	1061
Vineland	GREENBLATT, Ruth	(609)794-4243	463
Warren	WEIL, Ben H.	(201)647-0892	1317
Wayne	FIRSCHEIN, Sylvia H.	(201)694-8600	379
West Long Branch	FISHER, Scott L.	(201)229-9222	381
Westfield	REGENBERG, Patricia B.	(201)232-4870	1017
Whippany	MUNSICK, Lee R.	(201)386-1920	879
Woodbridge	DE WITT, Benjamin L.	(201)634-1316	298

NEW MEXICO
Albuquerque	BERNSTEIN, Judith R.	(505)262-2320	89
	ROLLINS, Stephen J.	(505)277-5057	1051
	SHELSTAD, Kirsten R.	(505)266-8502	1126
	STRUB, Jeane E.	(505)262-7158	1203
Los Alamos	GODFREY, Lois E.	(505)662-7381	442
Los Lunas	HAYNES, Douglas E.	(505)841-5318	516

NEW YORK
Albany	COX, Richard J.	(518)486-4820	253
	DANIELS, Pam	(518)473-8177	273
	DENOTO, Dorothy E.	(518)449-3166	293
	MATTIE, Joseph J.	(518)474-4970	786
	MATTURRO, Richard C.	(518)454-5734	786
	VAILLANCOURT, Pauline M.	(518)489-6207	1271
Amherst	COOVER, James B.	(176)636-2935	244
APO New York	HAUSRATH, Donald C.		513
Ballston Lake	BOTTA, Jean C.	(518)399-2636	118
	FRALEY, Ruth A.	(518)399-9542	395
Bayside	IPPOLITO, Andrew V.	(718)224-9484	583
	SHER, Deborah M.	(718)225-3435	1127
Bethpage	BURDEN, John	(516)575-3912	158
Binghamton	COHEN, Ann E.	(607)724-9597	227
	MCKEE, George D.	(607)729-5490	810
Bronx	DAVIS, Mary B.	(212)829-7770	280
	WAGSCHAL, Sara G.	(212)601-1723	1292
Brooklyn	CANDELMO, Emily		178
	GARA, Otto G.	(718)875-1300	416
	GREENBERG, Roberta D.	(718)857-0146	463
	GUREWITSCH, Bonnie	(718)338-6494	478
	HOMMEL, Claudia	(718)237-0028	555
	JOHNSON, Sheila A.	(718)780-7744	609
	KIRWAN, Kathleen	(718)389-8033	656

SPECIAL LIBRARY CONSULTANT (Cont'd)
NEW YORK (Cont'd)
Brooklyn

	SEMKOW, Julie L.	(718)624-3189	1115
	WENGER, Milton B.	(718)252-5019	1324
	WOFSE, Joy G.	(718)788-5360	1359
Brookville	GRANT, Mary M.	(516)299-2832	458
Buffalo	HUANG, C K.	(716)831-3402	568
	KARCH, Linda S.	(716)827-2323	627
	KASE-MCLAREN, Karen A.	(716)838-6610	628
Croton-on-Hudson	COHEN, Aaron	(914)271-8170	227
Delanson	SOMERS, Betty J.	(518)864-5235	1166
Delhi	SEN, Joyce H.	(607)746-7350	1115
Delmar	BRESLIN, Ellen R.	(518)439-7568	133
	POLAND, Ursula H.	(518)439-6872	980
East Northport	DAVIDSON, Steven I.	(516)368-0841	276
Elmhurst	SALEY, Stacey		1076
Farmingdale	ARMSTRONG, Ruth C.		32
Flushing	COOPER, Marianne	(718)520-7194	243
	DUTIKOW, Irene V.	(718)939-7382	329
	KOSTER, Gregory E.	(718)575-4264	673
	SURPRENANT, Thomas T.	(718)520-7194	1210
Forest Hills	VAN BRUNT, Amy S.	(718)261-0313	1272
	WIENER, Sylvia B.	(718)263-9469	1336
Fresh Meadows	MULCAHY, Brian J.	(718)454-2157	876
Geneseo	CAREN, Loretta	(716)243-0438	181
Getzville	DENSMORE, Christopher	(716)688-2001	293
Glendale	SOSTACK, Maura	(718)417-8242	1169
Grand Island	WATERS, Betsy M.		1308
Hewlett	WILLER, Kenneth H.		1341
Hornell	SMITH, Brian D.	(607)324-0841	1153
Hudson	HENDRICKS, Elaine M.		527
Huntington	JASSIN, Raymond M.	(516)266-1093	595
	ROSAR, Virginia W.	(516)549-4576	1054
Huntington Station	MAUTER, George A.	(516)421-9291	787
Ithaca	EDDY, Donald D.	(607)255-5281	335
	OLSEN, Wallace C.	(607)255-2551	922
	ZASLAW, Neal	(607)257-1052	1386
Jacksonville	HILLMANN, Diane I.	(602)387-9207	541
Jamaica	MARKE, Julius J.	(718)990-6759	771
Jamaica Estates	CHANG, Daphne Y.	(718)297-2541	200
Kew Gardens	THAU, Richard	(718)847-7736	1234
Kirkwood	HAMLIN, Eileen M.	(607)775-1758	493
Lindenhurst	MILNES, Patricia C.	(516)957-7755	845
Little Neck	EDWARDS, Barnett A.	(718)425-2576	337
Lynbrook	HESSLEIN, Shirley B.	(516)887-5071	534
Massapequa Park	AKS, Gloria	(516)795-7297	9
	GIANNATTASI, Gerard E.	(516)541-6584	430
Mattituck	PERLMAN, Stephen E.	(516)298-4335	959
Miller Place	TODOSOW, Helen K.	(516)928-7174	1248
Mineola	LODATO, James J.	(516)747-4070	736
Nassau	VANNORTWICK, Barbara L.	(518)766-4190	1276
New Rochelle	HUMPHRY, James	(914)834-6941	574
New York	ALLENTUCK, Marcia E.		16
	ARMSTRONG, Joanne D.	(212)280-3743	32
	BADERTSCHER, David G.	(212)374-5615	44
	BATES, Ellen	(212)503-8007	63
	BENSON, Harold W.	(212)420-7652	83
	BOCKMAN, Eugene J.	(212)566-5398	109
	BOWLEY, Craig	(212)239-0827	121
	BRAUDE, Robert M.	(212)472-5919	129
	BURGALASSI, Anthony J.	(212)382-6668	159
	BUSSEY, Holly J.	(212)708-5181	165
	CIOPPA, Lawrence	(212)677-5688	214
	COHEN, Rochelle F.	(212)577-3333	229
	COPLEN, Ron	(212)869-3348	244
	D'ANGELO, Paul P.	(212)760-1600	272
	DEUSS, Jean	(212)924-0521	296
	DOOLING, Marie	(212)510-4375	312
	EPPES, William D.	(212)675-2070	351
	FEBLES, Mary T.	(212)210-3983	367
	FERGUSON, Russell	(212)219-1222	372
	FLOERSHEIMER, Lee M.	(212)787-3727	385
	FODY, Barbara A.	(212)713-3673	387
	GILLESPIE, John T.	(212)861-9294	435
	GILLIGAN, Mary A.	(212)790-9090	436
	GINSBURG, Carol L.	(212)850-1440	438
	GOSSAGE, Wayne	(212)869-3348	453
	GRELE, Ronald J.	(212)280-2273	467
	GREWENOW, Peter W.	(212)280-8656	467

SPECIAL LIBRARY CONSULTANT (Cont'd)
NEW YORK (Cont'd)
New York

	GURIEVITCH, Grania B.	(212)974-9507	478
	HASWELL, Hollee	(212)280-3786	511
	HERBERT, Annette F.	(212)371-6220	530
	HERMAN, Marsha	(212)679-6105	531
	HEWITT, Vivian D.		535
	HUTSON, Jean B.	(212)368-1515	579
	JANIAK, Jane M.	(212)466-4060	593
	JONES, Roger A.	(212)777-2959	615
	KAPNICK, Laura B.	(212)975-2917	626
	KASTNER, Arno A.	(212)998-2477	629
	KELLEY, Dennis L.	(212)210-7043	636
	KILBERG, Jacqueline L.	(212)536-3562	648
	KLECKNER, Simone M.	(212)877-2448	658
	KOENIG, Michael E.	(212)867-0489	668
	LAMANN, Amber N.	(212)677-4102	689
	LANDAU, Herbert B.	(212)705-7600	692
	LASKOWITZ, Roberta G.	(212)684-2089	700
	LASTRES, Steven A.	(212)486-9500	701
	LIN, Tung F.	(212)669-5178	728
	MARGALITH, Helen M.	(212)575-0190	770
	MARTIN, Richard	(212)760-7970	778
	MASSIS, Bruce E.	(212)595-2000	782
	MASYR, Caryl L.	(212)777-9271	783
	MAYER, George L.	(212)724-8057	789
	MILLER, Ellen L.	(212)406-3186	837
	MILLER, Sarah J.		842
	MINTZ, Anne P.	(212)620-2499	847
	MOSES, Julian M.	(212)688-8426	871
	NELOMS, Karen H.	(212)582-9239	893
	O'GRADY, Jean P.	(212)370-8690	918
	PANELLA, Nancy M.		938
	PARRIS, Angela P.	(212)836-7640	944
	PASQUARIELLA, Susan K.	(212)781-0324	946
	PHILLPOT, Clive J.	(212)708-9431	969
	PIDALA, Veronica C.		971
	PINEDA, Conchita J.	(212)371-5188	974
	POTEAT, James B.	(212)759-6800	986
	REGAN, Muriel	(212)869-3348	1017
	RICHARDS, Daniel T.	(212)678-0908	1028
	RODERER, Nancy K.	(212)305-6302	1047
	ROTHSTEIN, Pauline M.	(212)750-6008	1060
	ST. CLAIR, Guy	(212)515-5299	1075
	SANCHEZ, Eliana P.	(212)254-8829	1079
	SCIOLINO, Elaine T.	(212)371-5900	1106
	SHIROMA, Susan G.	(212)998-2602	1131
	SLATE, Ted	(212)350-4682	1148
	SPRUNG, George	(212)362-9389	1176
	STRINGFELLOW, William T.	(212)586-2000	1202
	TAYLOR, Patricia A.	(212)566-4285	1228
	TAYLOR, Robert N.	(212)664-9021	1228
	THOMAS, Dorothy	(212)799-0970	1236
	TOMASULO, Patricia A.	(212)472-6442	1249
	TRACY, Janet R.	(212)222-1157	1253
	WALKER, William B.	(212)595-7335	1296
	WATKINS, Dorothy	(212)668-0940	1309
	WERTSMAN, Vladimir F.	(212)246-8176	1325
	WOSH, Peter J.	(212)581-7400	1369
North Chatham	WELLS, Gladysann		1322
North Syracuse	AUSTIN, Ralph A.	(315)457-1799	40
Oceanside	ROGGENKAMP, Alice M.	(516)766-1397	1050
Pearl River	ABDULLAH, Bilquis	(914)735-5078	2
Plattsburgh	RANSOM, Christina R.	(518)563-5719	1007
Port Washington	SCHREIBMAN, Fay C.	(516)767-0081	1099
Poughkeepsie	LEE, Judy A.	(914)473-3719	710
Rensselaerville	STORMS, Kate	(518)797-5154	1198
Rochester	BALKIN, Ruth G.	(716)482-1506	52
	BARRETT, Lizabeth A.	(716)272-1905	59
	BLUM, Elaine G.	(716)423-1611	107
	GIGLIOTTI, Mary J.	(716)254-0621	433
	GLASER, June E.	(716)275-5010	439
	GRAY, Shirley M.	(716)475-2010	460
	HELBERS, Catherine A.	(716)594-9652	523
	JUNION, Gail J.	(716)275-4496	620
	MOUREY, Deborah A.	(716)724-6819	874
	ROBBINS, Diane D.	(716)473-2200	1038
Roslyn Harbor	CARTAFALSA, Joan C.	(516)671-7411	188
Rouses Point	CURRAN, George L.		266

SPECIAL LIBRARY CONSULTANT (Cont'd)
NEW YORK (Cont'd)

Scarsdale	COAN, Mary L.	(914)723-5325	224
	SEULOWITZ, Lois	(914)472-4097	1117
Schenectady	KLEMPNER, Irving M.	(518)393-5983	660
Somers	RIGNEY, Janet M.	(914)276-2641	1034
	RITTER, Sally K.	(914)232-7889	1037
Staten Island	BARTO, Stephen C.	(718)727-8940	61
	HOGAN, Kristine K.	(718)727-1135	549
	HOGAN, Matthew	(718)273-6245	549
	KRIEGER, Tillie		678
Syosset	CALVANO, Margaret	(516)92*-1674	174
	JENSEN, Dennis F.	(516)921-0418	598
Syracuse	DUNN, Mary B.	(315)476-0402	327
	MCCLURE, Charles R.	(315)423-2911	797
	REINSTEIN, Diana J.	(315)492-5500	1021
	SHELANDER, Frances R.	(315)469-8068	1125
Three Mile Bay	PIZER, Charles R.	(315)649-5086	977
	PIZER, Elizabeth F.	(315)649-5086	977
Watertown	GARVEY, Jeffrey M.	(315)782-2400	421
West Valley	CURRY, Lenora Y.	(716)942-4362	266
White Plains	BAXTER, Paula A.	(914)946-3275	67
	BOWLES, Edmund A.	(914)696-1900	121
	DAVIES, Carol A.	(212)754-7438	277
	HOUGHTON, Joan I.	(914)335-7839	562
Woodhaven	PAYNE, Linda C.	(718)849-1320	951
Wynantskill	CORSARO, James		248
Yonkers	SIKORSKI, Charlene S.	(914)968-2674	1137
Yorktown Heights	YURO, David A.	(914)962-5200	1384

NORTH CAROLINA

Angier	FISH, Paula H.	(919)639-4331	380
Asheville	THIBODEAU, Patricia L.	(704)257-4448	1235
Bahama	STINE, Roy S.	(719)471-8853	1194
Boone	BUSBIN, O M.	(704)264-7141	164
Cedar Grove	WRIGHT, Larry L.		1372
Chapel Hill	DANIEL, Evelyn H.	(919)962-8366	272
	DICKERSON, Jimmy	(919)962-1188	300
	GASAWAY, Laura N.	(919)962-1321	421
	PRILLAMAN, Susan M.	(919)962-3791	993
	ROBERTSON, W D.	(919)933-6894	1042
	TELFER, Margaret E.	(919)933-7563	1230
	TUCKER, Mary E.	(919)933-8982	1262
Charlotte	BERRY, Mary W.	(704)371-4258	90
	HOWARD, Susanna J.	(704)364-7987	564
Durham	BARROWS, William D.	(919)549-0517	60
	BOMARC, M D.	(919)683-6244	113
	LAVINE, Marcia M.	(919)684-2011	703
	SEMONCHE, Barbara P.	(919)489-7247	1115
	SOUTHERN, Mary A.	(919)684-8118	1170
	VARGHA, Rebecca B.	(919)544-6045	1278
Fayetteville	KRIEGER, Lee A.	(919)864-9349	678
Greensboro	HANHAN, Leila M.	(919)292-1115	495
	MCZORN, Bonita A.	(919)273-4886	819
Greenville	MELLON, Constance A.	(919)757-6870	822
	YORK, Maurice C.	(919)752-5260	1381
Matthews	BACKMAN, Carroll H.	(704)847-6055	44
Montreat	FERM, Lois R.	(704)669-5550	373
New Bern	KEE, Walter A.		634
Raleigh	RATHGEBER, Jo F.	(919)872-3323	1009
	TAYLOR, Raymond M.	(919)787-7824	1228
Research Triangle Pk	BEST-NICHOLS, Barbara J.	(919)544-3808	92
	THOMAS, Katharine S.	(919)541-8500	1237
	TUTTLE, Walter A.	(919)549-0661	1266
Spring Hope	LANEY, Elizabeth J.	(919)478-3836	695
Spruce Pine	AUSTIN, Mary C.		40
Washington	TIMOUR, John A.	(919)975-3355	1246
Winston-Salem	ANDERSON, Sherry	(919)748-2305	25
	EKSTRAND, Nancy L.	(919)765-4817	341
	MILLER, Barry K.	(919)777-5597	836
	STEELE, Tom M.	(919)761-5440	1184

NORTH DAKOTA

Bismarck	GRAY, David P.	(701)224-2668	459
	NEWBORG, Gerald G.	(701)224-2668	898
Ellendale	ZINK, Esther L.	(701)349-3609	1389
Fargo	NORDENG, Diane	(701)235-5354	908

SPECIAL LIBRARY CONSULTANT (Cont'd)
OHIO

Akron	STROZIER, Sandra L.	(216)379-8250	1203
Athens	LEE, Hwa W.	(614)592-5194	710
Bay Village	BACON, Agnes K.		44
Bedford	PARCH, Grace D.		939
Berea	MACIUSZKO, Jerzy J.	(216)234-9206	755
Bowling Green	MCCALLUM, Brenda W.		793
Canfield	GENAWAY, David C.	(216)533-2194	426
Canton	ERWIN, Nancy S.	(216)477-7309	353
Centerville	GARTEN, Edward D.		420
Cincinnati	CLASPER, James W.	(513)871-0969	219
	CONNICK, Kathleen D.	(513)474-4975	237
	HALIBEY-BILYK, Christine M.	(513)559-4320	486
	KUEHNLE, Emery C.	(513)421-4142	682
	LE BLANC, Judith E.		708
	LIPPERT, Margret G.	(513)821-8733	732
	MC CORMICK, Lisa L.	(513)369-2540	798
	NASRALLAH, Wahib T.	(513)475-2411	888
	PATIENCE, Alice	(513)841-8589	947
	SUHRE, Carol A.	(513)732-7109	1207
	WELKER, Kathy J.	(513)684-2678	1321
Cleveland	ABID, Ann B.	(216)421-7340	2
	BORUCKI, Jennifer A.	(216)696-1313	117
	CHESHIER, Robert G.	(216)368-3427	206
	DZIEDZINA, Christine A.	(216)459-4313	331
	JOHNSON, Stephen C.	(216)429-8245	609
	KANTOR, Paul B.	(216)321-7713	626
	PIKE, Kermit J.	(216)721-5722	972
	STANLEY, Jean B.	(216)368-6596	1180
Cleveland Heights	GIBSON, Sarah S.	(216)321-4295	432
	TRAMDACK, Philip J.	(216)371-3445	1254
Columbus	BRANN, Andrew R.	(614)221-4181	128
	CLEAVER, Betty P.	(614)292-1177	220
	D'AMORE, Denice M.	(614)221-3211	272
	DAVIS, Linda M.	(614)294-5429	280
	EVANS, Shirley A.	(614)860-2496	358
	FU, Paul S.	(614)466-2044	407
	HOLOCH, S A.	(614)292-6691	553
	HUNE, Mary G.	(614)224-3168	574
	MCDOWELL, Judith H.	(614)771-0273	804
	MIMNAUGH, Ellen N.	(614)486-7755	845
	RATLIFF, Priscilla	(614)488-1622	1009
	TANNEHILL, Robert S.	(614)488-7587	1222
	VANBRIMMER, Barbara A.	(614)292-9810	1272
Dayton	BALL, Diane A.	(513)293-7339	52
	KNASIAK, Theresa J.	(513)254-1433	663
	NOLAN, Patrick B.	(513)274-3424	907
	QUINTEN, Rebecca G.	(513)277-3598	1000
	ROBINSON, Elizabeth A.	(513)837-1534	1044
	SEXTON, Sally V.	(513)890-1421	1118
Fairfield	LUCAS, Jean M.	(513)829-5227	746
Findlay	DUDLEY, Durand S.	(419)423-1113	323
Gambier	WILT, Charles F.	(614)427-5681	1353
Jefferson	BROWN, Vicki L.	(216)576-9553	148
Kent	GALLICCHIO, Virginia G.	(216)373-5608	414
	MORRIS, Trisha A.	(216)673-3464	867
Lakewood	HOLCZER, Lolita B.	(216)226-7173	550
Mansfield	ROMARY, Michael P.	(419)755-4321	1052
Mentor	DUANE, Carol A.	(216)255-3323	321
New Albany	HERB, Elizabeth D.	(614)855-7441	530
Painesville	BRANCHICK, Susan E.	(216)357-3462	127
Richmond Heights	SIESS, Judith A.	(216)486-7443	1136
Shaker Heights	MCCONNELL, Pamela J.	(216)921-7457	798
Toledo	ELLENBOGEN, Barbara R.	(419)536-4538	343
	HANNAFORD, Claudia L.	(419)536-7539	496
	WEILANT, Edward		1317
	WOODRUFF, Brenda B.	(419)245-4747	1366
Westlake	CHAMIS, Alice Y.	(216)777-2198	198
	GALLANT, Jennifer J.	(216)835-6020	414
Youngstown	ROSENTHAL, Barbara G.	(216)746-7211	1057

OKLAHOMA

Bartlesville	ROBIN, Annabeth	(918)336-7240	1043
Norman	MCKNIGHT, Michelynn	(405)360-2080	812
	POLAND, Jean A.	(405)360-7095	980
Oklahoma City	CORNEIL, Charlotte E.	(405)235-7763	246
	DOBBERTEEN, Sara J.	(405)842-0890	307
	JORSKI, Sharon D.	(405)636-7087	617
	WEISS, Catharine H.	(405)424-3344	1320

SPECIAL LIBRARY CONSULTANT (Cont'd)
OKLAHOMA (Cont'd)

Tulsa	COOPER, Sylvia J.	(918)599-5298	243
	HILL, Linda L.	(918)584-0891	540

OREGON

Coos Bay	TASHJIAN, Sharon A.	(503)267-5605	1224
Corvallis	MURRAY, Lucia M.		882
Eugene	DUCKETT, Kenneth W.	(503)686-3068	322
	EMMENS, Thomas A.	(503)345-6439	348
	GRAHAM, Deborah L.		456
	KLOS, Sheila M.	(503)686-3637	662
	MORRISON, Perry D.	(503)342-2361	868
	SHAW, Elizabeth L.	(503)343-9569	1123
	SUNDT, Christine L.	(503)686-3052	1210
Portland	BURSON, Lorraine E.	(508)246-4097	163
	JUDKINS, Dolores Z.	(503)236-6743	619
	OLSON-URLIE, Carolyn T.	(503)233-3242	923
	PIPER, Larry W.	(503)232-1781	975
	SHAVER, Donna B.	(503)226-8695	1123
	SUDDUTH, Susan F.		1206
	TEICH, Steven	(503)225-8026	1230
Roseburg	MUNGER, Freda R.	(503)672-6489	879

PENNSYLVANIA

Allentown	IOBST, Barbara J.	(215)778-2263	583
Bala Cynwyd	KREMER, Jill L.	(215)667-6787	677
Beaver	DENGEL, Bette S.	(412)728-5700	292
Belle Vernon	KLEIN, Joanne S.	(412)929-8290	659
Bethel Park	MCGINNESS, Mary B.	(412)835-2207	806
Bloomsburg	ROCKWOOD, Susan M.	(717)784-8456	1046
Broomall	CLINTON, Janet C.	(215)356-1927	222
Bryn Mawr	MARKSON, Eileen	(215)645-5087	771
Carlisle	FOX, James R.	(717)243-4611	394
	WIWEL, Pamela S.		1359
Chambersburg	MARLOW, Kathryn E.	(717)264-2382	772
Clarion	DINGLE, Susan	(814)226-2271	304
Coatesville	BURTON, Mary L.	(215)383-0245	164
Easton	SHINER, Sharon L.	(215)258-8390	1130
Elkins Park	NEMEYER, Carol A.		895
Erie	ANDRICK, Annita A.	(814)455-8080	27
Franklin Center	HOWLEY, Deborah H.	(215)459-7049	566
Friedens	KLINE, Eve P.	(814)443-2903	661
Glen Rock	LIEBERMAN, Ronald	(717)235-2134	726
Glenside	NIEWEG, Clinton F.	(215)884-5878	904
Harleysville	LINN, Mott R.	(215)464-4500	731
Harrisburg	MALLINGER, Stephen M.	(717)783-5737	763
Hatfield	PAKALA, James C.	(215)368-5000	935
Haverford	ROBERTSON, Robert B.	(215)896-1273	1042
Hershey	WOOD, M S.	(717)531-8630	1364
	WOODRUFF, William M.	(717)534-5106	1366
Holsopple	SLICK, Myrna H.	(814)479-7148	1149
Johnstown	BRICE, Heather W.	(814)539-8153	134
King of Prussia	RICH, Denise A.	(215)935-7054	1027
Lansdale	BLAUERT, Mary A.	(215)822-2929	105
Lititz	GERLOTT, Eleanor L.	(717)627-0944	429
Mechanicsburg	TENOR, Randell B.	(717)763-1804	1231
Media	BURGESS, Rita N.	(215)565-7900	159
Mercer	ELY, Betty L.	(412)662-2543	347
Middletown	BARRY, James W.		60
Millersville	JUDGE, Joseph M.	(717)872-7590	619
Natrona Heights	HAUGH, Amy J.	(412)224-5004	512
North Wales	MAXIN, Jacqueline A.	(215)855-5675	787
Pennsylvania Furnace	WOLFE, Mary S.	(814)234-5660	1361
Philadelphia	BUTLER, Evelyn		166
	COUCH, Susan H.	(215)242-0265	250
	GRAY, Priscilla M.	(215)386-6276	460
	GRILIKHES, Sandra B.	(215)898-7027	470
	GROSSMAN, Robert M.	(215)893-1954	473
	KOHN, Roger S.	(215)438-5635	668
	LEVITT, Martin L.	(215)627-0706	721
	MILLER, Fredric M.	(213)787-8257	837
	MOWERY, Susan G.	(215)248-8206	874
	SAUNDERS, William B.	(215)224-0235	1085
	SNOWTEN, Renee Y.	(215)557-8295	1164
	SOULTOUKIS, Donna Z.	(215)922-5460	1169
	SOWICZ, Eugenia V.	(215)354-2110	1170

SPECIAL LIBRARY CONSULTANT (Cont'd)
PENNSYLVANIA (Cont'd)

Pittsburgh	ARJONA, Sandra K.	(412)821-2263	31
	BLAIR, William W.	(412)355-8071	103
	BOUTWELL, Barbara J.	(412)967-3131	119
	CASLIN, Adele	(412)687-7738	193
	DETLEFSEN, Ellen G.	(412)624-9444	296
	EPSTEIN, Barbara A.	(412)624-2378	351
	FREEDMAN, Phyllis D.	(412)784-8599	400
	FUCHS, Karola M.		408
	HLUHANY, Patricia	(412)364-3000	544
	HODGSON, Cynthia A.	(412)374-4816	546
	HORVATH, Patricia M.	(412)562-8966	561
	JOHNSTON, Bruce A.	(412)731-8800	610
	KANE, Angelika R.	(412)263-1397	624
	KERCHOF, Kathryn K.	(412)434-6000	643
	KIRCHER, Linda M.	(412)624-9444	654
	LEONARD, Peter C.	(414)422-5815	716
	MCCULLOCH, Elizabeth A.	(412)931-6931	801
	ROOT, Deane L.	(412)624-4100	1054
	SCHEETZ, Mary D.	(412)421-4297	1091
	SPIEGELMAN, Barbara M.	(412)824-2222	1174
	STERLING, Alida B.	(412)323-1430	1189
	VASILAKIS, Mary	(412)422-5694	1279
Reading	IZZO, Kathleen A.	(215)373-2981	586
Sanatoga	NIPPERT, Carolyn C.	(215)323-4829	904
Scranton	BABISH, Jo A.	(717)963-2145	43
Secane	CASINI, Barbara P.	(215)543-4309	192
Somerset	PLASO, Kathy A.	(814)445-6501	977
Springfield	MAIN, Annette Z.		761
	STESIS, Karen R.	(215)328-8749	1189
State College	CARR, Caryn J.	(814)234-4203	185
	MURPHY, Charles G.	(814)865-6621	880
	PIERCE, Miriam D.	(814)237-7004	971
	PIERCE, William S.	(814)237-7004	972
	STOUT, Leon J.	(814)238-4855	1198
Villanova	WEINER, Betty	(215)688-6950	1318
Wayne	ANTOS, Brian F.	(215)254-0754	29
	LAZARUS, Karin	(215)964-0477	706
Waynesboro	POSEY, Sussann F.	(717)762-3047	985
West Chester	DINNIMAN, Margo P.	(215)430-3080	305
	MILES, Donald D.	(215)431-7685	834
Yardley	DU BOIS, Paul Z.	(215)493-6882	322

PUERTO RICO

Hormiguerow	MARTINEZ-NAZARIO, Ronaldo		779
Miramar	CASAS DE FAUNCE, Maria		191
Ponce	PADUA, Flores N.	(809)844-4150	934
Rio Piedras	THOMPSON, Annie F.	(809)761-1851	1239

RHODE ISLAND

Kingston	MASLYN, David C.	(401)792-2594	780
Providence	BOWLBY, Raynna M.	(401)274-7224	121
	CASHMAN, Norine D.	(401)863-3218	192
	DUMAINE, Paul R.	(401)274-7200	325
	ILACQUA, Anne K.		581
	SVENGALIS, Kendall F.	(401)274-3196	1212
	WILMETH, Don B.	(401)863-3289	1349

SOUTH CAROLINA

Charleston	MOLTKE-HANSEN, David	(803)723-3225	853
Chester	MURDOCK, Everlyne K.	(803)377-8145	879
Clemson	ABRAMS, Leslie E.	(803)654-8753	3
	KOHL, Michael F.	(803)656-5176	668
	MCCULLEY, P M.	(803)654-8753	800
	MEYER, Richard W.	(803)656-3026	830
Columbia	BILLINSKY, Christyn G.	(803)777-3858	96
	CROSS, Joseph R.	(803)777-3365	260
	GABLE, Sarah H.	(803)733-3344	411
	HOWARD-HILL, Trevor	(803)777-6499	564
	KINTNER, Susan B.	(803)771-4077	653
	PEAKE, Luise E.	(803)777-3214	952
	WILLIAMS, Robert V.	(803)799-2324	1346
Greenville	AYARI, Kaye W.	(803)235-4883	42
	TOWELL, Fay J.	(803)232-2941	1252
Greenwood	HILL, Thomas W.	(803)227-4851	541
Summerville	MAY, Robert E.	(803)871-2201	789

SPECIAL LIBRARY CONSULTANT (Cont'd)
SOUTH DAKOTA

Rapid City	HAMILTON, Patricia J.	(605)341-7101	492
	MC CAULEY, Philip F.	(605)348-5124	795
Sioux Falls	MODICA, Mary L.	(605)388-3701	851
	THOMPSON, Harry F.	(605)336-4007	1239
Vermillion	JENSEN, Mary B.	(605)677-5259	599

TENNESSEE

Germantown	COOPER, Ellen R.	(901)755-7411	242
Harriman	OVERTON, Margaret C.		931
Kingsport	TILSON, Koleta B.	(615)245-6572	1245
Knoxville	BEAL, Gretchen F.	(615)521-2500	68
	BULL, Margaret J.	(615)632-6173	156
	JETT, Don W.	(615)922-2548	600
	LLOYD, James B.	(615)974-4480	735
	PICQUET, D C.	(615)974-4381	971
Memphis	BANNERMAN-WILLIAMS, Cheryl F.	(901)785-7350	54
	HALE, Relda D.		485
	MARTIN, Jess A.	(901)528-5636	776
	MCDONELL, W E.	(901)278-0330	803
	OWEN, Richard L.	(901)522-5557	932
	TERRY, Carol D.	(901)529-2782	1232
Murfreesboro	WELLS, Paul F.	(615)898-2449	1323
Nashville	GMEINER, Timothy J.	(615)297-7958	442
	GOODALE, Adebonojo L.	(615)327-6728	448
	HELGUERA, Byrd S.	(615)322-2299	524
	MARTIN, Laquita V.	(615)383-0953	777
	PATTERSON, Jennifer J.	(615)383-4251	948
	PILKINGTON, James P.	(615)322-2927	973
	SHOCKLEY, Ann A.	(615)353-0771	1132
Niota	BURN, Harry T.	(615)745-8590	161
Oak Ridge	EKKEBUS, Allen E.	(615)574-5485	341
	NORTON, Nancy P.	(615)574-7159	910
Sewanee	CAMP, Thomas E.	(616)598-5931	175

TEXAS

Amarillo	NEELEY, Dana M.	(806)354-5447	891
Austin	BICHTELER, Julie H.	(512)471-3821	94
	DIVELY, Reddy	(512)288-3371	306
	HARMON, Jacqueline B.	(512)343-0978	502
	HELBURN, Judith D.	(512)454-7229	523
	HOOKS, Michael Q.	(512)250-1419	556
	JACKSON, Eugene B.	(512)345-1653	587
	JACKSON, Ruth L.	(512)345-1653	588
	LEACH, Sally S.	(512)329-8677	706
	MARTIN, Jean K.	(512)346-2973	776
	MCADAMS, Nancy R.	(512)453-7177	792
	PAYNE, John R.	(512)478-7724	951
	TRANFAGLIA, Twyla L.	(512)472-8800	1254
	WISE, Olga B.	(512)244-8330	1357
Bedford	PETERS, Mary N.	(817)283-3739	962
Bellaire	HOLAB-ABELMAN, Robin S.		550
Cedar Park	MITTAG, Erika	(512)259-0569	850
Corpus Christi	HOUSTON, Barbara B.	(512)889-8517	563
	NEU, Margaret J.	(512)884-2011	896
Dallas	ARMES, Patti	(214)341-6675	32
	BIRD, H C.	(214)553-5995	98
	BROWN, Muriel W.	(214)348-7861	146
	CAMACHO, Nancy S.	(214)368-5602	174
	COMPTON, Erlinda R.	(214)506-3601	235
	DOBSON, Christine B.	(214)746-3646	307
	HAWLEY, Laurie J.	(214)907-2940	514
	JONES, Lois S.	(214)528-2732	613
	JORDAN, Travis E.	(214)692-3199	617
	KLEIN, Mindy F.	(214)701-4116	659
	LOVELL, Bonnie A.	(214)826-1924	743
	MASON, Florence M.	(214)358-5755	781
	MCCASLIN, Cheryl A.	(214)490-8701	795
	MIDGETT, Ann S.	(214)954-5966	833
	MITCHE, Cynthia R.	(214)692-6767	848
	MITCHELL, Cynthia R.	(214)692-6767	848
	SHAPLEY, Ellen M.	(214)692-6407	1122
	SMITH, Kraleen S.	(214)754-7985	1156
	WATERS, Richard L.	(214)826-6981	1308
Denton	CVELJO, Katherine	(817)565-2445	268
	SCHLESSINGER, Bernard S.	(817)898-2017	1094

SPECIAL LIBRARY CONSULTANT (Cont'd)
TEXAS (Cont'd)

Fort Worth	ARBELBIDE, Cindy L.	(817)877-3355	30
	CARTER, Bobby R.	(817)735-2380	189
	DE TONNANCOUR, P R.	(817)763-1790	296
Fredericksburg	YOUNG, Marjie D.	(512)997-2253	1382
Galveston	FREY, Emil F.	(409)761-2371	402
Groves	MCCONNELL, Karen S.	(409)963-1481	797
Houston	BREWER, Stanley E.		134
	CALDWELL, Marlene	(713)661-5787	172
	CARTER, Daniel H.	(713)665-5150	189
	CEBRUN, Mary J.	(713)965-4045	196
	CHAMPION, Walter T.	(713)527-7125	198
	CHUANG, Felicia S.	(713)791-6668	213
	DAVIS, Sara	(713)669-2426	281
	FIELDING, Raymond E.	(713)749-7444	376
	GOURLAY, Una M.	(713)528-3553	454
	HACKNEY, Judith G.	(713)496-5590	481
	KORKMAS, Carolyn C.	(713)953-7222	671
	MAGNER, Mary F.	(713)870-7011	759
	MCCANN, Debra W.	(713)691-0148	794
	MOORE, Guusje Z.	(713)680-0715	859
	MORRISSEY, Charles T.	(713)799-4510	869
	SINCLAIR, Rose P.	(713)452-5555	1143
	WILLIAMS, Ann T.	(713)792-4094	1342
	WORCHEL, Harris M.	(713)956-7361	1368
	WRIGHT, Craig W.	(713)968-3282	1371
Huntsville	HOFFMAN, Frank W.	(409)294-1152	548
Irving	OGDEN, William S.	(214)255-3470	918
Katy	POWELL, Alan D.	(713)392-9340	987
Liberty	SCHAADT, Robert L.	(409)336-7097	1088
Lubbock	LINDSEY, Thomas K.	(806)791-4770	730
	MARLEY, Judith L.	(806)799-3299	772
	SARGENT, Charles W.	(806)792-0754	1082
Midland	MIRANDA, Cecilia	(915)685-4557	847
Mont Belvieu	BAILEY, Linda S.	(713)383-3382	46
Richardson	MARTIN, Irmgarde D.	(214)231-6121	776
San Antonio	BELL, Joy A.	(512)496-2057	77
	CRINION, Jacquelyn A.	(512)691-4575	259
	HURT, Nancy S.	(512)225-5500	578
	LANG, Anita E.	(512)684-5111	695
	TODD, Fred W.	(512)826-8121	1248
	VELA-CREIXELL, Mary I.	(512)733-7109	1281
Sherman	GARCIA, Lana C.	(214)893-4401	417
Sugar Land	JOHNSON, Pat M.	(713)980-5350	608
The Woodlands	FRAMEL, Phyllis M.	(713)367-9522	395
Waco	COLEY, Betty A.	(817)754-6114	231
Wimberley	WAYLAND, Terry T.	(512)847-9295	1311

UTAH

Logan	SPYKERMAN, Bryan R.	(801)750-1643	1177
Salt Lake City	BUTTARS, Gerald A.	(801)466-6363	167
	DOGU, Hikmet S.	(801)486-3238	309
	HEYER, Terry L.	(801)321-1054	535
	JOHNSON, Jeffery O.	(801)533-5250	606
	NOEL, Eileen N.	(801)594-6182	907
	OLSEN, Katherine M.	(801)355-0301	921
	PARTRIDGE, Cathleen F.	(801)277-3486	945
	STODDART, Joan M.	(801)272-2749	1196
West Jordan	KARPISEK, Marian E.	(801)561-4676	628

VERMONT

Middlebury	POST, Jennifer C.	(802)388-6252	986
Milton	SEKERAK, Robert J.		1113
White River Junction	LERNER, Frederick A.	(802)295-6548	717

VIRGINIA

Alexandria	AUSTON, Ione	(703)549-4325	40
	HARTT, Richard W.	(703)960-8741	509
	KUHL, Danuta	(703)461-0234	682
	MICHAELS, Andrea A.	(703)360-1297	831
	OLIVETTI, L J.	(703)683-8190	921
	OSIA, Ruby R.	(703)549-3048	928
	WALDE, Norma J.	(703)642-4178	1294
Annandale	MATON, Joanne T.	(703)256-2288	784
Arlington	ALEXANDER, Carol G.		12
	BETTS, Ardith M.	(703)524-8384	92
	CLARKE, Robert F.		219
	COSKEY, Rosemary B.		248

SPECIAL LIBRARY CONSULTANT (Cont'd)
VIRGINIA (Cont'd)
Arlington

	DORNER, Steven J.	(703)841-8400	313
	HARRIS, Linda S.	(703)521-2541	505
	HIGBEE, Joan F.	(703)524-5844	537
	JOACHIM, Robert J.	(703)920-7721	600
	MEREK, Charles J.	(703)920-5050	825
	MOORE, Penelope F.	(703)979-5900	861
	PREBLE, Leverett L.	(703)528-1880	990
	PRICE, Joseph W.	(703)241-0447	992
	PYKE, Carol J.	(703)241-7731	999
	WELLS, Christine		1322
	YODER, William M.	(703)527-7225	1380
Charlottesville	JORDAN, Ervin L.	(804)924-4975	616
Chesapeake	KERSTETTER, Virginia M.	(804)483-6544	644
Fairfax	SCOTT, Mona F.	(703)378-8027	1107
	WALCH, Timothy G.	(703)273-3260	1293
Falls Church	HARRIS, Virginia B.	(703)698-6968	506
	HELGERSON, Linda W.	(703)237-0682	524
	KENNEDY, Lynne		641
Fredericksburg	BULLEY, Joan S.	(703)899-1597	156
	HUGHES, J M.		571
Great Falls	CYLKE, Frank K.	(703)759-2031	268
Hampton	LANKES, J B.	(804)722-7821	696
Harrisonburg	GILL, Gerald L.	(703)568-6898	435
Herndon	GUERRIERO, Donald A.	(703)860-1058	476
McLean	ADAMS, Judith A.	(703)241-0973	5
	MORRISON, M C.	(703)356-1797	868
Newport News	DANIEL, Mary H.	(804)599-7245	272
	HAMMOND, Theresa M.	(804)595-8179	494
Reston	LISZEWSKI, Edward H.	(301)648-4306	733
	MCCLAIN, Deborah C.	(703)689-5194	795
Richmond	JACOBY, Mary M.	(804)231-2545	590
	KIMBALL, Gregg D.	(804)649-0711	649
	MOSER, Emily F.	(804)355-3348	870
	MURPHY, Robert D.	(804)741-1311	881
	OWEN, Karen V.	(804)649-6132	931
Roanoke	CALHOUN, Clayne M.	(703)981-2268	172
Springfield	ALBIN, Michael W.	(703)978-3022	10
	GEHRINGER, Michael E.	(703)451-0334	425
	GEHRINGER, Susanne E.	(202)835-8040	425
	LEONARD, Lawrence E.	(703)569-1541	716
Williamsburg	BERG, Susan	(804)229-8799	85
	GROVE, Pearce S.	(804)220-2477	473
Woodbridge	MELVIN, Kay H.	(703)491-2055	823

WASHINGTON

Everett	VAN DYKE, Ruth L.	(206)335-2406	1275
Fort Steilacoom	VAN DER VOORN, Neal P.	(206)756-2518	1274
Kirkland	ROBERTSON, Ann	(206)821-0506	1041
	SUGGS, John K.	(206)823-6754	1206
Mercer Island	FIELDING, Carol J.	(206)232-8988	376
Mt Vernon	SAUTER, Sylvia E.	(206)336-2604	1085
Olympia	MOORE, Mary Y.	(206)866-8272	860
Renton	SIENDA, Madeline M.		1136
Richland	CARVER, Sue A.	(509)943-5478	191
Seattle	BURKE, Vivienne C.	(206)522-0478	160
	ENGEMAN, Richard H.	(206)325-3121	349
	HARBOLD, Mary J.	(206)764-2075	499
	HAZELTON, Penelope A.	(206)543-4089	517
	HILDEBRANDT, Darlene M.	(206)543-5818	538
	KETCHELL, Debra S.	(206)543-5530	645
	LIPTON, Laura E.	(206)543-8616	732
	MIDDLETON, Dale R.	(206)523-1915	833
	SLIVKA, Enid M.	(206)723-4846	1149
	STEERE, Paul J.	(206)367-0328	1184
	SY, Karen J.	(206)545-2873	1217
	TWENEY, George H.	(206)243-8243	1266
Spokane	MURRAY, James M.	(509)838-3680	882
	NOLAN, Edward W.	(509)456-3931	907
	SHIDELER, John C.	(509)838-5242	1129
	WADDEN, Emily E.	(509)455-9555	1290
Steilacoom	PARR, Loraine E.	(206)582-7557	943
Tacoma	GILDENHAR, Janet		434
	JONES, Faye E.	(206)564-9254	613
	SELING, Kathy A.	(206)756-5571	1113

WEST VIRGINIA

Clarksburg	GREATHOUSE, Brenda J.	(304)624-9649	461

SPECIAL LIBRARY CONSULTANT (Cont'd)
WISCONSIN

Appleton	BAYORGEON, Mary M.	(414)738-2325	68
	BOOHER, Craig S.	(414)738-3384	115
Beloit	THOM, Pat A.	(608)365-3311	1235
Brookfield	CHRISTMAN, Inese R.	(414)786-6700	212
De Forest	SAYRS, Judith A.	(608)846-9363	1087
Eau Claire	MERRIAM, Louise A.	(715)839-5003	826
Green Bay	GORSEGNER, Betty D.	(414)465-1529	452
	JOBELIUS, Nancy L.	(414)497-7508	601
	MUSICH, Gerald D.	(414)437-7623	883
Hales Corners	BARLOGA, Carolyn J.	(414)425-0355	57
Kewaunee	ECKERT, Daniel L.	(414)388-2176	335
Lake Geneva	CIBOCH, Lorraine A.	(414)245-5806	214
Madison	ANDERSON, Axel R.	(608)233-0659	21
	ARNOLD, Barbara J.	(608)263-2909	33
	BEHNKE, Charles	(608)244-3253	75
	KRUSE, Ginny M.		681
	MATTHEWS, Geraldine M.	(608)266-1164	785
	PARSONS, Patricia S.		945
	WALKER, Richard D.	(608)257-5574	1296
	WHITCOMB, Dorothy V.	(608)262-2402	1330
Marshfield	ALLEN, Margaret A.	(715)387-7271	15
Menasha	DIETZ, Kathryn A.	(414)725-3803	302
Menomonee Falls	SEUSS, Herbert J.	(414)251-7674	1117
Mequon	NOVOTNY, Lynn E.	(414)241-8957	911
Milwaukee	BLUE, Richard I.	(414)963-4707	107
	BRENNEN, Patrick W.	(414)257-8323	133
	DETWILER, Eve N.	(414)332-3367	296
	HOLST, Ruth M.	(414)961-3856	554
	HORNUNG, Susan D.	(414)359-2111	560
	JONES, Richard E.	(414)229-6457	614
	REITMAN, Jo	(414)224-2376	1022
	SCHLUGE, Vicki L.	(414)527-8477	1094
	SMITH-GREENWOLD, Kathryn R.	(414)445-3586	1162
	THIEL, Mark G.	(414)224-7256	1235
	WATERSTREET, Darlene E.	(414)964-2377	1309
Neenah	LAMB, Cheryl M.	(414)729-8169	689
Stoughton	DANKY, James P.	(608)873-8722	274
Twin Lakes	OPEM, John D.	(414)877-9539	925
Waukesha	MILLER, Julia E.	(414)548-0448	839
	ODDAN, Linda	(414)544-2150	916
Wauwatosa	BOCHTE, Terrence C.	(414)259-1414	109
	CHAPLOCK, Sharon K.	(414)778-2167	201
West Allis	GRUEL, Janice L.	(414)541-5222	474

WYOMING

Cheyenne	MCGOWAN, Anne W.	(307)777-6430	807
	MENDOZA, Anthanett C.	(307)778-8706	824
Laramie	MACK, Bonnie R.	(307)766-6537	756
	NORD, Kay	(307)745-7373	908

CANADA

ALBERTA

Calgary	GASHUS, Karin C.	(403)237-4508	421
	LEESMENT, Helgi	(403)251-2221	712
Edmonton	BATEMAN, Robert A.	(403)483-3432	63
	BAYRAK, Bettie	(403)478-8062	68
	COOKE, Geraldine A.	(403)439-5879	241
	JORDAN, Peter A.	(403)469-9473	616
	LOVENBURG, Susan L.	(403)435-0176	743
	MCLAUGHLIN, W K.	(403)427-3567	813
	SINCLAIR, John M.	(403)488-2646	1142
Red Deer	GISHLER, John R.	(304)340-3922	438
Sherwood Park	SCHMIDT, Raymond J.	(403)464-8234	1095
Tofield	LEE, Diana W.	(403)662-3607	709

BRITISH COLUMBIA

North Vancouver	ELROD, J M.	(604)929-3966	346
Prince George	MAYFIELD, Betty L.	(604)562-1929	790
Richmond	ELLIS, Kathy N.	(604)272-5389	344
Vancouver	AUFIERO, Joan I.	(604)325-2317	39
	BROOME, Diana M.	(604)684-5986	141
	CAMERON, Hazel M.	(604)224-8470	175
	CHAN, Diana L.	(604)224-8470	199
	NICHOL, Kathleen M.	(604)263-7081	901
	PEPPER, David A.	(604)664-4311	958
	ROBERTSON, Guy M.	(604)689-8494	1041

SPECIAL LIBRARY CONSULTANT (Cont'd)

BRITISH COLUMBIA (Cont'd)

Vancouver			
	STEPHENSON, Mary S.	(604)228-4991	1188
	WARREN, Lois M.	(604)687-1072	1306
Victoria	HAMILTON, Donald E.	(604)721-7899	492
	VAN REENEN, Johannes A.	(604)595-9612	1277

MANITOBA

Brandon	EAGLETON, Kathleen M.		331
Winnipeg	LINCOLN, Robert S.	(204)786-2387	728
	MARSHALL, Kenneth E.	(204)269-3243	774
	REINALDO DA SILVA, Joann T.	(204)237-4203	1021
	ROUTLEDGE, Patricia A.	(204)474-9445	1062

NEW BRUNSWICK

Riverview	ENNS, Carol F.	(506)386-1084	350

NOVA SCOTIA

Halifax	BANFIELD, Eilzabeth S.	(902)421-4570	54
Wolfville	TAYLOR, Hugh A.	(902)542-7825	1227

ONTARIO

Deep River	LEWIS, Leslie	(613)584-2605	723
Don Mills	FAIRLEY, Craig R.	(416)447-5336	361
Downsview	BERNSTEIN, Elaine S.	(416)638-1962	89
	ZVEJNIEKS, Laila R.	(416)235-4545	1391
Exeter	WILCOX, Linda M.	(519)235-2700	1338
Go-Home Bay	CAMPBELL, Harry	(705)756-1878	176
Kingston	FLOWER, M A.	(613)645-6122	386
	FORKES, David	(613)544-2630	390
London	LIN, Louise	(519)439-3271	727
	RUTHERFORD, Frederick S.	(519)471-4867	1070
Mississauga	MASEN, Naunihal S.	(416)897-6269	780
	WEI, Carl K.	(416)822-4111	1316
North York	CROXFORD, Agnes M.	(416)493-4188	262
	VARMA, Divakara K.	(416)736-5139	1278
	WILLIAMS, Lorraine O.		1344
Ottawa	BROWN, Mabel		145
	BUCHANAN, Zoe A.	(613)526-3287	153
	COONEY, Jane	(613)232-9625	241
	KIDD, Betty H.	(613)996-7605	646
	MCCALLUM, David L.	(613)237-4586	793
	PARE, Richard	(613)733-8391	940
	SCHRYER, Michel J.	(819)994-6827	1100
	SPICER, Erik J.	(613)995-1166	1174
	TAYLOR, Margaret P.	(613)232-6172	1227
	TSAI, Shaopan		1260
Sarnia	O'DONNELL, Rosemary F.	(519)337-8251	917
Scarborough	KEYS, Sandra A.		645
Sudbury	BERTRAND, Doreen M.	(705)675-3008	91
Thornhill	SPEISMAN, Stephen A.	(416)886-2508	1172
Toronto	ARMSTRONG, Jennifer E.	(416)466-8089	32
	BAYNE, Jennifer M.	(416)595-3429	67
	BEAUMONT, Jane	(416)922-9364	70
	CHOUDHURI, Kabita	(416)484-0441	211
	DAVEY, Dorothy M.	(416)485-0377	276
	DENIS, Laurent G.	(416)978-3111	292
	DYSART, Jane I.	(416)974-2780	331
	GIBSON, Elizabeth A.	(416)595-7894	432
	GOLD, Sandra	(410)782-7236	444
	GRODSKI, Renata	(416)965-6763	471
	KIRSH, Julie	(416)947-2257	655
	KLEMENT, Susan P.	(416)486-0239	660
	MELVILLE, Karen E.	(416)978-3035	823
	MERILEES, Bobbie	(416)485-4177	826
	MERRYWEATHER, J M.	(416)965-3281	827
	SELLERS, Alexander G.	(416)489-4908	1114
	SMITHIES, Roger	(416)466-6636	1162
	THODY, Susan I.	(416)762-1690	1235
	VEANER, Allen B.	(416)486-0239	1280
	WILLIAMSON, Nancy J.		1347
	WONG, Lusi	(416)922-5100	1363
	YANCHINSKI, Roma N.	(416)767-6781	1377
Willowdale	DANIEL, Eileen	(416)223-2495	272

SPECIAL LIBRARY CONSULTANT (Cont'd)

QUEBEC

Baie d'Urfe	KLOK, Buddhi	(514)457-2757	662
Chambly	ASSUNCAO, Isabel	(514)658-3882	37
Drummondville	JANIK, Sophie	(819)477-7100	593
Laval-des-Rapides	VONKA, Stephanie	(514)667-1947	1288
Montreal	AUBIN, Robert	(514)323-7260	38
	BISSON, Jacques	(514)482-9110	100
	CAN, Hung V.	(514)521-8201	177
	COURTEMANCHE, Pierre O.		251
	DUCHESNEAU, Pierre	(514)281-6166	322
	DUMONT, Monique	(514)288-0100	325
	GARNETT, Joyce C.	(514)398-4763	419
	HOWARD, Helen A.	(514)933-0893	564
	JOBA, Judith C.	(514)489-0117	601
	MARCIL, Louise	(514)333-6621	769
	MOHAMMED, Selima	(514)398-4780	852
	ORLANDO, Richard P.	(514)877-1470	926
	OUELLET, Louise M.		930
	PIGGOTT, Sylvia E.	(514)877-9383	972
	PROVOST, Paul E.	(514)598-5389	996
	SYKES, Stephanie L.	(514)870-7088	1217
	TEES, Miriam H.	(514)392-3362	1229
Pointe Claire	MACFARLANE, Judy A.	(514)697-9572	755
Pointe Claire			
Dorval	STAHL, Hella	(514)630-4100	1178
Quebec	BERNIER, Gaston	(418)643-4032	89
	TESSIER, Yves	(418)872-4304	1233
Repentigny	MERCIER, Diane	(514)582-3920	825
Sainte-Foy	FLORIAN, Trudel	(418)652-2210	385
Sherbrooke	CHOUINARD, Germain	(819)564-5297	211
	FONTAINE, Nicole	(819)569-2551	388
	GOODFELLOW, Marjorie E.	(819)562-1694	448
	SOKOV, Asta M.	(819)821-7566	1166
Verdun	DIMITRESCU, Ioana	(514)765-8219	304
Westmount	LEDOUX, Marc A.	(514)484-5951	708

SASKATCHEWAN

Regina	BALON, Brett J.	(306)586-1990	53
	POGUE, Basil G.	(306)586-6846	979
Saskatoon	FRITZ, Linda	(306)934-3785	405

AUSTRALIA

Kensington	WILSON, Concepcion S.		1350

BELGIUM

Brussels	VAN SLYPE, Georges		1277

BRAZIL

Sao Paulo	GROSSMANN, Pierre	(011)255-3053	473

COSTA RICA

San Jose	CROWTHER, Warren W.		262

EGYPT

Cairo	EL-DUWEINI, Aadel K.	(027)197-7200	342
Giza	EL-MASRY, Mohammed		345

FEDERAL REPUBLIC OF CHINA

Taidzi	CHENG, Sheung O.		206
Taipei	WANG, Sin C.		1303

FEDERAL REPUBLIC OF GERMANY

Berlin	ELSTE, R O.		346
Bremerhaven	GOMEZ, Michael J.		447

FRANCE

Paris	PILLET, Sylvaine M.		973
	WACHTER, Margery C.		1290

HUNGARY

Budapest	LAZAR, Peter		706

INDIA

Bangalore	KITTUR, Krishna N.		657

IRELAND

Dublin	ASTON, Jennefer		37
	SLINEY, Marjory T.		1149

SPECIAL LIBRARY CONSULTANT (Cont'd)

ISRAEL
Haifa	BLOCH, Uri	105

ITALY
Milan	FABRE DE MORLHON, Christiane	360
Rome	JOLING, Carole G.	610
	MENOU, Michel J.	824

JAMAICA
Kingston	MANSINGH, Laxmi	(809)927-2748	767

JAPAN
Chiba-ken	NASU, Yukio	889
Tokyo	KATAOKA, Yoko	629
	KISHIMOTO, Hiroko	656
	YAMAZAKI, Hisamichi	1377

KENYA
Nairobi	BOWEN, Dorothy N.	120

MEXICO
Mexico City	BARBERENA, Elsa	55
	DE WALERSTEIN, Linda S.	297
	RODRIGUEZ, Serafin L.	1048
Nuevo Leon	ARTEAGA, Georgina	35

NETHERLANDS
Amersfoort	VAN HALM, Johan	1275
Amsterdam	OVEREYNDER, Rombout E.	931
Rotterdam	SCHUURSMA, Ann B.	1103

NEW ZEALAND
Auckland	RICHARDS, Valerie	1028

POLAND
Poznan	CHOJNACKA, Jadwiga	210

PORTUGAL
Lisbon	DE MACEDO, Maria L.	290

SAUDI ARABIA
Jeddah	KHAN, Mohammed A.	646
Riyadh	BROWN, Biraj L.	142
	MARTIN, Nannette	777

SOUTH AFRICA
Bedfordview	ARMSTRONG, Denise M.	32

SWEDEN
Jarfalla	SHELTON, Anita L.	1126
Taeby	CNATTINGIUS, Claes M.	224

TRINIDAD
Saint Joseph	MCCONNIE, Mary	798

ZAMBIA
Chilanga	LUMANDE, Edward	748

STAFF DEVELOPMENT CONSULTANT

ALABAMA
Birmingham	OLIVE, J F.	(205)967-8481	921
	ROGERS, Nancy H.	(205)991-6600	1050
	STEWART, George R.	(205)226-3611	1192
Florence	CARR, Charles E.	(205)767-2310	185
Helena	GOODWYN, Betty R.	(205)988-0896	450
Mobile	BUSH, Nancy W.	(205)343-8121	165
	DAMICO, James A.	(205)460-7021	271
Montgomery	MEDINA, Sue O.	(205)269-2700	820
Tuscaloosa	COLEMAN, J G.	(205)348-1523	231

ALASKA
Delta Junction	JENKS, Arlene I.	(907)895-4253	597
Juneau	SMITH, George V.	(907)789-2559	1155

STAFF DEVELOPMENT CONSULTANT (Cont'd)

ARIZONA
Mesa	ANDERSON, Herschel V.	(602)839-2742	23
Phoenix	NIXON, Arless B.	(602)246-9196	906
Sedona	CHICORE!, Marietta S.	(601)602-2826	208
Tucson	DUFORE, Thomas H.	(602)296-3823	324
	FRANK, Donald G.	(602)742-9688	396
	GOLDBERG, Susan S.	(602)747-2663	445
	JOHNSON, Robert K.	(602)323-0418	608
	MILLER, Edward P.		837
	WILLIAMS, Karen B.	(602)621-4866	1344

ARKANSAS
Conway	HARDIN, Willie	(501)450-3129	500

CALIFORNIA
Alamo	PIPER, Paula	(412)837-2880	975
Arcata	CROSBY-MUILENBURG, Corryn		260
Belmont	LEWIS, Gretchen S.	(415)591-4336	723
	MEGLIO, Delores D.	(415)591-2333	821
Benicia	HUTCHESON, Don S.	(707)746-8021	578
Berkeley	FALANGA, Rosemarie E.	(415)524-5501	361
	FALK, Candace S.	(415)526-9591	362
	MINUDRI, Regina U.	(415)843-7242	847
	WILLIAMS, Mary S.	(415)649-2520	1345
Beverly Hills	ANNETT, Susan E.	(213)550-4720	28
Bridgeport	REVEAL, Arlene H.	(619)932-7031	1024
Burbank	SIGMAN, Paula M.	(818)840-5424	1137
Carmichael	PARSONS, Jerry L.	(916)966-2086	945
Claremont	ROSE, David L.	(714)624-9041	1054
Concord	REYES, Helen M.	(415)000-0000	1024
Corte Madera	FARMER, Lesley S.	(415)924-6633	364
Costa Mesa	MARLOR, Hugh T.	(714)631-5637	772
Cypress	MOSER, Jane W.	(213)643-0322	870
Davis	BLANK, Karen L.	(916)752-2110	104
Downey	PAIK, Nan H.	(213)922-4648	935
Fairfield	GOLD, Anne M.	(707)429-6601	444
Granado Hills	SINOFSKY, Esther R.	(818)360-2146	1144
Hayward	SASSE, Margo	(415)482-2770	1083
Hillsborough	ABILOCK, Debbie	(415)348-2272	2
Huntington Beach	BAUER, Caroline F.	(714)969-2777	65
Irvine	WEINTRAUB, D K.	(714)856-6079	1318
La Jolla	HURLBERT, Irene W.	(619)534-1261	577
	TOMMEY, Richard J.	(619)454-4873	1250
Lake View Terrace	NAVARRO, Frank A.		889
Long Beach	ADAMS, Linda L.	(213)590-7639	5
	BRITTON, Helen H.	(213)498-4047	137
	CONNOLLY, Betty F.	(213)494-5465	237
	WELLS, H L.	(213)598-3549	1322
Los Angeles	ALFORD, Thomas E.	(213)612-3333	13
	EVANS, G E.	(213)642-4593	357
	GREEN, Ellen W.	(213)855-3751	461
	HALE, Kaycee	(213)204-0793	485
	MCINDOO, Larry R.	(213)485-4142	809
	TERZIAN, Shohig S.	(213)478-5193	1232
	TOMPKINS, Philip	(213)743-2543	1250
	WONG, Cecilia	(213)736-1139	1362
Los Gatos	SZABO, Carolyn J.	(408)353-2502	1218
Mission Viejo	WIERZBA, Heidemarie B.	(714)859-5193	1337
Mountain View	PORTER-ROTH, Anne	(415)965-7799	985
	SLOCUM, Hannah R.	(415)969-8356	1150
Novato	HIRABAYASHI, Joanne	(415)897-4245	543
Oakland	DANTON, J P.	(415)653-4802	274
	RUBIN, Rhea J.	(415)339-1274	1064
	SYPERT, Clyde F.	(415)763-6046	1217
Ojai	MOORE, Phyllis C.	(805)646-8592	861
Palo Alto	ELLSWORTH, Dianne J.	(415)321-2253	345
Pleasanton	BUTLER, David W.	(415)846-3308	166
Riverside	DUNN, Kathleen K.	(714)359-8429	327
	KOSHER, Helene J.	(714)787-4628	672
Rowland Heights	SIGLER, Ronald F.	(818)965-9917	1137
Sacramento	BURNS, John F.	(916)445-4293	162
	JACKSON, Gloria D.	(916)427-1956	587
San Diego	LOOMIS, Barbara L.	(619)565-3172	740
	SANNWALD, William W.	(619)236-5870	1081
	THORNE, Marco G.		1242

STAFF DEVELOPMENT CONSULTANT (Cont'd)
CALIFORNIA (Cont'd)

San Francisco	CANTER, Judy A.	(415)777-7845	179
	CODER, Ann	(415)442-7000	226
	ELNOR, Nancy G.	(415)929-1948	346
	FOX, Marylou P.	(415)546-8466	395
	GUNDERSON, Jeffery R.	(415)929-1472	477
	HAIKALIS, Peter D.	(415)338-2188	484
	MAH, Jeffery	(415)552-4733	760
	MORRIS, Effie L.	(415)931-2733	866
	WILSON, Jacqueline B.	(415)476-2534	1351
San Jose	ROSEN, Elizabeth M.	(408)277-2270	1055
San Leandro	YEH, Irene K.	(415)483-4830	1379
San Luis Obispo	FOURIE, Denise K.	(805)544-5427	393
San Pedro	SCULLY, Patrick F.	(213)832-6526	1109
San Rafael	HAMMER, Sharon A.	(415)499-6051	493
Santa Barbara	DAY, Bettie B.	(805)964-4711	282
Santa Cruz	TURNER, Anne M.	(408)429-3532	1264
Santa Monica	ANDERSON, Dorothy J.	(213)394-1899	22
Sebastopol	CANT, Elaine N.	(707)823-3214	179
Sherman Oaks	KWAN, Julie K.	(818)784-8606	685
	MILLER, Margaret S.	(818)783-5264	840
South Gate	BUBOLTZ, Dale D.	(213)567-1431	152
Studio City	PLATE, Kenneth H.	(818)797-7654	977
Valencia	CURZON, Susan C.	(805)259-8946	267
Woodland	WEBBER, Steven L.	(916)661-1242	1313

COLORADO

Aurora	HUGHES, Brad R.	(305)699-6248	571
	MURRAY, William A.	(303)364-8208	882
Boulder	BANKHEAD, Jean M.	(303)497-5566	54
	COLLARD, R M.	(303)444-1355	232
	VARNES, Richard S.	(303)444-8051	1279
Denver	BRUNELL, David H.	(303)691-0550	150
	GOODYEAR, Mary L.	(303)556-2683	450
	MITCHELL, Marilyn J.	(303)556-2835	849
Evergreen	SHARER, E J.	(303)292-4458	1122
Fort Collins	CHAMBERS, Joan L.	(303)491-1833	198
Grand Junction	RICHMOND, Elizabeth B.	(303)241-4358	1030
Littleton	BETTENCOURT, Nancy J.	(303)771-0968	92
Pueblo	JANES, Nina	(303)542-4591	593
	JONES, Donna R.	(303)542-2156	612

CONNECTICUT

Bridgeport	MINERVINO, Louise	(203)576-7779	846
Bristol	LEAHY, Michael D.	(203)582-0608	707
Greenwich	LUSHINGTON, Nolan	(203)655-3632	749
Middletown	BECK, Arthur R.	(203)347-1387	71
	WHITE, Charles R.	(203)638-4110	1330
New Britain	LAWRENCE, Scott W.	(203)677-1659	705
New Canaan	ROCKMAN, Connie C.	(203)972-3731	1046
	SENATOR, Rochelle B.	(203)966-5645	1115
New Hartford	GIBSON, Barbara H.	(203)379-3548	431
New Haven	PROSTANO, Emanuel T.	(203)397-4532	995
	SIGGINS, Jack A.	(203)776-3808	1137
	SULLIVAN, Maureen	(203)776-3808	1208
New London	VANDERLYKE, Barbara A.	(203)442-2889	1274
Norwalk	BOHRER, Karen M.	(203)854-5275	111
Ridgefield	SAMUELS, Lois A.	(203)431-3342	1079
Stamford	DIMATTIA, Susan S.	(203)322-9055	304
	KEMP, Thomas J.	(203)323-2826	639
Stonington	WILLIAMS, Edwin E.	(203)535-0720	1343
West Hartford	BURGER, Leslie B.	(203)233-0478	159
Westport	SCHWARZ, Shirlee	(203)226-6606	1105

DELAWARE

Duver	TRYON, Roy H.	(302)674-4522	1260
Wilmington	TITUS, H M.	(302)656-1722	1247
	TOMAN, Jocelyn B.		1249

DISTRICT OF COLUMBIA

Washington	ACKERMAN, F C.	(202)398-1842	3
	ANGLE, Joanne G.	(202)682-1698	28
	ATKINSON, Rose M.	(202)955-2139	38
	BATTLE, Thomas C.	(202)636-7241	65
	BELLEFONTAINE, Arnold G.	(202)287-6587	78
	FRANKLIN, Hardy R.	(202)727-1101	397
	HAGEMEYER, Alice L.	(202)727-2255	483
	HALEY, Roger K.	(202)224-2976	486
	HORTON, Forest W.		561

STAFF DEVELOPMENT CONSULTANT (Cont'd)
DISTRICT OF COLUMBIA (Cont'd)

Washington	JOHANSON, Cynthia J.	(202)287-5261	601
	JUROW, Susan R.	(202)232-8656	620
	KITZMILLER, Virginia G.		657
	KUPERMAN, Agota M.		684
	LAWTON, Bethany L.	(202)651-5220	705
	LEE, Amy C.	(202)546-5539	709
	LITTLEJOHN, Grace M.	(202)291-6920	734
	MCKEAN, Joan M.	(301)443-8358	810
	PHELPS, Thomas C.	(202)786-0271	967
	STONE, Elizabeth W.	(202)338-5574	1197
	SUNG, Carolyn H.	(202)287-5543	1210
	WALKER, Heather C.	(202)544-2443	1295
	WEBB, Barbara A.	(202)797-8909	1313

FLORIDA

Avon Park	APPELQUIST, Donald L.	(813)453-6661	30
Boca Raton	WILER, Linda L.	(305)393-3781	1339
Chattahoochee	BEASLEY, Clarence W.		69
Dunedin	FIORE, Carole D.	(813)733-2595	379
Fort Lauderdale	ALGAZE, Selma B.	(305)357-7501	13
	BROWN, Jeanette L.	(305)523-9145	144
Gainesville	BADGER, Lynn C.	(904)392-0342	44
	GOGGIN, Margaret K.	(904)378-8144	444
Jacksonville	MCMICHAEL, Sandra C.	(904)731-8380	815
Melbourne	HENSON, Llewellyn L.	(305)768-8000	529
Miami	KASKEY, Sid		629
	SINTZ, Edward F.	(305)375-5026	1144
	WILLIAMS, Thomas L.	(305)547-5782	1347
Orlando	ARMSTRONG, Ruth C.	(305)422-7218	32
Pensacola	TERNAK, Armand T.	(904)479-7835	1232
Plant City	PINGS, Vern M.	(813)752-3884	974
Sarasota	JENKINS, Althea H.	(813)355-5003	597
	MOON, Ilse	(813)355-1795	857
Tallahassee	BUSTETTER, Stanley R.	(904)487-2667	166
	FLEMING, Lois D.		384
	SUMMERS, F W.	(904)644-5775	1209
Tampa	CRAIG, James P.	(813)238-5514	254
	EL-HADIDY, Bahaa	(813)974-3520	342
	EYLES, Heberle H.	(813)837-3896	359
	LIANG, Diana F.	(813)988-2406	725
	PFISTER, Fred C.	(813)971-0755	966

GEORGIA

Americus	PASCHAL, Eloise R.	(912)924-3168	945
Appling	WARNER, Wayne G.	(404)868-7412	1305
Athens	ANDERSON, Thomas G.	(404)542-0598	25
	LIBBEY, George H.	(404)542-2716	725
Atlanta	BRYANT, Nancy J.	(404)955-9550	152
	CLEMONS, John E.	(404)727-6840	221
	ENGLER, June L.	(404)727-6405	350
	HENDRIX, Linda S.	(404)252-5745	527
	JAMES, Stephen E.	(404)681-0251	592
	JOHNSON, Herbert F.	(404)727-6861	605
	LAWSON, A V.	(404)377-1142	705
	LAWSON, Venable A.	(404)377-1142	705
	MCIVER, Stephanie P.	(404)688-4636	809
	ROBISON, Carolyn L.	(404)658-2172	1045
	RUSSELL, Ralph E.	(404)658-2172	1069
	SMITH, Jane B.	(205)271-5163	1155
	TYLER, Audrey Q.	(404)753-5564	1266
Bremen	BROCK, Kathy T.	(404)537-4960	138
Doerun	BOWEN, Louise E.	(912)782-5408	120
Jonesboro	BAKER, Gordon N.	(404)961-9824	48
La Grange	LEWIS, Frank R.	(404)882-2911	723
Valdosta	CLARK, Tommy A.	(912)244-6124	218

HAWAII

Honolulu	GOVERNS, Molly K.		454
	LUSTER, Arlene L.	(808)737-8876	750

IDAHO

Boise	TAYLOR, Adrien P.	(208)385-1621	1225
Nampa	SIMMONS, Randall C.	(208)467-8609	1140
Post Falls	JONES-LITTEER, Corene A.	(208)773-1515	616
Rexburg	HART, Eldon C.	(208)356-4447	507

STAFF DEVELOPMENT CONSULTANT (Cont'd)
ILLINOIS

Arlington Heights	VONDRUSKA, Eloise M.	(312)392-7232	1288
Beardstown	WEST, L P.	(217)323-5788	1326
Bloomington	STROYAN, Susan E.	(309)827-4321	1203
Brookfield	IRONS, Carol A.	(312)485-3503	584
Cahokia	BEAN, Bobby G.	(618)875-6915	69
Carbondale	HARWOOD, Judith A.	(618)453-2818	510
	JENKINS, Darrell L.	(618)549-8053	597
Charleston	LUQUIRE, Wilson	(217)581-6061	749
Chicago	CHUNG, Alison L.	(312)222-9350	213
	DOWELL, David R.	(312)567-6844	315
	DOWNES, Valerie	(312)871-7559	316
	DREWETT, William O.	(312)281-3651	319
	FEINER, Arlene M.	(312)348-8382	369
	HAAS, Carolyn B.	(312)822-0809	480
	JACOBSEN, Teresa T.	(312)266-1265	590
	KIM, Chung S.	(312)588-3901	648
	KNOBLAUCH, Mark G.	(312)549-5247	665
	KUSZMAUL, Marcia J.	(312)929-7537	685
	MAYFIELD, Maurice K.	(312)281-0510	790
	MCCARTNEY, Elizabeth J.	(312)666-8262	794
	MCNEILL, Janice M.	(312)642-4600	816
	MUNOFF, Gerald J.	(312)702-8749	879
	PALMER, Raymond A.	(312)266-2456	936
	PETERSON, Randall T.	(312)427-2737	964
	ROMAN, Susan	(312)944-6780	1052
	SHAEVEL, Evelyn F.	(312)944-6780	1118
	VANCURA, Joyce B.	(312)822-0422	1273
Darien	BOWDEN, Philip L.	(312)887-1620	120
Downers Grove	STOFFEL, Lester L.	(312)964-2541	1196
East Peoria	WILFORD, Valerie J.	(309)694-4389	1339
Elgin	FORD, Jennifer D.	(312)742-1040	389
	LONG, Sara E.	(312)888-5090	739
Evanston	PRENDERGAST, Kathleen M.	(312)491-7298	990
	QUERY, Lance D.	(312)491-2882	999
	QUINN, Patrick M.	(312)869-2861	1000
	ROOSE, Tina	(312)491-0662	1053
Flora	HARRIS, Thomas J.	(618)662-2679	506
Glenview	HAFNER, Arthur W.	(312)291-1022	482
	MARTINAZZI, Toni	(657)775-6000	779
Highland Park	SHERRY, Diane H.	(312)433-3968	1129
Hinsdale	CZARNECKI, Cary J.	(312)986-1976	268
	MUELLER, Elizabeth	(312)323-8054	875
La Grange	HUSLIG, Dennis M.	(312)352-7671	578
	TUGGLE, Ann M.	(312)627-9250	1262
Manteno	MC LAUGHLIN, Terry L.	(815)468-6424	813
Mascoutah	GORDON, Diane M.	(618)566-4981	451
Maywood	LUDWIG, Logan T.	(312)531-3192	747
Oak Lawn	IHRIG, Alice B.		581
	KELLY, Raymond T.		638
Park Forest	OCHSNER, Renata E.	(312)748-5374	915
Quincy	TYER, Travis E.	(217)223-5024	1266
River Forest	DAVIS, Richard A.	(312)366-7383	280
Rockford	CHITWOOD, Julius R.	(815)962-4409	209
	ROSENFELD, Joel C.	(815)965-6731	1056
Rolling Meadows	HEMENWAY, Patti J.	(312)255-6197	525
St Charles	MORRISON, Carol J.	(312)377-2499	868
Silvis	SWATOS, Priscilla L.	(309)792-3306	1214
Skokie	KAPLAN, Paul M.		626
Springfield	BERK, Robert A.	(217)782-2658	87
Streamwood	DEUEL, Marlene R.	(312)837-8242	296
Sycamore	BERRY, John W.	(815)895-4225	90
Urbana	BINGHAM, Karen H.	(217)333-0317	97
	EDMONDS, M L.	(217)333-2306	336
	KIBBEE, Josephine Z.	(217)333-2290	646
	WILSON, Lizabeth A.	(217)333-3489	1351
	WRIGHT, Joyce C.	(217)333-1031	1372
Wheaton	BERGER, Carol A.	(312)653-1115	85
	WALSH, Deborah T.	(312)653-1115	1299
Wheeling	KANNER, Elliott E.	(312)459-1300	625
Williamsville	KELLERSTRASS, Amy L.	(217)566-3517	636
Wilmette	JONES, Adrian	(312)256-6202	610
Winnetka	BLACKBURN, Joy M.	(312)446-8697	102

INDIANA

Bloomington	CALLISON, Daniel J.	(812)335-5113	174
	LAUGHLIN, Sara G.	(812)334-8347	703
Columbus	MEREDITH, Meri	(812)372-3482	825
East Chicago	MILLER, Marcia M.	(219)397-1072	840

STAFF DEVELOPMENT CONSULTANT (Cont'd)
INDIANA (Cont'd)

Gary	GUYDON, Janet H.	(219)938-3376	479
Hobart	HUNT, Margaret M.	(219)962-1103	575
Indianapolis	BONNER, Robert J.	(317)283-7362	114
	CHAMPLIN, Constance J.	(317)845-9400	198
	FRANCQ, Carole	(317)274-1411	396
	GILL, John H.	(317)872-2045	435
	KONDELIK, John P.	(317)283-9226	670
	SIMON, Ralph C.	(317)875-5336	1141
Lafayette	BONHOMME, Mary S.	(317)448-1251	114
	TROUTNER, Joanne J.	(317)477-7306	1258
Marion	BOYCE, Harold W.	(317)674-5211	122
Muncie	BEILKE, Patricia F.	(317)284-2457	75
	WOOD, Michael B.	(317)289-5417	1364
Notre Dame	MILLER, Robert C.	(219)239-7790	841
Rochester	LASHER, Esther L.	(219)223-8407	700
South Bend	OSTROWSKI, Lawrence C.	(219)282-4608	929
Terre Haute	LEACH, Ronald G.	(812)237-3700	706

IOWA

Ames	BLACK, William K.	(515)294-1442	102
Bettendorf	MEIER, Patricia L.	(319)355-3895	821
Denver	DUTCHER, Terry R.	(319)984-6120	329
Des Moines	ELLIOTT, Kay M.	(515)281-6033	344
	GEORGE, Shirley H.	(515)281-4105	428
Iowa City	BAKER, Sharon L.	(319)335-5707	49
	CRETH, Sheila D.	(319)335-5868	258
	DEWEY, Barbara I.	(319)335-5867	298
Marion	DAVIS, Deanna S.	(319)377-7135	278

KANSAS

Emporia	BODART-TALBOT, Joni	(316)343-1200	109
	HALE, Martha L.		485
Great Bend	SWAN, James A.	(316)792-4865	1213
Kansas City	RIDDLE, Raymond E.	(913)621-3073	1032
Lawrence	JOHNSON, Ellen S.	(913)864-3496	604
Manhattan	QUIRING, Virginia M.	(913)532-5693	1000
Topeka	BRAND, Alice A.	(913)273-7500	127
	RICHMOND, Robert W.	(913)234-4704	1031
	VOSS, Ernestine D.	(913)269-3296	1289

KENTUCKY

Berea	KIRK, Thomas G.	(606)986-9341	654
Danville	GILMER, Wesley	(606)236-1323	437
Frankfort	NELSON, James A.	(502)875-7000	894
Highland Heights	SCHULTZ, Lois E.	(606)572-5275	1102
Lexington	SINEATH, Timothy W.	(606)257-8876	1143
	STEENSLAND, Ronald P.		1184
Louisville	AULD, Dennis B.		39
	SOMERVILLE, Mary R.	(502)893-8451	1167
Paducah	BOYARSKI, Jennie S.	(502)442-6131	122

LOUISIANA

Baton Rouge	BINGHAM, Elizabeth E.	(504)292-1038	97
	BLOOMSTONE, Ajaye	(504)767-0847	106
	MCKANN, Michael R.	(504)342-4922	809
	PERRY, Emma B.	(504)928-3622	960
Charenton	NEAU, Philip F.	(318)923-7261	891
Lafayette	KREAMER, Jean T.	(318)231-6780	677
Lake Charles	CUROL, Helen B.	(318)477-1780	266
Natchitoches	BUCHANAN, William C.	(318)357-4403	153
New Orleans	DANKNER, Laura R.	(504)865-2367	273
Ruston	LOWE, Joy L.	(318)255-4379	744
Shreveport	BRAZILE, Orella R.	(318)674-3400	130

MAINE

Lewiston	GROSS, Richard F.	(207)782-3958	472
North Anson	LYONS, Dean E.	(207)566-0511	753
Portland	SMITH, Barbara J.	(207)761-2932	1153
York	HARMON, James R.	(207)363-7833	502

MARYLAND

Baldwin	WASIELEWSKI, Eleanor B.	(301)557-7293	1308
Baltimore	BOURKOFF, Vivienne R.	(301)338-8914	119
	CHELTON, Mary K.	(301)355-0906	204
	LANDRY, Mary E.	(301)235-8067	693
	MCADAM, Paul E.	(301)747-5030	791
	MONTGOMERY, Paula K.	(301)685-8621	856
	STEPHAN, Sandra S.	(301)333-2118	1187

STAFF DEVELOPMENT CONSULTANT (Cont'd)
MARYLAND (Cont'd)

Baltimore

	WALLER, Madalyn M.	(301)342-3521	1298
	WILSON, Marjorie P.	(301)328-3970	1352
Bethesda	CONGER, Lucinda D.	(301)229-7716	236
	GAUJARD, Pierre G.	(301)652-0034	422
	LORENZ, John G.	(301)320-4651	741
Brookeville	ROBERTS, Lesley A.	(301)774-4471	1040
Cabin John	ROBINSON, Barbara M.	(301)320-6011	1043
Chevy Chase	GOLDSBERG, Elizabeth D.		446
College Park	APPLEBAUM, Edmond L.	(301)474-7322	30
	ASSOUAD, Carol S.	(301)935-5631	37
	MARCHIONINI, Gary J.	(301)454-3235	769
Columbia	DIENER, Carol W.	(301)381-2525	302
	DOVE, Samuel	(301)964-4189	315
	HILL, Norma L.	(301)997-8000	540
	KOSMIN, Linda J.	(301)997-8954	672
Fort Washington	KALKUS, Stanley	(301)839-5729	623
Glen Burnie	HACKMAN, Mary H.	(301)768-2569	481
Hyattsville	COOPER, Judith C.	(301)699-3500	243
La Plata	WILLIAMS, J L.	(301)932-6768	1343
Landover	BARTH, Edward W.	(301)773-9790	61
Laurel	OMAR, Elizabeth A.	(301)490-3871	923
	SWEETLAND, Loraine F.	(801)490-8231	1215
Pocomoke City	SMITH, Jessie C.	(301)957-3320	1156
Rockville	CHIANG, Ahushun	(301)251-5486	207
	KING, Donald W.	(301)881-6766	650
St Marys City	REPENNING, Julie A.	(301)862-0267	1023
Salisbury	CUNNINGHAM, Barbara M.	(301)742-1537	265
Seabrook	LARSEN, Lida L.	(301)459-3931	698
Severna Park	COURSON, M S.	(301)647-5522	251
Silver Spring	HENDERSON, Ronald L.	(301)588-2844	527
Towson	DRACH, Marian C.	(301)825-8877	317
Westminster	MCCARTY, Emily H.	(301)848-1825	795

MASSACHUSETTS

Amherst	KURKUL, Donna L.	(413)253-5975	684
Arlington	PLUNKET, Linda	(617)646-7825	979
Boston	EATON, Elizabeth K.	(617)523-7415	333
	MATARAZZO, James M.	(617)738-2220	783
	MCCARTHY, Germaine A.	(617)742-3958	794
Brighton	BRAUN, Robin E.	(617)789-2177	130
Burlington	MCLAUGHLIN, Lee R.	(617)272-5772	813
Cambridge	MOFFITT, Michael D.	(617)864-5770	852
Carver	NEUBAUER, Richard A.	(617)866-5186	896
Charlestown	CURTIN-STEVENSON, Mary C.	(617)241-9664	266
East Boston	SCHLAFF, Donna G.	(617)561-0153	1093
Ipswich	GRAY, Carolyn M.	(617)356-0773	459
Lexington	BERNSTEIN, D S.	(617)863-1284	89
	WALSH, Joanna M.	(617)863-1275	1299
Medford	SCHATZ, Natalie M.	(617)381-3273	1090
Needham	MARKUSON, Carolyn A.	(617)449-6299	772
Reading	MARCY, Henry O.	(617)944-2194	769
South Deerfield	CRAIG, James L.	(413)665-2041	254
Waban	CHERNIN, David A.	(617)731-6760	206
Waltham	STRAND, Bethany	(617)736-4645	1200
Watertown	REDDY, Sigrid R.	(617)924-3282	1014
Winchester	KEATS, Susan E.	(617)729-9317	633
Worcester	CHAMBERLAIN, Ruth B.	(617)244-3612	197
Yarmouthport	STEEVES, Henry A.		1184

MICHIGAN

Alpena	WILLIAMS, Susan S.	(517)356-1622	1346
Ann Arbor	BLOUIN, Francis X.	(313)764-3482	107
	DURRANCE, Joan C.	(313)763-1569	328
	SCHWARTZ, Diane G.	(313)763-2037	1104
	WERLING, Anita L.	(313)761-4700	1324
Auburn Hills	WILLIAMS, Calvin	(313)853-4226	1342
Bloomfield Hills	FRANKIE, Suzanne O.	(313)855-6149	397
	ST. AMAND, Norma P.	(313)644-1878	1075
Clarkston	D'ELIA, Joseph G.	(313)625-8274	289
Dearborn Heights	KIRKESY, Oliver M.	(313)278-4670	655
Detroit	BISSETT, Donald J.	(313)577-1615	100
	GRAZIER, Margaret H.	(313)862-7106	461
	JOHNSON, Veronica A.	(313)532-6715	609
	MIKA, Joseph J.	(313)577-1825	834
	MORROW, Blaine V.	(313)893-1746	869
East Lansing	WOODARD, Beth E.	(517)355-5774	1365

STAFF DEVELOPMENT CONSULTANT (Cont'd)
MICHIGAN (Cont'd)

Eaton Rapids	FLAHERTY, Kevin C.	(517)663-2362	383
Grand Blanc	KINGSTON, Jo A.	(313)694-7323	652
Grosse Pointe	CASEY, Genevieve M.		192
Grosse Pointe Farms	HANSON, Charles D.	(313)882-3627	498
Grosse Pointe Park	TOLMAN, Bonnie B.	(313)885-0764	1249
Holland	LIGHT, Lin	(616)335-2540	726
Jackson	LEAMON, David L.	(517)788-4199	707
Kalamazoo	APPS, Michelle L.	(616)375-3611	30
	NETZ, David H.	(616)383-1666	896
	NOBLE, Valerie	(616)323-6352	906
	RIZZO, John R.	(616)381-1323	1037
Lansing	CALLARD, Carole	(517)373-1593	173
	EZELL, Charlaine L.	(517)485-8019	360
Monroe	MARGOLIS, Bernard A.	(313)243-5213	770
Mt Pleasant	KRUUT, Evald	(517)773-5184	681
Northville	ROCKALL, Diane M.	(313)349-9005	1046
Port Huron	WU, Harry P.	(313)982-2765	1373
Troy	ZARYCZNY, Wlodzimierz A.	(313)879-7217	1386
West Bloomfield	SMITH, Nancy J.	(313)682-2120	1158
Ypsilanti	BOONE, Morell D.	(313)484-4384	115
	MARSHALL, Albert P.		773

MINNESOTA

Golden Valley	COLE, Jack W.		230
Hopkins	SMITH, David R.	(612)933-0199	1154
Mankato	BIRMINGHAM, Frank R.	(507)389-5210	98
	CHRISTENSON, John D.	(507)625-6169	211
	HITT, Charles J.	(507)625-4834	544
Minneapolis	ROHLF, Robert H.	(612)926-6105	1050
	YAHNKE, Robert E.	(612)625-0504	1376
Northfield	BRUCE, Robert K.	(507)645-9279	149
Pine River	O'BRIEN, Marlys H.	(218)587-2171	915
Robbinsdale	HERTHER, Nancy K.	(612)529-0115	533
St Paul	CLARKE, Charlotte C.	(612)645-7359	218
	MAHMOODI, Suzanne H.		760
	RICCI, Patricia L.	(612)771-4764	1026
St Peter	HAEUSER, Michael J.	(507)931-7556	482
	HERVEY, Norma J.	(507)931-7563	533
Worthington	SCOTT, Thomas L.	(507)376-5803	1108

MISSISSIPPI

Clinton	BUCHANAN, Gerald	(601)924-7511	153
Hattiesburg	HAUTH, Allan C.	(601)266-4126	513
	WILSON, Mary S.	(601)266-4240	1352
Liberty	BURKS, Alvin L.	(601)657-8920	161
Natchez	RANDAZZO, Corinne O.	(601)445-2848	1006
Raymond	WALL, Norma F.	(601)857-3253	1297

MISSOURI

Ballwin	TAYLOR, Arthur R.	(314)394-9973	1226
Columbia	SHAUGHNESSY, Thomas W.	(314)882-4701	1123
Jefferson City	BEHLER, Patricia A.	(314)635-0608	74
Kansas City	GARDNER, Laura L.	(816)741-4070	418
	JENKINS, Harold R.	(816)444-2590	597
	MILLS, Elaine L.	(816)333-1245	844
	NESBITT, John R.	(813)926-7616	896
Liberty	HOOVER, Jonnette L.	(816)781-7812	557
Saint Joseph	ELLIOTT, Dorothy G.	(816)232-7729	344
St Louis	ELSESSER, Lionelle H.	(314)725-4722	346
	NOBLE, Barbara N.	(314)367-6324	906
	PAGE, Jacqueline M.	(314)781-6352	934
	ROBERTS, Jean A.	(314)664-0939	1040
Springfield	MORROW, Paula J.	(417)887-8161	869

MONTANA

Billings	NEWBERG, Ellen J.	(406)245-5483	898
Bozeman	BRUWELHEIDE, Janis H.	(406)587-0405	151
Helena	SCHLESINGER, Deborah L.	(406)442-2373	1094
Missoula	CHANDLER, Devon	(406)243-4072	199

NEBRASKA

Omaha	LITTLE, Nina M.	(402)554-6282	733
	MEANS, Raymond B.	(402)280-2705	820

NEVADA

Henderson	TRASATTI, Margaret S.	(702)733-3613	1254
Las Vegas	WELLS, David B.	(702)733-3641	1322

STAFF DEVELOPMENT CONSULTANT (Cont'd)

NEW HAMPSHIRE

Concord	JOHNSON, Jean G.	(603)271-2429	605
Manchester	COMEAU, Reginald A.	(603)668-6706	234
	KENT, Jeffrey A.	(603)622-4408	642
	MCGINNIS, Joan M.	(603)624-4366	806

NEW JERSEY

Aberdeen	WEISBURG, Hilda K.	(201)566-1995	1319
Bridgewater	STUDDIFORD, Abigail M.	(201)725-5616	1204
Columbus	ALITO, Martha A.	(609)298-5848	13
Cranford	HALL, Homer J.	(201)276-4311	488
East Orange	GORMAN, Audrey J.	(201)676-2472	452
Edison	FERRERE, Cathy M.	(201)819-8924	373
Elizabeth	LATINI, Samuel A.	(201)354-6060	701
Flemington	MCGREGOR, Walter	(201)788-3025	808
Iselin	SILVA, Nelly H.	(201)321-0683	1138
Lakewood	HERBERT, Barbara R.	(201)364-2200	530
Madison	COUGHLIN, Caroline M.	(201)377-3000	250
Mahwah	MAYDET, Steven I.		789
	YUEH, Norma N.	(201)529-7578	1384
Maplewood	KRUPP, Robert G.	(201)763-8436	681
Marlton	RICHIE, Mark L.	(609)985-0436	1030
Montclair	HOROWITZ, Marjorie B.	(201)744-8697	560
Moorestown	LADOF, Nina S.	(609)235-1570	687
Morristown	BUCK, Anne M.	(201)829-5111	153
Neshanic	VANDERGRIFT, Kay E.	(201)369-8685	1274
New Brunswick	RUBEN, Brent D.	(201)932-7447	1064
	VARLEJS, Jana	(201)932-7169	1278
Nutley	GILHEANY, Rosary S.	(201)667-7013	434
Oceanport	WAITE, William F.	(201)542-7216	1293
Passaic	SCHEAR, Thomas W.	(201)777-6146	1090
Peapack	WHITING, Elaine M.	(201)234-0598	1333
Phillipsburg	HESS, Jayne L.	(201)454-3712	534
Plainsboro	QUINN, Ralph M.	(609)799-3072	1000
Point Pleasant	GREENE, Ellin P.	(201)899-2270	464
Princeton	BLASINGAME, Ralph	(609)987-0273	104
Short Hills	TALCOTT, Ann W.	(201)379-6721	1221
Spring Lake	GARVEY, Nancy G.	(201)449-4673	421
Summit	SOMMER, Ursula M.	(201)593-8526	1167
Trenton	BRODOWSKI, Joyce H.	(609)771-2343	139
Upper Montclair	PARR, Mary Y.	(201)746-0352	944
Warren	WEIL, Ben H.	(201)647-0892	1317
Washington Township	MAYNES, Kathleen R.	(201)358-0209	790

NEW MEXICO

Albuquerque	RASSAM, Cynthia K.	(505)277-4203	1009
Las Cruces	DRESP, Donald F.	(505)522-3627	319

NEW YORK

Albany	COX, Richard J.	(518)486-4820	253
	DANIELS, Pam	(518)473-8177	273
	VAILLANCOURT, Pauline M.	(518)489-6207	1271
	YAVARKOVSKY, Jerome	(518)473-1189	1378
Ballston Lake	EGAN, Mary J.	(518)399-5151	338
Bay Shore	HEINTZELMAN, Susan K.	(516)666-0177	522
Bellerose	GATNER, Elliott S.		422
Briarwood	BORRESS, Lewis R.	(718)441-6328	117
Bronx	WENDT, Mary E.	(212)220-6560	1324
Brooklyn	BRANDWEIN, Larry	(718)780-7803	128
	ROMALIS, Carl		1052
	SCHWABACHER, Sara A.	(718)388-0023	1104
	THOMAS, Lucille C.	(718)778-1585	1237
Brookville	MAILLET, Lucienne G.	(516)299-2855	761
Buffalo	DIBARTOLO, Amy L.	(716)878-6309	299
	ELLISON, John W.	(716)636-3069	345
	NEWMAN, George C.	(716)886-8132	899
	PALMIERI, Lucien E.	(716)882-9275	937
	VON WAHLDE, Barbara	(716)636-2967	1288
Croton-on-Hudson	COHEN, Aaron	(914)271-8170	227
Dewitt	ELY, Donald P.	(315)446-0259	347
Elmira	LAPIER, Cynthia B.	(607)739-3581	697
Flushing	COHEN, David	(718)520-7194	228
FPO New York	LANE, Elizabeth L.		694
Jamestown	LEE, Sylvia	(716)483-5415	711
Kirkwood	HAMLIN, Eileen M.	(607)775-1758	493
Lackawanna	BEDNAR, Sheila	(716)822-0840	73
Lindenhurst	MILNES, Patricia C.	(516)957-7755	845
Long Island City	MARTIN, Brian G.	(718)726-5885	775

STAFF DEVELOPMENT CONSULTANT (Cont'd)

NEW YORK (Cont'd)

Mamaroneck	O'CONOR, William C.	(914)698-4741	916
Massapequa Park	AKS, Gloria	(516)795-7297	9
Mexico	MAUTINO, Patricia H.	(315)963-7251	787
Mineola	KRATZ, Charles E.		676
New City	SIMON, Patricia B.	(914)634-4998	1140
New Rochelle	MITTELGLUCK, Eugene L.	(914)834-8739	850
New York	BADERTSCHER, David G.	(212)374-5615	44
	BRAUDE, Robert M.	(212)472-5919	129
	CIOPPA, Lawrence	(212)677-5688	214
	COHEN, Rochelle F.	(212)577-3333	229
	DAVILA, Daniel	(212)989-1732	277
	DYER, Esther R.	(212)777-9064	330
	ELLIS, Peter K.	(212)222-3274	345
	FODY, Barbara A.	(212)713-3673	387
	GOSSAGE, Wayne	(212)869-3348	453
	HALL, Alix M.	(212)536-3598	486
	HEWITT, Vivian D.		535
	LANDAU, Herbert B.	(212)705-7600	692
	NATHAN, Frances E.	(212)876-0269	889
	PALMER, Julia R.	(212)744-7202	936
	PELLOWSKI, Anne	(212)316-1170	955
	ST. CLAIR, Guy	(212)515-5299	1075
	SALY, Alan J.	(212)475-5400	1078
	SARRIS, Shirley C.	(212)473-2990	1083
	TICE, Margaret E.		1244
Niagara Falls	SHIELDS, Gerald R.	(716)284-2928	1130
North Chatham	WELLS, Gladysann		1322
Oneonta	CHIANG, Nancy	(607)432-4200	207
Oswego	JUDD, Blanche E.	(315)341-4267	618
Pearl River	BRISFJORD, Inez S.	(914)735-1567	136
	SPERR BRISFJORD, Inez L.	(914)735-1567	1173
Peekskill	SALUSTRI, Madeline	(914)739-2823	1077
Penfield	PARKE, Kathryn E.		941
Poughkeepsie	JEANNENEY, Mary L.	(914)452-7000	596
	STAINO, Rocco A.		1178
Rochester	HUNT, Suellyn	(716)428-6981	575
	JUNION, Gail J.	(716)275-4496	620
	MOUREY, Deborah A.	(716)724-6819	874
Rockville Centre	FRIEDLAND, Rhoda W.	(516)766-6387	403
Roslyn Heights	HARRIS, Martha	(516)484-0792	505
Saratoga Springs	DOE, Lynn M.	(518)584-5000	308
Scarborough	HOPKINS, Lee B.	(914)941-5810	558
Scarsdale	BERGER, Pam P.	(914)723-3156	86
Setauket	NICHOLS, Gerald D.	(516)689-7071	901
	VERBESEY, J R.	(516)751-6913	1282
Syracuse	EISENBERG, Michael B.	(315)423-4549	340
	JOHNSON, Nancy B.	(315)423-2911	608
	MCLAUGHLIN, Pamela W.	(315)476-7359	813
Water Mill	GROSSMAN, Adrian J.	(516)537-3623	473
White Plains	TREFRY, Mary G.	(914)761-5478	1255
Willow	LOWE, Mildred	(914)679-6222	744

NORTH CAROLINA

Chapel Hill	COGGINS, Timothy L.	(919)962-6202	227
	FEEHAN, Patricia E.	(919)962-8366	368
	MATER, Dee A.	(919)962-0700	783
	MORAN, Barbara B.	(919)962-8363	862
	OWEN, Willy	(919)962-1301	932
Durham	BRUCE, Nancy G.	(919)490-0069	149
	BURGIN, Robert E.	(919)683-6485	159
	SEMONCHE, Barbara P.	(919)489-7247	1115
	SPELLER, Benjamin F.	(919)683-6485	1172
Elkin	MACPHAIL, Jessica		758
Fairview	HUTTON, Jean R.	(704)628-1453	579
Greensboro	JARRELL, James R.	(919)273-7061	594
	MILLER, Marilyn L.	(919)334-5100	840
	RANCER, Susan P.	(919)288-2160	1006
	YOUNG, Tommie M.	(909)621-0032	1383
High Point	AUSTIN, Neal F.	(919)869-6260	40
Kinston	JONES, John W.	(919)527-7066	613
	SOUTHERLAND, Carol A.	(919)523-0819	1169
Montreat	BROOKS, Jerrold L.	(704)669-7661	140
	FOREMAN, Kenneth J.	(704)669-2782	390
Raleigh	BRADBURN, Frances B.	(919)878-4497	125
	ISACCO, Jeanne M.	(919)851-4703	584
	SMITH, Catherine	(919)851-4703	1153
Research Triangle Pk	BEST-NICHOLS, Barbara J.	(919)544-3808	92

STAFF DEVELOPMENT CONSULTANT (Cont'd)

NORTH CAROLINA (Cont'd)

Roanoke Rapids	JOYCE, Robert A.	(919)537-1324	618
Spring Hope	LANEY, Elizabeth J.	(919)478-3836	695
Wilmington	BEECH, Vivian W.	(919)763-3303	74

NORTH DAKOTA

Ellendale	ZINK, Esther L.	(701)349-3609	1389
Fargo	JANZEN, Deborah K.	(701)277-1865	594

OHIO

Bowling Green	MILLER, Ruth G.	(419)352-0817	842
	MILLER, William	(419)372-2857	843
	REPP, Joan M.		1024
	ZAPOROZHETZ, Laurene E.	(419)354-2101	1386
Canfield	LITTLE, Dean K.	(216)533-6703	733
Canton	ERWIN, Nancy S.	(216)477-7309	353
Centerville	GARTEN, Edward D.		420
Chesterland	CORBUS, Lawrence J.	(216)286-8941	245
Cincinnati	DICKMAN, Emmajane H.		301
	HEFFRON, Sheila F.	(513)891-4200	520
	KONKEL, Mary S.	(513)681-2074	670
	MC NAIR, Marian B.	(513)369-4750	815
Cleveland	BORUCKI, Jennifer A.	(216)696-1313	117
	PIKE, Kermit J.	(216)721-5722	972
	RADER, Hannelore B.	(216)687-2475	1002
Columbus	CHESKI, Richard M.	(614)462-6843	207
	PARSONS, Augustine C.	(614)895-3201	944
	WANG, Anna M.	(614)294-8035	1302
Dayton	BUCK, Jeremy R.	(513)227-9500	153
	COYLE, Christopher B.	(513)865-6882	253
Dublin	SHREWSBURY, Lynn D.	(614)764-6403	1133
Euclid	COLEMAN, Judith	(216)261-5300	231
Findlay	JANKY, Donna L.	(419)422-3211	593
Georgetown	TOMLIN, Marsha A.	(513)378-3154	1250
Hubbard	GROHL, Arlene P.	(216)759-7800	471
Kent	NELSON, Olga G.	(216)678-8236	895
Mansfield	KARRE, David J.	(419)526-1337	628
Mentor	DUANE, Carol A.	(216)255-3323	321
Middletown	PALMER, Virginia E.	(513)424-4263	937
New Albany	HERB, Elizabeth D.	(614)855-7441	530
Norwalk	DRAPP, Laureen	(419)668-6063	318
Oberlin	MOFFETT, William A.	(216)775-8285	852
Parma	ROBINSON, Doris J.	(216)888-3462	1043
Piqua	OVERHOLT, Maria B.	(513)773-3640	931
Toledo	CARY, Mary K.	(419)537-2833	191
Troy	CRAM, Mary E.	(513)334-5067	255
	MILLER, John E.	(513)335-8801	839
Waterford	TEPE, Ann S.	(614)749-3007	1231
Westlake	GALLANT, Jennifer J.	(216)835-6020	414
Yellow Springs	NEWMAN, Marianne L.		899
Youngstown	DONAHUGH, Robert H.	(216)788-6950	310
	YANCURA, Ann J.	(216)746-7042	1377

OKLAHOMA

Ada	COULTER, Cynthia M.	(405)332-8000	251
Edmond	ROADS, Clarice D.	(405)341-3660	1038
Norman	SHERMAN, Mary A.	(405)321-1481	1128
	WEAVER-MEYERS, Pat L.	(405)325-3341	1313
Oklahoma City	DAVIS, Denyvetta	(405)424-2106	278
	LITTLE, Paul L.	(405)789-9400	733
	SAULMON, Sharon A.	(405)634-3181	1084
Stillwater	JOHNSON, Edward R.	(405)372-2637	604
	ROUSE, Charlie L.	(405)372-4651	1061
Tahlequah	MADAUS, J R.		758
Tulsa	BUTHOD, J C.	(918)592-7894	166
	SMITH, Peggy C.	(918)592-6000	1159

OREGON

Ashland	PURCELL, V N.	(503)482-2629	998
Beaverton	JACOBS, Patt	(503)646-6959	590
Bend	BYRNE, Helen E.	(503)382-1621	169
Coos Bay	TASHJIAN, Sharon A.	(503)267-5605	1224
Eugene	HILDEBRAND, Carol I.	(503)344-4267	538
Portland	BURSON, Lorraine E.	(508)246-4097	163
Roseburg	COOK, Sybilla A.	(503)673-0504	240
	MUNGER, Freda R.	(503)672-6489	879

STAFF DEVELOPMENT CONSULTANT (Cont'd)

PENNSYLVANIA

Allentown	MOSES, Lynn M.		871
Ambler	MORROW, Ellen B.	(215)646-1755	869
Berwyn	BROWN, David E.	(215)644-5241	143
California	CARUSO, Nicholas C.	(412)938-9166	190
Camp Hill	ALBRECHT, Lois K.	(717)737-6111	10
Clarion	PERSON, Ruth J.	(814)226-5341	961
Coraopolis	SKOVIRA, Robert J.	(412)262-8257	1147
Harrisburg	MALLINGER, Stephen M.	(717)783-5737	763
Haverford	FREEMAN, Michael S.	(215)896-1272	401
Lancaster	WALKER, Sue A.	(717)396-6803	1296
Lansdale	NOLAN, Joan	(215)368-9800	907
	WEBER ROOCHVARG, Lynn E.	(215)368-8688	1314
Library	SALVAYON, Connie	(412)833-5585	1078
Mars	JOSEPH, Patricia A.	(412)776-9249	617
McKeesport	HORVATH, Robert T.	(412)672-0625	561
Middletown	TOWNLEY, Charles T.	(717)948-6079	1253
North Wales	MAXIN, Jacqueline A.	(215)855-5675	787
Philadelphia	AUGUST, Sidney	(215)985-2872	39
	AXAM, John A.	(215)549-6485	42
	BENDER, Evelyn	(215)634-0357	79
	CHILDERS, Thomas A.	(215)895-2479	208
	FISHER, Douglas A.	(215)587-4915	380
	FUSELER-MCDOWELL, Elizabeth A.	(215)423-9294	410
	MARCO, Guy A.		769
	MARVIN, Stephen G.	(215)895-1874	780
	MAYOVER, Steven J.	(215)686-5400	791
	NAISMITH, Patricia A.	(215)235-0256	887
	PROMOS, Marianne	(215)686-5351	995
	RIDGEWAY, Patricia M.	(215)898-7555	1032
	SNOWTEN, Renee Y.	(215)557-8295	1164
	STEINBERG, Eileen	(215)333-5536	1185
Pittsburgh	BEARMAN, David A.	(412)421-4638	69
	CASLIN, Adele	(412)687-7738	193
	CRONEBERGER, Robert B.	(412)622-3100	260
	FIDOTEN, Robert E.	(412)963-8785	375
	FITZGERALD, Patricia A.	(412)268-2428	382
	KING, Mimi	(412)237-2593	652
	LOCKE, Jill L.	(412)624-9435	736
	MITCHELL, Joan M.	(412)578-6137	849
	WOODSWORTH, Anne		1367
Slippery Rock	JOSEPH, Elizabeth T.	(412)794-4623	617
State College	CARR, Caryn J.	(814)234-4203	185
University Park	FORTH, Stuart	(814)865-0401	391
West Chester	AMICONE, Janice L.	(215)692-6889	20
West Point	MESSICK, Karen J.	(215)661-6026	828

PUERTO RICO

Ponce	PADUA, Flores N.	(809)844-4150	934

RHODE ISLAND

Kingston	FUTAS, Elizabeth	(401)792-2947	411
Providence	DANIELS, Bruce E.	(401)277-2726	273

SOUTH CAROLINA

Cayce	FREEMAN, Larry S.	(803)794-5370	401
Charleston	SEAMAN, Sheila L.	(803)795-4416	1109
	WOOD, Richard J.	(803)763-8532	1365
Clemson	HIPPS, Gary M.	(803)654-3934	543
Columbia	BARRON, Daniel D.	(803)777-4825	60
	NORRIS, Gale K.	(803)265-9920	909
Glendale	WHITE, Ann T.	(803)579-3330	1330
McCormick	TOWNSEND, Catherine M.	(803)465-3185	1253
Orangeburg	WILLIAMS-JENKINS, Barbara J.	(803)536-7045	1347

SOUTH DAKOTA

Sioux Falls	MODICA, Mary L.	(605)388-3701	851
	THOMPSON, Ronelle K.	(605)336-4921	1241

TENNESSEE

Clinton	GREESON, Judy G.	(615)457-0931	465
	SPATH, Charles E.	(615)457-8616	1171
Jackson	ROBERTSON, Billy O.	(901)668-1818	1041
Kingsport	FANSLOW, Malinda C.	(645)246-7171	363
	TILSON, Koleta B.	(615)245-6572	1245

STAFF DEVELOPMENT CONSULTANT (Cont'd)
TENNESSEE (Cont'd)

Memphis	CARD, Judy	(901)725-8851	180
	POURCIAU, Lester J.	(901)454-2201	987
	WEDIG, Eric M.	(901)454-2206	1315
Nashville	WILBURN, Clouse R.	(615)322-8050	1338
Sewanee	WATSON, Tom G.	(615)598-1213	1310

TEXAS

Abilene	DAHLSTROM, Joe F.		269
Amarillo	WELLS, Mary K.	(806)381-2435	1322
Austin	GAMEZ, Juanita L.	(512)837-6247	416
	HELBURN, Judith D.	(512)454-7229	523
	JACKSON, Eugene B.	(512)345-1653	587
	JUERGENS, Bonnie	(512)288-2072	619
	KAHLER, June	(512)463-9660	621
	SEIDENBERG, Edward	(512)463-5459	1112
	SMITH, Dorothy B.	(512)453-1384	1154
College Station	ST. CLAIR, Gloriana S.	(409)696-8982	1075
Dallas	JAGOE, Katherine P.	(214)931-8938	591
	MOLTZAN, Janet R.	(214)691-3267	854
	WETHERBEE, Louella V.	(214)750-6130	1327
Denton	GALLOWAY, Margaret E.	(817)565-3024	415
	SCHLESSINGER, Bernard S.	(817)898-2617	1094
	SHELDON, Brooke E.	(817)898-2602	1125
	SWIGGER, Keith	(817)898-2609	1216
	TOTTEN, Herman L.	(817)383-1902	1252
El Paso	GOODMAN, Helen C.	(915)584-4509	449
Fort Worth	ALLMAND, Linda F.	(817)870-7706	17
	ARD, Harold J.	(817)293-5474	31
	DE TONNANCOUR, P R.	(817)763-1790	296
	MUELLER, Peggy	(817)870-7701	875
Galveston	PHILLIPS, Carol B.	(409)740-1747	967
Garland	LARSON, Jeanette C.	(214)240-0661	699
Harlingen	CORBIN, John	(512)428-5475	245
Houston	BROWN, Freddiemae E.	(713)227-9177	144
	FORD, Delores C.	(713)631-7730	389
	HASKELL, Peter C.	(713)529-6681	510
	KLAPPERSACK, Dennis	(713)630-1130	657
Huntsville	PICHETTE, William H.	(409)291-2994	970
	YOUNG, J A.	(409)295-8766	1382
Irving	HAGLE, Claudette S.	(214)986-2343	483
Kingsville	MERCHANT, Cheryl N.	(512)592-9684	825
Lubbock	CARGILL, Jennifer S.	(806)792-2349	181
	WEBB, Gisela M.	(806)794-7359	1313
New Braunfels	SCHUMANN, Iris T.	(512)625-5656	1103
Palestine	SELWYN, Laurie	(214)723-1436	1114
Prairie View	YEH, Helen S.	(409)857-3192	1379
Round Rock	RICKLEFS, Dale L.	(512)255-3939	1032
San Antonio	TODD, Fred W.	(512)826-8121	1248
The Woodlands	MILLER, Carol A.	(713)367-7500	836
Tyler	LAMBERTH, Linda E.	(214)595-3481	690
Waco	PHILLIPS, Luouida V.		968
Weatherford	HEEZEN, Ronald R.	(817)599-0833	520

UTAH

Provo	MARCHANT, Maurice P.	(801)378-2976	768
	WILSON, D K.	(801)375-2770	1350
Salt Lake City	JENSEN, Charla J.	(801)533-5250	598

VERMONT

| Montpelier | KLINCK, Patricia E. | (802)828-3265 | 661 |

VIRGINIA

Alexandria	BROWN, Dale W.	(703)751-3236	143
Annandale	CHOBOT, Mary C.	(703)323-9402	210
Arlington	ARDEN, Caroline	(703)532-1548	31
	LEATHER, Deborah J.	(703)522-5600	707
	WOODALL, Nancy C.	(703)528-5128	1365
Burke	STEPHENSON, Richard W.	(703)323-7721	1188
Emory	JENNERICH, Elaine Z.	(703)944-3121	598
Falls Church	LEONARD, Lucinda E.	(703)536-2373	716
Farmville	STWODAH, M I.	(804)392-8925	1206
Hampton	BIGELOW, Therese G.	(804)727-6234	95
Harrisonburg	HABAN, Mary F.	(703)433-2183	480
	ROBISON, Dennis E.	(703)568-6578	1045
Lexington	HAYS, Peggy W.	(703)463-8643	517
Manassas	KILLEEN, Erlene B.	(703)369-7193	648
Norfolk	JONES-TRENT, Bernice R.	(804)632-8873	616
	MILLER, Ellen L.	(804)440-3283	837

STAFF DEVELOPMENT CONSULTANT (Cont'd)
VIRGINIA (Cont'd)

Portsmouth	LIN, John T.	(804)484-2121	727
Richmond	BAGAN, Beverly S.	(804)780-7691	45
	GWIN, James E.	(804)288-7602	479
	TYSON, John C.	(804)289-8456	1267
Vienna	DODSON, Whit	(703)938-2630	308
Williamsburg	SCHEITLE, Janet M.	(804)220-3104	1091
Winchester	BISCHOFF, Frances A.	(703)667-5350	99

WASHINGTON

Bellevue	SKELLEY, Cornelia A.	(206)747-6473	1145
Edmonds	STRONG, Sunny A.	(206)778-3804	1203
Ellensburg	SCHNEIDER, Frank A.	(509)963-1901	1097
Federal Way	WILSON, Anthony M.	(206)839-0496	1349
Kirkland	MACDONALD, Margaret R.	(206)486-8931	754
Lacey	WIEMAN, Jean M.	(206)491-4700	1336
Olympia	MOORE, Mary Y.	(206)866-8272	860
	SHAFFER, Maryann	(206)943-5001	1119
Redmond	WALLS, Francine E.	(206)333-4815	1299
Seattle	BAGG, Deborah L.	(206)621-7896	45
	HILL, Ann M.	(206)525-4212	539
	JENNERICH, Edward J.	(206)626-6320	598
	LEONARD, Gloria J.	(206)722-4828	716
	MADDEN, Susan B.	(206)684-6626	758
	STEERE, Paul J.	(206)367-0328	1184
	STOCK, Carole G.	(206)325-8364	1195
	TOLLIVER, Barbara J.	(206)684-6615	1248
	WEAVER, Carolyn G.	(206)543-5530	1312
Spokane	MURRAY, James M.	(509)838-3680	882
Tacoma	BECKER, Roger V.	(206)591-2703	72
	BUELER, Roy D.	(206)593-6860	155
	SELING, Kathy A.	(206)756-5571	1113

WEST VIRGINIA

| Athens | BROWN, Thomas M. | (304)384-3115 | 148 |
| Huntington | REENSTJERNA, Frederick R. | (304)523-9651 | 1016 |

WISCONSIN

Grafton	MORITZ, William D.	(414)377-6695	865
Green Bay	GORSEGNER, Betty D.	(414)465-1529	452
Madison	ARNOLD, Barbara J.	(608)263-2909	33
	BUNGE, Charles A.	(608)263-2900	157
	CAIN, Carolyn L.	(608)271-6198	171
	CRAWFORD, Josephine	(608)274-7984	256
	MATTHEWS, Geraldine M.	(608)266-1164	785
	WEINGAND, Darlene E.	(608)262-8952	1318
	WHITCOMB, Dorothy V.	(608)262-2402	1330
Menomonie	JAX, John J.	(715)232-1184	595
Middleton	ZWEIZIG, Douglas L.	(608)831-4364	1392
Milwaukee	AMAN, Mohammed M.	(414)239-4709	19
	BOTHAM, Jane	(414)278-3078	118
	KRCHMAR, Sandra L.	(414)961-8863	677
	SAGER, Lynn S.	(414)964-5940	1074
New London	DIEHL, Carol L.	(414)982-5040	301
Oshkosh	SHARMA, Ravindra N.	(414)424-0139	1122
Reedsville	OHLEMACHER, Janet H.	(414)754-4831	919
Ripon	MCGOWAN, Sarah M.	(414)748-8330	807
Twin Lakes	OPEM, John D.	(414)877-9539	925
Wauwatosa	CHAPLOCK, Sharon K.	(414)778-2167	201
West Allis	LUECHT, Richard M.	(414)321-3152	747

WYOMING

Cheyenne	JOHNSON, Wayne H.	(307)777-7283	609
Gillette	SIEBERSMA, Dan	(307)686-0786	1135
Laramie	COTTAM, Keith M.	(307)766-3279	250

CANADA

ALBERTA

Calgary	BAILEY, Madeleine J.	(403)240-6134	46
	BOUEY, Elaine F.	(403)284-4418	119
	MING, Marilyn	(403)284-8072	846
	WHITE, Valerie L.	(403)255-6419	1332
Sherwood Park	SCHMIDT, Raymond J.	(403)464-8234	1095

STAFF DEVELOPMENT CONSULTANT (Cont'd)

BRITISH COLUMBIA

Nanaimo	MEADOWS, Donald F.	(604)753-3662	819
Richmond	WEESE, Dwain W.		1316
Vancouver	AUFIERO, Joan I.	(604)325-2317	39
	HAABNIIT, Ene	(604)736-9335	480
	HAYCOCK, Carol A.	(604)734-0255	515
	HAYCOCK, Kenneth R.	(604)731-1131	515
	LEITH, Anna R.	(604)228-2762	714
Victoria	HAMILTON, Donald E.	(604)721-7899	492

MANITOBA

Winnipeg	COVVEY, H D.	(204)942-5335	252
	FOWLER, Margaret A.	(204)884-6593	394
	ROUTLEDGE, Patricia A.	(204)474-9445	1062
	SANTORO, Corrado A.	(204)474-8243	1082

ONTARIO

Belfountain	DE RONDE, Paula D.	(519)927-5156	294
Don Mills	TEMPLIN, Dorothy	(416)447-2380	1231
Go-Home Bay	CAMPBELL, Harry	(705)756-1878	176
Guelph	GILLHAM, Virginia A.	(519)824-4120	436
Hamilton	FLEMMING, Tom	(416)525-9140	384
Kitchener	SHEPHERD, Murray C.		1127
London	MILLER, Beth M.	(519)661-3542	836
Mississauga	DINEEN, Diane M.	(416)279-7002	304
Toronto	BAYNE, Jennifer M.	(416)595-3429	67
	DENIS, Laurent G.	(416)978-3111	292
	GREENWOOD, Jan	(416)963-9383	465
	HAYES, Janice E.	(416)480-7545	516
	KENDALL, Sandra A.		640
	PARKER, Arthur D.	(416)967-5525	941
	SELLERS, Alexander G.	(416)489-4908	1114
	SMITH, Anne C.	(416)423-9826	1152
	SMITH, Cynthia M.	(416)488-6117	1153
	VEANER, Allen B.	(416)486-0239	1280
	WILKINSON, John P.	(416)978-3167	1340
Windsor	WALSH, G M.	(519)253-7817	1299

QUEBEC

Baie d'Urfe	KLOK, Buddhi	(514)457-2757	662
Boucherville	NADEAU, Johan	(514)655-4858	885
Montreal	DARBON, Ginette	(514)343-7687	274
	SAVARD, Rejean	(514)343-6044	1085
	WALUZYNIEC, Hanna	(514)398-4759	1302

SASKATCHEWAN

North Battleford	RIDLER, Elizabeth A.		1032
Regina	VOHRA, Pran	(306)787-4321	1287

ARGENTINA

Entre Rios	HAMMERLY, Hernan D.		493

AUSTRALIA

Newcastle	NEAME, Roderick L.		891

COSTA RICA

San Jose	CROWTHER, Warren W.		262

CUBA

Havana	ASIS, Moises		36

EGYPT

Giza	MAHOUD ALY, Usama E.		761

ENGLAND

Harrogate	LINE, Maurice B.		730

FRANCE

Paris	ROBERTS, Kenneth H.		1040

HONG KONG

Kowloon	POON, Paul W.		983

IRELAND

Banger	DUFFIN, Elizabeth A.		323

ISRAEL

Birzeit	HADDAD, Aida N.		481
Haifa	WASERMAN, Barbara		1307

STAFF DEVELOPMENT CONSULTANT (Cont'd)

ITALY

Milan	CASIRAGHI, Edoardo		192
	FABRE DE MORLHON, Christiane		360

MEXICO

Nuevo Leon	ARTEAGA, Georgina		35

NETHERLANDS

Amersfoort	VAN HALM, Johan		1275

NIGERIA

Lagos	AFOLAYAN, Matthew A.	(018)001-6040	7

PHILIPPINES

Quezon City	VALLEJO, Rosa M.		1271

SAUDI ARABIA

Riyadh	MANSFIELD, Jerry W.		767

SCOTLAND

Glasgow	HEANEY, Henry J.		518

SOUTH AFRICA

Bedfordview	ARMSTRONG, Denise M.		32
Belhar Cape Province	SEPTEMBER, Peter E.		1115
Pretoria	WILLEMSE, John		1341

TRAINER

ALABAMA

Auburn	JONES, Allen W.	(205)826-4360	610
Birmingham	BRITT, Mary C.	(203)934-4475	137
Decatur	MORRIS, Betty J.	(205)773-6262	866
Mobile	NICHOLS, Amy S.	(205)694-3895	901
Montgomery	FRANKS, Janice	(205)271-6277	398
Tuscaloosa	LEE, Sulan I.	(205)752-6008	711

ALASKA

Delta Junction	JENKS, Arlene I.	(907)895-4253	597
Fairbanks	MUDD, Isabelle G.	(907)479-4522	875
	STEPHENS, Dennis J.	(907)479-5826	1187
Wasilla	TRIDLE, Jeanne A.	(907)376-5188	1256

ARIZONA

Flagstaff	JOHNSON, Harlan R.	(602)523-4408	605
Holbrook	ROTHLISBERG, Allen P.	(602)524-2257	1060
Sedona	CHICOREL, Marietta S.	(601)602-2826	208
Tempe	OETTING, Edward C.	(602)345-7636	917
Tucson	ALURI, Rao	(602)722-5678	19
	CARTER, Judith A.		189
	CROWE, Gloria J.	(602)792-9450	261
	GILREATH, Charles L.	(602)621-4865	437
	GOTHBERG, Helen M.	(602)887-2262	453
	HOLSINGER, Katherine	(602)621-3282	554
	LONG, Carla J.	(602)621-4869	739
	PHIPPS, Shelley E.	(602)621-2101	969
	WILLIAMS, Karen B.	(602)621-4866	1344

ARKANSAS

Prescott	WATSON, Morlyn		1310

CALIFORNIA

Alamo	PIPER, Paula	(412)837-2880	975
Albany	BLITZ, Ruth R.	(415)525-4186	105
	EWEN, Eric P.	(415)527-0894	359
Anaheim	KOGA, James S.	(714)630-0618	668
	WRIGHT, Betty A.	(714)998-1127	1370
Arcata	CROSBY-MUILENBURG, Corryn		260
Ben Lomond	CROWLEY, Terence	(408)336-5019	262
Berkeley	CASTRO, Rafaela G.	(415)526-0815	194
	FALANGA, Rosemarie E.	(415)524-5501	361
	FLUM, Judith G.	(415)486-0378	386
	OGDEN, Barclay W.	(415)642-4946	918
	PISANO, Vivian M.	(415)527-1959	975
	WEEDMAN, Judith	(415)642-9980	1315

TRAINER (Cont'd)
CALIFORNIA (Cont'd)

Berkeley			
	WHEELER, Helen R.	(415)549-2970	1329
	X, Laura	(415)548-1770	1376
Burbank	BROWNE, Jeri A.	(818)953-8770	148
Carmichael	O'NEILL, Diane J.	(916)965-0935	924
	PARSONS, Jerry L.	(916)966-2086	945
Castro Valley	OVERMYER, Elizabeth C.	(415)670-6281	931
Chico	BROWN, Carol G.	(916)861-2762	142
Claremont	ROSE, David L.	(714)624-9041	1054
Corte Madera	FARMER, Lesley S.	(415)924-6633	364
Costa Mesa	POARCH, Margaret E.	(714)662-1867	979
Cupertino	KERSHNER, Lois M.	(408)255-2719	644
Davis	DAVIS, Rebecca A.	(916)752-6204	280
	LEWIS, Alfred J.	(916)752-3325	722
Downey	PAIK, Nan H.	(213)922-4648	935
East Palo Alto	DERKSEN, Charlotte R.	(415)323-5386	294
El Cerrito	KATZ, Jeffrey P.		630
	KIRESEN, Evelyn M.	(415)526-6718	654
Fairfield	GOLD, Anne M.	(707)429-6601	444
Fresno	CARLSON, Alan C.	(209)445-0828	182
Fullerton	BRIL, Patricia L.	(714)773-3852	136
	MASTERS, Robin J.	(714)524-9696	782
Glendale	ECKLUND, Lynn M.	(818)242-2793	335
	PRIME, Eugenie E.	(818)243-5707	993
Hayward	SASSE, Margo	(415)482-2770	1083
Huntington Beach	BAUER, Caroline F.	(714)969-2777	65
	MACKINTOSH, Mary L.	(714)896-4639	757
Irvine	CLARY, Rochelle L.	(714)856-6531	219
	TSENG, Sally C.	(714)856-6832	1260
Kensington	MULVANY, Nancy	(415)524-4195	878
La Jolla	HUCKINS, Barbara W.	(619)453-7500	569
	ZYROFF, Ellen S.	(619)459-1513	1392
Livermore	HUNT, Richard K.	(415)443-5525	575
Long Beach	CONNOLLY, Betty F.	(213)494-5465	237
	WELLS, H L.	(213)598-3549	1322
Los Angeles	DEENEY, Kay E.	(213)479-6672	286
	GILMAN, Lelde B.	(213)825-6498	436
	GRASSIAN, Esther S.	(213)825-2138	458
	HALE, Kaycee	(213)204-0793	485
	JAFFE, Lee D.	(213)935-6770	591
	ROSE, Steven C.	(213)668-0444	1055
	SATER, Analya	(213)277-1969	1083
	SCHOTTLAENDER, Brian E.	(213)825-7785	1099
	STREIKER, Susan L.	(213)738-6727	1201
	SUGRANES, Maria R.	(213)201-3507	1207
	WAGNER, Sharon L.	(213)931-4048	1292
Manhattan Beach	MARKEY, Penny S.	(213)374-1838	771
Modesto	SHAMS, Kamruddin	(209)576-8585	1120
Monterey Park	WANG, Connie	(818)288-5518	1302
Mountain View	ALBUM, Bernie	(415)967-5593	11
Napa	CHAMBERLIN, Leslie A.	(707)253-1071	198
Oakland	SYPERT, Clyde F.	(415)763-6046	1217
Palo Alto	ANDREWS, Chris C.		26
	MAIN, Linda Y.	(415)328-4865	761
Palos Verdes Estates	UEBELE, Dorothy B.	(213)541-2559	1268
Petaluma	GORDON, Ruth I.	(707)778-4719	452
Pleasanton	BUTLER, David W.	(415)846-3308	166
Pomona	IVERSON, Diann S.	(714)624-4728	585
	REMKIEWICZ, Frank L.	(714)623-5251	1022
Rancho Palos Verdes	KATTLOVE, Rose W.	(213)544-0061	630
	WORMINGTON, Peggie		1369
Richmond	RYUS, Joseph E.	(415)222-0846	1072
	TURITZ, Mitch L.	(415)527-5109	1263
	VANDERBERG, Patricia S.	(415)237-1081	1273
Riverside	CUEVAS, John R.	(714)684-4636	263
	KOSHER, Helene J.	(714)787-4628	672
Rowland Heights	SIGLER, Ronald F.	(818)965-9917	1137
Sacramento	ANDERSEN, Thomas K.	(916)324-4863	21
	MCGOVERN, Gail J.	(916)446-2411	807
	SCRIBNER, Ruth B.		1108
	WILLIAMS, Joan F.	(916)927-4953	1344
Salinas	SHAFFER, Dallas Y.	(408)424-3244	1119
San Diego	BUSCH, Barbara	(619)224-8412	165
	HERON, Susan J.	(619)260-4800	532
	HOWARD, Pamela F.		564
	KAYE, Karen	(619)560-2695	632

TRAINER (Cont'd)
CALIFORNIA (Cont'd)

San Diego	SOETE, George J.	(619)453-3538	1165
	VEGA, Carolyn L.		1281
San Francisco	CODER, Ann	(415)442-7000	226
	ELNOR, Nancy G.	(415)929-1948	346
	FOX, Marylou P.	(415)546-8466	395
	GERSH, Barbara S.	(415)346-7882	429
	HAIKALIS, Peter D.	(415)338-2188	484
	JANK, David A.	(415)751-9958	593
	MAH, Jeffery	(415)552-4733	760
	MERRITT, Betty A.	(415)972-4294	827
	MOORE, Gregory B.	(415)753-2645	859
	MORRIS, Effie L.	(415)931-2733	866
	RUNYON, Steven C.	(415)386-5873	1067
	STROMME, Gary L.	(415)972-4293	1203
	TARTER, Blodwen	(415)346-8199	1224
San Luis Obispo	DOBB, Linda S.	(805)756-2389	307
Santa Barbara	FALK, Joyce D.	(805)687-7283	362
	GIBBONS, Carolbeth	(805)961-3320	431
Santa Rosa	HARRIS, Vallena D.		506
Sebastopol	CANT, Elaine N.	(707)823-3214	179
South Gate	BUBOLTZ, Dale D.	(213)567-1431	152
Stanford	WIBLE, Joseph G.	(415)723-1110	1335
Studio City	KAZLAUSKAS, Edward J.	(818)797-7654	632
Thousand Oaks	HOCKEL, Kathleen N.		545
Upland	MOSER, Judith E.	(714)982-8753	871
	THELIN, Sonya R.	(714)982-2336	1234
Valencia	CURZON, Susan C.	(805)259-8946	267
	HUSKEY, Janet S.	(805)259-0783	578
Walnut Creek	BECK, Diane J.	(415)939-9129	71
Westlake Village	TISE, Barbara L.	(818)991-0047	1247
Whittier	RODRIGUEZ, Ronald	(213)693-0585	1048

COLORADO

Aurora	HUGHES, Brad R.	(305)699-6248	571
Boulder	BOUCHER, Virginia P.	(303)492-6176	118
Colorado Springs	DOWLIN, Kenneth E.	(303)635-2236	316
	MALYSHEV, Nina A.	(303)531-6333	764
Denver	BRUNELL, David H.	(303)691-0550	150
	GOODYEAR, Mary L.	(303)556-2683	450
	HENSINGER, James S.	(303)691-0550	529
	KAVANAGH, Janette R.	(303)777-8971	631
	LUEVANE, Marsha A.	(303)989-1036	747
	RAINWATER, Barbara C.	(303)871-6206	1004
Golden	KENNEY, Brigitte L.	(303)278-8482	641
Grand Junction	HENDRICKSON, Charles R.	(303)248-1862	527
	RICHMOND, Elizabeth B.	(303)241-4358	1030
Lakewood	SMITH, Catherine C.	(303)987-2815	1153
Lamar	BURNETT, James H.	(303)336-4632	161
Littleton	ALSOP, Robyn J.	(303)779-1925	18
	STARK, Philip H.	(305)740-7100	1182

CONNECTICUT

Bridgeport	HUGHES, John M.	(203)576-4392	571
Bristol	LEAHY, Michael D.	(203)582-0608	707
	SENKUS, Linda J.	(203)589-1298	1115
Danbury	HORRIGAN, John J.	(203)797-2731	560
Fairfield	WARGO, Peggy M.	(203)259-8267	1305
Guilford	GAFFNEY, Maureen	(203)453-6533	412
Hartford	CORCORAN, Virginia H.	(203)524-2230	246
	PORTER, Kathryn W.	(203)727-4321	985
Middletown	BECK, Arthur R.	(203)347-1387	71
New Britain	TEMPLE, Leroy E.	(203)827-7263	1230
New Canaan	ROCKMAN, Connie C.	(203)972-3731	1046
New Haven	PROSTANO, Emanuel T.	(203)397-4532	995
	SPURGEON, Kathy R.		1176
	SULLIVAN, Maureen	(203)776-3808	1208
New London	VANDERLYKE, Barbara A.	(203)442-2889	1274
Ridgefield	MCMASTER, Deborah L.	(203)798-5574	815
Stamford	DIMATTIA, Susan S.	(203)322-9055	304
Stratford	ROTH, Alison C.	(203)378-8700	1059
Unionville	MOON, Peter S.	(203)675-6675	858
Wallingford	MCGREGOR, M C.	(203)284-6000	808
Waterbury	CARRINGTON, Virginia F.	(203)574-4702	186
	YOUNG, Marianne F.	(203)574-8216	1382
West Hartford	BURGER, Leslie B.	(203)233-0478	159
	HORAK, Ellen B.	(203)233-3164	558
Westport	LOWE, Ida B.	(203)255-8780	743

TRAINER (Cont'd)

CONNECTICUT (Cont'd)

Woodbridge	MILLER, Irene K.	(203)393-0458	838

DELAWARE

Frankford	HITCHENS, Howard B.	(302)539-2420	544
Newark	GLOGOFF, Stuart J.	(302)451-2234	441
Wilmington	DRUKKER, Alexander E.	(302)478-1746	320
	TOMAN, Jocelyn B.		1249

DISTRICT OF COLUMBIA

Washington	ACKERMAN, F C.	(202)398-1842	3
	AUSTIN, Monique C.	(202)546-7236	40
	BELLEFONTAINE, Arnold G.	(202)287-6587	78
	CALLINAN, Ellen M.	(202)624-2838	173
	CANNAN, Judith P.	(202)287-5263	178
	CARTER, Yvonne B.	(202)357-6315	190
	EDWARDS, Andrea Y.	(202)269-3449	337
	GARLICK, Karen	(202)287-5634	419
	GILLESPIE, Veronica M.	(202)287-5262	435
	HORTON, Forest W.		561
	JUROW, Susan R.	(202)232-8656	620
	KOSTINKO, Gail A.	(202)483-4118	673
	LANE, Elizabeth S.		694
	LAWTON, Bethany L.	(202)651-5220	705
	LEE, Amy C.	(202)546-5539	709
	MCGOWAN, Anna T.	(202)245-1235	807
	MILEVSKI, Robert J.	(202)287-5634	834
	MILLER, William S.	(202)775-4080	843
	MUSSEHL, Allan A.	(202)488-8162	883
	NOWAK, Geraldine D.	(202)475-9419	911
	PHELPS, Thomas C.	(202)786-0271	967
	STARCK, William L.	(202)234-6006	1181
	SUNG, Carolyn H.	(202)287-5543	1210
	SWEENEY, June D.	(202)427-1392	1215
	TERRY, Susan N.	(202)332-7120	1232
	TSCHERNY, Alexander	(202)723-5415	1260
	TSCHERNY, Elena	(202)727-1183	1260
	VASLEF, Irene	(202)342-3240	1279
	WEBB, Barbara A.	(202)797-8909	1313
	WILLSON, Elizabeth	(202)745-7722	1349

FLORIDA

Belle Glade	SNODGRASSE, Elaine	(305)996-3453	1163
Brooksville	TORNABENE, Charles	(904)686-9318	1251
Captiva	WALTON, Terence M.	(813)454-0410	1302
Coral Gables	LOWELL, Felice K.	(305)284-2250	744
	ROBAR, Terri J.	(305)284-4706	1038
Coral Springs	KORNITSKY, Judith M.	(305)753-7081	672
Fort Lauderdale	ALGAZE, Selma B.	(305)357-7501	13
	BROWN, Jeanette L.	(305)523-9145	144
Gainesville	BADGER, Lynn C.	(904)392-0342	44
	GOGGIN, Margaret K.	(904)378-8144	444
Jacksonville	FAHNERT, Elizabeth K.	(904)641-8649	361
	SMITH, Linda L.	(904)731-1065	1157
Miami	HALE, Kay K.	(305)271-3678	485
	KASKEY, Sid		629
	LIGHTERMAN, Mark	(305)279-5467	726
	ROVIROSA, Dolores F.		1062
	WRIGHT, Joseph F.	(305)379-3105	1372
Miami Beach	LESNIAK, Rose	(305)673-6309	718
Miami Shores	PINE, Nancy M.	(305)758-3392	974
Naples	BOULA, Lillian Y.		119
Orlando	BRIERTY, Carol A.	(305)275-2564	135
Pensacola	MOREIN, P G.	(904)474-2492	863
Plant City	PINGS, Joan G.	(813)752-3884	974
Ponte Vedra Beach	PECK, Brian T.	(904)246-1400	953
Tampa	EL-HADIDY, Bahaa	(813)974-3520	342
	EYLES, Heberle H.	(813)837-3896	359
	JOHNSTON, Judy F.	(813)974-2162	610
Winter Park	PFARRER, Theodore R.	(305)647-3294	966
Winter Springs	THOMAN, Nancy L.		1236

GEORGIA

Athens	RIEMER, John J.	(404)542-0591	1033
Atlanta	BARNETT, Becky L.	(404)529-3886	57
	DAVIS, Joy V.	(404)634-3511	279
	DEES, Leslie M.	(404)894-4523	287
	HENDRIX, Linda S.	(404)252-5745	527
	VIDOR, Ann B.	(404)894-4523	1283

TRAINER (Cont'd)

GEORGIA (Cont'd)

Decatur	HUGHES, Glenda J.	(404)636-0108	571
	LANDRAM, Christina L.	(404)321-0778	693
Lilburn	HOUGH, Leslie S.	(404)979-0270	562
Valdosta	CLARK, Tommy A.	(912)244-6124	218

HAWAII

Honolulu	GOVERNS, Molly K.		454
	LINVILLE, Marcia L.	(808)737-2511	731
	LUSTER, Arlene L.	(808)737-8876	750
	SHELDEN, Patricia R.	(808)538-6430	1125
	STEPHENS, Diana C.	(808)945-2837	1188
	URAGO, Gail M.	(808)949-6496	1269
Kailua	WRIGHT, John C.	(808)261-3714	1371
Kailua-Kona	KOLMAN, Roberta F.		669
Waiaulua	VEATCH, Laurie L.	(808)237-8411	1280

IDAHO

Moscow	STEINHAGEN, Elizabeth N.	(208)885-6260	1186
Rexburg	HART, Eldon C.	(208)356-4447	507

ILLINOIS

Addison	WRIGHT, Deborah L.	(312)628-3338	1371
Arlington Heights	VONDRUSKA, Eloise M.	(312)392-7232	1288
Beardstown	WEST, L P.	(217)323-5788	1326
Brookfield	IRONS, Carol A.	(312)485-3503	584
Charleston	RAO, Paladugu V.	(217)581-6061	1008
Chicago	BOLT, Janice A.	(312)233-9399	113
	CARLSON, Robert P.	(312)944-6780	182
	CARSON, James G.	(312)996-2742	188
	CHUNG, Alison L.	(312)222-9350	213
	CORNICK, Ron	(312)282-6579	247
	DOWNES, Valerie	(312)871-7559	316
	DUJSIK, Gerald	(312)225-1700	324
	FANG, Min L.	(317)842-0321	363
	FOUSER, Jane G.	(312)477-4712	393
	GLANZ, Lenore M.	(312)528-7817	439
	GRAVES, Karen J.	(312)348-0930	459
	HELGE, Barbara L.	(312)955-4545	524
	JACOBSEN, Teresa T.	(312)266-1265	590
	JAGODZINSKI, Cecile M.	(312)645-4860	591
	KARSTEN, Eileen S.	(312)583-2700	628
	KLEINMUNTZ, Dalia S.	(312)883-3580	660
	MANN, Vijai S.	(312)443-5423	766
	MCCARTNEY, Elizabeth J.	(312)666-8262	794
	MILLER, Thomas R.	(312)769-6159	843
	MOORE, Annie M.	(312)995-2254	858
	MUNOFF, Gerald J.	(312)702-8749	879
	PAIETTA, Ann C.	(312)996-2716	935
	RANDALL, Sara L.		1006
	SEGAL, Joan S.	(312)944-6780	1111
	SHAEVEL, Evelyn F.	(312)944-6780	1118
	SLAWNIAK, Patricia M.	(312)338-7589	1148
	SPARKS, Joanne L.	(312)728-5510	1171
	STRAIT, Constance J.		1199
	VIRGO, Julie A.	(312)751-1454	1285
	WILLIAMS, Charles M.	(312)275-2004	1342
Coal Valley	WALKER, Laura L.	(309)234-5483	1295
De Kalb	HURYCH, Jitka M.	(815)753-1947	578
Des Plaines	BURNS, Marie T.	(312)635-4732	162
Dow	HOLZBERLEIN, Deanne B.	(618)466-3015	555
Downers Grove	MIFFLIN, Michael J.	(312)963-9285	833
East Peoria	WILFORD, Valerie J.	(309)694-4389	1339
Elgin	FORD, Jennifer D.	(312)742-1040	389
Evanston	BRADY, Mary M.	(312)491-2929	127
	DAVIDSON, Lloyd A.	(312)491-2906	276
	ROOSE, Tina	(312)491-0662	1053
Evergreen Park	SOBKOWIAK, Emily J.	(312)425-1886	1165
Fox River Grove	CORCORAN, Frances E.	(312)639-5306	245
Glen Ellyn	FRADKIN, Bernard	(312)416-1199	395
Glenview	MARTINAZZI, Toni	(657)775-6000	779
Hinsdale	CZARNECKI, Cary J.	(312)986-1976	268
Lake Forest	MARSHALL, Deborah M.	(312)234-9220	774
	MIKOLYZK, Thomas A.	(312)295-6247	834
Lombard	EGAN, Elizabeth M.	(312)627-7130	338
Moline	KRAMER, Pamela K.	(309)797-5117	675
Oak Lawn	IHRIG, Alice B.		581
	ROCHE, Richard G.	(312)423-7110	1046
Oak Park	PAPPALARDO, Marcia J.	(312)848-5035	939

TRAINER (Cont'd)
ILLINOIS (Cont'd)

Park Forest	OCHSNER, Renata E.	(312)748-5374	915
	SHANNON, Kathleen L.	(312)481-1891	1120
Park Ridge	KNARZER, Arlene	(312)692-9550	663
	LOFTHOUSE, Patricia A.	(312)698-9731	737
River Forest	LI, Richard T.	(312)366-2490	725
Riverdale	PATEL, Jashu	(312)849-3959	947
Rockford	ROSENFELD, Joel C.	(815)965-6731	1056
St Charles	MORRISON, Carol J.	(312)377-2499	868
Springfield	BERK, Robert A.	(217)782-2658	87
	KELLEY, Rhona S.	(217)782-2658	636
Urbana	LOOMIS, Barbara	(217)333-7496	740
	RUBIN, Richard E.	(217)333-3280	1065
	WAJENBERG, Arnold S.	(217)333-6411	1293
	WILSON, Lizabeth A.	(217)333-3489	1351
Wauconda	SHENASSA, Daryoosh	(312)526-9123	1126
Wheaton	WALSH, Deborah T.	(312)653-1115	1299
Wilmette	MCGINN, Thomas P.	(312)256-5596	806

INDIANA

Bloomington	COPLER, Judith A.	(812)335-9255	244
	HENSON, Jane E.	(812)336-8288	529
	MURPHY, Marcy	(812)335-5113	881
	POPP, Mary F.	(812)335-9857	984
	SHAABAN, Marian F.	(812)335-6924	1118
Charlestown	WHALEY, Janie B.	(812)256-6363	1328
Evansville	TEUBERT, Lola H.	(812)428-8229	1233
Fort Wayne	DEANE, Paul D.	(219)424-7241	284
	WEICK, Robert J.	(219)478-1018	1316
Highland	ENGELBERT, Peter J.	(219)923-2173	348
Hobart	HUNT, Margaret M.	(219)962-1103	575
Indianapolis	ALLEN, Joyce S.	(317)929-8021	15
	BONNER, Robert J.	(317)283-7362	114
	BRADLEY, Johanna	(317)751-3779	126
	BRAHMI, Frances A.	(317)274-1401	127
	GILL, John H.	(317)872-2045	435
	GOODWIN, Vania M.	(317)274-0491	450
	GRIFFITTS, Joan K.	(317)297-3283	469
Lafayette	COLLINS, Mary E.		233
	TROUTNER, Joanne J.	(317)477-7306	1258
Mishawaka	STRATTON, Martha G.	(219)255-5262	1200
Muncie	BEILKE, Patricia F.	(317)284-2457	75
Terre Haute	KYKER, Penelope R.	(812)237-2540	685
West Lafayette	ADDISON, Paul H.	(317)463-2511	6
	HEWISON, Nancy S.	(317)463-0904	535
Westfield	VAN CAMP, Ann J.	(317)896-3537	1272

IOWA

Ames	SCHMIDT, Sandra L.	(515)292-1118	1096
Coralville	PEPETONE, Diane S.	(319)351-3922	957
Denver	DUTCHER, Terry R.	(319)984-6120	329
Iowa City	HAUSMAN, Julie	(319)337-1786	513
	NICKELSBURG, Marilyn M.	(319)351-2072	902
Vinton	SHEPHERD, Rex L.	(319)472-4721	1127

KANSAS

Derby	MATTOX, Rosemary S.	(316)268-5979	786
Fairway	CARVER, Jane W.	(913)236-8688	191
Hutchinson	HAWKINS, Paul J.	(316)663-5441	514
Leawood	LUNG, Mon Y.	(913)864-3025	748
Manhattan	MORELAND, Rachel S.	(913)539-8713	863
Overland Park	OJALA, Marydee P.		919
Topeka	CARROLL, James K.	(913)273-9156	187
	VOSS, Ernestine D.	(913)269-3296	1289
Wichita	BRADEN, Jan	(316)686-5954	125

KENTUCKY

Florence	BRATCHER, Perry R.	(606)371-5875	129
Frankfort	COOPER, Judy L.	(502)564-2672	243
Highland Heights	BREDEMEYER, Carol	(606)572-5395	131
	SCHULTZ, Lois E.	(606)572-5275	1102
Lexington	WALDHART, Thomas J.	(606)257-3771	1294
Louisville	BLACKBURN-FOSTER, Brenda	(502)582-4111	102
	LINCOLN, Carol S.	(502)568-7683	728
Maple Mount	BUSAM, Emma C.	(502)229-4103	164
Murray	BUSER, Robin A.	(502)762-2393	165

TRAINER (Cont'd)
LOUISIANA

Alexandria	JARRED, Ada D.	(312)445-5230	594
Baton Rouge	HOGAN, Sharon A.	(504)388-2217	549
	PERRAULT, Anna H.	(504)924-5790	959
	SMITH, Richard J.	(504)342-4942	1160
Lafayette	KREAMER, Jean T.	(318)231-6780	677
Lake Charles	CUROL, Helen B.	(318)477-1780	266
Metairie	SALVATORE, Gayle E.	(504)456-2660	1078
Saint Amant	HILL, Sue A.		540

MAINE

Alfred	ANDERSON, Marjorie E.	(207)324-6915	24
Boothbay	SEELEY, Catherine R.		1111
East Sebago	AIREY, Martha R.	(207)787-2817	9
Georgetown	LUDGIN, Donald H.	(207)371-2221	746
Lewiston	GROSS, Richard F.	(207)782-3958	472
York	HARMON, James R.	(207)363-7833	502

MARYLAND

Abingdon	ANDERSON, Della L.	(301)679-5720	22
Adelphi	YOST, F D.	(301)439-8544	1381
Baldwin	WASIELEWSKI, Eleanor B.	(301)557-7293	1308
Baltimore	ARRINGTON, Susan J.	(301)396-4042	34
	BLUTE, Mary R.	(301)889-4080	107
	CHELTON, Mary K.	(301)355-0906	204
	FREDENBURG, Anne M.	(301)377-9080	399
	GENUARDI, Michael T.	(301)235-1168	427
	HEISER, Jane C.	(301)396-5470	523
	HILDITCH, Bonny M.	(301)675-4333	539
	HOOFNAGLE, Bettea J.	(301)522-5447	556
	LANDRY, Mary E.	(301)235-8067	693
	MONTGOMERY, Paula K.	(301)685-8621	856
	PARTRIDGE, James C.	(301)664-4301	945
	SATTERTHWAITE, Rebecca K.	(301)955-3410	1084
	SMITH, Mary P.	(301)358-0356	1158
	STEPHAN, Sandra S.	(301)333-2118	1187
	TOOEY, Mary J.	(301)744-0521	1250
	WALLER, Madalyn M.	(301)342-3521	1298
	ZIMMERMAN, Martha B.	(301)668-5744	1389
Bethesda	HAWK, Susan A.	(301)897-8367	513
	MENNELLA, Dona M.	(301)652-0106	824
	TIFFT, Jeanne D.	(301)229-7415	1244
Bowie	EVANS, Frank B.	(301)464-8829	357
Cabin John	ROBINSON, Barbara M.	(301)320-6011	1043
Catonsville	STERLING, Judith K.	(301)455-3468	1189
Chevy Chase	GOLDSBERG, Elizabeth D.		446
	KENTON, Charlotte	(301)657-3855	642
College Park	MARCHIONINI, Gary J.	(301)454-3235	769
Columbia	DIENER, Carol W.	(301)381-2525	302
	DIENER, Richard A.	(301)381-2525	302
	DOVE, Samuel	(301)964-4189	315
	WOLTER, John A.	(301)730-6692	1362
Eldersburg	DAVIS, Denise	(301)795-3520	278
Fallston	SACK, Jean C.	(301)877-2825	1073
Frederick	BANKS, Jane L.	(301)695-6726	54
	KINNA, Dorothy H.	(301)898-5212	652
	NATHANSON, David	(301)662-4499	889
Gaithersburg	GROCKI, Daniel J.	(301)253-6044	471
	VAN BRUNT, Virginia	(301)762-6701	1272
Gamber	BOGAGE, Alan R.	(301)795-6167	110
Germantown	BUCHAN, Patricia C.	(301)540-1515	153
Glen Burnie	HACKMAN, Mary H.	(301)768-2569	481
Grasonville	SCHNEIDER, Karl R.	(301)827-9339	1097
Hillcrest Heights	CHAPMAN, Elwynda K.	(301)894-0963	202
Hyattsville	COOPER, Judith C.	(301)699-3500	243
	LOSINSKI, Julia M.	(301)699-3500	742
Kensington	CHAPUT, Linda J.	(703)683-8184	202
Laurel	BARKER, Lillian H.	(301)776-2260	56
	GOLDENBERG, Joan M.	(301)953-9253	445
	LEVINE, Emil H.	(301)776-3062	720
	SWEETLAND, Loraine F.	(801)490-8231	1215
Lusby	HUMMEL, Janice A.	(301)586-2200	573
Mount Airy	LISTON, David M.	(301)831-3008	732
New Market	WILSON, Susan W.	(301)831-6118	1353
Reisterstown	BRADLEY, Wanda L.		126
Rockville	HERIN, Nancy J.	(301)279-6101	531
	MARTINEZ-GOLDMAN, Aline		779
	WALL, Eugene	(301)881-4990	1297

TRAINER (Cont'd)

MARYLAND (Cont'd)

St Marys City	REPENNING, Julie A.	(301)862-0267	1023
Severna Park	COURSON, M S.	(301)647-5522	251
	FELDMAN, Eleanor C.	(301)647-6673	369
Silver Spring	BLIXRUD, Julia C.	(301)622-1904	105
	HARBISON, John H.	(801)589-4223	499
	HENDERSON, Ronald L.	(301)588-2844	527
	JACKSON, Carleton	(301)890-8594	587
	KADEC, Sarah T.	(301)598-7694	621
	RICHARD, Sheila A.	(301)438-4555	1028
	VAN CAMPEN, Rebecca J.	(301)890-8588	1272
Solomons	HEIL, Kathleen A.	(301)326-2967	521
Takoma Park	WRIGHT, Arthuree M.	(301)445-1220	1370
Upper Marlboro	HARBERT, Cathy E.	(301)868-9280	499
Upperco	RAND, Pamela S.	(301)429-2958	1006
Welcome	DUDLEY, Robyn A.	(301)934-4602	323
Wheaton	KAESSINGER, Carla S.	(301)949-1477	621

MASSACHUSETTS

Assonet	MEDEIROS, Joseph	(617)624-4094	820
Boston	ANDERSON, A J.	(617)738-2230	21
	BRITE, Agnes	(617)267-0369	137
	CAIN, Susan H.	(617)338-6553	171
	KORT, Richard L.	(617)266-3646	672
	MCCARTHY, Germaine A.	(617)742-3958	794
	O'TOOLE, James M.	(617)929-8110	930
	PRISTASH, Kenneth	(617)262-1120	993
	SCHATZ, Cindy A.	(617)732-2134	1090
	SCHWARTZ, Candy S.	(617)738-2223	1104
	SCHWARTZ, Frederick E.	(617)522-0234	1104
Brookline	SOVNER-RIBBLER, Judith	(617)277-2991	1170
Burlington	MCLAUGHLIN, Lee R.	(617)272-5772	813
Carlisle	HAMILTON, Fae K.	(617)369-1981	492
Dedham	LOSCALZO, Anita B.	(617)329-3964	741
Dover	WINQUIST, Elaine W.	(617)785-0816	1355
Lexington	PRUSAK, Laurence	(617)861-7580	996
Lincoln	COHEN, Martha J.	(413)259-9500	228
Marlborough	FERGUSON, Roberta J.	(617)481-5866	372
Medford	SCHATZ, Natalie M.	(617)381-3273	1090
Milton	OPPENHEIM, Roberta A.	(617)698-6268	925
Mount Hermon	LANGE, Clare M.	(413)498-5311	695
Needham Heights	ORENSTEIN, Ruth M.		925
Newton	CUNNINGHAM, Robert L.	(617)969-0400	265
	WALLAS, Philip R.	(617)527-1762	1298
Newtonville	INGERSOLL, Diane S.	(612)438-3978	582
North Abington	LAROSA, Sharon M.	(617)871-6288	698
Reading	MARCY, Henry O.	(617)944-2194	769
Revere	TATELMAN, Susan D.	(617)284-0154	1225
Roybury	SUTTON, Joyce A.	(617)427-4941	1211
Somerville	FELDT, Candice K.	(617)666-2745	369
Waltham	CHATTERTON, Leigh A.	(617)893-4807	204
Wellesley Hills	KENNEDY, Amy J.	(617)237-4013	640
Williamsburg	O'BRIEN, Marjorie S.	(413)268-7131	914
Winchester	KEATS, Susan E.	(617)729-9317	633
Worcester	NOAH, Carolyn B.	(617)799-1655	906

MICHIGAN

Ann Arbor	BEAUBIEN, Anne K.	(313)763-5060	70
	MOSEY, Jeanette	(313)973-8607	871
	SCHWARTZ, Diane G.	(313)763-2037	1104
	SLAVENS, Thomas P.	(313)665-6663	1148
	SMILLIE, Pauline A.	(313)665-0021	1151
	WILSON, Amy S.	(313)761-4700	1349
	WISE, Virginia J.	(313)663-5674	1357
	YOCUM, Patricia B.	(313)995-4644	1380
Berrien Springs	WALLER, Elaine J.	(616)473-3651	1298
Cedar Springs	RANSOM-BERGSTROM, Janette F.	(616)696-3428	1008
Dearborn	REID, Valerie L.	(313)278-1307	1019
Detroit	BARTKOWSKI, Patricia	(313)577-4024	61
	MA, Helen Y.	(313)833-1016	753
East Lansing	ACKERMAN, Katherine K.	(517)332-6818	4
	JIZBA, Laurel	(517)353-4526	600
	YARBROUGH, Joseph W.	(517)337-0693	1378
Farmington Hills	ROBBINS, Lora A.	(313)661-6957	1039
Grosse Pointe Park	TOLMAN, Bonnie B.	(313)885-0764	1249
Haslett	OLIVER, James W.	(517)339-0846	921

TRAINER (Cont'd)

MICHIGAN (Cont'd)

Kalamazoo	CARROLL, Hardy	(616)383-1926	187
	EVERITT, Janet M.	(616)385-7579	359
	RIZZO, John R.	(616)381-1323	1037
Lansing	CONWAY, Michael J.		239
	EZELL, Charlaine L.	(517)485-8019	360
Livonia	CHAKLOSH, Cynthia L.		197
Mt Clemens	CUNNINGHAM, Tina Y.	(313)286-5750	265
Northville	ROCKALL, Diane M.	(313)349-9005	1046
Romeo	NOWICKE, Carole E.	(313)752-6664	911
Southfield	SUMMERS, Sheryl H.	(313)357-0404	1209
Sturgis	BERKLUND, Nancy J.	(616)651-9361	87
Traverse City	SICILIANO, Peg P.	(616)947-1480	1135
Trenton	GREEN, Katherine A.		462
Ypsilanti	YEE, Sandra G.	(313)487-2220	1379

MINNESOTA

Eden Prairie	BILEYDI, Lois G.	(612)934-3576	96
Golden Valley	COLE, Jack W.		230
Mankato	BIRMINGHAM, Frank R.	(507)389-5210	98
Minneapolis	BEDOR, Kathleen M.	(612)823-3945	73
	BRANIN, Joseph J.	(612)624-5518	128
	OBERMAN, Cerise G.	(612)624-4520	914
	PANKAKE, Marcia J.	(612)331-2551	938
	ROSSMAN, Muriel J.	(612)624-4002	1059
	SANDNESS, John G.	(612)866-7033	1081
New Brighton	KEIM, Robert	(612)633-3393	635
Northfield	BRUCE, Robert K.	(507)645-9279	149
Rochester	HAWTHORNE, Dorothy M.	(507)284-8797	514
Saint Joseph	HYNES, Arleen M.		580
St Paul	ANDERSON, Rebekah E.	(612)733-9057	25
	CLARKE, Charlotte C.	(612)645-7359	218
	DAVIS, Emmett A.	(612)699-4367	279
	HARWOOD, Karen L.	(612)690-6653	510
	MAHMOODI, Suzanne H.		760
	STOKES, Claire Z.	(612)642-0120	1196
Scandia	HANSEN, Kathelen L.	(612)433-5477	497

MISSISSIPPI

Biloxi	VANCE, Mary L.		1273
Brandon	SELTZER, Ada M.		1114
Hattiesburg	LATOUR, Terry S.	(601)266-4345	701
Starkville	NETTLES, Jess	(601)323-5558	896

MISSOURI

Columbia	LENOX, Mary F.	(314)882-4546	715
Kansas City	DRAYSON, Pamela K.	(816)753-7600	318
	GARDNER, Laura L.	(816)741-4070	418
	LINSE, Mary M.	(816)765-0831	731
	MARCHANT, Thomas O.	(816)761-8873	768
	MILLS, Elaine L.	(816)333-1245	844
	RUBY, Carolyn M.		1065
Liberty	HOOVER, Jonnette L.	(816)781-7812	557
Maryville	MURPHY, Kathryn L.	(816)582-4768	880
Richmond	WALKER, Patricia A.	(816)776-2226	1296
Saint Joseph	ELLIOTT, Dorothy G.	(816)232-7729	344
St Louis	ELSESSER, Lionelle H.	(314)725-4722	346
	HELMS, Mary E.	(314)362-2787	525
	NOBLE, Barbara N.	(314)367-6324	906
	REHKOP, Barbara L.		1017
	WEITKEMPER, Larry D.	(314)353-6757	1320
Springfield	DUCKWORTH, Paul M.	(417)866-6978	322

MONTANA

Bozeman	BREMER, Thomas A.	(406)994-5295	132
	BRUWELHEIDE, Janis H.	(406)587-0405	151
	STACK, Laurie A.	(406)994-5310	1177
Great Falls	O'BRYANT, Alice A.		915

NEBRASKA

Lincoln	LEITER, Richard A.	(402)466-3468	714
Omaha	BROWN, Helen A.	(402)559-4326	144
	EARLEY, Dorothy A.	(402)333-5734	332

TRAINER (Cont'd)

NEVADA

Carson City	KERSCHNER, Joan G.	(702)887-2615	644
Henderson	TRASATTI, Margaret S.	(702)733-3613	1254
Las Vegas	HEATON, Shelley J.	(702)739-3512	519
	MORGAN, James E.	(702)384-4887	864
	WELLS, David B.	(702)733-3641	1322

NEW HAMPSHIRE

Concord	JOHNSON, Jean G.	(603)271-2429	605
Franconia	BJORNER, Susan N.	(603)823-8838	100
Hanover	ROLETT, Virginia V.	(603)643-3593	1051
Manchester	KENT, Jeffrey A.	(603)622-4408	642
	MCGINNIS, Joan M.	(603)624-4366	806
Nashua	EMOND, Kathleen A.		348
Peterborough	BOND, George	(603)924-9281	113
Twin Mountain	PALMATIER, Susan M.	(603)846-2239	936
Washington	HAMILL, Martha L.	(603)495-3994	491

NEW JERSEY

Basking Ridge	THOMPSON, Melia M.	(201)953-3326	1240
Butler	GARDNER, Sue A.	(201)838-3262	418
Cherry Hill	BECK, Susan J.	(609)354-7638	72
	BENSON, James A.	(609)354-7638	83
Cranford	HALL, Homer J.	(201)276-4311	488
Delanco	WOLFORD, Larry E.	(609)461-5667	1361
Dover	RYAN, Mary E.	(201)989-3079	1071
East Brunswick	TANG, Grace L.		1222
Elizabeth	LATINI, Samuel A.	(201)354-6060	701
Fort Lee	THIRD, Bettie J.	(201)461-6511	1235
Hoboken	SOLOMON, Geri E.	(201)420-8364	1166
Irvington	KNIGHT, Shirley D.	(201)371-9324	664
Kearny	HAWLEY, George S.	(201)997-5299	514
Lodi	KARETZKY, Stephen	(201)778-1190	627
Mahwah	MAYDET, Steven I.		789
Millburn	URKEN, Madeline	(201)379-2306	1270
Montclair	BROWN, Cynthia D.	(201)783-6420	142
New Brunswick	ANSELMO, Edith H.	(201)247-5610	28
	RUBEN, Brent D.	(201)932-7447	1064
Oceanport	WAITE, William F.	(201)542-7216	1293
Paramus	CESARD, Mary A.	(201)444-4389	196
Patterson	SAWYER, Miriam		1086
Pennington	KAZIMIR, Edward O.	(609)737-3582	632
Princeton	BAKES, Floy L.	(609)520-4631	50
	PASTER, Luisa R.	(609)452-5464	946
	THRESHER, Jacquelyn E.	(609)924-9529	1243
Saddle Brook	AUGHEY, Kathleen M.		39
Spring Lake	GARVEY, Nancy G.	(201)449-4673	421
Stratford	AVENICK, Karen	(609)784-8977	41
Upper Saddle River	DUDLEY, Debbra C.	(201)327-4006	323
	MICHAELS, Debbie D.	(201)327-5006	832
Voorhees	ROMISHER, Sivya S.	(609)772-1636	1053
West Milford	COURTNEY, Aida N.	(201)728-2823	251
West New York	BRITTON, Jeffrey W.	(201)868-2029	137
Woodbridge	SPANGLER, William N.	(201)634-4450	1171

NEW MEXICO

Albuquerque	KALE, Shirley W.	(505)298-5980	623
	KRUG, Ruth A.	(505)277-7213	680
	WHITLOW, Cherrill M.	(505)266-1472	1333
Farmington	JASSAL, Raghbir S.	(505)327-7813	595

NEW YORK

Albany	WALKER, M G.	(518)436-1975	1296
Alfred	CONNOLLY, Bruce E.	(607)871-2494	237
Amawalk	HANE, Paula J.	(914)962-2933	495
APO New York	NEUWILLER, Charlene		897
Armonk	DEVERS, Charlotte M.	(914)273-3887	297
Bayside	SHER, Deborah M.	(718)225-3435	1127
Briarwood	BORRESS, Lewis R.	(718)441-6328	117
Bronx	BARNETT, Philip	(212)549-5359	58
	CANNATA, Arleen	(212)295-5910	178
	LOCASCIO, Aline M.	(212)588-8400	735
	ROY, Diptimoy	(914)668-1840	1063
	SOPELAK, Mary J.	(212)588-2266	1168
Bronxville	HUEBNER, Mary A.	(914)337-9300	570
Brooklundy	HAMILTON, Reatha B.		492

TRAINER (Cont'd)

NEW YORK (Cont'd)

Brooklyn	BRANDEAU, John H.	(718)852-8700	128
	CANDELMO, Emily		178
	DINDAYAL, Joyce S.	(718)647-1624	304
	ESSIEN, Victor K.	(718)941-9020	354
	GENCO, Barbara A.	(718)499-8750	426
	GOODMAN, Rhonna A.	(718)965-2523	449
	HOMMEL, Claudia	(718)237-0028	555
	ROMALIS, Carl		1052
	SCHWABACHER, Sara A.	(718)388-0023	1104
	STRAM, Lynn R.	(718)434-7815	1200
	TUDIVER, Lillian	(718)789-7220	1262
Buffalo	ELLISON, John W.	(716)636-3069	345
	PERONE, Karen L.	(716)883-7000	959
	YERKEY, A N.	(716)636-3069	1380
Circleville	NELSON, James B.	(914)361-2415	894
Clarence Ctr	CHAPMAN, Renee D.	(716)741-9644	202
Cold Spring Harbor	FARAONE, Maria R.	(516)271-1771	363
Corona	KINYATTI, Njoki W.	(718)592-4782	653
Dewitt	ELY, Donald P.	(315)446-0259	347
East Meadow	CANDE, Lorraine N.	(516)794-1202	178
	MCCARTNEY, Margaret M.	(516)489-8136	794
Elmhurst	HSU, Elizabeth L.	(718)271-6623	567
	SALEY, Stacey		1076
Flushing	SAFRAN, Scott A.	(718)445-6752	1074
Forest Hills	WIENER, Sylvia B.	(718)263-9469	1336
Glen Falls	GRAMINSKI, Denise M.	(518)793-2927	457
Greenvale	YUKAWA, Masako	(516)299-2142	1384
Hicksville	EDWARDS, Harriet M.		337
Huntington	FALVEY, Genemary H.	(516)673-0015	363
	FOLCARELLI, Ralph J.	(516)271-0634	387
Ithaca	COONS, William W.	(607)255-7959	242
Jackson Heights	SPYROS, Marsha L.	(718)424-7849	1177
Jamaica Estates	BARTENBACH, Wilhelm K.	(718)658-3878	60
Larchmont	GILLIGAN, Julie		436
Long Beach	WASSERMAN, Ricki F.		1308
Long Island City	MARTIN, Brian G.	(718)726-5885	775
Lynbrook	HAYES, Jude T.	(516)887-2493	516
Macedon	WEMETT, Lisa C.	(315)986-3949	1323
Manlius	NAGLE, Ann	(315)682-8160	886
Mt Vernon	EARLE, Marcia H.		332
	OCKENE, David L.	(914)699-0949	915
New Windsor	SANKER, Paul N.	(914)562-0470	1081
New York	ARTHUR, Christine	(212)732-5964	35
	BERNAL, Rose M.	(212)674-6525	88
	BRAUDE, Robert M.	(212)472-5919	129
	BUTLER, Tyrone G.	(212)566-5367	167
	CIOPPA, Lawrence	(212)677-5688	214
	CURTIS, James A.	(212)222-9638	267
	DENNIS, Anne R.	(212)645-4500	292
	DEVERA, Rosalinda M.	(212)557-2570	297
	ELLIS, Peter K.	(212)222-3274	345
	ETZI, Richard		356
	FONTAINE, Sue	(212)533-7226	388
	FREIFELD, Roberta I.	(212)777-9271	401
	GREENBERG, Charles J.	(212)663-5526	463
	HAND, Sally C.	(212)940-3100	494
	HUNTER, Gregory S.	(212)940-1690	576
	KENDRIC, Marisa A.	(212)725-4550	640
	KENDRICK, Alice M.	(212)532-6350	640
	KILBERG, Jacqueline L.	(212)536-3562	648
	MACK, Phyllis G.	(212)926-2479	756
	MOORE, Sonia	(212)755-5120	861
	NATHAN, Frances E.	(212)876-0269	889
	NESTA, Frederick N.	(212)982-9672	896
	PALMER, Julia R.	(212)744-7202	936
	PELLOWSKI, Anne	(212)316-1170	955
	PERRY, Claudia A.	(212)876-8200	960
	POLLARD, Bobbie T.	(212)725-7648	981
	PRAVER, Robin I.	(212)214-1720	990
	QUAIN, Julie R.		999
	RAUCH, Anne	(212)906-8794	1010
	REID, Carolyn A.	(212)472-5919	1018
	RIVERA, Gregorio	(212)340-0949	1037
	SALVAGE, Barbara A.	(212)998-2463	1078
	SCHUMAN, Patricia G.	(212)925-8650	1103
	VAUGHAN, John	(212)924-3729	1279
	WOO, Janice	(212)662-3534	1363
North Chatham	WELLS, Gladysann		1322

TRAINER (Cont'd)
NEW YORK (Cont'd)

Oneonta	CHIANG, Nancy	(607)432-4200	207
Peekskill	SALUSTRI, Madeline	(914)739-2823	1077
Rhinebeck	NAVRATIL, Jean		890
Ridge	KINNEY, Daniel W.	(516)924-7338	653
Riverdale	CLANCY, Kathy	(212)796-2057	215
Rochester	BAILEY, Joe A.	(716)724-0212	46
	BALKIN, Ruth G.	(716)482-1506	52
	HUNT, Suellyn	(716)428-6981	575
	JUNION, Gail J.	(716)275-4496	620
	KATZ, Jacqueline E.	(716)254-7144	630
	REITANO, Maimie V.	(716)722-7067	1022
Saratoga Springs	RATZER, Mary B.		1010
Sayville	PAGELS, Helen H.	(516)589-2908	934
Scarsdale	BERGER, Pam P.	(914)723-3156	86
	COAN, Mary L.	(914)723-5325	224
Syracuse	EISENBERG, Michael B.	(315)423-4549	340
	KATZER, Jeffrey	(315)423-2911	630
	MCCLURE, Charles R.	(315)423-2911	797
Troy	BLANDY, Susan G.	(518)274-2098	104
Uniondale	BARTENBACH, Martha A.	(516)292-8920	60
West Nyack	SIVULICH, Sandra S.	(914)358-9298	1145
White Plains	DAVIES, Carol A.	(212)754-7438	277
	TREFRY, Mary G.	(914)761-5478	1255
Whitestone	RIECHEL, Rosemarie	(718)990-0714	1033
Willow	LOWE, Mildred	(914)679-6222	744
Yonkers	SIKORSKI, Charlene S.	(914)968-2674	1137

NORTH CAROLINA

Beulaville	FRAZELLE, Betty	(919)298-4658	399
Cedar Grove	WRIGHT, Larry L.		1372
Chapel Hill	MATER, Dee A.	(919)962-0700	783
	MEEHAN-BLACK, Elizabeth C.		821
Charlotte	MYERS, Carol B.	(704)523-1260	884
Durham	BOMARC, M D.	(919)683-6244	113
	FEINGLOS, Susan J.	(919)493-2904	369
	LAVINE, Marcia M.	(919)684-2011	703
	MIDDLETON, Beverly D.	(919)477-8497	833
	NYE, Julie B.	(919)471-1833	912
	SEMONCHE, Barbara P.	(919)489-7247	1115
Fairview	HUTTON, Jean R.	(704)628-1453	579
Greensboro	RANCER, Susan P.	(919)288-2160	1006
Greenville	DODGE, Michael R.		308
Kinston	MILLER, Sylvia G.		843
Matthews	CANNON, Robert E.	(704)847-0394	179
Raleigh	OSEGUEDA, Laura M.	(919)834-1024	927
	SMITH, Catherine	(919)851-4703	1153
Robbinsville	LARSON, Josephine	(704)479-8192	699
Sanford	MURCHISON, Margaret B.	(919)258-3277	879
Winston-Salem	RODNEY, Mae L.	(919)924-6992	1048

OHIO

Albany	CONLIFFE, Bobbi L.	(614)698-3336	236
Athens	HOUDEK, G R.	(614)593-5444	562
Bowling Green	REPP, Joan M.		1024
Canton	CLARK, Kay S.	(216)452-0665	217
	ERWIN, Nancy S.	(216)477-7309	353
Cincinnati	BAKER, Carole A.	(513)871-2042	48
	DICKMAN, Emmajane H.		301
	LIPPERT, Margret G.	(513)821-8733	732
	WILSON, Lucy	(513)745-4313	1351
Cleveland	DRACH, Priscilla I		318
	DZIEDZINA, Christine A.	(216)459-4313	331
	LOWELL, Virginia L.	(216)398-1800	744
Cleveland Heights	BOWIE, Angela B.	(216)291-5588	121
Columbus	BAYER, Bernard I.	(614)292-7895	67
	CHESKI, Richard M.	(614)462-6843	207
	KNOBLAUCH, Carol J.	(614)299-4020	665
	SMITH, Noralee W.	(614)299-0453	1159
	WAGNER, Judith O.	(614)451-7471	1292
	WILKS, Cheri L.	(614)253-3507	1341
Cuyahoga Falls	KLINGLER, Thomas E.	(216)923-5504	662
Dayton	BUCK, Jeremy R.	(513)227-9500	153
	COYLE, Christopher B.	(513)865-6882	253
	PURSCH, Lenore D.	(513)434-7064	998
	SEXTON, Sally V.	(513)890-1421	1118
Delaware	COHEN, Susan J.	(614)363-9433	229

TRAINER (Cont'd)
OHIO (Cont'd)

Dublin	HAYNES, Kathleen J.	(614)764-6000	516
	HURLEY, Geraldine C.	(614)764-6108	577
	MARSH, Elizabeth C.	(614)488-1942	773
	SCHUITEMA, Joan E.	(614)761-8827	1101
Fairborn	BAKER, Narcissa L.	(573)879-3638	49
Fairfield	LUCAS, Jean M.	(513)829-5227	746
Kent	GATTEN, Jeffrey N.	(216)672-2516	422
	NELSON, Olga G.	(216)678-8236	895
Lakewood	TAYLOR, Patricia L.	(216)226-8275	1228
Middlefield	GUMPPER, Mary F.	(216)632-1961	477
Middletown	PALMER, Virginia E.	(513)424-4263	937
Mogadore	SMITH, Cynthia A.	(216)678-0662	1153
Powell	RUSH, James E.	(614)881-5949	1068
Steubenville	BURKE, Ambrose L.	(614)283-3771	160
Toledo	HANNAFORD, Claudia L.	(419)536-7539	496
Upper Arlington	GRIEVE, Shelley	(614)442-1073	468
Westlake	GALLANT, Jennifer J.	(216)835-6020	414
Xenia	WALDER, Antoinette L.	(513)376-2995	1294
Yellow Springs	WESTNEAT, Helen C.	(513)767-1574	1327

OKLAHOMA

Ada	COULTER, Cynthia M.	(405)332-8000	251
Edmond	ALSWORTH, Frances N.	(405)341-2980	18
Norman	WEAVER-MEYERS, Pat L.	(405)325-3341	1313
Oklahoma City	DAVIS, Denyvetta	(405)424-2106	278
	SAULMON, Sharon A.	(405)634-3181	1084
Tahlequah	PATTERSON, Lotsee	(918)456-6882	948

OREGON

Ashland	PURCELL, V N.	(503)482-2629	998
Beaverton	JACOBS, Patt	(503)646-6959	590
Bend	BYRNE, Helen E.	(503)382-1621	169
Coos Bay	TASHJIAN, Sharon A.	(503)267-5605	1224
Eugene	GRIFFIN, Karen D.	(503)686-3064	468
	HILDEBRAND, Carol I.	(503)344-4267	538
Monmouth	JENSEN, Gary D.	(503)838-1220	598
Philomath	REEVES, Marjorie A.	(503)929-5354	1017
Portland	BURSON, Lorraine E.	(508)246-4097	163
	EDWARDS, Susan E.	(506)224-6812	338
	FELDMAN, Marianne L.	(503)292-2940	369
	SHAVER, Donna B.	(503)226-8695	1123
	SIMON, Dale	(503)227-7617	1140
Roseburg	GAULKE, Mary F.	(503)440-4036	423

PENNSYLVANIA

Allentown	ANDEL, June	(215)395-5168	21
	IOBST, Barbara J.	(215)778-2263	583
	SWARTZ, Patrice B.	(215)797-5696	1214
Bala Cynwyd	CORVESE, Lisa A.	(215)668-4930	248
Belle Vernon	KLEIN, Joanne S.	(412)929-8290	659
Berwyn	BROWN, David E.	(215)644-5241	143
Camp Hill	ALBRECHT, Lois K.	(717)737-6111	10
Catasauqua	SIMONE-HOHE, M J.	(215)262-1596	1141
Chambersburg	MARLOW, Kathryn E.	(717)264-2382	772
Cheltenham	ELSHAMI, Ahmed M.	(215)635-3823	346
Clarion	PERSON, Ruth J.	(814)226-5341	961
Clifton Heights	WHITMAN, Mary L.		1333
Coraopolis	SKOVIRA, Robert J.	(412)262-8257	1147
Easton	CRAWFORD, Gregory A.	(215)253-9459	256
Fleetwood	EMERICK, Michael J.	(215)944-8486	347
Franklin Center	CUTLER, Judith	(215)459-6032	208
Glenside	NIEWEG, Clinton F.	(215)884-5878	904
Greensburg	DUCK, Patricia M.	(412)836-9689	322
	SCHEEREN, William O.	(412)834-9000	1090
Hershey	ULINCY, Loretta D.	(717)531-8634	1268
Johnstown	BRICE, Heather W.	(814)539-8153	134
King of Prussia	RICH, Denise A.	(215)935-7054	1027
Lancaster	BROWN, Charlotte B.	(717)291-4225	142
Malvern	QUINTILIANO, Barbara		1000
McKeesport	KISH, Veronica R.	(412)678-1749	656
Middletown	TOWNLEY, Charles T.	(717)948-6079	1253
Mt Lebanon	WEISFIELD, Cynthia F.	(412)831-8225	1319
Norristown	PRITCHARD, Barbara		994
Philadelphia	ADAMS, Mignon S.	(215)596-8790	5
	AXAM, John A.	(215)549-6485	42
	BAUMGARTNER, Barbara W.	(215)686-5418	66
	BERWICK, Mary C.	(215)898-4112	91
	BOWDEN, Gail L.	(215)574-4417	120

TRAINER (Cont'd)
PENNSYLVANIA (Cont'd)

Philadelphia			
	CHILDERS, Thomas A.	(215)895-2479	208
	FARREN, Ann L.	(215)848-8146	365
	FENICHEL, Carol H.	(215)448-7185	371
	FISHMAN, Lee H.	(215)564-3521	381
	PAGELL, Ruth A.	(215)898-5922	934
	RIDGEWAY, Patricia M.	(215)898-7555	1032
	ROHDY, Margaret A.	(215)387-5768	1050
	SNOW, Bonnie		1164
	WRIGHT, Irene R.	(215)923-1726	1371
	YERGER, George A.	(215)587-4887	1379
	ZOGOTT, Joyce	(215)596-8994	1390
Pittsburgh	BEARMAN, David A.	(412)421-4638	69
	BROADBENT, H E.	(412)441-6409	138
	DOW, Elizabeth H.		315
	FIDOTEN, Robert E.	(412)963-8785	375
	GREEN, Joyce M.	(412)234-5039	462
	HLUHANY, Patricia	(412)364-3000	544
	LEIBOWITZ, Faye R.	(412)421-7974	713
	METZLER, Douglas P.	(412)624-9414	829
	MITCHELL, Joan M.	(412)578-6137	849
	PIETZAK, Stephen D.	(412)227-6839	972
	ROSS, Nina M.	(412)624-9475	1058
	SOUDER, Edith I.	(412)343-9325	1169
	WEBRECK, Susan J.	(412)624-5230	1314
Shippensburg	CROWE, Virginia M.	(717)532-1463	261
Slippery Rock	JOSEPH, Elizabeth T.	(412)794-4623	617
State College	LINDSAY, Ann M.	(814)237-0714	729
Tamaqua	EVERHART, Nancy L.	(717)668-3334	358
Trafford	FETKOVICH, Malinda M.	(412)373-0799	374
University Park	FREIVALDS, Dace I.	(814)865-1818	402
	RICE, Patricia O.	(814)865-1858	1027
	ROE, Eunice M.	(814)863-0140	1048
Upper Darby	SILVERMAN, Karen S.	(215)734-0146	1138
Wayne	ANTOS, Brian F.	(215)254-0754	29
	CRAUMER, Patricia A.	(215)687-6777	255
West Chester	AMICONE, Janice L.	(215)692-6889	20
	FIDISHUN, Dolores	(215)692-6806	375
West Point	MESSICK, Karen J.	(215)661-6026	828
Youngwood	SCHEEREN, Judith A.	(412)925-4126	1090

PUERTO RICO

Guaynabo	LEON, Carmencita H.	(809)792-7873	716

RHODE ISLAND

Providence	BOWLBY, Raynna M.	(401)274-7224	121
Warwick	BRYAN, Susan M.	(401)737-3300	152
Woonsocket	LEVEILLEE, Louis R.	(401)762-4440	719

SOUTH CAROLINA

Charleston	ANDERSON, Marcia	(803)792-2371	24
	NEVILLE, Robert F.	(803)792-8024	898
Clemson	HIPPS, Gary M.	(803)654-3934	543
Columbia	GABLE, Sarah H.	(803)733-3344	411
	UPHAM, Lois N.	(803)777-6938	1269
Greenville	TOWELL, Fay J.	(803)232-2941	1252
Greenwood	GOING, Susan C.	(803)229-7448	444

SOUTH DAKOTA

Madison	SMITH, Rise L.	(605)256-5319	1160
Pierre	HILMOE, Deann D.	(605)224-3178	541
Sioux Falls	DERTIEN, James L.	(605)339-7115	294

TENNESSEE

Kingsport	PRESLAR, M G.	(615)229-6117	991
	TILSON, Koleta B.	(615)245-6572	1245
Knoxville	HASTINGS, Constance M.	(615)690-0368	511
	LEACH, Sandra S.	(615)579-1315	706
	PEMBERTON, J M.	(615)690-5598	956
	PHILLIPS, Linda L.	(615)687-6734	968
	PONNAPPA, Biddanda P.	(615)675-4545	982
Memphis	CO, Francisca	(901)324-2453	224
	MADER, Sharon B.	(901)454-2208	759
Murfreesboro	NEAL, James H.	(615)895-1383	890
Nashville	RICHARDS, Timothy F.	(615)385-1858	1028
	SWIFT, David L.	(615)352-0308	1216
	WATTS, Adalyn	(615)321-1332	1310
	WILLIAMS, Marsha D.	(615)832-0704	1345

TRAINER (Cont'd)
TENNESSEE (Cont'd)

Norris	DYER, Barbara M.	(615)494-9555	330
Oak Ridge	PFUDERER, Helen A.	(615)574-5350	966

TEXAS

Abilene	GILLETTE, Robert S.	(915)677-5103	435
Amarillo	RUDDY, Mary K.	(806)353-1534	1065
Arlington	LOWRY, Charles B.	(817)273-3391	745
Austin	BRIDGE, Frank R.	(512)328-6006	135
	JUERGENS, Bonnie	(512)288-2072	619
	MATHIS, Rama F.	(512)343-7521	784
	PELOQUIN, Margaret I.		955
	WALTON, Robert A.	(512)346-1426	1301
	WEBSTER, Linda	(512)458-1852	1314
Bangs	WEEKS, Patsy L.	(915)752-7315	1315
Brownsville	VAUGHN, Frances A.	(512)544-8220	1280
Bryan	THOMAS, Barbara C.	(409)774-1273	1236
College Station	KELLOUGH, Jean L.	(409)845-2551	637
Corpus Christi	HOUSTON, Barbara B.	(512)889-8517	563
Dallas	CLEE, June E.	(214)941-3375	220
	CLEMENTS, Cynthia L.	(214)238-6153	221
	GALBRAITH, Paula L.	(214)680-3782	413
	KRALISZ, Victor F.	(214)247-7944	675
	RYDESKY, Mary M.	(214)339-3349	1071
Denton	ALMQUIST, Sharon G.	(817)387-1703	17
	KHADER, Majed J.		645
	SHELDON, Brooke E.	(817)898-2602	1125
El Paso	GOODMAN, Helen C.	(915)584-4509	449
	LABODDA, Marsha J.	(915)859-1956	686
Fort Worth	MUELLER, Peggy	(817)870-7701	875
Galveston	WYGANT, Alice C.		1375
Houston	BAGHAL-KAR, Vali E.	(213)667-4336	45
	BROWN, Carol J.	(713)247-2227	142
	CALDWELL, Marlene	(713)661-5787	172
	CRAIG, Marilyn J.	(713)749-4762	254
	GOLEY, Elaine P.	(713)467-5784	447
	HASKELL, Peter C.	(713)529-6681	510
	KIMZEY, Ann C.	(713)488-9280	649
	MULLINS, James R.	(713)522-8131	878
	WELCH, C B.	(713)749-4245	1321
	WILLIAMS, Ann T.	(713)792-4094	1342
	WILSON, Barbara A.	(713)797-1230	1349
	WILSON, Thomas C.	(713)995-8401	1353
Huntsville	BURT, Lesta N.	(409)295-1001	164
Irving	HAGLE, Claudette S.	(214)986-2343	483
Kingsville	MERCHANT, Cheryl N.	(512)592-9684	825
Lewisville	MARMION, Daniel K.	(214)436-5125	772
	MCCOY, Judy I.	(214)221-9251	799
Lubbock	WEBB, Gisela M.	(806)794-7359	1313
Mesquite	GIBSON, Timothy T.	(214)289-2479	432
Midland	MIRANDA, Cecilia	(915)685-4557	847
New Braunfels	SCHUMANN, Iris T.	(512)625-5656	1103
Palacios	WOLL, Christina B.	(512)972-2166	1361
San Antonio	BADING, Kathryn E.	(512)655-4120	44
	HOOD, Elizabeth	(512)736-7292	556
	MANEY, Lana E.	(512)496-7754	765
	NOLAN, Christopher W.	(512)736-7429	907
Seguin	KOOPMAN, Frances A.	(512)379-4161	671
The Woodlands	PEYTON, Janice L.	(713)292-4441	966
Waco	KEATTS, Rowena W.	(817)753-6415	633
Wichita Falls	GRIMES, John F.	(817)855-0463	470

UTAH

Logan	SPYKERMAN, Bryan R.	(801)750-1643	1177
Provo	NIELSON, Paula I.	(801)375-9241	903
Salt Lake City	BURKS, C J.	(801)466-2183	161
	DAY, J D.	(801)363-5733	282
	HEFNER, Loretta L.	(801)485-2005	520
	NASH, Cherie A.	(801)533-5250	888
	SCOTT, Patricia L.	(801)533-5250	1107
West Jordan	KARPISEK, Marian E.	(801)561-4676	628

VIRGIN ISLANDS

St Thomas	MILLS, Fiolina B.	(809)776-8396	844

TRAINER (Cont'd)
VIRGINIA

Alexandria	CASSEDY, James G.	(703)768-2070	193
	DRUMMOND, Louis E.		321
	OLIVETTI, L J.	(703)683-8190	921
	OMARA, Marie T.	(703)960-3981	923
	ROTHSCHILD, M C.	(202)274-7206	1060
	WANG, Ann C.	(703)751-4536	1302
Annandale	CHOBOT, Mary C.	(703)323-9402	210
	MCGINN, Ellen T.	(703)280-5085	806
Arlington	ARDEN, Caroline	(703)532-1548	31
	BETTS, Ardith M.	(703)524-8384	92
	CAPUTO, Anne S.	(703)534-3433	180
	CAPUTO, Richard P.	(703)553-8455	180
	HARRIS, Linda S.	(703)521-2541	505
	HIRONS, Jean L.	(703)243-9437	543
	KNIGHT, Nancy H.	(703)522-2604	664
	LEATHER, Deborah J.	(703)522-5600	707
	MCKENNEY, Linda S.	(703)247-7829	811
	WIENER, Theodore		1336
Blacksburg	EASTMAN, Ann H.	(703)951-4770	333
Burke	GOUDREAU, Ronald A.	(703)569-0994	454
Charlottesville	BADER, Susan G.	(804)973-2397	44
Dale City	MARTIN, Elaine R.	(703)680-0164	776
Fairfax	CONIGLIO, Jamie W.	(703)323-2877	236
	WALCH, Victoria I.	(703)273-3260	1293
Falls Church	REID, Judith P.	(703)379-0739	1018
Fort Monroe	LUH, Lydia Y.	(804)727-4292	747
Harrisonburg	HABAN, Mary F.	(703)433-2183	480
	STEINBERG, David L.	(703)433-1572	1185
Herndon	SINWELL, Carol A.	(703)689-0086	1144
McLean	MORISSEAU, Anne L.	(703)821-9171	865
	WINIARSKI, Marilee E.	(800)421-7229	1355
Newport News	HAMMOND, Theresa M.	(804)595-8179	494
Norfolk	BREWER, Helen L.	(804)444-7951	134
	JONES-TRENT, Bernice R.	(804)632-8873	616
Quantico	BROWN, David C.	(703)221-1586	143
Reston	MCLANE, Kathleen	(703)620-3660	813
	WILTSHIRE, Denise A.	(703)391-0505	1354
Richmond	VAN SICKLEN, Lindsay L.	(804)320-9691	1277
Springfield	FOURNIER, Susan K.	(703)569-9468	393
Triangle	GAUDET, Jean A.	(703)221-6434	422
Vienna	COCHRANE, Maryjane S.	(703)938-2037	226
	DODSON, Whit	(703)938-2630	308
Virginia Beach	BARKLEY, Carolyn L.	(804)431-3070	56
	CAYWOOD, Carolyn A.	(804)464-9320	195
	WHYTE, Sean	(804)481-6096	1335
Winchester	BISCHOFF, Frances A.	(703)667-5350	99

WASHINGTON

Auburn	GOLDSTEIN, Cynthia N.	(206)931-3018	446
Bellevue	SKELLEY, Cornelia A.	(206)747-6473	1145
Bellingham	SYMES, Dal S.		1217
East Wenatchee	BELT, Jane		78
Edmonds	STRONG, Sunny A.	(206)778-3804	1203
Everett	GRINSTEAD, Beth K.	(206)258-1951	471
Federal Way	WILSON, Anthony M.	(206)839-0496	1349
Friday Harbor	MILLER, Jerome K.	(206)378-5128	839
Kent	CHAPMAN, Kathleen A.	(206)630-0538	202
Lacey	PUZIAK, Kathleen M.	(206)491-0347	998
	WIEMAN, Jean M.	(206)491-4700	1336
Marysville	WILSON, Evie		1350
Mt Vernon	SAUTER, Sylvia E.	(206)336-2604	1085
Richland	SAMPLE, Charles R.	(509)376-1506	1078
Seattle	BAGG, Deborah L.	(206)621-7896	45
	HENSLEY, Randall B.	(206)543-2060	529
	JENNERICH, Edward J.	(206)626-6320	598
	JEWELL, Timothy D.	(206)524-8820	600
	KETCHELL, Debra S.	(206)543-5530	645
	LEONARD, Gloria J.	(206)722-4828	716
	MADDEN, Susan B.	(206)684-6626	758
	PRESS, Nancy O.	(206)367-6568	991
	ROWBERG, Alan H.	(206)548-6250	1062
	STOCK, Carole G.	(206)325-8364	1195
	TOLLIVER, Barbara J.	(206)684-6615	1248
Spokane	REHMS, Jane C.	(509)536-7049	1017
	TYSON, Christy	(509)624-9744	1267
	WEBER, Joan L.	(509)489-6959	1314
Tacoma	GILDENHAR, Janet		434
	SELING, Kathy A.	(206)756-5571	1113

TRAINER (Cont'd)
WASHINGTON (Cont'd)

Vancouver	HUTTON, Emily A.	(206)695-1566	579

WEST VIRGINIA

Clarksburg	GREATHOUSE, Brenda J.	(304)624-9649	461

WISCONSIN

Hales Corners	BARLOGA, Carolyn J.	(414)425-0355	57
Madison	ARNOLD, Barbara J.	(608)263-2909	33
	CONNER, P Z.	(608)256-4440	237
	CRAWFORD, Josephine	(608)274-7984	256
	MCCONNELL, Shirley M.	(608)274-7222	798
	MONROE, Margaret E.	(608)263-2900	855
	ROBBINS, Jane B.	(608)263-2908	1038
	WEINGAND, Darlene E.	(608)262-8952	1318
Marshfield	ALLEN, Margaret A.	(715)387-7271	15
Menomonie	GRAF, David L.	(715)232-1202	455
Middleton	ZWEIZIG, Douglas L.	(608)831-4364	1392
Milwaukee	ANTHONY, Rose M.	(414)384-6535	29
	GILLETTE, Meredith	(414)351-3501	435
	KRCHMAR, Sandra L.	(414)961-8863	677
	STRUBE, Kathleen	(414)257-8326	1203
	THIEL, Mark G.	(414)224-7256	1235
Rosholt	ADAMS, Helen R.	(715)592-4614	5
West Allis	LUECHT, Richard M.	(414)321-3152	747
Wisconsin Rapids	WILSON, William J.	(715)424-4272	1353

WYOMING

Gillette	SIEBERSMA, Dan	(307)686-0786	1135
Laramie	COTTAM, Keith M.	(307)766-3279	250

CANADA

ALBERTA

Calgary	BAILEY, Madeleine J.	(403)240-6134	46

BRITISH COLUMBIA

Richmond	WEESE, Dwain W.		1316
Vancouver	AUFIERO, Joan I.	(604)325-2317	39
	HAABNIIT, Ene	(604)736-9335	480
	HAYCOCK, Carol A.	(604)734-0255	515
	HAYCOCK, Kenneth R.	(604)731-1131	515
	LEITH, Anna R.	(604)228-2762	714
	NICHOL, Kathleen M.	(604)263-7081	901
	ROBERTSON, Guy M.	(604)689-8494	1041
	WARREN, Lois M.	(604)687-1072	1306

MANITOBA

Winnipeg	FOWLER, Margaret A.	(204)884-6593	394

NORTHWEST TERRITORIES

Yellowknife	ALBRIGHT, Donald A.	(403)873-8347	10

ONTARIO

Aqimeont	JAGIELLOWICZ, Jadzia	(410)492-8341	591
Belfountain	DE RONDE, Paula D.	(519)927-5156	294
Deep River	ALBURGER, Thomas P.		11
Don Mills	TEMPLIN, Dorothy	(416)447-2380	1231
Downsview	JONES, B E.	(416)244-3621	611
Hamilton	BROWNRIDGE, James R.	(416)572-2981	149
Mississauga	OLMSTEAD, Marcia E.	(416)848-9403	921
North York	HOFFMANN, Ellen J.	(416)736-2100	548
	WILLIAMS, Lorraine O.		1344
Ottawa	KANNEL, Ene	(819)994-7966	625
	KARCICH, Grant J.	(416)723-6068	627
	MACDONALD, Marcia H.	(819)994-6947	754
	MACDONALD, Patricia A.	(819)997-7066	754
	MCCALLUM, David L.	(613)237-4586	793
	VALENTINE, Scott	(819)994-6946	1271
	VEEKEN, Mary L.	(613)523-2169	1280
Thornhill	HARE, Judith E.	(416)881-4804	501
Toronto	ARDERN, Christine M.		31
	ARMSTRONG, Jennifer E.	(416)466-8089	32
	ATTINGER, Monique L.	(416)699-2530	38
	BAYNE, Jennifer M.	(416)595-3429	67
	CAMPBELL, Bonnie	(416)323-3566	176
	DE STRICKER, Ulla	(416)593-5211	296
	FRITZ, Richard J.	(416)923-0890	405
	GREENWOOD, Jan	(416)963-9383	465

TRAINER (Cont'd)
ONTARIO (Cont'd)
Toronto

	KING, Olive E.	(416)979-5081	652
	LAVERTY, Corinne Y.	(416)393-7024	703
	OLSHEN, Toni	(416)488-5321	922
	SELLERS, Alexander G.	(416)489-4908	1114
	TUDOR, Dean F.	(416)767-1340	1262
	WONG, Lusi	(416)922-5100	1363
Willowdale	DANIEL, Eileen	(416)223-2495	272
Windsor	SINGLETON, Cynthia B.	(519)253-4232	1143

QUEBEC

Chambly	ASSUNCAO, Isabel	(514)658-3882	37
Gatineau	ST. AMANT, Robert	(819)561-4988	1075
Greenfield Park	RICHARDS, Stella	(514)672-1008	1028
Montreal	CHALIFOUX, Jean P.	(514)285-7007	197
	CORBEIL, Lizette	(514)332-9854	245
	FINN, Julia P.	(514)487-9804	378
	MITTERMEYER, Diane	(514)398-4204	850
	MOHAMMED, Selima	(514)398-4780	852
	PROVOST, Paul E.	(514)598-5389	996
	TOUCHETTE, Francois G.	(514)524-7878	1252
Quebec	FOERTIN, Yves P.	(418)649-0811	387
St Laurent D'Orleans	BOLDUC, Yves		112

SASKATCHEWAN

Regina	VOHRA, Pran	(306)787-4321	1287

AUSTRALIA

Kensington	WILSON, Concepcion S.	1350
Magill	BEATTIE, Kathleen M.	70
Newcastle	NEAME, Roderick L.	891

BELGIUM

Brussels	VAN SLYPE, Georges	1277

COSTA RICA

San Jose	CROWTHER, Warren W.		262
	MIRABELLI, Gerardo	(506)315-0540	847

EGYPT

Cairo	EL-DUWEINI, Aadel K.	(027)197-7200	342
Giza	EL-MASRY, Mohammed		345
	MAHOUD ALY, Usama E.		761

FEDERAL REPUBLIC OF GERMANY

Berlin	WALTER, Raimund E.	1300
Bremerhaven	GOMEZ, Michael J.	447

FRANCE

Guyancourt	COURRIER, Yves G.	251
Paris	CHAUMIER, Jacques	204
	DEROODE, Clifford H.	294
	GRATTAN, Robert	458

GUATAMALA

Guatamala City	MARBAN, Ricio	768

HUNGARY

Budapest	LAZAR, Peter	706

INDONESIA

Jakarta	STONE, Clarence W.	1197

IRAN

Shiraz	MEHRAD, Jafar	821

ITALY

Rome	MENOU, Michel J.	824

JAMAICA

Kingston	DOUGLAS, Daphne R.		314
	MANSINGH, Laxmi	(809)927-2748	767

JAPAN

Kanagawa-ken	TETSUYA, Inoue	1233
Tokyo	MIWA, Makiko	850

TRAINER (Cont'd)
KENYA

Nairobi	BROCKMAN, Norbert C.	138

MEXICO

Benito	MACIAS-CHAPULA, Cesar A.	755
Mexico City	BARBERENA, Elsa	55

NIGERIA

Akure	ONONOGBO, Raphael U.	924
Ibadan	ABOYADE, Beatrice O.	2

PAKISTAN

Lahore	TRAINER, Leslie F.	1253

PHILIPPINES

Manila	DE CASTRO, Elinore H.	285
Quezon City	PICACHE, Ursula D.	970
	VALLEJO, Rosa M.	1271

SAUDI ARABIA

Jeddah	ALSANARRAI, Hafidh S.	17
Riyadh	MARTIN, Nannette	777

SCOTLAND

Glasgow	HEANEY, Henry J.	518

SOUTH AFRICA

Tygerberg	ROSSOUW, Steve F.	1059

SWEDEN

Jarfalla	SHELTON, Anita L.	1126

SWITZERLAND

Geneva	OHLMAN, Herbert	919

TRINIDAD

Saint Joseph	MCCONNIE, Mary	798

ZAMBIA

Chilanga	LUMANDE, Edward	748

TRANSLATOR (Afrikaans)

NEW YORK

Syracuse	PRINS, Johanna W.	(315)475-5534	993

CANADA

BRITISH COLUMBIA

Victoria	VAN REENEN, Johannes A.	(604)595-9612	1277

TRANSLATOR (Akan)

NEW YORK

Brooklyn	ESSIEN, Victor K.	(718)941-9020	354

TRANSLATOR (Arabic)

CALIFORNIA

Pasadena	ZEIND, Samir M.	(818)440-5161	1387
Santa Monica	YASSA, Lucie M.	(213)458-9811	1378

ILLINOIS

Champaign	DESSOUKY, Ibtesam	(217)333-4956	296

MICHIGAN

Sterling Heights	SAHYOUN, Naim K.	(313)939-6425	1075

NEVADA

Las Vegas	MOUJAES, Sylva S.	(702)454-0559	873

NEW JERSEY

Princeton	HIRSCH, David G.	(609)683-7502	543

TRANSLATOR (Arabic) (Cont'd)

NEW YORK
Roslyn | SIAHPOOSH, Farideh T. .... (516)627-1919 | 1134

NORTH CAROLINA
Greensboro | HANHAN, Leila M. .... (919)292-1115 | 495

PENNSYLVANIA
Pittsburgh | NASRI, William Z. .... (412)276-3234 | 888

WISCONSIN
Milwaukee | AMAN, Mohammed M. ...... (414)239-4709 | 19

EGYPT
Cairo | EL-DUWEINI, Aadel K. ...... (027)197-7200 | 342
Giza | MAHOUD ALY, Usama E. | 761

KUWAIT
Salmiyah | ABDEL-MOTEY, Yaser Y. | 2

SAUDI ARABIA
Jeddah | ALSANARRAI, Hafidh S. | 17
Riyadh | ALI, Farooq M. .... (467)615-7000 | 13

TRANSLATOR (Armenian)

FLORIDA
St Petersburg | FUSTUKJIAN, Samuel Y. .... (813)893-9125 | 410

NEVADA
Las Vegas | MOUJAES, Sylva S. .... (702)454-0559 | 873

NEW YORK
New York | CAPRIELIAN, Arevig .... (718)459-2757 | 180

TRANSLATOR (Ashanti)

LOUISIANA
New Orleans | SARKODIE-MENSAH, Kwasi . (504)483-7306 | 1083

TRANSLATOR (Bengali)

NEW YORK
Bronx | ROY, Diptimoy .... (914)668-1840 | 1063

TRANSLATOR (Bulgarian)

NEW YORK
Dewitt | POPOVIC, Tanya V. .... (315)446-7488 | 983

TRANSLATOR (Catalan)

ILLINOIS
Dwight | MCCLAREY, Catherine A. ... (815)584-3703 | 796

TRANSLATOR (Chinese)

ALABAMA
Tuscaloosa | LEE, Sulan I. .... (205)752-6008 | 711

ARIZONA
Tempe | WU, Ai H. .... (602)965-3354 | 1373

CALIFORNIA
Chico | HUANG, George W. .... (916)891-3455 | 568
 | LO, Henrietta W. .... (916)895-6406 | 735
Pasadena | YEUNG, Esther Y. | 1380
Pomona | HSIA, Ting M. .... (714)869-3107 | 567

CONNECTICUT
West Hartford | LI, Hong C. .... (203)523 5948 | 724

TRANSLATOR (Chinese) (Cont'd)

FLORIDA
Palm Harbor | HO, Paul J. .... (813)785-1874 | 545
Tampa | LIANG, Diana F. .... (813)988-2406 | 725

IDAHO
Moscow | WAI, Lily C. .... (208)882-0506 | 1292

ILLINOIS
Chicago | WONG, Mabel K. .... (312)938-1000 | 1363
De Kalb | HUANG, Samuel T. .... (815)756-2296 | 568
Macomb | TING, Lee H. .... (309)298-1770 | 1246
Round Lake | TAN, Elizabeth L. .... (312)546-6311 | 1222
Urbana | LEONG, Carol L. .... (217)333-3399 | 717
 | MAKINO, Yasuko .... (217)244-2048 | 762
 | WEI, Karen T. .... (217)344-5647 | 1316

INDIANA
Bloomington | MCCLOY, William B. .... (812)335-9666 | 797

KANSAS
Leawood | LUNG, Mon Y. .... (913)864-3025 | 748

MARYLAND
Baltimore | HSIEH, Rebecca T. .... (301)522-1481 | 567
 | KUAN, David A. .... (301)256-9044 | 681
Potomac | CHANG, Frances M. .... (301)258-0772 | 200
 | HO, James K. | 545

MASSACHUSETTS
Marshfield | TU, Shu C. .... (617)837-8607 | 1261
Needham | TSENG, Louisa .... (617)449-3630 | 1260

MICHIGAN
Ann Arbor | WILSON, Amy S. .... (313)761-4700 | 1349
Midland | CHEN, Catherine W. ...... (517)631-9724 | 205
Port Huron | WU, Harry P. .... (313)982-2765 | 1373
Rochester | KROMPART, Janet A. ...... (313)651-4738 | 679

MINNESOTA
St Paul | MARION, Donald J. .... (612)624-6379 | 770

MISSOURI
Fenton | CHAN, Jeanny T. .... (314)343-0929 | 199

NEW JERSEY
Cape May Court
House | HSU, Hsiu H. .... (609)465-4500 | 567
East Brunswick | TANG, Grace L. | 1222
Hoboken | LIN, Fumei C. .... (201)795-5066 | 727
Springfield | CHANG, Joseph I. .... (201)467-2037 | 200
Upper Montclair | LUNG, Chan S. .... (201)746-6733 | 748

NEW MEXICO
Albuquerque | HSU, Grace S. | 567

NEW YORK
Manlius | WU, Painan R. .... (315)682-2472 | 1373
New York | HSIAO, Shu Y. .... (212)749-2873 | 567
 | HSU, Karen M. .... (212)930-0703 | 567

NORTH CAROLINA
Fayetteville | CHAN, Moses C. .... (919)483-5022 | 190
Greenville | CHENG, Chao S. .... (929)756-4543 | 206
Monroe | ABBOTT, Chien N. .... (704)283-7996 | 1

OHIO
Columbus | CHANG, Tony H. .... (614)292-2664 | 201
 | WANG, Anna M. .... (614)294-8035 | 1302

PENNSYLVANIA
Bensalem | CHU, John S. .... (215)639-0768 | 212
Dresher | FU, Clare S. .... (215)641-1978 | 407
Reading | YU, Lorraine L. .... (215)374-4548 | 1384

SOUTH CAROLINA
Columbia | HUYGEN, Eva | 580

TENNESSEE
Memphis | CO, Francisca .... (901)324-2453 | 224

TRANSLATOR (Chinese) (Cont'd)

TEXAS
Arlington	SHIH, Chia C.	(817)860-5475	1130
Dallas	DOMA, Tshering		310
Houston	CHANG, Robert H.	(713)221-8181	201
	CHUANG, Felicia S.	(713)791-6668	213
Pharr	LIU, David T.	(512)787-1491	734

VIRGINIA
Arlington	KECSKES, Lily C.	(703)528-0730	633
Fort Monroe	LUH, Lydia Y.	(804)727-4292	747

WASHINGTON
Ellensburg	YEH, Thomas Y.	(509)925-9257	1379
Seattle	BRZUSTOWICZ, Richard J.	(206)527-9357	152
	YONGMAN, Zhang	(206)522-6701	1380

WISCONSIN
Milwaukee	FONG, Wilfred W.	(414)229-4707	388
Oshkosh	FU, Tina C.	(414)424-2206	407

CANADA

ALBERTA
Edmonton	HU, Shih S.	(403)436-9716	568

QUEBEC
Montreal	NGUYEN, Vy K.	(514)494-1480	901

FEDERAL REPUBLIC OF CHINA
Taidzi	CHENG, Sheung O.		206
Taipei	HU, James S.		567
	WANG, Sin C.		1303

HONG KONG
Jardine's Lookout	LEE, Betty W.		709
Kowloon	POON, Paul W.		983

JAPAN
Tokyo	KATAOKA, Yoko		629

TRANSLATOR (Croatian)

TEXAS
Denton	CVELJO, Katherine	(817)565-2445	268

TRANSLATOR (Czechoslovakian)

ARIZONA
Phoenix	BOROVANSKY, Vladimir T.		117

MARYLAND
Fort Washington	KALKUS, Stanley	(301)839-5729	623

NEW YORK
New York	PEHE, Jana	(718)278-0630	954
	RAJEC, Elizabeth M.	(212)690-4151	1004

CANADA

BRITISH COLUMBIA
Victoria	ROMANIUK, Elena	(604)592-8819	1052

TRANSLATOR (Danish)

CALIFORNIA
Menlo Park	BOYE, Inger	(415)325-8077	123

MINNESOTA
Minneapolis	TIBLIN, Mariann E.	(612)624-5860	1244

NEW MEXICO
Albuquerque	CARLSON, Kathleen A.	(505)883-1924	182

TRANSLATOR (Danish) (Cont'd)
CANADA

ALBERTA
Camrose	INGIBERGSSON, Asgeir	(403)672-9750	582

TRANSLATOR (Dutch)

DELAWARE
Wilmington	DRUKKER, Alexander E.	(302)478-1746	320

ILLINOIS
Hinsdale	SLIEKERS, Hendrik	(312)887-9368	1149

INDIANA
Goshen	SPRINGER, Joe A.	(219)534-5357	1176

MINNESOTA
St Paul	BLUMBERG-MCKEE, Hazel	(612)292-1680	107

NEBRASKA
Lincoln	WOOL, Gregory J.	(402)475-0391	1368

NEW YORK
New York	FOLTER, Roland	(212)687-4808	388
Syracuse	PRINS, Johanna W.	(315)475-5534	993

OHIO
Xenia	OVERTON, Julie M.	(513)376-4952	931

VIRGINIA
Blacksburg	BAER, Eberhard A.	(703)951-3480	44

CANADA

BRITISH COLUMBIA
Victoria	VAN REENEN, Johannes A.	(604)595-9612	1277

BELGIUM
Kraainem	WALCKIERS, Marc A.		1293

FEDERAL REPUBLIC OF GERMANY
Heidelberg	SOKOLOWSKI, Denise G.		1166

INDONESIA
Jakarta	ADITIRTO, Irma U.		6

TRANSLATOR (Esperanto)

DISTRICT OF COLUMBIA
Washington	VON PFEIL, Helena P.		1288

TRANSLATOR (Estonian)

CONNECTICUT
New Haven	KOEL, Ake I.	(203)432-1825	667

MICHIGAN
Mt Pleasant	KRUUT, Evald	(517)773-5184	681

PENNSYLVANIA
Philadelphia	ANDRILLI, Ene M.	(215)725-3660	27

TRANSLATOR (Finnish)

CALIFORNIA
Palo Alto	BRUGUERA, Eva A.	(415)494-2862	150
Santa Rosa	BALOGH, Leeni I.	(707)539-8955	53

CONNECTICUT
Guilford	HELENIUS, Majlen	(203)453-1744	523

MICHIGAN
Galesburg	MOSHER, Robin A.	(616)665-4409	871
Hancock	PENTI, Marsha E.	(906)482-5300	957
Mt Pleasant	TIMBERS, Jill G.		1245

TRANSLATOR (Finnish) (Cont'd)

NEW YORK
New York	LINDGREN, Arla M.	(212)662-6386	729

PENNSYLVANIA
Indiana	RAHKONEN, Carl J.	1003

RHODE ISLAND
Kingston	SIITONEN, Leena M.	(401)792-2878	1137

CANADA

ALBERTA
Edmonton	KUJANSUU, Asko J.	(403)435-1563	683

TRANSLATOR (French)

ALABAMA
Auburn	CANTRELL, Clyde H.	(205)826-4500	179
	PEDERSOLI, Heleni M.	(207)821-7168	954

ALASKA
Chugiak	PUTZ, Paul D.	(907)688-4894	998

ARIZONA
Flagstaff	BAUM, Ester B.	(602)774-8878	66
Mesa	MAIN, Isabelle G.	(602)962-4310	761
Tucson	FAHY, Terry W.	(602)621-6446	361
	WOLFSON, Catherine L.	(602)884-8305	1361

CALIFORNIA
Berkeley	BENIDIR, Samia	(415)644-1129	80
	GRIFFIN, Thomas E.	(415)643-6196	469
	MITCHELL, Annmarie D.		848
Claremont	ALLEN, Susan M.		16
Davis	COLLINS, William J.	(916)758-4989	233
El Cerrito	BERLOWITZ, Sara B.	(415)524-7257	88
Encino	WOOD, Raymund F.		1364
Fair Oaks	HILL, Kristin E.	(916)966-6024	540
Long Beach	SINCLAIR, Lorelei P.	(213)423-6399	1142
Los Angeles	MAACK, Mary N.	(213)475-7962	753
	SZEGEDI, Laszlo	(213)469-7030	1218
Moreno Valley	SWAFFORD, William M.	(714)242-7719	1212
Palo Alto	BRUGUERA, Eva A.	(415)494-2862	150
	MARANGONI, Eugene G.	(415)858-4053	768
Pasadena	HICKS, Cynthia S.	(818)792-6830	536
	ZEIND, Samir M.	(818)440-5161	1387
Pomona	LAMONTAGNE, Therese	(714)623-2716	691
Riverside	SELTH, Jefferson P.	(714)787-3703	1114
San Diego	JACOBS, Horace	(619)746-4005	589
San Francisco	FREEMAN, Kevin A.	(415)922-1296	401
	TREGGIARI, Arnaldo	(415)469-1649	1255
Santa Barbara	KINNELL, Susan K.	(805)965-1294	653
Santa Monica	YASSA, Lucie M.	(213)458-9811	1378
Sunland	CLARK, Patricia A.	(818)353-6820	217
Upland	GRAUE, Luz B.	(714)982-7574	458

COLORADO
Aurora	LAMBERT, Shirley A.	(303)770-1220	690
Denver	GIGNAC, Solange G.	(303)575-3751	433
Littleton	WHITBY, Thomas J.	(303)798-7049	1330

CONNECTICUT
Bloomfield	BROQUE, Suzanne	(203)242-3473	141
Hartford	WILKIE, Everett C.	(203)236-5621	1340
Lakeville	RESTOUT, Denise T.	(203)435-9308	1024
Stamford	BERLIET, Nathalie B.	(203)359-9359	87
Westport	MUTTER, Letitia N.	(203)227-1992	883

DELAWARE
Wilmington	DRUKKER, Alexander E.	(302)478-1746	320

DISTRICT OF COLUMBIA
Washington	BEDARD, Laura A.	(202)662-9172	73
	BEDARD, Laura A.	(202)662-9172	73
	CASSEDY, Barbara S.	(202)576-3279	193
	ELSASSER, Katharine K.	(202)544-0552	346
	GAMSON, Arthur L.	(202)382-5921	416
	GREENE, Danielle L.	(202)543-6461	463

TRANSLATOR (French) (Cont'd)
DISTRICT OF COLUMBIA (Cont'd)
Washington			
	HOPPER, Mildry S.		558
	HORCHLER, Gabriel F.	(202)547-6792	559
	KUPERMAN, Agota M.		684
	MCNAMARA, Emma J.	(202)382-5922	816
	PETERSON, Charles B.		963
	REITH, Louis J.	(202)686-0131	1022
	TSUNEISHI, Warren M.	(202)287-5543	1260
	VASLEF, Irene	(202)342-3240	1279

FLORIDA
Gainesville	LEONARD, Louise F.	(904)373-2705	716
Jacksonville	RANDTKE, Angela W.	(904)646-2550	1007
Miami	BOLDRICK, Samuel J.	(305)443-2216	112
	SANCHEZ, Sara M.	(305)854-7752	1079
Winter Park	SEBRIGHT, Terence F.	(305)678-8846	1110

GEORGIA
Atlanta	CAMP, John F.	(404)875-4373	175
	MILLER, Anthony G.	(404)688-4636	835
	VIDOR, Ann B.	(404)894-4523	1283

ILLINOIS
Champaign	DESSOUKY, Ibtesam	(217)333-4956	296
Chicago	BYRE, Calvin S.	(312)341-3643	169
	COTILLAS, Therese G.	(312)856-8341	250
	MCCOY, Patricia S.	(312)274-0370	799
	MCELWAIN, William	(312)248-5564	804
	STENGER, Brenda E.	(312)782-1442	1187
	STEWART, Richard A.	(312)269-2930	1193
	TAYLOR, Terry S.	(312)372-2000	1229
	TYLMAN, Wieslawa T.	(312)666-7193	1266
Evanston	FINEMAN, Charles S.	(312)866-7428	377
Geneseo	REDINGTON, Deirdre E.	(309)944-3311	1014
Glen Ellyn	PEISER, Richard H.	(312)790-3293	955
Oak Park	CAREY, Kevin J.	(312)848-0682	181
Rock Island	WESTERBERG, Kermit B.	(309)794-7221	1326
Urbana	GUSHEE, Marion S.	(217)367-9610	478
Wauconda	FERME, Paul H.	(312)526-9123	373
Wilmette	MCGINN, Thomas P.	(312)256-5596	806

INDIANA
Bloomington	MCCLOY, William B.	(812)335-9666	797
	SMITH, Lary		1156
	TALALAY, Kathryn M.	(812)335-2970	1220
Goshen	SPRINGER, Joe A.	(219)534-5357	1176
Indianapolis	BRAHMI, Frances A.	(317)274-1401	127
	GOODWIN, Vania M.	(317)274-0491	450
South Bend	WARREN, Lois B.	(219)287-6481	1306
West Lafayette	POLIT, Carlos E.	(317)463-6404	980

IOWA
Des Moines	DAGLEY, Helen J.	(515)281-3063	269
Iowa City	GORMAN, Lawrence R.	(319)335-5884	452

KANSAS
Hays	MILLER, Melanie A.	(913)625-9014	841

LOUISIANA
New Orleans	SARKODIE-MENSAH, Kwasi	(504)483-7306	1083

MAINE
Orono	MCCALLISTER, Myrna J.		793

MARYLAND
Baltimore	DAVISH, William	(301)323-1010	281
	MCADAM, Paul E.	(301)747-5030	791
	SMITH, Mary P.	(301)358-0356	1158
	THIES, Gail M.	(301)597-8918	1235
Beltsville	COLLINS, Donna S.	(301)344-3728	232
Bowie	MATHEWS, Mary P.	(301)262-0732	784
Greenbelt	AUSTIN, Rhea C.	(301)345-0750	40
Hyattsville	RHEAUME, Irene M.	(301)434-8805	1025
Rockville	MARTINEZ-GOLDMAN, Aline		779
Silver Spring	AMATRUDA, William T.	(301)585-3570	19

TRANSLATOR (French) (Cont'd)

MASSACHUSETTS

Boston	BEST, Eleanor L.	(617)552-4421	92
	KORT, Richard L.	(617)266-3646	672
Gloucester	RHINELANDER, Mary F.	(617)281-2439	1025
Pembroke	ROBINSON, Phyllis A.	(617)293-2193	1044
Plymouth	HORN, Joseph A.	(617)746-6172	559
Wendell	HOLMBERG, Olga S.	(617)544-2706	553
West Springfield	PECK, Ruth M.	(413)736-0989	953
	SMITH, Barbara A.	(413)736-4561	1152
Worcester	GONNEVILLE, Priscilla R.	(617)752-5615	447

MICHIGAN

Birmingham	IRWIN, Lawrence L.	(313)626-5339	584
Detroit	STREETER, Linda D.		1201
Mt Pleasant	KRUUT, Evald	(517)773-5184	681
	TIMBERS, Jill G.		1245

MINNESOTA

Minneapolis	HALLEWELL, Laurence	(612)724-6565	489
	WITT, Kenneth W.	(612)871-4262	1358
St Paul	NEVIN, Susanne	(612)625-1898	898
Worthington	SPILLERS, Roger E.	(507)372-2981	1174

MISSOURI

Afton	WOHLRABE, John C.	(314)843-8131	1359
Columbia	SHIRKY, Martha H.	(314)882-6324	1131
Kansas City	LONDRE, Felicia H.	(816)444-1878	738
St Louis	AMELUNG, Richard C.	(314)658-2754	19
	KISSANE, Mary K.	(314)727-8865	656

NEW HAMPSHIRE

Hanover	REED, Barbara E.	(603)646-3831	1014

NEW JERSEY

Caldwell	SKIDANOW, Helene	(201)226-4458	1146
Cherry Hill	KUAN, Jenny W.	(609)667-0300	681
East Orange	STICKEL, William R.	(201)678-4289	1193
Highland Park	NIGRIN, Albert G.		904
New Brunswick	ANSELMO, Edith H.	(201)247-5610	28
	MAMAN, Marie	(201)932-9407	764
Paramus	CESARD, Mary A.	(201)444-4389	196
Park Ridge	WERNER, Edward K.	(201)391-4934	1324
Passaic	RUIZ-VALERA, Phoebe L.	(201)471-1770	1067
Pennington	KAZIMIR, Edward O.	(609)737-3582	632
Princeton	BENEDUCE, Ann K.	(609)921-6624	80
	CRITCHLOW, Therese E.	(609)924-9529	259
	FARRELL, Mark R.		365
	PASTER, Luisa R.	(609)452-5464	946
Short Hills	HENRY, Mary K.	(201)379-4082	529
Wayne	BIDDEN, Julia E.	(201)831-7801	94

NEW YORK

Albany	NEAT, Charles M.	(518)482-0469	891
Bronx	FOLTER, Siegrun H.	(212)960-8831	388
	LOCASCIO, Aline M.	(212)588-8400	735
Brooklyn	ESSIEN, Victor K.	(718)941-9020	354
	HOFFMAN, Allen	(718)736-8306	547
	PRUITT, Brenda F.	(718)287-1681	996
Croton-on-Hudson	CLARKE, Elizabeth S.	(914)271-3729	218
Delmar	KRAMER-GREENE, Judith	(518)439-7028	675
Farmingdale	SALITA, Christine T.		1076
Fulton	REED, Catherine A.	(315)598-3435	1015
Hempstead	LOUISDHON-WALTER, Marie L.	(718)990-0767	742
Ithaca	SLOCUM, Robert B.	(716)255-4247	1150
	STEWART, Linda G.	(607)255-7959	1192
New Rochelle	KONOVALOFF, Maria S.		670
New York	ALLENTUCK, Marcia E.		16
	BULLOCK, Frances E.	(212)666-9037	156
	CAMBRIA, Roberto		174
	DEMANDY, Claire	(212)960-8575	291
	D'ONOFRIO, Erminio	(212)930-0586	311
	FOLTER, Roland	(212)687-4808	388
	GITNER, Fred J.	(212)355-6100	439
	GRANDE, Paula G.	(212)536-3229	457
	HEUMAN, Rabbi F.	(212)505-2174	535
	MERKIN, David	(212)837-6588	826
	MOORE, Sonia	(212)755-5120	861
Oneonta	ROUGEUX, Debora A.	(607)432-0290	1061

TRANSLATOR (French) (Cont'd)

NEW YORK (Cont'd)

South Salem	BIRO, Juliane		99
Stony Brook	VOLAT-SHAPIRO, Helene M.	(516)632-7100	1287
Syracuse	PRICE, Susan W.	(315)423-2093	992
Westhampton	BARR, Janet L.	(516)288-5539	58
Williamsville	SCHUTT, Dedre A.	(716)633-6384	1103

NORTH CAROLINA

Belmont	MAYES, Susan E.	(704)825-3711	789
Fayetteville	KRIEGER, Lee A.	(919)864-9349	678
Greensboro	HANHAN, Leila M.	(919)292-1115	495
Wilmington	SEXTON, Spencer K.	(919)799-0177	1118

OHIO

Ashland	ROEPKE, David E.		1048
Cincinnati	ALBERT, Stephen G.	(513)541-9119	10
	SCHUTZ, Robert S.	(513)948-7518	1103
Cleveland	PRYSZLAK, Lydia M.	(216)459-2043	996
Cleveland Heights	TRAMDACK, Philip J.	(216)371-3445	1254
Columbus	GOLDING, Alfred S.		445
	MIMNAUGH, Ellen N.	(614)486-7755	845
	OLSZEWSKI, Lawrence J.		923
	O'NEIL, Rosanna M.	(614)761-5057	924
	PLATAU, Gerard O.	(614)457-1687	977
	STOBAUGH, Robert E.	(614)451-3271	1195
	WANG, Anna M.	(614)294-8035	1302
Cuyahoga Falls	OSTERFIELD, George T.	(216)929-9470	928
Kent	BIRK, Nancy	(216)672-2270	98
Oberlin	GREENBERG, Eva M.	(216)774-1383	463
Oxford	ZASLOW, Barry J.	(513)523-3980	1386
Terrace Park	SEIK, Jo E.	(513)831-0780	1112
Xenia	OVERTON, Julie M.	(513)376-4952	931

OKLAHOMA

Harrah	MELIK, Ella M.	(405)391-2438	822

PENNSYLVANIA

Greensburg	KREDEL, Stephen F.		677
Hatfield	PAKALA, Denise M.	(215)368-5000	935
Haverford	ROBERTSON, Robert B.	(215)896-1273	1042
Jenkintown	MONTOYA, Leopoldo	(215)886-2299	856
	SEVY, Barbara S.	(215)884-8275	1117
Kennett Square	MORSE, Alfred W.	(215)444-3444	869
Lancaster	FRANCOS, Alexis	(717)397-9655	396
Malvern	QUINTILIANO, Barbara		1000
	VANDOREN, Sandra S.	(215)640-9809	1275
New Hope	CROWN, Faith W.	(215)794-8932	262
New Milford	MAASS, Eleanor A.	(717)465-3054	753
Philadelphia	BOISCLAIR, Regina A.	(215)438-0173	111
	CALDWELL, John M.	(215)545-2809	172
	DONOVAN, Judith G.	(215)928-0577	312
	KING, Eleanor M.		650
	YOLTON, Jean S.	(215)878-7548	1380
Pittsburgh	NASRI, William Z.	(412)276-3234	888
Upper Saint Clair	FULMER, Dina J.	(412)831-8664	409

PUERTO RICO

Ensenada	MEJILL-VEGA, Gregorio	(809)821-4734	822

RHODE ISLAND

Barrington	COULOMBE, Dominique C.	(401)245-4018	250
Kingston	SIITONEN, Leena M.	(401)792-2878	1137
Lincoln	DESMARAIS, Norman P.	(401)333-3275	295

SOUTH CAROLINA

Newberry	HAMILTON, Ben	(803)276-6870	491

SOUTH DAKOTA

Vermillion	SPRULES, Marcia L.	(605)624-6764	1176

TENNESSEE

Memphis	BAKER, Bonnie U.	(901)324-6536	48

TEXAS

Abilene	ALLEN, Peggy G.	(915)695-4939	15
Arlington	SHIH, Chia C.	(817)860-5475	1130
Austin	WISE, Olga B.	(512)244-8330	1357
College Station	COOK, C C.	(409)845-3731	239
Dallas	DOMA, Tshering		310

TRANSLATOR (French) (Cont'd)
TEXAS (Cont'd)

El Paso	LABODDA, Marsha J.	(915)859-1956	686
	RAMSEY, Donna E.	(915)855-1218	1005
Galveston	FREY, Emil F.	(409)761-2371	402
	NEALE, Marilee	(409)765-5575	891
Houston	CARRINGTON, Samuel M.	(713)527-4022	186
	CHANG, Robert H.	(713)221-8181	201
Pasadena	CATES, Susan W.	(713)487-1714	195
San Marcos	HUSTON, Susan S.	(515)396-3374	578

UTAH

Provo	MATHIESEN, Thomas J.	(801)378-3688	784
Salt Lake City	CASADY, Richard L.	(801)533-9607	191

VERMONT

Castleton	LUZER, Nancy H.	(802)468-5611	750

VIRGINIA

Arlington	WOLF, Richard E.	(703)276-0270	1360
Norfolk	PEREZ-LOPEZ, Rene	(804)423-7655	958

WASHINGTON

Seattle	BRZUSTOWICZ, Richard J.	(206)527-9357	152
Spokane	SHIDELER, John C.	(509)838-5242	1129
Walla Walla	BLACKABY, Sandra L.	(509)527-4292	102

WISCONSIN

Cudahy	KLAUSMEIER, Arno M.	(414)744-0268	658
Fond Du Lac	EBERT, John J.	(414)929-3616	334
Madison	CLARK, Peter W.	(608)257-4861	217
Milwaukee	AMAN, Mohammed M.	(414)239-4709	19
	POPESCU, Constantin C.	(414)332-5909	983
Wausau	CLARK, Margaret E.	(715)845-5097	217

CANADA

ALBERTA

Airdrie	WAUGH, Alan L.	(403)948-7921	1310
Edmonton	BERNARD, Marie L.	(403)455-2436	88
	COMPRI, Jeannine L.	(403)474-0577	235
	RIDGE, Alan D.		1032
Lethbridge	JONES, Winstan M.	(403)327-0765	615

MANITOBA

Winnipeg	DIVAY, Gabriele	(204)474-8926	306

NEWFOUNDLAND

Mt Pearl	MORGAN, Pamela S.	(709)368-5926	864
St John's	MILNE, Dorothy J.	(709)737-8270	845

NOVA SCOTIA

Halifax	BIANCHINI, Lucian	(902)445-2987	94

ONTARIO

Leamington	NICHOLSON, Jill A.	(519)326-3441	902
London	CLOUSTON, John S.	(519)679-2111	223
Nepean	KAYE, Barbara J.	(613)225-9920	632
Ottawa	BREGAINT, Bernard J.	(613)741-0242	131
	DUSSIAUME, Robert	(613)234-2824	329
	GUILBERT, Manon M.	(613)233-8012	476
	HOUSTON, Louise B.	(519)993-7699	563
	KIRKWOOD, Francis I.	(613)233-7592	655
	SPRY, Patricia		1176
	WARD, William D.	(613)225-7557	1304
Scarborough	KEYS, Sandra A.		645
Toronto	FRIEDLAND, Frances K.	(416)789-0741	403
	POWELL, Wyley L.	(416)965-3906	989

QUEBEC

Aylmer	MACKEY, Laurette	(819)684-0410	756
Boischatel	LUSSIER, Richard	(418)822-1904	749
Chomedey	ROY, Helene	(514)682-5221	1063
Hull	CHEVRIER, Francine	(819)777-4341	207
	DUHAMEL, Louis	(819)771-4453	324
	TESSIER, Richard	(819)595-0910	1233
Laval	AUGER, Bernard	(514)687-9730	39

TRANSLATOR (French) (Cont'd)
QUEBEC (Cont'd)

Montreal	BACHAND, Michelle	(514)484-1282	43
	BUTLER, Patricia	(514)283-9046	167
	CAN, Hung V.	(514)521-8201	177
	CAYA, Marcel	(514)398-7100	195
	CLARKE, Robert F.	(514)731-9211	219
	GIRARD, Luc	(514)343-7445	438
	GREENE, Richard L.	(514)343-7424	464
	MUKHERJEE, Yolande	(514)932-6161	876
	NGUYEN, Vy K.	(514)494-1480	901
	RATNER, Sabina T.		1010
	ROLLAND-THOMAS, Paule	(514)343-6046	1051
	THACH, Phat V.	(514)727-6817	1233
Pointe Claire	SMYTH, John	(514)697-3486	1162
Pointe Claire Dorval	COTE, Claire	(514)630-1218	249
Quebec	BERNIER, Gaston	(418)643-4032	89
	COLLISTER, Edward A.	(418)643-1515	233
	MCKENZIE, Donald R.	(418)691-6357	811
Rosemere	LAPIERRE, France	(514)621-8507	697
St-Bruno	LECOMPTE, Louis L.	(514)653-7290	708
St Laurent D'Orleans	BOLDUC, Yves		112
Sainte-Foy	GUILMETTE, Pierre	(418)658-0470	476
	PETRYK, Louise O.	(418)656-6921	965
Shawinigan-Sud	MATTE, Pierre V.	(819)536-3519	785
Stanstead	GRENIER, Serge	(819)876-2981	467
Touraine	MURRAY-LACHAPELLE, Rosemary F.	(819)568-0282	882
Westmount	LEDOUX, Marc A.	(514)484-5951	708

SASKATCHEWAN

Saskatoon	NELSON, Ian C.	(306)652-4934	893

BELGIUM

Kraainem	WALCKIERS, Marc A.		1293

BRAZIL

Pelotas	CASTAGNO, Lucio A.		194

ENGLAND

Bushey	SMITH, Margit J.		1157

FEDERAL REPUBLIC OF GERMANY

Heidelberg	SOKOLOWSKI, Denise G.		1166

FRANCE

Guyancourt	COURRIER, Yves G.		251
Paris	STONE, Toby G.		1197

HUNGARY

Budapest	LAZAR, Peter		706

SWITZERLAND

Villars Ollon	BURDET, Michele C.		158

TRANSLATOR (Gaelic)

CANADA

NEWFOUNDLAND

St John's	MILNE, Dorothy J.	(709)737-8270	845

TRANSLATOR (German)

ALABAMA

Auburn	PEDERSOLI, Heleni M.	(207)821-7168	954

ARIZONA

Flagstaff	BAUM, Ester B.	(602)774-8878	66
Mesa	MAIN, Isabelle G.	(602)962-4310	761
Phoenix	BOROVANSKY, Vladimir T.		117
Tucson	SABOVIK, Pavel	(602)885-9923	1073

TRANSLATOR (German) (Cont'd)

CALIFORNIA

Berkeley	GRIFFIN, Thomas E.	(415)643-6196	469
Chico	HUANG, George W.	(916)891-3455	568
Davis	COLLINS, William J.	(916)758-4989	233
El Cerrito	BERLOWITZ, Sara B.	(415)524-7257	88
Fair Oaks	HILL, Kristin E.	(916)966-6024	540
Long Beach	SINCLAIR, Lorelei P.	(213)423-6399	1142
Los Angeles	GOWAN, Christa I.		455
	SZEGEDI, Laszlo	(213)469-7030	1218
Menlo Park	FRANK, Peter R.	(415)329-1173	397
Mission Viejo	WIERZBA, Heidemarie B.	(714)859-5193	1337
Moreno Valley	SWAFFORD, William M.	(714)242-7719	1212
Newport Beach	SCHULTZ, Ute M.	(714)760-2308	1102
Palo Alto	MARANGONI, Eugene G.	(415)858-4053	768
San Diego	JACOBS, Horace	(619)746-4005	589

COLORADO

Denver	GERMOVNIK, Francis I.	(303)722-4687	429
Leadville	PARRY, David R.	(303)486-2626	944

CONNECTICUT

Guilford	HELENIUS, Majlen	(203)453-1744	523
New Haven	KOEL, Ake I.	(203)432-1825	667

DELAWARE

Wilmington	DRUKKER, Alexander E.	(302)478-1746	320

DISTRICT OF COLUMBIA

Washington	BEDARD, Laura A.	(202)662-9172	73
	BEDARD, Laura A.	(202)662-9172	73
	HOPPER, Mildry S.		558
	HORCHLER, Gabriel F.	(202)547-6792	559
	KUPERMAN, Agota M.		684
	PETERSON, Charles B.		963
	REITH, Louis J.	(202)686-0131	1022
	TSCHERNY, Alexander	(202)723-5415	1260
	TSUNEISHI, Warren M.	(202)287-5543	1260
	VASLEF, Irene	(202)342-3240	1279
	VON PFEIL, Helena P.		1288

FLORIDA

Jacksonville	RANDTKE, Angela W.	(904)646-2550	1007
Orlando	TREMBLAY, Gerald F.	(305)277-6944	1255
Winter Park	AHLIN, Nancy	(305)644-6424	8
	SEBRIGHT, Terence F.	(305)678-8846	1110

GEORGIA

Athens	WALD, Marlena M.	(404)549-5501	1294
Atlanta	VIDOR, Ann B.	(404)894-4523	1283

IDAHO

Moscow	STEINHAGEN, Elizabeth N.	(208)885-6260	1186

ILLINOIS

Chicago	BYRE, Calvin S.	(312)341-3643	169
	STEWART, Richard A.	(312)269-2930	1193
De Kalb	RIDINGER, Robert B.	(815)758-5070	1032
Evanston	FINEMAN, Charles S.	(312)866-7428	377
	PANOFSKY, Hans E.	(312)491-7684	938
Glen Ellyn	PEISER, Richard H.	(312)790-3293	955
Normal	MEISELS, Henry R.	(309)452-4485	822
Rock Island	WESTERBERG, Kermit B.	(309)794-7221	1326
Urbana	GUSHEE, Marion S.	(217)367-9610	478
	HUETING, Gail P.	(217)244-0481	570

INDIANA

Goshen	SPRINGER, Joe A.	(219)534-5357	1176

IOWA

Forest City	PALMER, Joy J.	(515)582-3513	936
Iowa City	GORMAN, Lawrence R.	(319)335-5884	452

LOUISIANA

New Orleans	HALFORD, Mary B.	(504)865-6865	486

MAINE

Orono	MCCALLISTER, Myrna J.		793

TRANSLATOR (German) (Cont'd)

MARYLAND

Bowie	MATHEWS, Mary P.	(301)262-0732	784
Catonsville	STERLING, Judith K.	(301)455-3468	1189
College Park	WELLISCH, Hans H.	(301)345-3477	1322
Fort Washington	KALKUS, Stanley	(301)839-5729	623
St Marys City	WILLIAMSON, John G.	(301)862-0256	1347
Silver Spring	BASA, Eniko M.	(301)384-4657	62

MASSACHUSETTS

Ayer	WILLIAMS, Carole C.	(617)433-6747	1342
Boston	HOSTAGE, John B.	(617)782-0910	562
West Springfield	PECK, Ruth M.	(413)736-0989	953
	SMITH, Barbara A.	(413)736-4561	1152

MICHIGAN

Alma	GERLACH, William P.	(517)463-7227	429
Benton Harbor	PELZER, Adolf	(616)926-7403	955
Clarkston	MEDER, Stephen A.	(313)625-5611	820
Dearborn	FORSYTH, Karen R.	(313)562-8830	391
Detroit	STREETER, Linda D.		1201
Mt Pleasant	KRUUT, Evald	(517)773-5184	681
	TIMBERS, Jill G.		1245
Traverse City	SICILIANO, Peg P.	(616)947-1480	1135

MINNESOTA

Minneapolis	BARRETT, Darryl D.	(612)370-0869	59
	TIBLIN, Mariann E.	(612)624-5860	1244
	WALDEN, Barbara L.	(612)624-5860	1294
St Paul	BLUMBERG-MCKEE, Hazel	(612)292-1680	107
	NEVIN, Susanne	(612)625-1898	898

MISSISSIPPI

Hattiesburg	BOYD, William D.	(601)266-4232	123
Jackson	WILSON, Ruth W.	(601)969-1013	1352

MISSOURI

Afton	WOHLRABE, John C.	(314)843-8131	1359
Jefferson City	TORDOFF, Brian G.	(314)893-3147	1251
Kansas City	CARSON, Bonnie L.		188
St Louis	SUELFLOW, August R.	(314)721-5934	1206

NEBRASKA

Lincoln	WOOL, Gregory J.	(402)475-0391	1368

NEW JERSEY

East Orange	STICKEL, William R.	(201)678-4289	1193
Flemington	MCGREGOR, Walter	(201)788-3025	808
Manalapan	FIELD, Jack	(201)431-7226	375
Park Ridge	WERNER, Edward K.	(201)391-4934	1324
Pennington	KAZIMIR, Edward O.	(609)737-3582	632
Princeton	FARRELL, Mark R.		365
Short Hills	HENRY, Mary K.	(201)379-4082	529
Springfield	CHANG, Joseph I.	(201)467-2037	200
Wayne	BIDDEN, Julia E.	(201)831-7801	94

NEW YORK

Albany	NEAT, Charles M.	(518)482-0469	891
APO New York	HAAS, Eva L.		480
Bronx	FOLTER, Siegrun H.	(212)960-8831	388
Brooklyn	HOFFMAN, Allen	(718)736-8306	547
Delmar	POLAND, Ursula H.	(518)439-6872	980
Garden City	DOCTOROW, Erica	(516)663-1042	307
Houghton	LAUER, Jonathan D.	(716)567-2211	702
Ithaca	SLOCUM, Robert B.	(716)255-4247	1150
	WALD, Ingeborg	(607)255-7047	1294
New York	ALLENTUCK, Marcia E.		16
	BURROUGHS, Christine M.	(212)751-3122	163
	FOLTER, Roland	(212)687-4808	388
	HEUMAN, Rabbi F.	(212)505-2174	535
	LIDSKY, Ella	(212)663-4949	725
	MEYER, Albert	(212)254-7031	829
	PEHE, Jana	(718)278-0630	954
	RAJEC, Elizabeth M.	(212)690-4151	1004
Oneonta	VON BROCKDORFF, Eric	(607)432-4200	1288
South Salem	BIRO, Juliane		99
Williamsville	SCHUTT, Dedre A.	(716)633-6384	1103

TRANSLATOR (German) (Cont'd)

NORTH CAROLINA
Broadway	CRANDALL, Elisabeth G.	(919)258-3553	255
Durham	FARKAS, Doina C.	(919)493-1890	364
Fayetteville	KRIEGER, Lee A.	(919)864-9349	678
Winston-Salem	HAUPERT, Thomas J.	(919)722-1742	512

OHIO
Ashland	ROEPKE, David E.		1048
Cincinnati	ALBERT, Stephen G.	(513)541-9119	10
	SCHUTZ, Robert S.	(513)948-7518	1103
Cleveland	SKUTNIK, John S.	(216)241-2141	1147
	VAN DER SCHALIE, Eric J.	(216)473-0350	1274
Columbus	GOLDING, Alfred S.		445
	MIMNAUGH, Ellen N.	(614)486-7755	845
	PLATAU, Gerard O.	(614)457-1687	977
	STOBAUGH, Robert E.	(614)451-3271	1195
Granville	MAURER, Charles B.	(614)587-6215	787
Oberlin	GREENBERG, Eva M.	(216)774-1383	463
Toledo	LERNER, Esther T.	(419)531-2269	717
Wooster	POWELL, Margaret S.	(216)263-2279	988
Xenia	OVERTON, Julie M.	(513)376-4952	931

OKLAHOMA
Harrah	MELIK, Ella M.	(405)391-2438	822

OREGON
Portland	FELDMAN, Marianne L.	(503)292-2940	369

PENNSYLVANIA
Bethlehem	METZGER, Philip A.	(215)866-1257	829
Greensburg	KREDEL, Stephen F.		677
Haverford	ROBERTSON, Robert B.	(215)896-1273	1042
Jenkintown	SEVY, Barbara S.	(215)884-8275	1117
Kennett Square	MORSE, Alfred W.	(215)444-3444	869
New Milford	MAASS, Eleanor A.	(717)465-3054	753
Philadelphia	CALDWELL, John M.	(215)545-2809	172
Swarthmore	LEHMANN, Stephen R.	(215)328-8492	713
University Park	FREIVALDS, Dace I.	(814)865-1818	402

RHODE ISLAND
Barrington	COULOMBE, Dominique C.	(401)245-4018	250
Kingston	SIITONEN, Leena M.	(401)792-2878	1137
Providence	LANDIS, Dennis C.	(401)863-2725	693

SOUTH CAROLINA
Columbia	HUYGEN, Eva		580
	PEAKE, Luise E.	(803)777-3214	952

SOUTH DAKOTA
Sioux Falls	DUNGER, George A.	(605)336-6588	326

TENNESSEE
Memphis	BAKER, Bonnie U.	(901)324-6536	48
	VILES, Elza A.	(901)454-4412	1284
Nashville	BRANTIGAN-STOWELL, Martha J.	(615)352-0787	129

TEXAS
Abilene	ALLEN, Peggy G.	(915)695-4939	15
Austin	WISE, Olga B.	(512)244-8330	1357
College Station	COOK, C C.	(409)845-3731	239
Dallas	SALL, Larry D.	(214)385-8528	1076
Galveston	FREY, Emil F.	(409)761-2371	402
Irving	WHITE, Lely K.	(214)721-5310	1331
Pasadena	CATES, Susan W.	(713)487-1714	195
San Marcos	HUSTON, Susan S.	(515)396-3374	578

UTAH
Provo	MATHIESEN, Thomas J.	(801)378-3688	784
Salt Lake City	CASADY, Richard L.	(801)533-9607	191

VIRGINIA
Arlington	KECSKES, Lily C.	(703)528-0730	633
	WOLF, Richard E.	(703)276-0270	1360
Blacksburg	BAER, Eberhard A.	(703)951-3480	44

WASHINGTON
Vancouver	GAGNON, Vernon N.	(206)694-2350	412
Walla Walla	BLACKABY, Sandra L.	(509)527-4292	102

TRANSLATOR (German) (Cont'd)

WISCONSIN
Cudahy	KLAUSMEIER, Arno M.	(414)744-0268	658
Milwaukee	POPESCU, Constantin C.	(414)332-5909	983
	RISTIC, Jovanka	(414)229-6282	1036
Wausau	CLARK, Margaret E.	(715)845-5097	217

CANADA

ALBERTA
Airdrie	WAUGH, Alan L.	(403)948-7921	1310
Camrose	INGIBERGSSON, Asgeir	(403)672-9750	582
Edmonton	KUJANSUU, Asko J.	(403)435-1563	683

BRITISH COLUMBIA
Victoria	VAN REENEN, Johannes A.	(604)595-9612	1277

MANITOBA
Winnipeg	DIVAY, Gabriele	(204)474-8926	306

ONTARIO
London	WHITE, Janette H.	(519)661-3542	1331
Nepean	KAYE, Barbara J.	(613)225-9920	632
Toronto	FRIEDLAND, Frances K.	(416)789-0741	403

QUEBEC
Blainville	JETTE, Monika E.	(514)430-4945	600

ENGLAND
Bushey	SMITH, Margit J.		1157

FEDERAL REPUBLIC OF GERMANY
Berlin	ULRICH, Paul S.		1268
Bremerhaven	GOMEZ, Michael J.		447
Heidelberg	SOKOLOWSKI, Denise G.		1166
Taufkirchen	ADENEY, Carol D.		6

HUNGARY
Budapest	LAZAR, Peter		706

TRANSLATOR (Greek)

COLORADO
Colorado Springs	SHERIDAN, John B.	(303)473-2233	1127

ILLINOIS
Chicago	BYRE, Calvin S.	(312)341-3643	169

MARYLAND
Bethesda	ROBINSON, Cathy A.		1043

MASSACHUSETTS
Boston	ZIMPFER, William E.	(617)353-3034	1389
Brookline	PAPADEMETRIOU, Athanasia	(617)731-3500	938

MISSOURI
Afton	WOHLRABE, John C.	(314)843-8131	1359
St Louis	SUELFLOW, August R.	(314)721-5934	1206

NEW YORK
New York	BULLOCK, Frances E.	(212)666-9037	156
	MEYER, Albert	(212)254-7031	829

NORTH CAROLINA
Winston-Salem	HAUPERT, Thomas J.	(919)722-1742	512

OHIO
Cuyahoga Falls	OSTERFIELD, George T.	(216)929-9470	928
Kent	BIRK, Nancy	(216)672-2270	98

SOUTH DAKOTA
Sioux Falls	DUNGER, George A.	(605)336-6588	326

TENNESSEE
Memphis	BAKER, Bonnie U.	(901)324-6536	48

UTAH
Provo	MATHIESEN, Thomas J.	(801)378-3688	784

TRANSLATOR (Greek) (Cont'd)

WISCONSIN
Cudahy   KLAUSMEIER, Arno M. ..... (414)744-0268   658

TRANSLATOR (Gujarati)

CALIFORNIA
Modesto   SHAMS, Kamruddin .... (209)576-8585   1120

TRANSLATOR (Hawaiian)

HAWAII
Honolulu   HORIE, Ruth H.   559
Kaneohe   ASHFORD, Marguerite K. .... (808)247-6834   36

TRANSLATOR (Hebrew)

DELAWARE
Wilmington   DRUKKER, Alexander E. ..... (302)478-1746   320

DISTRICT OF COLUMBIA
Washington   KUPERMAN, Agota M.   684

MARYLAND
Chevy Chase   FINE, Sandra R. .... (301)951-3453   377
College Park   WELLISCH, Hans H. .... (301)345-3477   1322

NEW JERSEY
Princeton   HIRSCH, David G. .... (609)683-7502   543

NEW YORK
Mineola   TISHLER, Amnon .... (516)294-7224   1247
New York   ALLENTUCK, Marcia E.   16
     HEUMAN, Rabbi F. .... (212)505-2174   535
     LIDSKY, Ella .... (212)663-4949   725

OHIO
Columbus   GOLDING, Alfred S.   445
Cuyahoga Falls   OSTERFIELD, George T. ..... (216)929-9470   928

OREGON
Portland   FELDMAN, Marianne L. ..... (503)292-2940   369

SOUTH DAKOTA
Sioux Falls   DUNGER, George A. .... (605)336-6588   326

CANADA

ONTARIO
Toronto   FRIEDLAND, Frances K. ..... (416)789-0741   403

ISRAEL
Ramat Gan   SNYDER, Esther M.   1164

TRANSLATOR (Hindi)

ILLINOIS
Chicago   MANN, Vijai S. .... (312)443-5423   766
Elk Grove Village   KALRA, Bhupinder S. .... (312)529-8607   623

MARYLAND
Aberdeen Proving
    Gnd   GOEL, Krishan S.   443

NEW HAMPSHIRE
Durham   KAPOOR, Jagdish C. .... (603)868-2504   626

NEW YORK
Bronx   ROY, Diptimoy .... (914)668-1840   1063

OHIO
Westchester   EMANI, Nirupama .... (513)777-5264   347

TEXAS
Houston   SIVARAM, Swaraj L.   1144

TRANSLATOR (Hindi) (Cont'd)
CANADA

ONTARIO
Mississauga   MASEN, Naunihal S. .... (416)897-6269   780

SAUDI ARABIA
Riyadh   ALI, Farooq M. .... (467)615-7000   13

TRANSLATOR (Hungarian)

CALIFORNIA
Los Angeles   ENYINGI, Peter .... (213)629-3531   351
     SZEGEDI, Laszlo .... (213)469-7030   1218

CONNECTICUT
Hamden   KOEL, Maria O. .... (203)281-3265   667

DISTRICT OF COLUMBIA
Washington   HORCHLER, Gabriel F. ...... (202)547-6792   559
     KUPERMAN, Agota M.   684
     VASLEF, Irene .... (202)342-3240   1279

MARYLAND
Silver Spring   BASA, Eniko M. .... (301)384-4657   62

NEW JERSEY
Englewood   HALASZ, Etelka B. .... (201)858-6970   484

NEW YORK
New York   DEMANDY, Claire .... (212)960-8575   291
     RAJEC, Elizabeth M. .... (212)690-4151   1004
     SZMUK, Szilvia E. .... (212)787-2573   1218

NORTH CAROLINA
Kinston   TABORY, Maxim .... (919)522-3830   1219

VIRGINIA
Arlington   KECSKES, Lily C. .... (703)528-0730   633

TRANSLATOR (Icelandic)

CANADA

ALBERTA
Camrose   INGIBERGSSON, Asgeir .... (403)672-9750   582

MANITOBA
Brandon   SIMUNDSSON, Elva D. ..... (204)728-7234   1142

TRANSLATOR (Indonesian)

TEXAS
Irving   WHITE, Lely K. .... (214)721-5310   1331

INDONESIA
Jakarta   ADITIRTO, Irma U.   6

TRANSLATOR (Italian)

ALABAMA
Auburn   CANTRELL, Clyde H. .... (205)826-4500   179

CALIFORNIA
Berkeley   CLARENCE, Judy .... (415)649-2400   216
     GRIFFIN, Thomas E. .... (415)643-6196   469
Davis   COLLINS, William J. .... (916)758-4989   233
San Francisco   TREGGIARI, Arnaldo ...... (415)469-1649   1255
Sunland   CLARK, Patricia A. .... (818)353-6820   217

COLORADO
Denver   GERMOVNIK, Francis I. ..... (303)722-4687   429

CONNECTICUT
Hartford   WILKIE, Everett C. .... (203)236-5621   1340

TRANSLATOR (Italian) (Cont'd)

DISTRICT OF COLUMBIA

Washington	ELSASSER, Katharine K.	(202)544-0552	346
	REITH, Louis J.	(202)686-0131	1022

FLORIDA

Miami	PARISE, Marina P.		940
	SANCHEZ, Sara M.	(305)854-7752	1079

GEORGIA

Atlanta	VIDOR, Ann B.	(404)894-4523	1283

ILLINOIS

Chicago	MARSHALL, Jerilyn A.		774
Urbana	GUSHEE, Marion S.	(217)367-9610	478

INDIANA

Bloomington	TALALAY, Kathryn M.	(812)335-2970	1220
West Lafayette	POLIT, Carlos E.	(317)463-6404	980

KANSAS

Wichita	IZBICKI, Thomas M.	(316)683-8157	586

MARYLAND

Baltimore	SMITH, Mary P.	(301)358-0356	1158
Beltsville	COLLINS, Donna S.	(301)344-3728	232
Chevy Chase	GOLDSBERG, Elizabeth D.		446
Silver Spring	AMATRUDA, William T.	(301)585-3570	19

MASSACHUSETTS

Gloucester	RHINELANDER, Mary F.	(617)281-2439	1025
West Springfield	SMITH, Barbara A.	(413)736-4561	1152

MISSOURI

St Louis	AMELUNG, Richard C.	(314)658-2754	19

NEW JERSEY

Manalapan	FIELD, Jack	(201)431-7226	375

NEW YORK

Albany	NEAT, Charles M.	(518)482-0469	891
Fulton	REED, Catherine A.	(315)598-3435	1015
New York	D'ONOFRIO, Erminio	(212)930-0586	311
	MOORE, Sonia	(212)755-5120	861

OHIO

Columbus	OLSZEWSKI, Lawrence J.		923
	O'NEIL, Rosanna M.	(614)761-5057	924
Oberlin	GREENBERG, Eva M.	(216)774-1383	463

PENNSYLVANIA

Haverford	ROBERTSON, Robert B.	(215)896-1273	1042
Jenkintown	MONTOYA, Leopoldo	(215)886-2299	856
	SEVY, Barbara S.	(215)884-8275	1117
Kennett Square	MORSE, Alfred W.	(215)444-3444	869
Malvern	QUINTILIANO, Barbara		1000
Philadelphia	CALDWELL, John M.	(215)545-2809	172
	GREEN, Rose B.	(215)828-7029	462

PUERTO RICO

San Juan	NADAL, Antonio	(809)724-6869	885

RHODE ISLAND

Lincoln	DESMARAIS, Norman P.	(401)333-3275	295

SOUTH CAROLINA

Newberry	HAMILTON, Ben	(803)276-6870	491

TEXAS

Bryan	MOUNCE, Clara B.	(409)779-1736	873

VIRGINIA

Arlington	WOLF, Richard E.	(703)276-0270	1360
Norfolk	PEREZ-LOPEZ, Rene	(804)423-7655	958

WISCONSIN

Cudahy	KLAUSMEIER, Arno M.	(414)744-0268	658
Milwaukee	POPESCU, Constantin C.	(414)332-5909	983

TRANSLATOR (Italian) (Cont'd)
CANADA

NOVA SCOTIA

Halifax	BIANCHINI, Lucian	(902)445-2987	94

QUEBEC

Hull	DUHAMEL, Louis	(819)771-4453	324
Montreal	DE LUISE, Alexandra	(514)871-1418	290

COSTA RICA

San Jose	MIRABELLI, Gerardo	(506)315-0540	847

ITALY

Rome	HUEMER, Christina G.		570

TRANSLATOR (Japanese)

CALIFORNIA

Burlingame	SHERMAN, Roger S.	(415)344-1213	1128
Chico	HUANG, George W.	(916)891-3455	568
Los Angeles	LEE, Hee J.	(213)391-4226	710
Pleasant Hill	FOWELLS, Fumi T.	(415)689-0754	393
Whittier	ASAWA, Edward E.	(213)698-4461	35

DISTRICT OF COLUMBIA

Washington	TSUNEISHI, Warren M.	(202)287-5543	1260

FLORIDA

Palm Harbor	HO, Paul J.	(813)785-1874	545

ILLINOIS

De Kalb	WELCH, Theodore F.	(815)758-6858	1321
Urbana	MAKINO, Yasuko	(217)244-2048	762
	WILLIAMS, Mitsuko	(217)333-3654	1345

INDIANA

Bloomington	MCCLOY, William B.	(812)335-9666	797

MARYLAND

Greenbelt	KOBAYASHI, Michiko		666

MINNESOTA

Owatonna	HOSLETT, Andrea E.	(507)451-0312	561

NEW JERSEY

Pennington	KAZIMIR, Edward O.	(609)737-3582	632
Plainsboro	QUINN, Ralph M.	(609)799-3072	1000
Springfield	CHANG, Joseph I.	(201)467-2037	200
Westwood	GINES, Noriko	(201)666-7042	437

NEW YORK

New York	CHO-PARK, Jaung J.	(212)280-2293	210

NORTH CAROLINA

Swannanoa	ALLEN, Christina Y.	(704)298-4742	14

OHIO

Cincinnati	SCHUTZ, Robert G.	(513)948-7518	1103
Columbus	MIMNAUGH, Ellen N.	(614)486-7755	845

PENNSYLVANIA

Bensalem	CHU, John S.	(215)639-0768	212

TEXAS

Arlington	SHIH, Chia C.	(817)860-5475	1130
Austin	SENG, Mary A.	(512)444-5148	1115

VIRGINIA

Arlington	KECSKES, Lily C.	(703)528-0730	633
Lynchburg	KAWAGUCHI, Miyako	(804)239-3071	632

WASHINGTON

Ellensburg	DOI, Makiko	(509)963-2101	309

TRANSLATOR (Japanese) (Cont'd)
CANADA

BRITISH COLUMBIA
Vancouver	GONNAMI, Tsuneharu	(604)224-4296	447

ONTARIO
Ottawa	OZAKI, Hiroko	(613)234-9064	932

JAPAN
Aichi	TOGUCHI, Eiko	1248
Aichi-ken	SANO, Hikomaro	1081
Ibaraki-ken	NOZOE, Atsutake	911
Tokyo	HOSONO, Kimio	562
	KISHIMOTO, Hiroko	656

TRANSLATOR (Korean)

CALIFORNIA
Costa Mesa	HAN, Kenneth P.	(714)557-4648	494
Los Angeles	KIM, Joy H.	(213)337-0794	649
	LEE, Hee J.	(213)391-4226	710
	ROH, Jae M.	(213)381-1453	1050

ILLINOIS
Chicago	AHN, Hyonah K.	(312)728-8652	8
	MILUTINOVIC, Eunhee C.	(312)472-9843	845

INDIANA
Bloomington	MCCLOY, William B.	(812)335-9666	797

NEW YORK
New York	CHO-PARK, Jaung J.	(212)280-2293	210

NORTH CAROLINA
Swannanoa	ALLEN, Christina Y.	(704)298-4742	14

OHIO
Dayton	NAM, Wonki K.	(513)890-7061	887
Dublin	PAK, Moo J.	(514)761-2174	935

TRANSLATOR (Latin)

ARIZONA
Mesa	MAIN, Isabelle G.	(602)962-4310	761

CALIFORNIA
Encino	WOOD, Raymund F.		1364
Los Angeles	SZEGEDI, Laszlo	(213)469-7030	1218

COLORADO
Colorado Springs	SHERIDAN, John B.	(303)473-2233	1127
Denver	GERMOVNIK, Francis I.	(303)722-4687	429
Leadville	PARRY, David R.	(303)486-2626	944

DISTRICT OF COLUMBIA
Washington	BEDARD, Laura A.	(202)662-9172	73
	BEDARD, Laura A.	(202)662-9172	73
	CASSEDY, Barbara S.	(202)576-3279	193

FLORIDA
Miami	BOLDRICK, Samuel J.	(305)443-2216	112

ILLINOIS
Chicago	BYRE, Calvin S.	(312)341-3643	169
Urbana	GUSHEE, Marion S.	(217)367-9610	478

INDIANA
Bloomington	TALALAY, Kathryn M.	(812)335-2970	1220

KANSAS
Wichita	IZBICKI, Thomas M.	(316)683-8157	586

MARYLAND
Baltimore	DAVISH, William	(301)323-1010	281

TRANSLATOR (Latin) (Cont'd)
MASSACHUSETTS
Boston	ZIMPFER, William E.	(617)353-3034	1389
Brookline	PAPADEMETRIOU, Athanasia	(617)731-3500	938
Gloucester	RHINELANDER, Mary F.	(617)281-2439	1025
Lowell	CAYLOR, Lawrence M.	(617)452-5000	195
Plymouth	HORN, Joseph A.	(617)746-6172	559
West Springfield	PECK, Ruth M.	(413)736-0989	953

MICHIGAN
Clarkston	MEDER, Stephen A.	(313)625-5611	820

MISSOURI
Afton	WOHLRABE, John C.	(314)843-8131	1359
St Louis	SUELFLOW, August R.	(314)721-5934	1206

NEW JERSEY
Princeton	FARRELL, Mark R.		365

NEW YORK
New York	FOLTER, Roland	(212)687-4808	388
	MEYER, Albert	(212)254-7031	829
Syracuse	PRICE, Susan W.	(315)423-2093	992

NORTH CAROLINA
Winston-Salem	HAUPERT, Thomas J.	(919)722-1742	512

OHIO
Columbus	GOLDING, Alfred S.		445
Cuyahoga Falls	OSTERFIELD, George T.	(216)929-9470	928
Kent	BIRK, Nancy	(216)672-2270	98
Oberlin	GREENBERG, Eva M.	(216)774-1383	463
Toledo	LERNER, Esther T.	(419)531-2269	717

OKLAHOMA
Norman	LARSEN, Nancy E.	(405)321-6795	698

PENNSYLVANIA
Greensburg	KREDEL, Stephen F.		677
Jenkintown	SEVY, Barbara S.	(215)884-8275	1117

RHODE ISLAND
Lincoln	DESMARAIS, Norman P.	(401)333-3275	295

TEXAS
San Marcos	HUSTON, Susan S.	(515)396-3374	578

UTAH
Provo	MATHIESEN, Thomas J.	(801)378-3688	784

VIRGINIA
Arlington	WOLF, Richard E.	(703)276-0270	1360

WISCONSIN
Fond Du Lac	EBERT, John J.	(414)929-3616	334
Madison	CLARK, Peter W.	(608)257-4861	217
Wausau	CLARK, Margaret E.	(715)845-5097	217

CANADA

ALBERTA
Edmonton	RIDGE, Alan D.	1032

NOVA SCOTIA
Halifax	BIANCHINI, Lucian	(902)445-2987	94

TRANSLATOR (Latvian)

NEW YORK
New York	GESKE, Aina S.	430

PENNSYLVANIA
University Park	FREIVALDS, Dace I.	(814)865-1818	402

TRANSLATOR (Malay)

CALIFORNIA
Culver City   NG, Carol S. . . . . (213)202-6523   900

TEXAS
Irving   WHITE, Lely K. . . . . (214)721-5310   1331

TRANSLATOR (Marathi)

OHIO
Westchester   EMANI, Nirupama . . . . (513)777-5264   347

TRANSLATOR (Nepali)

TEXAS
Dallas   DOMA, Tshering   310

TRANSLATOR (Norwegian)

ARIZONA
Flagstaff   BAUM, Ester B. . . . . (602)774-8878   66

CALIFORNIA
Fair Oaks   HILL, Kristin E. . . . . (916)966-6024   540
Menlo Park   BOYE, Inger . . . . (415)325-8077   123

DISTRICT OF COLUMBIA
Washington   HOPPER, Mildry S.   558

ILLINOIS
Dwight   MCCLAREY, Catherine A. . . . (815)584-3703   796
Evanston   FINEMAN, Charles S. . . . . . . (312)866-7428   377
Rock Island   WESTERBERG, Kermit B. . . . (309)794-7221   1326

MINNESOTA
Minneapolis   SPETLAND, Charles G. . . . . . (612)624-8060   1174
     TIBLIN, Mariann E. . . . . (612)624-5860   1244
St Paul   DANIELS, Paul A. . . . . (612)611-3205   273

NEW JERSEY
New Brunswick   MAMAN, Marie . . . . (201)932-9407   764

NEW YORK
New York   LINDGREN, Arla M. . . . . (212)662-6386   729
Penfield   PARKE, Kathryn E.   941

OHIO
Wooster   POWELL, Margaret S. . . . . . . (216)263-2279   988

TRANSLATOR (Old Norse)

INDIANA
Bloomington   SMITH, Lary   1156

TRANSLATOR (Persian)

NEW HAMPSHIRE
Durham   KAPOOR, Jagdish C. . . . . . . (603)868-2504   626

NEW YORK
Roslyn   SIAHPOOSH, Farideh T. . . . . (516)627-1919   1134

TEXAS
Houston   BAGHAL-KAR, Vali E. . . . . . . (213)667-4336   45

CANADA

QUEBEC
Montreal   WERYHO, Jan W. . . . . (514)392-5766   1325

SAUDI ARABIA
Riyadh   BUTT, Abdul W.   167

TRANSLATOR (Polish)

CALIFORNIA
Berkeley   MITCHELL, Annmarie D.   848

ILLINOIS
Chicago   TYLMAN, Wieslawa T. . . . . . (312)666-7193   1266

MARYLAND
Mt Rainier   STRANSKY, Maria . . . . (301)779-1627   1200

MASSACHUSETTS
Boston   KORT, Richard L. . . . . (617)266-3646   672
Cambridge   ALTENBERGER, Alicja . . . . . (617)495-4285   18

MINNESOTA
Worthington   SPILLERS, Roger E. . . . . (507)372-2981   1174

NEW YORK
Buffalo   SZEMRAJ, Edward R. . . . . . . (716)895-7675   1218
Ithaca   WAWRO, Wanda T. . . . . (607)255-9478   1311
New York   CAPRIELIAN, Arevig . . . . (718)459-2757   180
     LIDSKY, Ella . . . . (212)663-4949   725

OHIO
Berea   MACIUSZKO, Jerzy J. . . . . . . (216)234-9206   755

PENNSYLVANIA
Baden   JABLONOWSKI, Mary D. . . . . (412)869-2188   586
Devon   PIECHNICK, Katarzyna M. . . . (215)964-9348   971

VIRGINIA
Blacksburg   BAER, Eberhard A. . . . . (703)951-3480   44

TRANSLATOR (Portuguese)

ALABAMA
Auburn   CANTRELL, Clyde H. . . . . . . (205)826-4500   179
     PEDERSOLI, Heleni M. . . . . . (207)821-7168   954

CALIFORNIA
Nevada City   BISHOP, Diane   99
Palo Alto   GREEN-MALONEY, Nancy . . (415)858-3816   465
San Francisco   TREGGIARI, Arnaldo . . . . (415)469-1649   1255

DISTRICT OF COLUMBIA
Washington   ELSASSER, Katharine K. . . . . (202)544-0552   346
     SANCHEZ, Jose L. . . . . (202)387-7396   1079
     WELCH, Thomas L. . . . . (202)232-1706   1321

FLORIDA
Gainesville   LEONARD, Louise F. . . . . (904)373-2705   716
Miami   SANCHEZ, Sara M. . . . . (305)854-7752   1079

ILLINOIS
Chicago   STENGER, Brenda E. . . . . . . (312)782-1442   1187
Evanston   JAVONOVICH, Kenneth L. . . . (312)764-7713   595

INDIANA
Indianapolis   GOODWIN, Vania M. . . . . (317)274-0491   450

MARYLAND
Baltimore   SMITH, Mary P. . . . . (301)358-0356   1158

MASSACHUSETTS
Boston   BEST, Eleanor L. . . . . (617)552-4421   92

MINNESOTA
Minneapolis   HALLEWELL, Laurence . . . . . (612)724-6565   489

NEW JERSEY
Park Ridge   WERNER, Edward K. . . . . (201)391-4934   1324
Short Hills   HENRY, Mary K. . . . . (201)379-4082   529
South Orange   FAWCETT-BRANDON,
     Pamela S. . . . . (201)762-0230   367

TRANSLATOR (Portuguese) (Cont'd)

NEW YORK

New Rochelle	KONOVALOFF, Maria S.		670
New York	GRANDE, Paula G.	(212)536-3229	457
Old Brookville	HELLER, Jacqueline R.	(516)626-2700	524
Oneonta	ROUGEUX, Debora A.	(607)432-0290	1061

OHIO

Toledo	ELLENBOGEN, Barbara R.	(419)536-4538	343

PENNSYLVANIA

Philadelphia	DEWANE, Kathleen M.	(215)546-5600	298

PUERTO RICO

San Juan	NADAL, Antonio	(809)724-6869	885

RHODE ISLAND

Providence	MONTEIRO, George	(401)863-3266	856

SOUTH CAROLINA

Newberry	HAMILTON, Ben	(803)276-6870	491

TEXAS

El Paso	LABODDA, Marsha J.	(915)859-1956	686
Houston	ANDERSON, Eliane G.	(713)229-7276	22

VIRGINIA

Norfolk	PEREZ-LOPEZ, Rene	(804)423-7655	958
Springfield	ROARK, Robin D.	(703)644-7372	1038

CANADA

QUEBEC

Montreal	GAMEIRO, Maria H.	(514)848-7761	416

BRAZIL

Pelotas	CASTAGNO, Lucio A.		194

TRANSLATOR (Punjabi)

ILLINOIS

Elk Grove Village	KALRA, Bhupinder S.	(312)529-8607	623

MARYLAND

Aberdeen Proving Gnd	GOEL, Krishan S.		443

NEW MEXICO

Farmington	JASSAL, Raghbir S.	(505)327-7813	595

CANADA

ONTARIO

Mississauga	MASEN, Naunihal S.	(416)897-6269	780

TRANSLATOR (Romanian)

NEW JERSEY

Wayne	BIDDEN, Julia E.	(201)831-7801	94

NEW YORK

New York	KLECKNER, Simone M.	(212)877-2448	658

NORTH CAROLINA

Durham	FARKAS, Doina C.	(919)493-1890	364

WISCONSIN

Milwaukee	POPESCU, Constantin C.	(414)332-5909	983

TRANSLATOR (Russian)

ALASKA

Chugiak	PUTZ, Paul D.	(907)688-4894	998

ARIZONA

Phoenix	BOROVANSKY, Vladimir T.		117
Tucson	SABOVIK, Pavel	(602)885-9923	1073

CALIFORNIA

Chico	RYAN, Frederick W.	(916)895-5862	1071
Los Angeles	POPOVITCH-KREKIC, Ruzica	(213)476-2237	984
Palo Alto	MARANGONI, Eugene G.	(415)858-4053	768

COLORADO

Littleton	WHITBY, Thomas J.	(303)798-7049	1330

DISTRICT OF COLUMBIA

Washington	PETERSON, Charles B.		963

FLORIDA

Winter Park	AHLIN, Nancy	(305)644-6424	8

ILLINOIS

Chicago	MARSHALL, Jerilyn A.		774
	STEWART, Richard A.	(312)269-2930	1193
De Kalb	RIDINGER, Robert B.	(815)758-5070	1032
Urbana	LEONG, Carol L.	(217)333-3399	717

INDIANA

South Bend	WARREN, Lois B.	(219)287-6481	1306

IOWA

Iowa City	LORKOVIC, Tatjana B.	(318)351-5304	741

MARYLAND

Beltsville	COLLINS, Donna S.	(301)344-3728	232
Silver Spring	RAWSTHORNE, Grace C.	(301)949-0698	1011

MASSACHUSETTS

Boston	KORT, Richard L.	(617)266-3646	672
Wendell	HOLMBERG, Olga S.	(617)544-2706	553

MICHIGAN

Ann Arbor	PONOMARENKO, Ella	(313)996-5267	982
Birmingham	IRWIN, Lawrence L.	(313)626-5339	584
Traverse City	SICILIANO, Peg P.	(616)947-1480	1135

MISSOURI

Jefferson City	TORDOFF, Brian G.	(314)893-3147	1251
Kansas City	CARSON, Bonnie L.		188
	LONDRE, Felicia H.	(816)444-1878	738

NEW JERSEY

Caldwell	SKIDANOW, Helene	(201)226-4458	1146
Princeton	FARRELL, Mark R.		365
Union	AMRON, Irving	(201)688-4980	20

NEW YORK

Bronx	FOLTER, Siegrun H.	(212)960-8831	388
	LAMPORT, Bernard	(212)430-3747	691
Buffalo	SZEMRAJ, Edward R.	(716)895-7675	1218
Ithaca	WAWRO, Wanda T.	(607)255-9478	1311
Miller Place	TODOSOW, Helen K.	(516)928-7174	1248
New Rochelle	KONOVALOFF, Maria S.		670
New York	CAPRIELIAN, Arevig	(718)459-2757	180
	GOERNER, Tatiana	(212)222-3490	443
	LIDSKY, Ella	(212)663-4949	725
	MOORE, Sonia	(212)755-5120	861
	PEHE, Jana	(718)278-0630	954
	WERTSMAN, Vladimir F.	(212)246-8176	1325
Rhinebeck	MCCLELLAND, Bruce A.	(914)876-2230	796
Stony Brook	VOLAT-SHAPIRO, Helene M.	(516)632-7100	1287
Syracuse	PRICE, Susan W.	(315)423-2093	992
Williamsville	SCHUTT, Dedre A.	(716)633-6384	1103

TRANSLATOR (Russian) (Cont'd)

OHIO
Cincinnati	SCHUTZ, Robert S.	(513)948-7518	1103
Columbus	MIMNAUGH, Ellen N.	(614)486-7755	845
	STOBAUGH, Robert E.	(614)451-3271	1195
Oxford	ZASLOW, Barry J.	(513)523-3980	1386

PENNSYLVANIA
Greensburg	KREDEL, Stephen F.		677
New Milford	MAASS, Eleanor A.	(717)465-3054	753

RHODE ISLAND
Kingston	SIITONEN, Leena M.	(401)792-2878	1137
Providence	RAINWATER, Jean M.	(401)863-3723	1004

SOUTH DAKOTA
Vermillion	SPRULES, Marcia L.	(605)624-6764	1176

TEXAS
Denton	CVELJO, Katherine	(817)565-2445	268
Houston	IGNATIEV, Laura	(713)667-9558	581

VERMONT
Burlington	DAY, Martha T.	(802)863-0506	282

VIRGINIA
Blacksburg	BAER, Eberhard A.	(703)951-3480	44
Richmond	SARTAIN, Sara M.		1083

CANADA

ALBERTA
Airdrie	WAUGH, Alan L.	(403)948-7921	1310

ONTARIO
London	WHITE, Janette H.	(519)661-3542	1331
Ottawa	SCHNEIDER, Tatiana	(613)564-2640	1097
Toronto	YANCHINSKI, Roma N.	(416)767-6781	1377

QUEBEC
Montreal	SHLIONSKY, Anatoly	(514)861-1411	1132

INDIA
Hyderabad	SATYANARAYANA, Vadhri V.	(260)586-0000	1084

TRANSLATOR (Sanskrit)

NEW YORK
Bronx	ROY, Diptimoy	(914)668-1840	1063

TRANSLATOR (Serbian)

TEXAS
Denton	CVELJO, Katherine	(817)565-2445	268

TRANSLATOR (Serbo-Croatian)

CALIFORNIA
Los Angeles	POPOVITCH-KREKIC, Ruzica	(213)476-2237	984

IOWA
Iowa City	LORKOVIC, Tatjana B.	(318)351-5304	741

MASSACHUSETTS
Wendell	HOLMBERG, Olga S.	(617)544-2706	553

NEW YORK
Dewitt	POPOVIC, Tanya V.	(315)446-7488	983

TRANSLATOR (Slovak)

ARIZONA
Phoenix	BOROVANSKY, Vladimir T.		117

MARYLAND
Fort Washington	KALKUS, Stanley	(301)839-5729	623

NEW YORK
New York	PEHE, Jana	(718)278-0630	954
	RAJEC, Elizabeth M.	(212)690-4151	1004

CANADA

BRITISH COLUMBIA
Victoria	ROMANIUK, Elena	(604)592-8819	1052

TRANSLATOR (Slovenian)

COLORADO
Denver	GERMOVNIK, Francis I.	(303)722-4687	429

TRANSLATOR (Spanish)

ALABAMA
Auburn	CANTRELL, Clyde H.	(205)826-4500	179
	PEDERSOLI, Heleni M.	(207)821-7168	954

ARIZONA
Apache Junction	WHORTON, Pamela J.	(602)982-1110	1334
Mesa	MAIN, Isabelle G.	(602)962-4310	761
Tucson	HOOPES, Maria S.		557
	SABOVIK, Pavel	(602)885-9923	1073

CALIFORNIA
Berkeley	GRIFFIN, Thomas E.	(415)643-6196	469
	MITCHELL, Annmarie D.		848
	SCHNEIDER, Francisca M.	(415)644-6871	1097
Burlingame	SHERMAN, Roger S.	(415)344-1213	1128
Encinitas	SCLAR, Marta L.	(619)944-3963	1106
Encino	WOOD, Raymund F.		1364
Long Beach	SINCLAIR, Lorelei P.	(213)423-6399	1142
Los Angeles	SATER, Analya	(213)277-1969	1083
Nevada City	BISHOP, Diane		99
Oxnard	SMITH, Heather	(805)984-4637	1155
Palo Alto	BRUGUERA, Eva A.	(415)494-2862	150
	GREEN-MALONEY, Nancy	(415)858-3816	465
	MARANGONI, Eugene G.	(415)858-4053	768
Pasadena	HICKS, Cynthia S.	(818)792-6830	536
San Diego	JACOBS, Horace	(619)746-4005	589
San Francisco	TREGGIARI, Arnaldo	(415)469-1649	1255
Upland	GRAUE, Luz B.	(714)982-7574	458

COLORADO
Denver	BARELA, Lori A.	(303)871-3447	56

CONNECTICUT
Hartford	WILKIE, Everett C.	(203)236-5621	1340

DISTRICT OF COLUMBIA
Washington	ELSASSER, Katharine K.	(202)544-0552	346
	GAMSON, Arthur L.	(202)382-5921	416
	GREENE, Danielle L.	(202)543-6461	463
	HOPPER, Mildry S.		558
	HORCHLER, Gabriel F.	(202)547-6792	559
	MCNAMARA, Emma J.	(202)382-5922	816
	REITH, Louis J.	(202)686-0131	1022
	SANCHEZ, Jose L.	(202)387-7396	1079
	TSCHERNY, Alexander	(202)723-5415	1260
	TSCHERNY, Elena	(202)727-1183	1260
	TSUNEISHI, Warren M.	(202)287-5543	1260
	VASLEF, Irene	(202)342-3240	1279
	WEITZENKORN, Laurie	(202)842-6604	1320
	WELCH, Thomas L.	(202)232-1706	1321

TRANSLATOR (Spanish) (Cont'd)

FLORIDA
Apopka	RIVERA, Antonio	(305)869-7168	1037
Gainesville	LEONARD, Louise F.	(904)373-2705	716
Miami	BOLDRICK, Samuel J.	(305)443-2216	112
	CHAVES, Francisco M.	(305)385-2301	204
	LOPEZ, Silvia P.	(305)596-1695	741
	ROVIROSA, Dolores F.		1062
	SANCHEZ, Sara M.	(305)854-7752	1079
Winter Park	SEBRIGHT, Terence F.	(305)678-8846	1110

GEORGIA
Atlanta	PAYNE-BUTTON, Linda	(404)325-7188	951
	RAQUET, Jacqueline R.	(404)320-9727	1008
	VIDOR, Ann B.	(404)894-4523	1283
Augusta	BUSTOS, Roxann R.	(404)737-1748	166
Statesboro	BURGOON, Roger S.	(912)764-3195	159

IDAHO
Moscow	STEINHAGEN, Elizabeth N. . . .	(208)885-6260	1186

ILLINOIS
Chicago	COTILLAS, Therese G.	(312)856-8341	250
	HERNANDEZ, Hector R.	(312)523-2453	531
De Kalb	RIDINGER, Robert B.	(815)758-5070	1032
Dwight	MCCLAREY, Catherine A. . . .	(815)584-3703	796
Evanston	FINEMAN, Charles S.	(312)866-7428	377
	JAVONOVICH, Kenneth L. . . .	(312)764-7713	595
Evergreen Park	GARCIA-RUIZ, Maritza L. . . .	(312)425-6104	417
Hoffman Estates	CHAPA, Joan I.	(312)934-7032	201
Peoria	SWORSKY, Felicia G.	(309)672-8885	1217
Wilmette	MCGINN, Thomas P.	(312)256-5596	806

INDIANA
Indianapolis	GOODWIN, Vania M.	(317)274-0491	450
South Bend	TUCKER, Dennis C.		1261
West Lafayette	POLIT, Carlos E.	(317)463-6404	980

IOWA
Des Moines	DAGLEY, Helen J.	(515)281-3063	269
Iowa City	KELLEY, Ann C.	(319)335-5884	636

KENTUCKY
Bowling Green	ZIMMER, Connie W.	(502)781-4165	1388

LOUISIANA
New Orleans	SARKODIE-MENSAH, Kwasi .	(504)483-7306	1083

MAINE
Orono	MCCALLISTER, Myrna J.		793

MARYLAND
Baltimore	SMITH, Mary P.	(301)358-0356	1158
Greenbelt	AUSTIN, Rhea C.	(301)345-0750	40
Rockville	MARTINEZ-GOLDMAN, Aline		779

MASSACHUSETTS
Boston	BEST, Eleanor L.	(617)552-4421	92
Lowell	CAYLOR, Lawrence M.	(617)452-5000	195
West Springfield	SMITH, Barbara A.	(413)736-4561	1152
Winchester	SMITH, Ann M.	(617)729-7169	1152

MICHIGAN
Detroit	FRANTILLA, K A.	(313)972-0318	398
Traverse City	SICILIANO, Peg P.	(616)947-1480	1135

MINNESOTA
Minneapolis	HALLEWELL, Laurence	(612)724-6565	489
	MIRANDA, Esmeralda C.	(612)437-0245	847
Worthington	SPILLERS, Roger E.	(507)372-2981	1174

MISSOURI
Kansas City	LONDRE, Felicia H.	(816)444-1878	738
St Louis	AMELUNG, Richard C.	(314)658-2754	19

NEW JERSEY
Bloomfield	BETANCOURT, Ingrid T.	(201)743-9511	92
	SHEARIN, Cynthia E.	(201)338-6545	1124
Highland Park	BARZELATTO, Elba G.	(201)247-6248	62
Park Ridge	WERNER, Edward K.	(201)391-4934	1324

TRANSLATOR (Spanish) (Cont'd)

NEW JERSEY (Cont'd)
Passaic	RUIZ-VALERA, Phoebe L. . . .	(201)471-1770	1067
Princeton	PASTER, Luisa R.	(609)452-5464	946
Short Hills	HENRY, Mary K.	(201)379-4082	529

NEW YORK
Bayside	DE CUENCA, Pilar A.		286
Bronx	FOLTER, Siegrun H.	(212)960-8831	388
Brooklyn	HOFFMAN, Allen	(718)736-8306	547
Delmar	KRAMER-GREENE, Judith . . .	(518)439-7028	675
Fulton	REED, Catherine A.	(315)598-3435	1015
Ithaca	SLOCUM, Robert B.	(716)255-4247	1150
New York	ALICEA, Ismael	(212)220-6582	13
	D'ONOFRIO, Erminio	(212)930-0586	311
	GRANDE, Paula G.	(212)536-3229	457
	LASTRES, Steven A.	(212)486-9500	701
	SANCHEZ, Eliana P.	(212)254-8829	1079
	SZMUK, Szilvia E.	(212)787-2573	1218
Old Brookville	HELLER, Jacqueline R.	(516)626-2700	524
Oneonta	ROUGEUX, Debora A.	(607)432-0290	1061
Richmond Hill	BISSESSAR, Carmen T.	(718)835-6514	100
Selden	SALINERO, Amelia	(516)732-1268	1076
South Salem	BIRO, Juliane		99
Syracuse	BRAUN, Carl F.	(315)423-2091	129
White Plains	MOSLANDER, Charlotte D. . .	(914)428-1533	871
Williamsville	SCHUTT, Dedre A.	(716)633-6384	1103

NORTH CAROLINA
Maiden	CARDENAS, Mary E.		180
Wingate	ABBOTT, Kent H.	(704)233-8094	1

OHIO
Cincinnati	HALIBEY-BILYK, Christine M.	(513)559-4320	486
Columbus	OLSZEWSKI, Lawrence J.		923
Oxford	ZASLOW, Barry J.	(513)523-3980	1386
Terrace Park	SEIK, Jo E.	(513)831-0780	1112
Toledo	ELLENBOGEN, Barbara R. . . .	(419)536-4538	343

OKLAHOMA
Ada	HUESMANN, James L.	(405)332-7632	570

OREGON
Eugene	HADDERMAN, Margaret	(503)342-5457	482

PENNSYLVANIA
Carbondale	MCNABB, Corrine R.	(717)282-3151	815
Glenmoore	VOURVOULIAS, Sabrina M. .	(215)942-3421	1289
Haverford	ROBERTSON, Robert B.	(215)896-1273	1042
Jenkintown	MONTOYA, Leopoldo	(215)886-2299	856
Kennett Square	MORSE, Alfred W.	(215)444-3444	869
Philadelphia	DIAZ, Magna M.	(215)686-1994	299
	KING, Eleanor M.		650
	MORENO, Rafael	(215)898-7555	863
Pittsburgh	ARJONA, Sandra K.	(412)821-2263	31
West Chester	ASTORGA, Alicia M.	(215)793-2417	37

PUERTO RICO
Caparra Heights	FERNANDEZ, Josefina L.	(809)782-2618	373
Ensenada	MEJILL-VEGA, Gregorio	(809)821-4734	822
Guaynabo	LEON, Carmencita H.	(809)792-7873	716
Miramar	MCCARTHY, Carmen H.	(908)721-6574	794
San Juan	COLLAZO, Maria L.		232
	MAURA-SARDO, Mariano A. . .	(809)764-0000	787
	NADAL, Antonio	(809)724-6869	885
	RODRIGUEZ, Ketty		1048
Trujillo Alto	SABATER-SOLA, Rigel		1072

SOUTH CAROLINA
Newberry	HAMILTON, Ben	(803)276-6870	491

TENNESSEE
Memphis	CO, Francisca	(901)324-2453	224
Nashville	GLEAVES, Edwin S.	(615)741-3666	441

TRANSLATOR (Spanish) (Cont'd)

TEXAS

Austin	BECK, Alison M.	(512)263-5502	71
	WISE, Olga B.	(512)244-8330	1357
Dimmitt	AUTRY, Brick	(806)647-3666	41
El Paso	ANDERSON, Mark	(915)858-0905	24
	LABODDA, Marsha J.	(915)859-1956	686
Galveston	NEALE, Marilee	(409)765-5575	891
Houston	ANDERSON, Eliane G.	(713)229-7276	22
Huntsville	CULP, Paul M.	(409)294-1619	264
McKinney	CORREDOR, Javier	(214)548-9971	247
San Antonio	GONZALEZ, Sharon M.		448
	LOCH, Edward J.	(512)734-2620	735
San Benito	GARAZA, Noemi	(512)399-2311	417

VERMONT

Burlington	DAY, Martha T.	(802)863-0506	282

VIRGIN ISLANDS

St Thomas	MILLS, Fiolina B.	(809)776-8396	844

VIRGINIA

Alexandria	WOODWARD, Lawrence W.	(703)751-9426	1368
Norfolk	PEREZ-LOPEZ, Rene	(804)423-7655	958
Reston	LEWIS, Diane M.	(703)860-4475	723
	MCCLAIN, Deborah C.	(703)689-5194	795
Springfield	ROARK, Robin D.	(703)644-7372	1038

WISCONSIN

Eau Claire	CARROLL, Barbara T.		187
Kenosha	TRUPIANO, Rose M.	(414)553-2143	1259
Madison	CLARK, Peter W.	(608)257-4861	217
Platteville	SCHMITT, Madelaine M.	(608)342-1667	1096

CANADA

ALBERTA

Lethbridge	JONES, Winstan M.	(403)327-0765	615

NOVA SCOTIA

Halifax	BIANCHINI, Lucian	(902)445-2987	94

ONTARIO

London	CLOUSTON, John S.	(519)679-2111	223

QUEBEC

Aylmer	MACKEY, Laurette	(819)684-0410	756
Chomedey	ROY, Helene	(514)682-5221	1063
Hull	DUHAMEL, Louis	(819)771-4453	324
	TESSIER, Richard	(819)595-0910	1233
Quebec	BERNIER, Gaston	(418)643-4032	89

SASKATCHEWAN

Saskatoon	PAREDES-RUIZ, Eudoxio B.	(306)966-5969	940

BELGIUM

Kraainem	WALCKIERS, Marc A.	1293

BRAZIL

Pelotac	CASTAGNO, Lucio A.	194

COSTA RICA

Alajuela	MOSS, Loretta E.		872
San Jose	MIRABELLI, Gerardo	(506)315-0540	847

ENGLAND

Bushey	SMITH, Margit J.	1157

FRANCE

Guyancourt	COURRIER, Yves G.	251

PHILIPPINES

Manila	DE CASTRO, Elinore H.	285

TRANSLATOR (Swedish)

ARIZONA

Flagstaff	BAUM, Ester B.	(602)774-8878	66

CALIFORNIA

Menlo Park	BOYE, Inger	(415)325-8077	123
Santa Rosa	BALOGH, Leeni I.	(707)539-8955	53

CONNECTICUT

Guilford	HELENIUS, Majlen	(203)453-1744	523
New Haven	KOEL, Ake I.	(203)432-1825	667

ILLINOIS

Chicago	SVENSSON, C G.	(312)478-2939	1212
Dwight	MCCLAREY, Catherine A.	(815)584-3703	796
Rock Island	WESTERBERG, Kermit B.	(309)794-7221	1326

MARYLAND

College Park	WELLISCH, Hans H.	(301)345-3477	1322

MASSACHUSETTS

Boston	BEGG, Karin E.	74

MINNESOTA

Minneapolis	TIBLIN, Mariann E.	(612)624-5860	1244

NEW JERSEY

New Brunswick	MAMAN, Marie	(201)932-9407	764

NEW MEXICO

Albuquerque	CARLSON, Kathleen A.	(505)883-1924	182

NEW YORK

New York	LINDGREN, Arla M.	(212)662-6386	729
Tuckahoe	ANDERSON, Birgitta M.	(914)793-6830	21

WASHINGTON

Seattle	HILL, Ann M.	(206)525-4212	539

CANADA

ALBERTA

Edmonton	KUJANSUU, Asko J.	(403)435-1563	683

TRANSLATOR (Tagalog)

NEW YORK

Flushing	PASION, Betty D.	(718)746-6516	946

TENNESSEE

Memphis	CO, Francisca	(901)324-2453	224

PHILIPPINES

Manila	DE CASTRO, Elinore H.	285

TRANSLATOR (Tamil)

WISCONSIN

Madison	JESUDASON, Melba	(608)263-7464	600

TRANSLATOR (Telugu)

TEXAS

Houston	SIVARAM, Swaraj L.	1144

INDIA

Hyderabad	SATYANARAYANA, Vadhri V.	(260)586-0000	1084

TRANSLATOR (Thai)

NEW YORK

Ithaca	ASHMUN, Lawrence F.	36

TRANSLATOR (Turkish)

MINNESOTA
Eden Prairie   BILEYDI, Lois G. . . . . (612)934-3576   96

NEW YORK
Roslyn   SIAHPOOSH, Farideh T. . . . . (516)627-1919   1134

TRANSLATOR (Ukrainian)

MARYLAND
Mt Rainier   STRANSKY, Maria . . . . (301)779-1627   1200

MICHIGAN
Ann Arbor   PONOMARENKO, Ella . . . . . . (313)996-5267   982

NEW JERSEY
Cranford   SAWYCKY, Roman A. . . . . . . (201)276-3134   1086

NEW YORK
New York   CAPRIELIAN, Arevig . . . . (718)459-2757   180

OHIO
Cincinnati   HALIBEY-BILYK, Christine M. (513)559-4320   486
Cleveland   PRYSZLAK, Lydia M. . . . . . . (216)459-2043   996

CANADA

ONTARIO
Toronto   YANCHINSKI, Roma N. . . . . . (416)767-6781   1377

TRANSLATOR (Urdu)

CALIFORNIA
Modesto   SHAMS, Kamruddin . . . . (209)576-8585   1120

ILLINOIS
Chicago   MANN, Vijai S. . . . . (312)443-5423   766
Elk Grove Village   KALRA, Bhupinder S. . . . . . . (312)529-8607   623

NEW HAMPSHIRE
Durham   KAPOOR, Jagdish C. . . . . . . (603)868-2504   626

SAUDI ARABIA
Riyadh   ALI, Farooq M. . . . . (467)615-7000   13
                      BUTT, Abdul W.   167

TRANSLATOR (Vietnamese)

GEORGIA
Atlanta   MILLER, Anthony G. . . . . (404)688-4636   835

CANADA

QUEBEC
Montreal   CAN, Hung V. . . . . (514)521-8201   177
                      NGUYEN, Vy K. . . . . (514)494-1480   901

TRANSLATOR (Yiddish)

NEW YORK
New York   ALLENTUCK, Marcia E.   16
                      HEUMAN, Rabbi F. . . . . (212)505-2174   535

TRANSLATOR

CALIFORNIA
Manhattan Beach   MARKEY, Penny S. . . . . (213)374-1838   771
Stanford   HOMNACK, Mark . . . . (415)323-2244   555

CONNECTICUT
Hartford   KAIMOWITZ, Jeffery H. . . . . . (203)527-3151   622
Westport   RIBAROFF, Margaret F. . . . . . (203)849-0211   1026

TRANSLATOR (Cont'd)

DISTRICT OF COLUMBIA
Washington   SIPKOV, Ivan . . . . (202)287-9850   1144

MAINE
York   HARMON, James R. . . . . (207)363-7833   502

MARYLAND
Baltimore   TOPPAN, Muriel L. . . . . (301)837-9155   1251
Bethesda   KIM, Sunnie I. . . . . (301)496-8124   649
Silver Spring   ARANDA-COODOU, Patricio . (301)946-7859   30

MINNESOTA
Rochester   BEYNEN, Gijsbertus K.   93

NEW JERSEY
South Orange   VITART, Jane A. . . . . (201)763-2181   1286

NEW MEXICO
White Sands   BANICKI, Cynthia A. . . . . (505)678-5820   54

NEW YORK
Brooklyn   CORRSIN, Stephen D. . . . . . . (718)851-2317   247
Dewitt   SHRIER, Helene F. . . . . (315)446-5971   1133

NORTH DAKOTA
Fargo   JANZEN, Deborah K. . . . . (701)277-1865   594

PENNSYLVANIA
Cheltenham   ELSHAMI, Ahmed M. . . . . . . (215)635-3823   346

PUERTO RICO
Guaynabo   MOMBILLE, Pedro . . . . (809)783-8622   854
Ponce   GUILLEMARD DE COLON,
                        Teresita   476

TEXAS
San Antonio   SCHMELZIE, Joan C. . . . . . . (512)684-8430   1094
Seguin   HSU, Patrick K. . . . . (512)372-3868   567

WISCONSIN
Eagle Heights   HSIEH, Cynthia C. . . . . (608)238-7655   567

CANADA

NEW BRUNSWICK
Moncton   POTVIN, Claude . . . . (506)857-1932   987

ONTARIO
Ottawa   BRIERE, Jean M. . . . . (613)996-3817   135

QUEBEC
Quebec   GUERETTE, Charlotte M. . . . . (418)656-3017   476

FEDERAL REPUBLIC OF GERMANY
Saarbrucken   VON KEITZ, Wolfgang   1288

IRAN
Shiraz   MEHRAD, Jafar   821

JAPAN
Tokyo 105   YAMAKAWA, Takashi   1376

WRITER/EDITOR

ALABAMA
Auburn   ADAMS, Judith A. . . . . (205)826-4500   5
                      PEDERSOLI, Heleni M. . . . . . . (207)821-7168   954
                      VEENSTRA, Robert J. . . . . . . (205)826-4780   1281
Birmingham   BENTLEY, Elna J. . . . . (205)969-2326   83
                      BLEILER, Richard J. . . . . (205)934-6364   105
                      MCCARTHY, Sherri L. . . . . . . (205)226-3630   794
                      VENABLE, Douglas R. . . . . . . (205)871-3318   1282
                      WEATHERLY, Cynthia D. . . . . (205)939-0120   1312
                      WEED, Joe K. . . . . (205)991-6600   1315
Decatur   MORRIS, Betty J. . . . . (205)773-6262   866
Florence   MONTGOMERY, Kimberly K. . . (205)764-5392   856
Helena   GOODWYN, Betty R. . . . . (205)988-0896   450
Huntsville   KITCHENS, Philips H.   657

WRITER/EDITOR (Cont'd)
ALABAMA (Cont'd)

Maxwell AFB	GOODMAN, Anita S.	(205)293-2504	449
Mobile	SHEARER, Barbara S.	(205)471-7855	1124
Montgomery	ADAMS, Emily J.	(205)293-7691	4
	BREEDLOVE, Michael A. . . .	(205)262-6172	131
	DESSY, Blane K.	(205)277-7330	296
	GREGORY, Vicki L.	(205)277-1759	466
	MCCRANK, Lawrence J.	(205)244-9202	800
Northport	HAMILTON, Ann H.	(205)752-3830	491
Oneonta	WEAVER, Clifton W.	(205)274-9111	1312
Pelham	WRIGHT, Amos J.	(205)663-3403	1370
Tuscaloosa	COLEMAN, J G.	(205)348-1523	231
	NEAVILL, Gordon B.	(205)348-1520	891
	PRUITT, Paul M.	(205)348-1107	996
	WATTERS, Annette J.	(205)348-6191	1310

ALASKA

Anchorage	BRAUND-ALLEN, Julianna E.	(907)243-5947	130
	EGGLESTON, Phyllis A.	(907)337-0051	339
	KRAFT, Gwen L.		675
	LESH, Nancy L.	(907)786-1877	718
Central	OAKES, Patricia A.		913
Chugiak	PUTZ, Paul D.	(907)688-4894	998
Fairbanks	PARHAM, Robert B.	(907)479-5966	940
Juneau	KINNEY, John M.	(907)586-1857	653
Valdez	LEAHY, M J.	(907)835-2801	706
Wasilla	TRIDLE, Jeanne A.	(907)376-5188	1256

ARIZONA

Apache Junction	WHORTON, Pamela J.	(602)982-1110	1334
Chandler	MCGORRAY, John J.	(602)961-8016	807
	VATHIS, Alma C.	(602)899-7147	1279
Flagstaff	AWE, Susan C.	(602)523-6808	42
	JOHNSON, Harlan R.	(602)523-4408	605
Glendale	MOSLEY, Shelley E.	(602)939-5469	872
Holbrook	ROTHLISBERG, Allen P.	(602)524-2257	1060
Mesa	JOSEPHINE, Helen B.	(602)983-0237	617
	MEAD, Thomas L.	(602)892-3764	819
Phoenix	ALABASTER, Carol	(602)262-7360	9
	BERK, Nancy G.	(602)971-9264	87
	DOHERTY, Walter E.	(602)262-5303	309
	SLESINGER, Susan G.	(602)254-6156	1148
	TEVIS, Raymond E.	(602)255-4590	1233
	THOMPSON, Anne E.	(602)254-6156	1238
Scottsdale	FERRALL, J E.	(602)965-5167	373
	POTTER, William G.	(602)991-5578	987
Sun City	BERNINGHAUSEN, David K. .	(602)933-8439	89
Tempe	NILSEN, Aileen P.		904
	RIGGS, Donald E.	(602)965-3950	1034
Tucson	ALURI, Rao	(602)722-5678	19
	BUXTON, David T.	(602)621-2101	168
	ETTER, Patricia A.	(602)299-5199	355
	GOLDBERG, Susan S.	(602)747-2663	445
	GOTHBERG, Helen M.	(602)887-2262	453
	HOLLEMAN, Margaret	(602)884-6821	551
	HOOPES, Maria S.		557
	NICHOLS, Margaret M.		901
	OWENS, Clayton S.		932
	RIISE, Milton B.	(602)325-1348	1034
	ROBROCK, David P.	(602)743-7072	1045
	RULE, Amy E.	(602)621-6273	1067
	STOUT, Mary A.	(602)791-4368	1199
	STRICKLAND, Ann T.	(602)881-6244	1202
	TALLMAN, Karen D. . , , , . .	(602)577-3317	1221
	WHITE, Edward H.	(602)621-5455	1330
	WOLFSON, Catherine L.	(602)884-8305	1361

ARKANSAS

Conway	ALSMEYER, Henry L.	(501)450-1302	18
	GREEN, Douglas A.	(501)327-5611	461
Fayetteville	MILLER, Leon C.	(501)575-5577	839
Harrison	HAMBY, Tracy A.	(501)743-1203	491
Heber Springs	SEDELOW, Sally Y.	(501)362-3476	1110
Hope	TROMATER, Raymond B. . . .	(501)777-3361	1257
Little Rock	BRECK, Paul A.	(501)569-3121	131
	RAZER, Robert L.	(501)663-0789	1012
	SANDERS, Kathryn A.	(501)227-5581	1080
Mountain View	MCNEIL, William K.	(501)269-3851	816
North Little Rock	FOOS, Donald D.	(501)758-5112	388

WRITER/EDITOR (Cont'd)
ARKANSAS (Cont'd)

Springdale	GREESON, Janet S.	(501)751-4901	465

CALIFORNIA

Alameda	HOSEL, Harold V.	(415)522-5875	561
	HUNT, Deborah S.	(415)523-6518	575
Albany	BLITZ, Ruth R.	(415)525-4186	105
Altadena	GREGORY, Timothy P.	(818)798-1268	466
Aptos	HERON, David W.	(408)688-6994	532
Bakersfield	KIRKLAND, Janice J.		655
Belmont	LEWIS, Gretchen S.	(415)591-4336	723
Benicia	MILLER, Davic C.	(707)746-6728	836
Berkeley	ARONER, Miriam D.	(415)849-2711	34
	BASART, Ann P.	(415)848-7805	62
	CASTRO, Rafaela G.	(415)526-0815	194
	CLARENCE, Judy	(415)642-2400	216
	FALK, Candace S.	(415)526-9591	362
	GRIFFIN, Thomas E.	(415)643-6196	469
	HANDMAN, Gary P.	(415)524-9728	495
	HUMPHREYS, Nancy K.	(415)642-4786	574
	MAXWELL, Christine Y.	(415)644-4500	788
	MONTGOMERY, Teresa L. . .	(415)642-1752	856
	PISANO, Vivian M.	(415)527-1959	975
	RAFAEL, Ruth K.	(415)849-2710	1003
	RIGGS, Judith M.	(415)654-2809	1034
	ROBERT, Berring C.	(415)642-9980	1039
	VANYOUNG, Sayre	(415)848-2229	1278
	WOODBURY, Marda	(415)654-4810	1366
	X, Laura	(415)548-1770	1376
	ZBORAY, Ronald J.		1386
Beverly Hills	ANNETT, Susan E.	(213)550-4720	28
	WALDOW, Mitch		1294
Burbank	ELMAN, Stanley A.	(818)351-8245	345
	SIGMAN, Paula M.	(818)840-5424	1137
Campbell	HAZEKAMP, Phyllis W.	(408)379-1611	517
Carlsbad	KENNEDY, Charlene F.	(619)434-2871	640
Carmichael	O'NEILL, Diane J.	(916)965-0935	924
	STRONG, Gary E.	(916)966-2037	1203
Carphell	ALIX, Cleta M.	(408)371-3294	13
Carpinteria	ALLABACK, Patricia G.	(805)684-4127	13
Carson	KENNY-SLOAN, Linda		642
Chico	BROWN, Carol G.	(916)861-2762	142
	DWYER, James R.	(916)895-5837	330
Claremont	ALLEN, Susan M.		16
Concord	PUGH, Mary J.	(415)685-2133	997
Corona del Mar	DOSER, Virginia A.	(714)760-0148	313
Corte Madera	FARMER, Lesley S.	(415)924-6633	364
Costa Mesa	MARLOR, Hugh T.	(714)631-5637	772
	PETERMAN, Claudia A.	(714)650-9014	962
Cupertino	JAJKO, Edward A.	(408)446-1306	592
	MACEK, Rosanne M.	(408)973-3116	755
Davis	BENOIT, Gerald		82
	COLLINS, William J.	(916)758-4989	233
	ELLIOTT, C D.	(916)752-2110	343
	IRELAND, Laverne H.	(916)756-1105	583
	ROBINSON, Betty J.	(916)756-2187	1043
	TEBO, Jay D.	(916)758-8256	1229
Del Mar	HOLLEMAN, Marian P.	(619)755-4253	551
El Cerrito	HARDWICK, Bonnie S.	(415)237-7011	500
	KATZ, Jeffrey P.		630
	KIRESEN, Evelyn M.	(415)526-6718	654
	MACAULEY, C C.	(415)524-2762	754
	PRESSNALL, Patricia E.	(415)525-5186	991
Encino	WOOD, Raymund F.		1364
Fair Oaks	HILL, Kristin E.	(916)966-6024	540
Fairfax	DOWNEY, Lynn A.	(418)454-4290	316
Fallbrook	COMPTON, Joan C.	(619)723-2860	235
Fremont	DIBLE, Joan B.	(415)792-8736	299
Fresno	CARLSON, Alan C.	(209)445-0828	182
Fullerton	BRIL, Patricia L.	(714)773-3852	136
Garden Grove	HIXON, Donald L.	(714)638-9379	544
Glen Ellen	SCARBOROUGH, Katharine T.	(707)996-7993	1087
Glendale	BURNS, Nancy R.	(818)244-1994	162
	ECKLUND, Lynn M.	(818)242-2793	335
Granado Hills	SINOFSKY, Esther R.	(818)360-2146	1144
Grand Terrace	MARCHIANO, Marilyn C. . . .	(714)382-2353	768
Hayward	ARROWOOD, Donna J.	(415)881-2791	34

WRITER/EDITOR (Cont'd)
CALIFORNIA (Cont'd)

Huntington Beach	MACKINTOSH, Mary L.	(714)896-4639	757
	OPPENHEIM, Michael R.	(714)842-1548	925
Irvine	BLADEN, Marguerite	(714)551-6489	102
	POOLE, Jay M.	(714)856-6377	983
	PUGSLEY, Sharon G.	(714)856-7193	997
	SCHLACKS, Charles	(714)559-6184	1093
	TSANG, Daniel C.	(714)856-4978	1260
	WEINTRAUB, D K.	(714)856-6079	1318
Isla Vista	GALLERY, M C.	(805)968-6842	414
Jamul	SERDZIAK, Edward J.	(619)426-2253	1116
Kensington	LAWRENCE, Gary S.	(415)642-2370	704
	MULVANY, Nancy	(415)524-4195	878
La Canada-Flintridge	MORAN, William R.	(818)790-1529	862
La Jolla	ALLISON, Terry L.	(619)534-1256	17
	FISHER, Edith M.	(619)534-1258	380
	MCGILVERY, Laurence	(619)454-4443	806
	SMITH, Phillip A.	(619)534-1266	1159
	ZYROFF, Ellen S.	(619)459-1513	1392
La Mirada	ANJOU-DURAZZO, Martel T.	(213)944-5981	28
La Verne	HECKMAN, Marlin L.	(714)593-8680	520
Lafayette	NEWAY, Julie M.	(415)283-1862	898
	SVIHRA, S J.	(415)933-9549	1212
Livermore	PALLONE, Kitty J.	(415)447-2376	935
Lomita	BOWLING, Lance C.	(213)831-1322	121
Long Beach	AYALA, John L.	(213)599-8028	42
	WILLIAMS, Valencia	(213)434-9151	1347
Los Altos	FILES, Patricia T.		376
Los Angeles	ALFORD, Thomas E.	(213)612-3333	13
	CAMPBELL, Patricia J.	(213)666-6967	177
	CASE, Donald O.	(213)825-1379	191
	CONNOR, Billie M.	(213)660-6399	237
	DAVIS, Marianne W.	(213)397-7904	280
	GILMAN, Lelde B.	(213)825-6498	436
	GRANGER, Dorothy J.	(818)795-9161	457
	HASSAN, Abe H.	(213)649-2846	511
	HOFFMAN, Irene M.	(213)839-5722	548
	KAPLAN, Robin	(213)851-2480	626
	KRIKORIAN, Rosanne	(213)938-3621	678
	LAWRENCE, John R.	(213)206-1223	704
	MAACK, Mary N.	(213)475-7962	753
	MCCORMICK, Mona	(213)825-1693	798
	MCKENZIE, Harry	(213)934-7685	811
	MORRIS, Jacquelyn M.	(213)259-2671	866
	NEMCHEK, Lee R.	(213)621-9484	895
	PRINTZ, Naomi J.	(213)306-3573	993
	RITCHESON, Charles R.	(213)743-2543	1036
	ROSENBERG, Melvin H.	(213)612-3242	1056
	SCHOTTLAENDER, Brian E.	(213)825-7785	1099
	SCLAR, Herbert	(213)474-5900	1106
	STERLIN, Annette S.	(213)645-2406	1189
	SUGRANES, Maria R.	(213)201-3507	1207
	TERZIAN, Shohig S.	(213)478-5193	1232
	WAGNER, Sharon L.	(213)931-4048	1292
	WEISBAUM, Earl		1319
	WOOD, Elizabeth H.	(213)224-7234	1364
	YEE, Martha M.	(213)462-4921	1379
Malibu	CLARK, David L.	(818)888-9305	216
Menlo Park	BALES, F K.	(415)854-0115	52
	DENNETT, Stephen C.		292
	REDFIELD, Elizabeth	(415)859-6187	1014
Mill Valley	ASHLEY, Elizabeth	(415)388-8080	36
	ROBERTS, Justine T.		1040
Mission Viejo	WIERZBA, Heidemarie B.	(714)859-5193	1337
Modesto	MORAN, Irene E.	(209)576-2740	862
	SHAMS, Kamruddin	(209)576-8585	1120
Montclair	CARRIGAN, John L.	(714)621-5225	186
Montebello	GALLEGO, Bert H.	(213)721-5102	414
Monterey	BRUMAN, Janet L.		150
	SPINKS, Paul	(408)646-2341	1175
Moreno Valley	SWAFFORD, William M.	(714)242-7719	1212
Napa	CHAMBERLIN, Leslie A.	(707)253-1071	198
Northridge	ECKLUND, Kristin A.	(818)349-6115	335
Norton AFB	CROWTHER, Carol	(714)382-7119	262
Oakland	MULL, Richard G.	(415)841-2590	876
Ojai	MOORE, Phyllis C.	(805)646-8592	861
Orange	ERLICH, Martin		353
Oxnard	SMITH, Heather	(805)984-4637	1155

WRITER/EDITOR (Cont'd)
CALIFORNIA (Cont'd)

Palo Alto	ANDREWS, Chris C.		26
	GREEN-MALONEY, Nancy	(415)858-3816	465
	HAMILTON, David M.	(415)853-0197	491
	KAHN, Paul J.	(415)327-3135	622
	LEE, Judith C.	(415)494-0395	710
	MARANGONI, Eugene G.	(415)858-4053	768
	PEARSON, Judith G.	(415)856-2853	952
	WREDEN, William P.	(415)325-6851	1370
Pasadena	CHOUDHURY, Lori B.	(818)449-9468	211
	GOODSTEIN, Judith R.	(818)356-6433	450
	HOFFBERG, Judith A.	(818)797-0514	547
	KLINE, Victoria E.	(818)405-2100	661
	LONGO, Margaret K.	(818)793-7682	740
	WONG, Maida L.	(818)795-1255	1363
Penryn	ANDERSON, David C.	(916)663-3294	22
Petaluma	GORDON, Ruth I.	(707)778-4719	452
Placentia	CHRISTNER, Deborah S.	(714)996-2749	212
Pomona	ADAMSON, Danette	(714)869-3109	6
	IVERSON, Diann S.	(714)624-4728	585
	KUHNER, David A.	(714)593-2467	683
Poway	D'ADOLF, Steven P.	(619)451-2130	269
	DOLLEN, Charles J.	(619)748-5348	310
Redondo Beach	CASTONGUAY, Russell	(213)372-6281	194
	COYLE, Leslie P.	(213)543-5149	253
Redwood City	LEWARK, Kathryn W.	(415)364-1764	722
	SCHLACHTER, Gail A.	(415)594-0743	1093
Richmond	BENELISHA, Eleanor	(415)223-6417	80
	LAMBERT, Nancy	(415)620-3161	690
	TURITZ, Mitch L.	(415)527-5109	1263
	VANDERBERG, Patricia S.	(415)237-1081	1273
Ridgecrest	FRIEDMAN, Sandra M.	(619)375-8825	404
Riverside	DOUGLAS, Nancy E.	(714)787-5051	314
	MITCHELL, Steve		849
	PROSSER, Michael J.	(714)689-7273	995
	SELTH, Jefferson P.	(714)787-3703	1114
	STALKER, Laura A.	(714)787-5841	1178
	TANNO, John W.	(714)787-3221	1223
Sacramento	JACKSON, Gloria D.	(916)427-1956	587
	LOW, Kathleen	(916)322-4570	743
	MCGOVERN, Gail J.	(916)446-2411	807
	MILLER, Suzanne M.	(916)739-7010	842
	RUDDOCK, Velda I.	(916)921-0521	1065
	SCHEIBEL, Susan	(916)392-9461	1091
	WILLIAMS, Joan F.	(916)927-4953	1344
Saint Helena	STOCKWELL, Judith R.	(707)963-3533	1196
San Anselmo	BLUME, August G.	(415)457-0215	107
San Diego	CARTER, Nancy C.		189
	DAVISSON, Darell D.	(619)458-1544	281
	DERSHEM, Larry D.	(619)236-2409	294
	DYER, Charles R.	(619)236-2292	330
	FORMAN, Jack	(619)546-9250	390
	GIBSON, Joanne	(619)450-0333	432
	JACOBS, Horace	(619)746-4005	589
	LAGIES, Meinhart J.	(619)283-0608	688
	MAISEL, Merry W.	(619)587-8018	762
	MONROE, Shula H.	(619)222-1206	855
	MORRISON, Patricia	(619)292-2859	868
	PLOTSKY, Andrea G.	(619)695-1132	978
	ROBINSON, Michaele M.	(619)231-1515	1044
	TABORN, Kym M.	(619)232-3320	1219
	VOIGT, Melvin J.		1287
San Francisco	AVENEY, Brian H.	(415)338-2956	41
	BROWN, Barbara L.	(415)894-9896	142
	CODER, Ann	(415)442-7000	226
	DONOVAN, Diane C.	(415)587-7009	312
	GERSH, Barbara S.	(415)346-7882	429
	GRIFFIN, Michael D.	(415)664-2835	468
	HENKE, Dan	(415)565-4758	528
	KIRSHENBAUM, Sandra D.	(415)776-1530	655
	MOORE, Gregory B.	(415)753-2645	859
	MOYER, Barbara A.	(415)386-6297	874
	ROOS, Barbara J.	(415)567-0460	1053
	SCHNEIDER, Marcia G.	(415)584-8228	1097
	SHEW, Anne L.	(415)565-6352	1129
	STEFANCIC, Jean A.	(415)666-6678	1185
	TARTER, Blodwen	(415)346-8199	1224
	TREGGIARI, Arnaldo	(415)469-1649	1255

WRITER/EDITOR (Cont'd)
CALIFORNIA (Cont'd)

San Jose	BERCIK, Mary E.	(408)288-9798	84
	HARMON, Robert B.	(408)297-2810	502
	MULLEN, Cecilia P.	(408)265-8799	877
	ROSEN, Elizabeth M.	(408)277-2270	1055
San Leandro	WENDROFF, Catriona	(415)569-3491	1323
San Lorenzo	CARR, Richard D.	(415)276-9345	186
San Luis Obispo	FOURIE, Denise K.	(805)544-5427	393
	ROCKMAN, Ilene F.	(805)756-2273	1046
San Mateo	CROCKETT, Darla J.	(415)573-0494	259
	RAZE, Nasus B.	(415)345-9684	1012
San Rafael	TRZECIAK, William J.	(415)485-3319	1260
Santa Ana	HOFFMAN, Herbert H.	(714)667-3451	548
Santa Barbara	FALK, Joyce D.	(805)687-7283	362
	GEBHARD, Patricia	(805)969-1031	424
	KINNELL, Susan K.	(805)965-1294	653
	MACGREGOR, Raymond	(805)682-5654	755
Santa Cruz	COOPER, Susan C.	(408)426-2841	243
	LOMBARDI, Mary L.	(408)476-1131	738
	MARIE, Jacquelyn	(408)429-2802	770
	RITCH, Alan W.	(408)429-2802	1036
	STEVENS, Stanley D.	(408)475-9172	1191
	TURNER, Anne M.	(408)429-3532	1264
Santa Monica	BERMAN, Marsha	(213)399-3674	88
	DIRLAM, Dona M.	(213)452-1897	305
	FISHER, Alice J.	(213)459-0414	380
	KARR, Linda		628
	QUINT, Barbara E.	(213)451-0252	1000
Santa Rosa	WALSH, Donamarie F.		1299
	WATSON, Benjamin	(707)527-2668	1309
Sherman Oaks	KWAN, Julie K.	(818)784-8606	685
Sonoma	WINSON, Gail I.	(707)935-1546	1355
South Pasadena	WISE, Leona L.	(213)257-4020	1357
Stanford	CARSON, Susan A.	(415)723-2092	188
	CRAWFORD, Walt	(415)329-3551	257
	KRAKAUER, Elizabeth	(408)733-4611	675
	MUSEN, Mark A.	(415)723-6979	883
	SCHMIDT, C J.	(415)493-5280	1095
Stockton	LEONHARDT, Thomas W.	(209)946-2434	717
	NICHOLS, Elizabeth D.	(209)943-2484	901
Suisun	CISLER, Stephen A.	(707)422-5089	215
Turlock	PARKER, John C.	(209)634-9473	942
Upland	MOSER, Judith E.	(714)982-8753	871
Vacaville	ELDREDGE, Mary		342
Vallejo	LANE, David R.	(707)648-4265	694
Venice	EDELSTEIN, J M.	(213)827-8984	335
Walnut Creek	MORRIS, John	(415)933-3365	866
West Covina	RINGWALT, Arthur	(818)965-2598	1035
West Hollywood	BUTKIS, John F.	(213)000-0000	166
Westlake Village	TISE, Barbara L.	(818)991-0047	1247
Whittier	RODRIGUEZ, Ronald	(213)693-0585	1048
	WILLIAMS, Lisa B.	(213)693-0771	1344
Woodland Hills	NELSON-HARB, Sally R.		895
	REIFMAN, Deborah S.		1019

COLORADO

Aurora	HUGHES, Brad R.	(305)699-6248	571
	MURRAY, William A.	(303)364-8208	882
Boulder	BINTLIFF, Barbara A.	(303)492-2708	97
	COLLARD, R M.	(303)444-1355	232
	FINK, Deborah	(303)492-8302	378
	KOHL, David F.	(303)492-6897	668
	KRISMANN, Carol H.	(303)499-2977	678
	MEYER, Andrea P.		829
	MUELLER, Carolyn J.	(313)492-6788	875
	PORPA, Edythe C.	(303)442-2847	984
	ROTHMAN, Marilyn R.	(303)447-9938	1060
	VARNES, Richard S.	(303)444-8051	1279
Colorado Springs	LAZARUS, Josephine G.	(303)528-7609	706
	MAGRATH, Lynn L.	(303)473-2080	760
	MALYSHEV, Nina A.	(303)531-6333	764
	NEILON, Barbara L.	(303)574-6167	892
	STEWART, Anna C.	(303)472-0268	1192
	WYLIE, Nethery A.	(606)593-3290	1375
Denver	BOYER, Carol C.	(303)892-9404	123
	BREIVIK, Patricia S.	(303)556-2805	132
	BROCK, Laurie N.	(303)333-2772	138
	FORSMAN, Rick B.	(303)394-5125	391
	HENSINGER, James S.	(303)691-0550	529

WRITER/EDITOR (Cont'd)
COLORADO (Cont'd)

Denver			
	WAGNER, Barbara L.	(303)297-3611	1291
	WHITE, Joyce L.	(303)722-4687	1331
Englewood	OTTOSON, Robin D.	(303)761-2482	930
Evergreen	SHARER, E J.	(303)292-4458	1122
Fort Collins	AMAN, Ann L.	(303)484-9205	19
	ANDERSON, Lemoyne W.	(303)484-7319	24
	CHRISTENSEN, Erin S.	(303)224-4588	211
Greeley	KNEPEL, Nancy	(303)356-4357	664
	PITKIN, Gary M.	(303)339-2237	976
	SAVIG, Norman I.	(303)351-2251	1086
	SCHULZE, Suzanne S.		1102
Lafayette	MACARTHUR, Marit S.	(303)665-8237	754
Lamar	BURNETT, James H.	(303)336-4632	161
Leadville	PARRY, David R.	(303)486-2626	944
Littleton	GREALY, Deborah J.	(303)795-3156	461
	LOERTSCHER, David V.	(303)770-1220	737
Pueblo	MOFFEIT, Tony A.	(303)549-2751	852
Westminster	BOYD, Ruth E.	(303)450-4710	122

CONNECTICUT

Ansonia	MARTIN, Walter F.	(203)736-2601	779
Avery Point	HOLLOWAY, Patricia W.	(203)445-5577	552
Avon	BLOTNER, Linda S.	(203)677-0286	106
Bethany	ASH, Lee M.	(203)393-2723	35
Bridgeport	HUGHES, John M.	(203)576-4392	571
	PALMQUIST, David W.	(203)579-4397	937
Bristol	CALLAHAN, Helen H.	(203)584-7787	173
	SENKUS, Linda J.	(203)589-1298	1115
Collinsville	EICKENHORST, Joanna W.	(203)693-4315	339
Danielson	WEIGEL, James S.	(203)774-7755	1316
East Canaan	BYERS, Laura T.	(203)824-5971	168
Farmington	DEVINE, Marie E.	(203)677-2140	297
	WETMORE, Judith M.	(203)679-2942	1328
Hamden	DEL CERVO, Diane M.	(203)248-4815	289
	STRAKA, Kathy M.	(203)771-8383	1199
Hartford	KAIMOWITZ, Jeffery H.	(203)527-3151	622
	MCNULTY, Karen	(203)278-2670	817
	NEUFELD, Irving H.	(203)278-3202	897
	WILKIE, Everett C.	(203)236-5621	1340
Kent	CUSTER, Deborah P.	(203)927-3098	267
Lakeville	RESTOUT, Denise T.	(203)435-9308	1024
Madison	FALK, Peter H.	(203)245-2246	362
Middletown	BALAY, Robert E.	(203)347-6933	50
	BECK, Arthur R.	(203)347-1387	71
	FARRINGTON, James	(203)347-9411	365
	SABOSIK, Patricia E.	(203)347-6933	1073
Milford	BARGAR, Arthur W.	(203)783-3290	56
	WESTBROOK, Patricia C.	(203)878-3551	1326
New Britain	KASCUS, Marie A.	(203)827-7565	628
	LAWRENCE, Scott W.	(203)677-1659	705
New Haven	BROWN, William E.	(203)432-1749	148
	COLLIER, Bonnie	(203)432-1783	232
	ENSEL, Ellen H.	(203)782-2525	350
	HEINRITZ, Fred J.	(203)397-4530	522
	JOHNSON, Eric W.	(203)467-8721	604
	KOEL, Ake I.	(203)432-1825	667
	LAWRENCE, Carol A.	(203)785-4346	704
	PELTIER, Karen V.	(203)432-4794	955
	PROSTANO, Emanuel T.	(203)397-4532	995
	SPURGEON, Kathy R.		1176
	WALTER, Kenneth G	(203)307-4520	1300
New London	ROGERS, Brian D.	(203)447-7622	1049
Ridgefield	NORTON, Alice	(203)438-4064	910
	SWIFT, Janet B.	(203)438-5937	1216
Stamford	CASE, Ann M.	(203)322-3383	191
	DIMATTIA, Susan S.	(203)322-9055	304
	LIEBERMAN, Lucille N.	(203)353-2095	726
Storrs	BOGNAR, Dorothy M.		111
	JIMERSON, Randall C.	(203)486-2893	600
	KAGAN, Alfred	(203)429-6565	621
	ROLLIN, Marian B.	(203)429-4187	1051
	STEVENS, Norman D.	(203)429-7051	1190
Stratford	ROTH, Alison D.	(203)378-8700	1059
Wallingford	EBINGER, Meada G.	(203)269-5114	334
	MCGREGOR, M C.	(203)284-6000	808
Waterbury	CARRINGTON, Virginia F.	(203)574-4702	186
	FLANAGAN, Leo N.	(203)756-6149	383

WRITER/EDITOR (Cont'd)
CONNECTICUT (Cont'd)

West Hartford	HORAK, Ellen B.	(203)233-3164	558
	TALIT, Lynn	(203)233-7793	1221
Westport	MECKLER, Alan M.	(203)226-6967	820
	MUTTER, Letitia N.	(203)227-1992	883
	SELVERSTONE, Harriet S.	(203)226-6236	1114
Willimantic	EMBARDO, Ellen E.	(203)456-1952	347
Wilton	TRIFFIN, Nicholas	(914)681-4275	1256
Windsor	GAGNE, Susan P.	(203)285-3288	412
	URICCHIO, William J.	(203)549-0404	1269
Woodbridge	BOGENSCHNEIDER, Duane R.	(203)397-2600	110

DELAWARE

Frankford	HITCHENS, Howard B.	(302)539-2420	544
Milford	CARPENTER, Carole H.	(302)422-4290	184
New Castle	BROWN, Sarah C.	(307)328-3447	147
Newark	DANIEL, Alfred I.	(302)731-9723	272
	TEETER, Enola J.	(302)737-9621	1229
Odessa	JAMISON, Susan C.	(302)378-2158	593
Wilmington	BURDASH, David H.	(302)571-7402	158
	MINNICH, Nancy P.	(302)478-5291	846
	TITUS, H M.	(302)656-1722	1247
Winterthur	ADAMS, Barbara M.	(302)656-8591	4

DISTRICT OF COLUMBIA

Washington	ATKIN, Michael I.	(202)539-8252	37
	BALL, Alice D.	(202)362-6047	52
	BEDARD, Laura A.	(202)662-9172	73
	BEDARD, Laura A.	(202)662-9172	73
	BELLARDO, Trudi	(202)363-9614	78
	BERWICK, Philip C.	(202)543-3369	91
	BISHOP, Sarah G.	(202)244-6841	99
	BLUMER, Thomas J.	(202)543-7031	107
	COOPER, David J.	(202)544-3653	242
	COUGHLAN, Margaret N.		250
	DEUTSCH, James I.	(202)342-6175	296
	DOWD, Mary J.	(202)523-3174	315
	ELLIOT, Hugh	(202)333-8312	343
	ELSASSER, Katharine K.	(202)544-0552	346
	FAHERTY, Robert L.	(202)797-6250	361
	FALK, Diane M.	(202)291-3821	362
	FARINA, Robert A.	(202)287-5298	363
	FLYNN, Richard M.	(202)638-1956	387
	FOX, Ann M.	(202)244-6355	394
	GARLICK, Karen	(202)287-5634	419
	GRAY, Michael H.	(202)755-4799	460
	GREENE, Danielle L.	(202)543-6461	463
	HAGEMEYER, Alice L.	(202)727-2255	483
	HEAD, Anita K.	(202)994-7336	518
	HEARTY, John A.	(202)872-4533	519
	HORTON, Forest W.		561
	JAMES, Olive C.	(202)547-2157	592
	JENKINS, Lydia E.	(202)673-7263	597
	JONES, Elin D.		612
	KEHOE, Patrick E.	(202)885-2674	634
	KELLY, Mark M.	(202)625-4175	638
	KENDRICK, Brent L.	(202)543-7031	640
	KITZMILLER, Virginia G.		657
	KOSTINKO, Gail A.	(202)483-4118	673
	LATEGOLO, Meldie A.		701
	LAWTON, Bethany L.	(202)651-5220	705
	LUNIN, Lois F.	(202)965-3924	749
	LUSKEY, Judith	(202)357-4654	749
	MCCOY-LARSON, Sandra	(202)544-5520	799
	MCGOWAN, Anna T.	(202)245-1235	807
	MCGUIRE, Brian		808
	MCRAE, Alexander D.	(202)686-1788	818
	MILEVSKI, Sandra N.	(202)543-7145	835
	MISSAR, Margaret M.	(202)363-2751	847
	MORRIS, Timothy J.	(202)462-8209	867
	O'BRIEN, Kathleen	(202)331-8400	914
	PACIFICO, Michele F.	(202)253-3214	933
	PINKETT, Harold T.	(202)363-2742	974
	PORTER, Suzanne	(203)994-8906	985
	PREER, Jean L.	(202)635-5085	990
	PRUETT, Barbara J.	(202)362-1345	996
	PURDY, Virginia C.	(202)523-3105	998
	RADER, Ronald A.	(639)890-0000	1002

WRITER/EDITOR (Cont'd)
DISTRICT OF COLUMBIA (Cont'd)

Washington	REYNOLDS, Dennis J.	(202)745-7722	1025
	ROONEY, Eugene M.		1053
	ROSENBERG, Jane A.	(202)786-0358	1056
	ROSS, Rodney A.	(202)554-2272	1058
	RUSH, Candace M.	(202)393-4695	1068
	SANCHEZ, Jose L.	(202)387-7396	1079
	SAUVE, Deborah A.	(202)546-8770	1085
	SCOTT, Catherine D.	(202)357-3101	1107
	SERVERINO, Roberto	(202)625-4574	1116
	SIPKOV, Ivan	(202)287-9850	1144
	STONE, Elizabeth W.	(202)338-5574	1197
	TERRY, Susan N.	(202)332-7120	1232
	THOMPSON, Laurie L.	(202)994-2853	1240
	TRIPP-MELBY, Pamela	(202)676-9418	1257
	TSCHERNY, Alexander	(202)723-5415	1260
	TSCHERNY, Elena	(202)727-1183	1260
	VAN NIMMEN, Jane	(202)363-3664	1276
	VASLEF, Irene	(202)342-3240	1279
	WALKER, Heather C.	(202)544-2443	1295
	WEAVER, Thomas M.	(202)526-4262	1312
	WILLSON, Elizabeth	(202)745-7722	1349
	YARNALL, James L.	(202)234-6293	1378

FLORIDA

Atlantic Beach	URBANSKI, Verna P.	(904)246-3631	1269
Belle Glade	SNODGRASSE, Elaine	(305)996-3453	1163
Boca Raton	DONAHUE, Janice E.	(305)393-3774	310
	SKALLERUP, Amy G.		1145
Bradenton	JULIEN, Dorothy C.	(813)792-7899	619
	MORR, Lynell A.	(813)747-4319	866
Bunnell	MCKNIGHT, Jesse H.	(904)437-4151	812
Casselberry	BARAGER, Wendy A.	(305)699-6657	55
Clearwater	POTTER, Robert E.	(813)442-9061	987
Coral Gables	AHMAD, Carol F.	(305)284-3551	8
	ROBAR, Terri J.	(305)284-4706	1038
Coral Springs	KORNITSKY, Judith M.	(305)753-7081	672
Dade City	SPENCER, Albert F.		1173
Daytona Beach	BRANDON, Alfred N.	(904)677-5098	128
	MINOR, Dorothy C.	(904)253-6627	846
Fort Lauderdale	MILLER, Margaret R.	(305)791-1278	840
Gainesville	COVEY, William C.	(904)392-0796	252
	HOLE, Carol C.	(904)378-0270	550
	PRIMACK, Alice L.	(904)335-8525	993
	TEAGUE, Edward H.	(904)392-0222	1229
	WALTON, Carol G.	(904)392-0351	1301
	WILLETT, Charles	(904)378-1661	1341
	WOODS, Susan E.	(904)392-4018	1367
Indialantic	MELNICOVE, Annette R.		823
Jacksonville	BONFILI, Barbara J.	(904)725-5822	114
	FARKAS, Andrew	(904)646-2554	364
	GUNN, Thomas H.	(904)744-3950	477
	RANDTKE, Angela W.	(904)646-2550	1007
Key Biscayne	KIRBY, Diana G.	(305)361-3678	654
Lake Worth	MOFFETT, Martha L.	(305)964-7044	852
Lauderhill	HURTES, Reva	(305)735-8655	578
Melbourne	HENSON, Llewellyn L.	(305)768-8000	529
Miami	ADAMS, Gustav C.	(305)261-7031	4
	BYRD, Susan G.	(305)347-2068	169
	DANIELS, Westwell R.	(305)235-9484	273
	MILLER, Laurence A.	(305)554-2461	839
	PARISE, Marina P.		940
	PHILLIPS, Donald J.	(305)274-5724	968
	SEGOR, Phyllis L.	(305)940-6014	1112
	WILLIAMS, Thomas L.	(305)547-5782	1347
Miami Beach	LESNIAK, Rose	(305)673-6309	718
Miami Shores	PINE, Nancy M.	(305)758-3392	974
Oakland Park	WILLIAMS, Alexander	(305)565-2990	1341
Orlando	HUDSON, Phyllis J.	(305)275-2584	569
	TREMBLAY, Gerald F.	(305)277-6944	1255
Palm Harbor	HO, Paul J.	(813)785-1874	545
Pensacola	DEBOLT, W D.	(904)474-2213	284
	KIEFER, Rosemary M.	(904)438-2732	647
	TERNAK, Armand T.	(904)479-7835	1232
Pompano Beach	GULLETTE, Irene		477
	WHITESIDE, Lee A.	(305)782-0194	1333

WRITER/EDITOR (Cont'd)
FLORIDA (Cont'd)

St Petersburg	CATES, Jo A.	(813)522-1550	194
	HARDESTY, Larry L.	(813)867-1166	499
	WATERS, Sally G.	(813)345-1335	1308
Sanford	LINSLEY, Laurie S.	(305)323-1450	731
Sanibel	KLASING, Jane P.	(813)472-8391	657
Sarasota	MOON, Eric	(813)355-1795	857
	MOON, Ilse	(813)355-1795	857
	WEAVER, James B.	(813)378-1287	1312
Seminole	WEISS, Susan		1320
Tallahassee	FLEMING, Lois D.		384
	GIBLON, Charles B.	(904)893-3851	431
	HART, Thomas L.	(904)385-7550	507
	HUNT, Mary A.	(904)644-5775	575
	MCCRIMMON, Barbara S.		800
	MILLER, Betty D.	(904)335-4405	836
	PRATT, Darnell D.	(904)487-2651	990
	TOOLE, Gregor K.		1250
Tampa	EVANS, Josephine K.	(813)974-4471	357
	GATES, Jean K.	(813)974-3520	422
	MATHEWS, Richard B.	(813)253-3333	784
Tarpon Springs	O'BRIEN, Elizabeth M.	(813)942-3291	914
Venice	CARR, Mary L.	(813)497-0420	186
Vero Beach	KISER, Mary D.	(305)567-4111	656
West Palm Beach	FOSTER, Helen M.	(305)686-1776	392
	TAFFEL, Bobbe H.	(305)582-2539	1219
Winter Park	HUTCHINSON, Beck	(305)645-3608	579

GEORGIA

Acworth	STAHL, D G.	(404)924-8505	1178
Athens	BAKER, Barry B.	(404)542-2534	47
	CARPENTER, David E.	(404)542-8460	184
	HAAR, John M.	(404)549-7625	480
	ROWLAND, Lucy M.	(404)543-3690	1062
	WILLIAMS, Sara E.	(408)548-7519	1346
Atlanta	CAMP, John F.	(404)875-4373	175
	COURSEY, W T.	(404)264-0714	251
	DEES, Anthony R.	(404)355-0551	287
	FORSEE, Joe B.	(404)656-2461	391
	KLOPPER, Susan M.	(404)658-1776	662
	MCDAVID, Sara J.	(404)395-1605	801
	MILLER, Anthony G.	(404)688-4636	835
	MILLER, Jack E.	(404)892-3600	838
	QUINLIN, Margaret M.	(404)874-1589	1000
	SIMMONS, Hal	(404)451-0331	1140
	SMITH, Jane B.	(205)271-5163	1155
	STOWELL, Donald C.	(404)231-4414	1199
	TEMPLETON, Mary E.	(404)727-6875	1231
	TOPE, Diana R.	(404)656-2461	1251
	WILTSE, Helen C.	(404)451-4260	1353
Bremen	BROCK, Kathy T.	(404)537-4960	138
Carrollton	BEARD, Charles E.	(404)832-9458	69
Cartersville	HOWINGTON, Lee R.	(404)382-4203	566
Columbus	CLEMENTS, Betty H.	(404)327-3399	221
Dalton	LARY, Marilyn S.	(404)272-4527	700
Decatur	ALLEN, William R.	(404)284-2981	16
	BISHOP, Beverly D.	(404)371-8488	99
	BUDLONG, Thomas F.	(404)289-0583	155
	HATCHER, Nolan C.	(404)378-8282	511
	HUGHES, Glenda J.	(404)636-0108	571
	HULLUM, Cheri J.	(404)987-7473	573
	OVERBECK, James A.	(404)378-8821	931
	WENDEROTH, Christine	(404)378-8821	1323
Experiment	LEDFORD, Carole L.	(404)228-7238	708
Gainesville	VAUGHAN, Elinor F.	(404)534-6120	1279
Kennesaw	GRIFFIN, Martha R.	(404)422-9921	468
Lilburn	HOUGH, Leslie S.	(404)979-0270	562
Macon	HOWARD, Mary R.	(912)744-2960	564
	RANKIN, Jocelyn A.	(912)744-2515	1007
Milledgeville	SCOTT, Rupert N.	(912)453-5573	1108
Morrow	HENDERSON, Laurel E.	(404)961-7753	526
Richmond Hill	GLISSON, Patricia A.	(912)727-2592	441
Roswell	MARTIN, Clarece	(404)993-0625	775
Statesboro	JOHNSON, Jane G.	(912)681-1609	605
Stone Mountain	ENGERRAND, Steven W.	(404)469-5066	349
Sylvester	MEREY-KADAR, Ervin R.	(912)776-0723	825
Thomasville	CLARKE, Elba C.	(912)228-4280	218
Vidalia	HARTZ, Frederic R.	(912)537-0195	509

WRITER/EDITOR (Cont'd)
HAWAII

Aiea	TIMBERLAKE, Cynthia A.	(808)488-4507	1245
Honolulu	DILUCIA, Samuel J.	(808)955-1500	303
	LUSTER, Arlene L.	(808)737-8876	750
	MITCHELL, Jeanette E.	(808)949-5355	848
	NAJ, Linda M.	(808)946-5359	887
	SHELDEN, Patricia R.	(808)538-6430	1125
	SZILARD, Paula	(808)948-8263	1218
	TRAPIDO, Joel	(808)988-2068	1254
	UCHIDA, Deborah K.	(808)548-7915	1267
	URAGO, Gail M.	(808)949-6496	1269
	VAN NIEL, Eloise S.	(808)548-6283	1276
Kailua	NAHL-JAKOBOVITS, Diane	(808)261-2382	886
	WRIGHT, John C.	(808)261-3714	1371
Kailua-Kona	KOLMAN, Roberta F.		669
Pearl City	KAN, Katharine L.		624
Waiaulua	VEATCH, Laurie L.	(808)237-8411	1280

IDAHO

Boise	WELLS, Merle W.	(208)334-3356	1322
Moscow	ABRAHAM, Terry		3
	BAIRD, Lynn N.	(208)885-6713	47
	BRADY, Eileen E.	(208)883-0817	126
	CURL, Margo W.	(208)885-6260	265

ILLINOIS

Abbott Park	SWANSON, Ruth M.	(312)937-6959	1213
Arlington Heights	SHUMAN, Marilyn J.	(312)253-7752	1134
	VONDRUSKA, Eloise M.	(312)392-7232	1288
Aurora	MCKEARN, Anne B.	(312)892-4811	810
Blue Island	WOZNY, Jay	(312)388-1078	1370
Carbondale	BAUNER, Ruth E.	(618)457-5773	67
	BORUZKOWSKI, Lilly A.	(618)453-2365	117
	COX, Shelley M.	(618)457-8975	253
	DALE, Doris C.	(618)536-2441	270
	KOCH, David V.	(618)453-2516	667
	PERSON, Roland C.	(618)453-2818	961
	RAY, Jean M.	(618)549-1290	1011
	RYAN, Sheila	(618)549-7029	1071
	STARRATT, Joseph A.	(618)453-2683	1182
Champaign	BERGER, Sidney E.	(217)351-8140	86
	MCCLELLAN, William M.	(217)352-1893	796
	REPTA, Vada L.	(217)398-5728	1024
	WERT, Lucille M.	(217)356-6600	1325
Charleston	POLLARD, Frances M.	(217)345-5610	981
Chicago	ADAMSHICK, Robert D.	(312)353-1157	6
	BLOSS, Marjorie E.	(312)567-5265	106
	BREEN, Joanell C.	(312)929-1445	131
	BRICKMAN, Sally F.		135
	BROWN, Doris R.	(312)341-8066	143
	BYRE, Calvin S.	(312)341-3643	169
	CARSON, James G.	(312)996-2742	188
	COATSWORTH, Patricia A.	(312)947-2160	224
	CORNICK, Ron	(312)282-6579	247
	DOLNICK, Sandy F.	(312)944-6780	310
	DONOVAN, William A.	(312)947-9276	312
	DREWETT, William O.	(312)281-3651	319
	EPP, Ronald H.	(203)347-6933	351
	EPSTEIN, Dena J.	(312)373-0522	351
	FIEG, Eugene C.	(312)947-9640	375
	FLAGG, Gordon E.	(312)944-6780	383
	FRISBIE, Richard	(312)332-3984	405
	GERDES, Neil W.	(312)753-3196	428
	GLANZ, Lenore M.	(312)528-7817	439
	GODLEWSKI, Susan G.	(312)443-3936	442
	HAAS, Carolyn B.	(312)822-0809	480
	HARRINGTON, Margaret V.	(312)472-6543	504
	HOLLI, Melvin G.	(312)996-3141	552
	HUNT, Janis E.	(312)275-8439	575
	JACOBSEN, Teresa T.	(312)266-1265	590
	KALUZSA, Karen L.	(312)908-2859	623
	KAYAIAN, Mary S.	(312)245-2810	632
	KNOBLAUCH, Mark G.	(312)549-5247	665
	KOBASA, Paul A.	(312)944-6780	666
	KUSZMAUL, Marcia J.	(312)929-7537	685
	LANDRY, Ronald	(312)943-3282	694
	LEWIS, Sherman L.		724
	MACKEY, Denise R.	(312)407-1000	756
	MALINOWSKY, H R.	(312)329-1549	763

WRITER/EDITOR (Cont'd)
ILLINOIS (Cont'd)
Chicago

	MCDERMOTT, Patrice	(312)944-6780	802
	MCELWAIN, William	(312)248-5564	804
	MELTON, Emily I.	(312)944-6780	823
	MOORE, John R.	(312)763-7811	860
	MOORHEAD, John D.	(312)944-4020	862
	MORRISON, Samuel F.	(312)269-3053	868
	MUELLER, Julie M.	(312)645-4839	875
	O'HEARON, Doris M.	(312)221-0570	919
	OTT, Bill	(312)944-6780	930
	PARK, Chung I.	(312)942-3000	940
	PEARSON, Lois R.	(312)280-8957	952
	PERTELL, Grace M.	(312)286-5698	961
	PLOTNIK, Arthur	(312)929-8985	978
	REILLY, Jane A.	(312)764-2413	1020
	RETTIG, James R.	(312)996-2735	1024
	RICHMOND, Diane A.	(312)269-2864	1030
	ROBLING, John S.	(312)620-9600	1045
	ROCHMAN, Hazel P.	(312)944-6780	1046
	SCHRAMM, Mary T.	(312)248-7934	1099
	SHAW, Joyce M.	(312)294-4640	1123
	SPARKS, Joanne L.	(312)728-5510	1171
	STEWART, Richard A.	(312)269-2930	1193
	STONER, Ronald P.	(312)644-3100	1198
	STRAWN, Gary L.	(312)327-4930	1201
	SUTHERLAND, Zena B.	(312)702-8293	1211
	WELLS, James M.	(312)782-1172	1322
	WESTON, E P.	(312)996-2728	1327
	WIBERLEY, Stephen E.	(312)996-2730	1335
	WINGER, Howard W.	(312)748-1129	1355
	WRIGHT, Helen K.	(312)944-6780	1371
	WYLY, Mary P.	(312)477-5413	1375
	ZVIRIN, Stephanie H.	(312)944-6780	1392
Chicago Ridge	LOTZ, Marsha A.	(312)423-7753	742
Columbia	SUTTER, Mary A.	(618)281-7734	1211
Dawson	CHESLEY, Thea B.		207
De Kalb	KIES, Cosette N.	(815)753-1735	647
	LANIER, Donald L.	(815)753-0255	696
	LARSEN, John C.	(815)753-6269	698
	RIDER, Philip R.	(815)758-2181	1032
	RIDINGER, Robert B.	(815)758-5070	1032
	ROYLE, Maryanne	(815)753-9496	1063
	WELCH, Theodore F.	(815)758-6858	1321
Deerfield	CALLAGHAN, Linda W.	(312)945-3311	173
Des Plaines	MCKENZIE, Duncan J.	(312)967-8554	811
Downers Grove	BALCOM, Kathleen M.	(312)960-1200	51
Edwardsville	MOORE, Milton C.	(618)692-1638	860
Elk Grove Village	HOLBROCK, Mary A.	(312)439-4800	550
Evanston	BAUGH, L S.	(312)328-0243	65
	BEATTY, William K.	(312)328-5473	70
	BJORNCRANTZ, Leslie B.	(312)866-9112	100
	BRADY, Mary M.	(312)491-2929	127
	CLOUD, Patricia D.	(312)491-3136	223
	DAVIDSON, Lloyd A.	(312)491-2906	276
	GRISCOM, Richard W.	(312)491-3487	471
	HILL, Janet S.	(312)491-7587	540
	KAPLAN, Rosalyn L.	(312)869-1035	626
	METZLER, Valerie	(312)869-5992	829
	MICHAELSON, Robert C.	(312)491-3057	832
	PALMORE, Sandra N.	(312)328-5329	937
	PIRON, Alice M.	(312)864-3175	975
	PRENDERGAST, Kathleen M.	(312)491-7298	990
	QUINN, Patrick M.	(312)869-2861	1000
	ROOSE, Tina	(312)491-0662	1053
	SHERMAN, Sarah	(312)864-3801	1128
	STEWART, Donald E.	(312)475-5529	1192
	STUTZ, Patricia A.	(312)491-7630	1206
	WHITE, Matthew H.	(312)328-2221	1331
	WHITELEY, Sandra M.	(312)475-7931	1333
	WRIGHT, Donald E.	(312)866-0312	1371
Franklin Park	VOSS, Joyce M.	(312)678-1528	1289
Geneseo	REDINGTON, Deirdre E.	(309)944-3311	1014
Glen Ellyn	TEMPLE, Harold L.	(312)858-2800	1230
Grayslake	DIEHL, Mark	(312)680-5119	302
Highland Park	JANES, Virginia		593
Hinsdale	CZARNECKI, Cary J.	(312)986-1976	268
	GREGORY, Melissa R.	(312)325-2807	466
Hoffman Estates	MILLER, Deborah	(312)882-3698	837

WRITER/EDITOR (Cont'd)
ILLINOIS (Cont'd)

Itasca	HOGAN, Patricia M.	(312)773-1699	549
Jacksonville	ZUIDERVELD, Sharon R.	(217)243-6945	1391
Joliet	JOHNSTON, James R.	(815)729-3481	610
Kingston	SCHREIBER, Robert E.	(815)784-2280	1099
La Grange	HATTENDORF, Lynn C.	(312)579-0873	512
	TUGGLE, Ann M.	(312)627-9250	1262
Lake Forest	DANOFF, Fran	(312)234-2350	274
	MIKOLYZK, Thomas A.	(312)295-6247	834
Lena	FREY, Roxanne C.	(815)369-5372	403
Lisle	SHOTWELL, Richard T.	(312)665-9107	1133
Lockport	TROY, Shannon M.	(312)534-5000	1258
Lombard	MARSHALL, Mary G.	(312)932-1455	774
Macomb	TING, Lee H.	(309)298-1770	1246
Moline	KRAMER, Pamela K.	(309)797-5117	675
Monticello	ARNTZEN, Etta M.	(217)762-7827	34
Naperville	MEACHEN, Edward W.	(312)420-3425	819
Nashville	RUSIEWSKI, Charles B.	(618)327-8304	1068
Normal	DELOACH, Marva L.	(309)438-7463	290
	GOWDY, Laura E.	(309)438-7450	455
	MATTHEWS, Priscilla J.	(309)452-8514	785
Northfield	ANDERSON, Charles R.	(312)446-8259	22
Oak Lawn	DOBREZ, Cynthia K.	(312)422-4990	307
	IHRIG, Alice B.		581
Oak Park	BALCOM, William T.	(312)383-6824	51
	CAREY, Kevin J.	(312)848-0682	181
	MARSHALL, Maggie L.	(312)848-4432	774
	OLDERR, Steven	(312)383-8176	920
Palos Hills	TEO, Elizabeth A.	(312)974-4300	1231
Park Forest	BUCKLEY, Ja A.	(312)748-2536	154
	OCHSNER, Renata E.	(312)748-5374	915
	SHANNON, Kathleen L.	(312)481-1891	1120
Park Ridge	CRISPEN, Joanne	(312)696-6594	259
	JACKSON, William V.	(312)825-4364	588
	LOFTHOUSE, Patricia A.	(312)698-9731	737
Peoria	NIEHAUS, Barbara J.	(309)697-3798	903
	SWORSKY, Felicia G.	(309)672-8885	1217
Quincy	EGGERS, Thomas D.		339
	TYER, Travis E.	(217)223-5024	1266
Rock Island	OHRLUND, Ava L.	(309)786-0698	919
	WESTERBERG, Kermit B.	(309)794-7221	1326
Rockford	DALRYMPLE, Prudence W.	(815)968-9111	271
Rolling Meadows	SCHROEDER, Sandra J.	(312)303-0989	1100
Silvis	SWATOS, Priscilla L.	(309)792-3306	1214
Skokie	GROSSMAN, David G.	(312)673-9100	473
	KAPLAN, Paul M.		626
	SORENSON, Liene S.	(312)673-7774	1168
South Barrington	JUSTIE, Julie H.	(312)551-2093	620
Springfield	ALLEY, Brian	(217)522-8970	16
	BRADWAY, Becky J.	(217)753-4117	126
	ETTER, Constance L.	(217)546-5436	355
	FRISCH, Corrine A.	(217)753-4925	405
	HILDRETH, Charles R.		539
	LARISON, Brenda	(217)529-9233	697
	TEMPLE, Wayne C.	(217)528-6330	1230
Sullivan	ELDER, Nancy J.	(217)728-4832	342
Sycamore	BERRY, John W.	(815)895-4225	90
	STUDWELL, William E.	(815)895-9868	1204
	SULLIVAN, Peggy A.	(815)753-6155	1208
Urbana	ATKINS, Stephen E.	(217)244-1867	38
	BALACHANDRAN, Sarojini	(217)328-3577	50
	BINGHAM, Karen H.	(217)333-0317	97
	BURBANK, Richard D.	(217)333-2713	158
	CLARK, Barton M.	(217)333-0317	216
	DOWNS, Jane B.	(217)344-1714	317
	FAIRCHILD, Constance A.	(217)333-1900	361
	FORREST, Charles G.	(217)244-3770	390
	GUSHEE, Marion S.	(217)367-9610	478
	LANCASTER, Frederick W.	(217)384-7798	691
	MAHER, William J.	(217)333-0798	760
	O'BRIEN, Nancy P.	(217)333-2305	915
	ROLSTAD, Gary O.	(217)333-3280	1052
	RUBIN, Richard E.	(217)333-3280	1065
	SCHLIPF, Frederick A.	(217)367-4057	1094
	SCHMIDT, Karen A.	(217)333-1054	1095
	SIEGEL, Martin A.	(217)333-3247	1136
	TEMPERLEY, Nicholas	(217)333-8733	1230
	WATSON, Paula D.	(217)333-1116	1310
	WILLIAMS, James W.	(217)333-2305	1344

WRITER/EDITOR (Cont'd)
ILLINOIS (Cont'd)

Urbana			
	WILLIAMS, Mitsuko	(217)333-3654	1345
Villa Park	POINTON, Louis R.	(312)833-6555	980
Wauconda	HEITMAN, Lynn	(312)526-6225	523
West Chicago	KOSMAN, Joyce E.	(312)231-0774	672
	OLSEN, Sarah G.	(312)451-3078	922
Wheeling	HAMMER, Donald P.	(312)541-8149	493
	LAMB, Sara G.	(312)541-8114	690
Wilmette	ELSTEIN, Rochelle S.	(312)256-8484	346
	REIF, Lenore S.	(312)156-1100	1019
Wilmington	BOBAN, Carol A.	(815)458-3411	108
Winnetka	BLACKBURN, Joy M.	(312)446-8697	102

INDIANA

Anderson	KENDALL, Charles T.	(317)649-5039	640
Bloomington	BRISTOW, Ann	(812)335-8028	137
	COPLER, Judith A.	(812)335-9255	244
	FARRELL, David	(812)335-3403	365
	FLING, Robert M.	(812)335-2970	385
	HALPORN, Barbara	(812)335-1446	490
	LAUGHLIN, Sara G.	(812)334-8347	703
	MCCUNE, Lois M.	(812)339-0505	801
	MILLER, Constance R.	(812)335-5729	836
	MURPHY, Marcy	(812)335-5113	881
	SCHLESINGER, Louise D.	(812)334-2190	1094
	SELLBERG, Roxanne J.	(812)335-4626	1113
	TALALAY, Kathryn M.	(812)335-2970	1220
	WESTFALL, Gloria D.	(812)335-6924	1327
Bluffton	ELLIOTT, Barbara J.	(219)824-2315	343
Charlestown	WHALEY, Janie B.	(812)256-6363	1328
Chesterton	BECKING, Mara S.	(219)926-5618	73
Clinton	RAWLES-HEISER, Carolyn	(317)832-9969	1010
Evansville	BAKER, Donald E.	(812)425-4309	48
	MEEK, Janet E.	(812)479-2487	821
Fort Wayne	SANDSTROM, Pamela E.	(219)424-7241	1081
Frankfort	MUNDELL, Eric L.	(317)659-2027	878
Gary	MILLENDER, Dharathola	(219)882-4050	835
Highland	ENGELBERT, Peter J.	(219)923-2173	348
Hobart	CHRISTIANSON, Elin B.	(219)942-5536	212
Huntington	ISCA, Joseph J.	(219)672-8194	585
Indianapolis	ALLEN, Joyce S.	(317)929-8021	15
	BRADLEY, Johanna	(317)751-3779	126
	BRAHMI, Frances A.	(317)274-1401	127
	EBERSHOFF-COLES, Susan V.	(317)269-1815	334
	ELLSWORTH, Marlene A.	(317)274-7185	345
	GANN, Daniel H.	(317)299-9058	416
	HOOK-SHELTON, Sara A.	(317)274-7204	556
	SCHMIDT, Steven J.	(317)274-0470	1096
	STUSSY, Susan A.	(317)929-0343	1205
	THOMPSON, Anna M.		1238
	YOUNG, Philip H.	(317)788-3399	1383
Jeffersonville	HODGSON, Janet B.		546
La Porte	SMYERS, Richard P.	(219)324-2186	1162
Lafayette	TROUTNER, Joanne J.	(317)477-7306	1258
Muncie	BEILKE, Patricia F.	(317)284-2457	75
	DOLAK, Frank J.	(317)285-5141	309
	HODGE, Stanley P.	(317)285-8033	546
	WILLIAMS, Nyal Z.	(317)285-5065	1345
Noblesville	WILLIAMS, Maudine	(317)773-1763	1345
Notre Dame	CONNELLY, James T.	(219)233-9676	237
	DOELLMAN, Michael A.	(219)232-0778	308
	FUDERER, Laura S.	(219)239-5176	408
	MAXWELL, Jan C.	(219)239-6188	788
South Bend	BEATTY, R M.	(219)232-2349	70
	HARLAN, John B.	(219)288-0693	502
	HOHL, Robert J.	(219)289-8160	550
	TUCKER, Dennis C.		1261
	YATES, Donald N.	(219)289-3405	1378
Terre Haute	LITTLE, Robert D.	(812)237-2488	733
	MILLER, Marsha A.	(812)237-2605	840
	VANCIL, David E.	(812)237-2610	1273
Valparaiso	HOLTERHOFF, Sarah G.	(219)465-7866	555
	PERRY, Margaret	(219)464-5364	960
	RAYMAN, Ronald A.	(219)464-2060	1011
Warsaw	DETWILER, Susan M.	(219)269-5254	296

WRITER/EDITOR (Cont'd)
INDIANA (Cont'd)

West Lafayette	ANDERSON, Marilyn M.	(317)583-2586	24
	ANDREWS, Theodora A.	(317)463-6093	27
	BAILEY, Martha J.	(317)494-2910	46
	BAXTER, Pam M.	(317)494-2969	67
	BRANDT, Daryl S.		128
	CANGANELLI, Patrick W.	(317)494-2768	178
	HEWISON, Nancy S.	(317)463-0904	535
	PASK, Judith M.	(317)494-6735	946
	TUCKER, John M.	(317)494-2833	1261
	YOUNGEN, Gregory K.	(317)743-9893	1383
Westfield	VAN CAMP, Ann J.	(317)896-3537	1272
Winamac	SMITH, Robert E.	(219)946-6255	1160

IOWA

Ames	BLACK, William K.	(515)294-1442	102
	COLE, Jim E.	(515)294-0432	230
	KUHN, Warren B.	(515)294-1442	682
Bettendorf	MEIER, Patricia L.	(319)355-3895	821
Boone	ADAMS, Larry D.	(515)432-1931	5
Cedar Rapids	BLISS, David H.	(319)393-5892	105
	JANUS, Bridget M.	(319)365-5055	594
	LEAVITT, Judith A.	(319)390-3109	707
Davenport	PETERSON, Dennis R.	(319)391-3877	963
	STOUT, Robert J.	(319)326-6237	1199
Des Moines	CLAYBURN, Marginell P.	(515)279-6967	220
	GEORGE, Shirley H.	(515)281-4105	428
	JOHNSON, Nancy E.	(515)262-6714	608
Dubuque	KNEFEL, Mary A.	(319)589-3215	664
Iowa City	BROWN, Jeanine B.		144
	DUNLAP, Leslie W.		326
	EIMAS, Richard	(319)337-5538	340
	HOWELL, John B.	(319)335-5885	565
	KOHLER, Carolyn W.	(319)337-9839	668
	SCHERUBEL, Melody	(319)351-6264	1092
Manchester	CRAWFORD, Daniel R.		256
Muscatine	MATHER, Becky R.	(319)263-9049	783
	SORENSON, Debra J.	(319)263-1670	1168
Sioux City	PHILLIPS, Donna M.	(712)258-6981	968
Vinton	SHEPHERD, Rex L.	(319)472-4721	1127
West Branch	DENNIS, Mary R.	(319)643-2583	292

KANSAS

Alma	BIRNEY, Ann E.	(913)765-2370	98
Emporia	BODART-TALBOT, Joni	(316)343-1200	109
	BOGAN, Mary E.	(316)342-1394	110
Lawrence	HINTON, N E.	(913)842-8405	543
	RHODES, Saralinda A.		1026
	SNYDER, Fritz	(913)864-3025	1164
Lenexa	MCLEOD, Debra A.	(913)492-4512	814
Manhattan	WEISENBURGER, Patricia J.	(913)532-5968	1319
	WILLIAMS, Sara R.	(913)532-6516	1346
McPherson	OLSEN, Rowena J.	(316)241-0731	921
North Newton	HAURY, David A.	(316)283-2500	512
Overland Park	OJALA, Marydee P.		919
	SEVIER, Susan G.	(913)451-3111	1117
Pittsburg	DEGRUSON, Eugene H.	(316)231-7000	288
	LEE, Earl W.	(316)231-7000	709
	VOLLEN, Gene E.	(316)231-7000	1287
Salina	THOMAS, Evangeline M.	(913)827-1604	1236
Topeka	JOHNSON, Duane F.	(913)296-3296	603
	MICHAELIS, Patricia A.	(913)296-2624	831
	RICHMOND, Robert W.	(913)234-4704	1031
Valley Center	MEANS, E P.	(316)755-0414	820
Wichita	GERMANN, Malcolm P.	(316)689-3591	429
	MYERS, Robert C.	(316)689-3591	885
	SCHAD, Jasper G.	(316)685-6588	1088
	STRECK, Helen T.	(316)942-2201	1201
Winfield	ZUCK, Gregory J.	(316)221-4150	1391

KENTUCKY

Bowling Green	ZIMMER, Connie W.	(502)781-4165	1388
Danville	GILMER, Wesley	(606)236-1323	437
Edgewood	REESE, Virginia D.	(606)261-8211	1016
Elizabethtown	HOLT, David A.	(502)737-1473	554
Lexington	BIRCHFIELD, Martha J.	(606)257-6098	98
	CUNHA, George M.	(606)257-8876	265
	LEVSTIK, Frank R.	(606)266-9196	721
	MCANINCH, Sandra L.	(606)231-9279	792

WRITER/EDITOR (Cont'd)
KENTUCKY (Cont'd)

Lexington			
	STEPHENSON, Judy A.	(606)278-6316	1188
Louisville	HOUSE, Katherine L.	(502)459-2429	563
	JAMIOLKOWSKI, Nancy J.	(502)582-4111	593
	KEARNEY, Anna R.	(502)588-6744	633
	LINCOLN, Carol S.	(502)568-7683	728
	MAZUK, Melody	(502)897-4807	791
	NILES, Judith F.	(502)588-6756	904
	REDMON, Sherrill	(502)451-5907	1014
	SOMERVILLE, Mary R.	(502)893-8451	1167
	VOYLES, James R.	(502)589-4440	1289
Murray	WALL, Celia J.	(502)762-4990	1297
Richmond	MARTIN, June H.	(606)622-6176	777
Russel Springs	FOLEY, Mary D.	(502)866-5957	387
Southgate	FOX, Estella E.	(606)441-0743	394

LOUISIANA

Baton Rouge	BALL, Dannie J.	(504)388-3119	52
	BLOOMSTONE, Ajaye	(504)767-0847	106
	CARPENTER, Michael A.	(504)766-7385	185
	COE, Miriam M.		226
	HAMAKER, Charles A.	(504)388-8537	490
	HASCHAK, Paul G.	(504)766-9986	510
	HEIM, Kathleen M.	(504)388-3158	521
	HOGAN, Sharon A.	(504)388-2217	549
	KLEINER, Janellyn P.	(504)928-1960	660
	MARTIN, Robert S.	(504)767-7167	778
	MCKANN, Michael R.	(504)342-4922	809
	PHENIX, Katharine J.	(504)388-3158	967
	PHILLIPS, Faye	(504)388-6569	968
	REID, Marion T.	(504)388-2217	1019
	ROUNDTREE, Lynn P.	(504)336-1306	1061
	SHIFLETT, Orvin L.	(504)388-1462	1130
Houma	COSPER, Mary F.	(504)879-4243	249
Lake Charles	CAGLE, Robert B.	(318)437-5740	171
	CUROL, Helen B.	(318)477-1780	266
Metairie	KLEIN, Victor C.	(504)861-0488	659
Monroe	KONTROVITZ, Eileen R.		671
Natchitoches	HARRINGTON, Charles W.	(318)357-0813	504
	HUSSEY, Sandra R.	(318)352-2996	578
New Orleans	BARON, John H.	(504)865-5271	58
	DANKNER, Laura R.	(504)865-2367	273
	DAVIS, Margo	(504)488-1193	280
	DRAUGHON, Ralph B.	(504)891-1921	318
	FLEURY, Bruce E.	(504)865-5682	385
	GERICKE, Paul W.	(504)282-4455	428
	HARDY, D C.	(504)895-3981	500
	JUMONVILLE, Florence M.	(504)523-4662	619
	MCKNIGHT, Mark C.	(504)866-3394	812
	MCREYNOLDS, Rosalee	(504)866-9820	818
	RUSHING, Darla H.	(504)891-1127	1068
	SARKODIE-MENSAH, Kwasi	(504)483-7306	1083
	SKINNER, Robert E.	(504)483-7304	1146
Oakdale	LYNCH, Minnie L.	(318)335-3442	752
Plaquemines	MCCRAY, Evelina W.	(504)659-2541	800
Ruston	DICARLO, Michael A.	(318)257-3594	300
Shreveport	KING, Anne M.	(318)797-5738	650
	MCCLEARY, William E.	(318)865-9813	796
	MEADOR, Patricia L.	(318)797-5226	819
	SALTER, Jeffrey L.	(318)226-5871	1077

MAINE

Alfred	ANDERSON, Marjorie E.	(207)324-6915	24
Augusta	WISMER, Donald	(207)289-5600	1357
Bangor	BEISER, Karl A.	(207)947-4876	75
Bar Harbor	BAKER, Alison	(207)288-3371	47
	GOLBITZ, Peter	(207)288-4969	444
	KINGMA, Sharyn L.	(207)288-4969	652
Baritarbon	GOTTLIEB, Robert A.	(207)288-9574	453
Bath	MCKAY, Ann	(207)443-5524	809
Boothbay	LENTHALL, Franklyn	(207)633-4536	715
Brunswick	HEISER, Nancy E.	(207)725-4253	523
	SAEGER, Edwin J.	(207)729-5720	1074
Farmington	MCNAMARA, Shelley G.	(207)778-3501	816
Georgetown	LUDGIN, Donald H.	(207)371-2221	746
Kennebunkport	PEERS, Charles T.	(207)967-5764	954
Lewiston	GROSS, Richard F.	(207)782-3958	472
Orono	MCCALLISTER, Myrna J.		793

WRITER/EDITOR (Cont'd)
MAINE (Cont'd)

Portland	HUMEZ, Nicholas D.	(207)773-3405	573
	REIMAN, Anne M.	(207)774-4000	1020
Skowhegan	FRIDLEY, Russell W.	(207)474-7133	403
Westbrook	PARKS, George R.	(207)854-0355	943
York	HARMON, James R.	(207)363-7833	502

MARYLAND

Aberdeen	HADDEN, Robert L.	(301)272-1858	481
Adamstown	LIGHTBOWN, Parke P.		726
Adelphi	NITECKI, Danuta A.	(301)937-4791	905
Annapolis	MCKAY, Eleanor	(301)263-6526	809
	PRIMER, Ben	(301)974-3914	993
Arnold	OLSON, Christine A.	(301)647-6708	922
Baltimore	ANDREWS, Loretta K.	(301)396-5320	26
	BRENNAN, Edward P.	(301)675-8835	132
	CHELTON, Mary K.	(301)355-0906	204
	COUPE, Jill M.	(301)338-8357	251
	DAVISH, William	(301)323-1010	281
	EPSTEIN, Robert S.	(301)328-3928	351
	FLORANCE, Valerie	(301)383-9436	385
	FREDENBURG, Anne M.	(301)377-9080	399
	FRYER, Philip	(301)532-8787	407
	GENUARDI, Michael T.	(301)235-1168	427
	GWYN, Ann S.	(301)338-8325	479
	HILDITCH, Bonny M.	(301)675-4333	539
	KLEIN, Ilene R.		659
	LOWENS, Margery M.	(301)532-7422	744
	MONTGOMERY, Paula K.	(301)685-8621	856
	SLEEMAN, William E.	(301)346-5430	1148
	SMITH, Mary P.	(301)358-0356	1158
	TOOEY, Mary J.	(301)744-0521	1250
Beltsville	COLLINS, Donna S.	(301)344-3728	232
Bethesda	BYRNES, Margaret M.	(301)496-0382	169
	FISHBEIN, Meyer H.	(301)530-5391	380
	HENDERSON, Madeline M.	(301)530-6478	526
	LAKSHMAN, Malathi K.	(301)229-9287	689
	LAZAROW-STETTEN, Jane K.	(301)656-5471	706
	MILLENSON, Roy H.		835
	SCHWARTZ, Marla J.	(301)656-0043	1105
	TIFFT, Jeanne D.	(301)229-7415	1244
Bowie	EVANS, Frank B.	(301)464-8829	357
Brookeville	ROBERTS, Lesley A.	(301)774-4471	1040
Brooksville	BASCOM, James F.	(301)774-3175	62
BWI Airport	BUCHAN, Ronald L.	(301)859-5300	153
Cabin John	SEWELL, Winifred	(301)229-5008	1118
Cambridge	DEL SORDO, Jean S.	(301)228-7331	290
Cheverly	SILVESTER, June P.	(301)773-0407	1139
Chevy Chase	CHARTRAND, Robert L.		203
	CLEMMER, Dan O.	(301)654-4212	221
	ERLICK, Louise S.		353
	FINE, Sandra R.	(301)951-3453	377
	KENTON, Charlotte	(301)657-3855	642
	SEARS, Jonathan R.	(301)656-2306	1110
	SHAW, Renata V.	(301)654-3560	1123
College Park	APPLEBAUM, Edmond L.	(301)474-7322	30
	ASSOUAD, Carol S.	(301)935-5631	37
	SHULMAN, Frank J.	(301)935-5614	1133
	WILSON, William G.	(301)454-6003	1353
Columbia	AVERSA, Elizabeth S.	(301)992-3711	41
	GORDON, Martin K.	(301)992-7626	451
	GRUHL, Andrea M.	(301)596-5460	474
	JOHNSON, Elaine B.	(301)992-5502	604
	REIDER, William L.	(301)995-1639	1019
	RUSS, Kennetta P.	(301)381-0579	1068
Damascus	JOHNSON, Susan W.	(301)253-2759	609
Dundalk	MILLER, Everett G.	(301)522-5785	837
Ellicott City	LEVY, Sandra R.	(301)461-2409	722
Forestville	MOORE, Virginia B.	(301)568-8743	861
Fort Meade	KNICKERBOCKER, Wendy	(301)672-3057	664
Fort Washington	BRADSHER, James G.	(301)248-8884	126
Gaithersburg	GRIFFEN, Agnes M.	(301)340-3378	468
	GROCKI, Daniel J.	(301)253-6044	471
Garrett Park	PRATT, Laura C.	(301)942-1764	990
Germantown	MCQUEEN, Judith D.	(301)428-3400	817
	MOLINE, Judi A.	(301)972-5708	853
Greenbelt	ASHFORD, Richard K.	(301)982-5074	36
	SIMS, Sally R.	(301)345-0619	1142

WRITER/EDITOR (Cont'd)
MARYLAND (Cont'd)

Hyattsville	BURGESS, Eileen E.	(301)864-7223	159
Hydes	LANTZ, Louise K.	(301)592-2232	697
Kensington	PRICE, Douglas S.	(301)942-2091	992
Lanham	PUCCIO, Joseph A.	(301)459-0871	997
Laurel	GOLDENBERG, Joan M.	(301)953-9253	445
	LEVINE, Emil H.	(301)776-3062	720
Mount Airy	LISTON, David M.	(301)831-3008	732
	WETZBARGER, Cecilia G.	(301)829-0826	1328
New Carrollton	WILLIAMS, Helen E.	(301)454-6068	1343
New Market	WILSON, Susan W.	(301)831-6118	1353
Potomac	HO, James K.		545
Rockville	BRANDHORST, Wesley T.	(301)460-6932	128
	COSMIDES, George J.	(301)762-5428	249
	DOWD, Frank B.	(301)279-1098	315
	HERIN, Nancy J.	(301)279-6101	531
	LEWIS, Robert J.	(301)460-9145	724
	MICHAELS, Carolyn L.	(301)564-0509	831
	PEDAK-KARI, Maria	(301)279-1940	954
	WALL, Eugene	(301)881-4990	1297
	WHITMAN, Jean A.	(301)736-6804	1333
St Marys City	REPENNING, Julie A.	(301)862-0267	1023
Seabrook	LARSEN, Lida L.	(301)459-3931	698
Severn	JACK, Robert F.	(301)859-5300	586
Silver Spring	BASA, Eniko M.	(301)384-4657	62
	FELMY, John C.	(301)681-9069	370
	KIMMEL, Mark R.	(301)340-2100	649
	LEVITAN, Karen B.	(301)588-8139	721
	MERIKANGAS, Robert J.	(301)384-3449	826
	NORRIS, Loretta W.	(301)587-3470	909
	OVERTON, Kathryn R.	(301)236-9754	931
	PICKETT, Olivia K.	(301)434-7503	971
	PRITCHARD, Sarah M.	(301)588-8624	994
	RAWSTHORNE, Grace C.	(301)949-0698	1011
	SCHEIPS, Paul J.		1091
	STERN, Michael P.	(301)495-9413	1189
	TATUM, George M.	(301)236-9179	1225
	TAYLOR, Marcia E.	(301)942-6704	1227
	VAN CAMPEN, Rebecca J.	(301)890-8588	1272
	WALSH, Barclay		1299
Timonium	STUART, Karen A.	(301)561-4446	1204
Upper Marlboro	DICKSON, Katherine M.	(301)350-4035	301
	WOODY, Jacqueline B.		1368
Westminster	MCCARTY, Emily H.	(301)848-1825	795
Wheaton	KAESSINGER, Carla S.	(301)949-1477	621

MASSACHUSETTS

Amherst	DONOHUE, Joseph	(413)545-0498	312
Andover	GREENE, Cathy C.	(617)470-0902	463
Arlington	ENGLISH, Cynthia J.	(617)227-0270	350
	FORTIER, Jan M.	(617)646-5856	391
	LUKOS, Geraldine F.	(617)646-3439	748
Assonet	MEDEIROS, Joseph	(617)624-4094	820
Bedford	BERGIN, Dorothy O.	(617)275-7071	86
	HALE, Janice L.	(617)275-0377	485
Beverly	GAGNON, Ronald A.	(617)922-6722	412
Boston	ANDERSON, A J.	(617)738-2230	21
	BEGG, Karin E.		74
	BERNARD, Bobbi	(617)353-1568	88
	BUSH, Margaret A.	(617)262-2045	165
	CURLEY, Arthur	(617)536-5400	265
	FOX, Susan	(617)463-3178	395
	FRYDRYK, Teresa E.	(617)482-9485	407
	HEINS, Ethel L.	(617)527-2736	522
	HERNON, Peter	(617)738-2223	532
	HOLT, June C.	(617)727-1140	554
	MAIO, Kathleen L.	(617)573-8532	762
	MATIS, Lynn	(617)973-8000	784
	MURRAY, Lynn T.	(617)330-9000	882
	NESS, Arthur J.	(617)277-1776	896
	O'TOOLE, James M.	(617)929-8110	930
	PIGGFORD, Roland	(617)267-9400	972
	PRISTASH, Kenneth	(617)262-1120	993
	ROGAN, Michael J.	(617)536-5400	1049
	SHANNON, Marcia A.	(617)267-9400	1120
	SNIFFIN-MARINO, Megan G.	(617)738-3141	1163
	STEVENSON, Michael I.	(617)495-6374	1191
	TRIPP, Maureen A.	(617)578-8676	1257
	VOIGT, John F.	(617)266-1400	1287

WRITER/EDITOR (Cont'd)
MASSACHUSETTS (Cont'd)

Boston			
	ZIMPFER, William E.	(617)353-3034	1389
Brighton	BRAUN, Robin E.	(617)789-2177	130
Cambridge	DESIMONE, Dorothy H.	(617)495-2432	295
	DUNKLY, James W.	(617)868-3450	326
	EPPARD, Philip B.	(617)492-4157	351
	FERNALD, Anne C.	(617)491-4077	373
	KNAACK, Linda M.	(617)253-8462	663
	MANDEL, Debra H.	(617)497-0929	764
	PARKER, Susan E.	(617)495-3455	942
	WHITE, Chandlee	(617)576-9299	1330
Carlisle	MIELE, Madeline F.	(617)369-8582	833
Chestnut Hill	CONSTANCE, Joseph W.	(617)552-3698	238
Concord	JACKSON, Patience K.	(617)369-0586	588
	LEWONTIN, Amy	(617)369-9106	724
Douglas	COPPOLA, Peter A.	(617)476-2975	245
Easthampton	MELNICK, Ralph	(413)527-3036	823
Fitchburg	LAMBERT, Lyn D.	(617)345-6726	690
	WALSH, Jim	(617)342-9078	1299
Framingham	HANSSEN, Nancy E.	(617)875-0382	499
Gloucester	RHINELANDER, Mary F.	(617)281-2439	1025
Hanover	FRIEDMAN, Fred T.	(617)826-2972	403
Hanscom AFB	DUFFEK, Elizabeth A.	(617)377-4768	323
Heath	HOWLAND, Margaret E.	(413)337-4980	566
Hopedale	KANE, Jean B.	(617)473-9238	624
Ipswich	ANDERSON, Norman E.	(617)356-4623	24
Leverett	ZIPKOWITZ, Fay	(413)367-9573	1389
Lexington	CARTER, Walter F.	(617)860-6739	190
	TAUBER, Stephen J.	(617)861-6295	1225
	WARNER, Alice S.	(617)862-9278	1305
Lowell	KARR, Ronald D.	(617)452-5000	628
Medford	JONES, Frederick S.	(617)381-3345	613
	MARTIN, Murray S.	(617)776-3599	777
	MCDONALD, Ellen J.	(617)381-3273	802
Melrose	MURPHY, Eva B.	(617)665-7572	880
Monterey	INTNER, Sheila S.	(413)528-2698	583
Nahant	DESTEFANO, Daniel A.	(617)596-1767	296
Needham	CABEZAS, Sue A.	(617)449-3965	170
Newton	ALPERT, Hillel R.		17
	WALLAS, Philip R.	(617)527-1762	1298
Newton Highlands	FOX, Elyse H.	(617)443-4798	394
Newtonville	FRIEDMAN, Terri L.	(617)965-6310	404
North Abington	LAROSA, Sharon M.	(617)871-6288	698
North Dartmouth	DACE, Tish	(617)999-8304	269
North Quincy	NIELSEN, Sonja M.	(617)328-8306	903
Northampton	GRIGG, Susan	(413)584-2700	470
	MORTIMER, Ruth	(413)584-2700	870
	SCOTT, Alison M.	(413)584-2700	1106
	SLY, Margery N.	(413)584-2700	1150
Orange	PROUTY, Sharman E.	(617)544-6743	996
Petersham	MCMANAMON, Mary J.	(617)724-3407	814
Reading	MARCY, Henry O.	(617)944-2194	769
	O'CONNOR, Jerry	(617)944-6452	916
Roslindale	CLANCY, Catherine M.	(617)327-0013	215
Roybury	SUTTON, Joyce A.	(617)427-4941	1211
Sagamore	OLIANSKY, Joseph D.	(617)888-6189	920
Sharon	FRAZIER, James A.	(617)784-5642	399
Shrewsbury	CHANG, Isabelle E.	(617)845-4641	200
Somerville	FELDT, Candice K.	(617)666-2745	369
Springfield	DUNN, Donald J.	(413)782-1454	326
	MCLAIN, Guy A.	(413)739-3871	813
Stow	MOULTON, Lynda W.	(617)897-7163	873
Sudbury	KOVED, Ruth B.	(617)443-3591	674
Swampscott	BRENNER, Lawrence	(617)598-0370	133
Taunton	TURKALO, David M.	(617)824-8769	1263
Wakefield	BOZOIAN, Paula	(617)438-0779	124
Waltham	CHATTERTON, Leigh A.	(617)893-4807	204
Wareham	PILLSBURY, Mary J.	(617)295-2343	973
Watertown	BAKST, Shelley D.	(617)872-8200	50
	LANDESMAN, Betty J.	(617)924-7182	692
Wellesley Hills	KENNEDY, Amy D.	(617)237-4013	640
Wendell	HOLMBERG, Olga S.	(617)544-2706	553
West Newton	CHEN, Ching C.	(617)738-2224	205
Westhampton	LOMBARDO, Daniel J.	(413)527-1796	738
Westwood	KNAPP, Leslie C.	(617)329-3350	663
Williamsburg	LANCASTER, John	(413)268-7679	692
Winchester	SMITH, Ann M.	(617)729-7169	1152
Woods Hole	SHEPHARD, Frank C.	(617)548-2743	1127

WRITER/EDITOR (Cont'd)
MASSACHUSETTS (Cont'd)

Worcester	KASPERSON, Jeanne X.	(617)793-7133	629
	STANKUS, Tony	(617)793-2643	1180

MICHIGAN

Alpena	WILLIAMS, Susan S.	(517)356-1622	1346
Ann Arbor	BENSON, Peggy	(313)665-0651	83
	BOWEN, Jennifer B.	(313)663-6164	120
	CHASE, William D.	(313)663-5714	203
	CONWAY, Paul L.	(313)668-2218	239
	DAVIDSEN, Susanna L.	(313)995-7352	276
	DOUGHERTY, Richard M.	(313)764-9356	314
	DWOSKIN, Beth M.	(212)382-6727	330
	FINERMAN, Carol B.	(313)995-4485	378
	GATTIS, R G.	(313)936-1073	422
	HOUGH, Carolyn A.	(313)665-0537	562
	JASPER, Richard P.	(313)973-0747	595
	KOCHEN, Manfred	(313)764-2585	667
	KUSNERZ, Peggy A.		685
	MARTIN, Patricia W.	(313)665-3776	777
	REGAN, Lesley E.	(313)434-5530	1017
	SCOTT, Melissa C.	(313)764-7460	1107
	SIEVING, Pamela C.	(313)761-1418	1136
	SLAVENS, Thomas P.	(313)665-6663	1148
	SWEET, Robert E.	(313)246-6204	1215
	TAYLOR, Margaret T.	(313)747-3592	1227
	TERWILLIGER, Doris H.	(313)761-3912	1232
	WEST, Marian S.	(313)663-5907	1326
Auburn Hills	EL MOUCHI, Joan S.	(313)370-9466	346
Berkley	MARLOW, Cecilia A.	(313)547-3098	772
Berrien Springs	WILDMAN, Linda	(801)471-9764	1339
Birmingham	GOLDSTEIN, Doris R.	(313)626-9299	446
	JERYAN, Christine B.	(313)645-6268	600
	ROSE, Sharon G.	(313)647-4148	1055
Cheboygan	SMALLWOOD, Carol A.	(616)627-2308	1151
Clarkston	D'ELIA, Joseph G.	(313)625-8274	289
Dearborn	CRAWFORD, Geraldine H.	(313)271-2184	256
	FORSYTH, Karen R.	(313)562-8830	391
	LIMBACHER, James L.	(313)565-9687	727
	VINT, Patricia A.	(313)591-5073	1285
Dearborn Heights	KIRKESY, Oliver M.	(313)278-4670	655
Detroit	BRUNK, Thomas W.	(313)331-4930	150
	CONNORS, Martin G.	(313)961-2242	238
	GIGLIO, Linda M.	(313)872-4311	433
	HANNA, Hildur W.	(313)965-0150	496
	KNIFFEL, Leonard J.	(313)864-0982	664
	MENDELSOHN, Loren D.	(313)577-6317	823
	MORROW, Blaine V.	(313)893-1746	869
	NASSO, Christine	(313)961-2242	889
	STREETER, Linda D.		1201
	VELLIKY, Mary M.	(313)872-4311	1281
	WARD, Nancy E.	(313)256-9596	1304
East Lansing	ACKERMAN, Katherine K.	(517)332-6818	4
	BLATT, Gloria T.	(313)332-6817	104
	JIZBA, Laurel	(517)353-4526	600
	SANFORD, John D.	(517)355-2330	1081
Eaton Rapids	FLAHERTY, Kevin C.	(517)663-2362	383
Farmington Hills	RENKIEWICZ, Frank A.	(313)478-4506	1023
Ferndale	BORAM, Joan M.	(313)542-2523	116
Flint	ARNOLD, Peggy	(313)744-4040	34
	PALMER, David W.	(313)238-0166	936
Grand Haven	BROOKS, Burton H.	(616)842-2586	140
Grand Rapids	BOSE, Deborah L.	(616)453-1900	117
	DE KLERK, Peter	(616)957-6303	288
	FITZPATRICK, Nancy C.	(616)676-1568	383
	KING, Kathryn L.		651
	WEAVER, Clarence L.		1312
Grosse Pointe Farms	DRAPER, James P.	(313)881-4397	318
	HANSON, Charles D.	(313)882-3627	498
Grosse Pointe Woods	STRATELAK, Nadia A.	(313)886-1043	1200
Hancock	PENTI, Marsha E.	(906)482-5300	957
Huntington Woods	BINDSCHADLER, Valerie V.	(313)547-2962	97
Iron Mountain	SILVER, Gary L.	(906)774-3005	1138
Jackson	SMITH, Catherine A.	(517)784-7025	1153

WRITER/EDITOR (Cont'd)
MICHIGAN (Cont'd)

Kalamazoo	GROTZINGER, Laurel A.	(616)381-1865	473
	ISAACSON, David K.	(616)383-1562	584
	NESBURG, Janet A.	(616)349-7775	896
	VANDER MEER, Patricia F.	(616)383-1666	1274
Lansing	CALLARD, Carole	(517)373-1593	173
	EZELL, Charlaine L.	(517)485-8019	360
	FRYE, Dorothy T.	(517)393-7608	407
	HEINLEN, Bethany A.	(517)377-8389	522
Lincoln Park	HECK-RABI, Louise E.	(313)928-3967	520
Marquette	PAULIN, Mary A.	(906)228-6686	950
Mt Pleasant	MULLIGAN, William H.	(517)773-1374	877
	TIMBERS, Jill G.		1245
Novi	COREY, Marjorie	(313)344-1770	246
Olivet	COOPER, B L.	(616)749-7618	242
Otsego	PARK, Janice R.	(616)694-4546	941
Parchment	BOURGEOIS, Ann M.	(616)344-9097	119
Port Huron	YAEK, Larry A.	(313)484-3881	1376
Rochester	HILDEBRAND, Linda L.	(313)370-2483	538
Sault Sainte Marie	MICHELS, Fredrick A.	(906)635-2404	832
Southfield	COCOZZOLI, Gary R.	(313)443-8905	226
	JOSE, Phyllis A.	(313)355-9282	617
Springfield	BURHANS, Barbara C.	(616)965-4096	159
Traverse City	SICILIANO, Peg P.	(616)947-1480	1135
Warren	DOYLE, James M.	(313)445-7401	317
Wayne	WEISER, Douglas E.	(313)326-8910	1319
West Bloomfield	WREN, James A.	(313)682-6310	1370
Ypsilanti	KIRKENDALL, Carolyn A.	(313)482-7041	654
	MARSHALL, Albert P.		773

MINNESOTA

Braham	MCGRIFF, Ronald I.	(612)396-3957	808
Duluth	SCHROEDER, Janet K.	(218)723-3821	1100
Eden Prairie	BILEYDI, Lois G.	(612)934-3576	96
Grand Marais	GILLIS, Ruth J.		436
Grand Rapids	VALANCE, Marsha J.	(218)327-2336	1271
Hopkins	YOUNG, Margaret L.	(612)933-5062	1382
Mankato	PIEHL, Kathleen K.	(507)389-5961	971
Minneapolis	ALLISON, Brent	(612)624-4549	17
	ASPNES, Grieg G.	(612)926-1749	37
	BEAVEN, Miranda J.	(612)624-5860	71
	BOEDER, Thelma B.	(612)870-3657	109
	CARLSON, Stan W.	(612)571-2046	182
	DODGE, Christopher N.	(612)541-8572	308
	GASTON, Judith A.	(612)627-4277	421
	GUNTHER, Paul B.	(612)371-5622	478
	HALLEWELL, Laurence	(612)724-6565	489
	KELLY, Richard J.	(612)624-5860	638
	LACY, Lyn E.	(612)724-6110	687
	LATHROP, Alan K.	(612)789-4046	701
	OLSON, Lowell E.	(612)626-0824	923
	OVERMIER, Judith A.	(612)626-6881	931
	POQUETTE, Mary L.	(612)377-6691	984
	SANDNESS, John G.	(612)866-7033	1081
	WALDEN, Barbara L.	(612)624-5860	1294
	WEEKS, John M.	(612)624-6833	1315
	WITT, Kenneth W.	(612)871-4262	1358
	YAHNKE, Robert E.	(612)625-0504	1376
Red Wing	SWEEN, Roger	(612)388-5723	1214
Robbinsdale	HERTHER, Nancy K.	(612)529-0115	533
Saint Joseph	HYNES, Arleen M.		580
St Paul	BALDWIN, Jerome C.	(612)297-4532	51
	BLUMBERG-MCKEE, Hazel	(612)292-1680	107
	BROGAN, Martha L.	(612)698-1186	139
	COLOKATHIS, Jane	(612)297-4969	234
	DELOACH, Lynda J.	(612)627-4208	290
	HALES-MABRY, Celia E.	(612)645-2850	486
	HLAVSA, Larry B.	(612)699-7198	544
	MARION, Donald J.	(612)624-6379	770
	MCCLASKEY, Marilyn H.	(612)624-5333	796
	MINOR, Barbara G.	(612)698-4978	846
	OZOLINS, Karl L.	(612)645-2999	933
	STEINWALL, Susan D.	(612)690-5766	1186
	WHITE, William T.	(612)227-9531	1332
	WURL, Joel F.	(612)627-4208	1374
Waite Park	CLARKE, Norman F.	(612)253-2695	219

WRITER/EDITOR (Cont'd)

MISSISSIPPI

Clarksdale	GRAVES, Sid F.	(601)627-2322	459
Cleveland	STEWART, Jeanne E.	(601)843-2774	1192
Hattiesburg	VAN MELER, Vandelia L.	(601)266-4243	1276
Jackson	PARKS, James F.	(601)354-5201	943
Mount Olive	BOYD, Sandra E.	(601)797-3334	123
Prentiss	SMITH, Judy S.		1156
Starkville	NETTLES, Jess	(601)323-5558	896
University	FISHER, Benjamin F.		380
	TUCKER, Ellis E.	(601)232-7361	1261
Vicksburg	ABLES, Timothy D.	(601)636-8088	2

MISSOURI

Afton	WOHLRABE, John C.	(314)843-8131	1359
Ballwin	FORD, Gary E.	(314)225-6723	389
	TAYLOR, Arthur R.	(314)394-9973	1226
Boonville	JOB, Rose A.		601
Cape Girardeau	STIEGEMEYER, Nancy H.	(314)334-3674	1193
Columbia	ARCHER, Stephen M.	(314)442-0611	31
	ELS, Nancy T.	(314)882-9162	346
	MARTIN, Mason G.	(314)449-5798	777
	MULTER, Ell P.		878
	O'DELL, Charles A.	(314)445-6467	916
	POWELL, Ronald R.	(314)882-9545	988
	SHAUGHNESSY, Thomas W.	(314)882-4701	1123
	YOUNG, Virginia G.	(314)443-8413	1383
Fenton	DEKEN, Jean M.	(314)827-1717	288
Florissant	ANTHONY, Paul L.	(314)921-6158	29
Jefferson City	BEHLER, Patricia A.	(314)635-0608	74
	TORDOFF, Brian G.	(314)893-3147	1251
Kansas City	CARSON, Bonnie L.		188
	COX, Bruce B.		253
	GIBSON, Patricia A.	(816)333-9700	432
	HUDSON, Rosetta A.	(816)459-6606	570
	INGERSOL, Robert S.	(816)333-7000	582
	JENKINS, Harold R.	(816)444-2590	597
	KARNS, Kermit B.	(816)453-1294	627
	LINEBACH, Laura M.	(816)361-7031	730
	LONDRE, Felicia H.	(816)444-1878	738
	MEIZNER, Karen L.	(816)561-4000	822
	MILLS, Elaine L.	(816)333-1245	844
	NESBITT, John R.	(813)926-7616	896
	PETERSON, Paul A.	(816)363-5020	964
	PLUMB, Warren G.	(816)741-4824	978
	ROTH, Sally	(816)842-0984	1059
	SPALDING, Helen H.	(816)276-1531	1171
	SULLIVAN, Marilyn G.	(816)276-1871	1208
Kirkwood	SHALLENBERGER, Anna F.	(314)821-4169	1119
Marionville	MCCROSKEY, Marilyn J.	(417)463-7372	800
Ozark	WARNER, Wayne E.	(417)485-3972	1305
St Louis	BECK, Sara R.	(314)889-5483	71
	BETH, Dana L.	(314)721-0067	92
	BURCKEL, Nicholas C.	(314)889-5400	158
	CARGAS, Harry J.	(314)968-7014	181
	CRAWFORD, Susan Y.	(314)362-7080	257
	DELIVUK, John A.	(314)645-1324	289
	EIKEN, Mary A.	(314)385-8739	340
	GIETSCHIER, Steven P.	(314)993-7787	433
	KISSANE, Mary K.	(314)727-8865	656
	MILLES, James G.	(314)658-3991	843
	PLUTCHAK, T S.	(314)577-8605	979
	REHKOP, Barbara L.		1017
	ROBERTS, Jean A.	(314)664-0939	1040
	SIGALA, Stephanie C.	(314)721-0067	1137
	SMITH, Nancy M.	(314)241-2288	1159
	SUELFLOW, August R.	(314)721-5934	1206
	TIPSWORD, Thomas N.	(314)263-2345	1246
	WHITE, Cheryl L.	(314)367-0741	1330
Shelbyville	MASON, Laura L.	(816)762-4285	781
Springfield	MORROW, Paula J.	(417)887-8161	869
	SINCLAIR, Regina A.	(417)865-8731	1143
Sugar Creek	STEELE, Anitra T.	(816)836-4031	1184
Warrensburg	SADLER, Philip A.	(816)747-8726	1073

WRITER/EDITOR (Cont'd)

MONTANA

Billings	NERODA, Edward W.	(406)657-2320	895
Bozeman	MORTON, Bruce	(406)994-5313	870
Great Falls	O'BRYANT, Alice A.		915
Helena	CLARK, Robert M.	(406)444-4787	218
	JACKSON, George R.	(406)449-3935	587
	MORROW, Delores J.	(406)444-4714	869

NEBRASKA

Kearney	NORMAN, Ronald V.	(308)237-5133	909
Lincoln	ALLEN, Richard H.	(402)435-4052	16
	FELTON, John D.	(402)435-2146	370
	FROBOM, Jerome B.	(402)483-7129	405
	LEITER, Richard A.	(402)466-3468	714
	WOOL, Gregory J.	(402)475-0391	1368
Omaha	HOOVER, Clara G.	(402)895-3605	557
Ralston	OYER, Kenneth E.	(402)331-8843	932

NEVADA

Carson City	ROCHA, Guy L.	(702)885-5210	1045
Henderson	HARRISON, Susan E.		507
Las Vegas	GARDNER, Jack I.	(702)382-3493	418
	SAUNDERS, Laverna M.	(702)739-3069	1084
	VOIT, Irene E.	(702)361-5475	1287
Reno	MCNEAL, Betty	(702)325-5859	816
	ZINK, Steven D.	(702)345-0659	1389

NEW HAMPSHIRE

Amherst	SHERWOOD, Janet R.	(603)673-9242	1129
Concord	HIGGINS, Matthew J.	(603)228-3127	538
	MEVERS, Frank C.	(603)224-3896	829
Derry	HARDSOG, Ellen L.	(603)432-6140	500
Durham	KAPOOR, Jagdish C.	(603)868-2504	626
Franconia	BJORNER, Susan N.	(603)823-8838	100
Hampton	KORBER, Nancy	(603)926-6005	671
Hanover	BROWN, Stanley W.	(603)646-2037	147
Keene	VINCENT, Charles P.	(603)352-1909	1284
Merrimack	DENTON, Francesca L.	(603)424-8621	293
Milford	LISTOVITCH, Denise A.	(603)672-0899	733
Mirror Lake	SARLES, Christie V.	(603)569-4932	1083
Nashua	BARRETT, Beth R.	(603)880-3542	59
	EMOND, Kathleen A.		348
	FERRIGNO, Helen F.	(603)889-3042	373
North Chichester	NARDINI, Robert F.	(603)798-5751	888
Peterborough	BOND, George	(603)924-9281	113
	PERRON, Michelle M.	(603)924-9281	960
	TIERNAN, Linda M.	(603)924-7859	1244
Rindge	STEARNS, Melissa M.	(603)899-5111	1183

NEW JERSEY

Aberdeen	WEISBURG, Hilda K.	(201)566-1995	1319
Allenwood	ERBE, Evalina S.	(201)223-9388	352
Atlantic City	CROSS, Roberta A.	(609)345-2269	261
Audubon	VAUGHAN-STERLING, Judith A.	(609)546-0652	1280
Belle Mead	LEE, J S.	(201)359-5845	710
Belleville	JACKRELL, Thomas L.	(201)759-5318	586
Bergenfield	HILL, George R.	(201)384-4034	539
Bloomfield	LUSTIG, Joanne	(201)743-8777	750
	PICCIANO, Jacqueline L.	(201)743-9661	970
Bogota	MACKESY, Eileen M.		756
Bridgewater	STUDDIFORD, Abigail M.	(201)725-5616	1204
Butler	GARDNER, Sue A.	(201)838-3262	418
Caldwell	EDELSON, Ken		335
	HODGE, Patricia A.	(201)288-4424	546
	SKIDANOW, Helene	(201)226-4458	1146
Chatham	ETTLINGER, Sandra E.	(201)635-6407	356
Cherry Hill	ARROWOOD, Nina R.	(609)667-7653	35
	BROWN, Anita P.	(609)663-2247	142
	GLATT, Carol R.		440
	WALSH, Sharon T.	(609)243-1619	1300
Cliffside Park	PAWSON, Robert D.	(201)943-3228	951
	ROBERTSON, Betty M.	(201)894-0235	1041
Colts Neck	HIGGINS, Flora T.	(201)431-5656	537
Cranford	SAWYCKY, Roman A.	(201)276-3134	1086
Dumont	PAPAZIAN, Pierre	(201)385-8225	939
East Orange	GORMAN, Audrey J.	(201)676-2472	452
East Windsor	PINEL, Stephen L.	(609)448-8427	974

WRITER/EDITOR (Cont'd)
NEW JERSEY (Cont'd)

Edison	DINERMAN, Gloria	(201)906-1777	304
	FERRERE, Cathy M.	(201)819-8924	373
Elizabeth	MILLER, Virginia L.	(201)351-3288	843
Far Hills	SEAGLE, Janet M.	(201)234-2300	1109
Florham Park	BARRETT, Joyce C.	(201)765-1523	59
	BYOUK, Nancy K.	(201)377-2694	168
Forked River	ROYCE, Carolyn S.	(609)971-0665	1063
Green Village	KEON, Edward F.	(201)822-0062	643
Highland Park	MILLER, Lynn F.	(201)572-6563	840
Hightstown	BRODMAN, Estelle	(609)443-8094	139
Hoboken	PAULSON, Barbara A.	(201)420-8017	950
Iselin	FRANTS, Valery	(212)579-2496	398
Kearny	HAWLEY, George S.	(201)997-5299	514
Leonia	CIMBALA, Diane J.	(201)585-1921	214
	DAIN, Phyllis	(212)280-4032	270
Linden	PISKORIK, Elizabeth	(201)486-3888	976
Lodi	KARETZKY, Stephen	(201)778-1190	627
Madison	BROCKMAN, William S.	(201)377-3000	138
	LONG, Joanna R.	(201)377-2376	739
Mahwah	MAYDET, Steven I.		789
Manalapan	FIELD, Jack	(201)431-7226	375
Maplewood	AUSTIN, Fay A.		40
	BRYANT, David S.	(201)763-9294	152
	KRUPP, Robert G.	(201)763-8436	681
Mendham	MANTHEY, Carolyn M.	(201)543-2129	767
	MENNIE, Don	(201)543-9520	824
Metuchen	HIGGINS, Marilyn E.	(201)321-8745	538
Middletown	RILEY, Robert H.	(201)615-0900	1034
Millburn	URKEN, Madeline	(201)379-2306	1270
Montclair	FALK, Howard	(201)783-4050	362
	HOROWITZ, Marjorie B.	(201)744-8697	560
	TUROCK, Betty J.	(201)744-3354	1265
Montvale	REDRICK, Miriam J.	(201)573-9000	1014
Moorestown	SCHEPP, Brad J.	(609)778-1975	1091
Mount Holly	ALTERMAN, Deborah H.	(609)261-3458	18
	CARR, Charles E.	(609)267-9660	185
Neshanic	VANDERGRIFT, Kay E.	(201)369-8685	1274
New Brunswick	EDELMAN, Hendrik	(201)932-7836	335
	EUSTER, Joanne R.	(201)932-7505	356
	RICHARDS, Pamela S.		1028
	SWARTZBURG, Susan G.	(201)932-8573	1214
North Arlington	CASEY, Mary A.	(201)997-2141	192
Nutley	GILHEANY, Rosary S.	(201)667-7013	434
Ocean City	MASON, Michael L.	(609)398-0969	781
Oceanport	WAITE, William F.	(201)542-7216	1293
Park Ridge	LUXNER, Dick	(201)391-5935	750
	WERNER, Edward K.	(201)391-4934	1324
Patterson	SAWYER, Miriam		1086
Pennington	KAZIMIR, Edward O.	(609)737-3582	632
	PRIESING, Patricia L.	(609)737-1411	993
Piscataway	CALHOUN, Ellen	(201)932-4363	172
	CASSEL, Jeris F.	(201)752-0528	193
	FIGUEREDO, Danilo H.	(201)463-3725	376
	HOFFMAN, Helen B.	(201)932-3855	548
Plainfield	KRUSE, Theodore H.	(201)725-2294	681
	MCCOY, W K.	(201)753-0618	799
Plainsboro	QUINN, Ralph M.	(609)799-3072	1000
Point Pleasant	GREENE, Ellin P.	(201)899-2270	464
Princeton	BENEDUCE, Ann K.	(609)921-6624	80
	FERGUSON, Stephen	(609)452-3184	372
	JOHNSON, David K.	(609)924-2870	603
	LOGAN, Harold J.	(609)520-4066	737
	MORGAN, Paula M.	(609)452-3230	864
	PASTER, Luisa R.	(609)452-5464	946
	THRESHER, Jacquelyn E.	(609)924-9529	1243
Ramsey	SCARPELLINO, Rebecca A.	(201)825-1297	1088
Ridgewood	KOONTZ, John	(201)652-0185	671
Sewell	CROCKER, Jane L.	(609)468-5000	259
Somerset	GREENBERG, Linda	(201)846-8497	463
South Orange	BROWN, Ronald L.		147
	VITART, Jane A.	(201)763-2181	1286
Sparta	GUIDA, Pat	(201)729-8176	476
Springfield	SCOTT, Miranda D.	(201)467-7010	1107
Stanhope	KUTTEROFF, Ethel C.	(201)347-7600	685
Summit	JOHNSON, Minnie L.	(201)273-4952	607
	SOMMER, Ursula M.	(201)593-8526	1167
Trenton	WOODLEY, Robert H.	(609)771-2441	1366
Upper Montclair	STOCK, Norman	(201)893-7151	1195

WRITER/EDITOR (Cont'd)
NEW JERSEY (Cont'd)

Upper Saddle River	DUDLEY, Debbra C.	(201)327-4006	323
Voorhees	ROMISHER, Sivya S.	(609)772-1636	1053
Warren	WEIL, Ben H.	(201)647-0892	1317
Wayne	COHEN, Adrea G.	(201)696-8948	227
West Long Branch	FISHER, Scott L.	(201)229-9222	381
	HEDLUND, Dennis M.	(201)229-2343	520
West Orange	FICHTELBERG, Susan	(201)736-0198	374
Whippany	MUNSICK, Lee R.	(201)386-1920	879
Whitehouse Station	HOYT, Henry M.	(201)689-7717	566
Willingboro	PELLETIER, Karen E.		955

NEW MEXICO

Albuquerque	CARLSON, Kathleen A.	(505)883-1924	182
	ELDREDGE, Jonathan D.	(505)277-0654	342
	FREEMAN, Patricia E.		401
	KRUG, Ruth A.	(505)277-7213	680
	LOVE, Erika	(505)277-2548	743
	PRUETT, Nancy J.		996
	ROLLER, Twila J.	(505)884-7871	1051
	SEISER, Virginia	(505)842-5156	1113
	SUGNET, Christopher L.	(505)277-7162	1206
	THOMPSON, Janet A.	(505)277-7172	1240
	THORSON, Connie C.	(505)277-7201	1242
Farmington	RICHARD, Harris M.	(509)326-2936	1027
Las Cruces	MOORER, Jenny R.	(505)522-5126	862
Los Alamos	GODFREY, Lois E.	(505)662-7381	442
	SAYRE, Edward C.	(505)662-6889	1087
Los Lunas	HAYNES, Douglas E.	(505)841-5318	516
Santa Fe	LANCASTER, Kevin M.	(505)827-4854	692
	LOPEZ, Kathryn P.	(505)982-5683	741
	PIERSON, Robert M.	(505)982-0371	972

NEW YORK

Albany	BRISKA, Boniface	(518)465-5631	137
	COX, Richard J.	(518)486-4820	253
	DANIELS, Pam	(518)473-8177	273
	KNAPP, Sara D.	(518)442-3539	663
	LEWIS, Frances R.	(518)869-9317	723
	MATTIE, Joseph J.	(518)474-4970	786
	MATTURRO, Richard C.	(518)454-5734	786
	MCCOMBS, Gillian M.	(518)442-3633	797
	MILLER, Heather S.	(518)442-3626	838
	MOORE, Rue I.	(518)445-5197	861
	MOREHEAD, Joe	(518)442-5128	863
	NEAT, Charles M.	(518)482-0469	891
	NEVETT, Micki S.	(518)459-2178	897
	NICHOLS-RANDALL, Barbara L.	(518)489-7649	902
	NITECKI, Joseph Z.	(518)442-3568	905
	ROBERTS, Anne F.	(518)438-0607	1039
	SEVERINGHAUS, Ethel L.	(518)456-2110	1117
	SMITH, Audrey J.	(518)438-4316	1152
	VAILLANCOURT, Pauline M.	(518)489-6207	1271
Alfred	CONNOLLY, Bruce E.	(607)871-2494	237
	FREEMAN, Carla C.	(607)871-2492	400
Amherst	COOVER, James B.	(176)636-2935	244
	MAYER, Erich J.	(716)691-5554	789
APO New York	HAUSRATH, Donald C.		513
	RUDA, Donna R.		1065
Astoria	QUARTELL, Robert J.	(718)274-7568	999
Ballston Lake	FRALEY, Ruth A.	(518)399-9542	395
Bayside	BAKISH, David J.	(718)225-0475	50
	NOVIK, Sandra P.	(718)631-6271	911
	WEINER, Carolynn N.		1318
Bayville	SPIRT, Diana L.	(516)628-8341	1175
Beechhurst	CARVER, Mary		191
Bellport	KLAUBER, Julie B.	(516)286-1600	658
Bergen	FABRIZIO, Timothy C.	(716)494-2264	360
Binghamton	CHAMBERLAIN, Erna B.	(607)723-4064	197
	MCKEE, George D.	(607)729-5490	810
	WILLIAMS, Deborah H.	(607)723-6457	1342
Black River	MARSTON, Hope I.	(315)773-5847	775
Bronx	DECANDIDO, Graceanne A.		285
	GAROOGIAN, Rhoda	(212)588-2266	420
	GOLDBERG, Judy W.	(212)588-8400	444
	LAMPORT, Bernard	(212)430-3747	691
	LIEBER, Ellen C.	(212)920-4666	726
	MARK, Linda R.	(212)588-8400	770

WRITER/EDITOR (Cont'd)
NEW YORK (Cont'd)

Bronx
	PATRYCH, Joseph		947
	REIMAN, Donald H.	(212)549-4890	1020
	RUBEY, Daniel R.	(212)960-8580	1064
	SOPELAK, Mary J.	(212)588-2266	1168
	WEINBERG, Bella H.	(212)547-5159	1317

Bronxville
| | HUEBNER, Mary A. | (914)337-9300 | 570 |
| | ZIESELMAN, Paula M. | (914)337-0700 | 1388 |

Brooklyn
	ARMEIT, Marilyn	(718)209-1718	32
	BAKER, Zachary M.	(718)855-6318	50
	BLAKE-O'HOGAN, Kathleen E.	(718)625-2829	103
	BRANDEAU, John H.	(718)852-8700	128
	CLUNE, John R.	(718)680-7578	223
	CORRSIN, Stephen D.	(718)851-2317	247
	DOHERTY, Mary C.	(718)270-2106	309
	ESSIEN, Victor K.	(718)941-9020	354
	GARGAN, William M.	(718)780-5276	419
	GREENBERG, Roberta D.	(718)857-0146	463
	GUREWITSCH, Bonnie	(718)338-6494	478
	HOFFMAN, Allen	(718)736-8306	547
	KEAVENEY, Sydney S.	(718)636-3685	633
	KITT, Sandra E.		657
	KLEIMAN, Allan M.	(718)645-2396	658
	KRAMER, Allan F.	(718)857-7825	675
	MANBECK, Virginia B.	(718)253-9413	764
	NYREN, Dorothy E.	(718)780-7799	913
	PERSON, Diane G.	(718)596-2345	961
	PRUITT, Brenda F.	(718)287-1681	996
	ROGINSKI, James W.	(718)499-4850	1050
	SCHNEIDER, Adele	(718)743-7172	1096
	SEMKOW, Julie L.	(718)624-3189	1115
	SKROBELA, Katherine C.	(718)462-6749	1147
	SULTANOF, Jeff B.	(718)768-1611	1208
	SWIESZKOWSK, L S.	(718)383-8480	1216
	WEINRICH, Gloria	(708)998-9116	1318

Brooksville
| | O'HARA, Frederic J. | (516)299-2866 | 919 |

Brookville
| | GRANT, Mary M. | (516)299-2832 | 458 |

Buffalo
	COTY, Patricia A.	(716)636-3377	250
	DIBARTOLO, Amy L.	(716)878-6309	299
	HEPFER, Cynthia K.	(716)831-2139	530
	HEPFER, William E.	(716)636-2784	530
	KASE-MCLAREN, Karen A.	(716)838-6610	628
	KELLER, Sharon A.	(716)831-3337	635
	SZEMRAJ, Edward R.	(716)895-7675	1218
	WAGNER, Stephen K.	(716)837-1563	1292
	WELLS, Margaret R.	(716)636-2943	1322

Centerport
| | COOPER, Catherine M. | (516)754-9262 | 242 |

Chappaqua
| | CHEATHAM, Bertha M. | (914)238-3586 | 204 |

Cheektowaga
| | WITT, Susan T. | (716)686-3620 | 1358 |

Cobleskill
| | GALASSO, Nancy | (518)234-5841 | 412 |

Commack
| | ROFES, William L. | (516)499-4370 | 1049 |
| | SHAPIRO, Barbara S. | (516)368-4143 | 1121 |

Delhi
| | SEN, Joyce H. | (607)746-7350 | 1115 |

Deimar
| | KRAMER-GREENE, Judith | (518)439-7028 | 675 |
| | POLAND, Ursula H. | (518)439-6872 | 980 |

Dewitt
| | SHRIER, Helene F. | (315)446-5971 | 1133 |

Dobbs Ferry
| | BONE, Larry E. | (914)693-4500 | 113 |

East Patchogue
| | PLUMER, F I. | (516)289-3134 | 978 |

East Setauket
| | ALBERTUS, Donna M. | | 10 |
| | BLOHM, Laura A. | (516)444-3105 | 106 |

Elma
| | DRZEWIECKI, Iris M. | (716)683-0592 | 321 |

Elmhurst
| | NOLAN, John A. | (718)565-1627 | 007 |

Elmira
| | LAPIER, Cynthia B. | (607)739-3581 | 697 |

Elmsford
| | TRUDELL, Robert J. | (914)993-1608 | 1259 |

Fishkill
| | SHERWIG, Mary J. | (914)831-6600 | 1129 |

Flushing
	MCMORRAN, Charles E.	(718)358-4526	815
	RORICK, William C.	(718)520-7345	1054
	SURPRENANT, Thomas T.	(718)520-7194	1210

Forest Hills
	GELLER, Lawrence D.		426
	NERBOSO, Donna L.	(718)897-9826	895
	VAN BRUNT, Amy S.	(718)261-0313	1272

Freeport
| | VOLLONO, Millicent D. | (516)223-0838 | 1288 |

Fresh Meadows
| | MULCAHY, Brian J. | (718)454-2157 | 876 |

Garrison
| | BALDWIN, Geraldine S. | (914)424-3020 | 51 |

Geneseo
| | CAREN, Loretta | (716)243-0438 | 181 |

Glen Cove
| | WINCKLER, Paul A. | (516)671-0928 | 1354 |

Glen Falls
| | GRAMINSKI, Denise M. | (518)793-2927 | 457 |

WRITER/EDITOR (Cont'd)
NEW YORK (Cont'd)

Glendale	SOSTACK, Maura	(718)417-8242	1169
Glenmont	BAIN, Christine A.	(518)439-6664	47
Glens Falls	SMITH, Frederick E.	(518)792-8214	1155
Governors Island	GODWIN, Mary J.	(212)809-4351	443
Hamilton	BERGEN, Daniel P.	(315)824-2381	85
	WASHBURN, Keith E.	(315)824-3008	1307
Hastings on Hudson	JELLINEK, George	(914)478-1979	596
Hempstead	ANDREWS, Charles R.	(516)560-5940	26
Hicksville	EDWARDS, Harriet M.		337
Hollis Hills	GOLD, Renee L.	(718)479-9534	444
Hudson	MARTIN, Lyn M.	(518)828-1465	777
Huntington	NEWMAN, Eileen M.	(516)673-2023	899
	ROSAR, Virginia W.	(516)549-4576	1054
Ithaca	ASHMUN, Lawrence F.		36
	COONS, William W.	(607)255-7959	242
	ERICSON, Margaret D.	(607)274-3882	353
	SLOCUM, Robert B.	(716)255-4247	1150
	ZASLAW, Neal	(607)257-1052	1386
Jackson Heights	SPYROS, Marsha L.	(718)424-7849	1177
Jamaica	SHAPIRO, Martin P.	(718)990-0760	1121
Kenmore	RYBARCZYK, Barclay S.	(716)877-0605	1071
Kew Gardens	SALAZAR, Pamela B.	(718)441-2350	1076
	TANNENBAUM, Robin L.	(718)793-0372	1222
Kings Park	PANDIT, Jyoti P.	(516)269-1070	937
Lackawanna	BEDNAR, Sheila	(716)822-0840	73
Larchmont	GILLIGAN, Julie		436
Latham	BRUNELLE, Bette S.	(518)783-1161	150
	VEGTER, Amy H.	(518)783-1161	1281
Lockport	KLIMEK, Chester R.	(716)434-6167	661
Long Beach	WASSERMAN, Ricki F.		1308
Lynbrook	HAYES, Jude T.	(516)887-2493	516
Manlius	WU, Painan R.	(315)682-2472	1373
Massapequa	REID, Richard C.	(516)795-0262	1019
Massapequa Park	GIANNATTASI, Gerard E.	(516)541-6584	430
Mastic	MACINICK, James W.	(516)399-3281	755
Menands	LENZ, Millicent A.		716
Middletown	BAUM, Christina D.	(914)344-3615	66
Mt Kisco	NELSON, Nancy M.	(914)666-3394	894
Mt Vernon	O'DELL, Lorraine I.		916
	SEITZ, Robert J.	(914)699-6917	1113
Nanuet	MOLLO, Terry	(914)623-0531	853
New Hyde Park	LANG, Jovian P.	(516)352-1666	695
New Paltz	NYQUIST, Corinne E.	(914)255-2209	913
	O'CONNELL, Susan	(914)255-5987	915
New Rochelle	KONOVALOFF, Maria S.		670
	MITTELGLUCK, Eugene L.	(914)834-8739	850
New Windsor	SANKER, Paul N.	(914)562-0470	1081
New York	ALLENTUCK, Marcia E.		16
	AMISON, Mary V.	(212)666-9645	20
	ARKHURST, Joyce C.	(212)368-1788	31
	ARMSTRONG, Joanne D.	(212)280-3743	32
	AVALLONE, Susan	(212)315-4808	41
	BALKEMA, John B.	(212)876-8200	52
	BATES, Ellen	(212)503-8007	63
	BEALER, Jane A.	(212)355-0083	68
	BERNER, Andrew J.	(212)515-5299	88
	BOURKE, Thomas A.	(212)930-0838	119
	BOWLEY, Craig	(212)239-0827	121
	BRAUN, Robert L.		130
	BRODY, Catherine T.	(212)228-7863	139
	BRODY, Elaine	(212)535-9229	139
	BROWAR, Lisa M.	(212)930-0556	141
	BRUGNOLOTTI, Phyllis T.	(212)873-0677	150
	BUCKLEY, Virginia L.	(212)725-1818	154
	BUTLER, Tyrone G.	(212)566-5367	167
	CAMBRIA, Roberto		174
	CASSELL, Kay A.	(212)614-6551	193
	COHEN, Frederick S.	(212)594-9880	228
	COHEN, Rochelle F.	(212)577-3333	229
	COLBY, Robert A.	(212)787-3062	230
	COPLEN, Ron	(212)869-3348	244
	EBER, Beryl E.	(212)621-0635	334
	FLEISHMAN, Lauren Z.	(212)371-2000	384
	FLOERSHEIMER, Lee M.	(212)787-3727	385
	FOLTER, Roland	(212)687-4808	388
	FONTAINE, Sue	(212)533-7226	388
	FRANKLIN, Linda C.	(212)679-6038	398

FREIFELD, Roberta I.	(212)777-9271	401
GARDNER, Ralph D.	(212)877-6820	418
GERHARDT, Lillian N.	(212)463-6759	428
GESKE, Aina S.		430
GLASER, Gloria T.	(212)753-8694	439
GLASFORD, G R.	(212)669-3336	440
GOLLOP, Sandra G.	(212)770-7911	447
GOODMAN, Edward C.	(212)280-8407	449
GOTTLIEB, Jane E.	(212)362-8671	453
GRAY, Karen	(212)758-9663	460
GREENBERG, Charles J.	(212)663-5526	463
GREENFIELD, Stanley R.		464
GRELE, Ronald J.	(212)280-2273	467
GROTE, Janet H.	(212)627-1500	473
GUBERT, Betty K.	(212)362-4256	475
HAEFLIGER, Kathleen A.	(212)663-7857	482
HALL, Alix M.	(212)536-3598	486
HARVEY, John F.	(215)509-2612	509
HAVENS, Shirley E.	(212)463-6804	513
HAYNES, Patricia	(212)371-3200	516
HENDERSON, Brad	(212)666-2674	526
HEUMAN, Rabbi F.	(212)505-2174	535
HIGGINS, Steven	(212)674-2087	538
HOLTZE, Sally H.	(212)674-6973	555
HUDSON, Alice C.	(212)222-2835	569
HUNTER, Gregory S.	(212)940-1690	576
HYMAN, Richard J.	(212)865-7962	580
KARATNYTSKY, Christine A.	(212)420-1436	627
KENSELAAR, Robert	(212)870-1661	642
KULLESEID, Eleanor R.	(212)666-6013	683
LAWRENCE, Arthur P.	(212)505-7996	704
LEVINSON, Debra J.		721
LINDGREN, Arla M.	(212)662-6386	729
LOHF, Kenneth A.	(212)280-2231	737
LYONS, Ivan	(212)265-4995	753
MARKERT, Patricia B.	(212)925-4939	771
MARTIN, Jean F.	(212)928-4231	776
MASON, H J.	(212)505-3560	781
MASSIS, Bruce E.	(212)595-2000	782
MAYER, George L.	(212)724-8057	789
MCGLINCHEE, Claire	(212)737-1875	806
MEAGHER, Anne E.	(212)620-8462	819
MELKIN, Audrey D.	(212)850-6705	822
MILLER, Sarah J.		842
MOLZ, Redmond K.	(212)280-4787	854
MONACO, James	(212)254-8235	854
MOORE, Sonia	(212)755-5120	861
MOSES, Julian M.	(212)688-8426	871
NELOMS, Karen H.	(212)582-9239	893
OSTROW, Rona	(212)691-1672	929
PAVLAKIS, Christopher		950
PEDOLSKY, Andrea D.	(212)925-8650	954
PELLOWSKI, Anne	(212)316-1170	955
PERRY, Claudia A.	(212)876-8200	960
POTEAT, James B.	(212)759-6800	986
PRONIN, Monica		995
RACHOW, Louis A.	(212)228-7610	1001
RICHTER, Robert	(212)947-1395	1031
ROBERTS, Gloria A.	(212)535-2985	1040
ROSIGNOLO, Beverly A.	(212)962-4111	1057
ROTH, Claire J.	(212)755-6710	1059
SALVAGE, Barbara A.	(212)998-2463	1078
SALY, Alan J.	(212)475-5400	1078
SAUNDERS, Dorette	(212)371-4800	1084
SCHUMAN, Patricia G.	(212)925-8650	1103
SETTANNI, Joseph A.	(212)289-9059	1117
SHAPIRO, Fred R.	(203)432-1600	1121
SHERBY, Louise S.	(212)280-2241	1127
SHIROMA, Susan G.	(212)998-2602	1131
SLATE, Ted	(212)350-4682	1148
SMITH, David F.	(212)243-1753	1154
SPIER, Margaret M.	(212)337-6983	1174
STALKER, Dianne S.	(212)280-8484	1178
STILLMAN, Stanley W.		1194
STOLLER, Michael E.	(212)280-4356	1196
SULLIVAN, Stephen W.		1208
THOMAS, Dorothy	(212)799-0970	1236

	TOPEL, Iris N.	(212)337-6988	1251
	VINCENT-DAVISS, Diana	(212)598-2367	1284
	WERTSMAN, Vladimir F.	(212)246-8176	1325
	WILLNER, Channan P.	(212)870-1675	1348
	WOLFE, Allis	(212)496-0008	1360
	WOO, Janice	(212)662-3534	1363
	WOODS, Lawrence J.	(212)736-6629	1367
	WOSH, Peter J.	(212)581-7400	1369
	WRIGHT, Bernell	(212)866-3042	1370
	WRIGHT, Sylvia H.	(212)222-6148	1373
	YUSTER, Leigh C.	(212)337-7131	1385
Niagara Falls	SHIELDS, Gerald R.	(716)284-2928	1130
North Chatham	WELLS, Gladysann		1322
North Syracuse	AUSTIN, Ralph A.	(315)457-1799	40
North White Plains	SHADE, Ronald H.	(914)285-9583	1118
Oceanside	ROGGENKAMP, Alice M.	(516)766-1397	1050
Oneonta	CROWLEY, John V.	(607)431-2725	261
	JOHNSON, Richard D.	(607)432-0131	608
Ossining	LEW, Susan	(914)762-1154	722
	STAPLETON, Darwin H.	(914)762-8921	1181
Patchogue	NEUFELD, Judith B.	(516)289-6813	897
Pearl River	BRISFJORD, Inez S.	(914)735-1567	136
	SPERR BRISFJORD, Inez L.	(914)735-1567	1173
Peekskill	FALCONE, Elena C.	(914)528-2820	362
Pelham	FERRIBY, Peter G.	(914)738-3712	373
Penfield	PARKE, Kathryn E.		941
Pomona	GUBITS, Helen S.	(914)354-1340	475
Port Jervis	HOFMANN, Susan M.	(914)856-1513	548
Port Washington	EPSTEIN, Connie C.	(516)883-8177	351
Purchase	FREIDES, Thelma	(914)253-5096	401
Queens Village	HECKMAN, Lucy T.	(718)776-6285	519
Rensselaerville	STORMS, Kate	(518)797-5154	1198
Rhinebeck	MCCLELLAND, Bruce A.	(914)876-2230	796
Rochester	BAILEY, Joe A.	(716)724-0212	46
	BARRETT, Lizabeth A.	(716)272-1905	59
	BERKMAN, Robert I.	(716)461-3206	87
	CUMMINS, Julie A.	(716)428-7366	264
	GRAUER, Sally M.	(716)461-4380	458
	HOPE, Thomas W.	(716)458-4250	557
	ISGANITIS, Jamie C.	(716)461-1943	585
	KARNEZIS, Kristine C.	(716)482-3221	627
	LINDSAY, Jean S.	(716)428-7300	729
	LOCKE, William G.	(716)288-5422	736
	STOSS, Frederick W.	(716)436-8719	1198
Roslyn	WEINSTEIN, Judith K.	(516)627-6200	1318
Roslyn Harbor	CARTAFALSA, Joan C.	(516)671-7411	188
Rotterdam	SIMON, Anne E.	(518)355-8391	1140
St James	WIENER, Paul B.	(516)862-8723	1336
Saratoga Springs	DOE, Lynn M.	(518)584-5000	308
	LEWIS, Gillian H.	(518)587-0374	723
	ROBINSON, Jolene A.	(518)583-0208	1044
Scarborough	HOPKINS, Lee B.	(914)941-5810	558
Schenectady	HALSEY, Richard S.	(518)370-0902	490
	HODGES, Lois F.	(518)377-7738	546
	HOLT, Lisa A.	(518)370-1811	554
	SEEMANN, Ann M.	(518)370-6277	1111
Selden	SALINERO, Amelia	(516)732-1268	1076
Setauket	THOM, Janice E.	(516)751-1484	1235
Shoreham	WRIGHT-HESS, Anne H.	(516)929-8500	1373
Shrub Oak	TIFFEAULT, Alice A.	(914)528-4048	1244
Somers	RITTER, Sally K.	(914)232-7889	1037
	SHAPIRO, Lillian L.	(914)276-2269	1121
Sparkill	BARRIE, John L.	(914)359-7200	59
Staten Island	BARTO, Stephen C.	(718)727-8940	61
	KLINGLE, Philip A.	(718)390-5291	662
Stillwater	REEPMEYER, Marie C.	(518)785-6949	1016
Stony Brook	MASH, S D.		780
Sunnyside	WOOD, Sallie B.	(718)565-5490	1365
Syracuse	CASEY, Daniel W.	(315)468-0176	192
	JOHNSON, Nancy B.	(315)423-2911	608
	MINOR, Barbara B.	(315)425-9348	846
	SHELANDER, Frances R.	(315)469-8068	1125
	WASYLENKO, Lydia W.	(315)423-2585	1308
Three Mile Bay	PIZER, Elizabeth F.	(315)649-5086	977
Upton	LANE, Sandra G.	(516)282-7159	694
Utica	BROOKES, Barbara	(315)735-2279	140
	WEBER, Jerome F.	(315)732-4747	1314

WRITER/EDITOR (Cont'd)

NEW YORK (Cont'd)

Wantagh	LOMONACO, Martha S.	(516)783-9051	738
	NOVITSKY, Edward G.		911
Webster	DESMOND, Andrew R.	(716)671-7657	295
West Valley	CURRY, Lenora Y.	(716)942-4362	266
Westhampton Beach	KIRSCH, Anne S.	(516)288-2492	655
White Plains	BAXTER, Paula A.	(914)946-3275	67
	BOWLES, Edmund A.	(914)696-1900	121
	HESS, James W.	(914)592-4342	534
	HIGGINS, Judith H.	(914)949-2175	538
	MCELHANEY, William E.	(914)949-3270	804
	MOSLANDER, Charlotte D.	(914)428-1533	871
Whitestone	RIECHEL, Rosemarie	(718)990-0714	1033
Williamsville	SCHUTT, Dedre A.	(716)633-6384	1103
Yonkers	BERGER, Paula E.	(914)968-7906	86
	FRANK, Mortimer H.	(914)423-2304	397
	SIKORSKI, Charlene S.	(914)968-2674	1137
York	MACLEAN, Paul	(716)243-1069	757
Yorktown Heights	YURO, David A.	(914)962-5200	1384

NORTH CAROLINA

Albemarle	ESTES, Elizabeth W.	(704)983-7332	355
Angier	FISH, Paula H.	(919)639-4331	380
Asheville	BUCHANAN, William E.	(704)251-6436	153
Belmont	BAUMSTEIN, Paschal M.	(704)825-3711	66
	MAYES, Susan E.	(704)825-3711	789
Boone	BUSBIN, O M.	(704)264-7141	164
	WISE, Mintron S.	(704)262-2823	1357
	WORRELL, Diane F.		1369
Cary	BURCSU, James E.	(919)469-2731	158
Chapel Hill	ASHEIM, Lester E.	(919)967-1882	35
	BYRD, Gary D.	(919)966-2111	168
	CARMICHAEL, James V.		183
	DICKERSON, Jimmy	(919)962-1188	300
	KISER, Anita H.	(919)968-3946	656
	SEIBERT, Karen S.	(919)962-1301	1112
	TAYLOR, David C.	(919)962-1355	1226
	TUCKER, Mary E.	(919)933-8982	1262
	WILLIAMS, Wiley J.		1347
Charlotte	CARPENTER, Janella A.	(704)366-3955	184
	SUMMERFORD, Steven L.	(704)378-1032	1209
Cullowhee	LESUEUR, Joan K.	(704)456-3396	718
Durham	BALLARD, Robert M.	(919)489-6358	53
	BASEFSKY, Stuart M.	(919)684-2380	62
	BERGER, Kenneth W.	(919)684-2373	85
	EZZELL, Joline R.	(919)684-2034	360
	FEINGLOS, Susan J.	(919)493-2904	369
	LUBANS, John	(919)684-2034	745
	SHEARER, Kenneth D.	(919)683-6485	1124
	SOUTHERN, Mary A.	(919)684-8118	1170
	SPARKS, Martha E.	(919)489-6012	1171
	STRAUSS, Diane	(919)286-7895	1201
	VARGHA, Rebecca B.	(919)544-6045	1278
	WHITTINGTON, Erma P.	(919)489-9689	1334
	WOODBURN, Judy I.	(919)684-5987	1366
Eden	DAVIDSON, Laura B.	(919)627-1106	276
Elkin	MACPHAIL, Jessica		758
Elon College	JONES, Plummer A.	(919)584-2338	614
Fayetteville	FREEDMAN, Barbara G.	(919)868-1637	400
	HANSEL, Patsy J.	(919)484-7096	497
	KRIEGER, Lee A.	(919)864-9349	678
Garner	RICHARDSON, Beverly S.		1029
Greensboro	MCZORN, Bonita A.	(919)273-4886	819
	WINKEL, Lois	(919)275-4935	1355
	YOUNG, Tommie M.	(909)621-0032	1383
Greenville	COLLINS, Donald E.	(919)756-5469	232
	GLUCK, Myke H.	(919)757-6514	442
	MELLON, Constance A.	(919)757-6870	822
	SHIRES, Nancy P.	(919)758-8252	1131
	YORK, Maurice C.	(919)752-5260	1381
High Point	AUSTIN, Neal F.	(919)869-6260	40
Jefferson	FRANKLIN, Robert M.	(919)246-4460	398
Kinston	SOUTHERLAND, Carol A.	(919)523-0819	1169
	TABORY, Maxim	(919)522-3830	1219
Maiden	CARDENAS, Mary E.		180
Mars Hill	PETERSON, Cynthia L.	(704)689-2380	963
Matthews	CANNON, Robert E.	(704)847-0394	179

WRITER/EDITOR (Cont'd)

NORTH CAROLINA (Cont'd)

Montreat	BROOKS, Jerrold L.	(704)669-7661	140
	FOREMAN, Kenneth J.	(704)669-2782	390
New Bern	KEE, Walter A.		634
Newell	PENNINGER, Randy	(704)597-9248	957
Raleigh	BRADBURN, Frances B.	(919)878-4497	125
	DAVIS, Jinnie Y.	(919)737-2680	279
	HORTON, James T.		561
	LAMBERT, John W.	(919)833-8937	690
	PRICE, William S.	(919)733-7305	993
	PURYEAR, Pamela E.	(919)737-2836	998
	RATHGEBER, Jo F.	(919)872-3323	1009
	TAYLOR, Raymond M.	(919)787-7824	1228
Reidsville	GUNN, Shirley A.	(919)342-0951	477
Research Triangle Pk	MENDELL, Stefanie	(919)248-1842	823
Robbinsville	LARSON, Josephine	(704)479-8192	699
Sanford	BEAGLE, Donald R.	(919)776-8372	68
	MATOCHIK, Michael J.	(919)776-5737	784
	MURCHISON, Margaret B.	(919)258-3277	879
Washington	TIMOUR, John A.	(919)975-3355	1246
Wilmington	SEXTON, Spencer K.	(919)799-0177	1118
Winston-Salem	AHLERS, Glen P.	(919)761-5438	8
	EKSTRAND, Nancy L.	(919)765-4817	341
	FOLTZ, Faye D.	(919)748-2295	388
	HAUPERT, Thomas J.	(919)722-1742	512
	MILLER, Barry K.	(919)777-5597	836
	ROWLAND, Janet M.	(919)765-2081	1062
Yanceyville	MASSEY, Nancy O.	(919)968-0852	782

NORTH DAKOTA

Bismarck	MOREHOUSE, Valerie J.	(701)224-4658	863
Fargo	BIRDSALL, Douglas G.	(701)237-8878	98
	BRKIC, Beverly T.	(701)237-5865	138
Minot	BOARDMAN, Edna M.	(701)839-7424	108
Valley City	HOLDEN, Douglas H.	(701)845-4940	550

OHIO

Akron	LATSHAW, Patricia H.	(216)762-7621	701
	STROZIER, Sandra L.	(216)379-8250	1203
Ashland	ROEPKE, David E.		1048
Ashtabula	WARREN, Dorothea C.		1306
Athens	BETCHER, William M.	(614)593-2701	92
	MULLINER, Kent	(614)593-2707	878
Barberton	SWINEHART, Katharine J.	(216)745-1194	1216
Bay Village	DOMBEY, Kathryn W.	(216)871-5024	310
	LORANTH, Alice N.	(216)871-9014	741
Bedford	PARCH, Grace D.		939
Bowling Green	MCCALLUM, Brenda W.		793
	MILLER, William	(419)372-2857	843
Chardon	KLINGER, William E.	(216)564-9340	661
Cincinnati	DOBBS, David L.	(513)271-4827	307
	GILLILAND, Anne J.	(513)475-6459	436
	GROSVENOR, Philip G.	(513)683-0315	473
	HALIBEY-BILYK, Christine M.	(513)559-4320	486
	HILAND, Gerard P.	(513)231-0810	538
	HUDZIK, Robert T.	(513)369-6924	570
	KENT, Rose M.		642
	LE BLANC, Judith E.		708
	LEIBOLD, Cynthia K.		713
	MC CORMICK, Lisa L.	(513)369-2540	798
	NASRALLAH, Wahib T.	(513)475-2411	888
	PROPAS, Sharon W.	(513)475-2411	995
	RIFFEY, Robin S.	(513)871-3087	1033
	SIMMONS, Edlyn S.	(513)948-7829	1139
	SMITH, Maureen M.	(513)369-6917	1158
	WILSON, Lucy	(513)745-4313	1351
Cleveland	BALCAS, Georgianne	(216)368-2403	50
	EAGLEN, Audrey B.	(216)398-1800	331
	FINET, Scott	(216)687-2250	378
	ORR, Cynthia	(216)449-2049	926
	RAY, Laura E.	(216)844-3788	1011
	RICHMOND, Phyllis A.	(216)461-4948	1030
	ROM, Cristine C.	(216)229-0930	1052
	ROSENFELD, Joseph S.	(216)523-7323	1056
	SKUTNIK, John S.	(216)241-2141	1147

WRITER/EDITOR (Cont'd)
OHIO (Cont'd)

Cleveland Heights	BORCHERT, Catherine G.	(216)932-8324	116
	BOWIE, Angela B.	(216)291-5588	121
	GRABOWSKI, John J.	(216)932-8805	455
	TRAMDACK, Philip J.	(216)371-3445	1254
Columbus	ALLEN, Cameron	(614)237-1516	14
	ANDERSON, Carl A.	(614)486-9100	21
	BAYER, Bernard I.	(614)292-7895	67
	BETCHER, Melissa A.	(614)466-5511	92
	BRANCH, Susan	(614)267-3805	127
	BRANN, Andrew R.	(614)221-4181	128
	DALRYMPLE, Tamsen	(614)486-2109	271
	GOLDING, Alfred S.		445
	HADDOCK, Mable	(614)258-9052	482
	HECK, Thomas F.	(614)292-2310	519
	JAMISON, Martin P.	(614)895-8465	593
	KAWAKAMI, Toyo S.	(614)263-2278	632
	MCDOWELL, Judith H.	(614)771-0273	804
	MILLER, Dennis P.	(614)888-1886	837
	MIXTER, Keith E.	(614)263-7204	850
	MLYNAR, Mary	(614)486-7980	850
	MULARSKI, Carol A.	(614)292-9810	876
	NORMORE, Lorraine F.	(614)421-3600	909
	O'NEIL, Rosanna M.	(614)761-5057	924
	ORLANDO, Jacqueline M.	(614)262-6765	926
	PLATAU, Gerard O.	(614)457-1687	977
	POPOVICH, Charles J.	(614)292-2136	984
	RATLIFF, Priscilla	(614)488-1622	1009
	STOBAUGH, Robert E.	(614)451-3271	1195
	WALBRIDGE, Sharon L.	(614)274-4081	1293
Cuyahoga Falls	KLINGLER, Thomas E.	(216)923-5504	662
Dayton	BALL, Diane A.	(513)293-7339	52
	BANTA, Gratia J.	(513)277-4444	55
	COYLE, Christopher B.	(513)865-6882	253
	DISTEFANO, Marianne	(513)461-3740	305
	PEAKE, Sharon K.	(513)865-6958	952
	PURSCH, Lenore D.	(513)434-7064	998
	WYLLIE, Stanley C.	(513)252-8496	1375
Delaware	COHEN, Susan J.	(614)363-9433	229
Dublin	DITMARS, David W.	(614)761-7303	305
	HASKINS, Dawn A.	(614)761-7301	510
	JACOB, Mary E.	(614)764-6063	589
East Cleveland	KEENON, Una H.	(216)932-5090	634
Fairfield	LUCAS, Jean M.	(513)829-5227	746
Fairview Park	HYSLOP, Marjorie R.	(216)333-8645	580
Findlay	DICKINSON, Luren E.	(419)423-4934	301
Granville	RUGG, John D.		1066
Huron	CURRIE, William W.	(419)433-5560	266
Jackson	ANDERSON, Eric S.	(614)286-6685	22
Kent	BOLEK, Ann D.	(216)678-9429	112
	KREYCHE, Michael R.	(216)672-3024	678
	MORRIS, Trisha A.	(216)673-3464	867
	WYNAR, Lubomyr R.		1375
Lakewood	KEATING, Michael F.	(216)221-0608	633
Marion	GERWIN, Barbara L.	(614)387-0992	430
Mayfield Heights	RASKIN, Rosa S.	(216)442-3009	1009
Mentor	DUANE, Carol A.	(216)255-3323	321
Mogadore	SMITH, Cynthia A.	(216)678-0662	1153
Oberlin	CARPENTER, Eric J.	(216)775-2546	184
	RICKER, Alison S.	(216)775-8310	1031
	WEIDMAN, Jeffrey	(216)775-8635	1316
Oxford	WORTMAN, William A.	(513)529-3936	1369
Perrysburg	LOCKE-GAGNON, Rebecca A.	(419)874-1725	736
Reynoldsburg	WULKER, Clare	(614)866-5963	1374
Shaker Heights	BELKIN, Betsey B.		76
	MCCONNELL, Pamela J.	(216)921-7457	798
	MELTON, Vivian B.	(216)921-5803	823
	NISSENBAUM, Robert J.	(216)561-8168	905
South Euclid	BENSING, Karen M.	(216)932-0186	83
Springfield	ARK, Connie E.	(513)324-8470	31
	MONTAG, John	(513)327-7019	855
Toledo	HANNAFORD, Claudia L.	(419)536-7539	496
Troy	CRAM, Mary E.	(513)334-5067	255
University Heights	HECHT, Joseph A.	(216)291-5506	519
Upper Arlington	GRIEVE, Shelley	(614)442-1073	468
Walton Hills	POJMAN, Paul E.	(216)232-0527	980
Westchester	EMANI, Nirupama	(513)777-5264	347
Westerville	LOVEJOY, Eunice G.	(614)882-4791	743

WRITER/EDITOR (Cont'd)
OHIO (Cont'd)

Westlake	GALLANT, Jennifer J.	(216)835-6020	414
Wilmington	NICHOLS, James T.	(513)382-6661	901
Wooster	ESHELMAN, William R.	(216)345-8708	354
	POWELL, Margaret S.	(216)263-2279	988
Xenia	OVERTON, Julie M.	(513)376-4952	931
	WALDER, Antoinette L.	(513)376-2995	1294
Yellow Springs	NEWMAN, Marianne L.		899

OKLAHOMA

Ada	HUESMANN, James L.	(405)332-7632	570
Bartlesville	ROBIN, Annabeth	(918)336-7240	1043
Catoosa	FARLEY, Austin G.	(918)266-7367	364
Norman	BATT, Fred	(405)325-4231	64
	CLARK, Harry	(405)321-0352	217
	HOVDE, David M.	(405)325-4231	563
	MEACHAM, Mary	(405)321-8444	819
	PETERS, Lloyd A.		962
	POLAND, Jean A.	(405)360-7095	980
Oklahoma City	DOBBERTEEN, Sara J.	(405)842-0890	307
	JONES, Charles E.	(405)751-0574	611
	MEYERS, Duane H.	(405)946-2488	830
	ROACH, Eddie D.	(405)751-6400	1037
	SAULMON, Sharon A.	(405)634-3181	1084
Shawnee	ALDRIDGE, Betsy B.		11
Stillwater	MORRIS, Karen T.	(405)377-8114	867
	ROUSE, Roscoe	(405)377-1651	1061
Tahlequah	MCQUITTY, Jeanette N.	(918)456-5511	817
Tulsa	HILL, Linda L.	(918)584-0891	540
	MURPHY, Peggy A.	(918)743-7177	881
	WEAVER, Pamela J.	(918)592-6000	1312

OREGON

Albany	FELLA, Sarah C.	(503)928-2361	370
Ashland	OTNES, Harold M.	(503)482-6445	930
	PURCELL, V N.	(503)482-2629	998
Beaverton	POND, Patricia B.	(503)641-5524	982
Eugene	ALLEN, Alice J.	(503)686-3064	14
	BONAMICI, Andrew R.	(503)683-5194	113
	EMMENS, Thomas A.	(503)345-6439	348
	HADDERMAN, Margaret	(503)342-5457	482
	KNIEVEL, Helen A.	(503)345-2032	664
	MCDANIELS, Patricia R.	(503)343-4728	801
	MORRISON, Perry D.	(503)342-2361	868
	ROBERTSON, Howard W.	(503)686-3064	1042
	SHULER, John A.	(503)686-3048	1133
	WAND, Patricia A.	(503)686-3056	1302
Forest Grove	FALZON, Judith A.	(503)357-3023	363
Grants Pass	MCCOY, Joanne	(503)474-1739	799
Manzanita	LARSON, Signe E.	(503)368-6990	700
Monmouth	GORCHELS, Clarence C.	(503)838-1274	451
Portland	BURSON, Lorraine E.	(508)246-4097	163
	LEGER, Norissa	(503)246-2714	712
	SELLE, Donna M.	(503)629-5886	1113
	SHAVER, Donna B.	(503)226-8695	1123
	THENELL, Janice C.	(503)221-7726	1234
Roseburg	COOK, Sybilla A.	(503)673-0504	240
Salem	BAUER, Marilyn A.	(503)581-4292	65
	TURNBAUGH, Roy C.	(503)378-4241	1264

PENNSYLVANIA

Altoona	SHERIDAN, Margaret G.	(814)942-2565	1127
Ambler	SYEN, Sarah	(215)542-9967	1217
Ardmore	VLEDUTS-STOKOLOV, Natalia	(215)649-1148	1286
Berwyn	BROWN, David E.	(215)644-5241	143
Bethlehem	JARVIS, William E.	(215)758-3035	595
	METZGER, Philip A.	(215)866-1257	829
Bloomsburg	ROCKWOOD, Susan M.	(717)784-8456	1046
Blue Bell	TERRY, Terese M.	(215)641-6594	1232
California	NOLF, Marsha L.	(412)938-4048	908
Carbondale	MCNABB, Corrine R.	(717)282-3151	815
Center Square	SCHAEFER, John A.	(215)277-6386	1089
Center Valley	MCCABE, James P.	(215)282-1100	793
Chambersburg	EZELL, Johanna V.	(717)264-2269	360
Chester Heights	OWENS, Irene E.		932
Clarion	DINGLE, Susan	(814)226-2271	304
	HORN, Roger G.	(814)226-2490	559
	MCCABE, Gerard B.	(814)226-2343	792

WRITER/EDITOR (Cont'd)
PENNSYLVANIA (Cont'd)

City	Name	Phone	No.
Coraopolis	KASPERKO, Jean M.		629
	SKOVIRA, Robert J.	(412)262-8257	1147
Dalton	THOMAS, Scott E.	(717)563-2014	1238
Dresher	FU, Clare S.	(215)641-1978	407
Elizabethtown	BARD, Nelson P.	(717)367-1151	56
Elkins Park	NEMEYER, Carol A.		895
Erie	KAGER, Jeffrey F.	(814)825-3066	621
Franklin Center	CUTLER, Judith	(215)459-6932	268
Gettysburg	CHIESA, Adele M.	(717)334-1651	208
Gladwyne	FISHER, Daphne V.	(215)525-6628	380
Glenmoore	VOURVOULIAS, Sabrina M.	(215)942-3421	1289
Glenside	LOCKETT, Cheryl L.		736
Greensburg	BALAS, Janet L.	(412)836-4849	50
	SCHEEREN, William O.	(412)834-9000	1090
Harleysville	HILLEGAS, Ferne E.		541
	LINN, Mott R.	(215)464-4500	731
Harrisburg	FOUST, Judith M.	(717)787-8007	393
	SHULTZ, Suzanne M.	(717)782-4292	1133
	STAYER, Jonathan R.	(717)787-2701	1183
Hatboro	BURNS, Richard K.	(215)675-6762	162
Haverford	CORRIGAN, John T.	(215)896-7458	247
	FREEMAN, Michael S.	(215)896-1272	401
Havertown	HOFFMAN, Elizabeth P.	(215)446-3082	547
Holsopple	SLICK, Myrna H.	(814)479-7148	1149
Indiana	KROAH, Larry A.	(412)463-2055	679
	RAHKONEN, Carl J.		1003
Jenkintown	MONTOYA, Leopoldo	(215)886-2299	856
	SEVY, Barbara S.	(215)884-8275	1117
	WOODLOCK, Stephanie	(215)572-3564	1366
King of Prussia	RICH, Denise A.	(215)935-7054	1027
Kingston	PAUSTIAN, P R.	(717)283-2651	950
Lancaster	ZEAGER, Lloyd	(717)393-9745	1387
Lansdale	WEBER ROOCHVARG, Lynn E.	(215)368-8688	1314
Lewisburg	BOYTINCK, Paul	(717)524-2678	124
Macungie	BAHR, Alice H.	(215)821-1255	45
Malvern	QUINTILIANO, Barbara		1000
	VANDOREN, Sandra S.	(215)640-9809	1275
Mansfield	DOWLING, John	(717)662-4753	316
McKeesport	HORVATH, Robert T.	(412)672-0625	561
Meadville	STALLARD, Kathryn E.	(814)333-4363	1179
Media	ELLISON, J T.	(215)566-1699	345
Millersville	JUDGE, Joseph M.	(717)872-7590	619
Monroeville	BERGER, Lewis W.	(412)825-2284	85
	MURPHY, Diana G.	(412)327-5976	880
Mt Lebanon	WEISFIELD, Cynthia F.	(412)831-8225	1319
New Milford	MAASS, Eleanor A.	(717)465-3054	753
Norristown	PRITCHARD, Barbara		994
North Wales	MAXIN, Jacqueline A.	(215)855-5675	787
Philadelphia	ADAMS, Mignon S.	(215)596-8790	5
	BAKY, John S.	(215)951-1290	50
	BENDER, Evelyn	(215)634-0357	79
	BOISCLAIR, Regina A.	(215)438-0173	111
	CUTRONA, Cheryl	(215)844-9027	268
	DONOVAN, Judith G.	(215)928-0577	312
	DUCLOW, Geradline		322
	EVEY, Patricia G.	(215)848-3016	359
	FENICHEL, Carol H.	(215)448-7185	371
	FREEDMAN, Bernadette	(215)332-6937	400
	GREEN, Patricia L.	(215)724-5715	462
	GREEN, Rose B.	(215)828-7029	462
	GRILIKHES, Sandra B.	(215)898-7027	470
	HALLER, Douglas M.	(215)898-8304	489
	HOLUB, Joseph C.	(215)843-6220	555
	ICKES, Barbara J.	(215)745-9767	581
	KING, Eleanor M.		650
	LEVITT, Martin L.	(215)627-0706	721
	MILLER, Fredric M.	(213)787-8257	837
	MORRIS, Leslie A.	(215)985-4384	867
	MOWERY, Susan G.	(215)248-8206	874
	MYERS, James N.	(215)787-8231	884
	NIGHTINGALE, Daniel	(215)288-1151	904
	PITCHON, Cindy A.	(215)235-4486	976
	POST, Jeremiah B.	(215)748-2701	986
	POST, Joyce A.	(215)456-2971	986
	PROMOS, Marianne	(215)686-5351	995
	RIDGEWAY, Patricia M.	(215)898-7555	1032
	SCHAEFFER, Judith E.	(215)843-8840	1089

WRITER/EDITOR (Cont'd)
PENNSYLVANIA (Cont'd)

City	Name	Phone	No.
Philadelphia	SMIRAGLIA, Richard P.	(215)662-5699	1152
	SNOW, Bonnie		1164
	SNYDER, Theresa	(215)732-6200	1165
	SOULTOUKIS, Donna Z.	(215)922-5460	1169
	TANNER, Anne B.	(215)895-2483	1222
	VAN HORNE, John C.	(215)546-3181	1275
	WARTLUFT, David J.	(215)242-8746	1307
	WILLMANN, Donna S.		1348
	YERGER, George A.	(215)587-4887	1379
	ZIPF, Elizabeth M.	(215)587-4815	1389
	ZOGOTT, Joyce	(215)596-8994	1390
Phoenixville	SAUER, James L.	(215)933-2236	1084
Pittsburgh	ARJONA, Sandra K.	(412)821-2263	31
	BLEIER, Carol S.	(412)563-2712	105
	BOUTWELL, Barbara J.	(412)967-3131	119
	BROSKY, Catherine M.	(412)682-0837	141
	DETLEFSEN, Ellen G.	(412)624-9444	296
	ENGLERT, Mary A.	(412)795-1761	350
	EVANS, Nancy H.	(412)268-2114	357
	FORD, Sylverna V.	(412)268-2446	390
	FREEDMAN, Phyllis D.	(412)784-8599	400
	HARTNER, Elizabeth P.		508
	HOWARD, Elizabeth F.	(412)441-3753	564
	JOSEY, E J.	(412)624-9451	618
	KRZYS, Richard A.	(412)624-9459	681
	KURTIK, Frank J.	(412)687-3084	685
	LEIBOWITZ, Faye R.	(412)421-7974	713
	MAZEFSKY, Gertrude T.	(412)361-7582	791
	METZLER, Douglas P.	(412)624-9414	829
	NAISMITH, Rachael	(412)268-8896	887
	NASRI, William Z.	(412)276-3234	888
	ROOT, Deane L.	(412)624-4100	1054
	SCHEETZ, Mary D.	(412)421-4297	1091
	SCHUMACHER, Carolyn S.	(412)363-0190	1102
	SPIEGELMAN, Barbara M.	(412)824-2222	1174
	WEBRECK, Susan J.	(412)624-5230	1314
Reading	WEIHERER, Patricia D.	(215)376-7660	1317
Rosemont	SCHWALB, Ann W.	(215)527-3131	1104
Sanatoga	NIPPERT, Carolyn C.	(215)323-4829	904
Sarver	LIVENGOOD, Candice C.		734
Secane	CASINI, Barbara P.	(215)543-4309	192
Shippenville	EMERICK, Kenneth F.	(814)226-5775	347
Slippery Rock	JOSEPH, Elizabeth T.	(412)794-4623	617
South Williamsport	HICKEY, Kate D.	(717)322-2733	536
Springfield	MAIN, Annette Z.		761
State College	NADESKI, Karen L.	(814)238-7890	886
	PHILLIPS, Janet C.	(814)238-0254	968
Swarthmore	HAMILTON, Gloria R.	(215)544-1369	492
	LEHMANN, Stephen R.	(215)328-8492	713
Tamaqua	EVERHART, Nancy L.	(717)668-3334	358
University Park	CARSON, M S.	(814)865-1818	188
	CHAMBERLAIN, Carol E.	(814)865-1858	197
	FISHER, Kim N.	(814)865-1858	381
	FREIVALDS, Dace I.	(814)865-1818	402
	GARNER, Diane L.	(814)865-4861	419
	ROE, Eunice M.	(814)863-0140	1048
	SULZER, John H.	(814)866-4001	1209
	SWEENEY, Del	(814)863-3952	1215
	WESTERMAN, Melvin E.	(814)863-2898	1327
	ZABEL, Diane M.	(814)863-2898	1385
Upper Darby	REILLY, Rebecca S.		1020
Upper Saint Clair	FULMER, Dina J.	(412)831-8664	409
Villanova	ERDT, Terrence	(215)645-4670	352
Wayne	DRIEHAUS, Rosemary H.		320
West Chester	CHAFF, Sandra L.	(215)524-0547	197
Wexford	CARTER, Ruth C.	(412)935-1752	190
Yardley	DU BOIS, Paul Z.	(215)493-6882	322
	ROSE, Dianne E.	(215)493-2311	1054

PUERTO RICO

City	Name	Phone	No.
Hato Rey	NEGRON-GAZTAMBIDE, Olguita	(809)767-4192	892
San Juan	HAMEL, Eleanor C.	(809)765-4426	491

WRITER/EDITOR (Cont'd)

RHODE ISLAND

Barrington	BURKE, Lauri K.	(401)245-3741	160
Carolina	HULL, Catherine C.	(401)364-6100	572
Kingston	FUTAS, Elizabeth	(401)792-2947	411
	SCHNEIDER, Stewart P.	(401)792-2878	1097
	VOCINO, Michael C.	(401)789-9357	1286
	YOUNG, Arthur P.	(401)792-2666	1381
Lincoln	DESMARAIS, Norman P.	(401)333-3275	295
Newport	CHERPAK, Evelyn M.	(401)841-2435	206
Pawtucket	MILLS, Catherine H.	(401)728-9112	843
Providence	BRAUNSTEIN, Mark M.	(401)521-4771	130
	CASHMAN, Norine D.	(401)863-3218	192
	COOLIDGE, Arlan R.		241
	HENDERSON, Linda L.	(401)277-7887	526
	LAMAR, Christine L.	(401)331-8575	689
	LANDIS, Dennis C.	(401)863-2725	693
	MARSH, Corrie V.	(401)863-2954	773
	MONTEIRO, George	(401)863-3266	856
	RAINWATER, Jean M.	(401)863-3723	1004
	REEVES, Joan R.	(401)272-7745	1016
	SHERIDAN, Jean	(401)277-3818	1127
	SVENGALIS, Kendall F.	(401)274-3196	1212
	WAGNER, Albin	(401)277-2283	1291
	WILMETH, Don B.	(401)863-3289	1349
Saunderstown	BRENNAN, Deborah B.	(401)294-3175	132
Wakefield	BARNETT, Judith B.	(401)789-7435	57
Woonsocket	IMONDI, Lenore R.	(401)762-5165	582

SOUTH CAROLINA

Charleston	MOLTKE-HANSEN, David	(803)723-3225	853
	RUST, Roxy J.	(803)571-1443	1070
	SMITH, Nancy	(803)792-7672	1158
	STRAUCH, Katina P.	(803)723-3536	1200
Clemson	HIPPS, Gary M.	(803)654-3934	543
	JOHNSON, Steven D.	(803)654-3360	609
	MCCULLEY, P M.	(803)654-8753	800
	TAYLOR, Dennis S.	(803)656-3031	1226
Columbia	FRITZ, William R.		405
	GEOGHEGAN, Doris J.	(803)777-4206	427
	HELSLEY, Alexia J.	(803)781-8477	525
	HOLLEY, E J.	(803)774-4866	551
	HOWARD-HILL, Trevor	(803)777-6499	564
	MOSS, Patsy G.	(803)799-4349	872
	PEAKE, Luise E.	(803)777-3214	952
	SCHULZ, Constance B.	(803)777-4854	1102
	WASHINGTON, Nancy H.	(803)777-4206	1307
Denmark	BOOK, Imogene I.	(803)793-3660	115
Florence	HUX, Roger K.	(803)665-6121	579
Gaffney	EDEN, David E.	(803)489-4381	336
Greenwood	FECKO, Marybeth	(803)223-1810	367
	HARE, Ann T.	(803)229-8365	501
Greer	MESSINEO, Anthony	(803)268-7267	828
Irmo	BARDIN, Angela D.	(803)781-3138	56
Rock Hill	CHOPESIUK, Ronald J.	(803)366-5440	210
	MITLIN, Laurance R.	(803)329-5716	850
Spartanburg	FAWVER, Darlene E.	(803)596-9074	367
	SMITH, Stephen C.	(803)596-3505	1161
Surfside Beach	SALMON, Robin R.	(803)238-4655	1077
Timmonsville	WARR, Virginia M.		1306

SOUTH DAKOTA

Brookings	BROWN, Philip L.	(605)692-7735	146
Pierre	HILMOE, Deann D.	(605)224-3178	541
Rapid City	MC CAULEY, Philip F.	(605)348-5124	795
	MORGAN, Bradford A.	(605)394-1245	863
	SCHWARTZ, James M.	(605)394-1246	1104
Sioux Falls	LANG, Elizabeth A.		695
	THOMPSON, Harry F.	(605)336-4007	1239

TENNESSEE

Brentwood	NORTON, Tedgina	(615)371-0090	910
Chattanooga	BRUNER, Katharine E.	(615)266-0676	150
	REARDON, Elizabeth M.		1013
Clarksville	RIVES, Lydia L.	(615)647-9484	1037
	THWEATT, John H.	(615)647-0954	1243
Cleveland	NICOL, Jessie T.		902
Harriman	OVERTON, Margaret C.		931
Jackson	AUD, Thomas L.	(901)668-2896	39
Johnson City	SPEARS, Ross	(615)926-8637	1172

WRITER/EDITOR (Cont'd)

TENNESSEE (Cont'd)

Knoxville	BEAL, Gretchen F.	(615)521-2500	68
	CLELAND, Nancy D.	(615)588-5406	220
	GRADY, Agnes M.	(615)637-0008	455
	HASTINGS, Constance M.	(615)690-0368	511
	LLOYD, James B.	(615)974-4480	735
	MYERS, Marcia J.	(615)974-4465	884
	PHILLIPS, Linda L.	(615)687-6734	968
	PICQUET, D C.	(615)974-4381	971
	RADER, Joe C.	(615)523-6937	1002
	SAMMATARO, Linda J.	(615)521-7750	1078
Maryville	WORLEY, Joan H.	(615)982-6412	1369
Memphis	BAER, Ellen H.	(901)725-8853	45
	BAKER, Bonnie U.	(901)324-6536	48
	LASSLO, Andrew	(901)528-6080	700
	PERRY, Glenda L.	(901)527-4348	960
	RUDOLPH, N J.	(901)454-2208	1066
	VILES, Elza A.	(901)454-4412	1284
Murfreesboro	HUNTER, Joy W.	(615)893-1360	576
	MARSHALL, John D.	(615)893-2091	774
	NEAL, James H.	(615)895-1383	890
	WELLS, Paul F.	(615)898-2449	1323
	YOUREE, Beverly B.	(615)896-4911	1384
Nashville	ARMONTROUT, Brian A.	(615)320-3678	32
	EISENSTEIN, Jill M.	(615)327-8158	341
	HEARNE, Mary G.	(615)383-8989	518
	HODGES, Terence M.	(615)322-2299	546
	LEE, Geoffrey J.	(615)322-7390	710
	MANNING, Dale	(615)322-2407	766
	MOON, Fletcher F.	(615)833-1125	857
	RICHARDS, Timothy F.	(615)385-1858	1028
	SHOCKLEY, Ann A.	(615)353-0771	1132
	WHITEHEAD, Jane		1332
Norris	DYER, Barbara M.	(615)494-9555	330
Oak Ridge	MCDONALD, Ethel Q.	(615)482-5011	802
	SNYDER, Cathrine E.	(615)483-1228	1164
Sewanee	HAYMES, Don		516

TEXAS

Arlington	KERBY, Ramona A.	(817)478-9829	643
	LEATHERMAN, Donald G.	(817)459-6910	707
	LOWRY, Charles B.	(817)273-3391	745
Austin	BILLINGS, Harold W.	(512)442-8597	96
	BUCKNALL, Carolyn F.	(512)478-5129	154
	BURCH, David R.	(512)471-7726	158
	BURT, Eugene C.	(512)471-4777	164
	DAVIS, Donald G.	(512)471-3821	278
	DAYO, Ayo	(512)472-8980	283
	DEGRUYTER, M L.	(512)929-3086	288
	DIVELY, Reddy	(512)288-3371	306
	GOODWIN, Willard	(512)288-2373	450
	GOULD, Karen K.	(512)453-2602	454
	GRACY, David B.	(512)471-3821	455
	MARTIN, Jean K.	(512)346-2973	776
	MCCANN, Charlotte P.		793
	MIKSA, Francis L.	(572)346-6769	834
	PARKER, David F.	(512)450-1931	941
	PRATTER, Jonathan	(512)471-7726	990
	RODE, Shelley J.		1047
	ROY, Loriene	(512)471-6316	1063
	SKINNER, Vicki F.	(512)892-3997	1146
	SMITH, Nancy K.	(512)482-5137	1158
	SPRUG, Joseph W.	(512)448-8474	1176
	TAYLOR, Nancy L.	(512)346-1426	1228
	WALTON, Robert A.	(512)346-1426	1301
	WASSENICH, Red	(512)495-7151	1308
	WEBSTER, Linda	(512)458-1852	1314
	WESTBROOK, Jo L.		1326
Beaumont	HOLLAND, Mary M.	(409)892-8885	551
Bellaire	HOLAB-ABELMAN, Robin S.		550
Brazoria	RASKA, Ginny	(409)798-1628	1009
Brownfield	HAMILTON, Betty D.	(806)637-4213	491
Bryan	MOUNCE, Clara P.	(409)779-1736	873
	RABINS, Joan W.	(409)776-0374	1001
College Station	BROWN-WEBB, Deborah D.	(409)845-1636	149
	COOK, C C.	(409)845-3731	239
	RHOLES, Julia M.	(409)845-1952	1026
	ST. CLAIR, Gloriana S.	(409)696-8982	1075
	SCHULTZ, Charles R.	(409)845-1815	1101

WRITER/EDITOR (Cont'd)
TEXAS (Cont'd)
College Station

THOMPSON, Christine E. . . . . (409)845-8157 1239

Commerce CONRAD, James H. . . . . (214)886-5737 238
Conroe BALDWIN, Joe M. . . . . (409)756-4484 51
Corpus Christi SILVERMAN, Barbara G. . . . . (512)887-9225 1138
Dallas BIRD, H C. . . . . (214)553-5995 98
BROWN, Muriel W. . . . . (214)348-7861 146
CAMPBELL, Shirley A. . . . . . (214)330-0027 177
CLEE, June E. . . . . (214)941-3375 220
CLEMENTS, Cynthia L. . . . . . (214)238-6153 221
EATENSON, Ervin T. . . . . (214)521-4839 333
FARMER, David . . . . (214)692-3231 364
HOWINGTON, Tad C. . . . . . . (214)337-7779 566
LOVELL, Bonnie A. . . . . (214)826-1924 743
PEDEN, Robert M. . . . . (214)746-3646 954
RYDESKY, Mary M. . . . . (214)339-3349 1071
SACKETT-WILK, Susan A. . . . (214)307-1304 1073
SMITH, Michael K. . . . . (214)296-5187 1158
Denton ALMQUIST, Sharon G. . . . . . (817)387-1703 17
FOLLET, Robert E. . . . . (817)382-0037 388
LAVENDER, Kenneth . . . . . (817)565-2768 703
POPE, Betty F. . . . . (817)565-2609 983
SWIGGER, Keith . . . . (817)898-2609 1216
THOMAS, James L. . . . . (817)382-1697 1237
TURNER, Frank L. . . . . (817)898-2603 1264
El Paso ANDERSON, Mark . . . . (915)858-0905 24
CAMERON, Dee B. . . . . (915)566-1656 174
GEARY, Kathleen A. . . . . (915)533-5777 424
RAMSEY, Donna E. . . . . (915)855-1218 1005
Fort Worth DE TONNANCOUR, P R. . . . . (817)763-1790 296
DIXON, Catherine A. . . . . . . (817)870-7708 306
MONGOLD, Alice D. . . . . (817)457-9080 854
RICE, Ralph A. . . . . (817)626-7995 1027
VERNON, James R. . . . . (817)923-4901 1283
WESTBROOK, Brenda S. . . . (817)831-7232 1326
Georgetown SWARTZ, Jon D. . . . . (512)863-1214 1214
Glen Rose KENDALL, Lyle H. . . . . (817)897-4991 640
Harlingen CORBIN, John . . . . (512)428-5475 245
Houston ADAMS, Elaine P. . . . . (713)785-8703 4
BOOTHE, Nancy L. . . . . (713)667-1916 116
BUTLER, Marguerite L. . . . . . (713)726-9244 166
CHAMPION, Walter T. . . . . . (713)527-7125 198
CORBIN, John . . . . (713)749-4241 245
CRIST, Lynda L. . . . . (713)527-4990 259
GOLEY, Elaine P. . . . . (713)467-5784 447
GOTHIA, Blanche . . . . (713)266-5106 453
HACKNEY, Judith G. . . . . . . (713)496-5590 481
HOLIBAUGH, Ralph W. 550
JOITY, Donna M. . . . . (713)583-7160 610
KORKMAS, Carolyn C. . . . . . (713)953-7222 671
LYDEN, Edward W. . . . . (713)777-8212 750
LYDERS, Josette A. . . . . (713)728-3893 750
MCGOWN, Sue W. . . . . (713)850-0222 807
MORRISSEY, Charles T. . . . . (713)799-4510 869
ROBINSON, Kathleen M. 1044
SCHWARTZ, Charles A. . . . . (713)527-8101 1104
STUBBLEFIELD, J G. 1204
WEATHERS, Barbara H. . . . . (713)468-8211 1312
WELCH, C B. . . . . (713)749-4245 1321
WILSON, Ann Q. . . . . (713)871-0505 1349
WILSON, John W. . . . . (713)529-4301 1351
WILSON, Thomas C. . . . . . . (713)995-8401 1353
Huntsville BAILEY, William G . . . . (409)294-1614 47
HOFFMAN, Frank W. . . . . . . (409)294-1152 548
YOUNG, J A. . . . . (409)295-8766 1382
Irving BRAGG, William J. . . . . (214)556-1234 127
La Porte ATKINS, Winston . . . . (713)479-2421 38
Laredo BRESIE, Mayellen . . . . (512)722-8001 133
Leander BIGLEY, John E. 96
Lewisville MARMION, Daniel K. . . . . . . (214)436-5125 772
MCCOY, Judy I. . . . . (214)221-9251 799
TALLEY, Pat L. . . . . (214)434-2545 1221
Lubbock CARGILL, Jennifer S. . . . . . (806)792-2349 181
Odessa GROVES, Helen G. . . . . (915)363-9604 474
Palacios WOLL, Christina B. . . . . (512)972-2166 1361
Palestine SELWYN, Laurie . . . . (214)723-1436 1114
Pasadena CATES, Susan W. . . . . (713)487-1714 195
Pharr LIU, David T. . . . . (512)787-1491 734

WRITER/EDITOR (Cont'd)
TEXAS (Cont'd)
Plano DEILY, Carole C. . . . . (214)578-7175 288
PROKESH, Jane . . . . (214)754-6461 995
Richardson KRUSE, Luanne M. . . . . (214)680-9677 681
San Antonio BELL, Joy A. . . . . (512)496-2057 77
GONZALEZ, Sharon M. 448
GRUENBECK, Laurie . . . . . . (512)434-8938 474
NOLAN, Christopher W. . . . . (512)736-7429 907
RAY, Joyce M. . . . . (512)567-2470 1011
San Juan SIEMENS, Bessie M. 1136
Sugar Land JOHNSON, Pat M. . . . . (713)980-5350 608
The Woodlands PEYTON, Janice L. . . . . . . (713)292-4441 966
Uvalde KINGSBERY, Evelyn B. . . . . (512)278-4401 652
Waco HILLMAN, Kathy R. . . . . . . (817)755-2111 541
RICHARDS, James H. . . . . . (817)756-0602 1028
Weatherford HEEZEN, Ronald R. . . . . . . (817)599-0833 520
Wichita Falls GRIMES, John F. . . . . (817)855-0463 470
ROBERTS, Ernest J. . . . . . . (817)855-2390 1040
Wimberley FELSTED, Carla M. . . . . . . (512)847-5277 370

UTAH
Logan WEISS, Stephen C. 1320
Magna GOFORTH, Allene M. . . . . . (801)250-7507 444
Payson GILLUM, Gary P. . . . . (801)465-4527 436
Provo GOULD, Douglas A. . . . . . . (801)226-1469 454
HALL, Blaine H. . . . . (801)378-6117 487
LYMAN, Lovisa . . . . (801)378-3297 751
MATHIESEN, Thomas J. . . . . (801)378-3688 784
ROWLEY, Edward D. . . . . . . (801)378-6372 1063
Salt Lake City CASADY, Richard L. . . . . . . (801)533-9607 191
HEYER, Terry L. . . . . (801)321-1054 535
HINDMARSH, Douglas P. . . . (801)328-2609 542
HOLLEY, Robert P. . . . . (801)581-7741 551
OWEN, Amy . . . . (801)466-5888 931
SPERRY, Kip . . . . (801)255-9615 1174
West Jordan KARPISEK, Marian E. . . . . . (801)561-4676 628

VERMONT
Barre GRIFFIN, Marie E. . . . . (802)479-2810 468
Burlington DAY, Martha T. . . . . (802)863-0506 282
Chelsea BATTEY, Jean D. . . . . (802)276-3086 64
Putney THOMPSON, Jane K. . . . . . (802)387-4767 1240
Richmond REIT, Janet W. . . . . (802)482-2352 1022
Rutland SHERMAN, Jacob R. . . . . . (802)773-1860 1128
St Johnsbury BRYAN, Martin F. . . . . (802)748-9264 151
South Royalton SWIFT, Esther M. . . . . (802)763-7163 1216
White River
   Junction LERNER, Frederick A. . . . . . (802)295-6548 717

VIRGIN ISLANDS
St Croix VAUGHN, Robert V. . . . . . . (809)778-8465 1280
St Thomas MILLER, Veronica E. . . . . . (809)774-0059 843

VIRGINIA
Alexandria GOLDBERG, Jolande E. . . . . (703)765-4521 444
GRAY, Dorothy L. . . . . (703)684-8244 459
MARA, Ruth M. . . . . (703)765-0262 768
MICHAELS, Andrea A. . . . . . (703)360-1297 831
ROSENBERG, Kenyon C. . . . (703)642-5480 1056
ROTHSCHILD, M C. . . . . . . (202)274-7206 1060
STEIN, Karen E. . . . . (703)354-3154 1185
STEVENS, Roberta A. . . . . . (703)960-0464 1191
VAROUTSOS, Mary A. . . . . . (703)836-0156 1279
Amelia SMITH, Adeline M. 1152
Annandale MATON, Joanne T. . . . . (703)256-2288 784
MCGINN, Ellen T. . . . . (703)280-5085 806
Arlington ARDEN, Caroline . . . . (703)532-1548 31
ASHKENAS, Bruce F. . . . . . (301)763-7410 36
CARR, Timothy B. 186
DENNIE, David L. . . . . (703)685-0208 292
DESSAINT, Alain Y. . . . . (703)247-7750 295
GREEN, Randall N. . . . . (703)243-5631 462
JOACHIM, Robert J. . . . . . . (703)920-7721 600
POEHLMAN, Dorothy J. 979
STEVENS, Frank A. 1190
Blacksburg EASTMAN, Ann H. . . . . (703)951-4770 333
FOX, Edward A. . . . . (703)552-8667 394
JOHNSON, Bryan R. . . . . . . (703)552-0876 602
KENNEY, Donald J. . . . . (703)961-5069 641

WRITER/EDITOR (Cont'd)
VIRGINIA (Cont'd)

Charlottesville	BERKELEY, Edmund		87
	CAMPBELL, James M.	(804)924-4985	176
	COOPER, Jean L.	(804)978-4363	243
	FRANKLIN, Robert D.	(804)973-3238	398
	LOY, Dennis C.	(804)973-3410	745
	RODRIGUEZ, Robert D.		1048
	WHITE, William		1332
Chesapeake	KERSTETTER, Virginia M.	(804)483-6544	644
Chesterfield	WAGENKNECHT, Robert E.	(804)748-1601	1291
Fairfax	PFEIFFER, David A.	(703)425-4685	966
	ROBINSON, David F.	(703)273-6139	1043
	WALCH, Timothy G.	(703)273-3260	1293
	WALCH, Victoria I.	(703)273-3260	1293
Falls Church	BEAM, Christopher M.	(703)356-4908	69
	HELGERSON, Linda W.	(703)237-0682	524
	KAHLER, Mary E.		622
	VIOLA, Herman J.	(703)573-6211	1285
Fort Monroe	BYRN, James H.	(804)727-4491	169
Fredericksburg	MULVANEY, John P.	(703)899-4666	878
Harrisonburg	PALMER, Forrest C.	(703)568-6929	936
	RAMSEY, Inez L.	(703)568-6791	1006
	STEINBERG, David L.	(703)433-1572	1185
Hollins College	BECKER, Charlotte B.	(703)362-6235	72
Lynchburg	SIDDONS, James D.	(804)846-8129	1135
Manassas	CHRISTOLON, Blair B.	(703)369-3535	212
Martinsville	PEARL, Patricia D.	(703)632-9096	952
McLean	CHEVERIE, Joan F.	(703)893-3889	207
	WINIARSKI, Marilee E.	(800)421-7229	1355
Norfolk	BERENT, Irwin M.	(804)855-1272	84
	MAYER-HENNELLY, Mary B.	(804)441-2733	789
	NICHOLSON, Myreen M.	(804)627-6281	902
	SWAINE, Cynthia W.	(804)627-1115	1212
	TRASK, Benjamin H.		1254
North Springfield	AINES, Andrew A.	(703)569-4872	8
Portsmouth	BROWN, William A.	(804)483-2195	148
	BURGESS, Dean	(804)393-8501	159
Reston	JENSEN, Raymond A.	(703)648-6820	599
	JOSLYN, Camille	(703)471-1641	618
	LEWIS, Diane M.	(703)860-4475	723
	MONTGOMERY, Suzanne L.	(703)435-1974	856
	WILTSHIRE, Denise A.	(703)391-0505	1354
Richmond	DEBARDELEBEN, Marian Z.	(804)274-2876	284
	HALL, Bonlyn G.	(804)359-0409	487
	HUBBARD, William J.	(804)786-2331	568
	JACOBY, Mary M.	(804)231-2545	590
	KANE, Dorothea S.		624
	OWEN, Karen V.	(804)649-6132	931
	SHEPARD, E L.	(804)358-4901	1126
	TROTTI, John B.	(804)358-8956	1258
	WHALEY, John H.	(804)257-1108	1328
Roanoke	OBRIST, Cynthia W.	(703)362-6235	915
Springfield	CASWELL, Mary C.	(703)642-0340	194
	ROARK, Robin D.	(703)644-7372	1038
Vienna	DODSON, Whit	(703)938-2630	308
	SCHAEFER, Mary E.	(703)759-6339	1089
Virginia Beach	WELSH, Eric L.	(804)424-7000	1323
Williamsburg	GROVE, Pearce S.	(804)220-2477	473
Winchester	BISCHOFF, Frances A.	(703)667-5350	99
Wise	CHISHOLM, Clarence E.	(703)328-2431	209
Woodbridge	ENGLAND, Ellen M.	(703)670-2191	349
	MELVIN, Kay H.	(703)491-2055	823

WASHINGTON

Bellingham	BLUME, Scott	(206)671-8960	107
	SYMES, Dal S.		1217
Camas	BRENNAN, Cindy L.	(206)834-4692	132
Cheney	ALKIRE, Leland G.	(509)235-4669	13
	TRACY, Joan I.	(509)359-7892	1253
Clallam Bay	PEARSON, Barbara F.	(206)963-2369	952
Custer	HASELBAUER, Kathleen J.	(206)366-5063	510
Ellensburg	YEH, Thomas Y.	(509)925-9257	1379
Everett	GRINSTEAD, Beth K.	(206)258-1951	471
Kent	CHAPMAN, Kathleen A.	(206)630-0538	202
Kirkland	DIBIASE, Linda P.	(206)821-2863	299
Lacey	DEBUSE, Raymond	(206)491-7498	285
	PUZIAK, Kathleen M.	(206)491-0347	998
Longview	BAKER, Robert K.	(206)577-0756	49
Marysville	WILSON, Evie		1350

WRITER/EDITOR (Cont'd)
WASHINGTON (Cont'd)

Olympia	ZUSSY, Nancy L.	(206)786-9647	1391
Pullman	KEMP, Barbara E.	(509)334-5809	639
	KOPP, James J.	(509)335-9133	671
	ZIEGLER, Ronald M.	(509)335-2691	1388
Seattle	BAGG, Deborah L.	(206)621-7896	45
	BRZUSTOWICZ, Richard J.	(206)527-9357	152
	CLINE, Robert S.	(206)523-7268	222
	CRANDALL, Michael D.	(206)633-2530	255
	EULENBERG, Julia N.	(206)324-2605	356
	FASSETT, William E.	(206)545-2272	366
	HILDEBRANDT, Darlene M.	(206)543-5818	538
	LIPTON, Laura E.	(206)543-8616	732
	MCCORMICK, Jack M.	(206)526-6107	798
	MILLER, Carmen L.	(206)285-4248	836
	POLISHUK, Bernard	(206)524-8676	980
	ROWBERG, Alan H.	(206)548-6250	1062
	SILVA, Mary E.		1138
	STIRLING, Dale A.	(206)367-2728	1195
	THORSEN, Jeanne M.	(206)684-6606	1242
	WEAVER, Carolyn G.	(206)543-5530	1312
Spokane	MURRAY, James M.	(509)838-3680	882
	SHIDELER, John C.	(509)838-5242	1129
	TYSON, Christy	(509)624-9744	1267
Steilacoom	COHEN, Jane L.		228
	PARR, Loraine E.	(206)582-7557	943
Tacoma	GILDENHAR, Janet		434
	MENDELSON, Martin	(206)383-5855	823
Vancouver	CONABLE, Gordon M.	(206)694-0604	235
	CONABLE, Irene H.	(206)694-0604	235

WEST VIRGINIA

Charleston	HUMPHRIES, Joy D.		574
Glenville	FAULKNER, Ronnie W.	(304)462-7361	366
Huntington	STARKEY, Bonnie F.	(303)523-3109	1182
Morgantown	CUTHBERT, John A.	(304)293-3536	267
	ESKRIDGE, Virginia C.	(304)293-5300	354
	SHILL, Harold B.	(304)292-3762	1130
St Albans	PALMER, Marguerite C.	(304)722-6349	936
Salem	LANGER, Frank A.	(304)782-1007	695
Wheeling	JULIAN, Charles A.	(304)233-5900	619

WISCONSIN

Appleton	NADZIEJKA, David E.	(414)731-8904	886
Burlington	PROCES, Stephen L.	(414)763-7623	994
Caledonia	GRENDYSA, Peter A.	(414)764-3676	467
Cudahy	KLAUSMEIER, Arno M.	(414)744-0268	658
Eau Claire	CARROLL, Barbara T.		187
Green Bay	GORSEGNER, Betty D.	(414)465-1529	452
	MUSICH, Gerald D.	(414)437-7623	883
Hales Corners	BARLOGA, Carolyn J.	(414)425-0355	57
Iola	FOERSTER, Trey	(715)445-3838	387
Madison	ARNESON, Arne J.	(608)833-1617	33
	ARNOLD, Barbara J.	(608)263-2909	33
	BEHRND-KLODT, Menzi L.	(608)238-3966	75
	BOYER, Ann T.	(608)233-7252	123
	CLARK, Peter W.	(608)257-4861	217
	CONNER, P Z.	(608)256-4440	237
	CRAWFORD, Josephine	(608)274-7984	256
	DAHLGREN, Anders C.	(608)271-9148	269
	DRESANG, Eliza T.	(608)267-9357	319
	EDMONDS, Michael	(608)262-4672	336
	HERMAN, Gertrude B.		531
	KRUSE, Ginny M.		681
	MATTHEWS, Geraldine M.	(608)266-1164	785
	PARSONS, Patricia S.		945
	ROBBINS, Jane B.	(608)263-2908	1038
	SEARING, Susan E.	(608)263-5754	1109
	SHAFTMAN, Sarah	(608)241-7153	1119
	WEINGAND, Darlene E.	(608)262-8952	1318
	WELSCH, Erwin K.	(608)262-3195	1323
	WIEGAND, Wayne A.	(608)263-2914	1336
	WILLETT, Holly G.	(608)251-0633	1341
Marshfield	ZIMMERMANN, Albert J.	(715)387-2418	1389
Menomonie	GRAF, David L.	(715)232-1202	455
Mequon	AMAN, Mary J.	(414)242-9031	19

WRITER/EDITOR (Cont'd)
WISCONSIN (Cont'd)

Milwaukee	ANTHONY, Rose M.	(414)384-6535	29
	ASU, Glynis V.	(414)257-8339	37
	BJORKLUND, Edi		100
	BOULANGER, Mary E.	(414)229-4659	119
	EUKEY, Jim O.		356
	GILL, Norman N.	(414)352-1545	435
	GREENE, Victor R.	(414)963-7063	464
	SHUTKIN, Sara A.	(414)332-3321	1134
	ZIRBES, Colette M.	(414)483-1979	1390
Montello	TANNER, Linda L.	(608)297-2228	1223
New London	DIEHL, Carol L.	(414)982-5040	301
Oshkosh	SHARMA, Ravindra N.	(414)424-0139	1122
Racine	SCHINK, Sandra C.	(414)634-1495	1093
Reedsville	OHLEMACHER, Janet H.	(414)754-4831	919
Rhinelander	SLYGH, Gyneth	(715)362-3465	1151
Rosholt	ADAMS, Helen R.	(715)592-4614	5
Sheboygan	TOBIN, R J.	(414)459-7606	1247
Stoughton	DANKY, James P.	(608)873-8722	274
Superior	AXT, Randolph W.	(715)398-6767	42
Waukesha	TREBBY, Janis G.	(414)548-0261	1255
Wauwatosa	CHAPLOCK, Sharon K.	(414)778-2167	201
Whitefish Bay	LANK, Dannette H.	(414)225-2107	696

WYOMING

Cheyenne	MCGOWAN, Anne W.	(307)777-6430	807
	RAO, Dittakavi N.	(307)777-7509	1008
	SCHELL, Catherine L.	(307)637-7504	1091
Laramie	CHATTON, Barbara A.	(307)766-2167	204
	COTTAM, Keith M.	(307)766-3279	250
	OSTRYE, Anne T.	(307)766-5312	929

CANADA

ALBERTA

Airdrie	WAUGH, Alan L.	(403)948-7921	1310
Calgary	BAILEY, Madeleine J.	(403)240-6134	46
	GOODMAN, Henry J.	(403)220-6296	449
	MACRAE, Lorne G.	(403)294-8538	758
	ONN, Shirley A.	(403)282-5311	924
	ROBINS, Nora D.	(403)274-8837	1043
	VINE, Rita F.	(403)247-6524	1285
Edmonton	BAYRAK, Bettie	(403)478-8062	68
	BERNARD, Marie L.	(403)455-2436	88
	COMPRI, Jeannine L.	(403)474-0577	235
	LOVENBURG, Susan L.	(403)435-0176	743
	STARR, Jane E.	(403)466-6004	1182
Fort McMurray	BRUCE, Marianne E.	(403)743-5094	149
Lethbridge	DROESSLER, Judith B.	(403)381-2285	320
Red Deer	ARMSTRONG, Mary L.	(403)346-4491	32
Sherwood Pk	NOGA, Dolores A.	(403)467-4003	907
	SCHMIDT, Raymond J.	(403)464-8234	1095
Three Hills	JORDAHL, Ronald I.	(403)443-5511	616

BRITISH COLUMBIA

Abbotsford	HARRIS, Winifred E.	(604)853-7441	506
Clearbrook	SEARCY HOWARD, Linda M.	(604)859-7814	1109
North Vancouver	ASHCROFT, Susan M.	(604)984-8004	35
	DODSON, Suzanne C.	(604)988-4567	308
Vancouver	HALE, Linda L.	(604)321-0932	485
	HART, Elizabeth	(604)228-9031	507
	HAYCOCK, Carol A.	(604)734-0255	515
	LIGHTHALL, Lynne I.	(604)228-1480	727
	SALTMAN, Judith M.	(604)228-2587	1077
	STOKES, Roy B.	(604)261-4082	1196
	STUART-STUBBS, Basil F.	(604)731-1978	1204
Victoria	GIBB, Betty J.	(604)721-8234	431
	MOEHR, Jochen R.	(604)721-8581	851
	SIGNORI, Donna L.	(604)721-8247	1137
	VAN REENEN, Johannes A.	(604)595-9612	1277

MANITOBA

Brandon	SIMUNDSSON, Elva D.	(204)728-7234	1142
Winnipeg	BLANCHARD, Jim	(204)949-3360	103
	DIVAY, Gabriele	(204)474-8926	306
	LINCOLN, Robert S.	(204)786-2387	728

NEWFOUNDLAND

Grand Falls	MORTON, Elaine	(709)489-5935	870

WRITER/EDITOR (Cont'd)
NORTHWEST TERRITORIES

Yellowknife	O'KEEFE, Kevin T.	(403)873-5715	919

NOVA SCOTIA

Halifax	AMEY, Lorne J.	(902)422-8639	20
	TAYYEB, Rashid	(902)422-4684	1229

ONTARIO

Arnprior	BARKE, Judith P.	(613)623-5411	56
Bowmanville	MOON, Jeffrey D.	(416)263-8504	857
Fort Erie	PORTEUS, Andrew C.	(416)871-3814	985
Guelph	GILLHAM, Virginia A.	(519)824-4120	436
Hamilton	BROWNRIDGE, James R.	(416)572-2981	149
	FLEMMING, Tom	(416)525-9140	384
Keswick	MCCRACKEN, Ronald W.	(416)476-5556	799
Kingston	FLOWER, M A.	(613)645-6122	386
London	FYFE, Janet H.	(519)472-5201	411
	MILLER, Beth M.	(519)661-3542	836
Mississauga	DAVIS, Virginia K.	(416)673-2644	281
Nepean	KAYE, Barbara J.	(613)225-9920	632
North York	WILLIAMS, Lorraine O.		1344
Ottawa	AUBREY, Irene E.	(613)996-7774	38
	BANFILL, Christine	(613)235-8569	54
	BREGAINT, Bernard J.	(613)741-0242	131
	COOK, Terry G.	(613)996-7726	240
	EVANS, Gwynneth	(613)995-3904	357
	KIDD, Betty H.	(613)996-7605	646
	KIRKWOOD, Francis T.	(613)233-7592	655
	MCCALLUM, David L.	(613)237-4586	793
	MCKEEN, C E.	(613)996-7388	810
	PROULX, Steven D.	(613)596-3746	996
	REILLY, Brian O.	(613)993-9225	1020
	SCOTT, Judith W.	(613)232-0579	1107
	SPICER, Erik J.	(613)995-1166	1174
	SYLVESTRE, Guy	(613)521-8468	1217
	VALENTINE, Scott	(819)994-6946	1271
St Thomas	RHYNAS, Don M.	(519)631-6050	1026
Sault Ste Marie	BAZILLION, Richard J.	(705)949-4352	68
Scarborough	KEYS, Sandra A.		645
	MILLER, Ann M.	(416)694-3897	835
Sudbury	GOSS, Alison M.	(705)522-2883	453
Thornhill	SPEISMAN, Stephen A.	(416)886-2508	1172
Toronto	BELLAMY, Patricia C.	(416)595-0300	78
	BOITE, Mary E.	(416)461-2274	111
	BREGMAN, Alvan M.	(416)767-3625	131
	CARVALHO, Sarah V.	(416)979-2824	191
	DESOMOGYI, Aileen A.	(416)466-6572	295
	DE STRICKER, Ulla	(416)593-5211	296
	DOWDING, Martin R.	(416)925-7593	315
	FASICK, Adele M.	(416)978-7074	366
	FRITZ, Richard J.	(416)923-0890	405
	GREENWOOD, Jan	(416)963-9383	465
	GUNDARA, Jaswinder	(416)483-7810	477
	HAJNAL, Peter I.	(416)533-7338	484
	JOHNSON, John E.	(416)423-6979	606
	KLEMENT, Susan P.	(416)486-0239	660
	KOTIN, David B.	(416)531-2104	673
	LAND, Reginald B.	(416)965-3742	692
	LAVERTY, Corinne Y.	(416)393-7024	703
	MCCALLUM, Anita J.	(416)366-1921	793
	MERRYWEATHER, J M.	(416)965-3281	827
	MOORE, Lawrence A.	(416)363-3388	860
	MORRISON, Brian H.	(416)965-1641	867
	NIXON, Audrey I.	(416)531-0830	906
	NORTH, John A.	(416)979-5142	909
	OLSHEN, Toni	(416)488-5321	922
	POWELL, Wyley L.	(416)965-3906	989
	SABLJIC, John A.	(416)782-6754	1072
	TUDOR, Dean F.	(416)767-1340	1262
	VAN ORDER, Mary J.	(416)924-0671	1276
	WEAVER, Maggie	(416)925-5478	1312
	WILBURN, Gene	(416)586-5713	1338
	YANCHINSKI, Roma N.	(416)767-6781	1377
Willowdale	DANIEL, Eileen	(416)223-2495	272
	JOHNSON, James R.	(416)226-6380	605
	MARSHALL, Alexandra P.	(416)225-8193	773
	MCLEAN, Paulette A.	(416)636-4877	814

WRITER/EDITOR (Cont'd)

QUEBEC

Drummondville	JANIK, Sophie	(819)477-7100	593
Hampstead	FLUK, Louise R.	(514)488-3187	386
Laval	AUGER, Bernard	(514)687-9730	39
	SHANEFIELD, Irene D.	(514)688-9550	1120
Montebello	WENK, Arthur B.		1324
Montreal	AUBIN, Robert	(514)323-7260	38
	BACHAND, Michelle	(514)484-1282	43
	BERARDINUCCI, Heather R.	(514)255-2445	84
	BERNHARD, Paulette	(514)343-7408	89
	BERTRAND-GASTALDY, Suzanne	(514)343-6048	91
	BROCHU, Frederick	(514)598-1947	138
	CHAGNON, Danielle G.		197
	DE LUISE, Alexandra	(514)871-1418	290
	GARDNER, Richard K.	(514)343-6046	418
	MARRELLI, Nancy M.	(514)848-7775	773
	MOLLER, Hans	(514)398-4740	853
	MOLLER, Hans	(514)398-4740	853
	ORLANDO, Richard P.	(514)877-1470	926
	OUELLET, Louise M.		930
	PARKER, Charles G.	(514)282-3934	941
	RATNER, Sabina T.		1010
	ROUSSEAU, Denis	(514)843-3214	1061
	WALSH, Mary A.	(514)937-6633	1300
	WERYHO, Jan W.	(514)392-5766	1325
Montreal Oest	MORRISON, H D.	(514)488-9279	868
Outremont	LACROIX, Yvon A.	(514)273-7423	687
Pointe Claire	SMYTH, John	(514)697-3486	1162
Quebec	COLLISTER, Edward A.	(418)643-1515	233
	GUERETTE, Charlotte M.	(418)656-3017	476
Rosemere	LAPIERRE, France	(514)621-8507	697
St Lambert De Levis	HERLINGER, Peggy	(514)672-7360	531
St Laurent D'Orleans	SIMON, Marie L.	(514)744-7315	1140
Stanstead	GRENIER, Serge	(819)876-2981	467
Touraine	MURRAY-LACHAPELLE, Rosemary F.	(819)568-0282	882
Trois-Rivieres	SIMARD, Denis	(819)376-1721	1139

SASKATCHEWAN

North Battleford	RIDLER, Elizabeth A.		1032
Regina	BALON, Brett J.	(306)586-1990	53
Saskatoon	HANDE, D A.	(306)653-5692	494
	LAKHANPAL, Sarv K.	(306)966-5982	689
	NELSON, Ian C.	(306)652-4934	893

AUSTRALIA

Brisbane	COCHRANE, Thomas G.	226
Kensington	RAYWARD, W B.	1011
Magill	BEATTIE, Kathleen M.	70
Queensland	GOODELL, John S.	448
St Lucia	LAMBERTON, Donald M.	690
Turramurra	WILKINSON, Eoin H.	1340

BELGIUM

Kraainem	WALCKIERS, Marc A.	1293

CUBA

Havana	ASIS, Moises	36

ENGLAND

Letchworth Herts	AITCHISON, Thomas M.	9
London	ELLIOTT, Pirkko E.	344
Plymouth	PENGELLY, Joe	956
Sussex	GREEN, Jeffrey P.	462
Warwickshire	CHANDLER, George	200

FEDERAL REPUBLIC OF CHINA

Taidzi	CHENG, Sheung O.	206
Taipei	HU, James S.	567
	HUANG, Shih H.	568
	SENG, Harris B.	1115
	WANG, Sin C.	1303

WRITER/EDITOR (Cont'd)

FEDERAL REPUBLIC OF GERMANY

Berlin	ELSTE, R O.	346
	WALTER, Raimund E.	1300
Bonn	LOTZ, Rainer E.	742
Saarbrucken	VON KEITZ, Wolfgang	1288
Taufkirchen	ADENEY, Carol D.	6

FRANCE

Paris	ROBERTS, Kenneth H.	1040

HONG KONG

Jardine's Lookout	LEE, Betty W.	709

INDIA

New Delhi	AGRAWAL, Surendra P.	7

INDONESIA

Jakarta	STONE, Clarence W.	1197

IRAN

Shiraz	MEHRAD, Jafar	821

IRELAND

Dublin	FOX, Peter K.	395
	SLINEY, Marjory T.	1149

ISRAEL

Tel-Aviv	HOFFMANN, Eliahu W.	548

ITALY

Milan	CASIRAGHI, Edoardo	192
Rome	HUEMER, Christina G.	570

JAMAICA

Kingston	DOUGLAS, Daphne R.	314

JAPAN

Tokyo	HOSONO, Kimio		562
	KATAOKA, Yoko		629
	KISHIMOTO, Hiroko		656
	MIWA, Makiko		850
	YAMAZAKI, Shigeaki	(034)331-1110	1377

KUWAIT

Salmiyah	ABDEL-MOTEY, Yaser Y.	2

MALAWI

Lilongwe	SNYDER, Lisa A.	1165

MEXICO

Naucalpan	OROZCO-TENORIO, Jose M.	926

NETHERLANDS

Amersfoort	VAN HALM, Johan	1275
Rotterdam	SCHUURSMA, Ann B.	1103

NIGERIA

Ibadan	ABOYADE, Beatrice O.	2
Ogbomoso	TARPLEY, Margaret J.	1224

PAKISTAN

Lahore	TRAINER, Leslie F.	1253

PHILIPPINES

Manila	DE CASTRO, Elinore H.	285
Quezon City	OREJANA, Rebecca D.	925
	VALLEJO, Rosa M.	1271

SAUDI ARABIA

Jeddah	ALSANARRAI, Hafidh S.	17
Riyadh	BROWN, Biraj L.	142

SCOTLAND

Glasgow	HEANEY, Henry J.	518

SWITZERLAND

Geneva	FAGERLUND, M L.	361
	OHLMAN, Herbert	919
Villars Ollon	BURDET, Michele C.	158

Geographical Index

Professionals are indexed by state (Canadian province or country) and city, grouped by employers' names.

UNITED STATES

ALABAMA
AUBURN
Auburn Univ

ADAMS, Judith A. 5
CANTRELL, Clyde H. 179
COLSON, Harold G. 234
FRIEDMAN, Richard E. 404
GIBBS, Nancy J. 431
GIBBS, Robert C. 431
JONES, Allen W. 610
MARCINKO, Dorothy K. 769
NELSON, Barbara K. 893
NELSON, Michael B. 894
SABIN, Robert G. 1072
STRAITON, T H. 1199
VEENSTRA, Robert J. 1281
ZLATOS, Christy L. 1390

BIRMINGHAM
Alabama Power Co — KING, Karen H. 651
Birmingham Museum of Art — GRIFFITH, Ethel T. 469
Birmingham Pub Lib — DAY, Janeth N. 282
GUTHRIE, Virginia G. 479
HOGAN, Catherine R. 549
MCCARTHY, Sherri L. 794
STEWART, George R. 1192
VENABLE, Douglas R. 1282
Birmingham-Southern Coll — PENNINGTON, Walter W. . . . 957
Briarwood Christian High Sch — OLIVE, J F. 921
EBSCO Industries Inc — STEPHENS, James T. 1188
EBSCO Subscription Services — KETCHAM, Lee C. 645
MCKAY, Dashiell P. 809
ROGERS, Nancy H. 1050
VANDERPOORTEN, Mary
B. 1274
WEED, Joe K. 1315
Jefferson County Law Lib — HAND, Linda M. 494
Lange Simpson Robinson &
Somerville — FEENKER, Cherie D. 368
Mountain Brook City Schs — GOODWYN, Betty R. 450
RUST International Corp Lib — ATKINSON, Calberta O. 38
St Vincent's Hospital — SIMS, Joyce W. 1142
Samford Univ — CARTER, Selina J. 190
CLAPP, Laurel R. 216
JONES, Linda G. 613
NELSON, William N. 895
TAYLOR, Carol P. 1226
Sirote Permutt McDermott Slepian et
al — LEVINE, Patricia M. 720
Southern Alabama Junior Coll — HARRIS, Jay 504
Southern Progress Corp — NATHEWS, Ann 889
Univ of Alabama at Birmingham — BATTISTELLA, Maureen S. . . . 65
BLEILER, Richard J. 105
BRITT, Mary C. 137
CLEMMONS, Nancy W. 221
GRAMKA, Billie J. 457
HARRIS, Linda S. 505
LAING, Susan J. 688
LAUGHLIN, Steven G. 703
MCGARITY, Marysue 805
PFAU, Julia G. 966
SPENCE, Paul H. 1173
STEPHENS, Jerry W. 1188
WEATHERLY, Cynthia D. . . 1312

ALABAMA (Cont'd)
BIRMINGHAM (Cont'd)
Univ of Alabama at Birmingham

Univ of Montevallo
Veterans Administration Medical
Center
Woman's Missionary Union

BREWTON
Jefferson Davis State Junior Coll

COLUMBIANA
Alabama Lib Association
DADEVILLE
Tallapossa County Board of
Education
DAPHNE
Catholic Diocese of Mobile
US Sports Academy
DECATUR
Decatur High Sch Lib
Wheeler Basin Regional Lib
DOTHAN
Troy State Univ
FLORENCE
Univ of North Alabama

FORT MCCLELLAN
US Army
US Army Military Police Sch
FORT RUCKER
Lyster Hospital
GADSDEN
Baptist Memorial Hospital
GUNTER AFB
US Air Force
HELENA
Alabama Lib Association
HOMEWOOD
Homewood Pub Lib
HOOVER
Hoover Pub Lib
HUNTSVILLE
Alabama Lib Exchange Inc
Huntsville-Madison County Pub Lib

The Huntsville Times
Univ of Alabama at Huntsville

JACKSONVILLE
Jacksonville State Univ

JASPER
Walker Coll
MARION
Judson Coll
MAXWELL AFB
US Air Force

WRIGHT, Amos J. 1370
SCALES, Diann R. 1087

WILLIAMS, Nelle T. 1345
BENTLEY, Elna J. 83
HURTT, Betty D. 578

BIGGS-WILLIAMS, Evelyn
A. 95

WEBSTER, Sherry 1315

CANADY, Iris 177

ROBINSON, Gayle N. 1044
DANCE, Betty A. 272

MORRIS, Betty J. 866
LAND, Edward P. 692

SMITH, Julia L. 1156

CARR, Charles E. 185
O'NEAL, Kenneth W. 924
SLOAN, Tom W. 1150

AIDE, Kathryn S. 8
PARKS, Bernice Z. 943

PROTTSMAN, Mary F. 995

BUCKNER, Rebecca S. 154

LASETER, Ernest P. 700

SUTTON, Sandra K. 1211

GROOMS, Richard O. 472

ANDREWS, Linda R. 26

PIKE, Lee E. 973
COOPER, Regina G. 243
LIAW, Barbara C. 725
MCCANLESS, Christel L. . . . 793
KENDRICK, Aubrey W. 640
MCNAMARA, Jay 816
WILLIAMS, Delmus E. 1342

MERRILL, Martha 826
TAYLOR, Douglas M. 1226

ELLIOTT, Riette B. 344

YELVERTON, Mildred G. . . . 1379

GOODMAN, Anita S. 449
HARPER, Marie F. 503
LANE, Robert B. 694
LASETER, Shirley B. 700

ALABAMA (Cont'd)
MAXWELL AFB (Cont'd)
US Air Force

MAYTON, Regina A. 791
WISE, Kenda C. 1357

MOBILE
Mobile Coll

PARSLEY, Brantley H. 944
ROBERTS, Eddie F. 1039
WESTOVER, Mary L. 1327

Mobile Infirmary Medical Center — HALL, Patricia N. 488
Mobile Pub Lib — CALHOUN, Margie B. 172
CURRY, Janette M. 266
JEFFERY, Phyllis D. 596
LEFLORE, Walker B. 712
MCWHORTER, Jimmie M. . . 818

Spring Hill Coll — PEARSON, Peter E. 953
SELLEN, Mary K. 1114

US Court House — NICHOLS, Amy S. 901
Univ of South Alabama — BUSH, Nancy W. 165
DAMICO, James A. 271
ENGEBRETSON, Mary E. . . . 348
FINLEY, Vera L. 378
IRBY, Geraldine A. 583
MILLER, Hannelore A. 838
PERESICH, Mary G. 958
RODGERS, Patricia M. . . . 1047
SHEARER, Barbara S. 1124

MONTEVALLO
Univ of Montevallo — DUNMIRE, Raymond V. 326
WILLIAMS, Pauline C. 1346

MONTGOMERY
Alabama Christian Sch of Religion — LANCASTER III, Thomas A. . 692
Alabama Department of Archives & — BREEDLOVE, Michael A. 131
History — BRIDGES, Edwin C. 135
PENDLETON, Debbie D. . . . 956
Alabama Department of Education — SMITH, Jane B. 1155
Alabama Pub Lib Service — COLEMAN, James M. 231
DESSY, Blane K. 296
STEPHENS, Alice G. 1187
Alabama Regional Lib — BIVINS, Hulen E. 100
Alabama State Univ — PEDERSOLI, Heleni M. 954
Alabama Supreme Court & State Law
Lib — LEWIS, Timothy A. 724
Auburn Univ — BEST, Rickey D. 92
GREGORY, Vicki L. 466
HARRIS, Edwin R. 504
MARTIN, John B. 776
MCCRANK, Lawrence J. . . . 800
WRIGHT, Kathryn D. 1372
Faulkner Univ — NEWMAN, Sharon K. 900
Legal Services Corp of Alabama — FRANKS, Janice 398
Montgomery County Board of
Education — FELDER, Jimmie R. 369
Network of Alabama Academic Libs — MEDINA, Sue O. 820
United Methodist Church — PICKARD, Mary A. 970
US Air Force — ADAMS, Emily J. 4
GATLING, James L. 422

MOULTON
Lawrence County High Sch — SPILLERS, Doris H. 1174
MOUNTAIN BROOK
Emmet O'Neal Lib — MOORE, Patricia S. 861
MUSCLE SHOALS
Tennessee Valley Authority — CLARK, Wendolyn H. 218
GAMBRELL, Drucilla S. 416
MONTGOMERY, Kimberly
K. 856
NICHOLS, Shirley G. 901

ONEONTA
Blount County Commission — WEAVER, Clifton W. 1312
OPELIKA
Auburn Univ — FAIR, Kathy L. 361
PHENIX CITY
Mother Mary Mission Sch Lib — KLUESNER, Marvin P. 662
PRICHARD
Prichard Pub Lib Board — WILLIAMS, Gwendolyn 1343
REDSTONE ARSENAL
Redstone Arsenal — FOREMAN, Anne P. 390
Redstone Scientific Informaton Center — KITCHENS, Philips H. 657
US Army Missle Command — WARD, Dorothy S. 1303

ALABAMA (Cont'd)
SCOTTSBORO
Scottsboro Board of Education — ANDERSON, Ruby N. 25
TONEY
Madison County Board of Education — WILLIAMS, Patricia F. 1346
TROY
Troy State Univ — SOUTER, Thomas A. 1169
TUSCALOOSA
Tuscaloosa Pub Lib — MCKINLEY, Beebe M. 811
Univ of Alabama at Tuscaloosa — ATKINSON, Joan L. 38
BENHAM, Frances 80
COLEMAN, J G. 231
FIELD, Kathy M. 375
HAMILTON, Ann H. 491
KALYONCY, Adydan A. 623
KASKE, Neal K. 628
LEE, Sulan I. 711
LOWE, David 743
MOORE, Emily C. 859
MUIR, Scott P. 876
NEAVILL, Gordon B. 891
OSBURN, Charles B. 927
PRUITT, Paul M. 996
RAGSDALE, Kate W. 1003
RAMER, James D. 1005
RUSSELL, Lisa R. 1069
STEPHENS, Annabel K. . . . 1187
STEWART, Sharon L. 1193
STIEG, Margaret F. 1193
VISSCHER, Helga B. 1285
WATSON, Linda S. 1309
WATTERS, Annette J. 1310

TUSKEGEE INSTITUTE
St Joseph Sch — CLAVER, M P. 219
Tuskegee Inst — DAVIS, Frances F. 279
VALLEY
West Point Pepperell — DABBS, Mary L. 269

ALASKA
ANCHORAGE
Alaska Court Libs — ODSEN, Elizabeth R. 917
Alaska Health Sciences Lib — ANDRESS, Loretta M. 26
Alaska Pacific Univ — MORRISSETT, Elizabeth 868
Alaska State Lib — JENNINGS, Mary 598
Anchorage Municipal Libs — BRAUND-ALLEN, Julianna
E. 130
LUDWIG, J D. 746
MACLEAN, Barbara A. 757
PIERCE, Linda I. 971
PUTZ, Paul D. 998
WILLIAMS, Robert C. 1346
Anchorage Museum of History and
Art — BRENNER, M D. 133
Anchorage Sch District — TRIDLE, Jeanne A. 1256
WIGET, Laurence A. 1337
Hughes Thorsness Gantz Powell &
Brundin — ELAM, Kim A. 341
Information Resources Unlimited — EGGLESTON, Phyllis A. . . . 339
Municipality of Anchorage — FREDERIKSEN, Patience A. . 400
Univ of Alaska at Anchorage — INNES-TAYLOR, Catherine
E. 583
LESH, Nancy L. 718
SOKOLOV, Barbara J. 1165
BETHEL
Yukon-Kuskokwim Health Corp — EMMONS, Mary E. 348
CENTRAL
Circle District Historical Society — OAKES, Patricia A. 913
CHUGIAK
Polly's Book Repair — KALLENBERG, Mary E. 623
FAIRBANKS
Fairbanks North Star Borough Pub
Lib — GALBRAITH, William B. 413
Fairbanks North Star Borough Sch
Dist — THOMAS, Margie J. 1237
Professional Information Resources — PINNELL-STEPHENS, June
A. 975
Univ of Alaska at Fairbanks — GALBRAITH, Betty J. 413
GONIWIECHA, Mark C. 447
HALES, David A. 486
LAKE, Gretchen L. 688

ALASKA (Cont'd)
FAIRBANKS (Cont'd)
Univ of Alaska at Fairbanks

PARHAM, Robert B. 940
STEPHENS, Dennis J. 1187

FT GREELY
US Army   RICKS, Bonnie B. 1032
FORT RICHARDSONG
US Army   CHANEY, A V. 200
JUNEAU
Alaska Department of Administration   KINNEY, John M. 653
Alaska Department of Education   CRANE, Karen R. 255
                                           KOLB, Audrey P. 669
                                           MITCHELL, Micheal L. 849
Alaska State Archives & Records
  Service   NEWTON, Virginia A. 900
Alaska State Lib   SHELTON, Kathryn H. 1126
                                           SMITH, George V. 1155
City & Borough of Juneau Sch
  District   BELFLOWER, Elizabeth D. . . . 76
The Denali Press   SCHORR, Alan E. 1099
Univ of Alaska at Juneau   NICOLSON, Mary C. 903
NOME
Northwest Community Coll   ROSS, Rosemary E. 1058
PALMER
Matanuska-Susitna Community Coll   COLSON, Marcia B. 234
PETERSBURG
City of Petersburg   JENKINS, Joyce K. 597
SITKA
Sheldon Jackson Coll   BOEHMER, Elaine 109
Sitka Pub Schs   MCCLAIN, Harriet V. 795
SOLDOTNA
Kenai Peninsula Borough Sch District   MOHN, Kari 852
                                           PENDLETON, Kim B. 956
UNALAKLEET
Bering Strait Sch District   GOODMAN, Roslyn L. 449
VALDEZ
City of Valdez   LEAHY, M J. 706
                                           WEILAND, Karen B. 1317
WASILLA
Jenks & Associates, Lib Consultants   JENKS, Arlene I. 597

AMERICAN SAMOA
PAGO PAGO
Territory of American Samoa   MCDONNELL, Robert W. . . . 803

ARIZONA
APACHE JUNCTION
Apache Junction Unified Sch District
  43   GILSON, Myral A. 437
                                           WHORTON, Pamela J. 1334
CHANDLER
Intel Corp   MCGORRAY, John J. 807
Maricopa County Community Coll
  System   MILLER, Larry A. 839
COOLIDGE
City of Coolidge   FRANSEN, Gary K. 398
COTTONWOOD
Cottonwood-Oak Creek Elem Sch
  District 6   HERRON, Bettie J. 533
FLAGSTAFF
First Information Service   BAUM, Ester B. 66
Flagstaff City-Coconino County Pub
  Lib   DOWNUM, Evelyn R. 317
                                           GRANADE, Victoria A. 457
                                           MOHR, Mary C. 852
Northern Arizona Univ   AWE, Susan C. 42
                                           EGAN, Terence W. 338
                                           HASSELL, Robert H. 511
                                           JOHNSON, Harlan R. 605
                                           MULLANE, William H. 877
GILBERT
Gilbert Pub Schs   TRZICKY, Richard F. 1260
GLENDALE
Agua Fria Union High Sch   WHITNEY, Karen A. 1334
City of Glendale   MOSLEY, Shelley E. 872
Glendale Union High Sch District   MAJOR, Caryl M. 762
GLOBE
Globe Unified Sch District 1   DWAN, Sandra K. 330

ARIZONA (Cont'd)
GREEN VALLEY
Tucson Pub Lib   LEWIS, Jean R. 723
HOLBROOK
Northland Pioneer Coll   ROTHLISBERG, Allen P. . . . 1060
LUKE AFB
US Air Force   KESSLER, Katheryn M. 645
MESA
City of Mesa   ANDERSON, Herschel V. 23
Maricopa County Community Coll
  System   DAANE, Jeanette K. 269
                                           THEILMANN, James W. . . . 1234
Mesa Pub Lib   BECKER, Teresa J. 72
                                           CZOPEK, Vanessa 269
                                           GREGORY, Joan A. 466
                                           MURPHY, Ellen A. 880
Westwood High Sch   MAIN, Isabelle G. 761
PHOENIX
A R E Clinic   DIAL, Zona P. 299
Alhambra Elementary Schs   GILBERT, Betty H. 433
                                           STARRETT, Mildred J. 1182
Arizona Department of Economic
  Security   OLEARY, Jennie L. 920
Arizona Department of Education   EDGINGTON, Linda A. 336
                                           RIDGEWAY, Merrilyn S. . . . 1032
Arizona Dept of Lib, Archs & Pub
  Records   FRIEDMAN, Zena K. 404
                                           MCCOLGIN, Michael A. 797
Arizona State Capitol   TURGEON, Sharon 1263
Arizona State Univ West   KOLBER, Denise 669
Arthur Andersen & Co   STEPHENS, Stefanie N. . . . 1188
City of Phoenix   DIAL, Clarence M. 299
Deer Valley Unified Sch District   BROWN, I C. 144
Grand Canyon Coll   BRZOZOWSKI, Margery E. . . 152
                                           FEAZEL, Edythe J. 367
                                           GROSSNICKLE, Jane L. 473
GTE Communication Systems   LENNON, Suzanne 715
Humana Hospital   BERK, Nancy G. 87
Lewis & Roca   DOHERTY, Walter E. 309
Maricopa County Community Coll
  System   ALLEN, Stephanie O. 16
Maricopa County Law Lib   MEERIANS, Patti L. 821
Maricopa County Superior Court   SCHNEIDER, Elizabeth K. . . 1097
Mead Data Central   EWING, Alison L. 359
Ninth Circuit Court of Appeals   DANIELS, Delores E. 273
Oryx Press   DEBACHER, Richard D. 284
                                           SLESINGER, Susan G. 1148
                                           STECKLER, Phyllis B. 1183
                                           THOMPSON, Anne E. 1238
                                           WASCHLER, Merl E. 1307
Phoenix Art Museum   KIRKING, Clayton C. 655
Phoenix Newspapers Inc   LESHY, Dede 718
                                           STEVENS, Paula F. 1190
Phoenix Pub Lib   ALABASTER, Carol 9
                                           CHUNG, Catherine L. 213
                                           EDWARDS, Ralph M. 337
                                           FARNHAM, Shera M. 365
                                           MEYERS, Kathleen H. 831
                                           NORMAN, Nita V. 909
                                           ROATCH, Mary A. 1038
Ryley Carlock & Applewhite   HOUK, Douglas J. 563
St Joseph's Hospital & Medical
  Center   WELLIK, Kay E. 1321
Salt River Project   KLASSEN, Bonnie 657
Scottsdale Pub Lib   GOEBEL, Heather L. 443
Sergent Hauskins & Beckwith
  Engineers   JEROME, Susanne M. 599
State of Arizona   SHABERLY, Leanna J. 1118
                                           TEVIS, Raymond H. 1233
Streich Lang Weeks & Cardon   EDWARDS, Winifred 338
Superior Court of Arizona   EVANS, Iris I. 357
US Courts   WIEBELHAUS, Richard J. . . 1336
US Public Health Service   MEAD, Thomas L. 819
Valley National Bank of Arizona   GORMAN, Judith F. 452
Winston & Strawn   KLATT, Dixie K. 657
Xavier High Sch for Girls   HEINTZ, Mary L. 522
PRESCOTT
Prescott Unified Sch Dist 1   ELLIS, Caryl A. 344

ARIZONA (Cont'd)

SCOTTSDALE

City of Scottsdale	SAFERITE, Linda L. 1074
Scottsdale Community Coll	BIGLIN, Karen E. 96
Scottsdale Pub Lib	COLE, Christopher H. 230
	COLE, Mitzi M. 231
	KLIMIADES, Mario N. 661
	PILLOW, William H. 973

SELLS

Indian Oasis	CULL, Roberta 263

SIERRA VISTA

City of Sierra Vista	POSSNER, Roger D. 986

TEMPE

Arizona State Univ	ALCORN, Marianne S. 11
	BOROVANSKY, Vladimir T. . . 117
	FERRALL, J E. 373
	GEMPELER, Constance M. . . 426
	HAWKOS, Lise J. 514
	HOWARD, Pamela F. 564
	JOSEPHINE, Helen B. 617
	KNEPP, Kenneth B. 664
	MACHOVEC, George S. 755
	MILLER, Rosanna 842
	MOLLOY, Molly F. 853
	MULVIHILL, Joann 878
	NILSEN, Alleen P. 904
	OETTING, Edward C. 917
	POTTER, William G. 987
	RENEKER, Maxine H. 1023
	RIGGS, Donald E. 1034
	SCHON, Isabel 1098
	STEEL, Virginia 1183
	STEWART, Douglas J. 1192
	VATHIS, Alma C. 1279
	WU, Ai H. 1373
City of Tempe	JANSON, Sherryl A. 594
Tempe Pub Lib	PARK, Yong H. 941

TUCSON

Arizona Theatre Co	GOLDBERG, Susan S. 445
Art Libs Society of North America	PARRY, Pamela J. 944
Burr-Brown Corp	WOLF, Noel C. 1360
Carondelet Health Services Inc	DUFORE, Thomas H. 324
Catalina Foothills Sch District	DOOLEY, Sally J. 312
CDT Inc	SCHULTZ, Michael W. 1102
Center for Creative Photography	RULE, Amy E. 1067
Keramont Research & Advanced Ceramics	HUSBAND, Susan M. 578
National Optical Astronomy Observatories	VANATTA, Cathaleen E. . . . 1272
Ninth Circuit Court of Appeals	MAYNARD, Deo D. 790
Pima Community Coll	ALURI, Rao 19
	HOLLEMAN, Margaret 551
	NAMSICK, Lynn J. 887
Pima County	MATTY, Paul D. 786
Salpointe Catholic High Sch	MCBRIDE, Patricia A. 792
Summer Institute of Linguistics	HARRIS, Mary J. 505
Tucson Medical Center	KING, Christee 650
Tucson Planning Department	CROWE, Gloria J. 261
Tucson Pub Lib	BIERMAN, Kenneth J. 95
	GOODRICH, Nita K. 449
	HAMILTON, Rita 492
	MCLACHLAN, Ross W. 812
	STOUT, Mary A. 1199
	TYMCIURAK, Olya T. 1266
Univ of Arizona	ALTMAN, Ellen 18
	BAILEY, Tuuli T. 47
	BALDWIN, Charlene M. 51
	BUXTON, David T. 168
	CAMPBELL, Dierdre A. 176
	CARTER, Judith A. 189
	CHAPMAN, Jennalyn W. 202
	D'ANTONIO, Lynn A. 274
	DICKINSON, Donald C. 300
	DICKSTEIN, Ruth H. 301
	EAGLESON, Laurie E. 331
	ETTER, Patricia A. 355
	FAHY, Terry W. 361
	FIEGEN, Ann M. 375
	FORE, Janet S. 390
	FRANK, Donald G. 396

ARIZONA (Cont'd)

TUCSON (Cont'd)

Univ of Arizona	GILREATH, Charles L. 437
	GOTHBERG, Helen M. 453
	HAWBAKER, A C. 513
	HEIDENREICH, Fred L. 521
	HEITSHU, Sara C. 523
	HENDERSON, Joyce C. 526
	HIEB, Louis A. 537
	HOLSINGER, Katherine 554
	HOOPES, Maria S. 557
	HURT, Charlie D. 578
	JONES, Douglas E. 612
	KELLOGG, Rebecca B. 637
	KNIGHT, Rita C. 664
	LAIRD, W D. 688
	LAKE, Mary S. 689
	LEI, Polin P. 713
	LONG, Carla J. 739
	MAKUCH, Andrew L. 762
	MARSHALL, Thomas H. 775
	MAUTNER, Robert W. 787
	MAXWELL, Margaret F. 788
	MCCRAY, Jeanette C. 800
	MILLER, Edward P. 837
	MILLS, Victoria A. 844
	MINTON, James O. 846
	MOORE, Anne C. 858
	MOORE, Susan M. 861
	MOUNT, Jack D. 873
	MYERS, Roger 885
	NEWBY, Jill 898
	OLSRUD, Lois C. 923
	O'NEIL, Mary A. 924
	OWENS, Clayton S. 932
	PHIPPS, Shelley E. 969
	POWELL, Lawrence C. 988
	RAWAN, Atifa R. 1010
	REICHEL, Mary 1018
	RICE, Virginia E. 1027
	RIISE, Milton B. 1034
	ROBROCK, David P. 1045
	RUSSELL, Carrie 1068
	SABOVIK, Pavel 1073
	SCOTT, Sharon K. 1108
	SMITH, Dorman H. 1154
	SORENSEN, Lee R. 1168
	TALLMAN, Karen D. 1221
	TAYLOR, Patricia A. 1228
	TAYLOR, Trish A. 1229
	WHITE, Edward H. 1330
	WHITLEY, Katherine M. 1333
	WILLIAMS, Karen B. 1344
	WOLFSON, Catherine L. . . . 1361

YUMA

American Lib Trustee Association	WISENER, Joanne C. 1357
Arizona Western Coll	SHACKELFORD, Eileen R. . . 1118
Ravenstree Corp	STUART, Gerard W. 1204

ARKANSAS

ARKADELPHIA

Henderson State Univ	WOODS, L B. 1367
Ouachita Baptist Univ	CHILDRESS, Schelley H. . . . 208
	RICK, Jean A. 1031

BATESVILLE

Arkansas Coll	WATSON, Ellen I. 1309

BEEBE

Arkansas State Univ	GREEN, Douglas A. 461

BENTON

Saline County Library	ASHCRAFT, Carolyn A. 35

CONWAY

CCX Direct Marketing Network	WOMBLE, Jim 1362
Faulkner County Lib	VOSS, Ruth A. 1289
Hendrix Coll	ALSMEYER, Henry L. 18
Univ of Central Arkansas	DUDEK, Robert J. 323
	HARDIN, Willie 500
	MOORE, Gay G. 859
	MORRISON, Margaret L. 868
	ROYAL, Selvin W. 1063

ARKANSAS (Cont'd)
DE WITT
DeWitt Sch System .... HUDSPETH, Holly C. 570
EL DORADO
Barton Lib .... ARN, Nancy L. 33
El Dorado Sch District 15 ...... MISENHEIMER, Paula S. 847
EUREKA SPRINGS
Carroll County Pub Lib .... STOWE, Jean E. 1199
FAYETTEVILLE
Fayetteville Sch District 1 ...... DEWEESE, Don B. 298
Shane-Armstrong Information
  Systems .... SHANE, Charlotte J. 1120
Univ of Arkansas at Fayetteville .. CALLAHAN, Patrick F. 173
                             CHICK, Catherine P. 208
                             CLINKSCALES, Joyce M. ... 222
                             DABRISHUS, Michael J. 269
                             DEW, Stephen H. 297
                             EARNEST, Jeffrey D. 332
                             HARRISON, John A. 506
                             MCKEE, Elizabeth C. 810
                             MILLER, Leon C. 839
                             YOUNG, Juana R. 1382
FORREST CITY
East Arkansas Community Coll .... BERMAN, Arthur 88
FORT SMITH
Fort Smith Pub Lib .... LARSON, Larry 699
Westark Community Coll .... PIERSON, Betty 972
GREENWOOD
Scott Sebastian Regnl Lib .... CLEVENGER, Judy B. 221
GURDON
Gurdon Pub Schs .... WRIGHT, Pauline W. 1372
HARRISON
North Arkansas Regional Lib ..... HAMBY, Tracy A. 491
                             VAN ARSDALE, Dennis G. . 1272
HAZEN
Hazen Pub Sch .... JEFFCOAT, Phyllis C. 596
HEBER SPRINGS
Univ of Arkansas at Little Rock ... SEDELOW, Sally Y. 1110
                             SEDELOW, Walter A. 1110
HELENA
Phillips County Lib .... THOMAS, Cornel W. 1236
HOPE
Southwest Arkansas Regional Lib .. TROMATER, Raymond B. ... 1257
HOT SPRINGS
Garland County Community Coll ... MILLS, Peggy 844
JACKSONVILLE
Pulaski County Special Sch District . HENSON, Aleene E. 529
                             JONES, Wanda F. 615
JEFFERSON
Peters Technology Transfer Inc .... LANEY-SHEEHAN, Susan ... 695
JONESBORO
Arkansas State Univ .... BLAND, Janet A. 103
LITTLE ROCK
Arkansas Arts Center .... MCCOY, Evelyn G. 799
Arkansas History Commission .... BAKER, Russell P. 49
                             FERGUSON, John L. 372
                             IVEY, Frank 586
Arkansas Lib Association .... HALL, Deborah N. 487
Arkansas State Lib .... HALL, John J. 488
                             HONEYCUTT, Mary L. 556
                             MITCHAM, Janet C. 848
                             MULKEY, Jack C. 876
                             MURPHEY, John A. 880
                             PITTS, Cynthia F. 976
Arkansas Supreme Court .... WRIGHT, Jacqueline S. 1371
Central Arkansas Lib System ..... KASTANOTIS, William C. ... 629
                             MARTIN, Rosemary S. 778
                             RAZER, Robert L. 1012
Philander Smith Coll .... WILSON, Janora E. 1351
US Court of Appeals .... MAYS, Allison P. 791
Univ of Arkansas at Little Rock ... BASKIN, Jeffrey L. 63
                             BRECK, Paul A. 131
                             CASTLEBERRY, Crata L. ... 194
                             CLOUGHERTY, Leo P. 223
                             FOSTER, Lynn 392
                             GHIDOTTI, Pauline A. 430
                             HAWKS, Mary S. 514
                             KASALKO, Sally G. 628
                             RINGER, Sarah A. 1035
                             ROSE, Donna K. 1054

ARKANSAS (Cont'd)
LITTLE ROCK (Cont'd)
Univ of Arkansas at Little Rock
                             SANDERS, Kathryn A. 1080
                             STURGEON, Mary C. 1205
                             WALLS, Edwina 1298
                             WOLD, Shelley T. 1359
Veterans Administration Medical
  Center .... ZUMWALT, George M. 1391
LITTLE ROCK AFB
US Air Force .... GODBEY, Esther R. 442
LONOKE
Lonoke County Lib System ...... HOUGHTON, Sally L. 563
MAGNOLIA
Columbia-Lafayette-Ouachita-Calhoun
  Lib .... BRADLEY, Florene J. 125
MONTICELLO
Southeast Arkansas Regnl Lib .... LAWSON, Martha G. 705
MOUNTAIN VIEW
Arkansas Parks & Tourism
  Commission .... MCNEIL, William K. 816
NORTH LITTLE ROCK
Pulaski County Special Sch District . MCKINNEY, Barbara J. 812
William F Laman Pub Lib .... PACK, Nancy C. 933
ROGERS
City of Rogers .... KELLEY, Sally J. 637
Rogers-Hough Memorial Lib ..... LANGSAM, Christine E. 696
Rogers Pub Sch System .... COLCLASURE, Marian S. ... 230
RUSSELLVILLE
Arkansas Tech Univ .... VAUGHN, William A. 1280
SEARCY
Harding Univ .... BEARD, Craig W. 69
                             HAYES, Franklin D. 515
                             SPURRIER, Suzanne F. 1177
SPRINGDALE
Springdale Sch District .... GREESON, Janet S. 465
STATE UNIVERSITY
Arkansas State Univ .... BRENNER, Willis F. 133
SUBIACO
Subiaco Abbey & Academy ...... PIRRERA, Aaron C. 975
WALNUT RIDGE
Walnut Ridge Pub Schs .... ALLEN, Lucia W. 15

CALIFORNIA
AGOURA
Las Virgenes Unified Sch District .. ROGALSKY, Virginia R. 1049
ALHAMBRA
Santa Fe International Corp ...... KRAMER, Helen A. 675
Southern California Edison Co .... SCULLY, Patrick F. 1109
ALTADENA
Altadena Lib District .... TEMA, William J. 1230
ANAHEIM
Anaheim Pub Lib .... EARNEST, Patricia 332
Businessfacts .... ADAMS, Joyce A. 5
Servite High Sch .... RICHARDSON, Helen R. 1029
Simon Greenleaf Sch of Law ..... MONTGOMERY, John W. ... 856
ANGWIN
Pacific Union Coll .... RUHL, Taylor D. 1066
APO SAN FRANCISCO
CFSSCK .... LEE, Myung J. 711
US Air Force .... BALLOU, Eleanor F. 53
                             HEINES, Rodney M. 522
US Information Agency .... BOONE, Mary L. 115
ARCADIA
County of Los Angeles .... DEFATO, Joan 287
ARCATA
Humboldt State Univ .... CHADWICK, Sharon S. 197
                             CROSBY-MUILENBURG,
                               Corryn 260
                             KENYON, Sharmon H. 643
                             MAGLADRY, George C. 759
                             OYLER, David K. 932
                             WIMMER, Ted 1354
ARROYO GRANDE
County of San Luis Obispo ...... SCHLANSER, Deborah B. ... 1093
AUBURN
Auburn-Placer County Lib ...... SANBORN, Dorothy C. 1079
Placer Union High Sch District ... FROST, Shirley E. 406
AZUSA
Azusa Pacific Univ .... SZETO, Dorcas C. 1218

CALIFORNIA (Cont'd)

BAKERSFIELD

Bakersfield City Sch District — WICKEY, Marjorie J. 1335
California State Coll at Bakersfield — KIRKLAND, Janice J. 655
— WINTER, Eugenia B. 1356
California State Univ at Bakersfield — HERSBERGER, Rodney M. .. 533
Kern County — WADE, Sherry A. 1290
Kern County Lib System — COOPER, William E. 244
— GARDNER, Laura L. 418
— NICKERSON, Louann M. 902
— YOON, Sandra G. 1380

BELLFLOWER

Los Angeles County Pub Lib — CASTONGUAY, Russell 194
St John Bosco High Sch — PESTUN, Aloysius J. 961

BELMONT

Belmont Sch District — CHESSMAN, Rebecca L. ... 207
Coll of Notre Dame — GUEDON, Mary S. 475
— PELLE, Catherine A. 955
— RAMSEY, Robert D. 1006
Information Access Co — GRIFFIN, Michael D. 468
— MEGLIO, Delores D. 821
Peninsula Lib System — CROWE, Linda D. 261
— KERSHNER, Lois M. 644
San Mateo County Lib — BOWLES, Carol A. 121
Sisters of Notre Dame de Namur — STARK, Anne C. 1181
Wadsworth Inc — THORNTON, Jack N. 1242
Zift Davis Publishing — VARKENTINE, Aganita 1278

BENICIA

DCM Associates — MILLER, Davic C. 836
Randolph & Co — RANDOLPH, Kevin H. 1007
Solution Associates Inc — HUTCHESON, Don S. 578

BERKELEY

Alameda County Lib — CROOKS, Joyce M. 260
Alcohol Research Group — MITCHELL, Andrea L. 848
Berkeley Pub Lib — MINUDRI, Regina U. 847
— SCHNEIDER, Francisca M. . 1097
Berkeley Unified Sch District — FRANKEL, Kate M. 397
City of Berkeley — VANYOUNG, Sayre 1278
Graduate Theological Union — BERLOWITZ, Sara B. 88
— BISCHOFF, Mary L. 99
— BURDICK, Oscar C. 158
— CHOQUETTE, Diane L. 210
— CLARENCE, Judy 216
— WILLIAMS, Mary S. 1345
Information Counts — FALANGA, Rosemarie E. 361
Information for Business — MARKS, Larry 771
Information on Demand Inc — MAXWELL, Christine Y. 788
— PEARSON, Judith G. 952
Information Sources Inc — KOOLISH, Ruth K. 671
Innovative Interfaces Inc — FROHMBERG, Katherine A. ... 405
— SILBERSTEIN, Stephen M. . 1137
Judah L Magnes Museum — ARONER, Miriam D. 34
— RAFAEL, Ruth K. 1003
Lawrence Berkeley Laboratory — GRIFFIN, Hillis L. 468
— MCCARTHY, John L. 794
Magnes Museum — LEVY, Jane 721
McGraw-Hill Inc — BLAKE, Harry W. 103
Music & Arts Programs of America
Inc — MAROTH, Frederick J. 772
Ordered Word — RIGGS, Judith M. 1034
Prevention Research Center — FISHER, Leslie R. 381
— YANEZ, Elva K. 1377
The Ratcliff Architects — HUNT, Judy L. 575
US Department of Agriculture — SCHONBRUN, Rena 1098
Univ of California at Berkeley — BARKER, Joseph W. 56
— BASART, Ann P. 62
— BECK, Diane J. 71
— BENGSTON, Carl E. 80
— BENIDIR, Samia 80
— BERGER, Michael G. 85
— BERRING, Robert C. 90
— BESSER, Howard A. 91
— BOUCHE, Nicole L. 118
— BRAUNSTEIN, Yale M. 130
— BROWN, Diane M. 143
— BROWNRIGG, Edwin B. 149
— BUCKLAND, Michael K. 154
— BYRNE, Elizabeth D. 169
— COOPER, William S. 244
— COYLE, Karen E. 253

CALIFORNIA (Cont'd)

BERKELEY (Cont'd)

Univ of California at Berkeley — DANTON, J P. 274
— DEAN, Terry J. 284
— DONLEY, Leigh M. 311
— DUGGAN, Mary K. 324
— ELNOR, Nancy G. 346
— FALK, Candace S. 362
— FREEMAN, Kevin A. 401
— FULSAAS, Esther M. 409
— GERKEN, Ann E. 429
— GLENDENNING, Barbara J. ... 441
— GOLDMAN, Nancy L. 445
— GRIFFIN, Thomas E. 469
— HANDMAN, Gary P. 495
— HANFF, Peter E. 495
— HARDWICK, Bonnie S. 500
— HARLAN, Robert D. 502
— HECKART, Ronald J. 519
— HOEHN, Philip 547
— HORWITZ, Steven F. 561
— HOSEL, Harold V. 561
— HOWLAND, Joan S. 566
— HUMPHREYS, Nancy K. 574
— JENSEN, Ann M. 598
— JONES, Maralyn 614
— KATZ, Jeffrey P. 630
— KENEFICK, Mary L. 640
— KIRESEN, Evelyn M. 654
— KISLITZIN, Elizabeth H. 656
— KLEIBER, Michael C. 658
— KLUGMAN, Simone 662
— KOBZINA, Norma G. 666
— KOYAMA, Janice T. 674
— LARSON, Ray R. 699
— LAWRENCE, Gary S. 704
— LEISTER, Jack 714
— LEVIN, Marc A. 720
— LEVY, Judith B. 721
— MELTZER, Ellen J. 823
— MIKLOSVARY, Jozsef 834
— MITCHELL, Annmarie D. 848
— MONTGOMERY, Teresa L. .. 856
— MORENO, Catherine H. 863
— NICHOLS, Gail M. 901
— NOVAK, Gloria J. 910
— OGDEN, Barclay W. 918
— OGDEN, Dunbar H. 918
— OLIVARES, Jose A. 920
— ORTOPAN, Leroy D. 927
— RHEE, Susan F. 1025
— ROBERT, Berring C. 1039
— ROBERTS, John H. 1040
— ROSENTHAL, Joseph 1057
— RYUS, Joseph E. 1072
— SCHRIEFER, Kent 1100
— SIBLEY, Elizabeth A. 1135
— SNOW, Maryly A. 1164
— SO, Henry K. 1165
— SPOHRER, James H. 1175
— TENNANT, Roy 1231
— URBANIC, Allan J. 1269
— VANDERBERG, Patricia S. . 1273
— VAN HOUSE, Nancy A. 1275
— WANAT, Camille A. 1302
— WEEDMAN, Judith 1315
— WEIL, Beth T. 1317
— WHITSON, William L. 1334
— WILSON, Patrick 1352
— ZBORAY, Ronald J. 1386
Utlas International US Inc — LIGHTBOWN, Parke P. 726
— SPENCER, John T. 1173
Womanhood Media — WHEELER, Helen R. 1329
Women's History Research Center — X, Laura 1376
Wright Institute — PARKS, Mary L. 943

CALIFORNIA (Cont'd)

BEVERLY HILLS

Academy of Motion Picture Arts & Scis .... OKA, Susan Y. 919
.... STOCKSTILL, Patrick E. 1195

Beverly Hills Pub Lib .... ANNETT, Susan E. 28
.... GREGORY, Timothy P. 466
.... PIONTEK, Frank P. 975

Beverly Hills Unified Sch District .... DOUGLAS, Carolyn T. 314
.... GIRARD, Valerie V. 438

Finley Kumble Wagner Heine et al .... JEROME, Michael S. 599
.... PALMER, Catherine C. 936

KCOP Television Inc-Los Angeles .... WALDOW, Mitch 1294
Litton Industries .... RUNYON, Judith A. 1067
Nancy Escher Inc .... ESCHER, Nancy 354

BIEBER

Big Valley Joint Unified Sch District .... MAIN, Steven B. 761

BISHOP

Northern Inyo Hospital .... KRATZ, Gale G. 676

BLOOMINGTON

Bloomington High Sch .... MILLS, Denise Y. 844

BLYTHE

Palo Verde Valley Dist Lib .... MURPHY, Patricia A. 881

BODEGA BAY

Univ of California at Davis .... UHLINGER, Eleanor S. 1268

BREA

Unocal Corp .... OROSZ, Barbara J. 926

BRENTWOOD

Contra Costa County Lib .... ALEXANDER, Diane A. 12

BRIDGEPORT

Mono County Free Lib .... REVEAL, Arlene H. 1024

BRISBANE

Aircraft Technical Publishers .... DONINI, Elizabeth A. 311

BUENA PARK

Buena Park Lib District .... RITZ, Mary E. 1037

BURBANK

City of Burbank .... BROWNE, Jeri A. 148
.... MICHAELS, Joan M. 832
.... RICHARDS, Marcia M. 1028

Lockheed-California Co .... CRUM, Norman J. 262
The Walt Disney Co .... SIGMAN, Paula M. 1137

BURLINGAME

City of Burlingame .... BERGSING, Patricia M. 87
Mills-Peninsula Hospitals .... CHU, Sally C. 212
Theodon Books Inc .... BOWEN, Theodora 120

CALEXICO

City of Calexico .... MERKLEY, John P. 826

CAMARILLO

St John's Seminary .... RAMIREZ, Anthony L. 1005
System Development Corporation .... GILHEANY, Stephen J. 435

CANOGA PARK

Hughes Aircraft Co .... PAUL, Donald C. 949
Los Angeles Pub Lib .... LEWIS, Phyllis N. 724
Rockwell International .... HORACEK, Paula B. 558
.... RAINEY, Laura J. 1004

CARLSBAD

Carlsbad City Lib .... LANGE, Clifford E. 695
City of Carlsbad .... KENNEDY, Charlene F. 640

CARMICHAEL

Sacramento Pub Lib .... O'NEILL, Diane J. 924

CARPINTERIA

Cate Sch .... ALLABACK, Patricia G. 13

CARSON

California State Univ at Dominguez Hills .... BALDWIN, Claudia A 51
.... DUNKLEE, Joanna E. 326
.... OPPENHEIM, Michael R. 925
.... SUNDSTRAND, Jacquelyn K. 1210

CASTRO VALLEY

Alameda County Lib .... OVERMYER, Elizabeth C. ... 931

CHATSWORTH

NILS Publishing Co .... BOOTH, Barbara A. 116

CHICO

Butte County Lib .... BROWN, Carol G. 142
California State Univ at Chico .... ARIARATNAM, Lakshmi V. ... 31
.... DWYER, James R. 330
.... HUANG, George W. 568
.... LO, Henrietta W. 735
.... NISSLEY, Meta J. 905

CALIFORNIA (Cont'd)

CHICO (Cont'd)

California State Univ at Chico .... POST, William E. 986
.... POWER, Colleen J. 989
.... RYAN, Frederick W. 1071
.... SESSIONS, Judith A. 1117

CHINA LAKE

US Navy .... MAYES, Elizabeth A. 789

CHULA VISTA

City of Chula Vista .... BLUE, Margaret L. 107
.... BROWN, Paula D. 146

Grossmont Union High Sch District .... CURTIN, Mimi V. 266
Rohr Industries Inc .... TOMMEY, Richard J. 1250

CLAREMONT

Claremont Coll .... BAILEY, George M. 46
.... BARKEY, Patrick T. 56
.... KUHNER, David A. 683
.... MOSER, Judith E. 871
Claremont Unified Sch District .... ROSE, David L. 1054
Claremont Univ Center .... SAHAK, Judy H. 1075
Francis Bacon Foundation Inc .... WRIGLEY, Elizabeth S. 1373
Libs of the Claremont Colleges .... ALLEN, Susan M. 16
OCLC Online Computer Lib Center .... IVERSON, Diann S. 585
.... PRESLAN, Bruce H. 991
.... THELIN, Sonya R. 1234
Sch of Theology at Claremont .... COBB, Jean L. 224
.... FREUDENBERGER, Elsie L. . 402
Scripps Coll .... DRAKE, Dorothy M. 318

CLOVIS

Clovis Unified Sch District .... DICK, Norma P. 300

COALINGA

Coalinga-Huron Lib District .... GUIDINGER, Delmar J. 476

COLTON

Colton Pub Lib .... HOLM, Blair I. 552

COLUMBIA

Columbia Coll .... STEUBEN, Raymond L. 1190

COMMERCE

City of Commerce .... CONOVER, Robert W. 238

COMPTON

Compton Community Coll .... PANSKI, Saul J. 938

CONCORD

Bank of America .... GLYNN, Jeannette E. 442
.... REIST, Paul A. 1022
Mount Diablo Unified Sch District .... SKAPURA, Robert J. 1145

CORONADO

Coronado Pub Lib .... MURTEN, Holly T. 882

COSTA MESA

Susan Baerg Epstein Ltd .... EPSTEIN, Susan B. 351
Univ of Phoenix .... DOWNS, Sandra P. 317
.... SEGAL, Naomi R. 1112

CUPERTINO

Apple Computer Inc .... BIDWELL, Lynne H. 95
.... DEWEY, Barney L. 298
.... ERTEL, Monica 353
.... MACEK, Rosanne M. 755
.... VRATNY-WATTS, Janet M. 1289
Hewlett-Packard Co .... HUNG, Joanne Y. 574
.... RAZE, Nasus B. 1012
Tandem Computers .... DIFFERDING, Jane B. 302

CYPRESS

Anaheim Union High Sch District .... HALL, Howard L. 488
Orange County Pub Lib .... EVANS, Rina A, ... 358
US Air Force .... MOSER, Jane W. 870

DANVILLE

Crew-Noble Information Services .... CREW-NOBLE, Sara M. ... 258

DAVIS

Calgene Inc .... JOHNSON, Deanna L. 603
Davis Senior High Sch .... HALLBERG, Sharon P. 489
Petervin Press & Petervin Info Assocs .... IRELAND, Laverne H. 583
Robinson Information Service .... ROBINSON, Betty J. 1043
Univ of California at Davis .... ANDERSON, David C. 22
.... BLANCHARD, J R. 103
.... BLANK, Karen L. 104
.... BOORKMAN, Jo A. 115
.... CACCESE, Vincent 170
.... CASEMENT, Susan D. 192
.... DAILEY, Kazuko M. 270
.... DAVIS, Rebecca A. 280
.... ELDREDGE, Mary 342

CALIFORNIA (Cont'd)
DAVIS (Cont'd)
Univ of California at Davis

ELLIOTT, C D.	343
JESTES, Edward C.	600
KNOWLES, Em C.	665
LAMPRECHT, Sandra J.	691
LARUSSA, Carol J.	700
LEWIS, Alfred J.	722
LUNDQUIST, David A.	748
LUST, Vernon G.	750
MAWDSLEY, Katherine F.	787
PEATTIE, Noel	953
PIPER, Patricia L.	975
POPA, Opritsa A.	983
ROCKE, Reve P.	1046
ROSS, Johanna C.	1058
SHARROW, Marilyn J.	1122
SHERLOCK, John A.	1128
SHORT, Virginia	1132
SIBIA, Tejinder S.	1134
TEBO, Marlene	1229
WILLIS, Glee M.	1348
WINTER, Michael F.	1356

DEL MAR
Raymond M Holt & Associates — HOLT, Raymond M. 554
DOBBINS
Dorr Genealogy Lib — LE DORR, Lillian E. 708
DOWNEY
Los Angeles County Pub Lib

ASAWA, Edward E.	35
MARKEY, Penny S.	771
RODRIGUEZ, Ronald	1048
WAGNER, Sharon L.	1292

Rockwell International — CRANFORD, Theodore N. ... 255
PAIK, Nan H. 935
DUARTE
City of Hope National Medical Center — CARRIGAN, John L. 186
DUBLIN
National Food Processors Association — LAMANNA, Joan M. 689
EL CAJON
Grossmont Coll — LEVINE, Beryl 720
Grossmont-Cuyamaca Community
  Coll Dist — HEPP, Thomas A. 530
San Diego County Pub Lib System — SUBLER, Joyce A. 1206
EL CERRITO
CCM Associates — MACAULEY, C C. 754
Flower Films & Video — BLANK, Les 104
EL SEGUNDO
Aerospace Corp — HOCKING, Theresa R. 546
City of El Segundo — KIRBY, Barbara L. 653
Computer Sciences Corp — LEVINE, Warren D. 721
Ebsco Subscription Services — LOHNES, Richard B. 737
Hughes Aircraft Co

CAMPBELL, Bill W.	176
MORRISEY, Locke J.	867
PATTEN, Frederick W.	947
SEVIER, Jeffrey A.	1117
STERLIN, Annette S.	1189

Severy Inc — BARTH, Nancy L. 61
Xerox Corp — FELLER, Amy I. 370
EL TORO
Orange County Pub Lib — DENECOUR, Mary D. 291
ELDRIDGE
Sonoma Developmental Center — MOSIER, Eric M. 871
EMERYVILLE
Carlyle Systems Inc

BARANOWSKI, George V.	55
NASATIR, Marilyn	888
SALMON, Stephen R.	1077

Cetus Corp — KARCHER, Tracey L. 627
POKLAR, Mary J. 980
JHK & Associates — PAQUETTE, John F. 939
ENCINITAS
Data Trek Inc — PIERCE, Patricia J. 971
National Decision Systems — GAY, Thomas R. 423
ENCINO
Encino-Tarzana Friends of the Lib — BROWN, Marie H. 146
Financial Advice & Support Inc — ROSS, Ric 1058
ESCONDIDO
City of Escondido — BRIDGMAN, Amy R. 135
EUREKA
St Joseph Hospital — BROWN, Elizabeth E. 143

CALIFORNIA (Cont'd)
FAIR OAKS
Ellis Computer Services — ELLIS, Ruth M. 345
Imaging Update — HILL, Kristin E. 540
FAIRFIELD
Solano County Lib

CONDRA, Darrel A.	236
GOLD, Anne M.	444
MCCORMACK, Carolyn	798

FALLBROOK
CompTron Research Inc — COMPTON, Joan C. 235
San Diego State Univ — MCNALLY, Ruth C. 816
FOUNTAIN VALLEY
Fountain Valley Regional Hospital — SCHULZ, Judith H. 1102
FPO SAN FRANCISCO
US Naval Hospital, Guam — HADLEY, Alice E. 482
FREMONT
Alameda County Lib — PANTAGES, Sandra K. 938
California Department of Education — KLEINMAN, Elsa C. 660
Queen of Holy Rosary Coll — VANDERBECK, Maria 1273
FRESNO
California Sch of Professional Psy — KAUFFMAN, Inge S. 631
California State Univ at Fresno

BOCHIN, Janet S.	108
HILLMAN, Stephanie	541
RICHTER, Bertina	1031

Community Hospitals of Central CA
  Inc — NELSON, Iris N. 894
WARD, Penny T. 1304
Fresno County Pub Lib — CARLSON, Alan C. 182
COBB, Karen B. 225
Fresno Pacific Coll — BRANDT, Steven R. 128
PAULS, Adonijah 950
Mennonite Brethren Biblical Seminary — ENNS-REMPEL, Kevin M. ... 350
San Joaquin Memorial High Sch — LATIMER, Mary A. 701
Veterans Administration Medical
  Center — CONNOR, Paul L. 238
MEYER, Cynthia K. 830
FULLERTON
Beckman Instruments — MILLER, Jean R. 839
California State Univ at Fullerton

ANDERSEN, Leslie N.	21
BRIL, Patricia L.	136
STEPHENSON, Shirley E.	1189

City of Fullerton — JOHNSON, Carolyn E. 602
Dun & Bradstreet Corp — HARMON, Gary 502
Fullerton Pub Lib — MILO, Albert J. 845
MUELLER, Jane L. 875
Western State Univ at Fullerton

BECKER, Carol J.	72
PERKINS, Steven C.	959
THOMPSON, James A.	1240

GARDEN GROVE
Orange County Pub Lib — PENDLETON, Lynne G. 956
Orange County Transit District — MASTERS, Robin J. 782
Swedlow Inc — FORD, Marjorie F. 389
GARDENA
Professional Media Service Corp — HANSEN, Linda L. 497
JACOBS, Peter J. 590
GEORGE AFB
US Air Force — PAMINTUAN, Celia 937
GLENDALE
City of Glendale — FISH, Marie 380
RAMSEY, Jack 1006
Glendale Adventist Medical Center — GUPTA, Ann D. 478
PRIME, Eugenie E. 993
Glendale Community Coll — THOMAS, Mary C. 1237
Glendale Pub Lib — WONG, Maida L. 1363
Glendale Unified Sch District — BRACE, Joyce B. 124
Predicasts — HEDDEN, Judy A. 520
Project Completers Inc — BURNS, Nancy R. 162
NYBERG, Lelia J. 912
Seek Information Service — ECKLUND, Lynn M. 335
GRENIER, Myra T. 467
GOLETA
Paper Chaser — MUSICK, Nancy W. 883
Santa Barbara Research Center — GENTRY, Susan K. 427
GRANADO HILLS
Los Angeles Unified Sch District — SINOFSKY, Esther R. 1144
GRAND TERRACE
TRW Information Systems Group — MARCHIANO, Marilyn C. ... 768
GRASS VALLEY
Nevada County Lib — BAILEY, Darlene L. 46

CALIFORNIA (Cont'd)

HALF MOON BAY
Bowker Electronic Publishing — MALONEY, James J. 764

HARBOR CITY
Kaiser Foundation Hospital — SAWYER, Anne R. 1086

HAWTHORNE
California Book Supply — LUNSTEDT, Ralph A. 749
Northrop Corp — PRINTZ, Naomi J. 993

HAYWARD
Alameda County Lib — APPEL, Anne M. 29
— COOPER, Ginnie 242
— FLUM, Judith G. 386
— PISANO, Vivian M. 975
California State Univ at Hayward — CASTAGNOZZI, Carol A. ... 194
— REEDER, Ray A. 1015
— ROSE, Melissa M. 1055
Chabot Coll — BUTLER, David W. 166
— SASSE, Margo 1083
City of Hayward — EAGER, Nancy A. 331

HERMOSA BEACH
City of Santa Monica — MITCHELL, Betty J. 848

HILLSBOROUGH
Nueva Learning Ctr — ABILOCK, Debbie 2

HOLLYWOOD
Western Costume Co — NELSON-HARB, Sally R. ... 895

HUNTINGTON BEACH
Huntington Beach Pub Lib — HAYDEN, Ronald L. 515
McDonnell Douglas Corp — LO, Grace C. 735
— MACKINTOSH, Mary L. 757

INDIO
John F Kennedy Memorial Hospital — DICKINSON, Dan C. 300

INGLEWOOD
Inglewood Pub Lib — PETERSON, Anita R. 962

IRVINE
Allergan Inc — CURTIS, Richard A. 267
— NOVACK, Dona A. 910
— WIERZBA, Heidemarie B. ... 1337
Baxter Healthcare Corp — JACOBUS, Nancy M. 590
Charles Schlacks Jr Publisher — SCHLACKS, Charles 1093
Fluor Corp — LEE, William D. 711
McDonnell Douglas Corp — WORMINGTON, Peggie ... 1369
RMG Consultants Inc — WOODS, Lawrence A. 1367
Univ of California at Irvine — ARIEL, Joan 31
— BOYER, Calvin J. 123
— BROIDY, Ellen J. 139
— CLANCY, Stephen L. 215
— CLARY, Rochelle L. 219
— FALK, Joyce D. 362
— FINEMAN, Michael 377
— FORBES, Fred R. 389
— FRANK, Anne E. 396
— GELFAND, Julia M. 426
— HAN, Kenneth P. 494
— HIXON, Donald L. 544
— HORN, Judy K. 559
— LEUNG, Shirley W. 719
— LEWALLEN, David D. 722
— MYONG, Jae H. 885
— POOLE, Jay M. 983
— PUGSLEY, Sharon G. 997
— TSANG, Daniel C. 1260
— TSENG, Sally C. 1260
— WEINTRAUB, D K. 1318
— WOOLDRIDGE, Steven M. . 1368
— WYKLE, Helen H. 1375

JAMUL
Index & Information Srvs — SERDZIAK, Edward J. 1116

KENSINGTON
Bayside Indexing Service — MULVANY, Nancy 878

KING CITY
City of King — NOZICK, Sandy B. 911

LA CANADA-FLINTRIDGE
Flintridge Sacred Heart Academy — HA, Marie S. 480
La Canada Memorial Lib — MORAN, William R. 862

LA HABRA
Chevron Oil Field Research Co — COPPIN, Ann S. 245

CALIFORNIA (Cont'd)

LA JOLLA
Copley Newspapers — CARNES, Suzanne M. 183
Gabbert Information & Lib Services — GABBERT, Gretchen W. 411
James S Copley Lib — MCPHAIL, Martha E. 817
La Jolla Country Day Sch — VANSONNENBERG, Catherine 1277
La Jolla Museum of Contemporary Art — RICHARDSON, Gail 1029
San Diego Pub Lib — SHERWOOD, Judith 1129
Science Applications International Corp — GIBSON, Joanne 432
Scripps Clinic and Research Foundation — NEELY, Jesse G. 892
Scripps Clinic Medical Group Inc — DITO, William R. 305
Univ of California at Los Angeles — MILLER, James G. 838
Univ of California at San Diego — ALLISON, Terry L. 17
— BOWLES, Garrett H. 121
— BRUEGGEMAN, Peter L. 149
— COOLMAN, Jacqueline 241
— CREELY, Kathryn L. 257
— DAY, Deborah C. 282
— FEENEY, Karen E. 368
— FERGUSON, Chris D. 372
— FISHER, Edith M. 380
— GALLOWAY, Sue 415
— GREGOR, Dorothy D. 466
— HURLBERT, Irene W. 577
— KANTER, Elliot J. 625
— MARKWORTH, Lawrence L. . 772
— MILLER, R B. 841
— MIRSKY, Phyllis S. 847
— PARCHUCK, Jill A. 940
— SCHILLER, Anita R. 1093
— SMITH, Phillip A. 1159
— SPRAIN, Mara L. 1176
— STARR, Susan 1182
— SWEEDLER, Ulla S. 1214
— TALBOT, Dawn E. 1220
— TILLETT, Barbara B. 1245
— WILLHITE, Sherry 1341
— WILSON, Marilyn J. 1352
Veterans Administration Medical Center — HUCKINS, Barbara W. 569

LA MIRADA
Dymanic Bioreactors — ANJOU-DURAZZO, Martel T. 28

LA PUENTE
Hacienda La Puente Unified Sch District — SIGLER, Lorraine 1137
Los Angeles County Pub Lib — DEVEREAUX, Amy E. 297
— ROSENBERG, Stuart L. 1056

LA VERNE
Univ of La Verne — HECKMAN, Marlin L. 520
— KINMAN, Gay T. 652

LAFAYETTE
Teamsearch — NEWAY, Julie M. 898

LAGUNA HILLS
Saddleback Hospital and Health Center — KOPAN, Ellen K. 671

LAKEWOOD
Amtec Information Services Inc — KILKER, Paul V. 648
Los Angeles County Pub Lib — AMESTOY, Helen M 20

LIVERMORE
Chabot Coll — LUCAS, Linda L. 746
Lawrence Livermore National Laboratory — BURTON, Hilary D. 164
— FISHER, H L. 381
— HUNT, Richard K. 575
— KEIZUR, Berta L. 635
— LAI, Dennis 688
— LOVE, Sandra R. 743
Livermore Pub Lib — PALLONE, Kitty J. 935
North California Lib — MCLEAN, Janice A. 814
Ross McDonald Co — MCDONALD, Barbara J. 802
Univ of California at Livermore — GIRILL, T R. 438

LODI
City of Lodi — LACHENDRO, Leonard L. ... 686
Lodi Pub Lib — MAAS, Dorothy W. 753
— YAMAMOTO, Conrad S. ... 1376

CALIFORNIA (Cont'd)

LOMA LINDA

Loma Linda Univ	BUTLER, Randall R.	167
	WURANGIAN, Nelia C.	1374
Veterans Administration Medical Center	MAYERS, Deborah L.	789

LOMITA

Cambria Records & Publishing	BOWLING, Lance C.	121

LOMPOC

City of Lompoc	STARR, Carol L.	1182

LONG BEACH

California State Univ at Long Beach	AHOUSE, John B.	8
	BENSON-TALLEY, Lois I.	83
	BRITTON, Helen H.	137
	CULOTTA, Wendy A.	264
	DEBOER, Kee K.	284
	DUBOIS, Henry J.	322
	KOUNTZ, John C.	673
	LITTLEJOHN, Alice C.	734
	NESBITT, Renee D.	896
	PARKER, Joan M.	942
	SCEPANSKI, Jordan M.	1088
	SIMS, Sidney B.	1142
	SINCLAIR, Lorelei P.	1142
	SMITH, Gordon W.	1155
	WILLIAMS, Valencia	1347
City of Long Beach	NEWHARD, Eleanor M.	899
Douglas Aircraft Co	BREWSAUGH, Susan J.	134
Long Beach City Coll	AYALA, John L.	42
Long Beach Pub Lib	DARTT, Florence R.	275
	SALLSTROM, Marilee A.	1077
Long Beach Unified Schs	HECKLINGER, Ellen L.	519
St Anthony High Sch	CADY, Ruth A.	170
St Mary Medical Center	ATTARIAN, Lorraine B.	38
Star-Kist Foods Inc	JADWIN, Rochelle J.	591
TRW Information Systems Group	ADAMS, Linda L.	5
	HIATT, Jack	536
Veterans Administration Medical Center	CONNOLLY, Betty F.	237

LOS ALTOS

Cornerstone Technologies	RADWIN, Mark	1002
INFOUR	BUTLER, Brett B.	166
	CARSON, Susan A.	188
	CONDIT, Larry D.	235
Santa Clara County Lib		

LOS ALTOS HILLS

Foothill-De Anza Community Coll District	MCDONALD, Marilyn M.	803

LOS ANGELES

After Image Inc	HENDERSON, Ellen B.	526
AI&U	ROSE, Steven C.	1055
Alschuler Grossman & Pines	GRIGST, Denise J.	470
American Film Institute	SCHLOSSER, Anne G.	1094
Archdiocese of Los Angeles	WOLFF, Mary K.	1361
ARCO	BOWMAN, Frances A.	121
	HAUTH, Carol A.	513
	WRIGHT, Betty A.	1370
Artworks	PASCAL, Barbara R.	945
Bank of America	WAY, Kathy A.	1311
Bishop County High Sch	NAGY, Helen C.	886
Brobeck Phleger & Harrison	BESTE, Ian R.	92
California Department of Justice	RAFFALOW, Janet W.	1003
California Medical Center at Los Angeles	FITZGERALD, Diana S.	382
California Sch of Professional Psy	BERGMAN, Emily A.	86
	BIRCH, Tobeylynn	98
California State Court of Appeals	GOMEZ, Cheryl J.	447
California State Univ at Los Angeles	GREENBERG, Marilyn W.	463
	HOFFMAN, Irene M.	548
	ROLLING, George M.	1051
	SULLIVAN, Suzanne E.	1208
	WALTERS, Mary D.	1301
	WILKINSON, David W.	1340
Cathedral High Sch	GERARD, Sandra C.	428
CCH Computax Inc	PHILLIPS, Clifford R.	968
Cedars-Sinai Medical Center	GREEN, Ellen W.	461
City of Los Angeles	MCINDOO, Larry R.	809
Cleveland Chiropractic Coll	FOLLICK, Edwin D.	388
Cohen Brown Management Group	VARAT, Nancy L.	1278
Computer Business	HASSAN, Abe H.	511

CALIFORNIA (Cont'd)

LOS ANGELES (Cont'd)

Coopers & Lybrand	CROSS, Mabel L.	260
	MEARNS, Mary A.	820
Craft & Folk Art Museum	BENEDETTI, Joan M.	80
Cuadra Associates Inc	CUADRA, Carlos A.	262
	PELTO, Charles	955
DDB Needham Worldwide Inc	STEINMANN, Lois S.	1186
El Camino Coll	RONEY, Raymond G.	1053
El Pueblo de los Angeles State Park	STERN, Teena B.	1189
Fashion Inst of Design & Merchandising	HALE, Kaycee	485
First Church of God Christian Sch	GRAY, Tomysena F.	460
Gibson Dunn & Crutcher	HOLLINGSWORTH, Dena M.	552
Hennigan & Mercer	KARR, Linda	628
Hollywood Presbyterian Medical Center	KING, Joseph T.	651
Horizon Information Services	TONKERY, Dan	1250
House Ear Institute	CHARBONNEAU, Ronald P.	202
	MULE, Gabriel	876
Hufstedler Miller Carlson & Beardsley	DONALDSON, Maryanne T.	311
Hughes Aircraft Co	CLIFFORD, Susan G.	222
	GOUDELOCK, Carol V.	454
	TAYLOR, Alice J.	1226
Hughes Communications Inc	SUTTON, Joanna M.	1211
The Information Group	KAPLAN, Robin	626
Informed Sources	DALY, Eudice	271
International Technology Group	WARNOCK, Patric F.	1305
Irell & Manella	HAMOR, Monica E.	494
Jewish Federation Council	BEN-ZVI, Hava	84
Jones Day Reavis & Pogue	SCHIPPER, Joan A.	1093
Korn/Ferry International	HADLEY, Peter H.	482
LAC Health Services Administration	PRUHS, Sharon	996
Latham & Watkins	KACZOROWSKI, Monice M.	621
	WALLACE, Marie G.	1297
Lawry's Foods Inc	NEWCOMER, Susan N.	898
Library Management Systems	BALABAN, Robin M.	50
Los Angeles County Law Lib	BARROW, Jerry	60
	ENYINGI, Peter	351
	IAMELE, Richard T.	581
	MITTAN, Rhonda L.	850
	REYNOLDS, Diane C.	1025
	SNELL, Patricia P.	1163
Los Angeles County Medical Association	CRUMP, Joyce A.	262
	POTTER, Laurene	987
	TREISTER, Cyril C.	1255
Los Angeles County Pub Lib	CHAVEZ, Linda	204
Los Angeles Herald Examiner	SAUSEDO, Ann E.	1085
Los Angeles ORT Technical Institute	SATER, Analya	1083
Los Angeles Pub Lib	AHLSTROM, Romaine	8
	ALFORD, Thomas E.	13
	BEVERAGE, Stephanie L.	93
	BUCK, Donald	153
	CLARK, David L.	216
	COLLINS, Richard H.	233
	CONNOR, Anne C.	237
	CONNOR, Billie M.	237
	ELLISON, Bettye H.	345
	GAY, Elizabeth K.	423
	GINSBURG, Helen W.	438
	HICKS, Cynthia S.	536
	JONES, Wyman	615
	KHATTAB, Hosneya M.	646
	LEE, Hee J.	710
	MAZUR, Victoria P.	791
	NAVARRO, Frank A.	889
	NG, Carol S.	900
	NORDBY, Leslie L.	908
	PATRON, Susan H.	947
	REAGAN, Bob	1012
	ROH, Jae M.	1050
	ROSENBERG, Melvin H.	1056
	RUBEN, Jacquelen S.	1064
	SPENCER, Patricia O.	1173
	STREHL, Daniel J.	1201
	TESTA, Barbara E.	1233
	WALKER, Patricia A.	1296
	WALTER, Virginia A.	1300

CALIFORNIA (Cont'd)
LOS ANGELES (Cont'd)
Los Angeles Pub Lib

WILLIAMS, Sonja D.	1346
WINSTON, Gillian R.	1356
ZEIDLER, Patricia L.	1387

Los Angeles Times
BROWN, Patricia L.	146
SIMPSON, Mildred	1142

Los Angeles Unified Sch District
CROSS, Claudette S.	260
MULLINS, Carolyn J.	878
SKEHAN, Patricia A.	1145
SMITH, Margie G.	1157

Loyola Law Sch
HUFF-DUFF, Barbara	570
SZEGEDI, Laszlo	1218
WONG, Cecilia	1362

Loyola Marymount Univ
EVANS, G E.	357
SCHMIDT, Ford C.	1095

Marymount High Sch — TUOHY, Eileen M. 1263
McCutchen Black Verleger & Shea — ANNAND, Stewart S. 28
McKenna Connor & Cuneo — CHICK, Cynthia L. 208
McKinzie Publishing Co — MCKENZIE, Harry 811
Mercer Meidinger Hansen Inc — COSTELLO, Robert C. 249
Meserne Mumper & Hughes — ROLLINS, James H. 1051
Metropolitan Water Dist of Southern CA — LEE, Dora T. 709
Morrison & Foerster — NEMCHEK, Lee R. 895

Mount St Mary's Coll
CONDON, Erika M.	236
POPOVITCH-KREKIC, Ruzica	984

Natural History Musm of Los Angeles Cnty
DONAHUE, Katharine E.	310
EDWARDS, Jennifer L.	337

Northrop Corp — SUGRANES, Maria R. 1207
Northrop Univ — HALPIN, Jerome H. 490
Notre Dame Academy — JAIN, Celeste C. 591
Occidental Coll — MORRIS, Jacquelyn M. 866

O'Melveny & Meyers
SMITH, Catherine M.	1153
WANG, Connie	1302

Pacific Oaks Coll — GRANGER, Dorothy J. 457
Pasadena Pub Lib — POSTER, Susan E. 986
Peat Marwick Main & Co — LEE, Diane T. 709
Pepperdine Univ — LEUNG, Terry S. 719
Pertamina — MASWAN, Yurita 783
Price Waterhouse — VEASLEY, Mignon M. 1280
Proskauer Rose Goetz & Mendelsohn — MULLER, Malinda S. 877
Quotron Systems Inc — GRANT, George K. 458
Richards Watson & Gershon — BIRNIE, Elizabeth B. 98
St Vincent Medical Center — GELMAN-KMEC, Marsha 426
Security Pacific National Bank — SHEA, Ann W. 1124
Sidley & Austin — LAMARTINE, Elisabeth A. 689
Skadden Arps Slate Meagher & Flom — KUCZMA, Michelle 682
Southern California Gas Co — SANDVIKEN, Gordon L. 1081
Southern California Rapid Transit Dist — DEGOOD, S K. 288

Southwestern Univ of Los Angeles
MORRIS, George H.	866
STREIKER, Susan L.	1201
WEINER, Carole B.	1318
WHISMAN, Linda A.	1329

Steinmann Grayson Smylie — MERRIFIELD, Thomas C. 826
Stephen S Wise Temple — LEFF, Barbara Y. 712

Sydney Dataproducts Inc
CHASE, Jan	203
SANDELL, Judy L.	1079

Third Point Systems — COLLINS, Thomas F. 233
Times Mirror — HOLLY, James H. 552
Touche Ross & Co — TICE, Kathleen A. 1244
US Court of Appeals, Ninth Circuit — MAZZA, Joanne C. 791
US Food & Drug Administration — SNELL, Charles E. 1163

Univ of California at Los Angeles
ABRAMSON, Jenifer S.	3
ADAN, Adrienne	6
ANDERSON, Dorothy J.	22
ANDREWS, Karen L.	26
BATES, Marcia J.	64
BERMAN, Marsha	88
BIDWELL, John	95
BISOM, Diane B.	99
BORKO, Harold	116
CARAVELLO, Patti S.	180
CASE, Donald O.	191
CHAMMOU, Eliezer	198
CONTINI, Janice L.	239
COSTELLO, M R.	249

CALIFORNIA (Cont'd)
LOS ANGELES (Cont'd)
Univ of California at Los Angeles

COYLE, Leslie P.	253
DAVIS, James	279
DEENEY, Kay E.	286
EISENBACH, Elizabeth R.	340
FISHER, William	381
FRY, Stephen M.	407
FRY, Thomas K.	407
GILMAN, Lelde B.	436
GLITZ, Beryl	441
GOLDSMITH, Jan E.	446
GORAL, Miki	451
GRAHAM, Elaine	456
GRASSIAN, Esther S.	458
GULLION, Susan L.	477
HALL, Anthony	487
HAYES, Robert M.	516
HINCKLEY, Ann T.	542
INGEBRETSEN, Dorothy L.	582
JOHNSON, Jane D.	605
KUNSELMAN, Joan D.	684
KWAN, Julie K.	685
LAWRENCE, John R.	704
LEE, Don A.	709
MAACK, Mary N.	753
MARCUS, Sharon F.	769
MCCORMICK, Mona	798
MCGARRY, Dorothy	805
NOGA, Michael M.	907
NYHAN, Constance W.	912
PELZ, Bruce E.	955
PETERS, Marion C.	962
PORTILLA, Teresa M.	985
RAEDER, Aggi W.	1003
RANDALL, Michael H.	1006
RICHARDSON, John V.	1029
ROSENBERG, Betty	1056
SCHERREI, Rita A.	1092
SCHOTTLAENDER, Brian E.	1099
SEBO, Lorraine M.	1110
SHANK, Russell	1120
STERNHEIM, Karen	1189
SUBLETTE, Doris L.	1206
SVENONIUS, Elaine	1212
TIENHAARA, Kaarina I.	1244
TING, Eunice T.	1246
VOSPER, Robert	1289
WATERS, Marie B.	1308
WATSON, Janet L.	1309
WELLS, Dorothy V.	1322
WERNER, Gloria	1324
YEE, Martha M.	1379
ZEIDBERG, David S.	1387
ZIEGLER, Janet M.	1388
ZUCKERMAN, Arline	1391

Univ of Southern California
BELL, Christina D.	76
BENNION, Bruce C.	82
BOAZ, Martha T.	108
BRECHT, Albert O.	131
BROWN, Janis E.	144
CHRISTOPHER, Paul	212
CLINTWORTH, William A.	222
CRAMPON, Jean E.	255
GILMAN, Nelson J.	436
HAYES, Melinda K.	516
JAFFE, Lee D.	591
KARASICK, Alice W.	627
KAZLAUSKAS, Edward J.	632
KIM, Joy H.	649
KLEIN, Kenneth D.	659
MANNING, Phil R.	767
MANTHEY, Teresa M.	767
MORSE, David H.	869
REINHARDT, Alice L.	1021
RICE, Ronald E.	1027
RITCHESON, Charles R.	1036
SHERMAN, Judith E.	1128
SORGENFREI, Robert K.	1168

CALIFORNIA (Cont'd)

LOS ANGELES (Cont'd)

Univ of Southern California

	STAYNER, Delsie A.	1183
	THOMPSON, Don K.	1239
	TOMPKINS, Philip	1250
	TROTTA, Victoria K.	1258
	WETTS, Hazel H.	1328
	WILK, Wanda	1339
	WILLIAMS, Leonette M.	1344
	WINEBURGH-FREED, Margaret	1354
	WISE, Leona L.	1357
	WOOD, Elizabeth H.	1364
	WUERTZ, Eva L.	1373
	ZIAIAN, Monir	1387
Univ of West Los Angeles	BRISTOL, Arlen A.	137
Updata Publications Inc	SCLAR, Herbert	1106
Veterans Administration Medical Center	LEONARD, Jean E.	716
Veterans Administration W Los Angeles	DAVIS, Marianne W.	280
White Memorial Medical Center	MARSON, Joyce	775
Whittier Coll	GOWAN, Christa I.	455
	HAYTHORN, Joseph D.	517
	KRIKORIAN, Rosanne	678
	NOE, Christopher J.	906
	THAKER, Virbala M.	1234
Woodbury Univ	MOORE, Everett L.	859
Wyman Bautzer Christensen Kuchel Silbert	TAYLOR, Susan E.	1228

LOS GATOS

San Jose State Univ	SMITH, Edith	1154

MALIBU

Pepperdine Univ	FRASHIER, Anne E.	399
	HEATHER, Joleen	519
	HOLLAND, Harold E.	550
	SANDERS, Robert L.	1080
	STAHL, Ramona J.	1178

MARINA DEL REY

R&D Associates	KATZ, Janet R.	630
RDA/LOGICON	ANDERSON, Christine	22

MCKINLEYVILLE

North Humboldt Unified Sch District	MARVEL, Frances J.	780

MENLO PARK

Addison-Wesley Publishing Co	HALL, Elede T.	487
Heidrick & Struggles	LEWIS, Gretchen S.	723
Legal Infomation Management	DILORETO, Ann M.	303
Liposome Technology Inc	HARRIS, Nina M.	505
	JENSEN, Marilyn A.	599
Mead Data Central	TABKE, Robert	1219
Menlo Park Pub Lib	HOFLAND, Freda B.	548
Price Waterhouse	VEENKER, Linda J.	1281
Raychem Corp	HOFFKNECHT, Carmen L.	547
SRI International	DENNETT, Stephen C.	292
	KLEINER, Donna H.	660
	MYERS, Nancy J.	884
	REDFIELD, Elizabeth	1014
	ROLEN, Helen T.	1051
	STEELMAN, Lucille A.	1184

MERCED

Merced County Lib	KOBAYASHI, Deanna H.	666
	WILSON, Linda L.	1351

MILL VALLEY

Golden Gate Baptist Theological Seminary	ASHLEY, Elizabeth	36
	KUBIC, Joseph C.	682
	WHITE, Cecil R.	1330

MILPITAS

Santa Clara County Lib	COLBY, Diana C.	230

MISSION VIEJO

Saddleback Community Coll	GORDON, Wendy R.	452

MODESTO

Doctors Medical Center	LUEBKE, Margaret F.	747
Memorial Hospitals Association	HAMMETT, Susan A.	493
	SHAMS, Kamruddin	1120

MOFFETT FIELD

NASA/Ames Research Center Lib	SANDFORD, Betsy R.	1080

CALIFORNIA (Cont'd)

MONTEREY

City of Monterey	LAGIER, Jennifer B.	688
Inlex Inc	BRUMAN, Janet L.	150
	DOEHLERT, Irene C.	308
	MATTHEWS, Joseph R.	785
	SIDMAN, George C.	1135
	WEISS, William B.	1320
	WILLIAMS, Joan F.	1344
McDonnell Douglas Corp	BARKALOW, Pat A.	56
Monterey Bay Aquarium	MANKE, Merrill E.	765
Monterey Bay Area Coop Lib Syst	SERTIC, Kenneth J.	1116
Monterey Peninsula Coll	SMALLEY, Topsy N.	1151
Monterey Pub Lib	NEAL, Jan	890
Naval Postgraduate Sch	CLINE, Margery C.	222
	MARTIN, Roger M.	778
	SPINKS, Paul	1175
Publishers Data Service Corp	SQUIRE, Diane	1177

MORAGA

St Mary's Coll	GOODMAN, L D.	449
	O'CONNOR, Thomas F.	916
	SEEKAMP, Linda W.	1111

MOUNTAIN VIEW

Acurex Corp	STOCKS, Lee P.	1195
Advanced Information Management	CONDREY, Barbara K.	236
	PORTER-ROTH, Anne	985
Cooper Laboratories	HEMINGWAY, Beverly L.	525
Database Services Inc	SPIGAI, Fran	1174
El Camino Hospital	JAJKO, Pamela J.	592
Equatorial Communication Service	PARKER, Edwin B.	941
Info Consulting	POST, Linda C.	986
Knowledge Access International	BUTLER, Matilda L.	167
	PAISLEY, William J.	935
Nielsen Engineering & Research Inc	FALTZ, Judy A.	363
St Francis High Sch	SCHAFFER, Eamon	1089
SandCastles Inc	LEE, Judith C.	710
Semiconductor Equipment & Materials Inst	SHERMAN, Roger S.	1128
Whismmon Sch District	ALBUM, Bernie	11

NAPA

Napa City-County Lib	CHAMBERLIN, Leslie A.	198
	HERSH, Daniel	533

NATIONAL CITY

National City Pub Lib	MONROE, Shula H.	855
South Bay Family Practice	FIEDLER, Albert E.	375

NEVADA CITY

Nevada County Lib	HELLING, Madelyn	524

NEWPORT BEACH

City of Newport Beach	CHWEH, Steven S.	214
Hoag Memorial Hospital Presbyterian	SCHULTZ, Ute M.	1102
The Information Source	EVANS, Deborah L.	356
Kenneth Leventhal & Co	DOSER, Virginia A.	313
McDonnell Douglas Computer Systems	MARLOR, Hugh T.	772
Newport Beach Pub Lib	EASTMAN, Franklin R.	333
	JUNG, Soon J.	620
	POARCH, Margaret E.	979

NORTH HOLLYWOOD

California Family Study Center	GREENWOLD, Amy	465
Marshall/Plumb Research Associates	PLUMB, Carolyn G.	978
Oakwood Secondary Sch	KYROPOULOS, Mary S.	685

NORTHRIDGE

California State Univ at Northridge	CREAGHE, Norma S.	257
	DAVIS, Douglas A.	278
	DODSON, Snowdy D.	308
	DURAN, Karin J.	328
	ECKLUND, Kristin A.	335
	EICHELBERGER, Susan	339
	FINLEY, Mary M.	378
	PERKINS, David L.	959
	TANIS, Norman E.	1222
	WONG, Clark C.	1362

NORTON AFB

US Air Force	CROWTHER, Carol	262

NORWALK

Los Angeles County Pub Lib	PETERMAN, Claudia A.	962

CALIFORNIA (Cont'd)

NOVATO
Fireman's Fund Insurance Co	ALDRICH, Linda W.	11
	GHILOTTI, Linda L.	430
Harding Lawson Associates	HOTZ, Sharon M.	562
Marin County Free Lib	LAPERRIERE, Renee J.	697
	ZALE, Phyllis J.	1385
Novato United Sch District	HIRABAYASHI, Joanne	543

OAKDALE
Stanislaus County Free Lib	MOORE, Mary L.	860

OAKLAND
Alameda County Law Lib	KENSINGER, Colleen O.	642
	LOMAX, Ronald C.	738
	OWENS, Robert L.	932
Area Corp	YU, Simone	1384
Bay Area Lib & Information System	GUY, Patricia A.	479
Children's Hospital Medical Center	SHAPIRO, Leonard P.	1121
City of Oakland	WONG, Patricia M.	1363
Crosby Heafey Roach & May	SKRUKRUD, Nora L.	1147
Data Center	CHESTER, Claudia J.	207
DataCenter	HORN, Zoia	559
Enviroment Health Associates Inc	LONDON, Glenn S.	738
Highland Hospital	MORGAN, Linda M.	864
Holy Names Coll	HOWATT, Helen C.	565
	MAINELLI, Helen K.	761
Kaiser Engineers Inc	ZACHER, Elaine F.	1385
Mills Coll	PANDOLFO, Steven P.	937
	STOCKFLETH, Craig G.	1195
Oakland Pub Lib	BIBEL, Barbara M.	94
	CONMY, Peter T.	236
	GILDEN, Susanna C.	434
	LAMBREV, Garrett I.	691
	MILLER, Elissa R.	837
	MULL, Richard G.	876
	OSTROUMOV, Tatiana	929
	PAGE, Kathryn	934
	SWANSON, Clara M.	1213
	WHITE, Lelia C.	1331
Rubin Consulting	RUBIN, Rhea J.	1064
Univ of California at Berkeley	ECKMAN, Charles D.	335
Univ of California at Oakland	PRICE, Bennett J.	992
Visiting Nurse Association Inc	SIEBENMORGEN, Ruth	1135

OCEANSIDE
City of Oceanside	NELSON, Helen M.	893
Oceanside Pub Lib	ARNOLD, Donna W.	33
	CAPPADONNA, Mary S.	180
	WAZNIS, Betty	1311

OJAI
Ojai Unified Sch Dist	MOORE, Phyllis C.	861

ONTARIO
Ontario City Lib	GRAUE, Luz B.	458
Sunkist Growers Inc	NEMETH, Martha C.	895

ORANGE
Bergen Brunswig Corp	LA BORDE, Charlotte A.	686
Chapman Coll	SHAWL, Janice H.	1124
	WILSON, Wayne V.	1353
City of Orange	LEO, Karen A.	716
Orange County Pub Lib	JOHNSON, Mary L.	607
	MCSPARREN, Christine L.	818
	SMITH, Elizabeth M.	1154
St Joseph Hospital	RYAN, Ann	1070
	SMITH, Julie L.	1156

ORINDA
Mason-McDuffie Real Estate Inc	DOWNEY, Lynn A.	316

OROVILLE
Butte County Lib	TERRY, Josephine R.	1232
North State Cooperative Lib System	ALLENSWORTH, James H.	16

OXNARD
City of Oxnard	SMITH, Heather	1155
St John's Regional Medical Center	KENNEDY, Joanne	641

PACIFIC GROVE
Inlex Inc	HAY, Wayne M.	515
Stanford Univ	BALDRIDGE, Alan	51
Wadsworth Inc	NEEDHAM, Michael V.	891

PACIFIC PALISADES
Los Angeles Unified Sch District	HILLIS, Patricia K.	541
Pacific Research Associates	SCHRIBER, James E.	1100

PALMDALE
City of Palmdale	STORSTEEN, Linda L.	1198

CALIFORNIA (Cont'd)

PALO ALTO
DIALOG Information Services Inc	BOURNE, Charles P.	119
	CORCHADO, Veronica A.	245
	DEHN, Lydia A.	288
	FROST, Michelle	406
	GREEN-MALONEY, Nancy	465
	HOLLOWAY, Dona W.	552
	HUDNUT, Sophie	569
	MAR, Sandy	768
	MARANGONI, Eugene G.	768
	ROMERO, Georg L.	1052
	SHARP, Geoffrey H.	1122
	SIMONS, Robert A.	1141
	SUMMIT, Roger K.	1209
	TAOKA, Wesley M.	1223
	WOGGON, Michele	1359
	YODER, Susan M.	1380
Electric Power Research Institute	JUDY, Joseph R.	619
	PARKER, Stephen B.	942
Fairchild Research Center	COOK, Sherry M.	240
Fairchild Semiconductor	CRABTREE, Sandra A.	254
Hewlett-Packard Co	COFFIN, Theodore Q.	227
	DUNBAR, Miriam B.	325
	GUST, Kathleen D.	478
	VUGRINECZ, Anna E.	1289
Hoover Institution	HAWES, Grace M.	513
The Live Oak Press	HAMILTON, David M.	491
Lockheed Missiles & Space Co Inc	LEWIS, Ralph W.	724
	WOLF, Nola M.	1360
Palo Alto Pub Lib	DRIVER, Linda A.	320
	LEVY, Mary J.	722
	OLSON, Sharon L.	923
San Francisco Bay Socty for Adlerian Psy	KAHN, Paul J.	622
Syntex USA Inc	TRIMBLE, Kathy W.	1256
Varian Associates	FARMAR, Donna M.	364
	MURPHY, Joan F.	880
Veterans Administration Medical Center	BRUGUERA, Eva A.	150
William P Wreden Books & Manuscripts	WREDEN, William P.	1370
Wilson Sonsini Goodrich & Rosati	WILLIAMS, Donna S.	1342

PALOS VERDES ESTATES
Northrop Corp	WILLIS, Joan K.	1348
Palos Verdes Lib District	ELLIOTT, Linda P.	344
	UEBELE, Dorothy B.	1268
State of California	STEVENSON, Marilyn E.	1191

PALOS VERDES PEN
Palos Verdes Lib District	TSENG, Joan L.	1260

PANORAMA CITY
Los Angeles Pub Lib	CLARK, Patricia A.	217

PASADENA
Ambassador Coll	WALTHER, Richard E.	1301
Avery Fisher	STANLEY, Dale R.	1180
Avery International	KALVINSKAS, Louanne A.	623
California Institute of Technology	ANDERSON, Virginia	25
	BRUDVIG, Glenn L.	149
	CARD, Sandra E.	180
	CHANG, Min M.	200
	CHOUDHURY, Lori B.	211
	GOODSTEIN, Judith R.	450
	KNUDSEN, Helen Z.	666
	ROTH, Dana L.	1059
City of Pasadena	SZYNAKA, Edward M.	1219
Facts On File Inc	KLINE, Victoria E.	661
Fuller Theological Seminary	YEUNG, Esther Y.	1380
Huntington Memorial Hospital	ZEIND, Samir M.	1387
James M Montgomery Consulting Engineers	HELGESON, Duane M.	524
Jet Propulsion Laboratory	CASTAGNO, Judith M.	193
Kaiser Permanente Hospitals & Hlth Plan	CRAWFORD, Marilyn L.	257
Lockheed-California Co	ELMAN, Stanley A.	345
Pasadena Pub Lib	BISHOFF, Lizbeth J.	99
	CAIN, Anne H.	171
	GARNER, Carolyn L.	419
Unisys Corp	OLMSTEAD, Nancy L.	921
Univ of Southern California	HOROWITZ, Roberta S.	560

CALIFORNIA (Cont'd)

PASO ROBLES
City of El Paso de Robles — MARTIN, Ann F. 775
PATTON
Patton State Hospital — STUMBERG, Mary S. 1205
PEBBLE BEACH
Robert Louis Stevenson Sch — ANDRUS, Eloise A. 27
PETALUMA
Petaluma Secondary Sch District — GORDON, Ruth I. 452
PICO RIVERA
Los Angeles County Pub Lib — HAUSSMANN, Virginia D. ... 513
Northrop Corp — KILLIAN, Sandra L. 648
MOLLETT, Mike M. 853
SALM, Kay E. 1077
PLACENTIA
ABC Unified Sch District — PITLUK, Paula K. 976
PLACERVILLE
El Dorado County Free Lib — AMOS, Jeanne L. 20
BATTAGLIA, Bonnie J. 64
Herbert Green Middle Sch — KOSKY, Janet J. 672
PLEASANT HILL
Brown and Caldwell Consulting
Engineers — SPURLOCK, Pauline 1177
California Division of Mines &
Geology — BRUNTON, Angela 151
Contra Costa County Lib — KENNEDY, Rose M. 641
LARKIN, Sally S. 698
SIEGEL, Ernest 1136
Diablo Valley Coll — DOLVEN, Mary 310
PLEASANTON
Kaiser Aluminum & Chemical Corp — ROOSHAN, Gertrude I. 1053
POMONA
California State Polytechnic Univ — ADAMSON, Danette 6
DUNN, Kathleen K. 327
HSIA, Ting M. 567
KOGA, James S. 668
LAMONTAGNE, Therese 691
LIM, Sue C. 727
Kingsley Lib Equipment Co — KINGSLEY, Eleanor V. 652
Pomona Pub Lib — SHAPTON, Gregory B. 1122
STREETER, David 1201
Pomona Unified Sch Dist — REMKIEWICZ, Frank L. 1022
Pomona Valley Community Hospital — KLEIN, Deborah S. 659
PORT HUENEME
US Navy — THOMPSON, Bryan 1239
PORTERVILLE
Porterville Coll — NAUMER, Janet N. 889
PORTOLA VALLEY
San Mateo County Community Coll
District — ENGELBRECHT, Mary E. ... 349
POWAY
St Gabriel's Church — DOLLEN, Charles J. 310
PRESIDIO OF MONTEREY
Defense Language Institute — CHAN, Carl C. 199
RANCHO PALOS VERDES
Kattlove & Associates — KATTLOVE, Rose W. 630
WITTMANN, Cecelia V. 1358
REDDING
County of Shasta — MCCRACKEN, John R. 799
Redding Museum & Art Center — BARNARD, Sandra K. 57
Shasta County Lib — BIEK, David E. 95
REDLANDS
Univ of Redlands — HEARTH, Fred E. 519
NOLAND, Jon 908
REDWOOD CITY
City of Redwood City — DUFFY, Karen R. 324
Dynamic Information — MARSINKO, Randy 775
WLADAS, Edward 1359
Jerry FitzGerald & Associates — FITZGERALD, Ardra F. 382
Redwood City Pub Lib — BANGE, Stephanie D. 54
HIMMEL, Ned A. 542
LIGHT, Jane E. 726
Reference Service Press — SCHLACHTER, Gail A. 1093
San Mateo County Office of
Education — LATHROP, Ann 701
San Mateo County Superintendent of
Schs — MAY, Frank C. 788
Sequoia Hospital — HOUGHTON, Barbara H. 562

CALIFORNIA (Cont'd)

RICHMOND
Chevron Chemical Co — LOPEZ, Frank D. 741
Chevron Environmental Health Center
Inc — BURSON, Sherrie L. 164
KERNS, John T. 644
Chevron Research Co — DESOIER, Jacqueline J. 295
LAMBERT, Nancy 690
RILEY, Constance L. 1034
WAWRZONEK, Mary S. ... 1311
WHITE, Larry R. 1331
City of Richmond — CONTRERAS, Marie 239
Idox — O'CONNOR, Brian C. 915
Kaiser Permanente Medical Center — BALOGH, Leeni I. 53
Richmond Pub Lib — HOLTZMAN, Douglas A. 555
Stauffer Chemical Co — CHU, Insoo L. 212
PETERSON, Gretchen N. 963
SAYLOR, Linda 1086
Univ of California at Berkeley — SVIHRA, S J. 1212
Univ of California at Richmond — RUBENS, Charlotte C. 1064
STOCKTON, Gloria J. 1196
RIDGECREST
Martin Marietta Data Systems — FRIEDMAN, Sandra M. 404
RIVERSIDE
At Your Service, The Informative
Network — CUEVAS, John R. 263
Inland Lib System — AARON, Kathleen F. 1
Loma Linda Univ — DAVIS, Charles E. 278
HESSEL, William H. 534
WALKER, James J. 1295
Riverside City & County Pub Lib — JOHNSON, Thomas L. 609
SWAFFORD, William M. ... 1212
WOOD, Linda M. 1364
Riverside Community Coll — PROSSER, Michael J. 995
Riverside County Law Lib — WEBB, Gayle E. 1313
Riverside Unified Sch District — NEBEL, Jean C. 891
RUSSELL, Sandra W. 1069
Univ of California at Riverside — BRISCOE, Peter M. 136
CHURUKIAN, Araxie P. 213
DOUGLAS, Nancy E. 314
FLOWERS, Pat 386
FUSICH, Monica G. 410
HUNTER, David C. 576
JORDAN, Joan A. 616
JORGENSEN, Venita 617
KOSHER, Helene J. 672
MITCHELL, Steve 849
MOONEY, Margaret T. 858
SELTH, Jefferson P. 1114
SNYDER, Henry L. 1164
STALKER, Laura A. 1178
TANNO, John W. 1223
THOMPSON, James C. 1240
VIERICH, Richard W. 1284
ROHNERT PARK
Sonoma State Univ — HARRIS, Susan C. 506
WOLLTER, Patricia M. 1361
ROLLING HILLS ESTATE
Savage Information Services — GIFFORD, Becky J. 433
SAVAGE, Gretchen S. 1085
TUNG, Sandra J. 1263
ROSEMEAD
El Monte Union High Sch District — CONNELL, William S. 237
ROSEVILLE
City of Roseville — NICKERSON, Susan L. 902
SACRAMENTO
Aerojet Strategic Systems Co — MIRONENKO, Rimma 847
California Community Colls — MARRIOTT, Lois I. 773
California Dept of Food & Agriculture — KAWAMOTO, Chizuko 632
California Department of General Srvs — GRANADOS, Rose A. 457
California Department of
Transportation — HANEL, Mary A. 495
California Lib Association — FERRELL, Mary S. 373
CA Postsecondary Education
Commission — TESTA, Elizabeth M. 1233
California State Board of Equalization — AKEY, Sharon A. 9
California State Lib — ANDERSEN, Thomas K. 21
CUNNINGHAM, Jay L. 265
GILBERT, Carol L. 433
HAGEN, Dennis D. 483

CALIFORNIA (Cont'd)
  SACRAMENTO (Cont'd)
  California State Lib
    HUSTON, Esther L. 578
    LOW, Kathleen 743
    MCGOVERN, Gail J. 807
    SILVER, Cy H. 1138
    STRONG, Gary E. 1203
  California State Univ at Sacramento ANDREW, Karen L. 26
    DRUMMOND, Herbert 321
    GOFF, Linda J. 443
    GRAVES, Frances M. 459
    HICKS, Mary F. 537
    KONG, Leslie M. 670
    KRISTIE, William J. 679
    PARSONS, Jerry L. 945
    SNOW, Marina 1164
    TRIMINGHAM, Robert 1256
  California Training and Resource
    Network   RUDDOCK, Velda I. 1065
  Elk Grove Unified Sch District   SCRIBNER, Ruth B. 1108
  Kaiser Permanente Medical Center   BENNETT, Michael W. 82
  Radian Corp   SCHEIBEL, Susan 1091
  Sacramento City Unified Sch District JACKSON, Gloria D. 587
  Sacramento Pub Lib   EITZEN, Judy 341
    FERDUN, Georgenne M. 372
    JURGENS, Lann 620
    KILLIAN, Richard M. 648
    LARSON, Janet E. 699
    RICHARD, Robert J. 1028
    SHUMAKER, Lois 1134
  State of California   BURNS, John F. 162
    MARTINEZ, Barbara A. 779
  US Army Engineer District   NEWTON, Deborah A. 900
  US District Court   MURRAY, Roberta N. 882
  Univ of California at Davis   MALMGREN, Terri L. 763
    SEHR, Dena P. 1112
  Univ of the Pacific   MILLER, Suzanne M. 842
    NUNEZ-SCHALDACH, Ruth . 912

  SAINT HELENA
  George & Elsie Wood Lib   STOCKWELL, Judith R. . . . 1196
  Silverado Museum   SHAFFER, Ellen 1119
  SALINAS
  Hartnel Coll   DICKENS, Jan 300
  Monterey County   SHAFFER, Dallas Y. 1119
  Monterey County Lib   CHURCH, Sonia J. 213
  Salinas Pub Lib   GAMBLE, Mary J. 416
  SAN ANSELMO
  Augie Blume & Associates Inc   BLUME, August G. 107
  Butterfield Press   LEACH, Elizabeth A. 706
  San Domenico Sch   FARMER, Lesley S. 364
  Town of San Anselmo   WINGATE, Eliza C. 1354
  SAN BERNARDINO
  California State Univ at San
    Bernardino   PARISE, Marina P. 940
  Dement Research Assocs   DEMENT, Alice R. 291
  Don A Turner County Law Lib   WEBB, Duncan C. 1313
  Honeywell Inc   CARRICABURU, Robert 186
  Inland Lib System   SIMON, Vaughn L. 1141
  International Sch of Theology   MINDEMAN, George A. 845
  Record Lists   CHANDLER, Thomas V. 200
  San Bernardino Community Hospital   NOUROK, Marlene E. 910
  San Bernardino County Lib   WATTS, Richard S. 1310
  San Bernardino County Medical
    Center   WAKEFIELD, Jacqueline M. . 1293
  SAN DIEGO
  Boyce & Frausto APC   TABORN, Kym M. 1219
  California Western Sch of Law   BOOKHEIM, Louis W. 115
    GARCIA, Mary E. 417
  City of San Diego   DER PARSEGHIAN, Anahid
                                         A. 294
  Cubic Corp   COOK, Kathleen M. 240
    MOSER, Maxine M. 871
  Cubic Defense Systems   MOSER, Elizabeth C. 870
  DATA Inc   D'ADOLF, Steven P. 269
  Fashion Inst of Design &
    Merchandising   HARRIS, Kathryn S. 505
  General Dynamics Corp   ARNDAL, Robert E. 33
  Gray Cary Ames & Frye   MACLEOD, June F. 757
  Harcourt Brace Jovanovich   LAGIES, Meinhart J. 688

  CALIFORNIA (Cont'd)
  SAN DIEGO (Cont'd)
  Imed Corp   ALBRIGHT, Sue R. 10
  Imperial Corp of America   MORRISON, Patricia 868
  Imperial Savings Bank   GAGNON, Donna M. 412
  Info Webb   WEBB, Ty 1313
  Integrated Research & Information
    Srvs   PLOTSKY, Andrea G. 978
  Kelco Division of Merck & Co   WILLARD, Ann M. 1341
  Kratter Law Lib   BRISCOE, Georgia K. 136
  Latham & Watkins   VEGA, Carolyn L. 1281
  M/A-Com Government Systems   ROSS, Mary A. 1058
  Mead Data Central   KANJI, Zainab J. 625
  Merck & Co Inc   JENKINS, Ann A. 597
  Mercy Hospital & Medical Center   HABETLER, Anna M. 481
  Mesa Coll   FORMAN, Jack 390
  National Univ   LINDBERG, Susan J. 729
                                       NICKELSON-DEARIE,
                                         Tammy A. 902
  Naval Ocean Systems Center   WRIGHT, Kathleen J. 1372
  Pacific Naval Educ & Trng Support
    Ctr   BUSCH, Barbara 165
  Point Loma Nazarene Coll   POSEY, Vernell W. 985
  San Diego Community Coll   KAYE, Karen 632
  San Diego County Law Lib   CH'NG, Saw K. 209
    DERSHEM, Larry D. 294
    DYER, Charles R. 330
    EWING, Florence E. 359
    JOHNSRUD, Thomas E. 609
  San Diego County Lib   CLINE, Cheryl L. 222
    ESQUEVIN, Christian R. 354
    HESS, M S. 534
    LOOMIS, Barbara L. 740
    TRIVISON, Margaret A. 1257
    ZYROFF, Ellen S. 1392
  San Diego County Office of Education NIEMEYER, Kay M. 903
  San Diego Pub Lib   BOYLLS, Virginia W. 124
    FARMER, Marguerite E. 364
    KATKA, Patricia P. 629
    MARC-AURELE, Heidi L. 768
    MARTINEZ, Anna M. 779
    QUEEN, Margaret E. 999
    SANNWALD, William W. 1081
    SCHECTER, Fred 1090
    SCLAR, Marta L. 1106
    STANLEY, Sydney J. 1180
  San Diego State Univ   BOSSEAU, Don L. 117
    CHAN, Lillian L. 199
    DINTRONE, Charles V. 305
    LEERHOFF, Ruth E. 712
    PEASE, William J. 953
    PERKINS, Michael J. 959
    STRICKLAND, Muriel 1202
    WHITE, Phillip M. 1332
    WILSON, Carole F. 1350
  San Diego Supercomputer Center   MAISEL, Merry W. 762
  San Diego Unified Sch District   WYBORNEY, Charles E. 1374
  Sharp Memorial Hospital   WORTHINGTON, A P. 1369
  Sociological Abstracts Inc   CHALL, Miriam 197
  US International Univ   TEUTSCH, Walter 1233
  US Naval Ocean Systems Center   BUNTZEN, Joan L. 157
    SWEENEY, Urban J. 1215
  Univelt Inc Publishers   JACOBS, Horace 589
  Univ of California at San Diego   SLATER, Barbara M. 1148
    SOETE, George J. 1165
    VOIGT, Melvin J. 1287
  Univ of San Diego   CARTER, Nancy C. 189
    HERON, Susan J. 532
    HOLLEMAN, Marian P. 551
    HYDE, Mary L. 580
    RATHSWOHL, Eugene J. . . . 1009
  Vidionics International Database   DAVISSON, Darell D. 281
  Western State Univ at San Diego   CASTETTER, Karla M. 194
    SARRAINO, Kathleen A. . . . 1083
  Woodward-Clyde Consultants   ELLIOTT, Valerie E. 344
  Zoological Society of San Diego   ROBINSON, Michaele M. . . 1044

CALIFORNIA (Cont'd)
SAN FRANCISCO

Archives for the Performing Arts	VANSLYKE, Lisa M.	1277
Arthur Andersen & Co	FOX, Marylou P.	395
	MCDEVITT-PARKS, Kathryn B.	802
Bank of America	ANDERSON, Connie J.	22
	POLLACH, Karen F.	981
Bay Area Air Quality Management District	LENSCHAU, Jane A.	715
Bay Area Reference Center	SHOUSE, Richard	1133
Bechtel Civil Inc	SORROUGH, Gail L.	1169
Bechtel Power Corp	DUMLAO, Mercedes G.	325
	MAH, Jeffery	760
BHP Utah Minerals International	KIEFER, Karen N.	647
The Bookwatch	DONOVAN, Diane C.	312
Brick Row Book Shop	LOWMAN, Matt P.	744
Brobeck Phleger & Harrison	MCKENZIE, Alice M.	811
Bronson Bronson & McKinnon	SAWYER, Sandra	1086
California Academy of Sciences	MORITZ, Thomas D.	865
	TSAI, Sheh G.	1260
California State Lib	GLOVER, Frank J.	442
Chevron Corp	BROWN, Barbara L.	142
	HERDMAN, Elena	530
	LINDEN, Margaret J.	729
	WOO, Winnie H.	1363
City & County of San Francisco	GUARINO, John P.	475
	SCHMIDT, Robert R.	1096
City Coll of San Francisco	FEW, John E.	374
	SCHOLAND, Julia E.	1098
	SMYTH, Mary B.	1162
Davies Medical Center	SHEW, Anne L.	1129
Deloitte Haskins & Sells	MOORE-EVANS, Angela	862
Dolby Laboratories	EVANS, M R.	357
Farella Braun & Martel	MACKLER, Mark E.	757
Federal Home Loan Bank of San Francisco	GOVAARS, Inga	454
Federal Reserve Bank of San Francisco	ROSENBERGER, Diane C.	1056
Fine Print Publishing	KIRSHENBAUM, Sandra D.	655
Goethe Institute	BERNHART, Barbara M.	89
Golden Gate Univ	CODER, Ann	226
	WENDROFF, Catriona	1323
Gruen Gruen & Associates	SULLIVAN, Edward A.	1207
Hassard Bonnington Rogers & Huber	CONLEY, Linda A.	236
International Thomson Book	SMITH, Richard A.	1159
Kennedy Jenks Chilton Consltng Engineers	SANSOBRINO, Jean C.	1081
LeBoeuf Lamb Leiby & MacRae	WOODS, Marcia G.	1367
Lillick McHose & Charles	HARDIN, Betty N.	500
	SPATH, Linda C.	1171
Long & Levit	NEWMAN, Mark J.	899
Marakon Associates	GARDISER, Kathleen E.	417
McKinsey & Co	KRAEMER, Linda L.	674
Mechanic's Institute Lib	PABST, Kahleen T.	933
	SULLIVAN, Alice F.	1207
Meyer Boswell Books Inc	LUTTRELL, Jordan D.	750
Morrison & Foerster	OPPEDAL, Teresa A.	925
New Mills Law Lib	KOFF, Jacob	668
Niesar Kregstein & Cecchini	JONES, Michael D.	614
Northern California Health Center	DURSO, Angeline M.	329
Orrick Herrington et al	PAPERMASTER, Cynthia L.	939
Pacific Bell	MOYER, Barbara A.	874
	VENTURA, Dan L.	1282
Pacific Gas & Electric Co	MERRITT, Betty A.	827
	STROMME, Gary L.	1203
Pacific Presbyterian Medical Center	COLALILLO, Robert M.	230
	GIBSON, Harold R.	432
Pacific Telesis Corp	CHANDLER, James	200
	MILLER, Ralph D.	841
	TYERMAN, Vernon H.	1266
Pactel Properties	MULLIN, Jack A.	878
Peat Marwick Main & Co	MANN, Thomas	766
Peat Marwick Mitchell	CHAO, Yuan T.	201
Price Waterhouse	BLUM, Linda C.	107
Professional Sch of Psychology	DUZAK, Sandra J.	330
Rothchild Consultants	CARSCH, Ruth E.	187
Saint Francis Memorial Hospital	ZAREMSKA, Maryann	1386
St John Ursuline High Sch	SEGUNDO, Fe P.	1112
St Mary's Hospital & Medical Center	BENELISHA, Eleanor	80

CALIFORNIA (Cont'd)
SAN FRANCISCO (Cont'd)

St Rose Academy	KAUN, Thomas T.	631
San Francisco Art Institute	GUNDERSON, Jeffery R.	477
San Francisco Chronicle	CASTER, Suzanne	194
	GEIGER, Richard G.	425
	KIBBEE, Sally	646
San Francisco Examiner	CANTER, Judy A.	179
San Francisco Municipal Railway	HOFSTADTER, Marc E.	549
San Francisco Museum of Modern Art	CANDAU, Eugenie	178
	ERVITI, Debra L.	353
San Francisco Planning & Urban Research	HURLBERT, Roger W.	577
San Francisco Pub Lib	CADY, Steven R.	170
	COAKLEY, Dorothy J.	224
	COLBY, Michael D.	230
	FRANTZ, John C.	398
	GOLDMACHER, Sheila L.	445
	HUDSON, Jane	569
	KAVANAGH, Margaret M.	631
	KINCAID, Anne E.	649
	LANDGRAF, Mary N.	692
	LEWANDOWSKI, Joseph J.	722
	MURTHA, Edward J.	883
	NICHOLS, Elizabeth D.	901
	NYHAN, Catherine W.	912
	RAMIREZ, William L.	1005
	REGNER-HYATT, Anne L.	1017
	REILLY, James H.	1020
	SCHNEIDER, Marcia G.	1097
	TURITZ, Mitch L.	1263
San Francisco State Univ	AVENEY, Brian H.	41
	BONFIELD, Lynn A.	114
	GERSTLE, Steven M.	429
	HAIKALIS, Peter D.	484
	JACOBSEN, Lavonne	590
	JAMES, Olive C.	592
	MCQUOWN, Eloise	817
	TREGGIARI, Arnaldo	1255
	WHITSON, Helene	1334
Schs of the Sacred Heart	HAWKINS, Nina L.	514
	LESH, Jane G.	718
Sedgwick Deturt Moran & Arnold	BORKIN, Ann M.	116
Sierra Club	PRESBY, Richard A.	990
Strybing Arboretum Society	GATES, Jane P.	421
Taylor & Associates	TAYLOR, Kathryn E.	1227
Thelen Marrin Johnson & Bridges	HARMON, Marlene K.	502
	ZWEIFLER, Lynn A.	1392
U C Hastings Law Lib	PERITORE, Laura D.	958
US Court of Appeals	CELLE, Deborah A.	196
	MOORE, Gregory B.	859
US Department of Agriculture	SYPERT, Clyde F.	1217
US District Court	LUNDSTROM, Lynn E.	748
US Environmental Protection Agency	CIRCIELLO, Jean M.	215
US General Accounting Office	SHARP, Linda F.	1122
Univ of California at San Francisco	BELL, R E.	77
	COOPER, Richard S.	243
	DUNKEL, Lisa M.	326
	HENKE, Dan	528
	HOLLAND, Rebecca J.	551
	PERLMAN-STITES, Janice	959
	ROBERTS, Justine T.	1040
	TARCZY, Stephen I.	1224
	VANDEGRIFT, Glennda E.	1273
	WAKEFORD, Paul J.	1293
	WILSON, Jacqueline B.	1351
	WINSON, Gail I.	1355
	ZINN, Nancy W.	1389
Univ of San Francisco	BIRKEL, Paul E.	98
	EWEN, Eric P.	359
	GITLER, Robert L.	438
	KELSH, Virginia J.	639
	RUNYON, Steven C.	1067
	SHOSTROM, Marian L.	1133
	SONIN, Hille	1167
	STEFANCIC, Jean A.	1185
URS Corp	PRELINGER, Polly	990
Utah International Inc	DEWOLF, Timothy B.	298

CALIFORNIA (Cont'd)
  SAN FRANCISCO (Cont'd)
  Veterans Administration Medical
    Center   GOUVEIA, Sara C. 454
  Wells Fargo Bank   HUNSUCKER, Alice E. 574
     MERBACH, Peggy O. 825
  Whisler-Patri Architecture & Planning   CALDWELL, Kenneth R. 172
  Winguth Schweichler Associates   GERSH, Barbara S. 429
  World Affairs Council   BEESON, Lone C. 74
  Zoetrope Studios   NAZARIAN, Anahid 890
  SAN JOSE
  California State Court of Appeals   RODICH, Lorraine E. 1047
  City of San Jose   CARPIO, Virginia A. 185
     FLETCHER, Homer L. 384
  Class   ALIX, Cleta M. 13
     CHAMPANY, Barry W. 198
     SHIRASAWA, Sharon V. . . . 1131
  Cooperative Lib Agency for Systs &
    Srvs   ELLSWORTH, Dianne J. 345
     HAAS, Florence A. 480
     LEE, Doreen H. 709
     MILLER, Ronald F. 842
  Dataquest Inc   FINLEY, O R. 378
  East Side Union High Sch District   MCDONOUGH, Timothy M. . . 803
  Evergreen Sch District   SUTHERLAND, Helen G. . . . 1211
  FMC Corp   RANCATORE, Celeste L. . . 1006
  Franklin-McKinley Sch District   BERG, Charlene J. 84
     MERSHON, J L. 827
  General Electric Co   ROBINSON, Doris T. 1044
  Notre Dame High Sch   EGAN, Janet M. 338
  O'Connor Hospital   HAYES, Linda J. 516
  San Jose Bible Coll   LLOVIO, Kay M. 735
  San Jose Pub Lib   ABNEY, Timothy A. 2
     FOWLER, Brian R. 393
     JESSUP, Carrie 600
     RENDLER, Richard E. 1023
     ROSS, Ruth K. 1058
     SULLIVAN, Anne L. 1207
  San Jose State Univ   BELANGER, Sandra E. 75
     BRUNDAGE, Christina A. . . . 150
     CEPPOS, Karen F. 196
     COOVER, Robert W. 244
     CROWLEY, Terence 262
     ELLIOTT, Patricia G. 344
     EMMICK, Nancy J. 348
     HARMON, Robert B. 502
     HEALEY, James S. 518
     JOHNSON, Clifford R. 603
     LEONARD, Barbara G. 716
     LIU, Susanna J. 734
     MAIN, Linda Y. 761
     MARTIN, Rebecca R. 778
     MULLEN, Cecilia P. 877
     PAUL, Jeff H. 949
     REDFERN, Bernice I. 1014
     REYNOLDS, Judith L. 1025
     ROSEN, Elizabeth M. 1055
     WHITLATCH, Jo B. 1333
  Santa Clara Valley Medical Center   WILSON, Barbara A. 1350
  Sixty South Market Law Lib   DUNCAN, Rebecca 325
  SouthNet   KING, Kitty G. 651
  SAN LEANDRO
  Bissell & Karn Inc   HUNT, Deborah S. 575
  SAN LORENZO
  Life Chiropractic Coll West   CARR, Richard D. 186
     WOODBURY, Marda 1366
  SAN LUIS OBISPO
  California Polytechnic State Univ   DOBB, Linda S. 307
     HANSEN, Phyllis J. 498
     PRITCHARD, Eileen E. 994
     ROCKMAN, Ilene F. 1046
     STEWARD, Martha J. 1192
     WALCH, David B. 1293
  Library Concepts   FOURIE, Denise K. 393
  San Luis Obispo County Law Lib   BORRACCINO, Jean H. 117
  SAN MARCOS
  Palomar Coll   CATER, Judy J. 194
     ROTTER, Virginia B. 1061

CALIFORNIA (Cont'd)
  SAN MARINO
  Henry E Huntington Lib   SPIRO GREEN, Becky A. . . 1175
     ZALL, Elisabeth W. 1386
  Huntington Lib   HODSON, Sara S. 546
     MCLOONE, Harriet V. 814
     WOODWARD, Daniel 1368
  SAN MATEO
  Alumax Inc   LINDAHL, Ann L. 728
  Channelmark Corp   TARTER, Blodwen 1224
  Coll of San Mateo   ATKINS, Gregg T. 38
  EBSCO Subscription Services   CLINE, Sharon D. 222
  Market New Service Inc   MURPHY, Robert 881
  Peat Marwick Main & Co   MAYERS, Karen A. 789
  SAN PABLO
  Richmond Unified Sch District   RYUS, Phyllis K. 1072
  SAN PEDRO
  Logicon Inc   DAVENPORT, Constance B. . 275
     SPRUNG, Lori L. 1176
  SAN RAFAEL
  City of San Rafael   STRATFORD, Vaughn M. . . 1200
  Dominican Coll   DIENER, Margaret M. 302
  Lib Innovators   PLOTKIN, Nathan 978
  Lucasfild Ltd   FINE, Deborah J. 377
  Marin County Free Lib   EMERY, Frances D. 348
     HAMMER, Sharon A. 493
  Midwest Library Service   NAGEL, Lawrence D. 886
  San Rafael Pub Lib   TRZECIAK, William J. 1260
  SAN RAMON
  Chevron Information Technology Co   STAN, Gail A. 1179
  Chevron USA Inc   O'HEARN, Sarah A. 919
  Pacific Bell   RICHARDS, Jeff B. 1028
  Pacific Gas & Electric Co   BERCIK, Mary E. 84
     WALLEN, Jody H. 1298
  SANTA ANA
  City of Santa Ana   MORGAN, Ferrell 864
  Global Engineering Documents   AUSTIN, Stephen 40
  Orange County Register   OSTMANN, Sharon G. 929
  Orange County Transportation
    Commission   CHRISTNER, Deborah S. . . . 212
  Rancho Santiago College   HOFFMAN, Herbert H. 548
  Santa Ana Pub Lib   MINICK, Donna J. 846
  Santa Ana Unified Sch District   PINCOCK, Rulon D. 974
  Western Medical Center   SIMPSON, Evelyn L. 1141
  SANTA BARBARA
  ABC-CLIO   BOEHM, Ronald J. 109
     BYRNE, Pam 169
     KINNELL, Susan K. 653
  Cottage Hospital   FAY, Evelyn V. 367
  General Research Corp   BOWRIN-MARSH, Donna
     M. 122
  Kaman Tempo   GALLERY, M C. 414
  Office of County Superintendent of
    Schs   DAY, Bettie B. 282
  Presbyterian Univ of Santa Barbara   ANDERSON, John F. 23
  Santa Barbara Botanic Garden   HAWVER, Nancy 515
  Santa Barbara County Law Lib   MACGREGOR, Raymond . . . 755
  Santa Barbara High Sch District   MARR, Charles A. 773
  Santa Barbara Pub Lib System   HERZIG, Stella J. 534
     RICHARDSON, Bill 1029
  Univ of California at Santa Barbara   ANDERSON, Carol L. 22
     BOISSE, Joseph A. 111
     BULLARD, Sharon W. 156
     CRITTENDEN, Robert R. . . . 259
     DAVIDSON, Donald C. 276
     DOWELL, Connie V. 315
     GEBHARD, Patricia 424
     GIBBONS, Carolbeth 431
     GRAZIANO, Eugene 460
     HUBER, Charles F. 568
     JOHNSON, Diane D. 603
     KORENIC, Lynette M. 671
     LINVILLE, Herbert 731
     MARKHAM, James W. 771
     SILVER, Martin A. 1138
     TAI, Henry H. 1220
     WEIMER, Sally W. 1317
  Westmont Coll   BILYEU, David D. 97

CALIFORNIA (Cont'd)

SANTA CLARA
FMC Corp ... KOCH, Kathy R. 667
LUKE, Keye L. 747
SMOKEY, Sheila C. 1162
Intel Corp ... HAMBRIDGE, Sally L. 491
Mission Coll ... CARROLL, Lois E. 187
National Semiconductor ... HOLLAND, Mary 551
Santa Clara Univ ... BAZAN, Lorraine R. 68
EARHART, Marilyn N. 332
FRIEDRICH, Barbara J. 404
GOODWATER, Leanna K. ... 450
HOOD, Mary D. 556
JOHNSON, Linda B. 607
OKEEFE, Julia C. 919
SALZER, Elizabeth M. 1078
Stanford Telecommunications Inc ... NELSON, Alice R. 893
Unisys Corp ... SZABO, Carolyn J. 1218
Univ of Santa Clara ... BAILEY, Rolene M. 46
Versatec ... TYLER, Sharon R. 1266

SANTA CRUZ
Lombardi Indexing & Information
Services ... LOMBARDI, Mary L. 738
Santa Cruz City County Lib System ... ELGIN, Susan R. 342
SOUZA, Margaret A. 1170
TURNER, Anne M. 1264
Univ of California at Santa Cruz ... ANDERSON, Clifford D. 22
AUGUSTINE, Rolf S. 39
DYSON, Allan J. 331
GAREY, Anita I. 418
MARIE, Jacquelyn 770
MOKRZYCKI, Karen M. 852
PAQUETTE, Judith 939
RITCH, Alan W. 1036
ROBINSON, Margaret G. 1044
STEVENS, Stanley D. 1191
TAYLOR, Marion E. 1227

SANTA FE SPRINGS
Am Assn of Gynecologic
Laparoscopists ... PHILLIPS, Jordan M. 968

SANTA MONICA
Becker-Hayes Inc ... BECKER, Joseph 72
Crossroads Sch for Arts and
Sciences ... EVTUHOV, Tanya 359
Cuadra Associates Inc ... KURANZ, John 684
Gemological Institute Of America ... DIRLAM, Dona M. 305
Getty Center for the History of Art ... HERMAN, Elizabeth 531
REED, Marcia C. 1015
TIEMAN, Robert S. 1244
WHITE, Kathleen M. 1331
J Paul Getty Center ... EDELSTEIN, J M. 335
MENDENHALL, Bethany R. ... 824
NOBLE, Jean E. 906
SLEETER, Ellen L. 1148
YASSA, Lucie M. 1378
J Paul Getty Trust ... HALBROOK, Anne M. 485
Lear Siegler Inc ... BAGBY, Felicia R. 45
Meckler Publishing ... QUINT, Barbara E. 1000
Orbit Search Service ... LONGO, Margaret K. 740
Rand Corp ... BROPHY, Mary J. 141
GILL, Elizabeth D. 435
HELFER, Doris S. 523
JOHNSON, Mary E. 607
SHANMAN, Roberta 1120
Saint Johns Hospital & Health Center ... PINCKNEY, Cathey L. 974
Santa Monica Hospital Medical
Center ... ORFIRER, Lenore F. 925
Santa Monica Pub Lib ... FISHER, Alice J. 380
GRIFFITH, Virginia M. 469
SIMAS, Therese C. 1139
SDC Information Services ... BROOKS, Kristina M. 140
SCHWARTZ, A 1104
The TELCO Report ... PAEN, Alexander L. 934

SANTA ROSA
County of Sonoma ... SAYED, Joyce P. 1086
North Bay Cooperative Lib System ... BATES, Henry E. 64
The Press Democrat ... CANT, Elaine N. 179
Santa Rosa Junior Coll ... PETTAS, William A. 965
Santa Rosa Memorial Hospital ... HARRIS, Vallena D. 506
Sonoma County Law Lib ... WATSON, Benjamin 1309

CALIFORNIA (Cont'd)

SANTA ROSA (Cont'd)
Sonoma County Lib ... HARRIS, Roger L. 506
MORRISON, Deborah L. 868
PETTEY, Brent 965
ROSASCHI, Jim P. 1054
SABSAY, David 1073
SIMONS, Maurice M. 1141
STRIBLING, Lorraine R. ... 1202
Sonoma County Office of Education ... LEE, Mildred C. 711
Sonoma County Pub Lib ... WALSH, Donamarie F. 1299

SARATOGA
West Valley Coll ... BONNET, Janice M. 114

SAUSALITO
Pacific Energy & Resources Center ... RADEMACHER, Kurt A. ... 1002

SEAL BEACH
Orange County Pub Lib ... HOUSEL, Mary B. 563

SHERMAN OAKS
Davis & Schorr Art Books ... DAVIS, L C. 280
Info Mania ... LEWIS, Cookie A. 722

SOLEDAD
California Department of Corrections ... LEFFERS, Mary J. 712

SONOMA
Sonoma Valley Unified Sch District ... LUNARDI, Albert A. 748

SOUTH GATE
Los Angeles Unified Sch District ... BUBOLTZ, Dale D. 152

SOUTH SAN FRANCISCO
City of San Francisco ... GOODRICH, Jeanne D. 449
South San Francisco Unified Sch
District ... NIEBOLT, Henry C. 903

STANFORD
American Translators International ... HOMNACK, Mark 555
Ctr for Advanced Study in Behavioral
Sci ... AMARA, Margaret F. 19
Hoover Institution ... JAJKO, Edward A. 592
Research Libs Group Inc ... ALIPRAND, Joan M. 13
BALES, F K. 52
CRAWFORD, Walt 257
GLAZIER, Ed 440
JURIST, Susan 620
SCHMIDT, C J. 1095
STOVEL, Madeleine D. 1199
Stanford Medical Center ... YAU, Linda S. 1378
Stanford Univ ... ANDERES, Susan M. 21
ARROWOOD, Donna J. 34
BRIDGMAN, David L. 135
CLAEYS, Luisa T. 215
CROCKETT, Darla J. 259
DERKSEN, Charlotte R. 294
DIBLE, Joan B. 299
DIMUNATION, Mark G. 304
FORTSON, Judith 392
FRANK, Peter R. 397
GRIEDER, Elmer M. 467
HOGAN, Eddy 549
ITNYRE, Jacqueline H. 585
JOHNSON, Peter A. 608
KRASNER, Joan K. 676
LEGER, Norissa 712
MCELROY, Neil J. 804
MCPHERON, William 817
MIELKE, Marsha K. 833
MILFORD, Charles C. 835
MILLER, Dick R. 837
MUSEN, Mark A. 883
PAI, Herman H. 934
PALM, Miriam W. 935
REICH, Victoria A. 1018
ROSS, Alexander D. 1057
SLOCUM, Hannah R. 1150
STANGL, Peter 1180
SWEENEY, Suzanne 1215
THOMAS, Vivian 1238
TRUJILLO, Roberto G. ... 1259
VADEBONCOEUR, Elizabeth
J. 1270
WARD, Sandra N. 1304
WEBER, David C. 1314
WIBLE, Joseph G. 1335
WILSON, Karen A. 1351

CALIFORNIA (Cont'd)
STANFORD (Cont'd)
Stanford Univ

WU, Harriet 1373
YEH, Irene K. 1379
ZALEWSKI, Wojciech 1385

STOCKTON
San Joaquin County Office of
Education   DEAN, Martha L. 283
San Joaquin Delta Coll   CLARKE, Tobin D. 219
                                             MOORE, Evia B. 859

Stockton-San Joaquin County Pub
Lib   BROWN, Donna M. 143
                                             COLE, Gayle 230
                                             FRANCISCO, Marylynn 396
Univ of the Pacific   LEONHARDT, Thomas W. . . . 717
                                             SWANN, Arthur W. 1213
STUDIO CITY
Pacific Info Inc   PLATE, Kenneth H. 977
SUISUN
Contra Costa County Lib   CISLER, Stephen A. 215
SUN VALLEY
Masters Coll & Seminary   VOTAW, Floyd M. 1289
SUNNYVALE
City of Sunnyvale   BRITTAIN, Cynthia E. 137
                                             COMSTOCK, Evelyn B. 235
                                             DI MUCCIO, Mary J. 304
                                             SIMMONS, Beverley J. 1139
ESL Inc/Subsidiary of TRW   VAN VELZER, Verna J. 1277
Lockheed Missiles & Space Co Inc   STANEK, Suzanne 1179
                                             TYSON, Betty B. 1267
Palmer Coll of Chiropractic   HAZEKAMP, Phyllis W. 517
Philips Research Laboratories   TURK, Sally 1263
Sunnyvale Pub Lib   CANNON, Eleanor 179
Westinghouse Electric Corp   GESCHKE, Nancy A. 430
Xerox Corp   LEWARK, Kathryn W. 722
TEMECULA
Linfield Sch   BOWMAN, Kathleen A. 122
TEMPLE CITY
Los Angeles County Pub Lib   BUTTERWORTH, Linda M. . . 167
THOUSAND OAKS
City of Thousand Oaks   SMITH, Marvin E. 1158
                                             WALTERS, Roberta J. 1301
                                             WIGLEY, Marylou 1337
General Telephone of California   DENNISON, Lynn C. 292
Thousand Oaks Lib   BROOKS, Mary A. 140
                                             HOCKEL, Kathleen N. 545
                                             SULLIVAN, Kathleen A. 1207
TORRANCE
Copley Los Angeles Newspapers   ANDRADE, Rebecca 26
EBSCO Industries Inc   SPALA, Jeanne L. 1170
Torrance Memorial Hospital Medical
Ctr   KLECKER, Anita N. 658
Torrance Pub Lib   BEEBE, Richard J. 74
                                             BUCKLEY, James W. 154
                                             DOWNEY, Christine D. 316
                                             REEDER, Norman L. 1015
                                             SIEGEL, Jacquelin B. 1136
Torrance Unified Sch District   MOORE, Richard K. 861
TRACY
Tracy School Dist   WOBBE, Jean 1359
TRAVIS AFB
US Air Force   JACOBS, Nina F. . , , ... 580
TRUCKEE
Nevada County Lib   TORKELSON, Jon A. 1251
TURLOCK
California State Univ at Stanislaus   AMRHEIN, John K. 20
                                             BENNETT, Agnes H. 81
                                             PARKER, John C. 942
                                             SANTOS, Bob 1082
TUSTIN
St Jeanne de Lestonnac Sch   YOUNG, Eleanor C. 1381
UKIAH
Elinor Lindheimer Indexing Services   LINDHEIMER, Elinor 729
Mendocino Coll   MCGREEVY, Kathleen T. . . . 808
Shelfmark Original Cataloging   FELDMAN, Irwin 369
VACAVILLE
Vacaville Unified Sch District   MATTHIES, Donna K. 786

CALIFORNIA (Cont'd)
VALENCIA
California Institute of the Arts   HANFT, Margie E. 495
                                             HORIGAN, Evelyn A. 559
Coll of the Canyons   KELLER, Jan K. 635
Los Angeles County Pub Lib   CURZON, Susan C. 267
VALLEJO
California Maritime Academy   LANE, David R. 694
Mare Island Naval Shipyard   WONG, Carol Y. 1362
VAN NUYS
A Lib Service   DAVIS, Becky C. 277
ITT Gilfillan Inc   VILLERE, Dawn N. 1284
The Marquardt Company   LEE, Lydia H. 710
Smith Kline Bio-Science Laboratories   MACKEY, Lois M. 756
VANDENBURG AFB
US Air Force   ZEBROWSKI, Cheryl K. . . . 1387
VENTURA
Black Gold Cooperative Lib System   SOY, Susan K. 1170
Ventura County Lib Services Agency   ADENIRAN, Dixie D. 6
                                             BRONARS, Lori A. 140
                                             REDFIELD, Dale E. 1014
VIEJO
Saddleback Community Coll   TASH, Steven J. 1224
VISALIA
Golden West High Sch   PELOVSKY, Suzy A. 955
Tulare County Department of
Education   EBY, James F. 334
Tulare County Lib   PILLING, George P. 973
VISTA
National Univ   KELLY, Myla S. 638
WALNUT CREEK
John F Kennedy Univ   SMITH, Susan A. 1161
John Muir Memorial Hospital   REYES, Helen M. 1024
Pactel Publishing   OJALA, Rebecca A. 919
Woodward-Clyde Consultants   CRAWFORD, Margaret P. . . . 257
WEST COVINA
Los Angeles County Pub Lib   AROS, Andrew A. 34
Media Applications   HOFFMAN, William J. 548
WEST HOLLYWOOD
Los Angeles County Pub Lib   BUTKIS, John F. 166
WESTLAKE VILLAGE
Eaton Corp   LARSON, Donald A. 699
Reference Technology Inc   ALCOCK, Anthony J. 11
WHITTIER
Whittier Coll   DMOHOWSKI, Joseph F. . . . 306
                                             O'BRIEN, Philip M. 915
                                             WILLIAMS, Lisa B. 1344
WOODLAND
City of Woodland   KELLUM-ROSE, Nancy P. . . . 637
County of Yold   STEPHENS, Mary L. 1188
Legislative Intent Service   STALLARD, Thomas W. . . . 1179
Yolo County   WEBBER, Steven L. 1313
WOODLAND HILLS
Daily News of Los Angeles   REIFMAN, Deborah S. 1019
Littion Guidance & Control Systems   MASON, Elsbeth S. 781
Litton Systems Inc   CLIFTON, Joe A. 222
                                             GILBRIDE, Irene L. 434
YORBA LINDA
Yorba Linda Pub Lib   SCHWARZMANN, Diane D. 1105

COLORADO
ALAMOSA
Alamosa Southern Peaks Lib   SHELDON, L S, ... 1120
AURORA
Aurora Pub Lib   SMITH, Randolph R. 1159
Aurora Pub Schools   MURRAY, William A. 882
US WGST   HUGHES, Brad R. 571
BASALT
Basalt Regional Lib District   WINKLER, Jean J. 1355
BOULDER
The Alexandria Institute   KERR, Robert C. 644
Avalanche Development Co   ZOELLICK, Bill 1390
Ball Aerospace Systems Division   DAYHOFF, Judith A. 283
                                             PRESTON, Lawrence N. 991
Boulder Pub Lib   ELLISON, J T. 345
CareerTrack Inc   MEYER, Andrea P. 829
City of Boulder   BRADDOCK, Virginia O. 125
                                             GRALAPP, Marcelee G. 457
                                             VARNES, Richard S. 1279
                                             VOLC, Judith G. 1287

COLORADO (Cont'd)
BOULDER (Cont'd)
IBM Corp | WILLIAMS, Constance H. . . 1342
Library and Information Services | COLLARD, R M. 232
Library Information Specialist Inc | SUDOL, Barbara A. 1206
Mental Health Center of Boulder
  County | ROTHMAN, Marilyn R. 1060
National Center for Atmospheric
  Research | GAUSS, Nancy V. 423
  | KELLY, Karon M. 638
  | STRAND, Kathryn 1200
Native American Rights Fund | HARRAGARRA WATERS,
  | Deana J. 503
Reference Technology Inc | BARR, Arlene E. 58
  | BEFELER, Mike 74
  | MAIERHOFER, Ronald P. . . . 761
  | SMITH, Stephen S. 1161
Synergen Inc | HOFFMAN, Ann M. 547
US Department of Commerce | BANKHEAD, Jean M. 54
  | WATTERSON, Jane L. 1310
Univ of Colorado at Boulder | ANTHES, Susan H. 28
  | BINTLIFF, Barbara A. 97
  | BOUCHER, Virginia P. 118
  | BURKE, Marianne D. 160
  | BYRNE, Timothy L. 169
  | CARTER, Nancy F. 189
  | CHANAUD, Jo P. 199
  | ELLSWORTH, Ralph E. 345
  | FINK, Deborah 378
  | HENSLEY, Charlotta C. 529
  | JOST, Richard M. 618
  | KOHL, David F. 668
  | KRISMANN, Carol H. 678
  | MASON, Ellsworth G. 781
  | MUELLER, Carolyn J. 875
  | QUINLAN, Nora J. 1000
  | SANI, Martha J. 1081
  | WALTON, Clyde C. 1301
  | WERTHEIMER, Marilyn L. . . 1325
  | WYNNE, Allen 1375

CANON CITY
Colorado Department of Education | ROBERTS, Katherine M. . . . 1040
Fremont Sch District | HART, Karen L. 507
CASTLE ROCK
Douglas County Pub Lib | CONNOR, Evelyn 238
COLORADO SPRINGS
Air Academy High Sch | WILSON, M L. 1352
American Numismatic Association | GREEN, Nancy W. 462
Colorado Coll | JONES-EDDY, Julie 615
  | NEILON, Barbara L. 892
  | SHERIDAN, John B. 1127
Colorado Sch District 11 | DALBY, Richard F. 270
Colorado Springs Fine Arts Center | DEW, T R. 297
Falcon Sch District 49 | HELMAN, Sarah M. 524
Ford Microelectronics | LAZARUS, Josephine G. . . . 706
Harrison Sch District | SITTER, Clara M. 1144
Infotec Development Inc | MILLIGAN, Steven M. 843
McGraw-Hill Inc | HALL, Brian H. 487
Memorial Hospital of Colorado
  Springs | HANSON, Elana L. 498
Penrose Hospital | JANES, Nina 593
  | WATERS, W R. 1309
Pikes Peak Lib District | DOWLIN, Kenneth E. 316
  | MAGRATH, Lynn L. 760
  | MALYSHEV, Nina A. 764
  | MITCHELL, Carolyn 848
  | RITTEN, Karla J. 1036
  | WERNE, Kenneth L. 1324
Plains & Peaks Regional Lib Service
  Syst | OWEN, Mary J. 932
US Air Force Academy | BARRETT, Donald J. 59
  | KYSELY, Elizabeth C. 685
  | NELSON, Marie L. 894
  | STEWART, Anna C. 1192
Univ of Colorado at Colorado Springs | MANNING, Leslie A. 766
  | WYLIE, Nethery A. 1375

COLORADO (Cont'd)
DENVER
ABC-CLIO | BROCK, Laurie N. 138
American Humane Association | ALSOP, Robyn J. 18
American Medical International | GUTH, Karen K. 478
American Water Works Association | LUEVANE, Marsha A. 747
Association of Operating Room
  Nurses | BERG, Rebecca M. 84
  | KATSH, Sara 630
AT&T Bell Laboratories | ROSE, Phillip E. 1055
  | VARNER, James H. 1279
Auraria Lib | MACARTHUR, Marit S. 754
Bibliographical Center for Research | BRUNELL, David H. 150
  | GARZA, Rosario 421
  | HENSINGER, James S. 529
  | KAVANAGH, Janette R. . . . 631
Browne Bortz & Coddington Inc | MARSCHNER, Robyn J. . . . 773
Children's Hospital | KLENK, Anne S. 660
City and County of Denver | GEHRES, Eleanor M. 425
  | GIGNAC, Solange G. 433
Colorado Academy | YEN, Marilyn L. 1379
Colorado Alliance of Research Libs | GARRALDA, John C. 420
  | SHAW, Ward 1124
Colorado Department of Education | BOLT, Nancy M. 113
  | GORAL, Barbara J. 451
  | LANCE, Keith C. 692
Colorado Historical Society | KANE, Katherine 625
  | SHARP, Alice L. 1122
Colorado Lib Association | HAMILTON-PENNELL,
  | Christine 492
Colorado National Bankshares Inc | FUJII, Cynthia M. 408
Colorado State Lib | EATON, Barbara F. 333
  | HEMPSTEAD, John 525
  | LINSLEY, Priscilla M. 731
  | WAGNER, Barbara L. 1291
Davis Graham & Stubbs | BURNS, Linda L. 162
  | WOLFE, F M. 1360
Denver Art Museum | GOODRICH, Margaret 449
Denver Pub Lib | ASHTON, Rick J. 36
  | BOSWELL, Peggy B. 118
  | BOYER, Carol C. 123
  | CLOHESSY, Antoinette M. . . 223
  | CUMMING, Linda L. 264
  | FOLEY, Georgiana 387
  | TREFZ, Robert O. 1255
  | VOLZ, Edward J. 1288
  | WALTERS, Suzanne 1301
Denver Pub Schs | BEUTHEL, Ellengail 93
Division of State Archives & Pub
  Records | KETELSEN, Terry 645
Falsone Management Consultants | FALSONE, Anne M. 363
Holmes Roberts & Owen | ESTES, Mark E. 355
Iliff Sch of Theology | MYERS, Sara J. 885
Image Management Corp | DULAN, Peter A. 324
Information Professionals | ROESCH, Gay E. 1049
Info Srvs & Consulting | ZOOK, Ruth A. 1390
Manville Corp | CHANDLER, Constance P. . . 199
Martin Marietta Aerospace | REITER, Ellie W. 1022
Mead Data Central | CALVERT, Lois M. 174
Med-Info Search | GILBERT, Ruth E. 434
Mountain Bell | BOND, Bruce B. 113
  | BRUNER, Robert B. 150
Mullen High Sch | MILLER, Charles G. 836
Petroleum Information Corp | KELLER, Michael 635
Porter Memorial Hospital | BRITAIN, Karla K. 137
  | VERCIO, Roseanne 1282
Priscilla Kirshbaum Associates | KIRSHBAUM, Priscilla J. . . . 655
Roath & Brega | NORBIE, Dorothy E. 908
Rose Medical Center | SIMON, Nancy L. 1140
St Thomas Theological Seminary | GERMOVNIK, Francis I. 429
  | WHITE, Joyce L. 1331
Security Life Insurance Co of Denver | BENDER, Ruth 79
State of Colorado | CAMPBELL, Frances D. 176
United Engineers & Constructors Inc | MATTINGLY, Debra B. 786
  | OBERG, Judy M. 914
US Air Force | EIDSON, Alreeta 340
US Bureau of Land Management | BOWERS, Sandra L. 121
US Environmental Protection Agency | EDDY, Dolores D. 335
US Geological Survey | BIER, Robert A. 95
  | SHIELDS, Caryl L. 1129

COLORADO (Cont'd)
DENVER (Cont'd)

US West Knowledge Engineering Inc	BOSTON, Mary T.	118
	HARRIS, Michael A.	505
	KENLEY, Vernon F.	640
Univ of Colorado at Denver	BOTHMER, A J.	118
	BREIVIK, Patricia S.	132
	ESKOZ, Patricia A.	354
	FORSMAN, Rick B.	391
	GOODYEAR, Mary L.	450
	HEMPHILL, Jean F.	525
	INGUI, Bettejean	583
	MITCHELL, Marilyn J.	849
	SCHAFER, Jay G.	1089
	WITTHUS, Rutherford W.	1358
Univ of Denver	ABRAMS, Jeanne E.	3
	BARELA, Lori A.	56
	COCO, Al	226
	MOULTON, Suzanne L.	873
	RAINWATER, Barbara C.	1004
	SMITH, Sallye W.	1160

DURANGO
Fort Lewis Coll	PATERSON, Judy L.	947

EAGLE
Eagle County Pub Lib	ARMITAGE, Constance	32

ENGLEWOOD
Arapahoe Lib District	BRUNTON, David W.	151
Cherry Creek Pub Schs	BANKHEAD, Elizabeth M.	54
City of Englewood	WINKLE, Sharon L.	1355
Cyprus Minerals Co	SMART, Marriott W.	1151
Data General Corp	BETTENCOURT, Nancy J.	92
Denver Conservation Baptist Seminary	LYONS, Sarah P.	753
Denver Seminary	OTTOSON, Robin D.	930
Information Handling Services	SZABO, Kathleen S.	1218
	WHITE, Suellen S.	1332
IT Corp	HAMDY, Amira	491
Libraries Unlimited	WYNAR, Bohdan S.	1375
Medical Liability Consultants Program	THOMASSON, George O.	1238
Standard & Poor's Compustat Services Inc	HAMBRIC, Donna R.	491
	MCENTIRE, James E.	804
US West Inc	BIZZUL, Ash R.	100
	SMITH, Sally A.	1160
	SPANGLER, Bruce	1171

EVERGREEN
Advanced Systems Design Inc	HULL, Stephen P.	573
Colorado Endowment for the Humanities	SHARER, E J.	1122

FALCON AFS
TRW Defense Systems Group	QUINN, Candy L.	1000

FORT COLLINS
American Pub Works Association	CHRISTENSEN, Erin S.	211
Colorado State Univ	AMAN, Ann L.	19
	ANDERSON, Lemoyne W.	24
	BURNS, Robert W.	163
	CHAMBERS, Joan L.	198
	ERNEST, Douglas J.	353
	JOHNSON, K S.	606
	LANGE, Holley R.	695
	LINDGREN, William F.	729
	MOON, Myra J.	857
	NEWMAN, John	899
	SCHMIDT, Fred C.	1095
Platte River Power Authority	FELDMAN, Rosalie M	369
Poudre R-1 Sch Dist	LIRA, Judith A.	732

FORT LUPTON
Fort Lupton Pub Schs	MATSUNAGA, Fay L.	785

FORT MORGAN
Fort Morgan Pub Lib	KRUGLET, Jo A.	680

FOUNTAIN
Fountain-Ft Carson Sch District 8	POOLE, Rebecca S.	983

GOLDEN
Adolph Coors Co	BOND, Mary J.	113
Colorado Sch of Mines	FULMER, Russell F.	409
	LARSGAARD, Mary L.	698
	LEREW, Ann A.	717
	PHINNEY, Hartley K.	969
Graham Information Management Services	GRAHAM, Su D.	456

COLORADO (Cont'd)
GOLDEN (Cont'd)

Infocon Inc	KENNEY, Brigitte L.	641
J & A Assoc Inc	MONTAG, Diane	855
Rockwell International	MOOMEY, Margaret M.	857
Solar Energy Research Institute	CHERVENAK, Joseph F.	206
	MADDOCK, Jerome T.	759
X Press Information Services	BENNINGTON, Gerald E.	82

GRAND JUNCTION
Information Systems	RICHMOND, Elizabeth B.	1030
Mesa Coll	HENDRICKSON, Charles R.	527
Museum of Western Colorado	PROSSER, Judy A.	995
Rick Richmond Information Systems	RICHMOND, Rick	1030
St Mary's Hospital & Medical Center	PAINE, Joan E.	935
Veterans Administration Medical Center	BRAGDON, Lynn	127

GREELEY
Greeley Medical Clinic	CUTTS, William B.	268
High Plains Regional Lib Service System	KNEPEL, Nancy	664
Univ of Northern Colorado	FOX, Lynne M.	395
	HUGHES, Sondra K.	572
	JARAMILLO, George R.	594
	PITKIN, Gary M.	976
	ROBERTS, Francis X.	1040
	SAVIG, Norman I.	1086
	SCHULZE, Suzanne S.	1102
	SCHWEERS, Lucy	1105
	SERIS, Eileen J.	1116
Weld County Sch District 6	LANDRUM, Margaret C.	693

GUNNISON
Western State Coll	LANDRUM, Margaret C.	693

HAYDEN
Think Small Computers Inc	COSTA, Betty L.	249

IGNACIO
Southern Ute Indian Tribe	FROST, Debra R.	406

LAKEWOOD
COBE Laboratories Inc	HOLTON, Janet E.	555
Colonial Penn Information Service	CAMERON, Richard D.	175
Jefferson County Pub Lib	LAMPREY, Patricia M.	691
Medical Information Specialists	SMITH, Catherine C.	1153

LAMAR
City of Lamar	BURNETT, James H.	161

LEADVILLE
Lake County Lib	PARRY, David R.	944

LITTLETON
Arapahoe Lib District	WILDER, Mary K.	1339
Libraries Unlimited	LAMBERT, Shirley A.	690
	LOERTSCHER, David V.	737
Littleton Pub Schs	AKE, Mary W.	9
	SALLE, Ellen M.	1076
Marathon Oil Co	GREALY, Deborah J.	461
	STURDIVANT, Clarence A.	1205
Petroleum Information Corp	STARK, Philip H.	1182

MEEKER
Meeker Regional Lib District	NICKEL, Robbie L.	902
Wren Systems	NICKEL, Edgar B.	902

MONTE VISTA
Sargent Sch District	LUDWIG, Deborah M.	746

MONTROSE
Montrose County Sch District RE15	MACY, Edwin L.	758
Pathfinder Lib Syst	CAMPBELL, John D.	176

NEW CASTLE
Garfield County Pub Lib	CARYPIE, Renwick	421

NORTHGLENN
Adams County Pub Lib	DOBBS, Ann R.	307

PUEBLO
Arkansas Valley Regional Lib Srv System	JONES, Donna R.	612
Parkview Episcopal Medical Center	WILLIAMS, Alma	1341
Pueblo Community Coll	GARDNER, W J.	418
Pueblo County Sch District 70	DIRKSEN, Phyllis A.	305
Pueblo Lib District	BATES, Charles E.	63
Univ of Southern Colorado	GRATE, Jon F.	458
	MOFFEIT, Tony A.	852
	MOORE, Beverly B.	858

WALDEN
North Park Sch District	SWEET, Sally K.	1215

WESTMINSTER
Arabian Horse Trust	BOYD, Ruth E.	122

COLORADO (Cont'd)
WOODLAND PARK
Rampart Regional Lib District — LEITNER, Lavonne 714

CONNECTICUT
ANSONIA
Lower Naugatuck Valley Comunty Hlth Ctr — MARTIN, Walter F. 779
AVERY POINT
Southeastern Connecticut Lib Association — HOLLOWAY, Patricia W. 552
BERLIN
Berlin Board of Education — KATZ, Claire G. 630
BLOOMFIELD
Bloomfield Board of Education — CARLISLE, Carol A. 182
CIGNA Corp — CHEESEMAN, Bruce S. 204
Greenwich Lib — YARMAL, Ann 1378
BRANFORD
Yale Univ — KILLHEFFER, Robert E. 648
BRIDGEPORT
Bridgeport Hospital — STEMMER, Katherine R. ... 1186
Bridgeport Pub Lib — JOHMANN, Nancy 601
MINERVINO, Louise 846
MULAWKA, Chet 876
SLOMSKI, Monica J. 1150
Bridgeport Pub Schs — BERRYHILL, Ellen K. 90
City of Bridgeport — PALMQUIST, David W. 937
General Electric Co — FROST, Mary K. 406
Housatonic Community Coll — HARLOW, Aileen W. 502
Sacred Heart Univ — ROGERS, Mary E. 1050
Saint Vincent's Medical Center — GOERIG, Janet 443
Univ of Bridgeport — DELUCIA, Christina 290
FU, Theresa L. 407
HAMMOND, Harold A. 493
HUGHES, John M. 571
JOHNSON, Eric W. 604
MCELHANEY, William E. 804
PARISI, Judith A. 940
SATTERLUND, Lisa L. 1084
Wright Database Services — CONNOLLY, John F. 237
BRISTOL
Bristol Board of Education — LEAHY, Michael D. 707
Central High Sch — WARAKSA, Raymond P. 1303
City of Bristol — CALLAHAN, Helen H. 173
WILSON, Eleanor L. 1350
BROOKFIELD
Brookfield High Sch — SLONE, Eugenia F. 1150
BURLINGTON
Regional Sch District 10 — REILLY, Maureen E. 1020
CHESHIRE
Cheshire Pub Lib — POIRIER, Maria K. 980
WREGE, Ann S. 1370
Olin Corp — CAMPO, Lynn D. 177
CLINTON
Henry Carter Hill Lib Inc — CUMMINGS, Gary J. 264
COS COB
Hartley Film Foundation — HARTLEY, Elda E. 508
Mars & Co — ST. GEORGE, Susan M. ... 1075
CROMWELL
Town of Cromwell — BRANCIFORTE, Eileen G. ... 127
DANBURY
Connecticut State Lib — HORRIGAN, John J. 560
Grolier Educational Corp — HAYES, James L. 515
Leonard Burkat/Program Note Service — BURKAT, Leonard 160
Novo Laboratories Inc — CARNEGLIA, Anna L. 183
SAMUELS, Lois A. 1079
Union Carbide Corp — CONNER, Shirley D. 237
MARIANI, Carolyn A. 770
MCPHERSON, Mary A. 817
SHEA, Roseanne M. 1124
Western Connecticut State Univ — FOWLER, Louise D. 394
HURLEY, Trudy M. 577
LOOMIS, Mary K. 740
SHOLTZ, Katherine J. 1132
WARZALA, Martin L. 1307
DANIELSON
Killingly Junior High Sch — WEIGEL, James S. 1316

CONNECTICUT (Cont'd)
DARIEN
Darien Lib — BERRY, Louise P. 90
CARNAHAN, Anne D. 183
Darien Pub Sch System — GILBERT, Marion M. 433
SOUTHARD, Sarah T. 1169
Real Decisions Corp — COOKE, E P. 241
DERBY
Griffin Hospital — FINNUCAN, Louise A. 379
EAST HADDAM
Goodspeed Opera House — ROSENBURG, Betsy R. 1056
EAST HARTFORD
Pratt & Whitney — MOON, Mary G. 857
United Technologies Corp — MILLBROOKE, Anne 835
STEELE, Noreen O. 1184
WENDELL, Florence P. 1323
United Technologies Research Center — SIROIS, Valerie M. 1144
ENFIELD
Enfield Board of Education — DUBEAU, Marsha 321
FAIRFIELD
Fairfield Pub Lib — WARGO, Peggy M. 1305
Fairfield Univ — BRYAN, Barbara D. 151
COOMBS, Elisabeth G. 241
HAAG, Nancy R. 480
HEFZALLAH, Mona G. 521
General Electric Co — ESCARILLA, Jose G. 354
Sacred Heart Univ — KIJANKA, Dorothy M. 647
FARMINGTON
American Nuclear Insurers — SHERMAN, Dottie 1128
Farmington Village Green & Lib Assn — GIBSON, Barbara H. 431
Stauffer Chemical Co — EICKENHORST, Joanna W. . 339
Univ of Connecticut at Farmington — ARCARI, Ralph D. 30
RICHETELLE, Alberta L. ... 1030
WETMORE, Judith M. ... 1328
Univ of Connecticut Health Center — FREY, Barbara J. 402
LEVINE, Marion H. 720
Yale Univ — DEVINE, Marie E. 297
GALES FERRY
Gales Ferry Board of Education — HILLER, Catherine C. 541
GLASTONBURY
Futures Group — UBYSZ, Priscilla M. 1267
WILLSON, Katherine H. 1349
GREENWICH
AMAX Inc — DVORIN, Nancy T. 330
GRAYSON, Virginia S. 460
CNR Partners — STANKIEWICZ, Carol A. ... 1180
Greenwich High Sch — MARCHAND, Janet H. ... 768
Greenwich Lib — LUSHINGTON, Nolan 749
SKOP, Vera 1147
McPherson's America Inc — RICCOBONO, Joseph V. ... 1026
Penn Central Corporation — ZYGMONT, Carolyn A. 1392
Town of Greenwich — BIHLER, Charles H. 96
Wilson & McLane Inc — MCLANE, John F. 813
GROTON
Groton Public Lib & Information Center — REITER, Elizabeth A. 1022
Southeastern Connecticut Lib Association — BENN, James R. 81
US Navy — WILLIAMS, Edwin E. 1343
HAMDEN
American Worlds Books — SMITH, Nolan E. 1159
Hamden Lib — MAINIERO, Elizabeth T. 761
Quinnipiac Coll — LANG, Norma F. 695
Southen Connecticut Lib Council — HUPP, Sharon W. 577
Yale Univ — SAMUEL, Harold E. 1079
HARTFORD
Aetna Life & Casualty — DOMINIANNI, Beth S. 310
PORTER, Kathryn W. 985
TAYLOR, Melissa P. 1227
WEINSTEIN, Daniel L. 1318
Archdiocese of Hartford — JASKEL, Mary A. 595
Burgdorf Health Center — CONRAD, Celia B. 238
Cahill Larkin & Co — SHORE, Julia M. 1132
CIGNA Corp — BROQUE, Suzanne 141
LIU, Jessie 734
Connecticut Department of Education — HALE, Robert G. 485
Connecticut Historical Society — SCHMIDT, Alesandra M. ... 1095
WAIT, Gary E. 1293
WILKIE, Everett C. 1340
WILLARD, Anne H. 1341

CONNECTICUT (Cont'd)
  HARTFORD (Cont'd)

Connecticut Lib Association	SIMPSON, Jeanne	1142
Connecticut State Lib	AKEROYD, Richard G.	9
	BURGER, Leslie B.	159
	JERNIGAN, Denise D.	599
	JONES, Mark H.	614
	PRESEMPERE, Dominic A.	991
	SCHUTT, Cheryl M.	1103
Episcopal Diocese of Connecticut	CARROON, Robert G.	187
Hartford Courant	MCKULA, Kathleen S.	812
Hartford Hospital	CORCORAN, Virginia H.	246
	LAMB, Gertrude	690
Hartford Insurance Group	KLEMARCZYK, Laurice D.	660
	SMITH, Lydia K.	1157
	WOODWORTH, Bonnie J.	1368
Hartford Pub Lib	BERBERICH, Patricia L.	84
	BURGAN, John S.	159
	KING, Judith D.	651
	MARTIN, Vernon E.	778
	SCHULTZE, Salvatrice G.	1102
Industrial Risk Insurers	SASSO, Patricia A.	1083
Infotelligence	NEUFELD, Irving H.	897
Northeast Utilities Service Co	JOHNSON, Doris E.	603
Robinson & Cole	MATTHEWSON, David S.	786
Saint Francis Hospital	WILCOX, Carolyn G.	1338
Sorokin & Sorokin PC	BARNUM, Deborah C.	58
The Travelers Insurance Cos	ORLOSKE, Margaret Q.	926
Trinity Coll	BUNKER, Patricia J.	157
	KAIMOWITZ, Jeffery H.	622
	KNAPP, Peter J.	663
	MCKINNEY, Linda R.	812
	TALIT, Lynn	1221
	WARZALA, Allison B.	1307
Univ of Connecticut at Hartford	BENAMATI, Dennis C.	79
	STONE, Dennis J.	1197
Wadsworth Atheneum	MCNULTY, Karen	817

  KENT

Kent Lib Association	CUSTER, Deborah P.	267

  LITCHFIELD

Litchfield Pub Schs	VAN LEER, Jerilyn M.	1276

  MADISON

Sound View Press	FALK, Peter H.	362

  MANCHESTER

Manchester Community Coll	NATALE, Barbara G.	889
Manchester Memorial Hospital	GLUCK, Jeannine C.	442

  MERIDAN

Meriden Pub Lib	BOGATZ, June H.	110

  MIDDLEBURY

General Datacomm Industries	WIEHN, John F.	1336

  MIDDLETOWN

American Lib Association	BECK, Arthur R.	71
	SABOSIK, Patricia E.	1073
Choice Magazine	BALAY, Robert E.	50
Connecticut Department of Education	WHITE, Charles R.	1330
Connecticut State Lib	MERRILL, Mary G.	827
Connecticut Valley Hospital	ASBELL, Mildred S.	35
Middlesex Memorial Hospital	BRECK, Evelyn M.	131
Middletown Board of Education	POLOMSKI, Linda	982
NdS Information Consultants	DOUVILLE, Judith A.	314
Russell Lib	FERRO, Frank J.	374
	HERMAN, Felicia G.	531
	PORTER, Stuart T.	985
Wesleyan Univ	ADAMS, J R.	5
	FARRINGTON, James	365
	KONERDING, Erhard F.	670
	OSTROFF, Cynthia R.	929
Xavier High Sch	SAVAGE, Judith G.	1085

  MILFORD

IBM Corp	PRATT, Allan D.	989
Milford Hospital	WESTBROOK, Patricia C.	1326
Milford Pub Lib	BARGAR, Arthur W.	56

  MYSTIC

Groton Board of Education	LACKORE, Lois P.	686
Mystic Seaport Museum	STONE, Ellen C.	1197

  NAUGATUCK

Uniroyal Chemical Co Inc	HARMON, Patricia A.	502

CONNECTICUT (Cont'd)
  NEW BRITAIN

Central Connecticut State Univ	KASCUS, Marie A.	628
	PACKER, Joan G.	934
	TEMPLE, Leroy E.	1230
Farmington Pub Schs	LAWRENCE, Scott W.	705
St Thomas Aquinas High Sch	ANDRONIK, Catherine M.	27

  NEW CANAAN

New Canaan Lib	BLALOCK, Louise	103
	BUSCH, Kathleen M.	165
New Canaan Pub Schools	SENATOR, Rochelle B.	1115
News Bank Inc	ANDREWS, Chris C.	26
NewsBank Inc	DYER, Carolyn A.	330
Readex Microprint Corp	JONES, Daniel S.	612

  NEW HAVEN

Albertus Magnus Coll	KELLY, Thomas A.	638
	LYNCH, M W.	751
ArmTeis	CRUTCHER, Hope H.	262
Beinecke Lib	WYNNE, Marjorie G.	1375
City of New Haven	HAYNAM, Kenneth W.	516
Connecticut State Lib	SULLIVAN, Martha J.	1208
DATA Inc	GONZALEZ, Suzanna S.	448
Hospital of Saint Raphael	WALES, Patricia L.	1294
ITT Advanced Technology Center	DENMAN, Monica K.	292
New Haven Colony Historical Society	KOEL, Maria O.	667
New Haven Free Pub Lib	CLENDINNING, David	221
	ENSEL, Ellen H.	350
	KRITEMEYER, Ann C.	679
	ROSS, Carole L.	1058
R W Smith--Bookseller	SMITH, Raymond W.	1159
Southern Connecticut State Univ	CLARIE, Thomas C.	216
	HEINRITZ, Fred J.	522
	HILL, John R.	540
	HOLMER, Paul L.	553
	HUGHES, Frances M.	571
	KUSACK, James M.	685
	PROSTANO, Emanuel T.	995
	STODDARD, Charles E.	1196
	TRIOLO, Victor A.	1257
	WALTER, Kenneth G.	1300
Southern New England Telecommunications	HARRISON, Burgess A.	506
Southern New England Telephone Co	MACDOUGAL, Gary N.	754
	STRAKA, Kathy M.	1199
Tyler Cooper & Alcorn	LUBIN, Joan S.	745
William Reese Co	REESE, William S.	1016
Yale Center for British Art	FRIEDMAN, Joan M.	404
Yale Law Sch	COHEN, Morris L.	228
Yale Univ	ABELL, Millicent D.	2
	ARAKAWA, Steven R.	30
	BERSON, Bella Z.	90
	BOLLIER, John A.	112
	BROOKS, Robert E.	140
	BROWN, William E.	148
	COLLIER, Bonnie	232
	CROOKER, Cynthia L.	260
	FERGUSON, Elizabeth E.	372
	FERNANDEZ, Nenita	373
	FRANKLIN, Ralph W.	398
	FRYER, Regina K.	407
	HAHN, Boksoon	483
	HELENIUS, Majlen	523
	HUNENKO, Maria P.	574
	IANNUZZI, Patricia A.	581
	ICHINOSE, Mitsuko	581
	JARAMILLO, Ellen M.	594
	KANEKO, Hideo	625
	KAPLAN, Diane E.	626
	KELLER, Michael A.	635
	KELSEY, Mary J.	639
	KOEL, Ake I.	667
	LAEUCHLI, Ann J.	687
	LA FOGG, Mary C.	688
	LAWRENCE, Carol A.	704
	LOWELL, Gerald R.	744
	MANDOUR, Cecile A.	765
	MCCORKLE, Barbara B.	798
	MONTEE, Monty L.	856
	PARKS, Stephen	943
	PELTIER, Karen V.	955

CONNECTICUT (Cont'd)
  NEW HAVEN (Cont'd)
  Yale Univ

	PETERSON, Sandra K.	964
	PETERSON, Stephen L.	964
	ROBERTS, Susanne F.	1041
	ROGERS, Rutherford D.	1050
	SIGGINS, Jack A.	1137
	SILVERSTEIN, Louis H.	1139
	SPURGEON, Kathy R.	1176
	STEVENS, Hannah M.	1190
	STUEHRENBERG, Paul F.	1205
	SULLIVAN, Maureen	1208
	TIRRO, Frank P.	1247
	TRAINER, Karin A.	1253
	WALKER, Robin G.	1296
	WARREN, Richard	1306
	WOODS, Frances B.	1367

NEW LONDON
Connecticut Coll

	JOHNSON, Carolyn A.	602
	ROGERS, Brian D.	1049
	SORENSEN, Pamela	1168
	TARANOW, Gerda	1223
	WALDEN, Katherine G.	1294

Connecticut State Lib	BURKE, Jane D.	160
Edgerton Elem Sch	DAIGNEAULT, Audrey I.	270
Naval Underwater Systems Center	CAMPBELL, Barbara A.	176
New London Board of Education	MCKISSICK, Mabel F.	812

NEW MILFORD
Canterbury Sch	BOLSTER, Kathryn	113

NEW PRESTON
Trebizond Rare Books	BENEDICT, Williston R.	80

NEWINGTON
Loctite Corp	LERITZ, M K.	717

NEWTOWN
Connecticut Dept of Mental Health	KRUK, Pauline A.	680

NIANTIC
East Lyme Pub Lib	DEAKYNE, William J.	283

NORFOLK
Norfolk Pub Lib	SCHIMMEL, Louise S.	1093

NOROTON
Pathfinder Productions Inc	ECKRICH, Herman J.	335

NORTH HAVEN
Town of North Haven	BALDINI, Lois D.	51
	GLICK, Kenneth W.	441

NORWALK
Burndy Lib	WEIMERSKIRCH, Philip J.	1317
IBM Corp	LOWENSTEIN, Richard A.	744
Norwalk Board of Education	KNOPP, Marie L.	665
	LAPOLT, Margaret B.	697
	SELVERSTONE, Harriet S.	1114
Norwalk Community Coll	BAYLES, Carmen L.	67
	PIKUL, Diane M.	973
Norwalk Pub Lib	VAN DYKE, Aase S.	1275
Purdue Frederick Co	WALSH, Kathryn A.	1299
Time Sensitive Delivery Guide	SHARPE, Murem S.	1122
Videolog Communications	BRIGISH, Alan P.	136

NORWICH
State of Connecticut	TRAVER, Julia M.	1254

OLD GREENWICH
Old Greenwich Elementary Sch	THORNBURG, Joan S.	1242

OLD SAYBROOK
Town of Old Saybrook	NOVAK, Elaine L.	910

RIDGEFIELD
Alice Norton Pub Relations	NORTON, Alice	910
Behringer Ingelheim Pharmaceuticals Inc	HENTZ, Margaret B.	530
Boehringer Ingelheim Pharmaceuticals Inc	MCMASTER, Deborah L.	815
	MOYNIHAN, Mary B.	874
	SUPEAU, Cynthia	1210
The Jelem Co	MILSTEAD, Jessica L.	845
Ridgefield Board of Education	SULLI, Gerard C.	1207
Schlumberger Doll Research	BANKS, Mary E.	54

ROCKY HILL
Connecticut Department of Transportation	JUKNIS, Ann M.	619

SANDY HOOK
Univ of Connecticut at Storrs	JAY, Hilda L.	596

CONNECTICUT (Cont'd)
SHELTON
Richardson-Vicks Inc	SILVERMAN, Susanne	1139
	WEISS, Barbara M.	1319

SIMSBURY
Simsbury Board of Education	MICHAUD, Noreen R.	832

SOUTHPORT
Laurence Witten Rare Books	WITTEN, Laurence	1358
Pequot Lib	KEMP, Thomas J.	639

STAMFORD
American Connection	BERLIET, Nathalie B.	87
American Cyanamid Co	MOUNTFORD, Eve	873
	REITER, Martha B.	1022
Champion International Corp	COLUCCI, Mildred A.	234
Clairol Inc	KOLBIN, Ronda I.	669
Comp-U-Card International Inc	WALSH, Mark L.	1300
Connecticut State Lib	FAAS, Caroline	360
	O'BRIEN, Doris J.	914
Digital Information Group	ELWELL, Christopher S.	347
	SILVERSTEIN, Jeffrey S.	1139
Donnelley Marketing Information	HILL, Gary L.	539
Ferguson Lib	ARNOLD, Arleen B.	33
	DIMATTIA, Ernest A.	304
	FERRARI, Kathleen M.	373
	GOLOMB, Katherine A.	447
	ROCKMAN, Connie C.	1046
	WILLIAMS, Judy R.	1344
Gartner Group Inc	LAZINGER, Susan S.	706
	MASTERS, Kathy B.	782
Lloyd S Maritime Data Network	PFISTER, Lawrence T.	966
Maclean Hunter Media	PALMER, Shirley	937
Olin Corp	STANYON, Kelly	1181
Russell Reynolds Associates Inc	GAMBER, Deborah D.	416
St Joseph Hospital	LIEBERMAN, Lucille N.	726
Stamford High Sch	SERGEL, Carol K.	1116
Stamford Hospital	FARADAY, Joanna	363
Univ of Connicticut at Stamford	GILLIES, Nancy H.	436
Xerox Corp	ORRICO, James T.	926

STORRS
Univ of Connecticut at Storrs	BALMER, Mary	53
	BOGNAR, Dorothy M.	111
	EMBARDO, Ellen E.	347
	FORMAN, Camille L.	390
	JENSEN, Joan W.	598
	JIMERSON, Randall C.	600
	KAGAN, Alfred	621
	KLINE, Nancy M.	661
	MCDONALD, John P.	802
	MERRILL-OLDHAM, Jan	827
	ROLLIN, Marian B.	1051
	SCHIMMELPFENG, Richard H.	1093
	SCOTT, Joseph W.	1107
	SCURA, Georgia A.	1109
	STEVENS, Norman D.	1190

STRATFORD
Bibliomation Inc	ROTH, Alison C.	1059
Stratford Lib Association	JACOB, William	589
United Technologies Corp	SMALLWOOD, James R.	1151

TOLLAND
NERAC Inc	SENKUS, Linda J.	1115

TOLLARD
NERAC Inc	WILDE, Daniel U.	1338

TORRINGTON
Litchfield County Center for Higher Educ	JOY, Patricia L.	618

TRUMBULL
Cheseborough-Ponds Inc	SUPRYNOWICZ, Mary M.	1210
Town of Trumbull	BIRCH, Grace M.	97

WALLINGFORD
Bristol-Myers Products	MCGREGOR, M C.	808
Gaylord Hospital	EBINGER, Meada G.	334
	PENN, Elinor K.	957
Wallingford Pub Lib	SCHERER, Leslie C.	1092

WASHINGTON
Bancroft-Parkman Inc	LEAB, Katharine K.	706
Gunn Memorial Lib Board of Directors	COSTA, Shirley W.	249

CONNECTICUT (Cont'd)

WATERBURY

Carmody & Torrance	HODGES, Ann C. 546
Carrington Co	CARRINGTON, Virginia F. 186
City of Waterbury	YOUNG, Marianne F. 1382
Con Diesel Mobile Equipment	BARNES, Denise M. 57
Holy Cross High Sch	PARIKH, Kaumudi H. 940
	RECTOR, Wendell H. 1013
Region One Cooperating Lib Service Unit	FLANAGAN, Leo N. 383
	LOW, Jocelyn L. 743
Univ of Connecticut at Waterbury	SWIFT, Janet B. 1216

WATERFORD

Monte Cristo Coll	MCDONALD, Lois E. 803

WATERTOWN

Watertown High Sch	COGLISER, Luann L. 227

WEST HARTFORD

Focus Research Systems Inc	CHICHESTER, Gerald C. 208
	TALSKY, Gene R. 1221
Univ of Connecticut at Hartford	NORONHA, Marilyn S. 909
Univ of Connecticut at West Hartford	BRADBERRY, Richard P. 125
	LI, Hong C. 724
	MANNING, Beverley J. 766
Univ of Hartford	MILLER, Jean J. 838
	PIERCE, Anne L. 971

WEST HAVEN

City of West Haven	ABBOTT, Kathleen A. 1

WEST REDDING

Joel Barlow High Sch	CROWLEY, John D. 261
John Read Middle Sch	MITCHELL, Lucy A. 849

WESTON

Online Inc	PEMBERTON, Jeffery K. 956

WESTPORT

Greenwood Press	SIVE, Mary R. 1144
Lib Consulting Services	SCHWARZ, Shirlee 1105
Meckler Corp	MECKLER, Alan M. 820
Save the Children	FAESY, Nancy N. 361
Westport Board of Education	FISHER, Margery M. 381
Westport Pub Lib	BOHRER, Karen M. 111
	FADER, Ellen G. 360
	GORDON, Thelma S. 452
	POUNDSTONE, Sally H. 987
	WAGNER, George L. 1291
The Westport Publishing Group	RIBAROFF, Margaret F. ... 1026
Westport Research Group	REISMAN, Sydelle S. 1021

WETHERSFIELD

Donohue/McCaughtry Inc	DONOHUE, Christine N. 311
	MCCAUGHTRY, Dorothy H. . 795
	MOON, Peter S. 858
Wethersfield Board of Education	MEUCCI, Victoria F. 829
Wethersfield Pub Lib	KIRKPATRICK, Elizabeth M. . 655

WILLIMANTIC

Connecticut State Lib	VANDERLYKE, Barbara A. . 1274
Eastern Connecticut Lib Association	DAW, May B. 282
Eastern Connecticut State Univ	HOOSE, Beverly D. 557
	MOORHEAD, Kenneth E. 862
	NEWMYER, Joann C. 900
Mohegan Community Coll	KASPER, Barbara 629

WILTON

D&B Computing Service Inc	LEE, Frank B. 709
Dunsnet	MACHALE, Jesslyn C. 755
Wilton Lib Association Inc	GOLRICK, Michael A. 447

WINDSOR

Capitol Region Lib Council	PARKS, Amy N. 943
	SARGENT, Dency C. 1083
	URICCHIO, William J. 1269
Combustion Engineering Inc	CARTLEDGE, Ellen G. 190
	GAGNE, Susan P. 412

WINDSOR LOCKS

The Dexter Corp	MASTERS, Fred N. 782
Windsor Locks Public Lib Inc	HUBBS, Ronald B. 568

WOODBRIDGE

Research Publications	BOGENSCHNEIDER, Duane R. 110
	DEL CERVO, Diane M. 289
	GREENWAY, Helen B. 465
	KRAMER, Sheldon I. 675

DELAWARE

DOVER

Capital Sch District	FITZPATRICK, Barbara L. ... 382
City of Dover	MILLER, Paula J. 841
Delaware State Coll	COONS, Daniel E. 242
State of Delaware	TRYON, Roy H. 1260
	WYCHE, Louise E. 1374

FRANKFORD

Vanitch	HITCHENS, Howard B. 544

LAUREL

Laurel Pub Lib	STRANGE, Elizabeth B. 1200

LEWES

Cape Henlopen Sch District	ROBERTS, Judith M. 1040
Univ of Delaware	HALL, Alice W. 486

MILFORD

Milford Sch District	CARPENTER, Carole H. 184

NEW CASTLE

New Castle Pub Lib	BROWN, Sarah C. 147

NEWARK

Christina Sch District	BROWN, Atlanta T. 142
	MYERS, Victoria B. 885
	THORNTON, Alice J. 1242
Delaware Technical and Community Coll	TRUMBORE, Jean F. 1259
E I DuPont de Nemours & Co Inc	SELZER, Nancy S. 1114
Medical Center of Delaware	CHASTAIN-WARHEIT, Christine C. 203
New Castle County Lib Services	BEAMER, Lisa M. 69
	PUFFER, Yvonne L. 997
Stuart Pharmaceuticals	DANIEL, Alfred I. 272
Univ of Delaware	BRYNTESON, Susan 152
	CASON, Maidel K. 193
	CHOU, Vivian M. 210
	CLAYTON, John M. 220
	EVERETT, Amy E. 358
	GLOGOFF, Stuart J. 441
	KNIGHT, Rebecca C. 664
	PUFFER, Nathaniel H. 997
	ROBBINS, Rachel H. 1039
	RUDISELL, Carol A. 1065
	SCHREYER, Alice D. 1100
	SHAW, Richard N. 1124
	ULRICH, Sue 1268
	WANG, Margaret K. 1303
	WOLFF, Stephen G. 1361
	YOUNG, Kathryn A. 1382

ODESSA

Corbit-Calloway Memorial Lib	JAMISON, Susan C. 593

WILMINGTON

Alfred I Du Pont Institute	NOLTING, Carl E. 908
Breton & Associates Inc	BRETON, Ernest J. 133
Catholic Diocese of Wilmington	TRIBOLETTI, Kathleen 1256
Concord Pike Lib	TITUS, H M. 1247
Delaware Academy of Medicine	ELLIOTT, Gwendolyn T. 344
	PIFALO, Victoria 972
Delaware Law Sch Lib	PAUL, Jacqueline R. 949
Delaware Technical and Community Coll	ABED, Donna M. 2
E I DuPont de Nemours & Co Inc	GRILLO, Anthony L. 470
	MORTON, Dorothy J. 870
Family Court of the State of Delaware	FRANCIS, Diane S. 396
Goldey Beacom Coll	BEACH, Rose M. 68
	COE, Gloria M. 226
Hercules Inc	HENDERSON, Joanne L. 526
ICI Americas Inc	MECRAY, Freida S. 820
	THOMAN, Nancy L. 1236
MARLF	HUKILL, Jane E. 572
New Castle County Lib Services	SIMMONS, Elizabeth M. ... 1139
News Journal Co	WALKER, Charlotte J. 1295
Prickett Jones Elliott Kristol et al	YALLER, Loretta O. 1376
Richards Lauton & Finger	WINSTEAD, Jean D. 1356
Stuart Pharmaceuticals	DRUKKER, Alexander E. 320
	JOHNSON, Hilary C. 605
Tower Hill Sch	MCCARTHY, Carrol B. 794
	MINNICH, Nancy P. 846
Ursuline Academy High Sch	ASTORGA, Alicia M. 37
	RECHNITZ, Harriet L. 1013
The Wilmington Institute	BURDASH, David H. 158
Wilmington Institute Lib	MANUEL, Larry L. 767
Wilmington Lib	TITUS, Barbara K. 1247

DELAWARE (Cont'd)
WINTERTHUR
Joseph Downs Manuscript & Micofilm
Coll — ADAMS, Barbara M. 4
Winterthur Museum — MCKENNEY, Kathryn K. 811
THOMPSON, Neville M. ... 1241

DISTRICT OF COLUMBIA
APO WASHINGTON
US Army in Italy — BURNS, Dean A. 162
WASHINGTON
Academy for Educational
Development — BETTS, Ardith M. 92
MARA, Ruth M. 768
TIFFT, Jeanne D. 1244
Administrative Office of the US
Courts — ERICSON, Richard J. 353
HARRIS, Linda S. 505
THOMAS, Patricia A. 1238
Aerospace Industries Assn of
America Inc — RUTEMILLER, Annette M. ... 1070
Am Assn for the Advancement of
Science — ALDRICH, Michele L. 11
American Association of Retired
Persons — HARTZ, Mary K. 509
LATOUR, Catherine M. 701
LOVAS, Paula M. 743
RAFFERTY, Eve 1003
TABER, Sally A. 1219
American Assn of State Colls & Univs — STOCKTON, Ken R. 1196
American Association of Univ Women — MCGAUGHRAN, Roberta
W. 805
American Banker - Bond Buyer — TRIGAUX, Robert 1256
American Bankers Association — GERVINO, Joan 429
WENGEL, Linda 1324
American Chemical Society — HEARTY, John A. 519
Am Coll of Obstetricians &
Gynecologists — MEIKAMP, Kathie D. 822
VANHINE, Pamela M. 1275
American Council on Education — FONT, Mary M. 388
American Institute of Architects — KIMBERLIN, Robert L. 649
ROMEO, Sheryl R. 1052
American Lib Association — COOKE, Eileen D. 241
HEANUE, Anne A. 518
American Medical Association — BANKS, Jane L. 54
American Petroleum Institute — SCHUERMANN, Lois J. 1101
American Pharmaceutical Association — KUTTY, Lalitha M. 685
American Society for Information
Science — MORRISON, Steve 868
RATH, Charla M. 1009
RESNIK, Linda I. 1024
American Univ — CHASE, Linda S. 203
KEHOE, Patrick E. 634
SANDIQUE-OWENS, Amelia
A. 1080
ZICH, Joanne A. 1388
Archdiocese of Washington — BARRY, Paul J. 60
Architect of the Capitol — CARTLEDGE, Connie L. 190
Armed Forces Institute of Pathology — PATEL, Patricia C. 947
Army & Navy Club — SPONDER, Dorothy R. 1175
Arnold & Porter — SEELE, Ronald E. 1111
SHELAR, James W. 1125
Aspen Systems Corp — LOMAX, Denise W. 738
Association of American Publishers
Inc — RISHER, Carol A. 1036
Association of American Railroads — KOENEMAN, Joyce W. 668
Association of Research Libs — BARRETT, G J. 59
JUROW, Susan R. 620
REED-SCOTT, Jutta R. 1015
Assn of Teachers of Preventive
Medicine — ANGLE, Joanne G. 28
Beckerman Associates Inc — BECKERMAN, George 72
Benjamin Franklin Univ — LEWIS, Robert J. 724
BNA Inc — JENKINS, John A. 597
TAYLOR, George A. 1226
Bd of Governors of the Federal Rsv
Syst — CLARY, Ann R. 219
RATESH, Ioana 1009
VINCENT, Susan R. 1284
Broadcast Pioneers Lib — HEINZ, Catharine F. 522

DISTRICT OF COLUMBIA (Cont'd)
WASHINGTON (Cont'd)
Brookings Institution — FAHERTY, Robert L. 361
Brownstein Zeidman & Schoner — COUSINS, Richard F. 252
Bureau of National Affairs Inc — BALL, Thomas W. 52
DEGLER, Stanley E. 287
KING, Kamla J. 651
KLEIMAN, Helen M. 659
MODLIN, Marilyn J. 851
PILK, Emily G. 973
Business International Corp — MIDDLETON, Carl H. 833
CAPCON Lib Network — REYNOLDS, Dennis J. 1025
WILLSON, Elizabeth 1349
Carnegie Endowment for Intl Peace — LOWENTHAL, Jane E. 744
Casson Calligaro & Mutryn — JOHNSON, Maria S. 607
Catholic Univ of America — AVERSA, Elizabeth S. 41
BELLARDO, Trudi 78
CORTEZ, Edwin M. 248
HORNE, Esther E. 560
PREER, Jean L. 990
ROVELSTAD, Mathilde V. .. 1062
STANN, Patsy H. 1180
STONE, Elizabeth W. 1197
TOOHEY, Anne K. 1250
Charles E Simon & Co — GREEN, Randall N. 462
GRISDELA, Margaret 471
Children's Hospital National Medical
Ctr — INGERSOLL, Lyn L. 582
Cole & Corette — MCDONALD, Michael L. 803
Comsat Technology Products Co — BOYER, Nate 123
Congressional Quarterly Inc — ALITO, Martha A. 13
VEATCH, Laurie L. 1280
Congressional Research Services — BAUMGARDNER, Sandra A. .. 66
FLAM, Floris 383
Congressman Bill Archer — CARLSON, Julia F. 182
Consortium of Univs — LEMKE, Darrell H. 715
Coopers & Lybrand — HENEKS, Julia A. 528
Corcoran Gallery of Art — KOVACS, Katherine M. 673
Council on Lib Resources Inc — DEAN, Barbara C. 283
HAAS, Warren J. 480
KEMPNER, Maximilian 639
MARCUM, Deanna B. 769
THOMPSON, Mary A. 1240
Covington and Burling — MAHAR, Ellen P. 760
Crowell & Moring — CALLINAN, Ellen M. 173
Data Resources — FELMY, John C. 370
Daughters of the American Revolution — CRAWFORD, Elva B. 256
Davis Polk & Wardwell — MARTIN, Kathleen S. 777
Decision Resources Corp — CARR, Sallyann 186
Defense/Intelligence Agency — CRANOR, Alice T. 255
Dickstein Shapiro & Morin — DURAKO, Frances G. 328
DC General Hospital — MOORE, Sara L. 861
District of Columbia Pub Lib — BERGAN, Helen J. 85
CIMERMANIS, Ilze V. 214
DEANE, Roxanna 284
DOPP, Bonnie J. 312
FRANKLIN, Hardy R. 397
HAGEMEYER, Alice L. 483
JOHNSON, Brenda V. 602
JONES, Elin D. 612
MOLUMBY, Lawrence 854
RAPHAEL, Mary E. 1008
RAY, Kathryn C. 1011
ROBINSON, Cathy A. 1043
SALVADORE, Maria B. 1078
SWEENEY, June D. 1215
THOMPSON-JOYNER, Rita
S. 1241
TSCHERNY, Elena 1260
WALLACE, Michael T. 1298
WASHINGTON, Sigrid M. .. 1308
District of Columbia Pub Schs — EDWARDS, Andrea Y. 337
HARRIS, Marie 505
JENKINS, Lydia E. 597
LITTLEJOHN, Grace M. 734
MANOR, Lawanda 767
MOORE, Virginia B. 861
ROBINSON, Sandra N. 1044

DISTRICT OF COLUMBIA (Cont'd)
WASHINGTON (Cont'd)

Dominican House of Studies	NITZ, Andrew M.	905
	RZECZKOWSKI, Eugene M.	1072
	VANDEGRIFT, J R.	1273
Dumbarton Oaks Research Lib	BYERS, Laura T.	168
	VASLEF, Irene	1279
Dun & Bradstreet Corp	FRIEND, Gary I.	404
	MCGINTY, James P.	806
Edison Electric Institute	FARKAS, Susan A.	364
	JOHNSON, Jacqueline B.	605
Environmental Law Institute	LARSEN, Lynda L.	698
The Epstein Collection	VAN NIMMEN, Jane	1276
Executive Office of the US President	HOTCHKISS, Mary A.	562
	MCCOY-LARSON, Sandra	799
Export-Import Bank of the US	MCGILL, Theodora	806
	POSNIAK, John R.	985
Federal Deposit Insurance Corp	LEWIS, Noreen B.	724
	SMITH, Kathleen S.	1156
Federal Trade Commission	PERELLA, Susanne B.	958
FEDLINK	BEACHELL, Doria M.	68
Foley & Lardner	BARDE, Karla I.	56
Folger Shakespeare Lib	DOGGETT, Rachel H.	308
	KNACHEL, Philip A.	663
	KRIVATSY, Nati H.	679
	YEANDLE, Laetitia	1378
Food & Drug Administration	MCGOWAN, Anna T.	807
Food Marketing Institute	MCBRIDE, Barbara L.	792
Foster Associates Inc	BLANDAMER, Ann W.	103
Foundation of the Federal Bar Assn	FLYNN, Richard M.	387
Furash & Co	O'BRIEN, Kathleen	914
Gale Research Co	MISSAR, Margaret M.	847
Gallaudet Univ	CHANG, Helen S.	200
	DAY, John M.	282
	HARRINGTON, Thomas R.	504
	HURLEY, Faith P.	577
	LAWTON, Bethany L.	705
Gannett News Media Services	WOODHULL, Nancy	1366
Gen Conference of Seventh-day Adventists	SWEETLAND, Loraine F.	1215
General Conference/Seventh-Day Adventist	YOST, F D.	1381
George Washington Univ	APOSTLE, Lynne M.	29
	BADER, Shelley	44
	BARTHELL, Daniel W.	61
	DEUTSCH, James I.	296
	HEAD, Anita K.	518
	HOLLYFIELD, Diane S.	552
	KELLER, William B.	636
	LONG, Caroline C.	739
	MACEWEN, Virginia B.	755
	MARTIN, Elaine R.	776
	NIBLEY, Elizabeth B.	901
	PORTER, Suzanne	985
	ROGERS, Sharon J.	1050
	SANCHEZ, Jose L.	1079
	STEBELMAN, Scott D.	1183
	THOMPSON, Laurie L.	1240
	UNVER, Amira V.	1269
Georgetown Univ	BARRINGER, George M.	59
	BEDARD, Laura A.	73
	BEDARD, Laura A.	73
	BRAVY, Gary J.	130
	BROERING, Naomi C.	139
	CHAMBERS, Bettye T.	198
	CHEVERIE, Joan F.	207
	COLWELL, Carolyn J.	234
	DELANCEY, James F.	288
	DENHAM, Maryanne H.	292
	DOWLING, Shelley L.	316
	HELMINSKI, James C.	525
	JACKSON, Elisabeth S.	587
	JOINER, Mary J.	610
	KELLY, Mark M.	638
	MARSHALL, David L.	774
	MAXON, William N.	787
	NAINIS, Linda	886
	NOLEN, Anita L.	908
	OAKLEY, Robert L.	913
	POSTAR, Adeen J.	986

DISTRICT OF COLUMBIA (Cont'd)
WASHINGTON (Cont'd)

Georgetown Univ		
	REITH, Louis J.	1022
	REYNOLDS, Jon K.	1025
	SERVERINO, Roberto	1116
	SHAIMES, Karen	1119
	SMITH, Elizabeth W.	1154
	STACEY, Kathleen M.	1177
Gibson Dunn & Crutcher	DICKSON, Constance P.	301
Golembe Associates	GALLUP, Jane H.	415
Government of the District of Columbia	PROVINE, Dorothy S.	996
Groom & Nordberg Chartered	GREENE, Danielle L.	463
Group Health Association of America	SWANBERG, Lisa A.	1213
Harcourt Brace Jovanovich	CAROW, Marsha	184
Hogan & Hartson	DUVALL, John E.	329
Holy Trinity Sch	MORIARTY, Ann	865
Howard Univ	ACKERMAN, F C.	3
	BATTLE, Thomas C.	65
	HAITH, Dorothy M.	484
	HO, James K.	545
	JEFFERSON, Karen L.	596
	LEONARD, Angela M.	716
	MCCRAY, Maceo E.	800
	RICHARDSON, Deborra A.	1029
	SMITH, Clara M.	1153
	WRIGHT, Arthuree M.	1370
Howrey & Simon	BEALL, Barbara A.	68
	FELDMAN, Ellen S.	369
Hunton & Williams	FUTRELL, Iva M.	411
Independent Sector	BOHLEN, Jeanne L.	111
Information Consultants Inc	REGAN, William J.	1017
Information Inc	WEATHERSBY, Anne	1312
Information Industry Association	ALLEN, Kenneth B.	15
	ANGERMAN, Judith	27
	ATKIN, Michael I.	37
	CAUGHMAN, Alison Y.	195
	CUNNINGHAM, Linda	265
	PEYTON, David	966
	ZURKOWSKI, Paul G.	1391
Info Management	FREEMAN, Carla	400
Information Resources Management Service	CARR, Frank J.	185
	MCDONOUGH, Francis A.	803
	NEUSTADT, Margaret L.	897
Information Systems Consultants Inc	BOSS, Richard W.	117
Informative Design Group Inc	DAWSON, Barbara J.	282
Intelsat	LIU, Rosa	734
Intl Food Policy Research Institute	KLOSKY, Patricia W.	662
International Monetary Fund	ARANDA-COODOU, Patricio	30
	CUMMING, Leighton H.	264
	FRIERSON, Eleanor G.	404
	TURNER, Susan A.	1265
International Thomson	TAFT, James R.	1219
International Trade Commission	SCHNEIDER, Hennie R.	1097
Joint Center for Political Studies	PILGRIM, Auriel J.	973
	SYLVESTER, Carol	1217
Jones Day Reavis & Pogue	SHEELER, Harva L.	1125
Kirkpatrick & Lockhart	DATTALO, Elmo F.	275
Kluwer	EVERTS, Arjaan	359
Kutak Rock & Campbell	HARBISON, John H.	499
Labat-Anderson Inc	MCNAMARA, Emma J.	816
	PUGH, Thurman A.	997
Leffall Enterprises Inc	LEFFALL, Dolores C.	712
Legi-Slate Inc	GROVE, Curtis C.	473
Lewin & Associates Inc	ELLIOT, Hugh	343
	FEINBERG, Beryl L.	368
Lib of Congress	AGENBROAD, James E.	7
	ALBIN, Michael W.	10
	ALEXANDER, Virginia A.	12
	ANDERSON, Gillian B.	23
	ANDERSON, John M.	23
	AUSTIN, Judith P.	40
	AUSTIN, Monique C.	40
	AVDOYAN, Levon	41
	AVRAM, Henriette D.	42
	BARTLEY, Linda K.	61
	BASA, Eniko M.	62
	BEALL, Julianne	69

DISTRICT OF COLUMBIA (Cont'd)
WASHINGTON (Cont'd)
Lib of Congress

BEAN, Charles W. 69
BEATON, Barbara E. 70
BELLEFONTAINE, Arnold G. . . 78
BENJAMIN, Marilyn 81
BERNARD, Patrick S. 88
BLIXRUD, Julia C. 105
BLUMER, Thomas J. 107
BOORSTIN, Daniel J. 115
BOWMAN, James R. 122
BOYER, Larry M. 123
BRIDGE, Peter H. 135
BRODERICK, John C. 138
BROWN, Maxine M. 146
BURNEY, Thomas D. 162
CAHALANE, Edmond P. 171
CALDWELL, George H. 172
CANNAN, Judith P. 178
CARNAHAN, Stephanie B. . . 183
CARRINGTON, David K. 186
CASTRO-KLAREN, Sara 194
CHACE, Myron B. 196
CHANG, Roselyne M. 201
CHARTRAND, Robert L. 203
CHESTNUT, Paul I. 207
CHO, Sung Y. 209
CHRISTY, Ann K. 212
COLE, John Y. 231
COUGHLAN, Margaret N. . . . 250
CRISTAN, Anita L. 259
CURRAN, Donald C. 266
CYLKE, Frank K. 268
D'ALESSANDRO, Edward
    A. 270
DAVIS, Deta S. 278
DOBCZANSKY, Jurij W. 307
DRAGOVICH, Pamela M. 318
DRUMMOND, Louis E. 321
ELSASSER, Katharine K. 346
EWALD, Robert B. 359
FARINA, Robert A. 363
FAY, Peter J. 367
FELACO, Maja K. 369
FERRARESE, Mary A. 373
FILSTRUP, E C. 377
FLATNESS, James A. 384
FOX, Ann M. 394
GARLICK, Karen 419
GILLESPIE, Veronica M. 435
GLASBY, Dorothy J. 439
GOLDBERG, Jolande E. 444
GONZALEZ, Armando E. 448
GOUDREAU, Ronald A. 454
GUDE, Gilbert 475
GUILES, Kay D. 476
HAHN, Ellen 483
HARRISON, Harriet W. 506
HAWKINS, Sandra J. 514
HENDRICKSON, Norma K. . . 527
HERMAN, Steven J. 531
HERRICK, Judith M. 532
HIATT, Robert M. 536
HICKERSON, Joseph C. 536
HIGBEE, Joan F. 537
HILL, Victoria C. 541
HIRONS, Jean L. 543
HORCHLER, Gabriel F. 559
HSIA, Tao T. 567
HUGGENS, Gary D. 571
HUTSON, James H. 579
IBACH, Marilyn 581
JABBOUR, Alan 586
JAGUSCH, Sybille A. 591
JOHANSON, Cynthia J. 601
JOHNSON, Everett J. 604
JONES, Catherine A. 611
JWAIDEH, Zuhair E. 620
KAHLER, Mary E. 622

DISTRICT OF COLUMBIA (Cont'd)
WASHINGTON (Cont'd)
Lib of Congress

KENNEDY, Lynne 641
KENYON, Carleton W. 643
KESSINGER, Judith A. 644
KNOWLTON, John D. 665
KRAUS, David H. 676
LANE, Elizabeth S. 694
LEICH, Harold M. 713
LEVERING, Mary B. 719
LIGGETT, Suzanne L. 726
LISOWSKI, Andrew H. 732
LOO, Shirley 740
MARCUS, Stephanie M. 769
MARTON, Victor 779
MASTRANGELO, Marjorie
    J. 782
MATHESON, William 784
MCCAY, Lynne K. 795
MCGUIRE, Brian 808
MCGUIRL, Marlene C. 808
MCKINLEY, Sylvia J. 811
MCNELLIS, Claudia H. 817
MEDINA, Rubens 820
MICHENER, David H. 832
MILEVSKI, Robert J. 834
MILL, Rodney H. 835
MORRIS, Timothy J. 867
MWALIMU, Charles 884
MYERS, R D. 885
MYERS-HAYER, Patricia A. . . 885
NELSON, Marilyn L. 894
NEW, Gregory R. 898
NEWSOM, Jon 900
NYGREN, Deborah A. 912
OSTROFF, Harriet 929
OSTROVE, Geraldine E. 929
OSTROW, Stephen E. 929
OVERTON, Kathryn R. 931
PANITZ, Barbara R. 938
PANZERA, Donald P. 938
PEMPE, Ruta 956
PENKIUNAS, Ruta M. 956
PETERSON, Charles B. 963
PLETZKE, Linda 978
PRATT, Dana J. 990
PREBLE, Leverett L. 990
PRICE, Harry H. 992
PRICE, Joseph W. 992
PRICE, Mary S. 992
PRITCHARD, Sarah M. 994
PRUETT, James W. 996
PUCCIO, Joseph A. 997
RATHER, Lucia J. 1009
REID, Judith P. 1018
REIFSNYDER, Betsy S. 1020
RILEY, James P. 1034
RIMER, J T. 1035
SAUDEK, Robert 1084
SCHAAF, Robert W. 1088
SCHEEDER, Donna 1090
SCUKA, Aletta N. 1108
SEGEL, Bernard J. 1112
SETTLER, Leo H. 1117
SHAFFER, Norman J. 1119
SHAW, Renata V. 1123
SIPKOV, Ivan 1144
SMITH, Thomas E. 1161
SOLOMON, Alan C. 1166
SOLOMON, Arnold D. 1166
SPAANS, David N. 1170
SPARKS, Peter G. 1171
STANHOPE, Charles V. 1180
STARCK, William L. 1181
STARNER, James A. 1182
STEPHENSON, Richard W. . . 1188
STEVENS, Roberta A. 1191
STEWART, Ruth A. 1193
STREHL, Susan J. 1201

DISTRICT OF COLUMBIA (Cont'd)
WASHINGTON (Cont'd)
Lib of Congress

	STROUP, Elizabeth F.	1203
	STUBBS, Linda T.	1204
	SULLIVAN, Robert C.	1208
	SUNG, Carolyn H.	1210
	SWORA, Tamara	1217
	TABB, Winston	1219
	TAPPER, Bruce	1223
	TARR, Susan M.	1224
	THURONYI, Geza T.	1243
	TOTH, George S.	1252
	TRACZEWSKI, Elizabeth P.	1253
	TSCHERNY, Alexander	1260
	TSUNEISHI, Warren M.	1260
	VAN SYCKLE, Georgiana	1277
	VARGA, William R.	1278
	WANG, Ann C.	1302
	WANG, Chi	1302
	WARREN, Robert P.	1306
	WELSH, William J.	1323
	WIENER, Theodore	1336
	WIGGINS, Beacher J.	1337
	WISDOM, Donald F.	1356
	WITHERELL, Julian W.	1358
	WOLFE, Susan J.	1361
	WOLTER, John A.	1362
	WOMELDORF, Jack H.	1362
	WOOD, Karen A.	1364
	YASUMATSU, Janet R.	1378
	YOUNG, Peter R.	1383
	ZICH, Robert G.	1388
	ZIMMERMAN, Glen A.	1389
	ZIMMERMANN, Carole R.	1389
Lib Systems & Services	PERRONE, Jeanne M.	960
Linowes & Blocher	KOSLOSKE, Verleah B.	672
Lockheed Corp	SAWYER, Edmond J.	1086
Los Angeles Times	WALSH, Barclay	1299
Machinery & Allied Products Institute	DUFFY, Brenda F.	324
Maxima Corp	DEARNBARGER, Dennis	284
McGraw-Hill Inc	BECK, Douglas J.	71
	GIGLIO, William	433
	GRIMES, A R.	470
	MCKELVEY, Michael J.	811
MCI Communications Corp	BATES, Mary E.	64
McKinsey & Co	LEITCH, Karen E.	714
	TOCH, Terryann	1248
Mead Data Central	ROSS, Margery M.	1058
Milbank Tweed Hadley & McCloy	CAREY, Marsha C.	181
Miller Legislative Services	MILLER, William S.	843
Mintz Levin Cohr Ferris Glovsky & Popeo	PULVER, Thomas B.	997
Morgan Lewis & Bockius	WARD, Victoria M.	1304
Mount Vernon Coll	COCKE, Lucy S.	226
MPR Associates Inc	BERNSTEIN, Anna L.	89
Murdoch Magazines	GAZZOLA, Kenneth E.	424
	KINLEY, Jo H.	652
Museum Systems Enterprises	YARNALL, James L.	1378
National Academy of Sciences	MOBLEY, Arthur B.	851
National Aeronautics & Space Admin	HARGRAVE, Charles W.	501
National Air & Space Museum	SMITH, Martin A.	1158
National Archives & Records Admin	BEAM, Christopher M.	69
	BOHANAN, Robert D.	111
	BRADSHER, James G.	128
	BROWN, Linda	145
	BURKE, Frank G.	160
	BYRNE, John E.	169
	CALMES, Alan R.	174
	CASSEDY, James G.	193
	CHURCHVILLE, Lida H.	213
	DE ARMAN, Charles L.	284
	DOWD, Mary J.	315
	DOWNS, Charles F.	317
	EVANS, Frank B.	357
	GRAF, Thomas H.	456
	GUSTAFSON, Milton O.	478
	HARWOOD, James L.	510
	HEDLIN, Ethel W.	520
	JACOBS, Richard A.	590

DISTRICT OF COLUMBIA (Cont'd)
WASHINGTON (Cont'd)
National Archives & Records Admin

	MCREYNOLDS, R M.	818
	MEGRONIGLE, James C.	821
	MOORE, James W.	859
	PACIFICO, Michele F.	933
	PETERSON, David F.	963
	PFEIFFER, David A.	966
	PURDY, Virginia C.	998
	RICHTER, Pat	1031
	ROSS, Rodney A.	1058
	RUSH, James S.	1068
	RUSSELL, Marvin F.	1069
	SHERMAN, William F.	1128
	TRAUTMAN, Maryellen	1254
	WALCH, Timothy G.	1293
	WEIHER, Claudine J.	1316
National Association of Broadcasters	HILL, Susan M.	540
National Association of Home Builders	CAMPBELL, Doris	176
	CLARK, Margery M.	217
National Association of Letter Carriers	RUSH, Candace M.	1068
National Association of Manufacturers	LANEY, Helen B.	695
National Commission on Libs & Info Sci	CASEY, Daniel W.	192
	GRAY, Dorothy L.	459
	MILEVSKI, Sandra N.	835
	MOORE, Bessie B.	858
	YOUNG, Christina C.	1381
National Defense Univ	DAVIDSON, Dero H.	276
	JEMIOLA, Nancy E.	596
	RUSSELL, John T.	1069
	VAROUTSOS, Mary A.	1279
National Economic Research Associates	PAVEK, C C.	950
National Endowment for the Arts	MORRISON, M C.	868
National Endowment for the Humanities	COLETTI, Jeannette D.	231
	MARTZ, David J.	779
	PHELPS, Thomas C.	967
	ROSENBERG, Jane A.	1056
National Gallery of Art	DANIELS, Maygene	273
	DOUMATO, Lamia	314
	PHILBRICK, Ruth R.	967
	TURTELL, Neal T.	1265
	WEITZENKORN, Laurie	1320
	WISNIEWSKI, Julia L.	1357
National Geographic Society	BEVERIDGE, David C.	93
	BLOZIS, Jolene M.	107
	DREWES, Arlene T.	319
	FIFER-CANBY, Susan M.	376
	FLANNERY, Patrick D.	383
	SMITH, Mary P.	1158
	STORM, Jill	1198
Natl Histl Pubns & Records Commission	SAHLI, Nancy A.	1075
National League of Cities	PICKETT, Olivia K.	971
National Museum of American History	HASSE, John E.	511
National Museum of Women in the Arts	WASSERMAN, Krystyna	1308
National Press Club	VANDEGRIFT, Barbara P.	1273
National Pub Radio	MCGANN, Margot	805
	ROBINSON, Robert C.	1044
National Research Council of the US	BROWNE, Lynda S.	148
	LUKE, Lisbeth L.	747
National Restaurant Association	SMALLEY, Ann W.	1151
National Theatre Corp	SHOREBIRD, Thomas S.	1132
National Treasury Employment Union	STATTON, Thomas M.	1183
Naval Research Laboratory	KECK, Bruce L.	633
	STACKPOLE, Laurie E.	1178
Newman & Holtzinger P C	NEWTON, Stephanie K.	900
Newsweek Inc	FINE, Sandra R.	377
NMC Children's Hospital	KNOBLOCH, Shirley S.	665
Office of Management Studies	GARDNER, Jeffrey J.	418
Office of the Comptroller of Currency	KLEIN, Kristine J.	659
OMEC International Inc	RADER, Ronald A.	1002
O'Melveny & Meyers	OAKS, Robert K.	913
Organization of American States	FIGUERAS, Myriam	376
	WELCH, Thomas L.	1321

DISTRICT OF COLUMBIA (Cont'd)
WASHINGTON (Cont'd)

Overseas Development Council	BOYLE, James E.	123
Packard Press Corp	ARNSDORF, Dennis A.	34
Peat Marwick Mitchell	FRANKLIN, Brinley R.	397
Pentagon Lib	MINTER, Lyle	846
Phillips Corp	SCHNEIDER, Karen	1097
Pierson Semmes & Finley	WARRICK, Thomas S.	1307
Piper & Marbury	GEHRINGER, Susanne E.	425
Planned Parenthood	FORREST, Phyllis E.	391
Plymouth Congregational United Church	PINKARD, Ophelia T.	974
Prentice Hall Information Services	FATTIBENE, James F.	366
President's Committee	BROWN, Dale S.	143
Preston Thorgrimson Ellis & Holman	ASMUTH, Gretchen W.	36
Price Waterhouse	SHEERAN, Carole A.	1125
	WATERS, Susan S.	1309
Providence Hospital	LEONE, Rosemarie G.	717
Pub Technology Inc	JOHNSON, Elaine B.	604
Riggs National Bank	SAUNDERS, Vinette A.	1085
Rogovin & Lenzner PC	NEVIN, Barbara B.	898
Roy F Weston Inc	DOENGES, John C.	308
Russell Reynolds Associates Inc	MEADOWS, Beth W.	819
Sacred Heart Seminary	MAGRO, Emanuel P.	760
St Albans Sch	MOORE, Patsy H.	861
St Anselm's Abbey Sch	NAVE, Greer G.	890
Schiff Hardin & Waite	KELMAN, Rosalind S.	638
Schnader Harrison Segal & Lewis	SIKKEMA, Fern C.	1137
Senator Lloyd Bentsen	ODOM, Jane H.	917
Seyfarth Shaw Fairweather & Geraldson	QUINN, Susan	1000
Sidley & Austin	PACIFICI, Sabrina I.	933
Sidney Kramer Books/Lib Wholesale Srvs	KRAMER, William J.	675
SIRCO International	PFLEIDERER, Stephen D.	966
Smithsonian Institution	ADAMS, Robert	6
	AVERA, Victoria E.	41
	BROOKE, Anna	140
	CANICK, Maureen L.	178
	CHILD, Margaret S.	208
	CHIN, Cecilia H.	208
	DAVIES, Mary K.	277
	DERBYSHIRE, Richard	294
	FINK, Eleanor E.	378
	FLECKNER, John A.	384
	GRAY, Mary C.	460
	HARDING, Robert S.	500
	HEISS, Harry G.	523
	HENNESSEY, Christine	528
	HOBBINS, James M.	545
	JUNEAU, Ann	620
	KECSKES, Lily C.	633
	KENYON, Kay A.	643
	LEVIN, Amy E.	720
	LUSKEY, Judith	749
	LYNAGH, Patricia M.	751
	MALOY, Robert	764
	MAXWELL, Ted A.	788
	MOSS, William W.	872
	NEFF, William B.	892
	NIELSEN, Elizabeth A.	903
	PIETROPAOLI, Frank A.	972
	PRESLOCK, Karen	991
	RATNER, Rhoda S.	1010
	REED, Patricia A.	1015
	ROBINSON, Margaret L.	1044
	ROSENFELD, Mary A.	1056
	SCHALLERT, Ruth F.	1089
	SCOTT, Catherine D.	1107
	SEITZ, Phillip R.	1113
	SKARR, Robert J.	1145
	STANLEY, Janet L.	1180
	SZARY, Richard V.	1218
	VIOLA, Herman J.	1285
	VOGT-O'CONNOR, Diane L.	1287
	WELLS, Ellen B.	1322
	WILLIAMS, Martin T.	1345
Southeastern Univ at Washington	MUSSEHL, Allan A.	883
	RISHWORTH, Susan K.	1036

DISTRICT OF COLUMBIA (Cont'd)
WASHINGTON (Cont'd)

Special Libs Association	BATTAGLIA, Richard D.	64
	BENDER, David R.	79
	BRIMSEK, Tobi A.	136
	DOLAN, Beth C.	309
	HILL, Elaine	539
	MORTON, Sandy	870
	PALANIJIAN, Barbara	935
	RODRIGUEZ, Ruth	1048
	WARYE, Kathy	1307
	WELLINGTON, Carole E.	1322
States News Service	SCHWARTZ, Leland	1104
Steptoe & Johnson	FLEMING, Thomas B.	384
	FOWLIE, Linda K.	394
	KAHN, Victoria	622
Strategic Planning Associates Inc	CARDWELL, Diane O.	181
Strayer Coll	MOULTON, David A.	873
Supreme Court of the United States	JENSEN, Doris E.	598
Tax Foundation Inc	MARSHALL, Marion B.	774
Techworld	BOGATAY, Alan	110
Tobacco Institute	PICCIANO, Laura	970
Trinity Coll	LEIDER, Karen S.	713
Tucker Flyer Sanger & Lewis	MOTEN, Derryn E.	872
US Agency for Intl Devlpmnt, Lesotho	BERGQUIST, Christine F.	87
US Air Force	MAYHEW, Eileen G.	790
	ZELINKA, Mary A.	1387
US Army	KUBAL, Gene J.	681
US Army Center of Military History	ZEIDLICK, Hannah M.	1387
US Army Headquarters Services	CROSS, Dorothy A.	260
US Attorney's Office	STOCKTON, Sue T.	1196
US Bureau of the Census	CHAPMAN, Elwynda K.	202
US Claims Court	THOMPSON, Johanna W.	1240
US Congress	KLEIMAN, Gerald S.	659
US Copyright Office	HALL, Forest A.	487
	KENDRICK, Brent L.	640
US Court of Appeals	LOCKWOOD, David J.	736
	MCDERMOTT, Patricia M.	802
US Defense Communications Agency	GUERRIERO, Donald A.	476
US Defense Mapping Agency	GEE, Janet G.	424
US Department of Agriculture	BILLINGS, Edward S.	96
	PARSONS, John W.	945
	SPARKS, Richard M.	1171
US Department of Commerce	RANDOLPH, Susan E.	1007
	ROARK, Robin D.	1038
US Department of Defense	HOLLENBACH, Karen L.	551
US Department of Education	BUCK, Dayna E.	153
	CARTER, Yvonne B.	190
	FORK, Donald J.	390
	JONES, Milbrey L.	614
	KIRSCHENBAUM, Arthur S.	655
	KLASSEN, Robert L.	657
	STEVENS, Frank A.	1190
US Department of Energy	CUMMINGS, Helen H.	264
	KING, Hannah M.	651
US Department of Health & Human Services	HALPIN, Peter	490
US Dept of Housing & Urban Development	CHAPMAN, Susan E.	202
	STALLINGS, Elizabeth A.	1179
US Department of Interior	BARBEE, Norman N.	55
US Department of Justice	LEVINE, Emil H.	720
US Department of Labor	RILEY, Eileen V.	1034
US Department of State	CLEMMER, Dan O.	221
	CONGER, Lucinda D.	236
	STEERE, Paul J.	1184
	VON PFEIL, Helena P.	1288
US Department of the Interior	SLOCA, Sue E.	1150
US Department of the Treasury	KNAUFF, Elisabeth S.	663
US Department of Transportation	DOERNBERG, David G.	308
	LEONARD, Lawrence E.	716
	NORRIS, Loretta W.	909
	POEHLMAN, Dorothy J.	979
	REILLY, Francis S.	1020
US Department's Div of Info Management	FRAULINO, Philip S.	399
US Drug Enforcement Administration	DOLAN, Maura E.	309
	GOREN, Morton S.	452

DISTRICT OF COLUMBIA (Cont'd)		
WASHINGTON (Cont'd)		
US Environmental Protection Agency	BLALOCK, Charlotte R.	103
	GAMSON, Arthur L.	416
	NOWAK, Geraldine D.	911
US Food & Drug Administration	BERNSTEIN, Lee S.	89
	CHATFIELD, Michele R.	203
US General Accounting Office	PARMING, Marju R.	943
	RUGE, Audrey L.	1066
US Government	LATHAM, Donald C.	701
	PETERSON, Trudy H.	964
US Government Printing Office	DANIELSON, Wilfred D.	273
	GRUHL, Andrea M.	474
	HOA, Quynh N.	545
	KANELY, Edna A.	625
	SCULLY, Mark F.	1109
	TANSEY, Francis J.	1223
	WOODWARD, Lawrence W.	1368
US House of Representatives	OWENS, Major	932
US Information Agency	BORYS, Cynthia A.	117
	CHANG, Frances M.	200
	GRAY, Michael H.	460
	KUPERMAN, Agota M.	684
	LEE, Amy C.	709
	MANNING, Martin J.	766
	STONE, Marvin	1197
	TAYLOR, Joan R.	1227
	WICK, Charles Z.	1335
US International Trade Commission	KOVER, Steven J.	674
	PRUETT, Barbara J.	996
US National Guard Assn	WEAVER, Thomas M.	1312
US Navy	KALKUS, Stanley	623
US News & World Report	ATKINSON, Rose M.	38
	DENNIE, David L.	292
	TRIMBLE, Kathleen L.	1256
US Nuclear Regulatory Commission	SHELBURNE, Elizabeth C.	1125
US Patent & Trademark Office	CROCKETT, Martha L.	259
	GROOMS, David W.	472
	MAYKRANTZ, William J.	790
	RADUAZO, Dorothy M.	1002
US Postal Service	EAST, Catherine R.	332
	GERIG, Reginald R.	428
US Senate	HALEY, Roger K.	486
	PAUL, Karen D.	949
	PFUND, Leona I.	966
	WOMELDORF, Ann C.	1362
US Small Business Administration	LATEGOLO, Meldie A.	701
US Supreme Court	BAILEY, Marian C.	46
	SHERWIN, Rosalie L.	1129
US Tax Court	BONYNGE, Jeanne R.	115
US Treasury Department	UPDEGROVE, Robert A.	1269
Univ Club Lib	HUDGINS, Peggy	569
Univ of the District of Columbia	AUERBACH, Bob S.	39
	JORDAN, Robert T.	617
	PAGE, John S.	934
	SARANGAPANI, Chetluru	1082
	SHEN, I Y.	1126
	THOMPSON, Elizabeth M.	1239
Urban Institute	MOTTA, Camille A.	872
USA ITAC	ROBB, Thomas W.	1038
Veterans Administration Central Office	MASSAY, Mary K.	782
Veterans Administration Medical Center	RENNINGER, Karen	1023
VNU Amvest Inc	NYKS, Johannes M.	912
Walter Reed Army Institute of Research	CASSEDY, Barbara S.	193
Washington Assn of Realtors Inc	KITZMILLER, Virginia G.	657
Washington Hospital Center	COOK, Marilyn M.	240
	COOK, Mickey	240
The Washington Post	BELTON, Jennifer H.	78
	HAMACHEK, Ross F.	490
Washington Program & Annenberg Schs	DEHART, Odell	288
White & Case	TOWELL, Jane M.	1252
Willkie Farr & Gallagher	CILIBERTI, Nancy A.	214
Wilmer Cutler & Pickering	MITCHELL, Elaine M.	848
Winston & Strawn	BAXTER, Janet G.	67
Woodstock Theological Center	ROONEY, Eugene M.	1053
The World & I	FALK, Diane M.	362

DISTRICT OF COLUMBIA (Cont'd)		
WASHINGTON (Cont'd)		
The World Bank	GEHRINGER, Michael E.	425
	NEWTON, Robert C.	900
	ROBERTS, Lesley A.	1040
	TRIPP-MELBY, Pamela	1257
	WONG, Ming K.	1363
World Resources Institute	TERRY, Susan N.	1232
World Wildlife Fund/Conservation Fndtn	RODES, Barbara K.	1047
The Wyatt Co	MILLER, Herbert A.	838
FLORIDA		
APO MIAMI		
Lib of Congress	BALLANTYNE, Lygia M.	53
Panama Canal Coll	KANE, Joseph P.	624
AVON PARK		
South Florida Community Coll	APPELQUIST, Donald L.	30
	MOSLEY, Madison M.	871
BELLE GLADE		
Palm Beach County Pub Lib	SNODGRASSE, Elaine	1163
BOCA RATON		
CRC Press	SKALLERUP, Amy G.	1145
Florida Atlantic Univ	DONAHUE, Janice E.	310
	MOORE, Dahrl E.	859
	PELLEN, Rita M.	955
	SKALLERUP, Harry R.	1145
	WILER, Linda L.	1339
Social Issues Resources Series Inc	HARDT, James R.	500
BONIFAY		
Bonifay Elementary Sch	HOWELL, Wanda H.	565
BOYNTON BEACH		
City of Boynton Beach	COUP, William A.	251
	FARACE, Virginia K.	363
Ft Lauderdale Sun-Sentinel	ALBAIR, Catherine M.	9
Motorola Inc	LANGE, Joan K.	695
BRADENTON		
Manatee County Pub Lib System	O'CONNOR-LEVY, Linda L.	916
	PATTISON, Joanne	948
	PLACE, Philip A.	977
	TAYLOR, Rose M.	1228
Manatee County Sch Board	SHAMP, Mary J.	1120
Manatee Memorial Hospital	MOSHER, Jeanette M.	871
BRANDON		
Tampa-Hillsborough County Pub Lib System	CONKLIN, Candace V.	236
BROOKSVILLE		
Southwest FL Water Management District	TORNABENE, Charles	1251
BUNNELL		
Flagler County Abstract Co	MCKNIGHT, Jesse H.	812
CHATTAHOOCHEE		
Florida State Hospital	BEASLEY, Clarence W.	69
CLEARWATER		
City of Clearwater	MIELKE, Linda	833
Clearwater Pub Lib	HAMRELL, Larry G.	494
	RITZ, Paul S.	1037
	SCHMID, Cynthia M.	1094
Morton F Plant Hospital	DALLMAN, Glenn R.	270
St Petersburg Junior Coll	LICHTENFELS, David D.	725
COCOA BEACH		
Cocoa Beach Pub Lib	ARMSTRONG, Ruth C.	32
Patrick Air Force Base	CURRY, John W.	266
CORAL GABLES		
Miami-Dade Pub Lib System	CHIMERAKIS, Mary A.	208
	PEREZ, Maria L.	958
Papy Poole Weissenborn & Papy	MILLER, Jewell J.	839
Univ of Miami at Coral Gables	AHMAD, Carol F.	8
	DANIELS, Westwell R.	273
	DE VARONA, Esperanza B.	297
	GOLIAN, Linda M.	447
	KOBIALKA, Nancy C.	666
	LADNER, Sharyn J.	687
	LOWELL, Felice K.	744
	MESTRITS, Leila	828
	PETIT, Michael J.	965
	RABKIN, Judith R.	1001
	ROBAR, Terri F.	1038
	ROBARTS, Phyllis G.	1038
	RODGERS, Frank	1047

FLORIDA (Cont'd)

CORAL GABLES (Cont'd)

Univ of Miami at Coral Gables

SEILER, Susan L. 1112
WAXMAN, Jack 1311

CRAWFORDVILLE

Classic Software Inc — TODD, Hal W. 1248
Wakulla County — JONES, Douglas M. 612

DAVIE

Sch Board of Broward County — KLASING, Jane P. 657

DAYTONA BEACH

Atlantic Health Service Corp — CREERON, Carolyn E. 257
County of Volusia — WHEELER, James M. 1329
Father Lopez High Sch — DEANS, Janice P. 284
Florida Division of Blind Services — MINOR, Dorothy C. 846

DE LAND

Stetson Univ — EVERETT, David D. 358
JOHNSON, Betty D. 602

DELTONA

Blue Lake Elementary Sch — MOORE, Vivian L. 861

DUNEDIN

City of Dunedin — NOAH, Julia T. 906
SKUBISH, Barbara E. 1147
Dunedin Pub Lib — POTTER, Robert E. 987
SHINN, Sydniciel 1131
Mease Health Care — JENNINGS, Patricia S. 598

EASTPOINT

Florida State Univ — HOFFER, Thomas W. 547

FORT LAUDERDALE

Becker Poliakoff & Streitfeld — KOEING, Sherman 667
Broward Community Coll — DRAKE, Grady 318
Broward County Lib — ALGAZE, Selma B. 13
GOLDMAN, Ava R. 445
GRUBMAN, Donna Y. 474
HARTON, Pamela J. 508
KORNITSKY, Judith M. 672
MILLER, Margaret R. 840
MULLER, Charles W. 877
SOURS, Katherine M. 1169
Broward County Schs — JACKSON, Nancy I. 588
Center for Neurological Services — WHITESIDE, Lee A. 1333
Fort Lauderdale News/Sun-Sentinel — BROWN, Jeanette L. 144
Gould Inc — HAYES, L S. 516
Holy Cross Hospital — MCCLAIN, Mary P. 796
News/Sun-Sentinel Co — ISAACS, Bob 584
Nova Univ — HEMPHILL, Lia S. 525
KEMPER, Marlyn J. 639
TAYSOM, Daniel B. 1229
W Gozdz Enterprises Info — GOZDZ, Wanda E. 455

FORT MYERS

Edison Community Coll — FROSCHER, Jean L. 406
HUGHES, Joyce M. 572
SCHWENN, Janet M. 1105
Fort Myers Lee County Pub Lib
System — TIPPLE, Roberta L. 1246
Lee County Lib System — HOLSTINE, Lesa G. 554
WALTON, Terence M. 1302
Lee County Sch Board — ASFOUR, Karen R. 35

FORT PIERCE

St Lucie Board of County
Commissioners — HENEHAN, Alva D. 528
St Lucie County Lib System — BROOM, Susan E. 141
MITTLEMAN, Marilyn 850
POMERLEAU, Suzanne M. .. 982
Sch Board of Saint Lucie County — HARRIS, Martha J. 505

GAINESVILLE

Alachua County Lib District — BECKER, Josephine M. 72
HOLE, Carol C. 550
WILLIAMS, Ann W. 1342
Book Seminars Inc — GOGGIN, Margaret K. 444
CH2M Hill Inc — PROCTOR, Dixie L. 994
Environmental Science & Engineering
Inc — CIVITARESE, Kathleen A. ... 215
Florida Center for Lib Automation — DALEHITE, Michele I. 270
HOGUE, Margaret A. 549
Florida Department of Agriculture — JACOBSON, June B. 590
Online Connection Inc — CORCORAN, Maureen 246
Santa Fe Community Coll — LITTLER, June D. 734
State Univ System of Florida — COREY, James F. 246

FLORIDA (Cont'd)

GAINESVILLE (Cont'd)

Univ of Florida at Gainesville

BADGER, Lynn C. 44
BALDWIN, Ruth M. 52
BATTISTE, Anita L. 65
BENNETT, Richard F. 82
BROWN, M S. 145
CANELAS, Dale B. 178
COVEY, William C. 252
DRUM, Carol A. 320
FAIRBANKS, Deborah M. ... 361
FELTZ, Carol 370
FRANCIS, Barbara W. 396
HARRER, Gustave A. 503
HERBSMAN, Yael 530
HOPE, Dorothy H. 557
HSU, Pi Y. 567
IVES, Sidney E. 586
KONOP, Bonnie M. 670
LEONARD, Louise F. 716
MALANCHUK, Iona R. 762
MALANCHUK, Peter P. 762
MCKAY, Peter Z. 810
ORSER, Frank W. 927
PRIMACK, Alice L. 993
SPENCER, Deirdre D. 1173
TAYLOR, Betty W. 1226
TEAGUE, Edward H. 1229
WALTON, Carol G. 1301
WILLIAMS, Nancy L. 1345
WILLIAMS, Pamela D. 1345
WILLOCKS, Robert M. 1349
WOODS, Susan E. 1367

HAINES CITY

Haines City Pub Lib — BARTHE, Margaret R. 61

HIALEAH

City of Hialeah — COMRAS, Rema 235

HOLLYWOOD

Broward County Lib — BURKE, Donna J. 160
Temple Beth El — KURLAND, Roslyn S. 684

HOLMES BEACH

William W Gaunt & Sons Inc — GAUNT, James R. 423

HOMESTEAD

Miami-Dade Pub Lib System — WULF, Karlinne V. 1374
St John's Episcopal Day Sch — FOSTER, Candice L. 392

HOMESTEAD AFB

US Air Force — ROSEN, Bettylou 1055

HOWEY IN THE HILLS

DeSisto Schs — COHN, William L. 229

JACKSONVILLE

Blue Cross Blue Shield of Florida — JENKIN, Michael A. 596
City of Jacksonville — MARION, Gail E. 770
Duval County Pub Schs — BONFILI, Barbara J. 114
COTE, Sarah A. 249
MCMICHAEL, Sandra C. 815
YOUNG, Barbara A. 1381
Jackson Pub Libs — LITTON, Sally C. 734
Jacksonville Country Day School — STELBRINK, Mary H. 1186
Jacksonville Pub Libs — CARNAHAN, Mabel A. 183
CORNELL, Sylvia C. 247
DISMORE, Joan M. 305
GREEN, Madonna 462
SMITH, Margaret N. 1157
SUGDEN, Martin D. 1206
WILLIAMS, Judith L. 1344
Jacksonville Univ — GUNN, Thomas H. 477
Law Book Exchange — BROWN, G R. 144
Maytag Aircraft Corp — GOODIER, Darlene P. 448
Riverside Presbyterian Day Sch — PILLANS, Judith H. 973
TAD Technical Services — FAHNERT, Elizabeth K. 361
Univ of Florida at Jacksonville — HALL, M C. 488
Univ of North Florida — COHEN, Kathleen F. 228
FARKAS, Andrew 364
JONES, Robert P. 614
KAZLAUSKAS, Diane W. ... 632
RANDTKE, Angela W. 1007
SMITH, Linda L. 1157
URBANSKI, Verna P. 1269

JUPITER

Palm Beach County Sch Board — CONOVER, Kathryn H. 238

FLORIDA (Cont'd)

KENNEDY SPACE CTR
Kennedy Space Center .... ATKINS, Donna A. 37
New World Services Inc ...... RAPETTI, Vincent A. 1008
KEY WEST
Florida Keys Community Coll ... SOULE, Maria J. 1169
Monroe County Pub Lib .... MORSE, Pat B. 869
LAKE ALFRED
Univ of Florida at Lake Alfred ... RUSS, Pamela K. 1068
LAKE WORTH
Palm Beach Junior Coll .... RICHARDSON, Margaret B. 1029
LAKELAND
Lakeland Christian Sch .... VITELLO, Susan 1286
Lakeland Pub Lib .... SAGE-GAGNE, Waneta ... 1074
                            STAMPFL, Barbara A. 1179
Polk County Sch Board .... PAULSON, Mary E. 950
Southeastern Coll the Assemblies of
  God .... JONES, Linda L. 613
Watson Clinic Med Lib .... DEE, Cheryl R. 286
LANTANA
National Enquirer .... MOFFETT, Martha L. 852
LARGO
City of Largo .... MURPHEY, Barbara A. 880
Largo Lib .... BROMBERG, Johanna 139
LAUDERHILL
Florida Atlantic Univ .... HOLLMANN, Pauline V. 552
LEHIGH ACRES
Lee County Lib System .... DIAL, Carolyn E. 299
LIVE OAK
Suwannee River Regional Lib ... HALES, John D. 486
LOWELL
Florida Department of Corrections OVERSTREET, Allen J. 931
MADISON
North Florida Junior Coll ..... HISS, Sheila M. 544
MARGATE
Broward County Lib .... SMITH, Robyn H. 1160
MARIANNA
Chipola Junior Coll .... STABLER, William H. 1177
MELBOURNE
Brevard County .... HARRIS, Frank D. 504
Brevard County Law Lib ...... MELNICOVE, Annette R. 823
Florida Institute of Technology HENSON, Llewellyn L. 529
                            SHIAU, Ian L. 1129
Harris Corp Government Systems
  Sector .... CAREY, Jane G. 181
Krieger Publishing Co Inc .... KRIEGER, Robert E. 678
MIAMI
A T Kearney Inc .... CARR, Sallyann 186
Baptist Hospital of Miami ..... REAM, Diane F. 1013
Bascom Palmer Eye Institute ... HURTES, Reva 578
Dade County Pub Schs .... ADAMS, Gustav C. 4
                            CHAVES, Francisco M. 204
                            PHILLIPS, Donald J. 968
                            SEGOR, Phyllis L. 1112
Devon Aire Community Sch ..... BLOCK, Sandra S. 106
Florida International Univ ..... CARILLO, Sherry J. 181
                            MILLER, Laurence A. 839
                            MIRANDA, Salvador 847
                            MORRIS, Steve R. 867
Greenberg Traurig Askew Hoffman et
  al .... EFRON, Muriel C. 338
Historical Museum of Southern
  Florida .... SMITH, Rebecca A. 1159
Hmmm Corp .... LIGHTERMAN, Mark 726
Jackson Memorial Hospital .... TOWERS, Lynn C. 1252
Mercy Hospital .... HOLLOWAY, David R. 552
Mershon Sawyer Johnston Dunwody
  & Cole .... SNYDER, Jean 1165
Miami Children's Hospital ..... COSCULLUELA, Marta 248
Miami-Dade Community Coll .... BYRD, Susan G. 169
                            DEWAR, Jo E. 298
                            LEHMAN, Douglas K. 712
                            WINE, H E. 1354
Miami-Dade Pub Lib System .... BOLDRICK, Samuel J. 112
                            CARDEN, Marguerite 180
                            DONIO, Dorothy 311
                            LIANZI, Theresa L. 725
                            RYAN, Audrey H. 1070
                            SAMUELS, David H. 1079
                            SINTZ, Edward F. 1144

FLORIDA (Cont'd)

MIAMI (Cont'd)
Miami-Dade Pub Lib System
                            YOUNG, Barbara N. 1381
Miami Herald Publishing Co .... DONOVAN, Elizabeth L. 312
                            PAUL, Nora M. 949
The Miami News .... WRIGHT, Joseph F. 1372
Morgan Lewis & Bockius ...... LIPMAN, Renee E. 732
North Dade Regional Lib ...... KINNEY, Molly S. 653
Real Estate Data Inc .... JENKINS, George A. 597
Ryder System Inc .... OSWALD, Edward E. 929
St Brendan High Sch .... COPELAND, Mildred A. 244
St Thomas Episcopal Sch ..... LOPEZ, Silvia P. 741
St Thomas Univ .... WOLFE, Bardie C. 1360
Smathers Thompson .... KASKEY, Sid 629
South Miami Hospital .... STEINBERG, Celia L. 1185
Temple Beth American Lib ..... BERMAN, Margot 88
US Department of Defense
  Dependents Schs .... STAHLMAN, Cherry S. 1178
Univ of Miami .... BURROWS, Suzetta C. 163
                            SANCHEZ, Sara M. 1079
                            WILLIAMS, Thomas L. 1347
Univ of Miami at Coral Gables HALE, Kay K. 485
MIAMI BEACH
Metropolitan Dade Pub Lib System LYON, Bruce C. 752
                            STEPANICK, John R. 1187
Mount Sinai Medical Center ... EZQUERRA, Isabel 360
St Francis Hospital .... GROVER, Wilma S. 474
MIAMI SHORES
Barry Univ .... PINE, Nancy M. 974
Miami Shores Village .... ESPER, Elizabeth 354
                            KELLY, Anne V. 637
NAPLES
Barron Collier High Sch ...... HAINES, Nancy H. 484
NEW PORT RICHEY
Gulf Comprehensive High Sch ... GRADY, Alida J. 455
Pasco County Lib System ..... MCKENNA, Gerald M. 811
NICEVILLE
Okaloosa-Walton Junior Coll ... VINSON, B J. 1285
NORTH MIAMI
Florida International Univ ..... DOWNS, Antonie B. 317
                            MCCAMMON, Leslie V. 793
                            MEAD-DONALDSON,
                              Susan L. 819
Invest/Net Group Inc .... WRIGHT, John H. 1371
NORTH MIAMI BEACH
Adath Yeshurun Synagogue .... FRIEDMAN, Sylvia 404
OLDSMAR
City of Oldsmar .... MELLICAN, Nancy J. 822
ORLANDO
Academic Press Inc .... VANCE, Blake F. 1272
Akerman Senterfitt & Eidson ... SMITH, Mary D. 1158
Carlton Fields Ward Emmanuel Smith
  et al .... GEBET, Russell W. 424
City of Orlando .... AHLIN, Nancy 8
Florida Bankers Association ... BARAGER, Wendy A. 55
Florida Hospital .... BECKNER, Barbara J. 73
Harcourt Brace Jovanovich .... JOLINSKI, Jenny R. 610
Orange County Lib System .... BROOMALL, Susan G. 141
                            BUFKIN, Anne G. 155
                            MARTIN, John H. 776
                            PETERSON, Carolyn S. 963
Sentinel Communications Co ... GRIMSLEY, Judy L. 470
Univ of Central Florida ...... ALLISON, Anne M. 17
                            BAIN, Janice W. 47
                            BRIERTY, Carol A. 135
                            CRENSHAW, Tena L. 258
                            CUBBERLEY, Carol W. 263
                            HUDSON, Phyllis J. 569
                            LABRAKE, Orlyn B. 686
                            MAHAN, Cheryl A. 760
                            PFARRER, Theodore R. 966
                            STILLMAN, June S. 1194
Valencia Community Coll ...... HENDERSON, Patricia A. ... 526
                            HUTCHINSON, Beck 579
PALATKA
St Johns River Water Management
  District .... HUNTER, Judith G. 576
School Board of Putnam County MORGAN, Ina K. 864

FLORIDA (Cont'd)
  PALM BAY
Palm Bay Pub Lib   BOGGUS, Tamara K. 110
  PALM HARBOR
Florida Federal State Loan
  Association   GELEADI, Ruth H. 425
Liberty Publishing Co   HO, Paul J. 545
Palm Harbor Lib   RHODES, Debra S. 1026
Pinellas County Board of Education   JONES, Winona N. 615
                                             PASSARELLO, Nancy H. ... 946

  PALMETTO
Manatee County Sch Board   HUNT, Susan O. 576
  PANAMA CITY
Bay County Sch Board   MILLER, Merna B. 841
Northwest Regional Lib System   DANNECKER, Joyce H. 274
  PATRICK AFB
US Department of Defense   MISSAVAGE, Leonard 848
  PENSACOLA
Naval Aerospace Medical Institute   ROGERS, Ruth T. 1050
Naval Education & Training Program   HOMEYARD, Marjorie A. 555
Pensacola Christian Coll   BROWN, Lyn S. 145
                                             TERNAK, Armand T. 1232
Pensacola Junior Coll   BOWER, Beverly L. 120
Univ of West Florida   DEBOLT, W D. 284
                                             DOERRER, David H. 308
                                             JOHNSON, Theresa P. 609
                                             MOREIN, P G. 863
                                             PERDUE, Robert W. 958
                                             TOIFEL, Peggy W. 1248

  PERRY
Taylor County Junior High Sch   GROSS, James B. 472
  POMPANO BEACH
Pompano Beach City Lib   GALLAHAR, Christine M. ... 414
  PONTE VEDRA BEACH
Peck Research Group   PECK, Brian T. 953
  RIVERVIEW
Tampa-Hillsborough County Pub Lib
  System   RUDER, Clarice M. 1065
  ROYAL PALM BEACH
Palm Beach County Sch Board   TERWILLEGAR, Jane C. 1232
  RUSKIN
Tampa-Hillsborough County Pub Lib
  System   BRYAN, Michael G. 151
  SAFETY HARBOR
City of Safety Harbor   DE MEO, Mary A. 291
  SAINT LEO
Saint Leo Coll   NEUHOFE, M D. 897
  ST PETERSBURG
Bananas Records & Tapes   ALLEN, Douglas R. 14
Bayfront Medical Center Inc   CESANEK, Sylvia B. 196
E-Systems Inc   WEISS, Susan 1320
Eckerd Coll   HARDESTY, Larry L. 499
Florida Power Corp   CORNWELL, Douglas W. ... 247
Poynter Institute for Media Studies   CATES, Jo A. 194
St Petersburg Junior Coll   GOSS, Theresa C. 453
St Petersburg Times   ALZOFON, Sammy R. 19
                                             SCOFIELD, James S. 1106
Stetson Univ   WATERS, Sally G. 1308
                                             WOODARD, Joseph L. 1365
Tampa Bay Regional Planning
  Council   NOL, Maryke E. 907
Univ of South Florida   FUSTUKJIAN, Samuel Y. ... 410
  SANFORD
Seminole Community Coll   LINSLEY, Laurie S. 731
Seminole County Pub Lib System   RHEIN, Jean F. 1025
  SARASOTA
John & Mable Ringling Museum of
  Art   MORR, Lynell A. 866
Julie Rohr Academy   MITCHELL, Jan E. 848
Sarasota County   HOPKINS, Joan A. 558
                                             PINTOZZI, Chestalene 975
Sarasota Opera Association Inc   PETRIE, Mildred M. 965
Sch Board Sarasota County   DANIEL, Marianne M. 272
Selby Botanical Gardens   ALLEN, Francis P. 15
Selby Pub Lib   JULIEN, Dorothy C. 619
                                             STRADER, Helen B. 1199
Univ of Sarasota   HOLT, Ethel F. 554
Univ of South Florida   JENKINS, Althea H. 597
  SEBASTIAN
Indian River County Board   WALSH, Lynn R. 1299

FLORIDA (Cont'd)
  STUART
Martin County Pub Lib   HENNINGS, Leroy 528
  TALLAHASSEE
Department of State   KELLEY, Randall 636
                                             MORRELL, Ross 866
Florida Bar   DALLET, Jane L. 270
Florida Department of Education   SKINNER, L M. 1146
Florida State Univ   BILAL, Dania M. 96
                                             BURDICK, Lois B. 158
                                             CLACK, Doris H. 215
                                             CLARKSON, Jane S. 219
                                             CONAWAY, Charles W. 235
                                             DE PEW, John N. 293
                                             DONNELL, Marianne 311
                                             EVANS, Mark S. 357
                                             GAULT, Robin R. 423
                                             HART, Thomas L. 507
                                             HUNT, Mary A. 575
                                             LOGAN, Elisabeth L. 737
                                             MARTIN, James R. 776
                                             MILLER, Charles E. 836
                                             PATTON, Linda L. 949
                                             SCHROEDER, Edwin M. ... 1100
                                             SHINN, Allen E. 1130
                                             SRYGLEY, Sara K. 1177
                                             STONE, Alva T. 1196
                                             SUMMERS, F W. 1209
                                             TOOLE, Gregor K. 1250
                                             TREZZA, Alphonse F. 1256
                                             VAN ORDEN, Phyllis J. 1276
Holland & Knight   DOWLER, John W. 315
Leon County Pub Lib   BUSTETTER, Stanley R. 166
Leon County Pub Schs   HOLMES, Gloria P. 553
State Lib of Florida   BYRD, Beverly P. 168
                                             MAYO, Kathleen O. 790
                                             MILLER, Betty D. 836
                                             MOUNCE, Marvin W. 873
                                             PRATT, Darnell D. 990
                                             SUMMERS, Lorraine S. ... 1209
                                             WILKINS, Barratt 1340
Tallahassee Community Coll   GIBLON, Charles B. 431
Univ of Florida at Tallahassee   AHMAD, Saiyed A. 8
  TAMPA
Berkeley Preparatory Sch   MCCAMMON, Carol G. 793
Christ the King Sch   LOPEZ, Deborah A. 741
Greiner Inc   SCHWABEL, Lexie W. 1104
Hillsborough Community Coll   GIUNTA, Victoria J. 439
                                             WOOD, James F. 1364
MacFarlane Ferguson Allison & Kelly   GIBBS, Rosalyn D. 431
Price Waterhouse   TEW, Robin L. 1233
Reflectone Inc   KING, Elizabeth 650
Special Lib Service   EVERLOVE, Nora J. 359
Tampa Bay Lib Consortium Inc   MARTIN, Robert A. 778
Tampa-Hillsborough County Pub Lib
  System   APPELBAUM, Sara B. 29
                                             CHALLENER, Marcee M. ... 197
                                             FIORE, Carole D. 379
                                             HAWK, Susan P. 513
                                             LOSEY, Doris C. 742
                                             NICHTER, Alan 902
                                             STINES, Joe R. 1194
                                             STORCK, Bernadette R. ... 1198
Univ Community Hospital   TIBBS, Jo A. 1244
                                             WALTERS, Gwen E. 1301
Univ of South Florida   ABBOTT, Randy L. 1
                                             CHRISMAN, Larry G. 211
                                             CRAIG, James P. 254
                                             EL-HADIDY, Bahaa 342
                                             EVANS, Josephine K. 357
                                             GATES, Jean K. 422
                                             GRIMES, Maxyne M. 470
                                             HARKNESS, Mary L. 501
                                             JOHNSTON, Judy F. 610
                                             KETCHERSID, Arthur L. 645
                                             LIANG, Diana F. 725
                                             MCCROSSAN, John A. 800
                                             MCRAE, Linda 818
                                             MERCADO, Marilyn J. 825
                                             PFISTER, Fred C. 966

FLORIDA (Cont'd)
TAMPA (Cont'd)
Univ of South Florida

    SMITH, Alice G. 1152
Univ of Tampa
    ACOSTA, Lydia A. 4
    JOHNSON, Susan J. 609
    MATHEWS, Richard B. 784

TARPON SPRINGS
City of Tarpon Springs   O'BRIEN, Elizabeth M. 914
TAVARES
Lake County Bd of County
  Commissioners   BREEDEN, Wendy R. 131
TEMPLE TERRITORY
Florida Coll   TABOR, Curtis H. 1219
TITUSVILLE
Brevard County   MCFARLAND, George S. . . . 804
VENICE
Manatee Community Coll   CARR, Mary L. 186
Sarasota County   PIKE, Nancy M. 973
VERO BEACH
Indian River County Lib   KISER, Mary D. 656
WAUCHULA
Hardee County Pub Lib   MAPP, Erwin E. 768
WEST PALM BEACH
Gee & Jenson
  Engrng-Architects-Planners   FOSTER, Helen M. 392
Gunster Yoakley Criser & Stewart   PRITCHARD, Teresa N. 994
Palm Beach County   BROWNLEE, Jerry W. 148
Palm Beach County Pub Lib   ALLEN, Linda G. 15
Palm Beach County Sch Board   TAFFEL, Bobbe H. 1219
South Florida Water Management
  Dist   PLOCKELMAN, Cynthia H. . . 978
West Palm Beach Pub Lib   BAILEY, Sara G. 47
    MOJO, Anne Z. 852

WINTER PARK
Crow Segal Management Co Inc   STEALEY, Marjorie J. 1183
Rollins Coll   BLOODWORTH, Velda J. . . . 106
    GRANT, George C. 458
    MCCLELLAN, Edna S. 796
    SEBRIGHT, Terence F. 1110
Winter Park Pub Lib   ANDREWS, Janet C. 26
    BENNETT, Renae M. 82
    ELDER, Jane D. 342

GEORGIA
ALBANY
The Albany Herald   MEREY-KADAR, Ervin R. . . . 825
US Marine Corps   TOOKES, Amos J. 1250
ALPHARETTA
Fulton County Board of Education   SMITH, Judy B. 1156
AMERICUS
Americus City Board of Education   PASCHAL, Eloise R. 945
Georgia Southwestern Coll   MCLAUGHLIN, Laverne L. . . 813
APPLING
North Columbia Elem Sch   WARNER, Wayne G. 1305
ATHENS
Athens Regional Lib   TAYLOR, Prudence A. 1228
THEATRICANA   KAHAN, Gerald 621
US Forest Service   RUTHERFORD, Virginia L. . . 1070
Univ of Georgia   ANDERSON, Thomas G. 25
    ANDREW, Paige G. 26
    BAKER, Barry B. 47
    BERG, Elizabeth R. 84
    BISHOP, David F. 99
    BROWN, Steven A. 147
    CAMPBELL, John L. 176
    CARPENTER, David E. 184
    CLAYTON, William R. 220
    CLEMENS, Bonnie J. 220
    COMPTON, Lawrence E. . . . 235
    COONIN, Bryna R. 242
    COSCARELLI, William F. . . . 248
    ELLIS, Marie C. 345
    GUBISTA, Kathryn R. 475
    GULLEY, J L. 477
    HAAR, John M. 480
    HUGHES, Martha T. 572
    HUGHES, Neil R. 572
    KUHLMAN, James R. 682
    LIBBEY, George H. 725

GEORGIA (Cont'd)
ATHENS (Cont'd)
Univ of Georgia

    LUCHSINGER, Arlene E. 746
    MASSEY, Katha D. 782
    PADWA, David J. 934
    PARK, Margaret K. 941
    QUINLAN, Judy B. 1000
    RIEMER, John J. 1033
    ROWLAND, Lucy M. 1062
    RYSTROM, Barbara B. 1072
    SOMERS, Sally W. 1167
    SOUTHWICK, Mary L. 1170
    SURRENCY, Erwin C. 1210
    SUTHERLAND, Johnnie D. . . 1211
    VOGT, Sheryl B. 1287
    WALD, Marlena M. 1294
    WHEELER, Carol L. 1328
    WHITEHEAD, James M. . . . 1332
    WILLIAMS, Sara E. 1346

ATLANTA
Alston & Bird   STROUGAL, Patricia G. . . . 1203
Arnall Golden & Gregory   CAMBELL, Miriam A. 174
Arthur Andersen & Co   KLOPPER, Susan M. 662
Atlanta Arts Alliance   MILLER, Jack E. 838
Atlanta Board of Education   LOWERY, Phyllis C. 744
    ROSS, Theodosia B. 1059
Atlanta-Fulton Pub Lib   BRADLEY, Gail P. 125
    BRIGHTHARP, Wilma S. . . . 136
    CHUPP, Linda D. 213
    DAVIS, Joy V. 279
    HEID, Gregory G. 521
    HICKMAN, Michael L. 536
    JOHNSON, Beth 602
    JORDAN, Casper L. 616
    LANE, Linda A. 694
    LEE, Lauren K. 710
    MACK, Debora S. 756
    MCIVER, Stephanie P. 809
    MILLER, Anthony G. 835
    PICKENS, Lynne R. 970
    ROBERTS, Vann R. 1041
    SEARCY, David L. 1109
    SMITH-EPPS, E P. 1161
    TYLER, Audrey Q. 1266
    WILLIAMS, Howell M. 1343
Atlanta Historical Society   DICKENS, Rosa L. 300
    WIGHT, Nancy E. 1337
Atlanta Information Services   ROAN, Tattie W. 1038
Atlanta Journal Constitution   LYONS, Valerie S. 753
Atlanta Pub Schs   LINCOLN, Joanne 728
    PLOWDEN, Martha W. 978
Atlanta Univ   BROWN, Lorene B. 145
    COFFMAN, Joseph W. 227
    CRAFT, Guy C. 254
    JAMES, Stephen E. 592
    MISRA, Jayasri T. 847
    SPENCER, Albert F. 1173
    TROUTMAN, Joseph E. . . . 1258
Bellsouth Enterprises   CONLIN, Peter A. 236
Bellsouth Services   BARNETT, Becky L. 57
Bondurant Mixson and Elmore   KRONE, Judith P. 679
Cable News Network   ALLEN, William R. 16
Centers for Disease Control   STANSELL, Janet S. 1181
Children's Literature for Children   NIX, Kemie 905
CLSI Inc   HENDRIX, Linda S. 527
Cobb County Pub Lib   RHEAY, Mary L. 1025
Coca-Cola Co   CASSELL, Judy A. 193
    COOPER, Glenn 243
Creative Consulting & Design   STOWELL, Donald C. 1199
DeKalb County   BERGMANN, Sue A. 87
Document Conservation Center   MOORE, Harold H. 859
Emory Univ   AMMERMAN, Jackie W. . . . 20
    BENEVICH, Lauren A. 80
    BISHOP, Beverly D. 99
    BROWN, Carolyn M. 142
    CLEMONS, John E. 221
    DEEMER, Selden S. 286
    ELAM, Joice B. 341
    ENGLER, June L. 350

GEORGIA (Cont'd)
ATLANTA (Cont'd)
Emory Univ

JESCHKE, Channing	600
JOHNSON, Herbert F.	605
LAWSON, A V.	705
LAWSON, Venable A.	705
LESLIE, Elizabeth J.	718
MARKWELL, Linda G.	772
MILLS, Robin K.	844
MORTON, Ann W.	870
NITSCHKE, Eric R.	905
NITSCHKE, Marie M.	905
O'NEILL, Patricia E.	924
PIERCE, Sydney J.	972
TEMPLETON, Mary E.	1231
TORRENTE, Kathryn J.	1251
TUTTLE, Jane S.	1265
VISK, Linda S.	1285

Epstein School — REZNICK, Evi P. 1025
Equifax Inc — MCDAVID, Michael W. 801
Faxon Co — LUTHER, M J. 750
Federal Home Loan Bank of Atlanta — LAWLESS, Dorothy A. 704
Fernbank Science Center — LARSEN, Mary T. 698
Finder Information Tools Inc — SMITH, Judith A. 1156
Fulton County Government — PARKER, Dorothy J. 941
Georgia Department of Archives & History

BECHOR, Malvina B.	71
DEES, Anthony R.	287
ENGERRAND, Steven W.	349
FORSEE, Joe B.	391
TOPE, Diana R.	1251

Georgia Department of Education (above)

Georgia Department of Human Resources — CLARK, Jane F. 217
Georgia Division of Pub Lib Services — CORRELL, Emily N. 247
Georgia Institute of Technology

BAILEY, Dorothy C.	46
BRACKNEY, Kathryn S.	125
DEES, Leslie M.	287
DRAKE, Miriam A.	318
DREW, Frances K.	319
GARFINKLE, Gail J.	419
GRIFFIN, Martha R.	468
HALE, Ruth C.	485
KENNEDY, Joanna C.	641
KYLE, Robert J.	685
LONBERGER, Jana L.	738
SHERMAN, John R.	1128
TOMAJKO, Kathy L.	1249
VIDOR, Ann B.	1283
WALKER, Barbara J.	1295
WHITE, Carol A.	1330
WILTSE, Helen C.	1353

Georgia-Pacific Corp

GROOVER, Marion D.	472
HALL, Deanna M.	487
LONG, Linda E.	739
RAQUET, Jacqueline R.	1008

Georgia Power Co — INGLE, Bernita W. 582
— MANNING, Katherine J. 766
Georgia State Univ

ANDERSON, David G.	22
BANJA, Judith A.	54
CANN, Sharon F.	178
CHRISTIAN, Gayle R.	211
HOUGH, Leslie S.	562
HUGHES, Glenda J.	571
JOHNSON, Nancy P.	608
JONES, Helen C.	613
MENEELY, William E.	824
MORELAND, Virginia F.	863
MOSBY, Anne P.	870
PRESLEY, Roger L.	991
ROBISON, Carolyn L.	1045
RUSSELL, Ralph E.	1069
STILLWATER, Rebecca S.	1194
THAXTON, Lyn	1234

Georgia Technical Research Institute — GRELL, Holly J. 467
Hebrew Academy of Atlanta — KARP, Hazel B. 628
Heery Architects and Engineers — ALLEN, Laurie C. 15
Henrietta Egleston Children's Hospital — BELL, Mamie J. 77
Home Mission Board SBC — COURSEY, W T. 251

GEORGIA (Cont'd)
ATLANTA (Cont'd)
Hurt Richardson Garner Todd & Cadenhead — GUERIN, Roberta T. 476
ICD/CCNAA — CHERN, Jenn C. 206
Information America Inc — MADDEN, Mary A. 758
Intl Association for Financial Planning — MCDAVID, Sara J. 801
IBM Corp — MCDANIEL, Sara H. 801
Kilpatrick & Cody — LISI, Susan C. 732
King & Spalding — FRY, Mary A. 406
Lipshutz Frankel Greenblatt & King — LIPSHUTZ, Robert J. 732
Mac Farlane & Co Inc — GASKINS, Stephen D. 421
Mercer Univ

JACKSON, Elizabeth C.	587
SIMMONS, Hal	1140
WILLIAMS, Nancy F.	1345
SWANSON, Joe	1213

Morehouse Sch of Medicine — BRYANT, Nancy J. 152
MSL International Inc — ELZY, Martin I. 347
National Archives & Records Admin

FRENCH, Melodee J.	402
SCHEWE, Donald B.	1092

Northside Hospital — PAYNE-BUTTON, Linda 951
Office of the Secretary of State — WELDON, Edward 1321
Powell Goldstein Frazer & Murphy — FULLER, Ruth V. 409
— SCHEIN, Julia R. 1091
Rolls-Royce Inc — BELL, Karen L. 77
St Joseph's Hospital — WAVERCHAK, Gail A. 1311
Smith Currie & Hancock — BAUSCH, Donna K. 67
Southeastern Lib Network

HEITZ, Kathleen R.	523
BAUGHMAN, Steven A.	66
GRISHAM, Frank P.	471
ROBERTS, Lisa G.	1041
WILSON, Lesley P.	1351

State Library of Georgia — HALL, Richard B. 488
SunTrust Service Corp — BOZE, Lucy G. 124
TAPPI — STAHL, D G. 1178
Technl Assn of the Pulp & Paper Industry — BIBBY, Elizabeth A. 94
Techsouth Inc — CRIM, Dewey H. 258
Towers Perrin Forster & Crosby — BATTEN, Henry R. 64
— BAUER, Leslie L. 65
TPF&C/Tillinghast — REYNOLDS, Carol C. 1025
US Court of Appeals — FENTON, Elaine P. 371
— FISTE, David A. 382
Westminster Schs — DAYTON, Diane 283
— MCCLELLAND, Katherine L. 796

AUGUSTA
Augusta Coll — BUSTOS, Roxann R. 166
Augusta Genealogical Society — RANDALL, Gordon E. 1006
Augusta Regional Lib — CALHOUN, Wanda J. 172
Augusta-Richmond County Pub Lib — LAYMON, Diane L. 705
— WALKER, Alice O. 1295
Augusta Technical Institute — DUTTWEILER, Robert W. 329
Medical Coll of Georgia

ANDERSON, Gail C.	23
BASLER, Thomas G.	63
DAVIS, Shelley E.	281
DENNISON, Jacquelyn H.	292
FLAVIN, Linda M.	384
HENNER, Terry A.	528
MCCANN, Jett C.	794
MIMS, Dorothy H.	845
SCHLATTER, M W.	1093
TRAINOR, Donna J.	1253

Richmond County Board of Education — WILLIAMS, Anita 1342
Veterans Administration Medical Center — SCHNICK, Robert M. 1097

BAINBRIDGE
Georgia Department of Education — MARSHALL, Ruth T. 775
Southwest Georgia Regional Lib — MULCAHY, Bryan L. 876

BALL GROUND
Cherokee County Sch System — SALTER, Nellie C. 1077

BROOKLET
Bulloch County Board of Education — BURGOON, Roger S. 159

BRUNSWICK
Brunswick Junior Coll — BOYD, Ruth V. 123

CAIRO
Roddenberry Memorial Lib — DEENEY, Marian A. 286

CALHOUN
Gordon County Board of Education — OWINGS, Priscilla A. 932

GEORGIA (Cont'd)

CARROLLTON
West Georgia Coll — BEARD, Charles E. 69
BENNETT, Priscilla B. 82
FARMER, Nancy R. 364
JOBSON, Betty S. 601
West Georgia Regional Lib — WILLIS, Roni M. 1348

CARTERSVILLE
Bartow County Pub Lib System — HOWINGTON, Lee R. 566
LINKER, Rita S. 731

CLEVELAND
Truett-McConnell Coll — WILSON, Janice E. 1351

COLLEGE PARK
Fulton County Board of Education — HANSON, Kathy H. 498

COLUMBUS
Hughston Sports Medicine Foundation — CLEMENTS, Betty H. 221
Muscogee County Sch District — SELF, Sharon W. 1113
Valley Regional Lib Syst — BAKER, Rowena E. 49
W C Bradley Lib — SMITH, Matilda M. 1158

CONYERS
Rockdale County Schs — DURAND, Joyce J. 328

DAHLONEGA
North Georgia Coll — MALCOLM, Carol L. 762

DALTON
Dalton Coll — LARY, Marilyn S. 700
Whitfield County Board of Education — SPENCE, Rethia C. 1173

DECATUR
Columbia Theological Seminary — MARONEY, Daryle M. 772
OVERBECK, James A. 931
WENDEROTH, Christine . . . 1323
DeKalb County Sch System — BUFFALOE, Catherine S. . . . 155
HULLUM, Cheri J. 573
DeKalb Pub Lib System — HUNTER, Julie V. 576
LOAR, Barbara J. 735
LUKAS, Vicki A. 747
DeVry Institute of Technology — CHAMBERS, Shirley M. 198
Stone Mountain Regional Lib System — MANCINI, Donna D. 764
MOELLER, Edward R. 851
SKELLIE, Karen S. 1145

DOERUN
Colquitt County Board of Education — BOWEN, Louise E. 120

DORAVILLE
Doraville City Lib — DRAPER, James D. 318

DOUGLASVILLE
Douglas County Board of Commissioners — WARREN, Ruth M. 1307
Douglas County Board of Education — BISSELL, Susan J. 100
BROCK, Kathy T. 138
Tempo Enterprises Inc — WILLIAMS, Fred 1343

DULUTH
Lake Lanier Lib — SHELTON, John L. 1126
Missile Systems Division — DEWBERRY, Claire D. 298

DUNWOODY
DeKalb Coll — TIBBETS, Celeste 1243

EAST POINT
Atlanta Christian Coll — BAIN, Michael L. 47
Eltzroth-Gillette Research Services — ELTZROTH, Elsbeth L. 346

EASTMAN
Ocmulgee Regional Lib System — WILSON, David C. 1350

EXPERIMENT
Univ of Georgia — LEDFORD, Carole L. 708

FAIRBURN
Atlanta-Fulton Pub Lib — BUDLONG, Thomas F. 155

FITZGERALD
Fitzgerald-Ben Hill County Lib — HEFFINGTON, Carl O. 520
PAULK, Sara L. 950

FORT MCPHERSON
US Army — DOOLEY, Shelly Q. 312

FRANKLIN SPRINGS
Emmanuel Coll — HOWARD, Rachel L. 564

GAINESVILLE
Brehau Coll — VAUGHAN, Elinor F. 1279
Chestatee Regional Lib — BRONSON, Diane A. 140

GRIFFIN
Flint River Regional Lib — CHENEY, Philip M. 206
HATCHER, Nolan C. 511
STRAUTMAN, Randolph B. . . 1201
Griffin-Spalding Board of Education — ROGERS, Jan F. 1049
Griffin-Spalding County Schs — WILKINSON, Evalyn S. 1340

GEORGIA (Cont'd)

HAMPTON
Clayton County Board of Education — BAKER, Gordon N. 48

HARTWELL
Hart County Pub Lib — BISSO, Arthur J. 100

JONESBORO
Clayton County Lib System — STEWART, Carol J. 1192

LA FAYETTE
Cherokee Regional Lib — WOODLEE, Rick G. 1366

LA GRANGE
Callaway Educational Association — GIBSON, Ricky S. 432
La Grange Coll — LEWIS, Frank R. 723
Milliken & Co — KELLY, Patrick M. 638
Troup County Archives — LANNING, E K. 696
Troup-Harris-Coweta Regional Lib — BECHAM, Gerald C. 71

LITHONIA
DeKalb Sch System — DOUGLASS, Charlene K. . . . 314

LUTHERSVILLE
Meriweather County Board of Education — SHELTON, Elease B. 1126

MACON
Mercer Univ — BURKHART, Sue W. 161
CHANIN, Leah F. 201
COLLINS, Patrick 233
HARBER, Patty S. 499
HOWARD, Mary R. 564
RANKIN, Jocelyn A. 1007
Stetson Lib — HAMMOND, Elizabeth D. 493

MARIETTA
Cobb County Board of Education — SLOAN, Mary J. 1149
Cobb County Pub Lib System — COHRS, Joyce S. 229
LAZENBY, Gail R. 706
Kennesaw Coll — HARDIN, Barbara A. 500
Larlin Corp — BOYD, Kenneth W. 122
Marietta City Schs — KILPATRICK, Marguerite C. . . 648
STAVROLAKIS, Rachel G. . . 1183

MILLEDGEVILLE
Georgia Coll — FENNELL, Janice C. 371
SCOTT, Rupert N. 1108

MORROW
Clayton County Board of Education — GRANTHAM, Ann V. 458
Clayton State Coll — BROCKMEIER, Kristina C. . . . 138
Laurel Henderson & Associates — HENDERSON, Laurel E. 526

MOULTRIE
SW Georgia Health Scis Lib Consortium — STATOM, Susan T. 1183

MT VERNON
Brewton-Parker Coll — PHILLIPS, Don 968

MT ZION
Carroll County Board of Education — MITCHELL, Phyllis R. 849

MOUTTRIE
Colquitt County Board of Education — MOYE, Edna B. 874

RICHMOND HILL
Bryan County Board of Education — GLISSON, Patricia A. 441

RIVERDALE
Selective Dissemination of Information — LETT, Rosalind K. 719

ROME
Shorter Coll — MOSLEY, Mary M. 871

ROSWELL
City of Roswell — MARTIN, Clerece 775
National Lib Bindery Co — TOLBERT, Jack W. 1248

SAVANNAH
Armstrong State Coll — BALL, Ardella P. 52
C-E-L Regional Lib — ROEHLING, Steven R. 1048
Chatham-Effingham-Liberty Regional Lib — BROCKMAN, B D. 138
Savannah-Chatham County Board of Educ — BURKE, Grace W. 160

STATESBORO
Georgia Southern Coll — BROWN, Edna E. 143
HARRISON, James O. 506
JOHNSON, Jane G. 605
Statesboro Regional Lib — PATON, John C. 947
ROYAL, Henrietta 1063
WALKER, Terri L. 1296

STONE MOUNTAIN
Corpus Christi Catholic Church — SULLIVAN, Mary A. 1208

THOMASVILLE
South Georgia Neurological Institute — CLARKE, Elba C. 218

GEORGIA (Cont'd)

TIFTON
Abraham Baldwin Agricultural Coll SELLERS, Brenda A. 1114
Univ System of Georgia HENDERSON, Mary E. 526

TUCKER
Oglethorpe Power Corp HORAH, Richard H. 558
Southeastern Lib Association MEDORI, Claudia 820
Stone Mountain Regional Lib System WOLF, Melinda J. 1360

VALDOSTA
Valdosta State Coll CLARK, Tommy A. 218
  CRAWFORD, Sherrida J. . . . 257
  MONTGOMERY, Denise L. . . 856
  PAULK, Betty D. 950
  WRIGHT, Dianne H. 1371

VIDALIA
Ohoopee Regional Lib HARTZ, Frederic R. 509

WARNER ROBINS
Houston County Pub Libs MERK, P E. 826

WATKINSVILLE
Univ of Georgia CURTIS, Susan C. 267

WAYCROSS
Okefenokee Regional Lib System STANBERY, Nancy M. 1179

WINDER
Piedmont Regional Lib HOLMES, Nancy M. 553

GUAM

AGANA
Guam Territorial Law Lib WEINGARTH, Darlene 1318

MANGILAO
Univ of Guam DRIVER, Marjorie G. 320
  UYEHARA, Harry Y. 1270

HAWAII

AIEA
State of Hawaii KAN, Katharine L. 624

HICKAM AFB
US Air Force HASSLER, William B. 511

HILO
Hawaii State Department of Education HERRICK, Johanna W. 532
  TSUTSUMI, Carole K. 1261
Hawaii State Pub Lib System PLADERA, Lucretia 977
Hilo Hospital HAMASU, Claire 490
St Joseph High Sch EPIL, Charlene M. 351
Univ of Hawaii at Hilo HERRICK, Kenneth R. 532

HONOLULU
Ashford & Wriston REED, Carol R. 1014
Bank of Hawaii CHAFE, Douglas A. 197
  SCHULTZ, Elaine V. 1102
Belt Collins & Associates GOODY, Cheryl S. 450
Bernice P Bishop Museum ASHFORD, Marguerite K. . . . 36
  HORIE, Ruth H. 559
Cannon's Business Coll DILUCIA, Samuel J. 303
City & County of Honolulu AKAO, Pamela S. 9
Hawaii Institute of Geophysics PRICE, Patricia 992
Hawaii Judiciary KOTO, Ann S. 673
  TANAKA, Momoe 1222
Hawaii Medical Lib Inc BREINICH, John A. 132
  FETTES, Virginia M. 374
Hawaii Pub Radio CAMPBELL, R A. 177
Hawaii State Department of Archives ITAMURA, Ruth S. 585
Hawaii State Department of Education HARADA, Violet H. 499
  KANE, Bartholomew A. 624
  WARNER, Joyce E. 1305
Hawaii State Lib GOTANDA, Masae 453
Hawaii State Pub Lib System LINVILLE, Marcia L. 731
  SCHINDLER, Jo A. 1093
  SPENCER, Caroline P. 1173
  TAYLOR, Mary L. 1227
Hawaii Supreme Court WONG, Irene K. 1362
Hawaiian Electric Co Inc UCHIDA, Deborah K. 1267
Iolani Sch MITCHELL, Jeanette E. 848
Kaiser Permanente Medical Center FUKUDA, Jodel L. 408
Law Library Microfrom Consortium DUPONT, A J. 327
St Francis Medical Center SIROIS, Julie J. 1144
State of Hawaii FREITAS-OBREGON,
    Brenda J. 401
  VAN NIEL, Eloise S. 1276
Straub Clinic & Hospital MAZZOLA, Patricia R. 791
  SMITH, Frances P. 1155
US Air Force LUSTER, Arlene L. 750

HAWAII (Cont'd)

HONOLULU (Cont'd)
Univ of Hawaii at Honolulu AUSTIN, Mary C. 40
  BARD, Therese B. 56
  COLEMAN, David E. 231
  EHRHORN, Jean H. 339
  FURUMOTO, Viola G. 410
  HAAK, John R. 480
  JACKSON, Miles M. 588
  LUNDEEN, Gerald W. 748
  NAHL-JAKOBOVITS, Diane . 886
  POLANSKY, Patricia A. 980
  SAKAI, Diane H. 1076
  SHELDEN, Patricia R. 1125
  SZILARD, Paula 1218
  TAKAHASHI, Annabelle T. . 1220
  TRAPIDO, Joel 1254
  URAGO, Gail M. 1269
Univ of Hawaii at Manoa AYRAULT, Margaret W. 43
  ENOMOTO, Wanda H. 350
  MATSUMORI, Donald M. . . . 784
  NAJ, Linda M. 887
  NAKANO, Kimberly L. 887
  RIEDY, Allen J. 1033
  STEVENS, Robert D. 1190
  TRUETT, Carol A. 1259

KAILUA
State of Hawaii ELDREDGE, Jeffrey R. 342
  MORGAN, Sally W. 864
The Wright Consultants Inc WRIGHT, John C. 1371

KAILUA-KONA
BRS Information Technologies KOLMAN, Roberta F. 669

KANEOHE
Kaneohe Regional Lib CHAMBERS, Donald A. 198
Windward Community Coll STEPHENS, Diana C. 1188
  WILSON, Deetta C. 1350

KAUNAKAKAI
Hawaii State Pub Lib System TENCATE, Sri P. 1231

KIHEI
State of Hawaii USHIRODA, Christine H. . . . 1270

PEARL CITY
Hawaii State Department of Education FUJINO, Amy H. 408

WAILUKU
Wailuku Pub Lib TUPPER, Bobbie 1263

IDAHO

BOISE
Boise Pub Lib ROBERTSON, Naida 1042
Boise State Univ CRANE, David E. 255
  HANSEN, Ralph W. 498
  OSTRANDER, Gloria J. 929
  TAYLOR, Adrien P. 1225
Commtek Publishing Co GREEN, Carol A. 461
Idaho State Historical Society WELLS, Merle W. 1322
Idaho State Lib BOLLES, Charles A. 112
  FORD, Karin E. 389
  JOSLIN, Ann 618
The Idaho Statesman IRONS, Lynda R. 584
Joint Sch District 2 of Meridian DENNY, Mary C. 293
St Alphonsus Regional Medical
  Center STOLZ, Marty R. 1196
St Luke's Regional Medical Center SPICKELMIER, Pamela S. . . 1174

GARDEN CITY
Garden City Pub Lib SCHIFF, Margaret M. 1092

IDAHO FALLS
Eastern Idaho Regional Medical
  Center WINWARD, Coleen C. 1356
El Intl LOOP, Jacqueline N. 740
Idaho Falls Pub Lib ATWOOD, Virginia W. 38
  HOLLAND, Paul E. 551
The Post-Register VERHOFF, Patricia A. 1282

LEWISTON
Lewiston City Lib WILLIAMS, Brenda M. 1342

MOSCOW
Univ of Idaho ABRAHAM, Terry 3
  BAIRD, Dennis W. 47
  BAIRD, Lynn N. 47
  BECK, Richard J. 71
  CURL, Margo W. 265
  ECKWRIGHT, Gail Z. 335

IDAHO (Cont'd)
MOSCOW (Cont'd)
Univ of Idaho

FORCE, Ronald W. 389
FUNABIKI, Ruth P. 409
HANSON, Donna M. 498
HELLER, James S. 524
PIKE, George H. 972
STEINHAGEN, Elizabeth N. . . 1186
WAI, Lily C. 1292

NAMPA
Mercy Medical Center BALCERZAK, Judy A. 50
Northwest Nazarene Coll LANCASTER, Edith E. 691
RAMBO, Helen M. 1005
SIMMONS, Randall C. 1140

PINEHURST
Pinehurst-Kingston Free Lib District BREIDT, Cheryll K. 132
POCATELLO
Idaho State Univ WATSON, Peter G. 1310
Pocatello Pub Lib DOWNEY, Howard R. 316
POST FALLS
Post Falls Pub Lib JONES-LITTEER, Corene A. . . 616
REXBURG
Madison Memorial Hospital NELSON, Kathy J. 894
Madison Sch Dist 321 COVINGTON, Eddis E. 252
SODA SPRINGS
City of Soda Springs TATE, Karen E. 1225

ILLINOIS
ABBOTT PARK
Abbott Laboratories HOFF, Carole 547
LEWIS, Martha S. 724
MANDEL, Douglas J. 765
OPEM, John D. 925
SWANSON, Ruth M. 1213

ADDISON
Addison Trail High Sch JOHNSEN, Ellen I. 601
DuPage High Sch District 88 WRIGHT, Deborah L. 1371
ALGONQUIN
Algonquin Area Pub Lib VLCEK, Randall 1286
ALSIP
Alsip-Merrionette Park Lib BLIETZ, Cynthia S. 105
ARGO
CPC International Inc CARUSO, Joy L. 190
ARGONNE
Argonne National Laboratory DAVIDOFF, Gary N. 276
GREGORY, Melissa R. 466
WILSON, Majorie A. 1352
WOELL, Yvette N. 1359

ARLINGTON HEIGHTS
Arlington Heights Memorial Lib BROWN, Pamela P. 146
DEMPSEY, Frank J. 291
HANRATH, Richard A. 497
SHUMAN, Marilyn J. 1134
Memorial Lib RICKERT, Carol A. 1032
Northwest Community Hospital LIANG, Ching C. 725
Northwest Educational Cooperative PEISER, Richard H. 955
AURORA
Aurora Pub Lib ISELY, Megan M. 585
STEPHENS, Janet A. 1188
Aurora Univ MCKEARN, Anne B. 810
Mercy Center for Health Care
Services BEAN, Janet R. 69
West Aurora High School HOWREY, Mary M. 566
BARRINGTON
Barrington Area Lib ALLAN, Nancy P. 14
BRYAN, Mila 152
POLL, Diane R. 981
SUGDEN, Barbara L. 1206
Barrington Pub Schs KARON, Joyce E. 627
BARTONVILLE
Alpha Park Pub Lib District JACKSON, Susan M. 588
KAUTZ-WARTH, Linda S. . . . 631

BEARDSTOWN
Community Unit Sch District 15 LUKASIK, Marion F. 747
West Professional Services WEST, L P. 1326
BEDFORD PARK
Bedford Park Pub Lib District HAFFNER, Barbara 482

ILLINOIS (Cont'd)
BELLEVILLE
Belle Valley Sch District 119 DOMESCIK, Carol J. 310
Belleville Pub Lib KIRCHGRABER, Nancy B. . . 654
BELLWOOD
Bellwood Pub Lib HARRIS, Robert A. 506
BERWYN
MacNeal Hospital BEN-SHIR, Rya H. 83
FEDECZKO, Joyce L. 367
North Berwyn Sch Dist 98 KRAUSE, Roberta A. 676
BETHANY
Bethany Community Unit 301 SYFERT, Samuel R. 1217
BLOOMINGTON
Bloomington Pub Lib HUFFMAN, Carol P. 571
KELLEY, H N. 636
KUBIAK, Matthew C. 682
WOOD, Lois R. 1364
BroMenn Healthcare STROYAN, Susan E. 1203
Central Catholic High Sch JOHNSON, Keran C. 606
Illinois Farm Bureau OLSON, Rue E. 923
The Pantagraph MILLER, Diane C. 837
State Farm Insurance Companies JUSTICE, Sylvia H. 620
BLUE ISLAND
Blue Island Pub Lib WOZNY, Jay 1370
BOLINGBROOK
Fountaindale Pub Lib District ANDERSON, Karen T. 23
TODD, Alexander W. 1248
North View Elementary Sch SULLIVAN, Geraldine M. . . . 1207
BROOKFIELD
Brookfield Pub Lib TODD, Margaret 1248
BUFFALO GROVE
St Mary's Sch MADAY, Geraldine 758
BURBANK
Prairie Trails Pub Lib District WEST, Barbara G. 1326
BURR RIDGE
Suburban Lib System MUELLER, Elizabeth 875
SPENCER, Joan M. 1173
CAHOKIA
East St Louis Sch District 189 BEAN, Bobby G. 69
St Louis Univ ANTHONY, Paul L. 29
CAIRO
Cairo Unit Sch District 1 CASE, Doris A. 191
CALUMET CITY
Calumet City Pub Lib EDGREN, Gale R. 336
CANTON
Parlin-Ingersoll Lib WILSON, W R. 1353
CARBONDALE
Carbondale Pub Lib CAMPBELL, Ray 177
Morris Lib BLACK, George W. 101
Southern Illinois Univ MCCOY, Ralph E. 799
Southern Illinois Univ at Carbondale BAUNER, Ruth E. 67
BEDIENT, Douglas 73
BORUZKOWSKI, Lilly A. 117
COHN, Alan M. 229
COOK, Margaret K. 240
COX, Shelley M. 253
CRANE, Lilly E. 255
DALE, Doris C. 270
HARWOOD, Judith A. 510
HOUDEK, Frank G. 562
JENKINS, Darrell L. 597
KILPATRICK, Thomas L. 648
KOCH, David V. 667
MATTHEWS, Elizabeth W. . . 785
PALMER, Carole L. 936
PERSON, Roland C. 961
PETERSON, Kenneth G. 964
POTEET, Susan S. 986
RYAN, Sheila 1071
STARRATT, Joseph A. 1182
WILSON, Betty R. 1350
WITHEE, Jane S. 1358
CARLINVILLE
Blackburn Coll FORBES, Lydia B. 389
CAROL STREAM
Glenbard North High Sch SONDALLE, Barbara J. 1167
CARTERVILLE
John A Logan Coll BARRETTE, Linda J. 59
Shawnee Lib System UBEL, James A. 1267

ILLINOIS (Cont'd)
CARTHAGE
Carthage Pub Lib .... ROBISON, Diana E. 1045
CHAMPAIGN
Burnham Hospital .... BENNINGTON, April A. 82
Champaign Pub Lib & Information
  Center .... MCCABE, Ronald B. 793
Illinois Natural History Survey ... HEISTER, Carla G. 523
Illinois State Geological Survey .. SUIDAN, Randa H. 1207
.... WASSON, Patricia G. 1308
Illinois State Water Survey ...... DESSOUKY, Ibtesam 296
.... MEI, Angela L. 821
Lincoln Trail Libs System .... FREDERICK, Sidney C. 399
.... PACEY, Brenda M. 933
News-Gazette .... VANCE, Carolyn J. 1272
US Army .... BLAKE, Martha A. 103
Univ of Illinois at Urbana-Champaign CHAPLAN, Margaret A. 201
.... KOH, Siew B. 668
.... LIM, Peck B. 727
.... MANSFIELD, Fred 767
.... MCBRIDE, Ruth B. 792
.... MCCULLOH, Judith M. 801
.... MOSBORG, Stella F. 870
.... NOGUCHI, Sachie 907
.... NYBERG, Cheryl R. 912
.... WERT, Lucille M. 1325
Univ of Illinois Press .... DAVIS, Charles H. 278
CHANUTE AFB
US Air Force .... PROVINCE, William R. 996
CHARLESTON
Charleston Carnegie Pub Lib .... MCDOWELL, Myrnella J. 804
Eastern Illinois Univ .... CHEN, Robert P. 205
.... GRISSO, Karl M. 471
.... ISOM, Bill V. 585
.... KAPLAN, Sylvia Y. 626
.... LIBBEY, Maurice C. 725
.... LUQUIRE, Wilson 749
.... NESBIT, Angus B. 896
.... POLLARD, Frances M. 981
.... RAO, Paladugu V. 1008
CHICAGO
A T Kearney Inc .... LARSEN, Linda E. 698
Altheimer & Gray .... ANES, Joy R. 27
American Association of Law Libs . JEPSON, William H. 599
American Dental Association .... KOWITZ, Aletha A. 674
.... PILARSKI, James P. 973
American Hospital Association ... FOSTER, Eloise C. 392
.... PINKOWSKI, Patricia E. 975
.... POOLE, Connie 983
.... WENZEL, Duane E. 1324
American Lib Association .... BERRY, John W. 90
.... BRAWLEY, Paul H. 130
.... CARLSON, Robert P. 182
.... CLINE, Helen R. 222
.... DAVIS, Maryellen K. 280
.... EBERHART, George M. 334
.... ELLEMAN, Barbara J. 343
.... EPP, Ronald H. 351
.... ESTES, Sally C. 355
.... FLAGG, Gordon E. 383
.... GALVIN, Thomas J. 415
.... GUY, Jeniece N. 479
.... HANSEN, Andrew M. 497
.... HUCHTING, Mary 569
.... KAYE, Marilyn J. 632
.... KNUTSON, Linda J. 666
.... KOBASA, Paul A. 666
.... KRUG, Judith F. 680
.... KUSZMAUL, Marcia J. 685
.... LEE, Joel M. 710
.... LYNCH, Mary J. 752
.... MCDERMOTT, Patrice 802
.... MELTON, Emily I. 823
.... MULLER, Karen 877
.... MYERS, Margaret R. 884
.... OTT, Bill 930
.... PARENT, Roger H. 940
.... PEARSON, Lois R. 952
.... PLOTNIK, Arthur 978
.... ROBERTSON, Deborah G. . 1041

ILLINOIS (Cont'd)
CHICAGO (Cont'd)
American Lib Association
.... ROCHMAN, Hazel P. 1046
.... ROMAN, Susan 1052
.... SCARRY, Patricia A. 1088
.... SEGAL, Joan S. 1111
.... SHAEVEL, Evelyn F. 1118
.... WALLACE, Linda K. 1297
.... WHITE, Howard S. 1331
.... WHITELEY, Sandra M. 1333
.... WILSON, Phillis M. 1352
.... WOOD, Irene P. 1364
.... WRIGHT, Helen K. 1371
.... ZVIRIN, Stephanie H. 1392
American Medical Association ... FUNK, Carla J. 409
.... GRAVES, Karen J. 459
.... HAFNER, Arthur W. 482
.... JAGODZINSKI, Cecile M. ... 591
.... MUELLER, Julie M. 875
American Theological Lib Association FIEG, Eugene C. 375
.... HURD, Albert E. 577
.... MARKHAM, Robert P. 771
ATLA Religion Indexes .... TREESH, Erica 1255
Arnstein Gluck Lehr & Milligan .. DRAKE, Francis L. 318
Art Institute of Chicago .... BYRNE, Nadene M. 169
.... GODLEWSKI, Susan G. 442
.... HANSEN, Roland C. 498
.... WALSH, Susan E. 1300
Arthur Andersen & Co .... GUINEE, Andrea M. 476
.... HARRIS, Jeanne G. 504
.... JAMESON, Martha E. 592
.... MURRAY, Marilyn R. 882
.... O'BRIEN, Barbara E. 914
.... SWANTEK, Kathleen M. ... 1214
Arvey Hodes Costello & Burman .. HARRINGTON, Margaret V. . 504
Association of Coll & Research Libs BOURDON, Cathleen J. 119
Bank Marketing Association ..... CORNICK, Ron 247
.... JORDAN, Charles R. 616
.... REMEIKIS, Lois A. 1022
.... STENGER, Brenda E. 1187
Batten Barton Durstine Osborn .. DELANEY, Jerry 289
Benedictine Sisters of Chicago .. REILLY, Jane A. 1020
Blue Cross & Blue Shield Association AHRENSFELD, Jan 8
Boston Consulting Group .... EMBAR, Indrani M. 347
.... PEPLOW, Richard C. 958
BRS Information Technologies ... MIFFLIN, Michael J. 833
Cactus Software .... MOTTRAM, Geoffrey 873
Campbell Mithun Inc .... LELLENBERG, Nancy A. 714
The Carroll Group Inc .... CARROLL VIRGO, Julie 187
.... VIRGO, Julie A. 1285
Catholic Bishop of Chicago ..... GARBIN, Angelo U. 417
CBH Publishing Inc .... HAAS, Carolyn B. 480
Center for Research Libs .... HELGE, Brian L. 524
.... NARU, Linda A. 888
.... PETERSEN, Karla D. 962
.... SIMPSON, Donald B. 1141
CFS Continental Inc .... DEPKE, Robert W. 293
Chapman & Cutler .... KOWALEWSKI, Denis S. ... 674
.... STEWART, Jamie K. 1192
Charles E Merriam Center for Pub
  Admin .... COATSWORTH, Patricia A. .. 224
Charles P Young Management
  Services .... SMITH, Denis J. 1154
Checkers Simon & Rosner ...... JOHNSON, G V. 604
Chicago Board of Education ..... BAKER, Ethelyn J. 48
.... HANLON, Patricia S. 496
.... KELLY, Raymond T. 638
.... MUELLNER, John P. 875
Chicago Board Options Exchange . LAGRUTTA, Charles J. 688
The Chicago Defender .... ADKINS, Marjorie R. 6
Chicago Historical Society ...... EVANS, Linda J. 357
.... MCGILL, Sara L. 806
.... MCNEILL, Janice M. 816
.... MOTLEY, Archie 872
.... RYAN, Diane M. 1070
.... VISKOCHIL, Larry A. 1285
Chicago Mercantile Exchange ... FROST, Bruce Q. 406

ILLINOIS (Cont'd)
 CHICAGO (Cont'd)
  Chicago Pub Lib

AHN, Hyonah K. 8
AUSTIN, Sandra G. 40
BROWN, Eva R. 143
BYRNE, Janice M. 169
CAPANO, Laura M. 179
CARLSON, Claudette J. 182
CLAPP, David F. 215
COBURN, Morton 225
DAVIS, Sandra B. 281
DAWOOD, Rosemary 282
DONOVAN, William A. 312
DUFF, John B. 323
FLYNN, Barbara L. 386
GOMEZ, Martin J. 447
GUSS, Emily R. 478
HERNANDEZ, Hector R. 531
HOGAN, Thomas J. 549
HUDDLESTON, Marsha E. . . 569
HUSFELDT, Jerry J. 578
JAVONOVICH, Kenneth L. . . 595
JONES, Mary L. 614
KIM, Chung S. 648
KNOBLAUCH, Mark G. 665
LOCKRIDGE, Eunice A. 736
MCELWAIN, William 804
MEYER, Barbara G. 829
MILLER, Glenda G. 838
MILLER, Robert 841
MOORE, John R. 860
MORRISON, Samuel F. 868
OAKS, Claire 913
O'SHEA, Cornelius M. 928
REGNER, Erlinda J. 1017
REID, Margaret L. 1019
REID, Peg L. 1019
RICHMOND, Diane A. 1030
SADLER, Shirley L. 1073
SCHWEGEL, Richard C. 1105
SCOTT, Alice H. 1106
STEELE, Leah J. 1184
STEWART, Richard A. 1193
STRAIT, Constance J. 1199
STROUSE, Roger L. 1203
THORNHILL, Robert E. 1242
TIBBITS, George D. 1244
TREJO-MEEHAN, Tamiye . . 1255
TRIMMER, Keith R. 1256
TUTEUR, Civia M. 1265
VACCARO, William J. 1270

Chicago Research & Trading Group
 Ltd   REITER, Richard R. 1022
Chicago State Univ   BOLT, Janice A. 113
                                            CHANG, Sookang H. 201
                                            MANCUYAS, Natividad D. . . . 764
                                            MEEKER, Robert B. 821
                                            MEYER, Beverly R. 829
                                            MOORE, Annie M. 858
                                            ONGLEY, David C. 924
                                            PATEL, Jashu 947
Chicago Sun Times   PERLMAN, Michael S. 959
Chicago Transit Authority   CULBERTSON, Lillian D. 263
                                            GENESEN, Judith L. 427
                                            KERR, Kevin G. 644
Chicago Tribune   HUSCHEN, Mary 578
                                            JANSSON, John F. 594
                                            PAPPALARDO, Marcia J. . . . 939
                                            ROTT, Richard A. 1060
Children's Memorial Hospital   WARD, Meg 1304
City Colleges of Chicago   LOCKE, John W. 736
City of Chicago   BENIGNO, Linda A. 80
                                            STEWART, James A. 1192
                                            TIWANA, Shah J. 1247
Clausen Miller Gorman Caffrey &
 Witous   FINNER, Susan L. 378
Columbia Coll   HSIEH, Cynthia C. 567
Columbus Hospital   FINNERTY, James L. 379
Combs Moorhead Associates Inc   MOORHEAD, John D. 862
Commerce Clearing House Inc   GIERING, Richard H. 433

ILLINOIS (Cont'd)
 CHICAGO (Cont'd)
Commonwealth Edison Co   PERTELL, Grace M. 961
Consoer Townsend & Associates   SCHRAMM, Mary T. 1099
Continental Illinois National Bank   ALTGILBERS, Cynthia J. 18
                                            MOULTON, James C. 873
                                            REED, Janet S. 1015
Cook County Law Lib   HAMMOND, Louise H. 494
                                            LAM, Judy 689
                                            MANN, Vijai S. 766
                                            MARTIN, Bennie E. 775
                                            NARANJO-BOSCH, Antonio
                                             A. 888
Dastrup/Vondruska Associates Ltd   VONDRUSKA, Eloise M. . . . 1288
Data Resources   MUZZO, Steven E. 883
DataChase Inc   CURRY, John A. 266
                                            LANDRY, Ronald 694
Datalogics Inc   BROWN, Steven A. 147
Deloitte Haskins & Sells   COTILLAS, Therese G. 250
                                            JACOBSEN, Teresa T. 590
DePaul Univ   ACKER, Robert L. 3
                                            BADGER, Barbara 44
                                            BROWN, Doris R. 143
                                            CLARKE, Susan M. 219
                                            COOPER, Rosemarie A. 243
                                            DORST, Thomas J. 313
                                            GASKELL, Judith A. 421
                                            GORDON, Elaine H. 451
                                            KIRKLAND, Kenneth L. 655
                                            LINNANE, Mary L. 731
                                            MULHERIN, William S. 876
                                            OLSON, James 922
                                            SINKUS, Raminta 1144
DIALOG Information Services Inc   KAMINECKI, Ronald M. 624
                                            LEE, Ann H. 709
Dr William M Scholl Coll   KLEIN, Richard S. 659
Dun & Bradstreet Corp   MORROW, Murrey 869
Edgewater Hospital   JONES, Gwendolyn C. 613
Encyclopaedia Britannica Inc   HOTIMLANSKA, Leah D. . . . 562
                                            SCHROEDER, Anne M. 1100
                                            UDDIN, Shantha C. 1267
Federal Reserve Bank of Chicago   BECKER, John C. 72
                                            PHILLIPS, Dorothy E. 968
Felician Coll   GALLAGHER, Eileen M. 414
                                            MOCH, Mary I. 851
Felician Sisters   RUDNIK, Mary C. 1065
Field Museum of National History   CALHOUN, Michele 172
                                            MILLER, Janet 838
Film Comm   HEMPEL, Gordon J. 525
First National Bank of Chicago   ADLER, Naomi L. 7
                                            PROBST, Virginia M. 994
Fluor Daniel   SEABERG, Eileen J. 1109
Foote Cone & Belding
 Communication   NELSON, Dwayne L. 893
                                            WERNETTE, Janice J. 1325
Frankel & Co   KOVITZ, Nancy R. 674
Friends of the Libraries USA   DOLNICK, Sandy F. 310
Frisbie Communications   FRISBIE, Richard 405
Gardner Carton & Douglas   DONAHUE, Karin V. 310
Gas Research Institute   MICHAEL, Ann B. 831
                                            SUVARNAMANI, Nuj 1212
Gorman Publishing Co   INGISH, Karen S. 582
Grant Hospital of Chicago   KLEINMUNTZ, Dalia S. 660
Grant/Jacoby Inc   GATES, Carol M. 421
Greeley & Hansen Engineers   CICHON, Marilyn T. 214
Harrington Institute of Interior Design   SCHUSTER, Adeline 1103
Harza Engineering Co   IRONS, Carol A. 584
Heidrick & Struggles   MASON, Margaret E. 781
Heidrick Partners Inc   FELDMAN, Linda A. 369
Helene Curtis Inc   BECKER, Jacquelyn B. 72
                                            CLAGGETT, Laura K. 215
Hill & Knowlton Inc   KEELER, Janice S. 634
Hill Van Santen Steadman & Simpson PETERSON, Scott W. 964
I P Sharp Associates Limited   FOUSER, Jane G. 393
Illinois Coll of Optometry   BAIR, Alice E. 47
                                            DUJSIK, Gerald 324
Illinois CPA Society   HEIDKA, Patricia L. 521
Illinois Dept of Employment Security MILUTINOVIC, Eunhee C. . . . 845

ILLINOIS (Cont'd)
CHICAGO (Cont'd)

Illinois Institute of Technology

BLOSS, Marjorie E. 106
DOWELL, David R. 315
GLANZ, Lenore M. 439
JONES, Ann L. 611
PICKETT, Mary J. 970
STEVENS, Michael 1190
STRZYNSKI, John C. 1204
VANCURA, Joyce B. 1273

Institute of Gas Technology   RIX, Dolores M. 1037
Interior Planning Consultants   DAVIS, Glenn G. 279
Isham Lincoln Beale   RABAI, Terezia 1001
J Walter Thompson Co   HALVORSON, Eric H. 490
                                 KEARNEY, Sharon M. 633
                                 LOFTHOUSE, Patricia A. 737
                                 OWENS, Tina M. 932
                                 PICCOLI, Roberta A. 970

Jenner & Block   BAUMANN, Walter R. 66
                                 CHUNG, Alison L. 213
Jesuit-Krauss-McCormick Lib   HILGERT, Elvire R. 539
                                 PULVER, Emilie G. 997
                                 WHIPPLE, Caroline B. 1329
John F Kennedy Medical Center   SCHULTZ, Therese A. 1102
John M Wing Foundation   WELLS, James M. 1322
John Marshall Law Sch   KEISER, Mary P. 635
                                 LI, Dorothy W. 724
                                 PETERSON, Randall T. 964
                                 REDDY, Michael B. 1013
                                 WLEKLINSKI, William A. 1359
Johnson Publishing Co   MENZIES, Pamela C. 825
Kennedy-King Coll   OSGOOD, James B. 928
Kessler, Merci & Associates   KESSLER, Howard E. 645
Kirkland & Ellis Lib   TEGLER, Patricia 1230
Latham & Watkins   COLLINS, Janet 232
Latin Sch of Chicago   RUMNEY, Leslie W. 1067
Legal Assistance Foundation   RYDEN, John 1071
Leo Burnett Co   MORROW, Mary D. 869
                                 MUNSON, Kathleen J. 879
Lexecon Inc   SMITH, Judy E. 1156
Lib of the United States Courts YOUNG, Peter W. 1383
Lib Tech Reports   CAMP, John F. 175
Lincoln Park Zoological Society SHAW, Joyce M. 1123
Login Brothers Book Co   TAKACS, Sharon N. 1220
Louis A Weiss Memorial Hospital SACHS, Iris P. 1073
Loyola Univ of Chicago   BENNETT, Lee L. 82
                                 DELANA, Genevieve A. 288
                                 DOYLE, Francis R. 317
                                 FRY, Roy H. 406
                                 FULTON, Tara L. 409
                                 GIANGRANDE, Mark G. 430
                                 HOLZENBERG, Eric J. 555
                                 KLINK, Carol A. 662
                                 LEWIS, Sherman L. 724
                                 MCCOY, Patricia S. 799
                                 NEWMAN, Gerald L. 899
                                 NEWMAN, Lorna R. 899
                                 NUTTY, David J. 912
                                 RANDALL, Sara L. 1006
                                 STALZER, Rita M. 1179
                                 SVED, Alexander 1212
                                 WAITE, Ellen J. 1293
                                 WARRO, Edward A. 1307
                                 WICKREMERATNE, Swarna 1335
Lurie Sklar & Simon Ltd   MABANAG, Teresita R. 753
Lutheran Church in America   WITTMAN, Elisabeth C. 1358
Malcolm X Coll   PARK, Chung I. 940
McDermott Will & Emery   COVOTSOS, Louis J. 252
                                 TAYLOR, Terry S. 1229
Meadville/Lombard Theological Sch GERDES, Neil W. 428
Medical Lib Association   MAYFIELD, Maurice K. 790
                                 PALMER, Raymond A. 936
Merriam Center Lib   VALAUSKAS, Edward J. 1271
Midwest Stock Exchange   BREEN, Joanell C. 131
Moody Bible Institute Lib   OSBORN, Walter 927
Mother McAuley Liberal Arts High
Sch   O'HEARON, Doris M. 919
                                 RICH, Elisabeth 1027
Mount Sinai Hospital Medical Center SOBKOWIAK, Emily J. 1165

ILLINOIS (Cont'd)
CHICAGO (Cont'd)

Mundelein Coll   CURRY, Jean K. 266
                                 DONAHOE, Patricia A. 310
Museum of Contemporary Art   PIRON, Alice M. 975
National Association of Realtors WOOLSEY, Mary E. 1368
Natl Clearinghouse for Legal Srvs Inc STEVENSON, Katherine ... 1191
National Computer Network Corp   MCDONALD, Tom 803
National Live Stock & Meat Board SIARNY, William D. 1134
National Opinion Research Center BOVA, Patrick 120
National Safety Council   HALASZ, Marilynn J. 484
                                 MARECEK, Robert J. 770
                                 MORTON, Laura 870
Neuman Williams Anderson & Olson JACOBSON, William R. 590
Newberry Lib   BURROWS, Thomas W. 163
                                 CULLEN, Charles T. 263
                                 MARSHALL, Jerilyn A. 774
                                 MICKELBERRY, Mark B. 833
                                 WYLY, Mary P. 1375
North Park Coll   BODI, Sonia E. 109
                                 GROSS, Dorothy E. 472
                                 JOHNSON, Timothy J. 609
                                 KARSTEN, Eileen S. 628
                                 PEARSON, Karen L. 952
Northeastern Illinois Univ   ALTHAGE, Celia J. 18
                                 HIGGINBOTHAM, Richard
                                 C. 537
                                 HILBURGER, Mary J. 538
                                 KISTNER, Glen A. 657
                                 MCGREGOR, James W. 808
                                 MISTARAS, Evangeline 848
                                 REED, Virginia R. 1015
                                 SCOTT, Sharon E. 1108
                                 VILARO, Annette B. 1284
Northwestern Univ   BEATTY, William K. 70
                                 BERKEY, Irene 87
                                 KREINBRING, Mary 677
                                 OLSON, Anton J. 922
                                 SCHWERIN, Kurt 1106
                                 SHEDLOCK, James 1124
                                 TAWYEA, Edward W. 1225
                                 YOON, Choong N. 1380
O'Connor & Associates   LONGMAN, Judith J. 740
Online Access Publishing Group   CRIM, Elias F. 258
Park Ridge Pub Lib   BRICKMAN, Sally F. 135
Peat Marwick Main & Co   GROFT, Mary L. 471
                                 WONG, Mabel K. 1363
Photographic Conservation Assoc Ltd MATTENSON, Murray M. ... 785
Pub Lib Association   RODGER, Eleanor J. 1047
Quaker Oats Co   ROBSON, Amy K. 1045
Quigley Preparatory Seminary North NORTON, Margaret W. 910
R R Donnelly & Sons Co   HAMILTON, Dawn J. 492
Rehabilitation Institute of Chicago KALUZSA, Karen L. 623
                                 ZOROWITZ, Richard D. 1390
Resurrection High Sch   LOCKWOOD, Sally S. 736
Resurrection Hospital   WIMMER, Laura M. 1354
Richard Cady-Rare Books   CADY, Richard H. 170
RMG Consultants Inc   IDDINGS, Daniel H. 581
                                 MCCLINTOCK, Patrick J. 797
                                 MCGEE, Rob 805
Rooks Pitts & Poust   HENRY, Nancy J. 529
Roosevelt Univ   BYRE, Calvin S. 169
                                 JONES, Adrian 610
                                 EMRE, Serpil A. 348
Rosenthal & Schanfield
Rush-Presbyterian St Luke's Medical
Ctr   BOLEF, Doris 112
                                 DI MAURO, Paul 304
                                 GARDNER, Trudy A. 418
                                 MARSHALL, Maggie L. 774
                                 SPARKS, Joanne L. 1171
Rush Univ
Russell Reynolds Associates Inc DOLMON, Barbara N. 310
St Joseph Hospital & Health Care
Center   WIMMER, Katherine P. 1354
St Mary of Nazareth Hospital Center KEENAN, Mary T. 634
St Symphorosa Elementary Sch   GLEESON, Joyce M. 441
Santa Fe Railway   DREAZEN, Elizabeth P. 318
Santa Fe Southern Pacific Corp   ALFONSI-GIN, Mary A. 13
Schiff Hardin & Waite   MICKEY, Melissa B. 833
                                 PATTERSON, Patricia A. 948
Scholl Coll of Podiatric Medicine NAGOLSKI, Donald J. 886

ILLINOIS (Cont'd)
CHICAGO (Cont'd)

Sears Roebuck & Co   SYED, Mariam A. 1217
    WARNER, Claudette S. 1305
Sherwin-Williams Co   CIBULSKIS, Elizabeth R. 214
Shlaes & Co   MACKEY, Denise R. 756
Skadden Arps Slate Meagher & Flom   MORRIS, Ann 866
Society of American Archivists   NEAL, Donn C. 890
    WEBER, Lisa B. 1314
South Chicago Community Hospital   RAYMAN, Ronald A. 1011
South Shore Printers Inc   MITZIGA, Walter J. 850
Spertus Coll of Judaica   SALTZMAN, Robbin R. 1077
Standard Educational Corp   KING, David E. 650
Stein Roe & Farnham Inc   JANNUSCH, Celeste K. 593
    MARANO, Nancy H. 768
Telephone & Data Systems Inc   KAPLAN, Rosalyn L. 626
Touche Ross & Co   GIAMBRONE, Richard J. 430
Truman Coll   SKIDMORE, Gail 1146
United Charities of Chicago   BURNS, Marie T. 162
US Army Corps of Engineers   ADAMSHICK, Robert D. 6
US League of Savings Institutions   ENGRAM, Sandra K. 350
    STONER, Ronald P. 1198
    WILSON, Charlotte A. 1350
United Way - Crusade of Mercy   BARNUM, Sally J. 58
Univ of Chicago   BEZIRGAN, Basima 93
    BIBLO, Mary 94
    BLOSS, Alexander B. 106
    BOOKSTEIN, Abraham 115
    CLARK, Gerald L. 217
    CORSARO, Julie A. 248
    DEERWESTER, Scott C. 287
    DILLON, Howard 303
    HALIBEY, Areta V. 486
    HURD, Julie M. 577
    LENNEBERG, Hans H. 715
    MEYER, Daniel 830
    MUNOFF, Gerald J. 879
    NOWAK, Ildiko D. 911
    NYE, James H. 912
    OWNES, Dorothy J. 932
    RADER, Jennette S. 1002
    RUNKLE, Martin D. 1067
    SCHNOOR, Harriet E. 1098
    SINHA, Vaswati R. 1143
    SUTHERLAND, Zena B. 1211
    SWANSON, Don R. 1213
    SWANSON, Patricia K. 1213
    VITOLINS, Ilga 1286
    WINGER, Howard W. 1355
    WRIGHT, Judith M. 1372
Univ of Illinois at Chicago   AISTARS, Aivars 9
    BAMBERGER, Mary A. 53
    BENGTSON, Marjorie C. 80
    BLOOM, Stephen C. 106
    CARPENTER, Kathryn H. ... 185
    CARSON, James G. 188
    COCHRANE, Kerry L. 225
    CULLARS, John M. 263
    DAUGHERTY, Robert A. 275
    EASTERBROOK, David L. 333
    EDWARDS, Dana S. 337
    FANG, Min L. 363
    FRANKLIN, Annette E. 397
    GEROW, Sandra F. 429
    HATTENDORF, Lynn C. 512
    HOLLI, Melvin G. 552
    JOHN, Nancy R. 601
    JOHNSON, Judith M. 606
    JONES, William G. 615
    KUKAC, Denise A. 683
    LAMBRECHT, Jay H. 691
    LAUDERDALE, Diane S. 702
    LIMAYE, Asha A. 727
    LYNCH, Beverly P. 751
    MALINOWSKY, H R. 763
    MAY, Ruby S. 789
    MCCARTNEY, Elizabeth J. ... 794
    MOUW, James R. 874
    NAPSHA, Cheryl A. 887
    PAIETTA, Ann C. 935

ILLINOIS (Cont'd)
CHICAGO (Cont'd)

Univ of Illinois at Chicago   PIZER, Irwin H. 977
    RETTIG, James R. 1024
    SCHULTHEISS, Louis A. ... 1101
    SELMER, Marsha L. 1114
    STRAWN, Aimee W. 1201
    TYLMAN, Wieslawa T. 1266
    VAN HOUTEN, Stephen ... 1275
    WESTON, E P. 1327
    WHITE, Anne E. 1330
    WIBERLEY, Stephen E. 1335
    WILLIAMSON, Linda E. 1347
    WINNIKE, Mary E. 1355
Univ of Illinois at Urbana-Champaign   LOHRER, Alice 737
Urban Libs Council   LADENSON, Alex 687
Veterans Administration Lakeside
  Med Ctr   KINNAIRD, Cheryl D. 653
Veterans Administration Medical
  Center   TROFIMUK, Janette A. 1257
Veterans Admin West Side Medical
  Center   MORRIS, Lynne D. 867
Viskase Corp   PUPIUS, Nijole K. 998
VMS Realty Partners   GAYNON, David B. 424
Ward Howell International Inc   PEURYE, Lloyd M. 966
Wildman Harrold Allen & Dixon   KRUPKA, Karen K. 680
William Brinks Olds Hofer Gilson &
  Lions   HU, Robert T. 568
William M Mercer Meidinger Hansen
  Inc   FUKAI, Eiko 408
William Wrigley Jr Co   HANRATH, Linda C. 497
    KOSMAN, Joyce E. 672
Winston & Strawn   BURGH, Scott G. 159
World Book Inc   KAYAIAN, Mary S. 632
    NAULT, William H. 889

CHICAGO HEIGHTS
Prairie State Coll   BAYER, Susan P. 67
CHICAGO RIDGE
Chicago Ridge Pub Lib   LOTZ, Marsha A. 742
CHILLICOTHE
The American Botanist   CROTZ, D K. 261
CICERO
Cicero Pub Lib   MALLER, Mark P. 763
    WEBER, Julie A. 1314
J Sterling Morton High Schs   SHERMAN, William F. 1128
Morton High Sch District 201   DOWNES, Valerie 316
CLINTON
Clinton Community Sch District 15   ADCOCK, Betty L. 6
COAL VALLEY
River Bend Lib System   MCKAY, Robert W. 810
COLLINSVILLE
Good Shepherd Lutheran Sch   STELLING, Dwight D. 1186
CRYSTAL LAKE
Crystal Lake Pub Lib   SPRINGBORN, Janice T. ... 1176
Follett Library Book Co   RICHARDSON, Vickie W. ... 1030
Follett Software Co   MILLER, Randy S. 841
DANVILLE
Danville Area Community Coll   DUCHOW, Sally 322
    KESSINGER, Pamela C. 644
St Elizabeth Hospital   VAIL, Evelyn J. 1270
DARIEN
Darien Pub Lib   BOUGHTON, Ruth E. 119
DE KALB
De Kalb Pub Lib   GOLDEN, Urla M. 445
Northern Illinois Univ   ABBOTT, Craig S. 1
    ALEXANDER, Liz C. 12
    ANDERSON, Byron P. 21
    AUSTIN, John R. 40
    DEQUIN, Henry C. 293
    DUTTON, Lee S. 329
    GILDEMEISTER, Glen A. 434
    GRAHAM, Robert W. 456
    GROSCH, Mary F. 472
    HAMILTON, David A. 491
    HOLZBERLEIN, Deanne B. .. 555
    HORST, Stanley E. 561
    HUANG, Samuel T. 568
    HURYCH, Jitka M. 578
    JONES, Dorothy E. 612

ILLINOIS (Cont'd)

DE KALB (Cont'd)
Northern Illinois Univ

KAUFFMAN, S B.	631
KIES, Cosette N.	647
KISSINGER, Patricia A.	656
LANIER, Donald L.	696
LARSEN, John C.	698
MILLER, Doris A.	837
NAIMAN, Sandra M.	886
OSORIO, Nestor L.	928
RASMUSSEN, Gordon E.	1009
RAST, Elaine K.	1009
RENSHAW, Marita	1023
RIDER, Philip R.	1032
RIDINGER, Robert B.	1032
ROYLE, Maryanne	1063
SCHORMANN, Victor	1099
SCHREIBER, Robert E.	1099
SHAVIT, David	1123
SMITH, Lester K.	1157
STUDWELL, William E.	1204
TITUS, Elizabeth M.	1247
TOROK, Andrew G.	1251
VANDER MEER, Gary L.	1274
VARNER, Carroll H.	1278
WELCH, Theodore F.	1321
WRIGHT, H S.	1371

DECATUR
A E Staley Manufacturing Co	WALLACE, Richard E.	1298
Archer Daniels Midland Co	PERMAN, Karen A.	959
Decatur Memorial Hospital	ROGINSKI, Donna J.	1050
Decatur Pub Lib	SEIDL, James C.	1112
Herald & Review	HEARN, Geraldine B.	518
Millikin Univ	HALE, Charles E.	485
Richland Community Coll	BERGER, Sidney E.	86
Rolling Prairie Lib System	HICKS, Frederick M.	537
	WUNDERLICH, Nina M.	1374

DEERFIELD
Baxter Travenol Laboratories Inc	GARDNER, Margaret L.	418
Deerfield Pub Lib	BEAN, Rick J.	69
	CALLAGHAN, Linda W.	173
	MCCABE, Peggy J.	793
Premark International	HAMILTON, Meredith L.	492
Rolf Jensen & Associates Ltd	KIENE, Andrea L.	647
Travel Labs	LEE, Soon H.	711
Trinity Evangelical Divinty Sch	OSWALT, Karen K.	929
	PORCELLA, Brewster	984
	WELLS, Keith P.	1322

DES PLAINES
Allied Signal	GAUMOND, Suzanne M.	423
Community Consolidated Sch District 62	CORCORAN, Frances E.	245
Consolidated Sch District 62	MARTINAZZI, Toni	779
DeSoto Inc	KOZELKA, Catherine C.	674
	WHITT, Diane M.	1334
Forest Inst of Professional Psychology	LUNDGREN, Janan L.	748
Oakton Community Coll	BOROWSKI, Joseph F.	117
	HAWLEY, Marsha S.	514

DIXON
Dixon Pub Lib	GILLFILLAN, Nancy M.	435

DONOVAN
Community Unit Sch District 3	BOGARDUS, Roberta S.	110

DOWNERS GROVE
Downers Grove Pub Lib	BALCOM, Kathleen M.	51
	BOWEN, Christopher F.	120
	BROWN, Nancy E.	146
	KLEKOWSKI, Lynn M.	660
	NEAL, Karen F.	890
	SCHULTZ, Lois B.	1102
Professional Lib Consultants	STOFFEL, Lester L.	1196

DUNDEE
Dundee Township Pub Lib District	MECHTENBERG, Paul	820

EAST MOLINE
East Moline Pub Lib	WALKER, Laura L.	1295

EAST PEORIA
Fondulac District Lib	PIRES, Priscilla J.	975
Illinois Central Coll	LINDGREN, William D.	729

ILLINOIS (Cont'd)

EDWARDSVILLE
Southern Illinois Univ at Edwardsville

	ABBOTT, John C.	1
	CALCAGNO, Philip M.	172
	JOHNSON, Charlotte L.	603
	MCFARLAND, Mary A.	805
	MOORE, Milton C.	860

ELDORADO
Eldorado Memorial Lib	FUNKHOUSER, Brenda K.	410

ELGIN
Elgin Sch District 46	LONG, Sara E.	739
Gail Borden Pub Lib District	SOVANSKI, Vincent G.	1170
Great Lakes Industries	GORDON, Lewis A.	451
Illinois Dept of Mental Health	FORD, Jennifer D.	389
Juergensmeyer and Assocs	JUERGENSMEYER, John E.	619

ELK GROVE VILLAGE
Township High Sch District 214	HOLBROCK, Mary A.	550

ELMHURST
City of Elmhurst	STEWART, Virginia R.	1193
Elmhurst Coll	DARLING, Elizabeth A.	274
	KLATT, Melvin J.	658
	NG, Pauline	900
Elmhurst Memorial Hospital	CALTVEDT, Sarah C.	174
Elmhurst Pub Lib	MASON, John A.	781
Immaculate Conception High Sch		
Mumps Medical Info Management Systems	KRUSS, Daniel M.	681

ELMWOOD PARK
Elmwood Park Pub Lib	HOFFMANN, Maurine L.	548

ELSAH
Principia Coll	BURRUSS, Marsha A.	163

EUREKA
Eureka Public Lib	THOMAS, Marcia L.	1237

EVANSTON
American Academy of Dermatology	STLUKA, Thomas H.	1195
City of Evanston	WRIGHT, Donald E.	1371
Evanston Hospital	ANTON, Tess	29
	FEINBERG, Linda J.	368
Evanston Pub Lib	ANDERSON, Charles R.	22
	JOHNSON, Marjorie M.	607
	KRIIGEL, Barbara J.	678
	SCHOR, Abby R.	1099
	SCHWARZLOSE, Sally F.	1105
	SUNDELL, Elizabeth B.	1210
Evanston Township High Sch	GOLDBERGER, Virginia F.	445
	SHAFER, Anne E.	1119
Garrett-Evangelical, Seabury-Western Sem	HAGEN, Loren R.	483
	THOMPSON, John W.	1240
Garrett Seabury Seminaries	SMITH, Newland F.	1159
Grumman/Butkus Associates	GRUMMAN, David L.	475
Mary S Senn & Associates	SENN, Mary S.	1115
Northwestern Univ	AAGAARD, James S.	1
	BALL, Mary A.	52
	BENNETT, Scott B.	82
	BJORNCRANTZ, Leslie B.	100
	BOELKE, Joanne H.	110
	BRADY, Mary M.	127
	CAMPANA, Deborah A.	175
	CLOUD, Patricia D.	223
	DAVIDSON, Lloyd A.	276
	ELSTEIN, Rochelle S.	346
	FINEMAN, Charles S.	377
	FRIEDER, Richard D.	403
	GRISCOM, Richard W.	471
	HILL, Janet S.	540
	HORNY, Karen L.	560
	LEONARD, Kevin B.	716
	LOWMAN, Judith T.	744
	MAYLONE, R R.	790
	MCCARTHY, Mary C.	794
	MCGOWAN, John P.	807
	MCHENRY, Renee E.	808
	MCHUGH, William A.	809
	MICHAELSON, Robert C.	832
	NIELSEN, Brian	903
	PANOFSKY, Hans E.	938
	PRENDERGAST, Kathleen M.	990
	QUERY, Lance D.	999
	QUINN, Patrick M.	1000

ILLINOIS (Cont'd)
  EVANSTON (Cont'd)
    Northwestern Univ

	RAMM, Dorothy V.	1005
	ROBERTS, Donald L.	1039
	ROBERTS, Sally M.	1041
	SHAYNE, Mette H.	1124
	SHERMAN, Sarah	1128
	STAMM, Andrea L.	1179
	STRANGE, Michele M.	1200
	STRAWN, Gary L.	1201
	STUTZ, Patricia A.	1206
	WARD, Shirlene A.	1304
	WILLIAMS, Charles M.	1342
NOTIS Northwestern Univ	MILLER, Bruce A.	836
NOTIS Systems Inc	DREWETT, William O.	319
	MCGINN, Thomas P.	806
	SCHAPIRO, Benjamin H.	1090
Rotary International	HUNT, Janis E.	575
Saint Francis Hospital	GIBSON, Patricia M.	432
	VAN DYKE, Mary C.	1275
Shand Morahan & Co Inc	FIELD, Connie N.	375
Valerie Metzler Archivist & Historian	METZLER, Valerie	829
Washington National Insurance Co	BRYANT, Eugenia D.	152
	COX, Joyce M.	253
White & Janssen Inc	WHITE, Matthew H.	1331

  EVERGREEN PARK
    Little Co of Mary Hospital — KARNER, Rita — 627
  FAIRFIELD
    Fairfield Community High Sch — MAYNARD, Marilyn K. — 790
  FLORA
    Cumberland Trail Lib System — DOCKINS, Glenn — 307
                                  HARRIS, Thomas J. — 506
  FRANKFORT
    Frankfort Pub Lib Dist — NOVAK, Lorrine M. — 911
  FRANKLIN PARK
    Franklin Park Pub Lib — BOYLE, Lawrence C. — 124
                            VOSS, Joyce M. — 1289
                            WATSON, Robert E. — 1310
    Rich Inc — MURPHY, Therese B. — 881
  FREEPORT
    Freeport Pub Lib — LOCASCIO, John F. — 735
    Highland Community Coll — WELCH, Eric C. — 1321
    Plager Hasting & Krug Ltd — FREY, Roxanne C. — 403
  GALESBURG
    Galesburg Pub Lib — BABANOURY, Betty G. — 43
    Knox Coll — ROBISON, Carley R. — 1045
    Western Illinois Lib System — KIRK, Sherwood — 654
                                  WINNER, Ronald — 1355
  GARDNER
    Gardner-S Wilmington Township High
      Sch — MCCLAREY, Catherine A. — 796
  GENESEO
    Geneseo Pub Lib District — REDINGTON, Deirdre E. — 1014
    George B Dedrick Pub Lib — GILBORNE, Jean E. — 434
  GENEVA
    DuPage Lib System — FEINER, Arlene M. — 369
                        LUEDER, Dianne B. — 747
                        MORRISON, Carol J. — 868
                        SHURMAN, Richard L. — 1134
    Geneva Pub Lib Dist — HINTZ, Jeanne E. — 543
    Kane County 16th Circuit Court — POINTON, Louis R. — 980
  GLEN CARBON
    Village of Glen Carbon — DAVISON, Carol A. — 281
  GLEN ELLYN
    Coll of DuPage — BERGER, Marianne C. — 85
                    FRADKIN, Bernard — 395
                    GEYER, Robert I. — 430
                    TEMPLE, Harold L. — 1230
    Glen Ellyn Sch District 41 — ADCOCK, Donald C. — 6
  GLENDALE HEIGHTS
    Glendale Heights Community Hospital
      Inc — APOSTOLOPOULOS,
             Sophia S. — 29
    Glenside Pub Lib District — VOJTECH, Kathryn — 1287
  GLENVIEW
    Glenbrook Hospital — PERLES, Paul — 959
    Glenview Pub Lib — MOSS, Barbara J. — 872
    Kraft Inc — BIRKHOLD, Martha S. — 98
    Sch District 30 — WEISMAN, Kathryn M. — 1319

ILLINOIS (Cont'd)
  GLENVIEW (Cont'd)
    Scott Foresman & Co — HARRIS, Jane F. — 504
                          ROBERTSON, S D. — 1042
  GODFREY
    Lewis and Clark Community Coll — HUMPHRIES, Beverly H. — 574
  GRANITE CITY
    Lueders Robertson & Konzen — KONZEN, Brian E. — 671
  GREAT LAKES
    Naval Dental Research Institute — DIEHL, Mark — 302
  GREENVILLE
    Greenville Coll — HOPKINS, Jane L. — 558
  GURNEE
    Grayslake Community High Sch — ROBIEN, Eleanor K. — 1043
  HARVEY
    Harvey Pub Lib — AUFDENKAMP, Joann — 39
                     OCHSNER, Renata E. — 915
    Ingalls Memorial Hospital — FOLEY, Donna H. — 387
  HENNEPIN
    Putnam County Pub Lib — PITCHFORD, Martha K. — 976
  HIGHLAND PARK
    Baxter Travenol Laboratories Inc — SHERRY, Diane H. — 1129
    Highland Park Hospital — PRIOR, Janice L. — 993
    Highland Park Pub Lib — BRACHMANN, Kathleen A. — 124
                            GREENFIELD, Jane W. — 464
                            KAPLAN, Paul M. — 626
  HINSDALE
    Hinsdale High Sch District 86 — PETERS, Janet E. — 962
    Hinsdale Pub Lib — CZARNECKI, Cary J. — 268
                       SODERSTRUM, Ann L. — 1165
    Hinsdale Township High Sch Central — GRIFFIN, Thelma J. — 469
  HOFFMAN ESTATES
    Illinois Library Association — MILLER, Deborah — 837
  HOMEWOOD
    Dolton Pub Lib — FITZGERALD, Adena H. — 382
  ITASCA
    Itasca Community Lib — HOGAN, Patricia M. — 549
    Society of Actuaries — CHAPA, Joan I. — 201
  JACKSONVILLE
    Illinois Coll — ZUIDERVELD, Sharon R. — 1391
    Passavant Area Hospital — KNIGHT, Dorothy H. — 664
    Routt High Sch — MILLER, Stella M. — 842
  JOLIET
    Joliet Pub Lib — HALL, Clark J. — 487
                     JOHNSTON, James R. — 610
                     MOZGA, John P. — 874
                     MUNN, Patty L. — 879
    Valley View Sch District 365U
    Will County Law Lib — MOEN, Art J. — 851
  KANEVILLE
    Kaneville Pub Lib — HANKES, Janice R. — 496
  KANKAKEE
    Olivet Nazarene Univ — KINNERSLEY, Ruth T. — 653
  KEWANEE
    Kewanee Pub Lib — HARRIET, Conklin W. — 503
  LA GRANGE
    American Nuclear Society — WEBSTER, Lois S. — 1314
    La Grange Memorial Hospital — GRUNDKE, Patricia J. — 475
    Sch District 105 of La Grange — FERRO-NYALKA, Ruth R. — 374
    Suburban Lib System — HUSLIG, Dennis M. — 578
  LAKE BLUFF
    Lake Bluff Pub Lib — LAMB, Sara G. — 690
    Quality Books Inc — LEISNER, Anthony B. — 714
    Research Publications — DICK, John H. — 300
  LAKE FOREST
    Barat Coll — JEFFORDS, Rebecca J. — 596
    Chicago Research Group Inc — MARSHALL, Deborah M. — 774
    Lake Forest Coll — BRIGGS, Martha T. — 135
                       MIKOLYZK, Thomas A. — 834
                       MILLER, Arthur E. — 835
    Lake Forest Country Day Sch — DANOFF, Fran — 274
  LAKE ZURICH
    Dearborn Div of W R Grace & Co — MITCHELL, Martha M. — 849
    Ela Area Pub Lib District — DEMETRAKAKES, Jennifer
                                 B. — 291
                                 LARSON, Carol — 699
  LIBERTYVILLE
    Cook Memorial Pub Lib District — LAMBERT, Sandra L. — 690
                                     SULLIVAN, Eileen M. — 1207
    Hollister Incorporated — CUNNINGHAM, Elizabeth A. — 265
    Libertyville High Sch — KRAMER, Pamela K. — 675

ILLINOIS (Cont'd)

LIBERTYVILLE (Cont'd)
Libertyville United Methodist Church   HOOVER, Margaret R. 557
Winchester House   RING, Anne M. 1035
LINCOLNWOOD
Lincolnwood Pub Lib District   WHITNEY, Ruth 1334
LISLE
Bell Communications Research   IFFLAND, Carol D. 581
Illinois Benedictine Coll   THOMPSON, Bert A. 1239
The Morton Arboretum   HASSERT, Rita M. 511
  SHOTWELL, Richard T. 1133
R R Donnelley   MILLER, Thomas R. 843
LOCKPORT
Des Plaines Valley Pub Lib District   CHAPP, Debra R. 202
LOMBARD
DeVry Institute of Technology   BOWDEN, Philip L. 120
I S Grupe Inc   SCHIPMA, Peter B. 1093
Lombard Sch District 87   TUGGLE, Ann M. 1262
Mary Gaither Marshall Rare Book
  Consult   MARSHALL, Mary G. 774
Mid Con Corp   ELL, Elizabeth L. 343
Montini High Sch   RACZYNSKI, Mary K. 1002
National Coll of Chiropractic   IWAMI, Russell A. 586
  WHITEHEAD, Joyce E. 1332

MACOMB
Western Illinois Univ   CHANG, Roy T. 201
  CHU, Felix T. 212
  GOUDY, Allie W. 454
  NOLLEN, Sheila H. 908
  TING, Lee H. 1246
  WAGNER, Ralph D. 1292

MADISON
Madison Pub Lib   KERN, Frances L. 643
MARKHAM
Illinois Sch District 144   O'SHEA, Margaret A. 928
MASCOUTAH
Mascoutah Sch District 19   SCHAACK, Wilma J. 1088
MATTESON
Wei T'o Associates Inc   SMITH, Richard D. 1159
MATTOON
City of Mattoon   GRAFTON, Mona R. 456
Sarah Bush Lincoln Health Center   CLAYTON, Nina A. 220
MAYWOOD
Loyola Univ of Chicago   LUDWIG, Logan T. 747
MCCOOK
Akzo Chemic America   PETRY, Robyn E. 965
Akzo Chemie America   PACETTI, Karen C. 933
MCLEAN
Mount Hope Township   VAN HOORN, Audra G. . . . 1275
MELROSE PARK
Gottlieb Memorial Hospital   OSTERTAG, Ina 928
RHC-Spacemaster   TRELEASE, Robert J. 1255
Westlake Community Hospital   STRAUSS, Carol D. 1201
METAMORA
Illinois Prairie District Pub Lib   FREDERICKSEN, Grant A. . . 400
Metamora Township High Sch   WOOLARD, Wilma L. 1368
MIDLOTHIAN
Midlothian Pub Lib   PETERSON, Carolyn R. 963
MOLINE
Deere & Co   HAGBERG, Betty S. 482
  POLK, Diana B. 981
  STEGH, Leslie J. 1185
Moline Pub Lib   CHENOWETH, Rose M. 206
  SNYDER, Sherrie E. 1165
MOMENCE
Baker & Taylor   COOPER, Susan C. 243
MONMOUTH
Monmouth Coll   HAUGE, Harris R. 512
MONTICELLO
Allerton Pub Lib   LINTNER, Barbara J. 731
MORRIS
VSI Chemicals Co   VOSS, Ingrid M. 1289
MORRISONVILLE
John B Podeschi Bibliographer   PODESCHI, John B. 979
MORTON
Morton Pub Lib   SHERMAN, Janice E. 1128
MORTON GROVE
Morton Grove Pub Lib   GOLATA, John P. 444
  OSERMAN, Stuart 928

ILLINOIS (Cont'd)

MOUNDS
Meridian Community Unit Sch District
  101   SHAW, Louis P. 1123
MT MORRIS
McGregor Subscription Services Inc   LONG, Roger J. 739
MT PROSPECT
Mt Prospect Pub Lib   GRIEGER, Sharon L. 468
  MARABOTTI, Denise M. 768
  TIWANA, Nazar H. 1247
Mt Prospect Pub Schs   GUNDERSEN, Shirley S. . . . 477
MUNDELEIN
Fremont Pub Lib Dist   ROSE, Marta A. 1055
NAPERVILLE
Amoco Corp   AVERY, May S. 42
  BUNTROCK, Robert E. 157
  STRYCK, B C. 1203
AT&T Bell Laboratories   CHAPMAN, Ruby M. 202
  FURLONG, Robert E. 410
  ROMANO, Katherine V. . . . 1052
Edward Hospital   AMBROSE, Karen S. 19
Indian Prairie Sch District 204   YOUNG, Nancy J. 1382
Nalco Chemical Co   BOYLE, Stephen 124
  STUNKARD, Gilbert L. 1205
Nichols Lib   FIELDING, Susan K. 376
North Central Coll   MEACHEN, Edward W. 819
Packer Engineering Associates Inc   VAUGHAN, Ruth M. 1280
Pub Lib of Naperville   PEARSON, Roger L. 953
Sun Newspapers   KAGANN, Laurie K. 621
NASHVILLE
Nashville Community High Sch
  District 99   RUSIEWSKI, Charles B. . . . 1068
NEW LENOX
New Lenox Sch District 122   STARK, Colette G. 1181
NILES
Albert Whitman & Co   BOYD, Joseph W. 122
Chamberlain Manufacturing Corp   CARTER, Ida 189
Niles Pub Lib District   KALRA, Bhupinder S. 623
  MCKENZIE, Duncan J. 811
Notre Dame High Sch for Boys   SCHMID, Judith L. 1095
Triodyne Inc   HAMILTON, Beth A. 491
  HANSEN, Cheryl A. 497
NORMAL
Corn Belt Lib System   MC LAUGHLIN, Terry L. . . . 813
  MEISELS, Henry R. 822
  POULTNEY, Judy R. 987
Illinois State Univ   ALEXANDER, Lynetta L. 12
  BROWN, Mary J. 146
  DELOACH, Marva L. 290
  DELONG, Dianne S. 290
  DELONG, Douglas A. 290
  EASTON, William W. 333
  GOEHNER, Donna M. 443
  GOWDY, Laura E. 455
  MATTHEWS, Priscilla J. . . . 785
  NOURIE, Alan R. 910
  PETERSON, Fred M. 963
  THAKORE, Manhar 1234
NORTH RIVERSIDE
North Riverside Pub Lib   DAVIS, Carol L. 278
Robert W Mueller Rare Books   MUELLER, Robert W. 875
NORTHBROOK
A C Nielsen Co   STELK, W E. 1186
Allstate Insurance Co   BRUEMMER, Alice 149
Glenbrook North High Sch   WICKS, Jerry R. 1335
Northbrook Pub Lib   NICKELS, Judith L. 902
  REIMER, Elizabeth A. 1020
  REISNER, Susan 1021
  WESTON, Ann B. 1327
NORTHFIELD
Stepan Co   BROWN, Patricia L. 146
OAK BROOK
Official Airline Guides   JOHNSON, Carol 602
  OGREN, Mark S. 918
OAK FOREST
Acron Pub Lib District   NOVELLI, Jean L. 911
St Elizabeth's Hospital   CORDONI, Earl C. 246

ILLINOIS (Cont'd)

OAK LAWN
Christ Hospital & Medical Center ... KELLY, Janice E. 637
LLSC Inc ... MCGRAW, Scott C. 807
Oak Lawn Pub Lib ... DOBREZ, Cynthia K. 307
... MCMAHON, Judith L. 814
... MOORMAN, John A. 862
Oaklawn Pub Lib ... MCELROY, Beth A. 804
Suburban Lib System ... AMELING, Linda S. 19
... EGAN, Elizabeth M. 338
... GOULDING, Mary A. 454
... ROCHE, Richard G. 1046

OAK PARK
Histl Socty of Oak Park & River
Forest ... KELM, Carol R. 638
Libraries Inc ... DICK, Ellen A. 300
Oak Park Elementary Sch District 97 ... VOTH, Mary S. 1289
Oak Park Pub Lib ... STEVENSON, Sheila M. ... 1191
OBLONG
Oblong Community Unit Sch District 4 ... HEYDUCK, Marilyn J. 535
O'FALLON
US Air Force ... KNUDTSON, Gail L. 666
ORLAND PARK
Orland Park Pub Lib ... KRAMER, Ruth M. 675
OSWEGO
Oswego Pub Lib District ... FEATHER, Pamela P. 367
... PORTER, Carol 984

OTTAWA
Starved Rock Lib System ... WILLSON, Richard E. 1349
PALATINE
Palatine Pub Lib District ... BOURKE, Jacqueline K. 119
... BURNS, Mary F. 162
... MAGNUSSEN, Ruth A. 760
Township High Sch District 211 ... EVERHART, Paul R. 358
William Rainey Harper Coll ... FISHER, Marshall 381
PALOS HEIGHTS
Trinity Christian Coll ... SLIEKERS, Hendrik 1149
PALOS HILLS
Green Hills Pub Lib District ... CARY, Jan E. 191
... SODOWSKY, Kay M. 1165
Moraine Valley Community Coll ... D'AVERSA, Concettina M. ... 276
... HESSLER, Nancy R. 534
... TEO, Elizabeth A. 1231

PARIS
Paris Union Sch District 95 ... GERLACH, Gretchen J. 429
PARK FOREST
Park Forest Pub Lib ... MURRAY, Theresa A. 882
PARK RIDGE
American Farm Bureau Federation ... SCHULTZ, Susan 1102
Hospital Sisters Health Plan Inc ... KNARZER, Arlene 663
Lutheran General Hospital ... CRISPEN, Joanne 259
Park Ridge Pub Lib ... MCCULLY, William C. 801
Park Ridge Sch District 64 ... BOUMA, Ray H. 119
PEKIN
Dirksen Congressional Research
Center ... MACKAMAN, Frank H. 756
Illinois Valley Lib System ... NIEHAUS, Barbara J. 903
... WILFORD, Valerie J. 1339
Pekin Pub Lib ... WEISS, Paula K. 1320
PEORIA
Bradley Univ ... HANSEN, Eleanore E. 497
Methodist Medical Center ... WALTERS, Patsy M. 1301
Peoria Pub Lib ... GIBBS, Margareth 431
... KOSCIELSKI, Roberta L. 672
... NELSON, Maggie E. 894
... SWORSKY, Felicia G. 1217
Univ of Illinois at Chicago ... LANDWIRTH, Trudy K. 694
PHILO
Philo Township Pub Lib ... HIGHSMITH, June C. 538
PLAINFIELD
Plainfield Sch Dist 202 ... DIERCKS, Eileen K. 302
POLO
Polo Sch District 22 ... WOOD, Jonette E. 1364
PONTIAC
Pontiac Pub Lib ... HAMILTON, Patricia A. 492
PRAIRIE VIEW
Adlai E Stevenson High Sch ... KRUEGER, Sharon B. 680
PROSPECT HEIGHTS
Prospect Heights Pub Lib District ... MORGAN, Miriam M. 864
... ROZANSKI, Barbara 1064

ILLINOIS (Cont'd)

QUINCY
Blessing Coll of Nursing ... ROMANACE, Gisele R. 1052
Cooperative Services ... MORRIS, Susan M. 867
Great River Lib System ... ALBSMEYER, Betty J. 11
... GRAY, Karen S. 460
... TYER, Travis E. 1266
Illinois State Veterans Home ... EGGERS, Thomas D. 339
Quincy Coll ... KINGERY, Victor P. 652
... WEE, Lily K. 1315
Quincy Pub Lib ... CONROY, Margaret M. 238
... DECKER, Judy J. 286
... MCKIERNAN, Lester I. 811
St Mary Hospital ... RECKS, Dorcas E. 1013
RICHTON PARK
Richton Park Pub Lib District ... NEVINS, Patrick F. 898
RIVER FOREST
C Berger & Co ... FAUST, Julia B. 366
Concordia Coll ... LATZKE, Henry R. 702
Dominican Central Province ... WRIGHT, David F. 1371
Rosary Coll ... BLACK, Kenneth L. 101
... DAVIS, Richard A. 280
... FENSKE, Ruth E. 371
... LI, Richard T. 725
... NOONAN, Eileen F. 908
... TZE-CHUNG, Li 1267
St Vincent Ferrer Sch ... SCHAEFER, Elizabeth K. 1088
RIVERSIDE
Riverside Pub Lib ... OLDERR, Steven 920
Sch District 208 ... HELLER, Dawn H. 524
ROCK ISLAND
Augustana Coll ... BELAN, Judith A. 75
... CALDWELL, John 172
... CONWAY, Colleen M. 239
... MASON, Marjorie L. 781
... MILLER, Marian I. 840
... WESTERBERG, Kermit B. ... 1326
Modern Woodmen of America ... LEVIS, Gail A. 721
ROCKFORD
County of Winnebago ... LINDVALL, Robert J. 730
Jack Chitwood Consultant ... CHITWOOD, Julius R. 209
Legal Research Services ... HUTCHINS, Richard G. 579
Northern Illinois Lib System ... ANDERSON, Nancy E. 24
... HUTCHINS, Mary J. 579
... SCHOLTZ, James C. 1098
... WELCH, Steven J. 1321
... WINTER, Bernadette G. 1356
Rockford Board of Education ... NATHAN, Phyllis 889
Rockford Memorial Hospital ... LONG, Judith N. 739
Rockford Pub Lib ... NORWOOD, Pamela Z. 910
... PRESSING, Kirk L. 991
... ROSENFELD, Joel C. 1056
Rockford Sch District 205 ... LINDGREN, Beverly P. 729
Saint Anthony Medical Center ... DALE, Nancy 270
Sundstrand Aviation ... HAMILTON, D A. 491
Univ of Illinois at Rockford ... DALRYMPLE, Prudence W. ... 271
ROLLING MEADOWS
Item Data Inc ... LOWELL, Brian V. 744
... SINE, George H. 1143
Northrop Corp ... KONISHI, Sue S. 670
Northrop Sch District ... CAREY, Kevin J. 181
Rolling Meadows Pub Lib ... HEMENWAY, Patti J. 525
... SVENSSON, C G. 1212
Schroeder Editorial Services ... SCHROEDER, Sandra J. ... 1100
ROMEOVILLE
Fountaindale Pub Lib District ... HACKETT, Nancy J. 481
ROSEMONT
National Dairy Council ... CULBERTSON, Diana L. 263
... FARRELL, Patricia H. 365
ROUND LAKE
Baxter Healthcare Corp ... ALLEN, Dorothy L. 14
Baxter Travenol Laboratories Inc ... TAN, Elizabeth L. 1222
Travenol Laboratories Inc ... WORSTER, Carol L. 1369
ST CHARLES
St Charles Pub Lib ... BROWN, Diana M. 143
... HAULE, Laura M. 512
SANDWICH
Sandwich Township Pub Lib ... JOHNSON, Joanne D. 606
SAVOY
Illinois State Water Survey ... JOHNSON, Anita D. 602

ILLINOIS (Cont'd)

SCHAUMBURG
Ameritech Services Inc — METCALFE, Douglas N. 828
Keycom Electronic Publishing — AVERY, Cliff 41
Schaumburg Township Pub Lib — BRADLEY, Anne 125
MADDEN, Michael J. 758
SEAMAN, Sally G. 1109
Zurich-American Insurance Group — HORTON, Kathy L. 561

SCHILLER PARK
Schiller Park Elementary Sch District
81 — EFFERTZ, Rose 338

SCOTT AFB
Scott Air Force Base — GORDON, Diane M. 451
US Air Force — BURNSIDE, Diane B. 163
MARSHALL, Kathryn E. 774

SENECA
Seneca Pub Lib — HOGAN, Louise G. 549

SHOREWOOD
Bur Oak Lib System — SPEARMAN, Donna G. 1172
Shorewood-Troy Lib — POTENZIANI, Jo A. 986

SILVIS
Illini Hospital — SWATOS, Priscilla L. 1214

SKOKIE
G D Searle — SLAWNIAK, Patricia M. 1148
Joint Computer Programs for Libs — MITCHELL, Joyce P. 849
North Suburban Lib System — GRODINSKY, Deborah 471
ROOSE, Tina 1053
Packaging Corp of America — TRUE, Jacqueline J. 1259
Portland Cement Assn — SPIGELMAN, Cynthia A. ... 1174
Rand McNally & Co — GROSSMAN, David G. 473
Skokie Pub Lib — ANTHONY, Carolyn A. 28
CLELAND, Camille S. 220
GINSBURG, Coralie S. 438
JACOB, Merle L. 589
PALMORE, Sandra N. 937
SORENSON, Liene S. 1168

SMITHTON
Kaskaskia Lib System — CHAMBERLIN, Edgar W. ... 198
ENSLEY, Robert F. 350

SOUTH BARRINGTON
Allstate Insurance Co — JUSTIE, Julie H. 620

SOUTH HOLLAND
South Holland Pub Lib — NELSON, Barbara L. 893
Thornton Township High Sch District
205 — GIBBS, Mary E. 431
SHANNON, Kathleen L. 1120

SPRINGFIELD
City of Springfield — WHITAKER, Geraldine M. ... 1329
IL Coalition Against Sexual Assault — BRADWAY, Becky J. 126
Illinois Department of Corrections — CHESLEY, Thea B. 207
Illinois Historic Preservation Agency — BOWEN, Laurel G. 120
Illinois Secretary of State — SORENSEN, Mark W. 1168
TEMPLE, Wayne C. 1230
Illinois State Archives — MOORE, Karl R. 860
Illinois State Board of Education — SIVAK, Marie N. 1144
Illinois State Historical Lib — FERGUSON, Bonnie E. 372
Illinois State Lib — BOSTIAN, Irma R. 117
KELLERSTRASS, Amy L. ... 636
LAMONT, Bridget L. 691
PENCE, Cheryl S. 956
PENDERGRASS, Margaret
E. 956
SHERWOOD, Arlyn K. 1129
Legislative Research Unit — LARISON, Brenda 697
Lincoln Lib — FRISCH, Corrine A. 405
VETTER, Jean A. 1283
VOLKMANN, Carl W. 1287
Office of the Auditor General — ETTER, Constance L. 355
READ Ltd — HILDRETH, Charles R. 539
St John's Hospital — WRIGLEY, Kathryn J. 1373
Sangamon State Univ — ALLEY, Brian 16
ROBERTSON, Ina N. 1042
SHACKLETON, Suzanne M. 1118
Southern Illinois Univ Sch of Medicine — BERK, Robert A. 87
DILLEY, Richard A. 303
HITCHCOCK, Gail A. 544
HORNEY, Joyce C. 560
KELLEY, Rhona S. 636
KLESTINSKI, Martha A. 661
State Journal-Register — VANCE, Sandra L. 1273

ILLINOIS (Cont'd)

SPRINGFIELD (Cont'd)
State of Illinois — DALY, John E. 271
EFIRD, Frank K. 338
Supreme Court of Illinois — BRADLEY, Catherine 125

STICKNEY
Stickney-Forest View Lib District — WAGNER, Robin O. 1292

STREAMWOOD
Poplar Creek Pub Lib District — DEUEL, Marlene R. 296
KLOCKENGA, Gary R. 662

STREATOR
St Mary's Hospital — FLANIGAN, Anne J. 383

SULLIVAN
Sullivan Community Unit Schs Dist
300 — ELDER, Nancy J. 342

SUMMIT
Argo-Summit Bedford Park Pub Schs — WIRIG, Joan S. 1356

SUN CITY
BYLS Press — STUHLMAN, Daniel D. 1205

SYCAMORE
Northern Illinois Univ — SULLIVAN, Peggy A. 1208

TAYLORVILLE
Taylorville Pub Lib — PODESCHI, Gwen 979

TROY
Tri-Township Lib — HOLMES, Norman W. 553

UNIVERSITY PARK
Governors State Univ — TROY, Shannon M. 1258
VARNET, Harvey 1279

URBANA
Illinois State Geological Survey — KRICK, Mary 678
Mercy Hospital — WILLIAMSON, Harriet 1347
Music Lib Association — GUSHEE, Marion S. 478
Univ of Illinois at Urbana-Champaign — AGGARWAL, Narindar K. 7
ALLEN, Walter C. 16
ANDERSON, Nancy D. 24
ATKINS, Stephen E. 38
AULD, Lawrence W. 40
BINGHAM, Karen H. 97
BOAST, Carol 108
BOPP, Richard E. 116
BRICHFORD, Maynard J. 134
BROWN, Norman B. 146
BURBANK, Richard D. 158
CAROTHERS, Diane F. 184
CHOLDIN, Marianna T. 210
CLARK, Barton M. 216
CLARK, Sharon E. 218
CLOONAN, Michele V. 223
COBB, David A. 224
DAVIS, Elisabeth B. 278
DOWNS, Robert B. 317
EDMONDS, M L. 336
ESTABROOK, Leigh S. 355
FAIRCHILD, Constance A. ... 361
FAYNZILBERG, Irina 367
FORREST, Charles G. 390
GOLDHOR, Herbert 445
GRIFFITHS, Suzanne N. 469
HENDERSON, Kathryn L. ... 526
HENDERSON, William T. 527
HUETING, Gail P. 570
KIBBEE, Josephine Z. 646
KLINGBERG, Susan 661
KRUMMEL, Donald W. 680
LANCASTER, Frederick W. .. 691
LANDIS, Martha 693
LEONG, Carol L. 717
LITTLEWOOD, John M. 734
LOOMIS, Barbara 740
MAHER, William J. 760
MAKINO, Yasuko 762
MCCANDLESS, Patricia A. .. 793
MCCLELLAN, William T. 796
MONTANELLI, Dale S. 855
NASH, N F. 888
O'BRIEN, Nancy P. 915
PAUSCH, Lois M. 950
PENKA, Carol B. 956
PORTA, Maria A. 984
RAVENHALL, Mary 1010

ILLINOIS (Cont'd)
URBANA (Cont'd)
Univ of Illinois at Urbana-Champaign

RICHARDSON, Selma K. . . 1030
ROLSTAD, Gary O. 1052
RUBIN, Richard E. 1065
SCHMIDT, Karen A. 1095
SELF, David A. 1113
SHAW, Debora 1123
SIEGEL, Martin A. 1136
SMITH, Linda C. 1157
SMITH, Richard G. 1160
STENSTROM, Patricia F. . . 1187
STERN, David 1189
STEVENS, Rolland E. 1191
STUART, Mary P. 1204
TEMPERLEY, Nicholas . . . 1230
WAJENBERG, Arnold S. . . 1293
WATSON, Paula D. 1310
WEECH, Terry L. 1315
WEI, Karen T. 1316
WHEELER, Claudia J. 1328
WILLIAMS, James W. 1344
WILLIAMS, Martha E. 1345
WILLIAMS, Mitsuko 1345
WILSON, Lizabeth A. 1351
WONG, William S. 1363
WOODARD, Beth S. 1365
WRIGHT, Joyce C. 1372
YU, Priscilla C. 1384

Univ of Illinois Lab Sch   LAWSON, Mary L. 705
Urbana Free Lib   EDSTROM, James A. 337
                           HOGAN, Mary R. 549
                           REPTA, Vada L. 1024
                           SCHLIPF, Frederick A. 1094

VILLA PARK
Villa Park Pub Lib   BALCOM, William T. 51
                           RYAN, Marilyn P. 1071

WARRENVILLE
Warrenville Pub Lib District   STOCKNER, Patricia G. . . . 1195
WAUCONDA
Community Unit Sch District 118   RAKE, Anthony I. 1004
Lake County   FERME, Paul H. 373
Pars Information Design   SHENASSA, Daryoosh 1126
Wauconda Township Lib   HEITMAN, Lynn 523
WAUKEGAN
Dupont Critical Care Inc   KOZAK, Marlene G. 674
E I DuPont de Nemours & Co Inc   SYVERSON, Kathleen A. . . . 1217
Waukegan East High School   STEWART, Joanne R. 1192
Waukegan Pub Lib   CARNELLI, Sandra R. 183
                           LI, Grace Y. 724

WEST CHICAGO
West Chicago Community High Sch   OLSEN, Sarah G. 922
West Chicago Pub Lib District   SANDERS, Charlene R. 1079
WESTMONT
Westmont Pub Lib   MANNING, Mary J. 766
WHEATON
C Berger & Co   BERGER, Carol A. 85
                           BROWN, Patricia B. 146
                           JOHNSON, Linnea R. 607
                           KLINGBERG, Jane E. 661
                           RUSSELL, Janet 1069
                           STRABLE, Edward G. 1199
                           WALSH, Deborah T. 1299
DuPage County Health Department   ALECCIA, Janet A. 11
DuPage County Law Lib   EGGERT, Charlean D. 339
Wheaton Coll   ERICKSEN, Paul A. 352
                           SHUSTER, Robert D. 1134

WHEELING
Community Consolidated Sch District
  21   NEAL, Nancy J. 890
Indian Trails Pub Lib District   LEVIN, Joan E. 720
                           WRIGHT, Joanna S. 1371
North Suburban Lib System   KANNER, Elliott E. 625
                           MCCLARREN, Robert R. . . . 796

WILLOWBROOK
Willowbrook Pub Lib District   SCHACHT, Lenore A. 1088

ILLINOIS (Cont'd)
WILMETTE
Callaghan & Co   DANNE, William H. 274
                           GRIES, James P. 468
                           HACKNER, Barry M. 481
                           HUXSAW, Charles F. 580
                           KLAUS, Roger D. 658
                           LYNCH, Hugh J. 751
                           SCUDELLARI, Anthony E. . . 1108
Loyola Academy   REIF, Lenore S. 1019
Wilmette Pub Lib District   THOMPSON, Richard E. . . . 1241
WILMINGTON
Commonwealth Edison Co   BOBAN, Carol A. 108
Wilmington Unit Sch District 209-U   HANNON, Bobbie A. 497
WINFIELD
Central DuPage Hospital   ROWE, Dorothy B. 1062
WINNETKA
Lutheran General Hospital   BLACKBURN, Joy M. 102
New Trier High Sch   COBB, Marilyn R. 225
New Trier Township High Sch   DUNN, Lucia S. 327
                           FISHER, Lois F. 381
North Shore Country Day Sch   LUNDQUIST, Marie A. 748
Winnetka Pub Schs   TURCHI, Marilyn L. 1263
WOODRIDGE
Woodridge Pub Lib   GREIN, Mary L. 466
                           KELLER, Steven W. 636

INDIANA
ANDERSON
Anderson Coll   COTTINGHAM, Elsie E. 250
Anderson Univ   KENDALL, Charles T. 640
AUBURN
Eckhart Pub Lib   PENROD, Saundra K. 957
                           SMITH, Sirleine M. 1161
BLOOMINGTON
ERIC Clearinghouse   HENSON, Jane E. 529
Indiana Univ at Bloomington   AUCHSTETTER, Rosann M. . . 38
                           BAILEY, Joanne P. 46
                           BAUS, J W. 67
                           BECK, Erla P. 71
                           BRISTOW, Ann 137
                           CALLISON, Daniel J. 174
                           COPLER, Judith A. 244
                           CRIDLAND, Nancy C. 258
                           DAVISON, Ruth M. 281
                           FARRELL, David 365
                           FLING, Robert M. 385
                           FRY, Bernard M. 406
                           HALPORN, Barbara 490
                           HARTER, Stephen P. 508
                           HEISER, Lois 523
                           HENN, Barbara J. 528
                           IRVINE, Betty J. 584
                           JACKSON, Susan M. 588
                           JARBOE, Betty M. 594
                           KASER, David 628
                           KUDRYK, Oleg 682
                           LAIR, Nancy C. 688
                           LEE, Thomas H. 711
                           MARTIN, Fenton S. 776
                           MCCLOY, William B. 797
                           MCCUNE, Lois M. 801
                           MILLER, Constance R. 836
                           MURPHY, Marcy 881
                           MUSTO, Frederick W. 883
                           NELSON, Brenda 893
                           NIEKAMP, Dorothy R. 903
                           POPP, Mary F. 984
                           PUNGITORE, Verna L. 997
                           RABER, Nevin W. 1001
                           READ, Glenn F. 1012
                           RUDOLPH, Ellen T. 1066
                           RUDOLPH, L C. 1066
                           RUFSVOLD, Margaret I. . . . 1066
                           SELDIN, Daniel T. 1113
                           SELLBERG, Roxanne J. 1113
                           SEREBNICK, Judith 1116
                           SHAABAN, Marian F. 1118
                           SHEPARD, Clayton A. 1126
                           SHIPPS, Anthony W. 1131

INDIANA (Cont'd)
BLOOMINGTON (Cont'd)
Indiana Univ at Bloomington

SILVER, Joel B. 1138
SLOAN, Elaine F. 1149
SNYDER, Carolyn A. 1164
SORURY, Kathryn L. 1169
SOWELL, Steven L. 1170
SPULBER, Pauline 1176
STEELE, Patricia A. 1184
TALALAY, Kathryn M. 1220
THOMAS, Joseph W. 1237
TURCHYN, Andrew 1263
WALLACE, Danny P. 1297
WENNER, Alexander W. . . . 1324
WESTFALL, Gloria D. 1327
WHITBECK, George W. . . . 1329
WHITE, Herbert S. 1331
WIGGINS, Gary D. 1337
ZIMMERMAN, Brenda M. . . 1388

Monroe County Pub Lib   FARLEY, Janice S. 364
   KASER, Jane 628

St Charles Borromeo Sch   GLEASON, Ruth I. 440
Stone Hills Area Lib Services
   Authority   LAUGHLIN, Sara G. 703
BLUFFTON
Bluffton-Wells County Pub Lib   ELLIOTT, Barbara J. 343
BRAZIL
Brazil Pub Lib   PROCTOR, Judy C. 995
BROWNSBURG
Brownsburg Pub Lib   PEARSON, Wanda H. 953
CARMEL
Carmel Clay Schs   DANIELS, Ann A. 273
   NIEMEYER, Karen K. 903
Online Inc   GORDON, Helen A. 451
CHARLESTOWN
Charlestown-Clark County Pub Lib   MCCORMICK, Tamsie 799
Greater Clark County Schs   WHALEY, Janie B. 1328
CHESTERTON
Chesterton High Sch   BECKING, Mara S. 73
COLUMBUS
Cummins Engine Co Inc   MEREDITH, Meri 825
   POOR, William E. 983
Southeastern Indiana Area Lib   SCHLESINGER, Louise D. . . 1094
CRAWFORDSVILLE
Crawfordsville District Pub Lib   DAY, Thomas L. 283
Wabash Coll   FRYE, Larry J. 407
   RILE, B B. 1034
Wabash Valley Area Lib Srvs
   Authority   MARTHEY, Rebecca J. 775
CROWN POINT
Crown Point Community Sch Corp   SUTTINGER, Mary C. 1211
DANVILLE
Danville Pub Lib   KIBREAH, Golam 646
DONALDSON
Ancilla Coll   BOCKMAN, Glenda C. 109
EAST CHICAGO
East Chicago Pub Lib   BERRY, Marjorie L. 90
   SMYERS, Richard P. 1162
   TIMMER, Julia B. 1246
ELKHART
Associated Mennonite Biblical
   Seminaries   SANER, Eileen K. 1081
Church World Service   HUGHES, Rolanda L. 572
Elkhart Pub Lib   DOELLMAN, Michael A. . . . 308
   EILERS, Marsha J. 340
   MILLER, Junelle 839
Miles Laboratories   LE GUERN, Charles A. 712
   SAARI, David S. 1072
Miles Laboratories Inc   YATES, Donald N. 1378
EVANSVILLE
Evansville-Vanderburgh County Pub
   Lib   ALLEN, Patricia J. 15
   BICKEL, Bernice M. 94
   TEUBERT, Lola H. 1233
Evansville-Vanderburgh Sch Corp   BAIN, Leslie E. 47
   WINSLOW, Carol M. 1355
St Mary's Medical Center   SALTZMAN, E J. 1077
Univ of Evansville   MEEK, Janet E. 821

INDIANA (Cont'd)
EVANSVILLE (Cont'd)
Willard Lib   BAKER, Donald E. 48
   ELLIOTT, Joan M. 344
Williard Lib   SABA, Bettye M. 1072
FORT WAYNE
Allen County Pub Lib   BUDD, Anne D. 155
   CLEGG, Michael B. 220
   DEANE, Paul D. 284
   DICKMEYER, John N. 301
   KRULL, Jeffrey R. 680
   MCCAFFERY, Laurabelle . . 793
   REARDON, Ann L. 1013
   ROGERS, Martha J. 1050
   SANDSTROM, Pamela E. . . 1081
   STANLEY, Luana K. 1180
   VOORS, Mary R. 1289
   WITCHER, Curt B. 1358
Concordia Theological Seminary   WARTZOK, Susan G. 1307
Fort Wayne Area III Lib Srvs
   Authority
Fort Wayne Community Schs   LISTON, Karen A. 733
Indiana Institute of Technology   WEICK, Robert J. 1316
Indiana Univ-Purdue Univ at Fort   HICKLING, Jeanne 536
   Wayne   HUNSBERGER, Willard D. . . . 574
   SIEVERS, Arlene M. 1136
   TRUESDELL, Cheryl B. . . . 1259
   VIOLETTE, Judith L. 1285
Lutheran Hospital   AVEN, Lauralee 41
News Sentinel   MARTIN, Jody S. 776
St Joseph Medical Center   SHEETS, Michael T. 1125
FRANKFORT
Frankfort Community Pub Lib   CADDELL, Claude W. 170
FRANKLIN
Franklin Coll   FALLON, Marianna L. 362
GARY
Chief Judge Lake Superior Court   ENGELBERT, Peter J. 348
Gary Community Sch Cooperation   MCNAIR, James 815
Gary Public Lib   GUYDON, Janet H. 479
Indiana Univ Northwest   ARNOLD, Joann M. 33
   BAVER, Cynthia M. 67
   MCSHANE, Stephen G. . . . 818
   MORAN, Robert F. 862
   SUTHERLAND, Timothy L. . 1211
   WHITE, Lois A. 1331
St Mary Medical Center   MACKO, Lucinda M. 757
GOSHEN
Goshen Coll   AMSTUTZ, Mary 21
   MILNE, Sally J. 845
   SPRINGER, Joe A. 1176
Goshen Pub Lib   MCCARTNEY, Shirley R. . . . 795
GREENCASTLE
DePauw Univ   BRADLEY, Johanna 126
   GREMMELS, Gillian S. 467
Putnam County Pub Lib   SEDLACK, Ellen M. 1111
GREENFIELD
Eli Lilly & Co   WEHLACZ, Joseph T. 1316
GREENWOOD
Franklin & Johnson County Lib   EWICK, Joann 359
Greenwood Pub Lib   DAVIS, Bernice 277
HAMMOND
Bishop Noll Institute   BERG, Rita J. 85
Hammond Pub Lib   MEYERS, Arthur S. 830
   MILLER, Marcia M. 840
   ROONEY, Merilyn H. 1053
Hammond Sch City   HOLICKY, Bernard H. 550
Purdue Univ
HANOVER
Hanover Coll   MORRILL, Walter D. 866
   SOWARDS, Steven W. 1170
HOBART
Hobart Township Community Sch
   Corp   CHONCOFF, Joyce L. 210
   HUNT, Margaret M. 575
HOWE
Howe Military Sch   VANZUILEN, Darlene A. . . . 1278
HUNTINGTON
Our Sunday Visitor Inc   ISCA, Joseph J. 585

INDIANA (Cont'd)

INDIANAPOLIS

American Legion
AT&T Consumer Products   HOVISH, Joseph J. 563
Baker & Daniels   MASON, Dorothy L. 781
Barnes & Thornburg   SCHMIDT, Paula O. 1095
Bose McKinney & Evans   RIES, Steven T. 1033
Bureau of National Affairs Inc   BOOHER, William V. 115
Butler Univ   HAWKINS, John W. 514
   JONES, Deborah A. 612
   KONDELIK, John P. 670
   SCHOONOVER, Phyllis J. .. 1098
Christian Theological Seminary   GALBRAITH, Leslie R. 413
Commission on Pub Records   NEWMAN, John J. 899
Dann Pecar Newman Talesnick &
    Kleiman   WHITEMAN, Merlin P. 1333
Eli Lilly & Co   BERTRAM, Lee A. 91
Executive Telecom System Inc   GILL, John H. 435
   GUERRA, Angela M. 476
   HANKINS, John 496
   HASHEM, Judy A. 510
Golden Rule Insurance Co   SOWINSKI, Carolyn M. 1170
Ice Miller Donadia & Ryan   OVERSHINER, Barbara A. .. 931
Indiana Commission on Pub Records   JONES, Thomas Q. 615
Indiana Department of Education   CORNWELL, Linda L. 247
Indiana Historical Society   AUTRY, Carolyn 41
   DARBEE, Leigh 274
   KRASEAN, Thomas K. 676
   MUNDELL, Eric L. 878
Indiana House of Representatives   STAPLES, James A. 1181
Indiana Lib Association   MARTELLO, Joyce M. 775
Indiana State Lib   ASHER, Richard E. 36
   CONRADS, Douglas L. 238
   EWICK, Charles R. 359
   KAPOSTA, Joseph D. 626
   KONDELIK, Marlene R. 670
   LOGSDON, Robert L. 737
   ROBLEE, Martha A. 1045
   SCHMIDT, Kathy W. 1095
   SIMON, Ralph C. 1141
   SWANSON, Byron E. 1213
   WOODARD, Marcia S. 1366
   YOUNG, Noraleen A. 1382
Indiana Univ at Indianapolis   BRAHMI, Frances A. 127
   BROWN, Sandra S. 147
   CORBETT, Ann L. 245
   ELLSWORTH, Marlene A. ... 345
   FRANCQ, Carole 396
   HEHMAN, Jennifer L. 521
   HOOK-SHELTON, Sara A. .. 556
   JOHNTING, Wendell E. 610
   MATTS, Constance 786
   MUELLER, Jeanne G. 875
   RICHWINE, Margaret W. ... 1031
   SWITZER, Joann H. 1216
Indiana Univ-Purdue Univ at
    Indianapolis   BALDWIN, James A. 51
   BONNER, Robert J. 114
   FISCHLER, Barbara B. 380
   GNAT, Jean M. 442
   GOODWIN, Vania M. 450
   HUETTNER, Janet S. 570
   MATTHEW, Jeannette M. ... 785
   MAYLES, William F. 790
   SCHMIDT, Steven J. 1096
   STARKEY, Edward D. 1182
   STOCKER, Randi L. 1195
   WILLIAMS, Maudine 1345
Indianapolis-Marion County Pub Lib   ALLEN, Janice K. 15
   BRIDGE, Stephen W. 135
   COHEN, Harriet A. 228
   COLLINS, Marian M. 233
   DOLAN-HEITLINGER, Eileen . 309
   DOWNEY, Lawrence J. 316
   DUNCAN, Maureen E. 325
   EBERSHOFF-COLES,
     Susan V. 334
   FELTON, Barbara M. 370
   GANN, Daniel H. 416
   GNAT, Raymond E. 442
   LAUBE, Lois R. 702

INDIANA (Cont'd)

INDIANAPOLIS (Cont'd)

Indianapolis-Marion County Pub Lib
   LILES, William E. 727
   MCCANON, Marilyn 794
   THOMPSON, Anna M. 1238
Indianapolis Museum of Art   SU, Julie C. 1206
Information Outlet   GRIFFITTS, Joan K. 469
Locke Reynolds Boyd & Weisell   ENGLE, Madge 349
Marian Coll   STUSSY, Susan A. 1205
Marion County Pub Lib System   BADERTSCHER, Kimberlin
     H. 44
   COHEN, Karen S. 228
   TIMKO, Patricia A. 1246
Methodist Hospital   ANDERSON, Marilyn M. 24
   HOYT, Lester H. 566
Methodist Hospital of Indiana Inc   ALLEN, Joyce S. 15
Metropolitan Sch District of
    Washington   CHAMPLIN, Constance J. ... 198
Reilly Tar & Chemical Corp   GALOW, Donald G. 415
St Vincent Hospital & Health Care
    Center   DURKIN, Virginia M. 328
Sigma Theta Tau International   SPARKS, Marie C. 1171
South Wayne Junior High Sch   STEVENS, Deborah L. 1190
Tabbert Cremer & Capehart   ANDREWS, Sylvia L. 27
US Government   BROWN, Judith L. 145
Univ of Indianapolis   YOUNG, Philip H. 1383
Veterans Administration Medical
    Center   ALFRED, Judith C. 13
Winona Memorial Hospital   MONROE, Donald H. 855

JEFFERSONVILLE

Jefferson Township Pub Lib   BOLTE, William F. 113

KOKOMO

Kokomo-Howard County Pub Lib   KIDDIE, Jeanette A. 646
Purdue Univ   BONHOMME, Mary S. 114

LA PORTE

La Porte County Pub Lib   CLINE, James D. 222
   GUNNELLS, Danny C. 477

LAFAYETTE

Lafayette Sch Corp   NEWTON, Evah B. 900
Tippecanoe County Pub Lib   MITCHELL, Cynthia E. 848
   THOMAS, Victoria K. 1238

LEBANON

Lebanon Community Sch Corp   WESTFALL, Martha L. 1327

LOGANSPORT

Logansport Cass County Pub Lib   SHIH, Philip C. 1130

MADISON

Madison-Jefferson County Pub Lib   BABBITT, Dennis L. 43
   WILLIS, Ione P. 1348

MARION

Marion Coll   BOYCE, Harold W. 122

MERRILLVILLE

Lake County Pub Lib   CIUCKI, Marcella A. 215
   KETCHUM, Irene F. 645
   MOGLE, Dawn E. 852
   YAMAMOTO, M C. 1377
Northwest IN Area Lib Services
    Authority   SNOWDEN, Deanna 1164

MICHIGAN CITY

Michigan City Pub Lib   DEYOUNG, Charles D. 298

MISHAWAKA

Marian High Sch   BIANCHINO, Cecelia 94
Mishawaka Lib Services Authority   STRATTON, Martha G. 1200
Mishawaka-Penn Pub Lib   EISEN, David J. 340
   VOLLNOGLE, Leslie A. 1288

MITCHELL

Mitchell Community Pub Lib   HOLT, Vickie L. 554
Mitchell Community Schs   WOODRUFF, Gail R. 1366

MUNCIE

Ball State Univ   BEILKE, Patricia F. 75
   DOLAK, Frank J. 309
   FAUST, Mary H. 366
   HARLAND, Phyllis A. 502
   HODGE, Stanley P. 546
   KELLEY, Colleen L. 636
   KUO, Ming M. 684
   MCGINNIS, Mildred M. 806
   MOORE, Thomas J. 861
   RANSIL, M M. 1007
   SACZAWA, Rosemary 1073

INDIANA (Cont'd)
  MUNCIE (Cont'd)
  Ball State Univ
                                    TURNER, Nancy K. 1265
                                    WILLIAMS, Nyal Z. 1345
                                    WOOD, Michael B. 1364
  Muncie Pub Lib   KROEHLER, Beth A. 679
                                    SCHAEFER, Patricia 1089
  MUNSTER
  Lake County Pub Lib   PICHA, Charlotte G. 970
  NAPPANEE
  WaNee Community Schs   MATHEWS, Rosemary S. . . . 784
  NEW ALBANY
  Indiana Univ Southeast   BISHOP, Barbara N. 99
  NEW CASTLE
  New Castle-Henry County Pub Lib   JOHNSON, Marjorie J. 607
  NOBLESVILLE
  Noblesville-Southeastern Pub Lib COOPER, David L. 242
                                    MAXWELL, Donald W. 788
  NORTH MANCHESTER
  Heckman Bindery Inc   HECKMAN, Stephen P. 520
  Manchester Coll   STEPHENSON, Doris F. 1188
  NOTRE DAME
  Indiana Prov Congregation of Holy
    Cross   CONNELLY, James T. 237
  One World Publishing   KIANG, C K. 646
  Saint Mary's Coll   HOHL, Robert J. 550
                                    HOLLENHORST, Bernice M. . 551
                                    JONES, Marjorie 614
  Univ of Notre Dame   AMES, Charlotte A. 19
                                    DOLAN, Robert T. 309
                                    FUDERER, Laura S. 408
                                    GLEASON, Maureen L. 440
                                    HARLAN, John B. 502
                                    HAVLIK, Robert J. 513
                                    HAYES, Stephen M. 516
                                    JACOBS, Roger F. 590
                                    JORDAN, Louis E. 616
                                    KRIEGER, Alan D. 678
                                    LYSY, Peter J. 753
                                    MAXWELL, Jan C. 788
                                    MILLER, Robert C. 841
                                    MOON, Elizabeth A. 857
                                    PEC, Jean A. 953
                                    SLINGER, Michael J. 1149
                                    TANTOCO, Dolores W. 1223
                                    WITTORF, Robert H. 1359
                                    ZEUGNER, Lorenzo A. 1387
  PLAINFIELD
  Guilford Township Historical
    Collection   MILLER, Ida M. 838
  Indiana Law Enforcement Academy ZIMMERMAN, Donna K. . . . 1388
  Plainfield Pub Lib   CARTER, Susan M. 190
                                    MCMILLAN, Mary M. 815
  PORTAGE
  Portage Township Schs   DUHAMELL, Lynnette H. . . . 324
                                    KRAMER, Arlene H. 675
  PORTLAND
  Jay County Pub Lib   CLAMME, Rosalie A. 215
                                    FORD, Marcia K. 389
  RENSSELAER
  Saint Joseph's Coll   VIGEANT, Robert J. 1284
  RICHMOND
  Earlham Coll   FARBER, Evan I. 363
  Indiana Univ East   HUFFORD, Gordon L. 571
  Wayne Township Lib   SMYTH, Carol B. 1162
  ROCHESTER
  Fulton County Pub Lib   LASHER, Esther L. 700
  SAINT MEINRAD
  St Meinrad Coll and Sch of Theology DALY, Simeon 271
  SEYMOUR
  Seymour Pub Lib   OZINGA, Connie J. 933
  SOUTH BEND
  Bethel Coll   TUCKER, Dennis C. 1261
  Clark Equipment Co   EIGEMAN, Laurence E. 340
  Indiana Univ at South Bend   MARSHELEK, Sonja E. 775
                                    MULLINS, James L. 878
  Memorial Hospital of South Bend   MILLER, Jeanne L. 839
  R M B Productions   BEATTY, R M. 70
  Seventh Circuit Court of Appeals PIASECKI, Patricia S. 970

INDIANA (Cont'd)
  SOUTH BEND (Cont'd)
  South Bend Pub Lib   FUTA, Debra D. 411
                                    GUTSCHENRITTER,
                                      Victoria M. 479
                                    OSTROWSKI, Lawrence C. . . 929
                                    PIANE, Mimi 969
                                    WARREN, Hugh P. 1306
  TELL CITY
  Tell City-Perry County Pub Lib   HOLMAN, Mary J. 553
  TERRE HAUTE
  Indiana State Univ at Terre Haute ANDERSON, Virginia L. 25
                                    DAVIS, Betty B. 277
                                    DAVIS, H S. 279
                                    ENSOR, Pat L. 350
                                    GALE, Sarah E. 413
                                    LAMB, Robert S. 690
                                    LEACH, Ronald G. 706
                                    LITTLE, Robert D. 733
                                    LYLE, Jack W. 751
                                    MARTIN, Ron G. 778
                                    MCGIVERIN, Rolland H. 806
                                    MILLER, Marsha A. 840
                                    NORMAN, Orval G. 909
                                    SWARENS, Darrell F. 1214
                                    THOMPSON, Susan J. 1241
                                    TRIBBLE. Judith E. 1256
                                    VANCIL, David E. 1273
  International Minerals & Chemical
    Corp   SHANE, T C. 1120
  Pitman-Moore Inc   BAUMGARTNER, Kurt O. 66
  Rose-Hulman Institute of Technology ROBSON, John M. 1045
  Terre Haute Medical Education
    Foundation   KYKER, Penelope R. 685
  Vigo County Pub Lib   KASER, John A. 628
                                    RAWLES-HEISER, Carolyn . 1010
                                    WERT, Alice L. 1325
  Vigo County Sch Corp   BRETT, Lorraine E. 134
  UPLAND
  Taylor Univ   WOLCOTT, Laurie J. 1359
  VALPARAISO
  Valparaiso Univ   HOLTERHOFF, Sarah G. 555
                                    MEYER, Ellen R. 830
                                    MILLS, Richard E. 844
                                    PERRY, Margaret 960
                                    PERSYN, Mary G. 961
                                    WATTS, Tim J. 1310
  VINCENNES
  Vincennes Univ   PIEPENBURG, Scott R. 971
  WARSAW
  S M Detwiler & Associates   DETWILER, Susan M. 296
  WEST LAFAYETTE
  Great Lakes Chemical Corp   ADDISON, Paul H. 6
                                    CHANDIK, Barbara V. 199
                                    LINEPENSEL, Kenneth C. . . 730
  Purdue Univ   ANDREWS, Theodora A. 27
                                    BAILEY, Martha J. 46
                                    BAXTER, Pam M. 67
                                    BRACKEN, James K. 124
                                    BRANDT, Daryl S. 128
                                    CANGANELLI, Patrick W. . . . 178
                                    COLLINS, Mary E. 233
                                    CORYA, William L. 248
                                    DAGNESE, Joseph M. 269
                                    ERDMANN, Charlotte A. 352
                                    FUNKHOUSER, Richard L. . . 410
                                    GOLOVIN, Naomi E. 447
                                    HEWISON, Nancy S. 535
                                    LAW, Gordon T. 704
                                    MARKEE, Katherine M. 771
                                    MARTINO, Sharon C. 779
                                    MCKOWEN, Dorothy K. 812
                                    MOBLEY, Emily R. 851
                                    MURDOCK, J L. 879
                                    NEVILLE, Ellen P. 898
                                    NIXON, Judith M. 906
                                    OGLES, Lynn C. 918
                                    PASK, Judith M. 946
                                    POLIT, Carlos E. 980
                                    STEPHENS, Gretchen 1188

INDIANA (Cont'd)
    WEST LAFAYETTE (Cont'd)
    Purdue Univ
                                            TUCKER, John M. 1261
                                            YOUNGEN, Gregory K. 1383
    Tippecanoe Sch Corp   TROUTNER, Joanne J. 1258
    WESTFIELD
    Van Camp Information Associates   VAN CAMP, Ann J. 1272
    WHITING
    Calumet Coll   BROTON, Cecilianne S. 141
    WINAMAC
    St Luke Lutheran Church   SMITH, Robert E. 1160
    WINONA LAKE
    Grace Coll & Theological Seminary   DARR, William E. 275
    ZIONSVILLE
    Okey Research Inc   OKEY, Susan T. 920

IOWA
    AMES
    Ames Pub Lib   KENAGY, Charles R. 640
                                            LARSON, Teresa B. 700
                                            LAWSON, George T. 705
                                            RAILSBACK, Patsy S. 1003
                                            STUART, Kimberly A. 1204
    Bibliographical Center for Research   SCHMIDT, Sandra L. 1096
    Central Iowa Regional Lib   HILL, Fay G. 539
    Iowa State Univ   BLACK, William K. 102
                                            COLE, Jim E. 230
                                            DOBSON, Cynthia 307
                                            GALEJS, John E. 413
                                            HANTHORN, Ivan E. 499
                                            KLINE, Laura S. 661
                                            KUHN, Warren B. 682
                                            MADISON, Olivia M. 759
                                            MATHEWS, Eleanor R. 784
                                            MOODY, Marilyn K. 857
                                            MORRIS, Dilys E. 866
                                            ORR, Margaret H. 926
                                            OSMUS, Lori L. 928
                                            PARSONS, Kathy A. 945
                                            PETERSON, Lorna 964
                                            PETERSON, Sally R. 964
                                            TYCKOSON, David A. 1266
                                            VAN DE VOORDE, Philip E. 1274
    State Historical Society of Iowa   WORK, Dawn E. 1369
    ATLANTIC
    Atlantic Community Schs   CRAVER, Susan J. 256
    BELLEVUE
    Bellevue Pub Lib   KIEFFER, Marian L. 647
    BETTENDORF
    Bettendorf Community Sch District   MEIER, Patricia L. 821
    Bettendorf Pub Lib & Information
        Center   CLOW, Faye E. 223
    BOONE
    Mamie Doud Eisenhower Birthplace
        Fndtn   ADAMS, Larry D. 5
    BURLINGTON
    Burlington Pub Lib   FOWLER, Linda J. 394
                                            JOHNSON, Anne C. 602
    CARLISLE
    Carlisle Pub Lib   BERNING, Robert W. 89
    CEDAR FALLS
    Cedar Falls High Sch   KOLLASCH, Matthew A. 669
    Univ of Northern Iowa   ELIZABETH, Martin A. 343
                                            HIEBER, Douglas M. 537
                                            HILAND, Leah F. 538
                                            LETTOW, Lucille J. 719
                                            MARSHALL, Jessica A. 774
                                            MARTIN, Elizabeth A. 776
                                            RITCHIE, Verna F. 1036
                                            SHAW, James T. 1123
                                            WEEG, Barbara E. 1315
                                            WILKINSON, Patrick J. 1340
    CEDAR RAPIDS
    Brown Healey Bock Architects   HEALY, Edward H. 518
    Cedar Rapids Community Sch District   MCGREW, Linda L. 808
                                            WRIGHT, Dian A. 1371
    Cedar Rapids Gazette   JANUS, Bridget M. 594
    Cedar Rapids Medical Education
        Program   NELSON, Donald A. 893

IOWA (Cont'd)
    CEDAR RAPIDS (Cont'd)
    Cedar Rapids Pub Lib   DAVENPORT, Ronald D. 276
                                            HAYSLETT, Dawn C. 517
    Coe Coll   YU, Hsiao M. 1384
    Creswell Munsell Fultz & Zirbel Inc   PEARSON, Jo A. 952
    Mount Mercy Coll   DICKES, Janis H. 300
    Regis High Sch   DAVIS, Deanna S. 278
    Rockwell International   BLISS, David H. 105
                                            LEAVITT, Judith A. 707
    St Luke's Hospital   POHNL, Donald R. 980
    CHARLES CITY
    Charles City Pub Lib   STARK, Ted 1182
    CLARION
    Clarion Community Sch   FLETCHALL, Josephine V. . . 384
    CLINTON
    Clinton Pub Lib   SEGER, Robert M. 1112
    CONRAD
    Conrad Pub Lib   GALLENTINE, Richard J. 414
                                            MILLER, Pearl F. 841
    CORALVILLE
    Northwest Junior High Sch   LANGHORNE, Mary J. 696
    COUNCIL BLUFFS
    Free Pub Lib of Council Bluffs   NELSON, Mary L. 894
                                            PARROTT, Lynn K. 944
    CRESCO
    Cresco Pub Lib   HUISKAMP, Julie G. 572
    DAVENPORT
    Art Preservation Information Service   JONSON, Laurence F. 616
    Call-it Co Inc   ROSS, Robert D. 1058
    City of Davenport   MONTGOMERY, David E. . . . 856
    Davenport Pub Lib   MURRAY, Rochelle A. 882
                                            OHRLUND, Ava L. 919
                                            ROUDEBUSH, Lawanda C. . 1061
                                            RUNGE, Kay K. 1067
    Palmer Coll of Chiropractic   BUDREW, John 155
                                            PETERSON, Dennis R. 963
                                            STOUT, Robert J. 1199
                                            WIESE, Glenda C. 1337
    St Ambrose Univ   OHRLUND, Bruce L. 919
                                            POTTER, Corinne J. 987
    Southeastern Lib Srvs   NAVARRE, Emily L. 889
    DECORAH
    Luther Coll   FENSTERMANN, Duane W. . 371
                                            KEMP, Henrietta J. 639
    DES MOINES
    American Institute of Business   GRIFFIN, Kathryn A. 468
    Davis Hockenberg Wine Brown et al   KERN, Sharon P. 643
    Drake Univ   EDWARDS, John D. 337
                                            SKEERS, Timothy M. 1145
                                            STOPPEL, Ellen K. 1198
                                            STOPPEL, William A. 1198
    Iowa Department of Education   BUCKINGHAM, Betty J. 154
    Iowa Department of Human Services   ELLIOTT, Kay M. 344
    Iowa Hospital Association   TOVREA, Roxanna L. 1252
    Iowa Lib Association   STOVALL, Naomi 1199
    Iowa Lutheran Hospital   KROMMINGA, Patricia G. . . . 679
    Iowa State Archives   MCCONNELL, Edward 797
    Iowa State Lib   GEORGE, Shirley H. 428
    Pub Lib of Des Moines   BOGNANNI, Kathleen J. 111
                                            BROGDEN, Stephen R. 139
                                            CLAYBURN, Marginell P. . . . 220
                                            ESTES, Elaine G. 355
                                            GERSTENBERGER, Martha
                                            F. 429
                                            SHISLER, Shirley M. 1131
                                            STICK, Dorothy J. 1193
                                            TRUCK, Lorna R. 1259
    State Lib of Iowa   COCHRAN, William M. 225
                                            DAGLEY, Helen J. 269
                                            NICKELSBURG, Marilyn M. . . 902
                                            REES, Pamela C. 1016
                                            ROBERTSON, Linda L. 1042
    Univ of Osteopathic Medicine & Hlth
        Scis   MARQUARDT, Larry D. 772
    DIKE
    Dike Community Schs   MIDDLESWART, Patricia A. . 833

IOWA (Cont'd)

DUBUQUE

American Lutheran Church   WIEDERAENDE, Robert C. . 1336
Archdiocese of Dubuque Archives   KURT, Edgar 684
Carnegie-Stout Pub Lib   CLARK, Maeve K. 217
City of Dubuque   MINTER, Elizabeth D. 846
Loras Coll   GIBSON, Michael D. 432
                                            ZORDELL, Pamela K. 1390
Sisters of the Presentation   OFFERMAN, Mary C. 917
Univ of Dubuque   KNEFEL, Mary A. 664
                                            ROBINSON, Vera L. 1045
Wartburg Theological Seminary   HESS, Sandra K. 534

FAIRFIELD

Fairfield Community Sch District   DANIELSON, Connie S. 273
Maharishi International Univ   SHAW, Craig S. 1123

GARNER

Garner Pub Lib   GROTH, Robert E. 473

GRINNELL

Grinnell Coll   BONATH, Gail J. 113
                                            ENGEL, Kevin R. 348
                                            MCKEE, Christopher 810

IOWA CITY

American Coll Testing Program   RENTER, Lois I. 1023
Aqudas Achim Synagogue   GINSBERG, Marjorie E. 438
Hanson Lind Meyer Inc   PEPETONE, Diane S. 957
Iowa City Community Sch District   DONHAM, Jean O. 311
                                            KOSHATKA, Beverly V. 672
                                            PARK, Dona F. 941
                                            REHMKE, Denise M. 1017
Iowa City High Sch   HARMON, Charles T. 502
Iowa City Pub Lib   CARTER, Jeanette F. 189
                                            EGGERS, Lolly P. 339
                                            SPAZIANI, Carol 1172
Mercy Hospital   SNIDER, Jacqueline I. 1163
Neumann Monson PC   NEUMANN, Roy C. 897
Univ of Iowa   BAKER, Sharon L. 49
                                            BELGUM, Kathie G. 76
                                            BENTZ, Dale M. 84
                                            BIERBAUM, Esther G. 95
                                            BLOESCH, Ethel B. 106
                                            CRETH, Sheila D. 258
                                            DEWEY, Barbara I. 298
                                            EICHER, Thomas E. 339
                                            EIMAS, Richard 340
                                            EMDE, Susan J. 347
                                            ENGER, Kathy B. 349
                                            ERTL, Mary R. 353
                                            FALCONER, Joan O. 362
                                            GIAQUINTA, C J. 431
                                            GORMAN, Lawrence R. 452
                                            HAUSMAN, Julie 513
                                            HIRST, Donna L. 543
                                            HOWELL, John B. 565
                                            JORDAN, Robert P. 616
                                            KELLEY, Ann C. 636
                                            KOHLER, Carolyn W. 668
                                            KRANCH, Douglas A. 676
                                            LARSON, Catherine A. 699
                                            LITTLE, Margaret C. 733
                                            LORKOVIC, Tatjana B. 741
                                            MELROY, Virginia A. 823
                                            NEUFELD, Sue E. 897
                                            ORGREN, Carl F. 925
                                            RAWLEY, Wayne 1010
                                            RICE, James G. 1027
                                            ROBINSON, Caitlin M. 1043
                                            ROGERS, Earl M. 1049
                                            RUMSEY, Eric T. 1067
                                            SCHACHT, John N. 1088
                                            SHIPE, Timothy R. 1131
                                            WACHEL, Kathleen B. 1290
Veterans Administration Medical
  Center   BROWN, Jeanine B. 144
                                            KRAUS, Marilyn J. 676

JOHNSTON

Pioneer Hi-Bred International Inc   BEVERIDGE, Mary I. 93
                                            GOERS, Willona G. 443
                                            HOEVEN, Helen D. 547

KNOXVILLE

Knoxville Pub Lib   VINER, Mamie N. 1285

IOWA (Cont'd)

LAMONI

Graceland Coll   SHELTON, Diane E. 1126

LE GRAND

LDF Community Schs   WOOD, Marilyn R. 1364

LE MARS

Le Mars Pub Lib   SIMPSON, F T. 1141

MARSHALLTOWN

Marshalltown Area Education Agency
  6   TRAVILLIAN, Mary W. 1254
Marshalltown Community Schs   BURGESS, Barbara J. 159

MASON CITY

Mason City Community Schs   CHAPMAN-SIMPSON, Alisa
                                              M. 202
North Central Regional Lib System   SWANSON, P A. 1213

MT PLEASANT

Iowa Wesleyan Coll   SCHERUBEL, Melody 1092

MT VERNON

Cornell Coll   FALK, Mark F. 362

MUSCATINE

Muscatine Community Schs   MATHER, Becky R. 783
Musser Pub Lib   CHAUDOIN, Sheila M. 204
                                            SORENSON, Debra J. 1168

OTTUMWA

Ottumwa Pub Lib   GEIB, Jerry H. 425
Southern Prairie AEA 15   BRANDT, Garnet J. 128

PELLA

Central Coll   CAMP, Emily E. 175

SHENANDOAH

Shenandoah Pub Lib   JENSEN, Janet L. 598

SIOUX CENTER

Sioux Center Pub Lib   SIEBERSMA, Lois R. 1135

SIOUX CITY

Briar Cliff Coll   THEOBALD, Joanice 1234
Diocese of Sioux City   CUMMINGS, Kevin 264
Iowa Northwest Regional Lib   FALK, Louise G. 362
Marian Health Center   PHILLIPS, Donna M. 968
Morningside Coll   BOWEN, Kay 120
Northwest Regional Lib System   PLUEMER, Bonnie J. 978
Sioux City Pub Lib   HUNTING, Susan K. 576
                                            SCHEETZ, George H. 1090
                                            THOMPSON, Betsy J. 1239
Woodbury County Bar Association   DUNN, Susan M. 327

SPENCER

City of Spencer   MYRON, Victoria L. 885

SPIRIT LAKE

Spirit Lake Community Sch   KOEPP, Sara H. 668

VINTON

Vinton Community Schs   SHEPHERD, Rex L. 1127

WATERLOO

Waterloo Community Schs   DUTCHER, Terry R. 329
                                            TALLEY, Loretta K. 1221
Waterloo Pub Lib   ALLING, M P. 16
                                            BROWN, Darmae J. 143
                                            LIND, Beverly F. 728
                                            RIESBERG, Eunice L. 1033

WAVERLY

Century Companies of America   RIEKEN, Marietta K. 1033
Wartburg Coll   BECK, Marianne J. 71
Waverly Pub Lib   COFFIE, Patricia R. 227

WEBSTER CITY

Kendall Young Lib   WEISS, Cynthia A. 1320

WEST BRANCH

Herbert Hoover Presidential Lib Assn
  Inc   DENNIS, Mary R. 292
                                            FAWCETT, John T. 367
                                            KAUTZ, Richard C. 631
                                            MAYER, Dale C. 789
Hoover Presidential Lib   MATHER, Mildred E. 783
National Archives & Records Admin

WEST DES MOINES

West Des Moines Community Sch   KIRK, Mary L. 654

KANSAS

ABILENE

Eisenhower Foundation   STROWIG, Calvin 1203

ARMA

Arma Unified Sch District 246   ROBERTS, Linda A. 1041

ATCHISON

Benedictine Coll   BURBACH, Jude 158
                                            FENLON, Mary P. 371

KANSAS (Cont'd)

BELLE PLAINS
US District 357 — METTLING, Cora E. 828
CHANUTE
Chanute Pub Sch — TUNNELL, Mary D. 1263
Chanute Unified Sch District 413 — DRUSE, Judith A. 321
Neosho County Community Coll — VIERGEVER, Dan W. 1284
COFFEYVILLE
Coffeyville Community Coll — HENDERSON, Rosemary ... 527
Coffeyville Pub Lib — BUFFINGTON, Karyl L. 155
CONCORDIA
Concordia Unified Sch District 333 — BRADLEY, Susanne A. 126
DODGE CITY
Dodge City Community Coll — REEVES, Cathy L. 1016
St Mary of the Plains Coll — COOKE, Bette L. 241
DONNELLY, Lela M. 311
EL DORADO
Board of Trustees — BEATTIE, Brian 70
EMPORIA
Emporia State Univ — BEEZLEY, Jo A. 74
BIRNEY, Ann E. 98
BODART-TALBOT, Joni 109
BOGAN, Mary E. 110
GROVER, Robert J. 474
HALE, Martha L. 485
KLOSTERMANN, Helen M. .. 662
MEDER, Marylouise D. 820
STEWART, Henry R. 1192

FORT LEAVENWORTH
US Army Command & General Staff
Coll — SNOKE, Elizabeth R. 1163
FORT RILEY
Irwin Army Hospital — WHITESIDE, Phyllis J. 1333
GARDEN CITY
Garden City Community Coll — RUDDICK, Patsy R. 1065
GOODLAND
Goodland Pub Lib — WARREN, Janet B. 1306
GREAT BEND
Central Kansas Lib System — SWAN, James A. 1213
HAYS
Fort Hays State Univ — DIRKS, Martha W. 305
WARREN, G G. 1306
Hays Pub Lib — MILLER, Melanie A. 841
THOMPSON, Mary A. 1240

HESSTON
Hesston Coll — WIEBE, Margaret A. 1336
Hesston Pub Lib — EICHELBERGER, Marianne .. 339
HILLSBORO
Tabor Coll — JOHNSON, Georgina 604
HUTCHINSON
Hutchinson Pub Lib — CHRISTNER, Terry A. 212
RATZLAFF, Marcella J. 1010
SOLDNER, Nancy C. 1166
Hutchinson Pub Schs — GATTIN, Leroy M. 422
South Central Kansas Lib System — HAWKINS, Paul J. 514

INDEPENDENCE
ARCO Pipe Line Co — RYAN, Betsey A. 1070
INMAN
Inman Unified Sch District 448 — EIS, Myrna M. 340
KANSAS CITY
Donnelly Coll — VAN BENTEN, Virginia M. ... 1272
Kansas City Pub Lib — BENNETT, Samuel J. 82
GARRISON, Teresa J. 420
MILLS, Elaine L. 844
RIDDLE, Raymond E. 1032
RUSSELL, Marilyn L. 1069
VAN SICKLE, Mary L. 1277
Providence-St Margaret Health
Center — HOLLINGSHEAD, Mary A. .. 552
Shook Hardy & Bacon — WITMER, Tonya C. 1358
Univ of Kansas Medical Center — BINGHAM, James L. 97
CARVER, Jane W. 191
FARLEY, Alfred E. 364
HATCHER, Marihelen 511

KINGMAN
Kingman Unified Sch District 331 — HADA, Jerrianne 481

KANSAS (Cont'd)

LAWRENCE
Ergosyst Associates Inc — BURCH, John L. 158
HINTON, N E. 543
Lawrence Pub Lib — MAY, Cecilia J. 788
MAYO, Wayne 791
Univ of Kansas at Lawrence — BURCHILL, Mary D. 158
CRAIG, Susan V. 254
FRANKLIN, Janice C. 397
HAWKINS, Mary J. 514
HITCHENS, Susan H. 544
HOWARD, Clinton N. 564
HOWE, Priscilla P. 565
JOHNSON, Ellen S. 604
KOEPP, Donna P. 668
LUNG, Mon Y. 748
MASON, Alexandra 780
NEELEY, James D. 891
NEELEY, Kathleen L. 892
NEUGEBAUER, Rhonda L. .. 897
OTTO, Kathryn D. 930
RANZ, James 1008
RHODES, Saralinda A. 1026
SCHANCK, Peter C. 1090
SEAVER, James E. 1110
SNYDER, Fritz 1164
STUHR-ROMMEREIM,
Rebecca A. 1205
TRONIER, Suzanne 1258
WELLER, Leann C. 1321
WILLIAMS, Ann E. 1342
LEAVENWORTH
Saint Mary Coll — FINK, Madonna 378
HANNE, Anna R. 497
Veterans Administration Medical
Center — GOTTSHALL, Judith L. 454
LEAWOOD
Knight-Ridder Business Information — OWENS, Charles E. 932
LIBERAL
Seward County Community Coll — BROWN, Mary A. 146
US District 480 — JANTZ, Helen N. 594
LINNE
Linne Unified Sch District 223 — BACHAND, Alice J. 43
LYONS
Lyons Pub Lib — CRANE, Gerri G. 255
MANHATTAN
American Institute of Baking — HORTIN, Judith K. 561
Kansas State Univ — COFFEE, E G. 226
CRAWFORD, Anthony R. ... 256
GRASS, Charlene G. 458
MADSEN, Debora L. 759
MORELAND, Rachel S. 863
PRENTICE, Margaret A. 990
QUIRING, Virginia M. 1000
STUBBAN, Vanessa L. 1204
TALAB, Rosemary S. 1220
VANDER VELDE, John J. ... 1274
WEISENBURGER, Patricia
J. 1319
WILDE, Lucy E. 1338
WILLARD, Gayle K. 1341
WILLIAMS, Sara R. 1346
Manhattan High Sch — WHITSON, Joyce G. 1334
Manhattan Pub Lib — ATCHISON, Fres D. 37
MCCONNELL AFB
McConnell Air Force Base — DOMBOURIAN MOORE,
Ann 310
MCPHERSON
Central Coll — MCIRVIN, Jane P. 809
McPherson Coll — JOHNSON, H J. 605
OLSEN, Rowena J. 921
McPherson Pub Lib — OBERLY, Beverly R. 914
MONTEZUMA
Montezuma Unified Sch District 371 — CROTTS, Carolyn D. 261
NEWTON
Newton Pub Lib — EBERHARD, Neysa C. 334
NORTH NEWTON
Bethel Coll — SCHRAG, Dale R. 1099
Mennonite Lib & Archives — HAURY, David A. 512

KANSAS (Cont'd)

NORTON
Northwest Kansas Lib System — BUMBALOUGH, Bruce L. ... 157

OLATHE
Mid-America Nazarene Coll — GALLOWAY, Mary A. 415
Olathe Sch Dist — GOODRICH PETERSON, Marilyn 450

OVERLAND PARK
Johnson County Community Coll — KEMPF, Andrea C. 639
Ojala Associates — OJALA, Marydee P. 919
Planning Analysis Corp — POSTLEWAIT, Cheryl A. 986
Univ of Kansas at Overland Park — BURICH, Nancy J. 160
Utlas International US Inc — ALLEN, Norene F. 15
— ROTH, Sally 1059
— SEVIER, Susan G. 1117

PARSONS
Parsons Pub Lib — MAST, Jane E. 782

PITTSBURG
Pittsburg State Univ — COFFEE, Kathleen C. 226
— DEGRUSON, Eugene H. 288
— LEE, Earl W. 709
— VOLLEN, Gene E. 1287

SALINA
Marymount Coll — WHITE, George R. 1331
Salina Pub Lib — MCKENZIE, Joe M. 811
Salina Unified Sch District 305 — REED, Mary J. 1015
Sisters of St Joseph — THOMAS, Evangeline M. ... 1236

SCOTT CITY
Scott City Elementary Sch — BARTLETT, Gwenell J. 61

SENECA
Nemaha Valley Schools — PHILBRICK, Marcia 967

SHAWNEE MISSION
Johnson County Board of Commissioners — LANGWORTHY, Asher C. 696
Johnson County Lib — DRESSLER, Alta L. 319
— EVANS, Constance L. 356
— LAUFFER, Donna J. 702
— MCLEOD, Debra A. 814
— WAY, Harold E. 1311
North East Kansas Lib System — PLAISTED, Glen L. 977

STILWELL
Mobay Chemical Corp — YOUNG, Carolyn K. 1381

TOPEKA
American Companies Inc — LYNN, Barbara A. 752
City of Topeka — CARROLL, James K. 187
Kansas State Department of Education — LEVEL, M J. 719
Kansas State Historical Society — DECKER, Eugene 285
— MICHAELIS, Patricia A. 831
— RICHMOND, Robert W. 1031
Kansas State Lib — FLANDERS, Bruce L. 383
— JOHNSON, Duane F. 603
— VOSS, Ernestine D. 1289
Kansas Supreme Court — VINCENT, Claire E. 1284
Menninger Foundation — BRAND, Alice A. 127
St Francis Hospital & Medical Center — KINZIE, Lenora A. 653
Topeka Pub Lib — MARVIN, James C. 780
— MUTH, Thomas J. 883
— RUSTMAN, Mark M. 1070
Washburn Univ — ENSIGN, David J. 350
— MELICK, Cal G. 822
— REIMER, Sylvia D. 1021
— VUKAS, Rachel R. 1290

WAMEGO
Wamego Pub Lib — LEONARD, Leanne N. 716

WESTWOOD
United Telecommunications Inc — MOBLEY, Kathleen S. 851

WICHITA
Adorers of the Blood of Christ — STRECK, Helen T. 1201
Botanica The Wichita Gardens — WOOLF, Amy K. 1368
Diocese of Wichita — SHARMA, Shirley K. 1122
Foulston Siefkin Powers & Eberhardt — BERARD, Sue A. 84
Friends Univ — GAYNOR, Kathy A. 424
HCA Wesley Medical Center — BRADEN, Jan 125
Kansas Newman Coll — FORTE, Joseph E. 391
St Francis Regional Medical Center — MATTOX, Rosemary S. 786
Sisters of St Joseph of Wichita — HESCHMEYER, Laura 534
Wesley Medical Center — TANNER, Jane E. 1223
West High Sch — SCHEUERMAN, Luanne J. . 1092
Wichita Art Museum — CRANE, Lois F. 255

KANSAS (Cont'd)

WICHITA (Cont'd)
Wichita Eagle-Beacon Newspaper — TANNER, Allan B. 1222
Wichita Pub Lib — MESSINEO, Leonard L. 828
— RADEMACHER, Richard J. . 1002
Wichita Pub Schs — FORFIA, Linda S. 390
— MEANS, E P. 820
— MEYERS, Judith K. 831
Wichita State Univ — GERMANN, Malcolm P. 429
— IZBICKI, Thomas M. 586
— MYERS, Marilyn 884
— MYERS, Robert C. 885
— SCHAD, Jasper G. 1088
— TAGGART, Thoburn 1219
— WILKE, Janet S. 1339
— WILLIAMS, Brian W. 1342

WINFIELD
Southwestern Coll — DECKER, Ralph W. 286
— ZUCK, Gregory J. 1391

KENTUCKY

BEREA
Berea Coll — HAWLEY, Mary B. 514
— KIRK, Thomas G. 654
— ROBERTS, Gerald F. 1040

BOWLING GREEN
Warren County Board of Education — GRIFFIN, Charlene F. 468
— ZIMMER, Connie W. 1388
Western Kentucky Univ — COUTTS, Brian E. 252
— CUDD, John M. 263
— MILLS, Constance A. 844
— MOORE, Elaine E. 859
— STONE, Sue L. 1197
— WHICKER, Gene A. 1329

BROOKSVILLE
Bracken County Board of Education — TEEGARDEN, Maude B. ... 1229

BUCKNER
Oldham County High Sch — DIAMOND, Shela W. 299

COLD SPRING
Campbell County Pub Lib — LILLIE, Jean N. 727

COLUMBIA
Lindsey Wilson Coll — FOWLER, James W. 393

CORBIN
St Camillus Academy — TIPANE, Josephine 1246

COVINGTON
Covington Latin Sch — DECKER, Charlotte J. 285
Kenton County Pub Lib — AVERDICK, Michael R. 41
Online Inc — GARMAN, Nancy J. 419

CRESTVIEW HILLS
Thomas More Coll — ALBERT, Stephen G. 10

CYNTHIANA
Fort Thomas Board of Education — DOAN, Janice K. 307

DANVILLE
Danville-Boyle County Pub Lib — BENSON, Karl A. 83
— DEARUJO, Georgia R. 284

EDGEWOOD
Ludlow Board of Education — REESE, Virginia D. 1016

ELIZABETHTOWN
Hardin County Schs — DAY, Mary M. 283
Univ of Kentucky — THOMPSON, Ann B. 1238

FLORENCE
Boone County Pub Lib — BROWN, Lucinda A. 145

FORT CAMPBELL
US Army — RIVES, Lydia L. 1037

FORT KNOX
Patton Museum of Cavalry & Armor — HOLT, David A. 554

FRANKFORT
Commonwealth of Kentucky — NELSON, James A. 894
Department for Libs and Archives — HELLARD, Ellen G. 524
Kentucky Department for Libs & Archives — KLEE, Edward L. 658
— LEVSTIK, Frank R. 721
— WRIGHT, Paul L. 1372
Kentucky Department of Education — COOPER, Judy L. 243
Kentucky Department of Pub Advocacy — LYNES, Tezeta G. 752
Kentucky Historical Society — BELL, Mary M. 77
Kentucky Lib Association — UNDERWOOD, Mary S. ... 1269
Paul Sawyier Pub Lib — DOUTHITT, Rita C. 314
Pub Records Division — BELLARDO, Lewis J. 78

KENTUCKY (Cont'd)
FRANKFORT (Cont'd)
State of Kentucky

BARRISH, Alan S. 60
GILMER, Wesley 437

HAZARD
Southeast Area Health Education
Center

TURNER, Ray 1265

HENDERSON
Henderson Community Methodist
Hospital

ROYSTER, Jane G. 1063

HIGHLAND HEIGHTS
Northern Kentucky Univ

BENNETT, Donna S. 81
BRATCHER, Perry R. 129
BREDEMEYER, Carol 131
SCHULTZ, Lois E. 1102
STURM, Rebecca R. 1205
WHITTLE, Ann H. 1334

JEFFERSONTOWN
Interez Inc

HILL, Elizabeth C. 539

LEXINGTON
Ashland Oil

YOUNG, Sandra C. 1383

Council of State Governments

SIMS, Edward N. 1142

Eastern Kentucky Univ

FLAHERTY, Margaret P. 383

Fayette County Board of Education

MARTIN, Sandra D. 778

Greenebaum Doll & McDonald

FOGLE, Dianna L. 387

Kentucky Department for Libs &
Archives

PICKENS, Nancy C. 970

Lexington Community Coll

BIRCHFIELD, Martha J. 98

Lexington Herald-Leader

FARRAR, Lu A. 365
SMITH, Linda L. 1157

Lexington Pub Lib

MILLER, Norma B. 841
SCHABEL, Donald J. 1088
STEENSLAND, Ronald P. ... 1184

Lexington Theological Seminary

DARE, Philip N. 274

Transylvania Univ

BRYSON, Kathleen C. 152

Univ of Kentucky

BIRDWHISTELL, Terry L. 98
CHAN, Lois M. 199
CUNHA, George M. 265
CZARSKI, Charles M. 268
HILTON, Beverly A. 541
JAMES, William 592
KRESSE, Kerry L. 678
MCANINCH, Sandra L. 792
MESNER, Lillian R. 827
POLLARD, Richard 981
RIPLEY, Joseph M. 1035
ROBINSON, Christie M. 1043
ROGERS, Joann V. 1049
SEXTON, Ebba J. 1118
SINEATH, Timothy W. 1143
STEPHENSON, Judy A. 1188
WALDHART, Thomas J. ... 1294
WARTH, L T. 1307
WILLIS, Paul A. 1348
WIZA, Judith M. 1359
WILEY, Theresa K. 1339

Univ of Louisville
Veterans Administration Medical
Center

BAUGH, E S. 65

LOUISVILLE
Administrative Office of the US
Courts

COATES, Paul F. 224

Baptist Hospitals-Louisville

JOHNSON, Garry B. 604

Brown & Williamson Tobacco Corp

DIESING, Arthur C. 302
LINCOLN, Carol S. 728

The Filson Club

HOUSE, Katherine L. 563

Goldberg & Simpson P S C

VOYLES, James R. 1289

Greenebaum Doll & McDonald

CONNOR, Lynn S. 238

Jefferson Community Coll

SCHLENE, Vickie J. 1094

Jefferson County Board of Education

BING, Dorothy A. 97
CRACE, Sallye C. 254
JACOBSON-BEYER, Harry
E. 590
SMITH, Lena D. 1157

Jefferson County Pub Schs

KELLY, Sarah A. 638
LIVINGSTON, Sarah M. 735
TACKETT, Janet S. 1219

Kentucky Country Day Sch

GOLDBERG, Linda B. 444

Louisville Academy of Music

FRENCH, Robert B. 402

KENTUCKY (Cont'd)
LOUISVILLE (Cont'd)
Louisville Free Pub Lib

DIEMER, Irvin T. 302
GARNAR, William H. 419
JAMES, Karen G. 592
KING, Charles D. 650
PTACEK, William H. 996
ROBY, B D. 1045
SHEPHERD-SHLECHTER,
Rae 1127
SOMERVILLE, Mary R. 1167

Louisville Presbyterian Theological
Sem

COALTER, Milton J. 224
RICHARDSON, Susan C. .. 1030
WHITE, Ernest M. 1331

NKC Hospitals Inc

BUCHANAN, Holly S. 153

Southern Baptist Theological
Seminary

DEBUSMAN, Paul M. 285
DEERING, Ronald F. 287
GERON, Cary A. 429
MAZUK, Melody 791
POWELL, Martha C. 988
ROBINSON, Nancy D. 1044

Spalding Univ

CREAMER, Mary M. 257
FRANCK, Ilona G. 396
HUFF, James E. 570
STROHECKER, Edwin C. .. 1202

UMI Data Courier

ARNOLD, Stephen E. 34
AULD, Dennis B. 39
BLACKBURN-FOSTER,
Brenda 102
GASKINS, Betty 421
JAMES, Bonnie B. 592
JAMIOLKOWSKI, Nancy J. .. 593
MACLEOD, Valerie R. 757
SKLODOSKI, Terrance E. .. 1147

UMI Data Courier Inc

GORDON, Dena 451

Univ of Louisville

ANDERSON, James C. 23
ANDERSON, Patricia E. 25
BRINKMAN, Carol S. 136
CAMMARATA, Paul J. 175
COATES, Ann S. 224
DORR, Ralze W. 313
EDDY, Leonard M. 335
GILBERT, Gail R. 433
GRAY, Dorothy A. 459
HODGSON, Janet B. 546
KEARNEY, Anna R. 633
KORDA, Marion 671
MILLER, Robert H. 842
MORISON, William J. 865
NEELY, Glenda S. 892
NILES, Judith F. 904
OLMSTED, Elizabeth H. 921
PRIOR, Barbara Q. 993
REDMON, Sherrill 1014
SELMER, Sylvia A. 1114
TEITELBAUM, Gene W. ... 1230
TEN HOOR, Joan M. 1231

Ursuline Motherhouse

HEINTZMAN, Justina 522

Ursuline Sisters

WALLER, M C. 1208

Wyatt Tarrant & Combs

WOOD, Linda H. 1364

MAPLE MOUNT
Mount Saint Joseph Motherhouse

BUSAM, Emma C. 164

MARION
Crittenden County Board of Education

HERRON, Darl H. 533

MIDDLETOWN
Kentucky Baptist Convention Inc

YEISER, Doris B. 1379

MOREHEAD
Morehead State Univ

BESANT, Larry X. 91
HALL, Juanita J. 488
ISON, Betty S. 585
PRITCHARD, Elsie T. 994
WILLIAMS, Helen E. 1343

Rowan County Board of Education

WHITAKER, Sharon N. 1329

MUNFORDVILLE
Hart County Pub Lib

GRIDER, Patty B. 467

KENTUCKY (Cont'd)
MURRAY
Murray State Univ

BUSER, Robin A. 165
CULPEPPER, Jetta C. 264
HEIM, Keith M. 521
WALL, Celia J. 1297

OWENSBORO
Brescia Coll — RINEY, Judith N. 1035
Kentucky Wesleyan Coll — MCFARLING, Patricia G. 805
YATES, Dudley V. 1378

PADUCAH
Paducah Pub Lib — SUTHERLAND, Thomas A. . 1211
Univ of Kentucky — BOYARSKI, Jennie S. 122
Western Baptist Hospital — YOUNG, Stephanie O. 1383
PINEVILLE
Clear Creek Baptist Bible Coll — BROOKS, Carolyn B. 140
RICHMOND
Eastern Kentucky Univ

BARKSDALE, Milton K. 57
CRABB, George W. 254
HAY, Charles C. 515
KOLLOFF, Fred C. 669
MARTIN, June H. 777
STAPLETON, Diana L. 1181
THOMAS, Carol J. 1236
TURNER, Rebecca M. 1265

RUSSELL SPRINGS
Russell County Board of Education — FOLEY, Mary D. 387
ST CATHARINE
St Catharine Coll — WILLIAMSEN, Audrey M. . . 1347
SOUTHGATE
Southgate Pub Schools — FOX, Estella E. 394
WHITESBURG
Appalshop Inc — OLIVER, Scot 921
WILMORE
Asbury Theological Seminary

BUNDY, David D. 157
BUTTERWORTH, Donald Q. . 167
FAUPEL, David W. 366

WINCHESTER
Clark County Pub Lib — WILLIAMS, Danby O. 1342

LOUISIANA
ANGOLA
Louisiana State Penitentiary — LONG, Gary 739
BARKSDALE AFB
Barksdale Air Force Base — WOOD, Julienne L. 1364
BATON ROUGE
American Society of Artists Inc — COE, Miriam M. 226
Capitol City Press — MATTMILLER, C F. 786
City of Baton Rouge — HASCHAK, Paul G. 510
Earl K Long Memorial Hospital — FINLEY, Jean B. 378
East Baton Rouge Parish Lib — ABRAHAM, Sandra H. 3
BINGHAM, Elizabeth E. 97
MARCKS, Carol J. 769
East Baton Rouge Parish Sch Board — HEROY, Phyllis B. 532
ROBINSON, Joyce W. 1044
STEBEN, Florence E. 1183
Episcopal High Sch — CHEW, Susan M. 207
Ethyl Corp — FOOS, Ferol A. 388
LEMMON, Anne B. 715
Exxon Co USA — BIGGS, Barbara R. 95
Louisiana Lib Association — AUCOIN, Sharilynn A. 38
Louisiana State Lib — ANJIER, Jennifer S. 28
CRETINI, Blanche M. 258
MOORE, Grace G. 859
Louisiana State Senate — MCENANY, Arthur E. 804
Louisiana State Univ at Baton Rouge — ARNY, Philip H. 34
BALL, Dannie J. 52
BOYCE, Bert R. 122
BROWNING, Sandra B. 148
CARPENTER, Michael A. . . . 185
DANTIN, Doris B. 274
DUGGAN, James E. 324
FULLING, Richard W. 409
GIAMALVA, Lolah C. 430
HAMAKER, Charles A. 490
HEBERT, Madeline 519
HEIM, Kathleen M. 521
HOGAN, Sharon A. 549
JOHNS, Mary E. 601
KLEINER, Janellyn P. 660

LOUISIANA (Cont'd)
BATON ROUGE (Cont'd)
Louisiana State Univ at Baton Rouge

KRAFT, Donald H. 674
LANE, Mary J. 694
LOUBIERE, Sue 742
MARTIN, Norma H. 777
MARTIN, Robert S. 778
MAXSTADT, John M. 788
MERING, Margaret V. 826
MILLER, Susan E. 842
MOONEY, Sandra T. 858
NUCKLES, Nancy E. 912
PASKOFF, Beth M. 946
PATTERSON, Charles D. . . . 948
PERRAULT, Anna H. 959
PHENIX, Katharine J. 967
PHILLIPS, Faye 968
REID, Marion T. 1019
ROUNDTREE, Lynn P. 1061
SCULL, Roberta A. 1108
SHIFLETT, Orvin L. 1130
STANLEY, Eileen H. 1180
WANK, Paul G. 1303
WITTKOPF, Barbara J. 1358
Mary Bird Perkins Cancer Center — BLOOMSTONE, Ajaye 106
McCollister McCleary & Fazio — TOWLES, Anne S. 1252
Office of the Secretary of State — LEMIEUX, Donald J. 715
Office of the State Lib — MCKANN, Michael R. 809
Our Lady of Mercy Sch — BARTON, Miriam V. 62
Our Lady of the Lake Regional Med Center — WHITED, Diane D. 1332
Southern Univ and A&M Coll — POUNCY, Mitchell L. 987
Southern Univ of Baton Rouge — ROCHE, Alvin A. 1045
SMITH, Ledell B. 1157
State Lib of Louisiana — BRADLEY, Jared W. 126
FERGUSON, Anna S. 372
FERGUSON, Gary L. 372
JAQUES, Thomas F. 594
SMITH, Richard J. 1160
LANDRY, Denise C. 693
SANTA, Elizabeth C. 1082
State Times Morning Advocate
Sullivan High Sch
CHARENTON
St Mary Parish Sch Board — NEAU, Philip F. 891
COVINGTON
St Tammany Parish Lib — SOTO, Donna G. 1169
DESTREHAN
St Charles Parish — MIGUEZ, Betsy B. 833
EUNICE
Louisiana State Univ at Eunice — MARSHALL, Susan O. 775
FORT POLK
Bayne-Jones Army Community Hospital — HIGGINBOTHAM, Cecelia B. 537
US Army — JONES, Stephanie R. 615
GRETNA
Jefferson Parish Pub Sch System — FAVORITE, Grealdine J. . . . 366
HAMMOND
Holy Ghost Sch — WINFREE, Barbara S. 1354
Southeastern Louisiana Univ — CAIN, Charlene C. 171
GREAVES, F L. 461
PETERS, William W. 962
HARVEY
Jefferson Parish Pub Sch System — WASHINGTON, Idella A. . . . 1307
HOUMA
Terrebonne Parish Pub Lib — COSPER, Mary F. 249
SHAFFER, Margaret M. 1119
JEANERETTE
Allain-Le Breton Co — ALLAIN, Alexander P. 13
JENA
LaSalle Parish Police Jury — RAMBO, Gloria P. 1005
JENNINGS
Jefferson Davis Parish — PATTERSON, Trudy J. 948
LA PLACE
St John the Baptist Parish Pub Lib — DESOTO, Randy A. 295
LAFAYETTE
Bayouland Lib System — LAUGHLIN, Beverly E. 702
Cathedral-Carmel Sch — LONG, Marilyn B. 739
Episcopal Church — NOLAN, Peggy H. 907
Lafayette Pub Lib — DOMBOURIAN, Sona J. . . . 310

LOUISIANA (Cont'd)
LAFAYETTE (Cont'd)
Louisiana State Univ at Lafayette | RAMAKRISHNAN, T 1004
Univ of Southwestern Louisiana | CARSTENS, Jane E. 188
FOX, Willard 395
HAMSA, Charles F. 494
HIMEL, Sandra M. 542
KREAMER, Jean T. 677
RAGHAVAN, Vijay V. 1003
SCHMIDT, Jean M. 1095
SHAUGHNESSY, Megan ... 1123
STEWART, Mary E. 1193
TURNER, I B. 1264

LAKE CHARLES
Calcasieu Parish Pub Lib | LEE, Lynda M. 710
Lake Charles Memrl Hospital | SCHREMP, Mary J. 1100
McNeese State Univ | CAGLE, Robert B. 171
CUROL, Helen B. 266
KHOURY, Nancy L. 646
REID, Richard H. 1019

LULING
St Charles Parish | STROTHER, Garland 1203
MANY
Sabine Parish Lib | PICKETT, Joanne H. 970
METAIRIE
Jefferson Parish | BENOIT, Anthony H. 82
STUCKWICH, Chris E. 1204
STURCKEN, Rodney A. ... 1205
Orleans Parish School Board | KLEIN, Victor C. 659
MINDEN
Webster Parish Lib | SLACK, Barbara E. 1147
Webster Parish Sch Board | NOLES, Judy H. 908
MONROE
Monroe City Sch System | MEINEL, Nancy T. 822
Northeast Louisiana Univ | LARASON, Larry 697
Ouachita Parish Pub Lib | BURNS, Ollie H. 162
GODWIN, Tom P. 443
KONTROVITZ, Eileen R. 671

NATCHITOCHES
Northwestern State Univ of Louisiana | BUCHANAN, William C. 153
HUSSEY, Sandra R. 578
JARRED, Ada D. 594
LANDRY, Abbie V. 693
MAYEAUX, Thurlow M. 789
YOUNG, Amanda M. 1381

NEW ORLEANS
Brother Martin High Sch | SALVATORE, Gayle E. 1078
Chevron Geoscience | ROMALEWSKI, Robert S. ... 1052
Children's Hospital | KELLER, Nancy H. 635
Delgado Community Coll | CUMLET, Harolyn S. 264
REPMAN, Denise C. 1023
Gateway Productions Inc | YOUNG, Ruth H. 1383
Historic New Orleans Collection | DRAUGHON, Ralph B. 318
JUMONVILLE, Florence M. .. 619
LEMMON, Alfred E. 715
Hotel Dieu Hospital | CAFFAREL, Agnes 170
Law Lib of Louisiana | KERN, Elizabeth 643
SHULL, Janice K. 1133
Louisiana State Univ at Baton Rouge | NOLAN-MITCHELL, Patricia . 908
WOJKOWSKI, Suhad K. 1359
Louisiana State Univ at New Orleans | MARIX, Mary L. 770
STROTHER, Elizabeth A. 1203
Loyola Univ of New Orleans | BLAKE, Timothy J. 103
DANKNER, Laura R. 273
KELLY, Judy M. 638
MCKNIGHT, Mark C. 812
MCREYNOLDS, Rosalee 818
RUSHING, Darla H. 1068
SNOW, Maxine L. 1164
SWEAT, Mary L. 1214
McGlinchey Stafford Mintz Cellini & Lang | DAVIS, Margo 280
Mercy Academy | DU CARMONT, M C. 322
Milling Benson Woodward Hillyer et al | FISHER, Collette J. 380
MSU System Services Inc | STANLEY, Nelda J. 1180
New Orleans Baptist Theological Seminary | GERICKE, Paul W. 428
PONG, Connie K. 982

LOUISIANA (Cont'd)
NEW ORLEANS (Cont'd)
New Orleans Pub Lib | COADY, Reginald P. 224
WILKINS, Marilyn W. 1340
WILSON, C D. 1350
New Orleans Symphony | STRICKLAND, William C. ... 1202
Religious Sisters of Mercy | MULDREY, Mary H. 876
Southern Univ of New Orleans | GROSS, Mary D. 472
Texaco Inc | FLEURY, Mary E. 385
Tulane Univ | BARON, John H. 58
CARTEE, Lewis D. 188
COMBE, David A. 234
COPELAND, Patricia S. ... 244
CURTIS, Robert L. 267
FLEURY, Bruce E. 385
GOLDSTEIN, Cynthia H. 446
HAGEDORN, Dorothy L. 482
HALFORD, Mary B. 486
HAMORI, Annemarie R. 494
JERDE, Curtis D. 599
JONES, Philip L. 614
LEINBACH, Philip E. 714
MOORE, Mildred M. 860
NACHOD, Katherine B. 885
POSTELL, William D. 986
RENNIE, Margaret C. 1023
STAFFORD, Cecilia D. ... 1178
THOMPSON, Jeannette C. . 1240
WELSCH, Melissa W. 1323
ZULA, Floyd M. 1391
US Court of Appeals | DULEY, Kay E. 324
US Department of Agriculture | FLORENT, Marguerite R. 385
Univ of New Orleans | HANKEL, Marilyn L. 496
HARDY, D C. 500
HARRIS, Karen H. 505
PHELPS, Connie L. 967
SERBAN, William M. 1116
TIMBERLAKE, Phoebe W. ... 1245
Veterans Administration Medical Center | NEVEU, Wilma B. 897
Xavier Univ of Louisiana | SARKODIE-MENSAH, Kwasi 1083
SKINNER, Robert E. 1146

PEARL RIVER
St Tammany Parish Sch Board | HOLLEY, Rebecca M. 551
PINEVILLE
Louisiana Coll | SALLEY, Landrum 1076
Rapides Parish Lib | LEBLANC, Donna P. 708
PLAQUEMINES
Louisiana Retired Teachers | MCCRAY, Evelina W. 800
PORT ALLEN
Holy Family Sch | LAROSE, Louise K. 698
RUSTON
Lincoln Parish Lib | AVANT, Julia K. 41
Louisiana Technical Univ | BYERS, Cora M. 168
DICARLO, Michael A. 300
EVANS, James M. 357
HAMILTON, William F. 492
HENSON, Stephen 530
IRVIN, Judy C. 584
LOWE, Joy L. 744
MCFADDEN, Sue J. 804
SHORT, Peggy S. 1132
VIDRINE, Jacqueline M. ... 1283
WICKER, W W. 1335

SAINT AMANT
Ascension Parish | HILL, Sue A. 540
SHREVEPORT
Boots Pharmaceuticals Inc | TETTEH, Joseph A. 1233
Caddo Parish Schs | KENNEDY, Frances C. 641
Louisiana Southern Univ | TRIPLETT, Billy L. 1257
Louisiana State Univ at Baton Rouge | MCCLEARY, William E. ... 796
Louisiana State Univ at Shreveport | BROWN, Sue S. 147
KING, Anne M. 650
MEADOR, Patricia L. 819
MOSLEY, Mattie J. 871
Northwestern State Univ of Louisiana | MCCORMICK, Dorcas M. ... 798
Schumpert Medical Center | WILLIS, Marilyn 1348
Shreve Memorial Lib | COLON, Carlos W. 234
SALTER, Jeffrey L. 1077

LOUISIANA (Cont'd)

SHREVEPORT (Cont'd)

Southern Univ of Shreveport	BRAZILE, Orella R.	130
Veterans Administration Medical Center	JONES, Dixie A.	612

SLIDELL
St Tammany Parish Lib	TAYLOR, Rebecca A.	1228

TERRYTOWN
Professional Lib Services Inc	SMOTHERS, Alyce A.	1162

THIBODAUX
Nicholls State Univ	DESSINO, Jacquelyn A.	296
	MIDDLETON, Francine K.	833

WINNFIELD
Winn Parish Lib	STANDEFER, Steven R.	1179

ZACHARY
Nabors Bid Tabulations Service	JACKSON, Audrey N.	586

MAINE

AUBURN
Auburn Pub Lib	HILYARD, Nann B.	542
Mid-State Coll	GROSS, Richard F.	472

AUGUSTA
Central Maine Power Co	KING, Alan S.	650
Lithgow Pub Lib	CROSBY, Barbara A.	260
Maine Department of Educ & Cultural Srvs	TARANKO, Walter J.	1223
Maine State Archives	SILSBY, Samuel S.	1138
Maine State Lib	BOYNTON, John W.	124
	NICHOLS, J G.	901
	WISMER, Donald	1357

BANGOR
Bangor Pub Lib	WOODWARD, Robert C.	1368
Bangor Publishing Co	CAMPO, Charles A.	177
Eastern Maine Medical Center	JAGELS, Suellen T.	591
Maine State Lib	BEISER, Karl A.	75
Univ of Maine at Orono	BILODEAU, Judith M.	97

BAR HARBOR
The Jackson Laboratory	BAKER, Alison	47
Soyatech Inc	GOLBITZ, Peter	444
	GOTTLIEB, Robert A.	453
	KINGMA, Sharyn L.	652

BATH
Bath Memorial Hospital	MCKAY, Ann	809

BIDDEFORD
Univ of New England	GOLUB, Andrew J.	447

BOOTHBAY
Boothbay Playhouse Foundation Inc	LENTHALL, Franklyn	715

BRUNSWICK
Bowdoin Coll	SAEGER, Edwin J.	1074
	SHANKLAND, Anne H.	1120
Maine Sch Administrative District 75	BERRIE, Ellen T.	90

CARIBOU
Cary Medical Center	COTE-THIBODEAU, Donna E.	249

EAST SEBAGO
M R Airey & Associates	AIREY, Martha R.	9

FARMINGTON
Univ of Maine at Farmington	HOLMES, Richard C.	553
	MCNAMARA, Shelley G.	816

GEORGETOWN
The Electronic Scribe	LUDGIN, Donald H.	746

GORHAM
Univ of Southern Maine	KNOWLTON, Suzanne L.	666
	PERRY-BOWDER, Libbie E.	961

KITTERY
Kittery Sch Department	MOY, Agnes U.	874

LEWISTON
Central Maine Medical Center	GREVEN, Maryanne L.	467
St Mary's General Hospital	GREENLAW, Evelyn A.	465

MACHIAS
Univ of Maine at Machias	ALLEY, Katherine S.	16
	PHIPPS, Bert L.	969

NORTH ANSON
Maine Sch Administrative District 74	LYONS, Dean E.	753

ORONO
Univ of Maine at Orono	ALBRIGHT, Elaine M.	10
	CASSERLY, Mary F.	193
	GOODWIN, Bryan D.	450
	MCCALLISTER, Myrna J.	793
	THOR, Angela M.	1242

MAINE (Cont'd)

ORONO (Cont'd)
Univ of Maine at Orono		
	WHITE, Lucinda M.	1331
	WIHBEY, Francis R.	1337

PARIS
Hamlin Memorial Lib	MOTT, Schuyler L.	872

PITTSFIELD
Town of Pittsfield	NICHOLSON, Carol C.	902

PORTLAND
Bernstein Shur Sawyer & Nelson	STANTON, Linda J.	1181
E C Jordan Co	LAWSON, James R.	705
Mercy Hospital	ANDERSON, Marjorie E.	24
Nicholas D Humez Publishers' Services	HUMEZ, Nicholas D.	573
Portland Sch of Art	WAXMAN, Joanne	1311
State of Maine	PIERCE, Ann E.	971
Univ of Maine at Portland	MILLIGAN, Patricia M.	843
Univ of Southern Maine	DUVAL, Marjorie A.	329
	PARKS, George R.	943
Verrill & Dana	REIMAN, Anne M.	1020

PRESQUE ISLE
Univ of Maine at Presque Isle	VIGLE, John B.	1284

READFIELD
Maranacook Community Schs	BAYLISS, Edna M.	67

SANFORD
Goodall Memorial Lib	SMITH, Barbara J.	1153

SCARBOROUGH
Foundation for Blood Research	SPIEGEL, Nancy C.	1174

SKOWHEGAN
Northwood Institute	FRIDLEY, Russell W.	403

SOUTH PORTLAND
City of South Portland	ALEXANDER, William D.	12

WATERVILLE
Mid-Maine Medical Center	DAMON, Cora M.	272

WINDHAM
Town of Windham	KELLOGG, Joanne T.	637

WISCASSET
Temple Univ	HAMLIN, Arthur T.	492

MARYLAND

ABERDEEN PROVING GND
US Army	HADDEN, Robert L.	481
US Army Environmental Hygiene Agency	GOEL, Krishan S.	443

ANNAPOLIS
Annapolis & Anne Arundel County Lib	HALL, Edward B.	487
Anne Arundel County Board of Education	JACKSON, Doris G.	587
Anne Arundel County Circuit Court	SIMISON, Joan B.	1139
Anne Arundel County Pub Lib	PINDER, Jo A.	974
	PURCELL, Kathleen V.	998
Anne Arundel County Pub Sch System	LIVELY, Nancy J.	734
IN MOTION Film & Video Production Mag	LEHURAY, Stephen D.	713
Jackson Printing Inc	JACKSON, Elmer M.	587
Maryland Dept of Legislative Reference	CARMAN, Carol A.	183
Maryland State Archives	PRIMER, Ben	993
	THAPAR, Shashi P.	1234
St John's Coll	KINZER, Kathryn	653
State of Maryland	COLBORN, Robert J.	230
	PAPENFUSE, Edward C.	939
US Naval Academy	CREIGHTON, Alice S.	258
	CUMMINGS, John P.	264
	DICKSON, Katherine M.	301
	DURBIN, Ramona J.	328
	WAGNER, Susan C.	1292

ARNOLD
Anne Arundel Community Coll	STEINHOFF, Cynthia K.	1186
Anne Arundel County Board of Education	SMITH, Jan E.	1155
Chris Olson & Associates	OLSON, Christine A.	922

BALTIMORE
ALCOLAC Inc	BLUTE, Mary R.	107
Alex Brown & Sons Inc	QUINDLEN, Ruthann	999
AM Systems Inc	MEYER, Alan H.	829
Anne Arundel County Pub Lib	KELLER, Susan J.	636

MARYLAND (Cont'd)
BALTIMORE (Cont'd)
Baltimore City | HOLLOWAK, Thomas L. 552
Baltimore City Law Lib | COX, Irvin E. 253
Baltimore County Board of Education | HEINRICH, Lois M. 522
| MOLLENKOPF, Carolyn M. . . 853
Baltimore County Pub Lib | BAILEY, Carol A. 46
| LISS, Nancy J. 732
| MORRONE, Kay O. 869
| VALLAR, Cynthia L. 1271
Baltimore Sun | HARDNETT, Carolyn J. 500
Bryn Mawr Sch | SANDERS, Jacqueline C. . . 1080
Catonsville Community Coll | HILL, Suzanne P. 541
| PECK, Shirley S. 953
City of Baltimore | DULL, Karen A. 324
| LEDBETTER, Sherry H. 708
| NOTOWITZ, Joshua D. 910
Community Coll of Baltimore | BRADLEY, Wanda L. 126
| SHAPIRO, Burton J. 1121
Dundalk Community Coll | LANDRY, Mary E. 693
Enoch Pratt Free Lib | ANDREWS, Loretta K. 26
| ARRINGTON, Susan J. 34
| BENDER, Cynthia F. 79
| BLANK, Annette C. 104
| BLEGEN, John C. 105
| BROWN, Florence S. 144
| CURRY, Anna A. 266
| CYR, Helen W. 268
| DYSART, Marcia J. 331
| ELDER, Richard H. 342
| FINNERTY, Michael B. 379
| HEISER, Jane C. 523
| HIRSCH, Dorothy K. 543
| LAPIDES, Linda F. 697
| LOGAN, Mary A. 737
| SLEEMAN, William E. 1148
| SONDHEIM, John W. 1167
| WALLER, Madalyn M. 1298
Essex Community Coll | BROADY, Jessie 138
| HSIEH, Rebecca T. 567
| THOMAS, Fannette H. 1236
| RUFF, Martha R. 1066
Gilman Sch | BAVAR, Betty J. 67
Gordon Feinblatt Rothman et al | CONNOR, Elizabeth 237
Greater Baltimore Medical Center | BEARSS, Daniel H. 69
Johns Hopkins Univ | BOURKOFF, Vivienne R. . . . 119
| BRANCH, Katherine A. 127
| BUTTER, Karen A. 167
| COOPER, David J. 242
| COUPE, Jill M. 251
| FLORANCE, Valerie 385
| FLOWER, Kenneth E. 386
| GILLISPIE, James E. 436
| GWYN, Ann S. 479
| HALE, Dawn L. 485
| HEATH, Henry H. 519
| KIM, Chung S. 648
| KOEHLER, Barbara M. 667
| LOWENS, Margery M. 744
| LUCIER, Richard E. 746
| MARTIN, Susan K. 778
| MATHESON, Nina W. 783
| PERKINS, Earle R. 959
| PETTERSON, Marjorie M. . . 965
| PUGH, W J. 997
| QUIST, Edwin A. 1001
| ROBERTS, Cynthia H. 1039
| SATTERTHWAITE, Rebecca K. 1084
| SCHAAF, Elizabeth 1088
| SMITH, Mary P. 1158
| WOODS, Catharine C. 1366
Josephite Fathers and Brothers | HOGAN, Peter E. 549
Kennedy Inst for Handicapped Children | HOOFNAGLE, Bettea J. 556
Legal Aid Bureau Inc | BUTTS, Willie D. 168
Lib Co of the Baltimore Bar | FISHMAN, David H. 381
Lifecard International | SCHERER, Dieter 1092
LMTC | MCADAM, Paul E. 791
Loyola Coll | VARGA, Nicholas 1278

MARYLAND (Cont'd)
BALTIMORE (Cont'd)
Loyola-Notre Dame Lib | DAVISH, William 281
| FRYER, Philip 407
| RAY, John G. 1011
| TURKOS, Joseph A. 1263
Marshall Law Lib | GROSSHANS, Maxine Z. . . . 473
Martin Marietta | CHESLOCK, Rosalind P. . . . 207
| FELDMAN, Eleanor C. 369
| MORRIS, Sharon D. 867
| RICHTER, Mary L. 1031
| SCHWARTZ, Betsy J. 1104
Maryland Dept of Health & Mental Health | MUNSEY, Joyce E. 879
Maryland Dept of State Planning Lib | JENG, Helene W. 596
Maryland Historical Society | SILVER, Marcy L. 1138
| STUART, Karen A. 1204
Maryland Lib Association | GREENFIELD, Robert E. . . . 464
Maryland State Department of Education | BOLIN, Nancy C. 112
| HILDEBRANDT, Irene 539
| MONTGOMERY, Paula K. . . . 856
| PARTRIDGE, James C. 945
| STEPHAN, Sandra S. 1187
| TAYLOR, Nettie B. 1228
| WILLIAMS, J L. 1343
Maryland State Lib | SZCZCPANIAK, Adam S. . . 1218
Maryland State Lib for the Blind | FINNEY, Lance C. 379
Medical & Chirurgical Faculty | HARMAN, Susan E. 502
| JENSEN, Joseph E. 599
Mercy Hospital | KAISLER, Dolores H. 622
Miles & Stockbridge | COLE, Anna B. 230
Morgan State Univ | DE LERMA, Dominique R. . . . 289
| KUAN, David A. 681
Mueller Associates Inc | MENEGAUX, Edmond A. . . . 824
| TUCKER, Clark F. 1261
Niles Barton & Wilmer | HOLDEN, Nancy K. 550
Ober Kaler Grimes & Shriver | HINSON, Karen C. 543
Piper & Marbury | NIXON, Judith A. 906
| RASCHKA, Katherine E. . . . 1008
Record Collections Inc | LAZZARONI, Philip S. 706
RMS Associates | GENUARDI, Michael T. 427
St Agnes Hospital | SULLIVAN, Joanne L. 1207
St Mary's Seminary & Univ | CAREY, John T. 181
Semmes Bowen & Semmes | HARRIS, Helen Y. 504
Seton High Sch | RODDY, Ruth 1047
Social Security Administration | SMITH, Kathleen A. 1156
South Baltimore General Hospital | LAY, Shirley 705
Space Telescope Science Institute | STEVENS-RAYBURN, Sarah L. 1191
State Network Services | CUNNINGHAM, Barbara M. . 265
Towson State Univ | HOFSTETTER, Eleanore O. . . 549
| KALTENBORN, Helen P. 623
Tydings & Rosenberg | THIES, Gail M. 1235
Union Memorial Hospital | ZIMMERMAN, Martha B. . . . 1389
Union Memorial Lib | DAUGHERTY, Carolyn M. . . . 275
Univ of Baltimore | BEHLES, Patricia A. 74
| GREENBERG, Emily R. 463
| KLEIN, Ilene R. 659
| LABASH, Stephen P. 685
| YEAGER, Gerry 1378
Univ of Maryland at Baltimore | BRENNAN, Edward P. 132
| EPSTEIN, Robert S. 351
| FREIBURGER, Gary A. 401
| GONTRUM, Barbara S. 448
| HINEGARDNER, Patricia G. . 542
| HUMPHRIES, Anne W. 574
| RAND, Pamela S. 1006
| SMITH, Barbara G. 1152
| TEITELBAUM, Sandra D. . . 1230
| TOOEY, Mary J. 1250
| WILLIAMS, Mary A. 1345
| WILSON, Marjorie P. 1352
Univ of Maryland at Baltimore County | CREST, Sarah E. 258
| KULP, William A. 683
| LEBRETON, Jonathan A. . . . 708
| WILKINSON, Billy R. 1340
Veterans Administration Medical Center | STOUT, Deborah A. 1198

MARYLAND (Cont'd)
BALTIMORE (Cont'd)

Walters Art Gallery	KLEEBERGER, Patricia L.	658
	TOPPAN, Muriel L.	1251
Whiteford Taylor & Preston	SPIVEY, Lynne G.	1175

BEL AIR

Harford County Lib	CRISCO, Mary E.	259
	LEBRUN, Marlene M.	708
	MASSEY, James E.	782
	PITTMAN, Dorothy E.	976
	SEDNEY, Frances V.	1111
	SHAUCK, Stephanie M.	1123
	STREIN, Barbara M.	1201
	WASIELEWSKI, Eleanor B.	1308

BELTSVILLE

NALINET	CHEN, John H.	205
National Agricultural Lib	BROGDON, Jennie L.	139
	COLLINS, Donna S.	232
	ESMAN, Michael D.	354
	GELENTER, Winifred H.	426
	GOLDSBERG, Elizabeth D.	446
	MCCONE, Gary K.	797
	RAFATS, Jerome M.	1003
	RUSSELL, Keith W.	1069
	THOMAS, Sarah E.	1238
	WATERS, Samuel T.	1309
US Department of Agriculture	ANDRE, Pamela Q.	26
	DECKER, Leola M.	286
	DITXLER, Carol J.	306
	EDWARDS, Shirley J.	338
	FRANK, Robyn C.	397
	HANFMAN, Deborah A.	495
	HOOD, Martha W.	556
	HOWARD, Joseph H.	564
	KREBS-SMITH, James J.	677
	LARSON, Jean A.	699
	LEFEBVRE, Veronica A.	712
	LONGENECKER, William H.	740
	MACLEAN, Jayne T.	757
	MANGIN, Julianne	765
	MASON, Pamela R.	781
	PISA, Maria G.	975
	SCHNEIDER, Karl R.	1097
	STRANSKY, Maria	1200
	THOMPSON, Michael E.	1240
US Dept of Agriculture Forest Service	AYER, Carol A.	42

BETHESDA

American Coll of Cardiology	GOLDSTEIN, Helene B.	446
	LAFFREY, Laurel W.	687
American Hospital Association	KIGER, Anne F.	647
American Society of Hospital Pharmacists	HANES, Alice H.	495
	MORISSEAU, Anne L.	865
Atomic Industrial Forum	GOLDMAN, Patricia J.	445
Audio Response Services Inc	ELASIK, Ronald G.	341
Bethesda Naval Hospital	MEYER, Gerald E.	830
Booz Allen & Hamilton Inc	GRIMES, Judith E.	470
Cambridge Scientific Abstracts	SEARS, Jonathan R.	1110
Congressional Information Service Inc	JOHNSON, Richard K.	608
	MASSA, Paul P.	781
	MCRAE, Alexander D.	818
	STERN, Michael P.	1189
	TAYLOR, Marcia E.	1227
	VONDERHAAR, Mark N.	1288
Costabile Associates Inc	BOEHR, Diane L.	109
	COSTABILE, Salvatore L.	249
	PHILLIPS, Lena M.	968
	WINZER, Kathleen M.	1356
	YU, Pei	1384
Country Day Sch of the Sacred Heart	WILLIS, Susan C.	1348
Disclosure Information Group	HOFFMAN, Diane J.	547
	HYTLA, Sheila G.	581
	INKELLIS, Barbara G.	583
Dixon-Turner Research Associates	TURNER, Ellis S.	1264
Earle Palmer Brown Companies	MASTROIANNI, Richard L.	783
EDS Corp	PETERSON, George B.	963
Electronic Information Systems	GAUJARD, Pierre G.	422
ERIC Processing & Reference Facility	EUSTACE, Susan J.	356
Federation, Am Socty, Experimental Bio	ERLICK, Louise S.	353

MARYLAND (Cont'd)
BETHESDA (Cont'd)

Govt Relations Consultants	MILLENSON, Roy H.	835
Holton-Arms Sch	SMINK, Anna R.	1152
Landon Sch	BROWN, Judith B.	145
Logistics Management Institute	SHOCKLEY, Cynthia W.	1132
Martin Marietta	CARR, Margaret M.	186
MHF Consulting Service	FISHBEIN, Meyer H.	380
Montgomery County Pub Schs	DAVIES, Gordon D.	277
National Cancer Institute	DICKINSON, Patricia C.	301
	OSTROW, Dianne G.	929
	TINGLEY, Dianne E.	1246
National Heart Lung & Blood Institute	YORKS, Melissa L.	1381
Natl Information Standards Organization	HARRIS, Patricia R.	505
National Institutes of Health	CHU, Ellen M.	212
	COLLINS, Kenneth A.	233
	GLOCK, Martha H.	441
	HARRIMAN, Jenny F.	503
	KUNZ, Margarett N.	684
	MASYS, Daniel R.	783
	TAHIR, Mary M.	1220
	TEIGEN, Philip M.	1230
National Lib of Medicine	AINES, Andrew A.	8
	ALLEN, Cassandra	14
	ANDERSON, John E.	23
	ARENALES, Duane W.	31
	ARONSON, Jules	34
	BACKUS, Joyce E.	44
	BARNES, Alvin	57
	BECKELHIMER, Melvin	72
	BECKWITH, Frances	73
	BENNETT, Harry D.	81
	BLACK, Dennis E.	101
	BRAND, Jeanne L.	128
	BROWN, Sharon D.	147
	BUCHAN, Patricia C.	153
	BUCKNER, Donald	154
	BYRNES, Margaret M.	169
	CAIN, James	171
	CAMPBELL, Brian	176
	CARNEY, Kenneth G.	183
	CHARUHAS, Joseph	203
	CLEPPER, Peter A.	221
	COLAIANNI, Lois A.	229
	COLTON, Karin	234
	CONNER, P Z.	237
	COSMIDES, George J.	249
	COSTANZO, Sandra	249
	COX, John	253
	CURRY, Robert	266
	DAHLEN, Roger W.	269
	DOSZKOCS, Tamas	313
	DUFF, Judith A.	323
	DUTCHER, Gale A.	329
	FERGUSON, Tyrone	372
	GILKESON, Roger	435
	GOLDSMITH, James	446
	GOLDSTEIN, Charles M.	446
	GOODWIN, Linda	450
	GOSHORN, Jeanne C.	452
	HAWK, Susan A.	513
	HAZARD, George F.	517
	HENDERSON, B E.	525
	HERBERT, Charles E.	530
	HIRTLE, Peter B.	544
	HOFFMAN, Christa F.	547
	HORAN, Meredith L.	559
	HOWARD, Frances	564
	HSIEH, Richard K.	567
	HUMPHREY, Susanne M.	573
	HUMPHREYS, Betsy L.	573
	HUNT, Jennie P.	575
	JOHNSON, Frances E.	604
	JOHNSON, Gary M.	604
	KEISTER, Lucinda	635
	KENTON, David	643
	KIM, Sunnie I.	649
	KIRBY, Diana G.	654
	KISSMAN, Henry M.	656

MARYLAND (Cont'd)
BETHESDA (Cont'd)
National Lib of Medicine

KOTZIN, Sheldon 673
LACROIX, Eve M. 686
LAKSHMAN, Malathi K. 689
LINDBERG, Donald A. 728
LYON-HARTMANN, Becky
J. 752
MAIKAIL, Jackie 761
MAIN, James S. 761
MALCOMSON, Dennis 763
MCCUTCHEON, Dianne E. . . 801
MEHNERT, Robert B. 821
MERCHANT, Barbara 825
MEREDITH, Pam 825
PARASCANDOLA, John L. . . 939
PEGRAM, Bryant 954
PHILLIPS, Stanley J. 969
PINHO, Marie 974
RADA, Roy F. 1002
RAWSTHORNE, Grace C. . . 1011
ROBINSON, Arthur J. 1043
ROTARIU, Mark J. 1059
RUBEN, Patricia 1064
SAVAGE, Allan G. 1085
SCHOOLMAN, Harold M. . . 1098
SCHULMAN, Jacque L. 1101
SCHUYLER, Peri L. 1103
SEIGEL, Sidney 1112
SIEGEL, Elliot R. 1136
SILVERSTEIN, Bernard 1139
SINN, Sally 1144
SLATER, Susan B. 1148
SMITH, Kent A. 1156
SPANN, Melvin L. 1171
SWANSON, Brenda R. 1213
THOMA, George R. 1235
TILLEY, Carolyn N. 1245
UNGER, Carol P. 1269
VASTA, Bruno M. 1279
WALLINGFORD, Karen T. . . 1298
WEST, Richard T. 1326
WILLIAMS, Patricia D. 1346
WILLMERING, William J. . . . 1348
WOODSMALL, Rose M. . . . 1367
WORTHINGTON, Randall . . 1369
WRIGHT, Nancy D. 1372
National Standards Association   GILBERT, Mattana 433
Naval Medical Research Institute   COSKEY, Rosemary B. 248
Options & Choices Inc   POMERANTZ, Karyn L. 982
ORI Inc   BRANDHORST, Ted 128
                                    BRANDHORST, Wesley T. . . 128
                                    MISSAR, Charles D. 847
Path Services Inc   BEATTY, Samuel B. 70
The Resource Center   MENNELLA, Dona M. 824
US Department of Health & Human
    Services   BROWN, Carolyn P. 142
                                    LYNN, Kenneth C. 752
World Development Group Inc   GOLDSCHMIDT, Peter G. . . 446
BOWIE
Bowie State Coll   PENISTON, William A. 956
H & G Associates   GIGANTE, Vickilyn M. 433
Prince George's County Board of
    Educ   GERRING, Cheryl R. 429
Prince George's County Memorial Lib HARGROVE, Marion H. 501
BRENTWOOD
Dickinson-Higginson Press   MOREY, Frederick L. 863
BROOKLANDVILLE
St Paul's Sch for Girls   KELLY, Carol N. 637
BWI AIRPORT
NASA Scientific & Technl Info Facility BUCHAN, Ronald L. 153
                                    JACK, Robert F. 586
RMS Associates   FOURNIER, Susan K. 393
                                    SILVESTER, June P. 1139

CAMBRIDGE
Dorchester County Pub Lib   DEL SORDO, Jean S. 290
CAMP SPRINGS
St Philip the Apostle Sch   MC HALE, Mary M. 808

MARYLAND (Cont'd)
CATONSVILLE
American Society for Microbiology   SHAY, Donald E. 1124
Catonsville Community Coll   COOK, Daraka S. 239
Univ of Maryland at Baltimore County STERLING, Judith K. 1189
                                    WILT, Larry J. 1353

CHESTERTOWN
Kent County Pub Lib   BRIGGS, Anne F. 135
                                    REILLY, Deborah D. 1020
Washington Coll   HYMES, Judith I. 580
CHEVERLY
Prince George's Hospital Center   KLEMAN, Eleanor L. 660
CHEVY CHASE
Computer Data Systems Inc   ZYNJUK, Nila L. 1392
Kenton Assocs   KENTON, Charlotte 642
St Patrick's Episcopal Day Sch   PECK, Ann D. 953
Univ Research Corp   MARTINEZ-GOLDMAN,
                                    Aline 779

CHURCHTON
Systems Planning   TONEY, Stephen R. 1250
CLINTON
Federal Government   MEZZAPELLE, Alice S. 831
St John the Evangelist Sch   FITZGERALD, M A. 382
COLLEGE PARK
Litton-Amecom Div   O'DELL, M P. 916
Univ of Maryland at College Park   CUNNINGHAM, William D. . . 265
                                    CURTIS, Peter H. 267
                                    EBELING-KONING, Blanche
                                    T. 334
                                    EVANS, Sylvia D. 358
                                    FARREN, Donald 365
                                    HARRAR, H J. 503
                                    HEILPRIN, Laurence B. 521
                                    HEUTTE, Frederic A. 535
                                    JACKSON, Carleton 587
                                    KLAIR, Arlene F. 657
                                    KOBAYASHI, Michiko 666
                                    LARSEN, Lida L. 698
                                    MARCHIONINI, Gary J. 769
                                    MERIKANGAS, Robert J. . . . 826
                                    NITECKI, Danuta A. 905
                                    PITT, William B. 976
                                    ROBERTSON, Jack 1042
                                    SHEETS, Robin R. 1125
                                    SHULMAN, Frank J. 1133
                                    SIMS, Sally R. 1142
                                    SOERGEL, Dagobert 1165
                                    STIELOW, Frederick J. 1194
                                    VAN CAMPEN, Rebecca J. . . 1272
                                    WALSTON, Claude E. 1300
                                    WELLISCH, Hans H. 1322
                                    WILLIAMS, Helen E. 1343
                                    WILSON, William G. 1353
COLUMBIA
Allied Aerospace Co   DOVE, Samuel 315
Books Worth Buying   RUSS, Kennetta P. 1068
Howard County Lib   BOGAGE, Alan R. 110
                                    HILL, Norma L. 540
                                    JONES, Cynthia A. 612
Lib of Congress   JOHNSON, Bruce C. 602
The Rouse Co   SEMKO, Melanie J. 1115
Wasserman-Diener Associates Inc   DIENER, Carol W. 302
                                    DIENER, Richard A. 302
CROWNSVILLE
Crownsville Hospital Center   MERRILL, Susan S. 827
CUMBERLAND
Allegany County Lib System   NEAL, Robert L. 890
Bishop Walsh Middle/High School   PRICE, Consuelo 992
DENTON
Caroline County Pub Lib   SANDS, George A. 1081
DUNDALK
Dundalk Community Coll   MILLER, Everett G. 837
EASTON
Memorial Hospital of Easton Maryland MOLTER, Maureen M. 853
EDGEWATER
Anne Arundel County Board of
    Education   SHAMBARGER, Peter E. . . 1120
Smithsonian Institution   HAGGINS, Angela N. 483
ELDERSBURG
Carroll County Pub Lib   DAVIS, Denise 278

MARYLAND (Cont'd)

ELKTON
Cecil County Pub Lib BRAMMER, Linda A. 127
                      O'BRIEN, Lee A. 914
Cecil County Pub Schs THOMAS, Fred 1236
Morton Thiokol Inc IRWIN, Ruth A. 584

ELLICOTT CITY
Howard County Pub Schs O'LOUGHLIN, Marilyn L. 921

EMMITSBURG
Evaluative Technologies Inc POSEY, Sussann F. 985
Federal Emergency Management
  Agency CHIESA, Adele M. 208
Mount Saint Mary's Coll FITZPATRICK, Kelly 383

FALLSTON
Harford County Lib CLARK, David S. 216

FT MEAD
National Security Agency MEYER, William P. 830

FT MEADE
US Department of Defense WILLIAMS, Beth A. 1342

FORT WASHINGTON
Univ of Maryland at Fort Washington PHILLIPS, Gary B. 968

FREDERICK
Frederick County Board of Education FISHER, Eleanor W. 381
Frederick Cancer Research Facility KINNA, Dorothy H. 652
Frederick County Pub Libs FISHER, Joan W. 381
                          JOHNSON, Jerry D. 606
National Cancer Institute FRYSER, Benjamin S. 407
                          WILSON, Susan W. 1353
US Army GIBBONS, Katherine Y. 431
Univ Publications of America REINERSTEIN, Gail G. 1021

FROSTBURG
Frostburg State Coll GILLESPIE, David M. 435
                     WILLIAMS, Pamela S. 1346

GAITHERSBURG
Contel Federal Systems VAN BRUNT, Virginia 1272
General Electric Co HENDERSON, Susanne 527
John Sayer Associates SAYER, John S. 1086
National Bureau of Standards BAGG, Thomas C. 45
                             BERGER, Patricia W. 86
                             BOND, Marvin A. 113
                             JASON, Nora H. 595
                             KINGSTON, Mary L. 652
                             KLEIN, Sami W. 659
                             MOLINE, Judi A. 853
                             OVERMAN, Joanne R. 931
Resource Planning Inc PAUL, Rameshwar N. 949

GERMANTOWN
Lib Systems & Services MCQUEEN, Judith D. 817
Online Computer Systems Inc ALBRIGHT, John B. 10
                            BATOR, Eileen F. 64
                            MILLER, Kenda 839

GLEN BURNIE
Anne Arundel County Pub Lib SUMLER, Claudia B. 1209
Social Security Administration BREWER, Christina A. 134

GLENARDEN
Prince George's County Memorial Lib WOODY, Jacqueline B. 1368

GLENELG
Glenelg Country Sch PICKWORTH, Hannah S. . . . 971

GREENBELT
Lib of Congress VIRTA, Alan K. 1285
National Aeronautics & Space Admin BOGGESS, John J. 110
OAO Corp AUSTIN, Rhea C. 40
Prince George's County Pub Schs ASHFORD, Richard K. 36
Univ of Maryland at Baltimore PETERSON, William S. 965

HAGERSTOWN
Libra Associates Inc BAKER, Benjamin R. 48
Washington County Free Lib LIZER, Bonnie S. 735
                           MALLERY, Mary S. 763
                           SUTTON, Sharan D. 1212
Washington County Hospital
  Association BINAU, Myra I. 97

HUNT VALLEY
McCormick & Co Inc RILEY, Sarah A. 1035

HYATTSVILLE
Prince George's County Memorial Lib BURGESS, Eileen E. 159
                                    COOPER, Judith C. 243
                                    GORDON, William R. 452
                                    HALL, Mary A. 488
                                    LEVINE, Susan H. 721
                                    LOSINSKI, Julia M. 742

MARYLAND (Cont'd)

HYATTSVILLE (Cont'd)
Prince George's County Memorial Lib
                                    ROBINSON, Mark L. 1044
                                    SHIH, Walter D. 1130
Regina High Sch BEAULIEU, Yvette E. 70
Religions of Jesus and Mary RHEAUME, Irene M. 1025

INDIAN HEAD
Naval EOD Technology Ctr OMARA, Marie T. 923
Naval Ordnance Station GALLAGHER, Charles F. 413
USN EOD DAVIS, Bonnie D. 277

KENSINGTON
American Society for Training &
  Devlpmnt CHAPUT, Linda J. 202
Montgomery County Department of
  Pub Libs PILZER, Cecily R. 973
National Institutes of Health GALLAGHER, Elizabeth M. . . 414

LA PLATA
Southern Maryland Regional Lib HURREY, Katharine C. 577
                               TARAN, Nadia P. 1223
                               WILSEY, Charlotte A. 1349

LANDOVER
Prince George's County Pub Schs BARTH, Edward W. 61
Scientific Management Associates Inc OMAR, Elizabeth A. 923

LANHAM
Huffer Associates HUFFER, Mary A. 570
IIT Research Institute O'NEILL, Sue 924

LARGO
Prince George's Community Coll NEKRITZ, Leah K. 893

LAUREL
Johns Hopkins Univ DEBROWER, Amy M. 285
                   HILDITCH, Bonny M. 539
                   KOSMIN, Linda J. 672
                   NEWMAN, Wilda B. 900
Washington Suburban Sanitary
  Commission YUILLE, Willie K. 1384

LINTHICUM HEIGHTS
Booz Allen & Hamilton Inc WETZBARGER, Cecilia G. . 1328

LOTHIAN
Anne Arundel County Pub Sch
  System STIGALL, Judith N. 1194

LUSBY
Baltimore Gas & Electric Co HUMMEL, Janice A. 573

MOUNT AIRY
Lomond Publications Inc HATTERY, Lowell H. 512
                        JOHNSON, Susan W. 609

MOUNT SAVAGE
Allegany County Board of Education FAHERTY, Gladys W. 361

MYERSVILLE
The Data Brokers O'LEARY, Mick 920

NEW CARROLLTON
Prince George's County Memorial Lib GOODLETT, Doris R. 449
Prince George's County Pub Schs CAMPA, Josephine 175

NORTH EAST
Cecil Community Coll DENNEY, Christine A. 292

OXON HILL
Prince George's County Memorial Lib MOORE, Craig P. 859

PASADENA
Anne Arundel County Pub Lib MAZUREK, Adam P. 791

PATUXENT RIVER
US Naval Air Station SULLIVAN, Carol W. 1207

PERRY POINT
Veterans Administration Medical
  Center SCHULTZ, Barbara A. 1101

POTOMAC
Claritas Limited Partnership PATRICIU, Florin S. 947
Montgomery County Department of
  Pub Libs BUSH, Rhoda H. 165
            GALE, Roswita W. 413
Phillips Publishing Inc KIMMEL, Mark R. 649
                        MESHINSKY, Jeff M. 827
Smolian Sound Studios SMOLIAN, Steven J. 1162

PRINCE FREDERICK
Calvert County Pub Lib HAMMETT, Marcia G. 493
                       HOFMANN, Patricia P. 548

PRINCESS ANNE
Somerset County Board of Education SNYDER, Denny L. 1164
Univ of Maryland at Eastern Shore DADSON, Theresa E. 269
                                  PANDA, Rosamond E. 937
                                  SMITH, Jessie C. 1156

MARYLAND (Cont'd)

REISTERSTOWN

Baltimore County Board of Lib
  Trustees   TURNER, David E. 1264

Baltimore County Pub Lib   JONKE, Grace M. 616

ROCKVILLE

American Speech, Language &
  Hearing Assn   ZAHARKO, Nancy W. 1385

Aspen Publishers Inc   PATTERSON, Anne S. . 948

                      QUINLIN, Margaret M. 1000

Aspen Systems Corp   BATES, Ruthann I. 64

                      BYRD, Harvey C. 169

                      CHIANG, Ahushun 207

                      GAVIN, Andrew 423

                      GROCKI, Daniel J. 471

                      JOHNSON, Carol A. 602

                      JOHNSON, Emily P. 604

                      KNOERDEL, Joan E. 665

                      MCDONALD, Dennis D. 802

                      PEARSE, Nancy J. 952

                      USDIN, B T. 1270

                      VANCE, Julia M. 1273

Berul Associates Ltd   BERUL, Lawrence H. 91

Biospherics Inc   KNICKERBOCKER, Wendy .. 664

Chestnut Lodge Hospital   SMITH, Karen G. 1156

Electronic Data Systems   SLOAN, Cheryl A. 1149

FOI Services Inc   BOBKA, Marlene S. 108

Food & Drug Administration   ASSOUAD, Carol S. 37

Gillette Medical Evaluation
  Laboratories   DEXTER, Patrick J. 298

History Associates Inc   CANTELON, Philip L. 179

                      KELLS, Laura J. 637

                      MERZ, Nancy M. 827

Infax Corp   JONES, Gerry U. 613

King Research Inc   GRIFFITHS, Jose M. 469

                      KING, Donald W. 650

                      NOLAN, Deborah A. 907

Montgomery Coll

Montgomery County Department of
  Pub Libs   ALEXANDER, Estelle R. 12

                      CHELTON, Mary K. 204

                      DOWD, Frank B. 315

                      GRIFFEN, Agnes M. 468

                      PEDAK-KARI, Maria 954

                      PHIFER, Kenneth O. 967

                      SHAPIRO, Leila C. 1121

                      SOLOMON, Fern R. 1166

Montgomery County Pub Lib   MEIZNER, Kathie L. 822

Montgomery County Pub Schs BARALOTO, R A. 55

                      DEAN, Frances C. 283

                      KISSMAN, Elise C. 656

                      KNOX, Jo E. 666

National Assn of Securities Dealers
  Inc   WHITMAN, Jean A. 1333

National Clearinghouse for Alcohol
  Info   FREEDMAN, Lynn P. 400

National Oceanic & Atmospheric
  Admin   MCKEAN, Joan M. 810

Shady Grove Adventist Hospital HERIN, Nancy J. 531

US Food & Drug Administration KRUSE, Kathryn W. 681

US Pharmacopeial Convention WOLLAM, Martha A. 1361

US Pharmacopeial Convention Inc GRIFFITHS, Mary C. 469

Westat Inc   POTTER, Andrea K. 987

Young & Associates   YOUNG, Jean 1382

ST MARYS CITY

St Mary's Coll   BRITTEN, William A. 137

                      REPENNING, Julie A. 1023

                      WILLIAMSON, John G. 1347

SALISBURY

Peninsula General Hospital Medical
  Ctr   OGLE, Mary H. 918

Wicomico County Free Lib   GOETZ, Arthur H. 443

                      HOMAN, Frances M. 555

SEVERN

Anne Arundel County Pub Lib AUGER, Brian K. 39

SEVERNA PARK

Anne Arundel County Pub Lib COURSON, M S. 251

Severn Sch   TITCOMB, Anne S. 1247

MARYLAND (Cont'd)

SILVER SPRING

Agee Indexing Services   AGEE, Victoria V. 7

American Overseas Book Co   MARKS, Cicely P. 771

Assn for Information & Image
  Management   COURTOT, Marilyn E. 251

                      STEIGER, Bettie A. 1185

Automated Sciences Group Inc SPURLING, Norman K. 1177

CDB Enterprises Inc   BATTY, Charles D. 65

KADEC Info Management Co   KADEC, Sarah T. 621

The KBL Group Inc   LEVITAN, Karen B. 721

Linowes & Blocher   CAMILLO, Janet H. 175

Maryland Coll of Art & Design PRATT, Laura C. 990

Montgomery County Department of
  Pub Libs   LINTON, Linda A. 731

Montgomery County Lib   GIBBS, Beatrice E. 431

Montgomery County Pub Schs MORGAN, Betty J. 863

Morgan Lewis & Bockius   MERINGOLO, Joseph A. 826

Natl Center for Social Policy &
  Practice   REPPY, Charlotte D. 1024

Quinn's Records Management
  Service   QUINN, Sidney 1000

Ronald L Henderson Association HENDERSON, Ronald L. 527

Tax Analysts   AMATRUDA, William T. 19

US Department of Agriculture FORBES, John B. 389

Vitro Corp   MORRIS, Louis M. 867

SNOW HILL

Worcester County Lib   WELLS, Stewart L. 1323

SOLOMONS

Univ of Maryland at Solomons HEIL, Kathleen A. 521

SUITLAND

La Reine High Sch   SLANGA, Joanne 1147

National Archives & Records Admin DIMKOFF, Diane L. 304

Prince George's County Pub Schs MATHEWS, Mary P. 784

TAKOMA PARK

Special Information Services Inc VELLUCCI, Matthew J. 1282

Washington Adventist Hospital HINKEL, Jeannine M. 542

TOWSON

American Lib Trustee Association DAVIS, Herbert A. 279

Baltimore County Pub Lib   EICKHOFF, Jane S. 339

                      HAIRE, Jennifer C. 484

                      HEMPHILL, Franklin B. 525

                      MOLZ, Jean B. 854

                      ROBINSON, Charles W. ... 1043

                      WISOTZKI, Lila B. 1358

                      ZAIDEL, Jack N. 1385

Baltimore County Pub Schs   ANDERSON, Della L. 22

                      DRACH, Marian C. 317

                      HACKMAN, Mary H. 481

                      REIDER, William L. 1019

Goucher Coll   LANTZ, Louise K. 697

                      LEV, Yvonne T. 719

                      MAGNUSON, Nancy 759

Loyola-Blakefield Lib   RUSSELL, Rose M. 1069

Sheppard-Pratt Hospital   FREDENBURG, Anne M. 399

Towson State Univ   CHEEKS, Cellestine 204

                      GERHARDT, Edwin L. 428

                      HARER, John B. 501

UPPER MARLBORO

NAHB National Research Center HARBERT, Cathy E. 499

Prince George's County Pub Schs MURRAY, Bruce C. 881

WALDORF

Charles County Pub Lib   TRELEVEN, Richard L. 1255

DYNIX Inc   DUDLEY, Robyn A. 323

WESTMINSTER

Carroll County Pub Lib   MCCARTY, Emily H. 795

                      ROBERTS, Susan P. 1041

                      WOLF, Dorothy L. 1360

Western Maryland Coll   DENMAN-WEST, Margaret
                      W. 292

                      NEIKIRK, Harold D. 892

                      QUINN, Carol J. 1000

                      RICHWINE, Eleanor N. 1031

WHEATON

Actraining Services   KAESSINGER, Carla S. 621

GS Associates   SIEGMAN, Gita 1136

Montgomery County Department of
  Pub Libs   NITZBERG, Dale B. 905

WORTON

Kent County Pub Schs   HUNTINGTON, Joan L. 576

MASSACHUSETTS

ACTON
Sandra H Hurd Consultants . . . . HURD, Sandra H. 577

AHLEBORO
Leach & Garner Co . . . . MANGION, Barbara E. 765

AMHERST
Amherst Coll . . . . BAILEY, Leeta L. 46
BRIDEGAM, Willis E. 135
EVANS, Sally 358
LANCASTER, John 692
Jones Library Inc . . . . LOMBARDO, Daniel J. 738
Univ of Massachusetts at Amherst . . . . . . ADAMS, Leonard R. 5
CHADWICK, Alena F. 196
CRAIG, James L. 254
DONOHUE, Joseph 312
FELDMAN, Laurence M. . . . 369
FELLER, Siegfried 370
FRETWELL, Gordon E. 402
HOLM, Edla K. 552
JUENGLING, Pamela K. 619
KENDALL, John D. 640
KOCSIS, Jeanne 667
MERRIAM, Joyce 826
TALBOT, Richard J. 1220
TAUSKY, Janice 1225
WOOD, Ann L. 1363

ANDOVER
Advanced Library Systems Inc . . . . SAMMATARO, John A. 1078
Andover Pub Schools . . . . FREEDMAN, Annetta R. 400
Memorial Hall Lib . . . . JACOBSON, Nancy C. 590

ARLINGTON
Boston Athenaeum . . . . ENGLISH, Cynthia J. 350
Mitre Corp . . . . JENNINGS, Margaret S. 598

ATHOL
Athol Pub Lib . . . . ROSE, Christine P. 1054

ATTLEBORO
Attleboro Pub Lib . . . . STITT, Walter B. 1195

AUBURN
Auburn Pub Lib . . . . RAMSAY, John E. 1005

AVON
Winchester Industries Inc . . . . PILE, Deborah R. 973

BABSON PARK
Babson Coll . . . . MALLER, Alma L. 763

BEDFORD
Analysis & Computer Systems Inc . . . . . . ROSENTHAL, Marylu C. . . . 1057
Bedford Pub Lib . . . . MAIER, Robert C. 761
DEC Videotex Marketing Group . . . . PAGE, Bill 934
Digital Equipment Corp . . . . ADAMS, Michael Q. 5
Fisons Corp . . . . CAREY, Charlene E. 181
Middlesex Community Coll . . . . HALE, Janice L. 485
HORGAN, Laura A. 559
US Air Force . . . . MCLAUGHLIN, Lee R. 813
Veterans Administration Medical
Center . . . . KERN, Donald C. 643

BELCHERTOWN
Town of Belchertown . . . . PECK, Ruth M. 953

BELMONT
Belmont Pub Schs . . . . PHELAN, Mary C. 967
WOODS, Selina J. 1367
McLean Hospital . . . . LABREE, Rosanne 686

BEVERLY
Beverly Pub Lib . . . . SCULLY, Thomas F. 1109
Endicott Coll . . . . DUSCHATKO, Rebecca F. . . 329
North Shore Community Coll . . . . GAGNON, Ronald A. 412

BILLERICA
Aerodyne Research Inc . . . . MAST, Susan B. 782
Billerca Pub Lib . . . . FLAHERTY, Barbara A. 383
Cabot Corp . . . . DAVIS, Barbara M. 277
REID, Angea S. 1018
GTE Government Systems Corp . . . . TAUBER, Stephen J. 1225
Mobil Solar Energy Corp . . . . BERGIN, Dorothy O. 86

BOLTON
Bogart-Brociner Associates . . . . BOGART, Betty B. 110

BOSTON
ABC Schwann Publications Inc . . . . SCHWANN, William J. 1104
Agenda Technology . . . . BYRN, William H. 169
Art Institute of Boston . . . . DESJARDINS, Andrea C. . . . 295
Arthur Andersen & Co . . . . FISHER, Jean K. 381
Bain & Co Inc . . . . BLAKE, Michael R. 103
EISENMANN, Laura M. 341

MASSACHUSETTS (Cont'd)

BOSTON (Cont'd)
Bank of Boston-in-House Counsel . . . . . . VAN BEEK, Susan 1272
Barron & Stadfeld . . . . MOLONEY, Kevin F. 853
Battery March Financial Management
Co . . . . AVITABILE, Susan L. 42
Berklee Coll . . . . VOIGT, John F. 1287
Berwick Group . . . . BIANCANELLO, Anthony R. . . 93
Beth Israel Hospital . . . . DALY, Jay 271
Bingham Dana & Gould . . . . ANZALONE, Filippa M. 29
Boston Coll . . . . BEST, Eleanor L. 92
Boston Conservatory . . . . DIDHAM, Reginald A. 301
Boston Department of Health &
Hospitals . . . . BRENNER, Lawrence 133
Boston Edison Co . . . . HORN, David E. 559
Boston Globe Newspaper Co . . . . JOBE, Shirley A. 601
Boston Pub Lib . . . . BEECHER, Sally 74
BELANGER, Janet B. 75
BENDER, Helen F. 79
CEDERHOLM, Theresa D. . . . 196
CLANCY, Catherine M. 215
CORNWALL, Scot J. 247
CRIST, Margaret L. 259
CURLEY, Arthur 265
DOHERTY, John J. 309
GRIFFIN, Fredericia 468
HENRY, Susan L. 529
HORN, Joseph A. 559
KOLCZYNSKI, Charlotte A. . . 669
KORT, Richard L. 672
LANG, Rosalie A. 695
MOORACHIAN, Rose 858
MYLES, Bobbie 885
PARKS, P D. 943
ROGAN, Michael J. 1049
RUTKOVSKIS, Gunnars . . . 1070
ST. AUBIN, Arleen K. 1075
SCANNELL, Henry F. 1087
SCHLAFF, Donna G. 1093
SCHUELER, Dolores 1101
Boston Pub Schs . . . . ELAM, Barbara C. 341
KAUFMAN, Polly W. 631
Boston Redevelopment Authority . . . . SUTTON, Joyce A. 1211
Boston Univ . . . . ANDERSON, Wanda E. 25
CHRISTOPHER, Irene 212
CLIFT, Scott B. 222
FREEHLING, Dan J. 400
GATES, James L. 421
GRAMENZ, Francis L. 457
HARZBECKER, Joseph J. . . . 510
HUDSON, Robert E. 570
ILACQUA, Anne K. 581
LADD, Dorothy P. 687
LAUCUS, John 702
MOULTON, Catherine A. 873
PAYNE, Douglass B. 951
PERINO, Elaine S. 958
PETROFF, Loumona J. 965
PLUNKET, Linda 979
SAUER, David A. 1084
SESKIN, Ann H. 1116
SNYDER, David A. 1164
TOLMAN, Lorraine E. 1249
WEINSCHENK, Andrea 1318
ZIEPER, Linda R. 1388
ZIMPFER, William E. 1389
Bostonian Society . . . . BERGEN, Philip S. 85
Braxton Associates . . . . KING, Laurie L. 651
PREVE, Roberta J. 992
Brigham & Women's Hospital . . . . DUBNER, Nancy 321
Brown Rudnick Freed & Gesmer . . . . MURRAY, Lynn T. 882
Burns & Levinson . . . . HEACOCK, Pamela P. 518
Business Research Corp . . . . GALVIN, Carol K. 415
LEASON, Jane 707
Cambridge Analytical Associates . . . . DAMICO, Nancy B. 272
Camp Dresser & McKee Inc . . . . CARROLL, Virginia L. 187
Chamberlayne Junior Coll . . . . FRIEND, Ann S. 404
Chas T Main Inc . . . . MASON, Hayden 781
Children's Hospital . . . . GELLER, Miriam R. 426
Choate Hall & Stewart . . . . MURPHY, Eva B. 880

MASSACHUSETTS (Cont'd)
BOSTON (Cont'd)

Commonwealth of Massachusetts	CASO, Gasper	193
	CYPHERS, James E.	268
	MCLELLAN, Mary T.	814
	PIGGFORD, Roland	972
	SCHWALLER, Marian C.	1104
	WARNER, Marnie M.	1305
Dana-Farber Cancer Institute	BERNIER, Esta S.	89
The Data Desk	CAIN, Susan H.	171
E I DuPont de Nemours & Co Inc	LEEDS, Pauline R.	711
Eastern Massachusetts Regnl Lib System	HENEGHAN, Mary A.	528
	MONTANA, Edward J.	855
Emerson Coll	ALCORN, Cynthia W.	11
	BEZERA, Elizabeth A.	93
	CURTIN-STEVENSON, Mary C.	266
	MOSKOWITZ, Michael A.	871
	TRIPP, Maureen A.	1257
Federal Home Loan Bank of Boston	HAYES, Maureen L.	516
Fidelity Management & Research Co	CAHILL, Jack F.	171
First Church of Christ Scientist	HUENNEKE, Judith A.	570
Foley Hoag & Eliot	NORMAN-CAMP, Melody	909
Forsyth Dental Center	OPPENHEIM, Roberta A.	925
Franklin Institute	GIFFIN, Wendy L.	433
The Gillette Co	FOX, Susan	395
Goulston & Storrs	HAYES, Alison M.	515
Grand Lodge of Masons	HANKAMER, Roberta A.	496
Harvard Business Sch	EWING, Lydia M.	359
	JUDD, Eleanor M.	618
Harvard Sch of Pub Health	HAUSER, Betty W.	512
Harvard Univ	DUDA, Heidi E.	323
	PERRY, Emma B.	960
	SCHATZ, Cindy A.	1090
	STEVENSON, Michael I.	1191
	WEISS, Bernice O.	1320
	WINTERS, Wilma E.	1356
HBM/CREAMER Inc	ROSENBERG, Barbra E.	1055
Hemenway & Barnes	MOYER, Diane E.	874
Hill & Barlow	WELLINGTON, Carol S.	1321
Hill Holliday Connors Cosmopulos Inc	LEVINSON, Gail	721
Horn Book Magazine	SILVEY, Anita L.	1139
Houghton Mifflin Co	HOGAN, Margaret A.	549
	MURPHY, Marilyn S.	881
	PERRY, Guest	960
Ingalls Quinn & Johnson	MACIVER, Linda B.	756
John Hancock Mutual Life Insurance	RENDALL, Margot L.	1023
John Snow Inc	FRYDRYK, Teresa E.	407
Katharine Gibbs Sch	BUTLER, Ann S.	166
Laboure Coll	DESTEFANO, Daniel A.	296
Liberty Mutual Insurance Co	PROCOPIO, Concetta E.	994
Linguistics International Inc	PRINDLE, Paul E.	993
Massachusetts Archives at Columbia Point	WHITAKER, Albert H.	1329
Massachusetts Board of Lib Commissioners	DUGAN, Robert E.	324
	LEVITT, Irene S.	721
	SHANNON, Marcia A.	1120
Massachusetts Coll of Art	HOPKINS, Benjamin	557
Massachusetts Coll of Pharmacy	HILL, Barbara M.	539
Massachusetts Department of Pub Health	MOORE, Catherine I.	859
Massachusetts Dept of the Attorney Gen	MATZ, Ruth G.	786
Massachusetts Eye & Ear Infirmary	NIMS, Judith C.	904
Massachusetts Financial Service Center	MCGEE, Ruby T.	805
Massachusetts General Hospital	BUTTON, Katherine H.	167
	LEIGHTON, Helene L.	714
	SCHNEIDER, Elizabeth	1097
	SCULLIN, Janice A.	1109
	WESTLING, Ellen R.	1327
Massachusetts Horticultural Society	NESS, Pamela M.	896
Massachusetts Rehabilitation Commission	HOLT, June C.	554
Massachusetts State Lib	DONG, Tina	311
Massachusetts State Transportation Lib	PEARLSTEIN, Toby	952
Massachusetts Trial Court	KANE, Lois B.	625

MASSACHUSETTS (Cont'd)
BOSTON (Cont'd)

Massachusetts Water Resource Authority	LYDON, Mary E.	751
Mead Data Central	WALLAS, Philip R.	1298
Monosson Technology Enterprises	MONOSSON, Adolf S.	855
Museum of Fine Arts	ALLEN, Nancy S.	15
National Archives & Records Admin	DESNOYERS, Megan F.	295
	GOODRICH, Allan B.	449
	WHEALAN, Ronald E.	1328
The New England	KORMAN, Adrienne S.	671
New England Baptist Hospital	WOODARD, Paul E.	1366
New England Coll of Optometry	EPSTEIN, Lynne S.	351
New England Conservatory of Music	PRISTASH, Kenneth	993
New England Historic Genealogical Socty	HERMAN, Douglas C.	531
New England Sch of Law	ACTON, Anne M.	4
	STEARNS, Barry T.	1183
	TATELMAN, Susan D.	1225
Northeastern Univ	BENENFELD, Alan R.	80
	CAHALAN, Thomas H.	171
	CIANFARINI, Margaret	214
	HANSSEN, Nancy E.	499
	LEAHY, Lynda C.	706
	SCHALOW, John M.	1089
	STEINBERG, Marilyn H.	1185
Palmer & Dodge	LEONARD, Sharen C.	717
Parker Coulter Daley & White	ROFF, Jill R.	1049
Peat Marwick Main & Co	RAMSAY, Dorothy M.	1005
Perry Dean Rogers & Partners, Architects	FOOTE, Steven M.	388
The Pioneer Group Inc	DODSON, Nancy C.	308
Price Waterhouse	BUSCH, Joseph A.	165
	SCANLAN, Jean M.	1087
Prolepsis Inc	PLUNKET, Joy H.	978
PWS-KENT Publishing Co	BARCOMB, Wayne A.	55
Rich May Bilodeau & Flaherty	SWANN, Thomas E.	1213
Ropes & Gray	TRUBEY, Cornelia	1258
Simmons Coll	ANDERSON, A J.	21
	BAUGHMAN, James C.	66
	BUSH, Margaret A.	165
	CHEN, Ching C.	205
	HEINS, Ethel L.	522
	HERNON, Peter	532
	INTNER, Sheila S.	583
	LEONARD, Ruth S.	717
	MATARAZZO, James M.	783
	MCKIRDY, Pamela R.	812
	SCHWARTZ, Candy S.	1104
	SHARE, Donald S.	1122
	SNIFFIN-MARINO, Megan G.	1163
	STUEART, Robert D.	1205
Social Law Lib	FRANZEK, Karyn	398
	HAPIJ, Maria S.	499
	TAVARES, Cecelia M.	1225
	TURKALO, David M.	1263
Social Policy Research Group Inc	RUTTER, Nancy R.	1070
State Lib of Massachusetts	BEARDEN, Eithne C.	69
	NASON, Jennifer L.	888
	SIEGEL, Bette L.	1136
State Street Research & Management Co	LYNCH, Jacqueline	751
State Transportation Lib	MATIS, Lynn	784
Stone & Webster Engineering Corp	PELLINI, Nancy M.	955
Suffolk Univ	BANDER, Edward J.	54
	COLEMAN, James R.	231
	HAMANN, Edmund G.	490
	MAIO, Kathleen L.	762
Technical Data International	MILLS, Andrew G.	843
Teradyne Inc	BERNARD, Bobbi	88
Testa Hurwitz & Thibeault	DRISCOLL, Kathleen	320
Tufts Univ	EATON, Elizabeth K.	333
	STEARNS, Norman S.	1183
United Engineers & Constructors Inc	PRESTON, Margaret P.	992
US Court of Appeals	MILLER, Kristen L.	839
	MOSS, Karen M.	872
	RANDALL, Kristie C.	1006
US Environmental Protection Agency	NELSON, Margaret R.	894
	SARAVIS, Judith A.	1082

MASSACHUSETTS (Cont'd)
  BOSTON (Cont'd)
    Univ of Massachusetts at Boston   GROSE, B D. 472
                                    MAZURANIC, Joseph R. 791
                                    O'TOOLE, James M. 930
                                    SCHLESINGER, Frances C. 1094
                                    STIFFLEAR, Allan J. 1194
                                    TSENG, Louisa 1260
    Wentworth Institute of Technology   MANDEL, Debra H. 764
                                    PICCININO, Rocco 970
                                    SMITH, Ann M. 1152
  BRAINTREE
    Braintree Pub Schs   ROBINSON, Phyllis A. 1044
  BREWSTER
    Franklin Fixtures Inc   BAYLIS, Ted 67
  BRIDGEWATER
    Bridgewater State Coll   BATES, Susie M. 64
                                  CHANDRASEKHAR, Ratna .. 200
                                  NEUBAUER, Richard A. 896
                                  OAKLEY, Adeline D. 913
                                  TU, Shu C. 1261
                                  WEBBER, Cynthia J. 1313
    Commonwealth of Massachusetts   MCGOWAN, Owen T. 807
  BRIGHTON
    Archdiocese of Boston   EPPARD, Philip B. 351
    Boston Pub Lib   MCCORMICK, Sheila P. 799
    St Elizabeth's Hospital   BRAUN, Robin E. 130
  BROCKTON
    Brockton Hospital   KAMENOFF, Lovisa 623
    Brockton Pub Lib   WHITE, Sheree L. 1332
    Veterans Administration Medical
      Center   NOYES, Suzanne N. 911
  BROOKLINE
    Brookline Pub Schs   MARKUSON, Carolyn A. 772
    Hebrew Coll   TUCHMAN, Maurice S. 1261
    Hellenic Coll   PAPADEMETRIOU,
                                    Athanasia 938
                                    PAPADEMETRIOU, George
                                    C. 938
    Pub Lib of Brookline   STEINFELD, Michael 1186
    Pub Schs of Brookline Massachusetts   ZEIGER, Hanna B. 1387
    Searchline Associates Inc   SOVNER-RIBBLER, Judith . 1170
    Town of Brookline   ABRAHAM, Deborah V. 2
  BURLINGTON
    Arthur D Little Inc   ADAMOWICZ, Joanne C. 4
    Christian Center Elementary Sch   BERNSTEIN, D S. 89
    RCA Corp   HSU, Veronica 567
  BUZZARDS BAY
    Massachusetts Maritime Academy   RESSMEYER, Ellen H. 1024
  CAMBRIDGE
    The Architects Collaborative   GRIGORIS, Lygia 470
                                    HARTMERE, Anne 508
                                    TENNEY, Kimberly M. 1231
    Arthur D Little Inc   COLBY, Beverly 230
                                    HIBBERD, Cynthia M. 536
                                    MACKEY, Wendy W. 757
                                    MOFFITT, Michael D. 852
                                    REEDY, Martha J. 1015
                                    SACERDOTE, George S. 1073
                                    WOLPERT, Ann J. 1362
    BBN Communications Corp   DURHAM, Mary J. 328
    Biogen Research Corp   JONES, Rebekah A. 614
    Cambridge Pub Lib   CLOHERTY, Lauretta M. 223
                                    CRANE, Hugh M. 255
    Cambridge Research Institute   SMART, William R. 1151
    Caramics Process Systems Corp   SCHUTZBERG, Frances ... 1103
    Charles Stark Draper Laboratory Inc   COFFMAN, M H. 227
                                    ROTMAN, Laurie D. 1060
    City of Cambridge   SAKEY, Joseph G. 1076
    DIALOG Information Services Inc   HOCK, Randolph E. 545
                                    JACOBS, Leslie R. 589
    Dynatrend Inc   DRESLEY, Susan C. 319
                                    HUSSEY, Laurie L. 578
    Episcopal Divinity Sch   DUNKLY, James W. 326
    H W Wilson Co   LUKOS, Geraldine F. 748
    Harvard Coll   DAMES, Barbara B. 271
    Harvard Divinity Sch   WILSON, Virginia G. 1353

MASSACHUSETTS (Cont'd)
  CAMBRIDGE (Cont'd)
    Harvard Law Sch   DUCKETT, Joan 322
                                    HOSTAGE, John B. 562
                                    LEIGHTON, Lee W. 714
                                    RONEN, Naomi 1053
                                    THOMAS, Jonathan R. 1237
    Harvard Univ   ALTENBERGER, Alicja 18
                                    ASCHMANN, Althea 35
                                    BROW, Ellen H. 141
                                    BURG, Barbara A. 159
                                    CARPENTER, Kenneth E. 185
                                    CHILDERS, Martha P. 208
                                    COLLINS, John W. 232
                                    DESIMONE, Dorothy H. 295
                                    DI BONA, Leslie F. 299
                                    DOWLER, Lawrence E. 315
                                    DRAKE, Robert E. 318
                                    ELLIOTT, Clark A. 343
                                    ERICKSON, Alan E. 352
                                    FENG, Yen T. 371
                                    FREITAG, Wolfgang M. 401
                                    FUNG, Margaret C. 409
                                    HAIL, Christopher 484
                                    HAMILTON, Malcolm 492
                                    HOLDEN, Harley P. 550
                                    IRION, Millard F. 584
                                    ISHIMOTO, Carol F. 585
                                    JONES, Edgar A. 612
                                    KENT, Caroline M. 642
                                    MAHARD, Martha 760
                                    MCFARLAN, Karen N. 804
                                    MOCKOVAK, Holly E. 851
                                    MOREN, Harold M. 863
                                    OCHS, Michael 915
                                    PANAGOPOULOS, Beata D. .. 937
                                    PANTZER, Katharine F. 938
                                    PARKER, Susan E. 942
                                    PEDERSON, Daniel E. 954
                                    POLLARD, Russell O. 981
                                    ROBERTS, Helene E. 1040
                                    SKLAR, Hinda F. 1146
                                    SOLBRIG, Dorothy J. 1166
                                    STODDARD, Roger E. 1196
                                    VERBA, Sidney 1282
                                    WALSH, James E. 1299
                                    WARRINGTON, David R. ... 1307
                                    WICK, Constance S. 1335
                                    WUNDERLICH, Clifford S. ... 1374
                                    YACKLE, Jeanette F. 1376
    Index Group Inc   HAYWARD, Sheila S. 517
    Inmagic Inc   EDDISON, Elizabeth B. 335
    IBM Corp   WHITE, Chandlee 1330
    Keltoi Cybernetics   BISHOP, John 99
    Lesley Coll   DURANCEAU, Ellen F. 328
                                    STAVIS, Ruth L. 1183
    Lotus Development Corp   MCLAGAN, Donald L. 813
                                    SLAVIN, Vicky J. 1148
    Massachusetts Institute of Technology   BAKER, Shirley K. 49
                                    BELLO, Susan E. 78
                                    BIRD, Nora J. 98
                                    BJORNER, Susan N. 100
                                    CONNELLY, Ramona S. 237
                                    DAVY, Edgar W. 281
                                    GREEN, Kathleen A. 462
                                    GREENE, Cathy C. 463
                                    JACKSON, Arlyne A. 586
                                    KNAACK, Linda M. 663
                                    LUCKER, Jay K. 746
                                    MARCUS, Richard S. 769
                                    MCDOWELL, Sylvia A. 804
                                    WEBBER, Donna E. 1313
    Mount Auburn Hospital   LANDRY, Francis R. 693
    Polaroid Corp   LINGHAM, Laurie W. 730
                                    PRITCHARD, Robert W. 994
    Putnam Hayes & Bartlett Inc   HONESS, Mary E. 555
    Radcliffe Coll   ENGELHART, Anne D. 349
                                    KING, Patricia M. 652
                                    MOSELEY, Eva S. 870
    Rockford Research Inc   MOOERS, Calvin N. 857

MASSACHUSETTS (Cont'd)

CAMBRIDGE (Cont'd)

Simmons Coll	DANIELLS, Lorna M.	273
Smithsonian Institution	REY, Joyce	1024
Trans-World Visions	ALASTI, Aryt	9
Trial Court-Law Libs	LINDHEIMER, Sandra K.	729
W R Grace & Co	METCALF, Marjorie	828
Winthrop Group Inc	EDGERLY, Linda	336
Zipporah Films Inc	KONICEK, Karen B.	670

CANTON

Codex Corp	EDWARDS, Betty	337
	WRIGHT, Victoria L.	1373
Music Lib Association	BLOTNER, Linda S.	106
	HENDERSON, James P.	526

CHATHAM

Eldredge Pub Lib	GILLIES, Irene B.	436

CHELMSFORD

Appollo Computer Inc	MATTHEWS, Charles E.	785
Chelmsford Pub Lib	RAUCH, Ellen C.	1010
Digital Equipment Corp	DONOVAN, Paul	312

CHESTNUT HILL

Beaver Country Day Sch	SMITH, Zelda G.	1161
Boston Coll	BEGG, Karin E.	74
	CHANNING, Rhoda K.	201
	CHATTERTON, Leigh A.	204
	CONSTANCE, Joseph W.	238
	GROVE, Shari T.	474
	KHAN, Syed M.	646
	LIPPMAN, Anne F.	732
	MORNER, Claudia J.	865

CHICOPEE

Coll of Our Lady of the Elms	BRENNAN, Mary E.	132
	GALLAGHER, Mary E.	414
Elms Coll	STARKEY, Richard E.	1182

COHASSET

Paul Pratt Memorial Lib	HAYES, Richard E.	516

CONCORD

ERT Inc	ROBINSON, Deanna C.	1043
Joel R Pitlor Inc	ISAACS, Cynthia W.	584
Kazmaier Associates Inc	SAUNDERS, Leslie E.	1084

DEDHAM

Albany International Research Co	DAVIS, Jeannette	279
Dedham Board of Lib Trustees	ALLEN, Paul B.	15
Dedham Pub Lib	HARVEY, Paul W.	509
Massachusetts Sch of Professional Psy	WHELAN, Julia S.	1329
Town of Dedham	MCDONALD, Murray F.	803

DEERFIELD

Deerfield Academy	COHEN, Christina M.	228
	KELLY, Patricia M.	638
	VON KRIES, Beverley A.	1288
Historic Deerfield Inc	PROPER, David R.	995
	PROUTY, Sharman E.	996

DORCHESTER

Archdiocese of Boston	CLARK, Mary E.	217

DOUGLAS

Searchquest	COPPOLA, Peter A.	245

EAST LONGMEADOW

Town of East Longmeadow	CARVER, Gloria C.	191

EASTHAM

Eastham Pub Lib	ELDRIDGE, Jane A.	342

EASTHAMPTON

Williston Northampton Sch	MELNICK, Ralph	823

EDGARTOWN

Edgartown Pub Lib	NORTON, Linda N.	910

FALL RIVER

B M C Durfee High Sch	BETTENCOURT, Ronald J.	92

FALMOUTH

Falmouth Pub Lib	FOSTER, Joan	392

FITCHBURG

Commonwealth of Massachusetts	LAMBERT, Lyn D.	690
Fitchburg Pub Lib	KISSNER, Arthur J.	656

FORT DEVENS

US Army Intelligence Sch	PENSYL, Ornella L.	957

FOXBOROUGH

Town of Foxborough	MILLER, Barbara J.	835

MASSACHUSETTS (Cont'd)

FRAMINGHAM

Framingham Pub Lib	JAMES, Flaherty C.	592
Framingham State Coll	BOEHME, Richard W.	109
	KRIER, Mary M.	678
	MCDONALD, Stanley M.	803
Framingham Union Hospital	CLEVESY, Sandra R.	222
International Data Corp	BAKST, Shelley D.	50
	CAFFREY, Timothy J.	170
	KANE, Jean B.	624
	MCGOVERN, Patrick J.	807
Minuteman Lib Network	KUKLINSKI, Joan L.	683
	LINSKY, Leonore K.	731
New England Wild Flower Society Inc	WALKER, Mary M.	1296
Yankee Atomic Electric Co	HUGGINS, Dean A.	571

FRANKLIN

Dean Jr College	DACHS, Jerald K.	269

GARDNER

Levi Heywood Memorial Lib	HALES, Margaret L.	486
Mount Wachusett Community Coll	COOLIDGE, Christina L.	241

GLOUCESTER

Addison Gilbert Hospital	CHEVES, Vera L.	207

GREENFIELD

Commonwealth of Massachusetts	LEE, Marilyn M.	710
Greenfield Community Coll	HOWLAND, Margaret E.	566

HALIFAX

Holmes Public Lib	MCGRATH, Margaret A.	807

HANOVER

John Curtis Lib	FRIEDMAN, Fred T.	403

HANSCOM AFB

US Air Force	GERKE, Ray	428
	SEIDMAN, Ruth K.	1112

HARWICH

Vintage Jazz Inc	BRADLEY, Jack	126

HATFIELD

Western Massachusetts Regional Lib	GAUDET, Dodie E.	422
	RICH, Marcia A.	1027

HAVERHILL

Haverhill Pub Lib	HUTCHINS, Kathleen D.	579
Private Consult	JAFFARIAN, Sara	591

HOLBROOK

Holbrook Public Lib	MEAGHER, Janet H.	819

HOLDEN

Town of Holden	BAKER, Janet R.	48

HOLYOKE

Holyoke Community Coll	DUTCHER, Henry D.	329

HOPKINTON

Hopkinton Junior-Senior High Sch	FONTES, Patricia J.	388

HUDSON

Digital Equipment Corp	ANDREWS, Peter J.	27
	BAKER, Elizabeth A.	48
	MAGUIRE, Linda H.	760

HYANNIS

Cape Cod Hospital	FRAZIER, Nancy E.	399

KINGSTON

F C Adams Pub Lib	OLIANSKY, Joseph D.	920
Ship's Haven Environmental Info Srvs	FELICETTI, Barbara W.	370
Sisters of Divine Providence	HIRSCH, Elizabeth	543

LANCASTER

Lancaster Town Lib	FISCHER, Marge	380

LAWRENCE

Andrew Wilson Co	LEWIS, Thomas F.	724
Lawrence Pub Lib	WHITNEY, Howard F.	1334

LEE

Lee Lib Association	MASSUCCO, Georgia A.	782

LEOMINSTER

Leominster Pub Lib	THERIAULT, Susan L.	1234

LEXINGTON

Cary Memorial Lib	HILTON, Robert C.	541
	MCCARTHY, Germaine A.	794
Data Resources	BRINNER, Roger E.	136
	BROWN, George F.	144
	FELDMAN, Stanley J.	369
	HATFIELD, Philip A.	511
DRI/McGraw-Hill	WYSS, David A.	1376
Health Data Institute	WAKS, Jane B.	1293
The Information Guild	WARNER, Alice S.	1305
Instrumentation Laboratory	KATES, Jacqueline R.	629
Lexington Pub Lib	STANTON, Martha	1181
Lexington Pub Schs	BENDER, Nancy W.	79

MASSACHUSETTS (Cont'd)
LEXINGTON (Cont'd)

Litton Industries	LATHAM, Mary R.	701
Logicon Inc	EMOND, Kathleen A.	348
Massachusetts Institute of Technology	GREENBERG, Carolyn R.	463
MA Vocational Curriculum Research Center	DAY, Virginia M.	283
McGraw-Hill Inc	CARTER, Walter F.	190
	CATON, Christopher N.	195
	HARTMAN, David G.	508
	JAIN, Nem C.	592
	O'REILLY, Daniel F.	925
	PHILLIPS, Steven G.	969
	YACOUBY, Ray S.	1376
	YANCHAR, Joyce M.	1377
Raytheon Co	MAXANT, Vicary	787
	O'CONNOR, Jerry	916
Standard & Poor's Corp	COOPER, J P.	243
Temple Barker & Sloane	PRUSAK, Laurence	996
Town of Lexington	KELLSTEDT, Jenny	637
Walsh Associates	WALSH, Joanna M.	1299

LINCOLN

Massachusetts Audubon Society	COHEN, Martha J.	228

LITTLETON

Digital Equipment Corp	GARDNER, Catherine P.	417
	GILLIAM, Ellen M.	436
Inforonics Inc	BUCKLAND, Lawrence F.	154
	FINNI, John J.	379
Littleton Pub Schs	JENSEN, Kathryn E.	599
Reuben Hoar Pub Lib	DUNN, Jocelyn A.	327
Town of Littleton	WILLIAMS, Carole C.	1342

LOWELL

City of Lowell	O'BRIEN, Anne M.	914
Laserdata Inc	SHULSINGER, Don	1133
Lowell General Hospital	BEDARD, Martha A.	73
US Air Force	DUFFEK, Elizabeth A.	323
Univ of Lowell	CAYLOR, Lawrence M.	195
	DESROCHES, Richard A.	295
	FARAH, Barbara D.	363
	FORTIER, Jan M.	391
	KARR, Ronald D.	628
	SLAPSYS, Richard M.	1148
Wang Labs Inc	ARSENAULT, Patricia A.	35

LUDLOW

MA Municipal Wholestate Electric Co	MACDONALD, Wayne D.	754

LYNN

AtlantiCare Medical Center	ALMQUIST, Deborah T.	17
General Electric Co	MOLTZ, Sandra S.	854

MALDEN

Malden Hospital	O'BRIEN, Elizabeth J.	914

MARBLEHEAD

Marblehead Pub Schs	EHRICH, Joan C.	339
Town of Marblehead	DYER, Victor E.	330

MARION

Sippican Inc	ST. AUBIN, Kendra J.	1075

MARLBOROUGH

Digital Equipment Corp	GEER, Elizabeth F.	425
Raytheon Co	REILLY, Dayle A.	1020

MARSHFIELD

Ventress Memorial Lib	CORCORAN, Dennis R.	245

MAYNARD

Digital Equipment Corp	OWEN, Beth C.	931

MEDFORD

Lawrance Memorial Hospital of Medford	HARRIS, John C.	504
Medford Pub Lib	SHANK, Beverly C.	1120
Tufts Univ	BOYCE, Barbara S.	122
	FELDT, Candice K.	369
	GOLDMAN, Brenda C.	445
	JONES, Frederick S.	613
	KRUPANSKI, Pamela M.	680
	MARTIN, Murray S.	777
	MCDONALD, Ellen J.	802
	MCKIRDY, Colin	812
	PAISTE, Marsha S.	935
	SCHATZ, Natalie M.	1090
	STAACK, Katherine A.	1177
	WALSH, Jim	1299

MASSACHUSETTS (Cont'd)
METHUEN

Methuen Public School	JACOBS, Lois S.	589
Nevins Memorial Lib	WILLS, Lynda J.	1349

MILFORD

Data General Services Inc	COPPOLA, H P.	245

MILLIS

Perry Roe & Associates	ROE, Georgeanne T.	1048

MILTON

Curry Coll	KEYS, Marshall	645
Fontbonne Academy	UMANA, Christine J.	1268

MOUNT HERMON

Northfield Mount Herman Sch	LANGE, Clare M.	695

NAHANT

Nahant Pub Lib	CISNEY, Douglas S.	215

NANTUCKET

Nantucket Historical Assn	HARING, Jacqueline K.	501

NATICK

Business Information Services	DLOTT, Nancy B.	306
TRANSTECH International Corp	WANG, Gary Y.	1302

NEEDHAM

Duracell Inc	GEVIRTZMAN, Joyce L.	430
Glover Memorial Hospital	LOSCALZO, Anita B.	741
Leading Edge Products	ORENSTEIN, Ruth M.	925

NEW BEDFORD

St Luke's Hospital	WILDES, Elizabeth S.	1339

NEWBURYPORT

The Alexander Consulting Group Inc	JACQUES, Donna M.	591

NEWTON

Andover Newton Theological Sch	HARRISON, Sylvia E.	507
	O'NEAL, Ellis E.	923
	YOUNT, Diana	1384
Boston Coll	KIRK, Darcy	654
	SHEAR, Joan A.	1124
Harvard Sch of Pub Health	ALPERT, Hillel R.	17
Kenneth W Rendell Inc	RENDELL, Kenneth W.	1023
NELINET Inc	BOLAND, Mary J.	111
	CUNNINGHAM, Robert L.	265
	MOCKUS, Laima	851
Newton Free Lib	RASKIN, Susan R.	1009
Reed Publishing USA	URBACH, Peter F.	1269

NEWTON HIGHLANDS

Legal Information Services	FOX, Elyse H.	394

NEWTON LOWER FALLS

Newton Pub Schools	SLATTERY, Carole C.	1148

NEWTONVILLE

CLSI Inc	BRIAND, Margaret M.	134
	FRIEDMAN, Terri L.	404
	GLASSMAN, Penny L.	440
	GRIFFITH, William R.	469
	INGERSOLL, Diane S.	582
	LANDESMAN, Betty J.	692
	MIELE, Madeline F.	833
	SANTOSUOSSO, Joseph P.	1082
	SCHWARTZ, Frederick E.	1104

NONANTUM

CLSI Inc	JANK, David A.	593

NORTH ABINGTON

RDC Associates	LAROSA, Sharon M.	698

NORTH ADAMS

Sprague Electric Co	COGHLAN, Jill M.	227

NORTH ANDOVER

Aries Systems Corp	HOLMES, Lyndon S.	553
Bell Laboratories	CONDON, Mary M.	236
Town of North Andover	REEVE, Russell J.	1016

NORTH DARTMOUTH

Southeastern Massachusetts Univ	DACE, Tish	269
	GIBBS, Paige	431

NORTH EASTON

Stonehill Coll	BOUCHARD-HALL, Robert W.	118
	PEARCE, Jean K.	952

NORTH GRAFTON

Tufts Univ	SAFFER-MARCHAND, Melinda	1074

NORTH QUINCY

Thomson & Thomson	FERNALD, Anne C.	373

MASSACHUSETTS (Cont'd)

NORTHAMPTON
Forbes Lib	WIKANDER, Lawrence E.	1338
ResourceNets Telecommunications	MAZUR, Ronald M.	791
Smith Coll	BOZONE, Billie R.	124
	DAVIS, Charles R.	278
	GRIGG, Susan	470
	KURKUL, Donna L.	684
	MORTIMER, Ruth	870
	POIRRIER, Sherry	980
	SCOTT, Alison M.	1106
	SLY, Margery N.	1150
Veterans Administration Medical Center	DEWEY, Marjorie C.	298

NORTON
Wheaton Coll	HOVORKA, Marjorie J.	563
	STICKNEY, Zephorene L.	1193

NORWELL
Martinus Nijhoff International	JAGER, Conradus	591
Norwell Pub Lib	KADANOFF, Diane G.	621

NORWOOD
Morrill Memorial Lib	HIMMELSBACH, Carl J.	542
Northrop Corp	DELTANO, Pauline T.	290
Norwood Hospital	FOXMAN, Carole J.	395

PALMER
Palmer Pub Lib	HOLMBERG, Olga S.	553

PAXTON
C/W Mars Inc	ECKERSON, Gale E.	334

PEABODY
Bishop Fenwick High Sch	CODAIR, Frederick R.	226
Peabody Institute Lib	TRICARICO, Mary A.	1256

PETERSHAM
St Bede's Publications	MCMANAMON, Mary J.	814

PITTSFIELD
Berkshire Athenaeum	FUCHS, John M.	408
Berkshire Museum	MACE, Mary B.	754
Commonwealth of Massachusetts	SASS, Samuel	1083
G E Plastics	KANE, Nancy J.	625
St Joseph Central High Sch	BOSTLEY, Jean R.	117

PLYMOUTH
Commonwealth of Massachusetts	HOAGLAND, E L.	545
Plymouth Pub Lib	LEWIS, David D.	722
Town of Plymouth	BIBEAU, Janet A.	94

QUINCY
National Fire Protection Association	BARNHART, Arlene C.	58
Quincy Junior Coll	NIELSEN, Sonja M.	903

RANDOLPH
Turner Free Lib	MICHAUD, Charles A.	832
	WEISCHEDEL, Elaine F.	1319

READING
Austin Preparatory Sch	MILLER, George M.	837
Reading Pub Lib	FLANNERY, Susan M.	383
	FLANNERY, Susan M.	384

REVERE
Revere Pub Lib	DYGERT, Michael H.	331

SALEM
Christopher Burns Inc	BURNS, Christopher	162
Essex Institute	FOUNTAIN, Eugenia F.	393
Peabody Museum of Salem	TRINKAUS-RANDALL, Gregor	1257
Salem State Coll	ANDREWS, Margaret	27

SHARON
Kendall Whaling Museum	FRAZIER, James A.	399

SHEFFIELD
Berkshire Sch	CARVER, Jane C.	191

SHREWSBURY
DEC CD-ROM Publishing	HAYES, Kathleen M.	516
St John's High Sch	O'BRIEN, John F.	914
Town of Shrewsbury	CHANG, Isabelle E.	200

SOMERVILLE
Somerville Pub Lib	MINTON, Alix M.	846

SOUTH DARTMOUTH
Dartmouth Pub Lib	STANLEY, Ellen	1180

SOUTH HADLEY
Mount Holyoke Coll	CALLAHAN, Linda J.	173
	EDMONDS, Anne C.	336

SOUTH HAMILTON
Gordon-Conwell Theological Seminary	ANDERSON, Norman E.	24
	DVORAK, Robert	330

MASSACHUSETTS (Cont'd)

SOUTH LANCASTER
Atlantic Union Coll	PARSON, Lethiel C.	944
	SBACCHI, Margareta E.	1087

SOUTH LEE
J & J Lubrano	LUBRANO, Judith A.	745

SOUTH NATICK
Town of Natick	FEEN, Anne B.	368

SOUTHBRIDGE
Jacob Edwards Lib	LATHAM, Ronald B.	701

SPRINGFIELD
American International Coll	DELZELL, William R.	290
Baystate Medical Center	HUNTER, Isabel	576
Massachusetts Mutual Life Insurance Co	CLOUGH, Linda F.	223
Massachusetts Trial Court	FLYNN, Kathleen M.	386
Springfield City Lib	LAPIERRE, Barbe	697
	MCLAIN, Guy A.	813
	STEVENS, Michael L.	1190
Springfield Coll	TAUPIER, Andrea S.	1225
Springfield Lib & Museums Association	SKIPTON, Iris E.	1146
Springfield Pub Sch System	ERICKSON, Norma J.	352
Springfield Technical Community Coll	WURTZEL, Barbara S.	1374
Western New England Coll	ARCHAMBAUL, Christine	30
	DUNN, Donald J.	326
	GARBER, Suzanne	417
	KONESKI-WHITE, Bonnie L.	670
	STACK, May E.	1177
	WELLS, Susan C.	1323

STERLING
Conant Pub Lib	CORNELL, Barbara M.	246

STOCKBRIDGE
Austen Riggs Center	LINTON, Helen W.	731

STOUGHTON
Town of Stoughton	ANDERSON, Cheryl M.	22

STOW
Comstow Information Services	MOULTON, Lynda W.	873
Marlborough Pub Lib	GIULIANO, Lillian C.	439

STURBRIDGE
Old Sturbridge Village	ALLEN, Joan C.	15
	PERCY, Theresa R.	958

SUNDERLAND
Univ of Massachusetts at Sunderland	MCINTOSH, Nadia	809

SWAMPSCOTT
Marian Court Junior Coll	LINDSAY, Mary A.	729

TRURO
Truro Pub Libs	BRAINARD, Elsie K.	127

TYNGSBORO
Wang Institute of Graduate Studies	DENTON, Francesca L.	293

WAKEFIELD
Lucius Beebe Memorial Lib	MUNDY, Suzanne W.	879
Massachusetts Lib Association	BOZOIAN, Paula	124
Metcalf & Eddy Inc	CHAPDELAINE, Susan A.	201
	MUISE, Anita M.	876

WALTHAM
Bentley Coll	BELASTOCK, Tjalda N.	76
	LEWONTIN, Amy	724
Brandeis Univ	CARNAHAN, Paul A.	183
	COOPER WYMAN, Rosalind	244
	EVENSEN, Robert L.	358
	GELB, Linda	425
	GILROY, Rupert E.	437
	GRAY, Carolyn M.	459
	MASSEY-BURZIO, Virginia	782
	STRAND, Bethany	1200
Data Architects Inc	PUGH, Ann E.	997
Energy Research Group Inc	WINQUIST, Elaine W.	1355
Goulston & Storrs	MARX, Peter	780
Gregg Corp	HEACOCK, Gregg	518
GTE Laboratories	GRAHAM, Katherine I.	456
	REDFEARN, Linda E.	1014
Hewlett-Packard Co	SARAIDARIDIS, Susan B.	1082
Honeywell Bull Inc	BENDER, Elizabeth H.	79
	PAPALAMBROS, Rita G.	939
Teledyne Engineering Services	FINGERMAN, Susan M.	378

WAREHAM
Town of Wareham	PILLSBURY, Mary J.	973

MASSACHUSETTS (Cont'd)

WATERTOWN

City of Newton	TASHJIAN, Virginia A. 1224
Documentary Educational Resources Inc	CABEZAS, Sue A. 170
Watertown Free Pub Lib	REDDY, Sigrid R. 1014
	TUCHMAN, Helene L. 1261
Watertown Pub Schs	CLARK, Elizabeth K. 216
	GROSE, Rosemary F. 472
	SPROUL, Barbara A. 1176

WAYLAND

Raytheon Co	PORTSCH-SNOW, Joanne . . 985
Wayland Pub Lib	BROWN, Louise R. 145

WELLESLEY

Autex Systems Inc	LANDGREBE, George W. . . . 692
Babson Coll	MAGUIRE, Patricia V. 760
Massachusetts Bay Community Coll	SHERER, Elaine R. 1127
Minuteman Lib Network	BADEN, Diane G. 44
Silver Platter Information Inc	POOLEY, Christopher G. . . . 983
	RIETDYK, Ron J. 1033
Wellesley Coll	GUSTAFSON, Eleanor A. . . . 478
	HARDY, Eileen D. 500
	STOCKARD, Joan 1195
	WOOD, Ross 1365
Wellesley Free Lib	KELEHER, Carolyn P. 635
Wellesley Pub Schs	CAMPANELLA, Alice D. 175
Whitman & Howard Inc	FEIDLER, Anita J. 368

WELLESLEY HILLS

Agribusiness Associates Inc	KENNEDY, Amy J. 640
Corp Technology Information Services Inc	PEERS, Charles T. 954
	POMERANTZ, Michael H. . . . 982
Silver Platter Information Inc	CIUFFETTI, Peter D. 215
	HAMILTON, Fae K. 492
	HATVANY, Bela R. 512

WEST BOXFORD

Ingalls Memorial Library Association	LANE, Margaret 694

WEST BOYLESTON

Town of West Boyleston	STILES, Muriel H. 1194

WEST SPRINGFIELD

Town of West Springfield	WEEKS, Beverly J. 1315
West Springfield Pub Lib	HELO, Martin 525
	SMITH, Barbara A. 1152

WESTBORO

Data General Corp	FERGUSON, Roberta J. 372

WESTFIELD

Westfield State Coll	HANDY, Catherine H. 495
	UPPGARD, Jeannine 1269

WESTON

Cardinal Spellman Philatelic Museum	KOVED, Ruth B. 674
Liberty Mutual Insurance Co	CALLAHAN, Joan 173
Regis Coll	KEENAN, Elizabeth L. 634
Town of Weston	DOUGLAS, Alice W. 314
Weston Pub Schs	GOZEMBA, Frances E. 455

WESTWOOD

F W Faxon Co	KRUKONIS, Perkunas P. . . . 680
Faxon Co	BACON, Lois C. 44
	CLAPPER, Mary E. 216
	DEARBORN, Susan C. 284
	KNAPP, Leslie C. 663
	POSTLETHWAITE, Bonnie S. 986
Faxon Inc	ROWE, Richard R. 1062
John F Kennedy Lib Foundation Inc	CULLINANE, John J. 263

WILLIAMSTOWN

Clark Art Institute	ERICKSON, Peter B. 352
J Paul Getty Trust	PETERSEN, Toni 962
Sterling & Francine Clark Art Institute	GIBSON, Sarah S. 432
Williams Coll	GOLDBERG, Steven R. 444
	HAMMOND, Wayne G. 494
	SUDDUTH, William E. 1206

WILMINGTON

AVCO Systems Textron	HALL, Robert G. 488

WINCHESTER

Susan Keats & Associates	KEATS, Susan E. 633
Winchester Pub Schs	JOHNSON, Jean L. 606

WOBURN

Datex Inc	CUCCHIARO, Stephen J. . . . 263
Northern Research & Engineering Corp	BARRINGER, Nancy F. 59

MASSACHUSETTS (Cont'd)

WOODS HOLE

US Department of Commerce	BROWNLOW, Judith 148
Woods Hole Data Base Inc	SHEPHARD, Frank C. 1127
Woods Hole Oceanographic Instn	WINN, Carolyn P. 1355

WORCESTER

American Antiquarian Society	BARNHILL, Georgia B. 58
	BURKETT, Nancy H. 161
	MCCORISON, Marcus A. . . . 798
	WASOWICZ, Laura E. 1308
Assumption Coll	GONNEVILLE, Priscilla R. . . 447
Becker Junior Coll	VIDMANIS, Visvaldis E. 1283
Bowditch & Dewey	HILL, Byron C. 539
Central Massachusetts Regional Lib Syst	CHAMBERLAIN, Ruth B. 197
Clark Univ	KASPERSON, Jeanne X. . . . 629
	ROCHELEAU, Kathleen D. . . 1046
Coll of the Holy Cross	STANKUS, Tony 1180
	THISTLE, Dawn R. 1235
Databooks	ABRAMOFF, Lawrence J. 3
Norton Co	SILVERBERG, Mary E. 1138
Quinsigamond Community Coll	SHIH, Jenny 1130
Riley Stoker Corp	MILLIGAN, Jane M. 843
St Vincent Hospital	DAVITT, Theresa B. 281
Univ of Massachusetts Medical Sch	KANG, Wen 625
Worcester Art Museum	BOLSHAW, Cynthia L. 112
Worcester City Hospital	RIVARD, Timothy D. 1037
Worcester Memorial Hospital	SIMEONE, Therese A. 1139
Worcester Pub Lib	JOHNSON, Dorothy A. 603
	JOHNSON, Penelope B. 608
	MUSSER, Egbert G. 883
	NOAH, Carolyn B. 906
	PARSONS, Duncan A. 945

MICHIGAN

ADRIAN

Adrian Coll	ARNDT, Arleen 33
Siena Heights Coll	BAKER, Jean S. 48
	DOMBROWSKI, Mark A. 310

ALBION

Albion Coll	CARSON, Claudia A. 188
	OBERG, Larry R. 914
Albion Pub Lib	KNOTT, Joan Y. 665
Woodlands Lib Cooperative	JENNINGS, Martha F. 598

ALLEGAN

Allegan Pub Lib	ROOP, Donna K. 1053

ALLEN PARK

Veterans Administration Medical Center	DURIVAGE, Mary J. 328

ALLENDALE

Grand Valley State Coll	FORD, Stephen W. 390
	KING, Kathryn L. 651
	VANDERLAAN, Sharon J. . . 1274

ALMA

Alma Coll	DOLLARD, Peter A. 309
	GERLACH, William P. 429
	HALL, Lawrence E. 488
	PALMER, Catherine S. 936

ALPENA

Northland Lib Cooperative	WILLIAMS, Susan S. 1346

ANN ARBOR

American Mathematical Society	PONOMARENKO, Ella 982
Ann Arbor Pub Lib	CAPPAERT, Lael R. 180
	COFFEY, Dorothy A. 227
	DALY, Kathleen E. 271
Ann Arbor Pub Schs	HERNANDEZ, Ramon R. . . . 532
BASF Corp	SWEET, Robert E. 1215
Catherine McAuley Health Center	DEY, Anita C. 298
	LANSDALE, Metta T. 696
	MARTIN, Patricia W. 777
Chase's Annual Events	CHASE, William D. 203
Chi Systems Inc	TERWILLIGER, Doris H. . . . 1232
Concordia Coll	DAVIDSEN, Susanna L. 276
Domino's Farms Archives & Galleries Corp	MATTHEWS, Darwin C. 785
Domino's Pizza	ELLENBOGEN, Barbara R. . . 343
Ecology Center of Ann Arbor	STONE, Nancy Y. 1197
Environmental Research Institute	PUBLISKI, Patricia J. 996
Gelman Sciences Inc	BENSON, Peggy 83
Greenhills Sch	SANTINGA, Reda A. 1082

MICHIGAN (Cont'd)

ANN ARBOR (Cont'd)

Huron Valley Lib System CHAPMAN, Mary A. 202
Industrial Technology Institute KELLER, Karen A. 635
KMS Fusion Inc BENNETT, Christine H. 81
Lib Hi Tech News MCDERMOTT, Rebecca 802
WALL, C E. 1297
Mountainside Publishing Co DOUGHERTY, Ann P. 313
Mouzon Information Services MOUZON, Margaret W. 874
National Archives & Records Admin CONWAY, Paul L. 239
Parke-Davis COAN, La V. 224
CYGAN, Rose M. 268
Pierian Press REGAN, Lesley E. 1017
Univ Microfilms International BILLICK, David J. 96
BREITENWISCHER,
Rosalyn E. 132
FITZSIMMONS, Joseph J. . . . 383
FOWELLS, Fumi T. 393
KING, Kenneth E. 651
MALCOLM, J P. 762
MAXWELL, Bonnie J. 788
SMILLIE, Pauline A. 1151
WERLING, Anita L. 1324
WILSON, Amy S. 1349
WOOD, Richard T. 1365
Univ of Michigan at Ann Arbor ADLER, Robert J. 7
ANDERSEN, H F. 21
BEAN, Margaret 69
BEAUBIEN, Anne K. 70
BERGEN, Kathleen M. 85
BIDLACK, Russell E. 95
BIGGS, Debra R. 95
BJORKE, Wallace S. 100
BLOUIN, Francis X. 107
BOLES, Frank 112
BUTZ, Helen S. 168
CRAWFORD, David E. 256
CROOKS, James E. 260
DAUB, Peggy E. 275
DAVIS, Anne C. 277
DIDIER, Elaine K. 301
DOUGHERTY, Richard M. . . . 314
DOWNES, Virginia C. 316
DURRANCE, Joan C. 328
FINERMAN, Carol B. 378
FRIEDMAN, Bruce A. 403
GALIK, Barbara A. 413
GATTIS, R G. 422
GOSLING, William A. 453
GRIMM, Ann C. 470
HALL, Jo A. 488
HART, Patricia H. 507
JASPER, Richard P. 595
KARP, Nancy S. 628
KOCHEN, Manfred 667
KUSNERZ, Peggy A. 685
LEARY, Margaret R. 707
LOUP, Jean L. 742
MAHONY, Doris D. 761
MASLOW, Linda S. 780
MATZO, Deborah J. 786
MCDONALD, David R. 802
MOSEY, Jeanette 871
NICHOLS, Darlene P. 901
PAO, Miranda L. 938
POOLEY, Beverly J. 983
ROENZWEIG, Merle 1048
ROSEN, Barbara 1055
SALZER, Melodie A. 1078
SCHWARTZ, Diane G. 1104
SCOTT, Melissa C. 1107
SIEVING, Pamela C. 1136
SLAVENS, Thomas P. 1148
STOFFLE, Carla J. 1196
TAYLOR, Margaret T. 1227
VANCE, Kenneth E. 1273
WAGMAN, Frederick H. . . . 1291
WARNER, Robert M. 1305
WESTBROOK, Jo L. 1326
WHEATON, Julie A. 1328

MICHIGAN (Cont'd)

ANN ARBOR (Cont'd)

Univ of Michigan at Ann Arbor
WISE, Virginia J. 1357
YOCUM, Patricia B. 1380
YORK, Grace A. 1381
Veterans Administration Medical
Center SMITH, Victoria A. 1161
Ypsilanti Public Schools TRIM, Kathryn 1256
AUBURN HILLS
City of Auburn Hills EL MOUCHI, Joan S. 346
Oakland Community Coll WILLIAMS, Calvin 1342
BAD AXE
Bad Axe High Sch MAYES, Jane M. 789
BATTLE CREEK
Kellogg Community Coll SCHUCKEL, Sally B. 1101
Kellogg Co HULSEY, Richard A. 573
Leila Hospital & Health Center MOSHER, Robin A. 871
Veterans Administration Medical
Center BURHANS, Barbara C. 159
BAY CITY
Bay County Lib System PEARSONS, Sheila M. 953
Bay Medical Center KORMELINK, Barbara A. 671
BAY VIEW
Bay View Association DOERR, Jane P. 308
BELLEVILLE
Anotherplace Research Service STARESINA, Lois J. 1181
BENTON HARBOR
Benton Harbor Area Schs PELZER, Adolf 955
Benton Harbor Lib Board KIRBY, Frederick J. 654
Whirlpool Corp HEILEMAN, Gene C. 521
BERKLEY
City of Berkley KAPUR, Geraldine P. 626
MORSE, Celia B. 869
BERRIEN SPRINGS
Andrews Univ SOPER, Marley H. 1168
WALLER, Elaine J. 1298
WILDMAN, Linda 1339
Berrien County Intermediate Sch
District FITZGERALD, Ruth F. 382
BEULAH
John Stevens Robling Ltd ROBLING, John S. 1045
BIRMINGHAM
Baldwin Pub Lib KERSHNER, Stephen A. 644
MARTIN, John E. 776
ORMOND, Sarah C. 926
SWEENEY, Thomas F. 1215
BLOOMFIELD HILLS
Betsy Ross Publications BUZAN, Norma J. 168
Bloomfield Hills Schs ASHLEY, Roger S. 36
Bloomfield Township Pub Lib HERBST, Linda R. 530
RAFAL, Marian D. 1003
SANDY, Marjorie M. 1081
Cranbrook Academy of Art DYKI, Judy 331
GUNN, Diane M. 477
Cranbrook Educational Community COIR, Mark A. 229
ST. AMAND, Norma P. 1075
Cranbrook Institute of Science JERYAN, Christine B. 600
D'Arcy Masius Benton & Bowles ROCHLEN, Rita E. 1046
SIDEN, Harriet F. 1135
BLOOMINGSDALE
Bloomingdale Pub Schs POST, Roger 086
BRECKENRIDGE
Breckenridge Community Schs HOERGER, Helen L. 547
CADILLAC
Cadillac-Wexford County Pub Lib BEST, Donald A. 92
CANTON
Advanced Info Consult BRYANT, Barton B. 152
Plymouth Salem High Sch WEST, Marian S. 1326
CASSOPOLIS
Cass County Lib FEDEROWSKI, Marjorie S. . . 368
CLARKSTON
Colobiere Center MEDER, Stephen A. 820
Independence Township ROSE, Anne 1054
St Daniel Catholic Church Lib HIBLER, James P. 536
Univ of Detroit D'ELIA, Joseph G. 289
CLAWSON
Blair Memorial Lib LEVIN, Elizabeth A. 720

MICHIGAN (Cont'd)
DEARBORN

City of Dearborn	MARQUIS, Rollin P.	773
Dearborn Board of Education	MCCARTY, Linda A.	795
Dearborn Pub Schs	CRAWFORD, Geraldine H.	256
Ford Motor Co	BALOK, Becki	53
	ESTRY, Donna S.	355
Jayell Enterprises	LIMBACHER, James L.	727
Library Management Systems Inc	KILLIAN, Mary C.	648
Madonna Coll	VINT, Patricia A.	1285
Society of Manufactruing Engineers	GROEN, Paulette E.	471
Univ of Michigan at Dearborn	BROWN-MAY, Patricia A.	148
	LUKASIEWICZ, Barbara	747
	NUCKOLLS, Karen A.	912
	SCHNEIDER, Janet M.	1097
	STUCK, Judy K.	1204

DECATUR

Van Buren County Lib	TATE, David L.	1225

DETROIT

Arthur Andersen & Co	SNAY, Sylvia A.	1162
	STREETER, Linda D.	1201
Automobile Aerospace & Agricultural	KIBILDIS, Melba	646
Bodman Longley & Dahling	HEINRICH, Mark A.	522
Children's Hospital of Michigan	KLEIN, Michele S.	659
City of Detroit	MOSS, Josievet	872
Clark Klein & Beaumont	GAMACHE, Kathleen A.	416
CMP Associates Inc	PORTER, Jean F.	984
Comerica Inc	LILLEY, Barbara A.	727
	STANTON, Beth L.	1181
Detroit Board of Education	THOMAS, Laverne J.	1237
Detroit Coll of Law	HANNA, Hildur M.	496
	LORNE, Lorraine K.	741
Detroit Free Press	PEPPER, Alice A.	958
The Detroit News	HAVLENA, Betty W.	513
Detroit Pub Lib	BOWEN, Jennifer B.	120
	BUCKLEY, Francis J.	154
	CURTIS, Jean E.	267
	FRANCIS, Gloria A.	396
	GAREN, Robert J.	418
	GRIMES, Timothy P.	470
	HAUSMAN, Lisa M.	513
	HENSON, Ruby P.	530
	KNIFFEL, Leonard J.	664
	LAROSE, Margaret	698
	MA, Helen Y.	753
	MATZKE, Ellen S.	786
	OLDENBURG, Joseph F.	920
	TSAI, Fu M.	1260
	TUCKER, Florence R.	1261
	WISCHMEYER, Carol A.	1356
	ZARYCZNY, Wlodzimierz A.	1386
Detroit Pub Schs	BIELICH, Paul S.	95
	HUNTER, Dorothea A.	576
	WALL, Marilyn M.	1297
Detroit Receiving Hospital	MUDLOFF, Cherrie M.	875
Dickinson Wright Moon Van Dusen et al	DARGA, Carol M.	274
	HANAFEE, Valerie	494
Founders Society	WAGNER, Cherryl A.	1291
Fruehauf Corp	SCOTT, Jane	1107
Gale Research Co	BIANCO, David P.	94
	BREWER, Annie M.	134
	BRYFONSKI, Dedria A.	152
	CLARK, William E.	218
	CONNORS, Martin G.	238
	CROWLEY, Ellen T.	261
	DRAPER, James P.	318
	LABEAU, Dennis	685
	MARCACCIO, Kathleen Y.	768
	MARLOW, Cecilia A.	772
	NASSO, Christine	889
	PAUL, Thomas A.	949
	ROMIG, Thomas L.	1053
	RUFFNER, Frederick G.	1066
	RUNCHOCK, Rita M.	1067
	SAVAGE, Helen	1085
	SCHMITTROTH, John	1096
	SELLGREN, James A.	1114
	TARBERT, Gary C.	1224

MICHIGAN (Cont'd)
DETROIT (Cont'd)

General Motors Corp	COCHRAN, Catherine	225
	STEPHENS, Karen L.	1188
Henry Ford Hospital	REID, Valerie L.	1019
	STEVENS, Sheryl R.	1191
Henry Ford Museum and Greenfield Village	HEYMOSS, Jennifer M.	536
Hill Lewis Adams Goodrich & Tait	SERPENTO, Mary M.	1116
Honigman Miller Schwartz & Cohn	HEINEN, Margaret A.	522
Hutzel Hospital	BRENNAN, Jean M.	132
Indian Village Historical Collection Inc	BRUNK, Thomas W.	150
Information Coordinators Inc	STRATELAK, Nadia A.	1200
Lafayette Clinic	WARD, Nancy E.	1304
League Insurance Companies	ZYSKOWSKI, Dianne D.	1392
Market Opinion Research	KELLEY, Barbara C.	636
Michigan Bell	SPRAGUE, Karol S.	1176
Michigan Consolidated Gas Co	AMES, Kay L.	20
Michigan Osteopathic Medical Center	HOUGH, Carolyn A.	562
Miller Canfield Paddock & Stone	GREEN, Katherine A.	462
Motor Vehicle Manufacturers Association	GIGLIO, Linda M.	433
	SIEGEL, Marilyn	1136
	VELLIKY, Mary M.	1281
	WREN, James A.	1370
Mount Carmel Mercy Hospital	SKONIECZNY, Jill	1147
National Bank of Detroit Bancorp	WOODROW, Carolyn M.	1366
North Detroit General Hospital	BURSON, Barbara A.	163
Pepper Hamilton & Scheetz	STAJNIAK, Elizabeth T.	1178
Plunkett & Cooney	KONDAK, Ann	670
Province of St Joseph of Capuchin Order	WIEST, Donald H.	1337
Sacred Heart Seminary	RZEPECKI, Arnold M.	1072
St Hedwig High Sch	FORSYTH, Karen R.	391
St John Hospital	O'DONNELL, Ellen E.	917
	WAYLAND, Marilyn T.	1311
Unisys Corp	CARUSO, Genevieve O.	190
	FRANTILLA, K A.	398
	WHITE, Jane F.	1331
Univ of Detroit	AUER, Margaret E.	39
	BLACK, Shirley R.	101
	COOPER, Byron D.	242
	HOMANT, Sue J.	555
	HUPP, Stephen L.	577
	SMITH, Peter A.	1159
Wayne State Univ	ALLEN, Nancy H.	15
	BARTKOWSKI, Patricia	61
	BISSETT, Donald J.	100
	BOLLINGER, Robert O.	112
	BRAITHWAITE, Heather J.	127
	BUGG, Louise M.	155
	CHURCHWELL, Charles	213
	CLARK, Georgia A.	217
	EDWARDS, Willie M.	338
	ENGLE, Constance B.	349
	GRAZIER, Margaret H.	461
	GUNN, Arthur C.	477
	KAUL, Kanhya L.	631
	KIRKESY, Oliver M.	655
	LARONGE, Philip V.	698
	MENDELSOHN, Loren D.	823
	MIKA, Joseph J.	834
	PFLUG, Warner W.	966
	ROBBINS, Lora A.	1039
	ROSENBAUM, David	1055
	SELBERG, Janice K.	1113
	SHUMAN, Bruce A.	1134
	SMITH, Michael O.	1158
	SPYERS-DURAN, Peter	1177
	VAN TOLL, Faith	1277
	WILLIAMS, James F.	1343
Wayne State Univ Press	WEST, Donald	1326

EAST DETROIT

City of East Detroit	TODD, Suzanne L.	1248
East Detrcit Memorial Lib	REID, Bette C.	1018

EAST GRAND RAPIDS

Kent County Lib System	DEYOUNG, Gail O.	298

MICHIGAN (Cont'd)

EAST LANSING
East Lansing Pub Lib | POBANZ, Becky L. 979
Ingram-Rude Information Researchers | INGRAM, Elizabeth T. 583
Katherine Ackerman and Assoc | ACKERMAN, Katherine K. 4
Mayers & Associates | MAYERS, Henry L. 789
Michigan State Univ | ARMSTRONG, Carole S. 32
| BLACK-SHIER, Mary L. 102
| BURINSKI, Walter W. 160
| CHAPIN, Richard E. 201
| CLULEY, Leonard E. 223
| COOK, Kay A. 240
| COURTOIS, Martin P. 251
| FRYE, Dorothy T. 407
| HAKA, Clifford H. 484
| HONHART, Frederick L. 556
| JIZBA, Laurel 600
| KLOSWICK, John 662
| KOCH, Henry C. 667
| MANDERSCHEID, Dorothy
| H. 765
| MEAHL, D D. 819
| OLIVER, James W. 921
| OSTROM, Kriss T. 929
| REITER, Berle G. 1022
| RIVERA, Diana H. 1037
| SANFORD, John D. 1081
| SCOTT, Randall W. 1108
| SHAPIRO, Beth J. 1121
| THUNELL, Allen E. 1243
| WIEMERS, Eugene L. 1336
| WOODARD, Beth E. 1365

ECORSE
Ecorse Public Schs | MCKINNEY, Ceola S. 812
FARMINGTON
Farmington Community Lib | THEEKE, Tina M. 1234
FARMINGTON HILLS
Botsford General Hospital | ADAMS, Deborah L. 4
Digital Equipment Corp | BEICHMAN, John C. 75
Farmington Community Lib | PAPAI, Beverly D. 938
FLINT
Baker Coll | ARNOLD, Peggy 34
| VOELZ, Laura D. 1286
Charles Stewart Mott Foundation | BROWN, Eve C. 144
The Flint Journal | LARZELERE, David W. 700
Flint Pub Lib | CHAMBERS, E G. 198
| JAEGER, Sally J. 591
| KINGSTON, Jo A. 652
| OAKLANDER, Linda G. 913
| SCHAAFSMA, Roberta A. 1088
| STILLEY, Cynthia S. 1194
Genesee District Lib | ARVIN, Charles S. 35
| GAMBLE, Marian L. 416
GMI Engineering & Management
   Institute | MEADOWS, Brenda L. 819
Kearsley Community Schs | KIRN, Marjorie A. 655
McLaren General Hospital | MORELAND, Patricia L. 863
Univ of Michigan at Flint | GIFFORD, Paul M. 433
| HART, David J. 507
| PALMER, David W. 936
FRANKENMUTH
City of Frankenmuth | MCEWEN, Mary A. 804
GRAND BLANC
Grand Blanc High Sch | BERTRAND, Beverly P. 91
GRAND HAVEN
City of Grand Haven | AMES, Mark J. 20
Grand Haven Pub Schs | BROOKS, Burton H. 140
GRAND RAPIDS
Aquinas Coll | MARTIN, Rose M. 778
Arnold's Archives | JACOBSEN, Arnold 590
Calvin Coll & Seminary | CARLSON, Susan L. 182
| DE KLERK, Peter 288
| MONSMA, Marvin E. 855
Computer Aided Planning | FITZPATRICK, Nancy C. 383
Grand Rapids Pub Lib | BOSE, Deborah L. 117
| MATTESON, James S. 785
| RAZ, Robert E. 1012
Grand Rapids Pub Schs | COLYER, Judith A. 234
Kendall Coll of Art & Design | HORNBACH, Ruth M. 559
Kent County Lib System | GARCIA, Joseph E. 417

MICHIGAN (Cont'd)

GRAND RAPIDS (Cont'd)
Lear Siegler Inc | BRACKETT, Norman S. 124
Metropolitan Hospital | LOFTIS, Mary B. 737
NHPRC | SIEBERS, Bruce L. 1135
St Mary's Hospital | HANSON, Mary A. 498
| MATHIS, Yvonne L. 784
Smith Haughey Rice & Roegge | RANSOM-BERGSTROM,
| Janette F. 1008

GROSSE POINTE
Bon Secours Hospital | FRATIES, Marie L. 399
Grosse Pointe Pub Lib | HANSON, Charles D. 498
| MORROW, Blaine V. 869
Grosse Pointe Pub Sch System | GREGORY, Helen B. 466
| ROBERTS, Scott J. 1041
| STEPHENS, John H. 1188
Our Lady Star of The Sea High | PARTHUM, John W. 945
Wayne State Univ | CASEY, Genevieve M. 192
HANCOCK
Suomi Coll | PENTI, Marsha E. 957
HARPER WOODS
Bishop Gallagher High Sch | SLIVKA, Regina 1149
City of Harper Woods | ARRIVEE, Sally D. 34
Lutheran High Sch East | FRITZ, Donald D. 405
HARTLAND
Hartland Consolidated Schs | SCHERBA, Sandra A. 1092
HASTINGS
Hastings Pub Lib | SCHONDELMAYER,
| Barbara B. 1098
HICKORY CORNERS
Michigan State Univ | HAMMARSKJOLD, Carolyn
| A. 493
HIGHLAND PARK
Chrysler Corp | PERECMAN, Carol J. 958
City of Highland Park | NDENGA, Viola W. 890
HILLIDALE
Hillsdale Coll | KNOCH, Daniel L. 665
HOLLAND
Donnelly Corp | YETMAN, Nancy J. 1380
Herrick Pub Lib | CORRADINI, Diane M. 247
| LIGHT, Lin 726
Hope Coll | JENSEN, David P. 598
| MURRAY, Diane E. 881
Western Theology Seminary | SMITH, Paul M. 1159
Worden Co | GRANT, Robert S. 458
HOUGHTON
Michigan Technological Univ | MORROW, Deborah 869
| SPENCE, Theresa S. 1173
| THOMAS, David H. 1236
Michigan Tech Univ | KRENITSKY, Michael V. 677
HOWELL
Howell Carnegie Lib | ZAENGER, Kathleen L. 1385
HUNTINGTON WOODS
Oak Park Pub Lib | WASSERMAN, Sherry T. .. 1308
INKSTER
Wayne-Oakland Lib Federation | MURATA, Mabel M. 879
INTERLOCHEN
Interlochen Center for the Arts | WELIVER, E D. 1321
IRON MOUNTAIN
Mid-Peninsula Lib Cooperative | SILVER, Gary L. 1138
Veterans Administration Medical
   Center | DUROCHER, Jeanne M. 328
JACKSON
Consumers Power Co | SMITH, Catherine A. 1153
Gilbert Commonwealth Inc | HERBERT, Helen E. 530
Jackson District Lib | BUXBAUM, Sharolyn 168
| LEAMON, David L. 707
JENISON
Jenison Pub Schs | VELTEMA, John H. 1282
KALAMAZOO
American Latvian Association | BUNDZA, Maira 157
Borgess Medical Center | HARVEY, Norma L. 509
Cain Associates Architects | CAIN, Robert B. 171
Kalamazoo Coll | PINKHAM, Eleanor H. 974
| SMITH, Carol P. 1153
| SMITHSON, Paul G. 1162
Kalamazoo Institute of Arts | NESBURG, Janet A. 896
| SHERIDAN, Helen A. 1127
Kalamazoo Pub Lib | LARSON, Catherine A. 699
| RIFE, Mary C. 1033

MICHIGAN (Cont'd)

KALAMAZOO (Cont'd)
Kalamazoo Pub Schs	WILLIAMS, S J.	1346
Kalamazoo Regional Psychiatric Hospital	AEBLI, Carol L.	7
Kalamazoo Valley Community Coll	APPS, Michelle L.	30
KALSEC Inc	SAGAR, Mary B.	1074
The Upjohn Co	ALLRED, Paula M.	17
	EVERITT, Janet M.	359
	HOMAN, J M.	555
	MACKSEY, Julie A.	757
	NOBLE, Valerie	906
	POWELL, James R.	988
	SATTLER, Pauline	1084
	SLACH, June E.	1147
	WORDEN, Diane D.	1369
W E Upjohn Institute	CLEMENTS, Susan S.	221
Western Michigan Univ	BLEIL, Leslie A.	105
	BOURGEOIS, Ann M.	119
	BRUNHUMER, Sondra K.	150
	CARROLL, Hardy	187
	DRISCOLL, Jacqueline	320
	ENGELKE, Hans	349
	GROTZINGER, Laurel A.	473
	HEGEDUS, Mary E.	521
	ISAACSON, David K.	584
	LOWRIE, Jean E.	744
	NETZ, David H.	896
	PEREZ-STABLE, Maria A.	958
	RING, Donna M.	1035
	RIZZO, John R.	1037
	ROSS, Mary E.	1058
	SICHEL, Beatrice	1135
	SMITH, William K.	1161
	VANDER MEER, Patricia F.	1274

KENTWOOD
Kent County Lib System	CAMMENGA, Cheryl G.	175

LAKE ORION
Orion Township Pub Lib	SICKLES, Linda C.	1135

LANSING
Bureau of History	BIGELOW, Martha M.	95
	MILLER, Bertha H.	836
Ingham Medical Center	KEDDLE, David G.	634
Lansing Catholic Central High Sch	BROWN, Joan	145
Lansing Community Coll	MAJOR, Marla J.	762
	RADEMACHER, Matthew J.	1002
Lansing General Hospital	HEINLEN, Bethany A.	522
Lansing Pub Lib	CONWAY, Lauren K.	239
Lib of Michigan	DUKELOW, Ruth H.	324
	EZELL, Charlaine L.	360
	JOHNSON, Veronica A.	609
	WOLFE, Charles B.	1360
Michigan Lib Association	GESSNER, Marianne	430
Michigan Lib Consortium	CONWAY, Michael J.	239
	FLAHERTY, Kevin C.	383
St Lawrence Hospital	CLAYTOR, Jane B.	220
State of Michigan	CALLARD, Carole	173
	FRY, James W.	406
	SCHOLFIELD, Caroline A.	1098
Thomas M Cooley Law Sch	BONGE, Barbara M.	114
	LUCAS, Ann	745
	MICHAUD, John C.	832
Waverly Community Schs	YARBROUGH, Joseph W.	1378

LAPEER
Lapeer County Lib	STRAUSS, Laura C.	1201
Lapeer General Hospital	VIGES, R J.	1284

LAURIUM
Calumet Pub Hospital	BINONIEMI, Amanda M.	97

LIVONIA
City of Livonia	DELLER, A M.	289
	TRENNER, Claudine F.	1255
	VOIGHT, Nancy R.	1287
Libonia Pub Lib	FARHAT, Elizabeth M.	363
Livonia Pub Lib	BERRY, Charlene	90
Madonna Coll	MLODZIANOWSKI, Mary L.	850
Schoolcraft Coll	NUFFER, Roy A.	912

MADISON HEIGHTS
Bishop Foley High Sch	UZENSKI, Helen R.	1270
Madison Heights Pub Lib	YERMAN, Roslyn F.	1380

MICHIGAN (Cont'd)

MARCELLUS
Marcellus Community Schools	TATE, Carole A.	1225

MARQUETTE
Northern Michigan Univ	PETERS, Stephen H.	962
	WAGAR, Joanna M.	1291

MAYVILLE
Mayville District Pub Lib	GARNSEY, Alice M.	419

MIDLAND
Dow Chemical Co	JAZBINSCHEK, Jerri	596
	STEINER, Doris L.	1186
Dow Corning Corp	HORCHER, Ann M.	559
Grace A Dow Memorial Lib	DYKHUIS, Randy	331
	KOBEL, Rose A.	666
Northwood Institute	CHEN, Catherine W.	205

MONROE
Monroe County Historical Commission	KULL, Christine L.	683
Monroe County Lib System	MARGOLIS, Bernard A.	770

MONTAGUE
Montague Area Pub Schs	SCARBROUGH, S J.	1087

MT CLEMENS
Chippewa Valley Schs	MATECUN, Marilyn L.	783
Lib Cooperative of Macomb	CUNNINGHAM, Tina Y.	265
Macomb County Lib	LUFT, William	747
Macomb Intermediate Sch District	PALMER, Richard J.	936

MT PLEASANT
Central Michigan Univ	MULLIGAN, William H.	877
	SHIRLEY, David B.	1131
	TIMBERS, Jill G.	1245
	WEATHERFORD, John W.	1311
City of Mt Pleasant	KRUUT, Evald	681

MUSKEGON
Hackley Hospital	MARSHALL, Betty J.	773
Hackley Pub Lib	KIRKLAND, Ruth M.	655
Muskegon Community Coll	VANDERLAAN, Robert J.	1274
Muskegon County Lib	MCFERRAN, Warren A.	805
	VETTESE, Richard	1283
Muskegon Schs	HOUSEWARD, Bernice A.	563
Pub Schs of Muskegon	PRETZER, Dale H.	992

NEGAUNEE
Negaunee Pub Schs	PAULIN, Mary A.	950

NEWPORT
Detroit Edison Co	WOODLEY, Victoria B.	1366

NORTHVILLE
State of Michigan	SEFCIK, Delphine M.	1111

NOVI
Clayton Environmental Consultants	COREY, Marjorie	246
Kenneth King Associates	KING, Kenneth	651
Novi Community Schs	KIEFER, Marilyn V.	647
Novi Pub Lib	DRUSCHEL, Pauline H.	321

OAK PARK
Oak Park Pub Lib	BRANZBURG, Marian G.	129

OKEMOS
Okemos Pub Schs	TREGLOAN, Donald C.	1255

OLIVET
Olivet Coll	COOPER, B L.	242
	EVANS, Kathy J.	357
	STEVENS, Marjorie	1190

ORCHARD LAKE
St Mary's Coll	IRWIN, Lawrence L.	584

OXFORD
Oxford Pub Lib	DOUBLESTEIN, Judith A.	313

PAW PAW
Paw Paw Pub Lib	PRITCHARD, Mildred H.	994

PELLSTON
Pellston Pub Schs	SMALLWOOD, Carol A.	1151

PETOSKEY
Burns Clinic Medical Center	KELLY, Kay	638

PLAINWELL
Charles A Ransom District Lib	PARK, Janice R.	941
Plainwell High Sch	PARR, Michael P.	944

PLYMOUTH
Library Design Associates Inc	DE BEAR, Richard S.	284
	MCCLINTOCK, Janet	797
Plymouth District Lib	RAWLINSON, Pamela	1011
St John's Seminary	CARLEN, Claudia	181
	DE BEAR, Estelle G.	284
	MCGARTY, Jean R.	805
Unisys Corp	FEDER, Carol S.	367

MICHIGAN (Cont'd)

PONTIAC
Oakland County Reference Lib — JOSE, Phyllis A. 617
Oakland Schs — CROSS, Jennie B. 260
Pontiac General Hospital — SAHYOUN, Naim K. 1075
St Joseph Mercy Hospital — LYNCH, Mollie S. 752
PORT HURON
St Clair County Community Coll — YAEK, Larry A. 1376
St Clair County Lib System — ARNETT, Stanley K. 33
WU, Harry P. 1373
PORTAGE
Portage Pub Lib — HAENICKE, Carol A. 482
HEMPHILL, Frank A. 525
RIVERVIEW
City of Riverview — NAPOLITAN, Jacquetta 887
ROCHESTER
Crittenton Hospital — LEE, Lucy W. 710
Oakland Univ — BLATT, Gloria T. 104
DAVID, Indra M. 276
FRANKIE, Suzanne O. 397
GAYLOR, Robert G. 423
HILDEBRAND, Linda L. 538
KROMPART, Janet A. 679
Rochester Hills Pub Lib — BRAGLIA, Nancy L. 127
HAGE, Christine C. 482
HOWARTH, Mary K. 565
SATTERTHWAITE, Diane A. 1084
WILSON, Patricia L. 1352
ROMEO
Romeo District Lib — KRUSE, Marina B. 681
ROSEVILLE
Roseville Communtiy Schs — TOLMAN, Bonnie B. 1249
Roseville Pub Lib — KOLLMORGEN, Rose M. ... 669
ROYAL OAK
William Beaumont Hospital — EMAHISER, Joan A. 347
SAGINAW
Pub Libs of Saginaw — O'CONNELL, Catherine A. 915
REINKE, Carol R. 1021
Saginaw Cooperative Hospitals Inc — JOHN, Stephanie C. 601
Saginaw Pub Lib — SCHULTZ, Christine K. 1102
SAINT CLAIRE SHORES
Saint Clair Shores Pub Lib — WALKER, Joe L. 1295
WOODFORD, Arthur M. ... 1366
SAINT JOSEPH
Heath/Zenith Data Systems — WOJCIKIEWICZ, Carol A. .. 1359
SAULT SAINTE MARIE
Lake Superior State Coll — MICHELS, Fredrick A. 832
NAIRN, Charles E. 886
SOUTH LYON
South Lyon Public Lib — NIETHAMMER, Leslee 904
SOUTHFIELD
Allied Automotive — BLASCHAK, Mary M. 104
Eaton Corp — MONTGOMERY, Mary E. ... 856
Electronic Data Systems — MARGOLIS, Suzanne M. 770
Farmington Community Lib — SUMMERS, Sheryl H. 1209
Lawrence Institute of Tech — COCOZZOLI, Gary R. 226
Providence Hospital — GILBERT, Carole M. 433
Southfield Pub Lib — BENSON, Carol T. 83
HORN, Anna E. 559
SMOLER, Shelly 1162
VERGE, Colleen R. 1282
ZYSKOWSKI, Douglas A. .. 1392
Southfield Pub Schools — MOSKOWITZ, May K. 871
Thomas Consulting Inc — THOMAS, Margaret J. 1237
Tri-County Dental Health Council — BINDSCHADLER, Valerie V. .. 97
W B Doner and Co Advertising — LEB, Joan P. 707
SPRING ARBOR
Spring Arbor Coll — BURNS, David J. 162
SPRING LAKE
Spring Lake Township — SHERIDAN, Clare A. 1127
STERLING HEIGHTS
Sterling Heights Pub Lib — CURTIS, Kathleen W. 267
STEVENSVILLE
Lincoln Township Pub Lib — BEDUNAH, Virginia M. 74
STURGIS
Sturgis Pub Schs — BERKLUND, Nancy J. 87
TECUMSEH
Tecumseh Pub Lib — REASONER, Mary B. 1013

MICHIGAN (Cont'd)

TRAVERSE CITY
Center for the Gifted — HALSTED, Judith W. 490
Gerald R Ford Foundation — GRIFFIN, Robert P. 469
Traverse Area District Lib — KULIBERT, Marie M. 683
SCHAUB, Theresa F. 1090
TRENTON
County of Wayne — MISNER, Joyce V. 847
Riverside Osteopathic Hospital — SKOGLUND, Susan E. 1147
TROY
General Dynamics Corp — MAGUIRE, Shirley E. 760
Troy Sch District — COREY, Glenn M. 246
Walsh Coll of Accountancy & Bus Admin — ELLIS, Gloria B. 344
UNIVERSITY CENTER
Delta Coll — BROW, Judith A. 141
Saginaw Valley State Coll — JONES, Clifton H. 612
KOSCHIK, Douglas R. 672
WARREN
Bi-County Community — WILLIAMS, Gayle A. 1343
Campbell-Ewald Co — ROSE, Sharon G. 1055
STEPEK, Susan B. 1187
General Motors Corp — BRISTOR, Patricia R. 137
HORNE, Ernest L. 560
SHEPARD, Margaret E. 1127
VAN ALLEN, Neil K. 1271
Macomb Community Coll — DOYLE, James M. 317
GAURI, Kul B. 423
Warren Consolidated Schs — BAIRD, Patricia M. 47
WAYNE
Wayne-Oakland Lib Federation — MORGAN, Patricia L. 864
WEISER, Douglas E. 1319
WEST BLOOMFIELD
West Bloomfield Scns — MADDEN, Terence J. 759
West Bloomfield Township Pub Lib — FORD, Gale I. 389
KULBERG, Gretchen S. 683
SMITH, Nancy J. 1158
WHITE CLOUD
City of White Cloud — HARPER, Nancy L. 503
WIXOM
Wixom Pub Lib — GOLDSTEIN, Doris R. 446
WYANDOTTE
BASF Corp — SPECTOR, Janice B. 1172
WYOMING
Kent County Lib Board — THOMAS, Louise V. 1237
Kent County Lib System — STADELMAN, Kathleen M. . 1178
YPSILANTI
Eastern Michigan Univ — BEAL, Sarell W. 68
BECK, Mary C. 71
BLUM, Fred 107
BOONE, Morell D. 115
BULLARD, Rita J. 156
DRABENSTOTT, Jon D. 317
GLIKIN, Ronda 441
HANSEN, Joanne J. 497
KING, Carmen M. 650
KIRKENDALL, Carolyn A. 654
RACZ, Twyla M. 1001
STANGER, Keith J. 1180
YEE, Sandra G. 1379
Ypsilanti District Lib — LINDSTROM, Susan C. 730
ZEELAND
Herman Miller Inc — WAGENVELD, Linda M. ... 1291

MINNESOTA

ALBERT LEA
Independent Sch District 241 — LONNING, Roger D. 740
ALEXANDRIA
Alexandria Pub Lib — HELGESON, Victoria L. 524
Northern Lights Lib Network — LARSON, Joan B. 699
ANOKA
Anoka Pub Lib — SHANLEY, Dennis M. 1120
AUSTIN
Austin Pub Lib — HAYS, Robert M. 517
BEMIDJI
Bemidji State Univ — ELLIOTT, Gwendolyn W. 344
KISHEL, Deane A. 656
Kitchigami Regional Lib — WEISS, Kay M. 1320

MINNESOTA (Cont'd)

BLAINE
Anoka County Lib   WEEKS, Diane M. 1315
                                          YOUNG, Jerry F. 1382
BLOOMINGTON
Hennepin County Lib   ISMAIL, Noha S. 585
Normandale Community Coll   REIERSON, Pamela M. . . . 1019
CAMBRIDGE
East Central Regional Lib   BOESE, Robert A. 110
CANNON FALLS
City of Cannon Falls   WOLF, Joy G. 1360
CLOQUET
Independent Sch District 94   URBANSKI, Lawrence E. . . . 1269
COLD SPRING
St Cloud State Univ   WESTBY, Jerry L. 1326
COLUMBIA HEIGHTS
Columbia Heights Pub Schs   VAUGHAN, Janet E. 1279
CROOKSTON
Corbett Coll   HILBER, Leocadia 538
DULUTH
City of Duluth   SCHROEDER, Janet K. 1100
Duluth Pub Lib   OUSE, David J. 930
Univ of Minnesota at Duluth   EBRO, Diane C. 334
                                          ENRICI, Pamela L. 350
                                          JOHNSON, Deborah S. 603
EAGAN
Dakota County   MACDONALD, Roderick 754
EDEN PRAIRIE
Rosemount Inc   WELDON, Barbara J. 1321
EDINA
Edina Public Schs   DIMENT, Elna N. 304
Fairview Southdale Hospital   FEMAL, Mary B. 370
Hennepin County Lib   FISCHER, Catherine S. 379
Independent Sch District 271   VAN SOMEREN, Betty A. . . 1277
International Information Networks Inc   HANSEN, Kathelen L. 497
EMBARRASS
Esala Associates
   Information/Research   ESALA, Lillian H. 354
FARIBAULT
Faribault Regional Center   HELTSLEY, Mary K. 525
State of Minnesota   WRIGHT, Myrna F. 1372
FERGUS FALLS
Viking Lib System   HANKS, Gardner C. 496
GOLDEN VALLEY
Hennepin County Lib Board   COLE, Jack W. 230
Honeywell Inc   KAUFENBERG, Jane M. 630
                                          MUSUMECI, Joann 883
GRAND RAPIDS
Grand Rapids Pub Lib   VALANCE, Marsha J. 1271
HOPKINS
David Rexford Smith Consulting
   Librarian   SMITH, David R. 1154
LAKE CITY
Independent Sch District 813   POST, Diana 986
LITTLE FALLS
St Francis Convent   MARTHALER, Margaret K. . . 775
MANKATO
Mankato State Univ   ALLAN, David W. 14
                                          BIRMINGHAM, Frank R. . . . 98
                                          CARRISON, Dale K. 187
                                          FARNER, Susan G. 365
                                          HITT, Charles J. 544
                                          MCDONALD, Frances B. . . . 802
                                          MOORE, Barbara N. 858
                                          PEISCHL, Thomas P. 955
                                          PIEHL, Kathleen K. 971
                                          READY, Sandra K. 1012
                                          SCHWARTZKOPF, Rebecca
                                             B. 1105
                                          SUYEMATSU, Kiyo 1212
Minnesota Valley Regional Lib   GAVIN, Donna J. 423
                                          WEIKUM, James M. 1317
Southcentral Minnesota Interlib
   Exchange   LOWRY, Lucy J. 745
                                          TOHAL, Kate J. 1248
Traverse des Sioux Lib System   CHRISTENSON, John D. . . . 211
MENDOTA HEIGHTS
Cray Research Inc   LAPENSKY, Barbara A. 697

MINNESOTA (Cont'd)

MINNEAPOLIS
A Chance to Grow   DAVIS, Emmett A. 279
Arthur Andersen & Co   DINGLEY, Doris A. 305
Augsburg Coll   ANDERSON, Margaret J. . . . 24
                                          SIBLEY, Marjorie H. 1135
Augsburg Publishing Co   JANSSEN, Gene R. 594
Billy Graham Evangelistic Association   FERM, Lois R. 373
Breck Sch   TABAR, Margaret E. 1219
Cargill Inc   ANDERSON, Marcia L. 24
                                          PETERSON, Julia C. 963
Charles Babbage Institute   BRUEMMER, Bruce H. 149
Colle & McVoy Advertising   HARNDEN, Donna J. 502
Control Data Corp   AXDAL, Joan L. 42
                                          CLIFT, Crystal A. 222
                                          GRIFFITH, Cary J. 469
                                          JESSEE, W S. 600
                                          LEHMAN, Tom 713
Corporate Report   MINOR, Barbara A. 846
Cowles Information Services   FANARAS, William F. 363
Deloitte Haskins & Sells   REYNEN, Richard G. 1025
Experience Inc   BLUMENFELD, Judith K. . . . 107
Faegre & Benson   DUNN, Jamie N. 326
Fallon McElligott   OLSEN, Stephen 922
Federal Reserve Bank of Minneapolis   SWAN, Janet 1213
FluiDyne Engineering Corp   JOHNSON, Marlys J. 607
FMC Corp   MOE, Sandra J. 851
Gale Research Co   DARNAY, Brigitte T. 275
                                          YOUNG, Margaret L. 1382
General Mills Inc   ANGUS, Jacqueline A. 28
                                          GALT, Judith A. 415
                                          HALLSTROM, Curtis H. 489
                                          HONEBRINK, Andrea C. . . . 555
Hage Fundsearch   HAGE, Elizabeth A. 482
Hennepin County Law Lib   GRANDE, Anne W. 457
Hennepin County Lib   DODGE, Christopher N. 308
Honeywell Inc   BARTLETT, Vernell W. 61
I E Associates Inc   ABELES, Tom 2
Law Lib Consultants Inc   BEDOR, Kathleen M. 73
Leonard Street & Deinard   CUMMINGS, Patricia K. . . . 264
                                          ROLONTZ, Linda 1051
Lutheran Church Lib Asssociation   JENSEN, Wilma M. 599
Medtronic Inc   LO, Maryanne H. 735
MINITEX   DEJOHN, William T. 288
                                          ROSSMAN, Muriel J. 1059
                                          YOUNGHOLM, Philip 1383
Minneapolis Coll of Art & Design   MANNING, Mary L. 766
Minneapolis Community Coll   RINE, Joseph L. 1035
Minneapolis Pub Lib   BARRETT, Darryl D. 59
                                          BRUCE, Robert K. 149
                                          CORCORAN, Nancy L. 246
                                          FUGAZZI, Elizabeth B. 408
                                          GRIGGS, Cynthia B. 470
                                          HASENSTEIN, Virginia P. . . . 510
                                          HILL, Constance L. 539
                                          KANE, Dennis M. 624
                                          KIMBROUGH, Joseph 649
                                          KUKLA, Edward R. 683
                                          SELANDER, Lucy M. 1113
                                          SHANNON, Zella J. 1121
                                          SIMMONS, Antoinette S. . . . 1139
                                          SMISEK, Thomas P. 1152
                                          TERTELL, Susan M. 1232
                                          THEWS, Dorothy D. 1234
                                          VAN WHY, Carol B. 1277
                                          VETH, Terry R. 1283
Minneapolis Pub Schs   LACY, Lyn E. 687
Minnegasco Inc   FABIO, Janet L. 360
Minnesota Lib Association   TOWNE, Pamela 1252
Minnesota Orchestral Association   GUNTHER, Paul B. 478
Moore Data Database Publishing   RUBNIK, Louis J. 1065
Moore Data Management Services   BRUTON, Robert T. 151
Municipal Information Lib   RAFTER, Susan 1003
National City Bank of Minneapolis   MIRANDA, Esmeralda C. . . . 847
North Central Bible Coll   SHIRK, John C. 1131
Northern States Power Co   SOLSETH, Gwenn M. 1166
Onan Corp   NELSON, Catherine G. 893
                                          ROHRER, Valera E. 1051
Park Nicollet Medical Foundation   LATTA, Barbara K. 702

MINNESOTA (Cont'd)
MINNEAPOLIS (Cont'd)
Pillsbury Co

Poquette & Associates
Rulon-Miller Books
Shadduck & Sullivan Information
  Spclst
Super Valu Stores
United Methodist Church
US Department of Defense
Univ of Minnesota at Minneapolis

PEDERSEN, Dennis C. 954
SCHUMACHER, Patricia C. . 1103
POQUETTE, Mary L. 984
RULON-MILLER, Robert ... 1067

SHADDUCK, Gregg S. 1118
CANFIELD, Linda N. 178
BOEDER, Thelma B. 109
WITT, Kenneth W. 1358
ALLISON, Brent 17
ARTH, Janet M. 35
BAUM, Marsha L. 66
BEAVEN, Miranda J. 71
BILEYDI, Lois G. 96
BRANIN, Joseph J. 128
BROGAN, Martha L. 139
CHRISTIANSON, Ellory J. .. 212
COGSWELL, James A. 227
COLLINS, Mary F. 233
D'ELIA, George P. 289
FAGERLIE, Joan M. 361
FOREMAN, Gertrude E. 390
FULLER, Sherrilynne S. 409
GANGL, Susan D. 416
GASTON, Judith A. 421
GLASGOW, Vicki L. 440
GROSCH, Audrey N. 472
HALES-MABRY, Celia E. ... 486
HALLEWELL, Laurence 489
HOPP, Ralph H. 558
IMMLER, Frank 582
JOHNSON, Donald C. 603
KARON, Bernard L. 627
KELLY, Richard J. 638
KLAASSEN, David J. 657
KROSCH, Penelope S. 680
LA BISSONIERE, William R. . 686
LATHROP, Alan K. 701
LONG, John M. 739
LORING, Christopher B. 741
MARION, Donald J. 770
MONSON, Dianne L. 855
MUELLER, Mary G. 875
NEVIN, Susanne 898
OBERMAN, Cerise G. 914
OLSON, Lowell E. 923
OVERMIER, Judith A. 931
PANKAKE, Marcia J. 938
REES, Warren D. 1016
REISNER, Suzanne R. 1021
RUBENS, Donna J. 1064
SANDNESS, John G. 1081
SCHERER, Herbert G. 1092
SMITH, Eldred R. 1154
SPETLAND, Charles G. 1174
STEINKE, Cynthia A. 1186
STOKES, Claire Z. 1196
TIBLIN, Mariann E. 1244
TURNER, Patricia 1265
VAN CLEVE, Nancy J. 1273
WALDEN, Barbara L. 1294
WEEKS, John M. 1315
WEINBERG, Gail B. 1317
YAHNKE, Robert E. 1376

Veterans Administration Medical
  Center

Walker Art Center
MINNETONKA
Crane McDowell & Co Inc
Hennepin County Lib

Syntactic Analyzer Inc

SINHA, Dorothy P. 1143
STANKE, Judith U. 1180
FURTAK, Rosemary 410

HAM, Beverly V. 490
DESIREY, Janice M. 295
ENGBERG, Linda L. 348
FRYMIRE, Jane K. 407
GROSSMAN, Michael P. ... 473
ROHLF, Robert H. 1050
ROLF, Robert H. 1051
WRONKA, Gretchen M. 1373
SCHULTZ, Arnold J. 1101

MINNESOTA (Cont'd)
MOORHEAD
Concordia Coll
Lake Agassiz Regional Lib

Moorhead Pub Lib
Moorhead State Univ

St Ansgar Hospital
MOUND
Hennepin County Lib
NEW BRIGHTON
Bethel Theological Seminary
Keim Enteprises
United Theological Seminary
NORTHFIELD
Carleton Coll

Northfield Pub Lib
St Olaf Coll

OWATONNA
Owatonna Pub Lib
PINE RIVER
Kitchigami Regional Lib
PLYMOUTH
Robbinsdale Independent District 281
RED WING
City of Red Wing
ROBBINSDALE
North Memorial Medical Center

ROCHESTER
City of Rochester
Mayo Clinic

Rochester Area Schs
Rochester Pub Lib
ROSEMOUNT
Rosemount Sch Dist 196
ROSEVILLE
Ramsey County Pub Lib

Unisys Corp
ST CLOUD
Great River Regional Lib

Independent Sch District 742
St Cloud Hospital
St Cloud State Univ

Stearns County Historical Society
SAINT JOSEPH
St Benedict's Convent
ST PAUL
American Lutheran Church
Briggs and Morgan
City of St Paul
Coll of St Catherine

Coll of St Thomas
Concordia Coll
Cretin-Derham Hall

RUDIE, Helen M. 1065
JANZEN, Deborah K. 594
OLSON, Chris D. 922
OSTAZEWSKI, Theodore ... 928
BRUNTON, Marilyn H. 151
SHOPTAUGH, Terry L. 1132
SIBLEY, Carol H. 1134
MYHRE, Char 885

GELINAS, Jeanne L. 426

MAGNUSON, Norris A. 759
KEIM, Robert 635
MERRILL, Arthur L. 826

GREENE, Mark A. 464
METZ, T J. 828
NILES, Ann A. 904
SANFORD, Carolyn C. 1081
YOUNG, Lynne M. 1382
CHRISTENSEN, Beth E. 211
DITTMANN, Chrisma S. 306
HUBER, Kristina R. 569

HOSLETT, Andrea E. 561

O'BRIEN, Marlys H. 915

SCHEU, Jean W. 1092

BRANDT, Janet E. 128

BARBOUR-TALLEY, Donna
  L. 55

TAYLOR, Judith K. 1227
CARON, Theodore F. 184
ERWIN, Patricia J. 353
GINN, Marjorie J. 437
HAWTHORNE, Dorothy M. .. 514
KEY, Jack D. 645
KOPPER, John A. 671
PALMER, Joy J. 936
SANDE, Alice E. 1079
BENSON, Laurel D. 83
GODSEY, James M. 443

SKELLY, Laurie J. 1146

CLARKE, Charlotte C. 218
JONES, Mary A. 614
MICHEL, William D. 832
VINNES, Norman M. 1285
RASMUSSEN, Mary L. 1009

BERNDTSON, Janet L. 88
CARMACK, Mona 183
COLE, David H. 230
SORELL, Janice G. 1168
HEETER, Judith A. 520
BERLING, John G. 88
CLARKE, Norman F. 219
SCHULZETENBERG,
  Anthony C. 1102
DECKER, John W. 286

BLATZ, Imogene 104

DANIELS, Paul A. 273
MUNTEAN, Deborah E. 879
EPSTEIN, Rheda 351
HARWOOD, Karen L. 510
HOLT, Constance W. 554
KINNEY, Janet S. 653
MCINERNEY, Claire R. 809
OZOLINS, Karl L. 933
OFFERMANN, Glenn W. 917
BROOKS, S B. 141

MINNESOTA (Cont'd)
ST PAUL (Cont'd)
Doherty Rumble & Butler   TURNER, Ann S. 1264
Friends of the St Paul Pub Lib   MEISSNER, Edie A. 822
Hamline Univ   KING, Jack B. 651
Hennepin County Lib   BYRNE, Roseanne 169
Independent Sch District 621   HAJICEK, Nancy K. 484
Independent Sch District 625   ROTH, Alvin R. 1059
James Jerome Hill Reference Lib MARKHAM, Scott C. 771
                                 WHITE, William T. 1332
Legislative Reference Lib   CATHCART, Marilyn S. 195
Luther Northwestern Theological
   Seminary   OLSON, Carol A. 922
                                 OLSON, Ray A. 923
                                 WENTE, Norman G. 1324
Macalester Coll   CLEMMER, Joel G. 221
                                 FISHEL, Teresa A. 380
Metropolitan Lib Service Agency WELYGAN, Sylvia M. 1323
Midway Hospital   WINDHAM, Carol B. 1354
Midwest China Center   ASPNES, Grieg G. 37
Minnesota Attorney General   ANDERSON, Anita M. 21
Minnesota Department of Education ASP, William G. 37
                                 DALBOTTEN, Mary S. 270
                                 FEYE-STUKAS, Janice 374
                                 LEWIS, Alan D. 722
                                 MILLER, Robert H. 842
                                 SWEEN, Roger 1214
                                 TALLY, Roy D. 1221
Minnesota Dept of Energy & Econ
   Devlpmnt   FENTON, Patricia F. 371
Minnesota Department of Human
   Services   LINEWEAVER, Joe R. 730
Minnesota Department of Revenue SLAMKOWSKI, Donna L. . . 1147
Minnesota Department of
   Transportation   BALDWIN, Jerome C. 51
                                 CORNELL, Pamela J. 246
Minnesota Historical Society   BAKER, Tracey I. 50
                                 HOLBERT, Sue E. 550
                                 WALSTROM, Jon L. 1300
                                 WIENER, Alissa L. 1336
Minnesota Office of Lib Devlpmnt &
   Srvs   MAHMOODI, Suzanne H. . . . 760
Minnesota Pollution Control Agency DOLAN, Mary M. 309
Minnesota State Law Lib   COLOKATHIS, Jane 234
                                 GALLIGAN, Sara A. 414
                                 GJELTEN, Daniel R. 439
                                 HAASE, Gretchen E. 480
Minnesota State Legislature   GADE, Rachel P. 411
Oppenheimer Wolff & Donnelly   COVER, Teresa A. 252
Ramsey County Pub Lib   KATZUNG, Judith 630
St John's Hospital   GALT, Francis E. 415
St Paul Pioneer Press Dispatch   HLAVSA, Larry B. 544
St Paul Pub Lib   JACOB, Rosamond T. 589
                                 REHNBERG, Marilyn J. 1017
                                 KAISER, Sally A. 622
St Paul Pub Schs   JACKSON, Mildred E. 588
St Peter Claver Church   ANDERSON, Rebekah E. 25
3M   BOYD, Cheryl J. 122
                                 DUELTGEN, Ronald R. 323
                                 FOLLMER, Diane E. 388
                                 HUPPERT, Ramona R. 577
                                 LESLIE, Donald S. 718
Unisys Corp   ELFSTRAND, Stephen F. 342
                                 VAN HORN, Virginia A. 1275
US Army   SCHMIDT, Jean M. 1095
US Satellite Broadcasting   HEINERSCHEID, Paul R. 522
Univ of Minnesota at St Paul   CARLSON, Livija I. 182
                                 DELOACH, Lynda J. 290
                                 JOHNSON, Margaret A. 607
                                 LETNES, Louise M. 718
                                 MCCLASKEY, Marilyn H. . . . 796
                                 MCDIARMID, Errett W. 802
                                 MOODY, Suzanna 857
                                 SCHOLBERG, Henry 1098
                                 WURL, Joel F. 1374
West Publishing Co   MCKEE, James E. 810
Westlaw   MCLEOD, T J. 814

MINNESOTA (Cont'd)
ST PAUL (Cont'd)
William Mitchell Coll of Law   ANDERSON, E A. 22
                                 CHERRY, Anna M. 206
                                 MARION, Phyllis C. 770
                                 SATZER, Patricia A. 1084
ST PETER
Gustavus Adolphus Coll   ESSLINGER, Guenter W. . . . 355
                                 FISTER, Barbara R. 382
                                 HAEUSER, Michael J. 482
                                 HERVEY, Norma J. 533
                                 THORSTENSSON, Edith J. . . 1243
SPRING LAKE PARK
Independent Sch District 16   BURESH, Reggie F. 158
STAPLES
Staples High Sch   PRESTEBAK, Jane R. 991
THIEF RIVER FALLS
Lincoln High Sch   HOFSTAD, Alice M. 548
WILLMAR
Rice Memorial Hospital   CONRADI, Carol A. 238
Willmar Pub Sch District 347   PAULEY, Charles W. 950
WINONA
St Mary's Coll   MOXNESS, Mary J. 874
WORTHINGTON
Nobles County   SPILLERS, Roger E. 1174
Plum Creek Lib Syst   SCOTT, Thomas L. 1108

MISSISSIPPI
BAY ST LOUIS
US Navy   LOOMIS, Ann R. 740
BILOXI
Sun Herald Gulf Publishing Co   PUSTAY, Marilyn J. 998
BOONEVILLE
Booneville Sch System   BARAGONA, Lynn C. 55
BOYLE
Delta State Univ   BAHR, Edward R. 45
BROOKHAVEN
Lincoln Lawrence Franklin Regional
   Lib   LEDET, Henry J. 708
CARROLLTON
Carroll County Schools   NEILL, Laquita B. 892
CLARKSDALE
Clarksdale & Coahoma County   GRAVES, Sid F. 459
CLEVELAND
Bolivar County Lib   STEWART, Jeanne E. 1192
                                 WISE, Ronnie W. 1357
Delta State Univ   MACON, Myra 758
CLINTON
Mississippi Coll   HOWELL, John B. 565
                                 SMITH, Rachel H. 1159
COLUMBUS
Columbus Air Force Base   ZUMBERGE, Gloria A. 1391
Mississippi Univ for Women   PAYNE, David L. 951
GREENVALE
Washington County Lib System   SCHALAU, Robert D. 1089
GULFPORT
Mississippi Power Co   MCCREARY, Gail A. 800
HATTIESBURG
Forrest General Hospital   DUNCAN, Bettye M. 325
Hattiesburg Pub Lib System   SANFORD, Janice R. 1081
Univ of Southern Mississippi   BOYD, Sandra E. 123
                                 BOYD, William D. 123
                                 CARNOVALE, A N. 184
                                 DRAKE, Betty S. 318
                                 GRESSITT, Alexandra S. 467
                                 HARRIS, Ouida C. 505
                                 HAUTH, Allan C. 513
                                 JONES, Dolores B. 612
                                 KELLY, John M. 638
                                 LATOUR, Terry S. 701
                                 LAUGHLIN, Cheryl H. 703
                                 LAUGHLIN, Jeannine L. 703
                                 THOMPSON, Karolyn S. 1240
                                 VAN MELER, Vandelia L. . . 1276
                                 WILLIAMS, Eddie A. 1343
                                 WILSON, Mary S. 1352
                                 WITTIG, Glenn R. 1358
                                 YOUNG, Julia M. 1382

MISSISSIPPI (Cont'd)
HERNANDO
First Regional Lib ANDERSON, James F. 23
ROGERS, Margaret N. 1049
WARREN, Catherine S. 1306
WILROY, Joann 1349

INDIANAOLA
Sunflower County Lib POWELL, Anice C. 988
ITTA BENA
Mississippi Valley State Univ BOWEN, Ethel B. 120
JACKSON
Belhaven Coll ADAMS, Velma L. 6
Catholic Diocese of Jackson BOECKMAN, Frances B. 109
Department of Archives & History HILLIARD, Elbert R. 541
Jackson & Hinds Lib System BALLARD, Thomas H. 53
DUNAWAY, Charjean L. 325
Jackson State Univ GENTRY, Etherlene H. 427
SANDERS, Lou H. 1080
Millsaps Coll PARKS, James F. 943
Mississippi Baptist Medical Center BELL, Cecelia L. 76
Mississippi Coll MCMILLAN, Carnette R. 815
WEST, Carol C. 1326
Mississippi Dept of Archives and
History HENNEN, Earl M. 528
Mississippi Lib Association BELL, Bernice 76
Mississippi Lib Commission WOODBURN, David M. 1366
Reformed Theological Seminary REID, Thomas G. 1019
Univ of Mississippi SELTZER, Ada M. 1114
KEESLER AFB
US Air Force FREEDMAN, Jack A. 400
KOSCIUSKO
Mid-Mississippi Regional Lib System RODICH, Nancy A. 1048
LAUREL
Lauren Rogers Museum of Art CLARK, Diane E. 216
LIBERTY
Liberty High Sch BURKS, Alvin L. 161
LONG BEACH
Univ of Southern Mississippi BECK, Allisa L. 71
WILTSE, Elaine E. 1353
LUCEDALE
Jackson-George Regional Lib SMITH, Janet E. 1155
MERIDIAN
Meridian Junior Coll JOHNSON, Scott R. 609
RAINWATER, Mark T. 1004
Meridian Pub Lib MACNEILL, Daniel S. 758
MISSISSIPPI STATE
Mississippi State Univ BRELAND, June M. 132
CHRESSANTHIS, June D. .. 211
WELLS, Anne S. 1322
NATCHEZ
Natchez-Adams Pub Schs RANDAZZO, Corinne O. ... 1006
PASCAGOULA
Jackson-George Regional Lib System MAJURE, William D. 762
PEARL
Central Mississippi Regional Lib
System JOHNSON, Max C. 607
PONTOTOC
Dixie Regional Lib System HART, Julie C. 507
WILLIS, Jan L. 1348
PRENTISS
South Mississippi Regional Lib
System SMITH, Judy S. 1156
RAYMOND
Hinds Junior Coll MYRICK, Judy C. 885
WALL, Norma F. 1297
RIDGELAND
Holmes Junior Coll RICE, Joyce I. 1027
STARKVILLE
Mitchell Memorial Lib ELLSBURY, Susan H. 345
Oktibbeha County Pub Libs Syst NETTLES, Jess 896
TOUGALOO
Jackson State Univ MOMAN, Orthella P. 854
UNIVERSITY
Univ of Mississippi BUTLER, James C. 166
COCHRAN, J W. 225
FISHER, Benjamin F. 380
GRAVES, Gail T. 459
HARPER, Laura G. 503
STEEL, Suzanne F. 1183
TUCKER, Ellis E. 1261

MISSISSIPPI (Cont'd)
UNIVERSITY (Cont'd)
Univ of Mississippi
VERICH, Thomas M. 1282
WHITE, Elaine R. 1331
VICKSBURG
St Mary Jacqueline Tarrant BATTAGLIA, Mary H. 64
US Army ABLES, Timothy D. 2
US Army Corps of Engineers BLACK, Bernice B. 101
KIRBY, Donald J. 654
Warren County-Vicksburg Pub Lib MITCHELL, Deborah S. 848

MISSOURI
BOLIVAR
Southwest Baptist Univ VAN BLAIR, Betty A. 1272
Southwest Regional Lib KAISER, Patricia L. 622
BOONVILLE
Boonville Correctional Center JOB, Rose A. 601
BRIDGETON
DePaul Health Center LANEMAN, Joan A. 695
BUTLER
Butler R-V Sch District FISHER, Georgeann 381
CAMDEN POINT
Mid-Continent Pub Lib AMOS, Billie E. 20
CAPE GIRARDEAU
Cape Girardeau Pub Lib MAXWELL, Martha A. 788
Lutheran Family & Childrens Services STIEGEMEYER, Nancy H. ... 1193
Southeast Missouri State Univ BUIS, Edmund L. 156
CHESTERFIELD
Logan Coll of Chiropractic BUHR, Rosemary E. 156
Parkway Sch District NOBLE, Barbara N. 906
COLUMBIA
Columbia Daily Tribune SUMMERS, Janice K. 1209
Columbia Pub Schs FUCHS, Curt R. 408
WERNER, Laura L. 1325
Daniel Boone Regional Lib ANDREWS, Mark J. 27
BELCHER, Nancy S. 76
MARTIN, Mason G. 777
MILLSAP, Gina J. 844
WATERS, Bill F. 1308
Ellis Fischel State Cancer Center O'DELL, Charles A. 916
Mid-Missouri Lib Network RAITHEL, Frederick J. 1004
Missouri Lib Association MCCARTNEY, Jean A. 794
Natl Fisheries Contaminant Research
Ctr HINDMAN, Axie A. 542
State Historical Society of Missouri TUCKWOOD, Jo A. 1262
US Fish & Wildlife Service MULTER, Ell P. 878
Univ of Missouri at Columbia ALBRITTON, Rosie L. 10
ALLCORN, Mary E. 14
ALMONY, Robert A. 17
ARCHER, Stephen M. 31
BARNES, Everett W. 57
BHULLAR, Pushpajit D. 93
BREWER, O J. 134
CARROLL, C E. 187
DEL CASTILLO, Mireya 289
DEWEESE, June L. 298
ELS, Nancy T. 346
FAIR, Norma J. 361
GULSTAD, Wilma B. 477
HAVENER, Ralph S. 513
HOWELL, Margaret A. 565
HUFFMAN, Robert F. 571
JOHNSON, E D. 604
KOPP, Kurt W. 671
LENOX, Mary F. 715
LUH, Ming 747
MACEWAN, Bonnie J. 755
MCKININ, Emma J. 811
MITCHELL, Joyce A. 849
MYERS, Victor C. 885
PALLARDY, Judy S. 935
PARKER, Ralph H. 942
POWELL, Ronald R. 988
RACINE, John D. 1001
RICKERSON, George T. ... 1031
RIKLI, Arthur E. 1034
RILEY, Ruth A. 1034
SHAUGHNESSY, Thomas
W. 1123

MISSOURI (Cont'd)

COLUMBIA (Cont'd)
Univ of Missouri at Columbia

SHIRKY, Martha H.	1131
STEVENS, Robert R.	1191
STEVENSON, Marsha J.	1191
TIMBERLAKE, Patricia P.	1245
WADE, D J.	1290
WINJUM, Roberta J.	1355

EXCELSIOR SPRINGS
Excelsior Springs Sch District 40 — HOOVER, Jonnette L. 557

FAYETTE
Central Methodist Coll — HOCHSTETLER, Donald D. ... 545

FENTON
Maritz Inc — DEKEN, Jean M. 288

FLORISSANT
St Louis Preparatory Seminary North — LAWS, Janet E. 705

FULTON
Ovid Bell Press Inc — BELL, Ovid H. 77

HARRISONVILLE
Cass County Pub Lib — FRANKLIN, Jill S. 397

INDEPENDENCE
Independence Regional Health Center — VOSS, Kathryn J. 1289

Mid-Continent Pub Lib
HENRY, Peggy L.	529
MEYERS, Martha L.	831
MORALES, Milton F.	862
STEELE, Anitra T.	1184

National Archives & Records Admin
BRILEY, Carol A.	136
CURTIS, George H.	267

Temple Sch — HALLIER, Sara J. 489

JEFFERSON CITY
Coordinating Board for Higher Education
BEHLER, Patricia A.	74
MOORE, Barbara S.	858

Missouri Department of Health — TORDOFF, Brian G. 1251

Missouri State Lib
HIGHTOWER, Monteria	538
MILLER, Richard T.	841
PARKES, Darla J.	942
WATSON, Janice D.	1309

Office of the Secretary of State — BEAHAN, Gary W. 68

Thomas Jefferson Lib System
ATHY, Doris J.	37
READING, Barbara A.	1012

JOPLIN
Missouri Southern State Coll
CONNORS, Theresa	238
KEMP, Charles H.	639
NODLER, Charles E.	906
REIMAN, David A.	1020

Ozark Christian Coll — ABERNATHY, William F. 2

Post Foundation — SIMPSON, Leslie T. 1142

KANSAS CITY
American Family Records Association — KARNS, Kermit B. 627

Church of the Nazarene Headquarters — INGERSOL, Robert S. 582

Consolidated Sch District 1 — HARTMAN, Linda C. 508

Family Health Foundation of America
CRAIG, Marian D.	254
GIBSON, Patricia A.	432
RUBY, Carolyn M.	1065

Farmland Industries Inc — HUDSON, Rosetta A. 570

Glenn Books Inc — GLENN, Ardis L. 441

Gospel Missionary Union — JACOBS, Mildred H. 589

Hallmark Communications — KOE, Bruce G. 667

Harry S Truman Lib Institute — OLSON, James C. 922

Kansas City Art Institute — GAMER, May L. 416

Kansas City Pub Lib
BRADBURY, Daniel J.	125
BRETING, Elizabeth C.	133
HAMMOND, John J.	493
HANSEN, Charles A.	497
PARMENTER, Julie	943
TOMS, Merrill F.	1250

Linda Hall Lib
COX, Bruce B.	253
MARTIN, Louis E.	777
PETERSON, Paul A.	964

Lutheran High Sch of Kansas City — BOETTCHER, Joel W. 110

Metropolitan Community Coll — NELSON, Freda H. 893

Mid-Continent Pub Lib — PLUMB, Warren G. 978

Midwest Research Institute
CARSON, Bonnie L.	188
DRAYSON, Pamela K.	318

Morris Larson King and Stamper — GINGRICH, Linda K. 437

National Assn of Insurance Commissioners
GINDRA, Janice J.	437
SHIPLEY, Anne C.	1131

MISSOURI (Cont'd)

KANSAS CITY (Cont'd)
Nazarene Theological Seminary	MILLER, William C.	843
Nelson-Atkins Museum of Art	HESS, Stanley W.	534
	MEIZNER, Karen L.	822
North Kansas City Sch District	HAWKINS, Marilyn J.	514
Nursing Heritage Foundation	LINEBACH, Laura M.	730
Park Coll	SMITH, Harold F.	1155
Park Hill K-5 Sch District	GARDNER, Laura L.	418
Pembroke Hill Sch	ERICKSON, Anne E.	352
Polsinelli White Vardeman & Sheldon	KLEBBA, Lisa A.	658
Researcher's Data Bank	MARCHANT, Thomas O.	768
Rockhurst Coll	HUBBLE, Gerald B.	568
Rockhurst High Sch	DEACON, William W.	283
St Mary's Hospital	SERLING, Kitty	1116
St Paul's Episcopal Day Sch	AYLWARD, Judith A.	43
Shook Hardy & Bacon	HIBBELER, Sara J.	536
	HUNT, Lori A.	575
Stinson Mag & Fizzell	VIGLIATURO, Kristy	1284
Truman Medical Center East	DALTON, Richard R.	271
US General Services Administration	NESBITT, John R.	896
Univ of Missouri at Kansas City	BECK, Susan E.	71
	COURT, Patricia	251
	GERRITY, Marline R.	429
	HOHENSTEIN, Margaret L.	549
	LABUDDE, Kenneth J.	686
	LONDRE, Felicia H.	738
	SHELDON, Ted P.	1126
	SHIPLEY, Ruth M.	1131
	SPALDING, Helen H.	1171
	SULLIVAN, Marilyn G.	1208
Veterans Administration Medical Center	SMITH, Valerie K.	1161
Waddell & Reed Investment Management Co	HOWERTON, Betty J.	565

KIRKSVILLE
Kirksville Coll of Osteopathic Medicine	ONSAGER, Lawrence W.	924
Northeast Missouri State Univ	ELLEBRACHT, Eleanor V.	343
	LOCKHART, Carol A.	736
	OFSTAD, Odessa L.	917

KIRKWOOD
Kirkwood R-7 Sch District	LEWIS, Marilee V.	723
St Joseph Hospital	SHIEH, Monica W.	1129

LEBANON
Kinderhook Regional Lib — CRAVENS, Vickie L. 256

LEE'S SUMMIT
Metropolitan Community Colls — SCHWAAB, Beverly J. 1103

LEXINGTON
Lexington RV Sch District — ROSS, Shirley D. 1059

LIBERTY
William Jewell Coll — KNAUSS, Bonnie S. 663

MARYVILLE
Northwest Missouri State Univ
HANKS, Nancy C.	496
MURPHY, Kathryn L.	880

MOBERLY
Missouri Training Center for Men	BEQUETTE, V L.	84
Moberly Area Junior Coll	DARST, Valerie	275

NEOSHO
Crowder Coll — SCHADE, Barbara L. 1088

NEVADA
Cottey Coll — KIEL, Becky 647

NORTH KANSAS CITY
North Kansas City Pub Lib — HARTMETZ, Walter J. 508

O'FALLON
St Charles City-County Lib District	RADGINSKI, Martha E.	1002
St Charles Community Coll	SANDERS, John B.	1080

PERRYVILLE
Perry County Sch District 32 — TUCKER, Phillip H. 1262

POPLAR BLUFF
John J Pershing Veterans Administration	AKIYAMA, Wilfrid S.	9
Poplar Bluff Pub Lib	BECKEMEIER, Dewayne R.	72

RICHMOND
Richmond R-XVI Sch District — WALKER, Patricia A. 1296

ROLLA
Univ of Missouri at Rolla
STAUTER, Mark C.	1183
STEWART, J A.	1192

SAINT ANN
St Louis County Lib — JANKU, Margaret M. 593

MISSOURI (Cont'd)

ST CHARLES

St Charles City-County Lib System	DILLARD, Bonita D.	303
Sch District of the City of St Charles	TERRY, Virginia W.	1232

SAINT JOSEPH

Heartland Health Systems	HUGHES, Joan L.	571
Heartland Hospital West	GARNER, Sherril	419
Rolling Hills Consolidated Lib	HUMEL, Joyce A.	573
Saint Joseph Pub Lib	ELLIOTT, Dorothy G.	344

ST LOUIS

Alpha Byte & Co	WEAVER, Nancy B.	1312
American Association of Orthodontists	GILTINAN, Celia E.	437
American Optometric Association	DRAPER, Linda J.	318
American Soybean Association	GIBSON, Marianne	432
Anheuser Busch Co Inc	LAURENSTEIN, Ann G.	703
	VOLLMAR, William J.	1288
Archdiocese of St Louis	BEDAN, Lucille D.	73
Arthur Andersen & Co	KETTERING, Marguerite L.	645
Cardinal Glennon Coll	GLADIEUX, Mary B.	439
Coburn Croft and Putzell	KISSANE, Mary K.	656
Concordia Historical Institute	BODLING, Kurt A.	109
	WOHLRABE, John C.	1359
Concordia Publishing House	BOBB, Barry L.	108
Deaconess Hospital	IGLAUER, Carol	581
DMA Aerospace Center	BICK, Barbara K.	94
	MECHANIC, Margaret A.	820
Episcopal Diocese of Missouri	REHKOPF, Charles F.	1017
Fontbonne Coll Lib	BAER, Eleanora A.	45
Gardner Advertising Co	FINGERS, Deborah L.	378
Greensfelder Hemker et al	GIBSON, Helen R.	432
Harris-Stowe State Coll	GUENTHER, Charles J.	475
	KNORR, Martin R.	665
	SHAPIRO, Marian S.	1121
Health Sciences Communications Assn	ELSESSER, Lionelle H.	346
Hellmuth Obata & Kassabaum	BAERWALD, Susan M.	45
Incarnate Word Academy	EIKEN, Mary A.	340
InfoQuest	REHKOP, Barbara L.	1017
Kenrick Seminary	PAGE, Jacqueline M.	934
Lashly Baer & Hamel PC	TEANEY, Carol R.	1229
Lewis & Rice Law Firm	WHITE, Cheryl L.	1330
The Lutheran Church Missouri Synod	SUELFLOW, August R.	1206
Maryville Coll	MCKEE, Eugenia V.	810
McDonnell Douglas Corp	PRESTON, Jenny	991
	TOLSON, Stephanie D.	1249
Missouri Baptist Hospital	RENFER, Melissa	1023
Missouri Botanical Garden	NYSTROM, Kathleen A.	913
	RILEY, Martha J.	1034
	WOLF, Constance P.	1360
Missouri Lib Network Cooperation	MERCANTE, Mary A.	825
Monsanto Co	BACKES, Lynn B.	44
	CHUNG, Carolyn	213
	GAFFEY, Mary V.	411
	GELINNE, Michael S.	426
	KLEIN, Regina D.	659
	WILKINSON, William A.	1340
National Archives & Records Admin	DEWAELSCHE, Thomas M.	297
Norcliff Thayer Inc	ALDRIDGE, Gloria J.	11
Normandy Sch District	COURTNEY, Marjorie S.	251
Our Lady of Sorrows Sch	WINKLER, Carol A.	1355
Parkway Sch District	MERRELL, Sheila J.	826
Popkin & Stern	COSTELLO, Elaine	249
Principia Coll	FABIAN, William M.	360
Ralston Purina Co	SUTTER, Mary A.	1211
St John's Mercy Medical Center	BRENNER, Saundra H.	133
St Louis Art Museum	BETH, Dana L.	92
	SIGALA, Stephanie C.	1137
St Louis Board of Education	DOSS, Mamie	313
St Louis County Lib	DELIVUK, John A.	289
	GAERTNER, Donell J.	411
	SCHRAMM, Betty V.	1099
St Louis Metropolitan Police Dept	MIKSICEK, Barbara L.	834
St Louis Post-Dispatch	BROWN, Gerald D.	144
St Louis Pub Lib	GANYARD, Margaret E.	416
	LYONS, A J.	753
	MCKAY, Micheal W.	810
	REINHOLD, Edna J.	1021
	ROBERTS, Jean A.	1040
	SMITH, Nancy M.	1159
	WATTS, Anne	1310

MISSOURI (Cont'd)

ST LOUIS (Cont'd)

St Louis Regional Lib Network	TAYLOR, Arthur R.	1226
St Louis Univ	AGUILAR, Barbara S.	8
	AMELUNG, Richard C.	19
	ELAM, Kristy L.	341
	GALLAGHER, Kathy E.	414
	HEISER, W C.	523
	JOSEPH, Miriam E.	617
	MCKENZIE, Elizabeth M.	811
	MESSERLE, Judith R.	828
	MILLES, James G.	843
	MOODY, Carol A.	857
	NORTH, Daniel L.	909
	PLUTCHAK, T S.	979
	SEARLS, Eileen H.	1110
	TAYLOR, Carolyn L.	1226
Sisters of Mercy of St Louis	DEMUTH, Elizabeth J.	291
Sisters of St Joseph of Carondelet	DEUTSCH, N E.	297
	KELLY, Patricia J.	638
Southwestern Bell Corp	FORD, Gary E.	389
	MASHBURN, Ray	780
Spectrum Emergency Care	MUETH, Elizabeth C.	875
The Sporting News	GIETSCHIER, Steven P.	433
Thompson & Mitchell	HOLSTEN, Terri L.	554
Union Electric Co	GATLIN, Patricia F.	422
	VERBECK, Alison F.	1282
US Army	TIPSWORD, Thomas N.	1246
US Court of Appeals	FESSENDEN, Ann T.	374
	JUNG, Mary K.	620
US Courts	GREGORY, Kirk	466
Univ of Missouri at St Louis	CANN, Cheryle J.	178
	PERSHE, Frank F.	961
Utlas International US Inc	HANIFORD, K L.	496
Veterans Administration Medical Center	REPETTO, Ann M.	1023
	WEITKEMPER, Larry D.	1320
Villa Duchesne Sch	BREIMEIER, Lois	132
Washington Univ	ALLEN, Ronald	16
	ANDERSON, Paul G.	25
	BALACHANDRAN, Sarojini	50
	BECK, Sara R.	71
	BURCKEL, Nicholas C.	158
	CHAN, Jeanny T.	199
	CRAWFORD, Susan Y.	257
	EWING, Jerry L.	359
	FEDDERS, Cynthia S.	367
	FOX, Judith A.	395
	FRISSE, Mark E.	405
	GODT, Carol	443
	HALBROOK, Barbara	485
	HALL, Holly	487
	HELMS, Mary E.	525
	HUESTIS, Jeffrey C.	570
	KANAFANI, Kyung C.	624
	LEWIS, Ruth E.	724
	MCDERMOTT, Margaret H.	802
	MCFARLAND, Robert T.	805
	NELSON, Mary A.	894
	REAMS, Bernard D.	1013
Webster Univ	CARGAS, Harry J.	181

ST PETERS

St Charles City-County Lib District	HICKS, James M.	537
	SANDSTEDT, Carl R.	1081

SPRINGFIELD

Drury Coll	SINCLAIR, Regina A.	1143
General Council of the Assemblies of God	WARNER, Wayne E.	1305
Noble Communications	CARTER, Steva L.	190
St John's Regional Health Center	CRABTREE, Anna B.	254
Southwest Missouri State Univ	COOMBS, James A.	241
	FREEMAN, C L.	400
	GREEN, Walter H.	463
	HOWELLS, Joyce W.	565
	KOTAMRAJU, Sarada	673
	MACKEY, Neosha A.	756
	MALTBY, Florence H.	764
	MCCROSKEY, Marilyn J.	800
	MEADOR, John M.	819
	STEWART, Byron	1192

MISSOURI (Cont'd)
SPRINGFIELD (Cont'd)
Springfield-Greene County Lib   DROSS, Polly C. 320
   DUCKWORTH, Paul M. 322
   GLEASON, Virginia L. 440
   GLENN, Michael D. 441
   LEITLE, Barbara K. 714
   SANDERS, Jan W. 1080
   SMITH, Jewell 1156
UNION
East Central Coll   PARKS, Gary D. 943
WARRENSBURG
Central Missouri State Univ   GILBERT, Ophelia R. 434
   HELMICK, Aileen B. 525
   HUND, Flower L. 574
   NIEMEYER, Mollie M. 903
   SADLER, Philip A. 1073
   SCHELL, Rosalie F. 1091
   SLATTERY, Charles E. 1148
   WALKER, Stephen R. 1296
   WHITE, D J. 1330
WEBSTER GROVES
Webster Groves Pub Lib   BLANKENSHIP, Phyllis E. ... 104
Webster Groves Sch District   DOBRUNZ, Sally J. 307
   SMITH, Sharon M. 1160
   WEISENFELS, Marjorie A. ... 1319

MONTANA
BILLINGS
Bureau of Land Management   KOCH, Patricia J. 667
Eastern Montana Coll   HAUSE, Aaron H. 512
   NERODA, Edward W. 895
Parmly Billings Lib   NEWBERG, Ellen J. 898
BOZEMAN
Grand Ave Christian Church   FREEMAN, Lucile 401
Montana State Univ   ALLDREDGE, Noreen S. 14
   BRANDON, Janice R. 128
   BREMER, Thomas A. 132
   BRUWELHEIDE, Janis H. ... 151
   KAYA, Kathryn A. 632
   MORTON, Bruce 870
   STACK, Laurie A. 1177
   STEPHENS, Marian G. 1188
BROWNING
US Government   SPOTTED EAGLE, Joy 1175
BUTTE
Montana Coll of Mineral Sci and Tech   HUYGEN, Michaele L. 580
Montana Lib Association   MAXWELL, Lawrence 788
GREAT FALLS
Coll of Great Falls   LEE, Susan M. 711
Great Falls Pub Lib   O'BRYANT, Alice A. 915
Great Falls Pub Schs District 1   WILLIAMSON, Phyllis B. ... 1348
HAVRE
Havre-Hill County Lib   RITTER, Ann L. 1036
HAYS
St Paul's Indian Grade Sch   HARTMANN, M C. 508
HELENA
Lewis & Clark Lib   SCHLESINGER, Deborah L. 1094
Montana Historical Society   CLARK, Robert M. 218
   HIBPSHMAN, Lawrence 536
   MORROW, Delores J. 869
Montana Office of Pub Instruction   BERGERON, Cheri Y. 86
Montana State Lib   CATES, Sheila A. 195
   PARKER, Sara A. 942
Shodair Children's Hospital   HOLT, Suzy 554
State Law Lib of Montana   GRASMICK, Brenda 458
   MEADOWS, Judith A. 819
KALISPELL
Kalispell Regional Hospital   LONG, Susan S. 740
MILES CITY
Miles City Unified Sch District   STERLING, Linda L. 1189
MISSOULA
Missoula County   WYNNE, Tia J. 1375
Tamarack Federation of Libs   SCHMIDT, Theodore A. 1096
Univ of Montana   CHANDLER, Devon 199
   DRIESSEN, Karen C. 320
   OELZ, Erling R. 917
   PATRICK, Ruth J. 947
   SCHUSTER, Bonnie H. 1103
   VANHORNE, Geneva T. ... 1275

NEBRASKA
BEATRICE
Media Resource Center   DUX-IDEUS, Sherrie L. 330
BELLEVUE
Bellevue Pub Schs   KEEFE, Betty 634
City of Bellevue   JACKA, David C. 586
Eastern Lib System   BERNER, Karen J. 88
BLAIR
Dana Coll   PETERSON, Vivian A. 964
CHADRON
Chadron Pub Schs   HAMMITT, Margaret R. 493
Chadron State Coll   BRENNAN, Terrence F. 133
   SHRADER, Juanita J. 1133
COLUMBUS
Columbus City Schs   TAYLOR, Joie L. 1227
CRETE
City of Crete   HARDING, Margaret A. 500
FREMONT
Midland Lutheran Coll   BOYLE, Thomas E. 124
HASTINGS
Hastings Coll   GARDNER, Charles A. 417
Hastings Pub Lib   REA, Linda M. 1012
KEARNEY
Kearney Pub Lib & Information
   Center   NORMAN, Ronald V. 909
Kearney State Coll   MAYESKI, John K. 790
KIMBALL
Kimball Grade Schs   DATUS, Marie B. 275
LINCOLN
Bryan Memorial Hospital   ECHOLS, Susan P. 334
Ecumenical Music & Liturgy Resource
   Lib   BARRICK, Judy H. 59
Lincoln City Libs   DOW, Carolyn E. 315
   FELTON, John D. 370
Lincoln Telephone Co   CARNES, Mary J. 183
Nebraska Legislative Council   SLOAN, Patricia K. 1149
Nebraska Lib Commission   ALLEN, Richard H. 16
   KOPISCHKE, John 671
   MUNDELL, Jacqueline L. 878
   NAUGLE, Gretchen R. 889
   WAGNER, Rod G. 1292
Nebraska State Historical Society   DANIELS, Sherrill F. 273
   PAUL, Andrea I. 949
Nebraska Wesleyan Univ   LU, Janet C. 745
Olan Mills Portrait Studios   SCHUSTER, Mary F. 1103
Union Coll   NESMITH, Edmund D. 896
Univ of Nebraska at Lincoln   COOK, Anita I. 239
   FROBOM, Jerome B. 405
   HENDRICKSON, Kent H. 527
   HERZINGER, Sandra S. 534
   JOHNSON, Judy L. 606
   LANE, Alice L. 694
   LEITER, Richard A. 714
   LOGAN-PETERS, Kay E. 737
   SARTORI, Eva M. 1083
   STRIMAN, Brian D. 1202
   TIBBITS, Edith J. 1243
   WISE, Sally H. 1357
   WOMACK, Sharon K. 1362
   WOOL, Gregory J. 1368
Woodmen Accident & Life Co   SLOAN, Virgene K. 1150
MCCOOK
McCook Community Coll   RUBY, Irple P. 1065
MINATARE
Minatare Pub Schs   JOHNSON, Elizabeth L. 604
NORFOLK
Norfolk Pub Lib   HANWAY, Wayne E. 499
Northeast Technical Community Coll   WARNER, Karen R. 1305
OFFUTT AFB
US Air Force   SAUER, Mary L. 1084
OMAHA
Baird Holm McEachen Pedersen et al   LOMAX, Anne M. 738
City of Council Bluffs   BERNARDI, John V. 88
Creighton Univ   GRABE, Lauralee F. 455
   LEBEAU, Chris 707
   MEANS, Raymond B. 820
   MURDOCK, Douglas W. 879
Douglas County District Court   GENDLER, Carol J. 426
Kutak Rock & Campbell   FORSMAN, Avis B. 391
Mercy High School   REDDING, Kathleen A. 1013

NEBRASKA (Cont'd)
OMAHA (Cont'd)
Metropolitan Technical Community
  Coll   MARSH, Paul W. 773
Midcontinental Regnl Medical Lib
  Program   EARLEY, Dorothy A. 332
Millard Pub Schs   HOOVER, Clara G. 557
Northwestern Bell   BARTON, Laurel 62
Omaha Pub Lib   BIALAC, Verda H. 93
     KUBICK, Dan P. 682
     PHIPPS, Michael C. 969
     STEPHENS, Ann E. 1187
Omaha Pub Schs   CRAWFORD-ROSE,
       Kathleen J. 257
     LITTLE, Nina M. 733
     SJURSON, Gail M. 1145
Omaha World-Herald   PARISOT, Beverly J. 940
St James/Seton Elementary Sch   BENDA, Constance M. 79
Sisters of Mercy of the Omaha
  Providence   TURNER, Dorothea 1264
Union Pacific Railroad   OYER, Kenneth E. 932
Univ of Nebraska at Omaha   BOYER, Janice S. 123
     BROWN, Helen A. 144
     DICKSON, Laura K. 301
     FAWCETT, Georgene E. 367
     HASELWOOD, Eldon L. 510
     NEWCOMER, Audrey P. 898
     REIDELBACH, John H. 1019
     RUNYON, Robert S. 1067
     TOLLMAN, Thomas A. 1249
     WILLIS, Dorothy B. 1348

PAPILLION
Papillion-La Vista High Sch   ZANARINI, Linda S. 1386
SCOTTSBLUFF
Scottsbluff Pub Lib   OLTMANNS, Judith A. 923
SEWARD
Concordia Coll   MEIER, Marjorie A. 821
WAYNE
Wayne State Coll of Nebraska   EGBERS, Gail L. 339
     KENDRA, William E. 640
YORK
Kilgore Memorial Lib   SCHULZ, Stanley D. 1102
York Coll   VAN BAUCOM, Charles ... 1272

NEVADA
BOULDER CITY
Clark County Sch District   KEENE, Richard R. 634
     KEENE, Roberta E. 634
CARSON CITY
Carson-Tahoe Hospital   STURM, H P. 1205
Nevada State Lib & Archives   KERSCHNER, Joan G. 644
Nevada Supreme Court   DION, Kathleen L. 305
     SOUTHWICK, Susan A. ... 1170
State of Nevada   ROCHA, Guy L. 1045
ELKO
Elko County Lib   MADSEN, Carol 759
ELY
White Pine County Pub Lib   GRAY, Robert G. 460
HAWTHORNE
Walker-Wassac Art Alliance   PIERCE, Mildred L. 971
HENDERSON
Henderson District Pub Lib   CLARK, Janet L. 217
INCLINE
Washoe County Sch District   OSSOLINSKI, Lynn 928
LAS VEGAS
CER Corp   JACKSON, Ella J. 587
City of Las Vegas   ORTIZ, Diane 927
Clark County Lib District   MOUJAES, Sylva S. 873
Clark County Sch District   GROSSHANS, Merilyn P. ... 473
Inst of Advanced Law Study   KADANS, Joseph M. 621
Las Vegas-Clark County Lib District   BATSON, Darrell L. 64
     CUTLER, Marsha L. 268
     DAVENPORT, Marilyn G. ... 275
     GARDNER, Jack I. 418
     HUNSBERGER, Charles W. . 574
     LANGEVIN, Ann T. 695
     LAUB, Mary M. 702
     MORGAN, James E. 864
     TRASATTI, Margaret S. ... 1254
     VOIT, Irene E. 1287

NEVADA (Cont'd)
LAS VEGAS (Cont'd)
Las Vegas-Clark County Lib District
     WELLS, David B. 1322
Nevada State Museum & Historical
  Society   CAROLLO, Michael T. 184
Reynold Electrical & Engineering Co
  Inc   ORTIZ, Cynthia 927
Univ Medical Center of Southern
  Nevada   JONYNAS, Aldona I. 616
Univ of Nevada at Las Vegas   CLARK, Camille S. 216
     COVINGTON, Robert D. 252
     CURLEY, Elmer F. 265
     DEACON, Mary D. 283
     HEATON, Shelley J. 519
     POLSON, Billie M. 982
     SAUNDERS, Laverna M. ... 1084
MINDEN
Douglas County Lib   STURM, Danna G. 1205
NORTH LAS VEGAS
Clark County Community Coll   MASTALIR, Janet K. 782
RENO
Desert Research Institute   SMITH, Shirley M. 1161
Nevada Bell   BANTZ, K J. 55
     COWARD, J P. 252
     DAVID, B J. 276
     EPIFANI, R I. 351
     HANSEN, E G. 497
     HILL, D L. 539
     HOPKINS, Lloyd T. 558
     MATHSON, L J. 784
     MITCHELL, R G. 849
     ORIEN, C G. 925
     PIERSON, S M. 972
     STEWART, J W. 1192
     VAN ALLEN, R K. 1271
Nevada Sch of Law of Old Coll   MCNEAL, Betty 816
Reno Gazette-Journal   SPINA, Nan H. 1175
St Mary's Hospital   PRATT, Kathleen L. 990
Truckee Meadows Community Coll   COONEY, Mata M. 242
Univ of Nevada at Reno   BLESSE, Robert E. 105
     BUTLER, Barbara C. 166
     CONWAY, Susan L. 239
     DONOVAN, Ruth H. 312
     GREFRATH, Richard W. 465
     NEWMAN, Linda P. 899
     OTERO-BOISVERT, Maria .. 930
     PARKHURST, Carol A. 942
     RICE, Dorothy F. 1027
     ZENAN, Joan S. 1387
     ZINK, Steven D. 1389
Washoe County Lib   GOULD, Martha B. 454
     MANLEY, Charles W. 765
SPARKS
Washoe County Sch District   ZINK, Lois C. 1389

NEW HAMPSHIRE
AMHERST
New England Lib Association   RUPERT, Mary A. 1068
CHESTER
White Pines Coll   GAVRISH, Diane L. 423
CONCORD
Concord Sch District   KENT, Jeffrey A. 642
Franklin Pierce Law Center   LANDAU, Cynthia R. 692
New Hampshire State Lib   HIGGINS, Matthew J. 538
     JOHNSON, Jean G. 605
     MCDONOUGH, Kathleen C. . 803
     RINDEN, Constance T. 1035
     RYAN, Clare E. 1070
     WHITTIER, Ruth E. 1334
New Hampshire Technical Institute   HARE, William J. 501
Northern Telecom Inc   NELSON, David W. 893
State of New Hampshire   MEVERS, Frank C. 829
CONTOOCOOK
Yankee Book Peddler   DUCHIN, Douglas 322
     NARDINI, Robert F. 888
DERRY
Derry Pub Lib   BISSETT, Claudia K. 100
     HARDSOG, Ellen L. 500

NEW HAMPSHIRE (Cont'd)
DOVER
City of Dover .... TREMBLAY, Carolyn B. 1255
DURHAM
Univ of New Hampshire .... FINLAY, J A. 378
                                     GRIFFITH, Joan C. 469
                                     HENNESSEY, Barry J. 528
                                     JACOBS, Gloria 589
                                     KAPOOR, Jagdish C. 626
                                     LANE, David M. 694
                                     REIK, Constance 1020
                                     TEBBETTS, Diane R. 1229
EXETER
Exeter Hospital Inc .... REED, Alice 1014
Phillips Exeter Academy .... THOMAS, Jacquelyn H. 1236
FARMINGTON
Farmington High Sch .... GAGNON, Ruth 412
HANOVER
Dartmouth Coll .... BROWN, Stanley W. 147
                                     CRANE, John G. 255
                                     CRONENWETT, Philip N. ... 260
                                     FINNEGAN, Gregory A. 378
                                     FISKEN, Patricia B. 382
                                     MORAN, William S. 862
                                     OTTO, Margaret A. 930
                                     REED, Barbara E. 1014
                                     WALLIN, Cornelia B. 1298
Dartmouth-Hitchcock Medical Center .. BUNDY, John F. 157
ISU Inc .... ROLETT, Virginia V. 1051
Spectra Inc .... LERNER, Frederick A. 717
HOLLIE
Hollis Social Lib .... SHERWOOD, Janet R. 1129
KEENE
Keene High Sch .... PERLUNGHER, Richard A. .. 959
Keene Pub Lib .... LESSER, Charlotte B. 718
                                     PERLUNGHER, Jane R. 959
Keene State Coll .... MADDEN, Robert J. 758
                                     VINCENT, Charles P. 1284
LEBANON
Mark Mitchell Associates .... MITCHELL, Mark B. 849
LONDONBERRY
The Tucker Co .... TUCKER, Richard B. 1262
MANCHESTER
Elliot Hospital .... REINGOLD, Judith S. 1021
Hillsborough County .... THOMPSON, Debra J. 1239
Manchester Historic Association ..... LESSARD, Elizabeth B. ... 718
McLane Graf Raulerson & Middleton
 PA .... GUEDEA, Elizabeth J. 475
New Hampshire Vocational Technl
 Coll .... COMEAU, Reginald A. 234
St Anselms Coll .... BERTHIAUME, Dennis A. 90
Sheehan Phinney Bass & Green .... LIZOTTE, Jeanette S. 735
Veterans Administration Medical
 Center .... MCGINNIS, Joan M. 806
MEREDITH
Meredith Pub Lib .... TORR, Lydia M. 1251
MERRIMACK
Digital Equipment Corp .... AHERN, Camille P. 8
                                     FERRIGNO, Helen F. 373
                                     KORBER, Nancy 671
                                     VORBEAU, Barbara E. 1289
Kollsman .... RICE, Gerald W. 1027
Merrimack Pub Lib .... MARSHALL, Margaret E. 774
MILFORD
Wadleigh Memorial Lib .... BRYAN, Arthur L. 151
NASHUA
Daniel Webster Coll .... BARRETT, Beth R. 59
                                     JACKSON, Patience K. 588
                                     KOZIKOWSKI, Derek M. 674
Digital Equipment Corp .... GRANT, Nancy A. 458
Nashua Pub Lib .... WARREN, Ann R. 1306
St Joseph Hospital .... NOFTLE, Dorothy B. 907
Sanders Associates .... BERLIN, Arthur E. 87
NEW LONDON
Colby-Sawyer Coll .... TATE, Joanne D. 1225
PEASE AFB
US Air Force .... HATHAWAY, Teresa M. 512

NEW HAMPSHIRE (Cont'd)
PETERBOROUGH
BYTE Information Exchange .... BOND, George 113
McGraw-Hill Inc .... PERRON, Michelle M. 960
Peterborough Town Lib .... GEISEL, Ann M. 425
                                     TIERNAN, Linda M. 1244
PITTSFIELD
Pittsfield Middle High Sch .... DRUKE-STICKLER, Janet A. .. 320
PLYMOUTH
Plymouth State Coll .... FITZPATRICK, Robert E. 383
                                     KIETZMAN, William D. 647
PORTSMOUTH
City of Portsmouth .... PRIDHAM, Sherman C. 993
Portsmouth Pub Lib .... LE BLANC, Charles A. 708
                                     MCCANN, Susan F. 794
RINDGE
Franklin Pierce Coll .... GRISWOLD, Esther A. 471
                                     STEARNS, Melissa M. 1183
SALEM
Salem School District 57 .... GRAZIER, Dorothy W. 460
Sch Administrative Unit 57 .... BLESH, Tamara E. 105
TWIN MOUNTAIN
New Hampshire State Lib .... PALMATIER, Susan M. 936
WINDHAM
Castle Junior Coll .... BRANSWELL, Sr M. 129
WOLFEBORO
Wolfeboro Pub Lib .... GEHMAN, Louise A. 425

NEW JERSEY
ABERDEEN
Rutgers Univ .... ESPOSITO, Margaret 354
ANNANDALE
Baker & Taylor .... SUDEKUM, Katharine 1206
Exxon Research & Engineering Co ..... JOHNSON, David K. 603
ATCO
Waterford Township Pub Lib .... MCADOO, Jannifer C. 792
ATLANTIC CITY
Atlantic City Free Pub Lib .... CROSS, Roberta A. 261
BASKING RIDGE
AT&T Bell Laboratories .... GOLDSMITH, Carol C. 446
                                     MCDERMOTT, Ellen 801
Bernards Township Lib .... JIULIANO, Margaret C. 600
Crum & Forster Insurance Co .... MACKINTOSH, Pamela J. ... 757
                                     THOMPSON, Melia M. 1240
Ridge High Sch .... MCNALLY, Mary J. 815
BAYONNE
Bayonne Pub Lib .... CHUNG, Hai C. 213
Free Pub Lib of Bayonne .... DAYETTE, Patricia E. 283
National Archives & Records Admin ... BUCKWALD, Joel 155
                                     KINAHAN-OCKAY, Mary ... 649
BELLEVILLE
Belleville Pub Lib .... BRYANT, David S. 152
                                     COHEN, Adrea G. 227
BERGENFIELD
Marathon Software & Services Inc .... SKROBELA, Katherine C. .. 1147
BERKELEY HEIGHTS
Berkeley Heights Pub Lib .... LIND, Judith Y. 728
Berkeley Heights Pub Schs .... WICHELMAN, Ruthann 1335
Free Pub Lib of Berkeley Heights .... COHEN, Susan K. 229
BERNARDSVILLE
Bernardsville Pub Lib .... BURDEN, Geraldine R. 158
BLAIRESTOWN
Blair Academy .... JOHNSON, Holly P. 605
BLOOMFIELD
Bloomfield Coll .... GILLAN, Dennis P. 435
Lummus Crest Inc .... CIARAMELLA, Mary A. 214
Schering-Plough Corp .... BLUMENTHAL, Sidney L. ... 107
                                     NOCKA, Jean A. 906
BOONTON
Olde Tyme Music Scene .... DONAHUE, Louise 310
BOUND BROOK
Union Carbide Corp .... KLEMM, Carol B. 660
BRIDGEWATER
Baker & Taylor .... CAPOOR, Asha 180
                                     LAREW, Christian K. 697
                                     ROMANASKY, Marcia C. ... 1052
                                     SANDLER, Gary D. 1081
                                     STEVENS, Sharon G. 1191
DC Pickett Associates .... PICKETT, Doyle C. 970
Somerset County Lib .... ADAMS, June B. 5

NEW JERSEY (Cont'd)

BURLINGTON
Lib Co of Burlington   ZULEWSKI, Gerald J. 1391
BURLINGTON COUNTY
Memorial Hospital of Burlington
     County   O'CONNOR, Elizabeth W. ... 916
BUTLER
Butler Pub Lib   GARDNER, Sue A. 418
CALDWELL
Caldwell Coll   HODGE, Patricia A. 546
     STICKEL, William R. 1193
Children's House Inc   EDELSON, Ken 335
CAMDEN
Camden Free Pub Lib   DILLENSCHNEIDER,
         Patricia A. 303
     WEST, Shirley L. 1326
Campbell Soup Co   KESSLER, Selma P. 645
Helene Fuld Sch of Nursing   SOME, Barbara K. 1166
Our Lady of Lourdes Medical Center   KAFES, Frederick W. 621
RCA Corp   ARROWOOD, Nina R. ... 35
Rutgers Univ   BECK, Susan J. 72
     CHAO, Gloria F. 201
     COFFEY, James R. 227
     SWARTZ, Betty J. 1214
Univ of Medicine & Dentistry of NJ   SKICA, Janice K. 1146
CAPE MAY COURT HOUSE
County of Cape May   HSU, Hsiu H. 567
CARNEYS POINT
Salem Community Coll   BRANAN, Julia D. 127
CEDAR GROVE
Township of Cedar Grove   LUEHS, Jeanne M. 747
CEDAR KNOLLS
Berlex Laboratories Inc   LINGELBACH, Lorene N. ... 730
     MILLINGTON, Kathleen A. ... 843
     SKIDANOW, Helene 1146
CHERRY HILL
Camden Catholic High Sch   BROWN, Anita P. 142
Cherry Hill Free Pub Lib   KUAN, Jenny W. 681
ISI   JUNKINS, Katherine V. 620
Televents Corp   GREEN, Donald T. 461
CINNAMINSON
Rutgers Univ   CRESCENZI, Jean D. 258
CLARK
Clark Pub Lib   CHAPIN, Joan R. 201
     JONES, Sandra K. 615
CLIFTON
American Cyanamid Co   AUGHEY, Kathleen M. 39
Clifton Pub Lib   CHAMBERLIN, Cynthia C. ... 198
CLOSTER
Closter Pub Lib   DLUGOS, Carolyn M. 306
     LUXNER, Ann F. 750
COLTS NECK
Monmouth County Lib   HIGGINS, Flora T. 537
CONVENT STATION
Coll of St Elizabeth   ROUSEK, Marie B. 1061
CRANBURY
Carter-Wallace Inc   URENECK, Dolores 1269
General Foods Corp   TAYLOR, Donna I. 1226
CRANFORD
Cranford Board of Education   GERMINDER, Robin L. 429
DELRAN
Datapro Research Corp   LOMBARDO, William J. 738
     SCHEPP, Brad J. 1091
DOVER
Dover General Hospital & Medical
     Center   RYAN, Mary C. 1071
DUMONT
Dixon Homestead Lib   SCHUELER, Frances S. ... 1101
Dumont Board of Education   MAYNES, Kathleen R. 790
Papazian Associates   PAPAZIAN, Pierre 939
EAST BRUNSWICK
East Brunswick Pub Lib   KARMAZIN, Sharon M. 627
     KHEEL, Susan T. 646
     STONE, Jason R. 1197
Jean Walling Civic Center   BERGER, Brenda L. 85
EAST HANOVER
Sandoz Pharmaceuticals   KOELLE, Joyce G. 667
EAST MILLSTONE
Exxon Biomedical Sciences Inc   DEDERT, Patricia L. 286
     SEAGER, Janice R. 1109

NEW JERSEY (Cont'd)

EAST ORANGE
East Orange Board of Education   SHEARES, Ora M. 1124
East Orange Pub Lib   EISEN, Marc M. 340
     IRGON, Deborah A. 583
     JONES, Dorothy S. 612
     MATHAI, Aleyamma 783
EDISON
Edison Board of Education   SCOTT, Mellouise J. 1107
Engelhard Corp   FEDORS, Maurica R. 368
     SOBIN, Maryann D. 1165
General Cable Co   DE WITT, Benjamin L. 298
The Library CO-OP Inc   DINERMAN, Gloria 304
Middlesex County Coll   MILLER, Mary A. 840
Mobil Chemical Co   GURNEY, Eileen A. 478
North Edison Pub Lib   CULLUM, Carolyn N. 263
Revlon Resrch Ctr   TANEN, Lee J. 1222
ELIZABETH
Elizabeth Board of Education   RICE, Anna C. 1026
Elizabeth General Medical Center   BOSS, Catherine M. 117
Elizabeth Pub Lib   DEMYANOVICH, Peter 291
     LATINI, Samuel A. 701
     SKRAMOUSKY, Mary C. 1147
Free Pub Lib of Elizabeth   BOLL, Charles K. 112
     SAWYCKY, Roman A. 1086
ELMWOOD PARK
Elmwood Park Pub Lib   GROSSBERG, Aileen D. 473
EMERSON
Emerson Pub Lib   SPOHN, Veronica G. 1175
ENGLEWOOD
City of Bayonne   HALASZ, Etelka B. 484
Englewood Hospital   LINDNER, Katherine L. 729
Englewood Pub Lib   HECHT, James M. 519
ENGLEWOOD CLIFFS
CPC International Inc   AVERILL, M S. 41
ENGLISHTOWN
Monmouth County Lib   BERGER, Morey R. 86
ESSEX FELLS
Essex Fells Board of Education   ROTSAERT, Stefanie C. ... 1060
FAIR LAWN
Maurice M Pine Free Pub Lib   NEDSWICK, Robert 891
FAIRFIELD
Fairfield Pub Lib   WROBLEWSKI, Christine .. 1373
Ogden Projects Inc   COLLISHAW, Jackie J. 233
Pat Guida Associates   GUIDA, Pat 476
FAR HILLS
US Golf Assn   SEAGLE, Janet M. 1109
FLEMINGTON
Hunterdon Central High Sch   ROSENBERG, Harlene Z. ... 1056
Hunterdon Medical Center   WHITE, Joyce G. 1331
FLORHAM PARK
Automatic Switch Co   GABBIANELLI, Patrice A. ... 411
Exxon Research & Engineering Co   BARRETT, Joyce C. 59
     CHAPMAN, Janet L. 202
     LAVIN, Margaret A. 703
Florham Park Pub Lib   BYOUK, Nancy K. 168
Lear Siegler Inc   SHAFER, Leona M. 1119
FORT DIX
US Army   MARCO, Guy A. 769
FORT LEE
Broadview Associates   GOLDSTEIN, Bernard 446
     POPPEL, Harvey 984
Fort Lee Pub Lib   ALTOMARA, Rita E. 18
On-Line Software International   HUTCHINS, Pearl G. 579
FORT MONMOUTH
Analytics Inc   HENKEL, Grace E. 528
US Army   MICHAL, Judith A. 832
FRANKLIN LAKES
Becton Dickinson & Co   CHANG, Bernadine A. 200
     DYKMAN, Elaine K. 331
     MENZUL, Faina 825
Franklin Lakes Board of Education   GOLDBERG, Barbara W. 444
FREEHOLD
Freehold Area Hospital   SIEGEL, Robin D. 1136
St Rose of Lima Sch   SCHUMACHER, Nancy C. .. 1102
GLASSBORO
Glassboro State Coll   GARRABRANT, William A. .. 420
     GAYNOR, William A. 424
     KENNEDY, Kathleen A. 641
     SZILASSY, Sandor 1218

NEW JERSEY (Cont'd)

GLEN GARDNER
North Hunterdon High Sch Dist — HONTZ, M E. 556
GLEN RIDGE
Glen Ridge Pub Lib — LOOS, Jean E. 740
GLEN ROCK
Glen Rock Pub Lib — FADLALLA, Gerald J. 361
GREEN VILLAGE
E F Keon Co — KEON, Edward F. 643
HACKENSACK
Fairleigh Dickinson Univ — MAROUSEK, Kathy A. 772
Johnson Free Pub Lib — OLSON, Marilyn A. 923
HACKETTSTOWN
Centenary Coll — ACKROYD-KELLY, Elaine S. 4
STEEN, Carol N. 1184
HADDONFIELD
Haddonfield Board of Education — GULICK, Eleanor L. 477
HAMILTON
Hamilton Township Free Pub Lib — HOOKER, Joan M. 556
Township of Hamilton — MEYER, Mary L. 830
HAMMONTON
South Jersey Regional Lib
   Cooperative — HYMAN, Karen D. 580
HARRISON
Dresser Industries Inc — SZE, Melanie C. 1218
HIGHLAND PARK
Highland Park Pub Lib — JONES, Dorothy C. 612
HILLSIDE
Bristol-Myers Products — BONDAROVICH, Mary F. ... 113
HOBOKEN
Stevens Institute of Technology — LUXNER, Dick 750
HOLMDEL
AT&T Bell Laboratories — CANOSE, Joseph A. 179
ENGLISH, Bernard L. 350
GRANT, George E. 458
LUNAS, Leslie K. 748
SPAULDING, Frank H. 1172
Prudential Property & Casualty
   Insurance — HENRY, Mary B. 529
HOPATCONG
Hopatcong Board of Education — FEAKINS, Lois S. 367
HOPEWELL
AT&T Bell Laboratories — ODERWALD, Sara M. 916
IRVINGTON
Irvington Pub Lib — MCCONNELL, Lorelei C. 797
Township of Irvington — BUTLER, Patricia M. 167
ISELIN
Fordham Univ — FRANTS, Valery 398
ISLAND HEIGHTS
Ocean County Lib — BELVIN, Carolyn J. 78
JACKSON
Jackson Board of Education — REGAN, Barbara M. 1017
JERSEY CITY
Block Drug Co Inc — LEICHTMAN, Anne B. 713
Christ Hospital — PANDELAKIS, Helene S. 937
VARGO, Katherine J. 1278
The Davey Co — BROOKS, Alfred C. 140
Jersey City Pub Lib — BRYANT, Judith W. 152
Jersey City State Coll — AUSTIN, Fay A. 40
St Peter's Coll — ROMANKO, Karen A. 1052
SCHUT, Grace W. 1103
Unz & Co — KAZIMIR, Edward O. 632
SCOTT, Daniel T. 1107
KEARNY
Joni L Cassidy Cataloguing Services — CASSIDY, Joni L. 193
KENILWORTH
Kenilworth Pub Lib — FLICK, Susan E. 385
LAKEWOOD
Bathgate Wegener Wouters &
   Newmann — ERBE, Evalina S. 352
Georgian Court Coll — HERBERT, Barbara R. 530
HUTCHINSON, Barbara J. ... 579
Lakewood Pub Lib — ANDERSON, Janelle E. 23
LAWRENCEVILLE
Rider Coll — MONTAVON, Victoria A. 855
STEPHEN, Ross G. 1187
TILLMAN, Hope N. 1245

NEW JERSEY (Cont'd)

LEONIA
Columbia Univ — DAIN, Phyllis 270
F W Faxon Co — CIMBALA, Diane J. 214
Leonia Board of Education — SHERMAN, Louise L. 1128
Leonia Pub Lib — PAWSON, Robert D. 951
LINCROFT
Brookdale Community Coll — ANTCZAK, Janice 28
EBELING, Elinor H. 334
KEARNEY, Jeanne E. 633
REESE, Carol H. 1016
VLOYANETES, Jeanne M. .. 1286
LINDEN
Linden Free Pub Lib — CANAVAN, Roberta N. 178
PISKORIK, Elizabeth 976
LITTLE FALLS
Berkeley Sch — RANDALL, Lynn E. 1006
Little Falls Pub Lib — SAWYER, Miriam 1086
LITTLE SILVER
Little Silver Pub Lib — EDWARDS, Susan M. 338
LIVINGSTON
Bell Communications Research — GLADSTONE, Mark A. 439
Free Pub Lib of Livingston — ROBERTS, Leila J. 1040
Newark Academy — MALLALIEU, Robert K. 763
LODI
Felician Coll — KARETZKY, Stephen 627
Lodi Memorial Lib — TAORMINA, Anthony P. ... 1223
LONG BRANCH
Monmouth Medical Center — PACHMAN, Frederic C. 933
LYNDHURST
Lyndhurst Pub Lib — BAYLESS, Bernie J. 67
PORTUGAL, Rhoda 985
MADISON
Drew Univ — BROCKMAN, William S. 138
COPELAND, Alice T. 244
COUGHLIN, Caroline M. 250
FERRIBY, Peter G. 373
FRIEDMAN, Ruth 404
JONES, Arthur E. 611
SNELSON, Pamela 1163
WANGGAARD, Janice H. .. 1303
Drew Univ Lib — CONNORS, Linda E. 238
Fairleigh Dickinson Univ — SOMMER, Ursula M. 1167
Madison Borough Pub Lib — POVILAITIS, Leanna J. 987
MAHWAH
Ramapo Coll of New Jersey — HEISE, George F. 522
YUEH, Norma N. 1384
MANALAPAN
Monmouth County Lib — FIELD, Jack 375
FIELD, Margaret 375
SMOTHERS, Joyce W. 1162
MAPLEWOOD
Maplewood Memorial Lib — BENNETT, Rowland F. 82
MARLTON
Burlington County Lib — KALDENBERG, Katherine A. . 622
Lenape Regional High Sch District — DONOHUE, Nancy W. 312
RMS Technologies Inc — SANDERS, Mary C. 1080
MAYS LANDING
Atlantic County Lib — CAPELLA, Jeanne M. 179
PAULLIN, William D. 950
MEDFORD
Learned Information Inc — BAKER, Rita 49
BILBOUL, Roger R. 96
HOGAN, Thomas H. 549
SMITH, Bev 1153
STARRETT, Mary J. 1182
Lenape Regional High Sch District
Shawnee High School — DOMINESKE, Alice M. 310
MENDHAM
Coll of St Elizabeth — MANTHEY, Carolyn M. 767
Record Collector's Monthly — MENNIE, Don 824
METUCHEN
Metuchen Board of Education — MASSEY, Eleanor N. 782
Metuchen High Sch — HIGGINS, Marilyn E. 538
Metuchen Pub Lib — WANG, Hsi H. 1303
Scarecrow Press — DAUB, Albert W. 275
HORROCKS, Norman 561
MIDDLETOWN
AT&T Bell Laboratories — RIHACEK, Karen S. 1034
Middletown Township Lib — WOLFORD, Larry E. 1361
Robert H Riley & Assocs — RILEY, Robert H. 1034

NEW JERSEY (Cont'd)
MONTCLAIR
Glenfield Middle Sch .... HOROWITZ, Marjorie B. 560
Grimm-McPherson & Associates .... MCPHERSON, Kenneth F. ... 817
Montclair Kimberly Academy .... GREENSPAN, Vivi S. 465
Montclair Pub Lib .... GORMAN, Audrey J. 452
.... STRICKLAND, Patricia J. .. 1202
Mountainside Hospital .... REGENBERG, Patricia B. .. 1017
.... WATKINS, Elizabeth A. 1309

MONTVALE
National Association of Accountants .. REDRICK, Miriam J. 1014
Peat Marwick Main & Co .... BILES, Mark J. 96
.... BRAIMON, Margie S. 127
.... LAUB, Barbara J. 702

MOORESTOWN
Capehart and Scatchard .... WILLIAMSON, Carol L. 1347
Danyl Corp .... MERKERT, Robert J. 826
MORRISTOWN
Allied Signal .... MASILAMANI, Mary P. 780
AT&T Bell Laboratories .... CLARK, Joan 217
.... ENGLISH, Christopher C. 350
.... IMPERIALE, Karen P. 582
.... JONES, Deborah A. 612
.... KAUFFMAN, Betty G. 631
.... PRAQ, Lora B. 989
.... SINGER, Susan A. 1143
AT&T Communications .... SCHRIMPE, Janice E. 1100
Bell Communications Research ...... BEDDES, Marianne T. 73
.... BUCK, Anne M. 153
.... SUNDAY, Donald E. 1210
County of Morris .... LYNN-NELSON, Gayle 752
Joint Free Pub Lib of Morristown .... DENSKY, Lois R. 293
Morris County Board of Realtors .... HODNETT, Diane M. 546
Morristown Memorial Hospital ...... SEARLE, Jo A. 1110
Riker Danzig Scherer Hyland &
    Perretti .... BRUNNER, Karen B. 151
MOUNT FREEDOM
Books Unlimited Inc .... YANNOTTA, Peter J. 1377
MOUNT HOLLY
Burlington County Audiovisual Aids
    Ctr .... RICHIE, Mark L. 1030
Burlington County Lib .... ALEY, Judy M. 12
.... CARR, Charles E. 185
.... CRAWFORD, Lynn D. 257
.... RILEY, Marie R. 1034
Married Mettle Press .... ALTERMAN, Deborah H. 18
MOUNTAIN LAKES
Dun & Bradstreet Corp .... AMICO, Robert 20
.... BARTOS, Phil 62
.... BLOOM, Robert 106
.... CLARK, Rick 218
.... COLEMAN, Peggy 231
.... DOLAN, Joseph 309
.... EUSTIS, Peter 356
.... HACKETT, William F. 481
.... HANEY, Kevin M. 495
.... HORNE, Stephen 560
.... ITZ, Richard A. 585
.... KAHOFER, Stephen O. 622
.... KONTOGOURIS, Venetia ... 671
.... KREINER, Joseph 677
.... MCCARTHY, Thomas M. ... 794
.... REISBERG, Gerald 1021
.... WILKENING, Barry 1339
.... WOODS, William 1367
Dun's Marketing Services .... PIKE, Christine M. 972
MOUNTAINSIDE
Aromat Corp .... CHANG, Joseph I. 200
Children's Specialized Hospital ...... GLASSER, Anne 440
MURRAY HILL
AT&T Bell Laboratories .... BALLARD, Bruce W. 53
.... BROWN, Ina A. 144
.... HAWKINS, Donald T. 514
.... LEVY, Louise R. 721
.... LEWIS, Dale E. 722
.... PEABODY, Kenneth W. 951
.... PENNIMAN, W D. 957
.... QUINN, Ralph M. 1000
.... STANTON, Robert O. 1181
.... STEPIEN, Karen K. 1189

NEW JERSEY (Cont'd)
MURRAY HILL (Cont'd)
AT&T Bell Laboratories
.... ZIMMERMAN, Elisabeth K. .. 1388
Dun & Bradstreet Corp .... DONAHUE, Delaine R. 310
Dun & Bradstreet Credit Services .. ALDEN, Pamela V. 11
.... MILGRIM, Martin S. 835
.... OLD, Forrest R. 920
.... ROTHMAN, Joan 1060

NEPTUNE
Jersey Shore Medical Center .... PALMISANO-DRUCKER,
.... Elsalyn 937

NEW BRUNSWICK
E R Squibb & Sons Inc .... MCLAUGHLIN, Dorothy M. .. 813
Rutgers Univ .... ANDERSON, James D. 23
.... ANSELMO, Edith H. 28
.... BARTZ, Stephanie 62
.... BECKER, Ronald L. 72
.... BEEDE, Benjamin R. 74
.... BEETHAM, Donald W. 74
.... CAPARROS, Ilona S. 179
.... CASSEL, Jeris F. 193
.... CHEN, Chiou S. 205
.... EDELMAN, Hendrik 335
.... EUSTER, Joanne R. 356
.... FETZER, Mary K. 374
.... GRAHAM, Peter S. 456
.... GREENBERG, Evelyn 463
.... HALL, Homer J. 488
.... HARDGROVE, David J. 499
.... KING, Donald R. 650
.... KUHLTHAU, Carol C. 682
.... LANGSCHIELD, Linda S. .. 696
.... LI, Marjorie H. 724
.... MAMAN, Marie 764
.... MILLER, Lynn F. 840
.... MILLER, Sarah J. 842
.... MOTT, Thomas H. 872
.... NASH, Stanley D. 888
.... NIGRIN, Albert G. 904
.... OTA, Leslie H. 930
.... POLACH, Frank 980
.... PUNIELLO, Francoise S. ... 997
.... REELING, Patricia S. 1016
.... RICHARDS, Pamela S. 1028
.... RUBEN, Brent D. 1064
.... SARACEVIC, Tefko 1082
.... SIMMONS, Ruth J. 1140
.... SMITH, Beryl K. 1153
.... SWARTZBURG, Susan G. .. 1214
.... TUROCK, Betty J. 1265
.... VANDERGRIFT, Kay E. 1274
.... VARLEJS, Jana 1278
.... WATSON, Marjorie O. 1310
.... WEISBROD, David L. 1319
.... WILSON, Myoung C. 1352

NEW MILFORD
New Milford Pub Lib .... WALSH, Carol J. 1299
NEW PROVIDENCE
FSI Archives of Recorded Sound .... GERBER, Warren C. 428
Martindale-Hubbell Inc .... PECON, Sally N. 953
NEWARK
Clapp & Eisenberg .... BORCHERT, Janis L. 116
New Jersey Bell Telephone .... FOSKO, Maureen E. 392
New Jersey Historical Society .... COLLINS, Sarah F. 233
.... MEYERS, Elsa M. 831
New Jersey Institute of Technology .. CALLANAN, Ellen M. 173
.... VAN FLEET, James A. 1275
Newark Pub Lib .... BEIMAN, Frances M. 75
.... BETANCOURT, Ingrid T. 92
.... CUMMINGS, Charles F. 264
.... DANE, William J. 272
.... HAWLEY, George S. 514
.... KAHN, Leslie A. 622
.... KNIGHT, Shirley D. 664
.... MILLER, Charles W. 836
.... REDLICH, Barry 1014
.... RUPPRECHT, Leslie P. 1068
.... SCHWARTZ, Lawrence C. .. 1104
.... SHEARIN, Cynthia E. 1124

NEW JERSEY (Cont'd)
NEWARK (Cont'd)
Pub Service Electric & Gas Co   KRUSE, Theodore H. 681
Pub Services Electric & Gas Co   HUNT, Florine E. 575
Robinson Wayne Levin Riccio & La
   Sala   FISHER, Scott L. 381
Rutgers Univ   AU, Ka N. 38
   AXEL-LUTE, Paul 42
   MULLINS, Lynn S. 878
   PROFETA, Patricia C. 995
   SCHRIEK, Robert W. 1100
   TIPTON, Roberta L. 1247
Seton Hall Univ   HERRERA, Deborah D. 532
Stryker Tams & Dill   SKYZINSKI, Susan E. 1147
United Hospitals Medical Center   GILHEANY, Rosary S. 434
   NAGELE, Nancy C. 886
Univ of Medicine & Dentistry of NJ   IRWIN, Barbara S. 584
   ROSENSTEIN, Philip 1057
   SMITH, Reginald W. 1159
   SPRUNG, George 1176

NEWTON
Sussex County Lib System   RAFFERTY, Stephen P. 1003
NORTH ARLINGTON
Queen of Peace Church   CASEY, Mary A. 192
NORTH BRUNSWICK
North Brunswick Township   THONER, Jane T. 1242
NUTLEY
Hoffmann-LaRoche Inc   CORRADO, Margaret M. 247
ITT Defense Communications   REISMAN, Rita C. 1021
OAKLAND
Oakland Pub Lib   HANNON, Patricia A. 497
Ramapo Indian Hills Board of
   Education   GOLLA, Viola K. 447
Witco Corp   SMITH, Jo T. 1156
OAKLYN
Oaklyn Memorial Lib   WILINSKI, Grant W. 1339
OCEAN CITY
Ocean City Free Pub Lib   MASON, Michael L. 781
OLD BRIDGE
Bond System   STAMP, Raymond T. 1179
ORADELL
Film Audio Services Inc   SUMMERS, Robert A. 1209
Medical Economics Co Inc   MCGILL, Thomas J. 806
Patient Care   O'CONNOR, Christine T. 916
ORANGE
Orange Pub Lib   LIN, Fumei C. 727
PALISADES PARK
Palisades Park Free Pub Lib   CHELARIU, Ana R. 204
   RANIERI, Bernice A. 1007
PARAMUS
Archdiocese of Newark   REINHARDT, Eileen 1021
ASKMAC   CESARD, Mary A. 196
BCCLS Computer Consortium   ROUX, Yvonne R. 1062
Bergen County Coop Lib Syst Comp
   Cnsrtm   WHITE, Robert W. 1332
Bergen Pines County Hospital   GONZALES, Victoria E. 448
Borough of Paramus   MOORE, Jean B. 860
Paramus Pub Lib   WELLSMAN, Jennifer A. . . . 1323
Prentice Hall Information Services   SATTIBENE, James 1084
Seagate Associates   GENTNER, Claudia A. 427
PARK RIDGE
Borough of Park Ridge   LINNAVUORI, Julie R. 731
PARLIN
Sayreville Board of Education   WEISBURG, Hilda K. 1319
PARSIPPANY
BASF Corp   VOGT, Herwart C. 1287
Dun & Bradstreet Corp   DITMARS, Robert D. 305
   LEHMKUHL, Charles 713
   PAIGE, Richard 935
   POLUSZNY, Joseph P. 982
   SIMON, David H. 1140
Dun's Marketing Services   BROWNE, Pat 148
Parsippany Troy Hills Pub Lib   WEINSTEIN, Judith L. 1318
TRINET Inc   HANRAHAN, Geane 497
   STRYKER, Charles W. 1203
PASSAIC
Passaic Board of Education   LOTZ, Marilyn R. 742
Passaic Pub Lib   SCHEAR, Thomas W. 1090
PATERSON
Paterson Free Pub Lib   BROWN, Linda M. 145

NEW JERSEY (Cont'd)
PAULSBORO
Mobil Research & Development Corp   BITTER, Jane L. 100
PEAPACK
Somerset County Lib   WHITING, Elaine M. 1333
PENNINGTON
Hopewell Valley Regional Sch District   PRIESING, Patricia L. 993
PENNSAUKEN
Camden County Vocational Technical
   Sch   GORDON, Muriel C. 451
PHILLIPSBURG
Ingersoll-Rand Co   SHINER, Sharon L. 1130
Phillipsburg Board of Education   ROMBERGER, Alice J. 1052
Phillipsburg Free Pub Lib   HESS, Jayne L. 534
PICATINNY ARSENAL
US Army   VARIEUR, Normand L. 1278
PISCATAWAY
Bell Communications Research   KAPLAN, Susan J. 626
   MILLER, Virginia L. 843
   MOONEY, Jennifer M. 858
   SCHNEIDER, Lynette C. . . . 1097
Janssen Pharmaceutica Inc   MONDSCHEIN, Lawrence
   G. 854
   SILVA, Nelly H. 1138
Linx Union Middlesex Regional Lib
   Coop   ROSENBERG, Gail L. 1056
Nuodex Inc   CARNAHAN, Joan A. 183
Piscataway Board of Education   MENINGALL, Evelyn L. 824
Piscataway Pub Lib   DEL GUIDICE, M R. 289
   SERPICO, Margaret A. 1116
Reed & Carnrick Pharmaceuticals   DUTKA, Jeanne L. 329
Rutgers Univ   BOYLE, Jeanne E. 124
   CALHOUN, Ellen 172
   DESS, Howard M. 295
   DYKEMAN, Amy 331
   GUSTAFSON, Ruth 478
   HOFFMAN, Helen B. 548
   NIPP, Deanna 904
   PAGE, Penny B. 934
   PIERMATTI, Patricia A. 972
   WEGLARZ, Catherine R. . . . 1316
PITMAN
Pitman Board of Education   PELLETIER, Karen E. 955
PLAINFIELD
Lockheed Electronics Co   GABRIEL, Linda 411
Plainfield Pub Lib   TUTWILER, Dorothea F. . . . 1266
Wardlaw-Hartridge Sch   KOLAYA, Margaret B. 669
PLAINSBORO
Plainsboro Free Pub Lib   KAMEN, Francine B. 623
PLEASANTVILLE
Atlantic Electric   LEVINE, Riesa E. 721
POMONA
Stockton State Coll   GARZILLO, Robert R. 421
   MOLL, Joy K. 853
PORT MURRAY
Piano Research Association   YRIGOYEN, Robert P. 1384
PRINCE
Educational Testing Service   AMIRZAFARI, Jamileh A. . . . 20
PRINCETON
Ayerst Laboratories Research   ALLISON, Kenneth J. 17
   WALLMARK, John S. 1298
Carnegie Foundation Advancement   GREENBERG, Hinda F. 463
CUH2A   MOSS, Susan K. 872
David Sarnoff Research Center   CHU, Wendy N. 213
Dow Jones & Co Inc   BAKES, Floy L. 50
   GROSSMAN, Allen N. 473
   LOGAN, Harold J. 737
   PACE, Thomas 933
   RODEAWALD, Patricia M. . . 1047
   TURNER, Tim L. 1265
   VALENTI, Carl M. 1271
   WARD, Catherine J. 1303
E R Squibb & Sons Inc   GEORGE, Muriel S. 428
   PHILLIPS, Carol H. 967
Educational Testing Service   HALPERN, Marilyn 489
   SARETZKY, Gary D. 1082
   WILLIAMS, Janet L. 1344
ERIC Clearinghouse   OLSON, Lucie M. 923
FMC Corp   MAYER, June C. 789
General Electric Co   PFANN, Mary L. 966

NEW JERSEY (Cont'd)
PRINCETON (Cont'd)

The Hun Sch of Princeton	FOX, Mary A.	395
Jacobus Pharmaceutical Co	JACOBUS, David P.	590
Liposome Co	GARNER, Linda J.	419
Mobil Oil Corp	SMITH, Yvonne B.	1161
Mobil Research & Development Corp	BULYA, Larissa	157
Princeton Pub Lib	BARZELATTO, Elba G.	62
	CARLSON, Dudley B.	182
	GREENFELDT, Eric W.	464
	ROCK, Sue W.	1046
	STRATTON, Elizabeth G.	1200
	THRESHER, Jacquelyn E.	1243
Princeton Theological Seminary	IRVINE, James S.	584
	TAYLOR, Sharon A.	1228
Princeton Univ	BELCHER, Emily M.	76
	BIELAWSKI, Marvin F.	95
	BLACK, William R.	102
	CARLISLE, Scott G.	182
	CHAIKIN, Mary C.	197
	CINLAR, Anne	214
	COE, D W.	226
	CZIFFRA, Peter	269
	FARRELL, Mark R.	365
	FERGUSON, Stephen	372
	GEORGE, Mary W.	427
	HAJDAS, Susan A.	484
	HENNEMAN, John B.	528
	HIRSCH, David G.	543
	HOELLE, Dolores M.	547
	JENSEN, Mary A.	599
	JOYCE, William L.	618
	KLATH, Nancy S.	657
	KOEPP, Donald W.	668
	LITTLE, Rosemary A.	734
	MCARTHUR, Anne	792
	MONTGOMERY, Michael S.	856
	MORGAN, Paula M.	864
	NASE, Lois M.	888
	NEWHOUSE, Brian G.	899
	NEWMAN, Lisa A.	899
	ODELL, Glendon T.	916
	PASTER, Luisa R.	946
	PHILLIPS, Richard F.	969
	PRESTON, Jean F.	991
	ROTH, Stacy F.	1059
	SCHMIDT, Mary M.	1095
	TOMPKINS, Louise	1250
Recording for the Blind Inc	KELLY, John P.	638
Response Analysis Corp	FRIHART, Anne R.	404
Robert Wood Johnson Foundation	GALLAGHER, Philip J.	414
Rutgers Univ	BLASINGAME, Ralph	104
Stuart Country Day Sch of Sacred Heart	HAYASHI, Chigusa	515
Westminster Choir Coll	BENTON, Mary A.	84
	VELLUCCI, Sherry L.	1282
Woodrow Wilson Natl Fellowship Fndtn	COUPER, Richard W.	251
RAHWAY		
M & T Chemicals Inc	ESKA, Dorothy I.	354
	TORRE, Louis P.	1251
Rahway Pub Lib	SUDALL, Arthur D.	1206
RAMSEY		
Funk & Wagnalls Inc	BRAM, Leon L.	127
McGraw-Hill Information Systems	MAYDET, Steven I.	789
Ramsey Free Pub Lib	SCARPELLINO, Rebecca A.	1088
RANDOLPH		
Corp Mgmt & Marketing Consultants Inc	PAVELY, Richard W.	950
County Coll of Morris	COHN, John M.	229
	JONES, David E.	612
	KELSEY, Ann L.	639
RARITAN		
Johnson & Johnson	PARAS, Lucille P.	939
Ortho Pharmaceutical Corp	BENTE, June E.	83
RIDGEFIELD		
Ridgefield Park Pub Lib	SCHACHER, Betty C.	1088
RIDGEFIELD PARK		
Ridgefield Park Pub Lib	ROSENTHAL, Phyllis T.	1057

NEW JERSEY (Cont'd)
RIDGEWOOD

Cumberland Books	KOONTZ, John	671
Ridgewood New Jersey Board of Education	LATHAM, Candace	701
Ridgewood Pub Lib	ROSS, Robert D.	1058
Valley Hospital	ALLOCCO, Claudia	17
ROBBINSVILLE		
Mercer County Lib	GREENBERG, Ruth S.	463
ROCHELLE PARK		
Dun & Bradstreet Corp	GREENBERG, Charles	463
ROCKAWAY		
Rockaway Township Free Pub Lib	BOWERS, Alyce J.	120
Rockway Township Free Pub Lib	COHN, Jeanette	229
ROSELAND		
Parsippany Troy Hills Board of Education	MARTINEZ, Jane A.	779
ROSELLE		
Roselle Free Pub Lib	OLSON, Evelyn N.	922
ROSELLE PARK		
Roselle Park Veterans Memorial Lib	BRIANT, Susan	134
SEA GIRT		
Monmouth County Lib	PARR, Louise M.	943
SECAUCUS		
Murdoch Magazines	COVILL, Bruce	252
Network for Continuing Medical Educ	CONNICK, Kathleen D.	237
Warner Brothers Music Publications Inc	SULTANOF, Jeff B.	1208
SEWELL		
Gloucester County Coll	BOLESTA, Linda	112
	CROCKER, Jane L.	259
Gloucester County Lib	COUMBE, Robert E.	251
SHIP BOTTOM		
Ocean County Lib	ROYCE, Carolyn S.	1063
SHORT HILLS		
Budd Larner Gross Picillo et al	LEVEROCK, Lisa A.	719
SHREWSBURY		
Monmouth County Lib	KRANIS, Janet C.	676
Region Five Lib Cooperative	HIEBING, Dottie	537
SKILLMAN		
Johnson & Johnson Baby Products Co	RONDELLI, Marilyn H.	1053
McNeil Specialty Products Co	DOUGLASS, Leslie A.	314
SOMERVILLE		
Biomedical Information Services	KUSHINKA, Kerry L.	685
Ethicon Inc	LITTLE, Karen M.	733
	MCGREGOR, Walter	808
	STAVETSKI, Norma K.	1183
Hildebrandt Inc	MOYER, Holley M.	874
RCA Corp	KAN, Halina S.	624
Somerset County Law Lib	GENNETT, Robert G.	427
SOUTH AMBOY		
Dowdell Lib	MCCOY, W K.	799
SOUTH ORANGE		
Seton Hall Univ	FIELD, William N.	376
	TALAR, Anita	1220
Township of South Orange Village	FAWCETT-BRANDON, Pamela S.	367
SPARTA		
Sparta High Sch	THOMAS, Carren A.	1236
SPRING LAKE		
Garvey Associates	GARVEY, Nancy G.	421
SPRINGFIELD		
AT&T Technologies Inc	SCOTT, Miranda D.	1107
STANHOPE		
Lenape Valley Regional High Sch	KUTTEROFF, Ethel C.	685
STRATFORD		
Free Pub Lib of Stratford	RODERICK, Ruth C.	1047
Univ of Medicine & Dentistry of NJ	PLAZA, Joyce S.	978
	RAINEY, Kathleen O.	1004
	SCHUBACK COHN, Judith	1101
SUMMIT		
CIBA-GEIGY Corp	WAITE, William F.	1293
CIBA-GEIGY Pharmaceuticals Co	JUTERBOCK, Deborah K.	620
Hoechst Celanese Corp	PAPROCKI, Mary E.	939
	URKEN, Madeline	1270
Overlook Hospital	MOELLER, Kathleen A.	851
Sci-Tech Information Services	JOHNSON, Minnie L.	607
Summit Free Pub Lib	ELENAUSKY, Edward V.	342

NEW JERSEY (Cont'd)

TEANECK

Holy Name Hospital	HOVER, Leila M.	563
International Thomson Business Press Inc	DALY, Charles P.	271
	SCHAEFER, Donald A.	1088
Omnifacts Information Bureau Inc	ROSENSTEIN, Susan J.	1057
Teaneck Pub Lib	WILEN, Rosamond L.	1339

TENAFLY

Infoserv Associates	KORNFELD, Carol E.	672
Tenafly Pub Lib	WECHTLER, Stephen R.	1315

TOMS RIVER

Community Memorial Hospital	REISLER, Reina	1021
Ocean County Coll	GARELICK, Alexander L.	418
Ocean County Lib	JAROSLOW, Sylvia W.	594
	KERN, Stella V.	643
	SORRENTINO, Robert L.	1169
	WOLPERT, Scott L.	1362

TRENTON

Department of State	IAZOVONE, Cesear	581
Hamilton Township Pub Lib	ENGLE, Joyce C.	349
	PORTER, Eva L.	984
Mercer Medical Center	MARCHOK, Catherine W.	769
New Jersey Department of Education	GOLDSMITH, Maxine K.	446
	MADDEN, Doreitha R.	758
	ROUMFORT, Susan B.	1061
	VOSS, Anne E.	1289
	WEAVER, Barbara F.	1312
New Jersey Dept of Law & Pub Safety	ASSENHEIMER, Judy	37
New Jersey Education Association	VAN BUSKIRK, Elisabeth L.	1272
New Jersey Lib Association	MCDONOUGH, Roger H.	803
	STUDDIFORD, Abigail M.	1204
New Jersey Office of Legislative Srvs	MAZZEI, Peter J.	791
New Jersey State Lib	BREEDLOVE, Elizabeth A.	131
	CRAWFORD, Nola N.	257
	GORDON, Kaye B.	451
	LEE, J S.	710
	RAILSBACK, Beverly D.	1003
	RAZZANO, Barbara W.	1012
NIDEP	BARATTA, Maria	55
State of New Jersey	CONLEY, Gail D.	236
	STRONG, Moira O.	1203
	TOMAR, Jeanne	1249
Trenton State Coll	BRODOWSKI, Joyce H.	139
	BUTCHER, Patricia S.	166
	CORWIN, Dean W.	248
	DU BOIS, Paul Z.	322
	MCCULLOUGH, Jack W.	801
	WOODLEY, Robert H.	1366

UNION

Amron Information Services	AMRON, Irving	20
CPC International Inc	BROWN, Jeanne I.	145
	MALAKOFF, Diane L.	762
Free Pub Lib of Union	GARDINER, Judith R.	417
	MARYNOWYCH, Roman V.	780
Kean Coll of New Jersey	KALIF, Alexander J.	623
	SIMPSON, Barbara T.	1141
Township of Union	WALSH, Florence C.	1299
Union Hospital	TANNENBAUM, Aileen Z.	1222

UPPER MONTCLAIR

Montclair State Coll	HUGHES, Kathleen	572
	MINTZ, Donald M.	847
	RICHARDSON, Robert J.	1030
	STOCK, Norman	1195

UPPER SADDLE RIVER

Easylink Information Service	MCCARTHY, Martin	794
Tri-Meridian Inc	DUDLEY, Debbra C.	323
Upper Saddle River Pub Lib	NEWMARK-KRUGER, Barbara	900

VERONA

Verona Pub Lib	TRAFTON, William M.	1253

VINELAND

City of Vineland	GREENBLATT, Ruth	463

VOORHEES

Camden County Lib	AVENICK, Karen	41
	DENNIS, Deborah E.	292
	LADOF, Nina S.	687
	ROMISHER, Sivya S.	1053
	ROTHENBERG, Patricia	1060

NEW JERSEY (Cont'd)

VOORHEES (Cont'd)

South Jersey Regional Film Lib	SCHALK-GREENE, Katherine	1089
West Jersey Health System	BELSTERLING, Jean I.	78

WALDWICK

Waldwick Board of Education	SLOAN, Ruth C.	1149

WARREN

Chubb & Son Inc	LINNAMAA, Mari M.	731

WASHINGTON

Warren County Community Coll	ANDERMAN, Lynea	21

WASHINGTON TOWNSHIP

Immaculate Heart Academy	DONOHOE, Monica M.	311

WAYNE

American Cyanamid Co	JONES, Anita M.	610
	MOSENKIS, Sharon L.	870
Bernard M Baruch Coll	LEE, Minja P.	711
GAF Corp	GARCIA, Ceil K.	417
Neumann Prep High Sch	KLOZA, Paula P.	662
Wayne Board of Education	FIRSCHEIN, Sylvia H.	379
	ONELLI, Patricia M.	924
Wayne Pub Lib	BURNS, John A.	162
	DICKER, Joan F.	300
	PUNSHON, Bette	998
William Paterson Coll	HEGG, Judith L.	521
	MCCLEAN, Vernon E.	796
Woodward-Clyde Consultants	WALLACE, Wendy L.	1298

WEST CALDWELL

American Sound & Video	GRAY, Lee H.	460
West Caldwell Board of Education	CARMER, Ann R.	183

WEST LONG BRANCH

Kultur Home Video	HEDLUND, Dennis M.	520
Monmouth Coll	SUTTON, Robert F.	1211
	VAN BENTHUYSEN, Robert F.	1272
West Long Branch Pub Lib	OGONEK, Donna L.	918

WEST MILFORD

West Milford Township	COURTNEY, Aida N.	251
William Paterson Coll	JOB, Amy G.	601

WEST NEW YORK

JNB Associates	BRITTON, Jeffrey W.	137

WEST ORANGE

National Park Service	BURT, Leah	164
US Department of Interior	BOWLING, Mary B.	121
West Orange City	FICHTELBERG, Susan	374

WESTFIELD

Westfield Memorial Lib	HURLEY, John	577
	THIELE, Barbara J.	1235
	WILSON, Carol A.	1350

WESTWOOD

Pascack Valley Hospital	MICHAELS, Debbie D.	832

WHIPPANY

Knoll Pharmaceuticals	LUSTIG, Joanne	750
Morris County Free Lib	MENZEL, John P.	825
	OTT, Linda G.	930
	VAN WIEMOKLY, Jane G.	1277
Morris County Lib	CAUSLEY, Monroe S.	195
Yesteryear Museum	MUNSICK, Lee R.	879

WILLIAMSTOWN

Free Pub Lib of Monroe Township	BOGIS, Nana E.	110

WOODBRIDGE

DeVry Technical Institute	BOYLE, Jean E.	124
	LIOU, Pearl S.	732
Free Pub Lib of Woodbridge	BECKERMAN, Edwin P.	72
	SPANGLER, William N.	1171
Greenbaum Rowe Smith Raven Davis et al	SEADER, Jane M.	1109
Woodbridge Free Pub Lib	MADERE, Sue E.	759
Woodbridge Township	TAYLOR, Anne C.	1226

WOODBURY

Underwood-Memorial Hospital	TIEDRICH, Ellen K.	1244

WYCKOFF

Wyckoff Pub Lib	NELSON, Louise H.	894
	SCHMITT, Judy	1096

NEW MEXICO
ALAMOGORDO
New Mexico State Univ at
  Alamogordo   RUCKMAN, Stanley N. 1065
ALBUQUERQUE
Access Innovations Inc   HLAVA, Marjorie M. 544
Albuquerque Pub Lib   SABATINI, Joseph D. 1072
Albuquerque Pub Schs   AVERY, Linda S. 42
                         CARLSON, Kathleen A. . . 182
                         WHITLOW, Cherrill M. 1333
Archdiocese of Santa Fe   FALARDEAU, Ernest R. 361
Bernalillo County Pub Lib   TAFT, Patricia S. 1219
Computer Sciences Corp   HSU, Grace S. 567
Honeywell Inc   SPURLOCK, Sandra E. 1177
Independent Sch Lib Media Center FREEMAN, Patricia E. 401
Lovelace Biomedical & Environmental NEFF, Judy C. 892
Lovelace Medical Foundation STRUB, Jeane E. 1203
Modrall Sperling Roehl Harris & Sisk GREENWOOD, Miriam J. . . . 465
Reddy Communications Inc KLOS, Ann M. 662
Rodey Dickason Sloan Akin & Robb
  PA   MORLEY, Sarah K. 865
Sandia National Laboratories PASTERCZYK, Catherine E. . 946
                         PRUETT, Nancy J. 996
                         ZAMORA, Gloria J. 1386
Sunset Mesa Schs Inc   MATTER, Kathy L. 785
Sutin Thayer & Browne   MCGOEY, Richard P. 807
United Methodist Church   ROLLER, Twila J. 1051
US Court of Appeals, Tenth Circuit DEMPSEY, Pamela M. 291
Univ of New Mexico   ADAMS, Dena R. 4
                         BEJNAR, Thaddeus P. 75
                         BERNSTEIN, Judith R. 89
                         BROWN, Eulalie W. 143
                         DODSON, Carolyn 308
                         DUCHARME, Judith C. 322
                         ELDREDGE, Jonathan D. . . . 342
                         GROTHEY, Mina J. 473
                         IVES, Peter B. 586
                         KEMPF, Jody L. 639
                         KRUG, Ruth A. 680
                         LEWIS, Linda K. 723
                         LOVE, Erika 743
                         RASSAM, Cynthia K. 1009
                         REX, Heather 1024
                         ROLLINS, Stephen J. 1051
                         SEISER, Virginia 1113
                         SHELSTAD, Kirsten R. 1126
                         SOHN, Jeanne G. 1165
                         SUGNET, Christopher L. . . . 1206
                         THOMPSON, Janet A. 1240
                         THORSON, Connie C. 1242
                         VASSALLO, Paul 1279
Veterans Administration Medical
  Center   MYER, Nancy E. 884
ANTHONY
Gadsden Independent Sch Dist ODENHEIM, Claire E. 916
AZTEC
Altruruan Pub Lib   ANDERSEN-PUSEY,
                         Vavene J. 21
BAYARD
Cobre Consolidated Sch District KEIST, Sandra H. 635
CLOVIS
Eastern New Mexico Univ   HUMPHREY, Thomas W. . . . 573
                         MCBETH, Deborah E. 792
DEMING
Deming Pub Lib   GREEN, Bradley A. 461
EUNICE
Eunice Municipal Sch   ANDREWS, Lois W. 26
FARMINGTON
San Juan Coll   RICHARD, Harris M. 1027
HOBBS
Coll of the Southwest   TUBESING, Richard L. 1261
JAL
Jal Pub Schs   BRAMLETT, Suzanne M. . . . 127
                         GOODFELLOW, Jacklyn M. . . 448
KIRTLAND AFB
US Air Force   JOURDAIN, Janet M. 618
US Air Force Weapons Laboratory NEWTON, Barbara I. 900

NEW MEXICO (Cont'd)
LAS CRUCES
City of Las Cruces   DRESP, Donald F. 319
New Mexico State Univ at Las
  Cruces   BARBER, Helen M. 55
                         CHEN, Laura F. 205
                         DAVIS, Hiram L. 279
                         DUHRSEN, Lowell R. 324
                         MOORER, Jenny R. 862
Thomas Branigan Memorial Lib ATKINS, Gene D. 37
LOS ALAMOS
County of Los Alamos   BJORKLUND, Katharine B. . . 100
                         KRAEMER, Mary P. 674
Los Alamos County Lib   SAYRE, Edward C. 1087
Los Alamos National Laboratory BEYER, Ann H. 93
                         CARTER, Jackson H. 189
                         COMSTOCK, Daniel L. 235
                         FREED, J A. 400
                         GODFREY, Lois E. 442
Los Alamos Pub Schs   CROCKER, Judith A. 259
LOS LUNAS
New Mexico Dept of Health &
  Environment   HAYNES, Douglas E. 516
PORTALES
Eastern New Mexico Univ   DOWLIN, C E. 316
                         MCGUIRE, Laura H. 808
                         SCHOTT, Mark E. 1099
                         WALKER, Mary J. 1296
ROSWELL
New Mexico Military Institute KLOPFER, Jerome J. 662
                         MCLAREN, M B. 813
Roswell Independent Sch District KALER, Dorothy C. 623
SANTA FE
New Mexico Records Center &
  Archives   MILLER, Bryan M. 836
New Mexico Supreme Court LANCASTER, Kevin M. 692
Santa Fe Indian Sch   PIERSON, Robert M. 972
Santa Fe Pub Lib   BENNETT, Deborah L. 81
Santa Fe Pub Schs   LOPEZ, Kathryn P. 741
State of New Mexico   HENDLEY, Virginia 527
State Records Center & Archives GRAINTO, Mary 457
Zia Cine Inc   WILLIAMS, Carroll W. 1342
SHIPROCK
Navajo Community Coll   JASSAL, Raghbir S. 595
SILVER CITY
Western New Mexico Univ   LEON, Louise B. 716
SUNSPOT
National Solar Observatory   CORNETT, John L. 247
THOREAU
St Bonaventure Academy   SCHUBERT, Donald F. 1101
TOADLENA
Bureau of Indian Affairs   MCCAULEY, Elfrieda B. 795
TRUTH OR CONSEQUENCE
Truth or Consequences Pub Lib SAMPSON, Ellanie S. 1078
WHITE SANDS
US Army   SAUNDERS, Laurel B. 1084
US Army Tradoc Analysis Command GIBSON, Julie A. 432

NEW YORK
ALBANY
Albany Law Sch   PINSLEY, Lauren J. 975
Albany Medical Center Archives MOORE, Rue I. 861
Albany Medical Coll of Union Univ MARTIN, Lyn M. 777
                         POLAND, Ursula H. 980
Albany Pub Lib   BRODERICK, Therese L. . . . 139
                         DRATCH-KOVLER, Carol A. . 318
                         GILLESPIE, Gerald V. 435
                         LEWIS, Frances R. 723
                         MIDDLETON, Marcia S. 833
                         O'CONNOR, William J. 916
                         PATRICK, Patricia M. 947
                         SACCO, Gail A. 1073
Capital Newspapers   MATTURRO, Richard C. 786
Coll of St Rose   CORDING, A C. 246
                         NEAT, Charles M. 891
Community Reformed Church of
  Colonie   SEVERINGHAUS, Ethel L. . . 1117
Council of Family & Chld Caring
  Agencies   ROBINSON, Jolene A. 1044

NEW YORK (Cont'd)
ALBANY (Cont'd)

Daughters of Charity St Vincent
DePaul   WHEELER, Elaine 1328
Empire Blue Cross & Blue Shield   RUBIN, David S. 1064
Forest Press   KRAMER-GREENE, Judith .. 675
                                          PAULSON, Peter J. 950
Hospital Association of New York
State   ROTMAN, Elaine C. 1060
NY Division of Equalization &
Assessment   BEVERLEY, Barbara S. 93
New York State   BOTTA, Jean C. 118
                                          DWORKIN, Victoria G. 330
                                          GILSON, Robert 437
                                          STORMS, Kate 1198
                                          WESTHUIS, Judith A. 1327
New York State Archives   COX, Richard J. 253
                                          DEARSTYNE, Bruce W. 284
                                          WARD, Christine W. 1303
New York State Department of Health   YOCHYM, Cynthia M. ... 1380
New York State Department of Law   KOUO, Lily W. 673
                                          REEPMEYER, Marie C. 1016
New York State Education
Department   BARRON, Robert E. 60
                                          BURKETT, Donald E. 161
                                          HACKMAN, Larry J. 481
                                          MATTIE, Joseph J. 786
                                          ROSCELLO, Frances R. ... 1054
                                          SHUBERT, Joseph F. 1133
                                          SHUMAN, Susan E. 1134
                                          SIMON, Anne E. 1140
                                          SMITH, Frederick E. 1155
                                          SOMERS, Betty J. 1166
                                          SWARTZELL, Ann G. 1214
                                          WEBSTER, Patricia B. 1315
New York State Legislature   BRESLIN, Ellen R. 133
                                          MURRAY, Elizabeth F. 881
New York State Lib   BAIN, Christine A. 47
                                          CADE, Roberta G. 170
                                          CHAPERO, Alicia 201
                                          CORSARO, James 248
                                          DESCH, Carol A. 294
                                          ESPOSITO, Michael A. 354
                                          HOLT, Lisa A. 554
                                          JUDD, J V. 619
                                          NICHOLS-RANDALL,
                                           Barbara L. 902
                                          PASTERNACK, Marcia A. ... 946
                                          SMITH, Audrey J. 1152
                                          SMITH, Dorothy C. 1154
                                          STANTON, Lee W. 1181
                                          YAVARKOVSKY, Jerome .. 1378
New York State Office of Mental
Health   DANIELS, Pam 273
New York State Senate   VANNORTWICK, Barbara L. 1276
New York Unified Court System   FRALEY, Ruth A. 395
St Peter's Hospital   MIYAUCHI, Phyllis J. 850
State Univ of New York at Albany   ANDERSON, Carol L. 22
                                          BENEDICT, Marjorie A. 80
                                          BONK, Sharon C. 114
                                          HALSEY, Richard S. 490
                                          KATZ, William A. 630
                                          KLEMPNER, Irving M. 660
                                          KNAPP, Sara D. 663
                                          KNEE, Michael 663
                                          LENZ, Millicent A. 716
                                          LIPETZ, Ben A. 732
                                          MCCOMBS, Gillian M. 797
                                          MILLER, Heather S. 838
                                          MOREHEAD, Joe 863
                                          NITECKI, Joseph Z. 905
                                          ROBERTS, Anne F. 1039
                                          SAFFADY, William 1074
                                          SHAFFER, Kay L. 1119
                                          SMIRENSKY, Helen K. 1152
                                          VIA, Barbara J. 1283
                                          WALKER, M G. 1296
                                          WELLS, Gladysann 1322
                                          WHALEN, Lucille 1328
                                          WING, Judith G. 1354

NEW YORK (Cont'd)
ALBANY (Cont'd)

Union Univ at Albany   DUNCAN, Elizabeth C. 325
Urbach Kahn & Werlin PC   DENOTO, Dorothy E. 293
ALBERTSON
Human Resources Center   TISHLER, Amnon 1247
Shelter Rock Pub Lib   CONRAD, Frances M. 238
ALBION
Albion Central Sch District   MERRILL, Barbara P. 826
ALFRED
New York State Coll of Ceramics   CONNOLLY, Bruce E. 237
                                          CULLEY, Paul T. 263
                                          FREEMAN, Carla C. 400
                                          GULACSY, Elizabeth 477
State Univ of New York at Alfred   LASH, David B. 700
AMAGANSETT
Amagansett Elementary Sch   BRUNO, Frances J. 151
AMAWALK
OCLC Online Computer Lib Center   HANE, Paula J. 495
AMHERST
Buffalo & Erie County Pub Lib   COLLINS, Ruth A. 233
State Univ of New York at Buffalo   BERTUCA, David J. 91
                                          COOVER, James B. 244
AMITYVILLE
Amityville Pub Lib   PAVLAK, Anne C. 950
AMSTERDAM
Greater Amsterdam School District   TUNISON, Janice A. 1263
APO NEW YORK
Ansbach American High Sch   MEIGS, Carolyn R. 821
Central Texas Coll   SIEBL, Linda M. 1135
Hanau American High Sch   PRINZ, Jane A. 993
Holmes & Narver Services Inc   RUDA, Donna R. 1065
US Air Force   BURKE, Joseph A. 160
                                          GADBOIS, Frank W. 411
                                          HAAS, Eva L. 480
                                          LOMEN, Nancy L. 738
                                          ROWELL, Regina A. 1062
US Air Force Lib Service   ANDREWS, Margaret D. 27
US Army in Berlin   BLACKBURN, Clayton E. ... 102
                                          CHICARELLA, Joseph T. 207
US Army in Europe   HOUGH, Allen D. 562
US Army Lib System   MORRISON, J M. 868
US Dept, Defense Overseas
Dependent Schs   YANOFF, Marcy S. 1377
US Department of Defense   RIVERA, Antonio 1037
US Department of Defense
Dependents Schs   CUNNINGHAM, Mary A. 265
                                          GRIFFIN, Cheryl J. 468
                                          HAUSRATH, Donald C. 513
US Information Agency   MEDEIROS, Joseph 820
US Saudi Arabian Joint Economic
Com   SOKOLOWSKI, Denise G. ... 1166
Univ of Maryland
ARDSLEY ON HUDSON
Transnational Publishers Inc   FENTON, Heike 371
ARMONK
Byram Hills High Sch   BERGER, Pam P. 86
North Castle Pub Lib   DEVERS, Charlotte M. 297
                                          STARK, Li S. 1181
ASTORIA
St John's Prep Sch   GORMAN, Mary B. 452
ATHOL SPRINGS
St Francis High Sch   PFEIFFER, Mary A. 966
ATTICA
Wyoming Correctional Facility   BARTLE, Matthew W. 61
AUBURN
Auburn Memorial Hospital   TOMLIN, Anne C. 1250
Cayuga Community Coll   LOLLIS, Martha J. 738
                                          MICHAEL, Douglas O. 831
AVON
Livingston & Wyoming Co Lib
Systems   BARTLE, Susan M. 61
BAKERS MILLS
Johnsburg Central Sch   SULLIVAN, Linda R. 1208
BALDWIN
Baldwin Pub Lib   HOPKINS, Barbara A. 557
BALDWINSVILLE
Baldwinsville Pub Lib   LAUBACHER, Marilyn R. 702
BALLSTON SPA
Ballston Spa Pub Lib   HUMPHREY, Virginia S. 573

NEW YORK (Cont'd)
BARRYTOWN
Unification Theological Seminary · · · NAVRATIL, Jean 890
BATAVIA
Genesee Community Coll · · · LANE, Elizabeth J. 694
Notre Dame High Sch · · · STRANC, Mary C. 1200
BAY SHORE
Bay Shore Pub Schs · · · FLOWERS, Helen F. 386
Southside Hospital · · · TRAVERS, Jane E. 1254
BAYSIDE
LDA Publishing · · · IPPOLITO, Andrew V. 583
New York City Board of Education · · · SINGER, Phyllis Z. 1143
Queensborough Coll, City Univ of NY · · · DAVILA, Daniel 277
Queensborough Coll of CUNY · · · NOVIK, Sandra P. 911
BAYVILLE
Bayville Free Lib · · · BERTINO, Lorna L. 91
BEDFORD HILLS
Pen Kem Inc · · · GOETZ, Helen L. 443
BEECHHURST
Carver Associates · · · CARVER, Mary 191
BELLEROSE
Long Island Univ · · · GATNER, Elliott S. 422
Queens Borough Pub Lib · · · SIAHPOOSH, Farideh T. . . . 1134
BELLPORT
Suffolk Cooperative Lib System · · · CANTWELL, Mickey A. 179
EIDELMAN, Diane L. 340
KLAUBER, Julie B. 658
LEVERING, Philip 719
MULLER, Claudya B. 877
PLUMER, F I. 978
RICHARDSON, John A. . . . 1029
ROTHENBERG, Mark H. . . . 1060
Viva Tours USA · · · JANSEN, Guenter A. 593
BEMUS POINT
Maple Grove Junior-Senior High Sch · · · BJORKQUIST, Donna M. . . . 100
BETHPAGE
Grumman Aerospace Corp · · · BURDEN, John 158
WESTERLING, Mary L. 1327
Grumman Corp · · · LOVISOLO, Lois 743
BINGHAMTON
Binghamton Psychiatric Center · · · MASON, Martha A. 781
Broome County Pub Lib · · · COHEN, Ann E. 227
SEARS, Carlton A. 1110
WILLIAMS, Deborah H. 1342
Four County Lib System · · · HILL, Malcolm K. 540
New York State Supreme Court · · · LAUER, Judy 702
Our Lady of Lourdes Hospital · · · BRETSCHER, Susan M. 134
Singer Co · · · CARPENTER, Dale 184
HAMLIN, Eileen M. 493
VALLIANT, Robert B. 1271
State Univ of New York at
  Binghamton · · · BURNETTE, Michaelyn 162
CHAMBERLAIN, Erna B. 197
FINN, Margaret M. 378
GERACI, Diane 428
LINCOLN, Betty W. 728
LINCOLN, Harry B. 728
MCKEE, George D. 810
BLUE MOUNTAIN LAKE
Adirondack Museum · · · PEPPER, Jerold L. 958
BOHEMIA
The Connetquot Central Sch Dist of
  Islip · · · JENSEN, Patricia K. 599
BRENTWOOD
Academy of Saint Joseph · · · WALTER, Maria 1300
Brentwood Pub Schs · · · RAPPELT, John F. 1008
Copiague Pub Schs · · · ADAMS, Grover C. 4
Suffolk Community Coll · · · PETERMAN, Kevin 962
Suffolk County Community Coll · · · QUINN, David J. 1000
BRIARCLIFF MANOR
Benchmark Films · · · SOLIN, Myron 1166
Briarcliff Manor Pub Lib · · · FARKAS, Charles R. 364
Frank B Hall Consulting Company · · · CLARKE, Elizabeth S. 218
BRIGHTON
MFI Associates Inc · · · RAHN, Erwin P. 1003
BROCKPORT
State Univ of New York at Brockport · · · RAKSHI, Sri R. 1004

NEW YORK (Cont'd)
BRONX
Albert Einstein Coll of Medicine · · · LAMPORT, Bernard 691
LINDNER, Charlotte K. 729
NELSON, Norma 894
Archdiocese of New York · · · FERNANDEZ, M L. 373
Bronx High Sch of Science · · · SUSSMAN, Valerie J. 1210
Bronx Municipal Hospital Center · · · DAVIDSON, Silvia 276
Fordham Univ · · · HITT, Gail D. 544
KANE, Patrice M. 625
MURPHY, Anne M. 880
H W Wilson Co · · · BARTENBACH, Wilhelm K. . . . 60
BATTOE, Melanie K. 65
BRISTOW, Barbara A. 137
CARRICK, Bruce R. 186
CASE, Ann M. 191
CHEN, Barbara A. 205
CLAYBORNE, Jon L. 219
CORNELL, Charles R. 246
DEEBRAH, Grace J. 286
DOWNEN, Kathleen Z. 316
ENTIN, Paula B. 351
FISHER, Maureen C. 381
FORCE, Stephen 389
GAROOGIAN, Rhoda 420
GHOSH, Subhra 430
GODWIN, Mary J. 443
GOLDBERG, Judy W. 444
HEWITT, Mary L. 535
HILLEGAS, Ferne E. 541
HOWARD, Joyce M. 564
HSIAO, Shu Y. 567
KING, Trina E. 652
LEWICKY, George I. 722
LOCASCIO, Aline M. 735
MARK, Linda R. 770
MILLER, Frank W. 837
MOONEY, Martha T. 858
NELSON, Milo G. 894
PEDALINO, M C. 954
PEHE, Jana 954
REGAZZI, John J. 1017
RENTSCHLER, Cathy 1023
ROY, Diptimoy 1063
SCOFIELD, Andrea 1106
SHAH, Syed M. 1119
SOPELAK, Mary J. 1168
TRAGER, Phyllis H. 1253
Herbert H Lehman Coll · · · WORTZEL, Murray N. 1369
Horace Mann Sch · · · PEELE, Marla H. 954
Lehman Coll of the City Univ of New
  York · · · DIAMOND, Harold J. 299
FOLTER, Siegrun H. 388
GEE, Ka C. 424
RUBEY, Daniel R. 1064
SHANNON, Michael O. . . . 1120
Manhattan Coll · · · BARRY, Richard A. 60
O'DONNELL, Mary A. 917
Montefiore Medical Center · · · LIEBER, Ellen C. 726
Museum of the American Indian · · · DAVIS, Mary B. 280
New York City Board of Education · · · ARKHURST, Joyce C. 31
DE CUENCA, Pilar A. 286
New York City Criminal Court · · · ROONEY, Mary T. 1053
New York Pub Lib · · · BUELOW, Mary E. 155
CAMPAGNA, Roxane R. . . . 175
CASSEL, Susan D. 193
MARTIN, Brian G. 775
SALTUS, Winifred T. 1077
WENDT, Mary E. 1324
ZEIGLER, Susan A. 1387
New York Zoological Society · · · JOHNSON, Steven P. 609
Preston High Sch · · · MCCANN, Kathleen 794
St Barnabas Hospital · · · KLEIN, Penny 659
Veterans Administration Medical
  Center · · · BLAKE-O'HOGAN, Kathleen
    E. 103
Wave Hill · · · FRANK, Mortimer H. 397

NEW YORK (Cont'd)

BRONXVILLE

Concordia Coll

ANDERSON, Birgitta M. 21
HUEBNER, Mary A. 570

Lawrence Hospital
Sarah Lawrence Coll

LARKIN, Virgil C. 698
BURSTEIN, Rose A. 164
ZIESELMAN, Paula M. 1388

Village of Bronxville

SELVAR, Jane C. 1114

BROOKLYN

Art Museum Lib Consortium
Bishop Kearney High Sch
Brookdale Hospital Medical Center
Brooklyn Coll of the City Univ of NY

LUCKER, Amy E. 746
LANE, Mary K. 694
STRAUSMAN, Jeanne 1201
BRAUCH, Patricia O. 129
CORRSIN, Stephen D. 247
FEINBERG, Renee 369
GARGAN, William M. 419
HIGGINBOTHAM, Barbra B. . 537
HORNE, Dorice L. 560
KUPFERBERG, Natalie 684
LESTER, Lillian 718
LONEY, Glenn M. 739
MEISELES, Linda 822
VAUGHN, Susan J. 1280
WILD, Judith W. 1338

Brooklyn Law Sch
Brooklyn Museum

ROBBINS, Sara E. 1039
GUZMAN, Diane J. 479
KERR, Virginia M. 644

Brooklyn Pub Lib

AKEY, Stephen 9
AVERY, Theodore M. 42
BRANDWEIN, Larry 128
CANNING, Joan M. 178
DAVIS, Natalia G. 280
DUCHAC, Kenneth F. 322
GENCO, Barbara A. 426
HAMILTON, Reatha B. 492
HARKAVY, Ira B. 501
JOHNSON, Sheila A. 609
KALKHOFF, Ann L. 623
KIMMONS, Anita L. 649
KLEIMAN, Allan M. 658
KUPERMAN, Aaron W. 684
MILLER, Roy D. 842
MILLS, David L. 844
NYREN, Dorothy E. 913
ROYTMAN, Serafima 1063
SALPETER, Janice L. 1077
TUDIVER, Lillian 1262
VOGEL, Dorothy H. 1286
YOUNG, Dorothy B. 1381

Brooklyn Sch Districts
Ctr for Holocaust Std Documtn &
Research
City Univ of New York
Coney Island Hospital
Edward R Murrow High Sch
Halcyon Associates
International Trade Education
Associates
Kingsborough Coll of the City Univ of
NY

MEYERS, Charles 830

GUREWITSCH, Bonnie 478
BRODY, Catherine T. 139
MARK, Ronnie J. 770
ZAPPONE, William F. 1386
FLECK, Donald R. 384

MATTERA, Joseph J. 785

CLUNE, John R. 223
KARKHANIS, Sharad 627
ORR, Coleridge W. 926
SCHNEIDER, Adele 1096

Long Island Coll Hospital
Long Island Univ
Maimonides Medical Center
Medgar Evens Coll of the City Univ of
NY
Methodist Hospital
METRO NY
METRO NY Metropolitan Reference
& Resrch
New York City Board of Education
New York City Sch Lib System
NY Metropolitan Ref & Resrch Lib
Agency

WAHLERT, George A. 1292
WENGER, Milton B. 1324
FRIEDMAN, Lydia 404

BAKISH, David J. 50
TANNER, Ellen B. 1222
BRANDEAU, John H. 128

BARTEN, Sharon S. 60
PRUITT, Brenda F. 996
KENNEDY BRIGHT, Sandra . 641

GOODMAN, Rhonna A. 449
MANBECK, Virginia B. 764
NEUMANN, Joan 897

New York State Supreme Court
Poly Prep Country Day Sch

GARA, Otto G. 416
PERSON, Diane G. 961

NEW YORK (Cont'd)

BROOKLYN (Cont'd)

Polytechnic Preparatory Country Day
Sch
Polytechnic Univ

KAHN, Laura 622
ROGERS, Jonathan B. 1049
SWEENEY, Richard T. 1215
TURIEL, David 1263

Pratt Institute

CHICKERING, F W. 208
GREENBERG, Roberta D. . . 463
HUMPHRY, James 574
KEAVENEY, Sydney S. 633
MALINCONICO, S M. 763
MATTA, Seoud M. 785
MCSWEENEY, Josephine . . 818

Presentations
St Francis Coll
Sisters of Mercy of Brooklyn
State Univ of New York at Brooklyn

ROGINSKI, James W. 1050
TORRONE, Joan M. 1251
SULLIVAN, Majella M. 1208
COOMBS, Ronald L. 241
DOHERTY, Mary C. 309
POONITHARA, Pradee P. . . 983
SEMKOW, Julie L. 1115

Veterans Administration Medical
Center
Women's Occupational Health
Resource Ctr
Wycoff Heights Hospital

LISZCZYNSKYJ, Halyna A. . . 733

HOMMEL, Claudia 555
BLOKH, Basheva 106

BROOKPORT

State Univ of New York at Brockport

MADAN, Raj 758

BROOKSVILLE

Long Island Univ

O'HARA, Frederic J. 919

BROOKVILLE

Center for Business Research
Long Island Univ

COOPER, Catherine M. 242
BRISFJORD, Inez S. 136
GRANT, Mary M. 458
IRWIN, Iris 584
MAILLET, Lucienne G. 761
MANN, Amy S. 765
SPERR BRISFJORD, Inez L. 1173
SPIRT, Diana L. 1175
WINCKLER, Paul A. 1354

BUFFALO

Albright-Knox Art Gallery
Barrister Information Systems
Buffalo & Erie County Historical
Society
Buffalo & Erie County Pub Lib

SCHENK, Kathryn L. 1091
WAGNER, Stephen K. 1292

BELL, Mary F. 77
CHODACKI, Roberta A. 210
CHRISMAN, Diane J. 211
CLOUDSLEY, Donald H. . . . 223
DORFMAN, Ethel L. 312
GURN, Robert M. 478
MAYER, Erich J. 789
ROSENFELD, Jane D. 1056
ROUNDS, Joseph B. 1061
STELZLE, James J. 1186
WILLET, Ruth J. 1341

Buffalo News
Calspan Corp
Canisius Coll

SCHLAERTH, Sally G. 1093
MILLER, Betty 836
NELSON, Robert J. 895
PERONE, Karen L. 959
TELATNIK, George M. 1230
WOLFE, Theresa L. 1361

Ecology & Environment Inc
Mercy Hospital
Nardin Academy
Natl Ctr for Earthquake Engrng
Resrch
New York State Supreme Court
Nichols Sch

KARCH, Linda S. 627
BREEN, M F. 131

COTY, Patricia A. 250
SAHLEM, James R. 1075
JOHNSON, Guy M. 605
RYBARCZYK, Barclay S. . . 1071

Roswell Park Memorial Institute

ABLOVE, Gayle J. 2
FRANKE, Gail E. 397
HUTCHINSON, Ann P. 579

State Univ of New York at Buffalo

ALLERTON, Ellen M. 16
BOBINSKI, George S. 108
BRADLEY, Carol J. 125
BUSH, Renee B. 165
CHAPMAN, Renee D. 202
CIPOLLA, Wilma R. 215
DAVIS, Susan A. 281
DECKER, Jean S. 285
DENSMORE, Christopher . . . 293

NEW YORK (Cont'd)
BUFFALO (Cont'd)
State Univ of New York at Buffalo

DIBARTOLO, Amy L. 299
DONG, Alvin L. 311
EDENS, John A. 336
ELLISON, John W. 345
GARLAND, Kathleen 419
GIBSON, Ellen M. 432
HAAS, Marilyn L. 480
HARDY, Gayle J. 500
HEPFER, Cynthia K. 530
HEPFER, William E. 530
HERMAN, Edward 531
HOPKINS, Judith 558
HUANG, C K. 568
JONES, Martin J. 614
KELLER, Sharon A. 635
LYMAN, Helen H. 751
MCGRATH, Ellen T. 807
MILLER, Mary F. 840
NEUMEISTER, Susan M. . . . 897
NEWMAN, George C. 899
NUZZO, David J. 912
NUZZO, Nancy B. 912
ROSE, Pamela M. 1055
SCHUTT, Dedre A. 1103
SENTZ, Lilli 1115
SHIELDS, Gerald R. 1130
SMITH, Karen F. 1156
STIEVATER, Susan M. 1194
VON WAHLDE, Barbara . . . 1288
WEBSTER, James K. 1314
WELLS, Margaret R. 1322
YERKEY, A N. 1380
ZUBROW, Marcia L. 1391

Trocaire Coll   MULDOON, Jane K. 876
Veterans Administration Medical
    Center   HALL, Russell W. 488
Villa Maria Coll   DOBRZYNSKI, Terenita 307
Western New York Lib Resrcs
    Council   EVERINGHAM, Joyce D. 358
CAMPBELL
United Health Services   EDSALL, Shirley A. 336
CANADAIGUA
Wood Lib   CUMMINS, A B. 264
CANTON
Potsdam Coll   FINCH, Frances 377
St Lawrence Univ   LARSEN, Joan A. 698
CARLE PLACE
Board of Cooperative Educational
    Srvs   HABER, Elinor L. 480
CARTHAGE
Carthage Central Schs   MOSES, Camelia T. 871
CENTEREACH
Middle County Public Lib   HEINEMAN, Stephanie R. . . . 522
CHAPPAQUA
Chappaqua Central Sch District   DI BIANCO, Phyllis R. 299
Chappaqua Lib   PLATT, Mary L. 977
CHEEKTOWAGA
Buffalo & Erie County Pub Lib   REINSTEIN, Julia B. 1021
Cheektowaga Central Schs   WITT, Susan T. 1358
Cheektowaga Pub Lib   USTACH, Joanne B. 1270
Maryvale Sch District   SZEMRAJ, Edward R. 1218
CHURCHVILLE
Terra Firma   FABRIZIO, Timothy C. 360
CLIFTON PARK
Shenendehowa Central Sch   RATZER, Mary B. 1010
CLINTON
Donmar Associates   ANTHONY, Donald C. 28
Hamilton Coll   MALOY, Frances 764
                                    SWETMAN, Barbara E. 1216
COBLESKILL
State Univ of New York at Cobleskill GALASSO, Nancy 412
COLD SPRING
Blackwell's Periodicals Division   FEICK, Christina L. 368
LEXIK House Publishers   BARNHART, David K. 58
COLD SPRING HARBOR
Cold Spring Harbor Laboratory   FALVEY, Genemary H. 363
Quest Information Services   FARAONE, Maria B. 363

NEW YORK (Cont'd)
COMMACK
Ballen Booksellers International Inc   SCHRIFT, Leonard B. 1100
COOPERSTOWN
Willis Monie Books   MONIE, Willis J. 855
CORINTH
Corinth Sch System   KOCH, Fran C. 667
CORNING
Corning Community Coll   HORNICK-LOCKARD,
                                        Barbara A. 560
Corning Glass Works   DREIFUSS, Richard A. 319
St Patrick's Catholic Church   DAVIS, Francis R. 279
CORNWALL ON HUDSON
Cornwall Pub Lib   KONDZELA, Jeanette M. 670
CORONA
Queens Borough Pub Lib   BENZ, Lieselotte 84
CORTLAND
Cortland City Sch District   HATCH, Nancy W. 511
State Univ of New York at Cortland HEARN, Stephen S. 518
                                    RITCHIE, David G. 1036
                                    SCHAFFER, D J. 1089
                                    SCHROEDER, Eileen E. . . . 1100
COTTOES
National Education Assn of New York PINGITORE, Patricia E. 974
CROTON-ON-HUDSON
Aaron Cohen Associates   COHEN, Aaron 227
                                    COHEN, Elaine 228
Croton Free Lib   BURNHAM, Helen A. 162
Infolink   TUCKERMAN, Susan 1262
CUTCHOGUE
Cutchague Free Lib   MINERVA, Jane R. 846
DANSVILLE
Central Sch District   MINEMIER, Betty M. 845
Dansville Pub Lib   CANUTI, Teresa D. 179
DELHI
State Univ of New York at Oneonta   SORGEN, Herbert J. 1168
DELMAR
Bethlehem Central Schs   GRAVLEE, Diane D. 459
Bethlehem Pub Lib   CARLSON, Marie S. 182
DIX HILLS
Half Hollow Hills Community Lib   MOY, Clarence T. 874
                                    NICHOLS, Gerald D. 901
DOBBS FERRY
Mercy Coll   BONE, Larry E. 113
                                    KLAVANO, Ann M. 658
Stauffer Chemical Co   HASSAN, Mohammad Z. 511
DUNKIRK
Dunkirk Pub Schs   GEIBEN, Rodney F. 425
EARLTON
Greene County Department of Social
    Srvs   MAURER, Eric 787
EAST AMHERST
Williamsville East High Sch   ORGREN, Sally C. 925
EAST AURORA
Christ the King Seminary   HAYES, Bonaventure F. 515
St Matthias' Episcopal Church   GUINN, Patricia L. 477
EAST ISLIP
East Islip Pub Lib   HEINTZELMAN, Susan K. . . . 522
EAST MEADOW
East Meadow Pub Lib   EDWARDS, Harriet M. 337
                                    FRANZEN, John F. 398
Massao County Medical Center   MERRIGAN, Paul G. 826
EAST NORTHPORT
National Lib Relocations Inc   MILLER, Scott W. 842
EAST SETAUKET
State Univ of New York at Stony
    Brook   BLOHM, Laura A. 106
                                    KENEFICK, Colleen M. 640
EASTCHESTER
Jerry Alper Inc   OKERSON, Ann L. 920
ELMHURST
Diocese of Brooklyn   STAFFORD, Catherine H. . . 1178
Mount Sinai Affiliation   SALEY, Stacey 1076
St Francis Coll   TAN, Wendy W. 1222
ELMIRA
Elmira & Chemung County   BROUSE, Ann G. 141
Elmira City Sch District   KEEFER, Ethel A. 634
Schuyler-Chemung-Tioga BOCES   LAPIER, Cynthia B. 697
Steele Memorial Lib Syst   WEIDEMANN, Margaret A. . . 1316

NEW YORK (Cont'd)

ELMONT
Elmont Pub Lib   CORBIN, Evelyn D. 245
ELMSFORD
Greenburgh Pub Lib   GILES, Marta M. 434
    LEW, Susan 722
    TRUDELL, Robert J. 1259
    TYNES, Jacqueline K. 1267
    WENDOLSKI, Alice D. 1323
Pergamon Infoline Inc   GIBBINS, P J. 431
Pergamon Microforms International   RITTER, Sally K. 1037
Pergamon Press   SMITH-GREENWOLD,
    Kathryn R. 1162
Westchester Lib System   PARRAVANO, Ellen A. 944
    TABEN, Eva M. 1219
ENDICOTT
Village of Endicott   LOCKE, Stanley J. 736
FAIRPORT
Fairport Pub Lib   WEMETT, Lisa C. 1323
FAR ROCKAWAY
Peninsula Hospital Center   RUBINSTEIN, Edith 1065
FARMINGDALE
Fairfield Republic Co   MAUTER, George A. 787
Farmingdale Pub Lib   MASCIA, Regina B. 780
Farmingdale Sch District   MCNAMARA, Marie F. 816
Polytechnic Univ   SCHEIN, Lorraine S. 1091
FAYETTEVILLE
Fayetteville Free Lib   MOORE, Ann L. 858
FISHKILL
New York State Department of
   Corrections   SHERWIG, Mary J. 1129
FLORAL PARK
Bellerose Sch District   CANDE, Lorraine N. 178
FLUSHING
Queens Coll of the City Univ of New
   York   COHEN, David 228
    COHEN, Jackson B. 228
    COOPER, Marianne 243
    HARTMAN, Anne M. 508
    HYMAN, Richard J. 580
    KOSTER, Gregory E. 673
    MACOMBER, Nancy 758
    NORDSTROM, Virginia 908
    PENCHANSKY, Mimi B. 956
    REMUSAT, Suzanne L. 1023
    RONNERMANN, Gail 1053
    RORICK, William C. 1054
    SCOTT, Bettie H. 1106
    SURPRENANT, Thomas T. . . 1210
    THOMAS, Lucille C. 1237
    WALL, Richard L. 1297
Systems & Encoding Corp   MEDINA, Ildefonso M. 820
FOREST HILLS
Adelphi Univ   LIFSHIN, Arthur 726
Queens Lib   AXLER, Judith A. 42
FPO NEW YORK
Cairo American Coll   GAMAL, Sandra H. 416
Lib of Congress   JAY, Donald F. 595
US Naval Support Activity   JONES, Kevin R. 613
US Navy   LANE, Elizabeth L. 694
FREDONIA
State Univ of New York at Fredonia   BESEMER, Susan P. 91
FREEPORT
Freeport Memorial Lib   EDWARDS, Guy P. 337
    OPATOW, Dave 924
Marshall Cavendish Corp   GOSDEN, George 452
FRESH MEADOWS
St Francis Prep Sch Lib   PERGOLA, Desales 958
FULTON
Nestle Foods   REED, Catherine A. 1015
GARDEN CITY
Adelphi Univ   DOCTOROW, Erica 307
    EDWARDS, Rita F. 337
    KELLY, Donald V. 637
    SCHNEIDER, Judith A. 1097
Garden City Pub Lib   PIRODSKY, Nancy E. 975
    ROECKEL, Alan G. 1048
    SHERWOOD, Nancy 1129
Nassau Academy of Medicine   WESTERMANN, Mary L. . . . 1327

NEW YORK (Cont'd)
GARDEN CITY (Cont'd)
Nassau Community Coll   FRIEDMAN, Arthur L. 403
    GRUNDT, Leonard 475
GARRISON
Alice & Hamilton Fish Lib   BALDWIN, Geraldine S. 51
GENESEO
State Univ of New York at Geneseo   MACLEAN, Paul 757
    NEESE, Janet A. 892
    QUICK, Richard C. 999
    WEAS, Andrea T. 1311
GENEVA
Finger Lakes Times   BARNARD, Catherine A. 57
GERMANTOWN
Germantown Central Sch   LINDSLEY, Barbara N. 730
GLEN COVE
Pall Corp   LETTIS, Lucy B. 719
GLEN HEAD
New York Chiropractic Coll   STERN, Marilyn 1189
GLENS FALLS
Crandall Lib   KARGE, James R. 627
GLOVERSVILLE
Gloversville Free Lib   STREIT, Ann M. 1202
GRAND ISLAND
Moore Business Forms Inc   WATERS, Betsy M. 1308
Occidental Chemical Corp   WAGNER, A B. 1291
GREAT NECK
Great Neck Pub Lib   TRINKOFF, Elaine 1257
Hayt Hayt & Landau   MULCAHY, Brian J. 876
Unisys Corp   MONTALBANO, James J. . . . 855
GREENPORT
US Department of Agriculture   PERLMAN, Stephen E. 959
GREENVALE
Long Island Univ   PODELL, Diane K. 979
    SYWAK, Myron 1217
    WEINSTEIN, Ellen B. 1318
    YUKAWA, Masako 1384
Panel Publishers Inc   SIMMONDS, Ruth E. 1139
GUILDERLAND
New York State Nurses Association   HAWKES, Warren G. 513
HAMILTON
Colgate Univ   GREEN, Judith G. 462
    PILACHOWSKI, David M. . . . 973
    SIMCOE, Darryl D. 1139
Gallery Association of New York
   State   VOURVOULIAS, Sabrina M. 1289
Univ of Rhode Island   BERGEN, Daniel P. 85
HARRISON
Harrison Central Schs   WOOD, Arline L. 1363
HASTINGS ON HUDSON
Hastings Pub Schs   AFROMSKY, Ellen S. 7
HAVERSTRAW
Haverstraw Kings Daughters Pub Lib   GUBITS, Helen S. 475
HELMUTIS
Collins Correctional Facility   KING, Charles L. 650
HEMPSTEAD
Hempstead Public Lib   STEFANI, Carolyn R. 1185
Hofstra Univ   ANDREWS, Charles R. 26
    ARMSTRONG, Ruth C. 32
    CINQUE, Deborah G. 214
    COONEY, Joan D. 242
    COONEY, Martha D. 242
    FREESE, Melanie L. 401
    GIANNATTASI, Gerard E. . . . 430
    GRAVES, Howard E. 459
    JENNINGS, Vincent 598
    KRATZ, Charles E. 676
    STERN, Marc J. 1189
    WAGNER, Janet S. 1291
Queens Lib   LOUISDHON-WALTER,
    Marie L. 742
HERKIMER
Library Bureau Inc   VAN PELT, Peter J. 1277
HEWLETT
Hewlett-Woodmere Pub Lib   DESCIORA, Susan O. 294
    VOLLONO, Millicent D. 1288

NEW YORK (Cont'd)
HICKSVILLE
Briarcliffe Coll   NOTARSTEFANO, Vincent
                                                      C. 910
Hecksville High Sch Lib   MCCARTNEY, Margaret M. . . 794
Hicksville Pub Lib   SWORDS, Susan 1217
Hicksville Pub Schs   WICHMANN, Jane M. 1335
Our Lady of Mercy Sch   SCHMIDTMANN, Nancy K. . 1096
HIGHLAND
Highland Pub Lib   RANKIN, Carol A. 1007
Southeastern New York Lib   CRAWFORD-OPPENHIEM-
                                                      ER, Christine 257
                                                   LAWRENCE, Thomas A. 705

HIGHLAND FALLS
Constitution Island Association   MARTIN, Janet L. 776
HILLBURN
Bamado Central Sch District   BURGESON, Clair D. 159
HILLCREST
Rockefeller Univ   HESS, James W. 534
HOLBROOK
Sachem Pub Lib   ROMANELLI, Catherine A. . 1052
HORNELL
St James Mercy Hospital   SMITH, Brian D. 1153
HOUGHTON
Houghton Coll   DOEZEMA, Linda P. 308
                                                   LAUER, Jonathan D. 702

HUDSON
Hudson City Sch District   HENDRICKS, Elaine M. 527
HUDSON FALLS
Washington-Warren-Hamilton-Essex
  BOCES   GRAMINSKI, Denise M. 457
HUNTINGTON
Finley Junior High   NEWMAN, Eileen M. 899
Huntington Pub Lib   MCGRATH, Antoinette M. .. 807
                                                   ROSEN, Albert 1055
                                                   WULFING, Joyce 1374
Law Lib Management Inc   JASSIN, Raymond M. 595
Touro Coll   MARKOWITZ, Lois 771
HYDE PARK
National Archives & Records Admin   GRIFFITH, Sheryl 469
                                                   SEEBER, Frances M. 1111
                                                   TEICHMAN, Raymond J. 1230

IRVINGTON
Irvington Unified Sch District   GINSBERG, Barbara 438
Village of Irvington   PERILLO, Marie J. 958
ISLIP TERRACE
Islip Pub Lib   KLATT, Wilma F. 658
ITHACA
Cornell Univ   ASHMUN, Lawrence F. 36
                                                   AXTMANN, Margaret M. 42
                                                   CARSON, Anne R. 188
                                                   CASSARO, James P. 193
                                                   CHIANG, Katherine S. 207
                                                   CLARKE, D S. 218
                                                   COLMAN, Gould P. 233
                                                   COONS, William W. 242
                                                   CORAL, Lenore 245
                                                   DEMAS, Samuel G. 291
                                                   DIEFENBACH, Dale A. 301
                                                   EDDY, Donald D. 335
                                                   FINCH, C H. 377
                                                   HAMMOND, Jane L. 493
                                                   HASKO, John J. 510
                                                   HILLMANN, Diane I. 541
                                                   HUNTER, Carolyn O. 576
                                                   KENNEDY, Bruce M. 640
                                                   KIM, Chung N. 648
                                                   LAURENCE, Katherine S. 703
                                                   LIPPINCOTT, Joan K. 732
                                                   MILLER, J G. 838
                                                   OLSEN, Wallace C. 922
                                                   POWELL, Jill H. 988
                                                   SALTON, Gerard 1077
                                                   SCHNEDEKER, Donald W. .. 1096
                                                   SERCAN, Cecilia S. 1116
                                                   SLOCUM, Robert B. 1150
                                                   SPRAGG, Edwin B. 1175
                                                   STEWART, Linda G. 1192
                                                   WALD, Ingeborg 1294
                                                   WAWRO, Wanda T. 1311

NEW YORK (Cont'd)
ITHACA (Cont'd)
Cornell Univ
                                                   WEISS, Paul J. 1320
                                                   WILSON, Marijo S. 1352
                                                   ZASLAW, Neal 1386
Finger Lakes Lib System   MORRIS, Jennifer D. 866
                                                   PANZ, Richard 938
                                                   PARKHURST, Kathleen A. 942
Ithaca Coll   ERICSON, Margaret D. 353
                                                   HICKEY, John T. 536
National Planning Data Corp   SALTER, Douglas C. 1077
South Central Research Lib Council   PACKARD, Joan L. 933
                                                   STEINER, Janet E. 1186
Tompkins County   MCGINNIES, Nancy L. 806
JACKSON HEIGHTS
Queens Borough Pub Lib   KRAMER, Mollie W. 675
Robert R Walsh and Associates   WALSH, Robert R. 1300
JAMAICA
Catholic Med Center of Brooklyn &
  Queens   WOODS, Regina C. 1367
Jamaica Hospital   MANSBACH, Carolyn 767
Passionist Monastery   JOHNSON, James G. 605
Queens Borough Pub Lib   ALVAREZ, Ronald 19
                                                   BORRESS, Lewis R. 117
                                                   BREEN, Karen B. 131
                                                   COOKE, Constance B. 241
                                                   DICKERSON, D J. 300
                                                   FONTAINE, Sue 388
                                                   HARWOOD, Vern 510
                                                   HSU, Elizabeth L. 567
                                                   KUGLER, Sharon 682
                                                   LIU, Carol F. 734
                                                   MCMORRAN, Charles E. 815
                                                   RIECHEL, Rosemarie 1033
                                                   RUBINSTEIN, Roslyn 1065
                                                   SHAPIRO, Martin P. 1121
                                                   SIVULICH, Kenneth G. 1145
                                                   VENER, Lucille 1282
                                                   WASSERMAN, Ricki F. 1308
Queens Coll of the City Univ of New
  York   OHLE, William P. 919
St John's Univ   BENSON, James A. 83
                                                   CLARK, Philip M. 218
                                                   CORRY, Emmett 247
                                                   DOYAL, Patricia A. 317
                                                   GRANT, Mary A. 458
                                                   HABER, Mark N. 481
                                                   HECKMAN, Lucy T. 519
                                                   LANG, Jovian P. 695
                                                   LINDGREN, Arla M. 729
                                                   MARKE, Julius J. 771
                                                   MELTON RSM, Marie F. 823
                                                   NOLAN, John A. 907
                                                   PARR, Mary Y. 944
                                                   POWIS, Katherine E. 989
                                                   SZMUK, Szilvia E. 1218
                                                   TURLEY, Harriet M. 1264
                                                   WEINBERG, Bella H. 1317
JAMESTOWN
Chautauqua-Cattaraugus Lib System   HAYNES, Jean 516
                                                   LEE, Sylvia 711
James Prendergast Lib Association   KOCH, Judith L. 667
                                                   MORRIS, Kim 867
JERICHO
Covidea   REIS, Howard 1021
JOHNSON CITY
United Health Services   WESTERFIELD, Marjorie C. . 1327
JOHNSTOWN
Hamilton-Fulton-Montgomery BOCES   BAILIE, Donna L. 47
JORDAN
Jordan Elbridge Sch District   BERGEN, Dessa C. 85
KATONAH
Four Winds Hospital   STERN, Deborah S. 1189
Katonah Village Lib   KELLOGG, Marya S. 637
KENMORE
Buffalo & Erie County Pub Lib   MOHN, Wallace D. 852
Kenmore Mercy Hospital   TUBOLINO, Karen M. 1261
Sisters of St Mary of Namur   HEFNER, Xavier M. 520

NEW YORK (Cont'd)

KINGS PARK
New York State Office of Mental
  Health   MACINICK, James W. 755
KINGS POINT
US Merchant Marine Academy   BILLY, George J. 97
    BOVARNICK, Esther W. 120

LACKAWANNA
Lackawanna Sch District   BEDNAR, Sheila 73
LANCASTER
Lancaster Central Sch   DRZEWIECKI, Iris M. 321
LARCHMONT
Biblio-File Inc   LANDMAN, Lillian L. 693
Larchmont Pub Lib   BARRETT, John C. 59
    HESLER, June P. 534

LATHAM
BRS Information Technologies   BROWN, Jane E. 144
    BRUNELLE, Bette S. 150
    MCCLELLAND, Bruce A. 796
    PALMER, Lloyd G. 936
    RALBOVSKY, Edward A. 1004
    VEGTER, Amy H. 1281
    ZIRPOLO, Frank 1390

LEVITTOWN
Island Trees Pub Lib   KING, Dennis W. 650
LEWISTON
Coutts Lib Service   GRANTIER, John R. 458
    SCHMIEDL, Keith S. 1096

LINDENHURST
Lindenhurst Memorial Lib   MILNES, Patricia C. 845
    SALITA, Christine T. 1076
    WARD, Peter K. 1304

LIVERPOOL
Calocerinos & Spina Consulting   AUSTIN, Ralph A. 40
Liverpool Pub Lib   GOLDEN, Fay A. 445
    POLLY, Jean A. 981
    ROSSOFF, Judith H. 1059

LIVONIA
Livonia Pub Lib   DEUTSCH, Karen A. 296
LOCKPORT
NIOGA Lib System   KLIMEK, Chester R. 661
LOCUST VALLEY
Friends Academy   FOLCARELLI, Ralph J. 387
Portledge Sch   LAPIDUS, Lois E. 697
LONG BEACH
Allard K Lowenstem Pub Lib   FIRTH, Jennifer L. 379
Brookhaven National Laboratory   SERCHUK, Barnett 1116
Long Beach Pub Lib   PILLA, Marianne L. 973
LONG ISLAND
Adelphi Univ   SMITH, Adelaide M. 1152
Newsday Inc   HOFFMAN, David M. 547
LONG ISLAND CITY
LaGuardia Coll of the City Univ of NY   LOW, Frederick E. 743
LaGuardia Community Coll   GILSON, Barbara J. 437
New York City Board of Education   DONNELLY, Mary E. 311
Queens Borough Pub Lib   TANG, Grace L. 1222
LOUDONVILLE
Town of Colonie   NAYLOR, Richard J. 890
LYNBROOK
EBS Univ   FIEGAS, Barbara E. 375
Incorporated Village of Lynbrook   PARK, T P. 941
MACEDON
Pal-Mac Central Sch   WOLF, Catharine D. 1360
MANHASSET
Dodd Mead Publisher   DEE, Camille C. 286
Hanhasset Pub Schs   CAZZULINO, Clara P. 195
North Shore Univ Hospital   EISENBERG, Debra 340
    NAPOLITANO, Joan A. 887

MANLIUS
Manlius Lib   FERGUSON, Jane M. 372
MARLBORO
Marlboro Central Sch District   BAKER, Marie A. 49
MARYKNOLL
Maryknoll Sch of Theology   O'HALLORAN, James V. 918
MASSAPEQUA
Massapequa Pub Schs   SPIEGEL, Bertha 1174
Plainedge Pub Lib   EISNER, Joseph 341
MASTIC BEACH
William Floyd Sch District   SUDA, Rullie A. 1206

NEW YORK (Cont'd)

MELVILLE
Half Hollow Hills Community Lib   WOODS, Janice T. 1367
Holzmacher Mclendon & Murrell PC   UZZO, Beatrice C. 1270
Katharine Gibbs Sch   EDWARDS, Barnett A. 337
Newsday Videotex Services   RAYNOR, Julie M. 1011
United Technologies Corp   SLOAN, Carol L. 1149
MEXICO
Oswego BOCES   MAUTINO, Patricia H. 787
MIDDLE ISLAND
Longwood Central Sch District   NARBY, Ann E. 888
MIDDLE VILLAGE
Pub Sch 49 Queens   WIENER, Sylvia B. 1336
MIDDLETOWN
Orange County Community Coll   BAUM, Christina D. 66
Ramapo Catskill Lib System   ANGLIN, Richard V. 28
    NELSON, James B. 894
Times Herald Record   SCARANO, Lisa C. 1087
MINEOLA
New York State   LODATO, James J. 736
Winthrop-Univ Hospital   COOK, Virginia I. 240
MONTICELLO
E B Crawford Memorial Lib   DORN, Robert J. 313
MORRISVILLE
State Univ of New York at Morrisville   DREW, Wilfred E. 319
MT KISCO
Melin Nelson Associates   NELSON, Nancy M. 894
Mt Kisco Pub Lib   BIRO, Juliane 99
Northern Westchester Hospital Center   WILLOUGHBY, Nona C. . . . 1349
MT VERNON
Bob Seitz Communications   SEITZ, Robert J. 1113
Consumers Union   INGRAM, Saralyn 583
Mt Vernon Hospital   COAN, Mary L. 224
Mount Vernon Pub Lib   MITTELGLUCK, Eugene L. . . 850
    O'DELL, Lorraine I. 916
    ROSSWURM, K M. 1059

NANUET
GJM Associates   MOLLO, Terry 853
NAPLES
Marketing Intelligence Service   BROOK, Rick 140
NASSAU
Carabateas Responsive Information
  Srv   CARABATEAS, Clarissa D. . . 180
NESCONSET
Town of Smithtown   GRAVITZ, Ina A. 459
NEW CITY
New City Lib   O'CONNELL, Susan 915
    SIMON, Patricia B. 1140

NEW HYDE PARK
Herricks Pub Schs   HARRIS, Martha 505
Hillside Pub Lib   ITKIN, Stanley 585
Long Island Jewish Medical Center   ATKIN, Shifra 37
    KING, Esther 651
NEW PALTZ
State Univ of New York at New Paltz   CONNORS, William E. 238
    LEE, Chui C. 709
    NYQUIST, Corinne E. 913
Ulster County Board   STAINO, Rocco A. 1178
NEW ROCHELLE
Coll of New Rochelle   GRECO, Gloria T. 461
    MOSLANDER, Charlotte D. . . 871
    RUSSO, Mary 1070
Iona Coll   LARKIN, Patrick J. 698
Monroe Business Institute   KONOVALOFF, Maria S. . . . 670
New Rochelle Pub Lib   GIORDANO, Frederick S. . . 438
    ZINMAN, Sandra 1389

NEW YORK
A C Nielsen Co   BEHANNA, William R. 74
The Academy of American Poets   CAMMACK, Bruce P. 175
Access Publishing Co   STILLMAN, Stanley W. 1194
Alan Patricof Associates   RUBIN, Myra P. 1064
Ally Gargano M C A Advertising Ltd   COHEN, Marsha C. 228
The American Alpine Club   FLETCHER, Patricia A. 385
American Assn of Advertising
  Agencies   APPEL, Marsha C. 29
    FENTON, Joan T. 371
    HUBBARD, Susan E. 568
    MORRIS, Margaret J. 867
    ZILAVY, Julie A. 1388

NEW YORK (Cont'd)
NEW YORK (Cont'd)

American Banker - Bond Buyer
ALLAN, John 14
BURKE, Edward 160
CASEY, Robert W. 192
FINCH, Brian 377
FREY, Ned 402
HENDERSON, Brad 526
KRAUS, James 676
LEVINE, Margaret A. 720
MALKIN, Peter 763
NOVEMBER, Robert S. 911
RUSLING, Con A. 1068
TIERNEY, Richard H. 1244
TYSON, David 1267
VELLA, Carl 1281
ZIMMERMAN, William 1389

American Bible Society
WOSH, Peter J. 1369
YAKEL, Elizabeth 1376

Am Ctr for Stanislavski Theatre Art Inc
MOORE, Sonia 861

American Council for the Arts
EISENBERG, Alan J. 340

American Craft Council
SECKELSON, Linda E. 1110

American Field Services International
GELLER, Lawrence D. 426

American Film & Video Association
TROJAN, Judith L. 1257

American Foundation for the Blind
ELLIS, Peter K. 345

American Guild of Organists
LAWRENCE, Arthur P. 704

Am Inst of Aeronautics & Astronautics
BUSTAMANTE, Corazon R. . 166
LAWRENCE, Barbara 704
WORTON, Geoffrey P. 1369

Am Inst of Certified Pub Accountants
BEHAR, Evelyn W. 74
NELOMS, Karen H. 893
ROSENFELD, Lillian E. 1056

American Institute of Physics
HOWITT, Jeff 566
LERNER, Rita G. 717
MARKS, Robert H. 771
PARISI, Paul A. 940
WARNOW-BLEWETT, Joan N. 1305

American International Group
GOLLOP, Sandra G. 447
STRAZDON, Maureen E. ... 1201

American Jewish Committee
HOROWITZ, Cyma M. 560
RITTER, Helen 1036

American Journal of Nursing Co
PATTISON, Frederick W. 948

American Kennel Club
VESLEY, Roberta A. 1283

American Management Association
JONES, Anne 611
LAMBKIN, Claire A. 691

American Museum of Natural History
KITT, Sandra E. 657
SHIH, Diana 1130

American Numismatic Society
CAMPBELL, Francis D. 176

American Petroleum Institute
BRENNER, Everett H. 133
HOFFMAN, Allen 547
LINDER, Eliott 729
SHERRILL, Jocelyn T. 1129
TERLIZZI, Joseph M. 1232

American Reading Council
PALMER, Julia R. 936
SCHWABACHER, Sara A. . 1104

American Record Collector's Exchange
MOSES, Julian M. 871

American Society of Civil Engineers
EDWARDS, Melanie G. 337

Anderson Russell Killsolick
KAIN, Joan P. 622

Andrew W Mellon Foundation
MOTIHAR, Kamla 872

Anglo-American Sch of Moscow
VOSE, Deborah R. 1289

Archive Film Productions Inc
MONTGOMERY, Patrick 856

Aroh for Resrch In Archetypal Symbolism
RONNBERG, Annmari 1053

Archive of Contemporary Music
GEORGE, B 427
WHEELER, David 1328

Arthur Young & Co
CARLSON, Robert E. 182
MCBRIDE, Jessica W. 792

Aspen Systems Corp
BRINBERG, Herbert R. 136

Associated Lib Service Inc
WUNDERLICH, Penina 1374

Associated Press
PEDERSON, Christopher 954
PISTILLI, Susan A. 976
SHAPIRO, Barbara G. 1121

Association for Computing Machinery
WEINER, Carolynn N. 1318

Assn for Volntry Surgical Contraception
RECORD, William J. 1013

NEW YORK (Cont'd)
NEW YORK (Cont'd)

Assn of the Bar of the City of New York
BURGALASSI, Anthony J. ... 159
GRECH, Anthony P. 461
RUIZ-VALERA, Phoebe L. ... 1067
WILLIAMS, David W. 1342

AT&T Bell Laboratories
O'TOOLE, James F. 930
ROGGENKAMP, Alice M. ... 1050
SWINBURNE, Ralph E. 1216

Austrian Lance & Stewart
ROJAS, Alexandra A. 1051

Ayerst Laboratories
BARNETT, Philip 58
SCHNEIDER, Helen S. 1097

Baker Spielvogal Bates
SCHACHTER, Bert 1088

Bank of America
BATES, Ellen 63

Bank Street Coll of Education
KULLESEID, Eleanor R. 683

Bankers Trust Co of New York
GINSBURG, Carol L. 438
SHALLENBERGER, Anna F. 1119

Barnard College
TUCKER, Mary E. 1262

Barrett Smith Schapiro Simon & Armstrong
SULLIVAN, Stephen W. ... 1208

Baruch Coll of the City Univ of New York
BIDDLE, Stanton F. 94
DIMARTINO, Diane J. 303
HEUMAN, Rabbi J. 535
HILL, George R. 539
LOWE, Ida B. 743
MEANS, Spencer 820
OSTROW, Rona 929
POLLARD, Bobbie T. 981
PRAGER, George A. 989
SLUSS, Sara B. 1150

Baseline Inc
MONACO, James 854

BBDO
SANTORO, Tesse F. 1082

BEA Associates
HEFFRON, Betsy A. 520

Beauty Without Cruelty USA
THURSTON, Ethel H. 1243

Bessemer Trust Co N A
STOOPS, Louise 1198

Beth Israel Medical Center
GALLAGHER, Patricia E. 414
SCHWARTZ, Dorothy D. ... 1104

Bibliographical Society of America
TICHENOR, Irene 1244

BMG Music/RCA
WOOD, Sallie B. 1365

Books for Libraries
SHAPIRO, S R. 1121

Booz Allen & Hamilton Inc
LANDES, J C. 692
WILLNER, Richard A. 1349

Bowker Electronic Publishing
ALLEN, Robert R. 16
HUDES, Nan 569
VONZIEGESAR, Franz 1289

Bowne & Co Inc
BARRA, Carol H. 58

Breed Abbott & Morgan
GREENE, Margaret A. 464
NOVICK, Ruth 911
STRINGFELLOW, William T. 1202

Broadcast Music Inc
TICE, Margaret E. 1244

Brooklyn Pub Lib
BROUDE, Ronald 141

Broude Brothers Limited
GABOR, John M. 411

BRS Information Technologies
HULL, Debbie M. 572
KAHN, Martin F. 622
KELLY, Jane A. 637
QUAIN, Julie R. 999
RUGOFF, Iris L. 1066

Burson-Marsteller
MACCALLUM, Barbara B. 754

Business & Technology Online
SHELTON, Anita L. 1126

Business International Electronic
CAPPS, Ian M. 180

Business Week
MUNDER, Barbara 879

Cabrini Medical Center
KASSIN, Abby I. 629

Cahill Gordon & Reindel
CAHN, Mary Z. 171
DAVENPORT, Margaret J. ... 275
LUNG, Chan S. 748

Cahners Magazines
GERHARDT, Lillian N. 428

Carl & Lily Pforzheimer Foundation Inc
REIMAN, Donald H. 1020

Carnegie Corp of New York
HAYNES, Patricia 516

Catalyst
CROCKER, Susan O. 259

CBS Inc
D'ALLEYRAND, Marc R. ... 270
KAPNICK, Laura B. 626
SALZ, Kay 1078
WOLOZIN, Sara 1362

Chase Manhattan Bank
NEUBERG, Karen S. 897

Chemical Bank
O'DONNELL, Maureen D. ... 917
PENNELL, Peggy P. 957

Cineaste
CROWDUS, Gary A. 261

NEW YORK (Cont'd)
NEW YORK (Cont'd)

Citibank North America	SANCHEZ, Eliana P. 1079
	WILKINS, Peggy 1340
Citicorp	PINEDA, Conchita J. 974
Citicorp Development	GREENBERG, Walter E. 463
Citicorp Electronic Securities	CIRILLO, Kenneth 215
Citicorp Information Business	GREENHOUSE, Lee R. 464
City Coll of the City Univ of New York	ALLENTUCK, Marcia E. 16
	CLINE, Herman H. 222
	DOUGLAS, Jacqueline A. . . . 314
	DUNLAP, Barbara J. 326
	FRANKLIN, Laurel F. 398
	HINDS, Vira C. 542
	KUHNER, Robert A. 683
	MOORE, Jane R. 859
	PERKUS, Paul C. 959
	RAJEC, Elizabeth M. 1004
	WRIGHT, Sylvia H. 1373
City of New York	BOCKMAN, Eugene J. 109
	DISHON, Robert M. 305
City Univ of New York	ANGEL, Kenneth E. 27
	RA, Marsha H. 1001
Clark Boardman Co Ltd	MORSE, Alan L. 869
CNR Partners	UNNOLD, Terry 1269
Coll Board of New York	AUBRY, John C. 38
Coll of Insurance	ROSIGNOLO, Beverly A. . . . 1057
Collegiate Sch Inc	BRUGNOLOTTI, Phyllis T. . . . 150
Columbia Univ	ANDERSON, Rachael K. 25
	ARMSTRONG, Joanne D. . . . 32
	BAGNALL, Whitney S. 45
	BANKS-ISZARD, Kimberly
	K. 54
	BATTIN, Patricia 64
	BELANGER, Terry 76
	BERNSTEIN, Mark P. 89
	BERTCHUME, Gary 90
	BORRIES, Michael S. 117
	CHIBNIK, Katharine R. 207
	CHO-PARK, Jaung J. 210
	CRYSTAL, Bernard R. 262
	CURTIS, James A. 267
	DELLA-CAVA, Olha 289
	ELLENBOGEN, Rudolph S. . . 343
	FEDUNOK, Suzanne 368
	FRANCK, Jane P. 396
	GOODMAN, Edward C. 449
	GREENBERG, Charles J. . . . 463
	GRELE, Ronald J. 467
	GREWENOW, Peter W. 467
	HAEFLIGER, Kathleen A. . . . 482
	HAGSTROM, Jack W. 483
	HARRIS, Carolyn L. 504
	HASWELL, Hollee 511
	HOLLIDAY, Geneva R. 552
	HOOVER, James L. 557
	JACKSON, Charles G. 587
	KEMPE, Deborah A. 639
	LEARMONT, Carol L. 707
	LESNIK, Pauline 718
	LEWIS, David W. 723
	LOHF, Kenneth A. 737
	MANDEL, Carol A. 764
	MAY, Jonathan B. 788
	MENT, David M. 824
	MOLZ, Redmond K. 854
	MOUNT, Ellis 873
	PAGEL, Scott B. 934
	PALMER, Paul R. 936
	PASQUARIELLA, Susan K. . . 946
	PAULSON, Barbara A. 950
	PEARCE, Karla J. 952
	PETERS, Paul E. 962
	RAUCH, Theodore G. 1010
	RICHARDS, Daniel T. 1028
	RODERER, Nancy K. 1047
	SHERBY, Louise S. 1127
	SMIRAGLIA, Richard P. 1152
	STALKER, Dianne S. 1178
	STOLLER, Michael E. 1196

NEW YORK (Cont'd)
NEW YORK (Cont'd)

Columbia Univ	
	TAYLOR, Arlene G. 1226
	THOMAS, Catherine M. 1236
	THOMPSON, Susan O. 1241
	TOYAMA, Ryoko 1253
	WEDGEWORTH, Robert W. . . 1315
	WOO, Janice 1363
The Communication Studio Inc	VAUGHAN, John 1279
The Conference Board Inc	HERNANDEZ, Tamsen M. . . . 532
Consolidated Edison Co	JAFFE, Steven 591
Consolidated Edison of New York Inc	DIETRICH, Peter J. 302
Continental Insurance Co	GAINES, Irene A. 412
Cooper Union - Advancement of Sci	
& Art	VAJDA, Elizabeth A. 1271
Coopers & Lybrand	BATTINO, Bill 65
	BERGFELD, C D. 86
	GRANDE, Paula G. 457
	HALL, Alix M. 486
	KILBERG, Jacqueline L. 648
	PORTA, Catherine M. 984
	POWELL, Timothy W. 989
Coordinating Council of Literary Mags	CASSELL, Kay A. 193
Cornell Medical Center	TOMASULO, Patricia A. 1249
Cornell Univ	BRAUDE, Robert M. 129
	PICCIANO, Jacqueline L. . . . 970
	REID, Carolyn A. 1018
	THOMSON, Diane G. 1241
Coudert Brothers	RUBENS, Jane C. 1064
Council on Foreign Relations	ETHERIDGE, Virginia 355
	MILLER, Barbara K. 835
Cravath Swaine & Moore	ADAMO, Marilyn H. 4
	BONADIA, Roseann 113
	GRAY, Kevin P. 460
Creamer Dickson Basford Inc	BOTKIN, Karen R. 118
Cuadra Associates Inc	SMITH, David F. 1154
D'Arcy Masius Benton & Bowles	BURKE, J L. 160
Data Resources	CORVESE, Lisa A. 248
	ESSMAN, Tallaine G. 355
Davis Hoxie Faithfull & Hapgood	HAYWARD, Diane J. 517
Davis Markel & Edwards	BENNIN, Cheryl S. 82
Davis Polk & Wardwell	MAGEE, Patricia A. 759
	PERRY, Paula J. 960
DDB Needham Worldwide Inc	BROMLEY, Alice V. 140
Dean Witter Reynolds	DAVID, Julia A. 276
Debevoise & Plimpton	JAROSEK, Joan E. 594
Dechert Price & Rhoads	WIERZBA, Christine 1337
Deloitte Haskins & Sells	KRAUSS, Susan E. 676
	LIN, Tung F. 728
Designs for Information Inc	MILLER, Ellen L. 837
Dewey Ballantine Bushby Palmer &	
Wood	SEER, Gitelle 1111
DIALOG Information Services Inc	ESPO, Hal 354
	KACHALA, Bohdanna I. 621
Dillon Read & Co Inc	BOWLES, Nancy J. 121
	SCHAFFER, Rita K. 1089
Disclosure Information Group	ARTHUR, Christine 35
	GRUENBERG, Michael L. . . . 474
Donaldson Lufkin & Jenrette	CLOWE, Isabel B. 223
Dorothy Thomas Co	THOMAS, Dorothy 1236
Drama Book Publishers	PINE, Ralph 974
Drexel Burnham Lambert	RIPIN, Laura G. 1035
Dreyfus Corp	DIFEDE, Robert F. 302
Dun & Bradstreet Corp	GOOGINS, Jennifer J. 450
Dun & Bradstreet International	JURKOWICH, George J. 620
Dwight Sch	ELLIS, Kathleen V. 344
E F Hutton Co Inc	STERLING, Sheila 1189
E M Warburg Pincus & Co Inc	SOROBAY, Roman T. 1169
E P Dutton	BUCKLEY, Virginia L. 154
EBASCO Services Inc	AKS, Gloria 9
	NOGA, Susan D. 907
	VAN BRUNT, Amy S. 1272
Eberstadt Fleming Inc	THOM, Janice E. 1235
Educational & Industrial Television	DAMOTH, Douglas L. 272
Educational Broadcasting Corp	DAWSON, Victoria A. 282
Educational Film & Video Association	MACINTYRE, Ronald R. 755

NEW YORK (Cont'd)
NEW YORK (Cont'd)

EIC Intelligence Inc
JAMIESON, Peter V. 593
KOLLEGGER, James G. 669
PRONIN, Monica 995
VITART, Jane A. 1286
Elf Aquitaine Inc CAMBRIA, Roberto 174
Elsevier Science Publishers HUNTER, Karen A. 576
Empire Blue Cross & Blue Shield CHANG, Daphne Y. 200
DYER, Esther R. 330
ROSHON, Nina C. 1057
Engineering Information Inc BERGER, Mary C. 85
BERRYMAN, Karen L. 90
BROWN-SPRUILL, Debra K. . 149
CABEEN, Samuel K. 170
LANDAU, Herbert B. 692
MCCOY, Barbara S. 799
MOLINE, Gloria 853
English-Speaking Union GRAY, Karen 460
Equitable Archives MATTHEOU, Antonia 785
Ernst & Whinney REID, Richard C. 1019
Experimente Old and Rare Books RAMER, Bruce J. 1005
Facts On File Inc KNAPPMAN, Edward W. 663
Fashion Institute of Technology MARTIN, Richard 778
ROZENE, Janette B. 1064
SMITH, Sweetman R. 1161
Federal Home Loan Bank of New
York LEVINTON, Juliette 721
Federal Reserve Bank of New York CONGDON, Rodney H. 236
LASKOWITZ, Roberta G. . . . 700
TRUEBLOOD, Emily H. 1259
WOOTEN, Jean A. 1368
FEICO NEWCOMB, Jonathan 898
Feit & Ahrens HERBERT, Annette F. 530
Fiduciary Trust Co International ARMEIT, Marilyn 32
FIND/SVP Inc BINGHAM, Kathleen S. 97
DENNIS, Anne R. 292
GARVIN, Andrew P. 421
Finley Kumble Wagner Heine et al SCIOLINO, Elaine T. 1106
Firehouse Communications SALY, Alan J. 1078
First Boston Corp LANDOLFI, Lisa M. 693
First Manhattan Co SUSMAN, Beatrice 1210
First Manhattan Consulting Group TAPIERO, Judith 1223
Forbes Inc MINTZ, Anne P. 847
Forbes Magazine BENDES, Adele N. 79
Ford Foundation HARDING, Mary H. 500
LAIST, Sharon B. 688
SAYWARD, Nick H. 1087
Fordham Univ DINDAYAL, Joyce S. 304
ESSIEN, Victor K. 354
TRACY, Janet R. 1253
The Foundation Center CAVINESS, Ann N. 195
DERRICKSON, Margaret 294
Fndtn, Children With Lrng Disabilities GILLIGAN, Julie 436
Framework for Information Inc FREIFELD, Roberta I. 401
MASYR, Caryl L. 783
Franklin Furnace Archive Inc HOGAN, Matthew 549
Franklin Watts Inc VESTAL, Jeanne G. 1283
Fred Alger Management Inc HERMAN, Marsha 531
Frederic R Harris Inc CANDELMO, Emily 178
Frederick Cohen Productions COHEN, Frederick 228
French Institute-Alliance Francaise GITNER, Fred J. 439
Friends Seminary WARNER, Elaine 1305
Frost & Sullivan Inc BORKENSTEIN, Donald M. . . 116
NAPOLITANO, Wanda M. . . . 887
SULLIVAN, Daniel M. 1207
SULLIVAN, Diane M. 1207
G P Putnam Sons GAUCH, Patricia L. 422
Gale Research Co GEISER, Elizabeth A. 425
HUBBARD, Roy 568
Garland Publishing Inc BALK, Leo F. 52
Garvin Information Services PROSKE, James 995
General American Investors Co Inc JONES, Jennifer R. 613
General Theological Seminary HOOGAKKER, David A. 556
Goldman Sachs & Co KOLATA, Judith 669
POJE, Mary E. 980
Goldome Bank CALLINAN, Mary H. 174

NEW YORK (Cont'd)
NEW YORK (Cont'd)

Gossage Regan Associates Inc
COPLEN, Ron 244
GESKE, Aina S. 430
GOSSAGE, Wayne 453
REGAN, Muriel 1017
TURNER, Gurley 1264
Grey Advertising DAGATA, Marie 269
Grolier Electronic Publishing Inc ARGANBRIGHT, David 31
TOWNLEY, Richard L. 1253
Guggenheim Memorial Foundation TANSELLE, G T. 1223
H P Kraus Rare Books and
Manuscripts FOLTER, Roland 388
Haight Gardner Poor & Havens COMEAU, Amy R. 234
Haines Lundberg Waehler SPINA, Marie C. 1175
Handy Associates Inc KAZANJIAN, Donna S. 632
Harlem Hospital MANDAL, Mina R. 764
Harlequin Enterprises JACKSON, Nancy D. 588
Haworth Press Inc COHEN, Bill 228
FRALEY, Ruth A. 395
RIZZO, John D. 1037
Health Insurance Plan of Greater NY MOUNIR, Khalil A. 873
Hebrew Arts Sch FLOERSHEIMER, Lee M. . . . 385
Heidrick & Struggles Inc JONG, Jennifer L. 616
High Density Systems Inc PAVLAKIS, Christopher 950
Hill Beats & Nash RABER, Steven 1001
Historical Concepts Inc WOLFE, Allis 1360
Hospital for Special Surgery DIN, Munir U. 304
Hughes Hubbard & Reed GREEN, Charlene 461
RISH, Jennifer G. 1035
ROSS, Ellen T. 1058
VELLEMAN, Ruth A. 1281
Human Resources Sch
Hunter Coll of the City Univ of New
York AUFSES, Harriet W. 39
BRAUER, Regina 129
SALAZAR, Pamela R. 1076
SEGAL, Judith 1112
Huttonline E F Hutton GOLD, Susan L. 444
I M Pei & Partners BURROUGHS, Christine M. . . 163
IMNET SHAPP, Lenore 1122
Independent Schs Multi-Media Center
Inc FISHER, Carolyn H. 380
Informaco Inc BOWKER, Scott W. 121
Institute for East-West Security
Studies DEVERA, Rosalinda M. 297
Inst of Electrical & Electronic Engnrs FERRERE, Cathy M. 373
Insurance Information Institute GORDON, Marjorie 451
International Data Corp GROTE, Janet H. 473
International Society of Copier Artists NEADERLAND, Louise O. . . . 890
ITT Corp HUNTER, Gregory S. 576
NARCISO, Susan D. 888
International Theatre Institute BURDICK, Elizabeth B. 158
International Thomson Organization
Ltd HALL, Robert C. 488
JACHINO, Robert J. 586
Interpublic Group of Companies FEUERSTEIN, Robin 374
J C Penney Co Inc MOLITERNO, Daniel A. 853
J P Morgan Securities HUDAK, Barbara M. 569
J Pierpont Morgan Lib NEEDHAM, Paul 891
J Walter Thompson Co GOODSELL, Joan W. 450
KELLEY, Dennis L. 636
Jamaica National Investment EDWARDS, Diane H. 337
Jamaica National Investment
Promotion PHILLIPS, Angela B. 967
SAUNDERS, Dorette 1084
Janes Publishing Co Inc Ltd MCHALE, Joseph T. 808
Jazz Record Center COHEN, Frederick S. 228
Jennison Associates Capital Corp RANSOM, Cynthia E. 1007
Jewish Braille Institute of America Inc JAHR, Joanne B. 591
Jewish Guild for the Blind MASSIS, Bruce E. 782
John Jay Coll of Criminal Justice,
CUNY LUTZKER, Marilyn L. 750
MARGOLIES, Alan 770
ROWLAND, Eileen 1062
John Wiley & Sons Inc ARLINGTON, Bill 31
FORD, Andrew E. 389
HARMON, James R. 502
JOHNSON, Richard O. 608
KING, Timothy B. 652
LESURE, Alan B. 718

NEW YORK (Cont'd)
NEW YORK (Cont'd)

John Wiley & Sons Inc

MELKIN, Audrey D. 822
WILEY, Deborah E. 1339
WITSENHAUSEN, Helen A.   1358
Jones Day Reavis & Pogue   GOLDMAN, Martha A. 445
Joseph E Seagram Co   GROSS, Alice 472
Julliard Sch   GOTTLIEB, Jane E. 453
K G Saur Inc   COOPER, Carol D. 242
Kaye Scholer Fierman Hays &
  Handler   GOODHARTZ, Gerald 448
                                   PARRIS, Angela P. 944
Kenyon & Kenyon   CULLEN, Martin J. 263
Kidder Peabody & Co Inc   ANTONETZ, Dolores 29
                                   DARNOWSKI, Christina M. . . 275
                                   DOOLING, Marie 312
Kirkus Reviews   LONG, Joanna R. 739
Kluwer Law Book Publishers Inc   BERNSTEIN, Sidney 89
Kramer Levin Nessen Kamin &
  Frankel   CHICCO, Giuliano 208
                                   CINQUE, Douglas V. 214
Kummerfeld Associates Inc   MILLER-KUMMERFELD,
                                     Elizabeth 843
Kyodo News International Inc   NAKAZATO, Kazuo 887
                                   STEIN, Pamela H. 1185
Laser Magnetic Storage International MOES, Robert T. 852
Latham & Watkins   LEWIS, Anne 722
Lazard Freres & Co   BENJAMIN, R D. 81
                                   SMITH, Sharon M. 1160
Leading National Advertisers   KOURY, Kyra 673
Lebhar-Friedman Inc   KRAMER, Allan F. 675
                                   LAMBE, Michael 690
                                   WESELTEER, Ruth 1325
LeBoeuf Lamb Leiby & MacRae   CHICCO, Meg 208
                                   FRANKENSTEIN, Steven S. . 397
                                   COHEN, Rochelle F. 229
Legal Aid Society
Lehman Coll of the City Univ of New
  York   DEMANDY, Claire 291
                                   RIDER, William J. 1032
Lenox Hill Hospital   DANSKER, Shirley E. 274
Levine Huntley Schmidt & Beaver   LOVARI, John A. 743
Lib Automation Products   ERLAND, Virginia K. 353
Lib Journal   BERRY, John N. 90
                                   FLETCHER, Janet 384
                                   FOX, Bette L. 394
LINK Resources Corp   FISCHER, Margaret T. 379
                                   GAFFNER, Haines B. 412
                                   SIECK, Steven K. 1135
                                   WRIGHT, Bernell 1370
Long Island Univ   MOFFAT, Edward S. 852
Lord Day & Lord   FRANK, Penny G. 397
LSI   PISCITELLI, Rosalie A. 976
Lutheran Council in the USA   KENDRICK, Alice M. 640
Macmillan Publishing Co   BERNAL, Rose M. 88
                                   HOWELL, Josephine T. 565
                                   MCELDERRY, Margaret K. . . 804
                                   WHIPPLE, Judith R. 1329
Manhattan Coll   WELSH, Harry E. 1323
Manhattan Comunty Coll, City Univ of
  NY   LOWRY, Lina M. 745
Manhattan Eye Ear & Throat Hospital WOFSE, Joy G. 1359
Manhattan Punch Line Theatre   BOWLEY, Craig 121
Manhattan Sch of Music   BRISTAH, Pamela J. 137
                                   HOFFMAN, Christine A. 547
Mannes Coll of Music   DAVIS, Deborah G. 278
                                   VAN BIEMA, Mary E. 1272
Manufacturers Hanover   RAUM, Tamar 1010
Markscope Inc   ETZI, Richard 356
Marsh & McLennan Inc   AARON, Rina S. 1
                                   COOK, Pamela D. 240
                                   KUCSMA, Susan P. 682
McGraw-Hill Book Co   ALMAN, Richard D. 17
                                   BRAGG, Sanford B. 127
                                   MARKERT, Patricia B. 771
                                   SMITH, Richard L. 1160
                                   SOLOMON, Samuel H. 1166
McGraw-Hill Bookstores   BOWMAN, James K. 121
McGraw-Hill Information Systems   JENSEN, Fred O. 598
McGraw-Hill International Book Co   HARDEN, Jon B. 499

NEW YORK (Cont'd)
NEW YORK (Cont'd)

McGraw-Hill Publications Co   ROWLANDS, Marvin L. 1063
McKinsey & Co   BERGMANN, Allison M. 86
                                   CARICONE, Paul 181
                                   KLINE, Harriet 661
Media Center for Children   BRAUN, Robert L. 130
                                   GAFFNEY, Maureen 412
Memorial Sloan-Kettering Cancer
  Center   ABBITT, Viola I. 1
                                   BECKER, Jeanne 72
Mercantile Lib   ROTH, Claire J. 1059
Merrill Lynch   BONACORDA, James J. 113
                                   DREZEN, Richard 319
                                   GREENBERG, Linda 463
Merrill Lynch Pierce Fenner & Smith WALKER, Jeanette F. 1295
Metropolitan Business Systems Inc D'ANGELO, Paul P. 272
Metropolitan Museum of Art   COVERT, Nadine 252
                                   DAY, Ross 283
                                   PINES, Doralynn 974
                                   WALKER, William B. 1296
                                   WERNER, Edward K. 1324
Milbank Tweed Hadley & McCloy   RESCIGNO, Dolores S. 1024
                                   SANDERS, Robin S. 1080
Mobil Oil Corp   DIGIOVANNA, Josephine A. . 303
                                   MARSHALL, Patricia K. 775
                                   ROBERTSON, Betty M. 1041
Modern Language Association   MACKESY, Eileen M. 756
                                   SPEARS, Dee E. 1172
Moody's Investors Service   BING, Robert H. 97
                                   KOPPELMAN, William H. . . . 671
                                   LAMBERT, Sheila S. 690
                                   ZOTTOLI, Danny A. 1390
Morgan & Finnegan   CURCI, Lucy 265
Morgan Guaranty Trust Co   SMITH, Melanie W. 1158
Morgan Stanley & Co   DESSER, Darrilyn 296
                                   ENGLER, Gretchen 349
                                   JONES, Sarah C. 615
                                   LAWSON, George F. 705
                                   MAYOPOULOS, Karen L. . . . 791
                                   VAZQUEZ, Edward 1280
Moseley Associates Inc   MOSELEY, Cameron S. 870
Mount Sinai Medical Center   MORGAN, Lynn K. 864
MSL International Ltd   RATZABI, Arlene 1010
Mudge Rose Guthrie Alexander &
  Ferdon   BRILL, Krista C. 136
                                   MARTIN, Margaret B. 777
Municipal Art Society   SWIESZKOWSK, L S. 1216
Museum of Broadcasting   DAVIDSON, Steven I. 276
Museum of Jewish Heritage   SCHREIBMAN, Fay C. 1099
Museum of Modern Art   BAXTER, Paula A. 67
                                   EKDAHL, Janis K. 341
                                   PHILLPOT, Clive J. 969
                                   SLOAN, William J. 1150
                                   STARR, Daniel A. 1182
Museum of the American Indian   WEATHERFORD, Elizabeth . 1311
Museum of the City of New York   COLEMAN, Faith 231
                                   TAYLOR, Robert N. 1228
Mutual of New York Financial
  Services   GROSS, Gretchen 472
N W Ayer Inc   BUSSEY, Holly J. 165
Naremco Services Inc   CROCKETT, Denise J. 259
NAACP Legal Defense & Eductnl
  Fund Inc   GLOECKNER, Donna S. 441
National Broadcasting Co   FRIEDMAN, Judy B. 404
                                   KATZ, Doris B. 630
                                   LEVINSON, Debra J. 721
                                   MAYER, Vera 789
National Multiple Sclerosis Society CALVANO, Margaret 174
                                   LAMANN, Amber N. 689
Neal-Schuman Publishers Inc   PEDOLSKY, Andrea D. 954
                                   SCHUMAN, Patricia G. 1103
Neurosciences Institute   NARDUCCI, Frances 888
New Museum of Contemporary Art   FERGUSON, Russell 372
New School for Social Research   SETTANNI, Joseph A. 1117
New York Academy of Medicine   BALKEMA, John B. 52
                                   CLARE, Richard W. 216
                                   KIRKPATRICK, Brett A. 655
                                   PERRY, Claudia A. 960
                                   RICHARDSON, Emma G. . . 1029

NEW YORK (Cont'd)
  NEW YORK (Cont'd)
    New York Academy of Medicine
    WOLFE, N J. 1361
    New York City Board of Education
    KLEIMAN, Rhoda E. 659
    MORRIS, Irving 866
    PEARLMUTTER, Regina S. . . 952
    WONSEVER, Eithne C. 1363
    New York City Bureau of Building
      Design
    LEE, Sang C. 711
    New York City Dept of Records &
      Info Srv
    BUTLER, Tyrone G. 167
    KIRWAN, Kathleen 656
    TAYLOR, Patricia A. 1228
    New York City Health & Hospitals
      Corp
    GALVIN, Jeanne D. 415
    New York City Human Resources
      Admin
    BENSON, Harold W. 83
    PETTOLINA, Anthony M. . . . 965
    New York County Board of Education
    RABIN, Alan H. 1001
    New York County Lawyers
      Association
    GALGAN, Mary N. 413
    TANZER, Barbara 1223
    New York Daily News
    BROWNE, Scott M. 148
    ROSENTHAL, Faigi 1057
    NY Genealogical & Biographical
      Society
    POHL, Gunther E. 979
    New York Historical Society
    BARR, Jeffrey A. 58
    CAPRIELIAN, Arevig 180
    GOERNER, Tatiana 443
    MOONEY, James E. 858
    REMECZKI, Paul W. 1022
    New York Hospital
    LERNER, Adele A. 717
    New York Infirmary
    LEYDEN, Annette 724
    New York Law Sch
    KELLER, Katarina S. 635
    MASTRANGELO, Paul J. . . . 783
    MOLINARI, Joseph G. 853
    NEWMAN, Marie S. 899
    SHAPIRO, Fred R. 1121
    YIRKA, Carl A. 1380
    New York Lib Association
    LIAN, Nancy W. 725
    New York Post
    BOWEN, Christopher E. 120
    SHERR, Merrill F. 1129
    New York Psychoanalytic Inst &
      Socty
    ROSS, David J. 1058
    New York Pub Lib
    ALICEA, Ismael 13
    BAKER, John P. 48
    BEHRMANN, Christine A. 75
    BOURKE, Thomas A. 119
    BOWERS, Sherri 121
    BOZIWICK, George E. 124
    BROWAR, Lisa M. 141
    BUCK, Richard M. 154
    CASTRO, Julio E. 194
    CHRISTENSON, Janet S. . . . 211
    CIOPPA, Lawrence 214
    CLAYPOOL, Richard D. 220
    COHEN, Renee G. 229
    CORWIN, Betty L. 248
    DECANDIDO, Robert L. 285
    DE GENNARO, Richard 287
    D'ONOFRIO, Erminio 311
    DOTSON, Mildred E. 313
    EBER, Beryl E. 334
    FASANA, Paul J. 366
    FIGUEREDO, Danilo H. 376
    FRIEDMAN, Barbara S. 403
    FRIEDMAN, Estelle Y. 403
    GREGORIAN, Vartan 466
    GRUTCHFIELD, Walter 475
    GUBERT, Betty K. 475
    HARDISH, Patrick M. 500
    HOLMGREN, Edwin S. 553
    HSU, Karen M. 567
    HUDSON, Alice C. 569
    JACKSON, Richard H. 588
    JUHL, M E. 619
    KARATNYTSKY, Christine
      A. 627
    KENSELAAR, Robert 642

NEW YORK (Cont'd)
  NEW YORK (Cont'd)
    New York Pub Lib
    KLEIN, Stephen C. 659
    KOROLIK, Margarita N. 672
    LACHATANERE, Diana 686
    LADUE, Annette S. 687
    LEE, Lolly P. 710
    LEVIN, Peggy S. 720
    LUTZ, Alexandra 750
    LYNCH, Richard C. 752
    MACK, Phyllis G. 756
    MULIA, Gusti 876
    MYERS, Paul 884
    NATHAN, Frances E. 889
    OCKENE, David L. 915
    O'CONNELL, Brian E. 915
    O'KEEFE, Laura K. 919
    OSTROWSKY, Edith 929
    PASION, Betty D. 946
    PATRI, Daniel 947
    PERCELLI, Irene M. 958
    PURCELL, Marcia L. 998
    QUARTELL, Robert J. 999
    RAPPAPORT, Susan E. . . . 1008
    RIVERA, Gregorio 1037
    ROHMANN, Gloria P. 1050
    SHUMAN, Kristen K. 1134
    SOMMER, Susan T. 1167
    SPERLING, Robert B. 1173
    SPYROS, Marsha L. 1177
    SWERDLOVE, Dorothy L. . . 1215
    VAN DYKE, Stephen H. 1275
    VELEZ, Sara B. 1281
    WERTSMAN, Vladimir F. . . . 1325
    WILLIAMS, Richard C. 1346
    WILLNER, Channan P. 1348
    WOESTHOFF, Catherine F. . 1359
    WOOD, Thor E. 1365
    New York Pulse
    EISBERG, Jeffrey L. 340
    New York State Department of Labor
    WEINRICH, Gloria 1318
    New York State Department of Law
    SHEINWALD, Franette 1125
    New York State Supreme Court
    BADERTSCHER, David G. . . . 44
    GICK, Julie 432
    PENICH, Sonia S. 956
    New York Stock Exchange Inc
    HALEY, Thomas E. 486
    New York Times
    GREENGRASS, Alan R. 464
    HAYES, Jude T. 516
    HOLMES, Harvey L. 553
    ROTHMAN, John 1060
    New York Univ
    BIDDEN, Julia E. 94
    BOORMAN, Stanley H. 115
    BRODY, Elaine 139
    BROWN, Ronald L. 147
    CARRENO, Angela M. 186
    CHEN, Ching F. 205
    DEDONATO, Ree 286
    EARLY, Caroline L. 332
    FRUSCIANO, Thomas J. 406
    GHALI, Raouf S. 430
    HENRY, Mary K. 529
    HIGGINS, Steven 538
    IOANID, Aurora S. 583
    KASTNER, Arno A. 629
    KRANICH, Nancy C. 676
    KRONISH, Priscilla T. 680
    LEWIS, Margaret S. 723
    LOMONACO, Martha S. 738
    MIHRAM, Danielle 834
    MILLER, Michael D. 841
    MONROE, William S. 855
    MYERS, Maria P. 884
    PERSKY, Gail M. 961
    PETTIT, Marilyn H. 965
    ROCHELL, Carlton C. 1046
    SAGER, Naomi 1074
    SALVAGE, Barbara A. 1078
    SHIROMA, Susan G. 1131
    SHUMAN, Jay A. 1134
    SOLOMON, Geri E. 1166

NEW YORK (Cont'd)
NEW YORK (Cont'd)
New York Univ

SPORE, Stuart	1175
SULLIVAN, Cecil G.	1207
SWANSON, Dorothy T.	1213
TANNENBAUM, Robin L.	1222
VINCENT-DAVISS, Diana	1284
WISE, Matthew W.	1357
YUCHT, Donald J.	1384

Newman Schlau Fitch & Burns P C	COLE, Charles D.	230
Newsweek Inc	PIDALA, Veronica C.	971
	SALBER, Cecilia T.	1076
	SALBER, Peter J.	1076
	SLATE, Ted	1148
	SOUDERS, Marilyn N.	1169
	STEVENSON, Mata	1191
	TYLER, David M.	1266
92 St Young Men's & Women's Hebrew Assn	SIEGEL, Steven W.	1136
Norstar Data Services	DEFALCO, Joseph	287
North Central Bronx Hospital	CHITTAMPALLI, Padma S.	209
NYNEX Corp	BREGMAN, Joan R.	131
	ECKENRODE, Robert J.	334
	FOGARTY, Patricia C.	387
Ogilvy & Mather Advertising Agency	PODWOL, Sharon L.	979
OPL Resources Ltd	ST. CLAIR, Guy	1075
Oppenheimer & Co Inc	CRAWFORD, Carter	256
Oryx Press	BERKNER, Dimity S.	87
Out There Productions Inc	LESNIAK, Rose	718
Oxbridge Communications	HAGOOD, Patricia C.	483
Pace Univ	BIRNBAUM, Henry	98
Paine Webber	CAGAN, Penny M.	170
	FACKLER, June M.	360
	FODY, Barbara A.	387
	MINKOFF, Jerry R.	846
	NESTA, Frederick N.	896
	NOBLE, James K.	906
	SLUSSER, W P.	1150
Pan American World Airways	CHIU, Liwa J.	209
Parapsychology Foundation Inc	NORMAN, Wayne R.	909
Parsons Brinckerhoff Quade & Douglas Inc	EARLE, Marcia H.	332
	ETTLINGER, Sandra E.	356
Paul Weiss Rifkind Wharton & Garrison	BERGER, Paula E.	86
	PANELLA, Deborah S.	938
	SMITH, Mark J.	1158
	STEIN, Marsha	1185
	SULLIVAN, Patrick F.	1208
Peat Marwick Main & Co		
Peat Marwick Mitchell	FORD, George H.	389
	LIEBERFELD, Lawrence	726
Pennie & Edmonds	BURKEY, Lynne	161
	GILLIGAN, Mary A.	436
Petroleum Industry Research Associates	KAGAN, Ilse E.	621
Philips Subsystems	MESSERSCHMITT, John C.	828
Photosearch Inc	POLSTER, Joanne	982
Pierpont Morgan Lib	CAHOON, Herbert	171
	DUPONT, Inge	327
	MAYO, Hope	790
	WEINBERG, Valerie A.	1318
	WILSON, Fredric W.	1351
Planned Parenthood	ROBERTS, Gloria A.	1040
Plaspec	VONHASSELL, Agostino	1288
The Players	RACHOW, Louis A.	1001
Plenum Publishing Corp	MEAGHER, Anne E.	819
Population Council Lib	ZIMMERMAN, Hugh N.	1389
Port Authority of New York & New Jersey	JANIAK, Jane M.	593
	MARKER, Rhonda J.	771
	SCIATTARA, Diane M.	1106
Prentice Hall Information Services	SPEYER, Thomas W.	1174
Presbyterian Hospital	MOUNT, Albertina F.	873
Price Waterhouse	CROFT, Elizabeth G.	260
	FLEISHMAN, Lauren Z.	384
	SOSTACK, Maura	1169
	ZIPPER, Masha	1390
Private Satellite Network Inc	KNICKLE, James P.	664

NEW YORK (Cont'd)
NEW YORK (Cont'd)

Proskauer Rose Goetz & Mendelsohn	JOHNSON, David J.	603
	RAUCH, Anne	1010
	ROSEN, Nathan A.	1055
Prudential Bache	BUZZANGA, Heidi S.	168
Prudential Bache Securities	PRAVER, Robin I.	990
	SCHLUCKEBIER, Leslie F.	1094
Pub Affairs Information Service	PRESCHEL, Barbara M.	991
	SEKELY, Maryann	1113
	WOODS, Lawrence J.	1367
Queens Borough Pub Lib	SIMON, Anna E.	1140
	SPENSLEY, Malcolm C.	1173
Queens Coll of the City Univ of New York	COLBY, Robert A.	230
	GAYNOR, Joann T.	424
Quest Advisory Corp	AVALLONE, Susan	41
R R Bowker Co	BROOKS, Martin	140
	BUCENEC, Nancy L.	153
	CHEATHAM, Bertha M.	204
	DECANDIDO, Graceanne A.	285
	DE MAIO, M C.	291
	DIETLE, Craig I.	302
	FERRARO, Tony	373
	HAVENS, Shirley E.	513
	KOLTAY, Emery I.	670
	MACFARLAND, Scott D.	755
	MEYER, Andrew W.	829
	NYREN, Karl	913
	PETERS, Jean R.	962
	REDEL, Judy A.	1014
	SADER, Marion	1073
	SIMON, Peter E.	1140
	SPIER, Margaret M.	1174
	TOPEL, Iris N.	1251
	WILBUR, Helen L.	1338
	YUSTER, Leigh C.	1385
Radio Free Europe/Radio Liberty Inc	DUTIKOW, Irene V.	329
Radio Station WQXR	JELLINEK, George	596
Reader's Digest Magazines Ltd	MANNING, Jo A.	766
Readmore Publications	NASON, Stanley J.	888
	TONKERY, Thomas D.	1250
Reavis & McGrath	LASTRES, Steven A.	701
Reboul MacMurray Hewitt Maynar & Kristol	MEHL, Cathy A.	821
Records Revisited	SAVADA, Morton J.	1085
Reliance Grove Holdings	RUBIN, Ellen R.	1064
Richards O'Neil & Allegaert	HODGES, Phyllis	546
Richter Productions	RICHTER, Robert	1031
Robinson Siverman Pearce Aronsohn & Berm	HENDERSON, Janice E.	526
Rogers & Wells Esq	NICOL, Margaret W.	903
	PELLETIER, Daniel J.	955
Rolf Werner Rosenthal	LEE, Judy A.	710
Rosenman & Colin	LILLY, Elise M.	727
Russell Sage Foundation	ROTHSTEIN, Pauline M.	1060
Saatchi & Saatchi Compton	DAMON, Shirley J.	272
	MELITO, Joyce A.	822
St Bernard's Sch	MEYER, Albert	829
St Brigid Sch	DENNEHY, Margaret	292
St Luke's/Roosevelt Hospital Center	PANELLA, Nancy M.	938
St Vincent's Hospital & Medical Center	FRANK, Agnes T.	396
Salomon Brothers Inc	DI MEGLEO, Arthur J.	304
Salvation Army	JOHNSON, Judith	606
	WILSTED, Thomas P.	1353
Sarris Bookmarketing Service	SARRIS, Shirley C.	1083
Scholastic Inc	MASON, H J.	781
Sch Lib Journal	JONES, Trevelyn E.	615
Schwab Goldberg Price & Dannay	GOLDBERG, Morton D.	444
Science Associates/International Inc	LYONS, Ivan	753
SEC ONLINE Inc	BARRETT, Michael D.	59
Securities Data Corp	WATKINS, Dorothy	1309
Security Pacific Realty Advisory Srvs	LEVINE, Linda A.	720
Seward & Kissel	DAVIS, Robert J.	280
Seyfarth Shaw Fairweather & Geraldson	INGLIS, Catherine A.	582
Shea & Gould	KUMAR, C S.	684
	O'GRADY, Jean P.	918
	STRAM, Lynn R.	1200

NEW YORK (Cont'd)
NEW YORK (Cont'd)

Shearman & Sterling	ELLENBERGER, Jack S.	343
	HAND, Sally C.	494
	MERKIN, David	826
Shearson Lehman Brothers	RODDEN, Stephanie L.	1047
Shubert Foundation	CHACH, Maryann	196
	KUEPPERS, Brigitte	682
Sidley & Austin	KASPAR, Eileen	629
Simpson Thacher Bartlett	MARSH, John S.	773
Skadden Arps Slate Meagher & Flom	LOCHER, Cornelia E.	736
Skidmore Owings & Merrill	GRETES, Frances C.	467
SKP Associates	PAUL, Sandra K.	949
Smithsonian Institution	MARTINEZ, Katharine	779
Solomon R Guggenheim Museum	WOLF, Marion	1360
Spence Sch	CORSON, Cornelia M.	248
	GOODRICH, Carolyn B.	449
Springer-Verlag New York Inc	FUGLE, Mary E.	408
SSC&B Inc	CONNELLY, Marie	237
Standard & Poor's Corp	HERENSTEIN, Ira	530
	JENSEN, Dennis F.	598
	KIESER, Scott P.	647
	MEYER, Garry S.	830
	O'CONOR, William C.	916
	PAYNE, Linda C.	951
	REINGOLD, Celeste S.	1021
State Univ of New York at Brooklyn	GAFFNEY, Denis C.	412
Sterling Drugs Inc	ASTIFIDIS, Maria	37
	BROWN, Cynthia D.	142
Stone & Webster Mgmt Consultants Inc	ROBICHAUD, Marcel J.	1042
Strand Book Store	MONDLIN, Marvin	854
Strategic Intelligence Systems Inc	BARTLETT, Jay P.	61
	KENDRIC, Marisa A.	640
	RUBINSTEIN, Ed	1065
	STANAT, Ruth E.	1179
Syracuse Univ	PARKE, Carol R.	941
Taylor-Carlisle Booksellers Inc	FAST, Barry	366
Technical Lib Service Inc	HAAS, Elaine H.	480
Ted Bates Advertising	BEALER, Jane A.	68
Telerate Systems Inc	COWLES, Richard J.	253
Television Information Office	POTEAT, James B.	986
	SLOCUM, Leslie E.	1150
Thacher Proffitt Wood	OHMAN, Elisabeth T.	919
Theatre Lib Association	PALLY, Alan J.	935
Theresa M Burke Employment Agency Inc	MCMEEN, Frances E.	815
Thomas Publishing Co	ANDERSEN, Robert J.	21
	LEE, Douglas E.	709
	SAFRAN, Scott A.	1074
Thompson Medical Co Inc	HOYT, Henry M.	566
Time Inc	GOTTFRIED, Erika D.	453
	RHODES, Deborah L.	1026
	ZARCONE, Beth B.	1386
Times Mirror	RUBIN, James S.	1064
TOGG Films Inc	GURIEVITCH, Grania B.	478
Touche Ross & Co	BERNTSEN, Robert M.	90
	CONNER, Norma	237
Touro Coll	KINYATTI, Njoki W.	653
	MARGALITH, Helen M.	770
Towers Perrin Forster & Crosby	BORBELY, Jack	116
	FIORILLO, Barbara A.	379
	HINKSON, Colin S.	542
Tradenet	KOENIG, Michael E.	668
Turner Subscriptions	BASCH, N B.	62
	KOCHOFF, Stephen T.	667
Union Theological Seminary	KASTEN, Seth E.	629
United Hospital Fund of New York	WILLER, Kenneth H.	1341
United Nations	ERLANDSSON, Alf M.	353
	FRIED, Suzanne C.	403
	GINES, Noriko	437
	KJOLSTAD-ERLANDSSON, Britt S.	657
	MARTINEZ-RIVERA, Ivette	779
	MUTTER, Letitia N.	883
	WARD, Edith	1303
UNICEF	CANNATA, Arleen	178
US Army	LIN, Susan T.	728
US Court of International Trade	KLECKNER, Simone M.	658
	LIDSKY, Ella	725

NEW YORK (Cont'd)
NEW YORK (Cont'd)

Univ Club Lib	BERNER, Andrew J.	88
Value Line Inc	CLANCY, Kathy	215
VCH Publishers Inc	GRAYSON, Martin	460
Veronis Suhler & Associates Inc	BODDORF, James E.	109
	DRONZEK, Ronald	320
	HADLEY, J M.	482
	HALE, Paul E.	485
	HUNNEWELL, Walter	574
	LAMB, David C.	689
	SCHULTE, Anthony M.	1101
	SHAPIRO, Marvin L.	1121
	STEVENSON, Jeffery T.	1191
	SUHLER, John S.	1207
	VERONIS, John J.	1283
Veterans Administration Medical Center	WISEMAN, Karin M.	1357
Videodial Inc	THOMAS, Hilary B.	1236
Wall Street On-Line Publishing Co	YOUNG, Howard	1382
Walter Conston Alexander & Green PC	MENZEL, William H.	825
Ward Howell International Inc	TICKER, Susan L.	1244
Warshaw Burstein Cohen Schlesinger & Kuh	DOKS, Vija	309
Webster & Sheffield	COOPER, Jo E.	243
Weinzimmer Associates Inc	WEINZIMMER, William A.	1318
Werthein Schroder & Co Inc	SIMON, Beth J.	1140
White & Case	ALIFANO, Alison F.	13
	REID, Pauline	1019
	WAGSCHAL, Sara G.	1292
Whitehall Laboratories	ARAYA, Rose M.	30
Willkie Farr & Gallagher	O'DONNELL, Maryann T.	917
Winthrop Stimson Putnam & Roberts	GOLD, Hilary G.	444
WNYC-FM	GLASFORD, G R.	440
World Zionist Organization	GOLDSTEIN, Alicia P.	446
Xavier High Sch	AMISON, Mary V.	20
Yeshiva Univ	BRICKER, Naomi S.	135
	FEIGER, Cherie S.	368
	KOHN, Roger S.	668
	LUBETSKI, Edith E.	745
	WISHART, H L.	1357
Yivo Inst for Jewish Research	BAKER, Zachary M.	50
Young & Rubicam	FEBLES, Mary T.	367
	PINE, Maureen A.	974
YWCA of the City of New York	DOUET, Madeleine J.	313
Ziff Corp	GREENFIELD, Stanley R.	464
NEWARK		
Beta Comp Indexing	GARCIA, Kathleen J.	417
NEWBURGH		
Newburgh Free Lib	HALPIN, James R.	490
US Government	IRONS, Florence E.	584
NEWFANE		
Newfane Central Sch District	VONDERHEIDE, Scott T.	1288
NIAGARA UNIVERSITY		
Niagara Univ	BUDGE, William D.	155
	CONEY, Kim C.	236
	MORRIS, Leslie R.	867
NORTH BABYLON		
North Babylon Union Free Sch District	RING, Constance B.	1035
NORTH TARRYTOWN		
Rockefeller Univ	OAKHILL, Harold W.	913
	STAPLETON, Darwin H.	1181
NORTH WOODMERE		
Transnational Commerce Corp	NEWMAN, Jerald C.	899
NORTHPORT		
Veterans Administration Hospital	LEHNOFF-ONGIRSKI, Hannelore	713
Veterans Administration Medical Center	SHER, Deborah M.	1127
NORWICH		
Chenango Memorial Hospital	SLOCUM, Ann L.	1150
Norwich Eaton Pharmaceuticals	WINDSOR, Donald A.	1354
	WORTHEN, Dennis B.	1369
NYACK		
Nyack Coll & Alliance Theological Sem	BRIGHAM, Jeffrey L.	136
Nyack Pub Lib	GROTT, Joan	473
Nyack Pub Schs	SVIBRUCK, Jonathan	1212

NEW YORK (Cont'd)

OAKDALE
Dowling Coll — BEAUDRIE, Ronald A. 70
GUY, Wendell A. 479

OGDENSBURG
Ogdensburg Pub Lib — FRANZ, David A. 398
Wadhams Hall Seminary-Coll — MARTIN, Helen 776

OLD BROOKVILLE
New York Chiropractic Coll — HELLER, Jacqueline R. 524

OLD WESTBURY
State Univ of New York at Old Westbury — COLLANTES, Lourdes Y. . . . 232
JUNG, Norman O. 620

ONEONTA
Hartwick Coll — CHIANG, Nancy 207
VON BROCKDORFF, Eric . . 1288
WOLF, Carolyn M. 1359
State Univ of New York at Oneonta — ARNOLD, Linda A. 34
BENSEN, Mary L. 83
BULSON, Christine 156
CLARK, Diane A. 216
CROWLEY, John V. 261
DOWNING, Elaine L. 316
FRANCIS, Barbara B. 396
FRANCO, Kathryn C. 396
GERBERG, Andrea F. 428
ICE, Diana C. 581
JOHNSON, Richard D. 608
POTTER, Janet L. 987
QUINN, Sharon E. 1000
ROUGEUX, Debora A. 1061

ORANGEBURG
Dominican Coll — ARNEJA, Harbhajan S. 33
N S Kline Inst for Psychiatric Research — COHAN, Lois 227
New York State Office of Mental Health — ABDULLAH, Bilquis 2

ORCHARD PARK
Orchard Park Pub Lib — MAGUDA, Joyce M. 760

OSSINING
Bev Chaney Books — CHANEY, Bev 200
Ossining Pub Lib — DOW, Sally R. 315
Ossining Union Free Schs — SPIN-WEINSTEIN, Ellen . . . 1175

OSWEGO
State Univ of New York at Oswego — CHU, Sylvia 213
DIAL, Ron 299
JUDD, Blanche E. 618
OSBORNE, Nancy S. 927
RYAN, Constance V. 1070
SMILEY, Marilynn J. 1151

OZONE PARK
Queensborough Pub Lib — BISSESSAR, Carmen T. 100

PALISADES
Columbia Univ — KLIMLEY, Susan 661

PATCHOGUE
Brookhaven Memorial Hospital M C — BOROCK, Freddie 116
Patchogue-Medford Lib — GIBBARD, Judith R. 431
HOFFMAN, Barbara E. 547
HRYVNIAK, Joseph T. 567
PAGELS, Helen H. 934

PAUL SMITHS
Paul Smith's Coll — MACK, Theodore D. 756

PEARL RIVER
American Cyanamid Co — HOWELL, M G. 565

PEEKSKILL
Field Lib — FALCONE, Edward M. 362
Lakeland Sch District — SALUSTRI, Madeline 1077

PENFIELD
Penfield Pub Lib — O'NEIL, Margaret M. 924

PENN YAN
Penn Yan Pub Lib — OVERGAARD, Lynn H. 931

PERRY
Town of Perry — PARKER, Margaret S. 942

PIERMONT
Rockland County BOCES — LEVINSON, Barbara 721

NEW YORK (Cont'd)

PITTSFORD
Pittsford Central Sch District — RICHARDSON, Constance H. 1029
SOUTHCOMBE, Patricia A. . 1169
Pittsford Community Lib — DEMALLIE, Marjorie W. 291
SUMMERS, Ruth O. 1209

PLAINVIEW
Plainview Old Bethpage Pub Lib — ROSEN, Wendy L. 1055
Plainview Old Bethpage Sch District — WOLFE, Barbara M. 1360

PLATTSBURGH
City of Plattsburgh — MCCAUSLAND, Sharon H. . . 795
Clinton-Essex-Franklin Lib System — RANSOM, Stanley A. 1007
ROGERS, Elizabeth S. 1049
CVPH Medical Center — RANSOM, Christina R. . . . 1007
Plattsburgh Pub Lib — RICKETSON, Karen F. 1032
State Univ of New York at Plattsburgh — BURTON, Robert E. 164

PLEASANTVILLE
Pace Univ — MURDOCK, William J. 880
Reader's Digest Magazines Ltd — FRASENE, Joanne R. 399
VELARDI, Adrienne B. 1281

POMONA
Dr Robert L Yeager Health Center — GROSS, Elinor L. 472

PORT CHESTER
Port Chester Pub Lib — LAROSA, Thomas J. 698
LETTIERI, Robin M. 719

PORT JERVIS
Port Jervis Free Lib — CARRINGTON, Ruth 186

PORT WASHINGTON
Hofstra Univ — HIGGINS, Virginia A. 538

POTSDAM
Clarkson Univ — BERRY, Gayle C. 90
NOLTE, James S. 908
STAHL, J N. 1178
SUBRAMANIAN, Jane M. . . 1206
Potsdam Coll — FOSTER, Selma V. 392
State Univ of New York at Potsdam

POUGHKEEPSIE
Adriance Memorial Lib — WALSH, Robin S. 1300
Dutchess County — LAFEVER, C R. 687
Franklin D Roosevelt Four Freedoms Fndtn — GOODMAN, Frederica 449
VANDEN HEUVEL, William J. 1273
Mental Health Assn in Dutchess County — CARUSO, Janet A. 190
Mid-Hudson Lib System — MARKARIAN, Rita J. 771
SANKER, Paul N. 1081
VAN ZANTEN, Frank V. . . . 1278
VERDIBELLO, Muriel F. . . . 1282
WIGG, Ristiina M. 1337
Vassar Coll — DURNIAK, Barbara A. 328
HILL, Thomas E. 541
JEANNENEY, Mary L. 596
LACKS, Bernice K. 686
MACKECHNIE, Nancy S. . . 756
MAUL, Shirley A. 787
RANSOM, Sarah B. 1007
WEISS, Sabrina L. 1320
WILLIAMS, Esther L. 1343

PURCHASE
IBM Corp — RANKINE, L J. 1007
ROFES, William L. 1049
TAPHORN, Joseph B. 1223
Manhattanville Coll — NICKERSON, Donna L. 902
RAY, Donald L. 1011
State Univ of New York at Purchase — EVANS, Robert W. 358
FREIDES, Thelma 401
GARRETT, Margaret S. 420
HAIMOVSKY, Kira A. 484
LIE, David W. 725

RENSSELAER
St Anthony-on-Hudson Theological Sem — DOYLE, James J. 317
Sterling-Winthrop Research Institute — WEIS, Ann M. 1319

RIVERDALE
Manhattan Coll — DOWD, Philip M. 315
New York Pub Lib — LEFKOWITZ, Mona 712
SAR Academy — HERTZ, Cynthia L. 533

NEW YORK (Cont'd)

RIVERHEAD
Central Suffolk Hospital — KIRSCH, Anne S. 655
Riverhead Free Lib — RICHTER, Kathleen A. 1031
Suffolk Community Coll — KUUSKMAE, Mati 685

ROCHESTER
Balkin Lib Management Services — BALKIN, Ruth G. 52
Catholic Diocese of Rochester — MCNAMARA, Robert F. 816
Center for Environmental Information Inc — STOSS, Frederick W. 1198
Colgate Rochester Divinity Sch — BRENNAN, Christopher P. 132
KANSFIELD, Norman J. 625
VANDELINDER, Bonnie L. ... 1273
East Irondequoit Pub Lib — HULTZ, Karen W. 573
Eastman Dental Center — GLASER, June E. 439
Eastman Kodak Co — BAILEY, Joe A. 46
BARTL, Richard P. 61
MOUREY, Deborah A. 874
REITANO, Maimie V. 1022
SEASE, Sandra A. 1110
Gates Pub Lib — SWANTON, Susan I. 1214
General Railway Signal Co — ERICKSON, Sandra E. 352
Greece Central Sch District — CUSEO, Allan A. 267
Greece Pub Lib — SHAPIRO, June R. 1121
Harris Beach Wilcox Rubin & Levey — BARRETT, Lizabeth A. 59
Highland Hospital — ROBBINS, Diane D. 1038
Hope Reports Inc — HOPE, Thomas W. 557
I P Sharp Associates Limited — GENEREAUX, Peter R. 427
International Museum of Photography — SIMMONS, Rebecca A. 1140
Irondequoit Pub Lib — OLDERSHAW, Anne 920
Lawyers Co-Operative Publishing Co — HALE, William B. 486
KARNEZIS, Kristine C. 627
LOCKE, William G. 736
Library Binding Institute — GRAUER, Sally M. 458
Monroe County Lib System — CUMMINS, Julie A. 264
Monroe Developmental Center — HOWIE, Maryann 566
National Technical Institute for Deaf — RITTER, Audrey L. 1036
Nazareth Coll of Rochester — MATZEK, Richard A. 786
TUOHEY, Jeanne D. 1263
Our Lady of Mercy High Sch — CARSTATER, Mary E. 188
Penfield Pub Lib — SALUZZO, Mary S. 1078
Pennwalt — SCARFIA, Angela M. 1087
Praxis Biologics — HELBERS, Catherine A. 523
Roberts Wesleyan Coll — KROBER, Alfred C. 679
Rochester City Sch District — STEVENS, Elizabeth B. 1190
Rochester General Hospital — POND, Frederick C. 982
Rochester Institute of Technology — CAREN, Loretta 181
CHURCH, Virginia K. 213
DEGOLYER, Christine C. 288
GRAY, Shirley M. 460
LUNT, Ruth B. 749
TAYLOR, Gladys M. 1226
TOTH, Gregory M. 1252
Rochester Pub Lib — BARNES, Robert W. 57
EAMES, Robert W. 332
HUNT, Suellyn 575
KATZ, Jacqueline E. 630
LINDSAY, Jean S. 729
MCCLURE, Jean M. 797
PERRY, Rodney B. 961
ROSENBERG-NUGENT, Nanci B. 1056
SHIPPEY, Susan S. 1131
SULOUFF, Patricia T. 1208
State Univ of New York at Brockport — FRASER, Charlotte R. 399
Todd Hood Information Means Business — HOOD, Katherine T. 556
Total Information — GIGLIOTTI, Mary J. 433
Town of Gates — MACKNIGHT, Judith M. 757
Univ of Rochester — BUFF, Iva M. 155
BURNS, Violanda O. 163
JUNION, Gail J. 620
KABELAC, Karl S. 620
KAPLAN, Isabel C. 626
LINDAHL, Charles E. 728
MCGOWAN, Kathleen M. ... 807
METZ, Ray E. 828
NESBIT, Kathryn W. 896
PLAIN, Marilyn V. 977
RAME, Mary E. 1005

NEW YORK (Cont'd)

ROCHESTER (Cont'd)
Univ of Rochester — RICKER, Shirley E. 1031
ROBERTSON, Michael A. .. 1042
SOLLENBERGER, Julia F. .. 1166
SOMERVILLE, Arleen N. ... 1167
STRIFE, Mary L. 1202
THYM, Jurgen 1243
WATANABE, Ruth T. 1308
WYATT, James F. 1374
Veracorp — DESMOND, Andrew R. 295
The Winters Group — BERKMAN, Robert I. 87
KASE-MCLAREN, Karen A. . 628

ROCKVILLE CENTRE
Diocese of Rockville Centre — GRAHAM, Loretta 456
Mercy Hospital — REID, Carol L. 1018
Molloy Coll — MAYER, Mary C. 789
Rockville Centre Pub Lib — FRIEDLAND, Rhoda W. 403

ROME
Jervis Pub Lib — ESWORTHY, Lori L. 355
FOWLER, Carole F. 393
Rome City Sch District — BUSH, Dianne 165

ROSLYN
Bryant Pub Lib — WYDEN, Elaine S. 1374
St Francis Hospital — WEINSTEIN, Judith K. 1318

ROUSES POINT
Ayerst Laboratories — CURRAN, George L. 266

RUSSELL
Board of Cooperative Educational Srvs — WHEELER, Allison S. 1328
Edwards-Knox Central Sch — BRIZENDINE, Margaret K. ... 137

RYE
Rye Free Reading Room — GREENFIELD, Judith C. 464
READ, Jean B. 1012

SALAMANCA
Seneca Nation of Indians — BRAY, Ethel E. 130

SANBORN
Niagara County Community Coll — FARRELL, Michele A. 365

SARATOGA SPRINGS
Anglican Bibliopole — KEARNEY, Robert D. 633
Skidmore Coll — DOE, Lynn M. 308
EYMAN, David H. 359
LEWIS, Gillian H. 723
SMITH, Barbara E. 1152

SCARSDALE
Scarsdale Board of Education — FERRERO, Lucia N. 373
Scarsdale Junior High Sch — LEWIS, Marjorie 723
Scarsdale Pub Lib — NICHOLS, Joyce N. 901
Scarsdale Sch System — RABBAN, Elana 1001
Sydney Wolf Cohen Inc — ABEND, Jody U. 2
Work in America Institute Inc — ROWAN, Diane M. 1062
RUBINO, Cynthia C. 1065

SCHENECTADY
Adirondack Research Ctr — KING, Maryde F. 651
General Electric Co — HEWITT, Julia F. 535
OLIVER, Patricia A. 921
SMITH, Marian J. 1157
WARDEN, Carolyn L. 1304
Hammer Mountain Book Halls — SOMERS, Wayne F. 1167
Mohawk Valley Lib Association — PROVOST, Beverly A. 996
Schenectady County Community Coll — HELLER, Nancy M. 524
SCOTT, Frances Y. 1107
Schenectady County Pub Lib — ADAMS, Bruce A. 4
HODGES, Lois F. 546
OCHS, Phyllis E. 915
SULLIVAN, Robert G. 1208
Schenectady Gazette — DAZE, Colleen J. 283
Union Coll — EVANS, Ruth A. 358
RAHN, Suzanne M. 1003
SEEMANN, Ann M. 1111
SHEVIAK, Jean K. 1129

SCHOHARIE
State Univ of New York at Cobleskill — NELSON, Winifred S. 895

SCOTIA
Burnt Hills-Ballston Lake Central Schs — EGAN, Mary J. 338

SEAFORD
Seaford Pub Lib — FLUCKIGER, Adrienne N. ... 386

NEW YORK (Cont'd)

SELDEN
Suffolk County Community Coll — KANIA, Antoinette M. 625
SETAUKET
Emma S Clark Memorial Lib — COOK, Jeannine S. 240
Three Village Historical Society — PACKARD, Agnes K. 933
SHIRLEY
Mastics-Moriches-Shirley Community
  Lib — VERBESEY, J R. 1282
SHOREHAM
Shoreham-Wading River Sch District — BENNETT, James F. 81
  WRIGHT-HESS, Anne H. . . 1373
SHRUB OAK
John C Hart Memorial Lib — HALLINAN, Patricia R. 489
Town of Yorktown — STEWART, Betty F. 1192
SMITHTOWN
Smithtown Central Sch District — ROSAR, Virginia W. 1054
Smithtown Township — SHAPIRO, Barbara S. 1121
SODUS
Sodus Central Sch — BUTLER, Rebekah O. 167
SOMERS
Pepsi Cola USA — BURROWS, Shirley 163
SOUTH SALEM
South Salem Lib — FOGLESONG, Marilee 387
SOUTHAMPTON
Altana Films — KLUGHERZ, Dan 662
Long Island Univ — KETCHAM, Susan E. 645
Rogers Memorial Lib — BERKEBILE, Sue A. 87
SPARKILL
Long Island Univ — BARRIE, John L. 59
  ZUBARIK, Therese 1390
St Thomas Aquinas Coll — BARTH, John E. 61
SPENCERPORT
Spencerport Central Schs — HARRINGTON, Judith F. 504
STATEN ISLAND
Arthur Kill Correctional Facility — ROMALIS, Carl 1052
Bayley Seton Hospital — SHELDON, Marie A. 1126
Coll of Staten Island — O'DONNELL, Michael J. 917
  SVENNINGSEN, Karen L. . . 1212
County of Richmond — KLINGLE, Philip A. 662
CSI — KRIEGER, Tillie 678
Institute for Basic Research — BLACK, Lawrence 101
New York Pub Lib — JOHNSON, Patrelle E. 608
  PASSOFF, Barbara F. 946
St Vincent's Medical Center of
  Richmond — DIMATTEO, Lucy A. 304
Social Sciences Research Council — RICHIUSO, John P. 1030
Staten Island Historical Society — BARTO, Stephen C. 61
Staten Island Institute of Arts & Scis — HOGAN, Kristine K. 549
Wagner Coll — WAGNER, A C. 1291
STELLA NIAGARA
Sisters of St Francis Holy Name
  Province — SERBACKI, Mary 1116
STONY BROOK
Long Island Lib Resources Council — NEUFELD, Judith B. 897
State Univ of New York at Stony
  Brook — BAUM, Nathan 66
  HUFFORD, Jon R. 571
  KAUFMAN, Judith L. 631
  KENDRICK, Curtis L. 640
  KING, Christine E. 650
  KINNEY, Daniel W. 653
  PANDIT, Jyoti P. 937
  SALINERO, Amelia 1076
  SEWELL, Robert G. 1117
  SIMPSON, Charles W. 1141
  SMITH, John B. 1156
  VOLAT-SHAPIRO, Helene
    M. 1287
  WALCOTT, Rosalind 1294
  WIENER, Paul B. 1336
  WILLIAMS, Doris C. 1343
Stony Brook Sch — MASH, S D. 780
SUFFERN
Avon Products Inc — BOROSON, Sarah 116
State Univ of New York at Suffern — GLEASON, Robert W. 440
  PATTERSON, Grace L. 948

NEW YORK (Cont'd)

SYOSSET
Harris Corp — PIENITZ, Eleanor 971
Syosset Pub Lib — GOLDENKOFF, Isabel M. . . . 445
  KRISTIAN, Alice 679
SYRACUSE
Central New York Lib Resources
  Council — SMITHEE, Jeannette P. 1161
  WASHBURN, Keith E. 1307
Community General Hospital — REINSTEIN, Diana J. 1021
Continental Information Systems — GRANKA, Bernard D. 457
Crouse Irving Memorial Hospital — SHELANDER, Frances R. . . . 1125
Laubach Literacy International — RYAN, Jenny L. 1071
Le Moyne Coll — BARNELLO, Inga H. 57
  POPOVIC, Tanya V. 983
  SIMONIS, James J. 1141
New York State — DUNN, Mary B. 327
Onodaga-Cortland-Madison BOCFS — FUNK, Nancy J. 410
Onondaga-Cortland-Madison BOCES — ROSS, Kathleen A. 1058
Onondaga County Pub Lib — CLEMINSHAW, Barbara B. . . 221
  DEMARCO, Elizabeth A. . . . 291
  DEVENISH-CASSEL, Ann
    W. 297
  GAWLER, Ann C. 423
  KINCHEN, Robert P. 650
  LOMICKA, Janet 738
  NAGLE, Ann 886
  NOTTINGHAM, Sharon E. . . . 910
  PFOHL, Theodore E. 966
St Joseph's Hospital Health Center — SHRIER, Helene F. 1133
State Univ of New York at Syracuse — HULBERT, Linda A. 572
  JUCHIMEK, Dianne M. 618
  MURRAY, Suzanne H. 882
  ONSI, Patricia W. 924
  UVA, Peter A. 1270
Syracuse Univ — ABBOTT, George L. 1
  BRAUN, Carl F. 129
  COCHRANE, Pauline A. 226
  EISENBERG, Michael B. 340
  ELY, Donald P. 347
  FROEHLICH, Thomas J. 405
  HORRELL, Jeffrey L. 560
  JOHNSON, Nancy B. 608
  KATZER, Jeffrey 630
  LANTZY, M L. 697
  MARCHAND, Donald A. 768
  MARTIN, Thomas H. 778
  MCCLURE, Charles R. 797
  MCLAUGHLIN, Pamela W. . . . 813
  MINOR, Barbara B. 846
  MULLEN, Marion L. 877
  NAYLOR, David L. 890
  PRICE, Susan W. 992
  PRINS, Johanna W. 993
  SEIBERT, Donald C. 1112
  STAM, David H. 1179
  STAM, Deirdre C. 1179
  UCHTORFF, Barbara J. 1267
  WALTZ, Mary A. 1302
  WASYLENKO, Lydia W. 1308
TARRYTOWN
Chem Systems Inc — GRANDY, Maryann M. 457
Union Carbide Corp — GALBRAITH, Barry E. 413
THORNWOOD
IBM Corp — BEVERIDGE, Walter W. 93
  CYPSER, Rudy J. 268
  KOSTENBAUDER, Scott 673
  SHADE, Ronald H. 1118
THREE MILE BAY
Pizer Archives Music Lib — PIZER, Charles R. 977
  PIZER, Elizabeth F. 977
TICONDEROGA
Ticonderoga Central Sch — DAVIS, Bonnie V. 277
TROY
Hudson Valley Community Coll — BLANDY, Susan G. 104
  ROOT, Christine 1053
  WALSH, Daniel P. 1299
New York State Office of Court
  Admin — PILLAI, Karlye A. 973

NEW YORK (Cont'd)

TROY (Cont'd)

Norton Co

Rensselaer Polytechnic Institute | SUTHERLAND-NEHRING, Laurie A. 1211
KENNICK, Sylvia B. 642
LOCKETT, Barbara A. 736
MOLHOLT, Pat 852
RYAN, Donald L. 1070

Russell Sage Coll
Saint Mary's Hospital | CLUM, Audna T. 223
Samaritan Hospital | SMITH, Annie J. 1152
Troy Pub Lib | EVELAND, Ruth A. 358
GINSBURG, Joanne R. 438
JANOWSKY, Cara A. 593

TUCKAHOE

Village of Tuckahoe | STEIN, Arlene B. 1185

TUXEDO

New York Univ | SINGLETON, Christine M. ... 1143

UNIONDALE

Nassau Lib System | BARTENBACH, Martha A. 60
BOREK, Mary A. 116
GOTTLIEB, Delia 453
GREEN, Joseph H. 462

Rivkin Radler Dunne & Bayh | CARTAFALSA, Joan C. 188
MONACO, Ralph A. 854

Sisters of St Dominic-Amityville | MURTAGH, Mary B. 882
Uniondale Pub Lib | OPATOW, Judith 925

UPTON

Brookhaven National Laboratory | ALBERTUS, Donna M. 10
COHEN, Rosemary C. 229
GALLI, Marilyn C. 414
LANE, Sandra G. 694
TODOSOW, Helen K. 1248

UTICA

Discography Series | WEBER, Jerome F. 1314
Office of Court Administration | ANTHONY, Mary M. 28
State Univ of New York at Utica | SCHABERT, Daniel R. 1088
Syracuse Univ | WU, Painan R. 1373
Utica City Schs | SCHEU, Susan P. 1092
Utica Pub Lib | BROOKES, Barbara 140
MOUSTAFA, Theresa A. 874

VALHALLA

PEPSICO | FALCONE, Elena C. 362
Valhalla Pub Schs | HIGGINS, Judith H. 538
Westchester County | SIKORSKI, Charlene S. 1137

VALLEY STREAM

Henry Waldinger Memorial Lib | ENG, Mamie 348

VESTAL

Town of Vestal | HOLLEY, James L. 551
Vestal Pub Lib | LA SORTE, Antonia J. 700

VICTOR

Victor Free Lib | KELLY, Patricia A. 638

WALLKILL

Wallkill Central Sch District | RUBIN, Ellen B. 1064

WALTON

Walton Central Sch | LEPINNET, Nancy M. 717

WALWORTH

Walworth-Seely Pub Lib | VAN RIPER, Joy C. 1277

WANTAGH

Wantagh Sch District | LOPATIN, Edith K. 740
SCHOENBAUM, Rhoda A. . 1098

WATER MILL

A J G Associates | GROSSMAN, Adrian J. 473

WATERTOWN

Mercy Hospital | GARVEY, Jeffrey M. 421
Watertown City Sch District | MARSTON, Hope I. 775

WATERVLIET

US Amccom, ARDEC, CCAS | MACKSEY, Susan A. 757

WEBSTER

Xerox Corp | BELLI, Frank G. 78
MUELLER, Leta A. 875
RICE, Cecelia E. 1027
TUCKER, Laura R. 1262

WEST ISLIP

St John the Baptist High Sch | JOYCE, Therese 618
REIMAN, Anthony C. 1020
West Islip Pub Lib | CARTER, Darline L. 189
KEATING, Faith 633

WEST NYACK

Champion International Corp | COHEN, Hannah V. 228
RIGNEY, Shirley A. 1034

NEW YORK (Cont'd)

WEST POINT

US Military Academy | AIMONE, Alan C. 8
BARTH, Joseph M. 61
RANDALL, Lawrence E. ... 1006

WEST VALLEY

West Valley Nuclear Services Co Inc | CURRY, Lenora Y. 266

WESTBURY

Westbury Memorial Pub Lib | KRAMPITZ, Barbara E. 676

WESTFIELD

Patterson Lib | NYERGES, Michael S. 912

WESTHAMPTON BEACH

Board of Cooperative Educational Srvs | BARR, Janet L. 58

WHITE PLAINS

Database Directory Service | MILLER, Barbara 835
General Foods Corp | HOUGHTON, Joan I. 562
SEULOWITZ, Lois 1117
SWANSON, Mary A. 1213
VAJDA, Carolyn M. 1271
WEINSTEIN, Lois 1318

IBM Corp | BOWLES, Edmund A. 121
SJOGREN, Mack D. 1145
Knowledge Industry Publications Inc | CSENGE, Maragaret L. 262
Kraus-Thomson Organization Limited | GSTALDER, Herbert W. 475
Laser Resources Inc | CONTESSA, William B. 239
Mercy Coll | MCLAUGHLIN, Denis F. 813
National Economic Research Associates | RYAN, James J. 1071
New York Power Authority | SPARER, Saretta 1171
NYNEX Corp | MCGARVEY, Eileen B. 805
MUSKUS, Elizabeth A. 883
SCHARF, Davida 1090
TIBBETTS, David W. 1243
Pace Univ | PIDGEON, Alice C. 971
TRIFFIN, Nicholas 1256
Texaco Inc | ROCQUE, Bernice L. 1046
Trintex | SMITH, Harry E. 1155
VALANDRA, Kent T. 1271
United Nations | DAVIES, Carol A. 277
White Plains Hospital Medical Center | GIORDANO, Joan 438
White Plains Pub Lib | BUSH, Joyce 165
SIVULICH, Sandra S. 1145

WHITESBORO

Dunham Pub Lib | SHEFFER, Karen M. 1125

WILLIAMSVILLE

Amherst Pub Lib | ALLENBACH, Norma A. 16
BOBINSKI, Mary F. 108
Erie Community Coll North | MORAN, Sylvia J. 862
Lancaster Central Sch | NEELAND, Margaret A. 891
Town of Amherst | TAMMARO, James M. 1221

WINGDALE

Harlem Valley Psychiatric Center | LEWANDOWSKI, Virginia M. 722

YONKERS

City of Yonkers | SCHAVRIEN, Judith L. 1090
Elizabeth Seton Coll | SULLIVAN, Marion M. 1208
St Joseph's Seminary | GAFFNEY, Ellen E. 412
Yonkers Pub Lib | AMICK, Charles W. 20
MILLER, Jacqueline E. 838
ROGERS, Irene 1049

YORKTOWN HEIGHTS

Putnam-Northern Westchester BOCES | MORRISON, George J. 868
13D Research Inc | YURO, David A. 1384

NORTH CAROLINA

ALBEMARLE

Stanly County Pub Lib | ESTES, Elizabeth W. 355
PARRISH, Nancy B. 944

APEX

Almay Inc | RATHGEBER, Jo F. 1009

ASHEBORO

Randolph County Pub Schs | SPENCER, Sue R. 1173
Randolph Pub Lib | BRENNER, Nancy F. 133
Randolph Technical Coll | SMITH, Merrill F. 1158

NORTH CAROLINA (Cont'd)
ASHEVILLE
Appalachian Hall — MAYER, Barbara D. 789
Asheville-Buncombe Lib System — HEROLD, Virginia L. 532
— PERRY, Douglas F. 960
Asheville City Schs — BROWN, Nancy E. 146
Mountain Area Health Education
Center — BUTSON, Linda C. 167
— THIBODEAU, Patricia L. ... 1235
NOAA NESDIS/NCDC — SNODGRASS, Rex J. 1163
Univ of North Carolina at Asheville — BUCHANAN, William E. 153
Veterans Administration Medical
Center — LAMBREMONT, Jane A. 691
BEAUFORT
North Carolina Maritime Museum — BUMGARNER, John L. 157
BELMONT
Belmont Abbey Coll — BAUMSTEIN, Paschal M. 66
— MAYES, Susan E. 789
BOONE
Appalachian State Univ — ANTONE, Allen L. 29
— BARKER, Richard T. 56
— BUSBIN, O M. 164
— GOLDEN, Susan L. 445
— HATHAWAY, Milton G. 512
— NAYLOR, Alice P. 890
— OLSON, Eric J. 922
— WISE, Mintron S. 1357
Western North Carolina Lib Network — GREGORY, Roderick F. 466
BRYSON CITY
Fontana Regional Lib — MODLIN, John W. 851
BUIES CREEK
Campbell Univ — SORVARI, Kare C. 1169
— WEEKS, Olivia L. 1315
BURGAW
Pender County Lib — TAYLOR, Michael Y. 1228
CAMP LEJEUNE
Camp Lejeune Naval Hospital — FRAZELLE, Betty 399
CANTON
Haywood County Schs — LESUEUR, Joan K. 718
CARTHAGE
North Carolina Lib Association — MYRICK, Pauline F. 885
CARY
Wake County Dept of Pub Libs — COUSINS, Gloria D. 252
CHAPEL HILL
Cabarrus County Schs — KISER, Anita H. 656
Carolina Library Services Inc — METZGER, Eva C. 829
Chapel Hill Pub Lib — CAMERON, Mary T. 175
Triangle Research Libs Network — BENNETT, David B. 81
Univ of North Carolina at Chapel Hill — ASHEIM, Lester E. 35
— BAILEY, Charles W. 46
— BALLENTINE, Rebecca S. 53
— BERGUP, Bernice 87
— BROADUS, Robert N. 138
— BYRD, Gary D. 168
— CARPENTER, Raymond L. .. 185
— CHENAULT, Elizabeth A. 205
— COGGINS, Timothy L. 227
— COTTEN, Alice R. 250
— COTTEN, Jerry W. 250
— CRANDALL, Elisabeth G. ... 255
— DANIEL, Evelyn H. 272
— DARLING, John B. 275
— DEBRECZENY, Gillian M. ... 285
— DICKERSON, Jimmy 300
— FARKAS, Doina C. 364
— FEEHAN, Patricia E. 368
— FLOWERS, Janet L. 386
— FRANK, Linda V. 397
— GASAWAY, Laura N. 421
— GLEIM, David E. 441
— GLEIM, Sharon S. 441
— GOVAN, James F. 454
— GRENDLER, Marcella 467
— HEWITT, Joe A. 535
— HOLLEY, Edward G. 551
— JONES, H G. 613
— KESSLER, Ridley R. 645
— LANEY, Elizabeth J. 695
— LOSEE, Robert M. 742
— MATER, Dee A. 783

NORTH CAROLINA (Cont'd)
CHAPEL HILL (Cont'd)
Univ of North Carolina at Chapel Hill
— MCNAMARA, Charles B. 816
— MEEHAN-BLACK, Elizabeth
C. 821
— MORAN, Barbara B. 862
— NEAL, Michelle H. 890
— NYE, Julie B. 912
— OWEN, Willy 932
— PALO, Eric E. 937
— PRILLAMAN, Susan M. ... 993
— SAYE, Jerry D. 1086
— SAYE, Terri O. 1086
— SCHELL, Nancy S. 1091
— SEGAL, Jane D. 1111
— SEIBERT, Karen S. 1112
— SLOCUM, Charlotte A. 1150
— STIGLEMAN, Sue E. 1194
— STRAUSS, Diane 1201
— SUTTON, Ellen D. 1211
— SWINDLER, Luke 1216
— TALBERT, David M. 1220
— TAYLOR, David C. 1226
— TUCKER, Mary E. 1262
— TUTTLE, Marcia L. 1266
— WEBSTER, Deborah K. 1314
— WOOD, Judith B. 1364
CHARLOTTE
Arthur Andersen & Co — MOORE, Patricia R. 860
Central Piedmont Community Coll — OPLINGER, Mary P. 925
Charlotte Law Lib Associates — HANNUM-MCPHERSON,
Melissa A. 497
Charlotte-Mecklenburg Schs — CARPENTER, Janella A. 184
— MILLER, Gloria 838
Duke Power Co — SKINNER, Linda W. 1146
Hoyt Galvin & Associates — GALVIN, Hoyt R. 415
Information/Access On-Line — HOWARD, Susanna J. 564
Johnson C Smith Univ — SUMMERFORD, Steven L. . 1209
Kennedy Cooington Lobdell &
Hickman — FURST, Joyce P. 410
Presbyterian Hospital — BERRY, Mary W. 90
Pub Lib of Charlotte & Mecklenburg
Cnty — AULD, Hampton M. 39
— CANNON, Robert E. 179
— GUENTHER, Christine G. 475
— MCCORMICK, Emily S. 798
— MOYER, James M. 874
— MYERS, Carol B. 884
— SUTTON, Judith K. 1211
Smith Helms Mulliss & Moore — DUVAL, Barbara C. 329
SunHealth Inc — BACKMAN, Carroll H. 44
Univ of North Carolina at Charlotte — AVELEYRA, Luz M. 41
— FRANKLE, Raymond A. 397
— HUDSON, Donna T. 569
— PENNINGER, Randy 957
— STAHL, Wilson M. 1178
— WALKER, Judith A. 1295
CLAYTON
Johnston County Schools — KONNEKER, Rachel C. 670
CONCORD
Cabarrus Memorial Hospital — MILLER, Nancy H. 841
Charles A Cannon Memorial Lib — DILLARD, Thomas W. 303
— HULL, Laurence O. 572
CULLOWHEE
Western Carolina Univ — COHEN, Edward S. 228
— DORR, Lorna B. 313
— KIRWAN, William J. 656
— MILLER, Lewis R. 840
— OSER, Anita K. 928
— STETSON, Keith R. 1190
— YOUNG, Judith E. 1382
DALLAS
Gaston Coll — HUNSUCKER, David L. 575
DAVIDSON
Davidson Coll — PARK, Leland M. 941
— WOOD, Kelly S. 1364
DEEP RUN
Lenoir County Board of Education — SOUTHERLAND, Carol A. ... 1169

NORTH CAROLINA (Cont'd)

DOBSON
Surry County Schs — STRICKLAND, Mary L. 1202

DURHAM
Africa News Service — WHITMORE, Sharon S. 1334
Duke Univ — ADAMS, Elizabeth L. 4
BASEFSKY, Stuart M. 62
BERGER, Kenneth W. 85
BIRD, Warren P. 98
BREEZE, Hope 131
BYRD, Robert L. 169
CAMPBELL, Jerry D. 176
CARRINGTON, Bessie M. 186
CLARK, Marie L. 217
DENSON, Janeen J. 293
DRUESEDOW, John E. 320
DUNN, Elizabeth B. 326
EZZELL, Joline R. 360
FARRIS, Joyce L. 365
FEINGLOS, Susan J. 369
GARTRELL, Ellen G. 420
GERMAIN, Claire M. 429
HEBERT, Robert A. 519
HENSEN, Steven L. 529
HINSON, Doris M. 543
KLINE, Lawrence O. 661
LAVINE, Marcia M. 703
LUBANS, John 745
MIDDLETON, Beverly D. 833
MOORE, Scott L. 861
NELIUS, Albert A. 893
PORTER, Katherine R. 985
REES, Joe C. 1016
SMITH, Eric J. 1155
SOUTHERN, Mary A. 1170
STEAD, William W. 1183
TRUMBULL, Jane 1259
VOGEL, Jane G. 1286
WOODBURN, Judy I. 1366
YOUNG, Betty I. 1381
Durham Academy — OSBORN, Dorothy H. 927
Durham City Schs — CLEMONS, Kenneth L. 221
Durham County Lib — GADDIS, Dale W. 411
SIPPEN, Kathi H. 1144
Durham County Schs — FISH, Barbara M. 380
Durham Herald Co Inc — BARBEE, Lisa M. 55
SEMONCHE, Barbara P. 1115
Family Health International — BARROWS, William D. 60
North Carolina Central Univ — BALLARD, Robert M. 53
BOMARC, M D. 113
BRACY, Pauletta B. 125
BURGIN, Robert E. 159
HAZEL, Debora E. 517
LAWTON, Patricia J. 705
RICHMOND, Alice S. 1030
SHEARER, Kenneth D. 1124
SPELLER, Benjamin F. 1172

EDEN
Rockingham County Pub Lib — DAVIDSON, Laura B. 276
WRIGHT, Linda D. 1372

ELIZABETH CITY
Coll of the Albemarle — COOK-WOOD, Holly M. 241
LEE, Charles D. 709
East Albemarle Regional Lib — SANDERS, Anne D. 1079
Roanoke Bible Coll — GRIFFIN, Patricia S. 469

ELKIN
Northwestern Regional Lib — MACPHAIL, Jessica 758

ELON COLLEGE
Elon Coll — JONES, Plummer A. 614
SHEPHERD, Gay W. 1127

FAYETTEVILLE
Cape Fear Valley Medical Center — BEATTIE, Barbara C. 70
Cumberland County Pub Lib & Info Center — ASPINALL, David L. 37
DEVITO, Robert M. 297
FREEDMAN, Barbara G. 400
HANSEL, Patsy J. 497
HUNTER, Julie A. 576
KRIEGER, Lee A. 678
MCGRIFF, Mary E. 808

NORTH CAROLINA (Cont'd)

FAYETTEVILLE (Cont'd)
Cumberland County Pub Lib & Info Center — THRASHER, Jerry A. 1243
Cumberland County Sch System — GARDNER, Janet K. 418
Fayetteville Area Health Educ Fndtn Inc — WRIGHT, Barbara A. 1370
Fayetteville Publishing Co — MAXWELL, Daisy D. 788
North Carolina Foreign Language Center — CHAN, Moses C. 199

GASTONIA
Gaston County Schs — YARBROUGH, Doris A. 1378
Gaston-Lincoln Regional Lib — RITTER, Philip W. 1036

GOLDSBORO
State of North Carolina — TABORY, Maxim 1219
Wayne County Pub Lib — ALLEN, Lynne B. 15
SHEARY, Edward J. 1124

GREENSBORO
Brodart Co — WINKEL, Lois 1355
Center for Creative Leadership — HARDIE, Karen R. 499
CIBA-GEIGY Corp — JACQUES, Eunice L. 591
City of Greensboro — VIELE, George B. 1283
Dun & Bradstreet Corp — MCZORN, Bonita A. 819
East Carolina Univ — KESTER, Diane D. 645
Greensboro Pub Lib — WATT, Richard S. 1310
WINDHAM, Shirley L. 1354
Greensboro Pub Schs — SANDERS, Elizabeth S. 1080
Guilford Coll — POWELL, Lucy A. 988
Guilford County Schs — KLEM, Marjorie R. 660
Information Conservation Inc — FAIRFIELD, John R. 361
Information Research Center Inc — O'CONNOR, Sandra L. 916
Lorillard Inc — SKLADANOWSKI, Lawrence M. 1146
Moses H Cone Hospital — MACKLER, Leslie G. 757
North Carolina A & T State Univ — YOUNG, Tommie M. 1383
North Carolina A&T State Univ — JARRELL, James R. 594
North Carolina Dept of Pub Instruction — TUGWELL, Helen M. 1262
North Carolina State Univ — FLOYD, Rebecca M. 386
Smith Helms Mulliss & Moore — WASHBURN, Anne C. 1307
Univ of North Carolina at Greensboro — BOMAR, Cora P. 113
CHILDRESS, Eric R. 208
LEVINSON, Catherine K. 721
MILLER, Marilyn L. 840
MITCHELL, W B. 849
MOORE, Kathryn L. 860
PARROTT, Margaret S. 944
WRIGHT, Keith C. 1372
WURSTEN, Richard B. 1374
Wesley Long Community Hospital — FURR, Margaret H. 410

GREENVILLE
East Carolina Univ — BOCCACCIO, Mary A. 108
BOYCE, Emily S. 122
CHENG, Chao S. 206
COLLINS, Donald E. 232
COTTER, Michael G. 250
DALTON, Lisa K. 271
DODGE, Michael R. 308
GLUCK, Myke H. 442
KARES, Artemis C. 627
KATZ, Ruth M. 630
LANIER, Gene D. 696
LAPAS, Martha E. 697
LENNON, Donald R. 715
MCGLOHON, Leah L. 807
MELLON, Constance A. 822
SCOTT, Ralph L. 1108
SHIRES, Nancy P. 1131
SPEER, Susan C. 1172
STEPHENSON, Marilyn R. . 1188

HENDERSON
H Leslie Perry Memrl Lib — SHAFFER, Nancy R. 1119
Vance-Granville Community Coll — SINCLAIR, R F. 1142

HENDERSONVILLE
Henderson County — MARSHALL, Elizabeth C. ... 774

HIGH POINT
City of High Point — AUSTIN, Neal F. 40
DORNBERGER, Julie L. 313
HAWN, Elizabeth L. 514
MORRIS, R P. 867

NORTH CAROLINA (Cont'd)

HIGH POINT (Cont'd)
High Point City — ALSTON-REEDER, Lizzie A. . . 18
High Point Coll — GAUGHAN, Thomas M. 422
High Point Pub Lib — ELLIS, Kem B. 345
EVANS, June C. 357
HICKS, Michael 537
MOORE, Emily C. 859
SPOON, James M. 1175
TOMLINSON, Charles E. . . . 1250

JACKSONVILLE
Coastal Carolina Community Coll — MARTIN, Richard T. 778
Onslow County Pub Lib — VEITCH, Carol J. 1281

JEFFERSON
McFarland & Co Inc — FRANKLIN, Robert M. 398

KANNAPOLIS
Kannapolis City Schs — DAVIS, Judy R. 279

KENANSVILLE
Duplin County Lib — HADDEN, Linda W. 481

KINSTON
Kinston-Lenoir County Pub Lib — FICKES, Raymond C. 374
Neuse Regional Pub Lib — CAWLEY, Marianne 195
EARL, Susan R. 332
JONES, John W. 613

LAURINBURG
St Andrews Coll — HOLMES, Elizabeth A. 553

LEWISVILLE
Forsyth County Pub Lib — BROWN, Merrikay E. 146

LEXINGTON
Davidson Community Coll — THOMAS, John B. 1237

LILLINGTON
Harnett County Lib — COLLINS, Melanie H. 233

MARS HILL
Mars Hill Coll — CADLE, Dean 170
PETERSON, Cynthia L. 963

MCLEANSVILLE
Guilford County Schs — RANCER, Susan P. 1006

MOCKSVILLE
Davie County Pub Lib — HOYLE, Ruth A. 566

MONROE
Union County Pub Lib — ABBOTT, Chien N. 1

MONTREAT
Challenge House — FOREMAN, Kenneth J. 390
Histl Fndtn Presbyterian & Reform Church — BROOKS, Jerrold L. 140
STOCKDALE, Kay L. 1195

MORGANTON
Broughton Hospital — BUSH, Mary E. 165

MT OLIVE
Mt Olive Coll — BAREFOOT, Gary F. 56

MURPHY
Nantahala Regional Library — ABBOTT, Dorothy D. 1

NEWELL
Univ of North Carolina at Charlotte — BRABHAM, Robert F. 124

NEWTON
Catawba County Pub Lib System — PRITCHARD, John A. 994

OXFORD
Granville County Lib System — STEPHENS, Arial A. 1187

PINEHURST
Sandhills Community Coll — WILKINS, Alice L. 1340

PITTSBORO
Univ of North Carolina at Pittsboro — WHITENER, Betty L. 1333

POPE AFB
US Air Force — OLENDER, Karen L. 920

RALEIGH
Adams McCullough & Beard — WILLIAMS, Lisa W. 1344
Carolina Power & Light Co — FISH, Paula H. 380
Central Regional Education Center — BRADBURN, Frances B. 125
Department of Cultural Resources — HOY, Suellen N. 566
PRICE, William S. 993
Duke Univ — TUTTLE, Joseph C. 1266
General Assembly of North Carolina — HALPEREN, Vivian P. 489
Hall Hill O'Donnell Taylor Manning et al — TAYLOR, Raymond M. 1228
Hunton & Williams — MURPHY, Malinda M. 881
ITT Telecom — HAY, Gerald M. 515
Maupin Taylor Ellis & Adams PA — LAMBE, Catherine V. 690
The News & Observer Publishing Co — LEONARD, Teresa G. 717

NORTH CAROLINA (Cont'd)

RALEIGH (Cont'd)
North Carolina Dept of Cultural Resource — KAN, Irene E. 624
MCGINN, Howard F. 806
SMITH, Catherine 1153
WILLIAMS, M J. 1345
NC Department of Cultural Resources — WILLIAMS, Gene J. 1343
WILLIAMS, Mildred J. 1345
North Carolina Dept of Pub Instruction — BOWMAN, Gloria M. 121
BRUMBACK, Elsie 150
North Carolina Division of State Lib — DRUM, Eunice P. 321
WELCH, John T. 1321
North Carolina Hospital Association — SPENCER, Linda A. 1173
North Carolina State Government — OLSON, David J. 922
North Carolina State Lib — IRVING, Ophelia M. 584
North Carolina State Univ — BEST-NICHOLS, Barbara J. . . 92
BROWN, Kathleen R. 145
CARSTENS, Timothy V. 188
DAVIS, Jinnie Y. 279
GEBBIE, Janet L. 424
HIGH, Walter M. 538
HUNT, Margaret R. 575
KING, Ebba K. 650
LEVINE, Cynthia R. 720
LINK, Margaret A. 730
LITTLETON, Isaac T. 734
MCGEACHY, John A. 805
NUTTER, Susan K. 912
OSEGUEDA, Laura M. 927
PORTER, Jean M. 985
POZO, Frank J. 989
PURYEAR, Pamela E. 998
ULMSCHNEIDER, John E. . . 1268
WALTNER, Nellie L. 1301
North Carolina Supreme Court — HALL, Frances H. 487
Pathways Consultants — ISACCO, Jeanne M. 584
Rex Hospital — MCCALLUM, Dorothy T. 793
Shaw Univ — TOOMER, Clarence 1251
Smith Anderson Blount Dorsett et al — MATZEN, Constance M. 786
Spectator Magazine — LAMBERT, John W. 690
Univ of North Carolina at Chapel Hill — RHINE, Cynthia 1025
Wake Area Health Education Center — RICHARDSON, Beverly S. . . 1029
Wake County Dept of Pub Libs — HORTON, James T. 561
MOORE, Thomas L. 861
PARKER, Lanny C. 942
REILLY, Carol H. 1020
VAN HOY, Catherine S. 1276
WASILICK, Michael J. 1308
Wake County Sch District — TAYLOR, Christine M. 1226
Wake Medical Center — GRANDAGE, Karen K. 457

RANDLEMAN
Randolph County Pub Schs — CLARK, Patty C. 217

REIDSVILLE
Rockingham County Pub Schs — PENN, Lea M. 957

RESEARCH TRIANGLE PK
Burroughs Wellcome Co — BURCSU, James E. 158
CARPENTER, Vincent P. 185
MCCONNELL, Judith J. 797
THOMPSON, Reubin C. 1241
TROMBITAS, Ildiko D. 1258
WALTON, Carol G. 1301
CIBA-GEIGY Corp — THOMAS, Katharine S. 1237
Glaxo Inc — HULL, Peggy F. 573
Microelectronics Ctr of North Carolina — MENDELL, Stefanie 823
National Humanities Center — TUTTLE, Walter A. 1266
VARGHA, Rebecca B. 1278
National Inst of Environmental Hlth Scis — ROBERTSON, W D. 1042
WRIGHT, Larry L. 1372
North Carolina Biotechnology Center — BRUCE, Nancy G. 149
O'Brien-Atkins Association — RICE, Patricia A. 1027
Rhone-Poulenc Ag Co — LAVOY, Constance J. 704

RIEGELWOOD
Bladen County Board of Education — KERESEY, Gayle 643

ROANOKE RAPIDS
Roanoke Rapids Pub Lib — MITCHELL, Joyce L. 849

ROCKINGHAM
Sandhill Regional Lib System — WALTERS, Carol G. 1301

NORTH CAROLINA (Cont'd)
ROCKY MOUNT
Braswell Memorial Lib — ELKINS, Anne M. 343
Nash Technical Coll — FINCH, Lynette 377
North Carolina Wesleyan Coll — WILGUS, Anne B. 1339
Thomas Hackney Braswell Memorial Lib — HUGHES, Donna J. 571
SALISBURY
Livingstone Coll & Hood Theol Sem — ALDRICH, Willie L. 11
Rowan County Pub Lib — BARTON, Phillip K. 62
CARPENTER, Jennifer K. 184
LYTLE, Marian M. 753
Rowan Pub Lib — MOXLEY, Melody A. 874
Veterans Administration Medical Center — OWSLEY, Lucile C. 932
SANFORD
Lee County Lib System — BEAGLE, Donald R. 68
MATOCHIK, Michael J. 784
WWGP & WFJA Broadcasting Corp — MURCHISON, Margaret B. .. 879
SMITHFIELD
Johnston County & Smithfield Pub Lib — CLAYTON, Sue N. 220
SWANNANOA
Warren Wilson Coll — COOPER, Ruth K. 243
HUTTON, Jean R. 579
SWANQUARTER
Hyde County Board of Education — MANN, Sallie E. 766
SYLVA
Fontana Regional Lib — NEWSOM, Jeanette D. 900
TARBORO
Edgecombe County Memorial Lib — YORK, Maurice C. 1381
TAYLORSVILLE
Alexander County Lib — LAWRENCE, Virginia W. 705
STEPHENS, Doris G. 1188
TRINITY
Randolph County Pub Schs — CHANDRA, Jane H. 200
FREEMAN, Evangeline M. ... 400
WAKE FOREST
Southeastern Baptist Theological Sem — MCLEOD, Herbert E. 814
PHILBECK, Jo S. 967
WAYNESVILLE
Haywood County Pub Lib — ARMITAGE, Katherine Y. 32
WELDON
Weldon City Schools — JOYCE, Robert A. 618
WILMINGTON
New Hanover County Pub Lib — BEECH, Vivian W. 74
Wilmington Area Health Education Center — SEXTON, Spencer K. 1118
WILSON
Wilson County Pub Lib — VALENTINE, Patrick M. 1271
Wilson Memorial Hospital — EDWARDS, Rosa C. 338
WINGATE
Wingate Coll — ABBOTT, Kent H. 1
HEUBERGER, Karen W. 535
LACROIX, Michael J. 686
WINSTON-SALEM
Bowman Gray Sch of Medicine — EKSTRAND, Nancy L. 341
JOHNSTON, Rebecca M. ... 610
SIBLEY, Shawn C. 1135
Forsyth County Pub Lib — BELCHEE, Nancy O. 76
ELMORE, Lisa E. 346
FERGUSSON, David G. 372
ROBERTS, William H. 1041
ROWLAND, Janet M. 1062
WEEKS, Arthur L. 1315
WHITE, Sherry J. 1332
Forsyth Memorial Hospital — COBB, Margaret L. 225
Moravian Archives — HAUPERT, Thomas J. 512
North Carolina School of the Arts — VAN HOVEN, William D. ... 1276
R J Reynolds Tobacco Co — CHUNG, Helen S. 213
MILLER, Barry K. 836
RALPH, Randy D. 1004
Reynolda Manor Branch Lib — THOMPSON, Barbara F. ... 1239
Wake Forest Univ — AHLERS, Glen P. 8
ANDERSON, Sherry 25
BERTHRONG, Merrill G. 91
COBB, Mary L. 225
FOLTZ, Faye D. 388
GETCHELL, Charles M. 430
MOORE, Maxine B. 860
STEELE, Tom M. 1184

NORTH CAROLINA (Cont'd)
WINSTON-SALEM (Cont'd)
Wake Forest Univ — WOODARD, John R. 1365
Winston-Salem/Forsyth County Schs — CHAPMAN, Peggy H. 202
Winston-Salem Journal — ROLLINS, Marilyn H. 1051
Winston-Salem State Univ — RODNEY, Mae L. 1048
Womble Carlyle Sandridge & Rice — BOERINGER, Margaret J. ... 110
YANCEYVILLE
Hkyconeechee Regnl Lib — MASSEY, Nancy O. 782
ZEBULON
Glaxo Inc — MCKAY, Alberta S. 809

NORTH DAKOTA
BISMARCK
Bismarck State Coll — NELSON, Colleen M. 893
North Dakota State Historical Society — GRAY, David P. 459
North Dakota State Lib — HARRIS, Patricia L. 505
HENDRICKS, Thom 527
MOREHOUSE, Valerie J. 863
State Historical Society of North Dakota — NEWBORG, Gerald G. 898
VYZRALEK, Dolores E. 1290
Veterans Memorial Pub Lib — HILDEBRANT, Darrel D. 539
WALDERA, Katherine A. 1294
DEVIL'S LAKE
Lake Region Community Coll — EVENSEN, Sharon L. 358
DICKINSON
North Dakota State Univ — SORENSON, Lillian R. 1168
ELLENDALE
Trinity Bible Coll — ZINK, Esther L. 1389
FARGO
Fargo Pub Lib — SCHULTZ, Gary J. 1102
Fargo Pub Schs — QUAMME, Beverly J. 999
YLINIEMI, Hazel A. 1380
Neuropsychiatric Institute — NORDENG, Diane 908
North Dakota State Univ — BIRDSALL, Douglas G. 98
BLUE, Margaret R. 107
BRKIC, Beverly T. 138
NELSON, David N. 893
Shanley High Sch — SORNSIN, Kathleen R. 1168
FORT TOLLEN
Little Hoop Community Coll — BLACK, Lea J. 101
GRAND FORKS
City and County of Grand Forks — STEMME, Virginia L. 1186
Grand Forks Pub Lib — PAGE, Dennis N. 934
Grand Forks Pub Sch Dist — RENICK, Paul R. 1023
Univ of North Dakota — BOONE, Jon A. 115
ETTL, Lorraine R. 356
GARD, Betty A. 417
GOTT, Gary D. 453
NIENOW, Beth M. 904
PEDERSEN, Lila 954
PEDERSON, Randy L. 954
STRAHAN, Michael F. 1199
JAMESTOWN
Jamestown Coll — BRATTON, Phyllis A. 129
US Fish & Wildlife Service — ZIMMERMAN, Ann S. 1388
MAYVILLE
Mayville State Univ — KARAIM, Betty J. 627
MINOT
Minot Pub Lib — KAUP, Jermain A. 631
Minot Pub Schs — BOARDMAN, Edna M. 108
Minot State Univ — WIRTANEN, James 1356
US Department of Commerce — ROBERTSON, Pamela S. ... 1042
VALLEY CITY
Prairie Information & Research Services — HOLDEN, Douglas H. 550

NORTHERN MARIANNAS
MARIANNA ISLANDS
Government of Northern Mariannas Islands — TIGHE, Ruth L. 1244

OHIO

ADA
Ohio Northern Univ — LEONARD, James 716

AKRON
Akron Beacon Journal — TIERNEY, Catherine M. 1244
Akron City Hospital — CREELAN, Marilee M. 257
GEARY, Linda L. 424
PHILLIPS, Judith Z. 968
Akron Pub Schs — MAYER, Mary C. 789
Akron-Summit County Pub Lib — BERRY, Diana M. 90
HAWK, Steven 513
LATSHAW, Patricia H. 701
NOWAK, Leslie A. 911
REED, Elizabeth M. 1015
WAGNER, Evelyn M. 1291
Brouse & McDowell — MCDOWELL, C B. 803
Children's Hospital Medical Center — STROZIER, Sandra L. 1203
GenCorp — HOLLIS, William F. 552
Goodyear Tire & Rubber Co — SMITH, Cynthia A. 1153
Ohio Edison Co — MALUMPHY, Sharon M. 764
MOGREN, Diane A. 852
Southern Ohio Coll — MORRIS, Trisha A. 867
Uniroyal Goodrich Tire Co — GALLICCHIO, Virginia G. ... 414
Univ of Akron — BERRINGER, Virginia M. ... 90
BOLEK, Ann D. 112
BRINK, David R. 136
DURBIN, Roger 328
GUSS, Margaret B. 478
KLINGLER, Thomas E. 662
MCFARLAND, Anne S. 804
POPPLESTONE, John A. ... 984
RICHERT, Paul 1030

ALLIANCE
Babcock & Wilcox Research & Development — CARTER, James W. 189
Rodman Pub Lib — CLEM, Harriet M. 220
HAYS, George W. 517

ASHLAND
Ashland County Law Lib Association — RHOADES, Nancy L. 1025
First Presbyterian Church — ROEPKE, David E. 1048

ASHTABULA
Ashtabula County District Lib — WARREN, Dorothea C. 1306
Board of Trustees — BALOG, Rita J. 53

ATHENS
Ohio Univ — BAIN, George W. 47
BETCHER, William M. 92
COHEN, Steven J. 229
CONLIFFE, Bobbi L. 236
HOUDEK, G R. 562
LEE, Hwa W. 710
MILLER, David A. 836
MULLINER, Kent 878
OBERLE, Holly E. 914
ROBERTS, Sallie H. 1041
ROGERS, William F. 1050
SMITH, Timothy D. 1161
WEI, Yin M. 1316
WEINBERG, Wanda J. 1318
WILLIAMS, Karen J. 1344

BARBERTON
Barberton Pub Lib — KIRBAWY, Barbara L. 653
PAPA, Deborah M. 938
SWINEHART, Katharine J. ... 1216
PPG Industries — OBERLANDER, Deborah K. ... 914

BARNESVILLE
Barnesville Exempted Village Schs — THOMPSON, Myra D. 1240

BATAVIA
Clermont Coll — MARCOTTE, Frederick A. ... 769
Clermont County Law Lib — SUHRE, Carol A. 1207
Clermont County Pub Lib — POMERANTZ, Bruce F. 982
Clermont Mercy Hospital — STONE, Diane L. 1197

BAY VILLAGE
Bay Village Schs — SCHWELK, Jennifer C. 1105

BEACHWOOD
Beachwood City Schs — CHAMPLIN, Lydia F. 198

BEDFORD
Cuyahoga County Pub Lib — DZURENKO, Joann T. 331
St Mary Elementary Sch — POJMAN, Paul E. 980

BELLAIRE
Bellaire Pub Lib — KNIESNER, John T. 664

OHIO (Cont'd)

BELLEVUE
Bellevue Hospital — WAGAR, Elsa A. 1290

BEREA
Baldwin-Wallace Coll — HAMBLEY, Susan L. 490
MACIUSZKO, Jerzy J. 755

BOWLING GREEN
Bowling Green State Univ — BURLINGAME, Dwight F. ... 161
COLLINS. Evron S. 232
FIDLER, Linda M. 375
HARNER, James L. 503
KLOPFENSTEIN, Bruce C. .. 662
MCCALLUM, Brenda W. 793
MILLER, Ruth G. 842
MILLER, William 843
POVSIC, Frances F. 987
PURSEL, Janet E. 998
REPP, Joan M. 1024
SLOVASKY, Stephen 1150
ZAPOROZHETZ, Laurene E. 1386
Wood County — GILL, Judith L. 435

BRECKSVILLE
BF Goodrich Research & Developmnt Center — BUTCHER, Sharon L. 166

BURTON
Burton Pub Lib — DONALDSON, Timothy P. ... 311
VARGA, Carol C. 1278

CANFIELD
Better Business Bureau, NIA Publshg Co — LITTLE, Dean K. 733

CANTON
Malone Coll — ANDERSON, Janice L. 23
TERHUNE, R S. 1231
WHITEHEAD, Beatrice A. ... 1332
Stark County District Lib — CLARK, Kay S. 217
GREEN, Gary A. 461
PLUMMER, Karen A. 978
Walsh Coll — SUVAK, Daniel S. 1212

CEDARVILLE
Association of Christian Librarians — BROCK, Lynn A. 138
Cedarville Coll — BROWN, Stephen P. 147

CHARDON
Geauga County Pub Lib — CORBUS, Lawrence J. 245
O'CONNOR, Deborah F. ... 916
WINANS, Diane D. 1354
Law Lib Association of Geavga County — MOSELEY, Audrey 870

CHESTERLAND
Geauga County Pub Lib — ORR, Cynthia 926

CHILLICOTHE
Ohio Univ — PLANTON, Stanley P. 977

CINCINNATI
Anderson Publishing Co — GATES, Robert G. 422
KUEHNLE, Emery C. 682
Archdiocese of Cincinnati — HILAND, Gerard P. 538
ATE Management & Service Co Inc — FENDER, Kimber L. 371
Bethesda Oak Hospital — GITLIN, Rebecca A. 439
Bureau of Jewish Education — KATZ, Lawrence M. 630
Children's Hospital Medical Center — HALIBEY-BILYK, Christine M. 486
HILL, Barbarie F. 539
Cincinnati Ctr for Devlpmntl Disorders — GILROY, Dorothy A. 437
Cincinnati Law Lib Association — FRENCH, Thomas R. 402
Cincinnati Milacron Inc — CLASPER, James W. 219
PATIENCE, Alice 947
Cincinnati Pub Schs — MC NAIR, Marian B. 815
SHIVERDECKER, Darlene J. 1132
Cincinnati Technical Coll — TUCKER, Debbie B. 1261
Coll of Mt St Joseph — ALBRECHT, Cheryl C. 10
Deer Park Community Schools — HEFFRON, Sheila F. 520
Drackett Company — ENNIS, Mary J. 350
Finneytown Local Sch — KENT, Rose M. 642
Forest Hills Sch District — LEIBOLD, Cynthia K. 713
Frost & Jacobs — DAVIS, Yvonne M. 281
Grace Episcopal Church — CONNERS, Margaret S. 237
Greater Cincinnati Chamber — ROTTE, Marge E. 1060
Greater Cincinnati Lib Consortium — JOHNSON, Joann 606
Hebrew Union Coll — GILNER, David J. 437
ZAFREN, Herbert C. 1385

OHIO (Cont'd)
CINCINNATI (Cont'd)

James N Gamble Institute of Med
  Research   MC CORMICK, Lisa L. 798
KZF Inc   HAMILTON, Dennis O. 492
LaSalle Hig Sch   BLACK, Jeannie M. 101
Lloyd Lib & Museum   PERRY, Rebecca A. 960
Mead Data Central   LONG, Clare S. 739
Merrell Dow Pharmaceuticals Inc   CRETSOS, James M. 258
   DOBBS, David L. 307
   ROSENTHAL, Francine C. ... 1057
   SCHUTZ, Robert S. 1103
   SIMMONS, Edlyn S. 1139
Morton Thiokol Inc   WAID, Diana L. 1292
PEI Associated   LE BLANC, Judith E. 708
Princeton City Sch District   WOLFORD, Betty K. 1361
Procter & Gamble Co   WILSON, Sharon L. 1353
Providence Hospital   EMANI, Nirupama 347
Pub Lib of Cincinnati & Hamilton
  County   ABRAMS, Roger E. 3
   DAHMANN, Rosemary G. ... 270
   FERGUSON, George E. 372
   HETTINGER, Susan F. 534
   HORTON, Anna J. 561
   HUDZIK, Robert T. 570
   HUGE, Sharon A. 571
   HUNT, James R. 575
   JOHNS, John E. 601
   KRAMER, Sally J. 675
   LEE, Sooncha A. 711
   MCCOY, Betty J. 799
   POCKROSE, Sheryl R. 979
   RYAN, Richard A. 1071
   SMITH, Maureen M. 1158
   STONESTREET, R D. 1198
   WIEHE, Janet C. 1336
Purcell Marian High Sch   RIFFEY, Robin S. 1033
Random Corp   GROSVENOR, Philip G. 473
St Gertrude Sch   BAKER, Carol J. 48
St Rita Sch for the Deaf   DINNESEN, Peter H. 305
Senco Products   SEIK, Jo E. 1112
South-Western Publishing Co   SMITH, C L. 1153
US Court of Appeals   VOELKER, James R. 1286
   WELKER, Kathy J. 1321
Univ of Cincinnati   CAIN, Linda B. 171
   CORNELL, Alice M. 246
   DENHAM, Patricia K. 292
   DESCHENE, Dorice 294
   FROMMEYER, L R. 405
   GILLIAM, Susanne P. 436
   GILLILAND, Anne J. 436
   HEIDTMANN, Toby 521
   HEISHMAN, Eleanor L. 523
   HUGHES, Marcelle E. 572
   JOHNS, Jean B. 601
   JONES, Alice W. 610
   KONKEL, Mary S. 670
   KOVACIC, Mark E. 673
   LIPPERT, Margret G. 732
   LORENZI, Nancy M. 741
   NASRALLAH, Wahib T. 888
   NEWMAN, Linda D. 899
   PALKOVIC, Mark A. 935
   PARR, Virginia I I. 944
   PROPAS, Sharon W. 995
   RILEY, Jacquelene W. 1034
   ROMANOS, Vasso A. 1052
   SANKOT, Janice M. 1081
   THOMPSON, Ann M. 1238
   TOLZMANN, Don H. 1249
   WELLINGTON, Jean S. 1322
   WILSON, Lucy 1351
   WOOD, Elizabeth B. 1364
USI Chemicals Co   RUDY, Michelle M. 1066
Xavier Univ   PRESNELL, Jenny L. 991
CIRCLEVILLE
Circleville Bible Coll   BAILEY, Lois E. 46

OHIO (Cont'd)
CLEVELAND

Austin Co   MAKELA, Helen M. 762
Benesch Friedlander Coplan &
  Aronoff   DONNELLY, Kathleen 311
BP America   MCCONNELL, Pamela J. 798
   WAGNER, Louis F. 1292
Case Western Reserve Univ   BALCAS, Georgianne 50
   BELL, Gladys S. 77
   BENTLEY, Stella 83
   BOBICK, James E. 108
   CHESHIER, Robert G. 206
   COTE, Susan J. 249
   HANSON, Norma S. 498
   HARRISON, Dennis I. 506
   LEDOUX, Mary E. 709
   LEVINE, Lillian S. 720
   MAHOVLIC, Leanne M. 761
   PINCHES, Mary F. 974
   RAY, Laura E. 1011
   RICHMOND, Phyllis A. 1030
   ROBSON, Timothy D. 1045
   STANLEY, Jean B. 1180
   WELLS, Catherine A. 1322
Cleveland Area Metropolitan Lib
  System   WAREHAM, Nancy L. 1304
Cleveland Board of Education   MELTON, Vivian B. 823
Cleveland Clinic Foundation   DORNER, Marian T. 313
   ENGLANDER, Marlene S. ... 349
   HALLERBERG, Gretchen A. . 489
Cleveland Consulting Associates   GRAY, Elisabeth M. 459
Cleveland Health Sciences Lib   JENKINS, Glen P. 597
Cleveland Institute of Art   FOWLER, Michele R. 394
   ROM, Cristine C. 1052
Cleveland Institute of Music   MCMAHON, Melody L. 814
Cleveland Marshall Coll of Law   FINET, Scott 378
Cleveland Metropolitan General
  Hospital   BENSING, Karen M. 83
   DZIEDZINA, Christine A. 331
Cleveland Museum of Art   ABID, Ann B. 2
   ADREAN, Louis V. 7
   LANTZ, Elizabeth A. 697
   PEARMAN, Sara J. 952
   TOTH, Georgina G. 1252
Cleveland Museum of Natural History   FLAHIVE, Mary E. 383
Cleveland Orchestra   CALMER, Charles E. 174
Cleveland Psychiatric Institute   PETIT, J M. 965
Cleveland Pub Lib   BOWIE, Angela B. 121
   FARRELL, Maureen C. 365
   JUNEJA, Derry C. 620
   KOLLAR, Mary E. 669
   LORANTH, Alice N. 741
   MARTINES, Karen E. 779
   MASON, Marilyn G. 781
   PIETY, Jean Z. 972
   PRYSZLAK, Lydia M. 996
   SEELY, Edward 1111
   SHAMP, B K. 1120
   TIPKA, Donald A. 1246
Cleveland State Univ   DEAN, Winifred F. 284
   LUPONE, George 749
   MONGAN, Janet 854
   NISSENBAUM, Robert J. ... 905
   NOLAN, Marianne 907
   RADER, Hannelore B. 1002
   ROSENFELD, Joseph S. ... 1056
   SANTAVICCA, Edmund F. . 1082
   SWAIN, Richard H. 1212
Cuyahoga County Pub Lib   BERLIN, Susan T. 87
   DRACH, Priscilla L. 318
   EAGLEN, Audrey B. 331
   HUEBSCHER, Mary 570
   KOZLOWSKI, Ronald S. 674
   LOWELL, Virginia L. 744
   SILVER, Linda R. 1138
   VAN DER SCHALIE, Eric J. . 1274
Dyke Coll   TRIVISON, Donna 1257
East Cleveland Pub Lib   VENABLE, Andrew A. 1282
Federal Reserve Bank of Cleveland   MAYNARD, Elizabeth 790
Ferro Corp   FULLER, Kathleen B. 408

OHIO (Cont'd)
CLEVELAND (Cont'd)

The Foundation Center	PASQUAL, Patricia E.	946
Freedom-Gaiswold Sch	MICHNAY, Susan E.	832
The Freedonia Group	BAUMGARTNER, Robert M.	66
The Glidden Co	BACON, Agnes K.	44
Harcourt Brace Jovanovich	MACIUSZKO, Kathleen L.	755
Information Access Co	PORTUGAL, Dolores	985
Jones Day Reavis & Pogue	GREEN, Lynda C.	462
Lincoln Electric Co	KLINGER, William E.	661
Mayfield City Sch District	GILLMORE, Salley G.	436
McKinsey & Co	BORUCKI, Jennifer A.	117
	VICTORY, Karen M.	1283
Meldrum & Fewsmith Inc	SKUTNIK, John S.	1147
Metrics Research Corp	MCSPADDEN, Robert M.	818
Mount Sinai Medical Center	LANDAU, Lucille	692
	RASKIN, Rosa S.	1009
Musical Arts Association	ARNOLD, Judith M.	33
National Aeronautics & Space Admin	FACINELLI, Jaclyn R.	360
	JARABEK, Leona T.	594
NASA Lewis Research Center	LONG, Melanie C.	739
	OBERC, Susanne F.	913
North Coast Instruments	IRWIN, James W.	584
Ohio Coll of Podiatric Medicine	COWELL, Judy M.	252
Penton Publishing	KEATING, Michael F.	633
Plain Dealer Newspaper	PARCH, Grace D.	939
Predicasts	HARRIS, Richard	506
	HECHT, Joseph A.	519
	OWEN, Paul E.	932
	RICHARDSON, Ulrike L.	1030
Record Data Inc TRW	FELDER, Bruce B.	369
St Alexis Hospital Medical Center	JOHNSON, Stephen C.	609
St John Hospital	HOLCZER, Lolita B.	550
Sherwin-Williams Co	HSU, Helena S.	567
Solon City Schs	RODDA, Donna S.	1047
Standard Oil Co	FELL, Sally B.	370
	JANKOWSKI, Dorothy A.	593
	TURNER, Freya A.	1264
	YANCEY, Marianne	1377
Tantalus Inc	KANTOR, Paul B.	626
Thompson Hine & Flory	FISHER, Jo A.	381
Union Carbide Corp	RIFFLE, Linda	1034
Univ Hospitals of Cleveland	JANES, Jodith	593
	KUCHERENKO, Eugenia	682
Veterans Administration Medical Center	NOURSE, Mary E.	910
	TESMER, Nancy	1233
Western Reserve Historical Society	GRABOWSKI, John J.	455
	PIKE, Kermit J.	972
World Almanac Education	RARESHEID, Cynthia L.	1008
WVIZ-TV 25	SHELLENBARGER, Linda K.	1126

CLEVELAND HEIGHTS

Cleveland Heights Univ Heights Pub Lib	HORVATH, Camilla K.	561
Cleveland State Univ	TRAMDACK, Philip J.	1254
St Ann Sch	REESE, Kathleen A.	1016
Shaker Heights Pub Lib	JACOBER, Sheryl A.	589
Univ Heights Pub Lib	BORCHERT, Catherine G.	116

COLUMBUS

American Chemical Society	BAKER, Dale B.	48
Ashland Chemical Co	LANDIS, Kay A.	693
	MILLER, Dennis P.	837
	RATLIFF, Priscilla	1009
AT&T Conversant Systems	EVANS, Shirley A.	358
Baker & Hostetler	RODGERS, Judith P.	1047
Battelle Memorial Institute	FELTES, Carol A.	370
	GUBIOTTI, Ross A.	475
	TROVER, Larry E.	1258
	WARNER, Susan B.	1305
Bexley Pub Lib	CHADWICK, Janina A.	197
Capital Univ	ORLANDO, Jacqueline M.	926
Chemical Abstracts Service	BENINTENDI, Cheri	81
	COPENHAVER, Ida L.	244
	HODGES, Pauline R.	546
	LANGSTAFF, Elizabeth M.	696
	LEMASTERS, Joann T.	715
	MOORE, Maxwell J.	860
	NICHOL, Marian P.	901
	NORMORE, Lorraine F.	909
	PLATAU, Gerard O.	977

OHIO (Cont'd)
COLUMBUS (Cont'd)

Chemical Abstracts Service	RYERSON, George D.	1071
	SNIDER, Elizabeth M.	1163
	STEPP, Dena F.	1189
	STOBAUGH, Robert E.	1195
	TANNEHILL, Robert S.	1222
	WATSON, Judith E.	1309
Columbia Museum of Art	GENSHAFT, Carole M.	427
Columbus & Franklin County Pub Lib	FELLOWS, Barbara G.	370
	MAURER, Lewis R.	787
Columbus Diocesan Schs	FITZPATRICK, Janis M.	383
Columbus Dispatch	HUNTER, James J.	576
Columbus Law Lib Association	BLOUGH, Keith A.	106
	BRANN, Andrew R.	128
Columbus Pub Schs	SMITH, Noralee W.	1159
Columbus Sch for Girls	ALTAN, Susan B.	18
Coopers & Lybrand	IRELAND, Clara R.	583
Coronet Recording Co	BUCHSBAUM, Robert E.	153
Franklin Univ	EHRHARDT, Allyn	339
	HELSER, Fred L.	525
Grandview Heights Pub Lib	CANTWELL, Mary L.	179
	ROBINSON, David A.	1043
Grant Medical Center	COHEN, Nancy E.	228
Information Consulting Inc	MIMNAUGH, Ellen N.	845
Mount Carmel Health Center	CHEEK, Fern M.	204
	ELWELL, Pamela M.	347
National Black Programming Consultants	HADDOCK, Mable	482
Natl Ctr for Resrch in Vocational Educ	WAGNER, Judith O.	1292
Ohio Dominican Coll	BUTLER, Christina	166
Ohio Historical Center	BAGBY, Ross F.	45
Ohio Historical Society	ARNOLD, Gary J.	33
	EAST, Dennis	332
	GAIECK, Frederick W.	412
	LINCK, Bonnie J.	728
	VIOL, Robert W.	1285
Ohio Lib Foundation	PARSONS, Augustine C.	944
Ohio State Lib	MEAD, Catherine S.	819
Ohio State Univ	BAYER, Bernard I.	67
	BEYNEN, Gijsbertus K.	93
	BLOCK, Bernard A.	106
	BLOMQUIST, Laura G.	106
	BOOMGAARDEN, Wesley L.	115
	BRADIGAN, Pamela S.	125
	BRANSCOMB, Lewis C.	129
	CENTING, Richard R.	196
	CHANG, Tony H.	201
	CLEAVER, Betty P.	220
	COUCH, Nena L.	250
	CROWE, William J.	261
	DALRYMPLE, Tamsen	271
	GAUNT, Sandra L.	423
	GODWIN, Eva D.	443
	GOERLER, Raimund E.	443
	GOLDING, Alfred S.	445
	HAMILTON, Marsha J.	492
	HECK, Thomas F.	519
	HOLOCH, S A.	553
	IBEN, Glenn A.	581
	IVES, Jean E.	586
	JACKSON, George R.	587
	JAMISON, Martin P.	593
	KRUMM, Carol R.	680
	LINCOVE, David A.	728
	LOGAN, Susan J.	737
	LUDY, Lorene E.	747
	MERCADO, Heidi	825
	MIXTER, Keith E.	850
	MULARSKI, Carol A.	876
	MURPHY, James L.	880
	O'HANLON, Nancyanne	919
	POPOVICH, Charles J.	984
	POST, Phyllis C.	986
	PRONEVITZ, Gregory	995
	ROGERS, Sally A.	1050
	SANDERS, Nancy P.	1080

OHIO (Cont'd)
COLUMBUS (Cont'd)
Ohio State Univ

SAWYERS, Elizabeth J. . . . 1086
STRALEY, Dona S. 1200
STUDER, William J. 1204
VANBRIMMER, Barbara A. . 1272
WALDEN, Graham R. 1294
WANG, Anna M. 1302
WOODS, Alan L. 1366
YAGELLO, Virginia E. 1376

Ohio Supreme Court WEILANT, Edward 1317
OHIONET DIENER, Ronald E. 302
KENT, Joel S. 642
KIE, Kathleen M. 646
MLYNAR, Mary 850
SNIDER, Sondra L. 1163

Porter Wright Morris & Arthur CHRISTIAN, Patricia A. 211
SCHAEFGEN, Susan M. . . . 1089

Pub Lib of Columbus & Franklin
County BLACK, Larry D. 101
HOWARTH, Meribah G. 565
KYLES, Rubye R. 685
MCWILLIAM, Deborah A. . . . 818
SCHROEDER, Donna L. . . . 1100

Schottenstein Zox & Dunn LPA D'AMORE, Denice M. 272
Schwartz Kelm Warren & Rubenstein HUNE, Mary G. 574
State Lib of Ohio BETCHER, Melissa A. 92
CHESKI, Richard M. 207
HEARD, Jeffrey L. 518
HORDUSKY, Clyde W. 559
PHILIP, John J. 967
SMITH, Ellen A. 1154
WILKS, Cheri L. 1341

Strawser & Allen ALLEN, Cameron 14
Supreme Court of Ohio FU, Paul S. 407
Trinity Lutheran Seminary HUBER, Donald L. 569
Upper Arlington City Schs DRIESSEN, Diane 320
CUYAHOGA FALLS
Cuyahoga Falls City Schs KLAUS, Susan B. 658
Cuyahoga Falls General Hospital MAKIN, Mollie D. 762
DAYTON
Carlson Marketing Group QUINTEN, Rebecca G. 1000
Chaminade-Julienne High Sch DISTEFANO, Marianne 305
DAP Inc SULLIVAN, Frances L. 1207
Dayton & Montgomery County Pub
Lib BEY, Leon S. 93
BUCK, Jeremy R. 153
NEWMAN, Marianne L. 899
WALLACH, John S. 1298
WESTNEAT, Helen C. 1327
WILSON, Letitia A. 1351
WYLLIE, Stanley C. 1375

Dayton Art Institute DUNWOODIE, Jane A. 327
PINKNEY, Helen L. 975

Dayton Board of Education JOHNSON, Floy W. 604
Dayton City Schs TAYLOR, Orphus R. 1228
Dayton-Montgomery County Pub Lib LINDSTROM, Elaine C. 730
Dayton Newspapers Inc TRIVEDI, Harish S. 1257
Freelance Library Services EVANS, Stephen P. 358
Good Samaritan Hospital & Health
Center ROBINSON, Elizabeth A. . . . 1044
Mad River Township Local Schs BRUMIT, Nancy T. 150
Mead Data Central CHRISTOU, Corilee S. 212
COYLE, Christopher B. 253
HERRICK, Carol L. 532
JOHNSON, John R. 606
NERO, Robert A. 895
PEAKE, Sharon K. 952
PRICKETT, Dan S. 993
REED, Buzz 1014
SIMPSON, Jack W. 1142
SPOHR, Cynthia L. 1175
SEXTON, Sally V. 1118

Miami Valley Hospital BALL, Diane A. 52
Oakwood Board of Education MAYL, Gene 790
Professional Books & Services POWELL, Lane P. 988
Reynolds & Reynolds Interactive ARK, Connie E. 31
Spinning Hills Middle Sch

OHIO (Cont'd)
DAYTON (Cont'd)
United Theological Seminary BERG, Richard R. 84
O'BRIEN, Betty A. 914
O'BRIEN, Elmer J. 914
Univ of Dayton ARTZ, Theodora S. 35
GARTEN, Edward D. 420
HANLEY, Thomas L. 496
HECHT, Judith N. 519
JENKINS, Fred W. 597
KRIEGER, Michael T. 678
SIMONS, Linda K. 1141
WALKER, Mary A. 1296
WERNERSBACH, Geraldine
S. 1325
Washington Township Pub Lib KLINCK, Cynthia A. 661
Wright State Univ BAKER, Narcissa L. 49
BOX, Krista J. 122
MCNEER, Elizabeth J. 816
NOLAN, Patrick B. 907
THOMAS, Ritchie D. 1238
WEHMEYER, Jeffrey M. . . . 1316

DEFIANCE
Defiance Coll SEDLCOK, Barbara J. 1111
DELAWARE
Delaware County District Lib SAMPLES, Judith L. 1078
Methodist Theological Sch FOSTER, Julia A. 392
Ohio Wesleyan Univ COHEN, Susan J. 229
HARPER, Lucy B. 503
SCHLICHTING, Catherine N. 1094
WHITAKER, Constance C. . 1329

DOVER
Dover Pub Lib COOLEY, Daniel R. 241
DUBLIN
AT&T Technical Training Services GRIEVE, Shelley 468
Dublin Local Schs LOVELAND, Catherine R. . . . 743
Information Dimensions Inc BRINKMAN, Barry J. 136
DITMARS, David W. 305
HASKINS, Dawn A. 510
KNOBLAUCH, Carol J. 665
MOORE, Brian P. 858
OCLC Online Computer Lib Center BLANCHARD, Mark A. 103
BROWN, Rowland C. 147
BROWNELL, Barbara A. . . . 148
CALL, J R. 173
CONNELL, Christopher J. . . . 237
DAVIS, Carol C. 277
DAVIS, Linda M. 280
DILLON, Martin 303
DRONE, Jeanette M. 320
GRABENSTATTER,
Christine N. 455
HAYNES, Kathleen J. 516
HURLEY, Geraldine C. 577
JACOB, Mary E. 589
KILGOUR, Frederick G. 648
KISER, Betsy N. 656
LENSENMAYER, Nancy F. . . 715
MARSHALL, Mary E. 774
OLSZEWSKI, Lawrence J. . . . 923
O'NEIL, Rosanna M. 924
PAK, Moo J. 935
PATTON, Glenn E. 949
PRABHA, Chandra G. 989
SCHUITEMA, Joan E. 1101
SHALOIKO, John L. 1119
SHARP, Linda C. 1122
SHREWSBURY, Lynn D. . . . 1133
TAVENNER, Deborah A. . . . 1225
THOMAS, James M. 1237
VIZINE-GOETZ, Diane 1286
WALBRIDGE, Sharon L. . . . 1293
WALTERS, Clarence R. 1301
WEITZ, Jay N. 1320
Price Waterhouse SPEECE, Yvonne M. 1172
Software Smithy MARSH, Elizabeth C. 773
EAST CLEVELAND
East Cleveland Board of Education AVERY, Jacqueline R. 41
East Cleveland Municipal Court KEENON, Una H. 634
East Cleveland Pub Lib REESE, Gregory L. 1016

OHIO (Cont'd)

ELYRIA
Elyria Pub Lib   BURRIER, Donald H. 163
HCT Corp   BANKS, Marie M. 54
EUCLID
Euclid Pub Lib   COLEMAN, Judith 231
FAIRBORN
Caci Inc   MAXWELL, Marjo V. 788
SofTech Inc   O'GORMAN, Jack 918
FAIRVIEW PARK
Cuyahoga County Pub Lib   CHARVAT, Catherine T. 203
                                  ROBINSON, Doris J. 1043
FINDLAY
Findlay City Schools   HARDESTY, Vicki H. 499
Findlay Coll   SCHIRMER, Robert W. 1093
                                  STEVENS, Donna H. 1190
Findlay-Hancock County Pub Lib   DICKINSON, Luren E. 301
                                  DUDLEY, Durand S. 323
                                  HABINSKI, Carol A. 481
                                  JANKY, Donna L. 593
                                  LUST, Jeanette M. 749
Marathon Oil Co   WHIPPLE, Connie S. 1329
FREMONT
Memorial Hospital of Fremont   KELLER, Marlo L. 635
Rutherford B Hayes Presidential
  Center   SMITH, Thomas A. 1161
GALLIPOLIS
Dr Samuel L Bossard Memorial Lib GUTHRIE, Chab C. 479
GAMBIER
Kenyon Coll   GREENSLADE, Thomas B. . . 465
                                  QUIGLEY, Suzanne L. 999
                                  WILT, Charles F. 1353
GARFIELD HEIGHTS
Cuyahoga County Pub Lib   POTELICKI, Athalene O. . . . 986
                                  SLEEMAN, Linda E. 1148
GARRETTSVILLE
Portage County District Lib   FINAN, Patrick E. 377
GERMANTOWN
Germantown Pub Lib   BANTA, Gratia J. 55
GRAFTON
Grafton/Midview Pub Lib   DIAL, David E. 299
GRANVILLE
Denison Univ   MAURER, Charles B. 787
Dow Chemical Co   QUINN, Caroline E. 1000
Ohio Roots   RUGG, John D. 1066
Owens-Corning Fiberglas Corp   LEMON, Nancy A. 715
GREENBRIER COMMONS
Cuyahoga County Pub Lib   BINA, Marcella A. 97
GREENVILLE
Greenville Pub Lib   RUHL, Jodi S. 1066
GROVE CITY
Grove City Pub Lib   BARRICK, Susan K. 59
                                  BLACK, Frances P. 101
HAMILTON
Butler County Law Lib   SHEW, Anita K. 1129
Lane Pub Lib   TAVISS, Patricia A. 1225
HIRAM
Hiram Coll   DUFFETT, Gorman L. 323
                                  WANSER, Jeffery C. 1303
Portage County District Lib   SPEAR, Linda A. 1172
HURON
Bowling Green State Univ   CURRIE, William W. 266
INDEPENDENCE
LTV Steel Co   WOOLARD, Kathryn A. 1368
IRONTON
Briggs Lawrence County Pub Lib   REID, Margaret B. 1018
JEFFERSON
Ashtabula County Law Lib
  Association   BROWN, Vicki L. 148
KALIDA
Kalida Board of Educ   MILLER, Marian A. 840
KENT
Kent Free Lib   CELIGOJ, Carmen Z. 196
Kent State Univ   BIRK, Nancy 98
                                  BUTTLAR, Lois J. 167
                                  DU MONT, Rosemary R. 325
                                  GATTEN, Jeffrey N. 422
                                  GEARY, James W. 424
                                  GILDZEN, Alex J. 434
                                  JACKSON, Clara O. 587

OHIO (Cont'd)

KENT (Cont'd)
Kent State Univ
                                  KERSTETTER, John 644
                                  KIRKBRIDE, Amey L. 654
                                  KREYCHE, Michael R. 678
                                  NELSON, Olga G. 895
                                  SCHLOMAN, Barbara F. . . . 1094
                                  TOLLIVER, Don L. 1248
                                  WHYDE, John S. 1335
                                  WYNAR, Lubomyr R. 1375
KENTON
Mary Lou Johnson-Hardin County
  Dist Lib   PETTY, Sue W. 965
KETTERING
BDM Corp Inc   ROHMILLER, Thomas D. . . . 1051
LAGRANGE
Keystone Local Schools   SCHMUHL, Gayle B. 1096
LAKEWOOD
Lakewood Board of Education   COLEMAN, Barbara K. 231
                                  FREDERICKA, Theresa 400
                                  HUDSON, Jo A. 569
Lakewood Hospital   FARAGO, Kathleen M. 363
Lakewood Pub Lib   GIOFFRE, B J. 438
                                  HENDERSON, Shirley A. 527
                                  RYAN, Mary E. 1071
                                  SPERRY, Linda S. 1174
                                  TAYLOR, Patricia L. 1228
St James Sch   MULLER, Madeline A. 877
LANCASTER
Fairfield County Lib   NEEDHAM, George M. 891
Ohio Univ   MCCAULEY, Hannah V. 795
LEBANON
Warren County Genealogical Society FOLEY, Harriet E. 387
LIMA
Shawnee Local Schs   MCDANIEL, Deanna J. 801
Western Ohio Regional Lib Devlpmnt
  Syst   SCHNEIDER, J K. 1097
LISBON
Lepper Lib Association   MCPEAK, James J. 817
LORAIN
Lorain Community Hospital   GANGLOFF, Tory W. 416
Lorain Pub Lib   CROMER, Kenneth L. 260
                                  RUSSO, Stephen A. 1070
                                  SMITH, Valerie M. 1161
MADISON
MacKenzie Memorial Pub Lib   JOHNSON, Ruth E. 608
MANSFIELD
Mansfield General Hospital   BENISHEK, Kristine K. 81
Mansfield-Richland County Pub Lib GARRETT, Melinda R. 420
                                  KIECZYKOWSKI, Edward
                                    M. 647
North Central Lib Cooperative   KARRE, David J. 628
Ohio State Univ   ROMARY, Michael P. 1052
MAPLE HEIGHTS
Cuyahoga County Pub Lib   EVERETT, Janet J. 358
                                  GREENLEE, Joanne E. 465
                                  HARRIS, Margaret J. 505
                                  WYNN, Vivian R. 1375
MARIETTA
Marietta Coll   NEYMAN, Sandra B. 900
Marietta Memorial Hospital   KERBOW, Sandra C. 643
Washington County Pub Lib   BELL, Ellen 76
MARION
Marion Pub Lib   GERWIN, Barbara L. 430
MARTINS FERRY
Martins Ferry Pub Lib   STORCK, John W. 1198
MASSILLON
Massillon Pub Lib   LESLIE, Camille J. 718
MAYFIELD HEIGHTS
Hillcrest Hospital   LYNAM, Nancy J. 751
MEDINA
Medina County District Lib   SMITH, Robert S. 1160
MENTOR
Lake County Historical Society   ENGEL, Carl T. 348
Lakeland Community Coll   MAGNER, Mary J. 759
METALS PARK
American Society for Metals Intl WEIDA, William A. 1316
ASM International   BALDWIN, Eleanor M. 51
                                  SANDULEAK, Barbara 1081

OHIO (Cont'd)
MIAMISBURG
Mead Imaging   ROHMILLER, Ellen L. 1051
Monsanto Research Corp   MOORE, Susan J. 861
MIDDLEFIELD
Geauga County Pub Lib   GUMPPER, Mary F. 477
MILFORD
SENMED   BAKER, Carole A. 48
NELSONVILLE
Nelsonville Pub Lib   KURZ, David B. 685
NEW ALBANY
Columbus Pub Schs   HERB, Elizabeth D. 530
NEW CARLISLE
New Carlisle Bethel Schs   ROGERS, Cassandra J. 1049
NEW PHILADELPHIA
Kent State Univ   KOBULNICKY, Michael 666
Tuscarawas County Pub Lib   HAGLOCH, Susan B. 483
NEWARK
Licking Memorial Hospital   FREYTAG, Lindsay J. 403
NEWTON FALLS
Newton Falls Pub Lib   MC CLEAF-NESPECA, Sue
                                        E. 796
NILES
McKinley Memorial Lib   MCMURRAY, Sallylou 815
                                      STOUT, Chester B. 1198
Niles City Schs   THOMAS, Saraalice F. 1238
NORTH OLMSTED
Cuyahoga County Pub Lib   VANKE, Judith P. 1276
NORTH ROYALTON
Cuyahoga County Pub Lib   ALEXA, Cynthia M. 12
North Royalton City Schs   WEST, Loretta G. 1326
NORWALK
Norwalk Pub Lib   DRAPP, Laureen 318
OBERLIN
Ciba-Corning Diagnostics   MULDER, Marjorie M. 876
Oberlin Coll   BAUMANN, Roland M. 66
                                      BOYD, Alan D. 122
                                      CARPENTER, Eric J. 184
                                      COMER, Cynthia H. 234
                                      ENGLISH, Raymond A. 350
                                      GOULD, Allison L. 454
                                      KNAPP, David 663
                                      MOFFETT, William A. 852
                                      RICKER, Alison S. 1031
                                      SCHOONMAKER, Dina B. ... 1098
                                      WEIDMAN, Jeffrey 1316
                                      ZAGER, Daniel A. 1385
OREGON
St Charles Hospital   JOHNSON, Debbie L. 603
ORRVILLE
Univ of Akron   GEISEY, Barbara T. 425
OTTAWA
Putnam County District Lib   JONES, Robert M. 614
OXFORD
Lane Pub Lib   RHODES, Glenda T. 1026
Miami Univ   MILLER, Clayton M. 836
                                      OLSON, Joann D. 922
                                      QUAY, Richard H. 999
                                      SCHMALBERG, Aaron 1094
                                      WORTMAN, William A. 1369
                                      ZASLOW, Barry J. 1386
PAINESVILLE
Lake Hospital System Inc   SHELDON, Holly L. 1126
Morley Lib   GARDNER, John R. 418
Ricerca Inc   BRANCHICK, Susan E. 127
                                      DUANE, Carol A. 321
PARMA
Cuyahoga County Pub Lib   BLAHA, Linda N. 102
                                      GRANTS, Yvette M. 458
                                      OBLOY, Elaine C. 914
PENINSULA
Peninsula Lib and Historical Society BERGDORF, Randolph S. 85
PEPPER PIKE
Ursuline Coll   BELKIN, Betsey B. 76
PORTSMOUTH
Portsmouth Pub Lib   COOK, Charles T. 239
POWELL
James E Rush Assoc Inc   RUSH, James E. 1068
RAVENA
Ravenna City Schs   WISE, Martha K. 1357

OHIO (Cont'd)
REYNOLDSBURG
Reynoldsburg City Schs   MEESE, Jane E. 821
ROCKY RIVER
Rocky River Board of Education   SLANE, Barbara A. 1147
Rocky River Pub lib   GARRISON, Michael G. 420
ROOTSTOWN
Northeastern Ohio Univ Coll of
   Medicine   BREWER, Karen L. 134
                                      OSTERFIELD, George T. 928
                                      PORTER, Marlene A. 985
                                      UNGER, Monica A. 1269
ROSSFORD
Rossford Pub Lib   BURKE, Saretta K. 160
                                      FRENCH, Michael 402
ST CLAIRSVILLE
Ohio Univ   NOBLE, Susan E. 906
SANDUSKY
Firelands Community Hospital   BARNUM, Denise I. 58
Sandusky Lib   BRAUTIGAM, Faith J. 130
SHAKER HEIGHTS
Cleveland Area Metropolitan Lib
   System   FRY, Mildred C. 406
Hathaway Brown Sch   LARSON, Gretchen S. 699
Shaker Heights Board of Education   KAPLAN, Lois J. 626
URS Dalton   SPAHR, Cheryl L. 1170
SHELBY
Marvin Memorial Lib   BAVIN, Ann L. 67
                                      WOOD, Ann F. 1363
SIDNEY
Amos Memorial Pub Lib   BELVIN, Robert J. 78
                                      WILSON, Memory A. 1352
Amos Press   HESSELBEIN, Krista M. 534
SOUTH EUCLID
Cleveland Diocese   BRADEN, Carol A. 125
St Gregory the Great Elementary Sch GEORGE, Linda H. 427
SPRINGFIELD
Warder Libs of Springfield & Clark
   Cnty   MCCROSKY, Janet E. 800
Wittenberg Univ   MONTAG, John 855
STEUBENVILLE
Pub Lib of Steubenville   HALL, Alan C. 486
T O R Franciscans   BURKE, Ambrose L. 160
STOW
Polysar   VARA, Margaret E. 1278
STREETSBORO
Streetsboro Senior High   MCKEE, Barbara J. 810
STRONGSVILLE
Cuyahoga County Pub Lib   GREENBERG, Eva M. 463
The Glidden Co   STARRETT, Patricia L. 1182
Strongsville City Schools   CUCCIARRE, Barbara L. 263
TIFFIN
Tiffin City Board of Education   LEWIS, Gwen C. 723
TOLEDO
Central Catholic High Sch   MOHLER, Dorothy C. 852
Davis Coll of Business   BASILE, Anne J. 63
Fuller & Henry   SCOTT, Melvia A. 1107
Libbey Owens Ford Co   KEOGH, Jeanne M. 643
Mercy Hospital   SINK, Thomas R. 1143
Owens-Corning Fiberglas Corp   CHRISTY, Patricia A. 212
Owens Technical Coll   EMRICK, Nancy J. 348
Riverside Hospital   MALUCHNIK, Kathryn K. 764
St Michael's in the Hills Church   HANNAFORD, Claudia L. ... 496
Shumaker Loop & Kendrick   ESBIN, Martha P. 354
Teledyne Cae   DOWDELL, Marlene S. 315
Toledo Blade   REDDINGTON, Mary E. 1013
Toledo Hospital   TILLMAN, Linda M. 1245
Toledo Law Association   WOODRUFF, Brenda B. ... 1366
Toledo-Lucas County Pub Lib   AVERY, Galen V. 41
                                      BAKER, Paula J. 49
                                      CLARK, Marilyn L. 217
                                      DANZIGER, Margaret 274
                                      EASTERLY-POTTER, Anne
                                        P. 333
                                      KUCINSKI, B J. 682
                                      LOCKE-GAGNON, Rebecca
                                        A. 736
                                      SCOLES, Clyde S. 1106
Toledo Museum of Art   MORRIS, Anne O. 866
                                      SCOTT, Sharon A. 1108

OHIO (Cont'd)
TOLEDO (Cont'd)
Toledo Pub Schs   SHEPARD, Jon R. 1127
Univ of Toledo   BALDWIN, Julia F. 51
                                                BITTER, Diane S. 100
                                                CARY, Mary K. 191
                                                ERNST, Gordon E. 353
                                                GREEN, Denise D. 461
                                                LERNER, Esther T. 717
                                                ORAM, Richard W. 925
                                                VOIGT, Kathleen J. 1287
                                                WEAVER, Alice O. 1312
VLS Inc   CHRISTIANSEN, Eric G. 211
TROY
Hobart Brothers Company   BAKER, Martha A. 49
Troy City Schs   MILLER, John E. 839
Troy-Miami County Pub Lib   CRAM, Mary E. 255
                                                TUCKER, Mary C. 1262

TWINSBURG
Twinsburg Pub Lib   KAUER, Patricia M. 630
UNIONTOWN
Kent State Univ   MCCHESNEY, Kathryn M. . . . 795
UNIVERSITY HEIGHTS
John Carroll Univ   BALCON, William J. 51
                                                PIETY, John S. 972
                                                SWEENY, Mary K. 1215

UPPER ARLINGTON
Upper Arlington Pub Lib   ANDERSON, Carl A. 21
VERSAILLES
Versailles Exempted Village Schs   MINNICH, Conrad H. 846
WAPAKONETA
Auglaize County Pub Lib   FREW, Martha G. 402
                                                FURL, Michael 410

WARREN
Warren-Trumbull County Pub Lib   BRIELL, Robert D. 135
                                                JONES, Judykay 613
                                                TYSON, Edith S. 1267

WARRENSVILLE
Cuyahoga Community Coll   GORDON, Shirlee J. 452
                                                MEYER, Jimmy E. 830

WARRENSVILLE HEIGHTS
Cuyahoga County Pub Lib   NANCE, Lena L. 887
WATERFORD
Wolf Creek Local Sch District   TEPE, Ann S. 1231
WELLSTON
Ohio Valley Area Libs   ANDERSON, Eric S. 22
WESTENVILLE
Westenville City Schs   GILBERT, Donna J. 433
WESTERVILLE
Otterbein Coll   MACKENZIE, Alberta E. 756
                                                SALT, Elizabeth A. 1077
Westerville Pub Lib   GARDNER, Frank D. 417
                                                TUROCI, Esther M. 1265

WESTLAKE
Eveready Battery Co Inc   LANGKAU, Claire M. 696
Information Management Consultants
   Inc   CHAMIS, Alice Y. 198
Porter Pub Lib   ADAMS, Liese A. 5
                                                DOMBEY, Kathryn W. 310
St John & West Shore Hospital   GALLANT, Jennifer J. 414
WESTON
Weston Pub Lib   FLOWER, Eileen D. 386
WILMINGTON
Clinton Memorial Hospital   TOMLIN, Marsha A. 1250
Southwestern Ohio Rural Libs   JOHNSON, Corinne E. 603
Wilmington Coll   NICHOLS, James T. 901
                                                TOEDTMAN, Janet J. 1248
Wilmington Pub Lib of Clinton County   NOVAK, Mary S. 911
WOOSTER
Coll of Wooster   GUSTAFSON, Julia C. 478
                                                POWELL, Margaret S. 988
Ohio State Univ   BRITTON, Constance J. 137
Wayne County Pub Lib   MARCONI, Joseph V. 769
                                                MORRIS, Glenna E. 866

WORTHINGTON
Systems Engineering Associates Inc   RICHARDSON, Katherine A.   1029
Worthington Pub Lib   BRANCH, Susan 127
                                                SHAW, Debra S. 1123
                                                WILSON, Leigh K. 1351

OHIO (Cont'd)
WRIGHT PATTERSON AFB
Defense Inst of Security Assistance
   Mgmt   KNASIAK, Theresa J. 663
US Air Force   BOETTCHER, Barry J. 110
                                                NAM, Wonki K. 887
US Air Force Institute of Technology   CUPP, Christian M. 265
                                                HELLING, James T. 524
                                                PURSCH, Lenore D. 998

XENIA
Green County District Lib   MULHERN, Raymond A. 876
Greene County District Lib   KELTON, Jon D. 639
                                                OVERTON, Julie M. 931
                                                WALDER, Antoinette L. 1294

YOUNGSTOWN
Austintown Pub Schs   PORMEN, Paul E. 984
Nola Regional Lib System   YANCURA, Ann J. 1377
Pub Lib of Youngstown & Mahoning
   County   DONAHUGH, Robert H. 310
                                                TRUCKSIS, Theresa A. 1259
St Elizabeth Hospital   ROSENTHAL, Barbara G. . . 1057
Youngstown City Schs   GROHL, Arlene P. 471
Youngstown State Univ   GENAWAY, David C. 426
                                                JACOBSON, Susan D. 590
                                                LUTTRELL, Jeffrey R. 750
                                                ROUTH, Sheila J. 1061
                                                VARMA, Valsamani 1278
                                                WALL, Carol 1297

ZANESVILLE
Bishop Rosecrans High Sch   SIGRIST, Staci E. 1137
John McIntire Pub Lib   SMITH, Jacqueline 1155

OKLAHOMA
ADA
East Central Univ   COULTER, Cynthia M. 251
                                                HUESMANN, James L. 570
                                                ROBBINS, Louise S. 1039

ALVA
City of Alva   THORNE, Larry R. 1242
Northwestern Oklahoma State Univ   LAU, Ray D. 702
APACHE
Apache I-6 Sch District   HUSTED, Ruth E. 578
ARDMORE
Chickasaw Lib System   ROBINSON, Joel M. 1044
Mental Health Services of Southern
   OK   KIMBLE, Valerie F. 649
BARTLESVILLE
Independent Sch District 30   STEWART, Vicki 1193
Natl Inst for Petroleum & Energy
   Resrch   STROMAN, Josh H. 1202
Phillips Petroleum Co   ROBIN, Annabeth 1043
BETHANY
Intl Pentecostal Holiness Church   HARGIS-LYTLE, Betty L. 501
Southern Nazarene Univ   FLINNER, Beatrice E. 385
                                                PELLEY, Shirley N. 955
                                                REINBOLD, Janice K. 1021

BROKEN ARROW
Sisters of the Sorrowful Mother   UHL, M C. 1268
DEL CITY
Metropolitan Lib System   FEHRENBACH, Laurie A. . . . 368
DURANT
Southeastern Oklahoma State Univ   PARHAM, Kay B. 940
EDMOND
Central State Univ   ALSWORTH, Frances W. 18
                                                CURTIS, Ronald A. 267
                                                RYLANDER, Carolyn S. 1072
Oklahoma Lib Association   BOIES, Kay A. 111
ENID
Phillips Graduate Seminary   HAMBURGER, Roberta L. . . . 491
Phillips Univ   SAYRE, John L. 1087
FORT SILL
US Army   RELPH, Martha H. 1022
GUTHRIE
City of Guthrie   ROYSTER, Peggy K. 1063
LAWTON
Cameron Univ   RABURN, Josephine R. 1001
MCALESTER
McAlester Pub Schs   WRIGHT, Carolyn R. 1370
Southeastern Pub Lib System   SIMON, Bradley A. 1140

OKLAHOMA (Cont'd)

MIAMI
City of Miami   WALLEN, Joyce M. 1298
MIDWEST CITY
Data Search & Retrieval Inc   MOSLEY, Thomas E. 872
Rose State Coll   HUST, Carolyn R. 578
                                          SAULMON, Sharon A. 1084
MOORE
Pioneer Multi-County Lib System   GOLDSBERRY, Maureen E. . 446
MUSKOGEE
Eastern Oklahoma District Lib System   VARNER, Joyce 1279
Veterans Administration Medical
  Center   GUTIERREZ, Carolyn A. 479
NORMAN
Central State Griffin Memorial
  Hospital   PIERCE, Shirley M. 972
National Severe Storms Laboratory   MEACHAM, Mary 819
Norman Pub Sch System   PARKER, Eleanor V. 941
Norman Regional Hospital   MCKNIGHT, Michelynn 812
Pioneer Multi-County Lib System   JORDAN, Linda K. 616
                                          PETERS, Lloyd A. 962
                                          SHERMAN, Mary A. 1128
Readex Microprint Corp   LARSEN, Nancy E. 698
Southern Nazarene Univ   COCHENOUR, Donnice K. . . 225
Univ of Oklahoma at Norman   BATT, Fred 64
                                          BENDER, Nathan E. 79
                                          CLARK, Harry 217
                                          COCHENOUR, John J. 225
                                          FAIBISOFF, Sylvia G. 361
                                          FAW, Marc T. 366
                                          GOODMAN, Marcia M. 449
                                          HARRINGTON, Sue A. 504
                                          HOVDE, David M. 563
                                          KANCHANAKPAN, Pongsak . 624
                                          LATROBE, Kathy H. 701
                                          LAUGHLIN, Mildred A. 703
                                          LEE, Sul H. 711
                                          MATHIS, Barbara B. 784
                                          POLAND, Jean A. 980
                                          STOLT, Wilbur A. 1196
                                          VOGES, Mickie A. 1287
                                          WEAVER-MEYERS, Pat L. . . 1313

OKLAHOMA CITY
Crowe & Dunlevy   CORNEIL, Charlotte E. 246
Datatek Corp   PASCHAL, Linda P. 945
                                          ROACH, Eddie D. 1037
DATATIMES Corp   PASCHAL, John M. 945
Fellers Snider Blankenship Bailey et
  al   BOOTENHOFF, Rebecca J. . . 116
HTB Inc   ROBERTSON, Retha M. 1042
Melton Co Inc   MELTON, Howard E. 823
Metroplitan Lib System   MEYERS, Duane H. 830
Metropolitan Lib System   BRAWNER, Lee B. 130
                                          CORLEE, Lisa 246
                                          DAVIS, Denyvetta 278
                                          HERSTAND, Joellen 533
                                          LITTLE, Paul L. 733
                                          MELIK, Ella M. 822
                                          PETERSON, Denise D. 963
Oklahoma Arts Institute   DOBBERTEEN, Sara J. 307
Oklahoma City Univ   NASH, Helen B. 888
Oklahoma City Zoo   WEISS, Catharine H. 1320
Oklahoma Department of Libs   BELEU, Steve 76
                                          BITTLE, Christine M. 100
                                          CLARK, Robert L. 218
                                          JONES, Beverly A. 611
                                          LOWELL, Howard P. 744
                                          MCVEY, Susan C. 818
                                          SKVARLA, Donna J. 1147
                                          VESELY, Marilyn L. 1283
Oklahoma State Department of
  Education   COWEN, Linda L. 253
                                          ROADS, Clarice D. 1038
South Community Hospital   JORSKI, Sharon D. 617
Univ of Oklahoma at Oklahoma City   CALLARD, Joanne C. 173
                                          SHROUT, Sally J. 1133
OKMULGEE
Oklahoma State Univ   KIRKBRIDE, Rebecca M. 654
PONCA CITY
City of Ponca City   SKIDMORE, Stephen C. . . . 1146

OKLAHOMA (Cont'd)

PRYOR
Pryor City Schs   BARRETT, Lenna M. 59
SEMINOLE
Seminole Pub Lib   RYAN, Kathleen M. 1071
SHAWNEE
Oklahoma Baptist Univ   ALDRIDGE, Betsy B. 11
                                          COBB, Sylvia R. 225
Pioneer Multi-County Lib System   DICKSON, Theresa J. 301
STILLWATER
OK Dept of Vocational & Technical
  Educ   MURPHY, Peggy A. 881
Oklahoma State Univ   BAUER, Carolyn J. 65
                                          BLEDSOE, Kathleen E. 105
                                          CAROL, Barbara B. 184
                                          DAVIS, Joyce N. 279
                                          GAGE, Marilyn K. 412
                                          HILKER, Emerson W. 539
                                          HOLMES, Jill M. 553
                                          JOHNSON, Edward R. 604
                                          MORRIS, Karen T. 867
                                          NELSON, Norman L. 895
                                          ROUSE, Roscoe 1061
                                          WOLFF, Cynthia J. 1361
Stillwater Pub Schs   ROUSE, Charlie L. 1061
TMS Inc   BENGE, Bruce 80
                                          PHILLIPS, J R. 968
STILWELL
Flaming Rainbow Univ   FULK, Mary C. 408
TAHLEQUAH
Northeast State Univ   VEITH, Charles R. 1281
Northeastern Oklahoma State Univ   CHEATHAM, Gary L. 204
Northeastern State Univ   BRICK, Sarah E. 134
                                          HILL, Helen K. 540
                                          MADAUS, J R. 758
                                          MCQUITTY, Jeanette N. 817
                                          PATTERSON, Lotsee 948
                                          SUMNER, Delores T. 1209
TISHOMINGO
Murray State Coll   KENNEDY, James W. 641
TULSA
American Assn of Petroleum
  Geologists   SHANKS, Katherine N. 1120
Amoco Production Co   EGGERT, Paula A. 339
Hillcrest Medical Center   COOK, Peggy M. 240
Newspaper Printing Corp   FARLEY, Austin G. 364
Occidental Oil & Gas Corp   STAIR, Fred 1178
OK Coll of Osteopathic Medcn &
  Surgery   ROBERTS, Linda L. 1041
Oklahoma Junior Coll   BISHOP, Donna M. 99
Oklahoma Osteopathic Hospital   COOPER, Sylvia J. 243
Oral Roberts Univ   JUDKINS, Timothy C. 619
                                          MOORE, Maxwell L. 860
                                          YOUNG, Thomas E. 1383
Philbrook Art Center   HAYHURST, Carol A. 516
Pub Services Co of Oklahoma   DONOVAN, James M. 312
St John Medical Center   BUTHOD, J C. 166
Tulsa City-County Lib System   GRAHAM, John 456
                                          JENNINGS, Kathryn L. 598
                                          KEENE, Janis C. 634
                                          MEADOR, Joan S. 819
                                          SEARS, Robert W. 1110
                                          STURDIVANT, Nan J. 1205
                                          TAPPANA, Kathy A. 1223
                                          WOODRUM, Patricia A . . 1366
Tulsa Junior Coll   HACKER, Connie J. 481
                                          MANES, Estelle L. 765
                                          MCCALL, Patricia 793
                                          NORTON, Paula T. 910
Tulsa Pub Schs   WRIGHT, Patricia Y. 1372
Union Pub Schs   UNDERHILL, Jan 1268
Univ of Oklahoma at Tulsa   MINNERATH, Janet E. 846
Univ of Tulsa   DUCEY, Richard E. 322
                                          HILL, Linda L. 540
                                          HUGHES, Carol A. 571
                                          HUTTNER, Sidney F. 579
                                          KANE, Kathy 625
                                          KEARNS, Richard P. 633
                                          MURRAY, James T. 882
                                          NELSON, Melanie D. 894

OKLAHOMA (Cont'd)
TULSA (Cont'd)
Univ of Tulsa

PATTERSON, Robert H.	948
SANDERS, Melodie	1080
SARK, Sue	1083
SMITH, Donald R.	1154
SMITH, Peggy C.	1159
TOOLEY, Katherine J.	1250
WEAVER, Pamela J.	1312

WALTERS
Walters Pub Schools

ZACHARY, Patricia A.	1385

OREGON
ALBANY

City of Albany	SUGGS, Wayne L.	1206
Greater Albany Pub Schs	OLSEN, Clintena D.	921
Linn-Benton Community Coll	FELLA, Sarah C.	370
US Department of Interior	BROOKS, Harry F.	140

ALOHA
Washington County Cooperative Lib
Srvs

SELLE, Donna M.	1113

ASHLAND
Southern Oregon State Coll

BURKHOLDER, Sue A.	161
OTNES, Harold M.	930

ASTORIA

Astoria Sch District	KORPELA, Betty L.	672
Clatsop Community Coll	DUNN, Carolyn A.	326

BEAVERTON

A T and E Laboratories Inc	VIXIE, Anne C.	1286
Oregon Graduate Center	SLOAN, Maureen G.	1149
Ringgold Management Systems Inc	SHOFFNER, Ralph M.	1132
Servio Logic Corp	SUDDUTH, Susan F.	1206
Tektronix Inc	SOUCIE, Yan Y.	1169

BEND

Bend Research Inc	WEBER, Nola S.	1314
Central Oregon Community Coll	FISCHER, Karen	379
	HENDERSON, Carol G.	526
Deschutes County Lib	BYRNE, Helen E.	169

COOS BAY

Coos Bay Pub Lib	RASH, David W.	1009
Southwestern Oregon Community
Coll	TASHJIAN, Sharon A.	1224

CORVALLIS

CH2M Hill Inc	O'BRIEN, Mary C.	915
	SHANNON, Norma M.	1120
City of Corvallis	SALMON, Kay H.	1077
Good Samaritan Hospital	LIBERTINI, Arleen J.	725
Oregon State Univ	FILSON, Laurie	377
	GEORGE, Melvin R.	427
	KINCH, Michael P.	649
	LAWRENCE, Robert E.	705
	MANNARINO, Elizabeth R.	766
	OSHEROFF, Shiela K.	928
	PERRY, Joanne M.	960
	REEVES, Marjorie A.	1017
	ST. CLAIR, Gloriana S.	1075
	WILLIAMS, Janet L.	1344
US Environmental Protection Agency	MCCAULEY, Betty P.	795

EUGENE

Bailey Hill Sch	FEUERHELM, Jill A.	374
City of Eugene	HILDEBRAND, Carol I.	538
	MEEKS, James D.	821
Eugene Shool District 4J	THOMPSON, Paulette	1241
Lane Education Service District	MAXWELL, James G.	788
Max Robinson Institute	EMMENS, Thomas A.	348
Sacred Heart General Hospital	GRAHAM, Deborah L.	456
	TYLER, Kim E.	1266
Univ of Oregon	ALLEN, Alice J.	14
	BARNWELL, Jane L.	58
	BONAMICI, Andrew R.	113
	BYNON, George E.	168
	CARMIN, James H.	183
	CLAYTON, Mary E.	220
	CONNORS, Kathleen M.	238
	CRUMB, Lawrence L.	262
	CUMMINGS, Hilary A.	264
	D'ANDRAIA, Dana D.	272
	DUCKETT, Kenneth W.	322
	FARRIER, Kathy D.	365

OREGON (Cont'd)
EUGENE (Cont'd)
Univ of Oregon

FRANTZ, Paul A.	398
GRIFFIN, Karen D.	468
HADDERMAN, Margaret	482
HEINZKILL, J R.	522
HOTELLING, Katsuko T.	562
KLOS, Sheila M.	662
MORRISON, Perry D.	868
PYATT, Timothy D.	999
ROBERTSON, Howard W.	1042
SCHENCK, William Z.	1091
SHAW, Elizabeth L.	1123
SHIPMAN, George W.	1131
SHULER, John A.	1133
SMITH, Terry M.	1161
SOUTH, Ruth E.	1169
STARK, Peter L.	1181
STIRLING, Isabel A.	1195
SUNDT, Christine L.	1210
WALKER, Luise E.	1295
WAND, Patricia A.	1302
WANG, Hsiao G.	1303
WATSON, Mark R.	1310

FOREST GROVE

Forest Grove City Lib	FALZON, Judith A.	363
Pacific Univ	HUFFINE, Lucinda J.	571

GLIDE

Glide Sch District 12	COOK, Sybilla A.	240

HILLSBORO

Intel Corp	STARNES, Jane K.	1182
Tektronix Inc	THOMAS, Sandra L.	1238

HOOD RIVER

Hood River County Lib	KNUDSON, June	666

JACKSONVILLE

Jackson County Lib System	GORDON, Patricia H.	451

KLAMATH FALLS

Oregon Institute of Technology	CHASE, Judith H.	203
	PETERSON, Karen L.	964

LA GRANDE

City of La Grande	ELAM, Barbara J.	341

LAKE OSWEGO

Blackwell North America	SCHMIDT, Holly H.	1095

LINCOLN CITY

City of Lincoln	HERINGER, Patricia G.	531

MARYLHURST

Sisters of the Holy Names	GIMPL, Caroline A.	437

MCMINNVILLE

Linfield Coll	BENSON, Mary M.	83
	CHMELIR, Lynn K.	209
	ENGLE, Michael O.	349

MEDFORD

Jackson County Dept of Mgmt Info
Srvs	THELEN, Richard L.	1234
Jackson County Lib System	BILLETER, Anne M.	96
	PURCELL, V N.	998

MILTON-FREEWATER

City of Milton-Freewater	SARGENT, Phyllis M.	1083

MONMOUTH

Western Oregon State Coll	GORCHELS, Clarence C.	451
	JENSEN, Gary D.	598

NEWPORT

Lincoln County Sch District	KRABBE, Natalie	674

OAKRIDGE

Oakridge Sch District	MCCOY, Joanne	799

ONTARIO

Treasure Valley Community Coll	AMSBERRY, Dan F.	20

OREGON CITY

Willamette Falls Hospital	VONSEGEN, Ann M.	1288

PORTLAND

Bassist Coll	SCHIWEK, Joseph A.	1093
	THURSTON, Nancy W.	1243
Blackwell North America	MILLER, Daniel J.	836
Boise Cascade Corp	GAGNON, Vernon N.	412
Bonneville Power Admin	CONNORS, Jean M.	238
Catlin Gabel Sch	KENNEY, Ann J.	641
Church & Synagogue Lib Association	BURSON, Lorraine E.	163
City of Portland	VAN HORN, Neal F.	1275
Columbia Christian Coll	ELLSON, Linda R.	345

OREGON (Cont'd)
PORTLAND (Cont'd)
Fred Meyer Charitable Trust — FERGUSON, Douglas K. 372
Good Samaritan Hospital & Medical Center — BROWN, Patricia L. 146
Holladay Park Medical Center — OLSON-URLIE, Carolyn T. . . 923
Information Masters — LARSON, Signe E. 700
Lewis & Clark Coll — FLYNN, Lauri R. 387
GERITY, Louise P. 428
Lib Association of Portland — LARSON, Betty 699
MIKKELSEN, June L. 834
Mead Data Central — SIMON, Dale 1140
Multnomah County Lib — BARNETT, Jean D. 57
BURNS, Carol J. 162
JULAPHONGS, Martha M. . . 619
LONG, Sarah A. 740
RENFRO, Robert S. 1023
RHYNE, Barbara B. 1026
THENELL, Janice C. 1234
WRIGHT, Catherine A. 1370
Multnomah Law Lib — JURKINS, Jacquelyn J. 620
National Coll of Naturopathic Medicine — KIRCHFELD, Friedhelm 654
OCLC Online Computer Lib Center — BOES, Rachel M. 110
Oregon Health Sciences Univ — CABLE, Leslie G. 170
JOHNSON, Millard F. 607
JUDKINS, Dolores Z. 619
MORGAN, James E. 864
O'DONOVAN, Patricia A. . . . 917
TEICH, Steven 1230
Oregon Historical Society — WINROTH, Elizabeth C. 1355
Portland General Electric — SHAVER, Donna B. 1123
WEBER, Robert F. 1314
Portland Pub Schs — ANDERSON, C L. 21
JONES, Mary C. 614
PIERRE, Zenata W. 972
Portland State Univ — BRUSEAU, Laurence L. 151
GREEY, Kathleen M. 465
POWELL, Faye 988
SOOHOO, Terry A. 1167
TAMBLYN, Eldon W. 1221
WRIGHT, Janet K. 1371
Reed Coll — SAYRE, Samuel R. 1087
St Vincent Hospital & Medical Center — JACOBS, Patt 590
Schwabe Williamson Wyatt — DAVID, Kay O. 276
Stoel Rives Boley Fraser & Wyse — PIPER, Larry W. 975
Tri-Met — KAWABATA, Julie 632
US Court of Appeals — MCCURDY, Scott M. 801
Univ of Portland — BROWNE, Joseph P. 148
HORAN, Patricia F. 559
Western Evangelical Seminary — METZENBACHER, Gary W. . 828
Western Seminary — KRUPP, Robert A. 681
ROSEBURG
Douglas County Lib System — CLELAND, Mary V. 220
Roseburg Sch District 4 — GAULKE, Mary F. 423
Umpqua Community Coll — MUNGER, Freda R. 879
Veterans Administration Medical Center — JORDAN, Cathryn M. 616
SAINT HELENS
St Helens Sch District 502 — BARNETT, Donald E. 57
SALEM
Oregon Judicial Department — ANDRUS, Roger D. 27
Oregon State Lib — DOAK, Wesley A. 306
FORCIER, Peggy C. 389
GINNANE, Mary J. 437
MCHARG, Kathleen M. 808
MOBERG, F A. 851
WEBB, John 1313
Oregon Supreme Court — BAUER, Marilyn A. 65
Pacific Book Co — BUSHMAN, James L. 165
State of Oregon — TURNBAUGH, Roy C. 1264
SPRINGFIELD
Univ of Oregon — HALGREN, Joanne V. 486
THE DALLES
Dalles-Wasco County Pub Lib — DOOLEY, Sheila M. 312
TOLEDO
City of Toledo — JORGENSEN, Blythe M. 617
TUALATIN
City of Tualatin — HARDIE, Susan H. 500

OREGON (Cont'd)
WOODBURN
City of Woodburn — SPRAUER, Linda J. 1176

PENNSYLVANIA
ABINGTON
Abington Free Lib — GINSBURG, Mary L. 438
POSEL, Nancy R. 985
Abington Memorial Hospital — PASKOWSKY, Carol 946
Pennsylvania State Univ — BISSELL, Joann S. 100
DOLE, Wanda V. 309
ALCOA CENTER
ALCOA Laboratories — MOUNTS, Earl L. 873
Aluminum Co of America — SAPP, V J. 1082
ALLENTOWN
Air Products & Chemicals Inc — BURYLO, Michelle A. 164
SMITH, Robert B. 1160
TUCCI, Valerie K. 1261
The Allentown Hospital — IOBST, Barbara J. 583
Allentown Osteopathic Medical Center — SCHWARTZ, Linda M. 1104
Allentown Pub Lib — STEPHANOFF, Kathryn 1187
AT&T Bell Laboratories — WAGNER, Darla L. 1291
Cedar Crest and Muhlenberg Colls — BAHR, Alice H. 45
Dun & Bradstreet Information Resources — DONOHUE, Delaine R. 312
Information Connection — ANDEL, June 21
Lehigh County Historical Society — GRIFFITHS, June B. 469
Lehigh Valley Hospital Center — NIPPERT, Carolyn C. 904
The Morning Call — SWARTZ, Patrice B. 1214
Times Mirror — DONCEVIC, Lois A. 311
ALLISON PARK
Pickwick Publications — HADIDIAN, Dikran Y. 482
ALTOONA
Pennsylvania State Univ — RAJPAR, Shamin H. 1004
AMBLER
Wissahickon Sch District — LYTLE, Marguerite S. 753
PARSONS, Muriel W. 945
SACHS, Kathie B. 1073
Wissahickon Valley Pub Lib — MULLEN, Francis X. 877
AMBRIDGE
Trinity Episcopal School for Ministry — MUNDAY, Robert S. 878
ARCHBALD
Fairchild Weston Systems Inc — KOHL, Arlene F. 668
ARDMORE
Lower Merion Lib Assn — RYAN, Patricia M. 1071
Township of Lower Merion — PULLER, Maryam W. 997
ASTON
Neumann Coll — MUDRICK, Kristine E. 875
TOMAN, Jocelyn B. 1249
AVALON
Avalon Pub Lib — OSTRUM, Roxane M. 929
BADEN
Quigley High Sch — JABLONOWSKI, Mary D. . . . 586
BALA CYNWYD
Township of Lower Merion — KNAPP, Mabel J. 663
BEAVER
Beaver County Law Lib — DENGEL, Bette S. 292
Beaver County Times — DISANTE, Linda B. 305
Medical Center Inc — COGHLAN, Patricia M. 227
Michael Baker Jr Inc — WILLIAMS, Ruth J. 1346
BELLEFONTE
Central Pennsylvania District Lib — WOLFE, Gary D. 1360
BENSALEM
Bucks County Free Lib — BURSK, Mary A. 163
BENTON
Frank & Effa Laubach Memorial Lib — HESS, Marjorie A. 534
BERWYN
Library Management Services — MACBETH, Eileen M. 754
Lib Management Services Ltd — SCAMMAHORN, Lynne . . . 1087
BETHEL PARK
Bethel Park Pub Lib — MCGINNESS, Mary B. 806
BETHLEHEM
Bethlehem Pub Lib — BERK, Jack M. 87
THOMAS, Lynda H. 1237
Bethlehem Steel Corp — HENDLEY, David D. 527
Lehigh Univ — CADY, Susan A. 170
JARVIS, William E. 595
METZGER, Philip A. 829
Mid-Atlantic Preservation Service — JONES, C L. 611

PENNSYLVANIA (Cont'd)
BETHLEHEM (Cont'd)
Moravian Archives .... NELSON, Vernon H. 895
Moravian Coll ...... CRAWFORD, Gregory A. ... 256
BLOOMSBURG
Bloomsburg Univ of Pennsylvania ...... ENDRES, Maureen D. 348
FROMM, Roger W. 405
FROST, William J. 406
VANN, John D. 1276
Central Columbia Sch District ...... FROST, Rebecca H. 406
BLUE BELL
Certaintaid Corp ...... RAC-FEDORIJCZUK, Karola
C. 1001
Montgomery County Community Coll ...... MARTIN, Shelby A. 778
ROSENBERGER, Merry G. . 1056
TERRY, Terese M. 1232
BOYERTOWN
Boyertown Area Sch District ...... EMERICK, John L. 347
Cabot Corp ...... FU, Clare S. 407
BRACKENRIDGE
Allegheny Ludlum Steel ...... GALLAGHER, Eileen W. 414
BRADDOCK
Braddock General Hospital ...... SHAPIRO, Ruth T. 1121
BRISTOL
Rohm & Haas Co ...... WOOD, Barbara G. 1363
BRYN ATHYN
The Academy of the New Church ...... SULLIVAN, Jennifer B. 1207
BRYN MAWR
The American Coll ...... HILL, Judith L. 540
Bryn Mawr Coll ...... BILLS, Linda G. 96
LAZARUS, Karin 706
LEAHY, Mary S. 707
LUNDY, M W. 748
MARKSON, Eileen 771
PRINGLE, Anne N. 993
REED, Gertrude 1015
REGUEIRO, Judith E. 1017
SCHWIND, Penelope 1106
SILVERMAN, Scott H. 1138
TANIS, James R. 1222
Newsnet Inc ...... BUHSMER, John H. 156
ELSTON, Andrew S. 346
HUGHES, Marilyn A. 572
REIBSAMEN, Gary G. 1018
Telebase Systems Inc ...... HORWITZ, Seth 561
KOLLIN, Richard P. 669
NEUFELD, Lynne M. 897
BUTLER
Butler Area Pub Lib ...... POWERS, Beverly A. 989
CALIFORNIA
California Univ of Pennsylvania ...... BARREAU, Deborah K. 58
BECK, William L. 72
NOLF, Marsha L. 908
Caruso Associates Inc ...... CARUSO, Nicholas C. 190
CAMP HILL
Foresight Inc ...... ALBRECHT, Lois K. 10
Hospital Association of Pennsylvania ...... RICHARDSON, Alice W. ... 1029
CARLISLE
Dickinson Coll ...... JACOB, Scott J. 589
POE, Terrence C. 979
Dickinson Sch of Law ...... FOX, James R. 394
JONES, Debra A. 612
PARTIN, Gail A. 945
SWARTHOUT, Judy L. 1214
US Army Military History Institute ...... GILBERT, Nancy L. 434
WIWEL, Pamela S. 1359
CASTLE SHANNON
Community Lib of Castle Shannon ...... HENDERSON, John E. 526
CENTER VALLEY
Allentown Coll ...... MCCABE, James P. 793
WELLE, Jacob P. 1321
MSC Seminary Lib ...... CAMILLI, E M. 175
CHAMBERSBURG
Wilson Coll ...... SENECAL, Kristin S. 1115
CHESTER
Consortium for Health Info & Lib Srvs ...... VICK, Kathleen 1283
Internal Medicine Associates ...... GOLDMAN, Richard 446
Sacred Heart Medical Ctr ...... SOLLENBERGER, Wesley
L. 1166

PENNSYLVANIA (Cont'd)
CHESTER (Cont'd)
Widener Univ ...... CARTULARO, Teresa C. 190
DIXON, Rebecca D. 306
FIDISHUN, Dolores 375
O'NEILL, Philip M. 924
TABORSKY, Theresa 1219
CLARION
Clarion Univ of Pennsylvania ...... DECKER, Debra E. 285
DINGLE, Susan 304
EMERICK, Kenneth F. 347
HARTSOCK, Ralph M. 508
HEAD, John W. 518
HORN, Janice H. 559
HORN, Roger G. 559
MCCABE, Gerard B. 792
PERSON, Ruth J. 961
TOWNSEND, Silas H. 1253
CLINTONVILLE
Ski's Market Inc ...... CHERESNOWSKI, Linda M. . 206
COATESVILLE
Brandywine Hospital ...... KELLEY, John F. 636
Coatesville Area Pub Lib ...... NEWPORT, Dorothea D. 900
Veterans Administration Medical
Center ...... BURTON, Mary L. 164
COLUMBIA
Watch & Clock Collectors Museum ...... SUMMAR, Donald J. 1209
CONSHOHOCKEN
Quaker Chemical Corp ...... MORROW, Ellen B. 869
CORAOPOLIS
Robert Morris Coll ...... MILLER, Mary C. 840
SKOVIRA, Robert J. 1147
DALTON
Dalton Community Lib ...... THOMAS, Scott E. 1238
DARBY
Mercy Catholic Medical Center ...... CLINTON, Janet C. 222
DOWNINGTOWN
Downingtown Area Sch District ...... GREBEY, Betty H. 461
JAFFE, Lawrence J. 591
DOYLESTOWN
Bucks County Free Lib ...... GILMOUR, Marianne S. 437
STRAUSS, Richard F. 1201
WHITTAKER, Edward L. ... 1334
DU BOIS
Pennsylvania State Univ ...... EMMER, Barbara L. 348
EAST STROUDSBURG
East Stroudsburg Univ ...... FELLER, Judith M. 370
RIEBEL, Ellis F. 1033
SUMMERS, George V. 1209
EASTON
Easton Area Pub Lib ...... BAUER, Barbara B. 65
MOSES, Lynn M. 871
Lafayette Coll ...... NARBETH, Thomas G. 888
ELIZABETHTOWN
Elizabethtown Coll ...... BARD, Nelson P. 56
ERIE
Erie County Historical Society ...... ANDRICK, Annita A. 27
Erie County Lib System ...... GALLIVAN, Marion F. 414
WIRICK, Terry L. 1356
Gannon Univ ...... DAVIES, Grace A. 277
LAURITO, Gerard P. 703
Hammermill Paper Co ...... YAPLE, Deborah A. 1377
Hamot Medical Center ...... TAUBER, Jean A. 1225
Lord Corp ...... HOWARD, Dianne D. 564
Mercyhurst Coll ...... COOPER, Joanne S. 243
Metro Health Center ...... WELCH, Carol J. 1321
Millcreek Township Sch District ...... KOSTIS, Leigh W. 673
Veterans Administration Medical
Center ...... KAGER, Jeffrey F. 621
Villa Maria Coll ...... ONUFFER, Joachim 924
EXPORT
Bushy Run Research Center ...... ELY, Betty L. 347
EXTON
Chester County Lib & District Center ...... FISCHER, Anna M. 379
KEOGH, Judith L. 643
LINDBERG, Richard L. 728
SILVER, Diane L. 1138
Thomas Newcomen Memorial Lib &
Museum ...... ARNOLD, Nancy K. 34

PENNSYLVANIA (Cont'd)
FORT WASHINGTON
LRP Publications and Axon Group Co | LOCKETT, Cheryl L. 736
McNeil Consumer Products Co | BECKER, Linda C. 72
Tri Star Publishing | NICKEL, R S. 902
| STEPHENSON, Jon R. 1188

FRANKLIN
Franklin Regional Medical Center | GILLILAND, Lee P. 436
FRANKLIN CENTER
The Franklin Mint | CUTLER, Judith 268
| HOWLEY, Deborah H. 566
| PITCHON, Cindy A. 976

FREELAND
MMI Preparatory Sch | EVERHART, Nancy L. 358
GETTYSBURG
Gettysburg Coll | HEDRICK, David T. 520
GLEN ROCK
The Family Album ABAA | LIEBERMAN, Ronald 726
GLENSHAW
Shaler North Hills Lib | GRAHAM, Marilyn L. 456
| HAHN, Maureen 484
| YATES, Diane G. 1378

GLENSIDE
Cheltenham Township Pub Sch
  District | LIGGETT, Julie A. 726
GRANTHAM
Messiah Coll | POWELL, Virginia L. 989
GREAT VALLEY
Eastman Pharmaceuticals | MILES, Donald D. 834
GREENSBURG
Hempfield Area Sch District | SCHEEREN, William O. 1090
Seton Hill Coll | PAWLIK, Deborah A. 951
Sisters of Charity of Seton Hall | REILLY, Sara L. 1020
Univ of Pittsburgh | DUCK, Patricia M. 322
Westmoreland Hospital Association | PETRAK, Janet C. 965
GWYNEDD VALLEY
Gwynedd Mercy Coll | CRESCENT, Victoria L. 258
HALIFAX
Halifax Area Sch District | BLACKWAY, Madeline E. ... 102
HAMBURG
Hamburg Pub Lib | WINGLE, Rita M. 1355
HANOVER
Hanover Pub Lib | MCFERREN, Priscilla G. 805
HARLEYSVILLE
Philadelphia Flyers | LINN, Mott R. 731
HARRISBURG
Bureau of Archives & History | WHIPKEY, Harry E. 1329
Capital Area Health Foundation | CAPITANI, Cheryl A. 180
Commonwealth of Pennsylvania | DEIBLER, Barbara E. 288
| FOUST, Judith M. 393
| SMITH, Eugene J. 1155
Dauphin County Lib System | GIBLIN, Carol C. 431
| WEBSTER, Connie L. 1314
McNees Wallace & Nurick | ANDREWS, Evelyn F. 26
Pennsylvania Department of
  Education | BEDDOES, Thomas P. 73
| RICHVALSKY, Neil F. 1031
| SPRANKLE, Vicki S. 1176
| WOZNIAK, Grace I. 1369
Pennsylvania Histl & Museum
  Commission | STAYER, Jonathan R. 1183
| TALLMAN, Carol W. 1221
Pennsylvania Lib Association | BAUER, Margaret D. 65
Polyclinic Medical Center | SHULTZ, Suzanne M. 1133
Senate of Pennsylvania | DUSZAK, Thomas J. 329
State Lib of Pennsylvania | BROWN, Donald R. 143
| CAHILL, Colleen R. 171
| FELIX, Sally T. 370
| FUNK, Elizabeth A. 410
| HOFFMAN, David R. 547
| INGRAHAM, Alice L. 582
| MALLINGER, Stephen M. ... 763
| SONDEN, Mary L. 1167
| TENOR, Randell B. 1231

HATBORO
Legacy Books | BURNS, Richard K. 162
HATFIELD
Biblical Theological Seminary | PAKALA, Denise M. 935
| PAKALA, James C. 935
| RITTER, Ralph E. 1037

PENNSYLVANIA (Cont'd)
HAVERFORD
Catholic Lib Association | CORRIGAN, John T. 247
| CORRINGAN, John T. 247
| MORGAN, Dorothy H. 863
Free Lib of Philadelphia | MCGLINN, Frank C. 806
Harverford Coll | ROBERTSON, Robert B. ... 1042
Haverford Coll | FREEMAN, Michael S. 401
Haverford Sch | BROWN, David E. 143
| ROGERS, Linda S. 1049

HAVERTOWN
Haverford Township Free Lib | HOCKER, Justine L. 545
| HOFFMAN, Elizabeth P. ... 547
| LEE, Janis M. 710

HAZLETON
Pennsylvania State Univ | TYCE, Richard 1266
HERSHEY
Hershey Foods Corp | WOODRUFF, William M. 1366
Pennsylvania State Univ | LINGLE, Virginia A. 730
| MALCOM, Dorothy L. 763
| ULINCY, Loretta D. 1268
| WOOD, M S. 1364

HONESDALE
Highlights for Children | BROWN, Kent L. 145
HORSHAM
Rorer Group Inc | HESLIN, Catherine M. 534
HUNTINGDON
Huntingdon County Lib | TYNAN, Laurie F. 1267
Juniata Coll | WILSON, Martin P. 1352
Mutual Benificial Insurance Co | SWIGART, William E. 1216
INDIANA
Indiana Area Sch District | MILLER, Sheila K. 842
Indiana Univ of Pennsylvania | CHAMBERLIN, Richard R. ... 198
| ELLIKER, Calvin 343
| KROAH, Larry A. 679
| MICCO, Helen M. 831
| RAHKONEN, Carl J. 1003
| RAMBLER, Linda K. 1005
| SHIVELY, Daniel C. 1132
| ZORICH, Phillip J. 1390

JAMESTOWN
Jamestown Area Sch District | MCCONNELL, Robert D. 798
JEANNETTE
Jeannette Pub Lib | BALAS, Janet L. 50
JENKINTOWN
Gellman Research Associates | FINN, Dorothy K. 378
SPS Technologies Inc | WOODLOCK, Stephanie ... 1366
JOHNSONBURG
Johnsonburgh Pub Lib | NELSON, Wilburta B. 895
JOHNSTOWN
Bishop McCort High Sch | PORTA, Mary D. 984
Conemaugh Valley Memorial Hospital | WILSON, Fred L. 1351
Univ of Pittsburgh | BRICE, Heather W. 134
| KREITZBURG, Marilyn J. ... 677

KENNETT SQUARE
Longwood Gardens | TEETER, Enola J. 1229
KING OF PRUSSIA
Pennwalt | DONOVAN, Kathryn M. 312
Rittenhouse Book Distributors | PUALWAN, Emily 996
Smith Kline & French Laboratories | ANTOS, Brian F. 29
| PRITCHARD, Barbara 994
Upper Merion Township | HELICHER, Karl W. 524
KINGSTON
Bishop O'Reilly High Sch | FANUCCI, Mary M. 363
Luzerne Intermediate Unit 18 | FARRIS, Loretta 365
KUTZTOWN
Kutztown Area Sch District | EMERICK, Michael J. 347
Kutztown Univ | APOSTOLOS, Margaret M. ... 29
| GEARHART, Carol A. 424
| GOLDSTAUB, Curt S. 446
| SAFFORD, Herbert D. 1074
| SIMONE-HOHE, M J. 1141
| SPRANKLE, Anita T. 1176

LANCASTER
Armstrong World Industries Inc | FILLER, Mary A. 377
| JUDGE, Joseph M. 619
Franklin & Marshall Coll | BROWN, Charlotte B. 142
International Signal & Control Group | STEFANACCI, Michal A. ... 1185
Lancaster Bible Coll | ROBBINS, Stephen L. 1039
Lancaster County Law Lib | GERLOTT, Eleanor L. 429

PENNSYLVANIA (Cont'd)
LANCASTER (Cont'd)
Lancaster Mennonite Historical
  Society   ZEAGER, Lloyd 1387
Lancaster Newspapers Inc   BULLOCK, Jessie M. 156
Lancaster Theological Seminary   SALGAT, Anne M. 1076
Sch District of Lancaster   FRANCOS, Alexis 396
     WALKER, Sue A. 1296
Technomic Publishing Co Inc   DUNN, Richard L. 327
LANGHORNE
Philadelphia Coll of Bible   BLACK, Dorothy M. 101
LANSDALE
American Electronic Labs Inc   BLAUERT, Mary A. 105
Calvary Baptist Theological Seminary   KROLL, Anna L. 679
Lansdale Sch of Business   WEBER ROOCHVARG,
         Lynn E. 1314
North Pennsylvania School District   NOLAN, Joan 907
LATROBE
Saint Vincent Coll   BENYO, John C. 84
     HILL, Lawrence H. 540
     MACEY, John F. 755
LEBANON
Lebanon County Lib System   MOORE, Curtis P. 859
Veterans Administration   FALGER, David E. 362
LEESPORT
Berks County Pub Lib System   WAGGONER, Susan M. ... 1291
LEHIGH VALLEY
Inquiry Inc   WEBER, A C. 1313
LEWISBURG
Bucknell Univ   BOYTINCK, Paul 124
     DE KLERK, Ann M. 288
     JENKS, George M. 597
     JENKS, Zoya E. 597
     LEWIS, Karen E. 723
LIBRARY
South Park Township   SALVAYON, Connie 1078
LIGONIER
Ligonier Valley Lib   WHEELER, Martha M. 1329
LINCOLN UNIVERSITY
Lincoln Univ   OWENS, Irene E. 932
LOCK HAVEN
Lock Haven Univ of Pennsylvania   BRAVARD, Robert S. 130
     CARRIER, Esther J. 186
     PALMA, Nancy C. 935
LORETTO
St Francis Coll   BRUSH, Cassandra 151
     NEGHERBON, Vincent R. ... 892
MALVERN
American Inst for Property Liability   HOLSTON, Kim R. 554
Controlled Therapeutics Corp   MCSWAIN, Christy A. 818
Great Valley Sch District   BALDWIN, Janet M. 51
Shared Medical Systems   YOUNG, Dorothy E. 1381
MANSFIELD
Mansfield Univ   DOWLING, John 316
     NESBIT, Larry L. 896
     SEABORN, Frances L. 1109
MARCUS HOOK
Sun Co   MORPHET, Norman D. 865
MCKEESPORT
Carnegie Free Lib   HORVATH, Robert T. 561
McKeesport Hospital   ZUNDEL, Karen M. 1391
Pennsylvania State Univ   HERRON, Nancy L. 533
MEADVILLE
Allegheny Coll   BURTON, Cynthia R. 164
     STALLARD, Kathryn E. 1179
MEDIA
Delaware County Lib System   BELANGER, David L. 75
     COURTRIGHT, Harry R. 252
     DOW, Sally C. 315
     LARSON, Phyllis S. 699
Pennsylvania Institute of Technology   BURGESS, Rita N. 159
MERION
Merion Elem Sch   SILER, Marguerite S. 1138
MIDDLETOWN
Pennsylvania State Univ   SALINGER, Florence A. ... 1076
     STANLEY, Nancy M. 1180
     TOWNLEY, Charles T. 1253
     ZAGON, Eileen 1385
MILFORD
Delaware Valley Sch District   HOFMANN, Susan M. 548

PENNSYLVANIA (Cont'd)
MILLERSVILLE
Millersville Univ   GLASS, Catherine C. 440
     LOTLIKAR, Sarojini D. 742
     LYONS, Evelyn L. 753
     MERRIAM, Doris E. 826
     PEASE, Elaine K. 953
     SANDERS, Minda M. 1080
     TASSIA, Margaret R. 1224
     TRIBIT, Donald K. 1256
     ZUBATSKY, David S. 1390
MONACA
Beaver County Federated Lib System   BRUBAKER, Dale L. 149
MONESSEN
Monessen Pub Lib   FERYOK, Joseph A. 374
MONROEVILLE
US Steel   RICHARDSON, Joy A. 1029
USX Corp   BERGER, Lewis W. 85
     POLLIS, Angela P. 981
Westinghouse Electric Corp   NATHANSON, Esther M. 889
     REICHERT, Richard E. 1018
MONT ALTO
Pennsylvania State Univ   EZELL, Johanna V. 360
MORRISTOWN
Montgomery County Department of
  Pub Libs   PECK, Marian B. 953
MOUNT GRETNA
Philhaven Hospital   DOLL, Harriet A. 309
MT LEBANON
Advocate Computerization Services
  Inc   WEISFIELD, Cynthia F. 1319
Mt Lebanon Pub Lib   HURLEY, Doreen S. 577
MUNCY
Pennsylvania State Correctional Instn   HOSTRANDER, Craig D. 562
NEW CASTLE
Jameson Memorial Hospital   WHITMAN, Joan T. 1333
New Castle Pub Lib   GRAHAM, Anne M. 456
NEW CUMBERLAND
New Cumberland Pub Lib   DILLEN, Judith A. 303
NEW HOLLAND
Eastern Lancaster County Sch District   SCHREFFLER, Lynne W. ... 1099
New Holland Community lib   SNELGROVE, Pamela S. 1163
NEW HOPE
The Freedonia Gazette   WESOLOWSKI, Paul G. 1325
New Hope-Solebury Sch District   ACKLER, Susan 4
NEW KENSINGTON
Citizens General Hospital   TEOLIS, Marilyn G. 1231
People's Lib   STICHA, Denise S. 1193
NEW WILMINGTON
Westminster Coll   BOLGER, Dorita F. 112
     BRAUTIGAM, David K. 130
     SPINNEY, Molly P. 1175
NEWBURG
State Lib of Pennsylvania   BRYSON, Susan A. 152
NEWTOWN
Bucks County Community College   BRADLEY, John 126
Newtown Friends Sch   OGLETREE, Elizabeth H. 918
NEWTOWN SQUARE
ARCO Chemical Co   WHITEHURST, Dori A. 1333
NORRISTOWN
Law Lib of Montgomery County   ZANAN, Arthur S. 1386
Montgomery County Department of
  Pub Libs   CATHEY, Gail L. 195
     GRIFFITH, Dorothy A. 469
Montgomery Hospital   O'BRIEN, Alberta T. 914
Pennsylvania State Pub Welfare Dept   LIEM, Frieda 726
NORTH EAST
McCord Memorial Lib   TRIPP, Audrey J. 1257
NORTHAMPTON
Mary Immaculate Seminary   KOKOLUS, Cait C. 669
PALMERTON
Palmerton Lib Association   DEFASSIO, Sharon L. 287
PAOLI
Church Farm Sch   SHAW, Doris G. 1123
Paoli Lib   LANG, Anna M. 695
PENN WYNNE
Lower Merion Township Lib
  Association   SORET, Judith E. 1168
PERKASIE
Bucks County Free Lib   KALTWASSER, Patricia F. .. 623

PENNSYLVANIA (Cont'd)
PHILADELPHIA

Abstract/Info Retrieval	AUGUST, Sidney	39
Academy of Natural Scis of Philadelphia	BAKER, Sylva S.	49
	SPAWN, Carol M.	1172
	SCHANER, Marian E.	1090
Albert Einstein Medical Center		
American Law Institute	HOLUB, Joseph C.	555
	WALSH, Sharon T.	1300
American Philosophical Society	CARROLL-HORROCKS, Elizabeth	187
	LEVITT, Martin L.	721
American Society for Testing Materials	SHUPAK, Harris J.	1134
Antioch Univ	SAUNDERS, William B.	1085
Antiquarian Bookselling Firm	MCKITTRICK, Bruce W.	812
Arthur Andersen & Co	CARTELLI, Alessandra J.	188
	PLEFKA, Cathleen S.	978
Athenaeum of Philadelphia	LAVERTY, Bruce	703
	MOSS, Roger W.	872
Balch Institute for Ethnic Studies	ANDERSON, R J.	25
	SUTTON, David H.	1211
	VANDOREN, Sandra S.	1275
BioSciences Information Service	ELIAS, Arthur W.	342
	HODGE, Gail M.	546
	KIESEL, Bruce H.	647
	ZIPF, Elizabeth M.	1389
BIOSIS	FARREN, Ann L.	365
	FISHER, Douglas A.	380
	KELLY, Maureen C.	638
	KENNEDY, H E.	641
	SYEN, Sarah	1217
	TOWNSEND, Carolyn J.	1253
	VLEDUTS-STOKOLOV, Natalia	1286
	WALSH, James A.	1299
	WASERSTEIN, Gina S.	1307
	WEINER, Betty	1318
	YERGER, George A.	1379
Center for Forensic Economic Studies	DEWANE, Kathleen M.	298
Chestnut Hill Hospital	MOWERY, Susan G.	874
City of Philadelphia	ERTZ, Ginger E.	353
Clark Ladner Fortenbaugh & Young	HAAS, Carol C.	480
Clio Group Inc	GRAY, Priscilla M.	460
Cohen Shapiro Polisher Sheikman & Cohen	KREMER, Jill L.	677
	METZ, Betty A.	828
Coll of Physicians of Philadelphia	FULTON, June H.	409
	HORROCKS, Thomas A.	561
	NEUMANN, Pamela A.	897
	POSES, June A.	985
Community Coll of Philadelphia	BRADLEY, James S.	126
	DALE, Charles F.	270
	JOHNSON, Joan E.	606
	WEIS, Aimee L.	1319
Cooper Heller Research	COOPER, Linda	243
	HELLER, Patricia A.	524
Coopers & Lybrand	BOODIS, Maxine S.	115
Cozen & O'Connor	NANES, Evelyn M.	887
Curtis Institute of Music	EISENBERG, Peter L.	340
	MEYER, Kenton T.	830
	WALKER, Elizabeth	1295
DIALOG Information Services Inc	SNOW, Bonnie	1164
Dilworth Paxson Kalish & Kauffman	PARKER, Lettice M.	942
	WYATT, Patricia A.	1374
Drexel Univ	CHILDERS, Thomas A.	208
	DUVALLY, Charlotte F.	330
	GARRISON, Guy G.	420
	GARSON, Kenneth W.	420
	GRIFFITH, Belver C.	469
	LABORIE, Tim	686
	LYTLE, Richard H.	753
	MANCALL, Jacqueline C.	764
	MARVIN, Stephen G.	780
	PAUL, Thompson	949
	SNYDER, Richard L.	1165
	TANNER, Anne B.	1222
	TRUMPLER, Elisabeth	1259
	WELSH, Barbara W.	1323
Duane Morris & Heckscher	BERGER, Joellen	85

PENNSYLVANIA (Cont'd)
PHILADELPHIA (Cont'd)

Eastern Baptist Theological Seminary	GILBERT, Thomas F.	434
Eighteen East Consulting	CUTRONA, Cheryl	268
Federal Reserve Bank of Philadelphia	ALDRIDGE, Carol J.	11
	NAULTY, Deborah M.	889
First Judicial District of Pennsylvania	DIAZ, Nelson A.	299
Fox Chase Cancer Center	NISTA, Ann S.	905
Franford Hospital	ROSE, Dianne E.	1054
Free Lib of Philadelphia	AXAM, John A.	42
	BARR, Marilyn P.	58
	BAUMGARTNER, Barbara W.	66
	BLUM, Irma	107
	BOARDMAN, Richard C.	108
	BOND, Mary W.	113
	BRICKER, Will S.	135
	CARSON, Sheila M.	188
	CATTIE, Mary M.	195
	DIAZ, Magna M.	299
	DUCLOW, Geradline	322
	EVEY, Patricia G.	359
	FOY, Lorraine M.	395
	GENDRON, Michele M.	426
	GLOVER, Peggy D.	442
	GREEN, Rose B.	462
	HALE, Carolyn R.	485
	HANSEN, Paula J.	498
	HARKE, Toby H.	501
	HARRISON, Susan B.	507
	HELVERSON, Louis G.	525
	HINTON, Frances	543
	ICKES, Barbara J.	581
	JENGAJI-EL, Taifa	596
	KENT, Frederick J.	642
	KOREY, Marie E.	671
	LIGHTNER, Karen J.	727
	MAXWELL, Barbara A.	788
	MAYOVER, Steven J.	791
	MCCONKEY, Jill T.	797
	MCLAUGHLIN, Patricia A.	813
	MOODY, Marilyn D.	857
	MULLEN, Helen M.	877
	NEWCOMBE, Jack A.	898
	NIGHTINGALE, Daniel	904
	ORSBURN, Elizabeth C.	927
	POST, Jeremiah B.	986
	PROMOS, Marianne	995
	RAIVELY, Martha M.	1004
	REIFF, Harry B.	1019
	ROSENSTEEL, J R.	1057
	SHELKROT, Elliot L.	1126
	SNOWTEN, Renee Y.	1164
	SULLIVAN, Kathryn A.	1208
	TERRY, Joseph D.	1232
	VERHAAREN, John E.	1282
	WOOD, Linda L.	1364
	WRIGHT, Irene R.	1371
Friends Hospital	SOULTOUKIS, Donna Z.	1169
Friends Select Sch	PANCOE, Deborra S.	937
GE/RCA Astro Space Division	SOWICZ, Eugenia V.	1170
General Electric Co	RICH, Denise A.	1027
Glassboro State Coll	MEREDITH, Phyllis C.	825
Graduate Cardiology Consultants Inc	KREULEN, Thomas	678
The Graduate Hospital	FARNY, Diane M.	365
Gray Panthers Project Fund	HOPPER, Jean G.	558
Hahnemann Univ	BAKER, Judith M.	48
	DONOVAN, Judith G.	312
	FENICHEL, Carol H.	371
	HODGE, Margaret T.	546
Historical Society of Pennsylvania	PARKER, Peter J.	942
	SNYDER, Theresa	1165
Holy Family Coll	MCDONALD, Joseph A.	802
	MICIKAS, Lynda L.	832
Hospital of the Univ of Pennsylvania	CLEVELAND, Susan E.	221
Hoyle Morris & Kerr	SMITH, Linda D.	1157
Information Ventures Inc	KLEINSTEIN, Bruce H.	660

PENNSYLVANIA (Cont'd)
PHILADELPHIA (Cont'd)

Institute for Scientific Information
EDWARDS, David M. 337
FREEDMAN, Bernadette 400
FUSELER-MCDOWELL,
  Elizabeth A. 410
GARFIELD, Eugene 418
LEINBACH, Anne E. 714
MEYER, Daniel E. 830
ROSEN, Theresa H. 1055
SCHAEFFER, Judith E. 1089
SCHREIBER-COIA, Barbara
  J. 1099
VLADUTZ, George E. 1286
WALKER, Kate 1295
ZAJDEL, George J. 1385
Institute of Pennsylvania Hospital
STRICKLAND, F J. 1202
La Salle Univ
BAKY, John S. 50
Lankenau Hospital
KODER, Alma 667
Laventhol & Horwath
ABRAMS, Joan R. 3
ROSENBERGER, Constance
  G. 1056
SHELLENBERGER, Dawn
  M. 1126
Lib Co of Philadelphia
GREEN, James N. 462
VAN HORNE, John C. 1275
WOLF, Edwin 1360
Lutheran Theological Seminary at
  Phila
WARTLUFT, David J. 1307
Magee Rehabilitation Hospital
COUCH, Susan H. 250
Media & Methods Magazine
SOKOLOFF, Michele 1165
Medical Coll of Pennsylvania
CHAFF, Sandra L. 197
HORNIG-ROHAN, James E. . 560
KIRBY, Martha Z. 654
MILLER, Naomi 841
MONTOYA, Leopoldo 856
WIGGINS, Theresa S. 1337
Meritor Corporate Archives
KING, Eleanor M. 650
Mesirov Gelman Jaffe Cramer &
  Jamieson
PROCTOR, David J. 994
Microform Inc
RUOCCHIO, James P. 1068
Miriam I & William H Crawford Books
CRAWFORD, Miriam I. 257
Montgomery McCracken Walker &
  Rhoads
BROWN, Georgeanne H. . . . 144
Morgan Lewis & Bockius
BEARDWOOD, Louise B. . . . 69
ROACH, Linda 1038
Moss Rehabilitation Hospital
CASINI, Barbara P. 192
Natl Federation of Abstctng & Info
  Srvs
CORNOG, Martha 247
NFAIS
UNRUH, Betty 1269
Our Mother of Sorrows Elementary
  Sch
DALY, Sally A. 271
Packard Press Corp
SCULLIN, Frank E. 1109
PALINET
SCHOENUNG, James G. . . 1098
SILVERMAN, Karen S. 1138
Peat Marwick Mitchell
FISHMAN, Lee H. 381
Pennsylvania Academy of the Fine
  Arts
BUSHNELL, Marietta P. 165
LEIBOLD, Cheryl A. 713
Pennsylvania Coll of Optometry
KRIVDA, Marita J. 679
Pennsylvania Economy League
BRENNAN, Ellen 132
Pepper Hamilton & Scheetz
BEYER, Robyn L. 93
LEVY, Anne W. 721
Philadelphia Board of Education
MARNET, Carole M. 772
Philadelphia Coll of Pharmacy &
  Science
ADAMS, Mignon S. 5
BRIZUELA, B S. 138
HESP, Judith A. 534
RAINEY, Nancy B. 1004
SMINK, Marjorie M. 1152
ZOGOTT, Joyce 1390
Philadelphia Coll of Textiles &
  Science
PHALAN, Mary A. 967
Philadelphia Coll of the Arts
CALDWELL, John M. 172
HALL, Martha H. 488
Philadelphia Geriatric Center
POST, Joyce A. 986
Philadelphia Jewish Archives Center
GRACE, William M. 455
Philadelphia Museum of Art
ERDREICH, Gina B. 352
SEVY, Barbara S. 1117

PENNSYLVANIA (Cont'd)
PHILADELPHIA (Cont'd)

Philadelphia Orchestra
GROSSMAN, Robert M. 473
NIEWEG, Clinton F. 904
Philadelphia Rare Books &
  Manuscripts Co
MERZ, Lawrie H. 827
Phildelphia Print Shop Ltd
CRESSWELL, Donald H. . . . 258
Presbyterian Historical Society
HAAS, John O. 480
Presbyterian Univ of Pennsylvania
ROEDELL, Ray F. 1048
Rawle & Henderson
HARVAN, Christine C. 509
Reed Smith Shaw & McClay
MINES, Denise C. 846
Rohm & Haas Co
HOSTETTER, Sandra F. . . . 562
Rosenbach Museum & Lib
FULLER, Elizabeth E. 408
MORRIS, Leslie A. 867
Roxborough Memorial Hospital
BERNOFF, Barbara D. 89
Saint Basil Academy
ORZEL, Dolores 927
St Charles Borromeo Seminary
BOYLAN, Lorena A. 123
St Joseph's Univ
ANDRILLI, Ene M. 27
PENROSE, Anna M. 957
RATHBONE, Marjorie A. . . . 1009
REILLY, Rebecca S. 1020
THOMAS, Deborah A. 1236
Saul Ewing Remick & Saul
ABRISS, Judith W. 3
Schnader Harrison Segal & Lewis
GLOECKNER, Paul B. 441
Sch District of Philadelphia
BENDER, Evelyn 79
BUCK, Patricia K. 154
POLITIS, John V. 981
STEINBERG, Eileen 1185
USES, Ann K. 1270
Smith Kline & French Laboratories
SHALLEY, Doris P. 1119
Temple Univ
BOISCLAIR, Regina A. 111
BURSTEIN, Karen 164
CARINO, Leopoldo C. 181
DURIS, Richard M. 328
ELSHAMI, Ahmed M. 346
GRZESIAK, Margaret M. . . . 475
JACOBS, Mark D. 589
JACOBY, Beth E. 590
MCDONNELL, Janice M. . . . 803
MILLER, Fredric M. 837
MYERS, James N. 884
PATTELA, Rao R. 947
SWAN, Christine H. 1213
TUCKER, Cornelia A. 1261
WEINBERG, David M. 1317
WRIGHT, Barbara C. 1370
Theodore F Jenkins Memorial Law
  Lib
PIECHNICK, Katarzyna M. . . 971
SCHAEFER, John A. 1089
SPIVACK, Amy D. 1175
WEINGRAM, Ida 1318
Thomas Jefferson Univ
ARMISTEAD, Henry T. 32
DAVIS, Samuel A. 281
DEVLIN, Margaret K. 297
MIKITA, Elizabeth G. 834
RISSINGER, Michael 1036
TIMOUR, John A. 1246
WARNER, Elizabeth R. . . . 1305
United Engineers & Constructors Inc
KNUP, Marie S. 666
US Environmental Protection Agency
LEVIN, Pauline G. 720
MCCREARY, Diane M. 800
Univ of Pennsylvania
ADELMAN, Jean S. 6
AZZOLINA, David S. 43
BATISTA, Emily J. 64
BELL, Steven J. 77
BERWICK, Mary C. 91
BRYANT, Lillian D. 152
GAEBLER, Ralph F. 411
GREEN, Patricia L. 462
GRILIKHES, Sandra B. 470
HALLER, Douglas M. 489
HALPERIN, Michael 489
HOLMES, John H. 553
JACKSON, Mary E. 588
KEANE, John J. 633
MORENO, Rafael 863
MYERS, Charles J. 884
PAGELL, Ruth A. 934
RIDGEWAY, Patricia M. . . . 1032
ROHDY, Margaret A. 1050

PENNSYLVANIA (Cont'd)
PHILADELPHIA (Cont'd)
Univ of Pennsylvania

	RUGGERE, Christine A.	1066
	SLYHOFF, Merle J.	1151
	TARNAWSKY, Marta	1224
	TRAISTER, Daniel H.	1253
	VAUGHAN-STERLING, Judith A.	1280
	WICKEY, Colleen	1335
	YOLTON, Jean S.	1380
	YOUNG, James B.	1382
User Education ISI	TEMOS, Barbara	1230
VU/TEXT Information Services Inc	BOWDEN, Gail L.	120
	WHITMAN, Mary L.	1333
	WILLCOX, M C.	1341
	WILLMANN, Donna S.	1348
W B Saunders Co	MITCHEM, M T.	849
West Philadelphia Girls High Sch	COX, Carol A.	253
Westminster Theological Seminary	MUETHER, John R.	875
Wyeth Laboratories	CHU, John S.	212
Yardstick Associates	WALL, H D.	1297

PHOENIXVILLE

Valley Forge Christian Coll	REYNOLDS, Dorsey	1025

PITTSBURGH

Allegheny County Law Lib	MAST, Joanne	782
Aluminum Co of America	PETERSON, Barbara E.	962
	WHITAKER, Cynthia D.	1329
Archives & Museum Informatics	BEARMAN, David A.	69
Archives of Industrial Society	KURTIK, Frank J.	685
Baldwin Borough Pub Lib	HARKINS, Anna W.	501
Belle Vernon Area Sch District	PARADISE, Don M.	939
Berkman Ruslander Pohl Lieber & Engel	ORSAG, Ann	927
Buchanan Ingersoll P C	HORVATH, Patricia M.	561
Calgon Corp	KASPERKO, Jean M.	629
	SCHWARZ, Betty P.	1105
Carlow Coll	MITCHELL, Joan M.	849
Carnegie Lib of Pittsburgh	BLANCHFIELD, Georgette	103
	BROSKY, Catherine M.	141
	CRONEBERGER, Robert B.	260
	DILWORTH, Kirby D.	303
	FALGIONE, Joseph F.	362
	GREEN, Vera A.	462
	KAMPER, Albert F.	624
	KONOPKA, Amelia S.	670
	LEONARD, Peter C.	716
	MARON-WOOD, Kathy M.	772
	PEFFER, Margery E.	954
	POTTER, Donald C.	987
	REPP, Robert M.	1024
	SAUNDERS, Sharon K.	1084
	SCOTT, Lydia E.	1107
	SHAPERA, Gladys S.	1121
	STRAWBRIDGE, Donna L.	1201
	TACK, A C.	1219
	THOMPSON, Sandra K.	1241
Carnegie Mellon Univ	EVANS, Nancy H.	357
	FITZGERALD, Patricia A.	382
	FORD, Sylverna V.	390
	JOHNSEN, Mary C.	602
	LINKE, Erika C.	731
	MARCHETTI, Honey B.	768
	NAISMITH, Rachael	887
	PISCIOTTA, Henry A.	976
	RICHARDS, Barbara G.	1028
	STIEBER, Michael T.	1193
	THOMPSON, Dorothea M.	1239
	TINSLEY, Geraldine L.	1246
	WILES-HAFFNER, Meredith L.	1339
Children's Hospital of Pittsburgh	SCHEETZ, Mary D.	1091
Community Center & Lib Association	SCHNEIDER, Louise H.	1097
Community Coll of Allegheny County	KING, Mimi	652
Coopers & Lybrand	BLAIR, William W.	103
Duquesne Univ	KERCHOF, Kathryn K.	643
	PUGLIESE, Paul J.	997
	RISHEL, Joseph F.	1035
	ROBINSON, Agnes F.	1043
Eckert Seamans Cherin, & Mellott	BURKHARD, Polly S.	161

PENNSYLVANIA (Cont'd)
PITTSBURGH (Cont'd)

Eye & Ear Hospital of Pittsburgh	JOHNSTON, Bruce A.	610
Fox Chapel Area Sch District	MILLER, Marjorie M.	840
Genix Corp	PUPO, Raul	998
Graphic Arts Techical Foundation	LAMMERT, Diana P.	691
H J Heinz Co	WRIGHT, Nancy M.	1372
Information Research Analysts	SOUDER, Edith I.	1169
Kirkpatrick & Lockhart	VARGAS, Gwen S.	1278
Lauri Ann West Memorial Lib	RAO, Rama K.	1008
Mead Data Central	IVAK, Patricia A.	585
Mellon Bank	GREEN, Joyce M.	462
Mine Safety Appliances Co	BOUTWELL, Barbara J.	119
Mobay Chemical Corp	ALSTADT, Nancy A.	18
Montefiore Hospital	ROSEN, Gloria K.	1055
North Hills Passavant Hospital	TREVANION, Margaret U.	1255
Northland Pub Lib	SMITH, Mary M.	1158
NUS Corp	STERLING, Alida B.	1189
Penn Hills Sch District	MURPHY, Diana G.	880
Pennsylvania Economy League	EVES, Judith A.	359
Pitt-Des Moines Inc	FRANZ, N L.	398
Pittsburgh Post-Gazette	KANE, Angelika R.	624
Pittsburgh Pub Schs	MIZIK, Judy G.	850
	PASHEL, Susan M.	945
Pittsburgh Regional Lib Center	ANDERSON, Elizabeth M.	22
	BROADBENT, H E.	138
PPG Industries	FIDOTEN, Robert E.	375
Presbyterian Univ Hospital	HESZ, Bianka M.	534
Psychological Service of Pittsburgh	FULMER, Dina J.	409
Record-Rama Sound Archives	MAWHINNEY, Paul C.	787
Reed Smith Shaw & McClay	STEWART, Barbara R.	1192
Reformed Presbyterian Theological Sem	GEORGE, Rachel	428
Robert Morris Coll	PIETZAK, Stephen D.	972
St Bede Sch	TOWNSEND, Rita M.	1253
St Clair Hospital	HO, Carol T.	545
St Francis Health System	MCCULLOCH, Elizabeth A.	801
St Margaret Memorial Hospital	ARJONA, Sandra K.	31
Shadyside Hospital	FETKOVICH, Malinda M.	374
Sisters of Mercy of Pittsburgh	CASLIN, Adele	193
Software Engineering Institute	FUCHS, Karola M.	408
South Hills Health System	KISH, Veronica R.	656
Univ of Pittsburgh	AL SADAT, Amira A.	17
	BANDEMER, June E.	54
	BEARMAN, Toni C.	69
	CARTER, Ruth D.	190
	COHEN, Laurie J.	228
	DAILY, Jay E.	270
	DEBONS, Anthony	285
	DETLEFSEN, Ellen G.	296
	DIMMICK, Mary L.	304
	ENGLERT, Mary A.	350
	FREEDMAN, Phyllis D.	400
	GLABICKI, Paul	439
	GREENE, Nancy S.	464
	HALLOCK, Nancy L.	489
	JOSEY, E J.	618
	KENT, Allen	642
	KIMMEL, Margaret M.	649
	KIRCHER, Linda M.	654
	KRZYS, Richard A.	681
	LEIBOWITZ, Faye R.	713
	LOCKE, Jill L.	736
	LYNESS, Ann L.	752
	METZLER, Douglas P.	829
	MICHALAK, Jo A.	832
	MILLER, Mary E.	840
	MITTEN, Lisa A.	850
	NASRI, William Z.	888
	PAUL, Suzanne	949
	PIPER, Paula	975
	ROOT, Deane L.	1054
	ROSS, Nina M.	1058
	SAUNDERS, Allene W.	1084
	SILVERMAN, Marc B.	1138
	STEPHENS, Norris L.	1188
	SUOZZI, Patricia	1210
	WEBRECK, Susan J.	1314
	WESSEL, Charles B.	1325
	WHITMORE, Marilyn P.	1333

PENNSYLVANIA (Cont'd)
PITTSBURGH (Cont'd)
Univ of Pittsburgh

WILLIAMS, James G. 1344
WOO, Lisa C. 1363
WOODSWORTH, Anne 1367
WOOLLS, Esther B. 1368
WRAY, Wendell L. 1370
ZABROSKY, Frank A. 1385
USX Corp — CANTRALL, Rebecca J. 179
Vincentian Sisters of Charity — HLUHANY, Patricia 544
Western Pennsylvania Sch for the
Deaf — SCHAEFER, Mary A. 1089
Western Psychiatric Institute & Clinic — EPSTEIN, Barbara A. 351
Westinghouse Electric Corp — HODGSON, Cynthia A. 546
KLEIN, Joanne S. 659
MARLOW, Kathryn E. 772
SPIEGELMAN, Barbara M. . 1174
VASILAKIS, Mary 1279
Wilkinsburg Pub Lib — THOMPSON, Marian A. 1240
PLYMOUTH MEETING
Emergency Care Research Institute — KATUCKI, June P. 630
POTTSTOWN
Pottstown Memorial Medical Center — CHAPIS, Marilyn D. 201
POTTSVILLE
Diocese of Allentown — MORIARTY, Kathleen T. 865
Pottsville Free Pub Lib — SAXMAN, Susan E. 1086
TOWLE, Jean A. 1252
Pottsville Hospital & Warne Clinic — LEINHEISER, Diane R. 714
PRIMOS
Delaware County Daily Times — CHANCE, Peggy J. 199
RADNOR
Chilton Co — SWEELY, Christine A. 1214
Country Dance & Song Society of
America — KELLER, Kate V. 635
Wyeth Laboratories — TAYLOR, Larry D. 1227
READING
Albright Coll — DEEGAN, Rosemary L. 286
HANNAFORD, William E. .. 496
STILLMAN, Mary E. 1194
Alvernia Coll — JONES, M C. 614
Crompton & Knowles Corp — HANF, Elizabeth P. 495
Pennsylvania State Univ — MORGANTI, Deena J. 864
SMALL, Sally S. 1151
Reading Pub Lib — COURTNEY, June M. 251
WEIHERER, Patricia D. 1317
YU, Lorraine L. 1384
Saint Joseph Hospital — IZZO, Kathleen A. 586
MOREY, Carol M. 863
RIMERSBURG
Eccles-Lesher Memorial Lib — SCHILL, Julie G. 1092
ROSEMONT
Rosemont Coll — LYNCH, Mary D. 752
ST DAVIDS
BRS Information Technologies — NORRIS, Carole 909
SWOPE, Paula J. 1217
Eastern Coll — SAUER, James L. 1084
SAYRE
Guthrie Clinic Ltd — ANTES, E J. 28
SCHNECKSVILLE
Carbon Lehigh Intermediate Unit 21 — GOODMAN, John E. 449
Leigh County Community Coll — VOROS, David S. 1289
SCHUYLKILL HAVEN
Pennsylvania State Univ — LODER, Michael W. 736
SCRANTON
Commonwealth of Pennsylvania — FADDEN, Donald M. 360
Community Medical Center — MCNABB, Corrine R. 815
Lackawanna Bar Association — PAPARELLI, Marita E. 939
Lackawanna County Lib System — REES, G M. 1016
Lackawanna Junior Coll — CAMPION, Carol M. 177
Marywood Coll — FEDRICK, Mary A. 368
MILLER, Mary E. 840
SPEIRS, Gilmary 1172
Mercy Hospital — BRANDRETH, Elizabeth A. . 128
Moses Taylor Hospital — BABISH, Jo A. 43
Univ of Scranton — APPELBAUM, Judith P. 29
SELLERSVILLE
Grand View Hospital — BEACH, Linda M. 68
SHAMOKIN
Shamokin & Coal Township Pub Lib — LOWE, Mary E. 744

PENNSYLVANIA (Cont'd)
SHIPPENSBURG
Shippensburg Univ — CROWE, Virginia M. 261
CULBERTSON, Judith D. .. 263
HANSON, Eugene R. 498
SHONTZ, Marilyn L. 1132
SLIPPERY ROCK
Slippery Rock Univ — BACK, Andrew W. 43
JOSEPH, Elizabeth T. 617
JOSEPH, Patricia A. 617
SOMERSET
Somerset State Hospital — KLINE, Eve P. 661
PLASO, Kathy A. 977
SOUTHEASTERN
Unisys Corp — HAHN, Susan H. 484
SPRING HOUSE
McNeil Pharmaceutical — STANLEY, Kerry G. 1180
WICKS, Pamela J. 1335
Rohm & Haas Co — DOTTERRER, Ellen C. 313
OWENS, Frederick H. 932
STRONG, Darrell G. 1203
SPRINGFIELD
Metropolitan Hospital — STESIS, Karen R. 1189
Springfield Township Lib — NAISMITH, Patricia A. 887
Triadvocates Associated — KLETZIEN, S D. 661
STATE COLLEGE
Assn for Lib & Info Science Education — PHILLIPS, Janet C. 968
Lock Haven Univ of Pennsylvania — CHANG, Shirley L. 201
Pennsylvania State Univ — MURPHY, Charles G. 880
SWINTON, Cordelia W. 1216
Schlow Memorial Lib — LINDSAY, Ann M. 729
State College Area Sch District — WOLFE, Mary S. 1361
STROUDSBURG
Monroe County Pub Lib — KEISER, Barbara J. 635
SWARTHMORE
Swarthmore Academy — JONES, Annabel B. 611
Swarthmore Coll — FULLER, Edward H. 408
HUBER, George K. 569
LEHMANN, Stephen R. 713
WILLIAMSON, Susan G. 1348
Swarthmore Pub Lib — LICHTENBERG, Elsa R. 725
SWEDELAND
Smith Kline & French Laboratories — YOUNG, K P. 1382
TAMAQUA
Tamaqua Area Sch District — TUZINSKI, Jean H. 1266
TARENTUM
Valley News Dispatch — LANG, Audrey H. 695
THORNTON
Cassar Technical Services — WIDLUND, Harriet L. 1336
TOWANDA
Towanda Area Sch District — BURLINGAME, Connie 161
TREVOSE
Eastern State Sch & Hospital — SORG, Elizabeth A. 1168
TREXLERTOWN
Air Products & Chemicals Inc — DRAGOTTA, Linda L. 318
UNIVERSITY PARK
Pennsylvania State Univ — ATTIG, John C. 38
BONTA, Bruce D. 114
BURKHARDT, Marlene 161
CARR, Caryn J. 185
CARSON, M S. 188
CHAMBERLAIN, Carol E. ... 197
CLINE, Nancy M. 222
CONKLING, Thomas W. 236
FERRAINOLO, John J. 373
FERRIN, Eric G. 373
FISHER, Kim N. 381
FORTH, Stuart 391
FREIVALDS, Dace I. 402
GARNER, Diane L. 419
GERHART, Catherine A. 428
GRUBER, Linda R. 474
HENSHAW, Rod 529
JAMISON, Carolyn C. 593
JEAN, Lorraine A. 596
KAISER, John R. 622
KALIN, Sarah G. 623
KELLERMAN, Lydia S. 636
LARSON, Mary E. 699
MANN, Charles W. 766

PENNSYLVANIA (Cont'd)
UNIVERSITY PARK (Cont'd)
Pennsylvania State Univ

MARTIN, Noelene P. 777
MCCOMB, Ralph W. 797
MCKOWN, Cornelius J. 812
NADESKI, Karen L. 886
NEAL, James G. 890
OGBURN, Joyce L. 918
PASTER, Amy L. 946
PIERCE, Miriam D. 971
PIERCE, William S. 972
RAWLINS, Gordon W. 1010
RICE, Patricia O. 1027
ROE, Eunice M. 1048
SAMET, Janet S. 1078
SEEDS, Robert S. 1111
SEPP, Frederick C. 1115
SMITH, Barbara J. 1153
SMITH, Diane H. 1154
SMITH, Elizabeth J. 1154
STOUT, Leon J. 1198
STRIEDIECK, Suzanne S. . . 1202
SULZER, John H. 1209
SWEENEY, Del 1215
WESTERMAN, Melvin E. . . . 1327
WHITTINGTON, Christine A. 1334
ZABEL, Diane M. 1385

UPLAND
DIANE Publishing Co   BARON, Herman 58
UPPER DARBY
Metropolitan Data Services Group Inc BOWERS, Paul A. 120
Upper Darby Township & Seller
    Memrl Lib   JUSHCHYSHYN, Caroline
                                       B. 620

UPPER SAINT CLAIR
Baldwin-Whitehall Sch District   JENKINS, Georgann K. 597
UWCHLAND
Downingtown Area Sch District   AMICONE, Janice L. 20
VALLEY FORGE
E F Houghton & Co   SCHWEITZER, Margaret C. . 1105
VILLANOVA
Villanova Univ   ARMSTRONG, Nancy A. 32
                                    BARTZ, Alice P. 62
                                    BENGALI, Zarin P. 80
                                    CRIBBEN, Mary M. 258
                                    DREHER, Janet H. 319
                                    ERDT, Terrence 352
                                    GALLAGHER, Dennis J. 414
                                    GRIFFIN, Mary A. 468
                                    PENNELL, Charles 957
                                    QUINTILIANO, Barbara 1000
                                    WALSH, Carolyn C. 1299
WALNUTPORT
Northampton Area Sch District   PAGOTTO, Sarah L. 934
WARMINSTER
Centennial Sch District   FRENCH, Janet D. 402
Warminster General Hospital   GRAHAM, Betty R. 456
WARRENDALE
Society of Automotive Engineers   HAUGH, Amy J. 512
WAYNE
Comquest Inc   DRIEHAUS, Rosemary H. . . . 320
County of Chester   HOFFACKER, Antoinette C. . . 547
Data-Star   CRAUMER, Patricia A. 255
Tredyffrin Pub Lib   STEVENS, Marian A. 1190
WAYNESBURG
Greene County Lib System   TURNER, Sue E. 1265
WELLSBORO
Soldiers and Sailors Memorial
    Hospital   PATTERSON, Charlean P. . . 948
WERNERSVILLE
Reading Alloys Inc   SCHLOTT, Florenceann 1094
WESCOSVILLE
Blue Valley Information   FISLER, Charlotte D. 382
WEST CHESTER
Cassar Technical Services   CASSAR, Ann 193
Chester County Hospital   HARRINGTON, Anne W. 503
QVC Network   RUTKOWSKI, Hollace A. . . . 1070
Roy F Weston Inc   DINNIMAN, Margo P. 305
Sartomer Co   GILLEN, Bonnie J. 435

PENNSYLVANIA (Cont'd)
WEST CHESTER (Cont'd)
West Chester Univ   BURNS-DUFFY, Mary A. 163
                                    HELMS, Frank Q. 525
                                    MCCAWLEY, Christina W. . . 795
                                    TRUESDELL, Eugenia R. . . . 1259

WEST PITTSBURGH
Mobay Chemical Corp   SCHLUETER, Betsy W. 1094
WEST POINT
Merck Sharp & Dohme   MAXIN, Jacqueline A. 787
                                    MESSICK, Karen J. 828

WILKES-BARRE
King's Coll   MECH, Terrence F. 820
                                    TOMASOVIC, Evelyn 1249
Mercy Hospital   NANSTIEL, Barbara L. 887
Osterhout Free Lib   VAN DE CASTLE, Raymond
                                        M. 1273
Wilkes-Barre General Hospital   TAYLOR, Rosemarie K. 1228
Wilkes Coll   ERDICK, Joseph W. 352
                                    PAUSTIAN, P R. 950

WILLIAMSPORT
Bell of Pennsylvania   VEDDER, Harvey B. 1280
Brodart Co   FOGAL, Annabel E. 387
                                    SHEAFFER, Marc L. 1124
Williamsport Area Community Coll   HICKEY, Kate D. 536
YARDLEY
Grey Nuns of the Sacred Heart   FOGARTY, Catherine B. . . . 387
YORK
Buchart-Horn Inc   HARTLEY, Gloria R. 508
Martin Memorial Lib   FUNK, Ann L. 409
Memorial Hospital of York   HOMICK, Elaine 555
York Coll of Pennsylvania   CAMPBELL, Susan M. 177
York Hospital   EVITTS, Beth A. 359
YOUNGWOOD
Westmoreland County Community
    Coll   SCHEEREN, Judith A. 1090
                                    SHEFFO, Belinda M. 1125

PUERTO RICO
BAYAMON
Universidad Central de Bayamon   MOMBILLE, Pedro 854
CAPARRA HEIGHTS
Colegio Puertorriqueno de Ninas   FERNANDEZ, Josefina L. . . . 373
CAROLINA
Univ of Puerto Rico   MCCARTHY, Carmen H. 794
MAYAGUEZ
Antillian Coll   PEREZ, Sarai 958
Univ of Puerto Rico   GONZALEZ-VELEZ, Isaura . . 448
                                    MARTINEZ-NAZARIO,
                                        Ronaldo 779
                                    VALENTIN-MARTY,
                                        Jeannette 1271
MIRAMAR
Academia Perpetuo Socorro   DE DEL VALLE, Heida C. . . . 286
PONCE
Catholic Univ of Puerto Rico   DELGADO-NUNEZ, Milton . . . 289
                                    GUILLEMARD DE COLON,
                                        Teresita 476
                                    MEJILL-VEGA, Gregorio 822
                                    PADUA, Flores N. 934
                                    RODRIGUEZ, Vidalina 1048
                                    SANTIAGO, Maria 1082
RAMEY
Univ of Puerto Rico   CONCEPCION, Luis 235
                                    JARAMILLO, Juana S. 594
RIO PIEDRAS
Puerto Rico Legal Services   CASTRO, Maritza 194
Univ of Puerto Rico   CASAS DE FAUNCE, Maria . 191
                                    FIGUEROA, Almaluces 376
                                    MUNOZ-SOLA, Haydee 879
                                    RIVERA-ALVAREZ, Miguel
                                        A. 1037
                                    RODRIGUEZ, Ketty 1048
                                    THOMPSON, Annie F. 1239
Univ of Puetro Rico   MILLS, Rolland W. 844
SAN GERMAN
San Jose Coll   ALSTON, Jane C. 18

PUERTO RICO (Cont'd)

SAN JUAN
Commonwealth High Sch — HAMEL, Eleanor C. 491
General Archives of Puerto Rico — NIEVES, Miguel A. 904
Legislative Assembly of Puerto Rico — TORRES-TAPI, Manual A. ... 1251
Office of Legislative Services — NEGRON-GAZTAMBIDE,
      Olguita 892
Puerto Rico Attorney General — NADAL, Antonio 885
Univ of Puerto Rico — AYALA-ORTIZ, Orietta 42
    BERNAL-ROSA, Emilia ... 88
    BULERIN-LUGO, Josefina ... 156
    COLLAZO, Maria L. 232
    GARCIA-RUIZ, Maritza L. ... 417
    LOPEZ, Elsa M. 741
    MAURA-SARDO, Mariano
      A. 787

SANTURCE
Hidalgo Lib — HIDALGO, Nilda R. 537
Inter American Univ of Puerto Rico — SABATER-SOLA, Rigel 1072
Sacred Heart Univ — BARRERAS, Dolly M. 59

RHODE ISLAND

BARRINGTON
Barrington Pub Lib — BURKE, Lauri K. 160
BRISTOL
Bristol High Sch — ALDRICH, Linda S. 11
Roger Williams Coll — TRINKAUS, Tanya 1256
CAROLINA
Clark Memorial Lib — HULL, Catherine C. 572
CHEPACHET
Glocester Manton Free Pub Lib — LOXLEY, Donna J. 745
CUMBERLAND
Cumberland Pub Lib — LEVESQUE, Janet A. 719
Sisters of Mercy — LITTLE, Eleanor 733
EAST PROVIDENCE
City of East Providence — CAIRNS, Roberta A. 171
East Providence School Dist — LUBER, Arlene R. 745
JAMESTOWN
Jamestown Philomenian Lib — BELL, Judith H. 77
JOHNSTON
Johnston Sch Department — SHANLEY, Elaine 1120
KINGSTON
Univ of Rhode Island — CAMERON, Lucille W. 175
    DEVIN, Robin B. 297
    ETCHINGHAM, John B. 355
    FUTAS, Elizabeth 411
    GIEBLER, Albert C. 432
    GIOVENALE, Sharon 438
    KEEFE, Margaret J. 634
    KELLAND, John L. 635
    KRAUSSE, Sylvia C. 676
    MASLYN, David C. 780
    SCHNEIDER, Stewart P. ... 1097
    SIEBURTH, Janice F. 1135
    SIITONEN, Leena M. 1137
    TRYON, Jonathan S. 1259
    TYRON, Jonathan 1267
    VOCINO, Michael C. 1286
    YOUNG, Arthur P. 1381
NARRAGANSETT
Univ of Rhode Island — BARNETT, Judith B. 57
NAVAL EDUC TRNG CTR
Naval Education & Training Center — AYLWARD, James F. 42
NEWPORT
Naval War Coll — CHERPAK, Evelyn M. 206
Newport Pub Lib — WATERS, Shirley V. 1309
Syscon Corp — COHEN, Barbara S. 228
US Naval War Coll — HALL, Ann H. 487
    OTTAVIANO, Doris B. 930
NORTH PROVIDENCE
North Providence Union Free Lib — BIERDEN, Margaret W. 95
PAWTUCKET
Hillside Associates — MILLS, Catherine H. 843
PORTSMOUTH
Rauthem Co — BALDWIN, Mark F. 52
Transcom Electronics — HAMPTON, Sylvia S. 494

RHODE ISLAND (Cont'd)

PROVIDENCE
Adler Pollock & Sheehan — DUMAINE, Paul R. 325
American Mathematical Society — KUSMA, Taissa T. 685
Brown Univ — ADAMS, Thomas R. 6
    BELL, Carole R. 76
    BOWLBY, Raynna M. 121
    BUZZELL, Bonnie G. 168
    CASHMAN, Norine D. 192
    COULOMBE, Dominique C. ... 250
    DESJARLAIS-LUETH,
      Christine 295
    FARK, Ronald K. 364
    GALKOWSKI, Patricia E. 413
    HELLER, Betty D. 524
    KELLERMAN, Frank R. 636
    LANDIS, Dennis C. 693
    LYNDEN, Frederick C. 752
    MARSH, Corrie V. 773
    MONTEIRO, George 856
    RAINWATER, Jean M. 1004
    STONE, Howard P. 1197
    TAYLOR, Merrily E. 1227
    WILMETH, Don B. 1349
    WALTON, Linda J. 1301
Butler Hospital — ALEXANDER, Jacqueline P. .. 12
Edwards & Angell — CHENICK, Michael J. 206
Hinckley Allen Tobin & Silverstein — LABEDZ, Elizabeth K. 686
Moses Brown Sch — ODEAN, Kathleen F. 916
The Providence Athenaeum — DUPLAIX, Sally T. 327
Providence Ctr, Counseling &
  Psychiatric — VIGORITO, Patricia M. 1284
Providence Coll — DESMARAIS, Norman P. 295
    DOHERTY, Joseph H. 309
Providence Journal Co — HENDERSON, Linda L. 526
    MEHR, Joseph O. 821
Providence Pub Lib — BUNDY, Annalee M. 157
    COOPER, Jacquelyn B. 243
    JOHNSEN-HARRIS, Amy ... 602
    MCKEE, Virginia W. 810
    WADDINGTON, Susan R. ... 1290
Providence Pub Schs — MICHAEL, Richard T. 831
Rhode Island & Providence
  Plantations — WAGNER, Albin 1291
Rhode Island Coll — BRENNAN, Patricia B. 133
    HRYCIW-WING, Carol A. ... 566
    OLSEN, Richard A. 921
    SIBULKIN, Lucille 1135
Rhode Island Department of State Lib
  Srv — DANIELS, Bruce E. 273
    SHEA, Margaret 1124
    WILSON, Barbara L. 1350
Rhode Island Historical Society — LAMAR, Christine L. 689
Rhode Island Hospital — LATHROP, Irene M. 701
Rhode Island Sch of Design — AVERILL, Laurie J. 41
    BRAUNSTEIN, Mark M. 130
    TERRY, Carol S. 1232
Rhode Island State Archives — SILVA, Phyllis C. 1138
Rhode Island State Lib — PERRY, Beth I. 960
Rhode Island Supreme Court — SVENGALIS, Kendall F. ... 1212
State of Rhode Island — QUINN, Karen H. 1000
    ZIPKOWITZ, Fay 1389
Univ of Rhode Island — SHERIDAN, Jean 1127
Veterans Administration Medical
  Center — LLOYD, Lynn A. 735
RIVERSIDE
Emma Pendleton Bradley Hospital — WALLER, Carolyn A. 1298
SMITHFIELD
Bryant Coll — CAMERON, Constance B. ... 174
WARREN
Sisters of St Dorothy — SANTILLO, Mary E. 1082
WARWICK
Kent County Memorial Hospital — ASPRI, Jo A. 37
Warnick Pub Lib — PEARCE, Douglas A. 952
Warwick Pub Lib — LISTOVITCH, Denise A. ... 733
Warwick Sch Department — BRYAN, Susan M. 152
WEST WARWICK
West Warwick Pub Lib System — LAMOUREUX, Jacquelyn W. . 691
WESTERLY
Westerly Pub Lib — LIGHT, Karen M. 726

RHODE ISLAND (Cont'd)
WOONSOCKET
Woonsocket Education Department IMONDI, Lenore R. 582
LEVEILLEE, Louis R. 719
Woonsocket Harris Pub Lib MCDONOUGH, Douglas M. ... 803
Woonsocket Hospital GILDEA, Ruthann 434

SOUTH CAROLINA
AIKEN
ABBE Regional Lib System BOWLING, Carol L. 121
E I DuPont Co SUTHERLAND, Carl T. 1211
Univ of South Carolina CUBBEDGE, Frankie H. 262
ALLENDALE
Allendale-Hampton-Jasper Regional
Lib DRYDEN, Donald W. 321
Univ of South Carolina DRYDEN, Sherre H. 321
ANDERSON
Patrick B Harris Psychiatric Hospital REIMER, Mary S. 1021
BEAUFORT
US Department of Defense ELLIS, Janet L. 344
CAMDEN
Kershaw County Lib ALBRIGHT, Penny E. 10
OLSON, Joann M. 922

CENTRAL
Central Wesleyan Coll SABINE, Davida M. 1072
CHARLESTON
Archdiocese of Boston PARKER, Mary A. 942
Charleston County Lib RAINES, Thomas A. 1004
SINDEL, Amy C. 1143
TROWELL, Amy U. 1258
Charleston County Records Center HOLLINGS, Marie F. 552
Charleston County Sch District BRADLEY, Patricia L. 126
MITCHUM, Grace M. 850
Charleston Lib Society SADLER, Catherine E. 1073
The Citadel MAYNARD, James E. 790
WOOD, Richard J. 1365
City of Charleston MCCOY, Gail 799
Coll of Charleston NEVILLE, Robert F. 898
ROSS, Gary M. 1058
SCHMITT, John P. 1096
SEAMAN, Sheila L. 1109
STRAUCH, Katina P. 1200
Evening Post Publishing Co CROCKETT, Mary S. 259
INFO FLO MICHAELS, Carolyn L. 831
Medical Univ of South Carolina ANDERSON, Marcia 24
POYER, Robert K. 989
SAWYER, Warren A. 1086
TREMBLAY, Gerald F. 1255
Roper Hospital Inc MORSI, Pamela A. 869
South Carolina Historical Society MOLTKE-HANSEN, David ... 853
Univ of South Carolina SMITH, Nancy 1158
CHESTER
Chester County Pub Lib MURDOCK, Everlyne K. 879
CLEMSON
Clemson Univ ABRAMS, Leslie E. 3
ARMISTEAD, Myra A. 32
HARRIS, Maureen 505
JOHNSON, Steven D. 609
KOHL, Michael F. 668
LYLE, Martha E. 751
MEYER, Richard W. 830
MORGAN, Nancy T. 864
SILER, Freddie B. 1137
TAYLOR, Dennis S. 1226
THOMAS, Julie A. 1237

COLUMBIA
Chem-Nuclear Systems Inc KINTNER, Susan B. 653
Columbia Coll CROSS, Mary R. 260
VASSALLO, John A. 1279
Department of Archives & History MCDOWELL, William L. 804
Hammond Academy Lower Sch JACOCKS, Marcia W. 590
Lutheran Theological Southern
Seminary DERRICK, Mitzi J. 294
Midlands Technical Coll LAFAYE, Cary D. 687
Richland County Pub Lib FRIEDMAN, Amy G. 403
KAHN, Gerda M. 622
RAWLINSON, Helen A. 1011
WARREN, Charles D. 1306
Richland County Sch District One NORRIS, Gale K. 909
Richland Northeast High Sch KING, Evlyn J. 651

SOUTH CAROLINA (Cont'd)
COLUMBIA (Cont'd)
Richland Sch District 1 BASS, Carolyn M. 63
South Carolina Dept of Archs &
History HELSLEY, Alexia J. 525
South Carolina Department of
Education EHRHARDT, Margaret W. ... 339
South Carolina Dept of Health &
Envirom KRONENFELD, Michael R. .. 679
South Carolina Electric & Gas Co MOSS, Patsy G. 872
South Carolina State Lib CALLAHAM, Betty E. 173
FREEMAN, Larry S. 401
HERRON, Margie E. 533
LANDRUM, John H. 693
LAW, Aileen E. 704
MAZUR, Marjorie A. 791
MCGREGOR, Jane A. 808
NOLTE, Alice I. 908
WILLIAMS, Guynell 1343
South Carolina Supreme Court BARDIN, Angela D. 56
Sumter County Sch District 2 MILTON, Brenda R. 845
Univ of South Carolina BAKER, Augusta 47
BARRON, Daniel D. 60
BILLINSKY, Christyn G. 96
CHOI, Jin M. 210
CROSS, Joseph R. 260
EASTMAN, Caroline M. 333
GABLE, Sarah H. 411
GEOGHEGAN, Doris J. 427
GISSENDANNER,
Cassandra S. 438
HOLLEY, E J. 551
HOWARD-HILL, Trevor 564
LANGE, Elizabeth A. 695
LUCAS, Linda S. 746
MCQUILLAN, David C. 817
OSBALDISTON, Diana M. ... 927
PEAKE, Luise E. 952
PUKL, Joseph M. 997
RIDGE, Davy J. 1032
ROPER, Fred W. 1054
SCHULZ, Constance B. 1102
TOOMBS, Kenneth E. 1251
TYLER, Carolyn S. 1266
UPHAM, Lois N. 1269
WARREN, Karen T. 1306
WASHINGTON, Nancy H. ... 1307
WEATHERS, Virginia W. ... 1312
WILLIAMS, Robert V. 1346
W B Farrar, DDS Periodontics HUYGEN, Eva 580
William S Hall Psychiatric Institute SHAH, Neeta N. 1119
CONWAY
Horry County Memorial Lib LOWRIMORE, R T. 745
DARLINGTON
Darlington County Lib JAMES, Denise T. 592
LANGSTON, William E. 696
DENMARK
Denmark Technical Coll BOOK, Imogene I. 115
DUNCAN
W R Grace & Co EZELL, Margaret M. 360
MCCULLEY, P M. 800
EASLEY
School District of Pickens County BLAIR, Sharon K. 103
FLORENCE
Florence County Lib MCREE, John W. 818
Francis Marion Coll DOVE, Herbert P. 314
HUX, Roger K. 579
MARTIN, Neal A. 777
FORT JACKSON
Moncrief Army Community Hospital WETHERBY, Ivor L. 1328
GAFFNEY
Cherokee County Pub Lib EDEN, David E. 336
GLENDALE
Spartanburg County Sch District
Three WHITE, Ann T. 1330
GREENVILLE
Furman Univ CLAYTON, J G. 220
Greenville County Lib AYARI, Kaye W. 42
EISENSTADT, Rosa M. 341
MESSINEO, Anthony 828

SOUTH CAROLINA (Cont'd)
GREENVILLE (Cont'd)
Greenville Higher Education
  Consortium   HIPPS, Gary M. 543
Greenville Hospital System   TOWELL, Fay J. 1252
Greenville Technical Coll   OLINGER, Elizabeth B. 920
Holmes Coll of The Bible   SLIFE, Joye D. 1149
Sch District of Greenville County   SCALES, Pat R. 1087
GREENWOOD
Abbeville-Greenwood Regional Lib   HEIMBURGER, Bruce R. 521
Greenwood Sch District 50   BUIST, Elaine R. 156
Lander Coll   FECKO, Marybeth 367
    GOING, Susan C. 444
    HARE, Ann T. 501
    WILLIAMS, Betty H. 1342
Upper Savannah Area Health Educ
  Cnsrtm   HILL, Thomas W. 541
HARTSVILLE
Darlington County Lib   WARR, Virginia M. 1306
IRMO
South Carolina Lib Association   MAXIM, Virginia 787
LANCASTER
Lancaster County Lib   BAND, Richard A. 53
LAURENS
Laurens County Lib   COOPER, William C. 244
LIBERTY
Pickens County Sch District   DUSENBERRY, Mary D. . . . 329
LORIS
Horry County Sch District   BELL, David B. 76
MANNING
Harvin Clarendon County Lib   GILBERT, Sybil M. 434
MARION
Marion County Lib   MCAULAY, Louise S. 792
MCCORMICK
McCormick Middle Sch   TOWNSEND, Catherine M. . 1253
MURRELLS INLET
Brookgreen Gardens   SALMON, Robin R. 1077
MYRTLE BEACH
City of Myrtle Beach   BOONE, Shirley W. 115
NEWBERRY
Hampton Books   HAMILTON, Ben 491
Newberry Coll   DENNIS, Everett J. 292
ORANGEBURG
Orangeburg County Lib   ALLEN, Debra C. 14
    PAUL, Paula F. 949
South Carolina State Coll   JOHNSON, Minnie M. 607
    SMALLS, Mary L. 1151
    TAPLEY, Bridgette M. 1223
    WILLIAMS-JENKINS,
      Barbara J. 1347
PENDLETON
Anderson County District 4 Schs   DIXON, Linda A. 306
REMBERT
Sumter County Sch District 2   SHIRLEY, Iris C. 1131
ROCK HILL
Roddey Carpenter & White PA   LUPPINO, Julie B. 749
Winthrop Coll   CHOPESIUK, Ronald J. 210
    DAVIDSON, Nancy M. 276
    KELLEY, Gloria 636
    MITLIN, Laurance R. 850
    SILVERMAN, Susan M. 1139
    TARLTON, Shirley M. 1224
York County Lib   LYON, David A. 752
SPARTANBURG
Converse Coll   FAWVER, Darlene E. 367
Milliken Research Corp   CRAVEN, Trudy W. 256
Sherman Coll of Straight Chiropractic   BOWLES, David M. 121
Spartanburg County Pub Lib   BRUCE, Dennis L. 149
    GRIMLEY, Susan M. 470
    SMITH, Stephen C. 1161
Spartanburg Regional Medical Center   CAMP, Mary A. 175
Univ of South Carolina   PERRIN, Robert A. 959
SUMMERVILLE
Library Equipment/Space Design Inc   MAY, Robert E. 789
Westvaco Corp   RUST, Roxy J. 1070
SUMTER
Medical Logic International   COOK, Galen B. 240
Morris Coll   GORDON, Clara B. 451
Sumter County Lib   LINE, Faith A. 730

SOUTH CAROLINA (Cont'd)
TIGERVILLE
North Greenville Coll   BAKER, Steven L. 49
WALHALLA
Oconee County Lib   CHANDLER, Dorothy S. 199
WALTERBORO
Low Country Area Health Education
  Center   DAVIS, Patsy M. 280
WEST COLUMBIA
Lexington Sch District 2   BRANTON, Mildred M. 129
    HARDIN, Sue H. 500
Univ of South Carolina   LAWSON, James F. 705
WINNSBORO
Fairfield County Lib   MCMASTER, Sarah D. 815

SOUTH DAKOTA
ABERDEEN
Alexander Mitchell Pub Lib   RAVE, David A. 1010
Northern State Coll   LUGER, Mary J. 747
BOX ELDER
Univ of South Dakota   DEAN, Leann F. 283
BROOKINGS
South Dakota State Univ   BRONSON, Mark C. 140
    BROWN, Philip L. 146
    CASPERS, Mary E. 193
    HALLMAN, Clark N. 489
    HUDSON, Gary A. 569
    LISTER, Lisa F. 732
    RANEY, Leon 1007
    RICHARDS, Susan L. 1028
CROOKS
Minnehaha County Lib   REDDY, Joan L. 1013
MADISON
Dakota State Coll   SMITH, Rise L. 1160
MITCHELL
Dakota Wesleyan Univ   RITTER, Linda B. 1036
PIERRE
St Mary's Hospital   HILMOE, Deann D. 541
South Dakota State Archives   SOMMER, Linda M. 1167
South Dakota State Lib   DAGANAAR, Mark L. 269
    GILLILAND, Donna E. 436
State of South Dakota   KOLBE, Jane 669
RAPID CITY
Black Hills Regional Eye Institute   EVANS, Jane 357
Rushmore National Health System   HAMILTON, Patricia J. 492
SDSM & T   SCHWARTZ, James M. . . . 1104
South Dakota Sch of Mines and
  Technology   MORGAN, Bradford A. 863
SIOUX FALLS
Augustana Coll   HAGEMEIER, Deborah A. . . . 483
    THOELKE, Elisabeth A. 1235
    THOMPSON, Harry F. 1239
    THOMPSON, Ronelle K. . . . 1241
City of Sioux Falls   DERTIEN, James L. 294
Modern Talking Picture Service   MODICA, Mary L. 851
North American Baptist Conference   DUNGER, George A. 326
O'Gorman High Sch   OSTHUS, Mary J. 928
Sioux Falls Pub Lib   CRANMER, Donna C. 255
SPEARFISH
Black Hills State Coll   JONES, Dora A. 612
Spearfish Sch District 40-2   ASLESEN, Rosalie V. 36
VERMILLION
Univ of South Dakota   EDELEN, Joseph R. 335
    HULKONEN, David A. 572
    JENSEN, Mary B. 599
    LEGET, Max 712
    MYERS, Nancy L. 884
    SPRULES, Marcia L. 1176
Vermillion Pub Lib   LARSON, Jane A. 699

TENNESSEE
ARLINGTON
Shelby County Sch System   WILSON, Donna R. 1350
ARNOLD AFB
Schneider Services International   BOYD, Effie W. 122
BARTLETT
Shelby County Sch System   CONLEY, Janis E. 236

TENNESSEE (Cont'd)

BLOUNTVILLE
Sullivan County Department of
  Education   HASBROUCK, Clara H. 510
Sullivan County Sch   TILSON, Koleta B. 1245
BRENTWOOD
City of Brentwood   NORTON, Tedgina 910
BRISTOL
King Coll   HERRING, Mark Y. 533
CHATTANOOGA
Baylor Sch   HOOPER, James E. 557
Chattanooga-Hamilton County   GRIFFISS, M K. 469
   HARTUNG, Nancy F. 509
   MCFARLAND, Jane E. 805
Draughons Junior Coll   TURNER, Deborah M. 1264
Edmondson Junior Coll   TAMM-DANIELS, Ana L. . . . 1221
Girls Preparatory Sch   LAMBERT, Sarah E. 690
Hamilton County Department of
  Education   VANDERGRIFF, Kathleen E. 1274
McCallie Sch   REARDON, Elizabeth M. . . . 1013
Tennessee Valley Authority   MILLS, Debra D. 844
Univ of Tennessee at Chattanooga   JACKSON, Joseph A. 587
   MURGAI, Sarla R. 880
   NICOL, Jessie T. 902
CLARKSVILLE
Austin Peay State Univ   BERWIND, Anne M. 91
   CARLIN, Don 182
   JOYCE, Donald F. 618
   MCMAHAN, Elnor W. 814
CLEVELAND
Cleveland City Schs   SMITH, Judy R. 1156
Cleveland State Community Coll   BASKETT, D A. 63
CLINTON
Clinch-Powell Regional Lib   GREESON, Judy G. 465
COLLEGEDALE
Southern Coll of Seventh-Day
  Adventists   BENNETT, Peg E. 82
   GRACE, Loranne J. 455
COLUMBIA
Blue Grass Regional Lib Center   SLOAN, Lynette S. 1149
   WAGGENER, Jean B. 1291
Columbia State Community Coll   HARRISON, Richard H. 507
   LIGHT, Marvin J. 726
COOKEVILLE
Tennessee Technological Univ   JONES, Christine S. 611
   JONES, Roger G. 615
   KOHUT, David R. 669
   LAFEVER, Susan 687
   ROBERTS, Marica L. 1041
   TABACHNICK, Sharon 1219
   WALDEN, Winston A. 1294
Upper Cumberland Regional Lib   NICHOLS, Dolores D. 901
COWAN
Franklin County Sch System   WATSON, Gail H. 1309
DAYTON
Bryan Coll   WRIGHT, David A. 1371
FAYETTEVILLE
Fayetteville City Schs   YOUNG, Patricia S. 1383
HARRISON
Hamilton County Department of
  Education   BRUNER, Katharine E. 150
HENDERSONVILLE
Sumner County Board of Education   MILLS, Wanda R. 844
JACKSBORO
Campbell County Board of Education   HENSON, Susie K. 530
JACKSON
Jackson-Madison County General
  Hospital   FARMER, Linda G. 364
Jackson-Madison County Lib   AUD, Thomas L. 39
Lane Coll   COOKE, Anna L. 240
Union Univ at Jackson   ROBERTSON, Billy O. 1041
JEFFERSON CITY
Carson-Newman Coll   SELF, George A. 1113
   SNODDERLY, Louise D. . . . 1163
Jefferson County Board of Education   LINDSEY, Nancy L. 730
JOHNSON CITY
East Tennessee State Univ   ABOUSHAMA, Mary F. 2
   BORCHUCK, Fred P. 116
   FISHER, Janet S. 381
   NORRIS, Carol B. 909

TENNESSEE (Cont'd)

JOHNSON CITY (Cont'd)
East Tennessee State Univ   RIDENOUR, Lisa R. 1032
   SCHER, Rita S. 1092
   WILLIAMS, Elizabeth L. . . . 1343
Holy Spirit Association   CONVERY, Sukhont K. 239
James Agee Film Project   SPEARS, Ross 1172
Johnson City Medical Center Hospital   TRIVETT, Martha S. 1257
Johnson City Press   BROWN, Phyllis J. 147
Quillen-Dishner College of Medicine   MCLEAN, Martha L. 814
KINGSPORT
City of Kingsport   FANSLOW, Malinda C. 363
Eastman Chemicals Div of Eastman
  Kodak   WEHNER, Karen B. 1316
Eastman Kodak Co   CASSELL, Gerald S. 193
   PRESLAR, M G. 991
   UBALDINI, Michael W. 1267
MJE Infoservices   ERWIN, Mary J. 353
KNOXVILLE
Fort Sanders Regional Med Ctr   COOK, Nedra J. 240
Knox County Pub Lib System   CARTER, Barbara W. 189
   COTHAM, James S. 249
   DYER, Barbara M. 330
Knox County Schs   LOCKWOOD, Bonnie J. 736
Knoxville Journal   JACKSON, Phyllis J. 588
Metropolitan Planning Commission   BEAL, Gretchen F. 68
Philips International B V   GALL, Bert A. 413
St Mary's Medical Center   CLARK, Glenda C. 217
Tennessee Valley Authority   BEST, Edwin J. 92
   BULL, Margaret J. 156
   KNIGHTLY, John J. 664
   MYERS, William F. 885
   NOONAN, Patricia K. 908
Univ of Tennessee at Knoxville   BEINTEMA, William J. 75
   BENGTSON, Betty G. 80
   BEST, Reba A. 92
   CROWTHER, Karmen N. 262
   ESTES, Glenn E. 355
   GARRETT, Stuart 420
   GRADY, Agnes M. 455
   HEWLETT, Carol C. 535
   HILL, Ruth J. 540
   HUNT, Donald R. 575
   JETT, Don W. 600
   KARRENBROCK, Marilyn H. . 628
   LEACH, Sandra S. 706
   LLOYD, James B. 735
   MITCHELL, Aubrey H. 848
   MYERS, Marcia J. 884
   PEMBERTON, J M. 956
   PHILLIPS, Linda L. 968
   PICQUET, D C. 971
   PONNAPPA, Biddanda P. . . . 982
   PRENTICE, Ann E. 990
   RADER, Joe C. 1002
   ROBINSON, William C. 1045
   SAMMATARO, Linda J. . . . 1078
   SILCOX, Tinsley E. 1137
   SOLBERG, Judy L. 1166
   VIERA, Ann R. 1284
   WALLACE, Alan H. 1297
Webb Sch of Knoxville   TUDOR, Betty A. 1262
LAWRENCEBURG
E O Coffman Middle Sch   EDWARDS, Barbara T. 337
LEBANON
Cumberland Univ   KARL, Roger M. 627
   ROBERTSON, Sally A. 1042
MARTIN
Tennessee State Lib & Archives   WASH, Melba W. 1307
Univ of Tennessee at Martin   SMITH, Lori D. 1157
   STOWERS, Joel A. 1199
MARYVILLE
American Academy of Orthopedic
  Surgeons   HARALSON, Robert H. 499
Maryville Coll   WORLEY, Joan H. 1369

TENNESSEE (Cont'd)
MEMPHIS

Baptist Memorial Health Care System	OWEN, Richard L.	932
Buckman Laboratories	FITZER, Maureen D.	382
	MCDONELL, W E.	803
Christian Brothers Coll	DENTON, A W.	293
City of Memphis	JACKSON, Harriett D.	587
Commercial Appeal	TERRY, Carol D.	1232
Harding Univ	BAKER, Bonnie U.	48
	MEREDITH, Don L.	825
Histl Fndtn of the Cumberland Church	WILLIAMSON, Jane K.	1347
Memphis & Shelby County Pub Lib	BAER, Ellen H.	45
	BRADY, Josiah B.	126
	CARD, Judy	180
	DRESCHER, Judith A.	319
	LINDENFELD, Joseph F.	729
	RICHARDSON, Merle J.	1029
	SMITH, Robert F.	1160
	STRAWDER, Maxine S.	1201
Memphis City Schs	BANNERMAN-WILLIAMS, Cheryl F.	54
	FARRIS, Mary E.	365
Memphis State Univ	BEHRENS, Elizabeth A.	75
	CO, Francisca	224
	DENTON, Ann L.	293
	EVANS, David H.	356
	HENDRIX, Wilma P.	528
	HUGGINS, Annelle R.	571
	MADER, Sharon B.	759
	MENDINA, Guy T.	824
	PARK, Elizabeth H.	941
	POURCIAU, Lester J.	987
	RUDOLPH, N J.	1066
	SMITH, Philip M.	1159
	VILES, Elza A.	1284
	WANG, Hueychyi V.	1303
	WARD, Suzanne M.	1304
	WEDIG, Eric M.	1315
	WILLIAMS, Saundra W.	1346
Methodist Hospital-North	PORTER, William R.	985
Mid-America Baptist Theological Seminary	HAIR, William B.	484
	MABBOTT, Deborah D.	753
Mid-South Bible Coll	ADAMS, Paul R.	5
	PENNINGTON, Melanie L.	957
Rhodes Coll	BLAIR, Lynne M.	102
	SHORT, William M.	1132
St Joseph Hospital	IRBY, Patricia P.	583
St Jude Children's Research Hospital	WALKER, Mary E.	1296
Shelby County Pub Lib & Info Center	LEVINE, Fay E.	720
	WUJCIK, Dennis S.	1374
Univ of Tennessee at Memphis	BELLAMY, Lois M.	77
	BUNTING, Anne C.	157
	COOPER, Ellen R.	242
	GIVENS, Mary K.	439
	LASSLO, Andrew	700
	MARTIN, Jess A.	776
	SELIG, Susan A.	1113
Waring Cox	BAILEY, Barbara G.	46

MORRISTOWN

Hamblen County Lib Board	EDWARDS, Rela G.	337
Morristown Hamblen Pub Lib	BROOKS, Judy B.	140

MT JULIET

Wilson County Board of Education	HAMLIN, Lisa K.	493

MURFREESBORO

Alvin C York Veterans Admin Medical Ctr	HUNTER, Joy W.	576
Middle Tennessee State Univ	BURKHEART, Hilda S.	161
	CRAIG, James D.	254
	GILL, Linda S.	435
	MARSHALL, John D.	774
	NEAL, James H.	890
	SCOTT, Margaret W.	1107
	WELLS, Paul F.	1323
	YOUREE, Beverly B.	1384
Veterans Administration Medical Center	EUBANKS, Marie	356

TENNESSEE (Cont'd)
NASHVILLE

Belmont Coll	GMEINER, Timothy J.	442
	GRENGA, Kathy A.	467
Boult Cummings Connors & Berry	BOURNER, Elizabeth A.	119
Country Music Foundation Inc	BELL, Rebecca L.	77
	SEEMANN, Charles H.	1111
Creative Information Retrieval Services	MOON, Fletcher F.	857
David Lipscomb Coll	PERRY, Myrna G.	960
	WARD, James E.	1304
David Lloyd Swift Paper Preservation	SWIFT, David L.	1216
Dearborn & Ewing	JULIAN, Julie L.	619
Disciples of Christ Historical Society	MCWHIRTER, David I.	818
Ensworth School	BURKE, Mary E.	160
Fine Arts Center at Cheekwood	KNOWLES, Susan W.	665
Fisk Univ	SHOCKLEY, Ann A.	1132
George Peabody Coll for Teachers	ROTHACKER, John M.	1059
Holy Rosary Academy	CUNNINGHAM, Helen	265
Hospital Corp of America	PATTERSON, Jennifer J.	948
Ingram Distribution Group Inc	PRICE, Larry C.	992
Jewish Federation of Nashville	RATKIN, Annette L.	1009
LaQuita Martin Lib Management Inc	MARTIN, Laquita V.	777
Meharry Medical Coll	CAMERON, Sam A.	175
	EARL, Martha F.	332
	GOODALE, Adebonojo L.	448
	HAMBERG, Cheryl J.	490
	MCHOLLIN, Mattie L.	809
	WATTS, Adalyn	1310
	WILLIAMS, Marsha D.	1345
Metro Nashville Pub Schs	MCANALLY, Charlotte L.	792
Metropolitan-Nashville Bd of Education	DURHAM, Wanda J.	328
Metropolitan Nashville General Hospital	PERRY, Glenda L.	960
Northern Telecom Inc	PILCHER, Annette S.	973
Occupational Health Services Inc	BRANSFORD, John S.	129
Pub Lib of Nashville	HEARNE, Mary G.	518
Saint Thomas Hospital	FORBES, Evelyn H.	388
	FULTON, Dixie W.	409
St Vincent de Paul Sch	KILPATRICK, Barbara A.	648
Southern Baptist Convention	SUMNERS, Bill F.	1209
Southern Baptist Sunday Sch Board	SKELTON, William E.	1146
State of Tennessee	HUGHES, Marylin B.	572
Tennessean	MORRISON, Annette T.	867
Tennessee Lib Association	NANCE, Betty	887
Tennessee State Lib & Archives	FANCHER, Evelyn P.	363
	GLEAVES, Edwin S.	441
	HARRELL, Neal	503
	HOM, Sharon L.	555
	THWEATT, John H.	1243
Tennessee State Univ	ARMONTROUT, Brian A.	32
	CHEN, Helen M.	205
	HUDSON, Earline H.	569
	STEPHENS, Alonzo T.	1187
United Methodist Publishing House	LEWIS, Rosalyn	724
United Paperworkers International Union	GLAUS, Roberta I.	440
US Tobacco	BORRELLI, Barbara A.	117
Univ Sch of Nashville	EISENSTEIN, Jill M.	341
Vanderbilt Medical Center	LEWIS, Carol E.	722
Vanderbilt Univ	BRANTIGAN-STOWELL, Martha J.	129
	BROSS, Valerie	141
	CHENEY, Frances N.	206
	DAVIS, Susan W.	281
	ELDRIDGE, Virginia L.	342
	GETZ, Malcolm	430
	GRAHAM, Sylvia R.	456
	HARWELL, Sara J.	509
	HELGUERA, Byrd S.	524
	HODGES, Terence M.	546
	KAVASS, Igor I.	631
	LASATER, Mary C.	700
	LEE, Geoffrey J.	710
	LEISERSON, Annabelle	714
	LYNCH, Frances H.	751
	MANNING, Dale	766
	PARKS, Dorothy R.	943
	PILKINGTON, James P.	973

TENNESSEE (Cont'd)
NASHVILLE (Cont'd)
Vanderbilt Univ

QUINN, Joan M. 1000
RICHARDS, Timothy F. 1028
RIEKE, Judith L. 1033
ROMANS, Lawrence M. 1052
SHABB, Cynthia H. 1118
STEFFEY, Ramona J. 1185
TAYLOR, William R. 1229
WILBURN, Clouse R. 1338
WILSON, Florence J. 1351
WOLFE, Marice 1361

Veterans Administration Medical
Center   GAUDET, Susan E. 422
Watkins Institute   SCOTT, Willodene A. 1108

OAK RIDGE
Children's Museum of Oak Ridge   ALDERFER, Jane B. 11
Kaiser Engineers Inc   MCDONALD, Ethel Q. 802
Martin Marietta Energy Systems   ALEXANDER, Mary B. 12
                                   DELKER, Kathy M. 289
                                   EKKEBUS, Allen E. 341
                                   GOVE, N B. 454
                                   NORTON, Nancy P. 910
                                   ROBBINS, Gordon D. 1038
                                   SNYDER, Cathrine E. 1164
                                   STRICKLER, Candice S. ... 1202
                                   VEACH, Lynn H. 1280
Maxima Corp   CLELAND, Nancy D. 220
Oak Ridge Associated Univs   BURN, Harry T. 161
                                   YALCINTAS, Rana 1376
Oak Ridge National Laboratory   CATON, Gloria M. 195
                                   EWBANK, W B. 359
                                   JONES, Kendra A. 613
                                   MUNRO, Nancy B. 879
                                   PFUDERER, Helen A. 966
US Department of Energy   CARROLL, Bonnie C. 187
                                   COYNE, Joseph 254
                                   HARDIN, Nancy E. 500
                                   RUSHING, Jessie W. 1068
                                   SPATH, Charles E. 1171
                                   STUBER, Charles E. 1204

SAINT ANDREWS
St Andrews - Sewanee Sch   KENT, Candace D. 642
SEWANEE
Univ of the South   CAMP, Thomas E. 175
                                   HAYMES, Don 516
                                   PHILLIPS, Patricia A. 968
                                   RAWNSLEY, Virgilia I. 1011
                                   WATSON, Tom G. 1310

SPARTA
Caney Fork Regional Lib Center   HOLDREDGE, Faith A. 550
WHITE PINE
Jefferson County Pub Schs   JONES, Anne G. 611

TEXAS
ABILENE
Abilene Christian Univ   ALEXANDER, Shirley B. 12
                                   ANDERSON, Madeleine J. 24
                                   HARPER, Marsha W. 503
                                   WALKER, Bonnie M. 1295
Abilene State Sch   ALLEN, Peggy G. 15
City of Abilene   WOODALL, Cynthia P. 1365
Hardin-Simmons Univ   BRADLEY, C D. 125
                                   CAMPBELL, Mary K. 177
                                   DAHLSTROM, Joe F. 269
                                   DONALDSON, Anna L. 311
                                   SPECHT, Alice W. 1172
McMurry Coll   HAGGARD, Lynn 483
                                   SPECHT, Joe W. 1172
Valley View Elementary Sch   GILLETTE, Robert S. 435
ALPINE
Sul Ross State Univ   SPEARS, Norman L. 1172
AMARILLO
Amarillo Pub Lib   GROSS, Iva H. 472
                                   RUDDY, Mary K. 1065
City of Amarillo   DOYLE, Patricia A. 317
                                   SNELL, Marykay H. 1163
                                   THOMAS, Greg 1236
Texas Panhandle Lib System   WELLS, Mary K. 1322

TEXAS (Cont'd)
AMARILLO (Cont'd)
Texas Tech Regnl Academic Hlth Ctr   NEELEY, Dana M. 891
ANGELTON
Brazoria County Lib System   BROWN, Steven L. 147
ARLINGTON
Arlington Independent Sch District   KERBY, Ramona A. 643
City of Arlington   LEATHERMAN, Donald G. 707
Univ of Texas at Arlington   HULL, Mary M. 572
                                   KONDRASKE, Linda N. 670
                                   LEWIS, John S. 723
                                   LOWRY, Charles B. 745
                                   MORRIS, Pamela A. 867
                                   SAMSON, Robert C. 1079
                                   SHEETS, Shirley H. 1125
                                   STOAN, Stephen K. 1195
                                   WELLVANG, James K. 1323
AUSTIN
Austin Community Coll   AIROLDI, Melissa 9
                                   HISLE, W L. 544
                                   PELOQUIN, Margaret I. 955
                                   SOWELL, Cary L. 1170
                                   WASSENICH, Red 1308
Austin Independent Sch District   SMITH, Dorothy B. 1154
Austin Pub Lib   DAYO, Ayo 283
                                   DEGRUYTER, M L. 288
                                   GAMEZ, Juanita L. 416
                                   MIDDLETON, Robert K. 833
                                   SKINNER, Vicki F. 1146
Brown Maroney Rose Barber & Dye   BIERI, Sandra J. 95
Catholic Archives of Texas   BRYSON, Gary B. 152
Central America Resource Center   MCCANN, Charlotte P. 793
Clark Thomas Winters & Newton   TRANFAGLIA, Twyla L. ... 1254
Eanes Independent Sch District   BOEHME, Vada M. 109
                                   HOOVER, Gloria E. 557
                                   WIDENER, Sarah A. 1335
Episcopal Theol Sem of the
Southwest   BOOHER, Harold H. 115
GSD & M Advertising   POWERS, Sally J. 989
Justan Enterprises   JUERGENS, Bonnie 619
                                   STANDIFER, Hugh A. 1179
Library Management & Services   HELBURN, Judith D. 523
Lyndon Baines Johnson Foundation   REED, Lawrence D. 1015
Lyndon Baines Johnson Lib   FRANKUM, Katherine H. 398
Martin & Martin Info Consultants Inc   MARTIN, Jean K. 776
McAdams Planning Consultants Inc   MCADAMS, Nancy R. 792
McGinnis Lochridge & Kilgore   HILL, Susan E. 540
                                   O'MARA, Joan 923
Microelectronics & Computer Tech
Corp   HARMON, Jacqueline B. 502
National Archives & Records Admin   HUMPHREY, David C. 573
                                   SMITH, Nancy K. 1158
                                   TISSING, Robert W. 1247
Payne Assn   PAYNE, John R. 951
Pub Utility Commission of Texas   WILLIAMS, Suzi 1346
R Walton and Associates   TAYLOR, Nancy L. 1228
Round Rock Independent Sch District   SPAULDING, Nancy J. 1172
St Edward's Univ   FELSTED, Carla M. 370
                                   SPRUG, Joseph W. 1176
St Frances Sch   MACBETH, Helen L. 754
Tandem Computers   WISE, Olga B. 1357
Tarlton Law Lib   PRATTER, Jonathan 990
Texas Education Agency   KAHLER, June 621
Texas General Land Office   HOOKS, Michael Q. 556
Texas Instruments Inc   ARNOLD, Gaye C. 33
Texas Lib Association   HOWARD, Ada M. 563
Texas State Law Lib   HAMBLETON, James E. 490
                                   HARLOW, Sally S. 502
                                   SCHLUETER, Kay 1094
Texas State Lib   BLACK, J A. 101
                                   BRIDGE, Frank R. 135
                                   CARTER, Janet K. 189
                                   HOLLAND, Michael E. 551
                                   MATHIS, Rama F. 784
                                   SEIDENBERG, Edward 1112
                                   WALTON, Robert A. 1301
3M   MITTAG, Erika 850
Travis County   KESHISHIAN, Maria L. 644

TEXAS (Cont'd)

AUSTIN (Cont'd)

Univ of Texas at Austin

AIRTH, Elizabeth J.	9
ARTHUR, Donald B.	35
BARKAN, Steven M.	56
BECK, Alison M.	71
BICHTELER, Julie H.	94
BILLINGS, Harold W.	96
BRENNAN, Mary H.	132
BUCKNALL, Carolyn F.	154
BURCH, David R.	158
BURLINGHAM, Merry L.	161
BURT, Eugene C.	164
CABLE, Carole L.	170
CRONEIS, Karen S.	260
DALLAS, Larayne J.	270
DAVIS, Donald G.	278
EISENBEIS, Kathleen M.	340
ELDER, Nancy I.	342
GARNER, Jane	419
GOODWIN, Willard	450
GOULD, Karen K.	454
GRACY, David B.	455
GUTIERREZ, Margo	479
HARMON, Glynn	502
HARTNESS, Ann	508
HELFER, Robert S.	523
HENDERSON, Cathy	526
HERRING, Billie G.	533
IMMROTH, Barbara F.	582
JACKSON, William V.	588
LANDIS, Lawrence A.	693
LEACH, Sally S.	706
MARSHALL, Suzanne K.	775
MERSKY, Roy M.	827
MIKSA, Francis L.	834
MILLER, Karl F.	839
PERRYMAN, Wayne R.	961
POUND, Mary E.	987
ROY, Loriene	1063
SCHWARTZ, Philip J.	1105
SENG, Mary A.	1115
TONGATE, John T.	1250
WYLLYS, Ronald E.	1375

BANGS

Bangs Independent Sch District — WEEKS, Patsy L. — 1315

BAY CITY

Bay City Independent Sch District — HOWARD, Elizabeth A. — 564

BAYTOWN

City of Baytown	KLEHN, Victoria L.	658
Exxon Chemical Co	NEWMAN, Robert M.	899
Lee Coll	INKS, Cordelia R.	583

BEAUMONT

Beaumont Independent Sch District	NISBY, Dora R.	904
Gulf States Utilities Co	MCCONNELL, Karen S.	797
Lamar Univ	HOLLAND, Mary M.	551
	MURRAY, Kathleen R.	882
	SPARKMAN, Mickey M.	1171

BEDFORD

Hurst-Euless-Bedford ISD — MONTGOMERY, Wanda W. — 856

BELLAIRE

Access Information Associates	HOLAB-ABELMAN, Robin S.	550
City of Bellaire	ALFORD, Mary A.	13
	YAPLE, Marilyn V.	1378
Episcopal High Sch	HAND, M D.	494

BELTON

Belton Independent Sch District	MARKS, Mary L.	771
Univ of Mary Hardin at Baylor	KERLEY, Izoro D.	643

BERGSTROM AFB

US Air Force — ST. JOHN, Louise — 1075

BIG SANDY

Ambassador Coll — CRISSINGER, John D. — 259

BIG SPRING

Big Spring State Hospital — BRADBERRY, Anna L. — 125

TEXAS (Cont'd)

BROOKS AFB

School of Aerospace Medicine	FRANZELLO, Joseph J.	398
US Air Force	FRIDLEY, Bonnie J.	403
	TODD, Fred W.	1248
US Air Force Sch of Aerospace Medicine	BREWSTER, Olive N.	134

BROWNFIELD

Brownfield Independent Sch District — HAMILTON, Betty D. — 491

BROWNSVILLE

Texas Southmost Coll — VAUGHN, Frances A. — 1280

BROWNWOOD

Howard Payne Univ — PARTON, William A. — 945

BRYAN

City of Bryan	MOUNCE, Clara B.	873
Texas A&M Univ	HAMBRIC, Jacqueline B.	491

BURKVILLE

Burkville Independent Sch District — TEDDER, Dorothy L. — 1229

CANYON

West Texas State Univ — RIEPMA, Helen J. — 1033

CARRIZO SPRINGS

Carrizo Springs Independent Sch District — POWELL, Mary E. — 988

CARROLLTON

Carrollton-Farmers Branch	BLAIR, Elaine K.	102
Thomson Components-Mostek	OGDEN, William S.	918

CLEBURNE

Cleburne High Sch — CARDENAS, Martha L. — 180

CLEVELAND

City of Cleveland — SMITH, Barbara F. — 1152

CLUTE

Brazosports Facts — RICE, Margaret R. — 1027

COLLEGE STATION

Texas A&M Univ

BROWN-WEBB, Deborah D.	149
BUTKOVICH, Nancy J.	166
CLARK, Charlene K.	216
COOK, C C.	239
FACKLER, Naomi P.	360
GYESZLY, Suzanne D.	479
HALL, Halbert W.	487
HALVERSON, Jacquelyn A.	490
HOADLEY, Irene B.	545
KELLOUGH, Jean L.	637
KELLOUGH, Patrick H.	637
PAYNE, Leila M.	951
RABINS, Joan W.	1001
RHOLES, Julia M.	1026
SCHMIDT, Sherrie	1096
SCHULTZ, Charles R.	1101
SMITH, Charles R.	1153
THOMAS, Barbara C.	1236
THOMPSON, Christine E.	1239

Texas State Lib — SCOTT, Paul R. — 1108

COLORADO CITY

Colorado Independent Sch District — GODWIN, Frances L. — 443

COMMERCE

East Texas State Univ — CONRAD, James H. — 238

CONROE

Medical Center Hospital	NEELAND, Ellen L.	891
Montgomery County Lib System	BALDWIN, Joe M.	51

COPPELL

City of Coppel — BIGGERSTAFF, Judi L. — 95

CORPUS CHRISTI

City of Corpus Christi	GEORGE, Aubrey W.	427
Corpus Christi Caller-Times	NEU, Margaret J.	896
Corpus Christi Pub Libs	CANALES, Herbert C.	178
Corpus Christi State Univ	BUCHWALD, Donald M.	153
	TROMBLEY, Patricia A.	1258
Hoechst Celanese Corp	UMFLEET, Ruth A.	1268
Kleberg Dyer Redford & Weil	HOUSTON, Barbara B.	563
Reynolds Metals Co	PHEGAN, Dolores M.	967
Tuloso-Midway Independent School Dist	SILVERMAN, Barbara G.	1138

COTULLA

Cotulla Independent Sch District — BARBOUR, James C. — 55

CYPRESS

Tri-Tech Data Solutions Inc — ZYSK, John T. — 1392

DALHART

Dalhart Independent Sch District — YOUNG, Nancy M. — 1382

TEXAS (Cont'd)
DALLAS

All Saints Catholic Church   BELLAVANCE, Maria I. 78
AMIGOS Bibliographic Council Inc   CHIU, Ida K. 209
   DOWNINS, Jeffery G. 317
   MARMION, Daniel K. 772
   WETHERBEE, Louella V. . . . 1327
   WHITE, Douglas A. 1330
Arthur Young & Co   BARRETT, Carol A. 59
   HOPKINS, Terry F. 558
Association for Higher Educ   JAGOE, Katherine P. 591
Baylor Hlth Scis Lib   THOMAS, Donald L. 1236
Baylor Univ   GUENTHER, Jody 475
BRS Information Technologies   GALBRAITH, Paula L. 413
Central and South West Services   WHISMAN, Loyse B. 1329
Computer Ability   BIRD, H C. 98
Computer Industry Almanac Inc   KRUSE, Luanne M. 681
Dallas Area Rapid Transit   BLOECHLE, Marie K. 106
   KANE, Deborah A. 624
Dallas County   BENGE, Joy L. 80
Dallas County Community Coll District   BAKER, Linda L. 49
Dallas County Law Lib   CLEE, June E. 220
   HOOD, Lawrence E. 556
Dallas Independent Sch District   DANIELS, Cynthia E. 273
   MCCASLIN, Cheryl A. 795
   MCLAUGHLIN, Hilda S. 813
   SPENCER, Barbara L. 1173
   YOUNG, J A. 1382
Dallas Morning News   LOVELL, Bonnie A. 743
   METCALF, Judith A. 828
Dallas Pub Lib   ALLEN, Sarabeth 16
   BOCKSTRUCK, Lloyd D. . . . 109
   BOGIE, Thomas M. 110
   BROWN, Muriel W. 146
   CROW, Rebecca N. 261
   DAVIS, Carolyn 278
   EWUNES, Ernest L. 359
   FOUDRAY, Rita C. 393
   FOUTS, Judith F. 393
   GRAY, Wayne D. 460
   HARRIS, Andrea L. 504
   HERFURTH, Sharon M. 530
   JOHNSON, Johanna H. 606
   KRALISZ, Victor F. 675
   MENDRO, Donna C. 824
   MOLTZAN, Janet R. 854
   O'BRIEN, Patrick M. 915
   OSWALT, Paul K. 929
   SHUEY, Andrea L. 1133
   SLAUGHTER, William J. . . . 1148
   SMITH, Michael K. 1158
   STAMELOS, Ellen A. 1179
   STONE, Marvin H. 1197
Dallas Theological Seminary   HUNN, Marvin T. 574
   IBACH, Robert D. 581
Dallas Times Herald   WALDEN, Elaine B. 1294
Dresser Industries Inc   GIBSON, Timothy T. 432
E C Lively Elementary Sch   WHISENNAND, Cynthia S. . 1329
EBSCO Subscription Services   SWEARINGEN, Wilba S. . . . 1214
Edwin L Cox Sch of Business   MASON, Florence M. 781
Electronic Data Systems   WILDER, Nancy S. 1339
Federal Home Loan Bank of Dallas   TALLEY, Pat L. 1221
First Baptist Church   SCHMIDT, Mary A. 1095
Frito-Lay Inc   HAWLEY, Laurie J. 514
   OGDEN, Suzanne M. 918
Gardere & Wynne   GARDNER, Linda 418
   LUETHEMEYER, Kaethryn . . . 747
HBW Associates Inc   WATERS, Richard L. 1308
Hughes & Luce   RODAWALT, Valarie J. 1046
INFOMART   DOBSON, Christine B. 307
   PEDEN, Robert M. 954
   TRICKEY, Katherine M. . . . 1256
   ZABEL, Patricia L. 1385
Jackson Walker Winstead Cantwell et al   JETER, Ann H. 600
JDA Inc   DAHLGREN, Jean E. 269
Jeanne Byrne Lib Service Inc   BYRNE, Jeanne M. 169
Jesuit Coll Preparatory Sch   SULLIVAN, Janice L. 1207
Johnson & Swanson   DEWBERRY, Betty B. 298
   GATES, Diane E. 421

TEXAS (Cont'd)
DALLAS (Cont'd)

Jones Day Reavis & Pogue   GRIMES, Carolyn E. 470
   HOOTON, Virginia A. 557
   LEE, Frank 709
MARC Inc   COMPTON, Erlinda R. 235
McKinsey & Co   PORRAS, Susan M. 984
Mead Data Central   NEWMAN, Patricia O. 899
Media Projects & New Day Films   MONDELL, Cynthia B. 854
Methodist Medical Center   JARVIS, Mary E. 595
Mitchell Information Services   MITCHE, Cynthia R. 848
   MITCHELL, Cynthia R. 848
Mobil Exploration and Producing Srvs Inc   FREEMAN, Mary L. 401
Mobil Research & Development Corp   SCHOOLFIELD, Dudley B. . . . 1098
Moore & Peterson   TEMPLETON, Virginia E. . . . 1231
Peat Marwick Main & Co   MCCLURE, Margaret R. 797
Peat Marwick Mitchell   HARRISON, Karen M. 507
   WHITTLESEY, Jane M. 1334
Price Waterhouse   SMITH, Kraleen S. 1156
Purvin & Gertz Inc   KERWIN, Camillus A. 644
Reference Technology Inc   RUBIN, Lenard H. 1064
Regional Medical Lib Program   LEE, Regina H. 711
Richland Coll   CLEMENTS, Cynthia L. 221
   JESER-SKAGGS, Sharlee A. 600
Santa Fe Minerals   DILLARD, Lois A. 303
Solomon Schechter Academy   GREMONT, Joan C. 467
South Central Regnl Medical Lib Program   CAMACHO, Nancy S. 174
Southern Methodist Univ   BAILEY, Anne M. 46
   CASEY, Carol A. 192
   DOMA, Tshering 310
   FARMER, David 364
   HEIZER, Carolyn H. 523
   HOLLEMAN, Curt 551
   JORDAN, Travis E. 617
   KACENA, Carolyn 621
   LATTIMORE, Clare I. 702
   LETSON, Dawn E. 719
   LOYD, Roger L. 745
   MCTYRE, Ruthann B. 818
   MONGOLD, Alice D. 854
   MUCK, Bruce E. 874
   MURPHY, Kristine L. 881
   ORAM, Robert W. 925
   RANDALL, Laura H. 1006
   SKINNER, Robert G. 1146
   SNODGRASS, Wilson D. . . 1163
   SZARKA, Tamara J. 1218
   THOMAS, Page A. 1238
   TOLMAN, Kimberly S. 1249
   UMOH, Linda K. 1268
Standard Oil Production Co   DAVIS, Connie J. 278
   KLEIN, Mindy F. 659
   METIVIER, Donna M. 828
T U Electric   MIDGETT, Ann S. 833
Texas Instruments Inc   BARRUS, Phyl 60
   BELL, Charise F. 76
   POPE, Hermon L. 983
   WALDEN, Millicent F. 1294
   WEBB, Sue E. 1313
Texas Oil & Gas Corp   MALCOLM, Jane B. 762
Texas Scottish Rite Hospital   PETERS, Mary N 962
Town of Highland Park   CASE, Bonnie N. 191
Tracy-Locke Inc   SHAPLEY, Ellen M. 1122
Transition Management   RYDESKY, Mary M. 1071
Univ of Texas at Dallas   BANDELIN, Janis M. 53
   MILLER, Jean K. 838
   WILKERSON, Judith C. 1339
Univ of Texas Health Science Center   ARMES, Patti 32
   MAYO, Helen G. 790
Veterans Administration Medical Center   CAMPBELL, Shirley A. 177
W R Grace & Co   MILLER, Rea R. 841
Winstead McGuire Sechrest & Minick   COOKSEY, Martha L. 241
   DERMODY, Rita R. 294

DEER PARK

Deer Park Pub Lib   CATES, Susan W. 195

TEXAS (Cont'd)

DENISON
Denison Pub Lib — BAILEY, Alvin R. 46

DENTON
Affiliated Pathologists — FORD, Mary R. 389
City of Denton — ORR, Joella A. 926
Denton Pub Lib — TOURAINE, Linda S. 1252
North Texas State Univ — ALMQUIST, Sharon G. 17
CARROLL, Dewey E. 187
CVELJO, Katherine 268
FERSTL, Kenneth L. 374
FOLLET, Robert E. 388
GALLOWAY, Margaret E. 415
HIMMEL, Richard L. 542
HOGAN, Sarah T. 549
JONES, Lois S. 613
LAVENDER, Kenneth 703
MITCHELL, George D. 848
POPE, Betty F. 983
SASSEN, Catherine J. 1083
TOTTEN, Herman L. 1252
VONDRAN, Raymond F. ... 1288
Texas Woman's Univ — CALIMANO, Ivan E. 173
PEDEN, Rita Y. 954
SCHLESSINGER, Bernard S. 1094
SHELDON, Brooke E. 1125
SNAPP, Elizabeth M. 1162
SWIGGER, Keith 1216
THOMAS, James L. 1237
TURNER, Frank L. 1264
WAN, William W. 1302

DEVERS
Devers Independent Sch District — COKINOS, Elizabeth G. 229

DIMMITT
Castro County — AUTRY, Brick 41
HOWELL, Gladys M. 565

DUNCANVILLE
Duncanville Pub Lib — BRYAN, Carla W. 151

EDINBURG
City of Edinburg — HOPPER, Lorraine E. 558
NANCE, Betty L. 887
Edinburg Pub Lib — LEAHY, Sheila A. 707
Pan American Univ — GAUSE, George R. 423
HAYNIE, Altie V. 517
MYCUE, David J. 884
SHABOWICH, Stanley A. ... 1118
TINSMAN, William A. 1246
Reynaldo G Garga Sch of Law — CORBIN, John 245

EL PASO
Del Valle High Sch — LABODDA, Marsha J. 686
El Paso Community Coll — MALLORY, Elizabeth J. 763
TAYLOR, Anne E. 1226
El Paso Herald-Post — MCCARGAR, Susan E. 794
El Paso Independent Sch District — CAMERON, Dee B. 174
El Paso Pub Lib — ANDERSON, Mark 24
DILLINGER, Mary A. 303
DOWDLE, Glen L. 315
FISCHER, Beverly J. 379
ROBERTS, Glenda S. 1040
RODERICK, Mary P. 1047
Geary Consulting — GEARY, Kathleen A. 424
Scott Hulse Marshall Feuille et al — MCDONALD, Brenda D. 802
Socorro Independent Sch District — NORTH, Yvonne M. 910
Texas Tech Univ — KNOTT, Teresa L. 665
Texas Trans-Pecos Lib System — DAVIS, Joyce 279
Univ of Texas at El Paso — BROWN, Susan W. 147
GOODWIN, Charles B. 450
SEAL, Robert A. 1109
Wiggs Middle Sch — WELLS, Frances D. 1322
Ysleta Independent Sch District — BASS, Martha L. 63

FARMERS BRANCH
Farmers Branch Pub Lib — KELLEY, Betty H. 636

FERRIS
Ferris Independent Sch District — REECE, Sue A. 1014

FORT BLISS
US Army Air Defense Artillery Sch — RAMSEY, Donna E. 1005

FT HOOD
US Army Training & Doctrine Command — WILBUR, Sharon F. 1338

TEXAS (Cont'd)

FORT SAM HOUSTON
US Army — ARNN, Judith A. 33

FORT WORTH
Amon Carter Museum — HUGHSTON, Milan R. 572
ROARK, Carol E. 1038
Baptist Book Stores — VERNON, James R. 1283
City of Fort Worth — BRACEY, Ann E. 124
Crowley Independent Sch District — CRAIGHEAD, Alice A. 254
Fort Worth Museum of Science & History — MAULDIN, Lou A. 787
Fort Worth Pub Lib — ALLMAND, Linda F. 17
ARD, Harold J. 31
BALSAM, Frances G. 53
DAVIS, Philip M. 280
DIXON, Catherine A. 306
MUELLER, Peggy 875
SANDEFUR, Kristin T. 1079
Fort Worth Star-Telegram — DE TONNANCOUR, P R. ... 296
General Dynamics Corp — WESTBROOK, Brenda S. ... 1326
Information PLUS — DOWNING, Jeannette D. 316
Kimbell Art Museum — SHIH, Chia C. 1130
Lake Worth Independent Sch District — DUNCAN, Donna P. 325
Motorola Inc — MCVICAR, Ann L. 818
National Archives & Records Admin — SCHMIDT HACKER, Margaret H. 1096
Southwestern Baptist Theological Sem — PHILLIPS, Robert L. 969
RUSSELL, Barbara J. 1068
SIMS, Phillip W. 1142
WROTENBERY, Carl R. ... 1373
Sunny von Bulow Natl Victim Advocacy Ctr — ARBELBIDE, Cindy L. 30
Tarrant County — HOWINGTON, Tad C. 566
WAYLAND, Sharon L. 1311
Tarrant County Junior Coll — MCCRACKEN, Barbara L. ... 799
Tarrant County Law Lib — PERRY, Frances 960
Texas Christian Univ — DUBIEL, Laura R. 321
ECHT, Sandy A. 334
FREEMAN, John P. 401
KARGES, Joann 627
MACDONALD, Hugh 754
OLSEN, Robert A. 921
Texas Coll of Osteopathic Medicine — CARTER, Bobby R. 189
ELAM, Craig S. 341
MASON, Timothy D. 781
WOOD, Richard C. 1365
Texas Wesleyan Coll — CAGE, Willa F. 171
CORLEY, Carol W. 246
FERRIER, Douglas M. 373

FREEPORT
BASF Corp — TYLER-WHITE, Patricia G. . 1266
Dow Chemical USA — WOLFE, Carl F. 1360

GALVESTON
Rosenberg Lib — HYATT, John D. 580
KENAMORE, Jane A. 640
SHEPHERD, Antoinette 1127
SHIPMAN, Natalie W. 1131
Texas A&M Univ — FREY, Emil F. 402
Univ of Texas at Galveston — PHILLIPS, Carol B. 967
WYGANT, Alice C. 1375
WYGANT, Larry J. 1375

GARLAND
Amber Univ — HENDERSON, Lennijo P. 526
LOWRY, Andretta G. 745
City of Garland — CRABB, Elizabeth A. 254
Garland Independent Sch District — STAAS, Gretchen L. 1177
Michael Duren MD — DUREN, Norman 328
Northeast Texas Lib System — MURRAY, Margaret A. 882
QUEYROUZE, Mary E. 999

GEORGE WEST
George West Indpendent Sch District — ROBINS, Barbara D. 1043

GEORGETOWN
Southwestern Univ of Georgetown — BIGLEY, John E. 96
SWARTZ, Jon D. 1214

GLEN ROSE
Limestone Hills Book Shop — KENDALL, Lyle H. 640

GOODFELLOW AFB
US Air Force — PENNER, Elaine C. 957

TEXAS (Cont'd)

GRAHAM

Graham Independent Sch District ... HINSON, Susan K. 543

GRAPEVINE

City of Grapevine ... ROBERSON, Janis L. 1039

Grapevine Pub Lib ... MCCOY, Judy I. 799

GREGORY

Gregory-Portland Independent Sch Dist ... COOK, Anne S. 239

HARLINGEN

City of Harlingen ... MILLS, Helen L. 844

HARROLD

Harrold Independent Sch District ... MCIVER, Lynne A. 809

HENRIETTA

Henrietta Independent Sch District ... MCKAY, Mary F. 810

HOUSTON

Access Information Associates ... SMITH, Dayna F. 1154

Aldine Independent Sch District ... WALKER, Tamara E. 1296

Amerada Hess Petroleum ... MOORE, Guusje Z. 859

Amoco Production Co ... JOHANSEN, Priscilla P. 601

Ashland Exploration Inc ... MATLOCK, Teresa A. 784

Baker & Botts ... DAVIS, Cynthia V. 278

HOPKINS, Joyce A. 558

JOITY, Donna M. 610

Blackwell's ... ALESSI, Dana L. 11

Bracewell & Patterson ... YANCY, Susan M. 1377

Brentanoj ... LANDINGHAM, Alpha M. ... 692

Browning-Ferris Industries Inc ... MAGNER, Mary F. 759

Butler & Binion ... BULL, Margarita A. 156

Chamberlain Hrdlicka White Johnson et al ... TRAFFORD, Susan M. 1253

Chevron USA Inc ... BREWER, Stanley E. 134

RIEMANN, Frederick A. 1033

City of Houston ... DEPETRO, Thomas G. 293

RADOFF, Leonard I. 1002

Clear Creek Independent Sch District ... POWELL, Patricia K. 988

Conoco Inc ... WEST, Barbara F. 1326

CRSS Inc ... FLESHMAN, Nancy A. 384

Daniel Carter Consulting ... CARTER, Daniel H. 189

DIALOG Information Services Inc ... CAMP, Joyce H. 175

Duchesne Academy ... WEATHERS, Barbara H. ... 1312

Elf Aquitaine Petroleum ... POWELL, Alan D. 987

Exxon Production Research Co ... CEBRUN, Mary J. 196

PARRIS, Lou B. 944

Fulbright & Jaworski ... HOLLAND, Jane D. 550

Galena Park Independent Sch District ... SINCLAIR, Rose P. 1143

Gulf Publishing Co ... WILSON, John W. 1351

Harris County Law Lib ... EICHSTADT, John R. 339

Harris County Pub Lib ... GOLDBERG, Rhoda L. 444

NOREM, Monica R. 908

Houston Academy of Medicine ... BAXTER, Barbara A. 67

COLSON, Elizabeth A. 234

GARCIA, Beatriz H. 417

IGNATIEV, Laura 581

KANESHIRO, Kellie N. 625

LYDERS, Richard A. 751

MANN, Caroline E. 765

RAMBO, Neil H. 1005

WHITE, Elizabeth B. 1331

WILSON, Barbara A. 1349

Houston Baptist Univ ... NOBLE, Ann A. 906

Houston Community Coll ... KLAPPERSACK, Dennis ... 657

TEOH, George M. 1231

Houston Independent Sch District ... BLALOCK, Virginia D. 103

HOLDREN, Ann E. 550

MILES, Ruby A. 834

WU, Jean 1373

Houston Lighting & Power Co ... ANDERSON, Eliane G. 22

LOOS, Carolyn F. 740

Houston Museum of Fine Arts ... ROBINSON, Kathleen M. ... 1044

Houston Post ... WORCHEL, Harris M. 1368

Houston Pub Lib ... BROWN, Carol J. 142

BROWN, Freddiemae E. 144

BRYANT, James M. 152

CLARK, Jay B. 217

ENDELMAN, Sharon B. 348

GOLEY, Elaine P. 447

GUBBIN, Barbara A. 475

HANDROW, Margaret M. 495

HENINGTON, David M. 528

TEXAS (Cont'd)

HOUSTON (Cont'd)

Houston Pub Lib ... HOLMAN, Linda E. 553

HORNAK, Anna F. 559

MOORE, Sheryl R. 861

POTIER, Gwendolyn J. 986

SELLIN, Linda M. 1114

TIRRELL, Brenda P. 1247

WILSON, Michael E. 1352

WOHLSCHLAG, Sarah A. ... 1359

ZWICK, Louise Y. 1392

Jacobs Engineering Group ... DAVIS, Sara 281

Kinkaid Sch ... WILLIAMS, Suzanne C. 1346

Lakewood Elementary Sch ... FORD, Delores C. 389

M D Anderson Hospital ... JACKSON, Sara J. 588

Marathon Oil Co ... DICKERSON, Mary J. 300

GILBERT, Barry 433

Mark Producing Inc ... AULBACH, Louis F. 39

McClelland Engineers Inc ... ALIMOHAMMAD, Habiba 13

Mead Data Central ... WEGMANN, Pamela A. 1316

Methodist Hospital ... GIROUARD, J L. 438

Mobil Producing of Texas & New Mexico ... BISHOP, Daran L. 99

Morris Architects ... WIEGMAN, John H. 1336

Museum of Fine Arts ... MOST, Gregory P. 872

SHEAROUSE, Linda N. 1124

Neurofibrometusis Institute Inc ... RICCARDI, Vincent M. 1026

NLP Center of Texas ... HASKELL, Peter C. 510

North Harris County Coll ... PORTER, Exa L. 984

PB-KBB Inc ... HACKNEY, Judith G. 481

Peat Marwick Main & Co ... EMERSON, Beth A. 347

KOHRS, Charlotte A. 669

SHAW, Peggy 1123

Post Oak Quarters ... PHILLIPS, Ray S. 969

Price Waterhouse ... PENDRAK, Eileen 956

Rice Univ ... BABER, Elizabeth A. 43

BAGHAL-KAR, Vali E. 45

BOOTHE, Nancy L. 116

CARRINGTON, Samuel M. .. 186

CRIST, Lynda L. 259

FORD, Margaret C. 389

GOURLAY, Una M. 454

HOLIBAUGH, Ralph W. 550

HUNTER, John H. 576

HYMAN, Ferne B. 580

KECK, Kerry A. 633

SCHWARTZ, Charles A. 1104

SUDENGA, Sara A. 1206

St Agnes Academy ... GOTHIA, Blanche 453

St Francis Episcopal Day Sch ... KOBAYASHI, Lee P. 666

St John's Sch ... MCGOWN, Sue W. 807

San Jacinto Coll ... CRENSHAW, Jan C. 258

Sewell & Riggs ... MAULSBY, Tommie L. 787

WILSON, Ann Q. 1349

Shell Development Co ... BRUNNER, A M. 151

Shell Oil Co ... BAADE, Harley D. 43

CALDWELL, Marlene 172

COTE, Carolee T. 249

DORSETT, Anita W. 313

HOWE, Paula A. 565

KORKMAS, Carolyn C. 671

LYDEN, Edward W. 750

South Texas Coll of Law ... LANGSTON, Sally J. 696

SCHWERBEl, Jeannette E. .. 1105

THOMPSON, Frances H. ... 1239

Spring Branch Independent Sch District ... MEADOR, Cornie M. 819

Tenneco Inc ... BAILEY, Linda S. 46

MULLINS, James R. 878

Texas Allergy Research Foundation ... MCGOVERN, John P. 807

Texas Eastern Corp ... KIRTNER, R R. 655

LUECKENHOFF, Anne F. 747

Texas Instruments Inc ... MANNING, Helen M. 766

Texas Southern Univ ... BEAN, Norma P. 69

BUTLER, Marguerite L. 166

CHAMPION, Walter T. 198

SCHIELACK, Tricia J. 1092

Touche Ross & Co ... MCCANN, Debra W. 794

Union Pacific Resources ... WRIGHT, Craig W. 1371

Union Texas Petroleum

TEXAS (Cont'd)
HOUSTON (Cont'd)
Univ of Houston — ADDISON, Jane G. 6
BOWMAN, Laura M. 122
CHANG, Robert H. 201
CORBIN, John 245
CRAIG, Marilyn J. 254
DOWNES, Robin N. 316
FIELDING, Raymond E. 376
HALL, John D. 488
HOTVEDT, Eileen A. 562
KIMZEY, Ann C. 649
LOPICCOLO, Cathy J. 741
LYDERS, Josette A. 750
WEISBAUM, Earl 1319
WELCH, C B. 1321
WILSON, Thomas C. 1353
Univ of St Thomas — WALKER, Constance M. ... 1295
Univ of Texas at Houston — CHUANG, Felicia S. 213
TEUN, Rebecca L. 1233
WILLIAMS, Ann T. 1342
Utility Fuels Inc — PHILLIPS, Toni M. 969
Vinson & Elkins — GRUBEN, Karl T. 474
Vista Chemical Co — ATRI, Pushkala V. 38
Weil Gotshal & Manges — BLACK, Elizabeth A. 101
Westbury Christian Sch — STUBBLEFIELD, J G. 1204
HUFFMAN
Huffman Independent Sch District — SHARP, Betty L. 1122
HUNTSVILLE
Sam Houston State Univ — BAILEY, William G. 47
BURKS, Paula 161
BURT, Lesta N. 164
CARTER, Betty B. 189
CULP, Paul M. 264
HARNSBERGER, R S. 503
HOFFMAN, Frank W. 548
KIM, David U. 648
PARIS, Janelle A. 940
PICHETTE, William H. 970
THORNE, Bonnie B. 1242
WILSON, Craig A. 1350
HURST
Tarrant County Junior Coll — FITE, Vicki A. 382
IRVING
Caltex Petroleum Corp — HUMMEL, Muriel H. 573
City of Irving — LEVINE, Harriet L. 720
DeVry Institute of Technology — COCHRAN, Carolyn 225
Frito-Lay Inc — ARNOLD, Patricia K. 34
Irving Independent Sch District — LANKFORD, Mary D. 696
Irving Pub Lib — AYRES, Edwin M. 43
PALMER, Judith L. 936
National Museum of Communications
Inc — BRAGG, William J. 127
Univ of Dallas — BAKER, Nettie L. 49
HAGLE, Claudette S. 483
WHITE, Lely K. 1331
WORLEY, Larry J. 1369
JACKSONVILLE
Baptist Missionary Assn Theological
Sem — BLAYLOCK, James C. 105
KELLER
City of Keller — EASON, Lisa H. 332
Keller Independent Sch District — BERRY, Mary A. 90
KILGORE
Kilgore Junior Coll — CLAER, Joycelyn H. 215
JACKSON, Marian D. 588
KILLEEN
American Educational Complex — MOSS, Charmagne L. 872
American Technological Univ — GUTHRIE, Melinda L. 479
KINGSVILLE
Kingsville Independent Sch District — MERCHANT, Cheryl N. 825
Santa Gertrudis Independent Sch
District — HUNTER, Cecilia A. 576
KINGWOOD
North Harris County Coll — PEYTON, Janice L. 966
KIRBYVILLE
City of Kirbyville — SAULSBURY, Margie M. 1084
KRUM
Krum Independent Sch District — LANGA, Patricia A. 695

TEXAS (Cont'd)
LA MARQUE
City of La Marque — NEALE, Marilee 891
LA PORTE
San Jacinto Museum of History Assn — ATKINS, Winston 38
LACKLAND AFB
US Air Force — BLACK, Katherine S. 101
LAREDO
Laredo State Univ — BRESIE, Mayellen 133
US Information Agency — MULLER, Mary M. 877
LEANDER
Leander Independent Sch District — SMITH, Lorraine K. 1157
LEVELLAND
South Plains Coll — STRICKLAND, Jimmy R. 1202
LIBERTY
City of Liberty — PICKETT, Ellen W. 970
Texas State Lib — SCHAADT, Robert L. 1088
LITTLE ELM
Little Elm Independent Sch District — FRITSCH, Janet E. 405
LOCKHART
Lockhart Independent Sch Dist — HOLLAND, Deborah K. 550
LONGVIEW
LeTourneau Coll — GRAY, Paul W. 460
Longview Independent Sch District — NYLUND, Carol L. 912
LUBBOCK
City of Lubbock — CHAPMAN, Katherine 202
Lubbock City County Lib — HARP, Marlene M. 503
Texas Tech Univ — ANDREWS, Virginia L. 27
CARGILL, Jennifer S. 181
CASELLA, Roberta L. 192
CLUFF, E D. 223
DUFFY, Suzanne 324
KELLEY, Carol M. 636
LINDSEY, Thomas K. 730
LUIKART, Nancy B. 747
MARLEY, Judith L. 772
MARX, Patricia C. 780
OLM, Jane G. 921
PEDERSEN, Judy K. 954
SARGENT, Charles W. 1082
TROST, Theresa K. 1258
VAN SCHAIK, Jo A. 1277
VUGRIN, Margaret Y. 1289
WARD, Deborah H. 1303
WEBB, Gisela M. 1313
LUMBERTON
Lumberton Independent Sch District — POOL, Jeraldine B. 982
MARSHALL
East Texas Baptist Univ — MAGRILL, Rose M. 760
MCALLEN
McAllen Memorial Lib — MITTELSTAEDT, Gerard E. .. 850
MCKINNEY
City of McKinney — DOYLE, Patricia L. 317
Collin County Community Coll District — CORREDOR, Javier 247
Collin County Law Lib — BALCOMBE, Judith A. 51
MESQUITE
Dallas County Community Coll District — DUMONT, Paul E. 325
EWALT, Rosalind H. 359
Mesquite Independent Sch District — MANN, Carol A. 765
Mesquite Pub Lib — BYROM, Jeanne 170
LARSON, Jeanette C. 699
MIAMI
Miami Independent Sch District — LOTMAN, Marion O. 742
MIDLAND
Midland Coll — MIRANDA, Cecilia 847
MINERAL WELLS
Mineral Well Independent Sch
System — CHESHER, Joyce A. 206
MISSION
Mission Consolidated Independent
Schs — ANDIS, Norma B. 26
PONTIUS, Louise 982
MISSOURI
Fort Bend Independent Sch District — DIXON, Donna S. 306
NACOGDOCHES
Stephen F Austin State Univ — CAGE, Alvin C. 170
MUCKLEROY, Sue A. 875
SCAMMAN, Carol J. 1087

TEXAS (Cont'd)

NEW BRAUNFELS
Dittlinger Memorial Lib   MCENTEE, Mary F. 804
Sophienburg Museum & Archives   SCHUMANN, Iris T. 1103
NORTH RICHLAND HILLS
North Richland Hills Pub Lib   HALLAM, Arlita W. 489
                                                           MACFARLANE, Francis X. . . 755
                                                           STATTON, Alison H. 1183
ODESSA
Ector County Lib   COPELAND, David R. 244
Univ of Texas of the Permian Basin   GROVES, Helen G. 474
                                                           KLEPPER, Bobbie J. 660
                                                           LINDSAY, Lorin H. 729
PALESTINE
Palestine Independent Sch District   WILLIAMSON, Lanelle S. . . 1347
Palestine Pub Lib   SELWYN, Laurie 1114
PHARR
Pharr Memorial Lib   LIU, David T. 734
PLANO
ARCO Oil & Gas Co   PROKESH, Jane 995
Plano Pub Lib System   BONNELL, Pamela G. 114
                                                           DEILY, Carole C. 288
Texas Instruments Inc   ANDERSON, Margaret 24
                                                           HULSE, Phyllis 573
                                                           LUTZ, Linda A. 750
                                                           MURPHY, Pency G. 881
                                                           SHARP, Charlotte J. 1122
PORT ARKANSAS
Port Arkansas Independent Sch
 District   DAVIS, Joan C. 279
PRAIRIE VIEW
Prairie View A&M Univ   ADAMS, Elaine P. 4
                                                           KUJOORY, Parvin 683
                                                           WACHTER-NELSON, Ruth
                                                            M. 1290
                                                           YEH, Helen S. 1379
RICHARDSON
Anderson Clayton Foods   MARTIN, Irmgarde D. 776
Bell-Northern Research   CASTO, Lisa A. 194
F Y I Associates   SCHRAEDER, Diana C. 1099
Richardson Independent Sch District BELL, Jo A. 77
                                                           GRAY, Gloria M. 460
Rockwell International   COTTER, Stacy L. 250
Univ of Texas at Dallas   ALLEN, Joan W. 15
                                                           HENEBRY, Carolyn L. 528
                                                           KRATZ, Abby R. 676
                                                           NISONGER, Thomas E. 905
                                                           OLSSON, Margaret G. 923
                                                           SAFLEY, Ellen D. 1074
                                                           SALL, Larry D. 1076
                                                           SHEA, Kathleen 1124
                                                           SOUTHARD, Ruth K. 1169
Varix Corp   SACKETT-WILK, Susan A. . . 1073
RICHMOND
Fort Bend County   JARMUSZ, Ruth M. 594
ROCKDALE
Rockdale Independent Sch District   WORTHY, Annie B. 1369
ROPESVILLE
Ropes Independent Sch District   SHANNON, Jerry B. 1120
ROUND ROCK
City of Round Rock   RICKLEFS, Dale L. 1032
Round Rock Pub Lib   JOHNSTON, L J. 610
ROWLETT
County of Dallas & City of Rowlett   CROUCH, Vivian E. 261
SAGINAW
City of Saginaw   COPELAND, Sara O. 214
SAN ANGELO
Tom Green County Pub Lib System   LACY, Yvonne M. 687
SAN ANTONIO
Alamo Community Coll District   HOLLOWAY, Geraldine B. . . . 552
                                                           METZGER, Oscar F. 829
Archdiocese of San Antonio   LOCH, Edward J. 735
City of San Antonio   GRUENBECK, Laurie 474
                                                           MCCONNELL, Ruth M. 798
                                                           MYLER, Josephine P. 885
                                                           SEXTON, Irwin 1118
Daughters of the Republic of Texas   HOOD, Sandra D. 556
Edgar Allan Poe Middle Sch   THEISS, Diane M. 1234
Fulbright & Jaworski   VELA-CREIXELL, Mary I. . . 1281

TEXAS (Cont'd)

SAN ANTONIO (Cont'd)
Hispanic Baptist Theological
 Seminary   WALLACE, James O. 1297
Incarnate Word Coll   DUNCAN, Lucy E. 325
Kelbry Enterprises   HEWINS, Elizabeth H. 535
McCamish Ingram Martin & Brown
 PC   HURT, Nancy S. 578
Meta Micro Library Systems Inc   LEATHERBURY, Maurice C. . 707
Mind Science Foundation   MORTON, Diane E. 870
National Autonomous Univ of Mexico MANEY, Lana E. 765
North East Independent Sch District   HAAS, Ruth M. 480
                                                           MCBURNEY, Lynnea R. 792
Northside Independent Sch District   FRIEDMAN, Tevia L. 404
Oblate Sch of Theology   MANEY, James W. 765
Our Lady of the Lake Univ   SHAPIRO, Lenore M. 1121
St Mary's Univ   GOERDT, Arthur L. 443
                                                           HENRICKS, Duane E. 529
                                                           HICKEY, Lady J. 536
San Antonio Coll   BALCOM, Karen S. 51
                                                           DRUMMOND, Donald R. . . . 321
San Antonio Pub Lib   BENSON, Joyce 83
Sawtelle Goode Davidson & Troilo   SPRINGER, Michelle M. . . . 1176
Southwest Foundation   BROOKS, Ruth H. 140
Southwest Research Institute   LANG, Anita E. 695
Southwest Texas Methodist Hospital   HOUKE, Billy P. 563
Trinity Univ   BADING, Kathryn E. 44
                                                           BARRINGER, Sallie H. 60
                                                           CARMACK, Norma J. 183
                                                           CLARKSON, Mary C. 219
                                                           FORD, Barbara J. 389
                                                           HOOD, Elizabeth 556
                                                           LIKNESS, Craig S. 727
                                                           NOLAN, Christopher W. 907
                                                           WERKING, Richard H. 1324
United Services Automobile
 Association   PHILLIPS, Sylvia E. 969
Univ of Texas at San Antonio   CRINION, Jacquelyn A. 259
                                                           JOSEPH, Margaret A. 617
                                                           KRONICK, David A. 679
                                                           RAY, Joyce M. 1011
                                                           SCHMELZIE, Joan C. 1094
Univ of Texas Health Science Center HANKS, Ellen T. 496
                                                           JONES, Daniel H. 612
                                                           PEDERSEN, Wayne A. 954
USAA Group   TODD, Leslie N. 1248
SAN BENITO
City of San Benito   GARAZA, Noemi 417
SAN MARCOS
San Marcos Pub Lib   RODE, Shelley J. 1047
Southwest Texas State Univ   CAINE, William C. 171
                                                           HUSTON, Susan S. 578
                                                           MEARS, William F. 820
                                                           RILEY, Richard K. 1034
                                                           WEATHERS, Jerry D. 1312
SANTE FE
City of Santa Fe   MCLENNA, D S. 814
SCHERTZ
City of Schertz   DOUGLAS, Virginia G. 314
SEGUIN
Texas Lutheran Coll   HSU, Patrick K. 567
                                                           KOOPMAN, Frances A. 671
SHERMAN
City of Sherman   WALLER, Hope C. 1298
Law & Order   GARCIA, Lana C. 417
SILSBEE
City of Silsbee   JOHNSON, Cathy 603
SOUTHLAKE
Carroll Independent Sch District   BROWN, Judith A. 145
STEPHENVILLE
Tarleton State Univ   TEVEBAUGH, Joyce E. 1233
SUGAR LAND
Fort Bend Independent Sch District   LOCKETT, Iva 736
LSI   JOHNSON, Pat M. 608
SWEETWATER
County-City Lib   MCSWEENEY, Bonnie 818

TEXAS (Cont'd)

TEMPLE
City of Temple — TIME, Ming M. 1245
Dyess Grove Inc — RICE, Ralph A. 1027
Olin E Teague Veterans Center — HEMPEL, Ruth M. 525
Scott & White Memorial Hospital — WORLEY, Merry P. 1369

TEXAS CITY
City of Texas City — MONCLA, Carolyn S. 854

THE COLONY
City of The Colony — SVEINSSON, Joan L. 1212
Colony Pub Lib — DAVIS, Mary F. 280

THE WOODLANDS
Betz Libs Inc — WEST, Deborah C. 1326
Glen Loch Elementary Sch — MILLER, Carol A. 836
IR Concepts Inc — FRAMEL, Phyllis M. 395

TYLER
City of Tyler — ALBERTSON, Christopher A. 10
HARPER, Sarah H. 503
Tyler Independent Sch District — LAMBERTH, Linda E. 690
Tyler Junior Coll — KENNEDY, Johnnye 641
WILSON, George N. 1351
Univ of Texas Health Science Center — CRAIG, Thomas B. 254

UNIVERSAL CITY
Schertz Cibolo Universal City ISD — YOUNG, Marjie D. 1382

UVALDE
Southwest Texas Junior Coll — KINGSBERY, Evelyn B. 652

VICTORIA
Univ of Houston — ALLEN, Virginia M. 16
Victoria Coll & Univ of Houston — MCCORD, Stanley J. 798
Victoria Independent Sch District — FRANKSON, Marie S. 398

WACO
Baylor Univ — COLEY, Betty A. 231
GEARY, Gregg S. 424
HILLMAN, Kathy R. 541
HUGHES, Sue M. 572
KENDRICK, Susan 640
SEAMAN, Helen D. 1109
SHARP, Avery T. 1122
SHEETS, Janet E. 1125
SPARKMAN, Glenda K. 1171
TOLBERT, Jean F. 1248
City of Waco — PROGAR, Dorothy R. 995
Paul Quinn Coll — KEATTS, Rowena W. 633
Richards Piano Service — RICHARDS, James H. 1028
Waco Independent Sch — CARPENTER, Charlotte L. ... 184

WAUTAUGA
City of Watauga — MCCURDY, Sandra A. 801

WEATHERFORD
Weatherford Public Lib — HEEZEN, Ronald R. 520

WELCH
Dawson Independent Sch District — SPRADLING, Nancy L. 1175

WESLACO
Weslaco Indiana Sch District — JOHNSON, Patricia T. 608

WICHITA FALLS
Information Systems — GRIMES, John F. 470
Midwestern State Univ — COFFEY, Sue E. 227
HARVILL, Melba S. 509
Wichita Falls Pub Schs — MCCULLEY, Lois P. 800
Wichita Falls State Hospital — ROBERTS, Ernest J. 1040

WIMBERLEY
Info-Search — SHAW, Ben B. 1123
O'Connor Ranch Book & Historical Project — WAYLAND, Terry T. 1311

WYLIE
Wylie Independent Sch District — WEISLAK, Susan L. 1319

UTAH

AMERICAN FORK
American Fork City — TOMLIN, Celia K. 1250

FARMINGTON
Davis County Lib — GIACOMA, Pete J. 430
LAYTON, A J. 705

LOGAN
Intermountain Community Lrng & Info Srvs — SPYKERMAN, Bryan R. ... 1177
Utah State Univ — ANDERSON, Janet A. 23
HAYCOCK, Richard C. 515
NIELSEN, Steven P. 903
PIETTE, Mary I. 972

UTAH (Cont'd)

LOGAN (Cont'd)
Utah State Univ — WEISS, Stephen C. 1320

MAGNA
Hercules Inc — PARTRIDGE, Cathleen F. ... 945
Salt Lake County Lib System — KITE, Yvonne D. 657

MURRAY
Murray City Pub Lib — SLUSHER, Donna C. 1150

OGDEN
US Dept of Agriculture Forest Service — CLOSE, Elizabeth G. 223
Weber County Lib — WILSON, Brenda J. 1350
ZEDNEY, Francis L. 1387

PRICE
Price City — SOWER, Marjorie T. 1170

PROVO
Brigham Young Univ — ALBRECHT, Sterling J. 10
BROADWAY, Marsha D. 138
CHANDLER, Jody A. 200
FLAKE, Chad J. 383
GELDMACHER, Bonnie R. .. 425
GILLUM, Gary P. 436
GOULD, Douglas A. 454
HALL, Blaine H. 487
ISOBE, Darron T. 585
JONES, Ruth J. 615
LAMB, Connie 689
LARSEN, A D. 698
LYMAN, Lovisa 751
MARCHANT, Maurice P. 768
MATHIESEN, Thomas J. 784
NELSON, Veneese C. 895
NIELSEN, Paula I. 903
OLSEN, Randy J. 921
PURDY, Victor W. 998
ROWLEY, Edward D. 1063
SHIELDS, Dorthy M. 1130
SMITH, Nathan M. 1159
SWENSEN, Dale S. 1215
WIGGINS, Marvin E. 1337
YANG, Basil P. 1377
DYNIX Inc — PETERSON, Douglas L. 963
WILSON, D K. 1350

SAINT GEORGE
Washington County Free Lib — SHIRTS, Russell B. 1131

SALT LAKE CITY
American Express Co — POLLARD, Louise 981
Bonneville Telecommunications — MEIER, Joe 821
Church of Jesus Christ Latter-day Saints — CASADY, Richard L. 191
CLEMENT, Charles R. 221
CUMMINGS, Christopher H. . 264
KIESSLING, Mary S. 647
MAYFIELD, David M. 790
REED, Vernon M. 1015
Corp of the President — CLEMENT, Patsy 221
Deseret News Publishing Co — CLARK, Audrey M. 216
Division of State History — HAYMOND, Jay M. 516
Family History Lib — SPERRY, Kip 1174
Intermountain Health Care Inc — JAMES, Brent C. 592
LDS Hospital — HEYER, Terry L. 535
Mainstream Data — BENNION, John F. 82
Mountainwest Coll of Business & Tech — MCMURRIN, Jean A. 815
Norton Christensen Inc — LIU, Kitty P. 734
St Mark's Hospital — SKIDMORE, Kerry F. 1146
Salt Lake City Pub Lib — DAY, J D. 282
EDMUNDSON, Margaret B. .. 336
GIAUGUE, James A. 431
GOFORTH, Allene M. 444
Salt Lake City Sch District — BURKS, C J. 161
KARPISEK, Marian E. 628
OLSEN, Katherine M. 921
PETERSON, Francine 963
Salt Lake Community Coll — STECKER, Alexander T. ... 1183
Salt Lake County Lib System — ELLEFSEN, David 343
FUJIMOTO, Jan D. 408
MARCHANT, Cathy 768
SCHUURMAN, Guy 1103
TALBERT, Dorothy R. 1220

UTAH (Cont'd)
SALT LAKE CITY (Cont'd)

State of Utah — SCOTT, Patricia L. 1107
Third Judicial Court — CHENG, Nancy H. 206
Unisys Corp — NOEL, Eileen V. 907
US Court of Appeals — HUMMEL, Patricia A. 573
Univ of Utah — ANGIER, Jennifer J. 27
BAILEY, Clint R. 46
DOGU, Hikmet S. 309
HAGGERTY, Maxine R. 483
HANSON, Roger K. 498
HINZ, Julianne P. 543
HOLLEY, Robert P. 551
KRANZ, Ralph 676
MOGREN, Paul A. 852
MORRISON, David L. 868
PATTERSON, Myron B. 948
REDDICK, Mary J. 1013
RUHLIN, Michele T. 1066
STODDART, Joan M. 1196
THOMSON, Ralph D. 1242
VAN ORDEN, Richard D. ... 1276
ZEIDNER, Christine M. 1387
Utah State Archives & Records Service — HEFNER, Loretta L. 520
JOHNSON, Jeffery O. 606
MOORE, Gwen A. 859
NASH, Cherie A. 888
WOOD, Steven R. 1365
Utah State Government — JENSEN, Charla J. 598
Utah State Historical Society — EVANS, Max J. 357
Utah State Lib — BUTTARS, Gerald A. 167
DOWNEY REIDA, Linda K. ... 316
HINDMARSH, Douglas P. 542
OWEN, Amy 931

VERMONT
BATTLEBORO
Town of Brattleboro — MORRISON, Meris E. 868
BENNINGTON
Bennington Free Lib — PRICE, Michael L. 992
Hemmings Motor News — GILCHER, Edwin 434
BRATTLEBORO
Academy School — HAY, Linda A. 515
BROOKFIELD
Brookfield Publishing Co — GERARD, James W. 428
BURLINGTON
Ashley Book Company — SINGER, George C. 1143
Champlain Coll — POPECKI, Jeanne M. 983
Dinse Erdmann & Clapp — ABAZARNIA, Diane B. 1
Trinity Coll — YERBURGH, Mark R. 1379
Univ of Vermont — CASWELL, Jerry V. 194
CROUCH, Milton H. 261
DAY, Martha T. 282
DURFEE, Tamara 328
EATON, Nancy L. 334
GALLAGHER, Connell B. 413
LEE, Donna K. 709
REIT, Janet W. 1022
SEKERAK, Robert J. 1113
WEINSTOCK, Joanna S. 1318
CASTLETON
Castleton State Coll — LUZER, Nancy H. 750
CHESTER
Readex Inc — BOCK, Thomas A. 109
CRAFTSBURY COMMON
Sterling Coll — PATERSON, Elizabeth N. ... 947
FAIRFAX
Vermont Department of Libs — WARD, Robert C. 1304
MANCHESTER
Burr and Burton Seminary — ELLIS, Margaret D. 345
MIDDLEBURY
City of Middlebury — REED, Sally G. 1015
Middlebury Coll — ECKERT, Sharon S. 335
MCBRIDE, Jerry L. 792
POST, Jennifer C. 986
RAUM, Hans L. 1010
REHBACH, Jeffrey R. 1017
RUCKER, Ronald E. 1065

VERMONT (Cont'd)
MONTPELIER
Agency of Administration — YACAVONI, A J. 1376
State of Vermont — KLINCK, Patricia E. 661
Vermont Department of Libs — CASSELL, Marianne K. 193
GREENE, Grace W. 464
NORTHFIELD
Norwich Univ — LINDBERG, Sandra 728
PITTSFIELD
Infotech — SCHWERIN, Julie B. 1106
PROCTOR
Proctor Junior-Senior High Sch — SHERMAN, Madeline R. ... 1128
PUTNEY
Landmark Coll — THOMPSON, Jane K. 1240
RANDOLPH CENTER
Vermont Technical Coll — PATTERSON, Dewey F. 948
RUTLAND
Coll of St Joseph — MCCULLOUGH, Doreen J. .. 801
Ruthland Hospital — STANLEY, Donald E. 1180
Rutland Free Lib — SHERMAN, Jacob R. 1128
ST JOHNSBURY
Downs Rachlin and Martin — BROWNE, Wynne W. 148
New Amberola Phonograph Co — BRYAN, Martin F. 151
St Johnsbury Academy — THOMPSON, Judith H. 1240
SOUTH BURLINGTON
Green Mountain Power Corp — HERNDON, Stan J. 532
South Burlington Community Lib — KNEELAND, Marjorie H. ... 664
SOUTH ROYALTON
Vermont Technical Coll — LAMSON, Maria W. 691
SPRING HOLLOW LANE
Oral Hist Inst — MORRISSEY, Charles T. 869
SPRINGFIELD
Town of Springfield — MOORE, Russell S. 861
VERNON
Vernon Free Lib — EVANS, Nancy I. 357
WATERBURY
Waterbury Village Pub Lib — HIRSCH, Barbara S. 543
WILLIAMSTOWN
Orange North Supervisory Union — BATTEY, Jean D. 64
WOODSTOCK
Woodstock Foundation — SWIFT, Esther M. 1216
Woodstock Union High Sch — DICENSO, Jacquelyn C. 300

VIRGIN ISLANDS
CHARLOTTE AMALIE
Virgin Islands Government — BARZELAY, Mary S. 62
ST CROIX
Aye-Aye Press — VAUGHN, Robert V. 1280
Blind & Physically Handicapped Regnl Lib — HERZ, Michael J. 534
Virgin Islands Department of Health — BRONSTEIN, Dorothy J. 140
Virgin Islands Lib Association — WILLIAMS, Wallace D. 1347
ST THOMAS
Government of the US Virgin Islands — CHANG, Henry C. 200
SOUFFRONT, Blanche L. .. 1169
St Thomas Department of Education — MACLEAN, Ellen G. 757
MILLS, Fiolina B. 844
Saints Peter & Paul Schs — STEIN, Josephine M. 1185
Virgin Islands Department of Education — MILLER, Veronica E. 843
PHARES, Abner J. 967

VIRGINIA
ABINGDON
Washington County Pub Lib — JESSEE, Brenda J. 600
ALEXANDRIA
Alexandria City Pub Schools — BROWN, Dale W. 143
Alexandria Hospital — HAMILTON, Elizabeth J. 492
Alexandria Pub Lib — EFFRON, Barbara L. 338
HINDMAN, Pamela J. 542
MERRIFIELD, Mark D. 826
PLITT, Jeanne G. 978
RUDOLF, Christine T. 1066
American Assn for Counseling & Devlpmnt — NISENOFF, Sylvia 905
American Society for Training & Devlpmnt — OLIVETTI, L J. 921
American Trucking Associations — ROTHBART, Linda S. 1060
Atlantic Research Corp — WALDE, Norma J. 1294
Bechtel Information Services — JONES, Frank 613

VIRGINIA (Cont'd)
ALEXANDRIA (Cont'd)
Burns Doane Swecker & Mathis	VODRA, Carol	1286
CEAC Computers Inc	KAISER, Donald W.	622
Center for Naval Analyses	HANNA, Jill C.	496
Chadwyck-Healey Inc	HAMILTON, Wellington M.	492
	SEVERTSON, Susan M.	1117
Computer Corp of America	BERGMAN, Rita F.	86
Defense Technical Information Center	COTTER, Gladys A.	250
	LAHR, Thomas F.	688
	LESSER, Barbara	718
	ROTHSCHILD, M C.	1060
	RYAN, R P.	1071
	SCHLAG, Gretchen A.	1093
Editorial Experts Inc	MORSE, June E.	869
Fairfax County Board of Education	GIEGERICH, M P.	433
Fairfax County Pub Lib	CHAUVETTE, Catherine A.	204
Franklin Research Center	GOLDENBERG, Joan M.	445
GEAC Computers Inc	GATTONE, Dean R.	422
	WEIST, Melody S.	1320
Information Workstation Group	GALE, John C.	413
Institute for Defense Analyses	SWEENEY, Joan L.	1215
JHK & Associates	HATHAWAY, Kay E.	512
Lib of Congress	MORGAN, Robert C.	864
Michaels Associates Design Consultants	MICHAELS, Andrea A.	831
	MICHAELS, David L.	832
Mount Vernon Community Center Sch	OSIA, Ruby R.	928
Northern Virginia Community Coll	JORDAN, Katherine H.	616
	TERWILLIGER, Gloria P.	1232
United Fresh Fruit & Vegetable Assn	MCLAUGHLIN, Elaine C.	813
US Army	BONNETT, Mary B.	114
US Army Research Institute	CASWELL, Mary C.	194
US Department of Agriculture	DENGROVE, Richard A.	292
US Department of Defense	JACOBSON, Carol E.	590
US Navy	TEAL, Erika U.	1229
Virginia Lib Association	TROCCHI, Debbie	1257

ANNANDALE
Fairfax County Pub Schs	HUNT, Linda A.	575
	TYSINGER, Barbara R.	1267
Marine Technology Society	MATON, Joanne T.	784
Mary C Chobot and Associates	CHOBOT, Mary C.	210
Northern Virginia Community Coll	BERNHARDT, Frances	89

APPOMATTOX
Appomattox County Lib	KEMPTER, Albert H.	640

ARLINGTON
American Defense Preparedness Assoc	CLARKE, Robert F.	219
American Gas Association	DORNER, Steven J.	313
American Management Systems Inc	GLAMM, Amy E.	439
	YODER, William M.	1380
American Psychological Association	DESSAINT, Alain Y.	295
	GOSLING, Carolyn	453
	GRANICH, Lois	457
	KNIGHT, Nancy H.	664
	LARMOUR, Rosamond E.	698
	MCKENNEY, Linda S.	811
Arlington County Department of Libs	BRITTO, Mary M.	137
	BROWN, Charles M.	142
	COLLINS, Sara D.	233
	COOPER, Nancy C.	243
	FISHER, Carl D.	380
	HABERLAND, Jody	481
	WEILERSTEIN, Deborah E.	1317
Arlington County Pub Schs	LAM, Letitia E.	689
Arlington Pub Lib	SWICEGOOD, Mary R.	1216
Arlington Pub Schs	YAEGER, Luke R.	1376
Bishop Denis J O'Connell High Sch	MCKELVEY, Mary J.	810
Booz Allen & Hamilton Inc	CIPRIANI, Debra A.	215
Bush Hartt & Kingsbury Inc	HARTT, Richard W.	509
Department of State	SUMMERS, Kathy B.	1209
DIALOG Information Services Inc	CAPUTO, Anne S.	180
	CAPUTO, Richard P.	180
Gannett Co Inc	WELLS, Christine	1322
George Mason Univ	BERWICK, Philip C.	91
	MCGINN, Ellen T.	806
	SAUR, Cindy S.	1085

VIRGINIA (Cont'd)
ARLINGTON (Cont'd)
Herner and Co	DAY, Melvin S.	283
	LUNIN, Lois F.	749
	STEIN, Rene S.	1185
International Thomson Lib Service	ASLESON, Robert F.	36
Labat-Anderson Inc	BRUNER, Linda J.	150
Lib of Congress	JACKSON, Nancy G.	588
Marymount Junior Sch	PYKE, Carol J.	999
Marymount Univ	CARR, Timothy B.	186
	LEATHER, Deborah J.	707
National Archives & Records Admin	ASHKENAS, Bruce F.	36
Natl Assoc of Industrial & Office Parks	HAUCK, Janice B.	512
REMAC Info Corp	ALEXANDER, Carol G.	12
Research Publications	MEREK, Charles J.	825
Richard E Wolf and Associates	WOLF, Richard E.	1360
Science Applications International Corp	MOORE, Penelope F.	861
System Planning Corp	MERCURY, Nicholas E.	825
US Patent & Trademark Office	MELVIN, Kay H.	823
Vector Biology & Control Project	AUSTON, Ione	40
World Methodist Historical Society	CALKIN, Homer L.	173

ASHLAND
Randolph-Macon Coll	BEDSOLE, Dan T.	73

BLACKSBURG
Virginia Polytechnic Inst & State Univ	BAER, Eberhard A.	44
	COCHRANE, Lynn S.	225
	EASTMAN, Ann H.	333
	GLENNON, Irene F.	441
	HINKLE, Mary R.	542
	KOK, Victoria T.	669
	KRIZ, Harry M.	679
	NORSTEDT, Marilyn L.	909
	RASMUSSEN, Lane D.	1009
	RICHARDSON, Linda B.	1029
	SPAHR, Janet E.	1170
Virginia Tech	COSGRIFF, John C.	248
	ENGELBRECHT, Pamela N.	349
	FOX, Edward A.	394
	GHERMAN, Paul M.	430
	KENNEY, Donald J.	641
	METZ, Paul D.	828
VTLS Inc	ESPLEY, John L.	354
	LEE, Carl R.	709
The Walrus Press	JOHNSON, Bryan R.	602

BRIDGEWATER
Bridgewater Coll	GREENAWALT, Ruth A.	463
Rockingham County Sch Board	WAMPLER, Dorris M.	1302

BRISTOL
Bristol Pub Lib	POWERS, Linda J.	989
Virginia Intermont Coll	HANLON, Gloria L.	496

CENTREVILLE
Fairfax County Pub Lib	JONES, Sue P.	615

CHARLOTTESVILLE
Albemarle County	KEYSER, Sue C.	645
GE Fanuc Automation Inc	COX, Tina S.	253
Institute of Textile Technology	LAWRENCE, Philip D.	704
	LOY, Dennis C.	745
Jefferson-Madison Regional Lib	ANDERSON, Valerie J.	25
	BERNE, Beth	88
	EVERINGHAM, Neil G.	358
	MORRIS, Karen L.	867
Kelly Communications	CAHILL, Linda J.	171
National Radio Astronomy Observatory	BOUTON, Ellen N.	119
Piedmont Virginia Community Coll	EISENBERG, Phyllis B.	340
	GRANITZ, Adrienne D.	457
Univ of Virginia	BADER, Susan G.	44
	BADERTSCHER, David A.	44
	BERKELEY, Edmund	87
	BRAUN, Mina H.	129
	CAMPBELL, James M.	176
	COOPER, Jean L.	243
	DUNNIGAN, Mary C.	327
	FARMER, Frances	364
	FRANTZ, Ray W.	398
	HURD, Douglas P.	577
	IVES, Gary W.	585
	JORDAN, Ervin L.	616

VIRGINIA (Cont'd)

CHARLOTTESVILLE (Cont'd)
Univ of Virginia

KRAEHE, Mary A. 674
LESTER, Linda L. 718
LINDEMANN, Richard H. . . . 729
MALMQUIST, Katherine E. . . 763
PANCAKE, Edwina 937
RODRIGUEZ, Robert D. . . . 1048
SADOWSKI, Frank E. 1074
SELF, James R. 1113
SLEEMAN, Allison M. 1148
STUBBS, Kendon L. 1204
STURGIS, Marylee C. 1205
THORKILDSON, Terry A. . . 1242
WALKER, Diane P. 1295
WHITE, Lynda S. 1331
WYNNE, Joseph J. 1375

CHESAPEAKE
City of Chesapeake   FOREHAND, Margaret P. . . . 390
                                REID, Kendall M. 1018

CHESTERFIELD
Chesterfield County Pub Lib   DUNAWAY, Carolyn D. 325
                                WAGENKNECHT, Robert E. 1291

CHRISTIANSBURG
Montgomery-Floyd Regional Lib   COMPARIN, Ida 235
Virginia Polytechnic Inst & State Univ LINN, Cynthia S. 731

COURTLAND
Walter Cecil Rawls Lib & Museum JOHNSON, Kenneth P. 606

DAHLGREN
US Navy   HUGHES, J M. 571

DANVILLE
Averett Coll   GRANT, Juanita G. 458
Danville Community Coll   JOHNSON, Martha A. 607
Memorial Hospital of Danville   SASSER, Ann B. 1083

DELAPLANE
Davenport Films   DAVENPORT, Thomas R. . . . 276

DISPUTANTA
Prince George's County Pub Schs JACKSON, F C. 587

DUMFRIES
Prince William County Pub Schs GAUDET, Jean A. 422
                                HOSKINS, Sylvia H. 561

EDINBURG
Shenandoah County Lib   STEINBERG, David L. 1185

EMORY
Emory & Henry Coll   JENNERICH, Elaine Z. 598

FAIRFAX
Association for Recorded Sound Cols ROCHLIN, Phillip 1046
Caci Inc   HUCK, Dan 569
                                SULLIVAN, Michael M. 1208
Central Michigan Univ   KINGSLEY, Marcia S. 652
Fairfax County Pub Lib   DEWEY, Helen W. 298
                                EHLKE, Nancy K. 339
                                FESSLER, Vera F. 374
                                GOODWIN, Jane G. 450
                                LEVY, Suzanne S. 722
                                WEBB, Barbara A. 1313
                                WOODALL, Nancy C. 1365
Fairfax County Pub Schs   KNAPP, Marilyn S. 663
George Mason Univ   ALTHEN, Elsa E. 18
                                CONIGLIO, Jamie W. 236
                                HURT, Charlene S. 577
                                SCHWARTZ, Marla J. 1105
                                SONNEMANN, Gail J. 1167
                                TATUM, George M. 1225
Odin Feldman & Pittleman   FIENCKE, Elaine L. 376
                                TOSIANO, Barbara A. 1252
TRW Federal Systems Group   ROBINSON, David F. 1043
Vanguard Technologies Corp   STEIN, Karen E. 1185

FALLS CHURCH
Gershman Brickner & Bratton Inc GOLDBERG, Lisbeth S. 444
Harris-Hess Associates   HARRIS, Virginia B. 506
St Anthony Elementary & Junior High
  Sch   BROWN, Barbara B. 142
Solutions by Design   LEONARD, Lucinda E. 716

FARMVILLE
Longwood Coll   HOWE, Patricia A. 565
                                LAINE, Rebecca R. 688
                                STWODAH, M I. 1206

VIRGINIA (Cont'd)

FT BELVOIR
Defense Systems Management Coll TIPPER, Maryellen 1246
US Army Corps of Engineers   GORDON, Martin K. 451

FORT MONROE
US Army   LUH, Lydia Y. 747
                                SCHEITLE, Janet M. 1091

US Army Training & Doctrine
  Command   BURGESS, Edwin B. 159
                                BYRN, James H. 169
                                DOYLE, Frances M. 317

FREDERICKSBURG
Central Rappahannock Regional Lib FARR, Patricia A. 365
                                VANDERBERG, E S. 1273
Mary Washington Coll   ANDERSON, Kari D. 24
                                MULVANEY, John P. 878
                                STROHL, Leroy S. 1202
Mary Washington Hospital   BULLEY, Joan S. 156

GLENNS
Rappahannock Community Coll   ROGERS, Dean C. 1049

GLOUCESTER POINT
Coll of William & Mary   BARRICK, Susan O. 59

GREAT FALLS
Fairfax County Pub Schs   FILSON, Anne H. 377

GREENWAY
Madeira Sch   MYERS, Martha O. 884

HAMPDEN SYDNEY
Hampden-Sydney Coll   MORRISON, Jane B. 868
                                NORDEN, David J. 908

HAMPTON
Hampton Pub Lib   BIGELOW, Therese G. 95
                                JORDAN, Caroline D. 616
                                OGDEN, Howard A. 918
                                WINTERS, Sharon A. 1356
Hampton Univ   DENDY, Adele S. 291
Information Companies of America SMITH, David A. 1153
National Aeronautics & Space Admin PINELLI, Thomas E. 974

HARRISONBURG
Eastern Mennonite Coll Seminary LEHMAN, James O. 712
James Madison Univ   ARNESON, Rosemary H. 33
                                BLANKENBURG, Judith B. . . 104
                                FOX, Barbara S. 394
                                GILL, Gerald L. 435
                                HABAN, Mary F. 480
                                PALMER, Forrest C. 936
                                RAMSEY, Inez L. 1006
                                ROBISON, Dennis E. 1045
                                UPDIKE, Christina B. 1269
Rockingham County Pub Schs   SOLES, Elizabeth S. 1166
Rockingham Pub Lib   FANNON, Elizabeth L. 363

HERNDON
CH2M Hill Inc   MONTGOMERY, Suzanne L. . 856
Faxon Co   REID, Janine A. 1018
Group L Corp   DYER, Daniel 330

HIGHLAND SPRINGS
Henrico County Pub Schs   KANE, Dorothea S. 624

HOLLINS COLLEGE
Hollins Coll   BECKER, Charlotte B. 72
                                SCHNEIDER, Holle E. 1097
                                THOMPSON, Anthony B. . . . 1239

KING GEORGE
Lewis Egerton Smoot Memorial Lib SCHEPMOES, Rita D. 1091

LANGLEY AFB
St Leo Coll   VERNON, Christie D. 1283
US Air Force   ROY, Alice R. 1063

LEXINGTON
George C Marshall Foundation   JACOB, John N. 589
                                WEBER, Anita M. 1313
Rockbridge Regional Lib   KRANTZ, Linda L. 676
Virginia Military Institute   DAVIS, Wylma P. 281
                                DELONG, Edward J. 290
                                FUN, Winnie W. 409
                                GAINES, James E. 412
                                HOLLY, Janet S. 552
                                JACOB, Diane B. 589
                                PEARSON, Marilyn R. 953
Washington & Lee Univ   BISSETT, John P. 100
                                BROWN, Barbara J. 142
                                DANFORD, Robert E. 272
                                GREFE, Richard F. 465

VIRGINIA (Cont'd)
LEXINGTON (Cont'd)
Washington & Lee Univ

HAYS, Peggy W.	517
WIANT, Sarah K.	1335

LYNCHBURG
Liberty Univ   KAWAGUCHI, Miyako 632
Lynchburg Coll   SCUDDER, Mary C. 1108
Lynchburg General Hospital STURGIS, Sibyl A. 1205
Lynchburg Pub Schs   YOUNGER, Melinda M. 1383
Randolph-Macon Woman's Coll DEMARS, Patricia 291
                         JOHNSON, Jan 605

MANASSAS
Prince William Pub Lib System BARKALOW, Irene M. 56
                         BREEN, Catherine H. 131
                         CHRISTOLON, Blair B. 212
                         MURPHY, Richard W. 881

MARTINSVILLE
Blue Ridge Regional Lib   RITTER, Allison C. 1036
First Presbyterian Church   PEARL, Patricia D. 952
Memrl Hospital Martinsville & Henry
  Cnty   SHERRARD, Mary A. 1129
MCLEAN
BDM Corp Inc   WHITE, Ardeen L. 1330
Derwent Inc   DIXON, Michael D. 306
                         FORMAN, Jeffrey L. 390
Farm Credit Administration REDMER, Paul C. 1014
GTE Spacenet Corp   BROOKS, Terri A. 141
Langley Publications Inc   HELGERSON, Linda W. 524
Mitre Corp   JOACHIM, Robert J. 600
                         LIEBERMAN, Sharon A. 726
                         NIGAM, Alok C. 904
                         TATALIAS, Jean A. 1225
PergaBase   BRIGGUM, Joan 136
Pergamon Infoline Inc   JONES, Michael W. 614
                         POOL, Madlyn K. 982
                         TERRAGNO, P J. 1232
                         WINIARSKI, Marilee E. 1355
Planning Research Corp   TRAVIS, Irene L. 1254
Quest Research Corp   SCHAEFER, Mary E. 1089
Science Applications International
  Corp   HAHN, Margaret M. 483
Source Telecomputing Corp   BUSSMANN, Steve 166
                         EDWARDS, Wilmoth O. 338
                         FILIPPONE, Anne 377
                         KELLER, Jay 635
                         LITTLE, William 734
                         LOVETT, Bruce 743
                         MAJOR, Skip 762
                         NEWLAND, Barbara 899
                         RINALDI, Roberta 1035
                         RYAN, Maureen 1071
                         STRATT, Randy 1200

MIDDLEBURG
Currier Lib   MATTHEWS, Stephen L. 786
MILLWOOD
Project HOPE   BISCHOFF, Frances A. 99
                         WARPHEA, Rita C. 1306

NEWPORT NEWS
Christopher Newport Coll   DANIEL, Mary H. 272
City of Newport News   HENDERSON, Harriet 526
The Daily Press   HAMMOND, Theresa M. 494
Mariners' Museum   CREW, Roger T. 258
                         KELLY, Ardie L. 637

NORFOLK
Chrysler Museum   CICCONE, Amy N. 214
City of Norfolk   BOONE, Edward J. 115
                         DARDEN, Sue E. 274
                         GRAY, Patricia B. 460
                         MARSHALL, Jane C. 774
Dialogue Across America   BERENT, Irwin M. 84
Eastern Virginia Medical Sch   POLLOCK, Ethel L. 981
Medical Coll of Hampton Roads HARRIS, Richard J. 506
National Defense Univ   NICULA, J G. 903
Naval Education & Training Support
  Ctr   BREWER, Helen L. 134

VIRGINIA (Cont'd)
NORFOLK (Cont'd)
Norfolk Pub Lib   DRYE, Jerry L. 321
                         GRIFFLER, Carl W. 469
                         LEGO, Jane B. 712
                         MAYER-HENNELLY, Mary
                           B. 789
                         NICHOLSON, Myreen M. ... 902
                         PARKER, John A. 942
Norfolk State Univ   JONES-TRENT, Bernice R. .. 616
Old Dominion Univ   DUNCAN, Cynthia B. 325
                         ERICKSON, Lynda L. 352
                         LIU, Albert C. 734
                         MCCART, Vernon A. 794
                         MILLER, Ellen L. 837
                         SWAINE, Cynthia W. 1212
Sovran Financial Corp   REEVES, Lois H. 1017
Virginia Wesleyan Coll   PEREZ-LOPEZ, Rene 958
The Virginian-Pilot & Leadger-Star BASNIGHT, Clara P. 63
OAKTON
Chemcyclopedia   KUNEY, Joseph H. 684
ORANGE
Orange County Pub Lib   HOLLOWAY, Johnna H. 552
PETERSBURG
Petersburg Pub Lib   FRENCH, Randy A. 402
Richard Bland Coll   HUETER, Eike 570
St Vincent de Paul High Sch   CARTER, Ann M. 189
Southside Regional Medical Center POLLARD, Joan B. 981
Virginia State Univ   BERGELT, Robert L. 85
                         CLAYMAN, Ida H. 220
POQUOSON
City of Poquoson   TAI, Elizabeth L. 1220
PORTSMOUTH
Portsmouth Psychiatric Center KERSTETTER, Virginia M. ... 644
Portsmouth Pub Lib   BROWN, William A. 148
                         BURGESS, Dean 159
Portsmouth Pub Schs   TURNER, Virginia S. 1265
Tidewater Community Coll   LIN, John T. 727
US Navy   ANDERSON, Marcia M. 24
PRINCE GEORGE
Prince George's County Sch Board TUGGLE, Pamela C. 1262
QUANTICO
US Marine Corps   BROWN, David C. 143
RADFORD
Radford Univ   BRAINARD, Blair 127
                         GIBSON, Robert S. 432
                         TURNER, Robert L. 1265
                         WILLIAMS, Greta A. 1343
RESTON
American Coll of Radiology   RICHARD, Sheila A. 1028
American Newspaper Publishers
  Assn   EGERTSON, Yvonne L. 339
Council for Exceptional Children MCLANE, Kathleen 813
Fairfax County Pub Lib   PARNES, Daria M. 943
Fairfax County Pub Schs   GRIEVE, Karen R. 468
                         GUILFORD, Diane E. 476
International Data Corp   DODSON, Whit 308
Reston Regional Lib   SINWELL, Carol A. 1144
Telenet Communications Corp   ADAMS, Judith A. 5
                         COOK, Charlaine C. 239
                         HARRISTON, Victoria R. 507
                         HUFF, Patricia M. 570
                         MATHISON, Stuart 784
                         MCCLAIN, Deborah C. 795
US Department of the Interior   JENSEN, Raymond A. 599
US Geological Society   SELLIN, Jon B. 1114
US Geological Survey   CHAPPELL, Barbara A. 202
                         KARRER, Jonathan K. 628
                         LEWIS, Diane M. 723
                         LISZEWSKI, Edward H. 733
                         MERRYMAN, Margaret M. ... 827
                         MESSICK, Carol H. 828
                         SINNOTT, Gertrude M. 1144
                         WILTSHIRE, Denise A. 1354
US Sprint   GENNARO, John L. 427
XMCO Inc   SCOTT, Mona L. 1107

VIRGINIA (Cont'd)
RICHMOND
A H Robins Co   CLEMANS, Margaret H. 220
                                       VAN SICKLEN, Lindsay L. . . . 1277
AT&T Technology Systems   ZANG, Patricia J. 1386
Benedictine Society of Virginia   LIGGAN, Mary K. 726
City of Richmond   COSTA, Robert N. 249
Commonwealth of Virginia   BAXA, Jay W. 67
                                       SNAIR, Dale S. 1162
The Computer Co   CARNEY, Marillyn L. 183
County of Henrico   FINCH, Mildred E. 377
                                       SADLER, Graham H. 1073
                                       TEMPLE, Patricia C. 1230
E I DuPont de Nemours & Co Inc   WILLS, Luella G. 1349
Edward T Rabbit & Co Books for
   Children   REMICK, Katherine G. 1022
Federal Reserve Bank of Richmond   CANNON, Ruth M. 179
                                       CASH, Susan R. 192
                                       THOMPSON, Connie B. . . . 1239
Foreign Mission Board   CASEY, Wayne T. 192
                                       MACLEOD, James M. 757
Henrico County Pub Schs   GEORGE, Melba R. 427
Hirschler Fleischer Weinberg Cox &
   Allen   MOSER, Emily F. 870
J Sargeant Reynolds Community Coll   BLAKE, Mary K. 103
                                       MIAH, Abdul J. 831
Mays & Valentine   WARD, Brenda H. 1303
McGuire Woods Battle & Boothe   ROBERTS, Ann B. 1039
Media General Inc   DILLON, James L. 303
                                       OWEN, Karen V. 931
Memory Lane & Record Finder   SMITH, Walter H. 1161
Organ Historical Society Inc   PINEL, Stephen L. 974
Philip Morris USA   DEBARDELEBEN, Marian Z. . 284
                                       ROSENBERG, Murray D. . . . 1056
                                       SOUTHWICK, Margaret A. . 1170
Resources Inc   MURPHY, Robert D. 881
Reynolds Metals Co   GREGORY, Carla L. 466
Richmond Pub Lib   DECAMPS, Alice L. 285
Richmond Pub Schs   BAGAN, Beverly S. 45
                                       PRETLOW, Delores Z. 992
St Mary's Hospital   PARHAM, Sandra H. 940
Supreme Court of Virginia   LONG, Elizabeth T. 739
                                       WARREN, Gail 1306
Union Theological Seminary   AYOCK, Martha 43
                                       THOMASON, Dorothy G. . . 1238
                                       TROTTI, John B. 1258
US Court of Appeals   FREY, Peter A. 402
                                       WOODWARD, Elaine H. . . . 1368
United Virginia Bank   WEEKS, Linda F. 1315
Univ of Richmond   ENGLISH, Susan B. 350
                                       GWIN, James E. 479
                                       HALL, Bonlyn G. 487
                                       MAXWELL, Littleton M. . . . 788
                                       MCCULLEY, Lucretia 800
                                       TYSON, John C. 1267
                                       WILLIAMS, Lila E. 1344
Valentine Museum   KIMBALL, Gregg D. 649
Virginia Commonwealth Univ   BACHMAN, Katherine H. . . . 43
                                       CARTER-LOVEJOY, Steven
                                          H. 190
                                       DUKE, John K. 324
                                       HUMMEL, Ray O. 573
                                       JOHNSON, Jane W. 605
                                       MURDEN, Steven H. 879
                                       REAM, Daniel L. 1012
                                       THOMAS, Mary E. 1237
                                       TURMAN, Lynne U. 1264
                                       WHALEY, John H. 1328
                                       WOODY, Janet C. 1368
Virginia Department of Education   BARBER, Gloria K. 55
Virginia Dept of Information
   Technology   TERRELL, Jane A. 1232
Virginia Historical Society   SARTAIN, Sara M. 1083
                                       SHEPARD, E L. 1126
                                       WINFREE, Waverly K. 1354
Virginia Museum of Fine Arts   JACOBY, Mary M. 590
                                       STACY, Betty A. 1178
Virginia Power   ROYAL, Linda G. 1063

VIRGINIA (Cont'd)
RICHMOND (Cont'd)
Virginia State Lib   CHAMBERLAIN, William R. . . 197
                                       HUBBARD, William J. 568
                                       MANARIN, Louis H. 764
                                       YATES, Ella G. 1378
ROANOKE
Coll of Health Sciences   SEAMANS, Nancy H. 1109
Hayes Seay Mattern & Mattern   COLLINS, Mitzi L. 233
Hollins Coll   DIERCKS, Thelma C. 302
                                       HILL, Nancy A. 540
                                       OBRIST, Cynthia W. 915
Roanoke Catholic Sch   BANE, Madelyn R. 54
Roanoke County Pub Lib   GARRETSON, George D. . . . 420
                                       UMBERGER, Sheila S. 1268
Roanoke County Pub Schs   CHAMBERLAIN, M J. 197
Roanoke Law Lib   CALHOUN, Clayne M. 172
Roanoke Memorial Hospitals   GLENN, Lucy D. 441
Roanoke Times & World-News   HARRIS, Belinda J. 504
ROSSLYN
InterAmerica Research Associates
   Inc   SAUVE, Deborah A. 1085
SALEM
Roanoke Coll   UMBERGER, Stan 1268
SOUTH BOSTON
Halifax County-South Boston
   Regional Lib   ULBRICH, David E. 1268
SPRINGFIELD
EBSCO Industries Inc   CARSON, Howard C. 188
Fairfax County Pub Lib   CLAY, Edwin S. 219
                                       COLEMAN, Karen S. 231
                                       MONK, Joanne 855
Markon Inc   KUHL, Danuta 682
National Technical Information
   Service   FINCH, Walter 377
                                       KANE, Astor V. 624
                                       LAWALL, Marie 704
                                       ROSENBERG, Kenyon C. . . 1056
                                       SMITH, Ruth S. 1160
Times Journal Co   WHITE-WILLIAMS, Patricia . 1333
US Department of Commerce   ELSBREE, John J. 346
                                       LEHMANN, Edward J. 713
STAUNTON
Staunton Pub Lib   KOUTNIK, Charles J. 673
SWEET BRIAR
Sweet Briar Coll   JAFFE, John G. 591
VIENNA
Boeing Co   WARD, Carol T. 1303
Lewis Mitchell & Moore   MOORE, Dianne T. 859
National Wildlife Federation   LEVY, Sharon J. 722
Quantum Computer Service Inc   CASE, Stephen M. 192
VINTON
Roanoke County Pub Schs   SPRENGER, Suzanne F. . . . 1176
VIRGINIA BEACH
American Systems Engineering Corp   WISECARVER, Betty A. . . . 1357
CBN Univ   KIEWITT, Eva L. 647
                                       LEHMAN, Lois J. 713
                                       SIVIGNY, Robert J. 1144
                                       WELSH, Eric L. 1323
City of Virginia Beach   BARKLEY, Carolyn L. 56
                                       CARR, Jeanette A. 185
                                       CAYWOOD, Carolyn A. 195
                                       DUNLEAVY, Theresa G. . . . 326
                                       LOHMAN, Toni A. 737
                                       SIMS, Martha J. 1142
                                       ZWICK, Susan G. 1392
Department of Pub Libraries   STEWART, John D. 1192
Tidewater Community Coll   BILLERT, Julia A. 96
US Navy   POLLOK, Karen E. 981
Virginia Beach City Pub Schs   OWENS, Martha A. 932
Virginia Beach Department of Pub
   Libs   CALLAHAN, John J. 173
Virginia Beach Pub Lib   MILLER, Nancy M. 841
                                       SWAIN, Lillian A. 1212
                                       WHYTE, Sean 1335
WAYNESBORO
Waynesboro Pub Lib   RUFE, Charles P. 1066
WEYERS CAVE
Blue Ridge Community Coll   BUCCO, Louise F. 153

VIRGINIA (Cont'd)
WILLIAMSBURG
Coll of William & Mary   BLUE, Kathryn J. 107
BROWN, Charlotte D. 142
EDMONDS, Edmund P. 336
HASKELL, John D. 510
HAUSMAN, Patricia R. 513
HEDGES, Bonnie L. 520
HEYMAN, Berna L. 536
MAGPANTAY, J A. 760
MARSHALL, Nancy H. 775
YELICH, Hope H. 1379
Colonial Williamsburg Foundation   BERG, Susan 85
GROVE, Pearce S. 473
HASKELL, Mary B. 510
Walsingham Academy Upper Sch   SHANNON, Theresa M. 1121
Willamsburg Regional Lib   VAZQUEZ, Martha W. 1280
Williamsburg Regional Lib   PAISLEY, Anna S. 935
WINCHESTER
Handley Lib   MILLER, Richard A. 841
WISE
Clinch Valley Coll   BENKE, Robin P. 81
Univ of Virginia   CHISHOLM, Clarence E. 209
WOODBRIDGE
Northern Virginia Community Coll   ENGLAND, Ellen M. 349
Prince William County Pub Schs   KILLEEN, Erlene B. 648
ZIMMERMAN, Nancy P. 1389
Prince William Pub Lib System   GARBELMAN, Alicia D. 417
WYTHEVILLE
Bookworm & Silverfish-ABAA   PRESGRAVES, Jim 991
Wytheville Community Coll   MATTIS, George E. 786
YORKTOWN
York County   COLTON, Norma W. 234

WASHINGTON
AUBURN
Auburn Pub Lib   GOLDSTEIN, Cynthia N. 446
Auburn Sch District 408   WALBURN, Joyce M. 1293
BAINBRIDGE ISLAND
dba Info-Access   SPEARMAN, Marie A. 1172
BELLEVUE
Bellevue Community Coll   DECOSTER, Barbara L. 286
WALLS, Francine E. 1299
Bellevue Pub Schs   ERICKSON, Jane 352
SHERMAN-PETERSON,
Ronald A. 1128
SKELLEY, Cornelia A. 1145
King County Lib System   NELSON, Judy T. 894
Puget Sound Power & Light   BALL, Susan C. 52
St Louise Sch   BIANCHI, Karen F. 93
Sisters of St Joseph of Peace   PATTERSON, Mary E. 948
Tetra Tech Inc   FIELDING, Carol J. 376
Thousand Trails   SCHUTTE, Raymond R. . . . 1103
BELLINGHAM
Bellingham Pub Lib   BLUME, Scott 107
MCCAIN, Claudia J. 793
Bellingham Sch District 501   ANDERSEN, Eileen 21
Western Washington Univ   EDMONDS, Susan M. 336
HAAG, Enid E. 480
HASELBAUER, Kathleen J. . . 510
JOHNSON, Dana E. 603
PACKER, Donna E. 933
PARKER, Diane C. 941
RHOADS, James B. 1026
SYMES, Dal S. 1217
Whatcom Community Coll   GROVER, Iva S. 474
Whatcom County Lib System   HALLIDAY, John 489
BLAINE
Blaine Sch District 503   BACON, Carey H. 44
BOTHELL
Advanced Technology Laboratories   GRINSTEAD, Beth K. 471
Seattle Pub Lib   YEE, J E. 1379
BREMERTON
Harrison Memorial Hospital   KANNEL, Selma 625
Kitsap Regional Lib   CARLSON, Sandra L. 182
HENINGER, Irene C. 528
CAMAS
Camas Pub Lib   BRENNAN, Cindy L. 132

WASHINGTON (Cont'd)
CHENEY
Eastern Washington Univ   ALKIRE, Leland G. 13
BAUMANN, Charles H. 66
MUTSCHLER, Charles V. . . . 883
TRACY, Joan I. 1253
Spokane Pub Lib   BENDER, Betty W. 79
CLALLAM BAY
Washington State Lib   PEARSON, Barbara F. 952
COLFAX
Whitman County Lib   WARNER, Gail P. 1305
COWICHE
Highland Sch District   JORDAN, Sharon L. 617
DES MOINES
Highline Community Coll   BOSLEY, Dana L. 117
TURLEY, Georgia P. 1263
WILSON, Anthony M. 1349
EDMONDS
Dominican Sisters of Edmonds   HALEY, Marguerite R. 486
Sno-Isle Regional Lib System   BETZ-ZALL, Jonathan R. 92
TURNER, Kathleen G. 1264
Stevens Memorial Hospital   DICKERSON, Bea 300
ELLENSBURG
Central Washington Univ   ALEXANDER, Malcolm D. 12
DOI, Makiko 309
SCHNEIDER, Frank A. 1097
VILLAR, Susanne P. 1284
YEH, Thomas Y. 1379
Ellensburg Pub Lib   WILLBERG, Carolyn S. 1341
ENUMCLAW
Enumclaw Pub Lib   BAER, Robert L. 45
EVERETT
Everett Pub Lib   NESSE, Mark A. 896
Hewlett-Packard Co   VAN DYKE, Ruth L. 1275
Providence Hospital   CAMPBELL, Mary E. 177
Snohomish County Law Lib   SCOTT, Betty Z. 1106
FALL CITY
National Park Service   AROKSAAR, Richard D. 34
FEDERAL WAY
King County Lib System   DUBOIS, Delores M. 322
FORT LEWIS
BDM Management Services Corp   PARR, Loraine E. 943
US Army   COHEN, Jane L. 228
US Department of Defense   WOOSTER, Linda I. 1368
FORT STEILACOOM
Washington State Lib   VAN DER VOORN, Neal P. . . 1274
FPO SEATTLE
US Navy   BODKIN, Sharon C. 109
FRIDAY HARBOR
Copyright Information Services   MILLER, Jerome K. 839
HOQUIAM
Hoquiam Sch Dist 28   GREGORY, Mary L. 466
ISSAQUAH
Issaquah Sch Dist   FLETCHER, Robert A. 385
King County Lib System   PETTIT, Donna K. 965
KELSO
Waldenbooks   ARBUCKLE, Marybeth M. 30
KENNEWICK
Kennewick Sch District 17   KNOLL, Betty A. 665
KIRKLAND
King County Lib System   MACDONALD, Margaret R. . . 754
LACEY
St Martins Coll   WIEMAN, Jean M. 1336
Woodard Bay Co   DEBUSE, Raymond 285
LONGVIEW
Longview Sch District   DOLBEY, Mary B. 309
Lower Columbia Coll   BAKER, Robert K. 49
LYNNWOOD
Edmonds Community Coll   NELSON, Christine 893
Sno-Isle Regional Lib System   KAPLAN, Lesly A. 626
MARYSVILLE
Sno-Isle Regional Lib System   STRONG, Sunny A. 1203
WILSON, Evie 1350
MONROE
Washington State Dept of Corrections   SIENDA, Madeline M. 1136
MT VERNON
Mt Vernon Sch District   JONES, Sally L. 615
PACCAR Technical Center   WARD, Maryanne 1304
MOUNTLAKE TERRACE
Sno-Isle Regional Lib System   SCOTT-MILLER, Gwen 1108

WASHINGTON (Cont'd)

NEWPORT
Pend Oreille County Lib · REMINGTON, David G. 1022

OAK HARBOR
Oak Harbor Junior High · MERWINE, Glenda M. 827

OCEAN PARK
Easley Information Service · EASLEY, Janet T. 332

OLYMPIA
Office of the Secretary of State · MCAPLIN, Sidney 792
Timberland Regional Lib · CHRISTIANSEN, Claire B. .. 211
· DICKERSON, Lon R. 300
· GREENWOOD, Alma I. 465
· LOKEN, Sarah F. 738
· SHAFFER, Maryann 1119
Washington State Energy Office · ALEXANDER, Ginger H. 12
Washington State Lib · ANDRESEN, David 26
· DEBUSE, Judith S. 285
· HAMMOCK, Janice D. 493
· KREIMEYER, Vicki R. 677
· MOORE, Mary Y. 860
· ZUSSY, Nancy L. 1391
Western Lib Network · HOLLAND, Helen K. 550
· PUZIAK, Kathleen M. 998
WLN Bibliographic Center · NEWELL, Rick K. 898

PORT ANGELES
North Olympic Library Systems · DAVIES, Jo 277

PULLMAN
Washington State Univ · BRADY, Eileen E. 126
· BREKKE, Elaine C. 132
· CHISMAN, Janet K. 209
· FISHER, Rita C. 381
· KEMP, Barbara E. 639
· KOPP, Carol S. 671
· KOPP, James J. 671
· MCCOOL, Donna L. 798
· NOFSINGER, Mary M. 907
· PASTINE, Maureen D. 946
· ROBERTS, Elizabeth P. 1039
· VYHNANEK, Kay E. 1290
· VYHNANEK, Louis 1290
· WIERUM, Ann R. 1337
· ZIEGLER, Ronald M. 1388

PUYALLUP
Puyallup Sch District · BAZE, Mary P. 68

REDMOND
Golder Assocs · EIPERT, Susan L. 340
Microsoft Corp · YOUNT, Natalie W. 1384
Overlake Sch · GARRETSON, Laurie J. 420
Sundstrand Data Control Inc · SMART, Doris M. 1151

RENTON
PACCAR Defense Systems · CAMOZZI-EKBERG, Patricia L. 175

RICHLAND
Battelle Northwest Laboratory · DANIEL, Eunice L. 272
· SAMPLE, Charles R. 1078
On-Line Research · CARVER, Sue A. 191
Richland Pub Lib · FOLEY, Katherine E. 387
Richland Sch District 400 · CARRIGAN, Marietta R. 186
Rockwell Hanford Operations · KING, Betty J. 650
Westinghouse Hanford Co · TRAUB, Teresa L. 1254

SEATTLE
Betts Patterson & Mines PS · WILLIAMS, Janet M. 1344
Boeing Co · BAGG, Deborah L. 45
· CAMPBELL, Corinne A. 176
· CRANDALL, Michael D. 255
· LAUGHLIN, Catherine 703
· SILVA, Mary E. 1138
CGS · STOCK, Carole G. 1195
Children's Hospital & Medical Center · TURNER, Tamara A. 1265
City of Seattle · CLINE, Robert S. 222
Converse Consultants NW · CHAPMAN, Kathleen A. 202
Data Matrix · ERICKSON, Randall D. 352
Davis Wright & Jones Lib · ANDERSON, Christine M. 22
Department of Commerce · MCCORMICK, Jack M. 798
Diocese of Olympia · HANSEN, Peggy A. 498
Dusty Strings Dulcimer Co · KREPS, Lise E. 678
Elaine Day Latourelle & Associates · OMURA, Michael 923
Federal Home Loan Bank of Seattle · FEATHERS, John E. 367
First Covenant Church · STORDAHL, Beth A. 1198
Genetic Systems Corp/Oncogen · WILDER, Patricia A. 1339

WASHINGTON (Cont'd)

SEATTLE (Cont'd)
Graham & Dunn · DOWD, Mary M. 315
Hart Crowser Associates Inc · SMITH, Sophia A. 1161
Haworth Press Inc · GELLATLY, Peter 426
Heritage North · STIRLING, Dale A. 1195
Historical Society of Seattle · CALDWELL, Richard C. 172
Karr Tuttle Koch Campbell Mawer et al · HOLT, Barbara C. 554
· YONGMAN, Zhang 1380
King County Lib System · ARCHBOLD, Barbara C. 30
· BEN-SIMON, Julie E. 83
· GREGGS, Elizabeth M. 465
· JOHNSON, Carolynn K. 603
· MADDEN, Susan B. 758
· MORGAN, Erma J. 864
· MUTSCHLER, Herbert F. 883
· POLISHUK, Bernard 980
· RICKELTON, Esther G. 1031
· THOMPSON, Rosalind R. .. 1241
· THORSEN, Jeanne M. 1242
· TOLLIVER, Barbara J. 1248
· WAGNER, Sabina H. 1292
· WALTERS, Daniel L. 1301
Lane Powell Moss & Miller · LAWSON, Annetta 705
· MCFADDEN, Denyse I. 804
The Magus Bookstore · AUSTIN, Kristi N. 40
Moss Adams · HETZLER, Jill K. 534
Municipality of Metropolitan Seattle · MCBRIDE, Anne 792
National Archives & Records Admin · EDWARDS, Steven M. 338
North Seattle Community Coll · CHASE, Dale L. 203
Owl Mountain Associates · EULENBERG, Julia N. 356
Pacific Medical Center · SONG, Seungja Y. 1167
Pacific Northwest Bell · BOLEN, Sheila 112
Perkins Cole · STEWART, Jane 1192
Preston Thorgrimson Ellis & Holman · JACKSON, Cleta L. 587
Price Waterhouse · FROST, Roxanna 406
Program for Appropriate Tech in Health · WOOD-LIM, Eileen K. 1366
R W Beck & Associates · SLIVKA, Enid M. 1149
Rainier National Bank · BURKE, Vivienne C. 160
Riddell Williams Bullitt & Walkinshaw · ZIKE, Ruth D. 1388
Schick Shadel Hospital · MILES, Pamela W. 834
Seattle Country Day Sch · MOCKETT, Sara H. 851
Seattle First National Bank · PRIVAT, Jeannette M. 994
Seattle Pacific Univ · HILL, Ann M. 539
· MCDONOUGH, George E. 803
· REED, Marcia E. 1015
Seattle Pub Lib · CHEN, Yvonne 205
· COLDWELL, Charles P. 230
· FOX, Howard A. 394
· HAMILTON, Darlene E. 491
· LEONARD, Gloria J. 716
· MEYER, Laura M. 830
· MILLER, G D. 837
· MYERS, Antoinette B. 884
· PUDERBAUGH, Velma E. 997
· TAYLOR, James B. 1227
Seattle Trust and Savings Bank · HUGHES, Dorothy S. 571
Seattle Univ · JENNERICH, Edward J. 598
· THOMAS, Lawrence E. 1237
US Court of Appeals · NORWOOD, Deborah A. 910
US Department of Commerce · THAYER, Martha B. 1234
Univ of Washington · AUSTIN, Martha L. 40
· BENNE, Mae M. 81
· BERNARD, Molly S. 88
· BLASE, Nancy G. 104
· BOLLING, Thomas E. 112
· BOYLAN, Merle N. 123
· BRADT, Elizabeth J. 126
· BURSON, Scott F. 163
· CHADWICK, Leroy D. 197
· CHISHOLM, Margaret 209
· DENFELD, Kay F. 291
· DIBIASE, Linda P. 299
· ENGEMAN, Richard H. 349
· FASSETT, William E. 366
· FIDEL, Raya 374
· FRALEY, David B. 395
· FUGATE, Cynthia S. 408

WASHINGTON (Cont'd)
SEATTLE (Cont'd)
Univ of Washington

GREEN, Carol C. 461
HAZELTON, Penelope A. . . . 517
HENSLEY, Randall B. 529
HIATT, Peter 536
HILDEBRANDT, Darlene M. . . 538
HILLER, Steven Z. 541
JEWELL, Timothy D. 600
KETCHELL, Debra S. 645
LIPTON, Laura E. 732
LOPEZ, Loretta K. 741
LORD, Charles R. 741
MAACK, David J. 753
MAHONEY, Laura E. 761
MENGES, Gary L. 824
MIDDLETON, Dale R. 833
MOFJELD, Pamela A. 852
MURDOCH, Martha T. 879
PASSARELLI, Anne B. 946
PRESS, Nancy O. 991
PRITCHARD, Jackie L. 994
REDALJE, Susanne J. 1013
RICKERSON, Carla 1031
ROWBERG, Alan H. 1062
SCHUELLER, Janette H. . . . 1101
SENN, Sharon L. 1115
SERCOMBE, Laurel 1116
SKELLEY, Grant T. 1145
SOPER, Mary E. 1168
STEVENS, Peter H. 1190
SY, Karen J. 1217
VAN MASON, Patricia M. . . 1276
WALKER, Paula B. 1296
WEAVER, Carolyn G. 1312
WIREN, Harold N. 1356

Veterans Administration Medical
  Center   HARBOLD, Mary J. 499
Virginia Mason Medical Center   ROBERTSON, Ann 1041
Western Lib Network   MAIOLI, Jerry R. 762
Western Washington Univ   SAUTER, Sylvia E. 1085
Word Hoard Author's Consulting
  Services   BRZUSTOWICZ, Richard J. . 152
SHELTON
ITT Rayonier Inc   TOSTEVIN, Patricia A. 1252
SNOHOMISH
Sno-Isle Regional Lib System   BUCKINGHAM, Rebecca M. . 154
SPANAWAY
Bethel Sch District 403   ULRICH, Pamela L. 1268
SPANGLE
Upper Columbia Academy   MOLLER, Steffen A. 853
SPOKANE
City of Spokane   SHELDEN, Lucinda D. 1125
Eastern Washington State Histl
  Society   NOLAN, Edward W. 907
Futurepast: The Hist Co   SHIDELER, John C. 1129
Gonzaga Univ   MURRAY, James M. 882
                                 WYNN, Debra D. 1375
Lukins & Annis   WADDEN, Emily E. 1290
Spokane Community Coll   REHMS, Jane C. 1017
Spokane County Lib District   DEDAS, Madelyn W. 286
                                 ICE, Priscilla T. 581
                                 WIRT, Michael J. 1356
Spokane Pub Lib   FREDRICKSON, Dennis C. . . 400
                                 JONES, Charlotte W. 611
                                 LANE, Steven P. 694
                                 TYSON, Christy 1267
                                 WEBER, Joan L. 1314
                                 WOLFE, Lisa A. 1361
Veterans Administration Medical
  Center   JONES, Ruth A. 615
Washington State Univ   PRINGLE, Robert M. 993
Whitworth Coll   BYNAGLE, Hans E. 168
TACOMA
American Plywood Assn   PRESTON, Deirdre R. 991
Clover Park Vocational-Technical Inst SELING, Kathy A. 1113
Ernst & Whinney   UHLMAN, Carol K. 1268
Pacific Lutheran Univ   GILCHRIST, Debra L. 434
Pierce Coll   HAMMOND, Mary W. 494

WASHINGTON (Cont'd)
TACOMA (Cont'd)
Pierce County Rural Lib   KRUZIC, Evelyn D. 681
                                 THOMPSON, Diane M. . . . 1239
Tacoma Family Medicine   MENDELSON, Martin 823
Tacoma News Tribune   BRITTON, Pilaivan H. 137
Tacoma Pub Lib   HAGAN, Dalia L. 482
                                 REESE, Gary F. 1016
Tacoma Sch District   BUELER, Roy D. 155
Tacoma Sch District 10   THORNDILL, Christine M. . . 1242
Univ of Puget Sound   BECKER, Roger V. 72
                                 GILDENHAR, Janet 434
                                 HARVEY, Suzanne 509
                                 JONES, Faye E. 613
                                 MENANTEAUX, A R. 823
                                 RICIGLIANO, Lorraine M. . . 1031
                                 SCHREINER, Suzanne M. . . 1100
                                 TAYLOR, Desmond 1226
Veterans Administration Medical
  Center   LEVI, Dennis L. 720
Weyerhaeuser Co   MARTINEZ, Linda W. 779
                                 MOHOLT, Megan L. 852
VANCOUVER
Evergreen Sch District   CONABLE, Irene H. 235
Fort Vancouver Regional Lib   CONABLE, Gordon M. 235
                                 EDWARDS, Susan E. 338
                                 HUTTON, Emily A. 579
Southwest Washington Hospitals   MACWILLIAMS, Sylvia E. . . 758
US Department of Energy   FENKER, John A. 371
Vancouver Pub Schs   ZALESKI, Mary A. 1385
VASHON
King County Lib System   FOWLER, Ellen T. 393
WALLA WALLA
Walla Walla Community Coll   BLACKABY, Sandra L. 102
Walla Walla County Rural Lib District BREIT, Anitra D. 132
Walla Walla Pub Lib   HALEY, Anne E. 486
Whitman Coll   CARR, Carol L. 185
                                 YAPLE, Henry M. 1377
WENATCHEE
Central Washington Hospital   BELT, Jane 78
YAKIMA
Yakima Valley Regional Lib   OSTRANDER, Richard E. . . . 929

WEST VIRGINIA
ATHENS
Concord Coll   BROWN, Thomas M. 148
BLUEFIELD
Ednor Enterprises   MCQUAIL, Edward J. 817
Mercer County Service Center   DYE, Luella I. 330
BUCKHANNON
West Virginia Wesleyan Coll   CRESSWELL, Stephen 258
CHARLESTON
John XXIII Pastoral Center   HUMPHRIES, Joy D. 574
Kanawha County Pub Lib   FRASER, Elizabeth L. 399
                                 LEASURE, Lois A. 707
                                 MARTIN, June R. 777
                                 PALMER, Marguerite C. 936
                                 WRIGHT, Linda G. 1372
Spilman Thomas Battle & Kloster
  Meyer   ORLANDO, Karen T. 926
Univ of Charleston   BARNES, Jean S. 57
West Virginia Dept of Culture &
  History   ARMSTRONG, Fredrick H. . . . 32
West Virginia Department of
  Education   MOELLENDICK, M J. 851
West Virginia Lib Commission   COOPER, Candace S. 242
                                 GLAZER, Frederic J. 440
                                 PROSSER, Judith M. 995
West Virginia Univ   GRAHAM, Robert J. 456
CLARKSBURG
Clarksburg-Harrison Pub Lib   THACKER, Timothy M. 1233
Harrison County Board of Education DANNUNZIO, Rebecca T. . . 274
Informed Sources Inc   GREATHOUSE, Brenda J. . . . 461
FAIRMONT
Fairmont State Coll   HUPP, Mary A. 577
                                 POWELL, Ruth A. 988
GLENVILLE
Glenville State Coll   FAULKNER, Ronnie W. 366
                                 RUSSELL, Richard A. 1069
                                 VERMA, Prem V. 1282

WEST VIRGINIA (Cont'd)

HARPERS FERRY

National Park Service

HERIOT, Ruthanne 531
NATHANSON, David 889

HUNTINGTON

Cabell County Board of Education
Cabell County Pub Lib
Marshall Univ

APEL, Catherine D. 29
RULE, Judy K. 1067
DZIERZAK, Edward M. 331
FIDLER, Leah J. 375
REENSTJERNA, Frederick
R. 1016

INSTITUTE

West Virginia State Coll

SCOBELL, Elizabeth H. 1106
SCOTT, John E. 1107

KEYSER

West Virginia Univ

HOWARD, Betty J. 564

MARTINSBURG

Martinsburg Lib Commission

BEALL, C E. 68

MORGANTOWN

West Virginia Univ

CUTHBERT, John A. 267
ESKRIDGE, Virginia C. 354
HOWARD, Elizabeth F. 564
MCKEE, Jean A. 810
SHILL, Harold B. 1130

PHILIPPI

Alderson-Broaddus Coll

SIZEMORE, William C. 1145

POINT PLEASANT

Mason County Board of Education

WILLIAMSON, Judy D. 1347

SALEM

Front Free Lib

LANGER, Frank A. 695

SHEPHERDSTOWN

Shepherd Coll

GAUMOND, George R. 423
WATSON, Carolyn R. 1309

SOUTH CHARLESTON

Union Carbide Corp

BEHR, Alice S. 75

SPENCER

Alpha Regional Lib

RADER, H J. 1002

WELCH

McDowell Pub Lib

MULLER, William A. 877

WELLSBURG

Brooke County Pub Lib

ANTIGO, Dolores A. 29

WEST LIBERTY

West Liberty State Coll

LYLE, Heather A. 751

WHEELING

Ohio County Pub Lib
West Virginia Northern Community
Coll

KALLAY, Ernest R. 623

JULIAN, Charles A. 619

WILLIAMSBURG

Stroud Booksellers

STROUD, John N. 1203

WISCONSIN

ADAMS

Adams County Pub Lib

STEINKRAUS, Ann M. 1186

ANTIGO

Antigo Unified Sch District

RETZER, Cathy E. 1024

APPLETON

A A L
Appleton Pub Lib

KLAVER, Timothy J. 658
DAWSON, Terry P. 282
KELLY, Barbara J. 637
PENNINGTON, Jerome G. . . . 957

City of Appleton
Fox Valley Technical Institute
Institute of Paper Chemistry

VIGNOVICH, Ray L. 1284
PARSON, Karen L. 944
BOOHER, Craig S. 115
NADZIEJKA, David E. 886
TIMMERS, Debra A. 1246

St Elizabeth Hospital

BAYORGEON, Mary M. 68

ASHLAND

Northern Waters Lib Service
Northland Coll

PAULI, David N. 950
FENNESSEY, Mary D. 371

BELOIT

Beloit Corp
Beloit Pub Lib

THOM, Pat A. 1235
ALLEN, Christina Y. 14
BREDESON, Peggy Z. 131
SIMPSON, W S. 1142
STAINBROOK, Lynn M. . . . 1178

BROOKFIELD

Intl Foundation of Employee Benefit
Plan

BIRSCHEL, Dee B. 99
CHRISTMAN, Inese R. 212
KRAJNAK, Patricia A. 675

WISCONSIN (Cont'd)

BROOKFIELD (Cont'd)

Intl Foundation of Employee Benefit
Plan

MILLER, Julia E. 839

BURLINGTON

Burlington Pub Lib

PROCES, Stephen L. 994

CALEDONIA

Words on Music Ltd

GRENDYSA, Peter A. 467

CASSVILLE

Univ of Dubuque

FLIEGEL, Deborah A. 385

CEDARBURG

Cedarburg Pub Schs

PITEL, Vonna J. 976

COLFAX

Colfax Pub Schs

WASSINK, Patricia L. 1308

COLUMBUS

Columbus Pub Schs

CZARNEZKI, Mary E. 268

DE PERE

Sadlon's Ltd
St Norbert Coll

SADLON, Ramona J. 1074
PIETERS, Donald L. 972

EAST TROY

Divine Word Seminary Lib

KREINUS, Anthony A. 677

EAU CLAIRE

Eau Claire Sch District
Indianhead Federated Lib System
L E Phillips Memorial Pub Lib
Le Phillips Memorial Pub Lib
Regis High Sch
Univ of Wisconsin at Eau Claire

BUGHER, Kathryn M. 155
ROBBERS, Sandra M. 1038
MERRIAM, Louise A. 826
LARSON, Mildred N. 699
NASSET, M J. 889
ENGELDINGER, Eugene A. . . 349
FOSTER, Leslie A. 392
MARQUARDT, Steve R. 772
THOMPSON, Glenn J. 1239

FENNIMORE

Southwest Wisconsin Lib System

DAWSON, Lawrence 282

FOND DU LAC

Fond Du Lac Pub Lib

CONRAD, Kay A. 238
RINGER, Susan G. 1035

Univ of Wisconsin at Fon du Lac
Univ of Wisconsin at Fond du Lac

EBERT, John J. 334
FRICK, John W. 403

FORT ATKINSON

City of Fort Atkinson
Highsmith Co Inc

GATES, Mary D. 422
VAN ORSDEL, Darrell E. . . . 1276

FRANKLIN

Franklin Pub Lib

BELLIN, Bernard E. 78
SANCHEZ, Alexander J. . . . 1079

GREEN BAY

Diocese of Green Bay
Foth & Van Duke & Associates
Green Bay Board of Education
National Railroad Museum

LONG, Brideen 739
JOBELIUS, Nancy L. 601
MURTO, Kathleen A. 883
MUSICH, Gerald D. 883

GREENDALE

St Alphonsus Sch

SCHULTE, Teresa M. 1101

HALES CORNERS

Hales Corners Pub Lib

SIPOLA, Debra L. 1144

HUDSON

City of Hudson

TIETZ, Kathleen E. 1244

IOLA

Trey Foerster Ink Inc

FOERSTER, Trey 387

JANESVILLE

Janesville Pub Lib

ENGELBERT, Alan M. 348
HARFST, Linda A. 501
HELWIG, Karen A. 525
KRUEGER, Karen J. 680

KAUKAUNA

Kaukauna Area Schs

SWITZER, Catherine M. . . . 1216

KENOSHA

Gateway Technical Coll
Kenosha Memorial Hospital
Kenosha Pub Lib

KALVONJIAN, Araxie 623
PUHEK, Esther L. 997
BAKER, Douglas 48
JAMBREK, William L. 592
THOMSON, Kathleen R. . . . 1241

Snap-on Tools Corp
Univ of Wisconsin at Parkside

HALL, Elizabeth L. 487
BARUTH, Barbara P. 62
PIELE, Linda J. 971
TRUPIANO, Rose M. 1259

LA CROSSE

Gundersen-Lutheran Medical Center
Information Management Associates
La Crosse Pub Lib

CIMPL, Kathleen A. 214
ACCARDI, Joseph J. 3
GROSKOPF, Amy L. 472
WHITE, James W. 1331

WISCONSIN (Cont'd)
LA CROSSE (Cont'd)

Univ of Wisconsin at La Crosse	HILL, Edwin L. 539
	SECHREST, Sandra L. 1110

LADYSMITH

Sisters, Servant of Mary of Ladysmith	HENKE, Alice M. 528

MADISON

American Family Mutual Insurance Group	BELLOWS, Leslie A. 78
An Idea Place	WAITY, Gloria J. 1293
Credit Union National Assn	SAYRS, Judith A. 1087
Department of Pub Instruction	DREW, Sally J. 319
	FOLKE, Carolyn W. 387
Edgewood Coll	BEYENKA, Barbara L. 93
	CLARK, Peter W. 217
	COSTELLO, Janice M. 249
Edgewood High Sch	HOWDEN, Regis 565
	LAESSIG, Joan M. 687
Information Transform	EPSTEIN, Hank 351
La Follette High Sch	CAIN, Carolyn L. 171
LaFollette & Sinykin	HUMPHRIES, Lajean 574
Lake View Elementary Sch	DEES DAUGHERTY, Kristin . 287
Madison Area Technical Coll	JEFFCOTT, Janet B. 596
Madison Metropolitan Sch District	BACH, Nancy C. 43
	DRESANG, Eliza T. 319
	KEMPF, Arlys L. 639
	PARFREY, Hilda W. 940
	SCHULTZ, Cathern J. 1101
Madison Pub Lib	ABLEIDINGER, Rose A. 2
	BRAGER, Beverly J. 127
	HAWLEY, Joann C. 514
	NIEMI, Peter G. 903
Oscar Mayer Foods Corp	WHITEMARSH, Thomas R. . 1333
RMT Inc	KAYES, Mary J. 632
South Central Lib System	DAVIS, Phyllis B. 280
	LUND, Patricia A. 748
	MCCONNELL, Shirley M. . . . 798
State Historical Society of Wisconsin	DANKY, James P. 274
	EDMONDS, Michael 336
	MULLER, H N. 877
State of Wisconsin	MATTHEWS, Geraldine M. . . 785
US Department of Agriculture	SCHARMER, Roger C. 1090
US District Court	OBERLA, Janet L. 914
Univ of Wisconsin at Madison	ARNESON, Arne J. 33
	ARNOLD, Barbara J. 33
	BLANKENBURG, Julie J. . . . 104
	BOLL, John J. 112
	BOYER, Ann T. 123
	BUNGE, Charles A. 157
	CARR, Jo A. 185
	CENTER, Sue L. 196
	CRAWFORD, Josephine 256
	DAVIS, Sally A. 281
	DEWEY, Gene L. 298
	DILLON, John B. 303
	DIXON, Edith M. 306
	GALNEDER, Mary H. 415
	GAPEN, D K. 416
	GIEBEL, Thomas W. 432
	HERMAN, Gertrude B. 531
	HOPKINS, Dianne M. 557
	HSIEH-YEE, Ingrid P. 567
	JESUDASON, Melba 600
	KRIKELAS, James 678
	KRUSE, Ginny M. 681
	LIVNY, Efrat 735
	MCCLEMENTS, Nancy A. . . . 796
	MONROE, Margaret E. 855
	NEILL, Priscilla 892
	PAUL, Nancy A. 949
	POPE, Nolan F. 983
	POPLAWSKY, Diane M. 983
	REEB, Richard C. 1014
	ROBBINS, Jane B. 1038
	ROSENSHIELD, Jill K. 1057
	ROUSE, Kendall G. 1061
	SCHULTZ, Ellen A. 1102
	SEARING, Susan E. 1109
	SESSIONS, Robert 1117
	THOMPSON, Jean T. 1240

WISCONSIN (Cont'd)
MADISON (Cont'd)

Univ of Wisconsin at Madison	
	WALKER, Richard D. 1296
	WEINGAND, Darlene E. . . . 1318
	WELSCH, Erwin K. 1323
	WHITCOMB, Dorothy V. . . . 1330
	WIEGAND, Wayne A. 1336
	WILCOX, Patricia F. 1338
	WILLETT, Holly G. 1341
	WILLIAMSON, William L. . . 1348
	XIA, Hong 1376
	YOUNGER, Jennifer A. 1383
	ZOLLER, R T. 1390
	ZWEIZIG, Douglas L. 1392
WILDCARD * RESOURCES	BEHNKE, Charles 75
Wisconsin Department of Justice	BEMIS, Michael F. 79
	PAUL, Sara J. 949
Wisconsin Dept of Natural Resources	HYNUM, Jill A. 580
	PARSONS, Patricia S. 945
Wisconsin Department of Pub Instruction	DAHLGREN, Anders C. 269
	LAMB, Donald K. 689
	NIX, Larry T. 905
	SHIRES, Leslyn 1131
	SORENSEN, Richard J. 1168
Wisconsin Interlibrary Services	MICHAELIS, Kathryn S. 831
Wisconsin Lib Association	MIRACLE, Faith 847
Wisconsin State Cartographer's Office	REINHARD, Christine M. . . . 1021
Wisconsin Supreme Court	KOSLOV, Marcia J. 672

MANITOWOC

Holy Family Medical Center	ECKERT, Daniel L. 335
Manitowoc Pub Lib	BENDIX, Linda A. 79
	OHLEMACHER, Janet H. . . . 919
	SINGH, Rosemary A. 1143

MARINETTE

Univ of Wisconsin at Marinette	SCOFIELD, Constance V. . . 1106

MARSHFIELD

Marshfield Clinic	ZIMMERMANN, Albert J. . . 1389
Marshfield Pub Lib	BRANDEL, Pamela A. 128
St Joseph's Hospital	ALLEN, Margaret A. 15

MENASHA

Menasha Pub Lib	LOCH-WOUTERS, Marge . . . 736

MENOMONEE FALLS

EATON/Cutler-Hamer	SEUSS, Herbert J. 1117
Maude Shunk Lib	BAKULA, Patricia A. 50
Med Associates Health Center	MADSEN, Joyce 759

MENOMONIE

Univ of Wisconsin at Stout	GRAF, David L. 455
	JAX, John J. 595
	OLSON, Dennis H. 922
	SAWIN, Philip Q. 1086

MEQUON

Mequon-Thiensville Sch District	CASEY, Jean M. 192
Novotny Associates	NOVOTNY, Lynn E. 911

MILTON

Milton Pub Lib	MERCHANT, Thomas L. 825
Milton Pub Schs	HAY, Mary K. 515

MILWAUKEE

Agridata Network	WEENING, Richard W. 1315
Allen-Bradley Co	MILTON, Ardyce A. 845
Alverno Coll	DELAUCHE, Jean E. 289
	SAGER, Lynn S. 1074
	SHUTKIN, Sara A. 1134
Arthur Young & Co	HOOTKIN, Neil M. 557
Badger Infosearch	WATERSTREET, Darlene E. 1309
Borgelt Powell Peterson & Frauen SC	PERLSON, Beverly J. 959
Bruce Guadalupe Community Sch	MCKILLIP, Rita J. 811
Cardinal Stritch Coll	GILLETTE, Meredith 435
Columbia Hospital	HOLST, Ruth M. 554
Data Retrieval Corp	ERICKSON, Thomas 353
Double Joy Studios	EUKEY, Jim O. 356
Family Service America	HORNUNG, Susan D. 560
	MCGILL, Nancy A. 806
Foley & Lardner	LINK, Noreen M. 730
Frisch Dudek & Slattery Ltd	PETERSON, Christine E. . . . 963
IBM Corp	MCALLISTER, Caryl K. 792
Johnson Controls Inc	ALLSOP, Mary B. 17
	RAUSCH, Marian 1010

WISCONSIN (Cont'd)
  MILWAUKEE (Cont'd)
  Journal/Sentinel Inc   KRCHMAR, Sandra L. 677
                                           REITMAN, Jo 1022
  Lib Council of Metropolitan Milwaukee   TREBBY, Janis G. 1255
  Malcahy & Wherry S C   LINTNER, Mary K. 731
  Marquette Univ   GARDNER, William M. 418
                                           GILL, Norman N. 435
                                           HOPWOOD, Susan H. 558
                                           POLLARD, Margaret E. 981
                                           RUNKEL, Phillip M. 1067
                                           THIEL, Mark G. 1235
  Medical Coll of Wisconsin   ANTONIEWICZ, Carol M. 29
                                           ASU, Glynis V. 37
                                           BLACKWELDER, Mary B. . . . 102
                                           BRENNEN, Patrick W. 133
                                           HOUKOM, Susan L. 563
                                           KIRKALI, Meral 654
                                           STRUBE, Kathleen 1203
                                           WONG, Elizabeth M. 1362
  MGIC Investment Corp   MCKEE, Margaret J. 810
  Milwaukee Area Technical Coll   MEERDINK, Richard E. 821
  Milwaukee Board of Sch Directors   PINGEL, Carol J. 974
  Milwaukee County   GEISAR, Barbara J. 425
  Milwaukee County Federated Lib
    System   SAGER, Donald J. 1074
  Milwaukee County Historical Society   COONEY, Charles W. 241
  Milwaukee Institute of Art & Design   MARCUS, Terry C. 769
  Milwaukee Pub Lib   ALTMANN, Thomas F. 18
                                           BOTHAM, Jane 118
                                           CEBULA, Theodore R. 196
                                           KINNEY, Michael F. 653
                                           LOCKETT, Sandra B. 736
                                           MCKINNEY, Venora 812
                                           RAAB, Kathleen M. 1001
                                           SCHULLER, Susan M. 1101
                                           SCHWARTZ, Virginia C. . . . 1105
  Milwaukee Pub Museum   CHAPLOCK, Sharon K. 201
                                           OTTO, Susan J. 930
                                           TURNER, Judith C. 1264
  Milwaukee Sch of Engineering   SCHMIDT, Mary A. 1095
  Northwest General Hospital   MARKS, Coralyn 771
  Northwestern Mutual Life Insurance
    Co   BARLOGA, Carolyn J. 57
                                           HALL, Deborah A. 487
                                           MURPHY, Virginia A. 881
  Pharmacia P-L Biochemicals Inc   MENITOVE, Symie D. 824
  Quarles & Brady   JANKOWSKI, Susan H. 593
  Reinhart Boerner Van Deuren et al   BANNEN, Carol A. 54
  Rollins Burdick Hunter Inc   DETWILER, Eve N. 296
  St Charles Borromeo Sch   ANTHONY, Rose M. 29
  St Francis Seminary Sch   ZIRBES, Colette M. 1390
  St Joseph's Hospital   SHAIKH, Sunja L. 1119
  St Michael Hospital   SCHLUGE, Vicki L. 1094
  Sch Sisters of Notre Dame   GENIN, M S. 427
  Sch Sisters of St Francis   MISNER, Barbara 847
  Sisters of the Divine Savior   KINZER, Ferdinelle M. 653
  Southeastern WI Health Systems
    Agency   FLETCHER, Nancy S. 384
  Universal Foods Corp   MUNDSTOCK, Aileen M. 879
  Univ of Wisconsin at Milwaukee   AMAN, Mary J. 19
                                           AMAN, Mohammed M. 19
                                           BARUTH, Christopher M. 62
                                           BJORKLUND, Edi 100
                                           BLUE, Richard I. 107
                                           BOULANGER, Mary E. 119
                                           FONG, Wilfred W. 388
                                           GREENE, Victor R. 464
                                           HAENSEL, Kathrine C. 482
                                           HARTIG, Linda 508
                                           JONES, Richard E. 614
                                           KOVAN, Allan S. 673
                                           LUECHT, Richard M. 747
                                           MARKOWETZ, Marianna C. . . 771
                                           MORITZ, William D. 865
                                           PESCHEL, Susan M. 961
                                           POPESCU, Constantin C. . . . 983
                                           RISTIC, Jovanka 1036
                                           SABLE, Martin H. 1072
                                           SCHERDIN, Mary J. 1092

WISCONSIN (Cont'd)
  MILWAUKEE (Cont'd)
  Univ of Wisconsin at Milwaukee
                                           STANTON, Vida C. 1181
                                           SWEETLAND, James H. . . . 1215
                                           TOBIN, R J. 1247
  Village of Whitefish Bay   EGGUM, Janet M. 339
  W H Brady Co   GRUEL, Janice L. 474
  Wisconsin Gas Company   SIMPSON, Carolyn A. 1141
  Wisconsin Lutheran Coll   SIEGMANN, Starla C. 1136
MONTELLO
  City of Montello   TANNER, Linda L. 1223
NEENAH
  James River Corp   LAMB, Cheryl M. 689
  Kimberly-Clark Corp   DIETZ, Kathryn A. 302
                                           RYAN, Carol E. 1070
  Neenah Pub Lib   FLYNN, Kathryn J. 386
NEW LONDON
  Sch District of New London   DIEHL, Carol L. 301
NORTH FOND DU LAC
  Spillman Pub Lib   HANAMAN, Nancy J. 494
OAK CREEK
  City of Oak Creek   TASNADI, Deborah L. 1224
  Oak Creek-Franklin Joint Sch District   MORROW, Kathryn M. 869
  Oak Creek Pub Lib   TALIS, Ross M. 1221
                                           UTZINGER, Orchard L. 1270
OCONOMOWOC
  Oconomowoc Area Sch District   KILANDER, Ann H. 647
ONEIDA
  Oneida Tribe of Indians of Wisconsin   CORNELIUS, Charlene E. . . . 246
OSHKOSH
  EAA Aviation Foundation Inc   PARKS, Dennis H. 943
  Mercy Medical Center   GEBHARDT, Sharon E. 424
  Univ of Wisconsin at Oshkosh   FU, Tina C. 407
                                           JONES, Norma L. 614
                                           KRUEGER, Gerald J. 680
                                           SHARMA, Ravindra N. 1122
  Winneconne Community Schs   TERESINSKI, Sally S. 1231
  Winnefox Lib System   SCHWARZ, Joy L. 1105
PEWANKEE
  Waukesha County Technical Institute   AHL, Ruth E. 8
PLATTEVILLE
  Sch District of Platteville   KRENTZ, Roger F. 677
  Univ of Wisconsin at Platteville   DANIELS, Jerome P. 273
                                           GERLACH, Donald E. 429
                                           SCHMITT, Madelaine M. . . . 1096
PORTAGE
  Portage Free Lib   JENSEN, Hans W. 598
RACINE
  Racine Pub Lib   PATANE, John R. 946
                                           SCHINK, Sandra C. 1093
  S C Johnson & Son Inc   FREY, Luanne C. 402
                                           TERANIS, Mara 1231
  St Luke's Memorial Hospital   GRONHOLM, Shirley A. 472
RANDOLPH
  Village of Randolph   DEICH, Ione L. 288
RHINELANDER
  Nicolet Coll   BRANT, Susan L. 129
  Sch District of Rhinelander   SLYGH, Gyneth 1151
RICE LAKE
  Rice Lake Area Sch District   HOLLE, Arthur J. 551
                                           REINAGLE, Carol M. 1021
RIPON
  Ripon Coll   BURR, Charlotte A. 163
                                           MCGOWAN, Sarah M. 007
RIVER FALLS
  Univ of Wisconsin at River Falls   ADAM, Anthony J. 4
                                           FORTIN, Clifford C. 391
                                           STEINWALL, Susan D. 1186
ROSHOLT
  Rosholt Pub Schs   ADAMS, Helen R. 5
ST FRANCIS
  St Francis Pub Lib   HACHMEISTER, Helen M. . . . 481
  Western Information Services   WESTERN, Eric D. 1327
SHEBOYGAN
  Donohue & Associates Inc   CONDON, John J. 236
  Mead Pub Lib   PETZOLD, Mary E. 966
                                           VAN STRATEN, Daniel G. . . . 1277
SHOREWOOD
  Shorewood Pub Lib   WEISMAN, Suzy 1319

WISCONSIN (Cont'd)

SPARTA
Sparta Area Schs   HAUG, Pauline C. 512
STEVENS POINT
Portage County Pub Lib   SWIFT, Leonard W. 1216
Sentry Insurance A Mutual Co   WHELIHAN, Annette S. 1329
Sisters of St Joseph   GUZMAN, Mary C. 479
Univ of Wisconsin at Stevens Point   GILLESBY, John D. 435
     PAUL, Patricia J. 949
     STRUPP, Sybil A. 1203

SUN PRARIE
Sun Prairie Pub Lib   REANDEAU, Walter E. 1013
SUPERIOR
Sch District of Superior   AXT, Randolph W. 42
Univ of Wisconsin at Superior   CARMACK, Bob 183
     JOHNSON, Denise J. 603
     TORNQUIST, Kristi M. 1251

TWO RIVERS
Two Rivers Lib Board   HEITKEMPER, Elsie M. 523
VERONA
City of Verona   KNODLE, Shirley M. 665
WATERTOWN
Northwestern Coll   GOSDECK, David M. 452
WAUKESHA
Carroll Coll   EVANS, Russel C. 358
     VAN ESS, James E. 1275
Sch District of Waukesha   ROOZEN, Nancy L. 1054
Southeastern WI Regnl Plng
  Commission   KLAUSMEIER, Arno M. 658
Waukesha County Lib System   GOSZ, Kathleen M. 453
Waukesha Memorial Hospital   ODDAN, Linda 916
Waukesha South High Sch   MCGHEE, Patricia L. 806
WAUPUN
Waupun Pub Lib   GREEN, Thomas A. 462
WAUSAU
Marathon County Pub Lib   PETERSON, Diane S. 963
Wausau Hospital Center   LIBRO, Teresa M. 725
Wausau Insurance Co   NUERNBURG, Donna S. 912
Wisconsin Valley Lib Service   ELDRED, Heather A. 342
     ORCUTT, Linda S. 925

WAUWATOSA
Curative Rehabilitation Center   BOCHTE, Terrence C. 109
WEST ALLIS
West Allis Pub Lib   WASICK, Mary A. 1308
WEST BEND
United Church of Christ   CORBLY, James E. 245
WHITEFISH BAY
Milwaukee Metropolitan Sewerage
  District   LANK, Dannette H. 696
WHITEWATER
Univ of Wisconsin at Whitewater   MANDERNACK, Scott B. ... 765
     PAYSON, Evelyn H. 951
     SCHARFENBERG, George
      E. 1090
     WESTON, Karen A. 1327

WISCONSIN RAPIDS
McMillan Memorial Lib   WILSON, William J. 1353
Sch District of Wisconsin Rapids   LINDSAY, Jane A. 729

WYOMING

CASPER
Fort Caspar Museum   MENARD, Michael J. 823
Wyoming Lib Association   ANDERSON, Lynnette 24
CHEYENNE
Archives Museums & Historical
  Department   YELVINGTON, Julia A. 1379
Laramie County Lib System   BYERS, Edward W. 168
     OSBORN, Lucie P. 927
MD Software   SCHELL, Catherine L. 1091
Sch District 1 Laramie County   MIDDLETON, Dorothy J. 833
State of Wyoming   MCGOWAN, Anne W. 807
     MENDOZA, Anthanett C. ... 824
US Federal Courts   FERRALL, Bard R. 373
Univ of Wyoming   SEEBAUM, Carol J. 1111
Wyoming State   WALTERS, Corky 1301
WY State Archives Museums & Histl
  Dept   HALLBERG, Carl V. 489
Wyoming State Lib   JOHNSON, Wayne H. 609
Wyoming Supreme Court   RAO, Dittakavi N. 1008

WYOMING (Cont'd)

CODY
Buffalo Bill Historical Center   PINSON, Patricia A. 975
     STOPKA, Christina K. 1198

EVANSTON
Wyoming State Hospital   MATCHINSKI, William L. 783
GILLETTE
Campbell County Pub Lib   SIEBERSMA, Dan 1135
Campbell County Sch District   PROCTOR, Deborah K. 994
     WURBS, Sue A. 1374

GREEN RIVER
Sweetwater County Lib System   HIGBY, Helen E. 537
JACKSON
Teton County Lib   EFFINGER, Nancy E. 338
LANDER
Fremont County Lib   HEUER, William J. 535
Lander Valley Regional Medical
  Center   HEUER, Jane T. 535
LARAMIE
Albany County Pub Lib   SIMPSON, Susan M. 1142
Ivinson Memorial Hospital   JACKSON, Sue H. 588
Univ of Wyoming   BALDWIN, David A. 51
     BURMAN, Marilyn P. 161
     CHATTON, Barbara A. 204
     CHISUM, Emmett D. 209
     COLLIER, Carol A. 232
     CORS, Paul B. 248
     COTTAM, Keith M. 250
     EMERSON, Tamsen L. 347
     MACK, Bonnie R. 756
     MEALEY, Catherine E. 820
     NELSON, Michael L. 894
     OSTRYE, Anne T. 929
     ROOS, Tedine J. 1053
     STEWART, William L. 1193
     VANARSDALE, William O. . 1272
     WOODS, Janet R. 1367
Wyoming Lib Association   NORD, Kay 908
RAWLINS
Carbon County Sch District 1   HOFF, Vickie J. 547
ROCK SPRINGS
Western Wyoming Community Coll   KALABUS, Robert L. 622
SHERIDAN
Sheridan Coll   IVERSON, Deborah P. 585
WORLAND
Washakie County School District 1   HARRINGTON, Carolyn B. . . 504

CANADA

ALBERTA

AIRDRIE
Airdrie Municipal Lib   OTTOSEN, Charles F. 930
ATHABASCA
Athabasca Univ   DWORACZEK, Marian 330
BARRHEAD
County of Barrhead   SLEMKO, M Y. 1148
CALGARY
Access Information Services   LEESMENT, Helgi 712
Acres International Ltd   ROSS, Evelyn M. 1058
Calgary Board of Education   MACRAE, Lorne G. 758
Calgary Pub Lib   ANDERSON, Gail 23
     HARDMAN, Joye A. 500
     MANSON, Bill B. 767
     REID, Patricia M. 1019
     RHYNES, H B. 1026
     WAUGH, Alan L. 1310
     WHITE, Valerie L. 1332
     WING, Marjorie 1354
City of Calgary   KLUMPENHOUWER,
      Richard 662
Deloitte Haskins & Sells   KOENDERINCK, Myrla J. ... 668
Dome Petroleum Limited   HARDY, Kenneth J. 501
     HARVEY, Carl G. 509
Energy Resource Conservation Board   JOHNSON, Liz 607
Environment Canada-Parks   GUNSON, Murray J. 478
     LIGHTFOOT, Robert J. 726
Esso Resources Canada Ltd   GASHUS, Karin C. 421
Gulf Canada Resources Limited   PARKINSON, Susan L. 943

ALBERTA (Cont'd)
CALGARY (Cont'd)
Home Oil Co Limited

FRASER, Gail L.	399	
LANE, Barbara K.	694	

Inst of Sedimentary & Petroleum
Geology

HAU, Edward T. 512
Mount Royal Coll — BAILEY, Madeleine J. 46
Novacor Chemicals Ltd — JENKINS-PENDER,
Maureen 597
PanCanadian Petroleum Ltd — KENNEDY, Marcia G. 641
Peat Marwick Mitchell — OAKE, Rhena E. 913
Petroleum Recovery Inst — JANJUA, Zaytoon 593
Rural Lib Training Project — MING, Marilyn 846
Shell Canada Limited — ZUBA, Elizabeth J. 1390
Southern Alberta Institute of
Technology — MATHEZER, Pauline B. 784
Texaco Canada Resources — DURIE, Debbie L. 328
Thorne Ernst & Whinney — DEGINNUS, Roxie 287
Univ of Calgary — BOUEY, Elaine F. 119
BROWN, David K. 143
CARRIE, Judith A. 186
CRAMER, Eugene C. 255
DEBRUIJN, Deborah I. 285
GHENT, Gretchen K. 430
GOODWIN, C R. 450
HAYWARD, Edith C. 517
HERSCOVITCH, Pearl 533
HOGAN, Kathleen M. 549
KING, Marjorie H. 651
MACDONALD, Alan H. 754
MOFFAT, N L. 852
NASSERDEN, Marilyn D. 889
NECHKA, Ada M. 891
ONN, Shirley A. 924
ROBERTSON, Kathleen A. . 1042
ROBINS, Nora D. 1043
STEELE, Apollonia L. 1184
STEVELMAN, Sharon R. 1190
TENER, Jean F. 1231
VINE, Rita F. 1285
Western Gas Marketing Limited — VARSEK, Elizabeth A. 1279
CAMROSE
Camrose Lutheran Coll — INGIBERGSSON, Asgeir 582
CANMORE
Canmore Pub Lib — LUTHY, Jean M. 750
EDMONTON
Alberta Agriculture — BATEMAN, Robert A. 63
NOGA, Dolores A. 907
STARR, Jane E. 1182
Alberta Alcohol & Drug Abuse
Commission — REIMER, Bette J. 1020
Alberta Community & Occupational
Health — MCLAUGHLIN, W K. 813
Alberta Culture Lib Services — CLUBB, Barbara H. 223
Alberta Economic Development &
Trade — GORDON, Donna M. 451
Alberta Education — ANDREWS, Christina A. 26
KRATZ, Hans G. 676
Alberta Environment Lib — FRALICK, Deborah L. 395
Alberta Municipal Affairs — BAYRAK, Bettie 68
Alberta Research Council — GEE, Sharon 425
Canada Environment Canada — JORDAN, Peter A. 616
Caritas High Sch — COMPRI, Jeannine L. 235
Community & Occupational Hlth Lib — LAVKULICH, Joanne 704
Edmonton Pub Lib — BERNARD, Marie L. 88
DUFFUS, Sylvia J. 323
RICHARDS, Vincent P. 1029
SINCLAIR, John M. 1142
Edmonton Sun — HU, Shih S. 568
Government of Alberta — KUJANSUU, Sylvia S. 683
FELL, Anthony M. 370
Grant Macewan Community Coll — MCDOUGALL, Donald B. 803
Legislative Assembly of Alberta — LOVENBURG, Susan L. 743
Lovenburg Lib Consultation — ALLISON, Scott 17
Univ of Alberta — BERTRAM, Sheila K. 91
BOUCHER, Michel 118
BRUNDIN, Robert E. 150
BUSCH, B J. 165
CAMPBELL, Sandra M. 177
COOKE, Geraldine A. 241

ALBERTA (Cont'd)
EDMONTON (Cont'd)
Univ of Alberta

DANCIK, Deborah B. 272
DELONG, Kathleen M. 290
DE SCOSSA, Catriona 295
FETTERMAN, Nelma I. 374
FREEMAN, Peter 401
HEBDITCH, Suzan A. 519
HOBBS, Brian 545
HOWE, Ernest A. 565
JONES, David L. 612
KUJANSUU, Asko J. 683
LASKOWSKI, Seno 700
MACGOWN, Madge C. 755
OBERG, Dianne 913
OLSON, Hope A. 922
REICHARDT, Randall P. ... 1018
ROONEY, Sieglinde E. 1053
SCHRADER, Alvin M. 1099
SHORES, Sandra J. 1132
SMITHERS, Anne B. 1162
STARR, Lea K. 1182
STRATHERN, Gloria V. 1200
TRAICHEL, Rudolf D. 1253
WRIGHT, John G. 1371
YOUNG, Margo 1382
ZIEGLER, Fred 1388
FORT MCMURRAY
Fort McMurray Regional Hospital — BRUCE, Marianne E. 149
Keyand Coll — JARVIS, Marylea 595
Syncrude Canada Ltd — SLOAN, Stephen M. 1150
FORT SASKATCHEWAN
Fort Saskatchewan Municipal Lib
Board — REDFORD, Marcia E. 1014
GRANDE PRAIRIE
Grande Prairie Pub Lib — SMITH, Linda A. 1157
GROUARD
Alberta Vocational Center — BRUCE, Robert D. 149
LAC LA BICHE
Alberta Vocational Center — ENGLESAKIS, Marina F. 350
LETHBRIDGE
Agriculture Canada — CUTLER, C M. 268
Lethbridge Pub Lib — RAND, Duncan D. 1006
Univ of Lethbridge — DROESSLER, Judith B. 320
JONES, Winstan M. 615
SEYEDMAHMOUD, Donna
A. 1118
RED DEER
Gishler Group Lib & Info System
Consults — GISHLER, John R. 438
Red Deer Coll — ARMSTRONG, Mary L. 32
BOULTBEE, Paul G. 119
BUCKLEY, Joanna 154
Red Deer Regional Hospital Centre — KAVANAGH, Elizabeth G. ... 631
ST ALBERT
St Albert Pub Lib Board — KISSAU, Arlene M. 656
SHERWOOD PARK
Strathcona County Board of
Education — SCHMIDT, Raymond J. 1095
STRATHMORE
Marigold Lib System — LUNN, Rowena F. 749
THREE HILLS
Prairie Bible Institute — BRADLEY, Harold K. 126
JORDAHL, Ronald I. 616
VEGREVILLE
Alberta Environmental Centre — LEE, Diana W. 709
BRITISH COLUMBIA
ABBOTSFORD
Fraser Valley Coll — HARRIS, Winifred E. 506
SIFTON, Patricia A. 1137
Fraser Valley Regional Lib — GOW, Susan P. 454
RAY, Gordon L. 1011

BRITISH COLUMBIA (Cont'd)

BURNABY
British Columbia Institute of
  Technology ..... WEEKS, Gerald M. 1315
Greater Vancouver Lib Federation ..... CLANCY, Ron 215
Simon Fraser Univ ..... FERJUC, Joan A. 372
..... GROVES, Percilla E. 474
..... MALINSKI, Richard M. 763

CASTLEGAR
Selkirk Coll ..... DEON, Judy S. 293
..... MANSBRIDGE, John 767

CLEARBROOK
Farser Valley Regional Lib ..... GARRAWAY, Babs L. 420
Fraser Valley Regional Lib ..... HUDSON, Susan P. 570
..... KIERANS, Mary E. 647
..... SEARCY HOWARD, Linda
  M. 1109
..... VIIERANS, Mary E. 1284

COQUITLAM
Coquitlam Pub Lib ..... DUNCAN, Deborah J. 325
..... UTSUNOMIYA, Leslie D. 1270

CRANBROOK
East Kootenay Community Coll ..... WHITELEY, Catherine M. .. 1333

DELTA
Fraser Valley Regional Lib ..... CHAN, Mary L. 199

HOPE
Hope Sch District 32 ..... SCOTT, William H. 1108

KAMLOOPS
Cariboo Coll ..... LEVESQUE, Nancy B. 719

NANAIMO
Malaspina Coll ..... BRIDGES, Douglas W. 135
Pacific Biological Station ..... MILLER, Gordon 838
Vancouver Island Regional Lib ..... MEADOWS, Donald F. 819

PRINCE GEORGE
Coll of New Caledonia ..... MAYFIELD, Betty L. 790
..... PLETT, Katherine 978
Prince George Pub Lib ..... NICHOLSON, Dianne L. 902

RICHMOND
Richmond Pub Lib ..... KELNER, Gregory H. 638
..... WILLISON, Maureen I. 1348
..... WEESE, Dwain W. 1316
Sch District 38

SURREY
Kwantlen Coll ..... FRANCIS, Derek R. 396
Surrey Pub Lib ..... ASHCROFT, Susan M. 35
..... GUTTERIDGE, Paul 479
..... HAABNIIT, Ene 480
..... SMITH, Stan 1161

VANCOUVER
Asia Pacific Foundation of Canada ..... BROOME, Diana M. 141
Cancer Control Agy of British
  Columbia ..... NOBLE, David 906
Forintek Canada Corp ..... JOHNSON, Marione 607
G F Stron Rehabilitation Centre ..... TROWSDALE, Robert G. 1258
H A Simons Ltd ..... PEPPER, David A. 958
Human Resources Development
  Group ..... HAYCOCK, Carol A. 515
Insurance Corp of British Columbia ..... MAKAREWICZ, Grace E. ... 762
Kinsmen Rehabilitation Foundation of
  BC ..... ELLIS, Kathy M. 344
L M Warren Inc ..... WARREN, Lois M. 1306
Pacific Press Ltd ..... MOONEY, Shirley E. 858
Pemberton Houston Willoughby Bell,
  et al ..... BONIN, Denise R. 114
Registered Nurses Association of BC ..... AUFIERO, Joan I. 39
Russell & Du Moulin ..... INSELBERG, Diana E. 583
Shaughnessy Hospital ..... JONSSON, Ellenor A. 616
Univ of British Columbia ..... BEWLEY, Lois M. 93
..... CAMERON, Hazel M. 175
..... CHAN, Diana L. 199
..... CROOKS, Sylvia A. 260
..... DOBBIN, Geraldine F. 307
..... DODSON, Suzanne C. 308
..... DYKSTRA, Stephanie 331
..... EASTWOOD, Terence M. ... 333
..... GONNAMI, Tsuneharu 447
..... HOPKINS, Richard L. 558
..... KREIDER, Janice A. 677
..... LEITH, Anna R. 714
..... LIGHTHALL, Lynne I. 727
..... MCINNES, Douglas N. 809

BRITISH COLUMBIA (Cont'd)

VANCOUVER (Cont'd)
Univ of British Columbia ..... PITERNICK, Anne B. 976
..... ROTHSTEIN, Samuel 1060
..... SAINT, Barbara J. 1075
..... SALTMAN, Judith M. 1077
..... STEPHENSON, Mary S. ... 1188
..... STUART-STUBBS, Basil F. . 1204
Vancouver Board of Trade ..... MAROTZ, Karen V. 772
Vancouver Community Coll ..... ANASTASIOU, Joan D. 21
..... APPLETON, Brenda F. 30
..... CARTER, Charles R. 189
..... WIEBE, Frieda 1336
Vancouver General Hospital ..... TRIP, Barbara M. 1257
Vancouver Pub Lib ..... BELL, Barbara 76
..... CAMPBELL, Brian G. 176
..... CAPES, Judy L. 179
..... DURSTON, Corinne L. 329
Vancouver Sch Board ..... HAYCOCK, Kenneth R. 515
Vancouver Sch of Theology ..... HART, Elizabeth 507
Vancouver Vocational Inst ..... DEVAKOS, Elizabeth R. 297

VERNON
Vernon Sch District 22 ..... FUNK, Grace E. 410
..... GRABINSKY, Warren B. 455

VICTORIA
Acton Information Resources Mgmt
  Ltd ..... ACTON, Patricia 4
Greater Victoria Hospital Society ..... VAN REENEN, Johannes A. 1277
Legislative Assembly of British
  Columbia ..... BARTON, Joan A. 62
Ministry of Labor & Consumer
  Services ..... MURPHY, Joyce 880
Ministry of Tourism, Recreation,
  Culture ..... MORGAN, Anne E. 863
Univ of Victoria ..... EKLAND, Patricia A. 341
..... GIBB, Betty J. 431
..... HALLIWELL, Dean W. 489
..... HAMILTON, Donald E. 492
..... KOMOROUS, Hana J. 670
..... MOEHR, Jochen R. 851
..... ROMANIUK, Elena 1052
..... ROSE, Frances E. 1054
..... SALMOND, Margaret A. ... 1077
..... SCOTT, Priscilla R. 1108
..... SIGNORI, Donna L. 1137
..... SLADE, Alexander L. 1147
..... TAGGART, William R. 1220
..... WHITE, Donald J. 1330

WEST VANCOUVER
Department of Fisheries and Oceans ..... KELLER, Susan E. 636
West Vancouver Memorial Lib ..... MOUNCE, Jack 873

MANITOBA

BRANDON
Agriculture Canada ..... SIMUNDSSON, Elva D. 1142
Brandon General Hospital ..... EAGLETON, Kathleen M. 331
Brandon Univ ..... JONES, June D. 613
..... SZIVOS, Maria 1218

FLINFLON
Flinflon Sch Division 46 ..... HOBBS, Henry C. 545

PINAWA
Atomic Energy of Canada Limited ..... GIBSON, Gladys N. 432

PORTAGE LA PRAIRIE
Manitoba Research Council ..... WILTON, Greg J. 1353

SELKIRK
Lord Selkirk Sch Division ..... PETROWSKI, Stan M. 965
Selkirk Community Lib ..... REID, Marion I. 1019

WINNIPEG
Canada Department of Fisheries &
  Oceans ..... MARSHALL, Kenneth E. 774
Canadian Grain Commission ..... BLANCHARD, Jim 103
Canadian Wheat Board ..... EMOND, Lucille I. 348
..... REEDMAN, M R. 1015
City of Winnipeg ..... BENSON, Theodore L. 83
..... GRAHAM, Heather F. 456
..... MARTEN, Mary L. 775
..... REINALDO DA SILVA,
  Joann T. 1021
..... SMITH, John R. 1156

MANITOBA (Cont'd)
WINNIPEG (Cont'd)
Clinicom International — COVVEY, H D. 252
Government of Manitoba — TOOTH, John E. 1251
Legislative Lib of Manitoba — NIELSON, Paul F. 903
Manitoba Attorney-General — HERNANDEZ, Marilyn J. 531
Manitoba Education — TRAILL, Susan 1253
Manitoba Legislative Lib — IRVINE, Joyce 584
Province of Manitoba — MACLOWICK, Frederick B. . . . 757
Red River Community Coll — FOWLER, Margaret A. 394
PORTER, Patricia K. 985
River East Sch Division 9 — GUILBERT, N P. 476
Ukrainian Cultural & Educational
Centre — CHOMENKO, Tamara L. 210
Univ Manitoba — DIVAY, Gabriele 306
Univ of Manitoba — BUDNICK, Carol 155
FAWCETT, Patrick J. 367
FERGUSON, Earle C. 372
GODAVARI, S N. 442
HARPER, Judy A. 503
KERR, Audrey M. 644
LINCOLN, Robert S. 728
MARSHALL, Denis S. 774
NICHOLLS, Pat 901
ROUTLEDGE, Patricia A. . . . 1062
SANTORO, Corrado A. 1082
TULLY, Sharon I. 1262
WRIGHT, Patrick D. 1372
Univ of Winnipeg — CONVERSE, Wm R. 239
DELONG, Linwood R. 290
Winnipeg Pub Lib — EGAN, Bessie C. 338
Winnipeg Sch Division 1 — BROWN, Gerald R. 144

NEW BRUNSWICK
BATHURST
Bathurst Sch District 42 — RUSSELL, Sharon A. 1069
EDMUNDSTON
Haut-Saint-Jean Regional Lib Board — CHIASSON, Gilles 207
FREDERICTON
Government of New Brunswick — BEYEA, Marion L. 93
Legislative Lib of Fredericton — SWANICK, Eric L. 1213
Univ of New Brunswick at Fredericton — COLSON, Judith K. 234
POPE, Andrew T. 983
RAUCH, Doris E. 1010
York Regional Library Board — LE BUTT, Katherine L. 708
MONCTON
Albert Westmorland Kent Regional
Lib — POTVIN, Claude 987
Atlantic Lottery Corp — ENNS, Carol F. 350
District 15 Sch Board — WILLIAMS, Eve A. 1343
Hopital Dr G L Dumont — BRIDEAU, Marthe 135
Univ de Moncton — ARSENAULT, Alban 35
BOUDREAU, Berthe 118
DIONNE, Charlotte A. 305
LEBLANC, Amedee 708
SACKVILLE
Mount Allison Univ — EADIE, Tom 331
MCNALLY, Brian D. 815
ST-ANDREWS
Saint John Regional Lib — KISSICK, Barbara J. 656
ST-JEAN
Bibliotheque Regionale de Saint-Jean — NADEAU, Sylvie 886
SAINT JOHN
New Brunswick Museum — ROSEVEAR, E C. 1057
Saint John Regional Lib — COGSWELL, Howard L. 227
COWAN, Barbara M. 252
Univ of New Brunswick at Saint John — COLLINS, Susan H. 233
SHIPPAGAN
Univ de Shippagan — GAUTHIER, Rose M. 423

NEWFOUNDLAND
GRAND FALLS
Newfoundland Pub Libs Board — MORTON, Elaine 870
ST JOHN'S
Cabot Institute of Applied Arts & Tech — MORGAN, Pamela S. 864
RAHAL, M P. 1003
Canada Inst for Scientific & Technl
Info — TILLOTSON, Joy G. 1245
House of Assembly — RICHARDS, Norma J. 1028

NEWFOUNDLAND (Cont'd)
ST JOHN'S (Cont'd)
Memorial Univ of Newfoundland — BALSARA, Aspi 53
BROWN, Jean I. 144
DENNIS, Christopher J. 292
ELLIS, Richard H. 345
HEINO, Dan R. 522
MEWS, Alison J. 829
MILNE, Dorothy J. 845
TIFFANY, William C. 1244
WOOD, Alberta A. 1363
Newfoundland Pub Libs Board — CAMERON, H C. 174
PENNEY, Pearce J. 957
TORBAY
Roman Catholic Sch Board — MARTINEZ, Helen 779

NORTHWEST TERRITORIES
YELLOWKNIFE
Government of the Northwest
Territories — BAER, Susan E. 45
O'KEEFE, Kevin T. 919
Indian & Northern Affairs Canada — ALBRIGHT, Donald A. 10
Prince of Wales Northern Heritage
Centre — KOBELKA, Carolynn L. 666

NOVA SCOTIA
AMHERST
Maritime Resource Management
Service Inc — CAMPBELL, Margaret E. 177
BRIDGEWATER
South Shore Regional Lib — HIMMELMAN, Pauline 542
DARTMOUTH
Canada Department of Fisheries &
Oceans — SUTHERLAND, J E. 1211
Dartmouth District Sch Board — LYNCH, Darrell B. 751
Dartmouth Regional Lib — LEWIS, Aileen M. 722
Dartmouth Regional Vocational Sch — HUANG, Paul T. 568
HALIFAX
Atlantic Sch of Theology — GILCHRIST-DOBSON,
Norma J. 434
Dalhousie Univ — AMEY, Lorne J. 20
BIRDSALL, William F. 98
DYKSTRA, Mary E. 331
ETTLINGER, John R. 356
FRICK, Elizabeth A. 403
HAMILTON, Elizabeth 492
HSIUNG, Lai Y. 567
MACLENNAN, Oriel C. 757
MCNAIR, Alison T. 815
NOWAKOWSKI, Frances C. . . 911
READE, Judith G. 1012
SIEGERT, Lindy E. 1136
Halifax City Regional Lib — COLBORNE, Michael B. 230
MACKENZIE, Heather L. 756
Halifax District Sch Board — CURRIE, Bertha B. 266
Izaak Walton Killam Children's
Hospital — LOGAN, Penelope A. 737
Maritime Telephone & Telegraph — BANFIELD, Eilzabeth S. 54
Mount St Vincent Univ — BIANCHINI, Lucian 94
GLENISTER, Peter 441
PARIS, Terrence L. 940
Nova Scotia Attorney General Dept — DEYOUNG, Marie 298
Nova Scotia Legislative Lib — GURAYA, Harinder 478
Nova Scotia Provincial Lib — MORASH, Claire E. 862
Novatron Information Corp — POTTER, Daniel 987
THORSTEINSON, William
A. 1243
Province House — MURPHY, Margaret F. 881
Saint Mary's Univ — SMITH, Arthur M. 1152
TAYYEB, Rashid 1229
MULGRAVE
Eastern Counties Regional Lib — MACRURY, Mary E. 758
SYDNEY
Cape Breton Regional Lib — MACINTOSH, Ian R. 755
TRURO
Colchester-East Hants Regional Lib — FREVE, Reay H. 402
MARSH, Mary L. 773
WOLFVILLE
Acadia Univ — BATES, Iain J. 64

ONTARIO

ANCASTER
Redeemer Coll — SAVAGE, Daniel A. 1085

ARNPRIOR
Arnprior Pub Lib — BARKE, Judith P. 56

AURORA
Canada Law Book Inc — CAMPBELL, Catherine J. . . . 176
Electronic Information — FOSTER, Anne 392
Vp Electronic Info Srvs — FOSTER, Margaret A. 392

BARRIE
Barrie Pub Lib — ADDY, Kathryn J. 6
MULLEN, Gail C. 877

BRAMPTON
Brampton Pub Lib & Art Gallery — BURGIS, Grover C. 159
CHAN, Bruce A. 199

BROCKVILLE
Brockville Pub Lib Board — HOWELL, Raymond C. 565

BURLINGTON
Burlington Pub Lib — JARVIS, A W. 595

CAMBRIDGE
Cambridge Pub Lib — SKELTON, W M. 1146
Ontario Cad/Cam Center — LARSON, Anna M. 699

CHALK RIVER
Atomic Energy of Canada Limited — ALBURGER, Thomas P. 11
LEWIS, Leslie 723
Petawawa National Forestry Institute — MITCHELL, Mary H. 849

CHATHAM
Ontario Centre for Farm Machinery — KEARNS, Mary J. 633
MCNAUGHT, Hugh W. 816
Union Gas Ltd — WHALEY, E M. 1328

CORNWALL
Cornwall Pub Lib — HARSANYI, Nancy L. 507

DON MILLS
Canadian Gas Assn — KARCICH, Grant J. 627
IBM Canada Ltd — LAUER, Marjorie A. 702
Multipoint Communications Limited — SMITH, Iain 1155
Ontario Hospital Association — TAGG, John T. 1219
Ortho Pharmaceutical Canada Ltd — BODNAR, Marta 109
Proctor & Redfern Group — SPARK, Catherine L. 1171
Richard de Boo Publishers — HALPIN, Gerard B. 490
Southam Communications Limited — MAYNARD, John C. 790
WISE, Sunny 1357

DOWNSVIEW
Ontario Ministry of Transportation, Comm — PAVLIN, Stefanie A. 951
ZVEJNIEKS, Laila R. 1391
Univ of Toronto — JONES, B E. 611
MILLS, Judy E. 844
York-Finch General Hospital — KAKOSCHKE, Mona S. 622
York Univ — MONTY, Vivienne 857
STEVENS, Mary 1190

ETOBICOKE
Etobicoke Board of Education — CHURCHMAN, Alice M. 213
Etobicoke Pub Lib Board — BUNCE, Catherine J. 157
DETERVILLE, Linda C. 296
LAITMAN, Sheila 688
Hoffmann-LaRoche Ltd — HOARE, Colin G. 545

EXETER
South Huron Hospital — WILCOX, Linda M. 1338

FORT FRANCES
Fort Frances Rainy River Board of Educ — KITTS, T J. 657

GLOUCESTER
Gloucester Pub Lib — NEILL, Sharon E. 892
PICARD, Albert 970

GODERICH
Huron County Pub Lib — COX, Sharon P. 253

GRIMSBY
Grimsby Public Lib — CHURCH, Barry S. 213

GUELPH
Guelph Pub Lib — KEARNS, Linda J. 633
John F Ross Collegiate & Vocational Inst — WRIGHT, Jonathan C. 1371
Uniroyal Ltd — COLE, Lorna P. 231
Univ of Guelph — BECKMAN, Margaret L. 73
BLACK, John B. 101
GILLHAM, Virginia A. 436
GOODGER-HILL, Carol 448
KATZ, Bernard M. 630
PAL, Gabriel 935

ONTARIO (Cont'd)
GUELPH (Cont'd)
Univ of Guelph —
PAWLEY, Carolyn P. 951
ROURKE, Lorna E. 1061

HALIBURTON
Haliburton County Pub Lib — LEVIS, Joel 721

HAMILTON
Canadn Ctr for Occupational Hlth/Safety — LAM, Vinh T. 689
Canadian Center for Occupational Safety — BROWNRIDGE, James R. . . . 149
City of Hamilton Board of Education — PAPOUTSIS, Fotoula 939
Corp of the City of Hamilton — BROWN, Phyllis E. 147
Dofasco Inc — DUFF, Ann M. 323
Hamilton General Hospital — MCKINLAY, Bessie J. 811
Hamilton Law Association — HEARDER-MOAN, Wendy P. 518
Hamilton Pub Lib — LEHNERT, Sharon A. 713
McMaster Univ — BENDIG, Regina 79
FITZGERALD, Dorothy A. . . . 382
FLEMMING, Tom 384
HAYNES, Robert B. 517
HAYTON, E E. 517
HILL, Graham R. 539
PANTON, Linda A. 938
RIDLEY, A M. 1033
THOMSON, Donna K. 1241
Mohawk Coll — BLACK, Sandra M. 101
Wentworth Lib Board — CALBICK, Ian M. 172

ISLINGTON
Albright & Wilson American Inc — LOGAN, Nancy L. 737

KANATA
Mitel Corp — PHILLIPS, Rosemary 969
National Lib of Canada — TURNER, Sharon 1265

KINGSTON
Information Corner: Health Scis Lib Srvs — FLOWER, M A. 386
Kingston Psychiatric Hospital — MORLEY, Mae L. 865
Ontario Cancer Treatment & Resrch Fndtn — FORKES, David 390
Queen's Univ — MACDERMAID, Anne 754
MCBURNEY, Margot B. 792
MOON, Jeffrey D. 857
SKEITH, Mary E. 1145
St Lawrence College — LOVE, Barbara 743
St Mary's of the Lake Hospital — LEVI, Penelope G. 720

KITCHENER
Kitchener Pub Lib — CORSTON, Christine F. 248
HOFFMAN, Susan J. 548
Kitchener Waterloo Record — COATES, Penny A. 224
Univ of Waterloo — SHEPHERD, Murray C. 1127

LEAMINGTON
Leamington Pub Lib — NICHOLSON, Jill A. 902

LINDSAY
County of Victoria — GIBSON, Mary B. 432

LONDON
D B Weldon Lib — LEE, Robert 711
Labatt Brewing Co Limited — LEHWALDT, Marliese 713
London & Middlesex County — BENOIT, Ursula L. 83
London Pub Libs & Museums — MITCHELL, Margaret M. 849
London Pub Lib — CADA, Elizabeth J. 170
London Pub Lib Board — OSBORNE, Reed E. 927
Ontario Lib Service of Thames — SKRZESZEWSKI, Stan E. . . 1147
Parkwood Hospital — SINGER, Eleanore M. 1143
St Joseph's Health Centre of London — LIN, Louise 727
PARR, John R. 943
3M Canada Inc — STEPHENSON, Cheryl E. . . 1188
Univ of Western Ontario — CLOUSTON, John S. 223
CRAVEN, Timothy C. 256
FYFE, Janet H. 411
GALSWORTHY, Peter R. . . . 415
KATZER, Sylvia U. 630
LAW, Jean M. 704
LUTZ, Linda J. 750
MEERVELD, Bert 821
MILLER, Beth M. 836
NEILL, Sam D. 892
NELSON, Michael J. 894
RIPLEY, Victoria E. 1035

ONTARIO (Cont'd)
LONDON (Cont'd)
Univ of Western Ontario

SCHULTE-ALBERT, Hans G.	1101
SMITH, Louise	1157
TAGUE, Jean M.	1220
WHITE, Janette H.	1331

MAPLE
Vaughan Pub Libs — KOSTIAK, Adele E. ... 673
MARKHAM
Gear Computers International — MORTON, Robert E. ... 870
Magna International Inc — JACKSON, Agnes M. ... 586
MISSISSAUGA
Allelix Inc — ATHA, Shirley A. ... 37
Atomic Energy of Canada Limited — GALTON, Gwen ... 415
Canada Systems Group — BYERS, Cathy L. ... 168
Credit Valley Hospital — KORNUTA, Helen ... 672
The Learning Tree Ltd — DAVIS, Virginia K. ... 281
Mississauga Pub Lib System — DINEEN, Diane M. ... 304
RYAN, Noel ... 1071
Ontario Research Foundation — WEI, Carl K. ... 1316
Petro-Canada Products — DAVIS, Wendy A. ... 281
NEILSON, Ann ... 892
Univ of Toronto — MCLEAN-LOWE, Dallas ... 814
Xerox Research Center of Canada — BASSETT, Betty A. ... 63
MONTEBELLO
Univ of Illinois at Chicago — WARREN, Peggy A. ... 1306
NEPEAN
Algonquin Coll of Applied Arts & Tech — BREGAINT, Bernard J. ... 131
HAUCK, Danuta ... 512
Bell-Northern Research — BIRKS, Grant F. ... 98
NEWMARKET
Town of Newmarket — READ-STARK, Marilyn A. ... 1012
NIAGARA FALLS
Acres International Ltd — D'AMBOISE, Marion J. ... 271
John Coutts Lib Srvs — PORTEUS, Andrew C. ... 985
NIAGARA-ON-THE-LAKE
Niagara-on-the-Lake Pub Lib Board — MOLSON, Gerda A. ... 853
NORTH BAY
North Bay Pub Lib — NORRGARD, Don K. ... 909
NORTH YORK
C-I-L Inc — DUNBAR, Janet M. ... 325
WEAVER, Maggie ... 1312
Calligraphic Arts Guild of Toronto — FREEMAN, Elayne B. ... 400
North York Pub Lib Board — BURNETT, Wayne C. ... 162
WILLIAMS, Lorraine O. ... 1344
Seneca Coll of Applied Arts & Technology — DAVIDSON-ARNOTT, Frances E. ... 277
Sunnybrook Medical Center — ARMSTRONG, Jennifer E. ... 32
York Univ — HOFFMANN, Ellen J. ... 548
VARMA, Divakara K. ... 1278
WYMAN, Kathleen M. ... 1375
OAKVILLE
Sheridan Coll — MACKENZIE, Shirley A. ... 756
WILBURN, Marion T. ... 1338
Town of Oakville — LA CHAPELLE, Jennifer R. ... 686
OHAUA
National Energy Board — PARK, Nancy R. ... 941
ORILLIA
Orillia Pub Lib — MCKINNON, Katherine D. ... 812
OSHAWA
Durham Coll of Applied Arts — BARCLAY, Susan L. ... 55
Ontario Ministry of Revenue — CRAIG, Wendy E. ... 254
Oshawa Pub Lib Board — BROOKING, Ruth P. ... 140
OTTAWA
Agriculture Canada — BOISVENUE, Marie J. ... 111
GAZELEY, Joan E. ... 424
MORTON, Margaret L. ... 870
Bell Canada — COVIENSKY, Lana ... 252
Bell-Northern Research — MASON-WARD, Lesley ... 781
Canada Department of External Affairs — GUILBERT, Manon M. ... 476
Canada Employment Immigration Commission — SUNDER-RAJ, P E. ... 1210

ONTARIO (Cont'd)
OTTAWA (Cont'd)
Canada Inst for Scientific & Technl Info — IRELAND, Michael A. ... 583
LATYSZEWSKYJ, Maria A. ... 702
REILLY, Brian O. ... 1020
SAMSON, Mary ... 1079
SMITH, Elmer V. ... 1154
Canada Post Corp — WEERASINGHE, Jean Y. ... 1316
Canadian Association of Research Libs — MCCALLUM, David L. ... 793
Canadian Federal Government — KAYE, Barbara J. ... 632
Canadian Health Libs Association — KENT, Diana ... 642
Canadian Lib Association — BOWES, Laurie A. ... 121
COONEY, Jane ... 241
PORTER, David E. ... 984
Canadian Nurses Association — SHIFF, Linda S. ... 1130
Canadn Organz for Devlpmnt Through Educ — ST. AMANT, Robert ... 1075
Carleton Univ — BRIGGS, Geoffrey H. ... 135
CAMPBELL, Laurie G. ... 177
CLARKE, Bozena ... 218
ROGERS, Dorothy S. ... 1049
ROSSMAN, Linda ... 1059
SCHNEIDER, Tatiana ... 1097
Children's Hospital of Eastern Ontario — TAYLOR, Margaret P. ... 1227
Conference Board of Canada — BUCHANAN, Zoe A. ... 153
ROSTAMI, Janet ... 1059
Consumer & Corporate Affairs Canada — HEROUX, Rejean W. ... 532
Department of External Affairs — LAFRANCHISE, David ... 688
Economic Council of Canada — BONAVERO, Leonard C. ... 113
Energy Mines & Resources of Canada — JESKE, Margo ... 600
MAYRAND, Florian ... 791
SCOLLIE, F B. ... 1106
WILSON, Valerie E. ... 1353
Environment Canada — SAVIC, Edward I. ... 1086
Finance/Treasury Board Lib — FIRTH, Leslie ... 379
Fulcrum Technologies Inc — EDDISON, E P. ... 335
Government of Canada — RICHER, Suzanne ... 1030
VANDOROS, Z ... 1275
Health & Welfare Canada — STABLEFORD, Bonita A. ... 1177
House of Commons — TAYLOR, Loretta C. ... 1227
INET 2000 — SOLOSKY, A G. ... 1166
Info Globe — MILLER, Katherine J. ... 839
Information Management Services — KNOPPERS, Jake V. ... 665
International Development Research Ctr — MORIN-LABATUT, Gisele ... 865
Lib of Parliament — BROWN, Barbara E. ... 142
LEGAULT, Michel ... 712
LEGERE, Monique E. ... 712
MARLEAU, Gilles ... 772
PARE, Richard ... 940
STILES, William G. ... 1194
Ministry of the Solicitor General — MOORE, Heather J. ... 859
National Archives of Canada — COOK, Terry G. ... 240
GORDON, Robert S. ... 451
KIDD, Betty H. ... 646
ST. PIERRE, Normand ... 1075
National Energy Board — KRALIK, Jane M. ... 675
National Gallery of Canada — HUNTER, Jacqueline E. ... 576
National Lib of Canada — ALGAR, L E. ... 13
ARBEZ, Gilbert J. ... 30
AUBREY, Irene E. ... 38
BALATTI, David R. ... 50
BELL, Irena L. ... 77
BISHOP, Heather F. ... 99
BRIERE, Jean M. ... 135
BRODIE, Nancy E. ... 139
BRYCE, Maria C. ... 152
BURNS, Barrie A. ... 162
BURROWS, Sandra ... 163
CAMLIOGLU, Ergun ... 175
CLEMENT, Hope E. ... 221
COLQUHOUN, Joan E. ... 234
DAWE, Heather L. ... 282
DEAVY, Elizabeth A. ... 284
DELSEY, Thomas J. ... 290
DUCHESNE, Roderick M. ... 322

ONTARIO (Cont'd)
OTTAWA (Cont'd)
National Lib of Canada

DUNN, Mary J.	327
DUPRE, Monique	327
DURANCE, Cynthia J.	328
DUSSIAUME, Robert	329
EVANS, Gwynneth	357
FORGET, Louis J.	390
FOX, Rosalie	395
GOODMAN, Julia M.	449
KALLMANN, Helmut M.	623
KANNEL, Ene	625
KAVANAGH, Susan E.	631
KIRKWOOD, Francis T.	655
LANOUETTE, Marie	696
LAWLESS, Ruthmary G.	704
LEMOINE, Claude	715
LEUNG, Frank F.	719
LUNAU, Carrol D.	748
MACDONALD, Marcia H.	754
MACDONALD, Patricia A.	754
MACLELLAND, Margaret A.	757
MANNING, Ralph W.	767
MCKEEN, C E.	810
MCQUEEN, Lorraine	817
OKUDA, Sachiko E.	920
OZAKI, Hiroko	932
PARENT, Ingrid T.	940
QUEINNEC, Young H.	999
RENAUD, Monique M.	1023
ROBERTS, Nancy	1041
ROBINSON, W D.	1045
ROGERS, Helen F.	1049
SCHRYER, Michel J.	1100
SCOTT, Judith W.	1107
SCOTT, Marianne F.	1107
SIMARD, Luc	1139
SMALE, Carol	1151
TSAI, Shaopan	1260
VALENTINE, Scott	1271
VAN DER BELLEN, Liana	1273
WEBBER, Reginald N.	1313
WEIR, Leslie	1319
WELCH, Grace D.	1321
WILLIAMSON, Michael W.	1347
ZIELINSKA, Marie F.	1388

National Museums of Canada

BLACK, Jane L. 101
BOJIN, Minda A. 111

National Research Council of Canada

LEONARDO, Joan M. . . . 717
LOW, Mary 743
PARKKARI, John 943
SCHMIDT, Diana M. . . . 1095
VEEKEN, Mary L. 1280
WALLACE, Kathryn M. . . . 1297

Office of the Auditor General — RAY, Cathy J. 1011
Ontario Lib Service of Rideau — ARONSON, Marcia L. . . . 34
Ottawa Board of Education

PERRY, William B. 961
WILLIAMS, Shelagh C. . . . 1346

Ottawa Citizen — PROULX, Steven D. . . . 996
Ottawa Civic Hospital — BROWN, Mabel 145
Ottawa Pub Lib

CORDUKES, Laura L. . . . 246
FRAPPIER, Gilles 399
MATTE, Suzanne 785
MUTCH, Donald G. 883
SPRY, Patricia 1176

Ottawa Regional Cancer Centre — LEBRUN, Anne 708
Ottawa Roman Cath Separate Sch
Bd — DEVOE, Dan L. 297
Parliament of Canada — SPICER, Erik J. 1174
Peat Marwick Mitchell — BELL, Hope A. 77
Pub Archives of Canada

BATCHELDER, Robert . . . 63
BIRRELL, Andrew 99
STONE, Gerald K. 1197
VOSIKOVSKA, Jana 1289

Revenue Canada Customs & Excise — PARSONAGE, Dianne L. . . . 944
Royal Canadian Mounted Police — WALDRON, Nerine R. . . . 1294
Saint Paul Univ — HICKS, Barbara A. 536

ONTARIO (Cont'd)
OTTAWA (Cont'd)
Statistics Canada

BILLINGSLEY, Andrew G. . . . 96
COURNOYER, Joanne 251
JENSEN, L B. 599

Supreme Court of Canada — MURRAY-LACHAPELLE,
Rosemary F. 882

Telecom Canada — GROHN, Susan M. 471
Telesat Canada — FOSTER, Eileen F. 392
Transport Canada — ZIMMERMAN, Suzan E. . . . 1389
Univ of Ottawa

BANFILL, Christine 54
DUHAMEL, Marie 324
LEBLANC, Jean J. 708
OUIMET, Jacinthe 930
RATSOY, Marye G. 1010
RICHER, Yvon 1030
ST. JACQUES, Suzanne L. . . . 1075
SAURIOL, Guy L. 1085
THIBAULT, Jean 1235
THOMSON, Dorothy F. . . . 1241
WARD, William D. 1304

PEMBROKE
Pembroke Pub Lib — MEHTA, Subbash C. 821
PETERBOROUGH
Trent Univ

GENOE, Murray W. 427
WISEMAN, John A. 1357

PICKERING
Ontario Hydro

BELLEFONTAINE, Gillian . . . 78
HENDERSON, Deborah A. . . . 526

PORT ELGIN
Bruce County Pub Lib — FLEMING, Anne 384
REXDALE
Canadian Standards Association — MARSHALL, Alexandra P. . . . 773
Garrett Canada — THODY, Susan I. 1235
RICHMOND HILL
Ontario Lib Service of Trent — HARRISON, Karen A. 507
Richmond Hill Pub Lib

ABRAM, Persis R. 3
LLOYD, Mary E. 735

ROCKLAND
City of Rockland — DALRYMPLE, Odette 271
ST CATHARINES
Brock Univ — RUSSELL, Moira 1069
St Catherine's General Hospital — ARMBRUST, Susan P. 31
ST THOMAS
St Thomas Pub Lib — RHYNAS, Don M. 1026
SARNIA
Dow Chemical Canada Inc

CHAPMAN, Phyllis C. 202
RUTHERFORD, Frederick S. . 1070

Esso Petroleum Canada — GASPAR, Noel J. 421
Fiberglas Canada Inc — BICE, Lee A. 94
Lambton Coll — TURNER, Margaret A. 1264
Polysar — O'DONNELL, Rosemary F. . . . 917
SAULT MARIE
Algoma Univ Coll — BAZILLION, Richard J. 68
SCARBOROUGH
Bank of Montreal — BOSMA, Elske M. 117
Centennial Coll of Applied Arts &
Tech — WOOD, Ronald P. 1365
Consumers' Gas Co Ltd — IVEY, Donna M. 586
International Thomson Profsnl
Publshg — FLEMING, Jack C. 384
Scarborough Pub Lib — SOLTYS, Amy 1166
Scarborough Pub Lib Board

BASSNETT, Peter J. 63
MULLERBECK, Aino 877
O'NEILL, Louise N. 924

Univ of Toronto

BALL, John L. 52
HODGINS, Imelda J. 546

STRATFORD
Stratford Pub Lib Board — KIRKPATRICK, Jane E. 655
SUDBURY
Government of Ontario — WHALEN, George F. 1328
Lauentian Univ — GOLTZ, Eileen A. 447
Laurentian Hospital — HAMILTON, Simone 492
Laurentian Univ

KELLY, Glen J. 637
SLATER, Ronald J. 1148

Northeastern Ontario Oncology
Program — GOSS, Alison M. 453
Sudbury Board of Education — BERTRAND, Doreen M. 91
SUTTON
York Region Board of Education — MCCRACKEN, Ronald W. . . . 799

ONTARIO (Cont'd)

THORNHILL
Town of Markham Pub Libs — HARE, Judith E. 501

THUNDER BAY
Ontario Lib Service of Nipigon — HSU, Peter T. 567
V B Cook Co Limited — SENNETT, Judith A. 1115

TORONTO
Addiction Research Foundation — CHAN, Margy 199
Allen B Veaner Associates — VEANER, Allen B. 1280
Art Gallery of Ontario — ARDERN, Christine M. 31
Bank of Nova Scotia — NOKES, Jane E. 907
Bassel Sullivan & Leake — FOOTE, Martha L. 388
Bell-Northern Research — SELLERS, Alexander G. . . . 1114
Blake Cassels & Graydon — MORRIS, Sandra M. 867
URQUHART, Dawn M. 1270
Bonnie Campbell & Associates — CAMPBELL, Bonnie 176
Borden & Elliot — DENTON, Vivienne K. 293
Canadian Bankers' Association — LEAMEN, Nancy J. 707
Canadian Broadcasting Corp — EARLS, M L. 332
Canadian Geriatrics Research Society — SABLJIC, John A. 1072
YANCHINSKI, Roma N. . . . 1377
Canadian Imperial Bank of Commerce — MILLER, Ann M. 835
Canadian Mental Health Association — ROUP, Carol E. 1061
Canadian Natl Institute for the Blind — HAYES, Janice E. 516
Canadian Press — KHAN, Asma S. 646
Centre for Christian Studies — TELFORD, Shelagh S. 1230
CMQ Communications — BECHER, Henry 71
Coopers & Lybrand — ATTINGER, Monique L. 38
MCCALLUM, Anita J. 793
Data Resources — ZURBRIGG, Lyn E. 1391
Deloitte Haskins & Sells — MACDONALD, Yvonne M. . . . 754
Dun & Bradstreet Canada Ltd — LA MARCHE, David L. 689
SOMMERS, Patrick C. 1167
Espial Productions Ltd — CAMPBELL, Harry 176
Fenco Engineers Inc — BUISMAN, Maria J. 156
CROXFORD, Agnes M. 262
The Financial Post — GUHERIDGE, Allison A. 476
ODHO, Marc 917
George Brown Coll of Applied Arts & Tech — HARDY, John L. 500
The Globe and Mail — HYLAND, Barbara 580
VALPY, Amanda M. 1271
Goodman & Goodman — RODGER, Jane 1047
Government of Ontario — VANDERELST, Wil 1274
Hay Management Consultants — ABRAM, Stephen K. 3
Hospital for Sick Children — GREEN, Deidre E. 461
Hugh MacMillan Medical Center — BERNSTEIN, Elaine S. 89
Humber College — HOOGKAMER, Dawne 556
I P Sharp Associates Limited — KEITH, David A. 635
Imperial Oil Limited — CZARNOTA, Les 268
RYANS, Kathryn J. 1071
Industrial Accident Prevention Assn — HARMS PENNER, Dolores T. 502
INFOMART — BLOXAM, Gerald S. 107
Information Resources — KLEMENT, Susan P. 660
International Thomson — BROWN, Michael 146
Laventhol & Horwath — ASHTON, Margaret A. 36
Legislative Assembly of Ontario — LAND, Reginald B. 692
Lovel Information Services — SMITH, Anne C. 1152
Lyndhurst Hospital — CHONG, Jean L. 210
Maclean Hunter Limited — OLSHEN, Toni 922
Maclean's Magazine — GRANT, Roberta L. 458
Manufacturers Life Insurance Co — CITROEN, Julie M. 215
McKim Advertising Ltd — PETRUGA, Patricia L. 965
McMillan Binch — GULLIVER, Joanne V. 477
Mead Data Central — RODGER, Stephen J. 1047
Medical Information Services — DAVEY, Dorothy M 270
Merilees Associates Inc — MERILEES, Bobbie 826
Metro Toronto Reference Lib — FRIEDLAND, Frances K. 403
GUNDARA, Jaswinder 477
Metropolitan Separate Sch Board — BOWEN, Tom G. 120
SEBANC, Mark F. 1110
Metropolitan Toronto Lib Board — BEETON, Elizabeth O. 74
KOTIN, David B. 673
LORENTOWICZ, Genia 741
MACDONALD, Christine S. . . 754
MCCUBBIN, George M. 800
MILANICH, Melanie M. 834
SCHWENGER, Frances S. . 1105
TSUI, Josephine 1260

ONTARIO (Cont'd)

TORONTO (Cont'd)
Metropolitan Toronto Lib Board — WATSON, Joyce N. 1309
Metropolitan Toronto Management — SMITH, Pamela 1159
Metropolitan Toronto Reference Lib — ALSTON, Sandra 18
BAWA, Indira 67
BURCHELL, Patricia M. 158
FAIRLEY, Craig R. 361
JACKSON, Craig A. 587
LAVERTY, Corinne Y. 703
MCCANN, Judith B. 794
STANGL-WALKER, Teresa L. 1180
Micromedia Limited — CASEY, Victoria L. 192
DE STRICKER, Ulla 296
FAST, Louise 366
GAGNE, Frank 412
GIBSON, Robert 432
GRAY, Sandra A. 460
OLMSTEAD, Marcia E. 921
Ministry of Consumer/Commercial Relation — NIXON, Audrey I. 906
Municipality of Metropolitan Toronto — DANIEL, Eileen 272
Noranda Minerals Inc — GOODINGS, Sally A. 449
North York Board of Education — MOORE, May E. 860
Ontario Cancer Institute — MORRISON, Carol A. 868
VAN ORDER, Mary J. 1276
Ontario Hydro — MCCLYMONT, Karen A. 797
Ontario Institute for Studies — BREGZIS, Ilze 131
BULAONG, Grace F. 156
Ontario Legislative Assembly — BURTON, Donna M. 164
DICKERSON, Mary E. 300
POWELL, Wyley L. 989
SMITH, Cynthia M. 1153
Ontario Lib Association — MCKEE, Penelope 810
MOORE, Lawrence A. 860
Ontario Medical Association — GREENWOOD, Jan 465
Ontario Ministry — BONGARD, Nancy D. 114
Ontario Ministry of Agriculture & Food — GINSLER, Mindy F. 438
Ontario Ministry of Citizenship/Culture — GRODSKI, Renata 471
WIERUCKI, Karen A. 1337
Ontario Ministry of Education — SHIP, Martin I. 1131
Ontario Ministry of Health — STANDING, Doris A. 1179
Ontario Ministry of Housing — BREZINA, Jennifer R. 134
Ontario Ministry of Industry — SERMAT-HARDING, Kaili I. . 1116
Ontario Ministry of Labour — GOLD, Sandra 444
MORRISON, Brian H. 867
WALSH, Sandra A. 1300
Ontario Ministry of Natural Resources — LOUET, Sandra 742
Ontario Ministry of the Environment — TIPLER, Stephen B. 1246
Ontario Ministry of Treasury & Economics — WEATHERHEAD, Barbara A. 1312
Ontario Mncpl Employees Retirement Syst — FAIR, Linda A. 361
Ontario Police Commission — MERRYWEATHER, J M. 827
Parker Management Associates — PARKER, Arthur D. 941
Price Waterhouse — SEDGWICK, Dorothy L. 1111
WELLS, Nancy E. 1322
Quill & Quire — DOWDING, Martin R. 315
Reed Inc — DRAKE, James B. 318
Registered Nurses Association of Ontario — BOITE, Mary E. 111
Reteaco Inc — LESLIE, Nathan 718
LOWRY, Douglas B. 745
LOWRY, John D. 745
Royal Bank of Canada — DANCE, Barbara L. 272
DYSART, Jane I. 331
GRIMES, Deirdre E. 470
KEALEY, Catherine M. 632
Royal Ontario Museum — WILBURN, Gene 1338
Royal Trust — MITCHELL, Faye F. 848
Ryerson Polytechnical Institute — KENDALL, Sandra A. 640
KING, Olive E. 652
NORTH, John A. 909
PHELAN, Daniel F. 967
TUDOR, Dean F. 1262
St Michael's Hospital — WONG, Anita 1362
Sedgwick Tomenson Inc — CHOUDHURI, Kabita 211

ONTARIO (Cont'd)
TORONTO (Cont'd)
Southam Communications Limited | WISE, Eileen M. 1356
Strathy Archibald & Seagram | COLVIN, Alison J. 234
Sun Life Assurance Co of Canada | CARVALHO, Sarah V. 191
| GIBSON, Elizabeth A. 432
| LUCIANI, Ellie 746
Technical Services Group | WEIHS, Jean 1317
Thorne Ernst & Whinney | JOHNSON, John E. 606
Toronto Dominion Bank | PULLEYBLANK, Mildred C. .. 997
| SMITH, Ruth P. 1160
Toronto East General Hospital | SMITHIES, Roger 1162
Toronto General Hospital | BAYNE, Jennifer M. 67
Toronto Institute of Medical
  Technology | LADD, Kenneth F. 687
Toronto Pub Lib | CHAN, Arlene S. 199
| DE RONDE, Paula D. 294
| FOWLIE, Les 394
| KRYGSMAN, Nancy T. 681
| RODGER, Elizabeth A. 1047
Toronto Stock Exchange | JUOZAPAVICIUS, Danguole
  T. 620
Toronto Sun Publishing Co | KIRSH, Julie 655
Toronto Western Hospital | REID, Elizabeth A. 1018
Tory Tory DesLauriers & Binnington | DARBY, Janet M. 274
TPF&C Limited | BERCOVITCH, Sari 84
Trinity Coll | CORMAN, Linda W. 246
TV Ontario | VOLPATTI, Rechilde 1288
Univ of Toronto | ANNETT, Adele M. 28
| BELLAMY, Patricia C. 78
| BREGMAN, Alvan M. 131
| CHERRY, Joan M. 206
| COOK, C D. 239
| CUMMINS, Marlene 264
| DENIS, Laurent G. 292
| FASICK, Adele M. 366
| GARLOCK, Gayle N. 419
| GRANATSTEIN, M E. 457
| HAJNAL, Peter I. 484
| HEATON, Gwynneth T. 519
| HORNE, Alan J. 560
| HORNE, Bonnie L. 560
| LANDON, Richard G. 693
| MARSHALL, Joanne G. 774
| MEADOW, Charles T. 819
| MELVILLE, Karen E. 823
| MOORE, Carole I. 858
| RAE, E A. 1002
| SCHABAS, Ann H. 1088
| TURKO, Karen A. 1263
| VERYHA, Wasyl 1283
| VUKOV, Vesna 1290
| WILKINSON, John P. 1340
| WILLIAMSON, Nancy J. ... 1347
Utlans International of Canada Inc | BROWNING, Linda A. 148
Utlas International of Canada Inc | FRITZ, Richard J. 405
| TAYLOR, Karen E. 1227
Utlas International US Inc | CURTIS, Alison J. 267
Victoria Univ | BRANDEIS, Robert C. 128
W G Hutchison Co | JAGIELLOWICZ, Jadzia 591
Watts Griffis & McQuat Limited | STRACHAN, Pamela H. ... 1199
Wellesley Hospital | EMPEY, Verla 348
Weston Research Centre | WONG, Lusi 1363
William M Mercer Limited | CHIU, Lily F. 209
Winkler Filion & Wakely | MASEN, Naunihal S. 780
York Pub Lib | SHIRINIAN, George N. 1131
York Univ | QUIXLEY, James V. 1001
VINELAND STATION
Agriculture Canada | FRAUMENI, Michael A. 399
WATERLOO
Mutual Life of Canada | ELLERT, Barbara M. 343
Univ of Waterloo | BEGLO, Jo N. 74
| PARROTT, James R. 944
Wilfrid Laurier Univ | SKELTON, Brooke 1146
WELLAND
Niagara Coll of Applied Arts & Tech | BOWMAN, Robert J. 122
| HEWITT, Heather O. 535
Welland Pub Lib | HANNS, Stephen 497
WHITBY
Town of Pickering Pub Lib | LINTON, Linda J. 731

ONTARIO (Cont'd)
WILLOWDALE
Bloorview Children's Hospital | LAMBERT, Deborah B. 690
Canadian Federation of Independent
  Bus | COORSH, Katalin 244
Crawford Adventist Academy | MCLEAN, Paulette A. 814
Datapoint Canada Inc | KEYS, Sandra A. 645
Metropolitan Toronto Separate Sch
  Board | PEPE, Berenice A. 957
North York Board of Education | GREAVES, H P. 461
Ontario Bible Coll | BELDAN, A C. 76
| JOHNSON, James R. 605
Toronto Jewish Congress | SPEISMAN, Stephen A. ... 1172
WINDSOR
City of Windsor | WALSH, G M. 1299
Univ of Windsor | SINGLETON, Cynthia B. ... 1143
| SOULES, Aline E. 1169
| WOLFE, Martha K. 1361
Windsor Pub Lib Board | ISRAEL, Fred C. 585
| ISRAEL, Kathleen 585
The Windsor Star Southam Inc | HANDY, Mary J. 495
WOODSTOCK
Oxford County Lib | WEBB, Mary J. 1313
Woodstock Pub Lib | JONES, Nancy P. 614
WOODVILLE
Victoria County Board of Education | DEKKER, Barbara A. 288

PRINCE EDWARD ISLAND
CHARLOTTETOWN
Government of Prince Edward Island | YKELENSTAM, Priscilla I. ... 1380
Prince Edward Island Prfsnl Libns
  Assn | LEDWELL, Bill 709
Provincial Lib | SCOTT, Donald 1107
Queen Elizabeth Hospital | KIELLY, Marion J. 647
Univ of Prince Edward Island | MANOVILLE, Susanne 767

QUEBEC
ALMA
City of Alma | BOUCHARD, Martin 118
AYLMER
City of Aylmer | MACKEY, Laurette 756
BEACONSFIELD
Beaconsfield Pub Lib | HIRON, Barbara A. 543
City of Beaconsfield | BADGER, Carole 44
BEAUPORT
Centre Hospitalier Robert-Giffard | PLAMONDON, Yolande M. .. 977
BOUCHERVILLE
Canada Inst for Scientific & Technl
  Info | VENNE, Louise 1282
City of Boucherville | DUBOIS, Florian 322
Service de Recherche Documentaire
  DSI | DUVAL, Marc 329
BROMONT
Mitel Corp | RICHARD, Marie F. 1028
BROSSARD
Town of Brossard | LACROIX, Yvon A. 687
CHICOUTIMI
CEGEP at Chicoutimi | HARVEY, Serge 509
Coll of Chicoutimi | GAUDREAU, Louis 422
Univ of Quebec | BOULET, Paul E. 119
CHICOUTIMI NORD
Institut Roland-Saucier | SAUCIER, Danielle 1084
CHISASIBI
Cree Sch Board | GOSSELIN, Claude 453
COTE SAINT-LUC
Cote Saint-Luc Pub Lib | LONDON, Eleanor 738
COWANSVILLE
Cowansville Institution | FILIATRAULT, Sylvie 376
DORVAL
Bibliotheque Municipale de Dorval | DAUNAIS, Marie J. 275
City of Dorval | BOUMAN, Judith C. 119
Kativik Sch Board | FINN, Julia P. 378
Sandoz Canada Inc | BOISVERT, Diane 111
| BOLSVERT, Diane B. 113
DRUMMONDVILLE
Commission Scolaire de
  Drummondville | HEON, Gerard 530
Office for the Handicapped of Quebec | JANIK, Sophie 593

QUEBEC (Cont'd)

HULL
Bell Canada .... MALEK, Stanislaw A. 763
City of Hull .... BOYER, Denis P. 123
                                        CHEVRIER, Francine 207
Government of Canada .... MAILLOUX, Jean Y. 761
Univ of Quebec .... BERGERON, Gilles I. 86
                                        CHENIER, Andre 206

JOLIETTE
Ecole les Melezes .... LEMIEUX, Louise 715
JONQUIERE
CEGEP at Jonquiere .... LAPOINTE, Louise 697
KIRKLAND
City of Kirkland .... CLEMENT, Clarie 221
LA BAIE
City of La Baie .... LEBEL, Anne 707
LAVAL
Coll Montmorency .... CHAUMONT, Elise 204
                                        DANIS, Rolland J. 273
Government of Canada .... BERGERON, Pierrette 86
Jewish Rehabilitation Hospital .... SHANEFIELD, Irene D. 1120
LE GARDEUR
City of Le Gardeur .... MARTIN, Ginette 776
LENNOXVILLE
Bishop's Univ .... SHEERAN, Ruth J. 1125
LEVIS
C S R Louis Frechette .... GELINAS, Rene 426
City of Levis .... LAMOUREUX, Michele 691
LONGUEUIL
City of Longueuil .... OUIMET, Yves 930
Comission Scolaire Regnl de
    Chambly .... GELINAS, Sylvain 426
MASCOUCHE
City of Mascouche .... ALLARD, Diane 14
MONTEBELLO
The Sedbergh Sch .... WENK, Arthur B. 1324
MONTREAL
Abbott Laboratories .... HEROUX, Genevieve 532
Archives Traces de Montreal .... CHAGNON, Danielle G. 197
ASFETM .... MERCIER, Diane 825
Atomic Energy of Canada Limited ..... NISH, Susan J. 905
Bank of Montreal .... ORLANDO, Richard P. 926
                                     PIGGOTT, Sylvia E. 972
Bell Canada .... SYKES, Stephanie L. 1217
                                     YOUNG, Patricia M. 1383
Bell Canada Enterprises .... FOWLES, Alison C. 394
Byers Casgrain .... EDER, Sonya 336
Canada Cement Lafarge .... SHLIONSKY, Anatoly 1132
Canada Inst for Scientific & Technl
    Info .... SCHEPPER, Josee H. 1091
Canadian Centre for Architecture .... DE LUISE, Alexandra 290
Canadian Jewish Congress .... NEFSKY, Judith L. 892
Canadian Marconi Co .... GONZALEZ, Paloma 448
Canadian National Railway Co .... HAGOPIAN, Shake 483
Canadian Pacific Rail .... BERARDINUCCI, Heather R. ... 84
Canadian Tobacco Manufactures'
    Council .... CLARKE, Robert F. 219
                                     TREVICK, Selma D. 1255
CECM .... LAPOINTE, Georgette 697
Ctr Hospitalier
    Notre-Dame-de-la-Merci .... TESSIER, Mario C. 1233
Centrale des Bibliotheques .... PELLETIER, Rosaire 955
Centre d'Animation, de
    Developpement .... BRETON, Lise 133
Centre Doc .... PARE, Gilles G. 940
Centre Hospitalier Cote-des-Neiges .. JUNEAU, Jocelyne B. 620
Cinematheque Quebecoise .... BEAUCLAIR, Rene 70
City of Montreal .... MEUNIER, Pierre 829
                                     THACH, Phat V. 1233
City of St Leonard Pub Lib .... CORBEIL, Lizette 245
Coll Andre-Grasset .... LUSSIER, Jean P. 749
Coll des Eudistes de Rosemont ...... AUGER, Bernard 39
Coll Marie-Victorin .... CHARETTE, Rejean 203
Concordia Univ .... APPLEBY, Judith A. 30
                                     BOUCHER, Lorna M. 118
                                     GALLER, Anne M. 414
                                     GAMEIRO, Maria H. 416
                                     HAWKE, Susan J. 513
                                     HOFFMAN, Sandra D. 548
                                     KATZ, Solomon B. 630

QUEBEC (Cont'd)

MONTREAL (Cont'd)
Concordia Univ
                                     MAHARAJ, Diana J. 760
                                     MARRELLI, Nancy M. 773
                                     MATE, Albert V. 783
                                     WINIARZ, Elizabeth 1355
Conseillers en Information Inc .... DUBEAU, Pierre 321
Dawson Coll .... MOSER, Beryl R. 870
Department Regional Industrial
    Expansion .... LAPLANTE, Carole 697
Ecole Polytechnique .... LEMYRE, Nicole 715
                                     THIBAUDEAU, Louise 1235
Federal Business Development Bank .. MCINTOSH, Julia E. 809
                                     ROWE, David G. 1062
                                     THIVIERGE, Lynda M. 1235
Fraser Hickson Institute .... ACKERMAN, Frances W. 3
The Gazette .... MCFARLANE, Agnes 805
Hopital du Sacre-Coeur .... LESSARD, Josee 718
Hopital Notre-Dame .... ALLARD, Andre 14
Hopital Riviere-des-Prairies .... AUBIN, Robert 38
Hopital Saint-Luc .... DUCHESNEAU, Pierre 322
Hopital Sainte-Justine .... LECOMPTE, Louis L. 708
Imperial Tobacco .... MUKHERJEE, Yolande 876
Info-Recherche .... DARLINGTON, Susan 275
Institut de Readaptation de Montreal BOYER, Maryse 123
Institut de Recherche en Sante ...... GREGOIRE, Fleurette 466
Institut de Recherches Cliniques .... SMYTH, John 1162
Institut Philippe-Pinel .... BEAUDET, Normand 70
                                     LESAGE, Jacques 717
Institute of Canadian Bankers .... VONKA, Stephanie 1288
Jewish Pub Lib .... RABY, Eva F. 1001
KPMG Peat Marwick .... MACFARLANE, Judy A. 755
La Presse Newspaper .... CHALIFOUX, Jean P. 197
LavaLin Inc .... MARCOTTE, Marcel 769
Les Franciscains .... PAPILLON, Yves 939
Les Pretres de Saint-Sulpice de
    Montreal .... AUMONT, Gerard 40
Lib of Administrative Sciences ...... COURTEMANCHE, Pierre
                                        O. 251
Maimonides Hospital Geriatric Centre BRESING, Sheindel H. 133
Martineau & Walker .... AMNOTTE, Celine 20
McGill Univ .... CAYA, Marcel 195
                                     COUGHLIN, Violet L. 250
                                     CRAWFORD, David S. 256
                                     CURRAN, William M. 266
                                     EVANS, Calvin D. 356
                                     FERAHIAN, Salwa 371
                                     FINLAY, Barbara J. 378
                                     GARNETT, Joyce C. 419
                                     GROEN, Frances K. 471
                                     HOBBINS, Alan J. 545
                                     HOWARD, Helen A. 564
                                     LAMBROU, Angella 691
                                     LEIDE, John E. 713
                                     MACLEAN, Eleanor A. 757
                                     MITTERMEYER, Diane 850
                                     MOHAMMED, Selima 852
                                     MOLLER, Hans 853
                                     MOLLER, Hans 853
                                     MORRISON, H D. 868
                                     ORMSBY, Eric 926
                                     RICHARD, Marc 1028
                                     RIDER, Lillian M. 1032
                                     TEES, Miriam M. 1229
                                     WALUZYNIEC, Hanna 1302
                                     WERYHO, Jan W. 1325
McMaster Meighen .... CHAREST, Ronald 203
Ministry of Energy and Resources ... MARCIL, Louise 769
Monenco Consultants Ltd .... KAMICHAITIS, Penelope H. . . 624
Montreal Children's Lib .... WALSH, Mary A. 1300
Montreal General Hospital .... KOBER, Gary L. 666
                                     STAMBOULIEH, Nora 1179
National Bank of Canada .... SABOURIN, Agathe 1073
National Film Board of Canada ...... BIDD, Donald W. 94
                                     BUTLER, Patricia 167
                                     TODD, Rose A. 1248
Office of the French Language ...... ROBINSON, Chantal 1043
Paramax Electronics Inc .... RICHARDS, Stella 1028
Province of Quebec .... KLOK, Buddhi 662

QUEBEC (Cont'd)
MONTREAL (Cont'd)
Quebec Safety League — BISSON, Jacques 100
Quebec Secretary of State — MONDOU, Cecile 854
Quebec Univs — DUPUIS, Onil 327
Reader's Digest Magazines Ltd — NISHIZAKI, Colette 905
Residence Notre-Dame-de-la-Trinite — GAULIN, S D. 422
Royal Bank of Canada — O'SHAUGHNESSY, John M. . 928
RABCHUK, Gordon K. 1001

Sir Mortimer B Davis Jewish Gen
  Hospital — STILMAN, Ruth 1194
Societe Radio-Canada — BACHAND, Michelle 43
Sodarcan Inc — DUMONT, Monique 325
Solliciteur General du Canada — MARION, Guylaine 770
Southeast Asia Information & Resrch
  Ctr — CAN, Hung V. 177
Towers Perrin Forster & Crosby — CHIPPS, Heather D. 209
Univ of Montreal — ARAJ, Houda 30
BEDARD, Bernard J. 73
BERNHARD, Paulette 89
BERTRAND-GASTALDY,
  Suzanne 91
BOIVIN-OSTIGUY, Jocelyne . 111
BOUDREAU, Gerald E. 118
BROCHU, Frederick 138
BULL, Jerry J. 156
DARBON, Ginette 274
DESCHATELETS, Gilles H. .. 294
DESROCHERS, Monique 295
FLUK, Louise R. 386
GARDNER, Richard K. 418
GIRARD, Luc 438
GREENE, Richard L. 464
HETU, Sylvie 534
MAYRAND, Lise M. 791
ROLLAND-THOMAS, Paule 1051
SAVARD, Rejean 1085
VADNAIS, Martine 1270
Univ of Quebec — BEAUMIER, Renald 70
COTE, Jean P. 249
DUPUIS, Marcel 327
GARDNER, Lucie 418
LAFRENIERE, Myriam 688
LATOUR, Pierre 701
MENARD, Francoise 823
PARKER, Charles G. 941
ROUSSEAU, Denis 1061
Vanier Coll — RATNER, Sabina T. 1010
Via Le Monde Productions — NAGY, Cecile 886
Via Rail Canada Inc — DUSABLON-BOTTEGA,
  Nicole 329

MONTREAL-EST
City of Montreal-Est — KO, Jean S. 666
MONTREAL-NORD
City of Montreal-Nord — DENOMMEE, Celine 293
NICOLET
Coll Notre-Dame-de-L'Assomption — ROY, Lucille Y. 1063
OTTAWA
Lib of Parliament — TESSIER, Richard 1233
Ottawa Pub Lib — DUHAMEL, Louis 324
PIERREFONDS
Regie Intermunicipale des
  Bibliotheques — BROSSEAU, Lise 141
POINTE CLAIRE DORVAL
City of Pointe-Claire — COTE, Claire 249
LAPERRIERE, Celine 697
Lakeshore General Hospital — FIORE, Francine 379
Merck Frosst Canada Inc — KELLY, Claire B. 637
WACASEY, Mary M. 1290
Pfizer Canada Inc — HAYWARD, Miriam C. 517
Pulp & Paper Research Institute,
  Canada — FINNEMORE, Mary A. 378
STAHL, Hella 1178

PONT-VIAU
Ecole Demosthene — ROY, Helene 1063

QUEBEC (Cont'd)
QUEBEC
CEGEP at Limoilou — GODIN, Maud 442
Coll Francois-Xavier Garneau — PAGEAU, Denise 934
Fortin & Assoc — FOERTIN, Yves P. 387
Laval Univ — BONNELLY, Claude 114
CANTIN, Gemma 179
CARTIER, Celine 190
GUERETTE, Charlotte M. 476
TAILLON, Yolande A. ... 1220
TESSIER, Yves 1233

Lib of the National Assembly of
  Quebec — PREMONT, Jacques 990
L'Institut Canadien de Quebec — MARQUIS, Julien 773
MCKENZIE, Donald R. 811
Microfor Inc — DENIGER, Constant 292
LUSSIER, Richard 749
Ministry of Agriculture — BELANGER, Sylvie 76
Ministry of Communications — COLLISTER, Edward A. 233
Ministry of Education — CYR, Solange 268
Ministry of Law, Hunting & Fishing — SAVARD, Madeleine 1085
National Assembly of Quebec — BERNIER, Gaston 89
BOILARD, Gilberte 111
DIONNE. Guy 305
FORTIN, Jean 391
FORTIN, Jean L. 391
LEBEL, Clement 707
NADEAU, Johan 885
NGUYEN, Vy K. 901
WAIT, Elaine 1292
Revenue Canada Taxation — ROY, Christine 1063
RIMOUSKI
Univ of Quebec — BIELLE, Christian P. 95
ROSEMERE
City of Rosemere — LAPIERRE, France 697
Laupenval Sch Board — ADRIAN, Donna J. 7
ROUYN-NORANDA
Bibliotheque Centrale de Pret — FINK, Norman 378
Coll de l'Abitibi-Temiscamingue — TREMBLAY, Levis 1255
Univ of Quebec — ALLARD, Serge 14
ROXBORO
Sources Pub Lib — GOLDEN, Helene 445
ST-BRUNO
City of St-Bruno de Montarville — BERNARDIN, Luce 88
SAINT-EUSTACHE
City of Saint-Eustache — KHOUZAM, Monique 646
ST-FELICIEN
CEGEP at St-Felicien — LAMBERT, Yvan 690
ST HUBERT
City of St Hubert — DUMOULIN, Nicole L. 325
ST-JANVIER
Bell Helicopter Textron Canada — GRITZKA, Gerda M. 471
ST JEAN SUR RICHELIE
Oerlibon Aerospace Inc — JOBA, Judith C. 601
ST-JOVITE
Commission Scolaire des Laurentides — FILIATRAULT, Andre Y. 376
ST LAMBERT DE LEVIS
Champlain Regional Coll — HERLINGER, Peggy 531
ST-LAURENT
City of Saint-Laurent — DJEVALIKIAN, Sonia 306
FORTIN, Johanne 392

ST LAURENT D'ORLEANS
Centre Marie-Vincent — BAZINET, Jeanne 68
City of Saint-Laurent — SIMON, Marie L. 1140
SAINTE-FOY
Canadian Department of Agriculture — LUSSIER, Claudine 749
Ctr de Recherche Industrielle du
  Quebec — FLORIAN, Trudel 385
TRUDEL, Florian 1259
Champlain Regional Coll — PETRYK, Louise O. 965
City of Sainte-Foy — AUGER, Claudette 39
Laval Univ — GUILMETTE, Pierre 476
JULIEN, Guy 619
LALIBERTE, Madeleine A. ... 689
ROBIN, Madeleine 1043
Univ of Quebec — ALAIN, Jean M. 9
DU BREUIL, Laval 322
GELINAS, Michel R. 426

SEPT-ILES
City of Sept-Iles — BOUDREAU, Jocelyne 119

QUEBEC (Cont'd)
SHERBROOKE
Centre Hospitalier Hotel-Dieu
  Sherbrooke   FONTAINE, Nicole 388
Coll du Sacre-Coeur   DEMERS, Madeleine M. 291
Univ of Sherbrooke   CHASSE, Jules 203
   CHOUINARD, Germain 211
   SOKOV, Asta M. 1166
   TANGUAY, Guy 1222

SILLERY
Coll Jesus-Marie de Sillery   LAMONTAGNE, Jacqueline .. 691
STANSTEAD
Tomifobia Vallee Hi-Tech   GRENIER, Serge 467
STE ANNE DE BELLEVUE
John Abbott Coll   DE LIAMCHIN, Lana 289
   DOUGLAS-BONNELL,
     Eileen 314
McGill Univ   GRAINGER, Bruce 457
Spar Aerospace Ltd   GROSS, Margaret B. 472
STE-THERESE
City of Ste-Therese   NADEAU, Leonard 886
Coll Lionel-Groulx   PARADIS, Jacques 939
TRACY
CEGEP at Sorel-Tracy   RIOPEL, Jean M. 1035
TROIS-RIVIERES
Centre Hospitalier St-Joseph   DE-ROUYN, Solange 294
City of Trois-Rivieres   BESSETTE, Madeleine 91
CEGEP at Trois-Rivieres   BAILLARGEON, Daniele 47
   SIMARD, Denis 1139
Univ of Quebec   MANSEAU, Edith 767
VAL D'OR
Commission Scolaire Regnl La
  Verendrye   MARCHAND, Jacques 768
VAUDREUIL
RCA Corp   WALKER, Elizabeth A. 1295
VERDUN
Bell-Northern Research   DIMITRESCU, Ioana 304
CECV   VAILLANCOURT, Alain 1270
VILLE DE VANIER
Hopital Christ-Roi   GELINAS, Gratien 426
WESTMOUNT
Academic & General Book Shop   GLASS, Gerald 440
Dawson Coll   GILMORE, Carolyn 437
Inform II   LEDOUX, Marc A. 708
Institut Catholique de Montreal   LALONDE, Diane 689
JAI Info   WADE, C A. 1290
Westmount Pub Lib   LYDON, Rosemary E. 751

SASKATCHEWAN
ESTEVAN
Estevan Comprehensive Sch Board   ANDRIST, Shirley A. 27
NORTH BATTLEFORD
Lakeland Library Region   RIDLER, Elizabeth A. 1032
PRINCE ALBERT
Wapiti Regional Lib   LABUIK, Karen L. 686
REGINA
Buffalo Plains Sch Division 21   MCLEOD, Karen E. 814
City of Regina   BALON, Brett J. 53
Gabriel Dumont Institute   TURNBULL, Keith 1264
Government of Saskatchewan   ADAMS, Karen G. 5
   ARORA, Ved P. 34
Province of Saskatchewan   RUSSELL, Fraser 1069
Regina Pub Lib   DIRKSEN, Jean 305
   FIELDEN, Janet 376
   GAGNON, Andre 412
   GRAYBIEL, Luisa 460
   JENSEN, Ken 599
   VANDER LAAN, Lubbert ... 1274
SK Alcohol & Drug Abuse
  Commission   KING, Karen P. 651
Saskatchewan Education   DUPERREAULT, Marilyn J. .. 327
Saskatchewan Highways &
  Transportation   BASLER, Ellen L. 63
Saskatchewan Legislative Lib   POWELL, Marian 988
Saskatchewan Lib   CAMPBELL, Joylene E. 177
   IVANOCHKO, Robert W. 585
Saskatchewan Telecommunications   POGUE, Basil G. 979

SASKATCHEWAN (Cont'd)
REGINA (Cont'd)
Univ of Regina   AFFLECK, Delburt E. 7
   BROWNE, Berks G. 148
   FIELDEN, Stanley 376
   HAMBLETON, Alixe E. 490
   INGLES, Ernie B. 582
   MACK, A Y. 756
   RESCH, Peter T. 1024
   SWEENEY, Shelley T. 1215
   THAUBERGER, Marianne T.   1234
Wascana Institute of Applied Arts &
  Scis   VOHRA, Pran 1287
SASKATOON
Frances Morrison Lib   BUCKLE, Judith 154
National Research Council of Canada   CHEN, Flora F. 205
Saskatchewan Archives Board   HANDE, D A. 494
Saskatoon Pub Lib   BARLOW, Elizabeth A. 57
   RUSSELL, Vija 1069
   TOMCHYSHYN, Theresa M.   1249
Univ of Saskatchewan   CANEVARI DE PAREDES,
     Donna A. 178
   CHEN, William Y. 205
   FRITZ, Linda 405
   HAMMEL, Philip J. 493
   HUBBERTZ, Andrew P. 568
   KRISHAN, Kewal 678
   LAKHANPAL, Sarv K. 689
   NELSON, Ian C. 893
   PAREDES-RUIZ, Eudoxio B. . 940
   REID, Marianne E. 1019
   SALT, David P. 1077
   WIENS, Paul 1336
Wheatland Regional Lib   CAMERON, Bruce 174
SWIFT CURRENT
Chinook Regional Lib   KEASCHUK, Michael J. 633
YORKTON
Parkland Regional Lib   CALEF, Daniel C. 172

YUKON TERRITORY
WHITEHORSE
Whitehorse Department of Education   HISCOCK, Audrey M. 544

ARGENTINA
ENTRE RIOS
Colegio Adventista del Plata   HAMMERLY, Hernan D. 493

AUSTRALIA
ADELAIDE
South Australian Institute of
  Technology   FOSKETT, Antony C. 392
BARDON BRISBANE
Univ of Queensland   ROUTH, Spencer 1061
BEDFORD PARK
Flinders Univ of South Australia   BROWN, Pauline 146
BRISBANE
Queensland Dept of Educ   GOODELL, Paulette M. 448
Queensland Institute of Technology   COCHRANE, Thomas G. 226
   GOODELL, John S. 448
CANBERRA
Australian National Univ   STEELE, Colin R. 1184
KENSINGTON
Univ of New South Wales   RAYWARD, W B. 1011
   WILSON, Concepcion S. ... 1350
MAGILL
South Australian Coll of Advanced
  Educ   BEATTIE, Kathleen M. 70
NEWCASTLE
Univ of Newcastle   NEAME, Roderick L. 891
NORTH RYDE
Macquarie Univ   WILKINSON, Eoin H. 1340
ST LUCIA
Univ of Queensland   LAMBERTON, Donald M. ... 690
SEAFORTH
Seaforth Coll of Technl & Further
  Educ   TANNER, Elizabeth 1222

AUSTRALIA (Cont'd)
SYDNEY
St George Hospital   NGUYEN, Michael V. 900
Univ of Sydney   RADFORD, Neil 1002
SYDNEY NSW
New South Wales Parliamentary Lib   TILLOTSON, Greig S. 1245
ULTIMO
Australian Lib Journal   ADAMS, Jenny 5
                                      LEVETT, John 720
VICTORIA
C J Bellamy & Associates   BENNETT, David M. 81
Churches of Christ in Australia   SMITH, Lindsay L. 1157
Melbourne Coll of Advanced
    Education   POWNALL, David E. 989

BAHAMAS
GRAND BAHAMAS ISLAND
Bahamas Ministry of Education   BARTON, Barbara I. 61

BAHRAIN
AL MANAMAH
Univ of Bahrain   ALI, Syed N. 13

BELGIUM
BEERSE
Janssen Research Foundation   PEETERS, Marc D. 954
BRUSSELS
Bureau Marcel van Dijk   VAN SLYPE, Georges 1277
Universite Libre de Bruxelles   DARIS, Claude 274
Univ of Louvain   WALCKIERS, Marc A. 1293
ST NIKLAAS
Hedendaagse Dokumentatie   VAN GARSSE, Yvan 1275

BRAZIL
SAO PAULO
Publications Technical International   GROSSMANN, Pierre 473

COLOMBIA
BOGOTA
Colegio Nueva Granada   CARDENAS, Mary E. 180

COSTA RICA
ALAJUELA
Centro Adventista de Estudios
    Superiores   MOSS, Loretta E. 872
SAN JOSE
INFOMED   SMITH, Sharon 1160
Reditec   MIRABELLI, Gerardo 847
United Nations/Central Am Pub
    Admin Inst   CROWTHER, Warren W. . . . 262

CUBA
HAVANA
Ctr of Information & Land
    Documentation   ASIS, Moises 36

EGYPT
CAIRO
National Information & Documentation
    Ctr   EL-DUWEINI, Aadel K. 342
GIZA
Cairo Univ   EL-MASRY, Mohammed 345
                                      MAHOUD ALY, Usama E. . . . 761

ENGLAND
BUSHEY
US International Univ in Europe   SMITH, Margit J. 1157
CHESTER
Shell Research Ltd   THORP, Raymond G. 1242
ESSEX
Gage Postal Books   GAGE, Laurie E. 412

ENGLAND (Cont'd)
HITCHIN HERTS
Institution of Electrical Engineers   AITCHISON, Thomas M. 9
HUCHEN
The Indexer   BELL, Hazel 77
LONDON
American Sch in London   SERVENTE, Marcia M. 1116
Ballet Rambert   PRITCHARD, Jane E. 994
British Lib   LINE, Maurice B. 730
Bryan Cave McPheeters &
    McRoberts   SNYDER, Elizabeth A. 1164
Butterworth & Co Ltd   CUSWORTH, George R. . . . 267
City Univ of London   ROBERTSON, Stephen E. . . 1042
IME Ltd   NOERR, Kathleen T. 907
Library Association Publishing Limited ELLIOTT, Pirkko E. 344
Strategic Developments Limited   BUNCE, George D. 157
LONDON NW8ONP
American Sch in London   BRILL, Kathryn R. 136
MERSEYSIDE
Unilever Research   HOWARD, Theresa M. 564
OXFORD
Pembroke Coll   WINSHIP, Michael 1355
OXON
CAB International   COOK, Elaine 239
PLYMOUTH
Plymouth Magistrates' Court   PENGELLY, Joe 956
SUSSEX
Rabbit Press Ltd   GREEN, Jeffrey P. 462
WITHYHAM
Richard Macnutt Ltd   MACNUTT, Richard P. 758

FEDERAL REPUBLIC OF CHINA
TAICHUNG
Feng Chia Univ   YANG, Mei H. 1377
TAIDZI
China Evangelical Seminary   CHENG, Sheung O. 206
TAIPEI
China Evangelical Seminary   WANG, Sin C. 1303
National Central Lib   CHOU, Nancy O. 210
                                      OU-LAN, Nancy 930
National Taiwan Univ   HU, James S. 567
                                      HUANG, Jack K. 568
                                      LEE, Lucy T. 710
                                      SENG, Harris B. 1115
                                      SHAW, Shiow J. 1124
Taipei American Sch   BRAUNGER, Patricia M. . . . 130
Tamkang Univ   HUANG, Shih H. 568
Veterans General Hospital   CHUO, Josephine Y. 213
World Coll of Journalism   LIN, Chih F. 727

FEDERAL REPUBLIC OF GERMANY
BERLIN
Amerika-Gedenkbibliothek   ULRICH, Paul S. 1268
Free Univ of Berlin   WERSIG, Gernot 1325
Prussian Cultural Heritage Foundation ELSTE, R O. 346
                                      KREH, Fritz 677
                                      WALTER, Raimund E. 1300
BINNINGEN
Institute of Medieval Music Limited   DITTMER, Luther A. 306
BONN
Federal German Ministry for Econ
    Cooprtn   LOTZ, Rainer E. 742
BRAUNSCHWEIG
Technical Univ of Braunschweig   EVERSBERG, Bernhard 359
BREMERHAVEN
Alfred Wegener Institute   GOMEZ, Michael J. 447
DARMSTADT
European Stars & Stripes   NEUWILLER, Charlene 897
FRANKFURT
Metallgesellschaft AG   BECHTEL, Hans 71
MUNICH
Aktion Das Frohliche Krankenzimmer   ADENEY, Carol D. 6
SAARBRUCKEN
Univ of Saarlandes   VON KEITZ, Wolfgang 1288
ZWEIBRUCKEN
US Air Force   WHITEHILL, Margaret 1332

FIJI
  SUVA
  Univ of the South Pacific   WOODS, Richard F. 1367

FRANCE
  PARIS
  American Coll in Paris   STONE, Toby G. 1197
  The American Lib in Paris   GRATTAN, Robert 458
  Bibliotheque Nationale   GARRETA, J C. 420
  Bureau Marcel van Dijk   CHAUMIER, Jacques 204
  International Energy Agency   WACHTER, Margery C. 1290
  Schiller International Univ   DEROODE, Clifford H. 294
  UNESCO   COURRIER, Yves G. 251
  RUEIL-MALMAISON
  Institut Francais du Petrole   MOUREAU, Magdeleine 873
  VILLEURBANNE
  Ecole Natl Superieure des
    Bibliothecaire   COBOLET, Guy P. 225

GUATAMALA
  GUATAMALA CITY
  Central Am Research Inst for Industry MARBAN, Ricio 768

HONG KONG
  KOWLOON
  City Polytechnic of Hong Kong   POON, Paul W. 983
  Hong Kong Baptist Coll   CHU, Tat C. 213
                                         FU, Ting W. 407
  SHATIN
  Chinese Univ of Hong Kong   WU, Edith Y. 1373
                                         YEN, David S. 1379
  THE PEAK
  Information Systems International   SANDFELDER, Paula M. ... 1080

INDIA
  ANDHRA PRADESH
  International Crops Research Institute SINHA, Pramod K. 1143
  BANGALORE
  St John's Med Coll and Hospital   KITTUR, Krishna N. 657
  HYDERABAD
  Bharat Heavy Electricals Ltd   SATYANARAYANA, Vadhri
                                           V. 1084
  MUSSOORIE
  Woodstock Sch   EUSEBIUS, Nima V. 356
  NEW DELHI
  Indian Council of Soc Science
    Research   AGRAWAL, Surendra P. 7

INDONESIA
  JAKARTA
  Univ of Indonesia   ADITIRTO, Irma U. 6
  URS International-Trans Asia   STONE, Clarence W. 1197

IRAN
  SHIRAZ
  Shiraz Univ   MEHHAD, Jafar 821

IRELAND
  DUBLIN
  Allied Irish Banks Plc   LAMBKIN, Anthony 690
  Dublin Pub Libs   SLINEY, Marjory T. 1149
  General Council of the Bar of Ireland ASTON, Jennefer 37
  IDA Ireland   KELLY, Jerry 638
  SICA Innovation Consultants Ltd   SWEENEY, Gerald P. 1215
  Trinity Coll   FOX, Peter K. 395
  Univ of Dublin   DUFFIN, Elizabeth A. 323

ISRAEL
  BIRZEIT
  Birzeit Univ   HADDAD, Aida N. 481
  BRAK
  Mor Institute for Medical Data   CAREL, Rafael S. 181
  HAIFA
  Assn of Americans & Canadians in
    Israel   WASERMAN, Barbara 1307
  Baha'i World Centre   BEAVERS, Janet W. 71
                                         COLLINS, William P. 233
                                         MOULD, Edith L. 873
  RAFAEL   BLOCH, Uri 105
  JERUSALEM
  Biokoor   BORCK, Liba 116
  Hebrew Univ of Jerusalem   KASOW, Harriet 629
  Henrietta Szold Institute   LANGERMAN, Shoshana P. . 695
  Israel Film Arch Jerusalem
    Cinematheque   DIAMANT, Betsy 299
  RAMAT AVIV
  Tel Aviv Univ   ERES, Beth K. 352
  RAMAT GAN
  Bar Ilan Univ   SNYDER, Esther M. 1164
  REHOVOT
  Weizmann Institute of Science   WOLVSKY, Haya S. 1362
  TEL-AVIV
  Israeli Ministry of Energy   HOFFMANN, Eliahu W. 548

ITALY
  FLORENCE
  Proel Tecnologie ISC   FORRESTER, John H. 391
  MILAN
  CFM Documentazione   FABRE DE MORLHON,
                                           Christiane 360
  L'Orsa Maggiore SRL   PUSATERI, Liborio 998
  Univ of Milan   CASIRAGHI, Edoardo 192
  ROME
  Food & Agriculture Organization   JOLING, Carole G. 610
  ICCROM   HUEMER, Christina G. 570
  UN Food & Agriculture Organization   MENOU, Michel J. 824

JAMAICA
  KINGSTON
  Caribbean Graduate Sch of Theology   ERDEL, Timothy P. 352
  Univ of the West Indies   DOUGLAS, Daphne R. 314
                                         MANSINGH, Laxmi 767
  MANDEVILL
  West Indies Coll   BALDWIN, Robert D. 52

JAPAN
  AICHI-KEN
  Nagoya Univ of Commerce   TOGUCHI, Eiko 1248
  Toyota Central R & D Lab Inc   SANO, Hikomaro 1081
  HIROSHIMA
  Radiation Effects Research
    Foundation   YORIOKA, Jimmie Y. 1380
  IBARAKI-KEN
  Univ of Lib & Information Science   NOZOE, Atsutake 911
                                         TAKEUCHI, Satoru 1220
  SENDAI MIYAGI
  Tohoku Univ   HARADA, Ryukichi 499
  TOKYO
  Aoyama Gakuin Univ   KOGA, Setsuko 568
  Epoch Research Corp   MIWA, Makiko 850
  Goldman Sachs & Co   KATAOKA, Yoko 629
  Jikei Univ Sch of Medicine   URATA, Kazuo 1269
                                         YAMAZAKI, Shigeaki 1377
  Keio Univ   HOSONO, Kimio 562
                                         TAMURA, Shunsaku 1221
  Maruzen Co Ltd   YAMANAKA, Tai 1377
  Mitsubishi Research Institute Inc   NASU, Yukio 889
                                         YAMAZAKI, Hisamichi 1377
  National Archives of Japan   OGAWA, Chiyoko 918
  National Cancer Center   KAWASHIMA, Hiroko 632
  National Diet Lib   SAKAMOTO, Hiroshi 1076
  Tokyo Gakugei Univ   TETSUYA, Inoue 1233
  Tokyo Medical Coll   SUGA, Toshinobu 1206

JAPAN (Cont'd)
TOKYO (Cont'd)
Tokyo National Univ of Fine Arts &
  Music   KISHIMOTO, Hiroko 656
Tsuda Coll   KATO, Hisae 629
TOKYO 105
USACO Corp   YAMAKAWA, Takashi 1376

KENYA
NAIROBI
Nairobi Evangelical Grad Sch of
  Theology   BOWEN, Dorothy N. 120
National Council for Science & Tech   IRURIA, Daniel M. 584
United Nations   PILLET, Sylvaine M. 973

KUWAIT
KHALIDIAH
Kuwait Univ   HAMDY, Mohamed N. 491
SAHAT
Pub Authority for Applied & Training   ALTURKAIT, Adela A. 19
SALMIYAH
Coll of Basic Education   ABDEL-MOTEY, Yaser Y. 2

LEBANON
BEIRUT
American Univ of Beirut   HANHAN, Leila M. 495

LUXEMBOURG
LUXEMBOURG CITY
European Commission Host
  Organisation   CORNELIUS, Peter K. 246

MALAWI
LILONGWE
Peace Corp   SNYDER, Lisa A. 1165

MALAYSIA
PENANG
Univ of Sains Malaysia   LIM, Hucktee E. 727

MEXICO
BENITO
Ministry of Health & Welfare   MACIAS-CHAPULA, Cesar
                                   A. 755
DURANGO
Institutu Tecnologico de Durango   LAU, Jesus G. 702
MEXICO CITY
Instituto Tecnologico Autonomo de
  Mexico   OROZCO-TENORIO, Jose
                                   M. 926
National Archives of Mexico   ORTIZ MONASTERIO,
                                   Leonor 927
National Association of Universities   BOOM, Ramon A. 115
National Autonomous Univ of Mexico   BARBERENA, Elsa 55
                                 DE WALERSTEIN, Linda S. . . 297
                                 RODRIGUEZ, Serafin L. . . . 1048
Secretary of Pub Education   MAGALONI, Ana M. 759
NUEVO LEON
Montemorelos Univ   SIEMENS, Bessie M. 1136
Univ of Nuevo Leon   ARTEAGA, Georgina 35

NETHERLANDS
AMERSFOORT
Johan Van Halm & Associates   VAN HALM, Johan 1275
AMSTERDAM
Jewish Historical Museum   CAHEN, Joel J. 171
Nedbook International BV   OVEREYNDER, Rombout E. . 931
NOORDWIJK
European Space Agency-ESTEC   RAITT, David I. 1004
WAGENINGEN
PUDOC   KOSTER, Lieuwien M. 673

NEW ZEALAND
AUCKLAND
Auckland City Council   TWEEDALE, Dellene M. . . . 1266
Univ of Auckland   RICHARDS, Valerie 1028

NIGERIA
AKURE
Federal Univ of Technology   ONONOGBO, Raphael U. . . . 924
BENIN CITY
Bendel State Lib Board   IMOISI, Ann U. 582
IBADAN
Univ of Ibadan   ABOYADE, Beatrice O. 2
KANO
Bayero Univ   AJIBERO, Matthew I. 9
LAGOS
Yaba Coll of Technology   AFOLAYAN, Matthew A. 7
OGBOMOSO
Nigerian Baptist Theological Seminary   OKPARA, Ibiba M. 920
                                 TARPLEY, Margaret J. 1224
Southern Baptist Convention   GUNN, Shirley A. 477
OKIGWE
Imo State Univ at Okigwe   OGBAA, Clara K. 918

NORTHERN IRELAND
BELFAST
Queen's Univ   LINTON, William D. 731

PAKISTAN
LAHORE
Lahore American Society   TRAINER, Leslie F. 1253

PEOPLE'S REPUBLIC OF CHINA
CHENGDU, SICHUAN
Sichuan Univ   ZHU, Xiaofeng . . . . : 1387

PHILIPPINES
MAKATI
Ateneo de Manila Univ   MORAN, Teresita C. 862
MANILA
The Lawyers Review   OREJANA, Rebecca D. 925
Philippine Normal Coll   DE CASTRO, Elinore H. 285
Summer Institute of Linguistics COOK, Marjorie L. 240
QUEZON CITY
Univ of the Philippines   PICACHE, Ursula D. 970
                                 VALLEJO, Rosa M. 1271

POLAND
POZNAN
US Consulate in Poland   CHOJNACKA, Jadwiga 210

PORTUGAL
LISBON
Lisbon National Lib   DE MACEDO, Maria L. 290

SAUDI ARABIA
DHAHRAM
ARAMCO   BASCOM, James F. 62
JEDDAH
Computer Consultants   ALSANARRAI, Hafidh S. 17
King Abdulaziz Univ   KHAN, Mohammed A. 646
RIYADH
King Fahd Hospital   KIRKWOOD, Brenda S. 655
King Faisal Hospital & Research
  Center   BROWN, Biraj L. 142
King Khalid Eye Specialist Hospital   MARTIN, Nannette 777
King Saud Univ   ALI, Farooq M. 13
                                 BUTT, Abdul W. 167
                                 SIBAI, Mohamed M. 1134
Ministry of Finance & National
  Economy   MANSFIELD, Jerry W. 767
Ministry of Foreign Affairs   TAMEEM, Jamal A. 1221
US Treasury Department   OSIER, Donald V. 928

SCOTLAND
GLASGOW
Univ of Glasgow   HEANEY, Henry J. 518

SOUTH AFRICA
BELLVILLE
Univ of the Western Cape   SEPTEMBER, Peter E. 1115
JOHANNESBURG
Anglo American Corp of South Africa   ARMSTRONG, Denise M. 32
PRETORIA
Univ of South Africa   WILLEMSE, John 1341
ROUNDEBOSCH
Univ of Cape Town   BARBEN, Tanya A. 55
SOMERSET WEST
General Conference/Seventh-Day
    Adventist   LUSK, Betty M. 749
TYGERBERG
Medical Research Council   ROSSOUW, Steve F. 1059

SOUTH KOREA
SEOUL
Sookmyung Women's Univ   KIM, Soon C. 649

SPAIN
BARCELONA
Laboratorios Grifols SA   FUENTES, Ismael 408
Univ of Barcelona   VELA, Leonor G. 1281

SWEDEN
STOCKHOLM
Swedish National Radio Corp   CNATTINGIUS, Claes M. . . . 224

SWITZERLAND
GENEVA
Institut d'Etudes Sociales   ESTERMANN-WISKOTT,
                                                   Yolande 355
International Trade Centre   JONES, Roger A. 615
Univ of Geneva   JACQUESSON, Alain L. 591
World Health Organization   FAGERLUND, M L. 361

THAILAND
BANGKOK
Chulalongkorn Univ   MINAIKIT, Nonglak 845
Tilleke & Gibbins ROP   RUNGSANG, Rebecca J. . . 1067

TRINIDAD
PORT OF SPAIN
United Nations   ELLIOTT, Lirlyn J. 344
SAINT JOSEPH
Technical Lib Consultancy   MCCONNIE, Mary 798
VALSAYN
Univ of the West Indies   NANTON-COMISSIONG,
                                                   Barbara L. 887

TURKEY
IZMIR
Izmir Amerikan Lisesi   FRANK, Elizabeth W. 397

UGANDA
MUKONO
Bishop Tucker Theological Coll   MUKUNGU, Frederick N. 876

VENEZUELA
CARACAS
Colegio Internacional de Caracas   BERNAT, Mary A. 88

ZAMBIA
CHILANGA
Ministry of Agriculture & Water
    Devlpmnt   LUMANDE, Edward 748